Key to phonetic symbols

Vowels and diphthongs

1	i	*as in*	**see** /si/
2	ɪ	*as in*	**sit** /sɪt/
3	e	*as in*	**ten** /ten/
4	æ	*as in*	**hat** /hæt/
5	ɑ	*as in*	**arm** /ɑm/
6	o	*as in*	**got** /got/
7	ɔ	*as in*	**saw** /sɔ/
8	ʊ	*as in*	**put** /pʊt/
9	u	*as in*	**too** /tu/
10	ʌ	*as in*	**cup** /kʌp/
11			
12			
13			
14	əʊ	*as in*	**home** /həʊm/
15	ɑɪ	*as in*	**five** /fɑɪv/
16	ɑʊ	*as in*	**now** /nɑʊ/
17	ɔɪ	*as in*	**join** /dʒɔɪn/
18	ɪə	*as in*	**near** /nɪə(r)/
19	eə	*as in*	**hair** /heə(r)/
20	ʊə	*as in*	**pure** /pjʊə(r)/

Consonants

1	p	*as in*	**pen** /pen/
2	b	*as in*	**bad** /bæd/
3	t	*as in*	**tea** /ti/
4	d	*as in*	**did** /dɪd/
5	k	*as in*	**cat** /kæt/
6	g	*as in*	**get** /get/
7	tʃ	*as in*	**chin** /tʃɪn/
8	dʒ	*as in*	**June** /dʒun/
9	f	*as in*	**fall** /fɔl/
10	v	*as in*	**voice** /vɔɪs/
11	θ	*as in*	**thin** /θɪn/
12	ð	*as in*	**then** /ðen/
13	s	*as in*	**so** /səʊ/
14	z	*as in*	**zoo** /zu/
15	ʃ	*as in*	**she** /ʃi/
16	ʒ	*as in*	**vision** /ˋvɪʒn/
17	h	*as in*	**how** /hɑʊ/
18	m	*as in*	**man** /mæn/
19	n	*as in*	**no** /nəʊ/ *syllabic* n *as in* **happening** /ˋhæpn̩ɪŋ/
20	ŋ	*as in*	**sing** /sɪŋ/
21	l	*as in*	**leg** /leg/ *syllabic* l *as in* **settling** /ˋsetl̩ɪŋ/
22	r	*as in*	**red** /red/ *syllabic* ɾ *as in* **measuring** /ˋmeʒɾ̩ɪŋ/
23	j	*as in*	**yes** /jes/
24	w	*as in*	**wet** /wet/

/ˋ/ *represents* principal stress *as in* **about** /əˋbɑʊt/
/ˈ/ *represents* subordinate stress *as in* **academic** /ˈækəˋdemɪk/

(r) An 'r' in parentheses is heard in British pronunciation when the next word begins with a vowel sound and follows without pause. Otherwise it is omitted. In American pronunciation no 'r' of the phonetic or the ordinary spelling need be omitted.

/-/ Hyphens preceding and/or following parts of a repeated transcription indicate that only the repeated part changes.

⇨ the Introduction for a full explanation of the phonetic transcription.

OXFORD ADVANCED LEARNER'S DICTIONARY OF CURRENT ENGLISH

A S HORNBY
with the assistance of
A P Cowie
J Windsor Lewis

London
Oxford University Press
1974

Oxford University Press, Ely House, London W.1.
GLASGOW NEW YORK TORONTO MELBOURNE
WELLINGTON CAPE TOWN IBADAN NAIROBI
DAR ES SALAAM LUSAKA ADDIS ABABA DELHI
BOMBAY CALCUTTA MADRAS KARACHI LAHORE
DACCA KUALA LUMPUR SINGAPORE HONG KONG
TOKYO

First published 1948 (Twelve Impressions)
Second Edition 1963 (Nineteen Impressions)
Third Edition 1974

Computer typeset in
Times and Univers by
George Overs Ltd,
Oxford University Press,
Unwin Brothers Ltd
and Trade Spools.
Printed in Great Britain
at the University Press, Oxford
by Vivian Ridler
Printer to the University.

The publishers are grateful to the following for permission to reproduce the photographs:

Aerofilms Ltd; The Associated Press Ltd; The Australian High Commission; Barnaby's Picture Library; British International Photographic Press Agencies; British Rail; The British Tourist Authority; Camera Press Ltd; The Canadian High Commission; J Allan Cash Ltd; The Central Electricity Generating Board; The Controller of Her Majesty's Stationery Office (British Crown Copyright); Fox Photos Ltd; The Greek State Tourist Office; Will Green Ltd; The Japanese Embassy; The Keystone Press Agency Ltd; Quentin Lloyd; The London Museum; Madame Tussaud's Ltd; The Mansell Collection; The National Portrait Gallery, London; The New Charing Cross Hospital, London; The Novosti Press Agency; The Rev C E Pocknee; The Post Office; The Radio Times Hulton Picture Library; The Royal National Institute for the Blind; St George's Hospital Medical School, London; The Science Museum, London (British Crown Copyright); The Sport & General Press Agency Ltd; John Topham Ltd; The Trustees of the British Museum; The Trustees of the British Museum (Natural History); The Trustees of the Wallace Collection, London; The United States Information Service; The Victoria & Albert Museum, London (British Crown Copyright).

Illustrations: Artist: Carl James.
Graphics: Colin Newman
and Vyvyan Thomas
of Oxford Illustrators Ltd.

Contents

Inside covers:

Key to phonetic symbols

Abbreviations used in the text

INTRODUCTION i–xxvii

The content and arrangement of the entries i
The headword i
Derivatives, compounds and idiomatic expressions ii
The definitions iii
Example phrases and sentences iii
Nouns: singular and plural iv
Irregular plurals, conjugations, etc iv
Entries for the major verbs v
Adverbial particles vi
Anomalous verbs vii
American English viii
Word-division ix
Stylistic values and specialist English usage x

Pronunciation and stress xii

The Verb Patterns xvi

THE DICTIONARY 1–1021

Appendices 1023–55
1 Irregular verbs 1023
2 Common abbreviations 1027
3 Affixes 1032
4 Numerical expressions 1036
5 Weights and Measures 1041
6 Geographical names 1044
7 Common forenames 1049
8 Shakespeare's works 1052
9 Ranks in the armed forces 1053
10 Books of the Bible 1055

Acknowledgements

I continue to be indebted to correspondents in many parts of the world for calling attention to occasional misprints and errors in the second edition and for suggestions on possible additions. These suggestions have been carefully considered and acted on where I felt in agreement with them.

Professor V Gatenby and Mr H Wakefield shared the work of compiling the first edition (1942). The value of their contributions remains, although these were extensively revised and added to in the second edition (1963) and in this third edition.

The dictionaries of the Clarendon Press have been used again, with the generous permission of the Delegates. The publication (1972) of Volume I of the *Supplement to the Oxford English Dictionary* has made possible the inclusion in this third edition of many words which were not entered in the second edition.

My work on this third edition has been greatly helped by three lecturers from the University of Leeds.

Mr A P Cowie, of the School of English, made a thorough scrutiny of the complete revision and made valuable suggestions for new treatment of many entries. He was responsible for the arrangement of all the main verb entries and gave his expert attention to the phrasal verbs and the ordering of the patterns into which they enter. The style in which these verb entries appear, with bold type to make prominent the patterns and their possible alternatives, is his work.

Mr J Windsor Lewis, of the Department of Phonetics, undertook the task of providing new phonetic transcriptions for all entries and the stress patterns added to all compounds and collocations. He undertook, too, the exacting work of proof-reading these transcriptions. An account, by Mr Windsor Lewis, of his scheme will be found on pages xii–xv of the Introduction.

Miss Loreto Todd, of the School of English, provided much useful material on differences of usage between British English and American English, and made numerous suggestions for the treatment of words and phrases used in commerce, industry and technology.

Mr Leslie Aczel, who has for twenty years directed his own language institute and laboratory in Budapest, has made useful suggestions to me on the verb patterns as set out in the first edition. The revised patterns, and the new arrangement, owe much to his comments, and I am grateful to him for the interest he took.

The appendices of the second edition have been revised and new ones added. I am particularly grateful to Mr S Murison-Bowie for his contribution on numerical expressions and to Mr A Powell for his work on the appendix of geographical names.

Finally I pay tribute to the editors of the Oxford University Press at Ely House, especially Christina Ruse, who gave so willingly of their knowledge of computer setting, care in the reading of proofs, and their judgement in the selection of a completely new set of illustrations.

London 1974 A S Hornby

specialist English

clav·icle /ˈklævɪkl/ *n* (anat) collar-bone. ⇨ the illus at **skeleton.**

cross-references to group illustrations

numbered headwords with the same spelling

numbered definitions

compounds and idiomatic expressions in bold type

countable and uncountable uses of the noun

con·cert[1] /ˈkɒnsət/ *n* **1** [C] musical entertainment, esp one given in a public hall by players or singers. **ˈ~ grand,** grand piano of the largest size, for ~s. **ˈ~-hall,** hall for ~s. ⇨ **music-hall.** ***at ˈ~ ˈpitch,*** (fig) in a state of full efficiency or readiness. ⇨ *keyed up* at **key**[2]. **2** [U] combination of voices or sounds: *voices raised in* ~. **3** [U] agreement; harmony: *working in ~ with his colleagues.*

con·cert[2] /kənˈsɜt/ *vi* arrange with others. Chiefly in **~ed** *adj* planned, performed, designed (by two or more together): *to take ~ed action; to make a ~ed attack.*

drivel /ˈdrɪvl/ *vt* (-ll-, US -l-) [VP2A,C] talk nonsense; talk childishly: *What's he ~ling about? He's still ~ling on.* □ *n* [U] silly nonsense; foolish talk. **~·ler,** US **~er** /ˈdrɪvlə(r)/ *n* person who ~s.

doubling of consonants

a box to indicate a change in the part of speech

over·sleep /ˌəʊvəˈslip/ *vi* (*pt,pp* -slept /-ˈslept/) [VP2A] sleep too long; continue sleeping after the proper time for waking: *He overslept and was late for work.*

irregular conjugations with phonetics

verb patterns

phonetics

pretty /ˈprɪtɪ/ *adj* (-ier, -iest) **1** pleasing and attractive without being beautiful or magnificent; *a ~ girl/garden/picture/piece of music. Go and make yourself ~,* tidy yourself, make up your face, etc. **ˈ~-~** *adj* (colloq) superficially ~ or charming. **2** fine; good: *a ~ wit; A ~ mess you've made of it!* (ironic) *You're a ~ sort of fellow.* **3** (colloq) considerable in amount or extent. ***a ~ penny,*** quite a lot: *It will cost you a ~ penny.* ***come to a ~ pass,*** ⇨ **pass**[1](2). ***a ~ kettle of fish,*** ⇨ **fish**[1](1).

comparative and superlative forms

stylistic values

stress in idioms

cross-references to other entries

headword

roll[2] /rəʊl/ *vt,vi* (For special uses with *adverbial particles* and *preps,* ⇨ **11** below.) . . . .

. . . . **11** [VP2C,15B] (special uses with *adverbial particles* and *preps*):

roll sth back, turn or force back, e g enemy forces.

roll in, come, arrive, in large numbers or quantities: *Offers of help are ~ing in.* ***be ˈ~ing in,*** **(a)** have large quantities of: *He's ~ing in money.* **(b)** be living in: *~ing in luxury.*

roll on, **(a)** be capable of being put on by ~ing. **(b)** (of time) pass steadily: *Time ~ed on.* **(c)** (of time, chiefly *imper*) come soon: *R~ on the day when I retire from this dull work!* ***~ sth on,*** put on by ~ing over a part of the body: *She ~ed her stockings on.* **ˈ~-on** *n* (woman's) elastic foundation garment ~ed on to the hips.

roll up, arrive; join a group: *Two or three latecomers ~ed up.* ***R~ up! R~ up!,*** used as an invitation to join others, e g possible customers at a street stall. ***~ sth up,*** (mil) drive the flank of (an enemy line) back and round.

part of speech

special arrangement for verbs which have many uses with adverbial particles and prepositions

numerous example phrases and sentences

stress in compounds

simple definitions

word-division

stimu·lus /ˈstɪmjʊləs/ *n* (*pl* -li /-laɪ/) [C] sth that stimulates: *work harder under the ~ of praise; a ~ to further exertions.*

irregular plurals with phonetics

American English spelling and pronunciation

tu·mour (US = **tu·mor**) /ˈtjumə(r) *US:* ˈtu-/ *n* diseased growth in some part of the body.

The content and arrangement of the entries

Compilers and printers of a dictionary have the problem of setting out a mass of detailed text clearly and economically. The use of too many abbreviations and symbols may make reference difficult but some are necessary in order to save valuable space. The user of this dictionary will benefit if he familiarizes himself with the notes that follow.

The headword The headword is printed in **bold type** and is positioned to the left of the column of text. The headword, together with its article (including definitions, derivatives, pronunciations, examples of usage, etc) is called an *entry*. The entries in the dictionary are listed in alphabetic order regardless of whether the headword is printed as a single word, is hyphened or is two or more separate words. A headword may be used as more than one part of speech each of which needs a long or complicated entry. Or a headword may have the same spelling as another but have unrelated meanings, sometimes with different pronunciations. In all these cases, the entries are listed separately with raised numbers after the headwords.

Examples

any[1] **bear**[1] **row**[1] **rebel**[1]
any[2] **bear**[2] **row**[2] **rebel**[2]
any[3] **row**[3]

If a headword has more than one spelling these are both given, separated by a comma.

Examples

gaol, jail
hic·cup, hic·cough

If there is an American English variant, or a British variant that is more common in American English, this is given in parentheses after the first spelling.

Examples

de·fence (US = **de·fense**)
ar·chae·ol·ogy (also **ar·che·ol-**)

If an alternative spelling belongs to another place in the alphabetic order of the headwords which is more than a page away from the entry, it is repeated in its alphabetic position with a cross-reference to the main entry.

Examples

en·quire ⇨ inquire
es·thetic ⇨ aesthetic

The boxes □ □ When a headword functions as two parts of speech and both are related and can be dealt with conveniently together, there is only one entry. The change from one part of speech to another is indicated by a square box □.

Examples

ap·peal as a *verb* and a *noun*
as·so·ci·ate as an *adjective* and a *noun*
at·tack as a *noun* and a *verb*

When a derivative in an article functions as two parts of speech the change from one part of speech to another is indicated by a smaller box ▫.

Example

at **al·co·hol**: **al·co·holic** as an *adjective* and a *noun.*

Derivatives, compounds and idiomatic expressions

A derivative is a word formed by the headword and a suffix. A compound is a combination of the headword and another word (written as one word, two separate words or separated by a hyphen). An idiom is the use of the headword in a phrase which must be learnt as a group, or the headword used idiomatically with an adverbial particle or preposition.

Derivatives, compounds and idiomatic expressions are printed in bold type.

Examples

bit·ter

a) a compound: **'~ -'sweet**

b) idioms: ***a ~ pill to swallow; to the ~ end***

c) derivatives: **~·ly ~·ness**

Note the typographical distinctions used: derivatives and compounds are in ordinary **bold** type; idiomatic expressions are in ***bold italic*** type.

Derivatives in *-able*, *-ly*, *-ment*, *-ness*, etc are not entered as separate headwords unless a separate article is useful. The adverb *hardly* is entered as a headword because it has little relevance to the adjective and adverb *hard*. 'He hardly worked' does not mean 'He worked hard'.

Phonetic information is given for derivatives wherever doubt might occur. In the case of compounds, stress is indicated. Stress is also shown in idiomatic expressions where the stress is not predictable. If there is a shift of stress which results in a change in pronunciation (usually of the vowel or vowels) a phonetic transcription of the derivative or necessary part is provided.

Example

adore /ə'dɔ(r)/ *v* **ador·ation** /ˌædə'reɪʃn/ *n*

A phonetic transcription is also given where the derivative contains a suffix which has more than one pronunciation or where the user may be uncertain of the pronunciation of the derivative.

Examples

bore² /bɔ(r)/ *v;* **~·dom** /-dəm/ *n*

bother /'boðə(r)/ *v;* **~·some** /-səm/ *adj*

con·tract² /kən'trækt/ *v;* **con·trac·tor** /-tə(r)/ *n*

See the article on pronunciation and stress on pp xii–xv of this Introduction for a full explanation with examples.

Hyphenation

For many compounds there is no agreement about the use or non-use of hyphens. Many, long established and familiar, are accepted as single words, for example *blackbird*, *breakthrough*. Many which were formerly written with a hyphen are now often written without one, for example *aircraft*, *breadcrumb*, *cornerstone*. Others are still most frequently written with a hyphen, for example *motor-vehicle*, *apple-pie*, *age-group*, and others are usually written as separate words, for example *contact lens*, *bank holiday*, *grass widow*. When there is no general agreement, a compound may appear in different styles, for example *headmaster*, *head-master* and *head master*. Choice of style depends on an editor's or writer's decision on usage or on the decision of a printing house. There are differences between British and American usage. The important point is, having decided on a written style for a compound, to be consistent.

Pronunciation Each headword is followed by a full phonetic transcription inside slanted strokes /—/. Transcriptions are also given for all derivatives which are not completely regular and/or predictable, and stress is indicated for compounds, idiomatic expressions and in the example phrases and sentences where any uncertainty might be possible. See pp xii–xv of this Introduction for details.

The definitions The various senses of a headword are marked off by numerals in bold type **1, 2, 3,** etc. If a compound, idiomatic expression or phrasal verb has more than one meaning, each is introduced by a letter in bold type: **(a), (b), (c),** etc.

Examples

battle - **battle-axe** has two meanings.

bear[2] - **bear oneself** has two meanings.

be·lieve - **believe in** has three meanings.

Example phrases and sentences These are a very important part of the text and follow the definitions in *italic* type. These examples are included to demonstrate the position of the headword or derivative in sentence patterns. They also indicate the kinds of style and context in which the headword or derivative may be used. If the example phrase or sentence is accompanied by notes or an explanation this is shown in ordinary type, in parentheses if it occurs within the example or, if at the end, preceded by a comma and not usually in parentheses.

These phrases and sentences illustrate everyday informal English unless the context is a formal one. Wherever such information is useful, stress is indicated.

The Tilde ~ ~ When a headword of more than three letters is repeated in an article, for example in illustrative phrases and sentences, a tilde ~ replaces the letters of the headword in order to save space. Thus at *elevate* the example *an ~d railway* is to be read as *an elevated railway*. A bold tilde **~** is also used to replace the headword in derivatives, idiomatic expressions and compounds.

Examples

care[1]

take ~ of **ˈ~·taker**

~ of **ˈ~·free**

take into ~ **ˈ~·worn**

If the headword is used in a derivative which is spelt with a capital letter this is shown by putting the first letter in its capital form before the tilde.

Example

care[1]

Child C~ Officer

When the tilde is used in illustrative sentences and phrases it does not necessarily follow the indications for word-division shown in the printed headword or derivative. In particular, the tilde may be followed by 's' in a plural form or 'd' or 'ed' in a past tense form. For guidance on word-division, choose from the breaks offered in the printed headword or derivative. Do not use the tilde as a guide.

The use of the slanted stroke / The slanted stroke / between two words or phrases in an idiomatic expression, example sentence or phrase, and occasionally in a definition, indicates that they are alternatives. For example, at **by²** there is *by accident/mistake* indicating the alternative expressions *by accident* and *by mistake*. *by/land/sea/air* gives three alternatives, *by land, by sea, by air*. Words in parentheses ( ) in idiomatic expressions indicate a wider choice of words which are likely to occur but which are not an essential part of the expression.

Nouns: singular and plural

There are some language problems which are adequately treated neither in dictionaries nor in the majority of textbooks on grammar. For those to whom English is a foreign language the problem of whether (and when) a noun may be used in the plural is often difficult. In some languages little or no distinction is made between singular and plural. In other languages nouns that may have plural forms (as French *nouvelles*) are, in English, used only in the singular (as English *news*).

In order to help the student of English to avoid such errors as *interesting informations, useful advices, an interesting news, a valuable furniture*, indications are supplied in this dictionary with most noun entries. These show which nouns, and which semantic varieties of nouns, may be used in the plural, and which may not, except with a change or extension of meaning. If a noun entry is followed by [C], or if [C] is placed after one of the numerals marking semantic varieties, it is a noun standing for something that may be counted. It may, therefore, be used with the indefinite article, or with *many*, numerals, and the plural form. If [U] is used, the noun stands for something (a material, quality, abstraction, etc) that cannot be counted, though it may be measured. Such a noun is not normally used with the indefinite article and has no plural form.

Difficulty may be taken as an example. Definition **1** is marked [U] and there are examples to illustrate its use: *with difficulty; without any/much difficulty*. Definition **2** is marked [C], with examples of the plural: *to raise difficulties. If you knew the difficulties I'm in!*

Irregular plurals, conjugations, etc

Irregular (and sometimes semi-irregular) plurals, conjugations, etc are included in parentheses immediately after the part of speech in an entry. Phonetic information is also provided where necessary.

Examples

bac·terium /bækˋtɪərɪəm/ *n* (*pl* -ria /-rɪə/)
baby /ˋbeɪbɪ/ *n* (*pl* -bies)
axis /ˋæksɪs/ *n* (*pl* axes /ˋæksiz/)
choose /tʃuz/ *vt,vi* (*pt* chose /tʃəʊz/, *pp* chosen /ˋtʃəʊzən/)
ap·ply /əˋplɑɪ/ *vt,vi* (*pt* -lied)

When the final consonant of a word is doubled, most frequently when conjugating verbs, this is also given after the part of speech.

Examples

chop¹ /tʃop/ *vt,vi* (-pp-)
bar² /bɑ(r)/ *vt* (-rr-)

American English does not follow the British English form of doubling consonants in certain words, particularly those ending in 'l'. In these cases both the British and American forms are given.

Examples

kid·nap *vt* (-pp-, US: -p-)
level³ *vt,vi* (-ll-, US: -l-)

Comparative and superlative These forms are given after the part of speech.

Examples

ample /ˈæmpl/ *adj* (-r, -est)
cold /kəʊld/ *adj* (-er, -est)
pretty /ˈprɪtɪ/ *adj* (-ier, -iest)

Such indications must not be taken as rules. The use of *more* or *most* is equally possible in many cases, the choice being dependent on context. 'The most lively and intelligent girl at the party' may be preferred to a mixture of two styles ('The liveliest and most intelligent girl at the party').

Entries for major verbs Entries for such verbs as *be*, *bring*, *come*, *get*, *make*, *send*, *sit* and *work* tend to be long and complex, partly because of the range of distinct meanings expressed by each of them, partly because of the ease with which they combine with other words to form special expressions, many of them highly idiomatic. Both of these features are taken into account in the organization of the entries for major, or 'basic' verbs.

Example **sit**

The standard arrangement of the main senses and special uses is as follows:
The principal meanings of **sit** are treated separately in a series of numbered sections (**1** to **7**), the more literal senses being given first and the more figurative later. Each section contains, in order:
1 a reference, in square brackets [ ], to the Verb Pattern(s) appropriate to the meaning in question;
2 the definition;
3 one or more illustrative phrases or sentences.
e g **7** [VP2C] (of clothes) suit, fit, hang: *That dress sits well/loosely*.

The verb patterns, which are set out in tabular form on pp xvi–xxvii, should be carefully noted, as an important difference in meaning often corresponds to a difference in the verb pattern.
The definition may contain, within parentheses, notes commonly associated with the verb in the sense indicated:
3 ... (of Parliament, a law court, a committee, etc) hold meetings
4 ... keep one's seat on (a horse etc)
5 ... (of birds) perch

Fixed expressions containing **sit** and a *noun* or *adjective* are printed in ***bold italic*** type. They are placed in sections according to the 'literal' meanings and grammatical patterns to which they most closely correspond, and are listed alphabetically according to the first letter of the *n* (or *adj*):
1 ... take or be in a position in which the body is upright and supported.. *The child is not big enough to sit at table yet.* ***sit to an artist,*** ... ***sit for an examination,*** ... ***sit for one's portrait,*** ... ***sit tight,*** ...

When an entry for the verb contains a number of fixed phrases, all of one pattern (eg *verb* + *noun*) which are not clearly related to any meaning of the *verb* alone, the expressions are grouped together and placed in a separate section.
Compounds which include a *non-finite* form of **sit** are placed after the finite uses to which they are closest in meaning:
sit for (a borough, etc) represent it in Parliament. Hence, ***the sitting member,*** the candidate ... who held the seat before the dissolution of Parliament.

5 ... (of birds) perch: *sitting on a branch.* **sitting duck,** an easy target or victim.

Compounds which are not related in meaning to any *finite* use of **sit** are placed with other compounds which they resemble in form. Thus **sitting tenant**, though unrelated in meaning to **sitting duck**, is placed after it because the two compounds have the same form (*present participle + noun*).

Special, ie figurative or idiomatic, uses of **sit** with *adverbial particles* and *prepositions* are dealt with in a separate section at the end of the entry (section **8**). The different combinations of **sit** + *adverbial particle* or **sit** + *preposition* are alphabetically arranged according to the initial letter of the *particle* or *preposition*.

Expressions containing both a *particle* and a *preposition* (or a *particle* and other additional words) follow the simpler combinations:

sit down, ... ***sit-down strike,*** ... ***sit down under*** (insults etc), ...
sit in, ... ***sit in on sth,*** ...

The difference between *particle* and *prepositional* uses of *down*, *in*, *off*, etc is indicated by varying the form printed in bold type, as follows: when *down* (etc) is a *particle*, the abbreviated *pronouns* 'sb' and 'sth' are *not* placed after it:

sit down, ... ***sit in,*** ... ***sit sth out,*** ... ***sit (sb) up,*** ...

when *down* (etc) is a *preposition*, it is followed by 'sb' or 'sth' (occasionally by both 'sb' and 'sth'):

sit in on sth, ... ***sit on sth,*** ... ***sit (up)on sb,*** ...

The difference between the intransitive and transitive uses of **sit** is also shown by varying the bold-face form. Nothing appears between **sit** and its *particle* (or *preposition*) when the verb is *intransitive*:

sit back, ... ***sit down,*** ... ***sit in on sth,*** ... ***sit (up)on sth.***

'sb' or 'sth' is placed between **sit** and the *particle* (or *preposition*) when it is used *transitively*:

sit sth out, ...

Occasionally a *verb + particle*, etc in a particular sense may be either transitive or intransitive. In such cases the *pronoun* is inserted in parentheses:

sit (sb) up, ...

Nouns formed from *sit + particle* are placed after the particular expression from which they are derived:

sit in, (of workers students, etc) demonstrate by occupying a building ... Hence, **`sit-in** *n* such a demonstration.

Adverbial particles

The term *adverbial particle* is used to designate an adverb of a particular class differing in many ways from other adverbs. In most cases these adverbs (eg *about*, *by*, *down*, *in*, *off*, *on*, *over*, *round*, *through*, *up*) are also used as prepositions.

They are important because, as described above, they enter into combinations with verbs to form collocations such as *blow up* (explode), *leave off* (stop), *go on* (continue), *give in* (yield), *give up* (abandon), *make out* (understand).

Another important feature of the adverbial particles is their position in the sentence. The following points should be well known to all learners who wish to write good English.

1 When there is no direct object in the sentence, the adverbial particle follows the verb immediately.

eg *Come in. Don't give up, whatever happens.*

2 When there is a direct object which is a personal pronoun, the adverbial particle is placed after, not before, the personal pronoun.

eg *I can't make it out. Put them on. Throw him out.*

3 When there is a direct object which is not a personal pronoun, the adverbial particle may be placed either before or after the direct object.

eg *Put your coat on. He put on his coat.*

In sentences where the direct object is long (eg when it is a noun clause), it is preferable to place the adverbial particle with the verb, and before the direct object.

eg *He gave away every book that he possessed.*
(cf *He gave his books away.*)

4 The adverbial particles may be placed at the beginning of exclamatory sentences.

eg *In you go! Away they went! Off went John!*

Note that in sentences of this kind subject and verb are inverted if the subject is a noun but not inverted if the subject is a personal pronoun.

5 The adverbial particles are compounded with the preposition *with* in verbless exclamations.

eg *Down with work! Up with the Republic! Off with his head! Away with him!*

Anomalous Verbs Some of the verb entries in this dictionary are followed by *anom fin*, short for *anomalous finite*. The anomalous verbs and their finites are set out in the table below.

	Non-finite forms			Finite forms	
	Infinitive	Present Participle	Past Participle	Present Tense	Past Tense
1	*be*	*being*	*been*	*am, is, are*	*was, were*
2	*have*	*having*	*had*	*have, has*	*had*
3	*do*	*doing*	*done*	*do, does*	*did*
4	—	—	—	*shall*	*should*
5	—	—	—	*will*	*would*
6	—	—	—	*can*	*could*
7	—	—	—	*may*	*might*
8	—	—	—	*must*	—
9	—	—	—	*ought*	—
10	—	—	—	*need*	—
11	—	—	—	*dare*	—
12	—	—	—	—	*used*

The 24 finite forms on the right-hand side of this table are important in English syntax. The grammar mechanisms of Affirmation, Negation and Interrogation cannot clearly be explained without reference to them.

Negative The negative sentence is made by placing the adverb *not* after the anomalous finite.

Thus, *I am → I am not; you can → you cannot; they ought → they ought not.* If an affirmative sentence contains no anomalous finite, the non-anomalous finite must first be replaced by using the corresponding

expanded tense, thus introducing *do*, *does*, or *did* (anomalous finites).
Thus, *I go → I do go → I do not go; he went → he did go → he did not go.*

Interrogative The chief mechanism for expressing the formal interrogative in modern English (and many European languages) is inversion of subject and finite.

Thus, *I am → am I? you ought → ought you? they must → must they?*

In modern English only the anomalous finites are normally inverted with the subject to form the interrogative. (*Went you* is archaic or biblical, and such constructions as '*Yes*', *said he* are exceptional.) If an affirmative sentence contains no anomalous finite, the procedure described above for the negative is followed.

Thus, *he comes → he does come → does he come? they came → they did come → did they come?*

Other examples of subject and finite inversion (always with one of the 24 anomalous finites) may be seen in sentences which contain a front-shifted adverbial.

eg Not only *did they* expect us but . . .
In no other way *can the matter* be explained.
Never before *have I* heard such fine singing.

The 24 anomalous finites are used to avoid repetition. This is seen clearly in answers to questions requiring a *yes* or *no* in the answer, and answers in which the subject is the essential part.

eg Have you read that book? Yes, I *have*. (Instead of *have read that book*.)
Shall you be seeing him soon? Yes, I *shall*. (Instead of *shall be seeing him soon*.)
Who discovered America? Columbus *did*. (Instead of *discovered America*.)

The 24 anomalous finites are used in other ways, eg

a) In Disjunctive Questions:
You can't come, *can* you?
You can come, *can*'t you?
He arrived late, *did*n't he?

b) In constructions expressing *also* and *also not*:
I can go there and so *can* you.
I went there and so *did* you.
I can't go; nor *can* you.
I didn't go; nor *did* you.

c) In comments which confirm or contradict:
You told us that yesterday. . . . Oh, yes, so I *did*!
Why didn't you tell us that yesterday? . . . But I *did*!

For a further description of the functions of these finites, the reader may consult *A Guide to Patterns and Usage in English.*

American English American English variants are always preceded by 'US'. American spellings follow the British forms in parentheses.

Examples

centre (US = **center**); **fla·vour** (US = **-vor**); **dia·logue** (US also **dia·log**) (meaning the British spelling is also used). American meanings or comments on American usage are preceded by (US), (US sl), (esp US), etc.

Examples

check·ers (US) = draughts.
sure ... **3** (colloq, esp US) certainly.

When the word or phrase is British English and rarely used in American English (GB) is placed before the definition. For examples see the entry for **flat**[1].

American pronunciation is also given alongside the British English forms. For details and examples, see p xii of this Introduction.

Cross-references An arrow (⇨) is used to indicate a reference to another part of the dictionary. This may be to another entry, in which case the arrow is followed by its headword, for example ⇨ neck (in the entry for *breathe*). If the headword is numbered, this is included in the reference, for example ⇨ bat[1] (in *belfry*). If the reference is to a particular definition, the definition number is also given, for example ⇨ one[3](3) at *another* which means 'look at the third entry for the word *one*, definition three'. If the reference is to a derivative the formula ⇨ (the named derivative in *italics*) at (the headword) is used, for example ⇨ *cast-~* at cast[1](3).

The same arrow is used to indicate references to illustrations. These occur fairly frequently since there are many labels on some illustrations, particularly those grouped thematically, which have cross-references from the dictionary entry to the illustration. The formula used is '⇨ the illus at . . .', for example '⇨ the illus at insect' is given at the entry for *ant*.

There are occasional references to the appendices of the dictionary, to Shakespeare's plays or to the books of the Bible. These follow a similar pattern, for example ⇨ App 4; ⇨ Mer of Ven; ⇨ Exod 8 : 3. Abbreviations used are those given in the relevant appendix of this dictionary.

The illustrations Illustrations can often define or describe vocabulary more easily and more economically than words. Illustrations have been used in the dictionary wherever they make a useful contribution to the text. There are photographs of scenes, buildings, artifacts, life-like sketches of the natural world and line drawings of mathematical shapes, technological diagrams and simple everyday objects. Many illustrations have been grouped under lexical subjects or themes (animals, bridges, tools, etc) and the careful labelling of individual parts (eg at skeleton, domestic animals, etc) increases their educational value.

Word-division In all types of English, handwritten, typewritten and printed, it is common practice to divide words when they require more space than is left at the end of a line. This division is indicated by adding a hyphen (-) immediately after the incomplete portion at the end of the line.

The rules which decide where a word may be divided vary considerably. In handwriting and typewriting many people avoid word-division altogether. The broad basis for the decision is syllabification but other considerations, such as derivation and intelligibility of either part of the divided word, play a part.

The headwords and derivatives in the dictionary include indications of where a word may be divided. These are shown by a bold dot (·) within the printed word. A word of one syllable should not be divided. Word division is not recommended for syllables of one letter at the beginning or end of a word, for example *apart*, *above*, *windy*, *bloody*. In short words such as *city*, *aura* no break is recommended. No division is indicated for *-ed* in the past tense or participle whether or not these are syllables, for example *walked*, *charged*, *wanted*, *invented*. Word division is not recommended within suffixes as *-able*, *-ible*, *-ably*, *-ibly*.

Thus **bear·able, in·cred·ibly** are given, *not* bear·a·ble, in·cred·i·bly. In general, word division should be avoided when only two letters are left after the break. The suffix *-ly* is an exception because it does not affect the intelligibility or pronunciation of the first part of the divided word when carried over to the next line (unless it is part of a longer suffix such as *-cally*, when a division at *-ly* is not recommended). Division after the first two letters of a word is acceptable, particularly by printers, and is therefore indicated in this dictionary though it is usually avoided in handwriting.

If a headword or derivative is normally written with a hyphen, the hyphen is shown, as in *never-ending*, *anti-hero*. Word division may be indicated elsewhere in these compounds but a break at the existing hyphen is to be preferred.

Sometimes a *tilde* is used in a derivative in the text. If word-division is permissible before the letters following the tilde, it is indicated, for example **~·able, ~·ly, ~·ment.** When no break is recommended no dot is shown, for example **~ed, ~s, ~al.**

Example

as·ton·ish indicates the following possible divisions:

as-
tonish (or) *aston-*
-ish

The second example is to be preferred.

Its derivatives are shown as

~ed where no break is recommended before *-ed.*

~·ment where a division is permissible before the suffix *-ment*. Thus *astonish-*
ment

Stylistic values and registers of specialist English usage

It is difficult for anyone learning English as a foreign language to know the stylistic context of the words. An error of judgement may result in the use of a pedantic, literary style in everyday conversation or slang in a formal context. It would help if these could all be indicated in dictionaries. It is possible to label some words as archaic, obsolete, formal, slang, poetic, colloquial, dated, humorous, obscene, etc. It is also possible to indicate the contexts or *registers* in which particular words are likely to occur, for example in art, law, commerce, sport, journalism, science, etc. Such indications are given in this dictionary and a list of the stylistic values and specialist English registers used is provided inside the front and back covers of the book.

There are thousands of words which cannot easily be labelled in these ways. These are the words which have their place in what is called the *active* vocabulary. They are the words and phrases which must be used correctly and fluently, without doubt or hesitation. There are thousands of words which need to be known but which need not be used or which are unlikely to be used. These are the words which have their place in what is called the *passive* vocabulary.

Commence is a word which needs to be known but *begin* or *start* are the more usual words in an active vocabulary. *Commence* is more formal and is part of a passive vocabulary. In the fiction of the 18th or 19th centuries, the verbs *court* and *woo* may occur. It is not usual today to speak of a girl being *wooed* or *courted*; such words are dated. However, they need to be known. They may still be heard in a broadcast on English literature; they may be used humorously; they may have a modern extension of meaning, as when parliamentary candidates are said to *woo the voters* before an election.

Colloquial and slang words present particular problems. The word *lousy* has a colloquial meaning. In colloquial style it is permissible to speak of 'lousy weather' or a 'lousy dinner' but it would be abusive to use it about a person, except perhaps in the colloquial meaning of being 'well-provided with something', for example 'He's lousy with money'.

Nothing dates more quickly than slang. *Flapper* was used in the early years of this century to describe a girl in her teens. It is not used today. Words such as *bird* or *chick* which were current a few years ago are now better avoided. Most girls will not be pleased to be called by these names today. To use slang which is out of date, or to use it in an unsuitable situation, is to betray oneself as being far from competent in English. A word or phrase in the dictionary labelled as colloquial, slang, modern slang, etc should therefore be used with caution. Unless there is complete confidence about the meaning of the word or expression, that it is in current usage and that it will not offend the company in which it is to be used, it should not be used. There are some slang words and phrases which may be considered coarse or vulgar. *Bloody* is not slang in such phrases as 'a murderer's bloody hands'. It is slang in such phrases as 'a bloody idiot', 'a bloody nuisance', 'a bloody marvellous film'. Some uses of *bloody* as a slang word will not offend most people today, as in the last example. Other slang uses may be considered by many people as coarse or vulgar.

Some words and phrases in this dictionary have the sign ⚠. These are taboo words which may be met, particularly in contemporary prose and drama, but which it is best not to use. The likelihood is that you will cause consternation. These words were never heard outside extremely vulgar contexts unless used in a meaningless sense in coarse colloquial style. There used to be a ban on the use of such words, particularly in print or on radio and television. Today the ban has been lifted and these words are often heard or seen. This does not mean that their use has become generally acceptable. The foreign learner of English may need to understand them but will do well to avoid using them, especially in conversation.

Definition of obscene words is simple if restricted to meaning and this dictionary has defined the common taboo words. However, they are widely used with no reference to their lexical context and these uses are difficult to explain. Those who have English as their first language do not need such explanations since such uses are often a meaningless habit. There are some obscene words which are also considered to be more obscene than others but such differences of acceptance are also difficult to explain. Examples may help the foreign learner:

1 *What are you doing?*
2 *Whatever are you doing?*
3 *What on earth/in the world are you doing?*
4 *What the hell are you doing?*
5 *What the bloody hell are you doing?*
6 *What the sodding hell are you doing?*
7 *What the fucking hell are you doing?*

1 is a simple unemotive question; 2 and 3 are more emphatic; 4 and 5 are progressively more emphatic or intense, and 5 is already offensive to many people; 6 and 7 will offend most people. *Sodding* and *fucking* are obscene here but meaningless since those who use these words in this way do so with no thought of the lexical meaning of the word.

Other words having the sign ⚠ are those which are offensive to a particular class or race, for example *nigger*. These are to be avoided.

Pronunciation and stress

This dictionary is arranged in paragraphs each of which begins with a headword. For every one of these headwords a full pronunciation is given using phonetic symbols from the authorised alphabet of the International Phonetic Association. A complete list of these symbols, with explanatory keywords, is given on the inside covers of the dictionary for easy reference. Each keyword displays the most usual spelling for the sound it represents.

Many English words have more than one common pronunciation. The pronunciations we have selected are those which research has suggested are the most common ones or, occasionally, the most suitable from other considerations for adoption by those whose mother tongue is not English.

Varieties of pronunciation

In most cases the pronunciation shown is equally suitable for use with speakers from any part of the English speaking world but, where this is not so, a choice of two forms is given, one representing the best known variety of British English the other the best known variety of American English. These varieties of English pronunciation are the only two which have been adopted widely for the purposes of teaching English as a foreign or second language. One of them is known as General American; the other may be conveniently termed General British (abbreviated to 'GA' and 'GB' in these notes). In its own country each of them is the variety of English most associated with national broadcasting and least restricted in its geographical distribution.

American pronunciation

The General American pronunciations are preceded by the abbreviation *US:* (US is used to identify all specifically American usages in this dictionary). The GA pronunciation is not given separately when the only difference between GA and GB would be the American use of that 'r' which is never sounded by GB speakers. Users of GA are recommended to sound the letter 'r' wherever it occurs in the ordinary spelling of all words whether or not it is given in our transcription.

Thus at the entries *arm* and *quarter*, where the transcriptions /ɑm/ and /ˋkwɔtə(r)/ only will be found, users of GA are expected to understand that they are recommended to adopt the pronunciations /ɑrm/ and /ˋkwɔrtər/ . It will be noticed that the symbol /ɜ/ is to be interpreted by GA users as a sound very similar to /ər/ but usually longer and associated with stress. For GB speakers it represents a sound with no r-quality of its own. Thus *hurry* in its GA pronunciation has no /r/ in its transcription. (The GB form of the word is shown as /ˋhʌrɪ/, the GA form as /ˋhɜɪ/.) An /r/ is shown in the transcription of a few words which is superfluous for GA users but has to go into the common version for the benefit of GB users, e g in *furry* /ˋfɜrɪ/, *currish* /ˋkɜrɪʃ/.

Separate GB and GA pronunciations will be found at entries such as:

ate /et *US:* eɪt/ **new** /nju *US:* nu/
half /hɑf *US:* hæf/ **vase** /vɑz *US:* veɪs/.

Quite often only part of a word needs to be re-spelt phonetically for GA users as at:

ceremony /ˋserəmənɪ *US:* –məʊnɪ/ **versatile** /ˋvɜsətɑɪl *US:* –tl/
civilisation /ˈsɪvḷɑɪˋzeɪʃn *US:* –ḷɪˋz–/ **voluntary** /ˋvoləntrɪ *US:* –terɪ/

These mean that the GA recommended pronunciations are /ˋserəməʊnɪ/, /ˈsɪvḷɪˋzeɪʃn/, /ˋvɜsətl/ and /ˋvolənterɪ/.

Stress notation It will be seen that at every headword which consists of more than one syllable /ˋ/ occurs immediately *before* the syllable on which the *principal stress* falls, as at:

any /ˋenɪ/ **increase** *n* /ˋɪnkris/
domestic /dəˋmestɪk/ **increase** *v* /ɪnˋkris/

When any other syllable which is usually stressed comes earlier in the word than the principal stress it is preceded by the sign for subordinate stress /ˈ/, as at:

unseen /ˈʌnˋsin/ **examination** /ɪgˈzæmɪˋneɪʃn/
university /ˈjunɪˋvɜsətɪ/ **individuality** /ˈɪndɪˈvɪdʒʊˋælətɪ/

Syllable boundaries The hyphen (-) is also used in a few places to clarify the phonetic point of division between two parts of a compound word, as at *biped, cartridge, partridge* etc. For example **cartridge** /ˋkɑ-trɪdʒ/ is so shown to suggest that the junction between the two halves of the word should be pronounced as in *car-trip* and not as in *cart-ride*.

Inflections Plurals and past-tense forms are not provided with pronunciations unless they are *phonetically* irregular. They may be phonetically quite regular even though there is some irregularity in their spelling.

For example, the plural of *sky* is the semi-irregular *skies* but, since its spoken form is made in exactly the way it would be if there were no irregularity in its spelling, the pronunciation /skɑɪz/ is not offered. On the other hand the plural of *basis* is irregular both in sound and spelling so it appears as *bases* /ˋbeɪsiz/. Some words have alternative inflections, one regular and the other irregular. For instance at *abacus* the regular plural *abacuses* is not transcribed phonetically but the irregular form *abaci* is given: /ˋæbəsɑɪ/. The verb *lean* has a past form *leaned* which is regular in spelling and recommended to be given the regular pronunciation /lind/ which it would be a waste of space to show. It also has another irregular past form *leant* for which a pronunciation is provided /lent/. Those who would like to be reminded of the regular patterns of the formation of plurals and past participles in spoken English should note the following:

i. Plurals are formed by the addition of /-z/ except that
 a) if the final sound of the noun's singular is /p, t, k, f or θ/ the addition is /-s/.
 b) if the final sound of the noun's singular is /s, z, ʃ, ʒ, tʃ or dʒ/ the addition is /-ɪz/.

ii. Past participles are formed by the addition of /-d/ except that
 a) if the final sound of the verb's present tense is /p, k, f, θ, s, ʃ or tʃ/, the addition is /-t/;
 b) if the final sound of the verb's present tense is /t or d/ the addition is /-ɪd/.

Combinations Within most entries, running on from the treatment of the headword, combinations follow in alphabetical order. Since the pronunciation of the headword has already been made clear, and since the pronunciation of any other word with which it is combined can be found – if the reader is not certain of it – at its own entry as a headword, there is usually no need for full transcription of any of these combinations. However, if they consist of single new words, printed with the tilde (the sign ~, which is used to avoid repetition of the headword) followed without any intervening space by the next word or linked to it with a hyphen, then their full stress patterns are always indicated, as at:

hot: `hotbed 'hot-`blooded `hothouse `hot-plate hot-`water-bottle
play: `child's-~ `~-boy `~-mate `~-acting `~-wright

Invisible compounds, etc. Large numbers of the combinations into which our headwords enter consist of phrasal verbs, idiomatic fixed phrases, compound nouns and compound adjectives etc which, unlike the combinations printed in one solid piece or linked by hyphens, show no visible evidence of the fact that they may behave very much as they would if they were linked in spelling. Many of these compound adjectives and compound nouns etc exist in two or more printed forms (solid, hyphened or spaced) one of which is favoured by one group of writers and printing houses, one by another.

For most of the unlinked sequences of words the very important principal stress usually falls on the last 'non-grammatical' word of the combination.

A 'non-grammatical' word is usually easily distinguished from a 'grammatical' word. (They are sometimes also called 'form' and 'content' words). A grammatical word serves to show the relationships of the main parts of an expression to each other. Such words are chiefly the articles, monosyllabic prepositions, conjunctions, object pronouns and auxiliary verbs. The non-grammatical words such as main verbs, nouns, adjectives and most adverbs are usually stressed.

As even those with quite a slight knowledge of English will easily notice, all unlinked combinations are usually stressed on non-grammatical words with their principal stress on the last of these. Thus the stress values of enormous numbers of these headword combinations can be *conveyed* without our actually marking them. Nevertheless, whenever there might be doubt about the stress values of such sequences of words, stress markings are provided. This very wide coverage extends not only to the sub-headwords (shown in **bold** type) but to the idiomatic fixed phrases and phrasal verbs (shown in ***bold italic*** type) and also, where useful, to other fixed phrases and compound nouns etc appearing (in *italic* type) in the examples of the uses of headwords and sub-headwords in phrases and sentences.

However, within full sentences, the stress patterns of a great many words very often have to be adjusted to their surroundings. There stress is not usually indicated because it might distort rather than display properly the *basic* stress pattern which must be learnt as an integral feature of every English word.

For example, it will be seen at *circuit* that the fixed phrase *make a circuit of* is unmarked because its stress pattern is predictable. It has no stresses on the article or the preposition but subordinate stress on *make* and principal stress on the final non-grammatical word, and is thus to be taken as stressed *'make a `circuit of*. Under the headword *cling* the two alternative phrases shown as *cling to/together* are to be interpreted as having no stress on the preposition but principal stress on the final non-grammatical word *together*: thus conveying *`cling to* and *'cling to`gether*.

Under the headword *citrus* the example of its use attributively is the 'invisible' compound noun *`~ fruit* which is provided with a stress mark to show that it does not have the stress values of *'bitter `fruit* but those of *`grapefruit*. Similarly at *clerk* the examples *a `bank ~* and *a 'corre`spondence ~* are marked for stress whereas *the Town C~* needs no marking as it is to be interpreted as *the 'Town `Clerk*. At *clock* the fixed phrase *work against the clock* is unmarked because it has the highly predictable stress values ˈ*work a*ˈ*gainst the* ˋ*clock.* On the other hand the fixed phrase ˈ*put the* ˋ*clock back* has been stress-marked because it has irregular absence of stress on the adverb *back.* For further examples see:

in ˋ*that case, for the* ˋ*most part, to be* ˋ*coining money, (have)* ˋ*other fish to fry, a* ˋ*pretty kettle of fish, (have) a good* ˋ*head on one's shoulders, paddle one's* ˋ*own canoe,* etc.

No English Dictionary has ever seriously attempted to reflect the extent to which compound nouns etc occur in print in each of the three possible forms (a) fully joined (b) linked by hyphens (c) unlinked. Even if reliable information on their relative frequencies were available, it would hardly be possible to give space to it in a one-volume dictionary. What should be clear is that most English compound words are printed unlinked but, because they are to a great extent of self-evident meaning, only a selection of specimens of them can be admitted to any dictionary however large. These are items like *bank manager*, *exercise book*, *drama course*, *holiday plans*, *danger signal*, *traffic jam*, etc. Fortunately compound nouns of this sort (noun plus noun) which are so numerous in English can usually be safely spoken with principal stress on the first word.

Note: Probably the most frequent of all items occurring in combinations is the word *man*. If the compound is shown solid the pronunciation of *man* is regularly transcribed. Whenever the singular is /-mən/ the plural is to be taken to be /-mən/ also. If the compound is hyphenated or 'invisible' (ie shown as separate words) the pronunciation is to be taken to be /-mæn/ and the plural /–mən/. Examples:

fisher ... ... ˋ**~·man** /-mən/
laundry ... ... ˋ**~-man** (to be understood as /-mæn/)

Derivatives At the end of each entry appear any words derived from the headword by the addition of various endings which in most cases have no independent existence. The majority of these derivatives are formed by the addition of one or more of a mere dozen or so extremely well known suffixes. These are chiefly:

-able /-əbl/, *-er* /-ə(r)/, *-est* /-ɪst/, *-ing* /-ɪŋ/, *-ish* /-ɪʃ/, *-ism* /-ɪzm/, *-ist* /-ɪst/, *-ive* /-ɪv/, *-less* /-ləs/, *-ly* /-lɪ/, *-ment* /-mənt/, *-ness* /-nəs/, *-(a)tion* /-(ˋeɪ)ʃn/, *-y* /-ɪ/.

Almost all of these suffixes are invariable in pronunciation. When one of them takes a form other than the normal one shown above – eg when *-ment* is a verb not a noun suffix – its pronunciation is given. Various other similarly common suffixes which, however, are variable or may be liable to misinterpretation are regularly given phonetic transcriptions eg *-age, -ess, -et, -ine, -ful, -fully, -ically, -ible* etc. See Appendix 3 for a detailed list of suffixes and prefixes with pronunciations.

Since most of these very common derivative endings do not cause any change in the stress patterns of the headwords to which they are added, stress markings are not ordinarily shown on derivatives.

If the headword does not have exactly the same pronunciation or stress pattern as it does when it is part of a derivative, the pronunciation of the derivative is given, as at:

condemn /kənˋdem/ ... ... **condemnation** /ˈkondemˋneɪʃn/
restore /rɪˋstɔ(r)/ ... ... **restoration** /ˈrestəˋreɪʃn/

Summary of verb patterns

Notes on the main features of this list of Verb Patterns are given below together with examples of usage. Some patterns, for example [VP6C] and [VP6D] or [VP12A] and [VP12B], seem to be identical; the differences are explained in the notes but reference to *A Guide to Patterns and Usage*, second edition is advised for a complete description of the patterns. Abbreviations used: S = Subject *vi* = intransitive verb *vt* = transitive verb DO = Direct Object IO = Indirect Object anom fin = anomalous finite.

[VP1]	S + BE + complement/adjunct
[VP2A]	S + *vi*
[VP2B]	S + *vi* + (*for*) adverbial adjunct
[VP2C]	S + *vi* + adverbial adjunct, etc
[VP2D]	S + *vi* + adjective/noun/pronoun
[VP2E]	S + *vi* + present participle/participial phrase
[VP3A]	S + *vi* + preposition + noun/pronoun/gerund
[VP3B]	S + *vi* + (preposition + *it*) + clause, etc
[VP4A]	S + *vi* + *to*-infinitive (phrase)
[VP4B]	S + *vi* + *to*-infinitive (phrase)
[VP4C]	S + *vi* + *to*-infinitive (phrase)
[VP4D]	S + SEEM/APPEAR, etc + (*to be*) + adjective/noun
[VP4E]	S + SEEM/APPEAR/HAPPEN/CHANCE + *to*-infinitive (phrase)
[VP4F]	S + finite of BE + *to*-infinitive (phrase)
[VP5]	S + anom fin + infinitive (phrase)
[VP6A]	S + *vt* + noun/pronoun
[VP6B]	S + *vt* + noun/pronoun
[VP6C]	S + *vt* + gerund, etc
[VP6D]	S + *vt* + gerund, etc
[VP6E]	S + NEED/WANT, etc + gerund, etc (passive)
[VP7A]	S + *vt* + (*not*) + *to*-infinitive, etc
[VP7B]	S + HAVE/OUGHT, etc + (*not*) + *to*-infinitive
[VP8]	S + *vt* + interrogative pronoun/adverb + *to*-infinitive
[VP9]	S + *vt* + *that*-clause
[VP10]	S + *vt* + dependent clause/question
[VP11]	S + *vt* + noun/pronoun + *that*-clause
[VP12A]	S + *vt* + noun/pronoun (IO) + noun/pronoun (DO)
[VP12B]	S + *vt* + noun/pronoun (IO) + noun/pronoun (DO)
[VP12C]	S + *vt* + noun/pronoun + noun/pronoun
[VP13A]	S + *vt* + noun/pronoun (DO) + *to* + noun/pronoun (phrase)
[VP13B]	S + *vt* + noun/pronoun (DO) + *for* + noun/pronoun (phrase)
[VP14]	S + *vt* + noun/pronoun (DO) + preposition + noun/pronoun (phrase)
[VP15A]	S + *vt* + noun/pronoun (DO) + adverbial phrase
[VP15B]	S + *vt* + noun/pronoun (DO) + adverbial particle
	S + *vt* + adverbial particle + noun/pronoun (DO)
[VP16A]	S + *vt* + noun/pronoun (DO) + *to*-infinitive (phrase)
[VP16B]	S + *vt* + noun/pronoun (DO) + *as/like* + noun (phrase) or clause
[VP17]	S + *vt* + noun/pronoun + (*not*) + *to*-infinitive
[VP18A]	S + *vt* + noun/pronoun + infinitive (phrase)
[VP18B]	S + *vt* + noun/pronoun + infinitive (phrase)
[VP18C]	S + HAVE + noun/pronoun + infinitive (phrase)
[VP19A]	S + *vt* + noun/pronoun + present participle (phrase)
[VP19B]	S + *vt* + noun/pronoun + present participle (phrase)
[VP19C]	S + *vt* + noun/pronoun/possessive + *ing* form of the verb
[VP20]	S + *vt* + noun/pronoun + interrogative + *to*-infinitive (phrase)
[VP21]	S + *vt* + noun/pronoun + dependent clause/question
[VP22]	S + *vt* + noun/pronoun/gerund (DO) + adjective
[VP23]	S + *vt* + noun/pronoun (DO) + noun (phrase)
[VP24A]	S + *vt* + noun/pronoun (DO) + past participle (phrase)
[VP24B]	S + HAVE + noun/pronoun (DO) + past participle (phrase)
[VP24C]	S + HAVE/GET + noun/pronoun (DO) + past participle (phrase)
[VP25]	S + *vt* + noun/pronoun (DO) + (*to be*) + adjective/noun

Verb patterns

The verb patterns in this dictionary supply information on syntax. If the learner spends a few hours on them, he will be able to avoid numerous possible errors. Familiarity with them will enable him to use verbs in the ways that are in accordance with usage.

A person learning English as a foreign language may be tempted to form sentences by analogy. He hears and sees sentences of the type 'Please tell me the meaning' or 'Please show me the way' (ie with an indirect object followed by a direct object). By analogy he forms the incorrect sentence *'Please explain me the meaning'. He hears and sees such sentences as 'I intend to come', 'I propose to come', and 'I want to come', and by analogy he forms the sentence *'I suggest to come' (instead of 'I suggest that I should come'). He hears and sees such sentences as 'I asked him to come', 'I told him to come', and 'I wanted him to come', and by analogy he forms such sentences as *'I proposed him to come' and *'I suggested him to come' (instead of 'I proposed/suggested that he should come'). He notes that 'He began to talk about the matter' means the same as 'He began talking about the matter' and supposes, wrongly, that 'He stopped to talk about the matter' means the same as 'He stopped talking about the matter'. Such misapprehensions are natural. It is equally natural for the learner to use a verb pattern from his own language with the equivalent English verb. The ordinary grammar book and dictionary often fail to supply adequate information on such points. The patterns below, with the numbered indications given with the verb entries (eg [VP5], [VP6A], [VP21]) do give guidance.

A full treatment of these patterns may be found in *A Guide to Patterns and Usage in English*, second edition. This is a complete revision and renumbering of patterns of the first edition, as used in the first and second editions of the dictionary.

Note: The use of the asterisk * indicates that the phrase or sentence is an example of *incorrect* structure.

Explanation and demonstration of the verb patterns

The tables below give examples of the 25 patterns summarized above. The pattern given in the dictionary for *congratulate* is [VP14] and this is used as a model for [VP14]: *congratulate sb on sth*. One of the patterns for *lend* is [VP12A], and this is used as a model for [VP12A]: *lend sb sth.* These patterns, summarized in this way, are supplied with the verb entries in the body of the dictionary. Thus, after the entry **absolve,** there are the numbered references [VP6A,14], followed by **~ (from),** showing that the verb may be used in the pattern *absolve a man (from a vow)*. After the entry **accede** there are numbered references [VP2A, 3A], followed by **~ (to),** showing that the preposition required here is *to*, as in *to accede to a proposal.*

[VP1] This pattern is for the verb *be*. The subject complement may be a noun, a pronoun, an adjective, an adjective phrase (e g a prepositional group). There may be an adverbial adjunct or an infinitive phrase.

Subject + BE	complement/adjunct
1 *This is*	*a book.*
2 *This umbrella is*	*mine.*
3 *The children are*	*asleep.*
4 *This book is*	*for you.*
5 *This is*	*where I work.*

There are numerous variations with introductory *there/it*.

There/It + BE	subject
1 *There was*	*a large crowd.*
2 *It was impossible*	*to go further.*
3 *It was a pity*	*the weather was so bad.*

[VP2A] This pattern is for verbs which may be used without a complement. Such verbs are called complete intransitive verbs. Adjuncts are possible but not essential.

Subject	*vi*
1 *We all*	*breathe, drink and eat.*
2 *The moon*	*rose.*
3 *A period of political unrest*	*followed.*

There are variations with introductory *there/it*.

1 *There followed*	*a long period of political unrest.*
2 *It doesn't matter*	*whether we start now or later.*

That-clauses occur after *seem*, *appear*, *happen*, *chance* and *follow*.

1 *It seemed*	*(that) the day would never end.*
2 *It so chanced/happened*	*that we were out when she called.*
3 *It does not follow*	*that he was completely in the wrong.*

[VP2B] Verbs in this pattern are used with an adverbial adjunct of distance, duration, weight, cost, etc. *For* may occur before adverbials of distance and duration. An indirect object may occur after *cost*, *last* and *take* (meaning 'require').

Subject + *vi*	(*for*) + adverbial adjunct
1 *We walked*	*(for) five miles.*
2 *The meeting lasted*	*two hours.*
3 *The book cost (me)*	*£1.20.*
4 *This box weighs*	*five kilos.*

[VP2C] Many intransitive verbs are used with an adverbial adjunct (including an adverbial particle alone, or an adverbial particle followed by a preposition).

Subject + *vi*	adverbial adjunct, etc
1 *Go*	*away!*
2 *Please come*	*in.*
3 *I'll soon catch*	*up with you.*
4 *It's getting*	*on for midnight.*
5 *It looks*	*like rain/as if it were going to rain.*

[VP2D] Verbs in this pattern are followed by an adjective, a noun or, in the case of a reflexive verb, a pronoun. Inchoative verbs (see *A Guide to Patterns and Usage*) and verbs of the senses (*smell*, *taste*, *feel*) are among the many verbs used in this pattern.

Subject + *vi*	adjective/noun/pronoun
1 *Her dreams have come*	*true.*
2 *The fire has burnt*	*low.*
3 *She married*	*young.*
4 *He died*	*a millionaire.*
5 *Later he became*	*an acrobat.*
6 *You're not looking*	*yourself.*

[VP2E] In this pattern the predicative adjunct may be a present participle or participial phrase. After *come* a noun or adjective, always with the definite article, may be used.

Subject + *vi*	present participle, etc
1 *She lay*	*smiling at me.*
2 *Don't come*	*the bully/the artful/the high and mighty over me.*
3 *Do you like to go*	*dancing?*
4 *The children came*	*running to meet us.*

[VP3A] Verbs in this pattern are followed by a preposition and its object (which may be a noun, pronoun, gerund, phrase, or clause). The verb and preposition function as a unit.

Subject + *vi*	preposition + noun/pronoun/gerund
1 *You may rely*	*on that man/his discretion/his being discreet.*
2 *Can I count*	*on your help?*
3 *What has happened*	*to them?*

An infinitive phrase may follow the noun.

1 *We are waiting*	*for our new car to be delivered.*
2 *I rely*	*on you to be discreet.*
3 *She pleaded*	*with the judge to have mercy.*

[VP3B] The preposition is omitted before a *that*-clause, thus producing the same word order as in [VP9] (for transitive verbs).

He insisted on his innocence. [VP3A]
He insisted that he was innocent. [VP3B]
Cf He declared that he was innocent. [VP9]

The preposition may be retained in some cases if its object is a dependent question or clause.

Subject + *vi*	(preposition + *it*)	clause, etc
1 *I agree*		*that it was a mistake.*
2 *You must see*	*(to it)*	*that this sort of thing never occurs again.*
3 *I hesitated*	*(about)*	*whether to accept your offer.*
4 *Have you decided*	*(upon)*	*where you will go for your holidays?*
5 *Don't worry*	*(about)*	*how the money was lost.*

[VP4A] In this pattern the verb is followed by a *to*-infinitive of purpose, outcome, or result.

Subject + *vi*	*to*-infinitive (phrase)
1 *We stopped*	*to rest/to have a rest.*
2 *How did you come*	*to know her?*
3 *Will he live*	*to be ninety?*
4 *Someone has called*	*to see you.*

[VP4B] The infinitive may be equivalent to a clause.

Subject + *vi*	*to*-infinitive (phrase)
1 *He awoke*	*to find the house on fire.*
2 *The good old days have gone*	*never to return.*
3 *Electronic music has clearly come*	*to stay.*
4 *The drunken man awoke*	*to find himself in a ditch.*

[VP4C] The infinitive adjunct is used after some verbs which, in [VP3A], are used with prepositions.

Don't trouble/bother about that.
Don't trouble/bother to meet me.

Subject + *vi*	*to*-infinitive (phrase)
1 *She hesitated*	*to tell anyone.*
2 *She was longing*	*to see her family again.*
3 *He agreed*	*to come at once.*

[VP4D] The verbs *seem* and *appear* are used in this pattern. If the infinitive is *be* with an adjective or noun as complement, *to be* may be omitted (unless the adjective is one that is used only predicatively, as in [VP4E]).

Subject + SEEM/APPEAR	*(to be)* + adjective/noun
1 *He seemed*	*(to be) surprised at the news.*
2 *This seems*	*(to be) a serious matter.*
3 *I seem*	*(to be) unable to enjoy myself.*

There is a variation of this pattern with introductory *it*, when the subject is an infinitive or gerundial phrase, or a clause.

It + SEEM/APPEAR	adjective/noun	subject
1 *It seemed*	*reasonable*	*to try again.*
2 *It seems*	*a pity*	*to waste them.*
3 *It doesn't seem*	*much use*	*going on.*
4 *It appears*	*unlikely*	*that we'll arrive in time.*

[VP4E] If the adjective after *seem/appear* is used only predicatively (e g *awake*, *asleep*, *afraid*), *to be* is obligatory. (**The baby seems asleep*.) *Happen* and *chance* are also used in this pattern.

Subject + SEEM/APPEAR/ HAPPEN/CHANCE	*to*-infinitive (phrase)
1 *The baby seems*	*to be asleep/to be sleeping.*
2 *My enquiries seem*	*to have been resented.*
3 *She happened*	*to be out when I called.*
4 *We chanced*	*to meet in the park.*

[VP4F] The finites of *be* are used with a *to*-infinitive to indicate a variety of meanings. See *be*[4](3).

	Subject + finite of BE	*to*-infinitive (phrase)
1	*We're*	*to be married in May.*
2	*At what time am I*	*to come?*
3	*How am I*	*to pay my debts?*

[VP5] In this pattern the auxiliary verbs or anomalous finites *will/would, shall/should, can/could, must, dare, need* are followed by a bare infinitive (ie without *to*). The phrases *had better, had/would rather* and *would sooner* fit into this pattern.

	Subject + anom fin	infinitive (phrase)
1	*You may*	*leave now.*
2	*You needn't*	*wait.*
3	*You'll*	*find it in that box.*
4	*I didn't dare*	*tell anyone.*
5	*You'd better*	*start at once.*

[VP6A] The verbs in this pattern have a noun or pronoun as direct object. Conversion to the passive voice is possible.

	Subject + *vt*	noun/pronoun
1	*We all enjoyed*	*the film.*
2	*We all had*	*a good time.*
3	*Everyone likes*	*her.*

[VP6B] The verbs in this pattern have a noun or pronoun as direct object, but conversion to the passive voice is not possible. *Have*, meaning 'possess/take/eat/drink', follows this pattern. Reflexive verbs, and verbs with cognate objects, follow this pattern.

	Subject + *vt*	noun/pronoun
1	*Have you had*	*breakfast yet?*
2	*She has*	*green eyes.*
3	*Have you hurt*	*yourself?*
4	*She smiled*	*her thanks.*
5	*He dreamed*	*a very odd dream.*

[VP6C] In this pattern the object is a gerund.

	Subject + *vt*	gerund, etc
1	*She enjoys*	*playing tennis.*
2	*Have you finished*	*talking?*
3	*I resent*	*being spoken to so rudely.*

[VP6D] In this pattern the object is a gerund. This may be replaced by a *to*-infinitive. For the difference between *like swimming* and *like to swim*, see the notes in *A Guide to Patterns and Usage*.

	Subject + *vt*	gerund, etc
1	*She loves*	*going to the cinema.*
2	*I'll continue*	*working while my health is good.*
3	*He began*	*talking about his clever children.*

[VP6E] After *need, want* (= need) and *won't/wouldn't bear*, the gerund is equivalent to a passive infinitive.

Subject + NEED/WANT, etc	gerund, etc (passive)
1 *My shoes want*	*mending.*
2 *He'll need*	*looking after.*
3 *His language wouldn't bear*	*repeating.*

(3 = *His language wouldn't bear* (= was too bad) *to be repeated.*)

[VP7A] In this pattern the object of the verb is a *to*-infinitive or infinitive phrase. (For intransitive verbs with the same word order, see [VP4].)

Subject + *vt*	(*not*) + *to*-infinitive, etc
1 *Do they want*	*to go?*
2 *He pretended*	*not to see me.*
3 *We hope/expect/intend*	*to start a youth club.*
4 *I forgot/remembered*	*to post your letters.*

[VP7B] The finites of *have* in this pattern indicate obligation. In colloquial style *have got to* is more usual than *have to*. *Ought* is included in [VP7B]. It could be placed in [VP7A].

Subject + HAVE/OUGHT, etc	(*not*) + *to*-infinitive, etc
1 *Do you often have*	*to work overtime?*
2 *You don't have*	*to go to the office on Saturdays, do you?*
3 *You ought*	*not to waste your money there.*

[VP8] In this pattern the object of the verb is a conjunctive (an interrogative pronoun or adverb, except *why*, or *whether*), followed by a *to*-infinitive.

Subject + *vt*	interrogative pronoun/adverb + *to*-infinitive
1 *Do you know/see*	*how to do it?*
2 *I couldn't decide*	*what to do next.*
3 *I found out*	*where to turn off.*
4 *You must learn*	*when to give advice and when to be silent.*

[VP9] The object of the verb is a *that*-clause. *That* is often omitted, except after more formal verbs (eg *decide, intend*).

Subject + *vt*	*that*-clause
1 *I suppose*	*you'll be there.*
2 *I wish*	*you wouldn't interrupt.*
3 *Do you think*	*it'll rain?*
4 *We intended*	*that John should be invited.*

[VP10] In this pattern the object of the verb is a dependent clause or question. The clause is introduced by a conjunctive (a relative adverb or pronoun, *what*, or *whether/if*).

Subject + *vt*	dependent clause/question
1 *Does anyone know*	*how it happened?*
2 *Tell me*	*what you've bought.*
3 *I wonder*	*whether/if he'll come.*
4 *She asked*	*why I was late.*

[VP11] The verb is followed by a noun or pronoun and a *that*-clause.

	Subject + *vt*	noun/pronoun	*that*-clause
1	*He warned*	*us*	*that the roads were icy.*
2	*I convinced*	*him*	*that I was innocent.*
3	*We satisfied*	*ourselves*	*that the plan would work.*

[VP12A] The verb is followed by an indirect object (I O) and a direct object (D O). The indirect object is equivalent to a prepositional adjunct with *to*, as in [VP13A].

	Subject + *vt*	I O	D O
1	*Won't you lend*	*him*	*your car?*
2	*He doesn't owe*	*me*	*anything.*
3	*He denied/grudged*	*her*	*nothing.*

[VP12B] In this pattern the indirect object is equivalent to a prepositional adjunct with *for*, as in [VP13B].

	Subject + *vt*	I O	D O
1	*She made*	*herself*	*a new dress.*
2	*Will you do*	*me*	*a favour?*
3	*She cooked*	*her husband*	*some sausages.*

[VP12C] Verbs in this pattern are rarely or never convertible to [VP13]. The labels I O and D O are not used.

	Subject + *vt*	noun/pronoun	noun/pronoun
1	*Ask*	*him*	*his name.*
2	*I envy*	*you*	*your fine garden.*
3	*He struck*	*the door*	*a heavy blow.*

[VP13A] In this pattern the verb is followed by a direct object, the preposition *to*, and the prepositional object. It corresponds to [VP12A].

	Subject + *vt*	D O	*to* + noun/pronoun (phrase)
1	*She told*	*the news*	*to everyone in the village.*
2	*He sold*	*his old car*	*to one of his neighbours.*
3	*I've sent*	*presents*	*to most of my family.*

[VP13B] In this pattern the preposition is *for*. It corresponds to [VP12B].

	Subject + *vt*	D O	*for* + noun/pronoun (phrase)
1	*She made*	*a new dress*	*for her youngest daughter.*
2	*Will you do*	*a favour*	*for a friend of mine?*
3	*Can you cash*	*this cheque*	*for me?*

[VP14] In this pattern the verb is followed by a direct object and a preposition and its object. This pattern is not convertible to [VP12], as are [VP13A] and [VP13B]. 'Give somebody something' [VP13A] may be converted to 'Give something to somebody' [VP12A]. 'Explain something to somebody' cannot be converted to '*Explain somebody something'.

The preposition is linked to the verb and they must be learnt together, e g 'congratulate somebody *on* something', 'compare one thing *to/with* another'. Note that in [VP14] the prepositional phrase is variable, e g 'put something *on/under the table, in the drawer*'.

Subject + *vt*	DO	prep	noun (phrase/clause)
1 *We congratulated*	*him*	*on*	*his success.*
2 *Compare*	*the copy*	*with*	*the original.*
3 *He compared*	*the heart*	*to*	*a pump.*
4 *I explained*	*my difficulty*	*to*	*him.*

Variations are possible. If the DO is long, the prepositional phrase may precede it. Introductory *it* may be used when there is an infinitive phrase or a clause.

Subject + *vt*	prep + noun	DO
1 *I explained*	*to him*	*the impossibility of granting his request.*
2 *I must leave it*	*to your own judgement*	*to decide whether you should offer your resignation.*

Compare: Subject + *vt*	DO	prep + noun
1 *I explained*	*the problem*	*to him.*
2 *I must leave*	*the decision*	*to you.*

[VP15A] In [VP15] the DO is followed by an adverbial phrase of place, duration, distance, etc which is obligatory. 'I read the book' [VP6] is a complete sentence, but '*I put the book' is not. *Put* needs an adjunct. eg 'I put the book *down/away/on the shelf*'.

With verbs marked [VP15A] the adverbial is a prepositional phrase.

Subject + *vt*	DO	adverbial phrase
1 *Don't let the child put*	*his head*	*out of the car window/into that plastic bag.*
2 *The secretary showed*	*me*	*to the door/into the reception room.*
3 *Please put*	*these papers*	*in that drawer/on that file/in my briefcase.*

[VP15B] In this pattern the adverbial particles (see p vi above) are used. When the DO is a personal pronoun, the adverbial particle follows. When the DO is a noun or noun phrase, the adverbial particle may either follow or precede. If the DO is long, the adverbial particle usually precedes.

Subject + *vt*	DO	adverbial particle
1 *Take*	*them/your shoes*	*off.*
2 *Don't throw*	*it/that old hat*	*away.*
3 *Did you wind*	*it/the clock*	*up?*

Subject + *vt*	adverbial particle	DO
6 *Lock*	*up*	*all your valuables.*
8 *She gave*	*away*	*all her old school books.*
9 *Don't forget to*	*switch off*	*the lights in all the rooms downstairs.*

[VP16A] In this pattern there is an adverbial adjunct which is an infinitive phrase. This may be introduced by *in order to* or *so as to*. [VP16A] is to be distinguished from [VP17] (with the same word order).

Cf I sent	Tom	to buy some fruit. [VP16A]
I want	Tom	to buy some fruit. [VP17]

In [VP16A] the infinitive is one of purpose or intended result. In [VP17] the infinitive is part of the direct object.

Subject + *vt*	DO	*to*-infinitive (phrase)
1 *He brought*	*his brother*	*to see me.*
2 *He opened*	*the door*	*to let the cat out.*
3 *They left*	*me*	*to do all the dirty work.*

[VP16B] The DO is followed by an adjunct with *as* or *like*, or a clause introduced by *as if* or *as though*.

Subject + *vt*	DO	*as/like* + noun (phrase) or clause
1 *I can't see*	*myself*	*as a pop singer.*
2 *Her parents spoilt*	*her*	*as a child.*
3 *You mustn't treat*	*your wife*	*as if she were a servant.*

[VP17] In this pattern the verb is followed by a noun or pronoun and a *to*-infinitive or infinitive phrase. This is sometimes called the accusative and infinitive construction. The noun/pronoun + *to*-infinitive is the object of the verb.

Subject + *vt*	noun/pronoun	(*not*) + *to*-infinitive (phrase)
1 *He likes*	*his wife*	*to dress well.*
2 *They warned*	*us*	*not to be late.*
3 *Do you want/wish*	*me*	*to stay?*

[VP18A] In this pattern the verb is used with a noun or pronoun and a bare infinitive. The verbs indicate physical perceptions. These verbs are also used in [VP19]. [VP18] indicates completed activity and [VP19] activity in progress.

Subject + *vt*	noun/pronoun	infinitive (phrase)
1 *Did you see/notice*	*anyone*	*leave the house?*
2 *We felt*	*the house*	*shake.*
3 *I once heard*	*her*	*sing the part of Aida.*

[VP18B] A small number of verbs which do not indicate physical perceptions are used in [VP18]. *Make* and *let* are examples. Compare *force/compel* and *allow/permit*, which are used in [VP17].

Please let	me	go.	[VP18]
Please allow/permit	me	to go.	[VP17]

Subject + *vt*	noun/pronoun	infinitive (phrase)
1 *What makes*	*you*	*think so?*
2 *Let*	*me*	*go!*
3 *I've never known*	*him*	*behave so badly before.*

[VP18C] *Have* is used in this pattern when it means 'wish', 'experience' or 'cause'.

Subject + HAVE	noun/pronoun	infinitive (phrase)
1 *What would you have*	*me*	*do?*
2 *She likes to have*	*the house*	*clean and tidy.*

3 *I had*	*a frightening thing*	*happen to me yesterday.*
4 *We often have*	*our friends*	*visit us on Sundays.*

[VP19A] The verb is followed by a noun or pronoun and a present participle. The verbs are those used in [VP18A] and also the verb *smell*.

Subject + *vt*	noun/ pronoun	present participle (phrase)
1 *Can you smell*	*something*	*burning?*
2 *She could feel*	*her heart*	*beating wildly.*
3 *Did you notice*	*anyone*	*standing at the gate?*

[VP19B] This pattern is used for some verbs which do not indicate physical perceptions.

Subject + *vt*	noun/ pronoun	present participle (phrase)
1 *I found*	*John*	*working at his desk.*
2 *They left*	*me*	*waiting outside.*
3 *This set*	*me*	*thinking.*
4 *Please start*	*the clock*	*going.*
5 *He soon had*	*them all*	*laughing.*

[VP19C] In this pattern the noun or pronoun is followed by the *-ing* form of a verb, and this may be either the present participle or the gerund, depending upon whether it is preceded by a noun or pronoun, or a possessive. For fuller notes, see *A Guide to Patterns and Usage.*

Subject + *vt*	noun/pronoun/ possessive	*-ing* form of the verb
1 *I can't understand*	*him/his*	*behaving so foolishly.*
2 *Can you imagine*	*me/my*	*being so stupid?*
3 *Does this justify*	*you/your*	*taking legal action?*
4 *I can't remember*	*my parents/their*	*ever being unkind to me.*
5 *I admire*	*Tom('s)/him/his*	*standing his ground.*

[VP20] In this pattern the verb is followed by a noun or pronoun, a conjunctive, ie an interrogative adverb (except *why*) or pronoun, and a *to*-infinitive or infinitive phrase. The pattern may be compared to [VP12A].

Tell	me	your name.	[VP12A]
Tell	me	what to call you.	[VP20]

Subject + *vt*	noun/ pronoun	interrogative + *to*-infinitive (phrase)
1 *I showed*	*them*	*how to do it.*
2 *Tell*	*him*	*where to put it.*
3 *Ask*	*your teacher*	*how to pronounce the word.*

[VP21] This pattern is similar to [VP20]. A clause replaces the infinitive phrase.

Subject + *vt*	noun/pronoun	dependent clause/question
1 *Tell*	*me*	*what your name is.*
2 *Ask*	*him*	*where he put it.*
3 *Show*	*me*	*what you have in your pockets.*

[VP22] The DO is followed by an adjective which indicates result or manner.

Subject + *vt*	DO	adjective
1 *We painted*	*the ceiling*	*green.*
2 *The sun keeps*	*us*	*warm.*
3 *The mud made*	*walking*	*difficult.*

[VP23] In this pattern the predicative adjunct is a noun.

Subject + *vt*	DO	noun (phrase)
1 *They made*	*Newton*	*President of the Royal Society.*
2 *They named*	*the baby*	*Richard.*
3 *They usually call*	*him*	*Dick.*

[VP24A] The verb is followed by a noun or pronoun and a past participle.

Subject + *vt*	DO	past participle (phrase)
1 *You must make*	*your views*	*known.*
2 *Have you ever heard*	*this opera*	*sung in Italian?*
3 *We want*	*the work*	*finished by Saturday.*

[VP24B] *Have* is used in [VP24] to indicate what the subject of the sentence experiences, undergoes, or suffers (as in Nos 1–3), or what is held or possessed (as in Nos 4 and 5).

Subject + HAVE	DO	past participle (phrase)
1 *King Charles I had*	*his head*	*cut off.*
2 *I've recently had*	*my appendix*	*removed.*
3 *They have*	*scarcely any money*	*saved for their old age.*

[VP24C] *Have* and *get* are used in [VP24] meaning 'cause to be'.

Subject + HAVE/GET	DO	past participle (phrase)
1 *Can we get*	*the programme*	*changed?*
2 *Please have*	*these letters*	*translated into English.*
3 *I'll have/get*	*the matter*	*seen to.*

[VP25] Verbs marked [VP25] may be followed by a noun or pronoun and a complement after *to be* (often omitted). In spoken English [VP9] (ie with a *that*-clause) is preferred.

Subject + *vt*	DO	(*to be*) + adjective/noun
1 *Most people considered*	*him*	*(to be) innocent.*
2 *They all felt*	*the plan*	*to be unwise.*
3 *I've always found*	*Jonathan*	*friendly/a good friend.*
4 *In Britain we presume*	*a man*	*(to be) innocent until he is proved guilty.*

For 1, 'Most people consider that he was innocent' [VP9] is more usual. Introductory *it* is used if, instead of a noun, there is a clause, infinitive phrase, etc.

Cf Do you consider *long hair for men* strange?
Do you consider *it* strange *for men to let their hair grow long?*

Aa

A[1], **a** /eɪ/ (*pl* **A's, a's** /eɪz/) the first letter of the English alphabet: *He knows the subject from A to Z,* knows it thoroughly. **A1** /ˈeɪ ˋwʌn/ **(a)** (of ships) classified as first class. ⇨ **Lloyd's. (b)** (colloq) excellent: *an A1 dinner; feeling A1,* in excellent health.

a[2] /ə *strong form:* eɪ/, **an** /ən *strong form:* æn/ *indef art* (*det*) **1** one: *I have a pen* (*pl some pens*). *Have you a pen* (*pl any pens*)? Cf *some, any, several, a few* with *pl nn.* **2** (with *adjj* and *pronouns* of number and quantity): *a lot of money; a great many friends; a few books; a little more.* **3** (with possessives): *a friend of my father's,* one of my father's friends; *a book of John's,* one of John's books. **4** (placed after *many, what* and *such*): *Many a man would be glad of the opportunity/such an opportunity. What an opportunity you missed!* **5** (placed between *half* and a *n*): *half a dozen; half an hour;* (before 1971) *half a crown,* the sum of 2s 6d. Cf *a half-crown,* former coin worth 2s 6d. **6** (placed after an *adj* preceded by *so, as, too, how*): *He's not so big a fool as he looks. She's as clever a girl as you can wish to meet. It's too difficult a book for me.* **7** that which is called; any; every (zero *pl*): *A horse is an animal.* Cf *Horses are animals.* **8** (When two objects, articles, etc naturally go together and are thought of as a unit, the *indef art* is not repeated): *a cup and saucer; a knife and fork.* **9** (used with a person's name, and the title *Mr, Mrs,* etc to indicate that the person is perhaps unknown to the person addressed): *A Mr White has called. A Mrs Green is asking to see you.* **10** one like: *He thinks he's a Napoleon,* a man like Napoleon. **11** (after *of* and *at,* in some phrases) the same: *They're all of a size. Birds of a feather* (= of the same kind) *flock together. Carry them three at a time.* **12** (used distributively): *twice a month; 20p a pound; 50p an hour; sixty miles an hour.*

aback /əˋbæk/ *adv* backwards. ***be ˈtaken aˋback,*** be startled, disconcerted.

aba·cus /ˈæbəkəs/ (*pl* **-cuses** /-kəsɪz/ or **-ci** /ˈæbəsɑɪ/) *n* frame with beads or balls sliding on rods, for teaching numbers to children, or (still in the East) for calculating; early form of digital computer.

abaft /əˋbɑft *US:* əˋbæft/ *adv, prep* (naut) at, in, toward, the stern half of a ship; nearer the stern than; behind.

aban·don[1] /əˋbændən/ *vt* **1** [VP6A] go away from, not intending to return to; forsake: *The order was given to ~ ship,* for all on board to leave the (sinking) ship. *The cruel man ~ed his wife and child.* **2** [VP6A] give up: *They ~ed the attempt,* stopped trying. *They had ~ed all hope,* no longer had any hope. *The new engine design had to be ~ed for lack of financial support.* **3** [VP14] ***~ oneself to,*** give oneself up completely to, e g passions, impulses: *He ~ed himself to despair.* ***~ed*** *part adj* **1** given up to bad ways; depraved; profligate: *You ~ed wretch!* **2** deserted; forsaken. **~·ment** *n* [U].

aban·don[2] /əˋbændən/ *n* [U] careless freedom, as when one gives way to impulses: *waving their arms with ~.*

abase /əˋbeɪs/ *vt* [VP6B] ***~ oneself,*** humiliate or degrade oneself: *~ oneself so far as to do sth,* lower oneself in dignity to the extent of doing sth. **~·ment** *n* [U].

abash /əˋbæʃ/ *vt* [VP6A] (passive only) cause to feel self-conscious or embarrassed: *The poor man stood/felt ~ed at this display of wealth,* was confused, not knowing what to do or say.

abate /əˋbeɪt/ *vt, vi* **1** [VP6A,2A] (of winds, storms, floods, pain, etc) make or become less: *The ship sailed when the storm ~d.* **2** [VP6A] (legal) bring to an end; abolish: *We must ~ the smoke nuisance in our big cities.* **~·ment** *n* [U] abating; decrease.

ab·at·toir /ˈæbətwɑ(r) *US:* ˈæbəˋtwɑr/ *n* slaughter-house (for cattle, sheep, etc).

abbé /ˈæbeɪ *US:* ˈæˋbeɪ/ *n* (courtesy title for a) French priest, esp one without official duties.

ab·bess /ˈæbes *US:* ˋæbɪs/ *n* woman (*Mother Superior*) at the head of a convent or nunnery.

ab·bey /ˈæbɪ/ *n* (*pl* **-beys**) **1** building(s) in which men (*monks*) or women (*nuns*) live as a community in the service of God. **2** the whole number of monks or nuns in an ~. **3** church or house which was once an ~ or part of an ~. **the A~,** often used of Westminster A~, London.

ab·bot /ˈæbət/ *n* man (*Father Superior*) at the head of the monks in an abbey or monastery.

ab·brevi·ate /əˋbrivɪeɪt/ *vt* [VP6A,14] shorten (a word, title, etc): *~ January to Jan.* ⇨ **abridge. ab·brevi·ation** /əˈbrivɪˋeɪʃn/ *n* **1** [U] abbreviating or being ~d. **2** [C] shortened form (esp of a word).

ABC /ˈeɪ bi ˋsi/ *n* **1** the alphabet. **2** simplest facts of a subject, to be learnt first.

ab·di·cate /ˈæbdɪkeɪt/ *vt, vi* **1** [VP6A] give up, renounce, a high office, authority or control, responsibility. **2** [VP2A] give up the throne: *King Edward VIII ~d in 1937 and was created Duke of Windsor.* **ab·di·ca·tion** /ˈæbdɪˋkeɪʃn/ *n* **1** [U] abdicating. **2** [C] instance of this.

ab·do·men /ˈæbdəmən/ *n* **1** (= colloq *belly*) part of the stomach that includes the stomach and bowels. ⇨ the illus at **trunk. 2** last of the three divisions of an insect, spider, etc. ⇨ the illus at **insect. ab·domi·nal** /æbˋdomɪnl/ *adj* in, of, for, the ~: *abdominal pains; an abdominal belt/operation.* ⇨ **intestinal.**

ab·duct /æbˋdʌkt/ *vt* [VP6A] take or lead (esp a woman or child) away unlawfully, by force or fraud. ⇨ **kidnap. ab·duc·tion** /æbˋdʌkʃn/ *n*

an abacus

abeam /əˋbim/ *adv* (naut) on a line at a right angle to the length of a ship or aircraft: *The lighthouse was ~ of the ship.*
abed /əˋbed/ *adv* (old use) in bed.
ab·er·ra·tion /ˈæbəˋreɪʃn/ *n* **1** [U] (usu fig) straying away from the right path, from what is normal: *stealing sth in a moment of ~.* **2** [C] instance of this; defect: *The delay was caused by an ~ in the computer.* **ab·er·rant** /æˋberənt/ *adj* straying away from what is normal, expected or usual; not true to type.
abet /əˋbet/ *vt* (-tt-) [VP6A,14] (legal) help (sb) (*in* doing wrong); encourage (vice, crime): *~ sb in a crime.* ***aid and ~ sb,*** (legal) be an accomplice in his wrongdoing.
abey·ance /əˋbeɪəns/ *n* [U] condition of not being in force or in use for a time: *The question is in ~,* is suspended, e g until more information is obtained. ***fall/go into ~,*** (legal) (of a law, rule, custom, etc) be suspended; be no longer observed.
ab·hor /əbˋhɔ(r)/ *vt* (-rr-) [VP6A] think of with hatred and disgust; detest; *~ cruelty to animals.* **~·rence** /əbˋhɔrns *US:* -ˋhɔr-/ *n* [U] hatred and disgust: *hold sth in ~rence; his ~rence of flattery.* **~·rent** /-rnt/ *adj* hateful; causing horror (*to* sb, *to* his feelings).
abide /əˋbaɪd/ *vt,vi* (*pt,pp* -d(**1**), **abode(3)** /əˋbəʊd/) **1** [VP3A] *~* ***by,*** be faithful to; keep: *~ by a promise/decision. I ~ by* (colloq 'stick to') *what I said. You'll have to ~ by the consequences,* endure them. (Used only of undesirable consequences.) **2** [VP6A] (esp with *can/could* in neg and interr) endure; bear: *How can you ~ him? She can't ~ that man.* **3** [VP2C] (in old or liter use) rest, remain, stay: *~ at/in a place; ~ with sb.* **4** [VP6A] (liter) wait for: *~ the event; ~ sb's coming.* **abid·ing** *adj* (liter) never-ending; lasting.
abil·ity /əˋbɪlətɪ/ *n* **1** [U] (potential) capacity or power (to do sth physical or mental): *to the best of my ~,* as well as I can. *I do not doubt your ~ to do the work.* **2** [U] cleverness; intelligence: *a man of great ~.* **3** [C] (*pl* -**ties**) mental powers: *a man of great abilities.*
ab initio /ˈæb ɪˋnɪʃɪəʊ/ *adv* (Lat) from the beginning.
ab·ject /ˋæbdʒekt/ *adj* **1** (of conditions) wretched; miserable: *living in ~ poverty.* **2** (of persons, their actions, behaviour) degraded; deserving contempt because cowardly or self-abasing: *~ behaviour; an ~ apology.* **~·ly** *adv* **ab·jec·tion** /æbˋdʒekʃn/ *n*
ab·jure /əbˋdʒʊə(r)/ *vt* [VP6A] promise or swear solemnly on oath or in public to give up, e g a belief, a right, evil ways: *~ one's religion.* **ab·jur·ation** /ˈæbdʒʊəˋreɪʃn/ *n* [C,U] (action of) abjuring; state of being ~d: *(an) abjuration of faith.*
ab·la·tive /ˋæblətɪv/ *adj, n* (gram) name of a form in Latin nouns indicating an agent, instrument or cause.
ab·laut /ˋæblaʊt/ *n* (phil) systematic vowel changes in verb forms of Indo-European languages (as in *drive, drove, driven*).
ablaze /əˋbleɪz/ *pred adj, adv* **1** on fire, in a blaze: *set it ~. The whole building was soon ~.* **2** (fig) shining; bright; excited: *The streets were ~ with lights. Her face was ~ with anger.*
able /ˋeɪbl/ *adj* **1** ***be ~ to do sth,*** have the power, means or opportunity to do sth: *Shall/Will you be ~ to come? You are better ~ to do it than I am.* ⇨ **can**[2], **could**. **2** (-r, -st) clever; capable; having or showing knowledge or skill: *an ~ lawyer; an ~ speech; the ~st/most ~ man I know.* **ˈ~-bodied** /-ˋbɒdɪd/ *adj* physically strong. **ˈ~ ˋseaman, ˈ~-ˈbodied ˋseaman** *n* (GB abbr = AB) seaman trained and certified for all duties. **ably** /ˋeɪblɪ/ *adv* in an ~ manner.
ab·lu·tion /əˋbluʃn/ *n* (usu *pl*) ceremonial washing of the hands or the body, esp as an act of religion: *perform one's ~s,* (often joc or fac) wash oneself.
ab·ne·ga·tion /ˈæbnɪˋgeɪʃn/ *n* [U] self-denial; (often **ˈself-ˋ~**) self-sacrifice.
ab·nor·mal /ˈæbˋnɔml/ *adj* different, often in an undesirable way, from what is normal, ordinary or expected. **~·ly** *adv* **~·ity** /ˈæbnɔˋmælətɪ/ *n* [U] quality of being ~; [C] (*pl* -**ties**) sth that is ~.
aboard /əˋbɔd/ *adv, prep* on (to) or in(to) a ship, aircraft, or (US) a train or motor-coach: *It's time to go ~. All ~!* (i e Go or come ~.) *Welcome ~!* (e g as a greeting by a stewardess on an aircraft.)
abode[1] /əˋbəʊd/ *n* **1** (old or liter use) house; dwelling-place: *take up one's ~ with one's parents-in-law,* go and live with them. **2** (legal) *place of ~,* domicile; *of/with no fixed ~,* having no fixed dwelling-place.
abode[2] /əˋbəʊd/ *pt,pp* of **abide**.
abol·ish /əˋbɒlɪʃ/ *vt* [VP6A] put an end to, do away with, e g war, slavery, an old custom. **abol·ition** /ˈæbəˋlɪʃn/ *n* [U] ~ing or being ~ed (esp used, in the 18th and 19th cc, of Negro slavery). **abol·ition·ist** /ˈæbəˋlɪʃn̩ɪst/ *n* (esp) person who wished to ~ Negro slavery.
A-bomb /ˋeɪ bɒm/ *n* = atomic bomb.
abom·in·able /əˋbɒmɪnəbl/ *adj* **1** causing hatred and disgust (*to* sb). **2** (colloq) unpleasant; bad: *~ weather/food.* **abom·in·ably** /-əblɪ/ *adv*
abom·in·ate /əˋbɒmɪneɪt/ *vt* [VP6A,C] detest; feel hatred or disgust for; (colloq) dislike. **abom·in·ation** /əˈbɒmɪˋneɪʃn/ **1** [U] horror and disgust: *hold sth in abomination.* **2** [C] sth that arouses horror and disgust (*to* sb).
abo·rig·inal /ˈæbəˋrɪdʒnl/ *adj* (of races of people, living creatures, etc) belonging to, existing in, a region from earliest times, or from the time when the region was first known. □ *n* ~ inhabitant, plant, etc of a region. **abo·rig·ines** /ˈæbəˋrɪdʒɪniz/ *n pl* (with *def art*): the ~ inhabitants.
abort /əˋbɔt/ *vt,vi* [VP6A,2A] come to nothing, to miscarry; terminate prematurely: *~ a space mission,* cancel it in space, e g because of mechanical trouble.
abor·tion /əˋbɔʃn/ *n* **1** [U] (legal) expulsion of the foetus from the womb during the first 28 weeks of pregnancy; helping or causing this: *A~ was formerly a crime in Britain.* **2** [C] instance of this; miscarriage of birth: *have/procure an ~.* **3** [C] creature produced by ~; dwarfed or mis-shapen creature; (fig) plan, effort, etc that has failed to develop. **~·ist** /-ɪst/ *n* person who brings about an ~; person who favours and supports legal ~.
abort·ive /əˋbɔtɪv/ *adj* coming to nothing; unsuccessful; arrested in development: *plans that proved ~; an ~ rebellion.* **~·ly** *adv*
abound /əˋbaʊnd/ *vi* [VP3A] *~* ***in/with,*** have, exist, in great numbers or quantities: *The river ~s in fish. Fish ~ in the river. The hut ~ed with vermin. Vermin ~ed in the hut.*
about[1] /əˋbaʊt/ *adv of degree* (contrasted with *just* or *exactly*) a little more or less than; a little before or after: *~ as high as that tree; for ~ three miles; ~ six o'clock; on or ~ the fifth of May. I've had*

just ~ *enough* (colloq understatement for 'quite enough'). *It's* ~ *time you stopped being so rude* (colloq understatement for 'quite time'). *That's* ~ *it/*~ *the size of it,* (colloq) is how I assess it, how I see it.

about[2] /ə'baʊt/ *adv part* **1** (with *vv* of movement) here and there, in no particular direction: *The children were rushing* ~. *The boys were climbing* ~ *on the rocks. Don't drop cigarette ash* ~. *Don't leave waste paper and empty bottles* ~ *in the park. He's taking Jane* ~ *a lot these days,* e g to dances, cinemas, theatres. **2** (with other *vv*, indicating position, etc): *There were books lying* ~ *on the floor/people sitting* ~ *on the grass.* **3** (with *be*): *There was no one* ~, no one to be seen. *There's a lot of influenza* ~, many people have it. *Mr Green is (out and)* ~ *again,* able to get out, work, etc after an illness. *It's time you were up and* ~, out of bed and active. **4** ***bring sth* ~,** ⇨ bring(6). ***come* ~,** ⇨ come(15). **5** facing round; in the opposite direction: *It's the wrong way* ~. *A*~ *turn!* (GB), *A*~ *face!* (US), (mil commands) turn round to face the other way. **'~-'face** *v* turn and face the other way. □ *n* complete reversal of views, actions, etc: *He did a complete* ~*-face.* **6** (of two or more persons or groups) ***take turns* ~, *(do sth) turn and turn* ~,** ⇨ turn[2](4).

about[3] /ə'baʊt/ *prep* **1** (with *vv* of movement) here and there, in no particular direction: *walking* ~ *the town; travelling* ~ *the world.* **2** (with other *vv*, indicating position, state, etc): *idle men standing* ~ *street corners; books and papers lying* ~ *the room. I haven't any money* ~ *me,* i e with me, in my pockets. **3** near to: *I dropped the key somewhere* ~ *here.* **4** concerning; regarding; in connection with: *He is careless* ~ *his personal appearance. What do you know* ~ *him? What is he so angry* ~? *Tell me all* ~ *it.* ***How/What* ~...,** used to ask for information, to make a suggestion or to get sb's opinion: *What* ~ *his qualifications for the position? How* ~ *going to France for our holidays?* **5** concerned or occupied with: *What are you* ~? (= colloq 'up to?'). *And while you're* ~ *it...,* while you're doing that.... *Mind what you're* ~, Be careful what you do. ***go/set* ~ *sth,*** deal with it: *Do you know how to go* ~ *it,* deal with the task? **6** round (which is usu preferred in mod Eng): *the fields* ~ *Oxford. She hung* ~ *his shoulders. He has his wits* ~ *him,* ⇨ wit. **7** ~ ***to* + *(inf),*** on the point of (doing sth), just going to (do sth): *As I was* ~ *to say, when you interrupted me...; He was* ~ *to start.*

above[1] /ə'bʌv/ *adv* **1** at a higher point; overhead; on high: *My bedroom is just* ~. *Seen from* ~, *the fields looked like a geometrical pattern. A voice from* ~ *shouted a welcome.* **2** earlier (in a book, article, etc): *As was stated* ~*...; See the statement* ~*/the* ~ *statement.* **3** in Heaven: *the Powers* ~, the heavenly powers. **a'bove 'board** *adv* without deception or concealment; honourably. □ *pred adj* frank; open. ⇨ underhand. **a'bove-'mentioned, a'bove-'named** *adjj* mentioned, named, ~ (or earlier) in this book, article, etc.

above[2] /ə'bʌv/ *prep* (contrasted with *below;* ~ may sometimes be replaced by *over* or *beyond*) **1** higher than: *The sun rose* ~ *the horizon. We were flying* ~ *the clouds.* Cf We flew *over/across* the Sahara. *The water came* ~ *our knees. A captain in the Navy ranks* ~ *a captain in the Army.* **2** greater in number, price, weight, etc: *The temperature has been* ~ *the average recently. There is nothing in this shop* ~*/over fifty cents. It weighs* ~*/over ten tons. Applicants must be* ~*/over the age of 21.* **3** more than: *A soldier should value honour* ~ *life.* ~ ***all,*** more than anything else. ***over and* ~,** in addition to. **4** too great, good, difficult, etc for: *If you want to learn, you must not be* ~ *asking* (= not be too proud to ask) *questions. He is* ~ *meanness and deceit,* does not show meanness or practise deceit. *This book is* ~ (now more usu *beyond*) *me,* too difficult for me. **5** out of reach of (because too great, good, etc): *His heroism was* ~*/beyond all praise. His conduct has always been* ~ *suspicion.* **6** (various uses): *the waterfall* ~ (= up stream from) *the bridge; live* ~*/beyond one's means,* in a style too expensive for one's income; *be* ~ *oneself,* in high spirits; *get* ~ *oneself,* become conceited, too self-satisfied and lacking in self-control; *She married* ~ *her station,* married sb from a higher social class.

ab·ra·ca·dabra /'æbrəkə'dæbrə/ *n* [U] magic jargon; gibberish.

abrade /ə'breɪd/ *vt* [VP6A] rub or scrape off, wear away (skin, etc) by friction or hard rubbing.

ab·ra·sion /ə'breɪʒn/ *n* [U] rubbing, scraping, or wearing off; [C] area where sth has been worn or scraped away: *an* ~ *of the skin.* **ab·ras·ive** /ə'breɪsɪv/ *n* [C,U] substance (e g emery) used for rubbing or grinding down surfaces. □ *adj* causing ~; (fig) harsh, rough: *an abrasive voice/character.*

abreast /ə'brest/ *adv* (of persons, ships, etc) on a level, side by side, and facing the same way: *walking three* ~; *warships in line* ~. ***be/keep* ~ *(of/with),*** level with, not behind: *You should read the newspapers to keep* ~ *of the times,* to be informed of the latest events, ideas, discoveries, etc.

abridge /ə'brɪdʒ/ *vt* [VP6A] make shorter, esp by using fewer words: *an* ~*d edition of 'David Copperfield';* shorten (an interview, the time sth lasts). ⇨ abbreviate. **~·ment, abridg·ment** *n* [U] abridging; [C] sth, e g a book, that is ~d.

abroad /ə'brɔd/ *adv* **1** in or to a foreign country or countries; away from one's own country: *be/go/live/travel* ~; *visitors who have come from* ~. *Do you like (it)* ~*/being* ~? **2** far and wide; everywhere: *There's a rumour* ~ *that...,* People are saying that.... **3** (old use) out of doors: *You were* ~ *early this morning.*

ab·ro·gate /'æbrəgeɪt/ *vt* [VP6A] repeal or annul by authority. **ab·ro·ga·tion** /'æbrə'geɪʃn/ *n*

abrupt /ə'brʌpt/ *adj* **1** unexpectedly sudden: *The road is full of* ~ *turns.* **2** (of speech, writing, behaviour) rough; brusque; disconnected: *a man with an* ~ *manner,* i e rather impolite, gruff, blunt; *an* ~ *style,* e g of speaking or writing. **3** (of a slope) steep. **~·ly** *adv* **~·ness** *n*

ab·scess /'æbses/ *n* [C] collection of thick yellowish-white liquid (called *pus*) formed in a cavity in the body: ~*es on the gums.*

ab·scond /əb'skɒnd/ *vi* [VP2A,3A] ~ ***(with/from),*** go away, suddenly, secretly, and aware of having done wrong, esp to avoid arrest.

ab·sence /'æbsns/ *n* **1** [U] being away (*from*): ~ *from school; during his* ~ *in America,* while he was there. *In the* ~ *of the Manager* (i e while he is away) *Mr X is in charge of the business.* ***leave of* ~,** ⇨ leave[2](1). **2** [C] occasion or time of being away: *numerous* ~*s from school; a long* ~; *after* *an ~ of three months.* **3** [U] lack; non-existence: *in the ~ of definite information. Cold is the ~ of heat.* **4** **~ of mind,** absent-mindedness (⇨ below).

ab·sent[1] /ˈæbsnt/ *adj* **1** **~ from,** not present at: *~ from school/work.* **2** lost in thought; abstracted: *When I spoke to him he looked at me in an ~ way but did not answer.* **~·ly** *adv* = ~-mindedly. ˈ**~-ˈminded** /ˈmaɪndɪd/ *adj* so deep or far away in thought that one is unaware of what one is doing, what is happening around one, etc. **~-mind·ed·ly** *adv* **~-minded·ness** *n*

ab·sent[2] /əbˈsent/ *vt* [VP6B,14] **~ oneself (from),** stay away (from): *Why did you ~ yourself (from school) yesterday?*

ab·sen·tee /ˌæbsnˈti/ *n* person who is absent, e g a landowner who habitually lives away from the place where his land is: (attrib) *~ landowners.* **~·ism** /-ɪzm/ *n* [U] habitual failure to be present, e g the practice of being absent from work or regular duty frequently and without good reason.

ab·sinthe, ab·sinth /ˈæbsɪnθ/ *n* [U] bitter, green alcoholic drink made with wormwood and other herbs.

ab·so·lute /ˈæbsəlut/ *adj* **1** complete; perfect: *A child usually has ~ trust in its mother. When giving evidence in a law court, we must tell the ~ truth.* **2** unlimited; having complete or arbitrary power: *An ~ ruler need not ask anyone for permission to do anything.* **3** real; undoubted: *It is an ~ fact. He must not be punished unless you have ~ proof of his guilt.* **4** unconditional; unqualified: *An ~ promise must be kept whatever happens.* **5** not relative; not dependent on or measured by other things. **~ zero,** lowest temperature theoretically possible, = 273·15°C. **~·ly** *adv* **1** completely: *~ly impossible; ~ly right.* **2** unconditionally: *He refused ~ly.* **3** /ˌæbsəˈlutlɪ/ (colloq, in answer to a question, or as a comment) quite so; certainly. **ab·so·lut·ism** /ˌæbsəˈlutɪzm/ *n* (pol) ~ government; despotism.

ab·sol·ution /ˌæbsəˈluʃn/ *n* [U] (R C Church) forgiveness (through penance or a religious act) for wrongdoing or guilt; freeing from the consequences of sin: *~ from sin.*

ab·solve /əbˈzolv/ *vt* [VP6A,14] **~ (from),** declare free (from sin, guilt, a promise, duty, etc): *I ~ you from all blame/from your vows.*

ab·sorb /əbˈsɔb/ *vt* **1** [VP6A] take or suck in, e g a liquid; take in, e g heat, light, (fig) knowledge, etc: *Paper that ~s ink is called blotting-paper. Dry sand ~s water. The clever boy ~ed all the knowledge his teachers could give him.* **2** [VP6A] take up the attention, interest or time of: *His business ~s him. He is completely ~ed in his business. He was ~ed* (= engrossed) *in a book.* **~·ent** /-ənt/ *adj, n* (substance) capable of ~ing: *~ent cotton wool.* **ab·sorp·tion** /əbˈsɔpʃn/ *n* [U] ~ing or being ~ed; engrossment: *Complete absorption in sport interfered with his studies.*

ab·stain /əbˈsteɪn/ *vi* [VP3A,2A] **~ (from),** hold oneself back, refrain: *His doctor told him to ~ from beer and wine. At the last election he ~ed (from voting).* **~·er** *n* person who ~s, esp *total ~er,* one who never takes alcoholic drinks.

ab·stemi·ous /əbˈstimɪəs/ *adj* sparing or moderate, esp in taking food and drink; frugal: *~ habits; an ~ meal.* **~·ly** *adv* **~·ness** *n*

ab·sten·tion /əbˈstenʃn/ *n* [U] **~ (from),** abstaining, esp not using one's vote at an election, etc; [C] instance of this: *six votes for, three against and two ~s.*

ab·sti·nence /ˈæbstɪnəns/ *n* [U] **~ (from),** abstaining, e g from food, enjoyment, esp alcoholic drink. ˈ**total** ˈ**~,** refraining completely from alcoholic drink.

ab·stract[1] /ˈæbstrækt/ *adj* **1** separated from what is real or concrete; thought of separately from facts, objects or particular examples: *A flower is beautiful, but beauty itself is ~.* ˈ**~** ˈ**art,** art which does not represent objects, scenes, etc in an obvious way, but abstracts and isolates features of reality. ⇨ **realism(1).** ˈ**~** ˈ**noun,** (gram) one that is the name of a quality or state, e g *length, goodness, virtue.* **2** **in the ~,** regarded in an ideal or theoretical way.

ab·stract[2] /əbˈstrækt/ *vt* [VP6A,14] **~ (from),** take out; separate: *~ metal from ore;* (colloq) steal: *~ a wallet from sb's pocket.* **~ed** *adj* not paying attention; withdrawn in thought. **~·ed·ly** *adv* in an absent-minded way.

ab·stract[3] /ˈæbstrækt/ *n* [C] short account, e g of the chief points of a piece of writing, a book, speech, etc: *an ~ of a sermon.*

ab·strac·tion /əbˈstrækʃn/ *n* **1** [U] abstracting or being abstracted. **2** [U] absent-mindedness: *in a moment of ~; with an air of ~.* **3** [C] visionary idea; idea of a quality apart from its material accompaniments: *Whiteness is an ~. Don't lose yourself in ~s,* i e keep a firm hold on reality. **4** [U] formation of such an idea or ideas.

ab·struse /əbˈstrus/ *adj* whose meaning or answer is hidden or difficult to understand; profound. **~·ly** *adv* **~·ness** *n*

ab·surd /əbˈsɜd -ˈzɜd/ *adj* unreasonable; foolish; ridiculous: *What an ~ suggestion! It was ~ of you to suggest such a thing.* **~·ly** *adv* **~·ity** *n* (*pl* **-ties**) **1** [U] state of being ~; unreasonableness. **2** [C] ~ act or statement.

abun·dance /əˈbʌndəns/ *n* **1** [U] great plenty: *food and drink in ~; live in ~,* have plenty of those things that make life enjoyable. **2** (with *indef art*) quantity that is more than enough: *an ~ of good things.*

abun·dant /əˈbʌndənt/ *adj* **1** more than enough; plentiful: *We have ~ proof of his guilt.* **2** **~ in,** rich in; well supplied with: *a land ~ in minerals* (*with an abundance of* or *abounding in* are more usu).

abuse[1] /əˈbjus/ *n* **1** [U] **~ (of),** wrong use; [C] instance of this; *an ~ of trust.* **2** [C] unjust custom or practice that has become established: *remedy an ~; put an end to ~s.* **3** [U] angry or violent attack in words; bad language; cursing: *greet sb with a stream of ~; shower ~ on sb.*

abuse[2] /əˈbjuz/ *vt* [VP6A] **1** make a bad or wrong use of: *Don't ~ your authority/the confidence they have placed in you.* **2** say severe, cruel or unjust things to sb or about sb. **3** (old use) ill treat. **4** (old use, esp in the passive) deceive: *She has been much ~d.*

abus·ive /əˈbjusɪv/ *adj* using, containing, curses: *use ~ language to sb; become ~,* begin to curse. **~·ly** *adv*

abut /əˈbʌt/ *vi* (-tt-) [VP3A] **~ on,** (of land) have a common boundary with; border on. **~·ment** *n* (eng) structure that bears the structure of a bridge or an arch.

abysm /əˈbɪzm/ *n* [C] (poet) abyss.

abys·mal /əˈbɪzml/ *adj* (esp fig and colloq) bottomless; extreme: ~ *ignorance,* (colloq) complete absence of knowledge. **~·ly** *adv*

abyss /ə`bɪs/ *n* hole so deep as to appear bottomless; hell, or the lower world: (fig) *the ~ of despair.*

aca·cia /ə`keɪʃə/ *n* [C] **1** (sorts of) tree from which gum is obtained. **2** (*false ~* or *locust tree*) (sorts of) related tree grown as an ornament in parks and gardens.

aca·demic /ˌækə`demɪk/ *adj* **1** of teaching, studying; of schools, colleges, etc; scholarly, literary or classical (contrasted with technical or scientific): *~ subjects; the ~ year,* (usu Oct to June in GB and US); *~ freedom,* liberty to teach and to discuss problems without outside, e g Government, interference. **2** too much concerned with theory and logic; not sufficiently practical: *The question/issue is ~,* is of no practical consequence. **3** of an academy: *~ rank/costume.* □ *n* [C] professional scholar. **aca·demi·cally** /-klɪ/ *adv*

aca·dem·icals /ˌækə`demɪklz/ *n pl* academic costume (cap and gown), as worn on ceremonial occasions.

acad·emy /ə`kædəmɪ/ *n* (*pl* **-mies**) **1** school for higher learning, usu for a special purpose: *a `naval/^military ~; an ˈ~ of `music; a `riding/`fencing ~.* **2** society of distinguished scholars; society for cultivating art, literature, etc, of which membership is an honour: *The Royal A~ of Arts; the A~,* its annual exhibition of works of art. **aca·dem·ician** /əˌkædə`mɪʃn *US:* ˌækədə`mɪʃn/ *n* member of an ~(2), e g of the Royal A~ in GB or of the French A~.

ac·cede /ək`sid/ *vi* [VP2A,3A] *~ (to),* **1** assent or agree, e g to a request or proposal. **2** take or succeed to, e g an office, a post, a position of authority.

ac·cel·er·ando /ækˌselə`rændəʊ/ *adj* (music) (direction for) increasing speed gradually.

ac·cel·er·ate /ək`seləreɪt/ *vt,vi* **1** [VP6A] increase the speed of; cause to move faster or happen earlier. **2** [VP2A] (of a motion or process) become faster. **ac·cel·er·ation** /əkˌselə`reɪʃn/ *n* [U] making or being made quicker; rate of increase of speed per unit of time: *a car with good acceleration.* **ac·cel·er·ator** /ək`seləreɪtə(r)/ *n* **1** device, e g the pedal in a motor-vehicle, for controlling speed. **2** (phys) device for accelerating particles or nuclei, also called (colloq) an 'atom-smasher'.

ac·cent /^æksnt *US:* `æksent/ *n* [C] **1** (pros) prominence (by means of stress or intonation) given to a syllable: *In the word 'today' the ~ is on the second syllable.* **2** mark or symbol, usu above a letter, used in writing and printing to indicate the quality of a vowel sound or syllabic stress. ⇨ **acute(5), circumflex** and **grave³**. **3** [sometimes U] individual, local or national way of pronouncing: *a Cockney ~; speaking English with a foreign ~; speak without an ~.* **4** (*pl*) way of speaking which indicates a particular quality, etc: *in the tender ~s of love.* **5** (colloq) emphasis given to some aspect of a display, performance, etc: *At this year's Motor Show the ~ is on sports cars.* □ *vt* /æk`sent/ [VP6A] pronounce with an ~; put emphasis on (a syllable or word); make prominent or conspicuous.

ac·cen·tu·ate /ək`sentʃʊeɪt/ *vt* [VP6A] give more force or importance to; draw attention to. **ac·cen·tu·ation** /əkˌsentʃʊ`eɪʃn/ *n*

ac·cept /ək`sept/ *vt,vi* [VP6A,9,16B,2A] **1** (consent to) receive (sth offered): *~ a gift/an invitation. He asked her to marry him and she ~ed him/his proposal. I cannot ~ you as my assistant.* **2** agree; recognize; regard with favour or approval: *I ~ that the change may take some time. It is an ~ed truth/fact,* sth that everyone believes. **3** take responsibility for; (comm): *~ a bill of exchange; ~ delivery of goods.* **~·able** /-əbl/ *adj* worth ~ing; welcome: *if this proposal is ~able to you.* **ac·cepta·bil·ity** /əkˌseptə`bɪlətɪ/ *n* **ac·cept·ance** /-əns/ *n* [U] **1** ~ing or being ~ed. **2** approval; favourable reception: *The proposal met with/found general ~ance.* **3** (comm) agreement to pay; (legal) contract, bill of exchange, which has been offered and ~ed. **ac·cep·ta·tion** /ˌæksep`teɪʃn/ *n* generally ~ed meaning of a word or expression.

ac·cess /^ækses/ *n* [U] **1** way (in) to a place: *easy/difficult/of ~;* (attrib) *good ~ roads,* roads giving good ~. *The only ~ to the farmhouse is across the fields.* **`~ road,** = slip-road, ⇨ **slip²(10)**. **2** *~ to,* right, opportunity or means of reaching, using or approaching: *Students must have ~ to good books. Only high officials had ~ to the Emperor.* **3** (with *indef art*) attack (*of* fever, etc); sudden attack, outburst (*of* anger, rage, despair, etc). **~·ible** /ək`sesəbl/ *adj ~ (to),* able to be reached, used, visited, etc: *facts that are ~ible to all; a collection of paintings not ~ible to the public;* that can be influenced by: *a man who is not ~ible to argument.* **ac·cessi·bil·ity** /əkˌsesɪ`bɪlətɪ/ *n* [U].

ac·cess·ary /ək`sesərɪ/ *n* (*pl* **-ries**), *pred adj* (= US *accessory* (1)) (legal) person who helps in any act, esp a crime: *an ~ to a crime; He was made ~ to the crime.* ***~ before/after the fact,*** ⇨ **fact(1)**.

ac·cession /æk`seʃn/ *n ~ to,* **1** [U] reaching a rank, position or state: *the Queen's ~ to the throne; on his ~ to the estate/to manhood.* **2** [C, U] (an) addition; (an) increase: *recent ~s to the school library; the ~ of new members to a political party.*

ac·cess·ory /ək`sesərɪ/ *n* (*pl* **-ries**) [C] **1** accessary. **2** sth extra, helpful, useful, but not an essential part of: *the accessories of a bicycle,* e g the lamp, a pump; *the accessories of a woman's dress,* e g gloves, a handbag.

ac·ci·dence /^æksɪdns/ *n* [U] (gram) that part of grammar which deals with meaningful differences in the form of a word, e g *have, has, had; foot, feet,* etc. The more usu term is now *morphology.* ⇨ **syntax**.

ac·ci·dent /^æksɪdnt/ *n* **1** [C] sth that happens without a cause that can be seen at once, usu sth unfortunate and undesirable: *There have been many railway ~s this year. He was killed in a motoring ~. There has been an ~ to...; A~s will happen,* (prov) Some unfortunate events must be accepted as inevitable. *He has had/met with an ~.* ⇨ **prone**. **2** [U] chance; fortune: *by ~ of birth.* ***by ~,*** by chance: *You might cut yourself by ~; you would not cut yourself on purpose.* ***without ~,*** safely. **`~ insurance,** against injury, damage or death which is the result of an ~.

ac·ci·den·tal /ˌæksɪ`dentl/ *adj* happening unexpectedly and by chance: *an ~ meeting with a friend.* **~·ly** /-tlɪ/ *adv*

ac·claim /ə`kleɪm/ *vt* **1** [VP6A,16B] welcome with shouts of approval; applaud loudly: *~ the winner of a race; ~ sb as a great actor.* **2** [VP23] make (sb) ruler, salute (sb) by ~ing: *They ~ed him King.* □ *n* [U] applause; approval: *The play received great critical ~.*

ac·cla·ma·tion /ˈæklə`meɪʃn/ *n* **1** [U] loud and enthusiastic approval of a proposal, etc: *elected/carried by ~,* without voting. **2** (usu *pl*) shouts or applause of welcome, acceptance: *the ~s of the crowd.*

ac·cli·mate /`æklɪmeɪt *US:* ə`klaɪmeɪt/ *vt, vi* (US = *acclimatize*). **ac·cli·ma·tion** /ˈæklaɪ`meɪʃn/ *n*

ac·cli·mat·ize /ə`klaɪmətaɪz/ *vt, vi* [VP14,2A] ~ ***(to),*** get (oneself, animals, plants, etc) used to a new climate, or (fig) to a new environment, new conditions, etc: *You will soon get ~d.* **ac·cli·mat·iz·ation** /əˈklaɪmətaɪ`zeɪʃn *US:* -tɪ`z-/ *n*

ac·cliv·ity /ə`klɪvətɪ/ *n* (*pl* **-ties**) [C] upward slope.

ac·col·ade /`ækəleɪd *US:* ˈækə`leɪd/ *n* [C] **1** bestowal of a knighthood by a tap on the shoulder with the flat of a sword. **2** (fig) praise; approval: *the ~s of the literary critics.*

ac·com·mo·date /ə`komədeɪt/ *vt* [VP6A,14] **1** have, provide, lodging for: *This hotel can ~ 600 guests.* **2** ~ ***sb (with sth),*** grant sth to sb; do sb a favour: *The bank will ~ you with a loan.* **3** ~ ***sth to,*** change sth so that it fits with or is in harmony with (sth else): *I will ~ my plans to yours.* **ac·com·mo·dat·ing** *adj* willing to oblige others; easy to deal with.

ac·com·mo·da·tion /əˈkomə`deɪʃn/ *n* **1** [U] (GB) furnished, unfurnished room(s), e g in a flat, house, hostel or in a hotel, etc: *Wanted, ~ for a married couple with small child, in London,* e g as in a newspaper advertisement. *Hotel ~ was scarce during the Olympic Games.* **2** (*pl,* US) lodgings; room(s) and food. **3** [C] sth that helps; sth for convenience: **an `~ ladder,** (attrib) a portable one hung from the side of a ship. **4** [C,U] compromise; settlement or adjustment (of one thing *to* another): *come to an ~,* reach a compromise, e g in a dispute.

ac·com·pani·ment /ə`kʌmpnɪmənt/ *n* [C] **1** sth that naturally or often goes with another thing: *Disease is often an ~ of famine.* **2** (music) (usu) instrumental part to support a voice, choir or solo instrument: *a song with a piano ~.* **ac·com·pan·ist** /ə`kʌmpənɪst/ *n* person who plays a musical ~.

ac·com·pany /ə`kʌmpnɪ/ *vt* (*pt,pp* **-nied**) [VP6A,14] **1** go with: *Warships will ~ the convoy across the Atlantic. He was accompanied by his secretary.* **2** attend; characterize: *fever accompanied with delirium; lightning accompanied with thunder.* **3** occur or do at the same time as: *~ one's words with blows.* **4** (music) play an accompanied to: *The singer was accompanied at the piano by Gerald Moore.*

ac·com·plice /ə`kʌmplɪs *US:* ə`kom-/ *n* helper or companion (*in* wrongdoing).

ac·com·plish /ə`kʌmplɪʃ *US:* ə`kom-/ *vt* [VP6A] perform; succeed in doing; finish successfully: *~ a task; a man who will never ~ anything.* ***an ~ed fact,*** sth already done. **~ed** *adj* clever; skilled (*in*): *an ~ed dancer;* well trained or educated in such social arts as conversation, art and music: *an ~ed young lady.* **~·ment** *n* **1** [U] completion; finishing: *the ~ment of their aims; difficult of ~ment.* **2** [C] sth ~ed, esp sth well done. **3** [C] skill in a social or domestic art: *Among her ~ments were dancing, playing the piano, sewing and cooking.*

ac·cord[1] /ə`kɔd/ *n* **1** [U] ***of one's own ~,*** without being asked or forced; willingly. ***in/out of ~ (with),*** in/out of harmony (with), agreeing/not agreeing with. ***with one ~,*** everybody consenting. **2** [C] treaty, agreement (*between* countries; *with* a country).

ac·cord[2] /ə`kɔd/ *vi, vt* **1** [VP2A,2C,3A] ~ ***(with),*** match, agree (with); be in agreement or harmony (with): *His behaviour and his principles do not ~ (well together). His behaviour does not ~ with his principles. What you say does not ~ with the previous evidence.* **2** [VP13A,12A] (formal style) give; grant: *~ sb permission; ~ permission to sb. He was ~ed a warm welcome.*

ac·cord·ance /ə`kɔdns/ *n* ***in ~ with,*** in agreement or conformity with: *in ~ with your wishes; in ~ with custom/the regulations.*

ac·cord·ing /ə`kɔdɪŋ/ ~ ***as,*** *conj* in proportion as; in a manner that depends upon: *You will be praised or blamed ~ as your work is good or bad.* ~ ***to,*** *prep* **(a)** on the authority of: *A~ to the Bible, God created the world in six days.* **(b)** in a degree in proportion to: *He will be punished ~ to the seriousness of his crime.* **(c)** in a manner consistent with: *The books are placed on the shelves ~ to authors.* **~·ly** *adv* **1** for that reason; therefore. **2** as the (stated) circumstances suggest: *I have told you the circumstances, so you must act ~ly.*

ac·cord·ion /ə`kɔdɪən/ *n* portable musical instrument with a bellows, metal reeds and a keyboard; (attrib) having narrow folds like the bellows or an ~: *~ pleats in a skirt.*

ac·cost /ə`kost *US:* ə`kɔst/ *vt* [VP6A] go up to and speak to first, esp a stranger in a public place; (of a prostitute) solicit: *I was ~ed by a beggar/a prostitute.*

ac·couche·ment /ə`kuʃmõ/ *n* (F) lying in; confinement; childbirth. ⇨ *lie in* at **lie**[2]**(1)**.

ac·count[1] /ə`kaʊnt/ *n* **1** [C] (comm) statement of money (to be) paid or received (for goods, services, etc): *I have an ~ with the Midland Bank,* keep my money with the Bank, pay my debts, etc by means of cheques on the Bank, etc. ***open an ~, open a bank/post office, etc ~,*** start to keep one's money at a bank, etc. *ask a shop/shopkeeper/store to* **put sth down to one's ~,** ask him to note the price of what is bought, for payment later. ***settle one's ~ (with),*** pay what one owes (to a tradesman, etc); (fig) avenge oneself for an injury, etc. ***send in/render an ~,*** send a written statement of what is owed. Hence, **`~ `rendered,** an ~ previously sent in but not yet paid. ***balance/square ~s (with sb),*** receive or pay the difference between debit and credit; (fig) remove moral grievances between people by giving or taking punishment. **`budget ~,** (with a shop) one used for buying goods, paying bills, etc by making regular payments to the shop; (with a bank) special ~ with a bank which makes regular deductions for bills paid. **`current ~, de`posit ~, `joint ~, `private ~, `savings ~,** ⇨ **current(3), deposit**[1]**(1), joint**[2]**, private(1)** and **save**[1]**(2)**. **2** [C] counting; calculation: *He is quick at ~s,* can calculate quickly. ***money of ~,*** used of sums of money, not of coins or banknotes. ⇨ **guinea**. **3** (*sing* only) benefit; profit: *invest one's money to good ~.* ***turn/put sth to (good) ~,*** use money, abilities, talent, etc profitably. ***work on***

one's own* ~,** for one's own purposes and profit, and at one's own risk. **4** [U] ***call/bring sb to* ~,** require him to justify or explain his conduct; state that he is answerable for sth. **5** [C] ***give a good* ~ *of oneself, do well; act in a way that brings credit, e g by defeating opponents in contests. **6** [C] report; description; narrative: *Don't always believe newspaper ~s of events.* ***by one's own* ~,** according to what one oneself says. ***by/from all* ~s,** according to what everybody, all the papers, etc say. **7** [U] estimation. ***be/be reckoned of some/small* ~,** be considered of some/low value. ***take sth into* ~, *take* ~ *of sth,*** note or consider it; pay attention to it. ***leave sth out of* ~, *take no* ~ *of sth,*** pay no attention to it. **8** [U] reason; cause. ***on* ~ *of,*** because of. ***on this/that* ~,** for this/that reason: *He's angry on that ~. Don't stay away on ~ of John/on John's ~.* ***on no* ~, *not on any* ~,** in no case; not for any reason: *Don't on any ~ leave the baby alone in the house.*

ac·count[2] /əˋkaʊnt/ *vt,vi* **1** [VP3A] **~ *for,* (a)** serve as an explanation of; explain the cause of: *His illness ~s for his absence. Ah, that ~s for it! He has been asked to ~ for his conduct,* explain why he acted as he did. *There's no ~ing for tastes,* We cannot explain why people have different likes and dislikes. **(b)** give a reckoning of (money that has been entrusted to one): *The boy has to ~ (to his parents) for the money they give him for school expenses.* **(c)** (sport) kill; shoot: *We ~ed for a fine brace of partridges.* **2** [VP25] consider: *In English law a man is ~ed innocent until he is proved guilty.* **~·able** /-əbl/ *adj* **~able *to sb/for sth,*** responsible; expected to give an explanation: *I'll hold you ~able. A madman is not ~able for his actions.*

ac·count·ant /əˋkaʊntənt/ *n* (in GB) person whose profession is to keep and examine business accounts: *chartered ~*; (in US): *certified public ~.* **ac·count·ancy** /-ənsɪ/ *n* [U] profession of an ~.

ac·coutre·ments (US = **ac·cou·ter·ments**) /əˋkutəmənts/ *n pl* (mil) soldier's equipment excluding clothes and weapons.

ac·credit /əˋkredɪt/ *vt* [VP14] (usu passive) **1** appoint or send (sb) as an ambassador, with official letters of introduction: *He was ~ed to/at Lisbon.* **2** = credit. **~ed** *part adj* officially recognized (person); generally accepted (belief, opinion, etc). **ˈ~ed ˋmilk,** guaranteed to be of an approved quality.

ac·cre·tion /əˋkriʃn/ *n* **1** [U] increase by organic addition or growth; the growing of separate things into one. **2** [C] sth added; sth resulting from ~.

ac·crue /əˋkru/ *vi* [VP2A,3A] **~ *(to sb/from sth),*** come as a natural growth or development: *If you keep your money in the Savings Bank, interest ~s. A~d interest is interest due, but not yet paid or received.*

ac·cu·mu·late /əˋkjumjʊleɪt/ *vt,vi* [VP6A,2A] make or become greater in number or quantity; come or gather together; heap up: *By buying ten books every month, he soon ~d a library. Dust soon ~s if the rooms are not swept. By working hard you may ~ a fortune.*

ac·cu·mu·la·tion /əˈkjumjʊˋleɪʃn/ *n* **1** [U] accumulation; collection: *the ~ of money/useful knowledge.* **2** [C] material, etc accumulated: *an ~ of books /evidence / rubbish.* **ac·cu·mu·lat·ive** /əˋkjumjʊlətɪv *US:* -leɪtɪv/ *adj* arising from ~; growing by a succession of additions.

ac·cu·mu·la·tor /əˋkjumjʊleɪtə(r)/ *n* [C] **1** (GB) storage battery, e g for a motor vehicle: *charge/discharge/an ~,* cause a current to flow into/out of it. **2** (in a computer) device which stores numbers and progressively adds numbers.

ac·cu·rate /ˋækjərət/ *adj* **1** careful and exact: *be ~ in one's work/in what one says; quick and ~ at figures; take ~ aim.* **2** free from error: *~ scales. Clocks in railway stations should be ~.* **~·ly** *adv* **ac·cu·racy** /ˋækjərəsɪ/ *n* [U] exactness; correctness.

ac·cursed, ac·curst /əˋkɜst/ *adj* under a curse; detestable; hateful.

ac·cu·sa·tion /ˈækjʊˋzeɪʃn/ *n* **1** [U] accusing or being accused. **2** [C] charge of doing wrong, of having broken the law: *bring an ~ of theft against sb; be under an ~ of theft.*

ac·cus·ative /əˋkjuzətɪv/ *adj, n* **the ~ (case),** (gram) inflected form of a noun, etc in Greek, Latin, German, etc chosen for the object of a verb or preposition.

ac·cuse /əˋkjuz/ *vt* [VP6A,14] **~ *sb (of sth),*** say that (sb) has done wrong, broken the law, is to be blamed: *~ sb of theft/cowardice; be ~d of sth.* **the ~d,** the person(s) charged in a criminal case. **ac·cuser** *n* **ac·cus·ing·ly** /əˋkjuzɪŋlɪ/ *adv* in an accusing manner: *He pointed accusingly at me.*

ac·cus·tom /əˋkʌstəm/ *vt* [VP14] (esp in the passive) **~ *(oneself) to,*** make used to: *When he became a soldier, he had to ~ himself to long marches. The boy soon became ~ed to hard work and poor food. This is not the kind of treatment I am ~ed to,* not the kind I usually receive. **~ed** *part adj* usual; habitual: *in his ~ed seat.*

ace /eɪs/ *n* [C] **1** the one on dice, on (playing-)cards or dominoes (⇨ these words); card so marked: *the ~ of spades.* ***an ace in the hole,*** (US sl, from the game of poker) sth held in reserve, likely to turn failure into success. **2** (colloq) person who is first rate or expert at sth, esp an airman or a driver of racing cars. **3 *within an ace of,*** failing, escaping, by a narrow margin: *within an ace of death/of being killed.*

acerb·ity /əˋsɜbətɪ/ *n* **1** [U] bitterness of speech, manner, temper. **2** [C] (*pl* -ties) instance of this; bitter or acrimonious remark, etc.

acetic /əˋsitɪk/ *adj* of vinegar or ~ acid. **ˈ~ ˋacid,** the acid contained in vinegar. **acet·ate** /ˋæsɪteɪt/ *n* salt of ~ acid: *acetate silk,* artificial silk made from cellulose acetate.

acety·lene /əˋsetəlin/ *n* [U] (chem) colourless gas **(C_2H_2)** which burns with a bright light, used in carbide lamps and for welding and cutting metal.

ache /eɪk/ *n* [C] (*sing,* with or without the *def art*) dull continuous pain: *have ~s and pains all over; have a ˋhead~; suffer from head~s; suffering from (the) ˋtooth/ˋear/ˋstomach-~.* □ *vi* **1** [VP2A] have a steady or continuous dull pain: *My head ~s/is aching. After climbing the mountain, he ~d all over. It makes my heart ~,* makes me sad. **2** [VP3A,4A] **~ *(for),*** have a longing: *His heart ~ed for her. He was aching for home. He ~d to be free.*

achieve /əˋtʃiv/ *vt* [VP6A] **1** complete; accomplish; get (sth) done: *He will never ~ anything,* will not do anything successfully. *I've ~d only half of what I hoped to do.* **2** gain or reach by effort: *~ one's purpose; ~ success/distinction in* *public life.* **achiev·able** /-əbl/ *adj* that can be ~d. **~·ment** *n* **1** [U] achieving: *the ~ment of an undertaking/of one's aims; impossible of ~ment; an ~ment test* (of skills, etc). **2** [C] sth ~d; sth done successfully, with effort and skill: *The inventor was rewarded by the Government for his scientific ~ments.*

Achilles /əˋkɪliz/ *n* **the heel of ~, ~' heel,** (fig) small but weak or vulnerable point, e g in sb's character.

acid /ˈæsɪd/ *adj* **1** sour; sharp to the taste: *A lemon is an ~ fruit. Vinegar has an ~ taste.* **ˋ~ drops,** sweets of boiled sugar with an ~ flavour. **2** (fig) sharp; sarcastic: *an ~ wit; ~ remarks.* □ *n* **1** [C,U] (chem) substance that contains hydrogen, which may be replaced by a metal to form a salt: *Vinegar contains acetic ~. Some ~s burn holes in wood and cloth.* H_2SO_4 *stands for sulphuric ~.* **ˋ~ test** *n* (fig) test that gives conclusive proof of the value or worth of sth. **2** [U] (sl, L S D) ⇨ App 2. **~·ify** /əˋsɪdɪfaɪ/ *vt,vi* (*pt,pp* **-fied**) [VP6A,2] make or become ~. **~·ity** /əˋsɪdətɪ/ *n* [U] state or quality of being ~. **~u·lated** /əˋsɪdjʊleɪtɪd *US:* -ɪdʒʊl-/ *adj* made slightly ~. **~u·lous** /əˋsɪdjʊləs *US:* -ɪdʒʊl-/ *adj* sour in feeling or manner; sharp; bitter.

ack-ack /ˈæk ˋæk/ *n* (mil sl) anti-aircraft gun/fire, etc.

ac·knowl·edge /əkˋnolɪdʒ/ *vt* **1** [VP6A,C,9A,24A] confess; admit the truth, existence or reality of: *He refused to ~ defeat/that he was defeated. He would not ~ his mistake. He won't ~ himself beaten. He ~d having been frightened. Does he ~ the signature,* agree or admit that it is his? [VP25] (liter style): *We praise thee, O God, we ~ Thee to be the Lord.* [VP16B] *Stephen ~d Henry as his heir,* recognized his claim to be heir. [VP25] *They all ~d him master,* agreed that he was their master. **2** [VP6A] report that one has received (sth): *~ (receipt of) a letter. We should always ~ gifts promptly.* **3** [VP6A] express thanks for: *We must not fail to ~ his services to the town.* **4** [VP6A] indicate that one recognizes (sb) by giving a greeting, a smile, a nod of the head, etc: *I met her in town but she didn't even ~ me when I raised my hat.* **~·ment, ac·knowl·edg·ment** *n* **1** [U] act of acknowledging: *We are sending you a small sum of money in ~ment of your valuable help.* **2** [C] sth given or done to ~ sth: *We have had no ~ment of our letter,* no reply. *This basket of fruit is a slight ~ment of your kindness.*

acme /ˈækmɪ/ *n* (*sing* with *def art*) summit; highest point of development; point of perfection: *the ~ of his desires/skill.*

acne /ˈæknɪ/ *n* [U] disease (common among adolescents) in which there are pimples and blackheads on the face and neck.

aco·lyte /ˈækəlaɪt/ *n* person who helps a priest in some religious services, esp the celebration of Mass.

ac·on·ite /ˈækənaɪt/ *n* (bot) (sorts of) plant with blue or purple flowers; monkshood; drug from the dried poisonous root of one of these kinds, used to slow down the action of the heart.

acorn /ˈeɪkɔn/ *n* seed or fruit of the oak tree. ⇨ the illus at tree. **ˋ~-cup** *n* cuplike holder of an ~.

acous·tic /əˋkustɪk/ *adj* of sound, the science of sound and the sense of hearing. **ˈ~ ˋgramo·phone,** the older kind, before electric reproduction. □ *n* [C] studio, hall, etc from the consideration of its ~s (⇨ 2 below): *Try recording the music in a better ~.* **acous·tics** *n* **1** (with *sing v*) the scientific study of sound. **2** (with *pl v*) the physical properties of sound; the properties of a hall, etc, that make it good, poor, etc for hearing music, speeches, etc: *The ~s of the new concert hall are excellent.*

ac·quaint /əˋkweɪnt/ *vt* [VP14] **1 ~ *sb/oneself with,*** make familiar with, reveal to sb: *~ sb with the facts of the case; ~ oneself/become ~ed/make oneself ~ed with one's new duties.* **2 *be ~ed (with sb),*** have met (sb) personally: *I am not ~ed with the lady. We are not ~ed.*

ac·quaint·ance /əˋkweɪntəns/ *n* **1** [U] knowledge or information gained through experience: *He has some ~ with German, but does not speak it fluently.* ***have a bowing/nodding ~ with,*** have some ~ with (a person, a subject). ***make sb's ~, make the ~ of sb,*** get to know sb, e g by being introduced. ***upon (further) ~,*** when known for a (further) period of time. **2** [C] person with whom one is acquainted; person whom one knows (less intimate than a friend): *He has a wide circle of ~s.* **3** (older English, collective): *He has a wide ~,* many ~s. **~·ship** /-ʃɪp/ *n* (circle of) ~s(**2**).

ac·quiesce /ˈækwɪˋes/ *vi* **1** [VP2A] agree; accept silently or without protest. **2** [VP3A] **~ *in,*** accept an arrangement, a conclusion, etc without protest: *Her parents will never ~ in such an unsuitable marriage.* **ac·qui·escence** /ˈækwɪˋesns/ *n* (act of) acquiescing. **ac·qui·escent** /-ˋesnt/ *adj* disposed to ~.

ac·quire /əˋkwaɪə(r)/ *vt* [VP6A] gain by skill or ability, by one's own efforts or behaviour: *~ a good knowledge of English/a reputation for dishonesty/a taste for brandy.* ***an ~d taste,*** one that comes when one has experimented with sth and, in the end, comes to like it: *Retsina* (= the resin-flavoured Gk wine) *is an ~d taste for British people.* **~·ment** *n* **1** [U] acquisition (now the more usu word). **2** [C] accomplishment(**3**) (now the more usu word).

ac·qui·si·tion /ˈækwɪˋzɪʃn/ *n* **1** [U] acquiring: *He devotes his time to the ~ of knowledge.* **2** [C] sth acquired: *my most recent ~s,* e g books I have bought recently. *Mr A will be a valuable ~ to* (= a valuable new member of) *the teaching staff of our school.*

ac·quis·itive /əˋkwɪzətɪv/ *adj* fond of, in the habit of, acquiring: *~ of new ideas; the ~ society,* valuing the possession of more and more material things.

ac·quit /əˋkwɪt/ *vt* (**-tt-**) **1** [VP6A,14] **~ *sb (of/on sth),*** give a legal decision that (sb) is not guilty, e g of an offence: *He was ~ted of the crime/~ted on two of the charges.* **2** [VP16B] conduct (oneself): *He ~ted himself well/like a hero.* **~·tal** /əˋkwɪtl/ *n* [C,U] judgement that a person is not guilty: *a sentence of ~tal; three convictions and two ~tals.*

acre /ˋeɪkə(r)/ *n* measure of land, 4 840 sq yds or about 4 000 sq metres. **ˋGod's ~,** churchyard (for burials). **~·age** /ˋeɪkərɪdʒ/ *n* [U] area of land measured in ~s: *What is the ~age of the London parks?*

ac·rid /ˋækrɪd/ *adj* (of smell or taste) sharp; biting: *the ~ smell of burning feathers;* (fig) bitter in temper or manner.

ac·ri·mony /ˋækrɪmənɪ *US:* -məʊnɪ/ *n* [U] bitterness of temper, manner, language. **ac·ri·moni·ous**

/ˈækrɪˋmaʊnɪəs/ *adj* (of arguments, quarrels, words) bitter.

ac·ro·bat /ˋækrəbæt/ *n* person who can do clever things with his body, e g on a tightrope or trapeze. **~ic** /ˈækrəˋbætɪk/ *adj* of or like an ~: *~ic feats.* **~·ics** *n pl* (used with *sing v*) ~ic tricks or feats.

acrobats

ac·ro·nym /ˋækrənɪm/ *n* [C] word formed from the initial letters of a name, e g *NASA* /ˋnæsə/, National Aeronautics and Space Administration. ⇨ App 2.

acrop·olis /əˋkropəlɪs/ *n* fortified part of a Gk city in ancient times, esp **the A~,** that of Athens.

across[1] /əˋkros *US:* əˋkrɔs/ *adv* (used with *vv* in the senses of the *prep*): *Can you swim ~? Will you row me ~? I helped the blind man ~. Come ~ to my office this afternoon. The river is half a mile ~,* = wide. ***~ from.*** (US) opposite: *The bank is just ~ from the school.*

across[2] /əˋkros *US:* əˋkrɔs/ *prep* **1** from side to side of: *walk ~ the street; draw a line ~ a sheet of paper; a bridge ~ the river; row sb ~ a lake.* ***aˈcross-the-ˋboard,*** including all groups, members, etc esp in an occupation or industry: *an ~-the-board wage increase.* **2** on the other side of: *My house is just ~ the street. We shall soon be ~ the Channel. He addressed me from ~ the room.* **3** so as to form a cross; so as to cross or intersect: *He sat with his arms ~ his chest. The two lines pass ~ each other at right angles.* **4** (with *vv*) ⇨ come(15), drop[2](13), get(17), put[1](11) and run[2](26).

acros·tic /əˋkrostɪk *US:* -ˋkrɔs-/ *n* word puzzle, word arrangement, in which the first, or the first and last, letters of the lines make a word or words.

acryl·ic /əˋkrɪlɪk/ *n* (comm) **ˈ~ ˋfibre,** (kinds of) synthetic fibre used for making dress materials, etc. **ˈ~ ˋresin,** (kinds of) transparent colourless plastic widely used in industry, e g for plastic lenses, aircraft windows.

act[1] /ækt/ *n* [C] **1** sth done: *To kick a cat is a cruel act. It is an act of kindness to help a blind man across the street.* **Acts (of the Apostles),** (NT) accounts of the missionary work of the Apostles. **2** process of, instant of, doing; action. ***(catch sb) in the (very) act (of doing sth),*** while performing the action: *The thief was caught in the act of breaking into the house. In the act of* (= While) *picking up the ball, he slipped and fell.* **Act of God,** sth which is the result of uncontrollable natural forces, e g storms, floods, earthquakes. ⇨ also grace(3). **3** law made by a legislative body: *an Act of Parliament: the Acts of Congress.* **4** main division of a play: *a play in five acts; Hamlet, Act* I. **5** one of a series of short performances in a programme: *a circus/variety act.* ***put on an act,*** (colloq) behave in an affected way (to get one's own way, etc).

act[2] /ækt/ *vi, vt* **1** [VP2A,3A] perform actions, do sth: *The time for talking is past; we must act at once. The girl's life was saved because the doctors acted so promptly. You have acted* (= behaved) *generously.* ***act (up)on*** *(a suggestion/sb's advice/an order)*, do what is suggested, advised, etc. **2** [VP2A,3A] do what is required; function normally: *The brakes wouldn't act, so there was an accident. The pump is not acting well,* not performing its proper function. ***act (up)on,*** have an effect (up)on: *This medicine acts on the heart/the bowels.* **3** [VP2A,C,3A] perform in a professional or official capacity: *The police refused to act,* would not interfere. ***act as,*** be, perform, as an interpreter, mediator, etc. ***act for/on behalf of,*** represent (sb) as a solicitor, barrister in a legal case: *A solicitor acts for his clients.* **4** [VP2A,C, 6A] take part in a play on the stage; take the part of, e g a character in a play or cinema film, or in real life: *Who is acting (the part of) Hamlet? She acts well. Don't act the fool/ass/idiot,* Don't behave foolishly. *Browning's plays won't act,* are not suitable for the stage. *She's not really crying; she's only acting* (= pretending) *in order to gain your sympathy.* [VP15B] ***act sth out,*** perform actions which represent, and may help to release, the fears, inhibitions, etc of a neurotic person. ***act up,*** (colloq) behave badly so as to attract attention; cause pain, irritation, annoyance by functioning badly: *My leg/car/TV, etc has been acting* (now more usu *playing*) *up all week.* **act·ing** *adj* doing the duties of another person for a time: *The Acting Manager/Headmaster; Acting Captain.* □ *n* [U] (art of) performing in a play for the theatre, cinema, TV, etc: *She did a lot of acting while she was at college.* **ˋacting copy,** (of a script) one for the use of an actor or actress.

ac·tin·ism /ˋæktɪnɪzm/ *n* [U] property of light rays that produces chemical activity and changes (as in photographic films). **ac·tinic** /ækˋtɪnɪk/ *adj* of ~: *actinic rays,* e g of the sun's radiation.

ac·tion /ˋækʃn/ *n* **1** [U] process of doing things: movement: (way of) using energy, influence, etc: *The time has come for ~,* We must act now. *A man of ~ does things; he is not content to just talk.* ***bring/call (sth) into ~,*** cause (it) to operate. ***put/set (sth) in ~,*** cause (it) to start acting. ***put (sth) out of ~,*** stop (it) working; make (it) unfit for use. ***take ~,*** begin to act. **ˋ~ painting,** form of abstract painting in which paint is splashed, dribbled, etc on to the canvas. **2** [C] thing done; act: *We shall judge you by your ~s, not by your promises. She is impulsive in her ~s,* does things impulsively. *A~s speak louder than words.* **3** [C] **(a)** mechanism of a piano, gun or other instrument. **(b)** manner of bodily movement, e g of a horse when jumping, of an athlete. **4** [C] legal process. ***bring an ~ against sb,*** seek judgement against him in a law court. **5** [C,U] fight(ing) between bodies of troops, between warships, etc: *go into ~,* start fighting; *break off the ~,* stop fighting; *killed in ~.* **ˋ~ stations,** (mil) positions to which soldiers, etc go when fighting is expected to begin. **~·able** /-əbl/ *adj* giving just cause for legal ~.

ac·ti·vate /ˋæktɪveɪt/ *vt* [VP6A] make active; (chem) accelerate reaction in, e g by heat; (phys) cause radiation from. **ac·ti·va·tion** /ˈæktɪˋveɪʃn/ *n*

ac·tive /ˋæktɪv/ *adj* **1** doing things; able to do things; in the habit of doing things; energetic;

characterized by activity: *He's over 90 and not very ~. A boy with an ~ brain will be more successful than a dull boy. Mount Vesuvius is an ~ volcano,* is one that erupts. *She has an ~* (= lively) *imagination. He takes an ~ part in school affairs.* ***on ~ service,*** (Navy, Army, Air Force) (GB) engaged in actual service, esp in fighting during a war; (US) on full duty, not in the reserves. ***under ~ consideration,*** being considered or canvassed. **2** (gram) **~ voice, (a)** form of a *v phrase* not containing *be + pp,* as in: *He was driving.* Cf *He was being driven.* **(b)** sentence containing a *vt* in which the *n* or *pron* preceding the *v,* and agreeing with it (the grammatical subject), refers to the doer of the action, i e the agent: *The children finished off the cake.* Cf *The cake was finished off by the children.* **~·ly** *adv*

ac·tiv·ist /ˋæktɪvɪst/ *n* [C] person taking an active part, e g in a political movement.

ac·tiv·ity /ækˋtɪvətɪ/ *n* (*pl* **-ties**) **1** [U] being active or lively: *When a man is over 70, his time of full ~ is usually past.* **2** [C] thing (to be) done; occupation: *Classroom activities are things done by pupils in the classroom; outdoor activities are things done outside. My numerous activities leave me little leisure.*

ac·tor /ˋæktə(r)/ *n* **1** man who acts on the stage, TV or in films. **2** person who takes part in a notable event, etc. **ac·tress** /ˋæktrəs/ *n* woman ~.

ac·tual /ˋæktʃʊəl/ *adj* existing in fact; real: *It's an ~ fact; I haven't invented or imagined it. Can you give me the ~ figures,* the real figures, not an estimate or a guess? *What is the ~ state of affairs?* **~·ly** /ˋæktʃəlɪ/ *adv* **1** in ~ fact; really: *the political party ~ly in power. He looks honest, but ~ly he's a rogue.* **2** strange or surprising as it may seem: *He ~ly expected me to do his work for him! He not only ran in the race; he ~ly won it!* **~·ity** /ˈæktʃʊˋælətɪ/ *n* (*pl* **-ties**) **1** [U] ~ existence; reality. **2** [C, usu *pl*] ~ conditions or facts; realities.

ac·tu·ary /ˋæktʃʊərɪ *US:* -tʃʊerɪ/ *n* (*pl* **-ries**) expert who calculates notes of insurance (by studying rates of mortality, frequency of fires, accidents, etc). **ac·tu·ar·ial** /ˈæktʃuˋeərɪəl/ *adj* of an ~ or his work.

ac·tu·ate /ˋæktʃʊeɪt/ *vt* [VP6A] cause to act: *A great statesman is ~d by love of his country, not by love of power.*

acu·ity /əˋkjuətɪ/ *n* [U] acuteness.

acu·men /əˋkjumən/ *n* [U] sharpness and accuracy of judgement; ability to understand clearly: *business ~.*

acu·punc·ture /ˋækjʊpʌŋktʃə(r)/ *n* [U] (med) pricking or puncturing of the living tissues of the human body with fine needles to relieve pain and as a local anaesthetic.

acute /əˋkjut/ *adj* **1** (of the senses, sensations, intellect) keen, sharp, quick: *Dogs have an ~ sense of smell. Our anxiety became more ~. He felt ~ remorse for his wrongdoing. A bad tooth can cause ~ pain. He is an ~ observer.* **2** (of diseases) coming sharply to a crisis: *The patient has reached the ~ stage of the disease,* the brief period during which the disease is severe and at a turning point. *Pneumonia is an ~ disease,* one that comes quickly to a turning-point. ⇨ chronic. **3** (of sounds) high; shrill. **4 ~ angle,** angle of less than 90°. ⇨ the illus at angle. **5 ~ accent,** mark over a vowel (´), as over *e* in *café.* **~·ly** *adv* **~·ness** *n*

ad /æd/ *n* [C] (colloq abbr for) advertisement: *'Want ads',* in newspapers, etc.

ad·age /ˋædɪdʒ/ *n* [C] old and wise saying; proverb.

adagio /əˋdɑdʒɪəʊ/ *n* (*pl* **-gios** /-dʒɪəʊz/) *adj, adv* (music) (passage played) in slow time.

Adam /ˋædəm/ *n* **ˋ~'s apple,** part that projects in the front of the throat, esp in men, and moves up and down when one speaks. ⇨ the illus at head. **the old ~,** the unregenerate side of human nature. ***not know sb from ~,*** have no knowledge of what he looks like.

ada·mant /ˋædəmənt/ *n* [U] kind of stone that, it is said, cannot be cut or broken. □ *pred adj* unyielding; firm in purpose: *He was ~ to their prayers. On this point I am ~,* Nothing can change my decision. *I only wish he were less ~.* **ada·man·tine** /ˈædəˋmæntɑɪn/ *adj* unyielding; inflexible.

adapt /əˋdæpt/ *vt* [VP6A,14] make (sth) suitable for a new use, need, situation, etc: *When you go to a new country, you must ~ yourself to new manners and customs. Difficult books are sometimes ~ed for use in schools. This book is ~ed to the needs of beginners/~ed for beginners. The play has been ~ed from the French,* i e translated and changed to suit English audiences. *Novels are often ~ed for the stage, television and radio.* **~er, ~or** /-tə(r)/ *nn* person who ~s sth; device that enables sth to be used for a purpose, or in a way, different from that for which it was designed, e g a fitting for taking electric current from an outlet so that more than one piece of apparatus may be used. **~·able** /-əbl/ *adj* able to ~ oneself; able to be ~ed: *an ~able man,* one who can ~ himself to circumstances, etc. **~a·bil·ity** /əˈdæptəˋbɪlətɪ/ *n* [U] power of ~ing or being ~ed. **ad·ap·ta·tion** /ˈædæpˋteɪʃn/ *n* ***~ation (of sth) (to sth),*** **1** [U] state of being ~ed; ~ing. **2** [C] sth made by ~ing: *An ~ation (of a novel) for the stage/for broadcasting.*

add /æd/ *vt,vi* **1** [VP6A,14] join, unite, put (one thing to another): *If you add 5 and/to 5 you get 10. The house has been added to from time to time,* new rooms, etc have been built on to it. *If the tea is too strong, add some hot water.* **ˋadding-machine** *n* machine for calculating mechanically. **2** [VP15B] ***add sth together,*** combine two or more things. [VP15B] ***add sth up,*** find the sum of: *add up a column of figures; add up ten figures; add them up.* [VP2C] ***add up (to),*** **(a)** give as a result, when joined: *The figures add up to 365.* **(b)** (colloq) mean; indicate; amount to: *All that this adds up to is that you don't want to help, so why not say so at once?* **(c)** (colloq) make sense; be plausible: *It just doesn't add up.* [VP15B] ***add sth in,*** include. **3** [VP6A,9A] say further; go on to say: *'And I hope you'll come early,' he added. She added that....* **4** [VP3A] ***add to,*** increase: *This adds to our difficulties.*

ad·den·dum /əˋdendəm/ *n* (*pl* **-da** /-də/) thing (omitted) that is to be added.

ad·der /ˋædə(r)/ *n* any of several small poisonous snakes, e g the viper, common in the Old World; any of several non-poisonous snakes, e g the puff ~ of N America. ⇨ the illus at snake.

ad·dict /əˋdɪkt/ *vt* (usu passive) ***be ~ed to,*** be given to, habitually or compulsively: *He is ~ed to alcohol/smoking/vice/lying/study/drugs, etc.* □ *n* /ˋædɪkt/ person who is ~ed, esp to sth harmful: *A*

ˋ*drug* ~. **ad·dic·tion** /əˋdɪkʃn/ *n* [C,U] (instance of) being ~ed. **ad·dic·tive** /əˋdɪktɪv/ *adj* causing ~ion: *~ive drugs.*

ad·di·tion /əˋdɪʃn/ *n* **1** [U] process of adding: *The sign + stands for ~.* ***in ~ (to),*** as well (as). **2** [C] sth added or joined: *They've just had an ~ to the family,* another child. *He will be a useful ~ to the staff of the school,* a useful new teacher. **~al** /-ʃnl/ *adj* extra; added: *~al charges* **~·ally** /-ʃnlɪ/ *adv*

ad·di·tive /ˋædɪtɪv/ *n* [C] substance added in small amounts for a special purpose: *food ~s,* e g to add colour; *petrol ~s,* e g to reduce engine knocking.

addle /ˋædl/ *adj* (usu in compounds) confused; muddled. **ˋ~-brained, ˋ~-pated** /-peɪtɪd/, having confused ideas. **ˋ~-head,** person with confused ideas. □ *vt,vi* **1** [VP6A] confuse: *~ one's head/brains.* **2** [VP2A] (of eggs) become rotten: *~d eggs.*

ad·dress[1] /əˋdres *US:* ˋædres/ *n* **1** particulars of where a person may be found and at which letters, etc may be delivered: *What's your home/business ~? Let me know if you change your ~.* **2** speech or talk (to an audience). **ˈpublic ˋ~ system,** system using microphones, loudspeakers, etc for amplifying speeches. **3** [U] (formal) manner or behaviour, esp in conversation: *A man of pleasing ~.* **4** [U] ***form of ~,*** style of written or spoken communication: *polite forms of ~.* **5** (*pl*) (dated) polite attentions or courtship: *pay one's ~es to a lady,* seek to win her hand in marriage; *reject sb's ~es,* show that one does not welcome sb's wishes to be friendly. **~ee** /ˈædreˋsi/ *n* person to whom sth is ~ed(2). **A~o·graph** /əˋdresəʊgrɑf *US:* -græf/ *n* (P) machine for printing ~es(1) on circulars, etc.

ad·dress[2] /əˋdres/ *vt* **1** [VP6A,16B] make a speech to; speak to, using a title: *Mr Green will now ~ the meeting. Don't ~ me as 'Colonel'; I'm only a major.* **2** [VP6A] write a destination on (with the name of the person to whom sth is to be delivered): *The letter was wrongly ~ed.* **3** [VP14] ***~ sth to,*** send (a remark, complaint, etc) to: *Please ~ all enquiries to this office. Please ~ complaints to the manager, not to me.* **4** [VP14] ***~ oneself to,*** work at, apply oneself to, be busy with (a task, etc): *It's time we ~ed ourselves to the business in hand,* time we got busy with the business we are here for.

ad·duce /əˋdjus *US:* əˋdus/ *vt* [VP6A] put forward (as proof, as an example): *~ reasons/proof/authority.*

ad·en·oids /ˋædɪnɔɪdz *US:* -dn̩-/ *n pl* (path) soft, sponge-like growth between the back of the nose and the throat, in some cases making breathing and speech difficult: *Have one's ~ out,* i e by a surgical operation; *She's got ~,* (colloq) is suffering from inflammation of the ~. ⇨ the illus at head. **ad·en·oidal** /ˈædɪˋnɔɪdl/ *adj* of the ~: *an adenoidal youth,* one suffering from ~.

adept /ˋædept/ *adj* expert, skilled (*in* sth; *at* or *in* doing sth). □ *n* (formal) expert: *I'm not an ~ in photography.*

ad·equate /ˋædɪkwət/ *adj* satisfactory; sufficient; satisfying a requirement: *£10 a week is not ~ to support a family. Are you getting ~ recompense for the work you're doing?* **~·ly** *adv* **ad·equacy** /ˋædɪkwəsɪ/ *n* [U] state of being ~: *He often doubts his adequacy as a husband and father.*

ad·here /ədˋhɪə(r)/ *vi* [VP2A,3A] ***~ (to),*** **1** stick fast (to): *Glue and paste are used to make one surface ~ to another.* **2** remain faithful (to); support firmly: *~ to one's plans/to an opinion/to a political party/to a promise. We decided to ~ to the programme.* Cf *depart from the rules.* **ad·her·ence** /-əns/ *n*: *adherence to a plan.*

ad·her·ent /ədˋhɪərnt/ *n* supporter (of a party, etc, but not necessarily a member): *The proposal is gaining more and more ~s.*

ad·he·sion /ədˋhiʒn/ *n* **1** [U] adhering; being or becoming attached or united. **2** [U] support: *give one's ~ to a plan.* **3** [U] (path) joining together of tissues in the body, e g after an injury; [C] instance of this: *painful ~s resulting from a wound that did not heal.*

ad·hesive /ədˋhisɪv/ *adj* having the property of sticking: *~ tape/plaster.* □ *n* [C,U] ~ substance, e g *gum.*

ad hoc /ˈæd ˋhok/ (Lat) arranged for this purpose.

adieu /əˋdju *US:* əˋdu/ *n, int* (*pl* -s or -x /əˋdjuz *US:* əˋduz/) goodbye: *bid sb ~; make one's ~/~s,* say goodbye.

ad in·fi·ni·tum /ˈæd ˌɪnfɪˋnɑɪtəm/ (Lat) without limit; for ever.

ad in·terim /ˈæd ˋɪntərɪm/ (Lat) in the meantime.

adi·pose /ˋædɪpəʊs/ *adj* of animal fat; fatty: *~ tissue.*

ad·jac·ent /əˋdʒeɪsnt/ *adj* next (*to*), lying near (*to*) but not necessarily touching: *~ rooms; ~ angles,* ⇨ the illus at angle. *The house ~ to the church is the vicarage.*

ad·jec·tive /ˋædʒɪktɪv/ *n* word that names a quality, or that defines or limits a noun. **ad·jec·tival** /ˈædʒɪkˋtɑɪvl/ *adj* of or like an ~: *an adjectival phrase/clause.*

ad·join /əˋdʒɔɪn/ *vt,vi* [VP6A,2A] be next or nearest (*to*): *The playing-field ~s the school. The two houses ~.*

ad·journ /əˋdʒ3n/ *vt,vi* **1** [VP6A] break off, e g proceedings of a meeting, etc for a time: *The meeting was ~ed for a week/until the following week.* **2** [VP2C] (of a meeting, etc) be broken off in this way: *The meeting ~ed at five o'clock.* **3** [VP2A,C] (colloq, of persons who have met together) **(a)** break off proceedings and separate. **(b)** go to another place: *When dinner was over they ~ed to the sitting-room.* **~·ment** *n* ~ing or being ~ed.

ad·judge /əˋdʒʌdʒ/ *vt* **1** [VP25,9] decide officially, by law: *~ sb (to be) guilty; ~ that a man is insane.* **2** [VP14] award: *~ land and property to sb; ~ a prize/legal damages to sb.*

ad·ju·di·cate /əˋdʒudɪkeɪt/ *vt,vi* **1** [VP6A,14] (of a judge or court) give a judgement or decision upon: *~ a claim for damages.* **2** [VP2A,3A] sit in judgement in order to decide: *~ (up)on a question.* **3** [VP25] declare (sb to be): *~ sb bankrupt.* **ad·ju·di·ca·tion** /əˈdʒudɪˋkeɪʃn/ *n* **ad·ju·di·ca·tor** /-tə(r)/ *n* judge; member of a jury, e g in a musical competition.

ad·junct /ˋædʒʌŋkt/ *n* **1** sth extra but subordinate. **2** (gram) word(s) or phrase added to qualify or define another word in a sentence.

ad·jure /əˋdʒʊə(r)/ *vt* [VP17A] ask (sb) earnestly or solemnly; require (sb) to do sth as though on oath or under penalty: *I ~ you to tell the truth.* **ad·jur·ation** /ˈædʒʊəˋreɪʃn/ *n* [U] adjuring; [C] earnest or solemn request.

ad·just /əˋdʒʌst/ *vt* [VP6A,14] set right; put in order; regulate; make suitable or convenient for use: *The body ~s itself to changes in temperature. You can't see well through a telescope unless it is ~ed correctly to your sight. She will have to ~ herself to new conditions,* change her ways of living, thinking, etc. *Please do not ~ your sets,* warning on a TV screen that the controls need not be changed. *You should ~ your expenditure to your income.* **'well-`~ed,** (psych) in harmonious relations with other persons: *a well-~ed child.* **~·able** /-əbl/ *adj* that can be ~ed. **~er** *n* (comm) person from an insurance company whose business it is to settle amounts due when claims are made, e g for loss. **~·ment** *n* **1** [U] ~ing; settling of, e g insurance, claims; [C] act of ~ing. **2** [C] means of ~ing sth; part of an apparatus for ~ing sth.

ad·ju·tant /'ædʒʊtənt/ *n* **1** (mil) army officer responsible for general administration and discipline in a battalion. **2** (also **~ bird**) large Indian stork.

ad lib /'æd `lɪb/ *adv* (abbr of *ad libitum*) (colloq) freely; without restraint. □ **ad-lib** *vi* (-bb-) [VP2A] (colloq) improvise, e g by making additions to one's part in a play. □ *attrib adj* made by ~bing: *~ comments.*

ad libi·tum /'æd `lɪbɪtəm/ *adv* (Lat; abbr *ad lib*) (music) (to be) performed without restraint.

ad-man /'æd mæn/ *n* (colloq) man who composes commercial advertisements.

ad·mass /'ædmæs/ *n* [U] that part of the public easily influenced by the mass media. ⇨ **media.**

ad·min·is·ter /əd`mɪnɪstə(r)/ *vt, vi* **1** [VP6A] control, manage, look after business affairs, a household, etc: *~ a country,* govern it. **2** [VP6A,14] apply; put into operation; hand out; give: *~ the law; ~ punishment to sb; ~ relief/help to people who are suffering from floods; ~ a severe blow to the enemy; ~ justice,* do the work of a judge. **3** [VP6A,14] cause to take: *~ the last sacraments,* i e to a dying man. *The oath was ~ed to him.* **4 ~ to,** ⇨ **minister(2).**

ad·min·is·tra·tion /əd'mɪnɪ`streɪʃn/ *n* **1** [U] management of affairs, etc, esp public affairs, government policy, etc. **the A~,** (esp US) that part of the Government which manages public affairs. **2** [U] the administering of justice, an oath, a sacrament, relief, a remedy, a punishment. ⇨ **ministration.**

ad·min·is·tra·tive /əd`mɪnɪstrətɪv *US:* -streɪtɪv/ *adj* of the management of affairs: *an ~ post; lacking in ~ ability.*

ad·min·is·tra·tor /əd`mɪnɪstreɪtə(r)/ *n* person who administers; person with ability to organize; (legal) person officially appointed to manage the property of others, to take charge of an estate, etc.

ad·mir·able /'ædmrəbl/ *adj* excellent; causing admiration. **ad·mir·ably** /-əblɪ/ *adv*

ad·miral /'ædmṛl/ *n* officer in command of a country's warships, or of a fleet or squadron; naval rank above vice-~ and below (GB) ~ of the fleet or (US) fleet ~. ⇨ **App 9. ~·ty** /'ædmṛltɪ/ *n* **1** office of ~. **2** that branch of Government which controls the Navy. **the A~ty,** (GB) headquarters of the naval administration. **'Court of `A~ty,** court for deciding law questions concerning shipping.

ad·mir·ation /'ædmə`reɪʃn/ *n* [U] **1** feeling of pleasure, satisfaction, respect (or, formerly) wonder: *She speaks English so well that her friends are filled with ~. Everyone cried out in ~. We were lost in ~ of the scenery. My ~ for your skill is great.* **2** (*sing* with *indef art*) object that arouses ~.

ad·mire /əd`mɑɪə(r)/ *vt* [VP6A] **1** look at with pleasure or satisfaction; have a high regard for: *Visitors to Britain usually ~ our policemen.* **2** express admiration of: *Don't forget to ~ the baby.* **ad·mirer** *n* person who ~s; man who finds a woman attractive: *Mary and her many ~s.* **ad·mir·ing** *adj* showing or feeling admiration: *admiring glances; an admiring crowd.* **ad·mir·ing·ly** *adv*

ad·miss·ible /əd`mɪsəbl/ *adj* **1** (legal) that can be allowed as judicial proof: *~ evidence.* **2** that can be allowed or considered. **ad·missi·bil·ity** /əd'mɪsə`bɪlətɪ/ *n* [U].

ad·mission /əd`mɪʃn/ *n* **1** [U] admitting, being admitted, to a society, a school, a building such as a theatre, a museum, etc; fee, charge or condition for this: *A~ to the school is by examination only. Price of ~, 10p. A~ free.* **2** [C] statement admitting sth; confession or acknowledgement: *make an ~ of guilt; an ~ that one has done wrong. To resign now would be an ~ of failure.* **by/on his own ~,** as he himself admitted.

ad·mit /əd`mɪt/ *vt, vi* (-tt-) **1** [VP6A,14] allow (sb or sth) to enter; let in: *The servant opened the door and ~ted me (into the house). Only one hundred boys are ~ted to the school each year. I ordered that he was not to be ~ted. Children not ~ted. The windows are small and do not ~ enough light and air.* **2** [VP6A] (of enclosed spaces) have room enough for: *The harbour ~s large liners and cargo boats. The theatre is small and ~s only 300 people.* **3** [VP6A] acknowledge; confess; accept as true or valid: *~ a claim/an assumption.* **4** [VP6A,C,9,14,25] acknowledge; confess: *The accused man ~ted his guilt. I ~ my mistake/that I was mistaken. He ~ted having done wrong. You must ~ the task to be difficult.* (more usu, *that the task is difficult*). *It is generally ~ted that...,* Most people acknowledge or agree that.... **5** [VP3A] **~ of,** leave room for: *The words ~ of* (= can have) *no other meaning. It ~s of no excuse,* There can be no excuse for it. **~ to,** make an acknowledgement; confess: *I must ~ to feeling ashamed of my conduct.* **~·ted·ly** /əd`mɪtɪdlɪ/ *adv* without denial; by general admission: *He is ~tedly an atheist.*

ad·mit·tance /əd`mɪtns/ *n* [U] act of admitting, being admitted (esp to a place that is not public); right of entry: *I called at his house but was refused ~,* was not allowed to enter. *No ~ except on business.*

ad·mix /æd`mɪks/ *vt, vi* [VP6A,2A] mix; become mixed; add as an ingredient.

ad·mix·ture /'æd`mɪkstʃə(r)/ *n* [U] mixture; [C] sth which is mixed with another substance, etc.

ad·mon·ish /əd`monɪʃ/ *vt* [VP6A,14] give a mild warning or a gentle reproof to: *The teacher ~ed the boys for being lazy/~ed them against smoking.* **ad·mo·ni·tion** /'ædmə`nɪʃn/ *n* [C,U] (an) ~ing; (a) warning. **ad·moni·tory** /əd`monɪtrɪ *US:* -tɔrɪ/ *adj* containing admonition: *an admonitory letter.*

ad nau·seam /'æd `nɔsɪəm/ *adv* (Lat) to the point of being disgusted; (colloq) to a ridiculous degree, so as to cause (great) annoyance, e g because of long continuance or repetition.

ado /ə`du/ *n* [U] fuss; trouble and excitement: *Without more/much/further ado, he signed.*

adobe /əˋdəʊbɪ/ *n* [U] sun-dried brick (not fired in a kiln), of clay and straw: (attrib) *an ~ house.*

adobe houses

ado·lescence /ˈædəˋlesns/ *n* [U] period of life between childhood and maturity; growth during this period. **ado·lescent** /-ˋlesnt/ *adj, n* (person) growing up from childhood (age 12 or 13 to 18).

adopt /əˋdɒpt/ *vt* [VP6A] **1** take (sb) into one's family as a relation, esp as a son or daughter, with legal guardianship: *As they had no children of their own, they ~ed an orphan.* ⇨ **foster. 2** take, e g an idea or custom, and use: *European dress has been ~ed by people in many parts of the world.* **3** accept, e g a report or recommendation: *Congress ~ed the new measures.* **adop·tion** /əˋdɒpʃn/ *n* ~ing or being ~ed: *The country of his ~ion.* **adop·tive** *adj* taken by ~ion: *His ~ive parents.*

adore /əˋdɔ(r)/ *vt* **1** [VP6A] worship (God); love deeply and respect highly. **2** [VP6A,C] (colloq; not in progressive tenses) like very much: *The baby ~s being tickled.* **ador·able** /-əbl/ *adj* lovable; delightful. **ador·ably** /-əblɪ/ *adv* **ador·ation** /ˈædəˋreɪʃn/ *n* [U] worship; love: *his adoration for Jane.* **adorer** *n* person who ~s (sb). **ador·ing** *adj* showing love: *adoring looks.* **ador·ing·ly** *adv*

adorn /əˋdɔn/ *vt* [VP6A,14] add beauty or ornament(s) to; decorate (oneself *with* jewels, etc); add distinction to. **~·ment** *n* [U] ~ing; [C] sth used for ~ing; ornament; decoration.

ad·re·nal /əˋdrinl/ *adj* (anat) of or near the kidneys: *~ glands.* **ad·ren·alin** /əˋdrenəlɪn/ *n* [U] (med) hormones secreted by the ~ glands, prepared as a substance used in the treatment of heart failure, etc.

adrift /əˋdrɪft/ *adv, pred adj* (of ships and boats) afloat, not under control and driven by wind and water; loose: *cut a boat ~ from its moorings;* (fig) at the mercy of circumstances: *turn sb ~,* send him away, e g from home, without money or means of livelihood.

adroit /əˋdrɔɪt/ *adj* **~ *(at/in),*** clever; skilful; ingenious or resourceful when dealing with problems. **~·ly** *adv* **~·ness** *n*

adu·la·tion /ˈædjʊˋleɪʃn *US:* -dʒʊˋl-/ *n* [U] (the giving of) excessive praise or respect, esp to win favour.

adult /ˈædʌlt/ *adj* grown to full size or strength; (of persons) intellectually and emotionally mature. □ *n* person or animal grown to full size and strength; (legal) person old enough to vote, marry, etc: *education for ~s; ~ education.* **~·hood** /-hʊd/ *n* the state of being ~.

adul·ter·ate /əˋdʌltəreɪt/ *vt* [VP6A,14] make impure, make poorer in quality, by adding sth of less value: *~d milk,* milk with water added. **adul·ter·ant** /əˋdʌltərənt/ *n* sth used for adulterating. **adul·ter·ation** /əˈdʌltəˋreɪʃn/ *n*

adul·tery /əˋdʌltərɪ/ *n* (*pl* -ries) [U] voluntary sexual intercourse of a married person with sb who is not the person to whom he or she is married; [C] instance of this. **adul·terer** /əˋdʌltərə(r)/ *n* man who commits ~. **adul·ter·ess** /əˋdʌltərəs/ *n* woman who commits ~. **adul·ter·ous** /əˋdʌltərəs/ *adj* of ~.

ad·um·brate /ˋædəmbreɪt/ *vt* [VP6A] indicate vaguely, foreshadow (a coming event).

ad va·lorem /ˈæd vəˋlɔrəm/ (Lat) (of taxes) in proportion to the estimated value of the goods.

ad·vance[1] /ədˋvɑns *US:* -ˋvæns/ *n* [C,U] **1** forward movement; progress: *With the ~ of old age, he could no longer do the work well. Science has made great ~s during the last fifty years. The country's industrial ~ has been remarkable. Has there been an ~ in civilization during the 20th century?* ***in ~ (of),*** before(hand): *Send your luggage in ~,* before you yourself leave. *It's unwise to spend your income in ~. Galileo's ideas were (well) in ~ of the age in which he lived.* **2** (attrib use) in ~: *an ~ copy of a new book,* one supplied before publication; *an ~ party,* party, e g of explorers, soldiers, sent in ~; *have ~ notice,* e g of sb's arrival. **ˈ~ ˋbooking,** reservation (of a room in a hotel, a seat in a theatre, etc) in ~ of the time when it is needed.

ad·vance[2] /ədˋvɑns *US:* -ˋvæns/ *vi,vt* **1** [VP2A, B,3A] come or go forward: *Our troops have ~d two miles. He ~d (up)on me in a threatening manner. Has civilization ~d during this century? The forces of the enemy ~d against us.* **2** [VP2A] (of costs, values, prices) rise: *Stock market prices/Property values continue to ~.* **3** [VP6A, 14] move, put or help forward: *The date of the meeting was ~d from the 10th to the 3rd June.* ⇨ **postpone.** *May I ~ my opinion on the matter? He worked so well that he was soon ~d* (= promoted) *to the position of manager. Such behaviour is not likely to ~ your interests.* **4** [VP6A] increase, raise (prices); (= colloq, *put up*): *The shopkeepers ~d their prices.* **5** [VP12A,13A] pay (money) before the due date: *He asked his employer to ~ him a month's salary. The banks often ~ money to farmers for seed and fertilizer.* **ad·vanced** *part adj* far on in life or progress, etc: *~d in years,* very old; *~d courses of study. The professor is engaged in ~d studies.* ⇨ **elementary.** *He has ~d ideas,* ideas that are new and not generally accepted. **the ~d level** (abbr ˋ*A level*) (of the General Certificate of Education), securing admission, in GB, to a college or university. **~·ment** *n* [U] promotion; preferment; improvement: *The aim of a university should be the ~ment of learning.*

ad·van·tage /ədˋvɑntɪdʒ *US:* -ˋvæn-/ *n* **1** [C] sth useful or helpful, sth likely to bring success, esp in competition: *the ~s of a good education. Living in a big town has many ~s, such as good schools, libraries and theatres.* ***have/gain/win an ~ (over), give (sb) an ~ (over),*** (have, give, etc) a better position or opportunity: *Tom's university education gave him an ~ over boys who had not been to a university.* ***have the ~ of sb,*** know sb or sth that he does not know. **2** [U] benefit; profit: *He gained little ~ from his visit to London.* ***take ~ of sb,*** deceive him, play a trick on him. ***take (full) ~ of sth,*** use it profitably, for one's own benefit: *He always takes full ~ of the mistakes* *made by his rivals.* ***to ~,*** in a way that enables sth to be seen, used, etc in the best way: *The painting is seen to better ~ from a distance. You should lay out your money* (= decide how to spend or invest it) *to the best ~.* ***be/prove to sb's ~,*** be profitable or helpful to him. ***turn sth to ~,*** make the most of it; use it profitably. **3** (tennis) the first point scored after deuce. □ *vt* [VP6A] benefit: *In what way will it ~ them?*

ad·van·tageous /ˈædvənˋteɪdʒəs/ *adj* profitable; helpful. **~·ly** *adv*

ad·vent /ˋædvent/ *n* **1** (usu *sing* with *def art*) coming or arrival (of an important development, season, etc): *Since the ~ of atomic power, there have been great changes in industry.* **2 A~,** (eccles) the coming of Christ; the season (with four Sundays) before Christmas Day. **3** the second coming of Christ at the Last Judgement. **Ad·vent·ist** /ˋædvəntɪst/ *n* person who believes that Christ's second coming and the end of the world are near.

ad·ven·ti·tious /ˈædvenˋtɪʃəs/ *adj* coming by chance; accidental: *~ aid.*

ad·ven·ture /ədˋventʃə(r)/ *n* **1** [C] strange or unusual happening, esp an exciting or dangerous journey or activity: *A flight in an aeroplane used to be quite an ~. The explorer told the boys about his ~s in the Arctic.* **2** [U] risk; danger, e g in travel and exploration: *fond of ~; a story of ~.* □ *vt* (= *venture,* the usu word). **ad·ven·turer** *n* **1** person who seeks ~. **2** person who is ready to make a profit for himself by risky or unscrupulous methods. **ad·ven·tur·ess** /-əs/ *n* woman ~r, esp one who is ready to use guile to obtain benefits. **ad·ven·tur·ous** /-əs/ *adj* **1** fond of, eager for, ~s. **2** full of danger and excitement: *an adventurous voyage.* **~·some** /-səm/ *adj* (rare or liter) = adventurous.

ad·verb /ˋædvɜb/ *n* word that answers questions with *how, when, where* and modifies *vv, adjj* and other *advv,* etc, e g *soon, here, well, quickly.* **ad·verb·ial** /ædˋvɜbɪəl/ *adj* of the nature of an ~. □ *n* ~ or ~ial phrase. **ad·verbi·ally** /ædˋvɜbɪəlɪ/ *adv*

ad·ver·sary /ˋædvəsərɪ *US:* -serɪ/ *n* (*pl* **-ries**) enemy; opponent (in any kind of contest).

ad·verse /ˋædvɜs/ *adj* unfavourable; contrary or hostile (*to*): *~ weather conditions; ~ winds,* e g for a sailing-ship; *developments ~ to our interests.* **~·ly** *adv*

ad·ver·sity /ədˋvɜsətɪ/ *n* (*pl* -ties). **1** [U] condition of adverse fortune; trouble: *be patient/cheerful in ~. A brave man smiles in the face of ~.* **2** [C] misfortune; affliction.

ad·vert[1] /ədˋvɜt/ *vi* [VP3A] (liter) ***~ to,*** refer to (in speech or writing): *~ to a problem.*

ad·vert[2] /ˋædvɜt/ *n* (GB colloq abbr) advertisement(2).

ad·ver·tise /ˋædvətaɪz/ *vt,vi* **1** [VP6A,2A,3A] make known to people (by printing notices in newspapers, etc or by other means, e g TV): *~ one's goods; ~ in all the newspapers; ~ for an assistant in the local newspapers,* announce that one wishes to engage an assistant. **2** [VP11,14] ***~ sb of sth/that,*** (old use) inform; announce. **ad·ver·tiser** *n* person who ~s. **~·ment** /ədˋvɜtɪsmənt *US:* ˈædvərˋtaɪzmənt/ *n* **1** [U] advertising: (attrib) *the ~ment manager,* e g of a newspaper. *A~ment helps to sell goods.* **2** [C] public announcement (in the press, TV, etc): *If you want to sell your piano, put an ~ in the newspaper.*

ad·vice /ədˋvaɪs/ *n* **1** [U] (informed) opinion about what to do, how to behave: *You won't get well unless you follow your doctor's ~. If you take my ~ and study hard, you'll pass the examination. You should take legal ~,* consult a lawyer. ***act on sb's ~,*** do what he suggests. ***(give sb) a piece/bit/word/few words of ~,*** (give) an opinion about what to do, etc. **2** [C] (comm) (usu *pl*) news from a distance, esp commercial: *~s from our Tokyo branch.* **ˋ~-note, letter of ~,** (comm) formal notice of delivery of goods, a business call, etc.

ad·vis·able /ədˋvaɪzəbl/ *adj* wise; sensible; to be advised or recommended: *Do you think it ~ to wait?* **ad·visa·bil·ity** /ədˈvaɪzəˋbɪlətɪ/ *n* [U].

ad·vise /ədˋvaɪz/ *vt,vi* **1** [VP6A,C,17,20,21,14] give advice to; recommend: *The doctor ~d a complete rest. What do you ~ me to do? Please ~ me whether I should accept the offer. We ~d an early start/their starting early/them to start early. Her father ~d her against marrying in haste. Who is the best man to ~ me on this question?* **2** [VP6A,21,14] (comm) inform; notify: *Please ~ us when the goods are dispatched/ ~ us of the dispatch of the goods.* **3** [VP3A] ***~ with (sb),*** (old use) consult; take counsel with. **ad·viser** *n* person who gives advice, esp one who is habitually consulted: *~r to the Government.* **ad·vised** *adj* (old use) considered; carefully thought out; deliberate. ***ill ~d,*** unwise; injudicious. ***well ~d,*** wise; judicious. **ad·vis·ed·ly** /ədˋvaɪzɪdlɪ/ *adv* after careful thought. **ad·vis·ory** /ədˋvaɪzərɪ/ *adj* of advice; having the power to ~: *an advisory committee/council/panel.*

ad·vo·cate /ˋædvəkət/ *n* **1** person who speaks in favour of sb or sth (esp a cause): *an ~ of equal pay for men and women.* **2** (legal) person who does this professionally in a court of law (*A~* in Scotland, *Barrister* in GB): *the Faculty of A~s,* the Scots bar. **Lord A~,** principal law officer in Scotland. □ *vt* /ˋædvəkeɪt/ [VP6A,C] support; speak publicly in support of: *Do you ~ keeping all children at school till the age of sixteen?* **ad·vo·cacy** /ˋædvəkəsɪ/ *n* [U] pleading in support (*of* a cause or sb).

ad·vow·son /ˈædˋvaʊzn/ *n* (GB, eccles) right of presentation to a church benefice.

adze, adz /ædz/ *n* carpenter's tool (with a blade at right angles to the handle) for cutting or shaping wood.

aegis, egis /ˋidʒɪs/ *n* protection; sponsorship. ***under the ~ of,*** with the patronage or support of.

aeon, eon /ˋiən/ *n* [C] period of time too long to be measured.

aer·ate /ˋeəreɪt/ *vt* [VP6A] charge (a liquid) with air or gas; expose to the chemical purifying action of air: *~ the soil by digging. Blood is ~d in the lungs.* **aer·ation** /ˈeəˋreɪʃn/ *n*

aer·ial /ˋeərɪəl/ *adj* **1** existing in, moving through, the air: *an ~ railway/ropeway,* a system of overhead suspension for transport. **2** of or like air; immaterial. □ *n* that part of a radio or TV system which receives or sends out signals, usu a wire or rod, or number of wires or rods (= US *antenna*).

aerie, aery, eyrie, eyry /ˋeərɪ/ *n* eagle's nest; nest of other birds of prey which are built high up among rocks; eagle's brood.

aero·bat·ics /ˈeərəˋbætɪks/ *n* (*sing v*) [U] the performance of acrobatic feats by airmen, e g flying upside down.

aero·drome /ˋeərədrəʊm/ *n* (US = *airdrome*) flying-ground, with hangars, workshops, etc (*flying-field, airfield, airport* are the more usu words).

aero·dy·nam·ics /ˈeərəʊdaɪˋnæmɪks/ *n pl* (*sing v*) [U] science dealing with the flow of air and the motion of aircraft, bullets, etc through air.

aero·naut /ˋeərənɔt/ *n* person who pilots or travels in a balloon, airship or other aircraft.

aero·naut·ics /ˈeərəˋnɔtɪks/ *n* (*sing v*) [U] science and practice of aviation (the more usu word).

aero·plane /ˋeərəpleɪn/ *n* (= US *airplane*) heavier-than-air flying machine with one or more engines. ⇨ *aircraft, airliner* at air[1](7).

aero·sol /ˋeərəsol *US:* -sɔl/ *n* dispersion of fine solid or liquid particles, e g of scent, paint, insecticide, detergent, released (in a mist) by pressure from a container with compressed gas from a valve; (P) the container itself.

aero·space /ˋeərəʊspeɪs/ *n* the earth's atmosphere and the space beyond: *an ~ vehicle.*

aery /ˋeərɪ/ *n* ⇨ **aerie.**

aer·tex /ˋeəteks/ *n* (P) kind of loosely woven textile material (as used for underwear).

aes·thete, es·thete /ˋisθit *US:* ˋesθit/ *n* person who claims to have great love of and understanding of what is beautiful, esp in the arts.

aes·thetic, es·thetic /ˈisˋθetɪk *US:* ˈes-/ *adj* of the appreciation of the beautiful, esp in the arts; (of persons) having such appreciation: *~ standards.* **aes·thet·ical, es·thet·ical** /-kl/ *adj* = aesthetic. **aes·thet·ically** /-klɪ/ *adv* **aes·thet·ics, es·thet·ics** *n* (*sing v*) [U] branch of philosophy which tries to make clear the laws and principles of beauty (contrasted with morality and utility). □ *n* particular set of ~ principles: *the ~ to which he remained faithful.*

aether /ˋiθə(r)/ *n* ⇨ **ether.**

aeti·ol·ogy /ˈitɪˋolədʒɪ/ ⇨ **etiology.**

afar /əˋfɑ(r)/ *adv* far off or away: *from ~,* from a distance.

af·fable /ˋæfəbl/ *adj* polite and friendly; pleasant and easy to talk to: *~ to everybody; an ~ reply.* **af·fably** /-əblɪ/ *adv* **affa·bil·ity** /ˈæfəˋbɪlətɪ/ *n* quality of being ~ (*to* or *towards*).

af·fair /əˋfeə(r)/ *n* [C] **1** concern; sth (to be) done; business: *That's my ~, not yours.* **2** (*pl*) business of any kind; day-to-day concerns of organization, etc: *A prime minister is kept busy with ~s of state,* the task of government. *When he asked me how much I earned, I told him to mind his own ~s,* not to ask questions about my business, etc. *We can't afford a holiday in the present state of ~s,* while things remain as they are now. **Secretary of State for Foreign/Home/Welsh, etc A~s,** titles of Government Ministers in GB. **3** ***have an ~ (with sb),*** have an emotional (and sexual) relationship with sb to whom one is not married: *The doctor, they say, is having an ~ with the rector's wife.* ***~ of honour,*** duel. **4** (colloq) occurrence; event; object: *The railway accident was a terrible ~. Her hat was a wonderful ~. What a ramshackle ~ your old car is!*

af·fect[1] /əˋfekt/ *vt* [VP6A] **1** have an influence or impression on; act on: *The climate ~ed his health,* injured it. *Some plants are quickly ~ed by cold. Will the changes in taxation ~ you personally,* Will you have to pay more (or less) in taxes? *The rise in the price of bread will ~ us all.* **2** move the feelings of: *He was much ~ed by the sad news. His death ~ed us deeply.* **3** (of diseases) attack; cause a particular condition in: *The left lung is ~ed,* e g by cancer, tuberculosis. **4** ***well/ill ~ed (towards),*** well/ill disposed (the more usu word) or inclined (towards). **~·ing** *adj* moving or touching (the feelings): *an ~ing sight.* **~·ing·ly** *adv* tenderly; pathetically.

af·fect[2] /əˋfekt/ *vt* **1** [VP6A,7A] pretend to have or feel (ignorance, indifference); pretend (to do, etc): *He ~ed not to hear me.* **2** [VP6A] have a liking for and use (esp for ostentation): *He ~s long and learned words,* uses them instead of short and simple words. *She ~s bright colours,* wears brightly coloured clothes, etc. **~ed** *adj* pretended; not natural or genuine: *an ~ed politeness; ~ed manners; with an ~ed cheerfulness; written in an ~ed style,* showing a liking for an artificial style.

af·fec·ta·tion /ˈæfekˋteɪʃn/ *n* **1** [C,U] (kind of) behaviour that is not natural or genuine: *Her little ~s annoyed me. Keep clear of all ~,* Do not behave unnaturally. **2** [C] pretence (made on purpose, for effect): *an ~ of interest/indifference/ignorance.*

af·fec·tion /əˋfekʃn/ *n* **1** [U] kindly feeling; love: *Every mother has ~ for/feels ~ toward her children. He is held in great ~,* is much loved. **2** [U or *pl*] ***gain/win sb's ~(s),*** win the love of. **3** [C] (old use) disease; unhealthy condition: *an ~ of the throat.*

af·fec·tion·ate /əˋfekʃn̩ət/ *adj* loving; fond; showing love (*to* sb): *an ~ wife; ~ looks.* **~·ly** *adv* ***Yours ~ly,*** used at the close of a letter, e g from a man to his sister.

af·fiance /əˋfɑɪəns/ *vt* [VP6A] (usu passive; liter or old use) promise in marriage: *be ~d to (sb),* be engaged to marry him/her.

af·fi·da·vit /ˈæfɪˋdeɪvɪt/ *n* (legal) written statement, made on oath, (to be) used as legal proof or evidence: *swear/make/take an ~.*

af·fili·ate /əˋfɪlɪeɪt/ *vt,vi* [VP6A,14,2A] ***~ (to/with),*** (of society or institution, or a member) enter into association: *The College is ~d to the University. Is the Mineworkers' Union ~d with the TUC?*

af·fili·ation /əˈfɪlɪˋeɪʃn/ *n* [U] affiliating or being affiliated; [C] connection made by affiliating. **ˋ~ order,** (GB, legal) order made by a magistrate, determining the paternity of an illegitimate child and requiring the father to contribute towards its support.

af·fin·ity /əˋfɪnətɪ/ *n* (*pl* **-ties**) ***~ (between/to/for),*** **1** [C] close connection, structural resemblance (between animals and plants, languages, etc) (or of one thing to/with another). **2** [U] relationship; [C] relation (by marriage); similarity of character suggesting relationship. **3** [C] strong liking or attraction: *She feels a strong ~ to/for him.* **4** chemical or physical attraction: *the ~ of common salt for water.*

af·firm /əˋf3m/ *vt,vi* **1** [VP6A,9,14] declare positively: *~ the truth of a statement/~ that it is true; ~ to sb that....* ⇨ **deny. 2** [VP2A] (legal) (of a person who has conscientious objections to swearing on the Bible) declare solemnly but not on oath. **~·ation** /ˈæfəˋmeɪʃn/ *n* **1** [U] ~ing. **2** [C] sth ~ed; (legal) declaration made by ~ing(2). **~·ative** /əˋf3mətɪv/ *adj n* (answering) 'yes': *an ~ative answer. The answer is the ~ative,* is 'Yes'. ⇨ **negative(1).**

af·fix[1] /əˋfɪks/ *vt* [VP6A,14] fix; fasten; attach: *~ a*

seal/stamp to a document; add in writing: *~ your signature to an agreement.*
af·fix[2] /ˈæfɪks/ *n* suffix or prefix, e g *-ly, -able, un-, co-.* ⇨ App 3.
af·fla·tus /əˈfleɪtəs/ *n* [U] divine revelation; inspiration.
af·flict /əˈflɪkt/ *vt* [VP6A] cause bodily or mental trouble to: *~ed with rheumatism; feel much ~ed at/by the news.*
af·flic·tion /əˈflɪkʃn/ *n* **1** [U] suffering; distress: *help people in ~.* **2** [C] cause or occasion of suffering: *the ~s of old age,* e g deafness, blindness.
af·fluence /ˈæflʊəns/ *n* [U] wealth; abundance: *living in ~; rise to ~,* become wealthy.
af·fluent /ˈæflʊənt/ *adj* wealthy; abundant: *in ~ circumstances; the ~ society,* society which is prosperous and whose members are concerned with material improvement. □ *n* [C] stream flowing into a larger one (*tributary* is the more usu word).
af·ford /əˈfɔd/ *vt* **1** [VP6A,7] (usu with *can/could, be able to*) spare or find enough time or money for: *We can't ~ a holiday/can't ~ to go away this summer. Are you able to ~ the time for a holiday?* **2** [VP7] (with *can/could*) run a risk by doing sth: *I can't ~ to neglect my work. She couldn't ~ to displease her boss.* **3** [VP12A,13A,6A] (formal) provide; give: *The trees ~ a pleasant shade. It will ~ me great pleasure to have dinner with you.*
af·for·est /əˈfɒrɪst *US:* -ˈfɔr-/ *vt* [VP6A] make into forest land. **af·for·est·ation** /əˌfɒrɪˈsteɪʃn *US:* -ˌfɔr-/ *n*: *~ation projects,* projects for planting large areas with trees.
af·fran·chise /əˈfræntʃɑɪz/ *vt* [VP6A] free from servitude.
af·fray /əˈfreɪ/ *n* [C] fight in a public place, causing or likely to cause a disturbance of the peace: *The men were charged with causing an ~.*
af·front /əˈfrʌnt/ *vt* [VP6A] insult on purpose; hurt sb's feelings or self-respect, esp in public: *feel ~ed at having one's word doubted.* □ *n* [C] public insult; deliberate show of disrespect: *an ~ to his pride; suffer an ~; offer an ~ to sb.*
afield /əˈfild/ *adv* far away from home; to or at a distance: *Don't go too far ~.*
afire /əˈfɑɪə(r)/ *pred adj* on fire.
aflame /əˈfleɪm/ *pred adj* in flames; burning; red as if burning: (fig) *~ with passion; The autumn woods were ~ with colour.*
afloat /əˈfləʊt/ *pred adj* **1** floating; borne up, carried along, on air or water: *The ship stuck fast on the rocks and we couldn't get it ~ again.* **2** at sea; on board ship: *life ~,* the life of a sailor. **3** awash; flooded. **4** (business) started; solvent: *get a new periodical ~,* launch it. **5** (of stories, rumours) current; in circulation.
afoot /əˈfʊt/ *pred adj* **1** in progress or operation; being prepared: *There's mischief ~. There's a scheme ~ to improve the roads.* **2** (old use) on foot; walking.
afore /əˈfɔ(r)/ *adv, prep* (naut) before: *~ the mast.* **ˈ~-said** *pron, adj* (legal) (that has been) said or mentioned before. **ˈ~-thought,** ⇨ malice.
a forti·ori /ˈeɪ ˈfɔtɪˈɔrɑɪ/ *adv* (Lat) with stronger reason.
afoul /əˈfɑʊl/ *adv* **run/fall ~ of,** (more usu *run/fall foul of*) come into collision with; get mixed up with.
afraid /əˈfreɪd/ *pred adj* **~ (of)/that/to do sth, 1** frightened (of): *There's nothing to be ~ of. Are you ~ of snakes?* **2** apprehensive; doubtful or anxious about consequences: *I was ~ of hurting his feelings/that I might hurt his feelings. Don't be ~* (= Don't hesitate) *to ask for my help. She was ~ of waking her husband,* didn't want to wake him, perhaps because he was ill or in need of sleep. *She was ~ to wake her husband,* feared that he might be angry with her. **3 be ~,** (with *that* usu omitted) (often a polite formula used with a statement that may be unwelcome): *I'm ~ we shall be late. You'll get caught in the rain, I'm ~. I'm ~ I can't help.*
afresh /əˈfreʃ/ *adv* again; in a new way: *Let's start ~.*
Afri·kaans /ˌæfrɪˈkɑns *US:* ˈæfrɪkɑns -nz/ *n* language developed from Dutch, one of the two official European languages in the Republic of South Africa.
Afro- /ˈæfrəʊ/ *pref* (in compounds) of Africa: **ˌ~-ˈAsian** *adj* of Africa and Asia. **ˌ~-Aˈmerican** *n* American Negro/Negress of African descent. **ˈ~-wig** *n* wig (worn by a woman) in the style of hairdressing of some African women.
aft /ɑft *US:* æft/ *adv* (naut) at or near the stern of a ship, ⇨ the illus at ship: *go aft; fore and aft,* ⇨ fore.
after[1] /ˈɑftə(r) *US:* ˈæf-/ *adj* (attrib only) **1** later; following: *in ~ years.* **2** (naut) toward the stern of a ship: *the ˈ~ cabin; the ˈ~mast.*
after[2] /ˈɑftə(r) *US:* ˈæf-/ *adv* **1** later in time; behind in place: *He fell ill on Monday and died three days ~* (*later* is more usu). *What comes ~? Soon ~* (*afterwards* is more usu), *he went to live in Wales.* **2** (modifying a *n*): *in ~* (= later) *years.*
after[3] /ˈɑftə(r) *US:* ˈæf-/ *conj* at or during a time later than: *I arrived ~ he (had) left. I shall arrive ~ you leave/have left.*
after[4] /ˈɑftə(r) *US:* æf-/ *prep* **1** following in time; later than: *~ dinner; ~ dark; ~ two o'clock; soon/shortly ~ six.* Cf a little *before* six. *~ that,* then; next; *the day ~ tomorrow; the week ~ next;* (US) *half ~* (GB = *past*) *seven.* **2** next in order to; following: *Put the direct object ~ the verb. 'Against' comes ~ 'again' in the dictionary.* **3** behind: *Shut the door ~ you when you leave the room.* **4** in view of; as a result of: *I shall never speak to him again ~ what he has said about me.* **5** in spite of: *A~ all my care, it was broken. He failed ~ all,* in spite of all that had been done, etc. **6** (in the pattern: *n ~ n,* indicating succession): *day ~ day; week ~ week; time ~ time,* repeatedly, very often; *shot ~ shot. It's one damned thing ~ another,* a succession of unpleasant happenings, etc. **7** (indicating manner) in the style of; in imitation of: *a painting ~ Rembrandt; (do sth) ~ a fashion, a man ~ my own heart,* ⇨ fashion(1), heart(2). **8** (with *vv,* indicating pursuit, search, inquiry): *The policeman ran ~ the thief. Did they inquire ~ me,* ask for news of me? **be/get ~ sb,** look for, in order to reprimand, punish, etc according to context: *The police are ~ him. They'll be ~ you if you steal apples from this orchard.* ⇨ *look ~, name sb ~, take ~,* at look[1](6), name[2](1) and take(16). **9** (Irish usage) preceding a gerund, making an equivalent of a perfect tense: *He's ~ drinking,* has been drinking.
after- /ˈɑftə(r) *US:* ˈæf-/ *pref* second or later. **ˈ~-care** *n* further treatment given to a person or class of persons, e g sb who has been ill or offenders discharged from prison. **ˈ~-damp** *n* poisonous

mixture of gases after the explosion of firedamp in a coalmine. **`~-effect** *n* effect that occurs afterwards, e g a delayed effect of a drug used medically. **`~-glow** *n* glow in the sky after sunset. **(the) `~-life** *n* **(a)** the life believed to follow death. **(b)** the later part of sb's lifetime (esp after a particular event). **`~-math** /-mæθ/ *n* (of grass) crop from a second growth (after the hay harvest); (fig) outcome; consequence: *Misery is usually the ~math of war.* **`~-thought** *n* [U] reflection afterwards. [C] thought that comes afterwards.

after·noon /ˈɑftəˋnun *US:* ˈæf-/ *n* time between morning and evening: *in/during the ~; this/ yesterday/tomorrow ~; every ~; on Sunday ~; on the ~ of May 1st; one ~ last week; on several ~s;* (attrib) *an ~ sleep/concert.*

afters /ˋɑftəz *US:* ˋæf-/ *n pl* (colloq) last (usu sweet) course at a meal: *What's for ~? Is it fruit and custard?*

after·wards /ˋɑftəwədz *US:* ˋæf-/ *adv* after; later.

again /əˋgen/ *adv* **1** once more: *If you fail the first time, try ~. Say it ~, please. Do you think she will marry ~,* remarry? *You must type this letter ~,* retype it. ***now and ~,*** occasionally, ***~ and ~, time and (time) ~,*** repeatedly; very often. ***(the) same ~,*** formula for re-ordering drinks. **2** (with *not, never*) any more: *This must never happen ~. Don't do that ~.* **3** to or in the original condition, position, etc: *You'll soon be well ~. He was glad to be home ~. You won't get the money back ~,* won't regain it. ***be oneself ~,*** be restored to a normal (physical or mental) condition. **4 *as many/much ~,*** **(a)** the same number/ quantity. **(b)** twice as many/much; the same in addition. ***half as many/much/long, etc ~,*** half as many/much, etc in addition. **5** (often preceded by *and* or *and then*) furthermore, besides: *Then ~, I feel doubtful whether....*

against /əˋgenst/ *prep* **1** (indicating opposition): *Public opinion was ~ the proposal.* Cf *for, in favour of. We were rowing ~ the current.* Cf *with. It was a race ~ time,* an attempt to finish before a certain time, before a possible happening, etc. *She was married ~ her will. Is there a law ~ spitting in the streets in this country? His appearance is ~ him,* is such that people are unlikely to favour or support him. **2** (with *vv* indicating protest): *vote/ cry out/write/raise one's voice ~ a proposal.* **3** (with *vv*, to indicate collision or impact): *The rain was beating ~ the windows. He hit his head ~ the wall in the dark cellar.* ⇨ *run against* at run[1](21). **4** in contrast to: *The pine trees were black ~ the morning sky.* **5** in preparation for; in anticipation of: *take precautions ~ fire; an injection ~ rabies; save money ~ a rainy day,* (prov) for a time of possible need. **6** (indicating support or close proximity): *Place the ladder ~ the tree. Put the piano with its back ~ the wall. He was leaning ~ a post.* **7 *over ~,*** facing, opposite to.

agape /əˋgeɪp/ *pred adj* with the mouth wide open (due to wonder, surprise, or a yawn).

agar-agar /ˈeɪgɑr ˋeɪgɑ(r) *US:* ˈɑg- ˋɑg-/ *n* [U] (jelly-like substance prepared from) seaweed.

ag·ate /ˋægɪt/ *n* (sorts of) very hard stone, a form of silica, with bands or patches of colour.

agave /əˋgeɪvɪ *US:* əˋgɑvɪ/ *n* (bot) (kinds of) tropical fleshy-leaved plant (including *sisal*), cultivated for their fibres and as a source of intoxicating drinks, e g *pulque.*

age[1] /eɪdʒ/ *n* **1** length of time a person has lived or a thing has existed: *What's his age,* How old is he? *Their ages are 4, 7 and 9. At what age do children start school in your country? What's the age of that old church? When I was your age...; I have a son your age,* a son the same age as you. *She ought to be earning her own living at her age,* She's old enough now to do this. ***be/come of age,*** be/become old enough to be responsible in law. ⇨ *age of consent* at consent. ***be of an age,*** reach a stage in life when one ought to do sth: *He's of an age when he ought to be settling down,* e g get a good job, marry. ***over age,*** having passed a certain age or age limit: *He won't be called up for military service; he's over age.* ⇨ *age limit* at limit[1]. ***under age,*** too young; not yet of age. **`age-bracket** *n* period of life between two specified ages, e g between 20 and 30. **`age-group** *n* number of persons of the same age. **2** [U] later part of life (contrasted with *youth*): *His back was bent with age. If we could have the strength of youth and the wisdom of age,....* **3** great or long period of time, with special characteristics or events: *the age of machinery; the atomic age; the Elizabethan Age,* the time of Queen Elizabeth I of England (1558—1603). ⇨ *golden age, middle age, the Middle Ages, the Stone Age* at golden(2), middle(3), stone(1). **4** (colloq) very long time: *We've been waiting for ages.*

age[2] /eɪdʒ/ *vt,vi* (*pres part* ageing or aging, *pp* aged /eɪdʒd/) [VP6A,2A] (cause to) grow old: *He's ag(e)ing fast. I found him greatly aged,* looking much older. **aged** /ˋeɪdʒd/ *pred adj* of the age of: *a boy aged ten.* □ *attrib adj* /ˋeɪdʒɪd/ very old: *an aged man; the poor and the aged,* those who are poor and old. **`aging, `age·ing** *n* [U] process of growing old; changes that occur as the result of the passing of time. **`age·less** *adj* eternal; always young; not affected by time. **`age-long** *adj* lasting for centuries; handed down the ages. **ˈage-`old** *adj* that has been known, practised, etc for a long time: *age-old customs/ceremonies.*

agency /ˋeɪdʒənsɪ/ *n* (*pl* -cies) **1** business, place of business, of an agent(1): *The Company has agencies in all parts of Africa. He found a job through an employment ~. Not all travel agencies are reliable.* **2** [U] ***the ~ of,*** the operation, instrumentality of; *Rocks are worn smooth through the ~ of water. He obtained a position in a government office through/by the ~* (= with the help or influence) *of friends.*

agenda /əˋdʒendə/ *n* (collective *n*, usu with *sing v*) **1** (list of) things to be done, business to be discussed, e g by a committee: *the next item on the ~; item No 5 on the ~.* **2** (comp) set of operations which form a procedure for solving a problem.

agent /ˋeɪdʒnt/ *n* **1** person who acts for, or who manages the business affairs of, another or others: *a `house-~,* one who buys, sells, lets and rents houses; *a `literary ~,* one who helps authors to find a publisher; *a `shipping or `forwarding ~,* one who sends goods by rail, sea, road, etc for merchants, manufacturers, etc. **`law ~,** (in Scotland) solicitor. ⇨ free[1](1), secret(1). **2** person used to secure sth, to get a result; (science) substance, natural agent, etc producing an effect: *Rain and frost are natural ~s that wear away rocks.*

agent pro·voca·teur /ˈæʒõ prəˈvokəˋtɜ(r)/ *n* (*pl* agents provocateurs) (F) person employed to find suspected criminals or offenders by tempting them to commit an offence openly.

ag·glom·er·ate /əˋglɒməreɪt/ *vt,vi* [VP6A,2A] gather, collect, into a mass. □ *adj* /əˋglɒmərət/ collected into, forming or growing into, a mass. **ag·glom·er·ation** /əˌglɒməˋreɪʃn/ *n* [U] action of agglomerating; [C] (esp untidy) heap or collection of ~d objects, e g a sprawl of untidy suburbs.

ag·glu·tin·ate /əˋglutɪneɪt/ *vt* [VP6A,2A] join together as with glue; combine. **ag·glu·ti·nat·ive** /əˋglutɪnətɪv *US:* -tṇeɪtɪv/ *adj* (of languages) that combine simple words into compounds without change of form or loss of meaning.

ag·grand·ize·ment /əˋgrændɪzmənt/ *n* increase in power, rank, wealth, importance: *a man bent on personal ~.*

ag·gra·vate /ˋægrəveɪt/ *vt* [VP6A] **1** make worse or more serious: *~ an illness/offence.* **2** (colloq) irritate; exasperate: *He ~s her beyond endurance. How aggravating,* annoying! **ag·gra·va·tion** /ˌægrəˋveɪʃn/ *n* [U] aggravating or being ~d; [C] sth that ~s.

ag·gre·gate /ˋægrɪgeɪt/ *vt,vi* **1** [VP6A,2A] bring or come together in a mass. **2** [VP2E] amount to (specified total). □ *n* /ˋægrɪgət/ **1** total obtained by addition; mass or amount brought together. ***in the ~,*** as a whole; collectively. **2** materials (sand, gravel, etc) mixed with cement to make concrete. **ag·gre·ga·tion** /ˌægrəˋgeɪʃn/ *n* [U] number of separate things, materials, brought together into a mass or group.

ag·gression /əˋgreʃn/ *n* **1** [U] unprovoked attacking; beginning a quarrel or war: *It was difficult to decide which country was guilty of ~ (upon the other).* **2** [C] instance of this.

ag·gress·ive /əˋgresɪv/ *adj* **1** quarrelsome; disposed to attack: *an ~ man; a man with an ~ disposition.* **2** offensive; of or for attack: *~ weapons.* **3** pushing; not afraid of resistance: *A man who goes from door to door selling things has to be ~ if he wants to succeed.* **~·ly** *adv* **~·ness** *n* **ag·gressor** /-sə(r)/ *n* person, country, making an ~ attack: (attrib) *the aggressor nation.*

ag·grieve /əˋgriv/ *vt* (usu passive) grieve: *be ~d.* ***feel (oneself) much ~d (at/over sth),*** feel that one has been treated unjustly; be hurt in one's feelings.

ag·gro /ˋægrəʊ/ *n* [U] (GB sl) aggression as shown by gangs of teenagers towards other gangs, racial minorities, etc.

aghast /əˋgɑst *US:* əˋgæst/ *pred adj* filled with fear or surprise: *He stood ~ at the terrible sight.*

agile /ˋædʒɑɪl *US:* ˋædʒl/ *adj* (of living things) quick-moving; active. **~·ly** *adv* **agil·ity** /əˋdʒɪlətɪ/ *n* [U].

agin /əˋgɪn/ *prep* (used jocularly for) against, e g in: *~ the government.*

aging *n* = ageing. ⇨ **age**[2].

agi·tate /ˋædʒɪteɪt/ *vt,vi* **1** [VP6A] move or shake (a liquid); stir up (the surface of a liquid). **2** [VP6A] disturb; cause anxiety to (a person, his mind or feelings): *She was deeply ~d until she learnt that her husband was among the survivors. He was ~d about his wife's health.* **3** [VP3A] ***~ for,*** argue publicly in favour of, take part in a campaign for: *~ for the repeal of a law; workers who ~d for higher wages.* **agi·tated** *part adj* troubled. **agi·tat·ing** *part adj* causing anxiety. **agi·ta·tion** /ˌædʒɪˋteɪʃn/ *n* **1** [U] moving or shaking (of a liquid). **2** [U] excitement of the mind or feelings; anxiety: *She was in a state of agitation.* **3** [C,U] discussion or debate (for the purpose of bringing about a change); [U] social or political unrest or trouble caused by such discussion: *Small shopkeepers carried on a long agitation against the big department stores.* **agi·ta·tor** /-tə(r)/ *n* person who ~s, esp politically.

aglow /əˋgləʊ/ *pred adj* **1** bright with colour; in a glow: *The sky was ~ with the setting sun.* **2** (of persons) showing warmth from exercise or excitement: *~ with pleasure;* shining: *a face ~ with health.*

ag·nail /ˋægneɪl/ *n* [U] torn skin at the base of a finger nail.

ag·nos·tic /ægˋnɒstɪk/ *n* person who believes that nothing can be known about God or of anything except material things. □ *adj* of this belief. **ag·nos·ti·cism** /ægˋnɒstɪsɪzm/ *n* [U].

ago /əˋgəʊ/ *adv* (used to indicate time measured back to a point in the past; always placed after the word or words it modifies; used with the simple *pt*): *The train left a few minutes ago/not long ago. That was many years/a long while ago. How long ago is it that you last saw her? I met Mary no longer ago than* (= as recently as) *last Sunday. It was seven years ago that my brother died.* Cf It *is* seven years *since* my brother died.

agog /əˋgɒg/ *pred adj* eager; excited: *~ for news; ~ to hear the news. The whole village was ~. His unexpected return set the town ~,* e g was the cause of many rumours about the reasons for his return.

ag·ony /ˋægənɪ/ *n* (*pl* **-nies**) [C] (*sing* or *pl*) great pain or suffering (of mind or body): *She looked on in ~ at her child's sufferings. I've suffered agonies/have been in agonies with toothache. He was in an ~ of remorse.* ˋ**~ column,** newspaper column with advertisements for news of missing friends, etc. ***pile on the ~,*** (colloq) ⇨ **pile**[3](1). **ag·on·ized** /ˋægənɑɪzd/ *adj* expressing ~: *agonized shrieks.* **ag·on·iz·ing** /ˋægənɑɪzɪŋ/ *adj* causing ~.

agora /ˋægərə/ *n* (in ancient Greece) (place of) assembly; market-place. **~·phobia** /ˌægərəˋfəʊbɪə/ *n* [U] fear of (crossing) open spaces.

agrar·ian /əˋgreərɪən/ *adj* of land (esp farmland) or land ownership: *~ laws/problems/reforms/disputes.*

agree /əˋgri/ *vi,vt* **1** [VP2A,3A,B] ***~ (to),*** say 'Yes'; consent: *I asked him to help me and he ~d. Mary's father has ~d to her marrying John. He ~d to my proposal.* **2** [VP3A,B,4C,7A] (also with an *inf* or a *that*-clause without a *prep*) be of the same opinion(s); be in harmony (*with* sb *on/about* sth, *as to* how to do sth, etc): *We ~d to start early. I hope you will ~ with me that our teacher's advice is excellent. We all ~d on the terms. We ~d on an early start/on making an early start/that we should start early. We met at the ~d time,* at the time we had ~d on. *We are* (= have) *all ~d on finding the accused man innocent. We are all ~d that the proposal is a good one. We could not ~ (as to) how it should be done. Have you ~d about the price yet?* **3** [VP2A,C] (of two or more persons) be happy together; get on well with one another (without arguing, etc): *We shall never ~. Why can't you children ~ (together)?* **4** [VP3A] ***~ (with),*** match, conform (with): *Your story ~s with what I had already heard. This bill does not ~ with your original estimate,* the two are different. **5** [VP3A] ***~ with,*** suit, e g the health or constitution of: *The climate doesn't ~ with me. The mussels I had for lunch haven't ~d with me,* have upset my stomach. **6** [VP3A] ***~ with,*** (gram) correspond in number, person, etc with: *The verb ~s with its subject in number and person.* **7** [VP6A] (of figures, accounts, proposals, etc) accept or approve (as being correct): *The Inspector of Taxes has ~d your return of income.*

agree·able /ə`griəbl/ *adj* **1** pleasing; giving pleasure: *She has an ~ voice.* **2** ready to agree: *Are you ~ to the proposal? I'm ~ to doing what you suggest.* **agree·ably** /-əblɪ/ *adv*: *I was agreeably surprised,* surprised and pleased.

agree·ment /ə`grimənt/ *n* **1** [U] having the same opinion(s); thinking in the same way: *We are in ~ on that point. I'm quite in ~ with what you say. There is no ~ upon/about what should be done.* **2** [C] arrangement or understanding (spoken or written) made by two or more persons, groups, business companies, governments, etc: *sign an ~; an ~ to rent a house.* ***come to/arrive at/make/reach an ~ (with sb),*** reach an understanding.

ag·ri·cul·ture /`ægrɪkʌltʃə(r)/ *n* [U] science or practice of farming; cultivation of the soil. **ag·ri·cul·tural** /'ægrɪ`kʌltʃərl/ *adj* of ~: *agricultural workers.*

aground /ə`graʊnd/ *adv, pred adj* (of ships) touching the bottom in shallow water: *The ship went ~/was fast ~.*

ague /`eɪgju/ *n* [U] malarial fever.

ah /ɑ/ *int* cry of surprise, pity, etc.

aha /ɑ`hɑ/ *int* cry of surprise, triumph, satisfaction, etc.

ahead /ə`hed/ *adv* ***~ (of),*** in front; in advance: *Tom was a quick walker and soon got ~ of the others. Standard time in Turkey is two hours ~ of Greenwich Mean Time.* ***Full speed ~!*** i e go forward at full speed. ***go ~,*** **(a)** make progress: *Things are going ~.* **(b)** (colloq, also *fire ~*) continue (with what you're about to say or do). ***in line ~,*** (of warships) moving forward, anchored, in a column or file. ***look ~,*** think of and prepare for future needs.

ahem /ə`hem/ *int* (usu spelling form of the) noise made when clearing the throat; noise made to give a slight warning or to call sb's attention.

ahoy /ə`hɔɪ/ *int* greeting or warning cry used by seamen.

aid /eɪd/ *vt* [VP6A,17B,14] help: *aid one another; aid sb to do sth; aid sb with money.* □ *n* **1** [U] help: *aid programmes,* those designed to give help, e g to developing countries. *He came to my aid,* came to help me. *What is the collection in aid of,* What is the money to be used for? ⇨ **first**[1](2), **legal**. **2** [C] sth that helps. **visual aids,** pictures, films, film-strips, etc used in teaching. **`deaf-aid,** appliance that helps a deaf person to hear.

aide-de-camp /'eɪd də `kõ *US:* `kæmp/ *n* (*pl* **aides-de-camp**) naval or military officer who helps a superior by carrying orders, etc.

aide-mémoire /'eɪd 'mem`wɑ(r)/ *n* (in diplomacy) memorandum.

aigrette, aigret /`eɪgret 'eɪ`gret *US:* 'eɪ`gret/ *n* tuft of feathers worn as an ornament on the head; spray of gems or jewels in imitation of this.

ail /eɪl/ *vt, vi* **1** [VP6A] (old use) trouble: *What ails him,* What's wrong with him, What's troubling him? **2** [VP2A,B] be ill: *The children are always ailing,* always in poor health. **ail·ment** *n* [C] illness.

ail·eron /`eɪlərɒn/ *n* hinged part of the wing of an aircraft that helps to balance the aircraft and control ascent and descent. ⇨ the illus at **aircraft**.

aim[1] /eɪm/ *vt, vi* **1** [VP6A,14,2A] ***aim (at),*** **(a)** point (a gun, etc) towards: *aim a gun at sb. He aimed (his gun) at the lion, fired and missed.* **(b)** send, direct, e g a blow, object (*at* sb or sth): *Tom got angry with his brother and aimed a heavy book at his head.* (fig) *My remarks were not aimed at you.* **2** [VP3A, *aim at doing sth;* US VP4A, *aim to do sth*] have as a plan or intention: *Harry aims at becoming a doctor. What are you aiming at?*

aim[2] /eɪm/ *n* **1** [U] act of aiming, e g with a gun: *Take careful aim at the target. He missed his aim,* did not hit the target. **2** [C] purpose; object: *What's your aim in life,* what do you want to do or be? *He has only one aim and object in life—to make a fortune before he is fifty/to become famous.* **aim·less** *adj* having no aim or purpose: *an aimless sort of life.* **aim·less·ly** *adv*: *wandering about the town aimlessly.*

ain't /eɪnt/ (vulg) contracted form of *are/is/am not,* and *have/has not*: *I ain't going. We ain't got any.*

air[1] /eə(r)/ *n* **1** [U] the mixture of gases that surrounds the earth and which we breathe: *Let's go out and have some fresh air.* ***in the air,*** **(a)** uncertain: *My plans are still quite in the air.* **(b)** (of opinions, etc) spreading about: *There are rumours in the air that....* **(c)** (mil) uncovered, unprotected: *Their left flank was left in the air.* ***clear the air,*** **(a)** make the air (in a room, etc) fresh again. **(b)** (fig) get rid of suspicion, doubt, etc by giving facts, etc. ⇨ also **castle, hot**[1](8). **2** ***by air,*** in aircraft: *travel/send goods, etc by air;* (attrib) of flying, aircraft, etc: *air transport.* **`Air Arm, the `Air Force,** all the military aircraft, the officers and men, etc of a country. **3** [U] (radio) ***on the air,*** broadcast(ing): *The Prime Minister will be on the air* (= will be broadcasting) *at 9.15 p m.* ***go off the air,*** stop broadcasting: *Why has that station gone off the air?* **4** [C] (liter, naut) breeze: *light airs,* i e almost a state of calm. **5** [C] (music, dated) tune, melody. **6** [C] **(a)** appearance; manner: *He has an air of importance,* seems to be, looks, important. *The house has an air of comfort.* **(b)** (usu *pl*) ***give oneself/put on airs,*** behave in an unnatural way in the hope of impressing people. ***airs and graces,*** foolish, exaggerated ways of behaving. **7** (compounds and attrib uses) **`air·bed** *n* mattress inflated with air. **`air-bladder** *n* (in animals and plants, esp seaweed) bladder filled with air. **`air·borne** *adj* **(a)** transported by air. **(b)** (of an aircraft) having taken off; in flight: *We were soon airborne.* **(c)** (of troops) specially trained for air operations: *an airborne division.* **`air·brake** *n* brake worked by compressed air. **'Air 'Chief `Marshal, 'Air `Commodore** *nn* ranks in the R A F. ⇨ App 9. **'air-con`ditioned** *adj* (of a room, building, railway coach, etc) supplied with air that is purified and kept at a certain temperature and degree of humidity. **'air-con`ditioning** *n* this process. **'air-`cooled** *adj* cooled by a current of air. **`air cover** *n* force of aircraft used to protect a military or naval operation, e g an invasion. **`air·craft** *n* (*sing* or collective *pl*) aeroplane(s); airship(s). ⇨ the illus at the end of **air**[1]. **`air·craft car·rier** *n* ship built to carry aircraft, with a long, wide deck for taking off and landing. **`air·craft(s)·man** /-mən/ *n* rank in the R A F. ⇨ App 9.

air·crew *n* crew of an aircraft. **'air cushion** *n* one inflated with air. **'air-cushion vehicle** *n* vehicle or craft of the hovercraft type. ⇨ the illus at hovercraft. **'air·drome** *n* (US) aerodrome. **'air drop** *n* dropping (of men, supplies) by parachutes from aircraft. **'air duct** *n* device, e g in an aircraft or a ship's cabin, for directing a flow of air for the comfort of passengers. **'air·field** *n* area of open, level ground, with buildings, offices, etc for operations of (esp military) aircraft. **'air·flow** *n* flow of air over the surfaces of an aircraft in flight. **'air-frame** *n* complete structure of an aircraft without the engine(s). **'air gun** *n* gun in which compressed air is used to propel the charge. **'air hostess** *n* stewardess in an airliner. **'air letter** *n* sheet of light paper (to be) folded and sent, without an envelope, cheaply by airmail. **'air lift** *n* large-scale transport of persons or supplies by air, esp in an emergency. **'air·line** *n* regular service of aircraft for public use. **'air·liner** *n* passenger-carrying aircraft. **'air lock** *n* **(a)** (bubble of air in a pipe causing) stoppage in the flow of liquid. **(b)** compartment with airtight doors at each end. **'air·mail** *n* [U] mail (to be) carried by air: *'airmail edition,* (of newspapers, periodicals) printed on thin light paper for sending by airmail. **'air·man** /-mən/ *n* man who flies in an aircraft as a member of the crew, esp a pilot; (R A F) man of any rank up to and including a Warrant Officer. **'air mechanic** *n* rank in the R A F. ⇨ App 9. **'air-'minded** *adj* looking upon flying as a normal and necessary method of transport. **'air pillow** *n* air cushion. **'air·plane** *n* (US) aeroplane. **'air pocket** *n* atmospheric condition (partial vacuum) causing an aircraft to drop some distance: *We had a bumpy flight because of air pockets.* **'air·port** *n* public flying ground for commercial use by airliners. **'air-pump** *n* pump for exhausting a vessel of its air. **'air raid** *n* attack by aircraft that drop bombs; (attrib, with hyphen): *air-raid warnings/precautions; air-raid warden,* person in charge of air-raid precautions. **'air rifle** *n* = air gun. **'air-screw** *n* aircraft propeller as on light aircraft. **'air-'sea 'rescue** *n* organization for, work of, rescuing airmen and passengers from the sea, e g by the use of motor-boats or helicopters. **'air-shaft** *n* passage for air into a mine. **'air·ship** *n* lighter-than-air flying-machine with engine(s). ⇨ balloon. **'air space** *n* part of the earth's atmosphere above a country: *violation of our air space by military aircraft.* **'air speed** *n* speed of an aircraft relative to the air through which it is moving. **'air-strip** *n* strip of ground for the use of aircraft, esp one made for use in war or in an emergency. **'air terminal** *n* terminus (in a town or city centre) to or from which passengers, etc travel to or from an airport. **'air·tight** *adj* not allowing air to enter or escape. **'air umbrella** *n* = air cover. **'air·way** *n* route regularly followed by airliners; company operating a service of airliners: *British European Airways.* **'air·woman** *n* (W R A F) woman of any rank up to and including a Warrant Officer. **'air-worthy** *adj* (of aircraft) fit to fly; in good working order. **'air·worthi·ness** *n* **'air-to-'air** *adj* (of missiles) fired from one aircraft against another. **'air-to-'ground** *adj* fired from an aircraft to hit a target on the ground.

air² /eə(r)/ *vt* [VP6A] **1** put (clothing, bedding, etc) into the open air or into a warm place to make it quite dry: *The mattress needs to be aired.* **2** let air into (a room, etc). **3** cause others to know (one's opinions, a grievance, etc): *He likes to air his knowledge,* let people see how much he knows. **air·ing** /'eərɪŋ/ *n*: *give sth an airing,* expose it to the air or to a fire; *go for an airing, take the children for an airing,* out in the fresh air. **'airing-cupboard** *n* warmed cupboard in which to keep bed linen, towels, etc.

aircraft

LIGHT AIRCRAFT

COMBAT AIRCRAFT (jet-fighter and bomber)

AIRLINER

Aire·dale /ˈeədeɪl/ *n* large rough-coated terrier (kind of dog).

air·less /ˈeələs/ *adj* **1** not having enough fresh air: *an ~ room.* **2** (of the weather) calm; still: *Isn't it ~ this evening!*

airy /ˈeərɪ/ *adj* **1** having plenty of fresh air moving through it: *a nice ~ room.* **2** of or like air; immaterial. **3** not sincere; superficial: *~ promises,* unlikely to be kept; *an ~ manner,* careless and light-hearted. **air·ily** /ˈeərəlɪ/ *adv*

aisle /ɑɪl/ *n* **1** passage in a church, esp one that is divided by a row of columns from the nave; (in a small church) passage between rows of pews (= seats). ⇨ the illus at **church**. **2** (US) passage between any rows of seats, e g in a theatre or railway coach; any long and narrow passageway.

aitch /eɪtʃ/ *n* the letter H: *drop one's ~es,* fail to utter the sound /h/ at the beginning of a word, e g by saying *'at* for *hat.* **ˈ~-bone** *n* (cut of beef over the) bone of the rump.

ajar /əˈdʒɑ(r)/ *pred adj* (of doors) slightly open.

akimbo /əˈkɪmbəʊ/ *adv* ***with arms ~,*** with the hands on the hips and elbows bent outwards.

akin /əˈkɪn/ *pred adj* **~ *(to),*** of similar character; like: *Pity is often ~ to love.*

ala·bas·ter /ˈæləbɑstə(r) *US:* -bæs-/ *n* [U] soft, white stone like marble in appearance, used for ornaments. □ *adj* like ~ in smoothness and whiteness.

à la carte /ˈɑ lɑ ˈkɑt/ *adv* (F) (of meals) ordered from a list, course by course, not at a fixed price for the complete meal (as for *table d'hôte*).

alack /əˈlæk/ *int* (old use) cry of regret or sorrow.

alac·rity /əˈlækrətɪ/ *n* [U] eager and cheerful readiness.

à la mode /ˈɑ ˈlɑ ˈməʊd/ *adv* (F) according to the latest fashion, ideas, etc; (comm) served with ice-cream: *apple pie ~.*

alarm /əˈlɑm/ *n* **1** [C] (sound or signal giving a) warning of danger; apparatus used to give such a warning: *a ˈfire ~; sound an ~;* ring a bell or in other ways send out a warning signal: *give/raise the ~.* **ˈ~(-clock)** *n* clock that can be set to ring a bell or sound a buzzer at a fixed time to waken a sleeping person: *set the ~(-clock) for six o'clock.* ***~s and excursions,*** (joc) noise and bustle; petty quarrelling. **2** [U] fear and excitement caused by the expectation of danger: *He jumped up in ~. I hope you didn't take/feel ~ at the news.* □ *vt* [VP6A] give a warning or feeling of danger to; cause anxiety to: *The noise of the shot ~ed hundreds of birds. Everybody was ~ed at the news that war might break out.* **~·ing** *part adj* causing ~. **~·ist** /-ɪst/ *n* person who raises ~s with little cause.

alas /əˈlæs/ *int* cry of sorrow or regret.

alb /ælb/ *n* white vestment reaching to the feet, worn by some Christian priests at ceremonies. ⇨ the illus at **vestment**.

al·ba·tross /ˈælbətrɒs/ *n* large, white, web-footed seabird, common in the Pacific and Southern Oceans. ⇨ the illus at **water**.

al·beit /ˈɔlˈbiɪt/ *conj* (not colloq) though.

al·bino /ˈælˈbinəʊ *US:* -ˈbɑɪ-/ *n* (*pl* -**nos** /-nəʊz/) animal or human being born without natural colouring matter in the skin and hair (which are white) and the eyes (which are pink).

al·bum /ˈælbəm/ *n* **1** blank book in which a collection of photographs, autographs, postage stamps, etc can be kept. **2** holder for a set of discs; long-playing record with several pieces by the same musician(s), singer(s).

al·bu·men /ˈælbjʊmən/ *n* [U] **1** white of egg. **2** substance as in white of egg, part of animal and vegetable matter.

al·chem·ist /ˈælkəmɪst/ *n* person who studied or practised alchemy.

al·chemy /ˈælkəmɪ/ *n* [U] chemistry of the Middle Ages, the chief aim of which was to discover how to change ordinary metals into gold.

al·co·hol /ˈælkəhɒl *US:* -hɔl/ *n* [U] **1** (pure, colourless liquid as present in) such drinks as beer, wine, brandy, whisky. **2** [C,U] (chem) large group of compounds of the same type as the ~ in wine. **~ic** /ˈælkəˈhɒlɪk *US:* -ˈhɔl-/ *adj* of or containing ~. □ *n* person whose desire for drink is so great that his health is affected. **~·ism** /-ɪzm/ *n* action of ~ on the human system; diseased condition caused by this.

al·cove /ˈælkəʊv/ *n* recess; partially enclosed extension of a room, often occupied by a bed or by seats; similar space within a garden enclosure.

al·der /ˈɔldə(r)/ *n* tree of the birch family, usu growing in marshy places.

al·der·man /ˈɔldəmən/ *n* (*pl* -**men** /-mən/) senior member of a city or borough council in England and Ireland, next in rank to a mayor, elected by fellow councillors. **~ic** /ˈɔldəˈmænɪk/ *adj*

ale /eɪl/ *n* light-coloured beer; (old use) = beer. ⇨ also **ginger**. **ˈale-house** *n* (old name for) public house.

alee /əˈli/ *adv, pred adj* (naut) at, on, towards, the lee or sheltered side of a ship.

alert /əˈlɜt/ *adj* watchful; fully awake; lively: *~ in answering questions.* □ *n* **1** ***on the ~,*** on the look-out (*for* sth, *against* an attack, etc, *to do* sth). **2** [C] (period of) watchfulness under enemy attack, esp an air raid. **3** [C] notice to stand ready: *They received the ~ at 10 a m.* □ *vt* [VP6A] put (troops, etc) on the ~. **~·ly** *adv* **~·ness** *n* being ~ or prompt (*in* doing sth).

alex·an·drine /ˈælɪgˈzændrɪn/ *n* (pros) iambic line of six feet or twelve syllables.

alexia /əˈleksɪə/ *n* [U] (path) disease in which cerebral lesions cause inability to read (popularly called 'word blindness'). **alexic** /əˈleksɪk/ adj of ~: *alexic* children.

al·falfa /ˈælfˈælfə/ *n* [U] (US) ⇨ **lucerne**.

al·fresco /ˈælˈfreskəʊ/ *adj, adv* (of meals) in the open air; out of doors: *an ~ lunch; lunching ~.*

alga /ˈælgə/ *n* (*pl* **algae** /ˈældʒi/) water plant of very simple structure.

al·gebra /ˈældʒɪbrə/ *n* branch of mathematics in which signs and letters are used to represent quantities. **al·ge·braic** /ˈældʒɪˈbreɪk/, **al·ge·braic·al** /-kl/ *adj* of ~. **al·ge·braic·ally** /-klɪ/ *adv*

alias /ˈeɪlɪəs/ *n* (*pl* -**ses** /-sɪz/) name by which a person is called on other occasions: *The criminal had several ~es.* □ *adv* also called.

alibi /ˈælɪbɑɪ/ *n* (*pl* -**bis** /-bɑɪz/) **1** (legal) plea that one was in another place at the time of an alleged act, esp a crime: *The accused man was able to establish/prove an ~.* **2** (colloq) excuse (for failure, etc).

alien /ˈeɪlɪən/ *n* (legal or official use) foreigner who is not a subject of the country in which he is: *An Englishman is an ~ in the United States.* □ *adj* **1** foreign: *an ~ environment.* **2** differing in nature or character (*from*): *These principles are ~ from our religion.* **3** contrary or opposed (*to*): *Cruelty* *was quite ~ to his nature.* **~·ation** /ˌeɪlɪəˈneɪʃn/ *n* ~ating or being ~ated; estrangement; (theatre) critical detachment (of actors and audience) from, emotional non-involvement in, problems presented by a drama.

alien·ate /ˈeɪlɪəneɪt/ *vt* [VP6A,14] **1** cause (sb previously friendly) to become unfriendly or indifferent (by unpopular or distasteful actions): *The Prime Minister's policy ~d many of his followers. At various times artists have felt ~d from society.* **2** transfer ownership of (property): *Enemy property is often ~d in time of war,* i e seized by the Government.

alien·ist /ˈeɪlɪənɪst/ *n* **1** (US) expert on the mental competence of witnesses in a law court. **2** specialist in mental illness (now called a *psychiatrist*).

alight[1] /əˈlaɪt/ *pred adj* on fire; lighted up: *The sticks were damp and wouldn't catch ~.* (fig) *Their faces were ~* (= bright, cheerful) *with happiness.*

alight[2] /əˈlaɪt/ *vi* [VP2A,3A] **1** get down (*from* a horse, bus, etc). **2** (of a bird) come down from the air and settle (*on* a branch, etc). **3** *~ on,* (formal) (fig) find by chance.

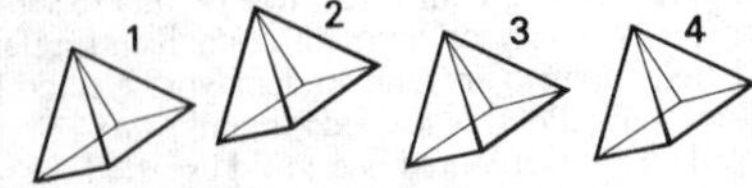

No 2 is out of alignment

align /əˈlaɪn/ *vt,vi* **1** [VP6A,2A] arrange in a line; bring into line (esp three or more points into a straight line); e g of soldiers, form in line: *~ the sights of a rifle.* **2** [VP14,3A] bring, come, into agreement, close co-operation, etc (*with*): *They ~ed themselves with us.* **~·ment** *n* [C,U] (an) arrangement in a straight line: *The desks are in/out of ~ment. There was a new ~ment of European powers,* a new grouping (colloq, *line-up*) of powers.

alike /əˈlaɪk/ *pred adj* similar; like one another: *The two sisters are very much ~. All music is ~ to him,* He has no ear for music, cannot distinguish one kind from other kinds. □ *adv* in the same way: *treat everybody ~;* the same: *summer and winter ~.*

ali·men·tary /ˌælɪˈmentrɪ/ *adj* of food and digestion. **the ˈ~ canal,** parts of the body through which food passes (from the mouth to the anus).

ali·mony /ˈælɪmənɪ *US:* -məʊnɪ/ *n* [U] money allowance (to be) paid by a man to his wife, or former wife, by a judge's order, e g after a legal separation or divorce.

alive /əˈlaɪv/ *pred adj* **1** living: *Who's the greatest man ~? You wouldn't like to be buried ~.* **2** in force; in existence: *If a claim is kept ~, it is more likely to be recognized. An awareness of the dangers of air-pollution should be kept ~ by the press and TV.* **3** *~ to,* conscious or aware of: *He is fully ~ to the dangers of the situation/public opinion.* **4** active; lively: *He is very much ~.* ***Look ~!*** Hurry up! Get busy! **5** *~ with,* full of (living or moving things): *The lake was ~ with fish.*

al·kali /ˈælkəlaɪ/ *n* (*pl* -lis /-laɪz/) (chem) one of a number of substances (such as soda, potash, ammonia) that combine with acids to form salts. **al·ka·line** /ˈælkəlaɪn/ *adj* of ~s: *soil of alkaline peat.*

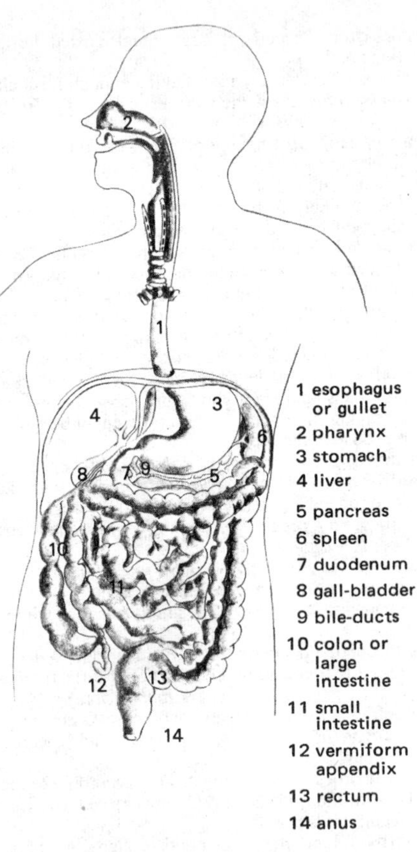

the alimentary canal

all[1] /ɔl/ *adj* **1** (with *pl nn*) the whole number of; (with *sing* material or abstract *nn*) the whole extent or amount of; (followed by the *def art,* demonstratives, possessives, and cardinal numbers): *All horses are animals but not all animals are horses. All five men/All five of them are hard workers. All you boys need to work harder. You've had all the fun and I've had all the hard work. He has lived all his life in London.* ***of all people***: *Of all people he should be the last to complain,* there is a strong reason why he shouldn't. *Why ask me to help, of all people?* I am the least likely person to be able to help, or the person to whom the speaker has the least right to apply for help. ***of all the idiots/nitwits,*** an expression of annoyance with sb who has behaved foolishly. ***on all fours,*** ⇨ four. **2** *He spent all (of) that year* (= the whole of that year) *in London.* ⇨ whole(3). **3** (Cf *all* and *every. All* suggests the whole; *every* points to each member of a group individually): *All (of) the boys enjoyed themselves.* Cf *Every one of the boys enjoyed himself.* **4** ***with all speed/haste,*** the utmost possible. **5** any: *beyond all doubt/argument/question,* there can't be any doubt, etc. *He hates all* (= any) *criticism of his work.* **6** **ˈAll ˈFools' Day,** 1 Apr; **ˈAll ˈHallows', ˈAll ˈSaints' Day,** 1 Nov; **ˈAll ˈSouls' Day,** 2 Nov.

all[2] /ɔl/ *adv* **1** quite; entirely: *They were dressed* *all in black.* Cf *They were all dressed* (i e all of them were dressed) *in black. Your hands are all tar,* (colloq) covered with tar. *She was all* (= greatly) *excited.* ***all alone,*** **(a)** not in the company of others. **(b)** without the help and company of other persons. ***all along,*** **(a)** for the whole length of: *There are trees all along the road.* **(b)** (colloq) all the time; from the start: *But I knew that all along!* ***all clear,*** ⇨ clear[1](5). ***all for,*** (colloq) strongly in favour of; anxious to have, etc: *I'm all for accepting the offer.* ***all the same,*** yet, nevertheless. ***all the same to,*** a matter not causing inconvenience to; a matter of indifference to: *If it's all the same to you...; It's all the same to me whether you go or stay.* ***all one to,*** a matter of indifference to: *Do as you like; it's all one to me.* ***all in,*** **(a)** (colloq) exhausted; *He was all in at the end of the race.* **(b)** inclusive of everything: *an all-in price.* **(c)** *all-in wrestling,* with no restrictions about methods or holds. ***all out,*** (colloq) using all possible strength, energy, etc: *He was going all out/was making an all-out effort.* ***all over,*** **(a)** in every part of: *He has travelled all over the world.* **(b)** at an end. ***all right,*** **(a)** satisfactory, satisfactorily; safe and sound; in good order: *I hope they've arrived all right.* **(b)** (as a response to a suggestion, etc) Yes, I consent. ***all there,*** (colloq) having one's wits about one; mentally alert. ***not all there,*** (colloq) not quite sane; mentally deficient. ***all told,*** altogether; as the total: *There were six people all told* (= in all). ***all up (with),*** at an end, over (with): *It's all up with him now,* He's likely to be ruined, to die, etc. **2** (with comparatives) much; so much: *You'll be all the better for a holiday.*

all[3] /ɔl/ *n* (in such phrases as) *my/his/their,* etc *all,* all that I/he/they, etc possess, value most, etc: *We must stake our all in this struggle. He had lost his all.*

all[4] /ɔl/ (in compounds) **1** (prefixed to many *adjj* and *participles*) in the highest degree; without limit: *'all-ˋmerciful; 'all-ˋpowerful; 'all-ˋembracing.* **2 'all-ˋmains** *attrib adj* (of a radio receiver) adaptable to all voltages: *an all-mains set.* **'all-ˋround** *adj* having ability in many different ways: *an all-round sportsman,* good at many different games and sports. Hence, **'all-ˋrounder** *n* ***an ˋall-star cast,*** (for a play, etc) one with star performers for all the chief parts. ***all-time high/low*** *n* (colloq) highest/lowest figure, level, etc on record. ***'all-'up ˋweight,*** total weight of an aircraft, including crew, passengers, cargo, etc when in the air.

all[5] /ɔl/ *pron* **1** everything: *He wanted all or nothing.* **2** ***all of,*** every one, the whole: *All of us want to go. Take all of it.* **3** (used in apposition, in the same way as *both* and *each*): *We all want to go. Take it all. They were all broken.* **4** (followed by a relative clause, *that* being omitted): *All I want is peace and quiet. He took all there was.* **5** (in prepositional phrases): ***above all,*** ⇨ above[2](3). ***after all,*** ⇨ after. ***(not) at all,*** /ə ˋtɔl/ (not) in any way, in the least degree: *if you are at all worried; not at all suitable for the post.* ***Not at all,*** polite formula in answer to an expression of thanks. Cf US: *You're welcome.* ***for all*** (*his wealth/great learning*), in spite of. ***for all I know/care, etc,*** (used to show ignorance or indifference): *He may be dead for all I know.* ***in all,*** ⇨ in[2](13). ***and all,*** as well; including: *The dog ate the whole rabbit, head, bones and all.* ***once (and) for all,*** now and for the last or only time. ***It was all I/he, etc could do not to*** (*laugh, etc*), I/he, etc could hardly refrain from (laughing, etc). ***all in all,*** of supreme or exclusive importance, interest, etc: *They were all in all to each other.* ***(taking it) all in all,*** considering everything. ***not as/so*** + ***adj*** or ***adv*** + ***as all that,*** to that extent; in that degree: *It's not so difficult as all that,* as is suggested, supposed, etc. ***not all that*** + ***adj*** or ***adv,*** (colloq or vulg): *It isn't all that dear,* not dear if all things are considered.

Allah /ˋælə/ *n* name of God among Muslims.

al·lay /əˋleɪ/ *vt* (*pt,pp* -layed) [VP6A] make, e g pain, trouble, excitement, fears, less.

al·lege /əˋledʒ/ *vt* [VP6A,9] declare; assist; put forward, esp as a reason or excuse, in support of a claim or in denial of a charge: *In your statement you ~ that the accused man was seen at the scene of the crime. The statement ~d to have been made by the accused is clearly untrue.* ***~d thief,*** person who is declared to be a thief. **al·le·ga·tion** /'ælɪˋgeɪʃn/ *n* [U] alleging; [C] statement, esp one made without proof: *You have made serious allegations, but can you substantiate them?* **al·leg·edly** /-ɪdlɪ/ *adv*

al·le·giance /əˋlidʒəns/ *n* [U] duty, support, loyalty, due (to a ruler or government): *Members of Parliament took the oath of ~ to the Queen.*

al·le·gory /ˋælɪgərɪ *US:* -gɔrɪ/ *n* (*pl* -ries) [C] story or description in which ideas such as patience, purity and truth are symbolized by persons who are characters in the story, e g Bunyan's *Pilgrim's Progress.* **al·le·goric** /'ælɪˋgorɪk *US:* -ˋgɔr-/, **al·le·gori·cal** /-kl/ *adj*

al·le·gretto /'ælɪˋgretəʊ/ *n, adj, adv* (I; music) (passage played) fast and lively, but not so brisk as allegro.

al·legro /əˋleɪgrəʊ/ *n, adj, adv* (I; music) (passage played) in quick time; fast and lively.

al·le·luia /'ælɪˋlujə/ *int* = hallelujah.

al·lergy /ˋælədʒɪ/ *n* (*pl* -gies) [C] (med) (condition of) being unusually sensitive to particular foods, kinds of pollen, insect stings, etc (as in the case of a person who begins to suffer from asthma when he gets a certain kind of dust or pollen into his nose or mouth). **al·ler·gen** /ˋælədʒen/ *n* (med, science) anything that causes an ~. **al·ler·gic** /əˋlɜdʒɪk/ *adj* of ~. ***allergic to,*** having an ~ to (sth); (colloq) having a dislike of; unable to get on well with.

al·levi·ate /əˋlivɪeɪt/ *vt* [VP6A] make (pain, suffering) less or easier to bear. **al·levi·ation** /ə'lɪvɪˋeɪʃn/ *n*

al·ley /ˋælɪ/ *n* (*pl* -leys) (also **ˋ~·way**) **1** narrow passage between houses or other buildings (often a narrow street in a slum quarter). **'blind ˋ~,** ~ closed at one end; (fig) occupation, e g that of an errand boy, that does not teach a trade or lead to a profession. **2** path or walk in a garden or park. **3** narrow enclosure for such games as bowls and skittles.

al·liance /əˋlaɪəns/ *n* **1** [U] association or connection. ***in ~ (with),*** joined or united (with). **2** [C] union of persons, families, e g by marriage, or states (by treaty): *enter into an ~ with a country.*

al·lied /əˋlaɪd/ ⇨ ally.

alli·ga·tor /ˋælɪgeɪtə(r)/ *n* reptile (like a crocodile) living in the lakes and rivers of the warm parts of America, ⇨ the illus at reptile; leather made from its skin. **~ pear,** avocado.

al·li·ter·ation /ə'lɪtə`reɪʃn/ *n* [U] repetition of the first sound or letter of a succession of words, e g *safe and sound; apt ~'s artful aid.* **al·lit·er·ative** /ə`lɪtrətɪv *US:* -təreɪtɪv/ *adj* **al·lit·er·ative·ly** *adv*

al·lo·cate /`æləkeɪt/ *vt* [VP6A,14] give, put on one side, as a share or for a purpose: *~ duties to sb; ~ a sum of money among several persons; ~ a sum of money to education.* **al·lo·ca·tion** /'ælə`keɪʃn/ *n* **1** [U] allocating or distributing. **2** [C] sth ~d or assigned (*to* or *for* a purpose, etc).

al·lot /ə`lot/ *vt* (-tt-) [VP6A,12A,13A,14] make a distribution of; decide a person's share of: *~ sth to sb for a purpose; ~ duties (to sb). Can we do the work within the time they have ~ted (to) us? They were ~ted a house to live in.* **~·ment** *n* **1** [U] division; distribution (of shares). **2** [C] part or share, esp (in GB) small area of public land rented as a vegetable garden.

allow /ə`laʊ/ *vt,vi* **1** [VP6A,C,17A,15B] permit: *Smoking is not ~ed here. No dogs ~ed,* It is forbidden to bring dogs into this place (building, park, etc). *Please ~ me to carry your bag. She is not ~ed out after dark.* **2** [VP12A,13A,14] give, let (sb or sth) have; agree to give: *How much money does your father ~ you for books? He ~s his wife £100 a year for clothes. She ~ed her imagination full play,* did nothing to control it. *The bank ~s 5 per cent interest on deposits. We can ~* (= take off, deduct) *5 per cent for cash payment.* **3** [VP6A] (legal) agree that sth is right or just: *The judge ~ed the claim.* **4** [VP25,9] admit (now the more usu word): *We must ~ him to be a genius/~ that he is a genius.* **5** [VP3A] ***~ for,*** take into consideration: *It will take thirty minutes to get to the station, ~ing for traffic delays.* ***~ of,*** admit of (now more usu): *The situation ~s of no delay.* **~·able** /-əbl/ *adj* that is or can be ~ed (by law, the rules, etc).

allow·ance /ə`laʊəns/ *n* **1** [C] sum of money, amount of sth, allowed to sb: *a dress ~ of £70 a year. The Director has an entertainment ~,* money for entertaining important customers, etc. **2** [C] (comm, fin) deduction or discount. **3** (*sing* or *pl*) ***make ~(s) for,*** allow for, ⇨ **allow(5)**. *We must make ~(s) for his youth,* remember that he is young, and not be too severe, etc.

alloy /`ælɔɪ/ *n* [C,U] mixture of metals, esp a metal of low value mixed with a metal of higher value: (used attrib) *~ steel.* □ *vt* /ə`lɔɪ/ [VP6A] mix (one metal) with a metal or metals of lower value; (fig) spoil; impair.

all·spice /`ɔlspɑɪs/ *n* [U] spice made from the dried berries of a W Indian tree called the pimento.

allude /ə`lud/ *vi* [VP3A] ***~ to,*** refer to; mention (now the more usu word): *In your remarks you ~ to certain sinister developments.*

allure /ə`lʊə(r)/ *vt* [VP6A,14,17A] tempt; entice; lure (now the more usu word). □ *n* [C,U] (liter) power to ~; fascination. **allur·ing** *part adj* charming; fascinating. **~·ment** *n* [C,U] that which ~s; charm, attraction (now the more usu words).

al·lu·sion /ə`luʒn/ *n* [C] ***~ (to),*** indirect reference to: *His speeches are full of classical ~s which few people understand. That man has a glass eye but he doesn't like people to make any ~ to it.* **al·lus·ive** /ə`lusɪv/ *adj* containing ~s.

al·luv·ial /ə`luvɪəl/ *adj* made of sand, earth, etc, left by rivers or floods: *~ soil/deposits.*

ally /ə`lɑɪ/ *vt* (*pt,pp* -lied) **1** [VP14] ***~ (oneself) with/to,*** unite by treaty, marriage, etc: *Great Britain was allied with the United States in both World Wars;* Hence: *the Allied* /`ælɑɪd/ *Powers.* **2** ***allied to,*** (of things) connected with: *The English language is allied to the German language.* □ *n* /`ælɑɪ/ (*pl* -lies) person, state, etc, allied to another; person who gives help or support.

Alma Mater /'ælmə `mɑtə(r)/ *n* (Lat) name used for the university or school that a person attended; (US) school song or anthem.

al·ma·nac /`ɔlmənæk/ *n* annual book or calendar of months and days, with information about the sun, moon, tides, anniversaries, etc.

al·mighty /'ɔl`mɑɪtɪ/ *adj* having all power; powerful beyond measure, esp *A~ God.* □ *n* **the A~,** God.

almond /`ɑmənd/ *n* (nut inside the) hard seed (stone-fruit) of a tree allied to the peach and plum: *ground ~s,* ~ nuts ground to powder. *shelled ~s,* ~ nuts removed from the shell or hard cover. **'~-`eyed** *adj* having eyes that appear to slant upwards and become narrower.

almoner /`ɑmənə(r) *US:* `ælm-/ *n* **1** (formerly) official who distributed money and help to the poor. **2** (GB, but not US) hospital official in charge of social service work for patients.

al·most /`ɔlməʊst/ *adv* **1** (with *vv, advv, adjj, nn*; replaceable by *nearly*): *He slipped and ~ fell. That's a mistake he ~ always makes. Dinner's ~ ready. It's ~ time to start.* **2** (with *no, none, nothing, never,* not replaceable by *nearly;* often replaced by *hardly* or *scarcely* with *any*): *A~ no one* (= Hardly anyone) *believed her. The speaker said ~ nothing* (= scarcely anything) *worth listening to.*

alms /ɑmz/ *n* (*sing* or *pl*) money, clothes, food, etc given to the poor: *give ~ to sb.* ***ask/beg (an) ~ of sb.*** **`~-box** *n* **`~-giving** *n* **`~-house** *n* (old use) house, founded by charity, in which poor people, no longer able to earn money, may live without paying rent.

aloe /`æləʊ/ *n* **1** plant with thick, sharp-pointed leaves. **2** (*bitter ~s*) juice from this plant, used in medicine.

aloft /ə`loft *US:* ə`lɔft/ *adv* high up, esp at the masthead of a ship, or up in the rigging.

alone /ə`ləʊn/ *pred adj, adv* ⇨ **lonely**. **1** (= by oneself, itself) without the company or help of others or other things: *He likes living ~,* by himself. *The house stands on the hillside all ~,* with no other houses near it. *You can't lift the piano ~,* without help. *His silence ~ is proof of his guilt.* **2** (following a *n* or *pron*) and no other: *Smith ~* (= Smith and no one else) *knows what happened. You ~* (= You and no other person) *can help me in this task.* **3** (in the *pred,* with *in*): *We are not ~ in thinking* (= not the only persons who think) *that.* **4** ***let ~,*** without referring to or considering: *He cannot find money for necessities, let ~ such luxuries as wine and tobacco.* ***let/leave sb/sth ~,*** abstain from touching, moving, interfering with: *You had better leave that dog ~; it will bite you if you tease it.* ***let well ~,*** do not go further than what is already satisfactory.

along /ə`loŋ *US:* ə`lɔŋ/ *adv* **1** (used with *vv* to indicate onward movement, often with the same sense as *on*): *Come ~! The dog was running ~ behind its master.* ***Move ~ please!*** e g a request by a policeman to people who are holding up the movement of others. **2** (used, as are *over, across,* up, down, in informal requests): *Come ~ and see me some time.* **3 all ~,** ⇨ all²(1). **get ~,** ⇨ get(17). □ *prep* **1** from one end of to the other end of; through any part of the length of: *We walked ~ the road. There are trees all ~ the river banks. Pass ~ the bus please!* (a request that passengers should move on so as to leave the entrance clear). **2 ~ here,** in this direction. **~·side** /əˈlɒŋˈsaɪd/ *adv, prep* close to, parallel with, the side of (a ship, pier, wharf).

aloof /əˈluf/ *adv* apart. ***stand/hold/keep (oneself) ~ (from),*** keep away from, take no part in sth: *Buyers are holding ~,* making no offers to buy. □ *adj* cool; remote (by nature): *I find him rather ~. He's a very ~ character.* **~·ness** *n*

aloud /əˈlaʊd/ *adv* **1** in a voice loud enough to be heard, not in a whisper: *Please read the story ~.* **2** loudly, so as to be heard at a distance: *He called ~ for help.*

alp /ælp/ *n* **1** high mountain, esp one of those (**the Alps**) between France and Italy. **2** (in Switzerland) green pasture-land on a mountain-side.

al·paca /ˈælˈpækə/ *n* **1** [C] sheep-like animal, kind of llama, of Peru. **2** [U] (cloth made from) its wool, often mixed with silk or cotton: *an ~ coat.*

alpen·stock /ˈælpənstok/ *n* long, iron-tipped stick used in climbing mountains.

al·pha /ˈælfə/ *n* the first-letter (A, α) in the Gk alphabet: *A~ and Omega,* the beginning and the end. ⇨ App 4. **ˋ~ particle,** helium nucleus given off by a radio-active substance. **~ *plus,*** (of marks in an examination) very good indeed.

al·pha·bet /ˈælfəbet/ *n* the letters used in writing a language, arranged in order: *the Greek ~;* the ABC. ⇨ App 4. **~i·cal** /ˈælfəˈbetɪkl/ *adj* in the order of the ~: *The words in a dictionary are in ~ical order.* **~i·cally** /-klɪ/ *adv*

al·pine /ˈælpaɪn/ *adj* of the Alps; of alps: *~ plants; an ~ hut.* **al·pin·ist** /ˈælpɪnɪst/ ~ climber.

al·ready /ˈɔlˈredɪ/ *adv* (usu with *v*, but may be placed elsewhere for emphasis) **1** by this/that time: *The postman has ~ been/has been ~. When I called, Tom was ~ dressed.* **2** (Cf *yet* which usu replaces *already* in neg and interr sentences. In neg and interr sentences *already* is used to show surprise.): *Have you had breakfast ~? Is it 10 o'clock ~? You're not leaving us ~, are you?* **3** previously; before now: *I've been there ~, so I don't want to go again.*

Al·sa·tian /ˈælˈseɪʃn/ *n* (US = *German shepherd*) large breed of dog, like a wolf, often trained for police work. ⇨ the illus at dog.

also /ˈɔlsəʊ/ *adv* too; besides; as well. (In spoken English, *too* and *as well* are often preferred to *also. Also* in an affirm sentence is replaced by *either* in a neg sentence.): *Tom has been to Canada. Harry has ~ been to Canada.* Cf *Tom has not been to Brazil. Harry has not been to Brazil, either.* **not only... but ~,** both... and: *He not only read the book but ~ remembered what he had read.* **ˋ~-ran** *n* (racing) horse not among the first three at the winning post; unsuccessful person in a contest.

al·tar /ˈɔltə(r)/ *n* **1** raised place (flat-topped table or platform) on which offerings are made to a god. **2** (in Christian churches) the Communion table, ⇨ the illus at church: *lead a woman to the ~,* marry her. **ˋ~-piece** *n* painting or sculpture placed behind an ~.

al·ter /ˈɔltə(r)/ *vt,vi* [VP6A,2A] make or become different; change in character, appearance, etc: *The ship ~ed course. That ~s matters/the case,* makes the situation different. *These clothes are too large; they must be ~ed. He has ~ed a great deal since I saw him a year ago.* **~·able** /-əbl/ *adj* that ~s or that can be ~ed. **~·ation** /ˈɔltəˈreɪʃn/ *n* [U] ~ing; making a change; [C] act of changing; change that is the result of ~ing: *There isn't much ~ation in the village; it's almost the same as it was twenty years ago. For making ~ations to a suit of clothes, £1.20.*

al·ter·ca·tion /ˈɔltəˈkeɪʃn/ *n* [U] quarrelling; [C] quarrel; noisy argument.

al·ter ego /ˈɔltər ˋegəʊ *US:* ˋigəʊ/ *n* (Lat) one's other self; very intimate friend.

al·ter·nate¹ /ɔlˈtɜnət/ *adj* **1** (of things of two kinds) by turns, first the one and then the other: *~ laughter and tears. Tom and Harry do the work on ~ days,* e g Tom on Monday, Harry on Tuesday, Tom on Wednesday, etc. **2** (of leaves along a stem) not opposite. **~·ly** *adv*

al·ter·nate² /ˈɔltəneɪt/ *vt,vi* **1** [VP6A,14] arrange or perform by turns; cause to take place, appear, one after the other: *He ~d kindness with severity,* was kind, then severe, then kind again, etc. *Most farmers ~ crops.* ⇨ rotation(2). **2** [VP3A] **~ *between,*** pass from one state, etc to a second, then back to the first, etc: *He ~d between high spirits and low spirits.* **~ *with,*** come one after the other, by turns: *Wet days ~d with fine days.* **ˈalternating ˋcurrent,** current that reverses its direction at regular intervals, the cycle being repeated continuously, the number of complete cycles per second being known as the *frequency.* ⇨ direct¹(5). **al·ter·na·tion** /ˈɔltəˈneɪʃn/ *n*

al·ter·na·tive /ɔlˈtɜnətɪv/ *adj* (of two things) that may be had, used, etc in place of sth else: *'Either' and 'or' are ~ conjunctions. There are ~ answers to $x^2 = 16$ (x = +4 or x = −4).* □ *n*[C] **1** choice between two things: *You have the ~ of working hard and being successful or of not working hard and being unsuccessful. Is there no ~ to what you propose?* **2** one of more than two possibilities. **~·ly** *adv* as an ~: *a fine of £10 or ~ly six weeks imprisonment.*

al·tho /ɔlˈðəʊ/ (US spelling for) although.

al·though /ɔlˈðəʊ/ *conj* ⇨ though.

al·tim·eter /ˈæltɪmitə(r) *US:* ˈælˋtɪmɪtər/ *n* barometer, e g as used in aircraft, for showing height above sea-level.

al·ti·tude /ˈæltɪtjud *US:* -tud/ *n* **1** (not of living things) height, esp above sea-level. **2** (usu *pl*) place high above sea-level: *It is difficult to breathe at these ~s.* **3** (astron) angular distance of a celestial object above the horizon.

alto /ˈæltəʊ/ *n* **1** (musical part for, a person having a) male singing voice between tenor and treble; counter(-)tenor; female voice of similar range (*contralto*). **2** instrument with the same range: *~-saxophone.*

al·to·gether /ˈɔltəˈgeðə(r)/ *adv* **1** entirely; wholly: *I don't ~ agree with him. It's ~ out of the question.* **2** (modifying a complete sentence) on the whole; considering everything: *The weather was bad and the trains were crowded; A~, it wasn't a very satisfactory excursion.*

al·tru·ism /ˈæltruɪzm/ *n* [U] principle of considering the well-being and happiness of others first; unselfishness; [C] instance of this. **al·tru·ist** /ˈæltruɪst/ *n* person who follows ~. **al·tru·is·tic**

/ˈæltruˋɪstɪk/ *adj* **al·tru·is·ti·cally** /-klɪ/ *adv*

alum /ˋæləm/ *n* white mineral salt, used medically, in dyeing, etc.

alu·min·ium /ˈæljʊˋmɪnɪəm/ (US = **alu·mi·num** /əˋlumɪnəm/) *n* [U] light white metal, extracted chiefly from bauxite, used for making hard, light alloys for cooking utensils, electrical apparatus, etc.

alumna /əˋlʌmnə/ *n* (*pl* -nae /-ni/) (US) girl or woman who was a pupil or student of a school, college or university.

alum·nus /əˋlʌmnəs/ *n* (*pl* -ni /-nɑɪ/) (US) boy or man who was a pupil or student of a school, college or university.

al·ve·olar /ˈælvɪˋəʊlə(r) *US:* ˈælˋvɪələr/ *n, adj* (phon) (consonant) made by the tongue against the gum behind the upper front teeth, e g /t, d, s/.

al·ways /ˋɔlwɪz/ *adv* **1** at all times; without exception: *The sun ~ rises in the east.* (*Always* may be modified by *almost, nearly* or *not.*) *He's nearly ~ at home in the evening.* Cf *not ~* and *hardly ever: I'm not ~ at home on Sundays,* i e I'm occasionally away from home. *I'm hardly ever* (= very seldom) *at home on Sundays.* **2** (usu with the continuous tenses) again and again; repeatedly: *He was ~ asking for money. Why are you ~ finding fault?*

am /*after 'I':* m *otherwise:* əm, *strong form:* æm/ ⇨ **be**[1].

amah /ˋɑmə/ *n* (in the East) nursemaid; maidservant.

amain /əˋmeɪn/ *adv* (old use, or poet) **1** violently. **2** in haste.

amal·gam /əˋmælgəm/ *n* **1** alloy of mercury. **2** soft mixture, e g one used for filling holes in decayed teeth.

amal·ga·mate /əˋmælgəmeɪt/ *vt, vi* [VP6A,2A] (of classes, societies, races of people, business companies) mix; combine; unite. **amal·ga·ma·tion** /əˈmælgəˋmeɪʃn/ *n* [U] mixing; combining. [C] combination; union.

am·anu·en·sis /əˈmænjʊˋensɪs/ *n* (*pl* **-ses** /-siz/) person who writes from dictation or copies what sb else has written.

ama·ryl·lis /ˈæməˋrɪlɪs/ *n* (kinds of) lily-like plant growing from a bulb.

amass /əˋmæs/ *vt* [VP6A] pile or heap up, collect (esp riches).

ama·teur /ˋæmətə(r)/ *n* **1** person who paints pictures, performs music, plays, etc, for the love of it, not for money; person playing a game, taking part in sports, etc, without receiving payment: (attrib) *an ~ painter/photographer.* ⇨ **professional.** **~·ish** /-rɪʃ/ *adj* inexpert; imperfect. **~·ism** /-ɪzm/ *n*

ama·tory /ˋæmətərɪ *US:* -tɔrɪ/ *adj* of or causing (esp sexual) love; of lovers; of making love.

amaze /əˋmeɪz/ *vt* [VP6A] fill with great surprise or wonder: *You ~ me! I was ~d at the news/~d to hear that....* **amaz·ing** *part adj* **amaz·ing·ly** *adv: He's doing amazingly well.* **~·ment** *n* [U] *I heard with ~ment that...; His ~ment at the news was immense. He looked at me in ~ment.*

Ama·zon /ˋæməzn *US:* -zon/ *n* **1** (in old Gk stories) female warrior. **2** (small *a*) tall, vigorous woman.

am·bas·sa·dor /æmˋbæsədə(r)/ *n* **1** minister representing the Government of his country in a foreign country: *the British A~ to Greece.* **2** (often *A~ Extraordinary*) minister sent by the Government of one State to the Government of another on a special mission. **3** authorized representative. **am·bas·sa·dress** /ˈæmˋbæsədrəs/ *n* female ~. **am·bas·sa·dorial** /æmˈbæsəˋdɔrɪəl/ *adj* ⇨ **diplomat, embassy.**

am·ber /ˋæmbə(r)/ *n* [U] hard, clear yellowish-brown gum used for making ornaments, etc; its colour (seen in traffic lights between red and green).

am·ber·gris /ˋæmbəgris *US:* -grɪs/ *n* [U] wax-like substance present in the intestines of whales and found floating in tropical seas, used as a fixative in perfumes.

am·bi·dex·trous /ˈæmbɪˋdekstrəs/, **-ter·ous** /-tərəs/ *adj* able to use the left hand or the right equally well.

am·bient /ˋæmbɪənt/ *adj* (of air, etc) on all sides; surrounding. **am·bience** /-əns/ *n* environment; atmosphere.

am·bi·guity /ˈæmbɪˋgjuətɪ/ *n* (*pl* **-ties**) **1** [U] state of being ambiguous. **2** [C] expression, etc that can have more than one meaning: *Let's clear up the ~ in this paragraph.*

am·bigu·ous /æmˋbɪgjʊəs/ *adj* of doubtful meaning; uncertain. **~·ly** *adv*

am·bit /ˋæmbɪt/ *n* (often *pl*) bounds; extent; range of power or authority.

am·bi·tion /æmˋbɪʃn/ *n* **1** [U] strong desire (*to be* or *do* sth, *for* sth): *A boy who is filled with ~ usually works hard. His ~ to become prime minister is likely to be realized.* **2** [C] particular desire of this kind: *He has great ~s.* **3** [C] object of such a desire: *achieve one's ~(s).*

am·bi·tious /æmˋbɪʃəs/ *adj* **1** full of ambition: *an ~ boy; ~ for fame; ~ for one's children; ~ to succeed in life.* **2** showing or needing ambition: *~ plans; an ~ attempt.* **~·ly** *adv*

am·biva·lent /æmˋbɪvələnt/ *adj* having either or both or two contrary or similar values, meanings, etc. **am·biva·lence** /-ləns/ *n*

amble /ˋæmbl/ *vi* [VP2A,C] (of a horse) move along without hurrying, lifting the two feet on one side together; (of a person) ride or walk at an easy pace. □ *n* slow, easy, pace: *He was coming along at an ~.*

am·brosia /æmˋbrəʊzɪə *US:* -əʊʒə/ *n* [U] (Gk myth) the food of the gods; anything that has a delightful taste or smell.

am·bu·lance /ˋæmbjʊləns/ *n* closed vehicle for carrying people who are ill, wounded in war or hurt in accidents.

am·bus·cade /ˈæmbəˋskeɪd/ *n, vt* = ambush.

am·bush /ˋæmbʊʃ/ *n* [C,U] (the placing of) troops, etc, lying in wait to make a surprise attack: *fall into an ~; be attacked from (an) ~.* □ *vt* [VP6A] *lie/wait in ~ (for sb).*

ameba = amoeba.

ameer /əˋmɪə(r)/ *n* = amir.

ameli·or·ate /əˋmilɪəreɪt/ *vt, vi* [VP6A,2A] (cause to) become better. **ameli·or·ation** /əˈmilɪəˋreɪʃn/ *n*

amen /ˈeɪˋmen *in liturgical use:* aˋmen/ *int* word used at the end of a prayer or hymn and meaning 'May it be so'.

amen·able /əˋminəbl/ *adj* **~ *(to),*** **1** (of persons) responsive; willing to be guided or controlled: *~ to kindness/advice/reason. Do you find your wife ~?* **2** (legal) (of persons) responsible (*to*); in a position where one must do certain things or be punished for not doing them: *We are all ~ to the law.* **3** (of cases, situations) able to be tested or dealt with: *The case is not ~ to ordinary rules.*

amend /əˋmend/ *vt,vi* **1** [VP6A,2A] make or become better; improve; free from faults or errors: *He'll have to ~ his style of living.* **2** [VP6A] make changes in the wording of a rule, a proposed law, etc. **~·able** /-əbl/ *adj* **~·ment** *n* [U] ~ing; [C] change proposed or made (*to* a rule, regulation, etc).

amends /əˋmendz/ *n pl* ***make ~/all possible ~ (to sb) (for sth),*** give compensation: *make ~ to sb for an injury.*

amen·ity /əˋminətɪ/ *n* (*pl* **-ties**) **1** (*pl*) things, circumstances, surroundings, that make life easy or pleasant: *an exchange of amenities,* of courtesies, polite expressions; *a town with many amenities,* e g a park, a public library, playing fields; *the amenities offered by a Bank,* e g the provision of travel cheques, payment of standing orders. **2** (*sing*) pleasantness: *the ~ of the climate.*

Ameri·can /əˋmerɪkən/ *adj* of America, esp the U S. **~ organ,** small organ with reeds but no pipes. **ˋ~ plan,** (at hotels) system of charges including room, all meals and service. □ *n* native or inhabitant of America; citizen of the U S. **~-ism** /-ɪzm/ *n* [C] word or phrase typical of ~ English; [U] loyalty to the U S or to things typically ~.

am·ethyst /ˋæmɪθɪst/ *n* precious stone, purple or violet.

ami·able /ˋeɪmɪəbl/ *adj* good-tempered; kind-hearted; easy and pleasant to talk to: *I've always found him a most ~ fellow.* **amia·bil·ity** /ˈeɪmɪəˋbɪlətɪ/ *n* [U] friendliness; (*pl;* **-ties**) friendly remarks: *after a few amiabilities.* **ami·ably** /-əblɪ/ *adv*

amic·able /ˋæmɪkəbl/ *adj* peaceable; done in a friendly way: *When countries cannot settle a dispute in an ~ way, they should settle it by arbitration.* **amica·bil·ity** /ˈæmɪkəˋbɪlətɪ/ *n* **amic·ably** /-əblɪ/ *adv*: *live together amicably,* peacefully, in a friendly way.

amid /əˋmɪd/, **amidst** /əˋmɪdst/ *preps* among, in, the middle of.

amid·ships /əˋmɪdʃɪps/ *adv* (naut) half-way between the bows and stern of a ship: *Our cabin is ~.*

amir, ameer /əˋmɪə(r)/ *n* (also **emir**) title used by some Muslim rulers.

amiss /əˋmɪs/ *pred adj, adv* wrong(ly); out of order: *There's not much ~ with it. Nothing comes ~ to him,* (colloq) He's ready to welcome, is able to use, anything that comes to him. ***take sth ~,*** take offence at it, be hurt in one's feelings: *Don't take it ~ if I point out your errors.*

am·ity /ˋæməti/ *n* [U] friendship; friendly relations (between persons or countries): *live in ~ with sb; a treaty of ~.*

am·me·ter /ˋæmɪtə(r)/ *n* meter that measures electric current in amperes.

am·monia /əˋməʊnɪə/ *n* [U] strong, colourless gas (NH_3) with a sharp smell, used in refrigeration and for the manufacture of explosives and fertilizers; solution of this gas in water. **am·moni·ated** /əˋməʊnɪeɪtɪd/ *adj* combined with ~.

am·mon·ite /ˋæmənɑɪt/ *n* coiled shell of an extinct mollusc.

am·mu·ni·tion /ˈæmjʊˋnɪʃn/ *n* [U] military stores, esp of explosives (shells, bombs, etc) to be used against the enemy.

am·nesia /æmˋnizɪə *US:* -iʒə/ *n* [U] (path) partial or total loss of memory.

am·nesty /ˋæmnəstɪ/ *n* (*pl* **-ties**) [C] general pardon, esp for offences against the State: *The rebels returned home under an ~.*

amoeba /əˋmibə/ *n* (*pl* **-bas** or **-bae** /-bi/) (zool) simple microscopic form of living matter, found in water, soil and animal parasites, always changing shape and too small to be seen except with the help of a microscope. **amoebic** /əˋmibɪk/ *adj* of, caused by, amoebae: *amoebic dysentery.*

amok /əˋmok/ *adv* (also **amuck**) ***run ~,*** run about wildly (with a desire to kill people).

among /əˋmʌŋ/, **amongst** /əˋmʌŋst/ *preps* **1** (showing position) surrounded by: in the middle of: *a village ~ the hills; sitting ~ her children; hiding ~ the bushes.* (Note that the *n* or *pron* after *among* must be *pl*) Cf Switzerland is situated *between* France, Italy, Austria and Germany. **2** (also with a *pl n* or *pron,* or a collective *n,* to show inclusion, association, connection): *You are only one ~ many who need help. A~ those present were the Prime Minister, the Bishop of Barchester and Mrs Proudie. I saw him ~ the crowd.* **3** (followed by a superl) one of: *Leeds is ~ the largest industrial towns in England.* **4** (indicating division, distribution, possession, joint activity, to, for or by more than two persons): *He divided his property ~ his sons. You must settle the matter ~ yourselves. They had less than £10 ~ them,* all of them together had less than £10. **5** (after a *prep*): *Choose one from ~ these.*

amoral /ˈeɪˋmorl *US:* -ˋmɔrl/ *adj* non-moral; not concerned with morals.

am·or·ous /ˋæmərəs/ *adj* easily moved to love; showing love; of (esp sexual) love: *~ looks; an ~ young man; ~ poetry.* **~·ly** *adv*

amor·phous /əˋmɔfəs/ *adj* having no definite shape or form.

amor·tize /əˋmɔtɑɪz *US:* ˋæmərt-/ *vt* [VP6A] end (a debt) by setting aside money regularly for future payments. ⇨ *sinking fund* at **sink¹(7)**. **amor·ti·za·tion** /əˈmɔtɪˋzeɪʃn *US:* ˈæmərtɪ-/ *n*

amount /əˋmaʊnt/ *vi* [VP3A] **~ to,** add up to; be equal to: *His debts ~ to £5 000. What he said ~ed to very little indeed,* didn't mean much, wasn't important. *Riding on a bus without paying the fare ~s to* (= is the same thing as) *cheating the bus company. It ~s to this, that…,* It means that…. □ *n* **1** total; whole: *He owed me £100 but could pay only half that ~,* could only pay £50. **2** [C] quantity: *A large ~ of money is spent on tobacco every year. He has any ~ of money,* is very rich. *There is still quite an ~ of prejudice against him.* **in large/small, etc ~s,** large/small, etc quantities at a time.

amour /əˋmʊə(r)/ *n* [C] (fac) love affair: *Don't bore us with accounts of your ~s.*

amour-propre /ˈæmʊə ˋpropr *with unsyllabic* r/ *n* (F) self-respect; self-esteem.

amp /æmp/ *n* (abbr) = ampere.

am·pere /ˋæmpeə(r) *US:* ˋæmpɪər/ *n* unit for measuring electric current.

am·pheta·mine /æmˋfetəmin/ *n* [U] (med) (trade name *Benzedrine*) (variety of) drug used medically, e g for slimming, and by drug addicts seeking euphoria.

am·phib·ian /æmˋfɪbɪən/ *n* **1** animal able to live both on land and in water, e g a frog. **2** aircraft designed to take off from and alight on either land or water. **3** flat-bottomed vehicle able to move in

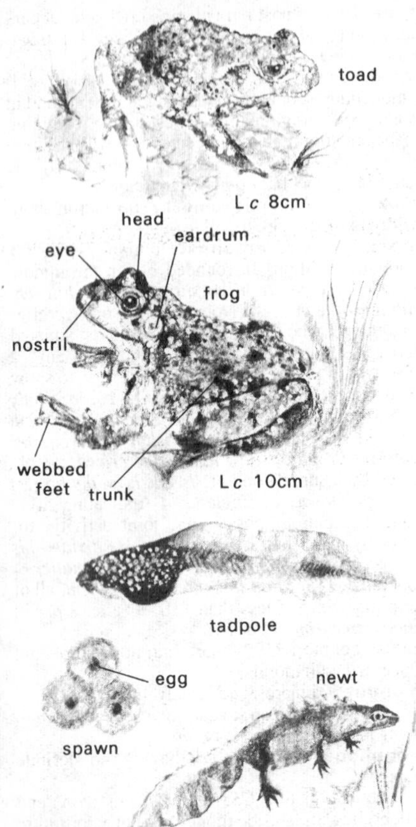

amphibians

water and on land: (attrib) ~ *tank*.

am·phibi·ous /æm`fɪbɪəs/ *adj* adapted for both land and water: ~ *vehicles*, vehicles that can cross rivers, etc as well as move on land; ~ *operations*, military operations in which land forces use ~ vehicles when making an invasion from the sea.

amphi·theatre (US = **-ter**) /`æmfɪθɪətə(r)/ *n* **1** round or oval unroofed building with rows of seats rising behind and above each other round an open space used for public games and amusements. **2** (not US) rows of seats similarly arranged in a half-circle in a theatre. **3** (*natural* ~) level space with hills rising on all sides.

an amphitheatre

am·phora /`æmfərə/ *n* (*pl* **-ras** or **-rae** /-ri/) two-handled jar, used in ancient Greece and Rome for holding wine or oil.

ample /`æmpl/ *adj* (**-r, -st**) **1** large-sized; with plenty of space: *This new car has an* ~ *boot. There's* ~ *room for the children on the back seat.* **2** plentiful: *He has* ~ *resources,* is wealthy. **3** sufficient; quite enough: *£5 will be* ~ *for my needs.* **am·ply** /`æmplɪ/ *adv*: *amply supplied with money,* having more than is needed; *amply rewarded,* well rewarded.

am·plify /`æmplɪfɑɪ/ *vt* (*pt,pp* **-fied**) [VP6A] **1** make larger or fuller, esp give fuller information, more details, etc, about: ~ *a story/an account.* **2** increase the strength of (voltage or current, etc). **am·pli·fi·ca·tion** /ˌæmplɪfɪ`keɪʃn/ *n* **am·pli·fier** /`æmplɪfɑɪə(r)/ *n* appliance for ~ing.

am·pli·tude /`æmplɪtjud *US:* -tud/ *n* [U] breadth; largeness, abundance.

am·poule (US also **am·pule**) /`æmpjul *US:* -pul/ *n* small container, esp for a hypodermic injection.

am·pu·tate /`æmpjʊteɪt/ *vt* [VP6A] cut off, e g an arm, a leg, by surgery. **am·pu·ta·tion** /ˌæmpjʊ`teɪʃn/ *n*

amuck /ə`mʌk/ *adv* ⇨ **amok.**

amu·let /`æmjʊlət/ *n* sth worn in the belief or hope that it will protect the wearer (*against* evil, etc).

amuse /ə`mjuz/ *vt* [VP6A] **1** make time pass pleasantly for: *The boys* ~*d themselves* (*by*) *drawing caricatures of their teacher. Keep the baby* ~*d with these toys.* **2** make (sb) laugh or smile: *His foolish mistakes* ~*d all of us. The children were* ~*d at/by the storyteller's jokes. We were* ~*d to learn that....* **amus·ing** *part adj* causing laughter or smiles: *an amusing story/storyteller.* **~·ment** *n* **1** [U] state of being ~d: *She couldn't hide her* ~*ment at his foolish mistake. To the great* ~*ment of everybody, the actor's beard fell off. He looked at me in* ~*ment.* **2** [C] sth that makes time pass pleasantly: *There are plenty of* ~*ments here—cinemas, theatres concerts, football matches, and so on.* **`~ment arcade,** room or hall containing pin-tables, gambling-machines, etc, esp in large towns, seaside resorts, etc. **`~ment park/grounds,** place with swings, roundabouts, shooting galleries, and other means of amusing oneself. ***places of ~ment,*** cinemas, theatres, etc. ***do sth for ~ment,*** do it as a means of passing time pleasantly, not for a serious purpose.

an[1] /ən *strong form:* æn/ *det* ⇨ **a**[2].

an[2] /æn/ *conj* (old use) if.

anach·ron·ism /ə`nækrənɪzm/ *n* [C] **1** mistake in dating sth; sth out of date now or in a description of past events: *In the sentence 'Julius Caesar looked at his wrist-watch and lifted the telephone receiver' there are two* ~*s.* **2** person, custom, attitude, etc regarded (unfavourably) as out of date: *Most young people in Britain regard Tory politicians who shoot grouse in Scotland as dreadful* ~*s.* **anach·ron·is·tic** /əˌnækrə`nɪstɪk/ *adj*

ana·conda /ˌænə`kondə/ *n* large snake, esp the kind that crushes its prey.

anaemia (US = **anemia**) /ə`nimɪə/ *n* [U] lack of enough blood; poor condition of the blood, causing paleness. **anaemic** (US = **anemic**) /ə`nimɪk/ *adj* suffering from ~.

an·aes·thesia (US = **an·es·thesia**) /ˌænɪs`θizɪə *US:* -`θiʒə/ *n* [U] state of being unable to feel (pain, heat, cold, etc); branch of chemistry concerned with substances producing this state. **an·aes·thetic** (US = **an·es·thetic**) /ˌænɪs`θetɪk/ *n* [C] substance, e g ether, chloroform, technique, that produces ~: *under an anaesthetic.* **`general anaesthetic,** one affecting the whole body, usu administered in hospital. **local anaesthetic,** one administered by injection and affecting only part of the body, e g into the gums by a dentist. **an·aes·the·tize** (US = **an·es·the·tize**) /ə`nisθətaɪz/ *vt* [VP6A] make insensible to pain, etc. **an·aes·the·tist** (US = **an·es·the·tist**) /ə`nisθətɪst/ *n* person trained to administer anaesthetics.

ana·gram /`ænəgræm/ *n* word made by changing the order of the letters in another word (e g plum —lump): *Let's play ~s,* make words of this kind.

anal /`eɪnl/ *adj* of the anus.

ana·lects /`ænəlekts/ (also **ana·lecta** /ˌænə`lektə/) *n pl* literary gleanings: *Confucian ~.*

an·al·gesia /ˌænl`dʒizɪə *US:* -ʒə/ *n* [U] (med) absence of, condition of not feeling, pain. **an·al·gesic** /ˌænl`dʒizɪk/ *n* substance, e g an ointment which relieves pain.

ana·logue (also **-log**) /`ænəlog *US:* -lɔg/ *n* **1** sth that is similar to another thing: *meat ~,* artificial prepared substitute for meat (usu of soya beans). **2** `~ **computer** *n* one which can perform operations on numbers, the numbers being represented by some physical quantity or electrical signal. ⇨ *digital computer* at **digit**.

anal·og·ous /ə`næləgəs/ *adj* similar or parallel: *The two processes are not ~ (with each other).* **~·ly** *adv*

anal·ogy /ə`nælədʒɪ/ *n* (*pl* **-gies**) **1** [C] partial likeness or agreement (*to* or *with* sth, *between* two things): *The teacher drew an ~ between the human heart and a pump.* **2** [U] process of reasoning between parallel cases: *argue by ~; argument by/from ~; on the ~ of.*

ana·lyse (US = **-lyze**) /`ænəlaɪz/ *vt* [VP6A] **1** examine (sth) in order to learn what it is made up of: *If we ~ water, we find that it is made up of two parts of hydrogen and one part of oxygen.* **2** (gram) split up (a sentence) into its grammatical parts. **3** study or examine in order to learn about: *The leader tried to ~ the causes of our failure.* **4** (esp US) = psychoanalyse.

analy·sis /ə`næləsɪs/ *n* (*pl* **-ses** /-siz/) **1** [U] (e g of a book, a character, a situation) separation into parts possibly with comment and judgement: *critical ~ of literary texts; expert ~ of market trends,* i e of how prices, sales, etc are likely to go; [C] instance of this; statement of the result of doing this. **2** (US) = psycho~. **ana·lyst** /`ænəlɪst/ *n* **1** person skilled in making (esp chemical) analyses: *a food analyst.* **2** (esp US) = psychoanalyst. **ana·lytic** /ˌænə`lɪtɪk/, **-i·cal** /-kl/ *adj* of ~; using ~. **ana·lyti·cally** /-klɪ/ *adv*

ana·lyze ⇨ **analyse.**

ana·paest (US = **-pest**) /`ænəpist *US:* -pest/ *n* (pros) foot consisting of two unaccented syllables followed by one accented syllable, e g 'I am 'mon/arch of 'all/I sur'vey'. **ana·paes·tic,** (US = **-pestic**) /ˌænə`pistɪk *US:* -`pest-/ *adj*

an·archy /`ænəkɪ/ *n* [U] absence of government or control; disorder; confusion. **an·arch·ism** /-ɪzm/ *n* [U] political theory that government and laws are undesirable. **an·arch·ist** /-ɪst/ *n* person who favours ~; person who wishes to overthrow all established governments. **an·archic** /ə`nɑkɪk/ *adj* **an·archi·cally** /-klɪ/ *adv*

anath·ema /ə`næθəmə/ *n* **1** (eccles) curse of the Church, excommunicating sb or condemning sth as evil. **2** sth that is detested. **~·tize** /ə`næθəmətaɪz/ *vt, vi* curse.

anat·omy /ə`nætəmɪ/ *n* [U] science of the structure of animal bodies; study of their structures by separation into parts. **ana·tomi·cal** /ˌænə`tomɪkl/ *adj* **a`nat·om·ist** /-ɪst/ *n* person who dissects corpses; person who studies or teaches ~.

an·ces·tor /`ænsɪstə(r) *US:* -ses-/ *n* any one of those persons from whom one is descended, esp one more remote than a grandparent: `~ *worship,* the worship of one's ~s as spirits or gods. **an·ces·tress** /-trəs/ *n* woman ~. **an·ces·tral** /æn`sestrl/ *adj* belonging to, having come from, one's ~s: *his ancestral home.* **an·ces·try** /`ænsɪstrɪ *US:* -ses-/ *n* (*pl* **-ries**) line of ~s.

an·chor /`æŋkə(r)/ *n* heavy piece of iron with a ring at one end, to which a cable is fastened, used for keeping a ship fast to the sea bottom or a balloon to the ground; anything that gives stability or security. ***let go/drop/cast the ~,*** lower it. ***weigh ~,*** raise it. ***come to ~, bring (a ship) to ~,*** stop sailing and lower the ~. ***lie/ride/be at ~,*** be made fast and held safe by the ~. **~·man** /-mən/, one who co-ordinates the work of a group of persons who work together, e g in a radio or T V studio. □ *vt, vi* [VP6A] make (a ship) secure with an ~; [VP2A] lower an ~. **~·age** /-rɪdʒ/ *n* place where ships may ~ safely.

an·chor·ite /`æŋkəraɪt/ *n* hermit.

an·chovy /`æntʃəʊvɪ/ *n* (*pl* **-vies**) small fish of the herring family; it has a strong flavour and is used for sauces, etc: (attrib) ~ *paste/sauce.*

ancient /`eɪnʃnt/ *adj* **1** belonging to times long past: ~ *Rome and Greece; the ~s,* the civilized people who lived long ago. **2** (often hum) very old: *an ~-looking hat.*

an·cil·lary /æn`sɪlərɪ *US:* `ænsḷerɪ/ *adj* **1** helping, providing a service to those carrying on the main business of an enterprise: *The transport corps is ~ to the infantry.* **2** subordinate (*to*): ~ *roads/undertakings/industries.*

and /*usu form:* ən *and* (*after* t, d, f, v, θ, ð, z, a, ʒ, ʃ) n; *strong form:* ænd/ *conj* **1** (connecting words, clauses, sentences): *a table and four chairs; learning to read and write.* (When two *nn* stand for things or persons closely connected, the determining word is not repeated before the second *n*): *a knife and fork.* Cf a knife and a spoon; *my father and mother.* Cf my father and my uncle. **2** (Note *twenty-five* but *five and twenty,* sometimes used in telling the time): *five and twenty to six.* **3** (In constructions replacing an *if*-clause): *Work hard and you will pass* (= If you work hard, you will pass) *the examination.* **4** (indicating intensive repetition or continuation): *for hours and hours; for miles and miles; better and better. We knocked and knocked,* continued to knock. **5** (colloq) to: *Try and come early. Go and buy one.*

an·dante /æn`dæntɪ/ *n, adv* (I; music) (piece of music to be played) in moderately slow time.

and·iron /`ændaɪən/ *n* iron support (usu one of a pair) for holding logs in a fireplace. Also called *firedog.*

an·ec·dote /`ænɪkdəʊt/ *n* short, usu amusing, story about some real person or event.

anemia, anemic ⇨ **anaemia, anaemic.**

anem·om·eter /ˌænɪ`momɪtə(r)/ *n* [C] (met) instrument for measuring the force and velocity of the wind.

anem·one /ə`nemənɪ/ *n* **1** (bot) (also called *wind-flower*) small star-shaped woodland flower; cultivated varieties of this flower. **2** `**sea ~,** popular name of a creature living in the sea. ⇨ p 30.

an anenome a sea anemone

anent /əˋnent/ *prep* (old use, or Scots) concerning; about.

an·er·oid /ˋænərɔɪd/ *adj, n* ~ **(barometer),** one that measures air-pressure by the action of air on the elastic lid of a box partly exhausted of air.

an·es·thesia *n* ⇨ **anaesthesia.**

anew /əˋnju *US:* əˋnu/ *adv* again; in a new or different way.

angel /ˋeɪndʒl/ *n* **1** (esp in Christian belief) messenger from God (usu shown in pictures as a human being in white with wings). **2** lovely or innocent person. **3** (as a compliment to sb who is kind, thoughtful, etc): *Thanks, you're an ~!* **an·gelic** /ænˋdʒelɪk/ *adj* of or like an ~. **an·geli·cally** /-klɪ/ *adv*

an·gelica /ˈænˋdʒelɪkə/ *n* [U] sweet-smelling plant, esp the kind used in cooking and medicine; its stem, boiled in sugar.

an·gelus /ˋændʒɪləs/ *n* (also **A~**) (bell rung in R C churches at morning, noon and sunset to call people to recite) prayer to the Virgin Mary.

anger /ˋæŋgə(r)/ *n* [U] the strong feeling that comes when one has been wronged or insulted, or when one sees cruelty or injustice; the feeling that makes people want to quarrel or fight: *filled with ~ at what he saw; speak in ~; do sth in a moment of ~.* □ *vt* [VP6A] fill (sb) with ~; make angry: *He is easily ~ed.*

an·gina pec·toris /ænˈdʒɑɪnə ˋpektərɪs/ *n* (Lat) (path) heart disease marked by sharp pain in the chest.

angle[1] /ˋæŋgl/ *n* **1** space between two lines or surfaces that meet. ˋ**~-dozer** *n* mechanical scraper used for levelling roads or ground surfaces. ⇨ **bulldozer.** ˋ**~-iron** *n* L-shaped length of iron or steel used to strengthen a framework. ˋ**~-parking** *n* the parking of cars at an angle to the side of the roadway, etc: *cars ~-parked as close as herring-bones.* **2** (fig) point of view: *Try looking at the affair from a different ~. What ~ are you writing the story from?* □ *vt* [VP6A] *~ the news,* present it to the public in a particular way (usu to suit the bias of the writer or his employer).

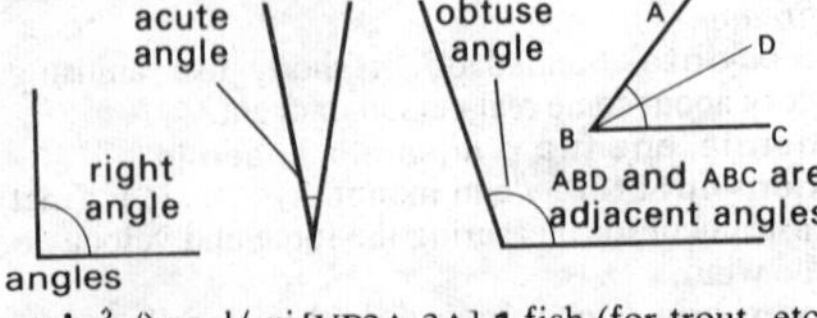

angles

angle[2] /ˋæŋgl/ *vi* [VP2A,3A] **1** fish (for trout, etc) with a hook and bait. **2** (fig) use tricks, hints, etc in order to get sth: *~ for compliments; ~ for an invitation to a party.* **angler** /ˋæŋglə(r)/ *n* person who fishes with a rod and line. Cf *fisherman* using nets, etc.

Angli·can /ˋæŋglɪkən/ *n, adj* (member) of the Church of England.

angli·cize /ˋæŋglɪsɑɪz/ *vt* [VP6A] make English or like English: *~ a French word.* **angli·cism** /ˋæŋglɪsɪzm/ *n* English way of saying sth.

Anglo /ˈæŋgləʊ/ *pref* English: *~-French relations,* between GB and France. ˈ**~-ˋCatholic** *n, adj* (member) of the party in the Anglican Church that insists upon its unbroken connection with the early Christian Church and that objects to being called Protestant. ˈ**~-ˋIndian** *n, adj* **(a)** of British birth, living or having lived, in India. **(b)** person of mixed European and Asian blood; Eurasian. ˈ**~-ˋSaxon** *n, adj* (person) of English descent; one of the race of people who settled in England (from N W Europe) before the Norman Conquest; their language (also called *Old English*).

Anglo·mania /ˈæŋgləʊˋmeɪnɪə/ *n* excessive love of and admiration for English customs, etc.

Anglo·phile /ˋæŋgləʊfɑɪl/ (also **-phil** /-fɪl/) *n* person who loves England or English things.

Anglo·phobe /ˋæŋgləʊfəʊb/ *n* person who hates England or English things.

Anglo·phobia /ˈæŋgləʊˋfəʊbɪə/ *n* excessive hatred of England and of English things.

an·gora /æŋˋgɔrə/ *n* **1** long-haired cat, goat or rabbit. **2** material made from wool of ~ goats.

an·gos·tura /ˈæŋgəˋstjʊərə/ *n* [U] bitter liquid, used as a tonic, made from the bark of a S American tree.

angry /ˋæŋgrɪ/ *adv* (-ier, -iest) **1** filled with anger (*with* sb, *at* what sb does or says, *about* sth): *He was ~ at being kept waiting. He was ~ with himself for having made such a foolish mistake. He will be ~ to learn* (= when he learns) *that you have disobeyed his orders.* **2** (of a cut, sore, wound) red; inflamed. **3** (of the sea, sky, clouds) stormy; threatening. **angri·ly** *adv*

angst /æŋst/ *n* [U] (G) feeling of anxiety (e g caused by considering the state of world affairs).

an·guish /ˋæŋgwɪʃ/ *n* [U] severe suffering (esp of mind): *She was in ~ until she knew that her husband's life had been saved.* **~ed** *adj* expressing ~: *~ed looks.*

angu·lar /ˋæŋgjʊlə(r)/ *adj* **1** having angles or sharp corners. **2** (of persons) with the shape of the bones showing under the skin; (of a person's nature, etc) rather stiff and awkward: *an ~ gait.* **~·ity** /ˈæŋgjʊˋlærətɪ/ *n* (*pl* **-ties**).

ani·line /ˋænɪlin *US:* ˋænḷɪn/ *n* substance obtained chemically from coal-tar, used in the manufacture of dyes, drugs, etc.

ani·mad·vert /ˈænɪmædˋvɜt/ *vi* [VP3A] make (esp critical) remarks, (*on* sb's conduct). **ani·mad·ver·sion** /ˈænɪmædˋvɜʃn *US:* -ˋvɜʒn/ *n* criticism.

ani·mal /ˋænəml/ *n* **1** living thing that can feel and move about. Men, dogs, birds, flies, fish and snakes are all ~s. **the** ˋ**~ kingdom,** one of three divisions (the others being *vegetable* and *mineral*). ⇨ the illus at **ape, cat, dog, domestic, large, reptile, sea, small. 2** four-footed ~ (e g a dog or a horse): *~ husbandry,* the breeding of cattle, sheep, horses, etc. **3** ~ other than man. **4** (used attrib) of the physical, not spiritual, side of man: *~ needs,* e g food; *~ desires.* **~ spirits,** natural lightheartedness. **~·cule** /ˈænɪˋmælkjul/ *n* microscopically small ~.

ani·mate /ˋænɪmət/ *adj* living; lively. □ *vt*

/ˈænɪmeɪt/ *v* [VP6A,14] give life to; make lively: *A smile* ~*d her face as she went to the gate to meet her husband. There was an* ~*d discussion. The news* ~*d* (= inspired) *us to greater efforts. All his life this great man was* ~*d* (= inspired, caused to act) *by love of his country.* **ˈ~d carˈtoon,** cinema film made by photographing a series of drawings. **ani·ma·tion** /ˌænɪˈmeɪʃn/ *n* [U] (esp) liveliness; ardour.

ani·mism /ˈænɪmɪzm/ *n* [U] belief that all objects (trees, stones, the wind, etc) have souls.

ani·mos·ity /ˌænɪˈmɒsətɪ/ *n* [U] strong dislike, active enmity (*against, towards,* sb, *between* persons); [C] (*pl* -**ties**) instance of this.

ani·mus /ˈænɪməs/ *n* [U] animosity; (with *indef art*) instance of this: *an* ~ *against me.*

an·ise /ˈænɪs/ *n* plant with sweet-smelling seeds. **ani·seed** /ˈænɪsid/ *n* [U] seed of ~, used for flavouring.

ankle /ˈæŋkl/ *n* joint connecting the foot with the leg; thin part of the leg between this joint and the calf. ⇨ the illus at **leg**. **ˈ~ socks,** short ones just covering the ~s. **ank·let** /ˈæŋklət/ *n* ornament for the ~.

anna /ˈænə/ *n* former copper coin in Pakistan and in India, a sixteenth part of a rupee.

an·nals /ˈænlz/ *n pl* story of events year by year; record of new knowledge or discoveries written year by year; yearly record of the work of a learned society. **an·nal·ist** /ˈænəlɪst/ *n* writer of ~.

an·neal /əˈnil/ *vt* [VP6A] cool (metals, glass, etc) very slowly after heating, in order to toughen and temper.

an·nex /əˈneks/ *vt* [VP6A,14] **1** take possession of (territory, etc). **2** add or join (sth) (as a subordinate part *to* sth). □ *n* /ˈænəks/ (also **an·nexe**) **1** smaller building added to, or situated near, a larger one: *an* ~ *to a hotel.* **2** addition (*to* a document). **an·nex·ation** /ˌænekˈseɪʃn/ *n* [U] ~ing; [C] instance of this, that which is ~ed.

an·ni·hi·late /əˈnaɪəleɪt/ *vt* [VP6A] destroy completely; end the existence of (e g an army, a fleet): *The invasion force was* ~*d;* (fig) *Radio communication has* ~*d space.* **an·ni·hi·la·tion** /əˌnaɪəˈleɪʃn/ *n* [U] complete destruction (of military or naval forces, etc).

an·ni·ver·sary /ˌænɪˈvɜsərɪ/ *n* (*pl* -**ries**) [C] yearly return of the date of an event; celebration of this: *my wedding* ~; *the* ~ *of Shakespeare's birth; an* ~ *dinner,* one held to celebrate an ~.

Anno Dom·ini /ˌænəʊ ˈdɒmɪnaɪ/ (Lat, shortened to AD /ˌeɪ ˈdi/) in the year of our Lord: *in* AD *250,* 250 years after the birth of Jesus. Cf *44* BC.

an·no·tate /ˈænəteɪt/ *vt* [VP6A] add notes (to a book, etc) explaining difficulties, giving opinions, etc: *an* ~*d text/version.* **an·no·ta·tion** /ˌænəˈteɪʃn/ *n* [U] annotating; [C] note or comment.

an·nounce /əˈnaʊns/ *vt* [VP6A,9,14] **1** make known: *Mr Green* ~*d (to his friends) his engagement to Miss White. It has been* ~*d that Mr Green and Miss White will be married in May. The book was* ~*d as in preparation. The Government* ~*d that the danger was past.* **2** make known the arrival of: *The servant* ~*d Mr and Mrs Brown,* spoke their names as they entered. **3** say that sb is about to speak, sing, etc (e g in a TV programme). **~·ment** *n* [C] sth said, written, or printed to make known what has happened or (more often) what will happen: *a broadcast* ~*ment. An* ~*ment will be made next week. A*~*ments of deaths, marriages and births appear in the newspapers.* **an·nouncer** *n* (esp) person who ~s speakers, singers, etc in a radio or TV broadcast.

an·noy /əˈnɔɪ/ *vt* [VP6A esp in passive] irritate; make rather angry: *He was* ~*ed with his wife because the dinner was badly cooked. I felt* ~*ed when he refused to help. Do stop* ~*ing your father! He was* ~*ed to learn that the train would be delayed. He felt/got/was* ~*ed with the boy for being so stupid/was* ~*ed at the boy's stupidity.* **~·ing** *part adj*: *It's* ~*ing to miss a train. How* ~*ing! The* ~*ing thing about it is that...,* What causes trouble or irritation is that.... **~·ance** /-əns/ *n* **1** [U] vexation; being ~ed: *with a look of* ~*ance; much to our* ~*ance; subject a person to* ~*ance,* worry him. **2** [C] sth that ~s: *All these little* ~*ances did not spoil her sweet temper.*

an·nual /ˈænjʊəl/ *adj* **1** coming or happening every year. **2** lasting for only one year or season. **3** of one year: *his* ~ *income; the* ~ *production.* □ *n* **1** plant that lives for one year or less. **ˌhardy ˈ~,** (joc) event, etc which often recurs (and is considered tiresome or monotonous). **2** book, etc that appears under the same title but with new contents every year. **~·ly** *adv*

an·nu·ity /əˈnjuətɪ *US:* -ˈnu-/ *n* (*pl* -**ties**) [C] fixed sum of money paid to sb yearly as income during his lifetime; form of insurance to provide such a regular, annual income. **an·nui·tant** /əˈnjuɪtənt *US:* -ˈnu-/ *n* person who receives an ~.

an·nul /əˈnʌl/ *vt* (-ll-) [VP6A] put an end to, e g an agreement, a law, etc; declare (that sth, e g a marriage, is) invalid, of no effect. **~·ment** *n*

an·nu·lar /ˈænjʊlə(r)/ *adj* ring-like.

an·nun·ci·ate /əˈnʌnsɪeɪt/ *vt* [VP6A] announce; proclaim.

an·nun·ci·ation /əˌnʌnsɪˈeɪʃn/ *n* **the A~,** (eccles) the announcement by the angel Gabriel to Mary that she was to be the mother of Jesus Christ; festival that commemorates this, 25 Mar.

an·ode /ˈænəʊd/ *n* (electr) (US also called *plate*) **1** positively charged electrode (from which current enters). ⇨ **cathode. 2** negative terminal of a battery.

ano·dyne /ˈænədaɪn/ *n, adj* (medicine, drug) able to lessen pain; (sth) able to give comfort to the mind.

anoint /əˈnɔɪnt/ *vt* [VP6A,23,14] apply oil or ointment to (esp as a religious ceremony): ~ *sb with oil. The Lord* ~*ed thee King over Israel* (⇨ I Sam 15:17). **~·ment** *n*

anom·al·ous /əˈnɒmələs/ *adj* irregular; different in some way from what is normal. **~ verb,** verb that forms its interr and neg without the helping verb *do* (e g *must, ought*). **~·ly** *adv* **anom·aly** /əˈnɒməlɪ/ *n* (*pl* -**lies**) ~ thing: *A bird that cannot fly is an anomaly.*

anon[1] /əˈnɒn/ *adv* (old use) soon. ***ever and* ~,** every now and then.

anon[2] /əˈnɒn/ (in footnotes, etc) short for *by an anonymous author.*

anony·mous /əˈnɒnɪməs/ *adj* without a name, or with a name that is not made known: *an* ~ *letter,* not signed; *an* ~ *gift,* from sb whose name is not known; *an author who remains* ~. **~·ly** *adv* **anon·ym·ity** /ˌænəˈnɪmətɪ/ *n* [U] state of being ~.

anoph·eles /əˈnɒfɪliz/ *n* (ent) (kinds of) mosquito.

esp the kinds that spread malaria. ⇨ the illus at **insect**.

an·orak /ˈænəræk/ *n* [C] jacket with a hood attached, worn as protection against rain, wind and cold; wind-cheater.

an·other /əˈnʌðə(r)/ *pron, adj* ⇨ **other**. **1** an additional (one): *Will you have ~ cup of tea? Where shall we be in ~ ten years*, ten years from now? *I don't like this hat; please show me ~ (one)*. **2** a similar (one): *This young man is very clever; he may be ~ Edison*, an inventor as clever as Edison. **3** a different (one): *We can do that ~ time. That's quite ~ matter. Taking one thing/ year, etc with ~*, on the whole, taking the average (of good and bad, etc). ***one ~***, ⇨ **one**[3](3).

answer[1] /ˈɑnsə(r) *US:* ˈæn-/ *n* ***~ to***, **1** sth done in return; reply: *Have you had an ~ to your letter? She gave no ~*, said nothing in return. *I have a complete ~ to the accusation*, can prove that it was wrongly made. ***in ~ to***: *in ~ to your letter. The doctor came at once in ~ to my telephone call*. **2** solution; result of working with figures, etc: *The ~ to* 3 × 17 *is* 51.

answer[2] /ˈɑnsə(r) *US:* ˈæn-/ *vt,vi* **1** [VP6A,9, 12A,2A] say, write or do, sth in return (to): *~ a question; ~ the teacher. He ~ed nothing. What shall I ~? Have you ~ed his letter? He ~ed that he knew nothing about it. No one ~ed. No one was able to ~ him a word* (⇨ Matt 22:48). *A~ me this question*. ***~ the door/the bell***, go to the door when sb has knocked or rung the bell. ***~ the telephone***, pick up the receiver and ~ the caller. [VP2C,15B] ***~ (sb) back***, ~ impolitely, interrupt, esp when being corrected or scolded. **2** [VP6A] fulfil; be suitable or satisfactory for: *Will this ~ your purpose?* **3** [VP2A] succeed; be satisfactory: *This plan has not ~ed; we must find a better one*. **4** [VP3A] ***~ to the name of***, (of a pet animal) have the name of: *The dog ~s to the name of Spot*. ***~ to a description***, correspond to it, be as described: *He doesn't ~ to the description of the missing man that appeared in the newspapers*. **5** [VP6A,3A] ***~ (to) the helm***, (of a ship) change course when the helm is moved: *The ship no longer ~s the helm*, cannot be steered. **6** [VP3A] ***~ for***, be responsible for: *I can't ~ for his honesty*, cannot guarantee that he is honest. *I will ~ for it* (= promise) *that the next one will be better. You will have to ~ for* (= suffer for) *your wrongdoing one day. He has a lot to ~ for*, is responsible for, to be blamed for, many things. **~·able** /-əbl/ *adj* **1** that can be ~ed. **2** (*pred* only) responsible (*to* sb *for* sth).

ant /ænt/ *n* (ent) small insect, proverbial for industry, that lives in highly organized societies. ⇨ the illus at **insect**. **ˈant-eater** *n* name of various animals that live on ants. **ˈant-hill** *n* pile of earth, etc, over an underground nest of ants; cone-shaped nest of white ants. **ˌwhite ˈant** *n* white ant-like insect (termite) that destroys wood, etc by eating it.

an·tag·on·ism /ænˈtægənɪzm/ *n* [C,U] (instance of) active opposition: *the ~ between the two men; feel a strong ~ for/toward sb*, find oneself strongly opposed to him.

an·tag·on·ist /ænˈtægənɪst/ *n* person struggling against another; opponent.

an·tag·on·is·tic /ænˌtægəˈnɪstɪk/ *adj* **1** adverse; opposed; contrary (*to*). **2** (of forces) acting against each other. **an·tag·on·is·ti·cally** /-klɪ/ *adv*

an·tag·on·ize /ænˈtægənɑɪz/ *vt* [VP6A] make an enemy of (sb); irritate into conflict: *I advise you not to ~ him*.

ant·arc·tic /ænˈtɑktɪk/ *adj* of the south polar regions. **the ˌA~ ˈCircle**, the line of latitude 66½°S.

ante /ˈæntɪ/ *n* stake in the game of poker that a player must put down after looking at his cards or before (*ante*) he can draw new cards. ***raise the ~***, increase one's stake (or contribution to sth).

ante- /ˈæntɪ/ *pref* before: *~nuptial*, before marriage.

ante·ced·ent /ˌæntɪˈsidnt/ *adj* previous (*to*). □ *n* **1** preceding event or circumstance. **2** (*pl*) ancestors; past history of a person or persons. **3** (gram) noun, clause or sentence, to which a following pronoun or adverb refers. **ante·ced·ence** /-dns/ *n* priority.

ante·cham·ber /ˈæntɪtʃeɪmbə(r)/ *n* room leading into a large room or hall.

ante·date /ˌæntɪˈdeɪt/ *vt* [VP6A] **1** put a date on, e g a letter, document, etc, earlier than the true one; give an earlier date than the true one to (an event). **2** come before in time: *This event ~s the arrival of Columbus by several centuries*.

ante·di·luv·ian /ˌæntɪdɪˈluvɪən/ *adj* of, suitable for, the time before the Flood, (Genesis); old-fashioned; out of date. □ *n* old-fashioned person.

ante·lope /ˈæntɪləʊp/ *n* deer-like, fast-running animal with thin legs. ⇨ the illus at **large**.

ante merid·iem /ˈæntɪ məˈrɪdɪəm/ (Lat) (shortened to *a m* /ˌeɪ ˈem/) time between midnight and noon: *7.30a m*.

ante·natal /ˌæntɪˈneɪtl/ *adj* existing or occurring before birth; pre-natal: *~ clinics*, for pregnant women.

an·tenna /ænˈtenə/ *n* (*pl* -nae /-ni/) **1** jointed organ found in pairs on the head of insects and crustaceans, used for feeling, etc. ⇨ the illus at **insect**. **2** (*pl* also **-nas**) (kind of) radio or T V aerial.

ante·nup·tial /ˌæntɪˈnʌpʃl/ *adj* before marriage: *an ~ contract*.

ante·pen·ul·ti·mate /ˌæntɪpɪˈnʌltɪmət/ *adj* last but two: *the ~ syllable*.

an·terior /ænˈtɪərɪə(r)/ *adj* coming before (in time or position).

ante·room /ˈæntɪrʊm *US:* -rum/ *n* antechamber; waiting-room.

an·them /ˈænθəm/ *n* musical composition, usu for choir and organ, to be sung in churches. **ˌnational ˈ~**, song or hymn of a country, e g 'God Save the Queen'.

an·ther /ˈænθə(r)/ *n* (bot) part of the stamen containing pollen. ⇨ the illus at **flower**.

an·thol·ogy /ænˈθɒlədʒɪ/ *n* (*pl* **-gies**) [C] collection of poems or pieces of prose, or of both, by different writers, or a selection from the work of one writer.

an·thra·cite /ˈænθrəsɑɪt/ *n* [U] very hard form of coal that burns with little smoke or flame.

an·thrax /ˈænθræks/ *n* [U] infectious, often fatal, disease of sheep and cattle that may be transmitted to human beings.

an·thro·poid /ˈænθrəpɔɪd/ *adj* man-like. □ *n* ~ animal, esp an ape, e g a gorilla.

an·thro·pol·ogy /ˌænθrəˈpɒlədʒɪ/ *n* [U] science of man, esp of the beginnings, development, customs and beliefs of mankind. **an·thro·pol·ogist** /ˌænθrəˈpɒlədʒɪst/ *n* expert in ~. **an·thro·po·logi·cal** /ˌænθrəpəˈlɒdʒɪkl/ *adj*

anti- /ˈæntɪ *US:* ˈæntaɪ/ *pref* against: ˈ~-balˋlistic; ˈ~-ˋclerical; ˈ~-ˋchristian, opposed to Christianity.

anti-air·craft /ˈæntɪ ˋeəkrɑft *US:* -kræft/ *adj* used against enemy aircraft: *~ guns.*

anti·biotic /ˈæntɪbɑɪˋotɪk/ *n, adj* (physiol) (substance, e g *penicillin*) produced by moulds and bacteria, capable of destroying or preventing the growth of bacteria.

anti·body /ˋæntɪbodɪ/ *n (pl* **-dies**) [C] (physiol) (kinds of) substance formed in the blood tending to inhibit or destroy harmful bacteria, etc.

an·tic /ˋæntɪk/ *n* (usu *pl*) grotesque movement, step, attitude, intended to amuse, e g by a clown at a circus; queer behaviour.

an·tici·pate /ˈænˋtɪsɪpeɪt/ *vt* [VP6A,C,9] **1** do, make use of, before the right or natural time: *Don't ~ your income,* order goods, etc before you receive your income. **2** do sth before sb else does it: *It is said that Columbus discovered America, but he was probably ~d by sailors from Norway who reached Labrador 500 years earlier.* **3** see what needs doing, what is likely to happen, etc and do what is necessary: *He tries to ~ all my needs,* satisfy them before I mention them. *A good general tries to ~ the enemy's movements.* **4** expect (which is the preferred word): *We don't ~ much trouble. The directors ~d a fall in demand/that demand would fall.* **an·tici·pa·tory** /ænˈtɪsɪˋpeɪtərɪ/ *adj*

an·tici·pa·tion /ænˈtɪsɪˋpeɪʃn/ *n* [U] action of anticipating; sth anticipated: *We bought an extra supply of coal in ~ of a cold winter. Thanking you in ~,* in advance and expecting you to do what I have asked.

anti·cli·max /ˈæntɪ ˋklɑɪmæks/ *n* [C] sudden fall from sth noble, serious, important, sensible, etc; descent that contrasts with a previous rise.

anti·cyc·lone /ˈæntɪˋsɑɪkləʊn/ *n* [C] (met) area in which atmospheric pressure is high compared with that of surrounding areas, with an outward flow of air; the area is characterized by quiet, settled weather. ⇨ **depression(4).**

anti·dote /ˋæntɪdəʊt/ *n* [C] medicine used against a poison, or to prevent a disease from having an effect: *an ~ against/for/to snakebite.*

anti·freeze /ˋæntɪfriz/ *n* [U] substance (usu a liquid) added to another liquid to lower its freezing point, e g as used in the radiator of a motor-vehicle.

anti-hero /ˋæntɪ hɪərəʊ/ *n (pl* **-roes** /-rəʊz/) (in fiction and drama) protagonist lacking the traditional characteristics of a hero, such as courage and dignity.

anti·knock /ˈæntɪˋnok/ *n* [U] substance added to the fuel in a motor-car engine to reduce noise. ⇨ **knock**[2]**(3).**

anti·log·ar·ithm /ˈæntɪˋlɔgərɪθm/ *n* number to which a logarithm belongs: *1 000, 100 and 10 are the ~s of 3, 2 and 1.*

anti·ma·cas·sar /ˈæntɪməˋkæsə(r)/ *n* covering to protect the back or arm of a chair or sofa from grease-marks.

anti·mony /ˋæntɪmənɪ *US:* -məʊnɪ/ *n* [U] easily broken silvery white metal, (symbol **Sb**) used in alloys, esp metal for type[1]**(3).**

an·tipa·thy /ænˋtɪpəθɪ/ *n* [U] strong and settled dislike (*to, towards, against,* sth, *between* two persons); [C] (*pl* **-thies**) instance or object of this: *feel/show a strong/marked ~ to a place/against sb.* **anti·pa·thetic** /ˈæntɪpəˋθetɪk/ *adj* having ~ (*to*).

anti-per·son·nel /ˈæntɪ ˈpɜsnˋel/ *adj* (usu of mines) designed to kill or wound human beings (not to destroy vehicles).

an·tipo·des /ænˋtɪpədiz/ *n pl* (usu **the ~**) (two) place(s) on the opposite sides of the earth, esp the region opposite our own.

anti·quar·ian /ˈæntɪˋkweərɪən/ *adj* connected with the study or sale of antiquities: *an ~ bookseller.* □ *n* antiquary.

anti·quary /ˋæntɪkwərɪ *US:* -kwerɪ/ *n (pl* **-ries**) person who studies, collects or sells, antiquities.

anti·quated /ˋæntɪkweɪtɪd/ *adj* obsolete; out of date; (of persons) having old-fashioned ideas and ways.

an·tique /ˈænˋtik/ *adj* belonging to the distant past; existing since old times; in the style of past times. □ *n* [C] material, (e g a piece of furniture, a work of art) of a past period (in GB at least 50 years old, in US 100 years) **the ~, ~** style in art. Cf *second-hand,* usu of things more recent.

an·tiquity /ænˋtɪkwətɪ/ *n* **1** [U] old times, esp before the Middle Ages; great age: *the heroes of ~; a city of great ~,* e g Athens; *in remote ~.* **2** (*pl;* **-ties**) buildings, ruins, works of art, remaining from ancient times: *Greek and Roman antiquities.*

an·tir·rhi·num /ˈæntɪˋrɑɪnəm/ *n* (bot) genus of plants; snapdragon.

anti-Sem·ite /ˈæntɪ ˋsimɑɪt *US:* ˋsem-/ *n, adj* (person) prejudiced against Jews, hating Jews. **anti-Sem·itic** /ˈæntɪ sɪˋmɪtɪk/ *adj* **anti-Semi·tism** /ˈæntɪ ˋsemətɪzm/ *n*

anti·sep·tic /ˈæntɪˋseptɪk/ *n, adj* (chemical substance) preventing putrefaction, esp by destroying germs.

anti·social /ˈæntɪˋsəʊʃl/ *adj* **1** opposed to social laws or to organized societies. **2** (recent colloq use) likely, tending to interfere with or spoil public amenities: *It is ~ to leave litter in public places/to play a transistor in public.*

anti·tank /ˈæntɪˋtæŋk/ *attrib adj* for use against military tanks: *~ guns/ditches.*

an·tith·esis /ænˋtɪθəsɪs/ *n (pl* **-ses** /-siz/) **1** [U] direct opposite (*of, to*). **2** [U] opposition (*of* one thing *to* another, *between* two things); [C] instance of this; contrast of ideas vividly expressed, as in 'Give me liberty, or give me death'. **anti·thetic** /ˈæntɪˋθetɪk/, **anti·theti·cal** /-ɪkl/ *adj* **anti·theti·cally** /-klɪ/ *adv*

anti·toxin /ˈæntɪˋtoksɪn/ *n* substance (usu a serum) able to counteract a toxin or disease.

anti·trade /ˈæntɪˋtreɪd/ *adj* ˋ**~ wind,** wind that blows in the opposite direction to a trade wind. □ *n* (usu *pl*) ~ wind.

ant·ler /ˋæntlə(r)/ *n* branched horn; branch of a horn (of a stag or other deer). ⇨ the illus at **large.**

an·to·nym /ˋæntənɪm/ *n* [C] word that is contrary in meaning to another: *Hot is the ~ of cold.* ⇨ **synonym.**

anus /ˋeɪnəs/ *n* (anat) opening at the end of the alimentary canal, through which waste matter passes out. ⇨ the illus at **alimentary.**

an·vil /ˋænvɪl/ *n* **1** large, heavy block of iron on which a smith hammers heated metal into shape. **2** (anat) bone in the ear. ⇨ the illus at **ear.**

anxiety /æŋˋzɑɪətɪ/ *n* **1** [U] emotional condition in which there is fear and uncertainty about the future: *We waited with ~ for news of her safe* *arrival. Tom's foolish behaviour caused his parents great* ~. **2** [C] (*pl* -**ties**) instance of such a feeling: *All these anxieties made him look pale and tired. The Budget statement removed all anxieties about higher taxes.* **3** [U] keen desire: ~ *for knowledge; his* ~ *to please his employers.*

anxious /ˈæŋkʃəs/ *adj* **1** feeling anxiety; troubled: *I am very* ~ *about my son's health. He is* ~ *for/about her safety/*~ *at her non-arrival.* **2** causing anxiety: *We have had an* ~ *time. His illness has been a very* ~ *business.* has caused us anxiety. **3** ~ ***to/for/about/that,*** strongly wishing: *He was* ~ *to meet you/*~ *for his brother to meet you. We were* ~ *that help should be sent promptly/*~ *for help to be sent.* **~·ly** *adv*

any[1] /ˈenɪ/ *adj* **1** ⇨ **some**[1](**1**) (in neg and interr sentences, and in clauses of condition, etc) **2** (in affirm sentences, with negation implied, e g with a *v* such as *'prevent'*, after the *prep 'without'*, after such *advv* as *'hardly'*): *We did the work without any difficulty. I have hardly any leisure nowadays. Please try to prevent any loss while the goods are on the way.* **3** (usu stressed; usu in affirm sentences) no matter which: *Come any day you like. You will find me at my desk at any hour of the day,* at all times. *We must find an excuse, any excuse will do.* **4** ***in any case,*** whatever happens, whatever the circumstances may be. ***at any rate,*** at least. **5** (colloq; used in affirm and neg sentences, with *sing* common *nn* for *a*(*n*) or *one*): *This bucket is useless—it hasn't any handle.*

any[2] /ˈenɪ/ *adv of degree* (used in neg, interr and conditional sentences, in contexts where negation or doubt is indicated or implied, and with comparatives. Cf the similar use of *no* and *none.*) at all; in any degree: *Is your father any better? They were too tired to go any further. The children didn't behave any too well,* i e they behaved rather badly. *If it's any good/use, I'll buy it.* ***(not) any the better/the worse/for,*** (not) at all better/worse for: *He got wet through in the rain yesterday but isn't any the worse for it,* has not suffered in any way.

any[3] /ˈenɪ/ *pron* ⇨ **some**[2].

any·body /ˈenɪbɒdɪ/ *n, pron* **1** (in neg, interr, etc sentences: ⇨ **somebody, someone**). **2** (in affirm sentences) no matter who: *A*~ *will tell you where the bus stop is. A*~ *who saw the accident is asked to communicate with the police. That's* ~*'s guess,* (colloq) is quite uncertain. ~ ***else,*** ⇨ **else. 3** person of importance: *You must work harder if you wish to be* ~. *Was she* ~ *before her marriage,* Had she any social position? *He'll never be* ~.

any·how /ˈenɪhaʊ/ *adv* **1** in any possible way; by any possible means: *The house was empty and I couldn't get in* ~. **2** carelessly; without order: *The work was done all* ~. **3** (*adv* or *conj*) in any case; at any rate: *A*~, *you can try,* even if there's not much chance of success. *It's too late now,* ~.

any·one /ˈenɪwʌn/ *n, pron* = anybody.

any·place /ˈenɪpleɪs/ *adv* (esp in US) = anywhere.

any·thing /ˈenɪθɪŋ/ *n, pron* **1** (in neg, interr, etc sentences: ⇨ **something**) (note the position of the *adj*): *Has* ~ *unusual happened?* **2** no matter what: *I want something to eat;* ~ *will do. He is* ~ *but mad,* far from being mad. **3** (used adverbially, to intensify a meaning): *The thief ran like* ~ *when he saw the policeman. It's (as) easy as* ~, (colloq) quite easy.

any·way /ˈenɪweɪ/ *adj* = anyhow.

any·where /ˈenɪweə(r) *US:* -hweər/ *adv* **1** (in neg, interr, etc sentences: ⇨ **somewhere**) (note the use of ~ with post-adjuncts): *I'll go* ~ *(that) you suggest. Are we going* ~ *(in) particular?* **2** (used as a *prep* object): *That leaves me without* ~ *to keep all my books.* **3** no matter where: *Put the box down* ~. *We'll go* ~ *you like.*

aorta /eɪˈɔtə/ *n* chief blood-vessel through which blood is carried from the left side of the heart. ⇨ the illus at **respiratory**.

apace /əˈpeɪs/ *adv* (old use, or liter) quickly: *Ill news spreads* ~.

apache /əˈpæʃ/ *n* (in Paris) hooligan; rough.

apa·nage (also **ap·pan·age**) /ˈæpənɪdʒ/ *n* **1** natural accompaniment; sth that necessarily goes with sth else. **2** property, etc coming to sb because of birth or office.

apart /əˈpɑt/ *adv* **1** distant: *The two houses are 500 metres* ~. *The negotiators are still miles* ~, show no signs of agreeing. **2** to or on one side: *He took me* ~ *in order to speak to me alone. Why does she hold herself* ~, i e not mix with other people? ***joking/jesting*** ~, speaking seriously. ***set/put (sth/sb)*** ~ ***(from),*** put (it) on one side; reserve it; make (sb) (appear) special: *His far-sightedness set him* ~ *from most of his contemporaries.* **3** separate(ly): *I can't get these two things* ~. *He was standing with his feet wide* ~. ~ ***from,*** independently of; leaving on one side: ~ *from these reasons.* **4** to pieces. ***tell/know two things or persons*** ~, distinguish one from the other. ⇨ **come(15), pull**[1]**(7), take**[1]**(16).**

apart·heid /əˈpɑtheɪt/ *n* (S Africa) (policy of) racial segregation; separate development of Europeans and non-Europeans.

apart·ment /əˈpɑtmənt/ *n* **1** single room in a house. **2** (*pl*) set of rooms, furnished or unfurnished, either owned or rented by the week or month, e g for a holiday at the seaside. **3** (US) set of rooms in a large building (called *an* ˈ~ *house*), usu on the same floor. (US ~ = GB *flat;* US ~ *house* = GB *block of flats;* US ~ *hotel* = GB *service flats.*) ⇨ **tenement.**

apa·thy /ˈæpəθɪ/ *n* [U] absence of sympathy or interest; indifference (*towards*). **apa·thetic** /ˌæpəˈθetɪk/ *adj* showing or having ~. **apa·theti·cally** /-klɪ/ *adv*

ape /eɪp/ *n* **1** tailless monkey (*gorilla, chimpanzee, orang-utan, gibbon*). **2** person who mimics others: *play the ape,* mimic. **3** (colloq) clumsy, ill-bred person. □ *vt* imitate (sb's behaviour, etc).

aperi·ent /əˈpɪərɪənt/ *n, adj* laxative.

aperi·tif /əˈperətɪf *US:* əˌperəˈtif/ *n* [C] alcoholic drink, (e g *vermouth*) taken before a meal.

ap·er·ture /ˈæpətʃʊə(r)/ *n* opening, esp one that admits light, e g to a camera lens.

apex /ˈeɪpeks/ *n* (*pl* **apexes** or **apices** /ˈeɪpɪsiz/) top or highest point: *the* ~ *of a triangle; at the* ~ *of his career/fortunes.*

aphasia /əˈfeɪzɪə *US:* -ʒə/ *n* [U] (path) loss of ability to use speech or to understand speech (as the result of brain injury).

aphid /ˈeɪfɪd/ *n* = aphis.

aphis /ˈeɪfɪs/ *n* (*pl* **aphides** /ˈeɪfɪdiz/) very small insect that lives by sucking juices from plants; plant louse.

aph·or·ism /ˈæfərɪzm/ *n* [C] short, wise saying; maxim.

aph·ro·dis·iac /ˌæfrəˈdɪzɪæk/ *n, adj* [C,U] (sub-

apes and monkeys

stance, drug) exciting sexual desire and activity.

api·ary /ˋeɪpɪərɪ *US:* -ɪerɪ/ *n* (*pl* -**ries**) place with a number of hives where bees are kept. **api·ar·ist** /ˋeɪpɪərɪst/ *n* person who keeps bees. **api·cul·ture** /ˋeɪpɪkʌltʃə(r)/ *n* bee-keeping.

apiece /əˋpis/ *adv* to, for or by, each one of a group: *They cost a penny* ~, each.

ap·ish /ˋeɪpɪʃ/ *adj* of or like an ape; foolishly imitative.

aplomb /əˋplom/ *n* [U] self-confidence; assurance (in speech or behaviour): *He answered with perfect* ~.

apoca·lypse /əˋpokəlɪps/ *n* revelation (esp of knowledge from God). **the A~,** the last book in the Bible, recording the revelation to St John. **apoca·lyp·tic** /əˈpokəˋlɪptɪk/ *adj* of or like an ~ or the A~.

Apoc·ry·pha /əˋpokrɪfə/ *n* (with *sing v*) those books of the Old Testament that are considered of doubtful authorship by the Jews and were excluded from the Bible at the time of the Reformation. **apoc·ry·phal** /əˋpokrɪfl/ *adj* of doubtful authority or authorship.

apo·gee /ˋæpədʒi/ *n* **1** position (in the orbit of the moon or any planet) when it is at its greatest distance from the earth. **2** (fig) highest point.

apolo·getic /əˈpoləˋdʒetɪk/ *adj* making an apology; expressing regret; excusing a fault or failure: *He was* ~ *for arriving late. He wrote an* ~ *letter.* **apolo·geti·cally** /-klɪ/ *adv* **apolo·get·ics** *n* (usu with *sing v*) the art or practice of explaining or justifying a religious belief, political creed, etc. **apolo·gist** /əˋpolədʒɪst/ *n* person who engages in ~s.

apolo·gize /əˋpolədʒɑɪz/ *vi* [VP2A,3A] ~ ***(to sb) (for sth),*** make an apology; say one is sorry: *You must* ~ *to your sister for being so rude.*

apol·ogy /əˋpolədʒɪ/ *n* (*pl* -**gies**) **1** [C] statement of regret (*for* doing wrong, being impolite, hurting sb's feelings): *offer/make/accept an* ~; *offer sb an* ~; *make an* ~ *to sb for sth; make one's apologies* (*to sb*), e g for being late, for not being able to come. **2** [C] explanation or defence (of beliefs, etc). ⇨ **apologetics. 3 *an*** ~ ***for,*** a poor specimen of, e g a dinner/letter.

apo·phthegm, apo·thegm /ˋæpəθem/ *n* [C] short, pointed or forceful, saying.

apo·plexy /ˋæpəpleksɪ/ *n* [U] loss of power to feel, move, think, usu caused by injury to blood-vessels in the brain. **apo·plec·tic** /ˈæpəˋplektɪk/ *adj* connected with, causing ~; suffering from ~: *an apoplectic stroke/fit;* (colloq) red in the face; easily made angry.

apos·tasy /əˋpostəsɪ/ *n* [U] giving up one's beliefs or faiths; turning away from one's religion; [C] (*pl* -**sies**) instance of this. **apos·tate** /ˋæpəsteɪt *US:* əˋposteɪt/ *n, adj* (person) guilty of ~.

a pos·teri·ori /ˋeɪ ˈpostɪərɪˋɔrɑɪ/ *adv, adj phrase* (Lat) (reasoning) from effects to causes, e g saying, *'The boys are tired so they must have walked a long way'.* ⇨ **a priori.**

apostle /əˋposl/ *n* **1** one of the twelve men chosen by Jesus to spread His teaching; missionary of the early Christian Church, e g St Paul, the A~ to the Gentiles. **2** leader or teacher of reform, of a new faith or movement. **apos·tolic** /ˈæpəˋstolɪk/ *adj* **1** of the ~s(**1**) or the times when they lived. **2** of the Pope.

apos·trophe[1] /əˋpostrəfɪ/ *n* the sign ' used to show omission of letter(s) or number(s), (as in *can't, I'm, '05,* for *cannot, I am, 1905*), for the possessive (as in *boy's, boys'*), and for the plurals of letters (as in *There are two l's in 'Bell'*).

apos·trophe[2] /əˋpostrəfɪ/ *n* passage in a public speech, in a poem, etc addressed to a particular person (who may be dead or absent). **apos·tro·phize** /əˋpostrəfɑɪz/ *vt* make an ~ to.

apoth·ecary /əˋpoθɪkərɪ *US:* -kerɪ/ *n* (*pl* -**ries**) (old use, but still in Scot) person who prepares and sells medicines and medical goods. **apothecaries' weight,** troy weight. ⇨ App 5.

apo·thegm ⇨ apophthegm.

apothe·osis /əˈpoθɪˋəʊsɪs/ *n* (*pl* **-ses** /-siz/) **1** (of a human being) making or becoming a god or a saint: *the ~ of a Roman Emperor.* **2** release from earthly life. **3** glorification; glorified ideal.

ap·pal (US also **ap·pall**) /əˋpɔl/ *vt* (-ll-) [VP6A] fill with fear or terror; dismay; shock deeply: *They were ~led at the news.* **~·ling** *adj*: *When will this ~ling war end?* **~·ling·ly** *adv*

ap·pa·nage ⇨ apanage.

ap·par·atus /ˈæpəˋreɪtəs *US:* -ˋrætəs/ *n* [C] (*pl* **-tuses**) (rarely *pl;* occ 'a piece of ~'). **1** set of instruments or other mechanical appliances put together for a purpose: *a heating ~,* e g for supplying steam heat throughout a building. **2** bodily organs by which natural processes are carried on: *Your digestive ~ takes the food you eat and changes it so that it can be used to build up the body.*

ap·parel /əˋpærl/ *n* [U] (old use, or liter) dress; clothing. □ *vt* (-ll-; US -l-) dress; clothe.

ap·par·ent /əˋpærnt/ *adj* **1** clearly seen or understood: *It was ~ to all of us...,* We all saw clearly...; *as will soon become ~,* as you will soon see. **2** seeming; according to appearances: *in spite of her ~ indifference,* although she seemed to be indifferent. **~·ly** *adv*

ap·par·ition /ˈæpəˋrɪʃn/ *n* [C] the coming into view, esp of a ghost or the spirit of a dead person.

ap·peal /əˋpil/ *vi* [VP2A,3A] **~ (to sb/for/from/against sth), 1** make an earnest request: *The prisoner ~ed to the judge for mercy. At Christmas people ~ to us to help the poor.* **2** (legal) take a question (to a higher court, etc) for rehearing and a new decision: *~ to another court; ~ against a decision; ~ from a judgement.* **3** go (to sb) for a decision: (football, etc) *~ to the linesman; ~ against the referee's decision;* (cricket) *The captain ~ed against the light,* said the light was too poor for further play. **4** attract; move the feelings of: *Bright colours ~ to small children. Do these paintings ~ to you?* □ *n* **1 an ~ for,** an earnest call for: *make an ~ for help.* **2** [C] act of ~ing(2): *an ~ to a higher court; an ~ from a decision; to lodge an ~;* [U] *to give notice of ~; acquittal on ~.* **3** [C] (esp in sport) act of ~ing: *an ~ to the referee.* **4** interest; (power of) attraction: *That sort of music hasn't much ~ for me/has lost its ~.* **5** [U] supplication: *with a look of ~ on her face,* asking for help or sympathy. **~·ing** *adj* **1** moving; touching the feelings or sympathy. **2** attractive. **~·ing·ly** *adv*

ap·pear /əˋpɪə(r)/ *vi* **1** [VP2A,C] come into view, become visible: *When we reached the top of the hill, the town ~ed below us. The ship ~ed on the horizon.* **2** [VP2A,C] arrive: *He promised to be here at four but didn't ~ until six.* **3** [VP2A,C] **(a)** (of an actor, singer, lecturer, etc) come before the public: *He has ~ed in every large concert hall in Europe.* **(b)** (of a book) be published: *When will your new novel ~?* **(c)** (legal) present oneself publicly: *The defendant failed to ~ before the court.* **4** [VP2A,4D,E] seem: *Why does she ~ so sad? He ~s to have many friends. You don't want to ~ a fool,* to look like a fool. *The house ~ed (to be) deserted. It would ~ that his intention was/His intention ~s to have been to arrive yesterday. There ~s to have been a mistake. So it ~s. It ~s not. It ~s to me that.../It begins to ~ that...,* It looks as though....

ap·pear·ance /əˋpɪərns/ *n* [C] **1** act of appearing: *make an ~; make one's first ~,* (of an actor, singer, etc) appear in public for the first time. ***put in an ~,*** show oneself, attend (a meeting, party, etc): *I don't want to go to the garden party but I'd better put in an ~.* **2** that which shows or can be seen; what sth or sb appears to be: *The child had the ~ of being* (= looked as if it were) *half starved. She has a slightly foreign ~. We mustn't judge by ~s,* by what can be seen outside, by outward looks. ***keep up ~s,*** maintain an outward show (in order to hide what one does not wish people to see, e g by buying smart clothes and spending little on food, etc). ***in ~,*** so far as ~ is concerned; outwardly: *In ~ it is a strong building.* ***to/by/from all ~(s),*** so far as can be seen: *He was to all ~(s) dead.*

ap·pease /əˋpiz/ *vt* [VP6A] make quiet or calm: *~ sb's anger; ~ sb's curiosity/hunger.* **~·ment** *n* [U] appeasing, e g by making concessions to potential enemies.

ap·pel·lant /əˋpelənt/ *adj* (legal) concerned with appeals. □ *n* (legal) person who appeals to a higher court.

ap·pel·la·tion /ˈæpəˋleɪʃn/ *n* [C] (formal) name or title; system of names.

ap·pend /əˋpend/ *vt* [VP6A,14] **~ to,** add in writing or in print; add (sth) at the end: *~ a clause to a treaty; ~ a seal or signature to a document.*

ap·pend·age /əˋpendɪdʒ/ *n* [C] sth added to, fastened to or forming a natural part of, a larger thing.

ap·pen·dix /əˋpendɪks/ *n* **1** [C] (*pl* **-dices** /-dɪsiz/) sth added, esp at the end of a book. **2** [C] (*pl* also **-dixes**) small out-growth on the surface of a bodily organ, esp (**vermiform ~**) a worm-like appendage of the large intestine. ⇨ the illus at alimentary. **ap·pen·di·ci·tis** /əˈpendəˋsaɪtɪs/ *n* [U] diseased condition of the vermiform ~, requiring in many cases a surgical operation. **ap·pen·dec·tomy** /ˈæpenˋdektəmɪ/ *n* (*pl* **-mies**) removal by surgery of the vermiform ~.

ap·per·tain /ˈæpəˋteɪn/ *vi* [VP3A] **~ to,** (formal) belong to as a right; be appropriate: *the duties ~ing to his office.*

ap·pe·tite /ˋæpətaɪt/ *n* [C, U] physical desire (esp *for* food): *The long walk gave him a good ~. She is suffering from lack of ~. If you eat a lot of chocolate before supper, it will spoil/take away your ~,* prevent you from enjoying your supper. (fig) *He had no ~ for the fight.* **ap·pe·tizer** *n* sth done (e g a walk) or served (e g olives, a short alcoholic drink) in order to stimulate the ~. **ap·pe·tiz·ing** *adj* pleasing to, exciting, the ~: *an appetizing smell from the kitchen.*

ap·plaud /əˋplɔd/ *vi,vt* **1** [VP6A,2A,B] show approval (of) by clapping the hands: *The audience ~ed (the singer) for five minutes. He was loudly ~ed.* **2** express approval of: *I ~ your decision.*

ap·plause /əˋplɔz/ *n* [U] loud approval; hand-clapping: *greeted with ~; win the ~ of the audience.*

apple /ˋæpl/ *n* (tree with) round fruit with firm juicy flesh and skin that is red, green or yellow when it is ripe. ⇨ the illus at fruit. ***the ~ of one's eye,*** sb or sth dearly loved. ***~ of discord,*** cause of quarrel. ***upset the/sb's ˋ~-cart,*** spoil his plans. ***in ˈ~-ˈpie ˋorder,*** in perfect order, with everything in the right place. '~**jack** *n* (US) brandy distilled from fermented cider. '~ '**sauce,** (US = '~**sauce**) *n* **(a)** sliced ~s stewed. **(b)** (US colloq) nonsense: insincere flattery. **Adam's ~,** ⇨ Adam.

ap·pliance /əˈplaɪəns/ *n* [C] instrument or apparatus: *an ~* (= tool) *for opening tin cans; an ~ for rescuing sailors from a wrecked ship,* e g a rope that can be fired from a gun; *household ~s,* e g a washing-machine, a food-mixer.

ap·pli·cable /ˈæplɪkəbl/ *adj* ~ ***(to),*** that can be applied; that is suitable and proper: *Is the rule ~ to this case?*

ap·pli·cant /ˈæplɪkənt/ *n* ~ ***(for),*** person who applies (esp for a position): *As the wages were low, there were no ~s for the job.*

ap·p·li·ca·tion /ˌæplɪˈkeɪʃn/ *n* **1** ~ ***(to sb) (for sth),*** [U] making of a request: *A list of new books may be had on ~ to the publishers;* [C] request (esp in writing): *The manager received twenty ~s for the position. We made an ~ to the court for an enquiry.* '~ **form,** form to be filled in when applying for sth. **2** ~ ***(of sth) (to sth),*** [U] putting one thing on to another: *This oil is for external ~ only,* to be used only on the surface; [C,U] substance used: *The doctor ordered ~(s) of ice to the forehead. Both cold and hot ~s are used to help people who are in pain.* **3** ~ ***(of sth) (to sth),*** [U] bringing a rule to bear on a case; putting to practical use: *the ~ of the rule to this case; the ~ of a discovery/a new process, etc to industry.* **4** [U] effort; attention: *If you show ~ in your studies* (= If you work hard) *you will succeed. My work demands close ~,* i e I have to concentrate my thoughts on it.

ap·plied ⇨ apply.

ap·pli·qué /əˈpliːkeɪ *US:* ˌæplɪˈkeɪ/ *n* [U] (esp in dress-making) ornamental work made of one kind of material, or material of one colour, applied to the surface of another. □ *vt* ornament in this way.

ap·ply /əˈplaɪ/ *vt, vi* (*pt, pp* -lied) **1** [VP2C,3A] ~ ***(to sb) (for sth),*** (formally) ask for: *~ to the Consul for a visa. You may ~ in person or by letter.* **2** [VP6A,14] lay one thing on or in another; cause (sth) to serve a purpose by doing this: *~ a plaster to a cut; ~ the brakes* (of a motor-vehicle, etc); *We intend to ~ economic sanctions.* **3** [VP6A,3A] ~ ***(to sth),*** (cause to) have a bearing (on); concern: *The rule cannot be applied in every case. What I have said does not ~ to you.* **4** [VP14] ~ ***oneself/one's mind/one's energies (to sth/to doing sth),*** concentrate one's thoughts, etc on a task, give all one's energy and attention to: *~ your mind to your work. We must ~ energies to finding a solution.* **5** [VP14] make practical use of (research, a discovery): *We can ~ his findings in new developments.* **ap·plied** *part adj* put to practical use: *applied mathematics,* e g as used in engineering; *applied art,* e g as used in textile designs, for pottery, etc.

ap·point /əˈpɔɪnt/ *vt* **1** [VP6A,14,16A] ~ ***(for sth, to do sth),*** fix or decide: *The time ~ed for the meeting was 8.30 p m. We must ~ a time to meet again/a time for the next meeting.* **2** [VP6A,25, 23,14] choose for a post; set up by choosing members: *They ~ed White (to be) manager. Smith was ~ed to the vacant post. The newly-~ed officials are all expert. We must ~ a committee.* **3** [VP9] (formal or older use) give orders: *~ that sth shall be done.* **4** ***well/badly ~ed,*** well/badly equipped. **~·ment** *n* **1** [U] ~ing: *meet sb by ~ment,* after fixing a time and place. **2** [C] arrangement to meet sb: *make/fix an ~ment with sb; keep/break an ~ment. I have an ~ment with my dentist at 3 p m.* **3** [C] position or office: *get a good ~ment in a business firm; an ~ment as manager.* **4** (*pl*) equipment; furniture. **~ee** /əˌpɔɪnˈtiː/ *n* person ~ed to an office or position.

ap·por·tion /əˈpɔːʃn/ *vt* [VP6A,12B,13B,14] divide; distribute; give as a share (*to*): *I have ~ed you different duties each day of the week. This sum of money is to be ~ed among the six boys.*

ap·po·site /ˈæpəzɪt/ *adj* strikingly appropriate for a purpose or occasion: *an ~ remark.* **~·ly** *adv*

ap·po·si·tion /ˌæpəˈzɪʃn/ *n* [U] addition of one word or group of words to another as an explanation. In the sentence, 'Herr Müller, our new teacher, is a German', *teacher* is in ~ to *Müller; teacher* and *Müller* are in ~.

ap·praise /əˈpreɪz/ *vt* [VP6A] fix a price for; say what sth is worth: *~ the ability of one's pupils; ~ property (at a certain sum) for taxation.* **ap·praisal** /əˈpreɪzl/ *n* valuation.

ap·preci·able /əˈpriːʃəbl/ *adj* that can be seen or felt: *an ~ change in the temperature.* **ap·preci·ably** /-əblɪ/ *adv*

ap·preci·ate /əˈpriːʃɪeɪt/ *vt, vi* **1** [VP6A] judge rightly the value of; understand and enjoy: *You can't ~ English poetry unless you understand its rhythm. We all ~ a holiday after a year of hard work.* **2** [VP6A] put a high value on: *We greatly ~ all your help.* **3** [VP2B] (of land, goods, etc) increase in value: *The land has ~d greatly since the new railway was built.*

ap·preci·ation /əˌpriːʃɪˈeɪʃn əˌpriːsɪ-/ *n* **1** [C, U] (statement giving) judgement, valuation: *Write an ~ of a new symphony. She showed little or no ~ of good music.* **2** [U] proper understanding and recognition: *in sincere ~ of your valuable help.* **3** [U] rise in value, e g of land, business shares. **ap·preci·ative** /əˈpriːʃətɪv/ *adv* feeling or showing ~(2): *an appreciative audience; appreciative of kindness.*

ap·pre·hend /ˌæprɪˈhend/ *vt* **1** [VP6A,9] (old use) understand: *You are, I ~, ready to....* **2** [VP6A,9] (formal) fear: *Do you ~ any difficulty/that there will be any difficulty?* **3** [VP6A] (legal) arrest, seize: *~ a thief.* **ap·pre·hen·sible** /ˌæprɪˈhensəbl/ *adj* capable of being ~ed(1).

ap·pre·hen·sion /ˌæprɪˈhenʃn/ *n* **1** [U] grasping (of ideas); understanding: *quick/slow of ~.* **2** [U] (also *pl*) fear; unhappy feeling about the future: *feel ~ for sb's safety; filled with ~; entertain some ~ of failure.* **3** (legal) seizing: *the ~ of a thief/deserter.*

ap·pre·hen·sive /ˌæprɪˈhensɪv/ *adj* uneasy; worried: *~ of further defeats; ~ for sb's safety; ~ that sb will be hurt.*

ap·pren·tice /əˈprentɪs/ *n* learner of a trade who has agreed to work for a number of years in return for being taught. □ *vt* ~ ***(to),*** [VP6A,14] bind as an ~: *The boy was ~d to a carpenter.* **~·ship** /-ʃɪp/ *n* (time of) being an ~: *serve one's ~ship (with sb).*

ap·prise /əˈpraɪz/ *vt* [VP14] ~ ***of,*** (formal) inform: *be ~d of sb's intentions; be ~d that....*

ap·pro /ˈæprəʊ/ *n* ***on ~,*** (comm sl) on approval: *goods on ~,* to be returned if not satisfactory.

ap·proach /əˈprəʊtʃ/ *vt, vi* **1** [VP6A,2A] come near(er) (to): *A boy of eighteen is ~ing manhood.*

As winter ~ed the weather became colder. (fig) *Few writers can even ~ Shakespeare in greatness.* **2** [VP6A] go to (sb) with a request or offer: *When is the best time to ~ my employer about an increase in salary? He is rather difficult to ~,* It is not easy to get on friendly terms with him. □ *n* **1** [U] act of ~ing: *The enemy ran away at our ~.* ***easy/difficult of ~,*** **(a)** (of a place) easy/difficult to get to. **(b)** (of a person) easy/difficult to meet and talk to. ***make ~es to sb,*** **(a)** try to obtain his interest, attract his attention. **(b)** offer, try, to enter into personal relations with (e g of a man who wants intimate friendship with a girl or woman). **2** [C] approximation: *an ~ to perfection.* **3** [C] way, path, road: *All the ~es to the Palace were guarded by soldiers.* **~·able** /-əbl/ *adj* (of a person or place) that can be ~ed; accessible.

ap·pro·ba·tion /ˈæprəˋbeɪʃn/ *n* [U] (formal) approval; sanction.

ap·pro·pri·ate[1] /əˋprəʊprɪət/ *adj* **~ *(for/to sth),*** suited to; in keeping with: *Sports clothes are not ~ for a formal wedding. Write in a style ~ to your subject.* **~·ly** *adv*

ap·pro·pri·ate[2] /əˋprəʊprɪeɪt/ *vt* [VP6A, 14] **1** put on one side for a special purpose: *£20 000 has been ~d for the new school buildings.* **2** take and use as one's own: *He often ~s my ideas.* **ap·pro·pri·ation** /əˈprəʊprɪˋeɪʃn/ *n* **1** [U] appropriating or being ~d; [C] instance of this. **2** [C] sth, esp a sum of money, that is ~d: *make an appropriation for payment of debts; Senate A~s Committee,* (US) one which deals with funds for defence, welfare, etc.

ap·proval /əˋpruvl/ *n* [U] feeling, showing or saying, that one is satisfied, that sth is right, that one agrees to sth: *Your plans have my ~. Does what I have done meet with your ~? She gave a nod of ~/nodded her ~.* ***goods on ~,*** to be returned if not satisfactory.

ap·prove /əˋpruv/ *vt,vi* **1 ~ *of (sth or sb),*** [VP3A] give one's approval of: *Her father will never ~ of her marriage to you. I cannot support a policy of which I have never ~d.* **2** [VP6A] confirm; agree to: *The minutes (of the meeting) were read and ~d. The expenditure has been ~d.* **~d school,** (GB) boarding school for training and educating children under 17 who are sent there by magistrates for juvenile offences or because in need of care and protection. (US = *reformatory, reform school*). **ap·prov·ing·ly** *adv*

ap·proxi·mate[1] /əˋproksɪmət/ *adj* very near (*to*); about right: *a sum of money ~ to what will be needed. The ~ area of my land is half an acre.* **~·ly** *adv*

ap·proxi·mate[2] /əˋproksɪmeɪt/ *vi,vt* **1 ~ *to,*** [VP3A] come near to (esp in quality or number): *His description of the event ~d to the truth but there were a few inaccuracies.* **2** [VP6A,3A] bring or come near to. **ap·proxi·ma·tion** /əˈproksɪˋmeɪʃn/ *n* [C] almost correct amount or estimate; [U] being or getting near (in number or quality).

ap·pur·ten·ance /əˋpɜtɪnəns/ *n* (usu *pl*) (legal) sth, that belongs to or usu goes with another thing: *the house and its ~s,* the lesser rights and privileges that go with ownership of the house.

après-ski /ˈæpreɪ ˋski/ *attrib adj* of the evening period after skiing: *~ fun and games; ~ clothes.*

apri·cot /ˋeɪprɪkot/ *n* (tree with) round, orange-yellow or orange-red fruit with soft flesh and a hard stone-like seed; colour of this fruit when ripe.

April /ˋeɪprl/ *n* fourth month of the year. **ˈ~ ˋfool,** person who is hoaxed on ˈAll ˋFools' Day (1 April).

a priori /ˈeɪ ˈpraɪˋɔraɪ/ *adv, adj* (Lat) (reasoning) from cause to effect. ⇨ a posteriori.

apron /ˋeɪprən/ *n* **1** loose garment worn over the front part of the body to keep clothes clean; any similar covering. ***tied to his mother's/wife's ˋ~-strings,*** too long or too much under her control. **2** hard-surfaced (tarmac, concrete, etc) area on an air-field, used for manœuvring and (un)loading aircraft. **3 ˋ~ stage,** (in some theatres) part of the stage jutting out into the audience. ⇨ proscenium.

apro·pos /ˈæprəˋpəʊ/ *adv, pred adj* to the purpose; well suited (to what is being said or done): *His suggestion is very much ~.* **~ *of*** *prep* concerning, with reference to.

apse /æps/ *n* semi-circular or many-sided recess, with an arched or domed roof, esp at the east end of a church. ⇨ the illus at church.

apt /æpt/ *adj* **1 *apt (at doing sth),*** quick-witted: *one of my aptest pupils; very apt at picking up a new subject.* **2** to the point; well suited: *an apt remark.* **3 *apt to do sth,*** having a tendency, likely to do sth: *Cast iron is apt to break. He's a clever boy but apt to get into mischief.* **apt·ly** *adv* suitably, justly. **apt·ness** *n*

ap·ti·tude /ˋæptɪtjud *US:* -tud/ *n* [C,U] **~ *for,*** natural or acquired talent: *He shows an ~ for languages. He has a singular ~ for dealing with a crisis. The pupils were given an ~ test.*

aqua·lung /ˋækwəlʌŋ/ *n* (P) breathing unit (face mask, valve unit and cylinder(s) of compressed air or oxygen) used for underwater swimming or diving. ⇨ the illus at frogman.

aqua·mar·ine /ˈækwəməˋrin/ *n* [C,U] bluish-green (jewel).

aqua·naut /ˋækwənɔt/ *n* person trained to live for a long period, in a structure submerged in the sea, to study marine life, etc.

aqua·plane /ˋækwəpleɪn/ *n* board on which a person stands while being pulled along by a fast motor-boat. □ *vi* ride on such a board.

aquar·ium /əˋkweərɪəm/ *n* (*pl* -riums, -ria /-rɪə/) (building with an) artificial pond or tank for keeping and showing living fish and water plants.

Aquar·ius /əˋkweərɪəs/ *n* the eleventh sign of the zodiac. ⇨ the illus at zodiac.

aquatic /əˋkwætɪk/ *adj* **1** (of plants, animals, etc) growing or living in or near water. **2** (of sports) taking place on or in water, e g rowing, swimming.

aqua·tint /ˋækwətɪnt/ *n* [U] process of etching on copper, the picture being made by letting acid bite into a plate covered with a layer of resin dust; [C] picture made in this way.

aqua·vit /ˋækwəvit/ *n* [U] strong Scandinavian liquor flavoured with caraway seed.

aque·duct /ˋækwɪdʌkt/ *n* artificial channel for supplying water, esp one built of stone or brick and higher than the surrounding land.

aque·ous /ˋeɪkwɪəs/ *adj* of or like water: *an ~ solution.*

aqui·line /ˋækwɪlɑɪn/ *adj* of or like an eagle: *an ~ nose,* hooked like an eagle's beak.

Arab /ˋærəb/ *n* name applied to any of those Semitic people who speak Arabic and claim des-

an aqueduct

cent from the inhabitants of the Arabian Peninsula who, in the 7th c, were conquerors of N Africa, Syria and Mesopotamia: *the military conquests of the ~s; the ~ League.*

ara·besque /ˌærəˈbesk/ *n* [C] (art) elaborate design of leaves, branches, scrolls, etc; (ballet) pose of a dancer on one leg, the other stretched backwards.

Arabian /əˈreɪbɪən/ *adj* of Arabia or the Arabs: *the ~ Nights,* famous stories of the Arabs in ancient times; *the ~ camel,* the dromedary.

Ara·bic /ˈærəbɪk/ *adj* of the Arabs: *~ numerals,* the signs 0, 1, 2, 3, etc. ⇨ **App 4.** □ *n* language of the Arabs.

Ara·bist /ˈærəbɪst/ *n* student or specialist in Arabic culture, language, etc.

ar·able /ˈærəbl/ *adj* (of land) suitable for ploughing; usually ploughed.

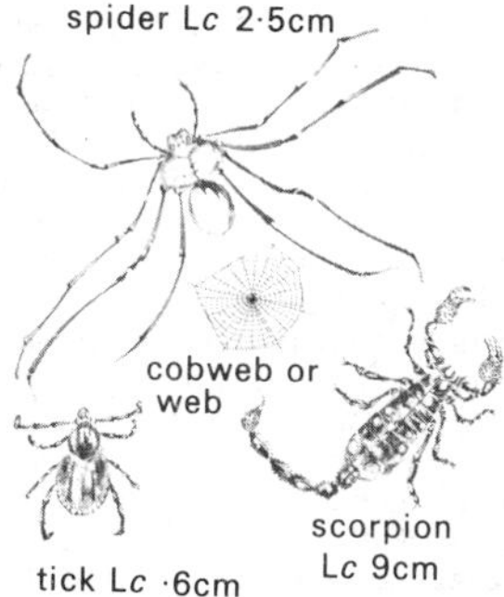

arachnids

arach·nid /əˈræknɪd/ *n* (zool) member of the genus including spiders, scorpions and mites.

ar·bi·ter /ˈɑbɪtə(r)/ *n* **1** person with complete control (*of* sth): *the sole ~ of their destinies.* **2** = arbitrator.

ar·bitra·ment /ɑˈbɪtrəmənt/ *n* [U] the deciding of a dispute by an arbiter; [C] decision made by an arbiter.

ar·bit·rary /ˈɑbɪtrərɪ *US:* -trerɪ/ *adj* **1** based on opinion or impulse only, not on reason. **2** dictatorial; using despotic power.

ar·bi·trate /ˈɑbɪtreɪt/ *vt, vi* [VP6A,2A] decide by arbitration; judge *between* two parties to a dispute (usu at the request of the two parties): *Mr X has been asked to ~ the dispute/to ~ between the employers and their workers. If countries would always ~ their quarrels, wars could be avoided.*

ar·bi·tra·tion /ˌɑbɪˈtreɪʃn/ *n* [U] settlement of a dispute by the decision of a person or persons chosen and accepted as judges or umpires: *refer a wage dispute to ~; submit a claim for ~. The Union agreed to (go to) ~,* i e for a settlement of their claims.

ar·bi·tra·tor /ˈɑbɪtreɪtə(r)/ *n* (legal) arbiter; person appointed by two parties to settle a dispute.

ar·bor ⇨ arbour.

ar·boreal /ɑˈbɔrɪəl/ *adj* of, living in, connected with trees: *~ animals,* e g squirrels, monkeys.

ar·bour (US = **ar·bor**) /ˈɑbə(r)/ *n* shady place among trees, esp one made in a garden, with climbing plants growing over a framework.

arc /ɑk/ *n* part of the circumference of a circle or other curved line. ⇨ the illus at **circle.** **ˈarc-lamp, ˈarc-light** *nn* brilliant light production by electric current flowing across a space between two carbon rods.

ar·cade /ɑˈkeɪd/ *n* covered passage, usu with an arched roof, e g a passage with shops or market stalls along one or both sides; covered market. **aˈmusement ~,** ⇨ amusement.

Ar·cad·ian /ɑˈkeɪdɪən/ *adj* of an ideal rustic simplicity; simple and innocent. □ *n* person with ~ tastes.

ar·cane /ɑˈkeɪn/ *adj* secret; mysterious.

arch[1] /ɑtʃ/ *n* **1** curved structure supporting the weight of what is above it, as in bridges, aqueducts, gateways, etc. ⇨ the illus of an aqueduct. **2** (also **ˈ~·way**) passageway under an ~, built as an ornament or gateway: *a triumphal ~.* **3** any curve in the shape of an ~, e g the curved under-part of the foot, ⇨ the illus at **leg**; a structure for supporting climbing roses, etc. □ *vt, vi* **1** [VP6A] form into an ~: *The cat ~ed its back when it saw the dog. Horses ~ their necks.* **2** [VP2C] be like an ~: *The trees ~ over the river.*

arch[2] /ɑtʃ/ *attrib adj* mischievous in an innocent or playful way (esp of women and children): *an ~ glance/smile.* **~·ly** *adv*

arch- /ɑtʃ/ *pref* chief; notable; extreme: *~-enemy.*

ar·chae·ol·ogy (also **ar·che·ol-**) /ˌɑkɪˈolədʒɪ/ *n* [U] study of ancient things, esp remains of prehistoric times, e g tombs, buried cities. **ar·chae·ologi·cal** /ˌɑkɪəˈlodʒɪkl/ *adj* of ~. **ar·chae·ol·ogist** /ˌɑkɪˈolədʒɪst/ *n* expert in ~.

ar·chaic /ɑˈkeɪɪk/ *adj* **1** (of languages) not now used except for special purposes. **2** of ancient times. **ar·chaism** /ɑˈkeɪɪzm/ *n* [C] ~ word or expression; [U] use or imitation of what is ~.

arch·angel /ˈɑkˈeɪndʒl/ *n* angel of highest rank.

arch·bishop /ˈɑtʃˈbɪʃəp/ *n* chief bishop. **~·ric** *n* position or rank of an ~; church district governed by an ~.

arch·deacon /ˈɑtʃˈdikən/ *n* (in the C of E) priest next below a bishop, superintending rural deans. **~ry** *n* (*pl* **-ries**) position, rank, residence, of an ~.

arch·dio·cese /ˈɑtʃˈdɑɪəsɪs/ *n* diocese of an archbishop.

arch·duke /ˈɑtʃˈdjuk *US:* -ˈduk/ *n* (title given to) son or nephew of former Emperors of Austria.

archer /ˈɑtʃə(r)/ *n* person who shoots with a bow and arrows. **arch·ery** /ˈɑtʃərɪ/ *n* [U] (art of) shooting with a bow and arrows. ⇨ **p 40.**

arche·type /ˈɑkɪtɑɪp/ *n* prototype; ideal form regarded as a pattern not to be changed. **arche·typal** /ˌɑkɪˈtɑɪpl/ *adj*

archi·man·drite /ˌɑkɪˈmændrɑɪt/ *n* head of a monastery or convent in the Gk Orthodox Church.

archi·pel·ago /ˌɑkɪˈpeləgəʊ/ *n* (*pl* **-gos, -goes** /-gəʊz/) (sea with a) group of many islands.

archi·tect /ˈɑkɪtekt/ *n* person who designs (and supervises the construction of) buildings, etc.

archi·tec·ture /ˈɑkɪtektʃə(r)/ *n* [U] art and science of building; design or style of building(s). **archi-**

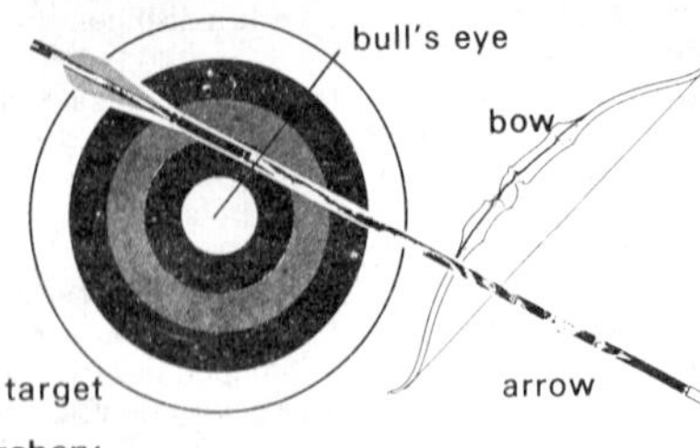

archery

tec·tural /ˌɑkɪˋtekʃərl/ *adj* of ~: *the architectural beauties of a city.*

ar·chives /ˋɑkaɪvz/ *n pl* (place for keeping) public or government records; other historical records. **archi·vist** /ˋɑkɪvɪst/ *n* person in charge of ~.

arch·way /ˋɑtʃweɪ/ *n* ⇨ arch¹(2).

arc·tic /ˋɑktɪk/ *adj* of the north polar regions: *the A~ Ocean; ~ weather,* very cold weather. **the 'A~ 'Circle,** the line of latitude 66½°N.

ar·dent /ˋɑdnt/ *adj* full of ardour: *~ supporters of the new movement.* **~·ly** *adv*

ar·dour (US = **-dor**) /ˋɑdə(r)/ *n* **~ *(for)*,** [C,U] warm emotion; enthusiasm.

ar·du·ous /ˋɑdjʊəs *US:* -dʒʊ-/ *adj* **1** (of work) needing and using up much energy. **2** (of a road, etc) steep; hard to climb. **~·ly** *adv*

are¹ /ə *strong form:* ɑ(r)/ ⇨ be¹.

are² /ɑ(r)/ *n* metric unit of area, 100 sq metres.

area /ˋeərɪə/ *n* [C] **1** surface measure: *If a room measures 3 5 metres, its ~ is 15 square metres/it is 15 square metres in ~.* ⇨ App 5. **2** region of the earth's surface: *desert ~s of North Africa; the postal ~s* (more usu *districts*) *into which London is divided.* **3** (fig) scope or range of activity: *the ~ of finance. The ~s of disagreement were clearly indicated at the Board Meeting,* The subjects on which members of the Board disagreed became clear. **4** small courtyard giving light to the windows of basement rooms, e g kitchen, scullery, in an old-fashioned town house, usu with stone steps from the street pavement: *sitting on the ~ steps.*

areca /ˋærɪkə/ *n* kind of palm-tree from which areca-nut (betel-nut) is obtained. ⇨ betel.

arena /əˋrinə/ *n* (*pl* **-nas**) central part, for games and fights, of a Roman amphitheatre; (fig) any scene of competition or struggle: *the ~ of politics.*

aren't /ɑnt/ = are not. *aren't I* (= a'n't I), am I not?

arête /æˋreɪt/ *n* (F) (esp of mountains in Switzerland) sharp ridge. ⇨ the illus at mountain.

ar·gent /ˋɑdʒənt/ *n, adj* (in heraldry and poetry) silver (colour).

ar·gon /ˋɑgon/ *n* [U] chemically inactive gas (symbol **Ar**), present in the atmosphere (0·8 per cent), used in some kinds of electric lamps.

Ar·go·naut /ˋɑgənɔt/ *n* (myth) one of the heroes who sailed in the ship Argo /ˋɑgəʊ/ with Jason in search of the Golden Fleece.

ar·gosy /ˋɑgəsɪ/ *n* (*pl* **-sies**) (poet) large merchant ship, esp one with valuable cargo.

ar·gue /ˋɑgju/ *vi, vt* **1** [VP2A,C,3A] **~ *(with sb) (about/over sth)*,** express disagreement; quarrel: *Don't ~ with me; my decision is final. Why are they always ~ing?* **2** [VP2A,3A,9] **~ *(for/against/that...)*,** maintain a case, give reasons (in support of, for, against, esp with the aim of persuading sb): *He ~s soundly. You can ~ either way, for or against. He was arguing that poverty may be a blessing.* **3** [VP14] ***~ sb into/out of doing sth,*** persuade by giving reasons: *They tried to ~ him into joining them.* **4** [VP6A] debate: *The lawyers ~d the case for hours.* **ar·gu·able** /ˋɑgjʊəbl/ *adj* that can be ~d about.

ar·gu·ment /ˋɑgjʊmənt/ *n* **1** [C] ***an ~ (with sb) (about/over sth)*,** (perhaps heated) disagreement; quarrel: *endless ~s about money; an ~ with the referee.* **2** [C,U] ***(an) ~ (for/against sth/that...)*,** reasoned discussion: *an ~ for not gambling. It is beyond ~ that...; I have no wish to engage in an ~ with you.* **3** [C] summary of the subject matter of a book, etc. **ar·gu·men·ta·tive** /ˌɑgjʊˋmentətɪv/ *adj* fond of arguing(1).

ar·gu·men·ta·tion /ˌɑgjʊmenˋteɪʃn/ *n* [U] process of arguing; debate.

Ar·gus /ˋɑgəs/ *n* (Gk myth) monster with a hundred eyes. **'~-'eyed** *adj* observant; vigilant.

aria /ˋɑrɪə/ *n* [C] melody for a single voice (esp in 18th c operas and oratorios).

arid /ˋærɪd/ *adj* **1** (of soil, land) dry, barren; (of climate, regions) having not enough rainfall to support vegetation. **2** (fig) uninteresting. **arid·ity** /əˋrɪdətɪ/ *n* [U] dryness.

Aries /ˋeəriz/ *n* the Ram, the first sign of the zodiac. ⇨ the illus at zodiac.

aright /əˋraɪt/ *adv* rightly: *if I heard ~.* (Before a *pp* use *rightly,* as in *to be rightly informed.*)

arise /əˋraɪz/ *vi* (*pt* **arose** /əˋrəʊz/, *pp* **arisen** /əˋrɪzn/) **1** [VP2A] come into existence; come to notice; present itself: *A new difficulty has ~n. If the need should ~...; Before they could start a mist arose.* **2** [VP3A] result from: *Serious obligations may ~ from the proposed clause.* **3** [VP2A] (old use) get up; stand up.

ar·is·toc·racy /ˌærɪˋstokrəsɪ/ *n* (*pl* **-cies**) **1** [U] government by persons of the highest social rank; [C] country or state with such a government. **2** [C] ruling body of nobles; the social class from which these nobles come. **3** best representatives in any class: *an ~ of talent.*

ar·is·to·crat /ˋærɪstəkræt *US:* əˋrɪst-/ *n* member of the class of nobles; person of noble birth. **~ic** /ˌærɪstəˋkrætɪk *US:* əˌrɪstə-/ *adj* of the aristocracy; having the ways and manners of an ~: *with an ~ic bearing.* **~i·cally** /-klɪ/ *adv*

arith·me·tic /əˋrɪθmətɪk/ *n* [U] science of numbers; working with numbers. **ar·ith·meti·cal** /ˌærɪθˋmetɪkl/ *adj* of ~. **~al progression,** series of numbers showing an increase, or decrease, by a quantity that is always the same, e g 1, 2, 3, etc, or 7, 5, 3, etc. **arith·me·tician** /əˌrɪθməˋtɪʃn/ *n* expert in ~.

ark /ɑk/ *n* (in the Bible) **1** covered ship in which Noah and his family were saved from the Flood. **2 Ark of the Covenant,** wooden chest in which writings of Jewish law were kept.

arm¹ /ɑm/ *n* **1** either of the two upper limbs of the human body, from the shoulder to the hand: *She was carrying a child in her arms. He was carrying a book under his arm,* between the arm and the body. *She had a basket on her arm,* with the handle supported on her arm. ***baby/child/infant in arms,*** child too young to walk. (*hold, carry sth*) ***at arm's length,*** with the arm fully extended. ***keep sb at arm's length,*** (fig) avoid becoming familiar with him. (*welcome sb/sth*) ***with open arms,*** warmly, with enthusiasm. ***walk***

ˈ*arm-in-ˋarm,* (of two persons) walk side by side, with the arm of one round the arm of the other. ˋ**arm-band** *n* armlet. ⇨ **brassard.** ˋ**arm·chair** *n* chair with supports for the arms: ˋ*armchair critic,* person who offers criticism but is not actively involved. ˋ**arm-hole** *n* hole (in a shirt, jacket, etc) through which the arm is put. ˋ**arm·let** /-lət/ *n* band (of cloth, etc) worn round the arm (on a sleeve). ˋ**arm·pit** *n* hollow under the arm near the shoulder. ⇨ the illus at **trunk. 2** sleeve: *The arms of this coat are too long.* **3** large branch of a tree. **4** sth shaped like or suggesting an arm: *an arm of the sea; the arms of a chair.* **5** (fig) ***the arm of the law,*** the authority or power of the law. **arm·ful** /ˈɑmfʊl/ *n* as much as one arm, or both arms, can hold: *He came into the library carrying books by the armful/with an armful of books.*

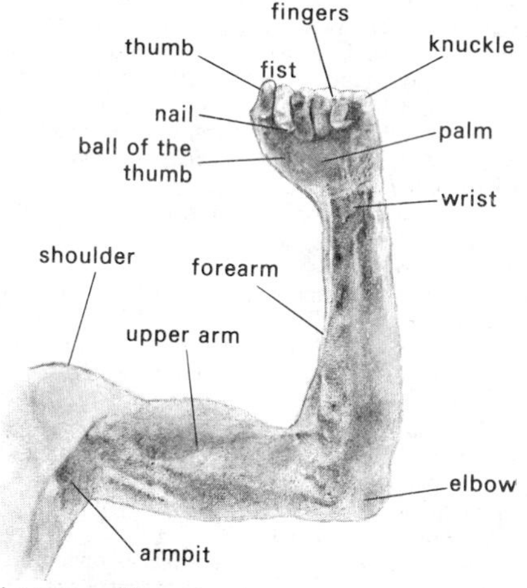

the arm and hand

arm[2] /ɑm/ *n* branch or division of a country's armed forces: *the infantry arm; the air arm.*

arm[3] /ɑm/ *vt,vi* [VP6A,14,2A] ***arm (with),*** supply, fit, weapons and armour; prepare for war: *a warship armed with nuclear weapons; armed with a big stick;* (fig) *armed with patience/with answers to all likely questions. Their former enemy is arming again* (= rearming). **the armed forces/services,** the military forces. **armed neutrality,** policy of remaining neutral but prepared for defence against aggression.

ar·mada /ɑˋmɑdə/ *n* great fleet of warships, esp **the A~,** the fleet sent by King Philip II of Spain against England in 1588.

ar·ma·dillo /ˈɑməˋdɪləʊ/ *n* (*pl* -los /-ləʊz/) small burrowing animal of S America, with a body covered with a shell of bony plates, and the habit of rolling itself up into a ball when attacked. ⇨ the illus at **small.**

Ar·ma·ged·don /ˈɑməˋgedn/ *n* **1** (biblical) (scene of) the last battle to be fought between the forces of good and evil, prophesied to happen at the end of the world. ⇨ Rev 16:16. **2** (fig) any similar conflict.

ar·ma·ment /ˋɑməmənt/ *n* **1** (usu *pl*) military forces and their equipment; navy, army, air force. **2** (usu *pl*) weapons, esp the large guns on a warship, military tank, etc: *the ~s industry.* **3** [U] process of getting military forces equipped; preparation for war.

ar·ma·ture /ˋɑmətʃə(r)/ *n* (electr) that part of a dynamo which rotates in a magnetic field and in which the current is developed; coil(s) of an electric motor.

ar·mis·tice /ˋɑmɪstɪs/ *n* agreement during a war or battle to stop fighting for a time. ˋ**A~ Day,** 11 Nov, kept as the anniversary of the ~ that ended fighting in the First World War (US = *Veterans' Day*). ⇨ **remembrance.**

ar·moire /ˋɑmwɑ(r) *US:* ɑmˋwɑr/ *n* [C] large cabinet or wardrobe.

ar·mor ⇨ **armour.**

ar·mor·ial /ɑˋmɔrɪəl/ *adj* of heraldry; of coats of arms. ⇨ **arms(2)**: *~ bearings,* a coat of arms.

ar·mour (US = **ar·mor**) /ˋɑmə(r)/ *n* [U] **1** defensive covering, usu metal, for the body, worn in fighting: *a suit of ~.* ⇨ the illus on p 42. **2** metal covering for warships, tanks, motor vehicles, etc. **3** (collective) tanks, motor-vehicles, etc protected with ~. ˋ**~-plate** *n* sheet of metal used as ~. **~ed** *part adj* **1** covered or protected with ~: *an ~ed cruiser/car.* **2** equipped with tanks, vehicles, guns, etc, that are protected with ~: *an ~ed column/division,* etc. **~er** *n* **1** manufacturer or repairer of arms and armour. **2** man in charge of fire-arms. **ar·moury** /ˋɑmərɪ/ *n* (*pl* -ries) place where arms are kept.

arms /ɑmz/ *n pl* **1** weapons (note, *fire-arm,* used in the *sing* form): (attrib) *an ~ depot; The soldiers had plenty of ~ and ammunition.* ˋ**fire-~,** those requiring explosives. ˋ**small ~,** fire-~ that can be carried by hand, e g revolvers, rifles, light machine-guns. ***lay down (one's) ~,*** stop fighting. ***take up ~, rise up in ~,*** (liter or fig) get ready to fight (*against*). ***under ~,*** provided with weapons and ready to fight. ***(be) up in ~ (about/over),*** (usu fig) be protesting vigorously. ˋ**~race,** competition among nations on military strength. **2** (heraldry) pictorial design used by a noble family, town university, etc. ˈ**coat of** ˋ**~,** such a design, e g on a shield. ⇨ the illus at **armour.**

army /ˋɑmɪ/ *n* (*pl* -mies) **1 the ~,** the military forces of a country, organized for fighting on land: *be in the ~,* be a soldier; *go into/join the ~,* become a soldier. ˋ**~ Act** *n* body of laws regulating the conduct of soldiers. ˋ**~ corps** *n* main subdivision of an ~. ˋ**~ list** *n* official list of commissioned officers. **2** organized body of persons: *the Salvation A~;* large number: *an ~ of workmen/officials/ants.*

ar·nica /ˋɑnɪkə/ *n* [U] medical substance (made from a plant) used for healing bruises and sprains.

aroma /əˋrəʊmə/ *n* [U] **1** sweet smell, fragrance: *the ~ of a cigar.* **2** (fig) quality or surrounding atmosphere considered typical: *the ~ of wealth.* **aro·matic** /ˈærəˋmætɪk/ *adj* fragrant; spicy: *the ~tic bark of the cinnamon tree.*

arose /əˋrəʊz/ *pt* of **arise.**

around /əˋraʊnd/ *adv, prep* **1** on every side, in every direction. **2** about; round; here and there: *I'll be ~* (= not far away) *if you should want me. From all ~ we heard the laughter of children. Take your arm from ~ my waist. He's been ~ a lot,* has had wide experience of life and the world, is sophisticated. ⇨ also **shop** *v* **(1), sleep**[2]**(2).**

arouse /əˋraʊz/ *vt* [VP6A,14] **1** awaken: *behaviour that might ~ suspicion; sufferings that ~d our sympathy; ~ sb from his sleep.* **2** cause (sb) to become active; stir (sb) up from inactivity; stimulate sexually: *fully ~d.*

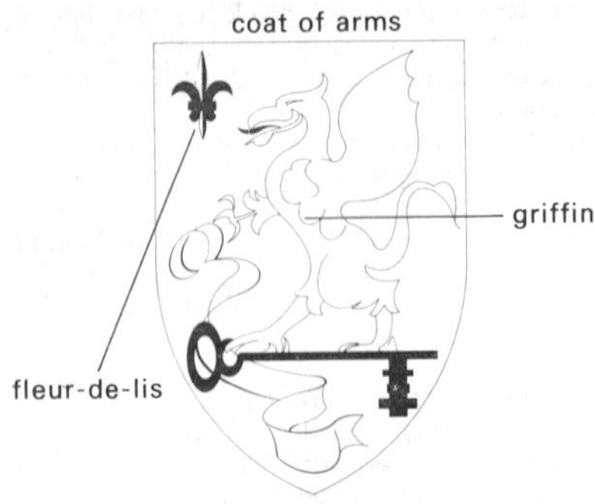

escutcheon or shield

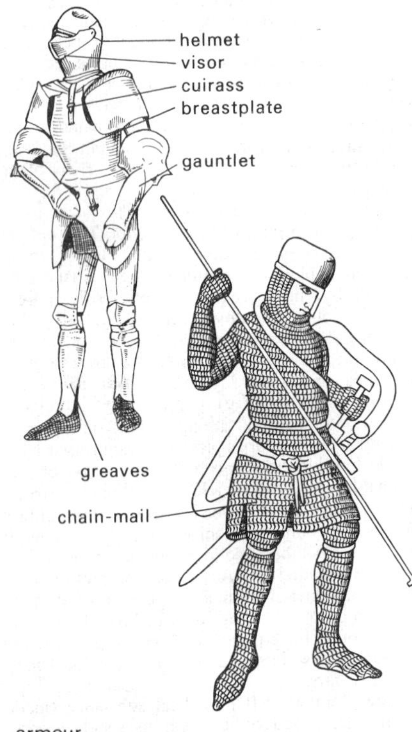

armour

ar·peg·gio /ɑˋpedʒɪəʊ/ *n* (*pl* -gios) (I; music) the playing of the notes of a chord in (usu upwards) succession.

ar·que·bus /ˋɑkwɪbəs/ *n* early kind of portable gun, supported on a tripod or a forked rest, used before muskets were invented.

ar·rack /ˋæræk/ *n* [U] strong alcoholic drink made in Eastern countries.

ar·raign /əˋreɪn/ *vt* [VP6A,14] (legal) bring a criminal charge against (sb); bring (sb) before a court for trial: *~ed on a charge of theft.* **~·ment** *n* ~ing or being ~ed.

ar·range /əˋreɪndʒ/ *vt,vi* **1** [VP6A] put in order: *She's good at arranging flowers. I ~d the books on the shelves. Before going away, he ~d his business affairs.* **2** [VP6A,15A,3A,4C] make plans in advance, see to the details of sth: *A marriage has been ~d between Mr Brown and Miss White. The Tourist Bureau ~d everything for our journey to Rome. I have ~d to meet her at ten o'clock. I have ~d for a car to meet you at the airport. The meeting ~d for tomorrow has been postponed. I can't ~ for everything.* **3** [VP3A] come to an agreement (*with* sb, *for* or *about* sth). **4** [VP6A,14] adapt (a piece of music): *~ a piece of music for the violin.* **5** [VP6A] settle, adjust (now the more usu words): *Mrs White often has to ~ disputes/differences between the two boys.*

ar·range·ment /əˋreɪndʒmənt/ *n* **1** [U] putting in order; arranging or being arranged: *The ~ of the furniture in our new house took a long time.* **2** (*pl*) plans; preparations: *Have you made ~s for your journey to Scotland? I'll make ~s for somebody to meet you/for you to be met at the airport.* **3** [U] agreement; settlement: *The price of the house is a matter for ~,* is a matter to be settled by discussion. *We can come to some sort of ~ over expenses.* **4** [C] result or manner of arranging: *an ~* (e g of orchestral music) *for the piano. I have an ~ by which I can cash my cheques at banks everywhere in Britain.*

ar·rant /ˋærənt/ *adj* (always of sth or sb bad) in the highest degree: *an ~ liar/knave/dunce/hypocrite/rogue; ~ nonsense.*

ar·ras /ˋærəs/ *n* tapestry, esp the kind formerly hung round the walls of rooms.

ar·ray /əˋreɪ/ *vt* (liter) [VP6A,15A] **1** place (esp armed forces, troops) in order for battle: *The Duke and his men ~ed themselves against the King,* took up arms against the King. **2** dress: *~ed in ceremonial robes; ~ed like a queen.* □ *n* (liter) **1** order: *troops in battle ~.* **2** clothes: *in holiday ~; in bridal ~.* **3** display (*of*): *a fine ~ of tools; an imposing ~ of statistics.*

ar·rears /əˋrɪəz/ *n pl* **1** money that is owing and that ought to have been paid: *~ of rent/wages.* ***be in/fall into ~ (with),*** be late in paying. Cf *be behindhand with.* **2** work still waiting to be done: *~ of correspondence,* letters waiting to be answered.

ar·rest /əˋrest/ *vt* [VP6A] **1** put a stop to (a process or movement): *Poor food ~s the natural growth of children.* **2** catch (sb's attention): *The bright colours of the flowers ~ed the child's attention.* **3** seize (sb) by the authority of the law: *The police ~ed the thief and put him in prison.* □ *n* act of ~ing (a wrongdoer, etc): *The police made several ~s.* ***under ~,*** held as a prisoner. ***be/place/put/under ~,*** be/be made a prisoner: *The officer was put under ~.* **~er** *n* **ˋ~er hook,** device for checking speed of aircraft as they land on the deck of a carrier. **~·ing** *adj* striking; likely to hold the attention.

ar·rière pensée /ˈærɪˈeə ˋpɔ̃seɪ *US:* pɔ̃ˋseɪ/ *n* (F) ulterior motive; mental reservation.

ar·rival /əˋraɪvl/ *n* **1** [U] act of arriving: *on ~ home; on his ~; waiting for the ~ of news; to await ~,* (on a letter, parcel, etc) to be kept until the addressee arrives. **2** [C] sb or sth that arrives: *There are several new ~s at the hotel. The new ~* (colloq = The newborn child) *is a boy.*

ar·rive /əˋraɪv/ *vi* [VP2A,C,3A] **1** reach a place, esp the end of a journey: *~ home; ~ at a port; ~ in harbour.* **2** come: *At last the day ~d. Her baby ~d* (= was born) *yesterday.* **3** [VP3A] **~ at,** reach (a decision, a price, the age of 40, manhood, etc). **4** [VP2A] establish one's position or reputation: *The flood of fan mail proved he'd ~d.*

ar·ro·gant /ˋærəgənt/ *adj* behaving in a proud, superior manner; (of behaviour, etc) showing too much pride in oneself and too little consideration for others: *speaking in an ~ tone.* **~·ly** *adv* **ar·ro·gance** /-əns/ *n* [U].

ar·ro·gate /ˋærəgeɪt/ *vt* [VP14] **1** ***~ to oneself,*** claim or take without right: *He ~d to himself the dignity of a chair,* claimed to be a university professor (although he was only a lecturer). **2** attribute unjustly; ascribe: *Don't ~ evil motives to me.*

ar·row /ˋærəʊ/ *n* **1** thin, pointed stick (to be) shot from a bow. ⇨ the illus at **archery**. **2** mark or sign (→) used to show direction or position, e g on a map or as a road sign. **ˋ~-head** *n* pointed end of an ~.

ar·row·root /ˋærəʊrut/ *n* [U] starchy food made from the powdered root of a plant.

arse /ɑs/ *n* (US = **ass** /æs/) (⚠, not in polite use) buttocks.

ar·senal /ˋɑsn̩l/ *n* government building(s) where weapons and ammunition are made or stored.

ar·senic /ˋɑsnɪk/ *n* [U] (chem) brittle, steel-grey crystalline chemical element (symbol **As**), used in glass-making, dyes, etc; white mineral compound of ~, a violent poison.

ar·son /ɑsn/ *n* [U] act of setting sth on fire intentionally and unlawfully, e g another person's property or one's own with the purpose of claiming under an insurance policy.

art[1] /ɑt/ *n* **1** [U] the creation or expression of what is beautiful, esp in visual form; fine skill or aptitude in such expression: *the art of the Renaissance; children's art; the art of landscape painting. The story is developed with great art.* **the ˈfine ˋarts,** drawing, painting, sculpture, architecture, music, ballet. **a ˈwork of ˋart,** a fine painting, piece of sculpture, etc. **an ˋart gallery,** one for the display of works of art. **an ˋart school,** one at which the arts of painting, etc are taught. **2** [C] sth in which imagination and personal taste are more important than exact measurement and calculation: *History and literature are among the arts/the arts subjects* (contrasted with science/science subjects). *Teaching/Public speaking is an art.* **ˈBatchelor/ˈMaster of ˋArts,** (abbr B A/M A) person who has passed the examination and fulfilled other conditions for the award of a university degree in this branch of learning. **3** [C, U] cunning; trickery; trick: *In spite of all her arts, the young man was not attracted to her.* **the black art,** magic (used for evil purposes). **4** (attrib) relating to art(1); of artistic design: *an ˋart historian/critic; art needlework/pottery.*

art[2] /ɑt/ *v* (*pres t* form of *be*) used with *thou*: *thou art,* you are.

ar·te·fact ⇨ **artifact.**

ar·terial /ɑˋtɪərɪəl/ *adj* of or like an artery: *~ blood: ~ roads,* important main roads; *~ railways/traffic.*

ar·tery /ˋɑtərɪ/ *n* (*pl* -ries) **1** one of the tubes carrying blood from the heart to all parts of the body. ⇨ the illus at **respiratory**. **2** main road or river; chief channel in a system of communications, etc: *arteries of traffic.*

ar·terio·scler·osis /ɑˈtɪərɪəʊˈsklɪəˋrəʊsɪs/ *n* [U] chronic disease with the hardening of the arteries, hindering blood circulation.

ar·tesian /ɑˋtizɪən *US:* -iʒn/ *adj*: *~ well,* perpendicular well producing a constant supply of water rising to the surface without pumping.

art·ful /ˋɑtfl/ *adj* cunning; deceitful; clever in getting what one wants. **~ly** /-flɪ/ *adv* **~·ness** *n*

ar·thri·tis /ˈɑˋθraɪtɪs/ *n* [U] inflammation of a joint or joints; gout. **ar·thri·tic** /ɑˋθrɪtɪk/ *adj*

ar·ti·choke /ˋɑtɪtʃəʊk/ *n* **1 globe ~,** plant like a large thistle, with a flowering head of thick, leaf-like scales used as a vegetable. ⇨ the illus at **vegetable. 2 Jerusalem ~,** plant like a sunflower, with tuberous roots used as a vegetable.

ar·ticle /ˋɑtɪkl/ *n* [C] **1** particular or separate thing: *~s of clothing,* e g shirts, coats; *toilet ~s,* e g soap, toothpaste. *'And the next ~, madam?'* (old use, in a shop) 'And what do you wish to buy next, madam?' **2** piece of writing, complete in itself, in a newspaper or other periodical: **ˈleading ˋ~,** (in a newspaper) ~ expressing the views of the editor(s). **3** (legal) separate clause or item in an agreement: *~s of apprenticeship.* **4** (gram): *definite ~,* 'the'; *indefinite ~,* 'a', 'an'. □ *vt* bind, e g an apprentice by ~s.

ar·ticu·late[1] /ɑˋtɪkjʊlət/ *adj* **1** (of speech) in which the separate sounds and words are clear. **2** (of a person) able to put thoughts and feelings into clear speech: *That man is not very ~.* **3** jointed. **~·ly** *adv*

ar·ticu·late[2] /ɑˋtɪkjʊleɪt/ *vt,vi* **1** [VP6A,2C] say (words) distinctly; speak (distinctly). **2** [VP15A, 2C] connect by joints: *bones that ~/are ~d with others.* **an ~d vehicle,** having parts joined in a flexible manner, e g a tractor flexibly joined to the part that carries the load.

ar·ticu·la·tion /ɑˈtɪkjʊˋleɪʃn/ *n* [U] **1** production of speech sounds: *The speaker's ideas were good but his ~ was poor.* **2** (connection by a) joint.

ar·ti·fact, ar·te·fact /ˋɑtɪfækt/ *n* [C] artificial product; something made by human being(s), esp a simple tool or weapon of archaeological interest.

ar·ti·fice /ˋɑtɪfɪs/ *n* **1** [C] skilful way of doing sth. **2** [U] cunning; ingenuity; trickery; [C] trick.

ar·tifi·cer /ɑˋtɪfɪsə(r)/ *n* skilled workman. **engine-room ~,** (rank in the Navy of a) skilled mechanic.

ar·ti·ficial /ˈɑtɪˋfɪʃl/ *adj* not natural or real; made by the art of man: *~ flowers/teeth/light; ~ silk,* (old name for) rayon; *~ manures,* chemical manures (not dung); *~ tears,* not caused by genuine sorrow; *~ manners,* affected, not natural manners; *~ respiration,* method of forcing air into the lungs, e g to a man nearly drowned. ⇨ also **insemination. ar·ti·fici'ally** /-ʃlɪ/ *adv*

ar·til·lery /ɑˋtɪlərɪ/ *n* [U] big guns (mounted on wheels, etc); branch of an army that uses these.

ar·ti·san /ˈɑtɪˋzæn *US:* ˋɑtɪzn/ *n* skilled workman in industry or trade; mechanic.

art·ist /ˋɑtɪst/ *n* **1** person who practises one of the fine arts, esp painting. **2** person who does sth with skill and good taste: *an ~ in words.*

art·iste /ɑˋtist/ *n* professional singer, actor, dancer, etc.

ar·tis·tic /ɑˋtɪstɪk/ *adj* **1** done with skill and good taste, esp in the arts; able to appreciate what is beautiful. **2** having or showing good taste. **3** of art or artists. **ar·tis·ti·cally** /-klɪ/ *adv*

art·istry /ˋɑtɪstrɪ/ *n* [U] artistic skill or work; qualities of taste and skill possessed by an artist.

art·less /ˋɑtləs/ *adj* (contrasted with *artful*) natural; simple; innocent: *as ~ as a child of 5.* **~·ly**

adv **~·ness** *n*

arty /ˋɑtɪ/ *adj* (colloq) pretending or falsely claiming to be artistic. **ˈ~-ˋcrafty,** (colloq) of, using, making, handmade articles, esp in a way that is considered affected.

arum /ˋeərəm/ *n* **~ lily,** tall white lily.

Aryan /ˋeərɪən/ *adj* of the family of languages called Indo-European, i e related to Sanskrit, Persian, Greek, Latin and the Germanic and Slavonic languages; of a race using an Aryan language. □ *n* person whose mother tongue is one of the ~ languages; (popular sense, now discredited) person of Germanic or Scandinavian ancestry.

as[1] /əz *strong form:* æz/ *adv* (followed by *as, conj*) in the same degree: *I'm as tall as you. Is it as difficult as they say it is?* (In a neg sentence *as* is often replaced by *so*): *It's not so difficult as I expected.*

as[2] /əz *strong form:* æz/ *conj* **1** when; while: *I saw him as he was getting off the bus. As a child, he lived in India. As he grew older he became less active.* **2** (expressing reason) since; seeing that: *As he wasn't ready in time, we went without him.* **3** (in comparisons of equality, in the patterns: *as* + adj or adv + *as, not so* + adj or adv + *as*): *I want a box twice as large as this. It isn't so/as big as you think it is.* (Used in numerous proverbial phrases): *as easy as ABC; as heavy as lead.* (Note the *pronouns* in these examples): *You hate him as much as I,* i e as much as I hate him; *You hate him as much as me,* i e as much as you hate me. (When there is no ambiguity, the object form of the *pronoun* is used in speech): *You can't expect to play tennis as well as me* (= as I do) *at your age.* **4** (introducing a concessive clause, usu replaceable by a construction with *although*): **(a)** with an *adj* or *adv*: *I know some of the family secrets, young as I am,* although I am young. *Much as I like you* (= Although I like you much), *I will not marry you.* **(b)** (with *vv*, esp *may, might, will, would*): *Try as he would* (= Although he tried, However hard he tried), *he could not lift the rock.* **5** (introducing adverbial clauses of manner) in the way in which: *Do as I do. Do it as I do it. Leave it as it is.* **6** (introducing a complement of manner) like: *Why is he dressed as a woman?* **7** (used to avoid repetition in the predicate): *Harry is unusually tall, as are his brothers,* and his brothers are also unusually tall. **8** in the capacity or character of: *He was respected both as a judge and as a man. Looking at Napoleon as a statesman, not as a soldier....* **9** [VP16B] (used after *regard, view, represent, treat, acknowledge,* and *vv* similar in meaning but not after *consider,* to introduce a predicative): *Most people regarded him* (= looked upon him) *as a fool.* Cf Most people *considered him (to be)* a fool. *Do you treat all men as your equals?* **10** (used to introduce illustrations or examples; usu preceded by *such;* replaceable by *for instance, for example* or *like*): *Countries in the north of Europe, such as Finland, Norway, Sweden,....* **11** ***as if, as though,*** (introducing a clause of manner, with a *pt* in the clause): *He talks as if he knew all about it. He looks as if he had seen a ghost. It isn't as though he were poor.* (followed by a *to*-infinitive): *He opened his lips as if to say something.* **12** ***as for,*** /ˈæz fə(r)/ with reference to (sometimes suggesting indifference or contempt): *As for you, I never want to see you here again.* ***as to,*** /ˈæz/ about; concerning (better avoided except when the words following *as to* are shifted to the beginning of a sentence for prominence): *As to your brother, I will deal with him later;* (with a gerund) *As to accepting their demand,....* **13** (used as a *conj* to introduce relative clauses, chiefly after *same* and *such*): *Such women as knew Tom* (= Those women who knew him) *thought he was charming. Such women as Tom knew* (= Those women whom Tom knew) *thought he was charming. You must show my wife the same respect as you show me,* the respect that you show me. *We drove out of the town by the same road as we had entered by.* **14** (introducing a non-defining relative clause, the antecedent being inferred): *Cyprus, as* (= which fact) *you all know, is in the Mediterranean. To shut your eyes to facts, as many of you do, is foolish.* **15** ***so as to,*** /ˈsəʊ əz/ **(a)** (introducing an infinitive of purpose): *He stood up so as to* (= in order to) *see better.* **(b)** (introducing an infinitive of manner): *It is foolish to behave so as to annoy* (= in ways that annoy) *your neighbours.* **16** ***as good as,*** the same thing as: *Will he be as good as his word?* Will he do what he promised? *He's as good as dead,* almost dead, sure to die soon. **17** ***as/so long as,*** **(a)** on condition that: *You can go where you like so long as you get back before dark.* **(b)** while: *You shall never enter this house as long as I live in it.* **18** ***as much,*** so; what really amounts to that: *I thought as much.* **19** ***as far as,*** ⇨ far[1](2). **20** ***(just) as soon, as soon as (not),*** ⇨ soon(3,5). ***as well (as),*** ⇨ well[2](8).

as·bes·tos /æsˋbestəs/ *n* [U] soft, fibrous, grey, mineral substance that can be made into fire-proof fabrics or solid sheeting and used as a heat-insulating material.

as·cend /əˋsend/ *vt, vi* **1** [VP6A,2C] go or come up (a mountain, river, etc): *We watched the mists ~ing from the valley. The path ~s here.* **2** ***~ the throne,*** become king or queen.

as·cend·ancy, -ency /əˋsendənsɪ/ *n* [U] (position of) having power. ***gain/have the ~ (over sb)***: *He has the ~ over his rivals/his party.*

as·cend·ant, -ent /əˋsendənt/ *n* ***in the ~,*** rising in power and influence.

as·cen·sion /əˋsenʃn/ *n* act of ascending. **the A~,** the departure of Jesus from the earth, on the fortieth day after the Resurrection.

as·cent /əˋsent/ *n* [C] act of ascending; way up; upward movement: *The ~ of the mountain was not difficult. I have never made an ~* (= have never been up) *in a balloon. The last part of the ~ is steep.*

ascer·tain /ˈæsəˋteɪn/ *vt* [VP6A,9,8,10,17] find out (in order to be certain about); get to know: *~ the facts; ~ that the news is true; ~ whether the train stops at X; ~ what really happened.* **~·able** *adj* that can be ~ed.

as·cetic /əˋsetɪk/ *adj* self-denying; austere; leading a life of severe self-discipline. □ *n* person who (often for religious reasons) leads a severely simple life without ordinary pleasures. **as·ceti·cally** /-klɪ/ *adv* **as·ceti·cism** /əˋsetɪsɪzm/ *n*

ascor·bic /əˋskɔbɪk/ *adj* **~ acid,** (also known as *vitamin C*) vitamin found in citrus fruits and vegetable products, used against scurvy.

as·cribe /əˋskraɪb/ *vt* [VP14] **~ to, 1** consider to be the cause, origin, reason or author, of: *He ~d his failure to bad luck. This play has been ~d to Shakespeare,* it has been said that Shakespeare was the author. **2** consider as belonging to: ~ *a wrong meaning to a word.* **as·crib·able** /-əbl/ *adj* that can be ~d: *His quick recovery is ascribable to his sound constitution.* **as·crip·tion** /əˈskrɪpʃn/ *n* ascribing: *The ascription of this work to Schubert may be false.*

as·dic /ˈæzdɪk/ *n* device using reflected sound-waves, for detecting submarines, etc.

asep·tic /əˈseptɪk/ *adj* (of wounds, dressings, etc) free from bacteria; surgically clean. **asep·sis** /əˈsepsɪs/ *n* [U] ~ condition.

asex·ual /ˌeɪˈsekʃʊəl/ *adj* **1** without sex or sex organs: ~ *reproduction.* **2** (of a person) showing no interest in sexual relations. **~·ity** /eɪˌseksʃʊˈælətɪ/ *n*

ash[1] /æʃ/ *n* forest-tree with silver-grey bark and hard, tough wood; [U] wood of this tree. **ˈash-key** *n* winged seed of the ash. ⇨ the illus at **tree**.

ash[2] /æʃ/ *n* [U or *pl*, but not with numerals] **1** powder that remains after sth has burnt: *Don't drop cigarette ash on the carpet. Remove the ash(es) from the stove once a day. The house was burnt to ashes.* **2** (*pl*) the burnt (= cremated) remains of a human body. **Ash Wednesday,** first day of Lent. **ˈash-bin, ˈash-can** *nn* (esp US; ⇨ **dustbin**) large rigid receptacle for ashes, cinders, kitchen waste, etc. **ˈash-pan** *n* tray (in a fireplace, stove, etc) into which ashes drop from a fire. **ˈash-tray** *n* small (metal, glass, etc) receptacle for tobacco ash.

ashamed /əˈʃeɪmd/ *pred adj* ~ ***(of/that/to do sth),*** feeling shame: *You should be ~ of yourself/of what you have done. He was/felt ~ to ask for help. He felt ~ that he had done/of having done so little. I feel ~ for you,* on your account, as if I were you. **asham·ed·ly** /əˈʃeɪmɪdlɪ/ *adv*

ashen /ˈæʃn/ *adj* of ashes; pale; ash-coloured: *His face turned ~ at the news.*

ashore /əˈʃɔ(r)/ *adv* on, on to, the shore. ***go ~,*** (of a sailor, etc) leave a ship to go on land. ***run/be driven ~,*** (of a ship) be forced to the shore, e g by bad weather.

ashy /ˈæʃɪ/ *adj* of or like ashes; covered with ashes; ash-coloured, pale.

Asian /ˈeɪʃn *US:* ˈeɪʒn/ *n adj* (native) of Asia.

Asi·atic /ˌeɪʃɪˈætɪk/ *n adj* (native) of Asia (*Asian* is the preferred word).

aside /əˈsaɪd/ *adv* on or to one side: *He laid the book ~,* put it down and stopped reading it. *We turned ~* (= away) *from the main road. The decision/verdict was set ~,* made of no effect. *Please put this ~ for me,* reserve it. *Joking ~,* i e speaking seriously,.... □ *n* words spoken ~, esp (on the stage) words that other persons (on the stage) are supposed not to hear.

as·in·ine /ˈæsɪnaɪn/ *adj* **1** of asses. **2** (colloq) stupid.

ask /ɑsk *US:* æsk/ *vt,vi* (*pt,pp* **asked**) **1** [VP6A, 12C,14 often with the indirect object omitted in 12C] call for an answer to; request information or service: *Did you ask the price? Ask (him) his name. May I ask (you) a question? Have I asked too much of you/asked you for too much? You asked of me more than you asked of the others. He asked a favour of me. We must ask him about it. He asked me for help.* [VP8,20] *I will ask (him) how to get there. Did you ask (her) which to buy?* [VP10,21] *They asked (me) what my name was, where I came from, and why I had come. Please ask (her) when she will be back.* [VP3A] ***ask after,*** ask for information about: *He asked after you/your health.* **2** [VP17A,15B,3A] invite: *We asked him to come again. I've been asked (out) to dinner. Mr Brown is at the door; shall I ask him in?* ***ask for trouble,*** (colloq) ***ask for it,*** behave in such a way that trouble is likely; invite trouble. **3** [VP17A,9] request to be allowed: *I must ask you to excuse me/ask to be excused. He asked permission to get up. He asked to get up/that he might get up.* **4** [VP6A,12C,14] demand as a price: *He asked (me) £25 a month as rent for that house. You're asking too much. What are they asking for the house?* **5** ***ask the banns,*** (old use; now usu *put up* or *publish*) publish them. **ask·ing** *n*: *You may have it/It's yours for the asking,* You have only to ask for it and it will be given to you.

askance /əˈskæns/ *adv* (only in) ***look ~ at (sb or sth),*** look at with suspicion.

as·kari /æˈskɑrɪ/ *n* European-trained African native soldier.

askew /əˈskju/ *adv, pred adj* out of the straight or usual (level) position: *hang a picture ~; have one's hat on ~: cut a plank ~,* aslant.

aslant /əˈslɑnt *US:* əˈslænt/ *adv, prep* in a slanting direction (*to*): *The wrecked coach lay ~ the railway track.*

asleep /əˈslip/ *pred adj* **1** sleeping: *He was fast ~. He fell/dropped ~ during the sermon.* **2** (of the arms or legs) without feeling (as when under pressure).

asp[1] /æsp/ *n* = aspen.

asp[2] /æsp/ *n* (zool) small poisonous snake of Egypt and Libya.

as·para·gus /əˈspærəgəs/ *n* [U] plant whose young shoots are cooked and eaten as a vegetable; the shoots.

as·pect /ˈæspekt/ *n* **1** look or appearance (of a person or thing): *a man of fierce ~; a man with a serious ~.* **2** front that faces a particular direction: *a house with a southern ~.* **3** (fig): *study every ~ of a subject,* study it thoroughly. **4** (gram) verb form which relates activity to passage of time. **as·pec·tual** /æˈspektʃʊəl/ *adj*: *the ~ual difference* between 'I saw him *cross* the road' and 'I saw him *crossing* the road'.

as·pen /ˈæspən/ *n* kind of poplar tree with leaves that move in the slightest wind.

as·per·ity /əˈsperətɪ/ *n* (*pl* **-ties**) **1** [U] roughness; harshness (of manner); severity; (of weather): *speak with ~.* **2** (with *pl*) instance of one of these qualities: *the asperities of winter in Labrador; an exchange of asperities,* e g of hard or bitter words.

as·perse /əˈspɜs/ *vt* [VP6A] slander; say false or unkind things about: ~ *sb's good name/honour/reputation.* **as·per·sion** /əˈspɜʃn *US:* -ʒn/ *n* (only in) ***cast aspersions (up)on sb/sb's honour, etc,*** slander him; say false things about him.

as·phalt /ˈæsfælt *US:* -fɔlt/ *n* [U] black, sticky substance like coal-tar used for making roofs, etc waterproof, and mixed with gravel or crushed rock, for making road surfaces. □ *vt* [VP6A] surface (a road) with ~.

as·pho·del /ˈæsfədel/ *n* **1** sort of lily. **2** (poet) immortal flower of the Gk Elysium /ɪˈlɪzɪəm/ (home of the dead).

as·phyxia /əsˈfɪksɪə/ *n* [U] condition caused by lack of enough air in the lungs; suffocation. **as·phyxi·ate** /əsˈfɪksɪeɪt/ *vt* [VP6A] make ill, cause the death of, through lack of sufficient air in the lungs: *The men in the coalmine were ~ted by bad gas.* **as·phyxi·ation** /əsˈfɪksɪˋeɪʃn/ *n* [U] = asphyxia; suffocation.

as·pic /ˋæspɪk/ *n* [U] clear meat jelly: *chicken in ~.*

as·pi·dis·tra /ˈæspɪˋdɪstrə/ *n* plant with broad, pointed leaves, usually grown as a house plant.

as·pir·ant /əˋspɑɪərnt/ *n* ~ ***(to/after),*** person who is ambitious for fame, etc: *an ~ to high office.*

as·pir·ate[1] /ˋæspərət/ *n* the sound of 'h'; sound with an 'h' in it: *Mind your ~s,* be careful to make the 'h' sounds where necessary.

as·pir·ate[2] /ˋæspəreɪt/ *vt* say with an 'h' sound: *The 'h' in 'honour' is not ~d.*

as·pir·ation /ˈæspəˋreɪʃn/ *n* [C,U] desire (*for* or *after* sth, *to be* or *do* sth): *his ~(s) for fame; his ~ to be an actor; the ~s of the developing countries.*

as·pire /əˋspɑɪə(r)/ *vi* [VP3A,4A] be filled with high ambition: *~ after knowledge; ~ to fame; ~ to become an author.*

as·pirin /ˋæsprɪn *US:* -pər-/ *n* [U] (P) medicine used to relieve pain and reduce fever; [C] tablet or measure of this: *Take two ~s for a headache.*

ass[1] /æs/ *n* **1** animal of the horse family with long ears and a tuft at the end of its tail; donkey; stupid person. **2** ***make an ass of oneself,*** behave stupidly so that one is ridiculed.

ass[2] /æs/ *n* (US vulg) = arse.

as·sa·gai /ˋæsəgɑɪ/ *n* = **assegai.**

as·sail /əˋseɪl/ *vt* [VP14] ~ ***(with),*** attack violently; pester: *~ sb with questions/insults; be ~ed with doubts.* **~·able** /-əbl/ *adj* that can be attacked. **~·ant** /-ənt/ *n* attacker.

as·sas·sin /əˋsæsɪn/ *n* person, often one hired by others, who assassinates. **as·sas·sin·ate** /əˋsæsɪneɪt *US:* əˋsæsn̩-/ *vt* [VP6A] kill sb (esp an important politician, ruler) violently and treacherously, for political reasons. **as·sas·sin·ation** /əˈsæsɪˋneɪʃn/ *n* [U] murder of this kind; [C] instance of this.

as·sault /əˋsɔlt/ *n* violent and sudden attack (*on*): *They made an ~ on/upon the enemy's positions. The sonic boom was an ~ on our nerves. The enemy's positions were taken by ~.* ***~ and battery,*** (legal) beating or hitting sb. **ˋ~ craft** *n* portable boat with an outboard motor, used for making attacks across rivers, etc. □ *vt* [VP6A] make an ~ on; attack (e g a fortress) by a sudden rush.

as·say /əˋseɪ/ *n* [C] test of the fineness, purity, or quality (*of* precious metals, ores, etc): *make an ~ of an ore.* □ *vt* **1** [VP6A] test, e g the purity of a metal, analyse, e g an ore, etc. **2** [VP6A,7A] (old use) attempt, e g sth difficult; try *to do* sth.

as·se·gai /ˋæsəgɑɪ/ *n* throwing-spear with a wooden haft, used by S African tribes.

as·sem·blage /əˋsemblɪdʒ/ *n* **1** [U] bringing or coming together; assembly (now the usu word): *the ~ of parts of a machine.* **2** [C] collection of things or (joc) persons.

as·semble /əˋsembl/ *vt,vi* **1** [VP6A,2A] gather together; collect: *The pupils ~d/were ~d in the school hall.* **2** [VP6A] fit or put together (the parts of): *~ a watch/car.*

as·sem·bly /əˋsemblɪ/ *n* (*pl* -lies) **1** [C] number of persons who have come together, esp a meeting of law-makers: *the Legislative A~; the school ~,* the daily ~ of staff and pupils. **ˋ~ room/s,** public hall in which meetings, balls, etc take place. **2 ˋ~ hall,** one where a school meets for prayers, etc; workshop where parts of large machines, e g aircraft, are put together. **ˋ~ line,** stage of mass production in which parts of a machine, vehicle, etc move along for progressive ~. **3** military call, by drum or bugle, for soldiers to assemble.

as·sent /əˋsent/ *n* official agreement, e g *to* a proposal; (royal) agreement (*to* a bill passed by Parliament): *by common ~,* everybody agreeing; *with one ~,* unanimously; nobody opposing. ⇨ **accord**[1](1). □ *vi* [VP2A,3A] give agreement (*to,* e g a proposal).

as·sert /əˋsɜt/ *vt* **1** [VP6A] make a claim to, e g one's rights. **2** [VP6A,9,25] declare: *~ one's innocence/that one is innocent; ~ sth to be true.* ***~ oneself,*** display authority, self-confidence.

as·ser·tion /əˋsɜʃn/ *n* **1** [U] insisting upon the recognition of one's rights: *self-~.* **2** [C] strong statement; claim: *make an ~.*

as·sert·ive /əˋsɜtɪv/ *adj* having or showing positive assurance: *speaking in an ~ tone.* **~·ly** *adv*

as·sess /əˋses/ *vt* [VP6A,14] **1** decide or fix the amount of (e g a tax or a fine): *Damages were ~ed at £100.* **2** appraise; fix or decide the value of (e g property), the amount of (e g income), for purposes of taxation; (fig) test the value of: *~ a speech at its true worth.* **~·ment** *n* [U] ~ing; [C] amount ~ed. **~or** /-sə(r)/ *n* **1** person who ~es property, income, taxes, etc. **2** person who advises a judge, magistrate or official committee, etc on technical matters.

as·set /ˋæset/ *n* **1** (usu *pl*) anything owned by a person, company, etc that has money value and that may be sold to pay debts. ⇨ **liability. 2** valuable or useful quality or skill: *Good health is a great ~.*

as·sev·er·ate /əˋsevəreɪt/ *vt* [VP6A,9] (formal) assert solemnly, e g *one's innocence, that....* **as·sev·er·ation** /əˈsevəˋreɪʃn/ *n*

as·si·du·ity /ˈæsɪˋdjuətɪ *US:* -ˋdu-/ *n* **1** [U] constant and careful attention to what one is doing: *He plans everything with unfailing ~.* **2** (*pl;* **-ties**) constant attentions (*to*).

as·sidu·ous /əˋsɪdjʊəs *US:* -dʒʊəs/ *adj* diligent; persevering: *~ in his duties.* **~·ly** *adv*

as·sign /əˋsɑɪn/ *vt* **1** [VP13A,12A] give (*to* sb) for use or enjoyment, or as a share or part in a distribution, e g of work, duty: *Those rooms have been ~ed to us. Your teacher ~s you work to be done at home.* **2** [VP13A,B] name, put forward as a time, place, reason, etc: *Has a day been ~ed for the trial? Can one ~ a cause to these events?* **3** [VP13B,17] appoint, name (sb *to* a task, *to do* sth): *A~ your best man to the job. Two pupils were ~ed to sweep the classroom.* **4** [VP14] (legal) transfer property, rights, etc *to.* **~·able** /-əbl/ *adj* that can be attributed or ~ed: *~able to several causes.* **~·ment** *n* [U] ~ing; [C] that which is ~ed.

as·sig·na·tion /ˈæsɪgˋneɪʃn/ *n* [C] (esp) appointment, e g of a time and place for a furtive meeting between lovers.

as·simi·late /əˋsɪməleɪt/ *vt,vi* **1** [VP6A,2A] absorb (food) into the body (after digestion); be thus absorbed: *We ~ some kinds of food more easily than others. Some kinds of food ~ easily.* **2** [VP6A,2A] (allow people to) become part of another social group or state: *The U S A has ~d people from many European countries,* has absorbed them, so that they are Americans. **3** [VP6A] absorb, e g ideas, knowledge. **4** [VP3A] ***~ to,*** make or become like. **as·simi·la·tion**

/əˈsɪməˈleɪʃn/ *n* [U] assimilating or being ~d.

as·sist /əˈsɪst/ *vt,vi* [VP6A,17A,14,2A] ~ ***(sb) with sth/in doing sth/to do sth,*** (formal) help: *~ (sb) with the form-filling; ~ sb to fill in the forms. Two men are ~ing the police in their enquiries,* are answering questions which may lead to the arrest of the criminal(s), or perhaps their own arrest as the criminals. **~·ance** /-əns/ *n* [U] *give/lend/render ~ance (to sb); come to sb's ~ance; be of ~ance (to sb),* help. **~·ant** /-ənt/ *n* helper: *an ~ant to the Manager; ~ant master,* in a school; *a ˈshop-~ant,* one who serves customers.

as·size /əˈsaɪz/ *n* **1** [U] trial by a judge and jury. **2** (*pl*) (until 1971) sessions held periodically in every English County to try civil and criminal cases before High Court Judges: (attrib, *sing*) *courts of ~; judges on ~; ~ towns.* ⇨ *Crown Court* at court[1](1) for the new system.

as·so·ci·ate[1] /əˈsəʊʃɪət/ *adj* joined in function or dignity: *an ~ judge.* □ *n* /əˈsəʊsɪət/ person who has been joined with others *in* work, business or crime; person given certain limited rights in an association; companion.

as·so·ci·ate[2] /əˈsəʊʃɪeɪt/ *vt,vi* **1** [VP14] ~ ***with,*** join or connect: *~ oneself with sb in a business undertaking; ~ one thing with another. We ~ Egypt with the Nile. I don't wish to ~ myself with what has been said,* don't want anyone to think that I have a part in it, or approve of it. **2** [VP3A] be often in the company of: *Don't ~ with dishonest boys.*

as·so·ci·ation /əˈsəʊʃɪˈeɪʃn/ *n* **1** [U] associating; being associated; companionship (*with*): *I benefited much from my ~ with him/from our ~. His English benefited through his long ~ with British children.* ***in ~ (with),*** together (*with*). **2** [C] group of persons joined together for some common purpose: *the ˈAutomobile A~; the ˈYoung Men's ˈChristian A~.* **3** **ˈA~ ˈfootball,** (common abbr *soccer*) game in which two teams of eleven players use a spherical ball that must not be handled except by the goalkeeper or when throwing in. ⇨ the illus at football. **4** connection (of ideas).

as·son·ance /ˈæsənəns/ *n* agreement between stressed vowels in two words, but not in the following consonants, as in *sharper* and *garter.*

as·sorted /əˈsɔtɪd/ *part adj* **1** of various sorts; mixed: *a pound of ~ toffees,* toffees of different kinds, mixed together. **2** matched, suited, one to another: *an ill-~ couple,* husband and wife who get on badly. **as·sort·ment** /əˈsɔtmənt/ *n* ~ collection of different examples of one class or of several classes: *This shop has a good assortment of goods to choose from.*

as·suage /əˈsweɪdʒ/ *vt* [VP6A] make, e g pain, suffering, feelings, desire, less.

as·sume /əˈsjum *US:* əˈsum/ *vt* **1** [VP6A,9,25] take as true before there is proof: *You ~ his innocence/him to be innocent/that he is innocent before hearing the evidence against him. He's not such a fool as you ~d* (= supposed) *him to be. Assuming this to be true....* **2** [VP6A] take up; undertake: *~ the direction of a business; ~ office; ~ the reins of government,* begin to govern. **3** [VP6A] take upon or for oneself sth not genuine or sincere: *~ a look of innocence; ~ a new name.*

as·sump·tion /əˈsʌmpʃn/ *n* **1** [C] sth taken for granted; sth supposed but not proved: *Their ~ that the war would end quickly was proved wrong. I am going on the ~ that...,* I am assuming (= supposing) that.... **2** [C] ~ ***of,*** the act of assuming(2): *his ~ of office/power/the presidency.* **3** ~ ***of,*** the adopting of a manner, etc which is not genuine: *with an ~ of indifference,* pretending not to be interested. **4** **the A~,** reception into Heaven in bodily form of the Virgin Mary; Church feast commemorating this.

as·sur·ance /əˈʃʊərns/ *n* **1** [U] (often *self-~*) self-confidence; belief and trust in one's own powers: *He answered all the questions with ~. A businessman, to be successful, should act with perfect (self-)assurance.* **2** [C] promise; statement made to give confidence: *He gave me a definite ~ that the repairs would be finished by Friday.* **3** [U] (chiefly GB) insurance on sth that is certain: *life ~,* because death is certain. ⇨ insurance. **4** [U] impudence (the much more usu word). **5** [U] certainty; confidence (*in*) (the much more usu word). ***make ~ doubly sure,*** remove all possible doubt.

as·sure /əˈʃʊə(r)/ *vt* **1** [VP11] say positively, with confidence: *I ~ you (that) there's no danger.* **2** [VP11,14] cause (sb) to be sure, to feel certain: *We tried to ~ the nervous old lady that flying was safe. He ~d me of his readiness to help.* **3** [VP6A] ensure (the more usu word): *Nothing can ~ permanent happiness.* **4** [VP6A] insure, esp against the death of sb or oneself. **as·sured** *part adj* sure: confident: *You may rest ~d that...,* feel confident that.... **as·sur·ed·ly** /əˈʃʊərɪdlɪ/ *adv* surely; confidently.

as·ter /ˈæstə(r)/ *n* garden plant with flowers that have white, pink or purple petals round a yellow centre.

as·ter·isk /ˈæstərɪsk/ *n* the mark *, used to call attention to something, e g a footnote, or to show that letters are omitted, as in *Mr J***s,* for *Mr Jones.*

astern /əˈstɜn/ *adv* **1** in or at the stern of a ship. ⇨ the illus at ship. **2** backward: *Full speed ~!* **3** ***fall ~ (of),*** fall behind (another ship).

as·ter·oid /ˈæstərɔɪd/ *n* [C] any of many small planets between the orbits of Mars and Jupiter. ⇨ the illus at planet.

asthma /ˈæsmə *US:* ˈæzmə/ *n* [U] chronic chest disease marked by difficulty in breathing. **asth·matic** /ˈæsˈmætɪk *US:* ˈæz-/ *adj* suffering from ~; of ~.

astig·ma·tism /əˈstɪgmətɪzm/ *n* [U] defect in an eye or lens that prevents correct focusing. **as·tig·matic** /ˈæstɪgˈmætɪk/ *adj*

astir /əˈstɜ(r)/ *adv, pred adj* **1** in motion; in a state of excitement: *The whole village was ~ when news came that the Queen was coming.* **2** (dated) out of bed and about: *You're ~ early this morning.*

as·ton·ish /əˈstonɪʃ/ *vt* [VP6A] surprise greatly: *The news ~ed everybody. You look ~ed at the news. I was ~ed to see him there. I am ~ed that he didn't come.* **~·ing** *part adj* very surprising: *It is ~ing to me that he should be absent.* **~·ment** *n* [U] great surprise: *I heard to my ~ment that...; He looked at me in ~ment. His ~ment at seeing me was amusing. What was my ~ment when I heard....*

astound /əˈstaʊnd/ *vt* [VP6A] overcome with surprise; shock.

as·tra·khan /ˈæstrəˈkæn *US:* ˈæstrəkən/ *n* [U] skin of young lambs with wool in tight little curls: (used attrib) *an ~ coat/cap.*

as·tral /ˈæstrəl/ *adj* of or from the stars.

astray /əˋstreɪ/ *adv, pred adj* out of, off, the right path, esp (fig) into wrongdoing: *The boy was led ~ by bad companions.*

astride /əˋstraɪd/ *adv, pred adj, prep* with one leg on each side (of): *riding ~; sitting ~ his father's knee.*

as·trin·gent /əˋstrɪndʒənt/ *n* (kind of) substance that shrinks soft tissues and contracts blood-vessels, thus checking the flow of blood. □ *adj* of or like an ~; (fig) harsh; severe. **as·trin·gency** /əˋstrɪndʒənsɪ/ *n*

as·tro·dome /ˈæstrədəʊm/ *n* small, transparent observation dome on the top of the fuselage of an aircraft, used by the navigator.

as·tro·labe /ˈæstrəleɪb/ *n* instrument used in the Middle Ages to determine the height of the sun, etc.

as·trol·ogy /əˋstrolədʒɪ/ *n* [U] art of observing the positions of the stars in the belief that they influence human affairs. **as·trol·oger** /-ədʒə(r)/ *n* student of ~. **as·tro·logi·cal** /ˈæstrəˋlodʒɪkl/ *adj*

as·tro·naut /ˈæstrənɔt/ *n* person who travels in a spacecraft. **~·ics** /ˈæstrəˋnɔtɪks/ *n pl* science and technology of travel through outer space.

as·tron·omy /əˋstronəmɪ/ *n* [U] science of the sun, moon, stars and planets. **as·tron·omer** *n* student of, authority on, ~. **as·tro·nomi·cal** /ˈæstrəˋnomɪkl/ *adj* of the study of ~: *an astronomical sum,* (colloq) an enormous figure.

as·tro·phys·ics /ˈæstrəʊˋfɪzɪks/ *n* (*sing v*) science of the chemical and physical conditions of the stars.

as·tute /əˋstjut *US:* əˋstut/ *adj* **1** quick at seeing how to gain an advantage. **2** shrewd; clever: *an ~ lawyer/businessman.* **~·ly** *adv* **~·ness** *n*

asun·der /əˋsʌndə(r)/ *adv* **1** (of two or more things) apart: *Parents and children were driven ~* (= separated) *by the war.* **2** into pieces: *tear sth ~.*

asy·lum /əˋsaɪləm/ *n* **1** [C,U] (place of) refuge or safety. **2** (formerly) institution where mentally ill people were cared for, now called a *mental home* or *mental institution.* **3** protection from persecution, etc: *ask for political ~.*

at /ət *strong form:* æt/ *prep* **1** (place and direction) **(a)** (indicating the place in or near which sth or sb was, is or will be): *at his office; at my uncle's; at the station.* Cf *in* for countries and large towns, and places important to the speaker. **(b)** (towards; in the direction of): *look at sth/sb; shoot/aim a gun at sth; rush at the enemy; laugh/growl at sb/sth; throw sth at sb,* i e intending to hit him. ⇨ *throw to* at **throw²(1)**; *talk at sb,* i e make an indirect attack on him, ⇨ *talk to* at **talk¹(1)**. **(c)** (indicating an attempt to get or reach sth, an uncompleted or imperfect action): *The drowning man clutched at the oar,* tried to seize it. *He had to guess at the meaning.* **(d)** (indicating distance): *hold sth at arm's length. It looks better at a distance.* **(e)** (indicating a point of entrance or exit) through; by: *What the teacher says often goes in (at) one ear and out (at) the other.* **2** (time and order) **(a)** (indicating a point of time): *at 2 o'clock; at sunset; at any moment; at this; at this point,* when this happened. **(b)** (of age): *He left school at (the age of) 15.* **(c)** (indicating order): *at the third attempt; at first; at last.* **(d)** (indicating frequency): *at (all) times; at regular intervals.* **3** (activity, state, manner) **(a)** (indicating occupation): *at work; at play. What is he at now,* What is he doing? ***ˈhard ˋat it,*** working hard. **(b)** (after *adjj*): *busy at his tasks; good at translation.* **(c)** (state, condition): *at war/peace; at leisure.* **(d)** (manner): *at a gallop; finish something at a sitting,* i e during one continuous period of activity. **4** (rate or degree, value, cost) **(a)** (rate): *at full speed; at a snail's pace.* **(b)** (value, cost, etc): *at immense cost, sell sth at a loss; buy articles at 20p and sell them at 25p.* **(c)** (with *superl*): *at its/his/their, etc best; at least; at the worst.* **5** (cause) **(a)** (after *vv*): *The pupils marvelled at the extent of their teacher's knowledge.* **(b)** (after *adjj* and *pp's*): *impatient at the delay; delighted at the idea of going to England.* ⇨ also *n* entries for *at hand, at last, in at the death* and others.

ata·brine /ˈætəbrin/ *n* [U] (P) bitter-tasting, anti-malarial drug.

ata·vism /ˈætəvɪzm/ *n* reappearance in a person of a characteristic or quality that has not shown itself for several or many generations. ⇨ **reversion, throwback. ata·vis·tic** /ˈætəˋvɪstɪk/ *adj*

ate /et *US:* eɪt/ *pt* of **eat**.

atel·ier /æˋtelɪəɪ *US:* ˈætlˋjeɪ/ *n* (F) workshop; studio.

athe·ism /ˈeɪθɪ-ɪzm/ *n* [U] belief that there is no God. **athe·ist** /ˈeɪθɪɪst/ *n* person who believes that there is no God. **athe·is·tic** /ˈeɪθɪˋɪstɪk/ *adj* of ~ or atheists.

athirst /əˋθɜst/ *pred adj* (liter) thirsty, eager *for* news, etc.

ath·lete /ˈæθlit/ *n* person trained for competing in physical exercises and outdoor games, e g a person good at running, jumping, swimming, boxing.

ath·letic /æθˋletɪk/ *adj* **1** of athletes. **2** physically strong, with well-balanced proportions between the trunk and limbs: *an ~-looking young man.* **ath·let·ics** *n pl* (usu with *sing v*) practice of physical exercises and sports, esp competitions in running, jumping, etc.

at-home /ət ˋhəʊm/ ⇨ **home¹(1)**.

athwart /əˋθwɔt/ *adv, prep* (naut) from one side to the other side (*of*).

atishoo /əˋtɪʃu/ *int* (hum) spelling form used to indicate a sneeze.

at·las /ˈætləs/ *n* book of maps.

at·mos·phere /ˈætməsfɪə(r)/ *n* **1** esp **the ~,** mixture of gases surrounding the earth. **2** air in any place. **3** feeling, e g of good, evil, that the mind receives from a place, conditions, etc: *There is an ~ of peace and calm in the country quite different from the ~ of a big city.*

at·mos·pheric /ˈætməsˋferɪk/ *adj* of, connected with, the atmosphere: *~ conditions.* **ˈ~ ˋpressure,** pressure at a point due to the weight of the column of air above that point, about 14½ lb or 6 6 kg per square inch at sea level. **at·mos·pher·ics** *n pl* electrical discharges that occur in the atmosphere and cause crackling sounds in radio receivers.

atoll /ˈætol/ *n* ring-shaped coral reef(s) almost or entirely enclosing a lagoon.

atom /ˈætəm/ *n* **1** smallest unit of an element that can take part in a chemical change: *A molecule of water* (H_2O) *is made up of two ~s of hydrogen and one ~ of oxygen.* ⇨ **electron, neutron, nucleus, proton. ˋ~ bomb,** = atomic bomb. **2** very small bit: *blow sth to ~s,* destroy it by explosion. *There's not an ~ of truth* (= no truth at all) *in what he said.*

an atoll

atomic /əˈtomɪk/ *adj* of an atom, or atoms. ˈ~ ˋ**bomb,** bomb of which the destructive power comes from the release of ~ energy in the shortest possible time. ˈ~ ˋ**energy,** energy obtained as the result of nuclear fission. ˈ~ ˋ**pile,** ⇨ reactor. ˈ~ ˋ**weight,** weight of an atom of an element expressed on a scale in which an atom of oxygen is 16. ⇨ nuclear.

at·om·ize /ˋætəmaɪz/ *vt* reduce to atoms. **at·om·izer** *n* device for producing a fine spray, e g of perfume.

atonal /æˋtəʊnl/ *adj* (music) not conforming to any system of key or mode. **~·ity** /ˈætəʊˋnælətɪ/ *n*

atone /əˋtəʊn/ *vi* [VP2A,3A] **~ *(for)*,** make repayment: ~ *(for) a fault by doing sth. How can I ~ for hurting your feelings? How can I ~?* **~·ment** *n* [U] atoning: *make ~ment for a fault.* **the A~ment,** the sufferings and death of Jesus.

atop /əˋtop/ *adv* (US) on top *(of).*

at·ra·bil·ious /ˈætrəˋbɪlɪəs/ *adj* melancholy; acrimonious.

atro·cious /əˋtrəʊʃəs/ *adj* **1** very wicked or cruel: *an ~ crime.* **2** (colloq) very bad: *an ~ dinner; ~ weather.* **~·ly** *adv*

atroc·ity /əˋtrosətɪ/ *n* (*pl* **-ties**) [U] wickedness; [C] wicked or cruel act: *the atrocities of which the enemy forces were guilty.*

atro·phy /ˋætrəfɪ/ *n* [U] wasting away (of the body or part of it, or (fig) of a moral quality). □ *vt, vi* [VP6A] cause ~ in; [VP2B] suffer ~.

atta·boy /ˈætəˋbɔɪ/ *int* (US colloq) (expressing encouragement or admiration) Bravo!

at·tach /əˋtætʃ/ *vt, vi* **1** [VP14] fasten or join (one thing *to* another): ~ *labels to the luggage; ~ a document to a letter; the sample ~ed to the letter; a house with a garage ~ed. A~ed you will find/A~ed please find...,* (business style) You will find, ~ed to this letter.... **2** [VP14] join (oneself *to*), e g as a junior, and perhaps unwelcome, member: ~ *oneself to a political party/to a travelling circus.* **3 *be ~ed to,*** be bound to by love or affection: *She is deeply ~ed to her young brother. He is foolishly ~ed to old customs.* **4** [VP14] consider to have; connect with: *Do you ~ much importance to what he says?* **5** [VP3A] go with, be joined (*to*): *No suspicion/blame ~es to him,* He cannot be suspected/blamed. **6** [VP6A] (legal) seize by legal authority: *Part of his salary was ~ed by shopkeepers to whom he owed money.* **7 *~ed to,*** (mil) appointed to another unit for specialist duties: *a gunnery officer ~ed to an infantry regiment.* **~·ment** *n* **1** [U] act of ~ing or joining; being ~ed. **2** [C] sth ~ed, esp an accessory ~ed to sth larger. **3** [C] affection; friendship: *have an ~ment for sb.* **4** legal seizing of goods, etc. **5 *on ~ment to,*** (temporarily) appointed to.

at·taché /əˋtæʃeɪ *US:* ˈætəˋʃeɪ/ *n* person who is attached to the staff of an ambassador: *the naval/military/press ~.* **~ case** /əˋtæʃɪ keɪs/ *n* small, flat, rectangular box or holder for documents.

at·tack /əˋtæk/ *n* **1** [C] violent attempt to hurt, overcome, defeat: *make an ~ upon the enemy;* [U] *The enemy came under ~. A~ is said to be the best form of defence.* **2** [C] adverse criticism in speech or writing: *a strong ~ against/on the Government's policy.* **3** [C] coming on, e g of disease: *an ~ of fever; a ˋliver ~; a ˋheart ~,* pain in the region of the heart, with irregular beating. **4** [U] way of beginning an activity, e g playing the violin, playing a stroke in cricket. □ *vt* [VP6A] make an ~ upon: ~ *the enemy; ~ the Prime Minister's proposals; a disease that ~s children. Rust ~s metals.* **~er** *n* person who ~s.

at·tain /əˋteɪn/ *vt, vi* **1** [VP6A] succeed in doing or getting: ~ *one's hopes/object/the end one has in view.* **2** [VP3A] **~ *to,*** reach, arrive at: ~ *to perfection/power/prosperity; ~ to man's estate,* reach manhood. **~·able** /-əbl/ *adj* that can be ~ed: *The goal is not yet ~able.* **~·ment** *n* **1** [U] act of ~ing: *easy/difficult/impossible of ~ment,* easy, etc to ~; *for the ~ment of* (= in order to ~) *his purpose.* **2** [C] (usu *pl*) sth ~ed; skill or accomplishment in some branch of knowledge, etc: *legal/linguistic ~ments; a scholar of the highest ~ments.*

at·tain·der /əˋteɪndə(r)/ *n* (legal) forfeiture of property and civil rights following sentence of death or outlawry. **Bill of A~,** Parliamentary Bill imposing this penalty without trial.

at·tar /ˋætə(r)/ *n* [U] ~ *of roses,* perfume from rose petals.

at·tempt /əˋtempt/ *vt* **1** [VP7A,6A] make a start at doing sth; try: *The prisoners ~ed to escape but failed. You have ~ed* (= made a start at performing) *a difficult task. Don't ~ impossibilities,* Don't try to do impossible things. **2** [VP6A] ~ *sb's life,* (old use) try to kill him. □ *n* [C] **1 ~ *to do sth,* ~ *at doing sth,*** ~ing; effort to do sth: *They made no ~ to escape/at escaping. His first ~ at English composition was poor. They failed in all their ~s to climb the mountain.* **2 ~ *at,*** sth not very well done: *Her ~ at a Christmas cake had to be thrown away.* **3 ~ *(up)on,*** attack: *make an ~ on sb's life; an ~ on the world speed record.*

at·tend /əˋtend/ *vi, vt* **1** [VP3A,2A] **~ *to,*** give care and thought to: ~ *to one's work; ~ to what sb is saying,* listen carefully; ~ *to the wants of customers,* try to supply them. *Are you being ~ed to?* (in a shop) Is anyone serving you? *You're not ~ing,* not listening, not paying attention. **2** [VP6A,3A] wait (*upon*); serve; look after: *Which doctor is ~ing you,* giving you medical care? *The patient has three nurses ~ing (on) him. She has many servants ~ing upon her. He had the honour of ~ing upon the Prince.* **3** [VP6A] go to; be present at: ~ *school/church; ~ a meeting/lecture. The lectures were well ~ed,* there were good audiences. **4** [VP6A] (formal) accompany: *a method that is ~ed by some risk; Our plans were ~ed with great difficulties. May good luck ~ you!,* (formal) May you have good luck!

at·tend·ance /əˋtendəns/ *n* **1** [U] ***in ~ (up)on,*** act of attending(2): *Major X was in ~ upon the Queen. Now that the patient is out of danger, the doctor is no longer in ~.* ⇨ dance²(2). **2** [C, U] being present, at school etc: *The boy was given a prize for regular ~,* for attending school regularly. *How many ~s has he made? Is ~ at school compulsory?* **3** [C] (with *adjj*) number of persons present: *There was a large ~ at church this morning.*

at·tend·ant /əˋtendənt/ *n* **1** servant or companion. **2** *medical ~,* doctor. **3** (*pl*) persons who accompany an important person: *the Prince and his ~s.* □ *adj* **1** accompanying: *famine and its ~ diseases,* the diseases that result from famine; *old age and its ~ evils,* e g deafness. **2** waiting upon: *an ~ nurse.*

at·ten·tion /əˋtenʃn/ *n* **1** [U] act of directing one's thoughts to sth: *Pay ~ to what you're doing,* Don't let your thoughts wander. *A teacher must know how to secure the ~ of his pupils. No ~ was paid to my advice,* no one took it. *Give your whole ~ to what you are doing,* i e think of nothing else. *He called/invited my ~ to some new evidence,* asked me to examine it. *He shouted to attract ~,* to make people notice him. *A~, Mr Roberts,* (in comm or official correspondence) This letter, memorandum, etc is to be dealt with by Mr Roberts. **2** (often *pl*) kind or polite act: *They showed the old lady numerous little ~s,* were kind and helpful in numerous ways. *A pretty girl usually receives more ~(s) than a plain girl,* finds men more willing to do things for her. ***pay one's ~s to a lady,*** (dated) court her, be polite and kind in the hope of winning her affections. **3** [U] drill position in which a man stands straight and still: *come to/stand at ~;* (as a military command): *A~!* (shortened to *'shun* /ʃʌn/).

at·tent·ive /əˋtentɪv/ *adj* giving or paying attention (*to*): *A speaker likes to have an ~ audience. Please be more ~ to your studies. A good host is ~ to (the needs of) his guests. She was always ~ to her young brother.* **~·ly** *adv*: *They listened ~ly to the teacher.*

at·tenu·ate /əˋtenjʊeɪt/ *vt* [VP6A] (formal) make thin or slender; weaken; reduce.

at·test /əˋtest/ *vt,vi* **1** [VP6A] be or give clear proof of: *The man's ability was ~ed by his rapid promotion,* His promotion was proof of his ability. *These papers ~ the fact that....* ***~ a signature,*** make it legal by witnessing it. **ˈ~ed ˋmilk/ˋcattle,** certified free of disease, esp tuberculosis. **2** [VP6A] declare on oath; put (a person) on oath; cause (sb) to declare solemnly: *I have said nothing that I am not ready to ~,* to say on oath. **3** [VP2A] enrol for military service (by taking the oath of allegiance). **4** [VP3A] ***~ to,*** bear witness to: *feats which ~ to his strength of will.*

at·tic /ˋætɪk/ *n* space within the roof of a house: *two small rooms in the ~.*

At·tic /ˋætɪk/ *adj* of Athens or Attica.

at·tire /əˋtaɪə(r)/ *n* [U] (liter or poet) dress: *in holiday ~.* □ *vt* [VP6A] (dated) dress: *~d in white/satin.*

at·ti·tude /ˋætɪtjud *US:* -tud/ *n* [C] **1** manner of placing or holding the body: *He stood there in a threatening ~.* ***strike an ~,*** suddenly and dramatically take up an ~. **2** way of feeling, thinking or behaving: *What is your ~ towards this question,* What do you think about it, how do you propose to act? *We must maintain a firm ~,* not show signs of weakness. **at·ti·tu·din·ize** /ˈætɪˋtjudɪnaɪz *US:* -ˋtudn̩-/ *vi* [VP2A] strike ~s; speak, write, behave in an affected way.

at·tor·ney /əˋtɜnɪ/ *n* (*pl* **-neys**) **1** person with legal authority to act for another in business or law: *letter/warrant of ~,* written authority by which a person appoints another to act for him; *power of ~,* authority so given. **2 ˈA~ ˋGeneral, (a)** legal officer with authority to act in all cases in which the State is a party, usu *district ~.* **(b)** (US, in some States) public prosecutor.

at·tract /əˋtrækt/ *vt* [VP6A] **1** pull towards (by unseen force): *A magnet ~s steel.* **2** get the attention of; arouse interest or pleasure in: *Bright colours ~ babies. Bright lights ~ moths. He shouted to ~ attention. Do you feel ~ed to her,* Do you like her?

at·trac·tion /əˋtrækʃn/ *n* **1** [U] power of pulling towards: *The ~ of the moon for the earth causes the tides. He cannot resist the ~ of the sea on a hot day/of a pretty girl. The cinema has little ~ for some people.* **2** [C] that which attracts: *the ~s of a big city,* e g theatres, concerts, cinemas, fine shops.

at·tract·ive /əˋtræktɪv/ *adj* having the power to attract; pleasing: *a most ~ girl; goods offered at ~ prices.* **~·ly** *adv*

at·trib·ute[1] /əˋtrɪbjut/ *vt* [VP14] **~ *to,*** consider as a quality of, as being the result of, as coming from: *He ~s wisdom to his teachers,* thinks they have wisdom. *He ~s his success to hard work,* says that his success is the result of hard work. *This comedy has been ~d to Shakespeare,* it has been said that Shakespeare was the author. **at·tribu·table** /əˋtrɪbjutəbl/ *adj* that can be ~d (*to*). **at·tri·bu·tion** /ˈætrɪˋbjuʃn/ *n* [U] act of attributing (*to*); [C] that which is ~d.

at·tri·bute[2] /ˋætrɪbjut/ *n* [C] **1** quality looked upon as naturally or necessarily belonging to sb or sth: *Mercy is an ~ of God. Politeness is an ~ of a gentleman.* **2** material object recognized as a symbol of a person or his position: *The crown is an ~ of kingship.*

at·tribu·tive /əˋtrɪbjʊtɪv/ *adj* **~ adjective,** (naming a quality and used with the *noun* as in *'old* man', *'red* hair', and contrasted with *predicative*). **~·ly** *adv*

at·tri·tion /əˋtrɪʃn/ *n* [U] wearing away by rubbing: *war of ~,* war in which each side waits for the other to wear itself out.

at·tune /əˋtjun *US:* əˋtun/ *vt* [VP14] bring into harmony or agreement with: *hearts ~d to worship;* make used to: *ears ~d to the sound of gunfire.*

auber·gine /ˋəʊbeʒin/ *n* [C] fruit of the eggplant, used as a vegetable. ⇨ the illus at **vegetable.**

aubrie·tia /ɔˋbriʃə/ *n* (kinds of) spring-flowering dwarf perennial grown on stone walls, rockeries, etc.

auburn /ˋɔbən/ *adj* (usu of hair) reddish-brown.

auc·tion /ˋɔkʃn/ *n* [C,U] public sale at which goods are sold to the persons making the highest bids or offers: *sale by ~; ~-sale; sell goods by ~; put sth up to/for ~; attend all the local ~s; ~ bridge,* ⇨ **bridge**[2]. □ *vt* [VP6A] sell by ~. ***~ sth off,*** [VP15B] get rid of sth by ~ing it. **~·eer** /ˈɔkʃəˋnɪə(r)/ *n* person who conducts an ~.

aud·acious /ɔˋdeɪʃəs/ *adj* **1** daring; bold. **2** foolishly bold. **3** impudent. **~·ly** *adv* **aud·ac·ity** /ɔˋdæsətɪ/ *n*

aud·ible /ˋɔdəbl/ *adj* loud enough to be heard: *in a scarcely ~ voice. The speaker was scarcely ~,* could be heard only with difficulty. **aud·ibly** /-əblɪ/ *adv* **audi·bil·ity** *n* /ˈɔdəˋbɪlətɪ/ *n* capacity for being heard.

audi·ence /ˋɔdɪəns/ *n* **1** gathering of persons for the purpose of hearing a speaker, singer, etc: *There was a large ~ in the theatre. He has* *addressed large* ~*s all over England.* **2** persons within hearing, whether they are together or not: *A broadcaster may have an* ~ *of several million.* **3** (of a book) readers: *His book has reached a wide* ~. **4** formal interview given by a ruler, the Pope, etc: *The Pope granted him an* ~. *The Prime Minister was received in* ~ *by the Queen.*

audio- /ˈɔdɪəʊ/ *pref* of hearing. **ˈ~-visual ˋaids,** teaching aids such as record players and film projectors. **ˈ~-lingual ˋmethods,** teaching methods making use of a language laboratory, tape recorders, etc. **ˈ~ ˋfrequency,** (radio) frequency which, when converted into sound waves by a loudspeaker, can be heard.

audit /ˋɔdɪt/ *n* official examination of accounts to see that they are in order. □ *vt* [VP6A] examine, e g accounts, officially.

aud·ition /ɔˋdɪʃn/ *n* **1** [C] trial hearing to test the voice of a singer, speaker, etc who is applying for employment or of an actor wishing to take part in a play. **2** [U] power of hearing; listening. □ *vt* [VP6A] give an ~ to.

audi·tor /ˋɔdɪtə(r)/ *n* **1** listener to a speaker, etc. **2** person who audits.

audi·tor·ium /ˈɔdɪˋtɔrɪəm/ *n* building, or part of a building, in which an audience sits.

audi·tory /ˋɔdɪtrɪ *US:* -tɔrɪ/ *adj* of the sense of hearing: *the* ~ *nerve.* ⇨ the illus at ear.

au fait /ˈəʊ ˋfeɪ/ *pred adj* (F) instructed: *put sb* ~ *of sth,* instruct him about it.

au fond /ˈəʊ ˋfõ/ *adv* (F) basically.

auger /ˋɔgə(r)/ *n* carpenter's tool for boring large holes in wood, with a handle at right angles; instrument for boring in soil.

aught /ɔt/ *n* **1** (liter) anything: *for* ~ *I know/care,* used to indicate that the speaker does not know/care at all. **2** (improperly, by confusion with *naught, nought*) zero: *read ·01 as point* ~ *one.*

aug·ment /ɔgˋment/ *vt,vi* [VP6A,2A] make or become greater; increase: ~ *one's income by writing short stories.* **aug·men·ta·tion** /ˈɔgmenˋteɪʃn/ *n* [U] ~ing or being ~ed; [C] sth added.

augur /ˋɔgə(r)/ *n* (in ancient Rome) religious official who claimed to foretell future events by omens from the entrails of birds, etc. □ *vi,vt* foretell, be a sign of: ~ ***well/ill (for sb/sth),*** be a good/bad sign for the future, for us: *Does this news* ~ *war?* **augury** /ˋɔgjʊrɪ/ *n* (*pl* -**ries**) [C] omen; sign.

au·gust /ɔˋgʌst/ *adj* majestic; causing feelings of respect or awe.

August /ˋɔgəst/ *n* the eighth month.

Au·gustan /ɔˋgʌstən/ *adj* of the best period of Latin literature; classical; of the period of English Literature including Dryden, Pope and Swift.

auk /ɔk/ *n* northern seabird, with short wings used in swimming.

auld lang syne /ˈɔld læŋ ˋzɑɪn, *Scot:* ˋsɑɪn/ (Scot, name of song) good times long ago.

aunt /ɑnt *US:* ænt/ *n* sister of one's father or mother; wife of one's uncle. **ˈA~ ˋSally,** wooden model of a woman's head, at which sticks are thrown, at fairs, etc; (fig) object, person, widely abused. **aun·tie, aun·ty** /ˋɑntɪ *US:* ˋæntɪ/ *n* (familiar for) aunt.

au pair /ˈəʊ ˋpeə(r)/ *adj* (F) (in GB) girl from overseas who, in return for light household duties, receives board and lodging, and facilities for study.

aura /ˋɔrə/ *n* atmosphere surrounding a person or object and thought to come from him or it: *There seemed to be an* ~ *of holiness about the Indian saint.*

aural /ˋɔrl/ *adj* of the organs of hearing: *an* ~ *surgeon.*

aure·ole /ˋɔrɪəʊl/ *n* halo.

au re·voir /ˈəʊ rəˋvwɑ(r)/ *int* (F) till we meet again; goodbye.

aur·icle /ˋɔrɪkl/ *n* **1** the external part of the ear. ⇨ the illus at respiratory. **2** either of the two upper cavities of the heart.

aur·icu·lar /ɔˋrɪkjʊlə(r)/ *adj* of or near the ear: ~ *confession,* made privately in the ear, e g of a priest.

aur·if·er·ous /ɔˋrɪfərəs/ *adj* yielding gold.

aur·ora /ɔˋrɔrə/ *n* **1 A~,** Roman goddess of dawn. **2** ~ **bor·ea·lis** /ɔˈrɔrə ˈbɔrɪˋeɪlɪs/ *n* display of coloured light, in streamers and bands, mainly red and green, seen in the sky in the regions of the North Pole; also called *Northern Lights.* **~ˈaus·tra·lis** /ɔˈrɔrə ɔˋstreɪlɪs/ *n* similar display seen in the southern hemisphere.

aus·pices /ˋɔspɪsɪz/ *n pl* ***under the*** ~ ***of,*** helped and favoured by: *under favourable* ~, with the omens in one's favour, with favourable prospects.

aus·picious /ɔˋspɪʃəs/ *adj* showing signs, giving promise, of future success; favourable; prosperous. **~·ly** *adv*

Aus·sie /ˋɔzɪ/ *n* (sl) Australian.

aus·tere /ɔˋstɪə(r)/ *adj* **1** of a person, his behaviour, severely moral and strict. **2** of a way of living, of places, styles, simple and plain; without ornament or comfort. **~·ly** *adv* **aus·ter·ity** /ɔˋsterətɪ/ *n* (*pl* -**ties**) **1** [U] quality of being ~. **2** (*pl*) ~ practices, e g fasting, living in a cell, for religious reasons.

aut·archy /ˋɔtɑkɪ/ *n* [C] (*pl*-chies) (country under) absolute sovereignty.

aut·arky /ˋɔtɑkɪ/ *n* [U] self-sufficiency, esp of a State in its economy.

auth·en·tic /ɔˋθentɪk/ *adj* genuine; known to be true: ~ *news; an* ~ *signature.* **auth·en·ti·cally** /-klɪ/ *adv* **auth·en·ti·cate** /ɔˋθentɪkeɪt/ *vt* [VP6A] prove to be ~; prove beyond doubt the origin, authorship, etc of. **auth·en·ti·ca·tion** /ɔˈθentɪˋkeɪʃn/ *n* **auth·en·tic·ity** /ɔˈθenˋtɪsətɪ/ *n* [U] genuineness; quality of being ~: *feel confident of the authenticity of a signature.*

author /ˋɔθə(r)/ *n* **1** writer of a book, play, etc: *Dickens is his favourite* ~. **2** person who creates or begins sth: *God, the A~ of our being.* **~·ess** /ˋɔθərəs/ *n* woman ~. **~·ship** /-ʃɪp/ *n* [U] **1** occupation of an ~: *It's risky to take to* ~*ship* (= begin to write books) *for a living.* **2** origin of a book, etc: *Nothing is known of the* ~*ship of the book,* about who wrote it.

auth·ori·tarian /ɔˈθɒrɪˋteərɪən/ *adj* supporting or requiring obedience to authority, esp that of the State, contrasted with individual liberty. □ *n* supporter of this principle. **~·ism** /-ɪzm/ *n*

auth·ori·tat·ive /ɔˋθɒrɪtətɪv/ *adj* **1** having, given with, authority: ~ *orders.* **2** having an air of authority; commanding: *in an* ~ *manner; speaking in* ~ *tones.* **3** that can be trusted because from a reliable source: *an* ~ *report;* ~ *information; from an* ~ *source.* **~·ly** *adv*

auth·or·ity /ɔˋθɒrətɪ/ *n* (*pl* -**ties**) **1** [U] power or right to give orders and make others obey: *The problem of how to cope with* ~, e g wrongdoers with the police, children with parents. *An officer* *has/exercises ~ over the soldiers under him. Who is in ~ here? These boys are under the ~ of the headmaster. He has made his ~ felt,* caused people to realize that he has power to make them obey. **2** [U] **~ *(for sth/to do sth),*** right given to sb: *Only the treasurer has ~ to make payments. He had the ~ of the Governor for what he did.* **3** [U] person or (*pl*) group of persons having ~: *the City, Municipal, County, etc authorities; the health authorities; the A'tomic 'Energy A~.* **4** [C,U] person with special knowledge; book, etc that supplies reliable information or evidence: *He is a great ~ on phonetics. The 'Oxford English Dictionary' is the best ~ on English words. What is your ~ for that statement? You should quote your authorities,* give the titles of books, etc, names of persons, etc used as sources for facts.

auth·or·ize /ˈɔθəraɪz/ *vt* **1** [VP17A] give authority to: *I have ~d him to act for me while I am abroad.* **2** [VP6A] give authority for: *The Finance Committee ~d the spending of £10 000 on a new sports ground. This payment has not been ~d.* **'A~d 'Version,** (common abbr *A V*) the English translation of the Bible, first published 1611. **auth·or·iz·ation** /ˌɔθəraɪˈzeɪʃn *US:* -rɪˈz-/ *n* [U] authorizing; giving legal right (*to do* sth, *for* sth); the right given.

aut·ism /ˈɔt-ɪzm/ *n* [U] (psych) severe form of mental illness in children. **aut·is·tic** /ɔˈtɪstɪk/ *adj* of ~: *autistic children.*

auto /ˈɔtəʊ/ *n* (US colloq) short for *automobile.*

auto- /ˈɔtəʊ/ *pref* (in compounds) self-, by oneself; independent(ly): *~-intoxication,* poisoning by substances produced within the body. **'~-changer,** device (on a record-player) that plays a number of discs in succession without attention.

auto·bahn /ˈɔtəbɑn/ (*pl* **-bahns** or (G) **-bahnen** /-nən/) *n* (G) = motorway.

auto·bi·ogra·phy /ˌɔtəbaɪˈɒgrəfɪ/ *n* (*pl* **-phies**) **1** [C] story of a person's life written by himself. **2** [U] the art and practice of this sort of writing. **auto·bio·graphic** /ˌɔtəˌbaɪəˈgræfɪk/, **auto·bio·graphi·cal** /-ɪkl/ *adj* of, engaged in, ~.

autoc·racy /ɔˈtɒkrəsɪ/ *n* (*pl* **-cies**) **1** [U] government by a ruler who has unlimited power. **2** [C] (country with a) government of this kind.

auto·crat /ˈɔtəkræt/ *n* ruler with unlimited power; person who requires things to be done without considering the wishes of others. **~ic** /ˌɔtəˈkrætɪk/ *adj* of or like an ~: *Don't be so ~ic,* Don't behave as if you were an ~. **auto·crati·cally** /-klɪ/ *adv*

auto-da-fé /ˌɔtəʊ dɑ ˈfeɪ *US:* ˌaʊtəʊ ˈdə/ *n* (*pl* **autos-da-fé** /ˌɔtəʊz *US:* ˌaʊtəʊz/) trial and sentence of a heretic by the Inquisition; carrying out of the sentence, esp by burning.

auto·giro, -gyro /ˌɔtəʊˈdʒaɪərəʊ/ *n* (P) early form of helicopter with a propeller in front and rotors above.

auto·graph /ˈɔtəgrɑf *US:* -græf/ *n* person's own handwriting, esp his signature: *~ book/album,* one in which signatures, e g of famous persons, are collected. □ *vt* [VP6A] write one's name on or in: *a book ~ed by the author; an ~ed photograph.*

auto·mat /ˈɔtəmæt/ *n* restaurant at which food and drink are obtained, by the customers themselves, from coin-operated closed compartments.

auto·mate /ˈɔtəmeɪt/ *vt* (science, comm) convert to, control by, automation.

auto·matic /ˌɔtəˈmætɪk/ *adj* **1** self-acting; self-moving; (of a machine) able to work or be worked without attention: *an ~ pilot,* (on an aircraft) maintaining altitude, course, etc; *~ gear-change* (in a motor vehicle); *~ weapons,* weapons that continue firing until pressure on the trigger is released. **2** (of actions) done without thought; unconscious: *Breathing is ~.* □ *n* small ~ firearm. **auto·mati·cally** /-klɪ/ *adv*

auto·ma·tion /ˌɔtəˈmeɪʃn/ *n* [U] (use of) methods and machines to save labour.

automa·ton /ɔˈtɒmətən *US:* -tɒn/ *n* (*pl* **-tons, -ta** /-tə/) person who appears to act involuntarily or without active intelligence; robot.

auto·mo·bile /ˈɔtəməbil *US:* ˌɔtəməˈbil/ *n* (esp US) motor-car.

auton·omous /ɔˈtɒnəməs/ *adj* (of states) self-governing. **auton·omy** /ɔˈtɒnəmɪ/ *n* (*pl* **-mies**) [U,C] (right of) self-government.

au·topsy /ˈɔtɒpsɪ/ *n* (*pl* **-sies**) [C] (med) post-mortem examination of a body (by cutting it open) to learn the cause of death.

auto·strada /ˌaʊtəʊˈstrɑdə/ *n* (*pl* **-das,** (I) **-de** /-ˈstrɑdeɪ/) (I) = motorway.

autumn /ˈɔtəm/ *n* (US = *fall*) third season of the year, between summer and winter (Sept, Oct and Nov in the northern hemisphere): *in ~; in the ~ of 1980; in (the) early/late ~;* (fig) *in the ~ of his life;* (attrib) *~ weather/fashions.* **autum·nal** /ɔˈtʌmnl/ *adj* of ~.

aux·ili·ary /ɔgˈzɪlɪərɪ/ *adj* helping; supporting: *~ troops; an ~ verb* (e g *is* in *He is working; has* in *He has gone*). □ *n* (*pl* **-ries**) **1** ~ verb. **2** (usu *pl*) ~ troops (esp troops hired from a foreign or allied country, e g in the Roman Empire in ancient times).

avail /əˈveɪl/ *vt,vi* **1** [VP14] **~ *oneself of,*** make use of, profit by, take advantage of: *You should ~ yourself of every opportunity to practise speaking English.* **2** [VP2A,3A] (liter) be of value or help: *Money does not ~ on a desert island. Nothing ~ed against the storm.* □ *n* ***of no/little ~,*** not helpful; not effective: *His intervention was of little ~.* ***without ~, to no ~,*** without regret; unsuccessfully: *We pulled him out of the river and tried to revive him, but to no ~. Of what ~ is it to...,* What use is it to...? **~·able** /-əbl/ *adj* capable of being used; that may be obtained: *These tickets are ~able for one month. There were no tickets ~able for Friday's performance.* **~·abil·ity** /əˌveɪləˈbɪlətɪ/ *n* [U].

ava·lanche /ˈævəlɑnʃ *US:* -læntʃ/ *n* great mass of snow and ice at a high altitude, caused by its own weight to slide down a mountain side, often carrying with it thousands of tons of rock, and sometimes destroying forests, houses, etc in its path: (fig) *an ~ of words/letters/questions.*

avant-garde /ˌævɔ̃ ˈgɑd/ *n* (F) vanguard of an army; (fig) radical leader(s) of any movement (in art, drama, literature, etc): (attrib) *~ writers/artists.*

av·ar·ice /ˈævərɪs/ *n* [U] greed (for money or possessions); great eagerness to get or keep. **av·ar·icious** /ˌævəˈrɪʃəs/ *adj* greedy (*of* money, power, etc). **av·ar·icious·ly** *adv*

avast /əˈvɑst *US:* əˈvæst/ *int* (naut) Stop!

ava·tar /ˌævəˈtɑ(r)/ *n* (Hindu myth) descent to earth of a deity in human or animal form.

avaunt /əˈvɔnt/ *int* (old use) Begone; Go away!

avenge /əˈvendʒ/ *vt* [VP6A,14] get or take vengeance for: ~ *an insult;* ~ *oneself/be* ~*d on an enemy* (*for* an injury, etc). *He* ~*d his father's death upon the murderer,* punished the murderer. **avenger** *n*

av·enue /ˈævənju *US:* -nu/ *n* **1** road with trees on each side, esp the private road going up to a large country house. **2** wide street with buildings on one or both sides. **3** (fig) way (*to* some object or aim): ~*s to success/promotion.*

aver /əˈvɜ(r)/ *vt* (-rr-) [VP6A,9] (old use) state positively (*that* sth is true).

av·er·age /ˈævərɪdʒ/ *n* **1** result of adding several quantities together and dividing the total by the number of quantities: *The* ~ *of 4, 5 and 9 is 6.* **2** standard or level regarded as ordinary or usual: *Tom's work at school is above the* ~, *Harry's is below the* ~ *and Jim's is about up to the* ~. *On an/the* ~, *there are twenty boys present every day.* □ *adj* **1** found by making an ~: *The* ~ *age of the boys in this class is fifteen. What's the* ~ *temperature in this town in August?* **2** of the ordinary or usual standard: *boys of* ~ *intelligence; men of* ~ *ability.* □ *vt,vi* **1** [VP6A] find the ~ of: *If you* ~ *7, 14 and 6, you get 9.* **2** [VP2B] amount to as an ~; do as an ~: ~ *200 miles a day during a journey. The rainfall* ~*s 36 inches a year.*

averse /əˈvɜs/ *adj* ~ ***from/to,*** opposed, disinclined: *He is* ~ *to hard work. We are* ~ *from taking action.*

aver·sion /əˈvɜʃn *US:* əˈvɜʒn/ *n* **1** [C,U] ~ ***to,*** strong dislike: *He has a strong* ~ *to getting up early. He took an* ~ *to me. Do you feel any* ~ *to hard study?* **2** [C] sth or sb disliked: *my pet* ~, sth I specially dislike.

avert /əˈvɜt/ *vt* **1** [VP14] ~ ***from,*** turn away (one's eyes, thoughts, etc): ~ *one's eyes/gaze from a terrible spectacle.* **2** [VP6A] prevent, avoid: ~ *an accident;* ~ *suspicion;* ~ *failure by hard work.*

avi·ary /ˈeɪvɪərɪ *US:* -vɪerɪ/ *n* (*pl* **-ries**) place for keeping birds, e g in a zoo.

avi·ation /ˈeɪvɪˈeɪʃn/ *n* (art and science of) flying in aircraft. ˈ~ **spirit,** high-octane motor spirit used in aircraft engines. **avi·ator** /ˈeɪvɪeɪtə(r)/ *n* airman (now usu *pilot* or *captain*) who controls an aircraft, airship or balloon.

avid /ˈævɪd/ *adj* ~ ***for,*** eager, greedy: ~ *for fame/applause.* ~**·ly** *adv* ~**·ity** /əˈvɪdətɪ/ *n* [U] eagerness: *He accepted the offer with* ~*ity.*

avo·cado /ˌævəˈkɑdəʊ/ *n* (*pl* -dos /-dəʊz/) (also *alligator pear*) pear-shaped tropical fruit. ⇨ the illus at **fruit**.

avo·ca·tion /ˌævəˈkeɪʃn/ *n* **1** occupation that is not a person's ordinary business. **2** (improperly) vocation.

avoid /əˈvɔɪd/ *vt* [VP6A,C] keep or get away from; escape: *Try to* ~ *danger. We only just* ~*ed an accident. You can hardly* ~ *meeting her if you both work in the same office.* ~**·able** /-əbl/ *adj* that can be ~ed. ~**·ance** /-əns/ *n* [U] act of ~ing: *the* ~*ance of bad companions;* ~*ance of taxation,* e g by not buying taxed goods such as tobacco and wine.

avoir·du·pois /ˌævədəˈpɔɪz/ *n* system of weights used, before metrication, in most English-speaking countries (1 pound = 16 ounces), used for all goods except precious metals and stones, and medicines. ⇨ App 5.

avouch /əˈvaʊtʃ/ *vt,vi* [VP6A,9,3A] (liter; now rare) assert; guarantee: ~ (*for*) *sth.*

avow /əˈvaʊ/ *vt* [VP6A,25 reflex] (formal) admit; declare openly: ~ *a fault. He* ~*ed himself* (*to be*) *a Christian.* ~**al** /-əl/ *n* [U] free and open confession; [C] instance of this: *make an* ~*al of one's sentiments.* ~**·ed·ly** /əˈvaʊɪdlɪ/ *adv* by confession; openly: *He was* ~*edly in the wrong.*

avun·cu·lar /əˈvʌŋkjʊlə(r)/ *adj* of or like an uncle (esp a benevolent uncle).

await /əˈweɪt/ *vt* [VP6A] **1** (of persons) wait for: *I* ~ *your instructions.* **2** be in store for; be waiting for: *A hearty welcome* ~*s you. Death* ~*s all men.*

awake[1] /əˈweɪk/ *vi* (*pt* awoke /əˈwəʊk/, *pp* awoke or ~d) **1** [VP2A] = wake. (*awake* is preferred for the fig uses, intrans, and *awaken* for the fig uses, trans) **2** [VP3A] ~ ***to,*** become conscious of, realize: *He awoke to his opportunities. You must* ~ *to the fact* (= You must realize) *that failure will mean disgrace. When he awoke to his surroundings...,* realized where he was.... [VP4B] *He awoke to find himself famous,* learnt, the next day, that he was famous.

awake[2] /əˈweɪk/ *pred adj* roused from sleep: *Is he* ~ *or asleep?* ~ ***to,*** aware of: *be* ~ *to what is going on/to a danger/to one's own interests.*

awaken /əˈweɪkən/ *vt* = awake. (*awaken* is preferred for fig uses, trans) [VP14] ~ ***sb to,*** make sb aware of: ~ *sb to a sense of his responsibility/to a sense of shame.* ~**·ing** /əˈweɪknɪŋ/ *n* act of becoming aware, of realizing, esp sth unpleasant: *It was a rude* ~*ing when he was told that he was to be dismissed for inefficiency.*

award /əˈwɔd/ *vt* [VP6A,12A,13A] give or grant (by official decision): *He was* ~*ed the first prize. The judge* ~*ed her £200 as damages. The gold medal was* ~*ed to Mr Brown for his fine show of vegetables.* □ *n* [C] **1** decision made by a judge or arbitrator. **2** sth given as the result of such a decision, e g a prize in a competition: *His horse was given the highest* ~ *at the show.* **3** money granted to a student at a university, etc.

aware /əˈweə(r)/ *pred adj* ~ ***of/that,*** having knowledge or realization: *Are you* ~ *that you're sitting on my hat? We are fully* ~ *of the gravity of the situation. Without being* ~ *of it...; I was not* ~ *(of) how deeply he had felt the death of his mother.* ~**·ness** *n* [U].

awash /əˈwɒʃ/ *pred adj* washed over by, level with, the waves: *rocks* ~ *at high tide. The ship's deck was* ~.

away /əˈweɪ/ *adv part* **1** to or at a distance (from the place, person, etc in question): *The sea is two miles* ~. *The shops are only a few minutes' walk* ~. *Is our next football match at home or* ~, on our ground or on the ground of our opponents? *It's an* ~ *match. Take these things* ~, remove them. *Keep the baby* ~ *from the fire. Don't look* ~ (i e in a different direction) *while I'm taking your photograph.* **2** (used in verbless exclamations before *with*): *A*~ *with them!* Take them ~! **3** continuously; constantly: *He was working* ~. *He was laughing / muttering / grumbling* ~ *all afternoon.* ⇨ laugh(2), mutter. **4** (used with *vv* to indicate loss, lessening, weakening, exhaustion): *The water has all boiled* ~, There is no water left. ⇨ blaze[2](4), boil[2](4), die[2](3), explain(2), melt(1). **5** (in phrases). ***far and*** ~, very much: *This is far and* ~ *better.* ***out and*** ~, beyond comparison: *This is out and* ~ *the best.* ***right/straight*** ~, at once, without delay.

awe[1] /ɔ/ *n* [U] respect combined with fear and reverence: *He had a feeling of awe as he was taken before the judge. Savages often live in awe of nature. The lazy boy stood in awe of his stern teacher.* **ˋawe-inspiring** *adj* filling with awe: *an awe-inspiring sight.* **ˋawe-stricken, ˋawe-struck** *adj* struck with awe. **ˋawe·some** /-səm/ *adj* causing awe.

awe[2] /ɔ/ *vt* [VP6A,14] **awe (into),** strike with awe, fill with awe: *I was awed by his solemn words. He awed them into obedience. The children were awed into silence.*

aweigh /əˈweɪ/ *adv* (naut, of an anchor) hanging just clear of the sea bottom.

aw·ful /ˋɔfl/ *adj* **1** terrible; dreadful: *He died an ~ death. His sufferings were ~ to behold.* **2** (colloq, intensive) very bad; very great; extreme of its kind: *What an ~ nuisance! What ~ handwriting/weather!* **~ly** /ˋɔflɪ/ *adv* (chiefly colloq) very (much): *It has been ~ly hot this week. I'm ~ly sorry. Thanks ~ly.*

awhile /əˋwɑɪl *US:* əˋhwɑɪl/ *adv* for a short time: *stay ~.*

awk·ward /ˋɔkwəd/ *adj* **1** (of objects, places) not well designed for use; (of circumstances, etc) likely to cause inconvenience or difficulty: *This is an ~ staircase. This is an ~ corner; there have been several road accidents here. The handle of this teapot has an ~ shape. The meeting was at 9 o'clock, which was an ~ time for many people. It's ~ that Brown should be unable to play in our team this week.* **an ~ customer,** (colloq) person or animal difficult or dangerous to deal with. **2** (of living things) clumsy; having little skill: *The child is still ~ with his knife and fork. Some animals are ~ on land but able to move easily in the water.* **the ˋ~ age,** years when adolescents are lacking in self-confidence. **3** embarrassed: *an ~ silence/pause.* **~·ly** *adv* **ˋ~·ness** *n*

awl /ɔl/ *n* small pointed tool for making holes, esp in leather or wood. ⇨ the illus at tool.

awn·ing /ˋɔnɪŋ/ *n* canvas covering (against rain or sun), e g over a ship's deck, over or before doors or windows.

awoke ⇨ awake.

awry /əˋrɑɪ/ *adv, pred adj* crooked(ly); wrong(ly): *Our plans have gone ~,* have gone wrong.

ax, axe /æks/ *n* (*pl* **axes** /ˋæksɪz/) tool for felling trees or splitting wood, ⇨ the illus at tool: *apply the axe to public expenditure,* reduce its cost by economies, etc. **ˈhave an ˋaxe to grind,** (fig) have private interests to serve. **get the axe,** (colloq) be dismissed from one's job. □ *vt* [VP6A] reduce, e g costs, public services; dismiss: *He's just been axed,* i e to save money.

ax·iom /ˋæksɪəm/ *n* statement accepted as true without proof or argument. **axio·matic** /ˈæksɪəˋmætɪk/ *adj* of the nature of an ~; clear and evident without proof: *It is ~atic that a whole is greater than any of its parts.*

axis /ˋæksɪs/ *n* (*pl* **axes** /ˋæksiz/) **1** line round which a turning object spins. **the earth's ~,** the imaginary line joining the North and South Poles through the centre of the earth, on which the earth rotates once in twenty-four hours. **2** line that divides a regular figure into two symmetrical parts, e g the diameter of a circle. **3** political connection (not always an alliance) between two or more states: *the Berlin—Rome—Tokyo A~* (before 1939); *A~ powers.*

axle /ˋæksl/ *n* **1** rod upon or with which a wheel turns. **2** bar or rod that passes through the centres of a pair of wheels: *the back ~ of a bus.*

ayah /ˋɑɪə/ *n* (In India and Pakistan) native nursemaid; lady's maidservant.

ay, aye /ɑɪ/ *int, adv* (Scot and regional) yes; (naval) usual reply to an order: *Aye, aye, sir!* □ *n pl* vote or person supporting a proposal: *The ayes have it,* Those for it are in the majority.

aye /eɪ/ *adv* (old use) always: *for ~.*

aza·lea /əˋzeɪlɪə/ *n* kinds of flowering shrub of the rhododendron genus.

azi·muth /ˋæzɪməθ/ *n* (astron) angular distance extending from the zenith to the horizon; (survey) angle measured clockwise from the south or north.

az·ure /ˋæʒə(r)/ *adj, n* (poet) bright blue: *an ~ sky.*

Bb

B, b /bi/ (*pl* **B's, b's** /biz/) the second letter of the English alphabet.

baa /bɑ/ *n* cry of a sheep or lamb. □ *vi* (**baaing, baaed** or *baa'd* /bɑd/) make this cry; bleat. **ˋ~-lamb** *n* child's word for a sheep or lamb.

baas /bɑs/ *n* (form of address used by S African non-European workmen to a European) boss.

babble /ˋbæbl/ *vi,vt* **1** [VP2A,B,C] talk in a way that is difficult to understand; make sounds like a baby; (of streams, etc) murmur. **2** [VP6A,15B] repeat foolishly; tell (a secret): *~ (out) nonsense/secrets.* □ *n* [U] **1** childish or foolish talk; confused talk not clearly to be understood (as when many people are talking at once). **2** gentle sound of water flowing over stones, etc. **bab·bler** *n* person who ~s, esp one who tells secrets.

babe /beɪb/ *n* **1** (liter) baby. **2** inexperienced and easily deceived person. **3** (US sl) girl or young woman.

babel /ˋbeɪbl/ *n* **1** *the Tower of B~,* tower built to reach heaven. (*Gen* 11). **2** (*sing* with *indef art*) scene of noisy and confused talking: *What a ~! A ~ of voices could be heard from the schoolroom.*

ba·boo, babu /ˋbɑbu/ *n* (as Hindu title) Mr; Hindu gentleman; Hindu clerk; (old use, pej) Hindu affecting English speech and manners.

ba·boon /bəˋbun *US:* bæ-/ *n* large monkey (of Africa and southern Asia) with a dog-like face.

baby /ˋbeɪbɪ/ *n* (*pl* **-bies**) **1** very young child: *She has a ˈ~-ˋboy/ˋgirl. Which of you is the ~* (= the youngest member) *of the family?* **(be left) carrying/holding/to carry/to hold the ~,** (colloq) be left responsible for sth one does not wish to be responsible for (because of its difficulty or distastefulness. **ˋ~ carriage,** (US) = (GB) pram. **ˋ~-farmer** *n* (often pej) woman who contracts to keep (esp unwanted) babies. **ˋ~-minder** *n* woman paid to look after a ~ for long periods (e g while the mother is out working). **ˋ~-sit·ter** *n* person paid to look after a ~ for a short time (e g while its parents are at the cinema). Hence, ˋ~-**sit** *vi*, ˋ~-**sit·ting** *n* ˋ~-**talk** *n* kind of speech used by or to babies with distorted vocabulary and syntax. **2** (used attrib) very small of its kind: *a* ˋ~ *car*, a small motor-car; *a* ~ *grand*, a small grand piano; ˋ~-*face* (*d*). **3** (sl) girl; sweetheart. □ *vt* [VP6A] (colloq) treat like a ~: *Don't* ~ *the boy!* ˋ~-**hood** *n* state of being a ~; time when one is a ~. ~-**ish** *adj* of or like a ~: ~*ish behaviour*.

bac·ca·laur·eate /ˌbækəˋlɔrɪət/ *n* (F) university degree of Bachelor.

bac·ca·rat, bac·cara /ˋbækərɑ/ *n* [U] gambling game with playing cards.

bac·cha·nal /ˋbækənæl/ *adj* **1** of or like Bacchus (the Gk god of wine) or his rites. **2** wild, excited, drunken: *a* ~ *feast*. □ *n* **1** follower of Bacchus; drunken reveller. **2** dance or song in honour of Bacchus; merrymaking. **bac·cha·na·lian** /ˌbækəˋneɪlɪən/ *adj* of ~s; noisy and drunken.

baccy /ˋbækɪ/ *n* [U] (colloq) tobacco.

bach·elor /ˋbætʃələ(r)/ *n* **1** unmarried man. ⇨ spinster; (attrib) of, suitable for, an unmarried person: *a* ~ (= independent unmarried) *girl*; ~ *flats*. **2** (man or woman who has taken the) first university degree: *B*~ *of Arts/Science*.

ba·cil·lus /bəˋsɪləs/ *n* (*pl* -cilli /-laɪ-/) rod-like bacterium, esp one of the types that cause disease.

back[1] /bæk/ *n* **1** (of the human body) surface of the body from the neck to the buttocks, ⇨ the illus at trunk: *If you lie on your* ~, *you can look up at the sky. He slipped and fell on his* ~. ***at the* ~ *of sb, at sb's* ~,** giving support or protection: *He knows that he has the head of the Department at his* ~, that the head is ready to support him. Cf *back sb up*. ***do/say sth behind sb's* ~,** without his knowledge (always in connection with sth unpleasant, such as slander). ***break sb's* ~,** give him too much to do. ***break the* ~ *of sth*** (e g a piece of work), finish the hardest or larger part of it. ***get off sb's* ~,** stop being a burden or hindrance. ***give sb a* ~, *make a* ~ *for sb*,** bend down in the game of leapfrog (or to enable sb to climb on one's ~ in order to get over a wall, etc). ***be glad to see the* ~ *of sb*,** feel pleased to see him go away. ***have/with one's* ~ *to the wall*,** in a difficult position, forced to defend oneself. ***be on one's* ~,** (esp) be ill in bed. ***put one's* ~ *into sth*,** work at it with all one's energy. ***put/get sb's* ˋ~ *up*,** make him angry. ***turn one's* ~ *on sb*,** turn away from him in an impolite way; avoid, shun, him. **2** upper surface of an animal's body: *Fasten the saddle on the horse's* ~. **3** that part of a chair or seat on which a person's ~ rests. **4** that surface of an object that is less used, less visible or important: *the* ~ *of one's hand*, (with the nails and knuckles, ⇨ the illus at hand). *You can't cut with the* ~ *of the knife. You can't see the* ~ *of your head. You write the address on the front of an envelope, not on the* ~. **5** that part of a thing that is farthest from the front: *a room at the* ~ *of the house; a garden at the* ~ *of a house*. **the B~s,** lawns and grounds (on the River Cam) of some Cambridge colleges. **6 *break her* ~,** (of a ship) break in two. **7** (football) (*centre*-ˋ~; *half*-ˋ~) player whose position is behind, near the goal. ⇨ the illus at football.

back[2] /bæk/ *adv part* **1** to or at the rear; away from the front: *Stand* ~, *please! The police held the crowd* ~. *Fasten the curtains* ~. *Sit* ~ *in your chair and be comfortable. The house stands* ~ (i e at some distance) *from the road*. ***go* ~ *(up)on/from one's word*,** fail to keep a promise. ***(in)* ~ *of*,** (US colloq) behind: *the houses* ~ *of the church*. **2** in (to) an earlier position or condition: *Put the dictionary* ~ *on the shelf. Throw the ball* ~ *to me. Call that boy* ~. *We shall be* ~ (= home again) *before dark. Shall we walk* ~ *or ride* ~? *How far is it there and* ~? *My brother is just* ~ (i e has just returned home) *from Paris. The company is now* ~ *on its feet*, has re-established itself after a period of financial, etc difficulties. **3** in return: *If I hit you, would you hit me* ~? *Don't answer* ~, Don't retort or argue. *When can you pay* ~ (= repay) *the money you borrowed?* ***have/get one's* ˋ*own* ~ *(on sb)*,** (colloq) have one's revenge. **4** (of time) ago; into the past: *some few years* ~; *far* ~ *in the Middle Ages*.

back[3] /bæk/ *vt, vi* **1** [VP6A,15A,2A,C] go or cause to go ~: *The horse* ~*ed suddenly. He* ~*ed the car into/out of the garage. The wind* ~*ed*, changed gradually in an anti-clockwise direction (e g from E through NE to N). ⇨ veer. **~ *the oars*, ~ *water*,** use the oars to reverse a boat's forward motion. **2** [VP6A,15B] support: ~ *a friend in an argument or quarrel*; ~ *a plan*; ~ *sb up*, support him in every way. **~ *a bill/note*,** endorse it as a promise to pay money if necessary. **3** [VP6A] bet money on (a horse, a greyhound): *The favourite was heavily* ~*ed*, much money was bet on its winning the race. **4** [VP2C] **~ *down (from)*,** give up a claim, etc: *I see he has* ~*ed down from the position he took last week*. Hence, ˋ~-**down** *n* **~ *off*,** give up a claim. **~ *out (of)*,** withdraw (from a promise or undertaking): *He promised to help and then* ~*ed out. He's trying to* ~ *out of his bargain*, escape from the agreement. **5** [VP6A] put or be a lining to; put on as a surface at the ~: ~*ed with sheet iron*. **6** [VP6A,3A] be situated at the ~ of: *Our garden* ~*s theirs. Their house* ~*s on to our garden*. ~**er** *n* **1** person who ~s a horse. **2** person who gives support or help (e g to a political movement); person who gives financial support to an undertaking. ~**·ing** *n* [U] **1** help; support; (with *indef art*) body of supporters: *The new leader has a large* ~*ing*. **2** material used to form a thing's ~ or support. **3** (pop music) musical accompaniment to a singer: *vocal/instrumental* ~*ing*.

back[4] /bæk/ (used attrib, and in compounds, with references to the articles on the *n*, *adv part* and *v* above) **1** ⇨ back[1](1,2). ˋ~**·ache** *n* [U] ache or pain in the ~. ˋ~**·band** *n* strap over a horse's cart-saddle, supporting the shafts of a cart or carriage. ˋ~**·bone** *n* **(a)** line of bones down the middle of the ~, ⇨ the illus at skeleton, from the skull to the hips; spinal column; (fig) chief support: *Such men are the* ~*bone of the country*. **(b)** [U] (fig) strength; firmness: *He hasn't enough* ~*bone*, is weak in character. **(c) *to the* ~*bone*,** (fig) completely; in every way: *He's British to the* ~*bone*. ˋ~-**break·ing** *adj* (of work) exhausting. **2** ⇨ back[1](4,5). ˈ~ˋ**hand(ed)** *adj*: ~-*hand blow/stroke*, one that is delivered with the ~ of the hand turned outwards, or in a direction different from what is usual or expected. Hence, (fig): *a* ~-*handed compliment*, one that is ambiguous (e g suggesting sarcasm). ˋ~**·scratcher** *n* **(a)** device with claws on a long handle for scratching the ~ (when there is an irritation, etc). **(b)** ⇨ scratch *v*(5). ˋ~-**stroke** *n* ~-handed stroke. ˋ~**·sword** *n* sword with only one cutting edge. **3** ⇨ back[1](5) and **back**²(**1**). '~-*to*-`~, (of housing) of two rows of terrace houses, often separated by a narrow alley, with the ~s facing. '~-`**bencher** *n* person occupying one of the seats in the House of Commons (or other law-making body) used by those members, who, because they do not or have not held office, are not entitled to a front-bench seat. ⇨ **bench(3)**. `~-**blocks** *n pl* (in Australia) areas of land a long way from a railway, river, the sea-coast, etc and thinly populated. `~·**board** *n* movable board at the ~ of a cart. `~·**cloth** *n* painted cloth or other material hung at the ~ of a stage in a theatre, as part of the scenery. '~-`**door** *n* door at the ~ of a house or other building; (attrib, fig) secret or indirect; clandestine: *~ influence.* `~·**drop** *n* = ~cloth. '~·**ground** *n* **(a)** that part of a view, scene (and, fig, a description) that serves as a setting for the chief objects, persons, etc. ⇨ **foreground. (b)** person's past experiences, education, environment. **(c)** contemporary condition(s): *the social and political ~ground;* (comm) details necessary to an understanding of company business: *B~ground information will be supplied at the Board meeting.* **(d)** obscurity: *be/keep/stay in the ~ground.* **(e)** *~ground music/effects, etc,* music, etc that accompanies dialogue, action, etc (e g in a radio or TV programme or a cinema film) but is not essential to the story, etc. **~·less** *adj* (of a dress), not covering the ~; cut to the waist at the ~: *a ~less gown.* `~·**most** *adj* farthest from the front. `~-**room** *n* room at the ~ of a building: *~room boys,* (colloq) scientists, engineers, research workers in offices and laboratories. '~·`**seat** *n* seat at the ~. ***take a ~seat,*** (fig) behave as if one were unimportant; humble oneself. '~·**seat** `**driver,** passenger (in a car) who corrects or advises the driver. `~·**side** *n* (not used in polite society) buttocks: *give sb a kick on the ~side.* '~·`**stage** *adv* **(a)** behind the scenes (in a theatre): *I was taken ~stage by the leading actor.* **(b)** (attrib): *~stage life,* of actors and actresses when not on the stage. '~·`**stair** *adj* secret; underhand: *~stair influence.* '~·`**stairs** *n* staircase from servants' quarters: (attrib) *~stairs gossip,* i e among servants. `~-**stays** *n pl* (naut) set of ropes from the mast-head to the sides of a ship, sloping towards the stern. `~·**wash** *n* movement of water going away in waves, esp the rush of water behind a ship; (fig) unpleasant after-effects of sth done. `~·**water** *n* **(a)** part of a river not reached by its current, where the water does not flow. **(b)** (fig) place, condition of mind, untouched by events, progress, etc: *living in an intellectual ~water,* untouched by new ideas, etc. `~·**woods** *n pl* uncleared forest land (esp in N America). '~·`**woodsman** /-mən/ *n* (*pl* -men) man who lives in the ~woods. ~ `**yard** *n* (esp of terraced houses) (usu paved) area at the ~ of a house: *The dustbin is kept in the ~ yard.* **4** ⇨ **back²(1).** to an earlier point in time; to a former place. '~·`**date** *vt* date ~ to a time in the past: *The wage increases are to be ~dated to the first of January.* '~·`**fire** *n* (sound caused by the) too early explosion of gas in an internal combustion engine, causing the piston to move in the wrong direction. □ *vi* produce, make the sound of, a ~fire; (fig) produce an unexpected or undesired result: *The plot ~fired.* `~-**formation** *n* [U,C] (process of making a) word that appears to be the root of a longer word (e g *televise,* from *television*). `~·**log** *n* accumulation of work or business (e g arrears of unfulfilled orders) not yet attended to. `~·**number** *n* **(a)** issue of a periodical of an earlier date, not now on sale. **(b)** (fig, colloq) out-of-date or old-fashioned method, thing, person, etc. `~ **pay/rent/taxes, etc,** *n* pay, etc in arrears; pay, etc that is overdue. '~·`**pedal** *vi* (on a bicycle, etc) pedal ~wards; (fig) retreat hurriedly from sth stated or promised. '~·`**slide** *vi* [VP2A] fall back from good ways into bad old ways of living; lose interest in religious practice, morality, etc. '~-`**space** *vi* move the carriage of a typewriter ~ one or more spaces by pressing the key (called the `~spacer key) used for this purpose. **5** ⇨ **back²(3).** in return; in reply. `~·**bite** *vt,vi* slander the reputation of (sb who is absent); speak slanderously about an absent person. Hence, `~·**biter** *n* person who ~bites. `~·**chat** *n* [U] (colloq) (exchange of) impertinent remarks: *I want none of your ~chat.* `~·**lash** *n* [U] **(a)** excessive movement caused by loose connections between mechanical parts (often causing ~ward movement). **(b)** (fig) antagonistic reaction (esp in social or race relations). `~·**talk** *n* [U] ~chat; insolent contradiction.

back·gam·mon /bæk`gæmən/ *n* [U] game for two players, played on a special double board with draughts and dice.

back·sheesh ⇨ **baksheesh**.

back·ward /`bækwəd/ *adj* **1** towards the back or the starting-point: *a ~ glance/movement; a ~ flow of water.* **2** having made, making, less than the usual or normal progress: *This part of the country is still ~; there are no railways or roads and no electricity. Because of his long illness, Tom is ~ in his studies.* Cf *well up in. Spring is ~ this year.* **3** shy; reluctant; hesitating: *Although he is clever, he is ~ in giving his views.* **~(s)** *adv* **1** away from one's front; towards the back: *He looked ~s over his shoulder.* **2** with the back or the end first: *It's not easy to walk ~s. Can you say the alphabet ~(s),* i e ZYXWV, etc? ***know sth ~s,*** know it perfectly; be quite familiar with it. it. ***~s and forwards,*** first in one direction and then in the other: *walking ~s and forwards; travelling ~s and forwards between London and the south coast.*

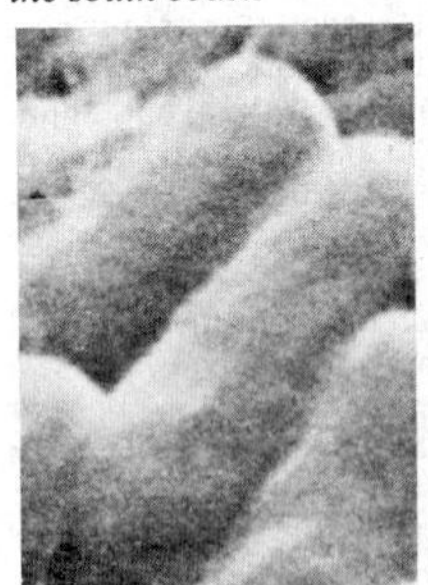
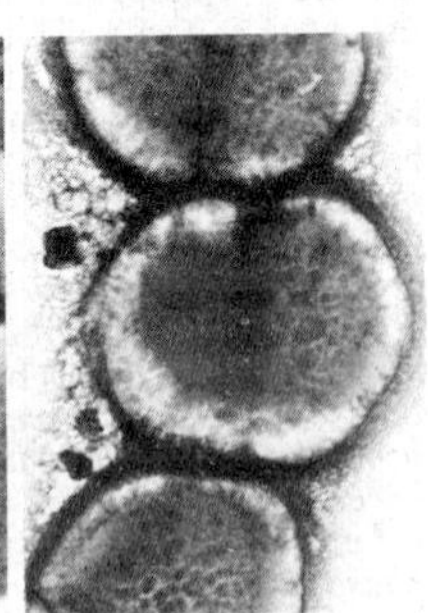

bacteria

bacon /`beɪkən/ *n* [U] salted or smoked meat from the back or sides of a pig. ***bring home the ~,*** (sl) succeed in one's undertaking. ***save one's ~,*** (colloq) escape death, injury, a reprimand.

bac·terium /bæk`tɪərɪəm/ *n* (*pl* -ria /-rɪə/) (kinds of) simplest and smallest form of plant life, existing in air, water and soil, and in living and dead creatures and plants, essential to animal life and sometimes a cause of disease. **bac·terial** /-rɪəl/ *adj* of bacteria: *bacterial contamination.* **bac·teri·ol·ogy** /bæk'tɪərɪ`olədʒɪ/ *n* science or study of bacteria. **bac·teri·ol·ogist** /-dʒɪst/ *n* student of, expert in, bacteriology.

bad[1] /bæd/ *adj* (**worse, worst**) **1** wicked, evil, immoral: *It is bad to steal. He leads a bad life.* ***act in bad faith,*** dishonestly, insincerely. ***bad language,*** swear words; the use of words connected with holy and sacred things in a wrong and disrespectful way. ***a bad lot/egg/hat,*** (dated sl) a good-for-nothing person. ***a bad word,*** a profane or obscene word. ***call sb bad names,*** call him insulting names. **2** unpleasant; disagreeable; unwelcome: *We've had bad news. What bad weather we're having! There's a bad smell here. The manner of his dismissal left a bad odour,* (fig) left unpleasant feelings. ***(be) in bad (with),*** (US colloq) in disfavour: *He's in bad with the boss.* **3** (of things, etc that are never good) definite; decided; notable: *That was a bad blunder/mistake. He has had a bad* (= serious) *accident. He had a bad headache. There has been a bad falling off in attendance at church.* **4** inferior; worthless; incorrect; of poor quality: *His pronunciation of English is bad. He speaks bad English. What a bad translation! You can't take photographs if the light is bad. The egg was bad and smelt horrible.* ***not bad/not so bad/not half bad,*** (colloq understatement) quite good. ***be in a bad way,*** be very ill or unfortunate; be in trouble or difficulty. ***go bad,*** become unfit to eat: *Fish and meat soon go bad in hot weather.* ***go from bad to worse,*** get worse every day. ***with bad grace,*** showing unwillingness. ***a bad business/job,*** (colloq) an unfortunate affair. ***a bad debt,*** one that is unlikely to be paid. ***bad law,*** law that cannot be sustained or held to be valid. ***bad shot,*** (fig) wrong guess. **`bad-lands** /-lændz/ *n pl* (US) barren infertile regions. **5** ***bad for,*** hurtful or injurious for; unsuitable for: *Smoking is bad for the health. Very small print is bad for the eyes. It's bad for him to live alone.* **6** in ill health, diseased: *a bad* (= sore) finger; a bad leg, causing pain; (colloq) *She feels bad today. She was taken bad* (= fell ill) *during the night.* **7** (colloq) unfortunate: *It's too bad she's so ill.* **8** (colloq) sorry; bothered: *I feel so bad about not being able to help you.* **bad·ly** *adv* (**worse, worst**) (Cf *well, better, best.*) **1** in a bad manner; roughly; untidily, etc: *badly made/dressed/wounded.* **2** by much: *badly beaten at football; badly in need of repair.* **3** (with *want, need*) very much: *She wants it badly.* **4** ***badly off,*** poor. **bad·ness** *n* quality of being bad: *the badness of the weather/climate.*

bad[2] /bæd/ *n* [U] **1** that which is bad: *take the bad with the good,* take bad fortune with good fortune. ***go to the bad,*** become completely immoral; become ruined. **2** ***to the bad,*** on the wrong side of the account: *I am £50 to the bad,* have lost £50 as the result (of the deal, etc).

bade /bæd/ ⇨ **bid**[1]**(3)**.

badge /bædʒ/ *n* **1** sth worn (usu a design on cloth or made of metal) to show a person's occupation, rank, etc or membership of a society. **2** (fig) sth that shows a quality or condition: *Chains are a ~ of slavery.*

badger[1] /`bædʒə(r)/ *n* small, grey animal living in holes in the earth and going about at night. ⇨ the illus at small.

badger[2] /`bædʒə(r)/ *vt* [VP6A,14,16A] worry or tease (*with* questions, requests, etc *for* sth): *Tom has been ~ing his uncle to buy him a camera. I was ~ed into doing what she wanted.*

ba·di·nage /`bædɪnɑʒ *US:* 'bædn̩`ɑʒ/ *n* [U] banter.

bad·min·ton /`bædmɪntən/ *n* game played with rackets and shuttlecocks across a high, narrow net.

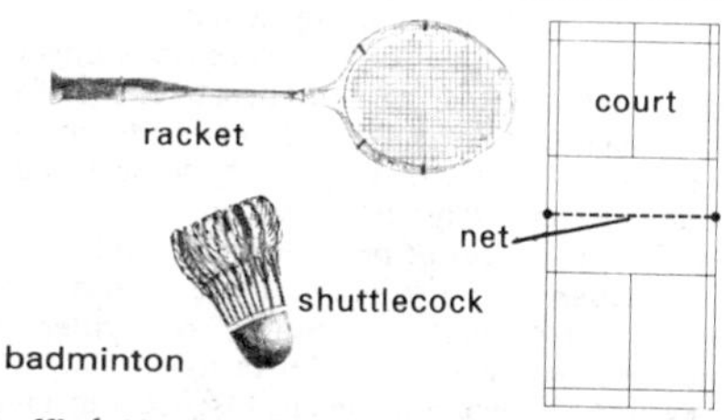

baffle[1] /`bæfl/ *vt* [VP6A] puzzle; prevent (sb) from doing sth; be too difficult to do, understand, etc: *One of the examination questions ~d me completely. They were ~d in their attempt. The scene ~d all description,* could not be described.

baffle[2] /`bæfl/ *n* plate, board, screen or other device, used to hinder or control the flow of a gas, a liquid or sound through an inlet or outlet.

bag[1] /bæg/ *n* **1** container made of flexible material (paper, cloth, leather) with an opening at the top, used for carrying things from place to place: *`money-bag; `travelling-bag; `handbag; `kitbag; `tool-bag; `mailbag,* ⇨ these words. ***bag and baggage,*** with all one's belongings (used esp of sb who is expelled). ***a bag of bones,*** a lean person or animal. ***let the cat out of the bag,*** tell a secret (without intending to do so). ***pack one's bags,*** pack (for a journey). ***the whole bag of tricks,*** (colloq) everything needed for a purpose; the whole lot. **2** (= *`game-bag*) contents of a game-bag; all the birds, animals, etc shot or caught: *They secured a good bag.* ***be in the bag,*** (colloq) (of results, outcomes, etc) be as desired: *The election is in the bag.* **3** ***bags of,*** (sl) plenty of: *There's bags of room. He has bags of money.* **4** ***bags under the eyes,*** (colloq) puffiness under the eyes. **`bag·man** /-mən/ *n* (*pl* **-men**) (colloq) commercial traveller. **`bag·pipes** *n pl* musical instrument with air stored in a wind-bag held under one arm and pressed out through pipes in which there are reeds. ⇨ the illus at kilt.

bag[2] /bæg/ *vt,vi* (**-gg-**) **1** [VP6A,15B] put into a bag or bags: *to bag* (*up*) *wheat.* **2** [VP6A] (of sportsmen) kill or catch: *They bagged nothing except a couple of rabbits.* **3** [VP6A] (colloq) take (sb else's property, etc without permission, but not intending to steal): *Who has bagged my matches? She bagged* (= occupied, sat in) *the most comfortable chair. Try to bag an empty table,* secure one (e g in a crowded restaurant). **4** [VP2A,C] hang loosely, looking like a cloth bag: *trousers that bag at the knees.*

baga·telle /'bægə`tel/ *n* **1** [U] kind of game like billiards, played on a board with holes instead of pockets. **2** [C] (often *a mere ~*) sth small and of no importance. **3** [U] musical trifle.

bag·gage /`bægɪdʒ/ *n* [U] **1** (more usu, except in US, *luggage*) all the bags, trunks, etc with which a person travels. **`~ room,** (US) = (GB) left luggage office. **2** tents, bedding, equipment, etc, of an army: '~ *animals,* '~ *train, etc,* animals, carts, trucks, etc, carrying ~. **3** (playfully) saucy girl: *You little ~!*

baggy /ˈbægɪ/ *adj* hanging in loose folds: *trousers ~ at the knees; ~ skin under the eyes.*

bagnio /ˈbɑnɪəʊ/ *n* (old use) **1** prison. **2** brothel.

bags /bægz/ *n pl* (colloq) baggy trousers: *Oxford ~.* ⇨ debag.

bah /bɑ/ *int* used as a sign of contempt.

bail[1] /beɪl/ *n* [U] sum of money demanded by a law court, paid by or for a person accused of wrongdoing, as security that he will appear for his trial, until which time he is allowed to go free. ***go/put in/stand ~ (for sb),*** pay money to secure his freedom in this way. ***(be) out on ~,*** free after payment of ~. ***forfeit one's ~,*** fail to appear for trial. ***refuse ~,*** (of a judge) refuse to accept ~ and give freedom to a prisoner. ***surrender to one's ~,*** appear for trial after being out on ~. □ *vt* [VP15B] ***~ sb out,*** obtain his freedom until trial by payment of ~. **~ee** /ˈbeɪˈli/ *n* (legal) person(s) to whom permission is given to have the goods of another (e g a laundry which accepts goods for washing or dry-cleaning). **~ment** *n* (legal) delivery of goods to a ~ee. **~or** /ˈbeɪlɔ(r)/ *n* (legal) one who delivers goods to a ~ee.

bail[2] /beɪl/ *n* (cricket) either of the two cross pieces over the three stumps. ⇨ the illus at cricket.

bail[3] /beɪl/ *vt,vi* **1** [VP6A,15B,2A,C] throw water out of a boat with buckets, etc: *~ing water (out); ~ing (out) the boat.* **2** (sometimes used for) bale[2].

bailey /ˈbeɪlɪ/ *n* outer wall of a castle; courtyard of a castle enclosed by strong walls. **Old B~,** London Central Criminal Court.

Bailey bridge /ˈbeɪlɪ brɪdʒ/ *n* bridge (in prefabricated sections) designed for speedy assembly, used for spanning rivers, etc. ⇨ the illus at bridge.

bail·iff /ˈbeɪlɪf/ *n* **1** law officer who helps a sheriff. **2** landowner's agent or manager.

bairn /beən/ *n* (Scot and N England) child.

bait[1] /beɪt/ *n* **1** food, or sth made in imitation, put on a hook to catch fish, or in nets, traps, etc to attract prey: *live ~,* small fish used as ~ to catch large fish. *The fish took/swallowed/rose to/nibbled at the ~.* **2** (fig) sth that allures or tempts.

bait[2] /beɪt/ *vt,vi* **1** [VP 6A] put food, real or imitation, (on a hook, etc) to catch fish, etc: *~ a hook with a worm.* **2** [VP6A,2A] give food to (horses on a journey); (of horses) take food. **3** [VP6A] worry (a chained animal) by making dogs attack it: *'bear-~ing; 'bull-~ing; ~ a bear with dogs.* **4** [VP6A] torment (sb) by making cruel or insulting remarks.

baize /beɪz/ *n* [U] thick woollen cloth, usu green, used for covering (tables, etc): *a ~-covered door; green ~ for the billiard-table.*

bake /beɪk/ *vt,vi* [VP6A,22,2A,C] **1** cook, be cooked, by dry heat in an oven: *~ bread/cakes; ~d beans. The bread is baking/being ~d.* **2** make or become hard by heating: *The sun ~d the ground hard. Bricks and earthenware articles are ~d in kilns.* **3** be warmed or tanned: *We are baking in the sun.* **ˈhalf-~d** *adj* (colloq) half-witted; lacking in experience or common sense: *half-~d ideas; a half-~d prophet.* **ˈbaking-ˈhot** *adj* very hot: *a baking-hot day.* **ˈbaking-powder** *n* mixture of powders used to make bubbles of gas in cakes, etc and so cause them to be light. **baker** *n* person who ~s bread, etc. **~r's dozen,** thirteen. **bak·ery** /ˈbeɪkərɪ/ *n* place where bread is ~d for many people.

bake·lite /ˈbeɪkəlɑɪt/ *n* [U] (P) synthetic resin compound as used for old fountain pens, trays, telephones, etc.

bak·sheesh /ˈbækʃiʃ/ *n* [U] (in the Middle East) money given as a tip or as alms: *The porter expects ~ from you.*

bala·laika /ˈbæləˈlɑɪkə/ *n* guitar-like musical instrument (triangular, with three strings), popular in Russia and other countries in eastern Europe. ⇨ the illus at string.

bal·ance[1] /ˈbæləns/ *vt,vi* **1** [VP6A,14] weigh (a question, etc); compare (two objects, plans, etc) (in order to judge the relative weight, value, etc). **2** [VP6A,15A] keep or put (sth, oneself) in a state of balance: *Can you ~ a stick on the end of your nose? How long can you ~ (yourself) on one foot?* **3** [VP6A] (accounts) compare debits and credits and record the sum needed to make them equal. ***~ the budget,*** arrange for income and expenditure to be equal. [VP2A] (of the two sides of a balance-sheet) be equal: *My accounts ~.* **4 *a ~d diet,*** one with the quantity and variety of food needed for good health.

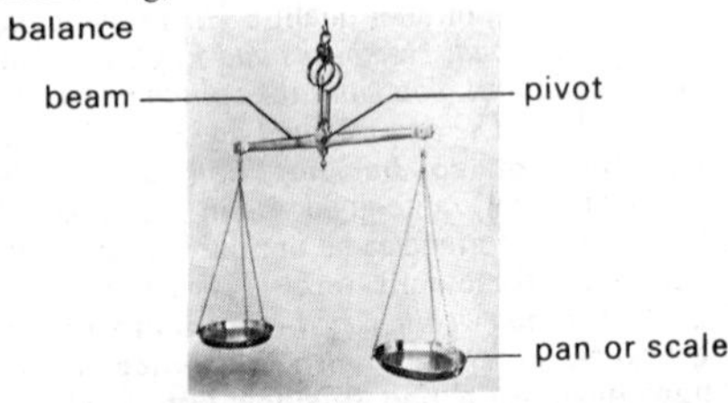

bal·ance[2] /ˈbæləns/ *n* **1** apparatus for weighing, with a central pivot, beam and two scales or pans. ***be/hang in the ~,*** (fig, of a result) be still uncertain: *For a long time his fate was in the ~.* **2** regulating apparatus of a watch or clock. **'~-wheel** *n* wheel, in a watch, that regulates the beat. **3** [U] condition of being steady; condition that exists when two opposing forces are equal. ***checks and ~s,*** ⇨ check[2](1). ***hold the ~,*** have the power to decide. ***in the ~,*** undecided. ***keep one's ~,*** keep steady, remain upright: *A small child has to learn to keep its ~ before it can walk far. Don't get excited; keep your ~,* (fig) keep calm. ***lose one's ~,*** become unsteady; fall; (fig) be upset mentally: *He was surrounded by so many dangers that he lost his ~,* became nervous and upset. ***throw sb off his ~,*** upset him; cause him to fall. ***~ of power,*** condition in which no one country or group of countries is much stronger than another. **4** [U] (in art) harmony of design and proportion: *a picture lacking in ~.* **5** (accounts) difference between two columns of an account (money received and money paid out, etc). ***on ~,*** taking everything into consideration. ***strike a ~ (between...),*** find this difference; (fig) reach a solution or adjustment considered to be fair to all; (fig) compromise; find a middle course. ***~ of payments,*** statement (for a stated period) of the total payments to foreign countries (for imports, outflow of capital and gold) and the total receipts from foreign countries (for exports, inflow of capital and gold). ***~ of trade,*** difference in value between exports and imports. **'~-sheet,** written statement of this difference, with details, showing credit and debit. **6** amount still owed after a part payment: *~ to be paid within one week.* **7 *the ~,*** (colloq) the remainder of anything; what is left.

bal·cony /ˋbælkənɪ/ *n* (*pl* **-nies**) **1** platform (with a wall or rail) built on an outside wall of a building, reached from an upstairs room. **2** (in a theatre or concert hall) series of rows of seats above floor-level and (usu) rising one above the other. (US = *gallery.*) ˋ**bal·conied** *adj* having a ~ or balconies: *a balconied house.*

bald /bɔld/ *adj* **1** (of men) having no or not much hair on the scalp; (of animals) hairless; (of birds) featherless; (of trees) leafless; (of land, hills, etc) without trees or bushes. **2** (fig) dull; without ornament: *a ~ style of writing: a ~ statement of the facts,* one that gives the facts in an uninteresting way. **3** ˋ**~-head,** ˋ**~-pate** *n* man with a ~ head. ***go at it*** ˈ***~-***ˋ***headed,*** (colloq) attack or deal with it in a reckless manner, using all one's energy. **~·ly** *adv* (always fig): *speaking ~ly; to put it ~ly,* plainly, without trying to soften what one says. **~·ness** *n*

bal·der·dash /ˋbɔldədæʃ/ *n* [U] foolish or meaningless talk or writing.

bal·dric /ˋbɔldrɪk/ *n* belt (passing over the right shoulder to the left hip) for a sword, bugle, horn, etc.

bale[1] /beɪl/ *n* [C] heap of material pressed together and tied with rope or wire: *~s of cloth,* (usu packed in canvas); *~s of hay,* (tied in string). □ *vt* [VP6A] make into, pack in, ~s: *to ~ hay.*

bale[2] /beɪl/ *vt* = bail³(2). **~ *out (of),*** (of an airman) jump with a parachute from a damaged aircraft or an aircraft out of control.

bale[3] /beɪl/ *n* (old use, liter) evil. **~·ful** /ˋbeɪlfl/ *adj* evil; sinister, harmful: *~ful looks/influences.* **~·fully** /-flɪ/ *adv*

balk, baulk[1] /bɔk/ *n* **1** thick, roughly squared beam of wood. **2** hindrance; obstacle; cause of delay.

balk, baulk[2] /bɔk/ *vt,vi* **1** [VP6A,14] purposely get in the way of: *~ sb's plans,* prevent him from carrying them out; *~ sb of his prey,* prevent him from getting it; *be ~ed in one's purpose.* **2** [VP2A,3A] **~ *(at),*** (e g of a horse) refuse to go forward; hesitate: *The horse ~ed at the high hedge. Her husband ~ed at the expense of the plans she had made.*

ball[1] /bɔl/ *n* **1** any solid or hollow sphere as used in games (ˋ*base~,* ˋ*foot~,* ˋ*tennis-~,* ˋ*cricket-~,* etc). ⇨ the illus at these *nn.* ***be on the ~,*** be alert, competent (in what one is doing). ***have the ~ at one's feet,*** have a good chance of attaining success. ***keep the ~ rolling,*** keep the conversation, etc going. ***play ~,*** (colloq) co-operate: *The management refused to play ~.* ***start/set the ~ rolling,*** start sth, esp conversation, going. ***The ~ is in your/his court, (is with you/him),*** The next move (in talks, etc) is yours/his. **three ~s,** pawnbroker's sign. ˈ**~-**ˋ**bearing(s),** bearings in which friction is lessened by the use of small steel ~s; (*sing*) one of these ~s. ˋ**~(-)cock** *n* device which regulates the supply of water in a tank or cistern by means of a floating ~ which shuts or opens a valve as the water rises and falls. ˋ**~-pen,** ˈ**~-point-**ˋ**pen,** nibless pen with a replaceable tube of ink (a *refill*); the ink flows round a ~-bearing that rotates on contact with the paper. **2** (cricket) single delivery of the ~ by the bowler. ***no ~,*** delivery that breaks the rules; (baseball) any strike or throw: *a foul ~;* (football) movement of the ~ by a player: *send over a high ~.* **3** material gathered, rolled or wound, into a round mass: *a ~ of wool/string; a* ˋ*snow~; a* ˋ*meat~,* of minced meat. **4** metal missile to be fired from a gun: ˋ*cannon-~,* (old fashioned, cf *shell*). ˋ**~-**ˈ**cartridge,** one containing a bullet (contrasted with blank cartridge). **5** round part: *the ~ of the thumb,* near the palm, ⇨ the illus at arm; *the ~ of the foot,* near the base of the big toe, ⇨ the illus at leg; ⚠ (*pl,* vulg) testicles. □ *int* ⚠ (*pl,* vulg) Nonsense! □ *vi* **1** form into a ~: *The snow ~ed under the horse's feet.* **2** wind or squeeze into a ~. **3 *~s up sth,*** (sl) ruin it. Hence, ˋ***~s-up*** *n*

ball[2] /bɔl/ *n* social gathering for dancing, with an organized programme, and (often) special entertainment. ***open the ~,*** set things going. ˋ**~-dress,** woman's frock to be worn at ~s. ˋ**~-room,** large room for ~s. **bal·lad** /ˋbæləd/ *n* simple song or poem, esp one that tells an old story.

bal·lade /bæˋlɑd/ *n* [C] **1** poem of one or more stanzas, each with 7, 8 or 10 lines, each ending with the same refrain line, followed by an envoy. **2** musical composition of a romantic nature.

bal·last /ˋbæləst/ *n* [U] **1** heavy material (e g rock, iron, sand) loaded into a ship to keep it steady. ***in ~,*** carrying ~ only. **2** sand or other material carried in a balloon, to be thrown out to make the balloon go higher. **3** (fig) mental stability. **4** gravel, crushed rock, etc used to make a foundation for a road, esp a railway. □ *vt* [VP6A] supply with ~.

bal·ler·ina /ˈbæləˋrinə/ *n* (I) woman ballet dancer, esp one who takes one of the chief classical roles.

bal·let /ˋbæleɪ/ *n* **1** dramatic performance, without dialogue or singing, illustrating a story by a group of dancers. **2** the dancers: *a member of the ~.* **3 *the ~,*** this kind of stage performance as an art. ˋ**~-dancer,** person who dances in ~s. ˋ**~-skirt,** short skirt worn by a ~ dancer.

bal·lis·tic /bəˋlɪstɪk/ *adj* of projectiles: *intercontinental ~ missiles,* long-range rockets for use in war. **bal·lis·tics** *n* (usu with *sing v*) study, science, of projectiles.

bal·locks /ˋbɔləks/ *n pl* ⚠ (vulg) **1** testicles. **2** nonsense.

bal·loon /bəˋlun/ *n* **1** bag or envelope filled with air, or with gas lighter than air: *captive ~,* one moored to the ground. ˋ**~ barrage,** barrier of steel cables, supported by captive ~s, intended to give protection against low-flying enemy aircraft. ˋ**barrage ~,** one of these captive ~s. **hot-air ~,** apparatus for travel in the air with a basket or car (for the passengers, etc) suspended beneath a large bag of hot gas. ˈ**~** ˋ**tyre,** low-pressure pneumatic tyre of great width. **2** (in a strip cartoon, etc) outline for dialogue, exclamations, etc. □ *vi* [VP2A, C] swell out like a ~. **~·ist** *n* person who goes up in ~s. ⇨ p 60.

bal·lot /ˋbælət/ *n* **1** [C] piece of paper (also ˋ~-*paper*), ticket or ball, used in secret voting; [U] secret voting; [C] instance of this: *take a ~,* decide by voting. **2** votes so recorded. ˋ**~-box,** box into which ~-papers are dropped by voters. □ *vi* [VP2A,3A] **~ *(for),*** give a vote; draw lots: *~ for precedence,* e g in moving resolutions in the House of Commons.

bally /ˋbælɪ/ *adj, adv* (GB sl, euphem for *bloody*) (used to show the speaker's strong feelings of like

balloons

or dislike, etc): *What a ~ nuisance! I'm too ~ tired to do any more.*

bally·hoo /ˈbælɪˈhu *US:* ˋbælɪhu/ *n* [U] (colloq) **1** noisy publicity or advertising; vulgar or misleading ways of attracting attention. **2** uproar.

balm /bɑm/ *n* [U] **1** sweet-smelling oil or ointment obtained from certain kinds of trees, used, for soothing pain or healing. **2** (fig) that which gives peace of mind; consolation. **~y** *adj* **1** (of air) soft and warm. **2** healing; fragrant. **3** (sl) = barmy.

bal·oney /bəˋləʊnɪ/ *n* (sl) nonsense.

balsa /ˋbɔlsə/ *n* [C,U] (light-weight wood of a) tropical American tree; raft of floats fastened to a framework: (attrib) *a ~ raft.*

bal·sam /ˋbɔlsəm/ *n* **1** = balm(1). **2** tree yielding balm. **3** flowering plant grown in gardens.

bal·us·ter /ˋbæləstə(r)/ *n* one of the upright posts supporting a handrail; (*pl*) bannisters. **bal·us·trade** /ˈbæləˋstreɪd/ *n* row of ~s with the stonework or woodwork that joins them on top, round a balcony, terrace, flat roof, etc.

bam·bino /bæmˋbinəʊ/ *n* (I) **1** baby. **2** representation in art of the infant Jesus.

bam·boo /ˈbæmˋbu/ *n* (*pl* **-boos**) [U] tall plant with hard, hollow, jointed stems, of the grass family; [C] stem, used as a stick or support.

bam·boozle /bæmˋbuzl/ *vt* (colloq) [VP6A,14] **1** mystify: *You can't ~ me.* **2** cheat, trick: *~ sb into/out of doing sth.*

ban /bæn/ *vt* (**-nn-**) [VP6A] order with authority that sth must not be done, said, etc: *a ban-the-bomb demonstration,* one calling for nuclear disarmament. *The play was banned by the censor.* □ *n* order that bans sth: *under a ban,* banned.

ba·nal /bəˋnɑl *US:* ˋbeɪnl/ *adj* commonplace; uninteresting: *~ remarks.* **~·ity** /bəˋnælətɪ/ *n* (*pl* **-ties**) [U] quality of being ~; [C] ~ remark, etc: *conversation that was chiefly ~ities.*

ba·nana /bəˋnɑnə *US:* bəˋnænə/ *n* [C] ⇨ the illus at fruit. long, finger-shaped, thick-skinned (yellow when ripe) fruit growing in bunches on the ~-tree in tropical and semi-tropical countries. ⇨ plantain.

band /bænd/ *n* **1** flat, thin strip of material, esp for fastening things together or for placing round an object to strengthen it: *iron ~s round a barrel; papers kept together with a rubber ~.* ˋ**~-saw** *n* (eng) machine-driven saw consisting of an endless steel belt. **2** flat, thin strip of material forming part of an article of clothing: *A man's shirt has a ˋneck~ and two ˋwrist~s.* **3** strip or line, different from the rest in colour or design, on sth: *a white plate with a blue ~ round the edge.* **4** group of persons doing sth together under a leader and with a common purpose: *a ~ of robbers/fugitives/revellers.* **5** group of persons who play music together, e g of wind-instrument performers (often *brass ~*): *the ˈRegimental ˋB~; a ˋdance ~; a ˋjazz ~; a ˋsteel ~.* ˋ**~·master** /ˋbændmɑstə(r)/ *n* conductor of a ~. ˋ**~s·man** /-mən/ *n* (*pl* -men) member of a ~. ˋ**~·stand** /ˋbændstænd/ *n* raised platform usu roofed, for a ~ playing in the open air. ˋ**~·wagon** *n* wagon carrying the ~ heading a march or procession (esp of a political party). ***climb/jump on/aboard the ~wagon,*** join in what seems likely to be a successful enterprise. **6** (radio; short for ˋ*wave-~*) range of frequencies that may be tuned in together: *the 19-metre ~.* □ *vt,vi* **1** [VP6A] put a ~, strip or line on. **2** [VP15,2C] unite in a group: *~ people together; ~ with others to do sth. They ~ed together to protest.*

ban·dage /ˋbændɪdʒ/ *n* strip of material for binding round a wound or injury, or for blindfolding sb. □ *vt* [VP6A,15B] tie up with a ~: *~ (up) a boy's leg; a man with a ~d hand.*

ban·danna /bænˋdænə/ *n* brightly coloured square of material with red or yellow spots, usu worn round the neck.

band·box /ˋbændbɒks/ *n* light, cardboard box for millinery: *She looks as if she had just come out of a ~,* She looks extremely smart and neat.

ban·deau /ˋbændəʊ/ *n* (*pl* **-deaux** /-dəʊz/) band for keeping a woman's hair in place.

ban·dit /ˋbændɪt/ *n* robber, one of an armed band (e g of brigands attacking travellers in forests or mountains or, today, banks and offices). **~ry** *n* [U] activity of ~s.

ban·do·leer, ban·do·lier /ˈbændəˋlɪə(r)/ *n* shoulder-belt with pockets for cartridges.

bandy[1] /ˋbændɪ/ *vt* [VP6A,14,15B] exchange (words, blows). ***have one's name bandied about,*** be talked about in an unfavourable way, be a subject for gossip. ***~ a story about,*** pass it from person to person. ***~ words with sb,*** exchange remarks quickly, esp when quarrelling.

bandy[2] /ˋbændɪ/ *adj* (of the legs) curving outwards at the knees. ˋ**~-legged** *adj* (of persons or animals) having ~ legs.

bane /beɪn/ *n* [U] **1** (only in compounds) poison: *ˋrat's-~.* **2** cause of ruin or trouble: *Drink was the ~ of his life. He has been the ~ of my life,* caused me constant trouble and anxiety. **~·ful** /-fl/ *adj* evil: *a ~ful influence.* **~·fully** /-flɪ/ *adv*

bang[1] /bæŋ/ *n* violent blow; sudden, loud noise: *a sonic ~* (= boom). *He fell and got a nasty ~ on the head. He always shuts the door with a ~. The firework went off with a ~.* ***go off with a ~,*** (GB colloq), ***go over with a ~,*** (US colloq) (of a performance, etc) be successful, be greatly liked. □ *vt,vi* **1** [VP6A,15B,2A,C] hit violently; give a ~ to; shut with a noise: *He ~ed at the door. He was ~ing on the door with his fist. He ~ed his fist on the table. She ~ed the keys on the piano. The teacher tried to ~ grammar into the heads of his pupils. Don't ~ the lid down. He ~ed the box down on the floor. A door was ~ing somewhere.*

The door ~*ed shut.* **2** [VP2A,C] make a loud noise: *The fireworks* ~*ed. The guns* ~*ed away. We were* ~*ing away* (= firing continuously) *at the enemy. Tell the children to stop* ~*ing about,* being noisy. □ *adv, int*: *go* ~, burst with a loud noise; ~ *in the middle,* exactly in the middle; *come* ~ *up* (= violently) *against sth.*

bang² /bæŋ/ *vt* cut (the front hair) squarely across the forehead: *She wears her hair* ~*ed.* □ *n* [C] fringe of ~ed hair.

banger /ˈbæŋə(r)/ *n* (sl) **1** sausage. **2** noisy firework. **3** old dilapidated car.

bangle /ˈbæŋgl/ *n* ornamental rigid band worn round the arm or ankle.

ban·ian, ban·yan /ˈbænɪən/ *n* **1** Hindu trader. **2** (also ˈ~*-tree*) Indian fig, whose branches come down to the ground and take root.

ban·ish /ˈbænɪʃ/ *vt* [VP6A,14] **1** ~ ***(from),*** send away, esp out of the country, as a punishment: *He was* ~*ed (from) the realm.* **2** put away from, out of (the mind): ~ *care.* **~·ment** *n* [U] *go into* ~*ment.*

ban·is·ter /ˈbænɪstə(r)/ *n* post supporting the hand-rail of a staircase; (*pl*) posts and handrail together.

banjo /bænˈdʒəʊ/ *n* (*pl* **-jos, -joes**) musical instrument played by plucking the strings with the fingers. ⇨ the illus at **string**.

bank¹ /bæŋk/ *n* **1** land along each side of a river or canal; ground near a river: *A river flows between its* ~*s. His house is on the south* ~ *of the river.* **2** sloping land or earth, often forming a border or division: *low* ~*s of earth between rice-fields. There were flowers growing on the* ~*s on each side of the country lanes.* **3** (also ˈ*sand*~) part of the sea-bed higher than its surroundings, but covered with enough water for ships except at low tide; (mining) coal-face. **4** flat-topped mass of cloud, snow, etc esp one formed by the wind: *The sun went down behind a* ~ *of clouds.* **5** artificial slope made to enable a car to go round a curve with less risk.

bank² /bæŋk/ *vt,vi* **1** [VP6A,15B,2C] ~ ***up,*** **(a)** make or form into ~s, ⇨ **4** above: *The snow has* ~*ed up.* **(b)** stop water (of a river, etc) from flowing by making a ~ of earth, mud, etc. **(c)** heap up (the fire in a fireplace or furnace) with coal-dust, etc so that the fire burns slowly for a long time. **2** [VP2A] (of a motor-car or aircraft) travel with one side higher than the other (e g when turning).

bank³ /bæŋk/ *n* **1** establishment for keeping money and valuables safely, the money being paid out on the customer's order (by means of cheques). **the B~,** the B~ of England, which is used by the British Government; *have money in the* ~, have savings; ˈ~ *clerk,* clerk working in a ~. ˈ**~-bill** *n* bill drawn by one ~ upon another ~. ˈ**~-book** *n* (also ˈ*pass-book*) book containing a record of a customer's account with a ~. ~ **giro,** ⇨ **giro.** ˌ**~** ˈ**holiday** *n* one of those days (not Sundays) on which ~s are closed by law, usu kept as general holidays (e g Good Fri, Easter Mon, Whit Mon, Christmas Day); (in US) any weekday on which ~s are closed. ˈ**~·note** *n* piece of paper money issued by a ~. ˈ**~-rate** *n* rate at which the B~ of England (or other national ~) will discount bills, ⇨ **bill³(5)**. ˈ**~-roll** *n* roll of paper money; (person's) ready cash. **2** (gambling) sum of money held by the keeper of the gaming table, from which he pays his losses. ***break the*** **~,** (e g at Monte Carlo) win all this money. **3** (place for storing) reserve supplies. ˈ**blood** ~ *n* place where blood or blood plasma is stored for use in hospitals, etc.

bank⁴ /bæŋk/ *vt,vi* **1** [VP6A] place (money) in a bank³(1): *He* ~*s half his salary every month.* **2** [VP3A] ~ ***(with),*** keep money in a bank: *Who do you* ~ *with,* With what firm of bankers do you keep your money? *Where do you* ~*?* **3** [VP3A] ~ ***(up)on,*** base one's hopes upon: *I'm* ~*ing on your help.* **~er** *n* person who owns or is a partner in a joint-stock bank, or is a governor or director; keeper of a bank³(2). **~er's order,** ⇨ **standing order.** **~·ing** *n* business of keeping a bank: ~*ing hours, 10a m to 3p m*

bank⁵ /bæŋk/ *n* **1** row of keys (on an organ or typewriter): *a three-*~*/four-*~ *typewriter.* **2** bench for rowers in a galley(**1**). **3** row of cylinders (in an engine).

bank·rupt /ˈbæŋkrʌpt/ *n* (legal) person judged by a law court to be unable to pay his debts in full, his property being distributed for the benefit of his creditors. □ *adj* **1** unable to pay one's debts. ***go*** **~,** become ~, insolvent. **2** ~ ***in/of,*** completely without: *The newspapers accused the Government of being* ~ *in ideas.* □ *vt* [VP6A] make ~. **~cy** /ˈbæŋkrəpsɪ/ *n* (*pl* **-cies**) [U] ~ condition; [C] instance of this: *There were ten* ~*cies in the town last year.*

ban·ner /ˈbænə(r)/ *n* **1** flag (now chiefly fig): *the* ~ *of freedom.* ***under the*** **~** ***(of),*** belonging to, supporting (a particular faith or movement). **2** flag or announcement, usu on two poles, carried in (e g religious or political) processions, making known principles, slogans, etc. ~ **headline,** (in a newspaper) prominent headline in large type.

ban·nis·ter *n* = banister.

ban·nock /ˈbænək/ *n* (Scot and N England) flat, oatmeal, home-made loaf.

banns /bænz/ *n pl* public announcement in church that two persons are to be married: *put up/publish the* ~*; have one's* ~ *called.* ***forbid the*** **~,** declare opposition to a proposed marriage.

ban·quet /ˈbæŋkwɪt/ *n* elaborate meal, usu for a special event, at which speeches are made: *a* ˈ*wedding* ~. □ *vt,vi* [VP6A] give a ~ to (sb); [VP2A] take part in a ~; feast.

ban·shee /ˈbænˈʃi *US:* ˈbænʃi/ *n* (Ireland and the Scottish Highlands) spirit whose cry is said to mean that there will be a death in the house where the cry is heard.

bant /bænt/ *vi* [VP2A] (dated) adopt a diet designed to reduce weight (*slim* and *reduce* are the usu words). **~·ing** *n* treatment of obesity by this means.

ban·tam /ˈbæntəm/ *n* **1** small-sized kind of domestic fowl, esp the cock, which is a fighter. **2** boxer between 112 and 118 lb.

ban·ter /ˈbæntə(r)/ *vt,vi* [VP6A,2A] tease in a playful way (by joking talk). □ *n* good-humoured teasing. **~·ing** *adj* **~·ing·ly** *adv*

Bantu /bænˈtu *US:* ˈbæntu/ *adj, n* used of many Central and S African Negro tribes and their languages.

ban·yan *n* = banian.

bao·bab /ˈbeɪəbæb *US:* ˈbaʊbæb/ *n* tree of tropical Africa with a trunk that grows to an enormous size. ⇨ the illus at **tree**.

bap·tism /ˈbæp-tɪzm/ *n* **1** [U] ceremony of sprinkling sb with, or immersing sb in, water, accepting him as a member of the Christian Church and (usu) giving him a name or names (in addition to the family name); [C] instance of this: *There were six ~s at this church last week.* **2** (fig) first experience of a new kind of life: *a soldier's ~ of fire,* his first experience of warfare. **bap·tis·mal** /bæpˋtɪzml/ *adj* of ~: *~al name/water/font.*

Bap·tist /ˋbæp-tɪst/ *n* one of those Christians who object to infant baptism and believe that baptism should be by immersion and at an age when a person is old enough to understand the meaning of the ceremony.

bap·tize /bæpˋtaɪz/ *vt* [VP6A,23] give baptism to (sb): *He had been ~d a Roman Catholic.*

bar[1] /bɑ(r)/ *n* **1** long-shaped piece of hard, stiff material (e g metal, wood, soap, chocolate). **2** rod or rail, rigid length of wood or metal, across a door, window or gate, or forming part of a grate (in a fireplace or furnace) or grid: *He was placed behind prison bars,* put into a prison cell. **3** barrier (across a road) that could not be passed (in former times) until a sum of money (called a *toll*) was paid: *a toll bar.* **4** bank or ridge of sand, etc across the mouth of a river or the entrance to a bay, deposited by currents or tides, often hindering navigation: *The ship crossed the bar safely. We stuck fast on the bar.* **5** (fig) barrier or obstacle; sth that hinders or stops progress: *Poor health may be a bar to success in life. Poverty is not always a bar to happiness.* **6** narrow band (of colour, light, etc): *As the sun went down, there was a bar of red across the western sky.* **7** strip of metal across the ribbon of (esp a military) medal to indicate either **(a)** that the holder has received the same award twice, or **(b)** that he has served in a particular field of operations. **8** (in music) vertical line across the stave marking divisions of equal value in time; one of these divisions and the notes in it: *the opening bars of the National Anthem.* ⇨ the illus at **notation**. **9** railing or barrier in a law court, separating the part where the business is carried on from the part for spectators: *be tried at (the) Bar,* be tried in open court, where everyone may see and hear, not secretly. ***the prisoner at the bar,*** the accused person. **10** (in Parliament) railing dividing off the space to which non-members are admitted (e g for examination by members); similar place in the US Senate, House of Representatives and State Legislatures. **11** (fig) sth that can be compared to a judge or examiner: *at the bar of public opinion; the bar of conscience.* **12 the Bar,** the profession of barrister; all those who have the right to act as barristers. ***be called to the Bar,*** be received as a member of the Bar. ***read for the Bar,*** study to become a barrister. **13 (a)** (in an inn or public house) room, counter, where drinks (such as beer and spirits) are served: *the Public Bar, the Private Bar,* for different classes of users. **(b)** (in a hotel, licensed restaurant or private house) room with such a counter. **ˋbarmaid** *n* woman who serves drinks at a bar(13). **ˋbarman** /-mən/ *n* (*pl* -men) man who does this. **ˋbartender** *n* barmaid or barman (⇨ *cocktail lounge*). **14** counter at which meals, etc are served and also eaten: *a milk bar; a quick-lunch bar.*

bar[2] /bɑ(r)/ *vt* (-rr-) **1** [VP6A] fasten (a door, gate, etc) with a bar or bars[1](2). **2** [VP15B] keep (sb) in or out: *He barred himself in,* fastened doors, windows, etc so that no one could enter the building. **3** [VP6A] obstruct: *bar a road/path. Soldiers barred the way and we couldn't go any farther.* **4** [VP6A,14] ***bar (from),*** prohibit: *bar sb from a competition,* order that he shall not take part. [VP6C] (colloq): *She bars smoking in the drawing-room,* does not permit it. *We bar playing cards for money.* [VP12C] *I will bar no honest man my house,* will let any honest man visit my house. **5** [VP6A] (usu passive) mark with a stripe or stripes: *a sky barred with clouds.*

bar[3] /bɑ(r)/, **bar·ring** /ˋbɑrɪŋ/ *prep* (colloq) except: *We shall arrive at noon barring accidents,* unless there are accidents. ***bar none,*** without exception. ***bar one,*** except one.

bar[4] /bɑ(r)/ *n* large Mediterranean fish.

barb /bɑb/ *n* back-turning or back-curving point of an arrow, spear, fish-hook, etc. **barbed** *adj* having a ~ or ~s: *~ed wire,* wire with short, sharp points, used for fences, etc: *~ed wire entanglements,* for defensive purposes in war.

a barb barbed wire

bar·bar·ian /bɑˋbeərɪən/ *adj, n* uncivilized or uncultured (person).

bar·baric /bɑˋbærɪk/ *adj* of or like barbarians; uncultivated; rough and rude (esp in art and taste): *the ~ splendour of Attila's court.*

bar·bar·ism /ˋbɑbərɪzm/ *n* **1** [U] state of being uncivilized, ignorant, or rude: *living in ~.* **2** [C] instance of this; (esp) misuse of language by mixing foreign or vulgar words into talk or writing.

bar·bar·ity /bɑˋbærətɪ/ *n* (*pl* -ties) [U] savage cruelty; [C] instance of this: *the barbarities of modern warfare,* e g the bombing of towns, sinking of passenger liners.

bar·bar·ize /ˋbɑbəraɪz/ *vt* [VP6A] make barbarous.

bar·bar·ous /ˋbɑbərəs/ *adj* uncivilized; cruel; savage; unrefined in taste, conduct, or habits. **~·ly** *adv*

bar·be·cue /ˋbɑbɪkju/ *n* grill, iron framework, for cooking an animal whole; ox, pig, etc roasted whole; (outdoor) social occasion at which meat cooked over a charcoal fire is eaten. □ *vt* roast (meat, etc) in this way.

bar·bel /ˋbɑbl/ *n* large European fresh-water fish.

bar·ber /ˋbɑbə(r)/ *n* (often *hairdresser*) person whose trade is shaving and men's hair-cutting. **~'s pole,** pole painted in coloured spirals and used as a sign. **ˋ~'s shop,** (US = **ˋ~ shop**) place where a ~ does his work.

bar·bi·can /ˋbɑbɪkən/ *n* fortified building, esp a double tower over a gate or bridge, used in olden times as an outer defence to a city or castle.

bar·bi·tone /ˋbɑbɪtəʊn/ *n* [U] drug used to soothe the nerves and cause sleep; veronal.

bar·bitu·rate /bɑˋbɪtʃʊrət/ *n* [C,U] (chem) (kinds of) organic compound with a (possibly dangerous) soporific effect; pill for settling the nerves or inducing sleep.

bar·ca·role, bar·ca·rolle /ˈbɑkəˋrəʊl/ *n* song of Venetian gondoliers.

bard /bɑd/ *n* **1** (esp Celtic) minstrel. **2** (liter) poet: *the ~ of Avon,* Shakespeare. **bar·dic** *adj* of ~s or their songs. **bar·dol·atry** /bɑˋdɒlətrɪ/ *n* [U] enthusiastic admiration of Shakespeare.

bare[1] /beə(r)/ *adj* **1** without clothing, covering, protection, or decoration: *fight with ~ hands*, without boxing gloves; *in his ~ skin*, naked; *~ to the waist; with his head ~*, not wearing a hat; *~ floors*, without carpets, rugs, etc; *a ~ hillside*, without shrubs or trees; *hills ~ of vegetation; trees that are already ~*, that have already lost their leaves; *sleeping on ~ boards*, without a mattress, etc. ***lay ~***, uncover, expose, make known (sth secret or hidden). **ˈ~·back** *adv* (of a horse) without a saddle: *ride ~back*. **ˈ~·ˈbacked** *adj* having the back ~. □ *adv* = ~back. **ˈ~·faced** *adj* insolent; shameless; undisguised: *It's ~faced robbery to ask £15 for such an old bicycle!* **~-faced·ly** *adv* **ˈ~·foot** *adv* without shoes and stockings. ***be/go/walk ~foot.*** **ˈ~·ˈfooted** *adj* with ~ feet. □ *adv* = ~foot. **ˈ~·ˈheaded** *adj* with a ~ head; not wearing a hat. **ˈ~·ˈlegged** *adj* with the legs ~; not wearing stockings. **2** empty or almost empty: *a room ~ of furniture; a larder ~ of food; ~ shelves. The garden looked ~ in winter*, had a few or no flowers. **3** not more than; mere: *the ~ necessities of life*, things needed merely to keep alive; *earn a ~ living*, only just enough money to live on: *approved by a ~ majority*, a very small one; *a ~ possibility*, a mere or very slight one. **~·ly** *adv* **1** in a ~ way: *~ly furnished rooms*, with little furniture. **2** only just; scarcely: *We ~ly had time to catch the train. He can ~ly read and write. I ~ly know her.* **~·ness** *n* ~ state.

bare[2] /beə(r)/ *vt* [VP6A] uncover; reveal: *~ one's head*, take one's hat off; *~ the end of a wire*, strip off the covering of rubber, etc (before making an electrical connection). *The tiger ~d its teeth.* ***~ one's heart,*** make known one's deepest feelings.

bar·gain /ˈbɑgɪn/ *n* **1** agreement to buy, sell or exchange sth, made after discussion; (in industry) agreement between management and labour over wages, hours, etc; sth obtained as the result of such an agreement. ***A ~'s a ~,*** When an agreement has been made, it must be kept. ***drive a hard ~,*** try to force an agreement favourable to oneself. ***a good/bad ~,*** one that favours/does not favour oneself. ***into the ~,*** as well; in addition; moreover. ***make/strike a ~ (with sb) (over sth***), reach agreement. ***ˈ~ing position,*** (in a debate, etc) state of affairs, arrangements, etc: *The Foreign Secretary was in a good/bad ~ing position in his dealings with his opposite number in France*, was in a favourable/unfavourable position when negotiating. **2** sth offered, sold or bought cheap: *a ˈ~ sale*, sale of goods at reduced prices; *ˈ~-basement*, lowest floor of a shop, where goods are offered at reduced prices; *ˈ~-counter*, counter at which ~s are displayed or sold; *~ price*, low price; *ˈ~-hunter*, person looking for ~s. □ *vi,vt* **1** [VP2A,3A] ***~ (with sb) (for sth),*** talk for the purpose of reaching an agreement (about buying or selling sth, doing a piece of work, etc): *We ~ed with the farmer for a supply of milk and butter.* **2** [VP3A] ***~ about,*** = ~ over. ***~ for,*** be ready or willing to accept or agree to: *He got more than he ~ed for*, (colloq) was unpleasantly surprised at the consequences. *I didn't ~ for John arriving so soon*, was surprised by this, didn't expect it. ***~ over sth,*** ~ with sb for sth. **3** [VP9] make a condition (*that*): *The men ~ed that they should not have to work on Saturday afternoons.* **4** [VP15B] ***~ away,*** give up in return for sth; sacrifice: *~ away one's freedom*, give it up in return for some advantage or other.

barge[1] /bɑdʒ/ *n* **1** large flat-bottomed boat for carrying goods and people on rivers and canals, in harbours, etc with or without sails, towed by a tug or horse; similar boat with its own engine. **2** warship's boat, for the use of the officers. **3** large rowing-boat for ceremonial occasions. **4** college house-boat at Oxford. **ˈ~-pole** *n* long pole used for guiding a ~: *I wouldn't touch it with a ~-pole*, I loathe it.

barge[2] /bɑdʒ/ *vi* (colloq) **1** [VP3A] ***~ into/against,*** rush or bump heavily into/against (sb or sth). **2** [VP2C,3A] ***~ about,*** move clumsily, without proper control of one's movements or without care (for persons or things). ***~ in/into,*** intrude; make one's way in, interrupt, rudely: *Stop barging into our conversation.*

bar·gee /bɑˈdʒi/ *n* master or member of the crew of a barge. ***swear like a ~,*** swear forcibly, and with a great variety of swear-words.

bari·tone, bary·tone /ˈbærɪtəʊn/ *n* male voice between tenor and bass.

bar·ium /ˈbeərɪəm/ *n* [U] **1** soft, silvery-white metal (symbol **Ba**) of which the compounds are used in industry. **2** chemical substance (~ sulphate) introduced into the intestines before an X-ray photograph of them is taken.

bark[1] /bɑk/ *n* [U] outer coverings or skin on the trunks, boughs and branches of trees. ⇨ the illus at **tree**. □ *vt* [VP6A] **1** take the ~ off (a tree). **2** scrape the skin off (one's knuckles, shin, knee, etc) (by falling against sth, etc).

bark[2] /bɑk/ *n* the cry made by dogs and foxes; (fig) sound of gunfire, or of a cough. ***His ~ is worse than his bite,*** He is bad-tempered but not dangerous. □ *vi,vt* **1** [VP2A,C,3A] (of dogs, etc) give a ~ or ~s: *The dog ~s at strangers.* ***~ up the wrong tree,*** (fig) direct one's complaint, accusation, etc wrongly. **2** [VP6A,15B] say (sth) in a sharp, commanding voice: *The officer ~ed out his orders. 'Come here!' he ~ed (out).*

bark[3], **barque** /bɑk/ *n* **1** sailing-ship with 3 to 5 masts and sails. **2** (poet) any ship or boat.

barker /ˈbɑkə(r)/ *n* (colloq) **1** person who stands outside a booth in a travelling show, or outside a shop, talking loudly to advertise the show, goods, etc. **2** (sl) pistol.

bar·ley /ˈbɑlɪ/ *n* [U] grass-like plant and its seed (called grain), used for food and for making beer and whisky. ⇨ the illus at **cereal**. **ˈ~-corn** *n* grain of ~; (colloq) malt liquor. **pearl ~** *n* ~ grain made smaller by grinding. **ˈ~-water** *n* drink made by boiling pearl ~ in water and then straining it. **ˈ~-sugar** *n* solid sweet substance, made from pure sugar.

barm /bɑm/ *n* [U] yeast.

barmy /ˈbɑmɪ/ *adj* (GB colloq) wrong in the head; foolish.

barn /bɑn/ *n* **1** covered building for storing hay, grain, etc on a farm. **ˈ~ dance** *n* kind of rustic dance. **ˈ~-door** *n* large door of a ~; (colloq) target too large to miss. **ˈ~-ˈdoor fowl** *n* ordinary kind of fowl kept on farms. **ˈ~·storm** *vi* (US) travel through the country making political speeches, presenting plays, etc. Hence, **ˈ~-stormer** *n* person who does this. **ˈ~-yard** *n* = farm-yard. **2** (contemptuous) any large, plain building: *What a ~ of a house!* **3** (US) building for sheltering cattle or horses; depot for trams, buses, etc.

bar·nacle /ˈbɑnəkl/ *n* small sea-animal that fastens itself to objects under water, rocks, the bottoms of ships, the timbers of wharves, etc.

ba·rom·eter /bəˈromɪtə(r)/ *n* instrument for measuring the pressure of the atmosphere, used for forecasting the weather and measuring height above sea-level; (fig) something which forecasts changes or fluctuations (e g in public opinion, market prices). **baro·met·ric** /ˌbærəˈmetrɪk/ *adj*

baron /ˈbærən/ *n* **1** (in GB) nobleman; lowest rank of Peer (called *Lord* —); holder of the non-British title (called *Baron* —). **2** (orig US) great industrial leader: *oil ~s; beer ~s.* **ˈ~·age** /-ɪdʒ/ *n* the ~s collectively; book with a list of the Peers. **~·ess** /ˈbærənes/ *n* ~'s wife; woman holding the rank of a ~ in her own right. **bar·o·nial** /bəˈrəʊnɪəl/ *adj* of, suitable for, ~s. **bar·ony** /ˈbærənɪ/ *n* rank of a ~: *confer a ~y on sb,* make him a ~.

bar·onet /ˈbærənɪt/ *n* member of the lowest hereditary titled order, lower in rank than a baron but above a knight; shortened to *Bart,* added to the name, as *Sir John Williams, Bart.* **~cy** /ˈbærənɪtsɪ/ *n* rank, title, of a ~.

ba·roque /bəˈrəʊk/ *n, adj* (of the) florid or extravagant style in the arts (esp architecture) in Europe in the 17th and 18th cc.

ba·rouche /bəˈruʃ/ *n* four-wheeled carriage, pulled by horses, with two seats facing each other and a folding top, for four occupants and a driver.

barque /bɑk/ *n* ⇨ bark[3].

bar·rack[1] /ˈbærək/ *n* **1** (often *a ~s,* with *sing v*) large building(s) for soldiers to live in: *The ~s are/is quite new.* **2** any building of plain or ugly appearance.

bar·rack[2] /ˈbærək/ *vt, vi* [VP6A,2A] jeer at; make cries of protest against (e g slow play in a cricket match). **~·ing** *n* slow clapping, etc.

bar·rage /ˈbærɑʒ *US:* bəˈrɑʒ/ *n* [C] **1** artificial obstacle built across a river (not across a valley) for storing water to be diverted into canals for irrigation (as on the Nile and the Indus). ⇨ dam. **2** (mil) barrier made by heavy, continuous gunfire directed onto a given area. **3** *balloon ~; ~ balloon,* ⇨ balloon.

barred /bɑd/ *pt, pp* of *bar* .

bar·rel /ˈbærl/ *n* **1** round container, made of wooden staves with bands or hoops, or of plastic; the amount that a ~ holds. **ˈ~-roofed ˈvault** *n* (semi-)cylindrical roof. **2** metal tube of a rifle, revolver or pistol. ⇨ the illus at rifle. **3** part of a fountain pen that holds the ink. **4 ˈ~-organ** *n* instrument from which music is produced by turning a handle and so causing a cylinder to act mechanically on keys; usu played by a man who goes round the streets, playing it for money. **bar·relled** *adj* stored in a ~: *~led beer.* □ *vt* (-ll-) put in a ~ or ~s.

bar·ren /ˈbærən/ *adj* **1** (of land) not good enough to produce crops. **2** (of plants, trees) not producing fruit or seeds. **3** (of women, animals) unable to have young ones. **4** (fig) without value, interest, or result: *a ~ subject/discussion; an attempt that was ~ of results.* **~·ness** *n*

bar·ri·cade /ˌbærɪˈkeɪd/ *n* barrier of objects (e g trees, carts, overturned or burnt-out cars, barrels) made across or in front of something as a defence. □ *vt* [VP6A,15B] block (a street, etc) with a ~: *They ~d themselves in.*

bar·rier /ˈbærɪə(r)/ *n* **1** sth (e g a wall, rail, fence, turnstile) that prevents, hinders or controls, progress or movement: *The Sahara Desert is a natural ~ that separates North and Central Africa. Show your ticket at the ~,* e g in a railway station. ⇨ also crash[1](1), half(3), heat[1](5) and sound[2](3). **2** (fig) hindrance: *Poor health and lack of money may both be ~s to educational progress.*

bar·ring /ˈbɑrɪŋ/ *prep* excluding.

bar·ris·ter /ˈbærɪstə(r)/ *n* (not US) lawyer who has the right to speak and argue as an advocate in higher law courts. ⇨ counsel.

bar·row[1] /ˈbærəʊ/ *n* **1** = wheel-~. **2** (also *ˈhand-~, ˈcoster's ~*) small cart with two wheels, pulled or pushed by hand. **~-boy/man** /-mən/ *n* costermonger. **3** (also *luggage-~*) metal frame with two wheels used by porters for luggage (at railway-stations, in hotels, etc).

bar·row[2] /ˈbærəʊ/ *n* (= tumulus) mound, dating from prehistoric times, built over a burial ground.

bar·ter /ˈbɑtə(r)/ *vt, vi* [VP15B,14,2A] **~ *(with sb/for sth),* ~ *sth away,*** exchange (goods, property, etc) (for other goods, etc): *~ wheat for machinery;* (fig) *~ away one's rights/honour/freedom.* □ *n* [U] exchange made in this way. **~·er** *n*

bary·tone /ˈbærɪtəʊn/ *n* ⇨ baritone.

ba·salt /ˈbæsɔlt/ *n* [U] sorts of dark-coloured rock of volcanic origin.

bas·cule /ˈbæskjul/ *n* **~ bridge,** (eng) kind of drawbridge of which the two halves can be raised and lowered with counter-weights.

base[1] /beɪs/ *n* **1** lowest part of anything, esp the part on which sth rests or is supported: *the ~ of a pillar,* ⇨ the illus at column. **ˈ~·board** *n* (US) = (GB) skirting board. **2** (geom) line or surface on which a figure stands or can stand: *BC is the ~ of the triangle ABC, ABCD is the ~ of the*

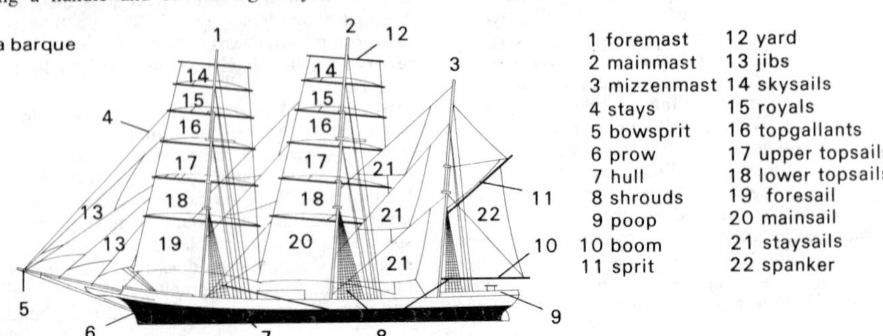

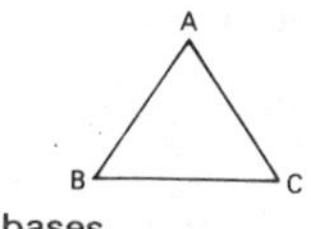

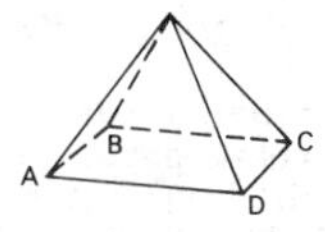

bases

pyramid. **3** (chem) substance capable of combining with an acid to form a salt and water only; substance into which other things are mixed. **4** place at which armed forces, expeditions, etc have their stores, hospitals, etc: *a* ˋ*naval* ~; *an* ˋ*air* ~; *a* ~ *of operations; a* ~ *camp,* e g for an Everest expedition. **5** (maths) the number (usu 10) which is the starting point for a logarithmic system. **6** (~ball) one of four stations or positions. ***get to first*** **~,** (US; fig) take a successful first step towards achieving sth. **~ hit** *n* hit on which a player gets to first ~. **7 ~-less** *adj* without cause or foundation: *~less fears.*

base[2] /beɪs/ *vt* [VP14] **~ *(up)on,*** build or place (*upon*); use as a basis for: *Direct taxation is usually ~d upon income. I ~ my hopes upon the news we had yesterday.*

base[3] /beɪs/ *adj* **1** (of persons, their behaviour, thoughts, etc) dishonourable: *acting from ~ motives.* **2 ~ metals,** non-precious metals. **~ coin,** mixed with inferior metals.

base·ball /ˋbeɪsbɔl/ *n* national game of the US, played with a bat and ball, by two teams of nine players on a field with four bases.

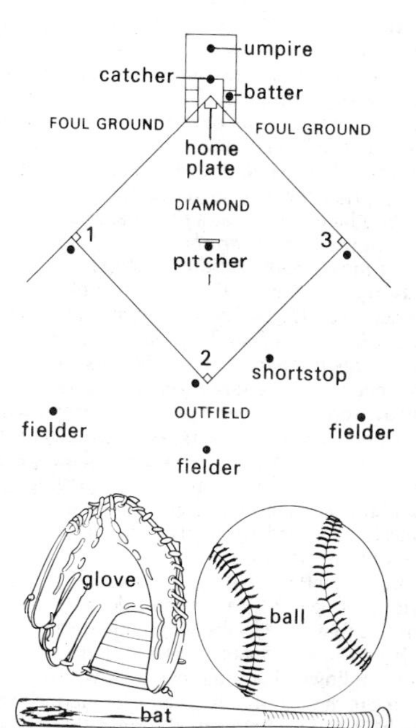

baseball

base·ment /ˋbeɪsmənt/ *n* lowest part of a building, partly or wholly below ground level; inhabited room(s) in this part.

bases 1 *pl* of basis. **2** *pl* of base[1].

bash /bæʃ/ *vt* [VP6A,15A,B] strike heavily so as to break or injure: *~ in the lid of a box; ~ sb on the head with a golf club; ~ one's head against sth in the dark.* □ *n* violent blow or knock: *give sb a ~ on the nose.* ***have a ~ at sth,*** (sl) attempt it.

bash·ful /ˋbæʃfl/ *adv* shy. **~ly** /-flɪ/ *adv*

basic /ˋbeɪsɪk/ *adj* of or at the base or foundation; fundamental: *the ~ processes of arithmetic,* e g adding, subtraction, multiplying; *the ~ vocabulary of a language,* the words that must be known. **B~ English,** artificial, simplified form of English. **~ slag** *n* fertilizer containing phosphates. **ba·si·cally** /-klɪ/ *adv* fundamentally.

basil /ˋbæzl/ *n* [U] sweet-smelling plant like mint, used in cooking.

ba·sil·ica /bəˋzɪlɪkə/ *n* oblong hall with a double row of columns and an apse at one end (used in ancient Rome as a law court); building of this type used as a church: *the ~ of St Peter's in Rome.*

bas·ilisk /ˋbæsɪlɪsk/ *n* **1** small American lizard with a hollow crest that can swell up with air. **2** fabulous reptile able to cause death by its look or breath.

basin /ˋbeɪsn/ *n* **1** round, open dish of metal, pottery, etc for holding liquids; contents of a ~. ⇨ wash-~. **2** bowl for preparing or serving food in. **3** hollow place where water collects (e g a stone structure at the base of a fountain, a deep pool at the base of a waterfall). **4** deep part of a harbour that is almost surrounded by land; dock with gates that control the inflow and outflow of water. **5** area of country drained by a river and its tributaries: *the Thames ~.*

basis /ˋbeɪsɪs/ *n* (*pl* **-ses** /-siz/) **1** substance into which others are mixed; most important part of a mixture. **2** foundation (usu fig): *the ~ of morality; on a solid ~; arguments that have a firm ~,* that are founded in facts; *On the ~ of our sales forecasts* (i e from what these indicate) *we may begin to make a profit next year.*

bask /bɑsk *US:* bæsk/ *vi* [VP2C] enjoy warmth and light: *sitting in the garden, ~ing in the sunshine*; (fig) *~ing in her favour/approval.*

bas·ket /ˋbɑskɪt *US:* ˋbæskɪt/ *n* **1** container, usu made of materials that bend and twist easily (osiers, canes, rushes) with or without a handle: *a* ˋ*shopping ~; a* ˋ*clothes ~; a waste-*ˋ*paper ~.* **2** as much as a ~ holds: *They ate a ~ of plums.* **~-ball** /ˋbɑskɪtbɔl *US:* ˋbæs-/ *n* game (resembling netball), played by two teams of five players (men) who try to throw a large inflated ball into an open-ended net fixed 10 ft above the ground. ⇨ netball.

basketball

bas-relief /ˈbæsrɪˋlif/ *n* [U] (= *low relief*) form of art in which a flat surface of metal or stone is cut away so that a design or picture stands out as on a coin but often to a greater degree; [C] example of this. ⇨ the illus at church.

bass[1] /bæs/ *n* (*pl* unchanged) (zool) kinds of fish (perch) used as food, caught in rivers, lakes and in the sea.

bass[2] /beɪs/ *adj* deep-sounding; low in tone. □ *n* lowest part in music (voice and instruments); singer or instrument with lowest notes: '~-ˋ*clarinet;* ~ *drum*, ⇨ the illus at percussion; double-ˋ~, ⇨ the illus at string; ~ *clef*.

bass[3] /bæs/ *n* [U] inner fibrous bark of the lime-tree, used for weaving baskets, mats, etc and for tying plants.

Bass /bæs/ *n* (P) beer made by the brewers named Bass.

bas·si·net /ˈbæsɪˋnet/ *n* baby's cradle or carriage made of woven wicker, with a hood.

bas·soon /bəˋsun/ *n* musical wind-instrument with double reeds made of wood, giving very low notes. ⇨ illus at brass.

bast /bæst/ *n* [U] **1** = bass[3]. **2** other fibrous barks (e g raffia) used for tying and weaving.

bas·tard /ˋbɑstəd *US:* ˋbæs-/ *n* **1** illegitimate child: (attrib) *a* ~ *child/daughter/son.* **2** ⚠ (also as *int*) ruthless insensitive person (used as a term of abuse): *You heartless* ~*! He's a real* ~*, leaving his wife in that way;* (also, not abusively, friendly colloq): *Harry, you old* ~*! fancy meeting you here!* **3** ⚠ unfortunate fellow: *Poor* ~*! He's been sacked and he won't find another job very easily;* (also of an unfortunate incident, state, etc): *this* ~ *of a headache/essay.* **4** (usu attrib) (of things) not genuine or authentic; spurious. ˋ**~·ize** *vt* **1** prove to be, pronounce as a ~. **2** make spurious: *a* ~*ized account of what happened.* **~y** *n* (legal) illegitimacy: *a* ~*y order,* one (made by a magistrate) for the support of an illegitimate by its father (now usu called a *maintenance order*).

baste[1] /beɪst/ *vt* [VP6A,15B] (in making clothes, etc) sew pieces together with long temporary stitches (so that adjustments are possible afterwards).

baste[2] /beɪst/ *vt* [VP6A] **~ *meat,*** pour over it the fat, juices, etc which come from it during cooking.

baste[3] /beɪst/ *vt* [VP6A] thrash; beat.

bas·ti·nado /ˈbæstɪˋnɑdəʊ/ *n* (*pl* -does) caning on the soles of the feet. □ *vt* [VP6A] punish by caning in this way.

bas·tion /ˋbæstɪən/ *n* (often five-sided) part of a fortification that stands out from the rest; (fig) military stronghold near hostile territory.

bat[1] /bæt/ *n* small mouse-like animal that flies at night and feeds on fruit and insects. ⇨ the illus at small. ***have bats in the belfry,*** (sl) be eccentric, have queer ideas. ***as blind as a bat,*** unable to see, not seeing, clearly.

bat[2] /bæt/ *n* **1** shaped wooden implement for striking the ball in games, esp cricket and baseball. ⇨ these entries. ***carry one's bat,*** (cricket) be 'not out' at the end of the innings. ***do sth off one's own bat,*** (fig) do it without help. ⇨ the illus at cricket. **2** = batsman: *He's a useful bat.* □ *vi,vt* (-tt-) **1** [VP2A,B,C] use a bat: *Green batted (for) two hours,* was at the wicket for two hours. **2** [VP6A] hit (with a bat); hit. **~s·man** /-smən/ *n* (*pl* -men) **1** (cricket) player who bats: *He's a good batsman but no good as a bowler.* **2** (aviation) man who uses a pair of bats (like those used in table-tennis) to guide an aircraft as and after it touches down (e g on the deck of an aircraft-carrier).

bat[3] /bæt/ *n* ***go off at a terrific/rare bat,*** (sl) at a fast rate.

bat[4] /bæt/ *vt* (-tt-) (sl) wink. ***not bat an eyelid,*** (a) not sleep at all. (b) not show any surprise.

batch /bætʃ/ *n* **1** number of loaves, cakes, etc baked together: *baked in* ~*es of twenty.* **2** number of persons or things receiving attention as a group: *a* ~ *of letters to be answered; a* ~ *of recruits for the army.*

bate /beɪt/ *vt* = abate. ***with ~d breath,*** with the voice lowered to a whisper (in expectancy, anxiety, etc).

bath /bɑθ *US:* bæθ/ *n* (*pl* ~s /bɑðz *US:* bæðz/) **1** washing of the body, esp by putting oneself completely in water: *I shall have a hot* ~ *and go to bed. He takes a cold* ~ *every morning.* ˋ**~·robe** *n* loose-fitting robe worn before and after taking a ~. **2** water for a ~: *Your* ~ *is ready.* ˋ**~·tub** *n* (usu *bath* in GB except in trade use) large (usu oblong) vessel (of porcelain or metal) in which ~s are taken. ˋ**~·room** *n* room in which there is a ~-tub (and usu a wash-hand-basin): *Every room in the hotel has a private* ~*room,* i e its own ~room. **3** (container for) liquid in which sth is washed or dipped (in chemical and industrial processes): *an oil* ~, (for parts of a machine); *a hypo* ~, (photography). **4** (*pl*) building, rooms, where ~s may be taken, often with a large indoor swimming pool: *public swimming* ~*s; the Turkish* ~*s.* □ *vt,vi* [VP6A,2A] give a ~ to: ~ *the baby;* take a bath.

Bath /bɑθ *US:* bæθ/ *n* (town in W England, with hot mineral springs). '**~-ˋchair** *n* three-wheeled chair for an invalid, pushed or pulled by hand.

bathe /beɪð/ *vt,vi* **1** apply water to; soak in water; put in water: *The doctor told him to* ~ *his eyes twice a day. The nurse* ~*d the wound.* **2** [VP6A] ***be ~d in,*** be made wet or bright all over: *Her face was* ~*d in tears. The countryside was* ~*d in brilliant sunshine. He was* ~*d in sweat,* ⇨ also sun(4). **3** [VP2A] go into the sea, a river, lake, etc for sport, swimming, to get cool, etc. □ *n* the taking of a bath in the sea, a river, lake, etc: *We had an enjoyable* ~ *before breakfast. Let's go for a* ~. Cf *have a bath.* **bather** /ˋbeɪðə(r)/ *n*

bath·ing /ˋbeɪðɪŋ/ *n* act or practice of going into the sea, etc: *The* ~ *here is safe,* It is safe to swim here. *He's fond of* ~*. There have been many fatal* ~ *accidents here,* Many bathers have been drowned here. ˋ**~-drawers/-dress/-suit,** (now dated) forms of swimming wear (replaced by *swimming-trunks* for men). ˋ**~-cap** *n* cap to cover a woman's hair while in the water. ˋ**~-costume** *n* (now usu female) worn for swimming. ˋ**~-machine** *n* cabin on wheels, pulled down to the water's edge and (formerly) used by bathers for dressing and undressing.

bathos /ˋbeɪθɒs/ *n* [U] (rhet) sudden change (in writing or speech) from what is deeply moving or sublime to what is foolish or unimportant.

bathy·sphere /ˋbæθɪsfɪə(r)/ *n* large, strongly built, hollow sphere that can be lowered to great depths in the sea, for observation of marine life.

ba·tik /ˋbætɪk/ *n* [U] method (originally in Java) of printing coloured designs on textiles by waxing the parts not to be dyed.

ba·tiste /bæˋtist/ *n* [U] fine thin linen or cotton cloth.

bat·man /ˋbætmən/ *n* (*pl* -men /-mən/) (GB mil) army officer's personal servant.

baton /ˋbætõ *US:* bəˋton/ *n* **1** policeman's short, thick stick, used as a weapon: *The police made a ~ charge,* drove the crowd back by using their ~s. **2** short, thin stick used by the conductor of a band or an orchestra. **3** staff of office: *a Field-Marshal's ~.*

bats /bæts/ *pred adj* (sl) mad; eccentric. ⇨ also bat.

bat·tal·ion /bəˋtælɪən/ *n* army unit made up of several companies and forming part of a regiment or brigade.

bat·ten[1] /ˋbætn/ *n* long board, esp one used to keep other boards in place, or to which other boards are nailed; (on a ship) strip of wood or metal used to fasten down covers or tarpaulins over a hatch. □ *vt* [VP6A,15B] ***~ down,*** make secure with ~s: *~ down the hatches.*

bat·ten[2] /ˋbætn/ *vi* [VP3A] ***~ (up)on,*** thrive, grow fat on (esp at the expense of others, or so as to injure others).

bat·ter[1] /ˋbætə(r)/ *vt,vi* [VP6A,15A,B,2C] strike hard and often; beat out of shape: *The heavy waves ~ed the wrecked ship to pieces. Let's ~ the door down. Someone was ~ing (away) at the door. He was driving a badly ~ed old car and wearing a ~ed old hat.* ˋ**~·ing ram** *n* /-trɪŋ/ (mil) big, heavy log with an iron head used in olden times for ~ing down walls.

bat·ter[2] /ˋbætə(r)/ *n* [U] beaten mixture of flour, eggs, milk, etc for cooking.

bat·tery /ˋbætrɪ/ *n* (*pl* -ries) **1** army unit of big guns, with men and vehicles. **2** group of big guns on a warship, or for coastal defence. **3** group of connected electric cells from which current will flow: *This transistor has four small batteries.* **4** set of similar utensils or instruments used together: *a ~ of lenses/ovens.* **5** ***assault and ~,*** (legal) attack upon or threatening touch (to sb). **6** series of boxes, etc in which hens are kept for laying eggs or for fattening: *~ hens.* ⇨ free-range.

bat·ting /ˋbætɪŋ/ *n* [U] cotton wool in flat wads.

battle /ˋbætl/ *n* **1** fight, esp between organized and armed forces (armies, navies, aircraft); (fig) any struggle: *the ~ of life.* **2** [U] victory; success: *The ~ is to the strong,* The strong are likely to win. *Youth is half the ~,* Youthful strength brings likelihood of success. **3** [U] *die in ~,* die fighting. ***give/offer ~,*** show readiness to fight. ***refuse ~,*** refuse to fight. □ *vi* [VP3A] ***~ (with/against) sb (for sth),*** struggle: *battling against adversity. They ~d with the winds and waves.* ˋ**~-axe** *n* (a) heavy axe with a long handle, formerly used as a weapon. (b) (colloq) domineering and assertive woman. ˋ**~-cruiser** *n* large fast cruiser with heavy guns and lighter armour than a ~ship. ˋ**~-dress** *n* soldier's uniform of belted blouse and trousers. ˋ**~·field** *n* place where a ~ is or was fought. ˋ**~·ground** *n* ~field. ˋ**~·ship** *n* large kind of warship, with big guns and heavy armour.

battle·dore /ˋbætldɔ(r)/ *n* bat or small racket used in the game called ~ and shuttlecock. ⇨ the illus at badminton.

battle·ments /ˋbætlmənts/ *n pl* flat roof of a tower or castle enclosed by parapets with openings through which to shoot.

bat·tue /bæˋtju *US:* -ˋtu/ *n* [C] driving of game[1](6) (by beating bushes, etc) towards the sportsmen; occasion when this is done.

batty /ˋbætɪ/ *adj* (sl) (of a person) crazy; slightly mad. ⇨ bats.

bauble /ˋbɔbl/ *n* pretty, bright and pleasing ornament of little value.

baulk /bɔk/ ⇨ balk.

baux·ite /ˋbɔksaɪt/ *n* [U] clay-like substance from which aluminium is obtained.

bawd /bɔd/ *n* (old use) woman who keeps a brothel. **~y** *adj* (of talk, persons) vulgar; humorously coarse: *~y talk/stories; a ~y old man.* □ *n* ~ talk, etc. **~·ily** *adv*

bawl /bɔl/ *vt,vi* [VP6A,15A,2C,3A] shout or cry loudly: *He ~ed out a curse. He ~ed to me across the street. The frightened child ~ed for help.* ***~ sb out,*** (US, sl) scold severely.

bay[1] /beɪ/ *n* **1** (also ˋ*bay-tree,* ˋ*bay laurel*) kind of tree or shrub with leaves that are used in cooking and are spicy when crushed. **2 bays,** ˋ**bay-wreath,** laurel wreath given in olden times to poets and heroes, victors in war and athletic contests; (fig) honour; glory. **3 bay rum,** for hair lotion, made from the leaves of a W Indian tree.

bay[2] /beɪ/ *n* part of the sea or of a large lake, enclosed by a wide curve of the shore: *the Bay of Biscay; Hudson Bay.*

bay[3] /beɪ/ *n* **1** compartment between columns and pillars that divide a building into regular parts. **2** extensions of a room beyond the line of one or two of its walls; recess. **ˈbay ˋwindow,** window, usu with glass on three sides, built in such a recess. ⇨ the illus at window. **3** side-line and platform in a railway station, used as a starting-point and terminus for local trains, separate from the main lines. **4** compartment in the fuselage of an aircraft: *the* ˋ*bomb bay;* part of a warship, college campus, etc for those who are ill or injured: *the* ˋ*sick-bay;* compartment in a warehouse, barn etc for storing things: *Clear No 3 bay to make room for new equipment.*

bay[4] /beɪ/ *n* deep bark, esp of hounds while hunting. ***at bay,*** (of a hunted animal) forced to face its attackers and show defiance; (fig) in a desperate position, compelled to struggle fiercely. ***keep/hold sb at bay,*** keep an enemy, etc at a distance; prevent him from coming too near. ***bring*** (a stag, an enemy) ***to bay,*** force (it, him) to make a final resistance; come to close quarters so that escape is impossible. □ *vi* [VP2A] (esp of large dogs, hounds) bark with a deep note, esp continuously, when hunting.

bay[5] /beɪ/ *adj, n* reddish-brown (horse): *He was riding a dark bay.*

bay·onet /ˋbeɪənɪt/ *n* dagger-like blade that can be fixed to the muzzle of a rifle and used in hand-to-hand fighting. □ *vt* [VP6A] stab with a ~.

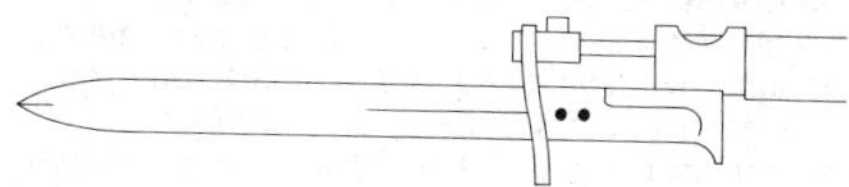

a bayonet

bayou /ˋbaɪu/ *n* (in N America) marshy offshoot of a river.

ba·zaar /bəˋzɑ(r)/ *n* **1** (in Iran, India and other Eastern countries) street of workshops and shops; that part of a town where the markets and shopping streets are. **2** (in GB, US) shop for the sale of cheap goods of great variety. **3** (place where there is a) sale of goods for charitable purposes: *a church ~.*

ba·zoo·ka /bəˈzukə/ *n* portable weapon for firing armour-piercing rockets.

be[1] /bi/ *vi* (*pres t* **am** /*after 'I':* m *otherwise:* əm *strong form:* æm/, **is** /z *but* s *after* p, t, k, f, θ *strong form:* ɪz/, **are** /ə(r) *strong form:* ɑ(r)/; *pt* **was** /wəz *strong form:* woz/, **were** /wə(r) *strong form:* wɜ(r)/; contracted forms, **I'm** /ɑɪm/, **he's** /hiz/, **she's** /ʃiz/, **it's** /ɪts/, **we're** /wɪə(r)/, **you're** /jʊə(r)/, **they're** /ðeə(r)/; neg **isn't** /ɪznt/, **aren't** /ɑnt *US:* ɑrnt/, **wasn't** /woznt/, **weren't** /wɜnt/; *Am I not* is contracted to *an't I*, usu written *aren't I* /ˈɑnt ɑɪ *US:* ˈænt/; *pres p* **being** /ˈbiɪŋ/, *pp* **been** /bin *US:* bɪn/) [VP1] (linking *v* (or *copula*), between the subject and various complements) **1** (with a *n* or *pron*, identifying or asking about the subject): *Today is Monday. Peter is a teacher/a Catholic. Who is that? It's me/him/her/the postman.* **2** (with an *adj* or a *prep*, indicating a quality, an attribute): *The world is round. He is ten years old. Short skirts are in/out of fashion.* ⇨ **fashionable, unfashionable. 3** (with a *prep* or *adverbial particle*, indicating a place): *The lamp is on the table. John's out in the garden. Mary's upstairs. The station is a mile away.* **4** (with a *n* or a *prep*, indicating possession, actual or intended): *The money's not yours, it's John's. The parcel is for father.*

be[2] /bi/ *vi* ⇨ **be**[1] [VP1] (linking *v*, indicating a change from one quality, place, etc to another): *He wants to be* (= become) *a fireman when he grows up. Give me a pound, and the skirt is* (= will be) *yours. You can be* (= get) *there in five minutes. Once more he was* (= again became) *the old John we used to know. Suddenly his face was* (= became) *scarlet.*

be[3] /bi/ *vi* ⇨ **be**[1] [VP1] **1** (with introductory *there*): *There's a bus-stop down the road. There were six of us. There are some stamps in that drawer. There's a letter for you.* (*A letter has come for you.* Cf *One of the letters is for you*). **2** (also with introductory *there*, meaning 'exist'): *There is a God. For there to be life there must be air and water.* **3** go; come (esp the *pp* **been**): *I've been to see* (= have paid a visit to) *my uncle. Have you ever been to Cairo? He has been to Paris.* Cf *He's gone to Paris*, i e is now either in Paris or on the way there. *Has the postman been* (i e called) *yet?* **4** ***been and...***, (vulg or hum) (used to indicate surprise, protest, etc): *You've been and bought a new hat! Who's been and taken my dictionary?* **the...to-ˈbe,** the future...: *the bride to-ˈbe.* **ˈwould-be,** who wishes to be or imagines himself to be: *a would-be poet.* **ˈmight-have-beens,** past possibilities. **ˈbe-all,** whole being: *the ˌbe-all and ˈend-all*, the supreme end or aim. ***for the time being,*** until some other arrangement, etc is made. ⇨ also **being.**

be[4] /bi/ *aux v* ⇨ **be**[1] **1** (used with *pres p* to form the progressive or continuous tenses): *They are/were reading. I shall be seeing him soon. What have you been doing this week?* **2** (used with a *pp* to form the passive voice): *He was killed in the war. Where were they made? He is to be pitied.* **3** [VP4F] (used with a *to*-infinitive) **(a)** (equivalent to *must* or *ought*, to indicate duty, necessity, etc): *I am to inform you* (= I have been told to inform you) *that... You are* (= ought, deserve) *to be congratulated.* **(b)** intention: *They are to be married in May.* **(c)** possibility: *The book was not to be* (= could not be) *found.* **(d)** a supposition or unreal condition: *If I were to tell you/Were I to tell you...; If it were to rain* (= If it rained) *tomorrow....* **(e)** (chiefly *pt*) destiny: *He was never to see his wife and family again,* Although he did not know this at the time, he did not see them again. **(f)** mutual arrangement: *We are to be married in May. Every member of the party was to pay his own expenses.* **(g)** the expressed wish of another person: *At what time am I* (= do you want me) *to be there?* **(h)** purpose: *The telegram was to say that she had been delayed.*

be- /bɪ-/ *pref* **1** all over; in every direction **(a)** (from *vv*): *besmear*, smear all over (with sth). **(b)** (from *nn*): *bedew*, cover with dew. **2** (making an intransitive *v* transitive): *bemoan.* Cf *bemoan one's fate*, moan about one's fate. **3** (making *adjj* in *-ed* from *nn*) wearing: *bewigged*; covered with: *bejewelled.* **4** (intensifying): *begrudge; belabour.*

beach /bitʃ/ *n* shore between high- and low-water mark, covered with sand or water-worn pebbles. **ˈ~ ball** *n* very large light-weight one used for games on the ~. **ˈ~ buggy** *n* motorized vehicle, smaller than a mini-moke, larger than a go-kart, used as a fun car for racing on waste ground, beaches, etc. **ˈ~·comber** /-kəʊmə(r)/ *n* **(a)** long wave rolling in from the sea. **(b)** man who makes a poor living on the waterfront in ports in the Pacific. **ˈ~·head** *n* fortified position established on a ~ by an invading army. ⇨ **bridgehead. ˈ~·wear** *n* [U] clothes for sunbathing, swimming, playing games, etc on the ~. □ *vt* [VP6A] push or pull (a boat, a ship) up on to the shore or ~.

bea·con /ˈbikən/ *n* **1** (old use; also *ˈ~-fire*) fire lit on a hill-top as a signal. **2** light on a hill or mountain, or on the coast, on rocks, etc to give warning of danger or for the guidance of ships, etc. **3** (also *~-light*) fixed lantern to warn or guide ships; flashing light to warn aircraft of high mountains, etc. **4** (in GB) seven-foot high post with a lamp, used to indicate a street-crossing for pedestrians: *flashing ~* or *Belisha* /bəˈliʃə/ *~*, one with a light that flashes, to warn motorists that pedestrians have priority over wheeled traffic. **5** (US) = beam**(4)**.

bead /bid/ *n* **1** small ball of wood, glass, etc with a hole through it, for threading with others on a string or wire; (*pl*) necklace of ~s. **2** ***tell one's ~s,*** (old use) say one's prayers (while counting ~s on a rosary). **3** drop of liquid: *His face was covered with ~s of sweat.* **~·ing** *n* wooden strip with a pattern of ~s, used for ornament; similar pattern on stonework; lace trimmings, etc with ~s on the threads.

beadle /ˈbidl/ *n* (formerly) parish officer who helped the priest by keeping order in church, giving out money to the poor, etc.

beady /ˈbidɪ/ *adj* (of eyes) small, round and bright.

beagle /ˈbigl/ *n* small, short-legged hound used for hunting hares when those who take part are on foot, not on horse-back. **beag·ling** *n* hunting hares with ~s.

beak[1] /bik/ *n* **1** hard, horny part of bird's mouth, esp when curved. ⇨ the illus at **prey. 2** ram at the prow of a warship in ancient times.

beak[2] /bik/ *n* **1** (sl) magistrate: *brought up before the ~.* **2** (old use; sl) schoolmaster.

beaker /ˈbikə(r)/ *n* **1** open glass vessel with a lip (as used for chemical experiments, etc). **2** (liter or archaic) large drinking vessel; goblet. **3** plastic vessel, shaped like and used as a drinking glass.

beam /bim/ *n* **1** long horizontal piece of squared timber, or of steel, light alloy, concrete, supported at both ends, used to carry the weight of a building, etc. **2** horizontal cross-timber in a ship, joining the sides and supporting the deck(s); the greatest width of a ship, ⇨ the illus at ship. ***on/off the port/starboard ~,*** on/at a distance from either side. ***on her '~-'ends,*** (of a ship) lying over to one side; almost capsizing. ***be on one's ~-ends,*** (of a person) at the end of one's financial resources; destitute. ***broad in the ~,*** (colloq, of a person) wide and stocky. **3 (a)** crosspiece of a balance, from which the scales hang. ⇨ the illus at balance. **(b)** chief piece of timber in an old-style plough, to which the share is fastened. **4 (a)** ray or stream of light (e g from a lamp or lighthouse, the sun or moon); (fig) bright look or smile, showing happiness, etc: *with a ~ of delight.* **(b)** directed electromagnetic waves: *the ~ system,* by which short waves are directed to a specific target. **(c)** radio signal used to direct an aircraft on its course. ***on/off the ~,*** (of an aircraft) following/not following the radio ~; (colloq) on the right/wrong track; behaving in a way likely/unlikely to be right. □ *vt,vi* **1** [VP2C] (of the sun, etc) send out light and warmth; (fig) smile happily and cheerfully: *~ing on his friends; ~ing with satisfaction.* **2** [VP6A,15] ***~ sth (to),*** (telegraphy) broadcast (a message, radio programme, etc) in a particular direction: *~ed from Britain to S America.*

bean /bin/ *n* **1** (any of several plants bearing) seed in long pods (all used as vegetables): *'broad ~s, 'kidney ~s, 'soya ~s.* ⇨ the illus at vegetable. **'~-stalk** *n* stalk of tall-growing varieties of ~. **2** seed similar in shape of other plants (esp coffee-~s, also called *berries*). **3** (sl uses) ***be without/not have a ~,*** be without any money. ***full of ~s,*** lively; in high spirits or vigour. ***give sb ~s,*** punish or scold him. ***old ~,*** (dated sl, as a familiar form of address) old boy/fellow. ***spill the ~s,*** give away information, esp sth not intended to be made known. **'~-feast/beano** /'binəʊ/ *nn* (dated colloq) feast; celebration; jolly time.

bear[1] /beə(r)/ *n* **1** large, heavy animal with thick fur. ⇨ cub, whelp. **'~-skin** *n* tall military headdress of black fur (worn by the Brigade of Guards in Britain). **2** rough, clumsy ill-mannered person. **3 the Great/Little B~,** names of two constellations in the northern hemisphere. **4** (stock exchange) person who sells stock for future delivery hoping before then to buy it cheap. ⇨ bull[1](3). **~ish** *adj* rough; clumsy.

bear[2] /beə(r)/ *vt,vi* (*pt* bore /bɔ(r)/, *pp* borne /bɔn/) **1** [VP6A,15B] carry: *~ a heavy load.* ***~ away,*** (now usu *carry off*): *~ away the palm,* excel in competition, by winning a prize, etc; *~ away* (i e win) *the prize.* **2** [VP6A] have; show: *~ the marks /signs /traces of blows/wounds/ punishment; a document that ~s your signature;* *~ arms,* be provided with weapons; *~ no/some/not much/little resemblance to sb or sth.* **3** [VP6A] have; be known by: *~ a good character; a family that bore an ancient and honoured name.* **4** [VP16B] ***~ oneself,*** **(a)** carry oneself in a specified way: *He ~s himself like a soldier,* stands, walks, etc like one. **(b)** behave; conduct oneself: *He bore himself with dignity in these difficult circumstances.* **5** [VP14,12C] have in the heart or mind: *~ a grudge (against sb); ~ (some/no) ill will/malice (towards sb); bear sb no malice; the love/hatred she bore him,* felt towards him. **6** [VP6A,14] bring; provide. ***~ a hand,*** help. ***~ witness to sth,*** (fig): *actions that ~ witness to* (= provide evidence of) *his courage.* ***~ false witness (against sb),*** give false evidence. **7** [VP6A,2A] support; sustain: *The ice is too thin to ~ your weight. The ice doesn't ~ yet. Who will ~ the responsibility/expense?* **8** [VP6A,6D,7A,17] (usu with *can/could,* and esp in neg and interr) endure; tolerate; put up with: *I can't ~ (the sight of) that old man. The pain was almost more than he could ~. There's no ~ing* (= It's impossible to ~) *such rude fellows. She couldn't ~ to see animals treated cruelly. She can't ~ to be laughed at/can't ~ being laughed at.* **9** [VP6E] be fit for: *His language won't ~ repeating. Your joke will ~ repeating,* is amusing enough to be heard again. **10** [VP6A,12C] give birth to: *~ a child. She has borne him six sons.* Cf *born*: The eldest son was born in 1932. **11** [VP2C] turn, include: *When you reach the top of the hill, ~ (to the) right.* **12** [VP15B,2C,3A] (with *adverbial particles* and *preps*):

bears

bear down, overcome; defeat: *~ down the enemy; ~ down all resistance.* ***~ down (up)on,*** (esp of a ship, car) move quickly towards.

(be) borne in on (sb), (of sb) be made to realize: *The terrible truth was borne in on him,* he had to realize it. *It was gradually borne in on me that...,* The idea that... was one that I gradually had to accept.

bear (sth or sb) out, confirm (sth); support (sb): *~ out a statement. John will ~ me out/~ out what I've said.*

bear up (against/under sth), be strong in the face of (sorrow, etc): *He bore up well against all these misfortunes. Tell her to ~ up,* to have courage, not give way.

bear (up)on, have relation to, have influence on, be relevant to: *How does this ~ upon the problem? These are matters that ~ upon the welfare of the community.* ***bring to ~ (up)on,*** make (sth) relate to, have influence on: *bring all one's energies to ~ upon a task; bring pressure to ~ on sb.* ***~ hard/heavily/severely, etc (up)on,*** be a burden on: *Taxation ~s heavily on all classes in Britain.*

bear with (sb), treat patiently or indulgently: *If you will ~ with me* (i e listen patiently to me) *a little longer....*

bear·able /ˈbeərəbl/ *adj* (from bear²(8)) that can be borne or endured.

beard /bɪəd/ *n* **1** hair of the lower part of the face (excluding the moustache): *a man with a ~; a week's (growth of) ~*; similar growth of hair on an animal: *a billy-goat's ~.* **2** ~-like sheath on the grain of barley, oats, etc. □ *vt* [VP6A] defy openly, oppose: *~ the lion in his den,* (fig) defy sb in his own stronghold. **~ed** *adj* having a ~. **~-less** *adj* having no ~: *a ~less youth.*

bearer /ˈbeərə(r)/ *n* **1** person who brings a letter or message: *the ~ of good news; the ~ of this letter;* person who helps to carry a coffin to a grave, who carries a stretcher, standard, etc; person who presents, at a bank, a cheque payable on demand. **ˈ~ bonds** *n pl* bonds, interest on which is payable to the ~, the owner's name not being written on them. **2** (in India, Pakistan, etc) male servant (originally one who helped to carry a palanquin). **3** (with *adjj*) plant, tree, etc that produces fruit, crops, etc: *a good/poor ~.*

bear·ing /ˈbeərɪŋ/ *n* **1** [U] way of behaving; way of standing, walking, etc: *a man of noble/soldierly ~. His kindly ~ caused all the children to like him.* ⇨ bear²(4). **2** [C,U] relation, aspect: *We must consider the question in all its ~s. What he said has no/not much ~ on* (i e is not connected with) *the subject.* ⇨ bear²(12). **3** [U] possibility of being endured; endurance: *His conduct was beyond (all) ~.* ⇨ bear²(8). **4** [C] direction in which a place, etc, lies (as measured, e g in degrees): *take a compass ~ on a lighthouse*; (*pl*) relative position; direction. ***get/take one's ~s,*** find the direction of a ship's course; find one's position by looking round for landmarks, etc. ***lose/be out of one's ~s,*** be lost; (fig) be puzzled. **5** (in a machine) device that supports moving parts and reduces friction (usu *pl ball-~s*). **6** (of a tree, etc): *in full ~,* producing fruit well. ⇨ child-~.

bear·ish /ˈbeərɪʃ/ *adj* ⇨ bear¹.

beast /bist/ *n* **1** four-footed animal (*animal* is the usu word; *beast* is used in fables). **2** (farming) cow or bullock; animal for riding or driving. **3** cruel or disgusting person. **4** (reproachfully or playfully) person who behaves badly: *Don't make a ~ of yourself!* (e g to sb who is over-eating). *They hate that ~ of a foreman!* (e g of a foreman who is very strict). **~·ly** *adj* **1** like a ~ or its ways; unfit for human use. **2** (colloq) nasty: *What ~ly weather!* □ *adv* (colloq; used to intensify *adjj* and *advv* used in a bad sense) very; unpleasantly: *He was ~ly drunk.* ⇨ jolly. *It was ~ly cold.* **~·li·ness** /-lɪnəs/ *n* [U]

beat¹ /bit/ *vt,vi* (*pt* beat, *pp* ~en /ˈbitn/) **1** [VP6A,14,2A,C] hit repeatedly (esp with a stick): *She was ~ing the carpet/~ing the dust out of the carpet. He was ~ing a drum. We heard the drums ~ing,* being ~en. *The boy was ~en until he was black and blue,* covered with bruises. *The hunters had to ~ a way through the undergrowth,* make a path by ~ing the branches, etc down. *Somebody was ~ing at/upon the door.* ***~ one's brains,*** ⇨ brain(4). ***~ a retreat,*** give the signal (by drum) to retreat; (fig) go back, retire. ***~ the woods,*** go into them to drive out game (for sport, shooting). **2** [VP2C] (of the sun, rain, wind, etc) strike: *The rain was ~ing against the windows.* **3** [VP6A,14] mix thoroughly and let air into by using a fork or similar utensil: *~ eggs; ~ cream* (to a froth); *~ flour, eggs, etc, to a paste.* ⇨ whip²(2). **4** [VP6A,22,15B] hammer, change the shape of by blows: *~ sth flat; ~ out gold,* hammer it flat; *~ the door in,* break it in by ~ing. **5** [VP6A,14,15A] defeat; do better than: *Our army was ~en. I'll ~ you to the top of that hill,* race you and get there first. *He ~ me at chess.* ***~ the record,*** break the record, make a new and better record. **6** [VP6A] be too difficult for; perplex: *That problem has ~en me.* **7** [VP6A,14] move up and down regularly: *The bird was ~ing its wings against the sides of the cage. His heart was still ~ing. Her heart was ~ing with joy.* ***~ time,*** measure time (in music) by making regular movements (with the hands, etc). **8** (various uses): ***~ about the bush,*** approach a subject without coming to the point. ***dead ~,*** tired out. ***~ it,*** (sl) go away. **9** [VP2C, 15B] (with *adverbial particles* and *preps*):

beat down (on), *The sun was ~ing down on our heads,* shining with great heat. ***~ sb/sth down:*** *He wanted £800 for the car but I ~ him down* (= made him lower his price) *to £600. I ~ down his price,* made him lower it. *The wheat had been ~en down* (= flattened) *by the rain.*

beat sb/sth off, *The attacker/attack was ~en off,* repulsed.

beat sth out, *The dry grass caught fire, but we ~ it out,* extinguished the fire by ~ing the burning grass. *He ~ out* (= drummed) *a tune on a tin can.*

beat sb up, *He was badly ~en up* (= beaten severely with cudgels, etc) *in a back alley.* ***~ sth up (into/to),*** mix thoroughly and let air into by using a fork or other utensil: *~ the mixture up to a creamy consistency; ~ the flour and eggs (up) to a paste.* **~·ing** *n* (esp punishment by hitting or striking repeatedly; defeat: *get/give sb a good ~ing.*

beat² /bit/ *n* **1** regular repeated stroke, or sound of this: *We heard the ~ of a drum. His heart ~s were getting weaker.* **2** recurring emphasis marking rhythm in music or poetry. **3** route over which sb goes regularly; appointed course of a sentinel or policeman: *The policeman was on his ~,* on the route he was ordered to patrol. ***be off/out of one's ~,*** (fig) be doing sth with which one is not familiar, sth different from one's usual work, etc.

beat³ /bit/ *adj* (attrib only) of or like beatniks: *the ~ generation.*

beaten /ˈbitn/ *adj* (esp) **1** shaped by beating: *~ silver.* **2** (of a path) worn hard by use: *a well-~ path.* ***go off/keep to the ~ track,*** do sth/not do anything unusual.

beater /ˈbitə(r)/ *n* **1** utensil used for beating: *a ˈcarpet-~; an ˈegg-~.* **2** man employed to drive birds, etc to those waiting with guns to shoot them.

bea·tif·ic /bɪəˈtɪfɪk/ *adj* showing great happiness; making blessed.

be·atify /bɪˈætɪfaɪ/ *vt* (*pt,pp* -fied) [VP6A] (in the R C church) announce that a dead person is among the Blessed (i e those who will live for ever with God in a state of supreme happiness). **be·ati·fi·ca·tion** /bɪˈætɪfɪˈkeɪʃn/ *n* ~ing or being beatified; first step before canonization.

be·ati·tude /bɪˈætɪtjud *US:* -tud/ *n* [U] great happiness; blessedness. **The B~s,** Christ's sermon on blessedness (in the Bible, Matt 5: 3-11).

beat·nik /ˋbitnɪk/ *n* (after World War II) person adopting unconventional manners and dress as a defiant protest against current morality and as a means of self-expression. Cf *hippy*, a later word.

beau /bəʊ/ *n* (*pl* **beaux** /bəʊz/) **1** (old use) rather old man who is greatly interested in the fashion of his clothes. **2** (now usu fac) men who pay great attention to women. **3** (now usu fac) girl's admirer or lover. **4** **~ ideal,** one's idea of what is most excellent or beautiful. **the ~ monde** /ˈbəʊ ˋmõd/ (F) fashionable society.

Beau·jolais /ˋbəʊʒəleɪ *US:* ˈbəʊʒəˋleɪ/ *n* [U] (F) light wine (usu red) of Burgundy.

beau·te·ous /ˋbjutɪəs/ *adj* (poet) beautiful.

beau·tician /bjuˋtɪʃn/ *n* person who runs a beauty-parlour.

beau·ti·ful /ˋbjutəfl/ *adj* giving pleasure or delight to the mind or senses: *a ~ face/flower/voice; ~ weather/music.* **~ly** /-fl̩ɪ/ *adv* in a ~ manner: *She plays the piano ~ly. That will do ~ly,* will be most satisfactory. **beau·tify** /ˋbjutəfaɪ/ *vt* (*pt, pp* **-fied**) [VP6A] make ~.

beauty /ˋbjutɪ/ *n* **1** [U] combination of qualities that give pleasure to the senses (esp the eye and ear) or to the moral sense or the intellect: *Everyone must admire the ~ of a mother's love. B~ is only skin deep,* We must not judge by outward appearance only. **2** [C] (*pl* **-ties**) person, thing, feature characteristic, that is beautiful or particularly good: *Isn't she a ~! Her smile is one of her beauties. Look at this peach. Isn't it a ~! We are always finding new beauties in Shakespeare's poetry. That's the ~ of it,* the point that gives satisfaction. **ˋ~-parlour** *n* establishment (now usu *ˋ~-salon*) in which women receive treatment (of the skin, hair, etc) to increase their ~. **ˋ~ queen** *n* girl voted the most beautiful in a ~ contest. **ˋ~-salon,** = ~-parlour. **ˋ~-sleep** *n* sleep before midnight. **ˋ~-spot** *n* **1** place with beautiful scenery. **2** birthmark or artificial patch on the face, said to heighten ~.

bea·ver[1] /ˋbivə(r)/ *n* **1** fur-coated animal that lives both on land and in water, with strong teeth with which it cuts down trees and makes dams across rivers. ⇨ the illus at **small**. **2** [U] its fur. **3** [U] heavy woollen cloth that looks like ~ fur. **4** [C] high hat made of ~ fur, formerly worn by men.

bea·ver[2] /ˋbivə(r)/ *n* (on the helmet worn by soldiers in olden times) movable lower part that guarded the lips and chin.

be·calmed /bɪˋkɑmd/ *pred adj* (of a sailing-ship) stopped because there is no wind.

be·came pt of **become**.

be·cause /bɪˋkoz *conj* **1** for the reason that: *I did it ~ they asked me to do it. Just ~ I don't complain, you mustn't suppose that I'm satisfied.* (Note that when the reason is obvious, or is thought to be known, it is preferable to use *as*, or a construction with *so: As it's raining, you'd better take a taxi.* After the noun *reason, that* is preferred to ~: *The reason* why we were late is *that...*) **2** ***~ of,*** *prep* by reason of; on account of: *B~ of his bad leg, he couldn't walk so fast as the others. I said nothing about it, ~ of his wife('s) being there.*

beck[1] /bek/ *n* (N England) mountain stream or brook.

beck[2] /bek/ *n* movement of the head, hand or arm, as a signal or sign, used only in: ***be at sb's ~ and call,*** be bound to obey his orders, to come and go, all the time. ***have sb at one's ~ and call,*** have sb always waiting to obey one's orders.

beckon /ˋbekən/ *vt,vi* [VP6A,15B,16A,2A] call sb's attention by a movement of the hand or arm, usu to show that he is to come nearer or to follow: *He ~ed (to) me to follow. He ~ed me on/in.*

be·come /bɪˋkʌm/ *vi,vt* (*pt* **became** /bɪˋkeɪm/, *pp* **become**) **1** [VP2D] come or grow to be; begin to be: *He became a doctor. He has ~ a famous man. The custom has now ~ a rule. He has ~ accustomed to his new duties. It's becoming much more expensive to travel abroad.* **2** [VP3A] **~ of,** happen to: *What will ~ of the children if their father dies? I don't know what has ~ of him.* **3** [VP6A] be well suited to: *Her new hat ~s her.* **4** [VP6A] be right or fitting; befit: *He used language* (e g vulgar language) *that does not ~ a man of his education.* **be·com·ing** *adj* **1** (of dress, etc) well suited to the wearer: *a becoming hat/dress/style of hair-dressing.* **2** suitable, appropriate: *with a modesty becoming to his low rank.* **be·com·ing·ly** *adv*

bed[1] /bed/ *n* **1** piece of furniture, or other arrangement, on which to sleep (Note omission and use of the articles): *go to bed; get into/out of bed; put the children to bed; sit on the bed; find a bed for sb; He thinks of nothing but bed,* (fig) love-making; *single bed,* for one person; *double bed,* for two persons: *I want a room with two single beds/a double bed. I want a double-bedded room; twin beds,* two exactly similar single beds; *spare bed(room),* one that is kept for an occasional visitor. ***bed and board,*** food and lodging; entertainment (at an inn, etc). ***make the beds,*** put the bedclothes (sheets, blankets, etc) in order, ready for use. ***As you make your bed so you must lie on it,*** (prov) you must accept the consequences of your acts. ***He got out of bed on the wrong side,*** said of sb who is bad-tempered for the day. ***take to/keep to one's bed,*** stay in bed because of illness. **2** mattress: *a ˋfeather bed; a ˋspring-bed.* **3** flat base on which sth rests: *The machine rests on a bed of concrete.* **4** bottom of the sea, a river, lake, etc; layer of rock, stone, etc, as a foundation for a road or railway; layer of clay, rock, etc, below the surface soil: *If you dig here, you will find a bed of clay.* **ˋbed-ˋrock,** solid rock below the soil, found at different depths in different places; (fig) ultimate facts or principles on which a theory, etc, is based: *reach/get down to bed-rock.* **5** garden plot, piece of ground (for flowers, vegetables, etc): *ˋseed-bed; ˋonion-bed; ˋflower beds.* **6** (compounds) **ˋbed-bug** *n* wingless, blood-sucking insect. **ˋbed-clothes** *n pl* sheets, blankets, etc for a bed. **ˋbed-fellow** *n* person with whom one shares a bed; (fig) companion. **ˋbed·pan** *n* vessel for waste matter from the body, used by an invalid in bed. **ˋbed·post** *n* upright support of a bedstead (esp the old-fashioned sort). **ˋbed·ridden** *adj* confined to bed by weakness or old age. **ˋbed-roll** *n* portable roll of bedding (e g as used by campers). **ˋbed·room** / *with -dr- as in 'dry', not separated as in 'head-room'*/ *n* room for sleeping in. **ˋbed·side** *n* side of (esp a sick person's) bed: *Dr Green has a good bedside manner,* is tactful, knows how to fill his patients with confidence in himself; (attrib) *bedside table; bedside books.* **ˈbed·ˋsitter** (colloq for) **ˈbed-ˋsitting-room** *n* room used (e g by students, single persons away from home) for both living in and sleeping in. **ˋbed·sore** *n* sore on the back, etc of an invalid, caused by lying in bed for a long time. **ˋbed·spread** *n* covering spread over a bed during the day. **ˋbed·stead** *n* framework of wood and metal to support the mattress. **ˋbed·time** *n* time for going to bed: *His usual bedtime is eleven o'clock.*

bed² /bed/ *vt* (-dd-) [VP6A,15A,B] **1** plant (seedlings, etc): *He was bedding out some young cabbage plants. He bedded the seedlings (in).* **2** place or fix in a foundation: *Bricks and stones are bedded in mortar or concrete. The bullet bedded itself in* (= went deep into) *the wall. Heavy guns have to be bedded in before they will fire accurately.* **3** *bed down a horse,* provide it with straw, etc on which to rest; *bed down a soldier/traveller, etc,* provide him with bedding. **ˋbed·ding** *n* [U] **1** bedclothes, e g blankets. **2** straw, etc, for animals to sleep on. **3** ***bedding out,*** planting out (of seedlings, young plants, etc).

be·daubed /bɪˋdɔbd/ *pred adj* ~ ***with,*** smeared (with sth dirty, wet, sticky, etc).

bed·ding /ˋbedɪŋ/ *n* [U] ⇨ bed².

be·decked /bɪˋdekt/ *pred adj* ~ ***with,*** adorned, decorated (with flowers, jewels, etc).

be·devil /bɪˋdevl/ *vt* (-ll-, US: -l-) (usu passive) confuse; complicate: *The issue is ~led by Smith's refusal to co-operate with us.* **~·ment** *n*

be·dewed /bɪˋdjud *US:* -ˋdud/ *pred adj* ~ ***with,*** (liter) sprinkled with, made wet with: *a face ~ with tears.*

be·dim·med /bɪˋdɪmd/ *pred adj* ~ ***with,*** (liter) (of the eyes, mind) made dim: *eyes ~ with tears; a mind ~ with sorrow.*

bed·lam /ˋbedləm/ *n* **1** (old use) asylum for mad people. **2** scene of noisy confusion: *When the teacher was called away the classroom was a regular ~.*

Bed·ouin, Bed·uin /ˋbedʊɪn/ *n* (*pl* unchanged) nomad desert Arab.

be·drag·gled /bɪˋdrægld/ *pred adj* (esp of a dress) made wet or dirty by being dragged in mud.

bee /bi/ *n* **1** small, four-winged, stinging insect that produces wax and honey after gathering nectar from flowers. ⇨ the illus at insect. ***have a bee in one's bonnet,*** be obsessed by an idea. ***make a ˋbee-line for,*** go towards by the shortest way, go quickly towards. **ˋbee·hive** *n* ⇨ hive. **2** (chiefly US) meeting for combined work and amusement (esp of neighbours and friends). **ˋspelling bee,** competition in spelling.

beech /bitʃ/ *n* [C] forest tree with smooth bark and shiny dark-green leaves and small triangular nuts; [U] its wood. **ˋ~ mast** *n* [U] ~ nuts.

beef /bif/ *n* **1** [U] flesh of an ox, bull or cow, used as meat. **~ cattle,** bred and reared for ~. ⇨ dairy cattle. **~ tea,** stewed juice from ~ (for people who are ill). **ˋ~·steak** *n* ⇨ steak. **ˋ~·eater** *n* yeoman of the guard; one of the warders of the Tower of London, dressed as in the days of the Tudor kings. **2** [U] (in men) muscle: *He's got plenty of ~.* **3** (with *pl* beeves /bivz/) fattened ox, considered as food. □ *vi* (sl) complain: *Stop ~ing so much!* **~y** *adj* (of a person) well covered with flesh; strong.

been ⇨ be¹.

beep /bip/ *n* repeated signal (as during a phone conversation, indicating that it is being recorded).

beer /bɪə(r)/ *n* [U] alcoholic drink made from malt and flavoured with hops; other drinks made from roots, etc: ˈ*ginger-ˋ~*, ˋ*nettle-~*. ***small ~,*** sth trifling and unimportant: *He thinks no small ~ of himself,* has a high opinion of himself. **~y** *adj* like ~ in taste or smell; (e g of a person) smelling of ~.

bees·wax /ˋbizwæks/ *n* [U] wax made by bees for honeycomb, used for polishing wood. □ *vt* polish with ~.

beet /bit/ *n* sorts of plant with a sweet root. **ˋred ~,** used as a vegetable, esp in salads. **ˋwhite ~,** used for making sugar. **ˈ~ ˋsugar,** sugar made from ~s, identical with cane sugar. **ˋ~·root** /ˋbitrut *with* tr *as in 'try'*/ *n* [C,U] root of ~; red ~.

beetle¹ /ˋbitl/ *n* tool with a heavy head and handle, used for crushing, ramming and smoothing.

beetle² /ˋbitl/ *n* insect with hard, shiny wing-covers. ⇨ the illus at insect.

beetle³ /ˋbitl/ *vi* [VP2A] overhang; project: *beetling cliffs.* **ˋ~-browed** *adj* having shaggy or projecting eyebrows.

beeves ⇨ beef(3).

be·fall /bɪˋfɔl/ *vt,vi* (*pt* befell /bɪˋfel/ *pp* befallen /bɪˋfɔlən/) [VP6A] (used only in the 3rd person) happen (to): *What has ~en him?*

be·fit /bɪˋfɪt/ *vt* (-tt-) [VP6A] be fitted for; be right and suitable for (used only in 3rd person): *It does not ~ a man in your position to....* **~·ting** *adj* right and proper. **~·ting·ly** *adv*

be·fog·ged /bɪˋfogd/ *pred adj* (fig, of a person) puzzled; muddle-headed.

be·fore¹ /bɪˋfɔ(r)/ *adv* **1** at an earlier time; in the past; already: *I've seen that film ~. It had been fine the day ~,* the previous day. *You should have told me so ~,* earlier. *That happened long ~,* a long time earlier. **2** (of space or position): *They have gone on ~,* in advance.

be·fore² /bɪˋfɔ(r)/ *conj* previous to the time when: *I must finish my work ~ I go home. Do it now ~ you forget. It will be five years ~ we meet again* (note the use of the *present t* here). Cf We *shall not meet again* until five years from now.

be·fore³ /bɪˋfɔ(r)/ *prep* **1** earlier than: *the day ~ yesterday; the year ~ last; two days ~ Christmas; in 55* B C (= ~ Christ, i e ~ the birth of Christ); *~ the holidays; since ~ the war; ~ now/then; ~ long,* soon. **2** in front of (esp with reference to order or arrangement): *B comes ~ C. Ladies ~ gentlemen,* ladies first. *Your name comes ~ mine on the list.* **3** in front of (with reference to position). (Except in a few phrases *in front of* is preferred to *before* in this sense, e g There are some trees *in front of* the house.) ***carry all ~ you,*** be successful in everything you attempt. ***sail ~ the mast,*** as an ordinary seaman, not as an officer. ***sail ~ the wind,*** with the wind behind. **4** in the presence of; face to face with: *He was brought ~ the judge. Don't hesitate to speak out ~ everyone* (i e in public) *about the way you've been treated.* **5** rather than; in preference to: *Death ~ dishonour.*

be·fore·hand /bɪˈfɔhænd/ *adv* earlier; before¹(1): *I knew what he would need, so I made preparations ~,* in advance, in readiness. *Please let me know ~. You ought to have told me ~.* □ *pred adj* early; in advance: *When you go on a journey, it's a good thing to be ~ with your packing. She's always ~ with the rent,* pays it, or is ready to pay it, before it is due.

be·foul /bɪˋfaʊl/ *vt* (liter) make dirty.

be·friend /bɪˋfrend/ *vt* [VP6A] make a friend of; be kind and helpful to (esp sb younger and needing help).

beg /beg/ *vt, vi* (-gg-) **1** [VP6A,2A,C,3A,14] ***beg (for sth) (from/of sb),*** ask for (food, money, clothes, etc); make a living by asking for money (in the streets, etc): *He begged a meal. He was so poor that he had to beg (for) his bread. He made a living by begging from door to door.* ***a begging letter,*** one that asks for help, esp money. **2** [VP6A,7A,17A,9,2C,15B] ask earnestly, or with deep feeling: *beg a favour of sb,* ask him to help to do sth; *beg (of) sb to do sth. They begged us not to punish them. I beg (of) you not to take any risks. I begged (of) him to stay/that he would stay. The children begged to come with us/that they might come with us.* ***beg the question,*** assume the truth of the matter that is in question. ***go begging,*** (of things) be unwanted: *If these things are going begging* (= if nobody wants them), *I'll take them.* ***beg off,*** ask to be excused. *He promised to come and help but has since begged off.* ***beg sb off,*** ask that sb may be excused or forgiven. ⇨ pardon. **3** [VP7A] take the liberty of (saying or doing sth): *I beg to differ. I beg to state/observe, etc that....*

be·gad /bɪˋgæd/ *int* (old use) by God!

be·gan ⇨ begin.

be·get /bɪˋget/ *vt* (-tt-) (*pt* begot /bɪˋgot/, old use begat /bɪˋgæt/, *pp* begotten /bɪˋgotn/) [VP6A] **1** give existence to (as father): (Bible) *Abraham begat Isaac. The only begotten of the Father,* the only Son of God the Father. **2** (liter) be the cause of: *War* ~*s misery and ruin.* **~·ter** *n* one who ~s.

beg·gar /ˋbegə(r)/ *n* **1** (also ~*man,* ~*woman*) person who lives by begging, e g for money, food; poor person. ***B~s can't be choosers,*** must take whatever is offered them. **2** person who begs for others, for charities, etc: *He's a good* ~, successful in collecting money for charity, etc. **3** (colloq; playful or friendly use) person; fellow: *You lucky* ~*! What a fine little* ~ *your boy is!* □ *vt* **1** [VP6A] make poor, ruin: *You'll* ~ *your family if you spend so much money on drink.* **2** ***~ description,*** make words seem poor and inadequate: *The scenery* ~*ed description.* **~·ly** *adj* very poor; mean; deserving contempt: *What a* ~*ly salary to offer me!* **~y** *n* [U] extreme poverty: *He complained that taxation was reducing him to* ~*y.*

be·gin /bɪˋgɪn/ *vt, vi* (-nn-, *pt* began /bɪˋgæn/, *pp* begun /bɪˋgʌn/) (For notes on the use of *begin* and *start,* ⇨ start.) **1** [VP6A,2A] start: *When did you* ~ *English,* learn your first English words? *It's time to* ~ *work. We shall* ~ *the meeting at seven o'clock. The meeting will* ~ *at seven o'clock. He has begun a new book,* is reading (or writing) the first few pages. ***~ (on),*** [VP3A the *v* being understood] *He has begun on* (= is reading, writing) *a new book. Has he begun (on) another bottle,* begun to drink another bottle? **2** [VP7A,6D] (used of activities and states that come into existence. The *inf* is preferred when the *pred* denotes a state of mind or a mental activity): *She began to feel dizzy/afraid. I'm* ~*ning to understand. I began to think you were never coming.* (The *inf* is preferred when the grammatical subject is lifeless, not a person): *The plaster was* ~*ning to fall from the walls. The barometer began to fall. The water is* ~*ning to boil. The snow began to melt when the sun came out.* (Either the *inf* or the *gerund* is used when the grammatical subject is a person and when the *pred* indicates an activity or process, not a state. Alternatives are given in the examples. Note that if *begin* is used in one of the progressive tenses, an *inf* follows, not a *gerund*): *When did you begin learning/to learn German? She began crying/to cry. It began raining/to rain. It is* ~*ning to rain/is* ~*ning raining.* **3** ***~ at,*** start from: *Today we* ~ *at page 30, line 12.* ***to ~ with,*** in the first place: *We can't give Smith the position; to* ~ *with, he's too young; secondly, I want my son to have the job.* ***~ life as,*** start one's life or career as: *He began life as a builder's labourer.* ***~ the world,*** (old use; liter) start in life, enter upon one's career. **~·ner** *n* (esp) person still learning and without much experience. **~·ning** *n* starting point: *I've read the book from* ~*ning to end. When learning a foreign language, it's important to make a good* ~*ning. Did democracy have its* ~*nings in Athens?*

be·gone /bɪˋgon/ *v* (imper only) (liter) go away (stronger than 'Go!'): *B~! B~ dull care!* ⇨ also woe~.

be·gonia /bɪˋgəʊnɪə/ *n* [C] garden plant with brightly coloured leaves and flowers.

be·gorra /bɪˋgorə/ *int* (Irish form of) by God!

be·got, be·got·ten ⇨ beget.

be·grimed /bɪˋgraɪmd/ *pred adj* made grimy: *hands* ~*d with oil and dirt.*

be·grudge /bɪˋgrʌdʒ/ *vt* (intensive form of *grudge*) [VP13A,12A,6C] feel or show dissatisfaction or envy at: *No one* ~*s you your good fortune. We don't* ~ *your going to Italy.*

be·guile /bɪˋgaɪl/ **1** [VP6A,14] ***~ sb (into),*** cheat, deceive: *They were* ~*d into forming an unwise alliance.* **2** [VP6A,14] ***~ (with),*** cause (time, etc) to pass pleasantly: *Our journey was* ~*d with pleasant talk.* **3** [VP6A,14] amuse: *We* ~*d the children with fairy tales.*

be·gum /ˋbeɪgəm/ *n* Muslim princess or lady of high rank.

be·gun ⇨ begin.

be·half /bɪˋhɑf *US:* -ˋhæf/ *n* ***in ~ of,*** (US) in the interest of. ***on ~ of,*** for, in the interest of, on account of, as the representative of. ***on my/his/our/John's, etc ~,*** for me/him/us/John, etc: *On* ~ *of my colleagues and myself,* speaking for them and me. *Don't be uneasy on my* ~, about me.

be·have /bɪˋheɪv/ *vi, reflex* **1** [VP2A,C,6B] act; conduct oneself: *He has* ~*d shamefully towards his wife,* has treated her in a shameful way. *Can't you make your little boy* ~ *(himself),* show good manners, be polite? *The troops* ~*d gallantly under fire.* **2** [VP2A,C] (of machines, etc) work; function: *How's your new car behaving?* **be·haved** *adj* (in compounds) **ˈwell-/ˈbadly ˋ~d,** behaving well/badly. *What badly* ~*d children!*

be·hav·iour (US = **-ior**) /bɪˋheɪvɪə(r)/ *n* [U] way of behaving, manners (good or bad); treatment shown towards others: *His* ~ *towards me shows that he does not like me. Tom won a prize for good* ~ *at school.* ***be on one's best ~,*** take great care to behave well. ***put sb on his best ~,*** advise or warn him to behave well. **~·ism** *n* [U] (psych) doctrine that all human actions could, if full knowledge were available, be analysed into stimulus and response. **~·ist** *n* believer in this doctrine.

be·head /bɪˋhed/ *vt* [VP6A] cut off the head of (as a punishment).

be·held ⇨ behold.

be·hest /bɪˋhest/ n (old use; only in) ***at sb's ~,*** on sb's orders: *at the King's ~.*

be·hind[1] /bɪˋhaɪnd/ *adv* **1** in the rear: *The dog was running ~. The others are a long way ~. The enemy attacked us from ~.* ***fall/lag ~,*** fail to keep up: *Harry was tired and fell ~.* ***stay/remain ~,*** stay after others have left. **2** ***be ~ with/in,*** be in arrears with: *Are you ~ with your work/studies, etc,* Have you done less than you ought to have done? *He was ~ in his payments,* had not made payments (e g of rent) when they were due.

be·hind[2] /bɪˋhaɪnd/ *n* (colloq) buttocks: *He kicked the boy's ~. He fell on his ~.*

be·hind[3] /bɪˋhaɪnd/ *prep* **1** to the rear of: *The boy was hiding ~ a tree. Come out from ~ the door. There is an orchard ~ the house. The sun was ~* (= hidden by) *the clouds. Walk close ~ me. He put the idea ~ him,* (fig) refused to consider it. ⇨ also **back**[1](1), **scene**(6) and **leave**[1](3). **2** not having made so much progress as: *~ other boys of his age; a country far ~ its neighbours. Mary is ~ the other girls in sewing.* **3** remaining after, when one has left a place: *He left nothing but debts ~ him. The storm left a trail of destruction ~ it.* **4** (of time): *Your schooldays will soon be far ~ you.* ⇨ also **time**[1](3, 10).

be·hind·hand /bɪˋhaɪndhænd/ *pred adj* **1** ***be/get ~ (with/in),*** be in arrears: *be ~ with the rent; get ~ in one's work.* **2** late; after others: *He did not want to be ~ in generosity,* later than others in being generous.

be·hold /bɪˋhəʊld/ *vt* (*pt,pp* **beheld** /bɪˋheld/) [VP6A] (old or liter use) take notice: see (esp sth unusual or striking). **~er** *n* spectator.

be·holden /bɪˋhəʊldn/ *pred adj* ***~ (to),*** under an obligation; owing thanks: *We are much ~ to you for your help.*

be·hove /bɪˋhəʊv/ (US = **be·hoove** /bɪˋhuv/) *vt* (impers) be right or necessary: *It ~s you to,* It is your duty to, You ought to…; *It does not ~ you to,* You must not or ought not to….

beige /beɪʒ/ *n* [U] colour of sandstone (brown, brownish grey or greyish yellow); soft fabric of undyed and unbleached wool.

be-in /ˋbi ɪn/ *n* (colloq) gathering of hippies.

be·ing /ˋbiɪŋ/ *n* **1** [U] existence. ***bring/call sth into ~,*** cause it to have reality or existence. ***come into ~,*** begin to exist: *We do not know when this world came into ~.* ***in ~,*** existing: *a fleet in ~,* not one that is planned for the future. **2** [C] human creature: *Men, women and children are human ~s.* **3 the Supreme B~,** God.

be·jew·el·led (US = **-eled**) /bɪˋdʒuld/ *part adj* decorated, adorned, with jewels.

be·la·bour (US = **-bor**) /bɪˋleɪbə(r)/ *vt* [VP6A] beat hard, give hard blows to: *The robbers ~ed him soundly.*

be·lated /bɪˋleɪtɪd/ *adj* coming very late or too late: overtaken by darkness: *~ apologies; ~ travellers who lost their way in the forest.*

be·lay /bɪˋleɪ/ *vt* [VP6A] (naut) make secure (a rope) round sth. **beˋlay·ing-pin** *n* fixed wooden or iron pin or cleat for ~ing. □ *n* turn of a rope in ~ing.

belch /beltʃ/ *vt,vi* **1** [VP6A,15B] send, e g smoke, flames, out or forth: *A volcano ~es out smoke and ashes.* **2** [VP2A] send out gas from the stomach noisily through the mouth. □ *n* act or sound of ~ing; sth ~ed out (e g a burst of flame from a furnace).

bel·dam, bel·dame /ˋbeldəm/ *n* (old use) old, esp bad-tempered, woman.

be·leaguer /bɪˋligə(r)/ *vt* [VP6A] besiege.

bel·fry /ˋbelfrɪ/ *n* (*pl* **-ries**) tower for bells, ⇨ the illus at **church**; part of a church tower in which bells hang. ***bats in the ~,*** ⇨ **bat**[1].

be·lie /bɪˋlaɪ/ *vt* [VP6A] **1** give a wrong or untrue idea of: *His cheerful appearance ~d his feelings.* **2** fail to justify or be equal to (what is hoped for or promised).

be·lief /bɪˋlif/ *n* **1** [U] ***~ (in),*** the feeling that sth is real and true; trust; confidence: *I haven't much ~ in his honesty,* cannot feel sure that he is honest. *He had no great ~ in his doctor,* had little confidence that his doctor could cure him. *He has lost his ~ in God,* no longer accepts the existence of God as true. *It is my ~ that,* I feel confident that…; *He came to me in the ~ that* (= feeling confident that) *I could help him.* ***to the best of my ~,*** in my genuine opinion. **2** [C] sth accepted as true or real; sth taught as part of a religion; religion: *the ~s of the Christian Church.*

be·lieve /bɪˋliv/ *vt,vi* **1** [VP6A,9,10,25] feel sure of the truth of sth, that sb is telling the truth; be of the opinion (*that*): *I ~ that man. I ~ what that man says. People used to ~ that the world was flat. They ~d him to be/~d that he was insane. I ~ it to have been a mistake. Nobody will ~ what difficulty there has been over this question/how difficult this question has been. Will they be ready tomorrow? Yes, I ~ so. No, I ~ not.* ***~ (you) me,*** I assure you. **2** [VP3A] ***~ in,*** **(a)** have trust in: *I ~ in that man.* **(b)** feel sure of the existence of: *~ in God.* **(c)** feel sure of the value or worth of: *He ~s in getting plenty of exercise. He ~s in old-fashioned remedies.* **3** ***make ~,*** pretend: *The boys made ~ that they were/made ~ to be explorers in the African forests.* Hence, **ˋmake-~** *n*: *Don't be frightened, it's all make-~,* is all pretence. **be·liever** *n* person who ~s, esp a person with religious faith. **be·liev·able** *adj* that can be ~d. **be·liev·ing** *n* ***Seeing is ~,*** You may ~ sth if you see it.

be·like /bɪˋlaɪk/ *adv* (old use) possibly.

be·little /bɪˋlɪtl/ *vt* [VP6A] cause to seem unimportant or of small value: *Don't ~ yourself,* be too modest about your abilities, etc.

bell /bel/ *n* **1** hollow vessel of cast metal, usu shaped like a cup, that makes a ringing sound when struck (usu by a tongue or clapper inside the ~ or, in an electric ~, by a small hammer). ***~, book and candle,*** ecclesiastical curse of excommunication. ***as sound as a ~,*** (fig) in first-rate condition. ***ring a ~,*** (colloq) recall to memory sth half forgotten. **2** (naut) ***one to eight ~s,*** ~ sounded every half hour: *eight ~s,* 12, 4 or 8 o'clock; *four ~s,* 2, 6 or 10 o'clock. **3** **ˋ~-boy, ˋ~-hop** *n* (US) boy or man employed in a hotel to carry luggage, messages, etc. ⇨ **buttons**(4) (GB). **ˈ~-ˋbottomed,** (of trousers) made very wide at the bottom of the leg (as worn by some sailors). **ˈ~-ˋbottoms** *n* trousers made this way. **ˋ~-buoy** *n* buoy with a ~ that is made to ring by the movement of the waves. **ˋ~-flower** *n* any plant of the genus *campanula*. **ˋ~-founder** *n* person whose trade is the casting of ~s. **ˋ~-foundry** *n* place where large ~s (for churches, etc) are cast. **ˋ~-metal** *n* [U] alloy of copper and tin used for making ~s. **ˋ~-push** *n* button pressed to ring an electric ~. **ˋ~-ringer** *n* person who rings church ~s. **ˋ~-tent** *n* ~-shaped tent. **ˋ~-**

wether *n* leading male sheep of a flock, with a ~ on its neck; (fig) ringleader. □ *vt* ~ ***the cat,*** (prov) do something dangerous in order to save others (from the fable of the mouse that suggested fastening a ~ round the cat's neck).

bella·donna /ˈbeləˋdɒnə/ *n* (drug prepared from) poisonous plant with red flowers and black berries.

belle /bel/ *n* beautiful girl or woman: *the ~ of the ball,* the most beautiful woman present.

belles-lettres /ˈbel ˋletr *with unsyllabic* r/ *n pl* (with *sing v*) (F) literary studies and writings (contrasted with commercial, technical, scientific, etc).

bel·li·cose /ˋbelɪkəʊs/ *adj* inclined to fighting; anxious to fight.

-bel·lied /-belɪd/ ⇨ belly.

bel·liger·ency /bɪˋlɪdʒərənsɪ/ *n* [U] being warlike; state of being at war.

bel·liger·ent /bɪˋlɪdʒərənt/ *adj, n* (state, party, nation) waging war: *the ~ Powers,* those that are waging war.

bel·low /ˋbeləʊ/ *vi,vt* **1** [VP2A] make a loud, deep noise (like a bull); roar; shout: *He ~ed before the dentist had started.* **2** [VP6A,15B] utter loudly or angrily: *They ~ed out a drinking song.*

bel·lows /ˋbeləʊz/ *n pl* ***a pair of ~,*** sometimes **a ~ 1** apparatus for blowing air into a fire, e g in a forge. **2** apparatus for forcing air through the pipes of an organ, e g in a church.

belly[1] /ˋbelɪ/ *n* (*pl* -lies) **1** ⇨ abdomen. **ˋ~-laugh** *n* loud, coarse laugh. □ *vi* give such a laugh. **2** the stomach: *with an empty ~,* hungry; *have the ˋ~-ache.* **ˋ~-ache** *vi* (colloq) grumble or complain bitterly, esp without good reason. **ˋ~ button** *n* (colloq) navel. **3** bulging part (concave or convex) of anything, e g the surface of a violin across which the strings pass. **ˋ~ landing** *n* landing made on the hull of an aircraft (when the under-carriage fails to operate). Hence, **ˋ~-land** *vi* **-bellied** *adj*: *ˈbig-ˋbellied,* having a big ~. **~-ful** /-fʊl/ *n* as much as one wants of anything: *He's had his ~ful of fighting,* doesn't want any more.

belly[2] /ˋbelɪ/ *vi,vt* (*pt,pp* -lied [VP6A,15B,2A,C] (cause to) swell out: *The wind bellied (out) the sails. The sails bellied (out).*

be·long /bɪˋlɒŋ *US:* -lɔŋ/ *vi* **1** [VP3A] **~ to, (a)** be the property of: *They ~ to me.* are mine. **(b)** be a member of, be connected with: *Which club do you ~ to?* **2** [VP2C] have as a right or proper place. *Do you ~ here,* live here? *Does this item of expenditure ~ under the head of office expenses,* is it rightly placed there? **~·ings** *n pl* (*personal ~ings*) movable possessions (not land, buildings, a business, etc): *I hope you've left none of your ~ings in the hotel.*

be·loved /bɪˋlʌvd/ *pp, pred adj* dearly loved: *~ by all; ~ of all who knew her.* □ *adj, n* /bɪˋlʌvɪd/ (person) dearly loved; darling: *his ~ wife.*

be·low[1] /bɪˋləʊ/ *adv* **1** (sometimes used after *from,* as if it were a *n*) at or to a lower level: *From the hilltop we saw the blue ocean ~. The people in the rooms ~ are very noisy. We heard voices from ~.* ***be/go ~,*** (in a ship) be/go ~ deck in (to) a cabin, saloon, etc. **2** at the foot of a page, etc; later (in a book, article, etc): *see paragraph six ~. Please affix your signature ~.* ***3 down ~,*** in the lower part of a building, in a ship's hold, etc (according to context). ***here ~,*** on earth.

be·low[2] /bɪˋləʊ/ *prep* (constrasted with *above.* ⇨ under, over[2](2); *below* can sometimes, but not always, be replaced by *under;* when *under* is possible, it is given in the examples) **1** lower than: *Skirts this year reach just ~ the knees. When the sun sets it goes ~ the horizon. Shall I write my name on, above or ~ the line? The temperature was five degrees ~ freezing-point. There is nothing ~/under 50p,* costing less than this. *The Dead Sea is ~ sea level. A captain in the army ranks ~ a captain in the Navy. Your work is ~ the average. He can't be much ~/under sixty,* i e years of age. ⇨ also belt(1), mark[1](8). **2** down stream from: *a few yards ~ the bridge.* **3 *(speak) ~ one's breath*** (more usu *under*), in a whisper. **4** (replaceable by *beneath*) unworthy of: *~ one's dignity.*

belt /belt/ *n* **1** band or strip of cloth, leather, etc worn round the waist or over one shoulder to support or keep in place clothes or weapons, or, like a corset, to support the abdomen: *He ate so much that he had to loosen his ~ two holes.* **hit below the ~,** give an unfair blow, fight unfairly. **2** endless strap, used to connect wheels and so drive machinery: *a ˋfan-belt,* in the engine of a car. **3** any wide strip or band, surrounding area, etc. **the comˋmuter belt,** residential area outside a large town, e g London, from which people commute to and from work. **the ˋCotton ~,** (US) area in which cotton is extensively grown. **green ~,** area of grassland, parks, etc, round a town. □ *vt* **1** [VP6A,15B] fasten with a ~: *The officer ~ed his sword on.* **2** [VP6A] thrash with a ~; (colloq) strike with the fist(s): *If you don't shut up, I'll ~ you.* **~·ing** *n*: *give the boy a good ~ing,* thrash him well. **3 *B~ up!*** (sl) Be quiet!

be·moan /bɪˋməʊn/ *vt* [VP6A] moan for; show great sorrow for: *~ one's sad fate; ~ing the loss of all her money.*

be·mused /bɪˋmjuzd/ *pred adj* preoccupied or stupid.

ben[1] /ben/ *n* (Scot) inner room (usu of a two-roomed house).

ben[2] /ben/ *n* (Scot) mountain peak (used with names as *Ben Nevis*).

bench /bentʃ/ *n* **1** long seat of wood or stone, e g in a public park, or across a rowing-boat; (in the House of Commons) seat occupied by certain classes of members. **ˋback-~es,** for members not entitled to a front ~. **ˋcross-~es,** for independent members who do not vote with either of the two main political parties. **front-~es,** reserved for ministers or ex-ministers. **the ˋTreasury B~,** for Ministers. **ˋ~ seat,** (in a car) seat (for 2 or 3 persons) extending the width of the car. ⇨ bucket seat. **2** (collective, with *def art*) judges; magistrates; judge's seat or office; law court. ***be raised to the B~,*** be made a judge or a bishop. **the King's B~ Division,** of the High Court of Justice. **3** work-table at which a shoemaker, carpenter, etc, works. **~er** *n* senior member of one of the Inns of Court.

bend[1] /bend/ *vt,vi* (*pt,pp* bent /bent/) **1** [VP6A, 15A,B] cause (sth rigid) to be out of a straight line or surface; force into a curve or angle: *It isn't easy to ~ a bar of iron. He heated the iron rod and bent it at a right angle. B~ the end of the wire up/down/back. Rheumatism prevents him from ~ing his back. Her head was bent over her book.* ***~ the knee (to),*** (rhet) bow, pray. ***on ~ed***

knees, (liter) kneeling; in an attitude of prayer or entreaty. ***~ a rule,*** (colloq) interpret it loosely (to suit the circumstances). **2** [VP2A,C] become curved or angular; bow; stoop: *The branches were ~ing (down) with the weight of the fruit. The branch bent but didn't break when the boy climbed on to it. Can you ~ down and touch your toes without ~ing your knees? The tall man bent forward to listen to the little girl. Sit up straight: don't ~ over your desk. The river ~s* (= turns) *several times before reaching the sea. The road ~s to the left here.* **3** [VP15A] direct: *It's time for us to ~ our steps homeward,* turn towards home. *All eyes were bent on me,* Every one was looking at me. *She stood there with eyes bent on the ground,* looking down. *He couldn't ~ his mind* (= give his attention) *to his studies.* **4** [VP2C,15A] submit: *~ to sb's will;* make (sb) submit: *~ sb to one's will.* **5** [VP6A] curve (a bow) in order to string it: *None of the suitors could ~ the bow of Odysseus.* **6** ***be bent on,*** have the mind set on, have as a fixed purpose: *He is bent on mastering English,* determined to learn it thoroughly. *He is bent on mischief,* has plans to do sth mischievous. **bent** *pred adj* (sl) dishonest; corrupt; mad.

bend[2] /bend/ *n* **1** curve or turn: *a sharp ~ in the road.* ***round the bend,*** (sl) mad. **2** sailor's knot (in a rope). **3 the ~s,** (colloq) pains in the joints, caused by working in compressed air, e g in a caisson(2).

be·neath /bɪˋniθ/ *prep, adv* **1** (old use, or liter) below, under(neath). **2** not worthy of: *His accusations are ~ contempt/notice,* should be ignored. *It is ~ you to complain,* unworthy of you to do so.

ben·edick /ˋbenɪdɪk/, (US = **ben·e·dict**) /ˋbenɪdɪkt/ *n* recently married man, esp one who has been a bachelor for many years.

Ben·edic·tine /ˈbenɪˋdɪktɪn/ *n, adj* (member) of the religious order founded in 529 A D by St Benedict; [U] /-tin/ liqueur made by monks of this order.

ben·edic·tion /ˈbenɪˋdɪkʃn/ *n* blessing (esp one given by a priest at the end of a church service): *pronounce the ~.*

ben·efac·tion /ˈbenɪˋfækʃn/ *n* [U] doing good; [C] good deed (esp the giving of money for charity); charitable gift: *That man's ~s now amount to £10 000.*

ben·efac·tor /ˋbenɪfæktə(r)/ *n* person who has given friendly help, esp financial help, to a school, hospital or charitable institution. **ben·efac·tress** /ˋbenɪfæktrəs/ *n* woman ~.

ben·efice /ˋbenɪfɪs/ *n* income-producing property (called a *church living*) held by a priest or clergyman (esp a vicar or rector). **ben·eficed** /-fɪst/ *adj* having a ~: *a ~d clergyman.*

be·nefi·cence /bɪˋnefɪsns/ *n* [U] doing good; active kindness. **be·nefi·cent** /bɪˋnefɪsnt/ *adj* doing good; kind.

ben·eficial /ˈbenɪˋfɪʃl/ *adj* having good effect, helpful: *Fresh air and good food are ~ to the health. I hope your holiday will be ~,* do you good. **~·ly** *adv*

ben·efici·ary /ˈbenɪˋfɪʃərɪ *US:* -ʃɪərɪ/ *n* (*pl* -**ries**) person who receives a benefit, esp one who receives money, property, etc under a will (at sb's death).

bene·fit /ˋbenɪfɪt/ *n* **1** [U] advantage; profit; help: *Did you get much ~ from your holiday,* did you feel better afterwards? *The book wasn't of much ~ to me,* didn't help me much. *The money is to be used for the ~ of the poor,* to help poor people. *It was done for your ~,* to help you. ***give sb the ~ of the doubt,*** assume that he is innocent because there is insufficient evidence that he is guilty. ***~ in kind,*** ⇨ kind[1](4). **~ performance/concert/match,** theatrical performance/concert/cricket or football match, etc, money for which is for the ~ of a charity, a particular player, etc. **2** [C] act of kindness; favour; advantage: *the ~s of a good education; the ~s we receive from our parents and teachers.* **3** [C] allowance of money to which a person is entitled as a citizen or as a member of an insurance society, etc: *medical/unemployment/sickness ~.* □ *vt,vi* **1** [VP6A] do good to: *The new railway will ~ the district. The sea air will ~ you.* **2 ~ *from/by,*** receive ~ from/by: *You will ~ by a holiday.*

ben·ev·ol·ence /bɪˋnevələns/ *n* [U] wish to do good; activity in doing good: *His ~ made it possible for many poor boys to attend college.* **ben·ev·ol·ent** /bɪˋnevələnt/ *adj* kind and helpful (*towards, to*). **ben·ev·ol·ent·ly** *adv*

be·nighted /bɪˋnɑɪtɪd/ *part adj* **1** (liter or old use) without the light of knowledge; in moral darkness. **2** (old use, of travellers) overtaken by darkness.

be·nign /bɪˋnɑɪn/ *adj* **1** (of persons) kind and gentle. **2** (of soil, climate) mild, favourable. **3** (of a disease, tumour) not dangerous. ⇨ malignant(2). **~·ly** *adv*

be·nig·nant /bɪˋnɪgnənt/ *adj* kind, gracious. **~·ly** *adv*

be·nig·nity /bɪˋnɪgnɪtɪ/ *n* [U] kindness of heart; [C] (*pl* -**ties**) kind act, favour.

beni·son /ˋbenɪsn/ *n* [C] (old use) blessing.

bent[1] /bent/ *n* **~ *(for),*** inclination or aptitude; natural skill in and liking: *She has a ~ for sewing/music.* ***follow one's ~,*** do what one is interested in and what one enjoys doing. ***to the top of one's ~,*** to one's heart's desire.

bent[2] ⇨ bend[1] esp (6).

be·numbed /bɪˋnʌmd/ *pred adj* made numb; with all feelings taken away: *My fingers were ~ with cold.*

Ben·za·drine /ˋbenzədrɪn/ *n* (P) brand of amphetamine.

ben·zene /ˋbenzin/ *n* [U] colourless liquid (C_6H_6) obtained from petroleum and coal-tar, used in the manufacture of numerous chemical products.

ben·zine /ˋbenzin/ *n* [U] colourless liquid (mixture of hydrocarbons) obtained from mineral oil, used for cleaning, etc.

ben·zol /ˋbenzol/ *n* [U] = benzene.

be·queath /bɪˋkwið/ *vt* [VP6A,12A,13A] **~ *(to)*** **1** arrange (by making a will) to give (property, etc to sb) at death: *He has ~ed me his gold watch.* **2** hand down to those who come after: *discoveries ~ed to us by the scientists of the last century.*

be·quest /bɪˋkwest/ *n* **1** [U] bequeathing. **2** [C] sth bequeathed: *He left ~s of money to all his servants.*

be·rate /bɪˋreɪt/ *vt* [VP6A] scold sharply.

be·reave /bɪˋriv/ *vt* (*pt,pp* **bereft** /bɪˋreft/ or **bereaved**; usu **bereft** in (1) and **bereaved** in (2)) [VP14] **1** rob or dispossess (of sth immaterial): *bereft of hope,* without hope; *bereft of reason,* mad. *Indignation bereft him of speech,* took away his power to speak. **2** (of death) leave sad by taking away (a relation, etc): *the accident that ~d him of his wife and child; the ~d husband,* the man whose wife had died. **~·ment** *n* [U] being ~d; loss by death: *We all sympathize with you in your ~ment;* [C] instance of this: *Owing to a recent ~ment she did not attend the concert.*

be·reft ⇨ bereave.

be·ret /ˋbereɪ *US:* bɪˋreɪ/ *n* flat, round cap of felt or cloth, worn with sports and holiday clothes, and as military head-dress.

berg /bɜg/ *n* = iceberg.

beri-beri /ˈberɪ ˋberɪ/ *n* [U] disease, common in oriental and tropical countries, caused by lack of vitamins, etc, essential to health.

berry /ˋberɪ/ *n* (*pl* **-ries**) **1** small seedy fruit: *holly berries; straw~; black~; rasp~.* ⇨ the illus at **fruit. 2** coffee bean.

ber·serk /bəˋsɜk/ *pred adj* ***be/go/send sb ~,*** be, go, etc uncontrollably wild: *He was absolutely ~/in ~ fury.*

berth /bɜθ/ *n* **1** sleeping-place in a train, a ship or an aircraft. **2** place at a wharf where a ship can be tied up; place for a ship to swing at anchor. ***give a wide ~ to,*** (fig) keep well away from, at a safe distance from. **3** (colloq) appointment. ***find a snug ~,*** an easy or pleasant job. □ *vt,vi* **1** [VP15A,2C] (naut) find, have, a sleeping-place (for): *Six passengers can be ~ed amidships.* **2** [VP6A] moor (a ship) in harbour, tie up (a ship) at a wharf, etc.

beryl /ˋberl/ *n* precious stone (usu green).

be·seech /bɪˋsitʃ/ *vt* (*pt,pp* **besought** /bɪˋsɔt/) [VP6A,17A,11,13B] (old use, or liter) ask earnestly or urgently: *He besought an interview. The prisoner besought the judge to be merciful/ besought him for mercy. Spare him, I ~ you.* **~-ing** *adj* (of a person's look, tone of voice, etc) entreating, appealing. **~·ing·ly** *adv*

be·seem /bɪˋsim/ *vt* (liter, old use; only in the 3rd person) be fitting or suitable: *It ill ~s you to refuse,* It is not fitting that you should refuse.

be·set /bɪˋset/ *vt* (-tt-, *pt,pp* **beset**) [VP6A] close in on all sides, have on all sides: *the temptations that ~ young people,* by which they are faced on all sides: *a problem ~ with difficulties; ~ by doubts,* troubled by doubts. **~·ting sin,** sin that most frequently tempts a person: *His ~ting sin is laziness.*

be·shrew /bɪˋʃru/ *vt* (archaic or joc): *B~ me!* May evil fall upon me!

be·side /bɪˋsaɪd/ *prep* **1** at the side of; close to: *Come and sit ~ me. She would like to live ~ the sea,* at the sea-side. **2** compared with: *You're quite tall ~ your sister.* ***set ~,*** put against; compare with: *There's no one to set ~ him as a general.* **3** ***~ the point/mark/question,*** wide of, having nothing to do with (what is being discussed, etc). **4** ***~ oneself,*** at the end of one's self-control: *He was ~ himself with joy/ excitement.*

be·sides /bɪˋsaɪdz/ *adv* moreover; also: *I don't like that new dictionary; ~, it's too expensive. It's too late to go for a walk now; ~, it's beginning to rain.* □ *prep* in addition to; as well as: *I have three other hats ~ this. There were five of us ~ John,* not including John. *He hadn't time to prepare his lecture, ~ which, he was unwell.*

be·siege /bɪˋsidʒ/ *vt* **1** [VP6A] surround (a place) with armed forces and keep them there; attack from all sides: *Troy was ~d by the Greeks for ten years.* **2** [VP14] ***~ with,*** crowd round (with requests, etc): *The teacher was ~d with questions and requests from her pupils.* **be·sieger** *n*

be·smear /bɪˋsmɪə(r)/ *vt* ***~ with,*** smear all over, e g with grease.

be·smirch /bɪˋsmɜtʃ/ *vt* make dirty: (fig) *His reputation was ~ed.*

be·som /ˋbizəm/ *n* broom made by tying a bundle of twigs to a long handle.

be·sot·ted /bɪˋsotɪd/ *part adj* stupefied (by alcoholic drink, drugs, love, etc).

be·sought ⇨ beseech.

be·spangled /bɪˋspæŋgld/ *pred adj* ***~ with,*** covered, decorated, with spangles.

be·spat·tered /bɪˋspætəd/ *pred adj* ***~ with,*** covered with spots of mud, etc.

be·speak /bɪˋspik/ *vt* (*pt* **bespoke** /bɪˋspəʊk/, *pp* **bespoke** or **bespoken** /bɪˋspəʊkən/) **1** [VP6A] (old use) order in advance; engage or reserve (a table in a restaurant, a room in a hotel). **bespoke bootmaker/tailor,** one who makes goods to order (contrasted with a seller of ready-made shoes, etc). ⇨ custom-built. **2** [VP6A,25] be evidence of: *His polite manners ~ the gentleman.*

best[1] /best/ *adj* (independent *superl;* ⇨ good, better) of the most excellent kind: *the ~ poetry/ poets; the ~ dinner I have ever had; the ~* (= quickest, most convenient, etc) *way from London to Paris.* ***the ~ part of,*** most of; the greater part of: *I've been waiting the ~ part of an hour.* ***the ~ thing to do,*** that which is most likely to bring about the desired result. ***make the ~ use of one's time/gifts/opportunities, etc,*** use one's time, etc in the most useful way. ***put one's ~ foot forward,*** ⇨ foot(1). ***with the ~ will in the world,*** even making every effort to be fair, etc. **ˈ~ ˋman,** bridegroom's friend, supporting him at his wedding.

best[2] /best/ *adv* (independent *superl;* ⇨ well, better) **1** in the most excellent way: *He works ~ in the morning. Do as you think ~. She was the ~-dressed woman in the village.* **2** most: *He is the ~-hated man in the village.* **ˈ~-ˋseller** *n* book that is sold in very large numbers: *His new novel is one of the season's ~-sellers.* **3** ***had ~,*** = had better. ⇨ better[2](2).

best[3] /best/ *pron* (independent *superl; the better* (*of*) ⇨ better[3]) the outstanding person, thing, etc among several; the most excellent part, aspect, of sth: *He's the ~ of husbands,* is distinguished among husbands for good qualities. *We're the ~ of friends,* very close friends. ***be all for the ~,*** be good in the end (although not at first seeming to be good). ***do sth all for the ~,*** act with good intentions (although it may not seem so). ***be/dress in one's (Sunday) ~,*** wear one's finest clothes: *They were (dressed) in their ~ for the occasion.* ***All the ~!*** (used when parting from sb) With warmest wishes! ***the ~ of it/the joke/etc,*** the amusing part (of what happened): *And the ~ of it/the ~ part of it was that....* ***at ~,*** taking the most hopeful view: *We can't arrive before Friday at ~.* ***at its/their/his, etc ~,*** in the ~ condition: *The garden is at its best this month,* looking most beautiful. *He was at his ~ yesterday evening and kept us all amused,* talked in his most amusing way. ***(even) at the ˋ~ of times,*** (even) when circumstances are most favourable. ***have/get the ~ of it/of the fight/quarrel/deal/bargain, etc,*** win; gain the advantage. ***have/get the ~ of everything,*** enjoy the ~ food, housing, etc. ***with the ~,*** as well as anyone: *Although he's nearly* *fifty, he can still play tennis with the ~.* **with the ~ of intentions,** intending only to help. **do one's ~/the ~ one can,** do one's utmost. **(do sth) to the ~ of one's ability/power,** use all one's ability/power when doing it. **make the ~ of a bad job/business,** do what one can, in spite of failure, misfortune, etc. **make the ~ of one's way home,** return home as quickly as possible, in spite of difficulties. **make the ~ of things,** be contented (although things are not satisfactory). **to the ~ of my knowledge/belief/recollection,** so far as I know/believe/recollect (though my knowledge, etc may be imperfect).

best[4] /best/ *vt* (colloq) [VP6A] get the better of; defeat.

bes·tial /ˈbestɪəl/ *adj* of or like a beast; brutish; savage. **~ly** *adv* **bes·ti·al·ity** /ˌbestɪˈælətɪ/ *n* (*pl* -ties) [U] quality of being ~; [C] ~ or brutal act.

bes·ti·ary /ˈbestɪərɪ *US:* -tɪerɪ/ *n* (*pl* -ries) medieval collection of moral stories about animals.

be·stir /bɪˈstɜ(r)/ *vt* (-rr-) **~ oneself,** busy oneself, be active.

be·stow /bɪˈstəʊ/ *vt* [VP6A,14] **1** give as an offering: *~ an honour/a title on sb; the praise that has been ~ed upon him.* **2** (old use) put, place. **~al** *n* ~ing.

be·strew /bɪˈstru/ *vt* (*pt* -ed, *pp* bestrewn /-ˈstrun/ or -ed) strew (a surface) (*with* sth); scatter (things) about.

be·stride /bɪˈstrɑɪd/ *vt* (*pt* bestrode /bɪˈstrəʊd/, *pp* bestridden /bɪˈstrɪdn/, bestrid /bɪˈstrɪd/, bestrode) [VP6A] sit, stand, with one leg on each side of: *~ a horse/chair/bidet/ditch/fence*, etc ⇨ astride.

bet /bet/ *vt,vi* (-tt-, *pt,pp* bet or occ betted) [VP9,11,12C,2A,3A] **1 bet on sth, bet (sb) that...,** risk money on a race or on some other event of which the result is doubtful: *He bet me a pound that Hyperion would win. It's foolish to bet on horses. Do you ever bet?* **2** (colloq uses): *I bet,* I'm certain; *you bet,* you may be certain. □ *n* agreement to risk money, etc on an event of which the result is doubtful; the money, etc offered: *make a bet; win/lose a bet; accept/take up a bet.*

beta /ˈbitə *US:* ˈbeɪtə/ *n* second letter (B, β) of the Greek alphabet. ⇨ App 4.

be·take /bɪˈteɪk/ *vt* (*pt* betook /bɪˈtʊk/, *pp* betaken /bɪˈteɪkən/) [VP14, reflex] (old use) **~ oneself to,** go to, apply oneself to.

betel /ˈbitl/ *n* leaf which is wrapped round bits of areca-nut and used by some Indians for chewing. **ˈ~ nut,** areca nut.

bête noire /ˌbeɪt ˈnwɑ(r)/ *n* (F) thing or person one dislikes greatly.

bethel /ˈbeθl/ *n* nonconformist chapel; (esp US) chapel for seamen.

be·think /bɪˈθɪŋk/ *vt* (*pt,pp* bethought /bɪˈθɔt/) **~ oneself,** (old use) reflect, consider (*of* sth, *how,* or *that*).

be·tide /bɪˈtɑɪd/ *vt* (only in) **woe ~ him/you, etc (if...),** may misfortune come to him/you, etc (if...).

be·times /bɪˈtɑɪmz/ *adv* (liter) early; in good time: *We must be up ~ tomorrow.*

be·token /bɪˈtəʊkən/ *vt* [VP6A] (old use) indicate, suggest: *Those black clouds ~ rain.*

be·took ⇨ betake.

be·tray /bɪˈtreɪ/ *vt* **1** [VP6A] be disloyal to; act deceitfully towards: *He ~ed his principles.* **2** [VP6A,14] **~ (to),** give away or sell treacherously: *Judas ~ed his master, Christ.* **3** [VP6A] allow (a secret) to become known, either by accident or on purpose. **4** [VP6A,25] be or give a sign of, show: *The boy's face ~ed the fact that he had been eating jam. His accent at once ~ed the fact that he was/~ed him to be a foreigner.* **~ oneself,** show what one really is, etc: *He had a good disguise, but as soon as he spoke he ~ed himself,* i e he was recognized by his voice. **~al** /bɪˈtreɪəl/ *n* [U] ~ing or being ~ed; [C] instance of this. **~er** *n*

be·troth /bɪˈtrəʊð/ *vt* (liter) **~ to,** [VP6A,14] engage (a woman) in contract of marriage (usu in *pp*): *His daughter was ~ed to a banker.* **be·trothed** *n* person engaged to be married. **~al** *n* engagement to be married.

bet·ter[1] /ˈbetə(r)/ *adj* (independent *comp*; ⇨ good, best) **1** *This is good but that is ~. He's a ~ man than his brother.* **~ than one's word,** more generous than one's promise. **(do sth) against one's ~ judgement,** despite feelings that it may be unwise. **no ~ than,** practically the same as: *He's no ~ than a beggar,* is, in spite of appearances, etc, almost a beggar. **no ~ than she should be,** (old use) is a woman of easy virtue. ⇨ virtue(2). **the ~ part of,** the larger part of: *Discretion is the ~ part of valour,* ⇨ discretion(1). **see ~ days,** be not so poor or unfortunate as at present: *He has seen ~ days.* **one's ~ feelings,** one's higher nature. **his ~ half,** (colloq) his wife. **2** (of health) recovering from illness (often contrasted with *ill* and unrelated to *well*): *The patient is ~ today but is still not well enough to get up. I'm quite ~ now,* am fully recovered.

bet·ter[2] /ˈbetə(r)/ *adv* (independent *comp*; ⇨ well, best) **1** *The ~* (= The more) *I know her the more I admire her abilities. You would write ~ if you had a good pen. You play tennis ~ than I do. You'll like it ~* (= more) *when you understand it more.* **be ~ off,** richer; more comfortable. **be ~ off without,** happier; more at ease: *We'd be ~ off without all that din from the children's room.* **know ~,** **(a)** be wise or experienced enough not to do sth: *You ought to know ~ than to go out without an overcoat on such a cold day.* **(b)** refuse to accept a statement (because one knows it is not true): *He says he didn't cheat, but I know ~,* feel sure that he did. **think (all) the ~ of sb,** have a higher opinion of him: *I shall think all the ~ of you after seeing you bear these misfortunes so bravely.* **think ~ of sth/of doing sth,** decide, after thought, not to do it. **2** [VP5] **had ~,** would find it more suitable, more to your advantage, etc: *You had ~ mind your own business. You'd ~ not say that,* I advise you not to say that. *I had ~ begin by explaining...,* It will be useful if I begin by...; *Hadn't you ~ take an umbrella?*

bet·ter[3] /ˈbetə(r)/ *n* **one's (elders and) ~s,** older, wiser, more experienced people: *Don't ignore the advice of your elders and ~s.* Cf *superior,* as in: *He's my superior at chess.* **get the ~ of sb or sth,** overcome; defeat; win (an argument, etc): *His shyness got the ~ of him,* he was overcome by shyness, was too shy to speak out. *She always gets the ~ of these quarrels.* **for ~ (f)or worse,** in both good and bad fortune. Cf *for good or ill.*

bet·ter[4] /ˈbetə(r)/ *vt* **1** [VP6A] improve; do better than: *The Government hopes to ~ the conditions of the workers. Your work last year was good; I* *hope you will* ~ *it, this year.* **2** ~ *oneself,* ~ *one's circumstances,* get a ~ position, higher wages, etc. **~·ment** *n* making or becoming ~.

bet·ter[5], **bet·tor** /ˈbetə(r)/ *n* person who bets; punter (the more usu word).

be·tween[1] /bɪˈtwin/ *adv* in(to) a place or time that is ~: *We visited the Museum in the morning and the Art Gallery later, with a hurried lunch* ~. ***far* ~,** at wide intervals. ***few and far* ~,** few and widely scattered or separate: *In this part of Canada houses are few and far* ~. ***in* ~,** spaced out among.

be·tween[2] /bɪˈtwin/ *prep* **1** (of place) *The letter B comes* ~ *A and C. The Mediterranean Sea is* ~ *Europe and Africa. A river flows* ~ *its banks.* (*Between* usu involves only two limits, but when boundaries are concerned, there may be more than two limits. *Switzerland lies* ~ *France, Italy, Austria and Germany.* ⇨ among.) **2** (of order, rank, etc): *An army major ranks* ~ *a captain and a colonel.* **3** (of time): ~ *the two world wars;* ~ *1 o'clock and 2 o'clock;* ~ *youth and middle age.* **4** (of distance, amount, etc): ~ *five and six miles;* ~ *thirty and forty tons;* ~ *5p and 10p;* ~ *freezing-point and boiling-point.* **5** to and from: *This liner sails* ~ *Southampton and New York.* **6** (showing connection): *after all there has been* ~ *us,* in view of our past friendship, the experiences we have shared, etc. ***There is no love lost* ~ *them,*** They dislike each other. ***There's nothing to choose* ~ *them,*** They are (both or all) alike. **7** (to show sharing; used of two only): *Divide/Share the money* ~ *you.* ~ ***ourselves,*** ~ ***you, me and the gatepost,*** ~ ***you and me,*** in confidence. **8** (to show combination, used of two, or more than two to show several and independent relationships): *The first five batsmen scored 253 runs* ~ *them. We* (two or more) *saved up for a year and bought a second-hand car* ~ *us. B*~ *them* (i e as the result of their combined efforts) *they soon finished the work.* **9** ~... ***and,*** because of... and... combined: *B*~ *astonishment and despair she hardly knew what to do. My time is fully taken up* ~ *writing and lecturing.* **10** (showing relationship): *the relation* ~ *teacher and pupil; the distinction* ~ *right and wrong; a comparison* ~ *two things; quarrels/wars/ill-feeling/rivalries/friendships, etc* ~ *nations.*

be·twixt /bɪˈtwɪkst/ *prep, adv* (old or liter use) between. ~ ***and between,*** (colloq) in an intermediate state; neither one thing nor the other.

bevel /ˈbevl/ *n* sloping edge; surface with such a slope, e g at the side of a picture frame or a sheet of plate glass. ˈ~ **gear,** either of a pair of gears with ~led teeth surfaces. □ *vt* (-ll-, US = -l-) give a sloping edge to.

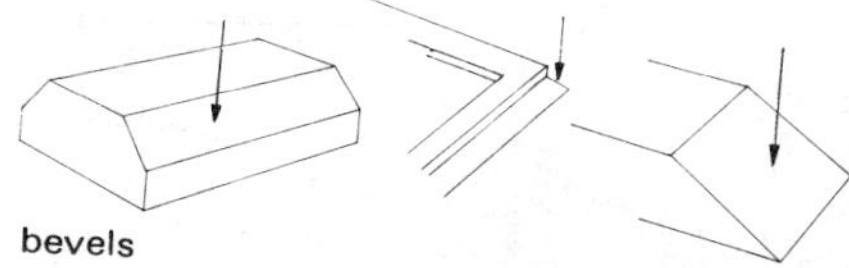

bevels

bev·er·age /ˈbevərɪdʒ/ *n* [C] any sort of drink except water, e g milk, tea, wine, beer.

bevy /ˈbevɪ/ *n* (*pl* -vies) **1** company or gathering (*of* women). **2** flock (*of* birds, esp quail).

be·wail /bɪˈweɪl/ *vt* [VP6A] express sorrow over; mourn for.

be·ware /bɪˈweə(r)/ *vi, vt* [VP2A in the imperative and infinitive only, 3A,10] be on guard, take care: *B*~ *of the dog! B*~ *of pickpockets! B*~ *(of) how you attempt it. B*~, *sir, (of) what you do.*

be·wil·der /bɪˈwɪldə(r)/ *vt* [VP6A] puzzle; confuse: *The old woman from the country was* ~*ed by the crowds and traffic in the big city. Tom was* ~*ed by the examination questions.* **~·ing** *adj*: *find something* ~*ing.* **~·ment** *n* [U] state of being ~ed: *He looked at me in open-mouthed* ~*ment.*

be·witch /bɪˈwɪtʃ/ *vt* [VP6A] **1** work magic on; put a magic spell on: *The old woman* ~*ed the cows so that they gave no milk.* **2** charm; delight very much: *She danced so well that she* ~*ed all the young men.* **~·ing** *adj*: *a* ~*ing smile.* **~·ing·ly** *adv*: *She smiled at him* ~*ingly.*

bey /beɪ/ *n* (Turkish word meaning) governor: *the Bey of Tunis.*

be·yond[1] /bɪˈjond/ *adv* at or to a distance; farther on: *India and the lands* ~. *What is* ~?

be·yond[2] /bɪˈjond/ *prep* **1** at, on or to, the farther side of: *The house is* ~ *the bridge. Don't go* ~ *the town boundary. We saw peak* ~ *peak,* a succession of peaks. **2** (of time) later than: *Don't stay out* ~ (*after* is the more usu word) *10 o'clock. He never sees* ~ *the present.* **3** surpassing, exceeding; out of reach of: *Your work is* ~ *all praise,* so good that it cannot be praised enough. *We succeeded* ~ *our hopes,* were more successful than we had hoped to be. *That's going* ~ *a joke,* passes the limits of what is reasonable as a joke. *He lives* ~ *his income,* spends more than he earns. *It's quite* ~ *me,* is more than I can understand. **4** (in neg and interr) except: *He has nothing* ~ *his pension.*

be·zique /bɪˈzik/ *n* [U] card-game for two or four players.

bhang /bæŋ/ *n* (kind of) narcotic made from hemp.

bi- /ˈbɑɪ/ *pref* **1** appearing twice (in the period given): *bi-monthly; bi-annual.* **2** lasting for two, appearing every two: *bi-ennial.* **3** having two: *bilateral; bilingual; biped, biplane.* **4** in two ways; doubly: *bi-concave.*

bias /ˈbɑɪəs/ *n* **1** leaning of the mind towards or away from sth; predisposition: *He has a* ~ *towards/against the plan,* is in favour of it/opposed to it without having full knowledge of it. *He is without* ~, is impartial, unprejudiced. **2** ***cut on the* ~,** (dress-making, etc) cut across, slantingly. **3** (esp of a ball in the game of bowls) tendency to swerve. □ *vt* (*pt,pp* biased or biassed) give a ~ to; influence (usu unfairly): *The government used newspapers and the radio to* ~ *the opinions of the people. He is* ~*(s)ed towards/against the plan,* is prejudiced. *He's clearly* ~*(s)ed.*

bib[1] /bɪb/ *n* **1** piece of cloth tied under a child's chin. **2** upper part of an apron.

bib[2] /bɪb/ *vi* (-bb-) drink too much or too often (rare except in *wine-bibbing, wine-bibber*).

Bible /ˈbɑɪbl/ *n* sacred writings of the Jews and the Christian Church. ˈ~ **puncher,** (colloq) evangelical preacher. **bib·li·cal** /ˈbɪblɪkl/ *adj* of, concerning, contained in, the ~: *biblical style,* the style used in (esp the Authorized Version of) the ~.

bib·li·ography /ˈbɪblˈogrəfɪ/ *n* (*pl* -phies) **1** [C] list of books and writings of one author or about one subject. **2** [U] study of the authorship, editions, etc of books. **bib·li·ogra·pher** /ˈbɪblɪˈogrəfə(r)/ *n* person who writes or studies bibliographies.

bib·lio·phile /ˋbɪblɪəfaɪl/ *n* person who loves and collects books.

bibu·lous /ˋbɪbjʊləs/ *adj* addicted to (alcoholic) drink.

bi·cam·eral /ˈbaɪˋkæmərl/ *adj* (of a legislature) having two chambers, e g House of Commons, House of Lords.

bi·car·bon·ate /ˈbaɪˋkɑbənət/ *n* [U] acid salt of carbonic acid, esp ~ *of soda* ($NaHCO_3$), used in cooking and in medicine.

bi·cen·ten·ary /ˈbaɪˈsenˋtinərɪ *US:* -ˋsentṇərɪ/ *n* (celebration of the) 200th anniversary of an event.

bi·cen·ten·nial /ˈbaɪˈsenˋtenɪəl/ *adj* **1** happening once in 200 years. **2** lasting for 200 years. **3** of a 200th anniversary. □ *n* 200th anniversary.

bi·ceps /ˋbaɪseps/ *n* (*pl* unchanged) large muscle in the front part of the upper arm: *His ~ is/are impressive.*

bicker /ˋbɪkə(r)/ *vi* [VP2A,C,3A] **~ *(with sb) (over/about sth),*** quarrel about sth small or unimportant: *Stop ~ing!*

bi·cycle /ˋbaɪsɪkl/ *n* two-wheeled machine propelled by using pedals, for riding on. □ *vi* (usu shortened to *cycle*) [VP2A,C] ride a ~; go (*to*) on a ~.

bid[1] /bɪd/ *vt,vi* (-dd-) **1** (*pt,pp* **bid**) [VP6A,14, 2A,3A] ***bid (for),*** (at an auction sale) make an offer of money; offer (a certain price): *Will anyone bid £5 for this painting? Mr X bid £20 for the horse so I bid £21. Is nobody else going to bid? What shall I bid? I hoped to get the house but a rich man was bidding against me,* offering higher prices. ⇨ **outbid**. *The politicians are bidding for popular support,* making offers, e g of tax reductions, in order to get support from the public. ***bid up,*** [VP15B] make the price higher by offering more money: *The goods were bid up far beyond their real value.* **2** (*pt,pp* **bid**) [VP2A,3A] ***bid on,*** (US) state a price (for doing sth); put in a tender for: *The firm decided to bid on the new bridge.* ⇨ **tender**[2]. **3** (old use; *pt* **bade** /bæd/, *pp* **bidden** /ˋbɪdn/, **bid**) [VP17,18B] **(a)** command; tell: *He bade me (to) come in. Do as you are bid. Soldiers must do as they are bidden. Bid him come in.* **(b)** (old use) invite: *the bidden guests; bid sb to a wedding.* **(c)** [VP12A,13A] say (as a greeting, etc): *bid farewell to sb; bid sb good morning.* **4 *bid fair to,*** seem likely to: *Our plan bids fair to succeed.* ***bid defiance to,*** (old use) announce that one defies (the enemy, etc). **5** (cards, bridge) made a bid: *bid 2 hearts.* ⇨ **bid**[2](4). **ˋbid·dable** *adj* (colloq) docile; ready to obey. **bid·ding** *n* **1** command. ***do sb's bidding,*** do what he commands. **2** [U] act of offering a price at an auction sale: *Bidding was brisk,* There were many bids, quickly made. **3** (at cards) the making of bids(4). **bid·der** *n* person who bids.

bid[2] /bɪd/ *n* **1** (at an auction sale) offer of a price: *Are there no bids for this very fine painting? Will no one make a higher/further bid?* **2** (US) statement of price for a piece of work, etc: *Bids were invited for the construction of a swimming-pool.* ⇨ **tender**[2]. **3 *make a bid for,*** try to obtain (by offering sth): *make a bid for popular support.* **4** (card games, esp bridge) statement of the number of tricks a player proposes to win: *a bid of 2 hearts/3 no-trumps; raise the bid.*

bide /baɪd/ *vt* (liter; old use) abide. (rare except in) ***~ one's time,*** wait for a favourable opportunity.

bidet /ˋbideɪ *US:* biˋdeɪ/ *n* (F) raised narrow bath (to be straddled) for washing the genitals and bottom.

bi-en·nial /baɪˋenɪəl/ *adj* lasting for two years; happening every alternate year. □ *n* plant that lives two years and has flowers and seeds in the second year. **~·ly** *adv*

bier /bɪə(r)/ *n* movable wooden stand for a coffin or a dead body.

biff /bɪf/ *n* (sl) sharp blow. □ *vt* (sl) strike: *~ sb on the nose.*

bi·focal /ˈbaɪˋfəʊkl/ *adj* (esp of lenses in spectacles for the eyes) designed for both distant and near vision. **bi·focals** *n pl* spectacles with ~ lenses.

bi·fur·cate /ˋbaɪfəkeɪt/ *vt,vi* [VP6A,2A] (of roads, rivers, boughs of trees, etc) divide into two branches, etc; fork. □ *adj* (also **~d**) forked. **bi·fur·ca·tion** /ˈbaɪfəˋkeɪʃn/ *n*

big /bɪg/ *adj* (-gg-) (antonym *little*; cf *large*, and *small*) of large size, extent, capacity, importance, etc. ***get/grow too big for one's boots,*** (colloq) become conceited. ***have big ideas,*** be ambitious. ***talk big,*** boast. **ˋbig bug** *n* (sl) ⇨ **bug(4)**. **ˈbig ˋbusiness,** commerce on a ~ financial scale. **ˋbig game,** ⇨ **game**[1]**(6)**. **big end** *n* (eng) part of a connecting shaft that bears on a crankshaft. **ˋbig noise** *n* (sl) ⇨ **noise**. **ˋbig shot** *n* (sl) ⇨ **shot**[2]**(8)**. **ˋbig stick,** = ~ shot. **ˋbig·wig** *n* (sl) important person.

big·amy /ˋbɪgəmɪ/ *n* [U] having two wives or husbands living, a sin and a crime in Christian countries. **big·am·ous** /ˋbɪgəməs/ *adj* guilty of, in-

a bicycle

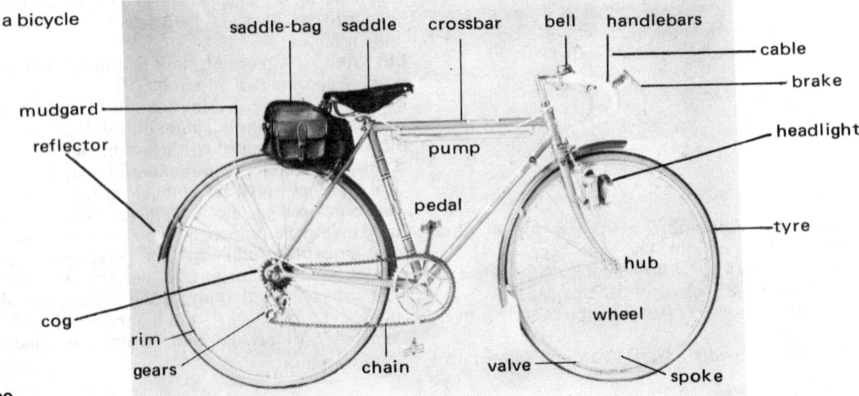

volving, ~: *a bigamous marriage.* **big·am·ist** /ˈbɪgəmɪst/ *n* person guilty of ~.

bight /baɪt/ *n* **1** loop made in a rope. **2** curve in a coast, larger than, or with not so much curve as, a bay.

bigot /ˈbɪgət/ *n* person who holds strongly to an opinion or belief in defiance of reason or argument. **~ed** /ˈbɪgətɪd/ *adj* intolerant and narrow-minded (in religion, etc). **ˈ~ry** *n* [U] state of being ~ed; [C] act, etc, of a ~.

bi·jou /ˈbiʒu/ *n* (F) jewel. □ *adj* small and elegant: *~ villas.*

bike /baɪk/ *n, vi* (colloq and common abbr for) bicycle.

bi·kini /bɪˈkinɪ/ *n* scanty two-piece garment (bra and briefs) worn by girls and women for swimming and sun-bathing: *~ top* (= bra); *~ briefs,* ⇨ briefs.

bi·labial /ˈbaɪˈleɪbɪəl/ *adj, n* (consonant) pronounced with both lips, e g /b, p, m, w/.

bi·lat·eral /ˈbaɪˈlætərl/ *adj* of, on, with two sides; (legal) (of an agreement, etc) made between two (persons, governments). **~·ly** *adv* **~ism** *n* principle based upon ~ agreements, esp of trade and financial agreements between countries.

bil·berry /ˈbɪlbrɪ *US:* -berɪ/ *n* (*pl* **-ries**) fruit of a dwarf hardy shrub growing on heaths, etc in N Europe (also called *blaeberry, whortleberry*).

bile /baɪl/ *n* [U] brownish-yellow bitter liquid produced by the liver to help in digesting food; (med) disorder of the ~; (fig) peevishness, bad temper. **ˈ~-duct,** (anat) tube carrying ~ to the duodenum. ⇨ the illus at alimentary.

bilge /bɪldʒ/ *n* [U] **1** almost flat part of a ship's bottom, inside or outside; (also **~-water**) the dirty water that collects in a ship's ~. **2** (sl) foolish or worthless talk or writing.

bil·har·zia /ˈbɪlˈhɑzɪə/ *n* tropical disease caused by parasites, flatworms in the blood and bladder.

bi·lingual /ˈbaɪˈlɪŋgwl/ *adj* **1** speaking, using, two languages (esp when these are learnt together in childhood): *a ~ country,* one in which two languages are used officially. **2** written, printed, in two languages. □ *n* ~ person.

bil·ious /ˈbɪlɪəs/ *adj* **1** caused by too much bile: *a ~ complaint/headache/attack;* suffering from such complaints: *~ patients.* **2** peevish; taking a gloomy view of life. **~·ness** *n*

bilk /bɪlk/ *vt* [VP6A,14] ***~ sb (out) of,*** escape paying money to; cheat (esp by running away): *He ~ed us out of the money.*

bill[1] /bɪl/ *n* (also **ˈ~hook**) long-handled tool with a curved blade used for cutting off branches of trees.

bill[2] /bɪl/ *n* horny part of the mouth of some birds. ⇨ the illus at bird. □ *vi* (of doves) stroke ~ with ~. ***~ and coo,*** exchange caresses.

bill[3] /bɪl/ *n* **1** written statement of charges for goods delivered or services rendered: *It's wrong to leave a place without paying all your ~s. There are some ~s to pay/to be paid.* ⇨ estimate[1], quotation(3). ***foot the ~,*** ⇨ foot. **2** written or printed notice, poster, placard: *a theatre/concert ~,* giving information about a play, concert, etc. ***fill the ~,*** (of an actor, etc) be, do, all that is required or expected. ***head/top the ~,*** be advertised at the head of the list, in large type, etc. **~ of fare,** list of dishes to be served at a hotel, restaurant, etc; menu. **ˈ~·board** *n* (US) structure for the display of advertisements, e g at the roadside. **ˈ~-poster, ˈ~-sticker** *n* person who pastes up ~s or placards (on walls, hoardings, etc). **3** (legal) proposed law, to be discussed by a parliament (and called an *Act* when passed). **4** (US) banknote: *a ten-dollar ~.* **ˈ~·fold** *n* pocket-book for banknotes. **5 B~ of Exchange,** order to a bank to pay a sum of money on a given date. **~s payable,** ~s of exchange due for payment by the holder. **~s receivable,** such ~s due for payment to the holder. **6** certificate. **~ of entry,** (comm) certificate from the Customs to indicate final clearance of imported goods. **~ of health,** (naut) certificate regarding infectious disease in a ship's crew: *clean ~ of health,* one certifying that there is no such disease. **~ of lading,** ⇨ lading. **~ of quantities,** ⇨ quantity(4). **~ of sale,** ⇨ sale(1). □ *vt* **1** [VP6A] make known by means of ~s(2) or placards; announce, put in, a programme: *Olivier was ~ed to appear as Lear,* It was announced that he would play the part of Lear. **2** [VP14] ***~ sb for sth,*** submit a ~(1) to: *~ a client for services rendered.*

bil·let /ˈbɪlɪt/ *n* **1** place (usu a private house) where soldiers are boarded and lodged: *The troops are in ~s,* in ordinary homes, not in camp or barracks. **2** (colloq) appointment or situation; job: *a soft/cushy ~,* one not needing much effort. □ *vt* [VP6A,14] ***~ (on),*** place (troops) in ~s: *~ soldiers on sb/on a town/on the villagers.*

bil·let-doux /ˈbɪleɪ ˈdu/ *n* (*pl* ~s-doux) (F) (joking style) love-letter.

bil·liards /ˈbɪlɪədz/ *n* (with *sing v*) game played with ivory or composition balls and long tapering sticks (called *cues*) on an oblong, cloth-covered table: *play ~; have a game of ~. B~ is played by women as well as by men.* **ˈbilliard-player/-room/-table/-marker** *nn* (*sing* in compounds).

bil·lings·gate /ˈbɪlɪŋzgeɪt/ *n* [U] (from the name of a London fish-market) abusive language full of swear-words.

bil·lion /ˈbɪlɪən/ *n* (GB) million millions or 10^{12}; (F, US) thousand millions or 10^9. ⇨ App 4.

bil·low /ˈbɪləʊ/ *n* (liter) great wave; (*pl,* poet) the sea; (fig) anything that sweeps along like a great wave. □ *vi* [VP2C] rise or roll like waves: *The flames ~ed over the prairie.* **~y** *adj* rising or moving like ~s.

billy /ˈbɪlɪ/ *n* (esp in Australia) tin can used as a kettle or cooking pot, esp in camping out.

billy-goat /ˈbɪlɪ gəʊt/ *n* male goat.

billy-(h)o /ˈbɪlɪ (h)əʊ/ *n* (colloq) ***like ~,*** vigorously: *raining/fighting like ~.*

bil·tong /ˈbɪltoŋ/ *n* [U] (in S Africa) sun-dried meat cut into strips.

bi·met·al·lism /ˈbaɪˈmetḷɪzm/ *n* system of having two metals, e g gold and silver, with a fixed ratio to each other as legal tender. **bi·met·al·lic** /ˈbaɪmɪˈtælɪk/ *adj*

bin /bɪn/ *n* large rigid container or enclosed space, usu with a lid, for storing coal, grain, flour, bread, etc: *ˈdustbin,* bin for rubbish, etc; *ˈlitter bin.*

bi·nary /ˈbaɪnərɪ/ *adj* of or involving a pair or pairs: *a ~ system,* (astron) two stars revolving round a common system or one round the other. *the ~ scale,* (maths) with two digits, 0 and 1, as the base of the notation:

1	2	3	4	5	6	7	8	9	10
1	10	11	100	101	110	111	1000	1001	1010

bind /baɪnd/ *vt,vi* (*pt,pp* bound /baʊnd/) **1** [VP6A,15B,14] ***~ sb or sth to sth/together***

(with sth), tie or fasten, with rope, etc: *They bound his legs (together) so that he shouldn't escape. Joan of Arc was bound to the stake and burnt to death. The prisoner was bound hand and foot,* His arms and legs were tied. (fig): *Commerce ~s the two countries together. We are bound to him by gratitude/by a close friendship.* **2** [VP6A, 14] secure the edge of sth with tape, braid, etc: *~ the edge of a carpet,* to prevent fraying; *~ the cuffs of a jacket with leather.* **3** [VP6A,15B] tie or wind sth round: *~ up a wound. Before sweeping the house she bound up her hair in a large handkerchief.* **4** [VP6A,15A,B] fasten (sheets of paper) into a cover: *~ a book; a well-bound book; bound in leather; ~ up two books into one volume.* [VP2A] *The new impression is ~ing,* is being bound. **5** [VP6A,15B,2A] hold or stick together in a solid mass: *Frost ~s the soil. The ground is frost-bound,* frozen hard. *Clay ~s* (= becomes hard) *when it is baked. Stones bound together with cement make good roads. Some kinds of food ~ the bowels/are ~ing,* cause constipation. **6** [VP17A,14,15B,16B] ***~sb to do sth/to sth,*** hold (sb) (by legal agreement, a promise, or under penalty) to a certain course of action: *~ sb to pay a debt; ~ sb to secrecy,* make him promise to keep sth secret. ***~ oneself to do sth,*** promise, undertake, guarantee, to do it. ***~ sb over*** (to keep the peace, etc), order that he must appear before the judge again (if he fails to keep the peace, etc). ***~ sb (over as an apprentice (to sb),*** make an agreement that he shall be one: *The boy was bound (as an) apprentice to a carpenter.* **7** [VP2A] (sl) complain; carp: *Oh, do stop ~ing!* **8** ⇨ bound[5] for special uses of the *pp.* **~er** *n* **1** person who ~s, esp *a `book-~er.* **2** thing that ties or holds things together, e g a machine, or part of a machine, that cuts and ~s grain; loose cover for unbound magazines; substance such as cement or bitumen for joining things. **`~ery** *n* place where books are bound. **~ing** *adj* (esp) that ~s(6) or obliges sb to do sth: *an agreement that is ~ing (up)on all parties.* ⇨ also bind(5). □ *n* (esp) **1** book-cover. **2** strip, braid, etc for protecting an edge or a seam (of a garment, etc).

bind·weed /`baɪndwid/ *n* [U] kinds of wild convolvulus.

bine /baɪn/ *n* flexible stem of various kinds of climbing plants, e g hops.

binge /bɪndʒ/ *n* (sl) ***have a ~, go on the ~,*** have a spree (drinking and making merry).

bingo /`bɪŋgəʊ/ *n* [U] popular gambling game, played with cards on which numbered squares are covered as the numbers are called at random: (attrib) *`~ halls.*

bin·nacle /`bɪnəkl/ *n* (naut) non-magnetic stand for a ship's compass (usu in front of the helm).

bin·ocu·lars /bɪ`nokjʊləz/ *n pl* field-glasses; instrument with lenses for both eyes, making distant objects seem nearer.

a pair of binoculars

bi·no·mial /baɪ`nəʊmɪəl/ *adj* (maths) made up of two numbers or algebraic expressions joined by + or − (e g $a^2 - 3b$).

bio·chem·is·try /'baɪəʊ`kemɪstrɪ/ *n* [U] chemistry of living organisms.

bio·de·grad·able /'baɪəʊ'dɪ`greɪdəbl/ *adj* (of substances) that can be broken down by bacteria: *Are these plastic substances indestructible or ~?*

bio·graph /`baɪəʊgrɑf *US:* -græf/ *n* = bioscope.

bi·ogra·phy /baɪ`ogrəfɪ/ *n* **1** [C] person's life-history written by another. **2** [U] branch of literature dealing with the lives of persons. **bi·ogra·pher** /baɪ`ogrəfə(r)/ *n* person who writes a ~. **bio·graphic, -i·cal** /'baɪəʊ`græfɪk, -ɪkl/ *adj* of ~.

bi·ol·ogy /baɪ`olədʒɪ/ *n* [U] science of the physical life of animals and plants. **bi·ol·ogist** /baɪ`olədʒɪst/ *n* student of, expert in, ~. **bio·logi·cal** /'baɪə`lodʒɪkl/ *adj* of ~: *a biological laboratory/experiment.* **'biological `warfare,** the deliberate

use of germs, etc for spreading disease.

bio·scope /ˋbɑɪəskəʊp/ *n* early name (still used in S Africa) for the cinema, or a film-projector.

bi·par·ti·san /ˈbɑɪpɑtɪˋzæn *US:* bɑɪˋpɑrtɪzn/ *adj* of, supported by, consisting of, two otherwise opposed (esp political) parties: *a ~ foreign policy.*

bi·ped /ˋbɑɪ-ped/ *n* two-footed animal, e g a man or a bird.

bi·plane /ˋbɑɪ-pleɪn/ *n* aircraft with two pairs of wings, one above the other.

birch /bɜtʃ/ *n* **1** [C] (kinds of) forest tree growing in northern countries; it has smooth bark and slender branches. **2** [U] its wood, e g as used for making canoes. **3** [C] (also ˋ**~-rod**) bundle of ~ twigs tied together and used formerly for punishing schoolboys. □ *vt* [VP6A] punish with a ~-rod.

bird /bɜd/ *n* **1** feathered creature with two legs and two wings, usu able to fly. ⇨ the illus opposite and at foul, prey, water. ***A ~ in the hand is worth two in the bush,*** (prov) Sth which one has, though small, is better than sth larger, which one has not. ***get the ~,*** be hissed, scorned or rejected. ***give sb the ~,*** hiss, scorn or reject him. ***kill two ~s with one stone,*** gain two ends at one. ˋ**~-cage** *n* cage for a ~ or ~s. ˋ**~-fancier** *n* person who knows about, collects, breeds or sells ~s. ˋ**~-lime** *n* sticky substance put on branches to catch ~s. ˈ**~'s-ˈeye ˋview** *n* wide view seen from high up; (fig) general survey of a subject. ˋ**~-nesting** *n* hunting for birds nests (to get the eggs). ˋ**~-watcher** *n* one who studies the habits of birds. ⇨ also feather[1], passage(1), prey. **2** (colloq) person: *He's a queer/rum ~. He's a cunning/wise/knowing old ~.* **3** (sl) young girl, esp a girl companion.

bir·etta /bɪˋretə/ *n* square cap worn by R C and some Anglican priests.

biro /ˋbɑɪərəʊ/ *n* (P) (kind of) ballpen.

birth /bɜθ/ *n* **1** [C,U] (process of) being born, coming into the world: *The baby weighed seven pounds at ~,* when it was born. *The boy has been delicate from (his) ~,* has been weak in health since he was born. *Cats sometimes have four or five young at a ~. There were 167 more ~s than deaths in the town last year.* ***give ~ to,*** bring into the world; (fig) produce: *give ~ to a child/a poem/a dispute.* **2** [U] origin, descent: *He's of good ~,* comes of a good family. *She is Russian by ~ and British by marriage.* ˋ**~-control** *n* [U] (method of) preventing unwanted conception(2). ˋ**~·day** *n* (anniversary of the) day of one's ~. ˋ**~·mark** *n* mark on the body at or from ~. ˋ**~-place** *n* house or district in which one was born. ˋ**~·rate** *n* number of ~s in one year for every 1 000 persons. ˋ**~·right** *n* any of various rights, privileges and properties to which a person has a right as a member of his family, a citizen of his country, etc.

bis·cuit /ˋbɪskɪt/ *n* [C] **1** flat, thin, crisp cake of many kinds, sweetened or unsweetened. ***take the ~,*** (sl) be the best/worst at something; be surprising. **2** (US) bread dough baked in small shapes. **3** light-brown.

bi·sect /ˈbɑɪˋsekt/ *vt* [VP6A] cut or divide into two (usu equal parts). **bi·sec·tion** /ˈbɑɪˋsekʃn/ *n* [U] division into two (equal) parts.

bi·sex·ual /ˈbɑɪˋsekʃʊəl/ *adj* of two sexes; having both male and female sexual organs; sexually attracted to either sex.

bishop /ˋbɪʃəp/ *n* **1** Christian clergyman of high rank who organizes the work of the Church in a city or district. ⇨ the illus at vestment. ⇨ diocese. **~·ric** /-rɪk/ *n* office of a ~; district under a ~. **2** chess piece, ⇨ the illus at chess.

bis·muth /ˋbɪzməθ/ *n* [U] reddish-white metal (symbol **Bi**), used in alloys; compound of this used medically, e g for stomach troubles.

bi·son /ˋbɑɪsn/ *n* European wild ox; American buffalo. ⇨ the illus at large.

bis·tro /ˋbistrəʊ/ *n* small bar or nightclub. ⇨ bar[1](13).

bit[1] /bɪt/ *n* **1** mouth-piece (metal bar) forming part of a horse's bridle. ⇨ the illus at harness. ***take the bit between one's teeth,*** (of a horse) run away out of control; (fig) get out of control. **2** part of a tool that cuts or grips when twisted; tool for boring or drilling holes (usu fitted into a *brace*). ⇨ the illus at brace.

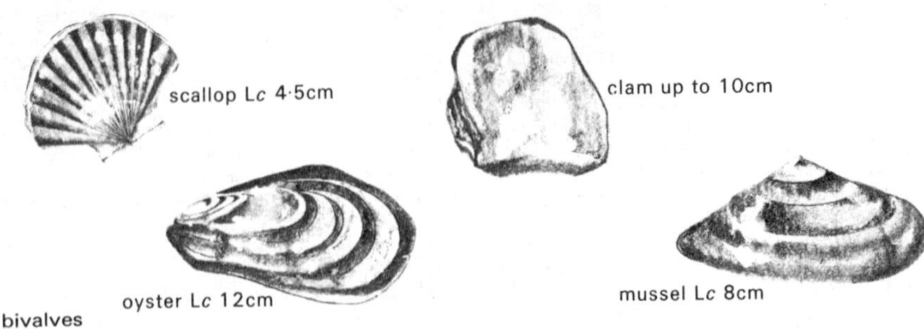

bit[2] /bɪt/ *n* **1** small piece of anything: *He took some paper and a few bits of wood and soon made a fire. He ate every bit of* (= all) *his dinner. He has saved a nice bit* (= a good sum) *of money.* ***bit by bit,*** slowly, gradually. ***a bit at a time,*** by degrees. ***every bit as good, etc,*** equally (good, etc). ***wait a bit,*** a short time. ***a bit,*** rather: *She's feeling a bit tired.* ***a bit of a,*** rather: *He's a bit of a coward.* ***not a bit,*** not at all; not in the least: *He's not a bit better. He doesn't care a bit. It's not a bit of use,* It's quite useless. ***not a bit of it,*** not at all (used as a strong denial): *You'd think she'd be tired after such a long journey, but not a bit of it!* ***pull/cut/tear sth to bits,*** into small pieces. ***go/come to bits,*** into small pieces. **2** (used colloq, like *piece,* with *news, advice, luck* and *mind*): *a bit of good advice.* **3** small coin: *threepenny bit,* (former) coin (GB) worth threepence; (US) 12 cents.

bit[3] /bɪt/ ⇨ **bite**[1].

bitch /bɪtʃ/ *n* **1** female dog, wolf or fox. **2** (colloq) spiteful woman or girl. □ *vi* [VP2A] (colloq) complain in a sour, carping way; speak spitefully to or about sb or sth too much. **~y** *adj* (colloq) spiteful.

bite[1] /baɪt/ *vt,vi* (*pt* **bit** /bɪt/, *pp* **bitten** /ˈbɪtn/). **1** [VP6A,15B,2A,3A] cut into with the teeth: *The dog bit me in the leg. Does your dog ~,* is it in the habit of biting people? ***~ at sth,*** try to get it with the teeth; snap at. ***~ off,*** cut off with the teeth: *He bit off a large piece of the apple.* ***~ off more than one can chew,*** attempt too much. ***(have) sth to ~ on,*** sth to get one's teeth into; (fig) sth definite to do, examine, etc. ***~ the dust,*** (fig) fall to the ground; be killed. ***~ one's lips,*** try to conceal one's anger or annoyance. ***once bitten twice shy,*** a person who has been cheated is likely to be cautious afterwards. ***the biter bitten,*** the person who intended to cheat was himself cheated. **2** [VP6A] **(a)** (of fleas, mosquitoes, etc) sting: *He was badly bitten by the mosquitoes.* **(b)** (of fish) accept the bait: *The fish wouldn't ~. I tried to sell him my old car but he wouldn't ~,* (fig) would not consider the suggestion. **3** [VP6A,2A,3A] cause a smarting pain to; injure: *His fingers were bitten by the frost/were frost-bitten. Mustard and pepper ~ the tongue. Strong acids ~ (into) metals,* make holes in them. **4** [VP6A,2A] take strong hold of; grip: *The rails were covered with ice and the wheels did not ~.* **bit·ing** *adj* sharp; cutting: *a biting wind; biting words.* **bit·ing·ly** *adv*

bite[2] /baɪt/ *n* **1** act of biting: *eating sth at one ~.* **2** injury resulting from a ~ or sting: *His face was covered with insect ~s.* **3** piece cut off by biting. **4** food to eat: *I haven't had a ~ since morning,* have eaten nothing. **5** taking bait from a hook by fish: *He had been fishing all morning but hadn't had a ~.* **6** [U] sharpness; sting: *There's a ~ in the air this morning.* **7** [U] grip; hold: *a file/screw with plenty of ~.*

bit·ten /ˈbɪtn/ ⇨ **bite**[1].

bit·ter /ˈbɪtə(r)/ *adj* **1** tasting like beer or quinine. **ˌ~-ˈsweet** *adj* sweet but with a ~ taste at the end; (fig) pleasant but with a mixture of sth unpleasant. **2** unwelcome to the mind; hard to bear; causing sorrow: *~ hardships/experiences. His failure to pass the examination was a ~ disappointment.* ***a ~ pill to swallow,*** sth unpleasant to accept. **3** filled with, showing, caused by, envy, hate, remorse, or disappointment: *~ quarrels/words/enemies/reproaches/tears.* **4** piercingly cold: *a ~ wind.* **5** ***to the ~ end,*** until all that is possible has been done: *fight to the ~ end.* □ *n* **1** bitterness. ***take the ~ with the sweet,*** accept misfortune as well as good fortune. Cf *take the rough with the smooth,* which is more usu. **2** [U] bitter beer: *a pint of ~.* **3** (*pl*) liquor made from herbs, fruits, etc taken to help digestion or used to flavour gin, etc: *orange ~s; gin and ~s.* **~·ly** *adv* **~·ness** *n*

bit·tern /ˈbɪtən/ *n* any of several kinds of wading birds that live on marshes, esp the kind known for its booming note. ⇨ the illus at **water**.

bitu·men /ˈbɪtʃʊmən/ *n* [U] black, sticky substance (from petroleum), used for making roads, etc; mineral pitch; asphalt. **bit·umi·nous** /bɪˈtjuːmɪnəs *US:* -ˈtu-/ *adj* containing ~ or tar: *bituminous coal,* burning with smoky yellow flames.

bi·valve /ˈbaɪvælv/ *n* (zool) water animal with a hinged double shell, e g an oyster, a mussel, a clam.

biv·ouac /ˈbɪvʊæk/ *n* soldiers' temporary camp without tents or other cover. □ *vi* (*pt,pp* **bivouacked**) [VP2A] make a ~; stay in a ~.

bi·week·ly /ˈbaɪˈwiklɪ/ *adj* lasting for two weeks; happening every alternate week.

biz /bɪz/ *n* (sl) business: *Good biz!* Well done! **ˈshow·biz,** (sl) (providing and managing) popular entertainment.

bi·zarre /bɪˈzɑ(r)/ *adj* grotesque; odd.

bi·zonal /ˈbaɪˈzəʊnl/ *adj* of two zones, e g of the British and American zones of occupation in Germany after 1947.

blab /blæb/ *vt,vi* (-bb-) [VP6A,15B,2A] talk foolishly or indiscreetly; tell (a secret): *~ out a secret. Don't ~.*

black /blæk/ *adj* **1** without light or almost without light; the colour of this printing-ink; opposite to white. ***be ~ and blue,*** covered with bruises. ***~ in the face,*** dark red or purple (with anger or because of making great efforts). ***be in sb's ~ book(s),*** ⇨ book[1](6). ***look ~ at sb, give sb a ~ look,*** look at him angrily. ***not so ~ as one is painted,*** not so bad as one is said to be. **2** (various uses, mostly to intensify the meaning of the *n*): *~ despair,* deep, dismal; *~ tidings,* sad news, causing despair; *~ deeds,* wicked; *in one of his ~ moods,* silent and bad-tempered. **3** (of work in a factory, shipyard, etc during a strike; of the materials, etc) not to be done, handled, etc: *The strikers declared the work/cargo ~.* **4** (compounds, etc) ***~ and white,*** ink drawing. ***(have sth down) in ~ and white,*** (have it) recorded in writing or print. **~ art, magic,** used for evil purposes. **ˋ~·ball** *vt* prevent (sb) from being elected a member of a club by voting against him at a secret ballot. **ˋ~-beetle** *n* cockroach. **ˋ~·berry** /ˋblækbrɪ *US:* -berɪ/ *n* (*pl* **-ries**) small berry, ~ when ripe, growing wild on bushes (called *brambles*): *go ~berrying* /-berɪɪŋ/, go out gathering ~berries. ⇨ the illus at fruit. **ˋ~·bird** *n* common European songbird. **ˋ~·board** *n* board used in schools for writing and drawing on with chalk. **ˈ~ ˋbox** *n* device for recording information about the performance of an aircraft during a flight. **ˈ~ ˋcap** *n* cap put on by a judge before sentencing a murderer to death. **ˈ~-ˋcoated** *adj*: *the ~-coated classes/workers,* (now called *white collar*) those who work in offices, etc (contrasted with those who work on farms, in mines, factories, etc). **ˈ~ ˋcoffee** *n* coffee without milk, usu strong. **the ˋB~ Country,** the smoky, industrial area in Staffordshire and Warwickshire. **ˋ~·cur·rant** *n* kind of currant with ~ fruit. ⇨ currant(2). **the ˈ~ ˋflag,** flag formerly used by pirates (sea-robbers); flag once used at prisons as a signal that a murderer had been executed by hanging. **ˈ~ ˋfrost** *n* hard frost without rime. **ˋ~guard** /ˋblægɑd/ *n* person who is quite without honour; scoundrel. □ *vt* call (sb) a ~guard; use very bad language about or to (sb). **ˋ~guard·ly** /ˋblægədlɪ/ *adj* dishonest and immoral: *a ~guardly track.* **ˋ~·head** *n* (kind of) pimple on the skin, the top being ~. **ˈ~ ˋice** *n* ice, esp on a road surface, which is almost invisible and dangerous to drive on. **ˈ~-ˋlead** *n* [U] soft, grey-black solid (plumbago, or graphite) used for lead pencils, polishing and as a lubricant. □ *vt* polish, e g a fireplace, with ~-lead. **ˋ~·leg** *n* person who offers to work when the regular workers are on strike; scab. □ *vi, vt* act as ~leg; betray (fellow workers) by doing this. **ˋ~·list** *n* list of persons who are considered dangerous or who are to be punished. □ *vt* enter the name of (sb) on a ~list. **ˈ~ ˋmagic** *n* witchcraft. **ˋ~·mail** *vt, n* [U] (force sb to make a) payment of money for not making known sth discreditable about him. Hence, **ˋ~·mailer** *n* person who does this. **ˈ~ Maˋria** /məˋraɪə/ *n* van for taking prisoners from and to jail. **ˈ~ ˋmarket** *n* unlawful buying and selling of goods, currencies, etc that are officially controlled; place where such trading is carried on. **ˈ~ ˈmarkeˋteer** /ˈmɑkɪˋtɪə(r)/, person carrying on this trade. **ˈ~ ˋmass,** travesty of the R C Mass, for Satan instead of God. **ˋ~·out** *n* **(a)** (during wartime) the keeping of all buildings, etc, dark (by curtains, etc, in windows, by having no street-lighting, etc) in order to prevent any light being seen, esp from the air. **(b)** temporary complete failure of the memory or consciousness; (esp flying) temporary blindness caused by a sudden turn or a change in speed. **(c)** extinguishing of all lights on the stage of a theatre, e g for a change of scenery. □ *vt, vi* [VP6A,2A] cause a ~out ((a) and (c) above); lose one's memory, etc, temporarily. **ˈB~ ˋPanther** *n* member of a revolutionary movement among Afro-Americans. **ˈB~ ˋPower,** militant movement with similar aims. **ˈ~ ˋpudding** *n* sausage made of blood, suet, barley, etc. **ˈ~ ˋsheep** *n* good-for-nothing person. **ˋB~-shirt** *n* member of the former Italian Fascist party. **ˋ~·smith** *n* man who makes and repairs things of iron, esp a shoer of horses. **ˋ~·thorn** *n* thorny shrub which has white blossom before the leaves appear and purple fruit (*sloes*) like small plums. **ˈ~·water ˋfever,** tropical disease with bloody urine. □ *n* **1** [U] ~ colour: *He was dressed in ~,* in ~ clothes. **2** [U] ~ paint or dye. **3** [C] particle of soot. **4** [C] Negro (formerly derog, but now widely used in US). □ *vt* [VP6A] **1** make ~, polish (boots, etc), with blacking. **2** declare ~(3): *The strikers ~ed the ship/the cargo.*

blacka·moor /ˋblækəmɔ(r)/ *n* (hum or derog) black-skinned person.

blacken /ˋblækən/ *vt, vi* **1** [VP6A,2A] make or become black. **2** [VP6A] speak evil of (sb's character).

black·ing /ˋblækɪŋ/ *n* [U] *black paste or liquid for polishing shoes* (*now usu shoe polish*).

blad·der /ˋblædə(r)/ *n* **1** bag of skin in which urine collects in human and animal bodies. ⇨ the illus at kidney. **2** such a bag, or a bag of rubber, etc, that can be filled with air, e g the rubber ~ in a football.

blade /bleɪd/ *n* **1** flattened cutting part of a knife, sword, chisel, etc: *a pocket-knife with two ~s; a packet of five razor ~s.* ⇨ the illus at razor. **2** sword; swordsman. **3** flat wide part of an oar (the part that goes into the water), bat, propeller, etc. **4** flat, long, narrow leaf, esp of grass and cereals (wheat, barley, etc).

blae·berry /ˋbleɪbrɪ *US:* -berɪ/ *n* = bilberry.

blah /blɑ/ *n* [U] (colloq) high-sounding but meaningless talk or writing.

blame /bleɪm/ *vt* [VP6A,14] ***~ sb (for sth), ~ sth on sb,*** fix on sb the responsibility for sth: *Bad workmen often ~ their tools. He ~d the teacher for his failure* (colloq) *He ~d his failure on his teacher. I have nothing to ~ myself for.* ***be to ~,*** deserve censure: *Who is to ~ for starting the fire,* Whom have we to find fault with? *I am in no way to ~,* am not in any way responsible. □ *n* [U] **1** responsibility for failure, etc: *Where does the ~ lie for our failure,* Who or what is responsible? ***bear/take the ~ (for sth),*** take the responsibility. ***put/lay the ~ on sb (for sth),*** make him responsible. **2** finding fault: *If you don't do the work well, you will incur ~,* people will find fault. **ˋ~·less** *adj* free from ~ or faults; innocent: *I am ~less in this matter.* **~·less·ly** *adv* **~·worthy** /ˋbleɪmwɜðɪ/ *adj* deserving ~.

blanch /blɑntʃ *US:* blæntʃ/ *vt, vi* [VP6A,2A] make or become pale or white, e g by taking the skin off almonds, by not letting light get to plants; make or become pale with fear, cold, etc.

blanc·mange /bləˋmɒnʒ/ *n* [C,U] jelly made in a mould with milk: *~ powder,* mixture of powdered milk, powdered gelatine, etc to make kinds of ~.

bland /blænd/ *adj* **1** gentle or polite in manner or talk (usu in order to ingratiate oneself). **2** (of air, food, drink) mild; comforting. **ˋ~·ly** *adv* **~·ness** *n*

bland·ish·ment /ˈblændɪʃmənt/ *n* (usu *pl*) soft and gentle ways and speech intended to make sb do sth; flattery; coaxing.

blank /blæŋk/ *adj* **1** (of paper) with nothing written, printed or drawn on it: *a ~ sheet of paper; a ~ page; fill in the ~s,* (e g on telegram forms) write names, addresses, messages, etc in the appropriate empty spaces. **2** (of a document) with spaces in which details, signature, etc are to be filled in. ˌ**~ ˈbill,** Bill of Exchange on which the name of the person to be paid is not stated. ˌ**~ ˈcheque,** one with the amount left for the payee to fill in. ***give sb a ~ cheque,*** (fig) full power to act as he thinks best. **3** empty; without interest or expression: *There was a ~ look on his face,* He seemed not to be interested, not to understand, etc. *He looked ~,* puzzled. *His future looks ~,* seems to be empty and dull. *My mind went ~,* I could not recall things, esp things I needed to be aware of. ˌ**~ ˈcartridge,** with a charge of powder, but no bullet. ˌ**~ ˈverse,** (usu lines of ten syllables) without rhyme. ˌ**~ ˈwall,** one with no door, window or other opening. ***come up against a ~ wall,*** be unable to find support, information, etc. □ *n* **1** space left empty or to be filled (in sth printed or written): *In a telegraph form there are ~s for the name and address, the message, etc. When Tom was doing his French translation, he left ~s for all the words he did not know.* **2** lottery ticket that does not win a prize. ***draw a ~,*** get nothing (after hoping to win or find sth). **3** empty surface; emptiness: *His mind/memory was a complete ~,* he could remember nothing. *The death of her husband in the war left a big ~ in her life.* **4** [C,U] ~ cartridge: *They fired twenty rounds of ~/twenty ~s.* **~·ly** *adv*

blan·ket /ˈblæŋkɪt/ *n* **1** thick, woollen covering used on beds, or for keeping a horse warm in a stable, etc: (fig) *a ~ of snow.* ***wet ~,*** (colloq) person who, by being gloomy himself, prevents others from enjoying themselves. **2** (used attrib) covering all cases or classes: *a ~* (= comprehensive) *insurance policy; ~ instructions,* intended to provide for everything. □ *vt* ***be ~ed with,*** be thickly covered with: *The valley was ~ed with fog.*

blare /bleə(r)/ *n* [U] sound or noise (of trumpets or horns): *the ~ of a brass band.* □ *vi,vt* **1** [VP2A,C] make such sounds: *The trumpets ~d (forth).* **2** [VP6A,15B] **~ *out,*** produce with such sounds; utter loudly: *The band ~d out a foxtrot. He ~d out a warning.*

blar·ney /ˈblɑnɪ/ *n* [U], *vt,vi* (use) the kind of talk that flatters and deceives people: *Not so much of your ~!*

blasé /ˈblɑzeɪ *US:* blɑˈzeɪ/ *adj* tired of pleasure.

blas·pheme /blæsˈfim/ *vi,vt* [VP2A,6A] speak in an irreverent way about God and sacred things; use violent language about (sb or sth): *~ the name of God.* **blas·phemer** *n* person who ~s. **blas·phem·ous** /ˈblæsfəməs/ *adj* (of persons) using blasphemy; (of language) containing blasphemy. **blas·phem·ous·ly** *adv* **blas·phemy** /ˈblæsfəmɪ/ *n* [U] contemptuous or irreverent talk about God and sacred things; [C] (*pl* **-mies**) instance of this.

blast /blɑst *US:* blæst/ *n* **1** strong, sudden rush of wind: *A ~ of hot air came from the furnace. When the window was opened an icy ~ came into the room.* **2** (often [U]) strong rush of air or gas spreading outwards from an explosion: *Thousands of windows were broken by ~ during the air raids.* ˈ**~-off,** ⇨ blast *v* (3). **3** stream of air used to intensify the heat in a furnace, etc. ***at full ~,*** (colloq) with the maximum activity. ***in/out of ~,*** (of a furnace) working/not working. ˈ**~-furnace** *n* furnace for melting iron ore by forcing into it a current of heated air. **4** sound made by a wind-instrument: *The hunter blew a ~ on his horn. The ship sounded a prolonged ~ on the siren.* **5** quantity of explosive (e g dynamite) used at one time (e g in a quarry). □ *vt* **1** [VP6A,2A] blow up (rocks, etc) with explosives: *Danger! B~ing in progress!* **2** [VP6A] cause (sth) to come to nothing; shrivel; injure: *blossom ~ed by frost. The tree had been ~ed by lightning. His hopes were ~ed.* **3** [VP6A] **~ *off,*** (of spacecraft, etc) be forced upwards by expanding gases. Hence, ˈ**~-off** *n* the (time of) launching of such a spacecraft: *the count-down to ~-off.* **4** [VP6A] (sl) reproach sb severely: *be ~ed by one's boss; get a ~ing from sb.* **5** (in curses, with *May God* understood) *B~ it/you!* **~ed** /ˈblɑstɪd *US:* ˈblæ-/ *attrib adj* (in curses) damnable.

bla·tant /ˈbleɪtnt/ *adj* noisy and rough; attracting attention in a vulgar and shameless way; too obvious. **~·ly** *adv*

blather /ˈblæðə(r)/ *n, v* ⇨ blether.

blaze[1] /bleɪz/ *n* **1** bright flame or fire: *We could see the ~ of a cheerful fire through the window. I put some wood on the fire and it soon burst into a ~,* began to burn brightly. **2** fire; burning building: *It took the firemen two hours to put the ~ out.* **3** (*pl*) hell: *Go to ~s! He was working like ~s,* working furiously. **4** glow of colour; bright light: *The red tulips made a ~ of colour in the garden. The main street of the town is a ~ of light(s) in the evening.* **5** violent outburst: *in a ~ of anger.*

blaze[2] /bleɪz/ *vi,vt* **1** [VP2A,C] burn with flame: *There was a fire blazing on the hearth. When the firemen arrived the whole building was blazing.* **~ *up,*** burst into flames. **2** [VP2A,C] be bright with colour; shine brightly or with warmth: *The garden was blazing with colour. The sun ~d down on us.* **3** [VP2A,C] burst out with strong feeling: *He was blazing with anger/indignation.* **4** [VP2C,15B] **~ *away,*** fire continuously with rifles, etc: *They ~d away at the enemy. He ~d away all his ammunition.* **blaz·ing** *adj*: *a blazing fire*; (fig) *a blazing* (= conspicuous) *indiscretion*; (foxhunting) *a blazing* (= very strong) *scent.*

blaze[3] /bleɪz/ *n* white mark on a horse's or an ox's face; mark made on a tree by cutting the bark. □ *vt* [VP6A] mark (a tree) by cutting off part of the bark. **~ *a trail,*** mark trees to show a path through a forest; (fig) do sth for the first time and show others how to do it.

blaze[4] /bleɪz/ *vt* [VP6A,15B] **~ *(abroad),*** make known far and wide: *~ the news (abroad).*

blazer /ˈbleɪzə(r)/ *n* loose-fitting jacket (often made of flannel, sometimes in the colours of a school, club, team, etc) for informal wear.

bla·zon /ˈbleɪzn/ *n* coat of arms, esp on a shield. ⇨ the illus at armour. □ *vt* = blaze[4]. **~ry** *n* bright display.

bleach /blitʃ/ *vt,vi* [VP6A,2A] make or become white (by chemical action or sunlight): *~ linen; bones of animals ~ing on the desert sand.* ˈ**~ing-powder** *n* (e g chloride of lime) substance used to remove colour from dyed materials. □ *n* (household ~) chemical for ~ing and sterilizing.

bleach·ers /ˋblitʃəz/ *n pl* (US) unroofed seats/planks at sports grounds.

bleak /blik/ *adj* **1** (of the weather) cold and cheerless; (of a place) bare, swept by cold winds: *a ~ hillside.* **2** (fig) dreary: *~ prospects.* **~·ly** *adv*

bleary /ˈblɪəˋri/ *adj* dim; blurred. **ˈ~-ˋeyed** /ˈblɪərˋaɪd/ *adj* having ~ eyes: *He got out of bed all ~-eyed.*

bleat /blit/ *n* cry of a sheep, goat or calf. □ *vi,vt* [VP2A] make a cry of this kind; [VP6A,15B] speak, say (sth) feebly: *He ~ed (out) a complaint.*

bleed /blid/ *vi,vt* (*pt,pp* **bled** /bled/) **1** [VP2A,C] lose, send out, blood; suffer wounds (for a cause, etc): *If you cut your finger it will ~. He was slowly ~ing to death.* **2** [VP2A,C, simple tenses only] feel great distress: *Our hearts ~ for homeless people during this cold winter.* **3** [VP6A] draw blood from: *Doctors used to ~ people when they were ill.* **4** [VP6A,14] force (sb) to pay money unjustly: *The blackmailers bled him for £500.* **5** [VP2A] (of a plant, tree, etc) lose sap or juice.

bleep /blip/ *n* (word used for a) high-pitched sound or signal sent out by radio (and used by sb carrying a small pocket radio, e g a doctor in a hospital, to summon him when needed). □ *vi* emit such sounds.

blem·ish /ˋblemɪʃ/ *n* [C,U] mark, etc that spoils the beauty or perfection of sb or sth; moral defect: *without ~*, faultless. □ *vt* [VP6A] spoil the perfection of.

blench /blentʃ/ *vi* [VP2A] make a quick movement of fear.

blend /blend *vt,vi* (*pt,pp* **~ed** or, liter, **blent** /blent/) **1** [VP6A] mix together, esp sorts of tea, tobacco, spirits, etc, to get a certain quality: *~ed whisky. A grocer used to need to know how to ~ tea. Our coffees* (i e varieties of coffee) *are carefully ~ed.* **2** [VP2A,3A] mix, form a mixture: *Oil and water do not ~. Oil does not ~ with water.* **3** [VP2A] go well together; have no sharp or unpleasant contrast: (esp of colours) pass by degrees into each other: *These two colours ~ well. How well their voices ~!* □ *n* [C] mixture made of various sorts (of tea, tobacco, etc): *This coffee is a ~ of Java and Brazil.*

blent ⇨ **blend.**

bless /bles/ *vt* (*pt,pp* **~ed** /blest/ and **blest**, as in (6) below) [VP6A] **1** ask God's favour for: *They brought the children to Jesus and he ~ed them. The priest ~ed the people/the crops.* **2** wish happiness or favour to: *B~ you, my boy!* **3** consecrate; make sacred or holy: *relics ~ed by the Pope; bread ~ed at the altar.* **4 *be ~ed with,*** be fortunate in having: *I am not greatly ~ed with worldly goods*, am not rich. *May you always be ~ed with good health.* **5** call (God) holy: *'We praise Thee, we ~ Thee,' 'We ~ Thy Holy Name.'* **6** (colloq, in exclamations): *B~ me! B~ my soul! Well, I'm blest!* (expressing surprise). *I'm blest if I know!* i e I don't know at all. **~ed** /ˋblesɪd/ *adj* **1** holy, sacred: **the B~ed Virgin,** the mother of Jesus. **the B~ed Sacrament,** Holy Communion. **2** fortunate: *B~ed are the poor in spirit.* **3 the B~ed,** those who are with God in paradise. **4** (sl, invective) cursed: *I've broken the whole ~ed lot.* **~ed·ness** /ˋblesɪdnəs/ *n* [U] happiness: *in single ~edness,* (joc) unmarried. **~·ing** *n* **1** the favour of God; prayer for God's favour; thanks to God before or after a meal: *ask a ~ing.* ⇨ **grace(5). 2** sth that one is glad of; sth that brings comfort or happiness: *What a ~ing it is you didn't get caught in the storm yesterday!* ***a ~ing in disguise,*** sth that seemed unfortunate, but that is seen later to be fortunate.

blether /ˋbleðə(r)/, **blather** /ˋblæðə(r)/ *n* [U] foolish talk. □ *vi* [VP2A,C] talk nonsense.

blew /blu/ ⇨ **blow**[1].

blight /blaɪt/ *n* **1** [U] (sorts of) plant disease; mildew. **2** [C] evil influence of obscure origin: *a ~ upon his hopes.* □ *vt* [VP6A] be a ~ upon: *His hopes were ~ed. Her life was ~ed by constant illness.* **~er** *n* (sl) **1** annoying person. **2** fellow: *You lucky ~er!*

Blighty /ˋblaɪtɪ/ *n* (GB army sl) home (during service abroad). ***a ~ wound,*** one severe enough for a soldier to be returned to GB.

bli·mey /ˋblaɪmɪ/ *int* (vulg) expressing surprise.

blimp /blɪmp/ *n* **1** small non-rigid airship. **2 (Colonel) B~,** pompous-looking reactionary person.

blind[1] /blaɪnd/ *adj* **1** without the power to see: *Tom helped the ~ man across the road. He is ~ in the right eye.* ***turn a/one's ~ eye to sth,*** pretend not to see it. **~ spot,** point on the retina insensible to light; (fig) inability to recognize sth. **2 ~ *(to),*** unable to see effects, to judge or understand well: *Mothers are sometimes ~ to the faults of their children. I am not ~ to the drawbacks of the method. A man would be ~ not to see that difficulty.* **3** reckless; thoughtless: *In his ~ haste he almost ran into the river.* **4** not ruled by purpose: *Some people think that the world is governed by ~ forces.* **5** (sl) drunk (also **~ *drunk***). **6 ~ alley,** ⇨ **alley(1). ~ date,** ⇨ **date**[1]**(4). ~ flying,** navigation, e g in cloud, fog, with the aid of instruments only. **~ turning,** (in a road) one that cannot easily be seen by drivers. **ˈ~·ˈman's ˋbuff** *n* game in which one player, who is ~folded, tries to catch and identify one of the others who push him about.

blind[2] /blaɪnd/ *vt* [VP6A,14] make ~; (fig) take away the power of judgement: *a ~ing light. The soldier had been ~ed in the war. His feelings for her ~ed him to her faults.* **~·ers** *n pl* (US) = blinkers. **~·ly** *adv* **~ness** *n*

blind[3] /blaɪnd/ *n* [C] **1** roll of cloth (usu strong linen) fixed on a roller and pulled down to cover a window (US = *window-shade*): *pull down/lower, draw up/raise the ~s.* **2** (fig) deception: *It was only a ~*, sth intended to hide the reality. **3** (US) = **hide**[1] *n*

blind·fold /ˋblaɪndfəʊld/ *vt* [VP6A] cover the eyes of (sb) with a bandage so that he cannot see. □ *n* such a cover. □ *adj* with the eyes bandaged, covered with a handkerchief, etc.

blink /blɪŋk/ *vi,vt* **1** [VP2A,C,6A,15B] shut and open the eyes quickly: *~ the eyes; ~ away a tear.* **2** [VP6A] ***~ the fact that,*** (fig) refuse to consider; ignore: *There's no ~ing the fact that....* **3** [VP2C] (of lights, esp when in the distance) come and go; shine in an unsteady way: *We saw the lights of a steamer ~ing on the horizon.* □ *n ~ing.* **~·ing** *adj* (vulg) bloody**(3)**: *It's a ~ing nuisance.*

blink·ers /ˋblɪŋkəz/ *n pl* (US = *blinders*) leather squares to prevent a horse from seeing sideways. ⇨ the illus at **harness.**

blip /blɪp/ *n* spot of light on a radar screen.

bliss /blɪs/ *n* [U] perfect happiness; great joy. **ˋ~·ful** /-fʊl/ *adj* **ˋ~·fully** /-flɪ/ *adv*

blis·ter /ˋblɪstə(r)/ *n* [C] **1** small bag-like swelling under the skin, filled with liquid (caused by rubbing, burning, etc): *If your shoes are too tight, you may get ~s on your feet.* **2** similar swelling on the surface of metal, painted or varnished wood, a plant, etc. □ *vt,vi* [VP6A,2A] cause, get, a ~ or ~s on: *He is not used to manual work and his hands ~ easily. The hot sun has ~ed the paint on the door.*

blithe, blithe·some /blaɪð, -səm/ *adj* (chiefly poet) gay and joyous. **~·ly** *adv*

blith·er·ing /ˈblɪðərɪŋ/ *adj* (colloq) utter; contemptible (esp in): *~ idiot.*

blitz /blɪts/ *n* rapid, violent attack (esp from the air). □ *vt* [VP6A] damage or destroy in this way (esp in *pp*): *~ed areas/towns,* destroyed by bombing during air-raids.

bliz·zard /ˈblɪzəd/ *n* [C] violent and heavy snowstorm.

bloated /ˈbləʊtɪd/ *adj* swollen; fat and large in an unhealthy way: *a ~ face; a fat, ugly man, ~ with over-eating;* (fig) *~ with pride,* puffed up with pride.

bloater /ˈbləʊtə(r)/ *n* salted and smoked herring: *~ paste,* paste made from ~s.

blob /blob/ *n* drop of liquid, e g paint; small round mass, e g of wax; spot of colour.

bloc /blok/ *n* combination of parties, groups, states, etc with a special interest: *the sterling ~,* of countries with currencies related to sterling.

block[1] /blok/ *n* **1** large, solid piece of wood, stone, etc: *A butcher cuts up his meat on a large ~ of wood. The ~s of stone in the Pyramids are five or six feet high. The statue is to be cut out of a ~ of marble. Children play with building ~s,* cubes of wood put together to make toy houses, etc. ⇨ **chip(1)**. **2** main part of a petrol engine, consisting of the cylinders and valves. **3 the ~,** (in olden times) large piece of wood on which a person put his neck to have his head cut off as a punishment. ***go/be sent to the ~,*** to death in this way. **4** shaped piece of wood on which hats are moulded. **5** pulley, or system of pulleys, in a wooden case (often referred to as ***~ and tackle***). **6** piece of wood or metal with designs, etc, cut (engraved) on it for printing. **7** mass of buildings (shops, offices, apartments, etc) joined together; (esp US) area of buildings bounded by four streets; the length of one side of such an area: *To reach the post-office, walk two ~s east and then turn left.* **~·buster** /ˈblok bʌstə(r)/ *n* bomb that can destroy a city ~. **8** division of seats in a theatre, concert hall, etc; large quantity of shares in a business. **9** obstruction; sth that makes movement or flow difficult or impossible: *There was a ~ in the pipe and the water couldn't flow away.* **ˈroad ~,** barrier across a road at which documents, etc are checked. **ˈtraffic ~,** (also *traffic jam*) large number of buses, cars, vans, trams, etc held up and unable to move on. **10 ~ grant,** fixed and non-recurring subsidy. **ˌ~ ˈletters/ˈwriting,** with each letter separate and in capitals: *Write your name in ~ letters.* **11** (cricket) spot on which a batsman rests his bat before playing a ball. **12** (sl) (person's) head: *I'll knock your ~ off!*

block[2] /blok/ *vt* **1** [VP6A,15B] make movement difficult or impossible; put sth in the way of: *All roads were ~ed by the heavy snowfall. They ~ed (up) the entrance to the cave with big rocks. The harbour was ~ed by ice.* **2** [VP6A] obstruct (progress); make (action) difficult or impossible: *The general succeeded in ~ing the enemy's plans.* **3** [VP6A] (chiefly in *pp*) restrict the use or expenditure of (currency, assets, etc): *~ed sterling.* **4** [VP6A] shape (e g hats) on a ~. ⇨ **block**[1]**(4)**. **5 ~ *in/out,*** make a rough sketch or plan of the general arrangement (of objects in a drawing, etc). **6** (cricket) stop (the ball) with the bat (kept upright in front of the wicket).

block·ade /bloˈkeɪd/ *n* the enclosing or surrounding of a place, e g by armies or warships, to keep goods or people from entering or leaving. ***run the ~,*** evade and get through the forces that are surrounding a place. ***raise the ~,*** end it. **ˈ~-runner** *n* ship, etc that gets through or past a ~. □ *vt* [VP6A] make a ~ of, e g a town, fort, etc.

block·age /ˈblokɪdʒ/ *n* state of being blocked; sth that blocks: *There's a ~ in the drain-pipe.*

block·head /ˈblokhed/ *n* slow and stupid person.

block·house /ˈblokhaʊs/ *n* military strongpoint with openings through which to shoot.

bloke /bləʊk/ *n* (sl) man.

blond /blond/ *n, adj* (man of European race) having fair complexion and hair. **blonde** /blond/ *n, adj* woman ~.

blood[1] /blʌd/ *n* [U] **1** red liquid flowing throughout the body of man and the higher animals: *The soldiers shed their ~* (= died) *for their country. It was more than flesh and ~* (= human nature) *could stand. He gave his ~ to help his sister,* gave ~ to be injected into his sister after a surgical operation or an accident. ***infuse new ~ (into sth),*** (fig) revive business, etc by introducing new talent. ***let ~,*** draw off ~ from a vein. ⇨ **7** below. **2** passion; temper: *His ~ is up,* he is angry, filled with passion. *His ~ ran cold,* he was filled with terror or horror. ***(kill sb) in cold ~,*** when one is not feeling angry or excited; deliberately. ***make bad ~ between persons,*** cause them to feel ill will towards one another. ***make one's ~ boil,*** make one very angry. ***make one's ˈ~ run cold,*** fill one with fear or horror. **3** relationships; family: *They are of the same ~,* have ancestors in common. **ˌblue ˈ~** *n* high birth or descent. ***of the (royal) ~,*** of royal race. ***one's own flesh and ~*** *n* one's relations. ***B~ is thicker than water,*** (prov) The ties of relationship are real. **ˈ~ feud** *n* deadly feud between families. **ˈ~-relation** *n* person related by ~, not by marriage. **4 *~ and iron,*** (fig) relentless use of force. **5** [C] (formerly) man of fashion; rich, pleasure-loving young man. **6 *~ and thunder*** *attrib adj* (of stories, dramas) melodramatic; full of exciting incidents. **7** (compounds) **ˈ~ bank** *n* ⇨ **bank**[1]**(3)**. **ˈ~-bath** *n* large-scale slaughter, e g in battle, or during a revolution. **~ brother,** one who swears to treat another as a brother (perhaps by mixing his ~ with the other person). **ˈ~ count** *n* (counting of the) number of red and white corpuscles in a certain volume of ~. **ˈ~-curdling** *adj* sending feelings of horror through the body. **ˈ~-donor** *n* person who gives ~ for ~ transfusions. **ˈ~-group/type** *n* any of several distinct classes of human ~. **ˌ~-ˈheat** *n* the normal temperature of human ~ (about 98·5°F, 37°C). **ˈ~-hound** *n* large dog able to trace a person by scent. ⇨ the illus at **dog**. **ˈ~-letting** *n* surgical drawing off of some of a patient's ~. **ˈ~-lust,** desire for killing sb. **ˈ~-money** *n* money obtained at the cost of a life, e g received by a murderer for killing someone or as a reward for betraying sb who is to be put to death.

'~-**poisoning** *n* condition that results when poisonous germs enter the ~, esp through a cut or wound. '~ **pressure** *n* the force exerted by ~ within the arteries. '~ '**red,** having the colour of ~. '~-**shed** *n* killing or wounding of people; putting to death: *There was great ~shed in Paris during the years after the Revolution in 1789.* '~-**shot** *adj* (of the white of the eyes) red. '~-**sports** *n pl* outdoor sports in which animals or birds are killed. '~-**stained** *adj* (a) stained with ~: *a ~stained shirt.* (b) disgraced by ~shed. '~-**stock** *n* (collective) thoroughbred horses. '~-**sucker** *n* (a) creature that sucks ~, esp a leech. (b) person who unjustly forces another or others to give him as much money as possible. '~-**thirsty** *adj* cruel and eager to take life; taking pleasure in killing. '~-**thirsti·ness** *n* '~-**transfusion** *n* transfer of ~ (originally taken) from the veins of one person to those of another. '~-**vessel** *n* tube (vein or artery) through which ~ flows in the body. ⇨ the illus at respiratory. ~-**less** *adj* **1** without ~shed: *a ~less victory.* **2** pale; unfeeling and coldhearted. ~-**less·ly** *adv*

blood[2] /blʌd/ *vt* [VP6A] allow the first taste of ~ to (foxhounds, etc).

bloody /ˈblʌdɪ/ *adj* **1** bleeding; covered with blood: *a ~ nose.* **2** with much bloodshed: *a ~ battle.* **3** (vulg, either intensive or expletive, derog or laud, but often with no meaning): *What a ~ shame!* (derog) *You're a ~ fool!* (laud) *You're a ~ genius!* '~-'**minded,** (sl) obstructive; unwilling to co-operate. □ *adv* (vulg sl): *Not ~ likely!* (= not at all likely).

bloom /blum/ *n* **1** [C] flower, esp of plants admired chiefly for their flowers (e g roses, tulips, chrysanthemums). ***in ~,*** (of plants) flowering: *The tulips are in full ~ now.* Cf *in blossom* for shrubs and trees. **2** (*sing* only) (time of) greatest beauty or perfection: *She was in the ~ of youth.* **3** [U] covering of fine dust or powder on plums, grapes, etc when they are at their best. ***take the ~ off sth,*** cause it to seem stale. □ *vi* [VP2A,C] **1** be in flower; bear flowers: *The roses have been ~ing all summer.* **2** (fig) be in full beauty and perfection. '~-**ing** *adj* **1** (in the senses of the *v*) **2** /ˈblʊmɪŋ/ (colloq euphem for *bloody*(**3**)): *You ~ing idiot!*

bloomer /ˈbluməә(r)/ *n* (sl) blunder: *He made a tremendous ~.*

bloom·ers /ˈbluməz/ *n pl* loose garment covering each leg to the knee and hanging from the waist, formerly worn by girls and women for games, cycling, etc, with or without a skirt.

blos·som /ˈblosəm/ *n* [C] flower, esp of a fruit-tree; [U] mass of flowers on a bush or tree. ⇨ the illus at flower. ***in ~,*** (of bushes and trees) having flowers: *The apple-trees are in ~.* ⇨ bloom(**1**). □ *vi* **1** [VP2A] open into flowers: *The cherry-trees will ~ next month.* **2** [VP2C] develop: *He ~ed out as a first-rate athlete.*

blot /blot/ *n* **1** mark caused by ink spilt on paper. **2** fault; disgrace; sth that takes away from the beauty or goodness of sth: *a ~ on his character; a ~ on the landscape,* e g an ugly building or advertisement. □ *vt* (-tt-) **1** [VP6A] make a ~ or ~s on (paper with ink). ~ ***one's copybook,*** (colloq) do sth that spoils one's good record. **2** [VP6A] dry up (wet ink) with ~ting-paper. '~-**ting-paper** *n* absorbent paper used to dry up wet ink quickly. **3** [VP15B] ~ ***out,*** (a) make a ~ over (words that have been written): *Several words in his letter had been ~ted out.* (b) hide from view: *The mist came down and ~ted out the view.* (c) destroy, exterminate (enemies, etc). ~-**ter** *n* **1** book containing sheets of writing-paper interleaved with sheets of ~ting-paper. **police ~ter,** (US) book in which the police enter records, e g of lost and found articles, missing persons. **2** piece or pad of ~ting-paper.

blotch /blotʃ/ *n* large, discoloured mark, usu irregular in shape (e g on the skin, or of ink on paper).

blotto /ˈblotəʊ/ *adj* (sl) fuddled or intoxicated with alcoholic drink.

blouse /blaʊz *US:* blaʊs/ *n* **1** outer garment from neck to waist, worn by women and girls (= US *shirtwaist*). **2** loose-fitting garment, often with a belt at the waist, worn by some workmen. **3** tunic as worn by some sailors and soldiers.

blow[1] /bləʊ/ *vi,vt* (*pt* blew /blu/, *pp* blown /bləʊn/, or, (**11**) below, ~ed) **1** [VP2A,C] (with *air, wind,* or *it* as the subject) move along, flow as a current of air: *It was ~ing hard,* there was a strong wind. *It was ~ing a gale/~ing great guns,* there was a (violent) gale. *The wind was ~ing round the street-corners. It's ~ing up for rain,* the wind seems likely to bring rain soon. **2** [VP15A,B] (of the wind) cause to move: *The wind blew my hat off. I was almost ~n over by the wind. The ship was ~n out of its course/on to the rocks. The wind blew the papers out of my hand.* [VP12A] *It's an ill wind that ~s nobody any good.* **3** [VP2,C,E] (of objects, etc) be moved or carried by the wind or other air current: *My hat blew off. The door blew open. The dust has ~n into the house.* **4** [VP6A,15B,2C] send or force a strong current of air upon, into or through: *~ (on) one's food* (to cool it); *~ the dust off a book; ~ one's nose,* in order to clear it; *~ (up) the fire,* make it burn better (e g by using a pair of bellows); *~ hot and cold,* (fig) vacillate. **5** [VP6A] make by ~ing: *~ bubbles,* by sending air through a pipe with soapy water, etc; shape by ~ing: *~ glass,* by sending a current of air into molten glass. **6** [VP6A] use (sth) to produce a current of air: *~ bellows;* work the bellows of: *~ an organ.* **7** [VP6A,2A] produce sound from (a trumpet, etc) by sending air into it; (of a wind-instrument, etc) produce sound: *The referee blew his whistle. Stop work when the whistle ~s. The huntsman blew his horn. We heard the bugles ~ing.* **8** [VP2A] breathe hard and quickly: *The old man was puffing and ~ing when he got to the top of the hill.* **9** [VP2A] (of whales) force up a stream of air and water: *There she ~s!* There is the fountain sent up by the whale! **10** [VP2A,C,6A,15B] (of a fuse) melt because the electric current is too strong; cause to do this: *The fuse has ~n. The fuse blew out. Don't ~ (out) the fuse.* **11** (sl uses) spend (money) recklessly or extravagantly: *~ £10 on a dinner with a girl friend.* ⇨ blue[3]. *B~ the expense,* Don't worry about it. *I'll be ~ed if.../B~ed if I will...,* I will certainly not.... *Well, I'm ~ed!* (indicating surprise). ~ ***one's top,*** (sl) lose one's temper; explode into angry words, etc. **12** (compounds from the *v*) '~-**back** *n* explosion of gas in a tube, etc. '~-**fly** *n* common meat fly. '~-**hole** *n* (a) opening for air, smoke, etc, in a tunnel. (b) hole (in rocks, etc near the seashore) through which air and water are forced by rising tides. '~-

ing-`up** *n* scolding: *give sb/get a ~ing-up.* **`~-lamp, `~torch** *nn* lamp for directing an intensely hot flame on to a surface. **`~-out *n* **(a)** sudden (often violent) escape of air, steam, etc; (esp) bursting of a tyre. **(b)** ~ing out of an electric fuse. **(c)** (sl) abundant meal; feast. **`~-pipe** *n* **(a)** tube for increasing the heat of a flame by forcing air into it. **(b)** tube through which some primitive people ~ poisoned darts. **`~-up** *n* greatly enlarged photograph: *The men in the procession carried ~-ups of their leader.* **13** [VP2C,3A,15B] (with *adverbial particles* and *preps*):

blow back, (of gas in a tube, etc) explode.

blow in/into, (colloq) arrive noisily, cheerfully, etc: *The door opened and John blew in/blew into the room.*

blow off steam, release tension by arguing, being noisy, etc: *Parents must let children ~ off steam sometimes.*

blow out, ~ sth out, (be) put out by ~ing: *The candle was ~n out by the wind. The light blew out.* ***~ itself out,*** lie down, exhaust itself: *The gale had ~n itself out.* ***~ one's brains out,*** kill oneself by shooting in the head.

blow over, pass by; be forgotten: *The storm/scandal will soon ~ over.*

blow up, **(a)** explode: *The barrel of gunpowder blew up.* **(b)** arise: *A storm is ~ing up.* **(c)** lose one's temper; work up to a crisis: *I'm sorry I blew up at you.* ***~ sb up,*** (colloq) scold severely: *The teacher blew John up for not doing his homework.* ***~ sth up,*** **(a)** break or destroy by explosion: *The soldiers blew up the bridge.* **(b)** inflate with air or gas: *~ up a tyre.* **(c)** enlarge greatly: *~ up a photograph.* **(d)** exaggerate: *His abilities have been greatly ~n up by the newspapers.*

blow[2] /bləʊ/ *n* blowing. ***have/go for a ~,*** go outdoors for fresh air. *Give your nose a good ~,* clear it thoroughly.

blow[3] /bləʊ/ *n* **1** hard stroke (given with the hand, a stick, etc): *He struck his enemy a heavy ~ on the head.* ***at one ~, at a (single) ~,*** in a single effort: *I killed six flies at a ~.* ***come to ~s, exchange ~s,*** fight. ***get a ~ in,*** succeed in placing a ~. ***strike a ~ for,*** (perform a single act of) support for; struggle for. ***without striking a ~,*** without having to fight. ***a ~-by-~ account,*** a detailed account (e g of a boxing match). **2** shock; disaster: *His wife's death was a great ~ to him. It was a ~ to our hopes.*

blow[4] /bləʊ/ *vi* (*pp* blown /bləʊn/) (chiefly in *pp* as) *full-blown roses,* wide open, with petals about to fall; *She has a complexion like a new-blown rose,* a delicate pink complexion.

blower /ˈbləʊə(r)/ *n* **1** apparatus for forcing air, etc into or through sth. **2** person who makes things by blowing (e g *a `glass-~*) or who pumps air into sth (e g *an `organ-~*). **3** (colloq) speaking-tube; (GB sl) telephone: *Get Jones on the ~ for me.*

blown /bləʊn/ *pp* of blow[1]. ⇨ also blow[4]. □ *adj* breathless (as the result of effort).

blowzy /ˈblaʊzɪ/ *adj* (usu of a woman) red-faced, dirty-looking and untidily dressed.

blub·ber[1] /ˈblʌbə(r)/ *n* [U] fat of whales and other sea-animals from which oil is obtained.

blub·ber[2] /ˈblʌbə(r)/ *vi,vt* [VP2A] weep noisily; [VP15B] ***~ (sth) out,*** say with sobs.

bludgeon /ˈblʌdʒən/ *n* short, thick stick with a heavy end, used as a weapon. □ *vt* [VP6A,14] strike repeatedly with a ~: *He had been ~ed to death. He was ~ed into doing it,* made to do it by the use of force.

blue[1] /blu/ *adj* coloured like the sky on a clear day or the deep sea when the sun is shining: *dressed in ~,* wearing ~ clothes; *His face was ~ with cold.* **'~ `blood(ed)** *adj, n* (of) high birth. **'~ `chips,** (fin) industrial shares considered valuable because of past records. **'~ `film,** obscene film. **'~ `jokes,** improper jokes. **'B~ `Peter,** ~ flag with a white square in the centre, used to show that a ship is about to sail. **'~ `ribbon,** sign of great distinction: *the ~ ribbon of the Atlantic,* held by the liner that has the record for the fastest crossing. ***look ~,*** (colloq) be sad or depressed. (*Things are*) ***looking ~,*** depressing. ***once in a ~ moon,*** very rarely.

blue[2] /blu/ *n* **1** ~ colour: *Oxford ~,* dark ~; *Cambridge ~,* light ~. **2** (the) sky. ***appear/come out of the ~,*** unexpectedly. ***a bolt from the ~,*** sth quite unexpected. **3** (at Oxford and Cambridge) right to wear a ~ cap, scarf, etc awarded to a person who has represented his University in athletics, etc: *a rowing ~.* ***win/get one's ~ (for sth).*** **4** (poet) (the) sea. **5** ***a true ~,*** a loyal member (of a political party, esp the Conservative). **6** (*pl*) (dances, dance tunes, for) haunting jazz melodies originally of Negroes in the southern US. ***the ~s,*** (colloq) condition of being sad, melancholy. **7** (compounds) **`~-bell** *n* (Scotland and N England) = harebell; (S England) wild hyacinth with ~ or white flowers growing in moist places and flowering in spring. **`~ book** *n* book published by the Government containing a report. **`~-bottle** *n* meat fly or blowfly. **`B~-coat,** schoolboy of Christ's Hospital (a charity school), who wears a long-skirted ~ coat. **'~-`collar(ed),** used of workers in factories, etc, who wear overalls (contrasted with *white-collar* workers). **`~-jacket** *n* seaman in the Navy. **'~-`pencil** *vt* mark, censor, with a ~ pencil. **`~-print** *n* photographic print, white on ~ paper, usu for building plans; (fig) plan, scheme: (attrib) *the ~print stage.* **`~-stock·ing** *n* woman who is regarded as having superior literary tastes and intellectual interests. **blu·ish** /ˈbluɪʃ/ *adj* tending towards ~: *bluish green.*

blue[3] /blu/ *vt* make blue; (sl) *~ one's money,* spend it recklessly.

bluff[1] /blʌf/ *n* headland with a broad and very steep face. □ *adj* **1** (of headlands, cliffs, a ship's bows) with a broad, perpendicular front. **2** (of a person, his manner, etc) abrupt; rough but honest and kind, simple and good-natured. **~·ly** *adv* **~-ness** *n*

bluff[2] /blʌf/ *vt,vi* [VP6A,14,15B,2A] deceive sb by pretending. ***~ sb into doing sth,*** lead sb to do sth or believe sth by deceiving him: *They were ~ed into supposing we were ill prepared.* ***~ it out,*** survive a difficult situation by pretence. ***~ one's way out of sth,*** escape from a situation by pretence. □ *n* [U] deception of this kind; (the use of) threats that are intended to get results without being carried out. ***call sb's ~,*** invite him to do what he threatened to do. **~er** *n* person who tries to ~ people.

blun·der /ˈblʌndə(r)/ *vi,vt* **1** [VP2A,C,3A] move about uncertainly, as if blind: *~ into a wall.* **2** [VP2A] make foolish mistakes: *Our leaders have ~ed again.* □ *n* [C] stupid or careless mistake. **~er** *n*

blun·der·buss /ˈblʌndəbʌs/ *n* old-fashioned gun with a wide mouth, firing many bullets or small shot at once at short range.

blunt /blʌnt/ *adj* **1** without a point or sharp edge: *a ~ knife.* **2** (of a person, what he says) plain; not troubling to be polite: *He's a ~ man. The ~ fact is that….* □ *vt* [VP6A] make ~: *If you try to cut stone with a knife, you will ~ the edge.* **~·ly** *adv*: *to speak ~ly*, plainly, without ceremony. **~·ness** *n*

blur /blɜ(r)/ *n* **1** dirty spot or mark; smear of ink. **2** confused or indistinct effect: *If, when you try to read small print, you see only a ~, you probably need glasses.* □ *vt,vi* (-rr-) [VP6A,2A] make a dirty mark or smear on (sth); make or become unclear, confused in appearance: *Tears ~red her eyes. Mists ~red the view. The writing was ~red. Rain ~red the windows of our car.*

blurb /blɜb/ *n* publisher's description of the contents of a book, printed on the paper jacket, etc.

blurt /blɜt/ *vt* [VP15B] **~ *sth out,*** tell sth, e g a secret, suddenly, often thoughtlessly.

blush /blʌʃ/ *vi* **1** [VP2A,C,3A] become red (in the face) from shame or confusion: *She ~ed for/with shame. She ~ed at the thought of…; I ~ for you,* i e because of what you have done, said, etc. *He ~ed as red as a peony.* **2** [VP4B] be ashamed: *~ to own that….* □ *n* **1** reddening of the face, e g from shame, etc: *She turned away to hide her ~es.* ***put sb to the ~,*** cause him to ~, to be embarrassed. **2** (old use) glimpse: *at first ~*, at the first look. **ˈ~·ing** *adj* **~·ing·ly** *adv*

blus·ter /ˈblʌstə(r)/ *vi,vt* **1** [VP2A,C] (of the wind, waves, etc) storm; be rough or violent. **2** [VP2A] (of persons) act and speak in a forceful but rather unsteady, often rather boastful way. **3** [VP15B] utter in this way: *~ out threats.* □ *n* [U] **1** noise of violent wind or waves. **2** ~ing talk and behaviour; noisy threats. **ˈ~y** *adj* (of the weather) rough and blowy.

bo(h) /bəʊ/ *int* ⇨ boo.

boa /ˈbəʊə/ *n* **1** (also **ˈboa-constrictor**) large non-poisonous snake that kills by crushing its prey. ⇨ the illus at snake. **2** (also **ˈfeather-boa**) feather stole (formerly) worn by women.

boar /bɔ(r)/ *n* **1** wild male pig. **2** uncastrated male domestic pig. ⇨ hog, sow[1].

board[1] /bɔd/ *n* **1** long, thin, flat piece of wood with squared edges, used in building walls, floors, boats, ship's decks, etc. **2** flat piece of wood or other material for a special purpose, sometimes bare, sometimes covered with cloth, leather, etc: *ˈsign~; ˈnotice~; a ˈdiving ~,* (at a swimming pool). **3** flat surface with patterns, etc on which games, e g chess, are played. ⇨ the illus at chess. **4** (from the ~s that form the stage of a theatre) **the ~s,** the theatre: *on the ~s*, employed as an actor; on the stage. **5** (from the ~s that form the deck of a ship) ***be on ~,*** be in a ship. ***go on ~,*** go on to a ship or into an airliner (in US, also of trains). ***go by the ~,*** (of masts, etc) fall over the ships side; (fig, of plans, hopes, etc) be given up or abandoned; fail completely. **6** (from the idea of *table*, used for gambling). ***above ~,*** openly, without deception. ***sweep the ~,*** win all the cards or the money staked; (fig) be completely successful. **7** (from the idea of *table*) council-table; councillors; committee; group of persons controlling a business, or a government department: *the B~ of Governors,* e g of a school; *the ˈB~ of ˈTrade; Local ˈGovernment B~; ˈSchool B~,* (in England until 1902) controlling elementary schools known as *ˈb~-schools; a ˈSelection B~,* one that selects (future officers, etc) from applicants or candidates. ***across-the-~,*** ⇨ across[2](1). **8** [U] food served at table, esp meals supplied by the week or month (e g at a lodging-house) or as part payment for service: *The hotel porter has £12 a week and free ~. B~ and lodging £15 weekly.* **9** thick, stiff paper, sometimes cloth-covered, used for book covers: *bound in cloth ~s.* ⇨ also card~, paste~. **10** (compounds) **ˈ~·room** *n* room in which meetings (of a B~ of Directors, etc) are held. **ˈ~-wages** *n pl* servant's extra pay instead of meals. **ˈ~walk** *n* (US) promenade, originally made of planks, esp along a beach.

board[2] /bɔd/ *vt,vi* **1** [VP6A,15B] make or cover with boards(1): *~ up a window; ~ (over) the stern of a boat,* cover it with boards to make a deck. *The floor was ~ed.* **2** (⇨ board[1](8)) [VP6A,3A,E] get, supply with, meals for a fixed weekly/monthly, etc payment: *In a university town, many people make a living by ~ing students. He ~s at his aunt's/with his aunt.* **~ *out,*** take meals at a different place from that in which one lives and sleeps. **3** [VP6A] get on or into (a ship, train, bus, etc); (in naval warfare, old style) go alongside (a ship) (usu to attack); force a way on board (a ship). **ˈ~ing-card,** embarkation card, esp for an airliner or ship. **~er** *n* person who ~s with sb. ⇨ 2 above; schoolboy or girl at a boarding-school (⇨ below). **~·ing** *n* [U] **1** structure of boards(1). **2** the providing or receiving of board(8). **ˈ~·ing-house** *n* private house that provides board and lodging. **ˈ~·ing school** *n* one at which pupils receive board and lodging as well as lessons.

boast /bəʊst/ *n* [C] **1** words used in praise of oneself, one's acts, belongings, etc: *It was the enemy's ~ that they could never be defeated.* **2** cause for satisfaction; sth of which one may rightly be proud: *It was his ~ that he had never failed in an examination.* □ *vt,vi* **1** [VP2A,3A,B] make a ~ or ~s: *He ~s of being/~s that he is the best tennis-player in the town. That's nothing to ~ of. He often ~s to his neighbours about the successes of his children.* **2** [VP6A] possess with pride: *Our school ~s a fine swimming-pool.* **~er** *n* person who ~s. **ˈ~·ful** /-fʊl/ *adj* (of persons) fond of ~ing; (of words, etc) full of self-praise. **ˈ~·fully** /-fḷɪ/ *adv*

boat /bəʊt/ *n* **1** small open vessel for travelling in on water, esp the kind moved with oars (*ˈrowing ~*), sails (*sailing ~*), or petrol or oil engines (*ˈmotor-~*); also used of fishing-vessels and small steamers: *We crossed the river by ~/in a ~. B~s for hire; 30p an hour.* ***be (all) in the same ~,*** have the same dangers to face. ***burn one's ~s,*** do sth that makes it impossible to retreat, to change one's plans, etc. ***take to the ~s,*** (of the crew and passengers of a ship) use the ship's ~s to escape, e g when the ship is sinking. **ˈ~-hook** *n* long pole for fending off or holding a ~, e g at a landing-stage. **ˈ~-house** *n* shed in which ~s are stored. **ˈ~·man** /-mən/ *n* (*pl* -men) man who rows or sails a small ~ for pay; man from whom rowing-~s may be hired. **ˈ~-race** *n* race between rowing-~s. **ˈ~-train** *n* train that takes people to or from a steamer, e g between London and Dover. ⇨ ferry, house[1](7), life(14), mail²(1). **2** ~-shaped dish used at table for gravy or sauce. □ *vi* [VP2A,C] travel in a ~, esp for pleasure: *We ~ed down the river.* ***go ~ing,*** go out (esp in a rowing-~) for pleasure.

boater /ˈbəʊtə(r)/ *n* hard straw hat (formerly worn in summer for boating).

boat·swain /ˈbəʊsn/ *n* senior seaman who controls the work of other seamen and is in charge of a ship's rigging, boats, anchors, etc.

bob¹ /bob/ *vi* (-bb-) [VP2C] **1** move up and down: *The cork on his fishing-line was bobbing on the water. That fellow bobs up like a cork,* (fig) cannot be 'kept down', always becomes active again after being in trouble, etc. *That question often bobs up,* is often asked. **2** ***bob to sb,*** also [VP6A] ***bob a curtsy,*** curtsy. □ *n* quick up and down movement; curtsy.

bob² /bob/ *vt* (-bb-) cut (a woman's or girl's hair) so that it hangs loosely and short of the shoulders: *She wears her hair bobbed. I shall have my hair bobbed.* □ *n* bobbed hair.

bob³ /bob/ *n* (*pl* unchanged; sl) former British coin, called 'shilling' (replaced by the 5p coin).

bob·bin /ˈbobɪn/ *n* small roller or spool for holding thread, yarn, wire, etc in a machine.

bob·bish /ˈbobɪʃ/ *adj* (colloq or dial) brisk, well: *looking/feeling pretty ~.*

bobby /ˈbobɪ/ *n* (GB colloq) policeman.

bobby pin /ˈbobɪ pɪn/ *n* (US) tight metal hair clip.

bobby-socks, sox /ˈbobɪ soks/ *n pl* (US, comm) girls' ankle socks.

bobby-soxer /ˈbobɪ soksə(r)/ *n* (US sl during the 1940's) teenage or adolescent girl.

bobo·link /ˈbobəlɪŋk/ *n* N American songbird.

bob·sled, bob·sleigh /ˈbobsled, -sleɪ/ *n* sleigh made by joining two short sleighs, used in tobogganing.

bobsleighing

bob·tail /ˈbobteɪl/ *n* (horse or dog with a) docked tail. ***the rag-tag and ~,*** the rabble.

Boche /boʃ/ *n adj* (old wartime sl) German.

bode /bəʊd/ *vt,vi* **1** [VP12,13] be a sign of; foretell: *This ~s us no good.* **2** ***~ well/ill for,*** be of good (bad) promise for: *His idle habits ~ ill for his future,* suggest that his future career will be a failure. **bod·ing** *n* feeling of coming evil.

bod·ice /ˈbodɪs/ *n* close-fitting part of a woman's dress or of an under-garment from the shoulders to the waist.

-bodied /bodɪd/ *adj* (with *adjj*): *big-~, strong-~,* having a big/strong body: *able-~,* ⇨ able.

bod·ily /ˈbodḷɪ/ *adj* of or in the human body or physical nature: *supply a person's ~ wants* (e g food); ~ (= physical) *assault.* □ *adv* **1** as a whole or mass; completely: *The audience rose ~* (= everyone rose at the same moment) *to cheer the speaker. The building was transported ~* (= as a whole, without being pulled down) *one hundred yards down the street.* **2** in person; in the body.

bod·kin /ˈbodkɪn/ *n* blunt, thick needle with a large eye (used for drawing tape, etc through a hem).

body /ˈbodɪ/ *n* (*pl* -dies) **1** ⇨ the illus at arm, head, leg, skeleton, trunk. The whole physical structure of a man or animal: *We wear clothes to keep our bodies warm.* ⇨ mind, soul, spirit. ***keep ~ and soul together,*** remain alive: *He earns scarcely enough to keep ~ and soul together.* **2** dead ~; corpse: *His ~ was brought back to England for burial.* **3** main portion of a man or animal without the head, arms and legs: *He received one wound in the left leg and another in the ~.* **4** main part of a structure: *the ~ of a motor-car; the ~ of a concert hall,* the central part where the seats are. **5** group of persons who do sth together or who are united in some way: *Large bodies of unemployed men marched through the streets demanding work. The affairs of the school are managed by the Governing B~. A legislative ~ is a group of persons who make laws.* ***the ~ politic,*** ⇨ politic(3). ***in a ~,*** all together; as a whole: *The staff resigned in a ~.* **6** person; human being: *She's a nice old ~.* (in compounds): *every~, any~, some~, no~.* **7** mass, quantity, collection: *A lake is a ~ of water. He has a large ~ of facts to prove his statements.* **8** distinct piece of matter: *the heavenly bodies,* the sun, moon and stars; *a foreign ~* (= a speck of dirt) *in the eye.* **9** [U] (of wine, etc) full, strong quality: *wine of good ~.* **10** (compounds) **ˈ~·guard** *n* group of men (sometimes a single man) guarding an important person. **ˈ~-servant** *n* valet. **ˈ~-snatcher** *n* person who exhumed corpses for dissection. **ˈ~-work** *n* main part, material, of (esp) a motor vehicle.

Boer /bɔ(r)/ *n* South African of Dutch descent. □ *adj* of Dutch South Africa.

bof·fin /ˈbofɪn/ *n* (sl) technician or scientist (esp one engaged in research).

bog /bog/ *n* **1** (area of) soft, wet, spongy ground (chiefly decayed or decaying vegetable matter). **2** (vulg sl) latrine. □ *vt,vi* (-gg-) [VP15,2E] ***~ down,*** (cause to) be stuck fast, unable to make progress: *The tanks (got) ~ged down in the mud. Our discussions have ~ged down.* **boggy** /ˈbogɪ/ *adj* (of land) soft and wet.

bo·gey ⇨ bogy.

Bo·gey /ˈbəʊgɪ/ *n* (golf score that a good player makes for a hole (or the whole course) and that other players try to equal.

boggle /ˈbogl/ *vi* **~ at sth,** be unwilling, hesitate, to do sth. *The mind/imagination ~s at the idea,* is alarmed at the idea.

bo·gie /ˈbəʊgɪ/ *n* (also **bogey, bogy**) **1** trolley. **2** four-wheeled undercarriage fitted under (the end of) a railway engine or wagon to enable it to go round curves.

bo·gus /ˈbəʊgəs/ *adj* sham; counterfeit.

bogy, bo·gey /ˈbəʊgɪ/ *n* (*pl* -gies, -geys) evil spirit; sb or sth that causes fear.

bo·he·mian /bəʊˈhimɪən/ *n adj* (person) not living in ways considered socially normal or conventional.

boil¹ /bɔɪl/ *n* hard (usu red, often painful) poisoned swelling under the skin, which bursts when ripe.

boil² /bɔɪl/ *vi,vt* **1** [VP2A,B,C,D] (of water or other liquid, also of the vessel that contains it and of the contents of the vessel) reach the temperature at which change to gas occurs; bubble up: *When water* ~*s it changes into steam. The kettle is* ~*ing. The potatoes are* ~*ing. Don't let the kettle* ~ *dry. Let the vegetables* ~ *gently.* ***keep the pot* ~*ing,*** earn or otherwise find enough money for food, etc. **'~ing-point** *n* temperature at which a liquid ~s. **~ing hot,** (colloq) very hot: *a* ~*ing hot day.* **2** [VP2A,C] (of the sea, of a person's feelings, etc) be agitated like ~ing water: *The boat was swallowed up by the* ~*ing waves. He was* ~*ing (over) with indignation. Cruelty to animals makes her blood* ~. **3** [VP6A,22] cause water or other liquid to ~; cook in ~ing water: *We* ~ *eggs, fish and vegetables. Please* ~ *my egg for three minutes. I like my eggs* ~*ed hard. My brother prefers soft-*~*ed eggs.* **4** [VP2C,15B] ***~ away,*** **(a)** continue to ~: *The kettle was* ~*ing away merrily on the fire.* **(b)** ~ until nothing remains: *The water had all* ~*ed away and the kettle was empty.* ***~ down,*** be reduced in quantity: *It all* ~*s down to this...,* (colloq) The essence (of the statement, proposal, etc) is.... ***~ sth down,*** make less by ~ing; (fig) condense: ~ *down a long article to two hundred words,* make a précis of it. ***~ over,*** flow over the side: *The milk had* ~*ed over.* □ *n* ~ing point: ***be on the ~,*** be ~ing. ***bring sth to the ~,*** heat it until it ~s. ***come to the ~,*** begin to ~.

boiler /ˈbɔɪlə(r)/ *n* **1** metal container in which water, etc is heated, e g for producing steam in an engine; tank forming part of a kitchen range for supplying hot water; tank for heating water for a laundry. **'~-suit** *n* one-piece garment, overalls, for rough or dirty work. **2** person whose trade is boiling sth: *a* '*soap-*~.

bois·ter·ous /ˈbɔɪstərəs/ *adj* rough, violent: ~ *weather; a* ~ *wind/sea*; (of a person, his behaviour) noisy and cheerful. **~·ly** *adv*

bold /bəʊld/ *adj* **1** without fear; enterprising; showing absence of fear. ***be/make so ~ as to do (sth),*** allow oneself to do it: *if I may be so* ~ *as to...,* If I may venture or presume to.... ***make ~ with (sth),*** (more usu *make free with*) take the liberty of using (it). **2** without feelings of shame; immodest. ***as ~ as brass,*** impudent. **3** well marked; clear: *the* ~ *outline of a mountain; a* ~ *headland; a painting made with a few* ~ (= free and vigorous) *brush strokes.* **~·ly** *adv* **~·ness** *n*

bole /bəʊl/ *n* trunk of a tree.

bol·ero /bəˈleərəʊ/ *n* **1** (music for a) Spanish dance. **2** /ˈbolərəʊ/ short jacket with no front fastening.

boll /bəʊl/ *n* round seed-vessel (of cotton and flax). **'~ 'weevil** /ˈwivl/ *n* small destructive insect that infests cotton-plants.

bol·lard /ˈboləd/ *n* **1** upright post (usu of iron) on a quay or a ship's deck for making ropes secure. **2** protective post on a traffic island, or a roadway, sometimes with an arrow to direct traffic.

bol·locks /ˈboləks/ *n pl* ⚠ = ballocks.

bo·lo·ney /bəˈləʊnɪ/ *n* [U] (GB sl) nonsense; humbug.

Bol·she·vik /ˈbolʃəvɪk/ *n* supporter of the system of government by soviets, as in the U S S R; person favouring Marxism or Communism.

Bol·shy /ˈbolʃɪ/ *n* (sl) Bolshevik □ *adj* rebellious; inclined to be against the established social order.

bol·ster¹ /ˈbəʊlstə(r)/ *n* long under-pillow for the head of a bed.

bol·ster² /ˈbəʊlstə(r)/ *vt* [VP6A,15B] ***~ (up),*** support; give (greatly needed, often undeserved) support to, e g a cause, theory, etc, that would otherwise fail.

bolt¹ /bəʊlt/ *n* **1** metal fastening for a door or window, consisting of a sliding pin or rod and a staple into which it fits. **2** metal pin with a head at one end and a thread (as on a screw) at the other, used with a nut for holding things together. **3** (old use) short heavy shot from a cross-bow. ***shoot one's (last) ~,*** make one's last effort. **4** discharge of lightning. ⇨ blue²(2), thunder-bolt. **5** (as a measure of cloth, canvas, etc) roll (as it comes from the loom). □ *vt, vi* [VP6A, 15B, 2A] fasten with a ~ or ~s(1): ~ *the doors and windows;* ~ *in,* shut him in by ~ing the door(s); ~ *sb out,* keep him out by ~ing the door(s). *The door* ~*s on the inside.*

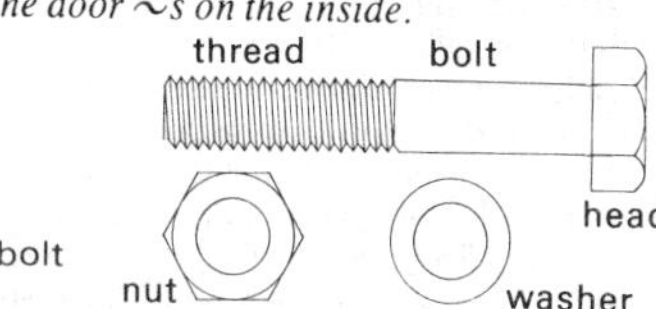

bolt² /bəʊlt/ *vi, vt* **1** [VP21,23] run away quickly; (esp of a horse) run off out of control: *As soon as I came downstairs the burglar* ~*ed through the back door.* **2** [VP6A] swallow (food) quickly: *We* ~*ed a few mouthfuls of food and hurried on.* **3** [VP2A] (of plants) grow quickly upwards and go to seed. □ *n* act of running away. ***make a ~ for it,*** run off quickly (usu to escape from sth). **'~-hole** *n* hole or burrow into which to ~ for safety.

bolt³ /bəʊlt/ *vt* [VP2A] sift (flour).

bolt⁴ /bəʊlt/ *adv* (only in) ***~ upright,*** quite upright.

bomb /bom/ *n* hollow metal ball or shell filled either with explosive for causing destruction or with smoke, gas, or incendiary material, now dropped from aircraft; (old use) hand-grenade. ***go like a ~,*** (sl) be very efficient, successful, etc: *My new car goes like a* ~. **'~ bay** *n* compartment (in an aircraft) for holding ~s. **'~-disposal squad,** squad for removing unexploded ~s and making them harmless. **'~-proof** *adj* giving protection against exploding ~s: *a* ~*-proof shelter.* **'~-shell** *n* (fig) sth that comes as a great surprise and shock. **'~-sight** *n* device (in an aircraft) for aiming ~s. **'~-site** *n* area (in a town) devastated by air-raids: *a car park on a* ~*-site.* □ *vt, vi* **1** [VP6A,15B] attack with ~s; drop ~s on. ***~ out,*** drive out (of buildings, etc) with ~s: ~*ed out families/factories.* **2** [VP15B,2C] ***~ up,*** load (an aircraft) with ~s. **~er** /ˈbomə(r)/ *n* aircraft used for ~ing; soldier trained in ~ing.

bom·bard /bomˈbɑd/ *vt* [VP6A,14] ***~ with,*** attack with shells from big guns; (fig) worry with questions, requests, complaints, etc; (nuclear physics) send a stream of high-speed particles against (an atom, etc). **~·ment** *n* ~ing or being ~ed: *after a long* ~*ment.*

bom·bar·dier /ˈbombəˈdɪə(r)/ *n* (in an artillery regiment) non-commissioned officer below a sergeant.

bom·bast /ˈbombæst/ *n* [U] insincere, high-sounding talk. **bom·bas·tic** /bomˈbæstɪk/ *adj* (of a person, his talk, behaviour) promising much but not likely to do much; using fine high-sounding words. **bom·bas·ti·cally** /-klɪ/ *adv*

bona fide /ˈbəʊnə ˈfɑɪdɪ/ *adj, adv* (Lat)

genuine(ly); sincere(ly); in good faith; (comm): *a ~ buyer.* **bona fides** /ˈbəʊnə ˋfɑɪdɪz/ *n pl* (legal) honest intention; sincerity.

bon·anza /bəˋnænzə/ *n* (US) sth, e g a gold-mine, an oil-well, that is prospering greatly; (attrib) bringing good luck and prosperity: *a ~ year.*

bon·bon /ˋbɒnbɒn/ *n* sweet; sth made of sugar in a fancy shape, etc.

bond /bɒnd/ *n* **1** agreement or engagement that a person is bound to observe, esp one that has force in law; document, signed and sealed, containing such an agreement. ***enter into a ~ with sb,*** agree a ~ with sb. ***His word is as good as his ~,*** He is so honest that his spoken promise is as good as a written agreement. **2** printed paper issued by a government or a corporation acknowledging that money has been lent to it and will be paid back with interest: *5% War B~s.* **ˋ~-holder** *n* person holding ~s. **3** sth that joins or unites (usu fig): *the ~(s) of affection. Common tastes form a ~ between the two men,* They are friends because they are interested in the same things. **4** the state of being joined: *Press the surfaces together to ensure a good, firm ~.* **5** (*pl*) prisoner's chains: *in ~s,* held as a prisoner or as a slave; *burst one's ~s,* win freedom. **6** (comm) ***in ~,*** (of goods) in a Customs warehouse (until duties are paid). ***place goods in/take goods out of ~.*** □ *vt* [VP6A] **1** put (goods) into a Customs warehouse. ***~ed goods,*** imported and placed in ~ until duty is paid. ***a ~ed warehouse,*** one in which goods are stored until duties are paid. **2** join securely (with glue, etc).

bond- /bɒnd-/ *pref* in slavery, not free: *ˋ~man, ˋbonds-man /-mən/; ˋ~maid; ˋ~servant; ˋ~-slave.*

bond·age /ˋbɒndɪdʒ/ *n* [U] slavery, servitude: *in hopeless ~ to his master.*

bone /bəʊn/ *n* **1** [C] one of the parts that make up the framework of an animal's body. ⇨ the illus at skeleton. *This fish has a lot of ~s in it. No ~s broken, I hope,* I hope you have not hurt yourself. ***~ of contention,*** subject of dispute. ***feel in one's ~s that,*** feel certain that. ***have a ~ to pick with sb,*** have sth to argue or complain about. ***make no ~s about doing sth,*** not hesitate to do it, do it without scruple: *They dismissed him and made no ~s about it.* ***(frozen) to the ~,*** completely in a penetrating way. ***will not make old ~s,*** will not live long. **2** [U] hard substance of which ~s are made: *Buttons are sometimes made of ~. He's all skin and ~,* is very thin. **3** (*pl*, old use) castanets; dice. **4** (compounds). **ˈ~ ˋdry** *adj* quite dry. **ˋ~-head** *n* (sl) stupid person. **ˈ~-ˋidle/-lazy** *adj* completely idle. **ˋ~-meal** *n* fertilizer of crushed and powdered ~s. **ˋ~-setter** *n* person who sets broken ~s. **ˋ~-shaker** *n* (colloq) old bicycle without rubber tyres; old, shaky bus, car or cart. **ˈbig-/ˈstrong-ˋ~d** *adj* having big/strong ~s. □ *vt* [VP6A] **1** take ~s out of (a chicken, a piece of meat, etc). **2** (old use) put ~s into (e g a corset). **3** (sl) steal. **4** ***~ up on*** (a subject), (sl) study hard.

boner /ˋbəʊnə(r)/ *n* (US sl) blunder.

bon·fire /ˋbɒnfaɪə(r)/ *n* large fire made out of doors either to celebrate some event or to burn up dead leaves, rubbish, etc: *make a ~ of,* get rid of.

bon·homie /ˋbɒnəmɪ/ *n* [U] (F) bluff, hearty; pleasantness of manner.

bo·nito /bəˋnitəʊ/ *n* large kinds of tunny of the Atlantic Ocean, esp the striped tunny.

bon·kers /ˋbɒŋkəz/ *pred adj* ***stark, raving ~,*** (sl) raving mad; completely insane.

bon mot /ˈbɒn ˋməʊ *US:* ˈbɔ̃/ *n* (*pl* **bons mots** /ˋməʊz/) witty saying or remark.

bon·net /ˋbɒnɪt/ *n* **1** small, round head-dress without a hard brim, usu tied under the chin, worn by children. **2** soft, flat cap worn by men in Scotland and by soldiers in some regiments. **3** protective cover of various sorts, e g over a chimney, or (US = *hood*) over the engine of a motor-car. ⇨ the illus at motor.

bonny /ˋbɒnɪ/ *adj* healthy looking; with a glow of health: *a ~ baby; her ~ face.* **bon·nily** *adj*

bo·nus /ˋbəʊnəs/ *n* (*pl* **bonuses**) payment in addition to what is usual, necessary or expected, e g an extra dividend to stockholders of a business company, (insurance) a share of profits to policy-holders, or an extra payment to workers: *cost-of-living ~,* addition to wages or salaries because of rising prices. **no claims ~,** percentage reduction in an insurance premium (for a motor-vehicle) if claims are not made.

bony /ˋbəʊnɪ/ *adj* (**-ier, -iest**) **1** full of bones: *a ~ fish,* e g a herring. **2** having big or prominent bones: *a tall, ~ man.* **3** with little flesh: *~ fingers.*

boo /bu/ *int* sound made to show disapproval or contempt; exclamation used to surprise or startle: *He can't say boo to a goose,* is timid. □ *vt,vi* [VP6A,15B,2A] make such sounds: *The speaker was booed off the platform. The crowd booed and hooted.*

boob /bub/ *n* (colloq) booby. □ *vi* make a silly mistake.

booby /ˋbubɪ/ *n* (*pl* **-bies**) silly or stupid person. **ˋ~ prize** *n* prize given as a joke to the person who is last in a race or competition. **ˋ~-trap** *n* sth balanced on the top of a door so that it will fall on the first person to pass through; (mil) apparently harmless object that will kill or injure sb when picked up or interfered with.

book¹ /bʊk/ *n* **1** number of sheets of paper, either printed or blank, fastened together in a cover; literary composition that would fill such a set of sheets: *write a ~.* **2 the B~,** the Bible: *swear on the B~,* take an oath. **3** main division of a large treatise or poem or the Bible: *the B~ of Genesis.* **4** packet of similar items fastened together, e g postage stamps, bus tickets, matches. **5** record of bets. ⇨ ~maker in **8** below. ***make/keep a ~ (on),*** take bets, etc. ***not suit one's ~,*** not be convenient. **6** (*pl*) business accounts, records, etc: *The firm has full order ~s,* orders for goods. ***be in sb's good/bad/black ~s,*** have/not have his favour or approval. ***bring sb to ~ (for sth),*** require him to explain his conduct. **7** libretto (of an opera). **8** (compounds): **ˋ~-case** *n* piece of furniture with shelves for ~s. **ˋ~-club** *n* organization that sells ~s at a discount to members who agree to buy a minimum number. **ˋ~-ends** *n pl* pair of props used to keep ~s upright, e g on a table. **ˋ~-keeper** *n* person who keeps accounts, e g of a business, public office. **ˋ~-keep·ing** *n* (art of) keeping (business) accounts. **ˋ~-maker** *n* person whose business is taking bets on horse-races. **ˋ~-mark(er)** *n* sth placed between the leaves of a ~ to mark the place. **ˋ~-mobile** /-məʊbil/ *n* (US) truck equipped as a mobile ~ store or lending library. **ˋ~-seller** *n* person who sells ~s retail. ˋ~-

stall *n* stall, kiosk, etc at which ~s are shown for sale outdoors, in a railway station, a hotel lobby, etc (= US *newstand*). '~ **token** *n* ⇨ token. '~**worm** *n* small maggot that eats holes in ~s; person who is very fond of reading ~s.

book² /bʊk/ *vt* [VP6A] **1** write down (orders, etc) in a notebook; (of the police) record a charge against (sb): *be ~ed for exceeding the speed limit.* **2** give or receive an order for, e g seats at a theatre, tickets for a journey; engage (sb) as a speaker, entertainer, etc: *Seats (for the theatre) can be ~ed from 10a m to 6p m. Have you ~ed your passage to New York,* arranged for a cabin? *Can I ~ (a ticket) through to Naples?* ***(fully) ~ed up,*** (of a restaurant, theatre, etc) no more tables, seats, available; (of a lecturer, singer, etc) unable to accept further engagements. '~**ing clerk** *n* person who sells tickets, e g at a railway station. '~**ing office** *n* office for the sale of tickets (for travel). '~**·able** /-əbl/ *adj* (of seats, etc) that can be reserved: *all seats ~able in advance.*

bookie /'bʊkɪ/ *n* (colloq) bookmaker. ⇨ book¹(8).

book·ish /'bʊkɪʃ/ *adj* of books and studies: *a ~ person,* one who gives much time to reading; *~ expressions,* found in books but not colloquial; *a ~ style,* literary, not colloquial. **~·ness** *n*

book·let /'bʊklət/ *n* thin book, usu in paper covers.

boom¹ /bum/ *n* **1** long spar used to keep the bottom of a sail stretched out. ⇨ the illus at barque. **2** ***derrick ~,*** pole fastened to a derrick, used for (un)loading cargo. **3** heavy chain, mass of floating logs, etc held in position across a river or harbour entrance, e g as a defence in time of war, or to prevent logs from floating away. **4** long, movable arm for a microphone.

boom² /bum/ *vt,vi* **1** [VP2A,C] (of big guns, the wind, an organ) make deep, hollow, or resonant sounds. **2** ***~ out,*** [VP15B] utter in a deep voice: *~ing out Shakespearian verses.* □ *n* deep, hollow sound: *the ~ of the guns/surf; a sonic ~.*

boom³ /bum/ *n* [C] sudden increase in trade activity, esp a time when money is being made quickly. ⇨ slump. '~ **town** *n* town showing sudden growth and prosperity. □ *vi* [VP2A,C] have a ~; become well known and successful: *Business is ~ing. Jones is ~ing as a novelist,* becoming famous.

boom·er·ang /'bumaræŋ/ *n* curved stick of hard wood (used by Australian aborigines), which can be thrown so that, if it fails to hit anything, it returns to the thrower; (fig) argument or proposal that comes back and harms its author.

boon¹ /bun/ *n* **1** (liter) request; favour: *ask a ~ of sb; grant a ~.* **2** advantage; blessing, comfort: *Parks are a great ~ to people in big cities. A vacuum cleaner is a tremendous ~ to busy housewives.*

boon² /bun/ *adj* (only in) **~ companion,** jolly, congenial, companion.

boor /bʊə(r)/ *n* rough, ill-mannered person. **~·ish** /-ɪʃ/ *adj* of or like a ~. **~·ish·ly** *adv* **~·ish·ness** *n*

boost /bust/ *vt* [VP6A] give (sb or sth) a push up; increase the value, reputation, etc of (sb or sth): *Seeing him there ~ed my morale.* □ *n* act of ~ing: being ~ed. **~er** *n* **1** thing that ~s: *His work got a welcome ~.* **~er rocket** *n* rocket used to give initial speed to a missile, after which it drops and leaves the missile to continue under its own power. **2** (also **~ injection**) supplementary dose of vaccine to strengthen the effect of an earlier dose; extra dose of morphine, etc (by drug addicts).

boot¹ /but/ *n* **1** outer covering for the foot and ankle, made of leather or rubber. ⇨ shoe. **high ~s,** reaching to the knee. '~**·leg** *vt* make, transport or sell illicit alcoholic drinks: (attrib) *~leg liquor.* '~**·leg·ger** *n* person who does this (as during the years when there was prohibition in US). ***die with one's ~s on/die in one's ~s,*** not in bed; die while still working, etc. ***get the ~,*** (sl) be dismissed, be kicked out. ***give sb the ~,*** (sl) dismiss him from his job. ***lick sb's ~s,*** behave in a servile way. ***put the ~ in,*** (sl) kick sb, e g in a brawl. '~**·lace** *n* string or leather strip for ~s. **2** (GB) place for luggage in a coach or at the back of a motor-car (= US *trunk*). □ *vt* [VP6A,15A,B] kick (sb): *He was ~ed out of the house.* **~ed** *adj* wearing ~s: *~ed and spurred,* ready for a journey.

boot² /but/ *n* (only in) ***to ~,*** as well, in addition.

boot³ /but/ *vt* (old use, usu with *it*): *What ~s it to..., that...,* what use is it to..., that...? ***It little ~s to, It ~s not to,*** It is of little/no avail to.

bootee /'buti/ *n* infant's knitted wool boot; kind of warmly lined boot for women.

booth /buð/ *n* **1** shelter of boards, canvas or other light materials, esp one where goods are sold at a market or a fair. **2** enclosure for a public telephone. ⇨ kiosk. **3** '**polling ~,** place for voting at elections. '**listening ~,** (in a shop) enclosure where customers may listen to records (discs).

boot·less /'butləs/ *adj* (liter) useless; unavailing: *It is ~ to complain.*

boots /buts/ *n* (formerly) hotel servant who cleans shoes and boots, carries luggage, etc.

booty /'butɪ/ *n* [U] things taken by robbers or captured from the enemy in war (and usu to be divided among those who take them).

booze /buz/ *vi* [VP2A,C] (colloq) drink (alcoholic liquor), esp in excess. □ *n* alcoholic drink; period of drinking. ***have a '~(-up), go on the ~,*** have a bout of drinking. **boozer** *n* one who ~s; (sl) pub. **boozy** *adj*

bo-peep /'bəʊ'pip/ *n* [U] game of hiding and suddenly showing oneself to a baby.

bor·acic /bə'ræsɪk/ *adj* of borax: *~ acid,* = boric acid.

bor·age /'bɒrɪdʒ/ *n* [U] blue-flowered, hairy-leaved plant of which the leaves are used as a seasoning.

borax /'bɔræks/ *n* white powder used to make porcelain enamels, in glass manufacture and other industries, and for cleaning.

Bor·deaux /bɔ'dəʊ/ *n* [U] (F) (often attrib) wine from the ~ area of France; claret.

bor·der /'bɔdə(r)/ *n* **1** edge; part near the edge of sth: *We camped on the ~ of a lake. A woman's handkerchief may have a lace ~. There is a ~ of flowers round the lawn.* **2** (land near the) line dividing two states or countries: *The criminal escaped over the ~.* (attrib): *a ~ town; ~ incidents,* e g small fights between armed forces of two neighbouring states. **the B~,** (esp) that between England and Scotland. '~**·land** /-lænd/ *n* **(a)** district on either side of a ~ or boundary. **(b)** (*sing* with *def art,* and attrib) condition between: *the ~land between sleeping and waking.* '~**·line** *n* line that marks a ~; (attrib) ***a ~line case,*** one that is dubious, e g sb who may or not pass an examination. □ *vt,vi* **1** [VP6A] put or be a ~ to: *Our garden is ~ed by a stream.* **2** [VP3A] **~ (up)on,** be next to: *My land ~s (up)on yours. The park ~s on the shores of the lake.* **3 ~ (up)on,** [VP3A] resemble; be almost the same as: *The proposal ~s upon the absurd.* **~er** *n* person living on or near a frontier, esp that between England and Scotland.

bore[1] /bɔ(r)/ *vt,vi* [VP6A,14,15] make a narrow, round deep hole in sth with a revolving tool; make (a hole, one's way) by doing this or by digging out soil, etc: *~ a hole in wood; ~ a well; ~ a tunnel through a mountain; animals* (e g moles) *that ~ their way under the ground.* □ *n* **1** (also **`~-hole**) hole made by boring, e g to find water. **2** hollow inside of a gun barrel; its diameter. **borer** *n* (kind of) insect that ~s.

bore[2] /bɔ(r)/ *vt* [VP6A] make (sb) feel tired by being dull or tedious: *I hope you're not getting ~d listening to me. I've heard all that man's stories before; they ~ me/he ~s me.* **~ sb to death/tears,** ~ him intensely. □ *n* person or thing that ~s. **bor·ing** *adj*: *a boring evening.* **~·dom** /-dəm/ *n* [U] state of being ~d.

bore[3] /bɔ(r)/ *n* high tidal wave, often many feet high, that advances up a narrow estuary.

bore[4] /bɔ(r)/ *pt* of bear.

boric /`bɔrɪk/ *adj* **~ acid,** used as an antiseptic and a preservative.

born /bɔn/ one of the *pp's* of bear. **1** *be* **~,** come into the world by birth. **~ *with a silver spoon in one's mouth,*** ⇨ silver(1). **2** (with a complement) destined to be: *He was ~ a poet. He was ~ to be hanged.* **3** (attrib) by natural ability: *a ~ orator.*

borne /bɔn/ *pp* of bear (except of birth). ⇨ bear[2](10).

boron /`bɔrən *US:* -ron/ *n* non-metallic element (symbol **B**).

bor·ough /`bʌrə *US:* `bɜəʊ/ *n* **1** (England) town, or part of a town, that sends one or more members to Parliament; town with a municipal corporation and rights of self-government conferred by royal charter. **2** (US) any one of the five administrative units of New York City.

bor·row /`borəʊ/ *vt,vi* **1** [VP6A,2A,14] **~ *(from),*** get sth, or the use of sth, on the understanding that it is to be returned: *May I ~ your pen? He fell into the river and had to go home in ~ed clothes. Some people are good at ~ing but bad at giving back.* ⇨ lend. **2** [VP6A] take and use as one's own: *~ sb's ideas/methods.* **~er** *n* person who ~s.

borsch, bortsch /bɔʃt/ *n* [U] (kinds of) E European soup, esp of beetroot.

bor·stal /`bɔstl/ *n* **~ institution,** place where young offenders live and receive training designed to reform them.

bor·zoi /`bɔzɔɪ/ *n* Russian wolf-hound.

bosh /boʃ/ *n, int* nonsense.

bosky /`boskɪ/ *adj* (liter) (of land) covered with trees and bushes.

bo'sn /`bəʊsn/ ⇨ boatswain.

bosom /`bʊzəm/ *n* **1** (old use) person's breast; part of dress covering this. **2** centre or inmost part, where one feels joy or sorrow; (attrib) ***a ~ friend,*** one who is dear and close. **3** midst: *in the ~ of one's family.*

boss[1] /bos/ *n* (sl) master; person who controls or gives orders to workmen: *Who's the ~ in this house,* Is the husband or the wife in control? □ *vt* [VP6A,15B] be the ~ of; give orders to: *He wants to ~ the show,* to make all the arrangements. **~ *sb about/around,*** order sb here and there. **~y** *adj* (-ier, -iest) fond of ~ing, fond of being in authority.

boss[2] /bos/ *n* round metal knob or stud on a shield or as an ornament.

boss[3] /bos/ *n* (sl) (also **`~ shot**) bad shot or guess; bungle; *make a ~ shot at sth; make a ~ of sth.* **`~-eyed** *adj* (sl) blind in one eyed; cross-eyed.

bo'sun /`bəʊsn/ ⇨ boatswain.

bot·any /`botənɪ/ *n* [U] science of the structure of plants. **botan·ical** /bə`tænɪkl/ *adj* of ~: *botanical gardens* (where plants and trees are grown for scientific study). **bot·an·ist** /`botənɪst/ *n* student of ~. **bot·an·ize** /`botənɑɪz/ *vi* go out studying and collecting wild plants.

botch /botʃ/ *vt* [VP6A,15B] **~ *sth (up),*** repair badly; spoil by poor, clumsy work: *a ~ed piece of work.* □ *n* piece of clumsy, badly done work; *make a ~ of sth;* clumsy patch. **~er** *n* person who ~es work.

both[1] /bəʊθ/ *adj* (of two things, persons, etc) the two; the one and also the other; (*both* precedes the *def art,* demonstrative *adjj,* possessives, and other *adjj*): *I want ~ books/the books/these books. I saw him on ~ occasions. Hold it in ~ hands. B~ his younger brothers are in the army. You can't have it ~ ways,* must decide on one or the other. Cf *both* and *neither*: *B~ these books are useful. Neither of these books is useful.* Cf *both* and *each*: *There are shops on ~ sides of the street. There is a butcher's shop on each side of the street.*

both[2] /bəʊθ/ *adv* **~... *and,*** not only... but also: *Queen Anne is ~ dead and buried. He is remarkable for ~ his intelligence and his skill. He is ~ a soldier and a poet.*

both[3] /bəʊθ/ *pron* **1** the two; not only the one: *B~ are good. B~ of them are good.* Cf *both* and *neither*: *B~ of us want to go. Neither of us wants to go.* **2** (used in apposition, in the same way as *each* and *all*): *We ~ want to go. They are ~ useful. Take them ~. You must ~ work harder.*

bother /`boðə(r)/ *vt,vi* **1** [VP6A,14,16A,3A] be or cause trouble to; worry: *Tell the children to stop ~ing their father. Don't ~ me with foolish questions. That man is always ~ing me to lend him money.* **~ *oneself/one's head/about,*** be/feel anxious about: *It's not important; don't ~ your head about it. We needn't ~* (*about*) *when it happened.* **2** [VP3A,4C,2A] take trouble: *Don't ~ about getting/~ to get dinner for me today; I'll eat out.* **3** (used as an exclamation of impatience or annoyance): *Oh, ~* (*it*)*! B~ the flies! Oh, ~ you!* □ *n* **1** [U] worry, trouble: *Did you have much ~* (*in*) *finding the house? It will be no ~* (*to me*), won't involve much work or inconvenience. *We had quite a lot of ~* (*in*) *getting here because of the fog. Don't put yourself to any ~,* inconvenience yourself. **2** (with *indef art*) sb or sth that gives trouble: *His lazy son is quite a ~ to him. This drawer won't shut; isn't it a ~!* **~·ation** /ˈboðə`reɪʃn/ *int* What a nuisance! **`~·some** /-səm/ *adj* causing ~; troublesome or annoying.

bottle /`botl/ *n* container, usu made of glass and with a narrow neck, for milk, beer, wine, medicine, ink, etc; the contents of a ~: *Mary drinks two ~s of milk a day.* **`~-fed,** *brought up on*

the ~, (of a child) given milk from a feeding ~, not fed from its mother's breast. ***too fond of the*** ***~,*** of alcoholic drinks. '~-'**green** *adj* dark green. '~-**neck** *n* (**a**) narrower strip of road, between two wide parts, where traffic is slowed down or held up. (**b**) that part of a manufacturing process, etc, where production is slowed down (e g by shortage of materials □ *vt* [VP6A] put into, store in, ~s: *~ fruit.* ***~ up,*** [VP15B] (fig) hold in, keep under control, e g anger.

bot·tom /ˈbɒtəm/ *n* **1** lowest part of anything, inside or outside: *There are some tea-leaves in the ~ of the cup. He fell to the ~ of the well. We were glad to reach the ~* (= foot) *of the mountain. Notes are sometimes printed at the ~* (= foot) *of the page.* **2** part farthest from the front or more important part: *at the ~ of the garden;* less honourable end of a table, class, etc: *The poor relations were seated at the ~ of the long table.* **3** bed of the sea, a lake, river, etc: *The ship went to the ~,* sank. *The lake is deep and a swimmer cannot touch ~,* touch the bed of the lake with his toes. **4** seat (of a chair); part of the body on which a person sits; buttocks: *This chair needs a new ~. She smacked the child's ~.* **5** horizontal part of a ship near the keel; (esp cargo-carrying) ship: *The ship was found floating ~ upwards. Goods exported from this country usually go in British ~s.* **6** foundation: *We must get to the ~ of this mystery,* find out how it began. *Who's at the ~ of this business,* Who's responsible? **7** (fig uses): *The ~ has fallen out of the market,* Trade has fallen to a very low level. ***at ~,*** in essential character: *He's a good fellow at ~.* ***from the ~ of my heart,*** genuinely, deeply. ***knock the ~ out of an argument,*** prove that it is worthless. **8** (attrib) lowest, last: *Put the book on the ~ shelf. What's your ~ price? Who's the ~ boy of the class?* ⇨ also **gear(1)**, **rock[1](6)**. **~-less** *adj* very deep: *a ~less pit.*

botu·lism /ˈbɒtjʊlɪzm/ *n* [U] food poisoning.

bou·doir /ˈbudwɑ(r)/ *n* woman's private sitting-room or dressing-room.

bou·gain·villea /ˈbugənˈvɪlɪə/ *n* tropical climbing shrub with tiny flowers surrounded by red, purple, etc bracts.

bough /bɑʊ/ *n* large branch coming from the trunk of a tree. ⇨ the illus at **tree**.

bought /bɔt/ *pt,pp* of **buy**.

bouil·lon /ˈbuɪjõ/ *n* [U] ⇨ **stock[1](9)**; clear thin soup or broth.

boul·der /ˈbəʊldə(r)/ *n* large piece of rock, large stone, esp one that has been rounded by water or weather.

boul·evard /ˈbuləvɑ *US:* ˈbʊləvɑd/ *n* (F) wide city street, often with trees on each side.

bounce /bɑʊns/ *vi,vt* **1** [VP2A,6A] (of a ball, etc) (cause to) spring or jump back when sent against sth hard: *A rubber ball ~s well. The ball ~ed over the wall. She was bouncing a ball.* ***~ back,*** [VP2C] (fig) recover jauntily from a setback. **2** [VP2C,6A] (cause to) move up and down violently or noisily; rush noisily or angrily: *The boy was bouncing (up and down) on the bed. He ~d into/out of the room. She ~d out of her chair. The old car ~d along the bad roads.* **3** [VP2A] (colloq) (of a cheque) be returned by a bank as worthless: *Don't worry — my cheque won't ~.* □ *n* **1** (of a ball) bouncing: *catch the ball on the ~.* **2** (of a person) [U] boasting behaviour or speech. **bouncing** *adj*: *a bouncing girl,* a big strong, healthy, bustling girl.

bound[1] /bɑʊnd/ *n* (usu *pl*) limit: *It is beyond the ~s of human knowledge,* Man can know nothing about it. *There are no ~s to his ambition. Please keep within the ~s of reason,* do not say foolish things, attempt impracticable things. *He sets no ~s to his desires. Is it within the ~s of probability?* ***out of ~s,*** outside the limits of areas that one is allowed to enter (used esp of places that schoolchildren at boarding-schools or that soldiers must not visit): *Most of the bars had been placed out of ~s to troops.* (US = *off limits*).

bound[2] /bɑʊnd/ *vt* [VP6A, usu passive] limit (lit, fig); set bounds to; be the boundary of: *England is ~ed on the north by Scotland.*

bound[3] /bɑʊnd/ *vt* [VP2A,C,4A] jump, spring, bounce; move or run in jumping movements: *The ball struck the wall and ~ed back to me. His heart ~ed with joy. His dog came ~ing to meet him. Big rocks were ~ing down the hillside.* □ *n* jumping movement upward or forward: *at one ~; hit a ball on the ~* (or *rebound* /ˈribɑʊnd/), after it has hit the ground and is in the air again. ***by leaps and ~s,*** very rapidly.

bound[4] /bɑʊnd/ *part adj* ***~ (for),*** ready to start, having started: *Where are you ~ (for),* Where are you going to? *The ship is ~ for Finland. If a British ship is going away from Britain, she is outward ~; if she is returning to Britain, she is homeward ~.*

bound[5] /bɑʊnd/ *pp* of **bind**. (special uses) *~ to win, etc,* certain to win, etc; *~ to come, etc,* obliged, compelled or destined to come, etc. ***~ up in,*** much interested in, very busy with: *He is ~ up in his work.* ***~ up with,*** closely connected with: *The welfare of the individual is ~ up with the welfare of the community.*

bound·ary /ˈbɑʊndrɪ/ *n* (*pl* **-ries**) **1** line that marks a limit; dividing line: *This stream forms a ~ between my land and his. A ~ dispute is a quarrel about where a ~ is or ought to be. If something is beyond the ~ of human knowledge, man can know nothing about it.* **2** (cricket) hit to or over the ~, scoring 4 or 6 runs.

boun·den /ˈbɑʊndən/ *adj* (only in) ***my ~ duty,*** what my conscience tells me I must do.

bounder /ˈbɑʊndə(r)/ *n* (GB dated colloq) cheerful and noisy ill-bred person.

bound·less /ˈbɑʊndləs/ *adj* without limits: *his ~ generosity.* **~·ly** *adv*

boun·te·ous /ˈbɑʊntɪəs/ *adj* generous; giving or given freely; abundant: *a ~ harvest.* **~·ly** *adv*

boun·ti·ful /ˈbɑʊntɪfl/ *adj* = bounteous. ˋ**~ly** /-flɪ/ *adv*

bounty /ˈbɑʊntɪ/ *n* (*pl* **-ties**) **1** [U] freedom in giving; generosity. **2** [C] sth given out of kindness (esp to the poor). **3** [C] reward or payment offered (usu by a government) to encourage sb to do sth (e g increase production of goods, kill dangerous wild animals).

bou·quet /bʊˈkeɪ/ *n* **1** bunch of flowers (to be) carried in the hand. **2** perfume of wine.

bour·bon /ˈbɜbən/ *n* [U] kinds of whisky distilled from maize and rye.

bour·geois /ˈbʊəʒwɑ *US:* ˈbʊəˈʒwɑ/ *n, adj* (person) of the class that owns property or engages in trade; (pej) (person) concerned chiefly with material prosperity and social status. **bourgeoisie** /ˈbʊəʒwɑˈzi/ *n* **the ~,** persons of the

class, collectively.

bourn /bʊən/ *n* (old use) stream.

bourn(e) /bʊən/ *n* (old use) boundary; limit; goal.

bourse /bʊəs/ *n* foreign money-market (esp that of Paris).

bout /baʊt/ *n* **1** period of exercise, work or other activity: *a ˋwrestling ~; a ~ of fighting; a ˋdrinking ~.* **2** fit (of illness): *a ~ of influenza; bad coughing ~s.*

bou·tique /buˋtik/ *n* small shop selling articles (clothes, cosmetics, hats, etc) of the latest fashion.

bov·ine /ˋbəʊvaɪn/ *adj* of, like, an ox: *~ stupidity.*

bov·ril /ˋbovrɪl/ *n* [U] (P) meat extract used like beef tea.

bov·ver /ˋbovə(r)/ *n* (sl from Cockney pronunciation of *bother*) violence (esp between gangs of boys or young men): *have a spot of ~;* (attrib) *ˋ~ boots,* heavy, steel-capped, boots, as worn by members of such gangs.

bow[1] /bəʊ/ *n* **1** piece of wood curved by a tight string, used for shooting arrows. ⇨ the illus at archer. ***draw the long bow,*** exaggerate. ***have two strings to one's bow,*** have more than one plan, more resources than one. **2** rod of wood with horse-hair stretched from end to end, used for playing the violin, etc. ⇨ the illus at string. **3** curve; rainbow. **4** knot made with a loop or loops; ribbon, etc, tied in this way: *Tie your shoe-laces in a bow. She had a bow of pink ribbon in her hair.* **ˈbow ˋlegged** *adj* with the legs curved outwards at the knees; bandy. **ˈbow ˋlegs** *n* **ˈbow ˋtie** *n* necktie made into a bow. **ˋbow·shot** *n* distance to which a bow can send an arrow. **ˋbow·man** /-mən/ *n* (*pl* -men) archer. □ *vt* use a bow on (a violin, etc). **bow·ing** *n*: *The violinist's bowing is excellent.*

bow[2] /baʊ/ *vi, vt* **1** [VP2A,C,6A,3A] bend the head or body (as a sign of respect or as a greeting, or in submission, or to indicate assent); bend (the head or body): *I raised my hat to her and she bowed in return. They bowed down to the idol. They bowed their heads in prayer. He bowed before the shrine. He bowed his thanks,* expressed his thanks by bowing. *We can never bow the neck to these cruel invaders of our country.* [VP15B] ***bow sb in,*** receive a visitor with low bows. [VP15B] ***bow sb out,*** bow low to sb as he leaves. ***bow oneself out,*** bow as one goes out. ***bow to sb's opinion, etc,*** submit to it. ***have a bowing acquaintance with,*** ⇨ acquaintance. **2** [VP6A,15B, usu passive] bend: *His father is bowed with age. The branches were bowed down with the weight of the snow.* □ *n* bending of the head or body (in greeting, etc): *He answered with a low bow. He made his bow to the company and left the room.*

bow[3] /baʊ/ *n* **1** (often *pl*) front or forward end of a boat or ship from where it begins to curve. ***on/off the (port, starboard) bow,*** said of objects within 45° of the point right ahead. ⇨ the illus at ship. **2** (in a rowing-boat) oarsman nearest the bow. ⇨ stroke.

Bow Bells /ˈbəʊ ˋbelz/ *n pl* the bells of Bow Church, London: *born within the sound of ~,* (said of a true Cockney) born in the City of London.

bowd·ler·ize /ˋbaʊdləraɪz/ *vt* take out of (a book, etc) words, scenes, etc that might be considered improper, unsuitable for young readers, etc.

bowel /ˋbaʊl̩/ *n* **1** (usu *pl* except in medical use and when attrib) division of the food canal below the stomach, ⇨ the illus at alimentary; intestine: *a ~ complaint. Keep your ~s open,* don't become constipated. **2** (always *pl*) innermost part: *in the ~s of the earth,* deep underground.

bower /ˋbaʊə(r)/ *n* **1** summer-house in a garden; shady place under trees or climbing plants. **2** (liter) boudoir.

bowie knife /ˋbəʊɪ naɪf/ *n* long knife with a blade that is double-edged at the point, used as a weapon.

bowl[1] /bəʊl/ *n* **1** deep, round, hollow dish; contents of such a dish: *She ate three ~s of rice;* (compounds): *ˋfinger-~, ˋsalad-~, ˋsugar-~.* **2** sth shaped like a ~: *the ~ of a spoon. He filled the ~ of his pipe,* put tobacco into it. *The electric light bulb is in an alabaster ~.* **3** (esp US) amphitheatre (for open-air concerts, etc): *The Hollywood B~.*

bowl[2] /bəʊl/ *n* **1** heavy, wooden or composition ball made so that it rolls with a bias. **2** (*pl*) game played with these balls: *have a game of ~s; play (at) ~s.*

bowl[3] /bəʊl/ *vi, vt* **1** [VP2A] play bowls. ⇨ bowl[2](2). **ˋ~ing-green** *n* area of fine, smooth grass for playing bowls. **ˋ~ing alley** *n* level area of wood, used for skittles, ninepins and tenpins. **2** [VP2A,6A] (cricket) send a ball to the batsman: *Smith ~ed ten overs.* ⇨ over[3]. ***~ (out),*** [VP6A,15B] dismiss (a batsman) by hitting the wicket or knocking the bails off: *The first two batsmen were ~ed (out).* **3** ***~ along,*** [VP2C] go quickly and smoothly on wheels: *Our car ~ed along over the smooth roads.* **4** ***~ (sb) over,*** [VP15B] **(a)** knock down. **(b)** make helpless, overcome: *He was ~ed over by the news. Her impudence ~ed me over,* left me speechless with surprise.

bow·ler[1] /ˋbəʊlə(r)/ *n* **1** person who plays bowls[2](2). **2** person who bowls in cricket.

bow·ler[2] /ˋbəʊlə(r)/ *n* (also **ˈ~ ˋhat**) hard, rounded, usu black hat.

bow·line /ˋbəʊlɪn/ *n* (also **ˋ~ knot**) simple but secure knot used by sailors.

bowls *n* ⇨ bowl[2](2).

bow·man /ˋbəʊmən/ *n* (*pl* -men) archer. ⇨ bow[1](1).

bow·ser /ˋbaʊzə(r)/ *n* (P) truck fitted with a tank for aviation spirit, etc used at airports for fuelling aircraft.

bow·sprit /ˋbəʊsprɪt/ *n* spar that extends from a ship's stem, to which ropes that support sails, etc are fastened. ⇨ the illus at barque.

bow win·dow /ˈbəʊ ˋwɪndəʊ/ *n* curved bay window. ⇨ the illus at window.

bow·wow /ˈbaʊ ˋwaʊ/ *int* imitation of a dog's bark. □ *n* /ˋbaʊ waʊ/ (young child's word for a) dog.

box[1] /boks/ *n* **1** container, usu with a lid, made of wood, cardboard, plastic, metal, etc used for holding solids: *a box of matches; a ˋtool-box. Packs the books in a wooden box.* **ˋbox-kite** *n* kite made in the form of a box (or two boxes) of light material. **ˋbox-number** *n* number used in a newspaper advertisement as an address to which answers may be sent (and forwarded from the newspaper office). **PO Box No** *n* number used as part of an address to which letters, etc may be directed. ⇨ also call-box, Christmas-box, letter-box, money-box, pillar-box. **2** separate compartment, with seats for several persons, in a theatre, concert hall, etc. **ˋbox-office** *n* office for booking

seats in a theatre, concert hall, etc: *The play was a box-office success,* a financial success. **3** compartment in a law court for a special purpose: *ˈjury-box, ˈwitness-box.* **4** small hut or shelter, e g for a sentry or railway signalman. **5** separate compartment in a stable or railway truck for a horse. **6** raised seat for the driver of a carriage(**1**) or coach(**1**). **box·ful** /-fʊl/ *n* full box[1](**1**) (*of* sth). □ *vt* [VP6A] put into a box. **box sb/sth up,** [VP15B] shut up in a small space.

box[2] /bɒks/ *vt,vi* [VP6A] ***box sb's ears,*** give him a blow with the open hand on the ears. **2** [VP6A, 2A] fight (sb) with the fists, usu with thick gloves, for sport. *Do you box,* Do you fight in this way (as a form of exercise)? **ˈboxing-gloves** *n pl* padded gloves for use in boxing. **ˈboxing-match** *n* fight between two boxers. □ *n* slap or blow with the open hand (on the ear(s)). **boxer** *n* **1** person who boxes. **2** breed of dog (like a bulldog).

box[3] /bɒks/ [U] **1** (kinds of) small, evergreen shrub, used in garden borders. **2** (also **ˈbox·wood**) wood of this shrub.

Box·ing Day /ˈbɒksɪŋ deɪ/ *n* first weekday after Christmas Day.

boy /bɔɪ/ *n* **1** male child up to the age of 17 or 18. **ˈ~friend,** favoured male companion of a girl or young woman. **2** son (colloq of any age): *He has two boys and one girl.* **3** male servant (any age): *a ˈhouseboy.* Cf the use of *maid,* female servant, in countries where domestic servants are usu women. **ˈboy·hood** /-hʊd/ *n* [U] time when one is/was a boy. **boy·ish** *adj* of, for, like, a boy.

boy·cott /ˈbɔɪkɒt/ *vt* [VP6A] (join with others and) refuse to have anything to do with, to trade with (a person, business firm, country, etc); refuse to handle (goods, etc). □ *n* ~ing; treatment of this kind: *put sb/his shop/goods under a ~; put a ~ on sb, etc.*

bra /brɑ/ *n* (colloq abbr of) brassiere.

brace[1] /breɪs/ *n* **1** sth used to clasp, tighten or support, e g the roof or walls of a building. **2** revolving tool for holding another tool, e g a *bit* for boring holes, driving in screws, etc. **3** (*pl* unchanged) pair or couple (of dogs, game-birds): *five ~ of partridge.* **4** (*pl*) (US = *suspenders*) straps passing over the shoulders, used to keep trousers up. **5** (often *pl*) appliance of bands and wires fastened to the teeth to correct their alignment.

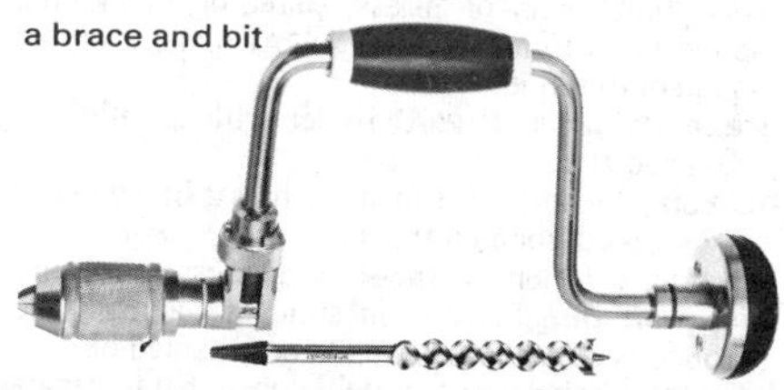
a brace and bit

brace[2] /breɪs/ *vt,vi* **1** [VP6A] support; give firmness to: *The struts are firmly ~d.* **2** [VP6A,15B, 16A] **~ *(up),*** steady oneself; stand firm: *B~ up! He ~d himself to meet the blow.* **3** (usu as *part adj*) enliven; stimulate: *bracing air; a bracing climate.*

brace·let /ˈbreɪslət/ *n* ornamental band or chain of metal for the wrist or arm.

bracken /ˈbrækən/ *n* [U] large fern that grows on hillsides/waste land, etc; mass of such fern.

bracket /ˈbrækɪt/ *n* **1** wood or metal support for a shelf; support on a wall for a gas or electric lamp. **2** (printing) either of the two symbols { } used for connecting lines of type. **3** grouping; classification: *income ~,* e g of incomes of £1 000 to £1 500; *age ~,* e g 20 to 30 years of age. □ *vt* [VP6A,15B] put inside, join with, ~s; put together to imply connection or equality: *Jones and Smith were ~ed together at the top of the list.*

brack·ish /ˈbrækɪʃ/ *adj* (of water) slightly salt; between salt and fresh water.

bract /brækt/ *n* [C] (bot) leaf-like part of a plant, often highly coloured, situated below a flower or cluster of flowers (as in bougainvillea, poinsettia).

brad /bræd/ *n* thin, flat nail with no head or a very small head.

brad·awl /ˈbrædɔl/ *n* small tool for piercing holes for brads or screws.

brae /breɪ/ *n* (Scot) slope; hillside.

brag /bræg/ *vi* (-gg-) **~ *(of/about),*** [VP2A,3A] boast: *~ of what one has done.* **brag·ging** *n* [U] **brag·gart** /ˈbrægət/ *n* person who ~s.

Brah·min /ˈbrɑmɪn/ *n* member of the highest Hindu priestly caste.

braid /breɪd/ *n* **1** [C] number of strands of hair woven together: *She wears her hair in ~s.* **2** [U] silk, linen, etc woven into a band, used for edging cloth or garments or (esp gold and silver ~) for decoration: *The uniforms of the generals were covered with gold ~.* □ *vt* [VP6A] make into ~(s); trim with ~; put (hair) into ~s.

braille /breɪl/ *n* [U] system of writing and reading (using raised dots) for blind people, to enable them to read by touch.

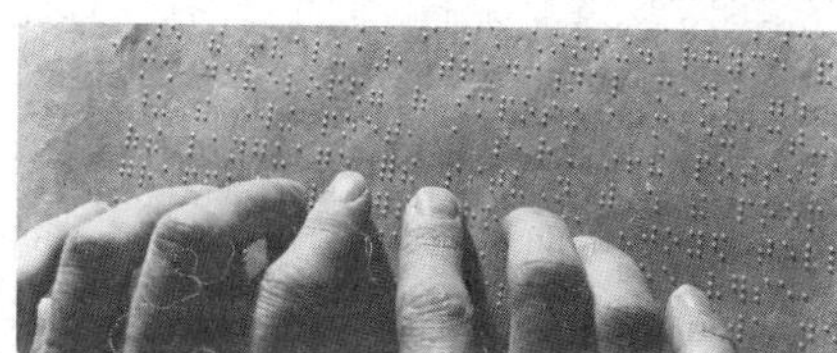
reading braille

brain /breɪn/ *n* **1** (*sing*) (in man and animals) the mass of soft grey matter in the head, centre of the nervous system: *The human ~ is a complex organ. The creature's ~ weighs a quarter of a kilo.* ⇨ the illus at **head**. **2** (as in **1** above, colloq and usu *pl*): *They dashed his ~s out on the rocks.* ***blow out one's ~s,*** ⇨ **blow**[1](**13**). **3** (*pl*) animal's ~s, eaten as food: *calf's/sheep's ~s.* **4** (colloq, usu *sing*) mind; intellect: *have a good ~; use one's ~(s).* ***beat/rack one's ~(s) (about sth),*** think very hard. ***have sth*** (e g money, sex) ***on the ~,*** think constantly about it. ***tax one's ~,*** strain or tire it. ***pick sb's ~(s),*** learn and use his ideas. **5** [C] clever, brilliant person: *He's the ~ of the school staff.* **6** (compounds) **ˈ~-child** *n* original idea, etc attributed to a person or group. **ˈ~ drain** *n* ⇨ **drain**[1](**2**). **ˈ~-fag** *n* mental exhaustion: *suffering from ~-fag.* **ˈ~ fever** *n* inflammation of the ~. **ˈ~-storm** *n* mental upset with uncontrolled emotion, e g weeping, and violence. **ˈ~-teaser** *n* difficult problem; puzzle. **ˈB~s Trust** *n* group of reputed experts giving advice, or answering questions put to them by members of an audience. **ˈ~-washing** *n* process of forcing a person to reject old beliefs and accept new beliefs by use of extreme mental pressure, e g persistent questioning. **`~-wave** *n* (colloq) sudden inspiration or bright idea. □ *vt* [VP6A] kill by a heavy blow on the head: *~ an ox.* **~·less** *adj* stupid. **~y** *adj* clever.

braise /breɪz/ *vt* [VP6A] cook (meat) slowly in a covered pan or pot: *~d beef/chicken.*

brake[1] /breɪk/ *n* device for reducing speed or stopping motion, e g of a bicycle, motor-car, train, etc: *put on/apply the ~s; act as a ~ upon (progress, initiative, etc)*, hamper it; control it. □ *vt,vi* [VP6A,2A] put on the ~(s) (to): *The driver ~d suddenly.*

brake[2] /breɪk/ *n* area or band or brushwood, thick undergrowth or bracken.

brake[3] /breɪk/ *n* large wagon or open carriage pulled by one or more horses, and with facing side seats, formerly used for pleasure outings. ⇨ shooting-brake.

bramble /ˈbræmbl/ *n* rough shrub with long prickly shoots; blackberry bush.

bran /bræn/ *n* [U] outer covering (husks) of grain (wheat, rye, etc) separated from flour by sifting.

branch /brɑntʃ *US:* bræntʃ/ *n* **1** ⇨ the illus at tree; armlike part of a tree, growing out from the trunk or a bough; smaller division growing from a large branch: *He climbed up the tree and hid among the ~es.* **2** (often attrib) ~-like division or subdivision of a river, road, railway, mountain range, etc; division or subdivision of a family, subject of knowledge, organization, etc: *There is a ~ post-office quite near. The bank has ~es in all parts of the country. English is a ~ of the Germanic family of languages.* ***root and ~,*** ⇨ root[1](1). □ *vi* [VP2A,C] send out, divide into, ~es: *The trees ~ (out) over the river. The road ~es here.* ***~ off,*** (of a car, road, train, etc) leave a main route and take a minor one. ***~ out,*** (of a person, business firm, etc) expand in a new direction, open new departments or lines of activities. **~y** *adj* with many ~es.

brand /brænd/ *n* **1** trademark (painted or printed on boxes, tins, packets, etc); particular kind of goods with such a mark: *the best ~s of cigars; an excellent ~ of coffee.* **ˈ~-ˈnew** *adj* quite new (as if freshly stamped with a ~). **2** piece of burning wood: *a ~ from the burning*, person rescued from the consequences of sin; converted sinner. **3** (also **`~·ing-iron**), iron used red-hot, for burning a mark into a surface; made in this way; (in olden times) mark burned on criminals, hence, (fig) mark of guilt or disgrace: *the ~ of Cain*, of a murderer. **4** (poet) torch. **5** (poet) sword. □ *vt* [VP6A,16B] **1** mark (cattle, goods, etc) with a ~: *On big farms cattle are usually ~ed. Criminals used to be ~ed.* (fig) *These frightful experiences are ~ed on his memory.* **2** give (sb) a bad name: *~ sb with infamy; ~ sb (as) a heretic.*

bran·dish /ˈbrændɪʃ/ *vt* [VP6A] wave about (to display, or before using): *~ing a sword.*

brandy /ˈbrændɪ/ *n* [C,U] (*pl*-**dies**) strong alcoholic drink distilled from wine of grapes: *two brandies and sodas*, two glasses of ~ mixed with soda water. **`~-ball** *n* kind of sweet. **`~-snap** *n* kind of gingerbread wafer.

bran-new /ˈbræn ˈnju *US:* ˈnu/ *adj* = brand-new.

brash /bræʃ/ *adj* (colloq) **1** saucy; cheeky. **2** hasty; rash.

brass /brɑs *US:* bræs/ *n* **1** [U] bright yellow metal made by mixing copper and zinc: *~ rods/buttons; a ~ foundry.* ***get down to ~ tacks,*** (rhyming sl for) facts, esp essential facts. **ˈ~ `hat,** (army sl) high-ranking officer. **ˈ~ `plate,** oblong plate of ~, on a door or gate, with the name, trade, occupation, etc, e g as used by doctors, lawyers, business firms. **ˈtop `~,** (colloq, collective) high-ranking officers (in the armed services). **2** [U] (and *pl*) things made of ~, e g candlesticks, bowls, ornaments: *clean/do the ~/the ~es.* **the ~,** (mus) musical instruments made of ~ (in a band). **ˈ~ `band,** band of musicians with ~ instruments. **4** [U] (GB sl) money. **5** [U] (sl) impudence. ⇨ brazen. **6** [C] ~ plate with an inscription, placed in a church in memory of a dead person. **~y** *adj* **1** like ~ in colour or sound. ⇨ **3** above. **2** impudent. □ *n* golf-club weighted with ~.

bras·sard /ˈbræsɑd/ *n* (arm-band bearing a) badge worn on the sleeve.

brass·erie /ˈbræsərɪ/ *n* beer-saloon or beer-garden (usu supplying food as well as drink).

brass·iere, ·ière /ˈbræzɪə(r) *US:* brəˈzɪər/ *n* (US usu *pl*) (usu shortened to *bra*) woman's close-fitting support for the breasts.

brat /bræt/ *n* (contemptuous) child.

bra·vado /brəˈvɑdəʊ/ *n* **1** [U] display of boldness or daring: *do sth out of ~*, in order to display one's courage. **2** (*pl* **-does, -dos**) instance of this.

brave /breɪv/ *adj* **1** ready to face danger, pain or suffering; having no fear: *as ~ as a lion. Be ~! It was ~ of him to enter the burning building.* **2** needing courage: *a ~ act.* **3** (old use) fine and splendid: *this ~ new world.* □ *n* Red-Indian warrior. □ *vt* [VP6A] face, go into, meet, without showing fear: *He had ~d death a hundred times. We decided to ~ the storm*, to go out in spite of the storm. ***~ it out,*** [VP15B] disregard, defy, suspicion or blame. **~·ly** *adv* **brav·ery** /ˈbreɪvərɪ/ *n* [U] **1** courage; being ~. **2** (old use) splendour (of dress, etc): *decked out in all their ~ry.*

bravo /ˈbrɑˈvəʊ/ *n, int* (*pl* **-voes, -vos**) (cry of approval) Well done! Excellent!

brawl /brɔl/ *n* noisy quarrel or fight. □ *vi* [VP2A] quarrel noisily; take part in a ~; (of streams) flow noisily (over stones and rocks). **~er** *n* person who takes part in a ~.

brawn /brɔn/ *n* [U] **1** muscle; strength. **2** (not US) meat (esp pork) cut up, spiced and pickled, and compressed. **~y** *adj* muscular: *The blacksmith has ~y arms.*

bray /breɪ/ *n* cry of an ass; sound of, or like the sound of, a trumpet. □ *vt* [VP2A] make a cry or sound of this kind.

braze /breɪz/ *vt* [VP6A] solder with an alloy of brass and zinc.

brazen /ˈbreɪzn/ *adj* **1** made of brass; like brass: *a ~ (= hard-sounding) voice; the ~ notes of a trumpet.* **2** (often **`~-faced**) shameless. □ *vt* (only in) ***~ it out,*** behave, in spite of having done wrong, as if one has nothing to be ashamed of.

braz·ier /ˈbreɪzɪə(r)/ *n* portable open metal framework (like a basket), usu on legs, for holding a charcoal or coal fire.

breach /britʃ/ *n* **1** breaking or neglect (*of* a rule, duty, agreement, etc): *a ~ of the peace*, unlawful fighting in a public place, e g the streets; *a ~ of contract* (in comm, etc); *a ~ of promise* (esp of a promise to marry); *a ~ of faith*, act of disloyalty; *a ~ of confidence; a ~ of security.* **2** opening, esp one made in a defensive wall, etc by artillery, attacking forces, etc: *step into/fill the ~*, come forward to help; *throw/fling oneself into the ~,*

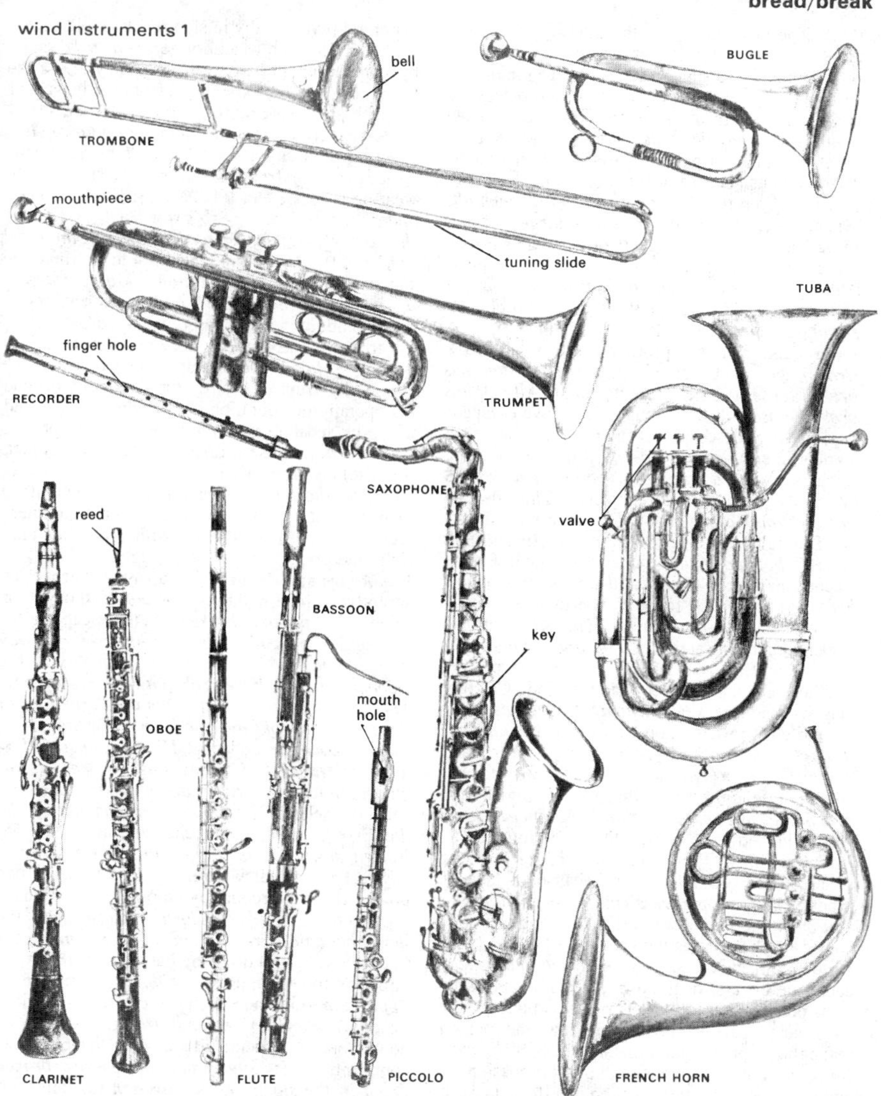

help those who are in trouble or danger; *stand in the ~*, bear the heaviest part of the attack; do most of the hard work. **3** broken place; gap: *The sheep got out of the field after one of them had made a ~ in the hedge. The waves made a ~ in the sea wall.* □ *vt* [VP6A] make a gap in, break through (a defensive wall, etc).

bread /bred/ *n* [U] food made by mixing flour with water and yeast, kneading, and baking in an oven: *a loaf/slice/piece of ~.* ***~ and butter*** /ˈbred n ˈbʌtə(r)/, **(a)** slice(s) of ~ spread with butter: *send one's hostess a ~-and butter note,* one of thanks for hospitality. **(b)** (GB sl) money: *earn one's ~ and butter* (= one's means of living) *by writing.* ***one's daily ~,*** one's means of living. ***earn one's ~,*** make enough money to live on. ***know which side one's ~ is buttered,*** know where one may have advantages, where one's interest lies. ***take the ~ out of sb's mouth,*** take away his means of living, e g by business competition. **ˈ~·crumb** *n* [C] tiny bit of the inner part of a loaf, esp crumbled for use in cooking. **ˈ~·fruit** *n* tree with starchy fruit, grown in the South Sea Islands and W Africa. **ˈ~·line** *n* line of people waiting for food given as charity or relief; (fig): *on the ~line,* very poor. **ˈ~·stuffs** *n pl* grain, flour. **ˈ~·win·ner** *n* person who works to support a family.

breadth /ˈbretθ/ *n* ⇨ broad[1](2). **1** distance or measure from side to side: *ten feet in ~.* ⇨ hair(2). **2** largeness (of mind or view); boldness of effect (in music or art). **ˈ~·ways, ˈ~·wise** *adv* so that the broad side is in front.

break[1] /breɪk/ *vt,vi* (*pl* broke /brəʊk/ old Eng brake /breɪk/, *pp* broken /ˈbrəʊkən/) (For uses with *adverbial particles* and *preps,* ⇨ 11 below.) **1** [VP6A,15B,2A,C] (of a whole thing) (cause to) go or come into two or more separate parts as the result of force, a blow or strain (but not by cutting): The boy fell out of the tree and broke his leg. Glass ~s easily. If you pull too hard you will ~ the rope. The string broke. **~ (in)to pieces, ~ in two,** *etc,* (cause to) come or go into pieces, in two, etc parts: *He broke the box into pieces. When I hit the ball, my bat broke in two.* **2** [VP6A,15B, 2A,C] (of a part or parts) (cause to) be separate or discontinuous because of force or strain: *He broke a branch from the tree. Don't ~ that branch off. The door-handle has broken off. A large part of it broke away,* came off. **~ sb/oneself of a habit,** succeed in getting him/oneself to give it up. **3** [VP6A] make (sth) useless by injuring an essential part (of a machine, apparatus, etc): *~ a clock/a sewing-machine.* **4** [VP2D,22] (with *adjj*): **~ even,** make neither a profit nor a loss. **~ loose (from),** get or become separate: *The dog has broken loose,* got free from its chain. *All hell has broken loose,* All the devils in hell have escaped; (fig) (used to describe a scene of confusion, e g a bombardment). **~ sth open,** get it open by using force: *~ open a safe/door/the lid of a desk.* **5** [VP2A,C] (with various subjects): *The abscess/blister/bubble broke,* burst. *Day was beginning to ~,* Daylight was beginning. ⇨ **daybreak.** *His voice is beginning to ~,* change in quality as he reaches manhood. *She was filled with emotion and her voice broke,* She faltered, was unable to speak clearly because of emotion. *The storm broke,* began, burst into activity. *The fine weather/The heat-wave/The frost broke,* The period of fine weather, etc ended after being settled. Cf How long will the fine weather *hold*? *The clouds broke* (= parted, showed an opening) *and the sun came through. The waves were ~ing* (= curling and falling) *over/on/against the rocks. The sea was ~ing* (= sending waves that were ~ing) *on the beach/over the wrecked ship. The enemy broke* (= developed gaps in their lines, fell into confusion) *and fled. When the bank broke* (= was unable to carry on business because of lack of funds), *many people were ruined. A good bowler can make the ball ~,* (in cricket) change from its course when it strikes the ground. **6** [VP6A] (with various objects): *~ sb's back/neck/nose, etc,* cause the bone(s) of the back, etc to be out of the right position. ⇨ **back[1](1).** *~ the bank,* exhaust its funds; win all the money that the person managing a public gaming-table has; *~ bounds,* (mil) go out of bounds without permission or authority; *~ one's fall,* weaken its effect, make it less violent; *~ the force of sth,* reduce its force by bearing part of it: *The tall hedge ~s the force of the wind.* ⇨ **windbreak;** *~ fresh/new ground,* (fig) start work at sth new; *~ sb's heart,* reduce him to despair; *~ a man,* ruin him; compel him to reveal a secret, etc; *~ the news,* make it known; *~ the (bad) news (to* sb), reveal the news in such a way that its effect is less of a shock; *~ an officer,* dismiss him, take his commission from him; *~ a path/way,* make one by pushing or beating aside obstacles; *~ prison/gaol,* escape from, make one's way out of, prison; *~ ranks,* (of soldiers) leave the ranks without permission; *~ a (Commonwealth/Olympic/World, etc) record,* do better than it, make a new record; *~ a set of books/china, etc,* cause it to be incomplete by giving away or selling a part or parts of it; *~ the skin on one's elbow/knees/knuckles, etc,* graze it, so as to cause bleeding; *~ step,* (of soldiers) stop marching rhythmically in step, e g to avoid excessive vibration on a weak bridge; *~ a strike,* end it by compelling the workers to submit. ⇨ **strike breaker;** *~ wind,* expel wind from the bowels or stomach. ⇨ also **code(3), cover[2](5), ice[1](1). 7** [VP6A,15A,B] train or discipline: *~ a horse (in),* bring it to a disciplined state: *a well-broken horse; ~ a horse to harness/to the rein,* accustom it to wearing harness, etc. **8** [VP6A,15B] subdue, keep under, end by force: *~ sb's spirit/will; ~ (down) the enemy's resistance; ~ the power of the rebel leader.* **9** [VP6A] act in opposition to; infringe: *~ the law/the rules/a regulation; ~ a contract/an agreement; ~ the Sabbath,* do things on a Sunday that should not be done; *~ one's word/a promise,* fail to keep a promise; *~ an appointment,* fail to keep it; *~ faith with sb,* betray or deceive him. **10** [VP6A] interrupt or destroy the continuity of; end the operation or duration of: *~ (the) silence,* end it, e g by speaking; *~ one's journey (at* a place); *~ the peace,* cause a disturbance; *~ one's fast,* (old use) take food after going without. ⇨ **breakfast;** *~ short (a conversation, etc),* end it; *a broken night's sleep,* one that is disturbed or interrupted. **11** [VP15B,2C,3A] (with *adverbial particles* and *preps*):

break away (from), go away suddenly or abruptly; give up (habits, modes of thought or belief): *The prisoner broke away* (= escaped after a struggle) *from his guards. Can't you ~ away from old habits? About twenty members of the Communist Party have broken away* (= seceded). *There has been a ~-away from the Party. One of the provinces broke away to form a new State.*

break down, (a) collapse: *His resistance will ~ down in time. Our plans have broken down. Negotiations have broken down.* **(b)** become disabled or useless: *The car/engine/machinery broke down,* i e because of a mechanical fault. *That old broken-down bus is not worth £5.* **(c)** suffer a physical or mental weakening: *His health broke down.* **(d)** be overcome by emotion, e g by bursting into tears: *She broke down when she heard the news, but quickly recovered.* **~ sth down, (a)** get (a door, wall, etc) down by battering it. **(b)** overthrow by force; suppress: *~ down all resistance/opposition.* **(c)** divide, analyse, classify (statistical material): *~ down expenditure,* give details of how money is spent. **(d)** change the chemical composition of: *Sugar and starch are broken down in the stomach.* **ˈ~-down** *n* **(a)** failure in machinery, etc: *There was a ~down on the railway and trains were delayed. The earthquake has caused a ~down of communications.* Hence: *ˈ~down gang,* men called to repair or remove a train, etc that has been derailed, smashed, etc. **(b)** collapse; weakening: *He's suffering from a nervous ~down.* **(c)** statistical analysis: *a ~down of expenditure.*

break forth, (esp fig, of anger, indignation) burst out.

break in, enter a building by force: *Burglars had broken in while we were away on holiday.* Hence, **ˈ~-in** *n*: *The police are investigating a ~-in at the local bank.* **~ (esp a horse) in,** ⇨ 7 above; train and discipline; accustom sb to a new routine. **~ in (up)on,** disturb; interrupt: *Please don't ~ in on our conversation.*

break into, (a) force one's way into (a building, etc): *His house was broken into* (i e by burglars or thieves) *last week.* **(b)** burst suddenly into: ~ (*out*) *into a loud laugh/into loud curses/into song/into praises of sb.* **(c)** change one's method of movement suddenly: ~ *into a run/trot/gallop.* **(d)** occupy, take up, undesirably: *Social duties* ~ *into my time/leisure.* **(e)** (of coins and notes): ~ *into a pound note,* use one to pay for sth costing less than this sum: *I can't pay you the 50p I owe you without ~ing into a £5 note.* **(f)** open and draw upon emergency supplies: *The garrison broke into their reserves of ammunition.*

break off, **(a)** stop speaking: *He broke off in the middle of a sentence.* **(b)** pause; stop temporarily: *Let's ~ off for half an hour and have some tea.* ***~ (sth) off,*** **(a)** (cause to) separate (a part of sth): *The mast broke off/was broken off.* **(b)** end abruptly: ~ *off relations (with sb);* ~ *off an engagement/conversation.*

break out, ⇨ **outbreak.** (of fire, disease, war, rioting, violence) appear, start, suddenly: *A fire broke out during the night. The quarrel broke out afresh. Riots and disorders have broken out. Plague broke out in several parts of the country.* ***~ out (of),*** escape: *Several prisoners broke out of the compound.* ***~ out in,*** **(a)** suddenly become covered with: *His face broke out in spots/a rash. He broke out in a cold sweat,* was struck with fear. **(b)** show sudden violence in speech or behaviour: *He broke out in a rage/in curses.*

break through, make a way through (an enclosure, obstacles, etc): *The enemy's defences were strong but our soldiers broke through. The sun broke through (the clouds).* ***~ through sth,*** overcome: ~ *through a man's reserve.* Hence, **'~-through** *n* **(a)** (mil) piercing (of the enemy's defences). **(b)** major achievement, e g in technology: *a ~through in cancer research.*

break up, **(a)** come to pieces; disintegrate: *The ship was ~ing up on the rocks. The gathering broke up in disorder.* **(b)** (fig, of persons) go to pieces; become weak: *He broke up under the strain.* **(c)** (of a school, etc) separate at the end of term for holidays: *When do you ~ up?* **(d)** (of a couple, a relationship) come to an end: *The marriage is ~ing up.* **(e)** divide: *Sentences ~ up into clauses.* ***~ sth up,*** **(a)** smash; demolish: ~ *up a box for firewood;* ~ *up an old ship for scrap metal.* **(b)** (cause to) split, or divide: ~ *up a piece of work (among several persons).* **(c)** (cause to) disperse: *The police broke up the crowd/meeting.* **(d)** bring to an end: *They broke up the alliance.* Hence, **'~-up** *n* (end of a marriage, coalition, etc). **(e)** (esp of a period of fine weather) change for the worse; end: *The weather is ~ing up.*

break with, **(a)** end a friendship with: ~ *with an old friend.* **(b)** give up; make an end of: ~ *with old habits;* ~ *with old ties,* e g when one leaves a district.

break[2] /breɪk/ *n* **1** breaking; broken place: *a ~ in the water mains.* **2** [U] ~ *of day (= day~),* dawn. **3** interval (in space of time): *a ~ in the conversation; an hour's ~ for lunch; the 'tea-~,* e g in an office or factory; *during a ~ at school,* during an interval between lessons. ***without a ~,*** continuously: *He has been writing since 2 o'clock without a ~.* **4** change, disturbance: *a ~ in one's way of living; a ~ in the weather.* **5** change of course of a cricket or tennis ball on first striking the ground: *a leg ~,* (cricket) one that breaks to the left. **6** (billiards) continuous score: *make a ~ of 450.* **7** ***give sb a ~,*** (colloq) an opportunity (to make a new start or remedy an error): *Give him a ~.* **8** (colloq) ***a bad ~,*** an unfortunate remark or ill-judged action; a piece of bad luck. ***a lucky ~,*** a piece of good fortune. **9** (= *'breakout*) (attempt to) escape (esp from prison): *He made a ~ for the gates.*

break[3] /breɪk/ *n* = **brake(3).**

break·able /'breɪkəbl/ *adj* easily broken. **breakables** *n pl* ~ objects, e g glasses, cups and saucers.

break·age /'breɪkɪdʒ/ *n* **1** act of breaking. **2** place in, part of, sth that has been broken. **3** (usu *pl*) broken articles; loss by breaking: *The hotel allows £150 a year for ~s,* for the cost of broken dishes, glasses, etc.

breaker /'breɪkə(r)/ *n* **1** large wave breaking into foam as it advances towards the shore; wave breaking against a rock, etc. **2** person or thing that breaks. **'ice-~** *n* strongly built ship used to break up ice in harbours, etc. ⇨ **house~** and other similar compounds.

break·fast /'brekfəst/ *n* first meal of the day: *Have a good ~. He hasn't eaten much ~. They were at ~ when I got down.* □ *vi* have ~.

break·neck /'breɪknek/ *adj* (usu) ***at (a) ~ speed,*** at a dangerous speed.

break·water /'breɪkwɔtə(r)/ *n* sth that breaks the force of waves, esp a structure built out into the sea to shelter (part of) a harbour.

a breakwater

bream /brim/ *n* (*pl* unchanged) **1** freshwater fish of the carp family. **2** (also **'sea-~**) salt-water variety of this.

breast /brest/ *n* **1** either of the milk-producing parts of a woman: *a child at the ~; give a child the ~.* ⇨ **suckle.** **'~-fed** *adj* (of a baby) fed with milk from the ~. Cf *bottle-fed.* **2** chest; upper front part of the human body, or of a garment covering this. **'~ 'pocket** *n* one in the ~ of a jacket, etc. **'~-stroke,** stroke (in swimming) in which both the arms are brought at the same time from in front of the head to the sides of the body. **'~-'high** *adv* high as the ~: *The wheat was ~-high.* **'~-'deep** *adv* deep enough to reach the ~: *In the middle of the stream the water was ~-deep.* **'~-plate** *n* piece of armour covering the ~. ⇨ the illus at **armour.** **'~-work** *n* low wall, e g of earth, sandbags, stones, put up as a temporary defence. **3** (fig) feelings; thoughts: *a troubled ~.* ***make a clean ~ of,*** confess (wrongdoing, etc). **4** part of an animal corresponding to the human ~. **5** (of a chimney) projection into the room for the fireplace and flue. □ *vt* [VP6A] present the ~(2) to, hence (fig), face, struggle with: ~ *the waves.*

breath /breθ/ *n* **1** [U] air taken into and sent out of the lungs; [C] single act of taking in and sending air out: *take a deep ~,* fill the lungs with air. ***bad ~,*** with an unpleasant smell. ***catch/hold one's ~,*** stop breathing for a moment (from fear, excitement, etc). ***get one's ~ (again),*** get back to the normal state. ***in the same ~,*** at the same moment: *They are not to be mentioned in the same ~*, cannot be compared. ***lose one's ~,*** have difficulty in taking in ~, e g while running or working hard. ***out of ~,*** unable to take in ~ quickly enough. ***speak/say sth below/under one's ~,*** in a whisper. ***take ~,*** get enough ~ (after exertion): *Half-way up the mountain we stopped to take ~.* ***take sb's ~ away,*** startle or surprise him. Hence, **'~-taking,** *adj* exciting; causing awe. ***waste one's ~,*** talk in vain. **'~ test** *n* test of the alcoholic contents of a person's ~. **breathalyser** /ˈbreθəlaɪzə(r)/ *n* device (into which a person breathes) for such a test. **2** air in movement; light breeze: *There wasn't a ~ of air/wind,* The air was quite still. **3** (fig) suggestion (*of*): *not a ~ of suspicion/scandal.* **~·less** *adj* **1** out of ~; panting; likely to cause shortness of ~: *in a ~less hurry; listening with ~less attention/in ~less expectation,* with the ~ held back. **2** unstirred by wind: *a ~less* (= calm) *evening.* **~·less·ly** *adv*

breathe /brið/ *vi,vt* **1** [VP2A,C,6A,15B] take air into the lungs and send it out again: *~ in/out. He was breathing hard when he finished the race. We ~ air. He ~d a sigh of relief. He's still breathing,* is still alive. ***~ again/freely,*** be at ease, be relieved (after exertion, excitement, fear, etc). ***~ down sb's neck,*** ⇨ neck. **2** [VP6A] utter; send out, e g a scent, feeling: *Don't ~ a word of this,* keep it secret. **3** [VP6A] allow (a horse) to ~ gently and rest. **breather** *n* **1** short pause for rest: *take/have a ~r.* **2** short period of exercise: *go for a ~r.* **breath·ing** *n* [U] **'breath·ing-space** *n* time to ~; pause; rest.

bred *pt,pp* of breed.

breech /britʃ/ *n* back part of a rifle or gun barrel, where the cartridge or shell is placed: *a '~-'loading 'gun,* loaded at the ~, not through the muzzle. **'~-block** *n* block of steel that closes the ~ of a gun.

breeches /ˈbrɪtʃɪz/ *n pl* **1** garment fitting round the waist and below the knees: *'knee-~, 'court-~,* worn at court or as part of official costume; riding-~, garment covering the hips and thighs, buttoned below the knee, worn by men and women for riding on horseback. **2** (colloq) trousers; knickerbockers. ***wear the ~,*** (said of a woman) rule her husband. **'~-'buoy** /ˈbritʃɪz/ *n* pair of canvas ~ fastened to a lifebuoy, pulled along a rope, used for saving life at sea.

breed /brid/ *vt,vi* (*pt,pp* bred /bred/) **1** [VP6A] keep (animals, etc) for the purpose of producing young, esp by selection of parents: *~ horses/cattle.* **2** [VP2A] give birth to young; reproduce: *Rabbits ~ quickly. Birds ~ in the spring.* **3** [VP6A] train, educate, bring up: *an Englishman born and bred; a well-bred boy,* one who has been trained to behave well. ***What's bred in the bone will come out in the flesh,*** (prov) Hereditary characteristics always show themselves. **4** [VP6A] be the cause of: *Dirt ~s disease. War ~s misery and ruin.* **~er** *n* **1** person who ~s animals. **2** apparatus (reactor) that produces more radioactive material than is put into it. **~·ing** *n* [U] **1** (in verbal senses): *the ~ing of horses; the ~ing season for birds.* **2** knowledge of how to behave resulting from training: *a man of good ~ing.* □ *n* [C] kind or variety (of animals, etc) with hereditary qualities: *a good ~ of cattle.* ⇨ cross~ half-~.

breeze[1] /briz/ *n* **1** [C,U] wind, esp a soft, gentle wind: *a land/sea ~,* one blowing from the land/sea at certain hours; *not much ~; not much of a ~; spring ~s.* **2** (colloq) display of temper; slight quarrel. □ *vi* [VP2C] (colloq) **~ in/out,** come in/go out in high spirits, or without warning, unexpectedly. **breezy** *adj* **1** pleasantly windy: *breezy weather.* **2** swept by ~s: *a breezy corner.* **3** (of persons) jovial; lively; good-humoured. **breez·ily** /ˈbrizəlɪ/ *adv* **breezi·ness** /ˈbrizɪnəs/ *n*

breeze[2] /briz/ *n* [U] (not US) small coal cinders. **'~ blocks,** light-weight concrete building blocks made of ~ and cement.

Bren /bren/ *n* (also **'~-gun**) light-weight, semi-automatic, light machine gun. **'~ carrier** *n* small armoured vehicle that moves on tracks(3).

breth·ren /ˈbreðrən/ *n pl* (old use) brothers.

breve /briv/ *n* (music) note equal to two semi~s. ⇨ the illus at notation.

bre·vet /ˈbrevɪt *US:* brɪˈvet/ *n* document that gives sb higher rank without corresponding increase in pay or authority: *~ rank,* given by ~; *~ major.*

brevi·ary /ˈbrivɪərɪ *US:* -ɪerɪ/ *n* (*pl* -ries) book with prayers to be said daily by priests of the R C Church.

brev·ity /ˈbrevətɪ/ *n* [U] shortness (of statements, human life and other non-material things).

brew /bru/ *vt,vi* **1** [VP6A] prepare (beer, tea, etc) by soaking or boiling grain, leaves, etc; [VP2A] make beer, etc. **2** [VP6A] (fig) bring about; [VP2A,C] gather, be forming: *Those boys are ~ing mischief. A storm is ~ing,* gathering force. *There's trouble ~ing between them,* They are likely to quarrel. □ *n* result of ~ing; liquid made by ~ing: *the best ~s of beer; a good, strong ~ of tea.* **~er** *n* person who ~s beer. **~·ery** /ˈbruərɪ/ *n* (*pl*·-ries) building in which ~ing of beer is carried on.

briar /ˈbrɑɪə(r)/ *n* **1** [U] hard wood (root of a bush) used esp for making tobacco pipes. **2** [C] pipe made of this wood. **3** = brier.

bribe /brɑɪb/ *n* [C] sth given, offered or promised to sb in order to influence or persuade him (often to do sth wrong) in favour of the giver: *offer/give/hand out/take ~s.* □ *vt* [VP6A,17,15] offer, give, a ~ to: *~ a judge/witness. The child was ~d to take the nasty medicine. He had been ~d into silence/~d to say nothing.* **bri·bable** /ˈbrɑɪbəbl/ *adj* **bri·bery** /ˈbrɑɪbərɪ/ *n* [U] giving or taking of ~s.

bric-a-brac /ˈbrɪk ə bræk/ *n* [U] bits of old furniture, china, ornaments, etc, esp old and curious, of no great value.

brick /brɪk/ *n* **1** [C,U] (usu rectangular block of) clay moulded and baked by fire or sun, used for building purposes: *a house made of red ~(s); a ~ wall.* ***drop a ~,*** (colloq) do or say sth indiscreet. ***make ~s without straw,*** attempt a difficult and fruitless task. **'~·bat** *n* piece of ~, esp as a missile: *The Minister collected a lot of ~bats,* (fig) much abuse. **'~-field, '~·kiln** *n* field, kiln, in which ~s are made. **'~·layer** *n* workman who builds with ~s. **'~·work** *n* (part of a) structure made of ~. **2** child's rectangular block (usu of wood) used for building toy houses, etc. **3** ~-shaped block of sth, e g ice-cream. **4** (colloq) generous or kind-hearted person: *You've behaved like a ~.* □ *vt* [VP15B] **~ up/in,** block (an opening) with ~s: *~ up a window.*

bri·dal /ˈbrɑɪdl/ *n* wedding-feast; wedding; (attrib)

bridges

a pontoon bridge

a trestle bridge

a Bailey bridge

an arch bridge

a suspension bridge

a cantilever bridge

of a bride or wedding: *the ~ party,* the bride and her attendants and friends.

bride /ˋbrɑɪd/ *n* woman on her wedding-day; newly married woman. ˋ**~-cake** *n* (old name for) wedding-cake.

bride·groom /ˋbrɑɪdgrum/ *n* man on his wedding-day; newly married man.

brides·maid /ˋbrɑɪdzmeɪd/ *n* girl or young unmarried woman (usu one of several) attending a bride at her wedding. Cf *best man* for the bridegroom.

bridge[1] /brɪdʒ/ *n* **1** structure of wood, stone, brickwork, steel, concrete, etc, providing a way across a river, canal, railway, etc. ˋ**~-head** *n* defensive post or area established on the enemy's side of a river, etc; (loosely) any military position occupied in the face of the enemy. ⇨ **beachhead.** **2** platform over and across the deck of a ship for the use of the captain and officers. **3** upper, bony part of the nose. **4** movable part over which the strings of a violin, etc are stretched. **5** small metal device for keeping false teeth in place, fastened to natural teeth. □ *vt* [VP6A] join by means of a ~; build a ~ over: *a bridging loan,* loan (esp from a bank) to cover a period of time, e g between the purchase of one house and the sale of another; [VP15B] (fig) overcome (obstacles, etc): *~ over difficulties.*

bridge[2] /brɪdʒ/ *n* [U] card game for four players in which one player looks on while his cards, placed face up on the table, are played by his partner. ˋ**auction ~,** in which the right to name the trumps goes to the player who undertakes to make the highest score. ˋ**contract ~,** variety of auction ~ with penalties for failure to make the score.

bridle /ˋbrɑɪdl/ *n* that part of a horse's harness that goes on its head, including the metal bit for the mouth, the straps and the reins. ⇨ the illus at **harness.** ˋ**~-path,** ˋ**~-road** *n* one fit for riders on horseback but not for cars, etc. □ *vt,vi* **1** [VP6A] put a ~ on (a horse). **2** [VP6A] (fig) control, check: *Try to ~ your passions.* **3** [VP2A,C] throw back the head and draw in the chin (showing pride, contempt, vanity, etc): *~ with anger; ~ up; ~ at sb's remarks.*

brief[1] /brif/ *adj* (of time, events, writing, speaking) lasting only for a short time: *to be ~,* to speak shortly. ***in ~,*** in a few words. ˋ**~·ly** *adv* ⇨ **brevity.**

brief[2] /brif/ *n* **1** [C] summary of the facts of a case, drawn up for a barrister: *have plenty of ~s,* (of a barrister) be busy with professional work. ***hold a ~ for (sb),*** argue in support or favour of. ***hold no ~ for,*** (fig) not be prepared to support. ˋ**~-case** *n* flat leather or plastic case, for documents, etc. **2** (also ˋ**~·ing**) information, instructions, advice, etc given in advance, e g to an aircraft crew before a combat mission. **3** (comm) instructions: *My ~ did not include the buying of new materials.* □ *vt* [VP6A] **1** instruct or employ (a barrister). **2** give a ~(2) to. ⇨ **debrief.** **3** (comm) summarize the facts, e g of a business programme: *The Chairman will ~ the Board on the most recent developments.*

briefs /brifs/ *n pl* close-fitting pants without legs, held in position by an elastic waistband.

brier, briar /ˋbrɑɪə(r)/ *n* thorn-covered bush, esp the wild rose.

brig /brɪg/ *n* two-masted ship with square sails and an extra fore-and-aft sail on the main-mast.

brig·ade /brɪˋgeɪd/ *n* **1** army unit, usu of three battalions, forming part of an army division; corresponding armoured unit. **2** organized body of persons in uniform with special duties (ˋ**fire ~**) or for giving discipline and spare-time occupation (*Boys'/Church, etc, B~*). **Briga·dier** /brɪgəˋdɪə(r)/ *n* (formerly ˈ*Brigadier*-ˋ*General*) officer commanding a ~.

brig·and /ˋbrɪgənd/ *n* member of a band of robbers, esp a band that attacks travellers in forests or mountains and lives by pillage and ransom. **~·age** /ˈbrɪgəndɪdʒ/ *n* [U] prevalence or behaviour of ~s.

brig·an·tine /ˈbrɪgəntin/ *n* = brig.

bright /braɪt/ *adj* **1** giving out or reflecting much light; shining: *Sunshine is ~. Polished steel is ~. The leaves on the trees are ~ green in spring.* **2** cheerful and happy; lit up with joy or hope: *~ faces; a ~ smile; see the ~ side of things.* **3** quick-witted, clever: *A ~ boy learns quickly.* □ *adv* (chiefly with *shine*) = ~ly. **~en** *vt,vi* [VP6A,15B,2A,C] make or become ~er or lighter, more cheerful, etc: *These flowers ~en the classroom. The sky is ~ening. His face ~ened up.* **~ly** *adv* **~·ness** *n*

brill /brɪl/ *n* flat fish like a turbot.

bril·liant /ˈbrɪlɪənt/ *adj* very bright; sparkling; splendid, causing admiration: *a week of ~ sunshine, a ~ scientist; ~ jewels.* **~·ly** *adv* **brilliance** /ˈbrɪlɪəns/, **bril·liancy** /ˈbrɪlɪənsɪ/ *nn* [U] radiance, splendour, intelligence.

bril·lian·tine /ˈbrɪlɪəntin/ *n* [U] cosmetic used to make the hair lie flat.

brim /brɪm/ *n* **1** edge of a cup, bowl, glass, etc: *full to the ~*, quite full. **2** out-turned part (rim) of a hat, that gives shade. □ *vi* (-mm-) [VP2A,C] be full to the ~. ***~ over,*** be so full that some spills over the ~; (fig) *~ming over with high spirits.* **~·ful(l)** /ˈbrɪmˈfʊl/ *adj* full to the ~: *He is ~ful of new ideas.*

brim·stone /ˈbrɪmstən/ *n* [U] (old name for) sulphur.

brindled /ˈbrɪndld/ *adj* (esp of cows and cats) brown with streaks of another colour.

brine /braɪn/ *n* [U] salt water, esp for pickling. **briny** /ˈbraɪnɪ/ *adj* salt. □ *n* **the briny,** (colloq) the sea.

bring /brɪŋ/ *vt* (*pt,pp* **brought** /brɔt/) (For uses with *adverbial particles* and *preps,* ⇨ **6** below.) **1** ⇨ take [VP6A,15B,13,12,14] ***~ (with),*** cause sb to come towards the speaker, writer, etc carrying sth or accompanying sb: *Take this empty box away and ~ me a full one. The soldiers came back ~ing ten prisoners (with them). B~ Mary to the party with you. B~ one for me. B~ me one.* **2** [VP6A, 19B,12C,14] cause to come; produce: *Spring ~s warm weather and flowers. The sad news brought tears to her eyes. His writings ~ him £700 a year. A phone call brought him hurrying to Leeds. A shower brought the players scurrying to the pavilion.* **3** [VP17A] ***~ sb/oneself to do sth,*** persuade, induce, lead: *They could not ~ themselves to believe the news. She couldn't ~ herself to speak about the matter. I wish I could ~ you to see the situation from my point of view.* **4** [VP14] (legal) start, put forward: *~ an action/charge/an accusation against sb.* **5** (phrases) *~ sb to book,* ⇨ book[1](6); *~ sth to an end,* cause it to end; *~ sth home to sb,* ⇨ home[2](2); *~ low,* reduce to a low condition; *~ sth to light,* cause it to be visible or known; *~ sth to mind; ~ sth to pass,* ⇨ pass[1](3); *~ sth into line/play,* ⇨ line[1](11), play[1](8); *~ sb to his senses,* ⇨ sense(2). **6** [VP15A] (with *adverbial particles* and *preps*):

bring about, (a) cause to happen: *~ about a war/reforms/sb's ruin.* (b) (naut) cause (a sailing-ship) to change direction: *The helmsman brought us about.*

bring back, (a) return: *Please ~ back the book tomorrow;* (with *indirect object*): *If you're going to the market, please ~ me back ten eggs.* (b) call to mind; cause to remember: *Your newsy letter brought back many memories.* (c) restore; reintroduce. ***~ back to,*** restore to: *Her stay among the mountains brought her back to health. How many MP's favour ~ing back capital punishment?*

bring down, (a) cause to fall; cause to be down: *~ down a hostile aircraft,* shoot it down; *~ down prices,* lower them; *~ down* (= overthrow) *a tyrant.* (b) continue (records, etc) up to: *a new history of Europe, brought down to modern times,* i e made up to date. (c) kill or wound: *He aimed, fired and brought down the antelope.* (d) (football) cause (an opponent) to fall by fouling; (Rugby) tackle. (e) (arith) transfer a digit from one part of a sum (from one column) to another: *~ down the next two figures.* ***~ the house down/~ down the house,*** ⇨ house(6). ***~ sb's wrath/fury on one's head,*** cause it to be aimed at oneself.

bring forth, produce (fruit); give birth to (young ones): *What will the future ~ forth?*

bring forward, (a) cause to be seen, discussed, etc: *Can you ~ forward* (= produce) *any proof of what you say? Please ~ the matter forward at the next meeting.* (b) advance: *The meeting has been brought forward from May 10 to May 3,* is to be a week earlier. ⇨ postpone. (c) (abbr **b/f**) (book-keeping) carry the total of a column of figures at the foot of one page to the top of the next page.

bring in, (a) yield; (of capital, investments, etc) produce as profit: *His orchards ~ (him) in £200 a year. He does odd jobs that ~ him in ten to twelve pounds a month. This investment ~s (me) in 7½ per cent.* (b) introduce: *~ in a new fashion/a new topic.* (c) introduce (legislation): *~ in a Bill on road safety.* (d) admit (as a partner, adviser, etc): *They've brought in experts to advise on the scheme.* (e) (of the police) arrest; ~ to a police station for questioning, etc: *Two suspicious characters were brought in.* (f) (of a jury) pronounce (a verdict): *~ in a verdict of guilty.*

bring off, (a) rescue (esp from a wrecked ship): *The passengers and crew were brought off by the Deal lifeboat.* (b) carry (an enterprise) to success; manage to do sth successfully: *It was a difficult task but we brought it off,* we succeeded.

bring on, (a) lead to, (help to) produce: *He was out all day in the rain and this brought on a bad cold.* (b) cause to develop or advance: *The fine weather is ~ing the crops on nicely.* (c) help (a pupil, learner, etc) to develop: *The coach is ~ing on some youngsters in the reserve team.*

bring out, (a) cause to appear, show clearly: *~ out the meaning of a passage of prose. The sunshine will ~ out the apple blossom,* cause it to open. (b) publish (a book, etc): *When are the publishers ~ing out his new book?* (c) introduce (a girl) to fashionable society: *Mrs X is ~ing out her youngest daughter this season.* (d) help to lose shyness or reserve: *She's a nice girl, but needs a lot of ~ing out.* (e) call forth (a quality): *Danger ~s out the best in him.* (f) cause to strike: *The shop-stewards brought out the foundrymen.*

bring over, (esp) convert (sb) (*to* a different way of thinking, to a cause, etc).

bring round, (a) cause (sb) to regain consciousness after fainting: *Several girls fainted in the heat but they were soon brought round.* (b) convert to one's views, etc: *He wasn't keen on the plan, but we managed to ~ him round.* (c) (naut) make boat face the opposite way: *B~ her* (i e the boat) *round into the wind.* **~ round to,** direct (discussion, etc) to sth new: *He brought the conversation round to his favourite subject.*

bring through, save (sb who is ill): *He was very ill but good doctors and careful nursing brought him through,* restored him to health.

bring to, (a) = ~ round(a): *They brought the girl to with smelling salts. They brought her to.* (b) (naut) (cause to) stop: *The ship was brought to,* e g by the firing of a gun across her bows. *The ship brought to,* came to a stop.

bring under, (a) subdue; discipline: *The rebels were quickly brought under.* (b) include (within a category): *The various points to be dealt with can be brought under three main heads.*

bring up, (a) educate; rear: *She has brought up five children. All children should be brought up to respect their parents and teachers. If children are badly brought up they behave badly.* (b) vomit: *~ up one's dinner.* (c) call attention to: *These are facts that can always be brought up against you,* used as evidence against you. *These are matters that you can ~ up in committee.* (d) (mil) summon to the front line: *We need to ~ up more tanks.* (e) ~ for trial: *He was brought up on a charge of drunken driving.* (f) cause to stop suddenly: *His remarks brought me up short/sharp/with a jerk.* **~ up the rear,** come last (in a line): *The cavalry brought up the rear of the column.* (g) (older use, esp of a ship) end a journey: *The ship brought up at a port in Greece.*

brink /brɪŋk/ *n* **1** upper edge of a steep place, a sharp slope, etc; border (of water, esp when deep): *He stood shivering on the ~,* hesitating to plunge into the water. *He's on the ~ of the grave,* will die soon. **2** (fig) edge of sth unknown, dangerous or exciting: *on the ~ of war/ruin/an exciting discovery.* **ˈ~·man·ship** /ˈbrɪŋkmənʃɪp/ *n* pursuit of a dangerous policy to the limits of safety.

briny ⇨ brine.

bri·oche /ˈbrioʃ *US:* -əʊʃ/ *n* (F) piece of pastry baked in a circular shape.

bri·quette, bri·quet /brɪˈket/ *n* block (brick- or egg-shaped) of compressed coal-dust.

brisk /brɪsk/ *adj* (of persons and movement) active; lively; quick-moving: *a ~ walk; a ~ walker; at a ~ pace; a ~ demand for cotton goods. Trade is ~.* **~·ly** *adv*

bris·ket /ˈbrɪskɪt/ *n* [U] breast of animals (sometimes eaten as a joint of meat).

bristle /ˈbrɪsl/ *n* one of the short stiff hairs on an animal; one of the short stiff hairs in a brush: *a toothbrush with stiff ~s.* □ *vi* **1 ~ (up),** [VP2A,C] (of hair) stand up, rise on end: *The dog was angry and ~d up/its hair ~d.* **2** [VP2A,C] (fig) show rage, indignation, etc: *~ with anger.* **3 ~ with,** have in large numbers (sth difficult, sth suggesting ~s): *The battle-front ~d with bayonets. The problem ~s with difficulties.* **brist·ly** /ˈbrɪslɪ/ *adj* like ~s; full of ~s; (of hair, etc) rough and coarse: *She doesn't like his bristly moustache. What a bristly, unshaven chin!*

Brit·ain /ˈbrɪtn/ *n* (also **ˈGreat ˈB~**) England, Wales and Scotland; *North B~,* Scotland. **Bri·tan·nic** /brɪˈtænɪk/ *adj* of B~ (chiefly in *Her/His Britannic Majesty*).

Brit·ish /ˈbrɪtɪʃ/ *adj* **1** of the ancient Britons. **2** of Great Britain, the British Commonwealth or its inhabitants: *the B~,* B~ people; *B~ citizenship; a Jamaican with a B~ passport.* **~er** *n*

Briton /ˈbrɪtn/ *n* **1** one of the native inhabitants of S Britain at the time of the Roman invasion about 2 000 years ago. **2** (liter) native of Britain.

brittle /ˈbrɪtl/ *adj* hard but easily broken (e g coal, ice, glass): (fig) *He has a ~ temper,* quickly loses his temper.

broach[1] /brəʊtʃ/ *vt* [VP6A] make a hole in (a cask of liquor) and put in a tap in order to draw the wine, etc; (fig) begin discussion of (a topic).

broach[2] /brəʊtʃ/ *vi,vt* [VP2C,15B] **~ to,** (naut) veer or cause (a ship) to veer so that its side is presented to the wind and waves.

broad[1] /brɔd/ *adj* **1** wide, large across: *The river grows ~er as it nears the sea.* **~ in the beam,** ⇨ beam(2). **2** (after a phrase indicating width) in breadth, from side to side: *a river fifty feet ~.* **3** extending in various or all directions: *the ~ ocean; ~ lands.* **4** full and complete. **in ~ daylight,** when it is unmistakably light: *a bank raid in ~ daylight.* **give sb a ~ hint,** a strong, unmistakable one. **5** general, not minute or detailed: *a ~ distinction.* **in ~ outline,** without details. **6** (of the mind and ideas) liberal; not kept within narrow limits: *a man of ~ views,* a tolerant man. **ˈ~-ˈminded** /-ˈmaɪndɪd/ *adj* willing to listen sympathetically to the views of others even though one cannot agree with them; having a liberal and tolerant mind. **7** (of speech) strongly marked, showing that the speaker is from a definite part of the country: *~ Scots; a ~ accent.* **8** improper; coarse: *the ~ humour of Rabelais.* **9** (phrase) ***It's as ~ as it is long,*** It's all the same, however you view the problem. **10** (compounds, etc) **ˈ~ bean** *n* the common flattened variety, growing in large pods. **B~ Church** *n* used of churchmen who do not insist upon dogma and doctrine.

broad[2] /brɔd/ *n* the ~ part (*of* sth): *the ~ of the back.* **the B~s** *n pl* name used of wide stretches of water in East Anglia (Norfolk), used for yachting holidays and barge traffic. **~·ly** *adv*: *~ly speaking,* speaking in a general way, without going into detail. **~·ness** *n* = breadth (the usu word). **~en** /ˈbrɔdn/ *vt,vi* [VP6A,15B,2A,C] ***~en (out),*** make or become ~(er): *His face ~ened (out) into a grin.*

broad·cast /ˈbrɔdkɑst *US:* -kæst/ *vt,vi* (*pt,pp* broadcast) **1** [VP6A] send out in all directions, esp by radio or TV: *~ the news/a speech/a concert.* **2** [VP2A] speak, sing, perform music, etc for ~ing: *The Prime Minister will ~ this evening.* **3** [VP6A,2A] sow (seed) by scattering it, not by sowing it in drills, etc. □ *n* (often attrib) ~ing; sth ~: *today's ~; a ~ of a football match.* ⇨ telecast. □ *adv* by ~ing: *sow seed ~.* **~·ing** *n, adj*: *the British B~ing Corporation,* the B B C; *a ~ing station.*

broad·cloth /ˈbrɔdkloθ/ *n* [U] fine, smooth, double-width black cloth, formerly used for men's clothes.

broad·sheet /ˈbrɔdʃit/ *n* popular ballad or tract printed on one side only of a large sheet of paper (as formerly sold in the streets).

broad·side /ˈbrɔdsaɪd/ *n* [C] **1** the whole of a ship's side above the water; (the firing on the same target of) all the guns on one side of a ship; (fig) strong attack of any kind made at one time against one person or group. **2 ~ on (to),** (of a ship) with one side presented to or facing: *a collision ~ on,* so that the ship's side collides with sth.

broad·ways, broad·wise /ˋbrɔdweɪz, -waɪz/ *adv* in the direction of the breadth.

bro·cade /brəˋkeɪd/ *n* [C,U] woven material richly ornamented with designs (e g in raised gold or silver thread). □ *vt* [VP6A] decorate (cloth) with raised patterns.

broc·coli /ˋbrɒkəlɪ/ *n* [C] hardy kind of cauliflower with numerous white or purple sprouts (flower-heads), each like a small cauliflower.

bro·chure /ˋbrəʊʃʊə(r) *US:* brəʊˋʃʊər/ *n* short, usu descriptive, printed article in a paper cover; pamphlet: *travel/holiday ~s.*

brogue[1] /brəʊg/ *n* strong, thick-soled, usu ornamented shoe for country wear.

brogue[2] /brəʊg/ *n* provincial way of speaking, esp the Irish way of speaking English.

broil[1] /brɔɪl/ *vt, vi* [VP6A,2A] cook, be cooked, by direct contact with fire or on a gridiron; grill; (fig) be very hot: *a ~ing day; sit ~ing in the sun.* **~er** *n* bird, e g a chicken, killed at the age of 10 to 12 weeks and suitable for being ~ed or roasted, esp one reared in a shed or concrete building (and contrasted with a free-range bird), ⇨ battery(6).

broil[2] /brɔɪl/ *n* [C] (old use) quarrel; noisy argument. **~er** *n* quarrelsome fellow.

broke /brəʊk/ *pt* of break; old *pp* of break. ***(stony/flat) ~,*** (sl) penniless.

bro·ken /ˋbrəʊkən/ *pp* of break: *a ~ marriage,* one that has failed; *a ~ home,* one in which the parents have separated or are divorced, so that the children lack proper care, security, etc; ~ (= imperfect) *English; a ~ man,* a man reduced to despair; ~ (= uneven) *ground;* ~ (= disturbed, intermittent) *sleep;* ˌ~-ˋ*hearted,* crushed by grief.

bro·ker /ˋbrəʊkə(r)/ *n* **1** (**ˋstock-~**), person who buys and sells (esp business shares, bonds, etc) for others. **2** official licensed to sell the goods of sb unable to pay debts. **~·age** /ˋbrəʊkərɪdʒ/ *n* [U] ~'s commission for services.

brolly /ˋbrɒlɪ/ *n* (colloq) umbrella.

bro·mide /ˋbrəʊmaɪd/ *n* **1** [U] chemical compound, e g potassium ~, esp as used in medicine to calm the nerves. **2** [C] (colloq) trite remark; dull, tiresome or boring person.

bro·mine /ˋbrəʊmin/ *n* [U] non-metallic element (symbol **Br**), compounds of which are used in photographic and other chemicals.

bron·chi /ˋbrɒŋkaɪ/ *n pl* (*sing* bron chus /-kəs/) the branches into which the windpipe divides before entering the lungs, also called bronchial tubes. ⇨ the illus at respiratory. **~al** /ˋbrɒŋkɪəl/ *adj* of or affecting the ~: *bronchial asthma.* **bron·chi·tic** /brɒŋˋkɪtɪk/ *adj* suffering from, prone to, bronchitis. **bron·chi·tis** /brɒŋˋkaɪtɪs/ *n* inflammation of the mucous membrane of the ~.

bronco /ˋbrɒŋkəʊ/ *n* (*pl* -cos) wild or half-tamed horse of Western N America.

bronze /brɒnz/ *n* **1** [U] alloy of copper and tin: *a ~ statue; a statue in ~.* **the ˋB~ Age,** period when men used tools and weapons made of ~ (between the Stone Age and the Iron Age). **2** [U] colour of ~, reddish brown. **3** [C] work of art, e g a vase, made of ~: *a fine collection of ~s and ivories.* □ *vt, vi* [VP6A,2A] make or become ~ colour: *faces ~d by the sun and wind.*

brooch /brəʊtʃ/ *n* ornamental pin for fastening or wearing on part of a woman's dress.

brood /brud/ *n* all the young birds hatched at one time in a nest; family of other egg-produced animals; (hum) young family of human beings. ˋ**~-hen** *n* hen for breeding. ˋ**~-mare** *n* mare for breeding. □ *vi* [VP2A,C] **1** (of a bird) sit on eggs to hatch them. **2** [VP3A] ~ ***(on/over),*** (fig) think about (troubles, etc) for a long time: *~ing over/on his misfortunes. She sat there ~ing on whether life was worth living.* **~y** *adj* (of hens) wanting to ~; (colloq, of women) feeling the desire to have children; (fig, of persons) moody; depressed.

brook[1] /brʊk/ *n* small stream.

brook[2] /brʊk/ *vt* [VP6A,B] (usu in neg and interr) put up with; tolerate: *He cannot ~ interference/being interfered with.*

broom /brum/ *n* **1** shrub with yellow or white flowers growing on sandy banks, etc. **2** long-handled implement for sweeping floors, etc. ***a new ~,*** (esp) a newly appointed official (who gets rid of old methods, traditions, etc): (prov) *A NEW SWEEPS CLEAN.* ˋ**~·stick** *n* handle (on which witches were said to ride through the air).

Bros ⇨ App 2.

broth /brɒθ/ *n* [U] water in which meat has been boiled; this, flavoured and thickened with vegetables, etc, served as soup.

brothel /ˋbrɒθl/ *n* house at which prostitutes may be visited.

brother /ˋbrʌðə(r)/ *n* **1** son of the same parents as another person: *my elder/younger ~; the ~s Smith, the Smith ~s; Smith Brothers* or (comm style) *Smith Bros.* ˋ**~-in-law** /ˋbrʌðər ɪn lɔ/ *n* (*pl* ~s-in-law) ~ of one's husband or wife; husband of one's sister. **2** person united to others by membership of the same society, profession, etc; fellow member of a socialist organization, trade union, etc: (esp attrib) *a ~ doctor; ~s in arms,* soldiers who are serving or have served together; *~ officers,* in the same regiment. **3** (*pl* brethren /ˋbreðrən/) fellow member of a religious society. **B~,** form of address: *B~ Luke.* **4** official of certain guilds and companies. ˋ**~·hood** /-hʊd/ *n* **1** [U] feeling of ~ for ~. **2** [C] (members of an) association of men with common interests and aims, esp a religious society or socialist organization. ˋ**~·ly** *adj* of or like a ~('s): *~ly affection.*

brougham /ˋbruəm/ *n* (19th c) four-wheeled closed carriage drawn by one horse.

brought *pt, pp* of bring.

brou·haha /ˋbruhɑhɑ/ *n* (colloq) fuss; excitement.

brow /braʊ/ *n* **1** (usu *pl*; also ˋ**eye·~**) arch of hair above the eye: *knit one's ~s,* frown. **2** forehead. ⇨ high~[1](12), low~(13). **3** top of a slope; steep slope; overhanging edge.

brow·beat /ˋbraʊbit/ *vt* (*pt* browbeat, *pp* browbeaten) [VP6A,14] ~ ***(into doing sth),*** intimidate by shouting or looking stern at; bully: *~ sb into doing sth; a poor, ~en little woman.*

brown /braʊn/ *adj, n* colour of toasted bread, or coffee mixed with milk: *~ bread,* made with wholemeal flour; ~ paper, coarse kind used for parcels, etc; *~ sugar,* half refined. ***in a ~ study,*** deep in thought; in a reverie. ˋ**~·stone** *n* [U] kinds of reddish-brown sandstone used for building. □ *vt, vi* [VP6A,2A] make or become ~. ˌ***~ed*** ˋ***off,*** (sl) bored; fed up.

brownie /ˋbraʊnɪ/ *n* **1** small, good-natured fairy or elf. **2** (GB) junior member (age 8 to 11) of the Girl Guides.

browse /braʊz/ *vi* [VP2A,C] **1** feed, as animals do (on grass, etc): *cattle browsing in the fields.* **2** read (parts of a book or books) without any definite plan, for interest or enjoyment: *browsing among*

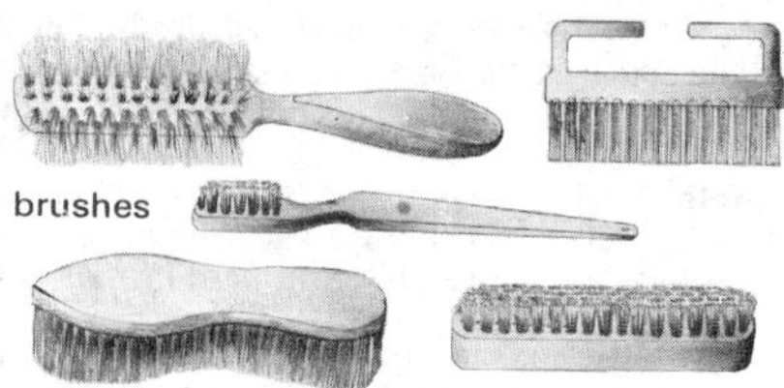

books in the public library. □ *n* (act, period, of) browsing: *have a good* ~.

bruin /ˈbruɪn/ *n* (pop name, e g in fairy tales, for) bear.

bruise /bruz/ *n* injury by a blow or knock to the body, or to a fruit, so that the skin is discoloured but not broken: *covered with* ~*s after falling off his bicycle.* □ *vt,vi* **1** [VP6A] cause a ~ or ~s to; batter, make dents in (wood or metal): *He fell and* ~*d his leg. Pack the peaches carefully so that they won't get* ~*d.* **2** [VP2A] show the effects of a blow or knock: *A child's flesh* ~*s easily.* **bruiser** *n* tough, brutal boxer.

bruit /brut/ *vt* [VP15B] (old use) spread (a rumour or report): ~ *it abroad*, spread the news everywhere.

brunch /brʌntʃ/ *n* late morning meal instead of breakfast and lunch.

bru·nette /bruˈnet/ *n* woman (of one of the white races) with dark skin and dark-brown or black hair.

brunt /brʌnt/ *n* chief stress or strain: *bear the* ~ *of an attack. The main* ~ *of their attack fell on us.*

brush[1] /brʌʃ/ *n* **1** implement of bristles, hair, wire, etc fastened in wood, bone, or other material, used for scrubbing, sweeping, cleaning (e g *ˈtooth*~, *ˈnail*~), or tidying the hair (*ˈhair*~); tuft of hair, etc set in a handle, used by painters and artists: *a paint-brush.* **2** (act of) using a ~: *He gave his clothes a good* ~, used a ~ on them. ⇨ also *ˈ*~*-up* at **brush**[2](**1**). **3** fox's tail. **4** [U] rough low-growing bushes; undergrowth: *a* ~ *fire.* ⇨ **bush**(**2**). **5** short, sharp fight or encounter: *a* ~ *with the enemy.* **ˈ~·wood** *n* [U] = brush(4). **ˈ~·work** *n* artist's style of using a paint-~.

brush[2] /brʌʃ/ *vt,vi* **1** [VP6A,15B,22] use a brush on; clean, polish, make tidy or smooth: ~ *your hat/clothes/shoes/hair/teeth;* ~ *sth clean;* remove with a brush: ~ *up the dust.* ***~ sth away/off,*** remove with a ~: *He* ~*ed away a fly from his nose,* used his hand to make the fly go away. *She* ~*ed the crumbs off the tablecloth.* ***~ sth aside/away,*** (fig) pay no or little attention to (difficulties, objections, etc). ***~ off,*** (colloq) reject, jilt; dismiss curtly: *He tries to get the girl to go out with him, but she always* ~*es him off.* Hence, **ˈ~-off** *n* (colloq) rejection or dismissal: *She gave him the* ~*-off.* ***~ up,*** study or practise (sth) in order to get back skill that has been lost: *If you're going to France you'd better* ~ *up your French.* Hence, **ˈ~-up** *n* act of ~ing: *Give your French a* ~*-up. Wash and* ~*-up, fivepence,* e g in a public lavatory. **2** [VP2A,C,6A] touch when passing: *He* ~*ed past/by/against me in a rude way. The leaves of the trees* ~*ed my face as I ran through the forest.* **3** [VP2C] ***~ off,*** come off as the result of being ~ed: *The mud will* ~ *off when it dries.*

brusque /brusk/ *adj* (of speech or behaviour) rough and abrupt. **~·ly** *adj* **~·ness** *n*

Brus·sels /ˈbrʌslz/ *n* of or from ~, Belgium: ~ *lace/carpets.* ˈ~ **ˈsprouts,** (plants with) buds growing thickly on the stem of a cabbage-like plant. ⇨ the illus at vegetable.

brutal /ˈbrutl/ *adj* savage; cruel. **~·ly** /-tlɪ/ *adv*

bru·tal·ity /bruˈtælətɪ/ *n* [U] cruelty; savagery; [C] cruel or savage act. **ˈ~·ize** *vt* [VP6A] make ~: *Years of warfare had* ~*ized the troops.*

brute /brut/ *n* **1** animal (except man). **2** stupid, animal-like or cruel person. **3** (attrib) animal-like; cruel and unthinking; unconscious or unreasoning; merely material: ~ *force/strength;* ~ *matter.*

brut·ish /ˈbrutɪʃ/ *adj* of or like a ~: *brutish appetites.* **ˈbrut·ish·ly** *adv*

bubble /ˈbʌbl/ *n* **1** (in air) floating ball formed of liquid and containing air or gas: *soap* ~*s; blowing* ~*s.* **2** (in liquid) ball of air or gas that rises to the surface, e g in boiling water, in sparkling wines. **3** air-filled cavity in a solidified liquid, e g glass. **4** (fig) visionary plan; idea, hope, etc that is not realized: *His* ~ *has burst.* **5** ˈ~ **car** *n* small car with a transparent dome as roof. ˈ~ **gum** *n* chewing gum which can be blown into bubbles on the lips. □ *vi* [VP2A,C] send up ~s; rise in ~s; make the sound of ~s: *The water* ~*d up through the sand. She was bubbling over with joy/high spirits/laughter.* **bub·bly** /ˈbublɪ/ *adj* full of ~s. □ *n* (hum) champagne.

bu·bonic plague /bjuˈbonɪk ˈpleɪg/ *n* plague that spreads quickly; it is spread by rats, and marked by chills, fevers and swelling in the armpits and groin.

buc·ca·neer /ˌbʌkəˈnɪə(r)/ *n* pirate; unscrupulous adventurer.

buck[1] /bʌk/ *n* **1** male of a deer, hare or rabbit. ⇨ doe. **ˈ~·skin** *n* [U] soft leather made from deerskin or goatskin, used for gloves, breeches, etc. **ˈ~·shot** *n* [U] large-size shot. **ˈ~·tooth** *n* (*pl* **-teeth**) (usu upper) tooth that projects. **2** (attrib) male.

buck[2] /bʌk/ *vi,vt* **1** [VP2A] (of a horse) jump up with the four feet together and the back arched; [VP6A] throw (the rider) to the ground by doing this. **2** ***~ (up),*** [VP2C, esp in the *imperative*] (colloq) make more vigorous or cheerful, ready for greater effort: *The good news* ~*ed us all up. We were greatly* ~*ed (up) by the news.*

buck[3] /bʌk/ *n* (sl) US dollar.

buck[4] /bʌk/ *n* ***pass the ~ (to sb),*** (sl) shift the responsibility (to). ***The ~ stops here,*** The responsibility cannot be shifted further.

buck·board /ˈbʌkbɔd/ *n* (US) four-wheeled open carriage with a single seat on a board connecting the front and rear axles.

bucket[1] /ˈbʌkɪt/ *n* **1** vessel of wood, metal, canvas, plastic, etc for holding or carrying water, milk, etc; (also **ˈ~·ful** /-fʊl/) the amount a ~ holds: *The rain was coming down in* ~*s,* was very heavy. **2** scoop of a dredging machine, grain-elevator, etc. ˈ~ **seat** *n* (in a car or aircraft) seat with a rounded back for one person (contrasted with a *bench* seat). **ˈ~-shop** *n* office or shop where persons who are not members of the Stock Exchange trade in stocks for gambling and speculating.

bucket[2] /ˈbʌkɪt/ *vi* ride a horse hard.

buckle /ˈbʌkl/ *n* **1** metal, plastic or bone fastener, with one or more spikes made to go through a hole in a strap, etc, to keep sth in place. **2** ornamental clasp on a shoe. □ *vt,vi* **1** [VP6A,15] ***~ (on),*** fasten with a ~: ~ *a belt;* ~ *on a sword/one's* *armour*. **2** [VP2C] (of a shoe, belt, etc) fasten (in a certain way). **3** [VP2C] **~ *to/down to*** (*work, etc*), begin (work) in earnest: *~ to a task. The sooner he ~s down to it, the better.* **4** [VP2A] (of metal work, etc) bend, become twisted, crumple up from strain or heat.

buck·ler /ˋbʌklə(r)/ *n* small round shield, usu held by a handle or worn on the arm.

buck·ram /ˋbʌkrəm/ *n* [U] stiff, rough cloth (esp as used for binding books).

buck·shee /ˈbʌkˋʃi/ *adj, adv* (GB sl) free; without charge.

buck·wheat /ˋbʌkwit *US:* -hwit/ *n* [U] (plant with) small triangular seed used for feeding horses and poultry. **ˋ~ flour,** flour made from this grain, used in US for breakfast cakes.

bu·colic /bjuˋkolɪk/ *adj* of country life and farming, esp of shepherds: *~ verse.* **bu·col·ics** *n pl* pastoral poems.

bud /bʌd/ *n* **1** leaf, flower or branch, at the beginning of its growth. ***in bud,*** having buds or sending out buds: *The trees are in bud.* ***nip sth in the bud,*** put an end to sth, e g a plot, while it is in the beginning stage. **2** partly opened flower. ⇨ the illus at tree. □ *vi* (-dd-) put out buds. **bud·ding** *adj* beginning to develop: *a budding lawyer/poet.*

Bud·dhism /ˋbʊdɪzm/ *n* the religion founded by Gautama /ˋgaʊtəmə/ or Siddhartha /sɪˋdɑtə/ Buddha /ˋbʊdə/ in N India, in about the 6th c. **Bud·dhist** /ˋbʊdɪst/ *n* follower of Buddha.

representations of Gautama Buddha

buddy /ˋbʌdɪ/ *n* (*pl* -dies) (sl, as a familiar form of address) chum; mate.

budge¹ /bʌdʒ/ *vt,vi* [VP6A, usu in *neg* and with *can, could*; VP2A,C, usu in *neg* with *won't, wouldn't*] (cause to) move very little, make the slightest movement; (fig) (cause to) change a position or attitude: *I can't ~ it. I won't ~ an inch.*

budge², budgie /bʌdʒ, ˋbʌdʒɪ/ *nn* (colloq *abbr*) budgerigar.

bud·geri·gar /ˋbʌdʒərɪgɑ(r)/ *n* Australian lovebird; kind of parakeet.

budget /ˋbʌdʒɪt/ *n* [C] **1** estimate of probable future income and expenditure, esp that made by the Chancellor of the Exchequer in the House of Commons; similar estimate made by a business company, society, private person, etc: *introduce/open the ~* (in the House of Commons). **ˋ~ account,** account with a bank maintained by monthly transfers from a current account, so that the Bank may pay regularly recurring expenses, e g gas, electricity, rates. **ˋ~ plan,** system of buying goods in (large) shops by making regular monthly payments to them. **2** collection of news, letters, etc. □ *vi* [VP3A] **~ *for,*** allow or arrange for (in a ~): *~ for the coming year.* **~·ary** /ˋbʌdʒɪtərɪ *US:* -terɪ/ *adj* of a ~.

buff /bʌf/ *n* [U] **1** thick, strong, soft leather; dull yellow colour. **2** the bare skin, esp in: *stripped to the ~,* without clothing. □ *vt* polish (metal) with ~.

buf·falo /ˋbʌfləʊ/ *n* (*pl* -los, US also -loes) kinds of ox in India, Asia, Europe and Africa; (incorrectly for) N American bison: *a herd of sixty ~/~es.*

buf·fer¹ /ˋbʌfə(r)/ *n* apparatus (either spring-loaded or hydraulic) for lessening the effect of a blow or collision, e g on a railway engine or van. **~ state,** state situated between two or more powerful states, lessening the risk of war between them.

buf·fer² /ˋbʌfə(r)/ *n* (sl, usu **old ~**) old-fashioned or foolish man.

buf·fet¹ /ˋbʊfeɪ *US:* bəˋfeɪ/ *n* counter where food and drink may be bought and consumed, e g in a railway station or on a train; sideboard or table from which food and drink are served, e g in a hotel; *cold ~,* (on a menu) cold cooked meat; *~ supper,* meal served to guests who do not sit at a table.

buf·fet² /ˋbʌfɪt/ *n* blow, generally one given with the hand; (fig) misfortune; blow delivered by fate. □ *vt,vi* **1** [VP6A] give a ~ or ~s to: *flowers ~ed by rain and wind; ~ed by the waves/misfortunes.* **2** [VP6A,3C] (rare) contend (*with*): *~ (with) the waves.*

buf·foon /bəˋfun *US:* bʌˋfun/ *n* clown; jester. ***play the ~,*** do and say foolish things to amuse others. **~·ery** /-nərɪ/ *n* [U] clowning; clown-like behaviour; (in *pl*) rough jokes and actions.

bug /bʌg/ *n* **1** small, flat, ill-smelling, blood-sucking insect that infests dirty houses and beds. ⇨ the illus at insect. **2** (esp US) any small insect (ˋ*harvest bug,* ˋ*mealy-bug,* etc). **ˋbug-hunter** *n* (colloq) entomologist. **3** (colloq) germ; virus infection: *You've got the Asian 'flu bug.* **4** (sl) ***big bug,*** important person. **5** (sl) defect; snag; (source of) malfunctioning, e g in a computer. **6** small hidden microphone (for listening to conversations, etc). □ *vt* (-gg-) [VP6A] **1** (colloq) use electronic devices (in a room, etc) in order to listen secretly to conversations: ˋ*bugging devices.* **2** (US colloq) cause to make mistakes. **3** (US sl) annoy: *That man really bugs me.*

buga·boo /ˈbʌgəˋbu/ *n* source of annoyance or fear.

bug·bear /ˋbʌgbeə(r)/ *n* sth feared or disliked, with or without good reason: *the ~ we all face today; the ~ of rising prices.*

bug·ger /ˋbʌgə(r)/ *n* **1** (legal) sodomite. **2** ⚠ used as a vulgar term of abuse: *You silly ~!* □ *vt,vi* ⚠ **1** [VP6A] commit ~y with. **2** [VP2C] **~ *off,*** go away! **~y** *n* sodomy.

buggy /ˋbʌgɪ/ *n* (*pl* -gies) **1** light carriage, pulled by one horse, for one or two persons: *the horse and ~ age,* period before motor vehicles came into use. **2** ˋ*beach ~,* ⇨ beach. **3** (US) baby carriage.

bugle /ˋbjugl/ *n* musical wind instrument of copper or brass (like a small trumpet but without keys or valves), used for military signals. ⇨ the illus at brass. **bugler** *n* ~ blower.

bugles /ˋbjuglz/ *n pl* tube-shaped glass or plastic beads stitched on a dress or ornament.

buhl /bul/ *n* [U] cabinet work (furniture) inlaid with brass, tortoise-shell and ivory: *a ~ cabinet.*

build¹ /bɪld/ *vt,vi* (*pt,pp* built /bɪlt/) **1** [VP6A

12B,13B,14] **~ sth (out of/from),** make by putting parts, materials, etc together (with what is made as the direct object): *~ a house/railway. Some birds ~ nests out of twigs. The school is built of wood. Mr Green is ~ing a garage for me/is ~ing me a garage.* **2** [VP14] **~ sth into,** put parts together to form a whole (with the material as the direct object): *He has built these scraps of metal into a very strange-looking sculpture.* **3** [VP15B,14] **~ in/into,** make (sth) form a firm and permanent part of sth larger; make (sth) a fixture: *Ask the carpenter to ~ in some cupboards/to ~ some cupboards into the walls.* Hence, **'built-'in**: *a bedroom with built-in wardrobes; a radio with a built-in aerial.* **4** [VP15B,2C] **~ up, (a)** accumulate; form a block: *Traffic is ~ing up* (= The number of vehicles is increasing steadily) *along the roads to the coast.* **(b)** come together (so as to increase or intensify): *One day your books will ~ up into a library. Their pressure on the enemy is ~ing up.* **~ sb/sth up, (a)** try to increase sb's reputation (through publicity, praise): *Don't ~ me up too much. I may disappoint you.* **(b)** make, acquire, steadily and gradually: *He has built up a good business/a good reputation for his goods. He went for an ocean voyage and soon built up* (= strengthened) *his health.* **(c)** (passive and as *adj*) become covered with buildings: *The district has been built up since I was last there.* Hence, **'built-up areas. (d)** bring together (so as to increase or intensify): *They are ~ing up their military forces.* Hence, **'~-up** *n* **(a)** increase: *a ~-up of forces/pressure.* **(b)** accumulation: *a ~-up of traffic.* **(c)** flattering publicity, etc: *the ~-up of a politician's image. The press gave him a tremendous ~-up.* **5** [VP15B,3A] **~ (up)on,** base (hopes, etc) on; rely on: *Don't ~ too many hopes upon his helping you. Don't ~ on his promises.* **6** (*pp* with *advv*): *a well-built man,* a man whose body has good proportions; *solidly built,* having a solid frame(work). **~er** *n* person who ~s, esp a contractor for ~ing houses; (fig) person who creates: *a great empire ~er.*

build² /bɪld/ *n* [U] general shape or structure: (of the human body) general characteristics of shape and proportion: *a man of powerful ~. We are of the same ~.*

build·ing /'bɪldɪŋ/ *n* **1** [U] (art of) constructing houses, etc: *~ operations; ~ materials; ~ land,* (to be) used for houses, etc. **'~ estate,** an area of land on which houses, etc are being built. **'~-society,** organization for making loans to members who wish to build or buy a house, using funds supplied by its members. **2** [U] house or other structure: *Houses, schools, churches, hotels, factories and sheds are all ~s.*

bulb /bʌlb/ *n* **1** almost round, thick, underground stem, sending roots downwards and leaves upwards, of such plants as the lily, onion, tulip. **2** sth like a ~ in shape, esp an electric lamp or the swollen end of a glass tube, e g in a thermometer.

bul·bous /'bʌlbəs/ *adj* of or having or like a ~; growing from a ~.

bul·bul /'bʊlbʊl/ *n* (in Persian poetry) songbird (perhaps a nightingale).

bulge /bʌldʒ/ *n* [C] irregular swelling; place where a swelling or curve shows; temporary increase in volume or numbers; (mil) salient. □ *vi,vt* [VP2A,C,6A] (cause to) swell beyond the usual size; curve outwards: *He ~d his pockets with apples. His pockets were bulging with apples. He ~d his cheeks.*

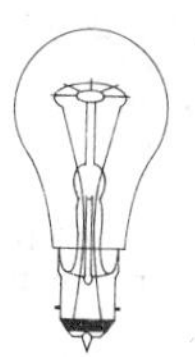

bulbs

bulk /bʌlk/ *n* [U] quantity, volume, esp when large. **in ~, (a)** in large amounts: *buy in ~; tankers carry petroleum in ~.* **(b)** loose, not packed in boxes, tins, etc. **~ buying,** purchase at one time of a very large quantity of goods, e g by the state during a war. **the ~ of,** the greater part or number of: *He left the ~ of his property to his brother.* □ *vi* **~ large,** appear large or important. **~y** *adj* taking up much space; clumsy to move or carry.

bulk·head /'bʌlkhed/ *n* [C] water-tight division or dividing wall in a ship; similar division in a tunnel, etc.

bull¹ /bʊl/ *n* **1** ⇨ the illus at **domestic.** uncastrated male of any animal of the ox family (⇨ **cow**): *a man with a neck like a ~,* with a thick neck. **a ~ in a china shop,** person who is rough and clumsy where skill and care are needed. **take the ~ by the horns,** meet a difficulty boldly instead of trying to escape from it. **'~-fight** *n* fight between men and a ~ for public entertainment, as in Spain. **'~-fighter** *n* **'~-ring** *n* arena for ~fights. **'~-shit** *n* ⚠ (vulg sl) nonsense; foolish and exaggerated talk. **2** male of the whale, elephant and other large animals. **3** (Stock Exchange; ⇨ **bear¹(4)**) person who tries to raise prices with a view to selling at a profit: *'~ market,* with rising prices. **4** (compounds) **'~-dog** *n* **(a)** large, powerful breed of dog, with a short, thick neck, noted for its strong grip and its courage. ⇨ the illus at **dog. (b)** university proctor's attendant. **'~-doze** *vt* [VP6A,14] **(a)** remove earth, flatten obstacles with a ~dozer. **(b) ~doze sb into doing sth,** force sb to do sth by using one's strength or by intimidating him. **~-dozer** /'bʊldəʊzə(r)/ *n* powerful tractor that pushes a broad steel blade or sheet in front, used for levelling land, shifting large quantities of earth, etc. **'~-finch** *n* small songbird with rounded beak and brightly coloured feathers. **'~-frog** *n* large American species of frog. **'~-'headed** *adj* clumsy, impetuous, obstinate. **'~'s-eye** *n* centre of target (for archers, etc). ⇨ the illus at **archery. '~-'terrier** *n* cross between a ~dog and a terrier.

a bulldozer

bull² /bʊl/ *n* official order or announcement from the Pope.

bull³ /bʊl/ *n* (also **Irish ~**) foolish or amusing mistake in language, usu because there is a contradiction in terms (e g 'If you do not get this letter, please write and tell me'): *It's a lot of* ~, nonsense.

bull[4] /bʊl/ *n* [U] (GB army sl) (insistence upon) excessive attention to cleaning and polishing equipment, etc; unnecessary routine.

bul·let /ˈbʊlɪt/ *n* shaped piece of lead, usu coated with another metal, (to be) fired from a rifle or revolver. Cf *shells* fired from guns. ⇨ the illus at cartridge. ˈ**~-headed** /-hedɪd/ *adj* having a small, round head. ˈ**~-proof** *adj* able to stop ~s: *a ~-proof jacket.*

bull·etin /ˈbʊlətɪn/ *n* **1** official statement of news: *During the king's illness the doctors issued ~s twice a day.* **2** printed sheet with official news or announcements.

bul·lion /ˈbʊlɪən/ *n* [U] gold or silver in bulk or bars, before manufacture.

bul·lock /ˈbʊlək/ *n* castrated bull.

bully[1] /ˈbʊlɪ/ *n* (*pl* -lies) person who uses his strength or power to frighten or hurt those who are weaker. □ *vt* [VP6A,14] **~ *sb (into doing sth),*** use strength, etc in this way to persuade sb to do sth.

bully[2] /ˈbʊlɪ/ *n* [U] (also ˈ**~ beef**) tinned beef.

bully[3] /ˈbʊlɪ/ *adj* (sl) fine; excellent: *B~ for you!*

bul·rush /ˈbʊlrʌʃ/ *n* [C] (kinds of) tall rush or reed with a thick velvety head.

bul·wark /ˈbʊlwək/ *n* **1** wall, esp one built of earth, against attack; earthwork; (fig) sth that defends or protects: *Law is the ~ of society,* gives us security. **2** (usu *pl*) wall round (esp a sailing) ship's deck.

bum[1] /bʌm/ *n* (colloq) part of the body on which one sits; buttocks.

bum[2] /bʌm/ *n* (sl) habitual beggar or loafer. □ *adj* of poor quality; worthless. □ *vi* (-mm-) [VP2C] **~ *around,*** loaf, wander about doing nothing.

bumble·bee /ˈbʌmbl biː/ *n* large kind of hairy bee with a loud hum.

bum·boat /ˈbʌmbəʊt/ *n* (naut) small boat carrying fresh provisions to ships lying offshore.

bump /bʌmp/ *vt,vi* **1** [VP6A,14,2C,3A] **~ *against/into,*** come with a blow or knock: *The room was dark and I ~ed (my head) against the door. The blind man ~ed into me. The car ~ed against the kerb/~ed into the car in front.* **~ *against/on,*** hurt (one's head, etc) by striking it on sth. **2** [VP2C] move with a jerky, jolting motion (like a cart on a bad road): *The heavy bus ~ed along the rough mountain road.* **3** [VP15B] **~ *sb off,*** (sl) murder him. □ *adv* suddenly; violently: *Our bus ran ~ into the wall.* □ *n* **1** blow or knock; dull sound made by a blow (as when two things come together with force). **2** swelling on the body caused by such a blow; natural bulge on the skull. ⇨ phrenology. **3** swelling or irregularity on a road surface made by traffic. **4** (jolt felt in an aircraft, caused by a) sudden change in air-pressure. **~y** *adj* with many ~s: *a ~y road/ride.*

bum·per[1] /ˈbʌmpə(r)/ *n* fender (usu a horizontal bar) on a bus, motor-car, etc (front and rear), to lessen the effect of a collision; fender (on the side of a boat or ship). ⇨ the illus at motor.

bum·per[2] /ˈbʌmpə(r)/ *n* **1** glass of wine, full to the brim. **2** (attrib) sth unusually large or abundant: *~ crops; a ~ harvest; ~ edition* (of a periodical).

bump·kin /ˈbʌmpkɪn/ *n* awkward person with unpolished manners, esp from the country.

bump·tious /ˈbʌmpʃəs/ *adj* conceited; self-important: *~ officials.* **~·ly** *adv* **~·ness** *n*

bun /bʌn/ *n* **1** small round, sweet cake, usu containing currants. **2 *in a bun,*** (of a woman's hair) twisted into a knot above the back of the neck. ⇨ chignon.

buna /ˈbuːnə/ *n* [U] (P) synthetic rubber.

bunch /bʌntʃ/ *n* **1** numbers of small, similar things naturally growing together: *a ~ of grapes/bananas.* **2** collection of things of the same sort placed or fastened together: *a ~ of flowers/keys.* **3** (sl) mob; gang. **4 *the best of the ~,*** (colloq) the best or pick of the lot. □ *vt,vi* [VP15B,2A,C] **~ *up,*** form into a ~; come or bring together into a ~ or ~es, or in folds: *Don't ~ up,* ie cluster together.

a bunch of keys

a bundle of sticks

bun·come = bunkum.

bundle /ˈbʌndl/ *n* number of articles fastened, tied, or wrapped together: *a ~ of sticks/firewood; a ~ of old rags. The books were tied up in ~s of twenty.* □ *vt,vi* **1** [VP15B] **~ *up,*** make into a ~ or ~s: *We ~d everything up.* **2** [VP15A] put together in a confused heap; put away without order: *We ~d everything into a drawer.* **3** [VP15A,B,2C] send or go in a hurry or without ceremony: *She ~d him into a taxi. They ~d off/out/away.*

bung /bʌŋ/ *n* large (usu wooden, rubber, cork or recently plastic) stopper for closing a hole in a cask or barrel. □ *vt* [VP6A,15B] put a ~ into (the hole in a cask). ˈ**~-hole** *n* hole for filling a cask. **~*ed up,*** (of the nose) stopped up with mucus; (of drains) clogged with dirt.

bun·ga·low /ˈbʌŋɡələʊ/ *n* small house with only one storey; (in India) such a house surrounded by a large verandah. ˈ**bun·ga·loid** /ˈbʌŋɡəlɔɪd/ *adj* of or like ~s: *bungaloid growth,* area of unsightly building development with many ~s.

bungle /ˈbʌŋɡl/ *vt,vi* [VP6A,2A] do (a piece of work) badly and clumsily; spoil (a task, etc) by lack of skill. □ *n* ~d piece of work. **bung·ler** /ˈbʌŋɡlə(r)/ *n* person who ~s.

bun·ion /ˈbʌnɪən/ *n* inflamed swelling, esp on the large joint of the big toe.

bunk[1] /bʌŋk/ *n* narrow **1** bed fixed on the wall, eg of a cabin in a ship or in a train; sleeping-berth. **2 ~ beds,** pair of single beds, one fixed above the other, usu for children.

bunk[2] /bʌŋk/ *vi, n* (sl) run away: *~ off.* ***do a ~,*** run away.

bunk[3] /bʌŋk/ *n* [U] abbr for bunkum.

bunker /ˈbʌŋkə(r)/ *n* **1** that part of a ship where coal or fuel oil is stored. **2** sandy hollow, made as an obstacle, on a golf-course. **3** (mil) underground shelter, fortified point, of steel and concrete. □ *vt,vi* **1** [VP6A,2A] fill a ship's ~s with fuel; (of a ship) obtain supplies of fuel. **2** (usu passive) ***be ~ed,*** get one's ball into a ~ at golf; (fig) be in difficulties.

bun·kum /ˈbʌŋkəm/ *n* [U] senseless or purposeless talk: *That's all ~!*

bunny /ˈbʌnɪ/ *n* (*pl* -nies) (child's word for) rabbit.

Bun·sen /ˈbʌnsn/ *n* ˈ~ **burner**, burner for gas, with an air-valve for regulating the mixture of gas and air.

bunt·ing /ˈbʌntɪŋ/ *n* [U] (bright-coloured cloth used for making) flags and decorations (for use in streets and on buildings on festive occasions).

buoy /bɔɪ/ *n* **1** floating object, anchored to the bottom, used to show a navigable channel or to indicate reefs, submerged wrecks, etc. **2** (also ˈ**life-~**) sth designed to keep a person afloat in the water, e g sth made of cork or sth that can be inflated with air. □ *vi* **1** [VP6A] mark the position of with a ~: *~ a wreck/channel.* **2** [VP15B] *~ up*, keep afloat; (fig) keep up hopes, etc: *~ed up with new hope.*

buoy·ancy /ˈbɔɪənsɪ/ *n* [U] **1** power to float or keep things floating: *Salt water has more ~ than fresh water.* **2** (fig) lightness of spirits; power to recuperate; (of the stock market) tendency of prices to rise.

buoy·ant /ˈbɔɪənt/ *adj* able to float or to keep things floating; (fig) light-hearted: *a ~ disposition;* springy: *with a ~ step;* (of the stock market, etc) maintaining high prices. **~·ly** *adv*

bur, burr /bɜ(r)/ *n* (plant with a) seed-case or flower-head that clings to the hair or fur of animals; sth or sb that sticks like a ~, esp a person who forces his company on others and is hard to shake off.

Bur·berry /ˈbɜbərɪ/ *n* (name of manufacturers of a) coat of waterproof cloth.

burble /ˈbɜbl/ *vi* make a gentle murmuring or bubbling sound: *burbling with mirth.*

bur·den /ˈbɜdn/ *n* **1** sth (to be) carried; load (esp one that is heavy); (liter and fig) sth difficult to bear: *the ~ of taxation (up)on industry; a ~ of sorrow/grief; the white man's ~,* (old use) his task of leading the world forward. ***be a ~ to sb,*** cause him expense and trouble: *He was always a ~ to his parents.* **beast of ~,** animal that carries packs on its back. **2** [U] ship's carrying capacity, tonnage; *a ship of 3 000 tons ~.* ***3 the ~ of proof,*** obligation to prove: *The ~ of proof rests with him,* He must prove the truth of his statement. **4** refrain or chorus (of a song); (with *def art*) chief theme of a statement, speech, etc: *The ~ of his remarks was that....* □ *vt* ***~ sb/oneself (with),*** [VP6A,14] load; put a ~ on: *~ oneself with a heavy overcoat; ~ one's memory with useless facts; ~ed with taxation.* **~·some** /ˈbɜdnsəm/ *adj* hard to bear; making (sb) tired; troublesome (*to* sb).

bur·dock /ˈbɜdok/ *n* wild plant with leaves like those of a dock and prickly flower-heads (*burrs*).

bureau /ˈbjʊərəʊ/ *n* (*pl* -reaux, /-rəʊz/) **1** (GB) writing desk with drawers. **2** government or municipal department or office: *ˈInforˈmation B~; ˈTourist B~.* **3** (US) chest of drawers for clothes, etc, usu with a mirror.

bureauc·racy /bjʊəˈrokrəsɪ/ *n* [U] government by paid officials not elected by the people; officials who keep their positions whatever political party is in power; [C] (*pl* -cies) this system of government; the officials as a body.

bureau·crat /ˈbjʊərəkræt/ *n* (often pej) official who works in a bureau or government department, esp one who obeys the rules of his department without exercising much judgement. **~ic** /ˈbjʊərəˈkrætɪk/ *adj* of or like a ~; too much attached to rules; carried on according to official rules and habits. **~i·cally** /-ɪklɪ/ *adv*

burette /bjʊəˈret/ *n* graduated glass tube with a tap for measuring small quantities of liquid run out of it.

burg /bɜg/ *n* (US colloq) town; city.

bur·geon /ˈbɜdʒən/ *vi* (poet) put out leaves; begin to grow.

bur·gess /ˈbɜdʒəs/ *n* person having the full rights of an English borough.

burgh /ˈbɜg/ *n* borough in Scotland.

bur·gher /ˈbɜgə(r)/ *n* (old use) citizen (esp of a Dutch or German town).

bur·glar /ˈbɜglə(r)/ *n* person who breaks into a house at night in order to steal. **bur·glary** /ˈbɜglərɪ/ *n* (*pl* -ries) [U] crime of breaking into a house by night to steal: [C] instance of this: *There have been numerous ~ies in this district recently.* ˈ**~-alarm** *n* device to give warning of ~s. ˈ**~-proof** *adj* made so that ~s cannot break in or into. **burgle** /ˈbɜgl/ *vt, vi* [VP6A] break into (a building) to commit ~y; [VP2A] commit ~y. **~i·ous** /bɜˈgleərɪəs/ *adj* (legal) of ~y: *guilty of a ~ious attempt.*

burgo·mas·ter /ˈbɜgəmɑstə(r) *US:* -mæs-/ *n* mayor of a Dutch or Flemish town.

Bur·gundy /ˈbɜgəndɪ/ *n* [U] kinds of (usu red) wine of Burgundy (in Central France).

burial /ˈberɪəl/ *n* [U] burying, [C] instance of this. ˈ**~-ground** *n* cemetery. ˈ**B~ Service,** the religious ceremony at a funeral.

burke /bɜk/ *vt* [VP6A] avoid (publicity, inquiry): *~ an issue.*

bur·lap /ˈbɜlæp/ *n* [U] coarse canvas (used for bags, wrappings, etc).

bur·lesque /bɜˈlesk/ *n* **1** [C] imitation, e g of a book, speech, person's behaviour, for the purpose of making fun of it or of amusing people. **2** [U] amusing imitation or parody. **3** (US) vaudeville entertainment. ⇨ variety(5). **4** (as *adj* or attrib) intended as a ~: *~ acting.* □ *vt* [VP6A] make a ~ of; parody; travesty.

burly /ˈbɜlɪ/ *adj* (of a person) big and strong; solidly built.

burn[1] /bɜn/ *n* (Scot) small stream.

burn[2] /bɜn/ *vt, vi* (*pt, pp* burnt /bɜnt/ occ burned /bɜnd/) (For uses with *adverbial particles* and *preps*, ⇨ 6 below.) **1** [VP6A,15B] use for the purpose of lighting or heating; *Most large steamships now ~ oil instead of coal. This lamp ~s oil. People used to ~ candles to get light. We have ~t (up) all our logs.* **2** [VP6A] damage, hurt, destroy by fire, heat or the action of acid: *Be careful not to ~ the meat. The coffee is very hot, don't ~ your mouth. I don't like ~t toast,* toast which has been heated too much, so that it is black. *The child ~t itself/its fingers while playing with matches. Some acids are strong enough to ~ wood.* ***~ one's fingers,*** ⇨ finger. ˈ**~ing glass** *n* lens used to concentrate the sun's rays (to set fire to sth). **3** [VP2A,B,C] be on fire or alight; be capable of giving out light and heat: *Wood ~s easily. Stone won't ~. All the lights were ~ing.* **4** [VP6A,14] make by heat; heat (a material) to make (sth): *~ bricks/lime/charcoal; ~ clay to make bricks; ~ a hole in a carpet,* e g by dropping a cigarette end. **5** [VP6A,C,4A] be hurt or spoilt by fire or heat; scorch; be or feel warm or hot; (fig) be filled with strong feeling: *The milk/sauce has ~t. She has a* *skin that* ~*s easily,* is quickly hurt by the sun. *Her cheeks were* ~*ing with shame. He was* ~*ing with anger. They were* ~*ing to avenge the death of their leader.* **6** [VP15B,2C] (with *adverbial particles* and *preps*):

burn away, **(a)** continue to ~: *The fire was* ~*ing away cheerfully. The gas-fire has been* ~*ing away all night.* **(b)** make, become less, by ~ing: destroy, be destroyed, by ~ing: *Half the candle had* ~*t away. An area of skin on his hand was* ~*t away.*

burn down, be destroyed, destroy to the foundations, by fire: *The house (was)* ~*t down.* ~ **down/low,** ~ less brightly as the material ~s or the fuel is used.

burn out, **(a)** become extinguished: *The fire* ~*t (itself) out. The candle* ~*t out.* **(b)** (of a rocket) use up its fuel. **(c)** (of an electric motor, coil) stop working because high current has caused electrical ~ing. **(d)** (usu passive) be destroyed, be reduced to a shell, by fire; be gutted: ~*t-out factories/tanks.* ~ **oneself out,** ruin one's health by overwork, dissipation, etc.

burn up, **(a)** burst into flames, flare up: *Put some wood on the fire and make it* ~ *up.* **(b)** consume, get rid of, by ~ing: *We* ~*t up all the garden rubbish.* **(c)** (of a rocket, etc, re-entering the atmosphere from space) catch fire and be destroyed. **ˋ~-up** *n* (GB sl) high-speed race on a public road between young people on motorcycles.

burn[3] /bɜn/ *n* **1** injury, mark, made by fire, heat or acid: *He died of the* ~*s he received in the fire.* **2** (aerospace) one firing of a rocket: *a two-minute* ~ *to correct course to the moon.* **~er** *n* **1** person who ~s sth or makes sth by ~ing: *a ˋcharcoal-~er.* **2** that part of a lamp, stove, etc from which the light or flame comes: *a four-~er oil-stove.* **~ing** *adj* **1** intense: *a* ~*ing thirst/desire.* **2** exciting; hotly debated: *a* ~*ing question.* **3** notorious, scandalous: *a* ~*ing disgrace/shame.*

bur·nish /ˋbɜnɪʃ/ *vt,vi* [VP6A] polish (metal) by, or as if by, rubbing; [VP2A] take a polish: *material that* ~*es well.*

bur·nouse /bɜˋnus/ *n* kind of cloak with a hood, worn by Arabs and Moors.

burp /bɜp/ *n* [C] (sl) belch; hiccup. □ *vi* [VP2A] give a ~ or ~s.

burr[1] *n* ⇨ **bur.**

burr[2] /bɜ(r)/ *n* **1** whirring sound made by parts of machines that turn quickly. **ˋ~-drill** *n* one used by dentists. **2** marked pronunciation of 'r'; marked (rural) accent: *speak with a soft West-country* ~.

bur·row /ˋbʌrəʊ *US:* ˋbɜəʊ/ *n* hole made in the ground (by foxes, rabbits, etc). □ *vi,vt* [VP6A,2C] make a ~: ~ *a hole;* (fig) investigate (sth hidden): ~ *into a mystery.*

bur·sar /ˋbɜsə(r)/ *n* **1** treasurer (esp of a college). **2** (person holding a) scholarship at a university of Scotland, or a grant for continuation of studies: *British Council* ~*s in Great Britain.* **~y** *n* **1** college ~'s office. **2** scholarship at a university in Scotland; grant for continuation of studies.

burst[1] /bɜst/ *vi,vt* (*pt,pp* **burst**) (For uses with *adverbial particles* and *preps,* ⇨ 5 below.) **1** [VP2A] (of a bomb, boiler, etc) fly or break apart from internal pressure; explode; (of river banks, a dam, an abscess, a boil) break outwards; (of a bubble) break; (of leaf and flower buds) open out. **be ~ing to,** be eager to: *He was* ~*ing to tell us the news.* **2** [VP6A,22] cause to fly apart, explode, open suddenly, give way under pressure: ~ *a tyre/balloon; The river* ~ *its banks. We had to* ~ *the door open. If you get much fatter you'll* ~ *your clothes. He* ~ *a blood-vessel,* suffered the ~ing of one; (fig) ~ *one's sides with laughing. Don't* ~ *yourself,* injure yourself by making too great an effort. **3** ~ **(with),** [VP2A,3A] be full to overflowing; be able to contain with difficulty: *storehouses* ~*ing with grain; sacks* ~*ing with corn. The greedy boy ate till he almost* ~. *They were* ~*ing with happiness/pride/excitement/impatience/health.* **4** [VP2C] make a way or entry suddenly or by force: *He* ~ *into the room. The oil* ~ (= gushed) *out of the ground. The sun* ~ *through the clouds,* appeared through an opening in the clouds. **5** [VP2C,3A] (with *adverbial particles* and *preps*):

burst forth, ⇨ ~ out.

burst in (upon), **(a)** interrupt: *Stop him* ~*ing in. He* ~ *in upon our conversation.* **(b)** appear or arrive suddenly: *He'll be* ~*ing in on us at any moment.*

burst into, **(a)** send out suddenly; break out into: *The oil-stove upset and* ~ *into flames.* **(b)** ~ *into tears/laughter, etc,* suddenly begin to cry (laugh, etc); ~ *into song,* begin to sing; ~ *into angry speech,* begin to speak angrily. **(c)** ~ *into bloom/blossom,* (of shrubs, trees) open out with blossom. **(d)** ~ *into view/sight,* (of a scene, spectacle) suddenly become visible.

burst out (into), exclaim; begin to speak: *'Why don't you behave?' he* ~ *out* (= ~ forth). *He* ~ *out into threats.* ~ **out laughing/crying,** suddenly begin to laugh/cry.

burst upon, come suddenly or unexpectedly to: *The view* ~ *upon our sight. The truth* ~ *upon him,* he suddenly realized it. *The cries of the mob* ~ *upon our ears.*

burst[2] /bɜst/ *n* **1** bursting explosion: *the* ~ *of a shell/bomb; a* ~ *in the water main.* **2** brief, violent effort: *a* ~ *of energy/speed; work in sudden* ~*s.* **3** outbreak: *a* ~ *of applause/anger/tears; a* ~ *of flame.* **4** short spurt: *a* ~ *of gunfire,* e g from a machine-gun. **5** ⇨ **bust**[2].

bur·then /ˋbɜðən/ *n, v* (liter) burden.

bur·ton /ˋbɜtn/ *n* beer brewed at Burton-on-Trent, Derbyshire. ***gone for a*** ~, (GB ex-armed forces sl) dead; missing.

bury /ˋberɪ/ *vt* (*pt,pp* **-ried**) **1** [VP6A] place (a dead body) in the ground, in a grave or in the sea; (of a clergyman) perform the Burial Service over; (of relatives) lose by death: *Many great Englishmen are buried in Westminster Abbey. He was buried at sea. Poor old Brown! He's dead and buried. She has buried five husbands.* **2** [VP6A, 22,15A] put underground; cover with earth, leaves, etc; cover up and forget; hide from view: *buried treasure. You wouldn't like to be buried alive. The dog buried the bone. The end of the post was buried in the ground. The house was half buried under snow. She buried* (= hid) *her face in her hands.* ~ ***oneself in the country,*** go to a place in the country where one will meet few people. ~ ***oneself in one's books/studies,*** give all one's time and attention to them. ***be buried in thoughts/memories of the past,*** etc, be deep in thought, etc, paying no attention to other things. **ˋ~ing-ground** *n* cemetery.

bus /bʌs/ *n* (*pl* **buses** /ˋbʌsɪz/) **1** (= omnibus which is now dated) public conveyance that travels along a fixed route and takes up and sets down passengers at fixed points: *Shall we walk or go by bus?* ***miss the bus,*** (sl) be too late to use an opportunity. **ˈbus·man** *n* bus-driver. **ˈ*busman's ˈholiday,*** leisure time spent in the same kind of occupation as one's ordinary work. **ˈ~ stop** *n* fixed stopping place for buses. **2** (sl) aeroplane; motor-car. □ *vi, vt* (-ss-) [VP2A,6A] go, take, by bus; (esp US) transport children to their schools: *the bussing of children to achieve racial integration,* e g by taking children from white areas to black areas and vice versa.

busby /ˈbʌzbɪ/ *n* (*pl* -bies) fur cap worn for ceremonial parades by soldiers of some British regiments.

bush /bʊʃ/ *n* **1** [C] low-growing plant with several or many woody stems coming up from the root. Cf *tree,* with a single trunk: *ˈrose-~; ˈfruit ~es,* e g currants, gooseberries. **2** [U] (often **the ~**) wild, uncultivated land, with or without trees or bushes, esp in Africa and Australia. ⇨ also telegraph. **ˈBush·man** /-mən/ *n* (*pl* -men) member of certain tribes in the desert regions of S Africa. **ˈ~y** *adj* **1** covered with ~es. **2** growing thickly; thick and rough: *~y eyebrows; a fox's ~y tail.*

bushel /ˈbʊʃl/ *n* (before metrication) measure for grain and fruit (8 gallons). ⇨ App 5. ***hide one's light under a ~,*** be modest about one's abilities, good qualities, etc.

busier, busiest, busily ⇨ busy.

busi·ness /ˈbɪznəs/ *n* **1** [U] buying and selling; commerce; trade: *We do not do much ~ with them. He's in the wool ~,* buys and sells wool. *He has set up in ~ as a bookseller. He is in ~ for himself,* works on his own account, is not employed by others. *Which do you want to do, go into ~ or become a lawyer?* ***on ~,*** for the purpose of doing ~: *Are you here on ~ or for pleasure?* **~ address,** address of one's shop, office, etc. Cf *home address.* **~ hours,** hours during which ~ is done: *~ hours, 8 a m to 5 p m.* **ˈ~-like** *adj* using, showing, system, promptness, care, etc. **~·man** /-mən/ *n* (*pl* -men) man who is engaged in buying and selling, etc (not a lawyer, doctor, etc). **2** [C] shop; commercial enterprise, etc: *He has a good ~ as a greengrocer. He is the manager of three different ~es. The newspapers advertise many small ~es for sale.* **3** [U] task, duty, concern; what has to be done: *It is a teacher's ~ to help his pupils. I will make it my ~* (= will undertake) *to see that the money is paid promptly. That's no ~ of yours,* is something about which you need not or should not trouble. ***get down to ~,*** start the work that must be done. ***mind one's own ~,*** attend to one's own duties and not interfere with those of others. ***mean ~,*** be in earnest. ***send sb about his ~,*** send him away and tell him not to interfere. **4** [U] right: *You have no ~ to do that.* **5** (with *indef art*) difficult matter: *What a ~ it is getting the children off to school!* **6** (often contemptuous) affair; subject; device: *I'm sick of the whole ~,* tired of the affair. **7** (colloq): *the ~ end of a pin/a chisel, etc,* the sharp end, the end to be used. **8** [U] (theatre) action, facial expression, etc of the actors in interpreting their parts (as distinct from the words they speak).

busker /ˈbʌskə(r)/ *n* person who entertains people, e g by singing or dancing, in public places, e g to queues outside cinemas.

bust[1] /bʌst/ *n* **1** head and shoulders of a person cut in stone, or cast in bronze, gypsum, etc. **2** woman's bosom; measurement round the bosom and back.

bust[2] /bʌst/ *vt, vi* (sl for burst) *~ sth,* smash it: *The business went ~,* failed. □ *n* ***have a ~, go on the ~,*** a period of wild revelry. **ˈ~-up** *n* (sl) quarrel.

bus·tard /ˈbʌstəd/ *n* large, swift-running bird.

bus·ter[1] /ˈbʌstə(r)/ *n* (in compounds) bomb or shell that wrecks completely: *ˈdam-~; ˈtank-~; ˈblock-~,* i e a bomb that may destroy a block of buildings.

bus·ter[2] /ˈbʌstə(r)/ *n* (US sl as a form of address) mate; chum: *Hi, ~!*

bustle[1] /ˈbʌsl/ *vi, vt* [VP2A,C,15B] (cause to) move quickly and excitedly: *Tell him to ~,* hurry. *Everyone was bustling about/in and out,* appearing to be very busy. *She ~d the children off to school.* □ *n* [U] excited activity: *Everybody was in a ~. Why is there so much ~?*

bustle[2] /ˈbʌsl/ *n* frame formerly used to puff out a woman's skirt at the back.

busy /ˈbɪzɪ/ *adj* (busier, busiest) **1** working; occupied; having much to do: *The doctor is a ~ man. He was ~ with/at/over his work. He was ~ getting ready for his journey. You'd better get ~,* start doing things. **ˈ~·body** *n* (*pl* -bodies) person who interferes in the affairs of other people, esp when his help is not wanted. **2** full of activity: *a ~ day;* (of places) filled with active people, traffic, etc: *The shops are ~ before Christmas. This is one of the busiest stations in London.* **3** (of a telephone line) in use. □ *vt* (*pt, pp* -sied) [VP14] ***~ oneself (with),*** keep ~, occupy oneself with: *He busied himself with all sorts of little tasks. She busied herself (in) tidying up her desk.* **busi·ly** /ˈbɪzlɪ/ *adv* in a ~ way: *busily engaged in doing sth.*

but[1] /bʌt/ *adv* only (now the usu word): *We can but try. He left but an hour ago. He's but a boy. If I could but see you for an hour!*

but[2] /bət *strong form:* bʌt/ *conj* **1** (co-ordinating): *Tom was not there but his brother was. We tried to do it but couldn't. He's a hardworking but not very intelligent boy.* **2** (subordinating, with a neg implication): *I never go past my old school but I think* (= without thinking) *of Mr Wilkins, the headmaster. No man is so old but he may learn,* No man is too old to learn. *Never a month passes but she writes* (= in which she does not write) *to her old parents.* **3** (with *cannot* or *could not* and an *inf;* formal use): *I cannot help but think that...,* am compelled to...; *I could not choose but go* (= had no alternative). *I cannot but admire* (= must admire, cannot help admiring) *your decision.*

but[3] /bət *strong form:* bʌt/ *prep* (The uses of *but* as a *prep* and as a *conj* are not always clearly to be distinguished. The subject forms of the *pers pronouns* are often used after *but* meaning 'except', as if it were a *conj.* The object forms are also used, as if *but* were a *prep*). (With negatives, e g *no one, none, nothing,* and interrogatives, e g *who,* and such words as *all, every one*) except, excluding: *Nothing but disaster would come from such a plan. They're all wrong but me. No one but he/him showed much interest in the proposal. Who but he would do such a thing?* **first/next/last but one/two/three**: *Take the next turning but one* (= the second turning) *on your left. I live in the* *last house but two* (= the third house from the end) *in this street. Smith was the last but one* (= second to last) *to arrive.* '**but for,** except for, without: *But for your help we should not have finished in time. But for the rain* (= If it had not rained) *we should have had a pleasant journey.* **but that,** except that: *He would have helped us but that* (= if it had not been for the fact that) *he was short of money at the time.* **but then,** on the other hand: *London is a noisy place, but then it's also the place where you get the best entertainment.*

but[4] /bʌt/ *rel pron* (rare; formal) who or that not: *There is not one of us but wishes* (= not one of us who does not wish) *to help you. There are few of us but* (= few of us who do not) *admire your determination.*

but[5] /bʌt/ *n* (Scot) outer room of a two-roomed cottage. ⇨ ben.

bu·tane /ˈbjuteɪn/ *n* [U] gas produced from petroleum supplied in metal containers for use in houses, etc, where there is no piped supply of gas (for cooking, heating, lighting, etc).

butch /bʊtʃ/ *adj* (of a woman) having tendencies towards masculine behaviour and clothes. □ *n* such a woman; lesbian.

butcher /ˈbʊtʃə(r)/ *n* **1** person who kills, cuts up and sells animals for food: *~'s meat,* meat excluding poultry, game and bacon; *the ~'s,* the ~'s shop. **2** person who has caused unnecessary death, e g a general who wastes the lives of soldiers; person who kills savagely and needlessly. □ *vt* [VP6A] kill violently, esp with a knife. ˋ**~y** *n* [U] **1** (attrib) ~'s trade: *He's in the ~y business.* **2** needless and cruel killing of people.

but·ler /ˈbʌtlə(r)/ *n* head manservant (in charge of the wine-cellar, pantry, valuables, etc).

butt[1] /bʌt/ *n* **1** large cask for wine or ale. **2** large barrel for storing rainwater, e g from roofs.

butt[2] /bʌt/ *n* **1** thicker (usu wooden) end (esp of a fishing-rod or rifle). **2** unburned end of a smoked cigar or cigarette, or of a used candle.

butt[3] /bʌt/ *n* **1** (usu *pl* with *def art*) shooting-range; the targets and the mound of earth behind them (used for practice in firing rifles). **2** person who is a target for ridicule, jokes, etc: *He is the ~ of the whole school.*

butt[4] /bʌt/ *vt,vi* **1** [VP6A,15A] push with the head (as a goat does): *~ man in the stomach.* **2** **~ in,** [VP2C] (colloq) force oneself into the conversation or company of others; interrupt sb: *May I ~ in.* [VP3A] ***~ into,*** run into, head or front first.

but·ter /ˈbʌtə(r)/ *n* [U] **1** fatty food substance made from cream by churning, used on bread, in cooking, etc: *She looks as if ~ would not melt in her mouth,* has a demure and innocent appearance. ˋ**~·bean,** large, dried haricot ~. ˋ**~·cup** *n* wild plant with yellow flowers. ˋ**~·fin·gers** *n* person unable to hold things well, esp one unable to catch a cricket-ball. ˋ**~·milk** *n* liquid that remains after ~ has been separated from milk. ˋ**~·scotch** *n* [U] sweet substance made by boiling sugar and ~ together. **2** substance similar to ~, made from other materials: *cocoa ~, peanut ~.* □ *vt* **1** [VP6A] spread ~ on (bread); cook with ~. ⇨ also bread. **2** [VP15B] ***~ sb up,*** flatter.

but·ter·fly /ˈbʌtəflɑɪ/ *n* (*pl* **-flies**) insect with four wings, often brightly coloured, and feelers. ˋ**~ (stroke)** *n* stroke used in swimming, both arms moving upward and outward at the same time as an up and down kick of the feet.

but·tery /ˈbʌtərɪ/ *n* (*pl* **-ries**) (in some GB universities) place where provisions (bread, butter, ale) are kept and from which they are served.

but·tock /ˈbʌtək/ *n* **1** ⇨ the illus at trunk. Either side of that part of the body on which a person sits: *an injection of penicillin in the left ~.* **2** (*pl*) **the ~s,** the rump, the bottom: *a smack on the ~s.*

but·ton /ˈbʌtn/ *n* **1** small, usu round, bit of bone, metal, etc for fastening articles of clothing, or sewn on as an ornament. ˋ**~·hole** *n* hole through which a ~ is passed; flower worn in a ~hole (e g in the lapel of a jacket or coat). □ *vt* [VP6A] hold sb by the ~hole (to get his attention). ˋ**~·hook** *n* hook for pulling a ~ into place through a ~hole. ˋ**~·wood** *n* tall tree with a ~-shaped fruit, related to the sycamore; its wood. **2** small, round ~-like object, esp one that, when pushed, makes an electrical contact, e g for a bell: *press/push/touch the ~.* **3** small, unopened mushroom. **4** (*pl*) (colloq) boy wearing uniform, employed as a page in a club, hotel, etc. ⇨ bell-hop. □ *vt,vi* [VP6A,15B,2A] fasten with a ~ or ~s: *~ (up) one's coat; a dress that ~s down the back. My collar won't ~,* I can't ~ it. '**~ed-ˋup,** **(a)** (colloq) (of a person) silent and reserved. **(b)** safely, at last, completed: *That's that job ~ed-up!*

but·tress /ˈbʌtrəs/ *n* support built against a wall; (fig) prop; sth that supports, ⇨ the illus at church: *the ~es of society/the constitution.* □ *vt* [VP6A,15B] ***~ (up),*** strengthen, hold up (by building a ~); (fig) support, strengthen: *~ up an argument.*

buxom /ˈbʌksəm/ *adj* (of women) good-looking, healthy-looking and well covered with flesh.

buy /bɑɪ/ *vt,vi* (*pt,pp* **bought** /bɔt/) [VP6A,15B,12B,13B,2A] **1** get in return for money, get by paying a price: *Can money buy happiness? I bought this car from Green. Buy one for me. Buy me one. I must buy myself a new hat. He bought it for £2. He bought them at 10p a piece.* **buy back:** *He sold his house and then bought it back again.* **buy in, (a)** buy a stock of: *buy in coal for the winter.* **(b)** (at an auction sale) bid for and obtain (one's own goods) by offering a higher price than the highest offered by others (when bids are considered too low. ***buy off,*** get rid of (an unjust claim, a blackmailer) by making a payment. ***buy out,*** pay (sb) to give up a post, property, etc or a share in one's own business. ***buy over,*** bribe or corrupt (sb). ***buy up,*** buy all or as much as possible of (sth). **2** [VP6A] obtain at a sacrifice: *He bought fame at the expense of his health and hap-*

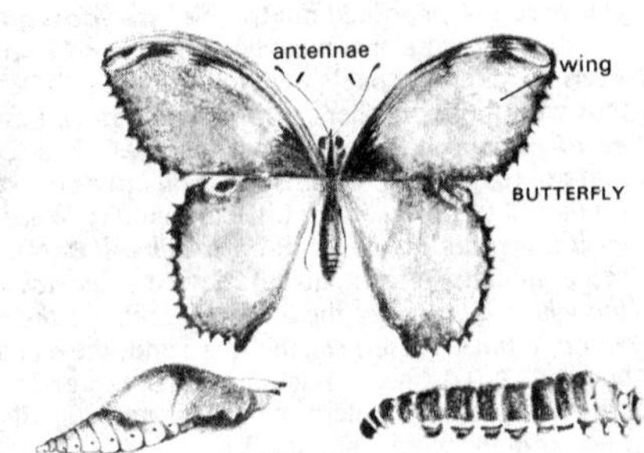

a butterfly

piness. Victory was dearly bought. □ *n* (colloq) purchase: *a good buy,* a bargain. **buyer** *n* person who buys. **buyers' market,** state of affairs when goods are plentiful and money scarce, so that low prices favour buyers.

buzz /bʌz/ *vi,vt* **1** [VP2A,C] make a humming sound (as of bees or machinery in rapid motion). **2** [VP2C] move rapidly or excitedly: *~ about/around; ~ing along the road.* **~ off,** (sl) go away. **3** [VP2A] (of the ears) be filled with a ~ing noise: *My ears ~.* **4** [VP6A] (of an aircraft) fly near to or low over (another plane) in a threatening manner: *Two fighters ~ed the airliner.* □ *n* humming (of bees or other insects); sound of people talking, of whirling machinery, etc. **~er** *n* **1** electrical device that produces a ~ing note when the current flows. **2** steam whistle; hooter (as used in factories as a time signal).

buz·zard /ˈbʌzəd/ *n* kinds of falcon.

by[1] /baɪ/ *adv part* **1** near: *He hid the money when nobody was by.* **standby,** ⇨ stand[2](11). **2** past: *He hurried by without a word. Fame passed him by. I can't get by,* can't pass. *The time is gone by* (= is past) *when....* **3** *lay/put/set sth by,* keep it, save it, for future use. **4** (in phrases) ***by and by,*** later on. ***by the by(e), by the way,*** (used to introduce a new topic, or sth that has been forgotten). ***by and large,*** on the whole; taking everything into consideration.

by[2] /baɪ/ *prep* **1** near; at or to the side of: *Come and sit by me/by my side. My house is by the river. We had a day by the sea.* ***by oneself,*** alone: *He was (all) by himself.* ⇨ 12 below. ***have sth by one,*** have it handy, within easy reach: *It's useful to have a good dictionary by you when you're reading.* ***stand by sb,*** support him. **2** (in reading the cardinal points) towards: *North by East,* one point towards the East from the North, i e between N and NNE: *East by North,* one point North of East, i e between E and ENE. ⇨ the illus at compass. **3** (showing direction of movement) through, along, across, over: *We came by the fields, not by the roads. Did you come by the nearest road? We travelled to Paris by Dover and Calais.* **4** past: *I go by* (= pass) *the post office every morning on my way to work. He walked by me without speaking.* **5** (of time, esp to indicate conditions and circumstances) during: *The enemy attacked by night.* (This emphasizes the circumstances: under cover of darkness, etc. Cf Everything was quiet *during* the night.) *Do you prefer travelling by night or by day? We went for a sail on the lake by moonlight. It's no use trying to escape by daylight.* **6** (of time) as soon as; not later than; when (the time indicated) comes: *Can you finish the work by tomorrow? He ought to be here by this time/by now. They were tired out by evening. By the time (that) you get there* (*that* is almost always omitted) *it will be dark.* **7** (in phrases indicating a unit of time, length, weights, measurements, etc): *rent a house by the year; hire a bicycle by the day,* e g 30p for one day's use; *engage a clerk by the month; pay a labourer by the day/the hour; buy/sell by retail; sell cloth by the yard/coal by the ton/eggs by the dozen, etc; freight charged by weight/volume; a room 20 ft by 30 ft.* **8** through the agency, means, or instrumentality, of: *The streets are lighted by electricity. This church was designed by Wren. He makes a living by teaching. He was shot by a sniper. The man was killed by a falling chimney. He was killed by lightning.* (*Lightning,* instrumentality, not instrument. Cf The rat was killed *by* Tom *with* a stick. ⇨ with(3).) **9** (indicating means of travel, transport, conveyance): *travel by land/sea/air; by bus/car/boat, etc; send sth by post/hand.* **10** (indicating a part of the body that is touched, etc): *take sb by the hand,* i e take his hand; *seize sb by the hair; grab sb by the scruff of his neck.* **11** ***know/learn sth by heart,*** so that one can repeat it from memory. ***know sb by name/reputation/sight,*** know only his name, etc but not know him personally. **12** (in adverbial phrases of manner) ***by accident/mistake,*** accidentally, not on purpose or intentionally. ***by chance/good fortune,*** as the result of chance or good fortune. ***by oneself,*** without help. ⇨ 1 above. **13** in accordance with; in agreement with: *by request of my employer; by your leave,* with your permission; *by (the terms of) Article 3 of the Treaty.* **14** according to: *judging by appearances; by rights,* rightly. *By my watch it is 2 o'clock. That's nothing to go by,* One should not form judgements by that. **15** to the extent of: *The bullet missed me by two inches. It needs to be longer by two feet. He's too clever by half,* much too smart. ⇨ far[3](2). **16** (in oaths) as surely as I believe in: *I swear by Almighty God that...; He swore by all that he held sacred that....*

bye /baɪ/ *n* **1** sth subordinate or incidental: *by the bye.* ⇨ by[1](4). **2** (cricket) run scored for a ball that passes the batsman and the wicket-keeper.

bye-bye /ˈbaɪ baɪ/ *n* (child's word for) sleep, bed: *go to ~s* /ˈbaɪ baɪz/. □ *int* /ˈbaɪ ˈbaɪ/ (colloq) goodbye.

by-elec·tion /ˈbaɪ ɪlekʃn/ *n* election made necessary by the death or resignation of a member during the life of Parliament. ⇨ general election.

by·gone /ˈbaɪgɒn/ *adj* past: *in ~ days,* in the time now past. □ *n* (*pl*) the past; past offences. ***Let ~s be ~s,*** Forgive and forget the past.

by-law, bye-law /ˈbaɪ lɔ/ *n* law or regulation made by a local authority (e g a town or railway company).

by-pass /ˈbaɪ pɑs *US:* pæs/ *n* new, wide road passing round a heavily populated urban area or village, to take through traffic. □ *vt* [VP6A] **1** provide with a ~: *~ a village/falls on a river.* **2** make a detour round (a town, etc); (fig) *Let's ~ that proposal,* ignore it.

by·path /ˈbaɪpɑθ *US:* -pæθ/ *n* indirect or retired path, less important or less direct path.

by·play /ˈbaɪ pleɪ/ *n* [U] (theatre) action apart from that of the main story; dumb-show of minor characters.

by-prod·uct /ˈbaɪ prɒdʌkt/ *n* [C] substance obtained during the manufacture of some other substance: *Ammonia, coal-tar and coke are valuable ~s obtained in the manufacture of coal-gas.*

byre /ˈbaɪə(r)/ *n* cow-house.

by-road /ˈbaɪ rəʊd/ *n* side road; road that is not much used.

by·stander /ˈbaɪ stændə(r)/ *n* person standing near but not taking part in an event or activity.

by-way /ˈbaɪweɪ/ *n* secondary or side road: (fig) *~s of history/literature, etc,* less known departments of history, etc.

by·word /ˈbaɪwɜd/ *n* person, place, etc regarded and spoken of as a notable example (usu bad): *She became the ~ of the village. The place was a ~ for iniquity.*

Cc

C, c /si/ (*pl* **C's, c's** /siz/) the third letter of the English alphabet.

cab /kæb/ *n* **1** horse carriage (e g *hansom cab*) or motor carriage (ˋ*taxi-cab*) that may be hired for short journeys: *Shall we go by bus or take a cab?* ˋ**cab·man** /-mən/ *n* (*pl* **-men**) driver of a cab. ˋ**cab-rank** *n* row of cabs waiting to be hired. ˋ**cab-stand** *n* place where cabs are authorized to wait for customers. **2** part of a railway engine for the driver and fireman; part of a bus, lorry, etc for the driver.

ca·bal /kəˋbæl/ *n* (group of persons who carry on) secret intrigue (esp in politics).

cab·aret /ˋkæbəreɪ/ *n* **1** French tavern. **2** (also ˋ**~ show**) entertainment (songs, dancing, etc) provided in a restaurant etc, while guests are at table.

cab·bage /ˋkæbɪdʒ/ *n* [U] (of kinds of) cultivated plant with a round head (often called the *heart*) of thick green leaves, ⇨ the illus at **vegetable**; [U] these leaves cooked as a vegetable or eaten (white ~) as salad.

cabby /ˋkæbɪ/ *n* (colloq) cab-driver.

ca·ber /ˋkeɪbə(r)/ *n* trunk of a roughly trimmed young fir-tree tossed in Highland games (Scotland) as a trial of strength and skill: *toss the ~.*

cabin /ˋkæbɪn/ *n* **1** room in a ship or aircraft, esp (in a ship) one for sleeping in. ˋ**~-boy** *n* boy who waits on officers and passengers. ˋ**~ class** *n* (in liners) class between first and tourist class. ˋ**~ cruiser** *n* large motor boat with a ~ or ~s. **2** small, usu roughly made house (e g of logs); railway signal-box.

cabi·net /ˋkæbɪnət/ *n* **1** piece of furniture with drawers or shelves for storing or displaying things: *a* ˋ*medicine ~; a* ˋ*filing ~*, for storing letters, documents; *a* ˋ*china ~*, often with a glass front, for displaying ornamental china. ˋ**~-maker** *n* skilled workman who makes fine furniture. **2** plastic, wooden or metal container for radio or record-playing equipment. **3** group of men (chief ministers of state) chosen by the head of the government (the prime minister in GB) to be responsible for government administration and policy: *C~ Minister*, one of these men; *~ council*, meeting of these men. **4** (old use) private room.

cable /ˋkeɪbl/ *n* **1** [C,U] (length of) thick, strong rope (of fibre or wire strands), used for making ships fast; rope or chain of an anchor. **2** ˋ**~('s)-length** *n* 100 fathoms, one-tenth of a nautical mile. **3** thick rope of wire strands for supporting a bridge, etc. ˋ**~-car,** ˋ**~-railway,** one up a steep hillside, worked by a ~ and a stationary engine; funicular railway. **4** protected bundle of insulated wires (laid underground or on the ocean bottom) for carrying messages by electric telegraph; message electric power overhead (⇨ the illus at **pylon**) or underground. □ *vt, vi* [VP6A,2A] send (a message), communicate, inform (sb) by ~. ˋ**~-gram** /ˋkeɪblgræm/ *n* ~d telegram.

ca·boodle /kəˋbudl/ *n* (sl) ***the whole ~,*** (of persons or things) all the lot.

ca·boose /kəˋbus/ *n* **1** room on a ship's deck in which cooking is done. **2** (US) small van at the end of a freight train for the use of the train men.

cab·ri·olet /ˈkæbrɪəˋleɪ/ *n* (old use) one-horse carriage with two wheels and a folding hood; (modern use) motor-car with fixed sides and folding top. ⇨ **convertible.**

ca' canny /ˈkɑˋkænɪ/ *n* workers' policy of restricting output (by working slowly).

ca·cao /kəˋkɑ-ʊ/ *n* **1** (also ˋ**~-bean**) seed of a tropical tree from which cocoa and chocolate are made. **2** (also ˋ**~-tree**) the tree.

cache /kæʃ/ *n* (hiding-place for) food and stores left (e g by explorers) for later use. □ *vt* place in a ~.

ca·chet /ˋkæʃeɪ *US:* kæˋʃeɪ/ *n* distinguishing mark (to prove excellence, authenticity).

ca·chou /ˋkæʃu *US:* kəˋʃu/ *n* scented sweet formerly used by smokers to disguise the odour of tobacco in the breath.

cackle /ˋkækl/ *n* [U] noise made by a hen after laying an egg; [C] loud laugh; [U] foolish talk. □ *vi* (of a hen) make this noise; (of a person) talk or laugh noisily. □ **cack·ler** *n*

ca·coph·ony /kəˋkofənɪ/ *n* discord. **ca·coph·onous** /kəˋkofənəs/ *adj* discordant.

cac·tus /ˋkæktəs/ (*pl* **-ses, cacti** /ˋkæktɑɪ/) (sorts of) plant from hot, dry climates with a thick, fleshy stem, usu with no leaves and covered with clusters of spines or prickles.

cactuses

cad /kæd/ *n* person guilty of or capable of dishonourable behaviour. **cad·dish** /ˋkædɪʃ/ *adj* of or like a cad: *a caddish trick.*

ca·da·ver /kəˋdeɪvə(r)/ *n* corpse, (usu human). **~·ous** /kəˋdævərəs/ *adj* looking like a corpse; deadly pale.

cad·die, caddy /ˋkædɪ/ *n* (*pl* **-dies**) person who is paid to carry a golfer's clubs for him round the course.

caddy /ˋkædɪ/ *n* (*pl* **-dies**) small box for holding the dried leaves used for making tea.

ca·dence /ˋkeɪdns/ *n* rhythm in sound; the rise and fall of the voice in speaking.

ca·denza /kəˋdenzə/ *n* ornamental passage to be played by the soloist, usu near the end of a movement, in an instrumental concerto.

ca·det /kəˋdet/ *n* **1** student at a naval, military or air force college. ˋ**~ corps** *n* (at some GB schools and colleges) organization that gives military training to older boys. **2** young person under training for a profession: ˋ*police ~s; British Council ~s.* **3** (formal) younger son.

cadge /kædʒ/ *vt, vi* [VP6A,14,2A] beg; (try to) get (*from* sb) by begging: *~ a meal; be always cadging.* **cad·ger** *n* person who ~s; beggar.

cadi /ˋkædɪ/ *n* civil judge (in a Muslim country).

cad·mium /ˋkædmɪəm/ *n* [U] soft, silvery-white tin-like metal (symbol **Cd**).

cadre /ˋkɑdə(r)/ *n* **1** framework. **2** (mil) permanent establishment of a regiment, that can be expanded when necessary.

Cæsar /ˋsizə(r)/ *n* title of the Roman emperors from Augustus to Hadrian; any Roman emperor. **~·ian** /sɪˋzeərɪən/ *adj* **~ian section/birth,** delivery of a child by cutting the walls of the abdomen and uterus.

cæsura /sɪˋzjʊərə *US:* -ˋzʊərə/ *n* point at which a pause naturally occurs in a line of verse.

café /ˋkæfeɪ *US:* kæˋfeɪ/ *n* (in Europe) place where the public may buy and drink coffee, beer, wine, spirits, etc; (in GB) tea-shop; small restaurant at which meals (but not alcoholic drinks) may be bought. **~-au-lait** /ˈkæfeɪ əʊ ˋleɪ/ *n* (F) coffee with milk.

cafe·teria /ˈkæfɪˋtɪərɪə/ *n* restuarant at which customers collect their meals on trays at counters and carry them to tables.

caff /kæf/ *n* (GB sl) café.

caf·feine /ˋkæfin/ *n* [U] organic compound in tea leaves and coffee beans, used in medicine.

caf·tan /ˋkæftən/ *n* long tunic with a girdle at the waist, worn by men in the Near East; woman's loosely hanging dress.

cage /keɪdʒ/ *n* **1** framework, fixed or portable, with wires or bars, in which birds or animals may be kept. **2** camp for prisoners of war. **3** framework in which cars are lowered or raised in the shaft of a mine. □ *vt* [VP6A] put, keep, in a ~: *a ~d bird.*

cagey /ˋkeɪdʒɪ/ *adj* (colloq) cautious about sharing confidences; uncommunicative; secretive. **cag·ily** *adv*

ca·hoots /kəˋhuts/ *n pl* ***be in ~ (with),*** (US sl) be planning sth (esp sth disreputable), be in league, with.

cai·man, cay·man /ˋkeɪmən/ *n* (*pl* -mans /-mənz/) S American reptile resembling an alligator.

ca·ique /kɑˋik/ *n* rowing-boat; small sailing ship or motor-boat (as used in the eastern Mediterranean).

cairn /keən/ *n* pyramid-shaped heap of rough stones set up as a landmark or a memorial.

cais·son /ˋkeɪsn/ *n* **1** chest or wagon for ammunition, usu attached to a big gun on wheels. **2** large watertight box or chamber in which men work under water (e g when building foundations): *~ disease,* ⇨ bend²(3).

cai·tiff /ˋkeɪtɪf/ *n* (old use) despicable or cowardly person.

ca·jole /kəˋdʒəʊl/ *vt* [VP14] ***~ sb (into/out of doing sth),*** use flattery or deceit to persuade or soothe, or to get information, etc from sb. **ca·jol·ery** *n*

cake /keɪk/ *n* **1** [C,U] sweet mixture of flour, eggs, butter, etc baked in an oven: *an assortment of fancy ~s; a slice of ~,* i e of a large one that is cut into pieces. ***a piece of ~,*** (sl) sth very easy and pleasant. ***~s and ale,*** merry-making. ***(selling) like hot ~s,*** very fast. ***take the ~,*** (colloq) surpass everything, become audacious, impudent, etc. **2** [C] mixture of other kinds of food, usu compressed and cooked in a round or ornamental shape: *ˋfish-~s; ˋoat-~s.* **3** [C] shaped piece of other materials or substances: *a ~ of soap/ tobacco.* □ *vt,vi* [VP6A,2A] coat thickly, become coated (*with* sth that becomes hard when dry); form into a thick hard mass: *His shoes were ~d with mud.*

cala·bash /ˋkæləbæʃ/ *n* (tree with) fruit or gourd of which the hard outer skin (or shell) is used as a container for liquids, grain, etc.

ca·lam·ity /kəˋlæmətɪ/ *n* (*pl* -ties) great and serious misfortune or disaster (e g a big earthquake or flood, becoming blind, the loss of all one's money). **ca·lami·tous** /kəˋlæmɪtəs/ *adj* marked by, causing, ~ (*to*).

cal·cify /ˋkælsɪfɑɪ/ *vt,vi* (*pt,pp* -fied) [VP6A,2A] change, be changed, into lime; harden by deposit of lime.

cal·cine /ˋkælsɪn/ *vt,vi* [VP6A,2A] make, be made, into quicklime or powder by roasting or burning; burn to ashes. **cal·ci·na·tion** /ˈkælsɪˋneɪʃn/ *n* conversion of metals into their oxides by burning.

cal·cium /ˋkælsɪəm/ *n* soft white metal (symbol **Ca**), the chemical basis of many compounds essential to life; occurs in bones and teeth, and forms part of limestone, marble and chalk. **ˈ~ ˋcarbide** *n* compound of ~ and carbon (**CaC_2**), used with water to make acetylene gas (**C_2H_2**). **~ hydroxide** *n* slaked lime.

cal·cu·lable /ˋkælkjʊləbl/ *adj* that may be measured, reckoned or relied upon.

cal·cu·late /ˋkælkjʊleɪt/ *vt,vi* **1** [VP6A,9,8,10,2A] find out by working with numbers: *~ the cost of a journey. Astronomers can ~ when there will be eclipses of the sun and moon.* **calculating machine** *n* one that works with numbers automatically. **2** ***be ~d to,*** be planned or designed to: *This advertisement is ~d to attract the attention of housewives.* ***a ~d insult,*** said or done on purpose. **3** [VP3A] ***~ (up)on,*** (US) depend, bank (the usu words in GB): *We cannot ~ upon having fine weather for the sports meeting.* **4** [VP9] (US) suppose, believe. **5** [VP9] weigh reasons, etc and be confident (*that* sth will happen, etc). **cal·cu·lat·ing** *adj* scheming; shrewd; crafty. **cal·cu·la·tor** /-tə(r)/ *n* person who ~s; calculating machine.

cal·cu·la·tion /ˈkælkjʊˋleɪʃən/ *n* [U] act of calculating: careful thought; [C] result of this: *After much ~, they decided to give Green the position of manager. I'm out in my ~s,* have made a mistake in them.

cal·cu·lus /ˋkælkjʊləs/ *n* (*pl* -li /-lɑɪ/ or -luses /-ləsɪz/) **1** branch or mathematics divided into two parts, *differential ~* and *integral ~,* that deals with variable quantities, used to solve many mathematical problems. **2** (med) stone in some part of the human body.

cal·dron *n* = cauldron.

cal·en·dar /ˋkælɪndə(r)/ *n* **1** list of the days, weeks, months, of a particular year; list with dates that are important to certain classes of people. **2** system by which time is divided into fixed periods, and marking the beginning and end of a year: *the Muslim ~: the Gregorian ~* (with every fourth year a leap year of 366 days). **ˈ~ ˋmonth** *n* month as marked on the ~ (contrasted with a lunar month of 28 days).

cal·en·der /ˋkælɪndə(r)/ *n* roller-machine for pressing and smoothing cloth or paper. □ *vt* [VP6A] put through a ~.

cal·ends, kal·ends /ˋkælendz/ *n pl* first of the month in the ancient Roman calendar: *on the Greek ~,* never.

calf¹ /kɑf *US:* kæf/ *n* **1** (*pl* calves /kɑvz *US:* kævz/) ⇨ the illus at domestic, young of the domestic cow; also of the seal, whale and some other animals for the first year. Cf *bull, cow, heifer, ox, steer*. **cow in/with ~,** pregnant cow. **'~-love** *n* childish love affair; love of a young or inexperienced person. **2** [U] (also **'~ skin**) leather from the skin of a ~, esp as used in bookbinding and shoemaking.

calf[2] /kɑf/ *US:* kæf/ *n* (*pl calves* /kɑvz *US:* kævz/) fleshy part of the back of the human leg, between the knee and the ankle. ⇨ the illus at **leg**.

cali·brate /ˈkælɪbreɪt/ *vt* [VP6A] determine or correct the calibre or scale of a thermometer/gauge or other graduated instrument. **cali·bra·tion** /ˈkælɪˈbreɪʃn/ *n* degree marks, etc on a measuring instrument.

cal·ibre (US = **cali·ber**) /ˈkælɪbə(r)/ *n* **1** [C] inside diameter of a tube/gun/barrel, etc. **2** [U] quality of mind or character; (person's) standing or importance: *a man of considerable ~*.

cal·ico /ˈkælɪkəʊ/ *n* (*pl* -cos, -coes /-kəʊz/) [U] cotton cloth, esp plain white cloth used for bed sheets, or with coloured designs printed on it, used for women's dresses.

cali·pers /ˈkælɪpəz/ *n pl* (US) = *callipers*.

ca·liph, ca·lif /ˈkeɪlɪf/ *n* title once used by rulers who were descendants and successors of Muhammad; chief civil and religious ruler: *the C~ of Baghdad*. **'~·ate** /ˈkeɪlɪfeɪt/ *n* ~'s position and residence.

cal·is·then·ics /ˈkælɪsˈθenɪks/ *n pl* (US) = *callisthenics*.

calk[1] /kɔk/ *vt, n* [VP6A] (provide with a) sharp iron plate in a horse-shoe or boot to prevent slipping.

calk[2] = caulk.

call[1] /kɔl/ *n* **1** shout; cry: *a ~ for help. They came at my ~,* when I shouted to them. ***within ~,*** within ~ing distance: *Please remain within ~,* close at hand. **2** characteristic cry of a bird; military signal (on a bugle, etc). **3** short visit (to sb's house, etc); short stop (at a place): *Pay a ~ on a friend. I have several ~s to make. I must return their ~,* visit them because they visited me. **port of ~,** one at which a ship stops for a short time. **place/house of ~,** (old use) one at which ~s are made regularly. **4** message; summons; invitation: *telephone ~s. I'll give you a ~. He answered the ~ of his country* (i e the summons to serve his country in some way). *Many Englishmen feel the ~ of the sea.* **'~-box** *n* small cabin (in GB more usu called a telephone kiosk) with a public telephone. **'~-boy** *n* person who summons actors from their dressing rooms when it is time for them to go on the stage. **'~-girl** *n* prostitute hired by telephone ~. **5** demand for money (esp unpaid capital from company shareholders); claim of any kind: *I have many ~s on my time,* many duties that need a lot of time. **'~-loan, '~-money, money on ~, money payable at/on ~,** money lent on condition that its return can be demanded without notice. **6** [U] (chiefly interr and neg) need; occasion: *There's no ~ for you to worry.* **7** (cards) player's right or turn to make a bid at auction bridge; bid thus made: *Whose ~ is it? Was the last ~ two spades?*

call[2] /kɔl/ *vt,vi* (For special uses with *adverbial particles* and *preps,* ⇨ 9 below.) **1** [VP2A,B,3A] say sth in a loud voice; cry; speak or shout to attract attention: *Why doesn't my son come when I ~? I thought I heard somebody ~ing. She ~ed to her father for help. I've been ~ing (for) ten minutes.* ***~ out,*** cry or shout when needing help, or from surprise, pain, etc. ⇨ 9 below. **2** [VP2A, C,3A,4A] ***~ (on sb/at a place),*** pay a short visit; go to sb's house/office etc; stop at: *I ~ed on Mr Green. I ~ed at Mr Green's house. I ~ed to see Mr Green. Mr Green was out when I ~ed. Does the steamer ~ at Naples? This train ~s at every station. A man has ~ed to read the electric light meter. The butcher's boy has ~ed to know whether you want any meat.* ***~ for,*** visit (a house, etc) to get sth, or to go somewhere with sb: *The grocer's boy ~s every Monday for orders. I'll ~ for you at 6 o'clock and we'll go to the cinema together.* **3** [VP23] name; describe as: *His name is Richard but we all ~ him Dick. What are you going to ~ the baby? He ~s himself a colonel,* claims that he has the right to this title. *You may ~ it what you like. He ~ed her a slut.* ⇨ also spade. ***~ sb names,*** abuse or insult him. ***~ sth one's own,*** claim as one's own property: *We have nothing that we can ~ our own.* ***~ into being,*** create. ***~ it a day,*** ⇨ day(3). ***~ into play,*** ⇨ play[2](8). **4** [VP22,23] consider; regard as: *Do you ~ English an easy language? I ~ that a shame. I ~ that dishonest. Shall we ~ it five quid,* (colloq) settle the price, sum, etc at five pounds? **5** [VP6A,15B] summon; wake; send a message to: *Please ~ a doctor. Please ~ me* (= wake me up) *at 6 tomorrow morning. The aircraft was ~ing* (i e sending radio signals to) *the control station at the airport. This is London ~ing,* is the BBC, London. *The doctor was ~ed away to an accident. My brother ~ed me (up)* (= telephoned to me) *from Leeds last night.* [VP12B,13B] (colloq): *Please ~ me a taxi/~ a taxi for me.* **6** (special uses, with *nouns*) ***~ sb's bluff,*** ⇨ bluff[2]. ***~ a halt (to),*** say that it is time to halt: *~ a halt to gambling,* forbid it. ***~ a meeting,*** announce that one will be held and summon people to attend. ***~ the roll,*** ⇨ roll[1](4). ***~ a strike,*** order workers to come out on strike. **7** (cards) bid or make a demand. ⇨ call[1](7). **8** (phrases) ***~ (sb) to account,*** ⇨ account[1](4). ***~ attention to,*** require (sb) to give his attention to. ***~ the banns,*** ⇨ banns. ***be ~ed to the bar,*** ⇨ bar[1](12). ***~ sth in question,*** declare that one has doubts about it. ***~ sb/a meeting to order,*** ask for orderly behaviour, ask that attention should be paid to the rules. **9** [VP15B,3A] (special uses with *adverbial particles* and *preps*):

call by, (colloq) visit briefly (usu when passing the house, etc).

call sb down, (US sl) reprimand him severely. ***~ sth down,*** invoke, ask for: *~ down curses on his head.*

call for, demand, require: *You must take such steps as seem (to be) ~ed for,* do what seems necessary. *The occasion ~s for prompt action.*

call sth forth, **(a)** be the cause of: *His behaviour ~ed forth numerous protests.* **(b)** produce and use: *You will have to ~ forth all your energy.*

call sth in, order or request the return of: *The librarian has ~ed in all books. Gold coins were ~ed in by the Government. He was so short of money that he had to ~ in the loans he had made.*

call sth off, **(a)** ~ away: *Please ~ your dog off,* ~ to your dog so that it stops worrying me. **(b)** decide, give orders, to stop sth: *The strike/attack was ~ed off,* was either not started or was

stopped. *You had better ~ the deal off,* not carry out what was agreed upon. *The engagement has been ~ed off,* ended.
call on, **(a)** make a short visit. **(b)** ⇨ call (up)on, below and call²(2).
call out, **(a)** summon, esp to an emergency: *The fire brigade was ~ed out twice yesterday. Troops had to be ~ed out.* **(b)** instruct (workers) to come out on strike: *The coalminers were ~ed out by the Union officials.*
call sth over, read (a list of names) to learn who is present. **'~-over** *n* (also **'roll-~**) reading of a list of names (e g in school, the army).
call sb/sth up, **(a)** telephone to: *I'll ~ you up this evening.* **(b)** bring back to the mind: *~ up scenes of childhood.* **(c)** summon for (military, etc) service: *If war breaks out, we shall be ~ed up at once.* Hence, **'~-up** *n*
call (up)on, appeal to; invite; require: *I ~ed (up)on him to keep his promise. I now ~ (up)on* (= invite) *Mr Grey to address the meeting. I feel ~ed upon* (= feel that I ought) *to warn you that....* **~er** *n* person who ~s on sb. **~ing** *n* (esp) occupation; profession or trade.

calla /ˈkælə/ *n* (also **'~ lily**) = arum.

cal·ligra·phy /kəˈlɪgrəfɪ/ *n* [U] handwriting: (art of) beautiful handwriting.

cal·li·ope /kəˈlaɪəpɪ/ *n* steam-organ; musical instrument with steam whistles played by pressing keys.

cal·li·pers /ˈkælɪpəz/ *n pl* **1** instrument for measuring the diameter of round objects or the calibre of tubes, etc. **2** metal supports attached to the legs of a disabled person to enable him to walk.

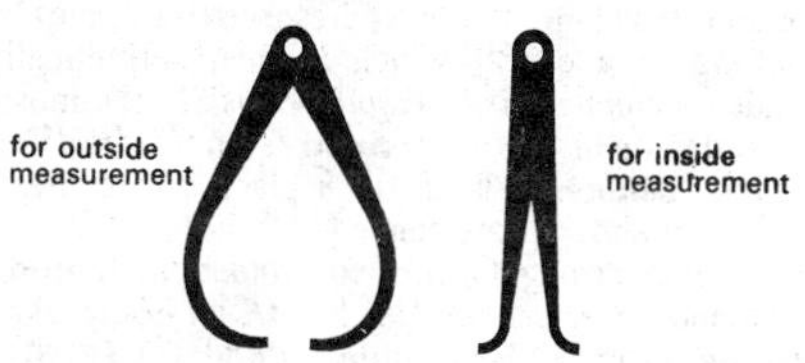

callipers

cal·lis·then·ics /ˌkælɪsˈθenɪks/ *n pl* (usu with a *sing v*) exercises designed to develop strong and graceful bodies.

cal·los·ity /kəˈlɒsətɪ/ *n* (*pl* **-ties**) area of hardened thick skin; callus.

cal·lous /ˈkæləs/ *adj* **1** (of the skin) made hard (by rough work, etc). **2** (fig) unfeeling; indifferent (*to* insults, *to* the suffering of others).

cal·low /ˈkæləʊ/ *adj* young; unfledged; inexperienced: *a ~ youth.* **~ness** *n*

cal·lus /ˈkæləs/ *n* (*pl* **-luses** /-ləsiz/) area of thick, hardened skin.

calm /kɑm/ *adj* **1** (of the weather) quiet; not windy; (of the sea) still; without large waves. **2** not excited; untroubled; quiet: *keep ~.* □ *n* **a ~,** a time when everything is quiet and peaceful. □ *vt, vi* [VP6A,15B,2C] **~ *(down),*** make or become ~: *C~ yourself! The sea ~ed down.* **~·ly** *adv* **~·ness** *n* ~ condition.

calo·mel /ˈkæləmel/ *n* [U] white, tasteless, insoluble substance used as a purgative.

Calor gas /ˈkælə gæs/ *n* [U] (P) butane.

cal·orie /ˈkælərɪ/ *n* unit of heat; unit of energy supplied by food: *An ounce of sugar supplies about 100 ~s.* **cal·or·ific** /ˌkæləˈrɪfɪk/ *adj* producing heat: *calorific value,* (of food or fuel) quantity of heat produced by a given quantity.

cal·umny /ˈkæləmnɪ/ *n* (*pl* **-nies**) [C] false statement about a person, made to damage his character; [U] slander. **ca·lum·ni·ate** /kəˈlʌmnɪeɪt/ *vt* [VP6A] slander.

Cal·vary /ˈkælvərɪ/ *n* hill outside Jerusalem where Jesus was crucified; (small *c*) carved representation of the Crucifixion.

calve /kɑv *US:* kæv/ *vi* give birth to a calf.

Cal·vin·ism /ˈkælvɪnɪzm/ *n* religious teaching of Calvin (1509-64). **Cal·vin·ist** *n* follower of Calvin's teachings.

ca·lyp·so /kəˈlɪpsəʊ/ *n* (*pl* **-sos** /-səʊz/) improvised song, as composed by West Indians, on a subject of current interest.

ca·lyx /ˈkeɪlɪks/ *n* (*pl* **-lyxes** or **calyces** /ˈkeɪlɪsiz/) ring of leaves (called *sepals*) forming the outer support of the petals of an unopened flower-bud. ⇨ the illus at **flower**.

cam /kæm/ *n* projection on a wheel or shaft, designed to change circular motion into up-and-down or back-and-forth motion. **cam·shaft** /ˈkæmʃɑft *US:* -ʃæft/ *n* ⇨ the illus at **motor**.

cama·raderie /ˌkæməˈrɑdərɪ/ *n* (F) [U] friendliness and mutual trust of comrades.

cam·ber /ˈkæmbə(r)/ *n* upwards slope (of a road surface) towards the edge of a curve. □ *vt, vi* (of a surface) have a ~; give a ~ to.

cam·bric /ˈkeɪmbrɪk/ *n* [U] fine, thin cloth of cotton or linen.

came *pt* of come.

camel /ˈkæml/ *n* long-necked animal, with either one or two humps on its back, used in desert countries for riding and for carrying goods. ⇨ the illus at **large**. **'~-'hair** *n* fine hair for making the brushes used by artists; soft, heavy cloth of this hair: *a ~-hair coat.*

ca·mellia /kəˈmilɪə/ *n* evergreen shrub from China and Japan with shiny leaves and white, red or pink rose-like flowers; the flower.

Cam·em·bert /ˈkæməmbeə(r)/ *n* (F) rich, soft cheese (of Normandy, France).

cameo /ˈkæmɪəʊ/ *n* (*pl* **-os** /-əʊz/) piece of hard stone with a raised design, often of a different colour, used as a jewel or ornament.

cam·era /ˈkæmr̩ə/ *n* **1** apparatus for taking still photographs or (**'film/'movie ~**) moving pictures, or, (**'T V ~**) for receiving light images and transforming them for broadcasting live or for receiving on video tape. **'~-man** /-mæn/ *n* (*pl* **-men**) person who operates a ~ for films or T V. **2 *in ~,*** (Lat) in the judge's private room, not in court; privately.

cami-knick·ers /ˈkæmɪnɪkəz/ *n pl* woman's undergarment (combining camisole and knickers).

cam·ion /ˈkæmɪən/ *n* (F) low, four-wheeled truck; lorry.

cami·sole /ˈkæmɪsəʊl/ *n* woman's sleeveless undergarment for the upper half of the body.

camo·mile, chamo·mile /ˈkæməmɑɪl/ *n* sweet-smelling plant with daisy-like flowers; [U] the dried flowers and leaves used in medicine as a tonic.

cam·ou·flage /ˈkæməflɑʒ/ *n* [U] **1** that which makes it difficult to recognize the presence or real nature of sth: *The white fur of the polar bear is a natural ~,* because the bear is not easily seen in the snow. **2** (in war) the use of paint, netting,

cameras

boughs of trees, smoke-screens, etc to deceive the enemy by giving a false appearance to things. □ *vt* [VP6A] try to conceal by means of ~.

camp[1] /kæmp/ *n* **1** place where people (e g people on holiday, soldiers, boy scouts, explorers) live in tents or huts for a time: *be in ~; pitch a ~; strike/break up ~*, pack up (the tents, etc). **'~-`bed/-`chair/-`stool** *n* that can be folded and carried easily. **`~-fire** *n* one of logs, etc, made in the open air. **`~-follower** *n* person (not a soldier) who follows an army to sell goods or services. **`~-meeting** *n* religious meeting (often extending over several days) held in the open air or in a large tent. ⇨ also **concentration ~**. **2** number of people with the same ideas (esp on politics or religion): *You and I belong to different political ~s. We're in the same ~*, are in agreement, are working together. □ *vi* [VP2A,C] **~ *(out)***, make, live in, a ~: *Where shall we ~ tonight? They ~ed out in the woods.* ***go ~ing,*** spend a holiday in tents, etc: *The boys have decided to go ~ing next summer.* **~er** *n* **~·ing** *n* (gerund) [U] *a ~ing holiday; Do you like ~ing?*

camp[2] /kæmp/ *adj, n* (colloq) **1** once thought of as fashionable, valid, etc but now considered to be absurdly or sentimentally old-fashioned: *high ~*, deliberately absurd affectation of this kind. **2** (of men) affectation of manners of dress, etc considered to be affected or feminine: *a ~ hairstyle*, e g curly and shoulder length; *a ~ shirt*, of brightly coloured flowery print material. □ *vi* ***~ it up,*** behave in a melodramatic or affected manner.

cam·paign /kæm`peɪn/ *n* [C] **1** group of military operations with a set purpose, usu in one area. **2** series of planned activities to gain a special object: *a political ~; an advertising ~; a ~ to raise funds.* □ *vi* [VP2A,3A] take part in, go on, a ~. **~er** *n* person who ~s or who ~ed: *He's an old ~er*, has much experience of adapting himself to circumstances.

cam·pa·nile /'kæmpə`nileɪ/ *n* bell tower, usu a separate building.

cam·pan·ula /kəm`pænjʊlə/ *n* (kinds of) plant with bell-shaped flowers, usu blue or white.

cam·phor /`kæmfə(r)/ *n* [U] strong-smelling white substance used medically and in the manufacture of celluloid. **`~ ball** *n* small ball of ~, used to keep moths, etc out of clothes. **~·ated** /`kæmfreɪtɪd/ *adj* containing ~: *~ated oil.*

cam·pion /`kæmpɪən/ *n* [C] (kinds of) common flowering plant that grows wild on roadsides and in fields.

cam·pus /`kæmpəs/ *n* (*pl* -puses /-pəsɪz/) grounds of a school, college or university.

can[1] /kæn/ *n* **1** metal container for liquids, etc: *`oil-can, `milk-can.* ***carry the can*** (*for sb*), (sl) take the blame. ***(be) in the can,*** (of film, videotape) exposed or recorded and stored ready for use. **2** (formerly US but now also GB) tin-plated airtight container (for meat, fish, fruit and other foods, also cigarettes, etc); contents of such a container: *a can of beer/peaches.* ⇨ **tin. 3** (US sl) prison. □ *vt* (-nn-) [VP6A] preserve (food, etc) by putting in a can(2) which is then hermetically sealed: *canned fish; canned music*, (sl) music recorded on discs, etc. **canned** /kænd/ *adj* (US sl) drunk. **can·nery** /`kænərɪ/ *n* place where meat, fish or other foods are canned.

can[2] /kən *strong form:* kæn/ *anom fin* (cannot /`kænət/, can't /kɑnt *US:* kænt/, *pt* could /kəd *strong form:* kʊd/, couldn't /`kʊdnt/) [VP5] **1** (indicating ability or capacity to do sth) be able to; know how to: *Can you lift this box? I can't get the lid off. She can speak French.* (*Could* refers to ability or capacity in past time; ⇨ below): *She could read Latin and Greek when she was ten.* (*Could* is used in *if-* clauses to indicate a condition, expressed or implied): *Could you lift that box* (i e now, if you tried)? *Could you have lifted that box* (i e if you had tried, e g yesterday)? (Note that *could* is not used except in conditions, for an isolated achievement in past time. Instead, *be able to, manage to* or *succeed in* (*doing sth*) are preferred): *When the boat upset, they were able/managed to swim/succeeded in swimming/to the bank* (not *they could swim to the bank* which is incorrect). **2** (*Can* is used with *vv* of perception in place of the simple tenses, which are less usual. Nothing is added to the meaning.): *I can see a sail on the horizon. I can hear people talking in the next room.* (*Could* is used for past time): *We could hear someone singing in the bathroom. She said she could smell something burning.* **3** (*Can* is used, colloquial style, to indicate permission. The use of *may* is more formal. In reported speech, *could* is used after a *v* in the *pt*. It may also replace *can* in a tentative request in question form): *You* *can* (= may) *go home now. The children asked whether they could* (= might) *go for a swim. Do you think we could* (= might) *start early?* (The negative *can't* indicates what is not allowed): *You can't travel first-class with a second-class ticket. Put that cigarette out! You can't smoke near a petrol pump!* **4** (*Can/could* are used to indicate what is possible or likely): *One of the prisoners escaped yesterday; he can/could* (= may) *be anywhere by now.* (*Can have* is used for past time): *He's an hour late: he can have been delayed by fog, of course,* that's a possibility. **5** (*Can/could* in questions (and esp with *what(ever), where, how*) indicate surprise, bewilderment, impatience, etc, according to context. The strong forms are used): *What 'can he `mean? What 'can we `do about it? Where 'can they have `got to? How 'can/'could you be so un`kind?* **6** (*Can/could* indicate what is considered characteristic, what sb or sth is considered capable of being or doing. Adverbials of frequency (e g *at times, sometimes*) often occur): *Children can sometimes be very trying. It can be very cold here, even in May. The Bay of Biscay can be very rough at times. When I first knew her she could be very sarcastic, but she's more tolerant now.* **7** (*Could* may mean 'feel inclined to'): *I could smack your face!*

Ca·nadian /kə`neɪdɪən/ *n, adj* (native) of Canada.

ca·naille /kæ`nɑɪ/ *n* (F) the rabble.

ca·nal /kə`næl/ *n* **1** channel cut through land for use of boats or ships (e g *the Suez C~*) or to carry water to fields for irrigation. ⇨ the illus at lock. **`~ boat** *n* long, narrow boat, some of which are pulled by horses, used on ~s. **2** tube or pipe (or system of these) in a plant or animal body for food, air, etc: *the alimentary ~.* ⇨ the illus at alimentary, ear. **~·ize** /`kænəlɑɪz/ [VP6A,14] make (a river) into a ~ (by straightening, building locks, etc); (fig) direct; channel: *~ize one's energies/efforts into charity work.* **~·iz·ation** /'kænəlɑɪ`zeɪʃn/ *US:* -lɪ`z-/ *n*

can·apé /`kænəpeɪ *US:* 'kænə`peɪ/ *n* (F) thin piece of bread or toast spread with seasoned fish, cheese, etc.

ca·nard /kæ`nɑd/ *n* (F) false report.

ca·nary /kə`neərɪ/ *n* (*pl* -ries) **1** (also **`~-bird**) small, yellow-feathered song-bird, usu kept in a cage; [U] its colour, light yellow. **2** (also **`~-wine**) sweet white wine from the C~ Islands.

ca·nasta /kə`næstə/ *n* card game (using two packs of 52 cards) of Uruguayan origin.

can·can /`kænkæn/ *n* lively high-kicking dance performed by a group of women in long skirts.

can·cel /`kænsl/ *vt, vi* (GB -ll-, US -l-) **1** [VP6A] cross out, draw a line through (words or figures); make a mark on (sth, e g postage stamps, to prevent re-use): *~led stamps.* **2** [VP6A] say that sth already arranged or decided upon will not be done, will not take place, etc: *He ~led his order for the goods,* said that he no longer wanted to receive them. *The sports meeting was ~led.* **3** [VP3A,15B] **~ out,** (arith) (of items from the numerator and denominator) neutralize, make up for, each other: *The arguments ~ (each other) out.* **4** [VP1] *~ an indicator/flasher,* (in a motor vehicle) switch off lights which indicate one is turning. **~·la·tion** /'kænsl`eɪʃn/ *n* [U] ~ling or being ~led; [C] instance of this; mark(s) used in, made by, ~ling (e g on postage stamps).

can·cer /`kænsə(r)/ *n* [C,U] diseased growth in the body, often causing death: *~ of the throat; lung ~*; (fig) pernicious evil (e g in Society). **~·ous** /`kænsərəs/ *adj* of or like ~; having ~.

Can·cer /`kænsə(r)/ *n* **Tropic of ~,** the parallel of latitude $32\frac{1}{2}$°N; fourth sign of the zodiac, ⇨ the illus at zodiac.

can·de·la·brum /'kændɪ`lɑbrəm/ *n* (*pl* -bra /-brə/) ornamental holder or support with branches for candles.

can·did /`kændɪd/ *adj* **1** frank, straightforward: *I will be quite ~ with you: I think you acted foolishly.* **2** *~ camera,* small camera for taking informal or unposed photographs of people. **~·ly** *adv*

can·di·date /`kændɪdət -deɪt/ *n* **1** person who wishes, or who is put forward by others, to take an office or position (e g for election to Parliament): *The Labour ~ was elected. He offered himself as a ~ for the position.* **2** person taking an examination. **can·di·da·ture** /`kændɪdətʃə(r)/ *n* being a ~(1).

can·died ⇨ candy.

candle /`kændl/ *n* round stick of wax, etc with a wick through it, for giving light. ***burn the ~ at both ends,*** use up too much energy; work very early and very late. ***can't/is not fit to hold a ~ to,*** is not to be compared to, is not nearly so good as. ***The game is not worth the ~,*** is more trouble and expense than it is worth. **`~-light** *n* light of ~s: *reading by ~light.* **`~-power** *n* unit of light measurement: *a ten ~-power lamp.* **`~-stick** *n* holder or support for (usu) a single ~.

can·dour (US = **-dor**) /`kændə(r)/ *n* [U] quality of being candid; saying freely what one thinks.

candy /`kændɪ/ *n* **1** (also **'sugar-`~**) [U] sugar made hard by repeated boilings; [C] (*pl* -dies) piece of this. **2** [C,U] (US only; GB = *sweets*) shaped piece(s) of cooked and flavoured sugar, syrup, etc usu with fruit juices, milk, nuts, etc added. □ *vt, vi* **1** [VP6A] preserve (e g fruit) by boiling or cooking in sugar: *candied plums/lemon peel.* **2** [VP2A] form into sugar crystals. **can·died** /`kændɪd/ (*pp* as *adj*) sweet or agreeable; flattering: *candied words.*

candy·tuft /`kændɪtʌft/ *n* garden plant with flat tufts of white, pink or purple flowers.

cane /keɪn/ *n* **1** long, hollow, jointed stem of tall reeds and grass-like plants (e g bamboo, sugar-~), either [U] collectively and as material for making furniture, etc or [C] of one stem or a length of it (e g used for supporting plants, as a walking-stick): *a chair with a ~ seat; raspberry ~s.* **`~ sugar** *n* sugar made from sugar-~, chemically the same as beet sugar. **2** length of ~ used as an instrument for punishing children. ***get the ~,*** be punished with a ~. □ *vt* [VP6A] punish with a ~(2).

ca·nine /`kænɑɪn *US:* `keɪnɑɪn/ *adj* of, as of, a dog or dogs. **`~ tooth** *n* (in a human being) one of the four pointed teeth. ⇨ the illus at mouth.

can·is·ter /`kænɪstə(r)/ *n* **1** small box (usu metal) with a lid, used for holding tea, etc. **2** cylinder which, when thrown, or fired from a gun, bursts and scatters its contents: *a `tear-gas ~.*

can·ker /`kæŋkə(r)/ *n* **1** [U] disease that destroys the wood of trees; disease that causes the formation of ulcers in the human mouth, in the ears of dogs and cats, etc. **2** (fig) evil influence or tendency that causes decay. □ *vt* destroy by ~; be a ~ to. **~·ous** /`kæŋkərəs/ *adj* of or like ~; causing ~.

canna /ˈkænə/ *n* plant with large, ornamental leaves and bright yellow, red or orange flowers; the flower.

can·na·bis /ˈkænəbɪs/ *n* [U] Indian hemp, a drug also known as *hashish* and *marijuana*, smoked or chewed as an intoxicant. ⇨ hemp.

canned, can·nery ⇨ can.

can·ni·bal /ˈkænəbl/ *n* person who eats human flesh; animal that eats its own kind; (attrib) of or like ~s: *a ~ feast.* **~·ism** /ˈkænəblɪzm/ *n* practice of eating the flesh of one's own kind. **~·is·tic** /ˌkænəblˈɪstɪk/ *adj* of or like ~s. **~·ize** /ˈkænəbl̩-aɪz/ *vt* use (one of a number of similar machines, engines, etc) to provide spare parts for others.

a cannon

can·non /ˈkænən/ *n* **1** (collective *sing* often used instead of *pl*) large, heavy gun, fixed to the ground or to a guncarriage, esp the old kind that fired a solid ball of metal (called a ˈ*~-ball*). (*Gun* and *shell* are the words used for modern weapons). **2** heavy, automatic gun, firing explosive shells, used in modern aircraft in war. ˈ**~-fodder** *n* men regarded as expendable material in war. **~·ade** /ˌkænəˈneɪd/ *n* continued firing of big guns.

can·not ⇨ can².

canny /ˈkænɪ/ *adj* (-nier, -niest) not prepared to take unknown risks, shrewd, esp about money matters. **can·nily** *adv*

ca·noe /kəˈnu/ *n* light boat moved by one or more paddles. □ *vt* [VP2A,C] travel by ~. **~·ist** *n* person who paddles a ~.

canoeing

canon /ˈkænən/ *n* **1** ecclesiastical decree: *~ law,* church law. **2** general standard or principle by which sth is judged: *the ~s of conduct/good taste.* **3** body of writings accepted as genuine; those books of the Bible accepted as genuine by the Christian Church; also of other sacred books, and of an author's works: *the Chaucer ~.* **4** official list (esp of R C saints). **5** priest (with the title *the Rev C~*) who is one of a group with duties in a cathedral. ⇨ chapter(3). **ca·noni·cal** /kəˈnonɪkl/ *adj* according to ~ law; authorized; regular: *~ical books; ~ical dress,* i e of priests. **~·ize** *vt* [VP6A] place (a person) in the ~(4); authorize. **~iz·ation** /ˌkænənaɪˈzeɪʃn *US:* -nɪˈz-/ *n* ~izing or being ~ized.

cañon ⇨ canyon.

ca·noodle /kəˈnudl/ *vt,vi* (dated sl) fondle; cuddle.

can·opy /ˈkænəpɪ/ *n* (*pl* -pies) (usu cloth) covering over a bed, throne, etc or held (on poles) over a person; cover for the cockpit of an aircraft, ⇨ the illus at air¹; (fig) any overhanging covering: *the ~ of the heavens,* the sky; *a ~ of leaves,* e g in a forest.

cant¹ /kænt/ *n* [U] **1** insincere talk (esp implying piety); hypocrisy. **2** special talk, words, used by a class of people, a sect, etc; jargon: *thieves' ~;* (attrib) *a ~ phrase.*

cant² /kænt/ *n* sloping or sideways surface or position. □ *vt,vi* [VP6A,15B,2A,C] give, have, a ~: *~ a boat for repairs.*

can't /kɑnt *US:* kænt/ = cannot, ⇨ can².

Can·tab /ˈkæntæb/ *n, adj* (member) of Cambridge University.

can·ta·loup, -loupe /ˈkæntəlup/ *n* kind of melon.

can·tank·er·ous /kænˈtæŋkərəs/ *adj* bad-tempered: quarrelsome. **~·ly** *adv*

can·tata /kænˈtɑtə/ *n* short musical work to be sung by soloists and a choir, usu a dramatic story, but not acted.

can·teen /kænˈtin/ *n* **1** place (esp in factories, offices, barracks) where food, drink and other articles are sold and meals bought and eaten. **2** box or chest of table silver and cutlery (knives, forks, spoons). **3** soldier's eating and drinking utensils; mess-tin. **4** soldier's water container (usu of metal).

can·ter /ˈkæntə(r)/ *n* (of a horse) easy gallop: *The horse won the race at a ~,* won easily. □ *vt,vi* (cause to) gallop gently.

can·ticle /ˈkæntɪkl/ *n* short hymn, esp one of the Prayer Book hymns.

can·ti·lever /ˈkæntɪlivə(r)/ *n* long, large, armlike bracket extending from a wall or base (e g to support a balcony). ˈ**~ bridge** *n* one built on supports from which ~s extend and join. ⇨ the illus at bridge.

canto /ˈkæntəʊ/ *n* (*pl* -tos /-təʊz/) chief division of a long poem.

can·ton /ˈkænton/ *n* subdivision of a country (esp of Switzerland).

can·ton·ment /kænˈtunmənt/ *n* (esp in India and Pakistan) permanent military station; place where soldiers live.

can·tor /ˈkæntə(r)/ *n* **1** leader of the singing in a church; precentor. **2** precentor in a synogogue.

Ca·nuck /kəˈnʊk/ *n* (sl) French Canadian.

can·vas /ˈkænvəs/ *n* [U] strong, coarse cloth used for tents, sails, bags, etc and by artists for oil-paintings; [C] (piece of this for an) oil-painting. ***under ~,*** **(a)** (of soldiers, scouts, etc) living in tents. **(b)** (of a ship) with sails spread.

can·vass /ˈkænvəs/ *vt,vi* **1** [VP2A,3A] ***~ (for),*** go from person to person and ask for votes, orders for goods, subscriptions, etc or to learn about people's views on a question: *He is ~ing for the Conservative candidate.* **2** [VP6A] discuss thoroughly; examine by discussion. □ *n* ~ing.

can·yon, cañon /ˈkænjən/ *n* deep gorge (usu with a river flowing through it).

cap /kæp/ *n* **1** soft head-covering worn by boys and men, by some sailors and soldiers, without a brim, but often with a peak; special cap awarded to members of football teams, etc or worn to show rank: *a cardinal's cap;* academic head-dress with a flat top and a tassel: *wearing his cap and gown.* ⇨ mortar-board. **2** indoor head-dress worn by nurses, some women servants, and formerly by old women. **3** cap-like cover (e g on a milk bottle). **4** *per'cussion cap,* small quantity of gunpowder in a wrapper of paper, etc, used as a detonator. **5** (phrases) ***cap and bells,*** cap trimmed with bells, as formerly worn by jesters. ***if the cap fits,*** if a person feels that the remark applies to him. ***cap in hand,*** humbly. ***set one's cap at sb,*** (of a girl or woman) try to attract as a suitor. □ *vt* (-pp-) [VP6A] **1** put a cap on; cover the top of. **2** do or say sth better than (what sb else has done or said). ***cap a story/joke,*** tell a more amusing one. **3** award (a player) a cap (as a member of a football team, etc): *He's been capped 36 times for England.* (Scottish universities) confer a degree on.

ca·pa·bil·ity /ˈkeɪpəˈbɪlətɪ/ *n* **1** [U] power (*of* doing things, *to do* things); fitness or capacity (*for* being improved, etc): *nuclear ~,* power, capacity, to wage nuclear war. **2** (*pl*) (-ties) undeveloped faculties; qualities, etc, that can be developed: *The boy has great capabilities.*

ca·pable /ˈkeɪpəbl/ *adj* **1** gifted; able: *a very ~ doctor/nurse/teacher.* **2** *~ **of,*** (**a**) (of persons) having the power, ability or inclination: *Show your teacher what you are ~ of,* Show him how well you can work. *He's quite ~ of neglecting his duty,* is the sort of man who might do so. *He's ~ of any crime.* (**b**) (of things, situations, etc) ready for; admitting of; open to: *The situation is ~ of improvement.* **ca·pably** /-əblɪ/ *adv*

ca·pa·cious /kəˈpeɪʃəs/ *adj* able to hold much: *a ~ memory; ~ pockets.* **~·ness** *n*

ca·pac·ity /keˈpæsətɪ/ *n* **1** [U] (and with *indef art*) ability to hold, contain, get hold of, learn things/qualities/ideas etc: *The hall has a seating ~ of 500,* has seats for 500 people. *The theatre was filled to ~,* was quite full. *He has a mind of great ~,* a mind well able to grasp ideas. *This book is within the ~ of* (= can be understood by) *young readers. Some persons have more ~ for happiness* (= a greater power of experiencing happiness) *than others.* **2** [C] (*pl* -ties) position; character: *I am your friend, but in my ~ as an officer of the law I must take you into custody.*

cap-à-pie /ˈkæp ə ˈpi/ *adv* ***armed ~,*** armed from head to foot, completely.

ca·pari·son /kəˈpærɪsn/ *n* (often *pl*; old use) ornamental covering for a horse, or for a horse and the knight who rode it. □ *vt* put a ~ on (a horse).

cape[1] /keɪp/ *n* loose sleeveless garment, hanging from the shoulders.

cape[2] /keɪp/ *n* high point of land going out into the sea; headland. **the C~,** (S Africa) the C~ of Good Hope; C~ Province.

ca·per[1] /ˈkeɪpə(r)/ *vi* jump about playfully. □ *n* ***cut a ~/~s,*** jump about merrily; act foolishly or fantastically.

ca·per[2] /ˈkeɪpə(r)/ *n* prickly shrub; (*pl*) pickled flower-buds of this shrub, used to make ~ sauce.

cap·il·lary /kəˈpɪlərɪ *US:* ˈkæpleri/ *n* (*pl* -ries) tube with a hair-like diameter (e g joining the arteries and veins) ⇨ the illus at respiratory: (attrib) *~ attraction,* attraction of the kind that causes blotting-paper to absorb ink, or oil to rise through the wick of an oil lamp.

capi·tal /ˈkæpɪtl/ *n* (often attrib) **1** town or city where the government of a country, state or county is carried on: *Melbourne is the ~ of Victoria. London, Paris and Rome are ~ cities.* **2** (of letters of the alphabet) not small: *The pronoun 'I' is written and printed with a ~ letter. Write your name in ~ letters/in ~s.* **3** [U] wealth/money/property that may be used for the production of more wealth; money with which a business, etc is started (e g for building or buying factories, buying machinery): *~ expenditure,* on equipment, etc; *fixed ~,* machinery, etc; *floating ~,* goods, etc; *C~ and Labour,* owners of ~ and those who work for them; *a ~ levy,* confiscation by the State of a part of all private property; *~ gain,* profit made from the sale of ~ assets or real property; *~ goods,* e g ships, railways, etc for use in producing other consumer goods. *The company has a ~ of £500 000.* ***make ~ of,*** turn to account, use to one's own advantage. **4** head, top part, of a column. ⇨ the illus at column. □ *adj* **1** punishable by death: *~ offences.* **2** (colloq) excellent, first-rate: *He made a ~ speech. What a ~ idea!* **~·ism** *n* economic system in which a country's trade and industry are organized and controlled by the owners of ~(3), the chief elements being competition, profit, supply and demand. ⇨ socialism. **~·ist** /-ɪst/ *n* person who controls much ~(3). **~·is·tic** /ˈkæpɪtlˈɪstɪk/ *adj*

capi·tal·ize /ˈkæpɪtlaɪz/ *vt,vi* **1** [VP6A] write or print with a capital letter. **2** convert into, use as, capital(3); (fig) take advantage of; use to one's advantage or profit. **3** [VP3A] *~ **on,*** profit by; exploit: *~ on the errors of a rival firm.* **capi·tal·iz·ation** /ˈkæpɪtlaɪˈzeɪʃn *US:* -lɪˈzeɪʃn/ *n*

capi·ta·tion /ˈkæpɪˈteɪʃn/ *n* (reckoning of) tax, fee, charge or grant of an equal sum per person.

Capi·tol /ˈkæpɪtl/ *n* building in which the United States Congress meets.

ca·pitu·late /kəˈpɪtʃʊleɪt/ *vt* [VP2A] surrender (on stated conditions). **ca·pitu·la·tion** /kəˈpɪtʃʊˈleɪʃn/ *n* **1** [U] surrendering (on stated conditions). **2** (*pl*) agreement by which foreign residents in a country have extra-territorial rights.

ca·pon /ˈkeɪpən *US:* -pon/ *n* cock (male domestic fowl) castrated and fattened for eating.

ca·price /kəˈpris/ *n* **1** (often sudden) change of mind or behaviour that has no obvious cause; tendency to change suddenly without apparent cause. **2** piece of music in a lively, irregular style.

ca·pri·cious /kəˈprɪʃəs/ *adj* often changing; irregular; unreliable; guided by caprice: *a ~ breeze,* often or suddenly changing in direction. **~·ly** *adv*

Cap·ri·corn /ˈkæprɪkɔn/ *n* **Tropic of ~,** the parallel of latitude 23½°S; tenth sign of the zodiac, ⇨ the illus at zodiac.

cap·si·cum /ˈkæpsɪkəm/ *n* kinds of plant with seed-pods containing hot-tasting seeds; such pods prepared for use in cooking, etc. ⇨ cayenne, pepper(2).

cap·size /kæpˈsaɪz/ *vt,vi* [VP6A,2A] (esp of a boat in the water) (cause to) overturn, upset.

cap·stan /ˈkæpstən/ *n* upright barrel-like object turned by men who walk round it pushing horizontal levers, or (more usu today) by steam, etc, power, used for raising anchors, sails, etc and for pulling a ship to a wharf, etc.

cap·sule /ˈkæpsjul *US:* ˈkæpsl/ *n* **1** seed-case that opens when the seeds are ripe. **2** tiny soluble container for a dose of medicine. **3** metal cap for a bottle. **4** (recoverable or non-recoverable) receptacle (for scientific instruments, or an astronaut) which can be ejected from a spacecraft.

a space capsule

cap·tain /ˋkæptɪn/ *n* **1** leader or chief commander: *the ~ of a ship/fire-brigade/football or cricket team.* **2** (in the army) officer (below a major and above a lieutenant) who commands a company; (in the navy) officer below an admiral and above a commander. ⇨ App 9. □ *vt* [VP6A] act as ~ of (a football team, etc).

cap·tion /ˋkæpʃn/ *n* short title or heading of an article in a periodical, etc; words printed with a photograph or illustration, etc; word(s) on a movie film to establish the scene of the story, etc (e g Dover 1940). Cf *sub-titles.*

cap·tious /ˋkæpʃəs/ *adj* (fond of) finding fault, making protests, etc esp about unimportant points. **~·ly** *adv*

cap·ti·vate /ˋkæptɪveɪt/ *vt* [VP6A] capture the fancy of; fascinate: *He was ~d by Helen/~d with her charm.*

cap·tive /ˋkæptɪv/ *n, adj* **1** (person, animal) taken prisoner, kept as a prisoner. ***be taken/hold sb ~,*** take or keep them prisoner. **ˈ~ ˋballoon,** one that is held to the ground by a cable. **2 ˈ~ ˋaudience,** one that cannot get away easily and is, therefore, open to persuasion (e g schoolchildren watching TV). **cap·tiv·ity** /kæpˋtɪvətɪ/ *n* [U] state of being held ~: *Some birds will not sing in captivity.*

cap·tor /ˋkæptə(r)/ *n* person who takes sb captive.

cap·ture /ˋkæptʃə(r)/ *vt* [VP6A] make a prisoner of; take or obtain as a prize by force, trickery, skill, etc: *Our army ~d 500 of the enemy. The police have not ~d the thief yet. Tom was so clever that he ~d most of the prizes at school. This advertisement will ~ the attention of readers everywhere.* □ *n* [U] act of capturing: *the ~ of a thief;* [C] thing that is ~d.

car /kɑ(r)/ *n* **1** motor-car or tram-car (street-car). ⇨ these words and the illus at motor. **ˋcar-ferry** *n* ferry (sea or air) for taking cars (e g across the English Channel). **ˋcar-port** *n* open-sided shelter for a motor vehicle. **2** (on a railway train) (in GB) coach: *ˋdining-car; ˋsleeping-car.* (in US also) wagon for goods: *ˋfreight-car* (= GB *goods-wagon*). **3** that part of a balloon, airship or lift (US *elevator*) used by passengers. **4** (poet) wheeled vehicle; chariot: *the car of the sun-god.*

ca·rafe /kəˋræf/ *n* water-bottle, or decanter for wine, for use at table.

cara·mel /ˋkærəml/ *n* **1** [U] burnt sugar used for colouring and flavouring. **2** [C] small, shaped piece of sticky boiled sugar; sweetmeat.

cara·pace /ˋkærəpeɪs/ *n* shell on the back of a tortoise and crustaceans. ⇨ the illus at crustacean, reptile.

carat /ˋkærət/ *n* **1** unit of weight (about three and one-fifth grains) for precious stones. **2** measure of the purity of gold, pure gold being 24 ~: *a gold ring of 20 ~,* i e 20 parts gold, 4 parts alloy.

cara·van /ˋkærəvæn/ *n* **1** company of persons (e g pilgrims, merchants) making a journey together for safety, usu across desert country. **2** covered cart or wagon used for living in, e g by gipsies or people on holiday, esp (today) the kind pulled behind a motor vehicle. ⇨ also trailer at trail. **~-ning** *n* (the practice of) taking holidays in a ~. **~·sary, ~·serai** /ˈkærəˋvæn-sərɪ, sərɑɪ/ *n* inn with a large inner courtyard where ~s put up in Eastern countries.

a caravan of camels

a gypsy caravan

a modern caravan

caravans

cara·way /ˋkærəweɪ/ *n* plant with spicy seeds used to flavour bread, cakes, etc.

car·bide /ˋkɑbɑɪd/ *n* compound of carbon. ⇨ calcium.

car·bine /ˋkɑbɑɪn/ *n* short rifle (originally for soldiers on horseback).

carbo·hy·drate /ˈkɑbəʊˋhɑɪdreɪt/ *n* [C,U] (kinds of) organic compound including sugars and starches; (*pl*) starchy foods, considered to be fattening.

car·bolic acid /ˈkɑˈbolɪk ˋæsɪd/ *n* [U] strong-smelling, powerful liquid used as an antiseptic and disinfectant.

car·bon /ˋkɑbən/ *n* **1** [U] non-metallic element (symbol **C**) that occurs in all living matter, in its pure form as diamonds and graphite and in an impure form in coal and charcoal. **ˋ~ black** *n* black powder obtained by partly burning oil, wood, etc. **ˋ~ dating,** method of dating prehistoric objects by measuring the decay by radioactive isotopes. **2** [C] stick or pencil of ~ used in an electric arc-lamp. **3** [C,U] (also **ˋ~-paper**) (sheet of) thin paper coated with coloured matter, used between sheets of writing paper for taking copies. **4** [C] (also **~ copy**) copy made by the use of ~-paper. **5 ˈ~ diˋoxide** *n* gas (CO_2) produced by animal bodies and breathed out from the lungs, used in canned beers and soft drinks, in aerosols, etc. '~ **mon'oxide** *n* poisonous gas (**CO**) produced when ~ burns, present in the exhaust gas of petrol engines and after explosions in coal mines. '~**·ated** /'kabəneɪtɪd/ *adj* containing ~ dioxide: *~ed beverages.* ~**·if·er·ous** /'kabə'nɪfərəs/ *adj* (geol) producing coal: *~iferous strata.* ~**·ize** *vt* [VP6A] convert into ~ by burning. ~**·iz·ation** /'kabənaɪ'zeɪʃn *US:* -nɪ'z-/ *n*

car·bonic acid /ka'bonɪk 'æsɪd/ *n* [U] carbon dioxide dissolved in water (e g giving the sharp taste to soda water).

car·bor·un·dum /'kabə'rʌndəm/ *n* (P) hard compound of carbon and silicon, used for polishing and grinding.

car·boy /'kabɔɪ/ *n* large, round glass or plastic bottle, usu enclosed in basketwork or a crate to protect it from being broken.

car·buncle /'kabʌŋkl/ *n* **1** bright-red jewel. **2** red (usu painful) inflamed swelling under the skin.

car·bu·ret·tor, -retor, -ret·ter /'kabjʊ'retə(r) *US:* 'kærbəreɪtər/ *n* that part of an internal-combustion engine in which petrol (US = gasoline) and air are mixed to make an explosive mixture. ⇨ the illus at motor.

car·cass, car·case /'kakəs/ *n* **1** dead body of an animal (esp one prepared for cutting up as meat): *~ meat,* meat from a ~ (contrasted with tinned or corned meat). **2** (contemptuous) human body. **3** shell(2).

card[1] /kad/ *n* **1** (usu small, oblong-shaped) piece of stiff paper or thin cardboard, as used for various purposes, e g *a visiting-~* (US *calling ~*), with a person's name, etc on it; *'Christmas/New 'Year/ 'Birthday ~s,* sent with greetings at Christmas, etc; *'record ~,* one for keeping records, notes, etc, and stored in a box or drawer; *~ index,* index on ~s. ~**-carrying member** *n* registered member of a group, political party, trade union, etc. '~ **vote** *n* vote taken at a trade union meeting at which each delegate has a ~ representing a certain number of workers. **2** programme for a race meeting or game, with details, and space for marking results: *a 'score ~,* e g for cricket. **3** (esp) one of the 52 cards (often *playing-~*) used for various games (whist, bridge, poker, etc) and for telling fortunes. ***have a ~ up one's sleeve,*** have a secret plan in reserve. ***hold/keep one's ~s close to one's chest,*** ⇨ chest(2). ***make a ~,*** take a trick (⇨ trick(5)) with it. ***on the ~s,*** (from fortune-telling by ~s) likely or possible. ***one's best ~,*** one's strongest argument, best way of getting what one wants. ***play one's ~s well,*** do one's business cleverly, with good judgement. ***play a sure/ safe/doubtful ~,*** use a plan or expedient that is sure, etc. ***put one's ~s on the table,*** make one's plans, intentions, etc, known. '~**-sharper** *n* person who makes a living by swindling at ~ games. **4** (dated hum) person who is odd or amusing.

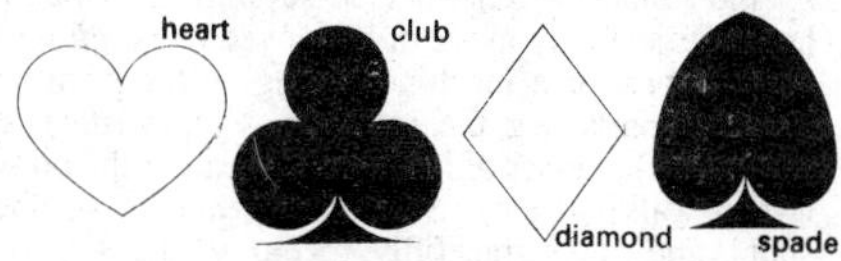

playing-card symbols

card[2] /kad/ *n* toothed instrument, wire brush, for combing or cleaning wool. □ *vt* clean or comb wool, hemp, etc with such an instrument.

car·da·mom /'kadəməm/ *n* [U] aromatic spice from seed-capsules of various East Indian plants.

card·board /'kadbɔd/ *n* [U] thick, stiff kind of paper or pasteboard, used for making boxes, binding books, etc.

car·diac /'kadɪæk/ *adj* of the heart: *~ muscle; ~ symptoms,* i e of heart, disease.

car·di·gan /'kadɪgən/ *n* knitted woollen jacket that buttons up the front, made with sleeves. ⇨ pullover, sweater.

car·di·nal /'kadnl/ *adj* chief; most important; on which sth depends: *the ~ virtues.* ~ **numbers,** e g 5, 17, 717,... (contrasted with *ordinal numbers*); *the ~ points,* of the compass (N, S, E and W). ⇨ the illus at compass. □ *n* **1** member of the Sacred College of the R C Church, which elects Popes. **2** bright red.

care[1] /keə(r)/ *n* **1** [U] serious attention or thought; watchfulness; pains: *You should take more ~ over your work. This is made of glass, so take ~ not to break it. Glass, with ~!* e g as a warning when goods are sent by rail. *Take ~ (that) you don't get run over when you cross the street. Do your work with more ~.* (Used with the *indef art*): *Have a ~* (= Take ~), be cautious. ***take ~ of,*** (colloq) deal with, be responsible for. **2** [U] protection; charge; responsibility: *The child was left in its sister's ~. The library is under the ~ of Mr Grey. I will leave this in your ~,* leave you responsible for it. **~ of,** (often written **c/o**) used in addresses before the name of the person(s) to whose house, office, etc a letter is sent. **Child C~ Officer** *n* (in GB but no longer current, now *social worker*) person appointed to look after children who are homeless or whose parents are neglectful, etc. ***take into ~,*** (of such an officer) take (a child lacking proper ~) to an institution. '~**·taker** *n* person paid to take ~ of a building during the owner's absence; person in charge of a public building such as an old castle, a small museum: *the school ~taker,* (US = *janitor*); *a ~taker Government,* administration that continues in office until a new one is formed to take over its work. **3** [U] sorrow; anxiety; troubled state of mind caused by doubt or fear: *free from ~. C~ had made him look ten years older.* '~**-free** *adj* free from ~. '~**·worn** *adj* (sometimes *'~-laden*) laden with, troubled by, anxiety. **4** [C] (usu *pl*) cause of sorrow and anxiety: *He was rich and free from ~s of every kind. He was poor and troubled by the ~s of a large family.*

care[2] /keə(r)/ *vi* **1** [VP2A,3A,B] (with *prep* usu omitted before a clause) ***~ (about),*** feel interest, anxiety or sorrow: *He failed in the examination but I don't think he ~s very much/he doesn't seem to ~. He doesn't ~ much (about) what happens to me. He doesn't ~ what they say. I don't ~ who you are/how soon you leave. He doesn't ~ a damn,* is not in the least interested, worried, etc. *I don't much ~ about going. Well, who ~s?* **2** [VP3A] ***~ for,*** like (to have): *Would you ~ for a drink? I shouldn't ~ for that man to be my doctor. He doesn't much ~ for television.* **3** [VP3A] ***~ for,*** have a taste for; like: *Do you ~ for modern music?* **4** [VP3A] ***~ for,*** look after, provide food, attendance, etc: *Who will ~ for the children if their mother dies? The State must ~ for the families of soldiers killed in the war.* **5** [VP4C] like; be willing or desirous (inter and neg only): *Would* *you ~ to go for a walk? I don't ~ to be seen in his company.*

ca·reen /kə`rin/ *vt, vi* **1** [VP6A] turn (a ship) on one side for cleaning, repairing, etc. **2** [VP6A,2A] (cause to) tilt, lean over to one side.

ca·reer /kə`rɪə(r)/ *n* **1** [C] progress through life; development and progress of a party/principle etc: *We can learn much by reading about the ~s of great men.* **2** [C] way of making a living; profession: *Should all ~s be open to women,* Should women be allowed to enter all occupations? (attrib) professional: *a ~ diplomatist; a `~ girl,* (esp) one who prefers a ~ to marriage. **3** [U] quick or violent forward movement: *in full ~,* at full speed; *stop (sb) in mid ~.* □ *vi* [VP2C,3A] **~ *about/along/past/through, etc,*** rush wildly. **~·ist** /-ɪst/ *n* person whose chief interest is personal advancement in his profession.

care·ful /`keəfl/ *adj* **1** (of a person) taking care; cautious; thinking of, paying attention to, what one does, says, etc: *Be ~ not to break the eggs. Be ~ what you do/where you go/how you carry it etc. Be more ~ with your work. Be ~ of your health. Be ~ (about) what you say.* **2** done with, showing, care: *a ~ piece of work; a ~ examination of the facts.* **~·ly** /-flɪ/ *adv* **~·ness** *n*

care·less /`keələs/ *adj* **1** (of a person) not taking care; thoughtless: *He is ~ about leaving the door unlocked when he goes to bed. A ~ driver is a danger to the public.* **2** done or made without care: *a ~ mistake.* **3** (liter) light-hearted; gay: *~ little songbirds.* **4** unconcerned about; uncomplainingly accepting: *He is ~ of his reputation. The soldiers were ~ of hardship.* **~·ly** *adv* **~·ness** *n: a piece of ~ness,* a ~ act.

ca·ress /kə`res/ *n* [C] loving or affectionate touch; kiss. □ *vt* [VP6A] give a ~ or ~es to. **~·ing** *adj* showing love. **~·ing·ly** *adv*

caret /`kæret/ *n* mark (‸) used (e g in correcting proofs) to show, in writing or print, where sth is to be inserted.

cargo /`kɑgəʊ/ *n* (*pl* -goes, US also -gos /-gəʊz/) [C,U] goods carried in a ship, aircraft or other vehicle.

cari·bou /`kærɪbu/ *n* (*pl* -bous or, collective *pl* -bou) N American reindeer.

cari·ca·ture /'kærɪkə`tʃʊə(r) *US:* `kærɪkətʃʊər/ *n* **1** [C] picture of sb or sth, imitation of a person's voice, behaviour, etc, stressing certain features in order to cause amusement or ridicule. **2** [C] art of doing this. □ *vt* [VP6A] make, give, a ~ of. **cari·ca·tur·ist** *n* expert in ~.

car·ies /`keərɪz/ *n* [U] decay (of bones or teeth): *dental ~.* **cari·ous** /`keərɪəs/ *adj* (of bone) affected with ~.

car·il·lon /`kærɪljən *US:* `kærl̩on/ *n* set of bells in a tower on which tunes may be played by some kind of mechanism (e g a keyboard).

Car·mel·ite /`kɑmɪlɑɪt/ *n* (also *White Friar*) member of an order of monks or friars founded in 1155 or of a community of nuns of this order.

car·mine /`kɑmɑɪn/ *n, adj* deep red colour, colouring matter.

car·nage /`kɑnɪdʒ/ *n* [U] killing of many people: *a scene of ~,* e g a battlefield.

car·nal /`kɑnl/ *adj* of the body or flesh; sensual (opp to spiritual): *~ desires.* **~·ly** *adv*

car·na·tion /kɑ`neɪʃn/ *n* garden plant with sweet-smelling white, pink or red flowers; the flower.

car·nel·ian /kɑ`nilɪən/ *n* = *cornelian.*

car·ni·val /`kɑnɪvl/ *n* [U] public merrymaking and feasting, usu with processions of persons in fancy dress, esp in R C countries during the week before Lent; [C] festival of this kind.

car·ni·vore /`kɑnɪvɔ(r)/ *n* flesh-eating animal. **car·ni·vor·ous** /kɑ`nɪvərəs/ *adj* flesh-eating.

carob /`kærəb/ *n* tree with horn-like edible pods.

carol /`kærl/ *n* song of joy or praise, esp a Christmas hymn: *~ singers,* singers who visit people's houses at Christmas to sing ~s (and usu to collect money for charity). □ *vt* (-ll-, in US also -l-) sing joyfully: celebrate with ~s. **~·ler** *n*

ca·rouse /kə`rɑʊz/ *vt* [VP2A] drink heavily and be merry (at a noisy feast, etc). **ca·rousal** /kə`rɑʊzl/ *n* noisy drinking-party or revelry.

carp[1] /kɑp/ *n* (*pl* unchanged) freshwater fish that lives in lakes and ponds.

carp[2] /kɑp/ *vt* [VP2A,3A] **~ *(at),*** make unnecessary complaints about small matters: *a ~ing tongue; ~ing criticism. She's always ~ing at her husband.*

car·pal /`kɑpl/ *adj* (anat) of the wrist. □ *n* (anat) bone in the wrist, ⇨ the illus at **skeleton**.

car·pen·ter /`kɑpɪntə(r)/ *n* workman who makes and repairs (esp) the wooden parts of buildings and other structures of wood. ⇨ **joiner**. **car·pen·try** *n* [U] work of a ~.

car·pet /`kɑpɪt/ *n* [C] **1** thick covering for floors or stairs, usu of wool, hair or synthetic fibres, often with a pattern or designs woven into it. ***on the ~,*** (colloq) being reprimanded. ***sweep sth under the ~,*** hide, ignore, sth, in order to delay action, escape blame, etc. **`~-bag** *n* (old fashioned) travelling bag made of ~. **`~-bag·ger** *n* (US) person, during the civil war, from northern U S A who went to the South to seek financial or political advantage. **`~-knight** *n* soldier who has not seen active service, stay-at-home soldier; ladies' man. **~-slippers** *n pl* old-fashioned kind of slippers with uppers of woollen cloth. **`~-sweeper** *n* device for sweeping ~s and rugs. **2** sth suggesting a ~: *a ~ of moss,* e g in a garden. □ *vt* [VP6A] **1** cover (as) with a ~: *to ~ the stairs; a lawn ~ed with fallen leaves.* **2** (colloq) reprimand: *He's been ~ed.*

car·riage /`kærɪdʒ/ *n* **1** [C] vehicle, esp one with four wheels, pulled by a horse or horses, for carrying people: *a ~ and pair,* one pulled by two horses. **`~-drive** *n* road through the grounds, park, etc. **`~·way** *n* (part of a) road used by vehicles: *Cars must not park on the ~way.* **'dual `~way,** road divided down the centre (by a barrier, a strip of pavement or grass) for traffic in each direction (= US *divided highway*). **2** [C] wheeled vehicle for passengers on a railway train (= US *car*); coach: *The first class ~s are in front.* **3** [U] (cost of) carrying of goods from place to place. **~ *forward,*** cost of ~ to be paid by the receiver. **~ *free/paid,*** ~ free to the receiver/paid by the sender. **4** [C] wheeled support on which a heavy object may move or be moved (e g a *gun ~*) moving part of a machine, changing the position of other parts (e g the roller of a typewriter). **5** (*sing* only) manner of holding the head or the body (when walking, etc): *She has a graceful ~,* She stands and walks gracefully. ⇨ **carry**[1]**(8)**.

car·rier /`kærɪə(r)/ *n* **1** person or company that carries goods or people for payment (e g a railway, steamship or aircraft company). **2** support for luggage, etc fixed to a bicycle, motor-car, etc. **3** per-

a carriage

son, animal, etc that carries or transmits a disease without himself or itself suffering from it. **4** vehicle, ship, etc used for the transport of troops, aircraft, tanks, etc. ⇨ aircraft-~, Bren-~, troop-~. **5** '~ **'bag** *n* strong paper or plastic bag for carrying away purchases from shops. '~-**pigeon** *n* pigeon used to carry messages because it can find its way home from a distant place.

car·rion /ˋkærɪən/ *n* [U] dead and decaying flesh. ˋ~-**crow,** crow that lives on ~ and small animals.

car·rot /ˋkærət/ *n* (plant with) yellow or orange-red root used as a vegetable, ⇨ the illus at vegetable: *the stick and the ~,* (fig) threats and bribes; *hold out/offer a ~ to sb,* entice by offering a reward or advantage. **~y** *adj* (esp of hair) orange-red.

carry[1] /ˋkærɪ/ *vt,vi* (*pt,pp* carried) (For uses with *adverbial particles* and *preps,* ⇨ 11 below.) **1** [VP6A,15A,B] support the weight of and move from place to place; take a person, a message, etc from one place to another: *He was ~ing a box on his shoulder. She was ~ing the baby in her arms. Railways and ships ~ goods. He carried* (= went round and told) *the news to everyone in the village. He ran off as fast as his legs could ~ him,* as fast as he could run. *This bicycle has carried me 500 miles. How far will five gallons of petrol ~ you? The farmers are ~ing corn this week,* ~ing it from the fields, after harvest, to the stacks, barns, etc. *Some kinds of seeds are carried by the wind for great distances. The raft was carried by ocean currents to a small island. Good soil is often carried out to sea by swift-flowing rivers. The police seized the spy and carried him off to prison. A spy carries his life in his hands,* takes the risk of death. ˋ~-**cot** *n* light cot with handles (but no wheels) for ~ing a baby. **2** [VP6A,15A] have with one; wear; possess: *Do you always ~ an umbrella? Ought the police to be allowed to ~ fire-arms? I never ~ much money with me. Can you ~ all these figures in your head,* remember them without writing them down? *The wound left a scar that he will ~ with him to the grave,* that will remain for life. **3** [VP6A] support: *These pillars ~ the weight of the roof. The girders are carried on trestles.* **4** [VP6A] involve; entail; have as a result: *The loan carries 3½% interest. That argument does not ~ conviction,* is not convincing. *Power carries responsibility with it. His word/promise carries weight,* is influential. **5** [VP6A,15A] (of pipes, wires, etc) conduct; take: *The oil is carried across the desert in pipe-lines. Wires ~ sound. Copper carries electricity.* **6** [VP15A] make longer; extend; take (to a specified point, in a specified direction, etc): *~ a fence round a field; ~ pipes under a street; ~ a joke too far,* be no longer amusing; *Don't ~ modesty too far.* **7** [VP6A,15A] win; capture; persuade; overcome: *The soldiers rushed forward and carried the enemy's position. He carried his audience with him,* won their sympathy and agreement. *The bill/motion/resolution was carried,* there were more votes for it than against it. **~ the day,** be victorious. **~ everything before one,** be completely successful. **~ one's point,** win approval for it. **8** [VP6A,15A,16B] hold oneself/one's head/one's body in a specified way: *He carries himself like a soldier,* stands and walks like one. *She carries herself badly,* e g by slouching or stooping. **9** [VP2B,C] (of guns) send (a shell, etc) a certain distance; (of missiles, sounds, voices, etc) have the power to go to: *Our guns do not ~ far enough. The sound of the guns carried many miles. The shot carried 200 metres. A public speaker must have a voice that carries well.* **10** [VP6A] (of a newspaper, etc) print in its pages: *a newspaper that carries several pages of advertisements.* **11** [VP15B,2C] (with *adverbial particles* and *preps*):

carry away, **(a)** (usu passive) cause to lose self-control: *He was carried away by his enthusiasm,* was so enthusiastic that he was unable to judge calmly, etc. **(b)** (naut) lose (masts, etc) by breaking: *The ship's masts were carried away during the storm.*

carry back, take back in the memory: *an incident that carried me back to my schooldays,* caused me to recall them.

carry forward, (comm, book-keeping) transfer (a total of figures on a page) to the head of a new column or page.

carry off, win: *Tom carried off all the school prizes.* **~ *it off (well),*** succeed in a difficult situation; cover a mistake, etc.

carry on, **(a)** conduct; manage: *Rising costs made it hard to ~ on the business. It's difficult to ~ on a conversation at a noisy party.* **(b)** talk volubly and complainingly; behave strangely or suspiciously: *How she does ~ on! Did you notice how they were ~ing on?* Hence, **~ings-on** *n pl*: *Such queer ~ings-on next door,* such queer happenings! **~ *on (with),*** continue (doing sth): *C~ on (with your work). They decided to ~ on in spite of the weather.* **~ *on (an affair) with,*** (often suggesting disapproval) flirt with; have a love affair with: *His wife is ~ing on with the postman.* ***(sth) to ~ on with,*** sth (to do or use) for the time being: *I can't give you all you need, but here's £5 to ~ on/be ~ing on with.*

carry through, **(a)** help (through difficulties, etc): *Their courage will ~ them through.* **(b)** complete sth: *Having made a promise, you must ~ it through.*

carry[2] /ˋkærɪ/ *n* **1** range of a gun, etc; distance that a shell, etc, goes. **2** portage; act of carrying boats, etc, from one river or lake to another; place where this must be done.

cart /kɑt/ *n* two-wheeled vehicle pulled by a horse, used in farming and for heavy goods (ˋ*coal-~,* etc) or for delivery of goods by tradesmen (*butcher's ~,* etc) (now usu replaced by motor-vans). ⇨ also hand~. ***be in the ~,*** (sl) be in an awkward or losing position. ***put the ~ before the horse,*** do or put things in the wrong order, take the effect for the cause (e g by saying 'I was lazy because I didn't study'). ˋ~-**horse** *n* strong horse for heavy work. ˋ~-**load** *n* as much as a ~ holds: *a ~-load of manure.* ˋ~-**road/-track,** rough unmetalled road. ***turn*** ˋ~-***wheels,***

turn somersaults sideways. □ *vt* [VP6A,15B] **1** carry in a ~: *~ing hay; ~ away the rubbish.* **2** (colloq) carry in the hands, etc: *Have you really got to ~ these parcels around for the rest of the day?* **~·age** /ˈkɑtɪdʒ/ *n* [U] (cost of) carting. **~er** *n* man whose work is driving ~s; carrier(**1**).

a cart

carte blanche /ˈkɑt ˈblɔ̃ʃ/ *n* (F) full authority or freedom (to use one's own judgement about how to proceed, etc).

car·tel /kɑˈtel/ *n* combination of traders, manufacturers, etc to control output, marketing, prices of goods, etc.

car·ti·lage /ˈkɑtlɪdʒ/ *n* [C,U] (structure, part, of) tough, white tissue attached to the joints, in animal bodies; gristle. **car·ti·lagi·nous** /ˈkɑtɪˈlædʒnəs/ *adj* of or like ~.

car·togra·pher /kɑˈtogrəfə(r)/ *n* person who makes maps and charts. **car·togra·phy** /kɑˈtogrəfɪ/ *n* [U] the drawing of maps and charts.

car·ton /ˈkɑtn/ *n* cardboard box for holding goods: *a ~ of 200 cigarettes,* with 10 packets of 20.

car·toon /kɑˈtun/ *n* **1** drawing dealing with current (esp political) events in an amusing way. **2** full-size preliminary drawing on paper, used as a model for a painting, a tapestry, a fresco, a mosaic, etc. **3** (*animated*) cinema film made by photographing a series of drawings: *a Walt Disney ~.* □ *vt* represent (a person, etc) in a ~. **~·ist** *n* person who draws ~s(**1**).

car·tridge /ˈkɑ-trɪdʒ/ *n* **1** case (of metal, cardboard, etc) containing explosive (for blasting), or explosive with bullet or shot (for firing from a rifle or shot gun). ⇨ **blank,** *adj* **3**. **ˈ~-belt** *n* one with sockets for holding ~s. **ˈ~-paper, (a)** paper for making ~ cases. **(b)** thick white paper for pencil and ink drawings. **2** detachable head of a pick-up (on a record-player), holding the stylus. **3** (US) = *cassette.*

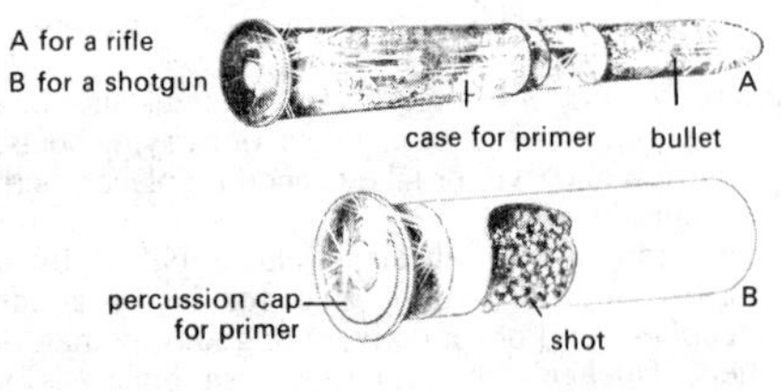

cartridges

carve /ˈkɑv/ *vt,vi* **1** [VP6A,14,15B] form (sth) by cutting away material from a piece of wood or stone: *~ a statue out of wood/a statue in oak; a figure ~d from marble; ~ out a career for oneself,* (fig) achieve one by great effort. **2** [VP6A,15A] inscribe by cutting on a surface: *~ one's initials/an inscription on a bench/a tree trunk.* **3** [VP6A,15B] cut up (cooked meat) into pieces or slices at or for the table: *~ a leg of mutton/a turkey.* **ˈcarving-knife/-fork** *n* knife, fork, used for carving meat. **carver** *n* carving-knife; person who ~s; (*pl*) carving-knife and fork. **carv·ing** *n* sth ~d in wood, etc. ⇨ **sculptor, sculpture.**

cary·atid /ˈkærɪˈætɪd/ *n* draped statue of a female figure used as a support (e g a pillar) in a building.

cas·cade /kæˈskeɪd/ *n* waterfall; one section of a large, broken waterfall; wave-like fall of lace, cloth, etc. □ *vi* fall like a ~.

cas·cara /kæˈskɑrə/ *n* (also ~ *tablet*) (kind of) laxative.

case[1] /keɪs/ *n* **1** instance or example of the occurrence of sth; actual state of affairs; circumstances or special conditions relating to a person or thing; (med) person suffering from a disease; instance of a diseased condition: *Is it the ~* (= Is it true) *that you have lost all your money? No, that's not the ~,* is not true. *If that's the ~* (= If the situation is as stated or suggested), *you'll have to work much harder. I can't make an exception in your ~,* for you and not for others. *Such being the ~* (= In view of, Because of, these facts, etc), *you can't go away. It's a clear ~ of cheating,* is clear that cheating has taken place. *There were five ~s of* (= five persons suffering from) *influenza. The worst ~s were sent to hospital.* ***a ~ in point,*** ⇨ **point**[1](**9**). ***(just) in ~,*** if it should happen that; because of a possibility: *It may rain; you'd better take an umbrella (just) in ~. In ~ I forget, please remind me of my promise.* ***in ~ of,*** in the event of: *In ~ of fire, ring the alarm bell.* ***in any ~,*** whatever happens or may have happened. ***in no ~,*** in no circumstances. ***in this/that ~,*** if this/that happens, has happened, should happen. **ˈ~-book** *n* record kept by a professional man (e g a doctor) of ~s dealt with. **ˈ~-ˈhistory** *n* record of the past history of sb suffering from a disease, social or mental trouble, etc. **ˈ~-work** *n* work involving personal study of individuals or families with social problems. **2** (legal) question to be decided in a law court; the facts, arguments, etc, used on one side in a law court: *the ~ for the defendant,* the statement of facts, etc in his favour. *When will the ~ come before the Court? State your ~,* Give the facts and arguments in your favour. *He has a strong ~.* ***make out a ~ (for),*** give arguments in favour of (sb, doing sth). ***make (out) one's ~,*** prove that one is right. **ˈ~-law** *n* law based on decisions made by judges. **3** (gram) (change in the) form of a noun or pronoun that shows its relation to another word: *The first person pronoun has three ~s, 'I', 'me' and 'my'.*

case[2] /keɪs/ *n* **1** box, bag, covering, container: *ˈpacking-~,* large box in which goods are packed; *ˈglass ~,* for the display of specimens, etc (e g in a museum); *a ˈwatch ~; a ˈjewel ~,* lined with velvet for keeping jewels in; *a ˈseed ~,* on a plant, in which the seeds ripen; *a ˈpillow-~,* of cloth for covering a pillow; *a ˈdressing-~,* a bag for hair-brushes, combs, razors, etc. ⇨ also **suit-~, book~** and other compounds. **ˈ~-ˈhardened** *adj* (fig or persons) made callous by experience. **2** (printing): *upper ~,* capital letters; *lower ~,* small letters. □ *vt* [VP6A] enclose in a ~ or casing.

casein /ˈkeɪsɪɪn/ *n* [U] body-building food (protein) found in milk, forming the basis of cheese. **ca·seous** /ˈkeɪsɪəs/ *adj*

case·ment /ˈkeɪsmənt/ *n* window that opens outwards or inwards like a door, not up or down or from side to side, ⇨ the illus at **window**; (poet) window. ⇨ **sash window**.

cash /kæʃ/ *n* [U] **1** money in coin or notes: *I have no ~ with me; may I pay by cheque? We sell goods for ~ only; we don't give credit.* **ˈ~ crops** *n* crops (e g coffee, sisal) to be sold for ~ (contrasted with *subsistence crops* such as millet, beans, grown for use by the growers). **ˈ~ desk,** desk or counter (in a shop, etc) where payments (by ~ or cheque) are made. **ˈ~ dispenser,** machine (outside some banks) which, by the use of a personal coded card, dispenses ~. ***~ down, ~ on delivery,*** payment on delivery of the goods. ⇨ **credit**[1](1). **ˈ~ price** *n* price for immediate payment. **~ register** *n* ~ box with a device for recording and storing ~ received. **~ and carry store** *n* one where goods are sold (usu at lower prices) for ~ payment if the buyer takes them away with him. **2** money in any form: *be short of ~; be rolling in ~; out of ~,* without money. **3** (kinds of) oriental coin of small denomination (esp one with a square hole in it). □ *vt,vi* **1** [VP6A, 12B,13B] give or get ~ for: *~ a cheque. Can you ~ this cheque for me/~ me a cheque?* **2** [VP2C] ***~ in (on),*** take advantage of; benefit from: *shopkeepers who ~ in on shortages by putting up prices.* **~·able** *adj* that can be ~ed.

a cash register

castanets

ca·shew /ˈkæʃu/ *n* (tropical American tree with) small kidney-shaped nut.

cash·ier[1] /kæˈʃɪə(r)/ *n* person who receives and pays out money in a bank, store, hotel, restaurant, etc.

cash·ier[2] /kəˈʃɪə(r) *US:* kæˈʃɪə(r)/ *vt* [VP6A] dismiss (a commissioned officer) with dishonour and disgrace.

cash·mere /kæʃˈmɪə(r)/ *n*: *a ~ shawl,* one made of the fine soft wool of Kashmir /kæʃˈmɪə(r)/ goats.

cas·ing /ˈkeɪsɪŋ/ *n* covering; protective wrapping: *copper wire with a ~ of rubber; ~s for sausages.*

ca·sino /kəˈsinəʊ/ *n* (*pl* -nos) public room or building for music, dancing, etc and (usu) for gambling.

cask /kɑsk *US:* kæsk/ *n* barrel for liquids: *a ~ of cider;* amount that a ~ holds.

cas·ket /ˈkɑskɪt *US:* ˈkæskɪt/ *n* **1** small box to hold letters, jewels, cremated ashes, etc. **2** (US) coffin.

casque /kæsk/ *n* (old use) military helmet.

cas·sava /kəˈsɑvə/ *n* [U] tropical plant with starchy roots from which tapioca is extracted. ⇨ the illus at **vegetable**.

cas·ser·ole /ˈkæsərəʊl/ *n* covered and heat-proof dish in which food is cooked and then served at table; food so cooked: *a ~ of lamb.*

cas·sette /kəˈset/ *n* [C] (US = *cartridge*) container for magnetic tape (for use with a ~ tape-recorder) or for photographic film (to be fitted into a camera). ⇨ the illus at **tape**.

cas·sock /ˈkæsək/ *n* long, close-fitting outer garment, worn by some priests. ⇨ the illus at **vestment**.

cas·so·wary /ˈkæsəwerɪ/ *n* (*pl* **-ries**) large bird, unable to fly, similar to, but smaller than, an ostrich.

cast[1] /kɑst *US:* kæst/ *vt,vi* (*pt,pp* **cast**) **1** [VP6A, 15A,B] throw; allow to fall or drop: *The fisherman ~ his net into the water. Snakes ~ their skins. His horse ~ a shoe,* one of its shoes came off. ***~ anchor,*** lower it. ***be ~ down,*** be depressed, unhappy. ⇨ **downcast**. ***~ lots, ~ in one's lot with,*** ⇨ **lot**[2](1,3). ***~ a vote,*** give a vote. **~·ing vote** *n* one given (e g by the chairman) to decide a question when votes on each side are equal. ***~ sth in a person's teeth,*** ⇨ **tooth(1)**. **2** [VP6A,15A, 2C] turn or send in a particular direction: *~ one's eye over sth,* look at, examine, it; *~ a gloom/shadow on sth,* make it seem gloomy, depressing; *~ a new light on a problem, etc,* make it clearer, easier to understand; *~ a rather wary glance at sb,* look at him warily; *~ a slur on someone's reputation,* say things to damage it. ***~ about for*** (allies, excuses, etc), (anxiously) look for, try to find. **3** [VP6A] pour (liquid metal) into a mould; make (e g a statue *in* bronze, etc) in this way: *a figure ~ in bronze.* **ˈ~ iron** *n* iron in a hard, brittle form, made by shaping in moulds after melting the ore in a blast furnace, and usually converted into wrought iron or steel before being used. Hence, **ˌ~-ˈiron** *adj* **(a)** made of ~ iron. **(b)** (fig) hard; untiring: unyielding: *a man with a ~-iron will/constitution.* **4** [VP6A,15B] ***~ up,*** add, calculate (more usu *add up* or *tot up*) *~ up a column of figures.* **5** [VP15B,2C] ***~ sb or sth aside,*** (= *cast off, (b)*) abandon; throw away as useless or unwanted. ***~ off,*** **(a)** unloose (a boat) and let go: **(b)** (fig) abandon; throw away as unwanted. **ˌ~-off ˈclothes, ˈ~-offs** *n pl* clothes that the owner will not wear again. **(c)** (knitting) remove the last row of stitches from the needles. ***~ on,*** (knitting) make the first row of stitches. **6** [VP6A] give (an actor) a part in a play: *He was ~ for the part of Hamlet.* **~·ing** *n* [C] sth shaped by being poured in a mould (e g a wheel or axle). ⇨ 3 above.

cast[2] /kɑst *US:* kæst/ *n* **1** act of throwing (e g a net or fishing line): *stake everything on a single ~ of the dice.* **2** sth made by casting(3) or by pressing soft material into a mould: *His leg was in a plaster ~.* **3** mould into which metal is poured or soft material pressed. **4** set of actors in a play; the distribution of the parts among these actors: *a play with an all-star ~.* **5** type or quality: *~ of features; ~ of mind.* **6** (of the eyes) slight squint.

cas·ta·nets /ˌkæstəˈnets/ *n pl* instruments of hardwood or ivory used in pairs on the fingers to make rattling sounds as a rhythm for dancing. ⇨ the illus at **cash**.

cast·away /ˈkɑstəweɪ *US:* ˈkæst-/ *n* shipwrecked person, esp one reaching a strange country or lonely island.

caste /kɑst *US:* kæst/ *n* one of the Hindu hereditary social classes; any exclusive social class; [U] this system. ***lose ~ with/among,*** lose the right to be respected; come down in social rank.

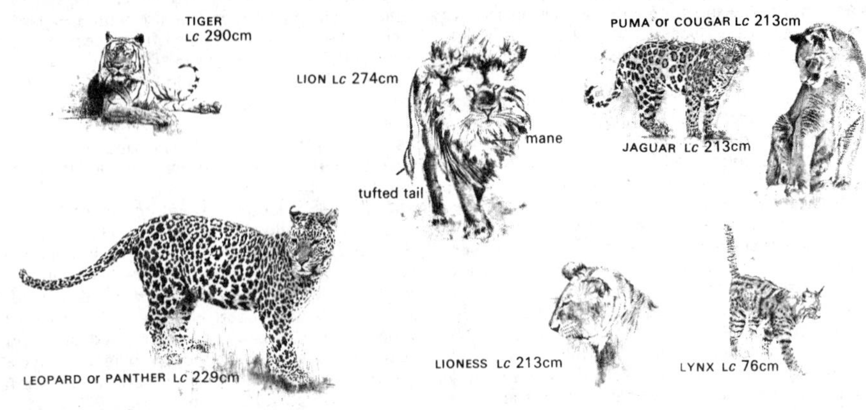

some wild cats

cas·tel·lated /ˈkæstəleɪtɪd/ *adj* having turrets or battlements (like a castle).

cas·ti·gate /ˈkæstɪgeɪt/ *vt* [VP6A] punish severely with blows or by criticizing. **cas·ti·ga·tion** /ˌkæs-tɪˈgeɪʃn/ *n* [C,U] (instance of) severe punishment.

castle /ˈkɑsl *US:* ˈkæsl/ *n* large building or group of buildings fortified against attack, esp as in olden times; house that was once such a fortified building; piece (also called *rook*) used in the game of chess. ⇨ the illus at **chess**. ***~s in the air, ~s in Spain,*** day-dreams; plans or hopes that are unlikely to be realized. □ *vi* (chess) move the king sideways two squares towards the ~ and place the ~ on the square the king moved across.

cas·tor, cas·ter /ˈkɑstə(r) *US:* ˈkæs-/ *n* **1** wheel (on a swivel) fixed to each leg of a piece of furniture (so that it may be turned and moved easily). **2** bottle or metal pot, with holes in the top, for sugar, salt, etc. ˈ**~ sugar** *n* white, finely powdered sugar.

cas·tor oil /ˌkɑstər ˈɔɪl *US:* ˈkæstər ɔɪl/ *n* [U] thick, yellowish oil, made from beans of the ~ plant, used as a purgative.

cas·trate /kæˈstreɪt *US:* ˈkæstreɪt/ *vt* [VP6A] remove the sex glands of (a male animal); make (a male animal) useless for breeding purposes. **cas·tra·tion** /kæˈstreɪʃn/ *n* castrating.

cas·ual /ˈkæʒʊəl/ *adj* **1** happening by chance: *a ~ meeting.* **2** careless; undesigned; unmethodical; informal: *a ~ glance; clothes for ~ wear,* for informal occasions, holidays, etc. *She's a very ~ person,* e g is careless and thoughtless about the convenience of others. **3** irregular; not continued: *earn a living by ~ labour; ~ labourers,* not permanently engaged by one employer. ˈ**~ ward** *n* (old use) division of a workhouse for persons who were for a time unable to support themselves. ⇨ **work**[1](11). **~·ly** *adv*

casu·alty /ˈkæʒʊəltɪ/ *n* [C] (*pl* **-ties**) **1** accident, esp one involving loss of life. **2** soldier or sailor who is killed, wounded or missing; person killed in war or seriously injured in an accident: *The enemy suffered heavy casualties. C~ lists were not published until months after the battle.* ˈ**C~ Ward/Department** *n* part of a hospital to which persons injured, e g in road accidents, are taken for urgent treatment.

casu·ist /ˈkæʒʊɪst/ *n* expert in ~ry. **~ry** *n* [U] judgement of right and wrong by reference to theories, social conventions, etc, (often with false but clever reasoning); [C] false but clever argument used in this way. **casu·is·tic, -ti·cal** /ˌkæʒʊ-ˈɪstɪk, -tɪkl/ *adj* of or like ~ry.

casus belli /ˌkeɪsəs ˈbelɑɪ/ *n* (Lat) act that is held to justify war.

cat[1] /kæt/ *n* **1** small, domestic, fur-covered animal often kept as a pet, to catch mice, etc; *wild cat,* any animal of the group that includes tigers, lions, panthers and leopards, (fig) excitable woman. ***bell the cat,*** ⇨ **bell**(2). ***let the cat out of the bag,*** ⇨ **bag**[1](1). ***like a cat on hot bricks,*** very nervous or jumpy. ***wait for the cat to jump, see which way the cat jumps,*** refuse to give advice, make plans, etc, until one sees what other people are thinking and doing. ***ˌcat-and-ˈdog life,*** one full of quarrels. **2** (short for) **ˌcat-o'-ˈnine-tails** *n* whip with many knotted cords, formerly used for punishing wrong-doers. ***not room to swing a cat in,*** very narrow space. **3** (compounds, etc). ˈ**cat burglar** *n* one who enters a building by climbing up walls, rainpipes, etc. ˈ**cat-call** *n, v* (make a) loud, shrill whistle expressing disapproval (e g at a political meeting). ˈ**cat-fish** *n* large fish without scales, with feelers around the mouth. ˈ**cat-nap,** ˈ**cat-sleep** *n* short sleep (in a chair, etc, not in bed). **ˌcat's ˈcradle** *n* children's game with a length of string looped over the fingers of both hands and transferred between the fingers of two players. ˈ**cat's eye** *n* reflector stud placed in roadways to guide traffic in darkness or on the rear of a vehicle (e g a bicycle). ˈ**cat's paw** *n* person who is used as a tool by another. ˈ**cat suit** *n* woman's or child's close-fitting one-piece garment for the whole body. ˈ**cat-walk** *n* narrow footway along a bridge, or through a mass of machinery, etc.

cat[2] /kæt/ *n* (colloq abbrev) caterpillar tractor.

cata·clysm /ˈkætəklɪzm/ *n* [C] sudden and violent change (e g a flood, an earthquake, a great war, a political or social revolution). **cata·clys·mic** /ˌkætəˈklɪzmɪk/ *adj*

cata·combs /ˈkætəkəʊmz/ *n pl* series of underground galleries with openings along the sides for the burial of the dead (as in ancient Rome).

cata·falque /ˈkætəfælk/ *n* decorated stand or stage

for a coffin at a funeral.

cata·lepsy /ˈkætəˋlepsɪ/ *n* [U] disease in which the sufferer has periods when he loses consciousness and sensation and his muscles become rigid. **cat·a·lep·tic** /ˈkætəleptɪk/ *adj* of, having, ~. □ *n* person who has ~.

cata·logue (US also **catalog**) /ˋkætəlog *US:* -lɔg/ *n* list of names/places/goods etc, in a special order: *a library* ~. □ *vt* [VP6A] make a ~ of; put in a ~.

ca·talpa /kəˋtælpə/ *n* (kinds of) tree with heart-shaped leaves and trumpet-shaped flowers.

ca·taly·sis /kəˋtæləsɪs/ *n* the process of aiding or speeding up a chemical process by a substance that does not itself undergo any change. **cata·lyst** /ˋkætḷɪst/ *n* [C] substance that causes ~. **cata·lyt·ic** /ˈkætəˋlɪtɪk/ *adj* of ~; causing ~.

cata·maran /ˈkætəməˋræn/ *n* boat with twin hulls; two boats or canoes fastened side by side (as used in the South Seas).

a catamaran

cat·a·pult /ˋkætəpʌlt/ *n* **1** Y-shaped stick with a piece of elastic, for shooting stones, etc from; (in ancient times) machine for throwing heavy stones in war. **2** apparatus for launching aircraft without a runway (e g from the deck of a carrier). □ *vt* launch (aircraft) with a ~; shoot (as) from a ~.

cata·ract /ˋkætərækt/ *n* **1** large, steep waterfall. **2** growth over the eyeball, that progressively obscures sight.

ca·tarrh /kəˋtɑ(r)/ *n* [U] inflamation of the mucous membrane, esp of the nose and throat, causing flow of liquid, as when one has a cold, or of the stomach and bowel.

ca·tas·trophe /kəˋtæstrəfɪ/ *n* [C] sudden happening that causes great suffering and destruction (e g a flood, earthquake, fire). **cata·strophic** /ˈkætəˋstrofɪk/ *adj*

catch[1] /kætʃ/ *vt,vi* (*pt,pp* caught /kɔt/) **1** [VP6A] stop (sth that is in motion) (e g by getting hold of it with the hands, by holding out sth into which it may come): *I threw the ball to him and he caught it. The dog caught the bit of meat in its mouth.* ~ ***sb out,*** (cricket) dismiss a batsman by ~ing the ball he has struck before it touches the ground. ⇨ also 3 below. **2** [VP6A] capture; seize; intercept: ~ *a rat in a trap;* ~ *a thief. How many fish did you* ~*? Cats* ~ *mice. I caught him* (= met him and stopped him) *just as he was leaving the house.* **3** [VP6A,19B,14,15B] come unexpectedly upon (sb) doing sth (esp sth wrong); surprise or detect (sb *at* or *in* sth): *I caught the boys stealing apples from my garden. I caught them at it,* came upon them while they were doing it. *They were caught in the act,* while actually doing it. *You won't* ~ *me* (= There's no likelihood of my being discovered) *doing that again! Let me* ~ *you at it again!* There will be trouble for you if I find you doing that again! ~ ***sb out,*** detect an offender. ~ ***sb napping,*** ⇨ nap[1] **4** [VP6A] be in time for: ~ *a train/the bus, etc;* ~ *the post,* post letters before the box is emptied by the postman. **5** [VP15B,2C] ~ ***sb up,*** ~ ***up with sb,*** (**a**) come up to sb who is going in the same direction; overtake: *Go on in front, I'll soon* ~ *you up/*~ *up with you.* (**b**) do all the work that has not yet been done: *Tom was away from school for a month so now he's got to work hard to* ~ *up with the rest of the class.* **6** [VP6A,2C,3A,14,15A] (cause to) become fixed or prevented from moving; (cause to) be entangled (*on* or *in* sth): *The nail caught her dress. Her dress caught on a nail. I caught my fingers in the door,* trapped them between the door and the doorpost. *This bolt doesn't* ~, cannot be fastened. *The latch has caught,* stuck fast. *The car was caught between two lorries. He caught his foot on a tree root and stumbled.* **7** [VP6A] get (the meaning of sth); hear (the sound of sth); receive (punishment, etc): *I don't quite* ~ *your meaning. I didn't* ~ *the end of the sentence. I don't quite* ~ (= understand) *the idea. I don't quite* ~ *on,* [VP2C] (colloq) don't see the meaning, purpose, etc. *You'll* ~ *it!* You'll be scolded, punished, etc! ~ ***sb's attention/fancy,*** succeed in getting it. ~ ***sb's eye,*** look at him to attract his attention when he looks in your direction. ~ ***sight/a glimpse of,*** see for a short time. **8** [VP6A] become infected with: ~ *a disease/a fever;* ~ *a cold.* **9** [VP3A] ~ ***at,*** try to grasp: *A drowning man will* ~ *at a straw. He will* ~ *at* (= take eagerly) *any opportunity of practising his English.* [VP15B] ~ ***up,*** grasp; seize: ~ *up a loose end of rope. They were caught up* (fig, carried away) *in the wave of enthusiasm.* ~ ***hold of,*** seize, grab. **10** ~ ***(fire),*** begin to burn: *The wood soon caught,* soon caught fire. **11** [VP6A,12C,15A] hit: ~ *sb a blow. She caught him one* (= gave him a blow) *on the cheek. He caught it* (= was struck) *right on the forehead. You'll* ~ *it if your father sees you!* **12** ~ ***one's breath,*** fail to breathe regularly for a moment (from surprise, etc). ˋ**~-crop** *n* quick-growing crop (e g lettuce) grown between rows of other crops. ˋ**~-penny** *adj* designed or intended merely to get sales: *a book with a ~penny title.* ˋ**~-word** *n* (**a**) word placed so as to draw attention to an article, the subject of a paragraph, etc; first or last word of a page in a dictionary, printed above the columns. (**b**) phrase or slogan in frequent current use. **~er** *n* (baseball) player who stands behind the batter to ~ the ball thrown by the pitcher. **~-ing** *adj* (esp of diseases) infectious. **~y** *adj* **1** (of a tune, etc) easily remembered. **2** tricky, deceptive.

catch[2] /kætʃ/ *n* **1** act of catching (esp a ball): *That was a difficult* ~. **2** that which is caught or worth ~ing: *a fine* ~ *of fish. He's a good* ~ *for some young woman,* is a good man to get as a husband. **3** sth intended to trick or deceive; cunning question or device: *There's a* ~ *in it somewhere. Does the teacher ever include* ~ *questions in examination papers?* **4** device for fastening or securing a lock, door, etc. **5** song for a number of voices starting one after another.

catch·ment /ˋkætʃmənt/ *n* ˋ**~-area** *n* district(s) from which a school draws its pupil's. ˋ**~-basin** *n* land from which rainfall flows into a river.

catch·up /ˋkætʃəp/ *n* = ketchup.

cat·echism /ˋkætɪkɪzm/ *n* [U] instruction (esp about religion) by question and answer; [C] number, succession of questions and answers designed for this purpose: *the Church C~*, that in the Book of Common Prayer; *put a person through his ~*, question him closely.

cat·echize /ˈkætɪkɑɪz/ *vt* [VP6A] teach or examine by asking many questions.

cat·egori·cal /ˌkætɪˈɡɒrɪkl/ *adj* (of a statement) unconditional; absolute; detailed; explicit. **~ly** /-ɪklɪ/ *adv*

cat·egory /ˈkætɪɡərɪ US: -ɡɔrɪ/ *n* (*pl* -**ries**) division or class in a complete system or grouping. **cat·egor·ize** /ˈkætɪɡərɑɪz/ *vt* [VP6A] place in a ~.

cater /ˈkeɪtə(r)/ *vi* **1** [VP3A] **~ *for***, provide food: *Weddings and parties ~ed for*. The advertiser will supply food for weddings, etc. **2** [VP3A] **~ *for/to***, supply amusement, etc: *TV programmes usually ~ for all tastes* (US = ~ *to* all tastes). Some tabloid newspapers ~ (= pander) *to low tastes*. **~er** *n* person who provides meals, etc brought from outside, to clubs, homes, etc; owner or manager of a hotel, restaurant, etc.

cat·er·pil·lar /ˈkætəpɪlə(r)/ *n* **1** larva of a butterfly or moth, ⇨ the illus at **butterfly**. **2** endless belt passing over toothed wheels, used to give vehicles, tanks, etc, a good grip on soft or uneven surfaces: *~ tractor*, one fitted with such belts.

cat·er·waul /ˈkætəwɔl/ *vi, n* (make a) cat's howling cry.

cat·gut /ˈkætɡʌt/ *n* [U] material used for the strings of violins, tennis rackets, etc (made by twisting the intestines of sheep and other animals).

ca·thar·sis /kəˈθɑsɪs/ *n* (*pl* -**ses** /-siz/) [U] **1** emptying of the bowels. **2** outlet for strong emotion (e g as given by the drama, or by a willing account of deep feelings given to another person). **ca·thar·tic** /kəˈθɑtɪk/ *adj, n* (med) (substance) giving ~(1).

ca·the·dral /kəˈθidrl/ *n* chief church in a diocese, in which is the bishop's throne, under the charge of a dean.

cath·ode /ˈkæθəʊd/ *n* negative electrode in the form of a filament which, when hot, releases negative electrons which are attracted towards the (+) anode. **ˈ~ ˈray** *n* invisible stream of electrons from the ~ in a vacuum tube (as used in radar, television, etc), called *a ˈ~ ˈray tube*.

cath·olic /ˈkæθl̩ɪk/ *adj* **1** liberal; general; including many or most things: *a man with ~ tastes and interests; ~ in his sympathies*. **2** (**C~**) *the C~ Church*, the whole body of Christians; *Roman C~*, of the Church of Rome. ⇨ **Protestant**. □ *n* member of the Church of Rome. **Ca·tholi·cism** /kəˈθɒləsɪzm/ *n* teaching, beliefs, etc, of the Church of Rome. **cath·ol·ic·ity** /ˌkæθəˈlɪsətɪ/ *n* [U] quality of being ~(1).

cat·kin /ˈkætkɪn/ *n* [C] spike of soft, downy flowers hanging down from twigs of such trees as willows and birches.

cat·sup /ˈkætsəp/ *n* = **ketchup**.

cat·tish, cat·ty /ˈkætɪʃ, ˈkætɪ/ *adj* (esp) sly and spiteful. **cat·ti·ness** *n*

cattle /ˈkætl/ *n pl* oxen (bulls, bullocks, cows): *twenty head of ~. C~ were allowed to graze on the village common*. **ˈ~-cake** *n* [U] food fed to ~, made from various materials.

Cau·casian /kɔˈkeɪzɪən US: kɔˈkeɪʒn/ *n, adj* (member) of the Indo-European race of people.

cau·cus /ˈkɔkəs/ *n* (*pl* -**cuses** /-kəsɪz/) (meeting of the) organization committee of a political party (making plans, decisions, etc).

cau·dal /ˈkɔdl/ *adj* of or at the tail.

caught /kɔt/ *pt,pp* of **catch**.

caul /kɔl/ *n* thin skin enclosing a foetus, part of which, when covering a baby's head, was once thought to be a charm against drowning.

caul·dron /ˈkɔldrən/ *n* large, deep, open pot in which things are boiled.

cauli·flower /ˈkɒlɪflɑʊə(r) US: ˈkɔlɪ-/ *n* [C,U] (cabbage-like plant with a) large, white flower-head, used as a vegetable. ⇨ the illus at **vegetable**.

caulk /kɔk/ *vt* [VP6A] make (joins between planks, etc) tight with fibre or a sticky substance.

causal /ˈkɔzl/ *adj* of cause and effect; of, expressing, cause. **~·ity** /kɔˈzæləti/ *n* (*pl* -**ties**) relation of cause and effect; the principle that nothing can happen without a cause: *the law of ~ity*, e g cause always precedes effect. **cau·sa·tion** /kɔˈzeɪʃn/ *n* ~ity; causing or being caused. **cau·sa·tive** /ˈkɔzətɪv/ *adj* acting as, expressing, cause.

cause /kɔz/ *n* **1** [C,U] that which produces an effect; thing, event, person, etc, that makes sth happen: *The ~ of the fire was carelessness. We can't get rid of war until we get rid of the ~s of war*. **2** [U] reason: *There is no ~ for anxiety. You have no ~ for complaint/no ~ to complain. Don't stay away without good ~*. **3** [C] purpose for which efforts are being made: *work in/for a good ~; fight in the ~ of justice*. ***make common ~ with sb***, help and support him (in a political, social, etc movement). □ *vt* [VP6A,17,12A,13A] be the ~ of; make happen: *What ~s the tides? What ~d his death? You've ~d trouble to all of us. This has ~d us much anxiety. What ~d the plants to die?* (What *made* them die? is preferred.) *He ~d the prisoners to be put to death*. (He *had* them put to death. — is preferred.) **~·less** *adj* without any natural or known ~.

caus·erie /ˈkəʊzərɪ/ *n* informal discussion.

cause·way /ˈkɔzweɪ/ *n* raised road or footpath, esp across wet land or swamp.

caus·tic /ˈkɔstɪk/ *adj* **1** able to burn or destroy by chemical action: *~ soda*. **2** (fig) biting; sarcastic: *~ remarks; a ~ manner*. **caus·ti·cally** /-klɪ/ *adv*

cau·ter·ize /ˈkɔtərɑɪz/ *vt* [VP6A] burn (e g a poisoned wound, a snake-bite) with a caustic substance or with a hot iron (to destroy infection).

cau·tion /ˈkɔʃn/ *n* **1** [U] taking care; paying attention (to avoid danger or making mistakes): *When crossing a busy street we must use ~*. **2** [C] warning words: *A sign with 'DANGER!' on it is a ~. The judge gave the prisoner a ~ and set him free*. **3** (*sing* with *indef art*) (sl) person whose appearance, behaviour or conversation causes amusement. □ *vt* [VP6A,17,14] give a ~ to: *I ~ed him against being late. We were ~ed not to drive fast. The judge ~ed the prisoner*, warned and reproved him. **~·ary** /ˈkɔʃnrɪ US: ˈkɔʃn̩erɪ/ *adj* conveying advice or warning: *~ary tales*.

cau·tious /ˈkɔʃəs/ *adj* having or showing caution: *~ of giving offence; ~ not to give offence*. **~·ly** *adv*

cav·al·cade /ˌkævlˈkeɪd/ *n* [C] company or procession of persons on horseback or in carriages.

cava·lier /ˌkævəˈlɪə(r)/ *n* **1** (old use) horseman or knight. **2** (in the Civil War, England, 17th c) supporter of Charles I. □ *adj* discourteous. **~·ly** *adv*

cav·alry /ˈkævlrɪ/ *n* (usu with *pl v*, collective) soldiers who fight on horseback: (attrib) *~ soldier/*

officer.

cave /keɪv/ *n* hollow place in the side of a cliff or hill; large natural hollow under the ground. **ˈ~-dweller** *n* person living in a ~, esp in prehistoric times. **ˈ~-man** /-mən/ *n* (*pl* -men) ~ dweller; (colloq) man of primitive instincts and behaviour. □ *vi, vt* [VP2C,15B] **~ *in,*** (cause to) fall in, give way to pressure: *The roof of the tunnel ~d in.* Hence, **ˈ~-in** *n*

ca·veat /ˈkeɪvɪæt/ *n* (legal) process to suspend proceedings: *put in/enter a ~ (against).*

cav·ern /ˈkævən/ *n* (liter) cave. **ˈ~·ous** *adj* like a ~; full of ~s; (of a person's eyes) deepset.

caviar, cavi·are /ˈkævɪɑ(r)/ *n* [U] pickled roe (eggs) of the sturgeon or certain other large fish. ***~ to the general,*** too good or delicate to be appreciated by ordinary people.

cavil /ˈkævl/ *vi* (-ll-, US also -l-) [VP2A,3A] **~ *(at),*** make unnecessary complaints against, find fault with.

cav·ity /ˈkævətɪ/ *n* (*pl* -ties) empty space; small hole, within a solid body: *a ~ in a tooth; ~ walls,* hollow, to provide insulation.

ca·vort /kəˈvɔt/ *vi* (colloq) prance or jump about like an excited horse.

caw /kɔ/ *n* cry of a raven, rook or crow. □ *vi, vt* **1** [VP2A] make this cry. **2** [VP15B] **~ *out,*** utter in a cawing tone.

cay·enne /keɪˈen/ *n* (also **~ pepper**) [U] very hot kind of red pepper.

cay·man ⇨ caiman.

cease /sis/ *vt, vi* [VP6A,D,7A,2A,3A] come or bring to an end; stop: *C~ fire! The old German Empire ~d to exist in 1918. The factory has ~d making bicycles. Since he ~d (from) working,....* **ˈ~-ˈfire** *n* signal to stop firing (guns); truce. □ *n* (only in) ***without ~,*** incessantly. **~·less** *adj* never ending. **~·less·ly** *adv*

cedar /ˈsidə(r)/ *n* [C] evergreen tree with hard, red, sweet-smelling wood used for making boxes, pencils, fences, etc; [U] the wood: *a ~ cigar box.*

cede /sid/ *vt* [VP6A,14] **~ *to,*** give up (rights, land, etc to another state, etc).

ce·dilla /sɪˈdɪlə/ *n* mark put under the c (ç) in the spelling of some French, Spanish and Portuguese words (as in *façade*) to show that the sound is /s/.

ceil·ing /ˈsilɪŋ/ *n* **1** under surface or overhead lining of a room. **2** cloud level; highest (practicable) level (to be) reached by an aircraft: *an aircraft with a ~ of 20 000 ft.* **3** maximum height, limit or level: *price ~s; wage ~s.*

cel·an·dine /ˈseləndɑɪn/ *n* small, wild plant with yellow flowers.

cel·ebrant /ˈselɪbrənt/ *n* priest who officiates at Mass.

cel·ebrate /ˈseləbreɪt/ *vt* [VP6A, but with the *direct object* sometimes to be understood] **1** do sth to show that a day or an event is important, or an occasion for rejoicing: *~ Christmas/one's birthday/a wedding anniversary/a victory; ~ Mass,* consecrate the Eucharist. *It's your birthday tomorrow, so we must celebrate (it).* **2** praise and honour: *The names of many heroes are ~d by the poets.* **cel·ebrated** *part adj* famous: *a ~d painter; ~d for its hot springs; ~d as a hot spring resort.*

cel·ebra·tion /ˈseləˈbreɪʃn/ *n* [C,U] (the act of, an occasion of) celebrating. **ce·leb·rity** /sɪˈlebrətɪ/ *n* **1** [U] being ~d; fame and honour. **2** [C] (*pl* -ties) ~d person: *all the celebrities of the London theatre,* all the famous actors and actresses performing in London.

ce·ler·ity /sɪˈlerətɪ/ *n* [U] quickness.

cel·ery /ˈselərɪ/ *n* [U] garden plant of which the stems are eaten raw as salad or cooked as a vegetable: *a bunch/stick/head of ~; ~ soup.*

ce·lestial /sɪˈlestɪəl *US:* -tʃl/ *adj* **1** of the sky; of heaven: *~ bodies,* e g the sun and the stars; *~ joys.* **2** divinely good or beautiful. **3** *the C~ Empire,* an old name for China.

celi·bacy /ˈselɪbəsɪ/ *n* [U] state of living unmarried, esp as a religious obligation. **celi·bate** /ˈselɪbət/ *adj, n* unmarried person (esp a priest who has taken a vow not to marry).

cell /sel/ *n* **1** small room for one person (esp in a prison or a monastery). **2** compartment in a larger structure, esp in a honeycomb. **3** unit of an apparatus for producing electric current by chemical action, e g of metal plates in acid, often part of a battery. **4** microscopic unit of living matter enclosing a nucleus with self-producing genes. **5** (of persons) centre or nucleus of (usu revolutionary) propaganda: *communist ~s in an industrial town.*

cel·lar /ˈselə(r)/ *n* underground room for storing coal, wine, etc; (person's) store of wine. **~·age** /ˈselərɪdʒ/ *n* amount of ~ space; charge for storing sth in a ~.

cello, 'cello /ˈtʃeləʊ/ *n* (*pl* -los) short for *violoncello.* ⇨ the illus at **string**. **cel·list** /ˈtʃelɪst/ *n* cello player.

cello·phane /ˈseləfeɪn/ *n* [U] (P) thin, moisture-proof, transparent, material used for wrapping and packing.

cel·lu·lar /ˈseljʊlə(r)/ *adj* **1** consisting of cells(**4**): *~ tissue.* **2** (of textile materials) loosely woven: *~ shirts.*

cel·lu·loid /ˈseljʊlɔɪd/ *n* [U] (P) flammable plastic substance used for making toys, toilet articles, etc (and formerly for photographic film).

cel·lu·lose /ˈseljʊləʊs/ *n* [U] **1** structural tissue that forms the chief part of all plants and trees; wood fibre. **2** (popularly, for ˈ*~ ˈacetate*) plastic substance used for many industrial purposes (e g paper, explosives, ornaments, toughened glass).

Cel·sius /ˈselsɪəs/ *n* (of thermometers) = centigrade.

Celt /kelt *US:* selt/ *n* member of the last group of immigrants to settle in Britain before the coming of the Romans; (loosely) one of the Irish, Welsh, Cornish and Highland Scots today. **~ic** *n, adj* **1** (language) of the ~s. **2** /ˈseltɪk/ name of a football team in Scotland.

ce·ment /sɪˈment/ *n* [U] **1** grey powder (made by burning lime and clay) which, after being wetted, becomes hard like stone and is used for building, etc. ⇨ concrete. **ˈ~-mixer** *n* revolving drum in which ~ is mixed with other material to make concrete. **2** any similar soft substance that sets firm, used for filling holes (e g in the teeth), or for joining things. □ *vt* [VP6A,15B] put ~ on or in; join with ~; (fig) strengthen; unite firmly: *~ a friendship.*

cem·etery /ˈsemətrɪ *US:* ˈsemøterɪ/ *n* (*pl* -ries) area of land, not a churchyard, used for burials.

ceno·taph /ˈsenətɑf *US:* -tæf/ *n* monument put up in memory of a person or persons buried elsewhere.

cen·ser /ˈsensə(r)/ *n* vessel in which incense is burnt in churches.

cen·sor /ˈsensə(r)/ *n* **1** official with authority to examine letters, books, periodicals, plays, films, etc and to cut out anything regarded as immoral or in other ways undesirable, or, in time of war, helpful to the enemy. **2** (ancient Rome) officer who prepared a register or census of citizens and supervized public morals. **3** title of various university officials. □ *vt* [VP6A] examine, cut out, parts of (a book, etc). **ˋ~·ship** /-ʃɪp/ *n* office, duties, etc of a ~.

cen·sori·ous /senˋsɔrɪəs/ *adj* fault-finding; severely critical: ~ *of one's neighbours.*

cen·sure /ˋsenʃə(r)/ *vt* [VP6A,14] **~ *sb (for),*** criticize unfavourably for: ~ *sb for being lazy.* □ *n* [U] rebuke; disapproval: *pass a vote of* ~ *(on sb); lay oneself open to public* ~; [C] expression of disapproval: *a review containing unfair* ~*s of a new book.*

cen·sus /ˋsensəs/ *n* (*pl* -suses) official counting of the population; counting of traffic, etc.

cent /sent/ *n* the 100th part of a dollar and some other metric units of currency; metal coin of this value. ***per* ~,** (%) in, by or for, every 100. ***(agree, etc) one hundred per* ~,** completely.

cen·taur /ˋsentɔ(r)/ *n* (Gk myth) fabulous creature, half man and half horse.

cen·ten·arian /ˈsentəˋneərɪən/ *n, adj* (person who is) (more than) 100 years old.

cen·ten·ary /ˈsenˋtinərɪ *US:* ˋsentn̩erɪ/ *adj, n* (*pl* -ries) (having to do with a) period of 100 years; 100th anniversary.

cen·ten·nial /senˋtenɪəl/ *adj, n* = centenary. **~·ly** /-nɪəlɪ/ *adv*

cen·ter /ˋsentə(r)/ *n* (US) = centre.

cen·ti·grade /ˋsentɪgreɪd/ *adj* in or of the temperature scale that has 100 degrees between the freezing-point and the boiling-point of water: *the* ~ *thermometer, 100°* ~ (100°C). ⇨ Fahrenheit and App 5.

cen·ti·gram(me) /ˋsentɪgræm/ *n* the 100th part of a gram(me). ⇨ App 5.

cen·time /ˋsontim/ *n* the 100th part of a franc (France, etc).

cen·ti·metre (US = **-meter**) /ˋsentɪmitə(r)/ *n* the 100th part of a metre. ⇨ App 5.

cen·ti·pede /ˋsentɪpid/ *n* small insect-like crawling creature with a long, thin body, numerous joints, and a pair of feet at each joint.

cen·tral /ˋsentrl/ *adj* **1** of, at, from or near, the centre. *My house is very* ~, is in or near the middle of the town. **~ heating,** method of warming a building by steam, hot air or water in pipes from a ~ source. **2** chief; most important: *the* ~ *idea of an argument; the* ~ *figures* (= the chief persons) *in a novel.* **the ~ government** *n* that of the whole country. □ *n* (US) telephone exchange. **~·ly** /ˋsentrəlɪ/ *adv*

cen·tral·ize /ˋsentrl̩ɑɪz/ *vt, vi* [VP6A,2A] bring to the centre; come, put, bring, under central control: ~ *the administration of the coal mines.* **cen·tral·iz·ation** /ˈsentrl̩ɑɪˋzeɪʃn *US:* ˈsentrl̩ɪˋzeɪʃn/ *n*

centre (US = **center**) /ˋsentə(r)/ *n* **1** middle part or point: *the* ~ *of London; the* ~ *of a circle.* ⇨ the illus at circle. **~ *of gravity,*** that point in an object about which the weight is evenly balanced in any position. **ˋ~-bit,** tool for boring holes in wood. ⇨ brace. **ˋ~-board,** movable board that can be raised or lowered through a slot in the keel of a sailing-boat to prevent drifting to leeward. **ˋ~-piece,** ornament for the ~ of a table, ceiling, etc. **2** place of great activity, esp one to which people are attracted from surrounding districts or from which they go out: *the ˋshopping* ~ *of a town; a* ~ *of commerce.* **3** person or thing that attracts interest, attention etc: *She loves to be the* ~ *of interest.* **4** that which occupies a middle position, e g in politics, persons with moderate views, between two extremes. □ *vt, vi* **1** [VP6A,14] place in, pass to, come to, be at, the ~: *The defender* ~*d the ball.* **2** [VP3A,15B] **~ upon,** *Our thoughts* ~ *upon/are* ~*d upon one idea.*

cen·trifu·gal /senˋtrɪfjʊgl/ *adj* moving, tending to move, away from the centre or axis: ~ *force,* the force which causes a body spinning round a centre to tend to fly off. **cen·tri·fuge** /ˋsentrɪfjudʒ/ *n* (mech) ~ machine, e g for separating small solid particles in a liquid by rotating motion.

cen·trip·etal /senˋtrɪpɪtl/ *adj* tending towards the centre or axis.

cen·tur·ion /senˋtʃʊərɪən/ *n* (in ancient Rome) leader of a unit of 100 soldiers.

cen·tury /ˋsentʃərɪ/ *n* (*pl* -ries) **1** 100 years. **2** one of the periods of 100 years before or since the birth of Jesus Christ: *in the 20th* ~, A D 1901-2000. **3** (cricket) 100 runs made by a batsman in one innings: *make/score a* ~.

ce·ramic /sɪˋræmɪk/ *adj* of the art of pottery. **ce·ram·ics** *n* **1** (*sing v*) art of making and decorating pottery. **2** (*pl v*) articles made of porcelain, clay, etc.

cer·eal /ˋsɪərɪəl/ *n* (usu *pl*) any kind of grain used for food: ~ *grasses,* e g wheat, rye, barley; food prepared from ~s: *breakfast* ~*s.*

cer·ebral /ˋserəbrl/ *adj* of the brain: ~ *hæmorrhage;* ~ *palsy.* ⇨ spastic.

cer·ebra·tion /ˈserəˋbreɪʃn/ *n* [U] (formal) working of the brain; thinking.

cer·emo·nial /ˈserəˋməʊnɪəl/ *adj* formal; as used for ceremonies: ~ *dress.* □ *n* [C,U] special order of ceremony, formality, for a special event, etc: *the* ~*s of religion.* **~·ly** *adv*

cer·emo·ni·ous /ˈserəˋməʊnɪəs/ *adj* fond of, marked by, formality. **~·ly** *adv*

cer·emony /ˋserəmənɪ *US:* -məʊnɪ/ *n* (*pl* -nies) **1** [C] special act(s), religious service, etc on an

cereals

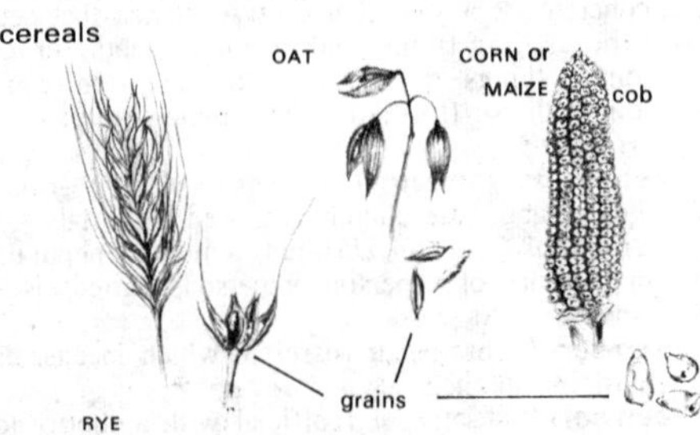

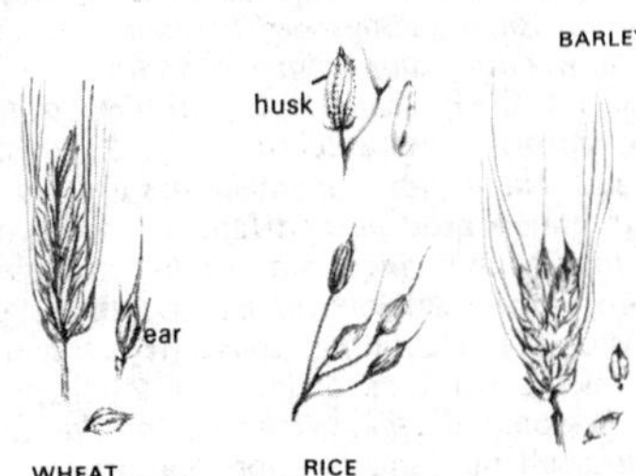

occasion such as a wedding, funeral, the opening of a new public building, etc. **'Master of 'Ceremonies** *n* person in charge of such formal proceedings. **2** [U] behaviour required by social customs, esp among officials, people of high class, etc: *There's no need for ~ between friends. There's too much ~ on official occasions.* ***stand on ~,*** pay great attention to rules of behaviour: *Please don't stand on ~,* i e please be natural and easy.

ce·rise /sə'riz/ *adj, n* (of a) light, clear red.

cert[1] /s3t/ *n* (sl) sth looked upon as certain to happen or that certainly has happened. ***a dead ~,*** an absolute certainty.

cert[2] /s3t/ *n* (colloq abbr) certificate: *get one's School C~* in the summer.

cer·tain /'s3tn/ *adj* **1** (pred only) settled; of which there is no doubt: *It is ~ that two and two make four.* **2** (pred only) ***~ that/of/about/to (+ infinitive),*** convinced; having no doubt; confident: *I'm ~ (that) he saw me. I'm not ~ who he is/ where he went, etc. You can be ~ of success. Are you ~ of/about that? He is ~ to come,* there is no doubt that he will come. ***for ~,*** without doubt: *I cannot say for ~* (= with complete confidence) *when he will arrive. I don't know for ~,* have no definite knowledge. ***make ~,*** **(a)** inquire in order to be ~: *I think there's a train at 8.20 but you ought to make ~.* **(b)** do sth in order to be assured: *I'll go to the theatre and make ~ of our seats,* e g by reserving them in advance. **3** assured; reliable; sure to come or happen: *There is no ~ cure for this disease. The soldier faced ~ death.* **4** (attrib only) not named, stated or described, although it is possible to do so: *for a ~ reason; on ~ conditions; a ~ person I met yesterday; a person of a ~ age* (usu = *middle-aged*). **5** (attrib only) some, but not much: *There was a ~ coldness in her attitude towards me. There is a ~ pleasure in pointing out other people's errors.* **~·ly** *adv* **1** without doubt: *He will ~ly die if you don't get a doctor.* ⇨ surely. **2** (in answer to questions) yes: *Will you pass me the towel, please? C~ly! Will you lend me your toothbrush? C~ly not!* **~·ty** *n* (*pl* -ties) **1** [C] sth that is ~: *Prices have gone up—that's a ~ty.* ***for a ~ty,*** for ~, without doubt: *I know for a ~ty that....* **2** [U] state of being ~: freedom from doubt: *I can't say with any ~ty where I shall be next week. We can have no ~ty of success. Would the ~ty of punishment deter criminals?*

cer·ti·fi·able /'s3tɪ'fɑɪəbl/ *adj* that can be certified: *a ~ lunatic,* a person who can be certified by a doctor as insane.

cer·tifi·cate /sə'tɪfɪkət/ *n* written or printed statement, made by sb in authority, that may be used as proof or evidence of sth: *a 'birth/'marriage ~; a health ~,* from a doctor; *~ of origin,* (comm) document stating the country or origin of imported goods. **cer·tifi·cated** /-keɪtɪd/ *adj* having the right or authority to do sth as the result of obtaining a ~: *~d teachers,* who have obtained teaching diplomas (now called *qualified teachers*).

cer·tify /'s3tɪfɑɪ/ *vt,vi* (*pt,pp* -fied) **1** [VP6A,9, 16B] declare (usu by giving a certificate) that one is certain of sth, that sth is true, correct, in order: *I ~ (that) this is a true copy of.... He was certified insane,* The doctor(s) wrote a certificate declaring that he was insane. *The accounts were certified (as) correct.* **certified cheque,** cheque the value of which is guaranteed by the bank. **2** [VP3A] ***~ to sth,*** attest it: *~ to sb's character,* declare that one is satisfied that it is reliable, etc.

cer·ti·tude /'s3tɪtjud *US:* -tud/ *n* [U] certainty (the more usu word).

ceru·lean /'serjʊ'lɪən/ *adj* sky-blue.

cer·vix /'s3vɪks/ *n* (anat) narrow part of an organ, esp of the womb. ⇨ the illus at reproduce. **cer·vi·cal** /s3'vɑɪkl *US:* 's3vɪkl/ *adj* of the neck: *~ smear,* smear taken from the neck of the womb, to test for cancer.

Cesar·ean = Caesarean.

Cesare·witch /sɪ'zærəwɪtʃ/ *n* horse-race run annually at Newmarket.

ces·sa·tion /se'seɪʃn/ *n* [U] ceasing: *the ~ of hostilities.*

cession /'seʃn/ *n* [U] (legal) act of ceding or giving up lands/rights etc by agreement; [C] sth ceded.

cess·pit /'sespɪt/, **cess·pool** /'sespul/ *nn* (usu covered) hole, pit or underground tank into which drains (esp for sewage) empty; (fig) filthy place.

cet·acean /sɪ'teɪʃn/ *n, adj* (member) of the order of aquatic mammals, e g whales.

Cey·lon·ese /'selə'niz *US:* 'silə'niz/ *adj* of or from Ceylon (now Sri Lanka). □ *n* native of Ceylon (now Sri Lanka). ⇨ Sinhalese.

Chab·lis /'ʃæblɪ/ *n* [U] dry, white wine of Burgundy.

Cha·conne /ʃæ'kon/ *n* (music for an) old stately Spanish dance.

chafe /tʃeɪf/ *vi,vt* **1** [VP6A] rub (the skin, one's hands) to get warmth. **2** [VP2A,6A] make or become rough or sore by rubbing: *A stiff collar may ~ your neck. Her skin ~s easily.* **3** [VP3A] ***~ at/under,*** feel long-continued irritation or impatience (because of sth): *~ at the delay/ hold-up/inefficiency; ~ under restraints/illness.* ⇨ also chafing dish below. □ *n* ~d place on the skin.

chaff[1] /tʃɑf *US:* tʃæf/ *n* [U] **1** outer covering (husks) of grain, removed before the grain is used as human food. **2** hay or straw cut up as food for cattle. □ *vt* [VP6A] cut up (hay, straw).

chaff[2] /tʃɑf *US:* tʃæf/ *n* [U] good-humoured teasing or joking. □ *vt* make good-humoured fun of: *~ sb about sth.*

chaf·fer /'tʃæfə(r)/ *vi* [VP2A,C,3A] argue, haggle, bargain (*with* a tradesman *about* prices, etc). □ *n* ~ing.

chaf·finch /'tʃæfɪntʃ/ *n* small European song-bird, sometimes kept as a pet.

chaf·ing dish /'tʃeɪfɪŋ dɪʃ/ *n* vessel with a heater under it, used at table for cooking food or keeping it warm.

chag·rin /'ʃægrɪn *US:* ʃə'grin/ *n* [U] feeling of disappointment and irritation (at having failed, made a mistake, etc): *Much to his ~, he did not win the race.* □ *vt* [VP6A] (formal; usu passive) affect with ~: *be/feel ~ed at/by.*

chain /tʃeɪn/ *n* **1** flexible line of connected rings or links for connecting, continuing, restraining, ornament, etc. ⇨ the illus at bicycle, dog; (*pl*) fetters of this kind, used for prisoners. ***in ~s,*** kept as a prisoner or slave. **2** number of connected things, events, etc: *a ~ of mountains/ideas/ events/proof.* **3** measure of length (66 ft). ⇨ App 5. **4** (compounds) **'~-armour/-mail,** armour made of metal rings linked together. ⇨ the illus at armour. **'~-gang,** gang of convicts fastened together with ~s while at work outside their prison. **`~-letter,** letter of which the recipient is asked to make copies to be sent to other persons, who will do the same. **`~ reaction,** chemical change forming products that themselves cause more changes so that the process is repeated again and again (as in the atomic bomb). **`~-smoker,** person who smokes cigarettes in continuous succession. **`~-stitch,** kind of sewing in which each stitch makes a loop through which the next stitch is taken. **`~-store,** one of many retail shops owned and controlled by the same company. □ *vt* [VP6A, 15A,B] make fast with a ~ or ~s: *The prisoners were ~ed to the wall. C~ up your dog.*

chair /tʃeə(r)/ *n* **1** separate movable seat for one person, usu with a back and in some cases with arms (*arm~*): *Won't you take a ~,* sit down? **`~-lift** *n* aerial ropeway with seats for carrying persons up and down mountain slopes, etc. Cf *ski-lift.* **2** seat, office, of a person who presides at a meeting. ***be in/take the ~,*** preside. ***leave the ~,*** end the proceedings. **3** position of professor: *the C~ of Philosophy.* **4** (old use) sedan ~. **5** (US) chair for the electrocution of criminals. □ *vt* [VP6A] **1** place in a ~, raise up and carry (sb who has won a contest): *The newly elected MP was ~ed by his supporters.* **2** *~ a meeting,* preside. **`~-man** /-mən/ *n* (*pl* -men) **1** person presiding at a meeting: *~man's report,* annual report of a company, signed by the ~man and presented at the annual general meeting. **2** (old use) one of the two men who carried a sedan ~.

chaise /ʃeɪz/ *n* low, usu four-wheeled horse-carriage (formerly) used by people driving for pleasure.

chalet /`ʃæleɪ/ *n* Swiss peasant's mountain hut or cottage built of wood and with sharply sloping and overhanging roof; summer cottage built in the same style; small hut in a holiday camp, etc.

chal·ice /`tʃælɪs/ *n* wine-cup, esp that used for the Eucharist.

chalices

chalk /tʃɔk/ *n* **1** [U] soft, white, natural substance (a kind of limestone) used for making lime. **`~-pit** *n* one from which ~ is dug. **2** [C,U] this material, or a material similar in texture, white or coloured, made into sticks for writing and drawing. **3** ***as different as ~ and cheese, as like as ~ to cheese,*** essentially unlike. ***by a `long ~,*** by far, by much. □ *vt* write, draw, mark, with ~; whiten with ~. [VP15B] ***~ sth up,*** write a score or record. **~y** *adj* of, containing, like, ~.

chal·lenge /`tʃæləndʒ/ *n* **1** invitation or call to play a game, run a race, have a fight, etc to see who is better, stronger, etc. **2** order given by a sentry to stop and explain who one is: *'Who goes there?' is the ~.* □ *vt* [VP6A,17A,14] give, send, be, a ~ to; ask for facts (to support a statement, etc): *~ sb to a duel; ~ sb to fight; ~ sb's right to do sth; ~ a juryman,* (legal) object to his being a member of the jury. **chal·lenger** *n* one who ~s.

cham·ber /`tʃeɪmbe(r)/ *n* **1** (old use) room, esp a bedroom. **`~ concert,** concert of ~ music. **'~ of `horrors,** place where gruesome objects are displayed. **`~-maid,** housemaid who keeps bedrooms in order (now chiefly in hotels). **`~ music,** music for a small number of players (e g a string quartet). **`~-pot,** vessel for urine, used in a bedroom. **2** (*pl*) judge's room for hearing cases that need not be taken into court; (not US) set of rooms in a large building to live in or to use as offices. **3** (hall used by a) group of legislators (e g in US, the Senate and the House of Representatives), often distinguished as the *`Upper C~* and the *`Lower C~.* **4** offices of barristers, etc esp in the Inns of Court. **5** group of persons organized for purposes of trade: *a C~ of Commerce.* **6** enclosed or walled space in the body of an animal or plant: *a ~ of the heart,* ⇨ **auricle, ventricle**; similar cavity in some kinds of machinery; enclosed space in a gun (where a shell or cartridge is laid).

cham·ber·lain /`tʃeɪmbəlɪn/ *n* officer who manages the household of a king or great noble.

cha·meleon /kə`miliən/ *n* ⇨ the illus at **reptile**. Small long-tongued lizard whose colour changes according to its background; person who changes his voice, manner, etc to match his surroundings.

chammy-leather /`ʃæmɪ leðə(r)/ *n* = chamois-leather.

cham·ois /`ʃæmwɑ *US:* `ʃæmɪ/ *n* small goat-like animal that lives in the high mountains of Europe and SW Asia. **~-leather** /`ʃæmɪ leðə(r)/ soft leather from the skin of goats and sheep.

champ[1] /tʃæmp/ *vt,vi* [VP6A,2A,C,4A] **1** (of horses) bite (food, the bit) noisily. **2** (fig) show impatience: *~ with rage. The boys were ~ing to start/~ing at the bit.*

champ[2] /tʃæmp/ *n* (colloq abbr) champion(**2**).

cham·pagne /ʃæm`peɪn/ *n* (kinds of) white sparkling (because charged with gas) French wine.

cham·paign /ʃæm`peɪn/ *n* (liter) (expanse of) open country.

cham·pion /`tʃæmpɪən/ *n* **1** person who fights, argues or speaks in support of another or of a cause: *a ~ of free speech/of woman's rights.* **2** person, team, animal, etc taking the first place in a competition: *a boxing/swimming/tennis, etc ~:* (attrib) *the ~ team; the ~ horse.* □ *adj, adv* (colloq) splendid(ly): *That's ~!* □ *vt* [VP6A] support; defend. **~ship** /-ʃɪp/ *n* [U] act of ~ing; [C] position of a ~: *to win a world swimming ~ship.*

chance[1] /tʃɑns *US:* tʃæns/ *n* **1** [U] the happening of events without any cause that can be seen or understood; the way things happen; fortune or luck: *Let's leave it to ~. Let ~ decide.* ***by ~,*** by accident, not by design or on purpose. ***game of ~,*** one that is decided by luck, not by skill. ***take one's ~,*** trust to luck, take whatever happens to come. **2** [C,U] possibility: *He has no/not much ~/a poor ~ of winning. I've had no ~ to get away/of getting away. What ~ of success is there? What is our ~/are our ~s of succeeding? What are the ~s that we shall succeed? The ~s are a hundred to one against you,* It's most unlikely that you will succeed. *If, by any ~,..., If, by some ~ or other...,* If it so happens that.... ***on the (off) ~ of doing sth/that,*** in view of the possibility, in the hope: *I'll call at his office on the ~ of seeing him before he leaves.* **3** [C] opportunity; occasion when success seems very probable:

This was the ~ he had been waiting for. It's the ~ of a lifetime, a favourable opportunity that is unlikely ever to come again. ***stand a (good, fair) ~ (of...),*** have a fair prospect (of sth). **the 'main '~** *n* opportunity of making money: *He always has an eye to the main ~,* sees when money can be made. **4** (attrib) coming or happening by ~(**1**): *a ~ meeting; a ~ companion.*

chance[2] /tʃɑns *US:* tʃæns/ *vi,vt* **1** [VP3A] ***~ (up)on,*** find or meet by chance. [VP4E,2A, after *it*] happen by chance: *I ~d to be there. It ~d that I was out/I ~d to be out when he called.* **2** [VP6A, C] take a risk, esp ***~ it, ~ one's arm,*** (colloq) take a chance of success although failure is probable.

chan·cel /'tʃɑnsl *US:* 'tʃænsl/ *n* eastern part of a church, round the altar, used by the priest(s) and choir. ⇨ the illus at church.

chan·cel·lery /'tʃɑnslrɪ *US:* 'tʃæns-/ *n* chancellor's position, department or residence; place of business of an embassy or legation.

chan·cel·lor /'tʃɑnslrɪ *US:* 'tʃæns-/ *n* **1** (in some countries, e g Germany) chief minister of state. **2** (of some universities) titular head or president (the duties being performed by the Vice-C~). **3** (GB) chief secretary of an embassy. **4** State or law official of various kinds: *the Lord C~ of England, the Lord High C~,* the highest judge (and chairman of the House of Lords); *the C~ of the Exchequer.*

chan·cery /'tʃɑnsərɪ *US:* 'tʃæns-/ *n* (*pl* -ries) **1** (GB) Lord Chancellor's division of the High Court of Justice. ***ward in ~,*** person (usu under age) whose affairs are in charge of the Lord Chancellor (e g because of the death of the ward's parents). **2** (US) court of equity for those cases with no remedy in common law. **3** office of public records.

chancy /'tʃɑnsɪ *US:* 'tʃænsɪ/ *adj* (-ier, -iest) (colloq) risky; uncertain.

chan·de·lier /'ʃændə'lɪə(r)/ *n* ornamental branched support (usu hanging from the ceiling) for a number of lights.

chan·dler /'tʃɑndlə(r) *US:* 'tʃænd-/ *n* **1** person who makes or sells candles, oil, soap, paint, etc. **2** ***ship's '~,*** dealer in canvas, ropes and other supplies for ships.

change[1] /tʃeɪndʒ/ *vt,vi* **1** [VP6A,14,2A] ***~ (from/out of) (to/into),*** leave one place and go to, enter, another; take off sth and put sth else on: *I must ~ these trousers—they've got oil on them. It won't take me five minutes to ~,* to put on different clothes. *He ~d out of his overalls (and into a lounge suit). We seldom ~ for dinner,* e g seldom ~ into formal evening dress. *I've ~d my address,* moved to a different house, flat, etc. *The house has ~d hands several times,* has been bought and sold several times. ***~ trains,*** leave one train and get into another during a journey: *~ (trains) at Crewe for Stockport. Where do we ~? All ~!* (a cry heard at stations when a train is going no further). ***~ up/down,*** (motoring) change to a higher/lower gear. **2** [VP6A,14] ***~ (sth for/into sth else).*** give and receive in return: *Can you ~ this five-pound note,* give me notes and/or coins of smaller denominations? *He ~d his Italian money before leaving Rome. Shall we ~ seats? I ~d places with her. He ~d his car for a foreign make.* **3** [VP6A,14,2A,C] ***~ (from) (into/to),*** make or become different: *That has ~d my ideas. My plans have ~d. Caterpillars ~ into butterflies or moths. The traffic lights ~d from amber to green. The wind has ~d from north to east. You've ~d since I last saw you. The weather often ~s in England.* ***~ one's mind,*** decide on a new plan, have a new opinion, etc. ***~ one's note/tune,*** become more humble, sad, etc. ***~ step,*** (when marching with a group) march so that the other foot is keeping time (e g with the beat of a drum). **~·able** *adj* likely to alter; often altering; able to be ~d: *~able weather; a ~able sort of person,* one whose moods often ~. **~·able·ness** *n*

change[2] /tʃeɪndʒ/ *n* **1** [C] changed or different condition(s); sth used in place of another or others; move from one place to another: *a welcome ~ from town to country life. We have a new house; it's a great ~ for the better. Take a ~ of clothes with you,* extra clothes to ~ into. *He had to make a quick ~* (i e of trains) *at Crewe.* ***a ~ of air/climate,*** e g a holiday away from home. ***ring the ~s,*** ⇨ ring[2](**11**). **2** [U] money in small(er) units; money that is the difference between the price or cost of sth and the sum offered in payment: *Can you give me ~ for a one-pound note? I have no small ~,* no coins of small value. *Don't leave your ~ on the shop counter!* ***get no ~ out of (sb),*** (colloq) get no help, information; or advantage from. **3** [C,U] alteration; changing: *C~ is not necessarily a good thing in itself. We shall have to make a ~ in the programme. Let's hope there will be a ~ in the weather.* ***for a ~,*** for the sake of variety; to be different from one's routine: *I usually have breakfast at 7.30, but during the holidays I'm having it at 8.30 for a ~.* ***~ of life,*** = menopause. **~·ful** /-fl/ *adj* continually changing; likely to change. **'~·less** *adj* unchanging.

change·ling /'tʃeɪndʒlɪŋ/ *n* child secretly substituted for another in infancy, esp (in old stories) a strange, ugly or stupid child left by fairies in place of one they have stolen.

chan·nel /'tʃænl/ *n* **1** stretch of water joining two seas; *the English C~,* between France and England. **2** natural or artificial bed of a stream of water; passage along which a liquid may flow. **3** deeper part of a waterway: *The ~ is marked by buoys. Keep to the ~; the river is shallow at the sides.* **4** (fig) any way by which news, ideas, etc may travel: *He has secret ~s of information.* ***through the usual ~s,*** by the usual means of communication (between persons, groups, etc): *A debate on this question can be arranged through the usual ~s,* e g, in Parliament, through the leaders of political parties. **5** (radio, TV) band of frequencies within which signals from a transmitter must be kept (to prevent interference from other transmitters). □ *vt* (-ll-, US also -l-) [VP6A,14] **1** form a ~ or ~s in, cut out (a way): *The river had ~led its way through the soft rock.* **2** cause to go through a ~ or ~s.

chant /tʃɑnt *US:* tʃænt/ *n* [C] often-repeated tune to which psalms and canticles are fitted; several syllables or words to one note. ⇨ hymn. □ *vi,vt* [VP2A,6B] sing; sing a ~; use a singing note (e g for a prayer in Church): *~ sb's praises,* (fig) praise constantly.

chantey /'ʃɑntɪ *US:* 'ʃæntɪ/ *n* (US) = chanty.

chan·ti·cleer /'tʃɑntɪklɪə(r) *US:* 'tʃæn-/ *n* (in fables, etc) (personal name for) domestic cock. ⇨ cock[1](**1**).

chan·try /'tʃɑntrɪ *US:* 'tʃæntrɪ/ *n* (*pl* -ries)

endowment(2) for a priest or priests to sing masses for the founder's soul; its chapel (often part of a church) or priests.

chanty, shanty /ˈʃæntɪ/ *n* (*pl* -ties) song sung by sailors in rhythm with their movements at work (esp hauling at ropes).

chaos /ˈkeɪos/ *n* [U] complete absence of order or shape; confusion: *The room was in a state of ~ when the burglars had left.* **cha·otic** /keɪˈotɪk/ *adj* in a state of ~; confused. **cha·oti·cally** /keɪˈotɪklɪ/ *adv*

chap[1] /tʃæp/ *vt,vi* (-pp-) **1** [VP2A] (of the skin) become sore, rough, cracked: *My skin soon ~s in cold weather.* **2** [VP6A] cause to become cracked or rough: *hands and face ~ped by the cold.* □ *n* crack, esp in the skin.

chap[2] /tʃæp/ *n* (also *chop*) (*pl*) jaws, esp of animals; cheeks. **ˈ~-fallen** *adj* dispirited, dejected.

chap[3] /tʃæp/ *n* (colloq) man; boy; fellow.

chap·book /ˈtʃæpbʊk/ *n* small book or pamphlet of popular tales, ballads, etc formerly sold on the streets by chapmen.

chapel /ˈtʃæpl/ *n* **1** place (not a parish church) used for Christian worship, e g in a large private house, school, prison, etc. **2** small place within a Christian church, used for private prayer, with an altar, and usually named (e g a ˈ*Lady C~*, one dedicated to Mary, the mother of Jesus). ⇨ the illus at **church**. **3** (GB; obsolescent use) place of worship used by those who do not belong to the established church: *the Methodist ~. Are you church or ~,* Do you belong to the Church of England or to one of the Free Churches? ⇨ **free**[1](3). **ˈ~-goer** /-gəʊə(r)/ *n* non-conformist (contrasted with a member of the Church of England). **4** [U] service held in a ~(3): *go to ~.*

chap·eron /ˈʃæpərəʊn/ *n* married or elderly person (usu a woman) in charge of a girl or young unmarried woman on social occasions. □ *vt* [VP6A] act as a ~ to.

chap·fallen /ˈtʃæpfɔlən/ *adj* ⇨ **chap**[2].

chap·lain /ˈtʃæplɪn/ *n* priest or clergyman, esp in the navy, army or air force, or officiating in a chapel(1). ⇨ **padre**.

chap·let /ˈtʃæplət/ *n* wreath (of leaves, flowers, jewels, etc) for the head; string of beads (a short rosary) for counting prayers.

chap·man /ˈtʃæpmən/ *n* (*pl* -men) (old use) pedlar.

chap·ter /ˈtʃæptə(r)/ *n* **1** (usu numbered) division of a book. ***~ of accidents,*** number of misfortunes closely following one another. ***~ and verse,*** exact reference to a passage, etc or authority (*for* a statement, etc) for. **2** period; epoch: *the most brilliant ~ in the history of the French court.* **3** (general meeting of the) whole number of canons of a cathedral church, or the members of a monastic order. **ˈ~-house** *n* building used for such meetings.

char[1] /tʃɑ(r)/ *vt,vi* (-rr-) [VP6A,2A] (of a surface) make or become black by burning: *~red wood.*

char[2] /tʃɑ(r)/ *vi* (-rr-) do the cleaning of offices, houses, etc with payment by the hour or the day: *go out ~ring.* □ *n* ~woman. **ˈ~·woman** *n* (*pl* -women) woman who earns money by ~ing, paid by the hour or the day. ⇨ **chore**.

char[3] /tʃɑ(r)/ *n* [U] (GB sl) tea: *a cup of ~.*

char-à-banc, char·a·banc /ˈʃærəbæŋ/ *n* (not US) long-distance single-decked (often unroofed) motor-coach (now usu called *coach*) with all seats facing forward, used for pleasure trips.

char·ac·ter /ˈkærɪktə(r)/ *n* **1** [U] (of a person, community, race, etc) mental or moral nature; mental or moral qualities that make one person, race, etc different from others: *a woman of fine/strong/noble, etc ~; the ~ of Julius Cæsar/of the French.* ***in/out of ~,*** appropriate/inappropriate to the actions, etc known to be in accord with a person's ~. **2** [U] moral strength: *a man of ~. Should ~ building be the chief aim of education?* **3** [U] all those qualities that make a thing, place, etc what it is and different from others: *the ~ of the desert areas of N Africa.* **4** [C] person who is well known: *a public ~*; person in a novel, play, etc: *the ~s in the novels of Charles Dickens;* person who is in some ways unusual: *He's quite a ~,* has peculiarities of his own, is not an average or typical sort of person. **5** [C] description of a person's abilities and qualities, esp in a letter by an employer, that may be used when applying for a position. **6** [C] reputation: *He has gained the ~ of a miser.* **7** [C] letter, sign, mark, etc used in a system of writing or printing: *Greek/Chinese, etc ~s.* **~·is·tic** /ˈkærɪktəˈrɪstɪk/ *adj* forming part of, showing, the ~ of: *with his ~istic enthusiasm. It's ~istic of him,* It's what people would expect him to do, because of his ~. □ *n* [C] special mark or quality: *What are the ~istics that distinguish the Chinese from the Japanese?* **ˈ~·ˈis·ti·cally** /-klɪ/ *adv* **ˈ~·ize** *vt* [VP6A] show the ~ of; give ~ to; mark in a special way: *Your work is ~ized by lack of attention to detail. The camel is ~ized by the ability to go for long periods without water.* **~·less** *adj* without ~; undistinguished; ordinary.

cha·rade /ʃəˈrɑd *US:* -ˈreɪd/ *n* [C] episode in a game in which a word is guessed by the onlookers after the word itself, and each syllable of it in turn, have been suggested by acting a little play; (*pl*, with sing *vb*) this game.

char·coal /ˈtʃɑkəʊl/ *n* [U] black substance, used as fuel, as a filtering material and for drawing, made by burning wood slowly in an oven with little air: *a bale/stick/piece, etc of ~.* **ˈ~-burner** *n* person who makes ~; stove, etc in which ~ is used as the fuel.

chard /tʃɑd/ *n* (often *Swiss ~*) variety of beet of which the leaves are used as a vegetable.

charge[1] /tʃɑdʒ/ *n* **1** accusation; statement that a person has done wrong, esp that he has broken a law: *arrested on a ~ of theft.* ***bring a ~ against sb,*** accuse him of (a crime). ***face a ~ (of sth),*** have to answer it in court: *He faces serious ~s.* ***lay sth to sb's ~,*** bring an accusation of sth against him. **ˈ~-sheet** *n* record of cases kept in a police station. **2** sudden and violent attack at high speed (by soldiers, wild animals, a football player, etc): *After a fierce bayonet ~, our soldiers drove the enemy from the hilltop.* **3** price asked for goods or services: *hotel ~s.* **ˈ~-account** *n* (US) = (GB) credit account. ⇨ **credit**[1](1). **4** amount of powder, etc (to be) used in a gun or for causing an explosion; amount of electricity (to be) put into an accumulator, contained in a substance, etc: *a positive/negative ~.* **5** [C] work given to sb as a duty; thing or person given or entrusted to sb to be taken care of; [U] responsibility; trust: *The baby was in Mary's ~. Mary was in ~ of the baby. The nurse took her young ~s/the children who were in her ~ for a walk. This ward of the hospital is in/under the ~ of Dr Green. I hope you'll never become a*

~ *on the public,* i e become a pauper, to be supported at public expense. ***give sb in ~,*** give him up to the police. ***take ~ of,*** be responsible for. **6** directions; instructions: *the judge's ~ to the jury,* instructions concerning their duty (in reaching a verdict).

charge[2] /tʃɑdʒ/ *vt, vi* **1** [VP6A,14] ***~ sb (with),*** accuse; bring a charge(**1**) against: *He was ~d with murder. He ~d me with neglecting my duty.* **2** [VP6A,2A,C] make a charge(**2**) against; rush forward and attack: *Our soldiers ~d the enemy. One of our strikers* (ie in a game of football) *was violently ~d by the defender. The wounded lion suddenly ~d at me.* **3** [VP12B,13B,14] ask as a price (*for*); ask in payment: *He ~d me fifty pence for it. How much do you ~ for mending a pair of shoes?* **4** [VP6A,14,15B] ***~ (up) to,*** make a record of (as a debt): *Please ~ these purchases to my account.* **5** [VP6A,2A] load (a gun); fill, put a charge(**4**) into: *~ an accumulator. Electrons are negatively ~d with electricity; protons are positively ~d.* **6** [VP14] ***~ with,*** give as a task or duty; give into sb's care: *He was ~d with an important mission. He ~d himself with* (= undertook) *the task of keeping the club's accounts in order.* **7** [VP6A,17A] (esp of a judge, a bishop or person in authority) command; instruct: *I ~ you not to forget what I have said. The judge ~d the jury,* gave them directions about how to perform their duty.

charge·able /tʃɑdʒəbl/ *adj* **1** that can be, is liable to be, charged: *If you steal, you are ~ with theft.* **2** that may be added (to an account): *sums ~ to a reserve.* **3** that may be made an expense: *Costs of repairs are ~ on the owner of the building.*

chargé d'affaires /ˈʃɑʒeɪ dæˋfeə(r)/ *n* (*pl* **chargés d'affaires**, pronunciation unchanged) official who takes the place of an ambassador or minister when the ambassador, etc is absent from his post.

charger[1] /ˋtʃɑdʒə(r)/ *n* (old use) army officer's horse.

charger[2] /ˋtʃɑdʒə(r)/ *n* (old use) large, flat dish; platter.

char·iot /ˋtʃærɪət/ *n* car with two wheels, used in ancient times in fighting and racing. **char·io·teer** /ˈtʃærɪəˋtɪə(r)/ *n* driver of a ~.

cha·risma /kəˋrɪzmə/ *n* **1** spiritual grace. **2** genius of an unusually high degree; capacity to inspire devotion and enthusiasm. **char·is·matic** /ˈkærɪzˋmætɪk/ *adj*: *the ~tic* (= divinely favoured) *position of the Emperor of Japan during the Meiji Era.*

chari·table /ˋtʃærɪtəbl/ *adj* showing, having, charity (*to*); for charity: *~ institutions,* for helping poor or suffering people; *~ to all men.* **chari·tably** /-blɪ/ *adv*

char·ity /ˋtʃærətɪ/ *n* **1** [U] (kindness in giving) help to the poor; money, food, etc so given; willingness to judge other persons with kindness; neighbourly love: *judge other people with ~. C~ begins at home,* (prov) A person's first duty is to help the members of his own family. *None of us would like to live on ~.* **ˋ~ school** *n* (in former times) one where poor children (esp orphans) are given free board, lodging and education. **ˈSister of ˋC~** *n* member of a religious society or organization for helping the poor. **2** [C] (*pl* **-ties**) society or organization for helping the poor: *He left all his money to charities,* to charitable institutions.

chari·vari /ˈʃɑrɪˋvɑrɪ *US:* ˈʃɪvəˋri/ *n* [U] hubbub; medley of noises and voices.

char·lady /ˋtʃɑleɪdɪ/ *n* (*pl* **-ladies**) (joc for) charwoman.

char·la·tan /ˋʃɑlətən/ *n* person who claims to have more skill, knowledge or ability than he really has, esp one who pretends to have medical knowledge.

Charles·ton /ˋtʃɑlstən/ *n* fast dance with side kicks from the knee (popular in the 1920's).

char·lock /ˋtʃɑlok/ *n* wild mustard, a weed with yellow flowers.

char·lotte /ˋʃɑlət/ *n* pudding of stewed fruit and breadcrumbs, baked in a dish: *apple ~.*

charm /tʃɑm/ *n* **1** [U] attractiveness; power to give pleasure; [C] pleasing quality or feature: *Her ~ of manner made her very popular. He fell a victim to her ~s,* her beauty, her attractive ways, etc. **2** [C] sth believed to have magic power, good or bad: *under a ~,* influenced in a magic way; *~s against evil spirits; a ~ to bring good luck,* e g a trinket worn on the body. ***work like a ~,*** with complete success. □ *vt, vi* **1** [VP6A,2A] attract; give pleasure to: *Does goodness ~ more than beauty? We were ~ed with the scenery. I'm ~ed* (*pleased* is more usu) *to meet you* (used as a polite formula). **2** [VP6A,15A] use magic on; influence or protect as if by magic: *He bears a ~ed life,* has escaped dangers, as if protected by magic. *She ~ed away his sorrow,* caused him to forget his troubles. **~·ing** *adj* delightful: *a ~ing young lady.* **~·ing·ly** *adv* **~er** *n* (usu joc) young man or woman with ~. **ˋsnake ~er** *n* person able to ~(**2**) snakes.

char·nel house /ˋtʃɑnl haʊs/ *n* place where dead human bodies or bones are stored.

chart /tʃɑt/ *n* **1** map used by sailors, showing the coasts, depth of the sea, position of rocks, lighthouses, etc. **2** sheet of paper with information, in the form of curves, diagrams, etc (about such things as the weather, prices, business conditions, etc): *a weather/temperature ~.* □ *vt* [VP6A] make a ~ of; show on a ~.

char·ter /ˋtʃɑtə(r)/ *n* **1** (written or printed statement of) rights, permission to do sth, esp from a ruler or government (e g to a town, city or university). **2** hiring or engagement (of an aircraft, a ship, etc): *a ˋ~ flight. C~s of oil-tankers may be by time or for the voyage.* □ *vt* [VP6A] **1** give a ~ to; grant a privilege to. **ˈ~ed acˋcountant,** (in GB) member of the Institute of Accountants (with a royal ~). **2** hire or engage a ship/an aircraft, etc for an agreed time, purpose and payment: *travel in a ~ed aircraft.* **ˋ~-party** *n* (comm) agreement between a shipowner and merchant for the use of a ship.

Chart·ism /ˋtʃɑt-ɪzm/ *n* early 19th c working class movement for democratic reform. **ˋChart·ist** *n*

char·treuse /ʃɑˋtrɜz *US:* -ˋtruz/ *n* (kinds of) liqueur (green, yellow) made by Carthusian /kɑˋθusɪən/ monks (of an austere monastic order founded in S France in 1086).

char·woman /ˋtʃɑwʊmən/ *n* ⇨ **char**[2].

chary /ˋtʃeərɪ/ *adj* ***~ (of),*** cautious, wary, careful: *~ of catching cold; a teacher who is ~ of giving praise,* who seldom praises his pupils. **char·ily** *adv*

Cha·ryb·dis /kəˋrɪbdɪs/ *n* ⇨ **Scylla**.

chase[1] /tʃeɪs/ *vt, vi* **1** [VP6A,15A,B] run after in order to capture, kill, overtake or drive away: *Dogs like to ~ rabbits. C~ that dog out of the garden. The letter had been chasing him for* *weeks*, e g had been following him from place to place during his travels. **2** [VP2C] (colloq) hurry; rush: *The children all* ~*d off after the procession.* □ *n* **1** act of chasing: *After a long* ~, *we caught the thief.* ***give*** ~ ***(to),*** run after; start in pursuit (of). ***in*** ~ ***of sb/sth,*** pursuing, running after. ***a*** **'*wild* `*goose* ~,** a search, expedition, etc that can have no success. **2 the** ~, hunting as a sport. **3** hunted animal, person or thing being pursued. **4** (area of) open ground where game[1](6) is bred and hunted: *Chevy C*~. **chaser** *n* (in compounds) person or thing that ~s (e g enemy submarines); (sl) drink taken after another or others: *He drank beer with whisky* ~*rs.*

chase[2] /tʃeɪs/ *vt* [VP6A] cut patterns or designs on (metal or other hard material); engrave: ~*d silver.*

chasm /`kæzm/ *n* deep opening or crack in the ground; abyss; gorge; (fig) wide difference (of feeling or interests, *between* persons, groups, nations, etc).

chas·sis /`ʃæsɪ/ *n* (*pl* unchanged) **1** framework of a motor-car or carriage on which the body is fastened or built; landing gear of an aircraft. **2** framework in which parts of radio or TV equipment are mounted.

chaste /tʃeɪst/ *adj* **1** virtuous in word, thought and deed; (esp) abstaining from unlawful or immoral sexual intercourse. **2** (of style, taste) simple; without ornament; pure. **~·ly** *adv*

chas·ten /`tʃeɪsn/ *vt* [VP6A] **1** punish in order to correct; discipline by inflicting suffering. **2** make chaste(**2**).

chas·tise /tʃæ`staɪz/ *vt* [VP6A] punish severely. **~·ment** *n* [U] punishment.

chas·tity /`tʃæstətɪ/ *n* [U] state of being chaste.

chas·uble /`tʃæzjʊbl/ *n* loose, sleeveless garment worn over all other vestments by a priest at Mass or Eucharist. ⇨ the illus at **vestment**.

chat /tʃæt/ *n* [C] friendly talk (usu about unimportant things): *I had a long* ~ *with him.* □ *vi, vt* (-tt-) **1** [VP2A,C] have a ~: *They were* ~*ting (away) in the corner.* **2** [VP15B] ~ ***sb up,*** (colloq) ~ to in order to win friendship, or for fun: ~ *up a pretty barmaid.* **~ty** *adj* fond of ~ting.

châ·teau /`ʃætəʊ/ *n* (*pl* -teaux /-təʊz/) castle or large country house in France.

a château

chat·el·aine /'ʃætə`leɪn/ *n* (old use) set of short chains fastened to a woman's belt for carrying keys, etc; mistress of a large country house or castle.

chat·tel /`tʃætl/ *n* (legal) article of personal movable property (e g a chair, a motor-car, a horse): *a person's goods and* ~*s.*

chat·ter /`tʃætə(r)/ *vi* [VP2A,C] **1** (of a person) talk quickly or foolishly; talk too much. **2** (of the cries of monkeys and some birds, of typewriter keys, of a person's upper and lower teeth striking together from cold or fear) make quick, indistinct sounds. □ *n* [C] sounds of the kind noted above: *the* ~ *of sparrows/children.* **`~·box,** person who ~s, esp a small child.

chauf·feur /`ʃəʊfə(r) *US:* 'ʃəʊ`fɜr/ *n* man paid to drive a privately-owned motor-car. **chauf·feuse** /`ʃəʊfɜz *US:* ʃəʊ`fɜz/ *n* woman ~.

chau·vin·ism /`ʃəʊvɪnɪzm/ *n* [U] unreasoning enthusiasm (esp for the military glory of one's own country); extreme patriotism. **chau·vin·ist** /-ɪst/ *n* person with such enthusiasm. **chau·vin·is·tic** /'ʃəʊvɪn`ɪstɪk/ *adj* of ~ or chauvinists.

chaw /tʃɔ/ *n, vt* (vulg) chew. **`~-bacon** *n* (dated) ignorant bumpkin.

cheap /tʃip/ *adj* **1** low in price; costing little money: *the* ~ *seats in a theatre; travel by the* ~*est route;* ~ *tickets/trips,* at specially reduced fares; *buy/get/sell sth* ~. ***on the*** ~, (colloq) ~ly: *buy sth on the* ~. **`~ jack** *n* pedlar or hawker selling ~ goods. **2** worth more than the cost; of good value for the money. **3** of poor quality: ~ *and nasty.* **4** shallow; insincere: ~ *emotion;* ~ *flattery.* **5** ***feel*** ~, (colloq) feel ashamed. ***hold sth*** ~, put a low value on it, despise it. ***make oneself*** ~, behave so that one's reputation goes down. **~·ly** *adv* **~·ness** *n*

cheapen /`tʃipən/ *vt, vi* [VP6A,2A] make or become cheap; lower the price of: *You mustn't* ~ *yourself,* behave so that you lower your reputation.

cheat /tʃit/ *vi, vt* [VP6A,2A,C,14] act in a dishonest way to win an advantage or profit: ~ *the customs,* e g by not declaring dutiable goods; ~ *sb out of his money;* ~ *at cards;* ~ *in an examination.* □ *n* person who ~s; dishonest trick.

check[1] /tʃek/ *vt, vi* **1** [VP6A,15B,2C] examine in order to learn whether sth is correct: ~ *a bill;* ~ *sb's statements. Will you please* ~ *these figures?* ~ ***sth off,*** mark it as having been found correct. ~ ***sth up,*** ~ ***up on sth,*** examine or compare it to learn whether it is correct. ~ ***up on sb,*** examine his credentials to see whether he is what he claims to be. **2** [VP6A] hold back; cause to go slow or stop: *We have* ~*ed the enemy's advance. He couldn't* ~ *his anger. This extravagant spending must be* ~*ed.* **3** [VP6A] restrain; rebuke. **4** [VP6A] (in the game of chess) threaten an opponent's king. **5** [VP2C] ~ ***in,*** arrive and register at a hotel/a factory etc. ~ ***out,*** pay one's bill and leave (a hotel, etc): `~*-out time,* time at which a room must be vacated. **`~·out** *n* (esp) place (e g in a supermarket) where one pays the bill, wraps one's goods and leaves. **6** (US) [VP6A] get a ticket, a piece of wood, metal, etc that shows a right to sth (e g hat and coat at a theatre, luggage sent by train or left at a railway station): *Have you* ~*ed all your baggage?* **~er** *n* person who ~s stores, orders, etc.

check[2] /tʃek/ *n* [U] **1** control; person or thing that checks or restrains: *Wind acts as a* ~ *upon speed. Our forces have met with a* ~, Their advance has been stopped, they have suffered a reverse. *We are keeping/holding the enemy in* ~, are preventing their advance. *I advise you to keep a* ~ *on* (= control) *your temper.* **'~s and `balances** *n pl* (methods of) control or supervision by Government, or other authorities, to guard against misuse of power. **2** examination to make certain of accuracy; mark or tick (usu written ✓) to show that sth has been examined and proved to be correct: *If we both add up the figures, your result will be a ~ on mine.* **'~-list** *n* list of items, titles, etc, used in checking sth. **'~·out** *n* ⇨ check[1](5). **'~·point** *n* (esp) place where traffic is halted for inspection. **'~·room,** (US) left-luggage office. **'~·up** *n* (esp a medical) examination made to certify sth. **3** receipt (bit of paper, piece of wood or metal with a number on it, etc) given in return for sth handed over to sb (e g a hat and coat at a theatre, luggage sent by train). **4** ***in ~,*** (chess) position of an opponent's king when it is exposed to direct attack. **5** (US) = cheque. **'~·book,** (US) = chequebook. **6** (US) = bill[3](1): *I'll ask the waiter for my ~.*

check[3] /tʃek/ *n* **1** pattern of crossed lines forming squares (often of different shades or colours); cloth with such a pattern: *Which do you want for your new dress, a stripe or a ~?* **2** (attrib) *a ~ tablecloth; a ~ pattern.* **checked** /tʃekt/ *adj* with a ~ pattern: *~ed material.*

checker /'tʃekə(r)/ *n, vt* (US spelling of) chequer. **check·ers** *n* (US) = draughts.

check·mate /'tʃekmeɪt/ *vt* [VP6A] **1** (chess) make a move that prevents the opponent's king from being moved away from a direct attack (and so win the game). **2** obstruct and defeat (a person, his plans). □ *n* complete defeat.

Ched·dar /'tʃedə(r)/ *n* [U] kind of firm cheese.

cheek /tʃik/ *n* **1** either side of the face below the eye. ⇨ the illus at head. ***say sth with one's tongue in one's ~,*** say one thing and mean another thing. ***~ by jowl,*** close together. **'~-bone** *n* the bone below the eye. **2** [U] impudence; saucy talk or behaviour: *He had the ~ to ask me to do his work for him! No more of your ~!* □ *vt* [VP6A] be impudent to: *Stop ~ing your mother!* **-cheeked** *suffix* (with an *adj*): *'rosy-'~ed 'boys,* boys with rosy ~s. **~y** *adj* (-ier, -iest) saucy; impudent. **~·ily** *adv*

cheep /tʃip/ *vi, n* [VP2A,C] (make a) weak, shrill note (as young birds do).

cheer[1] /tʃɪə(r)/ *vt, vi* **1** [VP6A,15B] ***~ sb (up),*** fill with gladness, hope, high spirits; comfort: *Your visit has ~ed (up) the sick man. Everyone was ~ed by the good news.* **2** [VP2C] ***~ up,*** take comfort, become happy: *He ~ed up at once when I promised to help him.* **3** [VP6A,15B,2A,C] give shouts of joy, approval or encouragement: *The speaker was loudly ~ed. The crowds ~ed as the Queen rode past. Everyone ~ed the news that the war was over. The boys ~ed their football team. The officer ~ed his men on.* **~·ing** *n* [U] *The ~ing could be heard half a mile away.* □ *adj*: *That's ~ing news.*

cheer[2] /tʃɪə(r)/ *n* **1** [U] state of hope, gladness: *words of ~,* of encouragement. **2** [U] *good ~,* good food and drink. **3** [C] shout of joy or encouragement: *give three ~s for,* cry or shout 'Hurrah!' three times. **'~-leader** *n* (US) one who leads organised cheering by a group or crowd. **4** (colloq) *C~s!* Word used when one drinks to sb's health, etc.

cheer·ful /'tʃɪəfl/ *adj* **1** bringing or suggesting happiness: *a ~ day/room/smile; ~ conversation.* **2** happy and contented; willing: *~ workers.* **~ly** /-flɪ/ *adv* **~·ness** *n*

cheerio /'tʃɪərɪ'əʊ/ *int* (colloq) **1** (at parting) goodbye. **2** (not US; dated) (in drinking) To your health!

cheer·less /'tʃɪələs/ *adj* without comfort; gloomy; miserable: *a wet and ~ day; a damp, cold and ~ room.* **~·ly** *adv* **~·ness** *n*

cheery /'tʃɪərɪ/ *adj* lively; genial; merry: *a ~ smile/greeting.* **cheer·ily** /'tʃɪərɪlɪ/ *adv*

cheese /tʃiz/ *n* [U] solid food made from milk curds; [C] shaped and wrapped portion or ball of this: *two cream ~s.* **'~-cake, (a)** tart filled with a sweet mixture of curd, eggs, etc. **(b)** (sl) photograph displaying a woman's physical charms (as in popular newspapers). ⇨ *pin-up* at pin[2](1). **'~-cloth,** thin cotton cloth (gauze) put round some kinds of ~; similar (thicker) cloth used to make shirts, etc. **'~-paring,** excessive carefulness in the spending of money: *~-paring economies.*

chee·tah /'tʃitə/ *n* kind of leopard that can be trained to hunt deer.

chef /ʃef/ *n* head male cook in a hotel/restaurant etc.

chef-d'œuvre /'ʃeɪ 'dʒvr *with unsyllabic* r/ *n* (*pl* chefs d'œuvre, pronunciation unchanged) (F) (person's) masterpiece.

chemi·cal /'kemɪkl/ *adj* of, made by, chemistry: *~ warfare,* using poison gas, smoke, incendiary bombs, etc. □ *n* (often *pl*) substance used in, or obtained by, chemistry. **~·ly** /-klɪ/ *adv*

che·mise /ʃə'miz/ *n* loose-fitting article (like a shirt) of underwear (now old-fashioned) worn by women and girls.

chem·ist /'kemɪst/ *n* **1** person who is expert in chemistry. **2** (US = druggist) person who prepares and sells medical goods, toilet articles, etc: *~'s shop,* pharmacy.

chem·is·try /'kemɪstrɪ/ *n* [U] branch of science that deals with how substances are made up, how they (their elements) combine, how they act under different conditions.

chemo·ther·apy /'keməʊ'θerəpɪ/ *n* [U] treatment of disease by drugs that attack microbes.

che·nille /ʃə'nil/ *n* velvety cord used for trimming dresses and furniture.

cheque /tʃek/ *n* (US = **check**) written order (usu on a printed form) to a bank to pay money: *a ~ for £10; pay by ~.* Cf *pay in cash.* **'~-book** *n* number of blank ~s fastened together.

chequer /'tʃekə(r)/ *vt* (US = **checker**) (usu passive) mark with a pattern of squares or patches of different colours or shades; (fig) mark by changes of good and bad fortune, etc: *a lawn ~ed with sunlight and shade; a ~ed career,* full of ups and downs of fortune, with variety of incident.

cher·ish /'tʃerɪʃ/ *vt* [VP6A] **1** care for tenderly. **2** keep alive (hope, ambition, feelings, etc) in one's heart: *For years she ~ed the hope that her husband might still be alive. Don't ~ the illusion that your father will always pay your debts.*

che·root /ʃə'rut/ *n* cigar with both ends open.

cherry /'tʃerɪ/ *n* (*pl -ties*) ⇨ the illus at **fruit**. (tree with) soft, small, round fruit, red, yellow or black when ripe and with a stone-like seed in the middle; [U] the wood of this tree. □ *adj* red: *~ lips.*

cherub /'tʃerəb/ *n* **1** (*pl* ~s) small beautiful child; (in art) such a child with wings. **2** (*pl* ~im /'tʃerəbɪm/) one of the second highest order of angels. ⇨ seraph. **cheru·bic** /tʃɪ'rubɪk/ *adj* (esp) sweet and innocent looking; roundfaced.

cher·vil /'tʃɜvɪl/ *n* [U] garden herb used to flavour soups, salads, etc.

chess /tʃes/ *n* [U] game for two players with sixteen pieces each (called **'~·men** /-men/), on a

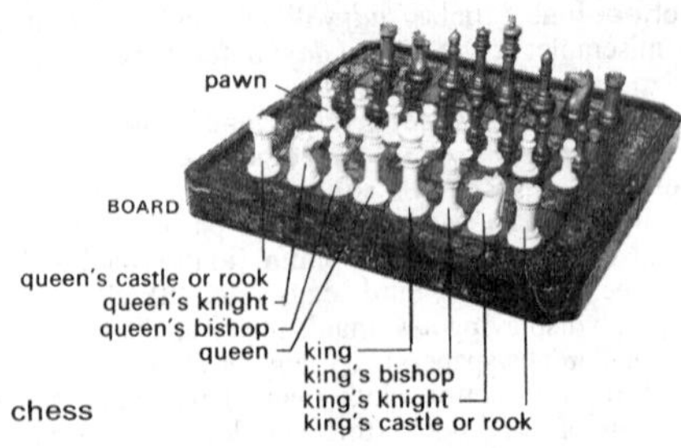

board with sixty-four squares (called a ˋ~-**board**).

chest /tʃest/ *n* **1** large, strong (usu wooden) box with a lid for storing, e g clothes, tools, money, medicine, tea, etc. ˈ**~ of ˋdrawers,** large ~ with drawers for clothes. **2** (anat) upper front part of the body, enclosed by the ribs, containing the heart and lungs. ⇨ the illus at trunk. ***get sth off one's ~,*** (sl) say sth one is anxious to say. ***(hold/keep one's cards) close to one's/the ~,*** (be) secretive. **3** (US) (funds of the) treasury of a public institution: *the community ~*, for charitable purposes.

ches·ter·field /ˋtʃestəfild/ *n* **1** single-breasted overcoat with a flap that covers the buttonholes. **2** long padded couch with sides and a back.

chest·nut /ˋtʃesnʌt/ *n* **1** [C,U] (sorts of, wood of) tree with smooth, bright reddish-brown nut (those of the Spanish or sweet ~ being edible). ⇨ the illus at tree. **2** colour of the nut. **3** horse of this colour. **4** (colloq) story or joke that is too old or well known to be amusing.

cheval glass /ʃəˋvæl glɑs *US:* glæs/ full-length mirror mounted on upright supports on which it can be tilted.

che·val·ier /ʃəˋvælɪeɪ/ *n* member of certain orders of knighthood, the French Legion of Honour, etc.

chev·ron /ˋʃevrən/ *n* bent line or stripe (∨ or ∧) worn on the sleeve by soldiers, policemen, etc to show rank, etc.

chevy, chevvy /ˋtʃevɪ/ *vt* (*pt,pp* -vied) = chivy (the more usu spelling).

chew /tʃu/ *vt,vi* **1** [VP6A,15B,2A,C] work (food, etc) about between the teeth in order to crush it: *C~ your food well before you swallow it.* ˋ**~-ing-gum** *n* [U] sticky substance sweetened and flavoured for ~ing. ⇨ also bite[1](1) and cud. **2** [VP15B,3A] ***~ sth over, ~ (up)on sth,*** (colloq) think over, consider. ***~ the rag,*** (sl) discuss matters (esp old grievances). □ *n* act of ~ing; sth (to be) ~ed: *a ~ of tobacco.*

Chi·anti /kɪˋæntɪ/ *n* [U] dry red or white Italian wine.

chi·aro·scuro /kɪˈɑrəˋskjʊərəʊ/ *n* (I) distribution of light and shade (esp in a painting).

chic /ʃik/ *n* [U] (of clothes, their wearer) style that gives an air of superior excellence. □ *adj* stylish.

chi·can·ery /ʃɪˋkeɪnərɪ/ *n* [U] (use of) legal trickery; [C] (*pl* -ries) false argument.

chi-chi /ˋʃiʃi/ *adj* (colloq) pretentious; affected.

chick /tʃɪk/ *n* **1** young bird just before or after hatching, esp a young chicken. ˋ**~·pea,** (plant with) edible yellow pea-like seeds. ˋ**~·weed,** common small weed whose leaves and seeds are eaten by birds. **2** small child; (sl) girl.

chicken /ˋtʃɪkɪn/ *n* **1** young bird, esp a young hen: *She's no ~,* (sl) is no longer young. ⇨ the illus at fowl. ***(Don't) count one's ~s before they are hatched,*** (Don't) be too hopeful of one's chances of success, etc. ˋ**~·feed** *n* (fig, sl) sth of relatively small value. ˈ**~-ˋhearted** /-hɑtɪd/ *adj* lacking in courage. ˋ**~·pox** *n* [U] disease (esp of children) accompanied by red spots on the skin. ˋ**~-run** *n* fenced-in area for ~s to run in. **2** [U] its flesh as food.

chicle /ˋtʃɪkl/ *n* [U] chief ingredient of chewing-gum.

chic·ory /ˋtʃɪkərɪ/ *n* [U] plant used as a vegetable and for salad; the root is roasted and made into a powder (used with or instead of coffee). ⇨ the illus at vegetable.

chide /tʃɑɪd/ *vt,vi* (*pt* chided /ˋtʃɑɪdɪd/ or chid /tʃɪd/, *pp* chided, chid or chidden /ˋtʃɪdn/) [VP6A,14] ***~ sb (for),*** scold; complain to (sb) as an anxious but not very firm parent might complain: *She was chiding her son for not being more dutiful to her.*

chief /tʃif/ *n* **1** leader or ruler: *a Red Indian ~; the ~ of the tribe.* **2** head of a department; highest official. ***C~ of Staff,*** senior staff officer. ***in ~,*** most of all, especially: *for many reasons, and this one in ~.* **-in-ˋ~,** supreme: *the Commander-in-~.* □ *adj* (attrib only; no comp or superl) **1** principal; most important: *the ~ rivers of India; the ~ thing to remember.* **2** first in rank: *the C~ Justice; the ~ priest.* **~·ly** *adv* **1** above all; first of all. **2** mostly; mainly: *It is ~ly composed of....*

chief·tain /ˋtʃiftən/ *n* **1** chief of a highland clan or of a tribe. **2** leader of a band of robbers. **~cy** /ˋtʃiftənsɪ/ *n* position or rank of a ~.

chif·fon /ˋʃɪfon *US:* ʃɪˋfon/ *n* [U] thin, transparent silk material used for scarves, veils, etc.

chif·fon·ier /ˈʃɪfəˋnɪə(r)/ *n* **1** (GB) movable low cupboard with a flat top used as a table. **2** (US) high chest of drawers. Cf (GB) *tallboy.*

chig·ger ⇨ jigger.

chi·gnon /ˋʃinjõ *US:* -njon/ *n* (F) knot or roll of hair worn at the back of the head by women.

chil·blain /ˋtʃɪlbleɪn/ *n* [C] painful swelling, esp on the hand or foot, caused by exposure to cold. **chil·blained** *adj* having ~s.

child /tʃɑɪld/ *n* (*pl* children /ˋtʃɪldrn/) unborn or newly born human being; boy or girl; son or daughter (of any age). ˋ**~'s play,** sth very easily done. ***be with ~,*** be pregnant. ˋ**~·bed,** ˋ**~·birth** *n* the process of giving birth to a ~: *She died in ~birth.* ˋ**~-bearing,** giving birth to children: *Ten years of ~-bearing exhausted her strength.* ˋ**~-hood** /-hʊd/ *n* [U] state of being a ~; time during which one is a ~: *have a happy ~hood.* ***second ~hood,*** dotage (in extreme old age). **~·ish** *adj* of, behaving like, suitable for, a ~: *~ish games/arguments.* **~·less** *adj* having no child(ren): *a ~less couple.* ˋ**~·like** *adj* simple, innocent.

chile, chili /ˋtʃɪlɪ/ *n* (US) = chilli.

chill /tʃɪl/ *n* **1** (*sing* only) unpleasant feeling of coldness: *There's quite a ~ in the air this morning. Take the ~ off the water,* warm it a little. **2** (fig) (*sing* only) depressing influence; sth that causes a downhearted feeling: *The bad news cast a ~ over the gathering.* **3** [C] illness caused by cold and damp, with shivering of the body: *catch a ~; have a ~ on the liver.* □ *adj* unpleasantly cold (liter, fig): *a ~ breeze; a ~ welcome.* □ *vt,vi* [VP6A,2A,C] make or become cold or cool: *He was ~ed to the bone. Don't ~ their enthusiasm.* **~ed beef,** beef preserved in cold storage at a moderately low temperature but not frozen. **~y** *adj* (-ier, -iest) **1** rather cold: *a ~y room; feel ~y. It's rather ~y this morning.* **2** (fig) unfriendly: *a ~y welcome; ~y politeness.*

chilli, chilly, chile, chili /ˋtʃɪlɪ/ *n* dried pod of red pepper, often made into powder and used to give a hot flavour to sauces, etc.

chime /tʃɑɪm/ *n* (series of notes sounded by a) tuned set of bells: *a ~ of bells; ring the ~s; listen to the ~s.* □ *vi,vt* **1** [VP6A,15A,2A,C] (of bells, a clock) make (bells) ring; ring (~s) on bells; show (the hour) by ringing: *The bells/The ringers ~d out a tune. The bells are chiming. The church clock ~d midnight.* **2** [VP2C] **~ in,** break in on the talk of others, usu to express agreement: *'Of course,' he ~d in.* **~ (in) with,** be in agreement with suit: *I think your plans will ~ in with mine.*

chim·era, chim·æra /kɑɪˋmɪərə/ *n* **1** (Gk myth) monster with a lion's head, a goat's body, and a serpent's tail. **2** horrible creature of the imagination. **3** (fig) wild or impossible idea or fancy. **chim·eri·cal** /ˈkɑɪˋmerɪkl/ *adj* unreal; visionary: *chimerical ideas/schemes.*

chim·ney /ˋtʃɪmnɪ/ *n* **1** structure through which smoke from a fire is carried away through the wall or roof of a building. **ˋ~-breast,** projecting wall in a room that contains the ~. **ˋ~ corner,** seat in an old-fashioned fireplace. **ˋ~-piece,** = mantel. **ˋ~-pot,** pipe (earthenware or metal) fitted to the top of a ~. **ˋ~-stack,** group of ~ tops. **ˋ~-sweep(er),** man who sweeps soot from ~s. **2** glass tube that protects the flame of an oil-lamp from draughts. **3** (mountaineering) narrow cleft or opening by which a cliff face may be climbed. ⇨ the illus at mountain.

chimneys

chimp /tʃɪmp/ *n* (colloq abbr of) chimpanzee.

chim·pan·zee /ˈtʃɪmpænˋzi/ *n* African ape, smaller than a gorilla. ⇨ the illus at ape.

chin /ˋtʃɪn/ *n* part of the face below the mouth; front of the lower jaw. ⇨ the illus at head. ***keep one's ˋ~ up,*** (colloq) show determination to face trouble without betraying fear or sorrow. **ˋ~-strap** *n* strap (on a helmet) held on the ~. **ˋ~-wagging** *n* (colloq) talking, gossiping.

china /ˋtʃɑɪnə/ *n* [U] baked and glazed fine white clay; articles (e g cups, saucers, plates) made from this. **ˋ~-closet,** cupboard in which ~ is kept or displayed. **ˋ~-ware,** [U] dishes, ornaments, etc made of ~ clay.

chin·chilla /tʃɪnˋtʃɪlə/ *n* [C] small S American animal that looks sth like a squirrel; [U] its soft grey fur.

chin-chin /ˈtʃɪn ˋtʃɪn/ *int* (not US) (dated colloq) word used as a greeting, and when drinking sb's health.

chine /tʃɑɪn/ *n* animal's backbone or part of it as a joint of meat.

chink¹ /tʃɪŋk/ *n* narrow opening or crack (e g between boards in the wall of a shed, through which the wind blows or through which one may peep).

chink² /tʃɪŋk/ *vt,vi, n* [VP6A,15B,2A,C] (make the) sound of coins, glasses, etc striking together; cause (coins, etc) to make such sounds: *I heard the ~ of coins.*

chintz /tʃɪnts/ *n* [U] kind of cotton cloth (usu glazed) with printed designs in colours; used for curtains, furniture covers, etc.

chip /tʃɪp/ *n* **1** small piece cut or broken off (from wood, stone, china, glass, etc). **ˋ~-board** *n* building material made from compressed ~s of waste wood, sawdust, etc and glue. ***~ off/of the old block,*** son who is very like his father. ***have a ~ on one's shoulder,*** have a defiant air, as if expecting and ready to accept a challenge; resent prejudice against oneself as (often incorrectly) perceived in other people. **2** strip cut from an apple, a potato, etc: *fish and ~s,* fried fish and potato ~s. **3** place (e g in a cup) from which a ~ has come. **4** thin strip cut from wood, palm-leaf, etc, used in making baskets, hats, etc: (usu attrib) *~ bonnets; ~ baskets.* **C~s,** (colloq nickname for) ship's carpenter. **5** flat plastic counter used as a money token (esp in gambling). ***(when) the ~s are down,*** (when) a crisis point is reached. □ *vt,vi* (-pp-) **1** [VP6A,15B] cut or break (a piece *off* or *from*): *~ a piece from the edge of a cup; ~ old paint from the side of a ship. All the plates have ~ped edges.* **2** [VP6A] make into ~s(2): *~ped potatoes.* **3** [VP2A] (of things) be easily broken at the edge: *These cups ~ if you are not careful.* **4** [VP2C] **~ in,** (colloq) **(a)** interrupt; join in (a conversation). **(b)** contribute money (to a fund). **5** [VP6A] shape (sth) by cutting the edge or surface (with an axe or a chisel). **ˋ~-pings** *n pl* bits of stone, marble, etc made by ~ping: *road ~pings,* for making a road surface.

chip·munk /ˋtʃɪpmʌŋk/ *n* small, striped N American squirrel-like rodent.

Chip·pen·dale /ˋtʃɪpəndeɪl/ *n* light style of drawing-room furniture (18th c in England): *~ chairs.*

chi·rop·odist /kɪˋropədɪst/ *n* person who is expert in the treatment of troubles of the feet and toenails. **chi·rop·ody** /kɪˋropədɪ/ *n* [U] work of a ~.

chiro·prac·tor /ˋkɑɪərəʊpræktə(r)/ *n* person who treats diseases by manipulating the joints (esp the spinal column).

chirp /tʃɜp/ *vi,vt, n* [VP2A,C,6A] (make) short, sharp note(s) or sound(s) (as of small birds or insects); utter in this way: *the ~s of the sparrows/cicadas; grasshoppers ~ing all day.*

chirpy /ˋtʃɜpɪ/ *adj* (-ier, -iest) lively, cheerful. **chirp·ily** /ˋtʃɜpɪlɪ/ *adv* **chirpi·ness** *n*

chir·rup /ˋtʃɪrəp/ *vt, n* (make a) series of chirps.

chisel /ˋtʃɪzl/ *n* steel tool with a bevelled edge for shaping wood, stone or metal. □ *vt* (-ll-, also -l-in US) [VP6A,15B,14] **1** cut or shape with a ~: *~led features,* (of a person's appearance) clear cut; well modelled. **2** (colloq) cheat; swindle. **~ler** /ˋtʃɪzḷə(r)/ *n* person who ~s(2).

chit¹ /tʃɪt/ *n* young child; young, small, slender woman (often used rather contemptuously): *a mere ~ of a child; only a ~ of a woman.*

chit² /tʃɪt/ *n* (esp in the East) short note or letter; note of sum of money owed (e g for drinks, etc at a club).

chit-chat /ˋtʃɪt tʃæt/ *n* [U] light, informal conversation.

chiv·alry /ˈʃɪvlrɪ/ *n* [U] **1** laws and customs (religious, moral and social) of the knights in the Middle Ages; the qualities that knights were expected to have (courage, honour, courtesy, loyalty, devotion to the weak and helpless, to the service of women). **2** (old use) all the knights of a country. **chiv·al·rous** /ˈʃɪvlrəs/ *adj* of, as of, the age of ~; of, as of, the knights of the Middle Ages; honourable; courteous.

chive /tʃɑɪv/ *n* small plant of the onion family, of which the slender leaves are used as a seasoning (in salads, etc).

chivy, chivvy /ˈtʃɪvɪ/ *vt* (*pt,pp* -vied) [VP15B] (colloq) ~ ***sb up/about,*** pester; chase; harass.

chlor·ide /ˈklɔrɑɪd/ *n* [U] compound of chlorine: *~ of lime/soda/potash.*

chlor·ine /ˈklɔrin/ *n* (chem) greenish-yellow, bad-smelling poisonous gas (symbol **Cl**), obtained from common salt (sodium chloride), used as a sterilizing agent and in industry. **chlor·in·ate** /ˈklɔrɪneɪt/ *vt* treat, sterilize, with ~: *chlorinated water,* water purified from disease germs by this treatment. **chlori·na·tion** /ˈklɔrɪˈneɪʃn/ *n*

chloro·form /ˈklɔrəfɔm *US:* ˈklɔr-/ *n* [U] thin, colourless liquid given, in the form of vapour, to make a person unconscious during a surgical operation. □ *vt* [VP6A] make (sb) unconscious by means of ~.

chloro·phyl(l) /ˈklɔrəfɪl *US:* ˈklɔr-/ *n* [U] (bot) green colouring matter in the leaves of plants.

chock /tʃok/ *n* block or wedge of wood used to prevent sth (e g a wheel, barrel, door) from moving; wedge on a ship's deck to support a boat. □ *vt* [VP6A,15B] ~ ***(up),*** **1** make fast with, support on, a ~ or ~s. **2** (colloq) *a room ~ed up with furniture,* filled up with far too much furniture. ˈ**~-a-ˋblock,** jammed together, packed tight (*with*). ˈ**~-ˋfull** /-ˋfʊl/ stuffed, as full as possible.

choc·olate /ˈtʃoklət/ *n* **1** [U] substance (powder or slab) made from the crushed seeds of the cacao tree; drink made by mixing this with hot water or milk; [C,U] sweet substance made from this, usu sweetened and often flavoured: *a bar of ~; a box of ~s;* (attrib) ~ *biscuit,* covered with ~; ~ cream, sweet paste covered with ~. **2** the colour of this substance, dark brown. **choc-ice** /ˈtʃok ɑɪs/ *n* (colloq) slab of ice-cream coated with chocolate.

choice /tʃɔɪs/ *n* **1** act of choosing: *make a careful ~; be careful in your ~; take your ~.* **2** [U] right or possibility of choosing: *I have no ~ in the matter,* cannot choose, must act in this way. ***for ~,*** by preference; if one must select: *I should take this one for ~.* ***Hobson's ~,*** no ~ at all because there is only one thing to take or do. **3** variety from which to choose: *This shop has a large ~ of hats.* **4** person or thing chosen: *This is my ~.* □ *adj* carefully chosen; uncommonly good: *~ fruit.*

choir /ˈkwɑɪə(r)/ *n* company of persons trained to sing together, esp to lead the singing in church; part of a church building for the ~. ˋ**~-school** *n* grammar school (attached to or connected with a cathedral) for ~-boys. ˋ~ **screen** *n* screen between the nave and the ~.

choke[1] /tʃəʊk/ *vi,vt* **1** [VP2A,3A] be unable to breathe because of sth in the windpipe, or because of emotion: *~ over one's food; ~ with anger.* **2** [VP6A,14] stop the breathing of, by pressing the windpipe from outside or blocking it up inside, or (of smoke, etc) by being unfit to breathe: *~ the life out of sb. The smoke almost ~d me. Her voice was ~d with sobs. Anger ~d his words. He swallowed a plum-stone and (was) almost ~d.* **3** [VP15B] ~ ***up (with),*** fill, partly or completely, a passage, space, etc that is usually clear: *a chimney/drain ~d (up) with dirt. The garden is ~d with weeds. The room was ~d up with useless old furniture.* **4** [VP15B] ~ ***sth back/down,*** hold or keep back/down: *~ back one's tears/indignation; ~ down one's anger.* ~ ***sb off,*** (colloq) discourage him (from doing sth); reprimand him for doing sth wrong: *He got ~d off for being late.* ˋ**~-damp,** carbon dioxide gas, left after an explosion in a coal-mine.

choke[2] /tʃəʊk/ *n* valve in a petrol engine to control the intake of air: *pull out the ~,* i e the ~ control.

choker /ˈtʃəʊkə(r)/ *n* **1** (hum) stiff, high collar; clerical collar. **2** close-fitting necklace (e g of pearls) or scarf.

chokey, choky /ˈtʃəʊkɪ/ *n* (sl dated) prison.

choler /ˈkolə(r)/ *n* (old use, or poet, liter) anger. **~ic** /ˈkolərɪk/ *adj* easily made angry; often angry.

chol·era /ˈkolərə/ *n* [U] infectious and often fatal disease, common in hot countries, with vomiting and continual emptying of the bowels.

choose /tʃuz/ *vt,vi* (*pt* chose /tʃəʊz/, *pp* chosen /ˈtʃəʊzn/) **1** [VP6A,16A,B,23,2A,C,3A] ~ ***(from/out of/between),*** pick out from a greater number; show what or which one wants by taking: *She took a long time to ~ her new hat. The greedy boy chose the largest apple in the dish. There are only five to ~ from. C~ your friends carefully. You have chosen well. They chose Green as their leader/to be their leader. Green was chosen (as) leader. He had to ~ between death and dishonour. There's nothing/not much/little to ~ between them,* They are about equal, are equally good/bad, etc. **2** [VP7A,2A] decide; be pleased or determined: *I do not ~ to be a candidate. He chose to stay where he was. Do just as you ~,* whatever pleases you. ***cannot ~ but,*** must, have to: *He cannot ~ but obey.*

choosy, choosey /ˈtʃuzɪ/ *adj* (-ier, -iest) (colloq, of persons) careful and cautious in choosing; difficult to please.

chop[1] /tʃop/ *vt,vi* (-pp-) [VP6A,15A,B] ~ ***(up) (into),*** cut into pieces by blow(s) with an axe or other edged tool: *He was ~ping wood,* cutting wood into sticks. *Meat is often ~ped up before being cooked. He ~ped a branch off the tree. I'm going to ~ that tree down. We had to ~ a way* (= make a path by ~ping) *through the undergrowth.* [VP3A] ~ ***at sth,*** aim a cutting blow at.

chop[2] /tʃop/ *n* **1** chopping blow. **2** thick slice of meat with bone in it, (to be) cooked for one person. ˋ**~-house** *n* (now usu *steak-house*) restaurant serving chops and steaks. **3** (colloq) the sack[2]: *get the ~.* **4** (boxing) short downward blow.

chop[3] /tʃop/ *n* (esp in India and China) official seal or stamp; (in China) trademark; brand of goods.

chop[4] /tʃop/ *vi* (-pp-) **1** [VP2A] ~ ***and change,*** (emphatic for *change*) be inconsistent: *He's always ~ping and changing,* always changing his opinions, plans, etc. **2** [VP2C] ~ ***about,*** (of the wind) change direction.

chop[5] /tʃop/ *n* ⇨ chap[2].

chop-chop /ˈʃop ˋtʃop/ *adv* (sl) quickly.

chop·per[1] /ˈtʃopə(r)/ *n* heavy tool with a sharp edge for chopping meat, etc. ⇨ the illus at tool.

chop·per[2] /ˋtʃopə(r)/ *n* (colloq) helicopter.

choppy /ˋtʃopɪ/ *adj* (**-ier, -iest**) (of the sea) moving in short, broken irregular waves; (of the wind) continually changing.

chop·sticks /ˋtʃopstɪks/ *n pl* pair of sticks (wood, ivory, etc) used by the Chinese and Japanese for lifting food to the mouth.

chopsticks

chop suey /ˈtʃop ˋsuɪ/ *n* [U] dish of meat or chicken served with rice, onions, etc (as in a Chinese restaurant).

choral /ˋkɔrl/ *adj* of, for, sung by or together with, a choir: *a* ˋ~ *society; a* ~ *service; Beethoven's* ~ *symphony*.

chorale /kəˋrɑl/ *n* simple hymn tune, usu sung by the choir and congregation together.

chord /ˋkɔd/ *n* **1** straight line that joins two points on the circumference of a circle or the ends of an arc. ⇨ the illus at **circle**. **2** (music) combination of three or more notes sounded together in harmony. ⇨ **discord**. **3** (also spelt *cord*) (anat) string-like structure, as in the throat (*the vocal* ~*s*) or the back (*the spinal* ~). ⇨ the illus at **head**. **4** string (of a harp, etc): *touch the right* ~, (fig) appeal cleverly to emotion.

chore /tʃɔ(r)/ *n* small duty or piece of work, esp an ordinary everyday task (in the home, on a farm, etc); unpleasant or tiring task. Cf *char*.

chor·eogra·phy /ˈkorɪˋogrəfɪ *US:* ˈkɔr-/ *n* [U] art of designing ballet. **chor·eogra·pher** *n*

chor·is·ter /ˋkorɪstə(r) *US:* ˋkɔr-/ *n* member of a choir, esp a choir-boy.

chortle /ˋtʃɔtl/ *vi, n* (give a) loud chuckle of glee.

chorus /ˋkɔrəs/ *n* **1** (music for a) group of singers. ˋ**~-girl** *n* one of a group of girls who sing and dance in a musical play. **2** (part of a) song for all to sing (after solo verses): *Mr White sang the verses and everybody joined in the* ~. **3** sth said or cried by many people together: *The proposal was greeted with a* ~ *of approval*. **in** ~, all together: *sing/answer in* ~. ⇨ **unison**. **4** (in old Gk drama) band of singers and dancers whose words and actions are a commentary on the events of the play. **5** (e g in Shakespeare's plays) actor who recites the prologue and epilogue. □ *vt* sing, speak, in ~.

chose, chosen ⇨ **choose**.

chow /tʃaʊ/ *n* **1** dog of a Chinese breed. **2** (sl) food.

chow·der /ˋtʃaʊdə(r)/ *n* thick soup or stew of fish or clams with vegetables.

Christ /kraɪst/ *n* title (= anointed one) given to Jesus, now used as part of or alternatively to His name. ˋ**~like** *adj* of or like ~; showing the spirit of ~.

christen /ˋkrɪsn/ *vt* [VP6A,23] **1** receive (an infant) into the Christian church by baptism; give a name to at the baptism. *The child was* ~*ed Mary*. **2** give a name to (a new ship when it is launched). ˋ**~ing** *n* ceremony of baptizing or naming: *There were ten* ~*ings at this church last month*.

Christen·dom /ˋkrɪsndəm/ *n* all Christian people and Christian countries.

Chris·tian /ˋkrɪstʃən/ *adj* of Jesus and his teaching; of the religion, beliefs, church, etc based on this teaching. ˋ~ **era**, time reckoned from the birth of Jesus. ˋ~ **name**, name given at baptism. Cf *family name*. ˈ~ ˋ**Science**, church and religious system of healing through spiritual means. □ *n* person believing in the religion of Christ. **Chris·ti·an·ity** /ˈkrɪstɪˋænətɪ/ *n* [U] the ~ faith or religion; being a ~; ~ character.

Christ·mas /ˋkrɪsməs/ *n* (also ˈ~ ˋ**Day**) yearly celebration (25 Dec) of the birth of Jesus Christ; week beginning on 24 Dec: (attrib) *the* ~ *holidays*. ˋ**~-box** *n* (not US) money given at ~ to the postman, tradesmen's delivery boys, etc for their services during the year. ˋ~ **card**, sent to friends at ~ to wish them 'A Merry ~ and a Happy New Year', etc. ˈ**Father** ˋ~, traditional figure who is supposed to give children gifts at ~. ˋ**~-tide/-time**, the ~ season. ˋ**~-tree** *n* small evergreen tree set up at ~ and decorated with tinsel, candles, presents, etc.

chro·matic /krəˋmætɪk/ *adj* **1** of, in, colour(s): ~ *printing*. **2** (music) of, having notes of the ~ scale, that is, the succession of semitones, twelve to the octave, normal in Western music.

chrome /krəʊm/ *n* yellow pigment, colouring matter, obtained from chromium salts, used in paints, rubber, ceramics, etc. ˋ~ **steel** *n* alloy of steel and chromium.

chro·mium /ˋkrəʊmɪəm/ *n* [U] element (symbol **Cr**) used for plating taps, hardware, motor-car fittings, etc and in steel alloys (including stainless steel): ~ *plating;* ˈ~-ˈ*plated* ˋ*fittings*.

chro·mo·some /ˋkrəʊməsəʊm/ *n* [C] (biol) one of the minute threads in every nucleus in animal and plant cells, carrying genes.

chronic /ˋkronɪk/ *adj* **1** (of a disease or condition) continual, lasting for a long time: ~ *rheumatism; a* ~ *invalid*, a person with a ~ illness. **2** (sl) intense; severe. **chroni·cally** /-klɪ/ *adv*

chron·icle /ˋkronɪkl/ *n* [C] record of events in the order of their happening. □ *vt* [VP6A] make a ~ of; record in a ~.

chrono·logi·cal /ˈkronəˋlodʒɪkl/ *adj* in order of time: *Shakespeare's plays in* ~ *order*, in the order in which they were written. **~ly** /-klɪ/ *adv*

chron·ol·ogy /krəˋnolədʒɪ/ *n* [U] science of fixing dates; [C] (*pl* **-gies**) arrangement of events with dates; list or table showing this.

chron·ometer /krəˋnomɪtə(r)/ *n* kind of watch that keeps very accurate time, esp as used for fixing longitude at sea.

chrysa·lis /ˋkrɪsəlɪs/ *n* (*pl* **-lises** /-lɪsɪz/) form taken by an insect during the torpid stage of its life (i e between the time when it creeps or crawls as a larva and the time when it flies as a moth, butterfly, etc); the sheath that covers it during this time. ⇨ the illus at **butterfly**.

chry·san·the·mum /krɪˋsænθɪməm/ *n* (flower of) garden plant blooming in autumn and early winter.

chub /tʃʌb/ *n* (*pl* usu unchanged, esp collective) thick coarse-fleshed fresh water fish.

chubby /ˋtʃʌbɪ/ *adj* (**-ier, -iest**) plump: ~ *cheeks;* round-faced: *a* ~ *child*.

chuck[1] /tʃʌk/ *vt* (colloq) **1** [VP15,A,B,12A,13A] throw: ~ *away rubbish;* ~ *a drunken man out of a pub*. ˈ**~er-**ˋ**out** *n* (sl) person whose duty it is to throw out troublesome people (from public-houses, political meetings, etc). **2** [VP6A,15B] ~ **(up)**, abandon, give up (in disgust): ~ *up one's job;* ~ *work*. *C*~ *it*, (sl) Stop doing that! **3** ~ *sb under the chin*, touch him or her playfully with the

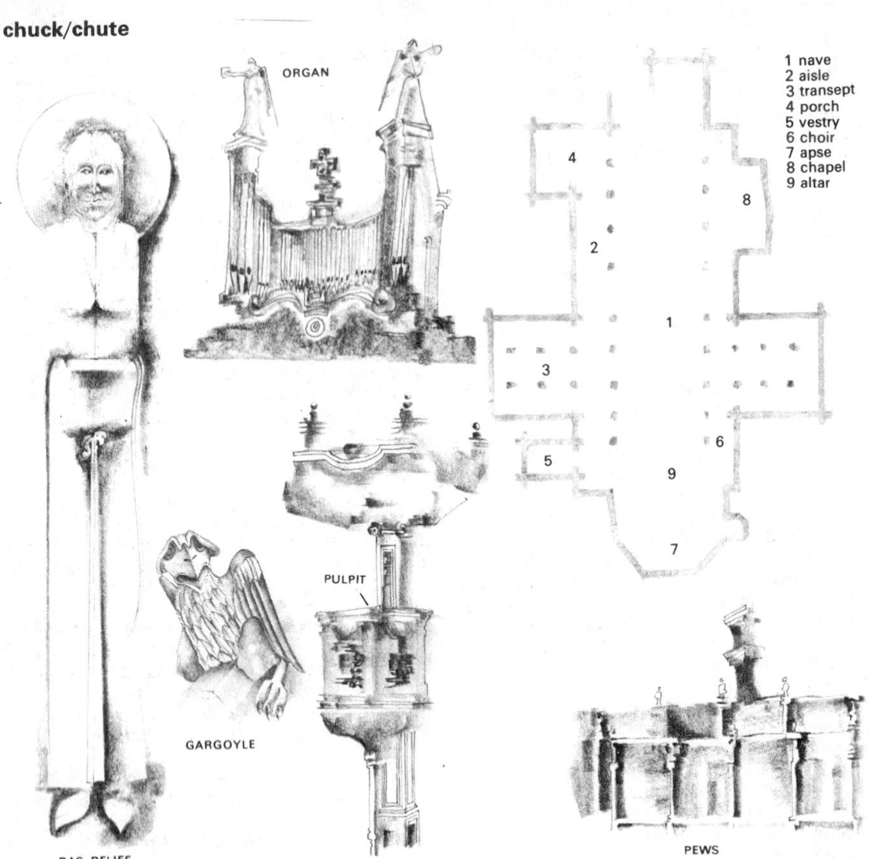

church architecture

back of the fist under the chin. □ *n* (sl) dismissal from one's job: *get the* ~, be dismissed; *give sb the* ~, dismiss him.

chuck[2] /tʃʌk/ *n* that part of a lathe which grips the work to be operated on or which grips the bit on a drill.

chuckle /ˈtʃʌkl/ *n* low, quiet laugh with closed mouth (indicating satisfaction or amusement). □ *vt* [VP2A,C] laugh in this way: *He was chuckling to himself over what he was reading.*

chug /tʃʌg/ *vi* (-gg-) [VP2C] make the short explosive sound (of an oil-engine or small petrol-engine running slowly): *The boat ~ged along.* □ *n* this sound.

chuk·ker /ˈtʃʌkə(r)/ *n* one of the periods into which the game of polo is divided.

chum /tʃʌm/ *n* close friend (esp among boys); (Australia): *new* ~, new arrival; recent immigrant; (US) room-mate. □ *vi* (-mm-) [VP2C] ***~ up (with sb),*** form a friendship (with). **~my** *adj* (-ier, iest) friendly; like a ~.

chump /tʃʌmp/ *n* **1** short, thick block of wood. **2** thick piece of meat: *a ~ chop.* **3** (sl) fool; blockhead. **4** (sl) head, esp. ***off one's ~,*** **(a)** wild with excitement. **(b)** out of one's right senses.

chunk /tʃʌŋk/ *n* thick, solid piece or lump cut off a loaf/a piece of meat/cheese etc. **~y** *adj* (-ier, -iest) short and thick.

church /tʃɜtʃ/ *n* **1** building for public Christian worship. ⇨ chapel. **ˈ~ ˈregister** *n* records of births, marriages and deaths in a parish. **ˈ~-yard** *n* burial ground round a ~. ⇨ cemetery. **2** [U] service in such a building: *What time does ~ begin? They're in/at* ~, attending a service. Cf *They're in the* ~, inside the building. *How often do you go to ~?* **ˈ~-goer** /-gəʊə(r)/ *n* person who attends ~ services regularly. **3** [C] *the C~ of Christ*, the whole body of Christians; *the C~ of England; the Methodist C~.* **4** ***enter the C~,*** become a minister of religion. **ˈ~ˈwar·den** *n* **1** elected representative of a C~ of England parish, not a priest, who helps to manage the business, funds, etc of a ~. **2** (not now used) clay tobacco pipe with a long stem.

churl /tʃɜl/ *n* **1** (old use) person of low birth, peasant. **2** bad-tempered person. **~·ish** *adv* bad tempered; ill bred. **~·ish·ly** *adv*

churn /tʃɜn/ *n* **1** tub in which cream is shaken or beaten to make butter. **2** (not US) very large can in which milk is carried from the farm. □ *vt,vi* **1** [VP6A] make (butter), beat and shake (cream) in a ~. **2** [VP6A,15B,2A,C] ***~ to/up,*** stir or move about violently: *The ship's propellers ~ed the waves to foam/~ed up the waves.*

chute /ʃut/ *n* **1** long, narrow, steep slope down which things may slide (e g for coal, barrels, etc into a cellar, logs down a hillside, letters, refuse, etc from the upper storeys of a high building): *an escape* ~, canvas tunnel by which passengers

A GOTHIC CHURCH

A BAROQUE CHURCH

leave an aircraft in an emergency. **2** smooth, rapid fall of water over a slope. **3** (colloq abbr of) parachute.

chut·ney /ˋtʃʌtnɪ/ *n* [U] hot-tasting mixture of fruit, peppers, etc eaten with curry, cold meat, etc.

cic·ada /sɪˋkɑdə/ *n* winged insect with transparent wings. The male chirps shrilly in hot, dry weather. ⇨ the illus at insect.

ci·cala /sɪˋkɑlə/ *n* = cicada.

cica·trice /ˋsɪkətrɪs/, **cica·trix** /ˋsɪkətrɪks/ *n* scar left by a healed wound.

cice·rone /ˈtʃɪtʃəˋrəʊnɪ/ *n* (*pl* -ni) (I) guide who understands and describes to sightseers places and objects of interest.

cider /ˋsɑɪdə(r)/ *n* [U] fermented apple juice. ˋ**~-press** *n* machine for pressing juice from apples.

cigar /sɪˋgɑ(r)/ *n* tight roll of tobacco leaves with pointed end(s) for smoking. ˋ**~-shaped,** shaped like a cylinder with pointed ends.

ciga·rette /ˈsɪgəˋret *US:* ˋsɪgəret/ *n* roll of shredded tobacco enclosed in thin paper for smoking. ˋ**~-case** *n* one in which a supply of ~s may be carried in the pocket or handbag. ˋ**~-holder** *n* tube in which a ~ may be put for smoking. ˋ**~-paper,** that used to make ~s.

cinch /sɪntʃ/ *n* (US sl) something that is certain; something easy and sure.

cin·chona /sɪŋˋkəʊnə/ *n* tree from whose bark quinine is obtained.

cinc·ture /ˋsɪŋktʃə(r)/ *n* (liter) belt or girdle.

cin·der /ˋsɪndə(r)/ *n* small piece of coal, wood, etc partly burned, no longer flaming, and not yet ash: *burnt to a ~,* (of a cake, etc) cooked so that it is hard and black. ˋ**~-track** *n* running track made with fine ~s.

Cin·de·rella /ˈsɪndəˋrelə/ *n* girl or woman whose attraction, merits, etc have not been recognized; (fig) sth long neglected.

cine- /sɪnɪ/ *pref* form used for *cinema* in compounds. ˋ**~-cam·era** *n* camera used for taking moving pictures. ⇨ the illus at camera. ˋ**~-film** *n* film used in ~-cameras. ˋ**~-loop** *n* continuous belt of film projected on to a screen (used esp in teaching). ˋ**~-pro·jec·tor** *n* machine for showing ~-films on a screen.

cin·ema /ˋsɪnəmə/ *n* **1** theatre in which films are shown. **2** (*sing,* with or without the *def art*) moving pictures as an art-form or an industry. *Are you interested in* (*the*) *~?* Cf the drama.

cine·mato·graph /ˈsɪnəˋmætəgrɑf *US:* -græf/ *n* (old name for) cine-projector.

cin·na·mon /ˋsɪnəmən/ *n* [U] spice from the inner bark of an E Indian tree, used in cooking; its colour, yellowish brown.

cinque·foil /ˋsɪŋkfɔɪl/ *n* plant with leaves divided into five parts and with small yellow flowers.

cipher, cypher /ˋsɑɪfə(r)/ *n* **1** the symbol 0, representing nought or zero. **2** any Arabic numeral, 1 to 9. **3** (fig) person or thing of no importance. **4** (method of, key to) secret writing: *a message in ~; a ~ key; the `~ officer,* officer who codes and decodes messages. □ *vt, vi* **1** [VP6A] put into secret writing. **2** [VP6A,2A] (colloq) do arithmetical problems; add up, divide, etc; work out a problem in figures.

circa /`s3kə/ *prep* (Lat, abbr *c, ca* or *circ*) about (with dates): *born ~ 150* B C.

circle /`s3kl/ *n* **1** (geom) space enclosed by a curved line, every point on which is the same distance from the centre; the line enclosing this space. ⇨ also the illus at concentric. **2** sth like a ~; ring: *a ~ of trees/hills; standing in a ~;* ***a vicious ~,*** ⇨ vicious. **3** block of seats in curved rows, one above the other, between the highest part (the gallery) and the floor of a cinema, theatre or concert hall. theatre. **4** number of persons bound together by having the same or similar interests: *in theatrical ~s,* among actors, etc; *moving in fashionable ~s,* among those in fashionable society; *business ~s. He has a large ~ of friends. They are newcomers to our ~.* **5** complete series: *the ~ of the seasons,* the four seasons in succession. ***come full ~,*** end at the starting-point. □ *vt, vi* [VP6A,2A,C] move in a ~; go round: *The aircraft ~d (over) the landing-field. Drake ~d the globe,* sailed round the world. *The news ~d round,* was passed round.

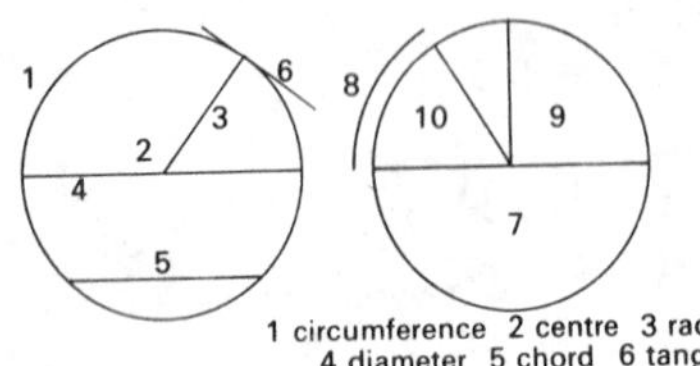

parts of a circle

circ·let /`s3klət/ *n* round band (e g of gold or flowers) worn as an ornament on the head, neck or arm.

circs /s3ks/ *n pl* (colloq abbr of) circumstances.

cir·cuit /`s3kɪt/ *n* **1** journey round, from place to place: *The ~ of the city walls is three miles.* ***make a ~ of,*** go round. **2** regular journey or itinerary made by judges and barristers to towns in England and Wales to county towns (*~ towns*) to hear civil and criminal cases, replaced in 1972 by Crown Courts ⇨ court[1]. One of six areas in the country, each having a number of Crown Courts: *Judges go on ~ for part of the year.* **3** chain of cinemas, theatres, etc under a single management: *Some theatrical companies travel over regular ~s,* visit certain towns in succession. **4** closed path for an electrical current; apparatus with a sequence of conductors, valves, etc for using an electric current: *~ diagram,* one that shows the connections in such an apparatus. ***closed ~ (TV),*** ⇨ close[3](2). ***short ~,*** faulty shortening of such a path by defective insulation. **5** regional group of Methodist churches sharing preachers.

cir·cu·itous /s3`kjuɪtəs/ *adj* indirect; going a long way round: *a ~ route.*

cir·cu·lar /`s3kjʊlə(r)/ *adj* round or curved in shape; moving round: *a ~ building; the North C~ Road,* round the north of London, for through traffic; *a ~ tour/trip,* ending at the starting-point without visiting a place more than once. **a ~ letter** *n* one sent out to many persons. '**~ `saw** *n* disc-shaped saw that revolves by machinery. □ *n* printed letter, advertisement, announcement, etc of which many copies are made and distributed. **~·ize** /`s3kjʊləraɪz/ *vt* [VP6A] *send ~s to.*

cir·cu·late /`s3kjʊleɪt/ *vi, vt* **1** [VP2A,C] go round continuously; move from place to place freely: *Blood ~s through the body. In many buildings hot water ~s through pipes to keep rooms warm. Bad news ~s quickly. In times of prosperity money ~s quickly; during a depression it ~s slowly.* **circulating library,** one from which books may be borrowed, usu on payment of a subscription. **2** [VP6A] cause to ~: *People who ~ false news are to be blamed.*

cir·cu·la·tion /'s3kjʊ`leɪʃn/ *n* **1** [U] circulating or being circulated, esp the movement of the blood from and to the heart: *He has a good/bad ~. The ~ of rumours is common in wartime.* **2** [U] state of being circulated: *Are there many forged banknotes in ~? That book has been withdrawn from ~,* cannot now be obtained. *When were the decimal coins put into ~?* **3** [C] number of copies of a newspaper or other periodical sold to the public; *a newspaper with a (daily) ~ of more than one million.*

cir·cum·cise /`s3kəmsaɪz/ *vt* remove the foreskin of (a male) or the clitoris of (a female). **cir·cum·cision** /'s3kəm`sɪʒn/ *n* circumcising, esp (of males) as a religious rite among Jews and Muslims.

cir·cum·fer·ence /s3`kʌmfərns/ *n* (geom) line that marks out a circle or other curved figure; distance round sth: *The ~ of the earth is almost 25 000 miles.* ⇨ the illus at circle.

cir·cum·flex /`s3kəmfleks/ *n* (also **~ accent**) mark placed over a vowel to indicate how it is to be sounded (as in French *rôle*).

cir·cum·lo·cu·tion /'s3kəmlə`kjuʃn/ *n* [C,U] (instance of) saying in many words what may be said in few words.

cir·cum·navi·gate /'s3kəm`nævɪgeɪt/ *vt* [VP6A] sail round (esp the world). **cir·cum·navi·ga·tion** /'s3kəm'nævɪ`geɪʃn/ *n*

cir·cum·scribe /`s3kəmskraɪb/ *vt* [VP6A] draw a line round; mark the limit(s) of; narrow down, restrict: *~ one's interests.* **cir·cum·scrip·tion** /'s3kəm`skrɪpʃn/ *n* **1** [U] circumscribing or being ~d. **2** [C] words inscribed round a coin.

cir·cum·spect /`s3kəmspekt/ *adj* paying careful attention to everything before taking action; cautious. **~·ly** *adv* **cir·cum·spec·tion** /'s3kəm`spekʃn/ *n* [U] prudence; caution.

cir·cum·stance /`s3kəmstæns/ *n* **1** (usu *pl*) conditions, facts, etc connected with an event or person: *Don't judge the crime until you know the ~s.* ***C~s alter cases,*** (prov) What may be good, wise, praiseworthy, etc in some ~s may be bad, foolish or blameworthy in other ~s. ***in/under the ~s,*** the ~s being so; such being the state of affairs. ***in/under no ~s,*** never; whatever may happen. **2** fact or detail: *There is one important ~ you have not mentioned. He has plenty of money, which is a fortunate ~.* **3** (*pl*) financial condition: *in easy/good/flourishing ~s,* having enough or plenty of money: *in reduced/straitened ~s,* poor. **4** (*sing* used only in) ceremony: *too much pomp and ~.*

cir·cum·stan·tial /ˈsɜkəmˋstænʃl/ *adj* **1** (of a description) giving full details. **2** (of evidence) based on, consisting of details that strongly suggest sth but do not provide direct proof. **~·ly** /-nʃlɪ/ *adv*

cir·cum·vent /ˈsɜkəmˋvent/ *vt* [VP6A] get the better of (sb); defeat (sb's plans); prevent (a plan) from being carried out; find a way to get round (a law, rule, etc). **cir·cum·ven·tion** /ˈsɜkəmˋvenʃn/ *n*

cir·cus /ˋsɜkəs/ *n* **1** (round or oval) place with seats on all sides for public games (in ancient Rome) or (in modern times) a show of performing animals, clever horse-riding, etc; persons and animals giving such a show. **2** (esp in proper names) open space where a number of streets converge: *Piccadilly C~*, in London.

cir·rho·sis /sɪˋrəʊsɪs/ *n* [U] chronic (and often fatal) disease of the liver.

cir·rus /ˋsɪrəs/ *n* type of cloud, high in the sky, delicate and feathery in appearance.

cissy /ˋsɪsɪ/ *adj, n* (sl) effeminate or cowardly (boy or man).

cis·tern /ˋsɪstən/ *n* water tank, e g as above the bowl of a *WC*, or for storing water in a building, with pipes to taps on lower storeys.

cita·del /ˋsɪtədl/ *n* fortress for protecting a town; (fig) place of refuge or safety.

cite /sɑɪt/ *vt* [VP6A] **1** give or mention as an example (esp by quoting from a book, to support an argument, etc). **2** (US) mention for bravery in war: *~d in dispatches.* **3** (legal) summon to a law court: *be ~d in divorce proceedings.* **ci·ta·tion** /sɑɪˋteɪʃn/ *n* [U] citing; [C] sth, esp a statement, that is ~d; (US) mention in an official record (e g for a brave act in war).

citi·zen /ˋsɪtɪzn/ *n* **1** person who lives in a town, not in the country: *the ~s of Paris.* **2** person who has full rights in a State, either by birth or by gaining such rights: *immigrants who have become ~s of the United States.* Cf *British subject; ~ of the world,* cosmopolitan person. **ˋ~·ship** /-ʃɪp/ *n* being a ~; rights and duties of a ~.

cit·ric /ˋsɪtrɪk/ *adj* (chem): *~ acid,* acid from such fruits as lemons and limes.

cit·ron /ˋsɪtrən/ *n* (tree with) pale yellow fruit like a lemon but larger, less acid, and thicker skinned.

cit·rous /ˋsɪtrəs/ *adj* of the citrus fruits.

cit·rus /ˋsɪtrəs/ *n* (bot) genus of trees that includes the lemon, lime, citron, orange and grapefruit; (attrib) of these trees: *ˋ~ fruit.*

city /ˋsɪtɪ/ *n* (*pl* **-ties**) **1** large and important town; town given special rights in self-government (in GB by royal charter, in US by a charter from the State). **the C~,** the oldest part of London, now the commercial and financial centre. **2** people living in a ~. **3** (attrib): *ˈ~ ˋcentre,* central area of a city; *ˈ~ ˋeditor,* (GB) one who deals with financial news; (US) one in charge of local news; *ˈ~ ˋhall,* building for transaction of the official business of a ~; *a ˋC~ man,* engaged in commerce or finance; *~ state,* city that is also an independent sovereign state (e g Athens in ancient times).

civet /ˋsɪvɪt/ *n* **1** (also **ˋ~-cat**) small spotted cat-like animal of Africa, Asia and Europe. **2** [U] strong-smelling substance from certain glands of this animal.

civic /ˋsɪvɪk/ *adj* of the official life and affairs of a town or a citizen: *~ duties; ~ pride; a ~ centre,* where the official buildings, e g the town hall, library, hospitals, etc, are grouped together. **civ·ics** *n pl* (*sing v*) study of city government, the rights and duties of citizens, etc.

civ·ies /ˋsɪvɪz/ *n pl* (sl) civilian clothes.

civil /ˋsɪvl/ *adj* **1** of human society; of people living together: *We all have ~ rights and ~ duties.* **ˈ~ ˈdisoˋbedience,** organized refusal to obey the laws (esp as part of a political campaign). **ˈ~ ˈengiˋneering,** the design and building of roads, railways, canals, docks, etc. **ˈ~ ˋlaw,** law dealing with private rights of citizens, not with crime. **ˈ~ ˋmarriage,** without religious ceremony but recognized by law. **ˈ~ ˋrights,** rights of a citizen to political, racial, legal, social freedom or equality. **ˈ~ ˋrights movement,** organized movement aiming to secure for minorities the enjoyment of constitutional rights. **ˈ~ ˋwar,** war between two parties of the same State. **2** not of the armed forces. **ˈC~ Deˋfence Corps,** organization to deal with results of attack (esp from the air). **ˈ~ ˋservant,** official in the C~ Service. **the ˈC~ ˋService,** all government departments except the Navy, Army and Air Force. **3** politely helpful: *The boy gave me a ~ answer. Can't you be ~? It was ~ of them to offer to help us.* **4 ˋ~ list,** (GB) allowance of money made by Parliament for the royal household and royal pensions. **~·ly** /ˋsɪvlɪ/ *adv* politely. **ci·vil·ity** /sɪˋvɪlətɪ/ *n* [U] politeness (*to*); (*pl;* **-ties**) polite acts.

ci·vil·ian /sɪˋvɪlɪən/ *n adj* (person) not serving with the armed forces: *I asked the soldier what he was in ~ life. He left the army and returned to ~ life. In modern wars ~s as well as soldiers are killed.*

civi·li·za·tion /ˈsɪvlɑɪˋzeɪʃn *US:* -lɪˋz-/ *n* **1** [U] civilizing or being civilized; state of being civilized: *The ~ of mankind has taken thousands of years.* **2** [C] system, stage of, social development: *the ~s of ancient Egypt, Babylon and Persia.* **3** [U] civilized States collectively: *acts that horrified ~.*

civi·lize /ˋsɪvlɑɪz/ *vt* [VP6A] **1** bring from a savage or ignorant condition to a higher one (by giving education in methods of government, moral teaching, etc). **2** improve and educate; refine the manners of: *Many a rough man has been ~d by his wife.*

civ·vies /ˋsɪvɪz/ *n pl* = civies.

Civvy Street /ˋsɪvɪ strit/ *n* (GB sl) civilian life.

clack /klæk/ *vi, n* (make the) short, sharp sound of objects struck together: *the ~ of her knitting needles; ~ing typewriters; ~ing tongues at the Women's Institute.*

clad /klæd/ old *pp* of clothe: *poorly ~,* dressed in poor clothes; (poet): *hills ~ in verdure;* (in compounds): *ˋsteel-~; ˋiron-~.*

claim /kleɪm/ *vt,vi* [VP6A,7A,9,2A] **1** demand recognition of the fact that one is, or owns, or has a right to (sth): *Does anyone ~ this umbrella? Every citizen in a democratic country may ~ the protection of the law. He ~ed to be the owner of/~ed that he owned the land. Have you ~ed yet?* e g made a ~ under an insurance policy. ***~ damages,*** (legal) ⇨ damage. ⇨ also bonus. **2** assert; say that sth is a fact: *He ~ed to have/~ed that he had done the work without help. He ~ed to be the best tennis player in the school.* **3** (of things) need; deserve: *There are several matters that ~ my attention.* □ *n* **1** [C] act of ~ing(**1**): *Does anyone make a ~ to* (but more usu *Does anyone claim*) *this purse,* say that it is his? *His ~ to own the house is invalid. He set up a ~ to the throne,* said he was the rightful king. **lay ~ to,**

demand (sth) as one's due: *If the land really belongs to you, why don't you lay ~ to it,* say so and try to get it? **2** [C] sum of money demanded under an insurance agreement (for loss, damage, etc): *make/put in a ~ (for sth).* **3** [U] right to ask for: *You have no ~ on my sympathies.* **4** [C] sth that is ~ed; piece of land (esp in a gold-bearing region) allotted to a miner: *stake out a ~,* mark boundaries to assert ownership. **'~·ant** /ˈkleɪmənt/ *n* person who makes a ~, esp in law.

clair·voy·ance /kleəˈvɔɪəns/ *n* [U] abnormal power of seeing in the mind what is happening or what exists at a distance; exceptional insight. **clair·voy·ant** /kleəˈvɔɪənt/ *n* person with such power.

clam /klæm/ *n* large shell-fish, with a shell in two halves, used for food. ⇨ the illus at **bivalve**. **~-bake** /ˈklæmbeɪk/ *n* (US) sea-shore picnic at which ~s and other foods are baked. □ *vt* (-mm) dig for, go out for, ~s.

clam·ber /ˈklæmbə(r)/ *vi* [VP2C] climb with some difficulty, using the hands and feet: *~ up/over a wall.* □ *n* awkward or difficult climb.

clammy /ˈklæmɪ/ *adj* (-ier, -iest) damp; moist; cold and sticky to the touch: *~ hands; a face ~ with sweat.* **clam·mi·ly** *adv*

clam·our (US = **clamor**) /ˈklæmə(r)/ *n* [C,U] loud confused noise or shout, esp of people complaining angrily or making a demand. □ *vi,vt* [VP2A,C,4A] make a ~: *The foolish people were ~ing for war. The newspapers ~ed against the government's policy. The troops were ~ing to go home.* **clam·or·ous** /ˈklæmərəs/ *adj* noisy: *a clamorous mob.*

clamp¹ /klæmp/ *n* **1** appliance for holding things together tightly by means of a screw. **2** band of iron, etc for strengthening or tightening. □ *vt,vi* **1** [VP6A,15B] put a ~ or ~s on; put in a ~. **2** [VP2C] ***~ down (on),*** (colloq) put pressure on; exert pressure against (in order to stop sth): *They ~ed down on the news.* Hence, **'~-down** *n*

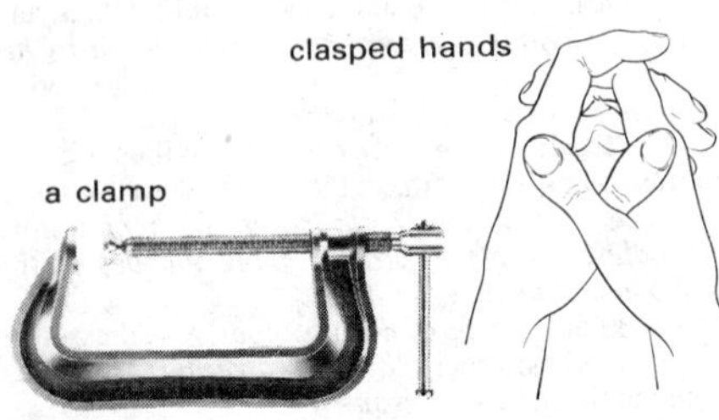

clamp² /klæmp/ *n* mound of potatoes, etc stored under straw and earth.

clan /klæn/ *n* large family group, as found in tribal communities, esp Scottish Highlanders with a common ancestor: *the Campbell ~.*

clan·des·tine /klænˈdestɪn/ *adj* secret; done secretly; kept secret: *a ~ marriage.*

clang /klæŋ/ *vt,vi, n* [VP6A,2A] (make a) loud ringing sound (e g a hammer striking an anvil): *The tramdriver ~ed his bell. The ~ of the firebell alarmed the village.* **~er** *n* (sl) ***drop a ~er,*** say sth indiscreet or embarrassing.

clan·gour (US = **-gor**) /ˈklæŋə(r)/ *n* continued clanging noise; series of clangs. **clangor·ous** /ˈklæŋərəs/ *adj*

clank /klæŋk/ *vt,vi, n* [VP6A,2A] (make a) ringing sound (not so loud as a clang) (e g armour, chains or swords striking together): *Prisoners ~ing their chains.*

clan·nish /ˈklænɪʃ/ *adj* showing clan feeling: (of people) in the habit of supporting one another against outsiders. **~·ly** *adv*

clans·man /ˈklænzmən/ *n* (*pl* -men) member of a clan.

clap¹ /klæp/ *vt,vi* (-pp-) **1** [VP6A,2A,B] show approval, applaud, by striking the palms of the hands together; do this as a signal (e g to summon a servant, a waiter, etc): *When the violinist finished the audience ~ped for five minutes. The baby ~ped its hands.* **2** [VP14] strike or slap lightly with the open hand, usu in a friendly way: *~ sb on the back.* **3** [VP15A,B] put quickly or energetically: *~ sb in prison; ~ one's hat on; ~ on sail,* spread more sail. ***~ eyes on sb,*** (colloq, esp in neg) catch sight of: *I haven't ~ped eyes on him since 1960.* □ *n* **1** loud explosive noise (of thunder). **2** sound of the palms of the hands brought together. (*Clapping* is the usu word for applause, not *claps*).

clap² /klæp/ *n* [U] (vulg) gonorrhea.

clap·board /ˈklæpbɔd *US:* ˈklæbɔd/ *n* weather-board.

clap·per /ˈklæpə(r)/ *n* tongue or striker of a bell; noisy hand rattle (used, for example, to scare birds from crops). **'~·board** *n* (filming) divided, hinged board which is sharply closed to mark the start of filming.

clap·trap /ˈklæptræp/ *n* [U] ideas, remarks, that are intended merely to attract attention or win applause.

claque /klæk/ *n* [C] number of persons hired to applaud at a theatre, concert, etc.

claret /ˈklærət/ *n* [U] (kind of) red table wine from Bordeaux; (also *adj*) its colour, dark red.

clar·ify /ˈklærɪfaɪ/ *vt,vi* (*pt,pp* -fied) [VP6A,2A] make or become clear; make (a liquid, etc) free from impurities. **clari·fi·ca·tion** /ˌklærɪfɪˈkeɪʃn/ *n* [U] ~ing or being clarified.

clari·net /ˌklærɪˈnet/ *n* musical wood-wind instrument, with finger holes and keys. ⇨ the illus at **brass**. **~·ist, ~·tist** *n* person who plays the ~.

clar·ion /ˈklærɪən/ *n* loud, shrill call made to rouse and excite; (attrib) loud and clear: *a ~ call; a ~ voice.*

clar·io·net /ˌklærɪəˈnet/ *n* = **clarinet**.

clar·ity /ˈklærətɪ/ *n* [U] clearness.

clash /klæʃ/ *vi,vt* **1** [VP6A,15B,2A,C] make a loud, broken, confused noise (as when metal objects strike together): *Their swords ~ed. She ~ed the pans down on the stone floor. The cymbals ~ed.* **2** [VP2A,C] come suddenly together; meet in conflict: *The two armies ~ed outside the town.* **3** [VP2A,C] (of events) interfere with each other because they are (to be) at the same time on the same date: *It's a pity the two concerts ~, I want to go to both.* **4** [VP3A,2A,C] ***~ (with),*** be in disagreement or at variance: *I ~ed with him/We ~ed at the last meeting of the Council. The colour of the curtains ~es with the colour of the carpet. The date of your party ~es with another engagement.* □ *n* **1** ~ing noise: *the ~ of weapons/of pots on a stove; the ~ of cymbals.* **2** disagreement; conflict: *a ~ of views/opinions; a ~ of colours.*

clasp /klɑsp *US:* klæsp/ *n* **1** device with two parts that fasten, used to keep together two things or two parts of one thing (e g the ends of a necklace or belt). '\~-**knife,** folding knife with a \~ for fixing the blade when open. **2** bar of silver, etc on a medal-ribbon (with the name of the battle, campaign, etc at which the person to whom the medal was awarded was present). **3** firm hold (with the fingers or arm); handshake; embrace. □ *vt,vi* **1** [VP6A,15A] hold tightly or closely: *\~ed in each other's arms; \~ sb by the hand. The thief was \~ing a knife in his hand.* **\~ hands,** shake hands with sb (showing more emotion than in the usual handshake). ***\~ one's hands,*** press them together with the fingers interlaced: *with hands \~ed in prayer; with his hands \~ed behind him.* **2** [VP6A,15A] fasten with a clasp(**1**): *\~ a bracelet round one's wrist.* **3** [VP2A] *This bracelet won't \~,* cannot be \~ed.

class /klɑs *US:* klæs/ *n* **1** group having qualities of the same kind; kind, sort or division: *There used to be first-\~, second-\~ and third-\~ carriages on the trains in Britain. The highest division of the animal or vegetable kingdom is a \~.* ⇨ family, genus, order[1](15), species. *As an actor A is not in the same \~ with B,* is not so good as B. **2** [U] system of ranks in society; caste system: *It will be difficult to abolish \~;* (used attrib): *\~ conflicts; the \~ struggle.* '\~-**conscious,** realizing one's \~ in society and the differences between social \~es. '\~-**feeling,** feeling of envy, etc of one \~ for another. '\~-'**warfare,** struggle, enmity, between \~es. **3** [C] all persons in one of these ranks: *Society may be divided into upper, middle and lower \~es.* **4** group of persons taught together; their course of teaching. '\~-**fellow/-mate,** *n* present or past member of the same \~: *Green and I were \~-mates last term.* '\~-**room,** room where a \~ is taught. **5** (US) group of pupils or students who enter school or college in the same year and leave together: *the \~ of 1973,* those who finished their school course in that year. **6** all those men conscripted for service in the armed forces in a year: *the 1970 \~.* **7** (not US) grade or merit after examination: *take a first/second-\~ degree.* '\~-**list,** honours list issued by examiners. **8** (colloq; often attrib) distinction; excellence; style: *He's a \~ tennis player. There's not much \~ about her.* □ *vt* [VP6A,14] place in a \~(**1**): *a ship \~ed A1; to \~ one thing with another.* **\~less** *adj* without distinctions of \~(**2**): *Is a \~less society possible?*

clas·sic /'klæsɪk/ *adj* **1** of the highest quality; having a value or position recognized and unquestioned. **2** of the standard of ancient Greek and Latin literature, art and culture. **3** with qualities like those of \~(**2**) art, i e simple, harmonious and restrained. **4** famous because of a long history: *a \~ event,* e g the Oxford and Cambridge boat race or the Derby. **5** (of style in costume, etc) traditional; not new. □ *n* **1** writer, artist, book, etc of the highest class: *Milton is a \~. 'Robinson Crusoe' is a \~.* **2** ancient Greek or Latin writer. **3** (*pl* with *def art*) (literature of the) ancient languages of Greece and Rome; (without *def art*) university course in these subjects: *He read \~s at Oxford.* **4** \~ event. ⇨ the *adj* **4** above.

clas·si·cal /'klæsɪkl/ *adj* **1** in, of, the best (esp ancient Gk and Roman) art and literature: *\~ studies; a \~ education; a '\~ scholar.* **2** of proved value because of having passed the test of time: *\~ music,* usually taking traditional form as a concerto, symphony, etc, e g of Haydn and Mozart. ⇨ light[4](4). **3** simple and restrained; not over-ornamented. **\~·ly** /-klɪ/ *adv*

clas·si·cist /'klæsɪsɪst/ *n* follower of classic style; classical scholar: *Milton was a \~.*

clas·si·fi·ca·tion /ˌklæsɪfɪ'keɪʃn/ *n* [U] classifying or being classified; [C] group into which sth is put.

clas·sify /'klæsɪfaɪ/ *vt* (*pt,pp* -fied) [VP6A] arrange in classes or groups; put into a class(**1**): *In a library books are usually classified by subjects.* **clas·si·fied** *adj* arranged in classes(**1**): *classified advertisements* (also, colloq, *classified ads*); *classified directory,* one in which the entries (e g of business firms) are entered in classes (e g builders, electricians, plumbers); (US) put in a group that is officially secret: *classified information.* **clas·si·fi·able** /'klæsɪfaɪəbl/ *adj* that can be classified.

classy /'klɑsɪ *US:* 'klæsɪ/ *adj* (colloq) stylish; superior; upper-class.

clat·ter /'klætə(r)/ *n* (*sing* only) **1** long, continuous, resounding noise (as of hard things falling or knocking together): *the \~ of a horse's hoofs on a hard road; the \~ of machinery; the \~ of cutlery.* **2** noisy talk: *The boys stopped their \~ when the teacher came into the classroom.* □ *vi,vt* [VP6A, 2A,C] make a \~(**1**): *Pots and pans were \~ing in the kitchen. Don't \~ your knives and forks. Some of the dishes \~ed down during the earthquake.*

clause /klɔz/ *n* **1** (gram) component of a (complex) sentence, with its own subject and predicate, esp one doing the work of a noun, adjective or adverb: *dependent/subordinate \~.* **2** (legal) complete paragraph in an agreement, legal document, etc.

claus·tro·pho·bia /ˌklɔstrə'fəʊbɪə/ *n* [U] morbid fear of confined places (e g a lift, cave or coal-mine).

clave /kleɪv/ old *pt* form of cleave[2].

clavi·chord /'klævɪkɔd/ *n* stringed instrument with a keyboard, predecessor of the piano.

clav·icle /'klævɪkl/ *n* (anat) collar-bone. ⇨ the illus at skeleton.

claw /klɔ/ *n* **1** one of the pointed nails on the feet of some animals, reptiles and birds; foot with such nails. ⇨ the illus at bird. **2** pincers of a shell-fish (e g a lobster). ⇨ the illus at crustacean. **3** instrument or device like a \~ (e g a steel hook on a machine for lifting things). '\~-**hammer** *n* hammer with one end of the head bent and divided for pulling nails out of wood. □ *vt* [VP6A,15B] get hold of, pull, scratch, with \~s or hands.

clay /kleɪ/ *n* [U] stiff, sticky earth that becomes hard when baked; material from which bricks, pots, earthenware, etc are made: (attrib) *\~ soil; a \~ pipe,* tobacco pipe made of white \~. **\~ey** /'kleɪɪ/ *adj* of, like, containing, covered with, \~.

clay·more /'kleɪmɔ(r)/ *n* heavy two-edged sword, formerly used in Scotland.

clean[1] /klin/ *adj* **1** free from dirt: *\~ hands; \~ air,* free from smoke; *a \~ bomb,* atomic or hydrogen bomb that, it is claimed, explodes without fall-out. ⇨ fall[1](1). *Keep the classroom \~. Wash it \~.* ⇨ heel[1](1). **2** not yet used; fresh: *Put some \~* (e g after having been washed) *sheets on the bed. Give me a \~ sheet of paper.* **3** pure; innocent; free from wrongdoing or indecency: *You must lead a \~ life. He has a \~ record,* is not known to have done wrong; *a \~ joke; Keep the party \~,* (colloq) Don't use bad language or tell improper stories. **4** well-formed; of good shape: *a motor-car/ship with \~ lines.* ⇨ *streamlined* at stream. '\~-

ˈlimbed *adj* having well-shaped limbs. **5** even; regular; with a smooth edge or surface: *A sharp knife makes a ~ cut. C~ timber has no knots in it.* **6** skilful; smart: *a ~ boxer;* (cricket) *~ fielding; a ~ stroke/blow.* **7** having ~ habits: *a ~ waitress.* **8** fit for food: *~/un~ animals,* those that are/are not considered fit for food (by religious custom). **9** thorough, complete. ***make a ~ sweep of,*** ⇨ sweep²(1). ⇨ also breast and slate(2). □ *adv* completely; entirely: *I ~ forgot about it. The bullet went ~ through his shoulder.* ***come ~,*** make a full confession. **ˈ~-ˈbowled** *adj* (cricket) bowled with no possibility of doubt. **ˈ~-ˈcut** *adj* sharply outlined. **ˈ~-ˈliving** *adj* chaste. **ˈ~-ˈshaven** *adj* with the hair of the face shaved off; not having a moustache or beard.

clean² /klin/ *vt,vi* **1** [VP6A] make clean (of dirt, etc): *Wash your hands and ~ your nails. I must have this suit ~ed,* sent to the dry-cleaner's. ⇨ dry¹(13). *C~ your shoes before you come into the house,* i e remove the mud, etc. ⇨ **brush, polish. 2** [VP2A] *A porcelain sink ~s easily,* is easy to ~. **3** [VP15B,2C] (with *adverbial particles* and *preps*): ***~ down,*** ~ by brushing or wiping: *~ down the walls.* ***~ sb out,*** win or take all the money of: *They really ~ed me out at Las Vegas,* I lost all my money gambling there. ***~ sth out,*** ~ the inside of, remove dirt, dust, etc from: *It's time you ~ed out your bedroom.* ***be ~ed out,*** (colloq) have no money left. ***~ up,*** make clean or tidy; put in order: *You should always ~ up after a picnic,* burn wastepaper, collect litter, empty bottles, etc. ***~ sth up,*** **(a)** get rid of criminal and immoral elements, etc: *The mayor has decided to ~ up the city,* end corruption, etc. **(b)** (colloq) make money (as gain or profit). **ˈ~-up** *n* (esp) (process of) ending or reducing crime, corruption, etc. □ *n* ~ing: *Give it a good ~,* ~ it well. **~er** *n* person or thing that ~s; tool, machine, etc for ~ing; substance that removes dirt, stains, grease, etc: *send/take a suit to the (ˈdry) ˈ~ers; ˈwindow-~er; ˈvacuum-~er.*

clean·ly /ˈklenlɪ/ *adj* (-ier, -iest) habitually clean; having clean habits: *Are cats ~ animals?* **clean·li·ness** *n*

clean·ly /ˈklinlɪ/ *adv* exactly, sharply; neatly: *He caught the ball ~,* without fumbling.

cleanse /ˈklenz/ *vt* [VP6A] make thoroughly clean; make pure: *~ the heart of/from sin.* **cleanser** *n* [C,U] substance that ~s (e g a synthetic detergent).

clear¹ /klɪə(r)/ *adj* (-er, -est) **1** easy to see through: *~ glass; the ~ water of a mountain lake;* free from cloud: *a ~ sky;* bright, pure: *a ~ light; a ~ fire,* burning without much smoke; distinct; easily seen: *a line of hills ~ in the morning sky; a ~ photograph; a ~ reflection in the water.* **2** free from guilt or blame: *a ~ conscience,* knowledge that one is innocent. **3** (of sounds, etc) easily heard; distinct; pure: *a ~ voice; the ~ note of a bell; speak so that one's words are ~.* **4** (of and to the mind) free from doubt or difficulty: *a ~ thinker/statement. My memory is not ~ about/on that point. It was ~ (to everyone) that the war would not end quickly.* ***make oneself/one's meaning ~,*** make oneself understood: *Now, do I make myself ~?* **ˈ~-ˈheaded,** having good understanding. **ˈ~-ˈsighted,** able to see, think, understand well. **5** easy or safe to pass along; free from obstacles, dangers, etc: *Is the road ~? It is sometimes difficult to keep the roads ~ of snow. The coast is ~,* (fig) There is no one about (so one can escape, etc). *Is the sea ~ of ice yet? The signal 'All ~' was sounded,* e g after an air raid, to inform people that the raiders had left. **ˈ~·way** *n* (in GB) section of the public highway on which vehicles must not stop or park on the carriageway. **6** confident; certain: *I want to be quite ~ on this point. I am not ~ as to what you expect me to do.* **7** free (from debt, suspicion, a charge): *I wish I were ~ of debt. You are now ~ of suspicion.* **8** complete: *for three ~ days;* without limitations; with nothing (to be) deducted: *a ~ profit of £5; passed by a ~ majority of ten.* □ *n* ***in the ~,*** free from suspicion, danger, etc.

clear² /klɪə(r)/ *adv* **1** distinctly: *speak loud and ~.* **ˈ~-ˈcut** *adv* well defined; distinct; having ~ outlines. **2** quite; completely: *The prisoner got ~ away.* **3** apart; without touching; at or to a distance: *He jumped three inches ~ of the bar. Stand ~ of the gates of the lift.* ***keep/stay ~ of,*** avoid; have nothing to do with: *You should keep ~ of that fellow. You should keep ~ of alcohol if you're driving.* **~·ness** *n* [U] state of being ~: *the ~ness of the atmosphere; ~ness of vision.*

clear³ /klɪə(r)/ *vt,vi* **1** [VP6A,14] ***~ sth (of/from),*** remove, get rid of, what is unwanted or unwelcome: *~ the streets of snow; ~ a canal of obstructions/~ obstructions from a canal; ~ a desk,* of papers, etc; *~ the table,* after a meal; *~ land of trees,* esp before cultivation; *~ a country of bandits; ~ one's mind of doubt; ~ oneself (of a charge),* prove one's innocence. ***~ the air,*** ⇨ air¹(1). ***~ the decks (for action),*** get a ship ready for a fight; (fig) make ready for any kind of struggle or activity. ***~ one's throat,*** e g by coughing. **2** [VP6A] get past or over without touching: *The winner ~ed six feet,* jumped this without touching the bar. *Can your horse ~ that hedge? Our car only just ~ed the gatepost. Jack up that wheel until it ~s* (= no longer rests on) *the ground.* **3** [VP6A] make as a net gain or profit: *~ £50; ~ expenses,* make enough money to cover them. **4** [VP6A] get (a ship or its cargo) free by doing what is necessary (signing papers, paying dues, etc) on entering or leaving a port; *~ goods through customs,* deal with requirements of the customs (e g by paying any necessary duties); leave (a port) after doing this. **5** [VP6A] pass a cheque/bill of exchange etc through a clearing-house. **6** [VP15B,2C] (with *adverbial particles* and *preps*): ***~ away,*** **(a)** take away, get rid of: *~ away the tea-things.* **(b)** pass away: *The clouds have ~ed away.* ***~ off,*** **(a)** get rid of, make an end of: *~ off a debt; ~ off arrears of work.* **(b)** (of unwanted persons) go away: *We don't give money to beggars. C~ off!* ***~ out,*** **(a)** empty; make clear by taking out the contents of: *~ out a drain/a cupboard. All these hospital expenses have ~ed me out,* (colloq) have left me without money. **(b)** (colloq) go away; leave: *The police are after you, you'd better ~ out!* ***~ up,*** become clear: *The weather/The sky is ~ing up.* ***~ sth up,*** **(a)** put in order; make tidy: *C~ up your desk before you leave the office. Who's going to ~ up the mess?* **(b)** make clear; solve (a mystery, etc): *~ up a difficulty/misunderstanding.*

clear·ance /ˈklɪərns/ *n* **1** clearing up, removing, making tidy: *a ~ sale,* a sale to clear out unwanted or superfluous stocks of goods. *You've* *made a tremendous ~ in the flat,* made it tidy, etc by getting rid of what was unwanted. **2** [C,U] free space; space between, for moving past: *a ~ of only two feet,* e g for a ship moving through a canal. *There is not much/not enough ~ for large lorries passing under this bridge.* ⇨ head-room. **3** (certificate of) clearing a ship. ⇨ clear³(4).

clear·ing /ˈklɪərɪŋ/ *n* open space from which trees have been cleared in a forest. **ˈ~-house,** office at which banks exchange cheques, etc and settle accounts, the balance being paid in cash. **ˈ~-hospital,** field hospital where sick and wounded soldiers get temporary treatment before being sent farther.

clear·ly /ˈklɪəlɪ/ *adv* **1** distinctly: *speak ~; state one's facts ~. It is too dark to see ~. You must ~ understand that....* **2** (in answers) undoubtedly: *'Was he mistaken?' 'C~'.*

cleat /klit/ *n* **1** strip of wood, etc fastened to a gangway, etc to prevent slipping. **2** piece of wood, metal, etc bolted on to sth, on which ropes may be fastened (by winding). **3** piece of material fastened to the underside of a shoe or boot (e g for football) to prevent slipping. **4** V-shaped wedge.

cleav·age /ˈklivɪdʒ/ *n* split or division; direction in which sth tends to split or divide; place where there is a split or cleft; (colloq) the cleft between a woman's breasts as seen above a low neckline of a dress.

cleave[1] /kliv/ *vt,vi* (*pt* clove /kləʊv/, cleft /kleft/ or cleaved /klivd/, *pp* cleft or cloven /kləʊvn/) **1** [VP6A,22,15] cut into two (with a blow from a heavy axe, etc); split: *~ a block of wood in two; ~ a man's head open with a sword.* **2** [VP2A] come apart; split: *This wood ~s easily.* **3** [VP6A, 14] make by cutting: *~ one's way through the crowd; ~ a path through the jungle.* ***in a cleft stick,*** (fig) in a tight place where neither advance nor retreat is possible. **ˌcleft ˈpalate** *n* malformation in the roof of the mouth because the two sides of the palate did not join before birth. **ˌcloven ˈhoof** *n* divided hoof of an ox, a sheep, a goat (and a devil). **cleaver** *n* heavy knife used by a butcher for chopping up meat.

cleave[2] /kliv/ *vi* (*pt* ~d or, old use, clave /kleɪv/, *pp* ~d) [VP3A] ***~ to,*** stick fast to: (fig) be faithful to.

clef /klef/ *n* (music) symbol placed at the beginning of a stave to show the pitch of the notes. ⇨ the illus at notation.

cleft[1] /kleft/ *n* crack or split (e g in the ground or in rock); opening made by a cleavage.

cleft[2] /kleft/ *pt,pp* of cleave¹.

clema·tis /ˈklemətɪs/ *n* [U] (kinds of) climbing plant with clusters of white, yellow or purple flowers.

clem·ency /ˈklemənsɪ/ *n* [U] mercy; mildness (of temper or weather).

clem·ent /ˈklemənt/ *adj* showing mercy; (of the weather, a person's temper) mild.

clench /klentʃ/ *vt* **1** [VP6A] press firmly together, close tightly: *~ one's teeth/jaws; ~ one's fingers/fist; a ~ed-fist salute.* **2** [VP14] grasp firmly: *~ sth in/with one's hand(s).* **3** = clinch.

clere·story /ˈklɪəstɔrɪ/ *n* (*pl* -ries) upper part of a wall in a large church, with windows in it above the aisle roofs.

clergy /ˈklɜdʒɪ/ *n* (collective *n* with *pl v*) persons ordained as priests or ministers of the Christian Church: *Thirty of the ~ were present at the ceremony. The ~ are opposed to the plan.* **ˈ~·man** /-mən/ *n* (*pl* -men) (not used of a bishop) ordained minister, esp of the Church of England.

cleric /ˈklerɪk/ *n* clergyman.

cleri·cal /ˈklerɪkl/ *adj* **1** of the clergy: *~ dress; a ~ collar.* **2** of, for, made by, a clerk or clerks(1): *~ work; a ~ error,* one made in copying or writing.

cleri·hew /ˈklerɪhju/ *n* witty or nonsensical piece of verse, usu two rhyming couplets of varying length.

clerk /klɑk *US:* klɜk/ *n* **1** person employed in a bank, office, shop, etc to keep records and accounts, copy letters, etc: *a ˈbank ~; a ˌcorreˈspondence ~.* **2** officer in charge of records, etc: *the Town C~; the C~ to the Council,* (usu a lawyer); *~ of the works,* having charge of materials, etc for building done by contract. **3** (US) shop-assistant; salesman or saleswoman. **4** (formal or legal): *~ in holy orders,* clergyman. **5** lay officer of the church with various duties: *the parish ~.* **6** (old use) person who can read and write: *I'm no great ~,* am not much good at writing. □ *vt* (US only) work as a ~(3): *She not only ~ed but also helped in the home.*

clever /ˈklevə(r)/ *adj* **1** quick in learning and understanding things; skilful: *He's ~ at arithmetic/at making excuses. How ~ of you to do that! He's a ~ workman.* **2** (of things done) showing ability and skill: *a ~ speech/book.* **3** nimble: *~ fingers.* **4** smart: He was too *~ for us,* he outwitted us. **~·ly** *adv* **~·ness** *n*

clew /klu/ *n* **1** (less common spelling of) clue(1). **2** ball of thread or yarn. **3** (naut) metal loop attached to the lower corner of a sail; loop holding the strings of a hammock. □ *vt* (also *clue*) (naut) haul a sail up or down.

cli·ché /ˈkliʃeɪ *US:* kliˈʃeɪ/ *n* [C] idea or expression that has been too much used and is now out-dated; stereotyped phrase: *a ~-ridden newspaper article.*

click[1] /klɪk/ *vi, n* [VP6A,2A,C] (make a) short, sharp sound (like that of a key turning in a lock): *The door ~ed shut. The soldier ~ed his heels and saluted. Don't snort and ~ your tongue at me! Some African languages contain several ~s, ~ing* sounds.

click[2] /klɪk/ *vi* [VP2A] (sl; not US) be lucky; (of two persons of the opposite sex) strike up an acquaintance, become friends, at once.

cli·ent /ˈklaɪənt/ *n* **1** person who gets help or advice from a lawyer or any professional man: *a successful lawyer with hundreds of ~s.* **2** customer (at a shop). **cli·en·tele** /ˌkliənˈtel/ *n* (collective) customers; supporters of a restaurant, theatre, etc.

cliff /klɪf/ *n* steep face of rock, esp at the edge of the sea. **ˈ~-hanger** *n* episode in a story or contest of which the end is uncertain, so that the reader or spectator is held in suspense.

cli·mac·teric /klaɪˈmæktərɪk/ *n* critical turning-point in (the body's) physical development.

cli·mac·tic /ˌklaɪˈmæktɪk/ *adj* forming a climax.

cli·mate /ˈklaɪmɪt/ *n* **1** weather conditions of a place or area; conditions of temperature, rainfall, wind, etc. **2** [C] area or region with certain weather conditions: *A drier ~ would be good for her health.* **3** prevailing condition: *the political ~; ~ of opinion,* general attitude of people to an aspect of life, policy, etc. **cli·mat·ic** /ˌklaɪˈmætɪk/

adj of ~. **cli·mati·cally** /-klɪ/ *adv* **cli·ma·tol·ogy** /ˌklaɪmə`tolədʒɪ/ *n* [U] science of ~.

cli·max /`klaɪmæks/ *n* event, point, of greatest interest or intensity (e g in a story or drama): *bring matters to a ~; work up to a ~; as a ~ to the evening's entertainment.* □ *vt, vi* bring or come to a ~.

climb /klaɪm/ *vt, vi* [VP6A,2A,C] go or get up (a tree, wall, rope, mountain, etc) or down; (of aircraft) go higher, gain height; (of plants) grow upwards by turning round a support, or with the support of tendrils, etc; rise by effort in social rank, position, etc: *~ a tree; ~ up a tree; ~ a wall; ~ over a wall. Monkeys ~ well.* ***~ down,*** (fig) admit that one has been mistaken, unreasonable, boastful, etc. Hence, **`~-down** *n* such an admission. **`~·ing irons** *n* spikes (to be) fastened to the boots for ~ing trees, ice-slopes, etc. □ *n* ~ing; place (to be) ~ed: *a hard ~. Have you done that ~?* **~er** *n* person who ~s; person who tries to advance socially; ~ing plant.

clime /klaɪm/ *n* (poet) climate(**2**).

clinch /klɪntʃ/ *vt, vi* **1** [VP6A] make (a nail or rivet) fast by hammering sideways the end that protrudes. **2** [VP6A] settle (a bargain, an argument) conclusively: *That ~es the argument,* ends all doubt. **3** [VP2A] (boxing) come to grips, with one or both arms round the opponent's body: *The boxers ~ed and the referee intervened.* □ *n* (boxing) the act, an instance, of ~ing: *get into a ~; break a ~.* **~er** *n* (colloq) ~ing argument.

cling /klɪŋ/ *vi* (*pt, pp* **clung** /klʌŋ/) [VP2C,3A] ***~ to/together,*** hold tight; resist separation: *~ to one's possessions; ~ to a hope of being rescued. They clung together when the time came to part. The ship clung to* (= did not go far from) *the coast. The child clung to its mother's skirt/garments. She's the ~ing sort,* is prone to depend upon others. **`~·ing clothes** *n* showing the shape or outline of the body or limbs.

clinic /`klɪnɪk/ *n* **1** (part of a) hospital or institution where medical advice and treatment are given and where students are taught through observation of cases; teaching so given; class of students taught in this way. **2** medical establishment for a specified purpose: *a `birth-control ~; an ˌante-`natal ~; an a`bortion ~.*

clini·cal /`klɪnɪkl/ *adj* (of medical teaching given) at the hospital bedside: *~ thermometer,* one for measuring the temperature of the body.

clink[1] /klɪŋk/ *vi, vt, n* [VP6A,2A,C] (make the) sound of small bits of metal, glass, etc knocking together: *the ~ of keys/glasses. They ~ed glasses,* brought their glasses together before drinking each other's health.

clink[2] /klɪŋk/ *n* (sl) prison: *be in ~; be put in ~; go to ~.*

clinker /`klɪŋkə(r)/ *n* [C,U] (piece of the) mass of rough, hard, slag-like material left in a stove, furnace, etc after coal has been burned.

clinker-built /`klɪŋkə bɪlt/ *adj* (of boats) made with the outside planks or metal plates overlapping downwards.

clip[1] /klɪp/ *n* [C] **1** wire or metal device for holding things (e g papers) together. **2** holder (with loops) for cartridges (to be used in a magazine rifle). □ *vt* (-pp-) [VP6A,15B,2C] put or keep together with a ~ or ~s: *~ papers together; ~ one paper to another.* **`~-on** attrib *adj* that can be attached with a ~: *a ~-on tie/brooch.*

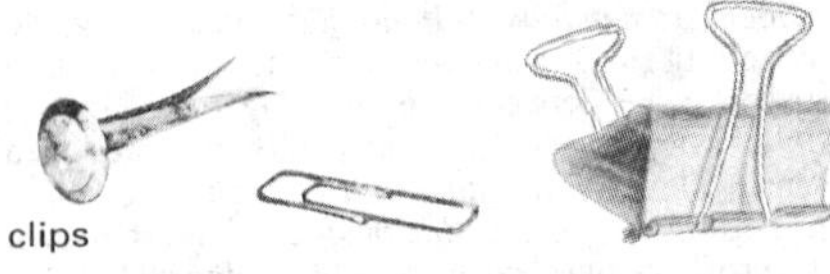
clips

clip[2] /klɪp/ *vt* (-pp-) **1** [VP6A,22,15A,B] cut with scissors or shears; make short or neat; cut off wool from (a sheep, etc): *~ a hedge; ~ a bird's wings; ~ sb's wings,* (fig) prevent him from doing what he is ambitious to do. ***~ sth out (of),*** remove by ~ping: *~ an article out of a newspaper.* **2** [VP6A] damage (a coin) by cutting off part of the edge. **3** [VP6A] omit or abbreviate (esp the end of) sounds of (words) (e g by saying *shootin'* /`ʃutn/ instead of *shooting* /`ʃutɪŋ/). **4** [VP6A] punch a hole in (a bus, tram or train ticket). **5** (sl) hit or punch sharply: *~ sb's ear; ~ sb on the jaw.* □ *n* **1** operation of shearing. **2** amount of wool cut from (a flock of) sheep at one time. **3** smart blow: *a ~ on the jaw.* **4** (US) fast speed. **~·ping** *n* (in verbal senses) (esp) sth ~ped off or out; *newspaper ~pings.*

clip·per /`klɪpə(r)/ *n* **1** (*pl*) (also *pair of ~s*) instrument for clipping: *`hair-~s; `nail-~s.* **2** sailing ship built for speed and used formerly esp in the tea-trade; (before jet aircraft) propeller-driven air-liner.

clique /klik/ *n* group of persons united by common interests (esp in literature or art), members of which support each other and shut out others from their company. **cliquish** /`klikɪʃ/ *adj* of or like a ~; tending to form a ~.

clit·oris /`klɪtərɪs/ *n* (anat) erectile organ at the upper end of the vulva, analogous to the penis.

cloak /kləʊk/ *n* loose outer garment, without sleeves; (fig) sth used to hide or keep secret: *use patriotism as a ~ for violence; under the ~ of darkness.* ***~ and dagger,*** (used attrib) in the style of, concerning, espionage, melodramatic intrigue, etc. **`~·room** *n* place where hats, coats, parcels, etc may be left for a short time (e g in a theatre or a railway station). □ *vt* [VP6A] (chiefly fig) conceal (thoughts, purposes, etc).

clob·ber /`klobə(r)/ *vt* [VP6A] (sl) **1** strike violently and repeatedly; hurt badly: *~ the taxpayer,* by heavy taxation. **2** defeat thoroughly: *Our team got ~ed on Saturday.*

cloche /kloʃ/ *n* [C] **1** glass or clear plastic protection, placed in long rows over tender plants; (older use) bell-shaped glass cover for a plant. **2** woman's close-fitting hat.

clock[1] /klok/ *n* instrument (not carried or worn like a watch) for measuring and showing the time. ***put the `~ back,*** **(a)** move the hands of the ~ back (e g when Summer Time ends). **(b)** (fig) take reactionary measures. ***work against the ~,*** work fast to finish before a certain time. ***(work) round the ~,*** (work) all day and night. Hence, **ˌround-the-`~,** (used attrib): *a round-the-~ watch/guard on sth,* all day and night. **`~-face/-dial,** surface of a ~ showing figures marking the hours, etc. **~-`golf,** game in which a golf-ball is putted on greens arranged in a circle. **`~-tower,** tall structure (forming part of a building, e g a church) with a ~ high up on an outside wall. **`~-watching,** practice (of some workers) of thinking constantly of how soon work will end. **`~·wise/ˌcounter-`~wise** *adv* moving in a curve in the direction/in the direction opposite to that taken by the hands of a ~. '~·**work,** (often attrib) mechanism with wheels and springs like a ~: *~work toys; a ~work driven train; with ~work precision; like ~work,* smoothly, without trouble. □ *vt,vi* **1** [VP6A] measure the time of; do sth (e g run a race) in a measured period of time: *He ~ed 9·6 seconds for the 100 metres.* **2** [VP2C] ***~ in/out, ~ on/off,*** record the time of (e g the arrival and departure of workers): *Workers in this factory are required to ~ in and out.* **3** [VP6A] (GB sl) strike; hit: *If you don't shut up, I'll ~ you one.*

clock[2] /klok/ *n* design sewn or woven on the side of a sock or stocking, at the ankle.

clod /klod/ *n* lump (of earth, clay, etc). '~·**hop·per** /-hopə(r)/ *n* clumsy, heavy-footed person, esp a rough farm worker.

clog[1] /klog/ *n* **1** shoe with a wooden sole; shoe carved out of a block of wood. '~-**dance** *n* dance in which the dancer wears ~s or wooden-soled shoes. **2** block of wood fastened to the leg of an animal to prevent its straying; (fig) encumbrance: *a ~ on his movements.*

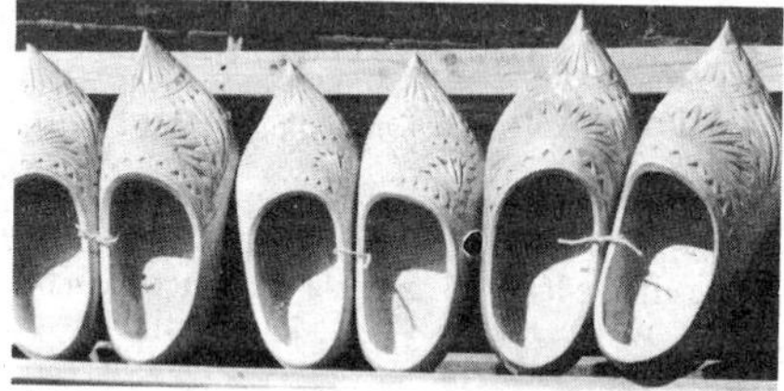

clogs

clog[2] /klog/ *vt,vi* (-gg-) [VP6A,15B,2A,C] **1** (cause to) be or become blocked with waste matter, dirt, grease, etc so that movement, flow of liquid, etc is difficult or prevented: *pipes ~ged with dirt; machinery ~ged (up) with grease.* **2** encumber; burden: *Don't ~ your memory with useless facts.* '~**gy** *adj* (-ier, -iest) lumpy; sticky.

cloi·sonné /'klwɑ'zoneɪ *US:* 'kleɪzn'eɪ/ *n* [U] enamel ware, in which the colours of the design are kept apart by thin metal strips.

clois·ter /'klɔɪstə(r)/ *n* **1** covered walk, usu on the sides of an open court or quadrangle, with a wall on the outer side and columns or arches on the inner side, esp within a convent, cathedral or college building. ⇨ the illus at church. **2** (life in a) convent or monastery. **the ~** *n* the seclusion of a convent, etc. □ *vt* [VP6A] put in, live in, a ~(2): *live a ~ed life,* a life of seclusion.

clone /kləʊn/ *n* (member of a) group of organisms produced asexually from one ancestor.

close[1] /kləʊs/ *adj* (-r, -st) **1** near (in space or time): *fire at ~ range; in ~ combat; in ~ proximity,* almost touching. ***a ~ call/thing,*** almost an accident, disaster or failure. ***a ~ shave,*** (fig) a narrow escape from collision or accident. '~-**up** *n* (a) photograph, esp as shown on a cinema or television screen, taken at ~ range and showing the subject on a large scale. (b) close view. **2** (in *adv* or *prep* phrases): ***~ at hand,*** not far away. ***~ to/by,*** near: *He lives ~ by the church. There's a bus-stop ~ to the school. The ship kept ~ to the coast.* ***(hold/keep one's hand) ~ to one's chest,*** ⇨ chest(2). ***~ upon,*** almost: *He is ~ upon sixty. It was ~ upon midnight. There are ~ upon fifty boys in the class.* **3** with little or no space in between: *~ writing; material of ~ texture,* e g woven with the threads ~ together. *The soldiers advanced in ~ order,* with little space between them. **4** strict; severe; rigorous: *a ~ blockade/siege; in ~ confinement; be (kept) under ~ arrest.* ***keep a ~ watch on sb,*** watch him carefully. **5** detailed; leaving no gaps or weak points; showing each step clearly: *a ~ argument; ~ reasoning; a ~ reasoner.* **6** thorough; concentrated: *after ~ consideration; on ~r examination. You must give me your ~ attention. Please make a ~* (= faithful and exact) *translation.* **7** intimate: *a ~ friend/friendship.* **8** restricted; limited: *a ~ scholarship,* open only to a restricted category of candidates. **9** (of competitions, games, their results) in which the competitors are almost equal: *a ~ contest/match/election/finish.* **10** (of vowels) pronounced with only a small opening of the lips (e g the *e* of 'they' but not the *e* of 'there', which is an 'open' vowel): *The English vowels /i/ and /u/ are ~.* **11** (also '~-'**fisted**) stingy; niggardly. **12** **~ season,** time (the breeding season) during which the killing of certain wild birds and animals, and the catching of certain fish, is illegal. **13** (of the weather) stifling; (of a room, etc) unventilated; having little fresh air; (of the air) difficult to breathe because heavy: *Open the windows; This room/The air here is too ~. The atmosphere in a steam-heated building is often ~.* **14** concealed; secret; not in the habit of talking about one's affairs: *keep/lie ~ for a while,* keep one's whereabouts secret, not show oneself; *keep sth ~,* say nothing about it, keep it secret; *be ~* (= secretive) *about sth,* Cf *keep sth to oneself.* □ *adv* in a ~ manner; near together; tightly: *follow ~ behind sb; stand/sit ~ against the wall; come ~r together; ~ shut.* ⇨ ~ly below. ***sail ~ to the wind,*** sail almost against the wind; (fig) almost break a law or a moral principle. '~-'**cropped/'cut** *adj* (of hair, grass, etc) cut very short. '~-'**fitting** *adj* fitting ~ (to the body, etc): *a ~-fitting dress.* '~-'**grained** *adj* (esp of wood) having a grain in which the lines in the pattern made by growth are ~ together (e g mahogany). '~-'**hauled** *adj* (of a sailing-ship) with the sails set for sailing as nearly as possible in the direction from which the wind is blowing. '~-'**set** *adj* set, placed, ~ together: *~-set eyes/teeth.* ~·**ly** *adv* in a ~ manner: *listen ~ly; follow an argument ~ly; watch ~ly; a ~ly contested election. She ~ly resembles her mother.* ~·**ness** *n*: *the ~ness of a resemblance/friendship/translation/pursuit.*

close[2] /kləʊs/ *n* **1** grounds round a cathedral, abbey or school, usu with its buildings (houses of the clergy, etc) round it. **2** cul-de-sac.

close[3] /kləʊz/ *vt,vi* **1** [VP6A,2A] shut: *If you ~ your eyes, you can't see. Did you ~ all the doors and windows? This box/The lid of this box doesn't ~ properly,* The lid does not fit properly. *Many flowers open in the morning and ~ at night.* ***~d book,*** (fig) subject about which one knows nothing; *Nuclear physics is a ~d book to most of us.* **2** [VP6A,2A] (not usu replaceable by *shut*) be, declare, be declared, not open: *This road is ~d to heavy motor traffic. The theatres have ~d for the summer. It's Sunday, so the shops are ~d. Wednesday is early-closing day here,* the day on which shops ~ for a half-holiday. *When is closing time,* the time at which shops, etc, stop doing business? *The inquiry was held behind/with ~d doors,* the public being excluded. **'~d 'circuit** *n* (in TV) circuit by which the current from the camera to the screen has its path along wires all the way (instead of being transmitted through the air): (attrib) *'~d-'circuit 'television.* **'~d 'shop** *n* trade or profession, workshop, factory, establishment, etc in which employment is open only to members of an approved trade union. **3** [VP6A,2A] bring or come to an end: *~ a discussion; the closing days of the year; the closing* (= last, final) *day for applications. The chairman declared the discussion ~d. I want to ~ my account,* settle it by paying or receiving money that is due. ***~ a deal,*** complete it, by agreeing to the terms, etc. **'closing prices,** (comm) prices of shares quoted at a Stock Exchange at the end of a day's business. **4** [VP6A,2C] bring or come together by making less space or fewer spaces between: *~ the ranks; ~ up,* (of soldiers, etc) come ~r together in line or lines. **5** [VP15B,2A,3A] (with *adverbial particles* and *preps*): ***~ down,*** **(a)** (of a factory, business, etc) stop production, shut completely: *The factory (was) ~d down because of a lack of orders.* **(b)** (of a broadcasting station) stop transmitting: *The time is just after midnight and we are now closing down.* Hence, **'~-down** *n* ***~ in,*** *The days are closing in,* getting shorter. ***~ in (up)on,*** **(a)** envelop. *Darkness ~d in on us.* **(b)** come near(er) and attack: *The enemy ~d in upon us.* ***~ with,*** **(a)** come within striking distance of (an enemy, etc). **(b)** accept (an offer); make a bargain with.

close[4] /kləʊz/ *n* (*sing* only) end (of a period of time); conclusion (of an activity, etc): *at the ~ of the day; towards the ~ of the 17th century; (at) ~ of play,* (cricket) (at the) end of play for the day. *Day had reached its ~.* ***draw/bring sth to a ~,*** end.

closet /ˈklozɪt/ *n* **1** (now chiefly US) small room for storing things. ⇨ **cupboard, storeroom. 2** (old use) small room for private interviews. **3** (old use) water-closet. ⇨ **water**[1]**(7).** □ *vt* (usu passive) ***be ~ed with/together,*** have private discussions with: *He was ~ed with the manager/They were ~ed together for two hours.*

clo·sure /ˈkləʊʒə(r)/ *n* **1** (in Parliament) device to end debate by taking a vote on a question: *apply the ~ to a debate; move the ~.* ⇨ **guillotine. 2** [C] act of closing: *pit ~s,* e g of coal-mines which are no longer economic.

clot /klot/ *n* [C] **1** half-solid lump formed from liquid, esp blood. **2** (sl) (often *clumsy ~*) idiot, fool. □ *vt,vi* (-tt-) [VP6A,2A] form into ~s: *~ted cream,* made by scalding it; *~ted hair,* stuck together by dirt or blood, etc.

cloth /kloθ *US:* klɔθ/ *n* (*pl* ~s /kloθs *US:* klɔðz/) **1** [U] material made by weaving (cotton, wool, silk, linen, etc): *three yards of ~; a book with a ~ binding.* **2** [C] piece of this material for special purpose: *a 'floor~; a 'dish~.* **3** [U] profession (esp clerical) as shown by the clothes worn: *the respect due to the ~,* to the clergy.

clothe /kləʊð/ *vt* (*pt,pp* clothed /kləʊðd/, old style clad /klæd/) [VP6A] **1** wear clothes; put clothes on, supply clothes for: *warmly ~d; ~d in wool. He has to work hard in order to ~ his family,* earn money for their clothes. **2** (fig) express: *His sentiments were ~d in suitable language.*

clothes /kləʊðz *US:* kləʊz/ *n pl* (no *sing*; not used with numerals) **1** coverings for a person's body; dress: *a baby in long ~; a ~-brush.* **2 'bed-~,** sheets, blankets, etc, for or on a bed. **'~-basket,** one for ~ which are to be, or have been, washed. **'~-horse,** frame for airing ~ that have been washed and dried. **'~-line,** rope (stretched between posts) on which ~ are hung to be dried after being washed. **'~-peg/-pin,** one used for fastening ~ to a ~-line.

cloth·ier /ˈkləʊðɪə(r)/ *n* dealer in cloth or clothes.

cloth·ing /ˈkləʊðɪŋ/ *n* [U] (collective) clothes: *articles of ~.*

cloud /klaʊd/ *n* **1** [C,U] (separate mass of) visible water vapour floating above the earth: *The top of the mountain was covered with/hidden under ~. Large, black ~s announced a coming storm.* **'~-bank** *n* thick mass of low ~. **'~-burst** *n* sudden and violent rainstorm. **'~-capped** *adj* (e g of mountains) having the top enveloped in ~. **~-'cuckoo-land** *n* imaginary and ridiculously ideal place. **2** mass of things in the air moving together: *a ~ of arrows/insects/horsemen, etc.* **3** mass (*of* smoke, dust, sand, etc) in the air. **4** vague patch on or in a liquid or a transparent object. **5** something that causes unhappiness or fear: *the ~s of war.* ***under a ~,*** out of favour, under suspicion, in disgrace. **6** (*pl*) ***(have one's head) in the ~s,*** (fig) with one's thoughts far away, not paying attention (to one's surroundings, etc). □ *vi,vt* [VP2A,C,6A] become, make, indistinct (as) through ~: *The sky ~ed over. Her eyes were ~ed with tears. All these troubles have ~ed his mind,* have affected his reason. **~·less** *adj* free from ~s; clear: *a ~less sky.* **~y** *adj* (-ier, -iest) **1** covered with ~s: *a ~y sky.* **2** (esp of liquids) not clear.

clout /klaʊt/ *n* **1** (colloq) blow or knock (on the head, etc, given with the hand). **2** piece of old cloth used for housework, etc: *a 'dish-~.* **3** (old use) article of clothing. □ *vt* (colloq) hit: *~ sb on the head.*

clove[1] ⇨ **cleave**[1].

clove[2] /kləʊv/ *n* dried, unopened flower-bud of a tropical tree, used as a spice. **'oil of '~s,** oil extracted from ~s and used in medicine.

clove[3] /kləʊv/ *n* one of the small, separate sections of a compound bulb: *a ~ of garlic.*

clove hitch /ˈkləʊv hɪtʃ/ *n* knot for fastening a rope round a pole, etc.

clo·ven ⇨ **cleave**[1].

clo·ver /ˈkləʊvə(r)/ *n* [U] low-growing plant with (usu) three leaves on each stalk, purple, pink or white flowers, grown as food for cattle, etc. ***be/live in ~,*** in great comfort and luxury. **'~-leaf,** highway intersection with flyovers, etc forming the pattern of a leaf of ~.

clown /klaʊn/ *n* man (esp in a circus or pantomime) who makes a living by performing foolish tricks and antics; person acting like a ~; rude, clumsy man. □ *vt* [VP2A] behave like a ~: *Stop all this ~ing.* **~·ish** *adj* of or like a ~.

cloy /klɔɪ/ *vt,vi* [VP6A,2A] make or become distasteful by excess, sweetness, richness (of food, pleasure, etc); satiate: *~ed with pleasure; ~ the appetite by eating too much sweet food.*

club[1] /klʌb/ *n* **1** heavy stick with one thick end, used as a weapon. **2** stick with a curved head for driving or putting the ball in golf and hockey. □ *vt* (-bb-) hit with a ~: *He had been ~bed to death. They ~bed him with their rifles.* **'~-'foot** *n* foot that is (from birth) thick and badly formed, hence, **'~-'footed** *adj*

club[2] /klʌb/ *n* one of the thirteen playing-cards

with one or more black leaf-like designs printed on it: *the ace/ten of ~s; play a small ~; C~s are trumps.* ⇨ the illus at card.

club³ /klʌb/ *n* **1** society of persons who subscribe money to provide themselves with sport, e g football, golf, social entertainment, etc, sometimes in their own grounds, buildings, etc where meals and bedrooms are available; the rooms or building(s) used by such a society. **2** (*benefit ~*) society for mutual insurance against illness, old age, etc. □ *vi* (-bb-) [VP2C] **~ together,** join or act (together, with others) for a common purpose: *The villagers ~bed together to help the old pensioners whose house had been burnt down.* **'~·bable** /'klʌbəbl/ *adj* fit for membership of a ~(1); sociable.

cluck /klʌk/ *vi, n* [VP2A] (make the) noise made by a hen, e g when calling her chickens.

clue /klu/ *n* **1** fact, idea, etc that suggests a possible answer to a problem: *get/find a ~ to a mystery. He hasn't a ~,* (colloq) is completely ignorant of, unable to understand or explain (what is in question). **2** ball of thread or yarn. ⇨ clew.

clump¹ /klʌmp/ *n* group or cluster (*of* trees, shrubs or plants): *growing in ~s.* □ *vt* plant in ~s.

clump² /klʌmp/ *vi* [VP2A,C] tread heavily: *~ about,* walk about putting the feet down heavily.

clumsy /'klʌmzɪ/ *adj* (-ier, -iest) **1** heavy and ungraceful in movement or construction; not well designed for its purpose: *The ~ workman put his elbow through the window and broke it. An axe would be a ~ tool to open a tin of milk with.* **2** tactless; unskilful: *a ~ apology/forgery; ~ praise.* **'clum·sily** /-səlɪ/ *adv* **'clum·si·ness** *n*

clung /klʌŋ/ *pt,pp* of cling.

clunk /klʌŋk/ *vi, n* (make the) sound of dull heavy metals striking together.

clus·ter /'klʌstə(r)/ *n* **1** number of things of the same kind growing closely together: *a ~ of flowers/berries/curls; hair growing in thick ~s.* **2** number of persons, animals, objects, etc in a small, close group: *a ~ of bees/spectators/islands; consonant ~s,* (in phonetics; e g *str* in *strong*)*; houses here and there in ~s.* □ *vi* [VP2A,3A] **~ (a)round,** be in, form, a close group round: *roses ~ing round the window. The village ~s round the church.*

clutch¹ /klʌtʃ/ *vt,vi* [VP3A,15A] **~ (at),** seize; take hold of tightly with the hand(s); attempt to seize: *He ~ed (at) the rope we threw to him. A drowning man will ~ at a straw,* will make a last, desperate but hopeless attempt to be saved. *Mary ~ed her doll to her breast.* □ *n* **1** the act of ~ing: *make a ~ at sth.* **2** (esp in *pl*) control; power. ***be in/out of, get into/out of the ~es of,*** e g of moneylenders. **3** device, e g a pedal, in a machine or engine for connecting and disconnecting working parts: *let in/disengage/withdraw the ~; put the ~ in/out. The ~ is in/out.* ⇨ the illus at motor.

clutch² /klʌtʃ/ *n* set of eggs placed under a hen to hatch at one time; number of young chickens hatched from these.

clut·ter /'klʌtə(r)/ *vt* [VP6A,15B] **~ (up),** make untidy or confused: *a desk ~ed up with papers; ~ up a room with unnecessary furniture.* □ *n*: *in a ~,* in disorder or confusion.

co- /ˌkəʊ/ *pref* together with (another or others): *ˌco-'author; ˌco-'heir; ˌco-ex'ist; ˌco-bel'ligerents; ˌco-pros'perity.*

coach¹ /kəʊtʃ/ *n* **1** four-wheeled carriage pulled by four or more horses, used to carry passengers and mail before railways were built (*'stage-~* and *'mail-~* for public use; *'state-~* used by a king or queen on ceremonial occasions). ***drive a ~ and horses through (sth),*** defeat the intention of (a regulation, etc) by finding serious faults in its wording. **2** (US = *car*) railway carriage, often divided into compartments. **3** (*'motor-~*) long-distance, single-decked motor-bus: *travel by ~; a ~-tour of Europe; leave by ~ for Edinburgh.* **'~-builder** *n* craftsman who builds the bodywork of motor-vehicles.

a state-coach

coach² /kəʊtʃ/ *n* teacher, esp one who gives private lessons to prepare students for a public examination; person who trains athletes for contests: *a baseball ~.* □ *vt,vi* [VP6A,14,2A] teach or train: *~ sb for an exam; ~ the crew for the boat race.*

co·agu·late /ˌkəʊ'ægjʊleɪt/ *vt,vi* [VP6A,2A] (of liquids) change to a thick and solid state, as blood does in air. **co·agu·lation** /ˌkəʊˌægjʊ'leɪʃn/ *n*

coal /kəʊl/ *n* [U] black mineral that burns and supplies heat, and from which ~-gas is made; [C] piece of this material, esp (*a live ~*) one that is burning: *A hot ~ fell from the fire and burnt a hole in the carpet.* ***carry ~s to Newcastle,*** take goods to a place where they are already plentiful. ***heap ~s of fire on sb's head,*** return good for evil and so induce remorse. **'~·face** *n* part of a ~ seam from which ~ is being cut. **'~·field** *n* district in which ~ is mined. **'~-gas** *n* the mixture of gases made from ~, used for lighting and heating. **'~-hole,** cellar for storing ~. **'~-house,** shed for storing ~. **'~-mine/-pit** *n* mine from which ~ is dug. **'~-scuttle** *n* container for a supply of ~ near a fireside. **'~-seam,** underground layer of ~. **'~-tar** *n* [U] (sometimes *'gas-tar*) thick, black, sticky substance produced when gas is made from ~. □ *vt,vi* [VP6A,2A] put ~ (into a ship, etc); take in ~: *The ship called at Gibraltar to ~. Coaling (a ship) is a dirty job.* **'~-ing-station** *n* port where ships can obtain ~.

co·alesce /ˌkəʊə'les/ *vi* come together and unite into one substance, group, etc. **co·alescence** /ˌkəʊə'lesns/ *n*

co·ali·tion /ˌkəʊə'lɪʃn/ *n* [U] uniting; [C] union of political parties for a special purpose: *a ~ government; the left-wing ~; form a ~.*

coam·ing /'kəʊmɪŋ/ *n* raised rim round a ship's hatches to keep water out.

coarse /kɔs/ *adj* **1** (of material) not fine and small; rough and lumpy: *~ sand/sugar;* having a rough surface or texture: *a dress made of ~ cloth; a ~ skin/complexion.* **2** (of food) common; inferior: *~ fish; ~ fishing,* e g for chub, roach, pike. **3** vulgar; not delicate or refined: *~ manners/language/words/laughter/jokes/tastes; ~ of speech.* **coarsen** /'kɔsn/ *vt,vi* [VP6A,2A] make or become ~. **~·ly** *adv* **~·ness** *n*

coast[1] /kəʊst/ *n* [C] land bordering the sea; seashore and land near it: *The ship was wrecked on the Kent ~. There are numerous islands off the ~. The village is on the south ~.* **'~·guard** *n* officer on police duty on the ~ (to prevent or detect smuggling, report passing ships, etc). **'~-line** *n* shoreline, esp with regard to its shape: *a rugged ~line.* **~al** /'kəʊstl/ *adj* of the ~: *~al navigation.* **'~·wise** *adj, adv* along the ~.

coast[2] /kəʊst/ *vi,vt* **1** [VP2A,6A] go in, sail, a ship along the coast. **2** ride or slide down a hill or slope without using power (e g along a road on a bicycle). **~er** *n* **1** ship that sails from port to port along the coast. **2** small mat, etc (for a drinking-glass, etc) to protect a polished table, etc from drips or moisture.

coat /kəʊt/ *n* **1** outer garment with sleeves, buttoned in the front. ***turn one's ~,*** change one's side or principles, desert one army or party and join the other. ⇨ **dress-~**, **frock-~**, **great-~**, **over~**, *top-~* at **top**[1]**(8)**. **'~-tails** *n pl* ⇨ **tail-coat** at **tail**. **'~ of 'arms,** ⇨ **arms**. **'~ of 'mail,** piece of armour of metal rings or plate for the upper part of the body. **2** (*~ and skirt*) woman's tailor-made garment for the upper part of the body; jacket. **3** any covering that is compared to a garment, e g an animal's hair or wool. **4** layer of paint or other substance put on a surface at one time: *The woodwork has had its final ~ of paint.* □ *vt* [VP6A,14] cover with a ~ or layer: *furniture ~ed with dust; ~ pills with sugar. Tinplate is made by ~ing sheets of iron with tin.* **'~·ing** *n* **1** thin layer or covering: *two ~ings of wax.* **2** [U] cloth for **~s(1,2)**.

coatee /kəʊ'ti/ *n* short coat.

coax /'kəʊks/ *vt,vi* **1** [VP6A,17A,15B,14,2A] get sb or sth to do sth by kindness or patience: *~ a child to take its medicine; ~ a fire to burn; ~ (up) the fire; ~ sb into/out of doing sth.* **2** [VP14] ***~ sth from/out of,*** get by ~ing; *~ a smile from the baby.* **~·ing** *n*: *He took a lot of ~ing before he agreed to take her to the theatre.* **'~·ing·ly** *adv*

cob /kob/ *n* **1** male swan. **2** strong short-legged horse for riding. **3** (also **'cob-nut**) large kind of hazel-nut. **4** (also **'corn-cob**) central part of an ear of corn (= maize) on which the grain grows: *corn on the cob.* ⇨ the illus at **cereal**.

co·balt /'kəʊbɔlt/ *n* hard silvery-white metal (symbol **Co**) used in many alloys; deep blue colouring matter made from its compounds, used to colour glass and ceramics.

cob·ber /'kobə(r)/ *n* (Australia; colloq) comrade; mate; chum.

cobble[1] /'kobl/ *n* (also **'~-stone**) stone worn round and smooth by the water and used for paving. □ *vt* pave with these stones: *~d streets.*

cobble[2] /'kobl/ *vt* [VP6A] mend, patch (esp shoes), or put together roughly.

cob·bler /'koblə(r)/ *n* **1** mender of shoes. (*shoe-repairer* is now the usu word). **2** clumsy workman.

co·bra /'kəʊbrə/ *n* poisonous snake of Asia and Africa. ⇨ the illus at **snake**.

cob·web /'kobweb/ *n* [C] fine network or single thread made by a spider. ⇨ the illus at **arachnid**.

coca-cola /'kəʊkə 'kəʊlə/ *n* (= colloq **coke**) (P) popular non-alcoholic carbonated drink.

co·caine /kəʊ'keɪn/ *n* [U] product (from a shrub) used by doctors as a local anaesthetic, and also used as a stimulant by drug addicts.

cochi·neal /'kotʃɪ'nil/ *n* [U] bright red colouring-matter made from the dried bodies of certain insects.

coch·lea /'koklɪə/ *n* spiral-shaped part of the inner ear. ⇨ the illus at **ear**.

cock[1] /kok/ *n* **1** (used alone) adult male bird of the domestic or farmyard fowl (US = *rooster*) ⇨ the illus at **fowl**. **'~-crow** *n* early dawn. **'~-a-'hoop** *adj, adv* with boastful crowing; exultant(ly). **~-a-doodle-doo** /'kok ə 'dudl 'du/ *n* the crow of the **~(1)**: child's name for a **~(1)**. ***'~-and-'bull story,*** foolish story that one should not believe. **'~-fighting** *n* fighting by game-~s as a sport for onlookers. ⇨ **game**[1]**(6)**. ***live like fighting-~s,*** live on the best possible food. ***~ of the walk/school,*** person who dominates others. **2** (in compounds) male of other kinds of bird: *'pea~; '~-'sparrow; '~-'robin.*

cock[2] /kok/ *n* **1** tap and spout for controlling the flow of a liquid or a gas, e g from a pipe, barrel. **2** lever in a gun; position of this lever when it is raised and ready to be released by the trigger. ***at half/full ~,*** half ready/quite ready to be fired. ***go off at half ~,*** of schemes, ceremonies, etc, begin before the arrangements are complete. **3** ⚠ (vulg sl) penis.

cock[3] /kok/ *vt* [VP6A,15B] ***~ (up),*** **1** turn upwards, cause to be erect (showing attention, inquiry, defiance, etc): *The horse ~ed its ears. The horse stopped with its ears ~ed up. He ~ed his eye at me,* glanced or winked at me knowingly, or raised his eyebrow. **'~ed 'hat** *n* triangular hat, pointed front and back, worn with some uniforms. ***knock sb/sth into a ~ed hat,*** knock shapeless, or so that recognition is impossible; beat thoroughly. **2** [VP6A] raise the cock of (a gun) ready for firing. ⇨ **cock**[2]**(2)**. **3** (vulg) make a mess of; upset: *They completely ~ed up the arrangements for our holiday.* Hence, **'~-up** *n*

cock[4] /kok/ *n* small, cone-shaped pile of straw or hay. □ *vt* pile (hay) in ~s.

cock·ade /ko'keɪd/ *n* knot of ribbon worn on a hat as a badge.

cocka·too /'kokə'tu/ *n* crested parrot. ⇨ the illus at **rare**.

cock·chafer /'koktʃeɪfə(r)/ *n* large beetle that flies with a loud whirring sound and is destructive to vegetation.

cocker /'kokə(r)/ *n* breed of spaniel.

cock·erel /'kokrl/ *n* young **cock**[1]**(1)**, not more than one year old.

cock-eyed /'kokɑɪd/ *adj* (sl) **1** squinting; crooked; turned or twisted to one side. **2** wild, ill-judged: *a ~ scheme.*

cock·horse /'kok'hɔs/ *adv* (children's word): *ride a ~,* ride on horseback or on a rocking-horse. ⇨ **rock(2)**.

cockle /'kokl/ *n* **1** edible shellfish; (also **'~-shell**) its shell. **2** small, shallow boat. **3** (warm, delight, etc) *the ~s of one's heart,* one's feelings.

cock·ney /'koknɪ/ *adj, n* (characteristic of a) native esp working-class, of London: *a ~ accent; ~ humour.*

cock·pit /'kokpɪt/ *n* **1** enclosed space where game-cocks fought. ⇨ *cock-fighting* at **cock**[1]**(1)**; (fig) area where battles have often been fought: *Belgium, the ~ of Europe.* **2** compartment in a small aircraft for the pilot. Cf *flight deck* of an air-liner; driver's seat in a racing-car. ⇨ the illus at **air**[1]. **3** (old use) part of a warship used as quarters for junior officers and for those wounded in action.

cock·roach /ˈkokrəʊtʃ/ *n* large, dark-brown insect that comes out at night in kitchens and places where food is kept. ⇨ the illus at **insect**.

cocks·comb /ˈkokskəʊm/ *n* **1** red crest of a cock[1](**1**). ⇨ the illus at **fowl**. **2** jester's cap. **3** plant with clusters of red or yellow feather-like flowers. ⇨ also **coxcomb**.

cock·sure /ˌkokˈʃʊə(r)/ *adj* presumptuously or offensively sure (*of* or *about* sth); confident.

cock·tail /ˈkokteɪl/ *n* [C] **1** mixed alcoholic drink, esp one taken before a meal, e g gin and vermouth. **ˈ~ lounge,** (in a hotel) where ~s may be bought and drunk. ⇨ **bar**[1](**13**). **2** mixture of fruit juices, or spiced tomato juice, served in a glass as an appetizer; quantity of crab meat or shrimps, similarly served. **3** mixed fruit salad served in a glass.

cocky /ˈkokɪ/ *adj* (**-ier, -iest**) (colloq) cocksure; pert; conceited.

coco /ˈkəʊkəʊ/ *n* (also **ˈ~-palm, ˈ~-nut palm**) tropical seaside palm-tree. **~·nut** /ˈkəʊkənʌt/ *n* large hard-shelled seed of this palm-tree, filled with milky juice and a solid white lining from which oil is extracted; ⇨ **copra**. ⇨ the illus at **palm**. **ˌ~nut ˈmatting,** made from the tough fibre of the ~nut's outer covering.

co·coa /ˈkəʊkəʊ/ *n* [U] powder of crushed cacao seeds; hot drink made from this with water or milk.

co·coon /kəˈkun/ *n* silky covering made by a caterpillar to protect itself while it is a chrysalis, esp that of the silkworm. ⇨ the illus at **silk**. □ *vt* [VP6A] protect (an aircraft, engine, car, etc) by covering completely with a plastic material (to prevent rust, etc during storage).

co·cotte /koˈkot/ *n* (F) (dated) fashionable prostitute.

cod[1] /kod/ *n* **1** [C] (*pl* unchanged) (also **ˈcod·fish**) large sea fish. **2** [U] its flesh as food. **~-liver oil** /ˈkod lɪvər ˈɔɪl/ *n* [U] used as a medicine.

cod[2] /kod/ *vt, vi* (**-dd-**) [VP6A,2A] (colloq) hoax; make a fool of: *You're codding (me)!*

cod·piece /ˈkodpis/ *n* (15th and 16th cc) bag or flap concealing the opening in the front of a man's close-fitting hose.

coda /ˈkəʊdə/ *n* passage (often elaborate in style) that completes a piece of music.

coddle /ˈkodl/ *vt* [VP6A] **1** (also **ˈmolly ~**) treat with great care and tenderness; pamper: *~ a child because it is in poor health.* **2** cook, e g eggs, in water just below boiling-point.

code /kəʊd/ *n* [C] **1** collection of laws arranged in a system. **2** system of rules and principles that has been accepted by society or a class or group of people: *a high moral ~; a ~ of honour. You must live up to the ~ of the school,* accept its unwritten rules of honour and conduct. **3** system of signs, secret writing, etc used to ensure secrecy, e g in war or economy, in sending cables or for a computer: *a telegraph ~; a ~ telegram; a five-letter ~,* e g one in which B X Y M A stands for a phrase or sentence. ***break a ~,*** discover how to interpret a secret ~. **the Morse ~,** using dots and dashes for letters and numerals. □ *vt* (also **en~** /enˈkəʊd/) put in a ~(**3**).

co·deine /ˈkəʊdin/ *n* [U] narcotic derived from opium.

co·dex /ˈkəʊdeks/ *n* (*pl* **codices** /ˈkəʊdɪsiz/) manuscript volume (esp of ancient or classical texts).

codger /ˈkodʒə(r)/ *n* (colloq) queer old person; fellow.

codi·ces ⇨ **codex**.

codi·cil /ˈkəʊdɪsɪl *US:* ˈkodəsl/ *n* appendix to a will, esp sth modifying or revoking part of it.

codi·fy /ˈkəʊdɪfaɪ *US:* ˈkodəfaɪ/ *vt* (*pt,pp* **-fied**) [VP6A] put into the form of a code(**1**): *~ the laws.* **codi·fi·ca·tion** /ˌkəʊdɪfɪˈkeɪʃn *US:* ˌkod-/ *n*

cod·ling[1] /ˈkodlɪŋ/ *n* young codfish.

cod·lin /ˈkodlɪn/, **cod·ling**[2] /ˈkodlɪŋ/ *n* kind of apple.

co-ed /ˈkəʊ ed/ *n* (colloq) (girl or woman at a) co-educational college or school.

co-edu·ca·tion /ˌkəʊ ˌedʒʊˈkeɪʃn/ *n* [U] education of boys and girls together. **~al** /-ˈkeɪʃnl/ *adj*

co-ef·ficient /ˌkəʊɪˈfɪʃnt/ *n* **1** (maths) number or symbol placed before and multiplying another quantity, known or unknown. (In *3xy,* 3 is the ~ of *xy*). **2** (physics) multiplier that measures some property.

co·equal /ˌkəʊˈikwl/ *adj* (emphatic for) equal.

co·erce /ˌkəʊˈɜs/ *vt* [VP6A,14] ***~ sb (into doing sth),*** use force to make (sb) obedient, etc; compel to (a course of action). **co·ercion** /ˌkəʊˈɜʃn *US:* -ˈɜʒn/ *n* [U] coercing or being ~d; government by force: *He paid the money under coercion.* **co·ercive** /ˌkəʊˈɜsɪv/ *adj* of coercion; using coercion: *coercive methods/measures.*

co·eter·nal /ˌkəʊɪˈtɜnl/ *adj* equally eternal with another.

co·eval /ˌkəʊˈivl/ *adj, n* ***~ (with),*** (person) of the same age; (person, things) existing at, lasting for, the same period of time.

co·execu·tor /ˌkəʊɪgˈzekjʊtə(r)/, **co·execu·trix** /ˌkəʊɪgˈzekjʊtrɪks/ *n* joint executor or executrix (with another or others).

co·exist /ˌkəʊɪgˈzɪst/ *vi* ***~ (with),*** exist at the same time. **co·exist·ence** /-təns/ *n* (esp) peaceful existence side by side of states with opposed political systems.

cof·fee /ˈkofɪ *US:* ˈkɔfɪ/ *n* [U] bush or shrub with berries containing seeds (called *beans*) which, when roasted and ground to powder, are used for making a drink; the seeds; the powder; [C,U] the drink: *three black ~s,* three cups of ~ without milk; *white ~,* ~ with milk. **ˈ~ bar** *n* small café serving ~ beverages and light refreshments. **ˈ~-house** *n* (formerly, in England) place frequented by literary men as a sort of club. **ˈ~-mill** *n* device for grinding roasted ~-beans. **ˈ~-stall** *n* movable stand selling hot ~ and food in the streets (esp at night).

cof·fer /ˈkofə(r)/ *n* **1** large, strong box, esp one for holding money or other valuables; (*pl*) place for storing valuables: *the ~s of a bank.* **2** ornamental panel in a ceiling, etc. **3** (also **ˈ~ dam**) caisson(**2**).

cof·fin /ˈkofɪn/ *n* box or case for a dead person to be buried in. ***drive a nail into sb's ~,*** do sth that will bring his death or ruin nearer.

cog /kog/ *n* one of a series of teeth on the rim of a wheel which transfers motion by locking into the teeth of a similar wheel. ⇨ the illus at **bicycle, gear**. ***be a cog in the machine,*** (fig) an unimportant part of a large enterprise. **ˈ~·wheel** *n* toothed wheel.

co·gent /ˈkəʊdʒənt/ *adj* (of arguments) strong and convincing. **co·gency** /ˈkəʊdʒənsɪ/ *n* [U] force or strength (of arguments).

cogi·tate /ˈkodʒɪteɪt/ *vi, vt* [VP2A,3A,6A,14] meditate; think deeply: ~ *upon sth;* ~ *mischief against sb.* **cogi·ta·tion** /ˈkodʒɪˋteɪʃn/ *n* **1** [U] cogitating: *after much cogitation.* **2** (*pl*) thoughts; reflections.

cognac /ˋkonjæk/ *n* [U] fine French brandy.

cog·nate /kogˋneɪt/ *adj* **1** ~ **(with),** having the same source of origin: *English, Dutch and German are* ~ *languages.* **2** related; having much in common: *Physics and astronomy are* ~ *sciences.* □ *n* [C] word, etc that is ~ with another.

cog·ni·tion /kogˋnɪʃn/ *n* [U] (phil) knowing; awareness (including sensation but excluding emotion).

cog·ni·zance /ˋkognɪzns/ *n* [U] **1** (legal) being aware, having conscious knowledge (of sth). ***take* ~ *of,*** become officially aware of. **2** (right of) dealing with a matter legally or judicially. ***fall within/go beyond one's* ~,** be sth one can/cannot deal with. **cogni·zant** /ˋkognɪznt/ *adj* ~ ***of,*** (also, legal) having knowledge, being fully aware of.

cog·no·men /ˋkognəʊmən/ *n* [C] **1** surname. **2** descriptive nickname, e g Aristides *the Just.*

co·habit /ˈkəʊˋhæbɪt/ *vi* (usu of an unmarried couple) live together and behave as, like, husband and wife. **co·habi·ta·tion** /ˈkəʊˈhæbɪˋteɪʃn/ *n*

co·here /ˈkəʊˋhɪə(r)/ *vi* [VP2A] stick together; be or remain united; (of arguments, etc) be consistent. **co·her·ence** /ˈkəʊˋhɪərns/ *n* **co·her·en·cy** /-rnsɪ/ *n* **co·her·ent** /-rnt/ *adj* **1** sticking together. **2** consistent; (esp of speech, thought, ideas, reasoning) clear; easy to understand. **co·her·ent·ly** *adv*

co·he·sion /ˈkəʊˋhiʒn/ *n* cohering; tendency to stick together; force with which molecules cohere. **co·he·sive** /ˈkəʊˋhisɪv/ *adj* having the power of cohering; tending to cohere.

co·hort /ˋkəʊhɔt/ *n* **1** (in the ancient Roman armies) tenth part of a legion. **2** number of persons banded together.

coif /kɔɪf/ *n* (old use) close-fitting cap covering the top, back and sides of the head. **coif·feur** /kwæˋfɜ(r)/ *n* (F) hairdresser. **coif·fure** /kwæˋfjʊə(r)/ *n* style of hairdressing.

coign /kɔɪn/ *n* ~ **of vantage** /ˈkɔɪn əv ˋvɑntɪdʒ *US:* ˋvæn-/ (formal, usu fig) place from which one has a good view of sth.

coil /kɔɪl/ *vt, vi* [VP6A,15A,B,2A,C] wind or twist into a continuous circular or spiral shape; curl round and round: ~ *a rope. The snake* ~*ed (itself) round the branch/*~*ed itself up.* □ *n* **1** sth ~ed; a single turn of sth ~ed: *the thick* ~*s of a python.* ⇨ the illus at **snake. 2** length of wire wound in a spiral to conduct electric current. **3** (colloq) an intra-uterine contraceptive device in the shape of a ~.

coin /kɔɪn/ *n* [C,U] (piece of) metal money: *a small heap of* ~*(s); gold and silver* ~*s; false* ~, imitation ~ in metal of low value. ***pay a man back in the same/his own* ~,** treat him as he has treated you. □ *vt* [VP6A] make (metal) into ~s; invent (esp a new word). ***be* ˋ~*ing money,*** be making money fast, be making large profits. **~·age** /ˋkɔɪnɪdʒ/ *n* **1** [C] making ~s; the ~s made; [C] system of ~s in use: *a decimal* ~*age.* **2** [U] inventing (of a new word); [C] newly invented word. **~er** *n* maker of counterfeit ~.

co·in·cide /ˈkəʊɪnˋsaɪd/ *vi* [VP2A,3A] ~ ***(with),*** **1** (of two or more objects) correspond in area and outline. **2** (of events) happen at the same time; occupy the same period of time: *They could not go to the theatre together because his free time never* ~*d with hers.* **3** (of ideas, etc) be in harmony or agreement: *The judges did not* ~ *in opinion. His tastes and habits* ~ *with those of his wife.*

co·in·ci·dence /ˈkəʊˋɪnsɪdəns/ *n* [U] the condition of coinciding; [C] instance of this, happening by chance: *by a curious* ~. *What a* ~*!* How curious, etc that these two events should come together! **co·inci·dent** /-ndənt/ *adj* coinciding. **co·inci·den·tal** /ˈkəʊˈɪnsɪˋdentl/ *adj* of the nature of a, exhibiting ~.

coir /ˋkɔɪə(r)/ *n* fibre from coconut shells, used for making ropes, matting, etc.

co·itus /ˋkəʊɪtəs/, **co·ition** /ˈkəʊˋɪʃn/ *n* [U] sexual intercourse between two human beings; the insertion of the penis into the vagina.

coke[1] /kəʊk/ *n* [U] rough, light substance that remains when gas has been taken out of coal by heating it in an oven, used as a fuel in stoves and furnaces. □ *vt* turn (coal) into ~.

coke[2] /kəʊk/ *n* (colloq for) coca-cola.

coke[3] /kəʊk/ *n* (sl) cocaine.

coker·nut /ˋkəʊkənʌt/ *n* = coconut.

col /kol/ *n* depression or pass in a mountain range. ⇨ the illus at **mountain.**

col·an·der, cul·len·der /ˋkʌləndə(r)/ *n* bowl-shaped vessel or dish with many small holes, used to drain off water from vegetables, etc in cooking.

cold[1] /kəʊld/ *adj* **(-er, -est) 1** of low temperature, esp when compared with the human body: ~ *weather; a* ~ *wind; feel* ~*; a hotel with hot and* ~ *water in every bedroom.* ***give sb the* ~ *shoulder,*** (fig) snub him; show distaste for his company. Hence: ~ **ˋshoulder** *n, vt.* ***have* ~ *feet,*** feel afraid or reluctant (to do sth involving risk or danger. ***leave one* ~,** leave one unmoved, unimpressed. ***(kill sb) in* ~ *blood, make one's blood run* ~,** ⇨ **blood**[1]. ***pour/throw* ~ *water on,*** ⇨ **water**[1]**(1).** ˋ~ **chisel,** one for cutting soft metals while they are ~. ˋ~ **comfort,** poor consolation. ˋ~ **cream,** ointment for cleansing and softening the skin. ˈ~ ˋ**front,** ⇨ **front.** ˈ~ ˋ**meat,** meat that has been cooked and cooled: ~ *meat for supper.* ˈ~ ˋ**steel,** [U] cutting or stabbing weapon (e g a sword or bayonet contrasted with firearms). ˈ~ ˋ**turkey,** ⇨ **turkey.** ˈ~ ˋ**war,** struggle for superiority waged by hostile propaganda, economic measures, etc without actual fighting. ˈ~-ˋ**blooded** *adj* **(a)** having blood that varies with the temperature (e g fish, reptiles). **(b)** (fig of persons, their actions) without feeling; pitiless. ˈ~-ˋ**hearted** /-ˋhɑtɪd/ *adj* without sympathy; indifferent. **2** (fig) **(a)** unkind; unfriendly: *a* ~ *greeting/welcome, etc.* **(b)** sexually unresponsive. **3** (of colours) suggesting ~, e g grey and blue. **~·ly** *adv* **~·ness** *n* state of being ~: *Because of the* ~*ness of the weather, we stayed indoors.*

cold[2] /kəʊld/ *n* **1** [U] (often with *def art*) relative absence of heat; low temperature (esp in the atmosphere): *He was shivering with* ~. *He disliked both the heat of summer and the* ~ *of winter. Don't stay outside in the* ~, *come indoors by the fire.* ***(be left) out in the* ~,** (fig) (be) ignored or neglected. **2** (phys) [U] freezing-point of water or below: *five degrees of* ~. **3** [U] illness (catarrh) of the nose or throat: *have a* ~*; catch (a)* ~. *Half the boys in the school were absent with* ~*s.*

cole·slaw /ˋkəʊlslɔ/ *n* [U] finely shredded raw cabbage (as a salad).

colic /ˋkolɪk/ *n* [U] severe pain in the stomach and bowels without diarrhoea.

co·li·tis /kəˋlaɪtɪs/ *n* [U] (med) inflammation of the mucous membrane of the colon.

col·lab·or·ate /kəˋlæbəreɪt/ *vi* **1** [VP2A,3A] **~ *(on sth) (with sb),*** work in partnership, esp in literature or art: *~ on a biography with a friend.* **2** [VP3A] **~ *with,*** work treasonably, esp with enemy forces occupying one's country. **col·lab·or·ator** /kəˈlæbəˋreɪtə(r)/ *n* person who ~s(1,2). **col·lab·or·ation** /kəˈlæbəˋreɪʃn/ *n* [U] collaborating: *working in collaboration with others.* **col·lab·or·ation·ist** /kəˈlæbəˋreɪʃn̩ɪst/ *n* person who ~s(2).

col·lage /ˋkolɑʒ *US:* kəˋlɑʒ/ *n* [C] (art) picture made by an unusual combination of bits of paper, cloth, photographs, etc.

col·lapse /kəˋlæps/ *vi, vt* [VP2A,6A] **1** fall down or in; come or break to pieces suddenly: *The weight of the snow on the roof caused the shed to ~. The roof ~d under the weight of the snow. If you cut the ropes of a tent, it will ~.* **2** lose physical strength, courage, mental powers, etc; break down: *If you work too hard you/your health may ~. Our plans will ~ unless we get more help. The price of copper ~d,* dropped to a low level. **3** (of apparatus) close or fold up. □ *n* collapsing: *the ~ of a table/tent/tower, etc;* (fig): *the ~ of their plans/hopes; suffer a nervous ~.* **col·ˋlaps·ible, -able** /-səbl/ *adj* that can be ~d(3) (for packing, etc): *a collapsible boat/chair.*

col·lar /ˋkolə(r)/ *n* **1** part of a garment that fits round the neck; turned-over neckband of a shirt, dress, etc: *The wind was so cold that he turned his coat ~ up.* ***blue/white ~ workers,*** ⇨ blue, white. **2** separate article of clothing (linen, lace, etc) worn round the neck and fastened to a shirt or blouse. **ˋ~ stud** *n* small button-like device for fastening a ~ to a shirt. **3** band of leather, etc put round the neck of a dog, horse or other animal. ⇨ the illus at harness. **4** metal band joining two pipes, rods or shafts, e g in a machine. **5 ˋ~·bone** *n* bone joining the shoulder and the breast bone. ⇨ the illus at skeleton. □ *vt* [VP6A] **1** seize (sb) by the ~; take hold of roughly: *The policeman ~ed the thief.* **2** (colloq) take without permission: *Who's ~ed my pen?*

col·late /kəˋleɪt/ *vt* [VP6A] make a careful comparison between (copies of texts, manuscripts, books, etc) to learn the differences between them: *~ a new edition with an earlier edition.*

col·lat·eral /kəˋlætərl/ *adj* **1** secondary or subordinate but from the same source: *~ evidence; ~ security,* property, e g stocks or bonds, pledged as security for repayment of a loan. **2** descended from a common ancestor but in a different line, i e through different sons or daughters. □ *n* ~ security.

col·la·tion /kəˋleɪʃn/ *n* [C] (formal) light meal, (usu *cold ~*), often one served at a time different from usual meal times.

col·league /ˋkolig/ *n* one of two or more persons working together and (usu) having similar rank and duties: *the Prime Minister and his ~s,* the other members of the Cabinet.

col·lect[1] /ˋkolekt/ *n* short prayer of the Church of Rome or the Church of England, to be read on certain appointed days.

col·lect[2] /kəˋlekt/ *vt, vi* **1** [VP6A,15B] bring or gather together; get from a number of persons or places: *The teacher told the boys to ~ all the waste paper lying about after the picnic and burn it. If he could ~ all the money people owe him, he would be a rich man. A man who ~s taxes is called a tax-~or.* **2** [VP6A] obtain specimens of (books, stamps, etc), e g as a hobby or in order to learn things: *~ foreign stamps/old china.* **3** [VP2A] come together: *A crowd soon ~s when there's a street accident.* **4** [VP6A] fetch: *~ a child from school.* **5** [VP6A] gather together, recover control of (one's thoughts, energies, oneself): *Before you begin to make a speech, you should ~ your thoughts and ideas.* **6** (US comm): *I'll pay for the goods ~,* when they are delivered. **~ed** *adj* (esp of a person) calm; not distracted. **~ed·ly** *adv*

col·lec·tion /kəˋlekʃn/ *n* **1** [U] collecting; [C] instance of this: *How many ~s of letters are there every day,* How often does the postman empty the boxes? **2** [C] group of objects that have been collected and that belong together: *a fine ~ of old swords/paintings/postage stamps.* **3** heap of materials or objects that have come together: *a ~ of dust/rubbish.* **4** [C] money collected at a meeting, a Church service, etc. ***make/take up a ~:*** *The ~ will be taken up after the sermon.*

col·lec·tive /kəˋlektɪv/ *adj* **1** of a group or society (of persons, nations, etc) as a whole: *~ leadership,* (emphasis on) government by a group rather than an individual. *~ ownership of the land/of means of production, etc,* by all citizens for the benefit of all; *~ security,* security of a State or States against aggression by means of common military, etc preparedness. **~ farm,** (e g in a Socialist State) one owned by the State and run by the workers for the benefit of all the citizens. **2 ~ noun,** (gram) one that is singular in form but stands for many individuals, as *cattle, crowd, audience.* In 'to catch fish', *fish* is a ~ noun. **col·lec·tiv·ize** /kəˋlektɪvaɪz/ *vt* [VP6A] change, e g farm lands, from private ownership to a system of State control. **col·lec·tiv·iz·ation** /kəˈlektɪvaɪˋzeɪʃn *US:* -vɪˋz-/ *n*

col·lec·tor /kəˋlektə(r)/ *n* person who collects: *a ˋstamp-~; a ˋtax-~; a ˋticket-~,* e g at a railway station; *a ˋ~'s piece,* an article sought by ~s, e g a book, a piece of china or furniture, because of its beauty, rarity, etc.

col·leen /ˋkolin/ *n* (Irish) young girl.

col·lege /ˋkolɪdʒ/ *n* **1** school for higher or professional education; body of teachers and students forming part of a university; their building(s): *go to ~; be at ~; a C~ of Agriculture/Pharmacy, etc; the Oxford and Cambridge ~s; Heads of C~s,* ⇨ for their titles Master[1](9), President, Principal, Provost, Warden. **2** union of persons with common purposes and privileges: *the C~ of Surgeons; the C~ of Cardinals,* who elect and advise the Pope. **col·le·giate** /kəˋlidʒɪət/ *adj* of or like a ~ or ~ student: *collegiate life,* life in ~s and universities.

col·lide /kəˋlaɪd/ *vi* [VP2A,C,3A] **~ *(with),*** **1** come together violently; meet and strike: *As the bus came round the corner, it ~d with a van. The bus and the van ~d. The ships ~d in the fog.* **2** be opposed; be in conflict: *If the aims of two countries ~, there may be war.*

col·lie /ˋkolɪ/ *n* Scottish sheepdog with shaggy hair. ⇨ the illus at dog.

col·lier /ˋkolɪə(r)/ *n* **1** coal-miner. **2** ship that carries coal as cargo.

col·liery /ˈkɒljərɪ/ *n* (*pl* -ries) coal-mine (and the buildings, etc connected with it).

col·li·sion /kəˈlɪʒn/ *n* [U] colliding; [C] instance of this: *a head-on ~ between two buses; a railway ~; on (a) ˈ~ course,* likely to collide. ***be in/come into ~ (with),*** have collided/collide (with): *The liner is reported to have been in ~ with an oil-tanker. The two ships were in/came into ~. People with revolutionary ideas may find themselves in ~ with the forces of the law,* get into trouble with the police.

col·lo·cate /ˈkɒləkeɪt/ *vi* [VP2A,3A] ***~ (with),*** (of words) combine in a way characteristic of language: *'Weak' ~s with 'tea' but 'feeble' does not.* **col·lo·ca·tion** /ˌkɒləˈkeɪʃn/ *n* [C,U] coming together; collocating of words: *'Strong tea' and 'heavy drinker' are English collocations. So are 'by accident' and 'so as to'.*

col·loquial /kəˈləʊkwɪəl/ *adj* (of words, phrases, style) belonging to, suitable for, ordinary conversation; not formal or literary. **~·ly** *adv* **~·ism** *n* [C] ~ word or phrase.

col·loquy /ˈkɒləkwɪ/ *n* (*pl* -quies) [C,U] (formal) conversation: *engage in ~ with sb.*

col·lu·sion /kəˈluʒn/ *n* [U] secret agreement or understanding for a deceitful or fraudulent purpose: *act in ~ with sb; ~ between persons who appear to be opposed to each other.* **col·lus·ive** /kəˈlusɪv/ *adj*

colly·wobbles /ˈkɒlɪwɒblz/ *n* (colloq) stomach-ache; slight feeling of fear.

co·lon[1] /ˈkəʊlən/ *n* lower and greater part of the large intestine. ⇨ the illus at **alimentary**.

co·lon[2] /ˈkəʊlən/ *n* punctuation mark (:) used in writing and printing.

colonel /ˈkɜnl/ *n* army officer above a lieutenant-~ (and in US) commanding a regiment; (abbr for) lieutenant-~. ⇨ App 9.

co·lo·nial /kəˈləʊnɪəl/ *adj* **1** of a colony or colonies(1). **C~ Office,** (GB) former State department in charge of colonies. **2** (esp US) in the style of architecture in the British colonies in N America before and during the Revolution. □ *n* inhabitant of a colony(1), esp one who helps or helped to found and develop it. **~·ism** *n* [U] policy of having colonies(1) and keeping them dependent. **~·ist** *n* supporter of ~ism; one who favours the retention of colonies(2).

col·on·ist /ˈkɒlənɪst/ *n* pioneer settler in a colony(1).

col·on·ize /ˈkɒlənaɪz/ *vt* [VP6A] establish a colony; establish in a colony: *The ancient Greeks ~d many parts of the Mediterranean.* **col·on·iz·ation** /ˌkɒlənaɪˈzeɪʃn *US:* -nɪˈz-/ *n* [U] colonizing: *the colonization of N America by the British, Dutch and French.* **col·on·izer** *n* one who helps to establish a colony(1).

col·on·ade /ˌkɒləˈneɪd/ *n* row of columns(1) set (usu) at equal distances. **col·on·naded** /ˌkɒləˈneɪdɪd/ *adj* having a ~.

col·ony /ˈkɒlənɪ/ *n* (*pl* -nies) **1** country or territory extensively settled by migrants from a mother country, and, for a time, controlled by it, e g (formerly) Canada and Australia. **2** country, territory, controlled, administered, and (often) developed by another, e g Hong Kong and (formerly) Sierra Leone (now an independent State). **3** group of people from another country, or of people with the same trade, profession or occupation, living together: *the American ~ in Paris; a ~ of artists,* e g one living in a place famous for its scenic beauty. **4** (biol) number of animals or plants, living or growing together: *a ~ of ants.*

color US spelling of **colour**.

col·ora·tura /ˌkɒlərəˈtjʊərə *US:* -tʊərə/ *n* [U] flowery or ornamental passages in vocal music; (*attrib*) *~ soprano.*

co·los·sal /kəˈlɒsl/ *adj* immense.

co·los·sus /kəˈlɒsəs/ *n* (*pl* -si /-saɪ/, -suses /-səsɪz/) immense statue (esp of a man, much greater than life-size); immense person or personification of sth.

col·our[1] (US = **color**) /ˈkʌlə(r)/ *n* **1** [U] sensation produced in the eye by rays of decomposed light; [C] effect produced by a ray of light of a particular wavelength, or by a mixture of these: *~ films; ~ TV; Red, blue and yellow are ~s. There isn't enough ~ in the picture.* **ˈ~-blind** *adj* unable to distinguish between some ~s, or to see certain ~s. **ˈ~ scheme** *n* scheme for combination of ~s in a design (e g for the furnishing and decoration of a room, the planting of a flower garden). **ˈ~-wash** *n* coloured distemper. **2** [U] redness of the face: *She has very little ~,* has a pale face. ***change ~,*** grow pale or redder than usual. ***have a high ~,*** have a red complexion. ***lose ~,*** become pale. ***be/feel/look off ~,*** (colloq) be unwell; in low spirits. **3** (*pl*) materials used by artists; paint: *ˈwater-~s; ˈoil-~s;* appearance produced by their use: (fig) *paint sth in bright/dark ~s,* make it appear (un)favourable. ***(appear/see sth) in its true ~s,*** as it really is. **4** [U] (of events, descriptions) appearance of reality or truth; pretext. ***give/lend ~ to,*** give an appearance of probability to: *His torn clothing gave ~ to his story that he had been attacked and robbed.* ***give a false ~ to,*** give a wrong character or tone to: *Newspapers often give a false ~ to the news they report,* twist the meaning to suit their aims. **5** (in literature) ***local ~,*** [U] use of details to make a description of a place, scene or time realistic. **6** (in music) [U] quality; variety of expression. **7** (*pl*) ribbon, dress, cap, etc, worn as a symbol of a party, a club, a school, etc, or to show ownership of a race-horse, etc: *The owner of a horse is always glad to see his ~s get to the winning-post first,* to see his horse win a race. ***get/win one's ~s,*** (at college, etc) be awarded a place in an athletic team. **8** (*pl*) flag (of a ship); ensign or standard of a regiment: *salute the ~s; serve with/join the ~s,* the Navy, Army or Air Force. ***come off with flying ~s,*** make a great success of sth. ***lower one's ~s,*** give up one's demands or position; surrender. ***nail one's ~s to the mast,*** make a decision, announce it, and show strong determination not to change it. ***sail under false ~s,*** be a hypocrite or impostor. ***show one's true ~s,*** show what one really is. ***stick to one's ~s,*** (fig) refuse to change one's opinion or party. **9** race or race-mixture other than European: *a man/woman of ~,* of non-white race. **ˈ~-bar,** legal and/or social distinction between white and coloured races. **~·ful** /-fl/ *adj* full of ~; bright; gay; exciting; vivid, etc: *a ~ful scene; a ~ful style of writing; lead a ~ful life.* **~·less** *adj* without ~; pale; (fig) lacking in interest, character, vividness: *a ~less style; leading a ~less existence.*

col·our[2] (US = **color**) /ˈkʌlə(r)/ *vt,vi* **1** [VP6A,22] give colour to; put colour on: *~ a wall green.* **2**

[VP2A,C] take on colour; blush: *The leaves have begun to* ~, to take on their autumn colours of yellow, brown, etc. *The girl is so shy that she* ~*s (up) whenever a man speaks to her.* **3** [VP6A] change or misrepresent in some way: *News is often* ~*ed*, changed to suit the views of those who supply it or those who will read it. *Travellers' tales are often highly* ~*ed*, exaggerated. **col·oured** *adj* **1** (in compounds) having the colour specified: *ˈcream-*~*ed; ˈflesh-*~*ed.* **2** (of persons) not wholly of white or European descent; (esp) of the Negro race: *Cape C*~*eds*, South African people of mixed race. **~·ing** *n* [U] (esp) style in which sth is ~ed; style in which an artist uses colour: ~*ing matter*, material used to ~ food, etc.

col·por·teur /ˈkolpɔtə(r)/ *n* person employed by a society to travel and distribute Bibles and religious tracts.

colt[1] /kəʊlt/ *n* young horse (male) up to the age of 4 or 5. ⇨ **filly**; (fig) young man with little experience. **~·ish** /ˈkəʊtɪʃ/ *adj* like a ~; frisky.

colt[2] /kəʊlt/ *n* (P) (US) early type of revolver or pistol.

col·ter /ˈkəʊltə(r)/ (US) spelling of **coulter**.

col·um·bine /ˈkoləmbaɪn/ *n* garden plant with spur-shaped flowers and petals.

col·umn /ˈkoləm/ *n* **1** tall, upright pillar, usu of stone, either supporting or decorating part of a building, or standing alone as a monument. **2** sth shaped like or suggesting a ~: *a* ~ *of smoke* (rising straight up); *the spinal* ~, the backbone; *a* ~ *of mercury* (in a thermometer); *a refining* ~, one in which oil, heated to vapour, is refined into fuel oil, petrol, etc. **3** vertical division of a printed page, (e g of this page or of a newspaper, occupied regularly by one subject): *the correspondence* ~*s of 'The Times'; the advertising* ~*s.* **4** series of numbers arranged under one another: *add up a long* ~ *of figures.* **5** line of ships following one another; deep arrangement of soldiers in short ranks, one behind the other. **fifth** ~, ⇨ **fifth**. **col·um·nist** /ˈkoləmnɪst/ *n* (US) journalist who regularly writes a ~ of miscellaneous news, political comment, etc for a newspaper.

coma /ˈkəʊmə/ *n* ***in a*** **~**, in an unnatural deep sleep usu from injury or illness. ***go into a*** **~**, pass into such a sleep. **~·tose** /ˈkəʊmətəʊs/ *adj* in a ~; unconscious.

comb /kəʊm/ *n* **1** piece of metal, rubber, plastic, etc with teeth for cleaning the hair, making it tidy, keeping it in place, etc or as an ornament. **2** part of a machine with a ~-like look or purpose, esp for tidying and straightening wool, cotton, etc for manufacture. **3** wax structure made by bees for honey. ⇨ **honey~**. **4** red fleshy crest of fowl. ⇨ **cocks~**. **5** crest of a large wave. □ *vt,vi* [VP6A, 15B] **1** use a ~ on (the hair). **2** prepare (wool, flax, etc) with ~s for manufacture. **3** search thoroughly: *The police* ~*ed the whole city in their efforts to find the murderer.* **4** **~ out**, (fig) take out (unwanted things, persons) from a group: ~ *out a government department*, get rid of officials who are not really needed, who are inefficient, etc. Hence, **ˈ~-out** *n* act of getting rid of (unnecessary officials, etc). **5** [VP2C] (of a wave) break, curl: *waves* ~*ing over the ship.*

com·bat /ˈkombæt/ *n* fight; struggle. **single ~**, fight between two persons only: (attrib) *a* ~ *mission.* □ *vt,vi* [VP6A,3A] fight; struggle: ~ *the enemy;* ~ *error; a ship* ~*ing with the wind and waves.* **~·ant** /ˈkombətənt/ *adj* fighting. □ *n* one who fights: *In modern wars both* ~*ants and non-*~*ants are killed in air attacks.* **~·ive** /ˈkombətɪv/ *adj* fond of fighting; ready to fight. **~·ive·ly** *adv*

com·bi·na·tion /ˈkombɪˈneɪʃn/ *n* **1** [U] joining or putting together; state of being joined: *in* ~ *with; enter into* ~ *with; every possible* ~ *and permutation*, every possible arrangement. **2** [C] number of persons or things that are joined: *The college is supported by a* ~ *of income from endowments and fees from students.* ~ *room*, (at Cambridge) common-room. ⇨ **common**[1]**(1)**. **3** motor-bike with sidecar attached. **4** (*pl*) one-piece undergarment covering body and legs. **5** (also **~-lock**) formula, complicated arrangement, for the lock of a safe, strong-room, etc: *How did the thieves learn the* ~ *used to open the safe?*

com·bine[1] /kəmˈbaɪn/ *vt,vi* [VP6A,14,2A,3A] ~ ***(with)***, (cause to) join together; possess at the same time: *We can't always* ~ *work with pleasure. Hydrogen and oxygen* ~*/Hydrogen* ~*s with oxygen to form water. Some films* ~ *education with recreation. Everything* ~*d against him*, Circumstances, etc made his task difficult or impossible. **~d operations/exercises**, in which air, sea and land forces work together.

com·bine[2] /ˈkombaɪn/ *n* **1** group of persons, trading companies, etc joined for a purpose (such as

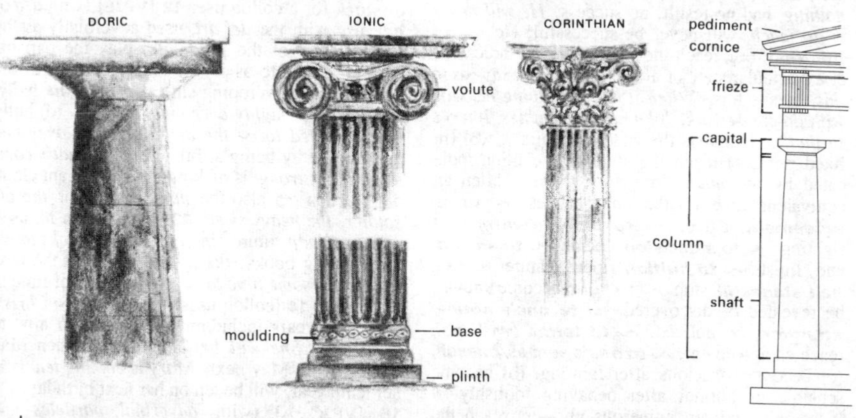

columns

a combine harvester

controlling prices). **2 '~-'harvester** machine that both reaps and threshes grain.

com·bust·ible /kəm'bʌstəbl/ *adj* catching fire and burning easily; (fig, of people) excitable. □ *n* (usu *pl*) ~ material.

com·bus·tion /kəm'bʌstʃən/ *n* [U] process of burning; destruction by fire. ⇨ **spontaneous.**

come /kʌm/ *vi* (*pt* came /keɪm/, *pp* come) (For uses with *adverbial particles* and *preps*, ⇨ **15** below). **1** [VP2B,C,3A] move towards or nearer to, the speaker; arrive where the speaker is, was or will be: *C~ here! Are you coming to my party this evening? He has just ~ from Leeds.* ⇨ **15** below. *He hasn't ~ yet. Help came at last. They came to a river.* ~ ***(with),*** **(a)** [VP3A] move towards, arrive, etc in sb's company: *She'll ~ to the party with John. Who are the children coming with?* ⇨ *bring (with) at* bring(1). **(b)** [VP4A] (with infinitive of purpose): *He has ~ here to work. They've ~ all the way from London to look for jobs. He's ~ to get/~ for his book.* **(c)** [VP2E] (with a *pres part* to indicate two activities or states that occur together): *The children came running to meet us. He came hurrying to her bedside as soon as he heard she was ill.* **2** [VP2C,E] ~ ***(into/onto/in/on, etc),*** move into, etc the place where the speaker is: *C~ into the hallway out of the rain. The train came puffing into the station. Can you ~ out with me for a walk? He came back to have a word with me. The sunshine came streaming through the windows.* **3** [VP3A] **(a)** ~ ***to,*** reach; rise to; fall to (a particular level, figure, point): *Your bill ~s to £20. His earnings ~ to more than £5000 a year.* ***(not) ~ to much/little/nothing,*** (not) amount to much, etc: *All his plans came to nothing*, had no result, no success. *He will never ~ to much*, will never be successful, etc. ~ ***to this/that, etc,*** reach the state of affairs indicated, or a particular state of affairs: *What you say ~s to this*, means this. *When it ~s to helping his wife with the housework, John never grumbles. If it ~s to that...*, If that is the state of affairs.... **(b)** (in fixed phrases) reach the state or condition indicated by the *nouns* for which there is often an equivalent *verb*. ⇨ the *noun* entries. ~ ***to an agreement,*** agree. ~ ***to blows (with),*** start fighting. ~ ***to a decision,*** decide. ~ ***to an end,*** end, finish. ~ ***to fruition,*** ripen, mature. ~ ***to a halt/standstill,*** stop. ~ ***to light,*** become known; be revealed or discovered. ~ ***to one's notice/attention,*** be noticed. ~ ***to terms (with sb),*** reach an agreement. ~ ***to one's senses/oneself,*** **(a)** become conscious after fainting. **(b)** become sensible or normal after behaving foolishly. **4** (used with *into* in numerous phrases) reach the state or condition indicated by the *nouns*. ⇨ the *nouns* in the phrases. ~ ***into blossom/bud/flower/leaf,*** begin to have blossom, buds, etc. ~ ***into contact (with sb/sth),*** meet sb, touch sth. ~ ***into focus,*** (of an object) be sharply defined; (of a problem) become prominent. ~ ***into a fortune/money,*** receive, inherit a fortune, etc. ~ ***into operation,*** start to operate. ~ ***into one's own,*** receive the credit, fame, etc that one deserves, what rightly belongs to one, etc. ~ ***into power,*** (of a political party, etc) form the Government. Cf *go into Opposition.* ***come into sight/view,*** appear. ⇨ also **collision, effect,** *existence* at **exist, fashion, force**[1]**(5), play**[2]**(8), possession,** *prominence* at **prominent, question**[1]**(2), use**[2]**(1). 5** ~ ***to sb (from sb),*** be left, willed, to sb (by Will and Testament, on death): *He has a lot of money coming to him*, will receive it when sb dies. *The farm came to him on his father's death.* **6** ~ ***to sb,*** occur to, strike (sb); befall (sb): *The idea came* (= occurred) *to him in his bath. No harm will ~ to you if you're careful. He had it coming to him,* (sl used only of unpleasant events) what happened was fated, and probably deserved. **7** [VP4A] reach a point where one sees, understands, etc: *He came to realize that he was mistaken. He had ~ to see the problem in a new light. I have ~ to believe that...*, I now believe that...; *When we ~ to know them better....* **8** [VP4A] (usu with *how*, and sometimes, in older English, with inversion of subject and finite instead of interr with *aux do*) asking for an explanation or reason: *How did you ~* (or, old style, *How came you*) *to find out where she's living? How did you ~ to be so foolish? Now that I ~* (= happen) *to think of it....* ***How ~ (that),*** (sl) How does/did sth happen: *How ~ (that) you just sat there doing nothing?* **9** [VP2C] occur; be found; have as its place: *May ~s between April and June. On what page does it ~?* **10** [VP2D] be; become; prove to be: *Your dream will one day ~ true*, be realized. *It ~s easy with practice. The handle has ~ loose. It ~s cheaper if you buy things in bulk. Everything will ~ all right in the end. That sort of thing ~s natural to her*, she does it without having to learn or make an effort. **11** [VP2D] (with *part adj* prefixed with *un-*, denoting undesirable conditions, etc) be; become: *My shoe laces have ~ undone. The seam came unstitched. The flap of the envelope has ~ unstuck.* ⇨ **unstuck** for a colloq use. **12** [VP2E] (with a *n* or *adj*, usu with the *def art*, used adverbially as the nominal part of the *predicate*) play the part of; behave, talk, etc as if one were (often with the suggestion of overdoing sth): *Don't ~ the bully, the high and mighty over me*, Don't (try to) bully me. *He tried to ~ the artful/virtuous over me*, impress me by being artful/virtuous. *That's coming it a bit strong*, is making an extravagant claim or assertion. ⇨ also the *noun* entries for *the old soldier, the heavy swell.* **13** (the *inf* with *to*, used as a *pred adj*) future: *in years to ~; books to ~*, forthcoming books; *the life to ~*, life in the next world; *for some time to ~*, for a period of time in the future. **14** (colloq uses): *two years ~ Christmas*, two years including the time from now to Christmas. *She will be 21 ~ May*, when May comes, i e in May next. *Mary is coming ten*, is in her tenth year, will be ten on her next birthday.

15 [VP2C,3A] (with *adverbial particles* and

preps):
come about, happen: *It came about in this way. How does it ~ about that...?* ⇨ 8 above.
come across (sb/sth), (a) find or meet by chance: *I came across this old brooch in a curio shop.* (b) occur to: *The thought came across my mind that...*, occurred to me.... Cf *It crossed my mind that....* **~ across (with),** (sl) pay (money owing); agree to give information.
come after sb, follow in pursuit of: *The farmer came after the intruders with a big stick.*
come along, (a) (*imper*) try harder; make more effort: *C~ along, now! Someone must know the answer.* (b) progress: *The garden is coming along quite nicely.* (c) appear; arrive: *When the right opportunity ~s along, he'll take it.* (d) (*imper*). hurry up; make haste: *C~ along, we'll be late for the theatre!*
come apart, ~, fall, to pieces: *The teapot just came apart in my hands.*
come at sb/sth, (a) reach; get access to: *The truth is often difficult to ~ at* (*get at* is more usu). (b) attack: *The man came at me with a big stick.* Hence, **~-at-able** /ˈkʌm ˋæt əbl/ *adj* (colloq) accessible (*get-at-able* is more usu).
come away (from), become detached: *The light switch came away from the wall.*
come back, return; (of fashions) become popular again: *Will ruffs ~ back?* **~ back at,** retort; retaliate: *He came back at the speaker with some sharp questions.* **~ back (to one),** return to the memory: *Their names are all coming back to me now,* I'm beginning to remember them. Hence, **ˋ~-back** *n* (a) (e g of actors, politicians, boxers, etc) successful return to, reinstatement in, a former position: *Can he stage a ~-back?* (b) retort; repartee. (c) redress; recompense (for a loss, etc): *If you're uninsured and you're burgled, you'll have no ~-back.*
come before sb/sth, (a) be dealt with by: *The complaint will come before the United Nations Assembly next week.* (b) have precedence over: *Baronets ~ before knights.*
come between, (a) interfere with a relationship: *It is not advisable to ~ between a man and his wife.* (b) prevent sb from having sth: *He never lets anything ~ between him and his evening paper.*
come by sth, (a) obtain by effort; become possessed of: *Was the money honestly ~ by? Jobs were hard to ~ by.* (b) receive by accident or chance: *How did you ~ by that cut on your wrist?*
come down, (a) collapse: *The ceiling came down on our heads.* (b) (of rain, snow, hail) fall: *The rain came down in bucketfuls.* (c) (of prices, temperature, etc) fall. (d) ~ from a city or large town to a smaller locality: *She came down last year and settled in the village.* (e) pay money: *My rich uncle came down generously,* made a generous gift of money. **~ down (from),** leave university (esp Oxford or Cambridge): *His son has just ~ down from Oxford.* **~ down in the world,** lose social position; become poor. Hence, **ˋ~-down** *n* fall in social position; humiliation: *He has had to sell his house and furniture. What a ~-down for him!* **~ down in favour of sb/sth, ~ down on the side of sb/sth,** decide to support: *He came down on the side of a more flexible trade policy.* **~ down on sb,** (colloq) rebuke severely: *The headmaster came down on the boy like a ton of bricks.* **~ down on sb for sth,** demand payment of money owing: *Tradesmen came down on him for prompt settlement of his accounts.* **~ down to,** (a) reach to: *Her hair ~s down to her waist.* (b) can be reduced to: *Your choices in the matter ~ down to these.* (c) (of traditions, etc) be handed down: *legends that have ~ down to us,* i e from our ancestors. **~ down to earth,** return to reality: *Now that his money has all been spent, he's had to ~ down to earth.* **~ down to doing sth,** be forced, e g by poverty, to doing sth humiliating: *He had ~ down to begging.* **~ down with,** (colloq) contribute: *I had to ~ down with £10 to her favourite charity.*
come forward, (a) offer or present oneself: *Will no one ~ forward as a candidate? No witness of the accident has ~ forward.* (b) (comm) become available: *the number of cattle coming forward for slaughter,* brought to market to be sold.
come from, (a) (not with progressive tenses) have as a birthplace, place of origin, etc: *He ~s from Kent. Much of the butter eaten in England ~s from New Zealand.* (b) = ~ of (b).
~ home to, ⇨ home²(2).
~ in, (a) (of the tide) rise: *The tide is coming in.* (b) become seasonable: *When do oysters ~ in?* (c) become fashionable: *When did mini-skirts first ~ in?* (d) (of a batsman in cricket) take his stand at the wicket: *When the next man came in,....* (e) take a place in the result of a race: *Which horse came in first?* (f) be elected; come into power: *If the Democrats ~ in,....* (g) be received as income, etc: *There's not much money coming in at present.* (h) have a part to play; gain an advantage: *Here is the plan of attack, and this is where you ~ in. Where do I ~ in,* (according to context) What is my share, How do I benefit, etc? **~ in handy/useful (for sth),** happen to be useful, serve a purpose: *Don't throw it away; it may ~ in handy one day.* **~ in for,** (a) receive (as an inheritance, a share, etc): *She has ~ in for a fortune.* (b) attract; be the object of: *Their handling of the case has ~ in for a great deal of criticism.* **~ in on,** join; take part in: *If you want to ~ in on the scheme, you must decide now.*
come of, (a) be descended from: *She ~s of a good family.* (b) be the result of: *He promised his help, but I don't think anything will ~ of it. No harm can ~ of trying.* **~ of age,** ⇨ age¹(1).
come off (sth), (a) become detached or separated (from): *A button has ~ off my coat. Please use lipstick that doesn't ~ off on the wine glasses. When we came off the gold standard...,* abandoned it.... (b) fall (from): *~ off a horse/bicycle. Don't ~ off!* (c) get down (from): *C~ off that wall before you fall off (it).* ⇨ also perch²(2). (d) **~ off it,** (colloq, *imper*) stop pretending, or talking nonsense: *Oh, ~ off it! What do you know about horse racing?* **~ off,** (a) take place: *The marriage did not ~ off. Did the proposed visit to Rome ever ~ off?* (b) (of plans, attempts) succeed: *The experiment did not ~ off. The play doesn't quite ~ off.* (c) (of persons) fare; prosper; acquit oneself: *They came off well/badly. Who came off best,* who won?
come on, (a) follow: *You go first, I'll ~ on later.* (b) (as a challenge): *C~ on! Let's race to the bottom of the hill.* (c) make progress; develop: *How's your garden coming on? The baby is coming on well.* (d) (of rain, the seasons, night, illness, etc) start; arrive: *Night/Darkness came on. It came on*

to rain. The rain came on again worse than ever. He said he felt a cold coming on, was beginning to suffer from a cold. **(e)** (of questions, lawsuits) arise for discussion: *When does the case ~ on for trial,* When will the court deal with it? **(f)** (cricket, of a bowler) begin to bowl. **(g)** (of an actor) appear on the stage; (of a play) be performed: *'Macbeth' is coming on again next month.* **~ on to** × *infinitive,* begin to: *It came on to rain.*

come out, **(a)** appear; become visible: *The sun/stars came out. The buds/flowers are coming out,* are opening. **(b)** become known: *When the news came out; if the truth ever ~s out....* **(c)** be published: *When will his new book ~ out?* **(d)** (of workmen) strike: *The car workers have all ~ out again.* **(e)** (of details, etc in a photograph; of qualities) appear: *You have ~ out well in that photograph,* It is a good likeness. *He always ~s out well,* Photographs of him are good. *His arrogance ~s out in every speech he makes.* **(f)** (of stains, etc) be removed: *These ink stains won't ~ out.* **(g)** (of dyes, etc) fade; disappear: *Will the colour ~ out if the material is washed?* **(h)** (of problems) be solved: *I can't make this sum/equation ~ out,* can't solve it. **(i)** make a début in (high) society: *When does your daughter ~ out?* **(j)** (of meaning, sense) become clear: *The meaning of the passage ~s out clearly in his interpretation.* ***~ out at,*** (of totals, averages, etc) amount to: *The total ~s out at 756,* is 756. ***~ out first/last, etc,*** (in examinations) have a certain position: *Tom came out first.* ***~ out in,*** be partially covered in (pimples, a rash, etc): *She's ~ out in spots!* ***~ out with,*** utter; say: *He came out with a most extraordinary story/a string of oaths.* **'coming-'out** *n* début: *a coming-out ball,* one given for a girl's first appearance in high society.

come over, **(a)** ~ from a distance: *a family that came over with William the Conqueror in 1066. Won't you ~ over to England for a holiday?* **(b)** change sides or opinions: *He will never ~ over to our side. ~ over sb,* (of feelings, influences) take possession of: *What has ~ over you,* Why have you changed in this way? *A fit of dizziness came over her,* She suddenly felt dizzy. ***~ over queer/funny/dizzy,*** (colloq) suffer a feeling of faintness/sickness/dizziness.

come round, **(a)** ~ by a circuitous route: *The road was blocked so we had to ~ round by the fields.* **(b)** pay an informal visit to: *Won't you ~ round and see me some time?* **(c)** recur: *Christmas will soon ~ round,* be here again. **(d)** change views, etc: *He will never ~ round to our way of thinking,* change his views and adopt ours. *He has ~ round,* has accepted/agreed. **(e)** regain consciousness: *Pour a jug of water on his face. He'll soon ~ round.* **(f)** recover from ill temper, etc: *Don't scold the boy; he'll ~ round in time.*

come through, **(a)** recover from a serious illness, from risk of injury: *With such a weak heart, he was lucky to ~ through. How did you manage to ~ through without even a scratch,* to escape even a slight injury? **(b)** arrive (by telephone, radio, etc): *Listen; a message is just coming through.* **(c)** pass through official channels: *Your posting has just ~ through: it's Hong Kong!* ***~ through sth,*** survive: *He has ~ through two world wars,* has lived safely through them.

come to, recover (consciousness). ⇨ come round (e), and 2 above.

come under sth, **(a)** be classed among; be in (a certain category, etc): *What heading does this ~ under?* **(b)** be subjected to: *~ under sb's notice/influence.*

come up, **(a)** (of seed, herbaceous plants, etc): show above the ground: *The seeds/snowdrops haven't ~ up yet.* **(b)** arise; be put forward: *The question hasn't ~ up yet,* has not been raised or discussed. *Her divorce case ~s up next month,* will be dealt with then. **(c)** (sl) be drawn (in a lottery): *My sweepstake ticket came up; I won £100.* **(d)** occur; arise: *We shall write to you if a vacancy ~s up.* **(e)** rise in social position: *He came up the hard way,* succeeded through his own, unaided efforts. ***~ up against,*** meet (difficulties, opposition). ***~ up (to),*** **(a)** reach: *The water came up to my waist.* **(b)** equal: *Your work has not ~ up to my expectations/to the required standards.* ***~ up with,*** **(a)** draw level with: *We came up with a party of hikers.* **(b)** produce; find (a solution, an answer).

come upon, **(a)** attack by surprise; strike: *the disaster that came upon them. Fear came upon us.* **(b)** make a demand (for): *She came upon him for alimony.* **(c)** be a burden to: *In former times paupers came upon* (= had to be supported by) *the parish.* **(d)** = come across (e).

com·edian /kəˋmidɪən/ *n* actor who plays comic parts in plays, broadcasts and TV; person who behaves in a comic way and who cannot be taken seriously. **com·edienne** /kəˌmidɪˋen *US:* kəˌmidɪen/ *n* female ~.

com·edy /ˋkomədɪ/ *n* **1** [U] branch of drama that deals with everyday life and humorous events: *He prefers ~ to tragedy;* [C] (*pl* **-dies**) play for the theatre, of a light, amusing kind. **ˌmusical ˋ~,** such a play, with music, songs and dancing. **2** [C, U] amusing activity or incident in real life: *There's not much ~ in modern war.*

come·ly /ˋkʌmlɪ/ *adj* **(-ier, -iest)** (usu of a person) pleasant to look at. **come·li·ness** *n*

comer /ˋkʌmə(r)/ *n* (chiefly in compounds) one who comes: *the first comer; the late-comers; all comers.*

com·est·ible /kəˋmestəbl/ *n* (usu *pl*) thing to eat.

comet /ˋkomɪt/ *n* heavenly body (looking like a star with a bright centre and a less bright tail) that moves round the sun in an eccentric orbit.

a comet

com·fit /ˋkʌmfɪt/ *n* sweetmeat; fruit (eg a plum) preserved in sugar.

com·fort /ˋkʌmfət/ *n* **1** [U] state of being free from suffering, anxiety, pain, etc; contentment; physical well-being: *become fond of ~ as one grows old; living in great ~.* **2** [U] help or kindness to sb who is suffering: *a few words of ~; news that brought ~ to all of us. Be of good ~,* cheer up, take courage. *That is cold ~,* not much consolation. **3** [C] person or thing that brings relief or help: *Your letters have been a great ~ to me. It's a ~ to know that she is safe. The hotel has every modern ~/all modern ~s.* **public ~ station,**

(US) public convenience station, lavatory, etc. □ *vt* [VP6A] give ~ to: *~ those who are in trouble. The child ran to its mother to be ~ed. The insurance money ~ed her for the tragic death of her husband.* **~er** *n* person who ~s; warm scarf to be worn round the neck; dummy teat for a baby. **'~less** *adj* without ~: *a ~less room.*

com·fort·able /ˈkʌmftəbl *US:* -fərt-/ *adj* **1** giving comfort to the body: *a ~ chair/bed.* **2** having or providing comfort: *a ~ life/income. Please make yourself ~.* **3** at ease; free from (excessive) pain, anxiety, etc: *to be/feel ~.* **com·fort·ably** /-əblɪ/ *adv* in a ~ manner: *a car that holds six people comfortably. They are comfortably off,* have enough money to live in comfort.

com·frey /ˈkʌmfrɪ/ *n* [U] tall wild plant with rough leaves and purple or white flowers.

comfy /ˈkʌmfɪ/ *adj* (**-ier, -iest**) (colloq) comfortable.

comic /ˈkomɪk/ *adj* **1** causing people to laugh: *a ~ song;* intended to amuse: *~ strips,* strips of humorous drawings, as printed in newspapers, etc. **2** of comedy: *~ opera.* □ *n* **1** music-hall comedian. **2 the ~s,** (those pages of) periodicals, or supplements to them, with ~ drawings.

comi·cal /ˈkomɪkl/ *adj* amusing; odd: *a ~ old hat.* **~ly** /-klɪ/ *adv*

Com·in·form /ˈkomɪnfɔm/ *n* bureau set up in 1947 for exchange of information, etc among Communist countries of eastern Europe.

com·ing /ˈkʌmɪŋ/ *n* arrival: *He believes in the Second C~,* the return of Jesus Christ when the world ends. □ *adj* which is to come or which will come: *in the coming years; the coming generation.* **a ~ man,** a man who is likely to be important, famous, etc.

Com·in·tern /ˈkomɪntɜn/ *n* (third) Communist Internationalist Party of the USSR (dissolved in 1943).

com·ity /ˈkomətɪ/ *n*: *the ~ of nations,* friendly recognition, shown by one nation, of the laws, customs, etc of other nations.

comma /ˈkomə/ *n* punctuation mark (,) to indicate a slight pause or break between parts of a sentence. **in'verted '~s,** the marks (" " or ' ').

com·mand[1] /kəˈmɑnd *US:* -ˈmænd/ *vt,vi* **1** [VP6A,17A,9,2A] order (usu with the right to be obeyed): *Do as I ~ (you). The officer ~ed his men to fire. The pirate chief ~ed that the prisoners should be shot. God ~s and man obeys.* **2** [VP6A,2A] have authority over; be in control of: *The captain of a ship ~s all the officers and men. Who ~s the army? Who ~s here?* **3** [VP6A] restrain; hold back; control (the more usu word): *~ oneself/one's temper/passions.* **4** [VP6A] be in a position to use; have at one's service: *He ~s great sums of money,* is able to use them if he so wishes. *A Minister of State ~s the services of many officials.* **5** [VP6A] deserve and get: *Great men ~ our respect. He ~s the sympathy of all who have heard the story of his sufferings.* **6** [VP6A] (of a place) be in a position that overlooks (and may control): *The fort ~ed the entrance to the valley. The hill ~s a fine view,* a fine view can be obtained from the top. **~ing** *adj* that ~s: *the ~ing officer; in a ~ing tone; in a ~ing position.*

com·mand[2] /kəˈmɑnd *US:* -ˈmænd/ *n* **1** [C] order: *His ~s were quickly obeyed. Give your ~s in a loud, confident voice.* **at the word of ~,** (mil) when the ~ is given. **2** [U] authority; power (to control): *General X is in ~ of the army. The army is under the ~ of General X. He has twenty men under his ~.* **have/take ~ of,** have/take authority: *When the major was killed, the senior captain took ~ of the company.* **do sth at/by sb's ~,** on sb's authority: *It was done by the Queen's ~.* **be at sb's ~,** ready to obey: *I am at your ~,* ready to obey you. **'~ paper,** (usu abbr *Cmd,* with a number), paper laid before Parliament by Royal ~. **~ performance,** (at a theatre) one given at the request of a head of State. **3** [C] part of an army, air force, etc under separate ~: *Western C~; Bomber C~.* **4** [U] possession and mastery: *He has a good ~ of the English language,* is able to use it well. *He has no ~ over himself,* cannot control his feelings, temper, etc. *He offered me all the money at his ~,* all the money he controlled.

com·man·dant /ˌkomənˈdænt/ *n* officer in command of a fortress or other military establishment.

com·man·deer /ˌkomənˈdɪə(r)/ *vt* [VP6A] seize (horses, stores, buildings, etc) for military purposes under martial law.

com·man·der /kəˈmɑndə(r) *US:* -ˈmæn-/ *n* person in command: *the ~ of the expedition; C~, Lieu'tenant-Com'mander,* naval officers (above lieutenant and below captain); *Wing-C~,* rank in the RAF; *'~-in-'chief, ~* of all the military forces of a State, or all those in a colony, etc. ⇨ **App 9.**

com·mand·ment /kəˈmɑndmənt *US:* -ˈmænd-/ *n* divine command, esp one of the ten laws given by God to Moses. ⇨ **Exod 20: 3 7.**

com·mando /kəˈmɑndəʊ *US:* -ˈmæn-/ *n* (*pl* **-dos** or **-does**) (member of a) body of men specially picked and trained for carrying out raids and making assaults.

com·mem·or·ate /kəˈmeməreɪt/ *vt* [VP6A] keep or honour the memory of (a person or event); (of things) be in memory of: *Christmas ~s the birth of Christ. A monument was built to ~ the victory.* **com·mem·or·ative** /kəˈmemṛətɪv *US:* -ˈmeməreɪt-/ *adj* serving to ~: *commemorative stamps/medals.*

com·mem·or·ation /kəˌmeməˈreɪʃn/ *n* [U] act of commemorating: *in ~ of;* [C] (part of a) service in memory of a person or event.

com·mence /kəˈmens/ *vt,vi* [VP6A,C,2A,3A] (formal) begin; start (the more usu words). **~ment** *n* **1** beginning. **2** (in US universities, and at Cambridge and Dublin) ceremony at which degrees are conferred.

com·mend /kəˈmend/ *vt* **1** [VP6A,14] praise; speak favourably of: *~ someone upon his good manners; ~ a man to his employers. His work was highly ~ed.* **2** [VP14] **~ sth to,** entrust for safekeeping to: *~ one's soul to God.* **3** [VP14] **~ to,** (*reflex*) be to the liking of; be acceptable to: *This book does not ~ itself to me. Will the proposal ~ itself to the public?* **~able** *adj* worthy of praise. **com·men·da·tion** /ˌkomənˈdeɪʃn/ *n* [U] praise; approval.

com·men·sur·able /kəˈmenʃʊrəbl/ *adj* **~ (to/with),** that can be measured by the same standard: *Their achievements are not ~.*

com·men·sur·ate /kəˈmenʃʊrət/ *adj* **~ (to/with),** in the right proportion: *Was the pay you received ~ with the work you did?*

com·ment /ˈkoment/ *n* [C,U] opinion given briefly in speech or writing about an event, or in explanation or criticism of sth: *Have you any ~s* *to make upon my story? Her strange behaviour caused a good deal of ~*, of talk, gossip, etc. ***No ~!*** I've nothing to say on this subject. □ *vi* [VP3A] ***~ (on/upon),*** make ~s on; give opinions.

com·men·tary /ˈkoməntrɪ *US:* -terɪ/ *n* (*pl* **-ries**) **1** collection of comments, e g on a book: *a Bible ~*. **2** series of continuous comments (on an event): *a broadcast ~ on a football match.* ***a running ~,*** number of remarks following one another continuously while an event is taking place: *He kept up a running ~ on the race.* **com·men·tate** /ˈkomənteɪt/ ***~ on,*** give a ~ on. **com·men·ta·tor** /ˈkomənteɪtə(r)/ *n* eye-witness who gives a broadcast ~ on an event, e g a horse-race or football match; writer of a ~**(1)**.

com·merce /ˈkomɜs/ *n* [U] trade (esp between countries); the exchange and distribution of goods: *a Chamber of C~.*

com·mer·cial /kəˈmɜʃl/ *adj* of commerce: *~ education; ~ travellers,* persons who travel with samples of goods to obtain orders. **~ TV/radio,** financed by charges made for ~ advertising in programmes. **~ vehicles,** vans, lorries, etc, for the transport of goods. □ *n* [C] advertisement inserted in a T V or radio programme. **~·ly** /-ʃl̩ɪ/ *adv* **~·ize** /kəˈmɜʃl̩ɑɪz/ *vt* [VP6A] (try to) make money out of: *Is it wise to ~ize sport?*

com·mie /ˈkomɪ/ *n* (colloq, usu pej) communist.

com·mi·na·tion /ˈkomɪˈneɪʃn/ *n* [C,U] threatening of divine vengeance. **com·mina·tory** /ˈkomɪnətrɪ *US:* -tɔrɪ/ *adj* threatening.

com·mingle /kəˈmɪŋgl/ *vt,vi* [VP6A,2A] mingle together.

com·miser·ate /kəˈmɪzəreɪt/ *vt,vi* [VP6A,3A] ***~ (with),*** feel, say that one feels, pity for: *~ (with) a friend on his misfortunes.*

com·miser·ation /kəˈmɪzəˈreɪʃn/ *n* [C,U] (expression of) pity or sympathy (*for* sb).

com·mis·sar /ˈkomɪsɑ(r)/ *n* **1** official of the Communist Party in charge of the enforcement of party loyalty. **2** (formerly) head of a Government Department of the U S S R.

com·mis·sar·iat /ˈkomɪˈsɑrɪət/ *n* **1** (formerly) major Government Department of the U S S R. **2** (formerly) department that supplied food and other stores to troops. **3** food supply. **com·mis·sary** /ˈkomɪsrɪ *US:* -serɪ/ *n* (*pl* **-ries**) (formerly) officer responsible for supplying food to troops. **ˈ~ ˈgeneral,** head of a ~**(2)**.

com·mission /kəˈmɪʃn/ *n* **1** [U] the giving of authority to sb to act for another; [C] instance of this; [C] action or piece of business that is done: *He has secured two ~s to design buildings for a local authority.* **2** [U] performance or committing (*of* crime). **3** [U] payment to sb for selling goods, etc, rising in proportion to the results gained: *to sell goods on ~,* draw a percentage of the receipts. *He receives a ~ of 10 per cent on sales, as well as a salary.* **4** [C] official paper (called a *warrant*) giving authority; (esp) (in GB) warrant signed by the Sovereign appointing an officer in the armed services: *get/resign one's ~.* **5** [C] body of persons given the duty of making an inquiry and writing a report: *a Royal C~ to report on betting and gambling.* **6** group of people legally authorized to discharge a task. **ˈC~ of the ˈPeace,** Justices of the Peace collectively. **7** ***in ~,*** (of a warship) with crew and supplies complete; ready for sea. ***out of ~,*** kept in reserve; (fig) not working, not available. □ *vt* [VP6A,17A] give a ~ to: *~ an artist to paint a portrait; be ~ed to buy books for a friend.* **com·mis·sioned** *adj* (of officers) holding rank by ~**(4)**. ⇨ non-~ed.

com·mission·aire /kəˈmɪʃnˈeə(r)/ *n* uniformed porter at the entrance to a cinema, theatre, hotel, large shop, etc.

com·missioner /kəˈmɪʃn̩ə(r)/ *n* **1** member of a commission**(5,6)**, esp one with particular duties: *the C~s of Inland Revenue,* who control Income Tax; the Civil Service C~s, who conduct the Civil Service examinations. **2** person who has been given a commission: *a C~ for Oaths,* solicitor (given commission by the Lord Chancellor) before whom documents are sworn on oath. **3** representative of high rank: *the High C~ for Canada,* e g representing the Canadian Government in London; *the British High C~ in Accra.*

com·mit /kəˈmɪt/ *vt* (**-tt-**) **1** [VP6A] perform (a crime, foolish act, etc): *~ murder/suicide/an offence.* **2** [VP14] ***~ sb/sth (to),*** entrust, give up, hand over to, for safe keeping or treatment: *~ a prisoner for trial; ~ a man to prison; ~ a patient to a mental hospital; ~ sth to paper/to writing,* write it down. *The body was ~ted to the flames,* was cremated. ***~ to memory,*** learn by heart. **3** [VP6A,14,16A] ***~ oneself (to...),*** make oneself responsible; undertake: *He has ~ted himself to support his brother's children. He refused to ~ himself by talking about the crime,* refused to say anything because it might get him into trouble. **4** [VP6A,14] (often *reflex*) pledge; bind (oneself): *I won't ~ myself to that course of action.* ⇨ uncommitted. **~·ment** *n* [C] (esp) sth to which one has ~ted oneself**(3)**; promise: pledge; undertaking: *If you have agreed to give a number of lectures, help to pay your brother's school expenses and give your sister £100 a year for clothes, you have quite a lot of ~ments.*

com·mit·tee /kəˈmɪtɪ/ *n* group of persons appointed (usu by a larger group) to attend to special business: *to attend a ˈ~ meeting; to be/sit on the ~; a Parliamentary C~,* one appointed by the House of Commons (or Lords) to examine a Bill or to inquire into a breach of privileges; *a ~ of the whole House,* one of all the members (for constitutional and financial matters).

com·mode /kəˈməʊd/ *n* **1** chest of drawers. **2** piece of bedroom furniture to hold a chamber-pot.

com·modi·ous /kəˈməʊdɪəs/ *adj* having plenty of space for what is needed: *a ~ house/cupboard.*

com·mod·ity /kəˈmodətɪ/ *n* (*pl* **-ties**) [C] useful thing, esp an article of trade: *household commodities, e g pots and pans.*

com·mo·dore /ˈkomədɔ(r)/ *n* naval officer having rank above a captain and below a rear-admiral; president of a yacht club; senior captain of a shipping line: *the ~ of the Cunard Line; Air C~,* officer in the Air Force. ⇨ App 9.

com·mon[1] /ˈkomən/ *adj* **1** belonging to, used by, coming from, done by, affecting, all or nearly all members of a group or society: *The husband is French, the wife German, and the servant Italian, but they have English as a ~ language,* they can all use English. *It is to the ~ advantage* (= to everyone's advantage) *that street traffic should be well controlled.* **ˈ~ ˈground,** (fig) basis for argument accepted by persons in a dispute, etc. **ˈ~ ˈknowledge,** what is known to most persons, esp in a group: *It was ~ knowledge among bankers that....* Cf *general knowledge.* **ˈ~ land,** land that belongs to, or may be used by, the community, esp in a village. ⇨ **common**²**(1)**. **ˈ~ ˈlaw,** (in England) unwritten law developed from old customs, e g in Saxon and Danish times, and decisions made by judges. ⇨ *statute law* at **statute**. **~-law wife,** woman with whom a man lives, as if she were his wife, but without marrying her. **the ˈC~ ˈMarket** *n* (officially *the European Economic Community*), economic, social and political union, established in 1958 of Belgium, France, Italy, Luxembourg, the Netherlands and West Germany, since enlarged in 1973 by the inclusion of Britain, Eire and Denmark with associate membership (for economic preferences) by other countries. **a ~ nuisance,** an offence that is harmful to the community and for which there is legal remedy. ⇨ also **cause** and **prayer**. **ˈ~-room (a)** (at Oxford) Fellows' room in some colleges. **(b)** room for use of the teachers or professors at a school, college, etc, or (in some schools and colleges) of pupils or students. **2** usual and ordinary; happening or found often and in many places: *a ~ flower; a ~ experience. Pine-trees are ~ in many parts of the world. Is this word in ~ use?* **the ˈ~ ˈman/ˈpeople,** the ordinary or average citizen(s): *The ~ man in every country wants peace.* **ˈ~ ˈsense,** practical good sense gained by experience of life, not by special study. **3** (of persons, their behaviour and possessions) vulgar; of inferior quality or taste: *~ manners; speak with a ~ accent; a girl who looks ~/who wears ~ clothes.* **4** (maths) belonging to two or more quantities: *~ factor/multiple.* **ˈ~ ˈnoun,** (gram) name that can be used for any member of a class, e g *book* or *knife; ~ gender,* masculine or feminine; (music) *~ time/measure,* two or four beats in a bar; *~ metre,* hymn stanza of 4 lines, with 8, 6, 8, 6 syllables. **~·ly** *adv* **1** usually: *That very ~ly happens. Thomas, ~ly called Tom.* **2** in a **~(3)** way: *~ly dressed.*

com·mon² /ˈkomən/ *n* **1** [C] area (usu in or near a village) of unfenced grassland for all to use: *Saturday afternoon cricket on the village ~.* **2** [U] ***right of ~,*** right (of a person, parish, etc) to use land: *The parish has right of ~ in the forest.* **3 *out of the ~,*** unusual. ***in ~,*** for or by all (of a group). ***have in ~ (with),*** share (with): *They have nothing in ~ with one another,* have no similar interests, etc. *In ~ with* (= Like) *many people he prefers classical music to pop.*

com·mon·alty /ˈkomənltɪ/ *n* **the ~,** the common people (contrasted with the upper classes).

com·moner /ˈkomənə(r)/ *n* one of the common people, not a member of the nobility.

com·mon·place /ˈkomənpleɪs/ *adj* ordinary or usual: *a ~ kind of man.* □ *n* remark, event, etc that is ordinary or usual: *conversation full of mere ~s. Travel by air is now a ~.*

com·mons /ˈkomənz/ *n pl* **1** (old use) the common people. ⇨ **aristocracy, nobility. the ˈHouse of ˈC~,** assembly (lower house) of those elected by the common people. **2** provisions shared in common. ***be on short ~,*** not have enough to eat.

com·mon·wealth /ˈkomənwelθ/ *n* **1** State; group of States (e g *the C~ of Australia*) associating politically for their common good. **2 the C~,** a free association of sovereign independent states (formerly colonies and dominions of GB) with their dependencies.

com·mo·tion /kəˈməʊʃn/ *n* [U] noisy confusion; excitement; [C] instance of this; violent uprising or disturbance: *You're making a great ~ about nothing.*

com·mu·nal /ˈkomjʊnl/ *adj* **1** of or for a community: *~ disturbances,* e g in countries were there are antagonisms between people of different races and religions. **2** for common use: *~ land/kitchens.*

com·mune¹ /kəˈmjun/ *vi* [VP2C,3A] **~ *(with/together),*** feel at one with; feel, be, in close touch with; talk with in an intimate way: *~ with nature/one's friends/God in prayer; friends communing together.*

com·mune² /ˈkomjun/ *n* **1** (in France, Belgium, Italy, Spain) smallest territorial district for purposes of administration, with a mayor and council. **2** organized group of people promoting local interests. **3** group of people living together and sharing property and responsibilities.

com·muni·cable /kəˈmjunɪkəbl/ *adj* (of ideas, illness, etc) that can be communicated or imparted.

com·muni·cant /kəˈmjunɪkənt/ *n* **1** one who (regularly) receives Holy Communion. **2** informer (the more usu word).

com·muni·cate /kəˈmjunɪkeɪt/ *vt, vi* **1** [VP6A,14] **~ *sth (to),*** pass on (news, information, feelings, heat, motion, an illness, etc). **2** [VP3A] **~ *with,*** share or exchange (news, etc): *We can ~ with people in most parts of the world by telephone. Young people sometimes complain of not being able to ~ with their parents.* **3** [VP2A,3A] **~ *(with),*** (of rooms, gardens, roads, etc) be connected: *My garden ~s with the garden next door by means of a gate. We asked the hotel to let us have communicating rooms,* rooms with a connecting door.

com·muni·ca·tion /kəˈmjunɪˈkeɪʃn/ *n* **1** [U] the act of communicating: *Among the deaf and dumb ~ may be carried on by means of the finger alphabet. Spitting in public places may lead to the ~ of disease. I am/must get into ~ with him on this subject.* **2** [C] that which is communicated (e g news): *This ~ is confidential.* **3** [C,U] means of communicating; roads, railways, telephone or telegraph lines connecting places, radio and TV: *a world ~s network; ~ satellites; mass ~s media. Telegraphic ~/~s between Amman and Baghdad has/have been restored. All ~ with the north has been stopped by snowstorms.* **ˈ~ cord,** cord that passes along the length of a train inside the coaches, to be pulled (to stop the train) in an emergency.

com·muni·cat·ive /kəˈmjunɪkətɪv *US:* -keɪtɪv/ *adj* ready and willing to talk and give information. ⇨ *reserved* at **reserve**¹.

com·mu·nion /kəˈmjunɪən/ *n* **1** [U] sharing in common; participation (*with*). **2** [U] exchange of thought and feelings; intercourse. ***hold ~ with oneself,*** think deeply (esp about moral or religious problems). **self-~,** thinking about oneself. **3** [C] group of persons with the same religious beliefs: *We belong to the same ~.* **4 Holy C~,** (in the Christian Church) celebration of the Lord's Supper. ***go to C~,*** attend church for this celebration.

com·mu·nique /kəˈmjunɪkeɪ/ *n* official announcement, e g as issued to the press.

com·mu·nism /ˈkomjʊnɪzm/ *n* [U] **1** (belief in a) social system in which property is owned by the community and used for the good of all its members. **2** (usu **C~**) political and social system (as in

USSR) in which all power is held by the highest members of the Communist Party, which controls the land and its resources, the means of production, transport, etc, and directs the activities of the people. **com·mu·nist** /ˈkomjʊnɪst/ *n* believer in, supporter of, ~. □ *adj* of ~.

com·mun·ity /kəˈmjunətɪ/ *n* (*pl* -ties) **1** (with *def art*) the people living in one place, district or country, considered as a whole: *work for the good of the* ~. ~ **centre,** building(s), etc where people meet for adult education classes, amateur dramatics, informal social intercourse, etc. ~ **chest,** (US) welfare fund for helping people in distress. **2** [C] group of persons having the same religion, race, occupation, etc or with common interests: *a* ~ *of monks; the Jewish* ~ *in London; the European* ~ *in Karachi.* **3** [U] condition of sharing, having things in common, being alike in some way: ~ *of race/religion/interests.* ~ **singing,** organized singing in which all present take part.

com·mut·able /kəˈmjutəbl/ *adj* that can be exchanged or compounded for. ⇨ compound[2](2).

com·mu·ta·tion /ˈkomjʊˈteɪʃn/ *n* **1** [U] commuting; making one kind of payment instead of another, e g money instead of service. **2** [C] payment made in this way. **3** [C] reduced punishment: *a* ~ *of the death sentence to life imprisonment.* **4** ~ **ticket,** (US) = (GB) season ticket.

com·mu·ta·tor /ˈkomjʊteɪtə(r)/ *n* device for altering the direction of an electric current.

com·mute /kəˈmjut/ *vt,vi* **1** [VP6A,14] ~ ***sth (into/for),*** exchange one thing (esp one kind of payment) for another: ~ *one's pension;* ~ *an annuity into/for a lump sum.* **2** [VP6A,14] reduce the severity of a punishment: ~ *a death sentence (to one of life imprisonment).* **3** [VP3A] travel regularly, e g by train or car, between one's work in a town and one's home in the country or suburbs. **com·muter** *n* person who ~s(3).

com·pact[1] /ˈkompækt/ *n* agreement between parties; contract; covenant.

com·pact[2] /kəmˈpækt/ *adj* closely packed together; neatly fitted; (of literary style) condensed. □ *vt* (usu passive) join firmly together. **~·ly** *adv* **~·ness** *n*

com·pact[3] /ˈkompækt/ *n* small, flat container for face-powder (and often with a mirror), made for carrying in a woman's handbag.

com·pan·ion[1] /kəmˈpænɪən/ *n* **1** person who goes with, or is often or always with, another: *my* ~*s on the journey.* **2** person who shares in the work, pleasures, misfortunes, etc of another: ~*s in arms,* fellow soldiers; ~*s in misfortune,* associated in it; *a faithful* ~ *of 50 years,* e g a man speaking of his wife. **3** person with similar tastes, interests, etc: *He's an excellent* ~. *His brother is not much of a* ~ *for him.* **4** one of two things that go together; thing that matches another or is one of a pair: *Here's the glove for my left hand, but where's the* ~? (also attrib): *the* ~ *volume.* **5** woman paid to keep another (usu old or ill) person company. **6** handbook or reference book: *the Gardener's C*~. **7** **C~,** member of some Orders: *C*~ *of the Bath.* ⇨ **order**[1](10). **~·able** *adj* friendly; sociable. **~·ship** /-ʃɪp/ *n* state of being ~s: *enjoy sb's* ~*ship; a* ~*ship of many years.*

com·pan·ion[2] /kəmˈpænɪən/ *n* (usu **~·way**) staircase from the deck of a ship to the saloon or cabins.

com·pany /ˈkʌmpənɪ/ *n* **1** [U] being together with another or others: *I shall be glad of your* ~ (= to have you with me) *on the journey.* ***be good/poor/bad/excellent, etc*** **~,** be a good, etc, companion(3). ***for*** **~,** to provide companionship: *I'll go with you as far as the station for* ~. ***in*** **~ *(with),*** together (with): *He came in* ~ *with a group of boys. We went in* ~. **keep ~ *(with)* sb,** be or go with him: *He stayed at home to keep his wife* ~. **keep ~ *(with),*** (older use) be friendly (with) (esp sb of the other sex, as an admirer). **part ~ *(with),*** separate; leave: *I was sorry to part* ~ *with such a pleasant fellow. It's sad that we have to part* ~. **2** [U] group of persons; number of guests: *I sin in good* ~, Better men have done what I have done. *We're expecting* ~ (= guests, visitors) *next week. He's not well enough to receive a great deal of* ~, many visitors. ˈ~ **manners,** behaviour of unusual politeness used in the presence of visitors. **3** [U] persons with whom one spends one's time: *You may know a man by the* ~ *he keeps,* judge his character by his friends. *Don't keep/get into bad* ~, Don't mix with, become friendly with, bad persons. **4** [C] (*pl* -nies) number of persons united for business or commerce: *a steamship* ~. **a ˈLimited ˈLiaˈbility C~,** partner(s) not named in the title of a firm: *ˈT ˈS ˋSmith & Co.* **5** number of persons working together: *a* ~ *of players,* actors who perform plays together; a theatrical ~; the ship's ~, the crew. **6** subdivision of an infantry battalion, commanded by a captain or major.

com·par·able /ˈkomprəbl/ *adj* ~ ***to/with,*** that can be compared: *The sets of figures are not* ~. *His achievements are* ~ *with the best.*

com·para·tive /kəmˈpærətɪv/ *adj* **1** having to do with comparison or comparing: *the* ~ *method of studying,* i e by finding out what is similar and different in two or more branches of knowledge; ~ *religion;* ~ *linguistics.* **2** measured or judged by comparing: *living in* ~ *comfort,* e g comfortably compared with others, or with one's own life at an earlier period. **3** (gram) form of adjectives and adverbs expressing 'more', as in *worse, more likely, more prettily.* □ *n* ~ degree: *'Better' is the* ~ *of 'good'.* **~·ly** *adv*

com·pare /kəmˈpeə(r)/ *vt,vi* **1** [VP6A,14] ~ ***sb/sth (with),*** examine, judge to what extent persons or things are similar or not similar: ~ *two translations;* ~ *your translation with the model translation on the blackboard.* ~ **notes,** exchange observations, ideas or opinions. **2** [VP14] ~ ***sb/sth to,*** point out the likeness or relation between: *Poets have* ~*d sleep to death. Mine cannot be* ~*d to yours,* is quite different. **3** [VP3A] ~ ***with,*** bear comparison: *He cannot* ~ *with Shakespeare as a writer of tragedies,* is not nearly so great. *This cannot* ~ *with that,* no comparison is possible because they are so different. **4** (gram) form the comparative and superlative degrees (of adjectives and adverbs). □ *n* comparison (but only in) ***beyond/past/without*** **~**: *She is lovely beyond* ~, so lovely that none can be ~d to her.

com·pari·son /kəmˈpærɪsn/ *n* **1** [U] ***by/in*** **~ *(with),*** when compared (with): *This one costs more but is cheaper by/in* ~, is plainly better value when you compare them and examine the quality, etc. *The tallest buildings in London are small in* ~ *with those of New York.* **the ~ of X**

and/with Y, the act of comparing: *the ~ of texts.* **2** [C] ***a ~ between X and Y/of X to Y,*** an act of comparing; an instance of this: *It is often useful to make a ~ between two things. The ~ of the heart to a pump/between the heart and a pump has often been made. There's no ~ between them,* They cannot be compared, one being clearly much better than the other. **3** ***bear/stand ~ with,*** be able to be compared favourably with: *That's a good dictionary, but it won't/can't stand ~ with this.* **4** ***degrees of ~,*** (gram) position, comparative and superlative (of adjectives and adverbs), e g *good, better, best.*

com·part·ment /kəmˋpɑtmənt/ *n* one of several separate divisions of a structure, esp of a railway carriage or coach: *The first-class ~s are in front. The ship's hold is built in watertight ~s.* **com·part·men·tal·ize** /ˈkompɑtˋmentḷɑɪz/ *vt* divide into ~s or categories.

com·pass[1] /ˋkʌmpəs/ *n* **1** device with a needle that points to the magnetic north: *the points of the ~* (N, NE, E, SE, S, SW, W, NW, etc); similar device, e g *a radio ~*, for determining direction. **2** (*pl*) **(a 'pair of) ˋ~es,** V-shaped instrument with two arms joined by a hinge, used for drawing circles, measuring distances on a map or chart, etc. **3** extent; range: *beyond the ~ of the human mind; outside the ~* (= range) *of her voice; in a small ~.*

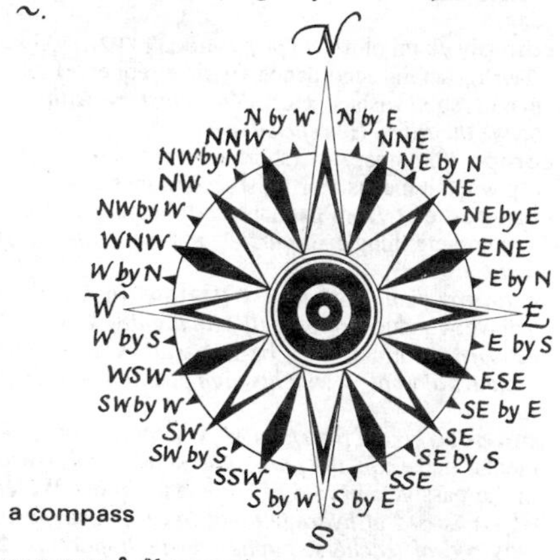

a compass

com·pass[2] /ˋkʌmpəs/ *vt* = encompass (the more usu word).

com·passion /kəmˋpæʃn/ *n* [U] pity; feeling for the sufferings of others, prompting one to give help: *have/take ~ on sufferers; be filled with ~ for the refugees; look at someone in/with ~; give a man money out of ~.* **~·ate** /kəmˋpæʃn̩ət/ *adj* showing or feeling ~: *The soldier was granted ~ate leave,* given leave(1), e g because personal affairs made necessary his presence at home.

com·pat·ible /kəmˋpætəbl/ *adj* ***~ (with),*** (of ideas, arguments, principles, etc) suited to, in accord with, able to exist together with: *pleasure ~ with duty; driving a car at a speed ~ with safety.* **com·pat·ibly** /-əblɪ/ *adv* **com·pati·bil·ity** /kəmˈpætəˋbɪlətɪ/ *n* [U] the state of being ~.

com·patriot /kəmˋpætrɪət *US:* -ˋpeɪt-/ *n* person born in or citizen of the same country as another; fellow-countryman.

com·peer /ˋkompɪə(r)/ *n* person equal in rank or capacity.

com·pel /komˋpel/ *vt* (-ll-) **1** [VP17] ***~ sb/sth to do sth,*** force (sb or sth to do sth); get, bring about, by force: *His conscience ~led him to confess. He was ~led by illness to resign.* **2** [VP14, 6A] ***~ (from),*** obtain by pressure: *Can they ~ obedience from us,* force us to obey?

com·pen·di·ous /kəmˋpendɪəs/ *adj* (of authors, books, etc) giving much information briefly.

com·pen·dium /kəmˋpendɪəm/ *n* concise and comprehensive account; summary.

com·pen·sate /ˋkompənseɪt/ *vt,vi* [VP6A,14,3A] ***~ (sb) (for sth),*** make a suitable payment, give something to make up (*for* loss, injury, etc): *Do employers in your country ~ workers for injuries suffered at their work? Nothing can ~ for the loss of one's health.* **com·pen·sa·tory** /kəmˋpensətərɪ *US:* -tɔrɪ/ *adj* compensating.

com·pen·sa·tion /ˈkompənˋseɪʃn/ *n* [U,C] compensating; sth given to compensate: *He received £5000 in ~/by way of ~ for the loss of his right hand.*

com·père /ˋkompeə(r)/ *n* (F) organizer of a cabaret or broadcast entertainment who introduces the performers, speakers, etc. □ *vt* act as ~ for.

com·pete /kəmˋpit/ *vi* [VP2A,3A] take part in a race, contest, examination, etc: *to ~ in a race* (*with others, for a prize, for the first place,* etc); *to ~ against/with other countries in trade.*

com·pet·ence /ˋkompɪtəns/ *n* **1** [U] being competent; ability: *his ~ in handling money/to handle money.* **2** (usu *sing* with *indef art*) income large enough for a person to live on in comfort: *have/enjoy a small ~.* **3** (of a court, a magistrate) legal capacity: *business that is within/beyond the ~ of the court.*

com·pet·ent /ˋkompɪtənt/ *adj* **1** (of persons) having ability, power, authority, skill, knowledge, etc (to do what is needed): *Is Miss X ~ in her work/~ as a teacher/~ to teach French?* **2** (of qualities) sufficient, adequate: *Has she a ~ knowledge of French?* **~·ly** *adv*

com·pe·ti·tion /ˈkompəˋtɪʃn/ *n* **1** [U] competing; activity in which persons compete: *trade ~ between countries; keen ~ for positions in commerce. At the Olympic Games our representatives were in ~* (= were competing) *with the best swimmers from all parts of the world.* **2** [C] instance of competing; contest; meeting(s) at which skill, strength, knowledge, etc is tested: *boxing/chess ~s.*

com·peti·tive /kəmˋpetətɪv/ *adj* in or for which there is competition: *~ examinations for government posts. Our firm offers you ~ prices,* prices that compete with those of other firms.

com·peti·tor /kəmˋpetɪtə(r)/ *n* person who competes.

com·pile /kəmˋpɑɪl/ *vt* [VP6A] collect (information) and arrange (in a book, list, report, etc): *~ a dictionary/a guide book/an index.* **com·piler** *n* **com·pi·la·tion** /ˈkompɪˋleɪʃn/ *n* [U] compiling: [C] thing that is ~d.

com·placence /kəmˋpleɪsns/ *n* [U] self-satisfaction; quiet contentment. **com·placency** /-ˋpleɪsnsɪ/ *n*

com·placent /kəmˋpleɪsnt/ *adj* self-satisfied: *with a ~ smile/air.* **~·ly** *adv*

com·plain /kəmˋpleɪn/ *vi* [VP2A,3A,B] ***~ (to sb) (about/of sth),*** say that one is not satisfied, that sth is wrong, that one is suffering: *She ~ed to me of his rudeness/that he had been rude to her. We have nothing to ~ of/about. He never ~s of not* *having enough work.* **~·ing·ly** *adv*

com·plain·ant /kəm`pleɪnənt/ *n* (legal) plaintiff.

com·plaint /kəm`pleɪnt/ *n* **1** [U] complaining: [C] statement of, grounds for, dissatisfaction: *You have no cause/grounds of ~. Have you any ~s to make? Some children are full of ~s about their food. Why don't you lodge a ~ against your noisy neighbours?* **2** [C] illness; disease: *a heart/liver ~; childish ~s,* illnesses common among children.

com·plais·ance /kəm`pleɪzns/ *n* [U] easy-going habit of mind; readiness and willingness to do what pleases others: *do sth out of ~.* **com·plais·ant** /-znt/ *adj* obliging; disposed to please: *a complaisant wife.*

com·ple·ment /`komplɪmənt/ *n* **1** that which makes sth complete; the full number or quality needed: *the ship's ~,* the full number of officers and men. **2** (gram) word(s) esp *adjj* and *nn,* used after *vv* such as *be* and *become* and qualifying the subject. □ *vt* [VP6A] complete; form the ~ to.

com·ple·men·tary /'komplə`mentrɪ/ *adj* serving to complete: *~ colours,* making white or grey when mixed; *~ angles,* together making up 90°; *two books that are ~ to one another.*

com·plete[1] /kəm`plit/ *adj* **1** having all its parts; whole: *a ~ edition of Shakespeare's plays.* **2** finished; ended: *When will the work be ~?* **3** thorough; in every way: *He's a ~ stranger to me. It was a ~ surprise to me,* I wasn't expecting it and hadn't even thought of it. **4** (rather archaic, of persons) accomplished; skilful: *He's a ~ horseman.* **~·ly** *adv* wholly; in every way: *~ly successful.* **~·ness** *n*

com·plete[2] /kəm`plit/ *vt* [VP6A] finish; bring to an end; make perfect: *The railway is not ~d yet. This ~s my happiness. I need one volume to ~ my set of Dickens.*

com·ple·tion /kəm`pliʃn/ *n* [U] act of completing; state of being complete: *You may occupy the house on ~ of contract,* when the contract of sale has been completed.

com·plex[1] /`kompleks *US:* 'kom`pleks/ *adj* made up of closely connected parts; difficult to understand or explain: *a ~ argument/proposal/situation; a ~ system of government; a ~ sentence,* (gram) one containing subordinate clauses. **~·ity** /kəm`pleksətɪ/ *n* [U] state of being ~; [C] (*pl* -ties) sth that is ~.

com·plex[2] /`kompleks/ *n* [C] complex whole; number of dissimilar parts intricately related; (psych) (abnormal) mental state which is the result of past experiences or suppressed tendencies; (colloq) obsessive concern or fear: *have a ~ about sth.* ⇨ *inferiority* at inferior, *superiority* at superior.

com·plexion /kəm`plekʃn/ *n* [C] **1** natural colour, appearance, etc of the skin, esp of the face: *a good/dark/fair ~.* **2** general character or aspect (of conduct, affairs, etc): *This victory changed the ~ of the war,* made the probable outcome different, gave hope of an early end, etc.

com·pli·ance /kəm`plaɪəns/ *n* [U] **1** action of complying: *in ~ with your wishes,* as you wish(ed) us (to do). **2** tendency to give way to others; unworthy submission.

com·pli·ant /kəm`plaɪənt/ *adj* ready to comply.

com·pli·cate /`komplɪkeɪt/ *vt* [VP6A] make complex; make (sth) difficult to do or understand: *This ~s matters.* **com·pli·cated** *adj* made up of many parts: *a ~d machine; ~d business deals.*

com·pli·ca·tion /'komplɪ`keɪʃn/ *n* [C] **1** state of being complex, confused, difficult; sth that adds new difficulties: *Here are further ~s to worry us.* **2** (med) new illness, or new development of an illness, that makes treatment more difficult: *influenza with ~s; if no ~s set in.*

com·plic·ity /kəm`plɪsətɪ/ *n* [U] **~ (in),** taking part with another person (in crime or other wrongdoing).

com·pli·ment /`komplɪmənt/ *n* [C] **1** expression of admiration, approval, etc, either in words or by action, e g by asking sb for his advice or opinions, or by imitating him. ***pay sb a ~/pay a ~ to sb (on sth)***: *They paid me a well-deserved ~.* **2** (*pl*) greetings: *My ~s to your wife,* Please give her a greeting from me. *With the ~s of the season,* phrase used at Christmas and the New Year. *With the author's/publisher's ~s,* phrase used when an author/publisher sends a gift of a book newly issued. □ *vi* /`komplɪment/ [VP6A,14] ***~ sb (on sth),*** pay a ~ to: *I ~ed him on his skill.*

com·pli·men·tary /'komplɪ`mentrɪ/ *adj* **1** expressing admiration, praise, etc. **2** given free, out of courtesy or kindness: *a ~ ticket/copy of a book, etc.*

com·plin, com·pline /`komplɪn/ *n* (in RC and Anglo-Catholic ritual) last (church) service of the day.

com·ply /kəm`plaɪ/ *vt* (*pt,pp* -lied) [VP2A,3A] ***~ (with),*** act in accordance (with a request, command, sb's wishes, etc): *You must ~ with* (= obey) *the rules. He refused to ~.*

compo /`kompəʊ/ *n* (short for) composition(**4**), esp when it means mortar, stucco or plaster.

com·po·nent /kəm`pəʊnənt/ *adj* helping to form (a complete thing): *~ parts.* □ *n* ~ part: *the ~s of a camera lens.*

com·port /kəm`pɔt/ *vt,vi* **1** [VP15A] (usu *reflex*) behave; conduct: *~ oneself with dignity.* **2** [VP3A] ***~ with,*** (formal) suit, be in harmony with: *His conduct did not ~ with his high position.* **~·ment** *n*

com·pose /kəm`pəʊz/ *vt,vi* **1** [VP6A] (of elements) make up: *the parts that ~ the whole;* (usu in the passive): be ~d of, be made up of: *Water* (H_2O) *is ~d of hydrogen and oxygen. Our party was ~d of teachers, pupils and their parents.* **2** [VP6A,2A] put together (words, ideas, musical notes, etc) in literary, musical, etc, form: *~ a poem/a song/an opera/a speech. He teaches music and also ~s,* writes music. **3** [VP6A] (printing) set up (type) to form words, paragraphs, pages, etc. ⇨ compositor. **4** [VP6A,16A] get under control; calm: *~ one's thoughts/passions. She ~d herself to answer the letter. Try to ~ your features,* make yourself look calm. **5** [VP6A] settle; bring to an end: *~ a quarrel/dispute.* **com·posed** *adj* calm; with feelings under control. **com·posed·ly** /-ɪdlɪ/ *adv* in a ~d manner.

com·poser /kəm`pəʊzə(r)/ *n* (esp) person who composes music.

com·pos·ite /`kompəzɪt/ *adj* made up of different parts or materials: *a ~ illustration,* made by putting together two or more drawings, etc.

com·po·si·tion /'kompə`zɪʃn/ *n* **1** [U] act or art of composing, e g a piece of writing or music, type for printing, objects for a picture: *He played a piano sonata of his own ~,* that he himself had composed. **2** [C] that which is composed, e g a poem, a book, a piece of music, an arrangement of objects to be painted or photographed; (esp) exercise in writing by one who is learning a language. **3** [U] the parts of which sth is made up: *Scientists study the ~ of the soil. He has a touch of madness in his ~*, There is an element of madness in him. **4** [C] substance composed of more than one material, esp an artificial substance: *~ floors.*

com·posi·tor /kəm`pozɪtə(r)/ *n* skilled person who composes type for printing.

com·pos men·tis /'kompəs `mentɪs/ *adj* (Lat) in one's right mind: *He's not quite ~*, is a little mad.

com·post /`kompost/ *n* [U] prepared mixture, esp of rotted organic matter, manure, etc, for use in horticulture. □ *vt* [VP6A] make into ~; treat with ~.

com·po·sure /kəm`pəʊʒə(r)/ *n* [U] condition of being composed in mind; calmness (of mind or behaviour): *behave with great ~.*

com·pote /`kompəʊt/ *n* [C,U] (dish of) fruit cooked with sugar and water.

com·pound[1] /`kompaʊnd/ *n, adj* **1** [C] (sth) made up of two or more combined parts: *Common salt is a ~ of sodium and chlorine.* **2** (gram) word composed of two or more parts, themselves usu words, e g *long-legged.* **'~ `sentence,** one containing two or more coordinate clauses (linked by *and, but,* etc). **3 '~ `interest,** interest on capital and on accumulated interest. **'~ `fracture,** breaking of a bone complicated by an open wound in the skin.

com·pound[2] /kəm`paʊnd/ *vt,vi* **1** [VP6A] mix together (to make sth new or different): *~ a medicine; a cake ~ed of the best ingredients.* **2** [VP6A,2A] **~ *(with sb) (for sth),*** settle (a quarrel, a debt) by mutual concession. **3** [VP3A] come to terms: *He ~ed with his creditors for a remission of what he owed.* **4** [VP6A] add to, increase (an offence or injury) by causing another: *That simply ~s the offence.*

com·pound[3] /`kompaʊnd/ *n* enclosed area with buildings, etc, e g a number of houses; (in India or China) a commercial or trading centre; an area for prisoners of war.

com·pre·hend /'komprɪ`hend/ *vt* [VP6A] **1** understand fully. **2** include.

com·pre·hen·sible /'komprɪ`hensəbl/ *adj* that can be understood fully: *a book that is ~ only to specialists.* **com·pre·hen·si·bil·ity** /'komprɪ'hensə`bɪlətɪ/ *n*

com·pre·hen·sion /'komprɪ`henʃn/ *n* [U] **1** the mind's act or power of understanding: *The problem is above/beyond my ~.* **2** [C,U] exercise aimed at improving or testing one's understanding of a language (written or spoken). **3** power of including: *a term of wide ~*, that includes many meanings, uses, etc.

com·pre·hen·sive /'komprɪ`hensɪv/ *adj* that comprehends(2) much: *a ~ description/review of the term's work, etc; a man with a ~ mind/grasp of ideas.* **`~ (school),** large school that combines all types of secondary education, i e grammar school, secondary modern and technical. **~·ly** *adv* **~·ness** *n*

com·press[1] /kəm`pres/ *vt* [VP6A,14] **1** press together; get into a small(er) space: *~ed air; ~ cotton into bales.* **2** put (ideas, etc) into fewer words; condense: *the poet ~ed many thoughts and emotions into a few well-chosen words.*

com·press[2] /`kompres/ *n* pad or cloth pressed on to a part of the body (to stop bleeding, reduce fever, etc): *a cold/hot ~.*

com·pression /kəm`preʃn/ *n* [U] compressing; being compressed: *~ of ideas.*

com·prise /kəm`praɪz/ *vt* [VP6A] be composed of; have as parts or members: *The committee ~s men of widely different views. The force ~d two battalions and a battery.*

com·pro·mise /`komprəmaɪz/ *n* [U] settlement of a dispute by which each side gives up sth it has asked for and neither side gets all it has asked for; [C] instance of this; settlement reached in this way: *The strike was not ended until they resorted to ~. A ~ agreement was at last arrived at. Can we effect a ~?* □ *vt,vi* **1** [VP6A,2A] settle a dispute, etc, by making a ~: *if they agree to ~.* **2** bring (sb, sth, oneself) under suspicion by unwise behaviour, etc: *You will ~ yourself/your reputation if you spend much time with these rogues.* **3** imperil the safety of (by folly or rashness, etc): *The position of the army was ~d by the general's poor judgement.*

comp·tom·eter /'komp`tomɪtə(r)/ *n* (P) calculating machine.

comp·trol·ler /kən`trəʊlə(r)/ *n* (in some titles) controller: *~ of accounts.*

com·pul·sion /kəm`pʌlʃn/ *n* [U] compelling or being compelled. ***under ~,*** because one must: *A defeated country usually signs a treaty of peace under ~.*

com·pul·sive /kəm`pʌlsɪv/ *adj* having a tendency or the power to compel; caused by an obsession: *a ~ eater/T V viewer,* one who feels compelled to eat/watch T V; *a ~ liar,* one who lies repeatedly. **~·ly** *adv*

com·pul·sory /kəm`pʌlsṛɪ/ *adj* that must be done; required: *Is military service ~ in your country? Is English a ~ subject?* **com·pul·sor·ily** /kəm`pʌlsṛlɪ/ *adv*

com·punc·tion /kəm`pʌŋkʃn/ *n* [U] uneasiness of conscience; feeling of regret for one's action: *She kept me waiting without the slightest ~.*

com·pu·ta·tion /'kompjʊ`teɪʃn/ *n* [U] computing; [C] result of computing; calculation: *It will cost £5 000 at the lowest ~. He has wealth beyond ~. Addition and division are forms of ~.*

com·pute /kəm`pjut/ *vt,vi* [VP6A,14,2A] reckon; calculate: *He ~d his losses at £50. What is the ~d horse-power of the engine?*

com·puter /kəm`pjutə(r)/ *n* electronic device which stores information on discs or magnetic tape, analyses it and produces information as required from the data on the tapes, etc. **~·ize** *vt* [VP6A] store (information) with or in a ~ or system of ~s; supply with a ~ or ~s.

com·rade /`komreɪd *US:* -ræd/ *n* **1** trusted companion; loyal friend: *~s in arms,* fellow soldiers; *~s in exile,* those who are exiled together. **2** fellow member of a trade union, a (left-wing) political party, etc. **~·ly** /`komrɪdlɪ/ *adv* **~·ship** /`komrɪdʃɪp/ *n*

con[1] /kon/ *vt* (-nn-) [VP2A,C] **~ *(over),*** learn by heart; study.

con[2] /kon/ *adv* ***pro and con,*** for and against: *argue pro and con for hours.* □ *n **the pros and cons,*** the arguments for and against.

con[3] /kon/ short for *confidence,* in attrib uses (sl): *a `con man; the `con game.* ⇨ **confidence(1).** □ *vt* (-nn-) [VP6A,14] **~ *sb (into doing sth),*** (colloq) swindle him after winning his confidence; persuade him to do sth in this way.

con·cat·ena·tion /ˈkonˌkætɪˋneɪʃn/ *n* [U] linking together; [C] series of things or events linked together.

con·cave /ˋkoŋkeɪv/ *adj* (of an outline or surface) curved inwards like the inner surface of a sphere or ball: *~ mirrors/lenses.* **con·cav·ity** /ˈkonˋkævətɪ/ *n* [U] ~ condition; [C] (*pl* -ties) ~ surface.

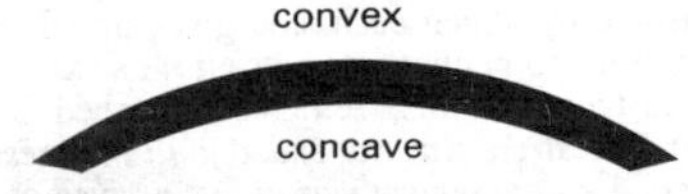

con·ceal /kənˋsil/ *vt* [VP6A,14] hide; keep secret: *~ sth from sb. He tried to ~ the fact that.... C~ed turning,* (as a road sign) warning that a turning into a road is hidden from view, e g by bushes or trees. **~·ment** *n* of ~ing; state of being ~ed: *stay in ~ment until the danger has passed.*

con·cede /kənˋsid/ *vt* [VP6A,9,13A,12A] ***~ sth (to sb),*** admit; grant; allow: *~ a point in an argument. He ~d ten points to his opponent/~d him ten points,* i e in a game. *They have ~d us the right to cross their land. You must ~ that I have tried hard. We cannot ~ any of our territory,* allow another country to have it.

con·ceit /kənˋsit/ *n* **1** [U] over-high opinion of, too much pride in, oneself or one's powers, abilities, etc: *He's full of ~.* ***(wise) in one's own ~,*** in one's own judgement. ***out of ~ with,*** (dated) no longer pleased with. **2** [C] humorous or witty thought or expression. **~ed** *adj* full of ~. **~·ed·ly** /-ɪdlɪ/ *adv*

con·ceive /kənˋsiv/ *vt,vi* **1** [VP6A,10,3A,9,14] ***~ (of),*** form (an idea, plan, etc) in the mind: *Who first ~d the idea of filling bags with gas to make balloons? I can't ~ why you allowed/can't ~ of your allowing the child to travel alone. I ~d that there must be some difficulties. Why have you ~d such a dislike for me?* **2** [VP2A,6A] (of a woman) become pregnant: *~ a child.* **con·ceiv·able** *adj* that can be ~d or believed: *It is hardly conceivable (to me) that....* **con·ceiv·ably** /-əblɪ/ *adv*

con·cen·trate /ˋkonsntreɪt/ *vt,vi* **1** [VP6A,14,2A] bring or come together at one point: *to ~ soldiers in a town. The troops were ordered to scatter and then ~ twenty miles to the south.* **2** [VP14,3A] ***~ on/upon,*** focus one's attention on: *You should ~ (your attention) (up)on your work. You'll solve the problem if you ~ upon it,* give all your attention to it. **3** [VP6A] increase the strength of (a solution) by reducing its volume (e g by boiling it). □ *n* product made by concentrating(3). **con·cen·trated** *adj* **1** intense: *~d hate; ~d fire,* the firing of guns all aimed at one point. **2** increased in strength or value by evaporation of liquid: *a ~d solution; ~d food.*

con·cen·tra·tion /ˈkonsnˋtreɪʃn/ *n* **1** [C] that which is concentrated: *~s of enemy troops.* **2** [U] concentrating or being concentrated: *a book that requires great ~; a child with little power of ~.* **~ camp,** place where civilian political prisoners or internees are brought together and confined.

con·cen·tric /kənˋsentrɪk/ *adj* ***~ (with),*** (of circles) having a common centre.

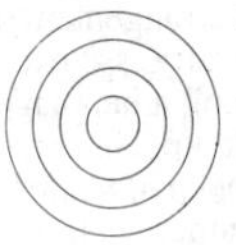
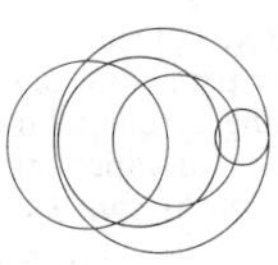

concentric circles   circles not concentric

con·cept /ˋkonsept/ *n* [C] idea underlying a class of things; general notion.

con·cep·tion /kənˋsepʃn/ *n* **1** [U] conceiving of an idea or plan; [C] idea or plan that takes shape in the mind: *A good novelist needs great powers of ~. I have no ~ of what you mean. An actor must have a clear ~ of the part he is to play.* **2** conceiving(2). **ˋ~ control,** more precise, but less common, term for *birth-control.*

con·cern[1] /kənˋsɜn/ *vt* **1** [VP6A] have relation to; affect; be of importance to: *Does this ~ me? Don't trouble about things that don't ~ you. He is said to have been ~ed in the crime,* to have had some connection with it. *So/As far as I'm ~ed...,* so far as the matter is important to me, or affects me.... *Where the children are ~ed...,* in matters where it is necessary to think of them.... ***as ~s,*** regarding. **2** [VP14] ***~ oneself with/in/about,*** be busy with, interest oneself in. **3** [VP6A] make unhappy or troubled: *Don't let my illness ~ you.* (esp in the passive): *Please don't be ~ed about me. We are all ~ed for/about her safety.* **~·ing** *prep* about.

con·cern[2] /kənˋsɜn/ *n* **1** [C] relation or connection; sth in which one is interested or which is important to one: *It's no ~ of mine,* I have nothing to do with it. *Mind your own ~s* (*business* is more usu), Don't interfere in other people's affairs. *What ~ is it of yours,* Why do you take an interest in it? **2** [C] business or undertaking: *The shop has now become a paying ~,* is making profits. *It's a going ~,* one that is active and in operation, not merely planned. **3** [C] share: *He has a ~ in the business,* is a part-owner. **4** [U] anxiety: *filled with ~; look at sb in ~. There is some cause for ~ but no need for alarm.* **con·cerned** *adj* anxious: *with a ~ed look.* **~·ed·ly** /-ɪdlɪ/ *adv*

con·cert[1] /ˋkonsət/ *n* **1** [C] musical entertainment, esp one given in a public hall by players or singers. **ˋ~ grand,** grand piano of the largest size, for ~s. **ˋ~-hall,** hall for ~s. ⇨ music-hall. ***at ˈ~ ˋpitch,*** (fig) in a state of full efficiency or readiness. ⇨ *keyed up* at key[2]. **2** [U] combination of voices or sounds: *voices raised in ~.* **3** [U] agreement; harmony: *working in ~ with his colleagues.*

con·cert[2] /kənˋsɜt/ *vi* arrange with others. Chiefly in **~ed** *adj* planned, performed, designed (by two or more together): *to take ~ed action; to make a ~ed attack.*

con·cer·tina /ˈkonsəˋtinə/ *n* musical wind instrument consisting of a pair of bellows, held in the hands and played by pressing keys at each end.

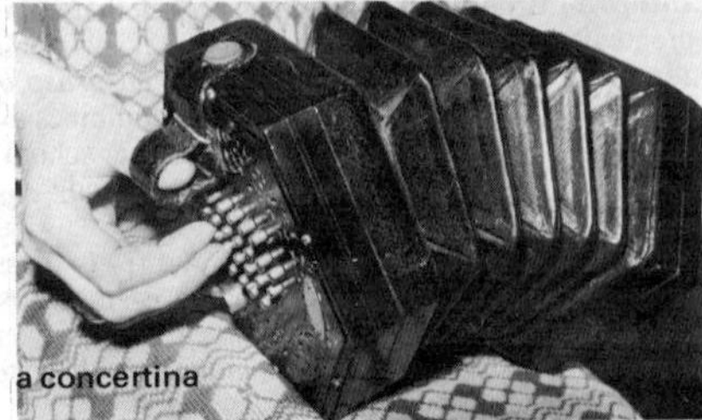

a concertina

con·certo /kənˋtʃɜtəʊ/ *n* (*pl* -tos) musical composition for one or more solo instruments supported by an orchestra: *a 'piano ~; a ~ for two violins.*

con·cession /kən'seʃn/ *n* **1** [U] conceding; [C] that which is conceded, esp after discussion, a difference of opinion, an argument, etc: *As a ~ to the public outcry, the Government reduced the tax on petrol.* **2** [C] (esp) right given by owner(s) of land, or by a Government, to do sth (e g take minerals from land): *American oil ~s in the Middle East.* **con·ces·sive** /kən'sesɪv/ *adj* (gram) expressing ~: *a concessive clause,* e g introduced by *as* or *although,* implying a contrast between circumstances, etc. **~·aire** /kən'seʃn'eə(r)/ *n* holder of a **~(2)**.

conch /kontʃ/ *n* large spiral shell of a mollusc, esp (in Roman myth) as the trumpet of a Triton. ⇨ the illus at **mollusc. con·chol·ogy** /'koŋ'kolədʒɪ/ *n* [U] study of shells and shell-fish.

con·chy /'konʃɪ/ *n* (*pl* **-chies**) (sl, 1914—18, derog) conscientious objector.

con·ci·erge /'kõsɪ'eəʒ *US:* 'kɔ̃sɪ'eərʒ/ *n* (F) (in France, etc) door-keeper, porter (of a block of flats, etc).

con·cili·ate /kən'sɪlɪeɪt/ *vt* [VP6A] win the support, goodwill or friendly feelings of; calm the anger of; soothe. **con·cili·atory** /kən'sɪlɪətrɪ *US:* -tɔrɪ/ *adj* tending or likely to ~: *a conciliatory act/spirit.*

con·cili·ation /kən'sɪlɪ'eɪʃn/ *n* [U] conciliating or being conciliated: *The dispute in the engineering industry is being dealt with by a ~ board,* a group of persons who arbitrate, etc.

con·cise /kən'saɪs/ *adj* (of a person, his speech or style, of writings, etc) brief; giving much information in few words. **~·ly** *adv* **~·ness** *n*

con·clave /'koŋkleɪv/ *n* [C] private or secret meeting (e g of cardinals to elect a Pope). ***sit in ~,*** hold a secret meeting.

con·clude /kən'klud/ *vt,vi* **1** [VP6A,14,2A,3A] come or bring to an end: *to ~ a speech/a lecture. He ~d by saying that.... The meeting ~d at 8 o'clock. The concert ~d with the National Anthem.* **2** [VP6A,14] **~ sth (with),** arrange; bring about: *to ~ a treaty with....* **3** [VP7A] arrive at a belief or opinion: *The jury ~d, from the evidence, that the accused man was not guilty.* **4** [VP7A] (esp US) decide, resolve (after discussion *We ~d not to go.*

con·clu·sion /kən'kluʒn/ *n* [C] **1** end: *at the ~ of his speech; bring a matter to a speedy ~.* ***in ~,*** lastly. **2** arrangement; decision; settling (*of*): *the ~ of a peace treaty.* **3** belief or opinion which is the result of reasoning: *to come to, reach the ~ that...; to draw a ~ from (evidence, etc).* ***a foregone ~,*** something settled or decided in advance, not to be doubted. **4** ***try ~s with,*** have a trial of skill with.

con·clus·ive /kən'klusɪv/ *adj* (of facts, evidence, etc) convincing; ending doubt: *~ evidence/proof of his guilt.* **~·ly** *adv*

con·coct /kən'kokt/ *vt* [VP6A] **1** prepare by mixing together: *to ~ a new kind of soup.* **2** invent (a story, an excuse, a plot for a novel, etc). **con·coc·tion** /kən'kokʃn/ *n* [U] ~ing; [C] sth that is ~ed.

con·comi·tant /kən'komɪtənt/ *adj* accompanying: *~ circumstances.* □ *n* [C] (usu *pl*) accompanying thing: *the infirmities that are the ~s of old age.*

con·cord /'koŋkɔd/ *n* **1** [U] agreement or harmony (between persons or things): *live in ~ (with...);* [C] instance of this. **2** (gram) [U] agreement between words in number, etc, e g between a *verb* and its subject in the present tense.

con·cord·ance /kən'kɔdns/ *n* **1** [U] agreement. **2** [C] arrangement in ABC order of the important words used by an author or in a book: *a 'Bible ~; a 'Shakespeare ~.*

con·cord·ant /kən'kɔdnt/ *adj* **~ (with),** agreeing, harmonious.

con·cor·dat /kən'kɔdæt/ *n* agreement, e g between a State and the Church, for settlement of ecclesiastical affairs.

con·course /'koŋkɔs/ *n* **1** coming or moving together of things, persons, etc: *an unforeseen ~ of circumstances.* **2** place (usu not enclosed) where crowds come together (esp US, the large hall of a railway station).

con·crete[1] /'koŋkrit/ *adj* **1** of material things; existing in material form; that can be touched, felt, etc: *A lamp is ~ but its brightness is abstract.* **~ noun,** name of a thing, not of a quality. **~ music,** composed of assorted electronic sounds. **2** definite; positive: *~ proposals/evidence/proof.* □ *n* [U] building material made by mixing cement with sand, gravel, etc: *roads surfaced with ~; a ~ wall; a '~ mixer* (usu a revolving drum). □ *vt* [VP6A] cover with ~: *~ a road.* **~·ly** *adv*

con·crete[2] /'konkrit/ *vi* [VP2A] form into a mass; solidify. **con·cretion** /kən'kriʃn/ *n* [U] process of forming into a mass; [C] mass formed in this way.

con·cu·bine /'koŋkjʊbaɪn/ *n* **1** (old use) woman who lives with a man as if she were his wife, without being lawfully married to him. **2** (in some countries, where polygamy is legal) lesser wife.

con·cu·pis·cence /kən'kjupɪsns/ *n* [U] sexual desire; lust.

con·cur /kən'k3(r)/ *vi* (-rr-) **1** [VP2A,3A] ***~ (with sb) (in sth),*** agree in opinion: *I ~ with the speaker in condemning what has been done.* **2** [VP3A,4A] (of circumstances, etc) happen together: *Everything ~red to produce a successful result.* **~·rence** /kən'kʌrns *US:* -'k3rəns/ *n* agreement; coming together: *~rence of ideas; ~rence in doing good.*

con·cur·rent /kən'kʌrnt *US:* -'k3rənt/ *adj* concurring; existing together; co-operating. **~·ly** *adv*

con·cuss /kən'kʌs/ *vt* [VP6A] injure (the brain) by concussion.

con·cussion /kən'kʌʃn/ *n* [C,U] (an) injury (to the brain); (a) violent shaking or shock (as caused by a blow, knock or fall).

con·demn /kən'dem/ *vt* **1** [VP6A,14,16B] say that sb is, or has done, wrong or that sth is wrong, faulty or unfit for use: *We all ~ cruelty to children. Everyone ~ed his foolish behaviour. The newspapers ~ed the Prime Minister for.... The meat was ~ed as unfit for human consumption. This old bridge is unsafe; it should be ~ed.* **2** [VP6A,14] ***~ sb (to),*** (legal) give judgement against: *~ a murderer to life imprisonment.* **~ed cell,** cell where a person ~ed to death is kept. **3** [VP6A,14,17] ***~ sb (to sth/to do sth),*** doom, send, appoint (to sth unwelcome or painful): *an unhappy housewife, ~ed to spend hours at the kitchen sink. He got well again, although the doctors had ~ed him,* said that he would not recover. **4** [VP6A] declare (smuggled goods, property, etc) to be forfeited: *Merchant ships captured in war were often ~ed,* taken from the owners without compensation. **5** [VP6A] show conviction of guilt: *His looks ~ed him.* **con·dem·na·tion** /'kondəm-

ˋneɪʃn/ *n* [U] ~ing or being ~ed.

con·den·sa·tion /ˈkondenˋseɪʃn/ *n* [U] condensing or being condensed: *The ~ of milk,* by taking out most of the water; *the ~ of steam to water;* [C,U] (mass of) drops of liquid formed when vapour condenses: *A cloud is a ~ of vapour.*

con·dense /kənˋdens/ *vt, vi* **1** [VP6A,14,2A,3A] (of a liquid) (cause to) increase in density or strength, to become thicker: *to ~ milk; ~ed milk;* (of a gas or vapour) (cause to) change to a liquid; (of light) focus; concentrate (by passing through a lens): *Steam ~s/is ~d to water when it touches a cold surface.* **2** [VP6A,14] put into fewer words: *a ~d account of an event.*

con·den·ser /kənˋdensə(r)/ *n* apparatus for cooling vapour and condensing it to liquid; apparatus for receiving and accumulating static electricity; mirror or lens that concentrates light, e g in a film projector.

con·de·scend /ˈkondɪˋsend/ *vi* [VP2A,3A,4A] **~ *to sb/sth,* ~ *to do sth*** **1** (in a good sense) do sth, accept a position, etc that one's rank, merits, abilities, etc do not require one to do: *The Duke has graciously ~ed to open the new playing field.* **2** (in a bad sense) stoop, lower oneself: *He occasionally ~ed to trickery/to take bribes.* **3** behave graciously, but in a way that shows one's feeling of superiority: *Mr X sometimes ~s to help his wife with the housework. Mrs X doesn't like being ~ed to.* **~·ing** *adj* **~·ing·ly** *adv* **con·de·scen·sion** /ˈkondɪˋsenʃn/ *n* [U] ~ing (all senses); [C] instance of this.

con·dign /kənˋdaɪn/ *adj* (of punishment, vengeance) severe and well deserved.

con·di·ment /ˋkondɪmənt/ *n* [C,U] sth used to give flavour and relish to food, e g pepper, salt, spices.

con·di·tion[1] /kənˋdɪʃn/ *n* **1** [C] sth needed before sth else is possible; sth on which another thing depends: *Ability is one of the ~s of success in life. Her parents allowed her to go, but made it a ~ that she should get home before midnight.* ***on ~ that,*** only if; provided that: *You can go swimming on ~ that you don't go too far from the river bank.* ***on this/that/no/what ~:*** *You must on no ~ tell him what has happened,* whatever he may say, do, ask, etc. *On what ~ will you agree,* What is necessary before you agree? **2** [U] the present state of things; nature, quality, character of sth or sb: *The ~ of my health prevents me from working. The ship is not in a ~ to make a long voyage.* ***in good ~,*** unspoiled, undamaged, etc: *Everything arrived in good ~,* undamaged, fit for use. ***in no ~ (to),*** unable to because ill, old, etc: *He's in no ~ to travel,* is not well or strong enough. ***in/out of ~,*** in good/poor health; physically (un)fit: *I can't go climbing this summer: I'm out of ~.* ***change one's ~,*** (archaic; fac) marry. **3** (*pl*) circumstances: *under existing/favourable ~s.* **4** [C] position in society: *persons of every ~/of all ~s.*

con·di·tion[2] /kənˋdɪʃn/ *vt* [VP6A] **1** determine; govern; regulate: *My expenditure is ~ed by my income.* **2** bring into a desired state or condition: *ˈill-/ˋwell-ˋ~ed;* bring (dogs, horses, etc) into good physical condition: *~ing powders,* for this purpose. *We'll never ~ the workers to a willing acceptance of a wage freeze.* **con·di·tioned** *part adj* subject to certain provisions or conditions; having a specified condition: *air-~ed cinemas.* ***~ed reflex,*** reflex action (one done normally in answer to a stimulus) that is a response, through practice or training, to a different stimulus not naturally connected with it.

con·di·tional /kənˋdɪʃnl/ *adj* **~ *(on/upon),*** depending upon, containing, a condition: *a ~ clause,* beginning with 'if' or 'unless'. *My promise to help you is ~ upon your good behaviour.* **~·ly** /-ʃnlɪ/ *adv*

con·dole /kənˋdəʊl/ *vi* [VP3A] **~ *with sb (on/upon sth),*** express sympathy, regret, at a loss, misfortune, etc. **con·dol·ence** /kənˋdəʊləns/ *n* (often *pl*) expression of sympathy: *Please accept my ~nces.*

con·do·min·ium /ˈkondəˋmɪnɪəm/ *n* joint control of a State's affairs by two or more other States.

con·done /kənˋdəʊn/ *vt* [VP6A,C] (of a person) overlook or forgive (an offence): *~ a husband's infidelity;* (of an act) atone for; make up for: *good qualities that ~ his many shortcomings.* **con·do·na·tion** /ˈkondəʊˋneɪʃn/ *n*

con·dor /ˋkondɔ(r)/ *n* large kind of vulture (in S America).

con·duce /kənˋdjus *US:* -ˋdus/ *vi* [VP3A] **~ *to/towards,*** (formal) contribute to; help to produce: *Does temperance ~ to good health?* **con·duc·ive** /kənˋdjusɪv *US:* -ˋdus-/ *adj* helping to produce: *Good health is conducive to happiness.*

con·duct[1] /ˋkondʌkt/ *n* [U] **1** behaviour (esp moral): *good or bad ~; the rules of ~; a good ~ prize,* given to a child at school; *~ sheet,* record of a soldier's offences and punishments. **2** manner of directing or managing affairs: *People were not at all satisfied with the ~ of the war,* the way in which the leaders were directing it.

con·duct[2] /kənˋdʌkt/ *vt, vi* **1** [VP6A,14,15] lead or guide: *Mr Y ~ed the visitors round the museum. Do you prefer ~ed tours or independent travel? The servant ~ed me in/out/to the door.* **2** [VP6A, 2A] control; direct; manage: *to ~ a meeting/negotiations; If he ~s his business affairs in the careless way he ~s his private affairs, they must be in confusion. Who is ~ing (the orchestra) this evening?* **3** (*reflex*) behave: *He ~s himself well.* **4** [VP6A,2A] (of substances) transmit; allow (heat, electric current) to pass along or through: *Copper ~s electricity better than other materials.* **con·duc·tion** /kənˋdʌkʃn/ *n* transmission or ~ing, e g of electric current along wires, of liquids through pipes, of heat by contact. **con·duc·tive** /kənˋdʌktɪv/ *adj* able to ~ (heat, electric current, etc). **con·duc·tiv·ity** /ˈkondʌkˋtɪvətɪ/ *n* (*pl* **-ties**) property or power of ~ing.

con·duc·tor /kənˋdʌktə(r)/ *n* **1** person who conducts esp one who conducts a group of singers, a band, an orchestra. **2** person who collects fares on a bus or tram; (US) person in charge of passengers on a train. ⇨ guard (GB). **3** substance that conducts heat or electric current: *~ rail,* rail (laid parallel to tracks) from which a locomotive picks up electric current. **con·duc·tress** /kənˋdʌktrəs/ *n* woman ~ (on a bus, etc).

con·duit /ˋkondɪt *US:* -duɪt/ *n* large pipe or waterway; tube enclosing insulated electric wires.

cone /kəʊn/ *n* **1** solid body which narrows to a point from a round, flat base. **2** sth of this shape whether solid or hollow, e g a ~ shaped basket hoisted as a storm signal, as an indication of road repairs, or an edible container for ice-cream. **3** fruit of certain evergreen trees (fir, pine, cedar). □ *vt* [VP15B] ***~ off,*** mark off with ~s: *~ off a section of the motorway during repairs.*

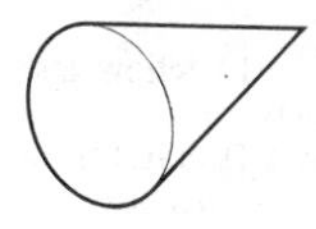

cones

co·ney *n* = cony.

con·fab /ˈkonfæb/ *n, vi* (-bb-) (colloq abbr of the two words below).

con·fabu·late /kənˈfæbjʊleɪt/ *vi* [VP2A,3A] **~ *(with)*,** have a confabulation. **con·fabu·la·tion** /kənˌfæbjʊˈleɪʃn/ *n* [C] friendly and private conversation.

con·fec·tion /kənˈfekʃn/ *n* **1** [C] mixture of sweet things; sweet cake. **2** [U] mixing; compounding. **3** [C] (dress-making trade) stylish or fancy ready-made article of dress (usu for a woman). **~er** *n* person who makes and sells pastry, pies, cakes, etc. **~·ery** /kənˈfekʃnrɪ *US:* -nerɪ/ *n* [U] sweets, chocolates, cakes, pies, pastry, etc; [C] (*pl* **-ries**) (place of) business of a ~er.

con·fed·er·acy /kənˈfedrəsɪ/ *n* (*pl* **-cies**) union of states, parties or persons: *the C~ of Delos,* in ancient Greece; *the Southern C~,* the eleven States that separated from the Union (US, 1860—61) and brought about the Civil War.

con·fed·er·ate[1] /kənˈfedrət/ *adj* joined together by an agreement or treaty: *the C~ States of America.* ⇨ above. □ *n* [C] **1** person or State joined with another or others. **2** accomplice (in a plot, etc).

con·fed·er·ate[2] /kənˈfedəreɪt/ *vt, vi* [VP6A,14, 2A,3A] **~ *(with)*,** bring into or come into alliance. **con·fed·er·ation** /kənˌfedəˈreɪʃn/ *n* [U] confederating or being confederated; [C] alliance; league.

con·fer /kənˈfɜ(r)/ *vt, vi* (-rr-) **1** [VP14] **~ *sth on/upon*,** give or grant (a degree, title, favour): *The Queen ~red knighthoods on several distinguished men.* **2** [VP2A,3A] **~ *(with sb) (on/about sth)*,** consult or discuss: *~ with one's lawyer.* **~·ment** *n*

con·fer·ence /ˈkonfrns/ *n* [C,U] (meeting for) discussion; exchange of views: *The Director is in ~ now. Many international ~s have been held in Geneva.*

con·fess /kənˈfes/ *vt, vi* **1** [VP6A,9,14,2A,3B,25] say or admit (that one has done wrong); acknowledge: *He ~ed that he had stolen the money. The prisoner refused to ~. She ~ed herself (to be) guilty. She ~ed to (having) a dread of spiders,* admitted that she was afraid of them. **2** [VP6A, 2A,3A] **~ *(to)*,** (esp in the RC Church) make known one's sins to a priest; (of a priest) listen to sb doing this: *~ one's sins. The criminal ~ed to the priest. The priest ~ed the criminal.* **~ed·ly** /-ɪdlɪ/ *adv* as ~ed; by one's own confession.

con·fession /kənˈfeʃn/ *n* **1** [U] confessing; [C] instance of this: *The accused man made a full ~. On his own ~ he has taken part in the robbery. She is a good Catholic and goes to ~ regularly. The priest is ready to hear ~s in Italian, French or English.* **2** [C] declaration (of religious beliefs, or of principles of conduct, etc): *a ~ of faith.*

con·fessional /kənˈfeʃnl/ *n* private place (stall) in a church where a priest sits to hear confessions: *the secrets of the ~.*

con·fes·sor /kənˈfesə(r)/ *n* priest who has authority to hear confessions.

con·fetti /kənˈfetɪ/ *n* (I) (*pl; sing v*) small bits of coloured paper showered on people at weddings and carnivals.

con·fi·dant /ˈkonfɪˈdænt/ *n* person who is trusted with private affairs or secrets (esp about love affairs).

con·fide /kənˈfaɪd/ *vt, vi* **1** [VP14] **~ *sth/sb to sb*,** tell secrets to sb; give (sth or sb to sb) to be looked after; give (a task or duty to sb): *He ~d his troubles to a friend. The children were ~d to the care of the ship's captain. She ~d to me that....* **2** [VP3A] **~ *in*,** have trust or faith in: *Can I ~ in his honesty? There's no one here I can ~ in.* **con·fid·ing** *adj* truthful; trusting: *The girl is of a confiding nature,* ready to trust others, unsuspicious. **con·fid·ing·ly** *adv*

con·fi·dence /ˈkonfɪdəns/ *n* **1** [U] (act of) confiding in or to. ***in strict ~*,** expecting sth to be kept, secret: *I'm telling you this in strict ~.* ***take a person into one's ~*,** tell him one's secrets, etc. **ˈ~ trick,** persuasion of a foolish person to entrust valuables to one as a sign of ~. **ˈ~ man/trickster,** one who swindles people in this way. **2** [C] secret which is confided to sb: *The two girls sat in a corner exchanging ~s about the young men they knew.* **3** [U] belief in oneself or others or in what is said, reported, etc; belief that one is right or that one is able to do sth: *to have/lose ~ in sb; to put little/complete/no ~ in sb/sth; Don't put too much ~ in what the newspapers say. There is a lack of ~ in the government,* People do not feel that its policies are wise. *I hope he will justify my ~ in him/my ~ that he will do well. The prisoner answered the questions with ~.*

con·fi·dent /ˈkonfɪdənt/ *adj* **~ *(of/that)*,** feeling or showing confidence; certain: *He feels ~ of passing/that he will pass the examination. The little girl gave her mother a ~ smile. We are ~ of success.* **~·ly** *adv*

con·fi·den·tial /ˌkonfɪˈdenʃl/ *adj* **1** (to be kept) secret; given in confidence: *~ information.* **2** having the confidence of another or others: *a ~ clerk/secretary.* **3** (of persons) inclined to give confidences: *Don't become too ~ with strangers.* **~·ity** /ˌkonfɪˌdenʃɪˈælətɪ/ *n* **~·ly** /-ʃlɪ/ *adv*

con·figur·ation /kənˌfɪgjʊˈreɪʃn/ *n* [C] shape or outline; method of arrangement: *the ~ of the earth's surface.*

con·fine /kənˈfaɪn/ *vt* **1** [VP14] **~ *to*,** keep or hold, restrict, within limits: *I wish the speaker would ~ himself to the subject. Please ~ your remarks to the subject we are debating.* **2** [VP6A, 14] keep shut up: *Is it cruel to ~ a lark in a cage? He is ~d to the house by illness. I should hate to be ~d within the four walls of an office all day.* **3** ***be ~d*,** (passive only) in bed to give birth to a child: *She expects to be ~d next month.* **con·fined** *adj* (of space) limited; narrow; restricted. **~·ment** *n* **1** [U] being ~d; imprisonment: *He was placed in ~ment,* in prison, in a mental hospital, etc. *The prisoner was sentenced to three months' solitary ~ment.* **2** [U] giving birth to a child; [C] instance of this: *Dr X has attended six ~ments this week. When does she expect her ~ment?*

con·fines /ˈkonfaɪnz/ *n pl* limits; borders; boundaries: *beyond the ~ of human knowledge; within the ~ of this valley.*

con·firm /kənˈfɜm/ *vt* [VP6A] **1** make (power, ownership, opinions, rights, feelings, etc) firmer or stronger: *Please ~ your telephone message by letter,* send a letter repeating the message. *The* *report of an earthquake in Greece has now been ~ed,* We now know that the report was true. *What you tell me ~s my suspicions.* **2** ratify; agree definitely to (a treaty, an appointment, etc). **3** admit to full membership of the Christian Church: *She was baptized when she was a month old and ~ed when she was thirteen.* **con·firmed** *part adj* (esp) unlikely to change or be changed: *a ~ed invalid,* one who is unlikely to be well again; *a ~ed drunkard,* one who cannot be cured of drunken habits.

con·fir·ma·tion /ˈkɒnfəˋmeɪʃn/ *n* [C,U] ~ ***(of),*** confirming or being confirmed (all senses): *We are waiting for ~ of the news. Evidence in ~ of his statements is lacking. C~ admits persons to full membership of the Church.*

con·fis·cate /ˋkɒnfɪskeɪt/ *vt* [VP6A] (as punishment or in enforcing authority) take possession of (private property) without compensation or payment: *If you try to smuggle goods into the country, they may be ~d by the Customs authorities.* **con·fis·ca·tion** /ˈkɒnfɪˋskeɪʃn/ *n* [U] confiscating or being ~d; [C] instance of this: *numerous confiscations of obscene books.*

con·fla·gra·tion /ˈkɒnfləˋgreɪʃn/ *n* [C] great and destructive fire, esp one that destroys buildings or forests.

con·flict[1] /ˋkɒnflɪkt/ *n* [C] **1** fight; struggle; quarrel: *a wordy ~,* a bitter argument; *a long-drawn-out ~ between employers and workers.* **2** (of opinions, desires, etc) opposition; difference: *the ~ between duty and desire; a ~ of evidence; a statement that is in ~ with other evidence.*

con·flict[2] /kənˋflɪkt/ *vi* [VP2A,3A] ~ ***with,*** be in opposition or disagreement: *Our accounts ~. Their account of the causes of the war ~s with ours.* **~·ing** *adj*: *~ing views/passions/evidence.*

con·flu·ence /ˋkɒnflʊəns/ *n* flowing together, esp a place where two rivers unite. **con·flu·ent** /ˋkɒnflʊənt/ *adj* flowing together; uniting.

con·form /kənˋfɔm/ *vi, vt* **1** [VP2A,3A] ~ ***to,*** be in agreement with, comply with (generally accepted rules, standards, etc): *You should ~ to the rules/ to the wishes of others, to the usages of society/to the usages of the Established Church.* **2** [VP14] ~ ***sth (to),*** make similar to: adapt oneself to: *~ one's life to certain principles.* **~·able** *adj* obedient; submissive: *~able to your wishes;* in agreement: *~able to custom/reason.*

con·for·ma·tion /ˈkɒnfɔˋmeɪʃn/ *n* way in which sth is formed; structure.

con·form·ist /kənˋfɔmɪst/ *n* one who conforms, e g to the usages of the Established Church. ⇨ *dissenter* at **dissent**[1], *nonconformist* at **non-**.

con·form·ity /kənˋfɔmətɪ/ *n* [U] **1** ~ ***(to),*** action, behaviour, in agreement with what is usual, accepted or required by custom, etc: *C~ to fashion* (= Having things of the latest fashions) *is not essential to the happiness of all women.* **2** agreement: *in ~ with your request. Was his action in ~ with the law?*

con·found /kənˋfaʊnd/ *vt* **1** [VP6A] fill with, throw into, perplexity or confusion: *His behaviour amazed and ~ed her. I was ~ed to hear that....* **2** [VP6A,14] mix up, confuse (ideas, etc): *Don't ~ the means with the ends.* **3** [VP6A] (rather old use) defeat; overthrow (enemies, plans, etc). **4** [VP6A] used to express annoyance or anger: *C~ it! C~ you!* **~ed** *part adj* (from **4** above; rather dated use): *You're a ~ed nuisance!* **~·edly** /-ɪdlɪ/ *adv* very: *~edly hot.*

con·frère /ˋkɒnfreə(r)/ *n* (F) fellow member of a profession, learned society, etc.

con·front /kənˋfrʌnt/ *vt* **1** [VP6A,14] ~ ***sb with,*** bring face to face: *The prisoner was ~ed with his accusers. When ~ed with the evidence of his guilt, he confessed at once.* **2** [VP6A] be or come face to face with: *The difficulties that ~ us seem insuperable. A soldier has to ~ danger.* **3** [VP6A] be opposite to: *My house ~s his.*

con·fron·ta·tion /ˈkɒnfrʌnˋteɪʃn/ *n* [C,U] (instance of) defiant opposition, of being face to face: *the ~ between Israel and the Arab world.*

Con·fu·cian /kənˋfjuʃn/ *adj, n* (follower) of Confucius /kənˋfjuʃəs/, the Chinese philosopher and teacher of morals (551–479 BC) who believed in the principles of true loyalty to friends, relatives, rulers, etc and that one should treat others as one would wish to be treated.

con·fuse /kənˋfjuz/ *vt* [VP6A,14] **1** put into disorder; mix up in the mind: *They asked so many questions that they ~d me/I got ~d.* **2** mistake one thing for another: *Don't ~ Austria with/and Australia.* **con·fus·edly** /-ɪdlɪ/ *adv* in a ~d manner.

con·fu·sion /kənˋfjuʒn/ *n* [U] being confused; disorder: *He remained calm in the ~ of battle. His unexpected arrival threw everything into ~. Everything was in ~. There has been some ~ of names; it was Mr Smythe who was to come, not Mr Smith.*

con·fute /kənˋfjut/ *vt* [VP6A] prove (a person) to be wrong; show (an argument) to be false. **con·fu·ta·tion** /ˋkɒnfjuˋteɪʃn/ *n*

congé /ˋkɔ̃ʒeɪ/ *n* **1** formal permission to depart: *give sb his ~.* **2** abrupt and unceremonious dismissal.

con·geal /kənˋdʒil/ *vt, vi* [VP6A,2A] make or become stiff or solid (esp as the effect of cold, or of the air on blood); thicken as if frozen: *His blood was ~ed,* (fig) e g through fear.

con·gen·ial /kənˋdʒinɪəl/ *adj* **1** (of persons) having the same or a similar nature, common interests, etc: *In this small village he found few persons ~ to him.* **2** (of things, occupations, etc) in agreement with one's tastes, nature: *a ~ climate; ~ work.* **~·ly** /-ɪəlɪ/ *adv*

con·geni·tal /kənˋdʒenɪtl/ *adj* (of diseases, etc) present, belonging to one, from or before birth: *~ idiocy.*

con·ger /ˋkɒŋgə(r)/ *n* (also **ˈ~-ˋeel**) ocean eel of large size. ⇨ the illus at **sea**.

con·gested /kənˋdʒestɪd/ *part adj* **1** too full; overcrowded: *streets ~ with traffic; ~ areas of a large town.* **2** (of parts of the body, e g the brain, the lungs) having an abnormal accumulation of blood.

con·ges·tion /kənˋdʒestʃən/ *n* [U] being congested: *~ of the lungs; delayed by the ~ of traffic in town.*

con·glom·er·ate[1] /kənˋglɒmərət/ *adj, n* (made up of a) number of things or parts stuck together in a mass or ball (e g rock made up of small stones held together).

con·glom·er·ate[2] /kənˋglɒməreɪt/ *vt, vi* [VP6A, 2A] collect into a round mass.

con·glom·er·ation /kənˈglɒməˋreɪʃn/ *n* [U] conglomerating or being conglomerated; [C] mass of conglomerated things.

con·gratu·late /kənˋgrætʃʊleɪt/ *vt* [VP6A,14] ~

sb (on/upon sth) **1** tell (sb) that one is pleased about sth happy or fortunate that has come to (him): *~ sb on his marriage.* **2** (*reflex*) consider (oneself) fortunate: *I ~d myself on my escape/on having escaped unhurt.* **con·gratu·la·tory** /kən'græt∫ʊˋleɪtərɪ/ *US:* -tɔrɪ/ *adj* that ~s: *a congratulatory letter/telegram.*

con·gratu·la·tion /kən'grætʃʊˋleɪʃn/ *n* (often *pl*) words that congratulate: *offer a friend one's ~s on/upon his success.*

con·gre·gate /ˋkɒŋgrɪgeɪt/ *vi,vt* [VP6A,2A,C] come or bring together: *People quickly ~d round the speaker.*

con·gre·ga·tion /'kɒŋgrɪˋgeɪʃn/ *n* [U] congregating; [C] gathering of people; (esp) body of people (usu except the minister and choir) taking part in religious worship. **~al** *adj* of a ~; **C~,** of the Union of Free Churches in which individual churches manage their own affairs.

con·gress /ˋkɒŋgres *US:* -grɪs/ *n* **1** [C] meeting, series of meetings, of representatives (of societies, etc) for discussion: *a medical ~; the Church C~.* **2 C~,** law-making body of US and some other republics in America; political party in India. **ˋ~-man** /ˋkɒŋgrɪsmən/ *n* (*pl* -men) **ˋ~-woman** *n* (*pl* -women) member of C~. Cf senator. **con·gressional** /kənˋgreʃnl/ *adj* of a ~: *~ional debates.*

con·gru·ent /ˋkɒŋgrʊənt/ *adj* **1** ***~ (with),*** suitable; agreeing (with). **2** (geom) having the same size and shape: *~ triangles.*

con·gru·ous /ˋkɒŋgrʊəs/ *adj* fitting; proper; harmonious (*with*).

conic /ˋkɒnɪk/ *adj* of a cone: *~ sections.* **coni·cal** /ˋkɒnɪkl/ *adj* cone-shaped. ⇨ the illus at projection.

coni·fer /ˋkɒnɪfə(r)/ *n* tree of the kind (e g *pine, fir*) that bears cones. **co·nifer·ous** /kəˋnɪfərəs/ *adj* (of kinds of trees) that bear cones.

con·jec·ture /kənˋdʒektʃə(r)/ *vi,vt* [VP6A,9,2A,25] guess; put forward an opinion formed without facts as proof: *It was just as I ~d. May we ~ that...?* □ *n* [C,U] guess; guessing: *I was right in my ~s. We had no facts, so were reduced to ~.* **con·jec·tural** /kənˋdʒektʃərl/ *adj* involving ~; inclined to ~.

con·join /kənˋdʒɔɪn/ *vt,vi* [VP6A,2A] join together; unite.

con·joint /'kɒnˋdʒɔɪnt/ *adj* united; associated. **~·ly** *adv*

con·ju·gal /ˋkɒndʒʊgl/ *adj* of marriage and wedded life; of husband and wife: *~ happiness/affection/infidelity.* **~·ly** /-gəlɪ/ *adv*

con·ju·gate /ˋkɒndʒʊgeɪt/ *vt* [VP6A] **1** give the forms of a verb (for number, tense, etc). **2** (of a verb) have these forms. **con·ju·ga·tion** /'kɒndʒʊˋgeɪʃn/ *n* [C,U] scheme or system of verb forms; [C] class of verbs ~d alike.

con·junc·tion /kənˋdʒʌŋkʃn/ *n* **1** [C] (gram) word that joins other words, clauses, etc, e g *and, but, or.* **2** [U] joining; state of being joined; *the ~ of skill and imagination in planning a garden.* ***in ~ with,*** together with. **3** [C] combination (of events, etc): *an unusual ~ of circumstances.*

con·junc·tive /kənˋdʒʌŋktɪv/ *adj* serving to join; connective. □ *n* ~ word.

con·junc·ture /kənˋdʒʌŋktʃə(r)/ *n* [C] combination of events or circumstances.

con·jur·ation /'kɒndʒʊˋreɪʃn/ *n* [C] solemn appeal, incantation.

con·jure /ˋkʌndʒə(r)/ *vt,vi* **1** [VP15A] do clever tricks which appear magical, esp by quick movements of the hands: *~ a rabbit out of a hat.* **2** [VP15B] ***~ up,*** cause to appear as if from nothing, or as a picture in the mind: *~ up visions of the past;* compel (a spirit) to appear by invocation: *~ up the spirits of the dead; a name to ~ with,* used of sb able to exercise great influence; *~ up a meal.* **3** /kənˋdʒʊə(r)/ [VP17] (formal) appeal solemnly to: *I ~ you not to betray me.* **con·jurer, con·juror** /ˋkʌndʒərə(r)/ *n* person who performs conjuring tricks. ⇨ 1 above.

conk[1] /kɒŋk/ *n* (GB sl) nose.

conk[2] /kɒŋk/ *vi* ***~ out,*** (colloq) (of a machine) fail or give signs of failing: *The car ~ed out.*

conker /ˋkɒŋkə(r)/ *n* (colloq) horse-chestnut.

con-man /ˋkɒn mæn/ *n* ⇨ confidence(1).

con·nect /kəˋnekt/ *vt,vi* **1** [VP6A,15A,B,14,2A,2C,3A] ***~ (up) (with),*** join, be joined (materially, by personal relationships, etc): *~ telephone subscribers; ~ (up) the cells of a battery. The two towns are ~ed by a railway. Where does the cooker ~ with the gas-pipe? Mr Y has been ~ed with this firm since 1950. He is ~ed with the Smiths/He and the Smiths are ~ed by marriage,* i e his wife is a member of the Smith family. *He is well ~ed,* has relatives who are high in society, or who hold important positions, etc. *The 9.00a m train from London ~s with the 12.05p m train at Crewe,* i e arrives at Crewe so as to enable passengers to continue their journeys by the 12.05p m train. **2** [VP14] ***~ (with),*** think of (different things or persons) as being related to each other: *to ~ Malaya with rubber and tin.*

con·nec·tion /kəˋnekʃn/ *n* **1** [C,U] connecting or being connected; point where two things are connected; thing which connects: *a bicycle pump ~. How long will the ~ of the new telephone take,* How long will it take to connect the house by telephone to the exchange? *What is the ~ between the two ideas?* ***in this/that ~,*** with reference to this/that. ***in ~ with,*** with reference to: *The meeting is in ~ with a proposal to construct a new swimming-pool.* **2** [C] train, boat, etc timed to leave a station, port, etc soon after the arrival of another, enabling passengers to change from one to the other: *The train was late and I missed my ~.* **3** [C] (collective noun) number of customers, clients, etc: *He set up in business and soon had a good ~. This dressmaker has good ~s among the well-to-do women of the town.* **4** [C] number of people united in a religious organization: *the Methodist ~.*

con·nect·ive /kəˋnektɪv/ *adj* serving to connect. □ *n* (esp) word that connects (e g a conjunction).

con·nexion /kəˋnekʃn/ occasional GB spelling for *connection.*

con·ning tower /ˋkɒnɪŋ taʊə(r)/ *n* (on a warship) superstructure from which steering, etc is directed (esp of a submarine on or near the surface).

con·nive /kəˋnaɪv/ *vi* [VP3A] ***~ at,*** take no notice of (what is wrong, what ought to be opposed) (suggesting that tacit consent or approval is given): *~ at an escape from prison.* **con·niv·ance** /kəˋnaɪvəns/ *n* [U] conniving (at or in a crime): *done with the connivance of/in connivance with....*

con·nois·seur /'kɒnəˋsɜ(r)/ *n* person with good judgement on matters in which taste is needed: *a ~ of/in painting/old porcelain/antique furni-*

ture/wine.

con·note /kəˋnəʊt/ *vt* [VP6A] (of words) suggest in addition to the fundamental meaning: *The word 'Tropics' means the area between about 23°N and 23°S; it ~s heat.* **con·no·ta·tion** /ˈkonəˋteɪʃn/ *n* [C] that which is ~d.

con·nu·bial /kəˋnjubɪəl *US:* -ˋnu-/ *adj* of marriage; of husband and wife.

con·quer /ˋkoŋkə(r)/ *vt* [VP6A] **1** defeat or overcome enemies/bad habits, etc. **2** take possession of by force: *~ a country.* **~or** /ˋkoŋkərə(r)/ *n* one who ~s: *William the C~or,* King William I of England.

con·quest /ˋkoŋkwest/ *n* **1** [U] conquering (e g a country and its people): *the (Norman) C~,* of England by the Normans in 1066. **2** [C] sth got by conquering: *the Roman ~s in Africa; make a ~ (of),* win the affections (of).

con·quista·dor /kənˈkwɪstəˋdɔ(r)/ *n* (16th c) one of the Spanish conquerors of Mexico and Peru.

con·san·guin·ity /ˈkonsæŋˋgwɪnətɪ/ *n* [U] relationship by blood or birth: *united by ties of ~.*

con·science /ˋkonʃns/ *n* [C,U] the consciousness within oneself of the choice one ought to make between right and wrong: *have a clear/guilty ~.* ***have no ~,*** be as ready to do wrong as right. ***(have sth) on one's ~,*** (feel) troubled about sth one has done, or failed to do. **ˋ~ money,** money that one pays (esp when no other person knows that it is owing) because one has a troubled ~. **ˋ~-smitten** /-smɪtn/ *adj* filled with remorse. ***for ~' sake,*** to satisfy one's ~. ***in all ~, upon my ~,*** (forms of emphatic declaration) surely; (colloq) by all that is fair: *I cannot in all ~/Upon my ~ I cannot agree.* ***make sth/be a matter of ~,*** make sth/be a question which one's ~ must decide.

con·scien·tious /ˈkonʃɪˋenʃəs/ *adj* **1** (of persons) guided by one's sense of duty: *a ~ worker; a ~ objector,* person who objects to doing sth (e g serving in the armed forces) because he thinks it is morally wrong. **2** (of actions) done carefully and honestly: *~ work.* **~·ly** *adv* **~·ness** *n*

con·scious /ˋkonʃəs/ *adj* **1** ***~ (of/that),*** (pred use) awake; aware; knowing things because one is using the bodily senses and mental powers: *They were ~ of being/that they were being watched. He was ~ of his guilt. Are you ~ (of) how people will regard such behaviour? A healthy man is not ~ of his breathing. The old man was ~ to the last,* aware of what was happening round him until the moment he died. **2** (of actions, feelings, etc) realized by oneself: *He spoke/acted with ~ superiority.* **~·ly** *adv*

con·scious·ness /ˋkonʃəsnəs/ *n* [U] **1** being conscious: *We have no ~ during sleep. The blow caused him to lose ~. He did not recover/regain ~ until two hours after the accident.* **2** all the ideas, thoughts, feelings, wishes, intentions, recollections, of a person or persons: *the moral ~ of a political party.*

con·script /kənˋskrɪpt/ *vt* [VP6A,14] ***~ (into),*** compel (sb) by law to serve in the armed forces; summon/call up for such service: *~ed into the army.* ⇨ draft¹(3). □ *n* /ˋkonskrɪpt/ person who is ~ed; (attrib) *~ soldiers.* **con·scrip·tion** /kənˋskrɪpʃn/ *n* ~ing (of men into the armed forces); system of, practice of, taxation of, or confiscation of property (as a penalty or for war needs).

con·se·crate /ˋkonsɪkreɪt/ *vt* [VP6A,14,23] ***~ (to),*** set apart as sacred or for a special purpose; make sacred: *to ~ one's life to the service of God/to the relief of suffering. The new church was ~d by the Bishop of Chester. He was ~d Archbishop last year.*

con·se·cra·tion /ˈkonsɪˋkreɪʃn/ *n* [U] consecrating or being consecrated; [C] instance of this: *the ~ of a church; the ~ of a bishop,* the ceremony at which a priest is made a bishop.

con·secu·tive /kənˋsekjʊtɪv/ *adj* following continuously; coming one after the other in regular order: *on five ~ days.* **~·ly** *adv*

con·sen·sus /kənˋsensəs/ *n* general agreement (*of* opinion, etc); collective opinion: *~ politics,* the practice of basing policies on what will gain wide support.

con·sent /kənˋsent/ *vi* [VP2A,3A,7A] ***~ (to sth/to do sth),*** give agreement or permission: *He ~ed to the proposal. Anne's father would not ~ to her marrying a foreigner.* □ *n* [U] ***~ (to),*** agreement; permission: *He was chosen leader by general ~,* when everyone agreed. *Her parents refused their ~ to the marriage. Silence gives ~,* If no one objects, it seems that ~ is given. ***with one ~,*** unanimously. **ˈage of ˋ~,** age at which the law recognizes a girl's responsibility for agreeing to sexual intercourse, a person's right to ~ to marry, etc.

con·se·quence /ˋkonsɪkwəns *US:* -kwens/ *n* **1** [C] that which follows or is brought about as the result or effect of sth: *If you behave so foolishly you must be ready to take the ~s,* accept what happens as a result. ***in ~ (of),*** as a result (of). **2** [U] importance *It's of no ~. Is it of any/much ~? He may be a man of ~* (= an important man, or a man of high rank) *in his own village, but he's nobody here.*

con·se·quent /ˋkonsɪkwənt/ *adj* ***~ on/upon,*** (formal) following as a consequence: *the rise in prices ~ upon the failure of the crops.* **~·ly** *adv*

conse·quen·tial /ˈkonsɪˋkwenʃl/ *adj* **1** = consequent. **2** (of a person) self-important. **~·ly** /-ʃlɪ/ *adv*

con·ser·vancy /kənˋsɜvənsɪ/ *n* (*pl* **-cies**) **1** [C] commission controlling a port, river, etc: *the Thames C~; the Nature C~.* **2** [U] official conservation (of forests, etc).

con·ser·va·tion /ˈkonsəˋveɪʃn/ *n* [U] preservation; prevention of loss, waste, damage, etc: *the ~ of forests/waterpower etc; the ~ of energy,* the principle that the total quantity of energy in the universe never varies.

con·serva·tism /kənˋsɜvətɪzm/ *n* tendency to maintain a state of affairs (esp in politics) without great or sudden change; the principles of the Conservative Party in British politics.

con·serva·tive /kənˋsɜvətɪv/ *adj* **1** opposed to great or sudden change: *Old people are usually more ~ than young people.* **2 the C~ Party,** one of the main political parties in Great Britain. ⇨ *Labour* at labour(3), *Liberal* at liberal(4), *Socialist* at socialism. **3** cautious; moderate: *a ~ estimate of one's future income.* □ *n* ~ person; member of the C~ Party. **~·ly** *adv*

con·serva·toire /kənˋsɜvətwɑ(r)/ *n* (F) (esp in Europe) public school of music.

con·serva·tory /kənˋsɜvətrɪ *US:* -tɔrɪ/ *n* (*pl* **-ries**) **1** building, or part of a building, with glass walls and roof in which plants are protected from cold. **2** school of music or dramatic art.

con·serve /kənˋsɜv/ *vt* [VP6A] keep from change,

loss or destruction: ~ *one's strength/energies/ health;* ~ *fruit,* e g by making it into jam. □ *n* (usu *pl*) fruit preserved in sugar; jam.

con·sider /kən`sɪdə(r)/ *vt* **1** [VP6A,C,8,10] think about: *Please* ~ *my suggestion. We are* ~*ing going to Canada. Have you* ~*ed how to get/how you could get there? Have you ever* ~*ed the fact that your pension will be inadequate?* ***one's ~d opinion,*** one's opinion arrived at after some thought: *It's my* ~*d opinion that you should resign.* **2** [VP6A] take into account; make allowances for: *We must* ~ *the feelings of other people. You should* ~ *his youth.* ***all things ~ed,*** taking into account, thinking of, all the events, possibilities, etc. **3** [VP25,9] be of the opinion; regard as: *They* ~*ed themselves very important. Do you* ~ *it wise to interfere? He will be* ~*ed a weak leader. C*~ *yourself* (= You are) *under arrest. We* ~ *that you are not to blame.*

con·sider·able /kən`sɪdrəbl/ *adj* great; much; important: *a* ~ *income/distance; bought at a* ~ *expense; a* ~ *man in local affairs.* **~·ably** /-əblɪ/ *adv* much; a great deal: *It's considerably colder this morning.*

con·sider·ate /kən`sɪdṛət/ *adj* ~ ***(of),*** thoughtful (of the needs, etc, of others): *It was* ~ *of you not to play the piano while I was having a sleep.* **~·ly** *adv* **~·ness** *n*

con·sider·ation /kən'sɪdə`reɪʃn/ *n* **1** [U] act of considering, thinking about: *Please give the matter your careful* ~. *The proposals are still under* ~. ***leave sth out of ~,*** neglect or fail to consider it: *There is one important fact that has been left out of* ~. ***take sth into ~,*** (esp) make allowances for: *When marking Tom's examination papers, the teacher took Tom's long illness into* ~. **2** [U] ~ ***(for),*** quality of being considerate; thoughtful attention to the wishes, feelings, etc, of others: *in* ~ *of/out of* ~ *for his youth. He has never shown much* ~ *for his wife's feelings.* **3** [C] sth which must be thought about; fact, thing, etc thought of as a reason: *Time is an important* ~ *in this case. Several* ~*s have influenced me in coming to a decision.* ***on no ~,*** in no circumstances; in no case. **4** [C] reward; payment: *He's the sort of man who would do anything for a* ~, if he were paid to do it. **5** [U] (rare use) importance: *It's of no* ~ *at all.*

con·sider·ing /kən`sɪdṛɪŋ/ *prep* in view of; having regard to: *She's very active,* ~ *her age. You've done very well,* ~, i e in view of the circumstances, etc.

con·sign /kən`saɪn/ *vt* ~ ***(to),*** **1** [VP6A,14] send (goods, etc) for delivery: *The goods have been* ~*ed by rail.* **2** [VP14] hand over, give up: ~ *a child to its uncle's care;* ~ *one's soul to God.* **~ee** /'konsaɪn`i/ *n* person to whom sth is ~ed. **~er, ~or** /-nər/ *nn* person who ~s goods. **~·ment** *n* [U] ~ing; [C] goods ~ed. ***on ~ment,*** with payment for goods to be made after they have been sold: *take/send/ship goods on* ~*ment.* **`~ment note,** one sent with a ~ment of goods.

con·sist /kən`sɪst/ *vi* [VP3A] **1** ~ ***of,*** (not in the progressive tenses) be made up of: *The committee* ~*s of ten members.* **2** ~ ***in,*** have as the chief/or only element: *The happiness of a country* ~*s in the freedom of its citizens.*

con·sist·ence /kən`sɪstəns/ *n* = consistency.

con·sist·ency /kən`sɪstənsɪ/ *n* **1** [U] the state of always being the same in thought, behaviour, etc; keeping to the same principles: *His actions lack* ~. **2** [C,U] (*pl* **-cies**) degree of thickness, firmness or solidity (esp of a thick liquid, or of sth made by mixing with a liquid): *mix flour and milk to the right* ~; *mixtures of various consistencies.*

con·sist·ent /kən`sɪstənt/ *adj* **1** (of a person, his behaviour, principles, etc) conforming to a regular pattern or style; regular: *a* ~ *friend of the working classes. The ideas in his various speeches are not* ~. **2** ~ ***(with),*** in agreement: *What you say now is not* ~ *with what you said last week.* **~·ly** *adv*

con·sis·tory /kən`sɪstərɪ/ *n* (*pl* **-ries**) court of priests, clergymen or presbyters to deal with church business.

con·so·la·tion /'konsə`leɪʃn/ *n* **1** [U] consoling or being consoled; sth that consoles: *a few words of* ~; *a letter of* ~. **`~ prize,** one given to a competitor who has just missed success or come last. **2** [C] circumstances or person that consoles: *That's one* ~. *Your company has been a great* ~ *to me.*

con·sola·tory /kən`solətrɪ *US:* -tɔrɪ/ *adj* comforting; intended to console: *a* ~ *letter.*

con·sole[1] /kən`səʊl/ *vt* [VP6A,14] give comfort or sympathy to (sb who is unhappy, disappointed, etc): ~ *sb for a loss;* ~ *oneself with the thought that it might have been worse.* **con·sol·able** *adj* that can be ~d.

con·sole[2] /`konsəʊl/ *n* **1** bracket to support a shelf. **`~ table,** narrow table held up by a bracket or brackets fixed to a wall. **2** frame containing the keyboards, stops, etc of an organ. **3** radio or TV cabinet made to stand on the floor (not a table model). **4** panel for the controls of electronic or mechanical equipment.

con·soli·date /kən`solɪdeɪt/ *vt,vi* **1** [VP6A,2A] make or become solid or strong: ~ *one's position/influence.* **2** [VP6A] unite or combine into one: ~ *debts/business companies/banks.* **~d annuities,** (also *consols*) Government securities of Great Britain, ~d in 1751 into a single stock. **C~d Fund** *n* fund from taxation, used for payment of interest on the national debt.

con·soli·da·tion /kən'solɪ`deɪʃn/ *n* [U] consolidating or being consolidated; [C] instance of this: *successive* ~*s of the national debt.*

con·sols /kən`solz/ *n pl* consolidated annuities. ⇨ consolidate(2).

con·sommé /kən`someɪ/ *n* (F) clear, meat soup.

con·son·ance /`konsənəns/ *n* [U] **1** agreement. **2** harmony.

con·son·ant[1] /`konsənənt/ *n* [C] speech sound produced by a complete or partial stoppage of the breath; letter of the alphabet or symbol (e g phonetic) for such a sound: *b, c, d, f,* etc.

con·son·ant[2] /`konsənənt/ *adj* ~ ***with,*** harmonious: *actions* ~ *with his beliefs; a position in the service* ~ *with your rank;* agreeable: ~ *to reason.*

con·sort[1] /`konsɔt/ *n* **1** husband or wife, esp of a ruler: *the queen* ~, the king's wife; *the prince* ~, the reigning queen's husband. **2** ship sailing with another (esp for safety during a war).

con·sort[2] /kən`sɔt/ *vi* [VP3A,2C] ~ ***with,*** **1** pass time in the company of: ~ *with criminals/one's equals.* **2** be in harmony, go well: *His practice does not* ~ *with his preaching,* He behaves in one way, but talks in another way.

con·sor·tium /kən`sɔtɪəm *US:* -`sɔrʃɪəm/ *n* (*pl* **-tia** /-tɪə *US:* -ʃɪə/) temporary co-operation of a number of powers, companies, banks, etc for a common purpose: *the* ~ *of Upper Clyde* *ship-builders/of oil companies in the North Sea.*

con·spec·tus /kən`spektəs/ *n* (*pl* -tuses /-təsɪz/) general view of a subject, scene, etc; synopsis (e g in the form of tables).

con·spicu·ous /kən`spɪkjʊəs/ *adj* easily seen; attracting attention; remarkable: *~ for his bravery. Traffic signs should be ~.* **make oneself ~,** attract attention by unusual behaviour, wearing unusual clothes, etc. **~·ly** *adv* **~·ness** *n*

con·spir·acy /kən`spɪrəsɪ/ *n* [U] act of conspiring; [C] (*pl* -cies) plan made by conspiring: *a ~ to overthrow the Government; a ~ of silence,* an agreement not to talk publicly about sth.

con·spire /kən`spɑɪə(r)/ *vi,vt* **1** [VP2C,3A,4A] make secret plans (*with* others, esp to do sth wrong): *~ against the Government. His enemies ~d to ruin him.* **2** [VP6A] plot: *~ sb's ruin.* **3** [VP4A] (of events) act together; combine: *events that ~d to bring about his downfall.* **con·spira·tor** /kən`spɪrətə(r)/ *n* person who ~s. **con·spira·tor·ial** /kən'spɪrə`tɔrɪəl/ *adj* of conspirators or a conspiracy: *with a conspiratorial air.*

con·stable /`kʌnstəbl *US:* `kon-/ *n* **1** (GB) (also **po`lice ~**) policeman: *Chief C~,* head of the police force of a county, etc; *special ~,* person who acts as a ~ on special occasions or for special duty. **2** (hist) principal officer in a royal household; governor of a royal castle, etc. **con·stabu·lary** /kən`stæbjʊlərɪ *US:* -lerɪ/ *n* (*pl* -ries) organized body of police ~s; police force.

con·stancy /`konstənsɪ/ *n* [U] quality of being firm, unchanging: *~ of purpose.*

con·stant /`konstənt/ *adj* **1** going on all the time; frequently recurring: *~ complaints.* **2** firm; faithful; unchanging: *a ~ friend. He has been ~ in his devotion to scientific studies.* □ *n* (maths, phys) number or quantity that does not vary. **~·ly** *adv* continuously; frequently.

con·stel·la·tion /'konstə`leɪʃn/ *n* named group of fixed stars (e g *the Great Bear*).

con·ster·na·tion /'konstə`neɪʃn/ *n* [U] surprise and fear; dismay: *filled with ~; looking back in ~.*

con·sti·pate /`konstɪpeɪt/ *vt* [VP6A] cause constipation: *to find some kinds of food constipating.*

con·sti·pated /`konstɪpeɪtɪd/ *part adj* having bowels that can be emptied infrequently or only with difficulty.

con·sti·pa·tion /'konstɪ`peɪʃn/ *n* [U] difficult or infrequent emptying of the bowels.

con·stitu·ency /kən`stɪtʃʊənsɪ/ *n* (*pl* -cies) [C] (body of voters living in a) town or district that sends a representative to Parliament.

con·stitu·ent /kən`stɪtʃʊənt/ *adj* **1** having the power or right to make or alter a political constitution: *a ~ assembly.* **2** forming or helping to make a whole: *a ~ part.* □ *n* **1** member of a constituency. **2** component part: *the ~s of happiness.*

con·sti·tute /`konstɪtjut *US:* -tut/ *vt* **1** [VP23] give (sb) authority to hold (a position, etc): *They ~d him chief adviser. What right have you to ~ yourself a judge of my conduct?* **2** [VP6A] establish; give legal authority to (a committee, etc). **3** [VP6A] make up (a whole); amount to; be the components of: *Twelve months ~ a year. He is so ~d* (= His nature is such) *that he can accept unjust criticism without getting angry.*

con·sti·tu·tion /'konstɪ`tjuʃn *US:* -`tuʃn/ *n* [C] **1** system of government; laws and principles according to which a state is governed: *Great Britain has an unwritten ~; the United States has a written ~.* **2** general physical structure and condition of a person's body: *Only men with strong ~s should climb in the Himalayas.* **3** general structure of a thing; act or manner of constituting: *the ~ of the solar spectrum; the ~ of one's mind and character.*

con·sti·tu·tional /'konstɪ`tjuʃnl *US:* -`tuʃnl/ *adj* **1** of a constitution(**1**): *~ government; a ~ ruler,* controlled or limited by a constitution: *~ reform.* ⇨ **absolute,** *autocratic* at **autocrat. 2** of a person's constitution(**2**): *a ~ weakness.* □ *n* (colloq) short walk for the health's sake: *take/go for a ~.* **~·ly** /-ʃnḷɪ/ *adv* **~·ism** *n* (belief in) ~ government or ~ principles. **~·ist** *n* supporter of ~ principles. **~·ize** /-ʃnḷɑɪz/ *vt* make ~.

con·sti·tut·ive /kən`stɪtjʊtɪv/ *adj* constructive; formative; essential.

con·strain /kən`streɪn/ *vt* [VP6A,17] make (sb) do sth by using force or strong persuasion; (of conscience, inner forces) compel: *I feel ~ed to write and ask for your forgiveness.* **con·strained** *part adj* (of voice, manner, etc) forced; uneasy; unnatural. **con·strain·ed·ly** /-ɪdlɪ/ *adv*

con·straint /kən`streɪnt/ *n* [U] constraining or being constrained: *to act under ~,* because one is forced to do so; *to feel/show ~ in a person's presence,* to hold back one's natural feelings.

con·strict /kən`strɪkt/ *vt* [VP6A] make tight or smaller; cause (a vein or muscle) to become tight or narrow; *a ~ed outlook,* one that is narrow or limited. **con·stric·tion** /kən`strɪkʃn/ *n* [U] ~ing; [C] feeling of being ~ed: *a ~ion in the chest;* [C] sth that ~s.

con·struct /kən`strʌkt/ *vt* [VP6A] build; put or fit together: *to ~ a factory/an aircraft/a sentence/a theory; a well-~ed novel.* **~or** /-tə(r)/ *n* person who ~s things: *motor-car-body ~ors.*

con·struc·tion /kən`strʌkʃn/ *n* **1** [U] act or manner of constructing; being constructed: *the ~ of new roads. The new railway is still under ~/in the course of ~. The new factory is of very solid ~.* **2** [C] sth constructed; structure; building. **3** [C] meaning; sense in which words, statements, acts, etc are taken: *Please do not put a wrong ~ on his action,* misunderstand its purpose. *The sentence does not bear such a ~,* cannot be understood in that way. **4** [C] arrangement and relationships of words in a sentence: *This dictionary gives the meanings of words and also illustrates their ~s.*

con·struc·tive /kən`strʌktɪv/ *adj* helping to construct; giving helpful suggestions: *~ criticism/proposals.* **~·ly** *adv*

con·strue /kən`stru/ *vt,vi* **1** [VP6A,2A] translate or explain the meaning of words, sentences, acts: *~ a passage from Homer. His remarks were wrongly ~d,* were misunderstood. **2** [VP6A] analyse (a sentence); combine (words with words) grammatically. **3** [VP2A] be capable of being analysed: *This sentence won't ~.*

con·sub·stan·ti·ation /'konsəb'stænʃɪ`eɪʃn/ *n* doctrine that the body and blood of Christ co-exist with the bread and wine in the Eucharist.

con·sul /`konsl/ *n* **1** State's agent living in a foreign town to help and protect his countrymen there. **2** (in ancient Rome) either of the two Heads of the State before Rome became an Empire. **3** any one of the three chief magistrates of the French Republic, 1799—1804. **~·ship** /-ʃɪp/ *n* position of a ~; period of time during which a ~ holds his position.

con·su·lar /ˋkɒnsjʊlə(r) *US:* -səl-/ *adj* of a consul or his work.

consu·late /ˋkɒnsjʊlət *US:* -səl-/ *n* consul's position; offices of a consul(**1**); period of consular government in France.

con·sult /kənˋsʌlt/ *vt,vi* **1** [VP6A,14] go to a person, a book, etc for information, advice, opinion, etc: *to ~ one's lawyer/a map/the dictionary; a ~ing engineer,* one with special knowledge of one or more branches of engineering. **2** [VP6A] (formal; *consider* is now preferred) take into consideration or account: *We must ~ his convenience,* cause him as little inconvenience as possible. **3** [VP3A] ***~ with,*** take counsel: *~ with one's fellow workers.*

con·sul·tant /kənˋsʌltənt/ *n* person who gives expert advice (e g in medicine, surgery, business): (attrib) *a ~ surgeon; a firm of ~s.*

con·sul·ta·tion /ˌkɒnslˋteɪʃn/ *n* **1** [U] consulting or being consulted: *in ~ with the director.* **2** [C] meeting for consulting: *The doctors held a ~ to decide whether an operation was necessary.*

con·sult·ative /kənˋsʌltətɪv/ *adj* of, for the purpose of, consulting: *a ~ committee.*

con·sume /kənˋsjum *US:* -ˋsum/ *vt,vi* **1** [VP6A] eat or drink. **2** [VP6A] use up; get to the end of; destroy by fire or wastefulness: *~ all one's energies. The flames quickly ~d the wooden huts. He soon ~d his fortune,* spent the money wastefully. *He was ~d* (= eaten, eaten up) *with envy/hatred/greed. This is time-consuming work,* work that takes up a lot of time. **3** ***~ away,*** waste away.

con·sumer /kənˋsjumə(r) *US:* -ˋsu-/ *n* (opp to *producer*) person who uses goods: *~/~'s goods,* those which directly satisfy human needs and desires (e g food and clothing) (opp to *capital goods,* e g factory equipment): *~ research; ~ sales resistance.* **con·sum·ing** *part adj* possessing or dominating: *consuming ambition.*

con·sum·mate[1] /kənˋsʌmət/ *adj* supremely skilled; perfect: *~ skill/taste.*

con·sum·mate[2] /ˋkɒnsəmeɪt/ *vt* [VP6A] **1** accomplish; make perfect: *Her happiness was ~d when her father took her to Paris.* **2** make complete (esp marriage by sexual intercourse).

con·sum·ma·tion /ˌkɒnsəˋmeɪʃn/ *n* [C,U] action, point of completing; perfecting, or fulfilling: *the ~ of a life's work/one's ambitions/a marriage.*

con·sump·tion /kənˋsʌmpʃn/ *n* [U] **1** using up, consuming (of food, energy, materials, etc); the quantity consumed: *The ~ of beer did not go down when the tax was raised.* **2** (popular name for) pulmonary tuberculosis.

con·sump·tive /kənˋsʌmptɪv/ *adj* suffering from, having a tendency to, consumption(**2**). □ *n* ~ person.

con·tact /ˋkɒntækt/ *n* **1** [U] (state of) touching or communication; (process of) coming together, esp in: ***be in/out of ~ (with), come/bring into ~ with***: *Our troops are in ~ with the enemy. The opposing forces are now in/out of ~ (with each other). A steel cable came into ~ with an electric power line. We can learn much by being brought into ~ with other minds/opposing opinions, etc.* ***make ~ (with),*** come into ~ (with), esp after searching, striving, etc: *I finally made ~ with him in Paris. We never really succeeded in making ~. They made ~ by radio/radio ~ with headquarters.* ***make/break ~,*** complete/interrupt an electric circuit. ˋ**~ lens,** one of thin plastic material made to fit closely over and in ~ with the eyeball to improve vision. **2** [C] (meeting with a) person: *He made many useful social ~s while he was in Canada,* met people who could be useful to him. **3** [C] connection (for electric current); device for effecting this. **4** [C] (med) person recently exposed to a contagious disease. □ *vt* [VP6A] get into touch with (sb): *Where can I ~ Mr Green?*

con·tagion /kənˋteɪdʒən/ *n* [U] the spreading of disease by contact or close association; [C] disease that can be spread by contact; (fig) the spreading of ideas, false rumours, feelings, etc: [C] influence, etc that spreads: *A ~ of fear swept through the crowd.*

con·tagious /kənˋteɪdʒəs/ *adj* **1** (of disease) spreading by contact: *Scarlet fever is ~.* **2** (of a person) in such a condition that he may spread disease. **3** (fig) spreading easily by example: *~ laughter/enthusiasm. Yawning is ~.* **~·ly** *adj*

con·tain /kənˋteɪn/ *vt* [VP6A] (not in the progressive tenses) **1** have or hold within itself: *The atlas ~s forty maps, including three of Great Britain. Whisky ~s a large percentage of alcohol.* **2** be equal to: *A gallon ~s eight pints.* **3** be capable of holding: *How much does this bottle ~?* **4** keep feelings, enemy forces, etc under control, within limits: *Can't you ~ your enthusiasm? He couldn't ~ himself for joy,* was so happy that his feelings burst out. *He couldn't ~ his wine,* was sick, became drunk, etc. *Has the cholera outbreak been ~ed,* prevented from spreading? **5** (geom) form the boundary of: *The angle ~ed by the lines A B and A C in the triangle A B C is a right angle.* **6** (maths) be divisible by, without a remainder: *12 ~s 2, 3, 4 and 6.* **~er** *n* **1** box, bottle, etc designed to ~ sth. **2** large metal box or other sealed ~er for transport of goods by road, rail, sea or air: ˋ*~er crane,* large crane mounted on a gantry, used on quays, etc to move ~ers(**2**). ˋ*~er train/liner,* one designed for such ~ers; ˋ*~er traffic;* ˋ*~er depot,* e g where ~ers are loaded and unloaded. **~·ment** *n* [U] policy of preventing a State from extending its sphere of influence.

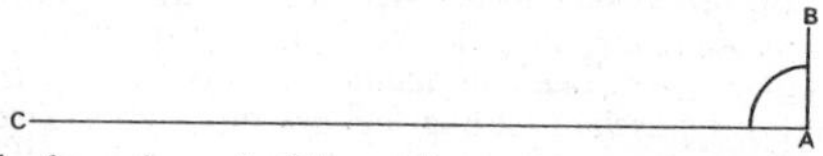

con·tami·nate /kənˋtæmɪneɪt/ *vt* [VP6A] make dirty, impure or diseased (by touching, or adding sth impure): *~d clothing,* e g by poison gas or radio-active materials. *Flies ~ food. His morals have been ~d by bad companions.*

con·tami·na·tion /kənˌtæmɪˋneɪʃn/ *n* **1** [U] contaminating or being contaminated: *contamination of the water supply.* **2** [C] that which contaminates.

con·temn /kənˋtem/ *vt* (liter) despise; disregard.

con·tem·plate /ˋkɒntəmpleɪt/ *vt* [VP6A,C,19C] **1** look at (with the eyes, or in the mind): *She stood contemplating her figure/herself in the mirror.* **2** have in view as a purpose, intention or possibility: *She was contemplating a visit to London. I hope your mother does not ~ coming to stay with us. I do not ~ any opposition from him,* do not think this is likely or possible.

con·tem·pla·tion /ˌkɒntəmˋpleɪʃn/ *n* [U] contemplating; deep thought; intention; expectation: *He sat there deep in ~.*

con·tem·pla·tive /kən`templətɪv *US:* `kontəmpleɪtɪv/ *adj* thoughtful; fond of contemplation; (of life in the Middle Ages) given up to religious contemplation.

con·tem·por·aneous /kən'tempə`reɪnɪəs/ *adj* originating, existing, happening, during the same period of time: *~ events; ~ with....* **~·ly** *adv*

con·tem·por·ary /kən`tempṛɪ *US:* -pərerɪ/ *adj* of the time or period to which reference is being made; belonging to the same time: *a ~ record of events,* one made by persons living at that time; *furniture in ~ style,* of the present time (contrasted with period furniture). *Dickens was ~ with Thackeray.* □ *n* (*pl* **-ries**) person ~ with another: *Jack and I were contemporaries at college.*

con·tempt /kən`tempt/ *n* [U] **1** condition of being looked down upon or despised: *to fall into ~ by foolish or bad behaviour. Such behaviour will bring you into ~. A man who is cruel to his children should be held in ~.* **2** mental attitude of despising: *We feel ~ for liars. Such an accusation is beneath ~,* not worth despising (because it is so ridiculous, etc). **3** disregard or disrespect; total disregard: *in ~ of all rules and regulations. He rushed forward in ~ of danger. He showed his ~ of death by rushing at the enemy.* ***Familiarity breeds ~,*** (prov) ⇨ **familiarity(1)**. **'~ of `court,** disobedience to an order made by a court; disrespect shown to a judge.

con·tempt·ible /kən`temptəbl/ *adj* deserving, provoking, contempt.

con·temptu·ous /kən`temptʃʊəs/ *adj* showing contempt: *~ of public opinion.* **~·ly** *adv*

con·tend /kən`tend/ *vi, vt* **1** [VP3A] ***~ with/ against/for,*** struggle, be in rivalry or competition: *~ing with difficulties; ~ing for a prize; ~ing passions,* strong feelings of different kinds (e g pity, a sense of justice) that make decision difficult. **2** [VP9] argue, assert (*that...*). **~er** *n* competitor, rival, e g one who challenges the holder of a boxing title.

con·tent[1] /kən`tent/ *adj* (not used attrib; ⇨ **contented** below) **1** ***~ with,*** not wanting more; satisfied with what one has: *Are you ~ with your present salary? She is ~ with very little.* **2** ***~ to do sth,*** willing or ready (to do sth): *I am ~ to remain where I am now. I should be well ~* (= quite pleased) *to do so.* □ *n* [U] the condition of being satisfied: *living in peace and ~; to one's heart's ~,* to the extent that brings satisfaction. □ *vt* [VP6A,14] ***~ sb/oneself (with),*** make ~; satisfy: *There's no ~ing some people,* It's impossible to please or satisfy them; *As there's no butter we must ~ ourselves* (= be satisfied) *with dry bread.* **~ed** *adj* satisfied; showing or feeling ~: *with a ~ed look/smile.* **~·ed·ly** *adv* **~·ment** *n* [C] state of being ~.

con·tent[2] /`kontent/ *n* **1** (*pl*) that which is contained in sth: *the ~s of a room/a book/a schoolboy's pockets, etc; the table of ~s,* list of the matter in a book, periodical, etc. **2** (*pl*) the amount which a vessel will hold: *the ~s of a barrel or cask.* **3** substance (of a book, speech, etc as opposed to its form): *Do you approve of the ~ of the article/speech?*

con·ten·tion /kən`tenʃn/ *n* **1** [U] contending(**2**); quarrelling or disputing: *This is not a time for ~.* ⇨ **bone(1)**. **2** [C] argument used in contending: *My ~ is that....*

con·ten·tious /kən`tenʃəs/ *adj* quarrelsome; likely to cause contention: *a ~ clause in a treaty.*

con·termi·nous /'kon`tɜmɪnəs/ *adj* = **coterminous.**

con·test /kən`test/ *vt, vi* **1** [VP6A,9] argue; debate; dispute: *~ a statement/point,* try to show that it is wrong: *~ sb's right to dó sth.* **2** [VP3A] contend(**1**). **3** [VP6A] fight or compete for; try to win: *~ a seat in Parliament. The enemy ~ed every inch of the ground,* fought with determination not to retreat. □ *n* /`kontest/ [C] struggle; fight; competition: *a keen ~ for the prize; a ~ of skill; a `speed ~;* (boxing) *a three-round featherweight ~.* **~ant** /kən`testənt/ *n* one who ~s.

con·text /`kontekst/ *n* [C,U] **1** what comes before and after a word, phrase, statement, etc helping to fix the meaning: *Can't you guess the meaning of the word from the ~? Don't quote my words out of ~,* e g so as to give a false impression of what I mean. **2** circumstances in which an event occurs. **con·tex·tual** /kən`tekstʃʊəl/ *adj* according to the ~.

con·ti·guity /'kontɪ`gjuətɪ/ *n* [U] the state of being contiguous.

con·tigu·ous /kən`tɪgjʊəs/ *adj* ***~ to,*** touching; neighbouring; near. **~·ly** *adv*

con·ti·nence /`kontɪnəns/ *n* [U] self-control; self-restraint (esp of passions and desires).

con·ti·nent[1] /`kontɪnənt/ *adj* self-controlled; having control of one's feelings and (esp sexual) desires; able to retain urine voluntarily.

con·ti·nent[2] /`kontɪnənt *US:* -tṇənt/ *n* one of the main land masses (Europe, Asia, Africa, etc): *the C~,* (as used by people in GB) the mainland of Europe. **con·ti·nen·tal** /'kontɪ`nentl *US:* -tn`entl/ *adj* **1** belonging to, typical of, a ~: *a ~al climate.* **2** of the mainland of Europe: *~al wars/alliances; the ~al Sunday,* as in Europe (with wider freedom for theatrical and other entertainments, sport, etc than formerly in GB). □ *n* inhabitant of the mainland of Europe.

con·tin·gency /kən`tɪndʒənsɪ/ *n* [U] uncertainty of occurrence; [C] (*pl* **-cies**) uncertain event; event that happens by chance; sth that may happen if sth else happens: *to be prepared for all contingencies; a result that depends upon contingencies;* (attrib) *~ arrangements/plans.*

con·tin·gent /kən`tɪndʒənt/ *adj* **1** uncertain; accidental. **2** ***~ upon,*** dependent upon (sth that may or may not happen): *a ~ advantage.* □ *n* [C] body of troops, number of ships, lent or supplied to form part of a larger force; group of persons forming part of a larger group.

con·tin·ual /kən`tɪnjʊəl/ *adj* going on all the time without stopping, or with only short breaks: *Aren't you tired of this ~ rain?* **~·ly** /-jʊlɪ/ *adv* again and again; without stopping.

con·tin·uance /kən`tɪnjʊəns/ *n* (*sing* only) **1** time for which sth continues; duration (the more usual word): *during the ~ of the war.* **2** remaining; staying: *a ~ of prosperity.*

con·tinu·ation /kən'tɪnjʊ`eɪʃn/ *n* **1** [U] continuing; starting again after a stop: *C~ of study after the holidays was difficult at first.* **2** [C] part, etc by which sth is continued: *The May number of the magazine will contain an exciting ~ of the story.*

con·tinue /kən`tɪnju/ *vi, vt* **1** [VP2A,B,D,E,6A,D,7A] go farther; go on (being); go on (doing); stay at/in; remain at/in: *The desert ~d as far as the eye could reach. How far does this road ~? I hope this wet weather will not ~. The king died but his* *work ~d. He hopes to ~ at school for another year. She still ~s in weak health. The weather ~d calm. If you ~ to be so obstinate,...; He ~d to live with his parents after his marriage. How long will you ~ working? You must ~ your study of French.* **2** [VP6A,2A] start again after stopping: *The story will be ~d in next month's issue. 'Well,' he ~d, 'when we arrived...'* **3** [VP14] retain (sb in office, etc): *The Colonial Secretary was ~d in office.*

con·ti·nu·ity /ˌkontɪˈnjuətɪ *US:* -ˈnu-/ *n* [U] **1** the state of being continuous: *There is no ~ of subject in a dictionary.* **2** (cinema, TV) scenario; arrangement of the parts of a story: *Moving pictures are often made out of ~,* e g a scene in the middle may be filmed before a scene near the beginning. ˈ**~ girl,** one who sees to the consistency and ~ of the different parts of a film. **3** connecting comments, announcements, etc, made between the parts of a broadcast programme.

con·tinu·ous /kənˈtɪnjʊəs/ *adj* going on without a break: *~ performance, 1.00p m to 11.30p m,* e g at a cinema. **~·ly** *adv*

con·tort /kənˈtɔt/ *vt* [VP6A,14] force or twist out of the usual shape or appearance: *a face ~ed with pain;* (fig) *~ a word out of its ordinary meaning.*

con·tor·tion /kənˈtɔʃn/ *n* [U] contorting or being contorted (esp of the face or body); [C] instance of this; contorted condition: *the ~s of an acrobat.* **~·ist** /-nˈtɔʃn̩ɪst/ *n* acrobat clever at contorting his body.

con·tour /ˈkontʊə(r)/ *n* [C] outline (of a coast, mountain range, etc); (on a map, design, etc) line separating differently coloured parts. ˈ**~ line,** line (on a map) showing all points at the same height above sea-level. ˈ**~ map,** one with ~ lines at fixed intervals (e g of 25 metres). ˈ**~ ploughing,** ploughing in which furrows follow ~ lines (on a hillside, etc) to prevent soil erosion. □ *vt* [VP6A] mark with ~ lines; make (a road) round the ~ of a hill.

contra- /ˈkontrə/ *pref* against.

contra·band /ˈkontrəbænd/ *n* [U] bringing into, taking out of, a country goods contrary to the law; (trade in) goods so brought in or taken out. ***~ of war,*** goods (e g ammunition) supplied by neutral countries to countries that are at war, which can be seized by any of the countries at war: (attrib) *~ goods; ~ trade.*

contra·bass /ˈkontrəbeɪs/ *n* = **double-bass.**

contra·cep·tion /ˌkontrəˈsepʃn/ *n* [U] practice, method, of preventing or planning conception(**2**). **contra·cep·tive** /ˌkontrəˈseptɪv/ *n* [C] device or drug intended to prevent conception(**2**). □ *adj* preventing conception: *~ pills/devices.*

con·tract[1] /ˈkontrækt/ *n* **1** [C] binding agreement (between persons, groups, states); agreement to supply goods, do work, etc at a fixed price: ***enter into/make a ~ (with sb) (for sth),*** make such an agreement. ***sign a ~,*** e g for the sale of land or buildings. ***exchange ~s,*** e g for the purchase of a house. [U] (phrases in which no article is used): *bind oneself by ~; work to be done by private ~; work on ~; breach of ~; conditions of ~;* (attrib use) *~ price/date,* price, date, agreed to. **2** ˈ**~ ˈbridge,** kind of bridge[2] in which only tricks bid[1](**5**) and won count towards game[1](**4**).

con·tract[2] /kənˈtrækt/ *vt,vi* **1** [VP6A,14,4A] ~ (with sb) for sth/to do sth: *~ a marriage; ~ to build a bridge; ~ with a firm for 1 000 tons of cement; ~ an alliance with another country.* [VP2C] ***~ out/out of sth*** /ˈkontrækt ˈaʊt/, reject, abandon, the terms of a ~: *~ out of an agreement/alliance.* **2** [VP6A] ***~ debts,*** become liable for them. **3** [VP6A] catch (an illness); form; acquire (e g bad habits). **~or** /-tə(r)/ *n* person, business firm, that enters into ~s: *engineering ~ors; army ~ors.* **con·trac·tual** /kənˈtræktʃʊəl/ *adj* of (the nature of) a ~.

con·tract[3] /kənˈtrækt/ *vt,vi* [VP6A,14,2A,C] **1** make or become smaller or shorter: *Metals ~ as they become cool. 'I will' is ~ed to 'I'll'.* **2** make or become tighter or narrower: *to ~ a muscle; to ~ the brows/forehead. The valley ~s as one goes up it.* **~·ible** *adj* that can be ~ed. **con·trac·tile** /kənˈtræktaɪl *US:* -tl/ *adj* that can ~ or be ~ed: *~ile wings,* e g of an insect, that can be folded over the body.

con·trac·tion /kənˈtrækʃn/ *n* **1** [U] contracting or being contracted: *the ~ of a muscle; the ~ of the mercury in a thermometer.* **2** [C] sth contracted; shortened form, as *can't* for *cannot.*

con·tra·dict /ˌkontrəˈdɪkt/ *vt* [VP6A] **1** deny the truth of (sth said or written); deny (the words of a person): *to ~ a statement. Don't ~ me.* **2** (of facts, statements, etc) be contrary to: *The reports ~ each other.* **con·tra·dic·tion** /ˌkontrəˈdɪkʃn/ *n* **1** [U] ~ing; [C] instance of this. **2** [U] absence of agreement; [C] instance of this: *Your statements today are in ~ion with what you said yesterday.* ***a ~ion in terms,*** statement that includes words that ~ each other (e g a generous miser). **con·tra·dic·tory** /ˌkontrəˈdɪktərɪ/ *adj* ~ing: *~ory statements/reports.*

contra·dis·tinc·tion /ˌkontrədɪˈstɪŋkʃn/ *n* (formal) distinction by contrast: *the crossing of the Atlantic by air in a few hours, in ~ to the longer journey by steamer.*

contra·dis·tin·guish /ˌkontrədɪˈstɪŋwɪʃ/ *vt* [VP14] distinguish (things *from...*) by contrast.

con·tralto /kənˈtræltəʊ/ (*pl* **-tos** /-təʊz/) *n* lowest female voice; woman with, musical part to be sung by, such a voice.

con·trap·tion /kənˈtræpʃn/ *n* (colloq) strange-looking apparatus or device.

contra·pun·tal /ˌkontrəˈpʌntl/ *adj* of or in counterpoint.

contra·riety /ˌkontrəˈraɪətɪ/ *n* [U] opposition or antagonism (in nature, quality or action); [C] (*pl* **-ties**) sth that is inconsistent or contrary: *contrarieties in nature.*

con·trari·wise /ˈkontrərɪwaɪz/ *adv* **1** on the contrary. **2** in the opposite way. **3** /kənˈtreərɪwaɪz/ perversely; in a manner showing opposition.

con·trary[1] /ˈkontrərɪ *US:* -trerɪ/ *adj* **1** **~ to,** opposite (in nature or tendency): *'Hot' and 'cold' are ~ terms. What you have done is ~ to the doctor's orders. The result was ~ to expectation.* **2** (of the wind and weather) unfavourable (for sailing): *The ship was delayed by ~ winds.* **3** (colloq, usu /kənˈtreərɪ/) obstinate; self-willed. **4** **~ to,** (compound prep) in opposition to; against: *to act ~ to the rules; events that went ~ to my interests.* **con·trar·ily** /ˈkontrərɪlɪ *US:* -rerl̩ɪ/ *adv* in a ~(**3**) manner. **con·trari·ness** /ˈkontrərɪnəs *US:* -rer-/ *n* being ~(**3**).

con·trary[2] /ˈkontrərɪ *US:* -trerɪ/ *n* (*pl* **-ries**) **1** (*sing* with *def art*) opposite: *The ~ of 'wet' is 'dry'.* ***on the ~,*** phrase used to make a denial or contradiction more emphatic: *'You've nothing to* *do now, I think.'—'On the ~, I have piles of work.'* **to the ~,** to the opposite effect: *I will come on Monday unless you write me to the ~,* telling me not to come. *I shall continue to believe it until I get proof to the ~,* proof that it is not true. **2 by contraries,** **(a)** ~ to expectation: *Many things in our lives go by contraries.* **(b)** by way of opposition: *She said that dreams go by contraries,* e g that a dream about bad fortune may foretell good fortune.

con·trast[1] /kən`trɑst *US:* -ræst/ *vt, vi* **1** [VP6A,14] **~ (with/and),** compare so that differences are made clear: *C~ these imported goods with/and the domestic product. It is interesting to ~ the two speakers.* **2** [VP2C,3A] show a difference when compared: *His actions ~ sharply with his promises. His actions and his promises ~ sharply.*

con·trast[2] /`kontrɑst *US:* -træst/ *n* **1** [U] the act of contrasting: *C~ may make something appear more beautiful than it is when seen alone.* **2** [C] difference which is clearly seen when unlike things are put together; sth showing such a difference: *The ~ between the two brothers is remarkable. The ~ of light and shade is important in photography. His white hair was in sharp ~ to/with his dark skin. Tom's marks* (e g 90 per cent) *by ~ with Harry's marks* (e g 35 per cent) *were excellent.*

con·tra·vene /'kontrə`vin/ *vt* [VP6A] **1** act in opposition to; go against (a law, a custom). **2** dispute, attack (a statement, a principle). **3** (of things) conflict with; be out of harmony with.

con·tra·ven·tion /'kontrə`venʃn/ *n* act of contravening (a law, etc): *in ~ of the rules,* so as to break or violate them.

contre·temps /`kontrətɔ̃/ *n* (*pl* unchanged) (F) unfortunate happening; unexpected hitch; setback.

con·trib·ute /kən`trɪbjut/ *vt, vi* **1** [VP6A,14,2A,3A] join with others in giving help, money, etc (to a common cause, *for* a purpose); give ideas, suggestions, etc: *~ food and clothing for the refugees; ~ to the Red Cross; ~ new information on a scientific problem.* **2** [VP3A] have a share in; help to bring about: *Drink ~d to his ruin.* **3** [VP14,3A] write (articles, etc) and send in (*to*): *Mr Green has ~d (poems) to the 'London Magazine' for several years.* **con·tribu·tor** /-tə(r)/ *n* person who ~s (money *to* a fund, articles *to* a periodical, etc).

con·tri·bu·tion /'kontrɪ`bjuʃn/ *n* **1** [U] act of contributing; [C] sth contributed: *~s to the relief fund. Do you consider ~s to the church funds a duty or a pleasure? The editor is short of ~s for the May issue.* **2** [C,U] compulsory payment for the support of an invading or occupying army: *lay a country under ~,* require ~s from the inhabitants.

con·tribu·tory /kən`trɪbjʊtərɪ *US:* -tɔrɪ/ *adj* **1** helping to bring about: *~ negligence,* e g that helped to cause an accident. **2** for which contributions are to be made: *a '~ `pension scheme.*

con·trite /`kontrɑɪt/ *adj* filled with, showing, deep sorrow for wrongdoing *a ~ heart.* **~·ly** *adv*

con·tri·tion /kən`trɪʃn/ *n* [U] deep sorrow (for sins, wrong-doing); repentance.

con·triv·ance /kən`trɑɪvəns/ *n* **1** [U] act or manner of contriving: *the ~s by which botanists fertilize flowers to obtain hybrids.* **2** [U] capacity to invent: *Some things are beyond human ~.* **3** [C] sth contrived; deceitful practice; invention or mechanical device: *a ~ to record both sides of a telephone conversation on magnetic tape.*

con·trive /kən`trɑɪv/ *vt, vi* [VP6A,7A,2A] invent; design; find a way of doing (sth), of causing (sth to happen): *to ~ a means of escape from prison; to ~ to live on a small income. He ~d to make matters worse,* made them worse by his efforts, even though this was not his intention. *Can you ~* (= manage) *to be here early? She finds it difficult to ~* (= manage her housekeeping economically) *now that prices are rising every month.* **con·triver** /kən`trɑɪvə(r)/ *n* (formal) one who ~s, esp one who manages household affairs: *His wife is a good ~r.*

con·trol /kən`trəʊl/ *n* **1** [U] power or authority to direct, order, or restrain: *children who lack parental ~,* who are not kept in order by parents. **be in ~ (of),** be in command, in charge. **be/come/bring/get under ~,** be, become, cause to be, under authority, restraint, in order, working properly: *get flood waters under ~.* **be/get out of ~,** in a state where authority, etc is lost: *The children are/have got out of ~.* **have/get/keep ~ (over/of),** have, get, keep authority, power, etc: *a teacher who has no ~ over his class; get ~ over a horse,* make it obey. **lose ~ of,** be unable to manage or contain: *lose ~ of one's temper.* **take ~ (of),** take authority: *We must find someone to take ~ of these bolshy children.* **2** [U] management; guidance: *~ of traffic/traffic ~; ~ of foreign exchange; `birth ~,* planning of the number of births, e g by the use of contraceptives. **3** [C] means of regulating, restraining, keeping in order; check: *Government ~s on trade and industry. The chairman's power to veto a proposal is a ~ over what the committee may do.* **4** [C] standard of comparison for results of an experiment: *The tests were given to three groups, Group Two being used as a ~. We must make more ~ experiments.* **5** (usu *pl*) means by which a machine, etc is operated or regulated: *the ~s of an aircraft,* for direction, altitude, etc; *the ~ column* (colloq *stick*), lever in an aircraft for ~ of direction, altitude, etc; *a car with dual ~s/a dual-~ car; the ~s of a transistor radio,* e g the volume ~, regulating the volume of sound; *the `~ tower of an airport,* for regulating air traffic. **6** [C] station at which cars taking part in a race may stop for overhaul, etc. **7** [C] (spiritualism) spirit actuating a medium**(4)**. □ *vt* (-ll-) [VP6A] **1** have ~ of: *to ~ one's temper/expenditure/a horse/oneself.* **2** regulate (prices, etc). **3** check; verify: *to ~ the accounts.* **~·lable** *adj* that can be ~led.

con·trol·ler /kən`trəʊlə(r)/ *n* **1** (also **comptroller**) person who controls expenditure and accounts. **2** person who controls or directs a department or division of a large organization: *C~ of BBC Radio/TV.*

con·tro·ver·sial /'kontrə`vɜʃl/ *adj* likely to cause controversy: *a ~ speech;* (of persons) fond of controversy. **~·ly** /-ʃlɪ/ *adv* **~·ist** *n*

con·tro·versy /`kontrəvɜsɪ, kən`trovəsɪ/ *n* (*pl* -sies) [C,U] prolonged argument, esp over social, moral or political matters: *engage in (a) ~ with/against sb* (*on* or *about* sth); *a question that has given rise to much ~; facts that are beyond ~,* that cannot be argued about.

con·tro·vert /'kontrə`vɜt/ *vt* [VP6A] dispute about; deny; oppose.

con·tu·ma·cious /'kontjʊmeɪʃəs/ *adj* stubborn and

rebellious; obstinate and disobedient. **~·ly** *adv*

con·tu·macy /ˈkontjʊməsɪ *US:* kənˈtuməsɪ/ *n* [U] obstinate resistance; stubborn disobedience; [C] (*pl* -cies) instance of this.

con·tu·meli·ous /ˈkontjʊˈmilɪəs *US:* -təˈm-/ *adj* insolent; opprobrious. **~·ly** *adv*

con·tume·ly /ˈkontjumlɪ *US:* kənˈtuməlɪ/ *n* [U] abusive language or treatment; [C] instance of this; humiliating insult.

con·tuse /kənˈtjuz *US:* -ˈtuz/ *vt* [VP6A] (med) bruise; injure (part of the body) by a blow, without breaking the skin. **con·tusion** /kənˈtjuʒn *US:* -ˈtu-/ *n* [C] bruise.

co·nun·drum /kəˈnʌndrəm/ *n* [C] puzzling question, esp one asked for fun; riddle.

con·ur·ba·tion /ˈkonɜˈbeɪʃn/ *n* [C] area of large urban communities where towns, etc have spread and become joined beyond their administrative boundaries.

con·va·lesce /ˈkonvəˈles/ *vi* [VP2A] regain health and strength after an illness: *She is convalescing after a long illness.*

con·va·les·cent /ˈkonvəˈlesnt/ *n, adj* (person who is) recovering from illness: *a ~ hospital*, one for ~s. **con·va·lescence** /ˈkonvəˈlesns/ *n* [U] gradual recovery of health and strength.

con·vec·tion /kənˈvekʃn/ *n* [U] the conveying of heat from one part of a liquid or gas to another by the movement of heated substances.

con·vec·tor /kənˈvektə(r)/ *n* apparatus (for heating a room, etc) by which air is warmed as it passes over hot surfaces.

con·vene /kənˈvin/ *vt, vi* **1** [VP6A] summon (persons) to come together (for a meeting, etc). **2** [VP2A] come together (for a meeting, council, etc). **con·vener** *n* member (of a society, etc) whose duty it is to ~ meetings.

con·veni·ence /kənˈvinɪəns/ *n* **1** [U] the quality of being convenient or suitable; freedom from difficulty or worry: *I keep my reference books near my desk for ~. The house was planned for ~, not for display,* ie planned so as to be easy to live and work in. *Please send the goods at your earliest ~,* at the earliest time that does not give you trouble. *Please do the work at your own ~,* how and when it best suits you. *It was a marriage of ~,* one in which material advantage was the chief consideration. *Come whenever it is to your ~.* **2** [C] appliance, device, arrangement, etc that is useful, helpful or convenient: *It was a great ~ to have the doctor living near us. The house has all modern ~s,* eg central heating, hot water supply, points for electric current. *The nearest public ~s* (= W C's, lavatories) *are in West Street.* ***make a ~ of sb,*** use his services unreasonably; take too much advantage of his good nature. ***flags of ~,*** ⇨ flag[1].

con·veni·ent /kənˈvinɪənt/ *adj* **~ *(for),*** suitable; handy; serving to avoid trouble or difficulty; easy to get to or at: *Will it be ~ for you to start work tomorrow? This is a ~ tool for the job. Will the 3.50 train be ~ for you? We must arrange a ~ time and place for the meeting.* **~·ly** *adv* in a ~ manner: *My house is ~ly near the bus-stop.*

con·vent /ˈkonvənt *US:* -vent/ *n* **1** society of women (called *nuns*) living apart from others in the service of God; (attrib) *'~ schools.* ⇨ monastery. **2** building(s) in which they live and work: *enter a ~,* become a nun.

con·ven·ticle /kənˈventɪkl/ *n* (building formerly used for) secret religious meeting of Nonconformists or Dissenters.

con·ven·tion /kənˈvenʃn/ *n* **1** [C] conference of members of a society, political party, etc devoted to a particular purpose (e g election of candidates); conference of persons in business, commerce, etc: *the Democratic Party C~.* Cf *conference* in GB. **2** [C] agreement between States, rulers, etc (less formal than a treaty): *the Geneva C~s,* about the treatment of prisoners of war, etc. **3** [U] general (usu tacit) consent (esp about forms of behaviour); [C] practice or custom based on general consent: *When men wore hats, ~ required them to raise them when they met a woman they knew. Does ~ allow women to smoke in public in your country? It is silly to be a slave to ~/to social ~s.* **4** [C] (in various card and board games, esp bridge) practice that is generally followed in bidding, leading cards, making an opening move in chess, etc.

con·ven·tional /kənˈvenʃnl/ *adj* **1** based on convention(3,4): *~ greetings; a few ~ remarks.* **2** following what has been customary; traditional: *a ~ design for a carpet; ~ art; ~ weapons,* ie excluding atomic and hydrogen bombs, etc; *a ~ power station,* using coal or oil as fuel (contrasted with heat from a nuclear reactor). **~·ly** /-ʃnlɪ/ *adv*

con·ven·tion·al·ity /kənˈvenʃnˈæləti/ *n* **1** [U] conventional quality or character: *the ~ of the paintings at the Academy Exhibition.* **2** [C,U] (*pl* -ties) convention(3).

con·verge /kənˈvɜdʒ/ *vi, vt* [VP2A,C,3A,6A,14] (of lines, moving objects, opinions) come, cause to come, towards each other and meet at a point; tend to do this: *armies converging on the capital.* **con·ver·gence** /kEnˈv3dZEns/ *n* **con·ver·gent** *adj*

con·ver·sant /kənˈvɜsnt/ *adj* **~ *with,*** having a knowledge of: *~ with all the rules.*

con·ver·sa·tion /ˈkonvəˈseɪʃn/ *n* [U] talking; [C] talk: *I saw him in ~ with a friend. No ~ while I'm playing the piano, please. I've had several ~s with him.* **~al** /-ʃnl/ *adj* (of words, etc) used in, characteristic of, ~; colloquial.

con·ver·sazi·one /ˈkonvəˈsætsɪˈəʊnɪ/ *n* (*pl* -nes, -ni /-ni/) social party given in the evening by or for a learned society.

con·verse[1] /kənˈvɜs/ *vi* [VP2A,C,3A] **~ *(with sb) (about/on sth),*** (formal) talk.

con·verse[2] /ˈkonvɜs/ *n* [U] (old use) conversation.

con·verse[3] /ˈkonvɜs/ *n, adj* **1** (idea, statement which is) opposite (to another). **2** (logic) form of words produced by transposing some of the words of another: *'He is happy but not rich' is the ~ of 'He is rich but not happy'.* **~·ly** *adv*

con·ver·sion /kənˈvɜʃn *US:* -ˈvɜʒn/ *n* [U] converting or being converted: *the ~ of cream into butter/of forest land into arable land/of pagans to Christianity; the improper ~ of public funds to one's own use,* eg by a government official; [C] instance of ~: *many ~s to Buddhism; building firms which specialize in house ~s,* eg of large houses into flats.

con·vert[1] /kənˈvɜt/ *vt* [VP6A,14] **1** change (from one form, use, etc into another): *to ~ rags into paper/securities into cash/pounds into francs; ~ club funds to one's own use,* use them unlawfully. **2** cause (a person) to change his beliefs, etc: *to ~ a man to Christianity.* **3** (Rugby football) complete (a try) by kicking a goal. **~ed** *part adj* that has been ~ed: *a ~ed mews,* stable(s) rebuilt, decorated, etc for use as a residence.

con·vert[2] /ˈkɒnvɜt/ *n* person converted, esp to a different religion (or from no religion), or to different principles: *a ~ to socialism.*

con·vert·ible /kənˈvɜtəbl/ *adj* that can be converted: *Banknotes are not usually ~ into gold nowadays.* □ *n* (esp US) touring car with a folding or detachable roof. **con·verti·bil·ity** /kənˌvɜtəˈbɪlətɪ/ *n*

con·vex /ˈkɒnveks/ (also, but not when used attrib /kənˈveks/) *adj* with the surface curved like the outside of a ball: *a ~ lens.* ⇨ **concave.** **~·ly** *adv* **~·ity** /kɒnˈveksətɪ/ *n* state of being ~.

con·vey /kənˈveɪ/ *vt* [VP6A,14] **~ *(to) (from)*** **1** take, carry: *Pipes ~ hot water from this boiler to every part of the building. This train ~s both passengers and goods.* **2** **~ *(to sb),*** make known ideas, views, feelings, etc to another person: *Words fail to ~ my meaning. This picture will ~ to you some idea of the beauty of the scenery.* **3** **~ *to,*** (legal) give full legal rights (in land or property): *The land was ~ed to his brother.* **~er, -or** /-veɪə(r)/ *n* person or thing that ~s: *a ˈcoal ~er.* **ˈ~er-belt,** (e g in a factory) flexible band or chain moving over wheels for ~ing packages, etc.

con·vey·ance /kənˈveɪəns/ *n* **1** [U] conveying. **2** [C] sth which conveys; carriage or other vehicle. **3** [C,U] (legal) (document) conveying property. **con·vey·ancer** *n* lawyer who prepares ~s.

con·vict[1] /kənˈvɪkt/ *vt* [VP6A,14] **~ *sb of sth*** **1** cause (sb) to be certain that he has done wrong, made a mistake: *to ~ sb of his errors; to be ~ed of sin.* **2** (of a jury or a judge) declare in a law court that (sb) is guilty (*of* crime): *He was ~ed of murder.*

con·vict[2] /ˈkɒnvɪkt/ *n* person convicted of crime and undergoing punishment.

con·vic·tion /kənˈvɪkʃn/ *n* **1** [U] the convicting of a person for a crime; [C] instance of this: *The ~ of the accused man surprised us. There were five acquittals and six ~s.* **2** [U] the act of convincing, of bringing certainty to the mind. ***(not) carry much ~,*** (not) be convincing. ***be open to ~,*** be ready to listen to evidence, etc that may convince one. **3** [C,U] firm or assured belief: *I speak in the full ~ that...,* firmly convinced that.... *Do you always act up to your ~s,* do what you are convinced is right, just, etc?

con·vince /kənˈvɪns/ *vt* [VP6A,11,14] **~ *sb (of sth/that...)*** make (sb) feel certain; cause (sb) to realize: *I am ~d of his honesty/that he is honest. We couldn't ~ him of his mistake.* **con·vinc·ing** *adj* that ~s: *a convincing speaker/argument.* **con·vin·cing·ly** *adv*: *to speak convincingly.* **con·vinc·ible** /kənˈvɪnsəbl/ *adj* willing, ready, to be ~d.

con·viv·ial /kənˈvɪvɪəl/ *adj* **1** gay; fond of drinking and merry-making: *~ companions.* **2** marked by drinking and merry-making: *a ~ evening.* **~ly** /-ɪəlɪ/ *adv* **~·ity** /kənˌvɪvɪˈælətɪ/ *n* (*pl* -ties) [C, U] merry-making; being ~.

con·vo·ca·tion /ˌkɒnvəˈkeɪʃn/ *n* **1** [U] convoking; calling together. **2** [C] legislative assembly of the Church, of graduates of some universities (e g Leeds, Durham, Oxford).

con·voke /kənˈvəʊk/ *vt* [VP6A] call together, summon (a meeting): *to ~ Parliament.*

con·vol·uted /ˈkɒnvəlutɪd/ *part adj* (zool, biol) coiled; twisted (e g a ram's horn).

con·vol·ution /ˌkɒnvəˈluʃn/ *n* [C] coil; twist: *the ~s of a snake.*

con·vol·vu·lus /kənˈvɒlvjʊləs/ *n* (*pl* -luses /-ləsɪz/) kinds of twining plant including bindweed and morning glory (with white, pink or blue flowers).

con·voy[1] /ˈkɒnvɔɪ/ *vt* [VP6A] (esp of a warship) go with, escort (other ships) to protect (them): *The troopships were ~ed across the Atlantic.*

con·voy[2] /ˈkɒnvɔɪ/ *n* **1** [U] convoying or being convoyed; protection: *The supply ships sailed under ~.* **2** [C] protecting force (of warships, troops, etc). **3** [C] ship, number of ships, under escort; supplies, etc under escort: *The ~ was attacked by submarines.*

con·vulse /kənˈvʌls/ *vt* [VP6A] cause violent movements or disturbances: *~d with laughter/anger/toothache; a country that has often been ~d by earthquakes/civil war.*

con·vul·sion /kənˈvʌlʃn/ *n* [C] **1** violent disturbance: *a ~ of nature,* e g an earthquake; *civil ~s,* riots, etc; *a political ~,* e g an attempt at revolution. **2** (usu *pl*) violent irregular movement of a limb or limbs, or of the body, caused by contraction of muscles: *The child's ~s filled us with fear.* **3** (*pl*) violent fit (of laughter): *The story was so funny that we were all in ~s.*

con·vul·sive /kənˈvʌlsɪv/ *adj* violently disturbing; having or producing convulsions: *~ movements.*

cony, coney /ˈkəʊnɪ/ *n* (*pl* **conies, coneys**) **1** (US) rabbit. **2** rabbit-skin, esp when dyed and prepared so as to resemble the fur of some other animal.

coo /ku/ *vi,vt, n* (*pt* **cooed** /kud/, *pres part* **cooing**) [VP2A] (make a) soft, murmuring sound (as of doves); [VP6A] say in a soft murmur: *to coo one's words.* ⇨ **bill**[2].

cook /kʊk/ *vt,vi* **1** [VP6A,2A,12B,13B] prepare (food) by heating (e g boiling, baking, roasting, frying). ***~ sb's goose,*** ⇨ **goose(1).** **2** [VP2A] undergo ~ing: *These apples ~ well.* **ˈ~ing apples/pears,** etc, suitable for ~ing. Cf *dessert/eating apples.* **3** [VP15B] **~ *up,*** concoct, invent a story, tale, etc: *Don't give me some ~ed-up yarn!* **4** [VP6A] tamper with; prepare fraudulently: *~ the books/the accounts,* falsify them. □ *n* person who ~s food. **ˈ~-book** *n* = cookery book. **ˈ~-house** *n* detached or outdoor kitchen (e g in a camp); ship's galley. **~·ing** *n* [U] *ˈ~ing lessons.*

cooker /ˈkʊkə(r)/ *n* **1** (esp in compounds, as *ˈoil-~, ˈgas-~*) apparatus, stove, for cooking food. **2** kind of fruit, etc (esp apples, pears, plums) grown for cooking: *These apples are good ~s.* Cf *dessert apples,* to be eaten uncooked.

cook·ery /ˈkʊkərɪ/ *n* [U] art and practice of cooking. **ˈ~-book,** one that deals with ~; book of cooking recipes.

cooky, cookie /ˈkʊkɪ/ *n* (*pl* -kies) (Scot) small, flat, thin, sweet cake (esp home-made); (US) biscuit.

cool[1] /kul/ *adj* (-er, -est) **1** between warm and cold: *~ autumn weather. Let's sit in the shade and keep ~. The coffee's not ~ enough to drink.* **2** providing or allowing a feeling between warm and cold: *a ~ room/dress.* **3** calm; unexcited: *Keep ~! He was always ~ in the face of danger. He has a ~ head,* doesn't get flurried. Hence, **ˌ~-ˈheaded** *adj* **4** impudent in a calm way; without shame: *What ~ behaviour—taking my lawnmower without asking my permission!* **5** (of behaviour) not showing interest or enthusiasm:

They gave the prime minister a ~ reception; play it ~, (colloq) deal calmly with a situation; be relaxed. **6** (of sums of money, distances, etc) putting emphasis on the figure, and perhaps suggesting complacency: *My new car cost me a ~ thousand. He suggested that we should walk a ~ twenty miles farther.* □ *n* **1** (usu *sing* with *def art*) ~ air or place; ~ness: *in the ~ of the evening; the ~ of the forest.* **2** (colloq) composure: *keep your ~,* remain calm, unworried. **~·ly** /ˈkulɪ/ *adv* **~·ness** *n*

cool² /kul/ *vt, vi* [VP6A,2A] make or become cool: *The rain has ~ed the air. Has his anger ~ed yet?* [VP3C] ***~ down/off,*** (esp fig) become calm, less excited or enthusiastic: *Her friendship for me has ~ed down.* ***a ˈ~ing ˋoff period,*** (in industrial disputes, etc) a compulsory delay (to ~ tempers) before a threatened strike. ***~ one's heels,*** be kept waiting: *Let him ~ his heels in the outer office; that will teach him to be more polite.*

cool·ant /ˈkulənt/ *n* [C,U] (kind of) fluid used for cooling (e g in nuclear reactors).

cooler /ˈkulə(r)/ *n* container in which things are cooled: *a wine/butter ~;* (sl) prison cell.

coolie /ˈkulɪ/ *n* unskilled workman or porter (esp in the East).

coon /kun/ *n* (chiefly US) raccoon; ⚠ (derog colloq) Negro: *a ˈ~-song,* a Negro melody.

coop /kup/ *n* cage, esp for hens with small chickens. □ *vt* [VP6A,15B] ***~ up,*** put in a ~; confine (a person): *How long are we going to stay ~ed up in here?*

co-op /ˈkəʊ op/ *n* **the ~,** (colloq) the co-operative society (shop, store): *She does all her shopping at the ~.*

cooper /ˈkupə(r)/ *n* maker of tubs, barrels, casks, etc.

co-op·er·ate /kəʊ ˋopəreɪt/ *vi* [VP2A,3A,4A] ***~ (with sb),*** work or act together in order to bring about a result: *~ with friends in starting a social club. Everything ~d to make our holiday a success.* **co-op·er·ator** /-tə(r)/ *n*

co-op·er·ation /kəʊ ˈopəˈreɪʃn/ *n* [U] working or acting together for a common purpose: *The workers, in ~ with the management, have increased output by 10 per cent.*

co-op·er·ative /kəʊ ˋopṛətɪv/ *adj* of co-operation; willing to co-operate: *a ~ society,* group of persons who co-operate, e g to buy machines and services for all to share, or to produce, buy and sell goods among themselves for mutual benefit, or to save and lend money: *the C~ Wholesale Society.* □ *n* (shop of a) ~ society; ~ group: *agricultural ~s in India and China.*

co-opt /kəʊ ˋopt/ *vt* [VP6A,14] (of a committee) add (a person) as a member by the votes of those who are already members: *~ a new member on to the committee.*

co-or·di·nate¹ /ˈkəʊ ˋɔdnət *US:* -dṇət/ *adj* equal in importance: *~ clauses,* clauses in a compound sentence. □ *n* ~ thing or person. **~·ly** *adv*

co-or·di·nate² /ˈkəʊ ˋɔdəneɪt *US:* -dṇeɪt/ *vt* [VP6A] make co-ordinate; bring or put into proper relation: *to ~ ideas; to ~ one's movements when swimming/~ the movements of the arms and legs.*

co-or·di·na·tion /ˈkəʊ ˈɔdnˋeɪʃn *US:* -dṇ-/ *n* the act of co-ordinating; the state of being co-ordinate.

coot /kut/ *n* name of several kinds of swimming and diving birds: *the bald ~,* one with a white spot on the forehead; hence: *as bald as a ~,* very bald.

cop¹ /kop/ *n* (sl) policeman.

cop² /kop/ *vt* (-pp-) (sl) catch: *You'll cop it,* be punished. □ *n* (sl) **1** capture (chiefly in): *It's a fair cop,* I have/He has, etc been caught and arrested in the act of committing the offence. **2** ***not much cop,*** nothing to value highly.

co-part·ner /ˈkəʊ ˋpɑtnə(r)/ *n* partner, e g an employee, who has a share in the profits of a business, etc in addition to his salary or wages. **~·ship** /-ʃɪp/ *n* system, practice, of having ~s in business or industry.

cope¹ /kəʊp/ *n* long, loose cloak worn by clergy on some special occasions. ⇨ the illus at **vestment.**

cope² /kəʊp/ *vi* [VP2A,3A] ***~ (with),*** manage successfully; be equal to: *~ with difficulties.*

co·peck /kəʊpek/ *n* (Russian coin worth) one-hundredth part of a rouble.

co·per /ˈkəʊpə(r)/ *n* horse-dealer.

Co·per·ni·can /kəˋpɜnɪkən/ *adj*: *the ~ system/theory,* of Copernicus /kəˋpɜnɪkəs/ (1473-1543), a Polish astronomer, that the planets, including the earth, move round the sun.

cop·ing /ˈkəʊpɪŋ/ *n* (archit) line of (sometimes overhanging) stonework or brickwork on top of a wall. **ˋ~-stone** *n* (fig) final act, crowning, of a piece of work.

copi·ous /ˈkəʊpɪəs/ *adj* plentiful: *a ~ supply; ~ tears;* (of a writer) writing much. **~·ly** *adv*

cop·per¹ /ˈkopə(r)/ *n* **1** [U] common reddish-brown metal (symbol **Cu**): (attrib) *~ wire/cable/alloy.* **2** [C] coin made of ~ or a ~ alloy. **3** [C] large vessel made of metal, esp one in which clothes are boiled. ⇨ **boiler(1).** **4** **ˋ~ beech** *n* kind of beech-tree with ~-coloured leaves. **ˈ~-ˋbottomed** *adj* **(a)** (of a ship) having the bottom plated with copper (and therefore seaworthy). **(b)** (fig) safe in every way: *~-bottomed guarantees.* **ˋ~·head** *n* poisonous snake of the US. **ˋ~·plate** *n* polished ~ plate on which designs, etc, are engraved: *~plate writing,* cursive, neat and clear. **ˋ~·smith** *n* one who works in ~. □ *vt* (also **ˈ~-ˋbottom**) sheathe (a ship's bottom, etc) with ~.

cop·per² /ˈkopə(r)/ *n* (sl) policeman.

cop·pice /ˈkopɪs/ *n* [C] small area of underwood and small trees (grown for periodical cutting, e g for bean and pea sticks).

copra /ˈkoprə/ *n* [U] dried kernels of coconuts, from which oil is extracted for making soap, etc.

copse /kops/ *n* coppice.

Copt /kopt/ *n* one of the direct descendants of the ancient Egyptians (about one-tenth of the population of modern Egypt). **Cop·tic** /ˈkoptɪk/ *n* language used in the lithurgy of the ~ Church, Egyptian Christian, (in Egypt and Abyssinia). □ *adj* of the Copts.

cop·ula /ˈkopjʊlə/ *n* (gram) verb form (esp a finite of *be*) that connects a subject and the complement.

copu·late /ˈkopjʊleɪt/ *vi* [VP2A,3A] ***~ with,*** (esp of animals) unite in sexual intercourse. **copu·la·tion** /ˈkopjʊˋleɪʃn/ *n* act or process of copulating. **copu·lat·ive** /ˈkopjʊlətɪv/ *adj* serving to connect. □ *n* (gram) word that connects (and which implies combination).

copy¹ /ˈkopɪ/ *n* (*pl* **-pies**) **1** thing made to be like another; reproduction of a letter, picture, etc: *rough ~,* the first (often imperfect) outline or draft of sth written or drawn; *fair ~,* the final form.

Make three carbon copies of the letter. '~**-book** *n* exercise book containing models of handwriting for learners to imitate: *~book maxims,* commonplace maxims (as formerly found in ~books). ⇨ also blot. '~**-cat** *n* (colloq) slavish imitator. **2** one example of a book, newspaper, etc of which many have been made: *If you can't afford a new ~ of the book, perhaps you can find a secondhand ~.* **3** [U] material to be sent to a printer: *The printers are waiting for more ~. The fall of the Cabinet will make good ~,* will make exciting news for the journalists to write about. '~ **boy** *n* boy in a newspaper office who carries ~ and runs errands. '~ **desk** *n* (US) desk in a newspaper office where ~ is edited and prepared for printing.

copy[2] /'kɒpɪ/ *vt,vi* (*pt,pp* -pied) **1** [VP6A,15A, B,14] make a copy of: *~ notes* (*out of a book, etc*) *into a notebook; ~ out a letter,* make a complete copy of it; *~ sth down* (*from the blackboard*). **2** [VP6A] do, try to do, the same as; imitate: *You should ~ his good points, not his bad points.* **3** [VP2A] cheat by looking at a neighbour's paper, etc: *He was punished for ~ing during the examination.* **~-ist** /'kɒpɪɪst/ *n* person who copies or transcribes (e g old documents); imitator.

copy·hold /'kɒpɪhəʊld/ *n* (GB) [U] the holding of land on conditions that were laid down in records of the manor; land held in this way. **~er** *n* person holding land in this way.

copy·right /'kɒpɪrɑɪt/ *n* [U] sole legal right, held for a certain number of years, by the author or composer of a work, or by someone delegated by him, to print, publish, sell, broadcast, perform, film or record his work or any part of it; (attrib) protected by ~. □ *vt* secure ~ for (a book, etc).

co·quet /kəʊ'ket/ *vi* (-tt-) flirt (*with*).

co·quetry /'kəʊkɪtrɪ/ *n* [U] flirting; [C] (*pl* -ries) instance of this; flirtatious act.

co·quette /kəʊ'ket/ *n* girl or woman who flirts. **co·quet·tish** /kəʊ'ketɪʃ/ *adj* of or like a ~: *coquettish smiles.* **co·quet·tish·ly** *adv*

cor·acle /'kɒrəkl/ *n* small, light boat made of wicker, covered with watertight material, used by fishermen on Welsh and Irish rivers and lakes.

cor an·glais /'kɔr 'ɒŋgleɪ *US:* ɒŋ'gleɪ/ *n* (music) wood-wind instrument (tenor oboe). ⇨ the illus at wind.

coral /'kɒrl *US:* 'kɔrl/ *n* **1** [U] hard, red, pink or white substance built on the sea bed by small creatures (*polyps*). '~ '**island,** one formed by the growth of ~. '~**-reef,** accumulation of ~. ⇨ the illus at atoll. [C] sea organism that makes this substance. **2** [C] baby's toy made of polished ~. □ *adj* like ~ in colour; red or pink: *~ lips.*

coral

cor·bel /'kɔbl/ *n* stone or timber projection from a wall to support sth (e g a cornice, an arch). ⇨ the illus at window.

cord /kɔd/ *n* **1** [C,U] (length of) twisted strands, thicker than string, thinner than rope. **2** [C] part of the body like a ~: *the spinal ~; the vocal ~s.* ⇨ chord. **3** [C] measure of wood cut for fuel (usu 128 cubic ft). □ *vt* put a ~ or ~s(1) round.

cord·age /'kɔdɪdʒ/ *n* [U] cords, ropes, etc, esp the rigging of a ship.

cor·dial /'kɔdɪəl/ *adj* **1** warm and sincere (in feeling, behaviour): *a ~ smile/welcome/handshake;* strongly felt: *~ dislike.* **2** (of food and drink, or medicine) making the heart beat faster. □ *n* (comm) sweetened, invigorating liquor: *lime juice ~.* **~ly** /-dɪəlɪ/ *adv* **~-ity** /'kɔdɪ'ælətɪ/ *n* [U] quality of being ~; [C] (*pl* -ties) expression of ~ feeling.

cor·dite /'kɔdɑɪt/ *n* [U] smokeless explosive substance.

cor·don /'kɔdn/ *n* [C] **1** line, ring, of police, soldiers, military posts, etc acting as guards: *a sanitary ~,* a guarded line separating infected and uninfected districts. **2** fruit-tree with all its branches pruned back so that it grows as a single stem (usu against a wall or along wires). **3** ornamental ribbon of an Order[1](10) (usu worn across the shoulder). '~ **bleu** /'kɔdɔ̃ 'blɜ/, (F) award to a cook or restaurant for high quality cooking. □ *vt* [VP15B] **~ *off,*** separate, keep at a distance, by means of a ~(1): *the crowd/area was ~ed off by the police.*

cor·du·roy /'kɔdərɔɪ/ *n* **1** [U] thick coarse, strong cotton cloth with raised lines on it. **2** (*pl*) trousers made of this cloth. **3** *~ road,* one made of tree trunks laid across low and wet land.

cords /kɔdz/ *n pl* (colloq abbr) corduroy trousers.

core /kɔ(r)/ *n* **1** (usu hard) centre, with seeds, of such fruits as the apple and pear. ⇨ the illus at fruit. **2** central or most important part of anything: *the ~ of an electromagnet* (a bar of soft iron). ***to the ~,*** right to the centre: *to get to the ~ of a subject. He is English to the ~,* completely English in manner, speech, dress, etc. ***rotten to the ~,*** (fig) thoroughly bad. □ *vt* [VP6A] take out the ~ of: *to ~ an apple.*

co-re·late ⇨ correlate.

co-re·ligion·ist /'kəʊ rɪ'lɪdʒənɪst/ *n* one of two or more persons who adhere to the same religion.

co-re·spon·dent /'kəʊ rɪ'spɒndənt/ *n* (legal) person charged with adultery with the spouse (husband or wife) of the respondent (petitioner or plaintiff) in a divorce suit.

corgi /'kɔgɪ/ *n* breed of small Welsh dog.

Co·rin·thian /kə'rɪnθɪən/ *n, adj* (native) of Corinth: *~ order,* (archit) one (of three types of column(1) in Grecian architecture) with a decoration of leaves on the capital. ⇨ the illus at column.

cork /kɔk/ *n* **1** [U] light, elastic, tough substance, the thick outer bark of the tree called the ~-oak: *~-tipped cigarettes;* (attrib) made of this material: *a ~ jacket.* **2** [C] round piece of this material used as a stopper for a bottle: *to draw/pull out the ~.* '~**-screw** *n* tool for drawing ~s from bottles. □ *vt,vi* move in spirals. □ *vt* [VP6A,15A] **~ *(up),*** stop with, or as with, a ~: *to ~ a bottle;* (fig): *to ~ up one's feelings.* **corked** *adj* (of wine) contaminated by decayed ~ or a bad ~: *~ed port.*

cork·age /'kɔkɪdʒ/ *n* [U] hotel-keeper's charge for serving wine not supplied by himself.

corker /'kɔkə(r)/ *n* (sl) **1** sth or sb remarkable or astonishing. **2** unanswerable argument.

corm /kɔm/ *n* bulb-like swelling on the underground stem of a plant (e g a crocus or a gladiolus), from the top of which buds sprout. Cf *bulb* which has scales.

cor·mor·ant /ˈkɔmərənt/ *n* large, greedy, long-necked seabird with a pouch under its beak for holding the fish it catches. ⇨ the illus at water.

corn[1] /kɔn/ *n* **1** [U] (collective) (seed of) any of various grain plants, chiefly wheat, oats, rye and (esp US) maize; such plants while growing: *a field of* ~; *a* ˋ~*-field; a sheaf of* ~. ⇨ the illus at cereal. ˋ**~-chandler** *n* retail dealer in ~. ˋ**~-bread,** made from ~ (maize) meal. ˋ**~-cob,** woody part of an ear of maize, on which the grains grow. ˋ**~-crake** /-kreɪk/, common European bird, the male of which has a loud, harsh cry. ˋ**~-exchange,** place where ~-chandlers do business. ˋ**~-flour (US** ˋ**~-starch)**, flour made from maize, rice or other grains. ˋ**~-flower,** name of various flowers growing wild in ~-fields, esp a blue-flowered kind (also grown in gardens). ˋ**C~ Laws,** (esp) laws in GB, repealed in 1846, regulating trade in ~. ˋ**~ pone** /-pəʊn/, (US) bread made of maize meal, milk, etc. ˋ**~-starch,** (US) = ~flour. **2** [C] single grain (of wheat, pepper, etc).

corn[2] /kɔn/ *n* small area of hardened skin on the foot, esp on a toe; often with a painful centre and root. ***tread on sb's ~s,*** (fig) hurt his feelings.

corn[3] /kɔn/ *vt* preserve (meat) in salt: *~ed beef.*

cor·nea /ˈkɔnɪə/ *n* tough transparent outer membrane protecting the iris of the eyeball. ⇨ the illus at eye.

cor·nel·ian /kɔˋnilɪən/ *n* semi-precious stone, reddish, reddish-brown or white.

cor·ner /ˈkɔnə(r)/ *n* **1** position (exterior or interior) of the angle where two lines, sides, edges or surfaces meet; angle enclosed by two walls, sides, etc that meet: *standing at a street* ~*; a shop situated on/at the corner; just round the* ~, (colloq) very near; *sitting in the* ~ *of the room.* ***cut off a ~,*** go across, not round, it; take a short cut. ***cut ~s,*** (of the driver of a motor vehicle) go across, not round them when travelling fast; (fig) simplify proceedings, ignore regulations, etc to get work done quickly: *We've had to cut a few ~s to get your visa ready in time.* ***drive sb into a ~,*** put him in a difficult situation from which escape is difficult. ***turn the ~,*** (fig) pass a critical point in an illness, a period of difficulty, etc. ***be in a tight ~,*** in an awkward or difficult situation. ˋ**~-stone** *n* **(a)** stone that forms a ~ of the foundation of a building (often laid in position at a ceremony). **(b)** (fig) foundation: *Hard work was the ~stone of his success.* **2** hidden, secret, or out-of-the-way place: *money hidden in odd ~s; hole-and-~ methods/transactions,* secret and underhand. **3** region; quarter: *to the four ~s of the earth.* **4** (comm) buying up all or as much as possible of the supply of an article of trade, a commodity, a stock, etc in order to secure a monopoly and control the price. ***make a ~ in sth,*** (e g wheat). **5** (Assoc football) (also ˋ**~-kick**) kick from the ~ of the field, allowed when the ball has been kicked by an opponent over his own goal-line. □ *vt, vi* **1** [VP6A] force into a ~; put into a difficult position: *The escaped prisoner was ~ed at last. That question ~ed me.* **2** [VP6A] make a ~**(4)** in (wheat, etc). **3** [VP2A] (of a vehicle, its driver) turn a ~ (on a road, etc): *My new car ~s/takes ~s well,* remains stable when going round ~s. **~ed** *adj* (in compounds) having ~s: *a three-~ed hat.*

cor·net[1] /ˈkɔnɪt/ *n* **1** small musical instrument of brass, like a trumpet. **2** piece of paper twisted into the shape of a cone, to hold sweets; cone-shaped container for ice-cream.

cor·net[2] /ˈkɔnɪt/ *n* (in former times) officer in a troop of cavalry who carried the colours[1]**(8)**.

cor·nice /ˈkɔnɪs/ *n* (archit) projecting part above the frieze in a column, ⇨ the illus at column; ornamental moulding (e g in plaster) round the walls of a room, just below the ceiling; horizontal strip of carved wood or stone along an outside wall; overhanging mass of snow above a precipice.

cor·nu·co·pia /ˈkɔnjʊˋkəʊpɪə *US:* -jʊkəˋpɪə/ *n* ornamental horn shown in art as overflowing with flowers, fruit and corn; (myth) horn of plenty; (fig) abundant supply.

corny /ˈkɔnɪ/ *adj* (-ier, -iest) (sl) hackneyed; often heard or repeated: ~ *jokes/music.*

co·rolla /kəˋrɒlə/ *n* (bot) ring of petals forming the cup of a flower. ⇨ the illus at flower.

co·rol·lary /kəˋrɒlərɪ *US:* ˋkɒrlerɪ/ *n* (*pl* -ries) [C] natural sequence or outcome of sth; sth self-evident after sth else has been proved.

co·rona /kəˋrəʊnə/ *n* (*pl* -nas /-nəz/, -nae /-ni/) ring of light seen round the sun or moon, e g during an eclipse. ⇨ the illus at eclipse.

cor·on·ary /ˈkɒrənrɪ *US:* ˋkɔrənerɪ/ *adj* (anat) of arteries supplying blood to the heart: ~ *thrombosis,* formation of a clot in a ~ artery. □ *n* (*pl* -ries) (colloq) attack of ~ thrombosis.

cor·on·ation /ˈkɒrəˋneɪʃn *US:* ˈkɔr-/ *n* ceremony of crowning a king, queen or other sovereign ruler: (attrib) *the queen's* ~ *robes.*

cor·oner /ˈkɒrənə(r) *US:* ˋkɔr-/ *n* official who inquires the cause of any death thought to be from violent or unnatural causes; *~'s inquest,* such an inquiry (held with a jury).

cor·onet /ˈkɒrənet *US:* ˋkɔr-/ *n* small crown worn by a peer or peeress; band of precious materials worn as (part of) a woman's head-dress; garland of flowers.

cor·poral[1] /ˈkɔprl/ *adj* of the human body: ~ *punishment,* e g whipping, beating.

cor·poral[2] /ˈkɔprl/ *n* (army) lowest non-commissioned officer (below a sergeant); (navy): *ship's* ~, one with police duties. ⇨ App 9.

cor·por·ate /ˈkɔpərət/ *adj* **1** of or belonging to a corporation: ~ *property;* ~ *bonds,* (Stock Exchange term for) bonds held by a group or company. **2** of, shared by, members of a group of persons: ~ *responsibility/action.* **3** united in one group: *a* ~ *body.*

cor·por·ation /ˈkɔpəˋreɪʃn/ *n* **1** group of persons elected to govern a town: *the Mayor and* ~*; the municipal* ~*;* (attrib) *the* ~ *tramways.* **2** group of persons authorized to act as an individual, e g for business purposes: *In Great Britain the Electricity Authority and the National Coal Board are public ~s.* (US *corporation* = GB *limited liability company*). **3** (colloq) large belly.

cor·por·eal /kɔˋpɔrɪəl/ *adj* **1** of or for the body: ~ *needs,* e g food and drink. **2** physical (contrasted with *spiritual*).

corps /kɔ(r)/ *n* (*pl* **corps** /kɔz/) **1** one of the technical branches of an army: *the* ˈ*Royal* ˈ*Army* ˋ*Medical C~.* **2** military force made up of two or more divisions. **3** **~ de ballet** /ˈkɔ də ˋbæleɪ/ (F) company of dancers in a ballet. **the C~ Diplomatique** /ˈkɔ ˈdɪpləʊmæˋtik/ (F) all the ambassadors, ministers and attachés of foreign states at a capital or Court.

corpse /kɔps/ *n* dead body (esp of a human being). ⇨ carcass.

cor·pu·lent /ˋkɔpjʊlənt/ *adj* (of a person or his body) fat and heavy. **cor·pu·lence** /ˋkɔpjʊləns/ *n*

cor·pus /ˋkɔpəs/ *n* (*pl* corpora /ˋkɔpərə/) body, collection, esp of writings on a specified subject or of material for study (e g for linguists, a collection of examples of spoken and written usages).

cor·puscle /ˋkɔpʌsl/ *n* one of the red or white cells in the blood.

cor·ral /kəˋrɑl *US:* -ˋræl/ *n* **1** enclosure for horses and cattle or the capture of wild animals. **2** = laager. □ *vt* (-ll-) [VP6A] drive (cattle, etc) into, shut up in, a ~; form (wagons) into a ~.

cor·rect[1] /kəˋrekt/ *adj* **1** true; right: *a ~ answer; the ~ time; ~ in every particular.* **2** (of conduct, manners, dress, etc) proper; in accord with good taste or convention: *the ~ dress for a ceremony; a very ~ young lady.* **~·ly** *adv* **~·ness** *n*

cor·rect[2] /kəˋrekt/ *vt* [VP6A,14] **1** make right; take out mistakes from: *I ~ed my watch by the time signal. Please ~ my pronunciation.* **2** point out the faults of; punish: *~ a child for disobedience.*

cor·rec·tion /kəˋrekʃn/ *n* **1** [U] correcting: *the ~ of schoolchildren's work.* **speak under ~,** speak while knowing that one may need to be corrected. **house of ~,** (old name for a) prison. **2** [C] sth put in place of what is wrong: *a written exercise with ~s in red ink.*

cor·rec·ti·tude /kəˋrektɪtjud *US:* -tud/ *n* [U] correctness (esp of conduct, e g in diplomacy).

cor·rect·ive /kəˋrektɪv/ *n, adj* (sth) serving to correct: *~ training,* e g for juvenile delinquents.

cor·re·late /ˋkorl̩eɪt *US:* ˋkɔr-/ *vt,vi* [VP6A,14, 2A,3A] **~ *with,*** have a mutual relation, bring (one thing) into such a relation (*with* another): *Results in the natural sciences seldom ~ with those in history or art. Research workers find it hard to ~ the two sets of figures/to ~ one set with the other.*

cor·re·la·tion /ˈkorɪˋleɪʃn *US:* ˋkɔr-/ *n* mutual relationship: *the ~ between climate and vegetation.*

cor·rela·tive /kəˋrelətɪv/ *n, adj* (word or thing) having a mutual relation: *'Either' and 'or' are ~ conjunctions.*

cor·re·spond /ˈkorɪˋspond *US:* ˋkɔr-/ *vi* [VP2A, 3A] **1 ~ *(with),*** be in harmony: *The house exactly ~s with my needs. His actions do not ~ with his words.* **2 ~ *to,*** be equal (to); be similar (in position, etc) (to): *His expenses do not ~ to his income. The American Congress ~s to the British Parliament.* **3 ~ *(with),*** exchange letters. **~·ing** *adj* that ~(s): *Imports for 1—10 July this year are larger by 10 per cent than for the ~ing period last year.* **~·ing·ly** *adv*

cor·re·spon·dence /ˈkorɪˋspondəns *US:* ˋkɔr-/ *n* **1** [C,U] agreement; similarity: *There is not much ~ between their ideals and ours.* **2** [U] letter-writing; letters: *I have been in ~ with him about the problem. Is commercial ~ taught in the school? He has a great deal of ~ to deal with.* **ˋ~ course,** course of academic study by posting essays, etc to one's tutor.

cor·re·spon·dent /ˈkorɪˋspondənt *US:* ˋkɔr-/ *n* **1** person with whom one exchanges letters: *He's a good/bad ~,* writes regularly/seldom. **2** *newspaper ~,* person regularly contributing local news or special articles to a newspaper: *our Hong Kong ~; a ˋwar-~.* **3** (comm) person, firm, bank, etc which has regular business relations with another (esp in a foreign country).

cor·ri·dor /ˋkorɪdɔ(r) *US:* ˋkɔr-/ *n* long narrow passages from which doors open into rooms or compartments. **ˋ~ train,** one with coaches having ~s which open into compartments.

cor·rie /ˋkorɪ *US:* ˋkɔrɪ/ *n* [C] (Scot) round hollow in a hillside.

corri·gen·dum /ˈkorɪˋdʒendəm *US:* ˈkɔr-/ *n* (*pl* -da /-də/) thing to be corrected (esp in a printed book).

cor·ri·gible /ˋkorɪdʒəbl *US:* ˋkɔr-/ *adj* (formal) capable of being corrected; (of persons) submitting to correction.

cor·rob·or·ate /kəˋrobəreɪt/ *vt* [VP6A] give support or certainty to (a statement, belief, theory, etc). **cor·rob·or·at·ive** /-ərətɪv/ *adj* tending to ~.

cor·rob·or·ation /kəˈrobəˋreɪʃn/ *n* [U] support or strengthening by further evidence; additional evidence: *in ~ (of),* giving further support (of).

cor·rode /kəˋrəʊd/ *vt,vi* [VP6A,2A] wear away, destroy slowly by chemical action or disease; be worn away thus: *Rust ~s iron. Iron ~s easily.* **cor·rosion** /kəˋrəʊʒn/ *n* [U] corroding or being ~d.

cor·ros·ive /kəˋrəʊsɪv/ *n, adj* (substance) that corrodes: *Rust and acids are ~.*

cor·ru·gate /ˋkorəgeɪt *US:* ˋkɔr-/ *vt,vi* [VP6A,2A] make into folds, wrinkles or furrows: *~ the forehead; ~d cardboard,* used for packing fragile goods; *~d roads in tropical countries,* with a furrowed surface caused by weather and use. **ˈ~d ˋiron,** sheet iron made into folds, used for roofs, fences, etc. **cor·ru·ga·tion** /ˈkorəˋgeɪʃn *US:* ˈkɔr-/ *n* [C,U] fold(s); wrinkle(s).

cor·rupt[1] /kəˋrʌpt/ *adj* **1** (of persons, their actions) immoral; depraved; dishonest (esp through taking bribes): *~ practices,* (esp) the offering and accepting of bribes. **2** impure: *~ air/blood.* **3** (of languages, texts, etc) debased by errors or alterations: *a ~ form of Latin.* **~·ly** *adv* **~·ness** *n*

cor·rupt[2] /kəˋrʌpt/ *vt,vi* [VP6A,2A] make or become corrupt: *young persons whose morals have been ~ed; to ~ the electorate,* e g try to win their votes by bribing them. *Does pornography ~?* **~·ible** /-əbl/ *adj* that can be ~ed: *~ible government officials.* **~i·bil·ity** /kəˈrʌptəˋbɪlətɪ/ *n*

cor·rup·tion /kəˋrʌpʃn/ [U] corrupting or or being corrupt; decay: *the ~ of the body after death; the ~ of a language; officials who are proof against ~,* who cannot be bribed.

cor·sage /kɔˋsɑʒ/ *n* upper part of a woman's dress (round the bust); (US) small bouquet of flowers to be worn on this part of the dress or at the waist.

cor·sair /ˋkɔseə(r)/ *n* pirate or pirate ship, esp of Barbary (N Africa in olden times), attacking ships of European countries.

corse /kɔs/ *n* (archaic or poet) corpse.

cor·set /ˋkɔsɪt/ *n* close-fitting reinforced undergarment confining the waist and hips, to shape the body to the current style (often named, in trade, a *foundation,* or *foundation garment*).

corse·let, cors·let /ˋkɔslət/ *n* tight-fitting coat of armour, esp a breast-plate.

cor·tege, cor·tège /kɔˋteɪʒ/ *n* (F) train of attendants; procession, e g at the funeral of a king or president.

cor·tex /ˋkɔteks/ *n* (*pl* cortices /ˋkɔtɪsiz/) outer shell or covering (e g the bark of a tree); outer layer of grey matter of the brain. **cor·ti·cal** /ˈkɔtɪkl/ *adj* of the ~.

cor·ti·sone /ˈkɔtɪzəʊn/ *n* (P) substance (a hormone from the adrenal gland) used medically in the treatment of arthritis and some allergies.

co·run·dum /kəˈrʌndəm/ *n* hard crystallized mineral used chiefly in abrasive, in powder form (for polishing).

cor·us·cate /ˈkorəskeɪt *US:* ˈkɔr-/ *vi* [VP2A] flash, sparkle: *coruscating wit.* **cor·us·ca·tion** /ˌkorəˈskeɪʃn *US:* ˌkɔr-/ *n*

cor·vée /ˈkɔveɪ/ *n* [C] (F) (in feudal times) day's unpaid work which had to be done by French peasants; (modern use) hard task or duty unwillingly performed.

cor·vette /kɔˈvet/ *n* (old use) warship with sails and one tier of guns; (modern use) small fast warship designed for escorting merchant ships.

cos[1] /kos/ *n* (kind of) long-leaved lettuce.

cos[2] /kos/ *n* (abbr of) cosine.

cos[3] /kəz/ *conj* (colloq abbr of) because.

cosh /koʃ/ *vt, n* (GB sl) (strike with a) length of lead pipe, flexible rubber tubing filled with metal, etc. **ˈ~-boy,** young criminal who uses a ~.

cosher /ˈkəʊʃə(r)/ *adj, n* = kosher.

co-signa·tory /ˌkəʊ ˈsɪgnətrɪ *US:* -tɔrɪ/ *adj, n* (*pl* **-ries**) (person) signing jointly with others.

co·sine /ˈkəʊsaɪn/ *n* (trig; abbr **cos**) sine of the complement of a given angle.

cos·metic /kozˈmetɪk/ *adj, n* [C] preparation, substance, esp one that adds colour, designed to make the skin or hair beautiful, e g *face-cream, lipstick.* **cos·me·tician** /ˌkozməˈtɪʃn/ *n* person employed in the preparation or sale of ~s.

cos·mic /ˈkozmɪk/ *adj* of the whole universe or cosmos: *~ rays,* radiations that reach the earth from outer space.

cos·mog·ony /kozˈmogənɪ/ *n* (*pl* **-nies**) (theory of) the origin, creation and evolution of the universe.

cos·mo·naut /ˈkozmənɔt/ *n* = astronaut.

cos·mo·poli·tan /ˌkozməˈpolɪtən/ *adj* **1** of or from all, or many different parts of, the world: *the ~ gatherings at the United Nations Assembly.* **2** free from national prejudices because of wide experience of the world: *a statesman with a ~ outlook.* □ *n* ~(2) person.

cos·mos[1] /ˈkozmos/ *n* the universe, all space, considered as a well-ordered system (contrasted with *chaos*).

cos·mos[2] /ˈkozmos/ *n* garden plant with white, pink or purple flowers.

cos·set /ˈkosɪt/ *vt* pamper.

cost[1] /kost *US:* kɔst/ *vi* (*pt,pp* **cost**) [VP2B] (the adverbial adjunct indicating price, etc may be preceded by an indirect object; not used in the passive voice). **1** be obtainable at the price of; require the payment of: *The house ~ him £8 000. It ~s them £300 a year to run a car. It ~s too much. Compiling a dictionary ~s much time and patience.* **2** result in the loss of: *Careless driving may ~ you your life.* **3** bring injury or disadvantage: *The boy's bad behaviour ~ his mother many sleepless nights.* **4** *vt* [VP6A] (*pt,pp* ~ed) (industry and comm) estimate the price to be charged for an article based on the expense of producing it. **~ing** *n* (industry) fixing of prices: *the ~ing department.*

cost[2] /kost *US:* kɔst/ *n* **1** [C,U] price (to be) paid for a thing: *the ~ of living; living ~s,* the general level of prices; the cost-of-living index, ⇨ **index(3)**; *the ~ price of an article,* the ~ of producing it or the price at which it may be bought wholesale. ⇨ **retail**; *to sell sth at ~,* i e at ~ price; *He built his house without regard to ~,* without considering how much money would be needed. **ˈ~ accountant/clerk,** one who keeps a record of every item of expense in a business, etc. **2** that which is used, needed or given to obtain sth: *The battle was won at a great ~ in human lives,* only after many soldiers had been killed. ***at all ~s,*** whatever the ~ may be. ***at the ~ of,*** at the loss or expense of: *He saved his son from drowning, but only at the ~ of his own life.* ***count the ~,*** consider the risks, possible losses, etc before doing sth. ***to one's ~,*** to one's loss or disadvantage: *Wasps' stings are serious, as I know to my ~,* as I know because of personal suffering from them. **3** (*pl*) (legal) expense of having sth settled in a law court: *He had to pay a £10 fine and £3 ~s.*

co-star /ˌkəʊ ˈstɑ(r)/ *vi, vt* (**-rr-**) **1** [VP6A] present (one star) as having equal status with another or others: *The film ~red John Wayne.* **2** [VP24] (of an actor or actress): *Lawrence Olivier ~s with Maggie Smith in this play.*

cos·ter·monger /ˈkostəmʌŋgə(r)/ *n* person who sells fruit, vegetables, etc from a barrow in the street.

cos·tive /ˈkostɪv/ *adj* constipated.

cost·ly /ˈkostlɪ *US:* ˈkɔst-/ *adj* (**-ier, -iest**) of great value; costing much: *a ~ mistake,* one involving great loss or sacrifice. **cost·li·ness** *n*

cos·tume /ˈkostʃum *US:* -tum/ *n* **1** [U] style of dress: *actors wearing historical ~,* clothes in the style of a period in the past; *Scotsmen in Highland ~,* wearing the kilt, etc; *a ˈ~ piece/play,* one in which the actors wear historical ~. **ˌ~ ˈjewellery,** artificial jewellery. **2** [C] woman's suit (short coat and skirt of the same material). ⇨ **bathing. cos·tumier** /koˈstjumɪə(r) *US:* -ˈstu-/ *n* maker of, dealer in, ~s.

cosy[1] /ˈkəʊzɪ/ *adj* (**-ier, -iest**) warm and comfortable: *a ~ little room.* **cosi·ly** *adv* **cosi·ness** *n*

cosy[2] /ˈkəʊzɪ/ *n* (*pl* **-sies**) covering for a teapot, or an egg in an egg cup.

cot[1] /kot/ *n* **1** small, narrow, easily moved bed; bed for a young child (usu with sides to prevent the child from falling out) (US = *crib*). **2** (US) camp bed; bunk bed on board ship.

cot[2] /kot/ *n* **1** small building for sheltering animals: *a sheep-cot.* **2** (poet) cottage.

cote /kəʊt/ *n* shed or shelter for domestic animals or birds: *a ˈdove-~; a ˈsheep-~.*

co-ten·ant /ˌkəʊ ˈtenənt/ *n* joint tenant.

co·terie /ˈkəʊtərɪ/ *n* group of persons associated by common interests, tastes, etc, esp one that tends to be exclusive: *a literary ~.*

co·termi·nous /ˌkəʊˈtɜmɪnəs/ *adj* having a common terminus or boundary.

co·til·lion, co·til·ion /kəˈtɪlɪən/ *n* name of several kinds of lively French dance originated in the 18th c; music for these.

cot·tage /ˈkotɪdʒ/ *n* small house, esp in the country: *farm labourers' ~s;* house at a summer resort; *~ industries,* those that can be carried on in ~s, e g knitting, pottery, some kinds of weaving. **ˈ~ piano,** small upright piano.

cot·tar, cot·ter /ˈkotə(r)/ *n* (Scot) man living in a cottage on a farm and working on the farm.

cot·ton /ˈkotn/ *n* [U] **1** soft, white fibrous substance round the seeds of the ~-plant, used for making thread, cloth, etc: (attrib) *~ yarn; ~ cloth; ~ goods.* **2** thread spun from ~ yarn: *a ˈneedle and ˋ~.* **ˋ~ batting** *n* (US) = **ˈ~ ˋwool.** **ˋ~-cake,** cattle food made by pressing out oil from seeds of the ~-plant. **ˈ~ seed ˋoil,** oil obtained from ~ seed. **ˈ~-ˋwool,** (GB) cleaned raw ~ or natural ~; absorbent ~ as used for padding, bandaging, etc. **ˋ~-tail** *n* (US) rabbit. □ *vi* ***~ up (to),*** make friendly advances (to). ***~ on (to),*** (sl) understand.

a cotton-plant

coty·ledon /ˌkotɪˋlidn/ *n* first leaf growing from a seed.

couch[1] /kaʊtʃ/ *n* **1** (liter) bed: *retire to one's ~.* **2** long bed-like seat for sitting on or lying on during the day: *studio-~.*

couch[2] /kaʊtʃ/ *vt,vi* [VP6A,14] **1** (formal) put (a thought, etc, *in* words): *The reply was ~ed in insolent terms.* **2** (of animals) lie flat (either in hiding, or ready for a jump forward). **3** lower (a spear or lance) to the position for attack. **4** (*pp* only; liter or poet): *a deer ~ed (= lying) on a grassy bank; ~ed in slumber.*

couch[3], **couch-grass** /ˋkaʊtʃ grɑs *US:* græs/ *n* [U] kind of grass with long creeping roots; quitch.

couch·ant /ˋkaʊtʃənt/ *adj* (heraldry, of animals in a coat of arms, etc) lying with the body resting on the legs and the head raised.

cou·chette /kuˋʃet/ *n* (F) sleeping berth (in a railway compartment).

cou·gar /ˋkugə(r)/ *n* large wild cat, also called a *puma.* ⇨ the illus at **cat**.

cough[1] /kof *US:* kɔf/ *vi,vt* **1** [VP2A] send out air from the lungs violently and noisily; [VP15B] *~ a speaker down,* (of an audience) prevent him by ~ing, from being heard. **2** [VP15B] ***~ up,*** get sth out of the throat by ~ing: *~ sth up,* (sl) say, produce (sth) reluctantly. **3** [VP6A,2A] (sl) confess a crime, esp to the police: *Jones refused to ~.*

cough[2] /kof *US:* kɔf/ *n* **1** act or sound of coughing: *He gave me a warning ~.* **2** condition, illness, that causes a person to cough often: *to have a bad ~; ˋ~-drop, ˋ~-lozenge,* taken to relieve a ~. **3** (sl) confession (of a crime).

could /kʊd/, *weak form* /kəd/ (neg **couldn't** /ˋkʊdnt/) *anom fin pt* of *can,* used in indirect speech in place of *can* if the main verb is *pt*; to express conditions, and to express occasional occurrence and inclination. ⇨ **can**.

couldst /kʊdst/ old form of *could,* used with *thou.*

coul·ter (US = **col·ter**) /ˋkəʊltə(r)/ *n* iron blade fixed vertically in front of a plough share (to cut the soil before it is lifted and turned by the share).

coun·cil /ˋkaʊnsl/ *n* group of persons appointed, elected or chosen to give advice, make rules, and carry out plans, manage affairs, etc, esp of government: *a city/county ~; the municipal ~; to be/to meet in ~; the C~ of the Republic,* upper house in the French legislature; *a ~ of war,* assembly of officers called by the Commander-in-Chief, etc; *the Privy C~.* **ˋ~-board,** table at which members of a ~ sit. **ˋ~-chamber,** in which a ~ meets. **ˋ~ estate,** housing estate built by a city, county, etc ~. ⇨ **housing. ˋ~-house,** house in a ~ estate.

coun·cil·lor (US also **coun·cil·or**) /ˋkaʊnslə(r)/ *n* member of a council.

coun·sel[1] /ˋkaʊnsl/ *n* **1** [U] advice; consultation; opinions; suggestions. ***keep one's own ~,*** keep one's views, plans, etc secret. ***hold/take ~ with sb,*** consult him. ***take ~ together,*** consult together. **2** (with *indef art* or in *pl* but not with numerals): *a ~/~s of perfection,* excellent advice that cannot be followed. **3** (*pl* unchanged) barrister, or group of barristers, giving advice in a law case: *when the jury had heard ~ on both sides,* the barristers for the prosecution and the defence. **Queen's/Kings ˋC~,** (abbr to QC, KC) barrister appointed to act for the State, higher in authority than other barristers.

coun·sel[2] /ˋkaʊnsl/ *vt* (-ll-, US also -l-) [VP6A,B,17] advise; give counsel to: *to ~ an early start; to ~ patience. Would you ~ our giving up/~ us to give up the plan?*

coun·sel·lor (US also **coun·sel·or**) /ˋkaʊnslə(r)/ *n* adviser; (in Ireland and US) lawyer.

count[1] /kaʊnt/ *vt,vi* **1** [VP2A,C] say or name (the numerals) in order: *to ~ from 1 to 20; to ~ up to 10. He can't ~ yet.* **2** [VP6A] find the total of: *Don't forget to ~ your change. Have the votes been ~ed yet?* **3** [VP6A,14,2A,C] include, be included, in the reckoning: *fifty people, not ~ing the children. That doesn't ~,* need not be considered or reckoned. **4** [VP25,16B] consider (sth or sb) to be: *I ~ myself fortunate in being here. I ~ it a great honour to serve you. I'm afraid we must ~ him as dead.* **5** [VP14,3A] ***~ (sth) against sb,*** be considered, consider to the disadvantage of: *His past record ~s against him. He is young and inexperienced, but please do not ~ that against him.* ***~ (sb) among,*** be regarded, regard sb, as one of: *You ~/You are ~ed among my best friends. I no longer ~ him among my friends.* **6** (uses with *adverbial particles* and *preps*): ***~ down,*** ~ seconds backwards (e g 10, 9, 8, 7...) as when launching a rocket, etc into space. Hence, **ˋ~-down** *n* ***~ for nothing/not much/little,*** be of no/little worth or importance: *Knowledge without common sense ~s for little. Such men do not ~ for anything.* ***~ in,*** include: *Go and see how many plates we have—but don't ~ in the cracked ones. If you're all going to the pub for a drink, you can ~ me in,* I will certainly be one of the party. ***~ on/upon,*** expect with confidence; rely upon. *We ~ (up)on your help/~ on you to help. You had better not ~ on an increase in your salary this year.* ***~ out,*** **(a)** ~ things (slowly), one by one: *The old lady ~ed out fifteen pence and passed it to the salesgirl.* **(b)** ~ up to ten over a boxer who has been knocked out: *The referee ~ed him out in the first round.* **(c)** not include: *If it's going to be a rowdy party, ~ me out,* I shall certainly not be there. ***~ the House out,*** (GB, House of Commons) ~ the members present and declare that, because enough members are not present, there must be an adjournment. ***~ up,*** find the total of:

Just you ~ up the number of times he has failed to keep a promise! **'~-ing-frame,** abacus. **'~-ing-house,** building or room for keeping accounts (e g in a bank). **~-able** *adj* that can be ~ed.

count[2] /kaʊnt/ *n* **1** act of counting; number got by counting: *Four ~s were necessary before we were certain of the total.* ***keep/lose ~ of,*** be aware/fail to know how many there are (of): *I've bought so many new books this year that I've lost ~ of them.* ***take the ~, be out for the ~,*** (boxing) be counted out. ⇨ count[1](6). **2** [U] account; notice: *to take no/some/any/not much, etc ~ of what people say.* **3** [C] (legal) one of a number of things of which a person has been accused: *He was found guilty on all ~s.*

count[3] /kaʊnt/ *n* title of nobility in France, Italy, etc (but not in GB). ⇨ countess, earl.

coun·ten·ance[1] /ˈkaʊntɪnəns/ *n* **1** face, including its appearance and expression: *a woman with a fierce ~; to change ~,* change one's expression because of emotion; *to keep one's ~,* maintain one's composure (esp by not laughing). ***put/stare sb out of ~,*** disconcert him, cause him to feel troubled or at fault (by looking at him steadily). **2** [U] support; approval: *to give ~ to a person/a plan.*

coun·ten·ance[2] /ˈkaʊntɪnəns/ *vt* [VP6A] give support or approval to: *to ~ a fraud. We can never ~ a war of aggression.*

coun·ter[1] /ˈkaʊntə(r)/ *n* table or flat surface on which goods are shown, customers served, in a shop or bank. ***under the ~,*** (of goods in shops) bought or sold surreptitiously, e g when they are scarce and difficult to obtain.

coun·ter[2] /ˈkaʊntə(r)/ *n* **1** small (usu round) flat piece of metal, plastic, etc used for keeping count in games, etc; piece used in draughts(7), etc. **2** (in compounds) device for keeping count (in machinery, etc): *'speed-~; 'revo'lution-~.*

coun·ter[3] /ˈkaʊntə(r)/ *adv* **~ to,** contrary; in the opposite direction (to); in opposition (to): *to act ~ to a person's wishes; requirements that run (go) ~ to one's inclinations.*

coun·ter[4] /ˈkaʊntə(r)/ *vt,vi* [VP6A,14,2A,3A] **~ *(with),*** oppose; meet an attack (with a return attack): *They ~ed our proposal with one of their own. The champion ~ed with the right,* (boxing) parried a blow and returned it with a right-handed blow.

coun·ter- /ˈkaʊntə(r)/ *pref* **1** opposite in direction: *~-attraction; ~-productive.* **2** made in answer to: *'~-attack; '~-'espionage/-in'telligence.* **3** corresponding: *'~part.*

coun·ter·act /ˈkaʊntəˈrækt/ *vt* [VP6A] act against and make (action, force) of less or no effect: *~ (the effects of) a poison/sb's bad influence.* **coun·ter·action** /ˈkaʊntərˈækʃn/ *n* ~ing.

coun·ter-at·tack /ˈkaʊntər ətæk/ *n* attack made in reply to an attack by the enemy. □ *vt,vi* make a ~ (upon).

coun·ter-at·trac·tion /ˈkaʊntər ətrækʃn/ *n* [C] rival attraction.

coun·ter·bal·ance /ˈkaʊntəbæləns/ *n* [C] weight, force, equal to another and balancing it. □ *vt* /ˈkaʊntəˈbæləns/ [VP6A] act as a ~ to.

coun·ter·blast /ˈkaʊntəblɑst *US:* -blæst/ *n* [C] violent retort.

coun·ter·claim /ˈkaʊntəkleɪm/ *n* claim made in opposition to another claim: *a ~ for damages,* by a defendant in a lawsuit.

coun·ter-clock·wise /ˈkaʊntə ˈklokwaɪz/ *adv* in the direction opposite to the movements of the hands of a clock.

coun·ter-espion·age /ˈkaʊntər ˈespɪənɑʒ/ *n* [U] spying directed against the enemy's spying.

coun·ter·feit /ˈkaʊntəfɪt/ *n, adj* (sth) made or done in imitation of another thing in order to deceive: *~ money/jewels/grief. This ten-dollar note is a ~.* □ *vt* [VP6A] copy, imitate (coins, handwriting, etc) in order to deceive. **~er** *n* person who ~s.

coun·ter·foil /ˈkaʊntəfɔɪl/ *n* section of a cheque, receipt, etc kept by the sender as a record. Cf US *stub.*

coun·ter-in·tel·li·gence /ˈkaʊntər ɪnˈtelɪdʒəns/ *n* [U] = counter-espionage.

coun·ter-ir·ri·tant /ˈkaʊntər ˈɪrɪtənt/ *n* sth used to produce a surface irritation and in this way relieve a more deeply seated pain, e g rheumatism.

coun·ter·mand /ˈkaʊntəˈmɑnd *US:* -ˈmænd/ *vt* [VP6A] take back, cancel, a command already given.

coun·ter·march /ˈkaʊntəmɑtʃ/ *vi,vt, n* [VP6A,2A] (cause to) march in the contrary direction.

coun·ter·mine /ˈkaʊntəmaɪn/ *n* (in war) mine (on land or sea) to counteract one of the enemy's; (fig) counter-plot. □ *vt,vi* oppose by ~; make a ~.

coun·ter-offer /ˈkaʊntər ofə(r) *US:* ɔf-/ *n* offer made in reply to an offer made by sb else.

coun·ter·pane /ˈkaʊntəpeɪn/ *n* covering for a bed; bedspread.

coun·ter·part /ˈkaʊntəpɑt/ *n* person or thing exactly like, or closely corresponding to, another.

coun·ter·plot /ˈkaʊntəplot/ *n* plot made to defeat another plot. □ *vt,vi* (-tt-) make a ~ (against).

coun·ter·point /ˈkaʊntəpɔɪnt/ *n* (music) **1** [C] melody added as an accompaniment to another melody. **2** [U] art or method of adding melodies as accompaniment according to fixed rules.

coun·ter·poise /ˈkaʊntəpɔɪz/ *n* **1** [C] weight used to balance another weight; force, power or influence that counterbalances another. **2** [U] the condition of being in balance; equilibrium. □ *vt* bring into, keep in, equilibrium.

coun·ter-rev·ol·ution /ˈkaʊntə ˈrevəˈluʃn/ *n* political movement directed against a revolution. **~-ary** /-ˈluʃṇərɪ *US:* -ṇerɪ/ *adj* characteristic of a ~. □ *n* (*pl* -ries) person engaged in ~(s).

counter·sign /ˈkaʊntəsaɪn/ *n* [C] password; secret word(s) to be given, on demand, to a sentry before he allows sb to pass: *'Advance and give the ~'.* □ *vt* [VP6A] add another signature to (a document) to give it authority.

coun·ter·sink /ˈkaʊntəsɪŋk/ *vt* (*pt* -sank /-sæŋk/, *pp* -sunk) **1** enlarge the top of (a hole) so that the head of a screw or bolt fits in level with or below the surface. **2** sink (the head of a screw or bolt) in such an enlarged hole.

coun·ter·tenor /ˈkaʊntətenə(r)/ *n* (music) (part for an) (adult person with a) male voice higher than tenor, alto.

coun·ter·vail /ˈkaʊntəveɪl/ *vt,vi* **1** [VP6A] counterbalance. **2** [VP2A] have equal or compensating power against: *~ing duties,* to be paid (as part of a tariff) on imports on which a subsidy is paid in the exporting country.

count·ess /ˈkaʊntɪs/ *n* wife or widow of a count or earl; woman to whom an earldom has descended.

count·less /ˈkaʊntləs/ *adj* that cannot be counted (because too numerous).

coun·tri·fied /ˈkʌntrɪfaɪd/ *adj* rural; rustic; having the unsophisticated ways, habits, outlook, etc, of those who live in the country(**4**), not of towns.

coun·try /ˈkʌntrɪ/ *n* (*pl* **-ries**) **1** [C] land occupied by a nation: *European countries.* **2** [C] land of a person's birth or citizenship: *to return to one's own* ~. **3** (*sing* with *def art*) the people of a ~(**1**); the nation as a whole: *Does the* ~ *want war?* ***go to the*** ~, (GB) appeal to the public by a general election for the right to form a government(**3**). **4** (*sing* with *def art*) land used for farming, land consisting of open spaces, etc; the contrary of town and suburb: *to live in the* ~; *to spend a day in the* ~. **5** (used attrib) of or in the ~(**4**): ~ *life;* ~ *roads; a* ~ *club,* club in the ~ or suburbs, where members may enjoy outdoor sports, etc; *a* ~ *cousin,* person who is unaccustomed to town life and ways; ~ *dance,* (esp in England) one in which couples are face to face in two long lines or face inwards from four sides; ~ *gentleman,* man who owns land in the ~ and has a house there; *ˈ~-ˈhouse, ˈ~-ˈseat,* house of a ~ gentleman; *ˈ~ party,* political party supporting agricultural interests (against manufacturing interests). **6** (*sing* only, with *attrib adj,* without *art*) area of land (esp considered with reference to its physical or geographical features): *We passed through miles of densely wooded* ~. *This is unknown* ~ *to me,* I have not been through it before (or, fig) This is a branch of learning, etc with which I am unfamiliar.

coun·try·man /ˈkʌntrɪmən/, **coun·try·woman** /ˈkʌntrɪwʊmən/ *n* (*pl* **-men, -women**) **1** person living in the country(**4**). **2** person of one's own (or a specified) country(**1**).

coun·try·side /ˈkʌntrɪsaɪd/ *n* [U] rural area(s) (contrasted with urban areas): *The English* ~ *looks its best in May and June. The preservation of the* ~ *is important.*

county /ˈkaʊntɪ/ *n* (*pl* **-ties**) **1** [C] division of GB, the largest unit of local government: *the* ~ *of York* (or *Yorkshire*); ~ *town,* (US = ~ *seat*) chief town of a ~, where administration is carried on; (GB) ~ *borough,* town having the right to send one or more representatives to Parliament and administrative powers similar to those of a ~ council. ~ *council,* body of persons elected to govern a ~; ~ *court,* local court for certain legal matters, e g recovery of debt; ~ *family,* family that has lived in a ~ for many generations and has an ancestral home in it; *the home counties,* those round London. **2** (in US and other countries) subdivision of a State. **3** (GB; collective *sing,* with *def art*) **the** ~, all the ~ families: *All the* ~ *was at the ball.* (Used *pred*): *The Hedons were* ~, were ~ families.

coup /ku/ *n* (*pl* **-s** /kuz/) (F) sudden action taken to get power, obtain a desired result, etc: *He made/pulled off a great* ~, succeeded in what he attempted. ~ **d'état** /ˈku deɪˈtɑ/, violent or unconstitutional change in government by persons in authority. ~ **de grâce** /ˈku də ˈgrɑs *US:* ˈgræs/, finishing stroke (that kills).

coupé /ˈkupeɪ *US:* kuˈpeɪ/ *n* (*pl* **-pés** /-peɪz/) **1** closed horse-drawn carriage with one inside seat for two people and an outside seat for the driver. **2** roofed two-door motor-car with a sloping back.

couple[1] /ˈkʌpl/ *n* **1** two persons or things, seen together or associated: *He came back with a* ~ *of rabbits and a hare.* ***go/hunt/run in*** ~***s,*** in pairs; two together. **2** man and his wife: *married* ~*s;* man and woman to be married: *courting* ~*s;* pair of partners in a dance: *Ten* ~*s took the floor,* went out into the middle of the room to dance.

couple[2] /ˈkʌpl/ *vt,vi* **1** [VP6A,14] fasten, join (two things) together: *to* ~ *two railway coaches. The dining-car was* ~*d on at Crewe. We* ~ *the name of Oxford with the idea of learning.* **2** [VP6A,2A] marry; [VP2A] (of animals) unite sexually; [VP2A] (of things) come together; unite.

coup·let /ˈkʌplət/ *n* two successive lines of verse, equal in length and with rhyme: *Heroic* ~, with lines of five feet and ten syllables.

coup·ling /ˈkʌplɪŋ/ *n* [U] act of joining; [C] link, etc that joins two parts, esp two railway coaches or other vehicles.

cou·pon /ˈkupɒn/ *n* ticket, part of a document, paper, bond, etc, which gives the holder the right to receive sth or do sth e g a voucher given with a purchase to be exchanged, taking trading stamps, for goods; entry form for a competition: *fill in the football* ~*s,* by forecasting results of matches.

cour·age /ˈkʌrɪdʒ *US:* ˈkɜ-/ *n* [U] bravery; quality that enables a person to control fear in the face of danger, pain, misfortune, etc. ***have the*** ~ ***of one's convictions,*** be brave enough to do what one feels to be right. ***not have the*** ~ ***to,*** not be brave enough to. ***lose*** ~, become less brave. ***take/pluck up/muster up/summon up*** ~, be brave. ***take one's*** ~ ***in both hands,*** summon up one's ~ for sth needing to be done.

cou·rageous /kəˈreɪdʒəs/ *adj* brave; fearless: *It was* ~ *of him to oppose his chief.* ~**·ly** *adv*

cour·gette /kʊəˈʒet/ *n* (US = *zucchini*) small green marrow(**3**) eaten as a vegetable. ⇨ the illus at **vegetable**.

cour·ier /ˈkʊrɪə(r)/ *n* **1** person who is paid to attend to details of travel (e g buying tickets, arranging for hotels, etc) and (sometimes) accompanying travellers. **2** messenger carrying news or important government papers.

course[1] /kɔs/ *n* **1** [U] forward movement in space or time: *the* ~ *of life from the cradle to the grave; a river in its* ~ *to the sea; the* ~ *of events.* ***in*** ~ ***of,*** in process of: *The railway is in* ~ *of construction,* being built. ***in due*** ~, in the natural order; at the normal time: *Sow the seed now and in due* ~ *you will have the flowers.* ***in the*** ~ ***of,*** during: *in the* ~ *of the discussion; in the* ~ *of conversation,* while we were talking; *in the* ~ *of centuries,* as the centuries pass. ***in the*** ~ ***of nature, in the ordinary*** ~ ***of events/things,*** normally; as part of the normal or expected sequence of events. ***in (the)*** ~ ***of time,*** at length; finally; when (enough) time has passed. **2** [C] direction taken by sth; line along which sth moves; line of action: *a map that shows the* ~*s of the chief rivers;* (liter) *the stars in their* ~*s. The ship is on/off her right* ~, is going/not going in the right direction. *The ship was blown off* ~. *Our* ~ *was due north. The* ~ *of the argument suddenly changed,* went in a different direction. *What are the* ~*s open to us,* the ways in which we may proceed to act? *He took to evil* ~*s,* formed bad ways of living. ***run/take its/their, etc*** ~, develop as is normal; proceed to the usual end: *The disease must run its* ~. *The law must take its* ~, the lawyers cannot save you from punishment. *We can do nothing except let matters run/take their* ~. ***(as) a matter of*** ~, that which one would expect to be or happen, for which no effort is needed: *You needn't ask him to come; he'll come as a matter of ~. Some people take my help as a matter of ~*, expect to get it without asking for it (or even thanking me for it). ***of ~,*** naturally; certainly: *'Do you study hard?' 'Of ~ I do'.* **3** [C] ground for golf: *a 'golf-~*; place for horse-races: *a 'race-~.* ***stay the ~,*** (liter, fig) continue going until the end; not give up. **4** [C] series of talks, treatments, etc: *a ~ of lectures/study/instruction; a ~ of X-ray treatment/pills; the high-school ~.* **5** [C] continuous layer of brick, stone, etc in a wall: *a 'damp-~*, layer of slate or other material to prevent damp rising from the ground. **6** [C] one of the several parts of a meal, e g soup, fish, dessert: *a dinner of five ~s/a five-~ dinner; the main ~.* **7** (naut) sail fastened to the lowest yard of a mast.

course² /kɔs/ *vt,vi* **1** [VP6A,2A] chase (esp hares) with dogs (greyhounds). **2** [VP2C] move quickly; (of liquids) run: *The blood ~d through his veins. Tears ~d down her cheeks.* **cours·ing** /ˈkɔsɪŋ/ *n* sport of chasing hares with greyhounds (by sight, not scent).

courser /ˈkɔsə(r)/ *n* (poet) swift horse.

court¹ /kɔt/ *n* **1** [C] place where law-cases are held; the judges, magistrates, and other officers who administer justice: *'~ of 'law/a 'law ~; '~-room; ~ of justice; po'lice-~; a (military or naval) ~ of inquiry*, one that deals with cases of indiscipline, etc; *The prisoner was brought to ~ for trial. The judge ordered the ~ to be cleared*, ordered members of the public to leave. *The case was settled out of ~*, a settlement was reached that made it unnecessary for the case to be decided in ~. ***be ruled/put out of ~, put oneself out of ~,*** do or say sth so that one is not entitled to be heard in ~. **~ of assize, ~ of quarter sessions,** ~s in England and Wales before 1971. **Crown C~,** (since 1971) one that may sit anywhere in England and Wales for all cases above magistrates' ~ level (replacing the former assize and quarter sessions). **2** (residence of a) great ruler, king, queen, emperor, his family and officials, councillors, etc; state gathering or reception given by a ruler: *The C~ of St James's*, the ~ of the British sovereign. *The C~ went into mourning when the Queen's uncle died. The Queen will hold several ~s during May and June. The C~* (= The royal household) *has gone to Windsor.* ***be presented at ~,*** (of a débutante) make one's first appearance at a state reception at the sovereign's ~ and pay respects to the sovereign. **'~ dress,** dress to be worn at ~ on ceremonial occasions. **'~ 'circular,** daily report of what happens at ~, published in the newspapers. **'~-card,** playing card with a king, queen or knave. **'~-guide,** book with names of those persons who have been presented at ~. **3** [C] space marked out for certain games: *a 'tennis-~. Do you prefer grass ~s or hard ~s?* ⇨ the illus at tennis. **4** (also **'~-yard**) unroofed space with walls or buildings round it, e g in a college at Cambridge, in a castle or an old inn; the buildings round such a space. Cf *quadrangle* at Oxford. ⇨ close². **5** [C] enclosed yard, usu opening off a street, often of poor, mean houses. **6** [U] *pay ~ to a woman*, (formal) try to win her affections.

court² /kɔt/ *vt,vi* **1** [VP6A,2A] try to win the affections of, with a view to marriage: *He had been ~ing Jane for six months. There were several ~ing couples in the park.* **2** [VP6A] try to win or obtain: *to ~ sb's approval/support; to ~ applause.* **3** [VP6A] act in such a way that one may meet or receive (sth disagreeable): *to ~ defeat/danger/disaster.*

cour·teous /ˈkɜtɪəs/ *adj* having, showing, good manners; polite and kind (*to*). **~·ly** *adv*

court·esan /ˈkɔtɪˈzæn *US:* ˈkɔtɪzn/ *n* (in former times, esp in court(2) circles) refined or high-placed prostitute who (because of her beauty, wit, success) could limit the number of men to whom she gave herself.

cour·tesy /ˈkɜtəsɪ/ *n* **1** [U] courteous behaviour. **2** [C] (*pl* -sies) courteous act. **3 '~ title,** (GB) title of nobility by ~ and not by right. ***by ~ of,*** by favour or permission, usu free of charge: *a radio programme presented by ~ of….*

court·ier /ˈkɔtɪə(r)/ *n* person in attendance at the court of a sovereign: *the King and his ~s.*

court·ly /ˈkɔtlɪ/ *adj* (-ier, -iest) polite and dignified. **court·li·ness** *n*

court-mar·tial /ˈkɔt ˈmɑʃl/ *n* (*pl* courts-martial) court for trying offences against military law; trial by ~. □ *vt* [VP6A] (-ll-) try (sb) in a court of this kind.

court·ship /ˈkɔtʃɪp/ *n* courting(1); period during which this lasts: *after a year's ~; after a brief ~.*

court·yard /ˈkɔtjɑd/ *n* court¹(4).

cousin /ˈkʌzn/ *n*: *first ~*, child of one's uncle or aunt; *second ~*, child of one's parent's first ~; *his ~ Mary; her ~ John.* **~·ly** *adj* of, suitable for, ~s: *~ly affection.*

cove¹ /kəʊv/ *n* small bay².

a cove

cove² /kəʊv/ *n* (GB, dated sl) fellow: *He's a queer ~.*

coven /ˈkʌvn/ *n* assembly (of witches).

cov·en·ant /ˈkʌvn̩ənt/ *n* **1** (legal) formal agreement that is legally binding. **'deed of '~,** written, signed and sealed and usu concerning property. **2** undertaking to make regular payments to a charity, trust, etc. □ *vt,vi* [VP6A,7A,9,14,3A] ***~ (with sb) (for sth/to do) sth/that,*** make a ~.

Cov·en·try /ˈkovntrɪ/ *n* town in Warwickshire, GB. ***send a person to ~,*** refuse to associate with him.

cover¹ /ˈkʌvə(r)/ *vt* [VP6A,15A,B] **1** place (one substance or thing) over or in front of (another); hide or protect (sth) in this way; lie or extend over; occupy the surface of: *C~ the table with a cloth. Pull your skirt down and ~ your knees. We shall ~ the seat of this old chair with chintz. Snow ~ed the ground. The floods ~ed large areas on both banks of the river. She ~ed her face in/with her hands. He laughed to ~* (= hide) *his nervousness.* ***~ in,*** complete the ~ing of: *The grave was* *quickly ~ed in,* filled with earth. **~ over,** spread sth over: *to ~ over a hole in a roof.* **~ up,** wrap up, hide: *C~ yourself up well,* Put on warm clothes, etc. *How can we ~ up our tracks/our mistakes?* **~ed wagon** *n* (US) large wagon with an arched canvas roof, used by pioneers for travel across the prairies. **2** (usu in the passive) ***be ~ed with,*** **(a)** have a great number or amount of: *trees ~ed with blossom/fruit; roses ~ed with greenfly.* **(b)** have as a natural coat: *Cats are ~ed with fur and dogs are ~ed with hair.* **(c)** (of non-material things) be overcome by: *~ed with shame/confusion.* **3** sprinkle or strew with: *A taxi went by and ~ed us with mud. The wind blew from the desert and ~ed everything with sand.* **4** (*reflex*) bring upon oneself: *~ oneself with glory/honour/disgrace.* **5** protect: *He ~ed his wife from the man's blows with his own body. Warships ~ed the landing of the invading army,* fired their guns to keep the enemy at a distance, etc. *Are you ~ed* (= insured) *against fire and theft?* **6** travel (a certain distance): *By sunset we had ~ed thirty miles.* **7** (of guns, fortresses, etc) command[1](6); dominate: *Our heavy artillery ~ed every possible approach to the town.* **8** keep a gun aimed at sb (so that he cannot shoot or escape): *C~ your man! Keep them ~ed!* **9** (of money) be enough for: *£10 will ~ my needs for the journey. We have only just ~ed our expenses,* made enough for our expenses, but no profit. **10** include; comprise; extend over; be adequate for: *Professor A's lectures ~ed the subject thoroughly. His researches ~ed a wide field. This book does not fully ~ the subject,* does not deal with all aspects of it. *Do the rules ~* (= Are they adequate for) *all possible cases?* **11** (in games such as cricket and baseball) stand behind (a player) to stop balls that he may miss: *The short-stop ~ed second base.* **12** (of a journalist) report (what is said and done at meetings, on public occasions, etc): *~ the Labour Party's annual conference.* **~·ing** *n* sth that ~s: *a leafy ~ing,* the trees. □ *part adj*: *~ing letter,* one sent with a document, or with goods, etc; *'~ing party,* number of soldiers to protect others who are working, digging trenches, etc.

cover[2] /ˈkʌvə(r)/ *n* **1** thing that covers: *When the water boils, take the ~* (= lid) *from the pan. Some chairs are fitted with loose ~s.* **2** binding of a book, magazine, etc; either half of this: *The book needs a new ~.* ***from ~ to ~,*** from beginning to end: *The child read the book from ~ to ~.* **'~ girl,** girl who poses for photographs to be used on the cover of a magazine. **3** wrapper or envelope. ***under plain ~,*** in a parcel or envelope which has no indication of the firm, the contents, etc: *The book of photographs of girls in the nude is being sent under plain ~.* ***under separate ~,*** (comm) in a separate parcel or envelope: *We are sending the goods under separate ~.* **4** [U] place or area giving shelter or protection: *The land was flat and treeless and provided no ~ for the troops. There was nowhere where we could take ~,* e g from rain. ***take ~,*** (mil) place oneself where one is concealed, or protected from enemy fire. ***under ~,*** sheltered from the weather. **5** [U] woods or undergrowth protecting animals, etc. ***break ~,*** (e g of a fox) come out of the undergrowth, etc. **6** [U] ***under ~ of,*** with a pretence of: *under ~ of friendship/religion; murders committed under ~ of patriotism.* **7** [U] force of aircraft protecting a land or sea operation: *give an operation fighter ~.* **8** place laid at table for a meal: *C~s were laid for six. There is a '~ charge of 25p,* 25p in addition to the cost of the food and drink. **9** (comm) money deposited to meet a liability or possible loss. **10** insurance against loss, damage, etc: *Does your policy provide adequate ~ against fire?* **'~ note,** document from an insurance company to provide temporary ~ between the acceptance and issue of a policy.

cover·age /ˈkʌvərɪdʒ/ *n* [U] covering of events, etc: *TV ~ of the election campaign,* e g by televising political meetings, interviews with candidates and voters. ⇨ **cover[1](12).**

cover·let /ˈkʌvələt/ *n* bed cover.

cov·ert[1] /ˈkʌvət/ *adj* (of glances, threats, etc) half-hidden; disguised. **~·ly** *adv*

cov·ert[2] /ˈkʌvət/ *n* area of thick undergrowth in which animals hide: *draw a ~,* search it (for foxes, etc). ⇨ **cover[2](5).**

covet /ˈkʌvɪt/ *vt* desire eagerly (esp sth that belongs to sb else).

covet·ous /ˈkʌvətəs/ *adj* ***~ of,*** eagerly desirous (esp of things belonging to sb else). **~·ly** *adv* **~·ness** *n*

covey /ˈkʌvɪ/ *n* (*pl* **-veys** /-vɪz/) brood, small flock (of partridges).

cow[1] /kaʊ/ *n* **1** ⇨ the illus at **domestic**. Fully grown female of any animal of the ox family, esp the domestic kind kept by farmers for producing milk; also female elephant, rhinoceros, whale, etc. ⇨ **bull[1](1), calf[1](1), heifer, steer[1]. 'cow·bell,** bell hung round a cow's neck to indicate her whereabouts. **'cow·boy,** man (usu on horseback) who looks after cattle in the western parts of the US. **'cow-catcher,** metal frame fastened to the front of a railway engine to push obstacles off the track. **'cow·hand, 'cow·herd,** person who looks after cattle at pasture. **'cow·hide,** leather (or a strip of leather as a whip) made from a cow's hide. **'cow·house, 'cow·shed,** building in which cows are kept when not at pasture, or to which they are taken to be milked. **'cow·man** /-mən/ (*pl* **-men**), man responsible for milking cows. **'cow·skin,** (leather from the) skin of a cow. **2** (pej) woman.

cow[2] /kaʊ/ *vt* [VP6A] frighten (sb) into submission: *The child had a cowed look,* looked frightened because of threats of violence, etc.

cow·ard /ˈkaʊəd/ *n* person unable to control his fear; person who runs away from danger. ***turn ~,*** become a ~. **~·ly** *adj* **1** not brave. **2** contemptible; of or like a ~: *a ~ly lie; ~ly behaviour.*

cow·ard·ice /ˈkaʊədɪs/ *n* [U] feeling, way of behaviour, of a coward; faint-heartedness.

cower /ˈkaʊə(r)/ *vi* [VP2A,C] lower the body; crouch; shrink back from cold, misery, fear, shame: *The dog ~ed under the table when its master raised the whip.*

cowl /kaʊl/ *n* **1** long, loose gown (as worn by monks) with a hood that can be pulled over the head; the hood itself. **2** metal cap for a chimney, ventilating pipe, etc, often made so as to revolve with the wind and improve the draught**(1)**. **'~·ing** *n* removable metal covering for an aircraft engine.

cow·pox /ˈkaʊpɒks/ *n* contagious disease of cattle, caused by a virus which, when isolated, is the source of vaccine for smallpox.

cow·rie /ˈkaʊrɪ/ *n* (*pl* **-ries**) small shell formerly used as money in parts of Africa and Asia.

cow·slip /ˈkaʊslɪp/ *n* small plant with yellow

flowers, growing wild in temperate countries.

cox /koks/ *n* (colloq abbr of) coxswain. □ *vt, vi* [VP6A,2A] act as coxswain (of a rowing-boat): *The Oxford boat was coxed by an American.*

cox·comb /ˈkokskəʊm/ *n* vain, foolish person, esp one who pays too much attention to his clothes.

cox·swain /ˈkoksn/ *n* person who steers a rowing-boat, esp in races; person in charge of a ship's boat and crew. ⇨ the illus at eight.

coy /kɔɪ/ *adj* (-er, -est) (esp of a girl) shy, modest; pretending to be shy; seeming more modest than one really is. **coy·ly** *adv* **coy·ness** *n*

coy·ote /ˈkɔɪəʊt *US:* ˈkɑɪəʊt/ *n* prairie wolf of western N America.

coypu /ˈkɔɪpu/ *n* S American rodent with webbed hind feet, kept on fur farms (*nutria fur*); it may be a pest when living in the wild state.

cozen /ˈkʌzn/ *vt* [VP6A,14] **~ *sb (out) of sth,*** (liter) defraud him of sth. **~ *sb into doing sth,*** (liter) beguile him into it.

cozy /ˈkəʊzɪ/ *adj* = cosy.

crab[1] /kræb/ *n* [C] ten-legged shellfish; [U] its meat as food. ⇨ the illus at crustacean. ***catch a ~,*** make a faulty stroke with one's oar.

crab[2] /kræb/ *n* (also ˈ**~-apple**) wild apple-tree; its hard, sour fruit.

crab[3] /kræb/ *vt* (-bb-) (colloq) decry; disparage.

crab·bed /ˈkræbɪd/ *adj* **1** bad-tempered; easily irritated. **2** (of handwriting) difficult to read; (of writings, authors) difficult to understand.

crack[1] /kræk/ *n* **1** line of division where sth is broken, but not into separate parts: *a cup with bad ~s in it. Don't go skating today—there are dangerous ~s in the ice. The ground was full of ~s after the hot, dry summer.* **2** sudden, sharp noise (as of a rifle or whip, or sth breaking): *the ~ of a pistol shot; the ~ of thunder; the ~ of doom,* the peal of thunder on the Day of Judgement. **3** sharp blow which can be heard: *give sb/get a ~ on the head.* **4** (sl) (= *wise~*) lively, forceful, or cutting comment or retort, esp one that causes laughter. **5** (sl) attempt. ***have a ~ at sth,*** try to do sth which is difficult. **6** (used attrib) first-rate; very clever or expert: *a ~ polo-player; a ~ regiment. He's a ~ shot,* expert at using a rifle. **7** ˈ**~-**ˈ**brained** *adj* crazy; foolish: *a ~-brained scheme.*

crack[2] /kræk/ *vt, vi* **1** [VP6A,14,2A,C] get or make a crack or cracks(1) in: *I can ~ it, but I can't break it. You've ~ed the window. The glass will ~ if you pour boiling water into it. He fell out of the window and ~ed his skull.* **2** [VP6A,2A] make, cause to make, a crack or cracks(2): *to ~ a whip/the joints of the fingers. The hunter's rifle ~ed and the deer fell dead. We heard a ~ing noise among the trees.* **~ *open,*** open with a ~ing sound: *~ open a safe.* **3** [VP2A] (of the voice) become harsh; (of a boy's voice when he is reaching puberty) undergo a change and become dissonant (*break* is more usu). **4** [VP6A] decompose (petroleum) by using heat and pressure so as to change thick oils into thinner oils. Hence, ˈ**~ing plant**. **5** (colloq and sl uses) **~ *up,*** **(a)** [VP2C] lose strength (in old age); suffer a mental collapse. Hence, ˈ**~-up** *n* failure; breakdown. **(b)** [VP2C, 15B] (of an aircraft) suffer damage, e g through a bad landing; cause an aircraft to suffer damage in this way. **~ *down on (sb/sth),*** take disciplinary action against: *~ down on gambling.* Hence, ˈ**~-down** *n* [VP15B] **~ *sb/sth up,*** praise highly, or in an exaggerated way: *He's not so clever as he's ~ed up to be.* **~ *a bottle (of wine),*** open one and drink the contents. **~ *a crib,*** (dated sl) break into, burgle, a house. **~ *a joke,*** make one. ⇨ crack[1](4). ***get ~ing,*** get busy (with work waiting to be done).

cracker /ˈkrækə(r)/ *n* **1** thin, flaky, dry biscuit (as eaten with cheese). **2** firework that makes cracking noises when set off: *The Chinese use ~s to frighten away evil spirits.* ˈ**Christmas ~,** one made of brightly coloured paper, which explodes harmlessly when the ends are pulled. **3** (*pl,* also ˈ**nut-~s**) instrument for cracking nuts.

crack·ers /ˈkrækəz/ *pred adj* (GB sl) mad; crazy.

crackle /ˈkrækl/ *vi* [VP2A,C] make a series of small cracking sounds, as when one treads on dry twigs, or when dry sticks burn: *A cheerful wood fire was crackling on the hearth; a crackling log fire.* □ *n* [U] **1** small cracking sounds, as described above: *the distant ~ of machine-gun fire.* **2** (also ˈ**~-china/~-ware**) china, etc covered with a network of what appear to be tiny cracks.

crack·ling /ˈkræklɪŋ/ *n* [U] **1** crackle(1). **2** crisp, well-cooked skin of roast pork.

crack·pot /ˈkrækpot/ *n* eccentric person with strange ideas: (attrib) *~ ideas.*

cracks·man /ˈkræksmən/ *n* (*pl* -men) burglar.

cradle /ˈkreɪdl/ *n* **1** small, low bed sometimes mounted on rockers, for a newborn baby: *from/in the ~,* from/during infancy; *from the ~ to the grave,* from birth to death. **2** (fig) place where sth is born or begins: *Greece, the ~ of Western culture.* **3** framework resembling a ~ of which is used like a ~, e g a structure on which a ship is supported while being built or repaired; framework like a trough, in which earth is shaken in water to separate any gold that may be in it; frame fastened to a scythe, used in harvesting, to lay the grain evenly; basket pulled along a line to rescue people from a wrecked ship; platform that can be moved up and down an outside wall by means of ropes and pulleys, used by workmen; part of a telephone apparatus on which the receiver rests. □ *vt* [VP6A,14] place, hold, in or as in a ~: *~ a child in one's arms: ~ the telephone receiver,* put it down.

craft /krɑft *US:* kræft/ *n* **1** [C] occupation, esp one in which skill in the use of the hands is needed; such a skill or technique: *the potter's ~; to learn the ~ of the woodcarver; a school for arts and ~s.* Used in many compounds, as ˈ**needle-~,** ˈ**wood-~,** ˈ**handi-~,** ˈ**stage-~. 2** (collective) those engaged in such an occupation, organized in a guild or union: *the ~ of masons; the C~,* brotherhood of Freemasons. **3** (*pl* unchanged) boat(s), ship(s): *a handy and useful little ~. The harbour was full of all kinds of ~/~ of all kinds.* ⇨ *air~* at air[1](7), *space~* at space. **4** [U] cunning; trickery; skill in deceiving: *Be careful when you do business with that man: he's full of ~. He got it from me by ~.* **~y** *adj* (-ier, -iest) full of ~(4): *a ~y politician; as ~y as a fox.* **~·ily** *adv* **~·i·ness** *n*

crafts·man /ˈkrɑftsmən *US:* ˈkræfts-/ *n* (*pl* -men) skilled workman who practises a craft. **~-ship** /-ʃɪp/ *n* skilled workmanship.

crag /kræg/ *n* [C] high, steep, sharp or rugged mass of rock. **~·ged** /ˈkrægɪd/ (poet), **~gy** (-ier, -iest) *adjj* having many ~s. ˈ**crags·man** /-mən/ *n* (*pl* -men) one who is clever at climbing ~s.

crake /kreɪk/ *n* kinds of bird. ⇨ *corncrake* at

corn¹(1).

cram /kræm/ *vt,vi* (-mm-) [VP6A,14,15B,2A] **1** **~ *into/with,*** make too full; put, push, very much or too much into: *to ~ food into one's mouth/~ one's mouth with food; to ~ papers into a drawer; an essay ~med with quotations.* **2** fill the head with facts (for an examination): to ~ pupils: to ~ up a subject, commit facts to memory (without serious study). **ˈ~-ˈfull** *adj,adv* as full as ~ming can make it. **~·mer** *n* special school where students are ~med; teacher paid to ~ students for examinations; textbook designed for ~ming; student who ~s for examinations.

cramp¹ /kræmp/ *n* [U] sudden and painful tightening of the muscles, usu caused by cold or overwork, making movement difficult: *writer's ~,* of the finger muscles. *The swimmer was seized with ~ and had to be helped out of the water.*

cramp² /kræmp/ *vt* [VP6A] **1** (liter, fig) keep in a narrow space; hinder or prevent the movement or growth of: *All these difficulties ~ed his progress.* (esp in the passive): *We are/feel ~ed for room here,* have insufficient space. ***~ one's style,*** (colloq) prevent one from doing sth as well as one could do it in more favourable circumstances. **2** cause to have, affect with, cramp¹. **3** fasten with a cramp³: *~ a beam.* **cramped** *part adj* (of handwriting) with small letters close together and for this reason difficult to read.

cramp³ /kræmp/ *n* (also **ˈ~-iron**) metal bar with the ends bent, used for holding together masonry or timbers.

cram·pon /ˈkræmpən/ *n* (usu *pl*) iron plate with spikes, worn on shoes for walking or climbing on ice.

cran /kræn/ *n* measure for fresh herrings (37½ gallons or 160·6 litres).

cran·berry /ˈkrænbrɪ *US:* -berɪ/ *n* (*pl* -ries) small, red, tart berry of a dwarf shrub, used for making jelly and sauce.

cranes

crane¹ /kreɪn/ *n* **1** large wading bird with long legs and neck. ⇨ the illus at water. **2** machine with a long arm that can be swung round, used for lifting and moving heavy weights.

crane² /kreɪn/ *vt,vi* [VP6A,16A,2A,C] stretch (the neck); stretch the neck (like a crane¹(1): *to ~ forward; to ~ one's neck to see sth.*

crane-fly /ˈkreɪn flɑɪ/ *n* (*pl* -flies) kind of fly with very long legs; daddy-long-legs.

cran·ial /ˈkreɪnɪəl/ *adj* of the skull.

cran·ium /ˈkreɪnɪəm/ *n* bony part of the head enclosing the brain. ⇨ the illus at head.

crank¹ /kræŋk/ *n* L-shaped arm and handle for transmitting rotary motion. **ˈ~·shaft** *n* shaft that turns or is turned by a ~. □ *vt* [VP6A,15B] move, cause to move, by turning a ~: *to ~ up an engine; to ~ a cine-camera.*

crank² /kræŋk/ *n* person with fixed (and often strange) ideas, esp on one matter: *a fresh air ~,* one who insists on having windows open, however cold, stormy, etc, it may be. **~y** *adj* (-ier, -iest) (of people) odd; eccentric; (of buildings, machines, etc) unsteady; shaky.

cranny /ˈkrænɪ/ *n* (*pl* -nies) small crack or opening, e g in a wall. **cran·nied** *adj* full of crannies.

crap /kræp/ *vi* (-pp-) ⚠ defecate. □ *n* ⚠ **1** excrement. **2** act of defecating: *have a ~.* **3** (sl) nonsense.

crape /kreɪp/ *n* black silk or cotton material with a wrinkled surface (formerly used for mourning). ⇨ **crêpe.**

craps /kræps/ *n* (*sing v*) (also **ˈcrap-shooting**) (sl) gambling game played with two dice: *shoot ~,* play this game.

crash¹ /kræʃ/ *n* **1** (noise made by a) violent fall, blow or breaking: *The tree fell with a great ~. His words were drowned in a ~ of thunder. He was killed in an ˈaircraft ~.* **ˈ~ barrier,** fence, rail, wall, etc designed to keep people, vehicles, etc apart where there is danger (e g one in the centre of a motorway). **ˈ~-dive,** sudden dive made by a submarine, e g to escape attack. □ *vi* dive in this way. **ˈ~-land** *vi,vt* (of aircraft) land, be landed, partly or wholly out of control, with a ~. Hence, **ˈcrash-landing** *n* **ˈ~-helmet,** padded helmet worn to protect the head in a ~, e g by a motorcyclist. **ˈ~ programme,** one made with intensive efforts to achieve quick results. **2** ruin; collapse (e g in trade, finance): *The great ~ on Wall Street in 1929 ruined international trade.* □ *adv* with a ~.

crash² /kræʃ/ *vt,vi* **1** [VP2A,C,6A] fall or strike suddenly, violently, and noisily (esp of things that break): *The bus ~ed into a tree. The tree ~ed through the window. The dishes ~ed to the floor. The aircraft ~ed.* **2** [VP2A,C] force or break through violently: *elephants ~ing through the jungle: ~ a cocktail party,* (colloq) intrude upon one uninvited. ⇨ *gatecrasher* at gate(2). **3** [VP2A] (of a business company, government, etc) come to ruin; meet disaster: *His great financial scheme ~ed.* **4** [VP6A] cause to ~: *to ~ an aircraft.*

crash³ /kræʃ/ *n* [U] coarse linen cloth (as used for towels, etc).

crass /kræs/ *adj* (of such qualities as ignorance, stupidity, etc) complete; very great.

crate /kreɪt/ *n* **1** large framework of light boards or basketwork for goods in transport. **2** (sl) old, worn-out motor-car or aircraft. □ *vt* put in a ~.

cra·ter /ˈkreɪtə(r)/ *n* mouth of a volcano; hole in the ground made by the explosion of a bomb, shell, etc: *~ lake,* lake in the ~ of an extinct volcano.

cra·vat /krəˈvæt/ *n* piece of linen, lace, etc loosely folded and worn as a necktie.

crave /kreɪv/ *vt,vi* [VP2A,3A] ***~ (for),*** ask earnestly for, have a strong desire for: *to ~ (for) mercy/forgiveness; to ~ for a drink.* **crav·ing** /ˈkreɪvɪŋ/ *n* [C] strong desire: *a craving for strong drink.*

cra·ven /ˈkreɪvn/ *n, adj* (person who is) cowardly.

craw·fish /ˈkrɔfɪʃ/ *n* = crayfish.

crawl /krɔl/ *vi* [VP2A,C] **1** move slowly, pulling the body along the ground or other surface (as worms and snakes do); (of human beings) move in this way, or on the hands and knees: *The wounded soldier ~ed into a shell-hole. Don't ~ to your boss,* (fig) ingratiate yourself with him, seek his favour. **2** go very slowly: *Our train ~ed over the damaged bridge.* **3** be full of, covered with, things that ~: *The ground was ~ing with ants. The child's hair was ~ing with vermin.* **4** (of the flesh) feel as if covered with ~ing things: *She says that the sight of snakes makes her flesh ~.* □ *n* **1** (with *indef art*) ~ing movement: *Traffic in Oxford St was reduced to a ~ during the rush hours.* (*go on a*) *'pub crawl,* visit and drink at several pubs in succession. **2** (usu with *def art*) high-speed swimming stroke in which the head is kept low in the water. **~er** *n* person or thing that ~s; (*pl*) overall garment made for a baby to ~ about in.

cray·fish /ˈkreɪfɪʃ/ *n* freshwater lobster-like shellfish.

crayon /ˈkreɪən/ *n* stick or pencil of soft coloured chalk, wax or charcoal. □ *vt* draw with crayons.

craze /kreɪz/ *vt* [VP6A] (usu in *pp*) make wildly excited or mad: *a ~d look/expression; a half-~d prophet.* □ *n* enthusiastic interest that may last for a comparatively short time; the object of such interest: *schoolboy ~s,* e g the making of paper darts as weapons; *the modern ~ for bingo.*

crazy /ˈkreɪzɪ/ *adj* **(-ier, -iest) 1** wildly excited or enthusiastic: *He is ~ about skiing. I'm ~ about/for you, darling.* **2** suffering from mental disorder; foolish: *You were ~ to lend that man your money. It was ~ of you to let such a young girl drive your car.* **3** (of buildings, etc) unsafe; likely to collapse. **4** (of quilts, pavements, etc) made up of irregularly shaped pieces fitted together: *~ paving.* **craz·ily** *adv* **crazi·ness** *n*

creak /krik/ *n, vi* [VP2A] (make a) sound like that of an unoiled door-hinge, or badly-fitting floorboards when trodden on. **~y** *adj* **(-ier, -iest)** making ~ing sounds: *~y stairs.* **~·ily** *adv*

cream /krim/ *n* [U] **1** fatty or oily part of milk which rises to the surface and can be made into butter. **2** kind of food containing or resembling ~: *~ cheese; ice-~; ~ ices; chocolate ~; ~ buns.* **3** substance like ~ in appearance or consistency, used for polishing, as a cosmetic, etc: *'furniture ~; 'shoe-~; 'face-~; 'cold-~.* **4** part of a liquid that gathers at the top: *~ of tartar/lime.* **5** best part of anything: *the ~ of society,* those of highest rank; *the ~ of the story,* the most amusing part, the point of it. **6** (attrib) yellowish-white: *~-laid/-wove paper,* smooth cream-coloured writing-paper. □ *vt* take ~ from (milk); make ~y; add ~ to: *~ed potatoes,* cooked so that they have the consistency of ~. **~y** *adj* **(-ier, -iest)** smooth and rich like ~; containing much ~. **~·ery** *n* (*pl* **-ries**) **1** place where milk, ~, butter, cheese, etc are sold. **2** butter and cheese factory.

crease /kris/ *n* **1** line made (on cloth, paper, etc) by crushing, folding or pressing: *~-resisting cloth,* which does not easily form into ~s. **2** (cricket) white line on the ground to mark the positions of certain players (bowlers, batsmen) ⇨ the illus at **cricket**. □ *vt, vi* [VP6A,2A] make a ~ or ~s in; fall into ~s; get ~s in: *Pack the dresses so that they won't ~. This material ~s easily.*

cre·ate /krɪˈeɪt/ *vt* **1** [VP6A] cause sth to exist; make (sth new or original): *God ~d the world. Dickens ~d many wonderful characters in his novels.* ***~ a part,*** (of an actor) be the first to play it. **2** [VP6A] give rise to; produce: *His behaviour ~d a bad impression. Her appearance ~d a sensation.* **3** [VP23,6A] invest (sb) with a rank: *He was ~d Baron of Bunthorp. Eight new peers were ~d.*

cre·ation /krɪˈeɪʃn/ *n* **1** [U] the act of creating (e g the world): *the ~ of great works of art/of an Empire. Economic conditions may be responsible for the ~ of social unrest. Is the ~ of the new life peers desirable?* **2** [U] all created things: *man, the lord of ~.* **the C~,** the world or universe as created by God. **3** [U] production of the human intelligence, esp one in which imagination has a part: *the ~s of poets, artists, composers and dramatists. The women were wearing the newest ~s of the Paris dressmakers.*

cre·ative /krɪˈeɪtɪv/ *adj* having power to create; of creation: *useful and ~ work,* i e requiring intelligence and imagination, not merely mechanical skill. **~·ly** *adv* **~·ness** *n*

cre·ator /krɪˈeɪtə(r)/ *n* one who creates. **the C~,** God.

crea·ture /ˈkritʃə(r)/ *n* **1** living animal: *dumb ~s,* animals. **2** (with an epithet, emotive use) living person: *a lovely ~,* a beautiful woman; *a poor ~,* a contemptible person, a person who is to be pitied; *a good ~,* a kindhearted person. **3** person who owes his position to another, esp one who is content to carry out another person's wishes without question: *mere ~s of the dictator.* **4** *~ comforts,* material needs such as food and drink.

crèche /kreɪʃ/ *n* **1** (GB) public nursery where babies are looked after while their mothers are at work. **2** (US) crib[1] **(3)**.

cre·dence /ˈkridns/ *n* [U] ***give/attach ~ to,*** (formal) believe (gossip, what is said, etc). ***letter of ~,*** letter of introduction.

cre·den·tials /krɪˈdenʃlz/ *n pl* letters or papers showing that a person is what he claims to be: *His ~ were so satisfactory that he was given the post of manager.*

cred·ible /ˈkredəbl/ *adj* that can be believed: *~ witnesses. It hardly seems ~,* seems almost impossible to believe. **cred·ibly** *adv* in a ~ manner: *We are credibly informed that....* **credi·bil·ity** /ˌkredəˈbɪlətɪ/ *n* (*pl* **-ties**): the credibility gap, the difference between what sb says and what is considered worthy of belief.

credit[1] /ˈkredɪt/ *n* **1** [U] belief of others that a person, business company, etc can pay debts, or will keep a promise to pay: *No ~ is given at this shop,* payment must be in cash. *His ~ is good for only £50. If you're very rich, you can probably get unlimited ~.* ***buy/sell on ~,*** buy/sell goods, payment being made later. **'~-worthy** *adj* accepted by tradesmen, hire-purchase companies, etc as safe for ~. Hence, **'~-worthiness** *n* **'~ account,** (US = *charge account*) account with a shop, store, etc under an agreement for payments at a later date (e g monthly or quarterly). **'~ card, (a)** card issued by a business firm enabling the holder to obtain goods and services on ~. **(b)** one issued by a bank, allowing the holder to draw money from its branches and use its cheques in payment for goods and services, with a maximum for each occasion. **'~ note,** (comm) one that gives ~ to a customer for goods returned or for overcharged goods. **'~ sales,** sales for which payment is made, by agreement, later. Cf *cash sales.* **ˌletter of '~,** letter from a bank to its agent(s) giving authority for credit to the holder. **2** [U] money shown as owned by a person, company, etc in a bank account: *How much have I standing to my ~? You have a ~ balance of £250. Please place this sum to my ~.* **3** [C] sum of money advanced or loaned (by a bank, etc): *The bank refused further ~s to the company.* '**~ squeeze,** (government) policy of making it difficult to borrow money (eg by raising interest rates), as part of a policy against inflation. **4** (book-keeping) record of payments received: *Does this item go among the ~s or the debits?* '**~-side,** right-hand side of an account for recording payment received. ⇨ debit(2). **5** [C] (US) entry on a record to show that a course of study has been completed: *~s in history and geography; a* '*~ course,* university course depending upon the number of grades and ~s received. **6** [U] honour, approval, good name or reputation: *a man of the highest ~.* ***get/take ~ (for sth),*** receive recognition, etc; take it: *He's cleverer than I gave him ~ for,* than I thought. *I gave you ~ for being more sensible,* You are less sensible than I thought. *Candidates will get additional ~* (ie marks) *for clearly labelled diagrams. One must give ~ where ~ is due. It is dishonest to take ~ for work done by others.* ***give ~ (to sb) (for sth),*** give recognition, praise, approval. **7** ***do sb ~/do ~ to sb; be to sb's ~, reflect ~ on sb,*** add to his reputation: *The work does you ~. His smart appearance does ~ to his tailors. It is greatly to your ~ that you have passed such a difficult examination. His fluency in Arabic reflects great ~ on/is greatly to the ~ of his teacher.* ***be a ~ to sb/sth,*** add to the good name of sb/sth: *The pupils are a ~ to their teacher. I hope you will be a ~ to your school.* '**~ titles,** names, shown on a cinema or TV screen, of persons responsible for the acting, direction, production, etc. **8** [U] belief; trust; confidence; credence: *The rumour is gaining ~.* ***lend ~ to,*** strengthen belief in: *The latest news lends ~ to the earlier reports.*

credit[2] /ˈkredɪt/ *vt* [VP6A,14] ***~ sb/sth with sth/~ sth to sb/sth,*** **(a)** believe that he/it has sth: *Until now I've always ~ed you with more sense. The relics are ~ed with miraculous powers. Miraculous powers are ~ed to the relics.* **(b)** enter on the ~ side of an account: *~ a customer with £10; ~ £10 to a customer/to his account.* ⇨ credit[1](4).

credi·table /ˈkredɪtəbl/ *adj* that brings credit(6,7): *a ~ attempt; conduct that was very ~ to him.* **credi·tably** /ˈkredɪtəblɪ/ *adv*

credi·tor /ˈkredɪtə(r)/ *n* person to whom one owes money: *run away from one's ~s.*

credo /ˈkreɪdəʊ/ *n* (*pl* -dos /-dəʊz/) creed.

cre·du·lity /krəˈdjulətɪ *US:* -ˈdu-/ *n* (*pl* -ties) too great a readiness to believe things.

credu·lous /ˈkredjʊləs *US:* -dʒʊ-/ *adj* (too) ready to believe things: *~ people who accept all the promises of the politicians.* **~·ly** *adv*

creed /krid/ *n* [C] (system of) beliefs or opinions, esp on religious doctrine. **the C~,** (formal) summary of Christian doctrine.

creek /krik/ *n* **1** (GB) narrow inlet of water on the sea-shore or in a river-bank. **2** (N America) small river.

creel /kril/ *n* angler's wicker basket for carrying the fish he catches.

creep /krip/ *vi* (*pt,pp* crept /krept/) [VP2A,B,C] **1** move along with the body close to the ground or floor; move slowly, quietly or secretly: *The cat crept silently towards the bird. The thief crept along the corridor.* **2** (of time, age, etc) come on gradually: *Old age ~s upon one unawares. A feeling of drowsiness crept over him.* **3** (of plants, etc) grow along the ground, over the surface of a wall, etc: *Ivy had crept over the ruined castle walls.* **4** (of the flesh) have the feeling that things are ~ing over it (as the result of fear, repugnance, etc): *The sight of the cold, damp prison cell, with rats running about, made her flesh ~.* ⇨ crawl(4). □ *n* **1** (sl) despicable person who tries to win favour by doing small favours, snooping, etc. **2** ***give sb the ~s,*** (colloq) cause the flesh to ~(4).

a crescent

creeper /ˈkripə(r)/ *n* insect, bird, etc that creeps; plant that creeps along the ground, over rocks, walls, etc.

creepy /ˈkripɪ/ *adj* (-ier, -iest) having or causing a creeping of the flesh, ⇨ creep(4): *The ghost story made us all ~.*

creese /kris/ *n* = kris.

cre·mate /krɪˈmeɪt/ *vt* [VP6A] burn (a corpse) to ashes: *He says he wants to be ~d, not buried.* **cre·ma·tion** /krɪˈmeɪʃn/ *n* [U] cremating; [C] instance of this. **cre·ma·tor·ium** /ˌkreməˈtɔrɪəm/ *n* furnace, building, place, for the cremating of corpses. **cre·ma·tory** /ˈkremətərɪ *US:* -tɔrɪ/ *n* (*pl* -ries) = crematorium.

crème de menthe /ˌkrem də ˈmonθ/ *n* [U] sweet, thick, green liqueur flavoured with peppermint.

cren·el·lated (US = **-el·ated**) /ˈkrenəleɪtɪd/ *adj* having battlements.

Cre·ole /ˈkriəʊl/ *n, adj* **1** (person) of pure European descent in the West Indies or Spanish America; (person) of mixed European and African blood in the West Indies, Mauritius, etc; (of a) language resulting from contact between a European language (esp English and French) and languages in West Africa, America and the Far East, and now spoken as a mother tongue. French dialect spoken in Louisiana, New Orleans, etc. **2** (in W Africa, esp Sierra Leone) descendant of the freed slaves who were returned to Africa from N America.

creo·sote /ˈkrɪəsəʊt/ *n* [U] **1** thick, brown, oily liquid obtained from coal-tar, used to preserve wood. **2** antiseptic obtained from wood-tar.

crêpe, crepe /kreɪp/ *n* [U] **1** name for kinds of crape-like cloth other than the black cloth formerly used for mourning. **2** *~ rubber,* raw rubber pressed into blocks. It has a wrinkled surface and is used for the soles of shoes, etc. **3** ˌ**~ ˈpaper,** thin paper with a wavy or wrinkled surface.

crepi·tate /ˈkrepɪteɪt/ *vi* [VP2A] make a series of sharp, crackling sounds. **crepi·ta·tion** /ˌkrepɪˈteɪʃn/ *n* crepitating (sound).

crept ⇨ creep.

cre·pus·cu·lar /krɪˋpʌskjʊlə(r)/ *adj* of, seen, heard or active during, twilight.

cres·cendo /krɪˋʃendəʊ/ *n* (*pl* **-dos** /-dəʊz/), *adj* (passage of music to be played, sth heard) with, of, increasing loudness; (fig) progress towards a climax.

cres·cent /ˋkresnt/ *n* **1** ⇨ the illus at **phase**. (sth shaped like) the curve of the moon in the first quarter; row of houses in the form of a ~. **2** (fig) faith and religion of Islam: *the Cross* (Christianity) *and the C~*. **3** (attrib) ~-shaped; increasing in size: *a ~ moon.*

cress /kres/ *n* [U] name of various plants, esp the kind with hot-tasting leaves (used in salads and sandwiches).

crest /krest/ *n* **1** tuft of feathers on a bird's head; cock's comb. ⇨ the illus at **fowl, water**. **ˋ~-fallen,** (fig) dejected, disappointed (at failure, etc). **2** ~-like decoration formerly worn on the top of a helmet; (poet) helmet. **3** design over the shield of a coat of arms, or used separately (e g on a seal, or on notepaper): *the family ~*, one used by a family. **4** top of a slope or hill; white top of a large wave. ***on the ~ of a wave,*** (fig) at the most favourable moment of one's fortunes. **~ed** *adj* having a ~**(3)**: *~ed note-paper;* (in compounds, as names of birds) *the golden-~ed wren.* □ *vt* reach the ~ of a hill, a wave.

cre·ta·cious /krɪˋteɪʃəs/ *adj* of (the nature of) chalk: *the ~ age,* when chalk-rocks were formed.

cre·tin /ˋkretɪn *US:* ˋkritn/ *n* deformed and mentally undeveloped person (diseased because of weakness of the thyroid gland). **~·ous** /ˋkretɪnəs *US:* ˋkritn̩əs/ *adj*

cre·tonne /kreˋton *US:* krə-/ *n* [U] cotton cloth with printed designs, used for curtains, furniture covers, etc.

cre·vasse /krɪˋvæs/ *n* deep, open crack, esp in ice on a glacier. ⇨ the illus at **mountain**.

crev·ice /ˋkrevɪs/ *n* narrow opening or crack (in a rock, wall, etc).

crew[1] /kru/ *n* **1** (collective noun) all the persons working a ship or aircraft; all these except the officers: *officers and crew.* **ˋground ~,** mechanics who service an aircraft on the ground. **2** (yachting) person or persons on a yacht or plane working under the direction of the helmsman or pilot. **3** group of persons working together; gang. **ˋ~-cut,** closely cropped style of hair-cut for men. □ *vi* act as ~**(2)**: *Will you ~ for me in tomorrow's race?*

crew[2] /kru/ *pt* of **crow**[2].

crib[1] /krɪb/ *n* **1** wooden framework (manger) from which animals can pull out fodder. **2** (US) bin or box for storing maize, salt, etc. **3** (US = *crèche*) representation (e g in a church at Christmas) of the nativity. **4** bed for a newborn baby. □ *vt* (**-bb-**) shut up in a small space.

crib[2] /krɪb/ *n* **1** sth copied dishonestly from the work of another. **2** word-for-word translation of a foreign text used by students of the language. □ *vt,vi* (**-bb-**) use a ~**(2)**; copy (another pupil's written work) dishonestly.

crib·bage /ˋkrɪbɪdʒ/ *n* [U] card-game for two, three or four persons, who use pegs and a board (**ˋ~-board**) with peg-holes in it for keeping the score.

crick /krɪk/ *n* (usu with *indef art*) stiff condition of the muscles of the neck or the back causing sudden, sharp pain: *to have/get a ~ in the neck.* □ *vt* produce a ~ in: *to ~ one's neck/back.*

cricket[1] /ˋkrɪkɪt/ *n* small, brown jumping insect which makes a shrill noise by rubbing its front wings together: *the chirping of ~s.* ⇨ the illus at **insect**.

cricket[2] /ˋkrɪkɪt/ *n* [U] ball game (**ˋ~-match**) played on a grass field by two teams of eleven players each, with bats and wickets. ***not ~,*** (colloq) unfair; unsportsmanlike. **~er** *n* ~ player.

cried /kraɪd/ ⇨ **cry**[1].

crier /ˋkraɪə(r)/ *n* **1** officer who makes public announcements in a court of law. **ˈtown-ˋ~,** man who goes round the streets to make proclamations and announcements. **2** person (esp a young child) who cries**(2)** a lot.

cries /kraɪz/ *pres t* of **cry**[1]; *pl* of **cry**[2].

cri·key /ˋkraɪkɪ/ *int* (colloq) exclamation of surprise.

crime /kraɪm/ *n* **1** [C] offence for which there is severe punishment by law; [U] such offences collectively; serious law-breaking: *to commit a serious ~; the ~s of which he was proved guilty. It is the business of the police to prevent and detect ~ and of the law courts to punish ~.* **ˋ~ fiction,** novels in which the detection of ~ is the chief interest. **2** foolish or wrong act, not necessarily an offence against the law: *It would be a ~ to send the boy out on such a cold, wet night.* **3** (in the

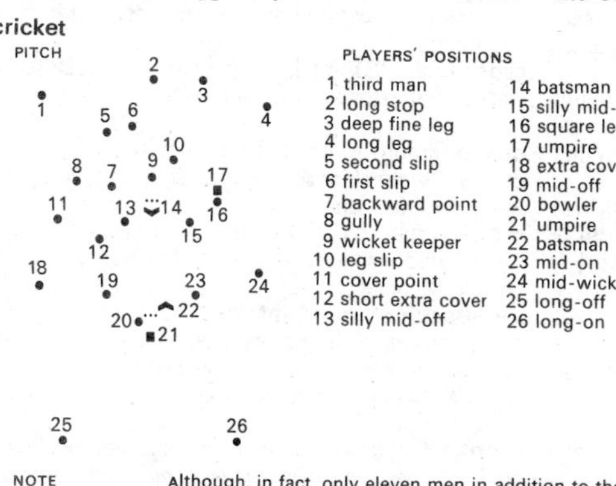

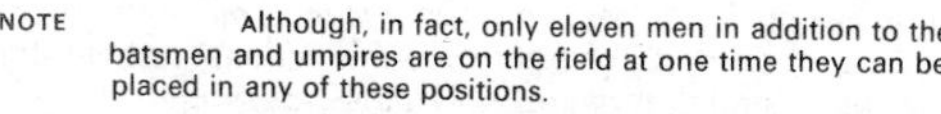
NOTE Although, in fact, only eleven men in addition to the batsmen and umpires are on the field at one time they can be placed in any of these positions.

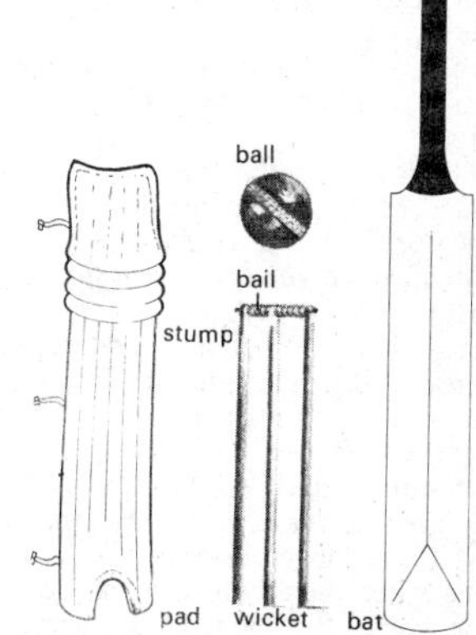

army) serious breaking of the regulations (not necessarily an offence against civil law). '~ **sheet,** record of a soldier's offences. □ *vt* charge (a man) with, convict (a man) of, a military offence.

crimi·nal /ˈkrɪmənl/ *adj* of crime: *a ~ act; a ~ offender; the ~ code.* Cf *the civil code.* □ *n* person who commits a crime or crimes. **~·ly** /-nəlɪ/ *adv*

crimi·nol·ogy /ˌkrɪmɪˈnɒlədʒɪ/ *n* [U] the study of crime.

crimp /krɪmp/ *vt* make (e g hair) wavy or curly (as with a hot iron).

crim·son /ˈkrɪmzn/ *adj, n* deep red. □ *vt, vi* make or become ~.

cringe /krɪndʒ/ *vi* [VP2A,C] **1** move (the body) back or down in fear: *The dog ~d at the sight of the whip.* **2** behave (towards a superior) in a way that shows lack of self-respect; be too humble: *a cringing beggar; to ~ to/before a policeman.*

crinkle /ˈkrɪŋkl/ *n* small, narrow wrinkle (in material such as foil or paper). □ *vt, vi* [VP6A,15, 2A,C] make or get a ~ or ~s in: *~d paper,* e g crêpe paper. **crin·kly** /ˈkrɪŋklɪ/ *adj* (**-ier, -iest**) (of materials) having ~s; (of hair) curly.

crino·line /ˈkrɪnəlɪn/ *n* [C] light framework covered with stiff material, as formerly worn to make a skirt swell out; skirt with a ~.

cripes /kraɪps/ *int* (vulg for Christ!) My Goodness!

cripple /ˈkrɪpl/ *n* person unable to walk or move properly, through injury or weakness in the spine or legs. □ *vt* [VP6A] (liter, fig) make a ~ of; damage or weaken seriously: *~d soldiers; ~d with rheumatism; a ship that was ~d in a storm; activities ~d by lack of money.*

cri·sis /ˈkraɪsɪs/ *n* (*pl* **-ses** /-siz/) turning-point in illness, life, history, etc; time of difficulty, danger or anxiety about the future: *a cabinet/financial ~. Things are coming to/drawing to a ~. Affairs have reached a ~. We must bring things to a ~,* do sth to reach the state when a definite decision must be taken.

crisp /krɪsp/ *adj* **1** (esp of food) hard, dry and easily broken: *~ toast/biscuits. The snow was ~ underfoot.* **2** (of the air, the weather) frosty, cold: *the ~ air of an autumn morning.* **3** (of hair) tightly curled. **4** (of style, manners) quick, precise and decided; showing no doubts or hesitation: *a man with a ~ manner of speaking.* □ *n* (US = *chips*) (also **ˈpotato ˈ~s**) thin slices of potatoes, fried and dried (usu sold in packets). □ *vt, vi* make or become ~. **~·ly** *adv* **~·ness** *n*

criss·cross /ˈkrɪsˈkrɒs *US:* -ˈkrɔs/ *adj* with crossed lines: *a ~ pattern/design.* □ *adv* crosswise. □ *vt, vi* move crosswise; mark with lines that cross.

cri·terion /kraɪˈtɪərɪən/ *n* (*pl* **-ria** /-rɪə/ *or* **-ions**) standard of judgement; principle by which sth is measured for value: *Success in money-making is not always a good ~ of real success in life.*

critic /ˈkrɪtɪk/ *n* **1** person who forms and gives judgements, esp about literature, art, music, etc: *musical/dramatic/literary, etc ~s.* **2** person who finds fault, points out mistakes, etc: *I am my own most severe ~.*

criti·cal /ˈkrɪtɪkl/ *adj* **1** of or at a crisis: *We are at a ~ time in our history. The patient's condition is ~,* He is dangerously ill. *This is a ~ moment,* e g one when there will be a change for the better or the worse. **2** of the work of a critic: *~ opinions on art and literature.* **3** fault-finding: *~ remarks. She looks on everything with a ~ eye.* **~·ly** /-ɪklɪ/ *adv* in a ~(**1**) manner: *He is ~ly ill.*

criti·cism /ˈkrɪtɪsɪzm/ *n* **1** [U] the work of a critic; the art of making judgements (concerning art, literature, etc). **2** [C] judgement or opinion on literature, art, etc. **3** [U] fault-finding; [C] remark, etc that finds fault: *He hates ~,* being criticized. *Your frank ~s of his attempts annoyed him.*

criti·cize /ˈkrɪtɪsaɪz/ *vt, vi* [VP6A,14,2A] form and give a judgement of; find fault with: *~ sb's work; ~ sb for doing/not doing sth.*

cri·tique /krɪˈtik/ *n* [C] critical essay or review.

croak /krəʊk/ *n* deep, hoarse sound (as made by frogs or ravens). □ *vt, vi* **1** [VP2A] make this kind of sound; speak in a ~ing voice. **2** [VP6A,15B, 2A] say (sth) in a ~ing voice; foretell (evil); express dismal views about the future. **3** [VP2A] (sl) = **die**[1].

cro·chet /ˈkrəʊʃeɪ *US:* krəʊˈʃeɪ/ *vt, vi* [VP6A,2A] make (needlework, e g a shawl) with a thread looped over others with the help of a small hooked needle (called a **ˈ~-hook**). □ *n* [U] material (e g lace) made or being made in this way.

crock[1] /krɒk/ *n* pot or jar made of baked earth, e g for containing water; broken piece of such a pot: *Fill the bottom of the flower-pot with ~s for drainage.*

crock[2] /krɒk/ *n* (colloq) horse that has become old, weak and useless; person who cannot work well because of bad health, lameness, etc; very old motor vehicle, etc. □ *vi, vt* [VP2C,15B] **~ up,** become, cause to become, a ~: *This attack of influenza has ~ed me up. The poor man is ~ing up.*

crock·ery /ˈkrɒkərɪ/ *n* [U] pots, plates, cups, dishes and other utensils (made of baked clay).

croco·dile /ˈkrɒkədaɪl/ *n* **1** large river reptile with a long body and tail, covered with a hard skin. ⇨ the illus at **reptile**. **ˈ~ tears,** insincere sorrow. **2** (GB colloq) school children walking in procession, two by two.

cro·cus /ˈkrəʊkəs/ *n* (*pl* **-ses** /-sɪz/) (kind of) small plant growing from a corm, with coloured flowers early in spring.

Croe·sus /ˈkrisəs/ *n* (6th c BC) wealthy king in Asia Minor; (with *indef art*) very wealthy person.

croft /krɒft *US:* krɔft/ *n* (not US) small, enclosed field; small farm. **~er** *n* person who rents or owns a small farm, esp a joint tenant of a divided farm in Scotland.

crom·lech /ˈkrɒmlek/ *n* prehistoric structure of large flat stones laid horizontally on upright stones.

crone /krəʊn/ *n* withered old woman.

crony /ˈkrəʊnɪ/ *n* (*pl* **-nies**) close friend; companion; close associate.

crook /krʊk/ *n* **1** stick or staff with a rounded hook at one end, esp such a stick used by a shepherd. ⇨ **hook**. **2** bend or curve, e g in a river or path. **ˈ~-back(ed),** hunch-back(ed). **3** (colloq) person who makes a living by dishonest or criminal means. **4** ***on the ~,*** (sl) dishonest(ly). □ *vt, vi* [VP6A,2A] bend into the shape of a ~; *to ~ one's finger/arm.*

crooked /ˈkrʊkɪd/ *adj* **1** not straight or level; twisted; bent: *a ~ little man. You've got your hat on ~.* **2** (of a person or his actions) dishonest; not straightforward. **~·ly** *adv* **~·ness** *n*

croon /krun/ *vt, vi* [VP6A,15,2C] hum or sing

gently in a narrow range of notes: *~ to oneself; ~ a lullaby; ~ the baby to sleep.* **~er** *n* (1930's and 1940's) person who ~s, esp a public entertainer who sings sentimental songs with a microphone held at the lips.

crop[1] /krop/ *n* [C] **1** yearly (or season's) produce of grain, grass, fruit, etc; (*pl*) agricultural plants in the fields: *the 'potato ~; a good ~ of rice; to get the ~s in;* (attrib) *~ failures. The land is in/under ~,* being cultivated. *The land is out of ~,* not being cultivated. **'~-dusting,** dusting of growing ~s with insecticides, e g from low-flying aircraft. **2** group of persons or things, amount of anything, appearing or produced together: *The Prime Minister's statement produced a ~ of questions.*

crop[2] /krop/ *n* [C] **1** bag-like part of a bird's throat where food is broken up for digestion before passing into the stomach. ***neck and ~,*** ⇨ neck. **2** handle of a whip; (also **'hunting-~**) handle with a loop instead of a lash. **3** very short haircut *You look as if you've had a prison ~,* had your hair cut very short, like men in prison.

crop[3] /krop/ *vt, vi* (-pp-) **1** [VP6A,22] (of animals) bite off the tops of (grass, plants, etc); graze: *The sheep had ~ped the grass short.* **2** [VP6A,22] cut short (a person's hair, a horse's tail or ears). **3** [VP6A,14] sow or plant: *to ~ ten acres with wheat.* **4** [VP2A] bear a crop: *The beans ~ped well this year.* ⇨ crop[1](1). **5** [VP2C] ***~ up/out,*** (of rock, minerals) show up above the earth's surface. ⇨ outcrop. **6** [VP2C] ***~ up,*** appear or arise (esp unexpectedly): *All sorts of difficulties ~ped up. The subject ~ped up in the course of conversation.*

crop·per /'kropə(r)/ *n* **1** (with *adjj*) plant yielding a crop: *These peas are good ~s,* yield good crops. **2** person or thing that crops. ⇨ *share-cropper* at share[1](1). **3** ***come a ~,*** (colloq) have a fall; meet with failure (e g in an examination).

cro·quet /'krəʊkeɪ *US:* krəʊ'keɪ/ *n* [U] game played on short grass with wooden balls which are knocked with wooden mallets through hoops.

cro·quette /krəʊ'ket/ *n* [C] ball of minced meat or fish, mixed with rice or potato, coated with breadcrumbs and cooked in fat.

crore /krɔ(r)/ *n* (India and Pakistan) ten millions; one hundred lakhs (e g of rupees).

cro·sier, cro·zier /'krəʊzɪə(r) *US:* -ʒər/ *n* bishop's staff, usu shaped like a shepherd's crook. ⇨ the illus at vestment.

cross[1] /kros *US:* krɔs/ *n* **1** mark made by drawing one line across another, thus: ×, +: *The place is marked on the map with a ~.* ***make one's ~,*** put a ~ on a document instead of one's signature (as in former times by illiterate persons). **2** line or stroke forming part of a letter (e g the horizontal stroke on a 't'). **3** stake or post with another piece of wood across it like T, † or X, as used in ancient times for crucifixion, esp **the C~,** that on which Christ died; model of this as a religious emblem; sth (esp a monument) in the form of a ~ (e g one in stone set up in the market-place of a village or town, called a **'market-~**); sign of a ~ made with the right hand as a religious act. **4** (fig) suffering; affliction; burden of sorrow: *to bear one's ~; to take up one's ~,* be ready to bear affliction or suffering. **5** emblem, in the form of a ~ or a star, (to be) worn by an order of knighthood; decoration for personal valour: *the Victoria C~; the Distinguished Service C~.* **6** (place of) crossing. ***(cut) on the ~,*** (dress-making) diagonally: *This skirt material was cut on the ~,* on the bias. **7** offspring of animals or plants of different sorts or breeds: *A mule is a ~ between a horse and an ass.*

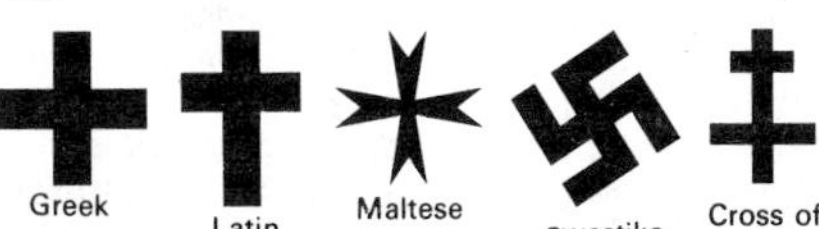

crosses

cross[2] /kros *US:* krɔs/ *vt, vi* **1** [VP6A,14,2A,C] go across; pass from one side to the other side of: *to ~ a road/river/bridge/the sea/the Sahara, etc; to ~ from Dover to Calais.* ***~ a person's path,*** meet him: *I hope I shall never ~ that man's path again.* ***~ one's mind,*** (of ideas, etc) occur to one: *The idea has just ~ed my mind that....* **2** [VP6A,15A,B] draw a line or lines across or through: *Two of the words had been ~ed out. I ~ed his name off the list.* ***~ a cheque,*** draw two lines across it so that payment can be made only through a bank. Hence, **'~ed 'cheque** *n* one that must be paid into a bank account, and cannot be cashed unless made out to 'self' or 'cash'. ***~ one's t's and dot one's i's,*** (fig) be careful and exact. **3** [VP6A,14] put or place across or over: *to ~ one's legs; to ~ one's arms on one's chest.* ***~ sb's palm with silver,*** give a coin to (esp a fortune-teller). ***to ~ swords (with sb),*** in fighting, or, (fig) argue with. ***keep one's fingers ~ed,*** (fig) hope for the best, that nothing will happen to upset one's plans, etc. **4** ***~ oneself,*** make the sign of the cross on or over oneself as a religious act, to invoke God's protection, or as a sign of awe. **5** [VP6A,2A] (of persons travelling, letters in the post) meet and pass: *We ~ed each other on the way. Our letters ~ed in the post. Your letter ~ed mine in the post.* **6** [VP6A] oppose or obstruct (sb, his plans, wishes, etc): *He was angry at having his plans ~ed. He ~es me in everything. He has been ~ed in love,* has failed to win the love of the woman he was in love with. **7** [VP6A,14] produce a cross(7) by mixing breeds; (cause to) interbreed; cross-fertilize (plants, etc). ⇨ crossbreed.

cross[3] /kros *US:* krɔs/ *adj* **1** (colloq) bad-tempered; easily or quickly showing anger: *Don't be ~ with the child for being late. I've never heard a ~ word from her lips. Don't pull the dog's tail, you'll make him ~.* ***as ~ as two sticks,*** (colloq) very bad-tempered. **2** (of winds) contrary; opposed: *Strong ~ winds made it difficult for the yachts to leave harbour.* **~·ly** *adv* **~·ness** *n*

cross·bar /'krosbɑ(r) *US:* 'krɔs-/ *n* bar going across, e g the bar joining the two upright posts of the goal (in football, etc) or the front and rear ends of a bicycle frame. ⇨ the illus at bicycle.

cross·beam /'krosbim *US:* 'krɔs-/ *n* beam placed across, esp one that supports parts of a structure; girder.

cross·benches /'krosbentʃɪz *US:* 'krɔs-/ *n pl* those benches in the House of Commons used by members who do not vote regularly with either the Government or the Opposition. Hence, **cross-bencher** *n*

cross·bones /'krosbəʊnz *US:* 'krɔs-/ *n pl* (design

of) two thigh bones laid across each other, usu under a skull, as an emblem of death (used as a warning of danger, and on the black flag once used by pirates).

cross·bow /ˋkrosbəʊ *US:* ˋkrɔs-/ *n* old kind of bow placed across a grooved wooden support, used for shooting arrows, bolts, stones, etc.

cross·bred /ˋkrosbred *US:* ˋkrɔs-/ *adj* produced by crossing breeds: *~ sheep.*

cross·breed /ˋkrosbrid *US:* ˋkrɔs-/ *n* (in farming, etc) animal, plant, etc, produced by crossing different kinds.

cross·coun·try /ˈkrosˋkʌntrɪ *US:* ˈkrɔs-/ *adj, adv* across the country or fields, not along roads: *a ~ race.*

cross-check /kros ˋtʃek *US:* krɔs/ *vt,vi* [VP6A, 2A] (comm) verify, e g a method, calculation, by using a different method, etc: *We ~ed the results twice.* □ *n* verification of this sort: *We'd better do a ~ on these figures.*

cross-cur·rent /ˋkros kʌrnt *US:* ˋkrɔs kɜənt/ *n* (fig) body of opinion contrary to that of the majority (on sth of public interest).

cross·cut /ˋkroskʌt *US:* ˋkrɔs-/ *adj* (of a saw) with teeth designed for cutting across the grain of wood. □ *n* diagonal cut or path; short cut.

cross-div·ision /ˈkros dɪˋvɪʒn *US:* ˈkrɔs/ *n* [C] division of a group according to more than one factor at the same time so that sub-divisions interrelate; instance of this.

crosse /kros *US:* krɔs/ *n* kind of long-handled racquet used in lacrosse.

cross-exam·ine /ˈkros ɪgˋzæmɪn *US:* ˈkrɔs/ *vt* [VP6A] question closely, esp to test answers already given to someone else, as in law court, by counsel, etc. **cross-exam·iner** *n* **cross-exam·in·ation** /ˈkros ɪgˈzæmɪˋneɪʃn *US:* ˈkrɔs/ *n*

cross·eyed /ˋkrosɑɪd *US:* ˋkrɔs-/ *adj* with one or both eyeballs turned towards the nose.

cross-fer·ti·lize /ˈkros ˋfɜtḷɑɪz *US:* ˈkrɔs/ *vt* (bot) carry pollen from the stamens of one plant to the pistil of another plant to produce hybrids. **cross-fer·ti·li·za·tion** /ˈkros ˈfɜtḷɑɪˋzeɪʃn *US:* ˈkrɔs -ḷɪˋz-/ *n*

cross·fire /ˋkrosfɑɪə(r) *US:* ˋkrɔs-/ *n* (mil) firing of guns from two or more points so that the lines of fire cross; (fig) situation in which questions are put to sb from persons in different places.

cross-grained /ˈkros ˋgreɪnd *US:* ˈkrɔs/ *adj* **1** (of wood) with the grain in crossing directions. **2** (fig) perverse; difficult to please or get on with.

cross-head·ing /ˈkros ˋhedɪŋ *US:* ˈkrɔs/ *n* (in a newspaper, etc) subordinate heading indicating briefly the contents of the passage that follows, inserted across the page or column to guide the reader.

cross-index /ˈkros ˋɪndeks *US:* ˈkrɔs/ *vt* [VP6A] supply with cross-references.

cross·ing /ˋkrosɪŋ *US:* ˋkrɔs-/ *n* **1** the act of going across, esp by sea: *We had a rough ~ from Dover to Calais.* **2** place where two roads, two railways, or (esp) a road and a railway cross. ˈ**level** ˋ**~**, one without a bridge (US = *grade ~*). **3** ˋ*street ~*, place on a street where pedestrians are requested to cross (often marked by studs or white lines and sometimes by traffic lights operated by pedestrians).

cross·keys /ˈkrosˋkiz *US:* ˈkrɔs-/ *n pl* (design of) crossed keys as Papal arms, and as an inn sign.

cross-leg·ged /ˈkros ˋlegd *US:* ˈkrɔs ˋlegɪd/ *adv* (of a person sitting) with one leg placed across the other.

cross·patch /ˋkrospætʃ *US:* ˋkrɔs-/ *n* (dated, colloq) cross, bad-tempered person.

cross-piece /ˋkros pis *US:* ˋkrɔs/ *n* piece (of a structure) lying across another piece.

cross-pur·poses /ˈkros ˋpɜpəsɪz *US:* ˈkrɔs/ *n pl* ***be at ~,*** (of two persons or groups) misunderstand one another; have different and conflicting purposes.

cross-ques·tion /ˈkros ˋkwestʃən *US:* ˈkrɔs/ *vt* [VP6A] = **cross-examine**.

cross-ref·er·ence /ˈkros ˋrefrns *US:* ˈkrɔs/ *n* [C] reference from one part of a book, index, file, etc to another, for further information.

cross·road /ˋkrosrəʊd *US:* ˋkrɔs-/ *n* **1** road that crosses another. **2** (*pl,* used with *sing v*) place where two or more roads meet: *We came to a ~s.* **3** ***at the ~s,*** (fig) at a critical turning-point (in life, etc).

cross-sec·tion /ˈkros ˋsekʃn *US:* ˈkrɔs/ *n* [C] (drawing of a) piece or slice made by cutting across, e g a tree trunk; (fig) typical or representative sample of the whole: *a ~ of the electors/the middle classes.*

cross-stitch /ˋkros stɪtʃ *US:* ˋkrɔs/ *n* stitch formed of two stitches that cross; needlework in which this stitch is used.

cross-talk /ˋkros tɔk *US:* ˋkrɔs/ *n* [U] (GB, colloq) rapid exchange of remarks, e g by comedians in a variety entertainment or in a quarrel; talk in which conversation is garbled, e g by crossed telephone lines.

cross·trees /ˋkrostriz *US:* ˋkrɔs-/ *n pl* two horizontal timbers bolted to a lower mast to support the mast above and to support ropes, etc.

cross·wind /ˋkroswɪnd *US:* ˋkrɔs-/ *n* [C] wind blowing at right angles, e g to an aircraft's line of flight or to traffic on a motorway.

cross-wise /ˋkros wɑɪz *US:* ˋkrɔs/ *adv* across; diagonally; in the form of a cross.

cross·word /ˋkroswɜd *US:* ˋkrɔs-/ *n* (also ˋ**~ puzzle**) puzzle in which words have to be written (from numbered clues) vertically and horizontally (up and down) in spaces on a chequered square or oblong.

crotch /krotʃ/ *n* **1** place where a branch forks from a tree: *The child was sitting in a ~ of a tree.* **2** place where a pair of trousers or a person's legs fork from the trunk.

crotchet /ˋkrotʃɪt/ *n* **1** (music) (US = *quarter note*) black-headed note with stem (♩), half of a minim. ⇨ the illus at **notation**. **2** strange, unreasonable idea. **~y** *adj* full of ~s(2).

crouch /krɑʊtʃ/ *vi* [VP2A,C,4A] ***~ (down),*** lower the body with the limbs together (in fear or to hide, or, of animals, ready to spring). □ *n* ~ing position.

croup[1] /krup/ *n* [U] children's disease in which there is inflammation of the windpipe, with coughing and difficulty in breathing.

croup[2] /krup/ *n* rump or buttocks of certain animals. ⇨ the illus at **domestic**.

crou·pier /ˋkrupɪeɪ/ *n* person who rakes in the money at a gaming table and pays out winnings.

crow[1] /krəʊ/ *n* (kinds of) large, black bird with a harsh cry. ⇨ the illus at **bird**. ⇨ also **carrion, jackdaw, raven, rook**[1]. ***as the*** ˋ***~ flies,*** in a straight line. ˋ**~'s-nest**, protected look-out platform fixed at the mast-head of a ship (e g a whaling ship) for the lookout man. **ˈ~'s-feet** *n pl* network of little lines on the skin near the outer corners of a person's eyes.

crow² /krəʊ/ *vi* (*pt* **crowed** or (archaic) **crew** /kru/, *pp* **crowed**) [VP6A,3A] **1** (of a cock) make a loud, shrill cry. **2** (of a baby) make sounds showing happiness. **3** ~ ***(over),*** (of persons) express gleeful triumph: *to ~ over an unsuccessful rival.* □ *n ~ing sound.*

crow·bar /ˈkrəʊbɑ(r)/ *n* straight, iron bar, often with a forked end, used as a lever for moving heavy objects.

crowd /kraʊd/ *n* [C] **1** large number of people together, but without order or organization: *There were large ~s of people in the streets on New Year's Eve. He pushed his way through the ~.* ***(would) pass in a ~,*** is not noticeably unsatisfactory or defective. **2 the ~,** the masses; people in general. ***follow/move with the ~,*** be content to do what most people do. **3** (colloq) company of persons associated in some way; set or clique of persons: *I can't afford to go about with that ~; they're too extravagant.* **4** large number (of things, usu without order): *a desk covered with a ~ of books and papers.* □ *vi,vt* **1** [VP2B,C,6A,14, 15A,B] come together in a ~: *Now, don't all ~ together!* ~ ***round,*** form a circle (round): *People quickly ~ round when there is a street accident. The pupils ~ed round the teacher to ask questions.* ~ ***through/in/into, etc,*** ~ ***(sth) with,*** (cause to) move through, etc in a ~; fill with: *They ~ed through the gates into the stadium. They ~ed the buses with passengers/~ed people into the buses. Let's not ~ the room with furniture. Memories ~ed in upon me,* came thick and fast into my mind. ~ ***sb/sth out (of),*** keep out by ~ing: *There was an overflow meeting for those who were ~ed out,* unable to obtain admission; *Your contribution to the school magazine was ~ed out,* There was no space for it. **2** (naut) ~ ***on sail,*** hoist many sails (so as to increase speed). **3** [VP6A] (colloq) put pressure on: *Don't ~ me; give me time to think!* **~ed** *part adj* having large numbers of people: *~ed cities/trains/buses.*

crown¹ /kraʊn/ *n* **1** ornamental headdress of gold, jewels, etc worn by a sovereign ruler; royal power: *to wear the ~,* rule as a sovereign; *succeed to the ~,* become the sovereign ruler; *an officer of the ~,* a State official: *a minister of the ~,* a Cabinet Minister; *a ~ appointment,* one made by the sovereign; *a C~ Colony,* one governed completely by the mother country; *~ prince,* next in succession to the throne; *~ princess,* wife of a ~ prince; *~ witness,* witness for the Prosecution in a criminal case. **ˌ~-ˈland,** land that belongs to the C~. **2** circle or wreath of flowers or leaves worn on the head, esp as a sign of victory, or as a reward: *a martyr's ~.* **3** (until 1971) *a ˌhalf-ˈ~,* British coin worth 2s 6d; *half a ~,* the sum of 2s 6d (= 12½ new pence). **4** top of the head or of a hat; part of a tooth that shows; (fig) perfection, completion: *the ~ of one's labours; the ~ of the year,* the autumn, season of harvests. **5** ~-shaped ornament (e g a crest or badge).

crown² /kraʊn/ *vt* **1** [VP6A,23] put a crown on (a king or queen): *the ~ed heads* (= kings and queens) *of Europe. They ~ed him king.* **2** [VP6A, 14] reward with a crown; give honour to; reward: *to be ~ed with victory; efforts that were ~ed with success.* **3** [VP6A,14] be or have at the top of: *The hill is ~ed with a wood.* **4** [VP6A] put a happy finishing touch to: *to open a bottle of wine to ~ a feast.* ***to ~ (it) all,*** to complete good/bad fortune, etc: *It rained, we had no umbrellas, and, to ~ all, we missed the last bus and had to walk home.* **5** [VP6A] put an artificial cover on a broken tooth. ⇨ **crown¹(4)**. **~·ing** *part adj* (attrib only) completing; making perfect: *the ~ing touch to the evening's entertainment. Her ~ing glory is her hair.*

cro·zier /ˈkrəʊzɪə(r) *US:* -ʒər/ *n* = **crosier**.

cru·cial /ˈkruʃl/ *adj* decisive; critical: *the ~ test/question; at the ~ moment.* **~·ly** /-ʃl̩ɪ/ *adv*

cru·cible /ˈkrusəbl/ *n* pot in which metals are melted; (fig) severe test or trial.

cru·ci·fix /ˈkrusɪfɪks/ *n* model of the Cross with the figure of Jesus on it.

cru·ci·fixion /ˌkrusɪˈfɪkʃn/ *n* [U] putting to death, being put to death, on a cross(**3**); [C] instance of this. **the C~,** that of Jesus.

cru·ci·form /ˈkrusɪfɔm/ *adj* cross-shaped.

cru·cify /ˈkrusɪfɑɪ/ *vt* (*pt,pp* **-fied**) put to death by nailing or binding to a cross.

crude /krud/ *adj* **1** (of materials) in a natural state; not refined or manufactured: *~ oil,* petroleum; *~ sugar; ~ ore.* **2** not having grace, taste or refinement: *the ~ life of our savage ancestors in the remote past; ~ manners.* **3** not finished properly; badly worked out: *~ schemes/methods/ideas; ~ paintings,* showing lack of skill; *~ facts,* presented in an undisguised way, with no attempt to make them less unpleasant; *a ~ log cabin in the mountains.* **~·ly** *adv*

crud·ity /ˈkrudətɪ/ *n* [U] the state or quality of being crude; [C] (*pl* **-ties**) instance of this; crude act, remark, etc.

cruel /krul̩/ *adj* **1** (of persons) taking pleasure in the suffering of others; ready to give pain to others: *a ~ master; a man who is ~ to animals. It was ~ of him to make the donkey carry such a heavy load.* **2** causing pain or suffering; showing indifference to the sufferings of others: *a ~ blow/punishment/disease/war; in a ~* (= distressing) *predicament.* **~·ly** /ˈkrʊəlɪ/ *adv*

cruel·ty /ˈkrul̩tɪ/ *n* **1** [U] readiness to give pain or cause suffering to others; delight in this; cruel nature: *C~ to animals is severely punished in England.* **2** [C] (*pl* **-ties**) cruel act.

cruet /ˈkruɪt/ *n* **1** small glass bottle for vinegar or oil for use at table. **2** (also **ˈ~-stand**) stand for oil and vinegar ~s, and for mustard and pepper pots.

cruise /kruz/ *vi* [VP2A,C] **1** sail about, either for pleasure, or, in war, looking for enemy ships. **2** (of cars, aircraft) travel at the speed (and of aircraft at the altitude) most economical of fuel, less than the top speed: *The car has a cruising speed of 50 miles an hour.* □ *n* cruising voyage: *to go on/for a ~. The liner is making a round-the-world ~ this year,* a pleasure voyage. **cruiser** /ˈkruzə(r)/ *n* **1** fast warship. **2 ˈcabin-~r,** motor-boat (with sleeping accommodation, etc) designed for pleasure ~s.

crumb /krʌm/ *n* **1** [C] very small piece of dry food, esp a bit of bread or cake rubbed off or dropped from a large piece: *sweep up the ~s;* [U] soft, inner part of a loaf of bread. ⇨ **crust(1)**. **2** (fig) small amount: *a few ~s of information/comfort.*

crumble /ˈkrʌmbl/ *vt,vi* [VP6A,2A,C] break, rub or fall into very small pieces: *to ~ one's bread,*

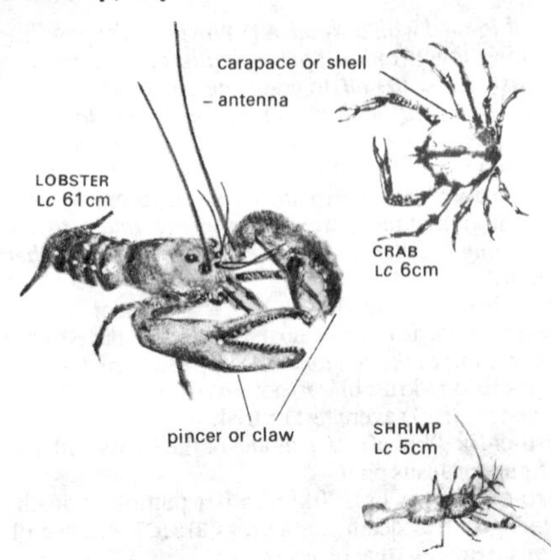

crustaceans

rub it into crumbs; *crumbling walls*, that are falling into ruin; *great empires that have ~d* (= decayed) *and fallen;* (fig) *hopes that ~d to dust,* came to nothing.

crum·bly /ˈkrʌmblɪ/ *adj* (-ier, -iest) *easily crumbled.*

crum·pet /ˈkrʌmpɪt/ *n* (GB) **1** flat, round, soft, unsweetened cake, usu toasted and eaten hot with butter spread on it. **2** (sl) head. **3** (sl) sexually attractive girl or woman.

crumple /ˈkrʌmpl/ *vt, vi* [VP6A,15B,2A,C] **1** press or crush into folds or creases: *to ~ one's clothes,* e g by packing them carelessly. **2** become full of folds or creases: *Some kinds of material ~ more easily than others. Do nylon sheets ~?* **3** *~ up,* (liter, fig) crush; collapse: *to ~ up a sheet of paper into a ball; to ~ up an opposing army. The wings of the aircraft ~d up.*

crunch /krʌntʃ/ *vt, vi* [VP6A,2A,C] **1** crush noisily with the teeth when eating: *The dog was ~ing a bone. People who ~ peanuts in the cinema can be very annoying.* **2** crush, be crushed, noisily under one's feet, under wheels, etc: *The frozen snow ~ed under the wheels of our car. Our feet ~ed the gravel.* □ *n* the act of ~ing; noise made by ~ing. ***when it comes to the ~,*** (colloq) when the moment of crisis or decision is reached.

crup·per /ˈkrʌpə(r)/ *n* leather strap fastened to the back of a saddle or harness and looped under the horse's tail; hindquarters of a horse. ⇨ the illus at **harness**.

cru·sade /kruˈseɪd/ *n* **1** any one of the military expeditions made by the Christian rulers and people of Europe during the Middle Ages to recover the Holy Land from the Muslims. **2** any struggle or movement in support of sth believed to be good or against sth believed to be bad: *a ~ against intemperance.* □ *vi* [VP2A,3A] *~* ***against/in favour of/for,*** take part in a ~. **cru·sader** *n* person taking part in a ~.

cruse /kruz/ *n* (old name for) earthenware pot for oil or water: *the widow's ~,* inexhaustible supply ⇨ **1 Kings 17: 12.**

crush¹ /krʌʃ/ *vt, vi* **1** [VP6A,15A,B] press, be pressed, so that there is breaking or injury: *Don't ~ this box; it has flowers in it. Wine is made by ~ing grapes. Several people were ~ed to death as they tried to escape from the burning theatre. We can't ~ any more people into the hall; it is crowded already.* ***~ up,*** make into powder by ~ing. ***~ out,*** force out by ~ing: *to ~ out the juice from oranges.* **2** [VP6A,15A,B,2A,C] (cause to) become full of creases or irregular folds; lose shape: *Her dresses were badly ~ed when she took them out of the suitcase. Some of the new synthetic dress materials do not ~.* **3** [VP6A] subdue; overwhelm: *He was not satisfied until he had ~ed his enemies. Our hopes have been ~ed. He smiled at her, but she ~ed him* (= made him feel abashed) *with a haughty look.* **4** [VP2C] (of persons) *~* ***in/into/through/past, etc,*** press or push in, etc: *They all tried to ~ into the front seats.* (With cognate *obj*) *We had to ~ our way through the crowd.* **~·ing** *adj* overwhelming: *a ~ing defeat;* in a manner intended to subdue or disconcert: *a ~ing reply.* **~·ing·ly** *adv*

crush² /krʌʃ/ *n* **1** (*sing* only, with *def* or *indef art*) crowd of people pressed together: *There was a frightful ~ at the gate into the stadium.* **ˈ~ barrier,** one erected to keep back crowds (e g along a pavement when crowds of people are expected). **2** (colloq) crowded social gathering. **3** (sl) ***get/have a ~ on sb,*** (usu of a young person) be, imagine oneself to be, in love with. **4** [U] fruit drink made by pressing out juice (e g from oranges).

crust /krʌst/ *n* **1** [C,U] (piece of the) hard-baked surface of a loaf; outer covering (pastry) of a pie or tart. **2** [C,U] hard surface: *a thin ~ of ice/frozen snow; the earth's ~,* the outer portion. **3** hard deposit on the inside of a bottle of wine. □ *vt, vi* [VP6A,2A,C] *~* ***over,*** cover, become covered, with a ~; form into a ~: *The snow ~ed over* (= froze hard on top) *during the night.*

crus·ta·cean /krʌˈsteɪʃn/ *n* any of a numerous class of animals, mostly living in water (and popularly called *shellfish*) with a hard shell (e g *crabs, lobsters*).

crusted /ˈkrʌstɪd/ *adj* **1** (fig) ancient; venerable. **2** fixed; engrained: *~ prejudices/habits.*

crusty /ˈkrʌstɪ/ *adj* (-ier, -iest) **1** having a crust; hard like a crust: *~ bread.* **2** (of persons, their behaviour) curt, harsh; quick to show irritation, etc.

crutch /krʌtʃ/ *n* **1** support used under the arm to help a lame person to walk: *a pair of ~es; to go about on ~es.* **2** support that is like a ~ in shape or use; (fig) any moral support. **3** crotch(**2**).

crux /krʌks/ *n* (*pl* -xes) part (of a problem) that is the most difficult to solve: *The ~ of the matter is this.*

cry¹ /krɑɪ/ *vi, vt* (*pt, pp* **cried**) **1** [VP2A,B,C,3A,4A] (of persons, animals, birds) make (usu loud) sounds that express feelings (e g pain, fear) but not ideas, thoughts, etc: *A baby can cry as soon as it is born. He cried with pain when the dentist pulled the tooth out.* **2** [VP2A,B,C,3A,6A,15B] (of persons) weep; shed tears (with or without sounds): *The boy was crying because he had lost his money. She was crying over her misfortunes. She was crying for joy,* because she was happy. *The child was crying for* (= because he wanted to be given) *some more cake. The boy was crying with pain/hunger. She cried hot tears.* ***cry one's ˈeyes/ˈheart out,*** weep very bitterly. ***cry oneself to sleep,*** cry until one falls asleep. ***give sb sth to cry for/about,*** punish him for crying without a good or obvious cause. **3** [VP6A,14,9,2C,3A,4A] exclaim; call out loudly in words: *'Help! Help!' he* *cried. The starving people cried to their chief for bread. He cried for mercy.* **cry for the moon,** demand sth impossible. ⇨ shame(3). **4** [VP6A, 15A,B] announce for sale; make known by calling out: *to cry one's wares; to cry the news all over the town.* **5 cry sth down,** suggest that it is worth little. **cry off,** withdraw from sth that one has undertaken: *I had promised to go, but had to cry off at the last moment.* **cry sth up,** praise it highly.

cry² /kraɪ/ *n* (*pl* cries) **1** loud sound of fear, pain, grief, etc; loud, excited utterance of words: *a cry for help; the cry of an animal in pain; a cry of triumph; angry cries from the mob; cries for the meeting to be/that the meeting should be adjourned. They raised/uttered/set up a cry of 'Thief! Thief!'* **a ˈfar/ˈlong cry,** a long way from; very different from: *Being a junior clerk is a far cry from being one of the Directors.* **in full cry,** (of a pack of hounds) barking together as they pursue or hunt (an animal); (fig) eagerly attacking (sb). ***much cry and little wool,*** (prov) much fuss with little result. ***within cry (of),*** within hearing; near enough to hear a call. ⇨ hue². **2** words spoken loudly to give information: *the cry of the night watchman;* call announcing sth for sale (by a person in the street): *the old (street) cries of London,* e g 'Fresh Herrings'. ⇨ crier(1). **3** watchword or phrase, used for a principle or cause: *a ˈwar-cry; a ˈbattle-cry. 'Asia for the Asians' was their cry.* **4** fit of weeping: *have a good cry,* find emotional relief by shedding tears. *Let her have her cry out,* let her weep until she becomes calm again. **ˈcry-baby,** child who cries often or easily without good or apparent cause.

cry·ing /ˈkraɪɪŋ/ *attrib adj* (esp of evils) demanding attention: *a ~ shame/evil/need.*

crypt /krɪpt/ *n* underground room, esp of a church.

a church crypt

cryp·tic /ˈkrɪptɪk/ *adj* secret; with a hidden meaning, or a meaning not easily seen: *a ~ remark.* **cryp·ti·cally** /-klɪ/ *adv*

crypto- /ˈkrɪptəʊ/ *pref* (in combination) hidden, secret: *a ˈ~-ˈcommunist,* person owing secret allegiance to the Communist Party.

crypto·gram /ˈkrɪptəgræm/ *n* [C] sth written in a secret code.

crypto·meria /ˈkrɪptəʊˈmɪərɪə/ *n* Japanese cedar-tree.

crys·tal /ˈkrɪstl/ *n* **1** [U] transparent, natural substance like quartz; [C] piece of this as an ornament: *a necklace of ~s;* (attrib) *~ ornaments; ~ detector,* type used in early radio sets (called *ˈ~ sets*). **ˈ~-gazing,** looking into a ~ ball in an attempt to see future events pictured there. **2** [U] glassware of best quality, made into bowls, vases, vessels, etc: *The dining-table shone with silver and ~.* **3** [C] (science) definite and regular shape taken naturally by the molecules of certain substances: *sugar and salt ~s; snow and ice ~s.* **4** (US) glass over the face of a watch.

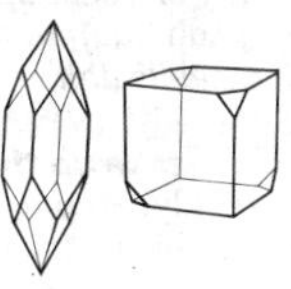

crystals

diamonds

cry·stal·line /ˈkrɪstəlaɪn/ *adj* made of crystal(s); like crystal; very clear.

cry·stal·lize /ˈkrɪstəlaɪz/ *vt,vi* **1** [VP6A,2A] form, cause to form, into crystals. **2** [VP6A] cover (fruit, etc) with sugar-crystals: *~d ginger.* **3** [VP6A,2A] (fig of ideas, plans) become, cause to be, clear and definite: *His vague ideas ~d into a definite plan.* **crys·tal·li·za·tion** /ˈkrɪstəlaɪˈzeɪʃn *US:* -lɪˈz-/ *n*

cub /kʌb/ *n* **1** young lion, bear, fox, tiger: *cub-hunting,* hunting of fox-cubs; *ˈwolf-cub,* junior boy scout; (fig) *a cub reporter,* young and inexperienced reporter. **2** ill-mannered young man. **cub·bing** *n* = cub-hunting.

cubby-hole /ˈkʌbɪ həʊl/ *n* small enclosed space; snug place.

cube /kjub/ *n* **1** solid body having six equal square sides; block of something so shaped or similarly shaped. **2** (maths) product of a number multiplied by itself twice: *The ~ of 5* (5^3) *is* 5 × 5 × 5 (*125*). *The ~ root of 64* ($\sqrt[3]{64}$) *is 4* (4 × 4 × 4 = 64). □ *vt* [VP6A] multiply a number by itself twice: *10 ~d is 1 000.*

cu·bic /ˈkjubɪk/ *adj* having the shape of a cube; of a cube: *one ~ metre,* volume of a cube whose edge is one metre; *~ content,* volume expressed in cubic metres, etc; *a motor vehicle with a 2 000 cc capacity,* i e 2 000 ~ centimetres.

cu·bi·cal /ˈkjubɪkl/ *adj* = cubic.

cu·bicle /ˈkjubɪkl/ *n* small division of a larger room, walled or curtained to make a separate compartment, e g for sleeping in, or for (un)dressing at a swimming-pool.

cub·ism /ˈkjub-ɪzm/ *n* [U] style in art in which objects are represented so that they appear to be largely of geometrical shapes. **cub·ist** /ˈkjubɪst/ *n* artist who practises ~.

cu·bit /ˈkjubɪt/ *n* old measure of length (18 to 22 inches or 45 to 56 centimetres).

cuck·old /ˈkʌkəʊld/ *n* man whose wife has committed adultery. □ *vt* [VP6A] (of a man) make (another man) a ~ by seducing his wife; (of a woman) make (her husband) a ~.

cuckoo /ˈkʊku/ *n* bird whose call is like its name, a migratory bird which reaches the British Isles in spring and lays its eggs in the nests of small birds. ⇨ the illus at bird. **ˈ~-clock,** one that strikes the hours with notes like the call of a ~.

cu·cum·ber /ˈkjukʌmbə(r)/ *n* [C,U] (creeping plant with) long, green-skinned fleshy fruit, usu sliced and eaten in salads, or made into pickle. ⇨ the illus at vegetable. ***as cool as a ~,*** unexcited; self-possessed.

cud /kʌd/ *n* [U] food which oxen, etc bring back from the first stomach and chew again. ***chew the cud,*** (fig) reflect; ponder.

cuddle /ˈkʌdl/ *vt,vi* [VP6A,15B,2C] **1** hold close and lovingly in one's arms: *The baby doesn't like being ~d herself, but she likes to ~ her doll.* **2 ~**

up (to/together), lie close and comfortably: *The children ~d up (together) under the blankets. She ~d up to him to get warm.* □ *n* act of cuddling; hug. **~-some** /-səm/, **cud·dly** /ˈkʌdl̩ɪ/ *adjj* suitable for, inviting, cuddling: *a nice cuddly doll.*

cud·gel /ˈkʌdʒl/ *vt, n* (-ll-; US also -l-) [VP6A] (hit with a) short, thick stick or club. ***take up the ~s for,*** (rhet) fight for; support strongly. ***~ one's brains,*** think hard on a difficult problem; try to think of (sth one has forgotten).

cue[1] /kju/ *n* [C] **1** sth (e g the last words of an actor's speech) which shows when sb else is to do or say sth. **2** hint about how to behave, what to do, etc: ***take one's cue from sb,*** observe what he does as a guide to one's own action.

cue[2] /kju/ *n* billiard-player's long, tapering, leather-tipped rod, for striking the ball.

cuff[1] /kʌf/ *n* **1** end of a shirt or coat sleeve at the wrist. ***play it off the ~,*** (colloq) use one's wits in a situation for which one is unprepared. **ˈ~-links,** used for fastening ~s. **2** (US) turned-up fold at the bottom of a leg of a pair of trousers. (GB = *turn-up*). **3** (*pl,* colloq) handcuffs.

cuff[2] /kʌf/ *vt, n* [VP6A] (give sb a) light blow with the open hand.

cuir·ass /kwɪˈræs/ *n* piece of armour to protect the body, breastplate and plate for the back, fastened together. ⇨ the illus at armour. **cuir·as·sier** /kwɪˈræsɪeɪ/ *n* horse-soldier wearing a ~.

cui·sine /kwɪˈzin/ *n* [U] **1** (F) style of cooking; cooking: *French ~; a hotel where the ~ is excellent.* **2** kitchen department; cooking arrangements.

cul-de-sac /ˈkʌl̩ də ˈsæk/ *n* street with an opening at one end only; blind alley.

cu·li·nary /ˈkʌlɪnṛɪ *US:* -nerɪ/ *adj* of cooking or a kitchen: *a ~ triumph,* a superbly cooked dish or meal; *~ plants,* suitable for cooking.

cull /kʌl/ *vt* [VP6A] pick (a flower); select: *extracts ~ed from the best authors.* □ *n* sth that is ~ed (e g a hen that no longer lays well, picked out and killed for food).

cul·len·der /ˈkʌləndə(r)/ *n* = colander.

cul·mi·nate /ˈkʌlmɪneɪt/ *vt* [VP3A] ***~ in,*** (of efforts, hopes, careers, etc) reach the highest point: *misfortunes that ~d in bankruptcy.* **cul·mi·na·tion** /ˌkʌlmɪˈneɪʃn/ *n* highest point: *the culmination of his career.*

culp·able /ˈkʌlpəbl/ *adj* (legal) blameworthy; deserving punishment: *hold a person ~; dismissed for ~ negligence,* wrongly neglecting to do sth. **culp·ably** /ˈkʌlpəblɪ/ *adv* **cul·pa·bil·ity** /ˌkʌlpəˈbɪlətɪ/ *n*

cul·prit /ˈkʌlprɪt/ *n* person who has done wrong; offender.

cult /kʌlt/ *n* [C] **1** system of religious worship. **2** devotion to a person or practice and ritual (esp of a single deity): *the ~ of archery; the ~ of Browning.* **3** (group of persons devoted to a) popular fashion or craze: (attrib) *a ˈ~ word,* one used because it is fashionable among members of such a group.

cul·ti·vable /ˈkʌltɪvəbl/ *adj* that can be cultivated.

cul·ti·vate /ˈkʌltɪveɪt/ *vt* [VP6A] **1** prepare (land) for crops by ploughing, etc; help (crops) to grow (e g by breaking up the soil around them, destroying weeds, etc). **2** give care, thought, time, etc in order to develop sth: *to ~ the mind/sb's friendship. He ~s* (= tries to win the good will of) *the sort of people who can be useful to him in his business.* **cul·ti·vated** *adj* (of a person) having good manners and education.

cul·ti·va·tion /ˌkʌltɪˈveɪʃn/ *n* [U] cultivating or being cultivated: *the ~ of the soil; land that is under ~; to bring land into ~; to allow land to go out of ~.*

cul·ti·va·tor /ˈkʌltɪveɪtə(r)/ *n* person who cultivates; machine for breaking up ground, destroying weeds, etc.

cul·tural /ˈkʌltʃərl/ *adj* having to do with culture: *~ studies,* e g art, literature; *a ~ institute.*

cul·ture /ˈkʌltʃə(r)/ *n* **1** [U] advanced development of the human powers; development of the body, mind and spirit by training and experience: *Physical ~ is important, but we must not neglect the ~ of the mind.* **2** [U] evidence of intellectual development (of arts, science, etc) in human society: *He is a man of considerable ~. Universities should be centres of ~.* **3** [U] state of intellectual development among a people; [C] particular form of intellectual development: *We owe much to Greek ~. He has studied the ~s of Oriental countries.* **4** [U] all the arts, beliefs, social institutions, etc characteristic of a community, race, etc: *the ~ of the South Sea Islanders.* **5** [U] cultivating; the rearing of bees, silkworms, etc: *He has five acres devoted to bulb ~,* to the growing of such flowers as daffodils, tulips, etc. **ˈ~(d) pearl,** pearl produced in an oyster shell into which a piece of grit has been introduced. **6** [C] (biol) growth of bacteria (for medical or scientific study): *a ~ of cholera germs.* **cul·tured** *adj* (of persons) cultivated; having ~ of the mind; (of tastes, interests, etc) refined.

cul·vert /ˈkʌlvət/ *n* sewer or drain that crosses under a road, railway or embankment; channel for electrical cables under the ground.

cum·ber /ˈkʌmbə(r)/ *vt* [VP6A,14] hamper; burden: *~ oneself with an overcoat on a warm day; ~ed with parcels.*

cum·ber·some /ˈkʌmbəsəm/ *adj* burdensome; heavy and awkward to carry: *A soldier today would find old-fashioned armour very ~.*

cum·brous /ˈkʌmbrəs/ *adj* = cumbersome.

cum·mer·bund /ˈkʌməbʌnd/ *n* (Anglo-Indian) sash worn round the waist.

cumu·lat·ive /ˈkjumjʊlətɪv *US:* -leɪtɪv/ *adj* increasing in amount by one addition after another.

cumu·lus /ˈkjumjʊləs/ *n* (*pl* -li /-lɪ/) cloud made up of rounded masses on a flat base.

cunei·form /ˈkjunɪɪfɔm/ *adj* wedge-shaped: *~ characters,* as used in old Persian and Assyrian writing.

cuneiform characters

cun·ning[1] /ˈkʌnɪŋ/ *adj* **1** clever at deceiving; showing this kind of cleverness: *a ~ old fox; a ~ trick.* **2** (old use) skilful: *a ~ workman.* **3** (US) attractive; cute: *a ~ smile/baby/kitten.* **~·ly** *adv*

cun·ning[2] /ˈkʌnɪŋ/ *n* **1** quality of being cunning(1): *The boy showed a great deal of ~ in getting what he wanted.* **2** (old use) skill: *My hand has lost its ~.*

cunt /kʌnt/ *n* ⚠ **1** vagina. **2** female pudenda. **3** (vulg; sl) (by transference) woman or girl, regarded as a sexual object. **4** (vulg; derog sl) despicable person.

cup[1] /kʌp/ *n* **1** small porcelain bowl, usu with a handle, used with a saucer, for tea, coffee or cocoa; contents of a cup: *a* `*teacup; a cup and saucer; a* '*cup of* `*coffee; two cups of flour* (used as a measure in cooking). ***not my cup of tea,*** (colloq) not what I like, not what suits me. **2** = chalice. **3** (fig) that which comes to a person; experience: *His cup of happiness was full.* **4** vessel (usu of gold or silver) given as a prize in competitions. **'cup-`final,** (football) final match to decide a competition. **`cup-tie,** (football) match to eliminate teams competing for a cup. **5** (from `*wine cup*) wine. ***in his cups,*** partly or wholly intoxicated. **`cup-bearer,** official of a royal or nobleman's household who serves wine at banquets. **6** sth shaped like a cup; *the cup of a flower; an* `*egg-cup;* `*acorn-cups; the cups of a bra.* **7** iced drink of wine, etc, usu flavoured: `*claret-cup;* `*cider-cup.* **cup·ful** /`kʌpfʊl/ *n* (*pl* **cupfuls**) as much as a cup will hold.

cup[2] /kʌp/ *vt* (-pp-) [VP6A] **1** put into the shape of a cup: *to cup one's hands,* e g to catch a ball; put round or over like a cup: *with her chin cupped in her hand.* **2** perform the operation of cupping on (a person). ⇨ **cupping** below.

cup·board /`kʌbəd/ *n* set of shelves with doors, either built into a room as a fixture, or a separate piece of furniture, used for dishes, provisions, clothes, etc: *a* `*kitchen-~; a* `*hanging-~,* one in which dresses, suits, etc may be hung on coat-hangers. Cf US *china-closet, linen-closet.* **`~-love,** affection that is shown in the hope of getting sth by it (e g a child hoping for cake).

Cu·pid /`kjupɪd/ *n* Roman god of love; (picture or statue of a) beautiful boy (with wings and a bow and arrows); symbol of love.

cu·pid·ity /kju`pɪdətɪ/ *n* [U] greed, esp for money or property.

cu·pola /`kjupələ/ *n* small dome forming (part of) a roof; ceiling of a dome.

cuppa /`kʌpə/ *n* (sl) cup of tea: *What about a ~?*

cup·ping /`kʌpɪŋ/ *n* [U] operation of drawing blood to or through the skin by creating a partial vacuum over the area by means of a glass cup (called a `*~-glass*).

cu·pric /`kjuprɪk/ *adj* containing copper.

cu·pro-nickel /'kjuprəʊ `nɪkl/ *n* [U] alloy of copper and nickel used for making coins.

cur /kɜ(r)/ *n* bad-tempered or worthless dog (esp low-bred); cowardly or badly behaved man.

cur·able /`kjʊərəbl/ *adj* that can be cured. **cura·bil·ity** /'kjʊərə`bɪlətɪ/ *n*

cura·çao, -çoa /`kjʊərəsəʊ *US:* -saʊ/ *n* liqueur (sweet and syrupy) flavoured with peel of bitter oranges.

cur·acy /`kjʊərəsɪ/ *n* (*pl* **-cies**) office and work of a curate.

curate /`kjʊərət/ *n* clergyman who helps a parish priest (rector or vicar).

cura·tive /`kjʊərətɪv/ *adj* helping to, able to, cure (disease or ill health): *the ~ value of sunshine and sea air.*

cu·ra·tor /kjʊ`reɪtə(r)/ *n* official in charge (esp of a museum or art gallery).

curb /kɜb/ *n* **1** chain or leather strap passing under a horse's jaw, used to control it. ⇨ the illus at **harness. 2** (fig) sth that holds one back or restrains: *put/keep a ~ on one's anger/passions.* **3** = **kerb.** □ *vt* [VP6A] **1** control (a horse) by means of a ~. **2** keep (feelings, etc) under control: *to ~ one's impatience.*

curd /kɜd/ *n* **1** (often *pl*) thick, soft substance, almost solid, formed when milk turns sour, used to make cheese. **2** [U] (in compounds) substance resembling ~: '*lemon-`~,* made from eggs, butter and sugar, flavoured with lemon.

curdle /kɜdl/ *vi,vt* [VP6A,2A] form, cause to form, into curds; become curd-like: *The milk has ~d;* (fig uses): *What a blood-curdling* (= horrifying) *yell! His blood ~d at the sight,* He was filled with horror.

cure[1] /kjʊə(r)/ *n* [C] **1** curing or being ~d(**1**): *The doctor cannot guarantee a ~. His ~ took six weeks.* **2** substance or treatment which ~s(**1**): *Is there a certain ~ for cancer yet? He has tried all sorts of ~s, but is still ill. You need a* `*rest-~,* a holiday from your work. **3** spiritual charge[1](**5**): *to obtain/resign a ~,* a position as a priest.

cure[2] /kjʊə(r)/ *vt,vi* [VP6A,14] **1** ***~ sb (of sth), ~ sth,*** bring (a person) back to health; provide and use successfully a remedy for a disease, ill health, suffering; get rid of (an evil): *to ~ a man of a disease; to ~ an illness; to ~ poverty/drunkenness; to ~ a child of bad habits; to try to ~ social discontent at home by making war abroad.* **`~-all,** sth which, it is claimed, ~s all ills. **2** treat meat, fish, skin, tobacco, etc in order to keep it in good condition by salting, smoking, drying, etc: *well-~d bacon.*

curé /`kjʊəreɪ *US:* kjʊ`reɪ/ *n* parish priest in France.

cur·few /`kɜfju/ *n* **1** (old use) ringing of a bell as a signal for lights to be put out and fires covered; bell for this; hour at which the bell was rung. **2** (modern use) time or signal (under martial law) for people to remain indoors: *to impose a ~ on a town; to lift/end the ~.*

curio /`kjʊərɪəʊ/ *n* (*pl* **-rios**) work of art of a strange or unusual character and valued for this reason.

curi·os·ity /'kjʊərɪ`ɒsətɪ/ *n* **1** [U] being curious(**1, 2**): *~ about/~ to learn about distant lands; to be dying of/burning with ~ to know what was happening. He yielded to ~ and opened the letter addressed to his sister.* **2** [C] (*pl* **-ties**) curious(**3**) thing; strange or rare objects.

curi·ous /`kjʊərɪəs/ *adj* **1** (in a good sense) eager (to learn, know): *I'm ~ to know what he said. If a boy is ~, he is always asking questions.* **2** meddlesome; having or showing too much interest in the affairs of others: *~ neighbours. Don't ask so many ~ questions. Hide it where ~ eyes won't see it. What is he so ~ about?* **3** strange; unusual; hard to understand: *What a ~ mistake! There was a ~ silence. Isn't he a ~-looking little man!* **4** (rather old use) showing the result of care and attention: *a jewel of ~ workmanship.* **~·ly** *adv*

curl[1] /kɜl/ *n* **1** [C] sth naturally like or twisted into a shape like the thread of a screw, esp a lock of hair of this shape: *~s (of hair) falling over a girl's shoulders; hair falling in ~s over the shoulder; a ~ of smoke rising from a cigarette; the ~ of a wave; a ~ of the lips,* expressing scorn. **2** [U] the state of being curly: *How do you keep your hair in ~?*

curl[2] /kɜl/ *vt,vi* [VP6A,15A,B,2A,C] make into curls; twist; grow or be in curls: *She has ~ed her hair. Does her hair ~ naturally? The smoke from* *the camp fire* ~*ed upwards. The frost made the young leaves* ~ *(up)/*~*ed up the young leaves. The dog* ~*ed (itself) up on the rug.* **~ (sb) up,** (cause to) collapse: *The cricket ball hit him on the head and he* ~*ed up* (= fell to the ground) *at once. She* ~*ed up (with laughter) at his joke. The blow* ~*ed him up completely.* **'~ing-tongs/-irons,** instruments (heated before use) for ~ing or straightening the hair. **'~ing-pins,** clips (used cold) for ~ing the hair.

cur·lew /ˈkɜlju/ *n* wading bird with a long, slender, down-curved bill. ⇨ the illus at **water.**

curl·ing /ˈkɜlɪŋ/ *n* [U] Scottish game played on ice with heavy, flat-bottomed stones (**'~-stones**) with handles, sent along the ice towards a mark.

curly /ˈkɜlɪ/ *adj* (**-ier, -iest**) having curls; arranged in curls: ~ *hair; a* '~*-headed girl.*

cur·mudgeon /kɜˈmʌdʒən/ *n* (colloq) bad-tempered or miserly person.

cur·rant /ˈkʌrənt *US:* ˈkɜ-/ *n* **1** small, sweet, dried seedless grape (grown in Greece and neighbouring countries) used in buns, cakes, puddings, etc. **2** (cultivated bush with) small black, red or white juicy fruit growing in clusters.

cur·rency /ˈkʌrənsɪ *US:* ˈkɜ-/ *n* **1** [U] the state of being in common or general use: *Many slang words have short* ~, soon go out of use. *The rumour soon gained* ~, was repeated until many people were aware of it. ***give ~ to,*** make ~; spread: *Do not give* ~ *to idle gossip.* **2** [C,U] (*pl* **-cies**) money that is actually in use in a country: *a gold/paper* ~*; foreign currencies; a decimal* ~.

cur·rent[1] /ˈkʌrənt *US:* ˈkɜ-/ *adj* **1** in common or general use; generally accepted: ~ *coin/money;* ~ *opinions/beliefs; words that are no longer* ~. **2** now passing; of the present time: ~ *expenses/prices; the* ~ *issue of a magazine; the* ~ *year,* this year; *a newsreel showing* ~ *events.* **3 '~ account,** (with a bank) one from which money may be drawn without previous notice. ⇨ *deposit account* at **deposit**[1](1). **~ assets,** (comm) assets which are not fixed but which change in the course of business (e g amounts owing). **~·ly** *adv* in a ~**(1,2)** manner: *It is* ~*ly reported that....*

cur·rent[2] /ˈkʌrənt *US:* ˈkɜ-/ *n* **1** stream of water, air, gas, esp one flowing through slower moving or still water, etc: *A cold* ~ *of air came in when the door was opened. Although he was a strong swimmer he was swept away by the* ~ *and was drowned. The warm* ~*s in the Atlantic influence the climate of Great Britain.* **2** flow of electricity through sth or along a wire or cable. ⇨ **alternate**[2]**(2), direct**[1]**(5).** **3** course or movement (of events, opinions, thoughts, etc): *Nothing disturbs the peaceful* ~ *of her life. The government used the radio to influence the* ~ *of thought.*

cur·ricu·lum /kəˈrɪkjʊləm/ *n* (*pl* **-lums** or **-la** /-lə/) course of study in a school, college, etc. **'~ vitae** /ˈvitɑɪ/ (Lat) brief written account of one's past history (e g education, employment), used when applying for a position, etc.

cur·rish /ˈkɜrɪʃ/ *adj* like a cur. **~·ly** *adv*

curry[1] /ˈkʌrɪ *US:* ˈkɜɪ/ *n* (*pl* **-ries**) [C,U] (dish of) meat (fish, eggs, etc) cooked with hot-tasting spices: *a chicken* ~*; Madras curries; to eat too much* ~. **'~-powder,** mixture of spices for a ~ ground or beaten to a powder. □ *vt* prepare (food) with hot-tasting spices; flavour (food) with ~-powder.

curry[2] /ˈkʌrɪ *US:* ˈkɜɪ/ *vt* (*pt,pp* **-ried**) [VP6A] rub down and clean (a horse); prepare (tanned leather) by soaking, scraping, etc. ***~ favour (with sb),*** try to win favour or approval (by using flattery, etc).

curse[1] /kɜs/ *n* **1** word, phrase or sentence calling for the punishment, injury or destruction of sth or sb. ***be under a ~,*** suffer as the result of a ~. ***call down ~s (from Heaven) upon sb,*** ask God or Heaven to punish him. ***lay sb under a ~,*** make him suffer as the result of a ~. **2** cause of misfortune or ruin: *Gambling is often a* ~. *The rabbits are a* ~ (i e do a lot of damage to crops, etc) *in this part of the country. His wealth proved a* ~ *to him.* **3** word or words used in violent language expressing anger. **4 the ~,** (colloq) menses.

curse[2] /kɜs/ *vt,vi* **1** [VP6A] use a curse against; use violent language against. **2** [VP2A,3A] utter curses (*at* sb): *to* ~ *and swear; to* ~ *at a stupid servant.* **3 be ~d with,** suffer misfortune, trouble, etc because of: *to be* ~*d with idle daughters/a violent temper.*

cursed /kɜst, ˈkɜsɪd/ *adj* damnable; hateful (often used colloq merely to show annoyance): *This work is a* ~ *nuisance.* **~·ly** /ˈkɜsədlɪ/ *adv*

cur·sive /ˈkɜsɪv/ *adj* (of handwriting) with the letters rounded and joined together. ⇨ **script.**

cur·sory /ˈkɜsərɪ/ *adj* (of work, reading, etc) quick; hurried; done without attention to details: *a* ~ *glance/inspection.* **cur·sor·ily** /ˈkɜsrɪlɪ/ *adv*

curst /kɜst/ *adj* = **cursed.**

curt /kɜt/ *adj* (of a speaker, his manner, what he says) short-spoken; hardly polite: *to give sb a* ~ *answer; a* ~ *way of speaking.* **~·ly** *adv* **~·ness** *n*

cur·tail /kɜˈteɪl/ *vt* [VP6A] make shorter than was at first planned; cut off a part of: *to* ~ *a speech/one's holidays; to* ~ *the allowance one has been making to sb,* give him less money. **~·ment** *n* act or result of ~ing.

cur·tain /ˈkɜtn/ *n* **1** piece of cloth or lace hung up at a window or door or (in former times) round a bed: *Please draw the* ~*s,* pull them across the window(s). ***draw a ~ over sth,*** (fig) say no more about it. **'~-lecture,** (old use) wife's scolding of her husband in private (originally in bed after the bed-~s were drawn). **2** sheet of heavy material to draw or lower across the front of the stage in a theatre before and after each scene of a play: *The* ~ *rises/is raised,* The play begins. *The* ~ *falls,* The play/act ends. **'~-call,** call (given by the audience) to an actor or actress to appear before the ~ for applause. **'~-raiser,** short piece performed before the chief play. **'safety-~,** one that is fire-proof. **3** (various senses indicating cover or protection): *A* ~ *of mist hid the view. The troops went forward behind a* ~ *of fire* (gun-fire from their artillery). □ *vt* **1** [VP6A] furnish or cover with ~s: ~*ed windows; enough material to* ~ *all the windows.* **2** [VP15B] **~ off,** separate or divide with a ~ or ~s: *to* ~ *off part of a room.*

curt·sey, curtsy /ˈkɜtsɪ/ *n* (*pl* **-seys, -sies**) gesture of respect (bending the knees) made by women and girls (e g to a queen): *to make/drop/bob a* ~ *(to sb).* □ *vi* (*pt,pp* **~ed, curtsied**) make a ~ *(to).*

cur·va·ture /ˈkɜvətʃə(r) *US:* -tʃʊər/ *n* curving; the state of being curved: *to suffer from* ~ *of the spine; the* ~ *of the earth's surface.*

curve /kɜv/ *n* line of which no part is straight and which changes direction without angles: *a* ~ *in the road. The driver of a car should not take/go* *round ~s at high speed.* □ *vt, vi* [VP6A,2A] have, cause to have, the form of a ~: *The river ~s round the town.*

cushion /ˈkʊʃn/ *n* **1** small bag filled with feathers or other soft material (e g foam rubber), to make a seat more comfortable, or to kneel on, etc; sth soft and like a ~ in shape or function: *a ~ of moss; a ˈpin-~; a ~ of air,* as for a hovercraft. **2** soft, resilient lining on the inner sides of a billiard-table where the balls hit. □ *vt* [VP6A,14] supply with ~s; protect from shock with ~s: *~ed seats;* (fig) protect from harmful changes: *farmers who are ~ed against falls in prices,* e g by subsidies.

cushy /ˈkʊʃɪ/ *adj* (-ier, -iest) (sl) (of a post, job, etc) not requiring much effort: *get a ~ job in the Civil Service.*

cusp /kʌsp/ *n* pointed end (esp of a leaf).

cus·pi·dor /ˈkʌspɪdɔ(r)/ *n* (US) spittoon.

cuss /kʌs/ *n* (sl) **1** curse. ***not give/care a ~,*** be quite unworried. ***not worth a tinker's ~,*** quite worthless. **2** person: *a queer old ~.*

cus·sed /ˈkʌsɪd/ *adj* (colloq) perverse; obstinate. **~·ly** *adv* **~·ness** *n*

cus·tard /ˈkʌstəd/ *n* [C,U] (ˈ**egg-**ˈ**~**) (dish of) mixture of eggs and milk, sweetened and flavoured, baked or boiled; mixture of powdered eggs, etc; (ˈ**~-powder**) prepared by adding sugar and milk to flavoured cornflour, eaten with fruit, pastry, etc.

cus·tod·ian /kəˈstəʊdɪən/ *n* person who has custody of sth or sb; caretaker of a public building.

cus·tody /ˈkʌstədɪ/ *n* [U] **1** (duty of) caring for, guarding: *A father has the ~ of his children while they are young. When Mary's parents died, she was placed in the ~ of her aunt. If you are going away for a long time you should leave your jewellery in safe ~,* e g with your bank. **2** imprisonment. ***(be) in ~,*** in prison (e g awaiting trial). ***give sb into ~,*** hand him over to the police. ***take sb into ~,*** arrest him.

cus·tom /ˈkʌstəm/ *n* **1** [U] usual and generally accepted behaviour among members of a social group (either small or large, e g a nation): *Does ~ still require us to stand when the national anthem is played? Don't be a slave to ~,* Do not do things merely because most people do them and have always done them. *It has become the ~* (= has become usual) *for English families to go to the seaside in summer.* **2** [C] particular way of behaving which, because it has been long established, is observed by individuals and social groups: *Social ~s vary in different countries. It was Tom's ~ to get up early and go for a walk before breakfast.* Cf *habit,* a word that means sth that a person does regularly, and that he cannot easily give up. **3** [U] regular support given to a tradesman by those who buy his goods: *We should very much like to have your ~,* would like you to buy our goods. *I shall withdraw my ~ from that shop,* not buy goods there in future. **4** (*pl*) taxes due to the government on goods imported into a country; import duties; department of government (*the C~s*) that collects such duties: *The officials in the C~s at London Airport were very polite. How long will it take us to pass* (= get through) *the C~s? The C~s formalities are simple.* ˈ**~ house,** office (esp at a port) where ~s are collected. ˈ**~s union,** agreement by States on a common policy on tariffs. **5** (US, attrib use only) made to order. ˈ**~-**ˈ**built,** as specified by the buyer. ˈ**~-**ˈ**made** *adj* (of clothes) made-to-measure, making things to order: *~ tailors/shoemakers.* ⇨ bespoke, tailor-made.

cus·tom·ary /ˈkʌstəmərɪ *US:* -merɪ/ *adj* in agreement with, according to, custom(**1,2**): *Is it ~ for guests at hotels in your country to tip the servants? There was the ~ vote of thanks to the chairman.* **cus·tom·ar·ily** /ˈkʌstəmr̩lɪ *US:* ˌkʌstəˈmerəlɪ/ *adv*

cus·tomer /ˈkʌstəmə(r)/ *n* **1** person who buys things, esp one who gives his custom(**3**) to a shop: *Mr X has lost some of his best ~s.* **2** (colloq) person or fellow, (esp): *a queer ~; an awkward ~,* person who is difficult to deal with.

cut[1] /kʌt/ *vt, vi* (-tt-; *pt, pp* cut) (For uses with *adverbial particles* and *preps* ⇨ **10** below; for uses with *adjj* ⇨ **7** below; for uses with *nouns* or *pronouns* ⇨ **6** below.) **1** [VP6A,12B,13B,15A,2A] make an opening, incision (with a sharp-edged instrument, e g a knife, a pair of scissors, or other edged tool); **(a)** make a mark, wound, in sth: *He cut his face/himself while shaving.* ⇨ *cut into sth* in **10** below. **(b)** sever; reap: *Don't pluck the flowers; it's better to cut them. Has the wheat been cut* (= harvested, reaped) *yet?* **(c)** shorten: *to cut one's nails; to cut a hedge; to have one's hair cut.* Hence, ˈ**hair-cut** *n* ⇨ also *cut sth short* in **7** below. **(d)** separate; remove from sth larger: *Please cut a slice of cake for me/cut me a slice of cake. Cut yourself some pineapple. Cut some pineapple for your sister. Two scenes/episodes were cut by the censor.* ⇨ also *cut off* and *cut out* in **10** below. **(e)** reduce sth by removing part: *Was your salary cut? The new jet service cuts the travelling time by half.* ⇨ *cut down* in **10** below. **(f)** divide into smaller pieces: *Will you cut the cake,* i e into pieces? *If you'll cut the bread* (i e into slices), *we'll make toast.* ⇨ *cut up* in **10** below. **(g)** divide, separate into two: *Don't cut the string, untie the knots. The Minister cut the tape to open a new section of motorway.* **(h)** make, fashion, by removing material with tools, machines, etc that cut: *to cut steps in the ice; to cut a tunnel through a hill; to cut a road up a hillside; to cut an inscription/one's initials.* ⇨ *cut out* in **10** below. **2** [VP2A,C] **(a)** (of a sharp tool, instrument, etc) be suitable to use: *This knife does not cut well.* **(b)** (of a material) be capable of being cut: *Sandstone cuts easily. This cloth is too narrow to cut well,* is narrow and difficult to cut into the shapes needed. **3** [VP6A] stay away from, be absent from (sth one ought to attend): *to cut a class/a lecture.* **4** [VP6A] (of lines) cross: *Let the point where AB cuts CD be called E.* **5** [VP6A] (sport, esp cricket, tennis, billiards) strike (a ball) so that it spins or is deflected; hit the edge of (a ball). **6** [VP6A] (used with *nouns* or *pronouns*) ***cut the cards/pack,*** lift part of a pack of playing-cards lying face downwards and turn it up to decide sth (e g who is to deal, who are to be partners). ***cut one's coat according to one's cloth,*** suit one's expenditure to one's income; not be too ambitious in one's plans. ***cut (off) a corner,*** go across, not round it. ***cut corners,*** (fig) take a short-cut. ***cut a disc/record,*** record music, etc on to a gramophone record. Cf *set up/break/establish a record,* when sporting events are in question. ***cut the ground from under sb/from under sb's feet,*** leave him in a weak or illogical position; destroy the foundation of his plan, argument, etc. ***cut no/not much ice (with sb),*** have little or no effect or influence (on). ***cut one's losses,***

abandon a scheme that has caused financial losses before one loses too much. ***cut a tooth,*** have a new tooth just begin to show itself above the gum. ***cut one's teeth on sth,*** learn, gain experience, from: *There's a job for you to cut your teeth on.* ***cut both ways,*** (of an action or argument) have an effect both for and against. ⇨ also **caper**[1], **dash**[1]**(6)**, **figure(5)**, **Gordian**. **7** [VP22] (with an *adj* as complement) ***cut sb dead,*** pretend not to have seen sb; treat as a complete stranger: *She cut me dead in the street,* ignored me completely. ***cut sb/sth free (from),*** make or get free by cutting: *He cut himself free from the ropes with which they had bound him.* ***cut sth/sb loose (from),*** make loose or separate by cutting: *cut loose a boat/cut a boat loose; cut oneself loose from one's family,* live an independent life. ***cut sth open,*** make an opening or split in: *He fell and cut his head open.* ***cut sth short,*** make shorter: *to cut a long story short; to cut short a person's remarks; a career cut short by illness.* ***cut it fine,*** (colloq) leave oneself only the minimum of what is needed (esp time): *He cut it rather fine,* e g by reaching the station half a minute before his train was due to leave. **8** (cinema; imper) Stop (shooting a scene). **9** *pp* ***cut and dried,*** (of opinions, etc) already formed and unlikely to be changed. **'cut 'flowers,** flowers cut for decoration (contrasted with flowers growing in the garden, in pots, etc). **'cut 'glass,** glass with patterns and designs cut on it, to reflect the light on the ends as well as on the uncut areas. **'cut 'price,** (esp) reduced, and below those of rivals or those recommended by the manufacturers, etc. **'cut-'rate,** (attrib) at a reduced price. **'cut to'bacco,** shredded (contrasted with *cake* tobacco). **cut·ting** *part adj* **(a)** sharp; piercing: *a cutting wind.* **(b)** sarcastic; wounding: *cutting remarks.* **10** [VP3A,15B,A,2C] (uses with *adverbial particles* and *preps*):

cut across sth, **(a)** take a shorter route across (a field, etc). **(b)** be contrary to: *Opinion on the Common Market in 1971 cut clean across normal political loyalties.*

cut at sb/sth, aim a sharp blow at (e g with a sword or whip): *cut at a hedge/a group of nettles with a stick.*

cut sth away, remove by cutting: *We cut away all the dead wood from the tree. The yacht was in danger of sinking until they cut away the broken mast and rigging.*

cut sth back, **(a)** (of shrubs, bushes, etc) prune close to the stem. **(b)** reduce: cut back production. Hence, **'cut-back** *n* **(a)** reduction: a cutback in expenditure. **(b)** flashback.

cut sth/sb down, **(a)** cause to fall by cutting: *to cut down a tree.* **(b)** kill or injure by striking with a sword or other edged weapon: *He cut down his enemy.* **(c)** deprive of life or health (by disease, etc): *He was cut down in the prime of manhood.* **(d)** reduce in quantity, amount, etc: *~ down expenses. I won't have a cigarette, thanks—I'm trying to cut down,* reduce the number of cigarettes I smoke. **(e)** persuade (sb) to reduce a price, charge, etc: *We managed to cut him down by £30.* **(f)** reduce the length of: *cut down a pair of trousers,* e g for sb who is shorter. *Cut down an article to make it fit the space available,* in a periodical, etc. ***cut down on,*** reduce one's consumption of: *He's trying to cut down on cigarettes and beer.* ***cut sb down to size,*** (colloq) show sb that he is not so important as he thinks he is: *Some of these so-called experts really need cutting down to size.*

cut in, (of the driver of a motor vehicle, etc, who has overtaken another vehicle) return too soon to his own side of the road (with possibility of collision, etc): *Accidents are often caused by drivers who cut in.* ***cut sb in,*** (colloq) include sb in a (profitable) venture: *If you'll contribute £500 we'll cut you in.* ***cut in/into,*** interrupt (a conversation, etc): *Don't cut into the story/cut in so rudely—let her finish.* ***cut in half/two/three, etc; cut into halves/quarters/thirds, etc,*** divide: *The submarine was cut in half by a destroyer. Cut the cable in two. Cut the apples into halves.*

cut into (sth), **(a)** make a cut in: *Mary cut into her birthday cake and everybody clapped.* **(b)** interfere with: *all this extra homework cuts into his weekends,* leaves him less free time.

cut sb/sth off (from), **(a)** remove (esp sth at an extremity) by cutting: *Don't cut your fingers off! Cut the chicken's head off. He cut off a metre of cloth from the roll.* **(b)** stop; interrupt; isolate: *be cut off while talking by telephone; cut off the gas/electricity supply,* e g because of unpaid accounts; *cut off an army from its base,* by getting in between; *cut off stragglers,* separate them from the main body and so capture them; *be cut off from all possibility of help; towns cut off* (= isolated) *by floods; cut off by the tide,* isolated on a rock, sandbank, etc by the incoming tide; *cut off sb's supplies/a son's allowance,* no longer allow him to receive them; *cut off sb with a shilling,* disinherit sb (e g a son who has behaved badly) except for a small sum (to show that the act is deliberate).

cut (off) a corner, ⇨ 6 above.

cut out, stop functioning: *One of the aircraft's engines cut out.* ***cut sth out,*** **(a)** remove by cutting (e g from a periodical): *That's an interesting article—I'll cut it out.* **(b)** make by cutting: *cut out a path through the jungle.* **(c)** shape (a garment) by cutting the outlines of the parts on cloth: *cut out a dress.* **(d)** (colloq) leave out; omit: *Let's cut out unimportant details.* **(e)** (colloq) stop doing or using (sth): *cut out all rivals for a lady's affections; My doctor told me I must cut out tobacco,* stop smoking. **(f)** separate (one animal) from a herd (as cowboys do). **(g)** (in naval warfare in the past) attack and seize (a ship) under the enemy's guns or in harbour by getting between the ships and the shore. ***cut sb out,*** defeat, eliminate (a rival, esp in competition for sth). ***cut it/that out,*** (colloq, imper) stop fighting, squabbling, etc: *Now just cut it out, you two!* ***cut out (the) dead wood,*** (colloq) remove unnecessary or unproductive parts: *There's a lot of dead wood to be cut out if the industry is to be efficient.* ***(not) be cut out for,*** (not) have the qualities and abilities needed for: *He's not cut out for that sort of work.* ***have one's work cut out (for one),*** be faced with as much work as one can manage: *It's a big job; he'll have his work cut out for him.* **'cut-out** *n* **(a)** design, figure, etc (to be) cut out from paper, cardboard, etc. **(b)** (electr) device that interrupts or disconnects a circuit (e g to avoid too heavy a load).

cut sb to the heart/quick, cause him pain or suffering: *His ingratitude cut her to the heart.* ***cut sb/sth to pieces,*** destroy by cutting, by gunfire, etc. *The enemy were cut to pieces.*

cut sth/sb up, (a) cut into pieces: *cut up one's meat.* (b) destroy: *cut up the enemy's forces.* (c) (colloq, usu passive) cause mental suffering to: *He was badly cut up by the news of his son's death. Don't be so cut up about it.* (d) (fig) criticize adversely; point out the faults of: *His latest novel has been cut up by the reviewers.* ***cut up (into),*** be capable of being cut up into: *This piece of cloth will cut up into* (= has enough material in it for) *three suits.* ***cut up well/for sth,*** be worth: *The turkey cut up well,* there was a lot of meat on it; leave at death: *The old man cut up well,* (of a man who has died) left a large estate to be divided among his heirs. ***cut up rough,*** (sl) behave aggressively; be violent and aggressive: *He'll cut up rough if you don't give him what he asked for.*

cut[2] /kʌt/ *n* **1** act of cutting; stroke with a sword, whip, etc; result of such a stroke; opening made by a knife or other sharp-edged tool, etc: *give a horse a cut across the flanks; a deep cut in the leg; cuts on the face,* e g after shaving. ***cut and thrust,*** (usu fig) vigorous argument, etc: *The cut and thrust of debate.* **2** reduction in size, amount, length, etc: *a cut in prices/salaries; a cut in expenditure/production; a power cut,* a reduction in the strength of electrical current, or a period for which current is cut off. **3** a cutting out; part that is cut out: *There were several cuts in the film,* Parts of it had been cut out (e g by the film censors). *Where can we make a cut in this long article?* **4** sth obtained by cutting: *a nice cut of beef; a cut off the joint,* a slice from a cooked joint of meat; *this year's cut of wool,* the wool sheared from the sheep. **5** style in which clothes, etc are made by cutting: *I don't like the cut of his beard.* ⇨ jib[1](1). **6** (cricket, tennis) quick, sharp stroke: *a cut to the boundary.* **7** remark, etc that wounds a person's feelings: *That remark was a cut at me,* was directed at me. **8** refusal to recognize a person: (usu) *give sb the cut direct.* ⇨ cut[1](7). **9** ***a `short cut,*** a way across (from one place to another) that shortens the distance. **10** ***a cut above,*** (colloq) rather superior to: *She's a cut above the other girls in the office,* is better educated, has wider interests, etc. *That's a cut above me,* above my range of interests, my abilities, etc. **11** railway cutting; canal. ⇨ cutting(1). **12** block or plate on which a design, illustration, etc has been cut; picture, etc, made from such a block. ⇨ *woodcut* at wood(4).

cute /kjut/ *adj* (-r, -st) **1** sharp-witted; quick-thinking. **2** (US colloq) attractive; pretty and charming. **~·ly** *adv* **~·ness** *n*

cu·ticle /ˋkjutɪkl/ *n* outer layer of hardened skin (esp at the base of a finger-nail or toe-nail).

cut·lass /ˋkʌtləs/ *n* (sailor's) short, one-edged sword with a slightly curved blade; cutting tool used by cacao-growers and copra-growers.

cut·ler /ˋkʌtlə(r)/ *n* man who makes and repairs knives and other cutting tools and instruments. **~y** *n* [U] trade of a ~; implements used at table (knives, forks, spoons, esp if made of stainless steel); things made or sold by ~s.

cut·let /ˋkʌtlət/ *n* slice of meat or fish for one person: *a veal ~.*

cut·purse /ˋkʌtpɜs/ *n* (hist) pickpocket.

cut·ter /ˋkʌtə(r)/ *n* **1** person or thing that cuts: *a tailor's ~,* who cuts out cloth; *`wire-~.* **2** sailing-vessel with one mast; ship's boat, for use between ship and shore.

cut-throat /ˋkʌtθrəʊt/ *n* **1** murderer. **2** (attrib uses) murderous: *~ competition,* likely to ruin the weaker competitors; *a ~ razor,* (hum) one with no guard on the long blade.

cut·ting /ˋkʌtɪŋ/ *n* **1** unroofed passage dug through the ground for a road, railway, canal, etc. **2** sth cut from a newspaper, etc and kept for reference: *`press ~s.* Cf US *clipping.* **3** short piece of the stem of a plant, to be used for growing a new plant: *chrysanthemum ~s; to take a ~.* **4** [U] process of editing cinema films, tape recordings, etc, by cutting out unwanted parts. Hence, **`~-room,** room where this is done. □ *part adj* (of words, etc) wounding the feelings, etc: *~ remarks.*

cuttle·fish /ˋkʌtlfɪʃ/ *n* sea-water animal with long arms (tentacles); it sends out a black liquid when attacked. ⇨ the illus at mollusc.

cut·worm /ˋkʌtwɜm/ *n* caterpillar that eats through the stems of young plants level with the ground.

cy·an·ide /ˋsaɪənaɪd/ *n* [U] poisonous compound substance: *potassium ~; sodium ~.*

cy·ber·net·ics /ˈsaɪbəˋnetɪks/ *n* (*sing v*) the science of communication and control in machines and animals (including man). **cy·ber·netic** *adj*

cyc·la·men /ˋsɪkləmən *US:* ˋsaɪk-/ *n* kinds of plant, wild and cultivated, with early-blooming flowers.

cycle /ˋsaɪkl/ *n* **1** series of events taking place in a regularly repeated order: *the ~ of the seasons.* **2** complete set or series: *a song ~,* e g by Schubert; *the Arthurian* /ɑˋθjʊrɪən *US:* -ˋθʊr-/ *~,* the stories of King Arthur and his knights. **3** (short for) bicycle or motor-cycle. □ *vi* [VP2A,B,C] ride a bicycle.

cyc·lic /ˋsɪklɪk/ *adj* recurring in cycles.

cyc·li·cal /ˋsɪklɪkl/ *adj* = cyclic.

cyc·list /ˋsaɪklɪst/ *n* person who rides a cycle.

cyc·lone /ˋsaɪkləʊn/ *n* violent wind rotating round a calm central area; violent windstorm. **cyc·lonic** /saɪˋklonɪk/ *adj* of or like a ~.

cyclo·pae·dia /ˈsaɪkləʊˋpidɪə/ *n* = encyclopaedia.

Cyclo·pean /saɪˋkləʊpɪən/ *adj* of or like a Cyclops /ˋsaɪklops/ (a one-eyed giant in Greek myth); huge; immense.

cyclo·style /ˋsaɪkləʊstaɪl/ *n* apparatus for printing copies from a stencil. □ *vt* reproduce (copies) with this.

cyclo·tron /ˋsaɪkləʊtron/ *n* apparatus used for producing heavy electric particles moving at high speed, used experimentally in nuclear research work.

cyder /ˋsaɪdə(r)/ *n* = cider.

cyg·net /ˋsɪgnɪt/ *n* young swan.

cyl·in·der /ˋsɪlɪndə(r)/ *n* **1** solid or hollow body as shown here. **2** ~-shaped chamber (in an engine) in which gas or steam works a piston: *a six-~ engine/motor-car;* ***(working) on all ~s,*** (colloq) with the maximum power or effort. **cy·lin·dri·cal** /sɪˋlɪndrɪkl/ *adj* ~-shaped. ⇨ also the illus at projection.

cym·bal /ˋsɪmbl/ *n* one of a pair of round brass plates struck together to make clanging sounds. ⇨ the illus at percussion.

cynic /ˋsɪnɪk/ *n* person who sees little or no good in anything and who has no belief in human progress; person who shows this by sneering and being sarcastic. **cyni·cism** /ˋsɪnɪsɪzm/ *n* [U] ~'s opinions or attitude of mind; [C] expression of this attitude.

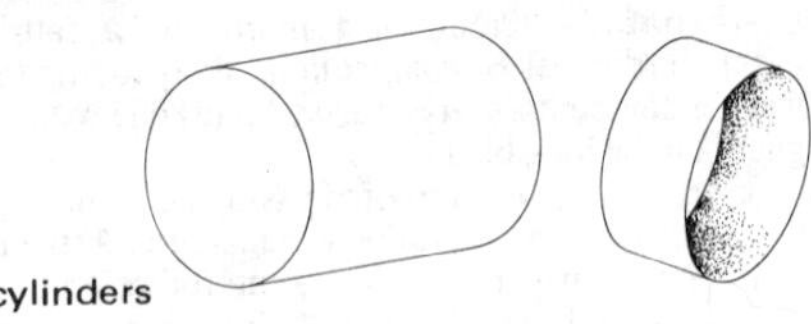
cylinders

cyni·cal /ˈsɪnɪkl/ *adj* of or like a cynic; sneering or contemptuous: *a ~ smile/remark.* **~·ly** /-klɪ/ *adv*
cyno·sure /ˈsɪnəzjʊə(r) *US:* ˈsaɪnəʊʃʊər/ *n* sth or sb that draws everyone's attention; centre of attraction.
cy·pher /ˈsaɪfə(r)/ *n* = **cipher**.
cy·press /ˈsaɪprəs/ *n* (kinds of) evergreen tree with dark leaves and hard wood.
Cyril·lic /sɪˈrɪlɪk/ *adj*: *~ alphabet*, that used for Slavonic languages (e g Russian).
cyst /sɪst/ *n* enclosed hollow organ in the body containing liquid matter.
czar /zɑ(r)/ *n* (also **tsar**) emperor (of Russia before 1917). **czar·ina** /zɑˈrinə/ *n* Russian empress.
Czech /tʃek/ *n* member of a branch of the Slavs; their language.

Dd

D, d /di/ (*pl* **D's, d's** /diz/) the fourth letter of the English alphabet; Roman numeral for 500. **'d,** used for *had* or *would* (esp after *I, we, you, he, she, they, who*).
dab[1] /dæb/ *vt,vi* (-bb-) [VP6A,14,15A,B,2C] touch, put on, lightly and gently: *dab one's eyes with a handkerchief; dab paint on a picture,* suggesting light, quick strokes of the brush. *She was dabbing (at) her cheeks with a powder-puff.* □ *n* [C] **1** small quantity (of paint, etc) dabbed on. **2** slight tap; brief application of sth to a surface (without rubbing): *A dab with a sponge won't remove the dirt, you'll have to rub it.*
dab[2] /dæb/ *n* kind of flat-fish.
dab[3] /dæb/ *n* (colloq) adept (at games, etc, at doing things): *She's a dab (hand) at tennis.*
dabble /ˈdæbl/ *vt,vi* **1** [VP6A,15A,B,2C] splash (the hands, feet, etc) about in water; put in and out of water. **2** [VP3] **~ at/in,** (art, politics, etc) engage in, study, as a hobby, not professionally. **dab·bler** /ˈdæblə(r)/ *n*
da capo /ˈdɑ ˈkɑpəʊ/ (I, music) (as a direction) repeat from the beginning.
dace /deɪs/ *n* (*pl* unchanged) small fresh-water fish.
dacha /ˈdætʃə/ *n* Russian country house or villa.
dachs·hund /ˈdækshʊnd/ *n* small short-legged breed of dog.
da·coit /dəˈkɔɪt/ *n* member of a band of armed robbers (formerly, in India, Burma). **~y** *n* (*pl* -ties) robbery by ~s.
dac·tyl /ˈdæktɪl/ *n* metrical foot of one long syllable followed by two short syllables (— ◡ ◡ e g ˈ*tenderly*). **~ic** /dækˈtɪlɪk/ *adj*
dad /dæd/ *n* (colloq) father.
daddy /ˈdædɪ/ *n* (*pl* -dies) child's word for 'father'. **'~-long-legs** *n* (popular name for the) crane-fly (a long-legged flying insect).
dado /ˈdeɪdəʊ/ *n* (*pl* -dos, US -does /-dəʊz/) lower part of a room wall, different from the upper part in colour or material.
dae·mon /ˈdimən/ *n* = demon.
daf·fo·dil /ˈdæfədɪl/ *n* yellow flower with long narrow leaves growing from a bulb. ⇨ the illus at flower.
daft /dɑft *US:* dæft/ *adj* (-er, -est) (colloq) silly; foolish; reckless. **~·ly** *adv*
dag·ger /ˈdægə(r)/ *n* **1** short, pointed, two-edged knife used as a weapon. ***at ~s drawn (with sb),*** about to fight. ***look ~s at sb,*** look with an expression of hatred and enmity. **2** (printing) mark of reference (†).
dago /ˈdeɪgəʊ/ *n* (*pl* -gos /-gəʊz/) ⚠ (term of contempt for an) Italian, Spaniard or Portuguese.
da·guerreo·type /dəˈgerətaɪp/ *n* portrait taken by an early photographic process.
dah·lia /ˈdeɪlɪə *US:* ˈdælɪə/ *n* garden plant with brightly coloured flowers, growing from tuberous roots.
Dail Eire·ann /ˈdɔɪl ˈeərən/ *n* Chamber of Deputies in the legislature of the Republic of Ireland (Eire).
daily /ˈdeɪlɪ/ *adj, adv* happening, done, appearing, every day (or every weekday): *Most newspapers appear ~. Thousands of people cross this bridge ~. He's done his ~ dozen,* his usual physical exercises. ***one's ~ bread,*** one's necessary food, etc. □ *n* newspaper published every day or every weekday; (colloq) non-resident woman servant who comes every day.
dainty[1] /ˈdeɪntɪ/ *adj* (-ier, -iest) **1** (of persons) pretty, neat and delicate(**1,3**) in appearance and tastes: *a ~ little lady.* **2** (of persons and animals) rather difficult to please because of delicate tastes: *She's ~ about her food. My cat is a ~ feeder.* **3** (of things) pretty; delicate(**3**), easily injured or broken: *~ cups and saucers; ~ spring flowers.* **4** (of food) delicate(**8**) and delicious. **dain·tily** *adv* in a ~ manner: *a daintily dressed young lady.* **dainti·ness** *n*
dainty[2] /ˈdeɪntɪ/ *n* (*pl* -ties) (usu *pl*) dainty morsel or dish of food: *There were dainties of every kind in the picnic basket.*
dairy /ˈdeərɪ/ *n* (*pl* -ries) **1** (part of a) building where milk and milk products are dealt with. **ˈ~-farm,** one that produces milk and butter. **~-ing, ˈ~-farming,** the business of a ~-farm. **ˈ~ cattle,** cows raised to produce milk, not meat. **ˈ~-maid,** woman who works in a ~. **2** shop where milk, butter, eggs, etc, are sold. **ˈ~-man** /-mən/ (*pl* -men) dealer in milk, etc.
dais /ˈdeɪɪs/ *n* (*pl* -sises /-sɪz/) platform (esp at the end of a hall) for a throne or for a desk (for a lecturer, etc).
daisy /ˈdeɪzɪ/ *n* (*pl* -sies) small white flower with a yellow centre, commonly growing wild; similar garden flower; other plants of various sorts (ˈ*Michaelmas ~*, etc) resembling it or of the same species. ***push up the daisies,*** ⇨ push[2](9).
dak-bun·ga·low /ˈdɑk ˈbʌŋgələʊ/ *n* (in India and Pakistan) house for use of government officials while on tour.
dale /deɪl/ *n* (esp in N England and in poetry) val-

ley. **dales·man** /ˈdeɪlzmən/ *n* (*pl* -men) person who lives in the ~s (in N England).

dal·li·ance /ˈdælɪəns/ *n* [U] trifling behaviour; love-making for amusement.

dally /ˈdælɪ/ *vi* (*pt,pp* -lied) **1** [VP2A,3A] ~ **(with)**, trifle; think idly about: *~ with an idea or proposal; ~ with a woman's affections*, flirt with her, not thinking seriously of marriage. **2** [VP2A, 3A] ~ **(over)**, waste time: *Don't ~ over your work.*

dam[1] /dæm/ *n* barrier built to keep back water and raise its level (e g to form a reservoir, or for hydro-electric power). Cf *barrage*, a barrier across a river, usu for irrigation purposes. □ *vt* (-mm-) [VP6A,15B] ~ **(up)**, make a dam across (a narrow valley, etc); hold back by means of a dam; (fig) hold back: *to dam up one's feelings/sb's eloquence.*

a dam

dam[2] /dæm/ *n* mother (of four-footed animals). ⇨ sire.

dam·age /ˈdæmɪdʒ/ *n* **1** [U] ~ **(to)**, harm or injury that causes loss of value: *The storm did great ~ to the crops. The insurance company will pay for the ~ to my car.* **2** (*pl*) (legal) money claimed from or paid by a person causing loss or injury: *He claimed £5 000 ~s from his employers for the loss of his right arm while at work.* **3 What's the ~?** (colloq) What's the cost? How much is there to be paid? □ *vt* [VP6A] cause ~(1) to: *furniture ~d by fire.*

dam·as·cene /ˈdæməsin/ *adj* of Damascus or damask.

dam·ask /ˈdæməsk/ *n* [U] **1** silk or linen material with designs shown up by reflection of light: (attrib) *~ table-cloths; ~ silk.* **2** steel with a pattern of wavy lines or with inlaid gold or silver: (attrib) ~ (or *damascene*) *steel.* **3** ˈ~ **rose**, variety originally brought from Damascus; its colour (bright pink).

dame /deɪm/ *n* **1** (old use) woman, esp a married woman. ˈ**~-school**, old-fashioned elementary school kept by a woman. **2** (title of a) woman who has been awarded the highest grade of the Order of the British Empire: *D~ Ellen Terry.* Cf the title *Lady*, used by the wife of a man who is a knight. **3** title used in: *D~ Nature, D~ Fortune*, nature, fortune, personified. **4** (US, sl) woman.

damn /dæm/ *vt* [VP6A] **1** (of God) condemn to everlasting punishment. **2** condemn; say that sth or sb is worthless, bad, etc: *The book was ~ed by the critics.* **3** (esp as *int*) used to express anger, annoyance, impatience, etc: *I'll be ~ed if I'll go*, I refuse to go. *D~ it all! D~ you/your impudence!* □ *n* negligible amount (esp) **not give a (tuppeny) ~**, not care at all. **not (be) worth a ~**, (be) worthless.

dam·nable /ˈdæmnəbl/ *adj* hateful; deserving to be damned; (colloq) very bad: *~ weather.* **dam·nably** /ˈdæmnəblɪ/ *adv*

dam·na·tion /dæmˈneɪʃn/ *n* [U] being damned; ruin: *to suffer eternal ~.* □ *int*: *May ~ take it/you!* Curse it/you! *Damn it!*

damned /dæmd/ *adj* **1** *the ~*, souls in hell. **2** (colloq) damnable: *You ~ fool!* □ *adv* (colloq) extremely: *~ hot/funny.*

Damocles /ˈdæməkliz/ *n* **sword of ~**, threatened danger in the midst of prosperity (from the old Greek story of a man who was feasted with a sword hanging by a thread over him).

damp[1] /dæmp/ *adj* (-er, -est) not thoroughly dry; having some moisture (in or on): *~ clothes; to wipe a window with a ~ cloth. Don't sleep between ~ sheets.* □ *n* [U] **1** state of being ~; ~ atmosphere; moisture on the surface of, or existing throughout, sth: *The ~ rising from the ground caused the walls to stain badly. Don't stay outside in the ~.* ⇨ *~-course* at course[1](5). **2 cast/strike a ~ over**, (fig) cause dejection or unhappiness: *Their mother's illness cast a ~ over the celebrations.* **3** (also ˈ**fire-~**) dangerous gas which may collect in coal-mines. **~·ish** *adj* rather ~. **~·ly** *adv* **~·ness** *n*

damp[2] /dæmp/ *vt,vi* **1** [VP6A] make damp(1): *to ~ clothes before ironing them.* **2** [VP6A] (also ˈ**dampen**) make sad or dull: *Nothing could ~ his spirits.* **3** [VP15A] ~ **down**, make (a fire) burn more slowly (e g by heaping ashes on it, or by controlling the draught of air entering a stove, etc). **4** [VP2C] ~ **off**, (of young plants) rot and die because of excessive damp(1).

dampen /ˈdæmpən/ *vt,vi* = damp[2](2).

damper /ˈdæmpə(r)/ *n* **1** movable metal plate that regulates the flow of air into a fire in a stove or furnace. **2** person or thing that checks or discourages. ⇨ damp[1](2).

dam·sel /ˈdæmzl/ *n* (old use) girl; young unmarried woman.

dam·son /ˈdæmzn/ *n* (tree producing) small dark-purple plum; dark-purple.

dance[1] /dɑns *US:* dæns/ *n* [C] **1** (series of) movements and steps in time with music; special form (e g a waltz), tune, piece of music, for such movements and steps: *May I have the next ~*, Will you be my partner in the next ~? *Shall we join the ~*, go out among the dancers? **lead sb a (pretty) ~**, cause him a lot of trouble, make him follow from place to place. **2** social gathering for dancing: *to give a ~*, arrange for and invite persons to such a gathering. **3** (attrib): *ˈ~-rhythm.* ˈ**~-band/-orchestra** *nn* providing music for dancing. ˈ**~-hall** *n* hall for public ~s, with a charge for admission. ⇨ *ballroom* at ball[2]. ˈ**~-hostess** *n* professional dancing-partner at a public ~-hall.

dance[2] /dɑns *US:* dæns/ *vi,vt* **1** [VP2A,C] move along in rhythmical steps, usu with music, either alone, or with a partner, or in a group: *Will you ~ with me? They went on dancing until after midnight.* **2** [VP6A] perform (a named kind of such movements or the named (style of) music for it): *to ~ a waltz/a ballet/Swanlake. Is the polka often ~d nowadays?* **~ attendance upon sb**, follow him about, pay great attention to his wishes, etc. **3** [VP2A,C] move in a lively way, quickly, up and down, etc: *The leaves were dancing in the wind. She ~d for joy. The sudden pain made him ~ up and down. Look at that boat dancing on the waves.* **4** [VP6A,15A] cause to ~(3): *to ~ a baby on one's knee.* **dancer** *n* person who ~s: *a clever*

~*r;* person who ~s in public for pay. ⇨ **ballerina, ballet-~r. danc·ing** *part adj* who or that ~s: *a 'dancing 'dervish.* □ *n* (gerund) [U] **1** (stress on the gerund only in): *'dancing-master,* professional teacher of dancing; *'dancing-partner,* person with whom one (usu) ~s; *'dancing-shoes,* light shoes for dancing; *'dancing-salon,* (US) public ~-hall. **2** (stress on the first element only): *'ballet-dancing; 'step-dancing; 'toe-dancing.*

dan·de·lion /ˈdændɪlɑɪən/ *n* small wild plant with bright-yellow flowers and deeply notched leaves.

dan·der /ˈdændə(r)/ *n* (colloq, only in) ***get sb's ~ up,*** make him angry. ***get one's ~ up,*** become angry.

dandle /ˈdændl/ *vt* [VP6A,15A,B] move (e g a child) up and down on one's knee(s) or in the arms.

dan·druff /ˈdændrʌf/ *n* [U] dead skin in small scales among the hair of the scalp; scurf.

dandy[1] /ˈdændɪ/ *n* (*pl* **-dies**) man who pays too much care to his clothes and personal appearance. **dan·di·fied** /ˈdændɪfɑɪd/ *adj* dressed up, etc like a ~: *a dandified appearance.*

dandy[2] /ˈdændɪ/ *adj* (sl) excellent; first-rate: *fine and ~.*

Dane /deɪn/ *n* native of Denmark.

dan·ger /ˈdeɪndʒə(r)/ *n* **1** [U] chance of suffering, liability to suffer, injury or loss of life: *Thin ice! D~! Is there any ~ of fire? In war a soldier's life is full of ~.* **at ~**: *The signal* (on a railway line) *was at ~,* in the position giving a warning of ~. ***in ~ (of)***: *His life was in ~. He was in ~ of losing his life.* **out of ~**: *He has been very ill, but the doctors say that he is now out of ~,* not likely to die. **'~ money,** extra pay for dangerous work. **2** [C] sth or sb that may cause ~: *He looked round carefully for hidden ~s. The wreck is a ~ to shipping. That man is a ~ to society.*

dan·ger·ous /ˈdeɪndʒərəs/ *adj* likely to cause danger or be ~ (*to*): *a ~ bridge/journey/illness. The river is ~ to bathe in. That dog looks ~,* looks as though it might attack people. **~·ly** *adv*

dangle /ˈdæŋgl/ *vi,vt* **1** [VP2A,C,6A,15A] hang or swing loosely; carry (sth) so that it hangs or swings loosely: *a bunch of keys dangling at the end of a chain; to ~ a toy in front of a baby;* (fig) *to ~ bright prospects* (e g of wealth, a well-paid position) *before a man.* **2** [VP2C] ***~ round/about,*** remain near (sb or sth) (as an admirer) hoping to obtain sth: *She always has half a dozen men dangling round her. She likes to keep her men dangling (about her).*

Dan·iel /ˈdænɪəl/ *n* upright judge; ⇨ **Dan 1 to 6**; person of great wisdom; ⇨ Mer of Ven, 4: 1.

Dan·ish /ˈdeɪnɪʃ/ *n, adj* (language) of Denmark or the Danes.

dank /dæŋk/ *adj* (**-er, -est**) damp in an unpleasant or unhealthy way: *the ~ undergrowth of a forest; a ~ and chilly cave.*

daphne /ˈdæfnɪ/ *n* kinds of flowering shrub.

dap·per /ˈdæpə(r)/ *adj* (usu of a small person) neat and smart in appearance; active in movement: *Isn't he a ~ little man!*

dapple /ˈdæpl/ *vt* [VP6A] (usu in *pp*) mark, become marked, with rounded patches of different colour or shades of colour, esp of an animal, or of sunlight and shadow: *~d deer; a ~d horse; ~d shade,* as when sunlight comes through the leaves of trees. **'~-'grey** *adj, n* (horse) of grey with darker patches.

Darby and Joan /ˈdɑbɪ ən ˈdʒəʊn/ *n* (GB) old, loving married couple: *a ~ club,* one for old couples.

dare[1] /deə(r)/ *anom fin* (*pt* **dared** /deəd/ or, less often, **durst** /dɜst/) (*dare not* is abbr to *daren't* /deənt/, *3rd pers sing* is *dare,* not *dares*) (Used with an *inf* without *to,* chiefly in neg sentences, including those with *hardly, never* and *no one, nobody,* and in interr and conditional sentences, and in sentences to indicate doubt.) [VP5] have the courage, impudence or effrontery to: *He wanted to fight me but he ~n't. Don't (you) ~ do that again! He ~n't have said such things to his boss! I wonder whether he ~ try. No one/Nobody ~d ask him about his intentions. He will hardly/never ~ go there again. How ~ he say such rude things about me!* ***I ~ say,*** It seems to me likely or possible: *You tried, I ~ say. I ~ say he'll come later.*

dare[2] /deə(r)/ *vt,vi* **1** [VP5,4A] (with or without *to*) be brave enough to: *He didn't ~ (to) go. I wonder how he ~s (to) say such things. I've never ~d (to) ask him. They wouldn't ~ (to be so rude)!* **2** [VP6A] take the risk of; face: *He will ~ any danger.* **3** [VP6A,17] ***~ sb (to do sth),*** challenge; suggest that sb has not the courage or ability to do sth: *I ~ you to say that again! He ~d me to jump from the bridge into the river. Go on, insult me! I ~ you!* **'~-devil** *n* (often attrib) person who is foolishly bold or reckless: *You ~-devil! What a ~-devil fellow he is!* □ *n* (only in) ***do sth for a ~,*** do sth because one is ~d(**3**) to do it.

dar·ing /ˈdeərɪŋ/ *n* [U] adventurous courage; audacity: *the ~ of the paratroops; lose one's ~.* □ *adj* brave; audacious: *a ~ robbery. What a ~ thing to do!* **~·ly** *adv*

dark[1] /dɑk/ *n* [U] **1** absence of light: *All the lights went out and we were left in the ~. Some children are afraid of the ~. Don't leave me alone in the ~.* ***before/after ~,*** before/after the sun goes down: *Try to get home before ~. The roads are so bad that we don't often go out after ~.* **2** (fig) ignorance. ***keep sb/be in the ~ (about sth),*** keep sb/be in ignorance: *We were completely in the ~ about his movements.*

dark[2] /dɑk/ *adj* (**-er, -est**) **1** with no or very little light: *a ~, moonless night; a ~ corner of the room. It's getting too ~ to take photographs.* **'~-lantern,** one that can have its light covered. **'~-room,** one that can be made ~ for photographic work. **2** (of colour) not reflecting much light; nearer black than white: *a ~ dress/suit; ~ blue/green/brown; ~-brown eyes.* **3** (of the skin) not fair: *a ~ complexion.* **4** (fig) hidden, mysterious: *a ~ secret,* one that is closely guarded; *the D~ Continent,* Africa (used of the time when most of it was unexplored and mysterious). ***a ~ horse,*** race-horse with unexpected or unknown capabilities; (fig) person whose capabilities may be greater than they are known to be. ***keep it ~,*** keep a secret. **5** hopeless; sad; cheerless: *Don't look on the ~ side of things.* **6** unenlightened (morally or intellectually): *the D~ Ages,* (in European history), from the 6th to the 12th cc; (also) between the end of the Roman Empire (A D 395) and the close of the 10th c. **7** not clear to or in the mind: *a ~ saying,* one that is obscure. **~·ly** *adv* **~·ness** *n* the state of being ~: *The room was in complete ~ness.*

Darkey, Darky /ˈdɑkɪ/ *n* ⚠ (colloq) (offensive term for a) Negro; Negress.

dark·some /ˈdɑksəm/ *adj* (poet or liter) dark; gloomy.

dar·ling /ˈdɑlɪŋ/ *n* **1** person or object very much loved: *She's a little ~. My ~!* **2** (attrib, colloq) charming; delightful: *What a ~ little cottage!*

darn[1] /dɑn/ *vt,vi* [VP6A,2A] mend (esp sth knitted, e g a sock) by passing thread in and out and in two directions: *My socks have been ~ed again and again.* □ *n* place mended by ~ing. **~·ing** *n* (esp) things needing to be ~ed. **ˈ~ing-needle,** large sewing needle used for ~ing.

darn[2] /dɑn/ *vt* [VP6A] (sl) damn(**3**): *Well, I'll be ~ed.*

dart[1] /dɑt/ *n* [C] **1** quick, sudden, forward movement: *The child made a sudden ~ across the road.* **2** small, sharp-pointed missile (feathered and pointed), to be thrown at a target (marked with numbers for scoring) in the game called ~s.

dart[2] /dɑt/ *vi,vt* [VP2A,C,6A,15A,B] (cause to) move forward suddenly and quickly; send suddenly and quickly: *The deer ~ed away when it saw us. The snake ~ed out its tongue. She ~ed an angry look at him. Swallows were ~ing through the air. She ~ed into the shop.*

dash[1] /dæʃ/ *n* **1** [C] sudden rush; violent movement: *to make a ~ for shelter/freedom; to make a ~ at the enemy.* **at a ~,** quickly and smartly: *The cavalry rode off at a ~.* **2** (usu *sing* with *def* or *indef art*) (sound of) liquid striking sth or being thrown or struck: *the ~ of the waves on the rocks; the ~ of oars striking the water. A ~ of cold water will revive a person who has fainted.* **3** [C] small amount of sth added or mixed: *a ~ of pepper in the soup; water with a ~ of whisky in it; red with a ~ of blue.* **4** [C] stroke of the pen or a mark (—) used in printing. **5** (*sing* with *def art*) short race: *the 100 metres ~.* **6** [U] (capacity for) vigorous action; energy: *an officer famous for his skill and ~.* **cut a ~,** make a brilliant show (in appearance and behaviour). **ˈ~·board, (a)** screen on the front part of a horse-drawn cart, wagon, etc to protect from mud splashed up from the road. **(b)** panel beneath the windscreen of a motor-car, with speedometer, various controls, etc. ⇨ the illus at motor.

dash[2] /dæʃ/ *vt,vi* **1** [VP6A,15A,B,2C] send or throw violently; move or be moved violently: *The boat was ~ed against the rocks. He ~ed the broken sword down and picked up another. The huge waves ~ed over the rocks. The elephants ~ed through the undergrowth. D~ a bucketful of water over this muddy floor. A motor-car ~ed past us/~ed mud all over us as it passed.* **~ sth off,** write or draw sth quickly: *I must ~ off a few letters before I go out.* **2** [VP6A] **~ sb's hopes,** destroy, discourage, them. **3** [VP6A] (colloq, used as a mild substitute for) Damn!: *D~ it!* **~·ing** *adj* impetuous; lively; full of, showing, energy: *a ~ing cavalry charge; a ~ing rider,* e g one who rides a horse boldly. **~·ing·ly** *adv*

das·tard /ˈdæstəd/ *n* (old use) bully; coward who is brutal when there is no risk to himself. **~·ly** *adj* of or like a ~.

data /ˈdeɪtə/ *n pl* (*pl* of Lat *datum*) **1** facts; things certainly known (and from which conclusions may be drawn): *unless sufficient ~ are available.* **2** (usu with *sing v*) information prepared for and operated on a computer programme: *The ~ is ready for processing.* **ˈ~ bank,** centre with a comprehensive file ~. **ˈ~ ˈprocessing,** the performing of operations on ~ to obtain information, solutions to problems, etc.

date[1] /deɪt/ *n* **1** statement of the time, day, month, year, one or all three of these, when sth happened or is to happen: *D~ of birth, 20 April 1974; the ~ of the discovery of America by Columbus (1492). What's the ~ today? Has the ~ for the meeting been fixed?* **ˈ~-line, (a)** (*International ~-line*) meridian 180° from Greenwich, east and west of which at any given time the calendar ~s differ by one day. **(b)** phrase giving the ~ and place of origin of an article in a periodical. **2** period of time, e g one to which antiquities belong: *Many ruins of Roman ~* (= of the time of ancient Rome) *are to be seen in the south of France.* **3** (phrases) ***(be/go) out of ~,*** obsolete; no longer used; old-fashioned: *out-of-~ ideas.* ***to ~,*** so far; until now. ***(be/bring) up to ~,* (a)** in line with, according to, what is now known, used, etc: *up-to-~ ideas/methods.* **(b)** up to the present time: *to bring a catalogue up to ~.* **4** (colloq) social meeting arranged with sb at a certain time and place; appointment: *I have a ~ with her next month.* **ˈblind ˈ~,** arrangement to meet sb socially, having not met him before. **5** (by extension; colloq) companion of the other sex with whom ~s(**4**) are arranged. **~·less** *adj* endless; immemorial.

date[2] /deɪt/ *vt,vi* **1** [VP6A] have or put a date(**1**) on: *Don't forget to ~ your letters. The letter is ~d from London, 24 May.* **2** [VP6A] give a date(**2**) to: *to ~ old coins/sth found in an excavation. That suit ~s you,* shows your age (because it is old-fashioned). ⇨ **4** below. **3** [VP2C,3A] ***~ from/back to,*** have existed since: *The castle ~s back to the 14th century,* was built then. *The prosperity of the family ~s from the war,* They became rich (e g by making munitions) during the war. **4** [VP2A] show signs of becoming out of date: *Isn't this textbook beginning to ~?* **5** [VP6A] make a date(**4**) with. **dated** *adj* out of fashion; (of words and phrases) used in the past but not now current. **dat·able** *adj* that can be dated(**2**).

date[3] /deɪt/ *n* small, brown, sweet, edible fruit of the date-palm, common in N Africa and S W Asia.

dat·ive /ˈdeɪtɪv/ *n* (in Latin and other inflected languages) form of a word showing that it is an indirect object of the verb; (in English, loosely used for) indirect object (e g *me* in 'Tell me your name').

datum /ˈdeɪtəm/ *n* ⇨ data.

daub /dɔb/ *vt,vi* **1** [VP6A,14,15A,B] put paint, clay, plaster, etc roughly on a surface: *to ~ plaster on a wall; to ~ a wall with paint. Don't ~ the paint on too thickly.* **2** [VP6A,2A] paint (pictures) without skill or artistry. **3** [VP6A,14] make dirty: *trousers ~ed with paint.* □ *n* **1** [C,U] (covering of) soft, sticky material, e g clay. **2** [C] badly painted picture. **~er** *n* person who paints unskilfully.

daugh·ter /ˈdɔtə(r)/ *n* one's female child. **~-in-law** /ˈdɔtr ɪn lɔ/ (*pl* **~s-in-law** /ˈdɔtəs ɪn lɔ/) wife of one's son. **~·ly** *adj* befitting a ~: *~ly affection.*

daunt /dɔnt/ *vt* [VP6A] discourage: *nothing ~ed,* not at all discouraged.

daunt·less /ˈdɔntləs/ *adj* not daunted; persevering. **~·ly** *adv*

dau·phin /ˈdɔfɪn/ *n* title of the King of France's eldest son (from 1349 to 1830).

dav·en·port /ˈdævnpɔt/ *n* **1** (GB, old use) piece of furniture with drawers and a hinged flap that opens so that it can be used as a writing-desk. **2** (orig US) long seat for two or three persons, with arms and a back. ⇨ **settee.**

davit /ˈdævɪt/ *n* one of a pair of small cranes(**2**), curved at the top, for supporting, lowering and raising a ship's boat.

daw /dɔ/ *n* = **jackdaw.**

dawdle /ˈdɔdl/ *vi, vt* [VP2A,C,15B] ~ ***(away),*** be slow; waste time: *Stop dawdling and do something useful! Don't ~ away your time! He's always dawdling.* **daw·dler** *n* person who ~s.

dawn[1] /dɔn/ *n* **1** first light of day; daybreak: *We must start at ~. He works from ~ till dark. It's almost ~.* **2** (fig) beginning; birth: *the ~ of intelligence/love/civilization. The war ended and we looked forward to the ~ of happier days.*

dawn[2] /dɔn/ *vi* [VP2A] **1** begin to grow light: *The day was just ~ing.* **2** begin to appear; grow clear (to the mind): *The truth began to ~ upon him. It has just ~ed on me that…,* I have just begun to realize that….

day /deɪ/ *n* **1** [U] time between sunrise and sunset: *He has been working all (the) day. We travelled day and night/night and day without stopping.* ***before day,*** before daylight comes. ***by day,*** during daylight: *We travelled by day and stayed at hotels every night.* ***pass the time of day (with sb),*** exchange greetings (e g by saying 'Good morning'). **2** [C] period of twenty-four hours (from midnight): *There are seven days in a week. I saw Tom three days ago. I shall see Mary in a few days' time,* a few days from now. *What day of the week is it? It's Monday.* ***the day after tomorrow***: *If today is Wednesday, the day after tomorrow will be Friday.* ***the day before yesterday***: *If today is Wednesday, the day before yesterday was Monday.* ***this day week***: *If today is 1 May, this day week will be 8 May.* ***this day fortnight***: *If today is 1 May, this day fortnight will be 15 May.* ***day after day, every day,*** for many days together. ***day in, day out,*** continuously. ***from day to day, from one day to the next***: *No one can be certain about what will happen from day to day.* ***one day,*** on a day (past or future). ***the other day,*** a few days ago. ***some day,*** on some day in the future. ***the day before/after the fair,*** too early/late to take advantage of a possible opportunity. ***one of these (fine) days,*** (used in making a promise or a prophecy) before long. ***to a/the day,*** exactly: *three years ago to the/a day.* **ˈdays of ˈgrace,** ⇨ **grace.** Note the omission of relatives after *day*: *the day (on which) I met you. We shall have many days (on which) to talk things over.* **3** the hours of the day given to work: *I've done a good day's work. His working day is eight hours. They want a six-hour day and a five-day week. Most workers are paid weekly, but some are paid by the day.* ***call it a day,*** decide that we have done enough (work) for one day: *Let's call it a day,* stop. ***all in the day's work,*** all part of the normal routine. **ˈday release,** (permission for a) worker who attends a technical college during a working day. **4** (often *pl*) time; period. ***better days,*** times when one was, or will be, richer, more prosperous, etc: *Let's hope we'll soon see better days.* ***fall on evil days,*** suffer misfortune. ***the present day,*** the time we are now living in: *present-day* (= modern) *writers; in these days* (= nowadays); *in those days* (= then); *in my schooldays; in his boyhood days; in the days of Queen Victoria; in days of old/in olden days,* in former times; *in days to come,* in future times; *the men of other days,* of past times; *in this day and age,* (cliché) in this present period. **5** (*sing* preceded by *his, her, their,* etc) lifetime; period of success, prosperity, power, etc: *Colonialism has had its day. She was a beauty in her day,* before she grew old. *Every dog has its day,* (prov) We all have good luck or a period of success at some time or other. **6** (*sing* with *def art*) contest: *We've won/carried the day/The day is ours.* We've won! *We've lost the day.* **7** (used attrib, and in compounds) **ˈday bed,** sofa or couch. **ˈday-boarder,** schoolchild who has meals at school, but sleeps at home. **ˈday-book** *n* (comm) record of purchases and sales as they take place, to be transferred to ledgers. **ˈday-boy/-girl,** one who attends school daily but sleeps at home. **ˈday·break,** dawn. **ˈday-dream** *vi, n* (have) idle and pleasant thoughts. **ˈday-labourer,** one who is hired by the day. **ˈday-long** *adj, adv* (lasting) for the whole day. **ˈday nursery,** place where small children may be left (while their mothers are at work). **ˈday-school,** used as the opp of *boarding-school, evening school,* and *Sunday school.* **ˈday shift,** (workers working a) period during the day, esp in a mine. **ˈday-spring,** (poet) dawn. **ˈday·time,** day(**1**), esp: *in the daytime.* **ˈday-ticket,** return ticket (often at a reduced rate) available both ways on one day only.

day·light /ˈdeɪlɑɪt/ *n* [U] **1** light of day: *Can we reach our destination in ~,* before it gets dark? **ˈ~-saving,** putting the hands of the clock forward so that darkness falls at a later hour. ⇨ **summer time. 2** dawn: *We must leave before ~.*

daze /deɪz/ *vt* [VP6A] make (sb) feel stupid or unable to think clearly: *If someone gave you a heavy blow on the head, you would probably feel ~d. He looked ~d with drugs/was in a ~d state.* □ *n* ***in a ~,*** in a bewildered condition. **dazed·ly** /ˈdeɪzɪdlɪ/ *adv* in a ~d manner.

dazzle /ˈdæzl/ *vt* [VP6A] make (sb) unable to see clearly or act normally because of too much light, brilliance, splendour, etc: *~d by bright lights; dazzling sunshine/diamonds. Such brilliant prospects almost ~d the young girl.* □ *n* [U] glitter.

D-day /ˈdi deɪ/ *n* (code name for the) day (6 June 1944) on which British and American forces landed in N France, during the Second World War; unnamed day on which (offensive) operations are to start.

dea·con /ˈdikən/ *n* minister or officer who has various duties in certain Christian churches (e g in the Church of England, below a bishop or priest; in nonconformist churches, a layman attending to secular affairs). **~·ess** /ˈdikənɪs/ *n* **~·ry** *n* (*pl* -ries) (office of) ~s.

dead /ded/ *adj, n* **1** (of plants, animals, persons) no longer living: *~ flowers/leaves. The hunter fired and the tiger fell ~.* ***D~ men tell no tales,*** (prov, used as an argument for killing sb whose knowledge of a secret may cause one loss or trouble). ***wait for a ~ man's shoes,*** wait for sb to die in order to step into his position. ***the ~,*** all those who have died or been killed: *to rise from the ~; the ~ and the wounded.* ***a ~ march,*** piece of slow, solemn music for a funeral. **2** never having had life: *~ matter,* e g rock. **3** without movement or activity: *in the ~ hours of the night,* when everything is quiet; (as *n*) *in the ~ of winter,* when there is no growth of vegetation, when the weather makes outdoor activity difficult, etc. ˈ~ ˋ**end** *n* cul-de-sac. ***be at/come to/reach a ~ end,*** (fig) the stage from which further progress appears impossible. ⇨ **deadlock. 4** (of languages, customs, etc) no longer used or observed: *a ~ language,* e g ancient Gk; *a regulation that has become a ~ letter,* one to which attention is no longer paid. ˋ~ **letter,** letter kept by the post-office because the person to whom it is addressed has not claimed it and neither he nor the sender cannot be found. **5** (of the hands, etc) numbed, e g by cold; unable to feel anything: *~ fingers.* ***~ to,*** unconscious of, hardened against: *~ to all feelings of shame; ~ to the world,* (fig) fast asleep. **6** complete; abrupt; exact: *to come to a ~ stop; runners on a ~ level,* running side by side; *a ~ calm,* not even a breath of wind. ***go into/be in a ~ faint,*** complete unconsciousness. ***a ~ heat,*** a race in which two or more runners reach the winning-post together. ***a ~ loss,*** a complete loss, with no compensation; (sl, of a person) one who is of no help or use to anyone. **the ~ centre,** the exact centre. **a ~ shot,** person who hits the target without fail; shot that goes to the exact point aimed at. **a ~ silence,** complete silence. **a ~ sleep,** a deep sleep (as if ~). **7** that can no longer be used: *a ~ match,* one that has been struck; *a ~ wire,* one through which electric current no longer passes. *The telephone went ~,* did not transmit sounds. **8** (of sound) dull, heavy; (of colours) lacking brilliance; (cricket, tennis, etc) (of the surface of the ground) such that balls move slowly: *a ~ pitch;* (of the ball, in various games) out of play. **9** (various uses) ˋ**~-line** *n* fixed limit of time for finishing a piece of work: *meet a ~line,* do, finish sth by the time assigned for it. ˋ**~-pan** *adj* (colloq) (of a person's face, looks) showing no emotion. ˋ~ **weight** *n* **1** (with *indef art*) heavy inert mass. **2** (comm) ship's loaded weight, including fuel and cargo. ***~ reckoning,*** ⇨ **reckon.** ***make a ~ set at sb,*** make a determined and deliberate attack on sb. □ *adv* completely; absolutely; thoroughly: *~ ˋbeat/ˋtired/exˋhausted; ~ ˋcertain/ˋsure; ~ ˋdrunk,* so drunk as to be incapable; *~ slow,* so slow as to be almost stopped; *~ ahead,* directly ahead. *The wind was ~ against us. You're ~ right!* ***cut sb ~,*** ⇨ **cut[1](7).**

deaden /ˋdedn/ *vt* [VP6A] take away, deprive of, force, feeling, brightness: *drugs to ~ the pain; thick walls that ~ street noises; thick clothing that ~ed the force of the blow.*

dead·lock /ˋdedlok/ *n* [C,U] ***be at/reach/come to (total) ~, fail completely to reach agreement, to settle a quarrel or grievance.***

dead·ly /ˋdedlɪ/ *adj* **(-ier, -iest) 1** causing, likely to cause, death: *~ weapons/poison. Fog is one of the sailor's deadliest enemies.* **2** filled with hate: *~ enemies.* **3** that may result in damnation: *the seven ~ sins.* **4** like that of death: *a ~ paleness.* **5** (colloq) excessive: *~ determination.* □ *adv* like that of death: *~ pale;* (colloq) excessively.

deaf /def/ *adj* **1** unable to hear at all; unable to hear well: *to become ~; the ~ and dumb alphabet,* one in which signs made with the hands are used for letters or words; to be ~ in one ear. ˋ**~-aid** *n* hearing aid; small device, usu electronic, that helps a ~ person to hear. ˈ~ ˋ**mute** *n* person who is ~ and dumb. **2** unwilling to listen: *~ to all advice/entreaty. He turned a ~ ear to* (= refused to listen to) *our requests for help.* **~·ness** *n*

deafen /ˋdefn/ *vt* [VP6A] make so much noise that hearing is difficult or impossible: *We were almost ~ed by the uproar. There were ~ing cheers when the speaker finished.*

deal[1] /dil/ *n* (board of) fir or pine wood: (chiefly attrib) *~ furniture; a ~ table; made of white ~.*

deal[2] /dil/ *n* [U] (usu) ***a (good/great) ~ (of),*** a large or considerable quantity; quite a lot: *He has had to spend a good ~ of money on medicines. I have spent a great ~ of trouble over the work. He has caused me a ~ of trouble.* □ *adv* very much: *She's a good ~ better today. They see each other a great ~.*

deal[3] /dil/ *vt,vi* (*pt,pp* **dealt** /delt/) **1** [VP6A, 15B,2A,12A,13A] ***~ (out),*** give out to a number of persons: *The money must be ~t out fairly. Who ~t the cards? He had been ~t four aces. It is the duty of a judge to ~ out justice.* ***~ sb a blow, ~ a blow at sb,*** **(a)** hit or strike him: *He ~t me a hard blow on the chin.* **(b)** (fig) hurt; upset: *The news ~t me a severe blow.* **2** [VP3A] ***~ in sth,*** stock, sell: *a shop that ~s in goods of all sorts.* **3** [VP3A] ***~ with sb/at a place,*** do business: *Do you ~ with Smith, the butcher? I've stopped ~ing at that shop—their prices are too high.* **4** [VP3A] ***~ with,*** **(a)** have relations with: *That man is easy/difficult/impossible to ~ with.* **(b)** behave towards; treat: *How would you ~ with an armed burglar? What is the best way of ~ing with young criminals,* How can we make them into good citizens? **(c)** (of affairs) manage; attend to: *How shall we ~ with this problem?* **(d)** be about; be concerned with: *a book ~ing with West Africa.* **5** ***~ well/badly by sb,*** treat him well/badly (usu in passive): *He has always ~t well by me. You've been badly ~t by.*

deal[4] /dil/ *n* [C] **1** (in games) distribution of playing cards: *It's your ~,* your turn to deal out the cards. ***a new ~,*** (orig) programme of social and economic reform (in US); any new plan that is thought to be just or fair. ***a raw ~,*** ⇨ **raw(7). 2** business transaction or agreement; (colloq) bargain: *Well, it's a ~,* I agree to do business with you on those terms. *I'll do a ~ with you,* make a bargain. ***get/give sb a square ~,*** fair treatment: *He gave me a square ~,* (colloq) treated me fairly.

dealer /ˋdilə(r)/ *n* **1** person who deals out playing-cards. **2** trader: *a ˋhorse-~; a ~ in* (= person who buys and sells) *stolen goods; a ˋcar ~.* Cf *a coal merchant.*

deal·ing /ˋdilɪŋ/ *n* **1** [U] dealing out or distributing; behaviour towards others: *He is well known for fair ~.* **2** (*pl*) business relations: *I've always found him honest in his ~s with me. I advise you to have no ~s with that fellow.*

dealt *pt,pp* of **deal[3]**.

dean /din/ *n* **1** clergyman at the head of a cathedral chapter. **2** ˋ**rural ~,** clergyman who, under an archdeacon, is responsible for a number of parishes. **3** (in some universities) person with authority to maintain discipline; head of a department of studies. **4** = doyen. **~·ery** /ˋdinərɪ/ *n* (*pl* **-ries**) office, house, of a ~; group of parishes under a rural ~.

dear /dɪə(r)/ *adj* **(-er -est) 1** loved; lovable: *Your mother is ~ to you. What a ~ little child!* ***hold sth/sb ~,*** (formal) love very much. **2** used as a form of address (polite or ironical) in speech, and at the beginning of letters: *My ~ Jones; D~ Madam/Sir; D~ Mr Green.* **3** high in price: (of a shop) asking high prices: *Everything is getting ~er. That's a ~ shop.* **`~ money,** (when loans are difficult to obtain) on which a high rate of interest must be paid. **4 *~ (to),*** precious (to); greatly valued: *He lost everything that was ~ to him.* □ *adv* at a high cost: *If you want to make money, you must buy cheap and sell ~.* □ *n* **1** lovable person: *Isn't she a ~! Aren't they ~s!* **2** (used to address a person): *'Come, my ~(est)' 'Yes, ~'*; (used with *indef art,* esp when coaxing sb): *'Drink your milk up, Anne, there's a ~'.* □ *int* used to express surprise, impatience, wonder, dismay, etc: *Oh ~! D~ me!* **~·ly** *adv* **1** very much: *He would ~ly* (= earnestly) *love to see his mother again. He loves his mother ~ly,* affectionately. **2** at great cost: *Victory was ~ly bought,* e g when hundreds of soldiers were killed. **~·ness** *n* being ~; great cost.

dearth /dɜθ/ *n* (*sing* only) scarcity; too small a supply (*of*): *in time of ~; a ~ of food.* ⇨ **shortage,** a much commoner word.

deary, dearie /ˈdɪərɪ/ *n* (*pl* **-ries**) (colloq) dear one; darling (used, esp by an elderly woman to a younger person, e g by a mother to address her child).

death /deθ/ *n* [C,U] (as shown in the examples) **1** dying; ending of life: *There have been several ~s from drowning here this summer. His mother's ~ was a great blow to him. Two children were burnt to ~ in the fire. He drank himself to ~. Don't work yourself to ~,* work so hard that you become ill and die. ***at ~'s door,*** dying; in danger of ~. **`~-bed,** bed on which one dies: *The criminal made a ~-bed confession,* confessed his crimes while dying. ***sick to ~ of sb/sth,*** extremely tired, bored, etc. ***bore sb to ~,*** bore him extremely. **`~-duties,** taxes (to be) paid on a person's property before it passes to his heir(s). **`~'s head,** human skull (as an emblem of ~). **`~-rate,** yearly number of ~s per 1 000 of population. **`~ rattle** *n* unusual rattling sound in the throat of a dying person. **2** killing or being killed: *The murderer was sentenced to ~,* to be executed. ***be in at the ~,*** (fox-hunting) see the fox killed; (fig) see the end of an enterprise, etc. ***put sb to ~,*** kill him; execute him. ***stone sb to ~,*** kill him by throwing stones at him. **`~-roll,** list of persons killed (in war, in an earthquake, etc). **`~-trap,** place where persons are likely to be killed (e g one where many fatal traffic accidents occur); place, set of circumstances, where people lose their lives (e g a burning building with no means of escape). **`~-warrant,** official paper giving authority for the execution of a criminal, traitor, etc; (fig) sth which destroys prospects of life or happiness, ends an old custom, etc. **3** [U] state of being dead: *eyes closed in ~; lie still in ~; united in ~,* e g of husband and wife in the same grave. ***(a fate) worse than ~,*** to be greatly dreaded. *D~ comes to all men.* **`~-mask,** cast taken of a dead person's face. **4 *be the ~ of sb,*** be the cause of sb's ~: *That old motor-bike will be the ~ of you one of these days,* you will have a fatal accident. *Don't make me laugh so much; you'll be the ~ of me,* make me die of laughing. ***catch one's ~ (of cold),*** (colloq) catch a cold that will be fatal. **`~-blow,** sth that causes ~; (fig) shock from which recovery is impossible: *a ~-blow to his hopes of success.* **the Black `D~,** pestilence in Europe in the 14th c. **5** (fig) destruction; end: *the ~ of one's hopes/plans.*

death·less /ˈdeθləs/ *adj* never dying or forgotten; immortal: *~ fame/glory.*

death·like /ˈdeθlaɪk/ *adj* like that of death: *a ~ silence.*

death·ly /ˈdeθlɪ/ *adj* like death: *a ~ stillness.* □ *adv* like death: *~ pale.*

deb /deb/ *n* (abbr of) débutante.

dé·bâcle /deɪˈbɑkl/ *n* (F) confused rush or stampede; sudden and great disaster; downfall.

de·bag /dɪˈbæg/ *vt* (**-gg-**) [VP6A] (colloq, dated) forcibly take off the trousers from, e g during rough play among students.

de·bar /dɪˈbɑ(r)/ *vt* (**-rr-**) [VP14] ***~ sb from,*** shut out; prevent (sb) by a regulation (from doing or having sth): *~ persons who have been convicted of crime from voting at elections.*

de·bark /dɪˈbɑk/ *vt, vi* **de·bark·ation** /ˌdibɑˈkeɪʃn/ *n* ⇨ **disembark.**

de·base /dɪˈbeɪs/ *vt* [VP6A] make lower in value, poorer in quality, character, etc: *to ~ the coinage,* e g by reducing the percentage of silver. **~·ment** *n*

de·bat·able /dɪˈbeɪtəbl/ *adj* that can be debated or disputed; open to question: *~ ground.*

de·bate /dɪˈbeɪt/ *n* [C,U] formal discussion, e g at a public meeting or in Parliament; contest between two speakers, or two groups of speakers, to show skill and ability in arguing: *After a long ~ the bill was passed by the House of Commons and sent to the House of Lords. After much ~ Harry was chosen captain of the football team. Who opened the ~,* was the first to speak? The question under ~ was.... □ *vt, vi* [VP6A,8,10,2A,C] have a ~ about; take part in a ~; think over in order to decide: *to ~ (upon) a question with sb; to ~ about sth; a debating society. We were debating whether to go to the mountains or to the seaside.* **de·bater** *n* one who ~s.

de·bauch /dɪˈbɔtʃ/ *vt* [VP6A] cause (sb) to lose virtue, to act immorally; turn (sb) away from good taste or judgement. □ *n* [C] occasion of excessive drinking, immoral behaviour, usu in company: *a drunken ~.* **~·ery** /dɪˈbɔtʃərɪ/ *n* [U] intemperance and indulgence in sensual pleasures: *a life of ~ery;* (*pl;* **-ries**) instances or periods of this. **~ee** /dɪˌbɔˈtʃi/ *n* ~ed person.

debbi /ˈdebɪ/ *n* four-gallon petrol tin, used in E Africa as a measure (and, flattened out, as roofing material).

de·ben·ture /dɪˈbentʃə(r)/ *n* [C] certificate given by a business corporation, etc as a receipt for money lent at a fixed rate of interest until the principal(4) is repaid.

de·bili·tate /dɪˈbɪlɪteɪt/ *vt* [VP6A] make (a person, his constitution) weak: *a debilitating climate.*

de·bil·ity /dɪˈbɪlətɪ/ *n* [U] weakness (of health, purpose): *After her long illness she is suffering from general ~.*

debit /ˈdebɪt/ *n* **1** (book-keeping) entry (in an account) of a sum owing. **2** (also **`~-side**) left-hand side of an account, on which such entries are made. ⇨ **credit[1](4).** □ *vt* [VP14] put on the ~ side of an account: *~ a person's account (with £5); to ~ £5 against his account. To whom shall I ~ this sum?*

deb·on·air /ˌdebəˈneə(r)/ *adj* cheerful; bright and

light-hearted.

de·bouch /dɪˋbaʊtʃ/ *vt,vi* [VP6A,2A] (cause to) emerge or issue.

de·brief /ˈdiˋbrif/ *vt* [VP6A] question, examine, e g persons who have returned from a mission, etc, to obtain information. ⇨ brief[2].

de·bris, dé·bris /ˋdeɪbri *US:* dəˋbri/ *n* [U] scattered broken pieces; wreckage: *searching among the ~ after the explosion.*

debt /det/ *n* [C,U] payment which must be, but has not yet been, paid to sb; obligation: *If I pay all my ~s I shall have no money left. I owe him a ~ of gratitude for all he has done for me.* **be in/out of ~,** owe/not owe money. ***get into/out of ~,*** reach a point where one owes/does not owe money: *It's much easier to get into ~ than to get out of ~.* **ˋNational D~** *n* money owed by the State to those who have lent it money. ⇨ bad[1](4), honour[2](2). **~or** /-tə(r)/ *n* person who is in ~ to another.

de·bug /ˈdiˋbʌg/ *vt* (-gg-) [VP6A] (colloq) search for and remove (possible causes of trouble, faults, errors, e g from a computer programme, engines on a production line).

de·bunk /diˋbʌŋk/ *vt* [VP6A] (colloq) reveal the truth about (a person, idea, institution) by stripping away false sentiments, traditions, etc.

debut, début /ˋdeɪbju *US:* deɪˋbju/ *n* (esp of a young woman) first appearance at adult parties and other social events; (of an actor, musician, etc) first appearance on a public stage: *to make one's ~.* **débu·tante** /ˋdebjʊtɑnt *US:* ˈdebjʊˋtɑnt/ *n* upper-class girl making her début into high society.

deca- /dekə/ *pref* ⇨ App 5 (the Metric System).

dec·ade /ˋdekeɪd/ *n* period of ten years: *the first ~ of the 20th century,* i e 1900—1909.

deca·dence /ˋdekədəns/ *n* [U] falling to a lower level (in morals, art, literature, etc esp after a period at a high level).

deca·dent /ˋdekədənt/ *adj* in a state of decadence. □ *n* person in this state.

deca·logue /ˋdekəlog *US:* -lɔg/ *n* (*sing* with *def art*) the Ten Commandments of Moses. ⇨ Exod 20: 2 17.

de·camp /dɪˋkæmp/ *vi* [VP2A,3A] ~ ***(with),*** go away suddenly (and often secretly).

de·cant /dɪˋkænt/ *vt* [VP6A] pour (wine, etc) from a bottle into another vessel slowly so as not to disturb the sediment. **~er** *n* vessel, usu of decorated glass with a stopper, into which wine is ~ed before being brought to table.

decanters

de·capi·tate /dɪˋkæpɪteɪt/ *vt* [VP6A] behead (esp as a legal punishment). **de·capi·ta·tion** /dɪˈkæpɪˋteɪʃn/ *n*

de·car·bon·ize /ˈdiˋkɑbənɑɪz/ *vt* remove carbon from, esp an internal combustion engine.

deca·syl·lable /ˋdekəsɪləbl/ *n* **deca·syl·labic** /ˈdekəsɪˋlæbɪk/ *adj* (line) of ten syllables.

de·cay /dɪˋkeɪ/ *vi* [VP2A] go bad; lose power, health: *~ing teeth/vegetables. Our powers ~ in old age. What caused the Roman Empire to ~?* □ *n* [U] decaying: *the ~ of the teeth. The house is in ~. Old civilizations may fall into ~,* lose strength.

de·cease /dɪˋsis/ *n* (esp legal) (a person's) death. □ *vi* die. **the ~d,** person who has, persons who have, recently died.

de·ceit /dɪˋsit/ *n* **1** [U] deceiving; causing a person to accept as true or genuine sth that is false: *She is incapable of ~,* would never tell lies, etc. **2** [C] lie; dishonest trick.

de·ceit·ful /dɪˋsitfl/ *adj* **1** in the habit of deceiving: *No one can admire a ~ boy.* **2** intended to deceive; misleading in appearance, etc: *~ words/acting.* **~ly** /-flɪ/ *adv* **~·ness** *n*

de·ceive /dɪˋsiv/ *vt* [VP6A,14] cause (sb) to believe sth that is false; play a trick on; mislead (on purpose): *You can't pass the examination without working hard, so don't ~ yourself. I've been ~d in you,* have found that you were not what I thought you were. *We were ~d into the belief/~d into believing that....* **de·ceiver** *n* person who ~s. **de·ceiv·ing·ly** *adv*

de·celer·ate /ˈdiˋseləreɪt/ *vt,vi* (cause to) diminish speed. ⇨ accelerate.

De·cem·ber /dɪˋsembə(r)/ *n* twelfth month of the year.

de·cency /ˋdisnsɪ/ *n* **1** [U] (the quality of) being decent; (regard for the) general opinion as to what is decent: *an offence against ~,* e g appearing naked in public. **2** (*pl;* -cies; with *def art*) requirements of respectable behaviour in society: *We must observe the decencies.*

de·cent /ˋdisnt/ *adj* **1** right and suitable; respectful: *Put on some ~ clothes before you call on the Smiths. Poor people cannot always live in ~ conditions.* **2** modest; not likely to shock or embarrass others (the only sense for which *indecent* is the opposite): *~ langauge and behaviour. Never tell stories that are not ~.* **3** (colloq) likeable; satisfactory: *He's a very ~ fellow. He gave us quite a ~ dinner.* **~·ly** *adv* in a ~(1,2) manner: *~ly dressed; behave ~ly. He's doing very ~ly,* e g making a good income.

de·cen·tra·lize /ˈdiˋsentrəlɑɪz/ *vt* [VP6A] give greater powers (for self-government, etc) to (places, branches, etc away from the centre). **de·cen·tra·liz·ation** /ˈdiˈsentrəlɑɪˋzeɪʃn *US:* -lɪˋz-/ *n*

de·cep·tion /dɪˋsepʃn/ *n* **1** [U] deceiving; being deceived: *to practise ~ on the public.* **2** [C] trick intended to deceive: *a gross ~.*

de·cep·tive /dɪˋseptɪv/ *adj* deceiving: *Appearances are often ~,* Things are not always what they seem to be. **~·ly** *adv*

deci- /desɪ/ *pref* ⇨ App 5 (the Metric System).

deci·bel /ˋdesɪbel/ *n* unit for measuring the relative loudness of sounds.

de·cide /dɪˋsɑɪd/ *vt,vi* **1** [VP6A,14,2A,3A] settle (a question or a doubt); give a judgement (*between, for, in favour of, against*): *We ~d the question by experiment. The judge ~d the case. It's difficult to ~ between the two. The judge ~d for/in favour of/against the plaintiff.* **2** [VP6A,7A,8,9,10,3A] think about and come to a conclusion; make up one's mind; resolve: *The boy ~d not to/~d that he would not become a sailor. It has been ~d that the exhibition shall not be open on Sundays. He could not ~ what to do/what he should do next. In the end she ~d on/~d to buy the green hat. We*

~d against/~d not to go for a holiday in Wales. **3** [VP17] cause to ~(2): *What ~d you to give up your job?* **de·cided** *part adj* **1** clear; definite: *There is a ~d difference between them. He's a man of ~d opinions.* **2** (of persons) having ~d opinions; determined: *He's quite ~d about it.* **de·cid·ed·ly** *adv* definitely; undoubtedly: *answer ~dly; ~dly better.*

de·cidu·ous /dɪˋsɪdʒʊəs/ *adj* (of trees) losing their leaves annually (esp in autumn).

deci·mal /ˋdesɪml/ *adj* of tens or one-tenths: *the ˋ~ system*, for money, weights, etc; *a ~ fraction*, e g 0·091; *the ~ point*, the point in 15·61. **~·ize** *vt* [VP6A] change to a ~ system: *~ize the currency.* **~·iz·ation** /ˌdesɪmḷaɪˋzeɪʃn *US:* -ḷɪˋz-/ *n*

deci·mate /ˋdesɪmeɪt/ *vt* [VP6A] kill or destroy one-tenth or a larger part of: *a population ~d by disease.*

de·cipher /dɪˋsaɪfə(r)/ *vt* [VP6A] find the meaning of (sth written in cipher, bad handwriting, sth puzzling or difficult to understand). **~·able** /dɪˋsaɪfrəbl/ *adj* that can be ~ed.

de·ci·sion /dɪˋsɪʒn/ *n* **1** [U] deciding; judging; [C] result of this; settlement of a question: *give a ~ on a case. Have they reached/come to/arrived at/taken/made a ~ yet? His ~ to retire surprised all of us.* **2** [U] ability to decide and act accordingly; the quality of being decided(**2**): *A man who lacks ~* (= who hesitates, cannot decide questions) *cannot hold a position of responsibility.*

de·cis·ive /dɪˋsaɪsɪv/ *adj* **1** having a decided or definite outcome or result; *a ~ battle*, deciding which side wins the war. **2** showing decision(**2**); definite: *He gave a ~ answer.* **~·ly** *adv*

deck[1] /dek/ *n* **1** any of the floors of a ship, usu of wooden planks, in or above the hull: *My cabin is on E ~. Shall we go up on ~*, up (from a cabin, saloon, etc) on to the main (or promenade) ~? ⇨ the illus at ship. ***clear the ~s,*** ⇨ clear[3](**1**). **ˋ~ cabin,** one on an open ~, not one that is below the main ~. **ˋ~ chair** *n* collapsible chair of canvas, on a wooden or metal frame, used out of doors, e g in parks, the sea front, and on the ~s of steamers. **ˋ~ hand** *n* member of a ship's crew who works on ~. **ˋ~ officers,** the captain and mates (contrasted with the engineers). **ˋ~ passenger,** one who does not use a cabin or the public rooms, but eats and sleeps on ~. **ˋ~ quoits** /kwɔɪts/, game played on a ~(**1**) in which a ring (*quoit*) is thrown. **2** any similar surface, e g the floor of a bus: *a single-~ bus; the top ~ of a double-~ bus.* **3** (chiefly US) pack of playing-cards; (comm) collection of punched cards from a particular file. **~er** *n* (in comb): *a three-~er*, ship with three ~s: *single/double-ˋ~er*, single/double deck bus; *double-/triple-decker sandwiches*, with two/three layers of bread.

deck[2] /dek/ *vt* [VP6A,14,15A] **1** ***~ (with/out in),*** decorate: *streets ~ed with flags. She was ~ed out in her finest clothes.* **2** cover, provide (a boat, ship) with a deck.

deckle-edged /ˌdekl ˋedʒd/ *adj* (of some kinds of paper, e g hand-made notepaper) having untrimmed edges.

de·claim /dɪˋkleɪm/ *vi, vt* **1** [VP2A,3A] ***~ against,*** speak with strong feeling; attack in words. **2** [VP6A,2A] speak in the manner of addressing an audience or reciting poetry; recite, e g a poem, rhetorically.

dec·la·ma·tion /ˌdekləˋmeɪʃn/ *n* [U] declaiming: [C] speech full of strong feeling: formal speech. **de·clama·tory** /dɪˋklæmətərɪ *US:* -tɔrɪ/ *adj* of ~.

dec·lar·ation /ˌdekləˋreɪʃn/ *n* [U] declaring; [C] that which is declared: *a ~ of war; the D~ of Independence*, that made by the N American colonies of Great Britain, on 4 July 1776, that they were politically independent; *a ~ of income*, one (to be) made to the Inspector of Taxes.

de·clare /dɪˋkleə(r)/ *vt, vi* **1** [VP6A,14,25] make known clearly or formally; announce: *to ~ the results of an election. I ~ this meeting closed.* ***~ (an innings closed),*** (cricket) (of the captain of the team) announce that the team will not continue batting although the innings is not finished: *Australia ~d when the score reached 500.* ***~ trumps,*** (in bridge[2]) say which suit(**5**) will be played as trumps. ***~ war (on/against),*** announce that a state of war exists. **2** [VP9,25] say solemnly; say in order to show that one has no doubt: *The accused man ~d that he was not guilty/~d himself innocent.* **3** [VP3A] ***~ for/against,*** say that one is/is not in favour of. **4** [VP6A] make a statement (to customs officials) of dutiable goods brought into a country, or (to a Tax Inspector) of one's income: *Have you anything to ~?* **5** (*int*) expressing surprise: *Well, I ~!* **de·clar·able** /dɪˋkleərəbl/ *adj* that must be ~d(**4**).

de·class·ify /ˌdiˋklæsɪfaɪ/ *vt* (*pt,pp* -fied) [VP6A] remove from a special class (esp sth hitherto secret): *~ information concerning nuclear fission.* **de·class·ifi·ca·tion** /ˌdiˌklæsɪfɪˋkeɪʃn/ *n*

de·clen·sion /dɪˋklenʃn/ *n* (gram) [U] varying the endings of *nouns, pronouns,* and *adjectives* according to their use in a sentence (e g in Latin). ⇨ case[1](**3**); [C] class of words whose endings for different cases are alike.

de·cli·na·tion /ˌdeklɪˋneɪʃn/ *n* deviation of the needle of a compass, E or W from the true north.

de·cline[1] /dɪˋklaɪn/ *vt, vi* **1** [VP6A,7A,2A] say 'No' (to); refuse (sth offered): *to ~ an invitation to dinner. He ~d to discuss his plans with the newspaper men.* **2** [VP2A,C] continue to become smaller, weaker, lower: *a declining birthrate; declining sales; an empire that has ~d. His strength slowly ~d. I wish prices would ~. He spent his declining years* (= the years when, in old age, he was losing strength) *in the country.* **3** [VP2A] (of the sun) go down. **4** [VP6A] give the cases of (a word). ⇨ case[1](**3**).

de·cline[2] /dɪˋklaɪn/ *n* [C] declining; gradual and continued loss of strength: *the ~ of the Roman Empire; a ~ in prices/prosperity.* ***fall into a ~,*** lose strength; (esp) suffer from consumption. ***on the ~,*** declining.

de·cliv·ity /dɪˋklɪvətɪ/ *n* (*pl* -ties) downward slope.

de·clutch /ˌdiˋklʌtʃ/ *vi* [VP2A] disconnect the clutch (of a motor vehicle) in readiness for changing gear.

de·code /ˌdiˋkəʊd/ *vt* [VP6A] decipher (sth written in code). **de·coder** *n* (esp) device for translating data from one code to another.

de·coke /ˌdiˋkəʊk/ *vt* (colloq) = decarbonize.

dé·colleté /ˌdeɪˋkolteɪ *US:* -kolˋteɪ/ *adj* (of a gown, etc) leaving the neck and shoulders uncovered; (of a woman) wearing such a gown.

de·col·on·ize /ˌdiˋkolənaɪz/ *vt* [VP6A] change from colonial to independent status. **de·col·on·iz·ation** /ˌdiˌkolənaɪˋzeɪʃn *US:* -nɪˋz-/ *n*

de·com·pose /ˌdikəmˋpəʊz/ *vt, vi* **1** [VP6A] separate (a substance, light, etc) into its parts: *A prism ~s light.* **2** [VP6A,2A] (cause to) become bad or rotten; decay. **de·com·po·si·tion** /ˌdiˈkompəˈzɪʃn/ *n*

de·com·press /ˈdikəmˋpres/ *vt* [VP6A] bring back (sb in compressed air, e g a diving suit) to normal pressure; reduce compression in (sth). **de·com·pres·sion** /ˈdikəmˋpreʃn/ *n*: *a ~ion chamber.*

de·con·tami·nate /ˈdikənˋtæmɪneɪt/ *vt* [VP6A] remove contamination from (e g what has been affected by poison-gas or radio-activity). **de·con·tami·na·tion** /ˈdikənˈtæmɪˋneɪʃn/ *n*

de·con·trol /ˈdikənˋtrəʊl/ *vt* (-ll-) [VP6A] *n* [C,U] release from control (e g of trade by the Government during a war).

dé·cor /ˋdeɪkɔ(r) *US:* deɪˋkɔr/ *n* all that makes up the general appearance, e g of a room or the stage of a theatre.

dec·or·ate /ˋdekəreɪt/ *vt* [VP6A,14] **1** put ornaments on; make (more) beautiful by placing adornments on or in: *to ~ a street with flags/the house with holly at Christmas.* **2** paint, plaster, etc the outside of (a building); put paint, wallpaper, etc on the inside rooms of (a building). **3** give (sb) a mark of distinction (e g a medal, an order): *Several soldiers were ~d for bravery.* **dec·or·ator** /-tə(r)/ *n* workman who ~s(2): *interior decorators.*

dec·ora·tion /ˈdekəˋreɪʃn/ *n* **1** [U] decorating or being decorated. **2** [C] sth used for decorating: *Christmas ~s.* **3** [C] medal, ribbon, etc given and worn as an honour or award.

dec·or·ative /ˋdekrətɪv *US:* ˋdekəreɪtɪv/ *adj* suitable for decorating(1): *Holly, with its bright red berries, is very ~.*

dec·or·ous /ˋdekərəs/ *adj* not offending. **~·ly** *adv*

de·corum /dɪˋkɔrəm/ *n* **1** [U] right and proper behaviour, as required by social custom. **2** (*pl*) requirements of polite society: *the little ~s that are supposed to mark a lady.*

de·coy /ˋdikɔɪ/ *n* **1** (real or imitation) bird (e g a duck) or animal used to attract others so that they may be shot or caught; place designed for this purpose (e g a sheet of water with nets in which birds are trapped). **2** (fig) person or thing used to tempt sb into a position of danger. □ *vt* /dɪˋkɔɪ/ [VP6A, 14] trick (sb or sth) into a place of danger by means of a ~: *He had been ~ed across the frontier and arrested as a spy.*

de·crease /dɪˋkris/ *vt,vi* [VP6A,2A] (cause to) become shorter, smaller, less: *Your hunger ~s as you eat. The population of the village has ~d by 150 to 500.* □ *n* /ˋdikris/ [U] decreasing; [C] amount by which sth ~s: *There has been a ~ in our imports this year.* ***on the ~,*** decreasing: *Is crime on the ~?*

de·cree /dɪˋkri/ *n* [C] **1** order given by a ruler or authority and having the force of a law: *issue a ~; rule by ~.* **2** judgement or decision of some law courts: *a ~ of divorce; a ~ in bankruptcy.* **~ nisi** /dɪˈkri ˋnɑɪsɑɪ/ *n* order for a divorce unless cause to the contrary is shown within a fixed period. □ *vt,vi* [VP6A,9,2A] issue a ~; order by ~: *It had been ~d that.... Fate ~d that....*

de·crepit /dɪˋkrepɪt/ *adj* made weak by old age or hard use: *a ~ horse.* **de·crepi·tude** /dɪˋkrepɪtjud *US:* -tud/ *n* the state of being ~.

de·cry /dɪˋkrɑɪ/ *vt* (*pt,pp* -cried) [VP6A] try, by speaking against sth, to make it seem less valuable, useful, etc.

dedi·cate /ˋdedɪkeɪt/ *vt* [VP6A,14] **~ to, 1** give up, devote (one's time, energy, etc, to a noble cause or purpose): *He ~d his life to the service of his country.* **2** devote with solemn ceremonies (to God, to a sacred use). **3** (of an author) write (or print) a person's name at the beginning of a book (to show gratitude or friendship to). **dedi·ca·tion** /ˈdedɪˋkeɪʃn/ *n* [U] dedicating: *the dedication of a church;* [C] words used in dedicating a book.

de·duce /dɪˋdjus *US:* dɪˋdus/ *vt* [VP6A,14,9] **~ *(from),*** arrive at (knowledge, a theory, etc) by reasoning; reach a conclusion: *If you saw a doctor leaving a house, you might ~ the fact that someone in the house was ill.*

de·duct /dɪˋdʌkt/ *vt* [VP6A,14] take away (an amount or part). ⇨ **subtract** for numbers. **~·ible** /dɪˋdʌktəbl/ *adj* that may be ~ed.

de·duc·tion /dɪˋdʌkʃn/ *n* **1** [U] deducting; [C] amount deducted: *~s from pay for insurance and pension.* **2** [U] deducing; [C] conclusion reached by reasoning from general laws to a particular case. **de·duct·ive** /dɪˋdʌktɪv/ *adj* of, using, reasoning by, ~(2).

deed /did/ *n* **1** sth done; act: *to be rewarded for one's good ~s. D~s are better than words when people are in need of help.* **2** (legal) written or printed signed agreement, esp about ownership or rights. **ˈ~ of ˋcovenant,** ⇨ **covenant(1). ˋ~-box** *n* one in which legal ~s are stored.

deem /dim/ *vt* [VP9,25] (formal) believe; consider: *He ~ed it/~ed that it was his duty to help.*

deep[1] /dip/ *adj* (-er, -est) **1** going a long way down from the top: *a ~ well/river.* ⇨ **shallow. ˈ~-ˈsea, ˈ~-ˈwater,** *attrib adjj,* of the deeper parts of the sea, away from the coastal water: *~-sea fishing.* ***go (in) off the ˋ~ end,*** ⇨ **end**[1]**(1).** ***in ~ water(s),*** (fig) in great difficulties, etc. **2** going a long way from the surface or edge: *a ~ shelf; a ~ wound;* (fig) *a ~ reader/thinker; a huge, ~-chested wrestler.* **3** placed or extending down, back or in (with words to indicate extent): *a hole two feet ~; with his hands ~ in his pockets; water six feet ~; ankle-~ in mud; to be ~ in debt; a plot of land 100 feet ~,* i e going back this distance from a street, road or other frontage. *The people were standing twenty ~ to see the Queen go past.* **4** (of sounds) low: *in a ~ voice: the ~ notes of a 'cello.* **5** (of sleep) profound: *in a ~ sleep,* from which one is not easily awakened. **6** (of colours) strong; intense: *a ~ red.* **7** brought from far down: *a ~ sigh;* strongly felt; coming from the heart: *~ sorrow/feelings/sympathy.* **8 ~ *in,*** absorbed in; having all one's attention centred on: *~ in thought/study/a book.* **9** (fig) difficult to understand or learn about: *a ~ mystery; a ~ secret;* (of a person) artful; concealing his real feelings, motives, etc: *He's a ~ one.* **10** (fig) going far; not superficial: *~ learning; a man with ~ insight.* **~en** /ˋdipən/ *vt,vi* make or become ~. **~·ly** *adv* profoundly; intensely: *He is ~ly interested in the subject. She felt her mother's death ~ly.* **~·ness** *n*

deep[2] /dip/ *adv* far down or in: *We had to dig ~ to find water. He went on studying ~ into the night.* ***Still waters run ~,*** (prov) said of a person whose real feelings, ideas, etc are not openly displayed. **ˈ~-ˋfreeze** *vt* freeze (food) quickly in order to preserve it for long periods: *~-frozen fish.* □ *n* special type of refrigerator (or a special part of an ordinary refrigerator) used for this purpose: *put surplus fruit and vegetables in the ~-freeze.* **'~-'laid,** (of schemes, etc) secretly and carefully planned. **'~-'mined,** (of coal) from ordinary coal-mines (contrasted with *open-cast;* ⇨ open[1](11)). **'~-'rooted,** not easily removed: *his ~-rooted dislike of hard work.* **'~-'seated,** firmly established: *The causes of the trouble are ~-seated.*

deep[3] /dip/ *n* (poet) **the ~,** the sea.

deer /dɪə(r)/ *n* (*pl* unchanged) (kinds of) graceful, quick-running animal, the male of which has horns. **'~·skin,** (leather made of) ~'s skin. **'~-stalker,** (**a**) sportsman who stalks ~. (**b**) cloth cap with two peaks, one in front and the other behind. **'~-stalking,** sport of hunting ~ by approaching them stealthily or from concealment.

de-esca·late /'di 'eskəleɪt/ *vt* [VP6A] decrease the area or intensity of, e g bombing. **de-esca·la·tion** /di'eskə'leɪʃn/ *n*

de·face /dɪ'feɪs/ *vt* [VP6A] spoil the appearance of (by marking or damaging the surface of); make engraved lettering (e g on a tombstone) illegible. **~·ment** *n* [U] defacing or being ~d; [C] sth that ~s.

de facto /'deɪ 'fæktəʊ/ *adj, adv* (Lat) in fact, whether by right (*de jure*) or not: *the ~ king.*

de·fal·ca·tion /'difæl'keɪʃn/ *n* [U] (legal) misappropriation of money entrusted to one; [C] instance of this; amount of money misappropriated.

de·fame /dɪ'feɪm/ *vt* [VP6A] attack the good reputation of; say evil things about. **defa·ma·tion** /'defə'meɪʃn/ *n* [U] defaming or being ~d; harm done to sb's reputation. **de·fama·tory** /dɪ'fæmətrɪ *US:* -tɔrɪ/ *adj* intended to ~: *defamatory statements.*

de·fault[1] /dɪ'fɔlt/ *n* [U] act of ~ing: *to win a case/a game by ~,* because the other party (team, player, etc) does not appear. ***in ~ of,*** in the absence of; if (sth) is not to be obtained, does not take place, etc. **~er** *n* **1** person who ~s. **2** soldier guilty of a military offence.

de·fault[2] /dɪ'fɔlt/ *vi* [VP2A] fail to perform a duty, or to appear (e g in a law court) when required to do so, or to pay a debt.

de·feat /dɪ'fit/ *vt* [VP6A] **1** overcome; win a victory over: *to ~ another school at football. They were ~ed in their attempt to reach the top of the mountain.* **2** bring to nothing; make useless; cause to fail: *Our hopes were ~ed.* □ *n* [U] ~ing or being ~ed: *a baseball team that has not yet suffered ~;* [C] instance of this: *six victories and two ~s.* **~·ism** /-ɪzm/ *n* [U] attitude, conduct, use of arguments, based on expectations of ~. **~·ist** *n* person with such an attitude, etc.

de·fe·cate /'defɪkeɪt/ *vi* [VP2A] (med) empty the bowels. **def·eca·tion** /'defə'keɪʃn/ *n*

de·fect[1] /'difekt/ *n* [C] fault; imperfection; shortcoming; sth lacking in completeness or perfection: *~s in a system of education.*

de·fect[2] /dɪ'fekt/ *vi* [VP2A,C] desert one's country, one's allegiance, etc: *the ballerina who ~ed to the West,* e g by asking for political asylum. **de·fec·tor** /-tə(r)/ *n* person who ~s: *~ors from the Republican Party.*

de·fec·tion /dɪ'fekʃn/ *n* [U] falling away from loyalty to a political party (or its leader), religion or duty; [C] instance of this: *~s from the Socialist Party.*

de·fec·tive /dɪ'fektɪv/ *adj* having a defect or defects; imperfect: *~ in workmanship/moral sense; mentally ~,* weak-minded; *a ~ verb,* e g *must.* **~·ly** *adv* **~·ness** *n*

de·fence (US = **de·fense**) /dɪ'fens/ **1** [U] defending from attack; fighting against attack: *money needed for national ~; to fight in ~ of one's country; weapons of offence and ~. We never fight except in self-~, you know.* **2** [C] sth used for defending or protecting; means of defending: *coastal ~s,* against attacks from the sea. *People used to build strong walls round their towns as a ~ against enemies. A thick overcoat is a good ~ against the cold.* **3** [C,U] (legal) argument(s) used to contest an accusation; the lawyer(s) acting for an accused person: *The accused man made no ~. Counsel for the ~ put in a plea for mercy. Counsel worked out a very convincing ~.* **~·less** *adj* having no ~; unable to defend oneself. **~·less·ly** *adv* **~·less·ness** *n*

de·fend /dɪ'fend/ *vt* [VP6A,14] **1** ~ ***(against/ from),*** guard; protect; make safe: *to ~ one's country against enemies; to ~ sb from harm. When the dog attacked me, I ~ed myself with a stick.* **2** speak or write in support of: ~ (= uphold) *a claim;* ~ (= contest) *a lawsuit. He made a long speech ~ing his ideas. You will need lawyers to ~ you.* **~er** *n* **1** person who ~s. Note legal term at **defence(3)**. **2** (in sport, e g football) player who guards his goal area against attacks from the other side.

de·fend·ant /dɪ'fendənt/ *n* person against whom a legal action is brought. ⇨ **plaintiff**.

de·fense ⇨ **defence**.

de·fens·ible /dɪ'fensəbl/ *adj* able to be defended.

de·fens·ive /dɪ'fensɪv/ *adj* used for, intended for, defending: *~ warfare/measures. Whether a gun is a ~ or an offensive weapon may depend upon whether you're behind it or in front of it.* □ *n* (usu) ***be/act on the ~,*** state or position of defence. **~·ly** *adv*

de·fer[1] /dɪ'fɜ(r)/ *vt* (-rr-) [VP6A,C] put off to a later time; postpone: *a ~red telegram,* one sent later at a cheaper rate; *a ~red annuity; to ~ one's departure for a week; to ~ making a decision; payment on ~red terms,* i e by instalments after purchase. ⇨ *hire-purchase* at **hire**. **~·ment** *n*

de·fer[2] /dɪ'fɜ(r)/ *vi* (-rr-) [VP3A] **~ to,** give way; yield (often to show respect): *to ~ to one's elders/to sb's opinions.*

def·er·ence /'defrəns/ *n* [U] giving way to the wishes, accepting the opinions or judgements, of another or others; respect: *to treat one's elders with ~; to show ~ to a judge.* ***in ~ to,*** out of respect for. **de·fer·en·tial** /'defə'renʃl/ *adj* showing ~. **de·fer·en·tially** /-ʃlɪ/ *adv*

de·fi·ance /dɪ'faɪəns/ *n* [U] open disobedience or resistance; refusal to recognize authority; defying. ***in ~ of,*** showing contempt or indifference of: *to act in ~ of orders,* do sth one has been ordered not to do. *He went swimming in the sea in ~ of the warning sign telling him not to.* ***bid ~ to,*** challenge, offer to fight. ***set sth at ~,*** treat with contempt; challenge: *If you set the law/public opinion at ~, you'll get into trouble.*

de·fi·ant /dɪ'faɪənt/ *adj* showing defiance; openly disobedient. **~·ly** *adv*

de·fi·ciency /dɪ'fɪʃnsɪ/ *n* (*pl* -**cies**) **1** [U] the state of being short of, less than, what is correct or needed; [C] instance of this: *suffering from a ~ of food; ~ diseases,* caused by a ~ of sth, e g vitamins, in diet. **2** [C] amount by which sth is short of what is correct or needed: *a ~ of £5.* **3** [C] sth imperfect: *Cosmetics do not always cover up the deficiencies of nature.*

de·fi·cient /dɪˈfɪʃnt/ *adj* not having enough of: *~ in courage; a mentally ~ person,* one who is weak-minded, mentally subnormal.

defi·cit /ˈdefəsɪt/ *n* [C] amount by which sth, esp a sum of money, is too small; amount by which payments exceed receipts. ⇨ **surplus.**

de·file[1] /dɪˈfaɪl/ *vt* [VP6A] make dirty or impure: *rivers ~d by waste from factories; to ~ one's mind by reading pornographic books.* **~·ment** *n* defiling or being ~d; pollution.

de·file[2] /ˈdifaɪl/ *n* narrow way, gorge, through mountains. □ *vi* (of troops) march in a single file or a narrow column.

de·fine /dɪˈfaɪn/ *vt* [VP6A] **1** state precisely the meaning of (e g words). **2** state or show clearly: *Please listen while I ~ your duties. The powers of a judge are ~d by law. When boundaries between countries are not clearly ~d, there is usually trouble. The mountain was clearly ~d against the eastern sky.* **de·fin·able** *adj* that can be ~d.

defi·nite /ˈdefnɪt/ *adj* clear; not doubtful or uncertain: *I want a ~ answer: 'Yes' or 'No'. I want an appointment for a ~ time and place.* **ˌ~ ˈarticle** *n* the word 'the'. **~·ly** /ˈdefnətlɪ/ *adv* **1** in a ~ manner. **2** (colloq, in answer to a question) yes, certainly.

defi·ni·tion /ˌdefəˈnɪʃn/ *n* **1** [U] defining; [C] statement that defines: *To give a ~ of a word is more difficult than to give an illustration of its uses.* **2** [U] clearness of outline; making or being distinct in outline; power of a lens (in a camera or telescope) to show clear outlines.

de·fini·tive /dɪˈfɪnətɪv/ *adj* final; to be looked upon as decisive and without the need for, or possibility of, change or addition: *a ~ offer/answer/edition of sb's poetry.*

de·flate /dɪˈfleɪt/ *vt* [VP6A] **1** make (a tyre, balloon, etc) smaller by letting out air or gas; (fig) lessen the conceit of: *~ a pompous politician.* **2** /ˈdiˈfleɪt/ take action to reduce the amount of money in circulation in order to lower or keep steady the prices of salable goods. **de·fla·tion** /dɪˈfleɪʃn *monetary:* ˈdiˈf-/ *n* [U] ⇨ **inflate. de·fla·tion·ary** /ˈdiˈfleɪʃnrɪ *US:* -nerɪ/ *adj* produced, designed or tending to produce deflation: *deflationary measures by the Chancellor.*

de·flect /dɪˈflekt/ *vt,vi* [VP6A,14,2A,3A] **~ *(from),*** (cause to) turn aside (from): *The bullet struck a wall and was ~ed from its course.* **de·flec·tion** /dɪˈflekʃn/ *n*

de·flower /dɪˈflaʊə(r)/ *vt* (liter or old use) deprive of virginity; ravage; spoil.

de·foli·ate /ˈdiˈfəʊlɪeɪt/ *vt* [VP6A] destroy the leaves of: *forests ~d by chemical means.* **de·foli·ation** /ˈdiˌfəʊlɪˈeɪʃn/ *n* **de·foli·ant** /ˈdiˈfəʊlɪənt/ *n* chemical used, e g by spraying, on vegetation to destroy the leaves.

de·for·est /ˈdɪˈforɪst *US:* -ˈfɔr-/ *vt* (esp US) = disafforest.

de·form /dɪˈfɔm/ *vt* [VP6A] spoil the form or appearance of; put out of shape. **de·formed** *part adj* (of the body, or a part of it; fig, of the mind) badly shaped; unnaturally shaped: *The boy has a ~ed foot and cannot play games.*

de·form·ity /dɪˈfɔmətɪ/ *n* [U] being deformed; [C] (*pl* **-ties**) deformed part (esp of the body).

de·fraud /dɪˈfrɔd/ *vt* [VP6A,14] **~ *(of),*** trick (sb) out of what is rightly his; get by fraud: *~ an author of his royalties by ignoring copyright.*

de·fray /dɪˈfreɪ/ *vt* [VP6A] supply the money needed for sth; pay (the cost or expenses of sth). **~al** /-ˈfreɪl/ *n* **~·ment** *n*

de·frock /ˈdiˈfrok/ *vt* = **unfrock.**

de·frost /ˈdiˈfrost *US:* -ˈfrɔst/ *vt* [VP6A] remove, get rid of, ice or frost (e g in a refrigerator, on the windscreen of a motor-car). **~er** *n*

deft /deft/ *adj* quick and clever (esp with the fingers). **~·ly** *adv* **~·ness** *n*

de·funct /dɪˈfʌŋkt/ *adj* (of persons) dead; (of things, e g laws) extinct: **the ~,** (legal) the dead person (who is being discussed).

de·fuse /ˈdiˈfjuz/ *vt* [VP6A] remove or render useless the fuse of, e g an unexploded bomb or shell.

defy /dɪˈfaɪ/ *vt* (*pt,pp* **-fied**) **1** [VP6A] resist openly; say that one is ready to fight. **2** [VP6A] refuse to obey or show respect to: *to ~ one's superiors. If you ~ the law, you may find yourself in prison.* **3** [VP6A] offer difficulties that cannot be overcome: *The problem defied solution,* could not be solved. *The door defied all attempts to open it.* **4** [VP17] ***~ sb to do sth,*** call on sb to do sth that one believes he cannot or will not do: *I ~ you to prove that I have cheated.* ⇨ **defiance.**

de·gauss /ˈdiˈgaʊs/ *vt* [VP6A] neutralize the magnetic field of, e g a T V screen.

de·gen·er·ate /dɪˈdʒenəreɪt/ *vi* [VP2A,3A] **~ *(into),*** pass from a state of goodness to a lower state by losing qualities which are considered normal and desirable: *Thrift is desirable, but do not let it ~ into avarice. He denied that the young men of today were degenerating,* e g that they were becoming less hard-working, less intelligent, less honest, than those of earlier times. □ *adj* /dɪˈdʒenərət/ having lost qualities (physical, moral or mental) that are considered normal and desirable: *He didn't let riches and luxury make him ~.* □ *n* ~ person or animal. **de·gen·er·acy** /dɪˈdʒenərəsɪ/ *n* [U] state or condition of being ~; process of degenerating. **de·gen·er·ation** /dɪˌdʒenəˈreɪʃn/ *n* [U] degenerating; the state of being ~d.

de·grade /dɪˈgreɪd/ *vt* [VP6A] **1** reduce in rank or status. **2** cause (sb) to be less moral or less deserving of respect: *to ~ oneself by cheating and telling lies.* **degra·da·tion** /ˌdegrəˈdeɪʃn/ *n* [U] degrading or being ~d: *a family living in degradation,* e g one that is content to live in slum conditions.

de·gree /dɪˈgri/ *n* **1** unit of measurement for angles: *an angle of ninety ~s,* (90°) a right angle; *a ~ of latitude,* about 69 miles. **2** unit of measurement for temperature: *Water freezes at 32 ~s Fahrenheit* (32°F) *or zero Centigrade* (0°C). **3** step or stage in a scale or process: *The boys show various ~s of skill in their use of carpentry tools. His work has reached a high ~ of excellence. He was not in the slightest ~ interested,* was completely uninterested. ***by ~s,*** step by step; gradually: *Their friendship by ~s grew into love.* ***to a ~,*** (colloq) = to the highest ~: *He is scrupulous to a ~.* ***to a high/the highest ~,*** intensively; exceedingly: *He is vain to a high ~.* ***to what ~,*** to what extent; how much: *To what ~ are you interested in botany?* ***first ~,*** stage of seriousness: *first ~ burns, first ~ murder.* ***third ~,*** severe and long examination (e g by the police) of an accused man to get information or a confession: *Are third-~ methods used in your country?* **4** position in society: persons of high ~. **5** academic title; rank or grade given by a university to one who has passed an examination: *studying for a ~; the ~ of Master of Arts* (M A). ⇨ **graduate, undergraduate. 6** (music) interval from one note to another on a stave. **7** (gram) one of the three forms of comparison of an *adj* or *adv*: *~s of comparison. 'Good', 'better' and 'best' are the positive, comparative and superlative ~s of 'good'. 'Rich', 'richer' and 'richest' are the positive, comparative and superlative ~s of 'rich'.*

de-horn /ˈdi ˋhɔn/ *vt* [VP6A] remove the horns from (cattle).

de·hu·man·ize /ˈdiˋhjumənɑɪz/ *vt* [VP6A] take away human qualities from.

de·hy·drate /ˈdiˋhɑɪdreɪt/ *vt* [VP6A] deprive (a substance) of water or moisture: *~d vegetables/eggs,* often in powdered form.

de-ice /ˈdi ˋɑɪs/ *vt* [VP6A] free, e g the surfaces of an aircraft, from ice.

de·ify /ˋdiɪfɑɪ/ *vt* (*pt,pp* **-fied**) [VP6A] make a god of; worship as a god. **de·ifi·ca·tion** /ˈdiɪfɪˋkeɪʃn/ *n* ~ing or being deified: *the deification of a Roman emperor.*

deign /deɪn/ *vi* [VP4A] ***~ to do sth,*** condescend; be kind or gracious enough to: *He passed by without ~ing to look at me.*

de·ism /ˋdi-ɪzm/ *n* belief in the existence of a Divine Being, but without acceptance of revelation or religious dogma. **de·ist** /ˋdiɪst/ *n* supporter of ~. ⇨ **theism.**

de·ity /ˋdeɪətɪ *US:* ˋdiətɪ/ *n* **1** [U] divine quality or nature; state of being a god or goddess. **2** [C] (*pl* **-ties**) god or goddess: *Roman deities,* e g Neptune, Minerva. **the D~,** God.

de·ject /dɪˋdʒekt/ *vt* (usu in *pp*) make sad or gloomy: *Why is she looking so ~ed,* in such low spirits? **de·ject·ed·ly** *adv* **de·jec·tion** /dɪˋdʒekʃn/ *n* [U] ~ed state; low spirits: *He left in ~.*

de jure /ˈdeɪ ˋdʒʊərɪ/ *adj, adv* (Lat) by right; according to law: *the ~ king; king ~.* ⇨ **de facto.**

dekko /ˋdekəʊ/ *n* (sl) ***have a ~,*** have a look (at sth).

de·lay /dɪˋleɪ/ *vt,vi* **1** [VP6A,2A] make or be slow or late: *The train was ~ed two hours. I was ~ed by the traffic; a ~ed-action bomb,* with a device causing it to explode after a pre-determined interval. *Don't ~.* **2** [VP6A,C] put off until later: *We must ~ our journey until the weather improves. Why have they ~ed opening the new school?* □ *n* **1** [U] ~ing or being ~ed: *We must leave without ~.* **2** [C] instance of this; time of being ~ed: *after several ~s; after a ~ of three hours.*

de·lec·table /dɪˋlektəbl/ *adj* (often ironical) delightful; pleasant.

de·lec·ta·tion /ˈdilekˋteɪʃn/ *n* [U] enjoyment; entertainment: *T V programmes suitable for the ~ of half-educated people.*

del·egacy /ˋdelɪgəsɪ/ *n* (*pl* **-cies**) system of delegating; body of delegates.

del·egate¹ /ˋdelɪgət/ *n* person to whom sth is delegated (e g an elected representative sent to a conference or convention). **del·ega·tion** /ˈdelɪˋgeɪʃn/ *n* **1** [U] delegating or being delegated. **2** [C] group of ~s.

del·egate² /ˋdelɪgeɪt/ *vt* [VP17,14] appoint and send (sb) as a representative to a meeting; entrust (duties, rights, etc *to* sb): *to ~ sb to perform a task; to ~ rights to a deputy.*

de·lete /dɪˋlit/ *vt* [VP6A] strike or take out (sth written or printed): *Several words had been ~d by the censor.* **de·le·tion** /dɪˋliʃn/ *n* [U] deleting; [C] sth deleted.

del·eteri·ous /ˈdelɪˋtɪərɪəs/ *adj* harmful (to mind or body).

delft /delft/, (also **delf** /delf/) *n* (also **ˋ~-ware**) [U] kind of glazed earthenware, usu with blue designs or decorations.

de·lib·er·ate¹ /dɪˋlɪbr̩ət/ *adj* **1** done on purpose; intentional: *a ~ lie/insult.* **2** slow and cautious (in action, speech, etc): *A statesman should be ~ in his speeches. He entered the room with ~ steps.* **~·ly** *adv*

de·lib·er·ate² /dɪˋlɪbəreɪt/ *vt,vi* [VP6A,8,10,2A,3A] consider, talk about, carefully: *We were deliberating what to do/how it might be done/whether to buy a new motor-car. They're still deliberating over/upon the question.*

de·lib·er·ation /dɪˈlɪbəˋreɪʃn/ *n* **1** [C,U] careful consideration and discussion; debate: *After long ~, they decided to send the boy to Oxford. What was the result of your ~(s)?* **2** [U] being deliberate(2); slowness of movement: *to speak/take aim/walk into a room with great ~.* **de·lib·er·ative** /dɪˋlɪbərətɪv *US:* -reɪtɪv/ *adj* for the purpose of ~(1): *a deliberative assembly.*

deli·cacy /ˋdelɪkəsɪ/ *n* (*pl* **-cies**) **1** [U] quality of being delicate (all senses): *Everyone admired the ~ of her features,* their fineness and tenderness. *Because of the ~ of her skin* (= because it is easily hurt by the sun), *she uses a sunshade. The girl's ~* (= the fact that she is delicate in health) *has always worried her parents. The political situation is one of great ~,* is very delicate, requires careful handling. *The violinist played with great ~,* with a very delicate touch. **2** [C] delicate(8) kind of food: *all the delicacies of the season.*

deli·cate /ˋdelɪkət/ *adj* **1** soft; tender; of fine or thin material: *as ~ as silk; the ~ skin of a young girl.* **2** fine; exquisite: *jewellery of ~ workmanship.* **3** easily injured; becoming ill easily; needing great care: *~ china/plants; a ~-looking child; in ~ health.* **4** requiring careful treatment or skilful handling: *a ~ surgical operation,* e g on sb's eyes. *The international situation is very ~ at present.* **5** (of colours) soft; not strong: *a ~ shade of pink.* **6** (of the senses, of instruments) able to appreciate or indicate very small changes or differences: *a ~ sense of smell/touch; the ~ instruments needed by scientists,* e g for weighing or measuring. **7** taking great care not to be immodest, not to hurt the feelings of others. **8** (of food, its flavour) pleasing to the taste and not strongly flavoured *Chicken is more ~ than beef. When people are ill they need ~ food. Some kinds of fish have a more ~ flavour than others.* **~·ly** *adv*

deli·ca·tessen /ˈdelɪkəˋtesn/ *n* [C,U] (shop selling) prepared foods ready for serving (esp cooked meat, smoked fish, pickles): *The ~ (shop) closes at 5.30.*

de·li·cious /dɪˋlɪʃəs/ *adj* giving delight (esp to the senses of taste and smell, and to the sense of humour): *a ~ cake. Doesn't it smell ~! What a ~ joke!* **~·ly** *adv*

de·light¹ /dɪˋlɑɪt/ *n* **1** [U] great pleasure; joy: *Concert parties gave great ~ to thousands of soldiers during the war. She looked a dream of ~. To his great ~ he passed the examination with first-class honours.* ***take ~ in,*** find pleasure in: *The naughty* *boy takes great ~ in pulling the cat's tail.* **2** [C] cause or source of great pleasure: *Dancing is her chief ~. He often thinks of the ~s of life in the country.* **~·ful** /-fl/ *adj* giving ~ (*to*): *a ~ful holiday.* **~·fully** /-flɪ/ *adv*

de·light[2] /dɪˋlɑɪt/ *vt,vi* **1** [VP6A] give great pleasure to; please greatly: *Her singing ~ed everyone.* **2** (passive): *be ~ed,* be greatly pleased: *I was ~ed to hear the news of your success/~ed at the news.../~ed that you were successful.* **3** [VP3A,4] **~ *in/to do sth,*** take or find great pleasure: *He ~s in teasing his young sister. He ~s to prove his brother wrong.*

de·limit /ˈdiˋlɪmɪt/, **de·limi·tate** /ˈdiˋlɪmɪteɪt/ *vt* [VP6A] determine the limits or boundaries of. **de·limi·ta·tion** /ˈdiˈlɪmɪˋteɪʃn/ *n* [C,U].

de·lin·eate /dɪˋlɪnɪeɪt/ *vt* [VP6A] show by drawing or by describing; portray. **de·lin·ea·tion** /dɪˈlɪnɪˋeɪʃn/ *n* [C,U].

de·lin·quency /dɪˋlɪŋkwənsɪ/ *n* **1** [U] wrongdoing; neglect of duty: *the problem of juvenile ~,* wrongdoing by young persons. **2** [C] (*pl* -cies) instance of this; misdeed.

de·lin·quent /dɪˋlɪŋkwənt/ *n, adj* (person) doing wrong, failing to perform a duty.

deli·quescent /ˈdelɪˋkwesnt/ *adj* (chem) becoming liquid in air (by absorbing moisture).

de·liri·ous /dɪˋlɪrɪəs/ *adj* **1** suffering from delirium; wildly excited: *The patient's temperature went up and he became ~. The children were ~ with joy.* **2** showing the effects of delirium: *~ speech.* **~·ly** *adv*

de·lirium /dɪˋlɪrɪəm/ *n* [U] violent mental disturbance, often accompanied by wild talk, esp during feverish illness; wild excitement. **ˈ~ ˋtremens** /ˋtremenz/ (usu **DT(S)** /ˈdi ˋti(z)/) *~ caused by extreme alcoholism.*

de·liver /dɪˋlɪvə(r)/ *vt* **1** [VP6A] take (letters, parcels, goods, etc) to houses, to the person(s) to whom they are addressed, to the buyer(s): *A postman is a man employed to ~ letters and parcels. Did you ~ my message to your father?* **2** [VP6A, 14] **~ *from,*** rescue, save, set free: *May God ~ us from all evil.* **3** [VP6A] give forth in words: *to ~ a sermon/a course of lectures; to ~ oneself of an opinion.* **4** (of a medical attendant, e g a midwife) help (a woman) in childbirth: *to be ~ed of a child,* give birth to one. **5** [VP6A,15B] **~ *up/over (to),*** surrender; give up; hand over: *to ~ up stolen goods; to ~ over one's property to one's son; to ~ (up) a fortress to the enemy.* **6** [VP6A] send against: (rhet) *to ~ a blow in the cause of freedom.* **~er** *n* one who ~s; rescuer; saviour.

de·liver·ance /dɪˋlɪvərns/ *n* **1** [U] **~ *from,*** delivering(2); rescue; being set free. **2** [C] formal or emphatic statement of opinion.

de·liv·ery /dɪˋlɪvrɪ/ *n* **1** [U] delivering (of letters, goods, etc); [C] (*pl* -ries) periodical performance of this: *We guarantee prompt ~ of goods. Freight charges are payable on ~,* when the goods are delivered. *How many deliveries are there in your town* (= How often does the postman deliver letters) *every day? Your letter came by the first ~. When can you take ~ of the new car we have obtained for you?* **ˋ~ note** *n* note, usu in duplicate, sent with goods, to be signed by the recipient. **ˋ~ truck** *n* (US) = (GB) goods van. **2** (*sing* only) manner of speaking (in lectures, etc): *His sermon was good, but his ~ was poor.*

dell /del/ *n* small valley, usu with trees on its sides.

de·louse /ˈdiˋlɑʊs/ *vt* rid (sb or sth) of lice or other vermin.

Del·phic /ˋdelfɪk/ *adj* of the oracle of Apollo /əˋpoləʊ/ at Delphi /ˋdelfɑɪ/ (in ancient Greece); obscure: ambiguous.

del·phin·ium /delˋfɪnɪəm/ *n* (kinds of) garden plant, usu with tall spikes of coloured flowers.

delta /ˋdeltə/ *n* Greek letter *d.* ⇨ App 4; land (alluvial deposits) in the shape of a capital ~ (Δ) at the mouth of a river between two or more branches: *the Nile D~; ˈ~-ˋwinged,* (of aircraft) having ~-shaped wings.

de·lude /dɪˋlud/ *vt* [VP6A,14] **~ *sb with sth/into doing sth,*** deceive; mislead (on purpose): *to ~ sb with promises one does not intend to keep; to ~ oneself with false hopes; to ~ sb/oneself into believing that....*

del·uge /ˋdeljudʒ/ *n* [C] **1** great flood; heavy rush of water; violent rainfall: *the D~,* the flood at the time of Noah ⇨ Gen 7. **2** anything coming in a heavy rush: *a ~ of words/questions/protests.* □ *vt* [VP6A,14] flood; come down on (sb or sth) like a ~: *He was ~d with questions.*

de·lusion /dɪˋluʒn/ *n* [U] deluding or being deluded: [C] false opinion or belief, esp one that may be a symptom of madness: *to be under a ~/under the ~ that...; to suffer from ~s.*

de·lus·ive /dɪˋlusɪv/ *adj* not real; deceptive. **~·ly** *adv*

de luxe /dɪ ˋlʌks/ *adj* (F) of very high quality, high standards of comfort, etc: *a ~ edition of a book.*

delve /delv/ *vt,vi* **1** [VP6A,2A] (old use) dig. **2** [VP3A] **~ *into,*** make researches into, e g old manuscripts: *~ for information into old books; to ~ into sb's past.*

de·mag·net·ize /ˈdiˋmægnɪtɑɪz/ *vt* [VP6A] deprive of magnetic properties. **de·mag·net·iz·ation** /ˈdiˈmægnɪtɑɪˋzeɪʃn *US:* -tɪˋz-/ *n*

dema·gogue /ˋdeməgog *US:* -gɔg/ *n* political leader who tries, by speeches appealing to the feelings instead of to reason, to stir up the people. **dema·gogy** /ˋdeməgodʒɪ/ *n* [U] principles and practices of a ~. **dema·gogic** /ˈdeməˋgodʒɪk/ *adj* of or like a ~.

de·mand[1] /dɪˋmɑnd *US:* -ˋmænd/ *n* **1** [C] **~ *(for),*** act of demanding(1); sth demanded(1): *The workers' ~s* (e g for higher pay) *were refused by the employers. It is impossible to satisfy all ~s. I have/People make many ~s on my time,* I am expected to do many things, etc. *There have been ~s for the prime minister to resign/for his resignation/that he should resign.* ***on ~,*** when demanded: *a cheque payable on ~.* **ˋ~ (note),** note that demands payment, e g of income tax. **2** [U] (or with an *indef art* and *adj*) desire, by people ready to buy, employ, etc (*for* goods, services, etc): *There is a great ~ for typists but a poor ~/not much ~ for clerks. There is little ~ for these goods. Our goods are in great ~. The ~ for fish this month exceeds the supply.*

de·mand[2] /dɪˋmɑnd *US:* -ˋmænd/ *vt* **1** [VP6A, 7A,9] ask for (sth) as if ordering, or as if one has a right to: *~ an apology from sb. The gatekeeper ~ed my business,* asked what I wanted. *The policeman ~ed his name and address/~ed to know where he lived. He came to my house and ~ed help/~ed that I should help him. He ~s that I shall tell him everything/~s to be told everything.* **2** [VP6A] need; require: *This sort of work ~s great patience. Does the letter ~ an im-*

mediate answer, Must it be answered at once?

de·mar·cate /ˋdimɑkeɪt/ *vt* [VP6A] mark or fix the limits of, e g a frontier.

de·mar·ca·tion /ˈdimɑˋkeɪʃn/ *n* [U] marking of a boundary or limit; separation: *a line of* ~*;* ~ *problems in industry,* e g settling the kind of work to be done by workers in different trades.

dé·marche /ˋdeɪmɑʃ/ *n* (F) political step or proceeding; diplomatic representation (to a foreign government).

de·mean /dɪˋmin/ *vt* [VP6A] ~ ***oneself,*** lower oneself in dignity, social esteem. **~·our** (US **-or**) /dɪˋminə(r)/ *n* [U] way of behaving: *I dislike his supercilious* ~*our.*

de·mented /dɪˋmentɪd/ *adj* mad; (colloq) wild with worry: *a poor,* ~ *creature. She'll become* ~ *if you don't stop asking silly questions.* **~·ly** *adv*

deme·rara /ˈdeməˋreərə/ *n* [U] ˋ~ **sugar,** A light brown raw cane sugar (from Guyana).

de·merit /ˈdiˋmerɪt/ *n* [C] fault; defect.

de·mesne /dɪˋmeɪn/ *n* [U] (legal) the holding of land as one's own property: *land held in* ~; [C] landed estate held in this way, not let to tenants.

demi·god /ˋdemɪgod/ *n* one who is partly divine and partly human; (in Gk myth, etc) the son of a god and a mortal woman, e g *Hercules.*

demi·john /ˋdemɪdʒon/ *n* large narrow-necked bottle, usu encased in wicker-work.

de·mili·tar·ized /ˈdiˋmɪlɪtərɑɪzd/ *part adj* (of a country, or part of it) required, by treaty or agreement, to have no military forces or installation in it.

demi·monde /ˈdemɪˋmɔ̃d *US:* -ˋmɔ̃d/ *n* (*sing* with the *def art*) (class of society made up of) women on the fringe of respectable society, often women maintained by rich men as mistresses. **demi·mon·daine** /ˈdemɪˈmɔ̃ˋdeɪn *US:* -ˈmɔ̃ˋd-/ *n* woman of this class.

de·mise /dɪˋmɑɪz/ *n* (legal) death.

de·mist /ˈdiˋmɪst/ *vt* remove the mist from, e g the windscreen of a motor vehicle. **~er** *n*

demo /ˋdeməʊ/ *n* [C] (colloq abbr for) demonstration(2).

de·mob /dɪˋmob/ *vt* (-bb-) and *n* (GB colloq abbr for) demobilize and demobilization: *When do you get* ~*bed/your* ~*?*

de·mo·bil·ize /dɪˋməʊbl̩ɑɪz/ *vt* [VP6A] release from military service. **de·mo·bil·iz·ation** /dɪˈməʊbl̩ɑɪˋzeɪʃn *US:* -l̩ɪˋz-/ *n*

democ·racy /dɪˋmokrəsɪ/ *n* (*pl* **-cies**) **1** [C,U] (country with principles of) government in which all adult citizens share through their elected representatives. **2** [C,U] (country with) government which encourages and allows rights of citizenship such as freedom of speech, religion, opinion and association, the assertion of the rule of law, majority rule, accompanied by respect for the rights of minorities. **3** [C,U] (society in which there is) treatment of each other by citizens as equals and absence of class feeling: *Is there more* ~ *in Australia than in Great Britain?*

demo·crat /ˋdeməkræt/ *n* **1** person who favours or supports democracy. **2 D~,** (US) member of the Democratic Party.

demo·cratic /ˈdeməˋkrætɪk/ *adj* **1** of, like, supporting, democracy(**1,2**). **2** (esp) of, supporting, democracy(**3**); paying no or little attention to class divisions based on birth or wealth. **3 the ˋD~ Party,** (US) one of the two main political parties. ⇨ Republican. **demo·crati·cally** /-klɪ/ *adv*

de·moc·ra·tize /dɪˋmokrətɑɪz/ *vt* [VP6A] make democratic. **de·moc·ra·tiz·ation** /dɪˈmokrətɑɪˋzeɪʃn/ *US:* -tɪˋz-/ *n*

dé·modé /ˈdeɪˋməʊdeɪ *US:* ˈdeɪməʊˋdeɪ/ *adj* (F) outmoded; out of fashion.

de·mogra·phy /dɪˋmogrəfɪ/ *n* [U] (study of) statistics of births, deaths, diseases, etc to show the condition of a community. **demo·graphic** /ˈdeməˋgræfɪk/ *adj*

de·mol·ish /dɪˋmolɪʃ/ *vt* [VP6A] pull or tear down, e g old buildings; destroy, e g sb's argument; make an end of. **demo·li·tion** /ˈdeməˋlɪʃn/ *n* [U] ~ing or being ~ed; [C] instance of this.

de·mon, dae·mon /ˋdimən/ *n* evil, wicked or cruel supernatural being or spirit; (colloq) fierce or energetic person: *a* ~ *bowler,* (cricket) very fast bowler. *He's a* ~ *for work,* (colloq) works with great energy.

de·monet·ize /ˈdiˋmonɪtɑɪz/ *vt* deprive (a metal) of its value as currency; withdraw (a metal) from use as currency. **de·monet·iz·ation** /ˈdiˈmonɪtɑɪˋzeɪʃn *US:* -tɪˋz-/ *n*

de·moni·acal /ˈdeməˋnɑɪəkl/ *adj* devilish; frenzied; fiercely energetic. **~·ly** /-klɪ/ *adv*

de·mon·strable /dɪˋmonstrəbl/ *adj* that can be logically proved. **de·mon·strably** /-blɪ/ *adv* **de·mon·stra·bil·ity** /dɪˈmonstrəˋbɪlətɪ/ *n*

dem·on·strate /ˋdemənstreɪt/ *vt,vi* **1** [VP6A,9] show clearly by giving proof(s) or example(s): *How would you* ~ *that the world is round? The salesman* ~*d the new washing-machine,* showed how it was used. **2** [VP2A,3A] take part in a demonstration(**2**): *The workers marched through the streets with flags and banners to* ~ *against the rising cost of living.*

dem·on·stra·tion /ˈdemənˋstreɪʃn/ *n* [C,U] **1** demonstrating(**1**): *to teach sth by* ~*; a* ~ *of affection,* e g when a child puts its arms round its mother's neck; *a* ~ *of a new car.* **2** public display of feeling by a group, e g of workers, students: *a* ~ *that ended in violence.*

de·mon·stra·tive /dɪˋmonstrətɪv/ *adj* **1** (of persons) showing the feelings: *Some children are more* ~ *than others,* readier to show affection, etc. **2** marked by open expression of feelings: ~ *behaviour.* **3** serving to point out; esp (gram) ˈ~ ˋ**pronoun,** (*this, these, that, those*). **~·ly** *adv*

dem·on·stra·tor /ˋdemənstreɪtə(r)/ *n* **1** person who demonstrates(**2**): *The* ~*s were dispersed by the police.* **2** person who teaches or explains by demonstrating(**1**).

de·moral·ize /dɪˋmorl̩ɑɪz *US:* -ˋmɔr-/ *vt* [VP6A] **1** hurt or weaken the morals of: *a boy who was* ~*d by bad companions; drugs that have a demoralizing effect.* **2** weaken the courage, confidence, self-discipline, etc of, e g an army. ⇨ morale. **de·moral·iz·ation** /dɪˈmorl̩ɑɪˋzeɪʃn *US:* -l̩ɪˋz-/ *n*

de·mote /ˈdiˋməʊt/ *vt* [VP6A] reduce to a lower rank or grade. **de·motion** /ˈdiˋməʊʃn/ *n*

de·motic /dɪˋmotɪk/ *adj* of, used by, the common people: ~ *Greek,* the colloquial form of modern Greek.

de·mur /dɪˋmɜ(r)/ *vi* (-rr-) [VP2A,3A] ~ ***(at/to),*** (formal) raise an objection: *to* ~ *to a demand; to* ~ *at working on Sundays.* □ *n* hesitation or objection: (chiefly in) *without* ~.

de·mure /dɪˋmjʊə(r)/ *adj* quiet and serious: *a* ~ *young lady;* pretending to be, suggesting that one is, ~: *She gave him a* ~ *smile.* **~·ly** *adv* **~·ness** *n*

den /den/ *n* **1** animal's hidden lying-place, e g a cave. **2** secret resort: *an opium den; a den of thieves.* **3** (colloq) room in which a person works and studies without being disturbed.

den·ary /ˈdinərɪ/ *adv* decimal.

de·nation·al·ize /ˈdiˈnæʃnḷɑɪz/ *vt* [VP6A] transfer (a nationalized industry, etc) to private ownership again. **de·nation·al·iz·ation** /ˈdiˈnæʃnḷɑrˈzeɪʃn *US:* -ḷɪˈz-/ *n*

de·na·tured /ˈdiˈneɪtʃəd/ *adj* that has been made unfit for eating and drinking (but may still be used for other purposes): *~ alcohol;* having lost natural qualities: *~ rubber,* no longer elastic.

de·ni·able /dɪˈnɑɪəbl/ *adj* that one can deny.

de·nial /dɪˈnɑɪḷ/ *n* ~ **of, 1** [U] denying; refusing a request; [C] instance of this: *the ~ of justice/a request for help.* **2** [C] statement that sth is not true: *the prisoner's repeated ~s of the charge brought against him.* ⇨ *self-~* at self-.

den·ier /ˈdenɪə(r)/ *n* unit of fineness for rayon, nylon and silk yarns: *30 ~ stockings.*

deni·grate /ˈdenɪgreɪt/ *vt* [VP6A] defame. **deni·gra·tion** /ˈdenɪˈgreɪʃn/ *n*

denim /ˈdenɪm/ *n* **1** [U] twilled cotton cloth (used for jeans, overalls, etc). **2** (*pl*) (colloq) jeans made from ~.

deni·zen /ˈdenɪzn/ *n* person, kind of animal or plant, living or growing permanently in the district, etc mentioned: *~s of the Arctic.*

de·nomi·nate /dɪˈnomɪneɪt/ *vt* [VP23] give a name to; call.

de·nomi·na·tion /dɪˈnomɪˈneɪʃn/ *n* [C] **1** name, esp one given to a class or religious group or sect: *The Protestant ~s include the Methodists, Presbyterians and Baptists.* **2** class or unit (in weight, length, numbers, money, etc): *The US coin of the lowest ~ is the cent. We can reduce fractions to the same ~,* e g $\frac{1}{2}$, $\frac{3}{16}$, $\frac{5}{8}$ = $\frac{8}{16}$, $\frac{6}{16}$ and $\frac{10}{16}$. **~al** /-ˈneɪʃnl/ *adj* of ~s(1): *~al schools.*

de·nomi·na·tor /dɪˈnomɪneɪtə(r)/ *n* number or quantity below the line in a fraction, e g 4 in $\frac{3}{4}$.

de·note /dɪˈnəʊt/ *vt* **1** [VP6A] be the sign or symbol of; be the name of: *In algebra the sign* x *usually ~s an unknown quantity.* **2** [VP6A,9] indicate: *The mark* (‸) *~s a place of omission/~s that something has been omitted.*

dé·noue·ment /ˈdeɪˈnumõ *US:* ˈdeɪnuˈmõ/ *n* final stage, where everything is made clear, in the development of the plot of a story, play, etc.

de·nounce /dɪˈnaʊns/ *vt* **1** [VP6A,16B] speak publicly against; give information against: *to ~ a heresy; to ~ sb as a spy.* **2** [VP6A] give notice that one intends to end (a treaty or agreement).

dense /dens/ *adj* **1** (of liquids, vapour) not easily seen through: *a ~ fog; ~ smoke.* **2** (of people and things) crowded together in great numbers: *a ~ crowd; a ~ forest.* **3** stupid; having a mind that ideas can penetrate only with difficulty. **~·ly** *adv*: *a ~ly populated country; ~ly wooded,* covered with trees growing close together. **~·ness** *n*

den·sity /ˈdensətɪ/ *n* **1** [U] the quality of being dense: *the ~ of a forest* (*the fog, the population*). **2** [C,U] (*pl* -ties) (phys) relation of weight to volume.

dent /dent/ *n* hollow, depression, in a hard surface made by a blow or by pressure; (fig, colloq): *a ~ in one's pride.* □ *vt,vi* **1** [VP6A] make a ~ or ~s in: *a motor-car badly ~ed in a collision.* **2** [VP2A] get ~s in: *metal that ~s easily.*

den·tal /ˈdentl/ *adj* **1** of or for the teeth: *a ~ plate, a denture; a ~ surgeon.* **2** (phon) with the tip of the tongue near or touching the upper front teeth: *~ sounds,* e g θ, ð.

den·ti·frice /ˈdentɪfrɪs/ *n* [U] tooth-powder or toothpaste (the usu word).

den·tist /ˈdentɪst/ *n* person whose work is filling, cleaning, taking out teeth and fitting artificial teeth. **~ry** /ˈdentɪstrɪ/ *n* [U] work of a ~.

den·ture /ˈdentʃə(r)/ *n* [C] plate (fitted on the gums) of artificial teeth.

de·nude /dɪˈnjud *US:* -ˈnud/ *vt* [VP6A,14] ~ **of, 1** make bare; take away covering: *trees ~d of leaves; hillsides ~d of trees.* **2** deprive: *~d by his creditors of every penny he had.* **de·nud·ation** /ˈdinjuˈdeɪʃn *US:* -nu-/ *n*

de·nunci·ation /dɪˈnʌnsɪˈeɪʃn/ *n* [C,U] denouncing: *the ~ of a traitor.*

deny /dɪˈnɑɪ/ *vt* (*pt,pp* -nied) **1** [VP6A,C,7,9,25] say that (sth) is not true: *The accused man denied the charge. I ~ that the statement is true. He denied this to be the case. He denied knowing anything about/denied any knowledge of their plans. It cannot be denied that.../There is no ~ing the fact that...,* Everyone must admit that.... **2** [VP6A] say that one knows nothing about; disown; refuse to acknowledge: *He denied the signature,* said that it was not his. *Peter denied Christ.* **3** [VP12A,13A] say 'no' to a request; refuse to give (sth asked for or needed): *He denies himself/his wife nothing. He gave to his friends what he denied to his family. She was angry at being denied admittance.*

deo·dar /ˈdɪədɑ(r)/ *n* Himalayan cedar.

de·odor·ize /ˈdiˈəʊdərɑɪz/ *vt* [VP6A] remove odour (esp bad smells) from. **de·odor·ant** /ˈdiˈəʊdərənt/ *n* substance that disguises or absorbs (esp body) odours.

de·part /dɪˈpɑt/ *vi* **1** [VP2A,3A] ~ ***from,*** go away; leave (esp in time-tables, as *dep* (= abbr for ~) *Leeds, 4.30p m*). **2** [VP3A] ~ ***from,*** behave in a way that differs from: *~ from routine/the usual procedure/old customs; ~ from the truth.* **3** [VP6A] ~ ***(from),*** (old use): *~ (from) this life,* die. **~ed** *part adj* byegone: *thinking of ~ed glories.* □ *n* **the ~ed,** (*sing*) person who has recently died; (*pl*) those who have died: *pray for the souls of the ~ed.*

de·part·ment /dɪˈpɑtmənt/ *n* **1** one of several divisions of a government, business, shop, university, etc: *the Education D~/D~ of Education; the shipping ~* (= of a business firm); *the men's clothing ~* (= in a large shop); *a ˈ~ store,* a large shop where many kinds of goods are sold in different ~s. **2** (F) administrative district. **~al** /ˈdipɑtˈmentl/ *adj* of a ~ (contrasted with the whole): *~al duties/administration.*

de·par·ture /dɪˈpɑtʃə(r)/ *n* **1** [U] departing; going away (*from*); [C] instance of this: *His ~ was unexpected. There are notices showing arrivals and ~s of trains near the booking-office. Which is the ~ platform,* that from which the train leaves? **2** [C,U] turning away or aside; changing: *a ~ from old custom; a new ~ in physics,* e g the discovery of nuclear fission.

de·pend /dɪˈpend/ *vi* [VP3A] ~ ***on/upon,*** **1** (not in the progressive tenses) need, rely on (the support, etc of) in order to exist or to be true or to succeed: *Children ~ on their parents for food and clothing. Good health ~s upon good food, exercise and getting enough sleep. He ~s on his pen* *for a living*, makes a living by writing. ***That ~s, It all ~s***, the result ~s on sth else; (colloq, with *prep* omitted): *It all ~s how you tackle the problem. It ~s whether....* **2** trust; be certain about: *You can always ~ upon John to be there when he is needed. You may ~ upon his coming/~ upon it that he will want to come. Can I ~ upon this railway guide or is it an old one?* ***~ upon it***, (at the beginning or end of a sentence) you can be quite certain: *The strike will ruin the country, ~ upon it.* **~·able** *adj* that may be ~ed upon.

de·pend·ant (also **-ent**) /dɪˋpendənt/ *n* sb who depends upon another or others for a home, food, etc; servant. ⇨ dependent *adv.*

de·pend·ence /dɪˋpendəns/ *n* ***~ on/upon***, [U] **1** the state of depending; being supported by others: *Why don't you find a job and end this ~ upon your parents?* **2** confident trust; reliance: *He's not a man you can put much ~ on*, you can't rely on him. **3** the state of being determined or conditioned by: *the ~ of the crops upon the weather; drug ~.*

de·pend·ency /dɪˋpendənsɪ/ *n* (*pl* **-cies**) country governed or controlled by another: *The Hawaiian Islands are no longer a ~ of the USA.*

de·pend·ent /dɪˋpendənt/ *n* = dependant. □ *adj* ***~ (up)on***, depending: *The man was out of work and ~ upon his son's earnings. Promotion is ~ upon your record of success.*

de·pict /dɪˋpɪkt/ *vt* [VP6A] show in the form of a picture; describe in words: *biblical scenes ~ed in tapestry.* **de·pic·tion** /dɪˋpɪkʃn/ *n*

de·pila·tory /dɪˋpɪlətrɪ *US:* -tɔrɪ/ *adj, n* (liquid, cream, etc) able to remove superfluous hair.

de·plane /ˈdiˋpleɪn/ *vi* (usu of troops, etc) disembark from an aircraft.

de·plete /dɪˋplit/ *vt* [VP6A] use up, empty until little or none remains: *to ~ a lake of fish; ~d supplies.* **de·pletion** /dɪˋpliʃn/ *n* depleting or being ~d.

de·plore /dɪˋplɔ(r)/ *vt* [VP6A] show, say, that one is filled with sorrow or regret for. **de·plor·able** /dɪˋplɔrəbl/ *adj* that is, or should be, ~d: *deplorable conduct; a deplorable accident.* **de·plor·ably** /-əblɪ/ *adv: deplorably ignorant children.*

de·ploy /dɪˋplɔɪ/ *vt,vi* [VP6A,2A] (mil of troops; also of warships) (cause to) spread out, e g into line of battle. **~·ment** *n*

de·pon·ent /dɪˋpəʊnənt/ *n* person who gives written testimony for use in a law court.

de·popu·late /ˈdiˋpopjʊleɪt/ *vt* [VP6A] lessen the number of people living in a place: *a country ~d by war/famine.* **de·popu·la·tion** /ˈdiˈpopjʊˋleɪʃn/ *n*

de·port[1] /dɪˋpɔt/ *vt* [VP6A] expel (an unwanted person) from a country: *The spy was imprisoned for two years and then ~ed.* **de·port·ation** /ˈdipɔˋteɪʃn/ *n* **~ing or being ~ed**: *Years ago criminals in England could be sentenced to ~ation to Australia.* **~ee** /ˈdipɔˋti/ *n* ~ed person.

de·port[2] /dɪˋpɔt/ *vt* [VP6A,16B] (*reflex*) behave: *to ~ oneself with dignity.* **~·ment** *n* [U] behaviour; way of holding oneself in standing and walking: *Young ladies used to have lessons in ~ment.*

de·pose /dɪˋpəʊz/ *vt,vi* **1** [VP6A] remove, esp a ruler such as a king, from a position of authority; dethrone. **2** [VP3A,9] ***~ to/that***, bear witness, give evidence, esp on oath in a law court: *to ~ that one saw...; to ~ to having seen....* ⇨ deposition.

de·posit[1] /dɪˋpozɪt/ *n* [C] **1** money that is deposited(2,3): *The shopkeeper promised to keep the goods for me if I left/paid/made a ~.* **money on ~**, money deposited in this way. **ˋ~ account**, money deposited in a bank, not to be withdrawn without notice, on which interest is payable. ⇨ *current account* at current[1](3). **ˋ~ safe**, safe in the strong-room of a bank, rented for the custody of valuables. **2** layer of matter deposited(4): *A thick ~ of mud covered the fields after the floods went down.* **3** layer of solid matter left behind (often buried in the earth) after having been naturally accumulated: *Valuable new ~s of tin have been found in Bolivia.*

de·posit[2] /dɪˋpozɪt/ *vt* [VP6A] **1** lay or put down: *He ~ed the books on the desk. Some insects ~ their eggs in the ground.* **2** put or store for safe-keeping: *to ~ money in a bank/papers with one's lawyer.* **3** make part payment of money that is or will be owed: *We should like you to ~ a quarter of the price of the house.* **4** (esp of a liquid, a river) leave (a layer of matter on): *When the Nile rises it ~s a layer of mud on the land.*

de·posi·tion /ˈdepəˋzɪʃn/ *n* **1** [U] deposing from office; dethronement. **2** [C] statement made on oath. **3** [U] depositing, e g of mud.

de·posi·tor /dɪˋpozɪtə(r)/ *n* person who deposits, e g money in a bank.

de·posi·tory /dɪˋposɪtrɪ *US:* -tɔrɪ/ *n* (*pl* **-ries**) place where goods are deposited; storehouse.

de·pot /ˋdepəʊ *US:* ˋdipəʊ/ *n* **1** storehouse, esp for military supplies; warehouse. **2** (US) railroad or bus station.

de·prave /dɪˋpreɪv/ *vt* [VP6A] make morally bad; corrupt (usu in *pp*): *~d persons; ~d* (= vicious or perverted) *tastes.*

de·prav·ity /dɪˋprævətɪ/ *n* [U] depraved state; viciousness: *sunk in ~;* [C] (*pl* **-ties**) vicious act.

dep·recate /ˋdeprəkeɪt/ *vt* [VP6A,C] (formal) feel and express disapproval of: *Hasty action is to be ~d. He ~s changing the rules at present.* **dep·reca·tion** /ˈdeprəˋkeɪʃn/ *n*

de·pre·ci·ate /dɪˋpriʃɪeɪt/ *vt,vi* [VP6A,2A] make or become less in value; say that (sth) has little value: *Shares in this company have ~d. Don't ~ my efforts to help.* **de·precia·tory** /dɪˋpriʃətərɪ *US:* -tɔrɪ/ *adj* tending to ~: *depreciatory remarks about my work.* **de·preci·ation** /dɪˈpriʃɪˋeɪʃn/ *n* [U] lessening of value or estimation.

dep·reda·tion /ˈdeprəˋdeɪʃn/ *n* (usu *pl*) (formal) destruction or pillaging of property.

de·press /dɪˋpres/ *vt* [VP6A] **1** press, push or pull down: *to ~ a lever/the keys of a piano.* **ˈ~ed ˋclasses**, classes of people who are prevented from rising, or unable to rise, socially or economically, e g by a rigid caste system. **2** make sad, low in spirits: *Wet weather always ~es her. The newspapers are full of ~ing news nowadays*, e g of war, crime, natural disasters, rising prices. **3** make less active; cause (prices) to be lower: *When business is ~ed there is usually an increase in unemployment.* **ˈ~ed ˋarea**, part of a country where industry is ~ed (with consequent poverty and unemployment).

de·pression /dɪˋpreʃn/ *n* **1** [U] being depressed(2); low spirits: *He commited suicide during a fit of ~.* **2** [C] hollow, sunk place, in the surface of sth, esp the ground: *It rained heavily and every ~ in the bad road was soon filled with water. The soldiers hid from the enemy in a slight ~.* **3** [C] time when business is depressed(3). **4** [C] lowering of atmospheric pressure: (esp) area of low barometric pressure: the system of winds round it: *a ~ over Iceland.*

de·prive /dɪˋpraɪv/ *vt* [VP14] **~ *sb/sth of sth,*** take away from; prevent from using or enjoying: *trees that ~ a house of light. What would a student do if he were ~d of his books?* **de·prived** *adj* = underprivileged. **depri·va·tion** /ˌdeprɪˋveɪʃn/ *n* [U] depriving or being ~d; [C] sth of which one is ~d: *deprivation of one's rights as a citizen.*

depth /depθ/ *n* **1** [C,U] being deep; distance from the top down, from the front to the back, from the surface inwards: *What is the ~ of the well? Water was found at a ~ of 30 feet. At what ~ is the wreck lying? The snow is three feet in ~.* ***in ~,*** thorough(ly): *explore a subject in ~; a study in ~.* ***be/go/get out of one's ~,*** **(a)** be in/enter water too deep to stand in: *If you can't swim, don't go out of your ~.* **(b)** (fig) attempt the study of sth that is too difficult: *When people start talking about nuclear physics I'm out of my ~.* **ˋ~-bomb/-charge,** bomb used against a submarine, for explosion under water. **2** deep learning, thought, feeling, etc: *a book that shows scholarship and ~ of thought. She showed a ~ of feeling that surprised us.* **3** (with *def art;* often *pl*) deepest or most central part(s): *in the ~ of one's heart; in the ~ of winter; in the ~s of despair; in the ~ of the country,* a long way from any town.

depu·ta·tion /ˌdepjʊˋteɪʃn/ *n* group of representatives; number of persons given the right to act or speak for others.

de·pute /dɪˋpjut/ *vt* [VP14,17] **~ *sth to sb/sb to do sth,*** give (one's work, authority, etc) to a substitute; give (another person) authority to act as one's representative.

depu·tize /ˋdepjʊtaɪz/ *vi* [VP2A,3A] **~ *(for sb),*** act as deputy.

deputy /ˋdepjʊtɪ/ *n* (*pl* **-ties**) **1** person to whom work, authority, etc is deputed: *I must find someone to act as (a) ~ for me during my absence.* **2** (in some countries, e g France) member of a legislative assembly.

de·rail /dɪˋreɪl/ *vt* [VP6A] cause (a train, etc) to run off the rails: (usu passive) *The engine was ~ed.* **~·ment** *n*

de·range /dɪˋreɪndʒ/ *vt* [VP6A] put out of working order; put into confusion; disturb: *He is mentally ~d,* insane. **~·ment** *n*

de·rate /ˌdiˋreɪt/ *vt* [VP6A] (GB) relieve (industries, etc) from a proportion of the local rates(**2**): *the Derating Act, 1929.*

Derby /ˋdɑbɪ *US:* ˋdɜbɪ/ *n* **1** annual horserace at Epsom, England: *ˋD~ Day,* day of the race (in June). **2** *a local ~,* sporting contest between local teams.

derby /ˋdɜbɪ/ *n* (US name for a) bowler (hat).

der·el·ict /ˋderəlɪkt/ *adj* abandoned; deserted and left to fall into ruin: *a ~ house; a ~ ship; ~ areas,* e g those made squalid by open-cast mining, gravel digging. **der·el·ic·tion** /ˌderəˋlɪkʃn/ *n* **1** making ~: *the dereliction caused by the armies of Genghis Khan.* **2** (wilful) neglect of duty.

de·requi·si·tion /ˌdiˌrekwɪˋzɪʃn/ *vt* [VP6A] free (requisitioned property, etc).

de·re·strict /ˌdirɪˋstrɪkt/ *vt* [VP6A] cancel a restriction upon: *~ a road,* remove a speed limit from it.

de·ride /dɪˋraɪd/ *vt* [VP6A,16B] mock; laugh scornfully at: *They ~d his efforts as childish.*

de rigeur /ˌdə rɪˋgɜ(r)/ *pred adj* (F) required by etiquette or custom: *Evening dress is ~ at the Casino.*

de·ri·sion /dɪˋrɪʒn/ *n* [U] deriding or being derided; sth that is derided: *hold sb/sth in ~; be/become an object of ~; make sb/sth an object of ~.*

de·ris·ive /dɪˋraɪsɪv/ *adj* showing or deserving derision: *~ laughter; a ~ offer,* e g £50 for a car that is worth £250.

de·ris·ory /dɪˋraɪsərɪ/ *adj* = derisive.

deri·va·tion /ˌderɪˋveɪʃn/ *n* **1** [U] deriving or being derived; origin; descent: *the ~ of words from Latin; a word of Latin ~.* **2** [C] first form and meaning of a word; statement of how a word was formed and how it changed: *to study the ~s of words.*

de·riva·tive /dɪˋrɪvətɪv/ *adj, n* [C] (thing, word, substance) derived from another; not original or primitive: *'Assertion' is a ~ of 'assert'.*

de·rive /dɪˋraɪv/ *vt,vi* **1** [VP14] **~ *sth from sth,*** get: *to ~ great pleasure from one's studies; medicine from which she has ~d little benefit.* **2** [VP14,3A] **~ *from,*** *have as a starting-point, source or origin: Thousands of English words are ~d from/~ from Latin.*

der·ma·tol·ogy /ˌdɜməˋtɒlədʒɪ/ *n* [U] medical study of the skin, its diseases, etc. **der·ma·tol·ogist** /ˌdɜməˋtɒlədʒɪst/ *n* expert in ~.

dero·gate /ˋderəgeɪt/ *vi* [VP3A] **~ *from,*** (formal) take away (a merit, good quality, right). **dero·ga·tion** /ˌderəˋgeɪʃn/ *n* [U] lessening (*of* authority, dignity, reputation, etc).

de·roga·tory /dɪˋrɒgətrɪ *US:* -tɔrɪ/ *adj* tending to damage or take away from (one's credit, etc): *remarks that are ~ to my reputation. Is the slang word 'cop' as ~ as 'pig' for 'policeman',* Are policemen likely to object to it as being insulting?

der·rick /ˋderɪk/ *n* **1** large crane for moving or lifting heavy weights, esp on a ship. **2** framework over an oil-well or bore-hole, to hold the drilling machinery, etc.

derrick cranes

an oil derrick

der·ring-do /ˌderɪŋ ˋdu/ *n* [U] (old use) desperate courage: *deeds of ~.*

derv /dɜv/ *n* [U] fuel oil for diesel engines (from *D*iesel *E*ngined *R*oad *V*ehicle).

der·vish /ˋdɜvɪʃ/ *n* member of an order of Muslim religious enthusiasts: *dancing ~es,* who engage in whirling dances; *howling ~es,* who shout loudly.

de·sali·nate /ˌdiˋsælɪneɪt/ *vt* [VP6A] = desalinize. **de·sali·na·tion** /ˌdiˌsælɪˋneɪʃn/ *n*

de·sali·nize /ˌdiˋsælɪnaɪz/ *vt* [VP6A] remove salt from (sea water or saline water). **de·salin·iz·ation** /ˌdiˌsælɪnaɪˋzeɪʃn *US:* -nɪˋz-/ *n*

de·salt /ˈdiˋsɔlt/ *vt* = desalinize.

de·scale /ˈdiˋskeɪl/ *vt* [VP6A] remove the scale[1](3) from, e g the inside of boiler tubes.

des·cant /ˋdeskænt/ *n* (music) additional independent accompaniment (often improvised) to a melody. □ *vi* /deˋskænt/ [VP3A] **~ on/upon, (a)** (music) sing or play a ~ on. **(b)** comment on, enlarge upon (a topic).

de·scend /dɪˋsend/ *vi,vt* **1** [VP2A,C,6A] (formal) come or go down: *On turning the corner, we saw that the road ~ed steeply. The balloon ~ed in Poland. He ~ed the stairs.* **2 be ~ed from,** have as ancestors: *According to the Bible, we are all ~ed from Adam.* **3** [VP2C] (of property, qualities, rights) pass (from father to son) by inheritance; come from earlier times. **4** [VP3A] **~ upon,** attack suddenly: *The bandits ~ed upon the defenceless village.* **5** [VP3A] **~ to,** lower oneself to: *You would never ~ to fraud/cheating.* **6 ~ to particulars,** pass on (in an argument, etc) to details, e g after a general introduction to a subject. **~·ant** /-ənt/ *n* person who is ~ed from (the person or persons named): *King Henry and his ~ants; the ~ants of Queen Victoria.*

de·scent /dɪˋsent/ *n* **1** [C,U] coming or going down: *The land slopes to the sea by a gradual ~,* slopes gradually. *The ~ of the mountain took two hours.* **2** [U] ancestry: *of French ~,* having French ancestors; *Darwin's 'D~ of Man',* i e his theory of evolution. *He traces his ~ from an old Norman family.* **3** [C] **~ upon,** sudden attack: *The Danes made numerous ~s upon the English coast during the 10th century.* **4** [U] handing down, e g of property, titles, qualities, etc by inheritance.

de·scribe /dɪˋskraɪb/ *vt* **1** [VP6,14,10,16B] say what (sb or sth) is like; give a picture of in words: *Words cannot ~ the beauty of the scene. Can you ~ it to/for me? Please ~ what you saw.* **2** [VP16B] **~ as,** qualify; say that (sb or sth) has certain qualities: *I hesitate to ~ him as really clever. He ~s himself as a doctor.* **3** [VP6A] mark out, draw (esp a geometrical figure): *It is easy to ~ a circle if you have a pair of compasses.*

de·scrip·tion /dɪˋskrɪpʃn/ *n* **1** [C,U] describing; picture in words: *He's not very good at ~. The scenery was beautiful beyond ~. Can you give me a ~ of the thief?* ⇨ answer[2](4). **2** [C] (colloq) sort: *The harbour was crowded with vessels of every ~.*

de·scrip·tive /dɪˋskrɪptɪv/ *adj* serving to describe; fond of describing: *There is some excellent ~ writing* (e g descriptions of scenery) *in Hardy's novels.*

des·cry /dɪˋskraɪ/ *vt* (*pt,pp* -cried) [VP6A] (formal) catch sight of; see (esp sth a long way off).

des·ecrate /ˋdesəkreɪt/ *vt* [VP6A] use (a sacred thing or place) in an unworthy or wicked way. **des·ecra·tion** /ˈdesəˋkreɪʃn/ *n* [U] desecrating or being ~d.

de·seg·re·gate /ˈdiˋsegrɪgeɪt/ *vt* [VP6A] abolish (esp racial) segregation in: *~ schools in Alabama.* **de·seg·re·ga·tion** /ˈdiˈsegrɪˋgeɪʃn/ *n*

de·sen·si·tize /ˈdiˋsensɪtaɪz/ *vt* [VP6A] render insensitive or less sensitive, e g to light or pain. **de·sen·si·tiz·ation** /ˈdiˈsensɪtaɪˋzeɪʃn *US:* -tɪˋz-/ *n*

de·sert[1] /dɪˋzɜt/ *vt,vi* **1** [VP6A] go away from: *The village had been hurriedly ~ed, perhaps because bandits were in the district. The streets were ~ed,* no people were to be seen. *We sheltered from the storm in a ~ed hut,* one that had been abandoned. **2** [VP6A] leave without help or support, esp in a wrong or cruel way: *He ~ed his wife and children and went abroad. He has become so rude that his friends are ~ing him.* **3** [VP6A,2A] run away from; leave (esp service in a ship, the armed forces) without authority or permission: *A soldier who ~s his post in time of war is punished severely. The Fourth Regiment ~ed in a body.* **4** [VP6A] fail: *His courage/presence of mind ~ed him.* **~·er** *n* person who ~s, esp in the sense of 3 above. **de·ser·tion** /dɪˋzɜʃn/ *n* [C,U] (instance of) ~ing or being ~ed.

des·ert[2] /ˋdezət/ *n* [C,U] (large area of) barren land, waterless and treeless, often sand-covered: *the Sahara D~.* □ *adj* **1** barren; uncultivated: *the ~ areas of N Africa.* **2** uninhabited: *wrecked on a ~ island.*

de·serts /dɪˋzɜts/ *n* (*pl*) what sb deserves: *to be rewarded/punished according to one's ~; to get/meet with one's ~.*

de·serve /dɪˋzɜv/ *vt,vi* (not used in the progressive tenses; ⇨ deserving. **1** [VP6A,7A] be entitled to (because of actions, conduct, qualities); merit: *Good work ~s good pay. He certainly ~s to be sent to prison. These people ~ our help.* **2 to ~ well/ill of,** to ~ to be well/badly treated by: *He ~s well of his country.* **de·serv·ed·ly** /dɪˋzɜvɪdlɪ/ *adv* according to what is ~d; rightly: *to be ~dly punished.*

de·serv·ing /dɪˋzɜvɪŋ/ *adj* having merit; worthy (*of*): *to give money to a ~ cause; ~ charities; to be ~ of sympathy; a ~ case,* a person who, because of his circumstances, etc, deserves interest, sympathy, help, etc.

dés·habillé /ˈdezəˋbileɪ/ = dishabille.

des·ic·cant /ˋdesɪkənt/ *n* (US) substance used to absorb moisture.

des·ic·cate /ˋdesɪkeɪt/ *vt* [VP6A] dry out all the moisture from, esp solid food, to preserve it: *~d fruit/coconut.*

de·sid·er·atum /dɪˈzɪdəˋreɪtəm/ *n* (*pl* -ta /-ˋrɑtə/) sth felt to be lacking and needed.

de·sign /dɪˋzɑɪn/ *n* **1** [C] drawing or outline from which sth may be made: *~s for a dress/garden;* [U] art of making such drawings, etc: *a school of ~.* **2** [U] general arrangement or planning (of a picture, book, building, machine, etc): *The building seats 2 000 people, but is poor in ~. A machine of faulty ~ will not sell well.* **3** [C] pattern; arrangement of lines, shapes, details, as ornament, e g on a bowl or carpet: *a vase with a ~ of flowers on it.* **4** [C,U] purpose; intention; mental plan: *Whether by accident or ~, he arrived too late to help us. Was the world made by ~ or did it come into existence by chance?* **have ~s on/against,** intend (selfishly or evilly) to get possession of: *That man has ~s on your money/your life;* (colloq) *He has ~s on that young girl,* wants to be intimate with her. □ *vt,vi* **1** [VP6A] prepare a plan, sketch, etc (of sth to be made): *~ a dress/garden.* **2** [VP2A,C] make ~s(1) from which sth will be made: *He ~s for a large firm of carpet manufacturers.* **3** [VP14,16B] **~ for,** set apart, intend, plan: *This course of study is ~ed to help those wishing to teach abroad. This room was ~ed for the children/~ed as a children's playroom.* **~·ed·ly** /-ɪdlɪ/ *adv* by ~; on purpose.

de·signer /dɪˋzɑɪnə(r)/ *n* person who designs, e g machinery, dresses.

de·sign·ing /dɪˋzɑɪnɪŋ/ *adj* (esp) artful and cunning; fond of intrigue. □ *n* art of making designs (for machinery, etc).

des·ig·nate¹ /ˈdezɪgneɪt/ *adj* (placed after the *n*) appointed to an office (but not yet installed): *the bishop* ~.

des·ig·nate² /ˈdezɪgneɪt/ *vt* **1** [VP6A] mark or point out clearly; give a name or title to: *to* ~ *boundaries.* **2** [VP6A,17,16B] appoint to a position or office: *He* ~*d Smith as his successor.*

des·ig·na·tion /ˌdezɪgˈneɪʃn/ *n* [U] appointing to an office; [C] name, title or description.

de·sir·able /dɪˈzaɪərəbl/ *adj* to be desired; causing desire; worth having: *This* ~ *property to be sold or let,* as in a house-agent's advertisement. *It is most* ~ *that he should attend the conference.* **de·sir·abil·ity** /dɪˌzaɪərəˈbɪlətɪ/ *n*

de·sire¹ /dɪˈzaɪə(r)/ *n* **1** [U] strong longing; strong sexual attraction; [C] instance of this; earnest wish: *He has no/not much* ~ *for wealth. He works hard from a* ~ *to become rich. He spoke about his country's* ~ *for friendly relations/that friendly relations should be established. It is impossible to satisfy all their* ~*s.* **2** (*sing*) request: *at the* ~ *of Her Majesty.* **3** [C] thing that is wished for: *I hope you will get all your heart* ~*s,* all you wish for.

de·sire² /dɪˈzaɪə(r)/ *vt* [VP6A,7A,17,9] **1** (formal) long for; wish; have a desire(**1**) for: *We all* ~ *happiness and health. Our rooms at the hotel were all that could be* ~*d,* were quite satisfactory. *What do you* ~ *me to do?* **2** (official style) request: *It is* ~*d that this rule shall be brought to the attention of the staff.*

de·sir·ous /dɪˈzaɪərəs/ *adj* (formal, official) feeling desire: ~ *of peace;* ~ *to do sth;* ~ *that....*

de·sist /dɪˈzɪst/ *vi* [VP2A,3A] ~ ***(from),*** (formal) cease; ~ *from gossiping.*

desk /desk/ *n* **1** piece of furniture (not a table) with a flat or sloping top and drawers at which to read, write or do business, e g one for office or school use. **2** = reception desk. ⇨ reception: *leave a message at the* ~ *(of the hotel).* ˈ~ **clerk** *n* (US) = reception clerk.

deso·late /ˈdesələt/ *adj* **1** (of a place) in a ruined, neglected state; (of land or a country) unlived in; unfit to live in; barren: *a* ~*, wind-swept moorland area.* **2** friendless; wretched; lonely and sad: *a* ~*-looking child; a* ~ *life.* ~**·ly** *adv* □ *vt* /ˈdesəleɪt/ [VP6A] make ~. **deso·la·tion** /ˌdesəˈleɪʃn/ *n* [U] making or being ~: *the desolation caused by war.*

des·pair¹ /dɪˈspeə(r)/ *n* [U] **1** the state of having lost all hope: *Your stupidity will drive me to* ~. *He gave up the attempt in* ~. *He was filled with* ~ *when he read the examination questions. The refugee's* ~ *of ever seeing his family again filled us with pity.* **2** ***the*** ~ ***of,*** sb or sth that causes loss of hope: *This boy is the* ~ *of all his teachers,* They no longer hope to teach him anything. *He is the* ~ *of all other pianists,* plays so well that they cannot hope to rival him.

des·pair² /dɪˈspeə(r)/ *vi* [VP2A,3A] ~ ***of,*** be in ~: *to* ~ *of success/of ever succeeding. His life was* ~*ed of,* All hope that he would live was lost. ~**·ing·ly** *adv*

des·patch /dɪˈspætʃ/ *n, v* = dispatch.

des·per·ado /ˌdespəˈrɑdəʊ/ *n* (*pl* -does; US also -dos /-dəʊz/) person ready to do any reckless or criminal act.

des·per·ate /ˈdesprət/ *adj* **1** (of a person) filled with despair and ready to do anything, regardless of danger: *The prisoners became* ~ *in their attempts to escape.* **2** lawless; violent: ~ *criminals.* **3** extremely serious or dangerous: *The state of the country is* ~. **4** giving little hope of success; tried when all else has failed: ~ *remedies.* ~**·ly** *adv* **des·per·ation** /ˌdespəˈreɪʃn/ *n* [U] the state of being ~(**1**): *The wretched people rose in desperation against their rulers. You'll drive me to desperation,* (colloq) fill me with despair, make me ready to do sth ~.

des·pic·able /dɪˈspɪkəbl/ *adj* deserving to be despised; contemptible. **des·pic·ably** /-əblɪ/ *adv*

des·pise /dɪˈspaɪz/ *vt* [VP6A] feel contempt for; consider worthless: *Strike-breakers are* ~*d by their workmates. A dish of strawberries and cream is not to be* ~*d,* is very good and should not be refused.

des·pite /dɪˈspaɪt/ *prep* in spite of: ~ *what she says....* □ *n* (obsolescent) ~ ***of, in*** ~ ***of,*** in spite of (which is the usu phrase). ~**·ful** /-fl/ *adj* (archaic) spiteful. ~**·fully** /-flɪ/ *adv*

de·spoil /dɪˈspɔɪl/ *vt* [VP6A,14] ~ ***sb (of),*** rob, plunder.

de·spon·dency /dɪˈspɒndənsɪ/ *n* [U] loss of hope; melancholy: *to fall into* ~. **de·spon·dent** /dɪˈspɒndənt/ *adj* having or showing loss of hope: *Don't become despondent.* **de·spon·dent·ly** *adv*

des·pot /ˈdespɒt/ *n* ruler with unlimited powers, esp one who uses these powers wrongly or cruelly; tyrant. ~**ic** /dɪˈspɒtɪk/ *adj of or like a* ~ *or tyrant.* ~**·ism** /ˈdespətɪzm/ *n* [U] the rule of a ~; tyranny; [C] country ruled by a ~.

des·sert /dɪˈzɜt/ *n* **1** course of fruit, etc, at the end of a meal. ˈ~**·spoon,** medium-sized spoon. ˈ~**·spoon·ful** /-fl/ *n* as much as a ~spoon will hold. ⇨ teaspoon, tablespoon. **2** (US) any sweet dish, e g pie, pudding, ice-cream, served at the end of a meal (GB also *the sweet, pudding*).

des·ti·na·tion /ˌdestɪˈneɪʃn/ *n* place to which sb or sth is going or is being sent.

des·tine /ˈdestɪn/ *vt* [VP17,14] (usu passive) ~ ***for,*** set apart, decide or ordain in advance: *He was a soldier's son and was* ~*d from birth for the army,* His father had decided, when the boy was born, that he should become a soldier. *They were* ~*d never to meet again,* Fate had determined that they should never meet again. *His hopes were* ~*d to be realized,* He realized his hopes, as we now see.

des·tiny /ˈdestɪnɪ/ *n* **1** [U] power believed to control events: *the tricks played on human beings by* ~. **2** [C] (*pl* -nies) that which happens to sb, thought of as determined in advance by fate, or a power that foreordains: *It was his* ~ *to die in a foreign country, far from his family.*

des·ti·tute /ˈdestɪtjut *US:* -tut/ *adj* **1** without food, clothes and other things necessary for life: *When Mr Hill died, his wife and children were left* ~. **2** ~ ***of,*** not having: *officials who are* ~ *of ordinary human feelings.* **des·ti·tu·tion** /ˌdestɪˈtjuʃn *US:* -ˈtuʃn/ *n* [U] being ~: *a war that brought desolation and destitution; reduced to destitution,* to complete poverty.

de·stroy /dɪˈstrɔɪ/ *vt* [VP6A] break to pieces; make useless; put an end to: *Don't* ~ *that box—it may be useful. The forest was* ~*ed by fire. All his hopes were* ~*ed.* ~**er** *n* person or thing that ~s, esp a small, fast warship for protecting larger warships or convoys of merchant-ships.

de·struc·tible /dɪˈstrʌktəbl/ *adj* that can be destroyed. **de·struc·ti·bil·ity** /dɪˈstrʌktəˈbɪlətɪ/ *n*

de·struc·tion /dɪˋstrʌkʃn/ *n* [U] destroying or being destroyed: *the ~ of a town by an earthquake;* that which ruins or destroys: *Gambling was his ~.*

de·struc·tive /dɪˋstrʌktɪv/ *adj* causing destruction; fond of, in the habit of, destroying: *a ~ storm; ~ criticism. Are all small children ~?* **~·ly** *adv* **~·ness** *n*

desue·tude /ˋdeswɪtjud *US:* -tud/ *n* [U] (formal, esp in) ***fall into ~,*** pass out of use: *customs/fashions/words that have fallen into ~.*

des·ul·tory /ˋdesltərɪ *US:* -tɔrɪ/ *adj* without system, purpose; not continuous: *~ reading.*

de·tach /dɪˋtætʃ/ *vt* **1** [VP6A,14] ***~ from,*** unfasten and take apart; separate: *to ~ a watch from a chain/a coach from a train.* ⇨ **attach. 2** [VP6A,16A] (armed forces) send (a party of men, ships, etc) away from the main body: *A number of men were ~ed to guard the right flank.* **de·tached** *part adj* **1** (of the mind, opinions, etc) impartial; not influenced by others: *to take a ~ed view of an event.* **2** (of a house) not joined to another on either side. ⇨ *semi-~ed* at **semi-**. **~·able** *adj* that can be ~ed: *a ~able lining in a coat.*

de·tach·ment /dɪˋtætʃmənt/ *n* **1** [U] detaching or being detached: *the ~ of a key from a key-ring.* **2** [U] the state of being detached**(1,2)**; being uninfluenced by surroundings, the opinions of others, etc; being indifferent and uninterested: *He answered with an air of ~.* **3** [C] group of men, ships, etc, detached**(2)** from a larger number (for a special duty, etc).

de·tail[1] /ˋditeɪl *US:* dɪˋteɪl/ *n* **1** [C] small, particular fact or item. *Please give me all the ~s. Don't omit a single ~. Every ~ of her dress was perfect.* **2** collection of such small facts or items: ***to go/enter into ~s, to explain sth in ~,*** to give the facts, item by item. **3** [U] (in art) the smaller or less important parts considered as a whole: *The composition of the picture is good but there is too much ~.* **4** [C] = **detachment(3).**

de·tail[2] /ˋditeɪl *US:* dɪˋteɪl/ *vt* **1** [VP6A,14] describe fully; give full ~s of: *a ~ed description,* given in ~; circumstantial: *The characteristics of the machine are fully ~ed in our brochure.* **2** [VP6A,16A] appoint for special duty: *Three soldiers were ~ed to guard the bridge.* ⇨ **detail**[1]**(4).**

de·tain /dɪˋteɪn/ *vt* [VP6A,16A] keep waiting; keep back; prevent from leaving or going forward: *He told his wife that he had been ~ed in the office by unexpected callers. This question need not ~ us long,* can be settled quickly. *The police ~ed the man to make further inquiries.* **~ee** /ˈditeɪˋni/ *n* person who is ~ed (esp by the authorities, as one who is suspected of wrong-doing, political agitation, etc).

de·tect /dɪˋtekt/ *vt* [VP6A] discover (the existence or presence of sb or sth, the identity of sb guilty of wrong-doing): *The dentist could ~ no sign of decay in her teeth. Can you ~ an escape of gas in this corner of the room?* **~·able** *adj* that can be ~ed. **~or** /-tə(r)/ *n* device for ~ing, e g changes of pressure, temperature or a radio signal. **ˋlie-~or,** ⇨ **lie**[1].

de·tec·tion /dɪˋtekʃn/ *n* [U] detecting: discovering: *the ~ of crime. He tried to escape ~ by disguising himself as an old man.*

de·tec·tive /dɪˋtektɪv/ *n* person whose business it is to detect criminals. **ˋ~ story/novel,** one in which the main interest is a puzzling crime and the process of solving it.

de·ten·tion /dɪˋtenʃn/ *n* [U] detaining or being detained, e g detaining a pupil in school after ordinary hours, as a punishment.

de·ter /dɪˋtɜ(r)/ *vt* (-rr-) [VP6A,14] ***~ from,*** discourage, hinder (sb from doing sth): *Failure did not ~ him from trying again.* **~·rent** /dɪˋterənt *US:* -ˋtɜ-/ *adj, n* (thing) tending to, intended to, ~: *Do you believe that the hydrogen bomb is a ~rent,* that it will ~ countries from making war?

de·ter·gent /dɪˋtɜdʒənt/ *adj, n* (substance) that removes dirt, esp from the surface of things: *Most synthetic ~s are in the form of powder or liquid.*

de·terio·rate /dɪˋtɪərɪəreɪt/ *vt,vi* [VP6A,2A] make or become of less value, or worse (in quality): *Leather quickly ~s in a hot, damp climate.* **de·terio·ra·tion** /dɪˈtɪərɪəˋreɪʃn/ *n*

de·ter·mi·nant /dɪˋtɜmɪnənt/ *adj, n* determining or deciding (agent, factor, element, etc).

de·ter·mi·nate /dɪˋtɜmɪnət/ *adj* limited; definite; fixed.

de·ter·mi·na·tion /dɪˈtɜmɪˋneɪʃn/ *n* [U] **1** ***~ of,*** determining or being determined; deciding: *The ~ of the meaning of a word is often difficult without a context.* **2** ***~ of,*** calculation or finding out (*of* an amount, etc): *the ~ of the amount of metal in a specimen of ore.* **3** ***~ (to do sth),*** firmness of purpose; resolution: *his ~ to learn English; to carry out a plan with ~; with an air of ~,* with a determined look.

de·ter·mi·nat·ive /dɪˋtɜmɪnətɪv/ *n, adj* (thing) having the power to direct, determine, limit; (gram) (*determiner* is now more usu) word that determines or limits the *noun* that follows.

de·ter·mine /dɪˋtɜmɪn/ *vt,vi* **1** [VP6A,10] decide; fix precisely: *to ~ the meaning of a word; to ~ a date for a meeting.* **2** [VP6A] calculate; find out precisely: *to ~ the speed of light/the height of a mountain by trigonometry.* **3** [VP6A,7A,9,8,10,3A] ***~ to do sth, ~ on/upon/sth,*** decide firmly, resolve, make up one's mind: *He ~d to learn Greek. We ~d to start early/~d on an early start. He has ~d on proving/~d to prove his friend's innocence. Have they ~d where the new school will be built? He has ~d that nothing shall/will prevent him. His future has not yet been ~d. but he may study medicine.* **4** [VP17,14] ***~ sb to do sth/against sth,*** cause to decide: *What ~d you to accept the offer? The news ~d him against further delay.* **5** [VP6A] be the fact that ~s: Do heredity and environment ~ a man's character? **de·ter·min·able** /-əbl/ *adj* that can be ~d. **de·ter·miner** *n* (gram) = **determinative.**

de·ter·rent ⇨ **deter.**

de·test /dɪˋtest/ *vt* [VP6A,C] hate strongly: *to ~ dogs; to ~ having to get up early.* **~·able** /-əbl/ *adj* hateful: deserving to be hated. **~·ably** /-əblɪ/ *adv* **de·tes·ta·tion** /ˈditeˋsteɪʃn/ *n* [U] strong hatred; [C] sth that is strongly hated.

de·throne /dɪˋθrəʊn/ *vt* [VP6A] remove (a ruler) from the throne, or (fig, a person) from a position of authority or influence. **~·ment** *n*

det·on·ate /ˋdetəneɪt/ *vt,vi* [VP6A,2A] (cause to) explode with a loud noise. **det·on·ator** /ˋdetəneɪtə(r)/ *n* **1** part of a bomb or shell that explodes first, causing the substance in the bomb, etc to explode. **2** fog-signal, e g as used on railways. **det·on·ation** /ˈdetəˋneɪʃn/ *n* explosion; noise of an explosion.

de·tour /ˋditʊə(r) *US:* dɪˋtʊər/ *n* roundabout way, e g a way used when the main road is blocked; diversion: *to make a ~.* □ *vt* [VP6A] make a ~.

de·tract /dɪˋtrækt/ *vi* [VP3A] ***~ from,*** take away (from the credit, value, etc, of): *to ~ from sb's merit,* make it less. **de·trac·tor** /-tə(r)/ *n* person who ~s; person who tries to make sb's reputation, etc, smaller. **de·trac·tion** /dɪˋtrækʃn/ *n* ~ing; disparagement.

de·train /ˈdiˋtreɪn/ *vt,vi* [VP6A,2A] (of troops, etc) (cause to) get out of a train.

de·tribal·ize /ˈdiˋtraɪbḷaɪz/ *vt* [VP6A] render (a person) no longer a member of a tribe; destroy the tribal customs of. **de·tribal·iz·ation** /ˈdiˈtraɪblaɪˋzeɪʃn *US:* -ḷɪˋz-/ *n*

det·ri·ment /ˋdetrɪmənt/ *n* [U] damage; harm: *I know nothing to his ~,* nothing against him. ***to the ~ of.*** *He works long hours to the ~ of his health.* **det·ri·men·tal** /ˈdetrɪˋmentl/ *adj* (*to*) harmful: *activities that would be ~al to our interests.* **det·ri·men·tally** /-tḷɪ/ *adv*

de·tri·tus /dɪˋtraɪtəs/ *n* [U] matter, e g sand, silt, gravel, produced by wearing away (from rock, etc).

de trop /də ˋtrəʊ/ *pred adj* (F) in the way; not wanted; unwelcome.

deuce[1] /djus *US:* dus/ *n* **1** the two on playing-cards or dice. **2** (tennis) the score of 40 all, or five games each, after which either side must gain two successive points (or games) to win the match (or set).

deuce[2] /djus *US:* dus/ *n* (dated colloq, in exclamations of annoyance) the devil, bad luck: *Who (Where, What) the ~...? D~ take it! There will be the ~ to pay,* a lot of trouble. **deuced** /djusɪd *US:* dus-/ *adj: in a ~d hurry,* in a great hurry. **deuced·ly** /ˋdjusɪdlɪ *US:* ˋdu-/ *adv* confoundedly; very: *~dly uncomfortable.*

Deu·ter·on·omy /ˈdjutəˋronəmɪ *US:* ˈdu-/ *n* fifth book of the Old Testament.

de·value /ˈdiˋvælju/ (US also **de·val·u·ate** /ˈdiˋvæljʊeɪt/) *vt* [VP6A] make (the value of a currency) less (esp in terms of gold): *to ~ the dollar/pound.* **de·valu·ation** /ˈdiˈvæljʊˋeɪʃn/ *n* (of currency) change to a new, lower fixed parity.

dev·as·tate /ˋdevəsteɪt/ *vt* [VP6A] ruin; make desolate: *towns ~d by fire/floods/war.* **dev·as·ta·tion** /ˈdevəˋsteɪʃn/ *n* devastating or being ~d.

de·velop /dɪˋveləp/ *vt,vi* **1** [VP6A,2A,3A] ***~ (from/into),*** (cause to) grow larger, fuller or more mature, organized; (cause to) unfold: *Plants ~ from seeds. A chicken ~s in the egg. Fresh air and exercise ~ healthy bodies. We must ~ the natural resources of our country,* make the minerals, forests, etc available for use. *The plot of the new novel gradually ~ed in the author's mind. Amsterdam ~ed into one of the greatest ports in the world.* **ˈ~ing ˋcountry,** one which is advancing to a higher (economic) state. **2** [VP6A,2A,C] (of sth not at first active or visible) come or bring into a state in which it is active or visible: *Symptoms of consumption ~ed,* appeared. *He ~ed a cough.* **3** [VP6A,2A] (photo) treat (an exposed film or plate) with chemicals so that the picture can be seen. **4** use (an area of land) for the building of houses (or shops, factories, etc) and so increase its value. **~er** *n* person who, authority which, ~s land, etc; substance used to ~ films and plates.

de·vel·op·ment /dɪˋveləpmənt/ *n* **1** [U] developing or being developed (all senses): *He is engaged in the ~ of his business. Which is more important, moral ~ or physical ~? The ~ of photographic films requires a dark-room. This land is ripe for ~,* for being developed(**4**). **ˋ~ area,** one to which new industries are directed as a means of increasing employment. **2** [C] new stage which is the result of developing: *The latest ~s in foreign affairs. We must await further ~s.*

de·vi·ant /ˋdivɪənt/ *n, adv* (person who is) different in moral and social standards from what is normal and accepted: *a sexual ~.*

de·vi·ate /ˋdivɪeɪt/ *vi* [VP3A] ***~ from,*** turn away, leave (what is usual, customary, right, etc): *to ~ from the truth/a rule/one's custom.*

de·vi·ation /ˈdivɪˋeɪʃn/ *n* [U] ***~ from,*** turning aside or away: *~ from the rules;* [C] instance or amount or degree of this: *slight ~s of the magnetic needle,* in a compass; *~s from the rules of syntax.* **~·ist** /-ɪst/ *n* person who deviates, esp from the principles of a social or political system, e g Marxism. **~·ism** /-ɪzm/ *n*

de·vice /dɪˋvaɪs/ *n* [C] **1** plan; scheme; trick: *a ~ to put the police off the scent.* ***leave sb to his own ~s,*** let him do as he wishes, without help or advice. **2** sth thought out, invented or adapted, for a special purpose: *a ~ for catching flies; a nuclear ~,* e g an atomic or hydrogen bomb. **3** sign, symbol or figure used in a decoration, e g a crest on a shield.

devil[1] /ˋdevl/ *n* **1** the spirit of evil; wicked spirit; cruel or mischievous person. **the D~,** the supreme spirit of evil, Satan. ***between the ~ and the deep sea,*** in a dilemma. ***give the ~ his due,*** be just, even to one who does not deserve much or who is unfriendly. ***go to the ~,*** be ruined; (imper) Be off! Go to hell! ***play the ~ with,*** harm, ruin. **2** (usu ***poor ~***) wretched or unfortunate person. **3** person who has to work hard for others and be abused by them. **printer's ~,** errand-boy in a printing-office. **4** (colloq) used in exclamations: *What (Who, Where, Why) the ~...? He has the ~ of a time,* i e according to context, a difficult, exciting, amusing, etc time. *He was working/running like the ~,* very hard. *There will be the ~ to pay,* trouble to be faced (as the result of sth done or said). **ˈ~-may-ˋcare,** reckless.

devil[2] /ˋdevl/ *vt,vi* (-ll-, US -l-) **1** [VP6A] grill with hot condiments: *~led kidneys/ham.* **2** [VP2A,3A] ***~ for,*** work (for a barrister).

devil·ish /ˋdevḷɪʃ/ *adj* wicked; cruel: *a ~ plot.* □ *adv* (colloq) very: *~ hot.*

devil·ment /ˋdevlmənt/, **dev·ilry** /ˋdevlrɪ/ *nn* **1** [C] mischief: *She's up to some ~ or other.* **2** [U] high spirits: *full of ~.*

de·vi·ous /ˋdivɪəs/ *adj* winding; roundabout; not straightforward: *to take a ~ route to avoid busy streets; to get rich by ~* (= cunning, underhand) *ways.* **~·ly** *adv* **~·ness** *n*

de·vise /dɪˋvaɪz/ *vt* **1** [VP14] leave (property) by will (*to*). **2** [VP6A,8] think out; plan: *to ~ a scheme for making money; to ~ how to do sth.* ⇨ device.

de·vital·ize /ˈdiˋvaɪtḷaɪz/ *vt* [VP6A] take away strength and vigour from. **de·vital·iz·ation** /ˈdiˈvaɪtḷaɪˋzeɪʃn *US:* -ḷɪˋz-/ *n*

de·void /dɪˋvɔɪd/ *adj* ***~ of,*** without; empty of: *~ of shame/sense.*

de·vol·ution /ˈdivəˋluʃn *US:* ˈdev-/ *n* [U] deputing, delegating (of power, authority); decentralization.

de·volve /dɪˈvɒlv/ *vi, vt* **1** [VP3A] **~ on/upon,** (of work, duties) be transferred or passed to: *When the President is ill, his duties ~ upon the Vice-President.* **2** [VP6A,14] pass, transfer (work, duties, *upon* or *to* sb).

de·vote /dɪˈvəʊt/ *vt* [VP14] **~ oneself/sth to,** give up (oneself, one's time, energy, etc) to: *to ~ one's spare time to sport. He ~d his life to mission work in Africa.* **de·voted** *adj* very loving or loyal: *the Queen's ~d subjects; a ~d friend. She is ~d to her children.* **de·vot·ed·ly** *adv*

devo·tee /ˌdevəˈti/ *n* person who is devoted to sth: *a ~ of sport/music;* zealous supporter (*of* a sect, etc). ⇨ votary.

de·vo·tion /dɪˈvəʊʃn/ *n* **1** [U] deep, strong love: *the ~ of a mother for her children.* **2** [U] devoting or being devoted (*to*): *~ to duty; a teacher's ~ to the cause of education.* **3** (*pl*) prayers: *The priest was at his ~s.* **~al** /-ˈvəʊʃnl/ *adj* of ~; used in ~s(3): *~al literature,* for use in worship.

de·vour /dɪˈvaʊə(r)/ *vt* [VP6A] **1** eat hungrily or greedily: *The hungry boy ~ed his dinner;* (fig) *She ~ed the new detective story. The fire ~ed twenty square miles of forest.* **2** **be ~ed by** (curiosity, anxiety, etc), be filled with, have all one's attention taken up by.

de·vout /dɪˈvaʊt/ *adj* **1** paying serious attention to religious duties: *a ~ old lady.* **2** (of prayers, wishes, etc) deepfelt; sincere: *a ~ supporter; ~ wishes for your success.* **~·ly** *adv* eagerly; sincerely. **~·ness** *n*

dew /dju *US:* du/ *n* [U] tiny drops of moisture condensed on cool surfaces between evening and morning from water vapour in the air: *The grass was wet with dew.* **ˈdew drop** *n* small drop of dew. **dewy** *adj* wet with dew.

dew·lap /ˈdjulæp *US:* ˈdu-/ *n* fold of loose skin hanging down from the neck of an animal such as a cow or ox.

dex·ter·ity /ˌdekˈsterətɪ/ *n* [U] skill, esp in handling things.

dex·ter·ous, dex·trous /ˈdekstrəs/ *adj* clever, skilful with the hands. **~·ly** *adv*

dex·trose /ˈdekstrəʊz *US:* -əʊs/ *n* [U] form of glucose.

dhobi /ˈdəʊbɪ/ *n* (in India) man whose trade is washing clothes.

dhoti /ˈdəʊtɪ/ *n* loin-cloth as customarily worn by male Hindus.

dhow /daʊ/ *n* single-masted ship, esp as used by Arab sailors for coastal voyages.

dia·betes /ˌdaɪəˈbitɪz/ *n* [U] disease of the pancreas in which sugar and starchy foods cannot be properly absorbed.

dia·betic /ˌdaɪəˈbetɪk/ *adj* of diabetes. □ *n* person suffering from diabetes.

dia·bolic /ˌdaɪəˈbɒlɪk/ *adj* of or like a devil; very cruel or wicked. **~al** /-kl/ *adj* **dia·boli·cally** /-klɪ/ *adv*

dia·critic /ˌdaɪəˈkrɪtɪk/ *n* [C] ~ mark. **~al** /-kl/ *adj*: *~ marks* (e g ´ ` ˆ ¨), used in writing and printing to indicate different sounds of a letter.

dia·dem /ˈdaɪədem/ *n* crown, worn as a sign of royal power; wreath of flowers or leaves worn round the head.

di·ær·esis, di·er·esis /ˌdaɪˈerəsɪs/ *n* (*pl* -eses /-əsiz/) mark (as in *naïve*) placed over a vowel to show that it is sounded separately from a preceding vowel.

di·ag·nose /ˈdaɪəgˈnəʊz *US:* -əʊs/ *vt* [VP6A,16B] determine the nature of (esp a disease) from observation of symptoms: *The doctor ~d the illness as diphtheria.*

di·ag·no·sis /ˌdaɪəgˈnəʊsɪs/ *n* (*pl* -noses /-ˈnəʊsiz/) [U] diagnosing; [C] (statement of the) result of this.

di·ag·nos·tic /ˌdaɪəgˈnɒstɪk/ *adj* of diagnosis: *symptoms that were of little diagnostic value,* that were not very useful in determining the disease.

di·ag·onal /daɪˈægənl/ *n, adj* ⇨ the illus at quadrilateral. (straight line) going across a straight-sided figure, e g an oblong, from corner to corner; slanting; crossed by slanting lines. **~·ly** /-nlɪ/ *adv*

dia·gram /ˈdaɪəgræm/ *n* drawing, design or plan to explain or illustrate something: *a ~ of a gearbox.* **~·matic** /ˌdaɪəgrəˈmætɪk/, **~·mati·cal** /-kl/ *adjj* **~mati·cally** /-klɪ/ *adv*

dial /ˈdaɪl/ *n* **1** face (of a clock or watch). **2** marked face or flat plate with a pointer for measuring (weight, volume, pressure, consumption of gas, etc). **3** plate, disc, etc on a radio set with names or numbers, for tuning into broadcasting stations. **4** part of an automatic telephone, with numbers and/or letters, used to make a connection. □ *vt* (-ll-) [VP6A] call by means of a telephone ~: *to ~ 01—230 1212; listen for the ~ling tone,* the sound showing that one may proceed to ~ the number wanted. **ˈ~ling code,** code of numbers for a telephone exchange to be ~led before the number of the person to whom the call is to be made: *The ~ling code for the London area is 01.*

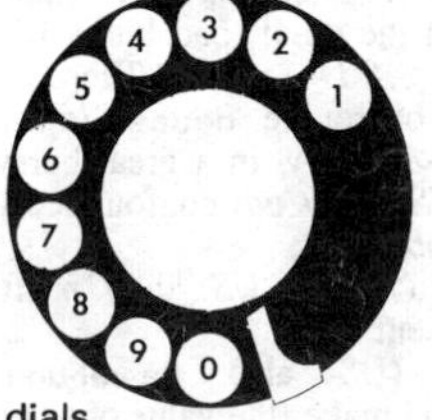

dials

dia·lect /ˈdaɪəlekt/ *n* [C,U] form of a language (grammar, vocabulary and pronunciation) used in a part of a country or by a class of people: *the Yorkshire ~; a play written in ~;* (attrib) *~ words/pronunciations.* **dia·lectal** /ˌdaɪəˈlektl/ *adj* of a ~ or ~s: *~al differences between two counties.*

dia·lec·tic /ˌdaɪəˈlektɪk/ *n* (also *pl* with *sing v*) critical analysis of mental processes; art of logical disputation. **di·a·lec·ti·cal** /-kl/ *adj* of ~: *the ~al conflict* (= the logical dispute) *between innovators and conservatives.* **ˌ~al maˈterialism,** theory, developed principally by Marx, combining traditional materialism(1) with a critical analysis of development by the conflict between an original direction, its direct opposite and their unification. **di·a·lec·tician** /ˌdaɪəlekˈtɪʃn/ *n* person skilled in ~.

dia·logue (US also **dia·log**) /ˈdaɪəlɒg *US:* -lɔg/ *n* **1** [U] (writing in the form of a) conversation or talk: *Plays are written in ~. There is some good descriptive writing in the novel, but the ~ is poor.* **2** [C] exchange of views (between leaders, etc): *a ~ between the two Prime Ministers.* **3** [C] talk: *long ~s between two comedians.*

di·am·eter /daɪˈæmɪtə(r)/ *n* ⇨ the illus at circle. Measurement across any geometrical figure or body; (length of a) straight line drawn from side to side through the centre, esp of a circular, spherical or cylindrical form: *the ~ of a tree-trunk; a lens that magnifies 20 ~s*, that makes an object look 20 times longer, wider, etc than it is.

dia·metri·cally /ˌdaɪəˈmetrɪklɪ/ *adv* completely; entirely: *~ opposed views.*

dia·mond /ˈdaɪəmənd/ *n* **1** brilliant precious stone of pure carbon in crystallized form, the hardest substance known: *a ring with a ~ in it;* (attrib) *a ~ ring/necklace.* **~ wedding** *n* sixtieth anniversary of a wedding. **rough ~,** person with rough manners but a kind heart. **2** piece of this substance (often artificially made) as used in industry, or as a stylus for playing gramophone records. **3** figure with four equal sides whose angles are not right angles; this shape (as printed in red on playing-cards): *the ten of ~s.* ⇨ the illus at **card. 4** (baseball) the space inside the lines that connect the bases. ⇨ the illus at **baseball.**

dia·per /ˈdaɪəpə(r)/ *n* **1** (linen fabric with) geometric pattern of lines crossing to make diamond shapes which are shown up by reflection of light. **2** (US) napkin(**2**) for a baby.

di·apha·nous /daɪˈæfənəs/ *adj* (of material for veils, dresses, etc) transparent; translucent.

dia·phragm /ˈdaɪəfræm/ *n* **1** wall of muscle between the chest and the abdomen. ⇨ the illus at **respiratory. 2** arrangement of thin plates that control the inlet of light, e g through a camera lens. **3** vibrating disc or cone in some instruments, e g a telephone receiver, a loudspeaker, producing sound-waves.

di·ar·chy /ˈdaɪɑkɪ/ *n* (*pl* **-chies**) government shared by two joint authorities or rulers.

di·ar·rhoea (also **-rrhea**) /ˌdaɪəˈrɪə/ *n* [U] too frequent and too watery emptying of the bowels.

diary /ˈdaɪərɪ/ *n* (*pl* **-ries**) (book for) daily record of events, thoughts, etc: *keep a ~.* **dia·rist** /ˈdaɪərɪst/ *n* person who keeps a diary.

Dia·spora /daɪˈæspərə/ *n* **the D~,** the dispersion of the Jews among the Gentiles after their period of exile: *People from every country of the ~ now live in Israel.*

dia·tribe /ˈdaɪətraɪb/ *n* [C] bitter and violent attack in words (*against* sb or sth).

dibble /ˈdɪbl/ *n* (also **dib·ber** /ˈdɪbə(r)/) short wooden tool with a pointed end for making holes in the ground (for tubers, young plants, etc). □ *vt* [VP15B] put (plants, etc, *in*) with a ~.

dice /daɪs/ *n pl* (*sing* **die**) small cubes of wood, bone, etc marked with spots, used in games of chance: *to play ~.* ***The die is cast,*** (prov) One's course is determined and cannot now be changed. Note: except in this prov, *die* is rarely used. 'One of the dice' is preferred to 'die'. **ˈ~-box** *n* deep, narrow box in which ~ are shaken and from which they are thrown. □ *vi, vt* **1** [VP2A] play ~. ***~ with death,*** (colloq) act dangerously and at the risk of death. **2** [VP6A] cut (food, e g carrots) into small cubes like ~.

dicey /ˈdaɪsɪ/ *adj* (colloq) risky; uncertain.

di·chot·omy /daɪˈkotəmɪ/ *n* (*pl* **-mies**) division into two (usu contradictory classes or mutually exclusive pairs): *the ~ of truth and falsehood.*

dick·ens /ˈdɪkɪnz/ *n* (colloq) used like **devil** and **deuce**: *'Who/What/Where the ~...?'*

dicker /ˈdɪkə(r)/ *vi* (colloq) [VP2A,3A] bargain or haggle (*with* sb, *for* sth).

dicky[1], **dickey** /ˈdɪkɪ/ *n* (colloq, sl) **1** (also **ˈ~-seat**) small, extra folding seat at the back of a two-seater motor-car. **2** false shirt-front. **3** **ˈ~-bird,** child's word for a bird.

dice

printer's dies

dicky[2] /ˈdɪkɪ/ *adj* (sl) unsound; weak: *a ~ heart;* liable to break or fall.

Dic·ta·phone /ˈdɪktəfəʊn/ *n* (P) office machine that makes a record of words spoken into it and then reproduces them (for transcription, etc).

dic·tate /dɪkˈteɪt *US:* ˈdɪkteɪt/ *vt, vi* **1** [VP6A,2A, 14] say or read aloud (words to be written down by another or others): *to ~ a letter to a secretary. The teacher ~d a passage to the class.* **2** [VP6A, 14] state with the force of authority: *to ~ terms to a defeated enemy.* **3** [VP3A] give orders (*to*): *I won't be ~d to,* I refuse to accept orders from you. □ *n* (usu *pl*) direction or order (esp given by reason, conscience, etc): *the ~s of common sense. Follow the ~s of your conscience,* Do what your conscience tells you to do.

dic·ta·tion /dɪkˈteɪʃn/ *n* **1** [U] dictating; being dictated to: *The pupils wrote at their teacher's ~.* **2** [C] passage, etc that is dictated.

dic·ta·tor /ˌdɪkˈteɪtə(r) *US:* ˈdɪkteɪtər/ *n* ruler who has absolute authority, esp one who has obtained such power by force or in an irregular way. **~-ship** /-ʃɪp/ *n* [C,U] (country with) government by a ~. **dic·ta·torial** /ˌdɪktəˈtɔrɪəl/ *adj* of or like a ~: *~ial government;* overbearing; fond of giving orders: *his ~ial manner.* **dic·ta·tori·ally** /-əlɪ/ *adv*

dic·tion /ˈdɪkʃn/ *n* [U] choice and use of words; style or manner of speaking and writing.

dic·tion·ary /ˈdɪkʃnrɪ *US:* -nerɪ/ *n* (*pl* **-ries**) book dealing with the words of a language, or with words or topics of a special subject, e g the Bible, architecture, and arranged in A B C order.

dic·tum /ˈdɪktəm/ *n* (*pl* **-tums, -ta** /-tə/) formal expression of opinion; saying.

did /dɪd/ ⇨ **do.**

di·dac·tic /dɪˈdæktɪk/ *adj* **1** intended to teach: *~ poetry.* **2** having the manner of a teacher: *A teacher should not be ~ outside the classroom.* **di·dac·ti·cally** /-klɪ/ *adv*

diddle /ˈdɪdl/ *vt* [VP14] (colloq) cheat (sb *out of* sth).

die[1] /daɪ/ *n* **1** (*pl* **dice**) ⇨ **dice. 2** (*pl* **dies** /dæɪz/) block of hard metal with a design, etc cut in it, used for shaping coins, type[1](**3**), medals, etc or stamping paper, leather, etc so that designs stand out from the surface. **ˈdie-cast** *adj* made by casting metal in a mould: *die-cast toys,* e g small models of cars.

die[2] /daɪ/ *vi* (*pt,pp* **died,** *pres part* **dying**) **1** [VP2A,C,D] come to the end of life; cease to live: *Flowers soon die if they are left without water.* (Note the *preps*): *to die of an illness/a disease/hunger/grief; to die by violence; to die by one's own hand,* i e commit suicide; *to die from a* *wound; to die for one's country; to die through neglect; to die in battle; to die happy/poor; to die a beggar/a martyr.* **2** (various phrases) ***die in one's bed,*** of old age or illness. ***die with one's boots on,*** *while still vigorous, while fighting.* ***~ in the last ditch,*** fighting desperately to defend sth. ***die game,*** facing death bravely. ***die hard,*** only after a struggle. ⇨ **6** below. ***die in harness,*** while still at one's usual occupation, still working. **3** [VP2C] (with various *adverbial particles*) ***die away,*** lose strength, become faint or weak: *The breeze died away. The noise died away.* ***die back,*** (of plants) die down to the roots, which remain alive and send up shoots the next growing season: *The dahlias died back when the frosts came.* ***die down,*** (of a fire in a fireplace, etc) burn with less heat; (of excitement, etc) become less violent; (of noise, etc) become less loud. ***die off,*** die one by one: *The leaves of this plant are dying off.* ***die out,*** become extinct; come to a complete end: *With the death of the fifth earl, this old family had died out. Many old customs are gradually dying out.* **4** [VP3A,4C] ***be dying for/to*** (*inf*), have a strong wish: *We're all dying for a drink. She's dying to know where you've been.* **5** [VP2A,C] pass from human knowledge; be lost: *His fame will never die. His secret died with him,* He died without telling it to anyone. **6** **ˈdie-hard,** (often attrib) person who obstinately resists being compelled to do anything; politician who obstinately opposes new policies and fights hard in defence of old policies.

die·sel /ˈdizl/ *n* (attrib) **ˈ~ engine,** oil-burning engine (as used for buses, locomotives) in which ignition is produced by the heat of suddenly compressed gas. **ˈ~ oil,** heavy fuel oil; *~-electric locomotive,* one that generates its own electric current from a ~ engine.

diet[1] /ˈdaɪət/ *n* series of meetings for discussion of national, international or church affairs: *the Japanese D~,* legislative assembly.

diet[2] /ˈdaɪət/ *n* **1** sort of food usually eaten (by a person, community, etc): *the Japanese ~ of rice, vegetables and fish. Too rich a ~* (= Too much rich food) *is not good for you.* **2** sort of food to which a person is limited, e g for medical reasons: *The doctor put her on a ~. No potatoes for me—I'm on a ~.* □ *vt,vi* [VP6A,2A] restrict (oneself, sb), be restricted, to a ~(2): *She became so fat that she had to ~ herself. My doctor is ~ing me very strictly. Is he still ~ing?* **die·tary** /ˈdaɪətərɪ *US:* -terɪ/ *adj* of ~: *~ary rules; ~ary taboos,* e g pork for Muslims. **die·tet·ics** /ˌdaɪəˈtetɪks/ *n* (*sing v*) science of ~. **diet·ician, diet·itian** /ˌdaɪəˈtɪʃn/ *n* expert in dietetics.

dif·fer /ˈdɪfə(r)/ *vi* [VP2A,C,3A] **1** be unlike; be distinguishable (*from*): *The two brothers are like each other in appearance, but ~ widely in their tastes. French ~s from English in having gender for all nouns. Tastes ~,* different people have different interests. **2** ***~ from sb (about/on...),*** disagree; have another opinion: *I'm sorry to ~ from you about/on/upon that question.* ***agree to ~,*** give up the attempt to convince each other.

dif·fer·ence /ˈdɪfrns/ *n* [C,U] **1** the state of being unlike: *the ~ between summer and winter.* **2** amount, degree, manner, in which things are unlike: *The ~ between 7 and 18 is 11. I can't see much ~ in them. What a great ~ there is in the temperature today! There are many ~s between the two languages.* ***split the ~,*** ⇨ split(3). **3** ***make a/some/no/any/not much/a great deal of ~,*** be of some/no, etc importance: *It won't make much ~ whether you go today or tomorrow. Does that make any ~,* Is it important, need we consider it? ***make a ~ between,*** treat differently. **4** disagreement: *Why can't you settle your ~s and be friends again?*

dif·fer·ent /ˈdɪfrnt/ *adj* **1** not the same: *They are ~ people with the same name. The two boys are ~ in their tastes. She is wearing a ~ dress every time I see her.* ***~ from/to,*** *Your method is ~ from/to mine.* ***~ than,*** used when ~ is not immediately followed by its *prep*: *How ~ life today is than what it was fifty years ago.* Cf *life today is ~ from life fifty years ago,* where ~ is followed immediately by *from.* **2** separate; distinct: *I called three ~ times, but he was out. They are made in ~ colours,* in a variety of colours. **~·ly** *adv*

dif·fer·en·tial /ˌdɪfəˈrenʃl/ *adj* **1** of, showing, depending on, a difference: *~ tariffs,* that differ according to circumstances. **2** *~ gear,* arrangement of gears (in a motor-car, etc) that allows the rear wheels to turn at different speeds on curves. □ *n* (*wage ~*) difference (expressed in a percentage) in wages between skilled and unskilled workers in the same industry: *They opposed a flat increase for all workers because that would upset the wage ~.*

dif·fer·en·ti·ate /ˌdɪfəˈrenʃɪeɪt/ *vt* [VP6A,14] **1** see as different; show to be different: *to ~ varieties of plants; to ~ one variety from another. The report does not ~ the two aspects of the problem. One aspect is not ~ed from the other.* **2** [VP3A] ***~ between,*** treat as different: *It is wrong to ~ between pupils according to their family background.* **dif·fer·en·ti·ation** /ˌdɪfəˌrenʃɪˈeɪʃn/ *n*

dif·fi·cult /ˈdɪfɪklt/ *adj* **1** not easy; requiring effort, strength, skill or ability: *a ~ problem/language. He finds it ~ to stop smoking. The sound is ~ to pronounce. It is a ~ sound to pronounce. The place is ~ to reach/~ of access. He was placed in ~ circumstances.* **2** (of persons) not easily pleased or satisfied: easily offended: *He's a ~ man to get on with. The famous actress was being rather ~,* was causing trouble, e g to the other members of the cast, the producer; *Please don't be so ~.*

dif·fi·culty /ˈdɪfɪkltɪ *US:* -kʌltɪ/ *n* **1** [U] the state or quality of being difficult: *Do you have any ~ in understanding spoken English? There was some ~ in getting everybody here in time. He did the work without ~/without any/much ~. He did it, but with ~.* **2** [C] (*pl* -ties) sth difficult, hard to do or understand: *the difficulties of Greek syntax; to be working under difficulties,* in difficult circumstances; *to be in financial difficulties,* short of money, in debt, etc. *If you knew the difficulties I am in! Mary's father raised/made difficulties when she said she wanted to marry a poor schoolteacher,* He objected to, opposed, the proposal.

dif·fi·dent /ˈdɪfɪdənt/ *adj* not having, not showing, much belief in one's own abilities; lacking in self-confidence: *to be ~ about doing sth; to speak in a ~ manner.* **~·ly** *adv* **dif·fi·dence** /-dəns/ *n* [U] being ~; shyness.

dif·fract /dɪˈfrækt/ *vt* [VP6A] break up (a beam of light) into a series of dark and light bands or the coloured bands of the spectrum. ⇨ the illus at prism. **dif·frac·tion** /dɪˈfrækʃn/ *n*

dif·fuse[1] /dɪˈfjuz/ *vt,vi* **1** [VP6A] send out, spread, in every direction: *to ~ learning/knowledge/good humour/light/heat/a scent or odour; ~d lighting,* contrasted with direct lighting. **2** [VP6A,2A] (of gases and liquids) (cause to) mix slowly. **dif·fusion** /dɪˋfjuʒn/ *n* [U] diffusing or being ~d: *the diffusion of knowledge through books and lectures; the diffusion of gases and liquids,* their mixing without external force.

dif·fuse[2] /dɪˋfjus/ *adj* **1** using too many words: *a ~ writer/style.* **2** spread out; scattered: *~ light.* **~·ly** *adv* **~·ness** *n*

dig[1] /dɪg/ *vt,vi* (*pt,pp* **dug** /dʌg/; (**-gg-**)) **1** [VP6A,15B,2C] use a tool (e g a spade), a machine, claws, etc to break up and move earth, etc; make a way (*through, into,* etc) by doing this; make (a hole, etc) by doing this; get (sth) by doing this: *It is difficult to dig the ground when it is frozen hard. They are digging through the hill to make a tunnel/digging a tunnel through the hill. He dug a deep hole. The soldiers were digging trenches.* **2** [VP6A] (sl) enjoy; appreciate; understand; follow: *I don't dig modern jazz.* **3** [VP15B, 3A,2C] (uses with *adverbial particles* and *preps*): ***dig in, dig into sth,*** serve oneself with food, begin eating, with appetite: *dig into a pie. The food's here, so dig in!* ***dig sth in,*** mix with the soil by digging: *The manure should be well dug in.* ***dig sth in/into sth,*** push, thrust, poke: *to dig a fork into a pie/a potato. The rider dug his spurs into the horse's flank/dug his spurs in.* ***dig oneself in,*** **(a)** protect oneself by digging a trench, etc. **(b)** (fig, colloq) establish oneself securely (in a position, etc). ***dig sb in the rib's*** poke one's elbow in his ribs, e g to call attention to sth funny. ***dig sb/sth out (of sth),*** **(a)** get out by digging: *They dug out the fox/dug the fox out of its hole. He was buried by the avalanche and had to be dug out.* **(b)** get by searching: *to dig information out of books and reports; to dig out the truth.* ***dig sth up,*** **(a)** break up (land) by digging: *to dig up land for a new garden.* **(b)** remove from the ground by digging: *We dug the tree up by the roots.* **(c)** bring to light (what has been buried or hidden) by digging: *An old Greek statue was dug up here last month.* **(d)** (fig): *The newspapers love to dig up scandals.*

dig[2] /dɪg/ *n* (colloq) **1** push or thrust: *give sb a dig in the ribs. That was a dig at me,* a remark directed against me. **2** site being excavated by archaeologists. **3** (*pl*) (GB, colloq) lodgings: *Are you living at home or in digs?*⇨ **digging** below.

di·gest[1] /ˋdaɪdʒest/ *n* [C] short, condensed account; summary: *a ~ of the week's news.*

di·gest[2] /daɪˋdʒest/ *vt,vi* [VP6A,2A] **1** (of food) change, be changed, in the stomach and bowels, so that it can be used in the body: *Some foods ~/are ~ed more easily than others.* **2** take into the mind; make part of one's knowledge; reduce (a mass of facts, etc) to order: *Have you ~ed everything that is important in the book?* **~·ible** /dɪˋdʒestəbl/ *adj* that can be ~ed. **~i·bil·ity** *n*

di·ges·tion /daɪˋdʒestʃən/ *n* [U] digesting: *food that is easy/difficult of ~*; (often used with *indef art* and an *adj*) power of digesting food: *to have a poor/good ~.*

di·ges·tive /daɪˋdʒestɪv/ *adj* of digestion (of food): *suffer from ~ trouble.* **the ˋ~ system,** the alimentary canal.

dig·ger /ˋdɪgə(r)/ *n* **1** (usu in compounds) person who digs: *ˋgold-~,* one who tries to find gold in a gold-field. **2** mechanical excavator. **3** (sl) Australian.

dig·ging /ˋdɪgɪŋ/ *n* **1** [U] action of digging; [C] (often *pl*) place where men dig or search for metal, esp gold. **2** (*pl*, GB dated colloq) lodgings.

digit /ˋdɪdʒɪt/ *n* **1** any one of the ten Arabic numerals 0 to 9: *The number 57306 contains five ~s.* **2** finger or toe. **digi·tal** /ˋdɪdʒɪtl/ *adj* of ~s. **ˋdigi·tal computer** *n* one that performs operations by representing quantities as ~s (binary or decimal).

dig·nify /ˋdɪgnɪfaɪ/ *vt* (*pt,pp* **-fied**) [VP6A,14] cause to appear worthy or honourable; give dignity to: *to ~ a small collection of books by calling it a library/~ it with the name library.* **dig·ni·fied** *part adj* having or showing dignity: *a dignified old lady.*

dig·ni·tary /ˈdɪgnɪtrɪ *US:* -terɪ/ *n* (*pl* **-ries**) person holding a high office, esp in the church, e g a bishop.

dig·nity /ˈdɪgnətɪ/ *n* **1** [U] true worth; the quality that earns or deserves respect: *the ~ of labour. A man's ~ depends not upon his wealth or rank but upon his character.* **2** [U] calm and serious manner or style: *If you're afraid of losing your ~* (e g of being made to look foolish), *you can't expect to learn to speak a foreign language.* **beneath one's ~,** below one's moral, social, etc standards: *It is beneath your ~ to answer such a rude remark.* ***stand (up)on one's ~,*** insist upon being treated with proper respect; refuse to do what one considers to be below one's moral, social, etc standard. **3** [C] (*pl* **-ties**) high or honourable rank, port or title: *The Queen conferred the ~ of a peerage on him.* **4** [C] (*pl* **-ties**) (old use) dignitary.

di·graph /ˋdaɪgrɑf *US:* -græf/ *n* two letters that represent a single sound (e g *sh* /ʃ/, *ea* /i/ in *seat*).

di·gress /daɪˋgres/ *vi* [VP2A,3A] **~ *(from),*** (esp in speaking or writing) turn or wander away (from the main subject). **di·gression** /daɪˋgreʃn/ *n* [U] ~ing; [C] instance of this.

digs /dɪgz/ *n pl* (GB, colloq) lodgings.

dike, dyke /daɪk/ *n* **1** ditch (for carrying away water from land). **2** long wall of earth, etc (to keep back water and prevent flooding). □ *vi* make ~s: *diking in the Fens.*

a dike

dil·api·dated /dɪˋlæpɪdeɪtɪd/ *adj* (of buildings, furniture, etc) falling to pieces; in a state of disrepair: *a ~-looking car; a ~ old house.* **dil·api·da·tion** /dɪˈlæpɪˋdeɪʃn/ *n* [U] being or becoming ~.

di·late /daɪˋleɪt/ *vi,vt* [VP6A,2A] (cause to) become wider, larger, further open: *The pupils of your eyes ~ when you enter a dark room. The horse ~d its nostrils.* **2** [VP3A] ***~ upon,*** speak or write comprehensively about: *If there were time, I could ~ upon this subject.* **di·la·tion** /ˈdaɪˋleɪʃn/ *n* dilating or being ~d.

dila·tory /ˋdɪlətrɪ *US:* -tɔrɪ/ *adj* slow in doing

things; causing delay.

di·lemma /dɪˋlemə/ *n* situation in which one has to choose between two things, two courses of action, etc both unfavourable or undesirable. ***be in/place sb in a ~***: *You place me in something of a ~.*

dil·et·tante /ˌdɪlɪˋtæntɪ/ *n* (*pl* -ti /-tɪ/) one who studies the arts, but not seriously and not with real understanding; one who merely dabbles in many things.

dili·gence /ˋdɪlɪdʒəns/ *n* [U] **1** steady effort; showing care and effort (*in* what one does). **2** (hist) public stage-coach.

dili·gent /ˋdɪlɪdʒənt/ *adj* hard-working; showing care and effort (*in* what one does). **~·ly** *adv*

dill /dɪl/ *n* herb with spicy seeds, e g as used for flavouring pickles.

dilly-dally /ˈdɪlɪ ˋdælɪ/ *vt* [VP2A] dawdle; waste time (by not making up one's mind).

di·lute /daɪˋljut *US:* -ˋlut/ *vt* [VP6A,14] **~ *(with),*** make (a liquid or colour) weaker or thinner (by adding water or other liquid): *to ~ wine with water;* (fig) weaken the force of (by mixing): *to ~ skilled labour,* e g by employing a proportion of unskilled workers. □ *adj* (of acids, etc) weakened by diluting. **di·lu·tion** /daɪˋljuʃn *US:* -ˋlu-/ *n* [U] diluting or being ~d; [C] sth that is ~d.

dim /dɪm/ *adj* (-mer, -mest) **1** not bright; not clearly to be seen: *the dim light of a candle; the dim outline of buildings on a dark night; dim memories/recollections of my childhood.* **2** (of the eyes, eyesight) not able to see clearly: *eyes dim with tears. His eyesight is getting dim.* ***take a dim view of,*** (colloq) regard with disapproval or pessimism. **3** (colloq, of persons) lacking keenness or intelligence. □ *vt,vi* (-mm-) [VP6A,2A] make or become dim: *The light of a candle is dimmed by sunlight.* **dim·ly** *adv* in a dim manner: *a dimly lit room.* **dim·ness** *n*

dime /daɪm/ *n* coin of US and Canada worth ten cents.

di·men·sion /dɪˋmenʃn/ *n* **1** measurement of any sort (breadth, length, thickness, height, etc): *What are the ~s of the room?* **2** (*pl*) size; extent: *a building of great ~s; the ~s of the problem.* **3** (algebra) number of unknown quantities contained as factors in a product: x^3, x^2y and *xyz are of three ~s.* **~al** /-ʃnl/ *adj*: ˈ*two-*, ˈ*three-*ˋ*~al,* having two, three, ~s: *three-~al films* (**3 D**), stereoscopic films, giving the illusion of depth in perspective (as well as height and breadth).

dim·in·ish /dɪˋmɪnɪʃ/ *vt,vi* [VP6A,2A] make or become less: *~ing food supplies; a war that seriously ~ed the country's wealth; a currency that has ~ed in value.*

dim·inu·endo /dɪˈmɪnjʊˋendəʊ/ *n* (*pl* -dos /-dəʊz/) [C] gradual decrease in loudness: *a sudden ~.*

dim·in·ution /ˈdɪmɪˋnjuʃn *US:* -ˋnuʃn/ *n* [U] diminishing or being diminished; [C] amount of this: *to hope for a small ~ in taxes.*

dim·inu·tive /dɪˋmɪnjʊtɪv *US:* -nʊ-/ *adj* **1** unusually or remarkably small. **2** (gram, of a *suff*) indicating smallness. □ *n* word formed by the use of a *suff* of this kind, e g *streamlet,* a small stream, *lambkin,* a small lamb.

dim·ity /ˋdɪmətɪ/ *n* [U] (kinds of) cotton cloth woven with raised strips or designs, used for bedroom hangings, etc.

dimple /ˋdɪmpl/ *n* small natural hollow in the chin or cheek (either permanent, or which appears, for example, when a person smiles); slight hollow on water (made, for example, by a breeze). □ *vt,vi* [VP6A,2A] make ~s on; form ~s.

din /dɪn/ *n* [U] (or with *indef art*) loud, confused noise that continues: *The children were making so much din/such a din that I couldn't study. They made/kicked up such a din at the party.* □ *vi,vt* (-nn-) **1** [VP2C] make a din: *The cries of his tormentors were still dinning in his ears.* **2 *din sth into sb,*** tell him again and again, in a forcible manner: *How much longer must I din into your ears the importance of hard work?*

dine /daɪn/ *vi,vt* **1** [VP2A,C,3A] have dinner: *to ~ off roast beef.* **~ *out,*** dine outside one's home (e g at the house of friends, or at a restaurant). **2** [VP6A] give a dinner for: *The great man was wined and ~d wherever he went,* People gave dinner-parties for him. **ˋdining-car,** railway coach in which meals are served. **ˋdining-room,** room in which meals are eaten. **ˋdining-table,** table used for dining.

diner /ˋdaɪnə(r)/ *n* **1** person who dines. **2** dining-car on a train. **3** (US) restaurant shaped like a ~(2).

ding-dong /ˈdɪŋ ˋdoŋ/ *n, adv* (with the) sound of bells striking repeatedly: (attrib) **a ~ struggle,** one in which each of two contestants has the advantage alternately.

din·ghy, din·gey /ˋdɪŋgɪ/ *n* (*pl* -ghies, -geys) (kinds of) small open boat; inflatable rubber boat (e g carried by an aircraft for use if forced down on water).

dingle /ˋdɪŋgl/ *n* deep dell, usu with trees.

dingy /ˋdɪndʒɪ/ *adj* (-ier, -iest) dirty-looking; not fresh or cheerful: *a ~ industrial town; a ~ hotel room.* **ding·ily** *adv* **dingi·ness** *n*

dining /ˋdaɪnɪŋ/ ⇨ dine.

dinky /ˋdɪŋkɪ/ *adj* (-ier, -iest) (GB, colloq) pretty; neat: *What a ~ little hat!*

din·ner /ˋdɪnə(r)/ *n* main meal of the day, whether eaten at midday or in the evening. Note the *preps* and the use and omission of the articles: *It's time for ~/ˋ~-time. Have you had* (US = *eaten*) *~ yet? They were at ~/having ~ when I called. He ate too much ~. The ~ was badly served. Shall we give a ~/ˋ~-party for her? Four ~s at £1 a head. Shall we ask him to ~?* **ˋ~-bell,** rung to announce that ~ is about to be served. **ˋ~-jacket,** black jacket worn by men in the evening for formal occasions. Cf *dress coat,* with tails, and US *tuxedo.* **ˋ~-service, ˋ~-set,** set of plates, dishes, etc for ~.

dino·saur /ˋdaɪnəsɔ(r)/ *n* (kinds of) large extinct reptile.

a dinosaur

dint /dɪnt/ *n* **1** [C] - dent. **2 *by ~ of,*** by means of: *He succeeded by ~ of hard work.*

dio·cese /ˋdaɪəsɪs/ *n* (*pl* -ceses /-sizɪz/) bishop's district. **di·ocesan** /daɪˋosɪsn/ *adj* of a ~.

di·ox·ide /ˈdaɪˋoksaɪd/ *n* (chem) oxide formed by

combination of two atoms of oxygen and one atom of a metal or other element: *carbon* ~, **(CO_2)**.

dip[1] /dɪp/ *vt, vi* (-pp-) **1** [VP6A,14] put, lower, (sth) *into* a liquid: *to dip one's pen into the ink; to dip sheep,* immerse them in a liquid that disinfects them, kills vermin; *to dip candles,* make them by dipping wick into melted fat; *dip a garment,* put it in a liquid dye to change its colour. **'~-stick,** stick or rod (to be) dipped into a tank or other container to measure the depth of liquid in it (e g oil in the sump of an engine). **2** [VP3A] ***dip into,*** (fig): *to dip into one's purse,* spend money; *to dip into the future,* try to imagine what it will be like; *to dip into a book/an author, etc,* make a cursory study. **3** [VP2A,C] go below a surface or level: *The sun dipped below the horizon. The birds rose and dipped in their flight.* **4** [VP6A,2A] (cause to) go down and then up again: *to dip a flag,* as a salute, e g to another ship; *to dip the headlights of a car,* lower their beams (in order not to dazzle the driver of another car). *The land dips gently to the south.* **5** [VP15A] ~ ***up/out,*** (obsolete) take or scoop up/out: *dip water out of a lake.*

dip[2] /dɪp/ *n* **1** [C] act of dipping, esp (colloq) quick bathe or swim: *to have/take/go for a dip.* **2** [U] cleansing liquid in which sheep are dipped. **3** [C] downward slope: *a dip in the road; a dip among the hills.* **4** position of a flag when it is dipped(4): *at the dip.*

diph·theria /dɪf'θɪərɪə/ *n* [U] serious contagious disease of the throat causing difficulty in breathing.

diph·thong /'dɪfθoŋ *US:* -θɔŋ/ *n* union of two vowel sounds or vowel letters, e g the sounds /ɑɪ/ in *pipe* /pɑɪp/, the letters *ou* in *doubt* (more usu *digraph*). ⇨ **digraph.**

di·ploma /dɪ'pləʊmə/ *n* [C] educational certificate of proficiency: *a* ~ *in architecture.*

di·plo·macy /dɪ'pləʊməsɪ/ *n* [U] **1** management of a country's affairs by its agents abroad (ambassadors and ministers), and their direction by the Ministry of Foreign Affairs at home; skill in this. **2** art of, skill in, dealing with people so that business is done smoothly.

diplo·mat /'dɪpləmæt/ *n* person engaged in diplomacy for his country (e g an ambassador).

diplo·matic /ˌdɪplə'mætɪk/ *adj* **1** of diplomacy: *the '~ service; the '~ corps/body,* all the ambassadors, ministers and their officers in the capital of a country. **2** tactful; having diplomacy(2): *a* ~ *answer; to be* ~ *in dealing with people.* **diplo·mati·cally** /-klɪ/ *adv*

di·ploma·tist /dɪ'pləʊmətɪst/ *n* **1** = **diplomat. 2** person clever at dealing with people.

dip·per /'dɪpə(r)/ *n* **1** cup-shaped vessel with a long handle, for dipping out liquids. **2** (US) *the Big D~, the Little D~,* groups of stars in the northern sky. ⇨ **bear**[1]**(3).**

dip·so·ma·nia /ˌdɪpsə'meɪnɪə/ *n* [U] insatiable craving for alcoholic drink. **dip·so·maniac** /ˌdɪpsə'meɪnɪæk/ *n* person suffering from ~.

dip·tych /'dɪptɪk/ *n* painting or carving, esp an altarpiece, on two hinged panels that can be closed like a book.

dire /'dɑɪə(r)/ *adj* (-r, -st) dreadful; terrible: ~ *news;* extreme: *to be in* ~ *need of help.*

di·rect[1] /dɪ'rekt/ *adj* **1** (going) straight; not curved or crooked; not turned aside: *in a* ~ *line; a* ~ *hit/shot,* not turned aside by hitting sth else first; *the* ~ *rays of the sun,* not reflected from sth. **2** with nothing or no one in between; in an unbroken line: *to be in* ~ *contact with sb; as a* ~ *result of this decision. He's a* ~ *descendant of the Duke of Bumford.* **3** straightforward; going straight to the point; frank; unhesitating: *He has a* ~ *way of speaking/doing things. He made a* ~ *answer to the charges brought against him.* **4** exact, diametrical: *a* ~ *contradiction; the* ~ *opposite/contrary.* **5** (various uses): **'~ action,** use of strikes by workmen to get their demands. **'~ current,** electric current flowing in one direction. ⇨ **alter|nate. '~ speech,** speaker's actual words. **'~ tax,** one levied on the person who pays it (e g income tax), not (e g value added tax) on goods, etc. □ *adv* without interrupting a journey; without going by a roundabout way: *The train goes there* ~. *He came* ~ *to London.* ⇨ **directly. ~·ness** *n*

di·rect[2] /dɪ'rekt/ *vt, vi* **1** [VP6A,14] tell or show (sb) how to do sth, how to get somewhere: *Can you* ~ *me to the post office? They* ~*ed me wrongly.* **2** [VP6A,14] address (a letter, parcel, etc): *Shall I* ~ *the letter to his business address or to his home address?* **3** [VP14] speak or write to: *My remarks were not* ~*ed to all of you.* **4** [VP6A, 2A] manage; control: *Who is* ~*ing the work? There was no one to* ~ *the workmen. Who* ~*ed (the orchestra) at yesterday's concert,* Who was the conductor? **5** [VP14] turn: *Please* ~ *your attention to what I am demonstrating. We* ~*ed our steps towards home. Our energies must be* ~*ed towards higher productivity.* **6** [VP17,9] order: *The officer* ~*ed his men to advance slowly. The general* ~*ed an advance to be made/*~*ed that an advance should be made the next morning.*

di·rec·tion /dɪ'rekʃn/ *n* **1** [C] course taken by a moving person or thing; point towards which a person or thing looks or faces: *Tom went off in one* ~ *and Harry in another* ~. *The aircraft was flying in a northerly* ~. *When the police arrived, the crowd scattered in all* ~*s.* (fig) *Reforms are needed in numerous* ~*s.* **'~-finder,** radio device that shows the ~ from which wireless signals are coming. **2** [U] *have a good/poor sense of* ~, be able/unable to determine well one's position with regard to one's surroundings when there are no known or visible landmarks. **3** (often *pl*) information or instructions about what to do, where to go, how to do sth, etc: *D~s about putting the parts together are printed on the card. He gave me full* ~*s to enable me to find his house.* **4** (usu *pl*) address on or for a letter, parcel, etc: *The parcel was returned to the sender because the* ~*s were insufficient.* **5** [U] management; control; guidance: ~ *of labour,* movement of workers from one area, or one kind of work, to another. *He did the work under my* ~. *She feels the need of* ~, wants sb to guide and advise her. **6** = **directorate(2). ~al** /-ʃnl/ *adj* of ~ in space (esp of radio signals transmitted over a narrow angle): *a* ~*al aerial.*

di·rec·tive /dɪ'rektɪv/ *n* [C] general or detailed instructions as given to staff to guide them in their work.

di·rect·ly /dɪ'rektlɪ/ *adv* **1** in a direct manner: *He was looking* ~ *at us.* **2** at once; without delay: *Come in* ~. **3** in a short time: *I'll be there* ~. □ *conj* (colloq) as soon as; *D~ I had done it, I knew I had made a mistake.*

di·rec·tor /dɪ'rektə(r)/ *n* person who directs, esp one of a group (called *the Board of D~s*) who manage the affairs of a business company;

(cinema) person who supervises and instructs the actors and actresses, the camera crew, etc. **~·ship** /-ʃɪp/ *n* position of a company ~; time during which he holds his position.

di·rec·tor·ate /dɪˋrektərət/ *n* **1** office or position of a director. **2** board of directors.

di·rec·tory /dɪˋrektṛɪ/ *n* (*pl* **-ries**) (book with a) list of persons, business firms, etc in a district; list of telephone subscribers (and usu addresses) in A B C order.

dire·ful /ˋdɑɪəfl/ *adj* (liter) dire; terrible. **~ly** /ˋdɑɪəfḷɪ/ *adv*

dirge /dɜdʒ/ *n* song sung at a burial or for a dead person.

diri·gible /ˋdɪrɪdʒəbl/ *adj* that can be steered. □ *n* ~ balloon.

dirk /dɜk/ *n* kind of dagger.

dirndl /ˋdɜrndl/ *n* full-skirted dress with a close-fitting bodice.

dirt /dɜt/ *n* [U] **1** unclean matter (e g dust, soil, mud) esp when it is where it is not wanted (e g on the skin, clothes, in buildings): *His clothes were covered with ~. How can I get the ~ off the walls?* **2** loose earth or soil: *a ~ road,* (US) unpaved, not macadamized. ***as cheap/common as ~,*** vulgar; low-class. ***fling/throw ~ at sb,*** say slanderous things about him. ***treat sb like ~,*** treat him as if he were worthless. **ˋ~ farmer,** (US) one who does all his own work. **ˈ~-ˋcheap,** very cheap, almost valueless. **ˋ~-track,** one made of cinders, etc, (for, e g motor-cycle ˈraces). **3** unclean thought or talk.

dirty[1] /ˋdɜtɪ/ *adj* (**-ier, -iest**) **1** not clean; covered with dirt: *~ hands/clothes;* causing one to be ~: *~ work.* **2** (of the weather) rough; stormy: *I'm glad I haven't to go out on such a ~ night.* **3** unclean in thought or talk; obscene: *scribble ~ words on lavatory walls.* **4** (colloq) mean, dishonourable, underhand: *play a ~ trick on sb,* play a mean trick on him; *get/give sb a ~ look,* one of severe disapproval or disgust. **dirt·ily** *adv*

dirty[2] /ˋdɜtɪ/ *vt,vi* (*pt,pp* **-tied**) [VP6A,2A] make or become dirty: *Don't ~ your new dress. White gloves ~ easily.*

dis- /dɪs/ *pref* App 3.

dis·abil·ity /ˈdɪsəˋbɪlətɪ/ *n* (*pl* **-ties**) **1** [U] state of being disabled; incapacity. **2** [C] sth that disables or disqualifies one: *Mr Hill has a ~ pension,* from the government, e g because he lost a leg while he was in the army.

dis·able /dɪsˋəɪbl/ *vt* [VP6A] make unable to do sth, esp take away the power of using the limbs: *~d ex-servicemen,* former soldiers, crippled in war. **~·ment** *n*

dis·abuse /ˈdɪsəˋbjuz/ *vt* [VP6A,14] **~ *(of),*** (formal) free (sb, his mind) from false ideas; put (a person) right (in his ideas): *to ~ a man of silly prejudices.*

dis·ad·van·tage /ˈdɪsədˋvɑntɪdʒ *US:* -ˋvæn-/ *n* **1** [C] unfavourable condition, sth that stands in the way of progress, success, etc: *It is a ~ to be small when you're standing in a crowd to look at a football game. His inability to speak English puts him at a ~ when he attends international conferences.* **2** [U] loss; injury: *rumours to his ~,* that hurt his reputation, etc. **~ous** /ˈdɪsˈædvənˋteɪdʒəs/ *adj* causing a ~ (*to*): *in a ~ous place.* **~ous·ly** *adv*

dis·af·fected /ˈdɪsəˋfektɪd/ *adj* unfriendly; (inclined to be) disloyal (esp *to* the government). **dis·af·fec·tion** /ˈdɪsəˋfektʃn/ *n* [U] political discontent; disloyalty.

dis·af·for·est /ˈdɪsəˋforɪst *US:* -ˋfɔr-/ *vt* [VP6A] (also *deforest*) cut down forests on. **dis·af·for·est·ation** /ˈdɪsəˈforɪˋsteɪʃn *US:* -ˈfɔr/ *n*

dis·agree /ˈdɪsəˋgri/ *vt* [VP2A,3A] **~ *(with) sb/sth,*** **1** take a different view; have different opinions; not agree: *Even friends sometimes ~. I'm sorry to ~ with you/with your statement/with what you say. The reports from Rome ~ with those from Milan.* **2** [VP3A] **~ *with sb,*** (of food, climate) have bad effects on; prove unsuitable: *The climate ~s with me.* **~·able** /-əbl/ *adj* unpleasant: *~able weather;* bad-tempered: *a ~able fellow.* **~·able·ness** *n* **~·ably** /-əblɪ/ *adv*

dis·agree·ment /ˈdɪsəˋgrimənt/ *n* **1** [U] act of disagreement; absence of agreement: *to be in ~ with sb or sth.* **2** [C] instance of this; difference of opinion; slight quarrel: *~s between husbands and wives.*

dis·al·low /ˈdɪsəˋlɑʊ/ *vt* [VP6A] refuse to allow or accept as correct: *The judge ~ed the claim.*

dis·ap·pear /ˈdɪsəˋpɪə(r)/ *vi* [VP2A] go out of sight; be seen no more: *Let's hope our difficulties will soon ~,* vanish. *The snow soon ~ed,* melted. **~·ance** /-rns/ *n* ~ing.

dis·ap·point /ˈdɪsəˋpɔɪnt/ *vt* [VP6A] **1** fail to do or be equal to what is hoped for or expected: *The book ~ed me. Please don't ~ me,* don't fail to do what you have promised. **2** prevent a hope, plan, etc from being realized: *I'm sorry to ~ your expectations.* **~ed** *part adj* sad at not getting what was hoped for, etc: *We were ~ed to learn/~ed when we heard that you could not come. We were ~ed that you could not come. I was ~ed at not finding/~ed not to find her at home. We were ~ed in our hopes. What are you looking so ~ed about? We were agreeably ~ed,* glad to find that there were no reasons for our fears. **~·ed·ly** *adv* **~·ing** *adj* causing sb to be ~ed: *The weather this summer has been ~ing.*

dis·ap·point·ment /ˈdɪsəˋpɔɪntmənt/ *n* **1** [U] being disappointed: *To her great ~, it rained on the day of the picnic.* **2** [C] sb or sth that disappoints: *He had suffered many ~s in love,* Many women had not returned his love.

dis·ap·pro·ba·tion /ˈdɪsˈæprəˋbeɪʃn/ *n* (formal) [U] disapproval.

dis·ap·prove /ˈdɪsəˋpruv/ *vi,vt* [VP2A,3A,6A] **~ *(of),*** have, express, an unfavourable opinion: *She wants to train for the theatre but her parents ~/~ of her intentions. Does he ~ of men wearing jewellery?* **dis·ap·proval** /-ˋpruvl/ *n* [U] disapproving: *He shook his head in disapproval,* to show that he ~ed. **dis·ap·prov·ing·ly** /-ɪŋlɪ/ *adv* in a way that shows disapproval: *When Mary lit a cigarette, her father looked at her disapprovingly.*

dis·arm /dɪsˋɑm/ *vi,vt* **1** [VP6A] take away weapons and other means of attack from: *Five hundred rebels were captured and ~ed.* **2** [VP2A] (of nations) reduce the size of, give up the use of, armed forces: *It is difficult to persuade the Great Powers to ~.* **3** [VP6A] make it difficult for sb to feel anger, suspicion, doubt: *By frankly admitting that he was not a scholar, he ~ed criticism. I felt angry, but her smiles ~ed me.* **dis·arma·ment** /dɪsˋɑməmənt/ *n* [U] ~ing or being ~ed(2): *~ament conferences; new proposals for ~ament.*

dis·ar·range /ˈdɪsəˋreɪndʒ/ *vt* [VP6A] disturb; upset; put into disorder: *to ~ sb's plans/hair.* **~·ment** *n*

dis·array /ˈdɪsəˋreɪ/ *n, vt* [VP6A] (put into) disorder: *The troops were in ~.*

dis·so·ci·ate /ˈdɪsəˋsəʊʃɪeɪt/ *vt* [VP14] = dissociate.

dis·as·ter /dɪˋzɑstə(r) *US:* -ˋzæs-/ *n* **1** [C] great or sudden misfortune; terrible accident (e g a great flood or fire, an earthquake, the loss of a large sum of money). **2** [U] great misfortune or suffering. ˋ**~ area,** area where a ~ is officially declared to have occurred. **dis·as·trous** /dɪˋzɑstrəs *US:* -ˋzæs-/ *adj* causing ~: *disastrous floods; a policy that was disastrous for the country.*

dis·as·trous·ly *adv*

dis·avow /ˈdɪsəˋvɑʊ/ *vt* [VP6A] (formal) deny belief in, approval or knowledge of: *He ~ed my share in the plot.* **~al** /-ˋvɑʊl/ *n*

dis·band /dɪsˋbænd/ *vt, vi* [VP6A,2A] (of organized groups) break up: *The army (was) ~ed when the war ended.* **~·ment** *n*

dis·be·lieve /ˈdɪsbɪˋliv/ *vt, vi* [VP6A,2A,3A] **~ in,** refuse to believe (sb or sth); be unable or unwilling to believe in. **dis·be·lief** /ˈdɪsbɪˋlif/ *n* [U] lack of belief; refusal to believe.

dis·bud /ˈdɪsˋbʌd/ *vt* (-dd-) [VP6A] remove buds from (a plant, etc) (e g to get stronger or better shoots from those that are left).

dis·bur·den /dɪsˋbɜdn/ *vt* [VP6A,14] relieve of a burden; unburden (the more usu word).

dis·burse /dɪsˋbɜs/ *vt, vi* [VP6A,2A] pay out (money). **~·ment** *n* [U] paying out (of money); [C] sum of money paid out.

disc, disk /dɪsk/ *n* **1** [C] thin, flat, round plate, e g a coin, a gramophone record; round surface that appears to be flat: *the sun's ~.* ˋ**~ brake,** brake which operates when a flat plate is brought into contact with another rotating, plate at the centre of a (car) wheel. ˋ**~ harrow,** one with ~s instead of teeth. ˋ**~ jockey,** radio or TV broadcaster who introduces performers and comments on records and tapes (esp) of light and popular music. **2** layer of cartilage between vertebrae: *a slipped ~,* one that is slightly dislocated.

dis·card /dɪˋskɑd/ *vt* [VP6A] throw out or away; put aside, give up (sth useless or unwanted): *to ~ one's winter underclothing when the weather gets warm; to ~ old beliefs.* □ *n* /ˋdɪskɑd/ card or cards ~ed in a card game.

dis·cern /dɪˋsɜn/ *vt* [VP6A] see clearly (with the eyes or with the mind); (esp) see with an effort: *We ~ed the figure of a man clinging to the mast of the wrecked ship. It is often difficult to ~ the truth of what we are told.* **~·ing** *adj* able to see and understand well. **~·ible** /-əbl/ *adj* that can be ~ed. **~·ment** *n* ~ing; ability to ~; keenness in judging, forming opinions.

dis·charge[1] /dɪsˋtʃɑdʒ/ *n* discharging or being discharged (all senses, the numbers refer to *discharge*[2]): *How long will the* ~**(1)** *of the cargo take? The* ~**(2)** *of water from the reservoir is carefully controlled. After his* ~**(4)** *from the army, he emigrated to Canada. The prisoners were glad to get their* ~s**(4)**. *He is faithful in the* ~**(5)** *of his duties. Will £50 be enough for the* ~**(5)** *of your liabilities?*

dis·charge[2] /dɪsˋtʃɑdʒ/ *vt, vi* [VP6A,14,21] **1** unload (cargo from) a ship. **2** give or send out (liquid, gas, electric current, etc): *Where do the sewers ~ their contents? The Nile ~s itself* (= flows into) *the Mediterranean. Lightning is caused by clouds discharging electricity. The wound is still discharging pus.* **3** fire (a gun, etc); let fly (an arrow or other missile). **4** send (sb) away; allow (sb) to leave: *to ~ a patient from hospital. The accused man was found not guilty and was ~d. The servant was ~d* (= dismissed) *for being dishonest. The members of the jury were ~d,* set free from their duties. **5** pay (a debt); perform (a duty): *a ~d bankrupt,* man who, after being made bankrupt, has done what the court requires and is now free to act as he wishes.

dis·ciple /dɪˋsɑɪpl/ *n* follower of any leader of religious thought, art, learning, etc; one of the twelve personal followers of Jesus Christ.

dis·ci·pli·narian /ˈdɪsəplɪˋneərɪən/ *n* person who maintains discipline(**2**): *a good/strict/poor ~. He's no ~,* does not or cannot maintain discipline.

dis·ci·pline[1] /ˋdɪsəplɪn/ *n* **1** [U] training, esp of the mind and character, to produce self-control, habits of obedience, etc: *school ~; military ~. Some teachers maintain ~ more strictly than others.* **2** [U] the result of such training; order kept (e g among schoolchildren, soldiers): *The soldiers showed perfect ~ under the fire of the enemy. The children were clever, but there was not much ~ in the school.* **3** [C] set rules for conduct; method by which training may be given: *Pronunciation drill and question and answer work are good ~s for learning a foreign language.* **4** [U] punishment. **5** [C] branch of knowledge; subject of instruction. **dis·ci·plin·ary** /ˈdɪsɪˋplɪnrɪ *US:* -nerɪ/ *adj* of or for ~: *to take disciplinary measures; disciplinary punishment.*

dis·ci·pline[2] /ˋdɪsəplɪn/ *vt* [VP6A] apply discipline(**1**) to; train and control the mind and character of; punish: *to ~ badly behaved children.*

dis·claim /dɪˋskleɪm/ *vt* [VP6A,C] say that one does not own, that one has no connection with: *to ~ responsibility for sth; to ~ all knowledge of an incident.* **~er** *n* statement that ~s: *to issue/send sb a ~er.*

dis·close /dɪˋskləʊz/ *vt* [VP6A,14] uncover; allow to be seen; make known: *to refuse to ~ one's name and address; to ~ a secret.* **dis·clos·ure** /dɪˋskləʊʒə(r)/ *n* [U] disclosing or being ~d; [C] that which is ~d (esp what has been kept secret).

dis·col·our (US = **-lor**) /dɪˋskʌlə(r)/ *vt, vi* **1** [VP6A] change, spoil, the colour of: *walls ~ed by damp.* **2** [VP2A] become changed in colour: *materials that ~ in strong sunlight.* **dis·colour·ation** (US = **-or-**) /dɪˈskʌləˋreɪʃn/ *n* [U] ~ing or being ~ed; [C] ~ed place; stain.

dis·com·fit /dɪˋskʌmfɪt/ *vt* [VP6A] baffle; confuse; embarrass. **dis·comfi·ture** /dɪˋskʌmfɪtʃə(r)/ *n* [U] ~ing or being ~ed.

dis·com·fort /dɪˋskʌmfət/ *n* **1** [U] absence of comfort; uneasiness of mind or body. **2** [C] sth that causes uneasiness; hardship: *the ~s endured by explorers in the Antarctic.*

dis·com·mode /ˈdɪskəˋməʊd/ *vt* [VP6A] (formal) put (sb) to inconvenience.

dis·com·pose /ˈdɪskəmˋpəʊz/ *vt* [VP6A] disturb the composure of: *Don't let their objections ~ you.* **dis·com·posure** /-ʒə(r)/ *n* [U] state of being ~d.

dis·con·cert /ˈdɪskənˋsɜt/ *vt* [VP6A] **1** upset the calmness or self-possession of: *The Manager was ~ed to discover that he had gone to the office without putting in his false teeth.* **2** spoil or upset (plans).

dis·con·nect /ˈdɪskəˋnekt/ *vt* [VP6A,14] detach

from; take (two things) apart: *You should ~ the TV set* (e g by pulling out the plug) *before you make adjustments inside it.* **~ed** *adj* (of speech or writing) having the ideas, etc badly connected.

dis·con·so·late /dɪˈskɒnsələt/ *adj* unhappy at the loss of sth; without hope or comfort; inconsolable. **~·ly** *adv*

dis·con·tent /ˈdɪskənˈtent/ *n* [U] dissatisfaction; absence of contentment; [C] cause of this; grievance. □ *vt* [VP6A] (usu in the *pp*) make dissatisfied: *to be ~ed with one's job.* **~·ed·ly** /-ɪdlɪ/ *adv*

dis·con·tinue /ˈdɪskənˈtɪnju/ *vt,vi* [VP6A,C,2A] cease; give up; put an end to; come to an end: *I'm so busy that I shall have to ~ (paying) these weekly visits.* **dis·con·tinu·ance** /-ˈtɪnjʊəns/ *n*

dis·con·tinu·ous /ˈdɪskənˈtɪnjʊəs/ *adj* not continuous.

dis·cord /ˈdɪskɔd/ *n* **1** [U] disagreement; quarrelling: *What has brought ~ into the family,* caused its members to be quarrelsome? **2** [C] difference of opinion; dispute. **3** [U] lack of harmony between sounds, notes, etc sounded together; [C] instance of this, offending the ear; clashing sound that lacks harmony. **dis·cor·dance** /dɪˈskɔdns/ *n* [U] want of harmony; disagreement. **dis·cor·dant** /dɪˈskɔdnt/ *adj* **1** not in agreement: *~ant opinions.* **2** (of sounds) not harmonious; harsh: *the ~ant noises of motor-car horns.* **dis·cor·dant·ly** *adv*

dis·co·theque /ˈdɪskəˈtek/ *n* club where people dance to amplified recorded music.

dis·count[1] /ˈdɪskaʊnt/ *n* amount of money which may be taken off the full price, e g of **(a)** goods bought by shopkeepers for resale, **(b)** an account if paid promptly, **(c)** a bill of exchange not yet due for payment: *We give 10 per cent ~ for cash,* for prompt payment instead of payment at a later date. **ˈ~ broker** *n* (comm) broker who gets a fee for acting as an intermediary between buyers and sellers. **ˈ~ house** (comm) establishment which specialises in the ~ing of bills of exchange. ⇨ discount[2](1). ***at a ~,*** (of goods) not in demand; easily obtained; (fig) not in high esteem: *Is honesty at a ~ today?*

dis·count[2] /dɪˈskaʊnt *US:* ˈdɪskaʊnt/ *vt* [VP6A] **1** (comm) purchase a bill of exchange for a sum less than its value when it will mature(2). **2** refuse complete belief to a piece of news, a story, etc; allow for exaggeration: *You should ~ a great deal of what appears in the daily press.*

dis·coun·ten·ance /dɪˈskaʊntɪnəns/ *vt* [VP6A] (formal) refuse to approve of; discourage.

dis·cour·age /dɪˈskʌrɪdʒ *US:* -ˈskɜ-/ *vt* **1** [VP6A] lessen, take away, the courage or confidence of: *Don't let one failure ~ you: try again.* **2** [VP14] **~ *sb from doing sth,*** put difficulties in his way; make it seem not worth while; try to persuade him not to do it: *We tried to ~ him from climbing the mountain without a guide. The wet weather is discouraging people from going to the sports meeting.* **~·ment** *n* [U] discouraging or being ~d; [C] sth that ~s.

dis·course /ˈdɪskɔs/ *n* **1** [C] speech; lecture; sermon; treatise. **2** [U] (old use) conversation: *to hold ~ with sb; in ~ with.* □ *vi* /dɪˈskɔs/ ***~ upon,*** (formal) talk, preach or lecture upon (usu at length).

dis·cour·teous /dɪˈskɜtɪəs/ *adj* not courteous; impolite: *It was ~ of you to arrive late.* **~·ly** *adv*

dis·cour·tesy /dɪˈskɜtəsɪ/ *n* [U] impoliteness; [C] (*pl* -**sies**) impolite act.

dis·cover /dɪˈskʌvə(r)/ *vt* [VP6A,9,8,10,25] find out; get knowledge of, bring to view (sth existing but not yet known); realize (sth new or unexpected): *Columbus ~ed America, but did not explore the new continent. Harvey ~ed the circulation of the blood. It was never ~ed how he died. We never ~ed who the man was. We suddenly ~ed that it was too late to catch the train. We have ~ed him to be* (more usu *that he is*) *quite untrustworthy.* **~er** /-vr̩ə(r)/ *n* person who has made a ~y.

dis·covery /dɪˈskʌvr̩ɪ/ *n* **1** [U] discovering or being discovered: *a voyage of ~; the ~ of new chemical elements; the ~ by Franklin that lightning is electricity.* **2** [C] (*pl* -**ries**) sth that is discovered: *He made wonderful scientific discoveries.*

dis·credit[1] /dɪˈskredɪt/ *vt* [VP6A] refuse to believe or have confidence in; cause the truth, value or credit of sth or sb to seem doubtful: *His theories were ~ed by scientists. The judge advised the jury to ~ the evidence of one of the witnesses. Such foolish behaviour will ~ him with the public.*

dis·credit[2] /dɪˈskredɪt/ *n* **1** [U] loss of credit or reputation: *If you continue to behave in this way, you will bring ~ upon yourself.* **2** (*sing* with *indef art;* rarely *pl*) person, thing, causing such loss: *a ~ to the school/to your family.* **3** [U] doubt; disbelief. **~·able** /-əbl/ *adj* bringing ~: *~able conduct.* **~·ably** /-əblɪ/ *adv*

dis·creet /dɪˈskrit/ *adj* careful, tactful, in what one says and does; prudent: *to maintain a ~ silence.* **~·ly** *adv*

dis·crep·ancy /dɪˈskrepənsɪ/ *n* (*pl* -**cies**) [C,U] (of statements and accounts) difference; absence of agreement: *There was considerable ~/There were numerous discrepancies between the two accounts of the fighting.*

dis·crete /dɪˈskrit/ *adj* discontinuous; individually distinct. **~·ness** *n*

dis·cre·tion /dɪˈskreʃn/ *n* [U] **1** being discreet; prudence: *You must show more ~ in choosing your friends.* ***years/age of ~,*** the age at which one is fit to judge and decide for oneself. ***D~ is the better part of valour,*** (prov) used jokingly to excuse oneself for not taking unnecessary risks. **2** freedom to act according to one's own judgement, to do what seems right or best: *Use your ~. It is within your own ~,* You are free to decide. *You have full ~ to act.* **~·ary** /dɪˈskreʃnr̩ɪ *US:* dɪˈskreʃnerɪ/ *adj* having ~(2): *an official with ~ary powers.*

dis·crimi·nate /dɪˈskrɪmɪneɪt/ *vt,vi* **1** [VP14,3A] ***~ one thing from another, ~ between two things,*** be, make, see, a difference between: *Can you ~ good books from bad/~ between good and bad books?* **2** [VP2A,3A] ***~ (against),*** treat differently; make distinctions: *laws which do not ~ against anyone,* that treat all people in the same way. **dis·crimi·nat·ing** *adj* **1** able to see or make small differences: *a discriminating taste in literature.* **2** giving special or different treatment to certain people, countries, etc; differential(1): *discriminating tariffs/rates/duties.*

dis·crimi·na·tion /dɪˈskrɪmɪˈneɪʃn/ *n* [U] discriminating; ability to discriminate: *Some people do not show much ~ in their choice of books. D~ against goods from foreign countries is usually done by means of tariffs. Is there racial ~ in your country?* **dis·crim·i·na·tory** /dɪˈskrɪmɪˈnətr̩ɪ *US:*

-tɔrɪ/ *adj* discriminating(2): *discriminatory legislation.*

dis·cur·sive /dɪˋskɜsɪv/ *adj* (of a person, what he says or does, his style) wandering from one point or subject to another. **~·ly** *adv* **~·ness** *n*

dis·cus /ˋdɪskəs/ *n* heavy, round plate of stone, metal or wood, thrown in ancient Roman and Greek athletic contests and in modern contests (e g the Olympic Games): *the ~ throw,* name used for this contest.

throwing the discus

dis·cuss /dɪˋskʌs/ *vt* [VP6A,8,10,14] **~ *with,*** examine and argue about (a subject): *to ~ a question with sb; to ~ (with one's friends) what to do/how to do it/how something should be done.*

dis·cussion /dɪˋskʌʃn/ *n* [U,C] discussing or being discussed; talk for the purpose of discussing: *after much ~; after several long ~s. We had a long ~ about the question. When will the matter come up for ~?* ***under ~,*** being discussed: *The question is still under ~.*

dis·dain /dɪsˋdeɪn/ *vt* [VP6A,C,7A] look on with contempt; think (it) dishonourable (to do sth); be too proud (to do sth): *A good man should ~ flattery. He ~ed to notice the insult. He ~ed my offer of help.* □ *n* [U] contempt; scorn: *No one likes to be treated with ~.* **~·ful** /-fl/ *adj* showing ~: *~ful looks.* **~·fully** /-flɪ/ *adv*

dis·ease /dɪˋziz/ *n* [U] illness; disorder of body or mind or of plants; [C] particular kind of illness or disorder: *The business of doctors is to prevent and cure ~. Measles, mumps and influenza are common ~s.* **dis·eased** /dɪˋzizd/ *part adj* suffering from, injured by, ~: *~d vines; ~d in body and mind.*

dis·em·bark /ˈdɪsɪmˋbɑk/ *vt,vi* [VP6A,14,2A,C] put, go, on shore (*from* a ship). **dis·em·bar·ka·tion** /ˈdɪsˈembɑˋkeɪʃn/ *n*

dis·em·bar·rass /ˈdɪsɪmˋbærəs/ *vt* [VP14] ***~ sb/ oneself (of),*** (formal) rid (sb, oneself) from embarrassment; rid (sb, oneself) of a burden: *to ~ oneself of a burden/charge/responsibility.* **~·ment** *n*

dis·em·body /ˈdɪsɪmˋbodɪ/ *vt* (*pt,pp* -died) [VP6A] (chiefly in *pp*) separate, set free (the soul or spirit) from the body: *a building haunted by a disembodied spirit.*

dis·em·bowel /ˈdɪsɪmˋbaʊl/ *vt* (-ll-) (US also -l-) [VP6A] cut out the bowels of.

dis·em·broil /ˈdɪsɪmˋbrɔɪl/ *vt* [VP6A] (formal) free from embroilment.

dis·en·chant /ˈdɪsɪnˋtʃɑnt *US:* -ˋtʃænt/ *vt* [VP6A] free from enchantment or illusion: *He is quite ~ed with the Tory Government.* **~·ment** *n*

dis·en·cum·ber /ˈdɪsɪnˋkʌmbə(r)/ *vt* [VP6A,14] (formal) free from encumbrance: *~ed of his heavy armour.*

dis·en·dow /ˈdɪsɪnˋdaʊ/ *vt* [VP6A,14] take away endowments (esp from a Church). **~·ment** *n*

dis·en·gage /ˈdɪsɪnˋgeɪdʒ/ *vt,vi* [VP6A,14,2A,C] ***~ (from),*** separate, detach (oneself or sth): *Two enemy battalions (were) ~d from the battle after suffering heavy casualties.* **dis·en·gaged** *pp* (of a person) free from engagements: *if the Manager is ~d,* if he is free. **~·ment** *n* (condition of) being ~d: *the military and economic ~ment of the USA from SE Asia.*

dis·en·tangle /ˈdɪsɪnˋtæŋgl/ *vt,vi* **1** [VP6A,14] ***~ from,*** free, from complications, tangles or confusion: *to ~ truth from falsehood.* **2** [VP2A] unravel; become clear of tangles: *This skein of wool won't ~,* cannot be ~d. **~·ment** *n*

dis·equi·lib·rium /ˈdɪsˈikwɪˋlɪbrɪəm/ *n* [U] absence, loss, of equilibrium; instability.

dis·es·tab·lish /ˈdɪsɪˋstæblɪʃ/ *vt* [VP6A] end, break up, an established state of affairs, esp the constitutional connection between a national Church (e g the Church of England) and the State. **~·ment** *n*

dis·fa·vour (US = **-favor**) /ˈdɪsˋfeɪvə(r)/ *n* [U] state of being out of favour; disapproval: *to regard sth with ~; to be in ~; to fall into ~; to incur sb's ~.* □ *vt* [VP6A] regard with ~; disapprove of.

dis·figure /dɪsˋfɪgə(r) *US:* -gjə(r)/ *vt* [VP6A] spoil the appearance or shape of: *beautiful scenery ~d by ugly advertising signs; a face ~d by a broken nose/an ugly scar.* **~·ment** *n* [U] disfiguring or being ~d; [C] sth that ~s.

dis·for·est /dɪsˋforɪst *US:* -ˋfɔr-/ *vt* = disafforest.

dis·fran·chise /dɪsˋfræntʃɑɪz/ *vt* [VP6A] deprive of rights of citizenship; (esp) deprive (a place) of the right to send a representative to parliament or (a citizen) of the right to vote for a parliamentary representative. **~·ment** /-ˋfræntʃɪzmənt/ *n*

dis·frock /dɪsˋfrok/ *vt* [VP6A] = unfrock (the usu word).

dis·gorge /dɪsˋgɔdʒ/ *vt* [VP6A] throw up or out from, or as from, the throat; (fig) give up (esp sth taken wrongfully).

dis·grace[1] /dɪsˋgreɪs/ *n* **1** [U] loss of respect, favour reputation: *A man who commits a crime and is sent to prison brings ~ on himself and his family. There need be no ~ in being poor.* **2** [U] state of having lost respect, etc: *He told a lie and is in ~. He has fallen into ~ with his companions.* **3** (*sing* with *indef art*) thing, state of affairs, person, that is a cause of shame or discredit: *These slums are a ~ to the city authorities. The continued use of armed forces to settle disputes is a ~ to the rulers of all countries.* **~·ful** /-fl/ *adj* bringing or causing ~: *~ful behaviour.* **~·fully** /-flɪ/ *adv: to behave ~fully.*

dis·grace[2] /dɪsˋgreɪs/ *vt* [VP6A] **1** bring disgrace on; be a disgrace to: *Don't ~ the family name.* **2** put (sb) out of favour.

dis·gruntled /dɪsˋgrʌntld/ *adj* discontented; in a bad mood (*at* sth, *with* sb).

dis·guise[1] /dɪsˋgɑɪz/ *vt* [VP6A,16B] **1** change the appearance, etc of, in order to deceive or to hide the identity of: *He ~d his looks but he could not ~ his voice. He ~d himself as a woman/~d himself by wearing a wig.* **2** conceal; cover up: *He ~d his sorrow beneath a cheerful appearance/by appearing cheerful. There is no disguising the fact that…,* The fact that… cannot be concealed.

dis·guise[2] /dɪsˋgɑɪz/ *n* **1** [U] disguising; disguised condition: *He went among the enemy in ~. He went to the ball in the ~ of a clown.* **2** [C,U] dress, actions, manner, etc used for disguising: *a clever ~. He had tried all sorts of ~s. She made no ~ of* *her feelings,* did not hide them.

dis·gust[1] /dɪsˋgʌst/ *n* [U] **~ *(at sth, with sb),*** strong feeling of dislike or distaste (e g caused by a bad smell or taste, a horrible sight, evil conduct): *He turned away in ~. To her great ~, she was given only a minor part in the play. His ~ at the government's policy caused him to resign.*

dis·gust[2] /dɪsˋgʌst/ *vt* [VP6A] cause disgust in: *His behaviour ~ed everybody. We were ~ed at/by/with what we saw.* **~·ing** *adj*: *behaviour that is ~ing to all decent folk.* **~·ing·ly** *adv*: *He is ~ingly mean with his money.* **~·ed·ly** /-ɪdlɪ/ *adv* with ~: *He looked ~edly at the dirty room.*

dish[1] /dɪʃ/ *n* **1** shallow, flat-bottomed (often oval or oblong) vessel, of earthenware, glass, metal, etc from which food is served at table: *a ˋmeat-~.* **~·ful** /-fʊl/ *n* as much as a ~ will contain. **2 the ~es,** all the crockery (plates, bowls, cups and saucers, etc) used for a meal: *to wash up the ~es.* **ˋ~-cloth,** cloth for washing ~es, etc. **ˋ~-washer,** power-operated machine for washing dishes, cutlery, etc. **ˋ~-water,** water in which ~es have been washed. **3** food brought to table on or in a ~: *His favourite ~ is steak and kidney pie.* **4** ~-shaped object, esp a large concave reflector for the reception of radio-waves from outer space, or in radio-telescopes, etc. ⇨ the illus at **radio-telescope. 5** (sl) attractive girl: *She's quite a ~.*

dish[2] /dɪʃ/ *vt* **1** [VP6A,15B] **~ *sth up,*** put on or into a ~ or ~es: *to ~ (up) the dinner,* get it ready for serving; (fig) prepare, serve up facts, arguments, etc: *to ~ up the usual arguments in a new form.* **~ *sth out,*** distribute. **2** [VP6A] (colloq) upset; thwart; outmanœuvre: *to ~ one's opponents. The scandal ~ed his hopes of being elected.* **~y** *adj* (-ier, -iest) (sl) (of a man or girl) attractive.

dis·habille /ˈdɪsəˋbil/ *n* [U] (usu *in* ~) (usu of a woman) the state of being negligently or partly dressed.

dis·har·mony /dɪsˋhɑmənɪ/ *n* [U] lack of harmony; discord. **dis·har·moni·ous** /ˈdɪshɑˋməʊnɪəs/ *adj*

dis·hearten /dɪsˋhɑtn/ *vt* [VP6A] cause to lose courage or confidence: *Don't be ~ed by a single failure.*

di·shev·el·led (US = **-eled**) /dɪˋʃevld/ *adj* with the hair uncombed; (of the hair and clothes) in disorder; untidy.

dis·hon·est /dɪsˋonɪst/ *adj* not honest; intended to cheat, deceive or mislead. **~·ly** *adv* **dis·honesty** /ˈdɪsˋonɪstɪ/ *n* [U] being ~; [C] ~ act, etc.

dis·hon·our (US = **-honor**) /dɪsˋonə(r)/ *n* **1** disgrace or shame; loss, absence, of honour and self-respect: *to bring ~ on one's family.* **2** (with *indef art*) person or thing that brings ~: *He was a ~ to his regiment.* □ *vt* [VP6A] **1** bring shame, discredit, loss of honour on (sb or sth). **2** (of a bank) *~ a cheque/bill of exchange,* refuse to pay money on it (because the bank's customer has not enough credit). **~·able** /dɪsˋonr̩əbl/ *adj* without honour; shameful. **~·ably** /dɪsˋonr̩əblɪ/ *adv*

dis·il·lu·sion /ˈdɪsɪˋluʒn/ *vt* [VP6A] set free from mistaken beliefs: *They had thought that the new colony would be a paradise, but they were soon ~ed.* □ *n* the state of being ~ed. **~·ment** *n* freedom from illusions: *in a state of complete ~(ment).*

dis·in·cen·tive /ˈdɪsɪnˋsentɪv/ *n* [C] act, measure, etc that tends to discourage efforts, production, etc: *Is high taxation a ~ to members of the managerial class?*

dis·in·cli·na·tion /ˈdɪsˈɪnklɪˋneɪʃn/ *n* (usu with *indef art*) unwillingness (*for* sth, *to do* sth): *Some schoolboys have a strong ~ for work. His ~ to meet people worries his wife, who is very sociable.*

dis·in·cline /ˈdɪsɪnˋklɑɪn/ *vt* [VP17,14] (usu passive) ***be ~d for sth, ~d to do sth,*** be reluctant or unwilling: *He was ~d to help me. The hot weather made him feel ~d for work.*

dis·in·fect /ˈdɪsɪnˋfekt/ *vt* [VP6A] make free from infection by bacteria: *The house was ~ed after Tom had had scarlet fever.* **dis·in·fec·tant** /ˈdɪsɪnˋfektənt/ *adj, n* ~ing (chemical). **dis·in·fec·tion** /ˈdɪsɪnˋfekʃn/ *n* [U] (act of) ~ing.

dis·in·fest /ˈdɪsɪnˋfest/ *vt* [VP6A] get rid of vermin. **dis·in·fes·ta·tion** /ˈdɪsˈɪnfeˋsteɪʃn/ *n*: *disinfestation officer,* person employed to get rid of vermin (e g a rat-catcher).

dis·in·fla·tion /ˈdɪsɪnˋfleɪʃn/ *n* (process of) returning from a state of inflation to a stable or more normal level (in which prices, wages, etc do not vary much).

dis·in·genu·ous /ˈdɪsɪnˋdʒenjʊəs/ *adj* insincere; not straightforward. **~·ly** *adv* **~·ness** *n*

dis·in·herit /ˈdɪsɪnˋherɪt/ *vt* [VP6A] take away the right (of sb) to inherit. **dis·in·heri·tance** /ˈdɪsɪnˋherɪtəns/ *n* [U] (act of) ~ing.

dis·in·te·grate /dɪsˋɪntɪgreɪt/ *vt, vi* [VP6A,2A] (cause to) break up into small parts or pieces: *rocks ~d by frost and rain.* **dis·in·te·gra·tion** /dɪsˈɪntɪˋgreɪʃn/ *n*

dis·in·ter /ˈdɪsɪnˋtɜ(r)/ *vt* (-rr-) [VP6A] dig up from the earth (e g from a grave). **~·ment** *n*

dis·in·ter·ested /dɪsˋɪntrəstɪd/ *adj* not influenced by personal feelings or interests: *His action was not altogether ~.* ⇨ **uninterested. ~·ly** *adv* **~·ness** *n*

dis·joint /ˈdɪsˋdʒɔɪnt/ *vt* [VP6A] separate at the joints; take to pieces: *to ~ a chicken.*

dis·jointed /dɪsˋdʒɔɪntɪd/ *adj* (e g of speech and writing) not connected; incoherent. **~·ly** *adv* **~·ness** *n*

dis·junc·tive /dɪsˋdʒʌŋktɪv/ *adj* (gram): *~ conjunction,* one expressing opposition of or contrast between ideas (e g *either… or*).

disk *n* ⇨ **disc.**

dis·like /dɪsˋlɑɪk/ *vt* [VP6A,C, rarely VP7] not like: *to ~ getting up early/being disturbed. If you behave like that, you'll get yourself ~d,* become unpopular. □ *n* [C] feeling of not liking; feeling against: *to have a ~ of/for cats; to take a ~ to sb,* begin to ~ him. ***likes and ~s*** /ˋdɪslɑɪks/, preferences and aversions: *He has so many likes and ~s that he is difficult to please.*

dis·lo·cate /ˋdɪsləkeɪt *US:* -ləʊk-/ *vt* [VP6A] **1** put (esp a bone in the body) out of position: *He fell from his horse and ~d his collarbone.* **2** put traffic, machinery, business, etc out of order: *Traffic was badly ~d by the heavy fall of snow.* **dis·lo·ca·tion** /ˈdɪsləˋkeɪʃn *US:* -ləʊˋk-/ *n* dislocating or being ~d: *the dislocation of trade caused by the blocking of the canal.*

dis·lodge /dɪsˋlodʒ/ *vt* [VP6A,14] **~ *(from),*** move, force (sb or sth) from the place occupied: *to ~ a stone from a building/the enemy from their positions.* **~·ment** *n*

dis·loyal /dɪsˋlɔɪl̩/ *adj* **~ to,** not loyal to. **~ly** /-ˋlɔɪl̩ɪ/ *adv* **~·ty** /-ˋlɔɪltɪ/ *n* [U] being ~ (*to*); [C] (*pl* -ties) ~ act, etc.

dis·mal /ˈdɪzml/ *adj* sad, gloomy; miserable; comfortless: ~ *weather; in a* ~ *voice.* **~·ly** /ˈdɪzmḷɪ/ *adv*

dis·mantle /dɪsˈmæntl/ *vt* [VP6A] **1** take away fittings, furnishings, etc from: *The old warship was ~d,* Its guns, armour, engines, etc were taken out. **2** take to pieces: *to* ~ *an engine.* **~·ment** *n* dismantling (now the usu word).

dis·mast /ˈdɪsˈmɑst *US:* -ˈmæst/ *vt* [VP6A] deprive (a ship) of its mast(s): *The schooner was ~ed in the storm.*

dis·may /dɪsˈmeɪ/ *n* [U] feeling of fear and discouragement: *The news that the enemy were near filled/struck them with* ~. *He looked at me in (blank)* ~. □ *vt* [VP6A] fill with ~: *We were ~ed at the news.*

dis·mem·ber /dɪsˈmembə(r)/ *vt* [VP6A] **1** tear or cut the limbs from: *Poor fellow! He was ~ed by a pack of wolves.* **2** (fig) divide up (a country, etc). **~·ment** *n*

dis·miss /dɪsˈmɪs/ *vt* [VP6A,14] **1** send away (from one's employment, from service): *The servant was ~ed for being lazy and dishonest. The officer was ~ed the service/~ed from the service for neglect of duty.* **2** allow to go: *The teacher ~ed his class when the bell rang.* **3** put away from the mind; stop thinking or talking about: *to* ~ *all thoughts of revenge.* **4** (cricket, of the team that is fielding) put a batsman/a team out: *The fast bowler ~ed Smith for ten runs. Cambridge were ~ed for only 75 runs.* **~al** /-ˈmɪsl/ *n* ~ing or being ~ed: *~al from the Navy.*

dis·mount /ˈdɪsˈmaʊnt/ *vi,vt* **1** [VP2A,3A] ~ ***(from),*** get down (from sth on which one is riding): *to* ~ *from one's horse/bicycle.* Cf *alight* from a bus, taxi, tram or train. **2** [VP6A] remove (sth) from its mount: *to* ~ *a gun* (from the gun-carriage). **3** [VP6A] cause to fall (from a horse, etc): *The knight ~ed his opponent.* ⇨ **joust. ~ed** *part adj* (of cavalry) fighting as infantry.

dis·obedi·ence /ˈdɪsəˈbidɪəns/ *n* [U] failure or refusal to obey: *acts of* ~; ~ *to orders.* **dis·obedi·ent** *adj* not obedient (*to*). **dis·obedi·ent·ly** *adv*

dis·obey /ˈdɪsəˈbeɪ/ *vt* [VP6A,2A] pay no attention to orders; not obey a person, a law, etc.

dis·oblige /ˈdɪsəˈblaɪdʒ/ *vt* [VP6A] (formal) refuse to be helpful or to think about another person's wishes or needs: *I'm sorry to* ~ *you, but last time I lent you money you did not repay me.*

dis·order /dɪsˈɔdə(r)/ *n* **1** [U] absence of order; confusion: *The burglars left the room in great* ~. *The enemy retreated in* ~. **2** [U] absence of order caused by political troubles; [C] angry outburst of rioting caused by political troubles, etc: *Troops were called out to deal with the ~s in the capital.* **3** [C,U] disturbance of the normal working of the body or mind: *a* ~ *of the digestive system; suffering from mental* ~; *~s of the mind.* □ *vt* [VP6A] put into ~: *a ~ed imagination/mind.*

dis·order·ly /dɪsˈɔdəlɪ/ *adj* **1** in disorder: *a* ~ *room/desk.* **2** causing disturbance; unruly; lawless: ~ *crowds; a* ~ *mob;* ~ *behaviour; keep a* ~ *house,* e g a brothel or one where illegal gambling is carried on.

dis·or·gan·ize /ˈdɪsˈɔgənaɪz/ *vt* [VP6A] throw into confusion; upset the working or system of: *The train service was ~d by fog.* **dis·or·gan·iz·ation** /ˈdisˌɔgənaɪˈzeɪʃn *US:* -nɪˈz-/ *n* [U].

dis·orien·tate /dɪsˈɔrɪənteɪt/ (also, esp US) **dis·orient** /dɪsˈɔrɪənt/ *vt* [VP6A] (liter, fig) confuse (sb) as to his bearings(**4**).

dis·own /dɪsˈəʊn/ *vt* [VP6A] say that one does not know (sb or sth), that one has not, or no longer wishes to have, any connection with (sb or sth): *The boy was so wicked that his father ~ed him.*

dis·par·age /dɪˈspærɪdʒ/ *vt* [VP6A] say things to suggest that (sb or sth) is of small value or importance. **~·ment** *n* **dis·par·ag·ing·ly** *adv* in a disparaging manner.

dis·par·ate /ˈdɪspərət/ *adj* that cannot be compared in quality, amount, kind, etc; essentially different. □ *n pl* things so unlike that comparison is impossible.

dis·par·ity /dɪˈspærətɪ/ *n* [U] inequality; difference; [C] (*pl* **-ties**) instance or degree of this: ~ *in age/rank/position; the disparities in the newspaper accounts of the accident.*

dis·passion·ate /dɪˈspæʃṇət/ *adj* free from passion; not taking sides, not showing favour (in a quarrel, etc between others). **~·ly** *adv* **~·ness** *n*

dis·patch[1], **des·patch** /dɪˈspætʃ/ *n* **1** [U] dispatching or being dispatched (all senses): *Please hurry up the* ~ *of these telegrams.* **2** [C] sth dispatched(**1**), esp, a government, military or newspaper report: *London newspapers receive ~es from all parts of the world. The soldier was mentioned in ~es,* had his name recorded in accounts of fighting, etc because of his bravery, etc. ⇨ *citation* at **cite**. **ˈ~-box,** one for official ~es. **ˈ~-rider,** man who carries military ~es (usu on a motor-bike). **3** [U] promptness; speed: *to act with* ~.

dis·patch[2], **des·patch** /dɪˈspætʃ/ *vt* **1** [VP6A,14] ~ ***(to),*** send off, to a destination, on a journey, for a special purpose: *to* ~ *letters/telegrams; to* ~ *a cruiser to the island to restore order.* **2** [VP6A] finish, get through, business, a meal quickly. **3** [VP6A] kill; give the death blow to: *The executioner quickly ~ed the condemned man.*

dis·pel /dɪˈspel/ *vt* (**-ll-**) [VP6A] drive away; scatter: *The wind soon ~led the fog. How can we* ~ *their doubts and fears?*

dis·pens·able /dɪˈspensəbl/ *adj* that can be done without; not necessary.

dis·pens·ary /dɪˈspensərɪ/ *n* (*pl* **-ries**) place where medicines are dispensed (e g in a hospital).

dis·pen·sa·tion /ˈdɪspenˈseɪʃn/ *n* **1** [U] the act of dispensing(**1**) or distributing: *the* ~ *of justice/charity/food.* **2** [U] ordering or management, esp of the world by Providence; [C] sth arranged by Nature or Providence: *A bereavement* (e g the death of a very old person) *is sometimes called a* ~ *of Providence.* **3** [C,U] permission to do sth that is usually forbidden, or not to do sth that is usually required, esp by ecclesiastical law: *to be granted* ~ *from fasting during a journey.* **4** [C] religious system prevalent at a period: *the Mosaic* ~, that of the time of Moses.

dis·pense /dɪˈspens/ *vt,vi* **1** [VP6A,14] deal out; distribute; administer: *to* ~ *charity/alms/one's favours to people;* (legal) *to* ~ *justice* (in law courts). **2** [VP6A] mix; prepare, give out (medicines): *to* ~ *a prescription; dispensing chemist,* one qualified to do this. **3** [VP3A] ~ ***with,*** **(a)** do without: *He is not yet well enough to* ~ *with the doctor's services.* **(b)** render unnecessary: *The new machinery ~s with hand-labour.* **dis·penser** *n* **1** person who ~s, esp medicines. **2** container from which sth can be withdrawn, ejected or otherwise obtained without removing a cover, lid, etc: *a ~r for liquid soap/ toilet powder/ paper cups.*

dis·perse /dɪˋspɜs/ *vt,vi* [VP6A,2A] (cause to) go in different directions; scatter: *The police ~d the crowd. The crowd ~d when the police arrived. The soldiers were ~d* (= stationed at different points) *along a wide front. A prism ~s light,* breaks it up into its coloured rays. **dis·per·sal** /dɪˋspɜsl/ *n* dispersing or being ~d. **dis·per·sion** /dɪˋspɜʃn *US:* -ʒn/ *n* = dispersal, esp of light. **the Dispersion,** the Jews ~d among the Gentiles. ⇨ Diaspora.

dis·pirit /dɪˋspɪrɪt/ *vt* [VP6A] discourage; dishearten (chiefly in *pp*): *to look ~ed.* **~·ed·ly** *adv*

dis·place /dɪˋspleɪs/ *vt* [VP6A] **1** put out of the right or usual position. **ˈ~d ˋperson,** refugee left homeless, unable or unwilling to return to his own country. **2** take the place of; put sth or sb else in the place of: *The volunteers were ~d by a professional army. Tom has ~d Harry in Mary's affections.*

dis·place·ment /dɪˋspleɪsmənt/ *n* [U] **1** displacing or being displaced: *the ~ of human labour by machines.* **2** amount of water displaced by a solid body in it, or floating in it: *a ship of 10 000 tons ~.*

dis·play[1] /dɪˋspleɪ/ *vt* [VP6A] **1** show; place or spread out so that there is no difficulty in seeing: *Department stores ~ their goods in the windows. The peacock ~ed its fine tail feathers.* **2** allow to be seen; show signs of having: *to ~ one's ignorance. She ~ed no sign of emotion when she was told of her son's death.*

dis·play[2] /dɪˋspleɪ/ *n* [C,U] displaying; show or exhibition: *a fashion ~,* a showing of new styles in clothes, etc; *a fine ~ of courage; a ~ of bad temper; to make a ~ of one's knowledge,* show what a lot one knows; *to make a ~ of one's affection,* show great affection (whether genuine or not). *Some newly rich people are fond of vulgar ~.*

dis·please /dɪˋspliz/ *vt* [VP6A] not please; offend; annoy; make indignant or angry: *to ~ one's wife; to be ~d with sb* (*for* doing sth); *to be ~d at sb's conduct.* **dis·pleas·ing** *adj* not pleasing (*to* sb). **dis·pleas·ing·ly** *adv*

dis·pleasure /dɪˋspleʒə(r)/ *n* [U] displeased feeling; dissatisfaction: *He incurred his father's ~. He looked with ~ at the meal that was set before him.*

dis·port /dɪˋspɔt/ *vt* [VP6A] (formal): *~ oneself,* play; amuse oneself, e g in the sea or in the sunshine.

dis·pos·able /dɪˋspəʊzəbl/ *adj* **1** made so that it may be (easily) disposed of after use: *~ nappies/ panties,* made of soft paper which disintegrates quickly in water. **2** available; at one's disposal.

dis·posal /dɪˋspəʊzl/ *n* [U] **~ *(of)*,** **1** the act of disposing(1,2): *the ~ of property,* e g by selling it, leaving it to sb in one's will; *the ~ of rubbish,* getting rid of it; *a waste-~ unit,* kind of machine that shreds waste products so that they can be washed away down the drains; *a bomb ~ squad,* group of men who, when unexploded bombs are found, try to make them harmless and remove them; *the ~ of troops,* the method of using them, placing them in position, etc; *the ~ of business affairs,* settling them. **2** control; management: *In time of war the government must have entire ~ of all material resources.* **at one's ~,** to be used as one wishes: *He placed £50 at my ~. My library is at your ~.*

dis·pose /dɪˋspəʊz/ *vi,vt* **1** [VP3A] **~ *of*,** finish with; get rid of; deal with: *to ~ of rubbish. He doesn't want to ~ of* (e g sell) *the land. I think we have ~d of all his arguments,* answered them, proved them unsound. *The dictator soon ~d of his opponents,* e g by putting them in prison. *We ~d of our opponents for 97 runs,* (cricket) got them all out for this total. **2** [VP6A,2A] place (persons, objects) in good order or in suitable positions: *The cruisers were ~d in line abreast. God ~s all things according to His will. Man proposes, God ~s,* (prov) Men may propose things, but God determines what shall happen. **3** [VP17] ***~ sb to do sth,*** (formal) make willing or ready: *Your news ~s me to believe that.... The low salary did not ~ him to accept the position. I'm not ~d/ don't feel ~d to help that lazy fellow.* ***be well/ill ~d (towards),*** be/not be friendly and helpful: *Most of the newspapers seem to be well ~d towards the new cabinet.*

dis·po·si·tion /ˈdɪspəˋzɪʃn/ *n* [C] **1** arrangement; placing in order: *the ~ of furniture in a room; a clever ~ of troops; ~s to withstand an attack.* **2** person's natural qualities of mind and character: *a man with a cheerful ~; a ~ to jealousy/to take offence easily.* **3** inclination: *There was a general ~ to leave early,* Most people seemed to wish to leave early. **4** power of ordering and disposing: *God has the supreme ~ of all things. Who has the ~ of this property,* the power or authority to dispose of it?

dis·pos·sess /ˈdɪspəˋzes/ *vt* [VP14] ***~ sb of sth,*** take away (property, esp land) from; compel (sb) to give up (the house he occupies): *The nobles were ~ed of their property after the Revolution.* **dis·pos·session** /ˈdɪspəˋzeʃn/ *n*

dis·proof /dɪˋspruf/ *n* [U] disproving; [C] that which disproves; proof to the contrary.

dis·pro·por·tion /ˈdɪsprəˋpɔʃn/ *n* [U] the state of being out of proportion: *~ in age.* **~·ate** /-ˋpɔʃn̩ət/ *adj* out of porportion; relatively too large or small, etc: *to give a ~ate amount of one's time to games; pay that is ~ate to the work done.* **~·ate·ly** *adv*

dis·prove /ˈdɪˋspruv/ *vt* [VP6A] prove to be wrong or false.

dis·put·able /dɪˋspjutəbl/ *adj* that may be disputed; questionable.

dis·pu·tant /dɪˋspjutənt/ *n* person who disputes.

dis·pu·ta·tion /ˈdɪspjʊˋteɪʃn/ *n* [U] disputing; [C] debate, controversy: *a medieval ~,* using syllogisms.

dis·pu·ta·tious /ˈdɪspjʊˋteɪʃəs/ *adj* fond of disputing; inclined to dispute. **~·ly** *adv*

dis·pute[1] /ˋdɪspjut/ *n* **1** [U] debate, argument: *The matter in ~* (= being disputed) *is the ownership of a house.* ***beyond/past (all) ~,*** unquestionably; undoubtedly: *This is beyond ~ the best book on the subject.* **in ~ with,** engaged in a ~ with: *The workers' union is in ~ with the management.* **without ~,** without fear of contradiction. **2** [C] quarrel; argument; controversy: *There were many religious ~s in England during the 17th century.*

dis·pute[2] /dɪˋspjut/ *vi,vt* **1** [VP2A,3A] ***~ (with/ against sb),*** argue, debate, quarrel in words: *Some people are always disputing.* **2** [VP6A,8,10] discuss, question the truth or validity of: *to ~ a* *statement/a claim/a decision. The election result was ~d,* e g it was said that the votes had been counted wrongly. *The will was ~d,* e g it was said that it had not been made in correct legal form. *They were disputing whether to start at once or wait. They ~d (about) how to get the best results.* **3** [VP6A] oppose; resist: *to ~ a landing/an advance by the enemy;* fight for, try to win: *Our team ~d the victory until the last minute of the game.*

dis·qual·ify /dɪˋskwolɪfɑɪ/ *vt* (*pt,pp* -fied) [VP6A,14] ***~ sb (for sth/from doing sth),*** make unfit or unable: *His weak eyesight disqualified him for military service. As he was a professional, he was disqualified from taking part in the Olympic Games.* **dis·quali·fi·ca·tion** /dɪˈskwolɪfɪˋkeɪʃn/ *n* [U] ~ing or being disqualified; [C] that which disqualifies.

dis·quiet /dɪˋskwɑɪət/ *vt* [VP6A] make troubled, anxious, uneasy: *~ed by apprehensions of illness.* □ *n* [U] anxiety; troubled condition: *The President's speech caused considerable ~ in some European capitals.* **~·ing** *adj* causing ~: *~ing news.* **~·ing·ly** *adv* in a way that causes ~: *a ~ingly high percentage of errors in the examination papers.* **dis·quiet·ude** /dɪˋskwɑɪətjud *US:* -tud/ *n* [U] state of ~; uneasiness.

dis·qui·si·tion /ˈdɪskwɪˋzɪʃn/ *n* [C] ***~ on sth,*** long, elaborate speech or piece of writing.

dis·re·gard /ˈdɪsrɪˋgɑd/ *vt* [VP6A] pay no attention to; show no respect for: *to ~ a warning/sb's objections to a proposal.* □ *n* [U] inattention; indifference; neglect: *~ of a rule; ~ for one's teachers.*

dis·rel·ish /dɪsˋrelɪʃ/ *vt* [VP6A] dislike. □ *n* [U] dislike, distaste.

dis·re·mem·ber /ˈdɪsrɪˋmembə(r)/ *vt* [VP6A] (regional, Irish) fail to remember.

dis·re·pair /ˈdɪsrɪˋpeə(r)/ *n* [U] the state of needing repair: *The building was in bad ~,* in great need of being repaired.

dis·repu·table /dɪsˋrepjʊtəbl/ *adj* having a bad reputation: *~ bars and dance-halls;* not respectable in appearance: *a ~-looking fellow; a ~ old hat,* dirty, worn out. ***~ to,*** reflecting badly on: *incidents ~ to his character as a priest.* **dis·repu·tably** /-təblɪ/ *adv*

dis·re·pute /ˈdɪsrɪˋpjut/ *n* [U] condition of being disreputable; discredit: *The hotel has fallen into ~,* no longer has a good reputation.

dis·re·spect /ˈdɪsrɪˋspekt/ *n* [U] rudeness; want of respect: *He meant no ~ by that remark,* did not intend to be impolite. *We must not show ~ for our seniors/treat our seniors with ~.* **~·ful** /-fl/ *adj* showing ~: *to be ~ful to sb.* **~·fully** /-flɪ/ *adv: to speak ~fully of/about sb.*

dis·robe /ˈdɪsˋrəʊb/ *vi,vt* [VP6A,2A] undress; take off (esp official or ceremonial robes): *The Queen ~d after the coronation ceremony.*

dis·rupt /ˈdɪsˋrʌpt/ *vt* [VP6A] break up, split, separate by force a State, an empire, communications, other non-physical things: *Their quarrels seem likely to ~ the Coalition.* **dis·rup·tion** /dɪsˋrʌpʃn/ *n* [U] ~ing or being ~ed: *the ~ion of the Roman Empire.* **dis·rup·tive** /dɪsˋrʌptɪv/ *adj* causing ~ion: *~ive forces.*

dis·sat·is·fac·tion /ˈdɪˈsætɪsˋfækʃn/ *n* [U] ***~ (with sb/sth/at an event),*** the state of being dissatisfied.

dis·sat·isfy /dɪˋsætɪsfɑɪ/ *vt* (*pt,pp* -fied) [VP6A] fail to satisfy; make discontented; (usu passive): *to be dissatisfied with one's salary/at not getting a better salary.*

dis·sect /dɪˋsekt/ *vt* [VP6A] **1** cut up (parts of an animal body, plant, etc) in order to study its structure. **2** (fig) examine (a theory, argument, etc) part by part, to judge its value. **dis·sec·tion** /dɪˋsekʃn/ *n* [U] ~ing or being ~ed; [C] (part of) sth that has been ~ed.

dis·semble /dɪˋsembl̩/ *vt,vi* [VP6A,2A] (formal) speak, behave, so as to hide one's real feelings, thoughts, plans, etc, or give a wrong idea of them: *to ~ one's emotions.* **dis·sembler** /-blə(r)/ *n* person who ~s; deceiver.

dis·semi·nate /dɪˋsemɪneɪt/ *vt* [VP6A] distribute or spread widely ideas, doctrines, etc. **dis·semi·na·tion** /dɪˈsemɪˋneɪʃn/ *n*

dis·sen·sion /dɪˋsenʃn/ *n* [U] angry quarrelling; [C] angry quarrel: *~(s) between rival groups in politics.*

dis·sent[1] /dɪˋsent/ *n* [U] dissenting; (expression of) disagreement: *to express strong ~. D~ used to be strong in this part of England* (esp in the sense of **dissent**[2](2)).

dis·sent[2] /dɪˋsent/ *vi* **1** [VP3A] ***~ from,*** have a different opinion from; refuse to assent to: *I strongly ~ from what the last speaker has said.* **2** [VP2A,3A] (esp) refuse to accept the religious doctrine of the Church of England: *a ~ing minister,* (formerly used of) a minister of a nonconformist church. **~er** *n* (often *D~*) one who ~s (esp as in **2** above).

dis·ser·ta·tion /ˈdɪsəˋteɪʃn/ *n* [C] long written or spoken account (e g as submitted for a higher university degree): *a ~ on/upon/concerning sth.*

dis·ser·vice /dɪˋsɜvɪs/ *n* ***~ (to),*** (*sing* with *indef art,* or [U]) harmful or unhelpful action; ill turn: *to do sb a ~. The spreading of such ideas is of great ~* (= is very harmful) *to the State.*

dis·sever /ˈdɪˋsevə(r)/ *vt* [VP6A] sever; divide.

dis·si·dent /ˋdɪsɪdənt/ *adj* disagreeing. □ *n* person who disagrees; dissenter. **dis·si·dence** /-dəns/ *n* [U] disagreement.

dis·simi·lar /dɪˋsɪml̩ə(r)/ *adj* ***~ (from/to),*** not the same; not similar: *people with ~ tastes.* **~·ity** /ˈdɪˈsɪml̩ˋærətɪ/ *n* [U] lack of similarity; [C] (*pl* -ties) point of difference. **dis·sim·ili·tude** /ˈdɪsɪˋmɪlɪtjud *US:* -tud/ *n* ~ity; unlikeness.

dis·simu·late /dɪˋsɪmjʊleɪt/ *vt,vi* [VP6A,2A] (formal) dissemble. **dis·simu·la·tion** /dɪˈsɪmjʊˋleɪʃn/ *n*

dis·si·pate /ˋdɪsɪpeɪt/ *vt,vi* **1** [VP6A,2A] (cause to) disperse, go away: *to ~ fear/doubt/ignorance.* **2** [VP6A] waste time, money foolishly: *He soon ~d his fortune. Don't ~ your efforts.* **3** [VP2A] engage in foolish or harmful pleasures. **dis·si·pated** *part adj* given up to foolish and often harmful pleasures: *to lead a ~d life; to fall into ~d ways.*

dis·si·pa·tion /ˈdɪsɪˋpeɪʃn/ *n* [U] dissipating or being dissipated: *a life of ~; unwise ~ of one's energy.*

dis·so·ci·ate /dɪˋsəʊʃɪeɪt/ *vt* [VP6A,14] ***~ from,*** separate (in thought, feeling); not associate with: *It is difficult to ~ the man from his position,* to think of the man without also thinking of his work and duties. *A politician's public and private life should be ~d. I wish to ~ myself from what has just been said.* **dis·so·ci·ation** /dɪˈsəʊʃɪˋeɪʃn/ *n* [U] dissociating or being ~d: *dissociation of ideas,* keeping them distinct.

dis·sol·uble /dɪˋsoljʊbl/ *adj* that can be dissolved or disintegrated; (of non-material things) that can be annulled: *The Roman Church says that no marriage is ~.* **dis·solu·bil·ity** /ˈdɪˈsoljʊˋbɪlətɪ/ *n*

dis·so·lute /ˋdɪsəljut *US:* -lut/ *adj* (of persons) given up to immoral conduct; (of behaviour, etc), evil; vicious: *to lead a ~ life; ~ conduct.* **~·ly** *adv*

dis·sol·ution /ˈdɪsəˋluʃn/ *n* [C,U] breaking up; undoing or ending (*of* a marriage, partnership, etc); (esp) ending of of Parliament before a general election.

dis·solve /dɪˋzolv/ *vt,vi* **1** [VP6A] (of a liquid) soak into a solid so that the solid itself becomes liquid: *Water ~s salt.* **2** [VP2A,3A] **~ *(in),*** (of a solid) become liquid as the result of being taken into a liquid: *Salt ~s in water.* **3** [VP6A,14] cause (a solid) to ~: *He ~d the salt in water.* **4** [VP2A, C] disappear; fade away: *The view ~d in mist.* **5** [VP6A,2A] bring to, come to, an end: *to ~ a business partnership/a marriage/Parliament. Parliament ~d.*

dis·son·ance /ˋdɪsənəns/ *n* [U] discord; [C] combination of notes that is discordant.

dis·son·ant /ˋdɪsənənt/ *adj* not harmonious; harsh in tone.

dis·suade /dɪˋsweɪd/ *vt* [VP6A,14] **~ *sb (from sth/from doing sth),*** advise against; (try to) turn (sb) away: *to ~ a friend from marrying on a small salary.* **dis·sua·sion** /dɪˋsweɪʒn/ *n* [U].

dis·taff /ˋdɪstɑf *US:* -tæf/ *n* stick round which wool, flax, etc, is wound for spinning by hand. ***on the ˋ~ side,*** on the mother's side of the family.

dis·tance /ˋdɪstəns/ *n* [C,U] **1** measure of space, between two points, places, etc; being far off: *In the USA ~ is measured in miles, not in kilometres. The house stands on a hill and can be seen from a ~ of two miles,* from two miles away. *The town is a great ~ off,* a long way off. *The station is no ~ at all,* is very near. *It's some ~* (= a fairly long way) *to the school. My house is within easy walking ~ of the shops,* near enough for me to walk to them easily. *The sound of the waterfall may be heard at a ~ of two miles. The picture looks better at a ~,* when not too near. *A ship could be seen in the ~,* far away. *We heard gunfire in the ~.* ***keep sb at a ~,*** refuse to let him become familiar; treat him with reserve. ***keep one's ~,*** (fig) not be too friendly or familiar. **ˈlong-ˋ~** *adj* **(a)** (of races, journeys, etc) covering an extensive length, area, etc: *ˋlong-~ runners.* **(b)** (of telephone calls) to/from a distant place. **ˋmiddle-~** *adj* (of races, etc) covering a medium-size length or area. □ *n* that part of a view between the foreground and the background. **2** space of time: *to look back over a ~ of fifty years; at this ~ of time.* □ *vt* [VP6A] (more usu **ˋout~**) leave behind in a race or competition: *The black horse soon (out)~d the others.*

dis·tant /ˋdɪstənt/ *adj* **1** far away in space or time: *The school is three miles ~ from the station. We had a ~ view of Mt Everest.* **2** far off in family relationship: *She is a ~ cousin of mine.* **3** (of degree of similarity) not easily seen: *There is a ~ resemblance between the cousins.* **4** reserved; not showing familiarity: *Instead of stopping to speak, she passed by with only a ~ nod.* **~·ly** *adv* in a ~ manner: *He is ~ly related to me.*

dis·taste /dɪˋsteɪst/ *n* [U] (*sing* with *indef art*) **~ *(for),*** dislike; aversion: *a ~ for hard work. He turned away in ~.* **~·ful** /-fl/ *adj* disagreeable; unpleasant: *It is ~ful to me to have to say this, but....* **~·fully** /-flɪ/ *adv* **~·ful·ness** /-flnəs/ *n*

dis·tem·per¹ /dɪˋstempə(r)/ *n* [U] (method of painting with) colouring matter (to be) mixed with water and brushed on walls and ceilings. □ *vt* [VP6A,22] colour with ~: *We ~ed the walls green.*

dis·tem·per² /dɪˋstempə(r)/ *n* [U] disease of dogs and some other animals, with coughing and weakness.

dis·tem·pered /dɪˋstempəd/ *adj* (old use) upset, deranged (in mind).

dis·tend /dɪˋstend/ *vt,vi* [VP6A,2A] (cause to) swell out (by pressure from within): *a ~ed stomache/vein.* **dis·ten·sion** (US = **-tion**) /dɪˋstenʃn/ *n* ~ing or being ~ed.

dis·til (US = **-till**) /dɪˋstɪl/ *vt,vi* (**-ll-**) **1** [VP6A, 15B,14] change (a liquid) to vapour by heating, cool the vapour and collect the drops of liquid that condense from the vapour; purify (a liquid) thus; drive *out* or *off* impurities thus; make (whisky, essences) thus: *Salt water can be ~led and made into drinking water.* **2** [VP6A,2A] fall, let fall, in drops: *flowers that ~ nectar.* **dis·til·la·tion** /ˈdɪstɪˋleɪʃn/ *n* **1** ~ling or being ~led: *the ~lation of malted barley* (to make whisky). **2** [C,U] substance obtained by ~ling.

dis·til·ler /dɪˋstɪlə(r)/ *n* person who distils (esp whisky). **dis·tillery** /-lərɪ/ *n* (*pl* -ries) place where liquids (e g whisky, gin) are distilled.

dis·tinct /dɪˋstɪŋkt/ *adj* **1** easily heard, seen, understood; plain; clearly marked: *a ~ pronunciation. The earth's shadow on the moon was quite ~. There is a ~ improvement in her typing.* **2 ~ *(from),*** different in kind; separate: *Keep the two ideas ~, the one from the other. Hares and rabbits are ~ animals.* **~·ly** *adv* in a ~ manner: *to speak/remember ~ly. He ~ly* (= clearly, leaving no room for misunderstanding) *told you what to do.* **~·ness** *n*

dis·tinc·tion /dɪˋstɪŋkʃn/ *n* **1** [U] being, keeping things, different or distinct(**2**); distinguishing, being distinguished, as different; [C] instance of this: *The President shook hands with everyone, without ~ of rank. The ~s of birth* (= The different classes of society into which people are born) *are less important than they used to be. It is difficult to make exact ~s between all the meanings of a word.* ***a ~ without a difference,*** no real difference at all. **2** [C] point of difference; that which makes one thing different from another: *The ~ between poetry and prose is obvious.* **3** [U] quality of being superior, excellent, distinguished: *a writer/novel of ~. He has great ~ of manner.* **4** [C] mark of honour; title; decoration; reward: *academic ~s,* e g a doctor's degree; *to win ~s for bravery. Her Majesty conferred a ~ upon the retiring prime minister,* e g made him an earl.

dis·tinc·tive /dɪˋstɪŋktɪv/ *adj* serving to mark a difference or make distinct: *Soldiers often have ~ badges on their caps. Scouts wear a ~ uniform.* **~·ly** *adv*

dis·tin·guish /dɪˋstɪŋgwɪʃ/ *vt,vi* **1** [VP14,3A] **~ *one thing from another, ~ between two things, etc,*** see, hear, recognize, understand well, the difference: *People who cannot ~ between colours are said to be colour-blind. The twins were so much alike that it was impossible to*

~ one from the other. *It is not easy to ~ cultured pearls from genuine pearls.* **2** [VP6A] make out by looking, listening, etc: *A person with good eyesight can ~ distant objects.* **3** [VP14] ~ ***from,*** be a mark of character, difference: *Speech ~es man from the animals. What ~es the hare from the rabbit?* **4** [VP6A] ~ ***oneself,*** behave so as to bring credit to oneself: *to ~ oneself in an examination. He ~ed himself by his courage.* **~·able** /-əbl/ *adj* that can be ~ed between: *Tom is hardly ~able from his twin brother. The coast was hardly ~able* (= could hardly be seen) *through the haze.* **dis·tin·guished** *adj* famous; well known; remarkable; showing distinction(**3**): *He is ~ed for his knowledge of economics/~ed as an economist. He has had a ~ed career in the diplomatic service.*

dis·tort /dɪˋstɔt/ *vt* [VP6A] **1** pull, twist, out of the usual shape: *a face ~ed by pain. A curved mirror ~s the features.* **2** give a false account of; twist out of the truth: *Newspaper accounts of international affairs are sometimes ~ed. You have ~ed my motives.* **dis·tor·tion** /dɪˋstɔʃn/ *n* [U] ~ing or being ~ed; [C] instance of this; sth that is ~ed.

dis·tract /dɪˋstrækt/ *vt* [VP6A,14] ~ ***from,*** draw away sb's attention from sth: *The noise in the street ~ed me from my reading. What can we do to ~ her mind from the sorrow caused by her child's death?* **~ed** *part adj* with the mind confused or bewildered: *to be ~ed between love and duty; to be ~ed with/by anxiety/grief.* **~·ed·ly** *adv* in a ~ed manner.

dis·trac·tion /dɪˋstrækʃn/ *n* **1** [U] distracting or being distracted. **2** [C] sth that distracts, sth annoying and unwelcome: *Noise is a ~ when you are trying to study.* **3** [C] sth that holds the attention and gives pleasure: *He complained that there were not enough ~s in the small village. There are plenty of ~s* (= interesting and amusing things to see and do) *in a large city.* **4** [U] wildness or confusion of mind: *He loves her to ~,* loves her wildly, passionately. *You will drive me to ~ with your silly questions.*

dis·train /dɪˋstreɪn/ *vi* [VP2A,3A] ~ ***upon,*** (legal) seize goods to compel a person to pay money due (esp rent): *to ~ upon a person's furniture for rent.* **dis·traint** *n* ~ing.

dis·trait /dɪˋstreɪ/ *adj* (fem *-traite* /-ˋstreɪt/) (F) absent-minded; not paying attention.

dis·traught /dɪˋstrɔt/ *adj* distracted; violently upset in mind: *~ with grief.*

dis·tress[1] /dɪˋstres/ *n* [U] **1** (cause of) great pain, discomfort or sorrow; (suffering caused by) want of money or other necessary things: *At the end of the Marathon race several runners showed signs of ~. His wild behaviour was a great ~ to his mother. He spent his fortune in relieving ~ among the poor.* **2** serious danger or difficulty: *The lifeboat went out to a ship in ~. The ship was flying a ~ signal.*

dis·tress[2] /dɪˋstres/ *vt* [VP6A] cause distress(**1**) to: *I am much ~ed to hear the news of your wife's death. What are you looking so ~ed about? Don't ~ yourself,* Don't get worried. **ˈ~ed ˋarea,** part of a country where there is serious and continued unemployment. **~·ful** /-fl/, **~·ing** *adjj* causing or experiencing ~. **~·fully** /flɪ/, **~·ing·ly** *advv* in a manner that causes distress.

dis·trib·ute /dɪˋstrɪbjut/ *vt* [VP6A,14] ~ ***(to/among),*** **1** give or send out: *The teacher ~d the books to the class. He left some money to be ~d among the hotel staff. The man had thirty parcels to be ~d at houses all over the town.* **2** spread out (over a larger area): *to ~ manure over a field.* **3** put into groups or classes. **dis·tribu·tor** /-tə(r)/ *n* person or thing (e g in a petrol engine) that ~s.

dis·tribu·tion /ˈdɪstrɪˋbjuʃn/ *n* [U] distributing or being distributed; manner of being distributed; [C] instance or occasion of distributing: *They could not agree about the ~ of the profits. Is the ~ of wealth uneven in your country? The pine-tree has a very wide ~,* is found in many parts of the world. *When will the prize ~ take place?*

dis·tribu·tive /dɪˋstrɪbjʊtɪv/ *adj* **1** of distribution: *the ~ trades,* e g railways, shop-keeping. **2** of each individual, each member of a class: *'Each', 'every', 'either' and 'neither' are ~ pronouns.* **~·ly** *adv*

dis·trict /ˋdɪstrɪkt/ *n* **1** part of a country: *a mountainous ~; the ˋlake D~,* in England; *purely agricultural ~s.* **2** part of a town or country marked out for a special purpose: *the London postal ~s,* e g NW5, EC4. ⇨ *postcode* at post[3](**3**); *rural and urban ~s,* for purposes of local government; *the ˈ~ ˋnurse,* one who visits people in their homes; *the D~ of Columbia,* Washington, the Federal government area of the US.

dis·trust /dɪˋstrʌst/ *n* [U] (occ with *indef art* for 'instance, variety or degree of ~') doubt or suspicion; want of trust or confidence: *The child looked at the big stranger with ~. He has a ~ of foreigners.* □ *vt* [VP6A] have no trust in; be doubtful about: *He would ~ his own friends. He ~ed his own eyes.* **~·ful** /-fl/ *adj* unwilling to trust; suspicious: *I was ~ful of his motives.* **~·fully** /-flɪ/ *adv* **~·ful·ness** *n*

dis·turb /dɪˋstɜb/ *vt* [VP6A] break the quiet, calm, peace or order of; put out of the right or usual position: *He put his oars in the water and ~ed the smooth surface of the lake. She opened the door quietly so as not to ~ the sleeping child. Don't ~ the papers on my desk. Please don't ~ yourself,* don't stop doing whatever you are now doing. *He was ~ed to hear of your illness/was ~ed by the news of your illness.* ~ ***the peace,*** (legal) cause disorder, rioting, etc.

dis·turb·ance /dɪˋstɜbəns/ *n* [U] disturbing or being disturbed; [C] instance of this; sth that disturbs; disorder (esp social or political): *Were there many political ~s in the country last year?*

dis·union /dɪsˋjunɪən/ *n* [U] breaking of what unites; want of union; dissension.

dis·unite /ˈdɪsjʊˋnaɪt/ *vt,vi* [VP6A,2A] (cause to) become separate.

dis·unity /dɪsˋjunətɪ/ *n* [U] lack of unity; dissension.

dis·use /dɪsˋjus/ *n* [U] state of no longer being used: *rusty from ~; words that have fallen into ~.* **dis·used** /dɪsˋjuzd/ *part adj* no longer used: *a ~d well.*

di·syl·labic (US = **dis·syl·labic**) /ˈdɪsɪˋlæbɪk/ *adj* of two syllables. **di·syl·lable** (US = **dis·syl·lable**), /ˈdɪˋsɪləbl/ *n* ~ word or metrical foot.

ditch /dɪtʃ/ *n* narrow channel dug in or between fields, or at the sides of a road, etc to hold or carry off water. ***dull as ˋ~ water,*** very dull(**3**) indeed. ⇨ die[2](**2**). □ *vt,vi* **1** [VP6A,2A] make, clean or repair ~es. **2** [VP6A] send or throw into a ~ (or, sl, the sea); (fig) abandon: *The drunken man ~ed his car,* drove it into one. *The pilot had to ~ his* *plane*, make a forced landing on the sea. *She's ~ed her boyfriend*, (colloq) put an (usu sudden) end to the relationship.

dither /ˋdɪðə(r)/ *vi* [VP2A,C] tremble; (colloq) hesitate about what to do; be unable to decide. □ *n* trembling: (colloq) *be all of a ~; have the ~s.*

ditto /ˋdɪtəʊ/ *n* (abbr *d°, do; pl* -tos /-təʊz/) the same. Used in lists to avoid writing words again: *One hat at £2.25; ~ at £4.50; say ~ to*, (colloq) say the same thing as; agree with.

ditty /ˋdɪtɪ/ *n* (*pl* **-ties**) short, simple song.

di·ur·nal /ˈdaɪˋɜnl/ *adj* (astron) occupying one day.

di·va·gate /ˋdaɪvəgeɪt/ *vi* [VP2A,3A] ~ ***(from)***, (formal) stray; wander from the point. **di·va·ga·tion** /ˈdaɪvəˋgeɪʃn/ *n*

di·van /dɪˋvæn *US:* ˋdaɪvæn/ *n* **1** long, low, soft, backless seat. ˋ**~-bed** such a seat that can be converted into a bed. **2** (in Muslim countries) public audience room; State council or council room.

dive[1] /daɪv/ *n* **1** the act of diving into water: *a graceful ~*. **2** (GB) underground room or basement where some special kind of food is sold or served: *an* ˋ*oyster-~*. **3** disreputable place for the sale of drink, or for gambling.

dive[2] /daɪv/ *vi* (US alternative *pt* **dove** /dəʊv/) [VP2A,C] ~ ***(off/from/into)***, **1** go head first into water: *He ~d from the bridge and rescued the drowning child.* **2** (of a submarine) go under water; (of divers) go under water in a special dress: *to ~ for pearls.* ˋ**diving-bell,** open-bottomed apparatus which can be lowered into water, supplied with air pumped through pipes, and used by underwater workers. **diving-board** /ˋdaɪvɪŋ bɔd/ *n* flexible board from which to ~ (e g into a swimming pool). ˋ**diving-dress/-suit,** suit with weighted boots and an airtight helmet into which air is pumped through tubes, used by divers. **3** go quickly to a lower level; move sth (e g the hand) quickly and suddenly downwards (into sth): *The aircraft ~d steeply. The rabbit ~d into its hole. He ~d into his pocket and pulled out a handful of coins.* ˋ**~-bomb** *vt,vi* (of an aircraft) drop bombs at the end of a steep dive. **diver** *n* person who ~s, esp a person who works under water in a diving-suit.

di·verge /daɪˋvɜdʒ/ *vi* [VP2A,3A] ~ ***(from)***, (of lines, paths, opinions, etc) get farther apart from a point or from each other as they progress; turn or branch away from: *to ~ from the beaten track.* **di·ver·gence** /daɪˋvɜdʒəns/, **-gency** /-dʒənsɪ/ *n* [U] diverging; [C] (*pl* **-ces, -cies**) instance of this: *divergencies from the normal.* **di·ver·gent** /-dʒənt/ *adj*

di·vers /ˋdaɪvəz/ *adj* (old use) several; more than one.

di·verse /daɪˋvɜs/ *adj* of different kinds: *The wild life in Africa is extremely ~.* **~·ly** *adv*

di·ver·sify /ˈdaɪˋvɜsɪfaɪ/ *vt* (*pt,pp* -fied) [VP6A] make diverse; give variety to: *a landscape diversified by hills and woods.* **di·ver·si·fi·ca·tion** /daɪˈvɜsɪfɪˋkeɪʃn/ *n*

di·ver·sion /daɪˋvɜʃn *US:* -ʒn/ *n* **1** [U] diverting; the act of turning sth aside or giving it a different direction: *the ~ of a stream;* [C] instance of this: *traffic ~s*, e g when traffic is directed by different routes because of road repairs. **2** [C] sth which turns the attention from serious things; sth giving rest or amusement: *Chess and billiards are his favourite ~s.* **3** [C] method used to turn the attention from sth that one does not wish to be noticed, as when, in war, the enemy's attention is drawn from one place by an unexpected attack at another place: *to create/make a ~.* **~ary** /daɪˋvɜʃnrɪ *US:* -ˋvɜʒnerɪ/ *adj*: *a ~ary raid.* **~·ist** *n* person who engages in disruptive or subversive activities.

di·ver·sity /ˈdaɪˋvɜsətɪ/ *n* [U] the state of being diverse; variety.

di·vert /ˈdaɪˋvɜt/ *vt* [VP6A,14] ~ ***(from)***, **1** turn in another direction: *to ~ the course of a river; to ~ a river from its course; to ~ water from a river into the fields.* **2** amuse; entertain; turn the attention away: *Some people are easily ~ed. How can we ~ her thoughts from her sad loss?* **~·ing** *adj* amusing. **~·ing·ly** *adv*

Dives /ˋdaɪviz/ *n* (typical name for a) rich man. ⇨ Luke 16: 19.

di·vest /daɪˋvest/ *vt* [VP14] ~ ***of***, **1** take off (clothes): *to ~ a king of his robes.* **2** take away from: *to ~ an official of power and authority.* **3** (*reflex*) get rid of; give up: *I cannot ~ myself of the idea*, It comes back to my mind.

di·vide[1] /dɪˋvaɪd/ *vt,vi* **1** [VP6A,15B,14,2A,C] separate, be separated (into); split or break up: *We ~d the money equally. They ~d the money between/among themselves. The river ~s my land from his. The Nile ~s near its mouth and forms a delta. He ~s his time between work and play. How shall we ~ the work up/~ up the work?* **2** [VP14] find out how often one number is contained in another: *If you ~ 6 into 30/~ 30 by 6, the answer is 5.* (With passive force): *12 ~s by 3*, can be ~d by 3. **3** [VP14] arrange in groups: *The teacher ~d the clever pupils from the stupid pupils.* **4** [VP6A] cause disagreement; cause to disagree: *Please don't let such a small matter ~ us. Opinions are ~d on the question*, There are opposed opinions. **5** [VP2A,6A] (in Parliament, at debates, etc) part in order to vote; cause to part for this purpose: *After a long debate, the House ~d*, voted on the question. *The Opposition does not propose to ~ the House on this question*, does not insist upon the taking of a vote.

di·vide[2] /dɪˋvaɪd/ *n* sth that divides, esp a watershed (a line of high land that separates two different river systems).

divi·dend /ˋdɪvɪdend/ *n* **1** (maths) number to be divided by another. ⇨ **divisor. 2** (usu periodical) payment of a share of profit, to shareholders in a business company, or of assets to creditors (e g of an insolvent company), or to a policy holder in a mutual insurance company: *to pay a ~ of 10 per cent.* ˋ**~-warrant,** order on a bank to pay a ~.

di·vid·ers /dɪˋvaɪdəz/ *n pl* pair of measuring-compasses, used for dividing lines or angles, measuring or marking distances, etc.

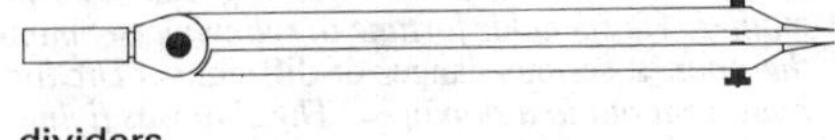

dividers

a compass

divi·na·tion /ˈdɪvɪˋneɪʃn/ *n* [U] divining, ⇨ **divine**[3]; discovery of the unknown or the future by supernatural means; [C] clever guess or forecast.

di·vine[1] /dɪˋvaɪn/ *adj* **1** of, from, or like God or a god: *D~ Service*, the public worship of God. *King Charles* I *claimed to rule by ~ right*, right given to him by God. **2** (colloq) excellent; very beautiful: *~ weather; a ~ hat. She looks ~ in that new dress.* **~·ly** *adv*

di·vine[2] /dɪˋvaɪn/ *n* person (usu a priest) learned in theology.

di·vine[3] /dɪˋvaɪn/ *vt,vi* [VP6A,10,2A] discover or learn (sth) about future events, hidden things, etc by means not based on reason: *to ~ sb's intentions; to ~ what the future has in store.*

di·viner /dɪˋvaɪnə(r)/ *n* person who divines, esp one who claims to have the power of learning the presence of subterranean water, metal, etc by using a Y-shaped stick or rod (called a *diˋvining-rod*). ⇨ **dowsing**.

div·ing ⇨ **dive**.

di·vin·ity /dɪˋvɪnətɪ/ *n* **1** [U] the quality of being divine, ⇨ **divine**[1]: *the ~ of Christ;* [C] (*pl* **-ties**) divine being. **2** [U] the study of theology: *the ~ school at Oxford; a doctor of ~* (abbr: D D).

di·vis·ible /dɪˋvɪzəbl/ *adj* (maths) that can be divided without remainder: *8 is ~ by 2.*

div·ision /dɪˋvɪʒn/ *n* **1** [U] dividing or being divided: *the ~ of time into months, weeks and days; a simple problem in ~* (e g 50 ÷ 5); *the ~ of labour,* sharing work, giving different kinds of work to different people, according to their capabilities. **2** [C] the effect of dividing; one of the parts into which sth is divided: *the export ~ of a business company; Is that a fair ~ of the money? He has a position in the second ~* (= the lower grade) *of the civil service.* **3** [C] (army) unit of two or more brigades. **4** [C] line that divides: *A hedge forms the ~ between his land and mine. The ~s between the various classes of society are not so sharply marked as they used to be.* **5** [C] disagreement; separation in thought, feeling, etc: *Agitators who stir up ~s in a nation are dangerous.* **6** [C] (Parliament, etc) separation into two groups for the counting of votes: *The Bill was read for the second time without a ~.* **ˋ~ bell,** bell rung to warn members (who are outside the House) that there is to be a ~.

div·isor /dɪˋvaɪzə(r)/ *n* (maths) number by which another number is divided. ⇨ **dividend(1)**.

di·vorce[1] /dɪˋvɔs/ *n* **1** [U] legal ending of a marriage so that husband and wife are free to marry again; [C] instance of this: *to sue for a ~; to take/start ~ proceedings; to obtain a ~ (from...).* **2** [C] ending of a connection or relationship: *the ~ between religion and science,* as when science claims or seems to show that religious beliefs have no foundation.

di·vorce[2] /dɪˋvɔs/ *vt* [VP6A,14] **1** put an end to a marriage by law: *Did Mr Hill ~ his wife or did she ~ him?* **2** (fig) separate (things usually together): *What happens to the soul when it is ~d from the body?* **di·vor·cee** /dɪˈvɔˋsi/ *n* ~d person.

divot /ˋdɪvət/ *n* piece of turf sliced off by a golf club in making a bad stroke.

di·vulge /daɪˋvʌldʒ/ *vt* [VP6A,14] **~ to,** make known (sth secret). **di·vul·gence** /-dʒəns/ *n*

divvy /ˋdɪvɪ/ *n* (*pl* **-vies**) (colloq abbr of) dividend(**2**), e g as formerly paid by a co-operative society.

dixie /ˋdɪksɪ/ *n* large iron pot in which tea, stew, etc is made or carried (by soldiers, campers, etc).

dizzy /ˋdɪzɪ/ *adj* (**-ier, -iest**) **1** (of a person) feeling as if everything were turning round, as if unable to balance; mentally confused. **2** (of places, conditions) causing such a feeling: *a ~ height.* □ *vt* make ~. **diz·zily** *adv* **diz·zi·ness** *n*

djinn /dʒɪn/ *n* = **genie**.

do[1] /du/ *anom v* (*1st person sing pres t* neg **don't** /dəʊnt/, *3rd person sing pres t* **does** /dʌz/, neg **doesn't** /ˋdʌznt/, *pt* **did** /dɪd/, neg **didn't** /ˋdɪdnt/, *pp* **done** /dʌn/) **1** used with the main *verb* **(a)** for neg sentences with *not*: *He didn't go. Don't go yet.* **(b)** for *interr* sentences: *Does/Did he want it?* **(c)** after a front-shifted *adverbial*, etc: *So hard did they work that...; Not only did they promise to help, but....* **(d)** to emphasize the positive or negative nature of a sentence (declarative, interr or imper), always stressed: *That's exactly what he ˋdid say. I tell you I ˋdon't like him. ˋDo stop that noise!* **2** used alone, to refer to a main *verb* or *verb* phrase: **(a)** in comparisons: *She plays the piano better now than she did* (i e played) *last year.* **(b)** in question phrases: *He lives in London, doesn't he? So you want to be a doctor, do you?* **(c)** in answers, comments, etc: *'They work hard'—'Oh, do they?' 'Who broke the window?'—'I did!'*

do[2] /du/ *vt,vi* ⇨ **do**[1] (For uses with *adverbial particles* and *preps* ⇨ **15** below.) **1 (a)** [VP6A] perform, carry out (an action); busy oneself with: *What are you doing now? What shall I do next? I will do what I can. What does he do for a living,* What is his occupation? *I have nothing to do. Are you doing anything tomorrow? There's nothing to do here,* i e no means of passing the time. *What's done cannot be undone. Try what kindness will do,* Try the effect of kindness. *That sort of thing isn't done,* is not considered right or suitable. *It's easier said than done,* easier to talk about than to do. *No sooner said than done,* done at once. *Well begun is half done,* A good start makes it easy to finish sth. *What must we do to keep well? Well done!* ***do it yourself,*** (abbr D I Y) (esp) do house decorating, upkeep, etc oneself (instead of by professional workers): (attrib) *do it yourself kits,* materials, etc for doing work of this kind. **(b)** [VP2C] act; behave: *When in Rome do as the Romans do. You would do well* (i e be wise) *to take your doctor's advice. You must do as the others do.* **2** [VP6A,12B,13B] (combined with *nouns* in many senses) **(a)** produce; make: *Patience and perseverance will do wonders,* produce remarkable results. *I have done* (i e made) *six copies. I will do* (i e make) *a translation for you/do you a translation.* **(b)** work at; be busy with: *She's doing her lessons/homework,* etc. **(c)** perform: *Do your duty. He still has to do his military service.* **(d)** study; learn: *Are you doing science at school? He has been doing engineering at Sheffield University.* **(e)** solve; find the answer to: *I can't do this sum/this problem in algebra.* **(f)** put in order; arrange: *Please do the flowers,* arrange them in vases, etc. **(g)** make tidy: *Go and do your hair.* **(h)** clean, sweep, brush, etc: *Tell the housemaid to do the bedrooms. Have you done* (i e brushed) *your teeth?* **(i)** deal with, attend to: *I will do you next, sir,* (e g at the barber's) I will attend to you next. *Mr A does the fiction* (i e reviews novels) *for the 'Spectator'. I have a lot of correspondence to do.* **(j)** use, exert: *do one's best/utmost; do all one can; do everything in one's power. He did his best to help us.* ⇨ also **credit**[1]**(7)**, **favour**[1]**(4)**, good²(1), harm, homage, honour¹(1), injury, justice, *kindness* at kind², mischief, service, *a good/bad turn* at turn, wrong. **do-gooder** /ˈdu ˋgʊdə(r)/ *n* (colloq; often *pej*) person who is over-zealous to improve people, conditions, etc. **3** (the *pp* and perfect tenses) bring to an end; finish: [VP6A] *It's done. I've done it. A woman's work is never done. Will he ever have/be done?* [VP3A] *Have you done* (ie finished) *with the writing materials?* [VP6C] *I've done talking—I'm going to act.* **4 do (for),** be good, satisfactory or convenient, enough (for a purpose, for sb); answer a purpose: *These shoes won't do* (ie are not strong enough) *for mountain-climbing. This log will do for a seat/do for us to sit on. This room will do me quite well,* will serve my needs. ***make sth do/ make do (with sth),*** make sth suffice, answer a need: *Can you make £5 do,* make this sum cover your expenses? *Can't you make that shirt do* (ie wear it) *for another day? It isn't much but I will make it do/make do with it,* manage with it. ⇨ make¹(14). **5** [VP2A] be fitting, suitable, tolerable: *This will never do,* cannot be accepted or allowed! *That will do!* You've said or done enough! *It doesn't do to be rude to your employer.* **6** [VP2A] (with passive force; colloq) happen: *He came to ask what was doing,* = being done, happening. *'Can you lend me 50p?'—'Nothing doing!'* (sl) No! **7** [VP2A] **(a)** fare; get on well, badly, etc: *Everything in the garden is doing* (= growing) *well. Roses do well in a clay soil. He's doing well at school.* **(b)** (esp of health) make progress: *The patient is doing quite well.* ***How do you do?*** (formula used when people are formally introduced). **8** [VP2B,15A] complete (a journey); travel (a distance); go (at a certain speed): *How many miles a day did you do during your tour? We've done eighty miles since lunch. We did the journey in six hours. The car was doing sixty miles an hour.* **9** [VP6A] play the part of: *He does Hamlet well. He does the host admirably,* is an admirable host. *I suppose we must do the polite thing,* (colloq) be sociable, chat, etc. **10** [VP6A,15B] cheat, swindle, get the better of: *Please don't think I'm trying to do you. I'm afraid you've been done. She was done out of her money. He once tried to do me out of my job,* supplant me. **11** ***do sb/ oneself well,*** (colloq) provide food, comforts, etc for: *They do you very well at the Bristol Hotel. He does himself well,* provides well for his own comfort. **12** [VP6A] (colloq) visit as a sightseer; see the sights of: *Some Americans think they can do England in a fortnight. Have you done the British Museum yet?* **13** [VP15A] cook in the right degree: *Mind you do the beef well. How would you like your mutton chop done?* ⇨ underdone, *overdone* at overdo. ˈ***done to a ˋturn,*** extremely well done: *The steak was done to a turn,* cooked perfectly. **14** [VP7B] (with *have*) ***have to do with,*** be connected with; result from: *I know he behaves badly—It all has to do with the way he was brought up.* ***have sth/nothing/not much/a great deal, etc to do with,*** be/not be connected or concerned with; contribute to: *He had something to do with* (= was in some way connected with, perhaps was responsible for) *my decision to teach English. Hard work had a great deal to do with* (= contributed greatly to) *his success.*

15 [VP2C,3A,15B] (uses with *adverbial particles* and *preps*):

do away with, abolish, get rid of: *That department was done away with two years ago. That's a practice that should be done away with. Our dog is getting so old and blind that we shall have to do away with him,* have him put to death.

do well/badly by sb, treat, deal with, well/ badly: *A good employer always does well by good workmen.* ***(be) hard done by,*** (be) treated unfairly: *He complains that he has been hard done by.* ***Do as you would be done by,*** (prov) Treat others as you would like to be treated.

do sb down, (colloq) **(a)** get the better of sb (by outwitting or cheating him). **(b)** speak ill of. ⇨ *run sb down* at run²(26).

do for, (colloq) **(a)** act as housekeeper for; perform, esp domestic services for: *Old Mrs Green has been doing for me since my wife died. He won't employ a housekeeper; he prefers to do for himself.* **(b)** manage: *What/How will you do for water* (= manage to have supplies of water) *while you're crossing the desert.* **(c)** (usu passive) ruin; destroy; kill: *These shoes are done for,* worn out, useless. *Poor fellow, I'm afraid he's done for,* according to context, ruined in his career, likely to die, etc. *The country's done for,* ruined.

do sb in, (sl) kill him. ***be done in,*** exhausted: *The horse was done in after the race.*

do sb out of sth, ⇨ 10 above.

do sth out, sweep or clean out; put in order: *Tell Tom to do out the stables. This room needs doing out.*

do over, redecorate: *The dining-room needs doing over.* ***do sb over,*** (sl) assault sb.

do sth up, **(a)** restore, repair, renovate: *The house needs to be done up/needs doing up,* repainted, restored, etc. **(b)** change the shape of, put new trimmings, etc on: *She has been doing up her last summer's hat.* **(c)** tie or wrap up; make into a bundle or parcel: *Please do up these books and post them to Mr Smith.* **(d)** fasten (a dress or other garment) with buttons, hooks and eyes, etc: *She asked her flatmate to do up her dress for her at the back.* **(e)** (of a dress, etc) fasten with buttons, etc: *This dress does up at the back.* **(f)** (usu passive) tire out: *He/His horse was done up* (*done in* is more usu) *after the long ride.*

do with, **(a)** (meanings as in the examples): *What did you do with my umbrella,* Where did you put it, leave it, etc? *What are we to do with* (= How shall we deal with) *this naughty boy? She didn't know what to do with herself,* how to occupy her time. *Tell me what you did with yourselves* (= how you passed the time) *on Sunday. The children didn't know what to do with themselves for joy/ excitement/impatience,* were so happy, excited, etc that they could not control their feelings. **(b)** get on with; tolerate; live or work with: *I can't do with him and his insolence.* **(c)** (with *can, could*) expressing a need or wish: *You look as if you could do with* (= as if you need) *a good night's sleep. That man could do with* (= would look better if he had) *a shave. I think we can do with* (= will need) *two extra loaves today. I could do with a cup of tea.*

do without, dispense with; manage without: *He can't do without the services of a secretary. We shall have to do without a holiday this summer. The hens haven't laid any eggs; we shall have to do without.*

do³ /du/ *n* (*pl* dos or do's /duz/) **1** (sl) swindle:

The scheme was a do from the start. **2** (colloq) entertainment; party: *We're going to a big do at the Green's this evening.* **3** customs, rules: *Some teachers have too many do's and don'ts.* **4** ***fair dos/do's*** (GB, sl) (as an exclamation) fair shares; Let's be fair, just (e g in sharing something).

do[4] /ˈdɪtəʊ/ (abbr of) ditto.

do[5], **doh** /dəʊ/ *n* (music) first of the syllables used in the scale *do, re, mi, fa, sol, la, ti, do.*

dob·bin /ˈdobɪn/ *n* (pet name for a) farm horse.

doc·ile /ˈdəʊsaɪl *US:* ˈdosl/ *adj* easily trained or controlled: *a ~ child/horse.* **do·cil·ity** /dəʊˈsɪlətɪ/ *n* [U] the quality of being ~.

dock[1] /dok/ *n* **1** place in a harbour, river, etc with gates through which water may be let in and out, where ships are (un)loaded or repaired: *to go into/enter/leave ~; to be in ~.* **ˈdry/ˈgraving ~,** one from which water may be pumped out. **ˈfloating ~,** floating structure that may be used as a dry ~. **ˈwet ~,** one in which the water may be kept at high-tide level. **ˈ~-dues,** money paid for the use of a ~. **2** (*pl*) number or row of ~s with the wharves, sheds, offices, etc round them. **ˈ~·yard,** enclosure with ~s and facilities for building and repairing ships: *the naval ~yard at Chatham.* **3** (US) wharf; ship's berth. **~er** *n* ~yard labourer.

dock[2] /dok/ *vi,vt* **1** [VP2A] (of a ship) come or go into a dock. **2** [VP6A] bring, take, (a ship) into a dock. **3** [VP6A] couple (two or more spacecraft) in space; [VP2A] perform this manœuvre.

dock[3] /dok/ *n* enclosure in a criminal court for the prisoner: *to be in the ~.*

dock[4] /dok/ *vt* [VP6A,14] **1** cut short (an animal's tail). **2** make wages, allowances, supplies, less: *to ~ a workman's wages; to have one's salary ~ed; to ~ the soldiers of part of their rations.*

dock[5] /dok/ *n* common weed with large leaves and small green flowers.

docket /ˈdokɪt/ *n* **1** summary of the contents of a letter, document, etc. **2** (comm) list of goods delivered, jobs done, etc; label on a package listing the contents, or giving information about use, method of assembly, etc. □ *vt* [VP6A] enter in or write on a ~; label.

doc·tor /ˈdoktə(r)/ *n* **1** person who has received the highest university degree: *D~ of Laws/Divinity, etc.* **2** person who has been trained in medical science. ⇨ **physician, surgeon.** □ *vt* [VP6A] **1** (colloq) give medical treatment to: *~ a cold/a child.* ***a ~ed tomcat,*** one that has been neutered, ⇨ **neuter(5). 2** make (esp food, drink) inferior by adding sth; add drugs to. **3** (fig) falsify accounts, evidence. **~·ate** /ˈdoktərət/ *n* ~'s degree.

doc·tri·naire /ˌdoktrɪˈneə(r)/ *n* person who wants his doctrines to be put into practice without allowing for circumstances, considering their suitability for particular cases, etc. □ *adj* theoretical; unpractical: *~ socialism.*

doc·trinal /ˌdokˈtraɪnl *US:* ˈdoktrɪnl/ *adj* of doctrine(s).

doc·tri·nar·ian /ˌdoktrɪˈneərɪən/ *n* = **doctrinaire.**

doc·trine /ˈdoktrɪn/ *n* [C,U] body of teaching; beliefs and teachings of a church, political party, school of scientists, etc: *a matter of ~; the ~ that the Pope is infallible.*

docu·ment /ˈdokjʊmənt/ *n* sth written or printed, to be used as a record or in evidence (e g birth, marriage and death certificate): *~ of title,* providing evidence of rights, ownership, etc; *a human ~,* number of facts or incidents that illustrate human nature. □ *vt* [VP6A] prove by, supply with, ~s: *to be well ~ed.* **doc·u·men·ta·tion** /ˌdokjʊmenˈteɪʃn/ *n* [U].

doc·u·men·tary /ˌdokjʊˈmentrɪ/ *adj* consisting of documents: *~ proof/evidence.* **ˌ~ ˈfilm,** cinema or TV film showing some aspect of human or social activity (e g the work of the post-office, the lives of fishermen). □ *n* ~ film.

dod·der /ˈdodə(r)/ *vi* [VP2A,C] (colloq) walk, move, in a shaky way, as from weakness or old age: *to ~ along.* **~er** *n* person who ~s. **~·ing, ~y** *adjj* trembling; weak and uncertain in movement.

dodge[1] /dodʒ/ *n* **1** quick movement to evade sth. **2** (colloq) trick; piece of deception: *He's up to all the ~s,* knows them all. **3** (colloq) plan; method; ingenious way of doing sth.

dodge[2] /dodʒ/ *vt,vi* [VP2A,3A,6A] **1** move quickly to one side, change position or direction, in order to escape or avoid sth: *He ~d cleverly when I threw my shoe at him. I ~d behind a tree so that he should not see me. You need to be quick in order to ~ the traffic in London nowadays.* **2** get round (difficulties), avoid (duties, etc) by cunning or trickery: *to ~ military service.* **dodger** *n* person who ~s, esp an artful or cunning person.

dodgy /ˈdodʒɪ/ *adj* (colloq) **1** artful. **2** involving risk or loss.

dod·gem /ˈdodʒəm/ *n* (colloq) (at fun fairs, etc) small car, electrically propelled, (to be) driven on a special platform where there are many others which have to be avoided or dodged. **Dodgem** = *Dodge them.*

dodo /ˈdəʊdəʊ/ *n* (*pl* **-does, -dos** /-dəʊz/) extinct, large, flightless bird of Mauritius.

doe /dəʊ/ *n* female fallow-deer, rabbit or hare. **ˈ~ skin** *n* skin of a ~; [U] soft leather made from this skin.

doer /ˈduə(r)/ *n* person who does things (contrasted with persons who merely talk, etc): *He's a ~, not a talker.* (Also in compounds, as *evil-doer*).

does /dʌz/, **doesn't** /ˈdʌznt/ ⇨ do[1].

doff /dof *US:* dɔf/ *vt* [VP6A] (old use) take off one's hat, coat, etc.

dog[1] /dog *US:* dɔg/ *n* **1** common domestic animal, (⇨ the illus at **domestic**) a friend of man, of which there are many breeds; male of this animal and of the wolf and the fox. ⇨ **bitch. 2** (phrases): ***a case of dog eat dog,*** situation, e g in business, where ruthless methods are used. ***die like a dog, die a dog's death,*** die in shame or misery. ***dressed like a dog's dinner,*** in the height of fashion. ***give/throw (sth) to the dogs,*** throw it away as worthless, or as a sacrifice to save oneself. ***give a dog a bad name (and hang him),*** (prov) give a person a bad reputation, slander him, and the bad reputation will remain. ***go to the dogs,*** be ruined. ***help a lame dog over a stile,*** help a person in trouble. ***lead a dog's life,*** be troubled all the time. ***lead sb a dog's life,*** give him no peace; worry him all the time. ***let sleeping dogs lie,*** (prov) let well alone; not look for trouble. ***love me, love my dog,*** (prov) if you want me as a friend, you must accept my friends as yours. ***a dog in the manger,*** person who prevents others from enjoying sth that is useless to himself. ***not stand (even) a dog's chance,*** have no chance at all of beating a stronger

dogs

enemy, surviving a disaster, etc. ***be top dog,*** be in a position where one rules. ***be (the) underdog,*** be in a position where one must always submit. **3** (colloq) **the dogs,** greyhound race-meetings. **4** (old use; of a man) worthless, wicked or surly person. **5** (with *adjj,* colloq) person: *He's a dirty/sly/lucky/gay dog.* **6** (kinds of) mechanical device for gripping, etc. **7** (*pl,* also *'fire-dogs*) metal supports for logs in a fireplace. **8** (compounds) **'dog-biscuit,** hard, thick biscuit for feeding dogs. **'dog-cart,** high, two-wheeled cart, pulled by a horse, with two seats back to back. **'dog-collar,** (colloq) clerical collar. **'dog-days,** period of very hot weather (July and August). **'dog-eared,** (of a book) having the corners of the leaves turned down with use. **'dog·fight,** (sl) fight in which two or more aircraft are involved. **'dog·fish,** small kind of shark. ⇨ the illus at **sea**. **'dog·house,** (sl) in disgrace or disfavour. **'dog paddle,** simple swimming stroke in which the arms and legs are moved in short, quick splashing movements. **'dogs·body,** drudge. **ˌdog 'tired,** tired out, exhausted. **'dog·tooth,** small pyramid-shaped ornament (in stonework, Norman and Early English architecture). **'dog's-tooth,** checked pattern (in cloth for men's suits, overcoats, etc). **'dog·trot,** gentle, easy trot. **'dog·watch,** (on ships) one of the two-hour watches (4 to 6p m, 6 to 8p m). **'dog·wood,** tree with large white or pinkish flowers in spring. **'dog-like** *adj* like or as of a dog, esp *dog-like devotion,* the kind of devotion given by a dog to its master. **doggy, doggie** /'dogɪ *US:* 'dɔgɪ/ *n* (child's word for a) dog.

dog[2] /dog *US:* dɔg/ *vt* (-gg-) [VP6A] keep close behind, in the footsteps of: *dog a suspected thief;* (fig) *dogged by misfortune.*

doge /dəʊdʒ/ *n* elected chief magistrate in the former republics of Venice and Genoa.

dog·ged /'dogɪd *US:* 'dɔg-/ *adj* obstinate; stubborn. **~·ly** *adv* **~·ness** *n*

dog·gerel /'dogərl *US:* 'dɔg-/ *n* [U] irregular, inexpert verse.

doggo /'dogəʊ *US:* 'dɔg-/ *adv* ***lie ~,*** (sl) lie without making a movement or sound.

dogma /'dogmə *US:* 'dɔg-/ *n* **1** [C] belief, system of beliefs, put forward by some authority (esp the Church) to be accepted as true without question. **2** [U] such beliefs collectively.

dog·matic /dog'mætɪk *US:* dɔg-/ *adj* **1** put forward as dogmas: *~ theology.* **2** (of a person) making purely personal statements as if they were dogmas; (of statements) put forward in this way without proof. **dog·mati·cally** /-klɪ/ *adv*

dog·ma·tism /'dogmətɪzm *US:* 'dɔg-/ *n* [U] the quality of being dogmatic; being dogmatic: *His ~ aroused their opposition.*

dog·ma·tize /'dogmətaɪz *US:* 'dɔg-/ *vi,vt* [VP2A] make dogmatic statements; [VP6A] express (a principle, etc) as a dogma.

doh ⇨ do[5].

doily /'dɔɪlɪ/ *n* (*pl* -lies) small, round piece of linen, lace, etc placed under a dish on a table or under an ornament on a shelf.

do·ings /'duɪŋz/ *n pl* (colloq) things done or being done: *Tell me about all your ~ in London.*

dol·drums /'doldrəmz/ *n pl: in the ~,* (fig) in low spirits.

dole[1] /dəʊl/ *vt* [VP15B] ***~ out,*** distribute food, money, etc in small amounts (e g to poor people). □ *n* [C] **1** sth ~d out. **2** (colloq term for) weekly payment made under various Insurance Acts in GB (from contributions made by workers, employers and the State) to an unemployed worker. ***be/go on the ~,*** receive/begin to receive, such payments.

dole[2] /dəʊl/ *n* (obsolete) grief.

dole·ful /'dəʊlfl/ *adj* mournful; dismal. **~ly** /-flɪ/ *adv*

doll[1] /dol/ *n* **1** model of a baby or person, usu for a child to play with. **2** (sl) pretty but empty-headed girl or woman.

doll[2] /dol/ *vt,vi* [VP15B,2C] ***~ up,*** (colloq) dress (oneself) up smartly: *She was all ~ed up for the party.*

dol·lar /'dolə(r)/ *n* unit of money (symbol $) in the US, Canada, Australia and other countries.

dol·lop /'doləp/ *n* (colloq) shapeless quantity of food, etc: *a ~ of cold rice pudding.*

dolly /ˈdolɪ/ *n* (*pl* -lies) **1** child's word for a doll. **2** small wheeled frame or platform for moving heavy objects; mobile platform for a heavy camera. **3** (sl) attractive, fashionably dressed girl or young woman.

dol·men /ˈdolmən/ *n* cromlech.

dol·our (US = **-lor**) /ˈdolə(r) *US:* ˈdəʊl-/ *n* (poet) grief; sorrow. **~·ous** /-rəs/ *adj* sorrowful; distressed; distressing.

dol·phin /ˈdolfɪn/ *n* sea animal like a porpoise. ⇨ the illus at sea.

dolt /dəʊlt/ *n* stupid fellow; blockhead. **~·ish** *adj* stupid.

do·main /dəʊˈmeɪn/ *n* lands under the rule of a government, ruler, etc; (fig) field or province of thought, knowledge, activity: *in the ~ of science.*

dome /dəʊm/ *n* **1** rounded roof with a circular base; sth shaped like a ~: *the rounded ~* (= summit) *of a hill.* **2** (poet) stately building. **domed** *adj* rounded: *a man with a ~d forehead.*

domes

Domes·day Book /ˈdumzdeɪ bʊk/ *n* record of the inquiry, made by King William I in 1086, into the ownership of all the lands in England.

do·mes·tic /dəˈmestɪk/ *adj* **1** of the home, family, household; *English girls today rarely enter ~ service,* rarely become servants in a home. *He has had a good many ~ troubles. What a charming ~ scene!* e g of members of a family happy together at home. *She's a very ~ sort of woman,* prefers home life to social activities outside the home. **2** not foreign; native; of one's own country: *~ commerce/trade; the ~ market; The government could get neither foreign nor ~ loans,* could not borrow money either abroad or at home. *This newspaper provides more foreign news than ~ news.* **3** (of animals, etc) kept by, living with, man: *Horses, cows and sheep are ~ animals.* ⇨ wild. □ *n* ~ servant; servant in a household. **do·mes·ti·cally** /-klɪ/ *adv*

do·mes·ti·cate /dəˈmestɪkeɪt/ *vt* [VP6A] **1** (chiefly in *pp*) make fond of, interested in, household work and duties: *She's not at all ~d,* is not fond of, skilled in, cooking, housekeeping, etc. **2** tame (animals). **do·mes·ti·ca·tion** /dəˌmestɪˈkeɪʃn/ *n*

do·mes·tic·ity /ˌdəʊmeˈstɪsətɪ/ *n* [U] home or family life.

domi·cile /ˈdomɪsaɪl/ *n* (formal) dwelling-place; (legal) place where a person lives permanently.

dom·i·cili·ary /ˌdomɪˈsɪlɪərɪ *US:* -lɪerɪ/ *adj* of or to a dwelling-place: *a ~ visit,* one made to a house, etc (e g by officials to search or inspect it, or, under the National Health Service, by medical specialists to a patient).

domi·nant /ˈdomɪnənt/ *adj* **1** having control or authority; dominating; most important or influential; *the ~ partner in a business.* **2** (of heights) overlooking others: *a ~ cliff.* **3** (music) fifth note of a scale. **~·ly** *adv* **domi·nance** /-nəns/ *n* being ~.

domi·nate /ˈdomɪneɪt/ *vt,vi* [VP6A,2A,3A] **~ *(over)*,** **1** have control, authority or influence: *A great man can ~ (over) others by force of character. The strong usually ~ (over) the weak. Love and duty struggled to ~ his mind.* **2** (of a place, esp a height) overlook: *The whole valley is*

PIG
snout
teat
horn
OX
DONKEY
WATER-BUFFALO
horn
COW
udder
teat
HORSE
crest
mane
withers
loins
hip
croup
chest
hind quarters
tail
muzzle
shoulder
breast
elbow
forearm
knee
hock
fetlock
heel
pastern
hoof
splint bone
SHEEP
fleece
GOAT

domestic animals

~d by this mountain. **domi·na·tion** /ˈdɒmɪˋneɪʃn/ *n* [U] dominating or being dominated.

domi·neer /ˈdɒmɪˋnɪə(r)/ *vi* [VP2A,3A] **~ *(over),*** act, speak, in a dominating manner; behave like a tyrant; be overbearing: *Big boys sometimes ~ over their small sisters.* **~·ing** *adj: He's a very ~ing sort of fellow,* likes to ~ over others. **~·ing·ly** *adv*

Dom·ini·can /dəˋmɪnɪkən/ *adj* of St Dominic (1170—1221, a Spanish priest) or the order of mendicant friars he founded in 1212, under vows of poverty and chastity. □ *n* ~ friar.

domi·nie /ˋdɒmɪnɪ/ *n* (Scot) schoolteacher.

do·min·ion /dəˋmɪnɪən/ *n* **1** [U] **~ *(over),*** authority to rule; control (over). **2** [C] territory of a sovereign government. **3** [C] one of the self-governing territories of the British Commonwealth of Nations: *the D~ of Canada.*

dom·ino /ˋdɒmɪnəʊ/ *n* (*pl* -noes or -nos /-nəʊz/) **1** small, flat, oblong piece of wood or bone, marked with spots. **2** (*pl* with *sing v*) table game played with 28 of these. **3** loose cloak with a mask for the upper part of the face, worn at parties, fancy-dress balls, etc.

don[1] /dɒn/ *n* **1** (at Oxford and Cambridge) senior resident member of university staff. **2** Spanish gentleman; Spanish title (used before a man's name): *Don Juan.* **don·nish** /ˋdɒnɪʃ/ *adj* of or like a don(1).

don[2] /dɒn/ *vt* (-nn-) [VP6A] (old use) put on clothing, etc. ⇨ doff.

do·nate /dəʊˋneɪt *US:* ˋdəʊneɪt/ *vt* [VP6A,14] **~ *to,*** give (e g money, to a charity, etc); contribute. **do·na·tion** /dəʊˋneɪʃn/ *n* [U] giving; [C] sth given: *donations to the Red Cross/the refugee fund.*

done /dʌn/ ⇨ do[1].

don·jon /ˋdʌndʒən/ *n* large, strongly fortified main tower (of a castle).

don·key /ˋdɒŋkɪ/ *n* (*pl* -keys /-kɪz/) (the common and usu word for an) ass. ⇨ the illus at domestic. ˋ**~ engine,** small auxiliary steam-engine, esp one on a ship's deck. ˋ**~-work** *n* drudgery.

do·nor /ˋdəʊnə(r)/ *n* person who gives sth, e g property or money: *blood ~,* person who gives his own blood for transfusion.

don't /dəʊnt/ **1** = *do not;* ⇨ do[1]. **2** ⇨ do[3](3).

doodle /ˋdudl/ *vi, n* [VP2A] (colloq) (make) meaningless scrawls or scribbles (while one is or ought to be paying attention to sth else).

doodle·bug /ˋdudlbʌg/ *n* (colloq) flying bomb (a pilotless guided missile) used by the Nazis against London in 1944.

doom[1] /dum/ *n* **1** (usu *sing*) ruin; death; sth evil that is to come: *to go to one's ~; to send a man to his ~.* **2** (also **Doomsday** /ˋdumzdeɪ/) the Day of Judgement; the end of the world: *from now till D~sday,* for ever.

doom[2] /dum/ *vt* [VP14] **~ *sb (to sth/to do sth),*** condemn (sb to some fate/to do sth): (esp in *pp*) *~ed to disappointment; ~ed to die; poems ~ed to oblivion,* certain to be forgotten.

door /dɔ(r)/ *n* **1** that which closes the entrance to a building, room, cupboard, safe, etc: *to open/close/lock, etc the ~; hinged/sliding/revolving ~s. The ~ opened/was opened and a man came out.* ˋ**back ~,** ~ at the back of the house (to the yard, garden, etc). ˋ**front ~,** chief ~ from a house to the street or road. ***next ~,*** (in, to) the next house: *Who lives next ~ (to you)? I'm just going next ~ to see Mrs Jones.* ***next ~ to,*** (fig) nearly, almost. ***two/three, etc ~s away/down/off,*** in the next house but one/two, etc: *My brother lives three ~s away.* ***from ~ to ~,*** (a) from the ~ of one building to the ~ of another: *It was raining heavily, but the taxi took us from ~ to ~.* (b) from house to house: *He went from ~ to ~ delivering the milk/selling encyclopaedias.* ***out of ~s,*** in the open air: *It's cold out of ~s; put an overcoat on.* ***within ~s,*** inside; in the house. ***at death's ~,*** near death. ***lay sth at sb's ~,*** say that he is responsible for it. ***show sb the ~,*** lead him out to it (esp when he is unwelcome). **2** (fig) means of obtaining or approaching sth: *a ~ to success; to close the ~ against an agreement upon disarmament,* make it impossible. **3** (compounds) ˋ**~·bell,** bell inside a building, operated by a button, etc outside. ˋ**~-case/-frame,** framework into which a ~ fits. ˋ**~·handle,** one which releases the latch to open a ~. ˋ**~-keeper,** person on duty or on guard at a ~ or other entrance. ˋ**~-knob,** round knob turned to release the lock on a ~. ˋ**~-knocker,** ⇨ knock[1]. ˋ**~·man** /-mən/ (*pl* -men) uniformed attendant at the entrance to a hotel, cinema, etc. ˋ**~-mat,** rough mat on which shoes may be wiped. ˋ**~-nail,** large-headed nail formerly used to decorate some ~s. ***dead as a ~-nail,*** certainly dead. ˋ**~-post,** upright post, part of a ~-frame. ***deaf as a (~-)post,*** quite deaf. ˋ**~-plate,** plate (usu brass) fastened to a ~ and with the name of the person living or working in the building or room. ˋ**~·step,** step up to (usu) an outer ~. ˋ**~·stopper,** heavy object placed in a ~way to prevent the ~ from closing. ˋ**~·way,** opening into which a ~ fits: *standing in the ~way.*

dope /dəʊp/ *n* [U] **1** thick, heavy liquid used as varnish. **2** (colloq) harmful drug (e g opium); narcotic. **3** (sl) information (e g on the probable winners at a race meeting). □ *vt* [VP6A] give ~(2) to; make unconscious with a drug or narcotic; stimulate (e g a race-horse) with a drug. **dopey, dopy** /ˋdəʊpɪ/ *adj* (sl) half asleep; (as if) drugged; stupid.

Doric /ˋdɒrɪk *US:* ˋdɔr-/ *adj: ~ order,* of the oldest and simplest forms of Greek architecture. ⇨ the illus at column.

dorm /dɔm/ *n* (schoolboy abbr of) dormitory.

dor·mant /ˋdɔmənt/ *adj* in a state of inactivity but awaiting development or activity: *a ~ volcano; ~ facilities,* mental powers capable of being developed; winter, alive but not growing.

dor·mer /ˋdɔmə(r)/ *n* (usu ˋ**~-window**) upright window built from a sloping roof. ⇨ the illus at window.

dor·mi·tory /ˋdɔmɪtrɪ *US:* -tɔrɪ/ *n* (*pl* -ries) sleeping-room with several or many beds, esp in a school or institution.

dor·mouse /ˋdɔmaʊs/ *n* (*pl* dormice /ˋdɔmaɪs/) small animal (like a mouse) that sleeps during cold weather in winter (and is often kept as a pet).

dor·sal /ˋdɔsl/ *adj* (anat) of, on, near, the back: *the ~ fin,* e g of a shark.

dory[1] /ˋdɔrɪ/ *n* (*pl* -ries) ship's light, flat-bottomed rowing-boat (e g as used by cod-fishers in N America).

dory[2] /ˋdɔrɪ/ *n* (also ˈ**John** ˋ**D~**) edible seafish.

dos·age /ˋdəʊsɪdʒ/ *n* [U] giving of medicines in doses; quantity of a single dose.

dose /dəʊs/ *n* [C] **1** amount (of medicine) to be taken at one time: *The bottle contains six ~s.* **2**

(fig, colloq) sth given or taken: *give sb a ~ of flattery.* **3** (sl) venereal disease: *give sb a ~.* □ *vt* [VP6A,15B,14] give ~(s) to: *to ~ oneself with quinine.*

doss /dos/ *vi* (GB sl) [VP2C] ***~ down,*** go to bed. **ˈ~-house** *n* cheap lodging-house.

dos·sier /ˈdosɪeɪ *US:* ˈdɔs-/ *n* set of papers giving information about a person or event, esp a person's record.

dost /dʌst/ *v* old form, used in *Thou ~,* You do.

dot[1] /dot/ *n* **1** small round mark (as over the letters i and j); decimal points: *dots and dashes,* the marks (e g · — · — — · · — · · ·) used for morse signals. ***on the dot,*** (colloq) at the precise moment. **2** sth like a dot in appearance: *We watched the ship until it was a mere dot on the horizon.* □ *vt* (-tt-) **1** mark with a dot. ***dot one's I's; dot the i's and cross the t's,*** (fig) make (sth) clear and definite. **2** make with, cover with, dots: *a dotted line,* e g on a document, for a signature. ***sign on the dotted line,*** (fig) agree without hesitation or protest; *dotted about,* scattered here and there: *a field dotted with sheep,* with sheep here and there.

dot[2] /dot/ *n* woman's dowry.

do·tage /ˈdəʊtɪdʒ/ *n* [U] weakness of mind caused by old age: *He is in his ~,* is growing foolish, is unable to remember things, fails to notice things, etc. **do·tard** /ˈdəʊtəd/ *n* person in his ~.

dote /dəʊt/ *vi* [VP3A] ***~ on/upon,*** show much, or too much, fondness; centre one's affections (on): *She ~s on her grandson. He's a doting* (= very loving) *husband.*

doth /dʌθ/ old form used for *does.*

dottle /ˈdotl/ *n* small quantity of tobacco left unsmoked in a pipe.

dotty /ˈdotɪ/ *adj* (-ier, -iest) (colloq) feeble-minded; idiotic; eccentric.

dou·ane /duˈɑn/ *n* (F) customs; custom-house.

double[1] /ˈdʌbl/ *adj* **1** twice as much, large, good, etc: *Is the material single width or ~ width,* i e is it folded lengthwise? *His partner is ill and he has to do ~ work. His income is ~ what it was five years ago. There was a ~ knock at the door,* two knocks in quick succession. *Two ~ whiskies, please,* two glasses of whisky, each with twice the usual portion. **2** having two like things or parts, ⇨ single: *a gun with a ~ barrel; a railway with a ~ track; ~ doors; ~-glazing/~ windows* (used in cold countries); *a man with a ~ chin,* with a fold of loose flesh below the chin; *a ship/box/trunk with a ~ bottom; a sword with a ~ edge; a ~ exposure,* (phot) two exposures on the same plate or section of film. **3** made for two persons or things: *a ~ bed; a ~ harness,* for two horses. **4** combining two things, qualities, etc: *a ~ advantage; a piece of furniture that serves a ~ purpose,* e g one that is a settee and can be opened out to make a bed; *a man with a ~ character,* e g Jekyll and Hyde; *to engage in ~ dealing,* be dishonest and deceitful. **5** (of flowers) having more than one set or circle of petals: *~ daffodils.*

double[2] /ˈdʌbl/ *adv* **1** twice (as much): *Many things now cost ~ what they did a few years ago.* **2** in twos; in a pair; in pairs or couples: *to see ~,* to see two things when there is only one; *to sleep ~,* two to a bed.

double[3] /ˈdʌbl/ *n* **1** twice the quantity: *Ten is the ~ of five.* ***~ or quits,*** the decision by chance (e g by throwing dice) whether a person shall pay twice what he owes, or nothing at all. **2** person or thing that looks exactly, or almost exactly, like another: *She is the ~ of her sister.* **3** a slow run (about twice as fast as ordinary walking): *The troops advanced at the ~.* **4** (tennis) game played with two on each side. ***mixed ~s,*** a man and woman against another man and woman. **5** sharp twist or turn. ⇨ double[4](3).

double[4] /ˈdʌbl/ *vt,vi* **1** [VP6A,2A] make or become twice as great: *to ~ one's income. Money earning good interest will ~ itself in time.* **2** [VP6A,15B] bend or fold in two: *Let me ~ the shawl and put it round you. He ~d his fists,* clenched them as if ready to fight. **3** [VP2A,C] ***~ (back),*** turn sharply back in flight (when running to escape pursuit): *The fox ~d (back) on its tracks.* **4** [VP15B,2C] ***~ back,*** turn or fold (sth) back. ***~ up,*** **(a)** fold (sth) up: *He ~d up his legs and kicked out,* e g when swimming. **(b)** be capable of folding up or rolling up: *This carpet is too thick to ~ up.* **(c)** (of persons) (cause to) bend the body with pain or in helpless laughter: *The stone struck him in the stomach and ~d him up. He ~d up with the pain of the blow.* **5** [VP2A] move at the double. ⇨ double[3](3). Chiefly as a military command: *Squad quick march! D~!* **6** [VP6A] go round: *The ship ~d Cape Horn.* **7** [VP6A] (of an actor) act two parts in the same play: *He's doubling the parts of a servant and a farm worker.*

double[5] /ˈdʌbl/ *adj, adv* (in compounds) **ˈ~-ˈbarrelled** *adj* (of a gun) having two barrels; (fig, of a compliment, etc) ambiguous; (of a surname) compound, hyphened (as *Armstrong-Jones*). **ˈ~-ˈbass** *n* largest and lowest-pitched instrument in the violin family. ⇨ the illus at string. **ˈ~-ˈbedded** *adj* (of a room) with two beds or a ~ bed. ⇨ *twin-bedded* at twin. **ˈ~-ˈbreasted** *adj* (of a coat or waistcoat) made so as to overlap across the front of the body. **ˈ~-ˈcheck** *vt* check[1](1), twice in order to be certain. **ˈ~-ˈcross** *vt* [VP6A] (colloq) cheat or betray (each of two parties, usu by pretended collusion with both). □ *n* act of this kind. **ˈ~-ˈdealer** *n* person who says one thing and means another; deceiver. **ˈ~-ˈdealing** *n, adj* deceit(ful) (esp in business). **ˈ~-ˈdecker** *n* ship (colloq, tram, bus) with two decks. ⇨ deck[1](2). **ˈ~-ˈdutch** *n* (colloq) gibberish. **ˈ~-ˈdyed** *adj* (chiefly fig) having certain qualities to a very high degree: *a ~-dyed scoundrel,* deeply stained with guilt. **ˈ~-ˈedged** *adj* with two cutting edges; (fig, of an argument, compliment) that can be understood as being either for or against. **ˈ~-ˈentry** *n* system of book-keeping in which each transaction is entered (written) on the debit side of one account and the credit side of another. **ˈ~-faced** *adj* (= *two-faced*) insincere. **ˈ~-first** *n* a first-class honours degree in two principal subjects gained at the same time. **ˈ~-ˈjointed** *adj* having joints that allow the fingers (or arms, legs) to move or bend in unusual ways. **ˈ~-ˈpark** *vt,vi* park a car at the side of a car already parked at the side of a street. **ˈ~-ˈquick** *adj, adv* very quick(ly): *in ~-quick time.* **ˈ~-talk** *n* kind of talk that really means the opposite of, or sth quite different from, what it seems to mean.

doub·let /ˈdʌblət/ *n* **1** close-fitting garment for the upper part of the body, worn by men (about 1400–1600). ⇨ p 264. **2** one of (esp) two words with the same origin but which have become different in form or meaning, e g *hospital* and *hostel.*

dou·bloon /dəˈblun/ *n* Spanish gold coin (not now in use).

doubly /ˈdʌblɪ/ *adv* (used before *adjj*) to twice the extent or amount: *to be ~ careful/sure.*

doubt[1] /daʊt/ *n* [U] uncertainty of mind; [C] feeling of uncertainty; uncertain state of things: *I have no ~ that you will succeed/no ~ of your ability. There is not much ~ about his guilt,* He is almost certainly guilty. *She had her ~s whether he would come. I have my ~s as to/about this being true. There is no room for ~,* We can be quite certain about it. *There is no ~ about it,* It is certain. *It became a matter of ~* (= became uncertain) *whether....* **in ~,** uncertain: *When in ~ about the meaning of a word, consult a dictionary. He is in ~ (about) what to do.* **beyond/past (all) ~, without (a) ~,** certainly: *Don't worry; he'll come back without ~.* **no ~,** certainly; (colloq) very probably: *He meant to help, no ~, but in fact he has been a hindrance.* **throw ~ upon** (sb's veracity, etc), suggest that (it) is not to be regarded as certain or reliable. ⇨ benefit.

doubt[2] /daʊt/ *vt,vi* [VP6A,9, *neg* and *interr,* 10, 6,3A] feel doubt about; hesitate to believe; question the truth of: *You cannot ~ your own existence. I ~ the truth of this report. Do you ~ my word,* think I am not telling the truth? *I don't ~ that he will come. Can you ~ that he will win? I ~ whether he will come. I ~ if that was what he wanted. Nor do we ~ being able to finish in time. They have never ~ed of success,* never had doubts about succeeding.

doubt·ful /ˈdaʊtfl/ *adj* feeling doubt; causing doubt: *I am/feel ~ (about) what I ought to do. The future looks very ~. The weather looks very ~. It's a ~ blessing,* may or may not be one. *Are you ~ of success? He's a ~ character,* perhaps dishonest. *It is a ~ neighbourhood,* one with a bad reputation, one where ~ characters live. **~ly** /-flɪ/ *adv*

doubt·less /ˈdaʊtləs/ *adv* without doubt; (colloq) very probably.

douche /duʃ/ *n* stream of water applied to a part of the body (outside or inside) for cleaning it or for medicinal purposes; instrument for forcing out such a stream of water.

dough /dəʊ/ *n* [U] mixture of flour, water, etc in a paste (for making bread, pastry, etc); (sl) money. **ˈ~·boy,** (sl) infantryman in the US army (World War I). **ˈ~·nut,** sweetened ~ cooked in deep fat, usu in the shape of a ring or a ball. **~y** *adj* of or like ~; soft; flabby.

doughty /ˈdaʊtɪ/ *adj* (old use, or, in mod Eng, jokingly) brave and strong; bold: *a ~ warrior; ~ deeds.*

dour /dʊə(r)/ *adj* severe; stern; obstinate: *~ looks; ~ silence.* **~·ly** *adv*

a doublet and hose   a jerkin

douse, dowse /daʊs/ *vt* [VP6A] put into water; throw water over; (colloq) extinguish (a light).

dove[1] /dʌv/ *n* **1** kind of pigeon; symbol of peace. **ˈ~·cote** *n* small shelter or house with nesting-boxes for ~s: *flutter the ~cotes,* (fig) alarm quiet people. **2** (colloq) member of a group promoting peace. ⇨ hawk[1](2).

dove[2] /dəʊv/ (US) alternative *pt* form of dive[2].

dove·tail /ˈdʌvteɪl/ *n* joint for two pieces of wood.

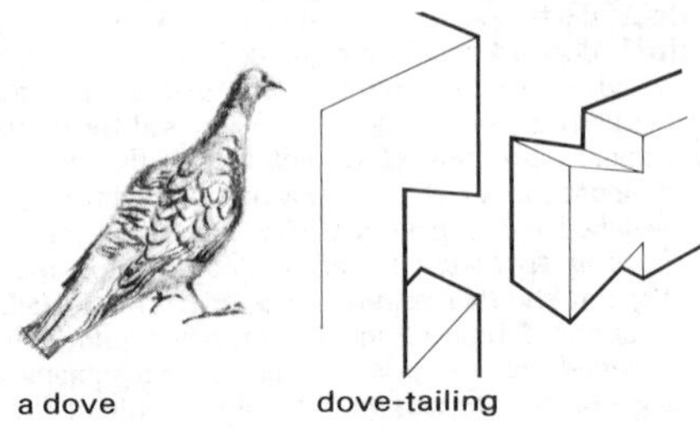

a dove   dove-tailing

□ *vt,vi* [VP6A,2A,C] join together by means of ~s; (fig) fit (together): *My plans ~ed with his.*

dowa·ger /ˈdaʊɪdʒə(r)/ *n* **1** woman with property or a title from her dead husband: *the ~ duchess.* **2** (colloq) dignified elderly lady.

dowdy /ˈdaʊdɪ/ *adj* (-ier, -iest) (of clothes, etc) shabby or unfashionable; (of a person) dressed in ~ clothes. **dow·di·ly** *adv* **dow·di·ness** *n*

dowel /ˈdaʊl̩/ *n* headless pin or peg for keeping two pieces of wood, metal, stone, etc together.

dower /ˈdaʊə(r)/ *n* **1** widow's share of her husband's property; dowry. **2** property brought by a woman to her husband; dowry. **3** gift of nature (e g beauty, intelligence). □ *vt* provide with a ~.

down[1] /daʊn/ *n* [U] first, soft feathers of young birds; soft under-feathers of birds (as used for pillows and cushions); fine soft hair, e g the first hair that comes on a boy's face; the soft hair on some plants and seeds (e g the thistle).

down[2] /daʊn/ *adv part* **1** (with *vv* indicating motion) from a high(er) level to a low(er) level: *The sun went ~. The flag was hauled ~ at sunset. If you can't jump ~, climb ~. Some kinds of food go ~* (= can be swallowed) *more easily than others.* (fig) *That story won't go ~,* will not be accepted, believed. **2** (with *vv* that indicate motion) from an upright position to a horizontal position: *He was knocked ~ by a bus. If you're tired, go and lie ~. He's ~* (= ill in bed) *with influenza. Don't hit a man when he's ~,* (fig) attack him when he has suffered misfortune, etc. **3** (with *vv* indicating change of attitude but not of position in space) to or in a lower position or direction: *Sit ~, please. The tall man bent ~ to speak to me.* **4** (with *vv* indicating position or station): *Mary isn't ~ yet,* is not yet dressed and downstairs. *We can't use the telephone—the lines are all ~,* on the ground, e g after a storm. *The river is ~,* back to its normal height, e g after a flood. *Use a book-mark; don't turn the corners of the pages ~. Can you get ~ here?* **5** from a more important place (e g the capital) to a less important place; from an inland place to the coast; from the university: *We went ~ to Brighton* (e g from London) *for the weekend. The Bill was sent ~* (from the House of Lords) *to the House of Commons. We're waiting for the ~ train,* the train from London. *Which is the ~ platform,* that at which ~

trains stop? *When did he come* ~ *from* (= leave, graduate at) *Oxford? He has been sent* ~, expelled from the University for misbehaving, etc. **6** (used with *vv* to indicate reduction to a smaller volume, a lower degree, a state of less activity, etc): *The heels of my shoes have worn* ~. *Boil the fat* ~. *The wind died* ~. *The sea is* ~/*has calmed* ~, is, has become, calm. *The fire is burning* ~, getting low. *One of the back tyres is* ~, is flat or getting flat. *The clock has run* ~, needs to be wound up. *The temperature has gone* ~. *The price of fruit is* ~. *The factory was closed* ~ (= Work was stopped) *because of a steel shortage.* **7** (used with reference to writing): *to write sth* ~; *to have/get sth* ~, have it written. *Please take* ~ *this letter,* write it (e g in shorthand) as I dictate it. *Put me* ~/*Put my name* ~ *for 50p,* e g as willing to give this sum to a charity or an appeal for a fund. *I see you're* ~ (= your name appears in the programme) *for a speech at the next meeting.* **8** from an earlier time (to a later time): *the history of Europe* ~ *to 1914; looking* ~ *through the ages; coming* ~ *to modern times.* **9** including the lower limit in a series: *everyone, from the queen* ~ *to the humblest of her subjects.* **10** (in various phrases) ***D~ with,*** let us be rid of: *D~ with the grammarians!* ***~ under,*** (colloq) in the antipodes (the other side of the world). ***up and ~,*** to and fro: *walking up and* ~. ***money/cash* '~, *a* '~ *payment,*** payment at the time of purchase (contrasted with credit): *You must pay 50p* ~. ***be ~ and out,*** (colloq) **(a)** (boxing) be knocked out, unable to resume the fight. **(b)** (fig) be beaten in the struggle of life; be unemployed and without money. Hence, **'~-and-'outs** *n* ***get ~ to work/business,*** start work in real earnest. **'~-to-'earth,** (attrib) concerned with realities; practical (contrasted with *impractical, vague, idealistic*): *He's a* ~*-to-earth sort of fellow.* ***be ~ on sb,*** feel ill-will towards him. ***be ~ in the dumps,*** (colloq) dejected; in low spirits. ***~ in the mouth,*** (colloq) sad-looking. ***~ on one's luck,*** (colloq) having suffered misfortune. ***come ~ in the world,*** fall to a lower social position. ***come ~ on sb,*** scold or rebuke him sharply.

down[3] /daʊn/ *prep* **1** from a high(er) to a low(er) level: *to run* ~ *a hill. The tears ran* ~ *her face. Her hair was hanging* ~ *her back.* **2** at a lower part of: *Oxford is farther* ~ *the river.* **3** along (not necessarily with reference to a lower level): *I was walking* ~ *the street. He has gone* ~ *town,* from one of the outlying parts, e g a suburb, to the business or shopping quarters of the town. ⇨ **downtown.** ***~ (the) wind,*** (of a boat) with the wind behind. **4** (of time) from a farther to a nearer period: ~ *the ages.*

down[4] /daʊn/ *vt* [VP6A] (colloq) bring, put, knock, down: *to* ~ *a player with a sliding tackle; to* ~ *a glass of beer,* empty the glass. ***~ tools,*** (of workers) refuse to work, go on strike.

down[5] /daʊn/ *n* (only in) ***ups and ~s,*** changes in fortune, prosperity, etc: *have one's ups and* ~*s, the ups and* ~*s of life; have a* ~ *on sb,* feel ill-will towards him.

down·beat /ˈdaʊnbit/ *n* (music) first beat of a bar (when the conductor's hand moves down).

down·cast /ˈdaʊnkɑst *US:* -kæst/ *adj* (of a person) depressed; discouraged; sad; (of eyes) looking downwards.

down·draught /ˈdaʊndrɑft *US:* -dræft/ *n* downward draught, esp one down a chimney into a room.

down·fall /ˈdaʊnfɔl/ *n* **1** heavy fall (of rain, etc). **2** (fig) ruin; fall from fortune or power: *His* ~ *was caused by gambling and drink.*

down·grade /ˈdaʊnˈgreɪd/ *vt* [VP6A] reduce to a lower grade or rank.

down·hearted /ˈdaʊnˈhɑtɪd/ *adj* in low spirits; depressed.

down·hill /ˈdaʊnˈhɪl/ *adv* in a downward direction. ***go ~,*** (fig) go from bad to worse (in health, fortune, etc).

Down·ing Street /ˈdaʊnɪŋ strit/ *n* street in London with official residences of the Prime Minister, Chancellor of the Exchequer, etc; (hence) the Government: *What does* ~ *think of the matter?*

down·pour /ˈdaʊnpɔ(r)/ *n* [C] heavy fall (esp of rain): *to be caught in a* ~.

down·right /ˈdaʊnrɑɪt/ *adj* **1** forthright; honest; frank: *He has a* ~ *manner. He is a* ~ *sort of person.* **2** thorough; out-and-out; nothing less than: *It's a* ~ *lie. It's* ~ *nonsense.* □ *adv* thoroughly: *He was* ~ *rude.* **~·ness** *n*

downs /daʊnz/ *n* **1** expanse of open, rolling land, esp the chalk uplands of S England: *The North/South D~s.* **2** the sea off the coast of Kent (S E England): *anchor in the D~s.*

down·stairs /ˈdaʊnˈsteəz/ *adv* **1** to, at, on, of, a lower floor; down the stairs: *He went* ~ *to breakfast. Our neighbours* ~ (= on the lower floor) *are very noisy. Your brother is waiting* ~. **2** (often without the final *s*) used as an *adj*: *the* ~*(s) rooms.*

down·town /ˈdaʊntaʊn/ *adv* (esp US) to or in the lower part of a town; to the main or business part of a town: (attrib) ~ *New York; a* ~ *movie theatre.*

down·trod·den /ˈdaʊnˈtrɒdn/ *adj* oppressed; kept down and treated badly.

down·ward /ˈdaʊnwəd/ *adj* moving, leading, going, pointing, to what is lower: *a* ~ *slope; on the* ~ *path; prices with a* ~ *tendency.* **down·wards** *adv* towards what is lower: *He laid the picture face* ~*s on the table. The monkey was hanging head* ~*s from the branch.*

downy /ˈdaʊnɪ/ *adj* of, like, covered with, down. ⇨ **down**[1].

dowry /ˈdaʊərɪ/ *n* [C] (*pl* **-ries**) property, money, brought by a bride to her husband.

dowse /daʊs/ *vt* ⇨ **douse.**

dows·ing /ˈdaʊzɪŋ/ *n* [U] searching for underground water or metals by using a **Y**-shaped stick or rod. ⇨ **diviner. dows·er** *n* person who does this.

dox·ol·ogy /ˈdɒksˈɒlədʒɪ/ *n* (*pl* **-gies**) words of praise to God, used in church services (e g 'Glory be to God...').

doyen /ˈdɔɪən/ *n* senior member of the diplomatic corps in a capital city, or a society, profession, etc.

doy·ley, doyly *n* = **doily.**

doze /dəʊz/ *vi* [VP2A,C] sleep lightly; be half asleep: *He* ~*d off* (= fell half asleep) *during the sermon.* □ *n* [C] short, light sleep.

dozen /ˈdʌzn/ *n* (also used attrib, *pl* unchanged) **1** twelve: *Eggs are 35p a* ~. *I want three* ~ *of these. Pack them in* ~*s,* in sets or groups of twelve. ***talk nineteen to the ~,*** talk incessantly. **2** (*pl*) ***~s of,*** a large number of: *I've been there* ~*s of times.*

drab /dræb/ *adj* **1** (also as *n*) dull muddy brown. **2** (fig) dull; uninteresting; monotonous: *a ~ existence.* □ *n* slut. **~·ly** *adv* **~·ness** *n*

drachm /dræm/ *n* = **(a)** drachma; **(b)** dram.

drachma /ˋdrækmə/ *n* ancient Greek silver coin; modern Greek unit of currency.

dra·co·nian /drəˋkəʊnɪən/ *adj* of a rigorous law or code of laws; harsh: *~ measures.*

draft[1] /drɑft *US:* dræft/ *n* [C] **1** outline (usu in the form of rough notes) of sth to be done: *a ~ for a speech/letter;* preliminary version: *a ~ for a Parliamentary Bill;* rough sketch: *a ~ for a machine.* **2** written order for payment of money by a bank; drawing of money by means of such an order: *a ~ for £500 upon London,* e g one written by a Paris bank upon its London branch. Hence, **ˋbank-~**. **3** (US) group of men chosen from a larger group for a special purpose, esp of men conscripted for the armed forces. **ˋ~ card,** card summoning a man to serve in the armed forces. **4** ⇨ **draught,** the usual GB spelling for many senses of *draft* as used in the US.

draft[2] /drɑft *US:* dræft/ *vt* [VP6A] **1** make a draft(1) of: *to ~ a speech.* **2** choose men for a draft(3); (US) conscript (a man) for the armed forces: *to be ~ed into the Army.* **~·ee** /ˈdrɑˋfti *US:* ˈdræˋfti/ *n* man ~ed for military service. **~·ing** *n* the act of ~ing; way in which sth is ~ed(1): *a ~ing committee,* e g of a Parliamentary Bill. *The ~ing of this section of the Bill is obscure.*

drafts·man /ˋdrɑftsmən *US:* ˋdræfts-/ *n* (*pl* -men) man who prepares drafts(1), esp in engineering and architecture; person responsible for the careful and exact wording of a legal document, or a (clause in a) parliamentary bill.

drafty /ˋdrɑftɪ *US:* ˋdræftɪ/ *adj* (-ier, -iest) (US) = draughty.

drag[1] /dræg/ *n* **1** sth that is dragged, e g a net (**ˋ~-net**) pulled over the bottom of a river to catch fish; a heavy harrow pulled over the ground to break up the soil. **2** (old use) heavy four-wheeled coach pulled by four horses. **3** (colloq) sth or sb that slows down progress because dull, etc: *His wife has been a ~ on him all his life,* has hindered him in his career. *Do we have to take your sister with us? She's such a ~.* ⇨ drag[2](3). **4** (sl) [U] woman's clothes worn by a man: *'As you Like It' performed in ~,* with the women's parts acted by men dressed as women. **5** (sl) puff at a cigarette or cigar.

drag[2] /dræg/ *vt,vi* (-gg-) **1** [VP6A,15B,14] pull along (esp with effort and difficulty): *to ~ a heavy box out of a cupboard. The escaped prisoner was ~ged out of his hiding-place.* ***~ sb into sth,*** involve him unwillingly in an undertaking: *He hates parties; we had to ~ him into going.* **2** [VP6A,15B,2A,C] (allow to) move slowly and with effort; (allow to) trail: *to walk with ~ging feet. He could scarcely ~ himself along. The ship ~ged its anchor/The ship's anchor ~ged during the night,* it failed to hold, was drawn along the sea bottom. ***~ one's feet,*** go forward slowly, unwillingly (often fig): *We suspect the Government of ~ging their feet.* ***~ up a child,*** (colloq) bring it up roughly and without proper training: *The children seem to have been ~ged up anyhow instead of being properly trained and educated.* **3** [VP2A,C] (of time, work, an entertainment) go on slowly in a dull manner: *Classwork often ~s towards the end of term,* pupils lose interest. *The performance ~ged (on). The soloist ~ged behind the orchestra. Time seemed to ~.* **4** [VP6A,2A] use nets, tools, etc to search the bottom of a river, lake, etc (usu for sth lost or missing): *They ~ged the river for the missing child.*

drag·gled /ˋdrægld/ *adj* (often ˋ*be~*) wet, dirty or muddy (as if dragged through mud, etc).

drago·man /ˋdrægəmən/ *n* (*pl* -mans) guide and interpreter (esp in Arabic-speaking countries).

dragon /ˋdrægən/ *n* fabulous creature like a crocodile or snake, but with wings and claws, able to breathe out fire, often guarding a treasure; vigilant woman, esp a severe chaperon of young girls.

a dragon

drag·on·fly /ˋdrægənflaɪ/ *n* (*pl* -flies) insect with a stick-like body and two pairs of large wings. ⇨ the illus at insect.

dra·goon /drəˋgun/ *n* horse-soldier; cavalryman. □ *vt* [VP6A,14] ***~ sb (into doing sth),*** force him to do sth, harass him.

drain[1] /dreɪn/ *n* **1** pipe, channel, trench, etc for carrying away water, sewage and other unwanted liquids; (*pl*) system of pipes and sewers for carrying away waste liquid, etc from buildings: *There's a bad smell; something wrong with the ~s, I suppose.* **ˋ~-pipe,** pipe used in a system of ~s. **2** (fig) sth that continually uses up force, time, wealth, etc; cause of weakening or loss: *Military expenditure has been a great ~ on the country's resources. All this extra work was a ~ on his strength.* **ˋbrain ~,** movement of trained technical and scientific personnel from one country to another (because of better opportunities, etc). **3** (colloq) small drink; mouthful: *Don't drink it all; leave me a ~!*

drain[2] /dreɪn/ *vt,vi* **1** [VP15B,2C] ***~ away/off,*** (of liquid) (cause to) run or flow away: *Dig trenches to ~ the water away/off. The water will soon ~ away/off.* **2** [VP2A,6A] (of land, etc) make, become dry as water flows away: *These swamps ought to be ~ed. Land must be well ~ed for some crops. These fields ~ into the river. Leave the dishes on the board to ~.* **ˋ~ing-board,** board at the side of a sink, on which dishes, etc are placed to ~. **3** [VP6A,15B,14,2C] (fig) (cause to) lose (strength, wealth, etc) by degrees: *The country was ~ed of its manpower and wealth by war. His life was slowly ~ing away,* e g of a man bleeding to death. **4** [VP6A,22] drink; empty (a glass, etc).

drain·age /ˋdreɪnɪdʒ/ *n* [U] **1** draining or being drained. **ˋ~-basin,** area drained by a river. **2** system of drains(1). **3** that which is drained away or off; sewage.

drake /dreɪk/ *n* male duck.

dram /dræm/ *n* **1** unit of weight: (apothecaries wt) 60 grains (8 drams = 1 oz or 28·35 grams); (avoirdupois) 27⅓ grains (16 drams = 1 oz or 28·35 grams). ⇨ App 5. **2** small drink of alcoholic spirits: *He's fond of a ~,* e g of whisky.

drama /ˋdrɑmə/ *n* **1** [C] play for the theatre, radio or TV; [U] composition, presentation and performance of such plays: *a student of (the) ~; to be interested in (the) ~.* **2** [C,U] series of exciting events.

dra·matic /drə`mætɪk/ *adj* **1** of drama(1): *~ performances; ~ criticism.* **2** sudden or exciting, like an event in a stage play: *~ changes in the international situation.* **3** (of a person, his speech, behaviour) exaggerating his feelings, etc in order to impress. **dra·mati·cally** /-klɪ/ *adv* in a ~ manner. **dra·mat·ics** *n* (usu with *sing v*) **1 ~ works or performances by amateurs:** *Are you interested in amateur ~s.* **2** ~(3) acts, speech, etc.

dra·matis per·sonae /ˈdræmətɪs pə`səʊnɑɪ/ *n pl* (Lat) (list of the) characters in a play.

drama·tist /`dræmətɪst/ *n* writer of plays.

drama·tize /`dræmətɑɪz/ *vt* [VP6A] put a story, novel, etc into the form of a drama. **2** be dramatic(3). **drama·tiz·ation** /ˈdræmətɑɪ`zeɪʃn *US:* -tɪ`z-/ *n* [C,U].

drank /dræŋk/ *pt* of drink.

drape /dreɪp/ *vt* [VP6A,14] ***~ round/over,*** **1** hang curtains, cloth, a cloak or other garment in folds round or over sth: *to ~ curtains over a window; to ~ a cloak over one's shoulders/a flag over the coffin.* **2** ***~ with,*** cover or decorate: *walls ~d with flags; a doorway ~d with a heavy curtain.* **3** allow to rest loosely: *He ~d his legs over the arms of his chair.* □ *n* [C] (chiefly US) cloth hung in folds; curtain.

dra·per /`dreɪpə(r)/ *n* (GB) shopkeeper who sells cloth, linen, clothing, etc. **~y** *n* **1** [U] ~'s trade; goods sold by a ~: (attrib) *a ~y business/store.* **2** [C,U] (*pl* -ries) materials used for garments, hangings, curtains, etc; such materials arranged in folds.

dras·tic /`dræstɪk/ *adj* (of actions, methods, medicines) having a strong or violent effect: *~ measures to cure inflation,* e g a steep increase in the bank rate; *~ remedies to cure an illness.* **dras·ti·cally** /-klɪ/ *adv*

drat /dræt/ *vt* (-tt-) (used chiefly in exclamations, colloq) confound; curse; bother: *Drat it all! Drat that child! That ~ted* (= cursed) *boy!*

draught (US = **draft**) /drɑft *US:* dræft/ *n* **1** [C,U] current of air in a room, chimney or other enclosed place: *You'll catch cold if you sit in a ~. Turn the electric fan on and make a ~. There's not enough ~ up the chimney; that's why the fire doesn't burn well.* **2** [C] the pulling in of a net of fish(es). **3** [U] depth of water needed to float a ship: *vessels of shallow ~; a ship with a ~ of ten feet.* ⇨ draw²(16). **4** [U] drawing of liquid from a container (e g a barrel): *beer on ~; ~ beer.* Cf *bottled beer.* **5** (amount drunk during) one continuous process of swallowing: *a ~ of water; to drink half a pint of beer at a ~.* **6** (of animals) used for pulling: *a `~-horse,* one that pulls heavy loads, ⇨ *pack-horse* at pack¹(1); *beasts of ~,* horses, oxen, etc. **7** (*pl, sing v*) (US = *checkers*) table game for two players using 24 round pieces (called `~s(men)) on a board with 32 black and 32 white squares. □ *vt* ⇨ draft². **draughts·man** /`drɑftsmən *US:* `dræ-/ *n* (*pl* -men) **1** = draftsman. **2** piece used in ~s, ⇨ 7 above.

draughty (US = **drafty**) /`drɑftɪ *US:* `dræftɪ/ *adj* (-ier, -iest) with draughts(1) blowing through: *a ~ room.*

draw¹ /drɔ/ *n* **1** the act of drawing (in various senses): *the ~ for the fourth round of the tennis tournament. When does the ~ take place,* When will the winning numbers for the lottery, etc, be drawn? *The game ended in a ~,* neither side won. *Our team has had five wins and two ~s this season.* **2** sb or sth that attracts attention, ⇨ draw²(6): *Mr A is always a great ~ at political meetings,* is a popular speaker. *The new play is a great ~,* many people are going to the theatre to see it. **3** *be quick/slow on the ~,* quick/slow at pulling out a sword, revolver, etc.

draw² /drɔ/ *vt,vi* (*pt* drew /dru/, *pp* drawn /drɔn/) **1** [VP6A,15B,14] move by pulling: *to ~ a boat (up) out of the water/on to the beach; to ~ one's chair up to the table; to ~ sb aside,* e g to speak to him quietly; *to ~ a curtain across a window; to ~ down the blinds* (of windows); *to ~* (= pull down) *one's hat over one's eyes; to ~ one's belt tighter; to ~ one's pen through a word,* cross it out. *The fisherman drew in his net. When you shoot an arrow, you ~ the bow,* bend it by pulling the string. ⇨ bow¹(1). *He drew the book towards him.* **2** [VP6A,15B] (esp) move by pulling after or behind: *a train ~n by two locomotives; tractor-~n ploughs. The wagon was being ~n by two horses.* ⇨ draught(6). **3** [VP6A,15B,14] take or get out by pulling; extract: *to ~ a cork,* out of a bottle; *to ~ nails from a plank/a sword from its scabbard; to ~ the sword,* (fig) declare war; start a war; *to have a tooth ~n; to ~ sb's teeth,* (fig) make him harmless; *to ~ stumps,* (cricket) pull them out at the end of play; *to ~ a chicken* (etc), remove the entrails before cooking it: *to ~ trumps,* (in card games such as bridge) cause them to be played; *to ~ cards from a pack; to ~ for partners,* e g when about to play a card game, allow this to decide the question; *to ~ lots,* ⇨ lot²(1); *to ~ the winner,* get a ticket, etc at a lottery, on which there is a payment, prize, etc; *to ~ a covert,* search it for game; *to ~ a blank,* find or obtain nothing; *to ~ a gun (on* sb), take it from its holster, ready for use. **4** [VP15B] ***~ on/off,*** (of gloves) pull on/off. **5** [VP6A,14] ***~ (from/out of),*** obtain from a source: *to ~ water from a well; to ~ cider/beer from a cask/barrel; to ~ one's salary; to ~ money from the bank/from one's account; to ~ rations,* get, receive, supplies (of food, etc) from a store; *to ~ inspiration from nature; to ~ facts/information from witnesses. What moral are we to ~ from this story?* ***~ it mild,*** (orig of beer; fig) be moderate; not exaggerate. ***~ tears/applause, etc,*** be the cause of: *Her singing drew long applause. Her pitiful story drew tears from all who heard it.* **6** [VP6A,14,15B,2A] attract: *Street accidents always ~ crowds. The film drew large audiences. The new play at the Queen's Theatre is ~ing well. He drew* (= called) *my attention to a point I had overlooked. She didn't feel ~n towards him,* There was nothing in his character, behaviour, etc that attracted her. **7** [VP6A,15B] take in: *to ~ a deep breath; stop to ~ breath,* to rest after exertion. ***~ one's first/last breath,*** be born/die. **8** [VP2A] (of a chimney, etc) allow a current of air to flow through; be built so that air and smoke pass up or through. *This chimney ~s badly. This cigar does not ~ well.* **9** [VP6A,15B] ***~ sb (out),*** cause, persuade, (a person) to talk, show his feelings, etc: *He was not to be ~n,* He refused to say anything about the matter. *He has many interesting stories* *of his travels if you can* ~ *him out.* **10** [VP6A,2C, 16B,14] **~ sth out,** stretch; (cause to) become longer: *He heated the metal and drew it out into a long wire. The battle was long ~n out. There was a long-~n-out discussion. He has ~n out the subject into three volumes.* **11** [VP2C,D] move; come (in the direction indicated by the *adv*, etc): *Christmas is ~ing near. The day drew to its close. The two ships drew level. The favourite began to ~* (= gain) *on the other runners. The Queen's horse quickly drew away from the others,* went ahead of them. *Everyone drew back in alarm. The taxi drew up at* (= reached and stopped at) *the station entrance. When the enemy saw how strong our forces were, they drew off,* went back. **~ back,** (fig) show unwillingness: *~ back from a proposal.* ⇨ drawback(1). **12** [VP6A,15B] cause to move or come (in the direction indicated by the *adv*, etc): *His promises drew me on,* caused me to proceed, follow his suggestions, etc. *Her indifference drew him on all the more,* made him even more determined to win her, etc. *He drew himself up to his full height,* stood in an erect, stiff attitude. **13** [VP6A,2A] make with a pen, pencil, chalk, etc; (fig) describe in words: *to ~ a straight line/a circle; to ~ a picture/plan/diagram;* (fig) *The characters in Jane Austen's novels are well ~n; to ~ a horse. She ~s well.* **~ a distinction (between),** point out differences; show the dividing line. **~ a parallel/comparison/analogy (between),** show how two things are alike. **~ the line (at),** set limits; declare what cannot be allowed; refuse to go as far as or beyond: *This noisy behaviour cannot be allowed; we must ~ the line somewhere. I don't mind lending him my razor, but I ~ the line at lending him my toothbrush.* **14** [VP6A,15B] write out: *to ~ a bill/cheque/order* (*on* a banker, etc, *for* a sum of money): *to ~ up* (= compose) *a document/a contract/an agreement; to ~ out a scheme,* set out the particulars in writing. **15** [VP3A] **~ on,** take or use as a source: *If newspaper men cannot get facts for their stories, they sometimes ~ on their imaginations. We mustn't ~ on our savings. You may ~ on me for any sum up to £500,* get sums up to this maximum from me or my agents. **16** [VP6A] (of a ship) require (a certain depth of water) in order to float, ⇨ draught(3): *The ship ~s 20 feet of water.* **17** [VP6A,2A] end (a game, etc) without either winning or losing: *to ~ a football or cricket match; a ~n game; to ~ 2—2. The teams drew.* **18** [VP2C] **~ in,** (a) (of a particular day) reach its end. (b) (of daylight in the temperate regions) become shorter: *The days begin to ~ in after midsummer.* **~ out,** (of days) become longer: *Christmas passed and the days began to ~ out.* **19** [VP15B] **~ up,** (usu passive) (of troops, etc) bring into regular order: *The troops were ~n up ready for the inspection.* **20** [VP6A,2A,B] extract the essence of: *to let the tea ~ for three minutes.* **21** (usu in *pp*) (of the features) pull out of shape: *a face ~n with pain/anxiety; with ~n features.*

draw·back /ˈdrɔbæk/ *n* **1** [C] sth which lessens one's satisfaction, or makes progress less easy; disadvantage (*to*). **2** [U] amount of import duty paid back when goods are exported again.

draw·bridge /ˈdrɔbrɪdʒ/ *n* bridge that can be pulled up at the end(s) by chains (e g across the moat of a castle in ancient times to prevent passage, or across a river or canal to allow ships to pass).

drawer /drɔ(r)/ *n* **1** box-like container (with a handle or handles) which slides in and out of a piece of furniture, etc. **ˈchest of ˈ~s,** piece of furniture consisting of a set of ~s. **2** (*pl*) old-fashioned two-legged undergarment for the lower part of the body; knickers. **3** (usu /ˈdrɔə(r)/) person who draws pictures; person who draws a cheque, etc.

draw·ing /ˈdrɔ-ɪŋ/ *n* [U] the art of representing objects, scenes, etc by lines, with a pencil, chalk, etc; [C] sth made in this way; a sketch, plan, etc. ***out of ~,*** incorrectly drawn. **ˈ~-board,** flat board on which to fasten paper for ~: *still on the ~-board,* in the planning stage. **ˈ~-pin,** (US = *thumb-tack*) flat-headed pin for fastening paper to a ~-board, notice-board, etc.

draw·ing-room /ˈdrɔ-ɪŋ rʊm *US:* rum/ *n* room in which guests are received.

drawl /drɔl/ *vi,vt* [VP2A,C,6A,15B] speak so that the sounds of the vowels are longer than usual: *The speaker ~ed on. Don't ~ (out) your words.* □ *n* slow way of speaking.

drawn /drɔn/ *pp* of draw². ⇨ esp **2, 9, 10, 17** and **21.**

dray /dreɪ/ *n* low, flat, four-wheeled cart, without sides, for heavy loads, e g barrels from a brewery.

dread /dred/ *n* [U] (or with *indef art*) great fear and anxiety: *to be in ~ of sb or sth; to live in constant ~ of poverty. Cats have a ~ of water.* □ *vt,vi* [VP6A,C,7A] fear greatly: *to ~ a visit to/~ having to visit the dentist. I ~ to think of what may happen.* **~ed** *part adj* greatly feared. **~·ful** /-fl/ *adj* **1** causing ~: *a ~ful disaster. What a ~ful story!* **2** (colloq) unpleasant: *What ~ful weather!* **~·fully** /-fl̩ɪ/ *adv* **~·ful·ness** *n*

dread·naught /ˈdrednɔt/ *n* type of battleship in the early years of the 20th century.

dream¹ /drim/ *n* [C] **1** sth which one seems to see or experience during sleep: *to have a ~ (about sth); to awake from a ~.* **ˈ~-land, ˈ~ world,** region outside the laws of nature, as experienced in sleep or in the imagination. **2** state of mind in which things going on around one seem unreal: *to live/go about in a ~.* **3** mental picture(s) of the future: *to have ~s of wealth and happiness.* **4** beautiful or pleasing person, thing, experience, etc: *His holiday by the sea was like a ~. She looked a perfect ~/a ~ of delight.* **~·less** *adj* without ~s. **~·like** /ˈdrimlɑɪk/ *adj* like a ~.

dream² /drim/ *vi,vt* (*pt,pp* ~ed or dreamt /drempt/) **1** [VP2A,3A,6A,15B,9,8,10] **~ about/of,** have ~s; see, experience, in a dream; imagine; suppose: *He often ~s. The soldier often ~t of/about home. He ~t that he was at sea. I*

a drawbridge

certainly didn't promise you £100; you must have ~t it. I wouldn't ~ of doing such a thing, The idea would never occur to me. *He little ~ed that...,* did not imagine or suppose that.... **2** [VP15B] *~ away one's time/the hours, etc,* pass one's time idly; *~ sth up,* (colloq) imagine, conceive (a plan, etc). **~er** *n* person who ~s; person with impractical ideas, plans, etc.

dreamy /ˈdrimɪ/ *adj* (-ier, -iest) **1** (of a person) with thoughts far away from his surroundings or work. **2** (of things, experiences) vague; unreal: *~ music; a ~ recollection of what happened.* **dream·ily** /-əlɪ/ *adv*

dreary /ˈdrɪərɪ/ *adj* (-ier, -iest) (poet **drear** /drɪə(r)/) dull; gloomy; causing low spirits: *~ work (weather).* **drear·ily** /-əlɪ/ *adv*

dredge[1] /dredʒ/ *n* apparatus for bringing up mud, oysters, specimens, etc from the bed of the sea, rivers, etc. □ *vt,vi* [VP6A,15B,2A,3A] ***~ up,*** bring up with a ~; clean with a ~: *to ~ (up) mud; to ~ (for) oysters; to ~ a channel/harbour.* **dredger** *n* boat carrying a ~.

dredge[2] /dredʒ/ *vt* [VP6A,14] sprinkle or scatter: *to ~ meat with flour; to ~ sugar over a cake.* **dredger** *n* box with holes in the lid for sprinkling flour, sugar, etc on food.

dregs /dregz/ *n pl* **1** bits of worthless matter which sink to the bottom of a glass, bottle, barrel, etc of liquid. ***drink/drain to the ~,*** drink and leave only the ~. **2** (fig) worst and useless part: *the ~ of society/humanity.*

drench /drentʃ/ *vt* [VP6A] make wet all over, right through: *to be ~ed with rain/~ed to the skin. They were caught in a downpour and came back ~ed.* **~ing** *n* thorough wetting: *We got a ~ing.*

dress[1] /dres/ *n* **1** [C] one-piece outer garment with a bodice and skirt worn by a woman or girl; gown or frock. **2** [U] clothing in general (for both men and women), esp outer garments: *Women usually pay more attention to ~ than men do. He doesn't care much about ~,* is not much interested in clothes. **ˈfull ˋ~,** kind of clothes worn on special occasions: *ambassadors, naval and military officers, all in full ~.* **ˋevening ~,** clothing worn at formal social occasions (e g dinners, evening parties). **ˋ~ circle,** lowest gallery in a theatre, in which evening ~ was formerly required. **ˋ~ coat,** black, swallow-tailed coat worn by men for evening ~. **ˋ~ rehearsal,** final rehearsal of a play, at which actors wear the costumes to be worn at actual performances. **ˋ~·maker,** woman who makes women's ~es.

dress[2] /dres/ *vt,vi* **1** [VP6A,2A] put on (clothes): *Mary was ~ing her doll. Jim isn't old enough to ~ himself. Have you finished ~ing? How long does it take you to ~ (yourself)?* [VP15B,2C] ***~ up,*** put on special clothes, as for a play, a fancy dress ball, etc: *The children ~ed (themselves) up as pirates.* **2** [VP2A,C] put on evening dress: *We don't ~ for dinner nowadays. You've just time to ~* (= change into evening dress) *before we leave for the theatre.* **3** [VP2C] (of what is habitual) wear clothes: *He has to ~ well in his position.* **4** ***be ~ed in,*** be wearing: *She was ~ed in white. They were ~ed in the height of fashion,* wearing the most fashionable clothes. **5** [VP6A] provide clothes for: *How much does it cost him to ~ his wife and daughters?* **6** [VP6A] make ready to use; prepare: *to ~ leather,* make it soft and smooth; *to ~ a salad,* ⇨ **dressing(3)**; *to ~ a chicken,* clean it ready for cooking. **7** [VP6A,15B] brush and comb, arrange (one's hair); *to ~ down a horse,* brush its coat well. **~ sb down,** (fig) scold him severely; thrash him. Hence, **ˈ~ing-ˋdown** *n* severe scolding. **8** [VP6A] clean and bandage a wound, etc. **9** [VP6A] make cheerful and attractive: *to ~ a shop-window* (with attractive goods); *to ~ the streets,* e g with flags; *to ~ a Christmas-tree.* **10** [VP6A,2A] (mil) get or bring (soldiers) into a straight line: *~ the ranks.*

dress·age /ˈdresɑʒ/ *n* [U] (F) training of horses (for show-jumping, etc).

dresser[1] /ˈdresə(r)/ *n* person who dresses, esp **(a)** one who helps a surgeon to dress wounds in a hospital; **(b)** person who helps actors and actresses to dress ready for the stage.

dresser[2] /ˈdresə(r)/ *n* **1** piece of kitchen furniture with shelves for dishes, and cupboards below, often with drawers for cutlery, etc. **2** (US) dressing-table.

dress·ing /ˈdresɪŋ/ *n* **1** [U] process of dressing (putting on clothes, cleaning and bandaging a wound, etc). **ˋ~-case,** one for brushes, bottles and other articles of toilet, when travelling. **ˋ~-gown,** loose gown worn over pyjamas, etc before dressing, etc. **ˋ~-table,** one with a mirror, used in a bedroom. **2** [C,U] sth used for dressing wounds, e g an ointment, bandage, etc. **3** [C,U] mixture of oil, vinegar, condiments, etc used as a sauce for salads and other dishes. **4** [U] substance used to stiffen silk, cotton, etc during manufacture.

dressy /ˈdresɪ/ *adj* (-ier, -iest) (colloq) (of persons) fond of, looking smart in, fine clothes; (of clothes) stylish.

drew /dru/ *pt* of **draw**[2].

dribble /ˈdrɪbl/ *vt,vi* [VP6A,2A] **1** (of liquids) flow, allow to flow, drop by drop or in a slow trickle (esp from the side of the mouth): *Babies often ~ on their bibs.* **2** (football) take (the ball) forward by means of quick, short kicks, either between the feet of one player, or by short passes from one player to another. **drib·bler** /ˈdrɪblə(r)/ *n* person who ~s.

drib·let /ˈdrɪblət/ *n* falling drop; small amount: *in ~s, by ~s,* a little at a time.

dribs and drabs /ˈdrɪbz n ˋdræbz/ *n pl* (colloq) small amounts.

dried /drɑɪd/ *pt,pp* of **dry**[2].

drier /ˈdrɑɪə(r)/ *adj* ⇨ **dry**[1] *n* ⇨ **dry**[2].

drift[1] /drɪft/ *n* **1** [U] drifting movement; being carried along by currents: *the ~ of the tide. The general ~ of the current was northerly.* **ˋ~·age** /-ɪdʒ/ *n* (of a ship) general movement off course due to currents, winds, tides, etc. **ˋ~-net,** large net into which fish ~ with the tide. **2** [C] sth caused by drifting: *Big ~s of snow/snow ~s made progress slow and difficult. It was buried in a ~ of dead leaves.* **ˋ~-ice,** broken ice carried along on the surface of the sea, a river, etc in masses by currents of water or air. **ˋ~-wood,** wood carried along by currents and washed up on beaches. **3** [U] general tendency or meaning: *I caught the ~ of what he said. Did you get the ~ of the argument?* **4** [U] the way in which events, etc tend to move: *The general ~ of affairs was towards war.* **5** [U] the state of being inactive and waiting for things to happen: *Is the government's policy one of ~?* **6** [U] (radio) drifting, ⇨ **drift**[2]**(3)**: *a tuning unit free from ~.*

drift[2] /drɪft/ *vi,vt* **1** [VP2A,C] be carried along by, or as by, a current of air or water; (fig, of persons) go through life without aim, purpose or self-control: *The boat ~ed out to sea. We ~ed down the stream. The snow had ~ed everywhere. Is the government/the country ~ing towards bankruptcy? She ~s from one job to another.* **2** [VP6A,15B,14] cause to ~: *The logs were ~ed down the stream to the saw-mills. The wind had ~ed the snow into high banks.* **3** [VP2A] (of the tuning unit in a radio set but rare in modern sets) move away from the wavelength to which it has been set. **~er** *n* **1** boat used in ~-net fishing and, during war, for mine-sweeping. ⇨ **drift**[1](1). **2** person who ~s(1).

drill[1] /drɪl/ *n* instrument with a pointed end or cutting edges for making holes in hard substances: *a dentist's ~.* □ *vt,vi* [VP6A] make a hole with a ~: *~ a hole in a stone wall;* [VP2A] use a ~. **'~ing rig,** ⇨ **rig**[1] *n*(2).

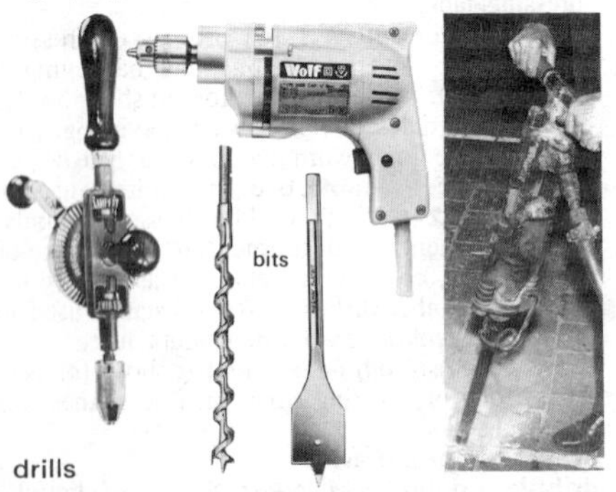

drills

drill[2] /drɪl/ *n* [C,U] **1** army training in the handling of weapons; formal movements, e g marching, turning, to develop alertness: *'bayonet ~; 'gun-~. The soldiers were at ~ in the barrack square.* **2** thorough training by practical experiences, usu with much repetition: *~s in the English vowel sounds.* **3** routine procedure to be followed, e g in an emergency: *'fire-~; 'lifeboat ~.* □ *vt,vi* [VP6A,14,2A] train, be trained, by means of ~s: *to ~ troops on a parade ground; a well-~ed crew.*

drill[3] /drɪl/ *n* furrow (long channel where seeds are to be sown); machine for making furrows, sowing seeds in them, and covering the seeds; row of seeds sown in this way. □ *vt* [VP6A] sow (seeds) in ~s.

drill[4] /drɪl/ *n* [U] heavy, strong linen or cotton cloth.

drill[5] /drɪl/ *n* kind of baboon.

drily /'draɪlɪ/ ⇨ **dry**[1].

drink[1] /drɪŋk/ *n* [C,U] **1** liquid for drinking: *We should die without food and ~. We have plenty of bottled ~s,* beer, lemonade, etc in bottles. **2** alcoholic liquor: *What about a ~? I'll bring in the ~s,* e g the gin, whisky, sherry. *He's too fond of ~.* ***take to ~,*** acquire the habit of drinking regularly and too much. ***be in ~/the worse for ~/ under the influence of ~,*** intoxicated: *He's a good husband except when he's in ~.* ***drive sb to ~,*** cause him to take to ~: *Mrs Bell's bad temper drove her husband to ~.* **3 the ~,** (sl) the sea.

drink[2] /drɪŋk/ *vt,vi* (*pt* **drank** /dræŋk/, *pp* **drunk** /drʌŋk/) **1** [VP6A,15B,2A] take (liquid) into the mouth and swallow: *to ~ a pint of milk.* ***~ sth down/off/up,*** ~ the whole of it (esp at once). **2** [VP6A,15B] (of plants, the soil, etc) take in, absorb (liquid): *The thirsty plants drank (up) the water I gave them. The parched soil drank (in) the rain.* **3** [VP15B] ***~ sth in,*** (fig) take into the mind eagerly or with pleasure: *The boy drank in every word of the sailor's story of his adventures.* **4** [VP6A,15B,2A] take alcoholic liquors, beer, wine, etc, esp in excess: *He ~s far too much. He ~s half his earnings,* spends it on alcoholic liquors. *He will ~ himself to death.* **5** [VP6A,3A] ***~ (to),*** wish good (to sb) while raising one's glass; ~ a toast to: *to ~ a person's health; to ~ to sb's success; to ~ to sb's health.* **~·able** /-əbl/ *adj* suitable or fit for ~ing. **~er** *n* (esp) person who ~s alcoholic liquor too often or too much: *He's a heavy ~er.* **~·ing** *n* process or habit of taking liquid(s), esp alcoholic liquor: *He's too fond of ~ing.* **'~·ing-bout,** long spell of ~ing. **'~-ing-fountain,** device for providing a supply of ~ing-water in a public place. **'~·ing-song,** one to be sung at a ~ing party; one celebrating the joys of ~ing. **'~·ing-water,** fit for ~ing.

drip /drɪp/ *vi,vt* (-pp-) [VP2A,C,6A] (of a liquid) fall, allow to fall, in drops: *The rain was ~ping from the trees. The tap was ~ping. Sweat was ~ping from his face. He was ~ping sweat. Blood was ~ping from his hand. His hand was ~ping blood.* ***~ping wet,*** very wet. **'~-'dry** *n* drying of laundered articles (of special texture) by allowing them to ~ until they are dry (without previous squeezing or wringing out): (attrib) *~-dry shirts.* □ *vt* dry in this way. □ *n* **1** the drop-by-drop falling of a liquid: *the ~s from the trees/of the rain.* **2** (sl) a dull, insipid person.

drip·ping /'drɪpɪŋ/ *n* **1** [U] (esp) fat melted out of roasted meat, used for frying, or spread on bread: *a slice of bread and ~.* **'~-pan,** pan in which ~ collects when meat is roasted. **2** (*pl*) liquid that drips or has dripped from sth: *the ~s from the roof.*

drive[1] /draɪv/ *n* **1** driving or being driven (in a car, etc, not in a public vehicle): *to go for a ~; to take sb for a ~. The station is an hour's ~ away.* **2** (in US also **'~·way**) private road through a garden or park to a house; approach from a public road to a garage. **3** (in games played with a ball, e g golf) [U] force given to a ball when it is struck; [C] stroke or hit: *a ~ to the boundary.* **4** [U] energy; capacity to get things done: *young men with brains, ~ and initiative. The new headmaster lacks ~/is lacking in ~.* **5** [C] organized effort or campaign: *a 'sales ~,* one made to increase sales, e g by reducing prices; *the 'export ~,* to increase exports; *The school made a great ~ to raise $20 000 for a new sports ground.* **6 'whist-~, 'bridge-~,** tournament. **7** (mech) apparatus for driving: *front/rear ~,* with power that operates the front/rear wheel(s); *a four-wheel ~,* with four wheels connected to the source of power; *right-/left-hand ~,* (of a motor vehicle) having the steering and other controls on the right/left side.

drive[2] /draɪv/ *vt,vi* (*pt* **drove** /drəʊv/, *pp* **driven** /'drɪvn/) **1** [VP6A,15B,14] cause animals, people to move in some direction by using cries, blows, threats or other means: *to ~ cattle to market; to ~ the enemy out of their positions.* ***~ sb into a corner,*** (fig) force him (e g during an argument) into a position from which escape will be difficult. **2** [VP6A,2A] operate, direct the course of a railway engine, tram, motor-car or other vehicle; control, direct the course of an animal or animals drawing a cart, plough, etc: *to ~ a taxi; to ~ a carriage and pair,* a carriage drawn by two horses; *to take driving lessons. D~ with caution.* **'driving licence,** licence to ~ a motor-vehicle. **'driving school,** one for teaching persons to ~ a motor vehicle. **'driving test,** test which must be passed to obtain a driving licence. **3** [VP2A,C] travel or go in a car, carriage, etc which is at one's disposal. Cf *ride* in a bus, train or other public vehicle: *We drove right up to the front door. Shall we ~ home or walk? We are merely driving through,* travelling through (the place) without intending to stay. **'~-in** *n* (and attrib) restaurant, cinema, etc at which persons get service while in their cars: *a ~-in cinema/bank.* **4** [VP15B,14] carry, convey, (sb) in a car, carriage, etc (not a public vehicle): *He drove me to the station.* **5** [VP6A] (usu passive) (of steam, electricity or other kind of power) set or keep going; be the power to operate: *The machinery is ~n by steam/water-power, etc.* **'driving-belt,** belt that carries motion from an engine, motor, etc to machinery. **'driving-wheel,** *one that communicates power to other parts of a machine.* **6** [VP15B,14] (of wind, water) send, throw, (lifeless things) in some direction: *The gale drove the ship on to the rocks. The ship was ~n out of its course. The wind was driving the rain against the window-panes.* **7** [VP2C] go or move along fast or violently: *The ship drove on the rocks/was driving along before the wind. The clouds drove across the sky. The rain was driving in our faces.* **8** [VP6A,15B,14] ***~ sth in/into sth,*** force a nail, screw, stake, etc into sth: *With one blow he drove the nail into the plank.* **9** [VP6A,15B,14,2A] hit or strike with force: (cricket) *to ~ a ball to the boundary;* (tennis) *to ~ a ball out of the court.* (golf) *He ~s well.* ***~ sth home,*** (fig) impress deeply on the mind. ***let ~ at,*** aim a blow at; send a missile at: *He let ~ at me with his left,* aimed a blow at me with his left fist. **10** [VP15B,17A,22B] cause (sb) to be (in a certain state); cause or compel (sb to do sth): *Failure drove him to despair. Her constant complaints drove him to desperation. You'll ~ me mad/to my wits' end. He was ~n by hunger to steal.* **11** [VP15,2C] (cause to) work very hard: *He was hard ~n. He ~s himself very hard. Don't ~ the workers too hard.* ***~ away at*** (one's work), work very hard at it. **12** [VP6A,15B,14] bore (a tunnel); make (a horizontal excavation): *to ~ a tunnel/gallery through a hill/a railway across a hilly district.* **13** [VP6A] carry on: *to ~ a roaring trade,* sell a lot of things very fast. ***~ a hard bargain,*** not give way easily to another person in a business deal. **14** [VP3A] ***~ at,*** (in the progressive tenses only) mean, intend: *What's he driving at,* What's he trying to do, explain, etc? **15** [VP14] postpone; defer: *Don't ~ it to the last minute.*

drivel /ˈdrɪvl/ *vt* (-ll-, US -l-) [VP2A,C] talk nonsense; talk childishly: *What's he ~ling about? He's still ~ling on.* □ *n* [U] silly nonsense; foolish talk. **~·ler,** US **~er** /ˈdrɪvl̩ə(r)/ *n* person who ~s.

driven /ˈdrɪvn/ *pp* of drive².

driver /ˈdraɪvə(r)/ *n* **1** person who drives (vehicles): *a 'taxi-~; a 'bus-~.* ⇨ chauffeur. **2** person who drives animals. ⇨ *drover* at drove², *slave-~* at slave. **3** (mech) part of a machine, etc that receives power directly, e g the driving-wheel of a locomotive. **4** (golf) wooden club for driving the ball long distances from the tee.

drizzle /ˈdrɪzl/ *vt* [VP2A] rain (in many small fine drops): *It ~d all day.* □ *n* [U] fine rain. **driz·zly** /ˈdrɪzl̩ɪ/ *adj* drizzling: *drizzly weather.*

drogue /drəʊg/ *n* **1** sea anchor (sth like a bag, dragged in the sea to steady a boat's movement). **2** wind-sock, ⇨ wind¹(8). **3** cone towed by one aircraft as a target for use by others in firing practice. **4** **'~ parachute,** small parachute used to pull a large parachute from its pack.

droll /drəʊl/ *adj* causing amusement (because strange or peculiar). **~·ery** /-ərɪ/ *n* [U] jesting; [C] (*pl* -ries) sth peculiar and amusing; amusing trick.

drom·edary /ˈdrʌmədərɪ *US:* ˈdromədərɪ/ *n* (*pl* -ries) fast, one-humped riding-camel.

drone /drəʊn/ *n* **1** male bee; person who does no work and lives on others. **2** [U] low humming sound (as) made by bees: *the ~ of an aeroplane high in the sky/of distant motorway traffic.* **3** [C] monotonous speech, sermon, speaker: *He's a boring old ~.* □ *vi,vt* **1** [VP15B,2C] make a ~(2). **2** [VP15B,2C] talk or sing, say (sth) in a low, monotonous way: *children droning through their lessons. The parson ~d out the psalm.*

drool /drul/ *vi* ***~ (over),*** dribble; slobber.

droop /drup/ *vi,vt* **1** [VP2A,C] bend or hang downwards (through tiredness or weakness): *The flowers were ~ing for want of water. Her head ~ed sadly. His spirits ~ed,* He became sad, low-spirited. **2** [VP6A] let (the head, face, eyes) move forward or down. □ *n* ~ing attitude or position. **~·ing·ly** *adv*

drop¹ /drop/ *n* **1** **(a)** very small quantity of liquid, usu round- or pear-shaped: *'rain~s.* **(b)** (*pl*) liquid medicine taken in ~s: *ear/eye/nose ~s. He emptied the glass to the last ~.* ***in ~s, ~ by ~,*** slowly, one ~ at a time. **2** very small quantity. ***only a ~ in the bucket/ocean,*** a negligible quantity. **3** (glass of) intoxicating liquor: *He has had a ~ too much,* is drunk. **4** sth like a ~ in shape or appearance: *'acid ~s,* of boiled sugar; *'ear~,* ⇨ ear¹(1). **5** movement from a higher to a lower level, esp distance of a fall: *a sudden ~ in the temperature,* e g from 30°C to 20°C; a ~ in the price of wheat. There was a ~ of 10 metres from the window to the ground. ***at the ~ of a hat,*** **(a)** as soon as a signal is given. **(b)** at once; readily or willingly. **6** thing that drops or is dropped(1): *a ~ in a gallows,* platform or trap-door which falls from under the feet of a person executed by hanging. **'~-curtain,** curtain lowered between the acts of a play in a theatre. **'~-kick,** (Rugby football) one in which the ball is dropped and kicked as it rises. **'~-hammer, '~-press,** machine for shaping or stamping, e g metal sheets for motor-car bodies, using the power of a dropped weight.

drop² /drop/ *vt,vi* (-pp-) (For uses with *adverbial particles* and *preps,* ⇨ 13 below.) **1** [VP2A,C,6A] (of liquids), fall, cause to fall, in drops. ⇨ drip. **2** [VP6A,2A,C,14,15B] fall (by the force of gravity, by not being held, etc); allow to fall: *It was so quiet you might hear a pin ~. The apple blossom is beginning to ~. The teapot ~ped out of her hand. She ~ped the teapot. Don't ~ the baby. He ~ped the letter into the pillar-box. The ewes are beginning to ~* (= give birth to) *their lambs.* ***~ anchor,*** lower the anchor; come to anchor. ***~ a***

brick, ⇨ brick. **~ *a stitch,*** (knitting) let it slip off the needle. **3** [VP2A,C,6A,15A,B] (allow to) become weaker or lower; (allow to) fall in amount, degree, pitch, condition, etc: *The wind/temperature has ~ped. His voice ~ped/He ~ped his voice to a whisper. Don't ~ your voice at the end of a sentence. Our boat gently ~ped* (= moved with the current) *downstream.* ⇨ drift[2](1). **4** [VP2A,C,6A,15] (cause to) fall or sink to the ground, etc: *They were ready to ~ with fatigue,* were so tired that they could scarcely stand. *She ~ped into a chair, utterly worn out. He ~ped (on) to his knees,* knelt down. *Supplies were ~ped by parachute.* Hence **'~ping-zone,** area where men, supplies, etc are ~ped by parachute. *The enemy were still ~ping* (= firing) *shells into the town. He ~ped a bird* (= hit one and caused it to fall) *with every shot. He ~ped* (= hit) *the ball to the back of the court.* **5** [VP6A,12A,13A] utter or send casually: *to ~ sb a hint,* give him one; *to ~ a word in sb's ear; to ~ sb a postcard (a few lines, a short note).* ⇨ let[1](4) for *let ~.* **6** [VP6A] omit; fail to pronounce, write or insert: *He ~s his h's,* e g by saying 'at for hat. *The printer has ~ped a letter here,* failed to insert, or replace, a type. *The relative pronoun is often ~ped if it is the object,* e g in 'the man (whom) we met yesterday'. **7** [VP15A] set down; stop (a car, etc) to allow sb to get out: *Where shall I ~ you? Please ~ me at the Post Office.* **8** [VP6A] cease to associate with (sb): *He seems to have ~ped most of his friends,* no longer meets them. **9** [VP6A] give up: *to ~ a bad habit.* **10** [VP6A,2A] (cause to) come to an end; no longer deal with or discuss: *The correspondence ~ped. We ~ped the subject. The subject (was) ~ped. We couldn't agree about the matter, so we decided to let it ~. Let's ~ it,* stop talking about it. **11** [VP6A] lose (money, esp in gambling or a risky enterprise): *He ~ped 100 francs at the Casino last night.* **12** (Rugby football) **~ *a goal,*** score a goal by a ~-kick, ⇨ drop[1](6). **13** [VP2C,3B,15B] (uses with *adverbial particles* and *preps*) **~ *across sb or sth,*** (= run across sb) (which is more usu) meet or find by chance; **~ *astern,*** (of a ship) fall to a position behind: *One of the cruisers had engine trouble and ~ped astern.* **~ *away,*** = ~ off(a). **~ *back,* ~ *behind,*** come to a position behind: *The two lovers ~ped back. They ~ped behind the rest of the party.* **~ *in (on sb),* ~ *by,*** pay a casual visit to: *I wish he wouldn't ~ in on me so often. Some friends ~ped in to tea/~ped by to see me.* **~ *off,*** **(a)** become fewer or less: *His friends ~ped off one by one. The doctor's practice has ~ped off,* He now has fewer patients. **(b)** fall asleep; doze: *He ~ped off during the sermon.* **~ *out,*** **(a)** (of persons taking part in a contest, etc) cease to compete: *Three of the runners ~ped out.* **(b)** (of persons engaged, or about to engage, in an activity, etc) not take part; give up the idea: *Smith has ~ped out of the (cricket) eleven. Two cars won't hold fifteen people in comfort; five of us had better ~ out,* not go with the others. **(c)** withdraw from conventional social activities, attitudes. Hence, **'~-out** *n* **(a)** person who ~s out, e g one who withdraws from a course of instruction: *the ~-out rate in a language course.* **(b)** person who drops out of society: *University ~-outs,* who do not finish their courses. **~ *through,*** (fig) come to nothing; be no longer discussed: *The big scheme he was busy with seems to have ~ped through.* **~·pings** *n pl* what is ~ped, esp dung of animals.

dropsy /ˈdropsɪ/ *n* [U] disease in which watery fluid collects in some part of the body, e g the legs. **drop·si·cal** /ˈdropsɪkl/ *adj* suffering from ~; of or like ~.

droshky /ˈdroʃkɪ/ *n* (*pl* -kies) light, four-wheeled, open horse-carriage, as formerly common in Russia.

dross /dros *US:* drɔs/ *n* [U] waste material rising to the surface of melted metals; (fig) anything considered to be worthless, mixed with sth else. **~y** *adj* worthless.

drought /draʊt/ *n* [C,U] continuous (period of) dry weather causing distress; want of rain.

drove[1] /drəʊv/ *pt* of drive[2].

drove[2] /drəʊv/ *n* large number of animals (a flock of sheep, a herd of cattle) being driven together; crowd of people moving together: *~s of sightseers; visitors in ~s.* **drover** *n* man who drives cattle, sheep, etc to market; cattle-dealer.

drown /draʊn/ *vt,vi* **1** [VP6A,2A] (cause sb to) die in water because unable to breathe: *a ~ing man. He ~ed the kittens. Do cats ~ easily? He fell overboard and was ~ed.* **2** [VP6A] (of sound) be strong enough to prevent another sound from being heard: *The noises in the street ~ed the teacher's voice.* **3** ***be ~ed out,*** be flooded out. **4** (fig): *a face ~ed in tears,* wet with tears; *~ed in sleep,* in a deep sleep (e g caused by exhaustion).

drowse /draʊz/ *vi,vt* [VP15B,2A,C] be half asleep; pass (time) *away* half asleep: *to ~ away a hot afternoon.* □ *n* half asleep condition: *in a ~.*

drowsy /ˈdraʊzɪ/ *adj* (-ier, -iest) feeling sleepy; half asleep; making one feel sleepy. **drows·ily** /-əlɪ/ *adv* **drow·si·ness** *n*

drub /drʌb/ *vt* (-bb-) [VP6A,14] give repeated blows to; hit with a stick; beat an idea, a notion *into* or *out of* sb. **~·bing** *n* beating: *give sb a good/sound ~bing,* beat him well.

drudge /drʌdʒ/ *n* person who must work hard and long at unpleasant tasks. □ *vi* [VP2A,C,3A] work as a ~ does: *to ~ at dictionary-making.* **drudg·ery** /-ərɪ/ *n* [U] hard, unpleasant, uninteresting work.

drug /drʌg/ *n* [C] **1** substance used for medical purposes, either alone or in a mixture; substance that changes the state or function of cells, organs or organisms. **'~·store** *n* (US) place where a wide variety of articles is sold, where prescriptions can be made up, and where food and drink may be bought and eaten. **2** substance (often habit-forming) inducing sleep or producing stupor or insensibility, e g opium, cocaine: *the ~ habit,* the habit of taking harmful ~s: *a '~ addict; '~ addiction; a '~ pedlar.* **3** ***a ~ on the market,*** an article that cannot be sold because there is no demand. □ *vt* [VP6A] **1** (-gg-) add harmful ~s to (food and drink): *His wine had been ~ged, and they stole his money while he was sleeping heavily.* **2** give ~s to, esp in order to make unconscious: *They ~ged the caretaker and then robbed the bank.*

drug·get /ˈdrʌgɪt/ *n* [C,U] (floor covering of) heavy coarse woollen material.

drug·gist /ˈdrʌgɪst/ *n* **1** (GB) tradesman who sells drugs; pharmacist. **2** (US) person who sells medicines, toilet articles and other goods, and usually food and drinks. ⇨ *drugstore* at drug(1).

Druid, druid /ˈdruɪd/ *n* member of the priesthood

among the Celts of ancient Gaul, Britain and Ireland.

drum[1] /drʌm/ *n* **1** (music) percussion instrument made of a hollow cylinder or hemisphere with parchment stretched over the open side(s), ⇨ the illus at **percussion**; sound of a ~ or ~s, or sound as of ~s. **ˋ~·fire,** heavy continuous rapid fire from big guns. **ˋ~·head service,** (mil) open-air service in which ~s form an altar. **ˋ~·head court-martial,** one held while military operations are in progress, in order to try an offender without delay. **ˈ~-ˋmajor,** sergeant in charge of drummers, and leader of a regimental band on the march; (US) (also **ˈ~-majorette** /ˈmeɪdʒəˋret/) leader of any marching band. **ˋ~·stick,** **(a)** stick for beating a ~. **(b)** lower part of the leg of a cooked chicken, turkey, etc. **2** sth like a ~ in shape, e g a cylindrical container for oil, a cylinder or barrel on which thick wire or cable is wound. ⇨ **ear**[1]**(1).**

drum[2] /drʌm/ *vt, vi* (-mm-) **1** [VP2A,C] play the drum. **2** [VP6A,14,2C,3A] make drum-like sounds; beat or tap continuously *on* sth, etc: *to ~ on the table with one's fingers; to ~ the floor with one's feet; ~ming on the piano/at the door.* **3** [VP15B] **~ up,** summon by ~ming; (fig) ~ up support for a cause. **4** [VP14] ***~ sth into sb/into sb's head,*** cause him to remember it by repeating it. **~·mer** *n* person who plays a drum; (colloq, esp US) commercial traveller.

drunk /drʌŋk/ *pred adj* (*pp* of **drink**[2]) *be ~*, be intoxicated, be overcome by drinking alcoholic liquor: *He was dead/blind/half ~. I've seldom seen him more ~.* **get ~,** become intoxicated: *It's easy to get ~ on brandy.* (fig) *He was ~ with joy/success.* □ *n* person who is ~; man charged (at a police-station) with drunkenness. **~·ard** /-kəd/ *n* man who is ~, or who often gets ~.

drunken /ˋdrʌŋkən/ *adj* (usu attrib, rarely *pred*) **1** intoxicated; in the habit of drinking; often drunk: *a ~ and dissolute man.* **2** caused by drinking; showing the effects of drinking: *a ~ frolic.* **~·ly** *adv* **~·ness** *n*

drupe /drup/ *n* (bot) fruit with juicy flesh, usu with a hard stone enclosing a seed, e g an olive, a plum, a peach.

dry[1] /drɑɪ/ *adj* (drier, driest) **1** not wet; free from moisture: *Is this wood dry enough to burn?* **ˈdry as a ˋbone, ˈbone-ˋdry,** quite dry. **2** not rainy: *dry weather;* having insufficient rainfall: *a dry climate.* **3** not supplying water: *a dry well;* not supplying milk: *The cows are dry.* **4** solid, not liquid: *dry goods* (contrasted with *meat, groceries,* etc), corn; (esp US) drapery. **dry measure,** measure of capacity for dry goods such as corn. **5** without butter: *dry bread/toast.* **6** (of wine, etc) not sweet, not fruity in flavour: *dry wines; a dry martini,* a kind of cocktail. **7** (colloq) thirsty; causing thirst: *to feel dry; dry work.* **8** uninteresting; dull: *a dry lecture/book/subject.* **9** expressed seriously or undemonstratively: *dry humour/sarcasm; a dry jest.* **10** plain; undisguised: *dry facts.* **11** not connected with liquid: *a dry cough,* without phlegm; *a dry death,* not by drowning; *a dry shampoo,* one in which water is not used. **12** (of a State, country, its legislation) prohibiting or restricting the sale of alcoholic liquor: *Will the country go dry,* Will it pass and accept legislation of this kind? **13** (compounds) **ˋdry battery,** electric battery with two or more dry cells. **ˋdry-bulb thermometer,** one of two thermometers, one dry and the other kept wet, used for measuring the humidity of the atmosphere **ˋdry cell,** cell in which the chemicals are in a moist paste which does not spill. **ˈdry-ˋclean** *v* clean (clothes, etc) by using spirits (e g petrol) instead of water. Hence **ˈdry-ˋcleaners, ˈdry-ˋcleaning. ˈdry ˋdock,** ⇨ **dock**[1]**(1). ˈdry ˋgoods,** (also called *ˋsoft goods*), (chiefly US) textiles, articles of clothing, etc. **ˈdry ˋice,** solid carbon dioxide (used for refrigerating). **ˈdry ˋnurse,** not suckling the baby she is caring for. **ˈdry ˋrot** *n* decay of wood (causing it to crumble to powder), occurring when there is no movement of air over its surface; (fig) hidden or unsuspected moral or social decay. **ˋdry-shod** *adj, adv* without wetting the feet; with dry feet or shoes. **ˈdry-ˋwalling,** building of stone walls (e g for a field) without mortar. **drily** /ˋdrɑɪlɪ/ *adv* **dry·ness** *n*

dry[2] /drɑɪ/ *vt, vi* (*pt, pp* dried) **1** [VP6A,15B,2A,C] make or become dry: *Dry your hands on this towel. We were drying our clothes in front of the fire. Our clothes soon dried.* **dry up,** make or become completely dry: *The long drought dried up all the wells. The stream dries up during the hot summer. His imagination seems to have dried up. Dry up!* (sl) Stop talking! Be quiet! **2** [VP6A] (usu the *pp*) preserve by extracting moisture: *dried eggs/milk.* **dryer, drier** *n* **1** substance mixed with oil-paints and varnish to quicken drying. **2** (in compounds) thing that dries: *an electric ˋhair-dryer;* thing on or in which clothes, etc are placed to dry: *a ˋclothes-drier; a ˋspin-drier.*

dryad /ˋdrɑɪəd/ *n* (Gk myth) tree nymph.

dual /ˋdjul *US:* ˋdul/ *adj* of two; double; divided in two: *~ control,* for or by two persons; *~ ownership; ˈ~ ˋcarriageway* (US = *divided highway*); *ˈ~-ˋpurpose,* adapted so as to, intended to, serve two purposes.

dub /dʌb/ *vt* (-bb-) **1** [VP22,23] make (sb) a knight by touching him on the shoulder with a sword; give (sb) a nickname: *They dubbed him 'Shorty' because he was so tall.* **2** [VP6A] replace or add to the sound-track of a film or magnetic tape, esp in a different language.

dub·bin /ˋdʌbɪn/ *n* [U] kind of thick grease used to make leather soft and waterproof.

du·biety /djuˋbɑɪətɪ *US:* du-/ *n* [U] (formal) feeling of doubt; [C] (*pl* -ties) doubtful affair.

du·bious /ˋdjubɪəs *US:* ˋdu-/ *adj* **1** ***~ (of/about),*** (of persons) feeling doubt: *I feel ~ of his honesty. I feel ~ about/as to what to do next.* **2** (of persons) causing doubt (because probably not very good or reliable): *He's a ~ character.* **3** (of things, actions, etc) causing doubt; of which the value, truth, etc is doubtful: *a ~ compliment; a ~ blessing. The result is still ~.* **~·ly** *adv* **~·ness** *n*

du·cal /ˋdjukl *US:* ˋdukl/ *adj* of or like a duke.

ducat /ˋdʌkət/ *n* gold coin formerly used in many European countries.

Duce /ˋdutʃeɪ/ *n* (I) leader (esp as used of Mussolini /ˈmʊsəˋlinɪ/ (1883—1945) Italian Fascist leader).

duch·ess /ˋdʌtʃɪs/ *n* wife or widow of a duke; woman whose rank is equal to that of a duke.

duchy /ˋdʌtʃɪ/ *n* (*pl* -chies) (also *dukedom*) land ruled by a duke or duchess.

duck[1] /dʌk/ *n* (*pl* ~s, but often unchanged when collective) **1** [C] common water-bird, both wild and domestic; female of this, ⇨ **drake;** ⇨ the illus at **fowl;** [U] its flesh as food. **ˈlame ˋ~,** disabled person or ship; business or commercial organization in financial difficulties. ***(take to sth) like a ~ to water,*** naturally, without fear, hesitation or difficulty. ***like water off a ~'s back,*** without producing any effect. ***~s and drakes,*** game in which flat stones are made to skip along water. ***play ~s and drakes with*** (one's money), squander, waste. **2** (colloq, also **~y**) darling; delightful person. **3** vehicle (also **DUKW** /dʌk/) able to travel on land and water, used as a landing-craft by troops. **4** (cricket, also sometimes **'~'s egg**) batsman's score of nought, 0: *to make a ~; be out for a ~.* **5** (compounds) **'~-bill, '~-billed 'platypus** /ˈplætɪpəs/, small Australian egg-laying water mammal with webbed feet and a beak like that of a ~. **'~-boards,** boards with narrow slats fixed across, for use on soft or muddy ground. **'~-weed,** small flowering plant growing on the surface of shallow water (e g on ponds). **'~-ling** /-lɪŋ/ *n* young ~: *ugly ~ling,* plain or stupid child who grows up to be attractive or brilliant.

duck[2] /dʌk/ *vt,vi* [VP6A,2A] **1** move quickly down (to avoid being seen or hit): *to ~ one's head.* **2** go, push (sb), quickly under water for a short time: *The big boy ~ed all the small boys in the swimming-pool.* □ *n* quick downward or sideways movement of the head or body; quick dip below water (when bathing in the sea, etc). **~·ing** *n* thorough wetting: *to give sb a ~ing,* e g by pushing him into or under the water.' *It rained heavily and we all got a ~ing.* **'~ing-stool,** one (attached to a pole) on which a person was tied and ~ed into a pond, river, etc, as a punishment.

duck[3] /dʌk/ *n* [U] strong linen or cotton cloth used for outer clothing of sailors; (*pl*) trousers made of this.

duct /dʌkt/ *n* **1** tube or canal through which liquid is conveyed, esp in the body: *'tear-~s.* **2** metal tube and outlet for air (to ventilate, e g an aircraft): *The air ~s above your seat may be adjusted to your convenience.*

duc·tile /ˈdʌktaɪl *US:* -tl/ *adj* **1** (of metals) that can be pressed, beaten or drawn into shape while cold, e g copper. **2** (fig of a person, his character) easily influenced, managed or directed; docile. **duc·til·ity** /dʌkˈtɪlətɪ/ *n* the quality of being ~(**1**).

dud /dʌd/ *n, adj* (sl) (thing or person) of no use, e g a shell or bomb that fails to explode or a bank-note or cheque of no value.

dude /djud *US:* dud/ *n* (US) dandy. **'~ ranch,** ranch organized for tourists.

dudg·eon /ˈdʌdʒən/ *n* ***in high ~,*** offended and feeling indignation, or sullen anger: *He went off in high ~.*

duds /dʌdʒ/ *n pl* (sl) clothes, esp old or ragged clothes.

due[1] /dju *US:* du/ *adj* **1** ***due (to),*** owing; to be paid: *When is the rent due? The wages due to him will be paid tomorrow.* **2** suitable; right; proper: *after due consideration; in due course,* at the right and proper time. **3** (to be) expected; appointed or agreed (for a certain time or date): *When is the steamer due? The train is due (in) at 1.30. Mr Hill is due to speak/lecture twice tomorrow.* **4** ***due to,*** that may be ascribed or attributed to: *The accident was due to careless driving.* Cf *'owing to': Owing to* (= Because of) *his careless driving, we had a bad accident.* □ *adv* (of points of the compass) exactly, directly: *due east/north.*

due[2] /dju *US:* du/ *n* **1** (*sing* only) that which must be given to sb because it is right or owing: *give the man his due.* ***give the devil his due,*** (prov) be fair to a person even though he is not a friend, or does not deserve much. **2** (*pl*) sums of money to be paid, e g for membership of a club, legal charges paid by ship-owners for the use of a harbour, etc.

duel /ˈdjuḷ *US:* ˈduḷ/ *n* (now illegal) fight (usu with swords or pistols) agreed between two persons, esp to decide a point of honour, at a meeting arranged and conducted according to rules, in the presence of two other persons called seconds; any two-sided contest: *a ~ of wits.* □ *vi* (-ll-, US also -l-) fight a ~ or ~s. **~·list, ~·ist** /ˈdjuəlɪst *US:* ˈdu-/ *n* person who fights ~s.

du·enna /djuˈenə *US:* du-/ *n* (esp in a Spanish or Portuguese family) elderly woman acting as governess and companion in charge of girls; chaperon.

duet /djuˈet *US:* du-/ *n* piece of music for two voices or for two players.

duff /dʌf/ *n* (dialect for) dough.

duf·fer /ˈdʌfə(r)/ *n* slow-witted, unintelligent or incompetent person.

duffle (also **duf·fel**) /ˈdʌfl/ *n* [U] coarse woollen cloth with a thick nap: *a '~ coat,* one of this material, usu with toggles instead of buttons; *a '~ bag,* a cylindrical kitbag (of cloth or canvas).

dug[1] /dʌg/ *pt,pp* of **dig.**

dug[2] /dʌg/ *n* udder or teat of a female mammal.

dug-out /ˈdʌg aʊt/ *n* **1** rough covered shelter made by digging, esp by soldiers for protection in war. **2** canoe made by hollowing a tree trunk. **3** (sl) retired officer called back to service.

duke /djuk *US:* duk/ *n* nobleman of high rank (next below a prince); (in some parts of Europe) independent sovereign ruler of a small State. **~·dom** /-dəm/ *n* **1** position and duties, rank of a ~. **2** (= *duchy*) land ruled by a ~ who is a sovereign ruler.

dul·cet /ˈdʌlsɪt/ *adj* (usu of sounds) sweet; pleasing.

dul·ci·mer /ˈdʌlsɪmə(r)/ *n* (often portable) musical instrument like a zither with strings struck with two hammers.

dull /dʌl/ *adj* (-er, -est) **1** not clear or bright: *a ~ colour/sound/mirror/day/sky; ~ weather; ~ of hearing,* unable to hear well. **2** slow in understanding: *~ pupils; a ~ mind.* **3** monotonous; uninteresting; not exciting or appealing to the imagination: *a ~ book/speech/sermon/play.* **4** not sharp: *a ~ knife; a knife with a ~ edge;* (of pain) not felt distinctly: *a ~ ache.* **5** (of trade) not active; (of goods) not in demand. □ *vt,vi* [VP6A, 2A] make or become ~: *to ~ the edge of a razor; drugs that ~ pain.* **~y** /ˈdʌllɪ/ *adv* **~·ness** *n*

dull·ard /ˈdʌləd/ *n* mentally dull person.

duly /ˈdjulɪ *US:* ˈdu-/ *adv* in a right or suitable manner; at the right time.

Duma /ˈdumə/ *n* Russian parliament from 1905 to 1917.

dumb /dʌm/ *adj* (-er, -est) **1** unable to speak: *~ from birth. We must be kind to ~ animals,* i e also to animals other than human beings. **2** temporarily silent: *The class remained ~ when the teacher asked a difficult question.* ***strike ~,*** make speechless, unable to talk because of surprise, fear, etc: *He was struck ~ with horror.* ***~ show,*** the communication of ideas by means of acting, etc but without words. **3** (US colloq) stupid; dull. **~·ly** *adv* **~·ness** *n*

dumb·bell /ˋdʌmbel/ *n* short bar of wood or iron with a metal ball at each end, used in pairs (one in each hand) for exercising the muscles of the arms and shoulders.

dumb·found (US also **dum·found**) /dʌmˋfaʊnd/ *vt* [VP6A] astonish; strike dumb with surprise.

dumb·waiter /ˈdʌmˋweɪtə(r)/ *n* **1** stand with (usu revolving) shelves for food, dishes, etc used at a dining-table. **2** (US; in GB *food-lift*) box with shelves, pulled up and down a shaft, to carry food, etc from one floor to another, e g in a restaurant.

dum·dum /ˋdʌmdʌm/ *n* **ˋ~ bullet,** soft-nosed bullet which expands on contact, causing a gaping wound.

dummy /ˋdʌmɪ/ *n* (*pl* **-mies**) **1** object made to look like and serve the purpose of the real person or thing: *a tailor's ~,* for fitting clothes; *a baby's ~,* sucked like the nipple of a mother's breast. **2** (attrib) sham, imitation: *a ~ gun.* **3** (in card games, esp bridge) player whose cards are placed upwards on the table and played by his partner; the cards so placed. **4** person who is present at an event, etc but who takes no real part, because he is acting for sb else. **5** (attrib) **ˈ~ ˋrun,** a trial or practice attack, shoot, performance, etc.

dump /dʌmp/ *n* **1** place where rubbish, etc may be unloaded and left; heap of rubbish, etc. **2** (place where there is a) temporary store of military supplies: *an ˈammuˋnition ~.* **3** (sl; pej) poorly cared for, dirty or ugly place (e g a village or town): *I should hate to live in a ~ like this.* □ *vt* [VP6A, 15A] **1** put on or into a ~(1); put or throw down carelessly; let fall with a bump or thud: *Where can I ~ this rubbish? They ~ed the coal outside the shed instead of putting it inside.* **2** (comm) sell abroad at low prices goods which are unwanted in the home market. **~er** *n* (also **ˋ~ truck**) vehicle with a bin that can be tilted, for carrying and emptying soil, rubble, etc (e g for road building).

dump·ling /ˋdʌmplɪŋ/ *n* **1** small round mass of dough steamed or boiled with meat and vegetables. **2** baked pudding made of dough with an apple or other fruit inside it.

dumps /dʌmps/ *n pl* ***(down) in the ~,*** (colloq) in low spirits; feeling gloomy.

dumpy /ˋdʌmpɪ/ *adj* (**-ier, -iest**) short and fat.

dun[1] /dʌn/ *adj, n* dull greyish-brown.

dun[2] /dʌn/ *vt* (**-nn-**) (continue to) demand payment of a debt or debts: *a dunning letter.* □ *n* person who duns; debt-collector; importunate demand for payment.

dunce /dʌns/ *n* slow learner (esp a child at school); stupid person. **ˋ~'s cap,** pointed paper cap which a ~ was formerly given to wear in class as a punishment.

dun·der·head /ˋdʌndəhed/ *n* blockhead; stupid person.

dune /djun *US:* dun/ *n* low stretch of loose, dry sand formed by the wind, esp near the sea-shore.

dung /dʌŋ/ *n* [U] waste matter dropped by animals (esp cattle), used on fields as manure: *to cart and spread ~.* **ˋ~-hill,** heap of ~ in a farmyard.

dun·ga·rees /ˈdʌŋgəˋriz/ *n pl* overalls or trousers (usu) of coarse calico.

dun·geon /ˋdʌndʒən/ *n* dark underground cell used (in olden times) as a prison.

dunk /dʌŋk/ *vt* [VP6A, 14] (US) dip (a piece of food) into a liquid: *~ a doughnut in one's coffee.*

duo·deci·mal /ˈdjuəˋdesɪml *US:* ˈduə-/ *adj* of twelve or twelfths; proceeding by twelves: *a ~ notation.*

duo·de·num /ˈdjuəˋdinəm *US:* ˈduə-/ *n* first part of the small intestine immediately below the stomach. ⇨ the illus at alimentary. **duo·denal** /ˈdjuəˋdinl *US:* ˈduə-/ *adj* of the ~: *a duodenal ulcer.*

duo·logue /ˋdjuəlog *US:* ˋduəlɔg/ *n* conversation between two persons.

dupe /djup *US:* dup/ *vt* [VP6A] cheat; make a fool of; deceive. □ *n* person who is ~d.

du·plex /ˋdjupleks *US:* ˋdu-/ *adj* double; twofold: *a ~ (oil-)lamp,* one with two wicks; *a ~ apartment,* (US) one with rooms on two floors with an inner staircase.

du·pli·cate[1] /ˋdjuplɪkət *US:* ˋdu-/ *adj* **1** exactly like: *~ keys for the front door of a house.* **2** with two corresponding parts; doubled; twofold. □ *n* [C] thing that is exactly like another. ***in ~,*** (of documents, etc) with a ~ copy.

du·pli·cate[2] /ˋdjuplɪkeɪt *US:* ˋdu-/ *vt* [VP6A] **1** make an exact copy of (a letter, etc); produce copies of. **2** multiply by two. **du·pli·ca·tor** /-tə(r)/ *n* machine, etc that ~s sth written or typed. **du·pli·ca·tion** /ˈdjuplɪˋkeɪʃn *US:* ˈdu-/ *n* [U] duplicating or being ~d; [C] copy.

du·plic·ity /djuˋplɪsətɪ *US:* du-/ *n* [U] deliberate deception.

dur·able /ˋdjʊərəbl *US:* ˋdʊə-/ *adj* likely to last for a long time: *a ~ pair of shoes,* not soon worn out or needing repair. □ *n* (usu *pl*) (often *ˋconsumer ~s*) goods bought and expected to last a long time (e g vacuum cleaners). **dura·bil·ity** /ˈdjʊərəˋbɪlətɪ *US:* ˋdʊə-/ *n* [U].

du·rance /ˋdjʊərəns *US:* ˋdʊ-/ *n* (old use) imprisonment.

dur·ation /djʊˋreɪʃn *US:* dʊ-/ *n* [U] time during which sth lasts or exists: *for the ~ of the war; of short ~.*

dur·bar /ˋdɜbɑ(r)/ *n* Indian ruler's court; reception given by a ruler in India.

dur·ess (also **-esse**) /djʊˋres *US:* dʊ-/ *n* threats, imprisonment, or violence, used to compel sb to do sth: *under ~,* compelled by such means.

dur·ing /ˋdjʊərɪŋ *US:* ˋdʊə-/ *prep* **1** throughout the continuance of: *The sun gives us light ~ the day.* **2** at some point of time in the continuance of: *He called to see me ~ my absence.*

durst /dɜst/ old *p* form of dare.

dusk /dʌsk/ *n* [U] time just before it gets quite dark: *scarcely visible in the ~.*

dusky /ˋdʌskɪ/ *adj* (**-ier, -iest**) rather dark; dark-coloured; dim.

dust[1] /dʌst/ *n* **1** [U] dry earth or other matter in the form of fine powder, lying on the ground or the surface of objects, or blown about by the wind: *The ~ was blowing in the streets. When it rains ~ turns into mud.* ***bite the ~,*** (rhet) fall wounded or killed. ***(humbled) in(to) the ~,*** humiliated (as if lying at the feet of an enemy). ***shake the ~ off one's feet,*** leave in anger or scorn. ***throw ~ in a person's eyes,*** mislead him; prevent him from seeing the truth. **ˋ~-bowl,** area that is denuded of vegetation by drought, unwise farming methods, etc. **ˋ~-coat,** coat worn to keep ~ off or out. **ˋ~-jacket/-wrapper,** removable paper cover to protect the binding of a book. **ˋ~-pan,** pan into which ~ is swept from the floor. **~-sheet** *n* one for covering furniture not in use. **2** (with *indef art*) cloud of ~: *What a ~!* ***make/raise/kick up a ~,*** (sl, fig) cause a commotion. **3** (compounds) (GB; Cf US *refuse, trash, garbage*) household refuse: **'~-bin,** rigid receptacle for this. Cf US *ash-can, garbage-box.* **'~-cart,** cart into which ~bins are emptied. **'~-man** /-mən/ (*pl* **-men**) man employed (by municipal authorities, etc) to empty ~bins and cart away refuse. **4** (old use, poet or liter) remains of a dead human body: *buried with the ~ of*(= in the same grave as) *one's ancestors.* **5** (from *gold ~*, sl) money. **6** confusion; turmoil: *the ~ and heat of the day,* the burden of a struggle or fight.

dust² /dʌst/ *vt* [VP6A] **1** remove dust from by wiping, brushing, flicking: *to ~ the furniture.* ***~ a person's jacket,*** beat him. **'~-up** *n* (colloq) fight; noisy argument. **2** sprinkle with powder: *to ~ a cake with sugar;* sprinkle (powder, etc): *to ~ sugar on to a cake.* **~er** *n* cloth for removing dust from furniture, etc.

dusty /'dʌstɪ/ *adj* (**-ier, -iest**) covered with dust; full of dust; like dust; dry as dust. ***a ~ answer,*** a vague, unhelpful answer.

Dutch /dʌtʃ/ *adj* **1** of or from the Netherlands (Holland), its people, their language: *~ cheese.* **2** (hist) of Germany or the Germans. **3** (colloq uses) ***~ auction,*** sale at which the price is reduced by the auctioneer until a buyer is found. ***~ courage,*** that obtained by drinking (spirits, etc). ***~ treat,*** meal, entertainment, etc at which each person pays for himself. ***go ~ (with sb),*** share expenses. ***talk to sb like a ~ uncle,*** lecture him candidly and severely. □ *n* **1 the ~,** the people of Holland. **2** their language. ***double ~,*** unintelligible language. **~-man** /-mən/ *n* (*pl* **-men**) native of Holland.

du·teous /'djutɪəs *US:* 'du-/ *adj* dutiful (the more usu word); obedient.

duti·able /'djutɪəbl *US:* 'du-/ *adj* on which customs duties must be paid: *~ goods. Tobacco is ~ in most countries.* ⇨ duty(3).

duti·ful /'djutɪfl *US:* 'du-/ *adj* doing one's duty well; showing respect and obedience (*to*): *a ~ son.* **~ly** /-flɪ/ *adv*

duty /'djutɪ *US:* 'dutɪ/ *n* (*pl* **-ties**) **1** [C,U] what one is obliged to do by morality, law, a trade, calling, conscience, etc; inner voice urging one to behave in a certain way: *When ~ calls, no man should disobey. Do not forget your ~ to your parents. His sense of ~ is strong. What are the duties of this post? The duty of a postman is to deliver letters and parcels.* ***on/off ~,*** actually engaged/not engaged in one's regular work: *He goes on ~ at 8am and comes off ~ at 5pm.* ***(as) in ~ bound,*** as required by ~. ***do ~ for,*** be used instead of; serve for: *An old wooden box did ~ for a table.* **2** (attrib) moral obligation: *a '~ call,* a visit one makes from a sense of duty, not because one expects to enjoy it. **3** [C,U] payment demanded by the government *on* certain goods exported or imported (*'customs duties*), or manufactured in the country (*'excise duties*), or when property, etc is transferred to a new owner by sale (*'stamp duties*) or death (*e'state ~*). **'~-'free,** (of goods) allowed to enter without the payment of customs duties; *~-free shops,* (e g at airports) selling ~-free goods.

duvet /'djuveɪ *US:* du'veɪ/ *n* bed quilt (filled with feathers, e g swan's-down, or an artificial substitute) used in place of blankets.

dwarf /dwɔf/ *n* (*pl* **~s**) person, animal or plant much below the usual size; (in fairy tales) small being with magic powers; (attrib) undersized. □ *vt* [VP6A] **1** prevent from growing to full size. **2** cause to appear small by contrast or distance: *The big steamer ~ed our little launch.*

dwell /dwel/ *vt* (*pt* **dwelt** /dwelt/) [VP3A] **1 ~ *in/at,*** etc, reside. **2 ~ *(up)on,*** think, speak or write at length about: *She ~s too much upon her past.* **~er** *n* (in compounds) inhabitant: *'town-~ers; 'cliff-~ers; 'cave-~ers.* **~ing** *n* place of residence (a house, flat, etc). **'~ing-house,** one used for living in, not as an office, workshop, etc.

dwindle /'dwɪndl/ *vt* [VP2A] become less or smaller by degrees.

dy·archy *n* = diarchy.

dye¹ /daɪ/ *vt,vi* (*3rd p sing pres t,* **dyes,** *pt,pp* **dyed,** *pres part* **dyeing**) **1** [VP6A,22] colour, usu by dipping in a liquid: *to dye a white dress blue; to have a dress dyed.* **dye in the wool/in grain,** dye while the material is in the raw state, so that the process is thorough. **'dyed-in-the-'wool** *adj* (fig) thorough; complete. **2** [VP6A] give colour to: *Deep blushes dyed her cheeks.* **3** [VP2A] take colour from dyeing: *This material does not dye well.*

dye² /daɪ/ *n* [C,U] substance used for dyeing cloth; colour given by dyeing; (fig) ***a villain/scoundrel of the blackest/deepest dye,*** of the worst kind. **'dye-stuff,** substance yielding a dye or used as a dye. **'dye-works,** one where dyeing is done. **dyer** *n* one who dyes cloth.

dy·ing ⇨ die².

dyke *n* = dike.

dy·namic /daɪ'næmɪk/ *adj* **1** of physical power and forces producing motion. ⇨ static. **2** (of a person) having energy, force of character. □ *n* **1** (*pl* with *sing v*) branch of physics dealing with matter in motion. **2** moral force that produces activity or change: *driven by an inner ~.* **dy·nami·cally** /-klɪ/ *adv*

dy·na·mism /'daɪnəmɪzm/ *n* [U] quality of being dynamic (esp(**2**)): *He's overflowing with ~.*

dy·na·mite /'daɪnəmaɪt/ *n* [U] powerful explosive (used in mining and quarrying). □ *vt* [VP6A] blow up with ~.

dy·namo /'daɪnəməʊ/ *n* (*pl* **-mos** /-məʊz/) machine for changing steam-power, water-power, etc into electrical energy. ⇨ the illus at bicycle.

dyn·ast /'dɪnəst *US:* 'daɪnæst/ *n* lord; hereditary ruler. **dyn·asty** /'dɪnəstɪ *US:* 'daɪ-/ *n* (*pl* **-ties**) succession of rulers belonging to one family: *the Tudor ~y* (in England). **dyn·astic** /dɪ'næstɪk *US:* daɪ-/ *adj* of a ~y.

dys·en·tery /'dɪsntrɪ *US:* -terɪ/ *n* [U] painful disease of the bowels, with discharge of mucus and blood.

dys·pep·sia /dɪs'pepsɪə/ *n* [U] indigestion. **dys·pep·tic** /dɪs'peptɪk/ *adj* of ~. □ *n* person suffering from ~.

Ee

E, e /i/ (*pl* **E's, e's** /iz/), fifth letter of the English alphabet.

each /itʃ/ *adj* (of two or more) every one, thing, group, person, etc taken separately or individually: *He was sitting with a child on ~ side of him. On ~ occasion I just missed the target. He had words of encouragement for ~ one of us.* □ *pron* **1** ~ thing, person, group, etc: *E~ of them wants to try. E~ of the boys had a try. He had good advice for ~ of us.* **2** used in apposition, like *all* and *both*: *We ~ took a big risk. Tom, Dick and Harry ~ put forward a different scheme.* **3** used *adverbially* meaning 'apiece': *He gave the boys 50p ~. The oranges are 6p ~.* **4** **~ other,** used as the object of a *v* or *prep*, often replaced by *one another* when the reference is to a number more than two: *We see ~ other* (= E~ of us sees the other) *on the beach every day. They are afraid of ~ other.*

eager /ˈigə(r)/ *adj* **~ (for sth/to do sth),** full of, showing, strong desire: *~ for success; ~ to succeed.* **ˈ~ ˈbeaver,** (colloq) hardworking and (over) enthusiastic person. **~·ly** *adv* **~·ness** *n*

eagle /ˈigl/ *n* **1** large, strong bird of prey of the falcon family with keen sight. ⇨ the illus at prey. **ˈ~-ˈeyed** *adj* keen-sighted. **2** (golf) score that is two below the number of strokes allowed as the average for the hole (except where the number allowed is three). **eag·let** /ˈiglət/ *n* young ~(1).

ear[1] /ɪə(r)/ *n* **1** organ of hearing. ⇨ the illus at head. ***be all ears,*** be listening eagerly. ***fall on deaf ears,*** pass unnoticed. ***feel your ears burning,*** imagine that you are being talked about. ***give one's ears*** (*for* sth *to do* sth), make any sacrifice, pay any price. ***go in at one ear and out (at) the other,*** said of sth that makes no impression. ***have an ear to the ground,*** be alert for what may be happening in secret. ***(have) a word in sb's ear,*** say sth in confidence: *May I have a word in your ear?* **have/win sb's ear(s),** his favourable attention. ***over head and ears*** (in debt, etc), deeply. ***prick up one's ears,*** look expectant. ***set (persons) by the ears,*** set them quarrelling. ***turn a deaf ear (to),*** refuse to help. ***up to one's ears in work,*** overwhelmed by work. ***wet behind the ears,*** naive. **ˈear·ache,** pain in the inner ear. **ˈear·drop,** earring with a hanging ornament. **ˈear·drum,** thin membrane (in the inner ear) which vibrates when sound-waves strike it. **ˈear·ful** /-fl/, as much (usu abusive or unsolicited) talk as one can endure. **ˈear·mark** *n* mark on the ear of a sheep, etc, to mark ownership. □ *vt* put an earmark on; (fig) set aside *for* a special purpose: *earmark a sum of money for research.* **ˈear·piece,** earphone of a telephone receiver. **ˈear·phone,** head-phone. **ˈear·ring,** ring worn in the lobe of the ear as an ornament. **ˈear·shot,** hearing distance: *within (out of) earshot.* **ˈear-trumpet,** trumpet-shaped tube formerly used by partly deaf people. ⇨ *hearing-aid* at hearing. **ˈear·wax,** waxy substance secreted in the ear. **2** sense of hearing. ***have a good ear for music,*** be able to discriminate sound. ***(play sth) by ear,*** (play) without printed music, or without having memorized it. **3** ear-shaped thing, esp the handle of a pitcher. **(-)eared** used in compounds: *ˈlong-ˈeared,* having long ears.

ear[2] /ɪə(r)/ *n* seed-bearing part of a cereal (corn, barley, etc): *corn in the ear,* with ears developed. ⇨ the illus at cereal.

earl /ɜl/ *n* (fem *countess*) title of a British nobleman of high rank. **~·dom** /-dəm/ *n* rank, lands, of an ~: *The queen conferred an ~dom on him.*

early /ˈɜlɪ/ (-ier, -iest) *adj, adv* near to the beginning of a period of time, sooner than usual or than others: *in the ~ part of this century; in ~ spring; an ~ breakfast,* e g 5 a m; *~ peaches,* ripening ~ in the season; *ˈ~-ˈclosing day,* on which shops, etc are closed during the afternoon. *He's an ~ riser,* gets up at an ~ hour. *Please come at your earliest convenience,* as soon as it is convenient for you to do so. *He keeps ~ hours,* gets up, goes to bed, ~. *It's better to be too ~ than too late. It's too ~; the cinema doesn't open until two o'clock. Come as ~ as possible.* ***The ~ bird gets/catches the worm,*** (prov) The person who arrives, etc ~ will (probably) succeed. ***earlier on,*** at an, earlier stage. Cf *later on* at late[2](1). ˈ~-

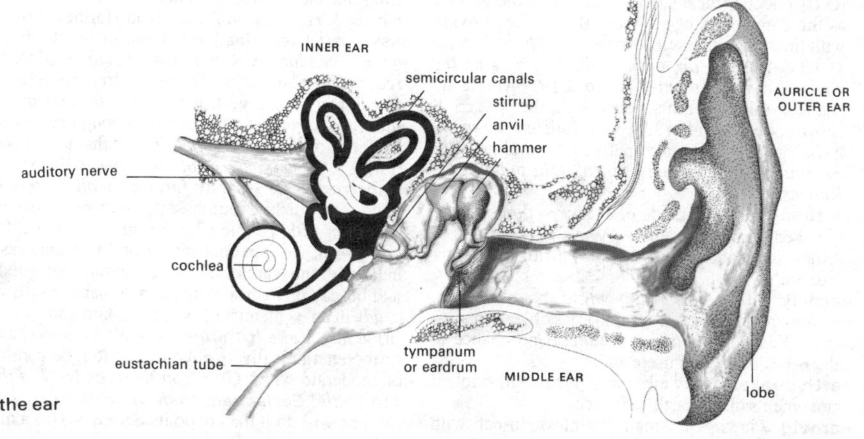

the ear

ˋ**warning** *adj* (of radar) giving early indication of the approach of enemy aircraft, missiles, etc: *an ~-warning system.*

earn /ɜn/ *vt* [VP6A,12B,13B] get in return for work, as a reward for one's qualities or in payment for a loan: *to ~ £2000 a year; to ~ one's living/one's livelihood/one's daily bread. The money ~s 7% interest. His achievements ~ed him respect and admiration. His eccentricities had ~ed for him the nickname 'The Madman'. I had a well-~ed rest.* **~·ings** *n pl* money ~ed: *He has spent all his ~ings.* ˋ**~ings yield,** (comm) ratio between annual profit and capital.

earn·est[1] /ˋɜnɪst/ *adj* serious; determined: *an ~ worker/pupil; an ~ Christian,* one who conscientiously practises beliefs: *a terribly ~ young man,* perhaps over-serious, over-conscientious. □ *n* **in ~,** in a determined manner; serious(ly): *If you work in ~, you will succeed. I'm perfectly in ~,* am not joking. *It is raining in real ~,* heavily, and likely to continue. **~·ly** *adv* in an ~ manner: *We ~ly hope that….* **~·ness** *n*

earn·est[2] /ˋɜnɪst/ *n* **1** (also ˋ**~-money**) part payment made as a pledge that full payment will follow. **2** sth coming in advance as a sign of what is to come after: *As an ~ of my good intentions I will work overtime this week.*

earth /ɜθ/ *n* **1** ⇨ the illus at planet. (*sing, def art*) this world; the planet on which we live: *The moon goes round the ~ and the ~ goes round the sun. Who do you think was the greatest man on ~?* **2** [U] land surface of the world; land contrasted with the sky: *The balloon burst and fell to ~.* ***come down/back to ~,*** stop day dreaming; return to practical realities. ***move heaven and ~*** (*to do sth*), make every possible effort. ***how/why/where/who, etc on ~,*** how/why, etc ever…. (used for emphasis; ⇨ ever). **3** [U] soil: *to fill a pit with ~; to cover the roots of a plant with ~.* ˋ**~-closet,** latrine; substitute for a lavatory in places where there is no supply of water from mains, etc. ˋ**~ nut,** groundnut. ˋ**~·work,** embankment of ~ used in fortifications as a defence. ˋ**~·worm,** common kind of worm that lives in the soil. **4** [C] hole of a fox, badger or other wild animal: *to stop an ~,* block it up so that the animal cannot return to it. ***run/go to ~,*** (of a fox) go into its hole. ***run sth/sb to ~,*** (fig) discover by searching; hunt (a fox) to its burrow. **5** [C,U] (electr) (means of) contact with the ground as the completion of a circuit. **6** [C] (chem) oxide with little taste or smell: *alkaline ~s; fuller's ~.* □ *vt* **1** [VP15B] **~ up,** cover with ~: *to ~ up the roots of a newly-planted shrub.* **2** [VP6A] (electr) connect (an apparatus, etc) with the ~. ⇨ 5 above. **~y** *adj* **1** of or like ~ or soil: *an ~y smell.* **2** (fig) grossly material; unaffected, unrefined: *the ~y and robust men and women in the paintings of Rubens.*

earthen /ˋɜθn/ *adj* made of earth: *~ floors;* made of baked clay: *an ~ jar.* ˋ**~·ware** /-weə(r)/ *n* [U] dishes, etc made of baked clay; (attrib) *an ~ware casserole.*

earth·ly /ˋɜθlɪ/ *adj* **1** of this world, not of heaven: *~ joys/possessions.* **2** (colloq) possible; conceivable: *You haven't an ~ (chance),* no chance at all. ***no ~ use,*** quite useless.

earth·quake /ˋɜθkweɪk/ *n* [C] sudden, violent movements of the earth's surface.

ear·wig /ˋɪəwɪg/ *n* small harmless insect with pincers at the rear end of its abdomen. ⇨ the illus at insect.

ease[1] /iz/ *n* [U] freedom from work, discomfort, trouble, difficulty, anxiety: *a life of ~; ~ of body and mind; to take one's ~,* stop working or worrying; *to do sth with ~,* without difficulty; *sitting at ~.* ***ill at ~,*** anxious or embarrassed. ***stand at ~,*** (as a mil command) with the legs apart and the hands behind the back. Cf *at attention, stand easy.*

ease[2] /iz/ *vt,vi* **1** [VP6A,14] give relief to (the body or mind) from pain, discomfort, anxiety: *~ sb's anxiety; ~ sb of his pain/trouble. Can I ~ you of your burden?* **2** [VP6A,15A,B,2C] make looser, less tight; lessen speed, efforts: *~ a coat under the armpits; ~ a drawer,* e g one that sticks fast or opens with difficulty: *~ (down) the speed of a boat. E~ off a bit, we're going too fast.* **3** [VP2A,C] ***~ (off),*** become less tense or troublesome: *the easing of tension between the two countries. The situation has ~d (off).*

easel /ˋizl/ *n* wooden frame to support a blackboard or a picture (while the artist is working at it).

east /ˋist/ *n* **1** (*sing* with *def art*) point of the horizon where the sun rises. ⇨ the illus at compass. **the ˈFar ˋE~,** China, Japan, etc. **the ˋMiddle E~,** countries from Egypt to Iran. **the ˈNear ˋE~,** Turkey, etc. **the E~, (a)** the Orient. **(b)** the eastern side of the USA ~ of the Allegheny /ˈæləˋgeɪnɪ/ Mountains and north of the Mason-Dixon /ˈmeɪsn ˋdɪksn/ line (the boundary between the states of Pennsylvania and Maryland). **2** (attrib): *an ~ wind,* one blowing from the ~; towards, at, in the direction of the ~: *on the ~ coast.* **the ˈE~ ˋEnd,** the eastern part of London (shipping and commercial areas). □ *adv* towards the ~: *to travel ~; to face ~; to sail due ~; a town that lies ~ of the Rhine.* **~·ward** /ˋistwəd/ *adj* towards the ~: *in an ~ward direction.* **~-ward(s)** *adv*: *to travel ~wards.*

Easter /ˋistə(r)/ *n* anniversary of the Resurrection of Christ, observed on the first Sunday (*~ Day, ~ Sunday*) after a full moon on or after 21 Mar. Used attrib in ˈ~-*week* (beginning on ~ Sunday); *the ~ holidays.* ˋ**~ egg,** egg with a painted or dyed shell, or an egg made of chocolate.

east·er·ly /ˋistəlɪ/ *adj, adv* in an eastern direction of position; (of the wind) coming from the east.

east·ern /ˋistən/ *adj* (attrib) of, from, living in, the east part of the world: *~ religions; the E~ Church,* the Greek Orthodox Church; *the E~ Hemisphere.* **~·most** /-məʊst/ *adj* farthest east.

easy /ˋizɪ/ (-ier, -iest) *adj* **1** not difficult: *an ~ book. The place is ~ to reach. It is an ~ place to reach. The place is ~ of access.* **2** free, from pain, discomfort, anxiety, trouble, etc: *to lead an ~ life; in ~ circumstances,* having enough money to live comfortably; *an ˋ~ chair,* one that is soft and restful; *~ manners, not showing stiffness or embarrassment; (to buy furniture) on ~ terms,* trade term for hire-purchase; *persons who are ~ to get on with,* people who are informal, not stiff. ˈ**~-ˋgoing,** (of persons) placid and tolerant; casual; lazy and careless; lax. **3** (comm) (of goods and money on loan) not much in demand. ⇨ **tight.** □ *adv* in an ~ manner: *E~!* (as a command) Move (it) gently. ***take it/things ~,*** don't work too hard or too energetically. ***go ~ on,*** (colloq) be careful or moderate with: *Go ~ on the brandy—it's the last bottle!* ***Easier said than done,*** It is easier to say one will do it than to do it. ***Stand ~!*** (as a mil command) Stand with more freedom of movement than when *at ease*, ⇨ ease¹. **eas·ily** /ˈizɫɪ/ *adv* **1** with ease. **2** without doubt: *easily the best TV programme.* **3** possibly: *That may easily be the case.*

eat /it/ *vt,vi* (*pt* ate or (very rarely) eat /et *US:* eɪt/, *pp* eaten /ˈitn/) **1** [VP6A,15B,2A,C,4A] take (solid food, also soup) into the mouth and swallow it: *to eat one's dinner; to eat up* (= finish eating) *one's food. Where shall we eat? He was too ill to eat. We should eat* (*in order*) *to live, not live to eat,* not make eating the most important thing in life. ***eat its head off,*** (a horse) cost more to feed than it is worth. ***eat one's heart out,*** suffer in silence; be very sad. ***eat one's words,*** take a statement back, say in a humble way that one was wrong. **2** [VP6A,3A,15B] destroy as if by eating: *Acids eat into metals. He is eaten up with pride. The river had eaten away the banks. The moths have eaten holes in my coat.* **ˈeating-apple** *n* suitable for eating uncooked. **ˈeating-house,** restaurant. **eats** *n pl* (sl) food: *There were plenty of eats, but not enough drinks.* **eat·able** /-əbl/ *adj* fit to be eaten: *The prison food was scarcely eatable.* □ *n* (usu *pl*) food. **~er** *n* **1** one that eats: *He's a big eater,* eats large quantities. **2** apple, pear, etc for dessert, good when eaten uncooked.

eau /əʊ/ *n* **eau de Cologne** /ˌəʊ də kəˈləʊn/ *n* (F) perfume made at Cologne. **eau-de-vie** /ˌəʊ də ˈvi/ *n* (F) brandy.

eaves /ivz/ *n pl* overhanging edges of a roof: *icicles hanging from the ~.* **ˈ~-drop** *vi* (-pp-) listen secretly to private conversation. **ˈ~-drop·per** /-dropə(r)/ *n* person who does this.

ebb /eb/ *vi* [VP2A,C] **1** (of the tide) flow back from the land to the sea. **2** (fig) grow less; become weak or faint: *His fortune's beginning to ebb. Daylight was ebbing away.* □ *n* **1** the flowing out of the tide: *the ebb and flow of the sea/the tide. The tide is on the ebb,* is going out. **2** (fig) low state; decline or decay: *at a low ebb.* **ˌebb-ˈtide** *n* = ebb.

eb·on·ite /ˈebənaɪt/ *n* [U] (comm) hard black insulating material made by vulcanising rubber.

eb·ony /ˈebənɪ/ *n* [U] hard, black wood. □ *adj* made of, black as, ~: *the ~ keys on a piano.*

ebul·lient /ɪˈbʌlɪənt/ *adj* exuberant. **ebul·lience** /-əns/ *n* exuberance; outburst (of feeling).

ec·cen·tric /ɪkˈsentrɪk/ *adj* **1** (of a person, his behaviour) peculiar; not normal. **2** ⇨ the illus at concentric. (of circles) not having the same centre; (of orbits) not circular; (of planets, etc) moving in an ~ orbit. □ *n* **1** ~ person. **2** (mech) device for changing circular motion into backward-and-forward motion.

ec·cen·tric·ity /ˌeksənˈtrɪsətɪ/ *n* **1** [U] quality of being eccentric; strangeness of behaviour, etc: *~ in dress.* **2** [C] (*pl* -ties) instance of this; strange or unusual act or habit: *One of his eccentricities is sleeping under the bed instead of in it.*

ec·clesi·as·tic /ɪˌklizɪˈæstɪk/ *n* clergyman. **ec·clesi·as·ti·cal** /-kl/ *adj* of the Christian Church; of clergymen. **ec·clesi·as·ti·cally** /-klɪ/ *adv*

eche·lon /ˈeʃəlon/ *n* step-like formation of troops, aircraft, ships, etc as shown here: *flying in ~.*

echo¹ /ˈekəʊ/ *n* (*pl* -oes /-əʊz/) **1** [C,U] sound reflected or sent back (e g from a wall of rock): *The speaker was cheered/applauded to the ~,* long and loudly. **ˈ~-sounding,** method of ascertaining distances (e g of the ocean bed or under-

flying in echelon

water objects) by measuring the time taken for waves of sound, etc to be echoed back. Hence, **ˈ~-sounder** *n* **2** person who, statement, etc which, is a copy or repetition of another.

echo² /ˈekəʊ/ *vi,vt* [VP6A,15B,2A,C] **1** (of places) send back an echo: *The valley ~ed as he sang. The hills ~ed back the noise of the shot.* **2** (of sounds) be sent back as an echo: *The shot ~ed through the woods.* **3** be an echo of; repeat the words, etc of another: *They ~ed every word of their leader.*

éclair /eɪˈkleə(r)/ *n* small cylindrical pastry iced on top and filled with cream.

éclat /ˈeɪklɑ *US:* eɪˈklɑ/ *n* brilliant, conspicuous success; applause from everyone: *with great ~.*

ec·lec·tic /ɪˈklektɪk/ *adj* (of persons, methods, etc) choosing, accepting, freely from various sources. **ec·lec·ti·cism** /-tɪsɪzm/ *n*

eclipse /ɪˈklɪps/ *n* [C] **1** total or partial cutting off of the light of the sun (when the moon is between it and the earth), or of the reflected light of the moon (when the earth's shadow falls on it). **2** (fig) loss of brilliance, power, reputation, etc: *After suffering an ~ he is now again famous. An author's reputation is often in ~ for some years after his death.* □ *vt* [VP6A] **1** (of a planet, etc) cause an ~; cut off the light from. **2** (fig) make (sb or sth) appear dull by comparison; outshine: *She was so beautiful that she ~d every other woman at the ball.*

a total eclipse of the sun

eclip·tic /ɪˈklɪptɪk/ *n* the orbit in which the sun seems to move.

ec·logue /ˈeklog *US:* -lɔg/ *n* short poem, esp a pastoral dialogue.

ecol·ogy /iˈkolədʒɪ/ *n* [U] branch of biology that deals with the habits of living things, esp their relation to their environment. **eco·logi·cal** /ˌikəˈlodʒɪkl/ *adj* of ~: *the ecological effects of industry,* e g the pollution of the atmosphere, of rivers, etc. **eco·logi·cally** /-klɪ/ *adv*

econ·omic /ˈikəˋnomɪk/ *adj* **1** of economics (⇨ below): *the government's ~ policy.* **2** designed to give a profit: *an ~ rent,* one that compensates the owner for the cost of the land, building, etc. **3** connected with commerce and the industrial arts: *~ geography,* studied chiefly in connection with industry.

econ·omi·cal /ˈikəˋnomɪkl/ *adj* careful in the spending of money, time, etc and in the use of goods; not wasteful: *to be ~ of time and energy; an ~ fire,* one that does not waste fuel. **~ly** /-klɪ/ *adv*

econ·omics /ˈikəˋnomɪks/ *n (sing v)* [U] science of the production, distribution and consumption of goods; condition of a country as to material prosperity. **econ·om·ist** /iˋkonəmɪst/ *n* **1** expert in ~; person who writes or lectures on ~ or political economy. **2** person who is economical or thrifty.

econ·om·ize /iˋkonəmɑɪz/ *vt, vi* [VP6A,2A,3A] **~ *(on sth),*** be economical; use or spend less than before; cut down expenses: *He ~d by using trams instead of taking taxis. We must ~ on light and fuel.*

econ·omy /iˋkonəmɪ/ *n (pl* **-mies***)* **1** [C,U] (instance of) avoidance of waste of money, strength or anything else of value: *to practise ~. In the long run, it is an ~ to buy good quality goods, even though they cost more. By various little economies, she managed to save enough money for a holiday.* **ˋ~ class,** cheapest class of travel (esp by air). **2** [U] control and management of the money, goods and other resources of a community, society or household: *political ~; domestic ~.* **3** [C] system for the management and use of resources: *the totalitarian economies of Germany and Italy before the Second World War.*

ecru /ˋeɪkru *US:* eɪˋkru/ *n* colour of unbleached linen; pale brown.

ec·stasy /ˋekstəsɪ/ *n (pl* **-sies***)* (feeling of) great joy and spiritual uplift: *in an ~ of delight; to be in/go/be thrown into ecstasies (over sth).* **ec·static** /ɪkˋstætɪk/ *adj* of, in, causing, ~. **ec·stati·cally** /-klɪ/ *adv*

ec·to·plasm /ˋektəplæzm/ *n* [U] substance supposed to be exuded from a spiritualistic medium during a trance.

ecu·meni·cal /ˈikjʊˋmenɪkl/ *adj* **1** of or representing the whole Christian world or universal Church: *an ~ Council,* e g as summoned by the Pope. **2** seeking to restore the unity of the Christian churches: *the ~ movement.*

ec·zema /ˋeksɪmə/ *n* [U] itching skin disease.

eddy /ˋedɪ/ *n (pl* **-dies***)* (of wind, smoke, fog, mist, dust, water) circular or spiral movement: *Eddies of mist rose from the valleys. The car went past in an ~ of dust.* □ *vi* [VP2A,C] move in small circles; move in or like eddies; whirl.

edel·weiss /ˋeɪdlvɑɪs/ *n* Alpine plant with white leaves and small flowers, growing among rocks.

Eden /ˋidn/ *n* (Bible) garden where Adam and Eve lived; place of delight.

edge[1] /edʒ/ *n* **1** sharp, cutting part of a knife, sword or other tool or weapon: *a knife with a sharp ~; to put an ~ on a knife,* sharpen it. ***be on ~,*** be excited or irritable. ***give sb the ~ of one's tongue,*** rebuke him sharply. ***have the ~ on sb,*** (colloq) have an advantage over him. ***set sb's teeth on ~,*** upset his nerves (as when a scraping sound or a sharp, acid taste causes physical revulsion). ***take the ~ off sth,*** dull or soften; reduce, e g one's appetite. **2** (line marking the) outer limit or boundary of a (flat) surface: *a cottage on the ~ of a forest; the ~ of a lake; trim the ~s of a lawn,* cut the grass there. *When you've finished eating, leave your knife and fork across the ~ of your plate. Don't put the glass on the ~ of the table; it may get knocked off. He fell off the ~ of the cliff.* **edgy** /ˋedʒɪ/ *adj* having one's nerves on ~.

edge[2] /edʒ/ *vt, vi* **1** [VP6A,14] supply with a border: *to ~ a handkerchief with lace/a garden path with plants;* form a border to: *a road ~d with grass.* **2** [VP6A] sharpen (a tool, etc). **3** [VP15A,B,2C] (cause to) move slowly forward or along: *~ oneself/~ one's way through a crowd; ~ along a narrow ledge of rock; ~ a piano through a door; ~ one's chair nearer to the fireplace.*

edge·ways, edge·wise /ˋedʒweɪz, -wɑɪz/ *adv* with the edge outwards or forwards. ***not get a word in ~,*** be unable to say anything when a very talkative person is speaking.

edg·ing /ˋedʒɪŋ/ *n* narrow border: *an ~ of lace on a dress.* **ˋ~-shears,** tool for trimming grass on the edges of a lawn.

ed·ible /ˋedəbl/ *adj* fit to be eaten. □ *n* (usu *pl*) things fit to be eaten. **edi·bil·ity** /ˈedəˋbɪlətɪ/ *n*

edict /ˋidɪkt/ *n* order or proclamation issued by authority; decree.

edi·fi·ca·tion /ˈedɪfɪˋkeɪʃn/ *n* [U] mental or moral improvement.

edi·fice /ˋedɪfɪs/ *n* [C] building (esp a large or imposing one); (fig) sth built up in the mind: *The whole ~ of his hopes was destroyed.*

edify /ˋedɪfɑɪ/ *vt (pt,pp* **-fied***)* [VP6A] improve in morals or mind: *~ing books.*

edit /ˋedɪt/ *vt* [VP6A] **1** prepare (another person's writing) for publication (esp in a newspaper or other periodical): *~ a newspaper; ~ a Shakespeare play for use in schools.* **2** do the work of planning and directing the publication of a newspaper, magazine, book, encyclopedia, etc. **3** prepare a cinema film, tape recording by putting together parts in a suitable sequence. **4** arrange data for computer processing.

edi·tion /ɪˋdɪʃn/ *n* **1** form in which a book is published: *a cheap ~; a ˋpocket ~.* **2** total number of copies (of a book, newspaper, etc) issued from the same types: *the first ~; a revised ~.* ⇨ **impression(3).**

edi·tor /ˋedɪtə(r)/ *n* person who edits (esp a newspaper, periodical, radio news programme) or who is in charge of part of a newspaper: *the ˋsports/fiˋnancial ~.*

edi·tor·ial /ˈedɪˋtɔrɪəl/ *adj* of an editor: *the ~ office; ~ work.* □ *n* [C] special article or discussion of news in a newspaper, etc usu written by the editor.

edu·cate /ˋedʒʊkeɪt/ *vt* [VP6A,15A,16A] give intellectual and moral training to; train: *The poor boy had to ~ himself in the evening after finishing his work. I was ~d for the law. You should ~ your children to behave well.* **edu·ca·tor** /-tə(r)/ *n* person who ~s.

edu·ca·tion /ˈedʒʊˋkeɪʃn/ *n* [U] **1** systematic training and instruction (esp of the young, in school, college, etc): *No country can afford to neglect ~. Is ~ free and compulsory in your country?* **2** knowledge and abilities, development of character and mental powers, resulting from such training. **~al** /-ʃnl/ *adj* of, connected with, ~: *~al work; an ~al magazine.* **~·ist** /-ʃn̩ɪst/, **~·al·ist** /-ʃnl̩ɪst/

n expert in ~.

educe /i`djus *US:* i`dus/ *vt* [VP6A] (formal) bring out, develop (from what is latent or potential).

eel /il/ *n* long, snake-like fish. ⇨ the illus at sea. ***as slippery as an eel,*** very difficult to hold.

e'en /in/ *adv* (poet) even.

e'er /eə(r)/ *adv* (poet) ever.

eerie, eery /`ɪərɪ/ *adj* (-ier, -iest) causing a feeling of mystery and fear: *an ~ shriek.* **eer·ily** /`ɪərɪlɪ/ *adv* **eeri·ness** *n*

eff /ef/ *vi* (euphem for ⚠ *fuck*): *I told him to eff off. What an effing nuisance!*

ef·face /ɪ`feɪs/ *vt* [VP6A] **1** rub or wipe out; make indistinct; (fig) obliterate: *~ an inscription; ~ unpleasant memories of the past.* **2** ***~ oneself,*** keep in the background in order to escape being noticed; make oneself appear to be unimportant. **~·ment** *n*

ef·fect /ɪ`fekt/ *n* **1** [C,U] ([U] for degree or extent) result; outcome: *the ~ of heat upon metals. The children were suffering from the ~s of the hot weather. Did the medicine have any ~/a good ~? Punishment had very little ~ on him,* did not reform him, frighten him, etc. *Our arguments had no ~ on them,* did not influence them. ***of no ~,*** useless, not doing what was intended or hoped for. ***in ~,*** **(a)** in fact, really; for practical purposes. **(b)** (of a rule, law, etc) in operation: *The rule is still in ~.* ***bring/carry/put sth into ~, come into ~,*** reach the stage of being operative: *The new tax regulations came into ~ last week;* cause it to operate: *The plans will soon be carried into ~.* ***give ~ to,*** cause to become active or have a result. ***take ~,*** **(a)** produce the result intended or required. **(b)** come into force; operate; become active. **2** [C] impression produced on the mind of a spectator, hearer, reader, etc: *wonderful `cloud ~s,* impressions produced by light on clouds, e g at sunset; *`sound ~s,* (in broadcasting, etc) sounds characteristic of a scene, or incidental to an event, e g the noise of a train. *Everything he says and does is calculated for ~,* designed to impress spectators or hearers. **3** [U] meaning: *That is what he said, or words to that ~,* words with the same general meaning. *I have received a cable to the ~ that...,* with the information that.... ***to the same ~,*** giving the same information: *I sent a telegram and wrote a letter to the same ~.* **4** (*pl*) goods; property: *The hotel-keeper seized her personal ~s because she could not pay her bill.* ***no ~s,*** written (often N/E) by bankers on a cheque which is dishonoured. □ *vt* [VP6A] bring about; accomplish: *~ one's purpose; ~ a cure; ~* (take out) *an insurance policy.*

ef·fec·tive /ɪ`fektɪv/ *adj* **1** having an effect; able to bring about the result intended: *~ measures to cure unemployment.* **2** making a striking impression: *an ~ scheme of decoration.* **3** actual or existing: *the ~ membership of the society;* (of a military force, soldiers, sailors, etc) fit for service: *the ~ strength of the army.* □ *n* (*pl* mil) ~ part of an army. **~·ly** *adv* **~·ness** *n*

ef·fec·tual /ɪ`fektʃʊəl/ *adj* (not used of persons) bringing about the result required; answering its purpose: *an ~ remedy/punishment; to take ~ steps.* **~·ly** /-lɪ/ *adv* **~·ness** *n*

ef·fec·tu·ate /ɪ`fektʃʊeɪt/ *vt* [VP6A] bring about; accomplish.

ef·femi·nate /ɪ`femɪnət/ *adj* womanish; unmanly. **ef·femi·nacy** /ɪ`femɪnəsɪ/ *n* [U] being ~; unmanly weakness.

ef·fendi /e`fendɪ/ *n* sir (as a title of respect in Turkey).

ef·fer·vesce /'efə`ves/ *vi* [VP2A] give off bubbles of gas; (of gas) issue in bubbles; (fig, of persons) be gay and excited. **ef·fer·vescence** /'efə`vesns/ *n* [U] **ef·fer·vescent** /-snt/ *adj*

ef·fete /e`fit/ *adj* exhausted; weak and worn out: *~ civilizations/empires.* **~·ness** *n*

ef·fi·ca·cious /'efɪ`keɪʃəs/ *adj* (not used of persons) producing the desired result: *an ~ cure for a disease.* **~·ly** *adv* **ef·fi·cacy** /`efɪkəsɪ/ *n* [U] state or quality of being ~.

ef·fi·cient /ɪ`fɪʃnt/ *adj* **1** (of persons) capable; able to perform duties well: *an ~ secretary/staff of teachers.* **2** producing a desired or satisfactory result: *~ methods of teaching.* **~·ly** *adv* **ef·fi·ciency** /ɪ`fɪʃnsɪ/ *n* [U] state or quality of being ~.

ef·figy /`efɪdʒɪ/ *n* (*pl* -gies) [C] representation of a person (in wood, stone, etc): *hang/burn a person in ~,* make an ~ and hang/burn it (as a sign of hatred, etc).

ef·flor·escence /'eflə`resns/ *n* [U] flowering; bursting out into flower. **ef·flor·escent** /-snt/ *adj*

ef·flu·ent /`eflʊənt/ *n* **1** stream flowing from a larger stream or from a lake. **2** discharge of waste liquid matter, sewage, etc, e g from a factory.

ef·flux /`eflʌks/ *n* [U] flowing out of liquid, gas, etc; [C] that which flows out.

ef·fort /`efət/ *n* **1** [U] trying hard; use of strength and energy (*to do* sth); [C] vigorous attempt: *He lifted the big rock without ~. It doesn't need much ~. Please make an ~ to arrive early. Does it require a great ~ of will to give up smoking? I will make every ~* (= do all I can) *to help you. His ~s at clearing up the mystery failed.* **2** [C] result of ~; sth done with ~: *That's a pretty good ~,* i e you have done well. **~·less** *adj* making no ~; without ~; easy: *done with ~less skill.*

ef·front·ery /ɪ`frʌntərɪ/ *n* [U] shameless boldness; impudence; [C] (*pl* -ries) instance of this: *How can you have the ~ to ask for another loan?*

ef·ful·gent /ɪ`fʌldʒənt/ *adj* radiant; resplendent. **ef·ful·gence** /-dʒəns/ *n* radiance.

ef·fu·sion /ɪ`fjuʒn/ *n* **1** [U] sending or pouring out (of liquid, e g blood); [C] quantity poured out. **2** [C] (esp unrestrained) outpouring of thought or feeling: *poetical ~s; ~s in love letters.*

ef·fu·sive /ɪ`fjusɪv/ *adj* (of the feelings, signs of pleasure, gratitude, etc) pouring out too freely: *~ thanks; ~ in one's gratitude.* **~·ly** *adv* **~·ness** *n*

eft /eft/ *n* newt.

egali·tar·ian /ɪ'gælɪ`teərɪən/ *n, adj* (person) favouring the doctrine of equal rights, benefits and opportunities for all citizens. Cf élitist. **~·ism** /-ɪzm/ *n*

egg[1] /eg/ *n* ⇨ the illus at fowl. Female reproducing cell; ovum, (esp an embryo enclosed in a shell, e g of a hen, used as food): *Birds, reptiles and insects come from eggs. Chickens are hatched from eggs. The hen laid an egg. Will you have your eggs boiled or fried?* [U] *You've got some egg* (i e a bit of a cooked egg) *on your chin.* ***a bad egg,*** (colloq) a worthless or dishonest person. ***as sure as eggs is eggs,*** (colloq) undoubtedly. ***in the egg,*** at an early stage; undeveloped. ***put all one's eggs in one basket,*** risk everything one has in a single venture, e g by investing all one's money in one business. ***teach one's grandmother to suck eggs,*** give advice to sb who has much more experience than oneself. **ˋegg-cup,** small cup for holding a boiled egg. **ˋegg-head** *n* (sl) intellectual person; theorist. **ˋegg·plant,** plant with large, purple (rather egg-shaped) fruit (aubergine), used as a vegetable. ⇨ the illus at vegetable. **ˋegg-shell,** shell of an egg: *egg-shell china*, very thin kind; *egg-shell paint*, kind that gives a finish that is neither glossy nor matt. **ˋegg-whisk,** utensil for beating eggs.

egg² /eg/ *vt* [VP15B] ***egg sb on,*** urge him (*to do* sth).

egis ⇨ aegis.

eg·lan·tine /ˋegləntaɪn/ *n* [U] kind of rose; sweet-briar.

ego /ˋegəʊ *US:* ˋigəʊ/ *n* (psych) individual's perception or experience of himself; individual's capacity to think, feel and act.

ego·cen·tric /ˈegəʊˋsentrɪk *US:* ˈig-/ *adj* self-centred; egoistic.

ego·ism /ˋegəʊɪzm *US:* ˋig-/ *n* [U] **1** (phil) theory that our actions are always caused by the desire to benefit ourselves. **2** systematic selfishness; state of mind in which one is always thinking of oneself. ⇨ altruism. **ego·ist** /-ɪst/ *n* believer in ~. **ego·istic** /ˈegəʊˋɪstɪk *US:* ˈig-/, **ego·isti·cal** /-kl/ *adj* of ~; of an egoist.

ego·tism /ˋegətɪzm *US:* ˋig-/ *n* [U] practice of talking too often or too much about oneself; self-conceit; selfishness. **ego·tist** /-tɪst/ *n* person who practises ~; selfish person. **ego·tis·tic** /ˈegəʊˋɪstɪk *US:* ˈig-/ *adj* of ~; of or like an egotist. **ego·tis·ti·cally** /-klɪ/ *adv*

egre·gi·ous /ɪˋgridʒɪəs/ *adj* outstanding, exceptional (used of sb or sth bad): *~ folly; an ~ blunder/idiot.*

egress /ˋigres/ *n* [U] (right of) going out; [C] way out; exit.

egret /ˋigret/ *n* kind of heron with beautiful long feathers in the tail and on the back; bunch of these feathers as an ornament.

Egyp·tian /ɪˋdʒɪpʃn/ *adj, n* (native) of Egypt.

eh /eɪ/ *int* used to express surprise or doubt, or to invite agreement.

eider·down /ˋaɪdədaʊn/ *n* (bed-covering filled with) soft breast feathers of large, wild duck (called ˋ*eider*).

eight /eɪt/ *adj, n* **1** the number 8. ⇨ App 4. ***have one over the ~,*** drink too much. **2** crew of ~ in a rowing-boat. ⇨ bow³(2), stroke¹(3). **eighth** /eɪtθ/ *adj, n* **~·pence** /ˋeɪtpəns *US:* -pens/ *n* **~-penny** /ˋeɪtpənɪ *US:* -penɪ/ *adj* **~·een** /ˈeɪˋtin/ *adj, n* 18. **~·eenth** /-ˋtinθ/ *adj, n* **~y** /ˋeɪtɪ/ *adj, n* 80: *during the eighties*, during the years '80 to '89 of the century. **~·ieth** /ˋeɪtɪəθ/ *adj, n*

a rowing eight

eight·some /ˋeɪtsəm/ *n* lively Scottish dance (a *reel*) for eight dancers.

eis·tedd·fod /ˈaɪˋsteðvod/ *n* (in Wales) annual gathering of poets and musicians for competitions.

either /ˋaɪðə(r) *US:* ˋiðər/ *adj, pron* **1** (Cf the use of *any*, or *any one of*, when the number is greater than two) one or the other (of): *Take ~ half; they're exactly the same. E~ of them/E~ one will be satisfactory. You must not favour ~ side in the dispute. In ~ event/~ of these events you will benefit.* **2** (Cf the use of *both* and *each*, which are more usu) one and the other (of two): *There was an armchair at ~ end of the long table.* □ *adv, conj* **1** used in statements after *not;* (Cf the use of *neither*): *I don't like the red one, and I don't like the pink one, ~,* i e I dislike both of them. *A: 'I haven't been to Paris yet.' B: 'I haven't been there yet, ~.'* (= Neither have I). **2** (used after a negative phrase) moreover; furthermore: *There was a time, and not so long ago ~, when she could walk twenty miles a day.* **3** (used to introduce the first of two or more alternatives, followed by *or*): *He must be ~ mad or drunk. Please ~ come in or go out: don't stand there in the doorway.*

ejacu·late /ɪˋdʒækjʊleɪt/ *vt* [VP6A] **1** say suddenly and briefly. **2** eject (fluid, e g semen) from the body. **ejacu·la·tion** /ɪˈdʒækjʊˋleɪʃn/ *n* **1** [C] exclamation; sth said suddenly. **2** discharge or ejection of fluid (e g semen) (from the body).

eject /ɪˋdʒekt/ *vt, vi* [VP6A] ***~ from,*** **1** compel (sb) to leave (a place); expel: *They were ~ed because they had not paid their rent for a year.* **2** send out (liquid, etc): *lava ~ed from a volcano.* **3** [VP2A] make an emergency exit, with a parachute, from an aircraft. **ejec·tion** /ɪˋdʒekʃn/ *n* **ejec·tor** /-tə(r)/ *n* sth that ~s. **eˋjector-seat,** one in an aircraft for ~ing the pilot so that he may descend by parachute.

eke¹ /ik/ *vt* [VP15B] ***~ sth out,*** make (small supplies of sth) enough for one's needs by adding sth; make (a living) by doing this: *eke out one's coal by saving the cinders for further use; eke out one's livelihood.*

elab·or·ate /ɪˋlæbrət/ *adj* worked out with much care and in great detail; carefully prepared and finished: *~ plans; an ~ design; an ~ dinner,* e g with many courses. □ *vt* /ɪˋlæbəreɪt/ [VP6A] work out, describe, in detail: *Please ~ your proposals a little.* **~ly** *adv* **~ness** *n* **elab·or·ation** /ɪˈlæbəˋreɪʃn/ *n* [U] elaborating or being ~d; [C] that which is added; detail that ~s.

élan /eɪˋlɔ̃/ *n* (F) vivacity; impetuosity; enthusiasm.

eland /ˋilənd/ *n* kind of S African antelope.

elapse /ɪˋlæps/ *vi* [VP2A] (of time) pass.

elas·tic /ɪˋlæstɪk/ *adj* **1** having the tendency to go back to the normal or previous size or shape after being pulled or pressed: *~ bands. Rubber is ~. Sponges are ~.* **2** (fig) not firm, fixed or unalterable; able to be adapted: *~ rules; an ~ temperament,* e g of a person who soon becomes cheerful again after being sad. □ *n* [U] cord or material made ~ by weaving rubber into it: *a piece of ~;* (attrib) *~ braces,* made of this material. **~·ity** /ˈelæˋstɪsətɪ *US:* ɪˈlæ-/ *n* [U] the quality of being ~: *elasticity of demand,* (comm) change in demand because of price changes.

elate /ɪˋleɪt/ *vt* [VP6A] stimulate; make high-spirited: (chiefly in passive) *He was ~d at the news/by his success.* **ela·tion** /ɪˋleɪʃn/ *n* high spirits: *filled with elation.*

el·bow /ˋelbəʊ/ *n* **1** ⇨ the illus at arm. (outer part of the) joint between the two parts of the arm; corresponding part of a sleeve (in a jacket, etc). ***at one's ~,*** close to; near by. ***out at ~s,*** **(a)** (of a garment) worn-out. **(b)** (of a person) in worn-out clothes. **'~ grease** *n* [U] vigorous polishing; hard work. **'~ room** *n* [U] room to move freely. **2** ~-shaped bend, corner or joint (e g in a pipe or chimney). □ *vt* [VP6A,15B,14] push or force (one's way *through, forward,* etc): *to ~* (also *shoulder*) *one's way through a crowd.*

el·der[1] /ˈeldə(r)/ *adj* **1** (of members of a family, esp closely related members, or of two indicated members) older; senior: *My ~ brother is in India. The ~ sister is called Mary.* Note that *elder* is used attrib. Cf *older.* **2** (before or after a person's name to distinguish that person from another of the same name): *Pliny the ~; the ~ Pitt.* **3 ˌ~ ˈstatesman** /-mən/ (*pl* -men), one (usu retired from office) whose unofficial advice is sought and valued because of his long experience. □ *n* **1** (*pl*) persons of greater age: *Should we always follow the advice of our ~s and betters?* **2** official in some Christian churches, member of a governing body (session) in Presbyterian churches. **3** older of two persons: *He is my ~ by several years.*

el·der[2] /ˈeldə(r)/ *n* (kinds of) bush or small tree with clusters of white flowers and red or black berries. **ˌ~·berry ˈwine,** wine made from these berries.

el·der·ly /ˈeldəlɪ/ *adj* getting old; rather old.

el·dest /ˈeldɪst/ *adj* first-born or oldest surviving (member of a family): *my ~ son/brother.*

El Dorado /ˌel dəˈrɑdəʊ/ *n* (*pl* -dos /-dəʊz/) fictitious country or city rich in precious metals.

elect[1] /ɪˈlekt/ *adj* **1** (after the *n*) chosen, selected: *the bishop ~,* not yet in office. **2** *the ~,* those persons specially chosen, or considered to be the best.

elect[2] /ɪˈlekt/ *vt* **1** [VP6A,25,23,14] choose (sb) by vote: *to ~ a president; to ~ Smith (to be) chairman; to ~ Green to the Academy.* **2** [VP7] choose; decide: *He had ~ed to become a lawyer.*

elec·tion /ɪˈlekʃn/ *n* [U] choosing or selection (of candidates for an office, etc) by vote; [C] instance of this: (attrib) *~ results.* **ˌgeneral ˈ~,** of representatives, members of the House of Commons, for the whole country. **ˈby-~,** of one member, to fill a vacancy. **~·eer·ing** /ɪˌlekʃnˈɪərɪŋ/ *n* [U] working in ~s, e g by canvassing, making speeches.

elec·tive /ɪˈlektɪv/ *adj* **1** having the power to elect: *an ~ assembly.* **2** chosen or filled by election: *an ~ office.* **3** (US) not compulsory; that may be chosen: *~ subjects in college.* ⇨ *optional* at **option.**

elec·tor /ɪˈlektə(r)/ *n* person having the right to elect (esp by voting at a parliamentary election). **~al** /ɪˈlektr̩l/ *adj* of an election; of ~s: *the ~al register,* the list of ~s. *The E~al college in the USA elects the President.* **~·ate** /ɪˈlektr̩ət/ *n* whole body of qualified ~s.

elec·tric /ɪˈlektrɪk/ *adj* of, worked by, charged with, capable of developing, electricity: *an ~ current/torch/iron/shock; ~ light; ~ flex/cord; the ~ chair,* used for electrocuting criminals; *~ blue,* steely blue; *an ~ guitar,* one that has amplifiers for the sound; *an ~ eye,* a photoelectric cell.

elec·tri·cal /ɪˈlektrɪkl/ *adj* **1** relating to electricity: *~ engineering.* **2** (fig) (e g of news) causing strong and sudden emotion. **~ly** /-klɪ/ *adv*

elec·tri·cian /ɪˌlekˈtrɪʃn/ *n* expert in setting up, repairing and operating electrical apparatus.

elec·tric·ity /ɪˌlekˈtrɪsətɪ/ *n* [U] **1** all the phenomena associated with electrons (negative charge) and protons (positive charge); the study of these phenomena. **2** supply of electric current: *When did ~ come to the village?*

elec·trify /ɪˈlektrɪfɑɪ/ *vt* (*pt,pp* -fied) [VP6A] **1** charge (sth) with electricity. **2** equip (a railway, etc) for the use of electric power. **3** (fig) excite, shock, as if by electricity: *to ~ an audience by an unexpected announcement.* **elec·tri·fi·ca·tion** /ɪˌlektrɪfɪˈkeɪʃn/ *n* ~ing, e g the conversion of a steam railway to an electric railway.

elec·tro- /ɪˈlektrəʊ/ *pref* in compounds: **ˌ~-ˈcardiogram** /-ˈkɑdɪəʊgræm/ curve traced by an ~ cardiograph, used in the diagnosis of heart disease. **ˌ~-ˈcardiograph** /-ˈkɑdɪəʊgrɑf *US:* -græf/ apparatus which detects and records electric activity in the muscles of the heart. **ˌ~-ˈchemistry,** electricity as applied to chemistry. **ˌ~-ˈmagnet,** piece of soft iron that becomes magnetic when an electric current is passed through wire coiled round it. **ˈ~-plate** *vt* coat with a thin layer of metal (e g silver) by electrolysis. □ *n* [U] articles plated with silver in this way.

elec·tro·cute /ɪˈlektrəkjut/ *vt* [VP6A] kill accidentally or put to death by means of an electric current. **elec·tro·cu·tion** /ɪˌlektrəˈkjuʃn/ *n*

elec·trode /ɪˈlektrəʊd/ *n* solid conductor by which an electric current enters or leaves a vacuum tube, etc. ⇨ **anode, cathode.**

elec·troly·sis /ɪˌlekˈtrɒləsɪs/ *n* [U] separation of a substance into its chemical parts by electric current.

elec·tron /ɪˈlektrɒn/ *n* [C] (phys) subatomic particle of matter having a negative electric charge. **~ic** /ɪˌlekˈtrɒnɪk/ *adj* of ~s; operated by, based on, ~s: *an ~ic microscope,* using ~s instead of visible light; *~ic music,* produced by manipulating natural or artificial sounds with tape recorders, etc. **ˌ~ic data ˈprocessing,** (abbr EDP) use of ~ic computers to derive information or to achieve a required order of data. **~·ics** *n* (with *sing v*) the science and technology of ~ic phenomena, devices and systems, as in radio, TV, tape recorders, computers, etc.

elee·mosy·nary /ˌelɪiˈmɒsɪnərɪ *US:* -nerɪ/ *adj* of, dependent upon, alms; charitable.

el·egant /ˈelɪgənt/ *adj* showing, having, good taste; beautiful; graceful; done with care, skill and taste: *an ~ young man; ~ manners; leading a life of ~ ease.* **~·ly** *adv* **el·egance** /-əns/ *n* [U].

el·egiac /ˌelɪˈdʒɑɪək/ *adj* **1** (of metre) suited to elegies: *~ couplets.* **2** mournful. □ *n pl ~ verses.*

el·egy /ˈelədʒɪ/ *n* (*pl* -gies) [C] poem or song of sorrow, esp for the dead; poem in elegiac metre.

el·ement /ˈeləmənt/ *n* **1** (science) substance which has not so far been split up into a simpler form by ordinary chemical methods: *Water is a compound containing the ~s hydrogen and oxygen.* **2** (according to the ancient philosophers): *the four ~s,* earth, air, fire and water (out of which the material universe was thought to be composed). ***in/out of one's ~,*** in/not in suitable or satisfying surroundings: *He's in his ~ when taking part in a political debate,* is doing sth that pleases and satisfies him. *I'm out of my ~ when people start talking about economics.* **3** (*pl*) **the ~s,** the forces of nature, the weather, etc: *exposed to the fury of the ~s,* to the winds, storms, etc. **4** (*pl*) beginnings or outlines of a subject of study; parts that must be learnt first: *the* ~*s of geometry.* **5** necessary or characteristic feature: *Justice is an important* ~ *in good government.* **6** suggestion, indication, trace: *There's an* ~ *of truth in his account of what happened.* ⇨ atom(2). **7** resistance wire in an electrical appliance (e g a heater). **8 the E~s,** the bread and wine of the Eucharist. **el·emen·tal** /ˈeləˋmentl/ *adj* of the four ~s(2); of the ~s(3): *the* ~*al fury of the storm.*

ele·men·tary /ˈeləˋmentrɪ *US:* -terɪ/ *adj* of or in the beginning stage(s); not developed; simple: *an* ~ (former type of State) *school;* ~ *arithmetic.* **ele·men·tar·ily** /ˈeləˋmentrɪlɪ/ *adv*

el·eph·ant /ˋeləfnt/ *n* largest four-footed animal now living, with curved ivory tusks and a long trunk (proboscis). ⇨ the illus at large. **ˈwhite ˋ~,** costly or troublesome possession useless to its owner. **el·ephan·tine** /ˈeləˋfæntɑɪn/ *adj* of or like ~s; heavy; clumsy: *an* ~*ine task;* ~*ine humour; an* ~*ine memory,* extremely reliable one.

el·ev·ate /ˋeləveɪt/ *vt* [VP6A,14] lift up; raise; (fig) make (the mind, morals) higher and better: ~ *the voice,* speak louder; ~ *a man to the peerage,* make him a peer; *an elevating book/sermon; an* ~*d railway/railroad,* one built on piers (usu in a town) to run overhead.

el·ev·ation /ˈeləˋveɪʃn/ *n* **1** [U] elevating or being elevated: ~ *to the peerage;* [C] instance of this. **2** [U] grandeur or dignity: ~ *of thought/style/language.* **3** [C] height (esp above sea-level); hill or high place: *an* ~ *of 2000 metres.* **4** [C] angle (e g of a gun) with the horizon. **5** [C] plan (drawn to scale) of one side of a building. ⇨ plan. ⇨ the illus at perspective.

el·ev·ator /ˋeləveɪtə(r)/ *n* **1** machine like a continuous belt with buckets at intervals, used for raising grain, etc. **2** store-house for grain. **3** thing that elevates, e g part of an aircraft that is used to gain or lose altitude. **4** (US) = lift *n*(2).

eleven /ɪˋlevn/ *adj, n* ⇨ App 4. a team of eleven players for football, hockey or cricket. **elev·enth** /ɪˋlevnθ/ *adj, n* **at the** ~**th hour,** at the latest possible time. **elev·enses** /ɪˋlevnzɪz/ *n pl* (GB) snack and drink taken during the morning.

elf /elf/ *n* (*pl* elves /elvz/) small fairy; mischievous little creature. **elfin** /ˋelfɪn/ *adj* of elves: *elfin dances/laughter.* **elf·ish** /ˋelfɪʃ/ *adj* mischievous.

elicit /ɪˋlɪsɪt/ *vt* [VP6A] draw out; cause to come out: *to* ~ *the truth/a reply.* **elici·ta·tion** /ɪˈlɪsɪˋteɪʃn/ *n*

elide /ɪˋlɑɪd/ *vt* [VP6A] omit (a vowel, syllable) in pronunciation. ⇨ elision.

eli·gible /ˋelɪdʒəbl/ *adj* ~ ***(for),*** fit, suitable, to be chosen; having the right qualifications: ~ *for promotion/a position/a pension/membership in a society; an* ~ *young man,* e g one who would be a satisfactory choice as a husband. **el·igi·bil·ity** /ˈelɪdʒəˋbɪlətɪ/ *n* [U] the state of being ~.

elim·in·ate /ɪˋlɪmɪneɪt/ *vt* [VP6A,14] ~ ***(from),*** remove; take or put away, get rid of (because unnecessary or unwanted): ~ *slang words from an essay;* ~ *a possibility,* set it aside and pay no consideration to it; ~ *waste products from the body,* excrete them. **elim·in·ation** /ɪˈlɪmɪˋneɪʃn/ *n*

eli·sion /ɪˋlɪʒn/ *n* (from elide) [U] leaving out or being left out; [C] instance of this; eliding of a vowel or syllable in speech.

élite /eɪˋlit/ *n* group in society considered to be superior because of the power, privileges, etc of its members: *the diplomatic* ~. ⇨ egalitarian. **élitism** /-ɪzm/ *n* belief that the education system, etc should aim at developing ~s. **élitist** /-ɪst/ *n*

elixir /ɪˋlɪksə(r)/ *n* [C] **1** preparation by which medieval scientists hoped to change metals into gold or (~ *of life*) to prolong life indefinitely. **2** remedy that cures all ills.

Eliza·bethan /ɪˈlɪzəˋbiθn/ *adj* of the time of Queen Elizabeth I of England: *the* ˋ~ *age;* ~ *drama.* □ *n* person who lived during her reign, e g Shakespeare.

elk /elk/ *n* one of the largest kinds of living deer, found in the Rocky Mountains, N America (where it is called a 'moose').

ell /el/ *n* old measure of length, 45 inches or about 112cm.

el·lipse /ɪˋlɪps/ *n* regular oval. **el·lip·tic** /ɪˋlɪptɪk/, **el·lip·ti·cal** /-kl/ *adj* shaped like an ~.

el·lip·sis /ɪˋlɪpsɪs/ *n* (*pl* -ses /-siz/) [U] omission from a sentence of words needed to complete the construction or meaning; [C] instance of this. **el·lip·ti·cal** /ɪˋlɪptɪkl/ *adj* containing ~: *an elliptical construction.*

elm /elm/ *n* (varieties of) common deciduous tree that grows to a great size and height; [U] its hard, heavy wood. ⇨ the illus at tree.

elo·cu·tion /ˈeləˋkjuʃn/ *n* [U] art or style of speaking well, esp in public. **~·ary** /-ʃṇərɪ *US:* -ʃṇerɪ/ *adj* of ~. **~·ist** /-ʃṇɪst/ *n* expert in ~; person who recites, e g poetry, usu memorized.

elon·gate /ˋiloŋgeɪt *US:* ɪˋlɔŋ-/ *vt, vi* [VP6A,2A] make or become long(er) spatially. **elon·ga·tion** /ˈiloŋˋgeɪʃn *US:* -lɔŋ-/ *n* [U] making longer; [C] the part (of a line, etc) produced this way.

elope /ɪˋləʊp/ *vi* [VP2A,C,3A] ~ ***(with),*** (of a woman) run away from home or a husband (with a lover). **~·ment** *n*

elo·quence /ˋeləkwəns/ *n* [U] skilful use of language to persuade or to appeal to the feelings; fluent speaking. **elo·quent** /-ənt/ *adj* having or showing ~. **elo·quent·ly** *adv*

else /els/ *adv* **1** (with *indef* or *interr pron* or *advv*) besides; in addition: *Did you see anybody* ~, any other person(s)? *Have you anything* ~ *to do? Ask somebody* ~ *to help you. That must be somebody* ~*'s* (= some other person's) *hat; it isn't mine. Nothing* ~ (= Nothing more), *thank you. We went nowhere* ~, to no other place. *How* ~ (= In what other way) *would you do it? Little* ~ (= Not much more) *remains to be done.* **2** otherwise; if not: *Run* (*or*) ~ *you'll be late. He must be joking, or* ~ *he's mad.*

else·where /ˈelsˋweə(r) *US:* -ˋhweər/ *adv* somewhere else; in, at or to some other place.

elu·ci·date /ɪˋlusɪdeɪt/ *vt* [VP6A] make clear; explain; throw light on (a problem, difficulty). **elu·ci·da·tion** /ɪˈlusɪˋdeɪʃn/ *n*

elude /ɪˋlud/ *vt* [VP6A] escape capture by (esp by means of a trick); avoid: ~ *one's enemies;* ~ *observation.*

elu·sive /ɪˋlusɪv/ *adj* tending to elude or escape: *an* ~ *criminal;* tending to escape from the memory; not easy to recall: *an* ~ *word.*

el·ver /ˋelvə(r)/ *n* young eel.

elves /elvz/ *pl* of elf.

elv·ish /ˋelvɪʃ/ *adj* = elfish.

Ely·sium /ɪˋlɪzɪəm/ *n* (Gk myth) home of the blessed after death; place or state of perfect happiness. **Ely·sian** /ɪˋlɪzɪən/ *adj* of ~;

heavenly; blissful.

'em /əm/ *pron* (colloq) = them.

em·aci·ate /ɪˋmeɪʃɪeɪt/ *vt* [VP6A] make lean (usu passive): *~d by long illness.* **emaci·ation** /ɪ'meɪʃɪˋeɪʃn/ *n* [U].

ema·nate /ˋemәneɪt/ *vi* [VP3A] *~ **from,*** come, flow, proceed from. **ema·na·tion** /'emәˋneɪʃn/ *n* [U] *emanating;* [C] sth that ~s.

eman·ci·pate /ɪˋmænsɪpeɪt/ *vt* [VP6A,14] set free (esp *from* legal, political or moral restraint): *~ slaves; an ~d young woman,* one who has freed herself from the conventions or restrictions of the community to which she belongs.

eman·ci·pa·tion /ɪ'mænsɪˋpeɪʃn/ *n* [U] emancipating or being emancipated: *the ~ of women,* giving or obtaining all or some of the rights, opportunities, etc that men have; *~ from the authority of one's parents.*

emas·cu·late /ɪˋmæskjʊleɪt/ *vt* [VP6A] deprive of manly vigour; make effeminate. **emas·cu·la·tion** /ɪ'mæskjʊˋleɪʃn/ *n*

em·balm /ɪmˋbɑm/ *vt* [VP6A] preserve (a dead body) from decay by using spices or chemicals; preserve from oblivion; fill with fragrance. **~-ment** *n*

em·bank·ment /ɪmˋbæŋkmәnt/ *n* [C] wall or mound of earth, stone, etc to hold back water or support a raised road or railway; roadway supported by such a wall: *the Thames E~.*

em·bargo /ɪmˋbɑgәʊ/ *n* (*pl* **-goes** /-gәʊz/) order that forbids trade, movement of ships, etc; stoppage of commerce, or of a branch of commerce: *a gold ~,* one that forbids or restricts the buying and selling of gold: *lift/raise/remove an ~ (from sth).* ***place/lay sth under (an) ~, put an ~ on sth.*** □ *vt* (*pt,pp* **-goed** /-gәʊd/) [VP6A] lay under an ~; seize (ships or goods) by government authority, for the service of the State.

em·bark /ɪmˋbɑk/ *vi,vt* **1** [VP2A,C,6A] go, put or take on board a ship: *The soldiers ~ed for Malta. The ship ~ed passengers and cargo.* **2** *~ **(up)on,*** [VP3A] start, take part in: *~ upon a new business undertaking.* **em·bar·ka·tion** /'embɑˋkeɪʃn/ *n* [U] ~ing; [C] instance of this; that which is ~ed.

em·bar·rass /ɪmˋbærәs/ *vt* [VP6A] **1** disconcert, cause mental discomfort or anxiety to: *~ing questions; ~ed by lack of money.* **2** hinder the movement of: *He fell into the river and, because he was ~ed by his heavy overcoat, only just managed to swim to the bank.* **~·ing·ly** *adv* **~·ment** *n* [U] ~ing or being ~ed; [C] sth that ~es: *financial ~ments; an ~ment* (= an over-abundance) *of riches.*

em·bassy /ˋembәsɪ/ *n* (*pl* **-sies**)duty and mission of an ambassador; his official residence; ambassador and his staff: *to go/come/send sb on an ~ (to sb); the French ~ in London;* (attrib) *~ officials.*

em·bat·tled /ɪmˋbætld/ *adj* (of an army, etc) drawn up ready for battle; (of a tower or building) having battlements.

em·bed /ɪmˋbed/ *vt* (**-dd-**) [VP6A,14] (usu passive) *~ **(in),*** fix firmly (in a surrounding mass): *stones ~ded in rock;* (fig) *facts ~ded in one's memory.*

em·bel·lish /ɪmˋbelɪʃ/ *vt* [VP6A,14] *~ **(with),*** make beautiful; add ornaments or details to: *~ a dress with lace and ribbons: ~ a story,* e g by adding amusing but perhaps untrue details. **~-ment** *n* [U] ~ing or being ~ed; [C] that which ~es; artistic addition.

em·ber¹ /ˋembә(r)/ *n* (usu *pl*) small piece of burning wood or coal in a dying fire; ashes of a dying fire.

em·ber² /ˋembә(r)/ *n* **'~ days,** (in some Christian Churches) twelve days of fasting and prayer.

em·bezzle /ɪmˋbezl/ *vt* [VP6A] use (money placed in one's care) in a wrong way for one's own benefit. **~·ment** *n* [U] embezzling; [C] instance of this.

em·bit·ter /ɪmˋbɪtә(r)/ *vt* [VP6A] arouse bitter feelings in: *~ed by repeated failures.* **~·ment** *n*

em·bla·zon /ɪmˋbleɪzn/ *vt* [VP6A,14] **1** adorn (e g a shield or banner) with heraldic devices: *~ed with the coat of arms of the family.* **2** extol; exalt.

em·blem /ˋemblәm/ *n* symbol; device that represents sth: *an ~ of peace,* e g a dove; *an ~ of kingship,* e g a crown or sceptre. **~·atic** /'emblәˋmætɪk/ *adj* serving as an ~ (*of* sth).

em·body /ɪmˋbodɪ/ *vt* (*pt,pp* **-died**) [VP6A,14] *~ **in,*** **1** give form to ideas/feelings, etc: *~ one's ideas in a speech.* **2** include; comprise: *The latest locomotives ~ many new features.* **3** clothe (a spirit) with a body: *an embodied spirit.* **em·bodi·ment** /ɪmˋbodɪmәnt/ *n* [C] that which embodies sth or is embodied: *She is the embodiment of kindness.*

em·bolden /ɪmˋbәʊldn/ *vt* [VP6A,17] give courage or confidence to: *Their sympathy ~ed me to ask them for help.*

em·bon·point /(F) 'ɔ̃bɔ̃ˋpwæ̃/ *n* (F) plumpness (used as a polite way of saying that sb, usu a woman, is very fat).

em·bosom /ɪmˋbʊzm/ *vt* [VP6A] (usu passive) (poet) enclose, embrace: *a house ~ed in trees,* surround: *a village ~ed with hills.*

em·boss /ɪmˋbos *US:* -ˋbɔs/ *vt* [VP6A,14] cause a pattern, figure, etc to stand out on (the surface of sth); raise the surface of sth into a pattern: *~ed notepaper,* with the address ~ed on it; *a silver vase ~ed with a design of flowers.*

em·bower /ɪmˋbaʊә(r)/ *vt* [VP6A] (usu passive) enclose in a bower.

em·brace /ɪmˋbreɪs/ *vt,vi* **1** [VP6A,2A] take (a person, etc) into one's arms, as a sign of affection: *~ a child. They ~d.* **2** [VP6A] accept; make use of: *~ an offer/opportunity.* **3** [VP6A] (of things) include: *~ many examples in a single formula.* □ *n* [C] act of embracing: *He held her to him in a warm ~.*

em·bra·sure /ɪmˋbreɪʒә(r)/ *n* [C] **1** bevelled opening in a parapet for a gun. **2** bevelled opening (esp interior side of a doorway or window), e g in an old stone castle.

em·bro·ca·tion /'embrәˋkeɪʃn/ *n* [U] liquid (a linament) for rubbing a bruised or aching part of the body.

em·broider /ɪmˋbrɔɪdә(r)/ *vt,vi* **1** [VP6A,2A] ornament (cloth) with needlework: *~ one's initials on a handkerchief; a design ~ed in gold thread.* **2** [VP6A] (fig) add fanciful details to a story. **~y** /-dәrɪ/ *n* [U] ~ed needlework: *What delicate ~!.*

em·broil /ɪmˋbrɔɪl/ *vt* [VP6A,14] *~ **sb/oneself in,*** cause (sb, oneself) to be mixed up in a quarrel: *I don't want to become ~ed in their quarrels.*

em·bryo /ˋembrɪәʊ/ *n* (*pl* **-yos** /-әʊz/) [C] offspring of an animal in the early stage of its development before birth (or before coming out of an egg); sth in its rudimentary stage. ***in ~,*** still undeveloped. **em·bry·onic** /'embrɪˋonɪk/ *adj* in

~: *an ~nic plan.*

emeer /e`mɪə(r)/ *n* = emir.

emend /ɪ`mend/ *vt* [VP6A] take out errors from: *~ a passage in a book.* **emen·da·tion** /ˈimən-`deɪʃn/ *n* [U] ~ing; [C] sth that is ~ed.

em·er·ald /`emr̩ld/ *n* bright green precious stone; colour of this.

emerge /ɪ`mɜdʒ/ *vi* [VP2A,3A] ~ *(from),* **1** come into view; (esp) come out (from water, etc): *The moon ~d from behind the clouds.* **2** (of facts, ideas) appear; become known: *No new ideas ~d during the talks.* **emerg·ence** /-dʒəns/ *n* emerging. **emerg·ent** /-dʒənt/ *adj* emerging: *(the ~d and) emergent countries of Africa,* those changing from dependence to independence, becoming modernized, etc.

emerg·ency /ɪ`mɜdʒənsɪ/ *n* (*pl* -cies) **1** [C] serious happening or situation needing prompt action: *This fire extinguisher is to be used only in an ~.* **2** (attrib use): *an ˈ~ `exit; an `~ fund,* one to be used in an ~.

emeri·tus /ɪ`merɪtəs/ *adj* (Lat) retired from service but retaining an honorary title: *~ professor.*

em·ery /`emr̩ɪ/ *n* [U] hard metal used (esp in powdered form) for grinding and polishing: *`~-cloth/-paper/-wheel,* with ~ on the surface.

em·etic /ɪ`metɪk/ *n* medicine causing a person to vomit, e g when suffering from food-poisoning.

emi·grate /`emɪgreɪt/ *vi* [VP2A,3A] ~ *(to) (from),* go away (from one's own country to another to settle there). **emi·grant** /`emɪgrənt/ *n* person who ~s: *emigrants to Canada;* (attrib) *emigrant labourers.* **emi·gra·tion** /ˈemɪ`greɪʃn/ *n* [U] emigrating; [C] instance of this.

émi·gré /`emɪgreɪ *US:* ˈemɪ`greɪ/ *n* person who has left his own country, usu for political reasons, esp a French Royalist exiled at the time of the Revolution.

emi·nence /`emɪnəns/ *n* **1** [U] state of being famous or distinguished; superiority of position; *reach ~ as a doctor; win ~ as a scientist.* **2** [C] area of high or rising ground. **3** *His/Your E~,* title used of or to a cardinal.

emi·nent /`emɪnənt/ *adj* **1** (of a person) distinguished: *~ for her virtues; ~ as a sculptor.* **2** (of qualities) remarkable in degree: *a man of ~ goodness.* **~·ly** *adv*

emir /e`mɪə(r)/ *n* Arab prince or governor; male descendant of Muhammad. **~·ate** /e`mɪəreɪt/ *n* rank, lands, etc of an ~: *the great Muslim ~ates of Northern Nigeria.*

em·iss·ary /`emɪsr̩ɪ/ *n* (*pl* -ries) person sent to deliver a message (often of an unpleasant and secret kind).

emission /ɪ`mɪʃn/ *n* [U] sending out or giving off (*of* light, heat, smell, etc); [C] that which is sent out or given off.

emit /ɪ`mɪt/ *vt* (-tt-) [VP6A] give or send out: *A volcano ~s smoke and ashes.*

emolu·ment /ɪ`moljʊmənt/ *n* [C] (usu *pl*) profit from official employment; fee; salary.

emo·tion /ɪ`məʊʃn/ *n* **1** [U] stirring up, excitement, of the mind or (more usu) the feelings; excited state of the mind or feelings: *He thought of his dead child with deep ~. He spoke in a voice touched with ~.* **2** [C] strong feeling of any kind: *Love, joy, hate, fear and grief are ~s. He appealed to our ~s rather than to our reason.* **~·less** *adj* without ~. **~al** /-ʃnl/ *adj* **1** of, directed to, the ~s: *an ~al appeal; ~al music.* **2** having ~s that are easily excited; capable of expressing ~s: *an ~al woman/actor/nature.* **~·ally** /-ʃnl̩ɪ/ *adv* **emot·ive** /ɪ`məʊtɪv/ *adj* of, tending to excite, the ~s.

em·pale /ɪm`peɪl/ *vt* = impale.

em·panel /ɪm`pænl/ *vt* (-ll-, US also -l-) [VP6A] enter (a person's name) on a panel; enrol (a jury).

em·pa·thy /`empəθɪ/ *n* [U] (psychol) (power of) projecting oneself into (and so fully understanding, and losing one's identity in) a work of art or other object of contemplation.

em·peror /`empərə(r)/ *n* ruler of an empire. ⇨ empress.

em·pha·sis /`emfəsɪs/ (*pl* -sises /-sɪsɪz/) *n* [C,U] force or stress laid on a word or words to make the significance clear, or to show importance; (the placing of) special value or importance: *Some schools lay/put special ~ on language study. I insist, with all the ~ at my command, that....* **em·pha·size** /`emfəsaɪz/ *vt* [VP6A] put ~ on; give ~ to: *He emphasized the importance of careful driving.* **em·phatic** /ɪm`fætɪk/ *adj* having, showing, using, ~: *an emphatic gesture/opinion; an emphatic person.* **em·phati·cally** /-klɪ/ *adv*

em·pire /`empɑɪə(r)/ *n* **1** [C] group of countries under a single supreme authority: *the Roman E~.* **2** [U] supreme political power: *the responsibilities of ~.* **the First E~,** (in France) period of the reign of Napoleon I (1804—15); (attrib) of the style of furniture or dress fashionable in this period. **the Second E~,** the period of the reign of Napoleon III (1852—70).

em·piric /ɪm`pɪrɪk/ *n, adj* (person) relying on observation and experiment, not on theory. **em·piri·cally** /-klɪ/ *adv* **em·piri·cism** /ɪm`pɪrɪsɪzm/ *n* **em·pir·i·cist** /-sɪst/ *n*

em·place·ment /ɪm`pleɪsmənt/ *n* prepared position for a heavy gun or guns.

em·plane /em`pleɪn/ *vi, vt* [VP2A,6A] go, put, on board an aircraft.

em·ploy /ɪm`plɔɪ/ *vt* [VP6A,16B,14] **1** give work to, usu for payment: *They ~ five waiters. He is ~ed in a bank.* **2** make use of: *How do you ~ your spare time?* □ *n* ***in the ~ of,*** ~ed by, working for. **~·able** /-əbl/ *adj* that can be ~ed. **~er** *n* person who ~s others. **~ee** /ˈemplɔɪ`i/ *n* person ~ed for wages.

em·ploy·ment /ɪm`plɔɪmənt/ *n* [U] employing or being employed; one's regular work or occupation: *to find ~; to give ~ to sb; the men in my ~; to be thrown out of ~.* **be in/out of ~,** have/not have a job. **`~ agency,** business establishment which helps persons (for a fee) to find ~. **`~ exchange,** Government office which puts employers and unemployed persons in touch with each other.

em·por·ium /ɪm`pɔrɪəm/ *n* centre of commerce; market; large retail store.

em·power /ɪm`pɑʊə(r)/ *vt* [VP17] ***~ sb to do sth,*** give power or authority to act.

em·press /`emprəs/ *n* woman governing an empire; wife of or widow of an emperor.

empty[1] /`emptɪ/ *adj* having nothing inside; containing nothing: *an ~ box; ~ promises,* not meaning anything, not giving satisfaction; *feeling ~,* (colloq) hungry: *words ~ of meaning,* meaningless words. *The house was ~,* unoccupied. **ˈ~-`handed** *adj* bringing back nothing; carrying nothing away. **ˈ~-`headed** *adj* witless; lacking in common sense □ *n* (usu *pl*) box, bottle, crate, etc that has been emptied: *Empties* (e g ~ beer bottles) *are not taken back,* The brewery will not accept them and allow credit for them. **emp·ti·ness** /ˋemptɪnəs/ *n*

empty² /ˋemptɪ/ *vt,vi* (*pt,pp* **-tied**) [VP6A,15B, 2A,C,3A] make or become empty, remove what is inside (sth): ~ *one's glass,* drink everything in it; ~ (*out*) *a drawer;* ~ *a box of rubbish into a rubbish-cart;* ~ *one's pockets of their contents. The streets soon emptied/were soon emptied when the rain started. The Rhone empties* (= flows) *into the Mediterranean. The water empties* (= flows out) *slowly. The cistern empties* (= becomes empty) *in five minutes.*

em·purpled /ɪmˋpɜpld/ *adj* made purple.

em·pyr·ean /ˈempɪˋrɪən/ *n* the highest heaven; the visible heavens. □ *adj* heavenly; celestial.

emu /ˋimju/ *n* large flightless Australian bird that runs well. ⇨ the illus at **rare**.

emu·late /ˋemjʊleɪt/ *vt* [VP6A] try to do as well as or better than.

emu·la·tion /ˈemjʊˋleɪʃn/ *n* [U] emulating: *in a spirit of* ~; *in* ~ *of each other.*

emu·lous /ˋemjʊləs/ *adj* (formal) wishing or anxious to do as well as or better than: ~ *of all rivals;* imitating (others) in a jealous spirit, desiring to obtain: ~ *of fame/honours.* **~·ly** *adv*

emul·sion /ɪˋmʌlʃn/ *n* [C,U] (kinds of) creamy liquid in which particles of oil or fat are suspended: ~ *paint,* in which the colour is in an ~-like liquid. **emul·sify** /ɪˋmʌlsɪfɑɪ/ *vt* (*pt,pp* **-fied**) [VP6A] make an ~ of.

en·able /ɪˋneɪbl/ *vt* [VP17A] make able, give authority or means (*to do* sth): *The collapse of the strike* ~*d the company to resume normal bus services.* **en·abling** /ɪˋneɪblɪŋ/ *part adj* making possible: *enabling legislation.*

en·act /ɪˋnækt/ *vt* **1** [VP6A,9] make (a law); decree ordain: *as by law* ~*ed. Be it further* ~*ed that....* (legal style). **2** [VP6A] perform on, or as though on, the stage of a theatre. **~·ment** *n* [U] ~ing or being ~ed; [C] law.

en·amel /ɪˋnæml/ *n* [U] **1** glass-like substance used for coating metal, porcelain, etc, for decoration or as a protection: ˋ~ *ware,* manufactured goods with ~ surfaces; ˋ~ *paint,* paint which dries to make a hard, glossy surface. **2** hard outer covering of teeth. □ *vt* (**-ll-**, US also **-l-**) cover, decorate, with ~ (esp with designs or decorations).

en·amour (US = **-amor**) /ɪˋnæmə(r)/ *vt* [VP6A] (usu in passive) ***be*** **~*ed of,*** fond of, delighted with and inclined to use: ~*ed of one's own voice.*

en·camp /ɪnˋkæmp/ *vt,vi* [VP6A,2A] settle in a camp; lodge in tents. **~·ment** *n* place where troops, etc are ~ed.

en·case /ɪnˋkeɪs/ *vt* [VP6A] put into a case; surround or cover as with a case: *a knight* ~*d in armour.*

en·caus·tic /ɪnˋkɔstɪk/ *adj* prepared by using heat: ~ *bricks/tiles,* inlaid with coloured clays that are burnt in.

en·ceinte /ɒ̃ˋsæ̃t/ *adj* (F) pregnant.

en·cepha·li·tis /ˈenˈsefəˋlɑɪtɪs/ *n* [U] inflammation of the brain.

en·chain /ɪnˋtʃeɪn/ *vt* [VP6A] fasten with chain(s); (fig) hold fast (the attention, etc).

en·chant /ɪnˋtʃɑnt *US:* -ˋtʃænt/ *vt* [VP6A] **1** charm; delight: *She was* ~*ed with/by the flowers you sent her.* **2** use magic on; put under a magic spell: *the* ~*ed palace,* e g in a fairy tale. **~er** *n* man who ~s. **~·ress** /-trəs/ *n* woman who ~s. **~·ing·ly** *adv* **~·ment** *n* **1** [U] being ~ed. **2** [C] sth which ~s; magic spell. **3** [U] charm; delight: *the* ~*ment of moonlight.*

en·circle /ɪnˋsɜkl/ *vt* [VP6A] surround; form a circle round: *a lake* ~*d by trees;* ~*d by enemy forces.* **~·ment** *n*

en clair /ˈɒ̃ˋ kleə(r) *US:* ˈɒn/ *phrase* (of telegrams, official dispatches, etc) (or *in clear*) in ordinary language, not in code or cipher.

en·clave /ˋenkleɪv/ *n* [C] territory wholly within the boundaries of another.

en·close /ɪnˋkləʊz/ *vt* [VP6A,14] **1** put a wall, fence, etc round; shut in on all sides: ~ *a garden with a wall;* ~ *common land,* put fences, etc round land which has been used by everyone. **2** put (sth) in an envelope, parcel, etc: *I'll* ~ *your letter with mine. A cheque for £5 is* ~*d. E*~*d, please find...,* (comm style) You will find, ~d with this....

en·clos·ure /ɪnˋkləʊʒə(r)/ *n* **1** [U] enclosing: ~ *of common land;* [C] instance of this. **2** [C] sth that is enclosed (esp with a letter).

en·co·mium /ɪnˋkəʊmɪəm/ *n* (usu *pl*) (formal) very high praise.

en·compass /ɪnˋkʌmpəs/ *vt* [VP6A] encircle; envelope; comprise.

en·core /ˋɒŋkɔ(r)/ *int* Repeat! Again! □ *vt, n* [VP6A] (call for a) repetition (of a song, etc) or further performance by the same person(s): *The violinist got an* ~. *The singer gave three* ~*s. The audience* ~*d the pianist.*

en·coun·ter /ɪnˋkɑʊntə(r)/ *vt* [VP6A] find oneself faced by (danger, difficulties, etc); meet (an enemy or enemies); meet (a friend, etc) unexpectedly. □ *n* [C] **~ *(with),*** sudden or unexpected (esp hostile) meeting.

en·cour·age /ɪnˋkʌrɪdʒ *US:* -ˋkɜ-/ *vt* [VP6A,14, 17] **~ *sb in sth/to do sth,*** give hope, courage or confidence to; support: ~ *a man to work harder;* ~ *a boy in his studies; feel* ~*d by the progress one has made. Don't* ~ *him in his idle ways.* **~·ment** *n* [U] encouraging: *cries of* ~*ment;* [C] sth that ~s: *Praise acts as an* ~*ment to the young.*

en·croach /ɪnˋkrəʊtʃ/ *vi* [VP3A] **~ *(up)on,*** beyond what is right or natural: ~ (*up*)*on sb's rights/time/land. The sea is* ~*ing* (*up*)*on the land,* washing it away. **~·ment** *n* [U] ~ing; [C] sth gained by ~ing; advance beyond the original limits: ~*ments made by the sea upon the land.*

en·crust /ɪnˋkrʌst/ *vt,vi* **1** [VP6A,14] cover with a crust; overlay (a surface) with a crust of ornamental or costly material: *a gold vase* ~*ed with precious stones.* **2** [VP2A] form into a crust.

en·cum·ber /ɪnˋkʌmbə(r)/ *vt* [VP6A,14] **1** get in the way of, hamper, be a burden to: *be* ~*ed with a large family; an estate* ~*ed with mortgages;* ~ *oneself with unnecessary luggage.* **2** crowd; fill up: *a room* ~*ed with old and useless furniture.* **en·cum·brance** /ɪnˋkʌmbrəns/ *n* [C] thing that ~s; burden: *An idle grown-up daughter may be an encumbrance to her parents.*

en·cyc·li·cal /ˈenˈsɪklɪkl/ *adj, n* (letter written by the Pope) for wide circulation.

en·cy·clo·pedia (also **-pædia**) /ɪnˈsɑɪkləˋpidɪə/ *n* book, or set of books, giving information about every branch of knowledge, or on one subject, with articles in ABC order. **en·cy·clo·pedic, -pædic** /ɪnˈsɑɪkləˋpidɪk/ *adj* dealing with, having knowledge of, a wide variety of subjects.

end¹ /end/ *n* **1** farthest or last part: *the end of a road/stick/line, etc; the house at the end of the street;* (attrib) *the end house; the end carriage,* the last carriage, e g in a railway coach or train; *the west/east end of a town,* the parts in the west/east; *the ends of the earth,* most remote parts, parts difficult of access. ***begin/start at the wrong end,*** in the wrong way, at a wrong point. ***get/have hold of the wrong end of the stick,*** have a completely mistaken idea of what is intended or meant. ***keep one's end up,*** (GB) continue cheerful, full of fighting spirit, in the face of difficulties, etc. ***at a loose end,*** unoccupied, having nothing important or interesting to do. ***on end,*** **(a)** upright: *Place the barrel/box on (its) end. His hair stood on end. The ghost story set their hair on end.* **(b)** continuously: *two hours on end.* ***end on,*** with the ends meeting: *The two ships collided end on,* The stern (or bows) of one struck the stern (or bows) of the other. ***end to end,*** in a line with the ends touching: *Arrange the tables end to end.* ***go in/off the deep end,*** express strong feeling without trying to control it. ***make (both) ends meet,*** live within one's income; balance one's income with one's expenditure. **2** small piece that remains; remnant: *candle ends; a cigarette end; a rope's end,* short piece of rope, e g as used for whipping sb; odds and ends. **ˈend·papers,** (usu) blank leaves pasted to the inside covers of a book. **3** finish; conclusion: *at the end of the day/the century; the end of a story/adventure. We shall never hear the end of the matter,* It will be talked about for a long time to come. ***(be) at an end, at the end (of):*** *The war was at an end,* finished. *She was at the end of her patience/tether,* had no patience left. *He was at the end of his resources.* ***come to an end,*** finish: *The meeting came to an end at last.* ***draw to an end:*** *As the year drew to its end....* ***make an end of sth, put an end to sth,*** finish it, get rid of it (according to context): *We must put an end to these abuses. Death put an end to his wicked career.* ***in the end,*** finally, at last: *He tried many ways of earning a living; in the end he became a farm labourer.* ***no end of,*** (colloq) very many or much, very great, etc: *We met no end of interesting people. He thinks no end of himself,* has a high opinion of his abilities, etc. ***without end,*** never reaching an end: *We had trouble without end.* **4** death: *He's nearing his end,* is dying. *She came to an untimely end,* died young. *If you don't give up crime, you'll come to a bad end,* e g be sent to prison for life as a murderer. **5** purpose, aim: *gain/win/achieve one's end(s); with this end in view; for/to this end; to the end that,* in order that; *to no end,* in vain. ***The end justifies the means*** (prov, used to suggest that for a good purpose even wrong or unfair methods may be allowed).

end² /end/ *vi,vt* [VP2A,C,3A,6A,15B] (cause to) come to an end; reach an end: *The road ends here,* goes no farther. *How does the story end? Let's end our quarrel. He ended his days in peace,* The last period of his life was peaceful. ***end in,*** have as a result: *The scheme ended in failure.* ***end (sth) off,*** finish: *He ended off his speech with some amusing stories.* ***end up,*** finish: *If you continue to steal, you'll end up in prison,* will one day be sent to prison. *We started with soup, and had fruit to end up with.* **end·ing** *n* [C] end, esp of a word or a story.

en·dan·ger /ɪnˈdeɪndʒə(r)/ *vt* [VP6A] put in danger; cause danger to: *~ one's chances of success.*

en·dear /ɪnˈdɪə(r)/ *vt* [VP14] ***~ sb/oneself to,*** make dear or precious: *~ oneself to everyone; an ~ing smile.* **~·ing·ly** *adv* **~·ment** *n* [C,U] act, word, expression, of affection: *a term of ~ment,* e g *darling; the ~ments that a wife expects from her husband.*

en·deav·our (US = **-vor**) /ɪnˈdevə(r)/ *n* [C] effort, attempt: *Please make every ~ to be early. His ~s to persuade her to go with him failed.* □ *vi* [VP4A] try: *~ to please one's wife.*

en·demic /enˈdemɪk/ *n, adj* (disease) prevalent or often recurring in a country or area, or among a particular class of people, e g miners. ⇨ epidemic.

en·dive /ˈendɪv *US:* -daɪv/ *n* [C] kind of curly-leaved chicory, used as salad.

end·less /ˈendləs/ *adj* having no end; never stopping: *a woman with ~ patience; an ~ belt/chain/cable,* one with the ends joined, to pass continuously over wheels, etc to transmit power in a machine. **~·ly** *adv*

en·dorse /ɪnˈdɔs/ *vt* [VP6A] **1** write one's name on the back of (a cheque); write comments, etc in, on the back of (a document): *His driving licence has been ~d,* A record of a motoring offence has been entered in it. **2** approve, support a claim, statement, etc. **~·ment** *n* [U] endorsing; [C] instance of this; statement, etc that ~s.

en·dow /ɪnˈdaʊ/ *vt* [VP6A,14] **1** give money, property, etc to provide a regular income for (e g a college): *~ a bed in a hospital; ~ a school.* **2** (usu passive) ***be ~ed with,*** possess naturally, be born with (qualities, etc): *be ~ed by nature with great talents.* **~·ment** *n* **1** [U] ~ing. **2** [C] money, property, etc given to provide an income: *The Oxford and Cambridge colleges have numerous ~ments.* **3** [C] talent: *natural ~ments,* e g a good ear for music.

en·due /ɪnˈdju *US:* -ˈdu/ *vt* [VP14] (usu passive) ***be ~d with,*** be furnished, supplied, with.

en·dur·ance /ɪnˈdjʊərns *US:* -ˈdʊə-/ *n* [U] ability to endure: *He showed remarkable powers of ~. He came to the end of his ~.* ***past/beyond ~,*** to an extent that can no longer be endured. **ˈ~ test,** test of how long sb or sth can endure sth.

en·dure /ɪnˈdjʊə(r) *US:* -ˈdʊər/ *vt,vi* **1** [VP6A,2A,C] suffer, undergo pain, hardship, etc: *~ toothache. If help does not come, we must ~ to the end,* suffer until death comes. **2** [VP6A,D,17, esp in *neg*] bear; put up with: *I can't ~ that woman. She can't ~ seeing/~ to see animals cruelly treated.* **3** [VP2A] last; continue in existence: *as long as life ~s; fame that will ~ for ever.* **en·dur·able** /-rəbl/ *adj* able to ~. **en·dur·ing** *adj* lasting: *an enduring peace.* **en·dur·ingly** *adv*

end·ways /ˈendweɪz/, **end·wise** /-waɪz/ *adv* with the end towards the spectator; end forward; end to end.

en·ema /ˈenəmə/ *n* (syringe used for an) injection of liquid into the rectum.

en·emy /ˈenəmɪ/ *n* (*pl* -mies) **1** one who tries or wishes to harm or attack; one who has ill feeling or hatred towards sb or sth: *A successful man often has many enemies. Don't make an ~ of him,* Do nothing that will cause him to be your ~. *He's an ~ to reform.* **2** (collective *pl* with *def art*) armed forces of a nation with which one's country is at war; ~-*occupied territory. The* ~ *were forced to retreat;* (attrib) of the ~: ~ *aircraft/ships.* **3** member of such a hostile force. **4** anything that harms or injures: *Laziness is his chief* ~. *Idleness is an* ~ *to discipline,* weakens discipline.

en·ergy /ˈenədʒɪ/ *n* (*pl* **-gies**) **1** [U] force, vigour; capacity to do things and get things done: *He had so much* ~ *that he did the work of three men. He's full of* ~. **2** (*pl*) (person's) powers available for working, or as used in working: *apply/devote all one's energies to a task.* **3** [U] (science) capacity for, power of, doing work: *electrical* ~; *kinetic* ~; *potential* ~. **en·er·getic** /ˈenəˈdʒetɪk/ *adj* full of, done with, ~(1). **en·er·geti·cally** /-klɪ/ *adv*

en·er·vate /ˈenəveɪt/ *vt* [VP6A] cause to lose physical, moral strength: *a country with an enervating climate.*

en famille /ˈõ fæˈmi *US:* ˈon/ *adv* (F) at home; among one's family.

en·fant ter·rible /ˈõfõ teˈribl *with unsyllabic* l/ *n* (F) child who is a nuisance because he asks awkward questions, tells tales, etc.

en·feeble /ɪnˈfibl/ *vt* [VP6A] make feeble.

en·fold /ɪnˈfəʊld/ *vt* [VP6A,14] ~ ***sb (in),*** enclose (esp in one's arms).

en·force /ɪnˈfɔs/ *vt* [VP6A,14] **1** compel obedience to; make effective; impose: ~ *a law;* ~ *discipline/silence;* ~ *a course of action upon sb.* **2** give force or strength to: *Have you any statistics that would* ~ *your argument?* ~**·able** /-əbl/ *adj* that can be ~d. ~**·ment** *n* [U] enforcing or being ~d: *strict* ~*ment of a new law.*

en·fran·chise /ɪnˈfræntʃɑɪz/ *vt* [VP6A] **1** give political rights to (esp, the right to vote at parliamentary elections): *In Great Britain women were* ~*d in 1918.* **2** set free (slaves). ~**·ment** /ɪnˈfræntʃɪzmənt/ *n*

en·gage /ɪnˈgeɪdʒ/ *vt,vi* **1** [VP6A,16B] obtain the right to employ: ~ *a typist;* ~ *sb as a guide/as an interpreter;* get the right to occupy: ~ *a taxi* (*hire* is the preferred word). **2** [VP7,17,9,3A] promise; undertake; bind (oneself); guarantee: *I will* ~ *to manage the business if you will* ~ (*yourself*) *to provide the capital. Can you* ~ *that all his statements are trustworthy? That is more than I can* ~ *for,* guarantee, take responsibility for. **3** [VP3A] ~ ***in,*** take part in; busy oneself with: ~ *in politics.* **4** (usu passive) promise, agree, to marry: *Tom and Anne are* ~*d. Tom is* ~*d to Anne.* **5** ***be*** ~***d (in),*** be busy (with), be occupied; be busy with; work at; take part in: *be* ~*d in business/in writing a novel. My time is fully* ~*d. The line/number is* ~*d,* (telephoning) Someone else is using the line. **6** [VP6A] (usu passive) attract: *Nothing* ~*s his attention for long. Her attention was* ~*d by the display of new hats in the shop window.* **7** [VP6A, 2A] attack; begin fighting with: *The general did not* ~ *the enemy. Our orders are to* ~ *at once.* **8** [VP2A,3A,6A,14] (of parts of a machine) lock together; (cause to) fit into: *The two cog-wheels* ~. *The teeth of one wheel* ~ *with those of the other.* (motoring) *E*~ *the clutch/the first gear.* **en·gag·ing** *adj* likely to ~ the attention; charming: *an engaging smile/manner.* **en·gag·ing·ly** *adv*

en·gage·ment /ɪnˈgeɪdʒmənt/ *n* [C] **1** (formal) promise or undertaking, esp one that is formal or made in writing: *He has only enough money to meet his* ~*s,* to make the payments he has undertaken to make. **2** agreement to marry: *Their* ~ *was announced in the papers.* ˈ~ **ring,** one given by a man to a woman when they agree to marry. **3** arrangement to go somewhere, meet someone or do sth, at a fixed time: *I have numerous* ~*s for next week.* **4** battle: *The admiral tried to bring about an* ~, to make the enemy fight. **5** [C,U] engaging (of part of a machine, etc): ~ *of first gear.*

en·gen·der /ɪnˈdʒendə(r)/ *vt* [VP6A] be the cause of (a situation or condition): *Crime is often* ~*ed by poverty.*

en·gine /ˈendʒɪn/ *n* **1** machine that converts energy into power or motion: *a* ˈ*steam-/*ˈ*oil-*~; *a new* ~ (petrol or diesel) *for a motor-vehicle, train, etc.* ˈ~**-driver** *n* (esp) man who drives a railway ~. **2** (old use) machine or instrument: ~*s of war,* e g cannons.

en·gin·eer /ˈendʒɪˈnɪə(r)/ *n* **1** person who designs machines, bridges, railways, docks, etc: *a civil/military/mining/electrical/sanitary, etc* ~; person who designs or makes machines or engines. **2** skilled and trained person in control of an engine or engines: *the chief* ~ *of a ship;* (US) man who drives a locomotive. **3** member of the branch of an army (called *the E*~*s*) that builds roads and bridges, controls communications, etc. □ *vt,vi* **1** [VP6A,2A] act as an ~; construct or control as an ~. **2** (colloq) arrange or bring about skilfully: ~ *a scheme/plot.* ~**·ing** *n* [U] the technology, work or profession of an ~: *a triumph of* ~*ing,* e g a magnificent bridge; *an* ~*ing works.*

Eng·lish /ˈɪŋglɪʃ/ *n* the ~ language. ***in plain*** ~, in language so simple that the meaning is quite clear. **the** ˈ**Queen's/**ˈ**King's** ˈ~, standard, educated English. **the** ~, ~ people. □ *adj* **1** of England. **2** of, written in, spoken in, the ~ language. ~**·man** /-mən/ (*pl* **-men**) *n* ~**·woman** /-wʊmən/ (*pl* **-women**) *n*

en·graft /ɪnˈgrɑft *US:* -ˈgræft/ *vt* [VP6A,14] insert (a shoot of one tree *into* or *upon* another); (fig) implant (principles *in* the mind or character).

en·grave /ɪnˈgreɪv/ *vt* **1** [VP6A,14] ~ ***(up)on,*** cut or carve (lines, words, designs, on, upon) a hard surface: ~ *a design on a metal plate* (for printing); *a name* ~*d on a tombstone.* **2** [VP14] ~ ***with,*** mark such surfaces with (an inscription, etc). **3** [VP14] ~ ***(up)on,*** (fig) impress deeply (*upon* the memory or mind). **en·graver** *n* person who ~s designs, etc on stone, metal, etc. **en·grav·ing** /ɪnˈgreɪvɪŋ/ *n* [U] art of cutting or carving designs on metal, stone, etc; [C] copy of a picture, design, etc printed from an ~d plate.

en·gross /ɪnˈgrəʊs/ *vt* **1** [VP6A] (usu passive) take up all the time or attention of: ~*ed in his work; an* ~*ing story.* **2** write (e g a legal document) in large letters or in formal style.

en·gulf /ɪnˈgʌlf/ *vt* [VP6A] swallow up (as in a gulf): *a boat* ~*ed in the sea/waves.*

en·hance /ɪnˈhɑns *US:* -ˈhæns/ *vt* [VP6A] add to (the value, attraction, powers, price, etc).

enigma /ɪˈnɪgmə/ *n* [C] question, person, thing, circumstance, that is puzzling. **enig·matic** /ˈenɪgˈmætɪk/ *adj* puzzling; mysterious. **enig·mati·cally** /-klɪ/ *adv*

en·join /ɪnˈdʒɔɪn/ *vt* [VP6A,17,9,14] give an order for; urge; prescribe; command: ~ *silence/obedience;* ~ *on sb the necessity for economy;* ~ *a duty on sb;* ~ *sb to obey the rules;* ~ *that sth should be done.*

en·joy /ɪnˈdʒɔɪ/ *vt* [VP6A,C] **1** get pleasure from;

take delight in: ~ *one's dinner. I've ~ed talking to you about old times.* **2** have as an advantage or benefit: ~ *good health/a good income.* **3** ~ ***oneself,*** experience pleasure; be happy. **~·able** /-əbl/ *adj* giving joy; pleasant. **~·ably** /-əblɪ/ *adv*

en·joy·ment /ɪn`dʒɔɪmənt/ *n* **1** [U] pleasure; joy; satisfaction: *to think only of/live for ~.* **2** [U] possession and use: *be in the ~ of the full possession of one's faculties,* be physically and mentally well. **3** [C] sth that gives joy and pleasure.

en·kindle /ɪn`kɪndl/ *vt* [VP6A] cause flame, passion, etc to flare up; inflame with passion.

en·large /ɪn`lɑdʒ/ *vt,vi* **1** [VP6A,2A] make or become larger: ~ *a photograph/one's house. Will this print ~ well,* Will it be good if it is reproduced on a larger scale? **2** [VP3A] ~ ***(up)on,*** say or write more about: *I need not ~ upon this matter; you all know my views.* **~·ment** *n* [U] enlarging or being ~d; [C] result of this, esp a photograph.

en·lighten /ɪn`lɑɪtn/ *vt* [VP6A,14] give more knowledge to; free from ignorance, misunderstanding or false beliefs: *Can you ~ me on this subject,* help me to understand it better? **~ed** *part adj* free from ignorance, prejudice, superstition, etc: *in these ~ed days.* **~·ment** *n* [U] ~ing or being ~ed: *living in an age of ~ment; work for the ~ment of mankind.* **the E~ment,** the period (esp 18th c) when men believed that reason and science (and not religion) would advance human progress.

en·list /ɪn`lɪst/ *vt,vi* **1** [VP6A,14,16B,2A,C] take into, enter, the armed forces: ~ *a recruit; ~ as a volunteer; ~ed men,* soldiers, etc; ~ *in the army.* **2** [VP6A,14] obtain; get the support of: ~ *sb's sympathy and help in a charitable cause/for the Red Cross.* **~·ment** *n* [U] ~ing or being ~ed; [C] instance of this.

en·liven /ɪn`lɑɪvn/ *vt* [VP6A] make lively: *How can we ~ the party?*

en masse /'õ `mæs *US:* 'on/ *adv* (F) in a mass; all together.

en·mesh /ɪn`meʃ/ *vt* [VP6A] take (as) in a net.

en·mity /`enmətɪ/ *n* [U] hatred: *be at ~ with one's neighbours;* [C] (*pl* **-ties**) particular feeling of hatred.

en·noble /ɪ`nəʊbl/ *vt* [VP6A] **1** make (sb) a member of the nobility. **2** (fig) make morally noble; make dignified. **~·ment** *n*

en·nui /on`wi/ *n* [U] (F) weariness of mind caused by lack of any interesting occupation; [C] instance of this.

enor·mity /ɪ`nɔmətɪ/ *n* **1** [U] great wickedness: *Does he realize the ~ of his offence?* **2** [C] (*pl* -ties) serious crime. **3** immense size: *the ~ of the problem of feeding the world's population in 2 000* AD.

enor·mous /ɪ`nɔməs/ *adj* very great; immense: *an ~ sum of money.* **~·ly** *adv* to an ~ extent: *The town has changed ~ly during recent years.* **~·ness** *n*

enough /ɪ`nʌf/ *adj, n, adv* (quantity or numbers) as great as is needed; as much or as many as necessary. (As an *adj enough* may either precede or follow a *noun;* as a *noun* it occurs in the pattern: **~ (of the/this/that/his, etc + noun) (for sb/to do sth)**: *There's ~ food/food ~ for everybody. Will £5 be ~ for you/~ to meet your needs? Have you had ~ of this TV programme? Thank you, I've had more than ~. I've had ~ of your impudence.* □ *adj* of degree (placed after *adjj, advv* and *pp;* also after a *noun* used as an *adj,* as when *fool* means *foolish.* Used in the pattern: ***adj ~ (for sb/to do sth)*** **1** to the right or necessary degree; sufficiently: *The meat is not cooked ~. Are you warm ~? You know well ~* (= quite well) *what I mean. I was fool* (= foolish) *~ to believe her. He wasn't man* (= manly) *~ to admit his mistake. You're old ~ to know better. This book is easy ~ for a six-year-old child to read.* **2** sometimes used in a disparaging way, suggesting that sth could be better, etc: It's well ~ in its way, moderately satisfactory. *She sings well ~,* indicating faint praise. **3** *oddly/curiously/strangely ~,* in a way that is odd, etc; *sure ~,* in a degree that satisfies doubt.

en·plane /en`pleɪn/ *vi,vt* ⇨ emplane.

en·quire, en·quiry /ɪn`kwɑɪə(r), ɪn`kwɑɪərɪ/ *v, n* ⇨ inquire, inquiry.

en·rage /ɪn`reɪdʒ/ *vt* [VP6A] fill with rage: *~d at/by sb's stupidity.*

en·rap·ture /ɪn`ræptʃə(r)/ *vt* [VP6A] fill with great delight or joy.

en·rich /ɪn`rɪtʃ/ *vt* [VP6A,14] ~ ***(with),*** make rich; improve in quality, flavour, etc: ~ *the mind (with knowledge); soil ~ed with manure.* **~·ment** *n*

en·roll, en·rol /ɪn`rəʊl/ *vt,vi* [VP6A,14,16B,2A,C] (cause to) become a member of a society or institute: *to ~ in evening classes; to ~ (sb) as a member of a society/club; to be ~ed in a register of electors; to ~ new students.* **~·ment** *n* [U] ~ing or being ~ed; [C] number ~ed: *a school with an ~ment of 800 pupils.*

en route /'õ `rut *US:* 'on `raʊt/ *adv* **~ *from/to,*** on the way: *We stopped at Paris ~ from Rome to London.*

en·san·guined /ɪn`sæŋgwɪnd/ *adj* (poet) bloodstained.

en·sconce /ɪn`skons/ *vt* [VP14] establish (oneself, in a safe, secret, comfortable, etc place).

en·semble /õ`sõbl *with unsyllabic* l *US:* on`sombl/ *n* [C] **1** sth viewed as a whole; general effect. **2** (music) passage of music in which all the performers unite; group of musicians who play together regularly (smaller than an orchestra). **3** (trade use) woman's matched clothing outfit (dress, coat, etc designed to be worn together).

en·shrine /ɪn`ʃrɑɪn/ *vt* [VP6A,14] ~ ***in,*** (formal) place or keep in, or as in, a shrine; serve as a shrine for: *the casket that ~s the relics; memories ~d in her heart; basic human rights ~d in the constitution.*

en·shroud /ɪn`ʃraʊd/ *vt* [VP6A] cover completely: *hills ~ed in mist.*

en·sign /`ensɑɪn/ (in the navy) *n* **1** flag or banner; (GB) *`white ~,* used by the Royal Navy; *`red ~,* used by British merchant ships; *`blue ~,* of the naval reserve. **2** badge or symbol (showing office, authority, etc). **3** (formerly) infantry officer who carried the regimental colours. **4** (US /`ensən/) lowest commissioned officer in the navy. ⇨ App 9.

en·si·lage /ɪn`sɑɪlɪdʒ/ *n* [U] green fodder stored in a silo or pit and fermented (to feed cattle in winter).

en·slave /ɪn`sleɪv/ *vt* [VP6A] make a slave of. **~·ment** *n*

en·snare /ɪn`sneə(r)/ *vt* [VP6A] catch in, or as in, a snare or trap.

en·sue /ɪn`sju *US:* -`su/ *vi* [VP2A,3A] ~ ***(from),***

happen later; follow, happen as a result: *the trouble that ~d from this misunderstanding; in the ensuing* (= next) *year.*

en·sure (US = **in·sure**) /ɪnˋʃʊə(r)/ *vt,vi* **1** [VP9] make sure; guarantee: *I can't ~ that he will be there in time.* **2** [VP14,3A] ***~ (sb) (against sth),*** make safe: *We ~d (ourselves) against possible disappointment. You should ~ (yourself) against loss of heat by having double glazing.* **3** [VP12A, 13A] secure; assure: *These documents ~ to you the authority you need. I cannot ~ you a good post.* **4** (formerly) = **insure.**

en·tail /ɪnˋteɪl/ *vt* **1** [VP6A,14] make necessary; impose (expense, etc *on* sb): *That will ~ an early start. Your plans ~ great expense.* **2** (legal) leave, settle, (land) to a line of heirs so that none of them can give it away or sell it: *~ an estate on sb.* □ *n* [U] settlement of landed property in this way; [C] the property so settled.

en·tangle /ɪnˋtæŋgl/ *vt* [VP6A,15A,14] **1** catch in a snare or among obstacles: *My fishing line got ~d in weeds. The duck flew into the nets and the more it struggled the more it ~d itself.* **2** (fig) put or get into difficulties, in unfavourable circumstances: *~ oneself with money-lenders.* **~·ment** *n* **1** [U] entangling or being ~d; [C] situation that ~s: *~ments with rogues; emotional ~ments.* **2** (*pl*) barrier of stakes and barbed wire to impede the enemy's advance.

en·tente /õˋtõnt *US:* onˋtont/ *n* [C] (group of States with a) friendly understanding. **ˈ~ cordiale** /ˈkɔdɪˋɑl/ *n* ~, esp between two governments.

en·ter /ˋentə(r)/ *vt,vi* **1** [VP6A,2A] come or go into: *~ a room. The train ~ed a tunnel. Where did the bullet ~ the body?* (Stage direction in a printed play) *E~ Hamlet,* Hamlet comes upon the stage. **2** [VP6A] become a member of; join: *~ a school/college; ~ the Army/Navy; ~ the Church,* become a priest; *~ a profession.* **3** [VP3A] ***~ into sth (with sb),*** begin, open: *~ into conversation with sb; ~ into negotiations with a business firm.* ***~ into sth,*** **(a)** *~ into details/particulars,* begin to deal with them. **(b)** sympathize with; be able to understand and appreciate: *~ into sb's feelings; ~ into the spirit of the occasion.* **(c)** form a part of: *a possibility that had not ~ed into our calculations.* **4** [VP3A] ***~ (up)on,*** **(a)** make a start on: *~ upon a new career/one's duties/another term of office.* **(b)** take possession of; begin to enjoy: *~ upon one's inheritance.* **5** [VP6A,14,15B] ***~ (in/up),*** unite, record names, details, etc in a book, etc: *~ (up) an item in an account-book.* **6** [VP14] ***~ (sb) (for),*** give the name of sb for a competition, race, etc: *~ oneself for an examination; ~ (one's name) for the high jump; ~ a horse for the Derby.*

en·teric /enˋterɪk/ *adj* of the intestines: *~ fever,* typhoid. **en·ter·itis** /ˈentəˋrɑɪtɪs/ *n* [U] inflammation of the intestines.

en·ter·prise /ˋentəprɑɪz/ *n* **1** [C] undertaking, esp one that needs courage or that offers difficulty. **2** [U] courage and willingness to engage in ~s(**1**): *We need a spirit of ~ if we are to overcome our difficulties. He is a man of great ~.* **3** [U] carrying on of ~s(**1**): *prefer private ~ to government control of commerce and industry.* **ˈfree ˋ~,** ⇨ **free**[1](**3**). **en·ter·pris·ing** *adj* having, showing, ~(**2**). **en·ter·pris·ing·ly** *adv*

en·ter·tain /ˈentəˋteɪn/ *vt* [VP6A,14,2A] **1** receive (people) as guests; give food and drink to: *~ friends to dinner. The Smiths ~ a great deal/do a great deal of ~ing,* often give dinner parties, etc. **2** amuse, interest: *We were all ~ed by his tricks.* **3** be ready to consider: *~ a proposal;* have in the mind: *~ ideas/doubts, etc.* **~·ing** *adj* pleasing; amusing. **~·ing·ly** *adv* **~·ment** *n* **1** [U] ~ing or being ~ed(**1**): *a hotel famous for its ~ment.* **2** [U] ~ing or being ~ed(**2**): *He fell into the water, much to the ~ment of the onlookers.* **3** [C] public performance (at a theatre, circus, etc). **~er** *n* person who ~s(**2**), esp professionally.

en·thral (also, esp US **en·thrall**) /ɪnˋθrɔl/ *vt* (-ll-) [VP6A] **1** take the whole attention of; please greatly: *~ed by an exciting story.* **2** enslave (usu fig): *~ed by a woman's beauty.*

en·throne /ɪnˋθrəʊn/ *vt* [VP6A] place a king, bishop on a throne; (fig) give a high place to, in one's judgement or affection: *a ruler ~d in the hearts of his subjects.* **~·ment** *n*

en·thuse /ɪnˋθjuz *US:* -ˋθuz/ *vi* [VP3A] ***~ over,*** (colloq) show enthusiasm for.

en·thusi·asm /ɪnˋθjuzɪæzm *US:* -ˋθu-/ *n* [U] strong feeling of admiration or interest: *arouse ~ in sb; a play that moved the audience to ~; feel no ~ for/about sth; an outburst of ~.* **en·thusi·ast** /ɪnˋθjuzɪæst *US:* -ˋθu-/ *n* person filled with ~ (*for* or *about* sth): *a sports enthusiast; an enthusiast for/about politics.*

en·thusi·as·tic /ɪnˈθjuzɪˋæstɪk *US:* -ˈθu-/ *adj* full of enthusiasm: *~ admirers of a film star; become ~ over sth.* **en·thusi·asti·cally** /-klɪ/ *adv*

en·tice /ɪnˋtɑɪs/ *vt* [VP6A,15A,17] tempt or persuade: *~ a young girl away from home; ~ sb into doing sth/to do sth wrong; ~ a man from his duty.* **~·ment** *n* [U] enticing or being ~d; [C] sth that ~s.

en·tire /ɪnˋtɑɪə(r)/ *adj* whole, complete; unbroken: *She was in ~ ignorance of what was being done. He enjoys our ~ confidence.* **~·ly** *adv* completely: *~ly unnecessary/different. My life is ~ly given up to work.* **~ty** /ɪnˋtɑɪərətɪ/ *n* (*pl* **-ties**) the state of being ~; completeness: *We must examine the question in its ~ty,* as a whole, not in parts only.

en·title /ɪnˋtɑɪtl/ *vt* **1** ***be ~d,*** have as a title: *a book ~d 'Adam Bede'.* **2** [VP14,17] ***~ sb to sth/to do sth,*** (of conditions, circumstances, qualities, etc) give a right (to): *If you fail three times, you are not ~d to try anymore.* **~·ment** *n*

en·tity /ˋentətɪ/ *n* (*pl* **-ties**) **1** [C] sth that has real existence; a thing's existence (contrasted with its qualities, relations, etc). **2** [U] being; existence.

en·tomb /ɪnˋtum/ *vt* [VP6A] place in a tomb; serve as a tomb for.

ento·mol·ogy /ˈentəˋmolədʒɪ/ *n* [U] the study of insects. **en·to·mol·ogist** /-dʒɪst/ *n* student of, expert in, ~. **en·to·mo·logi·cal** /ˈentəməˋlodʒɪkl/ *adj*

en·tour·age /ˈontʊˋrɑʒ/ *n* all those accompanying and attending on an important or high-ranking person: *the President and his ~.*

en·tr'acte /ˋõtrækt/ *n* [C] (performance in an) interval between acts in a play.

en·trails /ˋentreɪlz/ *n pl* bowels; intestines.

en·train /enˋtreɪn/ *vt,vi* [VP6A,2A] get, put troops, etc into a train.

en·trance[1] /ˋentrns/ *n* **1** [C] opening, gate, door, passage, etc by which one enters: *Visitors use the front ~; tradesmen and delivery boys use the back ~. The ~ to the cave had been blocked up.* **2** [C, U] coming or going in; coming of an actor upon the stage; entering: *the university ~ examination. E~ into/upon ministerial office requires a visit to the Queen. Actors must learn their ~s and exits,* when to come upon and leave the stage. **3** [C,U] right of entering: *to be refused ~.* **'~-fee, '~-money,** charge for admission.

en·trance² /ɪn'trɑns *US:* -'træns/ *vt* [VP6A] overcome, carry away as in a dream, with pleasure: *~d with the music. She stood ~d at the sight.*

en·trant /'entrnt/ *n* person who enters *to* a profession, *for* a competition, race, etc.

en·trap /ɪn'træp/ *vt* (-pp-) [VP6A] = trap (the usu word).

en·treat /ɪn'trit/ *vt* [VP6A,17,14] ask (sb) earnestly: *~ sb to show mercy; ~ a favour of sb. Stop pulling my hair, I ~ you.* **~·ing·ly** *adv*

en·treaty /ɪn'tritɪ/ *n* (*pl -ties*) [C,U] earnest request(ing): *deaf to all entreaties; with a look of ~.*

en·trée /'õtreɪ *US:* 'ontreɪ/ *n* **1** [U] right or privilege of admission. **2** [C] dish served between the fish and the meat course.

en·trench /ɪn'trentʃ/ *vt* [VP6A] **1** surround or protect with a trench or trenches: *The enemy were strongly ~ed on the other side of the river.* **~ *oneself,*** dig oneself into the ground. **2** establish firmly: *customs ~ed by tradition; ~ed clauses/provisions,* those (in a constitution(1)) which can be changed only by a special procedure. **~·ment** *n* trench made for defence.

entre·pot /'õtrəpəʊ/ *n* storehouse; commercial centre for the import, export, collection and distribution of goods.

entre·pre·neur /'õtrəprə'nɜ(r)/ *n* person who organizes and manages a commercial undertaking.

entre·sol /'õtrəsol/ *n* (F) = mezzanine.

en·trust /ɪn'trʌst/ *vt* [VP14] ***~ sth to sb, ~ sb with sth,*** trust sb to complete or safeguard sth: *Can I ~ the task to you/~ you with the task? Ought I to ~ to them such confidential and important plans?*

en·try /'entrɪ/ *n* [C] (*pl* **-ries**) **1** coming or going in: *the ~ of the USA into world politics. The army made a triumphal ~ into the town. Thieves had forced an ~ into the building.* **'~ visa,** ⇨ visa. **2** (place of) entrance; right of entering: *The sign ● means 'No ~'.* **3** item in a list; item noted in an account book: *dictionary entries; make an ~ of a transaction; book-keeping by double/single ~,* in which each item is entered twice (once) in a ledger. **bill of ~,** ⇨ bill³(6). **4** list, number, of persons, etc entering for a competition: *a large ~ for the 5000 metres race;* person or thing that is entered for a competition: *nearly fifty entries for the Marathon race.*

en·twine /ɪn'twɑɪn/ *vt* [VP6A,14] make by twining; curl (one thing) (*with* or *round* another).

enu·mer·ate /ɪ'njuməreɪt *US:* ɪ'nu-/ *vt* [VP6A] count, go through (a list of articles) naming them one by one. **enu·mer·ation** /ɪ'njumə'reɪʃn *US:* ɪ'nu-/ *n* [C] enumerating; [C] list.

enun·ci·ate /ɪ'nʌnsɪeɪt/ *vt,vi* **1** [VP6A,2A] say, pronounce (words): *He ~s (his words) clearly.* **2** express a theory, etc clearly or definitely. **enun·ci·ation** ɪ'nʌnsɪ'eɪʃn/ *n*

en·velop /ɪn'veləp/ *vt* [VP6A,14] ***~ (in),*** wrap up, cover, on all sides: *hills ~ed in mist; a baby ~ed in a shawl; ~ a subject in mystery.* **~·ment** *n*

en·vel·ope /'envələʊp/ *n* wrapper or covering, esp one made of paper for a letter; covering of a balloon or airship.

en·venom /ɪn'venəm/ *vt* [VP6A] put poison on or in, e g a weapon; (fig) fill with bitter hate: *~ed quarrels/tempers.*

en·vi·able /'envɪəbl/ *adj* causing envy; likely to excite envy (used both of the object and the person, etc, possessing it): *an ~ school record,* one of great success, etc; *an ~ woman,* e g one who has a kind, handsome and rich husband.

en·vi·ous /'envɪəs/ *adj* ***~ (of),*** full of envy; feeling envy; showing or expressing envy: *~ of sb's success; ~ looks; looking at sth with ~ eyes.* **~·ly** *adv*

en·viron /ɪn'vɑɪərn/ *vt* [VP6A] (formal) be in a position around; surround: *a town ~ed by/with forests.*

en·viron·ment /ɪn'vɑɪərnmənt/ *n* (collective *sing*) surroundings, circumstances, influences: *Students of social problems investigate the home, social and moral ~(s) of different classes of people.* **'Department of the 'E~,** (in GB, since 1971, formerly the Ministries of Housing and Local Government) department responsible for land planning, construction industries, transport, preservation of public amenities, control of air and water pollution, the protection of the coast and the countryside. **~al** /ɪn'vɑɪərən'mentl/ *adj* **~·ally** /-tlɪ/ *adv*

en·virons /'envɪrənz/ *n pl* districts surrounding a town, etc: *Berlin and its ~.*

en·vis·age /ɪn'vɪzɪdʒ/ *vt* [VP6A] face danger, facts, etc; picture in the mind (esp under a particular aspect): *He had not ~d the matter in that light.*

en·voy¹ (also **en·voi**) /'envɔɪ/ *n* [C] concluding part of a poem, esp a short stanza at the end of some archaic forms of poetry.

en·voy² /'envɔɪ/ *n* messenger, esp one sent on a special mission; diplomatic agent next in rank below an ambassador.

envy¹ /'envɪ/ *n* [U] **1** ***~ at sth/of sb,*** feeling of disappointment and ill will (at another's better fortune): *He was filled with ~ at my success. My success excited his ~. They say such scandalous things about you out of ~.* **2** object of such feeling: *His splendid new car was the ~ of all his friends/an object of ~ to all his friends.*

envy² /'envɪ/ *vt* (*pt,pp* **-vied**) [VP6A,12C] feel envy of: *I ~ you. I ~ your good fortune. I don't ~ him his bad-tempered wife,* am glad I am not married to her.

en·wrap /ɪn'ræp/ *vt* (-pp-) = wrap (the more usu word).

en·zyme /'enzɑɪm/ *n* [C] organic chemical substance (a catalyst) formed in living cells, able to cause changes in other substances without being changed itself.

eon /'ɪən/ *n* = aeon.

ep·aulet (also **ep·aul·ette**) /'epəlet/ *n* shoulder ornament on a naval or military officer's uniform.

épée /eɪ'peɪ/ *n* sharp-pointed slender sword used in fencing.

ephem·eral /ɪ'femrl/ *adj* living, lasting, for a very short time.

epic /'epɪk/ *n, adj* (poetic account) of the deeds of one or more great heroes, or of a nation's past history, e g Homer's *Iliad.*

epi·centre (US = **-center**) /'epɪsentə(r)/ *n* part of the earth's centre above the origin or focus of an earthquake.

epi·cure /ˈepɪkjʊə(r)/ *n* person who understands the pleasures to be had from delicate eating and drinking.

epi·cur·ean /ˈepɪkjʊˈrɪən/ *n, adj* (person) devoted to pleasure (esp refined sensuous enjoyment): *an ~ feast.*

epi·demic /ˈepɪˈdemɪk/ *n, adj* (disease) spreading rapidly among many people in the same place for a time: *an influenza ~.* ⇨ **endemic.**

epi·der·mis /ˈepɪdɜmɪs/ *n* [U] outer layer of the skin.

epi·dia·scope /ˈepɪˈdɑɪəskəʊp/ *n* optical lantern which projects on a screen transparent objects (e g film-strip) and opaque objects (e g coins, pictures).

epi·glot·tis /ˈepɪˈglotɪs/ *n* structure of tissue at the root of the tongue, lowered during swallowing to prevent food, etc from entering the windpipe. ⇨ the illus at **head.**

epi·gram /ˈepɪgræm/ *n* short poem or saying expressing an idea in a clever and amusing way. **~·matic** /ˈepɪgrəˈmætɪk/ *adj* short and witty in expression; (of a person) fond of making ~s.

epi·lepsy /ˈepɪlepsɪ/ *n* [U] nervous disease causing a person to fall unconscious (often with violent involuntary movements). **epi·lep·tic** /ˈepɪˈleptɪk/ *adj* of ~: *an epileptic fit.* □ *n* person suffering from ~.

epi·logue (US = **-log**) /ˈepɪlog *US:* -lɔg/ *n* last part of a literary work, esp a poem spoken by an actor at the end of a play; (radio, TV) religious programme at the end of the day's transmission.

Epiph·any /ɪˈpɪfənɪ/ *n* commemoration (6 Jan) of the coming of the Magi /ˈmeɪdʒɑɪ/ to Jesus at Bethlehem. Cf *Twelfth Night.*

epis·co·pal /ɪˈpɪskəpl/ *adj* of, governed by, bishops: *the E~ Church,* the Church of England; *the Protestant E~ Church in the US.* **epis·co·pa·lian** /eˈpɪskəˈpeɪlɪən/ *n, adj* (member) of an ~ church.

epi·sode /ˈepɪsəʊd/ *n* [C] (description of) one event in a chain of events. **epi·sodic** /ˈepɪˈsodɪk/ *adj*

epistle /ɪˈpɪsl/ *n* letter (but now only humorously of ordinary letters). **the E~s,** letters included in the New Testament, written by the Apostles. **epis·tol·ary** /ɪˈpɪstələrɪ *US:* -lerɪ/ *adj* of, carried on by, letters.

epi·taph /ˈepɪtɑf *US:* -tæf/ *n* [C] words describing a dead person (as cut on his tombstone).

Shakespeare's epitaph

epi·thet /ˈepɪθet/ *n* adjective or descriptive phrase used to indicate the character of sb or sth, as in 'Alfred the *Great*'.

epit·ome /ɪˈpɪtəmɪ/ *n* short summary of a book, speech, etc; sth which shows, on a small scale, the characteristics of sth much larger. **epit·om·ize** /ɪˈpɪtəmɑɪz/ *vt* [VP6A] make or be an ~ of.

ep·och /ˈipok *US:* ˈepək/ *n* (beginning of a) period of time in history, life, etc marked by special events or characteristics: *Einstein's theory marked a new ~ in mathematics.* **ˈ~-making,** beginning a new ~: *an ~-making discovery,* e g of America by Columbus.

Ep·som salts /ˈepsəm ˈsɔlts/ *n pl* hydrated magnesium sulphate **($MgSo_4$),** used medically to empty the bowels.

equable /ˈekwəbl/ *adj* steady; regular; not changing much: *an ~ climate/temper.* **equably** /ˈekwəblɪ/ *adv*

equal /ˈikwl/ *adj* **1** the same in size, amount, number, degree, value, etc: *~ pay for ~ work; ~ opportunity; ~ in ability; divide sth into two ~ parts; two boys of ~ height. He speaks English and Arabic with ~ ease. Things which are ~ to the same thing are ~ to one another.* **2 ~ to,** (with *n* or gerund) having strength, courage, ability, etc for: *He was ~ to the occasion,* was able to deal with it. *She did not feel ~ to receiving visitors.* □ *n* person or thing ~ to another: *Is he your ~ in strength? Mix with your ~s or betters, not your inferiors. Let x be the ~ of y.* □ *vt* (-ll-, US also -l-) [VP6A,15A] be ~ to: *He ~s me in strength but not in intelligence. He is ~led by no one in strength.* **~ly** /ˈikwlɪ/ *adv* in an ~ manner; in ~ shares: *~ly clever. Divide it ~ly.* **~·ity** /ɪˈkwolətɪ/ *n* [U] the state of being ~: *on an ~ity (with),* on ~ terms (with). **~i·tarian** /ɪˈkwoləˈteərɪən/ *n* = **egalitarian. ~·ize** /ˈikwəlɑɪz/ *vt* [VP6A] make ~: *~ize incomes.* **~·iz·ation** /ˈikwəlɑɪˈzeɪʃn *US:* -lɪˈz-/ *n*

equa·nim·ity /ˈekwəˈnɪmətɪ/ *n* [U] calmness of mind or temper: *bear misfortune with ~; disturb sb's ~.*

equate /ɪˈkweɪt/ *vt* [VP6A,14] **~ *with,*** consider, treat (one thing as being equal): (maths) *~ two quantities.*

equa·tion /ɪˈkweɪʒn/ *n* **1** (maths) [C] statement of equality between two expressions by the sign (=) as in: $2x + 5 = 11$. **2** [U] making equal, balancing, e g of demand and supply.

equa·tor /ɪˈkweɪtə(r)/ *n* imaginary line round the earth; line drawn on maps to represent points at an equal distance from the north and south poles. the illus at **projection. equa·tor·ial** /ˈekwəˈtɔrɪəl/ *adj* of or near the ~: *equatorial Africa.*

equerry /ɪˈkwerɪ/ *n* (*pl* -ries) officer in the court of a ruler; officer in attendance on a member of the royal family.

eques·trian /ɪˈkwestrɪən/ *adj* of horse-riding: *~ skill; an ~ statue,* of a person on horseback. □ *n* person clever at horse-riding: ~ performer.

equi·dis·tant /ˈikwɪˈdɪstənt/ *adj* separated by equal distance(s) (*from*).

equi·lat·eral /ˈikwɪˈlætrl/ *adj* having all sides equal: *an ~ triangle.*

equi·lib·rium /ˈikwɪˈlɪbrɪəm/ *n* [U] state of being balanced: *maintain/lose one's ~; scales* (on a balance) *in ~.*

equine /ˈekwɑɪn/ *adj* of, like, a horse; of horses.

equi·noc·tial /ˈikwɪˈnokʃl/ *adj* of, at or near, the equinox: *~ gales/tides.*

equi·nox /ˈikwɪnoks/ *n* time of the year at which the sun crosses the equator and when day and night are of equal length: *the spring* (= vernal) *~,* 20 Mar; *the autumnal ~,* 22 or 23 Sept.

equip /ɪˈkwɪp/ *vt* (-pp-) [VP6A,14] ***~ sb (with, sth) (for sth),*** supply (a person, oneself, a ship, etc) (with what is needed, for a purpose): *~ oneself for a task; ~ a ship for a voyage; ~ soldiers with uniforms and weapons.* **~·ment** *n* [U] **1** ~ping or being ~ped: *The ~ment of his laboratory took time and money.* **2** (collective *noun*) things needed for a purpose: *a factory with modern ~ment; 'radar ~ment.*

equi·page /'ekwɪpɪdʒ/ *n* [C] carriage, horses and attendants (of a rich person in former times).

equi·poise /'ekwɪpɔɪz/ *n* [U] equilibrium; [C] thing that counterbalances.

equi·table /'ekwɪtəbl/ *adj* fair; just; reasonable. **equi·tably** /-blɪ/ *adv*

equity /'ekwətɪ/ *n* **1** [U] fairness; right judgement; (esp, English law) principles of justice outside common law or Statute law, used to correct laws when these would apply unfairly in special circumstances. **2** (*pl*) (**-ties**) ordinary stocks and shares not bearing fixed interest.

equiv·al·ent /ɪ'kwɪvələnt/ *adj* equal in value, amount, meaning: *What is $5 ~ to in French francs?* □ *n* sth that is ~: *Is there a French word that is the exact ~ of the English word 'home'?* **equiv·al·ence** /-əns/ *n* [U] being ~; [C] sth that is ~.

equivo·cal /ɪ'kwɪvəkl/ *adj* **1** having a double or doubtful meaning; open to doubt: *an ~ reply.* **2** questionable; suspicious: *an ~ success.* **equivo·ca·tion** /ɪˌkwɪvə'keɪʃn/ *n* **1** [U] the use of ~ statements to mislead people. **2** [C] ~ expression.

era /'ɪərə/ *n* [C] period in history, starting from a particular time or event: *the Christian era.*

eradi·cate /ɪ'rædɪkeɪt/ *vt* [VP6A] pull up by the roots; destroy or put an end to: *~ crime/typhoid fever.* **eradi·ca·tion** /ɪˌrædɪ'keɪʃn/ *n*

erase /ɪ'reɪz *US:* ɪ'reɪs/ *vt* [VP6A] rub or scrape out: *~ pencil marks.* **eraser** *n* thing used to ~: *a pencil ~r* (usu *rubber*). **eras·ure** /ɪ'reɪʒə(r)/ *n* [U] erasing; [C] sth ~d; place where sth has been ~d.

ere /eə(r)/ *adv, prep* (old use, or poet) before.

erect[1] /ɪ'rekt/ *adj* upright; standing on end: *stand ~; hold a banner ~.* **~·ly** *adv* **~·ness** *n*

erect[2] /ɪ'rekt/ *vt* [VP6A] **1** build, set up: establish: *~ a monument; ~ a statue (to sb); ~ a tent.* **2** set upright: *~ a flagstaff (a mast).* **erec·tile** /ɪ'rektaɪl *US:* -tl/ *adj* (physiol) (capable of) becoming rigid from dilation of the blood-vessels: *~ tissue.* **erec·tion** /ɪ'rekʃn/ *n* **1** [U] act of ~ing; state of being ~ed; (med) hardening and swelling of the penis or clitoris. **2** [C] sth ~ed; building or structure.

ere·mite /'erɪmaɪt/ *n* hermit.

erg /ɜg/ *n* unit of energy in the centimetre/gramme system. ⇨ App 5.

ergo /'ɜgəʊ/ *adv* (Lat) (usu hum) therefore.

ergo·nom·ics /ˌɜgə'nomɪks/ *n pl* (*sing v*) study of the environment, conditions and efficiency of workers.

Erin /'erɪn/ *n* (old name for) Ireland.

er·mine /'ɜmɪn/ *n* **1** small animal whose fur is brown in summer and white (except for its black-pointed tail) in winter. **2** [U] its fur; garment made of this fur: *dressed in ~; a gown trimmed with ~.*

erode /ɪ'rəʊd/ *vt* [VP6A] (of acids, rain, etc) wear away; eat into: *Metals are ~d by acids.* **ero·sion** /ɪ'rəʊʒn/ *n* [U] eroding or being ~d: *soil erosion,* by wind and rain; *coast erosion,* by the sea. **ero·sive** /ɪ'rəʊsɪv/ *adj*

erogen·ous /ɪ'rodʒənəs/ *adj* (esp in): **ˌ~ 'zone,** area of the body particularly sensitive to sexual stimulation.

erotic /ɪ'rotɪk/ *adj* of sexual love or desire. **erot·ica** /ɪ'rotɪkə/ *n pl* books, pictures, etc intended to arouse sexual desire. **eroti·cism** /ɪ'rotɪsɪzm/ *n* [U] sexual excitement or desire.

err /ɜ(r) *US:* eər/ *vi* [VP2A,C] make mistakes; do or be wrong: (Biblical style) *We have erred from Thy ways like lost sheep. It is better to err on the side of mercy,* be too merciful than too severe.

er·rand /'erənd/ *n* **1** short journey to take or get sth, e g a message, goods from a shop: *to go on ~s for sb; to run ~s; send a child on an ~.* **'~-boy** *n* boy employed to run ~s. **2** object or purpose of such a journey. ***a fool's ~,*** one with no real or useful purpose.

er·rant /'erənt/ *adj* erring; mistaken: *an ~ husband,* one who is unfaithful to his wife.

er·ratic /ɪ'rætɪk/ *adj* **1** (of a person or his behaviour) irregular in behaviour or opinion; likely to do unusual or unexpected things. **2** (of things, e g a clock) uncertain in movement; irregular. **er·rati·cally** /-klɪ/ *adv*

er·ratum /e'rɑtəm/ *n* (*pl* **-ta** /-tə/) error in printing or writing: *an errata slip,* list of errors, misprints, etc in a printed book.

er·roneous /ɪ'rəʊnɪəs/ *adj* incorrect; mistaken. **~·ly** *adv*

er·ror /'erə(r)/ *n* **1** [C] sth done wrong; mistake: *spelling ~s; printer's ~s,* misprints; *an ~ of judgement; a clerical ~,* made in writing. **2** [U] condition of being wrong in belief or conduct: *fall/lead sb into ~; do sth in ~,* by mistake.

Erse /ɜs/ *n* name given by Lowland Scots to the dialect of Gaelic spoken in the West Highlands; sometimes used for Irish Gaelic.

eruc·ta·tion /ˌirʌk'teɪʃn/ *n* [C] belching, e g of a volcano.

eru·dite /'erʊdaɪt/ *adj* (formal) having, showing, great learning; scholarly. **~·ly** *adv* **eru·di·tion** /ˌerʊ'dɪʃn/ *n* [U].

erupt /ɪ'rʌpt/ *vi* [VP2A] (esp of a volcano) break out. **erup·tion** /ɪ'rʌpʃn/ *n* [C,U] outbreak of a volcano; (fig) of war, disease, etc: *~ions of ashes and lava; in a state of ~ion.*

ery·sip·elas /ˌerɪ'sɪpləs/ *n* skin disease that causes fever and produces deep red inflammation.

es·ca·late /'eskəleɪt/ *vt,vi* **1** [VP6A] intensify, enlarge, e g a war. **2** [VP2A] increase in intensity or extent. **es·ca·la·tion** /ˌeskə'leɪʃn/ *n*

es·ca·la·tor /'eskəleɪtə(r)/ *n* moving stairway carrying people up or down between floors or different levels.

es·ca·pade /ˌeskə'peɪd/ *n* [C] daring, mischievous or adventurous act, often one causing gossip or trouble.

es·cape[1] /ɪ'skeɪp/ *n* **1** [C,U] (act of) escaping; fact of having escaped: *E~ from Dartmoor prison is difficult. There have been very few successful ~s from this prison. I congratulate you on your ~ from the shipwreck. Don't look for an ~ of gas with a naked light.* **'~ velocity,** the speed at which a projectile or spacecraft must travel in order to leave (e g the earth's) gravitational field. **2** [C] means of escape: *a 'fire-~; an '~-pipe/-valve,* for carrying off steam or water. **3** (sth that provides) temporary distraction from reality or dull routine (e g through music, reading). **es·capee** /ɪˌskeɪ'pɪ/ *n* (esp) prisoner who has ~d. **es·cap·ism** /-ɪzm/ *n* [U] habit of escaping from unpleasant realities into a world of fancy. **es·cap·ist** /-ɪst/ *n* person whose conduct is characterized by escapism: (attrib) *escapist literature.*

es·cape[2] /ɪ'skeɪp/ *vi,vt* **1** [VP2A,3A] **~ *(from),*** get free; get away; (of steam, fluids, etc) find a way out: *Two of the prisoners have ~d. The* *canary has ~d from its cage. Is the gas escaping somewhere? Make a hole and let the water ~.* **2** [VP6A,C,2A] avoid; keep free or safe from: *You were lucky to ~ punishment/being punished. Where can we go to ~ the crowds? How can we ~ observation/being seen?* **3** [VP6A] be forgotten or unnoticed by: *His name ~s me for the moment,* I cannot recall it.

es·cape·ment /ɪˋskeɪpmənt/ *n* [C] device in a clock or watch to regulate the movement.

es·carp·ment /ɪˋskɑpmənt/ *n* steep slope or cliff separating two areas of different levels.

es·cha·tol·ogy /ˈeskəˋtolədʒɪ/ *n* [U] branch of theology concerned with last things (the final end of mankind, judgement, heaven and hell).

es·chew /ɪˋstʃu/ *vt* [VP6A] (formal) avoid (the more usu word); keep oneself away from, abstain from: *~ wine/evil.*

es·cort[1] /ˋeskɔt/ *n* [C] **1** one or more persons going with another or others, or with valuable goods, to protect them, or as an honour: *an ~ of soldiers; under police ~.* **2** one or more ships, aircraft, etc giving protection or honour: *When the Queen sailed, her yacht had an ~ of ten destroyers and fifty aircraft.* **3** person or persons accompanying sb for courtesy's sake: *Mary's ~ to the ball.*

es·cort[2] /ɪˋskɔt/ *vt* [VP6A,15B] go with as an escort: *a convoy of merchant ships ~ed by destroyers. Who will ~ this young lady home?*

es·cri·toire /ˈeskrɪˋtwɑ(r)/ *n* writing-desk with drawers for stationery.

es·cu·lent /ˋeskjʊlənt/ *n, adj* (in horticulture, etc) (thing) fit for food.

es·cutcheon /ɪˋskʌtʃən/ *n* shield with a coat of arms on it: *a blot on one's ~,* a stain on one's reputation. ⇨ the illus at armour.

Es·kimo /ˋeskɪməʊ/ *n* (*pl* -mos or -moes /-məʊz/), member of a race living in the Arctic regions of N America.

esopha·gus /iˋsofəgəs/ *n* (also **oes·oph·agus**) (anat) passage from the pharynx to the stomach; gullet. the illus at alimentary, head.

eso·teric /ˈesəˋterɪk/ *adj* intended only for those who are initiated, for a small circle of disciples or followers; abstruse.

es·palier /ɪˋspælɪeɪ/ *n* (tree or shrub trained on) a trellis or a wire framework.

es·pecial /ɪˋspeʃl/ *adj* particular; exceptional: *a question of ~ importance; for your ~ benefit.* **in ~,** above all. **~·ly** /-ʃlɪ/ *adv* to an exceptional degree; in particular: *She likes the country, ~ly in spring.*

Es·per·anto /ˈespəˋræntəʊ/ *n* [U] an artificial language designed for world use.

espion·age /ˋespɪənɑʒ/ *n* [U] practice of spying or using spies.

es·pla·nade /ˋespləneɪd/ *n* [C] level area of ground where people may walk or ride for pleasure, often by the sea.

es·pouse /ɪˋspaʊz/ *vt* [VP6A] **1** give one's support to (a cause, theory, etc). **2** (old use; of a man) marry. **es·pousal** /ɪˋspaʊzl/ *n* **1** espousing (of a cause, etc). **2** (old use; usu *pl*) marriage or betrothal.

es·presso /eˋspresəʊ/ *n* **ˈ~ ˋcoffee,** coffee made by forcing boiling water under pressure through ground coffee.

esprit /ˋespri *US:* ˈeˋspri/ *n* [U] lively wit. **~ de corps** /eˈspri də ˋkɔ(r)/ *n* spirit of loyalty and devotion which unites the members of a group or society.

espy /ɪˋspɑɪ/ *vt* (*pt,pp* -pied) [VP6A] catch sight of.

Es·qui·mau /ˋeskɪməʊ/ *n* (*pl* -maux /-məʊz/) = Eskimo.

Es·quire /ɪˋskwɑɪə(r) *US:* ˋes-/ *n* title of courtesy (used in GB and written *Esq*, esp in the address of a letter after a man's family name instead of *Mr* before it).

es·say /ɪˋseɪ/ *vt,vi* [VP6A,4A] try; attempt: *~ a task; ~ to do sth.* □ *n* /ˋeseɪ/ **1** piece of writing, usu short and in prose, on any one subject. **2** testing or trial of the value or nature of sth. **3** attempt. **~·ist** /-ɪst/ *n* writer of ~s(1).

es·sence /ˋesns/ *n* **1** [U] that which makes a thing what it is; the inner nature or most important quality of a thing: *Is the ~ of morality right intention? Caution is the ~ of that man's character. What you say is the ~ of nonsense. The two things are the same in outward form but different in ~.* **2** [C,U] extract obtained from a substance by taking out as much of the mass as possible, leaving all its important qualities in concentrated form: *meat ~s; ~ of peppermint.*

es·sen·tial /ɪˋsenʃl/ *adj* **1** necessary; indispensable; most important: *Is wealth ~ to happiness? Exercise, fresh air and sleep are ~ for the preservation of health. 'Wanted, a good cook: long experience ~.'* **2** of an essence(2): *~ oils.* **3** fundamental: *Love of fair play is said to be an ~ part of the English character.* □ *n* [C] fundamental element: *the ~s of English grammar. We've time to pack only the basic ~s,* the minimum amount (of clothes, etc) that is necessary. **~·ly** /ɪˋsenʃlɪ/ *adv* in an ~(3) manner: *We are an ~ly peace-loving people.*

es·tab·lish /ɪˋstæblɪʃ/ *vt* [VP6A,14,16B] **1** set up, put on a firm foundation: *~ a new state/government/business.* **2** settle, place a person, oneself in a position, office, place, etc: *We are now comfortably ~ed in our new house. Mr X was ~ed as governor of the province.* **3** cause people to accept a belief, claim, custom, etc: *He succeeded in ~ing a claim to the title. Newton conclusively ~ed the law of gravity. E~ed customs are difficult to change. His honesty is well ~ed.* **4** make (a church) national by law.

es·tab·lish·ment /ɪˋstæblɪʃmənt/ *n* **1** [U] establishing or being established: *the ~ of a new state.* **2** [C] that which is established, e g a large organized body of persons (in the army or navy, a civil service, a business firm, with many employees, a hotel and the staff in it): *He keeps a large ~,* a household with many servants, etc; a private ~, (usu small and) owned by individuals rather than shareholders. **3** *Church E~, the E~,* church system established by law. **4 the E~,** (GB) those persons in positions of power and authority, exercising influence in the background of public life or other field of activity.

es·tami·net /eˋstæmɪneɪ *US:* eˈstæmɪˋneɪ/ *n* (F) small French café selling beer, wine, coffee, etc.

es·tate /ɪˋsteɪt/ *n* **1** [C] piece of property in the form of land, esp in the country: *He owns large ~s in Scotland.* **ˋ~ agent,** person who buys and sells buildings and land for others. ⇨ (US) realtor. **ˋhousing ~,** area of land on which many houses are built, either by private enterprise or (*ˋcouncil ~*) by a public authority. **inˋdustrial ~,** area of land development for industrial use (factories, etc). **2** [U] (legal) a person's whole property. **ˈreal ~,** land and buildings. **ˈpersonal ~,** money and other kinds of property. **3** [C] political or social group or class: *the three ~s of the realm,* the Lords Spiritual (Bishops in the House of Lords), *the Lords Temporal* (other lords) *and the Commons* (the common people); *the fourth ~,* the press(3). **4** (old use) condition; stage in life: *reach man's ~; the holy ~ of matrimony.* **5 ˈ~ car,** saloon-type motor-vehicle with removable or collapsible rear seats and door(s) at the back, for easy loading of luggage, etc. Cf (US) *station-wagon.*

es·teem /ɪˈstim/ *vt* **1** [VP6A] have a high opinion of; respect greatly: *No one can ~ your father more than I do.* **2** [VP25] consider; regard: *I shall ~ it a favour if…; I ~ it a privilege to address this audience.* □ *n* [U] high regard: *He lowered himself in our ~ by this foolish behaviour. We all hold him in great ~.*

es·thetic ⇨ aesthetic.

es·ti·mable /ˈestɪməbl/ *adj* worthy of esteem.

es·ti·mate[1] /ˈestɪmət/ *n* [C] judgement; approximate calculation (of size, cost, etc): *I hope the builders don't exceed their ~. I do not know enough about him to form an ~ of his abilities. Can you give me a rough ~ of the cost?* ⇨ rough[1](3). **the E~s,** figures supplied each year by the Chancellor of the Exchequer showing the probable national expenditure, etc.

es·ti·mate[2] /ˈestɪmeɪt/ *vt,vi* [VP9,14,3A] form a judgement about; calculate the cost, value, size, etc of sth: *The firm ~d the cost of the new house at £8 000. We ~ that it would take three months to finish the work. Ask a contractor to ~ for the repair of the building.*

es·ti·ma·tion /ˌestɪˈmeɪʃn/ *n* [U] judgement; regard: *in my ~; in the ~ of most people.*

es·trange /ɪˈstreɪndʒ/ *vt* [VP6A,14] bring about a separation in feeling and sympathy: *foolish behaviour that ~d all his friends; ~ sb from his friends. He is ~d from his wife,* living apart from her. **~·ment** *n* [U] being ~d; [C] instance of this: *cause an ~ment between two old friends.*

es·tu·ary /ˈestʃʊərɪ *US:* -ʊerɪ/ *n* (*pl* **-ries**) [C] river mouth into which the tide flows: *the Thames ~.*

et cet·era /ɪt ˈsetrə *US:* et/ (Lat, usu shortened to **etc**) and other things; and so on.

etch /etʃ/ *vt,vi* [VP6A,2A] use a needle and acid to make a picture, etc on a metal plate from which copies may be printed; make (pictures, etc) in this way. **~er** *n* person who ~es. **~·ing** *n* [U] the art of the ~er; [C] copy printed from an ~ed plate.

eter·nal /ɪˈtɜnl/ *adj* **1** without beginning or end; lasting for ever: *the E~ God; the E~ City,* Rome. *The Christian religion promises ~ life.* **2** (colloq) unceasing; too frequent: *Stop this ~ chatter.* ***the ~ triangle,*** situation of conflict in which two men want the same woman or two women the same man. **~ly** /ɪˈtɜnļɪ/ *adv* throughout all time; for ever: (colloq) (too) frequently.

eter·nity /ɪˈtɜnətɪ/ *n* (*pl* **-ties**) **1** [U] time without end; the future life: *send a man to ~,* to his death. **2** [U] (with *indef art*) period of time that seems endless: *It seemed an ~ before news of his safety reached her.* **3** (*pl*) eternal truths.

ether /ˈiθə(r)/ *n* [U] **1** liquid made from alcohol, used in industry, and medically as an anaesthetic. **2** medium(3) through which, it was once believed, light waves were transmitted through all space. **3** (poet) the pure, upper air above the clouds.

eth·ereal /ɪˈθɪərɪəl/ *adj* **1** of unearthly delicacy; seeming too light or spiritual for this world: *~ beauty/music; the ~ figure of an angel.* **2** of the pure upper air above the clouds.

ethic /ˈeθɪk/ *n* (with *indef art*) system of moral principles, rules of conduct: *Was Islam in Turkey a traditional social code or an ~ for living?* **eth·ics** *n pl* **(a)** (with *sing v*) science of morals. **(b)** (with *pl*) moral soundness: *E~s is a branch of philosophy. The ~s of his decision are doubtful.* **ethi·cal** /-kl/ *adj* of morals or moral questions: *an ~ basis for education.* **ethi·cally** /-klɪ/ *adv*

eth·nic /ˈeθnɪk/, **eth·ni·cal** /-kl/ *adj* of race or the races of mankind. **eth·ni·cally** /-ɪklɪ/ *adv*

eth·nogra·phy /eθˈnogrəfɪ/ *n* [U] scientific description of the races of mankind. **eth·nogra·pher** /eθˈnogrəfə(r)/ *n* **eth·no·graphic** /ˌeθnəˈgræfɪk/ *adj*

eth·nol·ogy /eθˈnolədʒɪ/ *n* [U] science of the races of mankind, their relations to one another, etc. **eth·nol·o·gist** /-dʒɪst/ *n* student of, expert in, ~. **eth·no·logi·cal** /ˌeθnəˈlodʒɪkl/ *adj* of ~.

ethos /ˈiθos/ *n* characteristics of a community or of a racial culture; code of values by which a group or society lives.

ethyl /ˈeθɪl/ *n*: *~ alcohol,* anti-knock additive.

eti·ol·ogy /ˌitɪˈolədʒɪ/ *n* assignment of a cause; (med) study of the causes of disease.

eti·quette /ˈetɪket/ *n* [U] rules for formal relations or behaviour among people, or in a class of society or a profession: *medical/legal ~.*

ety·mol·ogy /ˌetɪˈmolədʒɪ/ *n* **1** [U] science of the origin and history of words. **2** [C] account of the origin and history of a word. **ety·mol·ogist** /-dʒɪst/ *n* student of ~. **ety·mo·logi·cal** /ˌetɪməˈlodʒɪkl/ *adj* of ~.

euca·lyp·tus /ˌjukəˈlɪptəs/ *n* sorts of tall evergreen tree (including the Australian gum tree) from which an oil, used for colds, is obtained.

Eu·char·ist /ˈjukərɪst/ *n* **the E~,** Holy Communion; the bread and wine taken at this.

Eu·clid·ean /juˈklɪdɪən/ *adj* of the geometric principles of Euclid /ˈjuklɪd/ (about 300 BC) the Greek mathematician.

eu·gen·ics /juˈdʒenɪks/ *n pl* (*sing v*) science of the production of healthy offspring with the aim of improving the human race.

eu·lo·gize /ˈjulədʒaɪz/ *vt* [VP6A] (formal) praise highly in speech or writing. **eu·logist** /ˈjulədʒɪst/ *n* person who does this. **eu·logis·tic** /ˌjuləˈdʒɪstɪk/ *adj* giving or containing high praise. **eu·logy** /ˈjulədʒɪ/ *n* (*pl* **-gies**) [C,U] (speech or writing full of) high praise.

eu·nuch /ˈjunək/ *n* castrated man, esp one formerly employed in some Oriental courts.

eu·phem·ism /ˈjufəmɪzm/ *n* [C,U] (example of the) use of other, usu less exact but milder or less blunt, words or phrases in place of words required by truth or accuracy: *'Pass away' is a ~ for 'die'. 'Queer' is a modern ~ for 'homosexual'.* **eu·phem·is·tic** /ˌjufəˈmɪstɪk/ *adj* of the nature of ~: *euphemistic language/expression.* **eu·phe·mis·ti·cally** /-klɪ/ *adv*

eu·phony /ˈjufənɪ/ *n* [U] pleasantness of sound; [C,U] (*pl* **-nies**) pleasant sound.

eu·phoria /juˈfɔrɪə/ *n* [U] state of well-being and pleasant excitement. **eu·phoric** /juˈforɪk *US:* -ˈfɔr-/ *adj*

eu·phu·ism /ˈjufjuɪzm/ *n* [C] (instance of) elaborately artificial style of writing and speaking (as fashionable in England in the late 16th and early 17th cc).

Eur·asia /jʊəˈreɪʒɪə *US:* -ʒə/ *n* Europe and Asia. **Eur·asian** /jʊəˈreɪʒn/ *n, adj* (person) of mixed European and Asian parentage; of Europe and Asia.

eu·reka /jʊˈrikə/ *int* (Gk = 'I have it!') cry of triumph at a discovery.

eu·rhyth·mics (also **eu·ryth-**) /juˈrɪðmɪks/ *n pl* harmony of bodily movement, esp as a system of physical training with music.

Euro·dollar /ˈjʊərəʊdolə(r)/ *n* U S A dollars put in European banks to act as an international currency and help the financing of trade and commerce.

Euro·pean /ˈjʊərəˈpɪən/ *n, adj* (native) of Europe; happening in, extending over, Europe: *~ countries; a ~ reputation.*

Euro·vision /ˈjʊərəvɪʒn/ *n* European T V network.

Eu·sta·chian tube /juˈsteɪʃn ˈtjub *US:* tub/ *n* (anat) duct extending from the middle ear to the pharynx. ⇨ the illus at **ear**.

eu·tha·nasia /ˈjuθəˈneɪzɪə *US:* -ˈneɪʒə/ *n* [U] (bringing about of a) mercifully easy and painless death (for persons suffering from an incurable and painful disease).

evacu·ate /ɪˈvækjʊeɪt/ *vt* **1** [VP6A] (esp of soldiers) withdraw from; leave empty: *~ a fort/town.* **2** [VP6A,14] *~ (from/to),* remove (a person) from a place or district, e g one considered to be dangerous in time of war: *The women and children were ~d to the country.* **3** [VP6A] empty (*of* its contents, esp defecate). **evacu·ation** /ɪˈvækjʊˈeɪʃn/ *n* [U] evacuating or being ~d; [C] instance of this. **evacuee** /ɪˈvækjuˈi/ *n* person who is ~d(2).

evade /ɪˈveɪd/ *vt* [VP6A,C] **1** get, keep, out of the way of; *~ a blow/one's enemies/an attack.* **2** find a way of not doing sth: *~ paying income tax; ~ military service;* avoid answering (fully or honestly): *~ a question.*

evalu·ate /ɪˈvæljʊeɪt/ *vt* [VP6A] find out, decide, the amount or value of. **evalu·ation** /ɪˈvæljʊˈeɪʃn/ *n*

evan·escent /ˈivəˈnesnt *US:* ˈev-/ *adj* quickly fading; soon going from the memory: *~ political triumphs.* **evan·escence** /-sns/ *n*

evan·gelic /ˈivænˈdʒelɪk/, **evan·geli·cal** /-kl/ *adj* **1** of, according to, the teachings of the Gospel: *~ preaching.* **2** (usu *evangelical*) of the beliefs and teachings of those Protestants who maintain that the soul can be saved only by faith in the atoning death of Jesus Christ, and who deny that good works and sacraments are enough, in themselves, for salvation. **evan·gel·i·cal·ism** /-ɪzm/ *n*

evan·gel·ist /ɪˈvændʒəlɪst/ *n* **1** one of the writers (Matthew, Mark, Luke or John) of the Gospels. **2** preacher of the Gospel, esp one who travels and holds religious meetings wherever he goes, preaching to any who are willing to listen. **evan·gel·is·tic** /ɪˈvændʒəˈlɪstɪk/ *adj*

evap·or·ate /ɪˈvæpəreɪt/ *vt,vi* **1** [VP6A,2A] (cause to) change into vapour: *Heat ~s water. The water soon ~d.* **2** [VP6A] remove liquid from a substance, e g by heating: *~d milk.* **3** [VP2A] disappear; die: *His hopes ~d,* He no longer felt any hope. **evap·or·ation** /ɪˈvæpəˈreɪʃn/ *n*

evas·ion /ɪˈveɪʒn/ *n* **1** [U] evading: *~ of responsibility.* **2** [C] statement, excuse, etc made to evade sth; act of evading: *His answers to my questions were all ~s.*

evas·ive /ɪˈveɪsɪv/ *adj* tending, trying, to evade: *an ~ answer; take ~ action,* do sth in order to evade danger, etc. **~·ly** *adv* **~·ness** *n*

Eve /iv/ *n* (in the Bible story of the Creation) the first woman.

eve /iv/ *n* day or evening before a Church festival or any date or event; time just before anything: *Christmas Eve,* 24 Dec; *New Year's Eve,* 31 Dec; *on the eve of great events.*

even[1] /ˈivn/ *adj* **1** level; smooth: *A billiard-table must be perfectly ~.* **2** regular; steady; of unchanging quality: *His ~ breathing showed that he had got over his excitement. His work is not very ~.* **3** (of amounts, distances, values) equal: *Our scores are now ~. The two horses were ~ in the race.* ***be/get ~ with sb,*** have one's revenge on him. ***~ odds,*** chances which are the same for or against. ***break ~,*** (colloq) make neither a profit nor a loss. **4** (of numbers) that can be divided by two with no remainder: *The pages on the left side of a book have ~ numbers.* ⇨ **odd**. **5** equally balanced: *~-handed justice.* **6** (of temper, etc) equable; not easily disturbed: *an ~-tempered wife.* □ *vt* [VP6A,15B] *~ (up),* make ~ or equal: *That will ~ things up,* make them equal. **~·ly** *adv* **~·ness** *n*

even[2] /ˈivn/ *adv* **1** (used to invite a comparison between what is stated and what might have been the case, what might have happened, been done, etc): *He never ~ opened the letter* (so he certainly did not read it). *He didn't answer ~ my letter* (not to mention letters from others). *It was cold there ~ in July* (so you may imagine how cold it was in winter). *E~ a child can understand the book* (so adults can certainly do so). **2** ***~ if/though,*** (used to call attention to the extreme nature of what follows): *I'll get there ~ if I have to pawn my watch to get the railway fare. She won't leave the T V set, ~ though her husband is waiting for his supper.* **3** (with comparatives) still, yet: *You know ~ less about it than I do. You seem ~ more stupid than usual today.* **4** ***~ as,*** just at the time when: *E~ as I gave the warning the car skidded.* ***~ now/then,*** in spite of these or those circumstances, etc: *E~ now he won't believe me. E~ then he would not admit his mistake.* ***~ so,*** though that is the case: *It has many omissions; ~ so, it is quite a useful reference book.*

even[3] /ˈivn/ *n* (poet) evening. **ˈ~-song** *n* Evening Prayer in the Church of England. **ˈ~·tide** /-taɪd/ *n* (poet) evening.

even·ing /ˈivnɪŋ/ *n* **1** that part of the day between afternoon and nightfall: *a cool ~; musical ~s,* evenings given to playing or listening to music; *two ~s ago;* (no *prep*) *this/tomorrow/yesterday ~; in the ~; on Sunday ~; on the ~ of the 8th; one warm summer ~.* **2** (attrib): *an ~ paper,* published after the morning papers; **ˈ~ ˈstar,** the planet Venus. **ˈ~ dress,** dress as worn for formal occasions in the ~. **ˈ~ ˈprayer,** church service; vespers.

even·song /ˈivnsoŋ *US:* -sɔŋ/ ⇨ **even**[3].

event /ɪˈvent/ *n* **1** happening, usu sth important: *the chief ~s of 1976. It was quite an ~* (often used to suggest that what happened was on an unusual scale, memorable, etc). ***in the natural/normal/usual course of ~s,*** in the order in which things naturally happen. **2** fact of a thing happening: *in* *the ~ of his death,* if he dies; *in that ~,* if that happens, if that is the case; *in either ~,* whichever happens. ***in any ~,*** whatever happens. ***at all ~s,*** in any case. **3** outcome; result. **4** one of the races, competitions, etc in a sports programme: *Which ~s have you entered for?* **~·ful** /-fl/ *adj* full of notable ~s: *He had had an ~ful life. The past year has been ~ful.*

even·tide /ˋivntaɪd/ *n* ⇨ even³.

event·ual /ɪˋventʃʊəl/ *adj* coming at last as a result; ultimate: *his foolish behaviour and ~ failure.* **~·ly** /-tʃʊlɪ/ *adv* in the end. **~·ity** /ɪˈventʃʊˋælətɪ/ *n* (*pl* **-ties**) [C] possible event.

ever /ˋevə(r)/ *adv* **1** (usu in *neg* and *interr* sentences, and in sentences expressing doubt or conditions; usu placed with the *v*) at any time: *Nothing ~ happens in this village. Do you ~ wish you were rich? She seldom, if ~, goes to the cinema. If you ~ visit London....* **2** (with the present perfect tense, in questions) at any time up to the present: *Have you ~ been up in a balloon?* (Note that *ever* is not used in the answer: either 'Yes, I have' or 'No, never', etc.) **3** after a comparative or superlative: *It is raining harder than ~,* than it has been doing so far. *It is more necessary than ~* (= than it has been so far) *for all of us to work hard. This is the best work you have ~ done.* **4** (chiefly in phrases) at all times; continuously: *~ after; for ~ (and ~); ~ since I was a boy.* **5** (colloq) (used as an intensifier): *Work as hard as ~ you can. I'll tell her as soon as ~ she arrives.* (non-standard colloq) ***~ so, ~ such (a),*** very: *~ so rich; ~ such a rich man.* **6** (used after interrogatives) in the way that 'in the world', 'on earth' and 'the devil' are used (written and printed as a separate word): *When/Where/How ~ did you lose it? What ~ do you mean?* **7** ***did you ~!*** used to express surprise, incredulity, etc: *Well, did you ~ hear such nonsense!* ***As if... ~,*** used in a similar way: *As if he would ~ do such a thing!* He would certainly not do it! **8** (old use) always: *You will find me ~ at your service.* **9** (modern use): ***Yours ~,*** used at the end of a letter, informal or familiar style.

ever·green /ˋevəgrin/ *n, adj* (tree, shrub) having green leaves throughout the year: *The pine, cedar and spruce are ~s.* ⇨ deciduous.

ever·last·ing /ˈevəˋlɑstɪŋ *US:* -ˋlæst-/ *adj* **1** going on for ever: *~ fame/glory.* **the E~,** God. **2** repeated too often: *I'm tired of his ~ complaints.*

ever·more /ˈevəˋmɔ(r)/ *adv* for ever.

every /ˋevrɪ/ *adj* (used attrib with *sing* countable *nouns*; cf the use of *all* with *plural nouns* and uncountable *nouns*) **1** all or each one of: *I have read ~ book* (= all the books) *on that shelf. Not ~ horse* (= Not all horses) *can run fast.* **2** (Cf *every* and *each*. When *every* is used as in **1** above, attention is directed to the whole; when *each* is used, attention is directed to the unit or individual): *E~ boy in the class* (= All the boys, The whole class) *passed the examination.* Cf: *Each boy may have three tries.* **3** (not replaceable by *all* and the *plural noun*) each one of an indefinite number (the emphasis being on the unit, not on the total or whole): *He enjoyed ~ minute of his holiday. Such things do not happen ~ day. He spends ~ penny he earns.* **4** (used with abstract *nouns*) all possible; complete: *You have ~ reason to be satisfied. I have ~ reason/There is ~ reason to believe that.... There is ~ prospect of success.* **5** (used with cardinal and ordinal numbers, and with *other* and *few,* to indicate recurrence, or intervals in time or space): *Write on ~ other line,* on alternate lines. *There are buses to the station ~ ten minutes. I go there ~ other day/~ three days/~ third day/~ few days, etc. He was stopped ~ dozen yards by friends who wanted to congratulate him.* ***~ now and then/again,*** from time to time. **6** (used with, and placed after, possessives; replaceable by *all* and the *plural* with *all* preceding): *His ~ movement was watched,* All his movements.... *He tries to meet her ~ wish,* all her wishes. **7** (in phrases) ***~ bit,*** quite: *This is ~ bit as good as that.* ***~ time,*** **(a)** always: *Our football team wins ~ time.* **(b)** whenever: *E~ time I meet him, he tries to borrow money from me.* ***~ one of them/us/you,*** (placed at the end) without exception: *You deserve to be hanged, ~ one of you.* ***in ~ way,*** in all respects: *This is in ~ way better than that.* **~·body** /ˋevrɪbodɪ/, **~·one** /ˋevrɪwʌn/ *pron* ~ person: *In a small village ~one knows ~one else.* **~·day** /ˈevrɪˋdeɪ/ *adj* (attrib only) happening or used daily; common and familiar: *an ~day occurrence; in his ~day clothes.* **ˋ~·place** (US) (informal) = *~where.* **~·thing** /ˋevrɪθɪŋ/ *pron* **1** all things: *This shop sells ~thing needed for camping. Tell me ~thing about it.* **2** (in the predicate) thing of the greatest importance: *Money is ~thing to him. She's beautiful, I agree, but beauty is not ~thing.* **~·where** /ˋevrɪweə(r) *US:* -hweər/ *adv* in, at, to, ~ place: *I've looked ~where for it. E~where seemed to be quiet.*

evict /ɪˋvɪkt/ *vt* [VP14] ~ ***(from),*** expel (a tenant) (from a house or land) by authority of the law: *They were ~ed for not paying the rent.* **evic·tion** /ɪˋvɪkʃn/ *n* [U] ~ing or being ~ed; [C] instance of this.

evi·dence /ˋevɪdəns/ *n* **1** [U] anything that gives reason for believing sth, that makes clear or proves sth: *There wasn't enough ~ to prove him guilty. Have you any ~ for this statement? We cannot condemn him on such slight ~. The scientist must produce ~ in support of his theories.* ***(be) in ~,*** clearly or easily seen: *She's the sort of woman who likes to be very much in ~,* who likes to be seen and noticed. *Smith was nowhere in ~,* could not be seen anywhere. ***give/bear ~ of,*** show signs of: *When the ship reached port, it bore abundant ~ of the severity of the storm,* i e signs of damage. ***turn Queen's/King's/State's ~,*** (US) (of a criminal) give ~ in court against accomplices. **2** (used in *pl*) indication, mark, trace: *There were ~s of glacial action on the rocks.* □ *vt* [VP6A] (rare) prove by ~; be ~ of. *His answer ~d a guilty conscience.*

evi·dent /ˋevɪdənt/ *adj* plain and clear (to the eyes or mind): *It must be ~ to all of you that...; He looked at his twelve children with ~ pride.* **~·ly** *adv*

evil /ˋivl/ *adj* **1** wicked, sinful, bad, harmful: *~ men/thoughts; live an ~ life; the ˋE~ One,* the Devil. **ˈ~-minded** /-ˋmaɪndɪd/, having ~ thoughts and desires. **2** likely to cause trouble; bringing trouble or misfortune: *in an ~ hour; fall on ~ days; an ~* (= slanderous) *tongue.* ***~ eye,*** malicious look; supposed power to cause harm by a look or glance. □ *n* **1** [U] sin; wrong-doing: *return good for ~; the spirit of ~.* **ˋ~-doer** /duə(r)/ *n* person who does ~. **2** [C] ~ thing; disaster: *War, famine and flood are terrible ~s.* ***be/***

choose the lesser of two ~s, the less harmful of two bad choices. **~ly** /ˈivḷɪ/ *adv* in an ~ manner: *He eyed her ~ly.*

evince /ɪˋvɪns/ *vt* [VP6A,9] (formal) show that one has a feeling, quality, etc: *a child who ~s great intelligence.*

evis·cer·ate /ɪˋvɪsəreɪt/ *vt* [VP6A] disembowel.

evoca·tive /ɪˋvokətɪv/ *adj* that evokes, or is able to evoke: *~ words,* that call up memories, emotions, in addition to their ordinary meanings.

evoke /ɪˋvəʊk/ *vt* [VP6A] call up, bring out: *~ a spirit from the other world; ~ admiration/surprise/a smile/memories of the past.* **evo·ca·tion** /ˈivəʊˋkeɪʃn/ *n*

evol·ution /ˈivəluʃn *US:* ˈev-/ *n* **1** [U] process of opening out or developing: *the ~ of a plant from a seed. In politics England had preferred ~* (= gradual development) *to revolution* (= sudden or violent change). **2** [U] (theory of the) development of more complicated forms of life (plants, animals) from earlier and simpler forms. **3** [C] movement according to plan (of troops, warships, dancers, etc). **~·ary** /ˈivəluʃnrɪ *US:* ˈevəluʃṇerɪ/ *adj* of, being produced by, ~; developing.

evolve /ɪˋvolv/ *vi,vt* [VP2A,6A] (cause to) unfold; develop; be developed, naturally and (usu) gradually: *The American constitution was planned; the British constitution ~d. He has ~d a new plan/theory.*

ewe /ju/ *n* female sheep. ⇨ **ram.**

ewer /ˋjuə(r)/ *n* large wide-mouthed pitcher for holding water, e g as used with a basin on a washstand in a bedroom without a piped supply of water.

ex·acer·bate /ɪgˋzæsəbeɪt/ *vt* [VP6A] (formal) irritate (a person); aggravate (= make worse) pain, disease. **ex·acer·ba·tion** /ɪgˈzæsəˋbeɪʃn/ *n*

ex·act[1] /ɪgˋzækt/ *adj* **1** correct in every detail; free from error: *Give me his ~ words. What is the ~ size of the room? I want ~ directions for finding your house.* **2** capable of being precise: *~ sciences; an ~ memory; an ~ scholar.* **~·ly** *adv* **1** correctly; quite: *Your answer is ~ly right. That's ~ly* (= just) *what I expected.* **2** (as an answer or confirmation) quite so; just as you say. **~·ness** *n* **~i·tude** /ɪgˋzæktɪjud *US:* -tud/ *n* = *~ness.*

ex·act[2] /ɪgˋzækt/ *vt* [VP6A,14] ***~ (from),*** **1** demand and enforce payment of: *~ taxes (from people); ~ payment from a debtor.* **2** insist on: *~ obedience.* **3** (of circumstances) require urgently; make necessary: *work that ~s care and attention.* **~·ing** *adj* making great demands; severe; strict: *an ~ing piece of work; an ~ing master.* **ex·action** /ɪgˋzækʃn/ *n* **1** [U] ~ing of money, etc. **2** [C] that which is ~ed, esp a tax which is considered to be too high; a great demand (on one's time, strength, etc).

ex·ag·ger·ate /ɪgˋzædʒəreɪt/ *vt,vi* [VP6A,2A] stretch (a description) beyond the truth; make sth seem larger, better, worse, etc than it really is: *You ~ the difficulties. If you always ~, people will no longer believe you. He has an ~d sense of his own importance,* thinks he is far more important than he really is. **exag·ger·ation** /ɪgˈzædʒəˋreɪʃn/ *n* [U] exaggerating or being ~d; [C] ~d statement: *a story full of exaggerations.*

ex·alt /ɪgˋzɔlt/ *vt* [VP6A] **1** make high(er) in rank, great(er) in power or dignity. **2** praise highly. **~ed** *adj* dignified; ennobled: *a person of ~ed rank.* **exal·ta·tion** /ˈegzɔlˋteɪʃn/ *n* [U] (fig) elation; state of spiritual delight.

exam /ɪgˋzæm/ *n* (colloq abbr of) examination.

ex·am·in·ation /ɪgˈzæmɪˋneɪʃn/ *n* **1** [U] examining or being examined: *On ~, it was found that the signature was not genuine. The prisoner is still under ~,* being examined. **2** [C] instance of this, esp **(a)** a testing of knowledge or ability: *an ~ in mathematics; ~ questions/papers; an oral ~.* **(b)** an inquiry into or inspection of sth: *an ~ of a botanical specimen; an ~ of business accounts; an ~ of one's eyes.* **(c)** questioning by a lawyer in a law court: *an ~ of a witness.*

ex·am·ine /ɪgˋzæmɪn/ *vt* [VP6A,14] **1** look at carefully in order to learn about or from: *~ old records; have one's teeth/eyes ~d; ~ a new theory. She needs to have her head ~d,* (colloq) is foolish or impudent. **2** put questions to in order to test knowledge or get information: *~ pupils in Spanish/on their knowledge of Spanish; ~ a witness in a court of law.* **exam·iner** *n* person who ~s.

ex·ample /ɪgˋzɑmpl *US:* -ˋzæmpl/ *n* [C] **1** fact, thing, etc which illustrates or represents a general rule: *This dictionary has many ~s of how verbs are used.* ***for ~,*** by way of illustration: *Many great men have risen from poverty—Lincoln and Edison, for ~.* **2** specimen showing the quality of others in the same group or of the same kind: *This is a good ~ of Shelley's lyric poetry.* **3** thing or person, person's conduct, to be copied or imitated: *follow sb's ~; set an ~ to sb; set sb a good ~.* **4** warning: *Let this be an ~ to you.* ***make an ~ of sb,*** punish him as a warning to others.

ex·as·per·ate /ɪgˋzɑspəreɪt *US:* -ˋzæs-/ *vt* [VP6A] irritate; produce ill feeling in; make ill feeling, anger, etc worse: *~d by/at sb's stupidity. It is exasperating to lose a train by half a minute.* **exas·per·ation** /ɪgˈzɑspəˋreɪʃn *US:* -ˈzæs-/ *n* state of being ~d: *'Stop that noise', he cried out in exasperation.*

ex·ca·vate /ˋekskəveɪt/ *vt* [VP6A] make, uncover, by digging: *~ a trench/a buried city.* **ex·ca·vator** /-tə(r)/ *n* person engaged in, machine used for, excavating. **ex·ca·va·tion** /ˈekskəˋveɪʃn/ *n* [U] excavating or being ~d; [C] place that is being or has been ~d.

ex·ceed /ɪkˋsid/ *vt* [VP6A] **1** be greater than: *Their success ~ed all expectations. London ~s Glasgow in size and population.* **2** go beyond what is allowed, necessary or advisable: *~ the speed limit,* drive faster than is allowed; *~ one's instructions,* do more than one has authority to do. **~·ing·ly** *adv* extremely; to an unusual degree: *an ~ingly difficult problem.*

ex·cel /ɪkˋsel/ *vi,vt* (-ll-) ***~ in/at,*** **1** [VP2C,3A] do better than others, be very good: *He ~s in courage/as an orator. The school ~s in/at sport.* **2** [VP6A,15A] do better than; surpass (the more usu word): *He ~s all of us in/at tennis.*

ex·cel·lence /ˋeksḷəns/ *n* **1** [U] the quality of being excellent; great merit: *a prize for ~ in French; his ~ in/at all forms of sport.* **2** [C] thing or quality in which a person excels: *They do not recognize her many ~s.*

Ex·cel·lency /ˋeksḷənsɪ/ *n* (*pl* -cies) title of ambassadors, governors and their wives, and some other officers and officials: *Your/His/Her ~.*

ex·cel·lent /ˋeksḷənt/ *adj* very good; of high quality. **~·ly** *adv*

ex·cel·sior /ekˋselsɪɔ(r)/ *n* [U] (US) soft, fine

wood shavings used for packing easily damaged goods, e g glassware.

ex·cept[1] /ɪkˋsept/ *prep* **1** not including; but not: *He gets up early every day ~ Sunday. Nobody was late ~ me.* Cf: Five others were late *besides* me. *My papers seem to be everywhere ~ where they ought to be.* **2** *~ for,* (used when what is excluded is different from what is included): *Your essay is good ~ for the spelling.* (The comparison is between the spelling, which is not good, and other things, e g ideas, grammar, which are satisfactory). Cf *All the essays are good ~ John's.* **3** *~ that,* apart from the fact that: *She knew nothing about his journey ~ that he was likely to be away for three months.* □ *conj* (old or liter use) unless: (biblical style) *E~ ye be born again.*

ex·cept[2] /ɪkˋsept/ *vt* [VP6A,14] exclude (from); set apart (from a list, statement, etc): *When I say that the boys are lazy, I ~ Tom. All those who took part in the plot, nobody ~ed, were punished.* ***present company ~ed,*** not including those here present. **~·ing** *prep, conj* (used after *not, always* and *without*) leaving out; excluding: *the whole staff, not ~ing the heads of departments.*

ex·cep·tion /ɪkˋsepʃn/ *n* **1** [C] sb or sth that is excepted (not included): *You must all be here at 8 a m; I can make no ~s,* cannot excuse any of you. *I enjoyed all his novels with the ~ of his last. All men between 18 and 45 without ~ are expected to serve in the army during a war.* **2** [C] sth that does not follow the rule: *~s to a rule of grammar.* **3** [U] objection. ***take ~ to,*** object to, protest against; be offended by: *He took great ~ to what I said. She took ~ to the statement.* **~-able** /-əbl/ *adj* objectionable. **~al** /-ʃnl/ *adj* unusual; out of the ordinary: *weather that is ~al for June; ~al advantages.* **~·ally** /-ʃnlɪ/ *adv* unusually: *an ~ally clever boy.*

ex·cerpt /ˊeksɜpt/ *n* [C] passage, extract, from a book etc, e g one printed separately.

ex·cess /ɪkˋses/ *n* **1** [U] (and in *sing* with *indef art*) fact of being, amount by which sth is, more than sth else, or more than is expected or proper: *an ~ of enthusiasm; an ~ of imports over exports.* ***in ~ of,*** more than. ***to ~,*** to an extreme degree: *Don't carry your grief to ~. She is generous to ~.* **2** [U] immoderation; intemperance (in eating and drinking): *drink to ~.* **3** (*pl*) personal acts which go beyond the limits of good behaviour, morality or humanity: *The ~es* (= acts of cruelty, etc) *committed by the troops when they occupied the capital will never be forgotten.* **4** /ˊekses/ (attrib) extra; additional: *~ fare,* e g for travelling farther than is allowed by one's ticket; *~ luggage,* weight above what may be carried free; *~ postage,* charged when a letter, etc is understamped: *~ profits duty,* extra tax on profits increased by, e g, war conditions. **~·ive** /ɪkˋsesɪv/ *adj* too much; too great; extreme: *~ive charges.* **~·ive·ly** *adv*

ex·change[1] /ɪksˋtʃeɪndʒ/ *n* **1** [C,U] (act of) exchanging: *Is five apples for five eggs a fair ~? There have been numerous ~s of views between the two governments. E~ of prisoners during a war is unusual. He is giving her French lessons in ~ for English lessons.* **2** [U] the giving and receiving of the money of one country for that of another; relation in value between kinds of money used in different countries: *the rate of ~* (between the dollar and the pound, etc). **ˋE~ Control,** system of protecting gold and reserves of foreign currency. **3** [C] place where merchants or financiers meet for business: *the ˋCotton E~.* **the ˋStock E~,** for the buying and selling of stocks, shares, bonds. **4 ˋlabour ~,** (GB) Government offices where unemployed workmen may be put in touch with prospective employers. **ˋtelephone ~,** control office where lines are connected.

ex·change[2] /ɪksˋtʃeɪndʒ/ *vt,vi* [VP6A,14A] give, receive (one thing) in place of another: *~ greetings/glances. The two drunken men ~d hats. The two girls ~d places. Mary ~d seats with Anne.* ***~ blows/words (with),*** quarrel. **~·able** /-əbl/ *adj* that may be ~d (*for*).

ex·chequer /ɪksˋtʃekə(r)/ *n* **1 the E~,** (GB) government department in charge of public money: *ˈChancellor of the ˋE~,* minister at the head of this department (= Minister of Finance in other countries). **2** supply of money (public or private); treasury.

ex·cise[1] /ˊeksɑɪz/ *n* [U] government tax on certain goods manufactured, sold or used within a country: *the ~ on beer/tobacco; ˋ~ duties; the Commissioners of Customs and E~.* **ˋ~·man** /-mən/ (*pl* -men), **ˋE~ Officer,** officer collecting ~ and preventing breaking of ~ laws.

ex·cise[2] /ɪkˋsɑɪz/ *vt* [VP6A] (formal) remove by, or as if by cutting (a part of the body, a passage from a book, etc). **ex·ci·sion** /ɪkˋsɪʒn/ *n* [U] excising or being ~d; [C] sth ~d.

ex·cite /ɪkˋsɑɪt/ *vt* [VP6A,14,17] **1** stir up the feelings of; cause (sb) to feel strongly: *Don't ~ yourself!* Keep calm! *Everybody was ~d by the news of the victory. It's nothing to get ~d about. Agitators were exciting the people to rebellion/to rebel against their oppressors.* **2** ***~ (in sb),*** get (a feeling) in motion; rouse; bring about: *~ admiration/envy/affection; ~ a riot.* **3** cause (a bodily organ) to be active: *drugs that ~ the nerves.* **ex·cit·able** /ɪkˋsɑɪtəbl/ *adj* easily ~d. **ex·cit·abil·ity** /ɪkˈsɑɪtəˋbɪlətɪ/ *n* quality of being excitable. **ex·cit·ed·ly** *adv* in an ~d manner.

ex·cite·ment /ɪkˋsɑɪtmənt/ *n* **1** [U] state of being excited: *news that caused great ~; jumping about in ~.* **2** [C] sth that excites; exciting incident, etc: *He kept calm amid all these ~s.*

ex·claim /ɪkˋskleɪm/ *vt,vi* [VP6A,2A] cry out suddenly and loudly from pain, anger, surprise, etc; say (*that*); say (the words quoted): *'What!' he ~ed, 'Are you leaving without me?'*

ex·cla·ma·tion /ˈekskləˋmeɪʃn/ *n* **1** [U] crying out or exclaiming. **ˋ~ mark,** the mark (!). **2** [C] sudden short cry, expressing surprise, pain, etc. *'Oh!' 'Look out!', and 'Hurrah!' are ~s.*

ex·clama·tory /ɪkˋsklæmətrɪ *US:* -tɔrɪ/ *adj* using, containing, in the nature of, an exclamation: *an ~ sentence.*

ex·clude /ɪkˋsklud/ *vt* [VP6A,14] ***~ (from),*** **1** prevent (sb from getting in somewhere): *~ a person from membership of a society/immigrants from a country.* **2** prevent (the chance of sth arising): *~ all possibility of doubt;* leave out of account, ignore as irrelevant: *We can ~ (from the reckoning) the possibility that the money won't arrive.* **ex·clu·sion** /ɪkˋskluʒn/ *n* [U] excluding or being ~d (*from*). ***to the exclusion of,*** so as to ~.

ex·clus·ive /ɪkˋsklusɪv/ *adj* **1** (of a person) not willing to mix with others (esp those considered to be inferior in social position, education, etc). **2** (of a group or society) not readily admitting new members: *He moves in ~ social circles and belongs to the most ~ clubs.* **3** (of a shop, goods sold in it, etc) of the sort not to be found elsewhere; uncommon. **4** reserved to the person(s) concerned; *~ privileges; have ~ rights/an ~ agency for the sale of Ford cars in a town: an ~ story/interview,* e g given to only one newspaper. **5 ~ of,** not including: *The ship had a crew of 57 ~ of officers.* **6** excluding all but what is mentioned: *Dictionary-making has not been his ~ employment.* **~·ly** *adv*

ex·cogi·tate /eksˋkodʒɪteɪt/ *vt* [VP6A] (often hum) think out (a plan). **ex·cogi·ta·tion** /ˈeks-kodʒɪˋteɪʃn/ *n*

ex·com·muni·cate /ˈekskəˋmjunɪkeɪt/ *vt* [VP6A] exclude (as a punishment) from the privileges of a member of the Christian Church, e g marriage or burial in church, Holy Communion. **ex·com·muni·ca·tion** /ˈekskəˈmjunɪˋkeɪʃn/ *n* [U] excommunicating or being ~d; [C] instance of this; official statement announcing this.

ex·cori·ate /ɪkˋskɔrɪeɪt/ *vt* [VP6A] (formal) strip, peel off (skin); (fig) criticize severely. **ex·cori·ation** /ɪkˈskɔrɪˋeɪʃn/ *n*

ex·cre·ment /ˋekskrəmənt/ *n* [U] solid waste matter discharged from the bowels.

ex·crescence /ɪkˋskresns/ *n* [C] abnormal (usu ugly and useless) outgrowth on an animal or vegetable body (also fig).

ex·creta /ɪkˋskritə/ *n pl* waste (excrement, urine, sweat) expelled from the body.

ex·crete /ɪkˋskrit/ *vt* [VP6A] (of an animal or plant) discharge from the system, e g waste matter, sweat. **ex·cre·tion** /ɪkˋskriʃn/ *n* [U] excreting; [C, U] that which is ~d.

ex·cru·ciat·ing /ɪkˋskruʃɪeɪtɪŋ/ *adj* (of pain, bodily or mental) acute. **~·ly** *adv*

ex·cul·pate /ˋekskʌlpeɪt/ *vt* [VP6A,14] (formal) free from blame; say that (sb) is not guilty of wrongdoing: *~ a person from a charge.*

ex·cur·sion /ɪkˋskɜʃn *US:* -ʒn/ *n* [C] short journey, esp one made by a number of people together for pleasure: *go on/make an ~ to the mountains; an ˋ~ train; an ˋ~ ticket,* one issued at a reduced fare. **~·ist** /-ɪst/ *n* person who makes an ~.

ex·cuse¹ /ɪkˋskjus/ *n* **1** [C] reason given (true or invented) to explain or defend one's conduct; apology: *He's always making ~s for being late. He had numerous ~s to offer for being late. Please give them my ~s.* **2** [U] ***in ~ of***: *Where the law is concerned, you cannot plead ignorance in ~ of your conduct.* ***without ~***: *Those who are absent without (good) ~ will be punished.*

ex·cuse² /ɪkˋskjuz/ *vt* **1** [VP6A,C,12B,13B,19C] give reasons showing, or intended to show, that a person or his action is not to be blamed; overlook a fault, etc: *~ sb's conduct. Nothing can ~ such rudeness. Please ~ my coming late/~ me for being late/~ my late arrival. E~ my interrupting you.* **2** [VP14,6A] ***~ from,*** set (sb) free from a duty, requirement, punishment, etc: *He was ~d (from) attendance at the lecture. They may be ~d from complying with this regulation.* **3** ***E~ me,*** used as an apology when one interrupts, disagrees, has to behave impolitely or disapprove: *E~ me, but I don't think that statement is quite true.* **ex·cus·able** /ɪkˋskjuzəbl/ *adj* that may be ~d: *an excusable mistake.* **ex·cus·ably** /-əblɪ/ *adv*

ex·ecrable /ˋeksɪkrəbl/ *adj* very bad; deserving hate: *~ manners/weather.*

ex·ecrate /ˋeksɪkreɪt/ *vt* [VP6A] express or feel hatred of. **ex·ecra·tion** /ˈeksɪˋkreɪʃn/ *n*

ex·ecute /ˋeksɪkjut/ [VP6A] *vt* **1** carry out (what one is asked or told to do): *~ sb's commands; ~ a plan/a piece of work/a purpose.* **2** give effect to: *~ a will.* **3** make legally binding: *~ a legal document,* by having it signed, witnessed, sealed and delivered. **4** carry out punishment by death on (sb): *~ a murderer.* **5** perform on the stage, at a concert, etc: *The piano sonata was badly ~d.* **ex·ecu·tant** /ɪgˋzekjʊtənt/ *n* person who ~s a design, etc; person who performs music, etc.

ex·ecu·tion /ˈeksɪˋkjuʃn/ *n* **1** [U] the carrying out or performance of a piece of work, design, etc: *His intention was good, but his ~ of the plan was unsatisfactory.* ***put/carry sth into ~,*** complete it, do what was planned. **2** [U] skill in performing music: *a pianist with marvellous ~.* **3** [U] (of weapons) destructive effect: *The artillery did great ~,* killed and wounded many. **4** [U] infliction of punishment by death; [C] instance of this: *~ by hanging; five ~s last year.* **~er** *n* public official who ~s criminals.

ex·ecu·tive /ɪgˋzekjʊtɪv/ *adj* **1** having to do with managing or executing(1): *~ duties; ~ ability.* **2** having authority to carry out decisions, laws, decrees, etc: *the ~ branch of the government; the ~ head of the State,* e g the President of the US. □ *n* **1 the ~,** the ~ branch of a government. ⇨ administration, judiciary, legislature. **2** (in the Civil Service) person who carries out what has been planned or decided. **3** person or group in a business or commercial organization with administrative or managerial powers.

ex·ecu·tor /ɪgˋzekjʊtə(r)/ *n* person who is appointed by a testator to carry out the terms of a will. **execu·trix** /ɪgˋzekjʊtrɪks/ *n* woman ~.

ex·egesis /ˈeksɪˋdʒisɪs/ *n* [U] exposition (esp of the Scriptures).

ex·emp·lary /ɪgˋzemplərɪ/ *adj* serving as an example or a warning: *~ conduct/punishment.*

ex·emp·lify /ɪgˋzemplɪfaɪ/ *vt* (*pt,pp* -fied) [VP6A] illustrate by example; be an example of. **exemp·lifi·ca·tion** /ɪgˈzemplɪfɪˋkeɪʃn/ *n* [U] ~ing; [C] example.

ex·empt /ɪgˋzempt/ *vt* [VP6A,14] ***~ (from),*** free from (an obligation): *Poor eyesight will ~ you from military service.* □ *adj* not liable to, free (*from*): *~ from tax.* **ex·emp·tion** /ɪgˋzempʃn/ *n* [U] ~ing or being ~ed (*from*); [C] instance of this.

ex·er·cise¹ /ˋeksəsaɪz/ *n* **1** [U] employment or practice (of mental or physical powers, of rights): *Walking, running, rowing and horse-riding are all healthy forms of ~. The doctor advised her to take more ~. E~ of the mental faculties is as important as bodily ~. The ~ of patience is essential in diplomatic negotiations. His excuses showed considerable ~ of the imagination.* **2** [C] activity, drill, etc designed for bodily, mental or spiritual training: *health/ vocal/ gymnastic/ deep-breathing, etc ~s; ~s for the harp/flute, etc; five-finger ~s for the piano; ~s in logic/ English composition; spiritual ~s,* e g prayer. *An ~ in clear thinking would benefit many public speakers.* **3** (*pl*) series of movements for training troops, crews of warships, etc: *military ~s; The third cruiser squadron has left for ~s in the North Sea.* **4** (*pl,* US) ceremonies: *graduation ~s; opening ~s,* e g speeches at the start of a conference.

ex·er·cise² /ˋeksəsaɪz/ *vt,vi* **1** [VP6A,15A,2A] take exercise; give exercise to, ⇨ **exercise¹(1)**: *Horses get fat and lazy if they are not ~d. He ~s himself in fencing. You don't ~ enough.* **2** [VP6A] employ; make use of: *~ patience; ~ authority over sb; ~ one's rights.* **3** [VP6A] (usu passive) perplex; trouble; worry the mind of: *The problem that is exercising our minds.... I am very much ~d about the future/about the shortcomings of my son.*

ex·ert /ɪgˋzɜt/ *vt* [VP6A,14,16A] **1** put forth; bring into use: *~ all one's strength/influence, etc (to do sth); ~ pressure on sb.* **2** (reflex) make an effort: *~ oneself to arrive early; ~ yourself on my behalf.*

ex·er·tion /ɪgˋzɜʃn/ *n* [U] exerting; [C] instance of this: *E~ of authority is not always wise; persuasion may be better. He failed to lift the rock in spite of all his ~s. Now that I am 90, I am unequal to the ~s of travelling.*

ex·eunt /ˋegzɪənt/ *vi* (Lat) (stage direction) they leave the stage.

ex gratia /eks ˋgreɪʃə/ *n* (Lat) **~ payment,** payment not legally binding but for which some moral obligation is felt.

ex·hale /eksˋheɪl/ *vt,vi* [VP6A,2A] breathe out; give off gas, vapour; be given off (as gas or vapour): *~ air from the lungs.* **ex·ha·la·tion** /ˈekshəˋleɪʃn/ *n* **1** [C] act of exhaling. **2** [U,C] sth ~d.

ex·haust¹ /ɪgˋzɔst/ *n* [C,U] (outlet, in an engine or machine, for) steam, vapour, etc that has done its work: (attrib) *ˋ~-wipe.*

ex·haust² /ɪgˋzɔst/ *vt* [VP6A] **1** use up completely: *~ one's patience/strength; ~ oneself by hard work; feeling ~ed,* tired out. **2** make empty: *~ a well; ~ a tube of air.* **3** say, find out, all there is to say about (sth): *~ a subject.*

ex·haus·tion /ɪgˋzɔst/ *n* [U] exhausting or being exhausted; total loss of strength: *They were in a state of ~ after climbing the mountain.*

ex·haus·tive /ɪgˋzɔstɪv/ *adj* thorough; complete: *an ~ inquiry.* **~·ly** *adv*

ex·hibit¹ /ɪgˋzɪbɪt/ *n* [C] **1** object or collection of objects, shown publicly, e g in a museum: *Do not touch the ~s.* **2** document, object, etc produced in a law court and referred to in evidence, e g a weapon said to have been used by the accused person.

ex·hibit² /ɪgˋzɪbɪt/ *vt* [VP6A] **1** show publicly for sale, in a competition, etc: *~ paintings in an art gallery/flowers at a flower show.* (used absolutely(4)): *Mr X ~s in several galleries.* **2** give clear evidence of (a quality): *The girls ~ed great powers of endurance during the climb.* **ex·hibi·tor** /-tə(r)/ *n* person who ~s at a show of pictures, a flower show, etc.

ex·hi·bi·tion /ˈeksɪˋbɪʃn/ *n* **1** [C] collection of things shown publicly (e g of works of art); display of commercial or industrial goods for advertisement; public display of animals, plants, flowers, etc (often shown in competition, for prizes, and colloq called a *'show'*). **2** (*sing* with *def* or *indef art*) act of showing: *an ~ of bad manners; an opportunity for the ~ of one's knowledge.* ***make an ~ of oneself,*** behave in public so that one receives contempt. **3** (GB) money allowance to a student from school or college funds for a number of years. **~er** *n* student to whom an **~(3)** is granted. **~·ism** /-ɪzm/ *n* [U] tendency towards extravagant behaviour designed to attract attention to oneself. **~·ist** /-ɪst/ *n* person given to ~ism.

ex·hil·ar·ate /ɪgˋzɪləreɪt/ *vt* [VP6A] (usu passive) fill with high spirits; make lively or glad: *exhilarating news.* **ex·hil·ar·ation** /ɪgˈzɪləˋreɪʃn/ *n*

ex·hort /ɪgˋzɔt/ *vt* [VP6A,14,17] ***~ sb to sth/to do sth,*** (formal) urge, advise earnestly: *~ sb to do good/to work harder/to give up bad ways; ~ one's listeners to good deeds.* **ex·hor·ta·tion** /ˈeksɔˋteɪʃn/ *n* [U] ~ing; [C] earnest request, sermon, etc that ~s sb.

ex·hume /ɪgˋzjum *US:* -ˋzum/ *vt* [VP6A] take out (a dead body) from the earth (for examination). **ex·hu·ma·tion** /ˈeksjʊˋmeɪʃn/ *n* [U] exhuming or being ~d; [C] instance of this.

exi·gency /ˈekˋsidʒənsɪ/ *n* (*pl* **-cies**) [C] condition of great need; emergency: *measures to meet the exigencies of this difficult period.* **exi·gent** /-dʒənt/ *adj* **1** urgent; pressing. **2** exacting.

ex·igu·ous /egˋzɪgjʊəs/ *adj* (formal) scanty: *an ~ diet.*

ex·ile /ˋegzɑɪl/ *n* **1** [U] banishment (being sent away from one's country or home), esp as a punishment: *be/live in ~; go/be sent into ~; a place of ~; after an ~ of ten years.* **2** [C] person who is banished in this way. □ *vt* [VP6A,15A] send (sb) into ~: ~ sb from his country; ~d for life.

ex·ist /ɪgˋzɪst/ *vi* **1** [VP2A,C] be; have being; be real: *The idea ~s only in the minds of poets. Do you believe that fairies ~,* that there really are fairies? *Does life ~ on Mars?* **2** [VP2A,C,3A] continue living: *We cannot ~ without food and water. She ~s on very little. How do they ~ in such wretched conditions?* **ex·ist·ence** /-əns/ *n* **1** [U] the state of ~ing: *When did this world come into ~ence? Do you believe in the ~ence of ghosts? This is the oldest Hebrew manuscript in ~ence.* **2** (with *indef art*) manner of living: *lead a happy ~ence.* **ex·ist·ent** /-ənt/ *adj* ~ing actual.

ex·is·ten·tial·ism /ˈegzɪˋstenʃḷɪzm/ *n* doctrine (deriving from Kierkegaard /ˋkɪəgɑd/ (1813—15), the Danish philosopher, and popularized by Sartre /ˋsɑtr/ (born 1905), the French writer and philosopher) that man is a unique and isolated individual in an indifferent or hostile universe, responsible for his own actions and free to chose his destiny.

exit /ˋeksɪt/ *n* **1** departure of an actor from the stage: *make one's ~,* go out or away. **2** way out, e g from a theatre or cinema. □ *vi* (as a stage direction) *E~ Macbeth,* Macbeth goes off the stage. ⇨ **exeunt.**

ex·odus /ˈeksədəs/ *n* (*sing* only) **1** going out or away of many people: *the ~ of people to the sea and the mountains for the summer holidays.* **2 E~,** the second book of the Old Testament, telling of the ~ of the Israelites from Egypt.

ex of·fi·cio /ˈeks əˈfɪʃɪəʊ/ *adv, adj* (Lat) because of one's office or position: *an ~ member of the committee; present at the meeting ~.*

ex·on·er·ate /ɪgˋzɒnəreɪt/ *vt* [VP6A,14] ***~ sb (from),*** free, clear: *~ sb from blame/responsibility.* **ex·on·er·ation** /ɪgˈzɒnəˋreɪʃn/ *n*

ex·or·bi·tant /ɪgˋzɔbɪtənt/ *adj* (of a price, charge or demand) much too high or great. **~·ly** *adv* **exor·bi·tance** /-təns/ *n*

ex·or·cize, -cise /ˋeksɔsaɪz/ *vt* [VP6A,14] ***~ sb/sth (from/out of),*** drive out, e g an evil spirit, by prayers or magic.

ex·otic /ɪgˋzɒtɪk/ *adj* **1** (of plants, fashions, words, ideas) introduced from another country. **2** foreign or unusual in style; striking or pleasing because colourful, unusual: *~ birds.*

ex·pand /ɪk'spænd/ *vt,vi* [VP6A,14,2A,C] **1** make or become larger: *Metals ~ when they are heated.* ⇨ contract³(1). *A tyre ~s when you pump air into it.* ⇨ shrink. *The river ~s* (= broadens) *and forms a lake. The small pocket dictionary was ~ed into a larger volume. Our foreign trade has ~ed during recent years.* **2** unfold or spread out: *His face ~ed in a smile of welcome. The petals of many flowers ~ in the sunshine.* **3** (of a person) become good-humoured or genial.

ex·panse /ɪk'spæns/ *n* [C] wide and open area: *the broad ~ of the Pacific; the blue ~ of the sky; a broad ~ of brow,* e g of a man with a high forehead and bald head.

ex·pan·sion /ɪk'spænʃn/ *n* [U] expanding or being expanded(1): *~ of the currency,* by putting more banknotes into circulation; *~ of territory,* e g by winning new territory; *the ~ of gases when heated.*

ex·pans·ive /ɪk'spænsɪv/ *adj* **1** able, tending, to expand. **2** (of persons, speech) unreserved, effusive. **~·ly** *adv* **~·ness** *n*

ex parte /'eks 'pɑtɪ/ *adv* (Lat) on, in the interests of, one side only. □ *adj:* (*exparte*)*: an ~ statement.*

ex·pati·ate /ɪk'speɪʃɪeɪt/ *vi* [VP3A] **~ *upon,*** (formal) write or speak at great length, in detail, about.

ex·patri·ate /eks'pætrɪeɪt *US:* -'peɪt-/ *vt* [VP6A] (reflex) leave one's own country to live abroad; renounce one's citizenship. □ *n* /-rɪət/ person living outside his own country: *American ~s in Paris;* (attrib) *~ Americans.*

ex·pect /ɪk'spekt/ *vt* [VP6A,17,7,9,14] think or believe that sth will happen or come, that sb will come; wish for and feel confident that one will receive: *We ~ed you yesterday. We were ~ing a letter from her. I ~ to be/~ that I shall be back on Sunday. You would ~ there to be/that there would be strong disagreement about this. You can't learn a foreign language in a week; it's not to be ~ed. You are ~ing too much of her. 'Will he be late?'—'I ~ so', 'Will he need help?'—'No, I don't ~ so'* (or) *'No, I ~ not'. They ~* (= require) *me to work on Saturdays. I ~* (= require) *you to be punctual. 'Who has eaten all the cake?'—'Oh, I ~* (colloq = suppose) *it was Tom.* **~·ancy** /-ənsɪ/ *n* the state of ~ing: *with a look/an air of ~ancy; life ~ancy.* **~·ant** /-ənt/ *adj* ~ing: *an ~ant mother,* woman who is pregnant. **~·ant·ly** *adv*

ex·pec·ta·tion /'ekspek'teɪʃn/ *n* **1** [U] expecting; awaiting: *He ate a light lunch in ~ of a good dinner.* **2** (often *pl*) thing that is expected. ***contrary to ~(s),*** in a way different from what was expected. ***beyond ~,*** in a way greater or better than was expected. ***fall short of/not come up to one's ~s,*** be less good than what was expected. **3** (*pl*) future prospects, esp sth to be inherited: *a young man with great ~s,* e g one who has a millionaire uncle who has promised to leave him his wealth. **4** [C] ***~ of life,*** years a person is expected to live: *A life assurance company can tell you the ~ of life of a man who is 40 years old.*

ex·pec·tor·ate /ɪk'spektəreɪt/ *vt,vi* [VP6A,2A] spit; send out (phlegm from the throat, blood from the lungs) by coughing.

ex·pedi·ent /ɪk'spidɪənt/ *adj* (usu *pred*) likely to be useful or helpful for a purpose; advantageous though contrary to principle: *In times of war governments do things because they are ~. Do what you think ~.* □ *n* [C] ~ plan, action, device, etc. **~·ly** *adv* **ex·pedi·ence** /-əns/, **ex·pedi·ency** /-ənsɪ/ *n* [U] suitability for a purpose; being ~; self-interest: *act from expediency, not from principle.*

ex·pedite /'ekspɪdɑɪt/ *vt* [VP6A] help the progress of; speed up (business, etc).

ex·pedi·tion /'ekspɪ'dɪʃn/ *n* **1** [C] (men, ships, etc making a) journey or voyage for a definite purpose: *a hunting ~; go/send a party of men on an ~ to the Antarctic; members of the Mount Everest ~.* **2** [U] promptness; speed. **~·ary** /-ʃnrɪ *US:* -ʃṇerɪ/ *adj* of, making up, an ~: *an ~ary force,* e g an army sent to take part in a war abroad.

ex·pedi·tious /'ekspɪ'dɪʃəs/ *adj* acting quickly; prompt and efficient. **~·ly** *adv*

ex·pel /ɪk'spel/ *vt* (-ll-) [VP6A,14] **~ *(from),*** send out or away by force: *~ the enemy from a town; ~ a boy from school,* as a punishment.

ex·pend /ɪk'spend/ *vt* [VP6A,14] **~ *(up)on,*** **1** spend: *~ all one's capital on equipment; ~ time and care in doing sth.* **2** use up: *They had ~ed all their ammunition.* **~·able** /-əbl/ *adj* that may be ~ed, esp that may be sacrificed to achieve a purpose: *The general considered that these troops were ~able.*

ex·pen·di·ture /ɪk'spendɪtʃə(r)/ *n* **1** [U] spending or using: *the ~ of money on armaments.* **2** [C,U] amount expended: *an ~ of £500 on new furniture. Limit your ~(s) to what is essential.*

ex·pense /ɪk'spens/ *n* **1** [U] spending (of money, time, energy, etc); cost: *Most children in Great Britain are educated at the public ~. I want the best you can supply; you need spare no ~,* you need not try to economize. ***at the ~ of,*** at the cost of: *He became a brilliant scholar, but only at the ~ of his health.* ***put sb/go to the ~ of,*** (cause sb to) spend money on: *It's foolish to go to the ~ of taking music lessons if you never practise. I don't want to put you to the ~ of engaging a private tutor for me.* ***at his/her/my, etc ~,*** **(a)** with him, her, me, etc paying: *We were all entertained at the director's ~.* **(b)** (fig) bringing discredit, ridicule or contempt on him, her, me, etc: *We had a good laugh at his ~,* We laughed at him because he had done sth ridiculous, been deceived, etc. **'~ account,** record of expenses incurred and either paid out of money supplied by, or to be refunded by, the employer, e g of a business man for travel, entertainment, etc. **2** (usu *pl*) money used or needed for sth: *travelling ~s. Illness, holidays and other ~s reduced his bank balance to almost nothing.*

ex·pens·ive /ɪk'spensɪv/ *adj* causing expense; high priced: *an ~ education; too ~ for me to buy.* **~·ly** *adv*

ex·peri·ence /ɪk'spɪərɪəns/ *n* **1** [U] process of gaining knowledge or skill by doing and seeing things; knowledge or skill so gained: *We all learn by ~. Has he had much ~ in work of this sort? He has not enough ~ for the position. A man of your ~ ought to do well. Only women with ~ of office work need apply for the position.* **2** [C] event, activity, which has given one ~(1); event that affects one in some way: *an unpleasant/trying/unusual ~.* □ *vt* [VP6A] have ~ of; feel; meet with: ~ *pleasure/pain/difficulty/great hardships.* **ex·peri·enced** *adj* having ~; having knowledge or skill as the result of ~: *an ~d nurse/teacher; a general ~d in warfare.*

ex·peri·ment /ɪk`sperɪmənt/ *n* [C] test or trial carried out carefully in order to study what happens and gain new knowledge: *perform/carry out an ~ in chemistry;* [U] *learn sth by ~.* □ *vi* [VP2A,C, 3A] make ~s: ~ *with new methods;* ~ *upon dogs.* **ex·peri·men·ta·tion** /ɪk'sperɪmen`teɪʃn/ *n* [U] ~ing.

ex·peri·men·tal /ɪk'sperɪ`mentl/ *adj* of, used for, based on, experiments: ~ *methods; an ~ farm.* **~ly** /-tlɪ/ *adv*

ex·pert /`ekspɜt/ *n* person with special knowledge, skill or training: *an agricultural ~; an ~ in economics; get the advice of the ~s.* □ *adj* trained by practice; skilful: *according to ~ advice/ opinions; men who are ~ at driving racing cars.* **~·ly** *adv* **~·ness** *n*

ex·pert·ise /'ekspɜ`tiz/ *n* [U] **1** (comm) expert appraisal; valuation. **2** expert's report. **3** expert knowledge and skill. ⇨ *know-how* at **know(6)**.

ex·pi·ate /`ekspɪeɪt/ *vt* [VP6A] make amends for, submit to punishment for (wrongdoing): ~ *sin/a crime.* **ex·pi·ation** /'ekspɪ`eɪʃn/ *n* [U].

ex·pir·ation /'ekspɪ`reɪʃn/ *n* [U] **1** ending (*of* a period of time): *at the ~ of the lease.* **2** breathing out (of air).

ex·pire /ɪk`spɑɪə(r)/ *vi* [VP2A] **1** (of a period of time) come to an end: *His term of office as President ~s next year. When does your driving licence ~?* **2** (liter) die.

ex·piry /ɪk`spɑɪərɪ/ *n* (*pl* **-ries**) end, termination, esp of a contract or agreement: *the ~ of a driving licence.*

ex·plain /ɪk`spleɪn/ *vt* **1** [VP6A,9,8,10,14] make plain or clear; show the meaning of: *A dictionary tries to ~ the meanings of words. Please ~ this problem to me. Please ~ to me what this means. He ~ed that he had been delayed by the weather. Please ~ yourself,* make your meaning clear. ⇨ 2 below. **2** [VP6A,15B] account for: *Can you ~ his behaviour? That ~s his absence. Please ~ yourself,* give reasons for your conduct. ~ ***sth away,*** show why one should not be blamed for a fault, mistake, etc: *You will find it difficult to ~ away your use of such offensive language.*

ex·pla·na·tion /'eksplə`neɪʃn/ *n* **1** [U] (process of) explaining: *Not much ~ will be needed. I had better say a few words by way of ~. Had he anything to say in ~ of his conduct?* **2** [C] statement, fact, circumstances, etc that explains: *an ~ of his conduct/of a mystery; after repeated ~s.*

ex·plana·tory /ɪk`splænətrɪ *US:* -tɔrɪ/ *adj* serving or intended to explain.

ex·ple·tive /ɪk`splitɪv *US:* `eksplətɪv/ *n* [C] violent (often meaningless) exclamation, e g 'My goodness', or an oath such as 'Damn'.

ex·plic·able /ek`splɪkəbl/ *adj* that can be explained.

ex·pli·cate /`eksplɪkeɪt/ *vt* [VP6A] (formal) explain and analyse in detail.

ex·plicit /ɪk`splɪsɪt/ *adj* (of a statement, etc) clearly and fully expressed; definite: *He was quite ~ about the matter,* left no doubt about what he meant. **~·ly** *adv* **~·ness** *n*

ex·plode /ɪk`spləʊd/ *vt,vi* **1** [VP6A,2A] (cause to) burst with a loud noise: ~ *a charge of gunpowder/a bomb. When the boiler ~d many people were hurt by the steam. The shell ~d in the barrel of the gun.* **2** [VP2A,C] (of feelings) burst out; (of persons) show violent emotion: *At last his anger ~d. He ~d with rage/jealousy.* **3** [VP6A] destroy, expose an idea, a theory, etc; show the falsity of: ~ *a superstition: an ~d idea.*

ex·ploit[1] /`eksplɔɪt/ *n* [C] bold or adventurous act; brilliant achievement.

ex·ploit[2] /ɪk`splɔɪt/ *vt* [VP6A] **1** use, work or develop mines, waterpower, other natural resources of a country. **2** use selfishly, or for one's own profit: ~ *child labour.* **ex·ploi·ta·tion** /'eksplɔɪ`teɪʃn/ *n* [U] ~ing or being ~ed (both senses): *the ~ation of a new country.*

ex·plore /ɪk`splɔ(r)/ *vt* [VP6A] **1** travel into or through (a country, etc) for the purpose of learning about it: ~ *the Arctic regions. Columbus discovered America but did not ~ the new continent.* **2** examine thoroughly problems, possibilities, etc in order to test, learn about, them. **ex·plorer** *n* person who ~s. **ex·plo·ra·tion** /'eksplə`reɪʃn/ *n* [U] exploring: *the exploration of the ocean depths;* [C] instance of this. **ex·plora·tory** /ɪk`splɔrətrɪ *US:* -tɔrɪ/ *adj* for the purpose of exploring.

ex·plo·sion /ɪk`spləʊʒn/ *n* [C] **1** (loud noise caused by) sudden and violent bursting: *a bomb ~. The ~ was heard a mile away.* **2** outburst or outbreak *of* anger, laughter, etc. **3** great and sudden increase: *the population ~ after the war.*

ex·plos·ive /ɪk`spləʊsɪv/ *n, adj* (substance) tending to or likely to explode: *a shell filled with high ~. Dynamite and gun-cotton are ~s. The old man has an ~ temper,* often explodes with anger, etc. *That's an ~ issue,* one likely to inflame feeling. **~·ly** *adv*

expo /`ekspəʊ/ *n* international exposition**(2)**: *E~ 70* (in Tokyo).

ex·po·nent /ɪk`spəʊnənt/ *n* **1** person or thing that explains or interprets, or is a representative or example (*of*): *Huxley was an ~ of Darwin's theory of evolution.* **2** (alg) symbol that indicates what power of a factor is to be taken. In a^3, the figure 3 is the ~; in x^n, the symbol ^{n} is the ~.

ex·port[1] /`ekspɔt/ *n* **1** [C] (business of) exporting: *a ban on the ~ of gold;* (attrib) *the `~ trade; `~ duties.* **2** [C] sth exported: *Last year ~s exceeded imports in value. What are the chief ~s of your country?*

ex·port[2] /ɪk`spɔt/ *vt* [VP6A] send (goods) to another country: ~ *cotton goods.* **~er** *n* trader who ~s goods. **~·able** /-əbl/ *adj* that can be ~ed. **ex·por·ta·tion** /'ekspɔ`teɪʃn/ *n* [U] the ~ing of goods; goods ~ed.

ex·pose /ɪk`spəʊz/ *vt* [VP6A,14,15A] ~ ***(to),*** **1** uncover; leave uncovered or unprotected: ~ *one's body to the sunlight;* ~ *soldiers to unnecessary risks/to the enemy's gunfire; ~d to the weather;* ~ *a newborn child,* leave it in the open, to die of cold or hunger (as was done in ancient Sparta); ~ *oneself to danger; be ~d to ridicule.* **2** display: ~ *goods in a shopwindow.* **3** disclose, make known: ~ *a plot/project/plan;* reveal the guilt or wrongdoing of; unmask: ~ *a villain/his villainy.* **4** (photo) allow light to reach (camera film, etc): ~ *30 metres of cinema film.*

ex·posé /'ek`spəʊzeɪ *US:* 'ekspə`zeɪ/ *n* orderly setting out or précis of a body of facts or beliefs.

ex·po·si·tion /'ekspə`zɪʃn/ *n* **1** [U] expounding or explaining; [C] instance of this; explanation or interpretation of a theory, plan, etc. **2** [C] (abbr *expo*) exhibition of goods, etc: *an industrial* ~.

ex·postu·late /ɪkˋspɒstʃʊleɪt/ *vi* [VP2A,3A] ~ ***(with sb) (on/about sth),*** make a friendly protest; reason or argue. **ex·postu·la·tion** /ɪkˈspɒstʃʊˋleɪʃn/ *n* [C,U] friendly protest(ing): *My expostulation(s) had no results.*

ex·po·sure /ɪkˋspəʊʒə(r)/ *n* **1** [U] exposing or being exposed (all senses): *The climbers lost their way on the mountain and died of* ~. *E~ of the body to strong sunlight may be harmful. The ~ of the plot against the President probably saved his life. The ~ of the criminal saved the innocent man from imprisonment.* **2** [C] instance of exposing or being exposed (all senses): *As a result of these ~s the government took strong measures against bribery and corruption. How many ~s have you made,* How many pictures have you taken on the (camera) film? *An ~ of one-hundredth of a second will be enough.* **3** aspect: *a house with a southern* ~, one that faces south, is exposed to sun, wind, etc from the south.

ex·pound /ɪkˋspaʊnd/ *vt* [VP6A,14] ~ ***(to),*** explain, make clear, by giving details: ~ *the Scriptures;* ~ *a theory/one's views* (*to* sb).

ex·press[1] /ɪkˋspres/ *adj* **1** clearly and definitely stated, not suggested or implied: *You cannot ignore such an ~ command. It was his ~ wish that you should not wait for him.* **2** going, sent, quickly; designed for high speed: *an* ˋ~ *train;* ~ *delivery,* by special postal messenger; *an ~ letter/messenger.* ˋ~ **way** *n* (US) major road for fast travel. ⇨ (GB) motorway. **3** (of likeness) exact: *He is the ~ image of* (= is exactly like) *his father.* □ *adv* by ~ delivery; by ~ train: *send a parcel* ~; *travel* ~. **~·ly** *adv* **1** plainly; definitely: *You were ~ly forbidden to touch my papers.* **2** specially; on purpose: *a dictionary ~ly compiled for foreign students of English.*

ex·press[2] /ɪkˋspres/ *n* **1** express train: *the 8.00a m ~ to Edinburgh.* **2** company that carries parcels, etc esp (US) a privately owned company: (attrib) *an ~ company; an ~ wagon/van,* one that collects and delivers goods quickly. **3** service rendered by the post office, railways, road services, etc for carrying goods: *send goods by* ~.

ex·press[3] /ɪkˋspres/ *vt* **1** [VP6A,10,15A] make known, show by words, looks, actions: *I find it difficult to ~ my meaning. A smile ~ed her joy at the good news. I cannot easily ~ (to you) how grateful I am for your help.* ~ ***oneself,*** communicate one's thoughts or feelings through words, gestures, etc: *He is still unable to ~ himself in English. He ~ed himself strongly* (= spoke in a forceful way) *on the subject.* **2** [VP6A] send a letter, goods, etc fast by special delivery: *The letter is urgent; you had better ~ it.* **3** [VP6A,14] press or squeeze out juices/oil *from/out of: juice ~ed* (*pressed* is more usu) *from grapes.*

ex·pression /ɪkˋspreʃn/ *n* **1** [U] process of expressing(**1**): *give ~ to one's gratitude,* say or show how grateful one is; *read* (aloud) *with* ~, in a way that shows feeling for the meaning. *There was an ~ of discontent on her face,* a discontented look. ˋ***beyond/past*** ~, in a manner that cannot be expressed: *The scenery was beautiful beyond* ~, indescribably beautiful. ***find ~ in,*** be expressed by means of: *Her feelings at last found ~ in tears.* **2** [C] word or phrase: *'Shut up'* (= Stop talking) *is not a polite ~. Slang ~s should be avoided in an essay.* **3** (maths) symbols expressing a quantity, e g $3xy^2$. **~·less** *adj* without ~(**1**): *in an ~less voice; an ~less face.*

ex·pression·ism /ɪkˋspreʃnɪzm/ *n* [U] (in art, music, etc) subordination of realism to the expression of emotional experience. **ex·pression·ist** /-ɪst/ *n: the expressionists;* (attrib) *the expressionist school.*

ex·press·ive /ɪkˋspresɪv/ *adj* ~ ***(of),*** serving to express: *looks ~ of despair/a cry ~ of pain; an ~ smile.* **~·ly** *adv*

ex·pro·pri·ate /eksˋprəʊprɪeɪt/ *vt* [VP6A,14] ~ ***(from),*** take away (property); dispossess (sb of an estate, etc). **ex·pro·pri·ation** /ˈeksˈprəʊprɪˋeɪʃn/ *n* [U].

ex·pul·sion /ɪkˋspʌlʃn/ *n* [U] ~ ***(from),*** expelling or being expelled; [C] instance of this: *the ~ of a student from college; an* ˋ~ *order,* official order expelling a person from a country.

ex·punge /ɪkˋspʌndʒ/ *vt* [VP6A,14] ~ ***(from),*** (formal) wipe or rub out words, names, etc from a book, etc.

ex·pur·gate /ˋekspəgeɪt/ *vt* [VP6A] take out from (a book, etc what are considered to be) improper or objectionable parts: *an ~d edition of a novel.* **ex·pur·ga·tion** /ˈekspəˋgeɪʃn/ *n*

ex·quis·ite /ekˋskwɪzɪt/ *adj* **1** of great excellence; brought to a high state of perfection: ~ *workmanship;* ~ *designs; a piece of ~ lace.* **2** (of pain, pleasure, etc) keenly felt. **3** (of power to feel) keen, delicate: ~ *sensibility.* **~·ly** *adv* **~·ness** *n*

ex-ser·vice /eks ˋsɜvɪs/ *adj* having formerly served in the armed forces. **~·man** /-mən/ *n* (*pl* -men) (GB): *an ~men's organization.*

ex·tant /ˈekˋstænt/ *adj* still in existence (esp of documents, etc): *the earliest ~ manuscript of this poem.*

ex·tem·por·ary /ɪkˋstempərərɪ *US:* -pərerɪ/ *adj* = extempore. **ex·tem·por·ar·ily** /-rərɪlɪ *US:* -ˋrerḷɪ/ *adv*

ex·tem·pore /ekˋstempərɪ/ *adv, adj* (spoken or done) without previous thought or preparation: *speak* ~, without notes; *an ~ address.* **ex·tem·por·aneous(·ly)** /ˈekˈstempəˋreɪnɪəs(lɪ)/ *adj, adv* in an ~ manner.

ex·tend /ɪkˋstend/ *vt, vi* **1** [VP6A] make longer (in space or time); enlarge: ~ *a railway/a fence/a wall/the city boundaries. Can't you ~ your visit for a few days,* stay a few days longer? *We are ~ing our premises;* ~ *credit,* (fin) prolong the time for which credit is given. **2** [VP6A,15A] lay or stretch out the body, a limb, or limbs at full length: ~ *one's arm horizontally;* ~ *one's hand to sb.* **3** [VP6A,14] ~ ***sth (to sb),*** offer, grant, accord: ~ *hospitality/an invitation/a greeting/a warm welcome to sb;* ~ *help to the poor.* **4** [VP2B,C] (of space, land, etc) reach, stretch: *a road that ~s for miles and miles. My garden ~s as far as the river.* **5** [VP6A,15A] cause to reach or stretch: ~ *a cable between two posts.* **6** [VP6A] (usu passive) tax or use the powers of a person, horse, etc to the utmost: *The horse was fully ~ed.* ⇨ *flat out* at flat[2] *adv* (**3**).

ex·ten·sion /ɪkˋstenʃn/ *n* **1** [U] extending or being extended: *the ~ of useful knowledge; University E~,* teaching for, examination of, non-resident students; *the ~ of Soviet influence in Africa.* **2** [C] additional part; addition or continuance; enlargement: *an ~ of one's summer holidays; build an ~ to a hospital; get an ~ of time,* e g for paying a debt; *an ~ to a sentence,* (gram) word or words amplifying the subject or predicate; *telephone No 01—629—8494, ~ 15,* i e a line extending from the switchboard to one of the rooms or offices.

ex·ten·sive /ɪk`stensɪv/ *adj* extending far; far-reaching: *an ~ view; ~ repairs/inquiries; a scholar with an ~ knowledge of his subject.* **~·ly** *adv*

ex·tent /ɪk`stent/ *n* [U] **1** ~ ***(of)***, length; area; range: *From the roof we were able to see the full ~ of the park. I was amazed at the ~ of his knowledge. They are building a new racing track, six miles in ~.* **2** degree: *to a certain ~,* partly; *to some ~; to such an ~ that...; to what ~; in debt to the ~ of £100.*

ex·tenu·ate /ɪk`stenjʊeɪt/ *vt* [VP6A] make (wrongdoing) seem less serious (by finding an excuse): *Nothing can ~ his base conduct. There are extenuating circumstances in this case.* **ex·tenu·ation** /ɪk'stenjʊ`eɪʃn/ *n* **1** [U] extenuating or being ~d: *He pleaded poverty in extenuation of the theft.* **2** [C] sth that ~s; partial excuse.

ex·terior /ek`stɪərɪə(r)/ *adj* outer; situated on or coming from outside: *the ~ surface of a hollow ball; the ~ features of a building.* ⇨ **interior.** □ *n* outside; outward aspect or appearance: *a good man with a rough ~.*

ex·terior·ize /ek`stɪərɪəraɪz/ *vt* [VP6A] (psych) visualize (a conception) in outward form. **ex·terior·iz·ation** /ek'stɪərɪəraɪ`zeɪʃn *US:* -rɪ`z-/ *n*

ex·ter·mi·nate /ɪk`stɜmɪneɪt/ *vt* [VP6A] make an end of (disease, ideas, people's beliefs); destroy completely. **ex·ter·mi·na·tion** /ɪk'stɜmɪ`neɪʃn/ *n*

ex·ter·nal /ek`stɜnl/ *adj* outside; situated on the outside; of or for the outside: *~ evidence,* obtained from independent sources, not from what is being examined; *alcohol for ~ use,* for use on the skin, not to be drunk; *~ examination,* one conducted by authorities outside the school, college, etc of the person(s) examined; *~ examiner,* person (not on the staff of those setting the examination) conducting such an examination. □ *n* (usu *pl*) ~ circumstances; outward features: *the ~s of religion,* acts and ceremonies (contrasted with inner and spiritual aspects); *judge people by ~s.* **~·ly** /ek`stɜnḷɪ/ *adv*

ex·ter·ri·tor·ial /'eks'terɪ`tɔrɪəl/ *adj* (e g of ambassadors, etc) free from the jurisdiction of the State in which one resides: *~ privileges and rights.*

ex·tinct /ɪk`stɪŋt/ *adj* **1** no longer burning; no longer active: *an ~ volcano.* **2** (of feelings, passions) dead. **3** no longer in existence; having died out: *an ~ species; become ~.*

ex·tinc·tion /ɪk`stɪŋkʃn/ *n* [U] **1** making, being, becoming, extinct: *a race threatened by ~; research that may lead to the ~ of a disease.* **2** act of extinguishing: *the ~ of a fire/of sb's hopes.*

ex·tin·guish /ɪk`stɪŋgwɪʃ/ *vt* [VP6A] **1** put out a light, fire. **2** end the existence of hope, love, passion, etc. **3** wipe out (a debt). **~er** *n* (kinds of) apparatus for discharging a jet of liquid chemicals for ~ing a fire.

ex·tir·pate /`ekstəpeɪt/ *vt* [VP6A] pull up by the roots; destroy utterly: *~ social evils.* **ex·tir·pa·tion** /'ekstə`peɪʃn/ *n* [U].

ex·tol /ɪk`stəʊl/ *vt* (-ll-) [VP6A,15A] praise highly: *~ sb to the skies,* greatly; *~ sb's merits; ~ sb as a hero.*

ex·tort /ɪk`stɔt/ *vt* [VP6A,14] ~ ***(from)***, obtain by violence, threats, etc: *~ money from sb. The police used torture to ~ a confession from him.* **ex·tor·tion** /ɪk`stɔʃn/ *n* [U] ~ing; [C] instance of this.

ex·tor·tion·ate /ɪk`stɔʃṇət/ *adj* in the nature of extortion; (of demands, prices) exorbitant. **~·ly** *adv*

extra /`ekstrə/ *adj* additional; beyond what is usual, expected or arranged for: *~ pay for ~ work; without ~ charge. There were so many people that the company put on ~ buses.* □ *adv* **1** more than usually: *an ~ strong box; ~ fine quality.* **2** in addition: *price £1.30, packing and postage ~.* □ *n* **1** ~ thing; sth for which an ~ charge is made: *Her regular school fees are £50 a term; music and dancing are ~s.* **2** (cricket) run not scored off the bat. **3** (cinema, T V, etc) person employed and paid (usu by the day) for a minor part, e g in a crowd scene.

ex·tract /ɪk`strækt/ *vt* [VP6A,14] ~ ***(from)***, **1** take or get out (usu with effort or by force): *~ a cork from a bottle; have a tooth ~ed; ~ a bullet from a wound;* (fig) *~ money/information from sb,* who is unwilling to give it. **2** obtain juices, etc) by pressing, crushing, boiling, etc: *~ oil from cotton-seed/olives.* **3** select and copy out words, examples, passages, etc (from a book. □ *n* /`ekstrækt/ [U,C] **1** that which has been ~ed(2) and concentrated: *vanilla ~; beef ~; ~ of malt.* **2** [C] passage ~ed(3): *~s from a long poem.* **ex·trac·tion** /ɪk`strækʃn/ *n* [U] **1** ~ing or being ~ed(1): *the ~ion of a tooth.* **2** descent; lineage: *Is Mr Mansion of French ~ion?*

extra·cur·ricu·lar /'ektrəkə`rɪkjʊlə(r)/ *adj* outside the regular course of academic work or studies: *~ activities,* e g in a dramatic society.

ex·tra·dite /`ekstrədaɪt/ *vt* [VP6A] **1** give up, hand over (a person) from the State where he is a fugitive to the State where he is alleged to have committed, or has been convicted of, a crime. **2** obtain (such a person) for trial. **ex·tra·di·tion** /'ekstrə`dɪʃn/ *n*

extra·ju·dicial /'ekstrədʒu`dɪʃl/ *adj* beyond the authority of a court; outside the (normal) authority of the law.

extra·mari·tal /'ekstrə`mærɪtl/ *adj* outside marriage: *~ relations,* adultery.

extra·mural /'ekstrə`mjʊərl/ *adj* **1** outside the walls and boundaries (of a town or city). **2** (of lectures, etc) from outside a university: *~ studies/students.*

ex·traneous /ɪk`streɪnɪəs/ *adj* not related (to the object to which it is attached); not belonging (to what is being dealt with); coming from outside: *~ interference.*

extra·ordi·nary /ɪk'strɔdnrɪ *US:* -dṇerɪ/ *adj* **1** beyond what is usual or ordinary; remarkable: *a man of ~ genius; ~ weather.* **2** (of officials) additional, specially employed: *envoy ~.* **ex·tra·ordi·nar·ily** /ɪk`strɔdnrlɪ *US:* -dṇerlɪ/ *adv*

extra·sen·sory /'ekstrə`sensərɪ/ *adj* (esp) ~ **perception** (abbr E S P), perception of external events without the use of any of the known senses.

extra·ter·ri·tor·ial /'ekstre'terɪ`tɔrɪəl/ *adj* = **exterritorial.**

ex·trava·gant /ɪk`strævəgənt/ *adj* **1** wasteful; (in the habit of) wasting (money, etc): *an ~ man; ~ tastes and habits.* **2** (of ideas, speech, behaviour) going beyond what is reasonable; not properly controlled: *~ praise/behaviour.* **~·ly** *adv* **ex·trava·gance** /-gəns/ *n* **1** [U] being ~: *His ex-*

travagance explains why he is always in debt. **2** [C] absurd statement, act, etc.

ex·trava·ganza /ɪkˈstrævəˋgænzə/ *n* **1** (music) irregular (often burlesque) and fanciful composition. **2** (theatre) burlesque; farce; spectacular entertainment. **3** wild behaviour and speech.

ex·treme /ɪkˋstrim/ *n* **1** either end of anything; highest degree: *annoying in the* ~, most annoying. **2** (*pl*) qualities, etc as wide apart, as widely different, as possible: *the* ~*s of heat and cold. Love and hate are* ~*s.* ***go/be driven to*** ~***s***, to ~ measures, to do more than is usu considered right or desirable. □ *adj* **1** at the end(s); farthest possible: *the* ~ *edge of a field; in* ~ *old age; the* ~ *penalty of the law* (in some countries) *is the death penalty.* **2** reaching the highest degree: ~ *patience/kindness; in* ~ *pain.* **3** (of persons, their ideas) far from moderate; going to great lengths in views or actions: *hold* ~ *opinions; the* ~ *left,* (in politics) those who support communism. ~**·ly** *adv* **ex·trem·ist** /-ɪst/ *n* person who holds ~ views (esp in politics). **ex·trem·ity** /ɪkˋstremətɪ/ *n* (*pl* -ties) [C] **1** ~ point, end or limit; (*pl*) hands and feet. **2** (*sing* only) ~ degree (of joy, misery, esp of misfortune): *an extremity of pain. How can we help them in their extremity?* **3** (usu *pl*) ~ measures, e g for punishing wrongdoers, taking revenge: *Both armies were guilty of extremities.*

ex·tri·cate /ˋekstrɪkeɪt/ *vt* [VP6A,14] ~ ***from,*** set free, get sb, oneself free: ~ *oneself from a difficulty.* **ex·tri·cable** /ekˋstrɪkəbl/ *adj* that can be ~d. **ex·tri·ca·tion** /ˈekstrɪˋkeɪʃn/ *n* [U].

ex·trin·sic /ekˋstrɪnsɪk/ *adj* ~ ***(to),*** (of qualities, values, etc) not a part of the real character; operating or originating from the outside; not essential.

ex·tro·vert /ˋekstrəvɜt/ *n* person more interested in what goes on around him than in his own thoughts and feelings; (colloq) lively, cheerful person. ⇨ introvert. **ex·tro·ver·sion** /ˈekstrəˋvɜʃn *US:* -ˋvɜʒn/ *n*

ex·trude /ɪkˋstrud/ *vt* [VP14] ~ ***(from),*** force sb or sth out; shape (e g plastic or metal) by forcing through a die. **ex·tru·sion** /ɪkˋstruʒn/ *n*

ex·uber·ant /ɪgˋzjubərənt *US:* -ˋzu-/ *adj* **1** growing vigorously; luxuriant: *plants with* ~ *foliage.* **2** full of life and vigour; high-spirited; overflowing: *children in* ~ *spirits; an* ~ *imagination.* ~**·ly** *adv* **ex·uber·ance** /-rəns/ *n* state or quality of being ~: *The speaker's exuberance won over an apathetic audience.*

ex·ude /ɪgˋzjud *US:* -ˋzud/ *vt, vi* [VP2A,C,6A] (of drops of liquid) come or pass out slowly; ooze out: *Sweat* ~*s through the pores.*

ex·ult /ɪgˋzʌlt/ *vi* [VP2A,3A,4C] rejoice greatly: ~ *at/in a success;* ~ *to find that one has succeeded;* ~ (= triumph) *over a defeated rival.* ~**·ant** /-ənt/ *adj* ~ing; triumphant. ~**·ant·ly** *adv* **ex·ul·ta·tion** /ˈegzʌlˋteɪʃn/ *n* [U] great joy (*at*); triumph (*over*).

ex voto /ˈeks ˋvəʊtəʊ/ *adv, n* (Lat) (offering made) in carrying out a vow.

eye[1] /ɑɪ/ *n* **1** organ of sight: *We see with our eyes. He opened/closed his eyes. He is blind in one eye.* ⇨ the illus on p 309. ***an eye for an eye,*** punishment as severe as the injury suffered; retaliation. ***eyes right/left/front,*** (mil command) Turn the head and look to the right, etc. ***if you had half an eye,*** if you were not so dull, unobservant. ***in the eye of the law,*** from the point of view of the law; as the law sees it. ***in the eyes of sb, in my/his, etc eyes,*** in the judgement of: *You're only a child in his eyes.* ***under/before one's very eyes,*** (a) in one's presence, in front of one. (b) with no attempt at concealment. ⇨ catch[1](7), dust[1](1). ***up to the eyes in*** (work, etc), deeply engaged in. ***with an eye to,*** with a view to, hoping for. ***be all eyes,*** be watching intently. ***be in the public eye,*** be often seen in public; be well known. ***close one's eyes to,*** refuse to see or take notice of. ***get one's eye in,*** (cricket and other ball games) become able, through practice, to follow with one's eyes the movement of the ball. ***give sb a black eye/black sb's eye,*** give him a blow so that there is a discoloured bruise round the eye. ***have an eye for,*** be a good judge of, have a due sense of: *He has a good eye for beauty/the picturesque.* ***have an eye to,*** have as one's object: *He always has an eye to business,* looks for possibilities of doing business. ***keep an eye on,*** (lit, fig) keep a watch on. ***make eyes at,*** look amorously at. ***make sb open his eyes,*** make him stare in surprise. ***mind your eye,*** (colloq) Take care, Look out. ***open sb's eyes to,*** cause him to realize. ***see eye to eye (with),*** agree entirely (with), have identical views. ***see sth with half an eye,*** see it at a glance. ***set/clap eyes on,*** see, behold: *I hope I shall never set eyes on her again.* ***never take one's eyes off,*** never stop watching. **2** thing like an eye: *the eye of a needle,* the hole for the thread; *a hook and eye,* fastening with a hook and loop for a dress, etc; *the eye of a potato,* point from which a leaf-bud will grow. **3** (compounds, etc) **ˋeye·ball** *n* the eye within the lids and socket. ***eyeball to eyeball,*** (colloq) face to face. **ˋeye-bath, ˋeye-cup** *nn* small glass for holding lotion, etc, in which to bathe the eyes. **ˋeye·brow** *n* arch of hair above the eye. ⇨ the illus at head. ***raise one's eyebrows,*** express surprise, doubt, etc. **ˋeye·ful** /-fl/ *n* as much as one is capable of viewing; as much as one can see at a glance. ***have/get an eyeful,*** have a good long look (at sth that has strongly attracted the attention because one is curious about it). **ˋeye-glass** *n* lens (for one eye) to help defective sight. **ˋeye-glasses** *n pl* pair of lenses in a frame; spectacles or glasses (the usu word). **ˋeye·lash** *n* hair, row of hairs, on the edge of the eyelid. **eye·less** *adj* without eyes. **ˋeye·lid** *n* upper or lower covering of the eye: *hang on by the eyelids,* have a very slight, insecure hold. **ˋeye-opener** *n* circumstance, etc that brings enlightenment and surprise. **ˋeye·piece** *n* lens at the end of a telescope or microscope, to which the eye is applied. **ˋeye·shot** *n* [U] seeing distance: *beyond/out of/in/within eyeshot.* **ˋeye·sight** *n* [U] power, faculty, of seeing: *to have good/poor eyesight.* **ˋeye·sore** *n* ugly object; sth unpleasing to look at. **ˋeye-strain** *n* [U] tired condition of the eyes (as caused, for example, by reading very small print). **ˋeye-tooth** *n* canine tooth. ⇨ the illus at mouth. **ˋeye·wash** *n* [U] (a) liquid for bathing the eyes. (b) (colloq) sth said or done to deceive; mere professions. **ˋeye-witness** *n* person who can bear witness from what he has himself seen: *an eye-witness account of a crime.* **-eyed** *suff* (in compounds): *a blue-eyed girl,* girl having blue eyes; *a ˋone-eyed man,* man having only one eye; *starry-eyed,* (colloq) idealistic.

eye[2] /ɑɪ/ *vt* [VP6A,15A] observe, watch: *He eyed me with suspicion. They were ey(e)ing us jealously.*

eye·let /ˈæɪlət/ *n* [C] small hole in cloth, in a sail, etc for a rope, etc to go through; metal ring round such a hole, to strengthen it.

eyrie, eyry /ˈɑɪərɪ/ *n* ⇨ aerie.

Ff

F, f /ef/ (*pl* **F's, f's** /efs/) the sixth letter of the English alphabet.

fa /fɑ/ *n* (music) fourth of the syllables used in the scale *do, re, mi, fa, sol, la, ti, do.*

fab /fæb/ *adj* (colloq abbr of) fabulous(**3**).

Fabian /ˈfeɪbɪən/ *adj* using cautious and slow strategy to wear out opposition: *a ~ policy.* □ *n* **the F~s,** left-wing political group in Great Britain.

fable /ˈfeɪbl/ *n* **1** [C] short tale, not based on fact, esp one with animals in it, e g *Aesop's ~s,* and intended to give moral teaching. **2** [U] (collective *sing*) myths; legends: *sort out fact from ~.* **3** [C] false statement or account. **fabled** /ˈfeɪbld/ *adj* celebrated in ~; legendary.

fab·ric /ˈfæbrɪk/ *n* [C,U] **1** kind, sheet, of textile material; *woollen/silk ~s; ~ gloves,* made of woven material, not of leather. **2** structure; sth put together: *the ~ of society; funds for the upkeep of the ~,* e g a church building.

fab·ri·cate /ˈfæbrɪkeɪt/ *vt* [VP6A] construct; put together; make up (sth false); forge (a document): *~ an accusation/a will: a ~d account of adventures.* **fab·ri·ca·tion** /ˈfæbrɪˈkeɪʃn/ *n* [U] fabricating; [C] sth ~d, e g a forged document, a false story of events.

fabu·lous /ˈfæbjʊləs/ *adj* **1** celebrated in fable(**2**): *~ heroes.* **2** incredible or absurd: *~ wealth.* **3** (colloq) wonderful; marvellous. **~·ly** *adv* incredibly: *~ly rich.*

fa·çade /fəˈsɑd/ *n* [C] front or face of a building (towards a street or open place); (fig) false appearance: *a ~ indifference.*

face[1] /feɪs/ *n* **1** the front part of the head (eyes, nose, mouth, cheeks, chin): *He fell on his ~. The stone struck him on the ~. Her ~ is her fortune,* said of a woman who has beauty, but no dowry or talents. ***bring two persons/parties ~ to ~, bring sb ~ to ~ with sb,*** bring them together so that they confront one another: *The two politicians were brought ~ to ~ in a T V interview.* ***come ~ to ~ with sb, meet sb ~ to ~,*** come into his presence, meet or confront him. ***look sb in the ~,*** look at him steadily. ***be unable to look sb in the ~,*** be unable to look at sb because of feeling ashamed, bashful, etc. ***set one's face against,*** oppose. ***show one's ~,*** appear, let oneself be seen: *How can you show your ~ here/in public after the way you behaved last time?* ***in (the) ~ of,*** (**a**) in the presence of; before. *What could he do in the ~ of all these difficulties?* (**b**) in spite of: *He succeeded in ~ of great danger.* ***fly in the ~ of sth,*** openly defy, disregard Providence/public disapproval/the facts. ***in one's ~,*** (**a**) straight against: *The sun was shining in our ~s.* (**b**) with no attempt at concealment: *Death stared him in the ~. She'll only laugh in your ~.* Cf *laugh up one's sleeve* at laugh(**1**). ***to one's ~,*** openly, in one's hearing. Cf *behind one's back: I'll tell him so to his ~,* i e I'm not afraid to tell him. **2** (compounds) **ˈ~-ache** *n* neuralgia. **ˈ~-card** *n* king, queen, or knave. **ˈ~-cloth,** (esp) small square towel for washing the ~ and hands. **ˈ~-cream,** cosmetic cream for the skin on the ~. **ˈ~-lift(ing)** *n* operation of tightening the skin to smooth out wrinkles and make the ~ look younger. **ˈ~-pack** *n* paste applied to clean and freshen the skin of the ~. **ˈ~-powder** *n* cosmetic powder for the ~. **3** look; expression: *a sad ~; smiling ~s. She is a good judge of ~s,* judges the character well from the expression of the ~. ***keep a straight ~,*** hide one's amusement (by not smiling or laughing). ***put on/wear/make/pull a ~/~s at sb/a long ~,*** look serious or dismal, pull the ~ out of shape; make grimaces. **4** (in various senses) ***have the ~ (to do sth),*** (more usu *the cheek*) be bold or impudent enough. ***lose ~,*** be humiliated, suffer loss of credit or reputation. ***put a new ~ on sth,*** alter its aspect, make it look different. ***put a good/bold ~ on sth,*** make it seem to be well; show courage in dealing with it. front(**4**). ***save (one's) ~,*** evade shaming oneself openly;

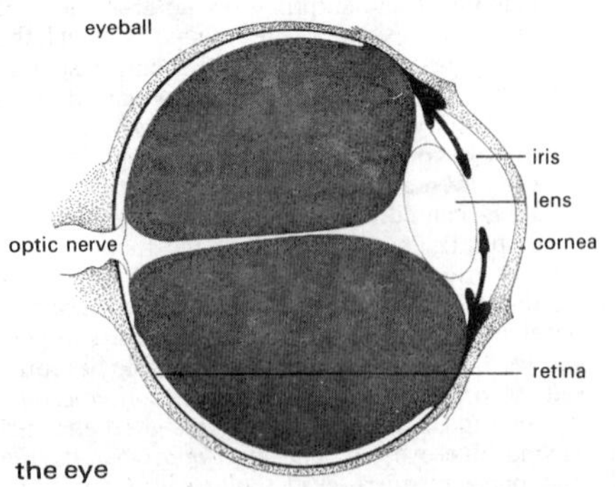

the eye

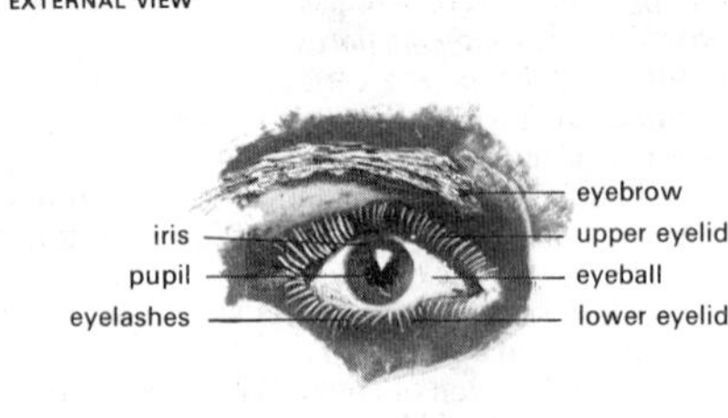

avoid losing one's dignity or suffering loss of one's reputation. Hence, **'~-saver** *n* **'~-saving** *n, part adj*: *~-saving moves.* ***on the ~ of it,*** judging by appearances, when first seen or heard: *On the ~ of it, his story seems unconvincing.* **5** ⇨ the illus at mountain. surface; façade (of a building); front: *the ~ of a clock. He laid the cards ~ down on the table. A dice has six ~s. A diamond crystal has many ~s. The team climbed the north ~ of the mountain. They disappeared from/off the ~ of the earth. The miner worked at the 'coal~ for six hours. The value of a coin or banknote is shown on its ~.* Hence, **'~ value,** the nominal value of a coin or banknote; (fig) what sth or sb seems to be from appearances: *take sth at its ~ value.* **6** size or style of the surface of a piece of type cast for printing: *bold-~ type.* **~less** *adj* (fig) anonymous; unknown to the general public: *the ~less men who have power in commerce and industry.*

face[2] /feɪs/ *vt, vi* **1** [VP6A,C] have or turn the ~ to, or in a certain direction; be opposite to: *Turn round and ~ me. Who's the man facing us? The window ~s the street. The picture ~s page 10. 'How does your house ~?' 'It ~s south.'* ***About/Left/Right ~!*** (US mil commands) Turn right round/to the left/right. Cf (GB) *About/Left/Right turn!* **2** [VP6A,15B,2C] meet confidently or defiantly: *~ the enemy; ~ dangers.* ***~ a matter out, ~ it out,*** refuse to give way, carry it through with courage. ***~ the music,*** show no fear at a time of trial, danger, difficulty. ***~ up to (sth),*** recognize and deal with, honestly and bravely: *~ up to the fact that one is no longer young.* **3** [VP6A] recognize the existence of: *~ facts/altered circumstances.* **4** [VP6A] present itself to: *the problem that ~s us.* **5** [VP6A,14] cover with a layer of different material: *~ a wall with concrete; a coat ~d with silk,* e g with silk on the lapels. **facer** *n* (GB colloq) serious difficulty by which one is suddenly or unexpectedly ~d: *Well, that's a ~r, isn't it!*

facet /ˈfæsɪt/ *n* one of the many sides of a cut stone or jewel; aspect, e g of a problem.

fa·cetious /fəˈsiʃəs/ *adj* (intended to be) humorous fond of, marked by, joking: *a ~ remark/young man.* **~·ly** *adv* **~·ness** *n*

facia /ˈfeɪʃə/ *n* = fascia.

fa·cial /ˈfeɪʃl/ *adj* of or for the face: *a ~ massage.* □ *n* ~ massage.

fa·cile /ˈfæsaɪl *US:* -sl/ *adj* **1** easily done or obtained: *a ~ victory.* **2** (of a person) able to do things easily; (of speech or writing) done easily but without attention to quality: *a ~ liar/remark; a man with a ~ pen/tongue.* **3** gentle; flexible: *a girl with a ~ nature/disposition.*

fa·cili·tate /fəˈsɪləteɪt/ *vt* [VP6A] make easy; lessen the difficulty of: *Modern inventions have ~d housework.* Note: ~ is never used when the subject is a word for a person.

fa·cil·ity /fəˈsɪlətɪ/ *n* (*pl* **-ties**) **1** [U] quality which makes learning or doing things easy or simple: *have great ~ in learning languages; show ~ in performing a task; write/play the piano with ~.* **2** (*pl*) aids, circumstances, which make it easy to do things: *facilities for travel,* e g buses, trains, air services; *facilities for study,* e g libraries, laboratories; *'sports facilities,* e g running tracks, swimming pools.

facing /ˈfeɪsɪŋ/ *n* **1** coating of different material, e g on a wall. **2** (*pl*) material of a different colour on a garment, e g on the cuffs, collar: *a purple jacket with green ~s.* ⇨ face[2](5).

fac·sim·ile /fækˈsɪməlɪ/ *n* [C] exact copy or reproduction of writing, printing, a picture, etc: *reproduced in ~,* exactly.

fact /fækt/ *n* **1** [C] sth that has happened or been done. ***accessary before the ~,*** accessary who is not present when a crime is committed. ***accessary after the ~,*** who knowingly helps another who has committed a crime. **2** [C] sth known to be true or accepted as true: *No one can deny the ~ that fire burns. Poverty and crime are ~s. I know it for a ~,* I know that it is really true. *A ~-finding commission has been appointed,* one to inquire into ~s, find out what is true and what is not true. **3** (*sing* without *indef art*) reality; what is true; what exists: *The story is founded on ~. It is important to distinguish ~ from fiction. The ~ of the matter is…,* The truth is…. ***in ~, as a matter of ~, in point of ~,*** really: *I think so; in ~, I'm quite sure.*

fac·tion /ˈfækʃn/ *n* **1** [C] discontented, often unscrupulous and self-interested group of persons within a party (esp political): *The party split into petty ~s.* **2** [U] quarrelling among such groups; party strife. **fac·tious** /ˈfækʃəs/ *adj* of, caused by, ~; fond of ~: *a factious spirit.*

fac·ti·tious /fækˈtɪʃəs/ *adj* unnatural; artificial; created or developed by design: *~ enthusiasm; a ~ demand for goods,* e g as the result of extensive advertising.

fac·tor /ˈfæktə(r)/ *n* **1** whole number (except 1) by which a larger number can be divided exactly: *2, 3, 4 and 6 are ~s of 12.* **2** fact, circumstance, etc helping to bring about a result: *evolutionary ~s,* environmental influences, etc that have caused sth to evolve or develop; *~s in the making of a nation; an unknown ~,* sth unknown, likely to influence a result; *the ~ of safety,* e g in engineering. Hence, **'safety-~.** **3** agent; person who buys and sells on commission; (in Scotland) land-agent, steward. **~·ize** /ˈfæktəraɪz/ *vt* [VP6A] find the ~s of (a number).

fac·tory /ˈfæktṛɪ/ *n* (*pl* **-ries**) **1** building(s) where goods are made (esp by machinery); workshop: (attrib) *~ workers; F~ Acts,* (in GB) dealing with safety regulations, working conditions of employees, etc. **2** (old use) merchant company's trading station abroad.

fac·to·tum /fækˈtəʊtəm/ *n* (often hum) servant doing all kinds of work.

fac·tual /ˈfæktʃʊəl/ *adj* concerned with fact.

fac·ulty /ˈfækltɪ/ *n* (*pl* **-ties**) [C] **1** power of mind; power of doing things: *the mental faculties,* the reason; *the ~ of making friends easily; have a great ~ for learning languages; the ~ of speech; be in possession of all one's faculties,* be able to see, hear, speak, understand, etc. **2** (in a university) department or grouping of related departments: *the F~ of Law/Science;* all the teachers, lecturers, professors, etc in one of these: *a member of (the) ~; a ~ meeting;* (US) the whole teaching staff of a university.

fad /fæd/ *n* [C] fanciful fashion, interest, preference, enthusiasm, unlikely to last: *Will Tom continue to collect foreign stamps or is it only a passing fad? She is full of fads and fancies,* has rather silly likes and dislikes. **faddy** /ˈfædɪ/ *adj* having fads; having silly likes and dislikes, e g about food. **fad·dily** /ˈfædəlɪ/ *adv*

fade /feɪd/ *vt,vi* **1** [VP6A,2A,C] (cause to) lose colour, freshness or vigour: *The strong sunlight had* ~*d the curtains. Flowers soon* ~ *when cut. Will the colour in this material* ~*? She is fading away*, losing strength. **2** [VP2A,C] go slowly out of view, hearing or the memory: *Daylight* ~*d away. As evening came the coastline* ~*d into darkness. The sound of the cheering* ~*d away in the distance. His hopes* ~*d. All memory of her childhood* ~*d from her mind.* **3** [VP15B,2C,3A] (cinema, broadcasting) (cause to) decrease or increase in strength: ~ *one scene into another* (on a cinema screen); ~ *a conversation out/in,* (in broadcasting) gradually reduce/increase the volume of sound to inaudibility/audibility.

fæces (US = **feces**) /fisiz/ *n pl* (med) waste matter excreted from the bowels.

faerie, faery /ˈfeərɪ/ *n* (old use) fairyland; (attrib) visionary; fancied.

fag[1] /fæg/ *n* **1** (*sing* only) tiring job: *What a fag! It's too much (of a) fag.* **2** (at public schools in England) junior pupil who performs duties for a senior pupil. **3** (sl) cigarette. **4** (sl) (= **faggot(3)**) homosexual.

fag[2] /fæg/ *vi,vt* (-gg-) **1** [VP2C] do very tiring work: *fag (away) at sth/at doing sth.* **2** [VP6A, 15B] (of work) make very tired: *Doesn't that sort of work fag you (out)? He was almost fagged out,* exhausted. *Your horse looks fagged.* **3** [VP2A,3A] (at public schools in England) act as a fag: *fag for a senior.* ⇨ **fag**[1](2).

fag-end /ˈfæg end/ *n* inferior or useless remnant; worthless part of anything; cigarette butt.

fag·got (US also **fagot**) /ˈfægət/ *n* **1** bundle of sticks or twigs tied together for burning as fuel. **2** meat ball for frying. **3** (sl) homosexual.

Fahr·en·heit /ˈfærənhaɪt/ *n* name of a thermometer scale with freezing-point at 32° and boiling-point at 212°. ⇨ **App 5**.

fa·ience /ˈfeɪˋɒ̃s/ *n* [U] decorated and glazed earthenware or porcelain.

fail[1] /feɪl/ *n* (only in) ***without*** ~***,*** for certain, no matter what difficulties, etc there may be: *I'll be there at two o'clock without* ~*.*

fail[2] /feɪl/ *vi,vt* **1** [VP2A,3A,4A,6A] be unsuccessful: ~ *(in) an examination;* ~ *to pass an examination. All our plans/attempts* ~*ed.* **2** [VP6A] (of examiners) reject (a candidate); decide that (a candidate) has ~ed: *The examiners* ~*ed half the candidates.* **3** [VP2A,C] (often with an *indir obj*) be not enough; come to an end while still needed or expected: *The crops* ~*ed because of drought. Our water supply has* ~*ed. The wind* ~*ed (us),* There was not enough wind for our sails. *Words* ~ *me,* I cannot find words (to describe my feelings, etc). *His heart* ~*ed him,* e g he lost courage. ˋ~**-safe** (attrib *adj*), (of a mechanical device, etc) designed to compensate automatically for a failure (thus eliminating danger, etc). **4** [VP2A,C] (of health, eyesight, etc) become weak: *His eyesight is* ~*ing. He has suffered from* ~*ing health/has been* ~*ing in health for the last two years.* **5** [VP4A] omit; neglect; not remember (or choose) (or, in many cases, simply making, with the *inf,* a neg of an affirm): *He never* ~*s to write* (= always writes) *to his mother every week. His promises* ~*ed to* (= did not) *materialize. He did not* ~ *to keep* (= he did keep) *his word.* **6** [VP2A] become bankrupt: *Several of the biggest banks* ~*ed during the depression.* **7** ~ ***in,*** [VP3A] be insufficiently equipped with; be lacking in: *He's a clever man, but* ~*s in perseverance.*

fail·ing[1] /ˈfeɪlɪŋ/ *n* [C] weakness or fault (of character); shortcoming: *We all have our little* ~*s.*

fail·ing[2] /ˈfeɪlɪŋ/ *prep* in default of; in the absence of: ~ *this,* if this does not happen; ~ *an answer,* if no answer is received; ~ *Smith,* if Smith is not available.

fail·ure /ˈfeɪljə(r)/ *n* **1** [U] failing; lack of success: *F*~ *in an examination should not deter you from trying again. All his efforts ended in* ~, were unsuccessful. **2** [C] instance of failing; person, attempt, or thing that fails: *Success came after many* ~*s. He was a* ~ *as a teacher.* **3** [U] state of not being adequate; non-performance of what is normal, expected or required; [C] instance of this: *ˋheart* ~*; ˋengine* ~*s. F*~ *of crops often results in famine. Crop* ~*s caused great hardship among the peasants.* **4** [C] bankruptcy: *numerous bank* ~*s.* **5** [C,U] neglect, omission, inability (*to do* sth): *His* ~ *to help us was disappointing. His* ~ *to answer questions made the police suspicious.*

fain /feɪn/ *adv* (poet, or old use after *would*) willingly; with pleasure: *I would* ~ *have stayed at home.*

faint[1] /feɪnt/ *adj* (-er, -est) **1** (of things perceived through the senses) weak; indistinct; not clear: *The sounds of the music grew* ~*er in the distance. She called for help in a* ~ *voice. Only* ~ *traces of the tiger's tracks could be seen. There was a* ~ *smell of incense in the church.* **2** (of things in the mind) weak; vague: *There is a* ~ *hope that she may be cured. I haven't the* ~*est idea (of) what you mean.* **3** (of the body's movements and functions) weak; failing: *His breathing became* ~*. His strength grew* ~*.* **4** (*pred* only) (of persons) likely to lose consciousness; giddy: *She looks/feels* ~*.* **5** (*pred* only) (of persons) weak, exhausted: ~ *with hunger and cold.* **6** (of actions, etc) weak; unlikely to have much effect: *a* ~ *show of resistance; make a* ~ *attempt to do sth.* **7** timid: *F*~ *heart never won fair lady.* ˈ~**-ˋhearted** *adj* lacking in courage. ~**·ly** *adv* ~**·ness** *n*

faint[2] /feɪnt/ *vi* [VP2A,C] **1** lose consciousness (because of loss of blood, the heat, shock, etc): *Several of the girls* ~*ed and had to be carried off the field. He* ~*ed from hunger.* **2** become weak: *He was* ~*ing with hunger.* **3** (= *fade*) become weak: *The sounds* ~*ed away.* □ *n* act, state, of ~ing(1): *She went off in a* ~, lost consciousness.

fair[1] /feə(r)/ *adj* (-er, -est) **1** just; acting in a just and honourable manner; in accordance with justice or the rules (of a game, etc): *Everyone must have a* ~ *share. It was a* ~ *fight,* e g the rules of boxing were observed. *We charge* ~ *prices and are content with* ~ (= reasonable) *profits.* ***give sb/get a*** ~ ***hearing,*** an opportunity to defend his conduct, etc, e g in a law court. ~ ***play,*** ⇨ play[1](2). ˈ~-ˋ**minded,** just. **2** average; quite good: *a* ~ *chance of success. His knowledge of French is* ~, *but ought to be better. The goods arrived in* ~ *condition. She has a* ~ *amount of sense.* **3** (of the weather) good; dry and fine; (of winds) favourable: *hoping for* ~ *weather. They set sail with the first* ~ *wind. The glass is at set* ~, The needle of the barometer is stationary (= set) at ~ (indicating a likelihood of good weather). ˈ~**-weather** ˋ**friends,** persons who cease to be friends when one is in trouble. **4** satisfactory; abundant: *a ~ heritage;* promising: *be in a ~ way to succeed,* be at the stage where success seems assured; *in a ~ way of business,* quite prosperous. **5** (of the skin, hair) pale; light in colour; blond: *a '~-haired girl; a ~ complexion.* **6** (of speeches, promises, etc) specious; plausible; carefully chosen to seem polite and gentle in order to please and persuade: *put sb off with ~ words/promises; the ~ speeches of the politicians,* e g before an election. **7** clean; clear; without blemish: *Please make a ~ copy of this letter,* a new one without the errors, corrections, etc. *Such behaviour will spoil your ~ name,* good reputation. **8** (old use) beautiful: *a ~ maiden; the ~ sex,* women. **~·ish** /ˈfeərɪʃ/ *adj* of ~(2) size or quality.

fair² /feə(r)/ *adv* **1** in a fair(1) manner: *play ~.* ***~ enough,*** (colloq) used to indicate that sb has acted reasonably, made a reasonable suggestion, etc. **2** *write/copy sth out ~,* write a fair copy of it. ⇨ fair¹(7). **3** straight, directly. **4** (old use) politely: *speak sb ~; a ~-spoken young man,* courteous.

fair³ /feə(r)/ *n* **1** market (esp for cattle, sheep, farm products, etc) held periodically in a particular place, often with entertainments: *(arrive) a day after the ~,* too late. **'~·ground,** open space for ~s. **2** large-scale exhibition of commercial and industrial goods: *a world ~.* **3** bazaar(3).

fair·ly¹ /ˈfeəlɪ/ *adv* **1** justly; honestly: *treat sb ~: come by* (= obtain) *sth ~,* by honest means. **2** (colloq) utterly; completely: *We were ~ caught in the trap,* had no chance of escape. *He was ~ beside himself with rage,* as angry as he could possibly be. *His suggestion ~ took my breath away,* left me quite breathless (with surprise, etc).

fair·ly² /ˈfeəlɪ/ *adv of degree* (Cf *rather,* which may be used with *too* and comparatives; *fairly* cannot be used in this way.) moderately: *This is a ~ easy book* (and is, therefore, perhaps suitable). Cf *This is a rather easy book,* suggesting 'rather too easy', and, therefore, perhaps unsuitable. *He wants a ~ large car,* not small, but not very large. Cf *That car is rather larger than he wants.*

fair·way /ˈfeəweɪ/ *n* **1** navigable channel for ships. **2** (golf) part of a golf-links, between a tee and a green, free from hazards.

fairy /ˈfeərɪ/ *n* (*pl* -ries) **1** small imaginary being with supernatural powers, able to help or harm human beings; (attrib) of or like fairies: *a ~ shape,* beautiful, small, delicate; *~ voices/footsteps; '~ lamps,* small lamps of coloured glass used for decoration. **2** (sl) homosexual. **'~-land** enchanted region; beautiful place. **'~-tale** *n* **(a)** tale about fairies. **(b)** untrue account, esp by a child.

fait ac·com·pli /ˈfeɪt əˈkomplɪ *US:* ˈəkomˈpli/ *n* (F) sth done and, for this reason, not reversible.

faith /feɪt/ *n* **1** [U] ***~ in sb/sth,*** trust; strong belief; unquestioning confidence: *have/put one's ~ in God. Have you any ~ in what he says? I haven't much ~ in this medicine. I've lost ~ in that fellow,* can no longer trust him. **'~ cure,** one (alleged to be) made through religious ~. **'~-healing,** (belief in) healing (of disease, etc) by prayer, appealing to and strengthening a person's religious ~, apart from the use of medicines, etc. **2** [C] belief in divine truth without proof; religion: *the Christian, Jewish and Muslim ~s.* **3** [U] promise; engagement. ***give/pledge one's ~ to sb,*** promise solemnly to support him. ***keep/break ~ with sb,*** be loyal/disloyal to sb, sth. **4** [U] loyalty; sincerity. ***in bad ~,*** with the intention of deceiving. ***in good ~,*** honestly; sincerely.

faith·ful /ˈfeɪθfl/ *adj* **1** keeping faith; loyal and true (*to* sb, *to* a cause, *to* a promise, etc): *a ~ friend; ~ to one's promise; ~ in* (= in respect of) *word and deed.* **2** true to the facts; accurate: *a ~ copy/description/account.* **3** *the ~,* (*pl*) the true believers, esp of Islam and Christianity. **~ly** /-flɪ/ *adv* in a manner. ***Yours ~ly,*** formula for closing a letter (esp in formal or business style). **~·ness** *n*

faith·less /ˈfeɪθləs/ *adj* false; disloyal. **~·ly** *adv* **~·ness** *n*

fake /feɪk/ *n* [C] story, work of art, etc that looks genuine but is not; person who tries to deceive by claiming falsely to be or have sth: (attrib) *a ~ picture.* □ *vt* [VP6A,15B] ***~ (up),*** make (e g a work of art, a story) in order to deceive: *~ an oil-painting. There wasn't a word of truth in what he said; the whole story had been ~d (up),* invented.

fakir /ˈfeɪkɪə(r) *US:* fəˈk-/ *n* Muslim or Hindu religious mendicant who is regarded as a holy man.

fal·chion /ˈfɔltʃən/ *n* short, broad, curved convex-edged sword.

fal·con /ˈfɔlkən *US:* ˈfælkən/ *n* small bird of prey trained to hunt and kill other birds and small animals. ⇨ the illus at prey. **~·ry** *n* [U] sport of hunting with ~s; art of training ~s.

fall¹ /fɔl/ *n* [C] **1** act of falling: *a ~ from a horse; the ~ of an apple from a tree; the F~ of man,* Adam's sin and its results; a ~ in the temperature; a ~ in prices; the ~ (= collapse) *of the Roman Empire.* **2** amount of rain that falls; distance by which sth falls or comes down: *The ~ of the river here is six feet.* **3** (often *pl*) place where a river falls over cliffs, etc: *Niagara F~s.* **4** (now US) autumn: *in the ~ of 1970;* (attrib) *~ fashions.*

fall² /fɔl/ *vi,vt* (*pt* fell /fel/, *pp* ~en /ˈfɔlən/) (For special uses with *adverbial particles* and *preps,* ⇨ 14 below.) **1** [VP2A,B,C,3A] come or go down freely (by force of weight, loss of balance, etc): *The book fell from the table to the floor. He fell into the water. The rain was ~ing steadily. The leaves ~ in autumn. He slipped and fell ten feet. This basket is full of eggs; don't let it ~,* don't drop it. *The lambs are beginning to ~,* be born. ⇨ drop²(2). *He fell into the trap. The river ~s* (= flows) *into the lake.* ***~ on one's feet,*** (fig) be fortunate; get out of a difficulty successfully: *Some people always seem to ~ on their feet,* be lucky and successful. ***~ short,*** (of a missile) not go far enough: *The arrow fell short.* ***~ short of,*** fail to equal; be inferior to: *Your work ~s short of my expectations.* **'~ing 'star,** object (e g a meteor) seen as a bright streak in the sky as it burns up. **2** [VP2A,C,3A] no longer stand; come to the ground; collapse; be overthrown: *Many trees fell in the storm. Babies often ~ when they are learning to walk. He fell over and broke his left leg. He fell full length. He fell on his knees* (= knelt down) *and begged for mercy. He fell in battle,* was killed. *They all fell fighting bravely. Six tigers fell to his rifle,* He shot six tigers. *Six wickets fell before lunch,* (cricket) Six batsmen were out. *The first wicket fell at eleven,* The first batsman was out when the score was eleven. ***~ flat (on one's face),*** (fig) fail to have the intended effect: *His best jokes all fell flat,* did not amuse his listeners. *The scheme fell flat,* was unsuccessful. ***~ to the ground,*** ⇨ ground¹(1). ***~ over***

oneself, **(a)** ~ because one is awkward, clumsy, or in too much of a hurry. **(b)** (fig) be very eager: *The big firms were ~ing over themselves/each other for the services of this brilliant young scientist.* **the ~en,** those killed in war. **3** [VP2C] hang down: *His beard fell to his chest. Her hair/cloak fell over her shoulders.* **4** [VP2A,B,C,3A] come or go to a lower level or point; become lower or less: *The barometer is ~ing. The temperature fell rapidly. His voice fell to a whisper. Her spirits fell at the bad news,* She became low-spirited, sad. *His face/jaw fell,* showed dismay. Cf *'make a long face'* at long[1](1). *His eyes fell,* looked downwards. *The wind fell during the night,* became less strong. **5** [VP2C,D,3A] become; pass into (the state indicated by the *adj* or phrase): *His horse fell lame. He fell silent. The old man fell asleep. He has ~en ill. When does the rent ~ due,* When must it be paid? *He fell into a doze,* began to doze. *He fell into a deep sleep. Do not fall into bad habits,* acquire or adopt them. *He fell into disgrace,* was disgraced. *They have ~en into poverty,* become poor. *She fell an easy prey to him.* ***~ in love (with),*** become filled with love: *He fell in love with an actress. I've ~en in love with your beautiful house.* ***~ out of love (with),*** cease to feel love (for). ⇨ foul[1](6). **6** [VP2A,C,3A] ***~ upon,*** descend upon: *Darkness fell upon the scene,* it became dark. *A great stillness had ~en upon everything,* Everything had become quiet and motionless. *Fear fell upon them,* They became frightened. **7** [VP2A,C] sin; give way to wrongdoing: *Eve tempted Adam and he fell.* **ˈ~en ˋwomen,** (old use) women who have lost their chastity. **8** [VP2A] be overcome or defeated; (of a city, fort, etc.) be captured: *The Government has ~en again.* **9** [VP3A] ***~ on,*** take the direction or position (indicated by the *adv* or phrase): *A shadow fell on the wall. His eye fell on* (= He suddenly saw) *a curious object. Strange sounds fell on our ears,* We heard strange sounds. *The lamplight fell on her face. In 'formidable' the stress may ~ on either the first or the second syllable.* **10** [VP3A] ***~ on/among,*** come by chance, design, or right: *All the expenses fell on me,* I had to pay them. *The responsibility/blame, etc fell upon me. Most of the fighting fell on the second regiment. It fell to my lot to open the discussion,* I had to speak first. *He has fallen on evil days,* is suffering misfortune. He fell among thieves. **11** [VP2C] (of land) slope: *The ground ~s towards the river.* **12** [VP2C] occur, have as date: *Easter ~s early next year. Christmas Day ~s on a Monday this year.* **13** [VP2A,C] be spoken: *Not a word fell from his lips. I guessed what she was going to do from the few words that she let fall,* from what she said. **14** [VP2C,3A,15B] (special uses with *adverbial particles* and *preps*):

fall about (laughing/with laughter), (colloq) laugh uncontrollably: *They fell about when dad slipped on the banana skin.*

fall among, get mixed up with, come by chance among: *~ among thieves, evil companions.*

fall astern, drop behind; not keep up with.

fall away, **(a)** desert: *His supporters began to ~ away.* **(b)** disappear, vanish: *In this crisis, prejudices fell away and all classes co-operated well.*

fall back, retreat; move or turn back: *Our attack was so vigorous that the enemy had to ~ back.* ***~ back on,*** have recourse to; turn to for support: *If you don't need the money now, bank it. It's always useful to have something to ~ back on.*

fall behind (with), fail to keep level with; lag: *He always ~s behind when we're going uphill. I've ~en behind with my correspondence,* have many unanswered letters. *Don't ~ behind with your rent, or you'll be evicted.*

fall down, (colloq) fail in a task, in expectation.

fall for, (colloq) yield to the charms, attractions or merits of (esp when deceived): *He ~s for every pretty face he sees. Did he ~ for your suggestion,* Did he decide that it was good, and agree to it? **ˋ~ guy** *n* (US sl) person who is easily deceived.

fall in, **(a)** collapse; give way: *The roof fell in. The (sides of the) trench fell in.* **(b)** (mil) take, cause to take, places in the ranks: *The sergeant ordered the men to ~ in.* **(c)** (of a single soldier) take his place in the ranks. **(d)** (of a lease) expire. **(e)** (of a debt) become due. ***~ sb in,*** (mil) cause to take a place in the ranks: *The sergeant fell his men in.* ***~ in with,*** **(a)** happen to meet. **(b)** agree to: *He fell in with my views at once.*

fall into, be naturally divisible into: *The subject ~s into four divisions.* ***~ into line (with),*** agree to (what others are doing or wish to do); accept a course of conduct, procedure, etc.

fall off, become smaller, fewer or less: *Attendance at church has ~en off this summer. The takings at the football stadium have ~en off,* Less money has been paid for admission. *The number of passengers by this line shows a slight ~ing off.*

fall on, attack; assault (the enemy).

fall out, **(a)** (mil) go off parade; leave one's place in the rank or file. **(b)** come to pass; happen: *It (so) fell out that I could not get there in time. Things fell out well. Everything fell out as we had hoped.* **(c)** discontinue; give up: *the ˋ~-out rate,* e g of pupils who give up a course of study. ⇨ *drop-out* at drop[2](13). ***~ out (with),*** quarrel (with): *The two men fell out. He has fallen out with the girl he was going to marry.* **ˋ~-out** *n* [U] radio-active dust in the atmosphere, after a nuclear explosion.

fall through, fail; miscarry; come to nothing: *His scheme fell through.*

fall to, begin to eat, fight, attack, etc: *They fell to with a good appetite. I fell to wondering where to go for my holidays.*

fall under, be classifiable under: *The results ~ under three heads.*

fal·lacy /ˈfæləsɪ/ *n* (*pl* -cies) **1** [C] false or mistaken belief. **2** [U] false reasoning or argument: *a statement based on ~.* **fa·lacious** /fəˋleɪʃəs/ *adj* misleading; based on error.

fal·lal /ˈfæˋlæl/ *n* [C] piece of finery, esp of clothing.

fallen *pp* of fall[2].

fal·lible /ˈfæləbl/ *adj* liable to error. **fal·li·bil·ity** /ˈfæləˋbɪlətɪ/ *n* (state of) being ~.

Fal·lo·pian tube /fəˈləʊpɪən ˋtjub *US:* ˋtub/ *n* (anat) = oviduct. ⇨ the illus at reproduce.

fal·low /ˈfæləʊ/ *adj, n* [U] (land) ploughed but not sown or planted: *allow land to lie ~; plough (up) ~ land.*

fal·low-deer /ˈfæləʊ dɪə(r)/ *n* (*pl* unchanged) small Eurasian deer with a reddish-yellow coat with, in the summer, white spots.

false /fɔls/ *adj* **1** wrong; incorrect: *a ~ alarm; ~ ideas; ~ weights,* e g one of 90 grammes marked as 100 grammes; *take a ˈ~ ˋstep,* stumble; (fig) make a social blunder; *sing a ~ note; ~ shame/pride*, based on wrong ideas, etc; *make a ~ start*, (athletics) start before the signal has been given. **2** deceitful; lying: *give a ~ impression; give ~ witness*, tell lies or deceive (e g in a law court); *be ~ to one's word*, fail to keep a promise. ***act under ~ pretences***, ⇨ pretence(2). ***be/put sb in a ~ position***, in circumstances that cause misunderstanding or make it necessary for sb to act contrary to principles. ***sail under ~ colours***, **(a)** (of a ship) with a flag which it has no right to use. **(b)** (fig) pretend or appear to be different from what one really is. ***a ~ bottom***, a secret compartment in a container such as a trunk. **3** not genuine; sham; artificial: *~ hair/teeth; ~ coins*. **4** improperly so called: *the ~ acacia* (not really an acacia tree). □ *adv* (only in) ***play sb ~***, cheat or betray him. **~·ly** *adv* in a ~ manner: *~ly accused*. **~·ness** *n*

false·hood /ˈfɔlshʊd/ *n* **1** [C] lie; untrue statement: *How can you utter such ~s?* **2** [U] telling lies; lying: *guilty of ~. Truth, if exaggerated, may become ~.*

fal·setto /fɔlˈsetəʊ/ *n* (*pl* -tos /-təʊz/) unnaturally high-pitched voice in men; (attrib) of or in such a voice: *in a ~ tone*.

fal·sies /ˈfɔlsɪz/ *n pl* (colloq) brassieres filled with soft material to exaggerate the size of the breasts.

fals·ify /ˈfɔlsɪfɑɪ/ *vt* (*pt,pp* -fied) [VP6A] **1** make false: *~ records/accounts;* tell falsely: *~ a story*. **2** misrepresent: *~ an issue*. **falsi·fi·ca·tion** /ˈfɔlsɪfɪˈkeɪʃn/ *n* [U] ~ing or being falsified; [C] change made in order to deceive.

fals·ity /ˈfɔlsətɪ/ *n* **1** [U] falsehood; incorrectness; error. **2** [C] (*pl* -ties) false or treacherous act, statement, etc.

fal·ter /ˈfɔltə(r)/ *vi,vt* **1** [VP2A,C] move, walk or act in an uncertain or hesitating manner, from either weakness or fear. **2** [VP2A] (of the voice) waver; [VP15B] (of a person) speak in a hesitating way or with a broken voice: *His voice ~ed as he tried to speak. He ~ed out a few words*. **~·ing·ly** /ˈfɔltŗɪŋlɪ/ *adv*

fame /feɪm/ *n* [U] (condition of) being known or talked about by all; what people say (esp good) about sb: *He was not anxious for ~. His ~ as a poet did not come until after his death*. **famed** *adj* famous: *~d for their courage*.

fam·il·iar /fəˈmɪlɪə(r)/ *adj* **1** ***~ with***, having a good knowledge of: *facts with which every schoolboy is ~. I am not very ~ with botanical names*. **2** ***~ to***, well known to: *facts that are ~ to every schoolboy; subjects that are ~ to you*. **3** common; usual; often seen or heard: *the ~ scenes of one's childhood; the ~ voices of one's friends*. **4** close; intimate; personal: *Are you on ~ terms with Mr Green?* (e g) Do you address him as 'Tom' or as 'Mr Green'? *Don't be too ~ with him; he's a dishonest man*. **5** claiming a greater degree of amorous friendship than is proper: *He made himself much too ~ with my wife*. □ *n* intimate friend. **~·ly** *adv* in a ~ manner; without ceremony.

fam·ili·ar·ity /fəˈmɪlɪˈærətɪ/ *n* (*pl* -ties) **1** [U] (the state of) being familiar: *His ~ with the languages used in Nigeria surprised me. You should not treat her with such ~*. ⇨ familiar(4,5). ***F~ breeds contempt***, (prov) When we know sth or sb very well, we may lose respect, fear, etc. **2** (*pl*) acts that lack ceremony; instance of familiar behaviour: *She dislikes such familiarities as the use of her first name by men she has only just met*.

fam·il·iar·ize /fəˈmɪlɪərɑɪz/ *vt* **1** [VP14] ***~ sb/oneself with***, make well acquainted (with): *~ oneself with a foreign language/the use of a new tool/the rules of a game*. **2** [VP6A] make well known: *The newspapers and radio have ~d the word 'automation'*.

fam·ily /ˈfæmļɪ/ *n* (*pl* -lies) **1** [C] parents and children: *Almost every ~ in the village has a man in the army* (Note *sing v* after collective *n*.); *My ~ are early risers* (Note *pl v* after *family*, as members of my family.) **2** (collective *n*) children: *He has a large ~. Has he any ~? Tom is the eldest of the ~*, the eldest child. **3** [C] all those persons descended from a common ancestor: *families that have been in Surrey for hundreds of years*. **4** [U] famous or distinguished ancestry: *a man of good ~; people of no special ~*. **5** [C] group of living things (plants, animals, etc) or of languages, with common characteristics and a common source: *animals of the cat ~*, e g lions and tigers; *the Germanic ~ of languages* (including German, Dutch, English). **6** (attrib) of or for a ~: *a ~ likeness*, i e between members of a ~; *a ~ doctor*, a general practitioner; *a ~ hotel*, one with lower rates for families; *a ~ man*, one who is fond of home life with his ~; *a ~ Bible*, a large one with pages for records of births, marriages and deaths; *the ~ estate/jewels, etc; a ~ tree*, a genealogical tree or chart; *~ planning*, (use of birth control, contraceptives, for) planning the number of children, intervals between births, etc in a ~; *~ name*, surname; *in the ~ way*, (sl; of a woman) pregnant.

fam·ine /ˈfæmɪn/ *n* **1** [U] extreme scarcity (esp of food) in a region: *Parts of India have often suffered from ~*. **2** [C] particular occasion when there is such scarcity: *a water/coal ~*. **3** (attrib) caused by ~: *~ prices*, high prices.

fam·ish /ˈfæmɪʃ/ *vi,vt* **1** [VP2A,3A] suffer from extreme hunger: *They were ~ing for food. I'm ~ing*, (colloq) very hungry. **2** [VP6A] (usu passive) cause (sb) to suffer from hunger: *The child looked half ~ed*.

fa·mous /ˈfeɪməs/ *adj* **1** known widely; having fame; celebrated: *a ~ scientist. The town is ~ for its hot springs/~ as a hot-spring resort*. **2** (obsolescent colloq) excellent; satisfactory: *He has a ~ appetite*. **~·ly** *adv* in a ~(2) manner: *getting on ~ly*.

fan[1] /fæn/ *n* object (waved in the hand, or operated mechanically, e g by an electric motor) for making a current of air (e g to cool a room, to blow dust, etc away); ⇨ p 314; sth that is or can be spread out flat, e g the tail of a peacock. **ˈfan belt** *n* rubber belt transferring circular motion to the cooling fan of an engine. **ˈfan·light** *n* fan-shaped window over a door. **ˈfan ˈvaulting** *n* (archit) style of vaulting in which ribs, like those of a folding fan, rise and spread from a single point.

fan[2] /fæn/ *vt,vi* (-nn-) **1** [VP6A] send a current of air on to: *fan oneself; fan a fire*, to make it burn up; *fan the flame*, (fig) increase excitement or emotion. **2** [VP6A] (of a breeze) blow gently on: *The breeze fanned our faces*. **3** [VP2C] ***~ out***, open in fan-shaped formation: *The troops stormed the enemy's trenches and fanned out across the fields*. **4** [VP6A] spread out (e g a number of playing cards) like a fan.

fan[3] /fæn/ *n* (colloq) fanatical supporter of sth:

fans

ˋ*baseball fans;* ˋ*fan mail*, letters from fans, e g to a popular T V star).

fa·natic /fəˋnætɪk/ *n* person filled with excessive (and often mistaken) enthusiasm, e g in religion: *food* ~*s*, willing to eat only certain kinds of food. □ *adj* (also **fa·nati·cal** /-kl/) excessively enthusiastic; of or like a ~: ~*(al) beliefs.* **fa·nati·cally** /-klɪ/ *adv* **fa·nati·cism** /-sɪzm/ *n* [U] violent, unreasoning enthusiasm; [C] instance of this.

fan·cier /ˋfænsɪə(r)/ *n* person with special knowledge of and love for some article, animal, etc (the name being prefixed): *a* ˋ*dog* ~; *a* ˋ*rose* ~.

fan·ci·ful /ˋfænsɪfl/ *adj* **1** (of persons) full of fancies(**2**); led by imagination instead of reason and experience: *a* ~ *writer.* **2** unreal; curiously designed: ~ *drawings.* **~·ly** /-flɪ/ *adv*

fancy[1] /ˋfænsɪ/ *n* (*pl* **-cies**) **1** [U] power of creating mental pictures (often a passive process). (⇨ **imagination**, in which the mind is more active): *He has a lively* ~. *By the power of* ~ *we may create an unreal world.* **2** [C] sth imagined; unfounded opinion or belief: *the fancies of a poet. Did I really hear someone come in or was it only a* ~? *I have a* ~ (= a vague idea) *that she will be late.* **3** [C] fondness, liking, desire (*for*): *I have a* ~ *for some wine with my dinner.* ***take a* ~ *to,*** become fond of: *The children have taken quite a* ~ *to their cousin.* ***take/catch the* ~ *of,*** please or attract: *The new musical play took the* ~ *of the public. She saw the hat in a shop window and it caught her* ~. ***a passing* ~,** sth that attracts one's attention and liking for a short period of time only. ˈ**~-ˋfree** *adj* not in love; not committed to anything; not taking things seriously: *footloose and* ~*-free.*

fancy[2] /ˋfænsɪ/ *adj* (usu attrib; not in the *comp* or *superl*) **1** (esp of small things) brightly coloured; made to please the eye: ~ *cakes;* ~ *goods; a* ~ *fair* (for the sale of ~ goods). **2** not plain or ordinary: ~ *bread;* ~ *dress,* i e unusual costume, often historical or exotic, as worn at balls, called ~*-dress balls.* ˋ**~ work,** ornamental sewing. **3** bred for particular points of beauty: ~ *dogs/pigeons;* ~ *pansies,* having two or more colours. **4** *a* ~ *price*, an unreasonably high or extravagent price. **5** (US, of goods) superior in quality: *'F~ Crab'* (on a label, etc). **6** based on imagination, not fact: *a* ~ *portrait.*

fancy[3] /ˋfænsɪ/ *vt* (*pt,pp* **-cied**) **1** [VP6A,16B, 19C] picture in the mind; imagine: *Can you* ~ *me as a pirate? I can't* ~ *his doing such a thing.* **2** [VP25,9] be under the impression that (without being certain, or without enough reason): *I rather* ~ *(that) he won't come. He fancied he heard footsteps behind him. Don't* ~ *that you can succeed without hard work. When she saw Tom, whom she had fancied (to be) dead,....* **3** [VP6A] have a fancy(**3**) for: *What do you* ~ *for your dinner? I don't* ~ *this place at all. Do you* ~ *that girl,* find her attractive, likeable? **4** ***~ oneself,*** have an excessively high opinion of oneself; be rather conceited: *He fancies himself as an orator.* **5** [VP6A,C] exclamatory style, expressing surprise: *F~ her saying such unkind things about you! F~ that, now! Just* ~! How strange! How surprising!

fan·dango /ˈfænˋdæŋgəʊ/ *n* (*pl* **-goes** /-gəʊz/) (music for a) lively Spanish or S American dance.

fane /feɪn/ *n* (poet) temple.

fan·fare /ˋfænfeə(r)/ *n* [C] flourish of trumpets or bugles.

fang /fæŋ/ *n* long, sharp tooth (esp of dogs and wolves); snake's poison-tooth.

fan·light fan[1].

fanny /ˋfænɪ/ *n* (*pl* **-nies**) (US sl) buttocks.

fan·tan /ˈfænˋtæn *US:* ˋfæntæn/ *n* Chinese gambling game.

fan·tasia /ˈfæntəˋzɪə *US:* fænˋteɪʒə/ *n* musical composition in which a fanciful style is more important than structure.

fan·tas·tic /fænˋtæstɪk/ *adj* **1** wild and strange; grotesque: ~ *dreams/shapes/fashions in dress*). **2** (of ideas, plans) impossible to carry out; absurd. **3** (sl) marvellous; wonderful: *Christina's a really* ~ *girl!* **fan·tas·ti·cally** /-klɪ/ *adv*

fan·tasy /ˋfæntəsɪ/ *n* (*pl* **-sies**) **1** [U] fancy(**1**); imagination, esp when extravagant. **2** [C] wild or fantastic product of the imagination. **3** [C] fantasia.

far[1] /fɑ(r)/ *adj* ⇨ **farther, farthest, further, furthest. 1** (usu in liter style) distant: *a far country.* ***a far cry,*** a long way. **2** *the Far East*, China, Korea, Japan, etc; *the Far West*, the Pacific coast area of the US. **3** (= *farther*) more remote: *at the far end of the street; on the far bank of the river.*

far[2] /fɑ(r)/ *adv* ⇨ **farther, farthest, further, furthest. 1** (indicating distance in space or time, commonly used in the interr and neg, but not usually, except as shown in **2** below in the affirm): *How far did you go? We didn't go far.* Cf (in the affirm): *We went a long way. We went only a short way.* **2** (with other *advv* and *preps*): *far away/off/out/back/in, far beyond the bridge; far above the clouds; not far from here; far into the night; far back in history; as far back as 1902.* ***far from,*** as in: *Your work is far from (being)* (= is not at all) *satisfactory. The newspaper accounts are far from being true,* are in many points false. *Far from* (= Instead of) *admiring his paintings, I dislike them intensely.* ***go far,*** (**a**) (of persons) be successful; do much: *He's clever and intelligent, and will go far.* (**b**) (of money) buy goods, services, etc: *A pound does not go so far today as it did five years ago.* ***go/carry sth too far,*** go beyond the limits of what is considered reasonable: *Don't carry the joke too far.* Cf It's beyond a joke. *Don't carry your modesty too far,* Don't be unnecessarily modest about your abilities, etc. ***go***

far towards/to doing sth, help or contribute greatly to: *The loan will go far towards overcoming our financial troubles.* ***far and near/wide,*** everywhere: *They searched far and wide for the missing child. People come from far and near to hear the famous violinist.* ***so far,*** until now: *So far the work has been easy.* ***So far, so good,*** up to now everything has gone well. ***as/so far as,*** (a) to the place mentioned: *He walked as far as the post office.* (b) the same distance: *We didn't go as/so far as the others.* (c) to the extent that (to indicate a limit of advance or progress): *So far as I know he will be away for three months. He will help you as far as he can/as far as is possible/as far as lies in his power. We have gone so far as to collect some useful statistics.* **3** (with qualifying *adjj* and *advv*) (by) much; considerably; to a great extent: *This is far better. It fell far short of our expectations.* ***far and away,*** very much: *He's far and away the best actor I've seen.* **far-away** *adj* (a) distant, remote: *far-away places/times.* (b) (of a look in a person's eyes) dreamy; as if fixed on sth far away in space or time. **ˈfar-ˋfamed** *adj* widely known. **ˈfar-ˋfetched** *adj* (of a comparison) forced; unnatural. **ˈfar-ˋflung** *adj* (rhet) widely extended. **far gone,** very ill, mad, drunk, in debt. **ˈfar-ˋoff** *adj* = far-away. **ˈfar-ˋreaching** *adj* likely to have many consequences; having a wide application: *far-reaching proposals.* **ˈfar-ˋseeing** *adj* seeing far into the future. **ˈfar-ˋsighted** *adj* (a) able to see distant objects more clearly than near objects. (b) (fig) prudent; having good judgement of future needs, etc.

far[3] /fɑ(r)/ *n* **1** distance: *Have you come from far?* **2** ***by far,*** (with a *comp* or *superl*) a large amount or degree: *This is better by far* (= far better).

farce /fɑs/ *n* **1** [C] play for the theatre, full of ridiculous situations intended to make people laugh; [U] this style of drama. **2** [C] series of actual events like a ~; absurd and useless proceedings: *The Disarmament Conference was a ~.* **far·ci·cal** /ˋfɑsɪkl/ *adj* of or like a ~; absurd. **far·ci·cally** /-klɪ/ *adv*

fare[1] /feə(r)/ *n* [C] **1** money charged for a journey by bus, ship, taxi, etc: *All ~s, please* (cried by the conductor of a bus, etc). **2** passenger in a hired vehicle: *The taxi-driver had only six ~s all day.*

fare[2] /feə(r)/ *n* [U] food provided at table: *good/simple/homely ~.* **ˈbill of ˋ~,** list of dishes; menu.

fare[3] /feə(r)/ *vi* [VP2C] **1** progress; get on: *How did you ~ during your journey,* What were your experiences? *It has ~d well with him,* He has done well, been fortunate. ***You may go farther and ~ worse,*** (prov, used to suggest that one should be content with one's present conditions). **2** (old use) go, journey. ***~ forth,*** start out.

fare·well /ˈfeəˋwel/ *int* goodbye. ***~ to,*** no more of. □ *n* leave-taking: *make one's ~s,* take one's leave; (attrib) *a ~ speech/dinner party.*

fari·na·ceous /ˈfærɪˋneɪʃəs/ *adj* starchy; of flour or meal: *~ foods,* e g bread, potatoes.

farm[1] /fɑm/ *n* **1** area of land (usu divided into fields) and buildings (e g barns), under one management (either owned or rented) for growing crops, raising animals, etc: *working on the ~.* Cf *in* the fields. **ˋ~·hand** *n* (US) ~ worker; agricultural labourer. **ˋ~·yard** *n* space enclosed by ~ buildings (sheds, barns, etc). **2** (also **ˋ~·house, ˋ~·stead** /-sted/) farmer's house on a ~.

farm[2] /fɑm/ *vt,vi* **1** [VP6A,2A] use (land) for growing crops, raising animals, etc: *He ~s 200 acres. He is ~ing in Africa. He is engaged in ˋsheep-~ing.* **2** [VP15B] ***~ out,*** send work out to be done by others. **~er** *n* man who owns or manages a ~. Cf *peasant,* a word not used of a ~er or farm worker in GB or US.

far·rago /fəˋrɑgəʊ/ *n* (*pl* **-gos, -goes** /-gəʊz/) medley, mixture: *a ~ of nonsense/useless knowledge.*

far·rier /ˋfærɪə(r)/ *n* smith who shoes horses.

far·row /ˋfærəʊ/ *vi* give birth to pigs: *When will the sow ~?* □ *n* litter of pigs; giving birth to pigs: *15 at one ~.*

fart /fɑt/ *vi, n* ⚠ (not in polite use) (send out, sending out of) wind through the anus.

far·ther /ˋfɑðə(r)/ *adv comp* of *far,* used chiefly for distance, and infrequently for *further* (when the idea of distance is absent): *We can't go any ~ without a rest. They went ~ into the forest.* □ *adj* more distant: *on the ~ bank of the river; at the ~ end of the street.*

far·thest /ˋfɑðɪst/ *adv, adj superl* of *far: Which village in England is ~ from London?* ***at (the) ~,*** (a) at the greatest distance: *It's five miles away at the ~,* is not more than five miles away. (b) (of time) at the latest.

far·thing /ˋfɑðɪŋ/ *n* (coin, not now in use in GB, worth) one-quarter of a penny: ***It doesn't matter/He doesn't care a ~,*** not in the least.

fas·cia (also **facia**) /ˋfeɪʃə/ *n* dashboard or panel on a motor-vehicle, etc (with gauges, dials, etc). ⇨ the illus at motor.

fas·ci·nate /ˋfæsɪneɪt *US:* -sn̩eɪt/ *vt* [VP6A] **1** charm or attract greatly: *The children were ~d by all the toys in the shop windows.* **2** take away power of movement by a fixed look, as a snake does. **fas·ci·nat·ing** *adj* having strong charm or attraction: *a fascinating smile/hat/shop-window/display.* **fas·ci·nat·ing·ly** *adv* **fas·ci·na·tion** /ˈfæsɪˋneɪʃn *US:* -snˋeɪʃn/ *n* [U] fascinating or being ~d; power to ~; [C] thing that ~s: *Girls have a fascination for Brian,* i e they ~ him. *Brian has a fascination for girls,* i e he ~s them.

Fas·cism /ˋfæʃɪzm/ *n* philosophy, principles and organization of the aggressive nationalist and anti-communist governmental system started in Italy in 1922 and dissolved in 1943. **Fas·cist** /ˋfæʃɪst/ *n* supporter of ~. □ *adj* of ~; extreme right-wing; reactionary.

fashion /ˋfæʃn/ *n* **1** (*sing* with *def* or *indef art*) manner of doing or making sth: *He was behaving in a strange ~. He walks in a peculiar ~.* ***after/in a ~,*** somehow or other, but not satisfactorily: *He can speak and write English, after a ~.* ***after the ~ of,*** like, in imitation of: *a novel after the ~ of Graham Greene.* **2** [C,U] (as shown in the examples) (of clothes, behaviour, thought, custom, etc) prevailing custom; that which is considered most to be admired and imitated during a period or at a place: *dressed in the latest ~; the Paris ~s; changes of ~. F~s for men's clothes change less frequently than ~s for women's clothes.* ***be all the ~,*** (of dress, behaviour, etc) be very popular. ***come into/go out of ~,*** become/no longer be in ~. *When did that style of dress come into/go out of ~?* ***follow/be in the ~,*** do what others do in matters of dress, behaviour, etc. ***set the ~,*** give the example by adopting new ~s. ***a man/woman of ~,*** one belonging to upperclass society and conforming to its usages. **ˈ~ plate** *n* picture showing a style of dress. □ *vt* [VP6A,15A] give form or shape to; mould: *~ a canoe out of a tree-trunk/a whistle from a piece of wood/a lump of clay into a bowl.*

fashion·able /ˈfæʃnəbl/ *adj* following the fashion(2); used by, visited by, many people, esp of the upper classes: *~ clothes; a ~ dressmaker/ hotel/summer resort.* **fashion·ably** /-əblɪ/ *adv* in a ~ manner: *fashionably dressed.*

fast[1] /fɑst *US:* fæst/ *adj* **1** firmly fixed; not easily moved: *The post is ~ in the ground. Make the boat ~,* Make it secure. *Take (a) ~ hold of the rope,* hold it tightly. ***hard and ~ rules,*** rigid rules. **2** steady; steadfast; loyal; close: *a ~ friend/friendship.* **3** (of colours) unfading. □ *adv* firmly, securely, tightly: *hold ~ to sth. The ship was ~ aground,* could not be refloated. *She was ~ asleep,* in a deep sleep. ***stand ~,*** not move or retreat; refuse to give way. ***stick ~,*** **(a)** = stand ~. **(b)** be unable to make progress. ***F~ bind, ~ find,*** (prov) If you make things secure, e g by locking them up, you will not lose them. ***play ~ and loose with,*** repeatedly change one's attitude towards; trifle with: *play ~ and loose with a girl's affections.*

fast[2] /fɑst *US:* fæst/ *adj* (-er, -est) **1** quick; rapid: *a ~ train/horse; a ~ trip; a ~ draw,* of a gun from a holster. **2** (now obsolescent) (of a person, his way of living) spending too much time and energy on pleasure and excitement; dissipated: *lead a ~ life; a ~ woman; ~ society.* **3** (of a watch or clock) showing time later than the true time: *My watch is five minutes ~,* e g showing 2.05 at 2.00. **4** (of a surface) promoting quick motion: *a ~ cricket pitch/billiard-table.* **5** (of photographic film) suitable for very brief exposures.

fast[3] /fɑst *US:* fæst/ *adv* **1** quickly: *Don't speak so ~. It was raining ~,* heavily. Her tears fell ~. **2** *live ~,* live in a dissipated way; use much energy in a short time. **3** (old use) close: *~ by/behind the church.*

fast[4] /fɑst *US:* fæst/ *vi* [VP2A,B] go without food, or without certain kinds of food, esp as a religious duty: *days devoted to ~ing and penitence,* e g in Lent. □ *n* **1** (period of) going without food: *a ~ of three days; break one's ~.* **2** day (**ˈ~-day**) or season of ~ing.

fasten /ˈfɑsn *US:* ˈfæsn/ *vt,vi* **1** [VP6A,15A,B] make fast[1]; fix firmly; tie or join together: *Have you ~ed all the doors and windows? He ~ed the two sheets of paper together. He ~ed up the box,* closed it and made it secure. **2** [VP14] ***~ (up)on,*** fix a nickname, accusation, etc upon sb; direct one's looks, thoughts, attention, etc, upon sb: *He ~ed his eyes (up)on me.* **3** [VP2A,C] became fast[1] or secured: *The door won't ~. This dress ~s down the back,* has buttons, etc down the back. **4** [VP3A] ***~ (up)on,*** lay hold of, seize upon; single (a person) out for attack: *He ~ed (up)on the idea.* **~er** *n* thing that ~s things together: *a paper ~er; a zip-~er.* **~·ing** *n* thing that ~s, esp a slide or a bolt.

fas·tid·ious /fəˈstɪdɪəs *US:* fæ-/ *adj* hard to please; quick to find fault: *He is ~ about his food/clothes, etc.* **~·ly** *adv* **~·ness** *n*

fast·ness /ˈfɑstnəs *US:* ˈfæs-/ *n* **1** [C] stronghold; fortress: *a mountain ~,* e g of bandits. **2** [U] the quality of being fast[1](3): *We guarantee the ~ of these dyes.*

fat[1] /fæt/ *adj* (fatter, fattest) **1** covered with, having much, fat: *fat meat: a fat man; fat cheeks; fat cattle,* made fat ready for slaughter. **ˈfat-head** *n* dull, stupid person. **2** thick; well filled: *a fat pocket-book,* one stuffed with banknotes. ***a fat lot,*** (sl) a great deal (usu ironic): *A fat lot you care,* i e you don't care at all. **3** rich, fertile: *fat lands.* **fat·tish** *adj* rather fat. **fat·ness** *n*

fat[2] /fæt/ *n* [C,U] (kinds of) white or yellow substance, oily or greasy, found in animal bodies; this substance purified for cooking purposes; oily substance obtained from certain seeds: *Give me red meat, please; I don't like fat. Fried potatoes are cooked in deep fat. Vegetable cooking fats are sold in tins.* ***chew the fat,*** continue to grumble about sth. ***live on the fat of the land,*** have the best of everything to eat. ***The fat's in the fire,*** What has been done (usu irrevocably) will cause a lot of trouble. **fat·less** *adj* ⇨ **fatty.**

fat[3] /fæt/ *vt* (-tt-) = fatten: *fatted cattle.* ***kill the fatted calf,*** receive (a returned prodigal) with joy.

fa·tal /ˈfeɪtl/ *adj* **1** causing, ending in, death or disaster (*to*): *a ~ accident. The cyclist was knocked down by a lorry and received ~ injuries. His illness was ~ to our plans,* caused them to fail. **2** like fate; of, appointed by, destiny: *the ~ day.* **~ly** /ˈfeɪtḷɪ/ *adv* in a ~ manner: *~ly injured/ wounded.*

fa·tal·ism /ˈfeɪtḷɪzm/ *n* [U] belief that events are decided by fate(1); submission to all that happens as inevitable. **fatal·ist** /ˈfeɪtḷɪst/ *n* believer in ~. **fatal·is·tic** /ˈfeɪtḷˈɪstɪk/ *adj* of ~: *a fatalistic attitude.*

fa·tal·ity /fəˈtælətɪ/ *n* (*pl* -ties) **1** [C] misfortune, calamity, esp one that causes death and destruction: *floods, earthquakes and other fatalities.* **2** [C] death by accident, in war, etc: *There have been numerous bathing fatalities this summer,* Many people have lost their lives while bathing. **3** [U] state of being subject to fate(1) or destiny. **4** [U] fatal infuence; deadliness: *the ~ of certain diseases,* e g cancer.

fate /feɪt/ *n* **1** [U] power looked upon as controlling all events in a way that cannot be resisted; destiny: *He had hoped to succeed to his father's estate, but ~ decided otherwise.* ***as sure as ~,*** quite certain(ly). **the F~s,** the three Greek goddesses of destiny. **2** [C] the future as decided by ~ for sth or sb; what is destined to happen: *They met their various ~s. They left/abandoned the men to their ~.* **3** (*sing*) death; destruction; person's ultimate condition: *go to one's ~; decide a person's ~,* e g whether he shall be killed or allowed to live; *meet one's ~,* be killed, die. □ *vt* (usu passive) ***be ~d to/that,*** be destined to/that: *He was ~d to be hanged. It was ~d that we should fail.*

fate·ful /ˈfeɪtfl/ *adj* **1** controlled by, showing the power of, fate(1); important and decisive: *a ~ decision; on this ~ day; these ~ events. When the judge pronounced the ~ words...,* e g sentence of death. **2** prophetic. **~ly** /-fḷɪ/ *adv*

fa·ther[1] /ˈfɑðə(r)/ *n* **1** male parent: *You have been like a ~ to me. The property had been handed down from ~ to son for many generations.* ***The child is ~ to the man,*** One's childhood decides the way in which one will develop in later years. ***The wish is ~ to the thought,*** (prov) We are likely to believe what we wish to be true. **ˈ~-in-law** /ˈfɑðr ɪn lɔ/ *n* (*pl* ~s-in-law) ~ of one's wife or husband. '~ **figure,** older man respected because of his concern for one's welfare. **2** (usu *pl*) ancestor(s): *sleep with one's ~s,* be buried in the ancestral tomb or grave. **3** founder or first leader: *the F~s of the Church,* Christian writers of the first five centuries; *the Pilgrim F~s,* English Puritans who founded the colony of Plymouth, Massachusetts, U S A in 1620; *the F~ of English poetry,* Chaucer. **4** *Our (Heavenly) F~,* God. **5** priest, esp one belonging to a religious order; head of a monastic house (⇨ **brother** for a monk): *the Holy F~,* the Pope. **6** title used in personifications: *F~ Christmas; F~ Time.* '**~-hood** /-hʊd/ *n* [U] state of being a ~. '**~-land** /-lænd/ *n* one's native country (*mother country* is the normal English usage). **~-less** *adj* without a living ~ or a known ~. **~-ly** *adj* of or like a ~: *~ly love/smiles.*

fa·ther[2] /ˈfɑðə(r)/ *vt* **1** [VP6A] be the originator of an idea, plan, etc. **2** [VP6A] admit oneself to be the father or author of a child, book, etc. **3** [VP14] **~ upon,** fix the paternity of (a child), the authorship of or responsibility for (sth *upon* sb): *Please don't ~ this magazine article on me,* don't lead people to think that I wrote it.

fathom /ˈfæðəm/ *n* measure (six feet or 1·8 metres) of depth of water: *The ship sank in six ~s. The harbour is four ~(s) deep.* □ *vt* [VP6A] find the depth of; get to the bottom of; comprehend: *I cannot ~ his meaning.* **~-less** *adj* too deep to ~.

fa·tigue /fəˈtig/ *n* **1** [U] condition of being very tired: *Several men dropped with ~ during the long march.* **2** [U] weakness in metals caused by prolonged stress. **3** [C] tiring task; non-military duty of soldiers, such as cleaning, cooking, etc. '**~-party** *n* group of soldiers given such duties. □ *vt* [VP6A] cause ~ to: *feeling ~d; fatiguing work.*

fat·ten /ˈfætn/ *vt,vi* [VP6A,15B,2A,C] **~ (up),** make or become fat: *~ cattle.*

fatty /ˈfætɪ/ *adj* (**-ier, -iest**) like fat; consisting of fat: *~ bacon.*

fatu·ous /ˈfætʃʊəs/ *adj* foolish; showing foolish self-satisfaction: *a ~ smile; a ~ young man.* **~·ly** *adv* **fa·tu·ity** /fəˈtjuətɪ *US:* -ˈtu-/ *n* [U] state of being ~; [C] (*pl* **-ties**) ~ remark, act, etc. **~-ness** *n*

fau·bourg /ˈfəʊbʊə(r)/ *n* (F) suburb; district within a city: *F~ St Germain,* in Paris.

fau·cet /ˈfɔsɪt/ *n* (esp US) device (*tap* in GB) for controlling the outflow of liquid from a pipe or container.

faugh /fɔ *spontaneously, as an explosive puffing sound/ int* expression of disgust.

fault /fɔlt/ *n* **1** [C] sth that makes a person, thing, etc imperfect; defect; blemish; flaw: *She loves me in spite of all my ~s. Her only ~ is excessive shyness. There is a ~ in the electrical connections.* **at ~,** in the wrong, at a loss; in a puzzled or ignorant state: *My memory was at ~.* **to a ~,** excessively: *She is generous to a ~.* **find ~ with,** complain about: *I have no ~ to find with your work. He's always finding ~.* Hence, '**~-finder,** '**~-finding.** **2** (*sing* only) responsibility for being wrong: *Whose ~ is it that we are late? It's your own ~. The ~ lies with you, not with me,* You are to blame. **3** [C] thing wrongly done; blemish; flaw; (tennis, etc) ball wrongly served. **4** [C] place where there is a break in the continuity of layers of rock, etc. □ *vt* [VP6A] find ~ with: *No one could ~ his performance.* **~-less** *adj* **~-less·ly** *adv* **~y** *adj* having a ~ or ~s. **~-ily** /-əlɪ/ *adv* in a ~y manner.

faun /fɔn/ *n* (Rom myth) one of a class of gods of the woods and fields, with a goat's horns and legs.

fauna /ˈfɔnə/ *n* all the animals of an area or an epoch: *the ~ of E Africa.*

faux pas /ˈfəʊ ˈpɑ/ *n* (*pl* unchanged) indiscreet action, remark, etc esp a social blunder: *to criticise his boss to his boss's wife was a dreadful ~.*

fa·vour[1] (US = **fa·vor**) /ˈfeɪvə(r)/ *n* **1** [U] friendly regard; willingness to help, protect, be kind to: *win a person's ~; look on a plan with ~,* approve of it; *be/stand high in sb's ~,* be well regarded by him. ***be in/out of ~ (with sb),*** have/not have his friendly regard, etc: *She's out of ~ with her employer,* has displeased him. ***find/lose ~ with sb/in sb's eyes,*** win/lose sb's ~. **2** [U] aid; support. ***in ~ of,*** **(a)** in sympathy with; on the side of: *Was he in ~ of votes for women?* **(b)** on behalf of; to the advantage or account of: *Cheques should be drawn in ~ of the Society, not in ~ of the Treasurer.* ***in sb's ~,*** to the advantage of: *The exchange rate is in our ~,* will benefit us when we change money. **3** [U] treatment that is generous, lenient; partiality: *He obtained his position more by ~ than by merit or ability.* ***without fear or ~,*** with impartial justice. **4** [C] act of kindness: *May I ask a ~ of you,* ask you to do sth for me? *I would esteem it a ~ if you would answer promptly.* ***do sb a ~/do a ~ for sb,*** do sth to help sb: *Do me a ~, darling—Please don't chatter while I'm listening to this music.* ***by ~ of...,*** words written on the envelope of a letter conveyed by the person whose name is written after, instead of by the post office. **5** [C] ornament or decoration, e g a badge, knot of ribbon, worn as a sign that one is a member or supporter of some organization, club or party. **6** (old use) *by your ~,* with your permission; if I may venture to say so. **7** (old use) looks, countenance. Hence, '*ill-'~ed,* having an unpleasing countenance.

fa·vour[2] (US = **fa·vor**) /ˈfeɪvə(r)/ *vt* **1** [VP6A] show favour to; support: *Fortune ~s the brave.* **2** [VP6A] treat with partiality; show more favour to one person, group, etc than to another: *most ~ed nation/clause,* clause (in a commercial treaty) agreeing that a nation shall be accorded the lowest scale of import duties. *A teacher should not ~ any of his pupils.* **3** [VP14] ***~ sb with sth,*** oblige; do something for: *Will you ~ me with an interview? Miss Sharp will now ~ us with a song,* will sing for us. **4** [VP6A] (of circumstances) make possible or easy: *The weather ~ed our voyage.* **5** [VP6A] resemble in features: *The child ~s its father,* looks more like its father than its mother.

a fault in rock

a faun

fa·vour·able (US = **-vor-**) /ˈfeɪvr̩əbl/ *adj* giving or showing approval; helpful: *a ~ report on one's work; ~ winds. Is he ~ to the proposal?* **fa·vour·ably** /-əblɪ/ *adv* in a ~ manner: *speak favourably of a plan; look favourably on sb.*

fa·vour·ite (US = **-vor-**) /ˈfeɪvr̩ɪt/ *n, attrib adj* **1** (person or thing) preferred above all others: *He is a ~ with his uncle/a ~ of his uncle's/his uncle's ~. This book is a great ~ of mine. Who is your ~ author?* **2** *the ~,* (racing) the horse, etc generally expected to win: *back the ~,* bet money on it. *The ~ came in third.* **3** person who receives too much favour, is given unfair advantages. **fa·vour·it·ism** (US = **-vor-**) /-ɪzm/ *n* [U] (practice of) having ~s(3).

fawn[1] /fɔn/ *n* **1** young fallow deer less than one year old. **2** (also ˋ*~-colour(ed)*) light yellowish brown.

fawn[2] /fɔn/ *vi* [VP2A,3A] *~ (on),* **1** (of dogs) show pleasure and affection by jumping about, tail-wagging, etc. **2** (of persons) try to win sb's favour by servile behaviour, flattery, etc: *~ on a rich relative.*

fay /feɪ/ *n* (poet) fairy.

fe·alty /ˈfiḷtɪ/ *n* (*pl* **-ties**) (in feudal times) tenant's or vassal's (acknowledgement of) fidelity to his lord: *do/make/swear ~* (*to* one's lord, *for* one's land); *take an oath of ~.*

fear[1] /fɪə(r)/ *n* **1** [C,U] feeling caused by the nearness or possibility of danger or evil; alarm: *They stood there in ~ and trembling,* frightened and shaking. *He was overcome with/by ~. The thief passed the day in ~ of discovery. Grave ~s are felt for the safety of the missing climbers. A sudden ~ came over him. He obeyed from ~. He was unable to speak for ~.* ***for ~ of,*** because of anxiety about: *She asked us not to be noisy, for ~ of waking the baby.* ***for ~ (that)/(lest)...,*** in order that... should not occur: *I daren't tell you what he did, for ~ (that) he should be angry with me.* **2** [U] anxiety for the safety (*of*): *He is in ~ of his life.* **3** [U] likelihood: *There's not much ~ of my losing the money. No ~!* (colloq) Certainly not! **4** [U] dread and reverence: *the ~ of God.* **~·ful** /-fl/ *adj* **1** causing ~; terrible: *a ~ful railway accident;* (colloq) annoying; very great: *What a ~ful mess!* **2** frightened; apprehensive: *~ful of wakening sb; ~ful that/lest the baby should wake up.* **~·fully** /-fḷɪ/ *adv* **~·ful·ness** *n* **~·less** *adj* without ~: *~less of the consequences.* **~·less·ly** *adv* **~·less·ness** *n* **~·some** /ˈfɪəsm/ *adj* (usu jokingly) frightening in appearance: *a ~some apparition.*

fear[2] /fɪə(r)/ *vt,vi* **1** [VP6A,C] feel fear of, be afraid of: *~ death. These men are not to be ~ed.* **2** [VP2A,4] feel fear; be afraid; hesitate: *Never ~! She ~ed to speak in his presence. He did not ~ to die.* **3** [VP3A] *~ for,* feel anxiety about: *We ~ed for his life/safety.* **4** [VP6A,9] have an uneasy feeling or anticipation of: *~ the worst,* be afraid that the worst has happened or will happen. *I ~ he has failed. 'Will he get well?'—'I ~ not.' 'Is he going to die?'—'I ~ so.'* **5** [VP6A] regard with awe and reverence: *F~ God and honour the Queen.*

feas·ible /ˈfizəbl/ *adj* **1** that can be done: *A counter-revolution is ~,* We can, if we choose, bring one about. **2** (colloq) that can be managed or that is convenient or plausible; that can be believed: *His story sounds ~,* may be true. **feasi·bil·ity** /ˌfizəˈbɪlətɪ/ *n*

feast /fist/ *n* **1** religious anniversary or festival, e g Christmas or Easter. ⇨ also movable. **2** splendid meal with many good things to eat and drink; (fig) sth that pleases the mind: *a ~ of reason,* intellectual talk. □ *vt,vi* **1** [VP6A,2A,B] take part in a ~; give a ~ to; pass (time) in ~ing: *~ one's friends; ~ all evening. He sat there ~ing (himself).* **2** [VP14] give sensuous pleasure to: *~ one's eyes on beautiful scenes.*

feat /fit/ *n* sth difficult well done, esp sth showing skill, strength or daring: *brilliant ~s of engineering; perform ~s of valour.*

feather[1] /ˈfeðə(r)/ *n* one of the light coverings that grow from a bird's skin. ⇨ the illus at bird, rare. ***a ~ in one's cap,*** sth one may justly be proud of. ***as light as a ~,*** very light indeed. ***in high ~,*** in high spirits. ***birds of a ~,*** people of the same sort. ***show the white ~,*** show fear. **ˈ~-ˈbed** *n* mattress stuffed with ~s. □ *vt* (**-dd-**) pamper by giving generous help; make things easy for: *~-bed the farmers,* e g by subsidizing them. **ˈ~-ˈbrained** *adj* empty-headed; flighty. **ˋ~·weight** *n* (esp) boxer weighing between 118 and 126 lb or (53·5 to 57 kg). **~y** *adj* light and soft like ~s: *~y snow.*

feather[2] /ˈfeðə(r)/ *vt* [VP6A] **1** supply with feathers: *~ an arrow.* ***~ one's nest,*** make things comfortable for oneself; enrich oneself. **2** *~ one's oar,* (rowing) turn it so as to pass along the surface of the water.

fea·ture /ˈfitʃə(r)/ *n* [C] **1** one of the named parts of the face: *Her eyes are her best ~.* **2** (*pl*) the face as a whole: *a man of handsome ~s.* **3** characteristic or striking part: *the geographical ~s of a district,* e g mountains, lakes; *unusual ~s in a political programme.* **4** (often attrib) prominent article or subject in a newspaper; full-length film in a cinema programme, etc: *a newspaper that makes a ~ of* (= gives special prominence to) *sport; a two-~ programme,* i e with two long films. □ *vt* [VP6A] be a ~(3) of; make (sb or sth) a ~(3,4) of; have a prominent part for: *a film that ~s a new French actress.* **~·less** *adj* uninteresting; with no obvious ~s(3).

feb·rile /ˈfibraɪl/ *adj* of fever; feverish.

Feb·ru·ary /ˈfebrʊərɪ *US:* -rʊerɪ/ *n* the second month of the year.

feces ⇨ fæces.

feck·less /ˈfekləs/ *adj* futile; inefficient. **~·ly** *adv* **~·ness** *n*

fec·und /ˈfikənd/ *adj* prolific, fertile. **fec·und·ity** /fɪˈkʌndətɪ/ *n* [U] fertility; productiveness.

fed *pt,pp* of feed.

fed·eral /ˈfedrl/ *adj* **1** of, based upon, federation: *In the USA foreign policy is decided by the ~* (i e central) *government, and ~ laws are made by Congress.* **F~ Bureau of Investigation** (abbr FBI), (US) department which is responsible for investigating violations of ~ law and safeguarding national security. ⇨ State[1](2). **2** relating to, supporting, central (as distinct from State) government. **~·ist** /ˈfedrḷɪst/ *n* supporter of ~ union or power. **ˋF~ist Party** (also **ˋF~ Party**), (US) political party, founded in 1787 after the American Revolution (1775—83) and prominent in the 1790's. **~·ism** /-ɪzm/ *n*

fed·er·ate /ˈfedəreɪt/ *vt,vi* [VP6A,2A] (of States, societies, organizations) combine, unite, into a federation.

fed·er·ation /ˌfedəˈreɪʃn/ *n* **1** [C] political system in which a union of States leave foreign affairs, defence, etc to the central (Federal) government but retain powers of government over some internal affairs. **2** [C] such a union of States, e g the US; similar union of societies, trade unions, etc. **3** [U] act of federating.

fee /fi/ *n* **1** [C] charge or payment for professional advice or services, e g private teachers or schools, examiners, doctors, lawyers, surveyors; entrance money for an examination, club, subscription library etc. **2** [U] (legal) inherited estate: *land held in fee simple/fee tail,* with the right to pass it to any class of heirs/one particular class of heirs. ⇨ entail. □ *vt* [VP6A] pay a fee to, engage for a fee: *fee a barrister.*

feeble /ˈfibl/ *adj* weak; faint; without energy: *a ~ old man; a ~ cry/argument. His pulse was very ~.* **ˈ~-ˈminded** /-ˈmaɪndɪd/ *adj* subnormal in intelligence. **feebly** /ˈfiblɪ/ *adv* **~·ness** *n*

feed[1] /fid/ *n* **1** [C] (chiefly of animals and babies; jokingly of persons) meal: *We stopped to let the horses have a ~.* **2** [U] food for animals: *There isn't enough ~ left for the hens.* **3** [C] pipe, channel, etc through which material is carried to a machine; [U] material supplied. **ˈ~·back** *n* **1** return of part of the output of a system to its source (so as to modify it). **2** (colloq) information, etc (about a product) given by the user to the supplier, maker, etc: *interesting ~back via the market research department.*

feed[2] /fid/ *vt,vi* (*pt,pp* fed /fed/) **1** [VP6A,14] give food to: *Have the pigs been fed yet? Have you fed the chickens? What do you ~ your dog on,* What kind of food do you give it? ***~ oneself,*** put food into the mouth: *The baby can't ~ itself yet.* [VP15B] ***~ up,*** give extra food to, give nourishing food to: *There are hundreds of poor children there who need ~ing up.* ***be fed up (with),*** (sl) have had too much of sth; be discontented: *I'm fed up with your grumbling.* **ˈ~ing-bottle** *n* bottle from which hand-fed infants are given milk, etc. **2** [VP14] give to as food: *~ oats to horses. I wouldn't ~ that stinking meat to my dog.* **3** [VP2A,C] (chiefly of animals, colloq or hum of persons) eat: *The cows were ~ing in the meadows. Have you fed yet?* **4** [VP3A] ***~ on,*** take as food: *Cattle ~ chiefly on grass.* **5** [VP6A,15A] supply with material; supply (material) to: *This moving belt ~s the machine with raw material/~s raw material into the machine. The lake is fed by two rivers.*

feeder /ˈfidə(r)/ *n* [C] **1** (of plants and animals, with *adjj*) one that feeds: *This plant is a gross ~,* needs much manure. **2** child's feeding-bottle or bib. **3** (often attrib) branch railway line, airline, canal, etc linking outlying areas with the main line, etc.

feel[1] /fil/ *n* (*sing* only) **1** *rough/smooth, etc to the ~,* when touched or felt. **2** sensation characteristic of sth when touching or being touched: *You can tell it's silk by the ~. The monk didn't like the ~ of the hair shirt they gave him.* **3** act of feeling: *Let me have a ~.*

feel[2] /fil/ *vt,vi* (*pt,pp* felt /felt/) **1** [VP6A,10] (try to) learn about, explore, by touching, holding in the hands, etc: *Blind persons can often recognize objects by ~ing them. The doctor felt my pulse. Just ~ the weight of this box! F~ whether there are any bones broken.* ***~ one's way,*** **(a)** go forward carefully, as in the dark, or as a blind man does. **(b)** be cautious in dealing with sth: *They were ~ing their way towards an agreement.* **2** [VP3A] ***~ (for),*** search (about) with the hand(s) (or the feet, a stick, etc): *He was ~ing about in the dark for the electric-light switch. He felt in his pocket for a penny. He felt along the wall for the door/to find the door.* **3** [VP6A,18A,19A] be aware of (through contact): *I can ~ a nail in my shoe. I felt something crawl(ing) up my arm.* **4** [VP6A,18A,19A] be aware of, perceive (not through contact): *Did you ~ the earthquake? He felt his heart beating wildly. She felt apprehension stealing over her.* [VP15B] ***~ sb out,*** try cautiously to learn the news of: *I'll ~ out the members of the committee.* **5** [VP2D,C] be consciously; be in a certain physical, moral or emotional state: *~ cold/hungry/comfortable/sad/happy, etc. How are you ~ing today? You will ~ better after a night's sleep. She doesn't ~ (quite) herself today,* is not as well, calm, self-possessed, etc as usual. *He ~s confident of success. He felt cheated. We don't ~ bound* (= obliged) *to accept this offer. Please ~ free* (= consider yourself welcome) *to call on us whenever you like.* **6** [VP2A] be capable of sensation: *The dead cannot ~.* **7** [VP3A] ***~ for/with,*** have sympathy (*with*), compassion (*for*): *I ~ with you in your sorrow. I ~ for you.* **8** ***~ as if/though,*** have, give, the impression that: *She felt as if her head were splitting. Her head felt as if it were splitting.* **9** [VP2D] give or produce the impression of being: *Your hands ~ cold. How does it ~ to be home again after twenty years abroad? This new suit doesn't ~ right.* **10** **ˈ~ like,** (of persons) be in the mood for: *I don't ~ like (eating) a big meal now. We'll go for a walk if you ~ like it.* ***~ equal to,*** (colloq) ***~ up to,*** be well enough to, be capable of: *I don't ~ equal to the task. He doesn't ~ up to a long walk.* **11** [VP6A,C] be sensitive to: suffer because of: *He doesn't ~ the heat at all,* is not troubled by it. *He felt the insult keenly. She will ~* (= be saddened by) *having to sell up her old home.* **12** [VP9,25] have the idea; be of the opinion: *He felt the plan to be unwise/felt that the plan was unwise. We all felt that our luck was about to turn. He felt in his bones that he would succeed.* **13** [VP6A] appreciate; understand properly: *We all felt the force of his arguments. Don't you ~ the beauty of this landscape?*

feeler /ˈfilə(r)/ *n* [C] **1** organ, e g an antenna, in certain animals for testing things by touch. ⇨ the illus at insect. **2** proposal, suggestion, made to test the opinions or feelings of others, before one states one's own views, esp in: ***put out ~s,*** test the views of others, by discreet inquiries.

feel·ing /ˈfilɪŋ/ *n* **1** [U] power and capacity to feel: *He had lost all ~ in his legs.* **2** [C] physical or mental awareness; emotion: *a ~ of hunger/well-being/discomfort/gratitude/joy;* idea or belief not based wholly on reason: *a ~ of danger/that something dreadful was about to happen;* (usu *sing*) general opinion: *The ~ of the meeting* (= The opinion of the majority) *was against the proposal.* **3** (*pl*) emotional side of a person's nature (contrasted with the intellect): *Have I hurt your ~s,* offended you? *The speaker appealed to the ~s of his audience rather than to their reason. No hard ~s, I hope!* i e no bitterness, no ill will. **4** [U] sympathy; understanding: *He doesn't show much ~ for the sufferings of others. She's a woman of ~.* ***good ~,*** friendliness.

ill/bad ~, bitterness. **5** [C,U] excitement of mind, esp of enmity and resentment: *His speech aroused strong ~(s) on all sides. F~ over the election ran high,* There was much bitterness. **6** [U] taste and understanding; sensibility: *He hasn't much ~ for natural beauty. She plays the piano with ~.* □ *adj* sympathetic; showing emotion: *a ~ remark.* **~·ly** *adv* so as to express ~: *speak ~ly on a subject.*

feet *n pl* of foot.

feign /feɪn/ *vt* **1** [VP6A,9] pretend: *~ illness/indifference/death; ~ that one is mad; ~ed modesty.* **2** [VP6A] invent: *~ an excuse.*

feint /feɪnt/ *n* **1** pretence (the more usu word): *make a ~ of doing sth.* **2** sham attack (in war and boxing) in one place to draw attention away from the place where the real attack is made. □ *vi* [VP2A,3A] make a ~ *at/upon/against.*

feld·spar, fel·spar /ˋfeldspɑ(r), ˋfelspɑ(r)/ *n* [U] (kinds of) crystalline rock forming mineral.

fel·ici·tate /fəˋlɪsɪteɪt/ *vt* [VP6A,14] ~ ***(up)on,*** (formal) congratulate (sb *on* sth). **fel·ici·ta·tion** /fəˈlɪsɪˋteɪʃn/ *n*

fel·ici·tous /fəˋlɪsɪtəs/ *adj* (of words, remarks) well chosen. **~·ly** *adv*

fel·ic·ity /fəˋlɪsətɪ/ *n* **1** [U] great happiness or contentment. **2** [U] pleasing manner of speaking or writing: *express oneself with ~;* [C] (*pl* -ties) well-chosen expression or phrase.

fe·line /ˋfilɑɪn/ *adj* of or like a cat: *walk with ~ grace.*

fell[1] *pt* of fall[2].

fell[2] /fel/ *adj* (poet) fierce, ruthless, terrible: *a ~ disease; with one ~ blow.*

fell[3] /fel/ *n* animal's hide or skin with the hair.

fell[4] /fel/ *n* stretch of rocky, bare moorland or bare hilly land (esp in N England): *the Derbyshire F~s.*

fell[5] /fel/ *vt* [VP6A] cause to fall; strike down; cut down (a tree): *He ~ed his enemy with a single blow.*

fel·lah /ˋfelə/ *n* (*pl* ~in, ~een /ˈfeləˋhin/) peasant (in Arab countries).

fel·low /ˋfeləʊ/ *n* **1** (colloq) man or boy: *He's a pleasant ~. Poor ~! A ~ must have a holiday occasionally* (used here for 'one' or 'I'). **2** (usu *pl*) comrade, companion: *ˋschool ~s; ˋbed-~s; ~s in good fortune/misery; ~s* (i e partners) *in crime.* ***be ˈhail-~-well-ˋmet with sb,*** be on friendly terms with him. **ˈ~-ˋfeeling** *n* sympathy. **3** (attrib) of the same class, kind, etc: *ˈ~ ˋcreatures; ˈ~ ˋsoldiers,* soldiers associated together; *ˈ~-ˋcitizen; ˈ~-ˋcountryman,* person from the same country or nation. **ˈ~-ˋtraveller** *n* **(a)** person travelling with one. **(b)** one who sympathizes with the aims of a political party (esp the Communist Party) but is not a member. **4** member of a learned society: *F~ of the British Academy;* member of the governing body of some university colleges; incorporated graduate member of a college. **5** one of a pair: *Here's one of my gloves, but where's its ~?*

fel·low·ship /ˋfeləʊʃɪp/ *n* **1** [U] friendly association; companionship: *offer sb the (right) hand of ~; enjoy cordial ~ with people; ~ in misfortune.* **2** [C] number of persons associated together; group or society; [U] membership in such a group: *admitted to ~.* **3** [C] position of a college fellow**(4)**.

fel·ony /ˋfelənɪ/ *n* (*pl* -nies) [C,U] major serious crime, e g murder, armed robbery, arson. ⇨ misdemeanour. **felon** /ˋfelən/ *n* person guilty of ~. **fel·oni·ous** /fɪˋləʊnɪəs/ *adj* criminal.

fel·spar ⇨ feldspar.

felt[1] *pt,pp* of feel[2].

felt[2] /felt/ *n* [U] wool, hair or fur, compressed and rolled flat into a kind of cloth: (attrib) *~ hats/slippers.*

fe·lucca /fɪˋlʌkə/ *n* narrow Mediterranean coasting vessel with oars or sails or both.

fe·male /ˋfimeɪl/ *adj* **1** of the sex that produces offspring: *a ~ child/slave/dog;* (of plants or their parts) fruit-bearing. **2** of women: *~ suffrage; ~ operatives,* girl or women factory workers. **3** (mech) having a hollow part designed to receive an inserted part, e g a plug. □ *n* ~ animal; (derog) ~ person.

femi·nine /ˋfemənɪn/ *adj* **1** of, like, suitable for, women: *~ pursuits and hobbies,* e g needlework; *a ~ voice/nature; ~ curiosity,* said to be typical of women. **2** (gram) of the gender proper to the names of females: *~ nouns and pronouns,* e g actress, lioness, she, her. **fem·i·nin·ity** /ˈfeməˋnɪnətɪ/ *n* [U] quality of being ~. ⇨ masculine.

fem·in·ism /ˋfemɪnɪzm/ *n* movement for recognition of the claims of women for rights (legal, political, etc) equal to those possessed by men. ⇨ lib. **fem·in·ist** /-ɪst/ *n* supporter of ~.

fe·mur /ˋfimə(r)/ *n* thigh-bone. ⇨ the illus at skeleton.

fen /fen/ *n* area of low marshy land: *the Fens,* low-lying districts in Cambridgeshire and Lincolnshire.

fence[1] /fens/ *n* [C] barrier made of wooden or metal stakes or rails, or wire, esp one put round a field, garden, etc to keep animals from straying or to keep out intruders. ***come down on one side or the other of the ~,*** give one's support to one side or the other. ***come down on the right side of the ~,*** join the winner. ***sit/be on the ~,*** not commit oneself; wait to see where one can win most advantage. □ *vt* [VP6A,15B] surround, divide, provide with a ~ or ~s: *Farmers ~ their fields. His land is ~d with barbed wire. The land is ~d in/round.* **fenc·ing** /ˋfensɪŋ/ *n* [U] material for making ~s.

fence[2] /fens/ *vt* [VP2A,C,3A] practise the art of fighting with long slender swords or foils; (fig) avoid giving a direct answer to a question(er): *~ with a question.* **fencer** *n* person who ~s. **fenc·ing** /ˋfensɪŋ/ *n* [U] art of fighting with swords.

fencing

fence[3] /fens/ *n* receiver of stolen goods; his place of business.

fend /fend/ *vt,vi* **1** [VP15B] ~ ***off,*** defend oneself from: *~ off a blow.* **2** ~ ***for oneself,*** look after oneself: *When his father died, Tom had to ~ for himself. Most animals let their young ~ for themselves from an early age.*

fender /ˋfendə(r)/ *n* **1** metal frame bordering an

open fireplace (to prevent burning coal, etc from rolling on to the floor). **2** (on the front of a tram-car, etc) sth used to lessen shock or damage in a collision. **3** log of wood, heavy mass of rope, old rubber tyre etc hung on the side of a boat to prevent damage, e g when the boat comes alongside a wharf or another ship. **4** (US) guard over the wheel of a motor-vehicle.

fen·nel /ˈfenl/ *n* [U] yellow-flowered herb, used as a flavouring.

feoff /fif/ *n* = fief.

fe·ral /ˈfɪərl/ *adj* wild; untamed; brutal.

fer·ment[1] /ˈfɜment/ *n* **1** [C] substance, e g yeast, that causes other substances to ferment. **2** ***in a ~,*** (fig) in a state of, e g social, political, excitement.

fer·ment[2] /fəˈment/ *vt, vi* [VP6A,2A] **1** (cause to) undergo chemical changes through the action of organic bodies (esp yeast): *Fruit juices ~ if they are kept a long time. When wine is ~ed, it gives off bubbles of gas.* **2** (fig) (cause to) become excited. **fer·men·ta·tion** /ˌfɜmenˈteɪʃn/ *n* [U] ~ing or being ~ed: *the ~ation of milk* (when cheese is being made); (fig) excitement and unrest.

fern /fɜn/ *n* [C] sorts of feathery, green-leaved flowerless plant: *hillsides covered with ~* (collective *sing*); *~s growing in pots.* **~y** *adj*

fer·ocious /fəˈrəʊʃəs/ *adj* fierce, cruel, savage. **~·ly** *adv*

fer·oc·ity /fəˈrosətɪ/ *n* [U] fierceness; savage cruelty; [C] (*pl* **-ties**) fierce, savage or cruel act.

fer·ret /ˈferɪt/ *n* small animal of the weasel family, used for driving rabbits from their burrows, killing rats, etc. □ *vt, vi* **1** [VP2A] hunt with ~s: *go ~ing.* **2** [VP15B,2C] ***~ out/about (for),*** discover by searching; search: *~ out a secret; ~ about among old papers and books for sth lost.*

fer·ro·con·crete /ˌferəʊˈkoŋkrit/ *n* [U] reinforced concrete.

fer·rous /ˈferəs/ *adj* containing or relating to iron: *~ chloride* (FeC_2).

fer·rule /ˈferul *US:* ˈferl/ *n* metal ring or cap placed on the end of a stick, etc, e g of an umbrella, or tube to prevent splitting; band strengthening or forming a joint.

ferry /ˈferɪ/ *n* (*pl* **-ries**) [C] (place where there is a) boat, hovercraft or aircraft that carries people and goods across a river, channel, etc. □ *vt, vi* [VP6A, 15A,B,2A,C] take, go, across in a ~: *~ people/a boat across a river; aircraft ~ing motor-cars between England and France.* **ˈ~-boat** *n* **ˈ~-man** /-mən/ (*pl* **-men**) *n*

fer·tile /ˈfɜtɑɪl *US:* ˈfɜtl/ *adj* **1** (of land, plants, etc) producing much; (of a person, his mind, etc) full of ideas, plans, etc: *~ fields/soil; a ~ imagination; ~ in expedients; a boy who is ~ in excuses,* able to produce plenty of them. **2** able to produce fruit, young; capable of developing: *~ seeds/eggs.* ⇨ sterile. **fer·til·ity** /fəˈtɪlətɪ/ *n* [U] state of being ~.

fer·til·ize /ˈfɜtḷɑɪz/ *vt* [VP6A] make fertile or productive: *~ the soil* (by using manure); *~ flowers* (as bees do when they collect nectar). **fer·ti·lizer** *n* [U] chemical plant food; artificial manure; [C] substance of this kind: *Bone meal and nitrates are common fertilizers.* **fer·ti·liz·ation** /ˌfɜtḷɑɪˈzeɪʃn *US:* -ḷɪˈz-/ *n* [U] fertilizing or being ~d.

fer·ule /ˈferul *US:* ˈferl/ *n* flat ruler for punishing children by striking them on the hand.

fer·vent /ˈfɜvənt/ *adj* **1** hot, glowing. **2** showing warmth of feeling; passionate: *~ love/hatred; a ~ lover/admirer.* **~·ly** *adv* **fer·vency** /ˈfɜvənsɪ/ *n*

fer·vid /ˈfɜvɪd/ *adj* fervent(2); spirited; showing earnest feeling: *a ~ orator.* **~·ly** *adv*

fer·vour (US = **-vor**) /ˈfɜvə(r)/ *n* [U] strength or warmth of feeling; earnestness.

fes·tal /ˈfestl/ *adj* of a feast or festival; festive (the more usu word): *a ~ occasion,* e g a wedding, a birthday party; *~ music.*

fes·ter /ˈfestə(r)/ *vi* [VP2A] **1** (of a cut or wound) (cause to) fill with poisonous matter (pus): *If the cut gets dirty, it will probably ~.* **2** (fig) act like poison in the mind; become resentful, embittered: *The insult ~ed in his mind.*

fes·ti·val /ˈfestɪvl/ *n* **1** (day or season for) rejoicing; public celebrations: *Christmas and Easter are Church ~s.* **2** series of performances (of music, ballet, drama, etc) given periodically (usu once a year): *the Saltsburg F~; a ~ of music.* **3** (attrib) festive; of a feast or feast-day.

fes·tive /ˈfestɪv/ *adj* of a feast or festival; joyous: *a ˈ~ season,* e g Christmas; *the ~ board,* a table on which a feast is spread.

fes·tiv·ity /feˈstɪvətɪ/ *n* (*pl* **-ties**) **1** [U] rejoicing; merry-making. **2** (*pl*) ~ proceedings; joyful events: *wedding festivities.*

fes·toon /feˈstun/ *n* [C] chain of flowers, leaves, ribbons, etc hanging in a curve or loop between two points, as a decoration. □ *vt* [VP6A] make into, decorate with, ~s: *a room ~ed with Christmas decorations.*

fetch /fetʃ/ *vt, vi* **1** [VP6A,15A,B,13A,12A] go for and bring back (sb or sth): *F~ a doctor at once. Please ~ the children from school. The chair is in the garden; please ~ it in. Shall I ~ your hat for you/~ you your hat from the next room?* ***~ and carry (for),*** be busy with small duties for; be a servant for: *He expects his daughter to ~ and carry for him all day.* **2** [VP6A,15A] cause to come out; draw forth: *~ a deep sigh/a dreadful groan; ~ tears to the eyes.* **3** [VP6A,12A] (of goods) bring in; sell for (a price): *These old books won't ~ (you) much.* **4** [VP12A] (colloq) deal, give (a blow) to: *She ~ed me a slap across the face/a box on the ears.* **~·ing** *adj* (dated colloq) attractive, delightful: *What a ~ing little hat! What a ~ing smile!*

fête /feɪt/ *n* (usu outdoor) festival or entertainment: *the village ~,* often one at which funds are raised, e g for the church or a charity. **ˈ~-day** *n* day of the saint after which a child is named, observed in R C countries as a birthday is observed in Great Britain. □ *vt* [VP6A] honour by entertaining; make a fuss of: *The hero was ~d wherever he went.*

fetid /ˈfetɪd/ *adj* stinking.

fet·ish, fe·tich /ˈfetɪʃ/ *n* **1** object worshipped by pagan people because they believe a spirit lives in it. **2** anything to which foolishly excessive respect or attention is given: *Some women make a ~ of clothes.*

fet·lock /ˈfetlok/ *n* (tuft of hair on a) horse's leg above and behind the hoof. ⇨ the illus at domestic.

fet·ter /ˈfetə(r)/ *n* chain for the ankles of a prisoner or the leg of a horse; (fig, usu *pl*) sth that hinders progress. □ *vt* [VP6A] put in ~s or chains; (fig) restrain.

fettle /ˈfetl/ *n* (usu) ***in fine/good ~,*** in good (physical) condition; in high spirits.

fe·tus ⇨ foetus.

feud /fjud/ *n* [C] bitter quarrel between two persons, families or groups, over a long period of time.

feu·dal /ˈfjudl/ *adj* of the method of holding land (by giving services to the owner) during the Middle Ages in Europe: *~ law; the ~ barons.* **~·ism** /-ɪzm/ *n* [U] the ~ system.

feuda·tory /ˈfjudətərɪ *US:* -tɔrɪ/ *adj* owing service to a lord: *~ obligations.* □ *n* vassal.

fe·ver /ˈfivə(r)/ *n* **1** [U] condition of the human body with temperature higher than usual, esp as a sign of illness: *She hasn't much ~. He has a high ~.* **ˈ~ heat,** high temperature of the human body in ~. **2** [U] one of a number of diseases in which there is high ~: *yellow/typhoid/rheumatic ~.* **3** (usu *sing* with *indef art*) excited state; nervous agitation: *in a ~ of impatience.* ***at/to ˈ~ pitch,*** at/to a high level of excitement: *The crowd was at ~ pitch.* **fe·vered** *adj* affected by a ~: *a ~ed imagination,* highly excited. **~·ish** /-rɪʃ/ *adj* having symptoms of ~; caused by ~; causing ~: *in a ~ish condition; ~ish dreams; ~ish swamps.* **~·ish·ly** *adv*

few /fju/ *adj* (-er, -est), *pron* (contrasted with *many*; ⇨ little, much) **1** (with a *pl n*) not many: *Few people live to be 100 and fewer still live to be 110. Which of you made the fewest mistakes,* the smallest number of mistakes? *He is a man of few words,* he says very little. ***no fewer than,*** as many as: *No fewer than twenty workers were absent through illness.* **2** (in the *pred*, rare in colloq style): *Such occasions are few. We are very few, fewer than at the last meeting of the society.* **3** (with the *indef art*) a small number (of) (Note that *few* is neg and *a few* is positive): *I know a few of these people. We are going away for a few days. I'd like a few more of the red roses.* ***some few, a good few, quite a few, not a few,*** a considerable number, a fair number. **4** *every few minutes/days, etc.* ⇨ every(5). **5 the few,** the minority. **few·ness** *n*

fey /feɪ/ *adj* (Scot) **1** having a feeling of approaching death. **2** clairvoyant.

fez /fez/ *n* red felt head-dress with a flat top and no brim, worn by some Muslim men.

fi·ancé, fi·ancée /fɪˈɒseɪ *US:* ˈfiɑnˈseɪ/ *n* man (*fiancé*) or woman (*fiancée*) to whom one is engaged to be married; one's betrothed.

fi·asco /fɪˈæskəʊ/ *n* (*pl* -cos, US also -coes /-kəʊz/) complete failure, breakdown, in sth attempted: *The pop concert at the Rainbow theatre was a ~.*

fiat /ˈfɑɪæt/ *n* [C] order or decree made by a ruler.

fib /fɪb/ *n* (colloq) untrue statement (esp about sth unimportant). □ *vi* (-bb-) [VP2A] tell a fib. **fib·ber** *n* person who tells fibs. **fib·bing** *n* telling fibs.

fibre (US = **fiber**) /ˈfɑɪbə(r)/ **1** [C] one of the slender threads of which many animal and vegetable growths are formed, e g cotton, wood, nerves, muscles. **2** [U] substance formed of a mass of ~s, for manufacture into various materials: *hemp ~,* for making rope; *cotton ~,* for spinning. **ˈ~·board** *n* board made of compressed ~. **ˈ~-glass** *n* [U] material of glass ~s in resin, used as an insulating material, and made into structural materials, e g for boat-building. **3** [U] structure; texture: *material of coarse ~;* (fig) character: *a person of strong moral ~.* **fi·brous** /ˈfɑɪbrəs/ *adj* made of, like, ~s.

fib·ula /ˈfɪbjʊlə(r)/ *n* outer of the two bones between the knee and the foot. ⇨ the illus at skeleton.

fickle /ˈfɪkl/ *adj* (of moods, the weather, etc) often changing; not constant: *~ fortune; a ~ lover.* **~·ness** *n*

fic·tion /ˈfɪkʃn/ *n* **1** [C] sth invented or imagined (contrasted with truth). ***a legal ~,*** sth assumed to be true, although it may be false, in order to avoid a difficulty. **2** [U] (branch of literature concerned with) stories, novels and romances: *works of ~; prefer history to ~. Truth is often stranger than ~.*

fic·ti·tious /fɪkˈtɪʃəs/ *adj* not real; imagined or invented: *The account he gives of his movements is quite ~.*

fiddle /ˈfɪdl/ *n* **1** violin; any instrument of the violin family, e g a 'cello or viola. ***have a face as long as a ~,*** look dismal. ***fit as a ~,*** very well; in good health. ***play second ~ (to),*** take a less important part (than). **ˈ~-stick** *n* bow[1](2). **ˈ~-sticks** *int* Nonsense! **2** instance of fiddling; ⇨ 3 below. □ *vt* **1** [VP6A,2A] play the ~; play a tune, etc on the ~. **2** [VP2A,C] make aimless movements; play aimlessly (*with* sth in one's fingers): *Stop fiddling! He was fiddling (about) with a piece of string.* **3** [VP6A] (sl) make or keep dishonestly inaccurate records of figures (in business accounts, etc): *~ an income-tax return,* prepare it so as to try to escape correct tax payments. **fid·dler** *n* person who plays the ~; person who ~s(3). **fid·dling** *adj* (colloq) trivial; futile: *fiddling little jobs.*

fi·del·ity /fɪˈdelətɪ/ *n* (*pl* -ties) [U] **1** loyalty, faithfulness (*to*): *~ to one's principles/religion/leader/wife.* **2** accuracy; exactness: *translate sth with the greatest ~; A high ~ equipment,* with high quality sound reproduction. ⇨ hi-fi.

fidget /ˈfɪdʒɪt/ *vi,vt* [VP2A,C,6A] (cause sb to) move the body (or part of it) about restlessly; make (sb) nervous: *Stop ~ing! The boy was ~ing with his knife and fork. What's ~ing you,* making you nervous or uneasy? *Hurry up, your father's beginning to ~,* show signs of impatience. □ *n* **1** (usu *the ~s*) ~ing movements: *Having to sit still for a long time often gives small children the ~s.* **2** person who ~s: *What a ~ you are!* **~y** *adj* having the ~s; restless: *a ~y child.*

fie /fɑɪ/ *int* (usu hum) for shame: *Fie upon you,* You ought to be ashamed!

fief /fif/ *n* [C] land held from a feudal lord.

field[1] /fild/ *n* [C] **1** area of land, either grassland for cattle, etc or arable land for crops, usu enclosed by means of hedges, fences, etc (not normally used of unenclosed land or uncultivated land): *working in the ~s.* Cf *on the farm. What a fine ~ of wheat!* **2** (usu in compounds) wide area or expanse; open space: *an ˈice-~,* e g round the North Pole; *a ˈflying-~, a ˈlanding ~* (for aircraft); *a ˈbaseball/ˈcricket/ˈfootball ~.* ⇨ the illus at these nouns. **ˈ~ sports** *n pl* hunting, shooting and fishing. **ˈ~ events** *n pl* athletic contests such as jumping and discus-throwing, but not races or other contests that take place on a track. **ˈ~ glasses** *n pl* long-distance binoculars for outdoor use. **3** (usu in compounds) area of land from which minerals, etc are obtained: *ˈgold-~s; a new ˈoil-~; ˈcoal-~s.* **4** province or department of study or activity: *the ~ of politics/art/science/medical research. That is outside my ~,* is not in the departments of knowledge that I have studied. **ˈ~ work,** scientific, technical or social investigation made outside laboratories, etc e g by surveyors, geologists or by students of social science who visit and talk to people. **5** range (of operation, activity, use); area or space in which forces can be felt: *a magnetic ~*, round a magnet: *a wide ~ of vision; an object that fills the ~ of a telescope; the earth's gravitational ~*, the space in which the earth's gravity is exerted. **6** place, area, where a battle or war is or was fought: *the ~ of battle* (*ˈbattle-~*)*; take the ~*, go to war. **ˈ~ artillery, ˈ~ gun** *nn* light and mobile, for use in battle. **ˈ~-hospital** *n* temporary hospital near the scene of fighting. **ˈ~ day** *n* day on which military operations are practised: (fig) great or special occasion. **ˈF~ ˈMarshal** *n* army officer of highest rank. **ˈ~-officer** *n* major or colonel. **ˈ~-work** *n* temporary fortification made by troops in the ~. **7** (sports and athletics) (in foxhunting) all those taking part in the hunt; (in a contest, esp a horse-race) all the competitors; (in cricket and baseball) team that is not batting; (cricket) the fielding side.

field[2] /fild/ *vt,vi* **1** [VP6A,2A] (cricket and baseball) (stand ready to) catch or stop (the ball): *He ~ed the ball smartly. He ~s well. Well ~ed, sir!* **2** [VP6A] (of football teams, etc) put into the ~: *The school is ~ing a strong team in their next match.* **~er, fields·man** /-mən/ *n* (*pl* -men) (cricket, etc) person who ~s: *He doesn't bat well, but he's an excellent ~er.* ⇨ the illus at baseball.

fiend /find/ *n* devil; very wicked or cruel person; (colloq) person devoted to or addicted to sth (indicated by the word prefixed: *a drug ~; a ˈfresh-ˈair ~*. **~·ish** /-ɪʃ/ *adj* savage and cruel. **~·ish·ly** *adv*: *~ishly clever*, (colloq) very clever.

fierce /fɪəs/ *adj* (-r, -st) **1** violent; cruel; angry: *~ dogs/winds; look ~; have a ~ look on one's face.* **2** (of heat, desire, etc) intense: *~ hatred.* **~·ly** *adv* **~·ness** *n*

fiery /ˈfɑɪərɪ/ *adj* (-ier, -iest) **1** flaming; looking like, hot as, fire: *a ~ sky; ~ eyes*, angry and glaring. **2** (of a person, his actions, etc) quickly or easily made angry; passionate: *a ~ temper/speech.* **~·ily** /-ɪlɪ/ *adv* **~i·ness** *n*

fi·esta /fɪˈestə/ *n* (Sp) religious festival; saint's day; holiday, festival.

fife /fɑɪf/ *n* small musical wind instrument like a flute, used with drums in military music: *a drum and ~ band.*

fif·teen /ˈfɪˈftin/ *n, adj* ⇨ App 4; team of Rugby (football) players. **fif·teenth** /ˈfɪfˈtinθ/ *n, adj*

fifth /fɪfθ *with* f *and* θ *simultaneous*/ *n, adj* ⇨ App 4. **ˈ~ ˈcolumn,** organized body of persons sympathizing with and working for the enemy within a country at war. **~·ly** *adv* in the ~ place.

fifty /ˈfɪftɪ/ *n* (*pl* -ties), *adj* ⇨ App 4. **the fifties,** the years between 49 and 60 (in a century, a person's life). ***go ~-~ (with) on a ~-~ basis,*** have equal shares. ***a ~-~ chance,*** equal chance. **fif·ti·eth** /ˈfɪftɪəθ/ *n, adj* ⇨ App 4.

fig[1] /fɪg/ *n* (broad-leaved tree having a) soft, sweet, pear-shaped fruit full of small seeds. ⇨ the illus at fruit. ***not care/give a fig (for),*** not care in the least; consider as valueless or unimportant. **ˈfig-leaf,** (with reference to the story of Adam and Eve) conventional device for concealing male genital organs in drawings, statues, etc.

fig[2] /fɪg/ *n* (sl) dress: *in full fig.* □ *vt* ***all figged up/out,*** dressed up, e g for a party.

fight[1] /fɑɪt/ *n* **1** [C] act of ~ing; struggle: *a ~ between two dogs; the ~ against poverty; a prize-~* (boxing). ***put up a good/poor ~,*** ~ with/without courage and determination. ***a free ~,*** ⇨ free[1](3). ***a stand-up ~,*** ⇨ stand[2](11). **2** [U] ~ing spirit; desire or ability for ~ing: *In spite of numerous defeats, they still had plenty of ~ left in them. The news that their leader had surrendered took all the ~ out of them.* ***show ~,*** show readiness to ~. **~er** *n* person or thing that ~s, esp a fast aircraft designed for attacking bombing-planes: (attrib) *a ˈ~er pilot/squadron.*

fight[2] /fɑɪt/ *vi,vt* (*pt,pp* fought /fɔt/) **1** [VP2A, B,C,3A,4A] struggle bodily against; struggle with the hands or with weapons; use physical force (as in war): *When dogs ~, they use their teeth. The dogs were ~ing over a bone/~ing for the possession of a bone. Great Britain has often fought against/with* (= against) *her enemies. Great Britain fought with* (= on the side of) *France. They were ~ing for* (= in order to secure or maintain) *their independence. They were ~ing to preserve their freedom.* ***~ to a finish,*** until there is a decision. ***~ shy of,*** keep away from, not get mixed up with. **2** [VP6A] (with cognate object): *~ a battle/a duel.* **3** [VP6A,15A,B] ***~ sth down,*** repress; overcome: *~ down a feeling of repugnance.* ***~ sb/sth off,*** drive away; struggle against: *~ off a cold*, e g by taking aspirin. ***~ one's way forward/out (of),*** advance, go forward, by ~ing. ***~ it out,*** ~ until a dispute is settled. **4** [VP6A] manœuvre (ships, etc) in battle: *The captain fought his ship well.* **8~** *ing n*: *ˈstreet ~ing.* □ *part adj*: *a ~ing chance*, a possibility of success if great efforts are made.

fig·ment /ˈfɪgmənt/ *n* [C] sth invented or imagined: *~s of the imagination.*

figu·rat·ive /ˈfɪgjʊrətɪv/ *adj* (of words and language) used not in the literal sense but in an imaginative way (as when *fiery* is used of a man who is easily made angry). **~·ly** *adv*

fig·ure /ˈfɪgə(r) *US:* ˈfɪgjər/ *n* **1** symbol for a number, esp 0 to 9: *He has an income of six figures*, £100 000 or more. *We bought the house at a high/low ~*, for a high/low price. **double ~s,** any number from 10 to 99 inclusive: *Only two of the batsmen reached double ~s, scored 10 or more.* **2** arithmetic: *Are you good at ~s?* **3** diagram; drawing to illustrate sth: *The blackboard was covered with geometrical ~s*, i e squares, triangles, etc. **4** person's ~ drawn or painted, or cut in stone, etc; drawing, painting, image, of the body of a bird, animal, etc. **ˈ~-head** *n* **(a)** carved image (either bust or full-length) placed for ornament at the prow of a ship. **(b)** person in high position but with no real authority. **5** human form, esp the appearance and what it suggests: *I saw a ~ approaching in the darkness. He has a good/poor/handsome, etc ~. She's a fine ~ of a woman*, is well-shaped. *I'm dieting to keep my ~*, in order not to grow stout. *She was a ~ of distress*, Her attitude and appearance suggested distress. ***cut a fine/poor/sorry, etc ~,*** make a fine, etc, appearance. **6** person, esp his influence: *Churchill, the greatest ~ of his era.* **7** ***~ of speech,*** expression, e g a simile or metaphor, that gives variety or force, using words out of their literal meaning. □ *vt,vi* **1** [VP15A] imagine; picture mentally: *~ sth to oneself.* **2** [VP2C] appear;

have a part; be prominent: *~ in history/in a play. He ~s in all the books on the subject.* **3** [VP15B] ***~ sth/sb out,*** calculate; think about until one understands: *I can't ~ that man out,* He puzzles me. **4** [VP3A] ***~ on sth,*** (US) reckon or count on: *They ~d on your arriving early.* **fig·ured** *adj* ornamented; decorated: *a ~d glass window,* with designs, e g in stained glass; *~d silk,* with patterns or designs on it.

fila·ment /ˈfɪləmənt/ *n* [C] slender thread, e g of wire in an electric light bulb: *a ~ lamp.*

fila·ture /ˈfɪlətʃə(r)/ *n* workshop in which raw silk is reeled from cocoons.

fil·bert /ˈfɪlbət/ *n* (nut of a) cultivated hazel.

filch /fɪltʃ/ *vt* [VP6A] pilfer; steal (sth of small value).

file[1] /faɪl/ *n* metal tool with roughened surface(s) for cutting or smoothing hard substances. ⇨ the illus at **tool**. □ *vt* [VP6A,22,15A] use a ~ on; make smooth with a ~; remove, cut through, with a ~: *~ one's fingernails; ~ sth smooth; ~ an iron rod in two.* **fil·ings** /ˈfaɪlɪŋz/ *n pl* bits ~d off or removed by a ~.

file[2] /faɪl/ *n* [C] holder, cover, case, box, drawer etc for keeping papers, etc together and in order for reference purposes, usu with wires, metal rods or other devices on which the papers, etc may be threaded: *Where's the ~ of 'The Times'? We have placed the correspondence on our ~s.* **on ~,** on or in a ~. □ *vt* [VP6A,15B] place on or in a ~; place on record: *~ an application; Please ~ (away) these letters; a ˈfiling clerk,* one who ~s correspondence, etc.

file[3] /faɪl/ *n* line of persons or things one behind the other; (mil) man in the front rank and the man or men straight behind him: *a single ~; in Indian ~,* in one line, one behind the other. ***the rank and ~,*** common soldiers (privates, corporals, 'other ranks'); (fig) ordinary, undistinguished persons. □ *vi* [VP2C] march in ~: *The men ~d in/out,* came or went in/out.

fil·ial /ˈfɪlɪəl/ *adj* of a son or daughter: *~ duty/piety.*

fili·bus·ter /ˈfɪlɪbʌstə(r)/ *n* (US) member of a legislature who tries to prevent the passage of a bill by making long speeches, etc. □ *vi* act as a ~.

fili·gree /ˈfɪlɪgri/ *n* [U] ornamental lace-like work of gold, silver or copper ware: (attrib) *a ~ brooch; ~ ear-rings.*

fil·ings /ˈfaɪlɪŋz/ *n pl* ⇨ **file**[1].

fill[1] /fɪl/ *n* **1** full supply; as much as is wanted: *eat/drink one's ~.* ***have one's ~ of sth,*** (colloq) have as much as one can bear. **2** enough to fill sth: *a ~ of tobacco,* enough to fill a pipe. **~·ing** *n* sth put in to ~ sth: *a ~ing in a tooth.*

fill[2] /fɪl/ *vt,vi* **1** [VP6A,14,15B,12B,13B,2A,C] ***~ (with),*** make or become full; occupy all the space in: *~ a hole with sand/a tank with petrol. Tears ~ed her eyes. I was ~ed with admiration. The smoke ~ed the room. Go and ~ this bucket with water for me/~ me* (less usu) *this bucket with water. The hall soon ~ed. The wind ~ed the sails. The sails ~ed* (= swelled out) *with wind.* ***~ in,*** add what is necessary to make complete: *~ in an application form,* write one's name, and other particulars required; *~ in an outline,* add details, etc. ***~ out,*** **(a)** make or become larger, rounded or fatter: *Her cheeks began to ~ out.* **(b)** (esp US) = ~ in. ***~ up,*** make or become quite full: *~ up with petrol; ~ up a tank. The channel of the river ~ed up with mud.* **ˈ~·ing station,** (US) place where petrol, oil, etc may be bought. Cf *service station,* where repairs may be done. **2** [VP6A] hold a position and do the necessary work; put (sb) in a position: *The vacancy has already been ~ed. He ~s the office satisfactorily,* performs the duties well. ***~ the bill,*** (colloq) meet one's needs: *These new machines really ~ the bill.* **3** [VP6A] execute, carry out an order/etc: *~ a doctor's prescription.*

fil·let /ˈfɪlɪt/ *n* **1** band (often ornamental) worn to keep the hair in place. **2** slice of fish or meat without bones. □ *vt* [VP6A] cut (fish) into ~s: *~ed plaice.*

fil·lip /ˈfɪlɪp/ *n* [C] quick, smart blow or stroke given with a finger; (fig) incentive or stimulus: *an advertising campaign that gave a fresh ~ to sales.*

filly /ˈfɪlɪ/ *n* (-lies) female foal. ⇨ **colt**[1].

film[1] /fɪlm/ *n* **1** [C] thin coating or covering: *a ~ of dust; a ~ of oil on water; a ~ of mist.* **2** [C,U] roll or sheet of thin flexible material for use in photography: *a roll* (US = *spool*) *of ~; expose 50 feet of ~; ~ stock,* cinema ~ not yet exposed; *ˈ~-strip,* length of ~ with a number of photographs (of scenes, diagrams, etc) to be shown on a screen separately (not as a motion picture). **3** [C] motion picture. **a ˈ~ première,** first showing of a cinema film. **ˈ~ test,** photographic test of sb who wishes to act for the ~s. **ˈ~ star,** well-known cinema actor or actress. **filmy** *adj* (-ier, -iest) like a ~(1): *~y clouds.*

film[2] /fɪlm/ *vt,vi* **1** [VP6A] take a motion picture of: *~ a play.* **2** [VP6A,2A,C] cover, become covered, with a film(1): *The scene ~ed over.* **3** [VP2A,C] be well, badly suited for reproduction on the ~s: *She ~s well.* **~·able** /-əbl/ *adj* (of a novel, etc) suitable for ~ing.

fil·ter /ˈfɪltə(r)/ *n* apparatus (containing, e g sand, charcoal, paper, cloth) for holding back solid substances in an impure liquid passed through it; coloured glass (as used on a camera lens) which allows light of certain wave-lengths to pass through; (in radio) device which separates alternating current of one frequency from others. **ˈ~ tip,** cigarette end containing material that acts as a ~ (for nicotine, etc). Hence, **ˈ~-tipped** *adj* □ *vt, vi* [VP6A,14,15B,2A,C] **1** (cause to) flow through a ~; purify (a liquid) by using a ~. **2** (fig, of a crowd, road traffic, news, ideas, etc) make a way, pass or flow: *new ideas ~ing into people's minds. The news of the defeat ~ed through.* **3** (of traffic in GB) be allowed to pass or turn to the left when traffic going straight ahead or to the right is held up by a red light.

filth /fɪlθ/ *n* [U] disgusting dirt; obscenity. **~y** *adj* (-ier, -iest) **~·ily** /-əlɪ/ *adv* **~i·ness** *n*

fin /fɪn/ *n* ⇨ the illus at **fish, sea.** one of those parts of a fish used in swimming; thing shaped like or used in the same way as a fin, e g the *ˈtail-fin* of an aircraft.

fi·nal /ˈfaɪnl/ *adj* **1** coming at the end: *the ~ chapter of a book.* **2** putting an end to doubt or argument: *a ~ decision/judgement.* □ *n* **1** (often *pl*) last of a series of examinations or contests: *the law ~(s); take one's ~s; the tennis ~s,* at the end of a tournament; *the Cup F~,* last football match in a series. **2** (colloq) edition of a newspaper published latest in the day: *'Late night ~'.* **~·ist** /-ɪst/ *n* **1** player who takes part in the last of a series of contests. **2** undergraduate in his ~ year.

~·ly /-nlɪ/ *adv* **1** lastly; in conclusion. **2** once and for all: *settle a matter ~ly.*

fi·nale /fɪˋnɑlɪ/ *n* (music) last movement of an instrumental composition, e g a symphony; closing scene of an opera; end.

fi·nal·ity /faɪˋnæləti/ *n* [U] state or quality of being final: *speak with an air of ~,* giving the impression that there is nothing more to be said or done.

fi·nal·ize /ˋfaɪnḷaɪz/ *vt* [VP6A] give a final form to.

fi·nance /ˋfaɪnæns/ *n* **1** [U] (science of) the management of (esp public) money: *an expert in ~; the Minister of F~* (in GB called the Chancellor of the Exchequer). **ˋ~ house/company,** one that provides ~ for hire-purchase sales. **2** (*pl*) money (esp of a government or a business company): *Are the country's ~s sound?.* □ *vt* [VP6A] provide money for (a scheme, etc).

fi·nan·cial /ˈfaɪˋnænʃl/ *adj* of finance: *in ~ difficulties,* short of money; *a ~ centre,* e g London or New York; *the ~ year,* the annual period for which accounts are made up. **fi·nan·cially** /-ʃḷɪ/ *adv*

fin·an·cier /faɪˋnænsɪə(r) *US:* ˈfɪnənˋsɪər/ *n* person skilled in finance; capitalist.

finch /fɪntʃ/ *n* kinds of small bird (usu with a distinctive epithet or prefix, as *ˋchaf~, ˋgreen~, ˋbull-~*).

find[1] /faɪnd/ *n* [C] finding; sth found, esp sth valuable or pleasing: *I made a great ~ in a second-hand bookshop yesterday,* found a rare or valuable old book. **~er** *n* **1** person who ~s sth: *Lost, a diamond ring: ~er will be rewarded.* **2** lens in a camera (*ˋview-~er*) or telescope used to ~ the object to be photographed, examined, etc. **~·ing** *n* (usu *pl*) **1** what has been learnt as the result of inquiry: *the ~ings of the Commission.* **2** what is determined by a jury, etc. ⇨ find[2](9).

find[2] /faɪnd/ *vt* (*pt,pp* found /faʊnd/) **1** [VP6A, 12B,13B] get back, after a search, (sth/sb lost, left behind, forgotten, etc): *Did you ever ~ that pen you lost? Please help Mary to ~ her hat. Please ~ Mary her hat/~ Mary's hat for her. The missing child has not been found yet.* **~ one's place** (in a book, etc), turn to the page where one wishes to continue reading etc. **~ one's voice/tongue,** be able to speak (after being silent because of shyness, etc). **2** [VP6A,12A,13A,15A,B] get or discover (sth/sb not lost, forgotten, etc) after search, experience or effort: *~ a cure/remedy (for sth); ~ a solution/an answer (to a problem); ~ (the) time to do sth. They dug five metres and then found water. I can ~ nothing new to say on this subject. Did you ~ him what he wanted? They couldn't ~ the way in/out/back. Where will they ~ money for the journey? She soon found favour with her employer.* ⇨ favour[1](1). *I can't ~ time to read. At last he found courage to ask Jane to marry him.* **~ fault (with),** ⇨ fault. **~ one's feet,** (a) be able to stand and walk, e g as a baby does: *How old was the baby when it began to ~ its feet?* (b) become able to act independently, without the help and guidance of others. **~ oneself,** discover one's vocation; learn one's powers and abilities and how to use them. ⇨ also 5 below. **~ it in one's heart to do sth,** (chiefly neg and interr with *can/could*) be so unkind or callous as to: *How can you ~ it in your heart to drown these little kittens?* **3** [VP6A,15A,B] arrive at naturally: *Rivers ~ their way to the sea. Water always ~s its own level.* **4** [VP6A,19B,22,15A] discover by chance; come across; fall in with: *He was found dying/dead/injured at the foot of a cliff. I found him in the cellar drinking my best brandy.* **5** [VP9,15A,22,25] become informed or aware of, by experience of trial: *We found the beds quite comfortable. We found him (to be) dishonest/found he was dishonest. They found him (to be) the right man for the job. Do you ~ that honesty pays/that it pays to be honest? I never ~ the best too good for me. You must take us as you ~ us,* accept us as we are, not expect special treatment or ceremony. *I ~ it difficult to understand him/~ him difficult to understand. I called at Smith's this morning and found him still in bed. I was disappointed to ~ her out* (i e not at home) *when I called.* **~ oneself,** discover, realize, that one is: *When he regained consciousness, he found himself in hospital,* e g after a motor accident. *How do you ~ yourself this morning,* How are you feeling? **6** [VP6A,15B,8, 10] learn by study, calculation, inquiry (often ~ **out**): *What do you ~ the total? Please ~ (out) when the train starts/whether there is an express train/how to get there. 'Where have you hidden my slippers?'—'F~ out!'* **~ sb out,** detect sb in wrongdoing or error: *Be sure your sins will ~ you out! Ah! I've found you out!* **7** [VP15A] equivalent to a construction with *there is/are,* etc with no suggestion of discovery or inquiry, the subject being *one* or *you*: *One doesn't/You don't ~* (= There isn't) *much vegetation in this area. Pine-trees are found* (= There are pine-trees) *in most European countries.* **8** [VP6A,15A] supply; furnish; provide: *Who will ~ the money for the expedition?* **~ sb/oneself in,** provide with: *He pays his housekeeper £25 a week and she ~s herself in clothes,* buys them herself, from her wages. **all found,** everything provided: *Wanted, a good cook, £50 a month and all found,* board, lodging, etc provided free in addition to wages. **9** [VP22, 25,9] (legal) determine and declare; give as a verdict: *How do you ~ the accused? The jury found the accused man guilty. They found* (= brought in) *a verdict of guilty. They found it* (= the offence) *manslaughter. The court found that the deceased* (= the dead person) *had been murdered by a person or persons unknown.* **~ for,** (elliptical use) decide in favour of: *~ for the defendant/ plaintiff.* ⇨ finding(2) in find[1].

fine[1] /faɪn/ *n* [C] sum of money (to be) paid as a penalty for breaking a law or rule. □ *vt* [VP6A,14] punish by a ~: *~ sb for an offence; ~ sb £5.* **~·able** (also **finable**) /ˋfaɪnəbl/ *adj* liable to a ~.

fine[2] /faɪn/ *n* (only in) **in ~,** (old use) in short, finally, to sum up.

fine[3] /faɪn/ *adj* (-r, -st) **1** (of weather) bright; clear; not raining: *It rained all morning, but turned ~ later.* **one ~ day,** (in story-telling) one day past or future. **one of these ~ days,** at some (vague) time in the future. **2** enjoyable; pleasing; splendid: *a ~ view; have a ~ time; ~ clothes. She has grown up to be a ~ young lady. That's a ~ excuse,* (ironic) a very poor excuse. **3** delicate; carefully made and easily injured: *~ workmanship; ~ silk.* **4** of very small particles: *~ dust. Sand is ~r than gravel.* **5** slender; thin; sharp: *~ thread; a pencil with a ~ point.* **not to put too ~ a point on it,** to express it plainly. ~ toothcomb, ⇨ tooth. **6** (of metals) refined; pure: *~ gold; gold 18 carats ~,* with 18 parts of pure gold and 6 of alloy. **7** (to be) seen only with difficulty or effort: *a ~ distinction;* capable of delicate perception, able to make delicate distinctions: *a ~ sense of humour; a ~ taste in art.* **the ~ arts, ~ art,** the visual arts that appeal to the sense of beauty, esp painting and sculpture. **8** (of speech or writing) too ornate; insincerely complimentary: *She likes to call things by ~ names,* e g *refuse collector* for *dustman. She thinks herself a ~ lady,* considers herself a lady of fashion, too superior to do housework, etc. **9** in good health: *I'm feeling ~.* **~·ly** *adv* **1** splendidly: *~ly dressed.* **2** into small particles or pieces: *carrots ~ly chopped up.* **~·ness** *n*

fine[4] /faɪn/ *adv* **1** (colloq) very well: *That will suit me ~.* **2** (in compounds) ˈ*~-ˋdrawn,* (drawn out) very thin; ˈ*~-ˋspoken,* insincerely complimentary; ˈ*~-ˋspun,* delicate. **3** ***cut it ~,*** ⇨ cut[1](7).

fin·ery /ˋfaɪnərɪ/ *n* [U] gay and elegant dress or appearance: *young ladies in their Sunday ~,* smart clothes; *the garden in its summer ~,* with its brightly coloured flowers, green lawns, etc.

fi·nesse /fɪˋnes/ *n* [U] artful or delicate way of dealing with a situation: *show ~ in dealing with people;* (cards) attempt to win a trick(5) using ~.

fin·ger /ˋfɪŋgə(r)/ *n* ⇨ the illus at arm. There are five ~s (or *four ~s and one thumb*) *on each hand.* ***his ~s are all thumbs,*** he is very clumsy. ***burn one's ~s,*** suffer because of incautious or meddlesome behaviour, etc. ***have a ~ in every/the pie,*** ⇨ pie. ***keep one's ~s crossed,*** ⇨ cross[2](3). ***lay a ~ on,*** touch (however slightly): *I forbid you to lay a ~ on the boy,* to punish him by hitting him, etc. ***lay/put one's ~ on,*** point out precisely (where sth is wrong, the cause of a trouble or evil). ***not lift a ~ (to help sb),*** do nothing to help when help is needed. ***put the ~ on sb,*** (sl) inform against (a criminal). ***slip through one's ~s,*** ⇨ slip[2](3). ***twist sb round one's (little) ~,*** cajole him; dominate him. ˋ**~-alphabet** *n* method (using the ~s in various ways) for talking with the deaf. ˋ**~-board,** wood (on a guitar, violin, etc) where the strings are held against the neck with the ~s. ˋ**~-bowl** *n* one for rinsing the ~s at meals. ˋ**~-mark** *n* mark, e g on a wall, made by a dirty ~. ˋ**~nail** *n* nail at the tip of the ~. ˋ**~-plate** *n* one fastened on a door near the handle or key-hole to prevent ~-marks. ˋ**~-post** *n* signpost giving directions with boards shaped like ~s. ˋ**~-print** *n* mark made by ~s when pressed on a surface, used for identifying criminals. ⇨ the illus at whorl. ˋ**~-stall** *n* protective cover (worn over an injured ~). ˋ**~-tip,** top of a ~. ***have sth at one's ~tips,*** be thoroughly familiar with it. □ *vt* [VP6A] touch with the ~s: *~ a piece of cloth,* touch, feel, it (to test its quality).

fini·cal /ˋfɪnɪkl/ *adj* too fussy or fastidious about food, clothing, etc.

fin·icky /ˋfɪnɪkɪ/ *adj* = finical.

fi·nis /ˋfɪnɪs/ *n* (*sing* only) (Lat) (at the end of a book) the end.

fin·ish /ˋfɪnɪʃ/ *vt,vi* **1** [VP6A,C,2A,C,15B,24] bring or come to an end; complete: *~ one's work; ~ reading a book. Have you ~ed that book yet,* read it to the end? *Term ~es next week. We have ~ed the pie,* eaten all of it. *That long climb almost ~ed me,* (colloq) almost caused my death. ***~ with sb/sth,*** no longer be engaged with sb or busy with sth: *I haven't ~ed with you yet,* still have sth to say. *Have you ~ed with that dictionary?* ***~ sth off/up,*** eat up completely: *We ~ed up everything on the table.* ***~ sb off,*** (sl) kill, destroy, him. *That fever nearly ~ed him off.* ***~ (up) with,*** have at the end: *We had an excellent dinner, with a glass of old brandy to ~ up with.* **2** [VP6A] make complete or perfect; polish: *The woodwork is beautifully ~ed,* smoothed and polished. *They gave a ~ed performance of the quartet. He gave the picture a few ~ing touches.* ˋ**~ing school,** private school preparing upper-class girls for social life. □ *n* (*sing* only) **1** last part: *the ~ of a race. It was a close ~,* The competitors were close together at the ~. ***be in at the ~,*** be present when the fox is killed at the end of the hunt; (fig) be present during the last stage (of a struggle, etc). ***a fight to the ~,*** until one side is defeated or exhausted. **2** the state of being ~ed or perfect; the manner in which sth is ~ed: *woodwork with a smooth ~. His manners lack ~.*

fi·nite /ˋfaɪnaɪt/ *adj* **1** limited; having bounds: *Human understanding is ~,* There are things that man cannot understand. **2** (gram) agreeing with a subject in number and person: *'Am', 'is', 'are', 'was', and 'were' are the ~ forms of 'be', and 'be', 'being' and 'been' are the non-~ forms.*

Finn /fɪn/ *n* native of Finland. **~·ish** *adj, n* (language) of the ~s.

fin·nan /ˋfɪnən/ *n* (also ˈ**~ ˋhaddock/haddie** /ˋhædɪ/) (kind of) smoked haddock.

fiord, fjord /fɪˋɔd/ *n* long, narrow arm of the sea, between high cliffs (as in Norway).

fir /fɜ(r)/ *n* ⇨ the illus at tree. conifer with needle-like leaves; [U] wood of this tree. ˋ**fir-cone** *n*

fire[1] /ˋfaɪə(r)/ *n* **1** [U] condition of burning: *F~ burns.* ***There is no smoke without ~,*** (prov) There is always some reason for a rumour. ***on ~,*** burning: *The house was on ~.* ***play with ~,*** take foolish risks. ***set sth on ~, set ~ to sth,*** cause it to begin burning: *He set the haystack on ~.* ***not/never set the Thames on ~,*** never do anything remarkable: *Tom's not the sort of boy who will ever set the Thames on ~,* distinguish himself. ***take/catch ~,*** begin to burn: *Paper catches ~ easily.* ***strike ~ from,*** get sparks from (by striking or rubbing): *strike ~ from flint.* **2** [U] destructive burning: *Have you insured your house against ~? ~ and sword,* burning and killing (in war). ˋ**~ risk(s),** possible or likely cause(s) of ~. **3** [C] instance of destructive burning: *forest ~s; a ~ in a coal-mine.* **4** [C] burning fuel in a grate, etc to heat a building, for cooking, etc: *The weather is too warm for ~s. There's a ~ in the next room.* ***lay a ~,*** put paper, wood, coal, etc together ready for use. ***make a ~,*** lay a ~ and light it. ***make up a ~,*** add fuel as it burns low. **5** [U] shooting (from guns). ***open/cease ~,*** start/stop shooting; ***between two ~s,*** shot at from two directions. ***under ~,*** being shot at. **running ~,** **(a)** a succession of shots from a line of troops. **(b)** (fig) succession of criticisms, hostile questions, etc. ***hang ~,*** ⇨ hang[2](4). **6** [U] strong emotion; angry or excited feeling; enthusiasm: *a speech that lacks ~,* is uninspiring; *eyes full of ~.* **7** (compounds) ˋ**~-alarm** *n* apparatus (bell, etc) for making known the outbreak of a ~. ˋ**~-arm** *n* (usu *pl*) rifle, gun, pistol or revolver. ˋ**~-ball** *n* (esp) centre of an exploding atomic bomb. ˋ**~-bird** *n* N American bird with orange and black plummage. ˋ**~-bomb** *n* one that burns fiercely and causes destruction by ~. ⇨ napalm. ˋ**~-box**

n fuel-chamber of a steam-engine. **'~-brand** *n* piece of burning wood; (fig) person who stirs up social or political strife. **'~-break** *n* **(a)** (in a forest) wide strip of land without trees (to lessen the risk of a forest ~ spreading). **(b)** wall or barrier of incombustible material in a warehouse, factory, etc. **'~-brick** *n* kind of brick, proof against ~, used in grates, furnaces, chimneys, etc. **'~-brigade** *n* organized team of men who put out ~s. **'~-bug** *n* (sl) person who commits arson. **'~-clay** *n* kind used for ~-bricks. **'~-control** *n* system of regulating the firing of guns. **'~-cracker** *n* small ~work that explodes with a cracking noise. **'~-damp** *n* [U] gas in coal-mines, explosive when mixed in certain proportions with air. **'~-dog** *n* andiron. **'~ drill** *n* practice of routine to be followed when ~ breaks out, e g on a ship. **'~-eater** *n* person who quickly gets angry and ready to fight. **'~-engine** *n* machine, manned by ~men, for throwing water on to a ~ or for pumping water from flooded buildings, etc. **'~-escape** *n* outside staircase by means of which people may leave a burning building; apparatus, kind of extending ladder, used by ~men to save people from a burning building. **'~-extinguisher** *n* portable metal cylinder with chemical substance, etc, inside, for putting out a small ~. **'~-fighter** *n* = ~man(**b**); (esp) man who fights forest ~s. **'~-fly** *n* (*pl* **-flies**) winged beetle that sends out phosphorescent light. **'~-guard** *n* protective metal framework or grating round a ~ in a room. **'~-hose** *n* hose-pipe used for extinguishing ~s. **'~-irons** *n pl* poker, tongs, shovel, etc (kept near a ~place). **'~-light** *n* light from the ~ in a ~place: *sitting in the ~light.* **'~-lighter** *n* piece or bundle of fuel for kindling a ~(**4**). **~-man** /-mən/ *n* (*pl* **-men**) **(a)** man who looks after the ~ in a furnace or steam-engine. **(b)** member of a ~-brigade. **'~-place** *n* grate or hearth for a ~ in a room, usu of brick or stone in the wall. **'~-power** *n* [U] capacity to fire(**6**), expressed as the total number and weight of shells fired per minute: *the ~-power of a cruiser.* **'~ plug** *n* connection in a water-main for a ~-hose. **'~-proof** *adj* that does not burn; that does not crack or break when heated. **'~-raising** *n* arson. **'F~ Service,** (now the official term for) ~-brigade(s). **'~-side** *n* (*sing* with *def art*) part of a room round the ~place: *sitting at the ~side;* (fig) home life; (attrib) *a ~side chair; a homely ~side scene.* **'~ station** *n* building for a ~-brigade and its equipment. **'~-stone** *n* ~proof stone (in a ~place, etc). **'~-walking** *n* ceremony of walking barefoot over stones heated by ~, or over white-hot wood-ash, etc. Hence, **'~-walker** *n* **'~-watcher** *n* (in World War II) person whose duty was to watch for fires started by bombs dropped from the air. Hence, **'~ watching** *n* **'~-water** *n* (colloq) spirits such as whisky, gin and rum. **'~-wood** *n* wood prepared for lighting ~s or as fuel. **'~-work** *n* [C] device containing gunpowder and chemicals, used for making a display at night, or as a signal; (*pl*) (fig) display of wit, anger, etc.

fire[2] /'faɪə(r)/ *vt, vi* **1** [VP6A] set fire to with the intention of destroying; cause to being burning: *~ a haystack.* **2** [VP6A] use artificial heat on sth in order to change it in some way: *~ (= bake) bricks/pottery in a kiln; ~ tea,* cure it, make green leaves dry and dark. **3** [VP6A] supply (a furnace) with fuel: *an oil-~d furnace.* **4 ~ up,** (of a person) (more usu *flare up*) become excited or angry: *She ~s up at the least thing.* **5** [VP6A] excite or stimulate; [VP14] ***~ sb with,*** fill with enthusiasm, zeal. **6** [VP6A] discharge (a gun, etc); send (a shell, etc) from a gun; explode (a charge of explosive): *~ a gun. They ~d a salute,* discharged guns as a salute. [VP2A] shoot: *The officer ordered his men to ~.* ***~ at/into/on/upon,*** [VP3A] direct fire towards: *~ at a target; ~ upon a fort/ship. The police ~d into the crowd.* ***~ away,*** [VP2C] continue firing: *They were firing away at the enemy.* [VP15B] **(a)** *They ~d away all their ammunition,* expended it all. **(b)** (fig) go ahead; begin: *I'm ready to answer questions; ~ away.* **'firing-line** *n* front line (of trenches) where soldiers ~ at the enemy. **'firing-party/-squad** *n* number of soldiers ordered to ~ volleys at a military funeral or to carry out a military execution. **7** [VP6A] (colloq) dismiss (an employee): *~ the sales-girl for being incompetent.*

fir·kin /'fɜkɪn/ *n* small cask.

firm[1] /fɜm/ *adj* (**-er, -est**) **1** solid; hard; not yielding when pressed: *~ flesh/muscles; ~ ground* (often fig, as *be on ~ ground,* be sure of one's facts); *as ~ as a rock.* **2** not easily changed or influenced; showing strength of character and purpose: *a ~ faith; take ~ measures; be ~ with children,* insist upon obedience and discipline; *~ in/of purpose; be ~ in one's beliefs.* **3** (of a person, his body, its movements, characteristics, etc) steady, stable: *walk with ~ steps. The baby is not very ~ on its feet yet,* does not stand or walk confidently. *He spoke in a ~ voice. He gave me a ~ glance.* □ *vt, vi* make or become ~. □ *adv* = ~ly: *stand ~; hold ~ to one's beliefs.* **~·ly** *adv* in a ~ manner. **~·ness** *n*

firm[2] /fɜm/ *n* [C] (two or more) persons carrying on a business.

fir·ma·ment /'fɜməmənt/ *n* (usu *sing* with *def art*) the heavens and all that is in them.

first[1] /fɜst/ *adj* **1** coming before all others in time or order: *January, the ~ month of the year; the ~ chapter* (or *Chapter One*)*; King Edward the F~* (often King Edward I); *a ~ edition copy of a book; the ~ man who arrived/the ~ man to arrive; (the) ~ thing tomorrow morning,* before anything else; *at the ~* (= earliest) *opportunity; the ~* (= the leading) *men in the country; ~* (= basic) *principles; not know the ~ thing* (= not even one thing) *about it.* **2** (special uses, compounds): **'~ aid** *n* treatment given at once to a sick or injured person before a doctor comes. **'~ base** *n* (baseball) ~ base[1](**6**) on the field. ***get to ~ base,*** make a successful start. **'~ 'class** *n* best accommodation in a train, steamer, aircraft, etc. **'~-'class** *adj* of the ~ class: *~-class hotels/cabins/passengers; a ~-class* (university) *degree.*

a firework display

□ *adv* by the ~ class: *travel* '~-'*class*. **~ cost** *n* (comm) cost not including profit. '**~ de'gree,** ⇨ degree. '**~ 'floor** *n* (GB) floor immediately above the ground floor; (US) ground floor. '**~ form** *n* (GB) lowest class in secondary schools. '**~-fruits** *n pl* earliest produce (crops, etc) of the season (offered to God); (fig) ~ results of one's work. '**~ 'gear,** lowest gear(1). '**~-'hand** *adj, adv* (obtained) directly from the source: *~-hand information; learn something* '*~-'hand*. **at ~ hand,** directly. '**~ 'lady** *n* (US) wife of a President or a Governor of a State. '**~ name** *n* given name (contrasted with family name): *be on ~ name terms with the boss* (suggesting lacking formality). '**~ 'night** *n* evening on which a play or opera is presented for the ~ time. Hence, '**~-'nighter,** person who regularly attends ~ nights. '**~ 'mate** *n* ⇨ mate[1](2) and App 9. '**~ of'fender,** one against whom no previous conviction has been recorded. '**~ 'person** (gram) the *pronouns I, me, we, us* (and the *verb* forms used with them). '**~-'rate** *adj* of the best class; excellent: *~-rate acting*. □ *adv* (colloq) very well: *getting on* '*~-'rate*. **at ~ sight,** when seen or examined for the ~ time: *fall in love at ~ sight. At ~ sight the problem seemed easy.* **~·ly** *adv* in the ~ place.

first[2] /fɜst/ *adv* **1** before anyone or anything else (often, for emphasis, *~ of all, ~ and foremost*): *Which horse came in ~*, won the race? *Women and children ~*, i e before men. ***F~ come, ~ served,*** Those who come ~ will be served ~. ***last in, ~ out,*** (esp) the last to be employed are the ~ to be dismissed when dismissals are necessary. ***~ and last,*** taking one thing with another; on the whole. '**~·born** *n, adj* eldest (child). **2** for the ~ time: *When did you ~ see him/see him ~?* **3** before some other (specified or implied) time: *I must finish this work ~*, i e before starting sth else. **4** in preference: *He said he would resign ~*, e g resign rather than do sth dishonest for his employers.

first[3] /fɜst/ *n* **1** ***at ~,*** at the beginning. ***from the ~,*** from the start. ***from ~ to last,*** from beginning to end; throughout. **2** (in examinations, competitions) place in the first class; person who takes this: *He got a ~ in Modern Languages.*

firth /fɜθ/ *n* narrow arm of the sea; (esp in Scotland) river estuary.

fis·cal /'fɪskl/ *adj* of public revenue.

fish[1] /fɪʃ/ *n* (*pl* ~ or ~es) **1** [C] ⇨ the illus at sea. cold-blooded animal living wholly in water and breathing through gills, with fins for swimming: *catch a ~/two ~es/a lot of ~.* ***a 'pretty kettle of ~,*** a state of confusion. ***have 'other ~ to fry,*** more important business to attend to. ***There's as good ~ in the sea as ever came out of it,*** (prov used to suggest that even if one chance, etc has not been seized, there will be plenty of others). **2** [U] ~ as food: *a ~ dinner; ~ and chips*, fried ~ with chipped potatoes; *~ fingers*, finger-shaped pieces of fish in batter, to be fried. **3** (compounds) '**~ ball,** '**~·cake** *nn* fried rissole of ~. '**~·bone** *n* bone of a ~. '**~-hook** metal hook used for catching ~. '**~-knife,** knife with which ~ is eaten. '**~·monger,** tradesman who sells ~. '**~·paste,** paste of ~ or shellfish (spread on sandwiches, etc). '**~-slice,** knife for carving and serving ~ at table. '**~·wife,** woman who sells ~ (esp in a market, or from a cart in the street). **~y** *adj* **1** smelling or tasting like ~: *a ~y smell.* **2** (colloq) causing a feeling of doubt: *a ~y story.*

fish[2] /fɪʃ/ *vi,vt* **1** [VP2A,C] try to catch fish: *go ~ing; ~ in the sea;* (fig) try to get, by indirect methods: *~ for information/compliments.* ***~ in troubled waters,*** try to win advantages for oneself from a disturbed state of affairs. **2** [VP6A] try to catch ~ in: *~ a river/a pool;* try to catch by ~ing: *~ trout.* **3** [VP15A,B] ***~ up, ~ out (of),*** draw or pull: *~ out a coin from one's pocket; ~ up a dead cat out of a canal.* **~·ing** *n* catching fish for a living or for pleasure. '**~·ing-line** *n* line[1](1) with a ~-hook attached for ~ing. '**~·ing-rod** *n* long tapered rod (often jointed) to which a ~ing-line is fastened. '**~ing-tackle** *n* [U] things needed for ~ing.

fisher /'fɪʃə(r)/ *n* (old use) fisherman. **~·man** /-mən/ *n* (*pl* **-men**) man who earns a living by fishing. ⇨ *angler* at angle[2].

fish·ery /'fɪʃərɪ/ *n* (*pl* **-ries**) part of the sea where fishing is carried on: *in-shore fisheries*, near the coast; *deep-sea fisheries.*

fish·plate /'fɪʃpleɪt/ *n* one of two iron plates used to fasten rails to a sleeper (on a railway track).

fis·sile /'fɪsaɪl *US:* 'fɪsl/ *adj* that tends to split: *~ material*, e g that can be split up in a nuclear reactor.

fission /'fɪʃn/ *n* splitting or division, e g of one cell into new cells; of the nucleus of certain atoms, e g uranium, when an atomic bomb is exploded. **~·able** /-əbl/ *adj* that can be split by ~; capable of atomic ~.

fis·sipar·ous /fɪ'sɪpərəs/ *adj* (of cells) reproducing by fission.

fis·sure /'fɪʃə(r)/ *n* [C] cleft made by splitting or separation of parts.

fist /fɪst/ *n* ⇨ the illus at arm. hand when tightly closed (as in boxing): *He struck me with his ~. He shook his ~ at me.* **~i·cuffs** /'fɪstɪkʌfs/ *n pl* (usu hum) fighting with the ~s.

fis·tula /'fɪstʃʊlə/ *n* long pipe-like ulcer with a narrow mouth.

fit[1] /fɪt/ *adj* **(fitter, fittest) 1** ***fit (for),*** suitable or suited; well adapted; good enough: *The food was not fit to eat*, was too bad to be eaten. *It was a dinner fit for a king. That man is not fit for the position. We must decide on a fit time and place for the meeting.* **2** right and proper: *It is not fit that*

fish

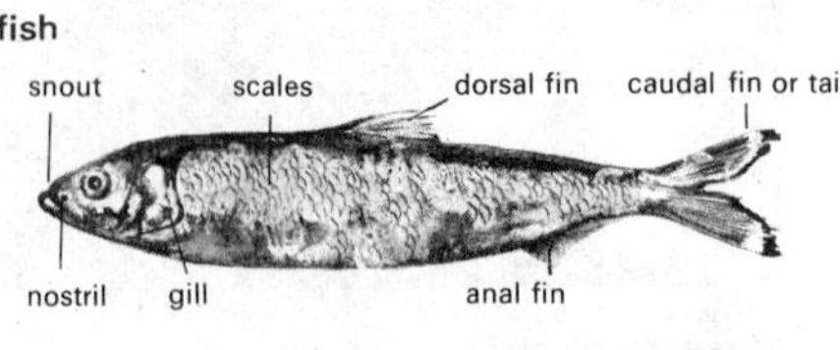

HERRING

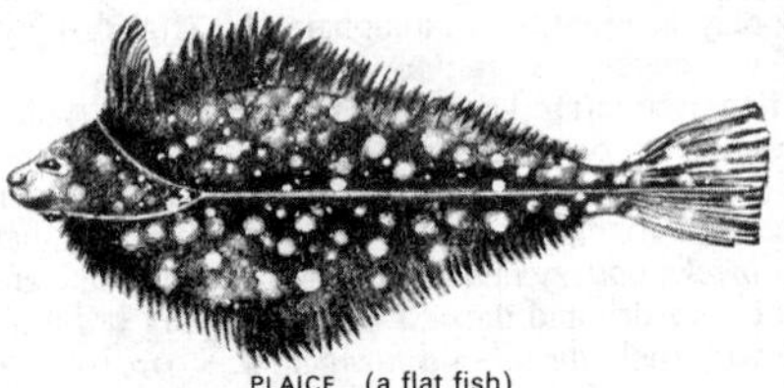
PLAICE (a flat fish)

you should make merry while your brother is seriously ill. **think/see fit (to do sth),** decide to: *He didn't see fit to adopt my suggestion. Do as you think fit.* **3** ready; in a suitable condition; (colloq, as an *adv*): *He was laughing fit to burst himself,* so violently that he seemed ready to burst. *They went on working till they were fit to drop,* ready to drop from exhaustion. **4** in good athletic condition; in good health: *I hope you're keeping fit.* ⇨ **keep**[1]**(14).** *He has been ill and is not fit for work/ fit to travel yet.* **fit·ly** *adv* **fit·ness** *n* **1** suitability (*for*): *the fitness of things,* what is right or suitable. **2** the state of being physically fit: *a national fitness campaign,* one for improving the nation's health.

fit[2] /fɪt/ *vt,vi* (-tt-) **1** [VP6A,2A] be the right measure, shape and size for: *shoes that fit well; a badly fitting door. This coat doesn't fit me. The key doesn't fit the lock.* **2** [VP15A,B] put on (esp clothing) to see that it is the right size, shape, etc: *have a new coat fitted.* **3** [VP15A,B] put into place: *fit a new lock on a door.* **4** [VP6A,14,16A] ***fit sb/oneself for sth/to do/be sth,*** make (sb, oneself) suitable or competent: *fit oneself for one's new duties. Military training fits men for long marches/to make long marches. Can we make the punishment fit the crime?* **5** [VP15B,2C] ***fit in (with),*** (cause to) be in a suitable or harmonious relation (with); find, be in, the right or a suitable time or place for: *I must fit my holidays in with yours. My holiday arrangements must fit in with yours.* ***fit sb/sth out,*** supply with what is needed; equip: *fit out a ship for a long voyage/a party for a polar expedition.* ***fit sb/sth up,*** supply: *a hotel fitted up with modern comforts and conveniences.* □ *n* (usu *sing* with *indef art* and *adj*) style, manner, in which sth, e g a garment, fits: *The coat is a tight/good/excellent fit.*

fit[3] /fɪt/ *n* **1** sudden (usu short) attack of illness: *a fit of coughing; a* ˋ*fainting fit.* **2** sudden attack of hysteria, apoplexy, paralysis, with loss of consciousness and violent movements: *fall down in a fit.* ***give sb a fit,*** (colloq) do sth that greatly shocks or outrages him. ***have a fit,*** (colloq) be greatly surprised or outraged: *She almost had a fit when she saw the bill.* **3** sudden onset lasting for a short time; outbursts: *a fit of energy/enthusiasm/ anger.* ***by/in fits and starts,*** in short periods, from time to time, not regularly. **4** mood: *when the fit was on him,* when he felt in the right mood (*for* sth). **fit·ful** /-fl/ *adj* occurring, coming and going, by fits and starts; irregular: *a fitful breeze.* **fit·fully** /-flɪ/ *adv*

fit·ment /ˋfɪtmənt/ *n* piece of furniture or equipment: *kitchen ∼s,* e g sinks, cupboards, working tables, esp when made as units in a series.

fit·ter /ˋfɪtə(r)/ *n* **1** (tailoring and dressmaking) person who cuts out, fits and alters garments. **2** (eng) workman who fits together and adjusts the finished parts of an engine, machine, etc.

fit·ting /ˋfɪtɪŋ/ *adj* proper; right; suitable. □ *n* **1** act of fitting: *go to the tailor's for a ∼.* **2** fixture in a building, esp (*pl*) things permanently fixed: *gas and electric light ∼s.* **3** furnishing: *office ∼s,* e g desks, chairs, filing cabinets.

five /faɪv/ *n, adj* 5, ⇨ App 4: *a ∼-day week,* one of ∼ working days. ˋ**∼-fold** *adj* with ∼ parts; ∼ times as much. **∼·pence** /ˋfaɪfpəns *US:* ˋfaɪvpens/ *n* ∼ pence; coin worth ∼ (new) pence. **∼·penny** /ˋfaɪfpənɪ/ *adj* costing ∼pence. **fiver** /ˋfaɪvə(r)/ *n* (colloq) £5 note; $5 bill.

fives /faɪvz/ *n* (GB) ball game played with the hands or a bat in a walled court.

fix[1] /fɪks/ *vt,vi* **1** [VP6A,15A,B] make firm or fast; fasten (sth) so that it cannot be moved: *fix a post in the ground/a shelf to a wall; fix bayonets* (as a mil command—put them in position on rifles); *fix facts/dates, etc in one's mind,* implant them deeply so that they will not be forgotten. **2** [VP14] ***∼ on,*** direct (the eyes, one's attention, etc) steadily on or to: *fix one's attention on what one is doing. He fixed his eyes on me. He has fixed his affections on a worthless woman.* **3** [VP6A] (of objects) attract and hold (the attention): *This unusual sight fixed his attention/kept his attention fixed.* **4** [VP6A] determine or decide: *fix the rent; fix a date for a meeting; sell goods only at fixed prices,* prices with no discount, with no possibility of bargaining; *a man with fixed* (= definite and decided) *principles.* **fixed odds,** ⇨ **odds(3).** **5** [VP6A] treat (photographic films, colours used in dyeing, etc) so that light does not affect them. **6** [VP15A] single out (sb) by looking steadily (at him): *fix a man with an angry stare.* **7** [VP15B] ***fix sb up (with),*** arrange; organize, provide for: *fix sb up with a job; fix up a friend for the night,* give him a bed. **8** [VP3A] ***fix (up)on,*** settle one's choice, decide to have: *They've fixed upon a little bungalow near Rye.* **9** [VP6A] (sl) **(a)** use bribery or deception, improper influence: *You can't fix a judge in Britain.* **(b)** get even with sb: *I'll fix him.* **10** [VP6A] (US colloq) put in order; prepare: *fix one's hair,* brush and comb it; *fix a watch,* repair it; *fix a salad,* mix and dress it. **fixed** /fɪkst/ *adj* unchanging: *fixed costs,* overhead expenses. ⇨ **overhead**; *a fixed idea,* one in which a person persists and which tends to occupy his thoughts too much; *a fixed star,* one that seems to keep the same position relative to others, not changing it as planets do. **fix·ed·ly** /ˋfɪksɪdlɪ/ *adv* in a fixed manner (esp of looking): *look/gaze fixedly at sb.*

fix[2] /fɪks/ *n* **1** ***be in/get oneself into a fix,*** a dilemma, an awkward situation. **2** finding of a position, position found, by taking bearings, observing the stars, etc. **3** (sl) hypodermic injection of a drug, e g heroin.

fix·ation /fɪkˋseɪʃn/ *n* **1** fixing or being fixed: *the ∼ of a photographic film.* **2** (psych) abnormal emotional attachment to another person, with difficulty in forming other, normal, attachments.

fixa·tive /ˋfɪksətɪv/ *n* substance which fixes specimens for study under a microscope; substance for keeping hair or dentures in position.

fix·ture /ˋfɪkstʃə(r)/ *n* [C] **1** sth fixed in place, esp (*pl*) built-in cupboards, electric-light fittings, etc which are bought with a building: *We were charged for ∼s and fittings.* **2** (day fixed or decided for a) sporting event: football and racing ∼s. **3** (colloq) person or thing that appears unlikely to move from or leave a place: *Professor Green seems to be a ∼ in the college.*

fizz /fɪz/ *vi* [VP2A,C] make a hissing sound (as when gas escapes from a liquid). □ *n* [U] this sound; (colloq) champagne. **∼y** *adj* (**-ier, -iest**).

fizzle /ˋfɪzl/ *vi* [VP2A,C] hiss or splutter feebly. ***∼ out,*** *end feebly; come to a weak, unsatisfactory end.*

fjord ⇨ **fiord.**

flab·ber·gast /ˋflæbəgɑst *US:* -gæst/ *vt* [VP6A] (colloq) overwhelm with amazement.

flabby /ˈflæbɪ/ *adj* **(-ier, -iest) 1** (of the muscles, flesh) soft; not firm: *A man who never takes exercise is likely to have ~ muscles.* **2** (fig) weak; without moral force: *a ~ will/character.* **flab·bily** /-əlɪ/ *adv* **flab·bi·ness** *n*

flac·cid /ˈflæksɪd/ *adj* flabby. **~·ity** /flækˈsɪdətɪ/ *n*

flag¹ /flæg/ *n* (usu square or oblong) piece of cloth, attached by one edge to a rope, used as the distinctive symbol of a country, or as a signal, ⇨ the illus on p **330**. *the national ~ of Great Britain,* the Union Jack; *the Red Cross ~; ~s of convenience,* ~, e g of Panama, Liberia, used to obscure actual ownership of ships and so evade taxation. ***lower/strike one's ~,*** take it down as a sign of surrender. **ˈ~-captain** *n* captain of a ~ship. **ˈ~-day (a)** day on which money is raised for a charitable cause by persons in public places, a small paper ~ being given to those who contribute. **(b)** (US) 14 June, anniversary of the day in 1777 when the Stars and Stripes became the national ~. **ˈ~ officer,** admiral. **ˈ~·pole,** pole on which a ~ is shown. **ˈ~·ship,** warship having an admiral on board. **ˈ~·staff,** pole on which a ~ is flown. ⇨ also **black, white²** and **yellow.** □ *vt* **(-gg-)** [VP6A] **1** place a ~ or ~s on; decorate with ~s: *streets ~ged to celebrate a victory.* **2** [VP6A,15B] ***~ (down),*** signal to (sb), stop a train, car, etc by moving one's outstretched arm up and down or waving a ~.

flags 1 St Andrew's 2 St George's 3 St Patrick's 4 the Union Jack

flag² /flæg/ *vi* **(-gg-)** [VP2A] (of plants, etc) droop, hang down, become limp; (fig) become tired or weak: *His strength/interest in his work/enthusiasm of the cause was ~ging.*

flag³ /flæg/ *n* (also **ˈ~·stone**) flat, square or oblong piece of stone for a floor, path or pavement.

flag⁴ /flæg/ *n* kinds of plant with blade-like leaves, growing in moist land, esp kinds of iris.

flagel·lant /ˈflædʒɪlənt/ *n* person who practises scourging (whipping) (as a religious penance). **flagel·late** /ˈflædʒɪleɪt/ *vt* [VP6A] flog, scourge. **flagel·la·tion** /ˈflædʒɪˈleɪʃn/ *n*

flageo·let /ˈflædʒəʊˈlet/ *n* small flute, like a whistle, with six stops.

flagon /ˈflægən/ *n* **1** large, rounded bottle in which wine, cider, etc is sold, usu holding about twice as much as an ordinary bottle. **2** vessel with a handle, lip and lid for serving wine at table.

fla·grant /ˈfleɪgrənt/ *adj* (of crime or a criminal, etc) openly and obviously wicked; glaring; scandalous: *~ offences/sinners.* **~·ly** *adv*

flail /fleɪl/ *n* old-fashioned tool for threshing grain, consisting of a strong stick hinged on a long handle. □ *vt* [VP6A] beat with (or as with) a ~.

flair /fleə(r)/ *n* natural or instinctive ability (to do sth well, to select or recognize what is best, most useful, etc): *have a ~ for languages,* be quick at learning them; *have a ~ for bargains,* be good at recognizing them.

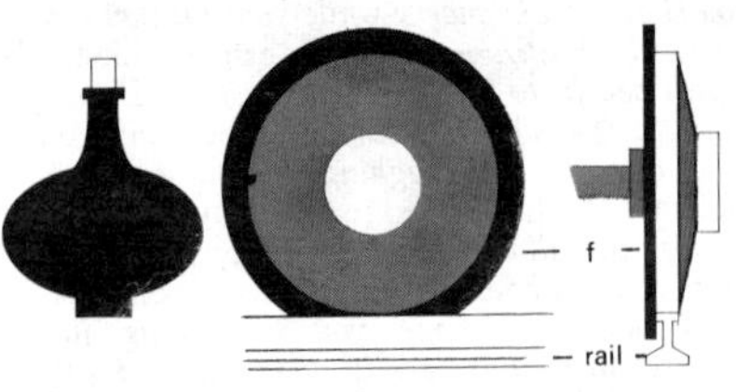

a flagon a flange

flak /flæk/ *n* (G) anti-aircraft guns or gunfire.

flake /fleɪk/ *n* [C] small, light, leaf-like piece: *ˈsnow~s; ~s of rust falling from old iron; ˈsoap-~s.* □ *vi* [VP2A,C] ***~ (off),*** fall off in ~s. **flaky** *adj* **(-ier, -iest)** made up of ~s: *flaky pastry.* **flaki·ness** *n*

flam·beau /ˈflæmbəʊ/ *n* (*pl* **-beaux** or **-beaus** /-bəʊz/) flaming torch.

flam·boy·ant /flæmˈbɔɪənt/ *adj* brightly coloured and decorated; (of a person, his character) florid, showy. **~·ly** *adv* **flam·boy·ance** /-əns/ *n*

flame¹ /fleɪm/ *n* **1** [C,U] (portion of) burning gas: *The house was in ~s,* was on fire, burning. *He put a match to the papers and they burst into ~(s).* **ˈ~·thrower** *n* weapon which projects a steady stream of burning fuel. **2** [C] blaze of light; brilliant colour: *the ~s of sunset.* **3** [C] passion: *a ~ of anger/indignation/enthusiasm.* **4** [C] (colloq) sweetheart: *She's an old ~ of his,* a woman with whom he was once in love.

flame² /fleɪm/ *vi* [VP2A,C] burn with, send out, flames; be or become like flames in colour: *make the fire ~ up; hillsides flaming with the colours of autumn,* e g of maple-trees. *His face ~d with anger. His anger ~d out. The boy's face ~d still redder,* became redder, with anger, embarrassment, etc. **flam·ing** *adj* burning; very hot: *a flaming sun;* (colloq, vulg) bloody**(3)**: *You flaming idiot!*

fla·mingo /fləˈmɪŋgəʊ/ *n* (*pl* **-gos, -goes** /-gəʊz/) large long-legged, long-necked wading bird with pink feathers. ⇨ the illus at **water.**

flam·mable /ˈflæməbl/ *adj* (= *inflammable,* but preferred in US and in technical contexts) having a tendency to burst into flames and to burn rapidly.

flan /flæn/ *n* [C] tart containing fruit, etc, not covered with pastry.

flange /flændʒ/ *n* projecting or outside rim or collar, e g of a wheel, to keep sth in position. ⇨ the illus at **flagon.**

flank /flæŋk/ *n* **1** fleshy part of the side of a human being or animal between the last rib and the hip. ⇨ the illus at **trunk. 2** side of a building or mountain. **3** right or left side of an army or body of troops: *attack the left ~; make a ~ attack.* □ *vt* [VP6A] **1** be situated at or on the ~ of. **2** go round the ~ of (the enemy).

flan·nel /ˈflænl/ *n* **1** [U] loosely woven woollen cloth: *a yard of ~; ~ trousers/shirts.* **2** (*pl*) ~ trousers used for summer sports and games, e g cricket. **3** [C] piece of ~ for cleaning, rubbing, etc: *a ˈface-~.* **~·ette** /ˈflænlˈet/ *n* [U] cotton material made to look like ~.

flap¹ /flæp/ *n* [C] **1** (sound of a) ~ping blow or movement: *A ~ from the tail of the whale upset* *the boat.* **2** piece of material that hangs down or covers an opening: *the ~ of a pocket; the gummed ~ of an envelope; the ~ of a table,* a hinged leaf that can hang down when not being used, ⇨ the illus at gate; *the upturned ~* (= brim) *of a hat.* **3** part of the wing of an aircraft that can be lifted in flight to alter its upward direction and speed. **4** ***be in/get into a ~,*** (sl) a state of nervous excitement or confusion (caused by fear of making errors, being incompetent, etc, e g while awaiting a visit from one's superiors).

flap[2] /flæp/ *vt,vi* (-pp-) **1** [VP2A,C,6A] (cause to) move up and down or from side to side: *The sails were ~ping against the mast. The wind ~ped the sails. The curtains were ~ping at the open window. The bird was ~ping its wings. The heron came ~ping over the water.* **2** [VP6A,15B] give a light blow to with sth soft and flat: *~ the flies off/away.* **3** [VP2A] (sl) get into a ~[1](3).

flap·jack /ˈflæpdʒæk/ *n* [C] small flat cake of batter fried in a pan.

flap·per /ˈflæpə(r)/ *n* **1** sth broad and flat (used to swat flies, etc). **2** (fish's) broad fin. **3** (sl use in the 1920's) teenage girl not yet old enough to attend social events with grown-ups.

flare[1] /fleə(r)/ *vi* **1** [VP6A] burn with a bright, unsteady flame: *The candle began to ~; flaring gas-jets.* **2** [VP2C] **~ up,** burst into bright flame; (fig) into rage; (of violence) suddenly break out: *When he was accused of lying, he ~d up. She ~s up at the least thing. Rioting ~d up again later.* Hence, **ˈ~-up** *n* sudden breaking into flame; short sudden outburst (of anger, etc). □ *n* **1** [U] flaring flame: *the ~ of torches; the sudden ~ of a match in the darkness.* **2** [C] device for producing a flaring light, used as a signal, etc: *The wrecked ship was using ~s to attract the attention of the coastguards.* **ˈ~-path** *n* lit-up landing strip for aircraft.

flare[2] /fleə(r)/ *vi,vt* [VP2A,6A] (of a woman's skirt, the sides of a ship) (cause to) spread gradually outwards; become, make, wider at the bottom. □ *n* gradual widening (of a skirt); upward bulge (in a ship's sides).

flash[1] /flæʃ/ *n* **1** sudden burst of flame or light: *a ~ of lightning; ~es of light from a mirror; ~es from the guns during a battle;* (fig) *a ~ of wit/merriment/inspiration.* **in a ~,** instantly, at once. **a ~ in the pan,** an effort that is quickly over or at once ends in failure. **ˈ~·back** *n* (also *cut back*) (cinema) part of a film that shows a scene earlier in time than the rest of the film (e g to the childhood days of the hero). **ˈ~·bulb** *n* (photo) bulb giving a momentary bright light. **ˈ~·gun** *n* (photo) device to synchronize the release of a ~bulb or electronic light source and a shutter in a camera. **ˈ~·light** *n* **(a)** light used for signals, in lighthouses, etc. **(b)** (also **ˈphoto-~** and ~ alone) any device for producing a brilliant ~ of light for taking a photograph indoors or when natural light is too weak. ⇨ the illus at camera. **(c)** small electric torch. **ˈ~-point** *n* temperature at which vapour from oil may be ignited. **2** formation, e g divisional, sign, esp on the shoulder of a uniform. Cf *a badge of rank.* **3** (also **ˈnews-~**) brief item of news received by telephone, cable, teleprinter, etc. **4** (attrib use; colloq) showy; smart: *a ~ sports car;* of the underworld of crime, etc.

flash[2] /flæʃ/ *vi,vt* **1** [VP2A,C] send, give out, a sudden bright light: *The lightning ~ed across the sky. A lighthouse was ~ing in the distance.* **2** [VP2C] come suddenly (into view, into the mind): *The idea ~ed into/through his mind. The express train ~ed past.* **3** [VP6A,15A,12C] send suddenly or instantly: *~ a light in sb's eyes; ~ a signal,* e g using a heliograph or lamp; *~ news across the world* (by radio or TV). *She ~ed him a despairing glance.* **4** [VP6A] send or reflect like a ~ or ~es: *Her eyes ~ed fire/defiance.*

flashy /ˈflæʃɪ/ *adj* (-ier, -iest) brilliant and attractive but not in good taste; given to (rather vulgar) display: *~ clothes/jewellery; ~ men.* **flash·ily** /-əlɪ/ *adv* in a ~ manner: *a flashily-dressed girl.*

flask /flɑsk *US:* flæsk/ *n* **1** narrow-necked bottle used in laboratories, etc. **2** narrow-necked bottle for oil or wine (often in wickerwork, as used in Italy). **3** (also **ˈhip-~**) flat-sided bottle of metal or (often leather-covered) glass for carrying spirits in the pocket.

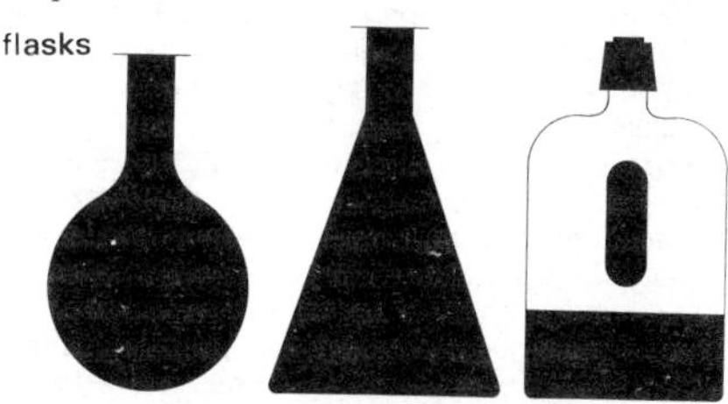

flat[1] /flæt/ *n* (GB) suite of rooms (living-room, bedroom, kitchen, etc) on one floor of a building as a residence: *an old house divided into ~s; a new block of ~s; ˈ~-dwellers,* people who live in ~s. ⇨ (US) apartment. **~·let** /-lət/ *n* tiny ~.

flat[2] /flæt/ *adj* (-ter, -test) **1** smooth and level; even; having an unbroken surface: *A floor must be ~. The top of a table is ~. People used to think that the world was ~; now we know that it is round. One of the tyres is ~,* has no or not enough air in it. **ˌ~-ˈbottomed** *adj* (of a boat) having a ~ bottom (for use in shallow water). **ˈ~-car** *n* (US) railroad car without a roof or sides, for carrying freight. **ˈ~·fish** *n* kinds of fish (including sole, plaice, turbot) having a ~ body and swimming on one side. ⇨ the illus at fish. **ˌ~-ˈfooted** *adj* **(a)** having feet with flat soles. **(b)** (colloq) downright; resolute. **ˈ~-iron** *n* iron tool with a ~ surface (*iron* is now the usu word) for smoothing linen, etc. **ˈ~ racing, the F~,** (horse-racing) over level ground with no obstacles. ⇨ *steeplechase* at steeple. **ˈ~·top** *n* (US colloq) aircraft-carrier. **2** spread out; (lying) at full length: *He fell ~ on his back. He knocked his opponent ~. The earthquake laid the city ~,* caused all the buildings to fall. **3** with a broad level surface and little depth: *~ plates/dishes/pans. The omelette was ~,* had failed to rise while cooking. **4** dull; uninteresting; monotonous: *Life seemed ~ to him. The party/conversation was rather ~. The soup is ~,* lacks flavour. *The beer tastes ~,* is tasteless because the gas has gone. ***fall ~,*** fail to win applause or appreciation: *His best jokes fell ~.* **5** (music) below the true pitch: *sing ~; a ~ note; A ~* (*A♭*), note half a tone lower than A. ⇨ sharp(10). **6** absolute; downright; unqualified: *give sb a ~ denial/refusal,* deny or refuse sth absolutely; *~ nonsense. And that's ~!* Let there be no doubt about that! **7** (comm) **ˈ~ rate,** common price paid for each of different things or services bought in quantity. **8** (of colours, coloured surfaces) uniform, without relief: *a ~ tint; ~ paint,* without a gloss. *His paintings all seem rather ~,* lack relief, shading, etc. **9** (of a battery) run down; needing to be recharged. **10** **ˌ~ ˈspin,** **(a)** (often uncontrolable) fast descent of an aircraft in a horizontal position and spinning. **(b)** (colloq) (mental) state of great confusion: *in a ~ spin.* □ *adv* **1** in a ~ manner: *sing ~.* **2** positively: *He told me ~ that.... He went ~ against orders.* ***~ broke,*** (colloq) with no money at all. **3** ***~ out,*** **(a)** (colloq) with all one's strength and resources: *He was working/running ~ out.* **(b)** exhausted. **~·ly** *adv* in a ~(6) manner: *The suggestions were ~ly opposed. He ~ly refused to join us.* **~·ness** *n*

flat[3] /flæt/ *n* **1** flat part of anything: *the ~ of the hand; with the ~ of his sword.* **2** stretch of low flat land, esp near water: *ˈmud ~s; ˈsalt ~s,* near the sea. **3** ⇨ the illus at notation. (music) flat note; the sign ♭: *sharps and ~s,* the black notes on a piano keyboard. **4** (esp US) deflated tyre, e g after a puncture. **5** piece of stage scenery on a movable frame.

flat·ten /ˈflætn/ *vt,vi* [VP6A,15A,B,2A,C] make or become flat: *a field of wheat ~ed by storms; ~ (out) a piece of metal by hammering it; ~ oneself against a wall,* e g to avoid being struck by a lorry in a narrow street.

flat·ter /ˈflætə(r)/ *vt* **1** [VP6A] praise too much; praise insincerely (in order to please). **2** [VP6A] give a feeling of pleasure to: *I feel greatly ~ed by your invitation to address the meeting.* **3** [VP6A] (of a picture, artist, etc) show (sb) as better looking than he is: *This photograph ~s you.* **4** ***~ oneself that...,*** be pleased with one's belief that...: *He ~ed himself that he spoke French with a perfect accent.* **~er** *n* person who ~s. **~y** *n* [U] ~ing; insincere praise; [C] (*pl* **-ries**) instance of this; ~ing remark: *Don't be deceived by her ~ies.*

flatu·lence /ˈflætʃʊləns/ *n* [U] gas in the alimentary canal; feeling of discomfort caused by an accumulation of this.

flaunt /flɔnt/ *vt,vi* **1** [VP6A] show off complacently; ostentatiously attract attention to: *~ oneself/one's new finery/riches, etc.* **2** [VP2A,C] wave proudly: *flags and banners ~ing in the breeze.*

flau·tist /ˈflɔtɪst/ *n* flute-player.

fla·vour (US = **-vor**) /ˈfleɪvə(r)/ *n* **1** [U] sensation of taste and smell: *When you have a cold, your food sometimes has very little ~.* **2** [C] distinctive taste; special quality or characteristic: *a ~ of garlic; various ~s in ice-cream; a newspaper story with a ~ of romance.* □ *vt* [VP6A] give a ~ to: *~ a sauce with onions.* **~·ing** *n* [C,U] sth used to give ~ to (food, etc): *too much vanilla ~ing in the cake. Many ~ings have little or no food value.* **~·less** *adj* having no ~.

flaw /flɔ/ *n* [C] crack; sth that lessens the value, beauty or perfection of a thing: *~s in a jewel/an argument/a person's character.* **~·less** *adj* perfect. **~·less·ly** *adv*

flax /flæks/ *n* [U] plant cultivated for the fibres obtained from its stems; these fibres (for making linen). **~en** /ˈflæksn/ *adj* (of hair) pale yellow.

flay /fleɪ/ *vt* [VP6A] take the skin or hide off (an animal); (fig) criticize severely or pitilessly: *The tutor ~ed the idle students.*

flea /flɪ/ *n* small wingless jumping insect that feeds on the blood of human beings and some animals. ⇨ the illus at insect. ***(go off/send sb off with a) ~ in his ear,*** (with a) stinging rebuke. **ˈ~-bite** *n* (fig) small inconvenience, sth not very troublesome. **ˈ~-bitten** *adj* **ˈ~ market,** open-air market selling cheap and second-hand goods. **ˈ~-pit** *n* (colloq) old and dirty place of entertainment, e g a cinema, theatre.

fleck /flek/ *n* [C] **1** small spot or patch: *~s of colour on a bird's breast; ~s of sunlight on the ground under a tree.* **2** small particles (of dust, etc). □ *vt* [VP6A] mark with ~s: *a sky ~ed with clouds.*

fled *pt,pp* of flee.

fledged /fledʒd/ *adj* (of birds) with fully grown wing feathers; able to fly. **ˌfully-ˈ~** *adj* trained and experienced: *a fully-~ engineer.* **fledg(e)·ling** /ˈfledʒlɪŋ/ *n* young bird just able to fly; (fig) young inexperienced person.

flee /fli/ *vi,vt* (*pt,pp* fled /fled/) [VP2A,C,6A] run or hurry away (from): *The enemy fled in disorder. The clouds fled before the wind. He killed his enemy and fled the country.*

fleece /flis/ *n* [C,U] **1** ⇨ the illus at domestic. woolly covering of a sheep or similar animal; quantity of wool cut from a sheep in one operation: *a coat lined with ~.* **2** ~-like head of hair. □ *vt* (usu fig) rob (sb) by trickery: *He was ~d of his money.* **fleecy** *adj* (-ier, -iest) like ~: *fleecy clouds/hair/falls of snow.*

fleet[1] /flit/ *n* [C] **1** number of warships under one commander; all the warships of a country. **2** number of ships, aircraft, buses, etc moving or working under one command or ownership.

fleet[2] /flit/ *adj* (poet, liter) quick-moving: *~ of foot, ~-footed.* **ˈ~ly** *adv* **ˈ~ness** *n*

Fleet Street /ˈflit strit/ *n* (street in central London where there are many newspaper offices, hence) the press; London journalism.

fleet·ing /ˈflitɪŋ/ *adj* passing quickly: *pay sb a ~ visit,* a short visit before one goes on to another place; *~ happiness,* lasting for a short time.

flesh /fleʃ/ *n* [U] **1** soft substance, esp muscle, between the skin and bones of animal bodies: *Tigers are ~-eating animals.* ***put on/lose ~,*** (more usu *weight*) become fat/thin. ***~ and blood,*** human nature with its emotions, weaknesses, etc: *more than ~ and blood can stand,* more than human nature can bear. ***one's own ~ and blood,*** one's near relatives. ***in the ~,*** in life, in bodily form. ***go the way of all ~,*** die. ***have/demand one's pound of ~,*** insist cruelly on repayment of what was borrowed. ⇨ Shakespeare's Mer of Ven IV, Sc 1. ***make a person's ˈ~ creep,*** frighten or horrify him (esp with dread of sth supernatural). **ˈ~-pots** *n pl* (places supplying) good food and material comforts. **ˈ~-wound** *n* one that does not reach the bone or vital organs. **2** **the ~,** physical or bodily desires; sensual appetites: *the sins of the ~.* **3** the body (contrasted with the *mind* and *soul*): ***The spirit is willing but the ~ is weak,*** (of a person who is willing to do sth, but is physically weak or lazy). **4** pulpy part of fruits and vegetables. **~·ly** *adj* of the body; sensual. **~y** *adj* fat; of ~.

flesh·ings /ˈfleʃɪŋz/ *n pl* flesh-coloured tights, e g as worn by ballet dancers.

fleur-de-lis, -lys /ˌflɜ də ˈli/ *n* (*pl* fleurs-de-lis, -lys pronunciation unchanged) heraldic lily; royal arms of France. ⇨ the illus at armour.

flew /flu/ *pt* of fly.

flex[1] /fleks/ *n* [C,U] (length of) flexible insulated cord for electric current.

flex[2] /fleks/ *vt* [VP6A] bend, e g a limb, one's muscles.

flex·ible /ˈfleksəbl/ *adj* easily bent without breaking; (fig) easily changed to suit new conditions; (of persons) adaptable. **flexi·bil·ity** /ˌfleksəˈbɪlətɪ/ *n* [U].

flib·ber·ti·gib·bet /ˌflɪbətɪˈdʒɪbɪt/ *n* frivolous person too fond of gossip.

flick /flɪk/ *n* [C] **1** quick light blow, e g with a whip or the tip of a finger. **2** short sudden movement; jerk. **ˈ~-knife** *n* knife with a blade (inside the handle) which can be brought into position with a ~ for use. □ *vt* **1** [VP6A,15A,22] strike with a ~, give a ~ with (a whip, etc); touch lightly: *He ~ed the horse with his whip/~ed his whip at the horse. He ~ed the switch,* e g for electric light. *He ~ed the knife open.* **2** [VP15B] ***~ sth away/off,*** remove with a ~: *She ~ed the crumbs off the table-cloth.* **the ~s** *n pl* (sl) cinema (films): *go to the ~s.*

flicker /ˈflɪkə(r)/ *vi* [VP2A,C] **1** (of a light; fig of hopes, etc) burn or shine unsteadily; flash and die away by turns: *The candle ~ed and then went out. A faint hope still ~ed in her breast.* **2** move back and forth, wave to and fro: *leaves ~ing in the wind; ~ing shadows; the ~ing tongue of a snake.* □ *n* (usu *sing*) ~ing movement: *a weak ~ of hope.*

flier /ˈflɑɪə(r)/ ⇨ flyer.

flight[1] /flɑɪt/ *n* **1** [U] flying through the air: *the art of ~; study the ~ of birds,* how they fly. ***in ~,*** while flying. **2** [C] journey made by air; distance covered: *a non-stop ~ from Paris to New York; ~s in a balloon; the spring and autumn ~s* (= seasonal migrations) *of birds.* **ˈ~ deck** *n* (on an aircraft-carrier) deck for taking off from and landing on; (in an airliner) compartment used by the pilot, navigator, engineer, etc. **3** [U] movement (and path) through the air: *the ~ of an arrow;* (attrib) *the ~ path of an airliner.* **4** [C] number of birds or objects moving together through the air: *a ~ of arrows/swallows.* ***in the first ~,*** taking or occupying a leading place. **5** [U] swift passing: *the ~ of time.* **6** [C] soaring; going up above the ordinary: *a ~ of the imagination/wit/fancy/ambition.* **7** [C] series (*of* stairs, etc without change of direction); stairs between two landings: *My bedroom is two ~s up. There was no lift and we had to climb six ~s of stairs.* **8** [C] group of aircraft in a country's Air Force. **ˈF~ Lieutenant, ˈF~ Sergeant,** etc, ⇨ App 9. □ *vt* [VP6A] move (the ball) sideways when bowling it, so as to deceive the batsman: *a well-~ed delivery.* **~·less** *adj* (of birds) unable to fly.

flight[2] /flɑɪt/ *n* **1** [U] (act of) fleeing of running away (from danger, etc): *seek safety in ~; put the enemy to ~,* defeat them and cause them to flee. ***take ~, take to ~,*** run away. **2** [C] instance of this: *the ~ into Egypt* (of Mary with the infant Jesus): *a ~ of capital,* e g when capital is sent abroad during a financial crisis.

flighty /ˈflɑɪtɪ/ *adj* (usu of a woman, her behaviour, character) influenced by whims; unsteady; fickle.

flimsy /ˈflɪmzɪ/ *adj* (-ier, -iest) (of material) light and thin; (of objects) easily injured and destroyed: *a ~ cardboard box;* (fig) *a ~ excuse/argument.* □ *n* [C] thin sheet of paper, e g as used when several carbon copies are made on a typewriter. **flims·ily** /-əlɪ/ *adv* **flim·si·ness** *n*

flinch /flɪntʃ/ *vi* [VP2A,3,3A] draw or move back; wince: *have a tooth pulled out without ~ing. You mustn't ~ from an unpleasant duty.*

fling /flɪŋ/ *vt,vi* (*pt,pp* flung /flʌŋ/) **1** [VP6A, 15A,B,22,12A,13A] throw violently: *~ one's hat up (in the air); ~ a stone at sb or sth; ~ one's clothes on,* dress hurriedly; *~ the doors and windows open,* open them quickly and forcibly; *be flung into prison; ~ caution to the winds,* act recklessly; *~ off one's pursuers,* escape from them. *She flung him a scornful look.* **2** [VP6A, 15A,B] move oneself, one's arms, etc violently, hurriedly, impulsively or angrily: *~ one's arms up/about; ~ oneself into a chair.* **3** [VP2C] go angrily or violently; rush: *She flung out of the room. He flung off without saying goodbye.* □ *n* [C] **1** act of ~ing; ~ing movement. ***have a ~ at,*** (*shot* is the more usu word) make an attempt at. **2** kind of impetuous dance: *the Highland ~,* as danced in Scotland. ***have one's ~,*** have a time of unrestricted pleasure.

flint /flɪnt/ *n* [U] hard kind of stone found in lumps like pebbles, steel-grey inside and white outside; [C] piece of this used with steel to produce sparks; [C] piece of hard alloy used in a cigarette-lighter to produce sparks. **ˈ~-lock** *n* old kind of gun in which ~ was used. **ˈ~·stone** *n* ~ pebbles used for building walls, etc. **~y** *adj* (-ier, -iest) very hard, like ~.

flip /flɪp/ *vt,vi* (-pp-) [VP6A,15A,B] put (sth) into motion by a snap of the finger and thumb; throw with a jerk: *~ a coin (down) on the counter.* □ *n* [C] quick, light blow; fillip. ***the ˈ~ side,*** (colloq) the reverse side (of a gramophone record).

flip·pant /ˈflɪpənt/ *adj* not showing deserved respect: *a ~ answer/remark.* **~·ly** *adv* **flip·pancy** /-ənsɪ/ *n* [U] being ~; [C] ~ remark, etc.

flip·per /ˈflɪpə(r)/ *n* **1** limb of certain sea animals (not fish) used in swimming. *Seals, turtles and penguins have ~s.* ⇨ the illus at sea. **2** device worn on the feet to increase the thrust of leg movements in swimming. ⇨ the illus at frogman.

flirt /flɜt/ *vi* [VP2A,3A] ***~ (with),*** **1** try to attract sb of the opposite sex; show affection for amusement, without serious intentions: *She ~s with every handsome man she meets.* **2** pretend to be interested in; think about, but not seriously: *He's been ~ing with the idea of going to Moscow.* □ *n* man or girl who ~s with many of the opposite sex. **flir·ta·tion** /flɜˈteɪʃn/ *n* [U] ~ing; [C] instance of this: *carry on a ~ation.* **flir·ta·tious** /flɜˈteɪʃəs/ *adj* fond of ~ing; of ~ing.

flit /flɪt/ *vi* (-tt-) **1** [VP2C] fly or move lightly and quickly: *bees ~ting from flower to flower; bats ~ting about in the dusk;* (fig) *fancies that ~ through one's mind.* **2** (Scot and N England) remove from one house to another; change one's abode, e g secretly, to avoid paying debts. □ *n* (colloq) act of ~ting(2): *do a (moonlight) ~.*

flitch /flɪtʃ/ *n* [C] side of bacon, salted and cured.

fliv·ver /ˈflɪvə(r)/ *n* (US obsolete sl) small, cheap motor-car.

float[1] /fləʊt/ *n* [C] **1** piece of cork or other light material used on a fishing-line (to indicate when the bait has been taken) or to support the edge of a fishing-net. **2** hollow ball or other air-filled container, e g to regulate the level of water in a cistern, or to support an aircraft on water. **ˈ~-plane** *n* seaplane with two ~s fastened below the fuselage to give the plane buoyancy on water. **3** low platform on wheels, used for showing things in a procession; kind of wagon or cart with a low floor.

float[2] /fləʊt/ *vi,vt* **1** [VP2A,C] be held up in air, gas or (esp) on the surface of liquid; move with moving liquid or air: *dust ~ing in the air. Wood ~s on water. A balloon ~ed across the sky. The boat ~ed down the river.* **2** [VP6A,15A,B] cause to ~; keep ~ing: *~ a raft of logs down a river. The ship was ~ed by the tide,* e g after sticking fast on a sand-bank. *There wasn't enough water to ~ the ship.* **3** [VP6A] (comm) get (esp financial) support in order to start (sth): *~ a new business company.* **4** [VP6A] (finance) allow the foreign exchange value (of a currency) to vary (usu within narrow limits): *~ the pound/dollar.* **~·ing** *adj* **1** fluctuating; variable: *the ~ing population,* that part which varies very much, e g sailors in a seaport; *the ˈ~ing vote,* the votes of those persons who are not committed to a political party. **2** **ˈ~ing bridge,** one made of boats or rafts. **ˈ~ing debt,** one of which part must be paid on demand, or at a stated time. **ˈ~ing rib,** (anat) one of the two lower pairs of ribs not attached to the breastbone.

floa·ta·tion, flo·ta·tion /fləʊˈteɪʃn/ *n* [C,U] floating(3) of a business company or enterprise.

flock[1] /flok/ *n* **1** number of birds or animals (usu sheep, goats) of one kind, either kept together or feeding and travelling together: *a ~ of wild geese; ~s and herds,* sheep and cattle. **2** crowd of people: *Visitors came in ~s to see the new bridge.* **3** Christian congregation; number of people together in sb's charge: *a priest and his ~.* □ *vi* [VP2C,4A] gather, come or go together in great numbers: *The children ~ed round their teacher. People ~ed to hear the new prophet.*

flock[2] /flok/ *n* [C] tuft of wool or hair; (*pl*) wool or cotton waste for stuffing mattresses, etc.

floe /fləʊ/ *n* [C] sheet of floating ice.

flog /flog/ *vt* (-gg-) [VP6A] **1** beat severely with a rod or whip. ***~ a dead horse,*** waste one's efforts. ***~ sth*** (e g a joke) ***to death,*** try to persuade people to accept or buy sth so persistently that they lose interest. **2** (sl) sell or exchange (esp sth illicitly obtained, or sth secondhand): *~ stolen goods/one's old car.* **~·ging** *n* [U] beating or whipping; [C] instead of this.

flood[1] /flʌd/ *n* [C] **1** (coming of a) great quantity of water in a place that is usually dry: *The rainstorms caused ~s in the low-lying parts of the town.* ***in ~,*** (of a river) overflowing its banks. **the F~, Noah's F~,** (biblical) that described in Genesis. **2** great outpouring or outburst: *~s of rain/tears; a ~ of light/anger/words/letters.* **3** (also **ˈ~-tide**) tide (⇨ **ebb**): *The tide is at the ~.* **ˈ~ gate** *n* gate opened and closed to admit or keep out water, esp the lower gate of a lock. **ˈ~·lights** *n pl* artificial lighting thrown in a bright and broad beam. **ˈ~·light** *vt* (*pt,pp* **-lighted, -lit** /-lɪt/) light up by this method: *The cathedral was ~-lit.*

flood[2] /flʌd/ *vt,vi* **1** [VP6A,14,16A] cover or fill with a flood (liter, fig): *The meadows were ~ed. The soldiers broke the dikes and ~ed the countryside to keep back the enemy. We have been ~ed with requests for help. The stage of the theatre was ~ed with light.* **2** (of rain) fill (a river) to overflowing: *rivers ~ed by heavy rainstorms.* **3** [VP15B] ***~ out,*** compel to leave because of a ~: *Thousands of people were ~ed out,* forced to leave their homes. **4** [VP3A] ***~ in,*** come in in great quantities or numbers: *Applications ~ed in.*

floor[1] /flɔ(r)/ *n* [C] **1** lower surface of a room; part on which one walks: *sitting on the ~; a bare ~,* one with no carpet, rugs or other covering. ***wipe the ~ with sb,*** utterly defeat him, e g in a fight or argument. **ˈ~·board** *n* plank of a wooden floor. **ˈ~·cloth** *n* piece of rough cloth for wiping or washing ~s. **ˈ~ show,** cabaret, entertainment. **2** number of rooms, etc on the same level in a building: *the ground ~* (level with the street); *the first ~* (in GB, above ground ~; US = ground ~); *the third and fourth ~s* (= US, second and third ~s). ***get in on the ground ~,*** ⇨ **ground**[1](10). **ˈ~-walker** *n* (= *shop-walker*) person employed in a large shop or store to direct customers, oversee sales, to detect shop-lifters, etc. **3** bottom of the sea, of a cave, etc. **4** part of an assembly hall, e g the Houses of Parliament, Congress, where members sit. ***take the ~,*** speak in a debate. **5** (opp of *ceiling*) lower limit (of prices). **~·ing** *n* [U] material, e g boards, used for making ~s.

floor[2] /flɔ(r)/ *vt* [VP6A] **1** put (a floor) in a building. **2** knock down: *~ a man in a boxing match.* **3** (of a problem, argument, etc) puzzle, defeat: *Tom was ~ed by two of the questions in the examination paper.*

floozy, floo·zie /ˈfluzɪ/ *n* (sl) slovenly woman, esp a prostitute.

flop /flop/ *vi,vt* (-pp-) **1** [VP2A,C] move, fall, clumsily or helplessly: *The fish we had caught were ~ping about in the bottom of the boat. He ~ped down on his knees and begged for mercy.* **2** [VP15A,B] put down or drop clumsily or roughly: *~ down a heavy bag.* **3** [VP2A] (sl) (of a book, a play for the theatre, etc) fail. □ *n* act or sound of ~ping; (sl) failure of a book, play, etc. □ *adv* with a ~: *fall ~ into the water.* **~py** *adj* (-ier, -iest) inclined to ~; hanging down loosely: *a ~py hat.*

flora /ˈflɔrə/ *n* all the plants of a particular area or period.

floral /ˈflɔrl/ *adj* of flowers: *~ designs.*

flori·cul·ture /ˈflɔrɪkʌltʃə(r)/ *n* [U] the cultivation of flowering plants.

florid /ˈflorɪd *US:* ˈflɔr-/ *adj* **1** very much ornamented; (too) rich in ornament and colour: *~ carving; a ~ style,* e g of writing. **2** (of a person's face) naturally red: *a ~ complexion.* **~·ly** *adv*

florin /ˈflorɪn *US:* ˈflɔr-/ *n* name of a former British coin worth one tenth of £1 (until 1971, two shillings; now ten (new) pence).

flor·ist /ˈflorɪst *US:* ˈflɔr-/ *n* person who grows or sells flowers.

floss /flos *US:* flɔs/ *n* [U] rough silk threads on the outside of a silkworm's cocoon; (also **ˈ~ silk**) silk spun from these for needlework.

flo·ta·tion ⇨ **floatation.**

flo·tilla /fləˈtɪlə/ *n* fleet of small warships, e g destroyers.

flot·sam /ˈflotsəm/ *n* [U] (legal) parts of a wrecked ship or its cargo floating in the sea. ⇨ **jetsam.**

flounce[1] /flaʊns/ *vi* [VP2C] move, go, with quick, agitated or impatient movements: *~ out of/about the room.* □ *n* [C] fling; jerk; sudden impatient movement of the body.

flounce[2] /flaʊns/ *n* [C] (often ornamental) strip of cloth or lace sewn by the upper edge to a woman's skirt. □ *vt* [VP6A] trim with a ~ or ~s.

floun·der[1] /ˈflaʊndə(r)/ *vi* [VP2A,C] make violent and usu vain efforts (as when trying to get out of deep snow, or when one is in deep water and

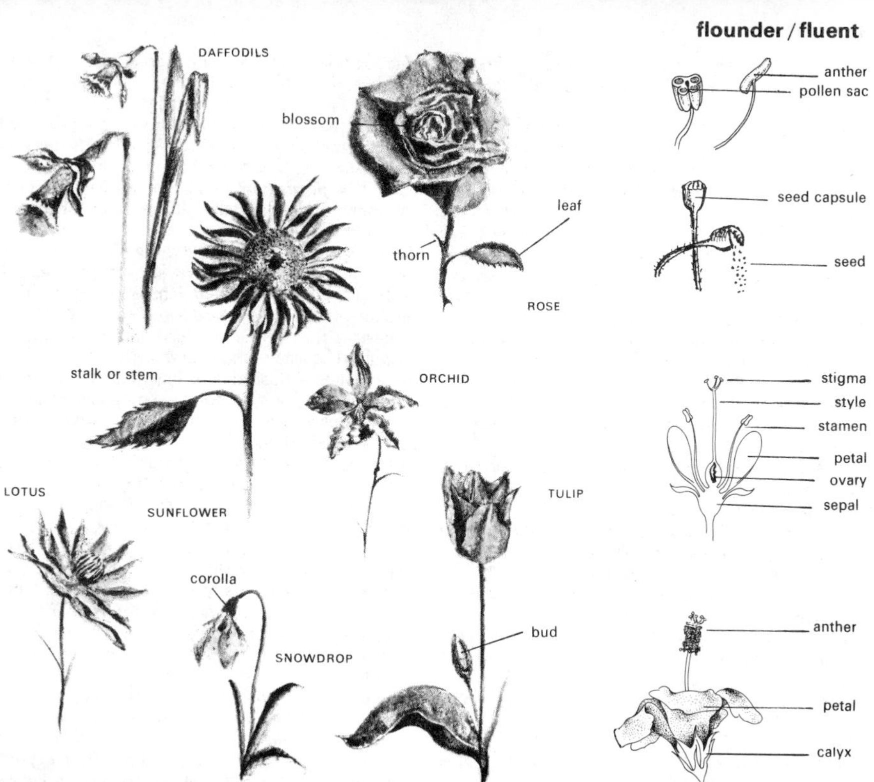

flowers

unable to swim); (fig) hesitate, make mistakes, when trying to do sth: ~ *through a speech*, e g in a foreign language.

floun·der[2] /ˈflaʊndə(r)/ *n* small flatfish, used as food.

flour /ˈflaʊə(r)/ *n* [U] fine meal, powder, made from grain, used for making bread, cakes, pastry, etc. □ *vt* [VP6A] cover or sprinkle with ~. **~y** *adj* of, like, covered with, ~.

flour·ish /ˈflʌrɪʃ *US:* ˋflɜ-/ *vi, vt* **1** [VP2A] grow in a healthy manner; be well and active; prosper: *His business is ~ing. I hope you are all ~ing*, keeping well. **2** [VP6A] wave about and show: ~ *a sword.* **3** [VP2A] (of famous writers, etc) be alive and active (at the time indicated): *Socrates ~ed about 400* B C. □ *n* [C] ~ing movement; curve or decoration, ornament in handwriting, e g to a signature; loud, exciting passage of music; fanfare: *a ~ of trumpets*, e g to welcome a distinguished visitor.

flout /flaʊt/ *vt* [VP6A] oppose; treat with contempt: ~ *sb's wishes/advice.*

flow /fləʊ/ *vi* (*pt, pp* ~ed) [VP2A,C] **1** move along or over as a river does; move smoothly: *Rivers ~ into the sea. The tears ~ed from her eyes. The river ~ed over* (= overflowed) *its banks. Gold ~ed* (= was sent) *out of the country.* **2** (of hair, articles of dress, etc) hang down loosely: *~ing robes; a ~ing tie; hair ~ing down her back.* **3** come from; be the result of: *Wealth ~s from industry and economy.* **4** (of the tide) come in; rise: *The tide began to ~.* ⇨ **ebb.** □ *n* (*sing* only) ~ing movement; quantity that ~s: *a good ~ of water; a ~ angry words; the ebb and ~ of the sea. The tide is on the ~*, coming in.

flower /ˈflaʊə(r)/ *n* **1** that part of a plant that produces seeds. ***in ~,*** with the ~s out. **ˋ~·bed** *n* plot of land in which ~s are grown. **ˋ~ garden,** one with ~ing plants, not vegetables, etc. **ˋ~-girl** *n* girl who sells ~s, e g in a market. **ˋ~ children/people,** (colloq, in the '60's) hippies dressed with ~s, bells, etc favouring universal love. **ˋ~ power,** the ideals of these people. **ˋ~·pot** *n* pot, e g of red earthenware or plastic, in which a plant may be grown. **ˋ~ show** *n* exhibition at which ~s are shown (often in competition for prizes). **2** (fig, *sing* only) finest part: *in the ~ of one's strength; the ~ of the nation's manhood*, the finest men. **3** ***~s of speech,*** ornamental phrases. □ *vi* [VP2A,C] produce ~s: *~ing bushes; late-~ing chrysanthemums.* **flow·ered** *adj* decorated with floral patterns: *~ed chintz.* **~y** *adj* (-ier, -iest) having many ~s: *~y fields;* (fig) full of ~s of speech: *~y language.* **~·less** *adj* not having, not producing, ~s: *~less plants.*

flown /fləʊn/ *pp* of **fly**.

flu /flu/ *n* (colloq abbr of) influenza.

fluc·tu·ate /ˈflʌktʃʊeɪt/ *vi* [VP2A,C] (of levels, prices, etc) move up and down; be irregular: *fluctuating prices; ~ between hope and despair.* **fluc·tu·ation** /ˈflʌktʃʊˋeɪʃn/ *n* [U] fluctuating; [C] fluctuating movement: *fluctuations of temperature; fluctuations in the exchange rates.*

flue /flu/ *n* [C] channel, pipe or tube for carrying heat, hot air or smoke to, from or through a boiler, oven, etc: *clean the ~s of soot.*

flu·ent /ˈfluənt/ *adj* (of a person) able to speak smoothly and readily: *a ~ speaker;* (of speech) coming smoothly and readily: *speak ~ French.* **~·ly** *adv* **flu·ency** /ˈfluənsɪ/ *n* [U] the quality of being ~.

fluff /flʌf/ *n* **1** [U] soft, feathery stuff that comes from blankets or other soft woolly material; soft fur or down[1]. **2** bungled attempt. ⇨ **2** below. □ *vt* **1** [VP6A,15B] **~ *(out),*** shake, puff or spread out: *~ out a pillow. The bird ~ed (out) its feathers.* **2** [VP6A] bungle (sth in games, in speaking one's lines in a play, etc): *~ a stroke,* e g in golf; *~ a catch,* e g fail to catch the ball in cricket. **~y** *adj* (**-ier, -iest**) of or like ~; covered with ~: *Newly hatched chickens are like ~y balls.*

fluid /ˈfluɪd/ *adj* able to flow (as gases and liquids do); (of ideas, etc) not fixed; capable of being changed: *~ opinions/plans.* □ *n* [C,U] (chem) ~ substance, e g water, air, mercury; (pop) liquid substance. **~ ounce,** ⇨ App 5. **~·ity** /fluˈɪdətɪ/ *n* quality of being ~.

fluke[1] /fluk/ *n* [C] sth resulting from a fortunate accident; lucky stroke: *win,* e g a game of billiards, *by a ~.*

fluke[2] /fluk/ *n* **1** broad, triangular flat end of each arm of an anchor; either lobe of a whale's tail. ⇨ the illus at **sea**. **2** (*pl*) whale's tail.

fluke[3] /fluk/ *n* parasite, a kind of flat worm, found in a sheep's liver.

flume /flum/ *n* [C] artificial channel for carrying water for industrial use, e g to a water-wheel in a mill, or for carrying logs.

flum·mox /ˈflʌməks/ *vt* [VP6A] (colloq) disconcert; confound.

flung /flʌŋ/ *pt,pp* of **fling**.

flun·key, flunky /ˈflʌŋkɪ/ *n* (*pl* **-keys, -kies** /-kɪz/) (contemptuous term for a) man-servant in uniform, e g a footman.

flu·or·escent /flʊəˈresnt/ *adj* (of substances) taking in radiations and sending them out in the form of light: *~ lamps/lighting.* **flu·or·escence** /-sns/ *n*

flu·or·ine /ˈflʊərin/ *n* (chem) non-metallic element (symbol **F**), a pale-yellow gas resembling chlorine. **flu·or·ide** /ˈflʊəraɪd/ *n* (chem) any binary compound of ~. **flu·ori·date** /ˈflʊərɪdeɪt/ *vt* [VP6A] add fluoride to (a water supply) in order to prevent dental decay. **flu·ori·da·tion** /ˈflʊərɪˈdeɪʃn/ *n* **flu·ori·dize** /ˈflʊəɪdaɪz/ *vt* = **fluoridate**. **flu·ori·diz·ation** /ˈflʊəɪdaɪˈzeɪʃn *US:* -dɪˈz-/ *n* = **fluoridation**.

flurry /ˈflʌrɪ *US:* ˈflɜ-/ *n* (*pl* **-ries**) [C] short, sudden rush of wind or fall of rain or snow; (fig) nervous hurry: *in a ~ of excitement/alarm.* □ *vt* [VP6A] cause (sb) to be confused, in a nervous hurry, etc: Keep calm! Don't get flurried.

flush[1] /flʌʃ/ *adj* **1 ~ *(with),*** even; in the same plane; level: *doors ~ with the walls.* **2** (pred) having plenty; well supplied: *~ with money.*

flush[2] /flʌʃ/ *n* **1** rush of water; rush of blood to the face; reddening caused by this; rush or emotion, excitement caused by this: *in the first ~ of victory.* **2** [U] fresh growth of vegetation, etc; high point or new access of strength: *the first ~ of spring,* the time when trees and plants send out new leaves; *in the first ~ of youth.*

flush[3] /dlʌʃ/ *n* (in card games) hand in which all the cards are of the same suit. **ˈroyal ~,** (poker) hand with the five highest cards of one suit.

flush[4] /flʌʃ/ *vi,vt* **1** [VP2A,C,D] (of a person, his face) become red because of a rush of blood to the skin: *The girl ~ed (up) when the man spoke to her. He ~ed crimson with indignation.* **2** [VP6A] (of health, heat, emotions, etc) cause (the face) to become red in this way; (fig) fill with pride; encourage: *Shame ~ed his cheeks. She was ~ed with exercise. The men were ~ed with success/joy/insolence.* **3** [VP6A] clean or wash with a ~ of water: *~ the drains; ~ the pan,* e g in a lavatory, by emptying the cistern. **4** [VP2A,C] (of water) rush out in a flood.

flush[5] /flʌʃ/ *vt,vi* **1** [VP6A,2A] (of birds) (cause to) rise suddenly and fly away: *~ a pheasant.* **2** [VP14] **~ *from/out of,*** chase, drive from a hiding-place: *snipers ~ed from fox-holes.*

flus·ter /ˈflʌstə(r)/ *vt* [VP6A] make nervous or confused. □ *n* nervous state: *all in a ~.*

flute[1] /flut/ *n* musical wind-instrument in the form of a wooden pipe with holes to be stopped by keys. ⇨ the illus at **brass**. □ *vi* play the ~. **flut·ist** /ˈflutɪst/ *n* (chiefly US) flautist.

flute[2] /flut/ *vt* [VP6A] make vertical grooves in (a pillar) etc: *~d columns.* **flut·ing** *n* (collective) grooves cut on a surface as a decoration.

flut·ter /ˈflʌtə(r)/ *vt,vi* **1** [VP2A,C,6A,15A,B] (of birds) move the wings hurriedly or irregularly without flying, or in short flights only; cause (the wings) to move in this way: *The wings of the bird still ~ed after it had been shot down. The bird ~ed its wings in the cage. The wounded bird ~ed to the ground.* **2** [VP2A,C,6A] (cause to) move about in a quick, irregular way; (of the heart) beat irregularly: *curtains ~ing in the breeze; apple-blossom petals ~ing to the ground. She ~ed nervously about the room.* □ *n* **1** (usu *sing*) ~ing movement: *the ~ of wings.* **2** (*sing* with *indef art*) state of nervous excitement: *in a ~; cause/make a ~.* **3** [U] vibration: *wing ~,* as a defect of an aircraft in flight; distortion in sound reproduced from a disc or tape caused by faulty recording or reproduction. **4** (colloq) gambling venture; spree: *go to the races and have a ~,* make a bet or bets.

flu·vial /ˈfluvɪəl/ *adj* of, found in, rivers.

flux /flʌks/ *n* **1** [U] continuous succession of changes: *in a state of ~.* **2** (*sing* only) flowing; flowing out. **3** substance mixed with metal to promote fusion.

fly[1] /flaɪ/ *n* (*pl* **flies**) ⇨ the illus at **insect**. two-winged insect, esp the common ˈ*housefly;* natural or artificial fly, used as a bait in fishing for trout, etc. Hence, **ˈfly-fishing.** ***a fly in the ointment,*** a small circumstance that prevents pleasure from being perfect. ***There are no flies on him,*** (sl) He is no fool, cannot be tricked, etc. **ˈfly-blown** *adj* (of meat) (going bad because) containing flies: eggs. **ˈfly·catcher** *n* kinds of bird; trap for catching flies. **ˈfly-fish** *vi* fish with artificial flies as bait. **ˈfly-paper** *n* strip of sticky paper formerly used for catching flies. **ˈfly-trap** *n* trap for catching flies. **ˈfly·weight** *n* boxer weighing 112 lb (50·8 kg) or less.

fly[2] /flaɪ/ *vi,vt* (*pt* **flew** */flu/, pp* **flown** /fləʊn/) **1** [VP2A,B,C,D,4A] move through the air as a bird does, or in an aircraft: *birds flying in the air; fly from London to Paris; fly (across) the Atlantic.* ***fly high,*** be ambitious. ***The bird is/has flown,*** The person wanted has escaped. **2** [VP6A,15A,B] direct or control the flight of (aircraft); transport goods/passengers in aircraft: *Five thousand passengers were flown to Paris during Easter weekend.* **3** [VP2A,C,D,4A] go or move quickly; rush along; pass quickly: *He flew down the road.*

The children flew to meet their mother. It's getting late; we must fly. The door flew open. He paid us a flying visit, a very short, fleeting visit. ***fly at sb,*** rush angrily at sb. ***let fly (at),*** ⇨ let[2](4). ***fly off the handle,*** ⇨ handle. ***fly in the face of,*** **(a)** defy openly: *You're flying in the face of Providence.* **(b)** be quite contrary to: *This version of what happened flies in the face of all the evidence.* ***fly into a rage/passion/temper,*** become suddenly angry. ***fly to arms,*** take up arms eagerly. ***fly to bits/in pieces,*** break to bits and scatter. ***make the feathers/fur fly,*** cause quarrelling or fighting. ***make the money fly,*** spend it quickly, recklessly. ***send sb flying,*** strike him so that he falls over or backwards. ***send things flying,*** send or throw them violently in all directions. **4** [VP6A] cause (a kite) to rise and stay high in the air; raise (a flag) so that it waves in the air. **5** flee from: *fly the country.*

fly[3] /flaɪ/ *n* **1** (colloq *flies*) flap of cloth on a garment to contain or cover a zip fastener or buttonholes, e g down the front of a pair of trousers: *John, your fly is undone!* **2** flap of canvas at the entrance to a tent or covered wagon. **3** (old use) one-horse hackney carriage. **4** outer edge of a flag farthest from the flagpole.

fly[4] /flaɪ/ *adj* (sl) knowing; wide-awake; not to be deceived or hoodwinked.

fly·leaf /ˈflaɪlif/ *n* blank leaf at the beginning or end of a book.

fly·over /ˈflaɪəʊvə(r)/ *n* **1** (US = *overpass*) roadway, bridge, etc which crosses above another roadway, etc (as on a motorway). **2** (GB) = fly-past.

a flyover

fly·past /ˈflaɪpɑst *US:* -pæst/ *n* flight of aircraft in formation, usu at a low altitude, as part of a military display.

fly·wheel /ˈflaɪwil *US:* -hwil/ *n* heavy wheel revolving on a shaft to regulate machinery.

flyer, flier /ˈflaɪə(r)/ *n* **1** animal, vehicle, etc going with exceptional speed. **2** airman.

fly·ing /ˈflaɪɪŋ/ *part adj, gerund* (in compounds): **ˈ~ boat** *n* form of seaplane without floats and with a fuselage that floats on water. **ˌ~-ˈbomb** *n* rocket filled with explosives that can be fired to a great distance. **ˌ~ ˈbuttress** *n* (archit) one slanting from a pier to a wall, the base not being joined to the wall. **ˈ~ club,** club for those who are interested in ~ as a sport. **ˌ~ ˈcolumn,** (mil) body of troops able to move rapidly and act independently. **ˌ~ ˈcolours,** flags on display (as during a ceremony). ***come off with ~ colours,*** ⇨ colour[1](8). **ˈ~ field,** airfield. **ˈ~-fish,** (kinds of) tropical fish able to rise out of the water and move forward. **ˌ~-fox,** (kinds of) large fruit-eating bat. **ˈF~ Officer,** rank in the Royal Air Force. ⇨ App 9. **ˌ~ ˈjump,** one made with a running start. **ˌ~ ˈsaucer,** unidentified flying object (abbr UFO) seen, or thought to have been seen, moving across the sky, e g one said to have come from another planet. **ˈ~-squad,** part of a police force organized (with fast cars) for pursuit of (suspected) criminals. **ˌ~ ˈvisit,** hasty visit made while passing.

foal /fəʊl/ *n* young horse (colt or filly). ***in/with ~,*** (of a mare) pregnant. □ *vi* [VP2A] give birth to a ~.

foam /fəʊm/ *n* [U] **1** white mass of small air bubbles formed in or on a liquid by motion, or on an animal's lips, e g after exertion. **2** (also **ˌ~-ˈrubber**) spongy rubber used in upholstery (e g in seats, mattresses). □ *vi* [VP2A,C] form ~; break into ~; send out ~ (at the mouth): *waves ~ing along the beach; a glass of ~ing beer*, beer with froth on it; *~ing with rage*, looking angry. **~y** *adj*

fob[1] /fob/ *vt* (-bb-) [VP15B] ***fob sth off on sb/fob sb off with sth,*** get a person to accept sth of little or no value by deceit or trickery. *He fobbed me off with promises that he never intended to keep.*

fob[2] /fob/ *n* (old use) small pocket for a watch, formerly made in the waistband of a pair of breeches.

fo·cal /ˈfəʊkl/ *adj* of or at a focus: *the ~ length/distance of a lens*, from the surface of a lens to its focus.

fo'c'sle /ˈfəʊksl/ *n* = forecastle.

fo·cus /ˈfəʊkəs/ *n* (*pl* focuses or foci /ˈfəʊsaɪ/) **1** meeting-point of rays of light, heat, etc; point, distance, at which the sharpest outline is given (to the eye, through a telescope, through a lens on a camera plate, etc): *The image is in/out of ~. Bring the object into ~ if you want a good photograph.* **2** point at which interests, tendencies, etc meet: *the ~ of attention; the ~ of an earthquake/storm/disease, etc.* □ *vt, vi* (-s- or -ss-) **1** [VP2A, C,6A,14] (cause to) come together at a ~; adjust (an instrument, etc) so that it is in ~: *~ the sun's rays on sth with a burning-glass; ~ the lens of a microscope.* **ˈ~ing screen/glass** *n* sheet of glass at the back of some kinds of camera, used for getting the right ~ before taking a photograph. **2** [VP14] ***~ on,*** concentrate: *~ one's attention/thoughts/efforts on a problem.*

fod·der /ˈfodə(r)/ *n* [U] dried food, hay, etc for farm animals, horses, etc.

foe /fəʊ/ *n* (poet) enemy. **foe·man** /-mən/ *n* (*pl* -men) (archaic) enemy in war.

foe·tus, fe·tus /ˈfitəs/ *n* fully developed embryo in the womb or in an egg. ⇨ the illus at reproduce. **foe·tal, fe·tal** /ˈfitl/ *adj* of, like, a ~: *the foetal position* (in the womb).

fog /fog *US:* fɔg/ *n* **1** [U] vapour suspended in the atmosphere at or near the earth's surface, thicker than mist and difficult to see through: *Fog is the sailor's worst enemy.* ***in a fog,*** (fig) puzzled; at a loss. **ˈfog·bank** *n* dense mass of fog on the sea. **ˈfog·bound** *adj* unable to proceed safely because of fog. **ˈfog·horn** *n* instrument used for warning ships in fog. **ˈfog·lamp,** head lamp (on a motor vehicle) providing a strong beam of light for use in foggy weather. **ˈfog·signal,** device placed on railway lines in fog to explode when a train passes over it and so warn drivers. **2** [C] period of fog; abnormal darkened state of the atmosphere: *London used to have bad fogs in winter.* **3** [C,U] (area of) cloudiness on a developed photographic plate or film. □ *vt* (-gg-) cover with, as with, fog, bewilder: *I'm a bit fogged,* puzzled. **foggy** *adj* (-ier, -iest) **1** dense, not clear, because of fog: *a foggy evening; foggy weather.* **2** obscure, confused: *have only a foggy idea of what something means.*

fogey (US = **fogy**) /ˈfəʊgɪ/ *n* (*pl* fogeys, US fogies) (usu *old* ~) person with old-fashioned ideas which he is unwilling to change.

foible /ˈfɔɪbl/ *n* [C] slight peculiarity or defect of character, often one of which a person is wrongly proud.

foil[1] /fɔɪl/ *n* **1** [U] metal rolled or hammered into a thin, flexible sheet: *lead/tin/aluminium* ~, e g as wrapped round chocolate or cigarettes. **2** [C] person or thing that contrasts with, and thus sets off, the qualities of another: *A plain old woman serves as a* ~ *to a beautiful young woman.*

foil[2] /fɔɪl/ *n* light sword without a sharp edge and with a button on the point, for fencing.

foil[3] /dɔɪl/ *vt* [VP6A] baffle; prevent (sb) from carrying out his plans; make plans/designs ineffective: *We* ~*ed him/his plans. He was* ~*ed in his attempt to deceive the girl.*

foist /fɔɪst/ *vt* [VP15B] ***~ sth (off) on sb,*** trick him into accepting (a useless article, etc).

fold[1] /fəʊld/ *vt,vi* **1** [VP6A,15B] bend one part of a thing back over on itself: ~ *a letter,* before putting it in an envelope; ~ *up a newspaper;* ~ *back the bedclothes.* **2** [VP2A,C] become ~ed; be able to be ~ed: ~*ing doors,* having hinged parts; *a* ~*ing boat/bed/chair,* made so as to occupy a smaller space when not in use. *The window shutters* ~ *back.* ***~ up,*** (fig; colloq) collapse; come to an end: *The business finally* ~*ed up last week.* **3** ***~ one's arms,*** across them over the chest. ***~ (sb or sth) in one's arms,*** hold to the breast. **4** [VP15A,B] cover, wrap up: ~ *sth (up) in paper;* ~ *sth round; hills* ~*ed in mist.* **5** (cooking) mix (an ingredient, e g beaten eggs, into another, e g flour, by turning them with a wooden spoon. □ *n* **1** part that is ~ed: *a dress hanging in loose* ~*s;* line made by ~ing. **2** hollow among hills or mountains. **~er** *n* **1** holder (made of ~ed cardboard or other stiff material) for loose papers. **2** ~ing card or paper with advertisements, railway timetables, etc printed on it, or (US) as a container, e g for matches.

fold[2] /fəʊld/ *n* [C] enclosure for sheep; (fig) body of religious believers; members of a Church. ***return to the ~,*** come or go back home (esp rejoin a body of believers). □ *vt* [VP6A] enclose (sheep) in a ~.

fo·li·age /ˈfeʊlɪɪdʒ/ *n* [U] all the leaves of a tree or plant.

fo·lio /ˈfəʊlɪəʊ/ *n* (*pl* -s) **1** sheet of paper numbered on one side only; page number of a printed book; (bookkeeping) two opposite pages of a ledger, used for both sides of an account. **2** large sheet of paper folded once to make two leaves or four pages (of a book); volume made of such sheets: ~ *volumes; in six volumes* ~.

folk /fəʊk/ *n* **1** (collective *n,* used with *pl v*) people in general: *Some* ~ *are never satisfied. Is there more honesty among country* ~ *than among towns*~*?* **2** (in compounds) of the common people of a country; of a tribe. **ˈ~-dance** *n* (music for a) traditional popular dance. **ˈ~·lore** *n* [U] (study of the) traditional beliefs, tales, etc of a community. **ˈ~ music/song** *nn* popular music/song handed down from the past. **ˈ~·tale** *n* popular story handed down orally from past generations. **3** (*pl*) (colloq) relatives: *the old* ~*s at home.*

folksy /ˈfəʊksɪ/ *adj* (colloq) unpretentious in manners; simple; friendly and sociable.

fol·low /ˈfoləʊ/ *vt,vi* **1** [VP2A,B,C,6A] come, go, have a place, after (in space, time or order): *You go first and I will* ~ *(you). Monday* ~*s Sunday. They* ~*ed us for miles. One misfortune* ~*ed (upon) another. His arguments were as* ~*s,* as now to be given. ***~ on,*** **(a)** ~ after a period of time. **(b)** (cricket, of a side) bat again after failing to get the necessary number of runs. Hence, **ˈ~-on** *n* second innings following the first at once. ***~ through,*** **(a)** (tennis, golf, etc) complete a stroke by moving the racker, club, etc after hitting the ball. Hence, **ˈ~-through** *n* **(b)** complete a task, carry out a promise. **2** [VP6A] go along, keep to (a road, etc): *F*~ *this road until you get to the church; then turn left.* **3** [VP6A,2A] understand (an argument, sth said, etc): *Do you* ~ *my argument? He spoke so fast that I couldn't* ~ *him/*~ *what he said.* **4** [VP6A] engage in as a business, trade, etc: ~ *the sea,* be a seaman; ~ *the plough,* be a ploughman; ~ *the law;* ~ *the trade of a hatter.* **5** [VP6A] take or accept as a guide, an example, etc: ~ *sb's advice;* ~ *the fashion;* ~ *suit,* do what has just been done by sb else. **6** [VP2A] be necessarily true: *Because he is good, it does not* ~ *that he is wise. It* ~*s from what you say that....* **7** [VP15B] ***~ sth up,*** pursue, work at further: ~ *up an advantage/a victory.* Hence, **ˈ~-up** *n* (esp) second letter, circular, visit, referring to an earlier one. ***~ sth out,*** keep to, carry out, to the end: ~ *out an enterprise.* **~er** *n* **1** supporter; disciple: *Robin Hood and his* ~*ers; ˈcamp-*~*ers,* persons who ~ an army. **2** pursuer. **3** (colloq, old use) man courting a maidservant. **~·ing** *adj* (esp as *pron*) *the* ~*ing,* the one or ones about to be mentioned. □ *n* body of supporters: *a political leader with a large* ~*ing.*

folly /ˈfolɪ/ *n* (*pl* -lies) [U] foolishness; [C] foolish act, idea or practice; ridiculous thing.

fo·ment /fəʊˈment/ *vt* [VP6A] **1** put warm water or clothes, lotions, etc on (a part of the body, to lessen pain, etc). **2** (fig) cause or increase (disorder, discontent, ill feeling, etc). **fo·men·ta·tion** /ˌfəʊmenˈteɪʃn/ *n* [U] ~ing; [C] that which is used for ~ing.

fond /fond/ *adj* **1** (*pred* only) ***be ~ of,*** like, be full of love for, take pleasure in: ~ *of music.* **2** loving and kind: *a* ~ *mother;* ~ *looks.* **3** foolishly loving; doting: *a young wife with a* ~ *husband.* **4** (of hopes, ambitions) held, but unlikely to be realized. **~·ly** *adv* **1** lovingly: *look* ~*ly at sb.* **2** in a foolishly optimistic manner: *He* ~*ly imagined that he could learn French in six weeks.* **~·ness** *n*

fon·dant /ˈfondənt/ *n* [C] kind of soft sweet that melts in the mouth.

fondle /ˈfondl/ *vt* [VP6A] touch or stroke lovingly: ~ *a baby/a doll/a kitten.*

font /font/ *n* **1** basin or vessel (often in carved stone) to hold water for baptism; basin for holy water. **2** = fount(2).

food /fud/ *n* [U] (except when used for 'a kind of ~') that which can be eaten by people or animals, or used by plants, to keep them living and for growth: ~ *and water; frozen* ~*s; packaged* ~*s;* (attrib) ~ *rationing;* (fig) ~ *for thought/reflection,* sth to think/reflect about. **ˈ~-stuff** *n* material used as ~. **~·less** *adj* without ~.

fool[1] /ful/ *n* **1** person without much sense; stupid or rash person; person whose conduct one considers silly: *What ~s we were not to see the joke! She was ~ enough* (= enough of a fool) *to believe him.* ***be a ~ for one's pains,*** do sth for which one gets neither reward nor thanks. ***be/live in a ~'s paradise,*** in happiness without any thought and that is unlikely to last. ***go/be sent on a ~'s errand,*** on an errand that is seen in the end to be useless. ***make a ~ of sb,*** trick him; cause him to seem like a ~. ***play the ~,*** behave stupidly. ***no ~ like an old ~,*** (prov) said of an aged lover. **2** (in the Middle Ages) man employed by a ruler or noble as a clown or jester. **3** **'April `~,** person deceived, or sent on a ~'s errand, on **'All `F~s' Day,** 1st April. **`~s-cap** *n* size of writing or printing paper (usu 17 in × 13½ in unfolded). **4** (used attrib, colloq) foolish; silly: *a scheme devised by some ~ politician.* □ *vi, vt* **1** [VP2A,C] behave like a ~; trifle; be idle and silly: *If you go on ~ing with that gun, there'll be an accident. Stop ~ing (about)!* **2** [VP6A,14,15B] cheat; deceive: *He ~ed her out of her money. You can't/don't ~ me! Don't ~ your time away!*

fool[2] /ful/ *n* creamy liquid of stewed fruit (esp gooseberries), crushed and mixed with cream or custard.

fool·ery /`fuləri/ *n* [U] foolish behaviour; (*pl;* -ries) foolish acts, ideas or utterances.

fool·hardy /`fulhadi/ *adj* foolishly bold; taking unnecessary risks. **fool·hardi·ness** *n*

fool·ish /`fulɪʃ/ *adj* without reason, sense or good judgement; silly: *How ~ of you to consent! It would be ~ for us to quarrel.* **~·ly** *adv* **~·ness** *n*

foot[1] /fʊt/ *n* (*pl* feet /fit/) **1** ⇨ the illus at **leg.** part forming the lower end of the leg, beginning at the ankle; part of a sock, etc covering the ~: *A dog has four feet. A dog's feet are called paws. He rose to his feet,* stood up. ***on ~,*** **(a)** walking, not riding. Cf go somewhere *on ~, by* bus, tram, etc. **(b)** in motion: *A project is on ~ to build a new tunnel here.* ***be on one's feet,*** **(a)** be standing: *I've been on my feet all day.* **(b)** rise (to speak): *The Minister was on his feet at once to answer the charge.* **(c)** (fig) be in good health after an illness: *It's nice to see you on your feet again.* ***fall on one's feet,*** (colloq) be fortunate, have good luck. ***find one's feet,*** ⇨ find[2](2). ***have one ~ in the grave,*** be near death, e g because of old age. ***keep one's feet,*** not fall, e g when walking on ice. ***put one's ~ down,*** (colloq) object; protest; be firm. ***put one's ~ in it,*** (colloq) say or do sth wrong or stupid; blunder. ***put one's feet up,*** (colloq) rest with the legs in a horizontal position. ***put one's best ~ forward,*** walk (fig, get on with one's work) as fast as one can. ***set sth/sb on his/its feet,*** make him/it self-supporting, no longer in need of help. ***set sth on ~,*** start it; get it going. ***under ~,*** on the ground: *wet under ~.* ***sweep sb off his feet,*** fill him with strong enthusiasm. ***wait on/bind sb hand and ~,*** ⇨ hand[1](1). **2** step, pace, tread: *light/swift/fleet of ~,* stepping or walking lightly, swiftly, etc. **3** lowest part; bottom: *at the ~ of the page/ladder/wall/mountain.* **4** lower end (opp *head*) of a bed or grave. **5** measure of length, 12 inches: *3 feet 6 inches;* (with *pl* unchanged) *George is very tall—he's six ~ two* (6′ 2″). **6** division or unit of verse, each with one strong stress and one or more weak stresses, as in: *for mén/may cóme/and mén/may gó.* **7** [U] (mil, old use) infantry: *the Fourth Regiment of F~; ~ and horse,* infantry and cavalry. **8** (compounds) **'~-and-`mouth disease,** disease of cattle and other cloven-hoofed animals. **`~-ball** *n* [C] inflated leather ball used in games; [U] the game played with it. ⇨ the illus on p 340 and at Rugby. **`~-bath** *n* (small bath used for a) washing of the feet. **`~·board** *n* sloping board for the feet of the driver (in a carriage, etc). **`~·bridge,** one for the use of persons on ~, not vehicles. **`~-fall,** sound of a ~step. **`~·fault,** (tennis) service not allowed because the server's feet are wrongly placed. **`~-hills** *n pl* hills lying at the ~ of a mountain or a range of mountains. **`~·hold** *n* support for the ~, e g when climbing on rocks or ice; (fig) secure position. **`~·lights** *n pl* row of screened lights at the front of the stage of a theatre; (fig) the profession of an actor. **`~·loose** (*and fancy free*), independent and without cares or responsibilities. **~·man** /-mən/ *n* (*pl* -men) manservant who admits visitors, waits at table, etc. **`~·mark** *n* = ~print. **`~·note,** one at the ~ of a page. **`~·pad,** (old name for) robber on ~ who attacked and robbed travellers on highways. ⇨ *highwayman* at **high**[1](12). **`~-path,** path for the use of persons on ~, esp one across fields or open country, or at the side of a country road. Cf US *trail.* ⇨ **pavement,** *sidewalk* at **side**[1](14). **`~·plate** *n* platform in a locomotive for the driver and fireman: *~plate workers,* drivers and firemen. **`~-pound,** unit of work (done in lifting 1 lb through 1 ft). **`~·print,** impression left on a soft surface (e~g mud, sand) by a ~. **`~-race,** running race between persons. **`~ rule,** ruler (strip of wood or metal) 12 inches long. **`~-slogger,** (colloq) person who walks or marches long distances. Hence, **`~-slogging** *n* **`~·sore** *adj* having sore feet, esp with walking. **`~·step** *n* (sound of a) step of sb walking; ~print: *follow in one's father's ~steps,* do as he did. **`~·stool** *n* low stool for resting the feet on. **`~·sure** *adj* not stumbling; not making false steps. **`~·wear** *n* [U] (tradesmen's term for) boots, shoes, etc. **`~·work** *n* [U] manner of using the feet, e g in boxing, dancing.

foot[2] /fʊt/ *vt, vi* **1** [VP6A] knit the ~ of, e g a stocking. **2** (colloq) ***~ it,*** go on ~; walk: *We've missed the last bus, so we'll have to ~ it.* ***~ the bill,*** (colloq) (agree to) pay it. **footed** (in compounds) having the kind of feet indicated: *'wet-`~ed; 'sure-`~ed, 'flat-`~ed.*

foot·age /`fʊtɪdʒ/ *n* length measured in feet, esp (cinema) length of exposed film.

footer /`fʊtə(r)/ *n* **1** (colloq) the game of football. **2** (in comb) *a 'six-`footer,* a person six feet tall.

foot·ing /`fʊtɪŋ/ *n* **1** placing of the feet; surface for

American football

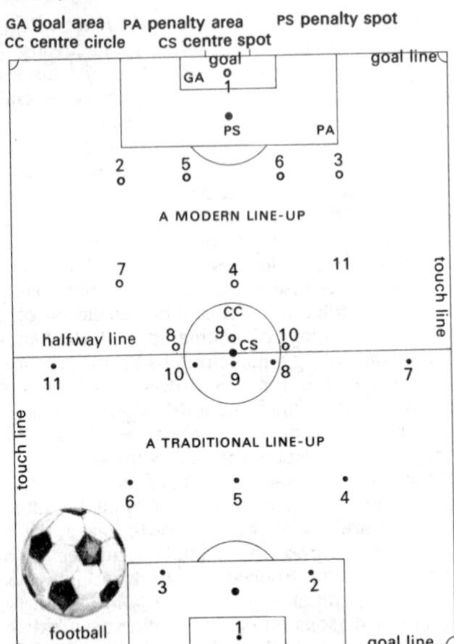

A TRADITIONAL LINE-UP 1 goalkeeper 2 right back 3 left back 4 right half (back) 5 centre half (back) 6 left half (back) 7 outside right or right winger 8 inside right 9 centre forward 10 inside left 11 outside left or left winger

A MODERN LINE-UP 1 goalkeeper 2 5 6 3 defenders or backs 7 4 11 midfield link men 8 9 10 strikers or forwards

Association football (soccer)

standing on: *He lost his* ~ (= stumbled, slipped) *and fell.* **2** (*sing* only) position in society, etc; relationships (with people): *get a* ~ *in society,* be accepted; *be on a friendly* ~ *with people.* **3** conditions; state of the army, etc: *on a peace/war* ~, in the state usual for peace/war.

footle /ˈfutl/ *vi, vt* (colloq) trifle; play the fool: ~ *about;* ~ *away one's time.* **foot·ling** *adj* insignificant, trifling: *footling little jobs.*

fop /fop/ *n* man who pays too much attention to his clothes and personal appearance. **fop·pish** /-ɪʃ/ *adj* of or like a ~.

for[1] /fə(r) *strong form:* fɔ(r)/ *prep* **1** (indicating destination, or progress or endeavours towards) **(a)** after *vv*: *set out for home; make for home,* turn one's steps towards home; *a ship bound for the Baltic. The ship was making for* (= sailing towards) *the open sea. The swimmers struck out for the shore.* **(b)** after *nn*: *the train for Glasgow; letters for the provinces; passengers for Cairo.* **2** (indicating what is aimed at, the attaining of what is shown by the *noun* after *for*): *He was educated for the law/trained for the priesthood. He felt that he was destined for something great.* **3** (indicating eventual possession): *Here's a letter for you. Are all these for me? Save it for me. She made some coffee for us.* **be ˈfor it,** (colloq) be likely to be punished, get into trouble, etc. **4** (indicating preparation to deal with a situation): *prepare/preparations for an examination; lay in supplies of coal for the winter; dress for dinner; get ready for school.* **5** (indicating purpose) **(a)** (used in place of an *inf*) in order to be, have, obtain, etc; with a view to: *go for a walk/ride/swim, etc; run for one's life; work for one's living; read for pleasure.* **what for,** for what purpose: *What's this tool for? What's this hole in the door for? It's for the cat to come in and out by.* ⇨ **24 (g)** below. *What did you do that for?* Why did you do that? **(b)** (followed by a gerund): *a mill for* (= for the purpose of) *grinding coffee; a room for sleeping in.* **6** (introducing a complement): *They were sold for slaves. They left him on the battlefield for dead. They chose him for* (= as, to be) *their leader.* **take sb/sth for,** mistakenly conclude that sb or sth is: *He took me for my brother.* **for certain,** as being certain: *I cannot hold it for certain that....* **7** (followed by an object of hope, wish, search, inquiry, etc): *hope for the best; pray for peace; fish for trout; ask for* (= to see) *the manager; go to sb for help; a cry for help; fifty applicants for a post.* **8** (indicating liking, affection, etc): *have a liking for sb or sth; a taste for art; no regret for the truth; a weakness for fine clothes.* **9** (indicating aptitude): *an aptitude for foreign languages; a good ear for music; an eye for the picturesque.* **10** (indicating suitability, fitness): *bad/good for your health; fit/unfit for food; clothes proper for the occasion. This is no place for a young, innocent girl. You are the very man for the job.* **11** (with *too* and *enough* and *adjj* not otherwise followed by *for*): *too beautiful for words; quite risky enough for me.* **12** considering (the circumstances, etc); in view of: *It's quite warm for January. Not bad for a beginner! She is tall for her age. For all the good you're doing, you may as well stop trying to help.* **for all that,** in spite of all that has been said, done, etc. **13** representing; instead of; in place of: *B for Benjamin; the member for Coventry,* the person representing Coventry in the House of Commons; *substitute one thing for another. Will you please act for me in the matter?* **stand for,** represent: *The letters MP stand for Member of Parliament and the letters PM stand for Prime Minister. What do you take me for?* You seem to have a mistaken or poor idea of my character, judging from what you say, etc. **14** in defence or support of; in favour of: *Are you for or against the proposal? The rate of exchange is for us,* in our favour. *Three cheers for the President! I'm all for an early start/for starting early.* **15** with regard to; so far as concerns: *hard up for money; anxious for sb's safety; for my part,* so far as it concerns me; *speaking for myself, and in the name of all my colleagues. You may take my word for it,* believe me so far as this is concerned. **16** because of; on account of: *for this reason; for my sake; for the sake of peace; for fear of discovery; noted/famous for its scenery; dance/cry for joy; suffer for one's sins; sent to prison for stealing; win a medal for bravery. She couldn't speak for laughing,* because she was laughing so much. *We trembled for their safety.* **17** (after a comparative) as the result of; because of: *My shoes are the worse for wear. Are you any the better for your long sleep?* **18** in spite of; notwithstanding: *For* (= In spite of) *all you say, I still like her. For all his wealth, he is unhappy.* **19** to the amount or extent of: *Put my name down for £5. He drew on his bank for £40.* (cricket) *The score is 157 for 8 wickets. They were all out for 80.* **20** in exchange for: *I paid 60p for the book. He did the job for nothing. Don't translate word for word. Plant a new tree for every tree you cut down.* **21** in contrast with: *For one enemy he has fifty friends.*

22 (indicating extent in time): *I'm going away for a few days. He will be a cripple for life. That's enough for the present.* **for good,** ⇨ good[2](2). **23** (indicating extent in space; *for* may be omitted if it occurs directly after the *v*): *We walked (for) three miles. For miles and miles there's not a house to be seen. The road is lined with trees for ten miles.* **24** (in the pattern, *for* + noun or pronoun + *to inf*) **(a)** (as the subject of a sentence, usu with preparatory *it*): *For a woman to divorce her husband is impossible in some countries. It's impossible for there to be a quarrel between us. It seemed useless for them to go on.* **(b)** (as a complement): *Their hope was for David to marry a wealthy girl.* **(c)** (after *adjj*, esp with *too* and *enough*, usu replaceable by a clause): *I am anxious for you and my sister to* (= anxious that you and my sister should) *become acquainted. This box is too heavy for her to lift.* **(d)** (after *nn*): *There's no need for anyone to know* (= that anyone should know). *It's time for little girls to be in bed. I'm in no hurry for them to do anything in the matter.* **(e)** (after *vv*, including some that normally take *for* and others that do not normally take *for*): *We didn't wait for the others to join us. She couldn't bear for Tom and Mary not to be friends.* **(f)** (after *than* and *as (if)*): *Is there anything more ridiculous than for a man of 80 to marry a girl of 18? She had her arms wide apart, as if for the child to run into them.* **(g)** indicating purpose, design, determination, etc: *I have brought the books for you to examine. The crowd made way for the procession to pass. I'd have given anything for this not to have happened. It's for you to decide. For production to be increased we must have efficient organization.*

for[2] /fə(r) *strong form:* fɔ(r)/ *conj* (rare in spoken English; not used at the beginning of a sentence) seeing that; since; the reason, proof, explanation, being that: *I asked her to stay to tea, for I had something to tell her.*

for·age /ˈforɪdʒ *US:* ˈfɔr-/ *n* [U] food for horses and cattle. ˈ**~ cap,** cap worn as informal headdress by British soldiers in the late '30's and early '40's. □ *vi* search (*for* food, etc).

for·as·much as /ˌfɔrəzˈmʌtʃ əz/ *conj* (legal) seeing that; since.

foray /ˈforeɪ *US:* ˈfɔreɪ/ *n* [C] raid; sudden attack (esp to get food, animals, etc): *make/go on a ~.* □ *vi* [VP2A] make a ~.

for·bad, for·bade /fəˈbæd *US:* -ˈbeɪd/ *pt* of forbid.

for·bear[1] /fəˈbeə(r)/ *vt,vi* (*pt* forbore /fɔˈbɔ(r)/, *pp* forborne /fɔˈbɔn/) [VP6C,7A,2A,3A] refrain, refrain from; not use or mention; be patient: *I ~ to go into details. I cannot ~ from going into details. We begged him to ~.* **~·ance** /fɔˈbeərns/ *n* [U] patience; self-control: *show ~ance towards sb; show ~ance in dealing with people.*

for·bear[2] (US = **fore·bear**) /ˈfɔbeə(r)/ *n* (usu *pl*) ancestor.

for·bid /fəˈbɪd/ *vt* (*pt* forbade or forbad /fəˈbæd *US:* -ˈbeɪd/, *pp* forbidden /fəˈbɪdn/ or forbid) [VP6A,17,12C] order (sb) not to do sth; order that sth shall not be done; not allow: *~ a girl to marry; ~ a marriage; ~ sb to leave; ~ his departure. Students are ~den the use of the office duplicator. I ~ you to use that word.* ***God ~ that...,*** used to express a wish that something may not happen. ˈ**~·den ˈfruit,** sth desired because it is not allowed (with reference to Eve and the apple). **~·ding** *adj* stern; repellent; threatening: *a ~ding appearance/look; a ~ding coast,* one that looks dangerous. **~·ding·ly** *adv*

for·bore, for·borne ⇨ forbear[1].

force[1] /fɔs/ *n* **1** [U] strength; power of body or mind; physical power: *the ~ of a blow/an explosion/argument; ~ of character; overcome by the ~ of her emotion; by ~ of contrast. The enemy attacked in (great) ~. He overcame his bad habits by sheer ~ of will. Owing to ~ of circumstances the plans had to be postponed.* **2** [C] person or thing that makes great changes: *the ~s of nature,* e g storms, earthquakes. *Christianity has been a ~ for good in the lives of many people. Fascism and Communism have been powerful ~s in world affairs.* **3** [C] organized body of armed or disciplined men: *the armed ~s of a country,* the Army, Navy, Air F~; *join the F~s;* (attrib) *a F~s newspaper,* one for members of the armed ~s: *the poˈlice ~; a small ~ of infantry.* ***join ~s (with),*** unite (with) in order to use combined strength. **4** [C,U] (intensity of, measurement of) pressure or influence exerted at a point, tending to cause movement. **5** (legal) authority; power of binding(**6**): *put a law into ~,* make it binding. *When does the new law come into ~? The rule/regulation is no longer in ~.*

force[2] /fɔs/ *vt* **1** [VP6A,15A,B,17A,22] compel, oblige; use force to get or do sth, to make sb do sth; break open by using force: *~ one's way through a crowd; ~ a way in/out/through; ~ an entry into a building,* e g by breaking a door; *~ (open) a door; ~ a confession from sb; ~ sb (oneself) to work hard; ~ sb into doing sth. They said that the war had been ~d upon them,* that they had not wanted to make war, but had been compelled to do so. ˈ**~d ˈlanding,** one that an aircraft is compelled to make, e g because of engine trouble. Hence, ˈ**~-ˈland** *vt,vi* ˈ**~d ˈmarch,** e~g by soldiers, one requiring special effort, made in an emergency. ***~ a person's hand,*** make him do sth unwillingly, or earlier than he wished or intended to do it. **2** [VP6A] cause plants, etc to mature earlier than is normal, e g by giving them extra warmth: (fig) *~ a pupil,* hurry on his education by making him do extra study. **3** [VP6A] produce under stress: *~ a smile,* e g when one is unhappy; *a ~d laugh,* one that is not the result of real amusement. *The singer had to ~ her top notes.*

force·ful /ˈfɔsfl/ *adj* (of a person, his character, of an argument, etc) full of force: *a ~ speaker/style of writing.* **~ly** /-flɪ/ *adv* **~·ness** *n*

force majeure /ˈfɔs mæˈʒɜ(r) *US:* məˈʒɜ/ *n* [U] (F) (legal) compulsion; superior force.

force·meat /ˈfɔsmit/ *n* [U] meat chopped up finely, mixed with herbs, etc used as stuffing, e g in a roast chicken.

for·ceps /ˈfɔseps/ *n sing, n pl* pincers or tongs used by dentists (when pulling out teeth) and by doctors for gripping things: *a ~ delivery* (of a child).

forc·ible /ˈfɔsəbl/ *adj* **1** done by, involving the use of, physical force: *a ~ entry into a building.* **2** (of a person, his acts, words, etc) convincing; persuasive. **forc·ibly** /-əblɪ/ *adj*

ford /fɔd/ *n* [C] shallow place in a river where it is possible to walk across. □ *vt* [VP6A] cross (a river) by walking through the water. **~·able** /-əbl/ *adj* that can be ~ed.

fore /fɔ(r)/ *adj* situated in the front (opp of *back, aft*): *in the ~ part of the train/boat; the ~ hatch,* (in a ship). □ *n* (*sing* only) **1** ~ part (of a ship). **2** ***to the ~,*** ready to hand; on the spot: *He has come to the ~ recently,* has become prominent. □ *adv* (naut) in front. ***~ and aft,*** at the bow and stern of a ship; lengthwise in a ship: *~ and aft sails/rigged,* with sails set lengthwise. ⇨ square-rigged. □ *int* (golf) warning (to people in front) that the player is about to drive the ball.

fore·arm[1] /ˈfɔrɑm/ *n* arm from the elbow to the wrist or finger-tips. ⇨ the illus at arm.

fore·arm[2] /ˈfɔrˋɑm/ *vt* [VP6A] (usu in passive) arm beforehand; prepare for trouble in advance: *To be forewarned is to be ~ed.*

fore·bear *n* = forbear[2].

fore·bode /fɔˋbəʊd/ *vt* (formal) **1** [VP6A] be a sign of warning of: *These black clouds ~ a storm.* **2** [VP6A,9] have a feeling of (usu sth evil); have a feeling (*that*): *~ disaster.* **fore·bod·ing** *n* [C,U] feeling that trouble is coming.

fore·cast /ˈfɔkɑst *US:* -kæst/ *vt* (*pt,pp* ~ or ~ed) [VP6A] say in advance what is likely to happen. □ *n* statement that ~s sth: *inaccurate weather ~s.*

fore·castle, fo'c'sle /ˈfəʊksl/ *n* (in some merchant ships) part under the bows where the seamen have their living and sleeping accommodation.

fore·close /fɔˋkləʊz/ *vt,vi* (legal) [VP6A,2A] use the right (given by a mortgage) to take possession of property (when interest or capital has not been paid at the required time): *The Bank ~d* (*the mortgage*). **2** [VP3A] ***~ on,*** = ~. **fore·clos·ure** /fɔˋkləʊʒə(r)/ *n* [C,U] (act of) foreclosing a mortgage.

fore·court /ˈfɔkɔt/ *n* enclosed space in front of a building.

fore·doom /ˈfɔˋdum/ *vt* [VP6A,14] (usu passive) ***~ to,*** destine (to): *an attempt that was ~ed to failure.*

fore·fathers /ˈfɔfɑðə(r)z/ *n pl* ancestors.

fore·fin·ger /ˈfɔfɪŋgə(r)/ *n* first finger, next to the thumb; index finger.

fore·foot /ˈfɔfʊt/ *n* (*pl* forefeet) one of the front feet of a four-legged animal.

fore·front /ˈfɔfrʌnt/ *n* (*sing* with *def art*) most forward part: *in the ~ of the battle.*

fore·gather ⇨ forgather.

fore·go /fɔˋgəʊ/ *vt,vi* (*pt* forewent /fɔˋwent/, *pp* foregone /fɔˋgɒn *US:* -ˋgɔn/) precede (but rarely used except in) **fore·going** *adj* preceding, already mentioned. **for·gone** /ˈfɔgɒn *US:* -gɔn/ *adj*: *a foregone conclusion,* ending that can be seen or could have been seen from the start.

fore·go ⇨ forgo.

fore·ground /ˈfɔgraʊnd/ *n* **1** part of a view (esp in a picture) nearest to the observer. **2** (fig) most conspicuous position: *keep oneself in the ~,* where one is most easily seen or noticed.

fore·hand /ˈfɔhænd/ *adj* (of a stroke at tennis, etc) made with the palm turned forward (*backhand* = stroke made with the back of the hand turned forward and from the left side of the body (by a right-handed player).

fore·head /ˈfɒrɪd *US:* ˋfɔrɪd/ *n* part of the face above the eyes. ⇨ the illus at head.

foreign /ˈfɒrən *US:* ˋfɔr-/ *adj* **1** of, in, from, another country, not one's own: *~ languages/countries; ~ trade; the ˋF~ Office,* the department of state dealing with ~ affairs; its building in London. **2** ***~ to,*** not natural to, unconnected with: *Lying is ~ to his nature.* **3** coming or introduced from outside: *a ~ body in the eye,* e g a bit of dirt blown into it by the wind. **~er** *n* person born in or person from a ~ country.

fore·knowl·edge /ˈfɔˋnɒlɪdʒ/ *n* [U] knowledge of sth before its occurrence or existence.

fore·land /ˈfɔlənd/ *n* cape; promontory.

fore·leg /ˈfɔleg/ *n* one of the front legs of a four-footed animal.

fore·lock /ˈfɔlɒk/ *n* lock of hair growing just above the forehead: *take time by the ~,* not let an opportunity slip by; use an opportunity promptly.

fore·man /ˈfɔmən/ *n* (*pl* -men /-mən/) **1** workman in authority over others. **2** chief member and spokesman of a jury.

fore·mast /ˈfɔmɑst *US:* -mæst/ *n* mast nearest the bow of a ship. ⇨ the illus at barque.

fore·most /ˈfɔməʊst/ *adj* first; most notable; chief: *the ~ painter of his period.* □ *adv* first in position. ***first and ~,*** before all else; in the first place.

fore·name /ˈfɔneɪm/ *n* (as used in official style, e g on forms) name preceding the family name.

fore·noon /ˈfɔnun/ *n* part of the day between sunrise and noon.

for·en·sic /fəˋrensɪk/ *adj* of, used in, courts of law: *~ skill,* skill as needed by barristers, etc; *~ medicine,* medical knowledge as needed in legal matters, e g a poisoning trial.

fore·or·dain /ˈfɔrɔˋdeɪn/ *vt* [VP6A,14,17] determine or appoint beforehand: *what God has ~ed.*

fore·part /ˈfɔpɑt/ *n* part in front.

fore·run·ner /ˈfɔrʌnə(r)/ *n* **1** sign of what is to follow: *swallows, the ~s of spring.* **2** person who foretells and prepares for the coming of another.

fore·sail /ˈfɔseɪl/ *n* principal sail on the foremast. ⇨ the illus at barque.

fore·see /fɔˋsi/ *vt* (*pt* foresaw /fɔˋsɔ/, *pp* foreseen /fɔˋsin/) [VP6A,9,10] see beforehand or in advance: *~ trouble; ~ what will happen/how things will turn out/that things will go well.*

fore·shadow /fɔˋʃædəʊ/ *vt* [VP6A] be a sign or warning of (sth to come).

fore·shore /ˈfɔʃɔ(r)/ *n* part of the shore between the sea and land that is cultivated, built on, etc.

fore·shorten /fɔˋʃɔtn/ *vt* [VP6A] (in drawing pictures) show (an object) with shortening of lines.

fore·sight /ˈfɔsaɪt/ *n* [U] ability to see future needs; care in preparing for these: *If you had had more ~, you would have saved yourself a lot of trouble.*

fore·skin /ˈfɔskɪn/ *n* fold of skin covering the end of the penis.

for·est /ˈfɒrɪst *US:* ˋfɔr-/ *n* **1** [C,U] (large area of) land covered with trees (and often undergrowth); the trees growing there: *~s stretching for miles and miles; ~ animals; ~ fires.* **2** area where game (e g deer) is or was hunted (and preserved), not necessarily wooded; (with proper name prefixed, as *Sherwood F~*) district that was formerly ~ but is now partly under cultivation: *the deer ~s in Scotland.* **3** (fig) sth that suggests ~ trees: *a ~ of masts,* e g in a harbour. **~er** *n* officer in charge of a ~ (protecting wild animals, watching for fires, etc); man who works in a ~. **~ry** *n* [U] (science of) planting and caring for ~s.

fore·stall /fɔˋstɔl/ *vt* [VP6A] do sth first and so prevent another from doing it; upset (sb, his plans) by doing sth unexpectedly early: *~ a competitor.*

fore·swear /fɔˋsweə(r)/ *vt* = forswear.

fore·taste /ˈfɔteɪst/ *n* partial experience of enjoyment or suffering (*of* sth) in advance.
fore·tell /fɔˋtel/ *vt* (*pt,pp* foretold /fɔˋtold/) [VP6A,9,10] tell beforehand; predict: *~ sb's future. Is this the prophet whose coming was foretold (to) us?*
fore·thought /ˈfɔθɔt/ *n* [U] careful thought or planning for the future.
fore·told *pt,pp* of foretell.
fore·top /ˈfɔtop/ *n* (naut) platform at the head of a foremast; (compounds), ⇨ the illus at barque.
for·ever /fəˋrevə(r)/ *adv* always; at all times; endlessly.
fore·warn /fɔˋwɔn/ *vt* [VP6A] warn beforehand.
fore·woman /ˈfɔwʊmən/ *n* (*pl* -women /-wɪmɪn/) woman in authority over other women workers.
fore·word /ˈfɔwɜd/ *n* [C] introductory remarks to a book, printed in it, esp by someone not the author of the book.
for·feit /ˈfɔfɪt/ *vt* [VP6A] (have to) suffer the loss of sth as a punishment or consequence, or because of rules: *~ the good opinion of one's friends; ~ one's health.* □ *n* [C] **1** sth (to be) ~ed: *His health was the ~ he paid for overworking.* **2** (*pl*) game in which a player gives up various articles if he made an error and can redeem them by doing sth ludicrous: *Let's play ~s.* **for·feit·ure** /ˈfɔfɪtʃə(r)/ *n* [U] ~ing; *(the) forfeiture of one's property.*
for·gather, fore·gather /fɔˋgæðə(r)/ *vi* [VP2A,C] come together.
for·gave /fəˋgeɪv/ *pt* of forgive.
forge[1] /fɔdʒ/ *n* [C] **1** workshop with fire and anvil where metals are heated and shaped, esp one used by a smith for making shoes for horses, repairing agricultural machinery, etc. **2** (workshop with) furnace or hearth for melting or refining metal.
forge[2] /fɔdʒ/ *vt* [VP6A] **1** shape by heating and hammering: *~ an anchor;* (fig) *Their friendship was ~d by shared adversity.* **2** make a copy of sth, e g a signature, a banknote, a will, in order to deceive. **forger** *n* person who ~s(2). **forg·ery** /ˈfɔdʒərɪ/ *n* **1** [U] forging(2) of a document, signature, etc. **2** [C] (*pl* -ries) ~d document, signature, etc. **forg·ing** *n* [C] piece of metal that has been ~d(1) or shaped under a press.
forge[3] /fɔdʒ/ *vi* [VP2C] **~ ahead,** make steady progress; take the lead (in a race, etc).
for·get /fəˋget/ *vt,vi* (*pt* forgot /fəˋgot/, *pp* forgotten /fəˋgotn/) **1** [VP6A,C,D,8,9,10,2A,3A] **~ (about),** lose remembrance of; fail to keep in the memory; fail to recall: *I ~/I've forgotten her name. I shall never ~ your kindness to me. Did you ~ (that) I was coming? I have forgotten how to do it/where he lives/whether he wants it. I forgot all about it. I shall never ~ hearing Chaliapin singing the part of Boris Godunov.* **forget-me-not** /fəˋget mɪ not/ *n* small plant with blue flowers. **2** [VP6A] neglect or fail (to do sth): *Don't ~ to post the letters. He has forgotten to pay me.* **3** [VP6A,2A] put out of the mind; stop thinking about: *Let's ~ our quarrels. Forgive and ~.* **4** [VP6A] omit to pay attention to: *Don't ~ the waiter,* give him a tip. **5 ~ oneself, (a)** behave thoughtlessly in a way not suited to one's dignity, to the circumstances. **(b)** act unselfishly, thinking only of the interests of others. **~·ful** /-fl/ *adj* in the habit of ~ting: *He's very ~ful of things. Old people are sometimes ~ful.* **~·fully** /-flɪ/ *adv* **~·ful·ness** *n*
for·give /fəˋgɪv/ *vt,vi* (*pt* forgave /fəˋgeɪv/, *pp* forgiven /fəˋgɪvn/) [VP6A,14,12C,2A] **1 ~ sb (sth/for doing sth),** say that one no longer has the wish to punish sb; no longer have the wish to punish sb for an offence, a sin; pardon or show mercy to (sb); no longer have hard feelings towards (sb): *~ sb for being rude/~ his rudeness. Am I ~n? F~ us our trespasses. Your sins will be ~n you.* **2** not demand repayment of (a debt), not demand repayment of a debt from (sb): *He forgave the debt. Will you ~ me the debt?* **for·giv·able** /-əbl/ *adj* **for·giv·ing** *adj* ready or willing to ~: *a forgiving nature.* **for·giv·ing·ly** *adv* **~·ness** *n* [U] forgiving or being ~n; willingness to ~: *ask for/receive ~ness; full of ~ness.*
for·go /fɔˋgəʊ/ *vt* (*pt* forwent /fɔˋwent/, *pp* forgone /fɔˋgon *US:* -ˋgɔn/) do without; give up: *~ pleasures in order to study hard.*
for·got, for·got·ten ⇨ forget.
fork /fɔk/ *n* [C] **1** implement with two or more points (prongs), used for lifting food to the mouth, carving, etc. **ˋ~ lunch/supper,** one (for more persons than can be seated at table) at which food is served as a buffet where guests serve themselves. **2** farm or gardening tool for breaking up the ground, lifting hay, straw, etc. **3** place where a road, tree-trunk, etc divides or branches; part of a bicycle to which a wheel is fixed. ⇨ also *tuning-~* at tune. **4 ˋ~-lift,** powered truck or trolley with mechanical means of lifting and lowering goods (to or from storage space, or for loading and unloading. □ *vt,vi* **1** [VP6A,15A,B] lift, move, carry, with a ~: *~ hay/straw; ~ in manure,* dig it into the ground with a ~; *~ the ground over,* turn the soil over with a ~. **2** [VP2A,C] (of a road, river, etc) divide into branches; (of persons) turn (left or right): *We ~ed right at the church.* **3** [VP15B,2C] **~ sth out, ~ up/out,** (colloq) hand over, pay: *I've got to ~ out a lot of money to the Collector of Taxes this year.* **forked** *adj* branching; dividing into two or more parts: *a ~ed road; the ~ed-tongue of a snake; a bird with a ~ed tail; ~ed lightning,* zigzagged.

a fork-lift truck

for·lorn /fəˋlɔn/ *adj* (poet or liter) unhappy; uncared for; forsaken. **~·ly** *adv* **~·ness** *n*
for·lorn hope /fəˈlɔn ˈhəʊp/ *n* [C] desperate enterprise; plan or enterprise which has very little likelihood of success.
form[1] /fɔm/ *n* **1** [U] shape; outward or visible appearance: *without shape or ~; take ~,* begin to have a (recognizable) shape; [C] person or animal as it can be seen or touched: *A dark ~ could be seen in the distance. Proteus was a Greek sea-god who could appear in the ~ of any creature he wished. He has a well-proportioned ~,* a well-shaped body. **2** [U] general arrangement or structure; way in which parts are put together to make a

whole or a group; style or manner of presentation: *a piece of music in sonata ~; have a sense of ~ in painting* (*form* being contrasted with colouring); *literary ~* (*form* being contrasted with subject-matter). **3** [C] particular kind of arrangement or structure; manner in which a thing exists; species, kind or variety: *~s of government; ~s of animal and vegetable life. Ice, snow and steam are ~s of water.* **4** (gram) [U] shape taken by a word: *change ~; different in ~ but identical in meaning;* [C] one of the shapes taken by a word (in sound or spelling): *The word 'brother' has two plural ~s, 'brothers' and 'brethren'. The past tense ~ of 'run' is 'ran'.* **5** [U] manner of behaving or speaking fixed, required or expected by custom or etiquette: *do sth for ~'s sake,* i e because it is usual, not because one wishes to do it or likes doing it; *say 'Good morning' as a mere matter of ~,* i e not because one is really pleased to see the person to whom the words are spoken. **'good/'bad ~,** behaviour according to/not according to custom or etiquette. **6** [C] particular way of behaving, etc greeting, utterance, act, as required by custom or etiquette; established practice or ritual: *the ancient ~s observed at the coronation of a sovereign; pay too much attention to ~s; a ~ of prayer used at sea; ~s of worship.* **7** [C] printed paper with space to be filled in: *'telegraph ~s; appli'cation ~s;* (also called **a ~ letter**); printed or typewritten letter sent out in great numbers. **8** [U] condition of health and training (esp of horses and athletes): *If a horse is not in good ~ it is unlikely to win a race. On ~* (= Judging from recent performances as evidence of condition and training), *the Aga Khan's horse is likely to win the race. Smith is out of ~/is not on ~ and is unlikely to run in the 100 metres race tomorrow.* **9** [U] spirits: *Jack was in great ~ at the dinner party,* in high spirits, lively. **10** [C] long wooden bench, usu without a back, for several persons to sit on. **11** [C] class in some GB (grammar and public) schools, the youngest boys and girls being in the first ~ and the oldest in the sixth ~. **~less** *adj* without shape. **~less·ly** *adv*

form² /fɔm/ *vt,vi* **1** [VP6A,15A] give shape or form to; make, produce: *~ words and sentences; ~ the plural of a noun by adding -s or -es; ~ one's style* (in writing) *on good models.* **2** [VP6A] develop, build up, conceive: *~ good habits; ~ a child's character/mind,* by training, discipline, etc: *~ ideas/images/judgements/opinions/plans/conclusions.* **3** [VP6A,15A] organize: *~ a class for beginners in French. The President invited M Mollet to ~ a Ministry. They ~ed themselves into a committee.* **4** [VP6A] be (the material of), be (*one* or *part of*): *What ~s the basis of this compound? This series of lectures ~s part of a complete course on French history.* **5** [VP14,2C] (mil) (cause to) move into a particular order: *~ a regiment into columns; ~ into line. The company was ~ed into three ranks.* **6** [VP2A,C] come into existence; become solid; take shape: *The idea ~ed in his mind. The words would not ~ on her lips,* She could not bring herself to speak them. *Ice ~s at the temperature of 0°C.*

for·mal /'fɔml/ *adj* **1** in accordance with rules, customs and convention: *pay a ~ call on the Ambassador; ~ dress,* as required by custom for certain occasions; *make a ~* (= ceremonious) *bow to sb; a ~ receipt,* according to commercial custom, regular and in good order. **2** regular or geometric in design; symmetrical: *~ gardens,* e g with flower beds, hedges, etc in geometrical patterns. **3** of the outward shape or appearance (not the reality or substance): *a ~ resemblance between two things.* **4 '~ 'grammar,** of the forms of words, of rules (of syntax, etc). **~ly** /-mḷɪ/ *adv* **~·ism** /-ɪzm/ *n* [U] exact observance of forms and ceremonies, e g in religious duties, in behaviour.

for·mal·de·hyde /fɔ'mældɪhaɪd/ *n* [U] (chem) colourless gas **(HcHo)** used, dissolved in water, as a preservative and disinfectant. **for·malin** /'fɔməlɪn/ *n* [U] (chem) solution of ~ used as a disinfectant.

for·mal·ity /fɔ'mæləti/ *n* (*pl* **-ties**) **1** [U] strict attention to rules, forms and convention: *There was too much ~ in the Duke's household.* **2** [C] formal act; sth required by custom or rules: *legal formalities; comply with all the necessary formalities.* **a mere ~,** sth one is required or expected to do, but which has little meaning or importance.

for·mat /'fɔmæt/ *n* shape and size of a book, including the type, paper and binding: *reissue a book in a new ~.*

for·ma·tion /fɔ'meɪʃn/ *n* **1** [U] forming or shaping: *the ~ of character/of ideas in the mind;* [C] that which is formed: *Clouds are ~s of condensed water vapour.* **2** [U] structure or arrangement: *troops/warships in 'battle ~; military aircraft flying in ~;* (attrib) *'~ flying;* [C] particular arrangement or order: *rock ~s;* the arrangement of the players (also *line-up*) in a (football, Rugby) match.

for·ma·tive /'fɔmətɪv/ *adj* **1** giving, or tending to give, shape to: *~ influences,* e g on a child's character. **2** pliable: *the ~ years of a child's life,* the years during which its character is formed.

for·mer /'fɔmə(r)/ *adj* **1** of an earlier period: *in ~ times; my ~ students; customs of ~ days. She looks more like her ~ self,* e g looks well again after her illness. **2** (also as *pron*) *the ~* (contrasted with *the latter*), the first-mentioned of two: *I prefer the ~ alternative to the latter. Of these alternatives I prefer the ~.* **~ly** *adv* in ~ times.

for·mic /'fɔmɪk/ *adj* **'~ 'acid,** the acid (used to make insecticides, fumigants, etc) contained in the fluid emitted by ants but now usu produced synthetically.

For·mica /fɔ'maɪkə/ *n* [U] (P) heat-resistant plastic made in sheets (for covering surfaces).

for·mi·dable /'fɔmɪdəbl/ *adj* **1** causing fear or dread: *a man with a ~ appearance.* **2** requiring great effort to deal with or overcome: *~ obstacles/opposition/enemies/debts.* **for·mi·dably** /-əblɪ/ *adv*

for·mula /'fɔmjʊlə/ *n* (*pl* **-las,** or, in scientific usage, **-lae** /-li/) **1** form of words used regularly (as 'How d'you do?', 'Excuse me', 'Thank you'); phrase or sentence regularly used in legal documents, church services, etc: *the ~ used in baptism.* **2** statement of a rule, fact, etc esp one in signs or numbers, as in chemistry, mathematics, etc, e g 'Water = H_2O'. **3** set of directions, usu in symbols, for a medical preparation: *a ~ for a cough mixture.*

for·mu·late /'fɔmjʊleɪt/ *vt* [VP6A] express clearly and exactly: *~ one's thoughts/a doctrine.* **for·mu·la·tion** /'fɔmjʊ'leɪʃn/ *n* [U] formulating; [C] exact and clear statement.

for·ni·ca·tion /ˌfɔnɪˈkeɪʃn/ *n* [U] voluntary sexual intercourse between persons not married to one another, esp when both are unmarried. ⇨ adultery. **for·ni·cate** /ˈfɔnɪkeɪt/ *vi* [VP21] commit ~.

for·ra·der /ˈforədə(r)/ *adv* (colloq) more forward: *can't get any ~*, can't make any progress.

for·sake /fəˈseɪk/ *vt* (*pt* forsook /fəˈsʊk/, *pp* forsaken /fəˈseɪkən/) [VP6A] give up; break away from; desert: *~ one's wife and children; ~ bad habits. His friends forsook him when he became poor.*

for·sooth /fəˈsuθ/ *adv* (old use, or used in irony) no doubt; in truth.

for·swear /fɔˈsweə(r)/ *vt* (*pt* forswore /fɔˈswɔ(r)/, *pp* forsworn /fɔˈswɔn/) [VP6A] **1** give up doing or using (sth): *~ bad habits/smoking.* **2** ***~ oneself,*** perjure oneself.

for·sythia /fəˈsɑɪθɪə *US:* -ˈsɪθ-/ *n* [U] shrub with bright yellow flowers in spring.

fort /fɔt/ *n* building or group of buildings specially erected or strengthened for military defence.

forte[1] /ˈfɔteɪ *US:* fɔrt/ *n* person's strong point; sth a person does particularly well: *Singing is not my ~*, I do not sing well.

forte[2] /ˈfɔteɪ/ *adj, adv* (music) (abbr *f~*) loud(ly).

forth /fɔθ/ *adv* **1** out (which is more usual). **2** onwards; forwards: *from this day ~; and so ~* (= and so on); *back and ~*, to and fro (which is more usu). **3** ***hold ~,*** ⇨ hold[1](14).

forth·com·ing /fɔθˈkʌmɪŋ/ *adj* **1** about to come out: *a list of ~ books*, books about to be published. **2** (pred) ready for use when needed: *The money/help we hoped for was not ~*, We did not receive it. **3** (colloq) ready to be helpful, give information, etc: *The girl at the reception desk was not very ~.*

forth·right /ˈfɔθrɑɪt/ *adj* outspoken; straightforward.

forth·with /fɔθˈwɪθ *US:* -ˈwɪð/ *adv* at once; without losing time.

for·ti·eth /ˈfɔtɪəθ/ ⇨ forty.

for·tify /ˈfɔtɪfɑɪ/ *vt* (*pt,pp* -fied) [VP6A,14] ~ ***(against),*** strengthen (a place) against attack (with walls, trenches, guns, etc); support or strengthen oneself, one's courage, etc: *~ a town against the enemy; a fortified city/zone; ~ oneself against the cold*, e g by having a good meal; *fortified with the rites of the Church*, prepared, by having received the Sacraments, for death. **ˈfortified wine,** wine, e g sherry, strengthened by the addition of grape brandy. **for·ti·fi·ca·tion** /ˈfɔtɪfɪˈkeɪʃn/ *n* [U] ~ing; [C] (often *pl*) defensive wall(s), tower(s), earthwork(s), etc.

for·tis·simo /fɔˈtɪsɪməʊ/ *adj, adv* (I; music) (abbr *ff~*) very loud(ly).

for·ti·tude /ˈfɔtɪtjud *US:* -tud/ *n* [U] calm courage, self-control, in the face of pain, danger or difficulty.

fort·night /ˈfɔtnɑɪt/ *n* period of two weeks: *a ~'s holiday; go away for a ~; a ~ today/tomorrow/next Monday; a ~ ago yesterday.* **~·ly** *adj, adv* happening or occurring every ~: *~ly sailings to Bombay; go ~ly.*

for·tress /ˈfɔtrəs/ *n* fortified building or town.

for·tu·itous /fɔˈtjuɪtəs *US:* -ˈtu-/ *adj* happening by chance: *a ~ meeting.* **~·ly** *adv*

for·tu·nate /ˈfɔtʃṇət/ *adj* favoured by fortune; lucky; prosperous; having, bringing, brought by, good fortune: *be ~ in life. You were ~ to escape being injured. He was ~ enough to have a good income. That was ~ for you. You were ~ in your choice/in winning his sympathy.* **~·ly** *adv* in a ~ manner: *~ly for everybody.*

for·tune /ˈfɔtʃun/ *n* **1** [C,U] chance; chance looked upon as a power deciding or influencing sb or sth; fate; good or bad luck coming to a person or undertaking: *have ~ on one's side*, be lucky. ***the ~(s) of war,*** what may happen in war. ***try one's ~,*** take a risky step. ***tell sb his ~,*** say, e g as gypsies do, from a reading of playing cards, or the lines on his palm, what will happen to him. **ˈ~ teller** *n* person who claims to be able to do this. **2** [C,U] prosperity; success; great sum of money: *a man of ~; seek one's ~ in a new country.* ***come into a ~,*** inherit a lot of money. ***make a ~,*** make a lot of money. ***marry a ~,*** marry sb who is or will be rich, e g an heiress. ***a small ~,*** a lot of money: *spend a small ~ on clothes.* **ˈ~ hunter** *n* man seeking a rich woman to marry.

forty /ˈfɔtɪ/ *adj, n* 40. ⇨ App 4: *a man of ~*, aged 40; *under/over ~; the forties*, years of life or of a century between 39 and 50. ***have ~ winks,*** ⇨ wink. **for·ti·eth** /ˈfɔtɪəθ/ *adj, n* ⇨ App 4.

fo·rum /ˈfɔrəm/ *n* (in ancient Rome) public place for meetings; any place for public discussion: *TV is an accepted ~ for the discussion of public affairs.*

for·ward[1] /ˈfɔwəd/ *adj* ⇨ backward. **1** directed towards the front; situated in front; moving on, advancing: *a ~ march/movement; the ~ ranks of a column of troops; ~ planning*, for future needs, etc; *be well ~ with one's work.* **2** (of plants, crops, seasons, children) well advanced; making progress towards maturity: *a ~ spring.* **3** eager or impatient; ready and willing: *~ to help others;* too eager; rather presumptuous: *a ~ young girl.* **4** advanced or extreme: *~ opinions.* **5** (comm) relating to future produce: *~ prices*, for goods to be delivered later; *a ~ contract.* □ *n* one of the first-line players in football (now often called a *striker*), hockey, etc. ⇨ the illus at football. **~·ness** *n* the state of being ~(2): *the ~ness of the season.*

for·ward[2] /ˈfɔwəd/ *vt* [VP6A,12A,13A,15A] **1** help or send forward; help to advance: *~ sb's plans.* **2** send, dispatch: *~ goods to sb. We have today ~ed you our new catalogue.* **ˈ~ing agent** *n* person or business company that ~s goods. **ˈ~ing instructions,** instructions concerning the destination, etc of goods. **3** send a letter, parcel, etc after a person to a new address: *Please ~ my letters to this address.*

for·ward(s) /ˈfɔwəd(z)/ *adv* (Note: ~*s* is rare or not much used except as in **4** below.) **1** onward so as to make progress: *rush/step ~; go ~.* ⇨ forrader. **2** towards the future; onwards in time: *from this time ~; look ~*, think ahead, think about the future. ⇨ carriage(3). **3** to the front; into prominence: *bring ~* (= call attention to) *new evidence; come ~*, offer oneself for a task, a post, etc. **4** ***backward(s) and ~(s),*** to and fro.

fosse /fos/ *n* [C] long, narrow ditch or trench, e g a moat, or as a fortification.

fos·sil /ˈfosl/ *n* [C] **1** recognizable (part, trace or imprint of a) prehistoric animal or plant once buried in earth, now hardened like rock: *hunt for ~s;* (attrib) *~ bones/shells.* ⇨ p 346. **2** person who is out of date and unable to accept new ideas: *Isn't Professor B an old ~!* **~·ize** /ˈfosḷɑɪz/ *vt,vi* [VP6A,2A] change or turn into stone; (fig) make or become out of date or antiquated. **~·iz·ation** /ˈfosļɑɪˋzeɪʃn *US:* -ļɪˋz-/ *n*

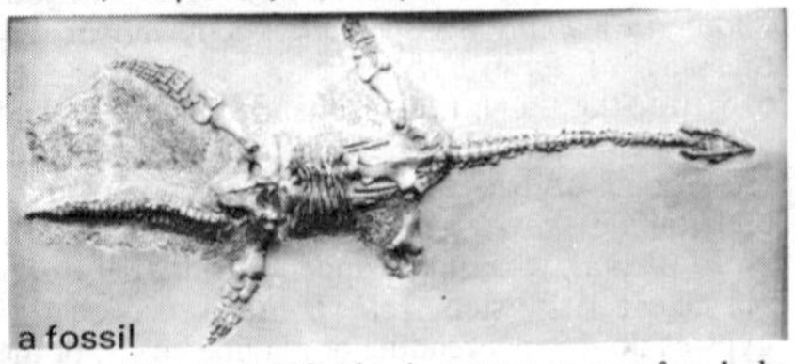
a fossil

fos·ter /ˋfostə(r) *US:* ˋfɔ-/ *vt* [VP6A] care for; help the growth and development of; nurture: *~ a child; ~ the sick; ~ musical ability; ~ evil thoughts/a desire for revenge.* **ˋ~-brother/-sister** *nn* one ~ed by one's parent(s). **ˋ~-child** *n* one brought up by ~-parents. **ˋ~-parent/-mother/-father** *nn* one who acts as a parent in place of a natural parent, but without legal guardianship. ⇨ **adopt.**

fought /fɔt/ *pt,pp* of **fight.**

foul[1] /fɑʊl/ *adj* **1** causing disgust; having a bad smell or taste; filthy: *a ~ prison cell; medicine with a ~ taste; ~-smelling drains; a ~ meal,* (sl) a poor meal. **2** wicked; evil; (of language) full of oaths; obscene: (of the weather) stormy; rough. **ˈ~-ˋspoken/-ˋmouthed** *adj* using ~ language. ***by fair means or ~,*** somehow or other, whether by good or evil methods. **3 ˈ~ ˋplay, (a)** (in sport) sth contrary to the rules. **(b)** violent crime, esp murder: *Is ~ play suspected,* Do the police think this is a case of murder? **4** entangled: *a ~ rope.* **5** (of a flue, pipe, gun-barrel, etc) clogged up, not clear: *The fire won't burn; perhaps the chimney is ~,* needs sweeping. **6 *fall ~ of,* (a)** (of a ship) run against, collide with, become entangled with. **(b)** (fig) get into trouble with: *fall ~ of the law.* □ *n* **1** [C] (sport) sth contrary to the rules; irregular stroke or piece of play. **2** [U] ***through fair and ~,*** through good and bad fortune; through everything. **~·ly** /ˋfɑʊlɪ/ *adv* in a ~ manner: *He was ~ly murdered.* **~·ness** *n*

foul[2] /fɑʊl/ *vt,vi* [VP6A,2A] **1** make or become foul: *factory chimneys that ~ the air with smoke; ~ one's name/reputation; ~ a drain/gun-barrel.* **2** collide; collide with; (cause to) become entangled: *The rope ~ed the anchor chain. His fishing-line ~ed the weeds.* **3** (sport) commit a ~(1) against: *~ an opponent.*

found[1] /fɑʊnd/ *pt,pp* of **find**[2].

found[2] /fɑʊnd/ *vt* **1** [VP6A] start the building of; lay the base of; establish: *~ a new city/a colony in a new country. The Methodist Church was ~ed by John Wesley.* **2** [VP6A] get sth started by providing money (esp endowments): *~ a new school.* **3** [VP14] ***~ sth (up)on,*** base on: *a novel ~ed on fact; arguments ~ed on facts.*

foun·da·tion /fɑʊnˋdeɪʃn/ *n* **1** [U] founding or establishing (of a town, school, church or other institution). **2** [C] sth that is founded, e g a college, monastery, hospital; fund of money for charity, research, etc: *the Ford F~.* **3** [C] (often *pl*) strong base of a building, usu below ground-level, on which it is built up: *the ~(s) of a block of flats. The huge lorries shook the house to its ~s.* **ˋ~-stone** *n* stone laid at a ceremony to celebrate the founding of a building. **4** [C,U] that on which an idea, belief, etc rests; underlying principle; basis; starting-point: *the ~s of religious beliefs; lay the ~(s) of one's career; a story that has no ~ in fact/is without ~.* **5 ˋ~ *garment,*** (trade use) woman's corset or other garment to shape and support the body (often with a bra attached); **ˋ~ *cream,*** (cosmetics) cream used on the skin before other cosmetics are applied.

foun·der[1] /ˋfɑʊndə(r)/ *n* person who founds or establishes a school, etc. **found·ress** /ˋfɑʊndrəs/ *n* woman ~.

foun·der[2] /ˋfɑʊndə(r)/ *vi,vt* [VP2A,6A] **1** (of a ship) (cause to) fill with water and sink. **2** (of a horse) fall or stumble (esp in mud) or from overwork; cause (a horse) to break down from overwork.

found·ling /ˋfɑʊndlɪŋ/ *n* deserted or abandoned child of unknown parents. **ˋ~ hospital,** (formerly) institution where ~s are taken in and cared for.

foun·dry /ˋfɑʊndrɪ/ *n* (*pl* -ries) place where metal or glass is melted and moulded: *a ˋtype ~,* where type for printing is made.

fount /fɑʊnt/ *n* **1** (poet) spring of water. **2** (also *font*) set of printer's type of the same size and face.

foun·tain /ˋfɑʊntɪn *US:* -tn/ *n* **1** spring of water, esp one made artificially with water forced through holes in a pipe or pipes for ornamental purposes. **ˋdrinking-~** *n* one that supplies drinking-water in a public place. **ˋ~-pen** *n* pen with a supply of ink inside the holder. **ˋsoda ~,** ⇨ **soda. 2** (fig) source or origin: *the ~ of honour.* **ˋ~-head** *n* original source.

four /fɔ(r)/ *n, adj* 4; ⇨ App 4: *a child of ~, ~ years old; an income of ~ figures,* from 999 to 9 999; *a coach and ~,* with ~ horses; *the ~ corners of the earth,* the farthest parts; *scatter sth to the ~ winds,* in all directions. **ˈ~-letter ˋword,** word of ~ letters, e g *shit,* which is regarded as obscene. ***on all ~s,*** on the hands and knees. ***a ~,*** a rowing-boat with a crew of ~; (cricket) hit for ~ runs. **ˈ~-in-ˋhand** *n* vehicle (coach or carriage) pulled by ~ horses and with no outrider. **ˋ~-part** *adj* (music) arranged for ~ voices to sing. **ˋ~-pence** *n* the sum of 4p: *apples, ~pence a pound.* **~·penny** /-pnɪ *US:* -penɪ/ *adj* costing 4p: *a ~penny loaf.* **ˋ~-ply** *adj* (of wool, wood, etc) having ~ strands or thicknesses. **ˈ~-ˋposter** *n* bed with ~ posts to support a canopy or curtains. **ˈ~-ˋpounder** *n* gun throwing a 4 lb shot. **ˋ~-score** *adj, n* 80; age of 80 years. **ˋ~-square** *adj* square-shaped; (fig) steady; solidly based. **ˈ~-ˋwheeler** *n* hackney carriage with ~ wheels (not a hansom cab). **~·fold** /ˋfɔfəʊld/ *adj* repeated ~ times; having ~ parts. □ *adv* ~ times as much or as many. **~·some** /ˋfɔsəm/ *n* game (esp of golf) between two pairs: *a mixed ~some,* with one man and one woman in each pair. **~·teen** /ˈfɔˋtin/ *n, adj* ⇨ App 4. **~·teenth** /ˈfɔˋtinθ/ *n, adj* ⇨ App 4; one of 14 equal parts. **fourth** /fɔθ/ *n, adj* ⇨ App 4. **fourth·ly** *adv* in the ~th place (esp in enumerations).

fowl /fɑʊl/ *n* **1** (old use) any bird: *the ~s of the air.* **2** (with a *pref*) one of the larger birds: *ˋwild~, ˋwater~.* **3** domestic cock or hen: *keep ~s.* **~-pest** /-pest/ *n* infectious disease of ~s. **ˋ~-run** *n* piece of (usu enclosed) land where ~s are kept. **4** [U] flesh of ~s as food: *roast ~ for dinner.* □ *vi* (usu as gerund) catch, hunt, snare, wild~: *go ~ing.* **ˋ~ing-piece** *n* light shot-gun used in ~ing. **~er** *n* person who shoots or traps wild birds for food.

fox /foks/ *n* (fem *vixen* /ˋvɪksn/) wild animal of the

birds 2

dog family, with (usu) red fur and a bushy tail, preserved in Britain for hunting, and proverbial for its cunning. ⇨ the illus at small. **ˈfox·glove** *n* plant with tall-growing spikes of purple or white flowers. **ˈfox·hole** *n* (mil) hole in the ground used as a shelter against enemy fire and as a firing-point. **ˈfox·hound** *n* kind of hound bred and trained to hunt foxes. **ˈfox·hunt** *n, vi* chasing of, chase, foxes with hounds. **ˌfox-ˈterrier** *n* small and lively short-haired dog used for driving foxes from earths, or kept as a pet. **ˈfox·trot** *n* (music for a) dance with short, quick steps. □ *vt* [VP6A] deceive by cunning; confuse; puzzle: *He was completely foxed.* **foxy** *adj* crafty; crafty-looking.

foyer /ˈfɔɪ-eɪ *US:* ˈfɔɪ-ər/ *n* large space in a theatre for the use of the audience during intervals; entrance hall of a cinema; large public room in a hotel.

fra·cas /ˈfrækɑ *US:* ˈfreɪkəs/ *n* (*pl* GB unchanged; US -cases) *noisy quarrel.*

frac·tion /ˈfrækʃn/ *n* **1** small part or bit. **2** number that is not a whole number (e g $\frac{1}{3}$, 5/8, 0·76). **~al** /-nl/ *adj* of or in ~s: *~al distillation,* partial separation of liquids, e g petroleum, having different boiling-points by gradual heating.

frac·tious /ˈfrækʃəs/ *adj* (usu of children, or senile persons) irritable; peevish; bad-tempered. **~·ly** *adv* **~·ness** *n*

frac·ture /ˈfræktʃə(r)/ *n* [U] breaking or being broken, e g of a bone, a pipe-line; [C] instance of this: *compound/simple ~s,* with/without skin wounds. □ *vt, vi* [VP6A,2A] break; crack: *~ one's leg; bones that ~ easily.*

frag·ile /ˈfrædʒɑɪl *US:* -dʒəl/ *adj* easily injured, broken or destroyed: *~ china/health/happiness.* **fra·gil·ity** /frəˈdʒɪlətɪ/ *n* [U].

frag·ment /ˈfrægmənt/ *n* [C] part broken off; separate or incomplete part: *try to put the ~s of a broken vase together; overhear ~s of conversation.* □ *vi* [VP2A] break into ~s: *The shell ~s on impact.* **frag·men·tary** /ˈfrægməntrɪ *US:* -terɪ/ *adj* incomplete: *a ~ary report of an event.* **frag·men·ta·tion** /ˌfrægmənˈteɪʃn/ *n*: *~ation bomb,* one that breaks up into small ~s.

fra·grant /ˈfreɪgrənt/ *adj* sweet-smelling: *~ flowers;* (fig) *~ memories.* **fra·grance** /-əns/ *n* [U] sweet or pleasing smell.

frail /freɪl/ *adj* (-er, -est) weak; fragile: *a ~ child,* one with a weak constitution; *a ~ support; ~ happiness.* **~ty** /ˈfreɪltɪ/ *n* [U] the quality of being ~: *the ~ty of human life;* [C] (*pl* -ties) fault; moral weakness: *He loved her in spite of her little frailties.*

frame[1] /freɪm/ *n* [C] **1** skeleton or main structure, e g steel girders, brick walls, wooden struts, of a ship, building, aircraft, etc which makes its shape, esp in the process of building. **ˈ~ aerial** *n* one in which the wire is round a ~ (instead of being stretched out between two poles, etc). **ˈ~ house** *n* one with a wooden skeleton covered with wooden boards or shingles. **2** border of wood or other material in which a picture, photograph, window or door is enclosed or set; structure that holds the lenses of a pair of spectacles. ⇨ the illus at window. **3** human or animal body: *a girl of slender ~. Sobs shook her ~.* **4** box-like structure of wood and glass for protecting plants from the cold: *a cold/heated ~.* **5** *~ of mind,* temporary state or condition of mind: *in a cheerful ~ of mind; in the ~ of mind to welcome any diversion.* **6** (more usu *ˈ~work*) established order or system: *the ~ of society.* **7** single exposure on a roll of photographic film. **ˈ~·work** *n* that part of a structure that gives shape and support: *a bridge with a steel ~works; the ~work of a government.*

frame[2] /freɪm/ *vt, vi* **1** [VP6A] put together; shape; build up: *~ a plan/theory/sentence; a man not ~d for severe hardships,* unable to endure them well. **2** [VP6A] put a frame(2) round; enclose in a frame: *~ a photograph; have an oil-painting ~d;* serve as a frame: *a landscape ~d in an archway.* **3** [VP2A,C] develop; give promise of developing: *plans that ~ well/badly.* **4** [VP6A] (sl) form a plan to make (sb) appear guilty of sth; put together a false charge against (sb): *The accused man said he had been ~d.* **ˈ~-up** *n* (colloq) scheme or conspiracy to make an innocent person appear guilty.

franc /fræŋk/ *n* standard unit of a decimal currency

in France, Belgium, Switzerland and other countries.

fran·chise /ˈfræntʃɑɪz/ *n* **1** (usu *sing* with *def art*) full rights of citizenship given by a country or town, esp the right to vote at elections. **2** [C] (chiefly US) special right given by public authorities to a person or company: *a ~ for a bus service.*

Fran·cis·can /frænˋsɪskən/ *n, adj* (friar) of the religious order founded in 1209 by St Francis of Assisi /əˋsisɪ/.

Franco- /ˈfræŋkəʊ/ *pref* (used in compounds) French: *the ˋ~-German War of 1870—71;* ˋ*~phile,* (one who is) friendly towards France; ˋ*~phobe,* (one who is) hostile towards France.

Frank /fræŋk/ *n* member of the Germanic tribes that conquered Gaul in the 16th c A D.

frank[1] /fræŋk/ *adj* showing clearly the thoughts and feelings; open: *a ~ look/smile/face; make a ~ confession of one's guilt; be quite ~ with sth* (*about* sth). **~·ly** *adv* **~·ness** *n*

frank[2] /fræŋk/ *vt* [VP6A] exempt (letters, etc) from postal charges (as, in former times, peers and Members of Parliament could, by putting their signature on the cover); stamp (letters with a ~ing-machine). ˋ**~ing-machine** *n* machine that automatically stamps letters passed through it, with a counting mechanism to show the total charge, locked and set by Post Office officials according to the sum paid in advance.

frank·furter /ˈfræŋkfɜtə(r)/ *n* seasoned and smoked sausage made of beef and pork.

frank·in·cense /ˈfræŋkɪnsens/ *n* [U] kind of resin from trees, giving a sweet smell when burnt.

frank·lin /ˈfræŋklɪn/ *n* (in GB, 14th and 15th cc) landowner not of noble birth, higher in rank than a yeoman.

fran·tic /ˈfræntɪk/ *adj* wildly excited with joy, pain, anxiety, etc: *~ cries for help; drive sb ~.* **fran·ti·cally** /-klɪ/ *adv*

fra·ter·nal /frəˋtɜnl/ *adj* brotherly: *~ love.* **~ly** /-nlɪ/ *adv*

fra·ter·nity /frəˋtɜnətɪ/ *n* (*pl* -ties) **1** [U] brotherly feeling. **2** [C] society of men, e g monks, who treat each other as equals; men who are joined together by common interests: *the ~ of the Press,* newspaper writers. **3** (US) society of students, with branches in various colleges, usu with names made up of Greek letters. ⇨ **sorority.**

frat·er·nize /ˈfrætənɑɪz/ *vi* [VP2A,C,3A] **~ *(with),*** become friendly (with): *Men from the two armies stopped fighting and ~d on Christmas Day.* **frat·er·niz·ation** /ˌfrætənɑɪˋzeɪʃn *US:* -nɪˋz-/ *n*

frat·ri·cide /ˈfrætrɪsɑɪd/ *n* [C,U] (person guilty of) wilful killing of one's brother or sister.

Frau /frɑʊ/ *n* (*pl* Frauen /ˈfrɑʊən/) (G) (of a German wife or widow) Mrs; German woman.

fraud /frɔd/ *n* **1** [U] criminal deception; [C] act of this kind: *get money by ~.* **2** [C] person or thing that deceives: *This hair-restorer is a ~; I'm as bald as ever.* **~u·lent** /ˈfrɔdjʊlənt *US:* -dʒʊ-/ *adj* acting with ~; deceitful; obtained by ~: *~ulent gains.* **~u·lent·ly** *adv*

fraught /frɔt/ *adj* (*pred* only) **1** involving; attended by; threatening (unpleasant consequences): *an expedition ~ with danger.* **2** filled with: *~ with meaning.*

Fräu·lein /ˈfrɔɪlɑɪn/ *n* (G) (of an unmarried German girl) Miss; German spinster.

fray[1] /freɪ/ *n* fight; contest: (liter, fig) *eager for the ~.*

fray[2] /freɪ/ *vt,vi* [VP6A,2A,C] (of cloth, rope, etc) become worn, make worn, by rubbing so that there are loose threads: *~ed cuffs,* e g on a coat sleeve; (fig) *Nerves/Tempers became ~ed,* strained, exasperated.

frazzle /ˈfræzl/ *n* completely worn or exhausted state: *worn to a ~.*

freak /frik/ *n* **1** absurd or most unusual idea, act or occurrence: (attrib) *a ~ storm.* **2** (also ˌ**~ of** ˋ**nature** person, animal or plant that is abnormal in form, e g a five-legged sheep. □ *vi* **~ *(out),*** (sl) have an intense emotional experience as from hallucinatory drugs. Hence, ˋ**~-out** *n* **~·ish** /-ɪʃ/ *adj* abnormal: *~ish behaviour.* **~·ish·ly** *adv* **~·ish·ness** *n* **~y** *adj* = ~ish.

freckle /ˈfrekl/ *n* one of the small light-brown spots on the human skin; (*pl*) such spots on the face and hands caused by sunburn. □ *vt,vi* [VP6A, 2A] (cause to) become covered with ~s: *a ~d forehead. Some people ~ more easily than others.*

free[1] /fri/ *adj* (freer, /ˈfriə(r)/, freest /ˈfriəst/) **1** (of a person) not a slave; not in the power of another person or other persons; not in prison; having personal rights and social and political liberty: *The prisoners were pardoned and set ~. Were the Pyramids built by slave labour or by ~ labour?* ⇨ also ~ labour. ˋ**~·born** *adj* inheriting liberty and rights of citizenship. **~·man** /-mən/ *n* (*pl* -men) person who is not a slave or a serf. ⇨ also ~man at **9** below. **2** (of a State, its citizens, and institutions) not controlled by a foreign government; having representative government in which private rights are respected: *America, the land of the ~; the ~ democracies of western Europe.* **3** not fixed or held back; able to move about without hindrance; unrestricted; not controlled by rules, regulations or conventions: *leave one end of the rope ~,* loose; *~ hydrogen,* not combined with another element. *You are ~ to go or stay as you please. Please feel free to ask questions. She is not ~ to marry,* cannot do so, e g because she has to look after her parents. *One of the parts has worked ~,* become loose, out of position. ***have/give/allow sb a ~ hand,*** permission or discretion to do what seems best without consulting others. ˈ**F~** ˋ**Church,** one not connected with the State. **the F~ Churches,** the noncomformists. ˈ**~** ˋ**enterprise,** the conduct of business and commerce with the minimum of government control. ˈ**~-and-**ˋ**easy** *adj* unceremonious. ˋ**~ fall** *n* fall from an aircraft at a great height without use of a parachute (until this is needed): *a ~-fall parachutist.* **a ~ fight,** one in which anyone present may join; one without rules. ˋ**~-for-all** *n* dispute, quarrel, etc in which all are allowed to express their views, fight for their own points of view, etc. ˋ**~·hand** *adj* (of drawings) done by hand with easy movements, no rules, compasses or other instrument being used: *a ~hand sketch.* ˈ**~-**ˋ**handed** *adj* generous; giving and spending money generously. ˋ**~·hold** *n* (legal) (holding of) land in absolute ownership. ⇨ *leasehold* at lease. ˋ**~·holder** *n* person who possesses ~hold estate. ˋ**~ house** *n* public-house not controlled by a brewery, and able, for this reason, to stock and sell all brands of beer, etc. ⇨ *tied house* at tie[2]. **~ labour** *n* workers not belonging to trade unions. ⇨ 1 above. **~·lance** /-lɑns *US:* -læns/ *n* **(a)** (in the Middle Ages) soldier ready to serve anyone for pay. **(b)** independent journalist, writer, etc earning his living by selling his services, wherever he can. □ *vi* work in this way: *He gave up his regular job in order to ~lance.* **'~-'liver** *n* person who indulges without restriction in pleasure (esp food and drink); hence, **'~-'living** *n, adj* **'~-'love** *n* agreed sexual relations without marriage. **'~ 'kick,** (football) kick allowed for a penalty without opposition from any other player. **'~ port** *n* port open to all traders alike, with no trade restrictions, taxes, import duties, etc. **'~-'range,** (of poultry) allowed to range freely (contrasted with *battery* birds). **'~ 'speech** *n* [U] right to speak in public without interference from the authorities. **'~-'spoken** *adj* not concealing one's opinions; speaking or spoken frankly. **'~-'standing** *adj* (of a piece of sculpture) standing independently so that it may be viewed from all sides. **'~·stone** *n* easily sawn sandstone and limestone. **'~·style,** (swimming) race where the competitors choose their own stroke, usually the crawl. **'~-'thinker** *n* person not accepting traditional religious teaching, but basing his ideas on reason; rationalist; hence, **'~-'thinking** *adj,* **'~-'thought** *n* **'~-'trade** *n* trade not hindered by customs duties to restrict imports or protect home industries. Hence, **'~-'trader** *n* supporter of this principle. **'~ translation** *n* not word for word, but giving the general meaning. **'~ 'verse** *n* without regular metre and rhyme. **'~·way** *n* (US) highway with several lanes; expressway. **'~-'wheel** *vi* move along on a bicycle with the pedals at rest (as when going downhill). **'~ 'will** *n* individual's power of guiding and choosing his actions (subject to limitations of the physical world, social environment, and inherited characteristics): *do sth of one's own ~ will,* without being required or compelled. □ *adj* voluntary: *a ~will offering.* **4 ~ from,** without: *~ from blame/error/anxiety;* released or exempt from: *~ from the ordinary regulations.* **~ of, (a)** outside: *as soon as the ship was ~ of the harbour.* **(b)** without: *a harbour ~ of ice. At last I am ~ of her,* have got away from her. **'~ 'agent,** person who is ~ to act without restrictions. **5** without payment; costing nothing: *~ tickets for the theatre; give sth away ~; 50p post ~,* 50p including cost of postage; *admission ~; ~ of income tax,* on which income tax need not be paid, or has been paid in advance (e g dividends on shares). ***(get sth) for ~,*** (colloq) without charge or payment. **'~-list** *n* **(a)** list of persons (to be) admitted ~, e g to a theatre or concert-hall. **(b)** list of goods (to be) admitted ~ of customs-duties. **'~ 'pass** *n* (for rail travel, etc) not paid for. **'~ on 'board,** (comm) where the exporter pays all the charges for putting the goods onto the ship. **6** (of place or time) not occupied or engaged; not being used; (of persons) not having time occupied; not doing anything: *There will be no rooms ~ in the hotel until after the holidays. Her afternoons are usually ~. She is usually ~ in the afternoon(s).* **have one's hands ~, (a)** have them empty, not being used. **(b)** be in a position to do as one likes; have no work or duties that demand attention. ⇨ tie²(5). **7** coming or given readily; lavish; profuse: *a ~ flow of water; ~ with his money; ~ bloomers,* plants that have a large number of blooms. *He is very ~ with his advice,* willingly gives plenty of advice. **8** without constraint: *He is somewhat ~ in his conversation,* not quite as proper or decent as he ought to be. ***make ~ with sth/sb,*** use property, persons as if they were one's own: *He seems to have made ~ with my whisky while I was away. He is/makes rather too ~ with the waitresses/the wives of his friends,* is too familiar or impudent in his behaviour. **9** ***make sb ~ of,*** give him the right to share in the privileges *of* a company, citizenship *of* a city; give him the unrestricted use *of* one's library, etc. **~·man** /-mən/ *n* (*pl* -men) one who has been given the privileges of a city, usu a distinguished person. ⇨ 1 above. **~·ly** *adv* in a ~ manner; readily.

free² /fri/ *vt* (*pt,pp* freed /frid/) [VP6A,14] make free (*from*); set at liberty: *~ an animal from a trap; ~ a country from oppression; ~ oneself from debt.* **freed·man** /'fridmən/ *n* (*pl* -men) slave set free.

free·booter /'fributə(r)/ *n* pirate; buccaneer.

free·dom /'fridəm/ *n* [U] condition of being free (all senses); [C] particular kind of ~: *the four ~s,* ~ of speech, ~ of religion, ~ from fear, ~ from want; *give slaves their ~; give sb ~ to do what he thinks best; speak with ~,* without constraint, fearing nothing; *the ~ of the seas,* (in international law) the right of ships of neutral countries to sail the seas without interference from warships of countries at war; *give a friend the ~ of one's house/library,* allow him to use it freely. ***give sb/receive the ~ of a town/city,*** full rights of citizenship (as an honour for distinguished services).

free·mason /'frimeɪsn/ *n* member of a secret society (with branches in many parts of Europe and America) for mutual help and fellowship. **~ry** *n* [U] system and institutions of the ~s; instinctive sympathy between people of similar interests, the same sex: *the ~ry of the Press.*

free·sia /'friziə/ *n* kinds of flowering bulbous plant.

freeze /friz/ *vt,vi* (*pt* froze /frəʊz/, *pp* frozen /'frəʊzn/) **1** [VP2A,C] (impers) be so cold that water turns into ice: *It was freezing last night. What freezing weather! It froze hard yesterday.* **'~ing-point** *n* temperature at which a liquid (esp water) ~s. **2** [VP2A,C] (of water) become ice; (of other substances) become hard or stiff from cold: *Water ~s when the temperature falls below 0°C (32°F). The lake froze over,* became covered with ice. ***make one's blood ~,*** fill one with terror. **3** [VP2A,C] be or feel very cold: *I'm freezing. Two of the men froze to death,* died of frost. **4** [VP6A, 15B] make cold; make hard; cover with ice: *frozen food,* preserved by being kept very cold, ⇨ *refrigeration* at refrigerate; *frozen roads,* with the surface of mud, snow, etc hardened by frost. *The lake was frozen over. If this frost lasts the ships in the harbour will be frozen in,* be fast in the ice. **'freezing-mixture** *n* one of salt, snow, etc used to ~ liquids. ***~ one's blood,*** fill one with terror. **5** [VP6A] make assets, credits, etc temporarily or permanently unrealizable; stabilize prices, wages: *'price-freezing* and *'wage-freezing* (as methods to cure inflation). **6** (sl) [VP15B] ***~ sb out,*** exclude him from business, society, etc by competition, cold behaviour, etc. **7** (sl) [VP3A] ***~ on to sth,*** take or keep a very tight hold of it. **8** [VP2A,C] become motionless, e g of an animal that stands quite still to avoid attracting attention. [VP2C] ***~ up,*** (of an actor) be unable to speak, move, etc on the stage. □ *n* **1** period of freezing weather. **2**

severe control, stabilization, of incomes, wages, dividends, etc: *a 'wage-~.* **3 'deep-'~,** (part of a) refrigerator where a very low temperature is used. ⇨ also deep². **freezer** *n* machine for freezing: *an ice-cream ~r;* compartment or room for freezing.

freight /freɪt/ *n* (money charged for) the carriage of goods from place to place by water (in US also by land); the goods carried: *'~liner,* ⇨ liner-train; (US) *~ train/car,* (= GB *goods train*). □ *vt* [VP6A,14] load (a ship) with cargo; send or carry (goods): *a ship ~ed with wheat; ~ a boat with fruit.* **~er** *n* ship or aircraft that carries mainly ~ (cargo).

French /frentʃ/ *adj* of France or the people of France. **'~ 'dressing** *n* salad dressing of oil and vinegar. **'~ fries** /frɑɪz/ *n pl* (US) = (GB) chips. **'~ 'horn** *n* brass wind instrument. ⇨ the illus at brass. **'~ 'window** *n* one that serves as both a window and a door, opening on to a garden or balcony. ⇨ the illus at window. ***take ~ leave,*** do sth; go away, without asking permission or giving notice. □ *n* the ~ language. **~·man** /-mən/ *n* (*pl* -men) man of ~ birth or nationality.

fren·etic /frə'netɪk/ *adj* frenzied; frantic.

frenzy /'frenzɪ/ *n* [U] violent excitement: *in a ~ of despair/enthusiasm; rouse an audience to absolute ~.* **fren·zied** /'frenzɪd/ *adj* driven to ~; wildly excited. **fren·zied·ly** *adv*

fre·quency /'frikwənsɪ/ *n* **1** [U] frequent occurrence: *the ~ of earthquakes in Japan.* **2** [C] (*pl* -cies) rate of occurrence; number of repetitions (in a given time): *a ~ of 25 per second,* e g of an alternating electric current.

fre·quent /fri'kwent/ *vt* [VP6A] go often to (a place); be often found in or at: *Frogs ~ wet places. He no longer ~s bars.* □ *adj* /'frikwənt/ often happening; numerous; common; habitual: *Hurricanes are ~ here in autumn. He's a ~ visitor.* **~·ly** *adv*

fresco /'freskəʊ/ *n* (*pl* -cos, -coes /-kəʊz/) **1** [U] pigment applied to moist plaster surfaces and allowed to dry; method of painting with this pigment: *painting in ~.* **2** [C] picture painted in this way: *the ~(e)s in St Peter's, Rome.* □ *vt* paint (a wall, etc) in ~.

fresh /freʃ/ *adj* (-er, -est) **1** newly made, produced, gathered, grown, arrived, etc. ⇨ stale, *faded* at fade: *~ flowers/fruit/eggs/milk; ~ paint* (= still wet); *a man ~ from the country; a boy ~ from school,* who has only recently finished his school course. **~·man** /-mən/ *n* (*pl* -men) student in his first year at a college or university. **2** (of food) not salted, tinned or frozen; *~ butter/meat;* (of water) not salt; not sea-water. **'~·water** *adj* of ~ water, not of the sea: *~water fish; ~water fishermen.* **3** new or different: *Is there any ~ news? Take a ~ sheet of paper and start again. He didn't throw much ~ light* (= give much new information) *on the subject.* ***break ~ ground,*** (fig) start sth new, find new facts. **4** (of the air, wind, weather) cool; refreshing: *a ~ breeze,* blowing rather strongly; *go out for some ~ air; in the ~ air,* out of doors. **5** bright and pure: *~ colours;* bright and pure in colour: *a ~ complexion.* **6** (US colloq) presumptuous, impudent (esp towards sb of the opposite sex): *Tell that young man not to get/be so ~ with your sister.* □ *adv* (in hyphened compounds) ~ly, newly: *~-caught fish; ~-killed meat; ~-painted doors.* **~·ly** *adv* (only with *pp,* without hyphen) recently: *~ly gathered peaches.* **~en** /'freʃn/ *vt,vi* make or become ~. **~er** *n* = ~man. **~·ness** *n*

fret¹ /fret/ *vi,vt* (-tt-) **1** [VP2A,C,6A,15A] worry; (cause to) be discontented or bad-tempered: *What are you ~ting about? Don't ~ over trifles. She ~s at even the slightest delays. Small babies often ~ in hot weather. She'll ~ herself to death one of these days.* **2** [VP6A] wear away by rubbing or biting at: *a horse ~ting its bit; ~ted rope; a channel ~ted through the rock by a stream.* □ *n* irritation; querulousness: *in a ~.* **~·ful** /-fl/ *adj* discontented; irritable; *a ~ful baby.* **~·fully** /-flɪ/ *adv*

fret² /fret/ *vt* (-tt-) [VP6A] decorate (wood) with patterns made by cutting or sawing. **'~·work** *n* [U] work in decorative patterns; wood cut with such patterns by using a ~saw. **'~·saw** *n* very narrow saw, fixed in a frame, for cutting designs in thin sheets of wood.

fret³ /fret/ *n* one of the metal ridges set at intervals across the fingerboard of a guitar, banjo, etc to act as a guide for the fingers to press the strings at the correct place.

Freud·ian /'frɔɪdɪən/ *adj* of the psychoanalytic theories of Sigmund Freud /frɔɪd/ (1856—1939), the Austrian psychoanalyst. **'~ 'slip,** (colloq) instance when a speaker accidentally says something contrary to what was intended and which seems to reveal his true thoughts.

fri·able /'frɑɪəbl/ *adj* easily crumbled. **fria·bil·ity** /'frɑɪə'bɪlətɪ/ *n*

friar /'frɑɪə(r)/ *n* man who is a member of one of certain religious orders, esp one who has vowed to live in poverty.

fric·assee /'frɪkə'si/ *n* [C,U] (dish of) meat or poultry cut up, fried or stewed, and served with sauce. □ *vt* make a ~ of.

frica·tive /'frɪkətɪv/ *adj, n* (consonant) produced with audible friction when the air is expelled through a narrowing of the air passage: *The sounds* /f, v, θ/ *are ~s.*

fric·tion /'frɪkʃn/ *n* **1** [U] the rubbing of one thing against another, esp when this wastes energy. **2** [C,U] (instance of a) difference of opinion leading to argument and quarrelling: *political ~ between two countries; ~(s) between parents with old-fashioned ideas and their children with newer ideas.*

Fri·day /'frɑɪdɪ/ *n* sixth day of the week. **'Good '~,** the ~ before Easter, the anniversary of the crucifixion of Jesus. **'man '~,** (from the story of Robinson Crusoe) faithful servant.

fridge /frɪdʒ/ *n* (abbr of) refrigerator.

fried /frɑɪd/ *pt,pp* of fry¹.

friend /frend/ *n* **1** person, not a relation, whom one knows and likes well; *my ~ Smith; some ~s of ours. We are great/good ~s. He has been a good ~ to me.* ***make ~s again,*** become ~s again after a disagreement, etc. ***make ~s with,*** become the ~ of. **2** helpful thing or quality: *Among these immoral young people, her shyness was her best ~.* **3** helper or sympathizer: *a good ~ of the poor.* **4 Friends,** members of the Society of F~s; Quaker. **~·less** *adj* having no ~s. **~-less·ness** *n*

friend·ly /'frendlɪ/ *adj* (-ier, -iest) acting, or ready to act, as a friend; showing or expressing kindness: *be ~ with sb; be ~ to a cause; a ~ smile; be on ~ terms with sb; a ~ match/game,* one not played in competition for a prize, etc. **F~**

Society, one for the mutual benefit of its members, e g during illness, unemployment, old age. **friend·li·ness** *n* [U] ~ feeling and behaviour.

friend·ship /ˈfrendʃɪp/ *n* **1** [U] being friends; the feeling or relationship that exists between friends: *live together in ~; my ~ for her.* **2** [C] instance or period of this feeling: *a ~ of twenty years; never to forget old ~s.*

frieze /friz/ *n* [C] ornamental band or strip along a wall (usu at the top), e g a horizontal band of sculpture on the outside of a building, or a strip of wallpaper with a special design just below the ceiling of a room.

frig·ate /ˈfrɪgət/ *n* fast sailing-ship formerly used in war; (modern use) fast escort vessel.

fright /frɑɪt/ *n* **1** [U] great and sudden fear: *die of ~; take ~ (at sth)*; [C] instance of this. ***get/have/give sb a ~.*** **2** [C] (colloq) ridiculous-looking person or thing: *What a ~ you look in that old hat!* □ *vt* (liter) frighten.

frighten /ˈfrɑɪtn/ *vt* [VP6A,15B,14] fill with fright or terror; alarm suddenly: *Did the noise ~ you? The barking of the dog ~ed the burglar away. She was nearly ~ed out of her life.* ***~ sb into/out of doing sth,*** cause him to do/not do sth by ~ing him. **fright·ened** *adj* (colloq) afraid: *be ~ed of sb or sth;* alarmed: *~ed at the idea of sth happening.* **~·ing** *adj* causing fright or terror: *a ~ing experience.*

fright·ful /ˈfrɑɪtfl/ *adj* **1** causing fear; dreadful: *a ~ accident.* **2** (colloq) very great; awful; unpleasant: *We had a ~ journey,* a very uncomfortable one. *What a ~ (= ugly) hat!* **~ly** /-flɪ/ *adv* **1** in a ~ way. **2** (colloq) very. **~·ness** *n*

frigid /ˈfrɪdʒɪd/ *adj* **1** cold: *~ weather; a ~ climate; the ~ zones,* those within the polar circles. **2** unfriendly; without ardour or sympathy; apathetic: *a ~ welcome; a ~ manner; ~ conversation; a ~ woman,* lacking in sexual desire. **~·ly** *adv* **frigid·ity** /frɪˈdʒɪdətɪ/ *n* [U].

frill /frɪl/ *n* **1** ornamental border on a dress, etc. **2** (*pl*) unnecessary adornments, e g to speech or writing; airs[1](6b), affectations. **fril·led** *adj* having ~s(1): *a ~ed skirt.* **frilly** *adj* having ~s; (colloq) too much ornamented.

fringe /frɪndʒ/ *n* [C] **1** ornamental border of loose threads, e g on a rug or shawl. **2** edge (of a crowd, forest, etc): *on the ~(s) of the forest; ˈ~ areas,* (esp) areas on the border of a district served by a broadcasting or television station (where reception may be poor); *ˈ~ group,* group of persons loosely attached to a larger group or party (but who may be rebellious or nonconformist in some respects); *~ benefits,* benefits, e g a rent-free house, the use of a car, additional to wages or salary. **3** part of (usu a woman's) hair cut short and allowed to hang over the forehead. □ *vt* [VP6A] put a ~ on; serve as a ~ to: *a roadside ~ed with trees.*

frip·pery /ˈfrɪpərɪ/ *n* [U] needless ornament, esp on dress; [C] (*pl* -ries) cheap ornament or useless trifle.

frisk /frɪsk/ *vi,vt* **1** [VP2A,C] jump and run about playfully. **2** [VP6A] pass the hands over (sb) to search for concealed weapons. **~y** *adj* (-ier, -iest) lively; ready to ~: *as ~y as a kitten.* **~·ily** *adv*

frit·ter[1] /ˈfrɪtə(r)/ *vt* [VP15B] ***~ away,*** waste on divided aims: *~ away one's time/energy/money.*

frit·ter[2] /ˈfrɪtə(r)/ *n* [C] piece of fried batter, usu with sliced fruit in it.

frivol /ˈfrɪvl/ *vi,vt* (-ll-) **1** [VP2A] behave in a silly, time-wasting way. **2** [VP15B] ***~ away,*** waste time, money, etc, foolishly.

friv·ol·ous /ˈfrɪvləs/ *adj* **1** not serious or important: *~ remarks/behaviour.* **2** (of persons) not serious; pleasure-loving. **~·ly** *adv* **friv·ol·ity** /frɪˈvolətɪ/ *n* **1** [U] ~ behaviour; lightness of character. **2** [C] (*pl* -ties) ~ act or utterance.

frizz /frɪz/ *vt* (of hair) form into masses of small curls. **~y** *adj* (-ier, -iest) (of hair) ~ed.

frizzle[1] /frɪzl/ *vt,vi* [VP6A,2A] cook, be cooked, with a spluttering noise: *bacon frizzling in the pan.*

frizzle[2] /frɪzl/ *vt,vi* [VP2C,15B] ***~ (up),*** (of hair) twist in small, crisp curls.

fro /frəʊ/ *adv* (only in) ***to and fro,*** backwards and forwards: *walking to and fro; journeys to and fro between London and Paris.*

frock /frok/ *n* **1** woman's dress or gown; dress for a girl or baby. **2** monk's long gown with loose sleeves. **3** **ˈ~-ˈcoat** *n* long coat, usu with square corners, formerly worn by men in the 19th c (now replaced by the *morning-coat*).

frog /frog *US:* frɔg/ *n* **1** small, cold-blooded, tailless jumping animal living in water and on land. ⇨ the illus at amphibian. **~·man** /-mən/ *n* (*pl* -men) person skilled in swimming under water with the aid of flippers on the feet and breathing apparatus. **ˈ~·march** *vt* carry (a prisoner) away, face downwards, by four men holding his arms and legs. **2** long button and loop for fastening to it, used to fasten cloaks, etc.

a frogman

frolic /ˈfrolɪk/ *vi* (*pt,pp* -icked) [VP2A,C] play about in a gay, lively way. □ *n* [C] outburst of gaiety or merrymaking; wild or merry prank. **~·some** /-səm/ *adj* inclined to ~; playful and merry.

from /frəm *strong form:* from/ *prep* **1** (used to introduce the place, point, person, etc that is the starting-point): *jump (down) ~ a wall; travel ~ London to Rome. bees going ~ flower to flower.* **2** (used to indicate the starting of a period of time): *~ the first of May; ~ childhood; ~ day to day; ~ beginning to end.* **3** (used to indicate the place, object, etc from which distance, absence, etc is stated): *ten miles ~ the coast; stay away ~ school; be/go away ~ home; far ~ blaming you,* not in any way doing so. **4** (showing the giver, sender, etc): *a letter ~ my brother; a present ~ his father. Tell him ~ me that....* **5** (showing the model, etc): *painted ~ nature/life,* with the actual scene, object, etc in front of the artist. **6** (showing the lower limit): *We have good Algerian wine ~ 80p a bottle,* at this price and at higher prices. *There were ~ ten to fifteen boys absent.* **7** (used to indicate the source from which sth is taken): *quotations ~ Shakespeare; draw water ~ a well; draw conclusions ~ the evidence; judge ~ appearances; ~ this point of view.* **8** (showing the material, etc used in a process, the material being changed as a result): *Wine is made ~ grapes. Steel is made ~ iron.* Cf *That bridge is made of steel.* **9** (used to indicate separation, removal, prevention, escape, avoidance, deprivation, etc. ⇨ *v* and *n* entries): *Take that knife (away) ~ the baby. When were you released ~ prison? What prevented/stopped/hindered you ~ coming?* **10** used to indicate change: *Things are going ~ bad to worse. The price has been increased ~ 20p to 25p.* **11** showing reason, cause or motive: *collapse ~ fatigue; suffer ~ starvation and disease; do sth ~ necessity, not ~ a sense of duty. F~ his looks you might think him stupid. F~ what I heard, the driver was to blame.* **12** (showing distinction or difference): *It differs ~ all the others. How would you know an Englishman ~ an American?* **13** (governing *advv* and *prep* phrases): *seen ~ above/below; looking at me ~ above/under her spectacles.*

frond /frond/ *n* leaf-like part of a fern or palm-tree.

front /frʌnt/ *n* **1** (usu *sing* with *def art;* used attrib) foremost or most important side: *the ~ of a building,* that with the main entrance; *the east/west ~ of the Palace; sitting in the ~ of the class,* in one of the foremost rows facing the teacher; *standing in ~ of the class,* facing the pupils; *a ~ seat; the ~ garden; a ~ room,* one in the ~ of a house: *the ~ page of a newspaper,* page 1; *~-page news,* news important enough for the ~ page: *a seat in the ~ part of the train.* ***(be) in the ~ rank,*** (fig) be well known or important. ***come to the ~,*** (fig) become conspicuous, well known, etc. **~ benches,** ⇨ bench. ***in ~,*** *adv* ***in ~ of,*** *prep: Please go in ~. There are some trees in ~ of the house.* **2** [C] (war) part where the fighting is taking place: *go/be sent to the ~; a ~ of 500 miles; successful on all ~s;* (fig) organized body or department of activity: *the home ~,* civilians as organized during a war. **3** road, promenade bordering the part of a town facing the sea; road or path bordering a lake: *have a walk along the (ˈsea)~; drive along the lake ~; a house on the ~,* facing the sea. **4** [U] ***have the ~ (to do sth),*** be impudent enough. ***put on/show/present a bold ~,*** face a situation with (apparent) boldness. **5** (**ˈshirt**) **~,** breast of a shirt (esp the starched ~ part of a man's (dress) shirt). **6** (theatre) auditorium; part where the audience sits. **7** (met) boundary between masses of cold and warm air: *a cold ~/warm ~.* **8** (poet, rhet) forehead; face. **9** apparent leader (*a ˈ~ man*) or group of persons (*a ˈ~ organization*) serving as a cover for the secret or illegal activities of an anonymous person or group. □ *vt,vi* **1** [VP6A,2A, C] face: *hotels that ~ the sea; windows ~ing the street; a house ~ing north, ~ing upon/towards the lake.* **2** [VP6A] (old use) confront; oppose: *~ danger.*

front·age /ˈfrʌntɪdʒ/ *n* [C] extent of a piece of land or a building along its front, esp bordering a road or river: *For sale, office buildings with ~s on two streets; factory premises with a good river ~; a building site with a road ~ of 500 metres.*

frontal /ˈfrʌntl/ *adj* of, on or to, the front: *a ~ attack.* ⇨ flank, rear; *full ~ nudity,* of the whole of the front of the body.

fron·tier /ˈfrʌntɪə(r) *US:* frʌnˈtɪər/ *n* [C] **1** part of a country bordering on another country; (land on each side of a) boundary: *a town on the ~;* (attrib) *~ disputes/incidents;* (esp US, in the past) farthest part of a country to which settlement has spread, beyond which there is wild or unsettled land. **~s·man** /-zmən/ *n* (*pl* -men) man who lives on a ~; pioneer in a newly settled district near the ~. **2** (fig) extreme limit: *the ~s of knowledge;* underdeveloped area (e g of scientific research).

front·is·piece /ˈfrʌntɪspis/ *n* illustration placed opposite the title-page of a book.

frost /frost *US:* frɔst/ *n* **1** [U] weather condition with temperature below the freezing-point of water; [C] occasion or period of such weather: *plants killed by ~; ten degrees of ~, early ~s,* i e in autumn; *late ~s,* i e in spring. **ˈJack F~,** ~ personified. **ˈ~-bite** *n* [U] injury to tissue in the body from freezing. **ˈ~-bitten** *adj* having, suffering from, ~-bite. **ˈ~-bound** *adj* (of the ground) made hard by ~. **2** [U] white powder-like coating of frozen vapour on the ground, roofs, plants, etc: *ˈwhite/ˈhoar ~,* with this coating: *ˈblack ~,* without it. **3** [C] (colloq) event which fails to come up to expectations or to arouse interest: *The entertainment was a ~,* no one enjoyed it. □ *vt,vi* **1** [VP6A] cover with ~(**2**): *~ed window-panes;* cover (a cake, etc) with finely powdered sugar. **2** [VP6A] injure or kill (plants, etc) with ~(**1**). **3** [VP6A] give a roughened surface to (glass) to make it opaque: *~ed glass.* **4** [VP2A,C] become covered with ~(**2**): *The windscreen of my car ~ed over during the night.* **~·ing** *n* [U] icing(**1**).

frosty /ˈfrostɪ *US:* ˈfrɔstɪ/ *adj* **1** cold with frost: *~ weather; a ~ morning.* **2** (fig) unfriendly; without warmth of feeling: *~ smiles/looks; a ~ welcome.* **frost·ily** *adv* **frosti·ness** *n*

froth /froθ/ *n* [U] **1** creamy mass of small bubbles; foam: *a glass of beer with a lot of ~ on it.* **2** light, worthless talk or ideas. □ *vi* [VP2A,C] have, give off, ~: *A mad dog may ~ at the mouth.* **~y** *adj* (-ier, -iest) of, like, covered with, ~: *~y beer/conversation.* **~·ily** /-əlɪ/ *adv* **~i·ness** *n*

fro·ward /ˈfrəʊəd/ *adj* (old use) perverse; not easily controlled.

frown /frɑʊn/ *vi* [VP2A,3A] draw the eyebrows together, causing lines on the forehead (to express displeasure, puzzlement, deep thought, etc): *~ at sb.* ***~ (up)on,*** disapprove of: *Gambling is very much ~ed upon here.* □ *n* [C] ~ing look; drawing together of the brows: *There was a deep ~ on his brow. He looked at her with a ~ of disapproval.* **~·ing·ly** *adv*

frowsty /ˈfrɑʊstɪ/ *adj* (of the atmosphere of a room) warm and musty; fuggy.

frowzy /ˈfrɑʊzɪ/ *adj* **1** ill-smelling; stuffy (like an overheated room). **2** slatternly; untidy; uncared for.

froze, frozen ⇨ freeze.

fruc·tify /ˈfrʌktɪfɑɪ/ *vt,vi* (*pt,pp* -fied) [VP6A,2A] make or become fruitful or fertile. **fruc·ti·fi·ca·tion** /ˌfrʌktɪfɪˈkeɪʃn/ *n*

fru·gal /ˈfrugl/ *adj* careful, economical (esp *of* food, expenditure); costing little: *a ~ meal; a ~ housekeeper; be ~ of one's time and money.* **~·ly** /-glɪ/ *adv* **~·ity** /fruˈgæləti/ *n* [U] being ~; [C] (*pl* -ties) instance of this.

fruit /frut/ *n* **1** (usu *sing* as a collective *n*) that part of a plant or tree that contains the seeds and is used as food, e g apples, bananas: *People are eating more ~ than they used to. Do you eat much ~?* **ˈ~-cake** *n* rich cake containing dried currants, peel, etc. **ˈ~-fly** *n* (*pl* -flies) (kinds of a) common small fly that feeds on fermenting ~. '~ **knife** *n* one with a silver blade, for cutting ~ at meals. '~ '**salad** *n* various ~s (= kinds of ~) cut up and mixed in a bowl. **2** [C] (bot) that part of any plant in which the seed is formed. **3** (*pl*) any plant or vegetable products that may be used for food: *the ~s of the earth,* including grain, etc. **4** (fig, often *pl*) profit, result or reward (of labour, industry, study, etc): *the ~s of industry. I hope your hard work will bear ~. His knowledge is the ~ of long study.* **5** '**~-machine** *n* (colloq) coin-operated gambling machine. □ *vi* (of trees, bushes, etc) bear ~: *These trees ~ well.* **~·erer** /'frutərə(r)/ *n* person who sells ~. **~·ful** /-fl/ *adj* producing ~ or (fig) good results; productive: *a ~ful career. The last session of Parliament was particularly ~ful,* much useful work was accomplished. **~·fully** /-flɪ/ *adv* **~·ful·ness** *n* **~·less** *adj* without ~ or (fig) results or success; profitless: *~less efforts.* **~·less·ly** *adv* **~·less·ness** *n* **~y** *adj* **1** of or like ~ in smell or taste. **2** (colloq) full of rough (often suggestive) humour: *a ~y novel.* **3** (colloq) rich; mellow; florid: *a ~y voice.*

fru·ition /fru'ɪʃn/ *n* [U] realization of hopes; getting what was wanted: *aims brought to ~; plans that come to ~.*

frump /frʌmp/ *n* person dressed in old-fashioned and dowdy clothes. **~·ish** /-ɪʃ/, **~y** *adjj*

frus·trate /frʌ'streɪt *US:* 'frʌstreɪt/ *vt* [VP6A,15A] prevent (sb) from doing sth; prevent (sb's plans) from being carried out: *~ an enemy in his plans/ the plans of an enemy; be ~d in an attempt to do sth.* **frus·tra·tion** /frʌ'streɪʃn/ *n* [U] frustrating or being ~d; [C] instance of this; defeat or disappointment: *embittered by numerous frustrations.*

fry[1] /fraɪ/ *vt,vi* (3rd pers sing *pres t* fries, *pt,pp* fried) [VP6A,2A] cook, be cooked, in boiling fat: *fried chicken. The sausages are frying/being*

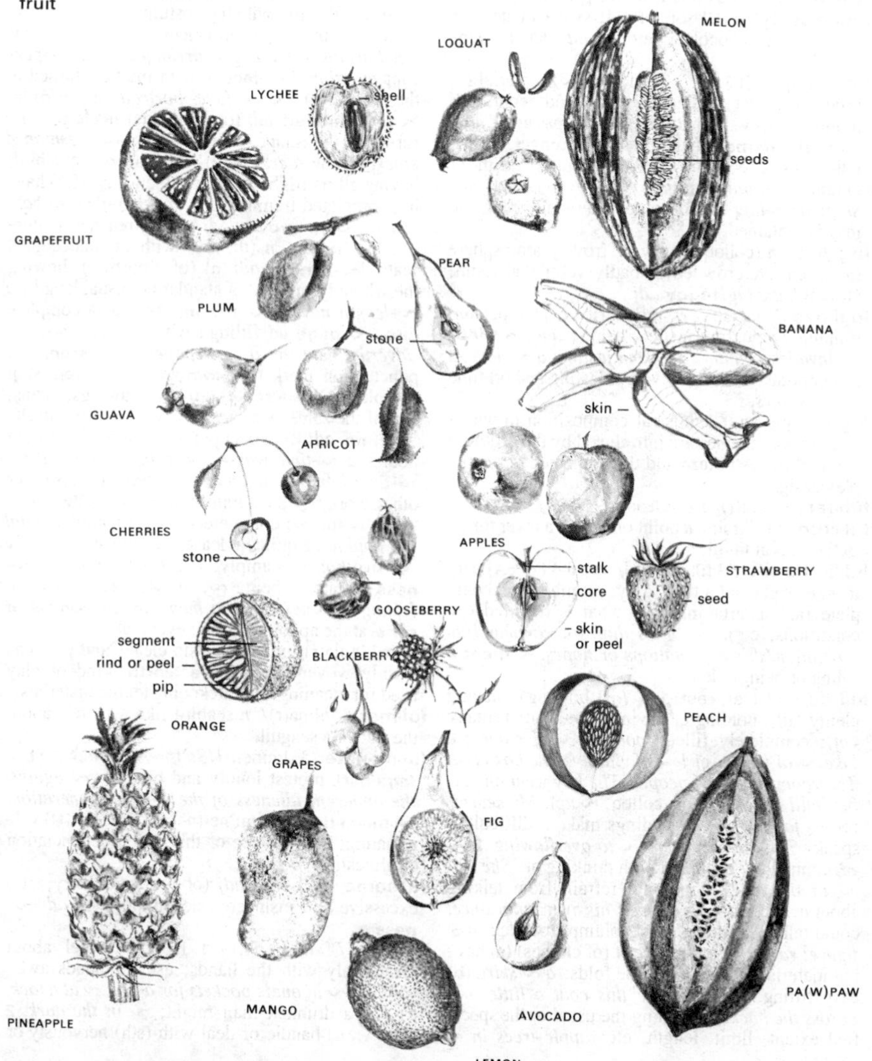

fried. ˋ~·**ing-pan,** US ˋ~**-pan** *n* shallow pan with a long handle used for frying. ***out of the frying-pan into the fire,*** from a bad situation to one that is worse. **fryer, frier** /ˋfraɪə(r)/ *n* small young chicken for frying.

fry[2] /fraɪ/ *n* (*pl* unchanged) newly hatched fishes. ***small fry,*** young or insignificant creatures; persons of no importance.

fuchsia /ˋfjuʃə/ *n* shrub with bell-like drooping flowers, pink, red or purple.

fuck /fʌk/ (⚠ taboo) *vt,vi* **1** [VP6A,2A] have sexual intercourse (with). **2** [VP2C] ~ ***off,*** (esp as an *imper*) go away. □ *int* expression of annoyance, etc. ~·**ing** *adj* used to indicate annoyance (but often meaningless): *What a ~ing nuisance!* ~**er** *n* fool; idiot.

fuddle /ˋfʌdl/ *vt* [VP6A,15A] make stupid, esp with alcoholic drink: *~ oneself/one's brain with gin; in a ~d state.*

fuddy-duddy /ˋfʌdɪ dʌdɪ/ *n* (*pl* -duddies) (colloq) fussy and old-fashioned person.

fudge /fʌdʒ/ *n* [U] sort of soft sweet made with milk, sugar, chocolate, etc. □ *int* (dated) Nonsense!

fuel /ˋfjuḷ/ *n* [U] (*pl* = kinds of ~) material for producing heat or energy, e g wood, coal, oil, uranium; (fig) sth that inflames the passions. ***add ~ to the flames,*** make passions stronger. □ *vt,vi* (-ll-, US also -l-) [VP6A,2A] supply with or obtain ~: *a power station ~led by uranium; ~ a ship; a* ˋ*~ling station,* one where oil, coal, etc may be obtained.

fug /fʌg/ *n* (colloq) frusty or frowzy atmosphere (as in an overcrowded or badly ventilated room, etc): *What a fug!* **fuggy** *adj*

fugi·tive /ˋfjudʒətɪv/ *n, adj* (attrib only) **1** (person) running away from justice, danger, etc: *~s from an invaded country; ~s from justice; a ~ slave.* **2** of temporary interest or value; lasting a short time only: *~ verses.*

fugue /fjug/ *n* [C] musical composition in which one or more themes are introduced by the different parts or voices in turn and then repeated in a complex design.

füh·rer /ˋfjʊərə(r)/ *n* (G) leader.

ful·crum /ˋfʌlkrəm/ *n* point on which a lever turns. ⇨ the illus at lever.

ful·fil (US also **ful·fill**) /fʊlˋfɪl/ *vt* (-ll-) [VP6A] perform or carry out a task, duty, promise, etc; complete (an undertaking); do what is required (by conditions, etc): *~ one's duties/a command/an obligation/sb's expectations or hopes.* ~·**ment** *n* ~ling or being ~led.

full /fʊl/ *adj* (-er, -est) **1** ~ ***(of),*** holding or having plenty (*of*), holding or having as much or as many (*of*); completely filled: *pockets ~ of money; a lake ~ of fish; a girl ~ of vitality. The box is ~. The room was ~ of people. The boy went on eating until he was ~* (or, colloq, *~ up*). *My heart is too ~ for words,* My feelings make it difficult to speak. *The drawers were ~ to overflowing.* **2** ~ ***of,*** completely occupied with thinking of: *She was ~ of the news,* could not refrain from talking about it. *He was ~ of himself/his own importance,* could talk of nothing else. **3** plump; rounded: *a ~ figure; rather ~ in the face.* **4** (of clothes) **(a)** having material arranged in wide folds: *a ~ skirt.* **(b)** easy fitting: *Please make this coat a little ~er across the back.* **5** reaching the usual or the specified extent, limit, length, etc: *apple-trees in ~ blossom; wait a ~ hour,* not less than an hour. *He fell ~ length,* so that he was lying stretched out on the floor/ground. *Her dress was a ~ three inches below the knee.* **6** (with *comp* and *superl*) complete: *A ~er account will be given later. This is the ~est account yet received.* **7** (phrases and compounds) ***in ~,*** without omitting or shortening anything: *write one's name in ~,* e g John Henry Smith, *not* J H Smith; *pay a debt in ~,* pay the whole of what is owed. ***at ~ speed,*** at the highest possible speed. ***to the ~,*** to the utmost extent; quite: *enjoy oneself to the ~.* ***in ~ career,*** while at the maximum rate of progress. ˋ~**-back** *n* player (defender) placed farthest from the centre line, behind the half-backs (in football, etc). ⇨ the illus at football. ˈ~-ˋ**blooded** *adj* **(a)** vigorous; hearty; virile. **(b)** of unmixed ancestry or race. ˈ~-ˋ**blown** *adj* (of flowers) completely open. ˈ~-ˋ**bottomed** *adj* (of wigs) covering the back and sides of the neck. ˈ~ ˋ**dress** *n* dress as worn on ceremonial occasions: *a ~-dress rehearsal,* (theatre) with the costumes, etc that are to be worn at public performances; *a ~-dress debate (in Parliament) one pre-arranged on an important question.* ˈ~ ˋ**face** *n* with the face turned to the viewer(s): *a ~-face portrait.* ⇨ profile. ˈ~**y-**ˋ**fashioned** *adj* (of garments) made to conform to the shape of the body: *~y-fashioned stockings/sweaters.* ˈ~**(y)-**ˋ**fledged** *adj* (of a bird) having all its flight feathers; able to fly; (fig) having completed training, etc: *a ~(y)-fledged barrister.* ˈ~**(y)-**ˋ**grown** *adj* having reached maturity. ˈ~ ˋ**house** *n* (theatre) with no unoccupied seats. ˈ~-ˋ**length** *adj* **(a)** (of a portrait) showing the whole figure. **(b)** of standard or usual length: *a ~-length novel.* ˈ~ ˋ**moon,** seem as a complete disc. ˋ~**-page** *adj* filling a whole page: *a ~-page advertisement in a newspaper.* ˈ~ ˋ**stop,** the punctuation mark (.). ***come to a ~ stop,*** stop completely. ˈ~-ˋ**scale** *adj* (of drawings, plans, etc) of the same size, area, etc of the object itself. ˋ~**-time** *adj, adv* occupying all normal working hours: *a ~-time worker; working ~-time; It's a ~-time job,* one that leaves no time for leisure or other work. ⇨ *part-time* at part[1](1). **fully** /ˋfʊlɪ/ *adv* **1** to the ~; completely: *~y satisfied; capital ~y paid up.* **2** quite; at least: *The journey will take ~y two hours.* **3** amply: *I feel ~y rewarded.* ~**-ness** *n* state of being ~; in ~ measure: *have a feeling of ~ness after a meal.* ***in the ~ness of time,*** at the appointed time; eventually.

fuller /ˋfʊlə(r)/ *n* person who cleans and thickens freshly woven cloth. ˈ~**'s** ˋ**earth,** kind of clay used for cleaning and thickening textile materials.

ful·mar /ˋfʊlmə(r)/ *n* seabird like a petrel, about the size of a seagull.

ful·mi·nate /ˋfʌlmɪneɪt *US:* ˋfʊl-/ *vi* [VP2A,3A] ~ ***(against),*** protest loudly and bitterly: *~ against the apparent idleness of the younger generation.* **ful·mi·na·tion** /ˈfʌlmɪˋneɪʃn *US:* ˈfʊl-/ *n* [U] fulminating; [C] instance of this; bitter denunciation or protest.

ful·some /ˋfulsəm/ *adj* (of praise, flattery, etc) excessive and insincere; sickening. ~·**ly** *adv* ~**-ness** *n*

fumble /ˋfʌmbl/ *vi,vt* **1** [VP2A,C] feel about uncertainly with the hands; use the hands awkwardly: *~ in one's pockets for a key; ~ at a lock,* e g, as a drunken man might; *~ in the dark.* **2** [VP6A,2A] handle or deal with (sth) nervously or incompetently: ~ *a ball*, e g in cricket. **fumbler** /ˋfʌmblə(r)/ *n* person who ~s.

fume /fjum/ *n* **1** (usu *pl*) strong-smelling smoke, gas or vapour: *air thick with the ~s of cigars; petrol ~s; ~s of incense.* **2** (liter) excited state of mind: *in a ~ of anxiety.* □ *vi,vt* **1** [VP2A,C,3A] ~ ***(at)***, given off ~s; pass away in ~s; (fig) betray repressed anger or irritation: ~ *because one is kept waiting; ~ at sb's incompetence.* **2** [VP6A] treat (wood, etc) with ~s (to darken the surface, etc): *~d oak.*

fu·mi·gate /ˋfjumɪgeɪt/ *vt* [VP6A] disinfect by means of fumes: ~ *a room used by someone with an infectious disease; ~ rose-bushes,* to kill insect pests. **fu·mi·ga·tion** /ˈfjumɪˋgeɪʃn/ *n*

fun /fʌn/ *n* [U] **1** amusement, sport; playfulness: *What fun the children had at the seaside,* How they enjoyed themselves! *He's full of fun. I don't see the fun of doing that,* do not think it is amusing. **ˋfun-fair** *n* = amusement park. ⇨ **amuse.** ***fun and games,*** (colloq) lively merry-making; pranks. ***make fun of, poke fun at,*** ridicule; cause people to laugh at: *It is wrong to make fun of a cripple.* ***for/in fun,*** as a joke, for amusement; not seriously: *He said it only in fun.* **2** that which causes merriment or amusement: *Your new friend is great fun,* is very amusing. *Sailing is good fun.* **3** (attrib, colloq): *a ˋfun car/hat/fur,* used, worn for amusement.

func·tion /ˋfʌŋkʃn/ *n* [C] **1** special activity or purpose of a person or thing: *the ~s of a judge/an officer of state; the ~ of the heart,* i e to pump blood through the body; *the ~s of the nerves; the ~ of education.* **2** public ceremony or event; social gathering or an important and formal kind: *the numerous ~s that the Queen must attend.* □ *vi* [VP2A,C] fulfill a ~**(1)**; operate; act: *The telephone was not ~ing,* was out of order. *Some English adverbs ~ as adjectives.* **~al** /-nl/ *adj* of a ~; having, designed to have, ~s**(1)**: *a ~al disorder,* an illness caused by the failure of an organ of the body to perform its ~; *~al architecture,* designed to serve practical purposes, beauty of appearance being secondary; *schools designed according to ~al principles.* **~·al·ism** /-nḷɪzm/ *n* principle that the ~ of objects, etc should determine their design, the materials used, etc. **~·al·ist** /-nḷɪst/ *n* adherent of ~alism.

func·tion·ary /ˋfʌŋkʃṇərɪ *US:* -ṇerɪ/ *n* (*pl* -ries) (often rather contemptuous) person with official functions.

fund /fʌnd/ *n* [C] **1** store or supply (of non-material things): *a ~ of common sense/humour/amusing stories.* **2** (often *pl*) sum of money available for a purpose: *a reˋlief ~,* e g to help sufferers from a flood or other disaster; *ˋmission ~s,* for the work of missionaries. **3** (*pl*) resources in the form of money: *the (public) ~s,* the stock of the national debt as a form of investment: *have £5 000 in the ~s.* ***no ~s,*** notice (given by a bank) that the person who has drawn a cheque on it has no money in his account. □ *vt* [VP6A] convert (short-term debts) into a long-term debt at fixed interest: *~ed debts,* part of the National Debt, with no fixed date for repayment; provide a sum of money for the payment of interest.

fun·da·men·tal /ˈfʌndəˋmentl/ *adj* ~ ***(to),*** of or forming a foundation; of great importance; serving as a starting-point: *the ~ rules of arithmetic,* those which must be learnt first and on which everything that follows depends. □ *n* (usu *pl*) ~ rule or principle; essential part: *the ~s of mathematics.* **~ly** /-tḷɪ/ *adv* **~·ism** /-ɪzm/ *n* [U] maintenance of the traditional beliefs of the Christian religion (such as the accuracy of everything in the Bible), in opposition to more modern teachings. **~·ist** /-ɪst/ *n* supporter of ~ism.

fu·neral /ˋfjunrəl/ *n* [C] **1** burial or cremation of a dead person with the usual ceremonies. **2** (attrib use) of or for a ~: *a ˋ~ procession; a ˋ~ march,* sad and solemn piece of music; *a ˋ~ pile/pyre,* pile of wood, etc on which a corpse is burnt; *a ˋ~ parlor,* (US) undertaker's offices. **fu·ner·eal** /fjuˋnɪərɪəl/ *adj* of or like a ~; gloomy; dismal; dark: *a funereal expression.*

fun·gus /ˋfʌŋgəs/ *n* (*pl* **-gi** /-gaɪ/) plant without leaves, flowers or green colouring matter, growing on other plants or on decaying matter, e g old wood: *Mushrooms, toadstools and mildew are all fungi.* **fun·gi·cide** /ˋfʌŋgɪsaɪd/ *n* substance that destroys fungi. **fun·goid** /ˋfʌŋgɔɪd/ *adj* of or like fungi. **fun·gous** /ˋfʌŋgəs/ *adj* of or like, caused by, fungi.

fungi

fu·nicu·lar /fjuˋnɪkjʊlə(r)/ *adj*: ~ *railway,* one on a slope, worked by a cable and a stationary engine. □ *n* ~ railway.

funk /fʌŋk/ *n* (colloq) **1** great fear: *be in a ~.* **2** coward. □ *vi,vt* [VP6A,2A] show fear; (try to) escape (doing sth) because of fear.

funnel /ˋfʌnl/ *n* **1** tube or pipe wide at the top and narrowing at the bottom, for pouring liquids or powders through small openings. **2** outlet for smoke (smoke stack, metal chimney) of a steamer, railway engine, etc. ⇨ the illus at **ship. ˈtwo-/ˈthree-ˋ~led** *adj* having two/three ~s. □ *vt,vi* (-ll-, US -l-) [VP6A,2A] (cause to) move through, or as if through, a ~.

funny /ˋfʌnɪ/ *adj* (-ier, -iest) **1** causing fun or amusement: ~ *stories.* **2** strange; queer; causing surprise: *There's something ~ about the affair,* sth strange, perhaps not quite honest or straightforward. **ˋ~-bone** *n* part of the elbow over which a very sensitive nerve passes. **the funnies,** *n* (colloq) comic strips. **fun·nily** /ˋfʌnḷɪ/ *adv* in a ~ way: *funnily* (= strangely) *enough.* **fun·ni·ness** *n*

fur /fɜ(r)/ *n* **1** [U] soft thick hair covering certain animals, e g cats, rabbits. ***make the fur fly,*** cause a disturbance. ***fur and feather,*** furred animals and birds. **2** [C] animal skin with the fur on it, esp when made into garments: *a fine fox fur; wearing expensive furs;* (attrib) *a fur coat,* one made of furs. **3** [U] rough coating on a person's tongue when ill; crust on the inside of a kettle, boiler, etc when the water heated in it contains lime. □ *vt,vi*

(-rr-) [VP6A,2A] cover, become covered, with fur(3): *a furred tongue/kettle.* **furry** /ˈfɜrɪ/ *adj* (-ier, -iest) of or like fur; covered with fur.

fur·be·low /ˈfɜbɪləʊ/ *n* (often ***frills and ~s***) (old-fashioned) piece of elaborate or unnecessary trimming (on a dress, etc).

fur·bish /ˈfɜbɪʃ/ *vt* [VP6A] polish, e g by removing rust from; make like new (esp sth that has not been used for a long time): *~ a sword; newly ~ed skills.*

furi·ous /ˈfjʊərɪəs/ *adj* violent; uncontrolled; full of fury: *a ~ struggle/storm/quarrel. running at a ~ pace; be ~ with sb/at what sb has done. The fun was fast and ~,* uproarious, wild. **~·ly** *adv*

furl /fɜl/ *vt,vi* [VP6A,2A] (of sails, flags, umbrellas, etc) roll up: *~ the sails of a yacht. This fan/umbrella doesn't ~ neatly.*

fur·long /ˈfɜlɒŋ *US:* -lɔŋ/ *n* 220 yards (= 201 metres); eighth of a mile.

fur·lough /ˈfɜləʊ/ *n* [C,U] (permission for) absence from duty (esp civil officials, members of the armed forces, missionaries, living abroad): *going home on ~; six months' ~; have a ~ every three years.* ⇨ leave².

fur·nace /ˈfɜnɪs/ *n* **1** enclosed fireplace for heating buildings with hot water or steam in pipes. **2** enclosed space for heating metals, making glass, etc.

fur·nish /ˈfɜnɪʃ/ *vt* [VP6A,14] ***~ sth (to sb), ~ sb with sth,*** supply or provide; put furniture in: *~ a library with books; ~ an army with supplies/~ supplies to an army; ~ a room/an office; a ~ed house/flat,* one rented with the furniture. **~·ings** *n pl* furniture and equipment.

fur·ni·ture /ˈfɜnɪtʃə(r)/ *n* [U] all those (usu) movable things such as chairs, beds, desks, etc needed in a house, room, office, etc.

fu·rore (US = **fu·ror**) /fjʊˈrɔrɪ *US:* fjuˈrɔ(r)/ *n* state of enthusiastic admiration: *The new play at the National Theatre created a ~,* was received with excited approval.

fur·rier /ˈfʌrɪə(r) *US:* ˈfɜ-/ *n* person who prepares, or who deals in, furs.

fur·row /ˈfʌrəʊ *US:* ˈfɜ-/ *n* [C] **1** long cut in the ground made by a plough: *newly turned ~s.* **2** wrinkle; line in the skin of the face, esp the forehead. □ *vt* [VP6A] make ~s in: *a forehead ~ed by old age/anxiety, etc.*

furry /ˈfɜrɪ/ ⇨ fur.

fur·ther /ˈfɜðə(r)/ *adv,adj* **1** (often used for *farther*): *It's not safe to go any ~.* **2** (not interchangeable in this sense with *farther*) more; in addition; additional: *We must get ~ information. The Museum will be closed until ~ notice. He sat down without ~ bidding,* without being invited again. *We need go no ~ into the matter,* need make no more inquiries. I'll offer you £50 but I can't go any ~, offer more. **3** (also *~more,* ⇨ below) moreover; also; besides: *He said that the key was lost and, ~, that there was no hope of its being found.* **4** at a distance (often euphem for *in hell,* used as a strong refusal of a request): *I'll see him/you, etc ~ first,* I refuse absolutely. □ *vt* [VP6A] help forward; promote: *~ sb's interests; ~ the cause of peace.* **~·ance** /-rns/ *n* [U] ~ing; advancement: *for the ~ance of public welfare; in ~ance of your aims.* **~·more** /ˈfɜðəˈmɔ(r)/ *adv* moreover; in addition. **~·most** /-məʊst/ *adj* most distant; furthest.

fur·thest /ˈfɜðɪst/ *adj, adv* = *farthest.*

fur·tive /ˈfɜtɪv/ *adj* done secretly so as not to attract attention; having or suggesting a wish to escape notice: *a ~ glance/manner; ~ behaviour; be ~ in one's movements.* **~·ly** *adv* **~·ness** *n*

fury /ˈfjʊərɪ/ *n* (*pl* -ries) **1** [U] violent excitement, esp anger; *filled with ~; the ~ of the elements,* wild storms, winds; *in the ~ of battle.* **2** [C] outburst of wild feelings: *She was in one of her furies. He flew into a ~ when I refused to lend him the money.* **3** [C] violently furious woman or girl: *What a little ~ she is!* **4 the Furies,** snake-haired goddesses in Greek mythology sent from the underworld to punish crime.

furze /fɜz/ *n* [U] = gorse.

fuse¹ /fjuz/ *n* [C] tube, cord, etc for carrying a spark to explode powder, etc, e g in a firecracker, bomb or blasting charge; (US = *fuze*) part of a shell or mine that detonates the explosive charge. **ˈtime-~** *n* one that does this after a pre-arranged interval of time.

fuse² /fjuz/ *vt,vi* **1** [VP6A,15A,B,2A] make or become liquid as the result of great heat; join, become joined, as the result of melting: *~ two pieces of wire together.* **2** [VP2A] (of an electric circuit, or part of it) be broken through melting of the ~: *The light has ~d.* ⇨ fuse¹. **3** [VP6A,15A,B] (fig) make into one whole. □ *n* [C] (in an electric circuit) short piece of wire which melts and breaks the circuit if the circuit is overloaded. **ˈ~ wire** *n* [U] kinds of wire used for this purpose.

fu·sel·age /ˈfjuzlɑʒ/ *n* body of an aircraft (to which the engine(s), wings and tail are fitted). ⇨ the illus at air.

fu·sil·ier /ˌfjuzlˈɪə(r)/ *n* soldier (of certain British regiments) formerly armed with a light musket.

fus·il·lade /ˌfjuzɪˈleɪd/ *n* [C] continuous discharge of firearms.

fu·sion /ˈfjuʒn/ *n* [C,U] mixing or uniting of different things into one: *the ~ of copper and tin; a ~ of races/political parties.* **ˈ~ bomb** *n* hydrogen bomb.

fuss /fʌs/ *n* [U] **1** unnecessary nervous excitement, esp about unimportant things; (with *indef art*) nervous state: *Don't make so much ~/get into such a ~ about trifles.* **2** ostentatious activity. ***make a ~ of,*** pay ostentatious attention to: *Don't make so much ~ of the children.* **ˈ~·pot** *n* (colloq) very ~y person. □ *vt,vi* [VP6A,2A,C] get into a ~; cause (sb) to be in a ~: *Stop ~ing. She ~ed about, unable to hide her impatience. Don't ~ over the children so much. Don't ~ me,* make me nervous. **~y** *adj* (-ier, -iest) **1** full of, showing, nervous excitement: be too ~y about one's clothes. **2** (of dress, style, etc) over ornamented; having too many unimportant details, etc. **~·ily** /-əlɪ/ *adv* **~i·ness** *n*

fus·tian /ˈfʌstɪən *US:* -tʃən/ *n* [U] **1** thick, strong, coarse cotton cloth; (attrib) made of this cloth. **2** (fig) high-sounding but empty talk; (attrib) worthless; bombastic.

fusty /ˈfʌstɪ/ *adj* stale-smelling; smelling of mould and damp; (fig) old fashioned in ideas, etc: *a ~ old professor,* e g one who has much book knowledge, but is out of touch with modern ideas, real life.

fu·tile /ˈfjutaɪl *US:* -tl/ *adj* **1** (of actions) of no use; without result: *a ~ attempt.* **2** (of persons) unlikely to accomplish much; vain or frivolous. **fu·til·ity** /fjuˈtɪlətɪ/ *n* (*pl* -ties) [U] the state of being ~; [C] ~ action or utterance.

fu·ture /ˈfjutʃə(r)/ *n, adj* **1** (time, events) coming after the present: *The ~ must always be uncertain. I hope you have a happy ~ before you. Have you provided for the ~*, saved money, taken out an insurance policy, etc? ***for the ~,*** with ~ time in mind: *Have you provided for the ~?* ***in ~,*** from this time onwards: *Try to live a better life in ~.* **2** (*adj*, or attrib use of the *n*) of or in the ~: *the ~ life*, after death of the body; *his ~ wife*, the woman he will marry; *the ~ tense*, with 'shall' and 'will'. *I've given up my job; there was no ~ in it*, no prospects of higher salary, advancement, etc. **3** (*pl*) (orders for) goods and stocks bought at prices agreed upon at the time of purchase, but to be paid for and delivered later. **~·less** *adj*

fu·tur·ism /ˈfjutʃərɪzm/ *n* [U] (early 20th c) movement in art and literature marked by a complete abandonment of tradition in favour of expressing the energy of contemporary life as influenced by modern machinery. **fu·tur·ist** /-ɪst/ *n* supporter of ~.

fu·tur·ity /fjuˈtjʊərətɪ *US:* -ˈtʊər-/ *n* (*pl* **-ties**) the future; (*sing* or *pl*) future events.

fuze /fjuz/ *n* ⇨ **fuse**[1].

fuzz /fʌz/ *n* [U] fluff, fluffy or frizzed hair; (sl) police.

fuzzy /fʌzɪ/ *adj* (**-ier, -iest**) blurred; indistinct (in shape or outline); frayed or fluffy.

Gg

G, g /dʒi/ (*pl* **G's, g's** /dʒiz/) the seventh letter of the English alphabet; (US sl) one thousand dollars.

gab /gæb/ *n* [U] (colloq) talk(ing): *Stop your gab*, (sl) be quiet. ***have the gift of the gab,*** be good at speaking.

gab·ar·dine /ˈgæbəˈdin/ *n* [U] dress material of cotton or silk with wool lining (as used for raincoats).

gabble /ˈgæbl/ *vt, vi* [VP6A,15B,2A,C] speak, say things, quickly and indistinctly: *The little girl ~d her prayers and jumped into bed. Listen to those children gabbling away.* □ *n* [U] fast, confused, unintelligible talk.

gab·er·dine /ˈgæbəˈdin/ *n* **1** = **gabardine**. **2** [C] long, loose gown or frock, esp as worn by Jews in the Middle Ages.

gable /ˈgeɪbl/ *n* [C] three-cornered part of an outside wall between sloping roofs. **gabled** /ˈgeɪbld/ *adj* having a ~ or ~s: *a ~d house.* ⇨ the illus at **window**.

gad[1] /gæd/ *vi* (**-dd-**) [VP2C] ***gad about,*** (colloq) go from place to place for excitement or pleasure. **ˈgad·about** *n* person who does this.

gad[2] /gæd/ *int* (also ***By ˈgad!***) (old-fashioned) used to express surprise, etc.

gad·fly /ˈgædflɑɪ/ *n* (*pl* **-flies**) fly that stings horses and cattle.

gadget /ˈgædʒɪt/ *n* (colloq) small (usu mechanical) contrivance or device: *a new ~ for opening tin cans.* **~ry** *n* [U] ~s collectively.

Gael /geɪl/ *n* Scottish or Irish Celt. **~ic** /ˈgeɪlɪk/ *adj, n* (language) of Scottish Celts; of the Scottish and Irish Celts.

gaff[1] /gæf/ *n* stick with an iron hook for landing fish caught with rod and line.

gaff[2] /gæf/ *n* ***blow the ~,*** (sl) let out a secret; disclose the plot.

gaffe /gæf/ *n* [C] blunder; indiscreet act or remark.

gaffer /ˈgæfə(r)/ *n* (colloq) elderly man, esp a countryman; foreman (of a gang of workmen). ⇨ **boss**[1], **guvnor**.

gag /gæg/ *n* [C] **1** sth put in a person's mouth to keep it open, e g by a dentist or into or over it to prevent him from speaking or crying out. **2** words or action added to his part by an actor in a play; jokes, funny story, esp as part of a comedian's act (in the theatre, or radio or TV). □ *vt, vi* (**-gg-**) **1** [VP6A] put a gag(**1**) into or over the mouth of; silence; (fig) deprive (sb) of free speech. **2** [VP2A] (of an actor, etc) use gags(**2**).

gaga /ˈgægɑ *US:* ˈgɑgɑ/ *adj* (sl) in senile dotage; fatuous.

gage[1] /ˈgeɪdʒ/ *n* **1** (old use) sth given as security or a guarantee; pledge. **2** (= *gauntlet*) glove thrown down (by knights in the Middle Ages) as a challenge to a fight. □ *vt* [VP6A] give or offer as a ~; pledge as a guarantee.

gage[2] /ˈgeɪdʒ/ ⇨ **gauge**.

gaggle /ˈgægl/ *n* flock (of geese); (hum) group (of talkative girls or women).

gai·ety /ˈgeɪətɪ/ *n* **1** [U] being gay; cheerfulness; bright appearance: *flags and bunting that added to the ~ of the scene.* **2** (*pl;* **-ties**) merrymaking; joyful, festive occasions: *the gaieties of the Christmas season.*

gaily /ˈgeɪlɪ/ *adv* ⇨ **gay**.

gain[1] /geɪn/ *n* **1** [U] increase of possessions; acquiring of wealth: *the love of ~; interested only in ~.* **2** (*pl*) **ill-gotten ~s,** dishonestly obtained profits, etc. **ˈcapital ~s,** ⇨ **capital**. **3** [C] increase in amount or power: *a ~ in weight/health; a ~ to knowledge.* **~·ful** /-fl/ *adj* yielding ~: *~ful occupations.* **~·fully** /-flɪ/ *adv* in a ~ful manner: *~fully employed.*

gain[2] /geɪn/ *vt, vi* **1** [VP6A,14,12B,13B] obtain (sth wanted or needed): *~ experience; ~ an advantage over a competitor; ~ strength*, e g become strong again after an illness; *~ ground*, make progress; *~ time*, improve one's chances by delaying sth, making pretexts, etc; *~ the upper hand*, be victorious. *What ~ed him such a reputation?* **2** [VP2A,B,C] make progress; be improved; benefit: *She is ~ing in* (more usu *putting on*) *weight. I have ~ed five pounds* (*in weight*). **3** [VP2A,B] (of a watch or clock) become fast, ahead of the correct time; *This watch neither ~s nor loses. The clock ~s three minutes a day.* **4** [VP3A] ~ ***(up)on,*** **(a)** get closer to (the person or thing pursued): *~ on the other runners in a race.* **(b)** go faster than, get farther in advance of: *~ on one's pursuers.* **(c)** (of the sea) advance gradually and eat away (the land). **5** [VP6A] reach, arrive at (a desired place, esp with effort): *~ the top of a mountain. The swimmer ~ed the shore.* **~·ings** *n pl* earnings; profits; winnings.

gain·say /ˈgeɪnˈseɪ/ *vt* (*pt,pp* **-said** /-ˈsed/) [VP6A] (chiefly in neg and interr) deny; contradict: *There is no ~ing his honesty,* We cannot deny that he is honest.

gait /geɪt/ *n* manner of walking or running: *an*

awkward/slouching ~.

gai·ter /ˈgeɪtə(r)/ *n* cloth or leather covering for the leg from knee to ankle, or for the ankle: *a pair of* ~*s.*

gal /gæl/ *n* (obs colloq or modern joc) girl.

gala /ˈgɑlə *US:* ˈgeɪlə/ *n* festive occasion: (attrib) *in* ~ *dress; a* ~ *night*, e g at a theatre, with special features.

ga·lac·tic /gəˈlæktɪk/ *adj* of the Galaxy: *extra-*~ *systems*, systems outside the Galaxy.

gal·an·tine /ˈgæləntin/ *n* white meat, boned, spiced, cooked in the form of a roll, and served cold.

gal·axy /ˈgæləksɪ/ *n* (*pl* **-xies**) **1** any of the large-scale clusters of stars in outer space. **the G~,** that which is our solar system, visible as a luminous band known as the Milky Way. **2** brilliant company of persons: *a* ~ *of talent/beautiful women.*

gale /geɪl/ *n* **1** strong and violent wind: *The ship lost her masts in the* ~. *It was blowing a* ~. **2** noisy outburst: ~*s of laughter.*

gall[1] /gɔl/ *n* [U] **1** bitter liquid (bile) secreted by the liver. ˈ~ **bladder** *n* (anat) vessel attached to the liver containing and discharging ~. ⇨ the illus at **alimentary**. ˈ~**-stone** *n* hard mass that forms in the ~ bladder. **2** bitter feeling: *with a pen dipped in* ~, used of a writer who makes bitter attacks. **3** (colloq) impudence: *Of all the* ~*!*

gall[2] /gɔl/ *n* [C] painful swelling on an animal, esp a horse, caused by rubbing (of harness, etc); place rubbed bare. □ *vt* **1** [VP6A] rub sore. **2** (fig) hurt the feelings of; humiliate: ~ *sb with one's remarks. It was* ~*ing to him to have to ask for a loan.*

gall[3] /gɔl/ *n* unnatural growth produced on a tree by insects, e g on the oak.

gal·lant /ˈgælənt/ *adj* **1** brave: *a* ~ *knight;* ~ *deeds.* **2** fine; beautiful; stately: *a* ~*-looking ship; a* ~ *display.* **3** (also /gəˈlænt/) showing special respect and courtesy to women: *He was very* ~ *at the ball.* □ *n* young man of fashion, esp one who is fond of and attentive to women. ~**·ly** *adv* ~**ry** *n* **1** [U] bravery. **2** [U] devotion, chivalrous attention, to women. **3** [C] (*pl* **-ries**) elaborately polite or amorous act of speech to a woman.

gal·leon /ˈgælɪən/ *n* Spanish sailing-ship (15th to 17th cc) with a high stern.

galleons

gal·lery /ˈgælərɪ/ *n* (*pl* **-ries**) **1** room or building for the display of works of art. **2** (people in the) highest and cheapest seats in a theatre, concert-hall, etc. ***play to the*** ~, try to win approval or popularity by appealing to the taste of the masses. **3** raised floor or platform extending from an inner wall of a hall, church, etc: *the* ˈ*press* ~ *of the House of Commons*, used by newspaper reporters. **4** covered walk or corridor, partly open at one side; colonnade. **5** long, narrow room: *a* ˈ*shooting-*~, for indoor target practice. **6** horizontal underground passage in a mine. ⇨ **shaft**.

gal·ley /ˈgælɪ/ *n* (*pl* **-leys**) **1** low, flat single-decked ship, using sails and oars, rowed by slaves or criminals; ancient Greek or Roman warship. ˈ~**-slave** *n* person condemned to row in a ~. **2** **ship's kitchen. 3** oblong metal tray in which type is assembled by compositors. ˈ~**-proof** *n* proof(**4**) on a long slip of paper, before division into pages.

Gal·lic /ˈgælɪk/ *adj* of Gaul or the Gauls; (often hum) French. **gal·li·cism** /ˈgælɪsɪzm/ *n* [C] French way of saying sth, used in another language.

gal·li·vant /ˈgælɪˈvænt/ *vi* [VP2C] (not used in the simple tenses) = gad about, ⇨ **gad[1]**: *Where are you* ~*ing off to now?*

gal·lon /ˈgælən/ *n* measure for liquids, four quarts. ⇨ App 5.

gal·lop /ˈgæləp/ *n* (of a horse, etc) fastest pace with all four feet off the ground at each stride; period of riding at such a pace: *He rode away at a* ~*/at full* ~. *Shall we go for a* ~*?* □ *vi,vt* **1** [VP2A,B,C,6A] (cause to) go at a ~: *He* ~*ed across the field.* **2** [VP2A,B,C] hurry: ~ *through one's work/lecture;* progress rapidly: *in a* ~*ing consumption*, ill with tuberculosis which is rapidly getting worse.

gal·lows /ˈgæləʊz/ *n* (usu with *sing v*) wooden framework on which to put criminals to death by hanging: *send a man to the* ~, condemn him to be hanged. *He'll end up on the* ~, will end by being hanged. ˈ~**-bird** *n* person who is thought by some to deserve hanging.

Gal·lup poll /ˈgæləp pəʊl/ *n* questioning of a representative sample of people to assess general public opinion about sth, e g how they will vote at a general election, esp as a means of making a forecast.

ga·lore /gəˈlɔ(r)/ *adv* in plenty: *a meal with beef and beer* ~.

ga·loshes /gəˈlɒʃɪz/ *n* rubber overshoes worn in wet weather: *a pair of* ~.

ga·lumph /gəˈlʌmf/ *vi* (made from *gallop* and *triumph*) prance in triumph.

gal·van·ism /ˈgælvənɪzm/ *n* [U] (science of, medical use of) electricity produced by chemical action from a battery. **gal·vanic** /gælˈvænɪk/ *adj* **1** of ~. **2** (fig) (of smiles, movements, etc) sudden and forced (as if produced by an electric shock).

gal·van·ize /ˈgælvənɑɪz/ *vt* **1** [VP6A] coat (sheet iron, etc) with metal, e g zinc, by galvanism: ~*d iron.* **2** [VP6A,14] ~ ***sb into doing sth,*** shock or rouse.

gam·bit /ˈgæmbɪt/ *n* kinds of opening move in chess (in which a player sacrifices a pawn or other piece to secure certain ends); (fig) any initial move: *His opening* ~ *at the debate was a direct attack on Government policy.*

gamble /ˈgæmbl/ *vi,vt* **1** [VP2A,B,C] play games of chance for money; take great risks for the chance of winning sth or making a profit: *He lost his money gambling at cards/gambling on the Stock Exchange/gambling in oil shares, etc.* **2** [VP15B] ~ ***sth away,*** lose by gambling: *He has* ~*d away half his fortune.* □ *n* [C] undertaking or attempt with risk of loss and chance of profit or advantage. **gam·bler** *n* person who ~s. **gamb·ling** *n* [U] playing games for money; taking risks for possible advantage: *fond of gambling.* ˈ**gambling-den/-house** *n* (formerly) place where gambling is carried on. ⇨ *gaming-rooms* at **game[3]**.

gam·boge /gæmˈbuʒ *US:* -ˈbəʊʒ/ *n* [U] deep yellow colouring matter used by artists.

gam·bol /ˈgæmbl/ *n* (usu *pl*) quick, playful, jumping or skipping movements, e g of lambs, children. □ *vi* (-ll-, US also -l-) [VP2A,C] make such movements.

game[1] /geɪm/ *n* **1** [C] form of play, esp with rules, e g tennis, football, cards: *play ~s; have a ~ of whist. He plays a good ~ at cards,* is a good player. ***be off one's ~,*** be out of form, not playing well. ***have the ~ in one's hands,*** be sure to win it, be able to direct it. ***play the ~,*** keep the rules; (fig) be straightforward and honest. **ˈgames-master/-mistress,** teacher in charge of ~s at a school. **games·man·ship** /ˈgeɪmzmənʃɪp/ *n* (colloq) the art of winning ~s by upsetting the self-possession of one's opponents. **2** [C] apparatus, etc needed for a ~, e g one played by children with a board and dice and counters, such as ludo and draughts. **3** (*pl*) athletic contests (in Scotland, today): *the Highland G~s;* (in Greece and Rome, ancient times) athletic and dramatic contests; (modern times) (international) athletic contests: *the Olympic/Commonwealth G~s.* **4** single round in some contests, e g whist, tennis: *win four ~s in the first set;* score needed to win; state of the ~; *the ~ is four all; ~ all, ~ and ~,* equal score; *~, set and match.* **5** [C] scheme, plan or undertaking; dodge or trick: *He was playing a deep ~,* engaged in a secret scheme of some sort. *I wish I knew what his ~ is,* what he is trying to do. *That's a ~ two people can play,* said when one person uses a scheme to win an advantage for himself. *So that's your little ~,* said when one discovers what sb is scheming to do. *The ~ is up,* Success is now impossible. *You're playing Smith's ~,* You are, unintentionally, helping to advance Smith's scheme. *None of your little ~s!* Don't try to play tricks on me! *You're having a ~ with me,* trying to trick me, deceive me, etc. ***ˈgive the ˈ~ away,*** reveal a secret trick, scheme, etc. ***make ~ of sb,*** ridicule him. **6** [U] (collective) (flesh of) animals and birds hunted for sport and food. **ˈbig ~** *n* the larger animals (elephants, lions, tigers). **ˈfair ~,** what may be lawfully hunted or shot; (fig) person or institution that may with reason be attacked or criticized. **ˈ~ bag,** bag for holding ~ killed by sportsmen. **ˈ~-cock,** of the kind bred for cock-fighting. **ˈ~-keeper,** man employed to breed and protect ~, e g pheasants, grouse, on a country estate. **ˈ~ laws** *n pl* laws regulating the killing and preservation of ~. **ˈ~-licence** *n* one to kill and deal in ~. **gamy** /ˈgeɪmɪ/ *adj* having the flavour and odour of ~(6), esp when high[1](8).

game[2] /geɪm/ *adj* **1** brave; ready to go on fighting; spirited: *die ~,* like a hero. **2** ***~ for/to do sth,*** spirited enough, willing: *Are you ~ for a 10-mile walk? He's ~ for anything you may suggest.* **~·ly** *adv*

game[3] /geɪm/ *vi,vt* [VP2A,C,15B] gamble. **ˈgaming-rooms,** rooms (usu licensed) for gambling.

game[4] /geɪm/ *adj* (of a leg, arm, etc) lame; crippled.

gamma /ˈgæmə/ *n* third letter of the Greek alphabet. ⇨ App 4. **ˈ~ rays** *n pl* rays of very short wave-length emitted by radio-active substances.

gam·mon[1] /ˈgæmən/ *n* [C] bottom piece of a flitch of bacon including a hind leg; [U] smoked or cured ham.

gam·mon[2] /ˈgæmən/ *n* [U] (old use) foolish talk; humbug. □ *int* (dated) Nonsense!

gammy /ˈgæmɪ/ *adj* (colloq) = game[4]: *a ~ leg.*

gamp /gæmp/ *n* (hum; dated) umbrella (esp a large, untidy one).

gamut /ˈgæmət/ *n* whole range of musical notes; (fig) complete extent or scope of anything: *the whole ~ of feeling,* e g from the greatest joy to the depths of despair or misery.

gan·der /ˈgændə(r)/ *n* male goose.

gang /gæŋ/ *n* **1** number of workmen, slaves or prisoners working together. **2** group of persons going about or working together, esp for criminal purposes. ⇨ gangster. **3** (colloq) group of persons going about together, disapproved of by the speaker: *Don't get mixed up with that ~; they spend too much time drinking and gambling.* □ *vi* [VP2C] **~ up,** act together as a ~(2): *They ~ed up on/against me.* **~er** /ˈgæŋə(r)/ *n* foreman of a ~(1).

gan·gling /ˈgæŋglɪŋ/ *adj* (of a person) lanky; tall, thin and awkward-looking.

gan·glion /ˈgʌŋglɪən/ *n* (*pl* -s or -lia /-lɪə/) group of nerve-cells from which nerve-fibres radiate; (fig) centre of force; activity or interest.

gang·plank /ˈgæŋplæŋk/ *n* movable plank placed between a ship or boat and the land, or between two boats or ships.

gan·grene /ˈgæŋgrin/ *n* [U] death and decay of a part of the body, e g because the supply of blood to it has been stopped: *G~ set in and his leg had to be amputated.* □ *vt,vi* [VP6A,2A] affect, become affected, with ~. **gan·gren·ous** /ˈgæŋgrɪnəs/ *adj*

gang·ster /ˈgæŋstə(r)/ *n* member of a gang of armed criminals: (attrib) *ˈ~ films.*

gang·way /ˈgæŋweɪ/ *n* **1** opening in a ship's side; movable bridge from this to the land. **2** passage between rows of seats, e g in the House of Commons, in a theatre or concert-hall, or between rows of people: *Clear the ~, please!* □ *int Make way!*

gan·net /ˈgænɪt/ *n* kind of large seabird.

gan·try /ˈgæntrɪ/ *n* (*pl* -ries) structure of steel bars to support a travelling crane, railway signals over several tracks, etc.

gaol, jail /dʒeɪl/ *n* (usu *jail* in US) [C] public prison; (without *art*) confinement in prison: *three years in ~; be sent to ~.* **ˈ~-bird** *n* prisoner, esp one who has often been in prison; rogue. □ *vt* [VP6A] put in ~. **~er, jailer, jailor** /ˈdʒeɪlə(r)/ *nn* man in charge of a ~ or the prisoners in it.

gap /gæp/ *n* **1** break or opening in a wall, hedge, etc: *The sheep got out of the field through a gap in the hedge. We must see that there is no gap in our defences.* **2** unfilled space; interval; wide separation (of ideas, etc): *a gap in a conversation,* interval of silence; *fill in the gaps in one's education,* study what one failed to learn while at school, etc: *a wide gap between the views of the two statesmen.* ***fill/stop a gap,*** supply sth lacking. ⇨ *stopgap* at stop[1](8). **ˈcrediˈbility gap,** failure of one person, group, etc to convince another that he or it is telling the truth. **ˈgeneˈration gap,** failure or inability of the younger and older generations to communicate, understand one another. **ˈgap-ˈtoothed** /ˈtuθt/ *adj* having teeth which are wide apart. **3** gorge or pass between mountains.

gape /geɪp/ *vi* [VP2A,C] ***~ (at sb/sth)*** **1** open the mouth wide; yawn; stare open-mouthed and in surprise: *country visitors gaping at the neon lights.* **2** open or be open wide: *a gaping chasm.* □ *n* yarn; open-mouthed stare. **the ~s, (a)** disease of poultry causing them to gape until they die (with the beak wide open). **(b)** (joc) fit of yawning.

garage /ˈgærɑʒ *US:* gəˈrɑʒ/ *n* **1** building in which to keep a car or cars. **2** roadside petrol and service station. □ *vt* [VP6A] put (a motor-vehicle) in a ~.

garb /gɑb/ *n* [U] (style of) dress (esp as worn by a particular kind of person): *a man in clerical ~.* □ *vt* [VP6A] (usu passive) dress: *~ed in motley.*

gar·bage /ˈgɑbɪdʒ/ *n* [U] **1** waste food put out as worthless, or for pigs, etc; (US) rubbish, refuse (of any kind). **ˈ~-can** *n* (US) = dustbin. **2** meaningless or irrelevant data in a storage device of a computer.

garble /ˈgɑbl/ *vt* [VP6A] make an incomplete or unfair selection from statements, facts, etc, esp in order to give false ideas: *a ~d report of a speech.*

gar·den /ˈgɑdn/ *n* **1** [C,U] (piece of) ground used for growing flowers, fruit, vegetables, etc: *a kitchen ~*, for vegetables; *a market ~*, for vegetables, fruit and flowers for sale in public markets; (attrib) *a ~ wall; ~ flowers/plants. We have not much ~/only a small ~.* ***lead sb up the ~ path,*** (colloq) mislead him. **ˈ~ party** *n* social gathering held out of doors on a lawn, in a ~ or park, etc. **ˈ~ ˈcity/ˈsuburb** *n* one laid out with many open spaces, and planted with numerous trees. **2** (usu *pl*) public park: *Kensington G~s*, in London; *botanical/zoological ~s.* **3** (*pl* with name prefixed) row(s) of houses with open spaces planted with bushes and trees: *Spring G~s.* □ *vi* [VP2A] cultivate a ~: *He's been ~ing all day.* **~er** *n* person who works in a ~, either for pay or as a hobby. **~·ing** *n* [U] cultivating of ~s: *fond of ~ing;* (attrib) *~ing tools.*

gar·denia /gɑˈdiniə/ *n* (kinds of) tree or shrub with large white or yellow flowers, usu sweet-smelling.

gar·gan·tuan /gɑˈgæntʃʊən/ *adj* enormous; gigantic.

gargle /ˈgɑgl/ *vt,vi* [VP6A,2A] wash the throat with liquid kept in motion by a stream of breath. □ *n* liquid used for this purpose; act of gargling.

gar·goyle /ˈgɑgɔɪl/ *n* stone or metal spout, usu in the form of a grotesque human or animal creature, to carry off rain-water from the roof of a building (esp Gothic-style churches) ⇨ the illus at **church**.

gar·ish /ˈgeərɪʃ/ *adj* unpleasantly bright; over-coloured or over-decorated: *~ clothes.* **~·ly** *adv*

gar·land /ˈgɑlənd/ *n* circle of flowers or leaves as an ornament or decoration; this as a prize for victory, etc. □ *vt* [VP6A] decorate, crown, with a ~ or ~s.

gar·lic /ˈgɑlɪk/ *n* [U] onion-like plant with strong taste and smell, used in cooking: *a clove of ~*, one of the small bulbs making up the compound bulb of a ~ plant; *too much ~ in the food; smelling of ~.*

gar·ment /ˈgɑmənt/ *n* [C] article of clothing: (US) *the ˈ~ industry; ˈ~ workers.*

gar·ner /ˈgɑnə(r)/ *n* (poet, rhet) storehouse for grain, etc (also fig). □ *vt* [VP6A,15B] ***~ (in/up),*** store, gather.

gar·net /ˈgɑnɪt/ *n* semi-precious gem of deep transparent red.

gar·nish /ˈgɑnɪʃ/ *vt* [VP6A,14] decorate, esp food for the table: *fish ~ed with slices of lemon.* □ *n* sth used to decorate a dish of food for the table.

gar·ret /ˈgærət/ *n* room (often small, dark, etc) on the top floor of a house, esp in the roof.

gar·ri·son /ˈgærɪsn/ *n* [C] military force stationed in a town or fort: (attrib) *a ~ town*, one in which a ~ is permanently stationed. □ *vt* [VP6A] supply a town, etc with a ~; place, troops, etc on ~ duty.

gar·rotte, ga·rotte /gəˈrot/ *vt* [VP6A] execute (a person condemned to death) by strangling or throttling (a stick being twisted to tighten a cord over the windpipe); murder (sb) in this way. □ *n* this method of capital punishment; apparatus used for it.

gar·ru·lous /ˈgærələs/ *adj* talkative; talking too much about unimportant things. **gar·ru·lity** /gəˈrulətɪ/ *n* [U].

gar·ter /ˈgɑtə(r)/ *n* (elastic) band worn round the leg to keep a stocking in place. **the G~,** (badge of) the highest order of English knighthood.

gas /gæs/ *n* (*pl* **gases** /ˈgæsɪz/) [C, but used with *indef art* or in *pl meaning 'kind(s) of gas'*] **1** any air-like substance, (used chiefly of those that do not become liquid or solid at ordinary temperatures): *Air is a mixture of gases. Hydrogen and oxygen are gases.* **2** [U] one of the gases or mixtures of gases used for lighting and heating, e g natural gas or the kind manufactured from coal; gas manufactured for use in war (*poison gas*), or occurring naturally, e g in a coalmine: *put the kettle on the gas*, i e on the gas-ring or cooker. **ˈgas-bag** *n* **(a)** bag for holding gas, e g in an airship. **(b)** (colloq) person who talks too much without saying anything useful or interesting. **ˈgas-bracket** *n* pipe with one or more burners projecting from a wall. **ˈgas chamber** *n* **(a)** room filled with gas for lethal purposes. **(b)** chamber filled with gas for preventing decay of apples, etc. **ˈgas-cooker** *n* stove (with gas-rings and an oven) for cooking by gas. **ˈgas fire** *n* one for heating a room by gas. **ˈgas-fitter** *n* workman who provides a building with **ˈgas-fittings** *n pl* apparatus, e g pipes, burners, etc for heating or lighting with gas. **ˈgas-helmet** *n* one used in coalmines, etc. **ˈgas-holder** *n* large, usu cylindrical tank for storing gas (= **gasometer**). **ˈgas-light** *n* [U] light produced by burning coal-gas. **ˈgas-mask** *n* breathing apparatus to protect the wearer against harmful gases. **ˈgas-meter** *n* meter for registering the amount of gas that passes through it. **ˈgas-oven** *n* **(a)** one heated by gas. **(b)** gas chamber(a). **ˈgas poker** *n* metal rod with holes in one end, connected to a supply of gas, used to light fires in a fireplace. **ˈgas-ring** *n* metal ring with numerous small holes and supplied with gas for cooking, etc. **ˈgas-stove** = gas cooker. **ˈgas tar,** [U] coal-tar produced during the manufacture of coal-gas. **ˈgas-works** *n* (*sing v*) place where coal-gas is manufactured. **3** (also *ˈlaughing-gas*) nitrous oxide (**N_2O**) used by dentists as an anaesthetic. **4** (orig US colloq) gasolene (petrol). ***step on the gas,*** press down the accelerator pedal; increase speed. **ˈgas-engine** *n* one from which power is obtained by the regular explosion of gas in a closed cylinder. **ˈgas-station,** (US) = petrol station. **5** (fig, colloq) empty talk; boasting. □ *vt,vi* (-ss-) **1** [VP6A] poison or overcome by gas. **2** [VP2A,C] (colloq) talk for a long time without saying much that is useful.

gas·eous /ˈgæsɪəs/ *adj* of or like gas: *a ~ mixture.*

gash /gæʃ/ *n* [C] long deep cut or wound. □ *vt* [VP6A] make a ~ in.

gas·ify /ˋgæsɪfɑɪ/ *vt,vi* (*pt,pp* **-fied**) [VP6A,2A] (cause to) change into gas. **gasi·fi·ca·tion** /ˈgæsɪfɪˋkeɪʃn/ *n*

gas·ket /ˋgæskɪt/ *n* **1** strip or soft, flat piece of material used for packing a joint, piston, etc to prevent steam, gas, etc from escaping. **2** (usu *pl*) small cords used for tying a furled sail to a yard.

gaso·line (also **-lene**) /ˋgæsəlin/ *n* [U] (US) petrol; motor spirit.

gas·ometer /gəˋsomɪtə(r)/ *n* large round tank in which gas is stored and measured (usu at a gas-works) and from which it is distributed through pipes.

gasp /gɑsp *US:* gæsp/ *vi,vt* **1** [VP2A,C] struggle for breath; take short, quick breaths as a fish does out of water: *~ing for breath; ~ing* (= breathless) *with rage/surprise.* **2** [VP6A,15B] ***~ (out),*** utter in a breathless way: *He ~ed out a few words.* □ *n* [C] catching of the breath through pain, surprise, etc: *at one's last ~,* exhausted; at the point of death.

gasper /ˋgɑspə(r) *US:* ˋgæs-/ *n* (dated GB sl) cheap cigarette.

gassy /ˋgæsɪ/ *adj* of or like gas; full of gas; (of talk, etc) empty; vain and boastful.

gas·tric /ˋgæstrɪk/ *adj* of the stomach: *a ~ ulcer; ~ fever; ~ juices.* **gas·tri·tis** /gæˋstrɑɪtɪs/ *n* [U] inflammation of the stomach.

gas·tron·omy /gæˋstronəmɪ/ *n* [U] art and science of choosing, preparing and eating good food. **gas·tron·omic** /ˈgæstrəˋnomɪk/ *adj* of ~.

gate /geɪt/ *n* **1** opening in the wall of a city, hedge, fence or other enclosure, capable of being closed by means of a barrier: *He opened the garden ~ and went up to the door of the house. He jumped over the ~ into the field.* **ˋ~-house** *n* house built at the side of, or over, a ~, e g at the entrance to a park, the house being used by a servant called the *ˋ~-keeper.* **2** barrier that closes such an opening, either of solid wood or of iron gratings or bars, usu on hinges; barrier used to control the passage of water, e g into or out of a lock on a canal. **ˋ~ money** *n* total sum paid for admission to a public spectacle in a stadium, etc, esp sport. **ˋ~-post** *n* post on which a ~ is hung or against which it is closed. ***between you (and) me and the ~-post,*** in strict confidence. **ˋ~-legged table,** table with legs that can be moved out to support a folding top. **ˋ~-way** *n* way in or out that can be closed by a ~ or ~s; (fig) means of approach: *a ~way to fame/knowledge.* **ˋ~-crash** *vt* [VP6A] enter (a building at which there is a private social occasion of some sort) without invitation or payment. Hence, **ˋ~-crasher** *n* **3** = ~ money, ⇨ 2 above. **4** *a starting ~,* barrier (either of horizontal ropes that are lifted or of rows of stalls with barriers) at the start of a horse or greyhound race. □ *vt* [VP6A] (at Oxford or Cambridge university) confine (a student) to college (as a penalty).

gâ·teau /ˋgætəʊ *US:* gɑˋtəʊ/ *n* (F) rich fancy cake, often served in slices.

gather /ˋgæðə(r)/ *vt,vi* **1** [VP6A,15A,B,2A,C] get, come or bring together: *He soon ~ed a crowd round him. A crowd soon ~ed round him. The clouds are ~ing; it's going to rain.* ***be ~ed to one's fathers,*** (liter or rhet) die. **2** [VP6A,12B,13B] pick (flowers, etc); collect: *~ one's papers and books together. Please ~ me some flowers/~ some flowers for me.* **3** [VP6A] obtain gradually; gain little by little: *~ information/impressions/experience. The train ~ed speed as it left the station.* **4** [VP6A,9] understand; conclude: *What did you ~ from his statement? I ~, from what you say, that....* **5** [VP6A,15A,B] (in sewing) pull together into small folds by putting a thread through; draw parts of material, a garment closer together: *a skirt ~ed at the waist.* **6** [VP2A] (of an abscess or boil) form pus and swell up; come to a head. **~·ing** *n* [C] **1** coming together of people; meeting. **2** swelling with pus in it.

a gate-legged table

gauche /gəʊʃ/ *adj* socially awkward; tactless. **gauch·erie** /ˋgəʊʃərɪ *US:* ˈgəʊʃəˋri/ *n* [U] ~ behaviour; [C] ~ act, movement, etc.

gaucho /ˋgɑʊtʃəʊ/ *n* cowboy of mixed European and American Indian descent.

gaud /gɔd/ *n* [C] showy ornament.

gaudy[1] /ˋgɔdɪ/ *adj* (**-ier, -iest**) too bright and showy; gay or bright in a tasteless way: *~ decorations; cheap and ~ jewels.* **gaud·ily** /-əlɪ/ *adv*

gaudy[2] /ˋgɔdɪ/ *n* (*pl* **-dies**) annual college dinner, given to former members.

gauge (US also **gage**) /geɪdʒ/ *n* **1** standard measure; extent: *take the ~ of,* e g sb's character, estimate; judge. **2** distance between rails (or between opposite wheels on a vehicle that runs on rails): *standard ~; broad ~,* more than 4 ft 8½ in; *narrow ~,* less than 3 ft 8½ in. **3** thickness of wire, sheet-metal, etc; diameter of a bullet, etc. **4** instrument for measuring, e g rainfall, strength of wind, size, diameter, etc of tools, wire, etc. □ *vt* [VP6A] measure accurately: *~ the diameter of wire/the contents of a barrel/the rainfall/the strength of the wind;* (fig) make an estimate, form a judgement, of: *~ a person's character.*

Gaul /gɔl/ *n* Celt of ancient ~ (the area now known as France and Belgium).

gaunt /gɔnt/ *adj* (of a person) lean, haggard, as from hunger, ill-health or suffering; (of a place) grim or desolate: *a ~ hillside.* **~·ness** *n*

gaunt·let[1] /ˋgɔntlət/ *n* **1** glove with metal plates worn by soldiers in the Middle Ages. ⇨ the illus at armour. ***throw down/pick up/take up the ~,*** give/accept a challenge to a fight. **2** strong glove with a wide cuff covering the wrist, used for driving, fencing, etc.

gaunt·let[2] /ˋgɔntlət/ *n* (only in) ***run the ~,*** run between two rows of men who strike the victim as he passes; (fig) be exposed to continuous severe criticism, risk, danger.

gauze /gɔz/ *n* [U] thin, transparent net-like material of silk, cotton, etc (for medical use) or of wire (for screening windows against insects, etc). **gauzy** *adj*

gave /geɪv/ *pt* of give.

gavel /ˋgævl/ *n* hammer used by an auctioneer or a chairman as a signal for order or attention.

ga·votte /gəˋvɒt/ *n* [C] (music for an) old French dance like the minuet but more lively.

gawk /gɔk/ *n* awkward or bashful person. **~y** *adj* (**-ier, -iest**) (of persons) awkward, bashful, ungainly. **~i·ness** *n*

gawp /gɔp/ *vi* [VP2A,3A] **~ (at sb),** look at in an intense, foolish way: *What are they all ~ing at?*

gay /geɪ/ *adj* (**-er, -est**) **1** light-hearted; cheerful; happy and full of fun: *the gay voices of young children; gay looks/laughter.* **2** suggesting happiness and joy: *gay music; gay colours; streets that were gay with flags.* **3** (in a bad sense) loose; irresponsible: *lead a gay life.* **4** (colloq) homosexual. **gaily** /ˋgeɪlɪ/ *adv* in a gay manner. **gay·ness** *n*

gaze /geɪz/ *n* (*sing* only) long, steady look: *with a bewildered ~.* □ *vi* [VP2A,C,3A] **~ (at),** look long and steadily: *What are you gazing at?* **~ (up)on,** (formal) set eyes on: *She was the most beautiful woman he had ever ~d upon.*

ga·zelle /gəˋzel/ *n* small, graceful kinds of antelope.

ga·zette /gəˋzet/ *n* **1** government periodical with legal notices, news of appointments, promotions, etc of officers and officials. **2** (as part of a title) newspaper: *the Marlowe G~.* □ *vt* (usu in the passive) *be ~d,* be published in the official ~: (of an army officer) *be ~d to a regiment.*

ga·zet·teer /ˌgæzəˋtɪə(r)/ *n* index of geographical names, e g at the end of an atlas.

ga·zump /gəˋzʌmp/ *vi,vt* [VP2A,6A] increase the price demanded for property between the date of acceptance of an offer and the date for signing the contract.

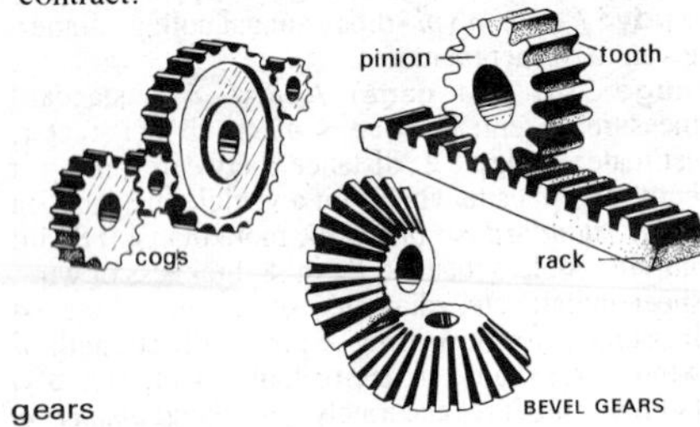

gears

gear /gɪə(r)/ *n* **1** ⇨ the illus at bicycle. [C] set of toothed wheels working together in a machine, esp such a set to connect the engine of a motor-vehicle with the road wheels: *Change ~; a car with four ~s, first, second, third and reverse.* ***high/low ~,*** mechanism causing the driven part to move relatively fast/slowly, low ~ being used when starting, or when driving on a steep hill. ***in/out of ~,*** engaged/disengaged from the mechanism. ***top/bottom ~,*** highest/lowest ~. **ˋ~-box/-case,** case that encloses the ~ mechanism. **ˋ~ shift/lever/stick,** device for engaging or disengaging ~s. **2** [C] apparatus, appliance, mechanism, arrangement, of wheels, levers, etc for a special purpose: *the ˋsteering-~ of a ship; the ˋlanding-~ of an aircraft.* **3** [U] equipment in general: *ˋhunting-~*; (modern colloq) clothes: *Carnaby Street ~.* □ *vt,vi* [VP15A,14,2A,C,3A] **~ up/down,** (= change up/down) put into a higher/lower ~. **~ to,** adjust one thing to the working of another, make dependent on: *The country's economics must be ~ed to wartime requirements.*

gecko /ˋgekəʊ/ *n* (*pl* **-ckos, -ckoes** /-kəʊz/) kind of small house lizard, found in warm countries.

gee[1] /dʒi/ (also **gee-up** /ˈdʒi ˋʌp/) *int* (command to a horse) go on; go faster. **gee-gee** /ˋdʒi dʒi/ *n* (child's word for a) horse.

gee[2] /dʒi/ *int* (US) (euphem for *Jesus*) mild exclamation indicating surprise, admiration, etc: *Gee, your shirt looks great!*

geese /gis/ *n pl* of goose.

geezer /ˋgizə(r)/ *n* (sl) old person, esp if eccentric.

Geiger /ˋgɑɪgə(r)/ *n* (esp **ˋ~ counter**) metal tube containing an electrode, used for detecting and measuring radio-activity.

geisha /ˋgeɪʃə/ *n* Japanese girl or woman trained to entertain men by singing and dancing at parties, etc.

gel /dʒel/ *n* semisolid like a jelly. □ *vi* (**-ll-**) **1** set into a jelly. **2** (colloq) come off; succeed: *That new idea has really gelled.*

gela·tine /ˈdʒeləˋtin *US:* ˋdʒelətɪn/ (also **gela·tin** /ˋdʒelətɪn/) *n* [U] clear, tasteless substance, made by boiling bones and waste parts of animals, dissolved in water to make jelly. **gel·ati·nous** /dʒɪˋlætɪnəs *US:* -tṇəs/ *adj* of or like ~; jelly-like in consistency, etc.

geld /geld/ *vt* [VP6A] castrate. **~·ing** *n* ~ed animal, esp a horse.

gel·ig·nite /ˋdʒelɪgnɑɪt/ *n* [U] explosive made from nitric acid and glycerine.

gem /dʒem/ *n* **1** precious stone or jewel, esp cut or polished. **2** sth valued because of great beauty; sth much prized: *the gem of the collection,* the most valued item in it. □ *vt* (**-mm-**) adorn with, or as with, gems: *the night sky gemmed with stars.*

Gem·ini /ˋdʒemɪnɪ/ *n* third sign of the zodiac. ⇨ the illus at zodiac.

gen /dʒen/ *n* (dated GB army sl) **the gen,** general or correct information.

gen·darme /ˋʒɒndɑm/ *n* (in France and some other countries, but not GB or US) member of a military force employed in police duties. **gen·darme·rie** /ʒɒnˋdɑmərɪ/ *n* (collective sing) force of ~s.

gen·der /ˋdʒendə(r)/ *n* grammatical grouping of words (nouns and pronouns) into classes (masculine, feminine and neuter).

gene /dʒin/ *n* [C] (biol) one of the factors controlling heredity.

gen·eal·ogy /ˈdʒinɪˋælədʒɪ/ *n* **1** [U] science of the development of plants and animals from earlier forms. **2** [C] (*pl* **-gies**) (diagram illustrating the) descent or line of development of a plant or animal from earlier forms: person's pedigree. **gen·eal·ogist** /ˈdʒinɪˋælədʒɪst/ *n* student of ~. **genea·logi·cal** /ˈdʒinɪəˋlɒdʒɪkl/ *adj* of ~: *a geneological tree,* a diagram (a table like a tree with branches) showing the descent of a family or species. **genea·logi·cally** /-klɪ/ *adv*

gen·era /ˋdʒenərə/ *n pl* of genus.

gen·eral /ˋdʒenrl/ *adj* **1** of, affecting, all or nearly all; not special, local or particular: *a matter of ~ interest,* one in which all or most people are likely to be interested; *a ~ meeting,* one to which all members (of a society, etc) are invited; *a ~ strike,* one by workmen of all, or nearly all, the trade unions; *a good ~ education,* in all the chief subjects; *a word that is in ~ use,* used by all people; *the ~ opinion on this subject,* what most people think about it. *The cold weather has been ~,* has been experienced in all or most parts of the country. ***as a ~ rule, in ~,*** in most cases; usually. **ˈ~ degree,** non-specialist university degree involving a course in two or more subjects. **ˈ~ ˈelection,** one for representatives in Parliament from the whole country. ⇨ by-election. **ˈ~ ˈknowledge,** of a wide variety of subjects. Cf *common knowledge*, knowledge (of a particular fact, etc) possessed by every member of a class or community of people. **ˈ~ post,** a change-around involving everybody, e g when ministers change positions in a government. **ˈ~ ˈpractitioner,** (GB) doctor who is not a specialist or consultant. **ˈ~ ˈstaff,** (mil) group of officers without command who assist superior officers at headquarters. **2** not in detail; not definite: *a ~ outline of a scheme; have a ~ idea of what a book is about; explain something in ~ terms.* **3** (after an official title) chief: *ˈpostmaster-ˈ~; ˈinspector-ˈ~.* □ *n* army officer with the highest rank below Field Marshal (and also, by courtesy, of *ˈLieutenant-ˈ~* and *ˈMajor-ˈ~*). ⇨ App 9.

gen·er·al·is·simo /ˌdʒenrəˈlɪsɪməʊ/ *n* (*pl* ~s) commander of combined military and naval and air forces, or of combined armies.

gen·er·al·ity /ˌdʒenəˈrælətɪ/ *n* (*pl* -ties) **1** [C] general rule or statement; vague or indefinite remark, etc: *I wish you would come down from generalities to particularities.* **2** ***the ~ (of),*** majority or greater part: *Is it wrong to say that the ~ of school children are lazy?* **3** [U] quality of being general: *a rule of great ~,* one with few exceptions.

gen·er·al·iz·ation /ˌdʒenrəlaɪˈzeɪʃn *US:* -lɪˈz-/ *n* **1** [U] generalizing: *It is unwise to be hasty in ~.* **2** [C] statement or proposition obtained by generalizing, esp one based on too few examples.

gen·er·al·ize /ˈdʒenrəlaɪz/ *vi,vt* **1** [VP2A,3A] ***~ from,*** draw a general conclusion; make a general statement. **2** [VP6A,14] state (sth) in general terms or principles (*from*): *~ a conclusion from a collection of instances or facts.* **3** [VP6A] bring into general use: *~ the use of a new invention.*

gen·er·ally /ˈdʒenrəlɪ/ *adv* (usu with the finite *v*) **1** usually; as a general rule: *I ~ get up at six o'clock.* **2** widely; for the most part: *The new plan was ~ welcomed,* was welcomed by most people. **3** in a general sense; without paying attention to details: *~ speaking.*

gen·er·ate /ˈdʒenəreɪt/ *vt* [VP6A] cause to exist or occur; produce: *~ heat/electricity; hatred ~d by racial differences.*

gen·er·ation /ˌdʒenəˈreɪʃn/ *n* **1** [U] generating; bringing into existence: *the ~ of electricity by steam or water-power; the ~ of heat by friction.* **2** [C] single stage or step in family descent: *three ~s,* children, parents, grandparents. **3** [C] average period (regarded as 30 years) in which children grow up, marry, and have children: *a ~ ago.* **ˈ~ gap,** ⇨ gap(2). **4** [C] all persons born about the same time, and, therefore, of about the same age: *the present/past/coming ~; the rising ~,* the young ~.

gen·er·at·ive /ˈdʒenrətɪv/ *adj* able to produce; productive.

gen·er·ator /ˈdʒenəreɪtə(r)/ *n* [C] machine or apparatus that generates (electricity, steam, gas, vapour, etc) (US = *dynamo*).

gen·eric /dʒɪˈnerɪk/ *adj* of a genus; common to a whole group or class, not special. **gen·eri·cally** /-klɪ/ *adv*

gen·er·os·ity /ˌdʒenəˈrɒsətɪ/ *n* **1** [U] the quality of being generous; nobility of mind; greatness of heart: *show ~ in dealing with a defeated enemy.* **2** [C] (*pl* -ties) generous act, etc.

gen·er·ous /ˈdʒenrəs/ *adj* **1** giving, ready to give, freely; given freely; noble-minded. *He is ~ with his money/~ in giving help. It was ~ of them to share their meal with their out-of-work neighbours. What a ~ gift! He has a ~ nature.* **2** plentiful: *a ~ helping of meat and vegetables; a ~ harvest.* **~·ly** *adv*

gen·esis /ˈdʒenəsɪs/ *n* **1** beginning; starting-point: *the ~ of civilization.* **2 G~,** the first book of the Old Testament.

gen·etic /dʒɪˈnetɪk/ *adj* of genes; of ~s. **gen·etics** *n pl* (with *sing v*) science (branch of biology) dealing with heredity, the ways in which characteristics are passed on from parents to offspring. **gen·eti·cist** /dʒɪˈnetɪsɪst/ *n* specialist in ~s.

ge·nial /ˈdʒiːnɪəl/ *adj* **1** kindly, sympathetic; sociable: *a ~ old man; ~ smiles; under the ~ influence of good wine.* **2** favourable to growth; mild; warm: *a ~ climate; ~ sunshine.* **~ly** *adv* **ge·nial·ity** /ˌdʒiːnɪˈælətɪ/ *n* [U] quality of being ~; [C] (*pl* -ties) ~ look, act, utterance, etc.

ge·nie /ˈdʒiːnɪ/ *n* (*pl* genies or genii /ˈdʒiːnɪaɪ/) (in Arabic stories) spirit or goblin with strange powers.

geni·tal /ˈdʒenɪtl/ *adj* of generation(1) or of animal reproductive organs. **geni·tals** *n pl* external sex organs.

geni·tive /ˈdʒenətɪv/ *adj*: *~ case,* (gram) showing source or possession.

gen·ius /ˈdʒiːnɪəs/ *n* (*pl* -ses, but ⇨ 6 below) **1** [U] great and exceptional capacity of the mind or imagination; creative or inventive capacity: *men of ~.* **2** [C] person having this capacity: *Einstein was a mathematical ~.* **3** (usu *sing* with *indef art,* followed by *for*) natural ability: *have a ~ for languages/acting/making friends.* **4** (usu *sing* with *def art*) guardian spirit of a person, place or institution, (hence, by extension) special and inborn character, spirit or principles of a language, a period of time, an institution, etc; prevalent feeling, opinions, taste, etc of a race of people: *the French ~; the ~ of the British Constitution/the Renaissance period in Italy.* **ˈ~ loci** /ˈləʊsaɪ/ (Lat) (with *def art*) associations, atmosphere, etc of a place. **5** ***one's good/evil ~,*** spirit or angel working for one's salvation or damnation; person who has a strong influence upon one for good or ill. **6** (*pl* genii /ˈdʒiːnɪaɪ/) demon; supernatural being. ⇨ genie.

geno·cide /ˈdʒenəsaɪd/ *n* [U] extermination of a race or community by mass murder, or by imposing conditions that make survival impossible.

genre /ʒɔ̃r *with unsyllabic* r/ *n* **1** kind; style; category (esp of literary form, e g poetry, drama, the novel). **2** (also **ˈ~-painting**) portrayal of scenes, etc, from ordinary life.

gent /dʒent/ *n* (vulg abbr of) gentleman. **gents** *n* (GB colloq) public toilet for men.

gen·teel /dʒenˈtiːl/ *adj* (usu ironic in modern use, but serious in former use) polite and well-bred; elegant; characteristic of, suitable for, the upper classes of society: *living in ~ poverty,* trying to maintain the style of the upper classes, although too poor to do so. **~·ly** *adv*

gen·tian /ˈdʒenʃn/ *n* (kinds of usu) blue-flowered plant growing in mountainous districts.

gen·tile /ˈdʒentaɪl/ *n, adj* (person) not of the Jewish race.

gen·til·ity /dʒenˈtɪlətɪ/ *n* [U] state of being genteel: *living in shabby ~*, trying, without real success, to keep up an appearance of being genteel.

gentle /ˈdʒentl/ *adj* (-r, -st) **1** kind, friendly; not rough or violent: *a ~ nature/heart/look/voice/call/touch; ~ manners; a ~ breeze; a ~ heat*, i e not too hot; *a ~ slope*, i e not steep. **2** (of a family) with good social position: *a person of ~ birth*. **ˈ~·folk** *n pl* persons of ~ birth. **~·ness** *n*

gentle·man /ˈdʒentlmən/ *n* (*pl* -men /-mən/) **1** man who shows consideration for the feelings of others, who is honourable and well-bred: *a fine old ~; a true ~*. **ˈ~'s agreement,** one that is binding in honour, but cannot be enforced at law. **2** (old use) man of good family attached to a court or the household of a great noble: *one of the king's gentlemen*. **ˌ~-at-ˈarms,** one of the sovereign's bodyguard. **3** (historical use) man entitled to bear arms but not a member of the nobility. **4** (dated use) man of wealth and social position, esp one who does not work for a living: *'What does he do for a living?' 'Nothing; he's a ~.'* **5** (polite synonym for) any man of any social position: *A ~ has called to see you. Who's the ~ in the corner?* **6** (*pl*) polite form of address to male members of an audience: *Gentlemen! Ladies and Gentlemen!* Also used instead of *Sirs* or *Dear Sirs* when writing to a business firm, etc. **~·ly** *adj* feeling, behaving, or looking like a ~; suitable or right for a ~(1): *a ~ly appearance*.

gentle·woman /ˈdʒentlwʊmən/ *n* (*pl* -women /-wɪmɪn/) lady: (in historical use) *the Queen and her gentlewomen*.

gen·tly /ˈdʒentlɪ/ *adv* in a gentle manner: *Hold it ~*, carefully. *Speak ~* (= softly, kindly) *to the child. The road slopes ~* (= gradually) *to the sea*.

gen·try /ˈdʒentrɪ/ *n* (collective pl, usu with *def art*) people of good social position next below the nobility; (ironic) people (of any class).

genu·flect /ˈdʒenjʊflekt/ *vi* [VP2A] bend the knee, esp in worship. **genu·flec·tion, genu·flexion** /ˌdʒenjʊˈflekʃn/ *nn*

genu·ine /ˈdʒenjʊɪn/ *adj* true; really what it is said to be: *a ~ picture by Rubens; ~ pearls; ~ sorrow; a ~ signature*. **~·ly** *adv* **~·ness** *n*

ge·nus /ˈdʒinəs/ *n* (*pl* genera /ˈdʒenərə/) **1** (science) division of animals or plants within a family: **ˌ~ ˈ***Homo* /ˈhəʊməʊ/, mankind. **2** sort; kind; class.

geo- /ˈdʒiəʊ/ *pref* form of Greek word for 'earth', used in combinations: **geo·cen·tric** /ˌdʒɪəʊˈsentrɪk/ *adj* having or representing the earth as centre. **geo·phys·ics** /ˌdʒɪəʊˈfɪzɪks/ *n pl* (*sing v*) study of the earth's magnetism, meteorology, etc. **geo-physi·cal** /-ˈfɪzɪkl/ *adj* **geo·poli·tics** /ˌdʒɪəʊˈpolətɪks/ *n pl* (*sing v*) country's politics as determined by its geographical position.

ge·ogra·phy /dʒɪˈogrəfɪ/ *n* [U] science of the earth's surface, physical features, divisions, climate, products, population, etc. **ge·ogra·pher** /dʒɪˈogrəfə(r)/ *n* authority on ~. **geo·graphi·cal** /ˌdʒɪəˈgræfɪkl/ *adj* of ~. **geo·graphi·cally** /-klɪ/ *adv*

ge·ol·ogy /dʒɪˈolədʒɪ/ *n* [U] science of the earth's history as shown by its crust, rocks, etc. **ge·ologist** /dʒɪˈolədʒɪst/ *n* authority on ~; student of ~. **geo·logic, -logi·cal** /ˌdʒɪəˈlodʒɪk(l)/ *adj* of ~. **ge·o·logi·cally** /-klɪ/ *adv*

ge·ometry /dʒɪˈomətrɪ/ *n* [U] science of the properties and relations of lines, angles, surfaces and solids. **geo·metric, -metri·cal** /ˌdʒɪəˈmetrɪk(l)/ *adj* of ~; of or like the lines, figures, etc used in ~: *geometrical patterns*. **ˌgeometrical proˈgression,** series of numbers with a constant ratio between successive quantities, the numbers either increasing by a common multiplier, or decreasing by a common divisor, as 1 : 3 : 9 : 27 : 81. **geo·met·ri·cally** /-klɪ/ *adv*

George /dʒɔdʒ/ *n* **1 St ~,** patron saint of England; *St ˈ~'s day*, 23 Apr; *St ˌ~'s ˈCross*, vertical and horizontal red bars crossing in the centre. **2** (sl) automatic pilot of aircraft. □ *int* **by ~!** exclamation of mild surprise, determination, etc.

geor·gette /dʒɔˈdʒət/ *n* [U] thin silk dress material.

Geor·gian /ˈdʒɔdʒən/ *adj* of the time of any of the first four Georges, Kings of England (18th c) or of George V and VI (20th c): *~ architecture*.

ger·anium /dʒəˈreɪnɪəm/ *n* kind of garden plant with red, pink or white flowers.

geri·atrics /ˌdʒerɪˈætrɪks/ *n pl* (*sing v*) medical care of old people. **geri·atric** *adj* of ~: *the geriatric ward*, of a hospital. **geria·tri·cian** /ˌdʒerɪəˈtrɪʃn/ *n* expert in ~.

germ /dʒɜm/ *n* [C] **1** portion of a living organism capable of becoming a new organism; (fig) beginning or starting-point (of an idea, etc). **2** microbe or bacillus, esp one causing disease: *~ warfare*, use of bacteria as a weapon in war.

Ger·man /ˈdʒɜmən/ *adj* of Germany and its people. **ˌ~ ˈshepherd** *n* (US) = Alsatian dog. □ *n* native of Germany; language of the ~ people. **~ic** /dʒəˈmænɪk/ *adj* of the group of languages now including German, English and Dutch.

ger·mane /dʒəˈmeɪn/ *adj* **~ *(to)*,** relevant, pertinent (to).

ger·mi·cide /ˈdʒɜmɪsaɪd/ *n* substance used to destroy germs (esp bacteria).

ger·mi·nate /ˈdʒɜmɪneɪt/ *vi,vt* [VP2A,6A] (of seeds) (cause to) start growth. **ger·mi·na·tion** /ˌdʒɜmɪˈneɪʃn/ *n* [U] germinating; sprouting.

ger·on·tol·ogy /ˌdʒeronˈtolədʒɪ/ *n* branch of science concerned with the processes of growing old, esp in human beings.

gerry·man·der /ˌdʒerɪˈmændə(r)/ *vt* [VP6A] manipulate (a constituency, etc by division into voting areas) so as to give unfair advantages to one party or class in elections; practise trickery. □ *n* such a falsification.

ger·und /ˈdʒerənd/ *n* **1** forms of Latin verb serving as cases of the infinitive in its noun use. **2** the *-ing* form of an English verb when used as a noun (as in 'fond of *swimming*').

Ges·tapo /geˈstɑpəʊ/ *n* German secret State police of the Nazi regime.

ges·ta·tion /dʒeˈsteɪʃn/ *n* carrying or being carried in the womb between conception and birth; this period.

ges·ticu·late /dʒɪˈstɪkjʊleɪt/ *vi* [VP2A] use movements of the hands, arms or head instead of, or to accompany, speaking. **ges·ticu·la·tion** /dʒɪˌstɪkjʊˈleɪʃn/ *n* [U] gesticulating; [C] movement used in this.

ges·ture /ˈdʒestʃə(r)/ *n* **1** [C] movement of the hand or head to indicate or illustrate an idea, feeling, etc; sth done to convey a friendly intention: *a ~ of refusal; make a friendly ~ to sb*. **2** [U] use of expressive movements: *an actor who is a master of the art of ~.* □ *vi* [VP2A] gesticulate.

get /get/ *vt,vi* (*pt* got /gɒt/, *pp* got or, in older English and in US gotten /ˈgɒtn/) (For uses with *adverbial particles* and *preps* ⇨ **15, 16, 17,** below.) **1** [VP2D] (cause oneself to) become; pass from one state to another: *get wet/tired/excited. He went out and got drunk. She soon got well again. You'll soon get used to the climate here. It's time you got married. Get lost!* (sl) Go away! ***get even with sb,*** ⇨ even[1](3). ⇨ also wise[1]. **2** [VP22,24C] bring to a certain condition; cause to be or become: *She soon got the children ready for school. I must get the breakfast ready/cooked. Did you get the sum right,* produce the correct answer? *He got his wrist broken,* broke it by accident. **3** [VP2E] reach the stage where one is doing something: *Get going!* Start! *It's time we got going,* made a start. *Things haven't really got going yet,* are not yet at the stage of full activity. *When these women get talking, they go on for hours.* **4** [VP19B] bring sb/sth to the point where he/it is doing sth: *Can you really get that old car going again,* restart or repair it? It's not hard to get the children talking; the problem is to stop them. We'll soon get things going. **5** [VP4A] reach the stage where one knows, feels, etc sth: *When you get to know him you'll like him. They soon got to be* (= become) *friends. After a time you get to realize that.... One soon gets to like it here. How did you get to know* (= learn) *that I was here?* **6** [VP17,24C] bring, persuade, cause (sb/sth) to do sth or act in a certain way: *You'll never get him to understand. I can't get this old radio to work. I can't get her to talk. I can't get anyone to do the work/can't get the work done by anybody.* Cf *I must get my hair cut/get somebody to cut my hair.* **7** [VP6A] receive; have; obtain; procure; acquire: *I got* (= now have) *your telegram. This room gets* (= receives, admits) *very little sunshine. I'll come as soon as I get time. The soldier got leave* (= permission) *to go home. He got* (= received) *a nasty blow on the head. The bullet got him/The soldier got it in the leg,* He was injured there. *Where did you get that hat? How does he get* (= earn) *his living? If we divide 12 by 4, we get 3. Can you get* (= receive) *distant stations on your transistor? Go and get* (= take, eat) *your breakfast.* [VP12A,13A] *Get me a ticket, please, and get some for yourself and your brothers. The book is not in stock, but we can get it for you. How did they get possession of it,* become the owner? ***get the better/best of,*** ⇨ better[3] and best[3]. ***get the boot,*** ⇨ boot[1](1). ***get a glimpse of,*** ⇨ glimpse. ***get hold of sth,*** ⇨ hold[2](1). ***get the sack,*** ⇨ sack[2]. ***get (a) sight of,*** ⇨ sight[1](2). ***get the upper hand (of),*** ⇨ upper. ***get one's own way,*** ⇨ way. ***get wind of,*** ⇨ wind[1](4). ***get the wind up,*** ⇨ wind[1](1). ***get the worst of,*** ⇨ worst. **8** [VP6A] catch (an illness): *get the measles; get religion,* (fig) be converted (from disbelief or indifference). **9** [VP6A] receive as a penalty: *get six months,* be sentenced to six months' imprisonment. ***get told off,*** (colloq) be admonished: *I daren't be late home again or I'll get told off.* **10** [VP6A] (colloq) understand: *I don't get you/your meaning. She didn't get my jokes. Get it?* Do you understand? *You've got it wrong,* have misunderstood it. *I didn't get* (= hear) *your name.* **11** [VP6A] (esp in the perfect tenses) puzzle; catch in an argument; bring an accusation against sb to which he cannot supply a good answer: *Ah! I've got you there! That's got him!* **12** [VP6A] ***has/have/had got,*** have, e g as a possession or characteristic: *We've got a new car. What ugly teeth he's got!* **13** [VP7B] ***has/have/had got to,*** must, be compelled or obliged: *It has got to* (= must) *be done today. She's got to work hard for her living. You haven't got to* (= needn't) *go to the office today, have you?* ⇨ have[3](1). **14** [VP7A] (US) be able: *Do you ever get to see him,* have opportunities of seeing him? **15** [VP2C,3A] (non-idiomatic uses with *adverbial particles* and *preps;* for idiomatic uses, ⇨ 17 below) move to or from a specified point or in a particular direction: *When did you get here,* arrive? *We didn't get to bed until 2am. Where have they got to? Where can it have got to?* Where can it be? *He gets about a good deal. A car makes it easier to get about. The bridge was destroyed so we couldn't get across,* couldn't cross the river. *Did you manage to get away* (= have a holiday) *this Easter? Get back!* (imper) Move backwards, e g away from danger. *When did you get back* (= return) *from the country? She got back into bed. Please let me get by,* pass. *He got down from his horse. Dust got into his eyes. I'm getting off* (= leaving the train) *at the next station. Get off the grass/my toes! Get a move on!* Hurry up! *Can you get over that wall?* ***get under one's skin,*** **(a)** annoy, irritate: *These harvest bugs/His remarks get under my skin.* **(b)** (colloq) be, become an infatuation: *I've got you under my skin.* ***get somewhere/anywhere/nowhere,*** obtain some/any/no result; make some/any/no progress. ***get there,*** (colloq) succeed; accomplish sth. **16** [VP15A,B] (non-idiomatic uses with *adverbial particles* and *preps;* for idiomatic uses, ⇨ 17 below) cause to move to or from a point, or be in a particular direction: *The general had to get his troops across the river. It was nailed to the wall and I couldn't get it off. He never lends books; he says it's too difficult to get them back. If you'll come and help me, I promise to get you back* (= see that you reach home again) *before dark. He's drunk again—we'd better call a taxi and get him home. Get* (= Put) *your hat and coat on. I can't get the lid on/off. We couldn't get the piano through the door.*

17 [VP2C,15B,3A,14] (idiomatic uses with adverbial particles and *preps*):

get about, **(a)** (of sb who has been ill) be no longer confined to bed, to the house: *He's getting about again after his accident.* **(b)** (of news, rumours, stories) spread from person to person, quietly, and usu by gossip: *The news of the defeat was censored, but it soon got about.*

get above oneself, have a feeling of self-satisfaction not in strict proportion to one's merits; have too high an opinion of oneself. ⇨ *swollen-headed* at swell(1).

get (sth) across (to sb), (colloq) (cause sth to) be understood (as when a comedian tries to get jokes across the footlights to an audience): *I spoke slowly, but my meaning didn't get across. He found it difficult to get his British jokes across to American audiences.*

get ahead (of sb), go forward and pass others; make progress: *Tom has got ahead of all the other boys in the class.*

get along, **(a)** manage: *We can't get along with-*

out money. **(b)** make progress: *How are you getting along? How is he getting along with his French?* **get along (with),** agree; be friendly or in harmony: *He gets along well with his boss. He and his boss get along well. Get along with you!* (colloq) imper) Go away! (or) Don't expect me to believe that!

get at sb/sth, reach; gain access to: *The books are locked up and I can't get at them.* Hence, **get-ˈat-able** *adj* accessible. **get at sb, (a)** bribe, corrupt: *One of the witnesses had been got at.* **(b)** taunt: *He's always getting at his wife.* **get at sth,** discover; lay bare: *get at the truth/the facts.* **be getting at,** (colloq) be implying; be trying to say or suggest: *What are you getting at?*

get away, manage to leave; escape: *Two of the prisoners got away.* Hence, **ˈget-away** *n: make one's get-away,* escape; (attrib) *The get-away car had been stolen.* **get away with sth,** pursue successfully a course of action which might usually be expected to result in blame, punishment or misfortune: *The thieves got away with the contents of the safe. If I cheat in the examination, do you think I might get away with it? Get away with you!* Get along with you. ⇨ get along above.

get back, return to power or prominence after losing it for a time: *The Democrats hope to get back at the next election.* **get back at sb/get one's ˈown back (on sb),** have one's revenge: *He tricked me this time but I'll get my own back one day.*

get by, (a) (fig) pass; be accepted, without comment or criticism: *I have no formal clothes for this occasion; perhaps I can get by in a dark suit.* **(b)** manage; survive: *How can he get by on such low wages? She can't get by without him.*

get down, leave the table: *May I get down (from the table), mummy?* (expression used by a small child, e g at the end of a meal). **get sb down,** (colloq) depress: *Don't let this wretched weather get you down.* **get sth down, (a)** swallow: *The medicine was horrid, and she couldn't get it down.* **(b)** write down: *Did you get that telephone message down?* **get down to sth,** deal seriously with; tackle: *get down to one's work after the holidays; get down to the facts,* deal with them, ignoring speculations, etc. **get down to brass tacks,** ⇨ brass.

get home (to) sb, (fig) be fully understood: *That remark of yours about Sally got home,* She understood (and reacted).

get in, (a) arrive: *The train got in five minutes early.* **(b)** be elected: *He got in* (= was elected MP) *for Islington.* **get sb in,** call sb to one's house, etc to perform a service: *We must get someone in to repair the TV.* **get sth in, (a)** collect: gather: *get in the crops/the harvest; get in debts/taxes.* **(b)** obtain a supply of sth: *get coal in for the winter; get in more wine for Christmas.* **get one's hand/eye in, not get a word in edgeways, get a blow in,** ⇨ hand[1](5), eye[1](1), edgeways, and blow[3](1).

get into, (a) put on: *I can't get into these shoes—they're two sizes too small!* **(b)** pass into a particular condition: *get into trouble/a rage/a temper; get into debt.* **get a girl into trouble,** (colloq) make her pregnant. ⇨ also get with below. **(c)** acquire: *get into bad habits.* **(d)** associate with: *get into undesirable company.* **(e)** learn by experience or experiment: *get into the way/habit/routine of doing something.* **get it into one's head that, get this into your head,** become convinced of sth.

get off, start: *We got off immediately after breakfast.* **get off lightly/cheaply,** escape severe punishment or suffering. **tell sb where to get off/where he gets off,** (colloq) tell him how far his misbehaviour, impudence, etc will be tolerated, or that it will no longer be tolerated (= put sb in his place). **get sb/sth off,** send: *get letters/parcels off in good time; get Ben off to school.* **get sth off one's chest,** ⇨ chest(2). **get sth/sb off one's hands,** ⇨ hand[1](1). **get sb off,** save from punishment or a penalty: *His youth and inexperience got him off. A clever barrister may be able to get you off.* **get sb off to sleep,** help him to fall asleep: *She got the baby off to sleep,* e g by rocking it. **get sth off,** remove: *get a ring off one's finger; get off one's gloves.* **get sth off (by heart),** learn it until the words can be repeated mechanically. **get off with sb,** (colloq) become acquainted with sb by chance or without an introduction: *She got off with a young doctor at a dance. She got off with her boss,* began an affair with him. **get off with sth,** escape more severe punishment or misfortune: *He got off with only a fine,* e g instead of possible imprisonment.

get on, make progress; advance: *He's sure to get on in life. Either get on or get out,* Either do something or leave. *Time is getting on,* is passing. **get on sth,** mount: *He got on his bike/horse/the train.* **get on one's feet,** stand; (fig) recover after a setback: *The industry will need time to get on its feet again.* **get on one's nerves,** ⇨ nerve(2). **be getting on for,** be approaching: *He's getting on for seventy,* will soon be 70 years old. *It's getting on for midnight.* **get on to sb, (a)** get in touch with, e g by telephone; make contact with: *If you're not satisfied with the firm's service get on to the manager.* **(b)** (colloq) succeed in recognizing, e g dishonesty, deceit: *He has tricked many of us but people are beginning to get on to him at last.* **get on (with sb),** work or live in a sociable way: *The new manager is easy to get on with. They don't get on at all well (together).* **get on (with sth),** continue: *Please get on with your work.*

get out, become known: *The secret got out. If the news gets out there'll be trouble.* **get sth out,** utter: *He managed to get out a few words of thanks.* **get out of (sth/doing sth), (a)** (fig) avoid; escape (from): *Don't try to get out of your duties, however unpleasant they are. I wish I could get out of going to that wedding.* **(b)** (fig) abandon gradually: *get out of bad habits.* **get sth out of sb,** extract: *The police will get a confession out of him,* will make him confess. *Just try getting money out of him!*

get over sb, (colloq) forget: *He never got over Jane, you know,* She stayed in his memory. **get over sth, (a)** recover from, e g illness, surprise, a loss: *I can't get over his rudeness. He never got over his big financial losses. Fred didn't remarry; he never got over the shock of losing Jane.* **(b)** overcome: *She can't get over her shyness.* **get sth over, (a)** get to the end of sth unpleasant or troublesome: *I have to see my dentist today; I'll be glad to get it over.* **(b)** = get sth across.

get round sb, persuade sb into some action to which he was at first opposed or indifferent; influence sb in one's favour; coax: *Alice knows how to get round her father.* **get round sth,** evade, e g a law or regulation, but without committing a legal offence; circumvent: *A clever lawyer might find ways of getting round that clause.* **get round to sth/to doing sth,** deal with it (when more important matters have been dealt with): *I'm very busy this week but I hope to get round to your request next week.*

get through, reach sb, arrive: *I started as soon as your message got through (to me). I rang you several times yesterday but couldn't get through.* **get through (sth),** pass, e g an examination: *Tom failed but his sister got through.* **get through sth,** reach the end of: *I've got through a lot of correspondence today. He has got through* (= spent) *all his money. As soon as I get through (with) my work, I'll join you.* **get sb through (sth),** help to pass an examination: *get pupils through (an examination).* **get sth through,** ensure that it is done; make it law: *get the proposal through the committee,* have it discussed and accepted; *get a Bill through Parliament.*

get to, reach a particular state. **get down to business,** ⇨ business(3). **get to work,** ⇨ work[1](1). **get to grips with sth,** ⇨ grip *n* (1). **get to the point,** ⇨ point[1](9).

get together, come or meet together, e g for discussion or social purposes: *Let's get together one evening and talk about old times.* Hence, **ˋget-together** *n* e g a social reunion of old friends. **get oneself together,** (colloq; more usu *pull*) get control of oneself, one's feelings, etc. **get people/things together,** collect; organise, put in order: *The rebel leader couldn't get an army together. I'll be able to entertain as soon as I've got the house together.*

get sth under, subdue; control; become the master of: *They soon got the fire under. The revolt was quickly got under.* **get under control,** ⇨ control. **get under way,** ⇨ way(8).

get up, (a) rise: *What time do you get up,* i e from bed? *He got up* (= stood up) *to ask a question.* **(b)** mount: *Get up behind me,* e g on a horse. **(c)** begin to be violent: *The wind/sea is getting up.* **get sb/oneself up, (a)** cause to rise, be out of bed: *Get the children up and dressed for school.* **(b)** make sb/oneself attractive, e g by the use of cosmetics, fine clothes: *She was beautifully got up. She was got up like a film star.* **(c)** dress in a certain style: *get oneself up as a sailor; get a child up as a fairy.* **get sth up, (a)** arrange or prepare the appearance of: *Please have these shirts got up well,* laundered, starched and ironed. *The book is well got up,* well printed and bound. **(b)** organize: *We're getting up a party for his birthday. They got up a dramatic performance for charity.* **(c)** make a special study of; work hard at: *What subjects do you have to get up for the exam*? Hence, **ˋget-up** *n* (colloq) **(a)** style or arrangement, e g of a book, periodical. **(b)** style of dress, esp if unusual: *I wouldn't be seen dead with you in that get-up!* **get up steam,** ⇨ steam(2). **get up to sth, (a)** reach: *We got up to page seventy-two last lesson. We soon got up to the others,* caught up with them. **(b)** become involved in; plan: *What will they get up to next?*

get sb with child, make her pregnant. **get with it,** (colloq) ⇨ with(12).

geum /ˋdʒiəm/ *n* [C] kinds of small garden plant.

gew·gaw /ˋgju gɔ/ *n* gaudy ornament or plaything.

gey·ser /ˋgizə(r) *US:* ˋgɑɪzə(r)/ *n* **1** natural spring sending up at intervals a column of hot water or steam. **2** /*US:* ˋgizə(r)/ apparatus for heating water, e g by gas, in a kitchen, bathroom, etc.

a geyser

gharry /ˋgærɪ/ *n* (*pl* -ries) (in India, etc) (horse-drawn) carriage.

ghast·ly /ˋgɑstlɪ *US:* ˋgæs-/ *adj* (-ier, -iest) **1** death-like; pale and ill: *looking* ~; (also as *adv*): ~ *pale.* **2** causing horror or fear: *a* ~ *accident.* **3** (colloq) very unsatisfactory or unpleasant: *a* ~ *dinner.* **4** (of a smile) painfully forced.

ghat, ghaut /gɔt/ *n* [C] (in India) flight of steps leading to a landing-place on a river bank: *burning* ~*s,* level areas at the top of ~s on which Hindus cremate their dead.

ghee /gi/ *n* [U] clarified Indian buffalo-milk butter.

gher·kin /ˋgɜkɪn/ *n* small, green cucumber for pickling.

ghetto /ˋgetəʊ/ *n* (*pl* -tos /-təʊz/) **1** (formerly, in some countries) Jewish quarter of a town. **2** section of a town, lived in by underprivileged classes, or people who are discriminated against, e g because of race or religion.

ghost /gəʊst/ *n* **1** spirit of a dead person appearing to sb still living: *He looked as if he had seen a* ~, looked frightened. *I don't believe in* ~*s. Do you like* ~ *stories?* **2** (old use) spirit of life. **give up the** ~, die **3** Spirit of God: (only in) **the Holy G**~, the Third Person of the Trinity. **4** sth shadowy or without substance: **ˋ~ town,** one now deserted, e g an area where gold was once mined, but is now abandoned. **not have the** ~ **of a chance,** no chance at all. **5** also **ˋ~-writer,** person who does literary or artistic work for which his employer takes the credit. **6** duplicated image on a television screen. □ *vt, vi* act as a ~-writer (for): ~*ed memoirs,* compiled by a ~-writer.

ghost·ly /ˋgəʊstlɪ/ *adj* **1** of, like, suggesting, a ghost: *vague shapes, looking* ~ *in the darkness.* **2** spiritual; from a priest: ~ *comfort/counsel.* **ghost·li·ness** *n*

ghoul /gul/ *n* **1** (in Eastern stories) spirit that robs graves and feeds on the corpses in them. **2** person with gruesome and unnatural tastes and habits. **~·ish** /-ɪʃ/ *adj* gruesome; revolting.

GI /ˈdʒi ˋɑɪ/ *n* enlisted soldier of the US army in World War II: *a GI bride,* bride (in or from a country other than the US) of such a soldier.

gi·ant /ˋdʒɑɪənt/ *n* **1** (in fairy tales) man of very great height and size. **2** man, animal or plant much larger than normal; (fig) person of extraordinary ability or genius. **3** (attrib) of great size or force: ~ *strength; a* ~ *cabbage.* **~·ess** /ˈdʒɑɪəntˋes/ *n* female ~.

gib·ber /ˋdʒɪbə(r)/ *vi* [VP2A,C] talk fast or make meaningless sounds (like an ape, or as when the

teeth knock together through cold or fear). **~·ish** /ˈdʒɪbərɪʃ/ *n* [U] meaningless sounds; unintelligible talk.
gib·bet /ˈdʒɪbɪt/ *n* wooden post with an arm, on which corpses of executed criminals were formerly exposed as a warning; death by hanging. □ *vt* put to death by hanging; (fig) hold up to contempt or ridicule.
gib·bon /ˈgɪbən/ *n* kinds of long-armed ape. ⇨ the illus at ape.
gib·bous /ˈdʒɪbəs/ *adj* **1** (of the moon) having the bright part greater than a semicircle and less than a circle. ⇨ the illus at phase. **2** humped; hunch-backed.
gibe, jibe /dʒaɪb/ *vi* [VP2A,3A] ***~(at),*** jeer or mock; make fun of: *~ at a boy's mistakes.* **gib·ing·ly** /ˈdʒaɪbɪŋlɪ/ *adv*
gib·lets /ˈdʒɪbləts/ *n pl* heart, liver, gizzard, etc of a goose, hen, etc taken out before the bird is cooked: *giblet soup,* soup made from these parts.
giddy /ˈgɪdɪ/ *adj* (-ier, -iest) **1** causing, having, the feeling that everything is turning round; feeling that one cannot stand firm: *look down from a ~ height. If you turn round quickly fifty times, you will feel ~.* **2** too fond of pleasure; not serious; without steady principles: *a ~ young girl; a ~ life of pleasure.* ***play the ~ goat,*** ⇨ goat. **gid·dily** *adv* **gid·di·ness** *n*
gift /gɪft/ *n* **1** [C] sth given: *~s to charities; ˈ~ vouchers/coupons.* Cf *birthday and Christmas presents.* **2** [C] natural ability or talent: *have a ~ for art/languages; a woman of many ~s,* talented by nature. ***look a ~-horse in the mouth,*** ⇨ mouth[1](1). **3** [U] right or power to give: *The living[2](3) is in the ~ of the squire,* He has the right to bestow it. *The property came to me by free ~,* was given to me. □ *vt* [VP6A] bestow, e g land, as a ~ to sb. **~ed** *adj* having great natural ability: *~ed with rare talents; a ~ed pianist.*
gig /gɪg/ *n* **1** small, light two-wheeled carriage pulled by one horse. **2** ship's small boat for oars or sails, e g for the captain's use.
gi·gan·tic /dʒaɪˈgæntɪk/ *adj* of immense size: *He has a ~ appetite, and eats ~ meals.*
giggle /ˈgɪgl/ *vi* [VP2A] laugh in a nervous and silly way; [VP6A] express by giggling: *She ~d her appreciation of my silly joke.* □ *n* laugh of this kind: *the ~s of schoolgirls.*
gig·olo /ˈʒɪgələʊ/ *n* (*pl* -los /-ləʊz/) professional male dancing-partner who may be hired by wealthy women; paid male companion of a wealthy older woman.
Gil·bert·ian /gɪlˈbɜtɪən/ *adj* ***a ~ situation,*** humorously topsy-turvy situation as in Gilbert and Sullivan operas.
gild[1] /gɪld/ *vt* (*pp* usu ~ed, but ⇨ gilt below) [VP6A] cover with gold leaf or gold-coloured paint; make bright as if with gold: *~ a picture-frame.* ***~ the lily,*** spoil the beauty of sth by garish embellishment. ***~ the pill,*** make an unpleasant necessity seem attractive. **~ed youth,** young men of fashion and wealth. **~er** *n* person who ~s (picture-frames, etc). **~ing** *n* [U] material with which things are ~ed.
gild[2] ⇨ guild.
gill[1] /gɪl/ *n* (usu *pl*) organ with which a fish breathes. ⇨ the illus at fish.
gill[2] /dʒɪl/ *n* one-quarter of a pint liquid measure. ⇨ App 5.
gil·lie /ˈgɪlɪ/ *n* man or boy attending a sportsman in Scotland while fishing or shooting.
gilt /gɪlt/ *n* (⇨ gild) gilding. ***take the ~ off the gingerbread,*** (prov) take away the most attractive feature. **ˈ~-ˈedged stocks/securities,** investments that are considered safe and to which (in England) trustees were formerly restricted.
gim·bals /ˈgɪmblz/ *n* (usu *pl*) contrivance (of rings and pivots) for keeping instruments, e g a compass, horizontal on a ship at sea.
gim·crack /ˈgɪmkræk/ *adj* worthless, flimsy and badly made: *~ ornaments.*
gim·let /ˈgɪmlət/ *n* small tool, with a handle usu fixed crosswise, used for boring holes in wood, etc. ⇨ the illus at tool.
gim·mick /ˈgɪmɪk/ *n* [C] (colloq, esp in film, broadcasting and journalistic circles) trick, device, catchword, mannerism, article of wear, etc used for publicity purposes, to identify sth or sb.
gin[1] /dʒɪn/ *n* **1** trap or snare for catching animals, etc. **2** machine for separating raw cotton from its seeds. □ *vt* (-nn-) [VP6A] **1** catch (animals, etc) in a trap or snare. **2** treat (cotton) in a gin.
gin[2] /dʒɪn/ *n* [U] colourless alcoholic drink distilled from grain or malt, often drunk with tonic water, and used in many kinds of cocktail. **ˈgin-palace** *n* flamboyant public-house.
gin·ger /ˈdʒɪndʒə(r)/ *n* [U] **1** (plant with) hot-tasting root used in cooking, as a flavouring and for making a kind of wine. **2** liveliness; spirit; energy: *a ˈ~ group,* (in Parliament) group of MP's that urges the Government to be more active. **2** (also as *adj*) light reddish-yellow colour: *~ hair.* **4** **ˈ~ ˈbeer/ˈale,** kinds of non-alcoholic aerated drink flavoured with ~. **ˈ~·bread** *n* dark-coloured cake or biscuit flavoured with ~. ⇨ gilt. **ˈ~ nut,** biscuit flavoured with ~. □ *vt* [VP6A, 15A] ***~ (up),*** make more vigorous or lively.
gin·ger·ly /ˈdʒɪndʒəlɪ/ *adv* with great care and caution to avoid harming oneself, what one touches, making a noise, etc: *set about sth ~.* □ *adj* cautious: *in a ~ fashion.*
ging·ham /ˈgɪŋəm/ *n* [U] printed cotton or linen cloth, usu with designs in stripes or checks.
gingko /ˈgɪŋkəʊ/ *n* (*pl* -kos, -koes /-kəʊz/) tree native to China and Japan with fan-shaped leaves.
gin·seng /ˈdʒɪnsəŋ/ *n* plant of which the aromatic root is used in medicine.
gipsy, gypsy /ˈdʒɪpsɪ/ *n* (*pl* -sies) **1** member of a wandering Asiatic race, now living in many parts of Europe, moving about in caravans and making camps from time to time, and earning a living by collecting scrap material, horse-dealing, fortune-telling, basket-making, etc: (attrib) *a ~ girl/camp/orchestra.* **2** (playfully) attractive or mischievous girl or woman, esp one with black, sparkling eyes.
gi·raffe /dʒɪˈrɑf *US:* -ˈræf/ *n* African animal with a very long neck and legs and dark patches on its coat. ⇨ the illus at large.
gird /gɜd/ *vt* (*pt,pp* girded or girt /gɜt/) (poet or rhet) **1** [VP15B] ***~ on,*** fasten, attach: *~ on a sword.* **2** [VP15B] ***~ up,*** raise and fasten, e g with a belt or sash: *~ up one's robe/clothes; ~ up one's loins,* (biblical) prepare for action. **2** encircle: *a sea-girt isle,* surrounded by the sea.
girder /ˈgɜdə(r)/ *n* wood, iron or steel beam to support the joists of a floor; compound structure of steel forming the span of a bridge, roof, etc.
girdle[1] /ˈgɜdl/ *n* **1** cord or belt fastened round the waist to keep clothes in position. **2** corset. **3** sth

that encircles like a ~: *a ~ of green fields round a town.* □ *vt* [VP15A,B] ***~ about/around/with,*** encircle: *a lake ~d with trees.*

girdle[2] /ˈgɜdl/ *n* (in Scotland) round iron plate for cooking cakes.

girl /gɜl/ *n* **1** female child; daughter; unmarried woman. **2** maidservant: *a new ~ to do the housework.* **3** girl or woman working in a shop, office, etc (irrespective of age): *ˈshop ~s; ˈfactory ~s; ˈoffice ~s.* **4** (often **ˈ~-friend**) regular companion with whom one may or may not be in love: *John and his ~.* **5 ˈG~ ˈGuide,** (GB) member of an organization for ~s, with principles and aims similar to those of the Boy Scouts (US = G~ Scout). **ˈ~·hood** /-hʊd/ *n* [U] state or time of being a ~. **~·ish** /-ɪʃ/ *adj* of, for, like a ~: *~ish games/behaviour/laughter.* **~·ish·ly** *adv* **~·ish·ness** *n*

giro /ˈdʒɑɪrəʊ/ *n* (comm) system of settling accounts operated by a number of Joint Stock banks collectively, the accounts being held at branches of the banks concerned. **National G~,** (GB) similar system operated by the Post Office.

girt /gɜt/ ⇨ gird.

girth /gɜθ/ *n* **1** leather or cloth band tightened round the body of a horse to keep the saddle in place. ⇨ the illus at **harness**. **2** measurement round anything that is roughly like a cylinder in shape: *a tree 10 metres in ~,* in circumference; *my ~,* my waist measurement.

gist /dʒɪst/ *n* (*sing* with *def art*) real or main points or substance, general sense: *Tell me the ~ of what he said.*

give[1] /gɪv/ *vt, vi* (*pt* **gave** /geɪv/, *pp* **given** /ˈgɪvn/) (For uses with *adverbial particles* and *preps,* ⇨ **13** below.) **1** [VP12A,13A,2A] ***~ (to),*** hand over (to sb) without payment or exchange, e g as a present or gift: *I gave David a book. I gave a book to each of the boys. Each of the boys was ~n a book. A book was ~n to each of them. I gave it him* (= to him). *G~ me one. G~ one to me. He ~s generously,* is generous in giving money, etc. **2** [VP12B,16A] ***~for, ~to + inf,*** cause (sb) to have (sth) in exchange for sth else, for payment, as compensation, etc: *How much will you ~ me for my old car? I gave a good price for this overcoat. I would ~ a lot to know where she is. I would ~ anything to know what happened.* **3** [VP12A,13A] ***~ (to),*** allow (sb or sth) to pass into the care or safekeeping or custody of; entrust (to): *G~ the porter your bags. G~ your money to the hotel manager to be looked after.* **4** [VP12A] allow (sb) to have, e g time; cause (sb) to have, e g trouble; concede; grant: *You'd better ~ yourself half an hour for the journey. G~ me five minutes and I'll change the wheel. They gave me a week to make up my mind.* ***~ sb (some/no/any, etc) trouble,*** cause or make trouble to: *Did you ~ your parents much trouble when you were young? 'The car has a good engine' 'OK, I'll ~ you that* (= concede that you're right on that point) *but the body's very rusty'.* **5** [VP6A,12A,13A] furnish; supply; provide: *The sun ~s us warmth and light. You should ~* (more usu *set*) *them a good example. You should ~ a good example to your young brothers and sisters.* **6** [VP12A,13A] be the source or origin of: *You've ~n me your cold,* I've caught a cold from you. **7** [VP6A,13A Note that 12A is not used] devote; dedicate: *He gave his life to the cause of peace.* **8** [VP12A] (used in the *imper* to show preference): *G~ me liberty or ~ me death,* If I cannot have liberty, I prefer to die. *G~ me Bach and Beethoven, not these very modern composers.* **9** [VP6A,12A,13A] (used with a *n* in a pattern that may be replaced by one in which the *n* is used as a *v*): *~ a groan/laugh/sigh/yell,* groan, laugh, sigh, yell; *~ a shrug of the shoulders,* shrug the shoulders; *~ three cheers,* cheer three times; *~ sb a kick/push/shove,* kick/push/shove him; *~ sb a ring,* phone him/her. **10** (in fixed phrases) ***~ birth (to),*** ⇨ birth. ***~ chase (to),*** ⇨ chase[1]. ***~ currency (to),*** ⇨ currency. ***~ my ears (to),*** ⇨ ear[1](1). ***~ evidence of,*** ⇨ evidence. ***~ ground,*** ⇨ ground[1](2). ***~ place to,*** ⇨ place[1](10). ***~ rise to,*** ⇨ rise[1](5). ***~ or take...,*** plus or minus: *She'll be here at 4 o'clock, ~ or take a few minutes. He's six feet tall, ~ or take an inch or two.* Cf *give and take* at give[2]. ***~ sb best,*** (old use) admit his superiority. ***~ sb to understand that,*** inform, assure him, that: *I was ~n to understand that you might help me to find employment.* ***~ it to him/her/them,*** (colloq) punish or reprimand him, etc. ***~ sb sth to cry for,*** ⇨ cry[1](2). ***~ sb what for/a piece of one's mind,*** (colloq) punish or scold him. ***~ way,*** **(a)** retire, retreat: *Our troops had to ~ way.* **(b)** fail to support: *The ice gave way and we all went through into the water. I felt the foundations giving way. The rope gave way,* broke, snapped. ***~ way (to sth/sb),*** **(a)** yield; allow priority to: *G~ way to traffic coming in from the right.* **(b)** be replaced by: *Sorrow gave way to smiles.* **(c)** abandon oneself to: *Don't ~ way to despair/grief/tears.* **(d)** make concessions (to): *We mustn't ~ way to these impudent demands.* **11** [VP2A] lose firmness; bend; yield to pressure: *The branch gave* (e g swung downwards) *but did not break. His knees seemed to ~,* to feel weak (so that he fell down). *This chair ~s comfortably,* is soft and springy. *The frost is beginning to ~,* is less severe. **12** (the *pp* ~n): **(a)** (in formal documents) delivered: *~n under my hand and seal in this fifth day of May, 1705.* **(b)** granting or assuming that one has, e g as a basis for reasoning: *G~n good health, I hope to finish the work this year.* **(c)** agreed upon; assigned: *under the ~n conditions. They were to meet at a ~n time and place.* **(d) ˈ~n name,** name ~n to a child in addition to its family name, e g *David* in David Hume. ***~n to sth/doing sth,*** devoted or addicted to; having as a habit or inclination: *He's ~n to boasting. I'm not much ~n to making forecasts.* **13** [VP2C,15B,3A] (Uses with *adverbial particles* and *preps*):

give sb away, (esp) hand over (the bride) to the bridegroom at a wedding: *The bride was ~n away by her father.* ***~ sth away,*** **(a)** allow sb else to have; sacrifice: *You've ~n away a good chance of winning the match.* **(b)** distribute: *The Mayor gave away the prizes at the sports meeting.* **(c)** ~ freely, not expecting anything in return: *He gave away all his money.* **(d)** reveal, intentionally or unintentionally: *Don't ~ away my secret. His accent gave him away,* made known who or what he was. Hence, **ˈ~-away** *n* **(a)** sth given without charge: *airlines which present ~-aways* (= gifts) *to their passengers. The last question on the exam paper was a ~-away,* so easy that it needed no effort, etc. **(b)** sth revealed, intentionally or unintentionally: *The expression on the thief's face was a ~-away,* showed his guilt. ***ˈ~ the ˈgame***

away, ⇨ game[1](5).
give sth back (to sb), ~ sb back sth, restore; return: *~ a thing back to its rightful owner; ~ a man back his liberty; a wall of rock that ~s back loud echoes.*
give sth forth, = ~ sth out.
give in (to sb), surrender; yield; submit: *The rebels were forced to ~ in. He has ~n in to my views,* has accepted them. *Mary usually has to ~ in to her big brother,* accept his plans, etc and abandon her own. ***~ sth in,*** **(a)** hand over (papers, etc) to the proper authorities: *Please ~ in your examination papers now.* **(b)** make known willingness or readiness for the: *~ in one's name,* e g for a duty, as a candidate, etc.
give sth off, emit, send out, e g smoke, vapour, etc: *This chemical ~s off an ill-smelling vapour.*
give on (to)/upon, look out on; overlook: *The windows ~ on to* (= look out on) *the courtyard.*
give out, come to an end; be exhausted: *Our food supplies began to ~ out. Her patience gave out at last. His strength gave out.* ***~ sb out/not out,*** (cricket, of the umpire) say that the batsman has been/has not been defeated. ***~ sth out,*** distribute; send out: *~ out books/handbills.* ***~ sb out to be, ~ it out that sb is,*** announce; reveal: *The newcomer gave himself out to be the son of Charles* I. It was ~n out that Mr Hall would be the chief speaker.
give upon, = ~ on.
give over, (sl) stop: *Please ~ over crying. Do ~ over!* ***~ sb/sth over (to sb),*** hand (the usu word) over; deliver: *~ sb over to the police.* ***be ~n over to sth,*** **(a)** be abandoned to (an undesirable state): *be ~n over to despair/evil courses.* **(b)** be devoted to: *The period after supper was ~n over to games.*
give up, abandon the attempt to do sth, find the answer to sth: *I can do nothing more; I ~ up. I can't answer that puzzle; I ~ up.* ***~ sb up,*** **(a)** say that one regards sb, or his estate, as hopeless: *The child is incorrigible—even his teachers have ~n him up,* have decided that he cannot be reformed. The doctors have ~n him up, say that they cannot cure him. **(b)** (colloq) stop keeping company with him/her: *She was tired of Tom's nagging so she gave him up.* **(c)** no longer expect sb: *She was so late that we had ~n her up.* ***~ sb up for lost,*** no longer expect him to be found or saved. ***~ sb/oneself/sth up (to sb),*** surrender; part with: *~ up a fortress; ~ up one's seat to sb,* e g in a crowded bus. *Shall we let the thief go or ~ him up* (= deliver him) *to the police? The escaped prisoner gave himself up.* ***~ sth up,*** stop (doing sth): *I wish I could ~ up smoking.* ***give up the ghost,*** die.

give[2] /gɪv/ *n* [U] quality of being elastic, of yielding to pressure: *A good dance floor should have a certain amount of ~ in it. A stone floor has no ~ in it;* (fig) (of a person) quality of yielding: *There's no ~ in him,* He does not concede anything, e g in negotiations, argument. ⇨ give[1](11). ***~ and take,*** compromise; mutual concession; willingness on both sides to give way: *There must be ~ and take if the negotiations to settle an industrial dispute are to succeed.* (attrib) *Is marriage a ~-and-take affair?*

giver /ˈgɪvə(r)/ *n* one who gives: *a generous/cheerful ~.*

given /ˈgɪvn/ *pp* of give[1].

giz·zard /ˈgɪzəd/ *n* bird's second stomach for grinding food; (fig) throat: *It sticks in my ~,* is a proposal, etc that I dislike intensely.

glacé /ˈglæseɪ *US:* glæˈseɪ/ *adj* (of fruits) iced, sugared; (of leather, cloth) smooth, polished.

gla·cial /ˈgleɪʃl/ *adj* of ice or the ice age: *the ~ era/epoch,* the time when large areas of the northern hemisphere were covered with ice; (fig) *a ~* (= icy) *manner/smile.*

gla·cier /ˈglæsɪə(r) *US:* ˈgleɪʃər/ *n* [C] mass of ice, formed by snow on mountains, moving slowly along a valley. ⇨ the illus at mountain.

glad /glæd/ *adj* (-der, -dest) **1** (*pred* only) pleased: *be/look/feel ~ about something; ~ to see someone. I am ~ of your success/that you have succeeded.* **2** causing or bringing joy; joyful: *Have you heard the ~ news/tidings? All nature seemed ~,* was bright and beautiful, as if rejoicing. ***give sb the ~ eye,*** (sl) give an amorous, inviting look. ***give sb the ~ hand,*** (sl) offer the hand of welcome. **ˈ~ rags,** (sl) clothes for a festive occasion. **~·den** /ˈglædn/ *vt* [VP6A] make ~. **~·ly** *adv* **~·ness** *n* **~·some** /-səm/ *adj* (liter) cheerful; joyful.

glade /gleɪd/ *n* clear, open space in a forest.

gladi·ator /ˈglædɪeɪtə(r)/ *n* (in ancient Rome) man trained to fight with weapons at public shows in an arena. **gladia·tor·ial** /ˌglædɪəˈtɔrɪəl/ *adj* of ~s: *~ial combats.*

gladi·olus /ˌglædɪˈəʊləs/ *n* (*pl* -li /-laɪ/ or -luses) plant with sword-shaped leaves and spikes of brightly coloured flowers.

glam·our (US also **glamor**) /ˈglæmə(r)/ *n* [U] **1** charm or enchantment; power of beauty or romance to move the feelings: *the ~ of moonlight on the sea; a scene full of ~.* **2** alluring beauty or charm, often with sex-appeal, e g of some film or TV stars. **~·ous** /-əs/ *adj* full of ~: *glamorous film stars.* **~·ize** /-aɪz/ *vt* [VP6A] make glamorous: *newspapers that glamorize the lives of film stars.* **~·iz·ation** /ˌglæmərаɪˈzeɪʃn *US:* -rɪˈz-/ *vt*

glance /glɑns *US:* ˈglæns/ *vi,vt* **1** [VP2C,3A] ***~ at/over/through/round,*** take a quick look: *~ at the clock; ~ over/through a letter; ~ round a room. She'd ~d shyly at him from behind her fan.* [VP15A] *He ~d his eye down the classified advertisements.* **2** [VP3A] ***~ off,*** (of a weapon or a blow) slip or slide: *The arrow ~d off his armour.* **3** [VP2C] (of bright objects, light) flash: *Their helmets ~d in the sunlight.* □ *n* **1** quick look: *take a ~ at the newspaper headlines; see something at a ~,* at once. **2** quick turning of the eyes: *a saucy ~; loving ~s.* **3** (sudden movement producing a) flash of light: *a ~ of spears in the sunlight.*

gland /glænd/ *n* simple or complex organ that separates from the blood substances that are to be used by or expelled from the body: *a snake's poison ~s; milk-producing ~s in a female; sweat ~s.* **~·ular** /ˈglændjʊlə(r) *US:* -dʒʊ-/ *adj* of or like a ~: *~ular fever;* containing a ~.

glan·ders /ˈglændəz/ *n* [U] contagious disease of horses with swellings below the jaw, and sores in the nose and throat.

glare[1] /gleə(r)/ *n* **1** [U] strong, fierce, unpleasant light: *the ~ of the sun on the water;* (fig) *in the full ~ of publicity,* with public attention directed towards one. **2** angry or fierce look; fixed look: *look at someone with a ~.*

glare[2] /gleə(r)/ *vi,vt* **1** [VP2A,C] shine in a dazzling or disagreeable way: *The tropic sun ~d down* *on us all the day.* **2** [VP2A,C,2A] ~ ***(at)***, stare angrily or fiercely: *They stood glaring at each other.* [VP6A,14] *They* ~*d defiance/hate at me.* **glar·ing** *adj* **1** dazzling: *a car with glaring headlights; glaring neon signs.* **2** angry; fierce: *glaring eyes.* **3** gross; conspicuous: *a glaring error/blunder; glaring injustice.* **4** (of colours) crude; gaudy.

glass /glɑs *US:* glæs/ *n* **1** [U] hard, brittle substance (as used in windows), usu transparent: *made of* ~*; a man with a* ~ *eye.* **2** [C] article made of this substance. **(a)** ~ drinking vessel or its contents: *drink a* ~ *of milk; have a* ~ *too much,* drink too much alcoholic liquor, be rather drunk. **(b)** (also **ˈlooking-~**) mirror made of ~. **(c)** telescope: *The sailor looked through his* ~. **(d)** barometer: *The* ~ *is falling.* **(e)** (*pl*) (rarely **ˈeye-~es**) spectacles: *She can't read without* ~*es.* **(f)** (*pl*) binoculars. **(g)** *ˈmagnifying* ~, ~ lens on a handle for making writing, etc appear larger. **3** [U] vessels and articles made of ~: *There's plenty of* ~ *in the house,* plenty of drinking ~es, wine ~es, ~ bowls and dishes, etc. *There are many acres of* ~ *in Jersey,* acres covered with ~houses (for growing plants). **4** (compounds) **ˈ~-blower** *n* workman who blows molten ~ to shape it into bottles, etc. **ˈ~-cutter** *n* workman who cuts designs on ~; tool for cutting ~. **ˈ~·house** *n* building with ~ sides and roof (for growing plants); (sl) military prison. ***People who live in ~houses shouldn't throw stones,*** (prov) People with faults shouldn't criticize those of others. **ˈ~·ware** /-weə(r)/ *n* [U] articles made of ~. **ˈ~-wool** *n* [U] fine ~ fibres used for filtering and in man-made fibres. **ˈ~·works** *n* factory where ~ is manufactured. □ *vt* [VP6A,15B] ~ ***in,*** fit with ~; glaze: *a* ~*ed-in veranda.* **~·ful** /-fʊl/ *n* as much as a drinking ~ will hold. **~y** *adj* (**-ier, -iest**) like ~ in appearance: *a* ~*y calm;* (of the sea, etc) smooth and shiny; *a* ~*y stare/look/eye,* lifeless, expressionless, fixed.

glau·coma /glɔˈkəʊmə/ *n* [U] eye disease involving gradual loss of sight.

glau·cous /ˈglɔkəs/ *adj* **1** dull greyish green or blue. **2** (of leaves, grapes, etc) covered with bloom(3).

glaze /gleɪz/ *vt,vi* **1** [VP6A,15B] ~ ***(in),*** fit glass into: ~ *a window/house;* ~ *in a porch/veranda,* enclose it with glass. **2** [VP6A,15B] cover with a glass-like surface: ~ *pottery/porcelain/bricks.* **3** [VP2A,C] (of the eyes) become glassy: *His eyes* ~*d over. His eyes were* ~*d in death.* □ *n* [C,U] (substance used for, surface obtained by giving, a) thin glassy coating: *a Satsuma vase with a fine crackle* ~.

glaz·ier /ˈgleɪzɪə(r) *US:* -ʒə(r)/ *n* workman who fits glass into the frames of windows, etc.

gleam /glim/ *n* [C] **1** beam or ray of soft light, esp one that comes and goes: *the* ~ *of a distant lighthouse; the first* ~*s of the morning sun.* **2** (fig) brief show of some quality or emotion: *an essay with an occasional* ~ *of humour/intelligence; a* ~ *of hope; a man with a dangerous* ~ *in his eye,* with a threatening look. □ *vi* [VP2A,C] send out ~s: *a cat's eyes* ~*ing in the darkness; glass reflector studs* ~*ing in the roadway.*

glean /glin/ *vi,vt* [VP2A,6A] pick up grain left in a harvest field by the workers; (fig) gather news, facts in small quantities: ~ *a field;* ~ *corn.* **~er** *n* person who ~s. **~·ings** *n pl* (usu fig) small items of knowledge ~ed from various sources.

glebe /glib/ *n* **1** (poet) earth; field. **2** portion of land that forms part of a clergyman's benefice.

glee /gli/ *n* [U] feeling of joy caused by success or triumph: *shout with* ~*. She was in high* ~ *when she learnt the news.* **2** [C] song for three or four voices singing different parts in harmony. **~·ful** /-fl/ *adj* full of ~; joyous. **~·fully** /-flɪ/ *adv*

glen /glen/ *n* narrow valley.

Glen·garry /ˈglenˈgærɪ/ *n* (*pl* **-ries**) kind of cap worn in the Highlands of Scotland.

glib /glɪb/ *adj* (**-ber, -best**) (of a person, what he says or how he says it) ready and smooth, but not sincere: *a* ~ *talker;* ~ *excuses;* ~ *in finding excuses; have a* ~ *tongue.* **~·ly** *adv* **~·ness** *n*

glide /glɑɪd/ *vi* [VP2A,C] move along smoothly and continuously: *The pilot of the sailplane* ~*d skilfully down to the landing-field. The ghost* ~*d out of the room. A boat* ~*d past.* □ *n* gliding movement: *The new dance consists of a series of* ~*s.* **glider** *n* aircraft without an engine, e g the kind towed behind a powered aircraft. ⇨ *sailplane* at sail[1](4). **glid·ing** *n* sport of flying in gliders.

glim·mer /ˈglɪmə(r)/ *vi* [VP2A,C] send out a weak, uncertain light: *lights* ~*ing in the distance.* □ *n* weak, faint, unsteady light: *a* ~ *of light through the curtains;* (fig) *a* ~ *of hope; not the least* ~ *of intelligence.*

glimpse /glɪmps/ *n* ***get/catch a ~ of sb/sth,*** quick, imperfect view: *get/catch a* ~ *of something from the window of a train;* short look (*at* sth or sb). □ *vt* [VP6A] catch a ~ of.

glint /glɪnt/ *vi* gleam. □ *n* gleam or flash: ~*s of gold in her hair.*

glis·sade /glɪˈsɑd/ *vi* (mountaineering) slide down a steep slope of ice or snow (usu with an ice-axe). □ *n* such a slide.

glis·sando /glɪˈsændəʊ/ *adv, adj* (music) passing quickly up or down the scale.

glis·ten /ˈglɪsn/ *vi* [VP2A,C] (esp of wet or polished surfaces, tear-filled eyes) shine brightly; sparkle: ~*ing dew-drops; eyes* ~*ing with tears.*

glis·ter /ˈglɪstə(r)/ *vi, n* (poet) glitter.

glit·ter /ˈglɪtə(r)/ *vi* [VP2A,C] shine brightly with flashes of light: *stars* ~*ing in the frosty sky;* ~*ing with jewels.* □ *n* [U] brilliant light: *the* ~ *of the Christmas tree decorations.* **~·ing** *adj* brilliant; attractive: ~*ing prizes.*

gloam·ing /ˈgləʊmɪŋ/ *n* (*sing* with *def art*) evening twilight.

gloat /gləʊt/ *vi* [VP2A,3A] ~ ***(over sth),*** look at with selfish delight: ~ *over one's wealth/the ruin of a rival; a miser* ~*ing over his gold.* **~·ing·ly** *adv*

glo·bal /ˈgləʊbl/ *adj* world-wide; embracing the whole of a group of items, etc.

globe /gləʊb/ *n* **1** objects shaped like a ball, esp a model of the earth; spherical chart of the earth or the constellations: *the use of the* ~*s,* (archaic for) the teaching of geography and astronomy by the use of spherical charts. **2** spherical glass vessel, esp a lampshade or a fishbowl. **3** **ˈ~ fish** *n* fish able to inflate itself into the shape of a ~. **ˈ~ trotter** *n* tourist who travels hurriedly through many foreign countries.

glob·ule /ˈglobjul/ *n* tiny drop, esp of liquid. **globu·lar** /ˈglobjʊlə(r)/ *adj* globe-shaped; made of ~s.

glock·en·spiel /ˈglokənspil/ *n* musical instrument consisting of metal bars which are struck with two light hammers. ⇨ the illus at **percussion**.

gloom /glum/ *n* [C] **1** semi-darkness; obscurity. **2** feeling of sadness and hopelessness: *The future seems to be filled with* ~. *The news cast a* ~ *over the village.*

gloomy /ˈglumɪ/ *adj* (-ier, -iest) **1** dark, unlighted. **2** depressed; depressing: *a* ~ *outlook over roofs and chimneys; feeling* ~ *about the future.* **~·ily** *adv*

glor·ify /ˈglɔrɪfɑɪ/ *vt* (*pt,pp* -fied) [VP6A] **1** give adoration and thanksgiving to (God); worship; give honour and glory to (a hero). **2** invest (sth common or simple) with charm or beauty; make (sth or sb) seem more imposing: *His weekend cottage is only a glorified barn.* **glori·fi·ca·tion** /ˌglɔrɪfɪˈkeɪʃn/ *n* ~ing or being glorified.

glori·ous /ˈglɔrɪəs/ *adj* **1** splendid; magnificent: *a* ~ *sunset/view.* **2** illustrious; honourable; possessing or conferring glory: *a* ~ *victory; the* ~ *reign of Queen Elizabeth* I. **3** (colloq) enjoyable: *have a* ~ *time;* ~ *fun.* **4** (ironic) dreadful: *What a* ~ *mess!* **~·ly** *adv*

glory /ˈglɔrɪ/ *n* [U] **1** high fame and honour won by great achievements. **2** adoration and thanksgiving offered to God: *'G~ to God in the highest.'* **3** quality of being beautiful or magnificent: *the* ~ *of a sunset.* **4** (sometimes [C] *pl* -ries) reason for pride; subject for boasting; sth deserving respect and honour: *the glories of ancient Rome.* **5** heavenly splendour: *the saints in* ~. **6** (colloq uses) *go to* ~, die; *send sb to* ~, kill him. **ˈ~-hole** *n* room, drawer, filled untidily with miscellaneous articles. □ *vi* [VP3A] **~ *in,*** rejoice in, take great pride in: ~ *in one's strength/in working for a good cause.*

gloss[1] /glos/ *n* **1** [U] smooth, bright surface: *the* ~ *of silk and satin; material with a good* ~. **ˈ~ paint** *n* paint which, when dry, leaves a ~ (usu washable) surface. **2** (fig, usu *sing* with *indef art*) deceptive appearance: *a* ~ *of respectability*, e g over a life of secret wrongdoing. □ *vt* [VP15A] **~ *over,*** give a ~ to; cover up or explain away (an error, etc): ~ *over sb's faults.* **~y** *adj* (-ier, -iest) smooth and shiny: *a* ~*y photographic print; serge trousers with a* ~ *seat;* ~*y periodicals*, those printed on high quality ~y paper, with photographs, coloured illustrations, etc, esp those periodicals dealing with clothes, fashions, etc. **~·ily** /-əlɪ/ *adv* **~i·ness** *n*

gloss[2] /glos/ *n* [C] explanation (in a footnote, or in a list at the end of an article, a book, etc) of a word in the text; comment; interpretation. □ *vt* [VP6A] add a ~ or ~es to (a text); write ~es on; make comments on.

gloss·ary /ˈglosərɪ/ *n* (*pl* -ries) [C] collection of glosses; list and explanations of special, e g technical, obsolete, words.

glot·tis /ˈglotɪs/ *n* opening between the vocal cords at the upper part of the windpipe. ⇨ the illus at **head**. **glot·tal** /ˈglotl/ *adj* of the ~. **glottal stop,** speech sound produced by a complete closure of the ~, followed by an explosive release of breath.

glove /glʌv/ *n* covering of leather, knitted wool, etc for the hand, usu with separated fingers. ⇨ the illus at **base**. ***fit like a* ~,** fit perfectly. ***be hand in* ~ *(with...)*,** be in close relations (with...). ***take off the* ~*s to sb, handle sb without* ~*s,*** argue or contend in earnest, without mercy. **ˈ~-locker/-compartment** *n* compartment in the dashboard of a car, for small articles.

glow /gləʊ/ *vi* [VP2A,C] **1** send out brightness or warmth without flame: ~*ing embers/charcoal;* ~*ing metal from the furnace.* **2** (fig) be, look, feel, warm or flushed (as after exercise or when excited): ~*ing with enthusiasm/health/pride.* **3** show strong or warm colours: *woods and forests* ~*ing with autumn tints.* □ *n* (*sing* only, with *def* or *indef art*) ~ing state; warm or flushed look; warm feeling: *in a* ~ *of enthusiasm; cheeks with the* ~ *of health on them;* (*all*) *in a* ~ *after a hot bath; the* ~ *of the sky at sunset.* **ˈ~-worm** *n* insect of which the wingless female gives out a green light at its tail. **~·ing** *adj* showing warm colour or (fig) enthusiasm: *give a* ~*ing account of what happened; describe an event in* ~*ing colours.* **~·ing·ly** *adv*

glower /ˈglɑʊə(r)/ *vi* [VP2A,3A] **~ at,** look in an angry or threatening way. **~·ing·ly** *adv*

glu·cose /ˈglukəʊs/ *n* [U] grape sugar.

glue /glu/ *n* [U] hard, brittle substance made by boiling hides and bones, used when softened by heat for joining (esp wooden) things; substance used for the same purpose, obtained from fish and other sources. □ *vt* (*pt,pp* glued; gluing) [VP6A, 15A,B] **1** stick, make fast, with ~: ~ *two pieces of wood together;* ~ *a piece of wood on to something.* **2** put tightly or closely: *His eyes were/His ear was* ~*d to the keyhole. Why must you always remain* ~*d to your mother,* Why can you never be separated from your mother? **gluey** /ˈgluɪ/ *adj* sticky, like ~.

glum /glʌm/ *adj* (-mer, -mest) gloomy; sad. **~·ly** *adv* **~·ness** *n*

glut /glʌt/ *vt* (-tt-) [VP6A,14] **~ *with,*** **1** supply too much to: ~ *the market* (*with fruit, etc*). **2** overeat; satisfy to the full; fill to excess: ~ *one's appetite;* ~ *oneself with rich food;* ~*ted with pleasure.* □ *n* [U] supply in excess of demand: *a* ~ *of pears in the market.*

glu·ten /ˈglutən/ *n* [U] sticky substance (protein) that is left when starch is washed out of flour. **glu·ti·nous** /ˈglutɪnəs *US:* -tṇəs/ *adj* of or like ~; sticky.

glut·ton /ˈglʌtn/ *n* person who eats too much: *You've eaten the whole pie, you* ~*! He's a* ~ *for work,* (fig) is always willing and ready to work. **~·ous** /ˈglʌtṇəs/ *adj* very greedy (for food). **~·ous·ly** *adv* **~y** /-tṇɪ/ *n* [U] habit or practice of eating too much.

gly·cer·ine (US = **gly·cer·in**) /ˈglɪsəˈrin *US:* ˈglɪsərɪn/ *n* [U] thick, sweet, colourless liquid made from fats and oils, used in medical and toilet preparations and explosives.

G-man /ˈdʒi mæn/ *n* (US colloq) federal criminal investigation officer.

gnarled /nɑld/ *adj* (of tree trunks) twisted and rough; covered with knobs: *a* ~ *old oak;* ~ (= knotty, deformed) *hands/fingers.*

gnash /næʃ/ *vi,vt* **1** [VP2A] (of the teeth) strike together, e g in rage. **2** [VP6A] (of a person) cause (the teeth) to do this: *wailing and* ~*ing of teeth.*

gnat /næt/ *n* small two-winged fly that stings; (fig) insignificant annoyance. ***strain at a* ~,** hesitate over a trifle.

gnaw /nɔ/ *vt,vi* **1** [VP6A,15B,3A] **~ *(at),*** bite steadily at (sth hard): *The dog was* ~*ing* (*at*) *a bone. The rats had* ~*ed away some of the woodwork. He was* ~*ing his finger-nails with impatience.* **2** [VP6A,3A] **~ *(at),*** torment; waste away: *fear and anxiety* ~*ing* (*at*) *the heart; the* ~*ing* *pains of hunger.*

gnome /nəʊm/ *n* (in tales) small goblin living under the ground (often guarding treasures of gold and silver).

gnu /nu/ *n* ox-like antelope (= wildebeest).

go[1] /gəʊ/ *vi* (*3rd pers pres t* goes /gəʊz/, *pt* went /went/, *pp* gone /gon *US:* gɔn/) (For idiomatic uses with *adverbial particles* and *preps,* ⇨ 28 below.) **1** [VP2A,C,3A,4A] (with a *prep* or *adv* of place or direction, present or implied ⇨ come) move, pass, from one point to another and away from the speaker, etc: *Shall we go (there) by train or by steamer? He has gone to China,* is now in, or on his way to, China. *He has gone to see his sister. Go and get your hat. Let's go to the cinema. Let's go,* Let's leave. *They came at six and went* (= left) *at nine. I must be going now,* must leave now. *I wish this pain would go (away). All hope is gone* (more usu today, *has gone*). *Be gone! Go away!* (the more usu expression today). *Who goes there?* (challenge from a sentry = Say who you are). **2** [VP2C] (**a**) be placed; have as a usual or proper position: *Where do you want your piano to go, Mister?* Where shall we put it? *'Where does this teapot go?' 'In that cupboard.' This dictionary goes on the top shelf.* (**b**) be fitted or contained in: *My clothes won't go into this small suitcase. 7 into 15 won't go,* 15 does not contain exact multiples of 7. **3** [VP2A,B,C,3A] reach, extend; last; (of a person's behaviour, remarks, achievements, etc) reach certain limits: *This road goes to London. I want a rope that will go from the top window to the ground. Differences between employers and workers go deep,* Their views are far apart. ***go a long way,*** (**a**) last: *She makes a little money go a long way,* buys many things, etc by careful spending. *A little of this paint goes a long way,* covers a large area. (**b**) (colloq) be as much as one can bear: *A little of his company goes a long way,* One can endure his company for a short time only. ***go a long way/far towards doing sth,*** make a considerable contribution towards: *The Prime Minister's statement went a long way towards reassuring the nation.* ***go (very) far,*** (**a**) last: *A pound doesn't go far nowadays,* doesn't last, doesn't buy much. (**b**) (of a person, future tense) succeed: *He will go far in the diplomatic service, will win promotion, etc.* ***go too far,*** go beyond acceptable limits: *That's going too far,* saying or doing more than is right. *You must apologize at once—you've gone too far,* exceeded the limits of accepted behaviour, etc. ***go (any) further,*** go beyond a certain point: *I'll give you £50, but I can't go any further. Need I go any further,* do or say anything more? ***go as/so far as to do sth,*** do or say sth to a certain limit: *I won't go as far as to say he's dishonest,* won't accuse him of this, even though I may suspect him of it. *I would go so far as to suggest that she deserves a higher salary.* ***as far as it goes,*** to a limited extent: *That's all very well as far as it goes,* the limitations of the statement, explanation, etc must be realised. *What he says is true as far as it goes,* suggesting that further information, knowledge, etc is needed or desirable. ***go to great lengths/trouble/pains (to do sth),*** take care to do sth well: *He went to great trouble to make his guests comfortable.* ***go to one's head,*** ⇨ head[1](19). ***go as low/high as,*** (of a price) reach a certain level: *I'll go as high as £250,* will offer this sum, e g at an auction. ***go one better (than sb),*** improve on what he has done: *I hit the target 17 times out of 20, but Tom went one better and scored 18. It all/just /just goes to show/prove that,* tends or helps to show/prove that. **4** ***go on a journey/trip/outing,*** make a journey, take a trip, have an outing, etc. ***go for a walk/swim, etc,*** go out in order to walk, swim, etc. ***go walking/swimming, etc,*** take part in the activity of walking, swimming, etc. Cf *Let's go for a walk* (referring to a specified occasion): *Do they often go sailing?* Is sailing sth they often engage in? *Mrs Green has gone (out) shopping,* has gone to buy things in the shops. **5** (in the pattern, *go + prep + n*) (**a**) pass into/from the state indicated by the *n.* ***go into abeyance,*** ⇨ abeyance. ***go from bad to worse,*** ⇨ bad[1](4). ***go into a coma/trance,*** ⇨ coma, trance. ***go out of fashion,*** ⇨ fashion(2). ***go into liquidation,*** ⇨ *liquidation* at liquidate. ***go (all) to pieces,*** ⇨ piece[1](1). ***go to pot,*** ⇨ pot[1](2). ***go to rack and ruin,*** ⇨ rack[4]. ***go into retirement,*** ⇨ *retirement* at retire. ***go to seed,*** ⇨ seed. ***go to sleep,*** ⇨ sleep[1](3). ***go out of use,*** ⇨ use[1](1). ***go to war,*** ⇨ war. (**b**) go to the place, etc indicated for the purpose associated with it. ***go to the block/stake,*** ⇨ block[1](3), stake(2). ***go to church,*** attend a church service. ***go to hospital,*** ⇨ hospital. ***go to market,*** ⇨ market. ***go to school/college/university,*** attend school, etc in order to learn or study. ***go to sea,*** become a sailor. ***go on the stage,*** ⇨ stage(1). ***go on the streets,*** ⇨ street. (**c**) have recourse to. ***go to the country,*** ⇨ country. ***go to law,*** ⇨ law(6). **6** [VP3A] ***go to sb,*** pass into sb's possession; be allotted to: *Who did the property go to when the old man died,* Who inherited it? *Honours do not always go to those who merit them. The first prize went to Mr Hill.* **7** [VP2D] become; pass into a specific condition: *go blind/mad, etc. He went purple with anger/grey with worry. Fish soon goes bad* (= rotten) *in hot weather. The children went wild with excitement. This material has gone a funny* (= strange) *colour. Tiverton went Liberal at the by-election,* changed politically by returning the Liberal candidate to Parliament. *Will the country go Democrat next year?* ***go berserk,*** ⇨ beserk. ***go broke,*** become penniless. ***go dry,*** ⇨ dry[1](12). ***go haywire,*** ⇨ hay. ***go native,*** (usu of sb of European race) adopt the mode of life of the natives of the country in which one is living. ***go phut,*** (colloq) (of machines) collapse: *The old car went phut half way up the hill.* ***go scot-free/unchallenged/unpunished,*** be free from penalty or punishment; escape being challenged. **8** [VP2A,C] be moving, working, etc: *This clock doesn't go. Is your watch going? Her tongue was going nineteen to the dozen,* ⇨ dozen. *The play went (down) like a bomb,* (colloq) was very favourably received. ***a going concern,*** a business in working order, operating well. **9** [VP2C,D] be or live habitually in a specific state or manner: *Refugees often go hungry. The men of this tribe used to go naked. He went in fear of his life. You'd better go armed* (= carry a weapon) *while in the jungle. She is six months gone,* pregnant. **10** [VP2C,D,E] (with an *adv* or *adv* equivalent, e g *adjj* such as *slow, easy,* indicating manner of progress) after 'How': *How's everything going* (= progressing)? *How's work going? How goes work? How goes it?* (colloq) How are you? **go well/badly,** (of work, events) proceed (un)satisfactorily: *All has gone well with our plans,* they've succeeded. *Things went better than had been expected.* **go easy (with sb/sth),** be less strenuous, less severe; handle gently or carefully: *Go easy with/on the butter, that's all we have,* don't be wasteful. *Go easy with her, she's too young to realise her mistake.* **go slow, (a)** (as a traffic signal) move forward slowly. **(b)** (of workers in factories, etc) work slowly esp to reduce output, as a protest against sth or to draw attention to demands: (attrib) *a go-slow (policy).* **be going strong,** be proceeding vigorously; be still flourishing: *He's ninety and/but still going strong.* **11** [VP2A,C] work; operate: *This machine goes by electricity. I've been going hard (at it) all day and I'm exhausted.* **12** [VP2C,3A] **go (to sb) for,** be sold (to sb) for: *The house went cheap. I shan't let mine go* (= sell it) *for less than £8 000.* **go for a song,** ⇨ song. **Going! Going! Gone!** (used at an auction to announce that the bidding has almost, quite, closed). **13** [VP24] **go on/in,** (of money) be spent on: *All his spare money goes on books. How much of your money goes on food and clothes/in rent? Half the money he inherited went in gambling debts.* **14** [VP2A,C] be given up, abandoned, lost: *Latin and Greek must go,* We must give up teaching them. *I'm afraid the car must go,* We can no longer afford to run it, so must sell it. *My sight is going,* I'm losing my ability to see. *We can no longer afford a gardener, he'll have to go,* be sacked. *The next wicket went for only two runs,* Only two runs were scored before the next batsman was out. **15** [VP2A,C] be current or accepted; be commonly thought of or believed: *When Britain had gold sovereigns they went everywhere,* were accepted everywhere (in payment) with confidence. *The story goes that....* It is said that.... **16** [VP2A] **as men/things, etc go,** considering the average men, etc: *They're good workers, as workers go nowadays,* judging them from the average or usual type today. *Five pounds for a pair of shoes is not bad as things go today,* in view of how much things cost today. **17** [VP2A] fail; collapse; give way; break off: *First the sails and then the mast went in the storm. The bank may go* (= fail) *any day. He's far gone,* is critically ill or (colloq) is mad. **let oneself go,** relax, enjoy oneself, etc. **18** (*pp* and phrases) die: *He has gone, poor fellow! dead and gone,* dead and buried. **19** [VP2A,C] be decided: *The case* (i e in a law court) *went against him,* he lost. *The case went in his favour,* he won. *How did the election go at Hull,* Who was elected? *Does promotion go by favour in your firm?* **20** (various phrases) **go bail (for sb),** ⇨ bail[1]. **go dutch (with sb),** ⇨ dutch. **go shares/halves (in sth with sb),** ⇨ share[1](1), half. **go sick,** ⇨ sick[1](2). **go it,** (colloq) act vigorously, indulge in wild spending, etc. **go it alone,** act by oneself, without support. **21** [VP2A,C] **(a)** have a certain wording or tune: *I'm not quite sure how the tune goes.* **(b)** (of a verse or song) be adaptable (to a certain tune): *It goes to the tune of 'Sur le pont d'Avignon'.* **22** (colloq) (followed by *and* and another *v*) proceed to do sth: *Go and shut the door, would you?* (as an informal request). *Don't go and ask that brainless doll to be your wife! Now you've been and gone and done it,* (sl) have made a mistake, blundered. **23** [VP2A,C] make a specific sound: *The clock goes 'tick-tock, tick-tock'. 'Bang! went the gun'.* **24** (in bridge[2]) bid; declare: *go two spades/three no trumps.* **25** [VP2A] begin an activity: *One, two, three, go!* or *Ready, steady, go!* (e g as a signal for competitors in a race to start). *Well, here goes!* (used to call attention to the fact that one is about to start to do sth). **26** **be going to do sth, (a)** indicating what is intended, determined or planned: *We're going to spend our holidays in Wales this year. I'm going to have my own way. We're going to buy a house when we've saved enough money.* **(b)** indicating what is considered likely or probable: *Look at those black clouds—we're going to have/there's going to be a storm. Is there going to be a (business) depression this year?* **(c)** forming an immediate or near future (= about to): *I'm going to tell you a story. I'm going to be twenty next month.* **27** (compounds) **'go-a`head** *n* ⇨ go ahead in 28 below. **go-as-you-please,** *attrib adj* untroubled by regulations. **`go-by,** ⇨ go by in 28 below. **go-`off** *n* start: *at the first go-off,* the first attempt. **'go-`slow,** ⇨ 10 above. **'go-to-`meeting,** *attrib adj* (dated colloq of hats, clothes, etc) worn on special occasions, e g for church: *wearing their Sunday go-to-meeting clothes.* **28** [VP2C,15B,3A] (idiomatic uses with *adverbial particles* and *preps*):

go about, (a) move from place to place; pay visits: *He's going about with that Polish girl now,* is often seen with her in public. **(b)** (of rumours, stories, etc) pass from person to person, usu verbally; be current: *A story/rumour is going about that....* **(c)** (of a ship) change course or tack(3). **go about sth, (a)** set to work at: *You're not going about that job in the right way. We'll have to go about it more carefully.* **(b)** deal with one's own affairs (rather than with sb else's): *Go about your business!*

go after sb/sth, try to win or obtain: *He's going after that pretty Swedish girl,* is trying to win her interest or affection. *He's gone after a job in the City.*

go against sb, (a) oppose: *Don't go against your father.* **(b)** have an unsatisfactory outcome: *The war is going against them,* They seem likely to be defeated. ⇨ also 19 above. **go against sth,** be contrary to: *It goes against my principles/interests.* **go against the grain,** ⇨ grain(4).

go ahead, (a) make progress: *He's going ahead fast. The Joneses are very go-ahead* (= progressive) *people; it's difficult to keep up with them.* **(b)** proceed without hesitation: *'May I start now?' 'Yes, go ahead'.* Hence, **`go-ahead** *n* permission to proceed: *give them the go-ahead.*

go along, proceed: *You may have some difficulty first but you'll find it easier as you go along.* **go along with sb, (a)** accompany: *I'll go along with you as far as the church.* **(b)** agree with: *I can't go along with you on that point. Go along with you!* (colloq) Don't expect me to believe that! Don't be so cheeky! etc, according to context.

go at sb/sth, (a) rush at; attack: *They went at each other furiously. They went at it tooth and nail/hammer and tongs,* fought furiously. **(b)** take sth in hand, deal with it energetically: *They were going at the job for all they were worth, making the utmost possible effort to do the work.*

go away, leave. **go away with sb/sth,** take with one, abscond with: *He has gone away with my razor, has taken it with him.*

go back, (a) return. (b) extend backwards in space or time: *His family goes back for hundreds of years/to the time of the Norman Conquest,* can be traced back for/to.... **go back (up)on,** fail to keep; break or withdraw from, e g a promise: *He's not the sort of man who would/to go back on his word.*

go before (sth), precede: *Pride goes before a fall.* **go behind sth,** search for sth: *go behind a person's words,* look for a hidden meaning in what he says. **go behind sb's back,** do or say sth without their knowledge. **go beyond sth,** exceed: *You've gone beyond your instructions. That's going beyond a joke,* is too serious to be amusing.

go by, pass: *Time went by slowly. We waited for the procession to go by.* **ˈgo by sth,** (a) be guided or directed by: *I shall go entirely by what my solicitor says,* shall follow his advice. *That's a good rule to go by,* to be guided by. (b) form an opinion or judgement from: *Have we enough evidence to go by? It's not always wise to go by appearances. I go by what I hear. He always goes by the book,* follows the advice, keeps to the rules, etc in it. **go by/under the name of,** be called: *My dog goes by the name of Rover.* **ˈgo-by** *n* **give sb/sth the go-by,** (colloq) ignore; disregard; slight or snub: *He gave me the go-by in the street yesterday,* ignored me completely.

go down, (a) (of a ship, etc) sink. (b) (of the sun, moon, etc) set. (c) (of food and drink) be swallowed: *This pill won't go down,* I can't swallow it. (d) leave a university for the vacation, having graduated, etc. (e) (of the sea, wind, etc) become calm: *The wind has gone down a little, is less strong.* (f) (of prices) go lower: *The price of eggs/The cost of living has gone down.* (g) **go down to the sea/country/cottage, etc,** pay a visit to the seaside, countryside, etc. **go down before sb,** be defeated or overthrown: *Rome went down before the barbarians.* **go down (in sth),** be written in; be recorded or remembered in: *It all goes down in his notebook. He'll go down in history as a great statesman.* **go down to,** be continued or extended as far as: *This 'History of Europe' goes down to 1970.* **go down with sb,** (a) (of an explanation or excuse, of a story, play, etc) be accepted or approved by the listener, reader, audience, etc: *The new play went down well/like a bomb* (= extremely well) *with provincial audiences. That explanation won't go down well with me. The new teacher doesn't go down well with his pupils.* (b) fall ill with: *Poor Peter—he's gone down with 'flu.*

go for sb, (a) go to fetch: *Shall I go for a doctor?* (b) attack: *The dog went for the postman as soon as he opened the garden gate. Go for him!* (said to a dog to urge him to attack). *They went for me in the correspondence columns of the papers.* (c) be applicable to: *What I have said about Smith goes for you, too.* **go for nothing/little,** be considered of no/little value: *All his work went for nothing.*

go forth, (formal) be published or issued: *The order went forth that....*

go forward, (a) advance: *A patrol went forward to investigate.* (b) make progress: *The work is going forward well.* (c) (old use, now *go on*) take place: *What's going forward here?*

go in, (a) enter: *The key won't go in (the lock). This cork's too big; it won't go in. She went in to cook the dinner.* (b) (of the sun, moon, etc) be obscured by clouds: *The sun went in and it grew rather cold.* (c) (cricket, etc) begin an innings: *Who goes in next?* (d) enter as a competitor: *Go in and win!* (used as a form of encouragement). **go in for sth,** (a) take, sit for: *go in for an examination.* (b) have an interest in, have as a hobby, etc: *go in for golf/stamp-collecting/growing orchids.*

go into sth, (a) enter: *go into business; go into society,* mix with people in high society; *go into the Army/the Church/Parliament. When did Britain go into Europe,* join the EEC? (b) busy or occupy oneself with: *go into (the) details/particulars,* deal with them closely; *go into the evidence; go deeply into a question. This problem will need a lot of going into,* will need thorough investigation. (c) (allow oneself to) pass into (a certain state): *go into fits of laughter/hysterical.* **go into mourning,** wear black clothes as a symbol of mourning.

go off, (a) explode; be fired: *The gun went off by accident. The pistol didn't go off.* (b) lose good quality; deteriorate: *This milk has gone off,* turned sour. *Meat and fish go off quickly in hot weather.* (c) become unconscious, either in sleep or in a faint: *Hasn't the baby gone off yet? She went off into a faint.* (d) (of goods) be got rid of by sale: *The goods went off quickly.* (e) (of events) proceed well, etc: *The performance/concert went off well. How did the sports meeting go off?* (f) (as a stage direction in a printed play) leave the stage; exit/exeunt: *Hamlet goes off.* **go off sb/sth,** lose interest in or one's taste for: *Jane seems to have gone off Peter. I've gone off beer.* **go off the beaten track,** ⇨ beaten. **go off the deep end,** ⇨ end[1](1). **go off one's head,** ⇨ head[1](19). **go off with sb/sth,** go away with, esp abscond with or steal: *He's gone off to Edinburgh with his neighbour's wife. The butler went off with some of the duke's treasured possessions.*

go on, (a) (of time) pass: *As the months went on, he became impatient.* (b) conduct oneself; behave, esp in a wrong, shameful or excited way: *If you go on like this you'll be expelled.* (c) happen; take place; be in progress: *What's going on there? There's nothing interesting going on here at present. Harvesting was going on in the south. Things are going on much as usual.* (d) (theatre) appear on the stage: *She doesn't go on until Act Two.* (e) take one's turn at doing sth; (e g cricket) begin bowling: *The captain told Snow to go on next.* **ˈgo on sth,** take or accept, e g as evidence: *What evidence have we got to go on,* to be guided by in reaching a decision, etc? **go on the dole/social security,** obtain, e g when unemployed, payments under various government schemes. **go on the parish,** (old use) accept payments, known as *Poor Relief,* from the parish. **go on the pill,** start using contraceptive pills. **go on about sth,** talk persistently and often irritatingly about: *I wish you'd stop going on about my little faults.* **go on (at sb),** rail; nag; scold: *She goes on at her husband terribly. Oh, you do go on!* **be going on for,** be approaching: *He's going on for seventy.* **be gone on,** (sl) be infatuated with: *It's a pity Peter's so gone on Jane.* **go on to sth/to do sth,** do or say next; proceed to: *Let's now go on to the next item on the agenda. He went on to say that...,* next said that.... *I shall now go on to deal with our finances.* **go on (with sth/doing sth),** continue, persevere, with: *Go on with your work. How much* *longer will this hot weather go on? That's enough to go on with/to be going on with,* enough for our immediate needs. *Go on trying. I hope it won't go on raining all day.* ***Go on (with you)!*** (colloq) Don't expect me to believe that! Don't be so silly! etc, according to context. **'goings-'on** *n pl* (colloq) ⇨ go on (b,c); (often with *such/strange/queer*) happenings; behaviour: *I've never seen such queer goings-on!*

go out, **(a)** leave the room, building, etc: *She was (all) dressed to go out,* wearing outdoor clothes. *Out you go! Do you often go out riding* (i e on a horse)? **(b)** attend social functions, go to parties, dances, etc: *She still goes out a great deal, even at seventy-five.* ***go out on a spree/on the town,*** ⇨ spree, town. **(c)** be extinguished: *The fire* (e g the fire burning in the grate) *has gone out. There was a power cut and all the lights went out.* **(d)** become unfashionable: *Has the fashion for mini-skirts/Have mini-skirts gone out?* **(e)** (of a government) retire from power: *The Ministry that has just gone out had become very unpopular.* **(f)** (formerly, esp of girls) leave home for employment in the house of others: *When she was eighteen she went out as a nursemaid/governess.* **(g)** (as used by workers of themselves) strike: *Are we likely to gain anything by going out?* ⇨ *come out* in come(15) (d). **(h)** (of a year, etc) end: *The year went out gloomily.* ***go out on a limb,*** ⇨ limb(2). ***go out to,*** leave, e g one's own country, and go to: *He couldn't get work at home* (e g in England) *so went out to Australia.* ***go out to sb,*** (of the heart, feelings) be extended to: *Our hearts/sympathies go out to those poor children orphaned by war.* ***go out with sb,*** (colloq) be regularly in sb's company: *How long has Jane been going out with David? How long have Jane and David been going out together?*

go over, (colloq) make an impression: *I wonder whether this new play will go over,* whether it will impress the public, be favourably received. *David didn't go over well with Jane's parents at the weekend.* ***go over sth,*** **(a)** examine the details of: *We must go over the accounts carefully before we settle them.* **(b)** look at; inspect: *We should like to go over the house before deciding whether we want to buy it.* **(c)** rehearse; study or review carefully: *Let's go over this chapter/lesson/the main facts/Scene 2 again.* Hence, **'going-'over** *n* (*pl* goings-over) **(a)** (colloq) process of examining or putting in good working order: *The document will need a careful going-over before we can make a decision. The patient was given a thorough going-over by/from the doctor.* **(b)** (sl): *The thugs gave him a thorough going-over,* struck him repeatedly. ***go over to sb/sth,*** change one's political party, side, a preference, etc: *He has gone over to the Democrats. I'm going over to a milder brand of cigarettes.*

go round, **(a)** be enough, in number or amount, for everyone to have a share: *There aren't enough apples/isn't enough whisky to go round.* **(b)** reach one's destination by using a route other than the usual or nearest way: *The main road to Worcester was flooded and we had to go (a/the long way) round.* ***go round (to a place/to do sth):*** *We're going round to my mother's/to see my mother at the weekend.* ***go round the bend,*** (colloq) become hysterical, enraged, mad, etc.

go through, **(a)** (= get through) be passed or approved: *The Bill* (i e in Parliament) *did not go through.* **(b)** be concluded: *The deal did not go through.* ***go through sth,*** **(a)** discuss in detail: *Let's go through the arguments again.* **(b)** search: *The police went through the pockets of the suspected thief.* **(c)** perform; take part in: *She made him go through both a civil and religious wedding. How long will it take to go through* (= complete) *the programme?* **(d)** undergo; suffer: go through hardships: *If you only knew what she has to go through with that husband of hers!* **(e)** (of a book) be sold: *The book went through ten editions,* Ten editions were sold out. **(f)** reach the end of; spend: *go through a fortune/all one's money.* ***go through with sth,*** complete; not leave unfinished: *He's determined to go through with the marriage in spite of his parents' opposition.*

go to sth, amount together to: *12 inches go to the foot.* ***go to/towards sth,*** contribute to, be contributed to: *What qualities go to the making of a statesman? This money can go towards the motorbike you're saving up for.*

go together, ⇨ go with (c) below.

go under, **(a)** sink. **(b)** (fig) fail; succumb; become bankrupt: *The firm will go under unless business improves.*

go up, **(a)** rise: *The barometer/temperature/thermometer is going up. Everything went up in the budget except pensions.* **(b)** be erected: *New office blocks are going up everywhere.* **(c)** be blown up; be destroyed by explosion or fire: *The bridge went up with a roar when the mine exploded. The whole building went up in flames.* **(d)** enter a university or travel to a town, esp the capital: *go up to London/to town. When will you go up* (e g to Cambridge)? ***go up sth,*** climb: *go up a tree/ladder/wall/hill.* ***go up the wall,*** ⇨ wall.

go with sb/sth, **(a)** accompany: *I'll go with you. We must go with the times/tide,* do as others do nowadays. *He always goes with his party,* votes, etc as the party does. **(b)** take the same view as: *I can't go with you on that,* can't agree with you. **(c)** be a normal accompaniment of: *Five acres of land go with the house,* become the property of the buyers or are for the use of the tenant. *Disease often goes with squalor, but it is wrong to say that crime always goes with poverty.* Disease often accompanies squalor, but crime does not always accompany poverty. **(d)** match; be fitting and suitable with: *These new curtains don't go well with your rugs,* don't suit them. I want a hat to go with this dress. **(e)** (colloq) (of a young man or girl) be often in the company of a person of the opposite sex possibly with a view to marriage: *go with a girl,* ⇨ go out with sb above.

go without (sth), endure the lack of: *The poor boy often has to go without supper. There's no money for a holday this year; we'll just have to go without.* ***go without saying,*** be understood without actually being stated: *It goes without saying that she's a good cook.*

go[2] /gəʊ/ *n* (*pl* goes /gəʊz/) (all uses colloq) ***all the go,*** very popular, fashionable: *Pop festivals were all the go last year.* ***be full of go, have plenty of go,*** be full of energy, enthusiasm. ***be on the go,*** be busy, active: *She's been on the go all day,* has had no rest. ***have a go (at sth),*** make an attempt: *He had several goes at the high jump before he succeeded in clearing it. The police* *warned the public not to have a go because the bank raiders were armed,* not to try to intercept, catch them. ***all systems (are) go,*** (of launching or operating a spacecraft, usu stated by ground control) proceed. ***no go,*** **(a)** (in games, sports/ spacecraft operations, etc) false start, attempt. **(b)** impossible: *It'll be no go to ask/asking for a rise when you arrive so late.* **'no-`go area,** one to which access is prohibited to those who do not live there. ***at one go,*** at one attempt: *He blew out all the candles on his birthday cake at one go.*

goad /gəʊd/ *n* pointed stick for urging cattle on; (fig) sth urging a person to action. □ *vt* [VP6A, 15B,14,17] ***~ sb on, ~ sb into doing sth,*** urge, drive forward: *~ sb into a fury; be ~ed by hunger into stealing.*

goal /gəʊl/ *n* **1** point marking the end of a race; (football) posts between which the ball is to be driven in order to score; point(s) made by doing this: *score/kick a ~; win by three ~s to one; keep ~,* protect the ~. **`~-keeper, ~ie** *n* (colloq) player whose duty is to keep the ball out of the ~. **2** (fig) object of efforts or ambition: *one's ~ in life; the ~ of his desires.*

goat /gəʊt/ *n* small, active horned animal, the *`she-~* (or *`nanny-~*) being kept for its milk: *`he-~* (or *`billy-~*), male goat. ⇨ **kid[1](1)**. ⇨ the illus at **domestic**. ***get one's ~,*** (sl) irritate or annoy one. ***play/act the giddy ~,*** play the fool; behave in a foolish and excited way. ***separate the sheep from the ~s,*** the good from the bad. **`~-herd** *n* person who looks after a flock of ~s. **`~-skin** *n* [C,U] (garment made of) skin of a goat. **~·ee** /gəʊ`ti/ *n* small tuft of hair on the chin like a ~'s beard.

gob[1] /gob/ *n* (vulg) clot or lump of slimy substance.

gob[2] /gob/ *n* (sl) mouth.

gob[3] /gob/ *n* (US sl) naval rating.

gob·bet /`gobɪt/ *n* [C] lump or chunk, esp of meat.

gobble[1] /`gobl/ *vt,vi* [VP6A,15B,2A] ***~ (up),*** eat fast, noisily and greedily.

gobble[2] /`gobl/ *vi* [VP2A,C] (of a turkeycock) make the characteristic sound in the throat; (of a person) make such a sound when speaking, because of rage, etc. □ *n* characteristic sound made by a turkeycock.

gobble·dy·gook /`gobldɪguk/ *n* [U] kind of jargon used by some bureaucrats.

gob·bler /`goblə(r)/ *n* (US) male turkey.

go-between /`gəʊ bɪtwin/ *n* person who acts as messenger or negotiator for two people or groups who do not or cannot meet: *in some countries marriages are arranged by ~s.*

gob·let /`goblət/ *n* glass or pottery drinking-vessel with a stem and base and no handle.

gob·lin /`goblɪn/ *n* mischievous demon; ugly-looking evil spirit.

go-cart /`gəʊ kɑt/ *n* **1** a light handcart. **2** small, often collapsible, baby's pushchair.

god /god/ *n* **1** being regarded or worshipped as having power over nature and control over human affairs; image in wood, stone, etc to represent such a being: *the blind god* (or *god of love*), Cupid /`kjupɪd/; *the god of the sea,* Neptune /`neptjun *US:* -tun/; *a feast/sight for the gods,* something extraordinary, exquisite, etc. **2 God,** the Supreme Being, creator and ruler of the universe. ***God willing,*** if circumstances permit. ***God knows,*** It is something that ordinary people cannot know. **3** person greatly adored or admired; very influential person; sth to which excessive attention is paid: *make a god of one's belly,* think excessively about food and drink. *He thinks he's a* (*little*) *tin god,* used e g of an official who expects undeserved and excessive respect. **4** (theatre) **the gods,** (persons in the) gallery seats. **5** (compounds) **`god·child, `god·daughter, `god·son** *nn* person for whom a godparent acts as sponsor at baptism. **`god·father, `god·mother, `god·parent** *nn* person who undertakes, when a child is baptized, to take an active interest in its welfare. **`god·fearing** *adj* reverent; living a good life and sincerely religious. **`god-for·saken** *adj* (of places) dismal; wretched. **God's-`acre** *n* (old use) churchyard. **god·send** /-send/ *n* piece of good fortune coming unexpectedly; sth welcome because it is a great help in time of need. **god·`speed** *n*: *bid/wish sb godspeed,* wish him success on a journey, etc. **god·dess** /`godɪs/ *n* female god, esp in Greek and Latin mythology: *Diana, the goddess of hunting.*

god·head /`godhed/ *n* [U] being God or a god; divine nature: *the G~,* God.

god·less /`godləs/ *adj* wicked; not having belief in God; not recognizing God. **~·ness** *n*

god·like /`godlaɪk/ *adj* like God or a god in some quality; like or suitable for a god.

god·ly /`godlɪ/ *adj* (-ier, -iest) loving and obeying God; deeply religious. **godli·ness** *n*

go·down /`gəʊdaʊn/ *n* (in the East) warehouse.

go-get·ter /ˈgəʊ `getə(r)/ *n* (colloq) pushing, enterprising person.

goggle /`gogl/ *vi* [VP2A,3A] ***~ at,*** roll the eyes about (or *at* sth); stare at with bulging eyes: *He ~d at her in surprise. The frog's eyes seemed to be goggling out of its head.* **`~-box** *n* (sl) T V set. **`~-eyed** *adj* having staring, prominent, or rolling eyes.

goggles /`goglz/ *n pl* large round glasses with hoods to protect the eyes from the wind, dust, etc (worn by racing motorists, etc).

go·ing /`gəʊɪŋ/ *n* ⇨ also **go[1]**. **1** [U] condition of the ground, a road, a race-course, etc, for walking, riding, etc: *The ~ is hard over this mountain road.* **2** [U] method or speed of working or travelling: *For a steam train, 70 miles an hour is good ~.* **3** (usu *pl*) ***comings and ~s,*** (liter or fig) arrivals and departures: *the comings and ~s in the corridors of power.* □ *adj* ***a ~ concern,*** ⇨ **go[1](8)**.

goitre (US = **goi·ter**) /`gɔɪtə(r)/ *n* diseased swelling of the thyroid gland (in the neck).

go-kart /`gəʊ kɑt/ *n* low, small, open framework vehicle with a petrol engine, used for racing by members of a 'kart club'.

gold /gəʊld/ *n* [U] **1** precious yellow metal used for making coins, ornaments, jewellery, etc: *currencies backed by ~; £500 in ~,* in ~ coins; (attrib) *a ~ watch/bracelet.* **2** money in large sums; wealth. **3** (fig) brilliant or precious things or qualities: *a heart of ~; a voice of ~.* **4** colour of the metal: *the red and ~ of the woods in autumn; old ~,* a dull, brownish-golden yellow. **5** (compounds) **`~-beater** *n* person whose trade is to beat ~ into ~-leaf. **`~-digger** *n* person who digs for ~; (sl) girl or woman who uses her attractions to extract money from men. **`~-dust** *n* ~ in the form of dust, as often found in ~fields. **`~-field** *n* district in which ~ is found. **`~-finch** *n* bright-coloured songbird with yellow feathers in the wings. `~-**fish** *n* small red carp kept in bowls or ponds. '~-`**foil,** '~-`**leaf** *n* [U] ~ beaten into thin sheets. `~-**mine** *n* place where ~ is mined; (fig) source of wealth, e g a shop that is very successful in making money. '~-`**plate** *n* [U] articles (spoons, dishes and other vessels) made of ~. `~-**rush** *n* rush to a newly discovered ~field. `~-**smith** *n* smith who makes articles of ~. `~ **standard,** ⇨ standard.

golden /`gəʊldn/ *adj* **1** of gold or like gold in value or colour: *~ hair.* **2** precious; excellent; important: *a ~ opportunity; ~ wedding,* fiftieth anniversary. **the** '~ `**rule,** any important rule of conduct (esp Matt 7: 12). **the** '~ `**mean,** the principle of moderation. **the** '~ `**age,** (in Gk stories) the earliest and happiest period in history; period in a nation's history when art or literature was most flourishing. '~ `**handshake,** (usu large) sum of money given to a high-ranking member of a company when he retires (in recognition of good work and loss of continuation of salary).

golf /golf/ *n* [U] game played by two or four persons with small, hard balls, driven with `~-clubs into a series of 9 or 18 holes on smooth greens(4) over a stretch of land called a `~-course or `~-links. □ *vi* play ~. **~er** *n* person who plays ~.

Gol·iath /gə`laɪəθ/ *n* giant. ⇨ 1 Sam 17.

gol·li·wog /`golɪwog/ *n* black-faced doll with thick stiff hair on end like a brush.

golly /`golɪ/ *int* (dated colloq) used to express surprise.

go·losh *n* ⇨ galosh.

gon·dola /`gondələ/ *n* **1** long, flat-bottomed boat with high peaks at each end, used on canals in Venice. **2** (old use) car suspended from an airship. **gon·do·lier** /'gondə`lɪə(r)/ *n* man who propels a ~.

a gondola

gone /gon *US:* gɔn/ *pp* of go[1].

goner /`gonə(r) *US:* `gɔn-/ *n* (sl) person or thing in desperate straits, ruined or doomed.

gong /goŋ/ *n* metal disc with a turned rim giving a resonant note when struck with a stick, esp as a signal, e g for meals. □ *vt* (of traffic police) direct (a motorist) to stop by striking a ~.

gon·or·rhea (also **-rhœa**) /'gonə`rɪə/ *n* [U] contagious veneral disease which causes an inflammatory discharge from the genital organs.

goo /gu/ *n* [U] (sl) sticky wet material; sentimentality. **gooy** /`guɪ/ *adj* sticky.

good[1] /gʊd/ *adj* (**better, best**) **1** having the right or desired qualities; giving satisfaction: *a ~* (e g sharp) *knife; a ~ fire,* one that is bright and cheerful, giving warmth; *~* (= fertile) *soil; ~* (= genuine) *money.* ***throw ~ money after bad,*** lose more ~ while trying to recoup oneself for money lost. *earning ~ money,* (colloq) high wages; *a woman of ~ family,* of a family with high social position; well born. *Is raw herring ~ eating,* Is it enjoyable to eat it? **2** beneficial; wholesome: *Is this water ~ to drink,* Is it clean and pure? *Milk is ~ for children. Exercise is ~ for the health.* **3** efficient; competent; able to do satisfactorily what is required: *a ~ teacher/driver/worker; a ~ man for the position; ~ at mathematics/languages/describing scenery. She has been a ~ wife to him.* **4** pleasing; agreeable; advantageous: *~ news. Here's a ~ fellow,* a friendly or sociable companion. *It's ~ to be home again.* ***have a ~ time,*** enjoy oneself. Hence, **a** `~-**time girl,** (colloq) one whose chief aim is enjoyment. ***(all) in ~ time,*** at a suitable or advantageous time. ***be a ~ thing,*** be sth that one approves: *Do you think lower taxes are a ~ thing?* ***be a ~ thing that,*** be fortunate that. ***have a good/bad night,*** sleep well/badly. ***put in/say a ~ word for sb,*** say sth in his favour. ***start/arrive/leave in ~ time,*** early. **5** kind; benevolent; willing to help others: *It was ~ of you to help them. Will you be ~ enough to/be so ~ as to come early? He's a very ~ fellow. How ~ of you!* Cf *do sb a ~ turn,* ⇨ turn[1](5); (in exclamations of surprise, shock, etc.) *'G~ `God! 'G~ `Gracious! 'G~ `Heavens!* **6** thorough; sound; complete: *give sb a ~ beating/scolding; have a ~ drink; find a ~ excuse; go for a ~ long walk.* ***have a ~ mind (to do sth),*** feel a strong desire to: *I've a ~ mind to report you to the police.* **7** strong; vigorous: *His eyesight is still ~. The children were in ~ spirits.* ⇨ *low spirits* at low[1](6). **8** amusing: *a ~ story/joke; as ~ as a play.* **9** fresh; eatable; untainted: *Fish does not keep ~ in hot weather. This meat doesn't smell quite ~.* **10** reliable; safe; sure: *a car with ~ brakes; ~ debts,* debts that will certainly be paid. ⇨ *bad debts* at bad[1](4). He's a ~ life, is healthy and is, therefore, likely to be acceptable for life assurance. ~ ***for,*** **(a)** safely to be trusted for (the amount stated): *His credit is ~ for £5 000.* **(b)** (of a draft, etc) drawn for (the amount stated): *~ for £5.* **(c)** having the necessary energy, inclination, etc: *He's ~ for several years' more service. My car is ~ for another five years. Are you ~ for a five-mile walk?* **(d)** valid: *The return half of the ticket is ~ for three months.* `~-**for-nothing,** `~-**for-naught** *adjj, nn* worthless (person). **11** (esp of a child) well behaved; not giving trouble: *Try to be a ~ boy. She's as ~ as gold.* **12** morally excellent; virtuous: *a ~ and holy man; live a ~ life.* '~ `**works,** charitable deeds, helping the poor, the sick, etc. **13** (rather archaic; biblical) right, proper; expedient: *He thought it ~ to offer his help.* (As an *int,* expressing approval): *'You will come with us?' 'G~!'* **14** in forms of greeting and farewell: *G~ morning/afternoon/evening/night.* **15** as a polite (but often ironical, patronizing or indignant) form of address: *my ~ sir/man/friend,* or as a polite (but often condescending) description: *How's your ~ man* (i e your husband)? *How's the ~ lady* (i e your wife)? ***the ~ people,*** the fairies. **16** as a form of commendation: *~ men and true. G~ old Smith! That's a ~ 'un!* /`gʊd n/ (colloq) an amusing lie or story. **17** considerable in number, quantity, etc: *a ~ deal of money; a ~ many people; a ~ few,* a considerable number. *We've come a ~ way,* quite a long way. **18** not less than; rather more than: *We waited for a ~ hour. It's a ~ three miles to the station. He ate a ~ half of the duck.* **19** ***as ~ as,*** practically, almost: *He as ~ as said I was a liar,* suggested that I was a liar without actually using the word 'liar'. *My car is as ~ as new, even though I've had it a year. The matter is as ~ as settled,* We may look upon it as being settled. **20 *make ~,*** accomplish what one attempts; prosper: *He went to Canada, where he soon made ~.* [VP22] ***make sth ~,*** **(a)** compensate for; pay for (sth lost or damaged): *make ~ a loss or theft.* **(b)** effect (a purpose): *make ~ one's escape.* **(c)** prove the truth of an accusation, a statement, etc. **(d)** restore to sound condition: *The plaster will have to be made ~ before you paint it.* **21** (phrases and compounds) **'~-'fellowship** *n* sociability. **'~ 'humour** *n* cheerful mood; happy state of mind. Hence, **'~-'humoured** *adj* **'~ 'looks** *n pl* personal beauty. **'~-'looking** *adj* (usu of persons) handsome. **'~-'natured** *adj* kind; ready and willing to help others, even by sacrificing one's own interests. **'~-'neighbourliness** *n* friendly conduct and relations. **'~ 'sense** *n* [U] soundness of judgement; practical wisdom. **'~-'tempered** *adj* not easily irritated or made angry.

good[2] /gʊd/ *n* [U] **1** that which is ~; what is morally right, beneficial, advantageous, profitable, etc; what has use, worth, value. ***do ~,*** help (through charitable works, etc): *The Salvation Army does a lot of ~.* ⇨ *do-gooder* at do[2](2). ***(do sth) for the ~ of,*** in order to benefit: *He works for the ~ of the country. I'm giving you this advice for your ~. Is it right to deceive people, even if it's for their own ~?* ***do (sb) ~,*** help or benefit him: *Eat more fruit: it will do you ~. Smoking does (you) more harm than ~. Much ~ may it do you,* (usu ironic, meaning) You won't get much benefit from it. ***be up to no ~,*** be engaged in sth wrong, mischievous, etc. ***be no/not much/any/some ~ (doing sth),*** be no, not much, etc use, of no, little, etc value: *It's no ~ (my) talking to him. Was his advice ever any ~? What ~ was it? This gadget isn't much ~.* **2** ***for ~ (and all),*** permanently; finally: *He says that he's leaving the country for ~,* intending never to return to it. **3** ***to the ~,*** as balance on the right side, as net profit: *We were £5 to the ~.* **4** (*adj* as *pl n*) good or virtuous persons: *G~ and bad alike respected the person.* **5** (*pl;* not used with numerals) movable property; merchandise: *He buys and sells leather ~s. Half his ~s were stolen.* **'~s and 'chattels,** (legal) personal belongings. **6** (*pl;* but not with numerals) things carried by rail, etc (contrasted with passengers): *a '~s agent/station; send sth by fast '~s train.* Cf (US) *freight.* **7 piece of ~s,** (colloq) female person: *She's a saucy little piece of ~s,* a saucy young girl.

good·bye /'gʊd'baɪ *fast or informal:* gə'baɪ/ *int n* (saying of) farewell: *'I must say ~ now',* It is time for me to leave. *Have you said all your ~s?*

good·ish /'gʊdɪʃ/ *adj* rather large, extensive, etc: *It's a ~ step from here,* quite a long way.

good·ly /'gʊdlɪ/ *adj* (-ier, -iest) (liter) **1** handsome; pleasant-looking. **2** of considerable size: *a ~ sum of money; a ~ heritage.*

good·ness /'gʊdnəs/ *n* [U] **1** quality of being good; virtue: *~ of heart.* ***have the ~ to,*** be kind enough to: *Have the ~ to come this way, please.* **2** strength or essence: *meat with the ~ boiled out.* **3** (in exclamations) used instead of *God!*: *G~ Gracious! G~ me! For ~' sake! Thank ~! I wish to ~ that...,* wish very strongly that.... ***G~ knows,*** **(a)** I do not know. **(b)** I appeal to Heaven to witness: *G~ knows I've tried hard.*

goods /gʊdz/ *n pl* ⇨ good[2](5,6).

good·will /'gʊd'wɪl/ *n* [U] **1** friendly feeling: *a policy of ~ in international relations.* **2** privilege of trading as the successor to a well-established business: *The ~ is to be sold with the business.*

goody[1] /'gʊdɪ/ *n* (colloq) sweetmeat.

goody-goody /'gʊdɪ 'gʊdɪ/ *adj, n* (person who is) primly or pretentiously virtuous.

gooey /'guɪ/ *adj* = gooy, ⇨ **goo.**

goofy /'gufɪ/ *adj* (-ier, -iest) (sl) silly.

goog·ly /'guglɪ/ *n* (*pl* -lies) (cricket) ball bowled as if to break in one way that actually breaks in the opposite way.

goon /gun/ *n* (sl) stupid or awkward person.

goose /gus/ *n* (*pl* **geese** /gis/) **1** ⇨ the illus at fowl. water bird larger than a duck; female of this, ⇨ gander; [U] its flesh as food. ***cook sb's ~,*** put an end to his hopes; prevent him from being a nuisance, etc. ***kill the ~ that lays the golden eggs,*** (prov) sacrifice future gains to satisfy present needs. ***be unable to say 'bo' to a ~,*** be very timid. ***All his geese are swans,*** He overestimates or exaggerates the good qualities of persons and things. **'~-flesh** *n* rough bristling skin caused by cold or fear. **'~-step** *n* way of marching without bending the knees. **2** simpleton: *You silly ~!*

goose·berry /'gʊzbrɪ *US:* 'gusberɪ/ *n* (*pl* -ries) [C] (bush with) green, smooth berry (used for jam, tarts, etc). ⇨ the illus at fruit. ***play ~,*** be present with two persons, e g lovers, who prefer to be alone.

go·pher /'gəʊfə(r)/ *n* burrowing rat-like animal in N America.

Gor·dian /'gɔdɪən/ *adj* (only in) **~ knot,** knot difficult or impossible to untie; difficult problem or task. ***cut the ~ knot,*** solve a problem by force or by disregarding the conditions.

gore[1] /gɔ(r)/ *n* [U] (liter, chiefly in descriptions of fighting) thickened blood from a cut or wound.

gore[2] /gɔ(r)/ *vt* [VP6A] pierce, wound, with the horns or tusks: *~d to death by an infuriated bull.*

gorge /gɔdʒ/ *n* **1** narrow opening, usu with a stream, between hills or mountains. **2** gullet; contents of the stomach: *His ~ rose at the sight/It made his ~ rise,* He was sickened or disgusted. □ *vi, vt* [VP6A,14,2A,C] ***~ (oneself) on/with sth,*** eat greedily; fill oneself: *~ on rich food; ~ oneself with meat.* □ *n* act of gorging; surfeit.

gorg·eous /'gɔdʒəs/ *adj* **1** richly coloured; magnificent: *a ~ sunset.* **2** (colloq) giving pleasure and satisfaction: *~ weather; a ~ dinner.* **~·ly** *adv*

Gor·gon /'gɔgən/ *n* (Gk myth) one of three snake-haired sisters whose looks turned to stone anyone who saw them.

Gor·gon·zola /'gɔgən'zəʊlə/ *n* [U] rich creamy cheese (from ~ in Italy).

gor·illa /gə'rɪlə/ *n* man-sized, tree-climbing African ape. ⇨ the illus at ape.

gor·man·dize /'gɔməndaɪz/ *vi* eat, devour, greedilyy for pleasure.

gorse /gɔs/ *n* [U] yellow-flowered evergreen shrub with sharp thorns, growing on waste land (also called *furze*).

gory /'gɔrɪ/ *adj* (-ier, -iest) covered with blood.

gosh /gɔʃ/ *int* (sl) (also **by ~**) by God.

gos·ling /'gozlɪŋ/ *n* young goose.

gos·pel /'gospl/ *n* **1 G~,** (the life and teachings of Jesus Christ as recorded in the) first four books of the New Testament; any one of these four books: *the G~ according to St John; go forth and preach the G~.* **'G~ 'oath,** oath sworn on the G~s. **'G~**

ˋtruth, truths contained in the G~; sth as true as the G~. **2** thing that may be believed with confidence; principle or set of principles that one acts upon or believes in: *the ~ of health; the ~ of soap and water,* (hum for) firm belief in the value of cleanliness.

gos·sa·mer /ˈgɒsəmə(r)/ *n* **1** [C,U] (thread of the) fine silky substance of webs made by small spiders, floating in calm air or spread on grass, etc. **2** [U] soft, light, delicate material: *as light as ~;* (attrib) *a ~ veil.*

gos·sip /ˈgɒsɪp/ *n* **1** [U] idle, often ill-natured, talk about the affairs of other people: *Don't believe all the ~ you hear. She's too fond of ~.* **2** [U] informal writing about persons and social happenings, e g in letters or in newspapers: (attrib) *the ˋ~ column,* of a newspaper; *a ˋ~ writer/columnist.* **3** [C] instance of this; friendly chat: *have a good ~ with a neighbour over the garden fence.* **4** [C] person who is fond of ~: *She's an old ~.* □ *vi* (-pp-) [VP2A,C] talk or write ~.

got *pt,pp* of get.

Goth /gɒθ/ *n* one of a Germanic tribe that invaded the Roman Empire in the 3rd and 4th cc; rough, uncivilized persons, esp one who destroys works of art. ⇨ vandal.

Gothic /ˈgɒθɪk/ *adj* **1** of the Goths or their language. **2** of the style of architecture common in Western Europe in the 12th to 16th cc, characterized by pointed arches, clusters of columns, etc. **3** of the 18th c style of romantic literature: *~ novels.* **4** (of printing type) thick or heavy, as used for German. □ *n* ~ language; ~ architecture; ~ type.

got·ten *pp* (in US) of get.

gouache /guˋɑʃ/ *n* opaque watercolour paint; method of painting using this material.

gouge /gaʊdʒ/ *n* tool with a sharp semicircular edge for cutting grooves in wood. □ *vt* [VP6A,15B] ***~ (out),*** cut with a ~; shape with a ~; force out with, or as with, a ~: *~ out a person's eye with one's thumb.*

gou·lash /ˈgulæʃ/ *n* [C,U] (dish of) stew of steak and vegetables, seasoned with paprika.

gourd /gʊəd/ *n* (large, hard-skinned fleshy fruit of) kinds of climbing or trailing plant; bottle or bowl consisting of the dried skin of this fruit.

gourds

gour·mand /ˈgʊəmənd/ *n* lover of food.

gour·met /ˈgʊəmeɪ/ *n* person who enjoys, and is expert in the choice of, delicate food, wines, etc.

gout /gaʊt/ *n* [U] disease causing painful swellings in joints, esp toes, knees and fingers. **~y** *adj suffering from ~.*

gov·ern /ˈgʌvn/ *vt,vi* **1** [VP6A,2A] rule (a country, etc); control or direct the public affairs of (a city, country, etc): *In Great Britain the sovereign reigns but does not ~.* **2** [VP6A] control: *~ one's temper.* **3** [VP6A] (usu passive) determine; influence: *be ~ed by the opinions of others. Don't be ~ed by what other people say.* **4** (gram, esp of a *v* or *prep*) require, make necessary (a certain case or form of another word). **~·ing** *adj* having the power or right to ~: *the ~ing classes of England; the ~ing body of a school/college, etc.*

gov·ern·ance /ˈgʌvṇəns/ *n* (archaic) act, fact, manner, of governing; sway, control.

gov·ern·ess /ˈgʌvṇɪs/ *n* woman who is employed to teach young children in a private family.

gov·ern·ment /ˈgʌvṃənt/ *n* **1** [U] governing; power to govern: *What the country needs is strong ~.* **2** [U] method or system of governing: *We prefer democratic ~.* **3** [C] ministry; body of persons governing a State: *The Prime Minister has formed a G~,* has chosen his colleagues, selected Ministers for the Cabinet. *The G~* (collectively) *has welcomed the proposal. The G~* (its members) *are discussing the proposal.* **G~ House,** official residence of the Governor (of a province, etc). **G~ securities,** bonds, exchequer bills, etc, issued by ~. **~al** /ˌgʌvnˋmentl/ *adj* connected with ~.

gov·ernor /ˈgʌvṇə(r)/ *n* **1** person who governs a province or colony or (US) a State: *the G~ of New York State.* Cf *the Mayor of New York City.* **ˌ~-ˋgeneral** *n* (in the British Commonwealth) representative of the Crown, having no special powers: *the G~-General of Canada.* **2** member of the governing body of an institution (e g a school in England, a college, a hospital). **3** (colloq) chief; employer; father. **4** regulator in a machine, automatically controlling speed or the intake of gas, steam, etc.

gown /gaʊn/ *n* **1** woman's dress, esp one for special occasions: *a ˋdressing-/ˈnight-~.* **2** loose, flowing robe worn by members of a university, judges, etc. ⇨ the illus at judge. □ *vt* (chiefly *pp*) dress in a ~: *beautifully ~ed women.*

grab /græb/ *vt,vi* (-bb-) [VP6A,3A] ***~ (at),*** take roughly; selfishly or eagerly snatch: *The dog ~bed the bone and ran off with it. Don't ~! He ~bed at the opportunity of going abroad.* □ *n* [C] **1** sudden snatch: *make a ~ at something.* **2** mechanical device for taking up and holding sth to be lifted or moved. **~·ber** *n* person who ~s; greedy person whose chief aim in life appears to be making money.

grace /greɪs/ *n* **1** [U] quality of being pleasing, attractive or beautiful, esp in structure or movement: *She danced with ~/with a ~ that surprised us.* **2** (usu *pl*) pleasing accomplishment; elegance of manner. ***airs and ~s,*** ways of speaking and behaving that are intended to impress and attract people. **3** [U] favour; goodwill. ***an act of ~,*** sth freely given, not taken as a right. ***days of ~,*** time allowed by the law or custom after the day on which a payment, e g of a bill of exchange, an insurance premium, is due. ***give sb a week's ~,*** allow him an extra week before requiring him to fulfil an obligation. ***be in sb's good ~s,*** enjoy his favour and approval. **4** [U] ***have the ~ to do sth,*** realize that it is right and proper, and do it: *He had the ~ to say that he was sorry.* ***do sth with a good/bad ~,*** do it willingly/reluctantly. **5** short prayer of thanks before or after a meal: *say (a) ~.* **6** [U] God's mercy and favour towards mankind;

influence and result of this: *in the year of ~ 1960*, in the 1960th year after the birth of Jesus. ***in a state of ~***, being influenced by the strength and inspiring power of God, having been pardoned; having received the Sacraments. ***fall from ~***, fall to a lower moral state after being in a state of ~. **7** as a title, used when speaking of or to an archbishop, duke or duchess: *His/Her/Your G~*. **8 the G~s**, (Gk myth) three beautiful sister goddesses who gave beauty, charm and happiness. □ *vt* [VP6A] add ~ to; confer honour or dignity on; be an ornament to: *The occasion was ~d by the presence of the Queen. Her character is ~d with every virtue.*

grace·ful /ˈgreɪsfl/ *adj* having or showing grace(1,4): *a ~ dancer; a ~ letter of thanks.* **~ly** /-fḷɪ/ *adv*

grace·less /ˈgreɪsləs/ *adj* without grace(4); without a sense of what is right and proper: *~ behaviour; a ~* (= depraved) *rogue.* **~·ly** *adv*

gra·cious /ˈgreɪʃəs/ *adj* **1** (of persons and their behaviour) pleasant; kind; agreeable: *her ~ Majesty the Queen. It was ~ of her to come.* **2** (of God) merciful. **3** (in exclamations) expressing surprise: *Good G~! G~ goodness! G~ me!* **~·ly** *adv* **~·ness** *n*

gra·da·tion /greɪˈdeɪʃn/ *n* [C,U] step, stage, degree in development; gradual change from one thing to another or from one state to another: *the ~s of colour in the rainbow.*

grade[1] /greɪd/ *n* [C] **1** step, stage or degree in rank, quality, value, etc; number or class of things of the same kind: *The rank of major is one ~ higher than that of captain. Milk is sold in ~s, and G~ A milk is the best quality. This pupil has a high ~ of intelligence.* **2** (US) division of the school course; one year's work; pupils in such a division: *An elementary school in the US has eight ~s and is called a 'ˈ~ school'. Its teachers are called 'ˈ~ teachers'.* **3** the mark, e g 80%, or rating, e g 'Excellent' or 'Fair', given to a pupil for his work in school. ***make the ~***, (colloq) reach a good standard; do as well as is required. **4** (US) slope of a road, railways, etc. Cf (GB) *gradient.* ***on the ˈup/ˈdown ~***, rising/falling: *Business is on the up ~*, is improving. **~ crossing**, (US) level crossing.

grade[2] /greɪd/ *vt* [VP6A] **1** arrange in order in grades or classes: *~ milk; ~d by size.* **2** make land (esp for roads) more nearly level by reducing the slope. **3** [VP6A,15B] *~ (up)*, cross (cattle) with a better breed.

gradi·ent /ˈgreɪdɪənt/ *n* degree of slope: *a ~ of one in nine; a steep ~.*

grad·ual /ˈgrædʒʊəl/ *adj* taking place by degrees; (of a slope) not steep: *a ~ increase in the cost of living.* **~·ly** /-dʒʊlɪ/ *adv* by degrees. **~·ness** *n*

grad·uate[1] /ˈgrædʒʊeɪt/ *n* **1** (GB) person who holds a university degree, esp the first, or Bachelor's, degree: *London ~s; a ~ student; post-~ studies.* **2** (US) one who has completed a course at an educational institution: *high school ~s; a ~ nurse*, one from a College or School of Nursing. Cf *trained nurse* in GB.

grad·uate[2] /ˈgrædʒʊeɪt/ *vt,vi* **1** [VP6A] mark with degrees for measuring: *a ruler ~d in both inches and centimetres; a ~d glass*, for measuring quantities of liquid. **2** [VP6A] arrange according to grade. **3** [VP2A,C] take an academic degree: *He ~d from Oxford/~d in law.* (US, of other institutions): *~ from the Boston School of Cookery.* **4** [VP6A] (chiefly US) give a degree or diploma to: *The university ~d 350 students last year. He had been ~d from Maryland College in the Class of 1868.* **gradu·ation** /ˈgrædʒʊˈeɪʃn/ *n* graduating or being ~d; (US) ceremony at which degrees are conferred.

graf·fito /grəˈfiːtəʊ/ *n* (*pl* -ti /-tiː/) (usu *pl*) (I) drawing, words, scratched on a hard surface, esp a wall.

graft[1] /grɑːft *US:* græft/ *n* **1** shoot from a branch or twig of a living tree, fixed in a cut made in another tree, to form a new growth. **2** (surgery) piece of skin, bone, etc from a living person or animal, transplanted on another body or another part of the same body. □ *vt,vi* [VP6A,15A,B,2A] put a ~ in or on (stock): *~ one variety on/upon/in/into another; ~ on briar roots; ~ new skin.*

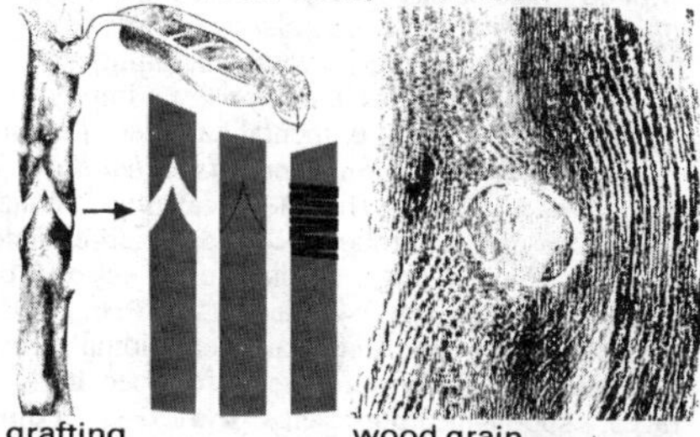
grafting wood grain

graft[2] /grɑːft *US:* græft/ *n* [C,U] (orig US) (instance of) getting business advantages, profit-making, etc by taking wrong advantage of connections in politics, municipal business, etc. □ *vi* practise ~.

grail /greɪl/ *n* (usu **the Holy G~**) platter or cup used by Jesus at the Last Supper and in which one of His followers is said to have received drops of His blood at the Crucifixion.

grain /greɪn/ *n* **1** [U] (collective *sing*) small, hard seed of food plants such as wheat and rice: *~ imports; a cargo of ~; a ˈ~ elevator*, storehouse for ~, with devices for lifting ~. ⇨ the illus at cereal. **2** [C] single seed of such a plant: *give a beggar a few ~s of rice; eat up every ~ of rice in one's bowl.* **3** [C] tiny, hard bit: *~s of sand/salt/gold;* (fig) small amount: *a boy without a ~ of sense; receive a few ~s of comfort.* **4** smallest unit of weight, 1/7 000 lb or 0·065 gr. ⇨ App 5. **5** [U] natural arrangement or pattern of the lines of fibre in wood, etc as seen on a surface that has been sawn or cut: *woods of fine/coarse ~.* ***be/go against the ~***, (fig) contrary to inclination.

gram /græm/ ⇨ gramme.

gram·mar /ˈgræmə(r)/ *n* [U] study or science of, rules for, the combination of words into sentences (*syntax*), and the forms of words (*morphology*): *a ˈ~-school*, (in GB) type of secondary school in which Latin was once the chief subject, now one which provides academic (contrasted with technical) courses. **~·ian** /grəˈmeərɪən/ *n* expert in ~.

gram·mati·cal /grəˈmætɪkl/ *adj* of, conforming to, the rules of grammar: *a ~ error/explanation/sentence.* **~ly** /-klɪ/ *adv*

gramme /græm/ *n* (also **gram**) metric unit of weight; weight of one cubic centimetre of water at maximum density. ⇨ App 5.

gramo·phone /ˈgræməfəʊn/ *n* (US = *phonograph*) machine for reproducing music and speech recorded on flat discs (*record-player* is now the usu word).

gram·pus /ˋgræmpəs/ *n* large dolphin-like sea animal; person who breathes loud.

gran·ary /ˋgrænərɪ/ *n* (*pl* -ries) storehouse for grain.

grand /grænd/ *adj* **1** (in official titles) chief; most important: *G~ Master,* e g of some orders of knighthood: *a ~ master,* chess champion; *G~ Vizier,* (former title of) chief minister of Turkey. **2** of most or greatest importance: *the ~ finale; the ~ question; the ~ staircase/entrance,* of a large building. **3** magnificent; splendid: *a ~ view; living in ~ style; ~ clothes.* **4** self-important; proud: *He puts on a very ~ manner/air.* **5** (colloq) very fine or enjoyable: *We had a ~ time. What ~ weather!* **6** full; complete: *a ~ orchestra,* one with all kinds of instruments (not strings only); *~ opera,* in which there are no spoken parts, everything being sung; *the ~ total,* including everything; *the ~ result of our efforts.* **7** impressive because of high moral or mental qualities: *Lincoln had a ~ character. Gladstone was called the G~ Old Man.* **8** (phrases) **the 'G~ ˋNational,** annual steeplechase at Liverpool. **'~ piˋano,** large piano with horizontal strings. ⇨ the illus at **keyboard.** **'baby ˋ~,** small-size ~ piano. **'G~ ˋPrix** /ˋpri/, (motor-racing) one of several international races. **ˋ~·stand,** rows of roofed seats for spectators at races, sports-meetings, etc. **the 'G~ ˋTour,** (formerly) tour of the chief towns, etc of Europe, completing the education of wealthy young men. **~·ly** *adv*

grand- *pref* **ˋ~·child, ˋ~·daughter, ˋ~·son** *nn* daughter or son of one's son or daughter. **ˋ~-parent, ˋ~·father, ˋ~·mother** *nn* father or mother of one's father or mother. **ˋ~·nephew, ˋ~·niece** *nn* son or daughter or one's nephew or niece. **ˋ~·uncle, ˋ~·aunt** *nn* uncle or aunt of either of one's parents. **ˋ~·father('s) ˋclock** *n* clock worked by weights in a tall wooden case.

gran·dad grand-dad /ˋgrændæd/ *n* (colloq for) grandfather.

gran·dee /'grænˋdi/ *n* Spanish or Portuguese nobleman of high rank.

gran·deur /ˋgrændʒə(r)/ *n* [U] greatness; magnificence: *the ~ of the Swiss Alps.*

gran·dilo·quent /grænˋdɪləkwənt/ *adj* using, full of, pompous words: *a ~ speaker; written in a ~ style.* **gran·dilo·quence** /-əns/ *n* [U].

gran·di·ose /ˋgrændɪəʊs/ *adj* planned on a large scale; imposing.

grand·ma /ˋgrænmɑ/ *n* (colloq for) grandmother.

grand·pa /ˋgrænpɑ/ *n* (colloq for) grandfather.

grand·sire /ˋgrændsɑɪə(r)/ *n* grandfather.

grange /greɪndʒ/ *n* country house with farm buildings attached.

gran·ite /ˋgrænɪt/ *n* [U] hard, usu grey, stone used for building.

granny, grannie /ˋgrænɪ/ *n* (*pl* -nies) (colloq) grandmother.

grant /grɑnt *US:* grænt/ *vt* **1** [VP6A,12A,13A] consent to give or allow (what is asked for): *~ a favour/request; ~ sb a request/permission to do sth. He was ~ed a pension.* **2** [VP6A,9,25] agree (that sth is true): *~ the truth of what someone says; ~ing this to be true/that this is true. I ~ his honesty/~ that he is honest. He's a good fellow, I ~ you.* **take sth for ~ed,** regard it as true or as certain to happen. □ *n* sth ~ed, e g money or land from a government: *~s towards the cost of a university education; ~-aided schools/students.*

granu·lar /ˋgrænjʊlə(r)/ *adj* of or like grains.

granu·late /ˋgrænjʊleɪt/ *vt, vi* [VP6A,2A] form into grains; roughen the surface of: *ˋ~d sugar,* sugar in the form of small crystals.

gran·ule /ˋgrænjul/ *n* [C] small grain.

grape /greɪp/ *n* ⇨ the illus at **fruit.** green or purple berry growing in clusters on vines, used for making wine: *a bunch of ~s.* **sour ~s, the ~s are sour,** said when sb says that sth he wants but cannot get has little or no value. **ˋ~ shot** *n* (hist) cluster of small iron balls fired together from a cannon to make a hail of shot. ⇨ **shrapnel. ˋ~-sugar** *n* dextrose or glucose, a kind of sugar found in ripe ~s and other kinds of fruit. **ˋ~-vine** *n* **(a)** kind of vine on which ~s grow. **(b)** means by which news gets about, e g in an office, school or a group of friends: *I heard on the ~-vine that Jill is to be promoted.*

grape·fruit /ˋgreɪpfrut/ *n* (*pl* with or without -s) [C] fruit like a large orange but with an acid taste. ⇨ the illus at **fruit.**

graph /græf/ *n* [C] diagram consisting of a line or lines (often curved) showing the variation of two quantities, e g the temperature at each hour. **ˋ~ paper,** paper with small squares of equal size.

graphic /ˋgræfɪk/ *adj* **1** of visual symbols (e g lettering, diagrams, drawings): *a ~ artist; ~ displays; the ~ arts.* **2** (of descriptions) causing one to have a clear picture in the mind: *a ~ account of the battle.* □ *n* (*pl*) lettering, drawings, etc. **graphi·cally** /-klɪ/ *adv* vividly; by writing or diagrams.

graph·ite /ˋgræfɑɪt/ *n* [U] soft, black substance (a form of carbon) used in lubrication, as a moderator in atomic piles, and in making lead pencils.

grap·nel /ˋgræpnl/ *n* **1** anchor with many flukes[2]; grappling instruments, e g as used for dragging along the bed of a river, lake, etc when searching for sth. **2** instrument like this formerly used in sea battles for holding enemy ships.

grapple /ˋgræpl/ *vi* [VP2A,C,3A] ~ ***with,*** seize firmly; struggle with sb/sth at close quarters; (fig) try to deal with (a problem, etc): *~ with an enemy. The wrestlers ~d together.* **ˋgrappling-iron** *n* grapnel.

grasp /grɑsp *US:* græsp/ *vt, vi* **1** [VP6A] seize firmly with the hand(s) or arm(s); understand with the mind: *~ sb's hand/a rope; ~ an argument/sb's meaning.* **2** [VP3A] **~ at,** try to seize; accept eagerly: *~ at an opportunity. A man who ~s at too much may lose everything.* □ *n* (usu *sing*) firm hold or grip; (power of) grasping: *in the ~ of a wicked enemy; have a thorough ~ of the problem; a problem within/beyond my ~,* that I can/cannot understand. **~·ing** *adj* eager to ~; greedy (for money, etc): *a ~ing rascal.*

grass /grɑs *US:* græs/ *n* **1** [U] kinds of common, wild, low-growing plant of which the green blades and stalks are eaten by cattle, horses, sheep, etc. ***not let the ~ grow under one's feet,*** (fig) waste no time in doing sth. **2** (with *pl* -ses) any species of this plant (including, in botanical use, cereals, reeds and bamboos). **3** [U] grazing land; pasture: (of animals) *at ~,* grazing. ***put/send/turn animals out to ~,*** put them to graze. **~-land** /-lænd/ *n* area of land covered with ~ where there are few trees. **'~ˋroots** *n pl* (often attrib) ordinary people remote from political decisions, but who are affected by these decisions: *a ~roots movement/rebellion. We must not neglect the ~roots.* ˈ~ ˋ**widow** *n* wife whose husband is temporarily not living with her. **~y** *adj* (-ier, -iest) covered with ~.

grass·hopper /ˋgrɑshɒpə(r) *US:* ˋgræs-/ *n* jumping insect which makes a shrill, chirping noise. ⇨ the illus at **insect**.

grate[1] /greɪt/ *n* (metal frame for holding coal, etc, in a) fireplace.

grate[2] /greɪt/ *vt,vi* **1** [VP6A,15A] rub into small pieces, usu against a rough surface; rub small bits off: *~ cheese into beaten eggs,* e g when making a cheese omelette. **2** [VP6A,2A,3A] ***~ on,*** make a harsh noise by rubbing; (fig) have an irritating effect (*on* a person, his nerves): *His bad manners ~d on everyone. Out-of-date slang ~s. The gate ~s on its hinges.* **grat·ing·ly** *adv* **grater** *n* device with a rough surface for grating food, etc: *a* ˋ*nutmeg ~r.*

grate·ful /ˋgreɪtfl/ *adj* **1** ***~ (to sb) (for sth),*** feeling or showing thanks: *We are ~ to you for your help.* **2** (liter) pleasant; agreeable; comforting: *trees that afford a ~ shade.* *~ly* /-flɪ/ *adv*

grat·ify /ˋgrætɪfɑɪ/ *vt* (*pt,pp* -fied) [VP6A] **1** give pleasure or satisfaction to: *We were all gratified with/at the result/to learn that you had been successful.* **2** indulge; give what is desired to: *~ a person's whims/his fancies for something; ~ a child's thirst for knowledge.* **~ing** *adj*: *It is very ~ing to learn that.* **grati·fi·ca·tion** /ˌgrætɪfɪˋkeɪʃn/ *n* **1** [U] ~ing or being gratified; state of being pleased or satisfied: *I have the gratification of knowing that I have done my duty.* **2** [C] that which causes one to feel gratified.

grat·ing /ˋgreɪtɪŋ/ *n* [C] framework of wooden or metal bars, either parallel or crossing one another, placed across an opening, e g a window, to keep out burglars or to allow air to flow through.

gra·tis /ˋgrætɪs/ *adv, adj* free of charge: *be admitted ~.*

grati·tude /ˋgrætɪtjud *US:* -tud/ *n* [U] ***~ (to sb) (for sth),*** thankfulness, being grateful.

gra·tu·itous /grəˋtjuɪtəs *US:* -ˋtu-/ *adj* **1** given, obtained or done, without payment: *~ service/information/help/advice.* **2** done or given, acting, without good reason: *a ~ insult; a ~ lie/liar.* **~ly** *adv*

gra·tu·ity /grəˋtjuətɪ *US:* -ˋtu-/ *n* (*pl* -ties) **1** gift (of money in addition to pay) to a retiring employee for services. **2** money given to a member of the armed forces at the end of his period of service. **3** tip (for service).

grave[1] /greɪv/ *adj* serious; requiring careful consideration: *~ news; make a ~ mistake; as ~ as a judge. The situation is more ~/is ~r than it has been since the end of the war.* **~ly** *adv*

grave[2] /greɪv/ *n* hole dug in the ground for a corpse; the mound of earth or the monument over it. ***have one foot in the ~,*** be nearing death, be very old. ˋ**~-clothes** *n pl* wrappings in which a corpse is buried. ˋ**~·stone** *n* stone over a ~, with the name, etc of the person buried there. ˋ**~·yard** *n* burial ground.

grave[3] /grɑv/ *n* (also **~ accent**) mark ˋ placed over a vowel to indicate how it is to be sounded (as in French *mère*).

grave[4] /greɪv/ *vt* (*pp* graven /ˋgreɪvn/) carve: *a ~n image,* an idol; *~n on my memory,* (liter style only) indelibly fixed.

gravel /ˋgrævl/ *n* [U] small stones with coarse sand, as used for roads and paths: *a load of ~;* (attrib) *a ~ path/pit.* □ *vt* (-ll-, US also -l-) [VP6A] **1** cover with ~: *~ a road; ~led paths.* **2** (colloq) perplex; puzzle.

grav·ing dock /ˋgreɪvɪŋ dɒk/ *n* dry dock in which the outside of a ship's hull may be cleaned.

gravi·tate /ˋgrævɪteɪt/ *vi* [VP3A] ***~ to/towards,*** move or be attracted: *Young people in the country districts seem to ~ towards the cities.* **gravi·ta·tion** /ˌgrævɪˋteɪʃn/ *n* [U] process of gravitating; gravity(**1**).

grav·ity /ˋgrævətɪ/ *n* [U] **1** force of attraction between any two objects, esp that force which attracts objects towards the centre of the earth. **2** weight: *centre of ~.* ˈ**specific** ˋ**~,** relation between the weight of a substance and that of the same volume of a standard substance (usu water for liquids and solids, and air for gases). **3** quality of being serious or solemn: *the ~ of the international situation; the ~ of his appearance. He could hardly keep his ~,* could with difficulty refrain from smiling or laughing.

gra·vure /grəˋvjʊə(r)/ *n* (also ˈ**photo** ˋ**~**) method of printing from copper plates on which text or photographic negatives are etched or engraved.

gravy /ˋgreɪvɪ/ *n* [U] **1** juice which comes from meat while it is cooking; sauce made from this. ˋ**~-boat** *n* vessel in which ~ is served at table. **2** (sl) money or profit easily or unexpectedly acquired: *get on the ~ train,* get a job where such money, etc is easily acquired.

gray /greɪ/ *adj, n* ⇨ **grey**.

graze[1] /greɪz/ *vi,vt* **1** [VP2A,C] (of cattle, sheep, etc) eat growing grass: *cattle grazing in the fields.* **2** [VP6A] put (cattle, etc) in fields to ~: *~ sheep;* use grassland for cattle: *~ a field.* ˋ**grazing-land** *n* land used for grazing cattle. **graz·ier** /ˋgreɪzɪə(r) *US:* ˋgreɪʒə(r)/ *n* person who feeds cattle for market.

graze[2] /greɪz/ *vt,vi* **1** [VP6A] touch or scrape lightly in passing; rub the skin from: *The bullet ~d his cheek.* **2** [VP2C] pass and touch while going *against/along/by/past.* □ *n* place where the skin is ~d.

grease /gris/ *n* [U] **1** animal fat melted soft. **2** any thick, semi-solid oily substance: ˋ*axle ~,* used to lubricate axles. ˋ**~-gun** *n* device for forcing ~ into the parts of an engine, machine, etc. ˋ**~-paint** *n* [U] mixture of ~ and paint used by actors to make up their faces. □ *vt* put or rub ~ on or in (esp parts of a machine). ***~ sb's palm,*** bribe him. **greaser** *n* man who ~s machinery, e g a ship's engines.

greasy /ˋgrisɪ/ *adj* (-ier, -iest) covered with grease; slippery: *~ fingers; a ~ road.* **greas·ily** /-əlɪ/ *adv* **greasi·ness** *n*

great /greɪt/ *adj* (-er, -est) **1** well above the average in size, quantity or degree: *take ~ care of sth; an essay that shows ~ ignorance of grammar; a ~ friend of mine,* one for whom I feel more than ordinary friendship. ***~ with child,*** (old use) pregnant. ˋ**~-coat** *n* heavy overcoat. **2** of remarkable ability or character: *~ men; a ~ painter/musician.* **3** important; noted; of high rank or position: *a ~ occasion; the G~ Powers of Europe; a ~ lady; Alexander the G~.* **4** (colloq, preceding another *adj* which is often weakly stressed) implying surprise, indignation, contempt, etc according to context: *See what a ~ big* *fish I've caught! Take your* ~ *big head out of my sight! What a* ~ *thick stick!* **5** (also **Greater**) used as a distinctive epithet of the larger of two. **the G~ Bear,** ⇨ bear[1](3); *the G~ War,* that of 1914—18. **G~ Britain**, England, Wales and Scotland, excluding Northern Ireland. **G~ Lakes,** series of five large lakes in N America along the boundary between Canada and the US. **'G~er 'London,** an administrative area of local government that includes inner London and the outer suburbs. **6** (attrib only) fully deserving the name of: *He's a* ~ *scoundrel. They are* ~ *friends.* **7** (with agent *nouns;* attrib only) doing or being sth to a high degree: *He's a* ~ *reader/eater,* reads/eats very much. *He's a* ~ *landowner,* owns a large area of land. **8** combined with words indicating quantity, etc: *a* ~ *deal,* very much; *a* ~ *number; a* ~ *while ago; the* ~ *majority,* much the larger part. **9** (colloq) splendid; satisfactory: *We had a* ~ *time in Paris. Wouldn't it be* ~ *if we could go there again!* **10** (colloq; predic only) ~ **at,** clever or skilful at. ~ ***on,*** having a good knowledge of. **11** prefixed to a kinship words in *grand-* to show a further stage in relationship: *'~-'grandfather,* one's father's or mother's grandfather; *'~-'grandson,* grandson of one's son or daughter. **12 Greats** *n pl* (colloq) (at Oxford) final B A examination, esp for honours in classical literature and philosophy. **~·ly** *adv* much; by much: *~ly amused.* **~·ness** *n*

greaves /grivz/ *n pl* pieces of armour to protect the shins. ⇨ the illus at armour.

grebe /grib/ *n* kinds of short-bodied diving bird. ⇨ the illus at water.

Gre·cian /'griʃn/ *adj* (e g of architecture, pottery, culture and features of the face) Greek.

greed /grid/ *n* [U] strong desire for more food, wealth, etc, esp for more than is right or reasonable.

greedy /'gridɪ/ *adj* (-ier, -iest) ~ ***for sth/to have sth,*** **1** filled with greed: *not hungry, just* ~*; looking at the cakes with* ~ *eyes;* ~ *for gain/honours.* **2** intensely desirous (*to do* sth). **greed·ily** /-əlɪ/ *adv* **greedi·ness** *n*

Greek /grik/ *n* member of the Greek race, either of ancient Greece or modern Greece; the Greek language: *It's* ~ *to me,* is beyond my understanding. □ *adj* of Greece, its people, or the Greek language.

green[1] /grin/ *adj* **1** of the colour between blue and yellow in the spectrum, the colour of growing grass, and the leaves of most plants and trees: *a* ~ *Christmas,* Christmas season when the weather is mild and there is no snow. **'~ 'belt,** wide area of land round a town, where building is controlled (by town-planning) so that there are ~ fields, woods, etc. ***give sb/get the ~ light,*** (colloq, from the ~ of traffic lights) permission to go ahead with a project, etc. **2** (of fruit) not yet ripe: ~ *apples;* ~ *figs,* young and tender figs; (of wood) not yet dry enough for use: *G~ wood does not burn well.* **3** inexperienced; undeveloped; gullible; untrained: *a boy who is still* ~ *at his job. I'm not so* ~ *as to believe that.* **4** (fig) flourishing; full of vigour: *live to a* ~ *old age; keep a person's memory* ~, not allow it to fade. **5** (of the complexion) pale; sickly looking. ~ ***with envy, '~-'eyed,*** jealous. **6** (special uses and compounds): **'~·back** *n* US banknote, the back printed in ~. **'~ fingers** *n* (colloq) skill in gardening. **'~·fly** *n* (collective *pl;* [U]) kinds of aphis. **~·gage** /-geɪdʒ/ *n* kind of plum with greenish-yellow skin and flesh and fine flavour. **'~·grocer** *n* shopkeeper selling vegetables and fruit. **'~-grocery** *n* (*pl* -ries) business of, things sold by, a ~grocer. **'~·horn** *n* inexperienced and easily deceived person. **'~·house** *n* building with sides and roof of glass, used for growing plants that need protection from the weather. **'~ room** *n* room in a theatre for actors and actresses when they are not on the stage. **'~-stuffs** *n* vegetables. **'~·sward** *n* [U] turf. **'~ 'tea** *n* tea made from steam-dried leaves. **'~·wood** *n* woodlands, esp in summer; forest in full leaf, esp as the home of outlaws in olden times.

green[2] /grin/ *n* **1** green colour; what is green: *a girl dressed in* ~*; a picture in* ~*s and blues,* with various shades of ~ and blue. **2** (*pl*) green leaf vegetables, e g cabbage, spinach, before or after cooking; vegetation: (US) *Christmas* ~*s,* e g branches of fir and holly for decoration. **3** area of land with growing grass. **(a)** public or common land: *the village* ~. **(b)** for the game of bowls: *a 'bowling-*~. **(c)** surrounding a hole on a golf course: *a 'putting* ~.

green·ery /'grinərɪ/ *n* [U] green foliage; verdure: *the* ~ *of the woods in spring.*

green·ish /'grinɪʃ/ *adj* somewhat green: (in compounds) *'~-'yellow; '~-'brown.* **~·ness** *n*

Greenwich /'grenɪtʃ/ *n* suburb of London east and west of which longitude is measured. ~ **(mean) time,** (abbr G M T), mean[2] time for the meridian of ~, used as a basis for calculating time in most parts of the world (now called *Universal time*).

greet /grit/ *vt* [VP6A,14] ~ ***sb with,*** **1** say words of welcome to; express one's feelings on receiving (news, etc); write (in a letter) words expressing respect, friendship, etc: ~ *a friend by saying 'Good morning!';* ~ *someone with a smile. The hero was* ~*ed with loud applause. They* ~*ed me with a shower of stones.* **2** (of sights and sounds) meet the eyes and ears: *the view that* ~*ed us at the hill-top.* **~·ing** *n* first words used on seeing sb or in writing to sb; expression or act with which sb or sth is ~ed: *'Good morning' and 'Dear Sir' are* ~*ings; a '*~*ings telegram,* one sent with, e g birthday, ~ings.

greg·ari·ous /grɪ'geərɪəs/ *adj* living in groups or societies; liking the company of others. **~·ly** *adv* **~·ness** *n*

Greg·or·ian /grɪ'gɔrɪən/ *adj* **1** of the kind of church music named after Pope Gregory I (540—604): ~ *chant.* **2** ~ **calendar,** the calendar introduced by Pope Gregory XIII (1502—85), with the days and months arranged as now.

grem·lin /'gremlɪn/ *n* goblin said to trouble airmen during World War II (by causing mechanical trouble).

gre·nade /grɪ'neɪd/ *n* small bomb thrown by hand or fired from a rifle.

grena·dier /'grenə'dɪə(r)/ *n* (formerly) soldier who threw grenades; (now) soldier in *the G~s, the G~ Guards,* British infantry regiment.

grew /gru/ *pt* of grow.

grey, gray /greɪ/ *adj* between black and white, coloured like ashes, or the sky on a dull, cloudy day: *His hair has turned* ~. **'~·beard** *n* old man. **'~-headed** *adj* old; of long service. **'~ matter,** material of the brain: *a boy without much* ~ *matter,* a not very intelligent boy. □ *n* ~ colour; ~ clothes: *dressed in* ~. □ *vt,vi* [VP6A,2A] make or become ~.

grey·hound /ˈgreɪhaʊnd/ *n* slender, long-legged, keen-sighted dog, able to run fast, used in chasing live hares and, as a modern sport, mechanical hares moved along a rail.

grey·ish /ˈgreɪɪʃ/ *adj* somewhat grey.

grid /grɪd/ *n* [C] **1** system of overhead cables carried on pylons, for distributing electric current over a large area. **2** network of squares on maps, numbered for reference. **3** grating: *a ˋcattle ~,* one placed at a gate, etc designed to prevent cattle from straying on to a road, etc. **4** frame of spaced parallel spirals or networks of wires in a radio valve. **5** gridiron.

griddle /ˈgrɪdl/ *n* circular iron plate used for baking cakes.

grid·iron /ˈgrɪdaɪən/ *n* **1** framework of metal bars used for cooking meat or fish over a clear fire. **2** field for American football (marked with numerous parallel lines).

grief /grif/ *n* **1** [U] deep or violent sorrow: *driven almost insane by ~; die of ~.* **2** [C] sth causing ~: *His failure to live a good life was a great ~ to his parents.* **3** ***bring sb/come to ~,*** cause sb to/meet with misfortune, injury or ruin.

griev·ance /ˈgrivns/ *n* [C] real or imagined cause for complaint or protest (*against*): *The trade union leader spoke about the ~s of the workers.*

grieve /griv/ *vt,vi* **1** [VP6A] cause grief to: *~ one's parents.* **2** [VP2A,C] feel grief: *~ for the dead/over sb's death; ~ about one's misfortunes/at bad news.*

griev·ous /ˈgrivəs/ *adj* **1** causing grief or suffering: *a ~ railway accident; ~ wrongs.* **2** severe: *~ pain.* **~·ly** *adv*

grif·fin /ˈgrɪfɪn/ (also **grif·fon, gry·phon** /ˈgrɪfən/) *n* (Gk myth) fabulous creature with the head and wings of an eagle and a lion's body. ⇨ the illus at armour.

grill /grɪl/ *n* [C] **1** = grating; grille; gridiron. **2** dish of meat, etc cooked directly over or under great heat: *a mixed ~,* steak, liver, bacon, etc. **3** (also ˋ**~-room**) room (in a hotel or restaurant) where ~s are cooked and served. □ *vt,vi* **1** [VP6A,2A,C] cook, be cooked, on a gridiron, or over great heat; expose oneself to great heat: *lie ~ing in the hot sun.* **2** [VP6A] e g of the police, question closely and severely.

grille /grɪl/ *n* screen of parallel bars used to close an open space, e g in a convent; similar screen over a counter, e g in a post office or bank as a protection.

grim /grɪm/ *adj* (-mer, -mest) stern; severe; forbidding; without mercy: *a ~ struggle; a ~ smile/expression; looking ~; a joke/story,* one with an element of cruelty in it. ***hold on like ~ death,*** very firmly. **~·ly** *adv* **~·ness** *n*

gri·mace /grɪˈmeɪs *US:* ˈgrɪmɪs/ *n* [C] ugly, twisted expression (on the face), expressing pain, disgust, etc or intended to cause laughter: *Only rude children make ~s.* □ *vi* [VP2A] make ~s.

grime /graɪm/ *n* [U] dirt, esp a coating on the surface of sth or on the body: *the soot and ~ of a big manufacturing town; a face covered with ~ and sweat.* □ *vt* [VP6A] make dirty with ~: *~d with dust.* **grimy** /ˈgraɪmɪ/ *adj* (-ier, -est) covered with ~: *grimy faces/roofs/windows.*

grin /grɪn/ *vi,vt* (-nn-) **1** [VP2A,C] smile broadly so as to show the teeth expressing amusement, foolish satisfaction, contempt, etc: *~ning with delight; ~ from ear to ear.* ***~ and bear it,*** endure pain, disappointment, etc, uncomplainingly. **2** [VP6A] express by ~ning: *He ~ned his approval.* □ *n* [C] act of ~ning: *the tigerish ~ on the madman's face; ~s of derision.*

grind /graɪnd/ *vt,vi* (*pt,pp* ground /graʊnd/) **1** [VP6A,15A,B] ***~ sth to/into,*** crush to grains or powder between millstones, the teeth, etc: *~ sth to pieces; ~ sth down; ~ coffee beans; ~ wheat in a mill; ~ corn into flour.* **2** [VP2A,C] be capable of ~ing: *This wheat ~s well. This wheat will not ~ fine,* cannot be ground fine. **3** [VP6A] produce in this way: *~ flour.* **4** [VP6A,15A] (usu passive) (fig) oppress or crush: *people who were ground (down) by poverty/taxation/tyranny; tyrants who ground the faces of the poor.* **5** [VP6A] polish or sharpen by rubbing on or with a rough, hard surface: *~ a knife/lens.* ***have an axe to ~,*** ⇨ axe. **6** [VP6A,15A,B] rub harshly together, esp with a circular motion: *~ one's teeth (together); a ship ~ing on the rocks; ~ one's heel into the ground; ~ to a halt,* (of a vehicle) stop noisily (with brakes that ~); (fig) (of a process) stop slowly: *The strikes brought industry ~ing to a halt.* **7** [VP6A,15A] work by turning; produce by turning: *~ a hand-mill/coffee-mill/barrel-organ; ~ out a tune on an organ;* (fig) *~ out some verses,* produce them slowly and with effort. **8** [VP2C,15B] (cause to) work or study hard and long (*at*); *~ away at one's studies; ~ for an exam.* □ *n* (colloq) long, monotonous task: *the examination ~,* the task of preparing for an examination. *Do you find learning English a ~?*

grinder /ˈgraɪndə(r)/ *n* **1** thing that grinds, e g a molar tooth, apparatus for grinding coffee: *~ ˋcoffee-~.* **2** (in compounds) person who grinds: *a ˋknife-~; an ˋorgan-~,* person who produces tunes by turning the handle of a barrel-organ.

grind·stone /ˈgraɪndstəʊn/ *n* stone shaped like a wheel, turned on an axle, used for sharpening tools. ***keep sb's nose to the ~,*** force him to work hard without rest.

grip /grɪp/ *vt,vi* (-pp-) [VP6A,2A] take and keep a firm hold of; seize firmly: *The frightened child ~ped its mother's hand. The brakes failed to ~ and the car ran into a wall. The speaker ~ped the attention of his audience. The film is a ~ping story of love and hate.* □ *n* **1** (*sing* only except as shown) act, manner, or power of ~ping: *let go one's ~ of sth; take a ~ on a rope; have a good ~* (fig, = understanding) *of a problem; have a good ~ on an audience,* hold their attention and interest. ***be at/come/get to ~s with,*** be attacking, begin to attack, in earnest; be in close combat: *get to ~s with a problem.* ***take a ~ on oneself,*** (colloq) stop being idle and inattentive. **2** [C] (in a machine, etc) part that ~s or clips; clutch; part that is to be ~ped. **3** [C] (also ˋ**~-sack**) (US) traveller's handbag: *a leather ~.*

gripes /graɪps/ *n pl* (colloq, usu with *def art*) violent pains in the abdomen.

grippe /grip/ *n* (with *def art*) influenza.

gris·ly /ˈgrɪzlɪ/ *adj* causing horror or terror; ghastly.

grist /grɪst/ *n* [U] grain to be ground, chiefly in fig phrases. ***It's all ~ to the mill/All is ~ that comes to his mill,*** (prov) He makes use of everything.

gristle /ˈgrɪsl/ *n* [U] tough, elastic tissue in animal bodies, esp in meat: *I can't eat this meat—it's all ~.*

grit /grɪt/ *n* [U] **1** (collective *sing*) tiny, hard bits of stone, sand, etc: *spread ~ on icy roads. I've got some ~ in my shoe.* **2** quality of courage and endurance: *The soldiers showed that they had plenty of ~.* □ *vt* (-tt-) **~ *the teeth,*** keep the jaws tight together. **~ty** *adj* (-ier, -iest) of or like ~ (1): *The sandstorm made the food ~ty. This spinach tastes ~ty.*

grits /grɪts/ *n pl* husked but unground oats; coarse oatmeal.

grizzle /ˈgrɪzl/ *vi* (colloq) (esp of children) cry fretfully.

griz·zled /ˈgrɪzld/ *adj* grey; grey-haired.

griz·zly /ˈgrɪzlɪ/ *n* (also ˈ~ **bear**) large, fierce grey bear of N America. ⇨ the illus at **bear**.

groan /grəʊn/ *vi, vt* **1** [VP2A,C] make a deep sound forced out by pain, or expressing despair or distress: *The wounded men lay there ~ing, with no one to help them. The teacher ~ed with dismay. The people ~ed under injustice.* **2** [VP2A,C] (of things) make a noise like that of ~ing: *The ship's timbers ~ed during the storm. The table ~ed with food,* (fig) was weighed down with large quantities of food. **3** [VP6A,15B] express with ~ing: *He ~ed out a sad story.* **4** [VP15B] silence by ~ing: *The speaker was ~ed down by his audience,* They prevented him from being heard. □ *n* [C] deep sound made in ~ing: *the ~s of the injured men; give a ~ of dismay; a speech interrupted by ~s of disapproval.*

groat /grəʊt/ *n* (hist) (14th to 17th cc) English silver coin worth fourpence.

groats /grəʊts/ *n pl* (crushed) grain, esp oats, that has been hulled.

gro·cer /ˈgrəʊsə(r)/ *n* shopkeeper who sells tea, sugar, butter, tinned and bottled food, household requirements such as soap, soap-powders, etc. **~y** *n* **1** [U] ~'s trade: *a ˈ~y business.* **2** (*pl;* -ries) things sold by a ~.

grog /grɒg/ *n* [U] (a word used by sailors) drink of spirits, rum, whisky, etc mixed with water.

groggy /ˈgrɒgɪ/ *adj* (-ier, -iest) **1** unsteady; likely to collapse or fall: *The legs of that chair look rather ~.* **2** weak and unsteady as the result of illness, shock, lack of sleep, etc: *That last attack of influenza left me rather ~.*

groin /grɔɪn/ *n* **1** depression between the stomach and the thigh. ⇨ the illus at **trunk**. **2** (archit) curved edge where two vaults meet (in a roof). □ *vt* build with ~s.

groom /grum/ *n* **1** person employed to look after horses. **2** bridegroom. □ *vt* [VP6A] **1** feed, brush and in other ways look after (horses); (of apes, monkeys) clean the fur and skin of: *a female ape ~ing her mate.* **2** (in the *pp*, of persons): *well/badly ~ed,* well/badly dressed (esp of the hair, beard and clothes). **3** (colloq) prepare (sb for a career, etc).

groove /gruv/ *n* **1** long, hollow channel in the surface of hard material, esp one made to guide the motion of sth that slides along it, e g a sliding door or window; spiral cut on a gramophone disc (in which the needle or stylus moves). **2** way of living that has become a habit. ***get into/be stuck in a ~,*** become set in one's ways, one's style of living. ***in the ~,*** (dated sl) in the right mood (for sth); exhilarated. □ *vt* make ~s in: *a ~d shelf.* **groovy** *adj* (sl) up-to-date; in the latest fashion (esp of young people): *a groovy restaurant: groovy clothes/people.* **~r** *n* groovy person.

grope /grəʊp/ *vi, vt* [VP2A,C,3A,15A] **~ *(about) (for/after) sth,*** feel about as one does in the dark; search: *He ~d for the door-handle. We ~d our way along the dark corridor.* **grop·ing·ly** *adv* in the manner of one who ~s.

gross[1] /grəʊs/ *n* (*pl* unchanged) twelve dozen; 144. ⇨ App 4.

gross[2] /grəʊs/ *adj* **1** vulgar; not refined; coarse in mind or morals: *~ language/jests/morals.* **2** (of food) coarse, greasy; liking such food: *a ~ feeder.* **3** (of the senses) heavy and dull. **4** flagrant; glaring; clearly seen: *~ injustice/negligence; a ~ error/overcharge.* **5** (of vegetation) luxuriant: *the ~ vegetation of the tropical rain-forest.* **6** (of persons) repulsively fat. **7** (opposite of *net*) total, whole: *the ~ amount; his ~ income.* **8** ***in (the) ~,*** wholesale; in bulk; in a general way. □ *vt* [VP6A] make as a total amount: *His last film ~ed five million pounds.* **~·ly** *adv* **~·ness** *n*

grot /grɒt/ *n* (poet) grotto.

gro·tesque /grəʊˈtesk/ *adj* **1** absurd; fantastic; laughable because strange and incongruous: *a ~ appearance; ~ manners.* **2** (in art) combining human, animal and plant forms in a fantastic way; made up of comically distorted figures and designs. □ *n* **1** ~ person, animal, figure or design. **2** *the ~,* painting, carving, etc in which the ~ style appears. **~·ly** *adv* **~·ness** *n*

grotto /ˈgrɒtəʊ/ *n* (*pl* -toes, -tos /-təʊz/) cave, esp one made artificially as a garden shelter.

grotty /ˈgrɒtɪ/ *adj* (sl) (of person, place, thing) unpleasing; useless; dirty.

grouch /graʊtʃ/ *vi* (colloq) complain. □ *n* fit of ill temper; sulky, discontented person. **~y** *adj* sullenly discontented.

ground[1] /graʊnd/ *n* **1** (*sing* with *def art*) solid surface of the earth: *lie on/sit on/fall to the ~; ~-to-air missiles,* fired from the ~ (at aircraft). ***fall/be dashed to the ~,*** (cause to) fail, be disappointed: *The scheme/Our plans fell to the ~. Our hopes were dashed to the ~. The airliner made a ~-controlled approach,* approached the runway under the direction (by radio-telephone) of sb in the control tower. ***get off the ~,*** (of an aircraft) rise into the air; (fig, of an undertaking or scheme) pass from the planning stage and make a start. ***above ~,*** alive. ***below ~,*** dead and buried. **2** [U] position, area or distance on the earth's surface. ***cut the ~ from under sb's feet,*** anticipate his plans, arguments, defences, etc and in this way embarrass him. ***cover (much, etc) ~,*** **(a)** travel: *We've covered a great deal of ~ today,* have come a long way. **(b)** (fig, of a lecture, report, inquiry, etc) deal with a variety of subjects; be far-reaching: *The committee's report covers much new ~,* deals with many new matters. ***gain ~,*** make progress; win a success or an advantage. ***give/lose ~,*** retreat; fail to keep one's position or advantage. ***hold/stand/keep one's ~,*** stand firm; not yield; maintain one's claim, intention, argument, etc. ***shift one's ~,*** change one's argument, etc. ***down to the ~,*** (colloq) thoroughly;

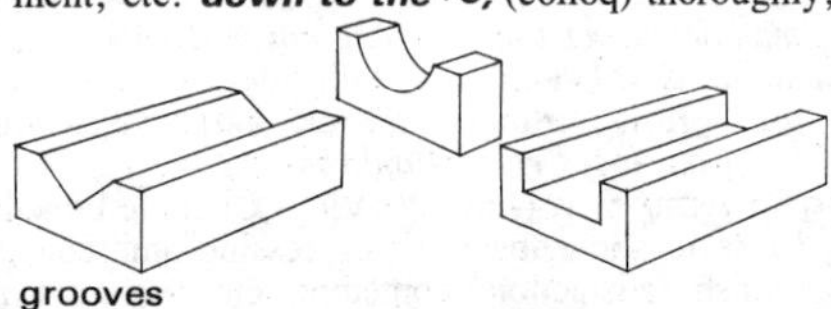
grooves

in all respects: *That will suit me down to the* ~. **common** ~, subject on which two or more persons or parties are in agreement or on which they have similar views. **forbidden** ~, (fig) subject that must be avoided. **3** [U] soil; earth: *till the* ~. *The frost has made the* ~ *hard.* ***break fresh*** ~, (**a**) cultivate land that has not been cultivated before. (**b**) (fig) do sth new; deal with a subject for the first time. **4** [C] area or piece of land for a special purpose or a particular use: *a 'football/'cricket/'sports* ~; *a 'parade/recre'ation* ~; *a 'play*~; *'hunting-*~*s; 'fishing-*~*s*, areas used for fishing. **5** (always *pl*) land, gardens, round a building, often enclosed with walls, hedges or fences: *the* ~*s of Buckingham Palace. The mansion has extensive* ~*s.* **6** [U] bottom of the sea or of any other body of water: (chiefly in) ***touch*** ~, (of a ship) strike the bottom. ⇨ **aground. 7** (*pl*) particles of solid matter that sink to the bottom of a liquid: (esp) *'coffee-*~*s.* **8** (*pl* or [U]) reason(s) for saying, doing or believing sth. ***on the*** ~***s of,*** because of: *excused on the* ~*s of youth; reject a man on 'medical* ~*s. On what* ~*s do you suspect him?* ***be*** ~***s for; have/give*** ~***s for,*** be, have, give a cause or reason for: *There are no* ~*s for anxiety. I have good* ~*s for believing his version of events. They don't give me much* ~*/many* ~*s for complaint. What are the* ~*s for divorce in this country,* What is recognized as a basis for an action of divorce? **9** [C] surface on which a design is painted, printed, cut, etc; undecorated part: *a design of pink roses on a white* ~. **10** (compounds) **'~-bait** *n* food thrown to the bottom of a fishing-~ to attract fish. **'~-fish** *n* fish living at or near the bottom. **'~ 'floor** *n* the floor of a building level with the ~. ***be/get in on the*** ~ ***floor,*** (colloq) be admitted, e g as a shareholder, on the same terms as the promoters. **'~·nut** *n* kind of pea with pods ripening under the ~ (also called *earthnut* and *peanut*). **'~-plan** *n* plan of a building at ~ level. **'~-rent** *n* rent paid for the use of land leased for building. **'~s·man** /-mən/ *n* (*pl* -men) man employed to look after a cricket ~. **'~·sheet,** waterproof sheet spread on the ~, e g under bedding in a tent. **'~ speed** *n* aircraft's speed relative to the ~ (contrasted with *air speed*). **'~ staff/crew** *n* mechanics who service aircraft on the ~; non-flying members of the staff of an airfield, etc. **'~ swell** *n* heavy, slow-moving waves caused by a distant or recent storm. **'~-work** *n* (usu fig) foundation; basis.

ground[2] /graʊnd/ *vt, vi* **1** [VP6A,2A] (of a ship) (cause to) touch the sea bottom; (of aircraft, airmen) compel to stay on the ground: *Our ship* ~*ed in shallow water. All aircraft at London Airport were* ~*ed by fog yesterday.* **2** [VP6A] ~ ***arms,*** (mil) lay (esp rifles) on the ground. **3** [VP14] ~ ***on sth,*** base (the more usu word) (a belief, etc) on: ~ *one's arguments on facts; a well-*~*ed theory.* **4** [VP6A,14] ~ ***sb in sth,*** give (sb) good teaching or basic training in: *The teacher* ~*ed his pupils in arithmetic.* **5** [VP6A] connect (a piece of electrical apparatus) with the ~ as conductor, as a safety precaution (*earth* is the usu word). **~·ing** *n* thorough teaching of the elements of a subject: *a good* ~*ing in grammar.*

ground[3] /graʊnd/ *pt,pp* of **grind**: ~ *rice,* reduced to fine powder. ~ ***glass,*** made non-transparent by grinding.

ground·less /'graʊndləs/ *adj* without foundation or good reason: ~ *fears/anxieties/rumours.* ⇨ **ground**[1](**3**).

ground·sel /'graʊndsl/ *n* [U] kinds of weed, the commonest kind of which is used as food for some cage-birds.

group /grup/ *n* [C] number of persons or things gathered or placed together, or naturally associated; number of jointly-controlled business companies, e g as the result of a merger: *a* ~ *of girls/trees/houses; people standing about in small* ~*s; the Germanic* ~ *of languages.* **'G~ captain,** Air Force officer. ⇨ App 9. □ *vt,vi* [VP6A,15A, B,2C] form into, gather in, a ~ or ~s: *The children* ~*ed (themselves) round their teacher. G*~ *the roses together.*

grouse[1] /graʊs/ *n* (*pl* unchanged) (sorts of) bird with feathered feet, shot for sport and food: *'*~ *shooting,* the shooting of red ~ on the moors of Scotland and northern England.

grouse[2] /graʊs/ *vi* [VP2A,C] (colloq) grumble; complain. □ *n* complaint.

grove /grəʊv/ *n* group of trees; small wood.

grovel /'grovl/ *vi* (-ll-; US also -l-) [VP2A,C] lie down on one's face, crawl, in front of sb whom one fears, (as if) begging for mercy; (fig) humble oneself; behave in a way that shows one has no self-respect: ~ *at the feet of a conqueror.* **~·ler** *n* person who ~s.

grow /grəʊ/ *vi,vt* (*pt* **grew** /gru/, *pp* **grown** /grəʊn/) **1** [VP2A,C,D] develop; increase in size, height, length, etc: *Rice* ~*s in warm climates. How quickly you are* ~*ing! How tall you've* ~*n! She has decided to let her hair* ~, not have it cut short. *A full-*~*n elephant is very large. He has* ~*n into a fine young man. Plants* ~ *from seeds. She has* ~*n in stature but not in wisdom.* ~ ***out of,*** (**a**) become too big for: ~ *out of one's clothes.* (**b**) become too old for; cease to practise; abandon: *He has* ~*n out of the bad habits of his boyhood days.* (**c**) have as a source: *His troubles grew out of his bad temper.* ~ ***up,*** (**a**) (of persons, animals) reach the stage of full development; become adult or mature: *When the boys* ~ *up,...; He has a* ~*n-up son.* (**b**) develop: *A warm friendship grew up between the two men.* **~·ing-pains** *n pl* (**a**) pains in the limbs of young children, popularly believed to be caused by rapid growth. (**b**) (fig) problems arising while a new enterprise is developing: *The business is still suffering from* ~*ing pains.* **'grown-'ups** *n pl* adult persons (contrasted with children). **2** [VP2D] become: ~ *older;* ~ *smaller. It began to* ~ *dark.* **3** [VP4A] ~ ***to be/like, etc,*** reach the point or stage where one is/likes, etc: *One* ~*s to like what one is accustomed to. My friendship with them grew to be* (= by degrees became) *considerable.* **4** [VP6A,12B,13B] cause or allow to ~: ~ *roses. He's* ~*ing a beard. Will you* ~ *some herbs for me/*~ *me some herbs this year?* **5** [VP3A] ~ ***(up)on,*** (**a**) become more deeply rooted: *a habit that* ~*s (up)on you.* (**b**) come to have a greater attraction for; win the liking of: *a book/a piece of music that* ~*s on you.* **~er** *n* **1** person who ~s things: *a 'fruit-*~*er; 'rose-*~*ers.* **2** plant, etc that ~s in a certain way: *a free/rapid* ~*er.*

growl /graʊl/ *vi,vt* **1** [VP2A,C] (of animals, men, thunder) make a low, threatening sound: *The dog* ~*ed at me. We heard thunder* ~*ing in the distance.* **2** [VP6A,15B] ~ ***(out),*** say in a ~ing manner: *He* ~*ed (out) his answer.* □ *n* [C] low threatening sound; angry complaint. **~·ing·ly** *adv*

growler /ˈgraʊlə(r)/ *n* (old colloq use) four-wheeled horse-drawn cab.

grown /grəʊn/ *pp* of **grow**: *a ~ man,* a mature man.

growth /grəʊθ/ *n* **1** [U] growing; development; process of growing: *the rapid ~ of our economy. At what age does an elephant reach full ~,* its greatest size? **2** [U] increase: *ˈ~ shares,* thought likely to increase in value. **3** [U] cultivation: *apples of foreign ~,* grown abroad. **4** [C] sth that grows or has grown: *a thick ~ of weeds; a three-days' ~ of beard.* **5** [C] diseased formation in the body, e g a cancer.

groyne /grɔɪn/ *n* [C] structure of wood, etc, or a low, broad wall of stone, concrete, etc built to prevent sand and pebbles from being washed away by the sea, the current or a river, etc.

grub[1] /grʌb/ *n* **1** [C] larva of insect. **2** [U] (sl) food.

grub[2] /grʌb/ *vt, vi* (**-bb-**) [VP6A,15B,2C] turn over the soil, esp in order to get sth up or out: *~bing up weeds. The pigs were ~bing about among the bushes.*

grubby /ˈgrʌbɪ/ *adj* (**-ier, -iest**) **1** dirty; unwashed. **2** having grubs in it.

grudge /grʌdʒ/ *vt* [VP12A,13A,6C] be unwilling to give or allow: *I don't ~ him his success,* I admit that he deserves it. *His cruel master ~d him even the food he ate,* gave him his food unwillingly. *I ~ paying £1 for a bottle of wine that is not worth 50p.* □ *n* [C] feeling of ill-will, resentment, envy or spite: *I bear him no ~. He has a ~ against me. I owe that man a ~,* think I have good reason to feel ill-will towards him. **grudg·ingly** *adv* in a grudging manner: *His employer grudgingly raised his salary.*

gruel /ˈgrul/ *n* [U] liquid food of oatmeal, etc boiled in milk or water: *have/get one's ~,* (dated colloq) be punished or defeated. **~·ling,** (US) **~·ing** *adj* severe; exhausting: *a ~ling race.*

grue·some /ˈgrusəm/ *adj* filling one with horror or disgust; frightful. **~·ly** *adv* **~·ness** *n*

gruff /grʌf/ *adj* (of a person, his voice, behaviour) rough; surly. **~·ly** *adv* **~·ness** *n*

grumble /ˈgrʌmbl/ *vi, vt* **1** [VP2A,C,3A] *~ (at/about/over sth),* complain or protest in a bad-tempered way: *He's always grumbling. He ~d at the low pay offered to him.* **2** [VP6A,15B] *~ (out),* say in a sullen, dissatisfied way: *~ (out) a reply.* **3** [VP2A,C] make a low, growling sound: *thunder grumbling in the distance.* □ *n* [C] (usu bad-tempered) complaint or protest: *That fellow is full of ~s.* **grum·bler** /ˈgrʌmblə(r)/ *n* person who ~s.

grumpy /ˈgrʌmpɪ/ *adj* (**-ier, -iest**) bad-tempered; surly. **grump·ily** *adv* **grumpi·ness** *n*

Grundy·ism /ˈgrʌndɪɪzm/ *n* [U] conventional propriety; prudery.

grunt /grʌnt/ *vi, vt* **1** [VP2A] (of animals, esp pigs) make a low, rough sound; (of persons) make a similar sound expressing disagreement, boredom, irritation, etc. **2** [VP6A,15B] utter in a ~ing way: *~ (out) an answer.* □ *n* [C] low, rough sound.

gry·phon /ˈgrɪfən/ *n* = **griffin**.

guano /ˈgwɑnəʊ/ *n* (*pl* **-nos** /-nəʊz/) [C] dung dropped by seabirds, used as fertilizer.

guar·an·tee[1] /ˌgærənˈti/ *n* [C] **1** (in law, **guaranty**) promise or undertaking (usu in writing or print) that certain conditions agreed to in a transaction will be fulfilled: *a year's ~ with a watch,* a promise to keep it in good repair, etc. **2** (in law, **guaranty**) undertaking given by one person to another that he will be responsible for sth to be done, e g payment of a debt, by a third person. **3** (in law, **guarantor** /-tɔ(r)/) person who gives such an undertaking: *be ~ for a friend's good behaviour. If I try to borrow £1 000 from the bank, will you be my ~?* **4** (in law, **guaranty**) sth offered, e g the deeds of a house or other document of ownership of property, as security for the fulfilling of conditions in a ~**(1,2)**: *'What ~ can you offer?' 'I can offer my house and land as a ~.'* **5** (colloq) sth that seems to make an occurrence likely: *Blue skies are not always a ~ of fine weather.*

guar·an·tee[2] /ˌgærənˈti/ *vt* [VP6A,7A,25,9,12A,13A] **1** give a guarantee**(1,2,3)** for (sth or sb): *~ a man's debts; ~ to pay a man's debts; ~ that the debts will be paid; ~ the payment of the debts. We cannot ~ the punctual arrival of trains in foggy weather. This clock is ~d for one year. We can't ~ our workers regular employment.* **2** (colloq) promise (without legal obligation): *Many shopkeepers ~ satisfaction to customers.*

guar·an·tor /ˌgærənˈtɔ(r)/ *n* (legal word for) guarantee. ⇨ **guarantee**[1]**(3)**.

guar·an·ty /ˈgærəntɪ/ *n* (*pl* **-ties**) (legal word for) guarantee. ⇨ **guarantee**[1]**(1,2,4)**.

guard[1] /gɑd/ *n* **1** [U] state of watchfulness against attack, danger or surprise: *The sentry/soldier is on ~,* at his post, on duty. *The soldier was ordered to keep ~.* **2** [U] attitude of readiness to defend oneself, e g in fencing, boxing, bayonet-drill. ***be on/off one's ~,*** be prepared/unprepared against attack or surprise: *Be on your ~ against pickpockets. He struck me while I was off my ~.* **3** [C] soldier or party of soldiers keeping ~; sentry. ***change ~,*** (mil) replace one ~ by another. Hence, ***the changing of the ~,*** e g at Buckingham Palace. ***mount ~,*** take up one's post as a sentry. ***relieve ~,*** take the place of a sentry who has finished his period of duty. ***stand ~,*** act as a sentry. **4** man (also called *warder*) or group of men in charge of a prison. **5** (GB, but not US) official in charge of a railway train (and formerly a stage-coach). **6** (*pl*) (in GB and some other countries) troops employed to protect the sovereign: *the G~s; the Royal Horse G~s; a G~s officer.* **ˈ~s·man** /-mən/ *n* (*pl* **-men**) soldier of the G~s. **7** [C] body of soldiers with the duty of protecting, honouring or escorting a person: *The Duke, on his arrival, inspected the ~ of honour at the station.* ⇨ also *rear~* at **rear**[1]**(4)**, *Home G~* at **home**[1]**(7)**. **8** (esp in compounds) (part of) an article or apparatus designed to prevent injury or loss: *a ˈfire-~,* in front of a fireplace; *a ˈmud~* (over the wheel of a bicycle, etc); *the ~ of a sword,* the part of the hilt that protects the hand. **9** (compounds) **ˈ~-boat** *n* one sent round a fleet of warships in harbour. **ˈ~-house** *n* (mil) building for a military ~ or one in which prisoners are kept. **ˈ~-rail** *n* rail, e g on a staircase, to prevent falling or (elsewhere) to prevent persons from danger, e g from traffic. **ˈ~-room** *n* room for soldiers on ~ or for soldiers under ~. **ˈ~-ship** *n* ship protecting a harbour.

guard[2] /gɑd/ *vt, vi* **1** [VP6A,15A] protect; keep from danger: *~ a camp; ~ one's life/one's reputation; ~ prisoners,* prevent them from escaping. **2** [VP3A] ***~ against,*** use care and caution to prevent: ~ *against disease/bad habits/suspicion.* **~ed** *adj* (of statements, etc) cautious: *a ~ed answer; be ~ed in what one says.* **~·ed·ly** *adv* cautiously.

guard·ian /ˈgɑdɪən/ *n* **1** (official or private) person who guards, esp (legal use) one who is responsible for the care of a young or incapable person and his property. **ˈ~ ˈangel,** spirit watching over a person or place. **2** (formerly in England): *~s of the poor,* members of Boards elected to administer the Poor Laws in a parish or district. **~·ship** /-ʃɪp/ *n* position or office of a ~.

guava /ˈgwɑvə/ *n* (tropical tree with) acid fruit used for making jelly. ⇨ the illus at **fruit**.

gudg·eon /ˈgʌdʒən/ *n* small freshwater fish used as bait.

guel·der rose /ˈgeldə rəʊz/ *n* plant with round bunches of white flowers; snowball tree.

guer·rilla, guer·illa /gəˈrɪlə/ *n* **1** (now usu ~ **war**) war carried on by fighters who are not members of a regular army. **2** man engaged in a ~ war: *urban ~s,* such men who engage in sporadic fighting in towns.

guess /ges/ *vt,vi* [VP6A,25,9,8,10,2A,C,3A] form an opinion, give an answer, make a statement, based on supposition, not on careful thought, calculation or definite knowledge: *Can you ~ my weight/what my weight is/how much I weigh? I should ~ his age at 50/~ him to be 50/~ that he is 50. Can't you even ~ at her age? G~ what I'm thinking. You've ~ed right/wrong. I ~ it's going to rain,* (US colloq) I think it's going to rain. □ *n* [C] opinion formed by ~ing: *make/have a ~ (at sth). One man's ~ is as good as another's.* ***it's anybody's ~,*** no one can be sure about it. ***at a ~,*** making a ~: *At a ~ I should say there were 50 people present.* ***by ~,*** by the use of ~ing: *Don't answer by ~; work the problem out.* **ˈ~-work** *n* [U] ~ing; result of ~ing.

guest /gest/ *n* person staying at or paying a visit to another's house or being entertained at a meal: *We're expecting ~s to dinner.* **ˈ~·room** *n* bedroom kept for the use of ~s. **ˈ~·house** *n* superior boarding-house. **ˈ~-night** *n* evening on which members of a club, college, mess[2], etc may bring in and entertain their friends as ~s. **ˈpaying ~** *n* boarder in a private house; person staying at an inn, a hotel or boarding-house, and paying for his entertainment.

guf·faw /gəˈfɔ/ *vi, n* (give a) noisy laugh.

guid·ance /ˈgɑɪdns/ *n* [U] guiding or being guided; leadership.

guide /gɑɪd/ *n* **1** person who shows others the way, esp a person employed to point out interesting sights on a journey or visit. **2** sth that directs or influences (conduct, etc): *Instinct is not always a good ~.* **ˈ~-lines** *n pl* advice (usu from sb in authority) on policy, etc: *~-lines on prices and incomes.* **3** (also **ˈ~·book**) book for travellers, tourists, etc with information about a place: *a ~ to the British Museum; a ~ to Italy.* **4** book of information; manual: *a ~ to Poultry Keeping.* **5** bar, rod or part of a machine or apparatus that keeps other parts, etc, moving as desired. **6 ˈGirl ˈG~,** ⇨ **girl(5)**. □ *vt* [VP6A,15A,B] act as ~ to: *~ sb to a place; ~ sb in/out/up, etc. You must be ~d by your sense of what is right and just.* **ˈ~d ˈmissile,** rocket (for use in war) which can be ~d to their destination while in flight by electronic devices.

guild /gɪld/ *n* (older spelling **gild**) society of persons for helping one another, forwarding common interests, e g trade, social welfare. **ˈG~-ˈhall** *n* hall in which members of a ~ met in the Middle Ages; *the G~-hall,* hall of the Corporation of the City of London, used for banquets, receptions, etc. **~ socialism,** system by which an industry is to be controlled by a council of its members.

guilder /ˈgɪldə(r)/ *n* unit of currency of the Netherlands (*gulden*) or *florin*.

guile /gɑɪl/ *n* [U] deceit; cunning: *a man full of ~; get sth by ~.* **~·less** *adj* **~·ful** /-fl/ *adj*

guille·mot /ˈgɪlɪmot/ *n* kinds of arctic seabird. ⇨ the illus at **water**.

guillo·tine /ˈgɪləˈtin/ *n* **1** machine for beheading (criminals in France) with a heavy blade sliding in grooves dropped from a height. **2** kind of machine for cutting the edges of books during manufacture, trimming sheets of paper, etc. **3** (in Parliament) method of stopping obstruction of a bill (by excessive debate) by fixing times for taking votes. □ *vt* [VP6A] use the ~ on.

guilt /gɪlt/ *n* [U] condition of having done wrong; responsibility for wrong-doing: *The ~ of the accused man was in doubt.* **~·less** *adj* innocent; without ~: *~less of the offence;* not having knowledge or possession (*of*). **~y** *adj* (-ier, -iest) **1** having done wrong: *plead ~y to a crime; be ~y of a crime.* **2** showing or feeling guilt: *look ~y; ~y looks; a ~y conscience.* **~·ily** /-əlɪ/ *adv* **~·iness** *n*

guinea /ˈgɪnɪ/ *n* (abbr *gns*) (money of account) formerly the sum of twenty-one shillings (now £1.05, or 105p), for which there was neither coin nor banknote, used in stating prices of goods, professional fees, charges, subscriptions, etc: *the 2000 Gns race,* horse-race with a prize of 2000 ~s.

guinea-fowl /ˈgɪnɪ fɑʊl/ *n* domestic fowl of the pheasant family, with dark grey feathers spotted with white.

guinea-pig /ˈgɪnɪ pɪg/ *n* ⇨ the illus at **small**. short-eared animal like a big rat, often used in experiments; sb allowing himself to be used in medical or other experiments.

Guin·ness /ˈgɪnɪs/ *n* (P) kind of bitter stout: *~'s stout;* bottle or glass of this: *one small ~, please.*

guise /gɑɪz/ *n* [C] **1** (old use) style of dress: *in the ~ of a monk.* **2** ***in/under the ~ of,*** assuming a particular manner or appearance: *under the ~ of friendship.*

guitar /gɪˈtɑ(r)/ *n* (usu) six-stringed musical instrument, plucked with the fingers or a plectrum. ⇨ the illus at **string**.

gulch /gʌltʃ/ *n* (US) deep, narrow, rocky valley.

gul·den /ˈgʊldən/ *n* = **guilder**.

gulf /gʌlf/ *n* **1** part of the sea almost surrounded by land: *the G~ of Mexico; the G~ Stream,* warm ocean current flowing north from the G~ of Mexico. **2** deep hollow; chasm; abyss; (fig) dividing line, division (*between* opinions, etc).

gull[1] /gʌl/ *n* (kinds of) large, long-winged seabird. ⇨ the illus at **water**.

gull[2] /gʌl/ *vt* [VP6A,15] cheat; deceive: *~ a fool out of his money.* □ *n* person who is easily ~ed. **~·ible** /-əbl/ *adj* easily ~ed. **~i·bil·ity** /ˈgʌləˈbɪlətɪ/ *n*

gul·let /ˈgʌlɪt/ *n* food passage from the mouth to the stomach; throat. ⇨ the illus at **head**.

gully /ˈgʌlɪ/ *n* (*pl* -lies) narrow channel cut or formed by rainwater, e g on a hillside, or made for carrying water away from a building.

gulp /gʌlp/ *vt,vi* [VP6A,15B] ***~ (down),*** swallow (food or drink) quickly or greedily: *~ down a cup of tea;* hold back or suppress (as if swallowing sth); make a ~ing motion. □ *n* [C] act of ~ing: *empty a glass at one ~;* amount that is ~ed; mouthful, esp of sth liquid: *a ~ of cold tea.*

gum[1] /gʌm/ *n* (usu *pl*) firm, pink flesh in which the teeth are rooted: *The dog bared its gums at me.* **gum·boil** /ˋgʌmbɔɪl/ *n* boil or abscess on the gums.

gum[2] /gʌm/ *n* **1** [U] sticky substance exuded from some trees, used for sticking things together. **2** [U] gum that has been specially prepared in some way: *chewing-gum;* [C] (also ˋ*gum-drop*) hard, transparent sweet made of gelatine, etc. **3** (also ˋ*gum-tree*) (kinds of) eucalyptus tree. ***up a gum-tree,*** (sl) in difficulties. **4** [U] rubber. **ˋgum boots,** (chiefly US) high rubber boots. □ *vt* (-mm-) [VP6A,15A,B] stick together with gum; spread gum on the surface of: *gum sth down; gum two things together.* **gummy** *adj* (-ier, -iest) sticky.

gum[3] /gʌm/ *n* (esp N England) (in oaths, etc) God: *By gum!*

gumbo /ˋgʌmbəʊ/ *n* (US) thick okra soup.

gump·tion /ˋgʌmpʃn/ *n* [U] (colloq) common sense and initiative; qualities likely to bring success: *The lad lacks ~.*

gun /gʌn/ *n* **1** general name for any kind of firearm that sends shells or bullets from a metal tube: *a warship with 16-inch guns; machine-guns.* ⇨ cannon, musket, rifle[1]. ***blow great guns,*** (of the wind) blow violently. ***stick to one's guns,*** maintain one's position against attack or argument. **ˋgun-boat** *n* small warship carrying heavy guns, or long-range missiles: *gun-boat diplomacy,* backed by the threat of force. **ˋgun-carriage** *n* wheeled support of a big gun, or part on which a gun slides when it recoils. **ˋgun-cotton** *n* [U] explosive of acid-soaked cotton. **ˋgun·man** /-mən/ *n* (*pl* -men) man who uses a gun to rob or kill people. **ˋgun-metal** *n* alloy of copper and tin or zinc. **ˋgun·powder** *n* explosive powder used in guns, fireworks, blasting, etc: *the Gunpowder Plot,* plot to blow up the Houses of Parliament, 5 Nov 1605. **ˋgun·room** *n* (in a warship) room for junior officers. **ˋgun-running** *n* [U] introduction of firearms, secretly and illegally, into a country, e g to help a revolt. **ˋgun-runner** *n* person engaged in this. **ˋgun·shot** *n* range of a gun: *be out of/within gunshot.* **ˋgun·smith** *n* person who makes and repairs small firearms. **2** person using a sporting gun, as a member of a shooting party. **3 big gun,** (colloq) important or powerful person. □ *vt* [VP6A,15B] ***~ sb (down),*** shoot with a gun.

gun·ner /ˋgʌnə(r)/ *n* (in the army) officer or man in the artillery; (official term) private soldier in an artillery regiment; (in the navy) warrant officer in charge of a battery of guns. **~y** *n* [U] construction and management or firing of large guns.

gunny /ˋgʌnɪ/ *n* [U] strong, coarse material used for making sacks, bales, bags, etc.

gun·wale /ˋgʌnl/ *n* upper edge of the side of a boat or a small ship. ⇨ the illus at row.

gurgle /ˋgɜgl/ *n* [C,U] bubbling sound as of water flowing from a narrow-necked bottle: *~s of delight.* □ *vi* make this sound: *The baby was gurgling happily.*

Gur·kha /ˋgɜkə/ *n* member of a ruling race in Nepal who became famous as soldiers in the British Indian army.

guru /ˋgʊru/ *n* Hindu spiritual teacher.

gush /gʌʃ/ *vi* [VP2A,C,3A] **1** burst, flow, out suddenly: *oil ~ing from a new well; blood ~ing from a wound.* **2** talk with excessive enthusiasm: *young mothers ~ing over their babies; girls who ~ over handsome film stars.* □ *n* sudden outburst or outflow: *a ~ of oil/anger/enthusiasm.* **~er** *n* oil-well with a strong natural flow (so that pumping is not needed). **~·ing** *adj*: *~ing compliments.* ⇨ 2 above. **~·ing·ly** *adv*

gus·set /ˋgʌsɪt/ *n* [C] (usu triangular or diamond-shaped) piece of cloth inserted in a garment to strengthen or enlarge it.

gust /gʌst/ *n* [C] sudden, violent rush of wind; burst of rain, hail, fire or smoke; (fig) outburst of feeling: *The wind was blowing in ~s.* **~y** *adj* (-ier, -iest) stormy; with wind blowing in ~s.

gus·ta·tion /gʌˋsteɪʃn/ *n* tasting.

gusto /ˋgʌstəʊ/ *n* [U] enjoyment in doing sth.

gut /gʌt/ *n* **1** (*pl*) intestines; bowels: *stick a bayonet into a man's guts. I hate his guts,* (sl) hate him intensely. **2** (*pl*) (colloq) contents of anything: *His speech had no guts in it,* no real arguments, force, etc. *The real guts* (= The essence) *of his speech is....* **3** (*pl*) (colloq) courage and determination: *a man with plenty of guts.* **4** [U] strong cord made from the intestines of animals, used for the strings of violins, etc. ⇨ *catgut.* □ *vt* (-tt-) [VP6A] **1** take the guts(1) out of (a fish, etc). **2** destroy the inside of or the contents of: *a building gutted by fire.* **gut·less** *adj* lacking in guts(3).

gutta-per·cha /ˈgʌtə ˋpɜtʃə/ *n* [U] rubber-like substance made from the juice of various Malayan trees.

gut·ter /ˋgʌtə(r)/ *n* [C] **1** channel or trough (usu metal) fixed under the edge of a roof to carry away rainwater; channel at the side of a road for the same purpose. **2** (fig) streets, esp of a poor district: *the language of the ~,* low and vulgar language. ***take a child out of the ~,*** remove it from poor and wretched conditions. ***the gutter press,*** newspapers giving much space to salacious stories, scandals, etc. **ˋ~·snipe** /-snɑɪp/ *n* poor, badly-dressed child who plays in slum streets. □ *vi* [VP2A] (of a candle) burn unsteadily so that the melted wax flows down the sides.

gut·tural /ˋgʌtərl/ *n, adj* (sound) produced in the throat: *~ consonants; the ~ speech of the Germans.*

guv·nor /ˋgʌvnə(r)/ *n* (GB sl) person who controls or gives orders to workmen.

guy[1] /gɑɪ/ *n* [C] rope or chain used to keep sth steady or secured, e g to hold a tent in place.

guy[2] /gɑɪ/ *n* **1** figure in the form of a man, dressed in old clothes (e g as burned on 5 Nov in memory of Guy Fawkes's Gunpowder Plot). **2** person dressed oddly. **3** (sl) man. ⇨ *fall-guy* at fall[2](14). □ *vt* (*pt,pp* guyed) [VP6A] ridicule; exhibit (sb) in effigy.

Guy's /gɑɪz/ *n* (colloq for) Guy's Hospital (in London).

guzzle /ˋgʌzl/ *vi,vt* [VP2A,6A,15] (colloq) eat or drink greedily: *be always guzzling; ~ beer.* **guz·zler** /-zlə(r)/ *n* person who ~s.

gym /dʒɪm/ *n* (sl) (short for) gymnasium, gymnastics: ˋ*gym-shoes; the* ˋ*gym mistress.* **ˋgym-slip** *n* sleeveless tunic worn in GB by some girls as part of school uniform.

gym·khana /dʒɪm`kɑnə/ *n* public display of athletics and sports competitions.
gym·na·sium /dʒɪm`neɪzɪəm/ *n* (*pl* -siums) room or hall with apparatus for physical training.
gym·nas·tic /dʒɪm`næstɪk/ *adj* of bodily training. **gym·nas·tics** *n pl* (forms of) exercises for physical training. **gym·nast** /`dʒɪmnæst/ *n* expert in ~.
gynae·col·ogy (US = **gyne-**) /ˈgɑɪnɪ`kolədʒɪ/ *n* [U] science of the diseases of women and pregnancies. **gynae·colo·gist** (US = **gyne-**) *n* **gynae·co·logi·cal** (US = **gyne-**) /ˈgɑɪnɪkə`lodʒɪkl/ *adj*
gyp[1] /dʒɪp/ *n* (male) college servant at Cambridge and Durham Universities.
gyp[2] /dʒɪp/ *n* ***give sb gyp,*** (sl) scold or punish him without mercy.
gyp·sum /`dʒɪpsəm/ *n* [U] mineral (a chalk-like substance) from which plaster of Paris is made; also used as a fertilizer.
gypsy, gipsy /`dʒɪpsɪ/ *n* = gipsy.
gy·rate /ˈdʒɑɪə`reɪt *US:* `dʒɑɪəreɪt/ *vi* move round in circles or spirals; revolve. **gy·ra·tion** /ˈdʒɑɪ`reɪʃn/ *n* [C,U] revolving; revolution.

a gyroscope

gyro /`dʒɑɪrəʊ/ *n* (colloq abbr of) gyroscope.
gyro·scope /`dʒɑɪərəskəʊp/ *n* heavy wheel which, when spinning fast, keeps steady the object in which it is fixed. **gyro·scopic** /ˈdʒɑɪərə`skopɪk/ *adj*
gyves /gɑɪvz/ *n pl* (arch) shackles: fetters.

Hh

H, h /eɪtʃ/ (*pl* H's, h's /`eɪtʃɪz/), the eighth letter of the English alphabet. ***drop one's h's,*** omit the sound /h/, e g by saying *'ot* for *hot.*
ha /hɑ/ *int* used to express surprise, joy, triumph, suspicion, etc. When repeated in print (*'Ha! Ha! Ha!'*) it indicates laughter.
ha·beas cor·pus /ˈheɪbɪəs `kɔpəs/ *n* (Lat) ***(writ of) ~,*** order requiring a person to be brought before a judge or into court, esp to investigate the right of the law to keep him in prison.
hab·er·dasher /`hæbədæʃə(r)/ *n* shopkeeper who sells clothing, small articles of dress, pins, cotton, etc. **~y** *n* [U] ~'s goods or business.
ha·bili·ments /hə`bɪlɪmənts/ *n pl* (rare) **1** dress suited to a certain event or to be worn by someone holding a special position. **2** (hum) clothing.
habit /`hæbɪt/ *n* **1** [C] sb's settled practice, esp sth that cannot easily be given up: *the ~ of smoking; ~-forming drugs.* ***be in/fall into the ~ of,*** have, acquire, the ~ of. ***fall/get into bad ~s,*** acquire them: *Don't let yourself get into bad ~s.* ***get sb into the ~ of,*** cause him to have the ~ of: *Don't let him get you into the ~ of taking drugs.* ***get out of a ~,*** abandon it. **2** [U] usual behaviour: *H~ is second nature. Are we all creatures of ~,* Do we do things from force of ~? ***do sth/act from force of ~,*** because one is in the ~ of doing it. **3** (old use) condition, general quality (of mind or body): *a cheerful ~ of mind.* **4** [C] dress worn by members of a religious order: *a monk's ~; a `riding ~,* woman's coat and skirt for horse-riding.
hab·it·able /`hæbɪtəbl/ *adj* fit to be lived in: *The old house is no longer ~.*
habi·tat /`hæbɪtæt/ *n* (of plants, animals) usual natural place and conditions of growth; home.
habi·ta·tion /ˈhæbɪ`teɪʃn/ *n* **1** [U] living in: *houses that were not fit for ~.* **2** [C] (dignified or liter) place to live in: *On these plains there was not a single human ~.*
ha·bit·ual /hə`bɪtʃʊəl/ *adj* **1** regular, usual: *He took his ~ seat at the dining-table.* **2** acting by habit; having a regular habit: *a ~ liar/drunkard/cinema-goer.* **~ly** /-tʃʊlɪ/ *adv* as a habit: *Tom is ~ly late for school.*
ha·bitu·ate /hə`bɪtʃʊeɪt/ *vt* [VP14] ***~ sb/oneself to sth,*** accustom; get (sb, oneself) used by (sth): *~ oneself to hard work/getting up early/a cold climate.*
habi·tude /`hæbɪtjud *US:* -tud/ *n* [U] custom; tendency; habitual way of acting or doing things.
ha·bitué /hə`bɪtʃʊeɪ/ *n* person who regularly goes to a place: *an ~ of the orchestral concerts/of the Café Royal.*
haci·enda /ˈhæsɪ`endə/ *n* (*pl* -das) (in Latin American countries) large landed estate with a dwelling house.
hack[1] /hæk/ *vt, vi* [VP6A,15A,B,2A,C,3A] cut roughly or clumsily; chop: *After the savage had killed his enemy, he ~ed the body to pieces. He ~ed at the branch* (i e struck heavy blows at it) *until it fell to the ground.* ***a ~ing cough,*** a short, dry cough. **`~·saw** *n* one with a replaceable blade in a frame, for cutting through metal. ⇨ the illus at tool.
hack[2] /hæk/ *n* **1** horse that may be hired. **2** person paid to do hard and uninteresting work as a writer: *publisher's ~s.* □ *vi* ride on horseback on roads, at an ordinary pace: *go ~ing.*
hackle /`hækl/ *n* (*pl* only) long feathers on the neck of the domestic cock: *with his ~s up,* (of a cock, dog or man) angry; ready to fight. ***have one's/get sb's ~s up,*** be, make sb angry, ready to fight, make him angry.
hack·ney /`hæknɪ/ *n* ordinary kind of horse for riding or driving. **`~ carriage,** one that may be hired. **hack·neyed** *adj* (esp of sayings) too common; repeated too often.
had /hæd/ ⇨ have[1].
had·dock /`hædək/ *n* (*pl* unchanged) seafish much used for food, esp *smoked ~.*
Hades /heɪdiz/ *n* (Gk myth) the underworld; place where the spirits of the dead go.
Hadji /`hædʒɪ/ *n* (title of a) Muslim pilgrim who has been to Mecca.
hæ·ma·tite /`hemətɑɪt/ *n* = hematite.
hæ·mo·glo·bin /ˈhimə`gləʊbɪn/ *n* = hemoglobin.
hæ·mo·philia /ˈhimə`fɪlɪə/ *n* = hemophilia.

hæm·or·rhage /ˈhemərɪdʒ/ *n* = hemorrhage.
hæm·or·rhoids /ˈhemərɔɪds/ *n* = hemorrhoids.
haft /hɑft *US:* hæft/ *n* handle of an axe, knife, dagger, etc.
hag /hæg/ *n* witch; ugly old woman, esp one who does, or is thought to do, evil. **ˈhag-ridden,** afflicted by nightmares; harassed.
hag·gard /ˈhægəd/ *adj* (of a person, his face) looking tired and lined, esp from worry, lack of sleep.
hag·gis /ˈhægɪs/ *n* Scottish dish of various parts of a sheep, cut up, mixed with oatmeal, and cooked in a sheep's stomach.
haggle /ˈhægl/ *vi* [VP2A,3A] ~ ***(with sb) (about/over) sth,*** argue, dispute, esp the price of sth or the terms of a bargain.
hagi·ol·ogy /ˈhægɪˈolədʒɪ/ *n* literature of the lives and legends of saints.
haha /ˈhɑhɑ/ *n* wall or fence bounding a park or garden, sunk in a hollow so as not to interfere with the view.
hail[1] /heɪl/ *n* **1** [U] frozen raindrops falling from the sky. **ˈ~·stone** *n* [C] small ball of ice: *~stones as big as peas.* **ˈ~·storm** *n* storm with fall of ~. **2** (usu with *indef art*) sth coming in great numbers and force: *a ~ of blows/curses.* □ *vi, vt* **1** (impers) (of ~) come down: *It ~ed during the morning.* **2** [VP2C,15B] ~ ***(down) (on sb),*** (of blows, etc) come, send down, hard and fast (on): *Blows ~ed down on his back. They ~ed curses down on us.*
hail[2] /heɪl/ *vt, vi* **1** [VP6A,16B] greet; give a welcoming cry to; call out to (so as to attract attention): *Cheerful voices ~ed us as we entered the hall. They ~ed him (as) king. He was ~ed as a hero. Let's ~ a taxi, shall we?* **2** [VP3A] ***~ from,*** come from: *Where does the ship ~ from,* Which is her home port? (colloq, of persons) *They ~ from all parts of the country.* □ *n* greeting; ~ing cry. ***within ~,*** (esp of ships) near enough to be ~ed. ***be ˈ~-fellow-well-ˈmet (with sb),*** be very familiar and friendly.
hair /heə(r)/ *n* **1** [U] (collective *sing*) ⇨ the illus at head. all the thread-like growths on the skin of animals, esp on the human head; thread-like growth on the stems and leaves of some plants; ~-like thing: *brush one's ~; have one's ˈ~ cut; a cat with a fine coat of ~;* [C] single thread of ~: *find a ~ in the soup; two grey ~s on his coat collar;* (archaic) (*pl*) in collective sense: *It will bring down my grey ~s in sorrow to the grave,* cause me, who am old, to die of sorrow. ***get sb by the short ~s,*** (sl) have him at one's mercy; get complete control of him. ***keep your ˈ~ on,*** (sl) keep cool; don't lose your temper. ***let one's ˈ~ down,*** (of a woman) remove the pins and allow the ~ to fall over the shoulders; (fig) relax after a period of being formal; behave with abandon. ***lose one's ~,*** **(a)** become bald. **(b)** lose one's temper. ***make one's ˈ~ stand on end,*** fill one with fright or horror. ***put up her ~,*** arrange or style it so that it is rolled up on the head. ***split ~s,*** make or pretend to see differences of meaning, distinctions, etc, so small as to be unimportant. Hence, **ˈ~-splitting** *n* ***tear one's ~,*** show great sorrow or vexation. ***not turn a ~,*** give no sign of being troubled. ***to a ~,*** (describe sth) exactly. **2** (compounds) **ˈ~('s)-breadth** *n* very small distance: *escape by a ~'s breadth, have a ~-breadth escape,* a very narrow one. **ˈ~·brush** *n* brush for grooming the ~. **ˈ~·cloth** *n* cloth made of a mixture of fabric and animal's ~ for facings and other uses. **ˈ~·cut** *n* act or style of cutting the ~ (by a barber or ~dresser): *~cut and shave, 80p.* **ˈ~-do** *n* (colloq) dressing of a woman's ~ by a ~dresser. **ˈ~·dresser** *n* person who dresses and cuts ~, esp for women. ⇨ barber. **ˈ~-dye** *n* dye for the ~. **ˈ~·line** *n* area where the roots of ~ join the forehead; width of a ~, very narrow: (attrib) *a ~line space/fracture.* **ˈ~·net** *n* net for keeping the ~ in place. **ˈ~-oil** *n* oil for dressing the ~. **ˈ~·piece** *n* tress of false ~. **ˈ~·pin** *n* (woman's) pin for keeping the ~ in place. **ˈ~pin ˈbend** *n* sharp bend on a road, esp on a steep road, so that the road doubles back. **ˈ~-raising** *adj* terrifying. **ˈ~-ˈshirt** *n* shirt made of ~cloth, uncomfortable to wear, for ascetics. **ˈ~-slide** *n* metal clip for keeping ~ tidily in place. **ˈ~·spring** *n* very delicate spring in a watch, controlling the balance-wheel. **ˈ~-trigger,** one that fires a gun, etc at the slightest pressure. **~-less** *adj* without ~; bald. **ˈ~-like** *adj* **~y** *adj* (-ier, -iest) of or like ~; covered with ~: *a ~y chest.* **~i·ness** *n*

hairpin bends

hake /heɪk/ *n* (*pl* unchanged) fish of the cod family, used as food.
hal·berd /ˈhælbəd/ *n* weapon used in the Middle Ages, a combined spear and battle-axe on a long handle. **hal·ber·dier** /ˈhælbəˈdɪə(r)/ *n* soldier armed with a ~.
hal·cyon /ˈhælsɪən/ *adj*: *~ days, ~ weather,* calm and peaceful.
hale[1] /heɪl/ *adj* (usu of old persons) (rare except in) ***~ and hearty,*** strong and healthy.
hale[2] /heɪl/ *vt* [VP15A,B] (archaic) take, drag, pull, by force: *~d off to prison.*
half /hɑf *US:* hæf/ *n* (*pl* **halves** /hɑvz *US:* hævz/) *adj, adv* **1** one of two equal or corresponding parts into which a thing is divided: *The ~ of 6 is 3/H~ of 6 is 3. Two halves make a whole. Two pounds and a ~/Two and a ~ pounds. H~ of the fruit is bad. H~ (of) the plums are bad. I want ~ as much again,* one and a ~ the amount. *Cut it in ~/into halves.* ***(do sth) by halves,*** incompletely, imperfectly. ***go halves (with sb) (in sth),*** share equally. ***too clever, etc by ~,*** far too clever, etc. ***one's better ~,*** (colloq) one's wife. **2** (as *adv*) to the extent of a ~; to a considerable degree: *meat that is only ~ cooked; ~-cooked cabbage; not ~* (= not nearly) *long enough; ~ dead,* (colloq) tired out, exhausted; *not ~ bad,* (colloq) not at all bad; quite good. ***not ~,*** (sl) to the greatest possible extent: *He didn't ~ swear,* He swore very violently. *'Was she annoyed?' 'Not ~!'* (i e she was intensely annoyed). **3** (in compounds) **ˈ~ a ˈcrown, ˈ~-ˈcrown** *n* (before 1971) the amount of *2s 6d.* **ˈ~ a ˈdozen** *n* six. **ˈ~ and ˈ~** *n* what is ~ one thing and ~ the other, e g a mixture of ale and porter. **ˈ~-back** *n* in football, hockey, etc: (position of) player (defender) between the for-

wards and the backs. ⇨ the illus at football. '~-'**baked** *adj* (colloq) dull-witted; crude and inexperienced: *a ~-baked young man;* foolish; of poor quality: *~-baked ideas.* '~-**barrier** *n* one extending ~way across, e g at a level crossing. '~-**blood** *n* (relationship of a) person having one parent in common with another. '~-**breed** *n* **(a)** person with parents of different races, esp differently coloured races. **(b)** offspring of two animals or plants of different species. '~-**brother** *n* brother by one parent only. '~-**caste** *n* ~-breed person. '~ '**cock** *n* position of the hammer of a gun when pulled ~way back. ***go off at ~ cock,*** (fig) act too soon and fail. '~-**hardy** *adj* (of plants) requiring protection from frost but otherwise suitable for growing in the open. '~-**hearted** *adj* done with, showing, little interest or enthusiasm: *a ~-hearted attempt.* Hence, '~-'**heartedly** *adv* '~-'**holiday** *n* day of which ~ (usu the afternoon) is free from work or duty. '~-'**hourly** *adj, adv* done, occurring every ~ hour: *a ~-hourly bus service.* '~-'**length** *adj* (of a portrait) of the upper ~ of a person. **at '~-'mast,** (of a flag) at the position, near the middle of a mast, to indicate mourning: *Flags were at ~-mast everywhere on the day of the President's funeral.* '~-'**pay** *n* reduced pay given to army or navy officers when not fully employed but not yet retired: *placed on ~-pay.* ~**penny** /'heɪpnɪ *US:* 'hæfpenɪ/ *n* British coin worth ~ a penny (½d before 1971, ½p now; either *one ~ p,* or *~ a new penny,* or *half a new pence*); *twopence ~penny* (2½d or 2½p, now usu *two and a half new pence*); *three ~pence* /θri 'heɪpəns *US:* 'hæfpens/, 1½d or 1½p, now usu *one and a half new pence.* ~·**penny·worth** /'heɪpnɪwɜθ *US:* hæf'penɪwɜθ/, **ha'p'orth** /'heɪpəθ/ *n* as much as ½d would buy before 1971; now chiefly fig. ⇨ App 5. '~-'**price** *adv* at ~ the usual price: *Children admitted ~-price.* '~-**seas**-'**over** *pred adj* (colloq) ~ drunk. '~-**sister** *n* sister by one parent only. '~-'**size** *adj* ~ the usual or regular size. '~-'**sovereign** *n* former British gold coin worth ~ a sovereign. '~-'**timbered** *adj* (of a building) having walls of a wooden framework filled in with brick, stone or plaster. '~-'**time** *n* **(a)** work and pay for ~ the usual time: *Owing to the business depression the workers are on ~-time this month.* **(b)** the interval between the two halves of a game of football, etc: *The score at ~-time was 2—2.* '~-**tone** *n* black and white photograph reproduced on paper, e g as an illustration in a book. '~-**track** *n* troop-carrying vehicle with tracks(5) on both sides at the rear and wheels at the front. Hence, '~-'**tracked** *adj* '~-**truth** *n* statement that conveys only a part of the truth. '~-'**way** *adj* **(a)** (of a house, an inn) situated at an equal distance from two towns, etc. **(b)** going ~ the way; not thorough: *In an emergency ~-way measures are usually unsatisfactory.* □ *adv* to or at ~ the distance: *meet a person ~-way,* be ready to make a compromise. '~-'**witted** *adj* weak-minded. Hence, '~-**wit** *n* '~-'**yearly** *adj, adv* (done, occurring) every ~ year.

hali·but /'hælɪbət/ *n* (*pl* unchanged) large, flat seafish used as food.

hali·tosis /'hælɪ'təʊsɪs/ *n* [U] bad-smelling breath.

hall /hɔl/ *n* **1** (building with) large room for meetings, concerts, public business, etc: *the Town/City H~; the County H~; the H~ of Justice; the Festival H~,* for concerts, in London; '*dance-~s; the ~s,* often used for '*music-~s.* **2** (in colleges at English universities) large room for meals: *dine in ~.* **3** building for university students: *a ~ of residence.* **4** (in England) large country house, usu one that belongs to the chief landowner in the district. **5** passage, space, into which the main entrance or front door of a building opens: *Leave your hat and coat in the ~.* '~-**stand** *n* piece of furniture for hats, coats, umbrellas, etc. **6** building of a guild: *Saddlers' H~.* '~-**mark** *n* mark used at Goldsmiths' H~ for marking the standard of gold and silver in articles (as a guarantee of quality). □ *vt* stamp a ~mark on.

hal·le·lu·jah /'hælɪ'lujə/ *n, int* praise to God.

hal·liard /'hæljəd/ *n* = halyard.

hallo /hə'ləʊ/ *int, n* cry to attract attention; greeting.

hal·loo /hə'lu/ *int, n* cry to urge on hounds; shout to attract attention. □ *vi* shout 'Halloo!', esp to hounds.

hal·low[1] /'hæləʊ/ *vt* [VP6A] (usu passive) make holy; regard as holy: *ground ~ed by sacred memories.*

hal·low[2] /'hæləʊ/ *n* (only in) ***All H~s,*** saints. ⇨ all[1](6).

Hal·low·e'en /'hæləʊ'in/ *n* 31 Oct, eve of All Saints' Day or All Hallows Day.

hal·luci·na·tion /hə'lusɪ'neɪʃn/ *n* [C,U] (instance of) seeming to see sth not present, sth imagined: *Drunken men are sometimes subject to ~s.* **hal·luci·na·tory** /hə'lusɪnətɔrɪ/, **hal·luci·no·genic** /hə'lusɪnəʊ'dʒenɪk/ *adjj* (of drugs) inducing ~.

halma /'hælmə/ *n* game played on a board of 256 squares where pieces are moved from one corner to the other.

halo /'heɪləʊ/ *n* (*pl* -loes, -los /-ləʊz/) circle of light round the sun or moon or (in paintings) round or above the heads of Christ or sacred figures.

halt[1] /hɔlt/ *n* **1** (chiefly mil, of soldiers) ***call a ~ (to),*** short stop on a march or journey: *The officer called a ~.* (fig) *It's time to call a ~ to vandalism,* end it. **2** (more general use) stop or pause: *The train came to a ~.* **3** (formerly) stopping-place (smaller than a station) on a railway-line, where trains stop for a short time only. □ *vi, vt* **1** [VP2A] (as a mil command) stop marching; come to a ~. **2** [VP6A] bring to a ~: *The officer ~ed his troops.*

halt[2] /hɔlt/ *vi* [VP2A,C] hesitate; walk in a hesitating way: *~ between two opinions; in a ~ing voice.* □ *adj* (archaic) lame: *the ~ and the blind.* ~·**ing·ly** *adv* in a ~ing way.

hal·ter /'hɔltə(r)/ *n* **1** rope or leather strap put round a horse's head (for leading or fastening the horse). **2** rope used for hanging a person.

halve /hɑv *US:* hæv/ *vt* [VP6A] **1** divide into two equal parts: *~ an apple.* **2** lessen by one half: *The newest airliners have ~d· the time needed for crossing the Atlantic.*

halves /hɑvz *US:* hævz/ *pl* of half.

hal·yard /'hæljəd/ *n* rope for raising or lowering a sail or flag.

ham /hæm/ *n* **1** [C] upper part of a pig's leg, salted and dried or smoked: *hams hanging on hooks;* [U] this as meat: *a slice of ham; a ham sandwich.* **2** [C] (chiefly used of animals) back of the thigh, thigh and buttock. **3** (sl) poor actor or performer; amateur who sends and receives radio messages; *a radio ham;* (attrib) *ham actors/acting.* '**ham**-'**handed/**-'**fisted** *adj* clumsy in using the hands. □

vt, vi (-mm-) (colloq) overact. ***ham (up),*** act in a (deliberately) artificial exaggerated way: *Oh, stop hamming it up!*

hama·dryad /ˈhæməˋdrɑɪəd/ *n* nymph living and dying with the tree she inhabited; poisonous Indian snake.

ham·burger /ˈhæmbɜgə(r)/ *n* **1** ground or chopped beef made into round flat cakes and fried. **2** sandwich or bread roll filled with this.

ham·let /ˈhæmlət/ *n* group of houses in the country; small village, esp one without a church.

ham·mer /ˈhæmə(r)/ *n* **1** tool with a heavy metal head used for breaking things, driving in nails, etc. ⇨ the illus at tool. ***be/go at it ~ and tongs,*** fight, argue, with great energy and noise. ***throwing the ~,*** athletic competition in which a heavy long-handled ~ is thrown as far as possible. **2** (in a piano, etc) one of the ~-like parts that strike the strings. **3** part of the firing device of a gun that strikes and explodes the charge. **4** wooden mallet used by an auctioneer. ***be/come under the ~,*** be sold by auction. **5** (anat) bone in the ear. ⇨ the illus at ear. □ *vt, vi* [VP6A,22,15B,2A,C,3A] **1** strike or beat with a ~, or as if with a ~: *~ nails into wood; ~ down the lid of a box,* fasten it down by ~ing; *~ in a nail/~ a nail in; ~ a piece of metal flat; ~ sth out,* make it flat or smooth by ~ing; *~ at the door,* e g with a stick, one's fists; *~ at the keys,* play the piano loudly, without feeling. **2** (fig) produce by hard work: *~ out a scheme;* work hard: *~ away at a problem/a solution/a compromise;* force: *~ an idea into sb's head.* **3** (colloq) inflict heavy defeats on (sb) in war or in games.

ham·mock /ˈhæmək/ *n* hanging bed of canvas or rope network, e g as used by sailors, or in gardens.

ham·per[1] /ˈhæmpə(r)/ *n* packing-case or basket with a lid, esp one used for sending food: *a Christmas ~,* one sent as a present, with food, wine, etc.

ham·per[2] /ˈhæmpə(r)/ *vt* [VP6A] hinder; prevent free movement or activity: *~ed by a heavy overcoat.*

ham·ster /ˈhæmstə(r)/ *n* rodent like a large rat, kept by children as a pet.

ham·string /ˈhæm-strɪŋ/ *vt* (-ed or -strung /ˈhæm-strʌŋ/) [VP6A] cripple (a person or animal) by cutting the tendon(s) at the back of the knee(s); (fig) destroy the power or efficiency of.

hand[1] /hænd/ *n* **1** part of the human arm beyond the wrist: *with his ~s in his pockets.* ⇨ the illus at arm. ***at ~,*** near; within reach: *He lives close at ~,* quite near. *The examinations are at ~.* ***at sb's ~,*** from sb: *I did not expect such unkind treatment at your ~s.* ***by ~,*** **(a)** without the use of machinery: *Are your socks knitted by ~/~-knitted or machine-made?* **(b)** without the use of the post office: *The note was delivered by ~,* by a messenger. ***bring up a baby/a calf, etc by ~,*** rear it by feeding from a bottle: *The lamb had to be brought up by ~.* ***from ~ to ~,*** directly, from one person to another: *Buckets of water were passed from ~ to ~ to put the fire out.* ***fight ~ to ~,*** at close quarters. Hence, *~-to-~ fighting.* ***live from ~ to mouth,*** precariously, spending money as soon as it is received. Hence, *a ~-to-mouth existence.* ***be ~ in glove (with sb),*** ⇨ glove. ***give/lend a ~ (with sth),*** help with, take a part in, doing sth: *Give (me) a ~ with the washing-up, please.* ***bind sb ~ and foot,*** (liter, fig) make him completely helpless. ***serve/wait on sb ~ and foot,*** attend to his every wish; perform every sort of service for him. ***eat/feed out of one's ~,*** **(a)** e g of a bird, be quite tame. **(b)** (fig) be ready to obey without question. ***give one's ~ on a bargain,*** take sb's ~ and clasp it to seal the bargain. ***have one's ˋ~s full,*** have all the work one can do; be fully occupied: *I have my ~s full just now/My ~s are full.* ***have/get the upper ~ (of sb),*** ⇨ upper. ***have a free ~, give/allow sb a free ~,*** ⇨ free[1](3). ***~ in ~,*** holding ~s; together: *They walked away ~ in ~.* (fig) *War and misery go ~ in ~.* ***H~s off!*** Don't touch or interfere! ***H~s up!*** Put your ~s up! Surrender! ***~ over ~,*** with each ~ used alternately (as when climbing, etc); (fig) rapidly and steadily. ***in ~,*** **(a)** in reserve, available for use: *I still have some money in ~. Cash in ~, £27.25.* **(b)** receiving attention; in course of completion: *The work is in ~ and will be finished by the end of the month. We have the situation well in ~,* are dealing with it satisfactorily. ***take sth/sb in ~,*** take control of; undertake to control: *These noisy children need to be taken in ~,* to be disciplined. ***in the ~s of,*** being looked after or managed by. ***in good ~s,*** being well cared for. ***lay (one's) ~s on sth/sb,*** ⇨ lay[1](2). ***lend a ~,*** ⇨ give a ~ above. ***not lift a ~, not do a ~'s turn,*** make not the least attempt to help. ***lift/raise a ~/one's ~ against sb,*** threaten, attack him. ***off-~,*** ⇨ *off-~.* ***off one's ~s,*** free from responsibility: *I'd be glad to get it off my ~s,* to rid myself of responsibility for it. ***on ~,*** available: *We have some new woollen goods on ~,* in our shop, warehouse, etc. ***on one's ~s,*** resting on one as a responsibility: *I have an empty house on my ~s,* one for which I want to find a buyer or tenant. *Time hangs heavy on his ~s,* seems burdensome, passes slowly. ***out of ~,*** **(a)** out of control; undisciplined: *The boys have got quite out of ~.* **(b)** at once, without hesitation: *The situation needs to be dealt with out of ~.* ***shake ~s with sb, shake sb's ~,*** grasp his ~ as a greeting, or to express agreement, etc. ***take a ~ (in),*** help; play a part (in sth). ***take sth/sb in ~,*** take charge of; undertake to control or manage. ***to ~,*** (comm style for) ***come to ~,*** be received: *Your letter is to ~,* has reached me and is receiving attention. ***wash one's ~s of,*** say that one will no longer be responsible for. ***win ~s down,*** win easily. ***(rule) with a heavy ~,*** oppressively; severely. ***win a lady's ~,*** win her consent to marriage. **2** (*pl*) power; possession; responsibility: *The property is no longer in my ~s,* It is no longer mine, or my responsibility. *The matter is in your ~s,* You must decide how to deal with it. *He's still in the ~s of the moneylenders.* ***change ~s,*** pass to another owner: *The property has changed ~s recently,* has been sold. **3** (*sing* only) influence or agency: *The ~ of an enemy has been at work here.* **4** (*sing* only) person from whom news, etc comes: (only in) ***at first ~,*** directly, without an intermediary: *I heard/learnt the news at first ~.* ***at second ~,*** indirectly. **5** (*sing* only) skill in using one's ~s: *She has a light ~ at pastry,* makes it with skill. *Why don't you try your ~ at editing the staff magazine,* see whether you have the skill needed? ***get one's ~ in,*** acquire or return to one's usual degree of skill by practice. ***keep one's ~ in,*** practise a skill, in order to retain it: *practise the piano every day to* *keep one's ~ in.* **6** [C] person who does what is indicated by the context; performer: *a good ~ at fencing,* a good fencer. *He's an old ~ at this sort of work,* has long experience of it. *He's an old parliamentary ~,* a person with long experience of parliamentary duties. **7** workman, e g in a factory or dockyard; member of a ship's crew: *The factory has taken on 200 extra ~s. All ~s on deck!* All seamen are needed on deck! **8** turn; share in an activity. ***have a ~ (in sth),*** have a share: *Let me have a ~ now. Do you think he had a ~ in it,* was involved? ***give/lend sb a ~,*** help: *Will you give me a ~ with this heavy box?* **9** [C] pointer or indicator on the dial of a watch, clock or other instrument: *the ˋhour/ˏminute/ˏsecond ~ of a watch.* **10** position or direction (to right or left). ***on every/either ~; on all ~s,*** to or from all quarters. ***on the one ~ (and) on the other ~,*** used to indicate contrasted points of view, arguments, etc. **11** (*sing* only) handwriting: *He writes a good/legible ~.* **12** (formal style) signature: *set one's ~ to a document. Given under my ~ and seal,* authenticated by my signature and seal. **13** (card games, e g bridge) **(a)** (number of) cards dealt to, held by, a player at one time. ***have a good/bad/poor ~,*** good/bad, etc cards. ***play a good/bad ~,*** play well/badly. ***take a ~ at whist/bridge,*** join in and play. ***play (for) one's own ~,*** (liter, fig) act for, look after, one's own interests. ***play into sb else's ~s/into the ~s of sb,*** do sth that is to his advantage. **(b)** player at cards: *We have only three players—we need a fourth ~.* **(c)** one round in a game of cards: *Let's play one more ~, shall we?* **14** [C] unit of measurement, about four inches (10·16 cm), the breadth of the ~, used for the height of a horse (from the ground to the top of the shoulder). **15** (colloq) applause by clapping. ***get/give sb a good ~,*** a lot of applause. **16** (compounds) ˋ**~-bag** *n* woman's bag for money, keys, handkerchief, etc. ˋ**~-barrow** *n* light two-wheeled barrow. ˋ**~-bill** *n* printed advertisement or announcement distributed by ~. ˋ**~-book** *n* small book giving useful facts; guide-book. ˋ**~-brake** *n* auxiliary brake in a motor vehicle, used when the vehicle is stationary. ˋ**~-cart** *n* small cart pushed or pulled by ~. ˋ**~-clap** *n* clapping: *a slow ~clap,* slow rhythmical clapping to show impatience. ˋ**~-cuff** *n* one of a pair of metal rings joined by a chain, fastened round a prisoner's wrists. □ *vt* put ~cuffs on. **~-ful** /-fʊl/ *n* (*pl* **~fuls**) **(a)** as much or as many as can be held in one ~. **(b)** small number: *Only a ~ful of persons came to the meeting.* **(c)** (colloq) person or animal difficult to control: *That young boy of hers is quite a ~ful,* is lively and unruly. ˋ**~-gun** *n* one (e g a pistol or revolver) that can be carried in and fired from the ~ (contrasted with e g a rifle). ˋ**~-hold** *n* (esp) anything a climber may grip, e g on a rock face. ˋ**~-loom** *n* loom worked by ~, not by machinery. ˋ**~-luggage** *n* light enough to be carried by hand. ˈ**~-ˋmade** *adj* made by ~ (contrasted with *machine-made*). ˋ**~-maid** *n* (archaic) woman servant or attendant. ˋ**~-me-down** *n* sth passed on (esp sth used and discarded, e g clothes) to another. ˋ**~-organ** *n* portable barrel-organ with a crank turned by ~. ˈ**~-ˋpicked** *adj* carefully selected. ˋ**~-rail** *n* railing along the edge of a staircase, etc. ˋ**~-shake** *n* greeting given by grasping a person's ~ with one's own. ˋ**~-stand** *n* acrobatic feat of supporting oneself in an upright position on the ~s: *do a ~stand.* ˋ**~-work** *n* [U] work done by ~, not by machinery. ˋ**~writing** *n* (person's style of) writing by ~: *Whose ~writing is this?*

hand² /hænd/ *vt* [VP12A,13A,15A,B] give or pass (to sb); help with the ~(s): *Please ~ me that book. He ~ed the book to the man at his side. He ~ed* (= helped) *his wife out of the railway carriage.* ***~ sth down (to sb),*** pass by tradition, inheritance, etc: *We cannot always observe the traditions ~ed down to us from the past.* ***~ sth on (to sb),*** send, give, to another: *Please ~ on the magazine to your friends.* ***~ sth out,*** distribute; (colloq) give as alms. Hence, ˋ**~-out** *n* **(a)** prepared statement given, e g by a politician, to newspaper men; leaflet, etc, distributed free of charge. **(b)** sth given as an alms, e g food or money to a beggar at the door. ***~ sb over,*** deliver a person to authority: *~ sb over to the police.* ***~ sth over (to sb),*** transfer: *You can't play with my gun, Tom! H~ it over at once. I've ~ed over my place on the committee.* ***~ it to sb,*** (colloq) give him the credit that is his due: *He's done well! You've got to ~ it to him.*

handi·cap /ˋhændɪkæp/ *n* [C] **1** (competition, race, in which there is a) disadvantage imposed on a competitor to make the chances of success more nearly equal for all, e g a weight to be carried by a horse: *win on ~,* as the result of ~s on competitors. **2** anything likely to lessen one's chance of success: *Poor eyesight is a ~ to a student.* □ *vt* (-pp-) [VP6A] give or be a ~ to: *~ped by ill health; ~ped children,* suffering from some disability.

handi·craft /ˋhændɪkrɑft *US:* -kræft/ *n* [C] art or craft needing skill with the hands, e g needlework, pottery, woodwork, weaving at a handloom.

handi·work /ˋhændɪwɜk/ *n* [U] work done, [C] thing made, by the hands; sth done by a named person: *That's some of Smith's ~.*

hand·ker·chief /ˋhæŋkətʃɪf/ *n* square piece of cotton, silk, linen, etc carried in the pocket or handbag, for blowing the nose into or wiping the face; similar square worn for ornament, e g round the neck.

handle /ˋhændl/ *n* **1** part of a tool, cup, bucket, door, drawer, etc by which it may be held in the hand. ˋ**~-bar** *n* (often *pl*) bar with a ~ at each end, for steering a bicycle, etc. ⇨ the illus at **bicycle**. ***fly off the ~,*** (colloq) get into a rage and lose self-control. **2** (fig) ***give a ~ against,*** provide an excuse or pretext that may be taken advantage of and used: *Your indiscreet behaviour may give your enemies a ~ against you.* **3** (sl) title: *have a ~ to one's name,* have, e g 'Sir' or 'Lord' as part of it. □ *vt* [VP6A] **1** touch with, take up in, the hands: *Gelignite is dangerous stuff to ~. Wash your hands before you ~ my books, please.* **2** manage; deal with; control (men): *An officer must know how to ~ men. Can you ~ the situation,* deal with it? **3** treat; behave towards: *The speaker was roughly ~d by the crowd.* **4** (comm) buy and sell: *This shop does not ~ imported goods.* **han·dler** /ˋhændlə(r)/ *n* person who trains and controls an animal, e g a police dog.

hand·some /ˋhænsəm/ *adj* **1** of fine appearance; (of men) good-looking; having virile beauty; (of women) having a fine figure, vigour and dignity: *What a ~ horse you have! What a ~ old building it is! He's a ~ fellow. Would you describe that* *woman as ~ or beautiful?* **2** (of gifts, behaviour) generous: *He said some very ~ things about you. £50 is quite a ~ birthday present.* ***H~ is that ~ does,*** (prov) A fine person is one who acts generously. **~·ly** *adv* in a ~(2) manner: *He came down ~ly,* made a generous gift.

handy /ˈhændɪ/ *adj* (-ier, -iest) **1** (of persons) clever with the hands. **~·man** /-mæn/ *n* (*pl* -men) person clever at doing odd jobs of various kinds. **2** (of things, places) convenient to handle; easily used: *A good toolbox is a ~ thing to have in the house. She's quite a ~ little sailing-boat,* is easily controlled. ***come in ~,*** be useful some time or other: *Don't throw that plastic bag away; it may come in ~.* **3** not far away; available for use: *Always keep a first-aid kit ~.* **hand·ily** /-əlɪ/ *adv* **handi·ness** *n*

hang[1] /hæŋ/ *n* (*sing* only) **1** way in which a thing hangs: *the ~ of a coat/skirt.* **2** ***get the ~ of sth,*** (a) see how sth, e g a machine, works or is managed: *I've been trying to get the ~ of this new electric typewriter.* (b) see the meaning or significance of sth said or written: *I don't quite get the ~ of your argument.* **3** ***not give/care a ~,*** (colloq) (euphem for *damn*) not care at all.

hang[2] /hæŋ/ *vt,vi* (*pt,pp* hung /hʌŋ/ or, for 2 below, ~ed) (For uses with *adverbial particles* and *preps,* ⇨ 7 below.) **1** [VP6A,15A,B,2A,C] support, be supported, from above so that the lower end is free: *~ a lamp from the ceiling; curtains ~ing over the window; windows hung with curtains; pictures ~ing on the wall. She hung the washing out in the garden. H~ your coat on that hook. A dog's tongue ~s out when it runs fast.* **2** (*pt,pp* ~ed) put, be put, to death by ~ing with a rope around the neck: *He was ~ed for murder. He said he would ~ himself,* commit suicide by ~ing. **3** (mild equivalent of *damn*—dated uses) *Oh, ~ it! I'll be ~ed if I know,* I don't know at all. *I'll be ~ed if I'll go,* I refuse absolutely to go **4** (various uses) *~ wallpaper,* attach it to a wall with paste: *~ bells,* fit them (e g in a belfry); *~ a door,* fasten it on hinges so that it swings freely to and fro. ***~ by a hair/a single thread,*** (of a persons's fate etc) be in a delicate state, depend upon sth small. ***~ the head,*** let it fall forward (e g when ashamed). ***~ fire,*** (a) (of a gun) be slow in going off. (b) (of events) be slow in developing. ***let things go ~,*** (colloq) be indifferent to them; take no interest in or care of them. ***~ in the balance,*** have an outcome that is doubtful. **5** [VP6A,2B] leave, e g meat, birds, ~ing until in the right condition for eating: *Hares and pheasants need to be well hung. How long has this meat hung for?* **6** (compounds) **~·man** /-mən/ *n* (*pl* -men) executioner who ~s criminals. **ˈ~·dog** *pred adj* (of sb's look) sly and ashamed. **ˈ~·over** *n* (a) unpleasant after-effects of excessive drinking. (b) (fig) survival of out-of-date news, rules, etc. **ˈ~-up** *n* (feeling of) frustration, etc ⇨ 7 below. **7** [VP2C,15A, B,3A] (with *adverbial particles* and *preps*):

hang about/(a)round, be standing or loitering about, doing nothing definite: *men ~ing about at street corners, waiting for the pubs to open.*

hang back, hesitate; show unwillingness to act or advance: *When volunteers were asked for, not one man hung back.*

hang on, (a) hold tight: *He hung on until the rope broke.* (b) persevere: *It's hard work, but if you ~ on long enough you'll succeed.* ***H~ on (a minute)!*** (colloq) Wait (a minute)! ***~ on to sth,*** hold it tightly.

hang out, (sl) live; lodge: *Where are you ~ing out now?* ***~ sth out,*** (a) hang (wet clothes, etc) out to dry: *She's in the yard, ~ing out the washing.* (b) display: *~ out flags for the Queen's visit.*

hang together, (a) (of persons) support one another; act in unison: *If we all ~ together, our plan will succeed: If we don't ~ together, we may all ~/be ~ed(2) separately.* (b) fit well together: *Their accounts of what happened don't ~ together,* are inconsistent, contradictory.

hang up, replace the receiver at the end of a telephone conversation: *She hung up on me,* (colloq) hung up the receiver before I had said all I wanted to say. ***be hung up,*** be delayed or frustrated; be mentally inhibited: *Everything seems to have gone wrong—I feel really hung up about things.*

hang upon sb's words/lips, listen eagerly.

hangar /ˈhæŋə(r)/ *n* building in which aircraft are housed.

hanger /ˈhæŋə(r)/ *n* device, loop, etc to, on or by which sth is hung (in compounds) **ˈdress-/ˈclothes-~,** device on which dresses, etc are hung. **~-on** /ˈhæŋər ˈon/ (*pl* ~s-on) *n* person who forces his company upon another or others in the hope of profit or advantage. **ˈpaper-~,** person who hangs (= pastes) wallpaper on to walls. **2** kind of short sword.

hang·ing /ˈhæŋɪŋ/ *n* **1** death by hanging: *There were three ~s here last month.* **2** (attrib) resulting in capital punishment: *a ˈ~ matter,* a crime punishable by ~. **3** (usu *pl*) curtains, drapery, etc with which walls are hung.

hang·nail /ˈhæŋneɪl/ *n* loose skin near the root of a finger-nail.

hank /hæŋk/ *n* (twisted) coil of wool, silk, etc thread: *wind a ~ of wool into balls.*

han·ker /ˈhæŋkə(r)/ *vi* [VP3A] ***~ after/for sth,*** have a strong desire: *~ for sympathy; ~ after wealth.* **~·ing** *n*: *have a ~ing for/after fame.*

hanky /ˈhæŋkɪ/ *n* (*pl* -kies) (child's word for) handkerchief.

hanky-panky /ˈhæŋkɪ ˈpæŋkɪ/ *n* [U] (colloq) underhand dealing; trickery.

Han·sard /ˈhænsɑd/ *n* official report of proceedings in Parliament.

han·som /ˈhænsəm/ *n* (also **ˈ-ˈcab**) (used in England 1835—1915) two-wheeled horse-drawn cab for two passengers, with the driver's seat high at the back and reins going over the roof.

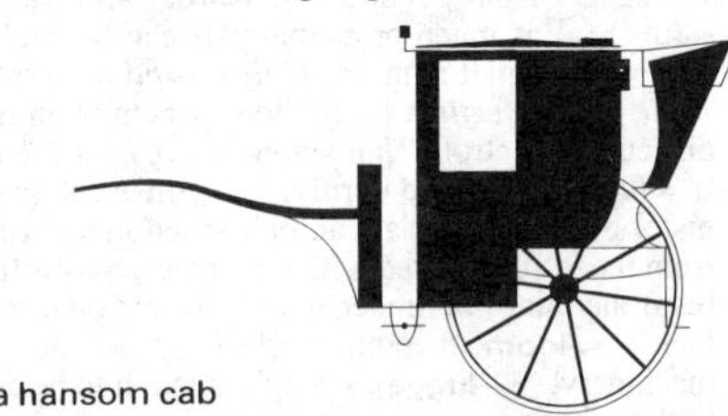

a hansom cab

hap /hæp/ *n* (archaic) chance; luck. □ *vi* (-pp-) come about by chance; happen.

hap·haz·ard /hæpˈhæzəd/ *adj, adv, n* accidental; (by) mere chance; (by) accident.

hap·less /ˈhæpləs/ *adj* (archaic) unlucky.

hap·ly /ˈhæplɪ/ *adv* (archaic) by chance; perhaps.

ha'p'orth /ˈheɪpəθ/ *n* (colloq) halfpennyworth.

hap·pen /ˈhæpn/ *vi* **1** [VP2A,3A] ***~ to,*** take

place; come about: *How did the accident ~? What ~ed next? Accidents will ~*, They are to be expected. *If anything ~s to him* (= If he meets with an accident), *let me know.* **2** [VP2A,4E] chance; have the fortune: *I ~ed to be out when he called. It so ~ed that I had no money with me.* ***as it ~s,*** by chance: *As it ~s, I have my cheque-book with me.* **3** [VP3A] ~ ***(up)on,*** find by chance: *I ~ed on just the thing I'd been looking for.* **~·ing** *n* **1** (often *pl*) event: *There have been strange ~ings here lately.* **2** (sl) usu improvised or spontaneous entertainment involving the audience in frenzied outbursts of excitement.

happy /ˈhæpɪ/ *adj* (**-ier, -iest**) **1** fortunate; lucky; feeling or expressing pleasure, contentment, satisfaction, etc: *Their marriage has been a ~ one. He is ~ in having congenial work. He's as ~ as the day is long,* very ~. **2** (in polite formulas) pleased: *We shall be ~ to accept your kind invitation.* **3** (of language, conduct, suggestions) well suited to the situation: *a ~ thought/idea, etc.* **~-go-lucky** /ˈhæpɪ gəʊ ˋlʌkɪ/ *adj* taking what fortune brings; carefree: *She goes through life in a ~-go-lucky fashion.* **hap·pily** /-pl̩ɪ/ *adv* **hap·pi·ness** *n*

hara-kiri /ˈhærə ˋkɪrɪ/ *n* suicide by disembowelment as practised in the past by Japanese men when they believed they had failed in their duty.

har·angue /həˋræŋ/ *n* long, loud (often scolding) talk or speech. □ *vt,vi* [VP6A,2A] make a ~ (to).

har·ass /ˈhærəs *US:* həˋræs/ *vt* [VP6A] **1** trouble; worry: *~ed by the cares of a large family; ~ed-looking housewives.* **2** make repeated attacks on: *In olden days the coasts of England were ~ed by the Vikings.* **~·ment** *n* [U] ~ing or being ~ed.

har·bin·ger /ˈhɑbɪndʒə(r)/ *n* sb or sth that foretells the coming of sb or sth: *The crowing of the cock is a ~ of dawn.*

har·bour (US = **-bor**) /ˈhɑbə(r)/ *n* **1** place of shelter for ships: *a natural ~*, e g an inlet of the sea: *an artificial ~*, one made with seawalls, breakwaters. ˋ**~ dues** *n pl* money (to be) paid for anchoring or mooring a ship in a ~. **2** (fig) any place of safety or shelter. □ *vt,vi* **1** [VP6A] give lodging or shelter to; protect; conceal: *~ an escaped criminal/a spy. My dog has long, thick hair that ~s fleas.* **2** [VP6A] hold in the mind: *~ thoughts of revenge.* **3** [VP2A] come to anchor (in a ~). **~·age** /ˈhɑbr̩ɪdʒ/ *n* (place of) shelter.

hard[1] /hɑd/ *adj* (**-er, -est**) **1** (contrasted with *soft*) firm; not yielding to the touch; not easily cut; solid: *as ~ as rock; ground made ~ by frost. Teak is a ~ kind of wood.* ***a ~ nut to crack,*** (fig) a difficult problem; person difficult to deal with or influence. **2** (contrasted with *easy*) difficult (to understand or explain); needing mental or moral effort: *~ words,* difficult for young learners or uneducated persons (in spelling or meaning); ⇨ 4 below; *a ~ problem/book/language; a subject that is ~ to understand. She found it ~ to make up her mind. That man is ~ to please/He is a ~ man to please. It's ~ to say which is better. It's ~ for an old man to change his way of living.* **3** causing unhappiness, discomfort, or pain; difficult to endure: *have/be given a ~ time,* experience difficulties, misfortunes, etc; *in these ~ times,* in these times of money shortage, unemployment, etc when life is difficult; *the ~ discipline of army life.* ***learn sth the ~ way,*** with perseverance and hardship. **4** severe; harsh: *a ~ father,* one who treats his children severely; *~ words,* harsh; showing lack of sympathy. ***be ~ on sb,*** treat him severely. ***drive a ~ bargain,*** ⇨ bargain. ***take a ~ line,*** be uncompromising. Hence, ˈ**~-ˋliner** *n* person who is uncompromising. ⇨ line[1](11). **5** (of the body) having ~ muscles and not much fat: *Regular physical exercises soon made the boys ~.* ***as ~ as nails,*** **(a)** strong and muscular. **(b)** (fig) without sentiment, or sympathy; ~-hearted. **6** done, doing (sth), with much effort or force; strenuous: *a ~ blow; go for a ~ gallop; a ~ worker;* **7** (of the weather) severe: *a ~ winter/frost.* **8** (of sounds) *The letter 'c' is hard in 'cat'. The letter 'g' is ~ in 'gun' and soft in 'gin'.* **9** (various uses) ***~ and fast (rules, etc),*** that cannot be altered to fit special cases. ***~ of hearing,*** rather deaf. ˋ**~·back,** ˋ**~·cover** *nn* book bound in a ~ (= stiff) cover (contrasted with paper-backed books): *The book has just appeared in ~back.* Hence, ˋ**~·backed/·covered/·bound** *adj* **~·board** /-bɔd/ *n* [U] kind of material like plywood in appearance and use, made by compressing waste wood that has been ground up finely. ˈ**~ ˋcash** *n* coins and notes, not a cheque or a promise to pay. ˋ**~ core** *n* **(a)** broken brick, rubble, etc (as used for foundations, roadmaking). **(b)** solid central, basic or underlying part; nucleus: *the ~ core of the opposition/rebellion.* ˋ**~ court** *n* (tennis) court with a ~ surface, not of grass. ˈ**~ ˋcurrency** *n* one which, because of an adverse balance of trade, a country has difficulty in getting enough of. ˈ**~ ˋdrugs,** those likely to lead to addiction, e g *heroin.* ˈ**~-headed** /ˈhedɪd/ *adj* practical; not sentimental; business-like. ˈ**~-hearted** /ˈhɑtɪd/ *adj* unfeeling; lacking in sympathy or the gentler emotions. ˈ**~ ˋlabour** *n* [U] imprisonment with ~ physical labour as a punishment. ˈ**~ ˋluck/ˋlines,** worse fortune than is deserved. Hence, ***a ~-luck story,*** one seeking pity, sympathy (for oneself). ˈ**~ ˋliquor/ˋdrinks,** with high alcoholic content e g *whisky.* ˈ**~ ˋshoulder,** ~ surface at the side of a motorway, to be used in an emergency: *The lorry driver pulled over to the ~ shoulder when one of the tyres burst.* ˈ**~ ˋstanding,** area of ~ surface, e g, concrete, for the parking of vehicles. ˋ**~·top** *n* car with a steel top and no sliding roof. ˋ**~·ware** *n* [U] **(a)** ironmongery; metal goods for domestic use, e g *pans, nails, locks.* **(b)** *military ~ware,* weapons and equipment, e g armoured vehicles. **(c)** *computer ~ware,* mechanical equipment (contrasted with information and programmes, called *software*). ˈ**~ ˋwater,** containing mineral salts that interfere with the lathering of soap. ˋ**~·wood** *n* [U] ~ heavy wood, e g *oak, ebony, teak,* contrasted with soft wood, such as pine and fir: (attrib) *~wood floors.*

hard[2] /hɑd/ *adv* **1** with great energy; strenuously; with all one's force: *work/study/think/pull/push ~; try ~ to succeed; drink/swear ~.* **2** severely; heavily: *freezing/raining ~.* **3** with difficulty; with a struggle; painfully: *my ~-earned money* ⇨ hardly(5). ***be ~ hit,*** be suffering severely, e g by financial losses, the death of sb much loved. ***be ~ pressed (for sth),*** be under pressure, strained. ***be ~ put to it (to do sth),*** find it difficult: *He was ~ put to it to explain what had happened.* ***run sb ~,*** pursue him closely. ***be ~ up,*** be short of money. ***be ~ up for (sth),*** in want of; at a loss for: *He's ~ up for ideas/something to do.* **4** so as to be ~(1), solid: *boil eggs ~; ~-boiled eggs; a*

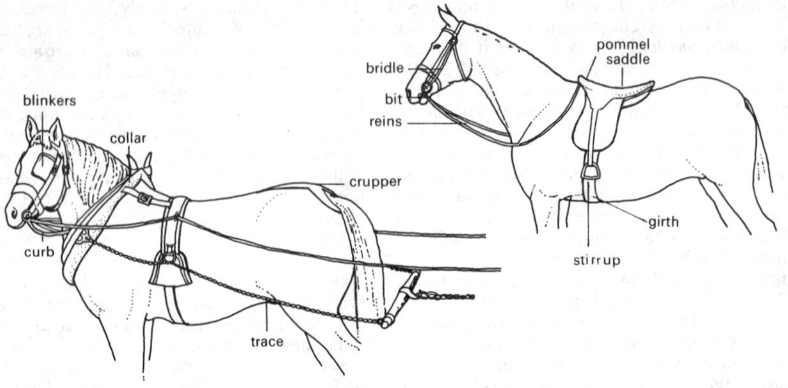

a harness

~-boiled woman, (fig) one lacking in the gentler feelings; one without sentiment or sympathy. **'~-'baked,** baked until ~. **'~-'boiled,** (e g of eggs) boiled ~; (fig) callous. **'~-'bitten** *adj* (of a person) stubborn in fighting; tough because of a difficult life, etc: *a ~-bitten colonel.* **5** closely; immediately: *follow ~ after/upon/behind someone.* **~ by,** close by: not far away.

harden /ˈhɑdn/ *vt,vi* [VP6A,2A] make or become hard, strong, hardy, etc: *~ steel; ~ the heart; a ~ed criminal,* one who is callous, who shows no signs of shame or repentance; *~ the body,* e g by taking exercise. ***be ~ed to,*** made insensitive to. [VP15B,2C] **~ off,** (of young plants, esp seedlings) make or become hardy and ready for planting out in the open.

hardi·hood /ˈhɑdɪhʊd/ *n* [U] boldness; audacity.

hard·ly /ˈhɑdlɪ/ *adv* **1** only just; not quite; scarely: *I ~ know her,* have only a very slight acquaintance with her. *We had ~ got/H~ had we got into the country when it began to rain.* Cf No sooner... than. *I'm so tired I can ~ walk.* **2** (used to suggest that sth is improbable, unlikely or unreasonable): *He can ~ have arrived yet. You can ~ expect me to lend you money again.* **3** (neg in meaning) almost no; almost not: *He ~ ever* (= very seldom) *goes to bed before midnight.* Cf His wife *almost always* goes to bed before midnight. *I need ~ say* (= It is almost unnecessary for me to say) *that I am innocent. There's ~ any coal left. H~ anybody* (= Very few people) *came to the meeting.* **4** (from hard²(3)) severely: *~ treated.* **5** (from hard¹(6)) with effort or difficulty. For this sense the *adv* 'hard' is usu preferred. Cf *hard-earned money* and *salary that was ~* (i e only just, barely) *earned.*

hard·ship /ˈhɑdʃɪp/ *n* **1** [C] circumstance that causes discomfort or suffering: *the ~s borne by soldiers during a war.* **2** [U] severe suffering: *bear ~ without complaining.*

hardy /ˈhɑdɪ/ *adj* (-ier, -iest) **1** strong; able to endure suffering or hardship: *A few ~ men broke the ice on the lake and had a swim.* (of plants) able to endure frost without being injured: *~ annuals.* **2** bold; ready to face danger. **hardi·ness** *n*

hare /heə(r)/ *n* fast-running field animal with long ears and a divided upper lip, like but larger than a rabbit. ***~ and hounds,*** paper-chase, a game in which two persons called the ~s run across country dropping torn-up bits of paper and are followed by others, called 'hounds', who try to catch them. ***run with the ~ and hunt with the hounds,*** try to keep the favour of both sides in a dispute; play a double game. ***mad as a (March) ~,*** very wild. ***start a ~,*** raise a topic, augment, etc unrelated to the main issue. **'~·bell** *n* round-leaved plant with blue bell-like flowers (in Scotland called *bluebell*). **'~-'brained** *adj* rash; wild. **'~·'lip** *n* person's upper lip divided (from birth) like that of a ~. □ *vi* [VP2C] run fast or away: *They ~d off.*

harem /ˈheərəm/ *n* women's part of a Muslim household: women living in it.

hari·cot /ˈhærɪkəʊ/ *n* (also **'~ bean**) kidney bean; French bean.

hark /hɑk/ *vi* **1** (chiefly imper) ***~ to/at,*** (colloq) listen to: *Just ~ at him!* **2** ***~ back (to),*** refer back to sth done or said earlier.

har·le·quin /ˈhɑləkwɪn/ *n* character in Italian comedy; mute character in English pantomime, full of tricks and very lively; (hence) person fond of practical jokes; buffoon. **~·ade** /ˈhɑləkwɪnˈeɪd/ *n* part of a pantomime in which a ~ plays the chief part.

Har·ley Street /ˈhɑlɪ strit/ *n* London street where many fashionable doctors and surgeons live.

har·lot /ˈhɑlət/ *n* (archaic, or as a term of abuse) prostitute.

harm /hɑm/ *n* [U] ***do sb ~,*** cause damage; injury: *It will do you no ~. He probably meant no ~,* did not intend to hurt anyone or anyone's feelings. *There's no ~ in your staying up late occasionally,* no reason why you should not do so. ***out of ~'s way,*** in a place of safety. □ *vt* [VP6A] cause ~ to: *It hasn't ~ed you, has it?* **~·ful** /-fl/ *adj* causing ~ *(to).* **~·fully** /-flɪ/ *adv* **~·less** *adj* **1** not doing ~ *(to): ~less snakes.* **2** innocent; inoffensive: *Several ~less spectators were wounded during the rioting.* **~·less·ly** *adv*

har·monic /hɑˈmɒnɪk/ *n* (music) higher note produced (by vibration of strings) with a note that is played, and having a fixed relation to it.

har·mon·ica /hɑˈmɒnɪkə/ *n* name of several musical instruments, esp (in GB) the mouth-organ.

har·moni·ous /hɑˈməʊnɪəs/ *adj* **1** pleasingly or satisfactorily arranged: *a ~ group of buildings.* **2** in agreement; free from ill feeling: *~ families/neighbours.* **3** sweet-sounding; tuneful; **~·ly** *adv*

har·mo·nium /hɑˈməʊnɪəm/ *n* musical instrument

with a keyboard like a small organ, supplied with wind by means of bellows worked by pedals, but with metal reeds instead of pipes.

har·mon·ize /ˈhɑmənɑɪz/ *vt,vi* **1** [VP6A,14] bring (one thing) into harmony (with another); (music) add notes (to a melody) to make chords. **2** [VP2A,C] be in harmony or agreement: *colours that* ~ *well* (*with the decorations/with each other.*) **har·mon·iz·ation** /ˌhɑmənɑɪˈzeɪʃn/ *n*

har·mony /ˈhɑmənɪ/ *n* (*pl* **-nies**) **1** [U] agreement (of feeling, interests, opinions, etc): *There was not much* ~ *in international affairs during those years.* ***be in* ~ *(with),*** match; agree (with): *His tastes are in* ~ *with mine.* **2** [C,U] (instance or example of) pleasing combination of related things: *the* ~ *of colour in nature,* e g the greens, browns, etc of trees in autumn. **3** [C,U] (music) pleasing combination of notes sounded together to make chords.

har·ness /ˈhɑnɪs/ *n* [U] (collective *sing*) all the leather-work and metal-work by which a horse is controlled and fastened to the cart, waggon, plough, etc, that it pulls. ***in* ~,** (fig) doing one's regular work. ***die in* ~,** die while engaged in one's regular work, not after retiring. ***work/run in double* ~,** work with a partner, or with a husband or wife. □ *vt* [VP6A] **1** put ~ on (a horse). **2** use (a river, waterfall, etc) to produce (esp electric) power.

harp /hɑp/ *n* freestanding musical instrument with vertical strings played with the fingers. ⇨ the illus at **string**. □ *vi* **1** play the ~. **2** ~ ***on sth,*** (fig) talk repeatedly or tiresomely about: *She is always* ~*ing on her misfortunes.* **~er, ~·ist** /-ɪst/ *nn* player on the ~.

har·poon /hɑˈpun/ *n* spear on a rope, thrown by hand or fired from a gun, for catching whales and other large sea animals. □ *vt* strike with a ~.

harp·si·chord /ˈhɑpsɪkɔd/ *n* piano-like instrument used from the 16th to the 18th cc (and today for music of these centuries). ⇨ the illus at **keyboard**.

harpy /ˈhɑpɪ/ *n* (*pl* **-pies**) **1** (old Gk stories) cruel creature with a woman's face and a bird's wings and claws. **2** cruel, greedy, hard-hearted woman.

har·ri·dan /ˈhærɪdən/ *n* worn-out, bad-tempered old woman.

har·rier /ˈhærɪə(r)/ *n* hound used for hunting hares; (*pl*) pack of these with huntsmen. **2** cross-country runner.

har·row /ˈhærəʊ/ *n* heavy frame with metal teeth or discs for breaking up ground after ploughing. □ *vt* [VP6A] pull a ~ over (a field, etc); (fig) distress (the feelings): *a* ~*ing tale of misfortunes.*

harry /ˈhærɪ/ *vt* (*pt,pp* **-ried**) [VP6A] **1** lay waste and plunder; attack frequently: *The Vikings used to* ~ *the English coast.* **2** annoy or worry: *money-lenders* ~*ing their debtors.*

harsh /hɑʃ/ *adj* (**-er, -est**) **1** rough and disagreeable, esp to the senses: *a* ~ *texture/voice/contrast;* ~ *to the ear.* **2** stern, cruel, severe: *a* ~ *judge/judgement/punishment.* **~·ly** *adv* **~·ness** *n*

hart /hɑt/ *n* adult male of (esp red) deer; stag.

har·tal /ˈhɑtɑl/ *n* (in India) closing of shops as a mark of sorrow or for a political reason.

harum-scarum /ˌheərəm ˈskeərəm/ *n* reckless, impulsive person.

har·vest /ˈhɑvɪst/ *n* **1** (season for) cutting and gathering in of grain and other food crops; quantity obtained: *this year's wheat* ~*; a succession of good* ~*s.* ˌ~ ˈ**festival** *n* service of thanksgiving in Christian churches after the ~ has been gathered. ˈ~ **home** *n* festival given by farmers to their workers when the ~ is gathered in. ˌ~ ˈ**moon** *n* full moon nearest to the autumn equinox. **2** (fig) consequences of action or behaviour: *reap the* ~ *of one's hard work,* be rewarded for it. □ *vt* [VP6A] cut, gather, dig up, a crop: ~ *rice/potatoes.* **~er** *n* **1** person who ~s; reaper. **2** machine for cutting and gathering grain, esp the kind that also binds it into sheaves or (ˌ**combine-**ˈ**~er**) threshes it. ⇨ the illus at **combine**.

has ⇨ **have**[1].

has-been /ˈhæz bin/ *n* (colloq) person who, or thing which, has lost a quality, skill, etc formerly possessed; sb or sth now out of date.

hash /hæʃ/ *vt* [VP6A,15B] ~ ***(up),*** chop or cut up (meat) into small pieces. □ *n* **1** [U] (dish of) cooked meat, ~ed and re-cooked. **2** ***make a* ~ *of sth,*** (fig) do it very badly, make a mess of it. ***settle sb's* ~,** deal with him in such a way that he gives no more trouble. **3** (colloq) hashish.

hash·ish, hash·eesh /ˈhæʃiʃ/ *n* [U] dried hemp leaves made into a drug for smoking or chewing; cannabis.

hasn't /ˈhæznt/ = has not. ⇨ **have**[1].

hasp /hæsp/ *n* metal fastening for a door, window, etc used with a staple. ⇨ the illus at **padlock**.

has·sock /ˈhæsək/ *n* cushion for kneeling on, e g in church.

hast /hæst/ (archaic): *thou* ~, you have.

haste /heɪst/ *n* [U] quickness of movement; hurry: *Why all this* ~*?* Why are you in such a hurry? *He went off in great* ~. ***Make* ~!** Hurry! ***More* ~, *less speed,*** (prov) The more you hurry, the less real progress you will make.

hasten /ˈheɪsn/ *vi,vt* **1** [VP2A,C,4A] move or act with speed: ~ *away/home/to the office;* ~ *to tell sb the good news.* **2** [VP6A] cause (sb) to hurry; cause (sth) to be done or to happen quickly or earlier: *Artificial heating* ~*s the growth of plants.*

hasty /ˈheɪstɪ/ *adj* (**- er, -iest**) **1** said, made or done (too) quickly: ~ *preparations for flight; a* ~ *departure;* ~ *words that are regretted afterwards.* **2** (older use) quick-tempered: *a* ~ *old colonel.* **hast·ily** /-əlɪ/ *adv* **hasti·ness** *n*

hat /hæt/ *n* covering for the head, usu (for men) with a brim, worn out of doors. Cf *cap* and *bonnet* without a brim. ***go/come hat/cap in hand,*** obsequiously, apologetically. ***send/pass round the hat,*** ask for, collect, contributions of money (usu for sb who has suffered a loss). ***take one's hat off to,*** (fig) express admiration for. ***talk through one's hat,*** (sl) talk foolishly. ***a bad hat,*** (sl) bad person. ˈ**hat-band** *n* band round the crown of a hat, above the brim. ˈ**hat-pin** *n* long pin used (formerly) by women to fasten a hat to the hair. ˈ**hat trick** *n* (cricket) taking of three wickets with successive balls; similar success in other sports or activities. **hat·ful** /-fʊl/ *n* as much as a hat holds. **hat·less** *adj* not wearing a hat. **hat·ter** *n* man who makes or sells hats. ***as mad as a hatter,*** very mad.

hatch[1] /hætʃ/ *n* **1** (movable covering over an) opening in a door or floor, esp (ˈ**~·way**) one in a ship's deck through which cargo is lowered and raised; opening in a wall between two rooms, esp a kitchen and a dining room, through which dishes, etc, are passed. ***under* ~*es,*** below deck. **2** lower half of a divided door.

hatch[2] /hætʃ/ *vt,vi* **1** [VP6A,2A] (cause to) break out (of an egg): ~ *an egg;* ~ *chickens. When will the eggs* ~? *Three chickens* ~*ed today.* ***Don't count one's chickens before they're*** ~***ed,*** Don't rely too much upon sth which is uncertain. **2** [VP6A] think out and produce (a plot, etc). **~·ery** /ˈhætʃərɪ/ *n* (*pl* -ries) place for ~ing (esp fish): *a* ˋ*trout-*~*ery.* Cf *incubator,* for chicks.

hatchet /ˈhætʃɪt/ *n* light, short-handled axe. ⇨ the illus at tool. ***bury the*** ~, stop quarrelling or fighting and be friendly.

hatch·ing /ˈhætʃɪŋ/ *n* [U] parallel lines drawn or engraved on a surface.

hatch·way /ˈhætʃweɪ/ *n* ⇨ hatch[1].

hate /heɪt/ *vt* [VP6A,D,7A,17A,19] have a violent dislike of or for; (colloq) regret: *My cat* ~*s dogs. I* ~ *to trouble you. I* ~ *you to be troubled. She* ~*s getting to the theatre late. She* ~*s anyone listening while she's telephoning.* □ *n* [U] extreme or violent dislike or ill-will: *He was filled with* ~ *for his opponent.*

hate·ful /ˈheɪtfl/ *adj* exciting hatred or strong dislike: *The sight of food was* ~ *to the seasick girl.* **~ly** /-flɪ/ *adv*

hath /hæθ/ (archaic) *3rd pers sing pres t* of *have.*

hatred /ˈheɪtrɪd/ *n* ~ ***of/for,*** hate; violent dislike: *He looked at me with* ~.

hat·ter /ˈhætə(r)/ *n* ⇨ hat.

hau·berk /ˈhɔbɜk/ *n* coat of chain mail (as worn by soldiers in the Middle Ages).

haughty /ˈhɔtɪ/ *adj* (-ier, -iest) arrogant; having or showing a high opinion of oneself: *The nobles used to treat the common people with* ~ *contempt.* **haught·ily** /-əlɪ/ *adv* **haugh·ti·ness** *n*

haul /hɔl/ *vt,vi* [VP6A,15A,B,2C,3A] pull (with effort or force): *elephants* ~*ing logs;* ~ *timber to a saw-mill;* ~ *at/upon a rope. They* ~*ed the boat up the beach.* ~ ***down one's flag/colours,*** surrender. ~ ***sb over the coals,*** scold him severely (for wrongdoing). □ *n* [C] **1** act of ~ing; distance along which sth is ~ed: *long* ~*s on the railways.* **2** amount gained as the result of effort, esp of fish ~ed up in a net: *a good* ~ *of fish. The thief made a good* ~, What he stole was valuable.

haul·age /ˈhɔlɪdʒ/ *n* [U] transport (of goods): *the road* ~ *industry,* concerned with carriage of goods by road in lorries, etc; *a* ~ *contractor.*

haul·ier /ˈhɔlɪə(r)/ *n* person or firm that owns lorries, and contracts to carry goods by road; haulage contractor.

haulm /hɔm/ *n* (collective *sing*) stems and stalks of peas, beans, potatoes, etc, esp after the crop is gathered.

haunch /hɔntʃ/ *n* (in man and animals) part of the body round the hips, or between the ribs and the thighs: *a* ~ *of venison. The dog was sitting on its* ~*es.*

haunt /hɔnt/ *vt* [VP6A] **1** visit, be with, habitually or repeatedly; (esp of ghosts and spirits) appear repeatedly in: *The old castle is said to be* ~*ed.* **2** return to the mind repeatedly: *A wrongdoer is constantly* ~*ed by fear of discovery.* □ *n* place frequently visited by the person(s) named: *a* ~ *of criminals; revisit the* ~*s of one's schooldays,* the places where one spent one's time then.

haut·boy /ˈ(h)əʊbɔɪ/ *n* = oboe.

hau·teur /əʊˈtɜ(r)/ *n* hautiness of manner.

Ha·vana /həˈvænə/ *n* cigar made at ~ or elsewhere in Cuba.

have[1] /*usu form after 'I, we, you, they':* v; *usu form after a pause:* həv; *usu form elsewhere:* əv; *strong form:* hæv/ *aux v* (*3rd pers sing* has /*usu forms:* z, *and after* p,t,k,f,θ *only:* s; *after* s,z,ʃ,ʒ, tʃ, dʒ *only:* əz; *after a pause:* həz; *strong form:* hæz/, *pp* had /*usu form after 'I, we, you, they':* d; *usu form after a pause:* həd; *usu form elsewhere:* əd; *strong form:* hæd/; neg forms haven't /ˈhævnt/, hasn't /ˈhæznt/, hadn't /ˈhædnt/) **1** used in forming the perfect tenses and the perfect inf: *I* ~*/I've finished. He has/He's gone. H*~ *you done it? Yes, I* ~. *No, I* ~*n't. I shall* ~ *done it by next week. You ought to* ~ *done it.* **2** (By inverting the finite *had* with the subject, the equivalent of an *if*-clause is obtained): *Had I* (= If I had) *known,....* ⇨ if(1).

have[2] /hæv/ *anom v* (*3rd pers sing* has /hæz/, *pp* had /hæd/; neg forms haven't /ˈhævnt/, hasn't /ˈhæznt/, hadn't /ˈhædnt/) (conjugated (for the neg and interr forms) without the *aux v* 'do' in GB usage, but not always in US usage; in colloq style often replaced by *have*[1] *got,* e g *I've got* for *I* ~) **1** (in sentences that can be recomposed with the *v* 'be'): [VP6A] *I* ~ *no doubt* (= There is no doubt in my mind) *that.... Has the house* (= Is there with the house) *a good garden?* **2** [VP6A] possess; own (sth concrete): *He's* (*got*) *a house in the country. How many books* ~ *you/do you* ~? **3** [VP6A] possess or show as a mental or physical characteristic (often equivalent to a construction with *be*): *Has she blue eyes or brown eyes?* Are her eyes blue or brown? *He hasn't a good memory.* His memory isn't good. Notes: In US usage aux *do* is common: *Does she* ~ *blue eyes? Do you* ~ *a good memory?* In GB colloq styles, the *pp got* is common: *Has she got blue eyes?* **4** [VP6A] used to indicate various connections: *How many children* ~ *they? He hasn't many friends here.* The notes above on GB and US usage apply here, too. **5** (followed by an abstract *n* and an *inf,* in a construction equivalent to *be* an *adj* and an *inf*): *Will you* ~ *the kindness/goodness, etc* (= Please be kind or good enough) *to hand me that book. How dare you* ~ *the impudence* (= be so impudent as) *to say that! Had she/Did she* ~ *the cheek* (= Was she cheeky enough) *to ask for more money?* **6** (in colloq style usu with *got*) hold or keep in the mind; exercise some quality of the mind; experience (some emotion): *H*~ *you* (*got*) *any idea where he lives? What reason* ~ *you* (*got*) *for thinking that he's dishonest? What kind of holiday* ~ *you in mind?* **7** [VP6A,18C,19B] (in the *inf* only and always stressed) allow; endure: *I won't* ˋ~ *such conduct. I won't* ˋ~ *you saying such things about my sister.*

have[3] (for pronunciations ⇨ have[2]) *vt* (Used in the neg and interr with or without the *aux v* 'do'. The distinction is not always clear and there can be recommendations only, not rules. When the reference is to sth regular or habitual, the use of *do* for neg and interr is to be preferred. When the reference is to a particular occasion, constructions without *do,* and, in colloq style, with *got,* are to be preferred.) **1** [VP7B] ~ ***to do sth,*** expressing obligation or necessity: *Do you often* ~ *to go to the dentist's? H*~ *you* (*got*) *to go to the dentist's today? The children don't* ~ *to go to school on Sundays, do they? You* ~*n't* (*got*) *to go to school today,* ~ *you? I* ~ *to be getting along* (= must leave) *now. He's so rich that he doesn't* ~ *to work. We had to leave early. Had you/Did you* ~ *to leave early? These shoes will* ~ *to be repaired.*

⇨ must[2], need[2]. **2** [VP6A] (in various senses as shown in these examples): *Do you often* ~ (= suffer from) *colds? H~ you* (*got*) (= Are you suffering from) *a cold now? Do you* ~ (i e as a rule, generally) *much time for reading? H~ you* (*got*) (i e now, or on the occasion specified) *time to come with me? Has your dog* (*got*) *any puppies yet? How often does your dog* ~ (i e give birth to) *puppies? Can you* ~ (= take and look after) *the children for a few days?*

have[4] (for pronunciations ⇨ have[2]) *non-anom v* (neg and interr always with the *aux v* 'do') **1** [VP6A] take; receive; accept; obtain: *There was nothing to be had,* obtained. *Do you* ~ *tea or coffee for breakfast? What shall we* ~ *for dinner?* **2** [VP6A] (with a *n*, so that *have* and the *n* are equivalent to a *v* identical with the *n*): ~ *a swim/walk/wash/rest. Let me* ~ *a try/look. Go and* ~ *a lie down. Do you ever* ~ *dreams?* **3** [VP6A] experience; undergo: *We didn't* ~ *much difficulty. Did you* ~ *a good holiday? You've never had it so good,* never before experienced such a high standard of living, enjoyed such prosperity, etc. ***let him/them ~ it,*** (sl) shoot, punish sb, etc according to the situation. ***~ had it,*** (sl) not be going to receive or enjoy sth: *Don't think you're going to get any money from me; you've had it!* **4** [VP24C] ***~ sth done,*** cause (sb to do sth): *You'd better* ~ *that bad tooth pulled out. I must* ~ *these shoes repaired. When did you last* ~ *your hair cut?* ⇨ get(2). ⇨ also 6 below. **5** [VP18C] ***~ sb to do sth,*** want: *I would* ~ *you know that…,* I want you to know that…. *What would you* ~ *me do? I wouldn't* ~ *you do that,* should prefer you not to do it. ***~ to do with,*** ⇨ do[2](14). **6** [VP24B] ***~ sth done,*** be effected in some way; experience or suffer: *He had his pocket picked,* sth stolen from his pocket. *Charles I had his head cut off. The Colonel had two horses shot under him.* **7** [VP6A] **(a)** trick; deceive: *I'm afraid you've been had. Mind he doesn't* ~ *you.* **(b)** beat; win an advantage over: *He had me in that argument. You had me there!* **8** (with *it* and a clause) express; maintain: *Rumour has it* (= There is a rumour) *that the Prime Minister is going to resign. He will* ~ *it* (= He insists) *that our plan is impracticable. … as Plato has it* (used when giving a quotation, etc). **9** [VP15B] (uses with *adverbial particles* and *preps*):

have at sb, (old use, chiefly imper) attack him.

have sth back: *You shall* ~ *it back* (= It will be returned to you) *next month. Let me* ~ *it back soon.*

have sb down, have sb as a visitor or guest: *We're having the Greens down* (e g from London) *for a few days.*

have sb in, have him in the room, house, etc: *We shall be having the decorators in next month,* the men will be decorating the house. ***~ sth in,*** have in the house, etc: *Do we* ~ *enough coal in for winter?*

have it off (with sb), ⚠ (sl) have sexual intercourse (with).

have sb on, (colloq) play a trick on him, deceive him. ⇨ 7 above. ***~ sth on,*** **(a)** be wearing: *He had nothing on,* was naked. **(b)** ~ an engagement: *I* ~ *nothing on tomorrow evening,* I am free.

have sth out, cause sth, to be out: ~ *a tooth out.* ***~ one's sleep out,*** continue sleeping until one wakes naturally: *Let her* ~ *her sleep out.* ***~ it out with sb,*** reach an understanding about sth by frank discussion.

have sb up, **(a)** have sb as a visitor (up to one's room, up from the country, etc). **(b)** (usu passive) (colloq) cause sb to appear before a magistrate, in a court of law, etc: *He was had up* (= was prosecuted) *for exceeding the speed limit.*

haves /hæv/ *n pl* ***the ~s and the ~-nots,*** the rich and the poor (of people and countries).

ha·ven /ˈheɪvn/ *n* harbour; (fig) place of safety or rest.

hav·er·sack /ˈhævəsæk/ *n* canvas bag, esp as used by soldiers, hikers and others, for carrying food, etc.

havoc /ˈhævək/ *n* [U] widespread damage; destruction: *The floods caused terrible* ~. ***play ~ with/among, make ~ of,*** destroy or injure.

haw[1] /hɔ/ *n* fruit (a red berry) of the hawthorn bush.

haw[2] /hɔ/ *vi, n* ⇨ hum(4).

haw-haw /ˈhɔ hɔ/ *n, int* boisterous laugh.

hawk[1] /hɔk/ *n* **1** strong, swift, keen-sighted bird of prey. ⇨ the illus at prey. **ˈ~-ˈeyed** *adj* having keen sight. **2** person who favours the use of military force in foreign policy. ⇨ dove.

hawk[2] /hɔk/ *vt* [VP6A,15B] go from house to house, street to street, with goods for sale; (fig) spread about: ~ *news/gossip about.* **~er** *n* person who ~s goods (usu from a barrow or cart). ⇨ pedlar.

haw·ser /ˈhɔzə(r)/ *n* thick, heavy rope; thin steel cable (used on ships).

haw·thorn /ˈhɔθɔn/ *n* thorny shrub or tree with white, red or pink blossom and small red berries (called *haws*), often used for hedges in GB.

hay /heɪ/ *n* [U] grass cut and dried for use as animal food. ***make hay,*** turn it over for exposure to the sun; (hence) **ˈhay-maker, ˈhay-making** *nn* ***make hay of,*** throw into confusion. ***make hay while the sun shines,*** (prov) make the earliest use of one's opportunities. **ˈhay·cock** *n* cone-shaped pile of hay in a field, to be carted away when dry. **ˈhay fever** *n* disease affecting the nose and throat, caused by pollen (dust) from various plants. **ˈhay-fork** *n* long-handled two-pronged fork for turning and lifting hay. **ˈhay·rick, ˈhay·stack** *nn* large pile of hay firmly packed for storing, with a pointed or ridged top. **ˈhay·wire** *n* wire for tying up bales of hay. □ *pred adj* (colloq) out of order: excited or distracted. ***go haywire,*** (of persons) become distraught; (of sth, e g a plan) become badly disorganised.

haz·ard /ˈhæzəd/ *n* **1** [C] risk; danger: *ˈhealth ~s,* e g smoking cigarettes; *a life full of ~s.* ***at all ~s,*** whatever the risks may be. **2** [U] game at dice, with complicated chances. □ *vt* [VP6A] **1** take the risk of; expose to danger: *Rock-climbers sometimes* ~ *their lives.* **2** venture to make: ~ *a guess/remark.* **~·ous** /-əs/ *adj* risky: *a ~ous climb.*

haze[1] /heɪz/ *n* [U] thin mist; (fig) mental confusion or uncertainty.

haze[2] /heɪz/ *vt* (US) harass (sb) by making him perform humiliating jobs; bully or persecute.

hazel /ˈheɪzl/ *n* [C] bush with edible nuts; [U] (esp of eyes) colour of the shell of the nut, reddish brown.

hazy /ˈheɪzɪ/ *adj* (-ier, -iest) misty: ~ *weather;* (fig) vague; slightly confused; uncertain: ~ *about what to do next.* **haz·ily** /-əlɪ/ *adv* **hazi·ness** *n*

H-bomb /ˈeɪtʃ bɒm/ *n* hydrogen bomb.

he /i *strong form:* hi/ *pron* **1** male person or animal previously referred to: *Where's your brother? He's in Paris.* **2** (as *pref*) male: *ˈhe-goat.* **he-man** /-mæn/ *n* (*pl* -men) masterful or virile man. **3** (liter style) ***he who,*** the one who, anyone who.

head[1] /hed/ *n* **1** that part of the body which contains the eyes, nose, mouth and brain: *They cut his ~ off. Hit him on the ~.* Note: *the ~,* not *his ~. It cost him his ~,* his life. *Many aristocrats lost their ~s during the French Revolution.* **2** (as a measure) ~'s length: *The Queen's horse won by a ~. Tom is taller than Harry by a ~.* ***be ~ and shoulders above sb,*** (fig) be considerably superior in intelligence or ability. **3** that side of a coin on which the ~ of a ruler appears, the other side being the *tail.* ***H~s or tails?*** (usu *pl* when spinning a coin to decide sth by chance): *H~s—I win!* ***be unable to make ~ or tail of sth,*** be unable to understand it in the least. **4** person: *50 dinners at £1.50 a ~.* **5** (*pl* unchanged) unit of a flock or herd: *50 ~ of cattle; a large ~* (= number) *of game.* **6** intellect; imagination; power to reason: *He made the story up out of his own ~,* It was an original story, not one that he had heard or read. **7** natural aptitude or talent: *He has a good ~ for business.* **8** sth like a ~ in form or position, e g the part that is pressed (*the ~ of a pin*), struck (*the ~ of a nail*), used for striking (*the ~ of a hammer*) or for cutting (*the ~ of an axe*); *tape recorder ~s,* attachment that holds or contains an electronic device to record, read or erase material on magnetic tape, disc, etc. **9** top; *at the ~ of the page; standing at the ~ of the staircase; at the ~ of the poll,* having received most votes at an election. **10** upper end: *the ~ of a lake,* the end at which a river enters it; *the ~ waters of the Nile,* its sources and upper streams; *the ~ of a bed,* where a person's ~ rests. **11** (of plants) mass of leaves or flowers at the top of a stem or stalk: *a fine ~ of cabbage; a ~ of lettuce; a ˈclover ~; a ˈflower ~.* **12** (often attrib) ruler; chief; position of command: *~s of government,* e g the President of the US, the Prime Minister of GB. Cf *summit; the crowned ~s of Europe, the kings and queens; the ~ of the family; at the ~ of the class,* at the top, having gained the highest marks; *the ~ office,* the chief or most important office (contrasted with *branch* offices); *the ~ waiter; at the ~ of the army; the ~ master/mistress of the school.* **13** front; front part: *at the ~ of the procession; marching at the ~ of the regiment. The ship was down by the ~,* with the bows deeper in the water than the stern. **14** (chiefly in proper names) cape or promontory: *Beachy H~.* ⇨ *headland* in **20** below. **15** body of water kept at a certain height (e g for a water-mill or a hydro-electric power station); pressure or force (per unit of area) of a confined body of steam, etc: *They kept up a good ~ of steam.* **16** main division in a discourse, essay, etc: *a speech arranged under five ~s; treat a question under several ~s.* ⇨ heading. **17** foam or liquid that has been poured out, esp liquor: *the ~ on a glass of beer.* **18** point rising from a boil or other swelling on the flesh, esp when the boil is ripening and about to burst: *The boil came to a ~.* ***come to a ~,*** (fig) reach a crisis, culminate: *Affairs have come to a ~.* **19** (various phrases) ***an old ~ on young shoulders,*** wisdom in a young person. ***bite sb's ~ off,*** scold them angrily. ***eat one's ~ off,*** (of a horse and, fig, a person) eat a great deal. ***give an animal/sb its/his ~,*** allow him to go freely; (fig, of a person) leave him to act freely, unchecked. ***go to one's ~,*** **(a)** (of liquor) intoxicate: *The whisky went to his ~.* **(b)** excite: *His successes have gone to his ~,* made him over-confident, conceited, etc. ***have a ˈgood ˈ~ on one's shoulders,*** have practical ability, common sense, etc. ***~ over heels,*** topsy-turvey; (fig) deeply or completely: *~ over heels in debt/in love.* ***keep one's ~,*** keep calm. ***keep one's ~ above water,*** (fig) out of debt. ***laugh/scream one's ~ off,*** laugh/scream loudly, with great energy. ***lose one's ~,*** become confused or excited. ***make some/no ~(way) against,*** resist successfully. ***(go) off one's ~,*** **(a)** (become) crazy; mad. **(b)** (become) wildly excited. ***(stand, etc) on one's ~,*** with feet in the air: *I could do it (standing) on my ~,* colloq It is very easy. ***on your (his, etc) own ˈ~ be it,*** the consequences will rest on you. ***(be promoted) over another's ~/over the ~s of others,*** before another or others with prior or stronger claims. ***put our/your, etc ~s together,*** consult together. ***put sth into a person's ~,*** suggest it to him. ***put sth out of one's ~,*** stop thinking about it; give up the idea: *You'd better put the idea of marriage out of your ~.* ***put sth out of sb's ~,*** make him forget it: *Something put it out of my ~.* ***take sth into one's ~,*** come to believe it: *He took it into his ~ that I was secretly opposing him.* ***talk sb's ~ off,*** weary him with talk. ***talk over a person's ~/ over the ~s of one's audience,*** talk in a way that is too difficult to understand. ***Two ~s are better than one,*** (prov) The opinions, advice, etc of a second person are valuable. ***turn sb's ~,*** make them conceited. ***(be) weak in the ~,*** (be) not very intelligent. **20** (compounds) **ˈ~ache** *n* [C,U] **(a)** continuous pain in the ~: *suffer from ~ache(s); have a bad ~ache.* **(b)** (sl) troublesome problem: *more ~aches for the Department of the Environment.* **ˈ~-band** *n* band worn round the ~. **ˈ~-dress** *n* covering for the ~, esp woman's ornamental kind. **ˈ~-gear** *n* hat, cap, ~dress. **ˈ~-hunter** *n* savage who cuts off and keeps as trophies the ~s of his enemies. **ˈ~-lamp** *n* powerful lamp fixed to the front of a motor vehicle, etc. ⇨ the illus at motor. **ˈ~-land** /-lənd/ *n* promontory, cape. **ˈ~-light** *n* large lamp on the front of a locomotive, motor-car, etc. ⇨ the illus at motor. **ˈ~-line** *n* newspaper heading; line at the top of a page containing title, etc; (*pl*) summary of broadcast news: *'Here are the news ~lines.'* **~-man** /-mæn/ *n* (*pl* -men) chief man of a village, tribe, etc. **ˈ~ˈmaster/ˈmistress** *nn* principal master (mistress) of a school. **ˈ~-on** *adj, adv* (of collisions) with the front parts (of vehicles) meeting: *a ~-on collision; meet/strike ~-on.* **ˈ~-phones** *n pl* receivers fitting over the ~ (for radio, etc); ear-phones. **ˈ~-piece** *n* **(a)** helmet. **(b)** (colloq) intelligence; brains. **ˈ~-ˈquarters** *n* (*sing* or *pl*) place from which (e g police, army) operations are controlled. **ˈ~-rest** *n* sth that supports the ~. **ˈ~-room** *n* = clearance(2). **ˈ~-set** *n* ~phones. **~-ship** /-ʃɪp/ *n* position of a ~master or ~mistress: *apply for a ~ship.* **ˈ~-stall** *n* part of a bridle or halter that fits round the ~. **ˈ~-stone** *n* stone set up at the ~ of a grave. **ˈ~-way** *n* [U] progress. ***make some/no ~way,*** ⇨ 19 above. **ˈ~-wind** *n* one that blows

the head and the neck

1 hair
2 forehead
3 eyebrow
4 bridge
5 temple
6 eye
7 ear
8 cheek
9 nose
10 nostril
11 mouth
12 jaw
13 chin
14 nape
15 neck
16 throat

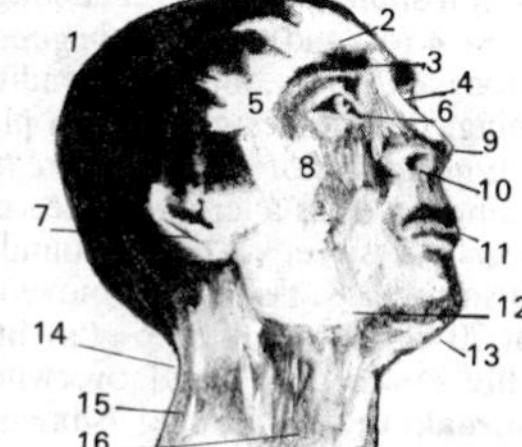

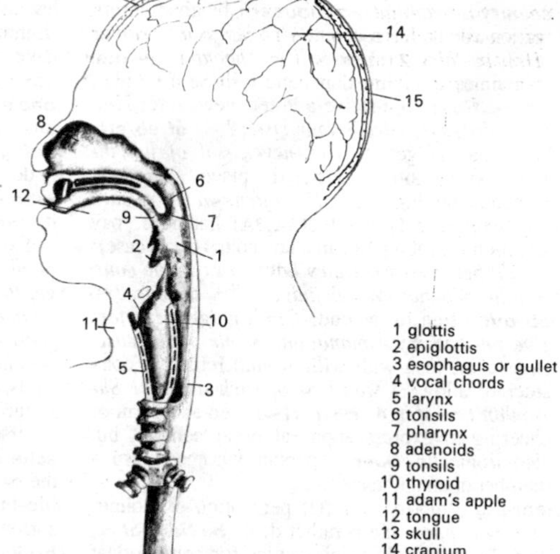

directly into one's face, or against the course of a ship, etc. **'~-word** *n* word used as a heading, e g the first word, in heavy type, of a dictionary entry. **~ed** *adj* (in compounds) *'three-'~ed,* having three ~s; *'long-'~ed,* having a long skull. **~less** *adj* having no ~.

head² /hed/ *vt,vi* **1** [VP6A] be at the head or top of: *~ a procession; ~ a revolt/rebellion,* act as the leader. *Smith's name ~ed the list.* **2** [VP6A] strike, touch, with the head (e g the ball in football). **3** [VP15B] **~ sth/sb off,** get in front of, so as to turn back or aside: *~ off a flock of sheep* (to prevent them from going the wrong way); (fig) prevent: *~ off a quarrel.* **4** [VP2C] move in the direction indicated: *~ south; ~ straight for home;* (fig) *be ~ing for disaster. Where are you ~ed (for)?*

header /'hedə(r)/ *n* **1** fall, dive or jump with the head first: *take a ~ into a swimming pool.* **2** (football) act of striking the ball with the head.

head·ing /'hedɪŋ/ *n* word or words at the top of a section of printed matter (to show the subject of what follows).

head·long /'hedlɒŋ *US:* -lɔŋ/ *adv, adj* **1** with the head first: *fall ~.* **2** thoughtless(ly) and hurried(ly): *rush ~ into danger; a ~ decision.*

head·strong /'hedstrɒŋ *US:* -strɔŋ/ *adj* self-willed; obstinate.

heady /'hedɪ/ *adj* (-ier, -iest) **1** acting, done, on impulse; headstrong. **2** (of alcoholic drink) having a quick effect on the senses; quickly causing intoxication: *a ~ wine;* (fig) (e g of sudden success) having an exciting effect.

heal /hil/ *vt,vi* **1** [VP6A,2A,C] (esp of wounds) (cause to) become healthy and sound: *The wound is not yet ~ed,* the new skin has not yet covered it. *The wound ~ed slowly. It soon ~ed up/over.* **2** [VP6A] (archaic or biblical) restore (a person) to health; cure (a disease): *~ sb of a disease* (*cure* is now the usu word). ⇨ also *faith-~ing* at faith. **3** [VP6A] (fig) *~ a quarrel,* end it. *Time ~s all sorrows.* **~er** *n* person or thing that ~s: *Time is a great ~er.* **~·ing** *adj*: *~ing ointments.*

health /helθ/ *n* **1** [U] condition of the body or the mind. ***have/enjoy/be in good/poor ~,*** *Fresh air and exercise are good for the ~* (more colloq *good for you*). **2** (in names of organizations, etc): *the 'World 'H~ Organisation* (abbr WHO); *the Department of H~ and Social Security* (in GB); *the 'National 'H~ Service* (in GB). **3** [U] (esp) state of being well and free from illness. **4** ***drink sb's ~, drink a ~ to (sb),*** (as a social custom) raise one's glass and wish good ~ to. **~·ful** /-fl/ *adj* ~-giving; good for the ~.

healthy /'helθɪ/ *adj* (-ier, -iest) **1** having good health; well, strong and able to resist disease: *The children look very ~. The children are quite ~, although they have slight colds at present.* (Note that *well* is the usu word when the reference is to a specific occasion: e g *I hope you're quite well*). **2** likely to produce good health: *a ~ climate; a ~ way of living.* **3** showing good health: *a ~ appetite.* **health·ily** /-əlɪ/ *adj* in a ~ way: *arrive home healthily tired.*

heap /hip/ *n* [C] **1** number of things, mass of material, piled up: *a big ~ of books; a ~ of sand; building material lying about in ~s.* ***be struck/knocked all of a ~,*** (colloq) be overwhelmed; be thrown into a state of bewilderment or confusion. **2** ***~s (of),*** (colloq) large number; plenty: *We have ~s of books/time. She has been there ~s of times,* very often. *There is ~s more I could say on this question.* **3** (as *adv;* colloq) much: *feeling ~s better.* □ *vt* **1** [VP6A,15A,B] ***~ (up),*** put in a ~: *~ (up) stones; ~ up riches.* **2** [VP14] ***~ sth (up)on sb/sth, ~ sb/sth with sth,*** fill; load: *~ a plate with food; ~ favours upon a person; ~ a person with favours; a ~ed spoonful,* more than a level spoonful.

hear /hɪə(r)/ *vt,vi* (*pt,pp* **heard** /hɜd/) **1** [VP2A, 6A,18A,19A,24A] perceive (sound, etc) with the ears: *Deaf people cannot ~. I ~d someone laughing. He was ~d to groan. Did you ~ him go out? Have you ever ~d that song sung in Italian? We listened but could ~ nothing. She doesn't/can't ~ very well.* Note the frequent use of *can-could* when an effort of perception is implied. **2** [VP6A, 9,3A] be told or informed: *Have you ~d the news?*

I ~d that he was ill. I've ~d (say) that your country is beautiful. ***~ about sth,*** be given information about; learn about: *I've just ~d about his dismissal/illness. You will ~ about this later,* sometimes implying that there will be a rebuke, etc. ***~ from sb,*** receive a letter, news, etc: *How often do you ~ from your sister?* ***~ of sb/sth,*** have knowledge of: *I've never ~d of her/the place,* know nothing of her/the place. ***~ tell of,*** ~ people talking about: *I've often ~d tell of such happenings.* **3** [VP6A,10,15A,3A] listen to; pay attention to; (of a judge in a law court) try (a case): *You'd better ~ what they have to say. The court ~d the evidence. Which judge will ~ the case?* ***~ sb out,*** listen to the end: *Don't judge me before I've finished my explanation: ~ me out, please.* ***not ~ of,*** (usu with *will, would*) refuse to consider or allow: *I won't ~ of such a thing! She wouldn't ~ of it.* **4** **'H~! 'H~!** used as a form of cheering to express approval or agreement, but also ironically. **~er** *n* person who ~s, esp a member of an audience.

hear·ing /ˋhɪərɪŋ/ *n* **1** [U] perception by sound: *Her ~ is poor,* she is rather deaf. ***be hard of ~,*** deaf. **ˋ~-aid** *n* electronic device for helping deaf people to hear. **2** [U] distance within which one can hear: *In some countries it is unwise to talk about politics in the ~ of strangers,* where strangers may hear. ***within/out of ~,*** near enough/not near enough to hear or be heard: *Please keep within ~.* **3** [C] opportunity of being heard (esp in self-defence). ***ˋgain a ~,*** an opportunity to be heard. ***give sb/get a fair ~,*** an opportunity of being listened to impartially. **4** (legal) trial of a case at law, esp before a judge without a jury.

hearken /ˋhɑkən/ *vi* (liter) listen (*to*).

hear·say /ˋhɪəseɪ/ *n* [U] common talk; rumour; what one has heard another person or other persons say: *I don't believe it; it's merely ~. H~ evidence is not accepted in law courts.*

hearse /hɜs/ *n* carriage, car, for carrying a coffin at a funeral.

heart /hɑt/ *n* **1** that part of the body which pumps blood through the system: *When a man's ~ stops beating, he dies. He had a ˋ~ attack,* a sudden illness with irregular and violent beating of the ~. ⇨ the illus at **respiratory**. **2** centre of the emotions, esp love; deepest part of one's nature: *a man with a kind ~; a kind-~ed man.* ***sb after one's own ~,*** of the sort one very much likes or approves of. ***at ~,*** deep down; basically. ***have sth at ~,*** be deeply interested in it, anxious to support or encourage it. ***from (the bottom of) one's ~,*** sincerely. ***in one's ~ of ~s,*** in one's inmost feelings. ***to one's ~'s content,*** as much as, for as long as, etc one wishes. ***with all one's ~,*** completely and willingly: *I love you with all my ~.* ***~ and soul,*** completely: *I'm yours ~ and soul.* ***break a person's ~,*** make him very sad. Hence, **'broken-ˋ~ed** *adj* ***cry one's ~ out,*** pine or brood over sth, esp in secret. ***do one's ˋ~ good,*** cause one to feel encouraged, cheerful, etc. ***(get/learn/know sth) by ~,*** from memory. ***have a ~,*** show sympathy, understanding. ***(have) a change of ~,*** change that makes one a better person. ***have the ~ to,*** (usu *neg,* or *interr* with *can-could*) be hard-~ed or unsympathetic enough to: *How can you have the ~ to drown such darling little kittens?* ***have one's ~ in sth,*** be interested in it and fond of it. ***have one's ~ in one's boots,*** be greatly discouraged, feel hopeless. ***have one's ~ in one's mouth,*** be badly frightened. ***have one's ~ in the right place,*** have true or kind feelings. ***have one's ~ set on sth,*** desire greatly. ***lose ~,*** be discouraged. ***lose one's ~ to sb/sth,*** become very fond of; fall in love with. ***set one's ~ on sth/having sth/doing sth, etc,*** be bent on, very anxious (to have, to do, etc). ***take (fresh) ~ (at sth),*** be confident. ***take sth to ~,*** be much affected by it; grieve over it. ***wear one's ~ (up)on one's sleeve,*** show one's feelings quite openly. **3** central part: *in the ~ of the forest; the ~ of the matter,* the essence; *get to the ~ of a subject/mystery; a cabbage with a good solid ~.* **4** (of land) fertility: *in good ~,* in good condition; *out of ~,* in poor condition. **5** ~-shaped thing, esp the design used on playing-cards: *the ten/queen/etc of ~s. H~s are trumps.* ⇨ the illus at **heart**. **6** (as a term of endearment to a person) *dear ~; ˋsweet~.* **7** (compounds) **ˋ~-ache** *n* deep sorrow. **ˋ~-beat** *n* [C] movement of the ~ (about 70 beats a minute). **ˋ~('s)-blood** *n* life-blood; life. **ˋ~-break** *n* [U] overwhelming sorrow. **ˋ~-breaking** *adj* causing ~break. **ˋ~-broken** *adj* crushed by ~break. **ˋ~-burn** *n* burning sensation in the lower part of the chest, caused by indigestion. **ˋ~-burning** *n* [U] (and also in *pl*) envious, discontented feeling(s), usu caused by disappointment. **ˋ~-disease** *n* disease of the ~. **ˋ~-failure** *n* failure of the ~ to function. **ˋ~-felt** *adj* sincere: *~felt emotion/thanks.* **ˋ~-rending** *adj* causing deep grief. **ˋ~'s-ease** *n* (old name for) pansy. **ˋ~-sick** *adj* low-spirited. **ˋ~-strings** *n pl* deepest feelings of love: *play upon sb's ~strings,* touch his feelings. **'~-ˋwhole** *adj* unmoved by love (for one of the opposite sex). **~ed** *adj* in compounds: *ˋhard-~ed; ˋsad-~ed; ˋfaint-~ed,* lacking in courage. **~-less** *adj* unkind; without pity. **~-less-ly** *adv* **~-less-ness** *n: I've never known such ~lessness.*

hearten /ˋhɑtn/ *vt* [VP6A] give courage to; cheer: *~ing news.*

hearth /hɑθ/ *n* floor of a fireplace; (fig) fireside as representing the home: *fight for ~ and altar,* (rhet) in defence of one's home and religion. **ˋ~-rug** *n* rug spread out in front of the ~.

heart·ily /ˋhɑtɪlɪ/ *adv* **1** with goodwill, courage or appetite: *set to work ~; eat ~.* **2** very: *~ glad that...; ~ sick of this wet weather.*

hearty /ˋhɑtɪ/ *adj* (-ier, -iest) **1** (of feelings) sincere: *give sb a ~ welcome; give one's ~ approval/support to a plan.* **2** strong: in good health: *still hale and ~ at eighty-five.* **3** (of meals, appetites) big: *a ~ meal.*

heat[1] /hit/ *n* **1** [U] hotness: *the ~ of the sun's rays. Cold is the absence of ~. She's suffering from the ~,* from the hot weather. **'prickly ˋ~,** ⇨ **prickle**. **2** [U] (fig) intense feeling: *speak with considerable ~; in the ~ of the debate/argument.* **3** [C] competition the winners of which take part in (the further competitions leading to) the finals: *trial/preliminary ~s.* ⇨ also *dead ~,* at **dead(6)**. **4** [U] (of female mammals) period or condition of sexual excitement. ***be in/on/at ~.*** **5** (compounds) **ˋ~ barrier** *n* = thermal barrier, ⇨ **thermal**. **ˋ~-flash** *n* intense ~, e g as released from the explosion of an atomic bomb. **ˋ~ pump** *n* machine that transfers ~ from a relatively low temperature liquid, e g river water, to a higher temperature, e g for ~ing a building. **ˋ~ shield** *n* device (esp on the nose-cone of a spacecraft) that gives protection against excessive ~. **'~·spot** *n* mark or point on the skin with a feeling of ~ in it. **'~-stroke** *n* sudden illness, prostration, caused by excessive ~. **'~·wave** *n* unbroken period of unusually hot weather.

heat[2] /hit/ *vt,vi* [VP6A,15B,2C] ~ ***(up)***, make or become hot: ~ *(up) some water; ~ up the cold meat for supper; a ~ed discussion*, one during which feelings are roused; *get ~ed with wine*. **~-ed·ly** *adv* in a ~ed (= passionate) manner. **~er** *n* device for supplying warmth to a room, or for ~ing water, etc: *a 'gas-~er; an 'oil-~er.*

heath /hiθ/ *n* **1** [C] area of flat waste land, esp if covered with the shrubs called ~. **2** [C,U] (kinds of) low evergreen shrub with small purple, pink or white bell-shaped flowers, e g *ling* and *heather*.

hea·then /'hiðn/ *n* **1** [C] (*pl* without *s* when used with *def art*) believer in a religion other than the chief world religions: *The Saxons who invaded England in olden times were ~s. He went abroad to preach Christianity to the ~.* **2** [C] person whose morals, etc are disapproved of: *They've allowed their daughter to grow up as a young ~*, wild, ill-mannered, without moral training. **3** (attrib): *a ~ land; ~ customs.* **~·ish** /-ɪʃ/ *adj* of or like ~s; barbarous.

heather /'heðə(r)/ *n* [U] variety of heath(2), with small light-purple or white flowers, common in Scotland. ***take to the ~,*** (in olden times) become an outlaw. **'~-mixture** *n* (of cloth) of mixed colours supposed to be like ~.

heave /hiv/ *vt,vi* (*pt,pp* ~d or 6 and 7 below nautical use hove /həʊv/) **1** [VP6A] raise, lift up (sth heavy): ~ *the anchor.* **2** [VP6A] utter: ~ *a sigh/groan.* **3** [VP6A,15A,B] (colloq) lift and throw: ~ *sth overboard; ~ a brick through a window.* **4** [VP2A,C,3A] ~ ***(at/on sth)***, pull (*at* a rope, etc): ~ *(away) at the capstan. H~ away! H~ ho!* (sailors' cries when pulling at ropes or cables). **5** [VP2A] rise and fall regularly; move up and down: *the heaving billows*, i e waves. **6** [VP2C,15B] (of a sailing-ship) (cause to) come to a standstill (without anchoring or mooring): *The barque hove to.* **7** ~ ***in sight,*** become visible. □ *n* act of heaving: *with a mighty ~*, a strong pull or throw.

heaven /'hevn/ *n* **1** home of God and the saints: *die and go to ~.* **2** (usu with cap H) God, Providence: *It was the will of H~. H~ forbid! Thank H~ you were not killed.* Also in exclamations: *By H~! Good H~s!* **'~·sent** *adj* providential: *a ~sent opportunity.* **3** place, state, of supreme happiness. **4** (often *pl*) the firmament: *the broad expanse of ~/the ~s.* ***move ~ and earth,*** do one's utmost. **'~·ward** /-wəd/ *adj* **'~·wards** *adv* towards ~.

heav·en·ly /'hevnlɪ/ *adj* **1** of, from, like, heaven: *a ~ angel/vision.* **the ~ bodies,** i e the sun, moon, planets, etc. **the ~ city,** Paradise. **2** of more than earthly excellence. **3** (colloq) very pleasing: *What ~ peaches!*

Heavi·side layer /'hevɪsaɪd leɪə(r)/ ⇨ *ionosphere* at ion.

heavy /'hevɪ/ *adj* **(-ier, -iest) 1** having weight (esp great weight); difficult to lift, carry or move: *It's too ~ for me to lift. Lead is a ~ metal.* **'~-weight** *n* boxer weighing 175 lb (79·3 kg) or more. **2** of more than usual size, amount, force, etc: ~ *guns/artillery*, of the largest class: ~ (= abundant) *crops; ~ rain; ~ work; a ~ blow*, one with great force behind it; *a ~ fall*, one likely to cause shock; *a ~ heart*, made sad; ~ *tidings*, bad news; ~ *soil*, difficult to cultivate; ~ *roads*, muddy and sticky, difficult to travel over; *a ~ sky*, dark with clouds; *a ~ sea*, rough, with big waves; ~ *food*, rich, difficult to digest; ~ *bread*, dense, sticky, like dough. ***find sth ~ going,*** find progress difficult. ***find sb (rather) ~ going,*** difficult or boring to listen to or follow. **,~ 'hydrogen,** isotope of hydrogen with atoms twice the normal weight. **,~ 'water,** water whose molecules consist of two ~ hydrogen atoms and one ordinary oxygen atom. **3** (of persons) slow in speech or thought; (of writing or painting) dull, tedious; (of parts in a play for the theatre) serious or solemn; *play the part of the ~ father;* (of bodily states) inactive: ~ *with sleep/wine.* **4** (compounds) **,~-'handed** *adj* awkward, clumsy. **,~-'hearted** *adj* melancholy. □ *adv* heavily: *The crime lies ~ on his conscience. Do you ever find time hangs ~ on your hands*, Does it ever pass too slowly? **,~-'laden** *adj* carrying a ~ load; (fig) having a ~ (= sad) heart. **heav·ily** /'hevl̩ɪ/ *adv* in a ~ manner: *a heavily loaded lorry.* **heavi·ness** *n*

heb·doma·dal /heb'domədl/ *adj* weekly: *H~ Council*, one that meets weekly.

He·braic /hi'breɪɪk/ *adj* Hebrew.

He·brew /'hibru/ *n* **1** Israelite; Jew. **2** language used by the ancient ~s (as in the Old Testament); language now spoken by the people of Israel. □ *adj* of the ~ language or people.

heca·tomb /'hekətum/ *n* (in ancient Greece) great public sacrifice; blood-offering (esp of 100 oxen).

heck /hek/ *n* (sl, euphem) hell (used in exclamations): *What the ~!* I don't care! etc.

heckle /'hekl/ *vt* [VP6A] interrupt and ask many troublesome questions at a public meeting: ~ *the Socialist candidate.* **heck·ler** /'heklə(r)/ *n*

hec·tare /'hektɑ(r) *US:* -teər/ *n* measure of area in the metric system, 10 000 sq metres (= 2·471 acres).

hec·tic /'hektɪk/ *adj* **1** unnaturally red; feverish; consumptive: ~ *cheeks; a ~ colouring.* **2** (colloq) full of excitement and without rest: *have a ~ time; lead a ~ life; for one ~* (= exciting) *moment.*

hecto- /'hektəʊ/ *pref* (in comb) hundred: *'~gram(me)*, 100 grammes.

hec·tor /'hektə(r)/ *vt,vi* bully; bluster.

he'd /hid/ = he had; he would.

hedge /hedʒ/ *n* **1** row of bushes, shrubs or tall plants, etc usu cut level at the top, forming a boundary for a field, garden, etc: *a 'beech-~. Will this ~ keep the sheep in the field?* **'~-hop** *vi* fly (an aircraft) not much above ground level, e g when spraying crops. **'~·row** *n* row of bushes forming a ~. **'~-sparrow** *n* common GB and US bird. **2** (fig) means of defence against possible loss: *buy gold/diamonds as a ~ against inflation.* □ *vt,vi* **1** [VP6A,15A,B] put a ~ or (fig) barrier round: ~ *a field; ~ a person in/round with rules and regulations*, restrict his freedom of action. **2** [VP2A] refuse to commit oneself; avoid giving a direct answer to a question: *Answer 'yes' or 'no'—don't ~!* **3** [VP2A,6A] (colloq) secure oneself against loss, esp when betting, by compensating transactions: ~ *one's bets.* **4** [VP2A] make or trim ~s.

hedge·hog /'hedʒhog *US:* -hɔg/ *n* insect-eating animal covered with spines, that rolls itself up into a ball to defend itself. ⇨ the illus at small.

he·don·ism /ˈhidənɪzm/ *n* [U] belief that pleasure is the chief good. **he·don·ist** /-ɪst/ *n* believer in ~. **he·don·is·tic** /ˌhidəˈnɪstɪk/ *adv*

heed /hid/ *vt* [VP6A] pay attention to: *~ a warning; ~ what a person says.* □ *n* [U] ***pay/give/take (no) ~ (of sb/sth),*** pay, etc (no) attention, notice: *pay no ~ to a warning.* **~·ful** /-fl/ *adj*: *be more ~ful of advice.* **~·less** *adj*: *~less of danger.*

hee·haw /ˈhihɔ/ *n* ass's bray; loud laugh.

heel¹ /hil/ *n* **1** back part of the human foot; part of a sock, stocking, etc covering this; part of a shoe, boot, etc supporting this. ⇨ the illus at leg. ***at ~, at/(up)on sb's ~s,*** close behind: *Famine often follows on the ~s of war. The thief ran off with an angry crowd at his ~s.* ***down at ~,*** (of shoes) with the ~s badly worn down; (of a person) wearing such shoes, or untidy and slovenly in appearance. ***under the ~ of,*** (fig) crushed by: *under the ~ of a cruel invader.* ***head over ~s,*** (rarely ***~s over head,***) upside down, in a somersault. ***come to ~,*** (of a dog) come, walk, close behind its master, under control; (fig, of a person) submit to discipline and control. ***kick/cool one's ~s,*** be kept waiting. ***kick up one's ~s,*** behave excitedly (esp to show joy at freedom). ***lay sb by the ~s,*** confine or imprison him. ***take to one's ~s,*** (less usu ***show a clean pair of ~s***), run away. ***turn on one's ~,*** turn sharply round. **2** (US sl) cad; low-down person. □ *vt* [VP6A] put a ~ on: *sole and ~ a pair of shoes.* **ˈwell-ˈ~ed** *adj* (sl) very rich.

heel² /hil/ *vi,vt* [VP2A,C,15B] ***~ over,*** (of a ship) (cause to) lean over to one side.

hef·ty /ˈheftɪ/ *adj* (-ier, -iest) (colloq) big and strong: *a ~ farm worker.*

he·gem·ony /hiˈgemənɪ *US:* hɪˈdʒemənɪ/ *n* (*pl* -nies) (formal) leadership, esp of one state in a group of states.

He·gira, He·jira /hɪˈdʒɑɪərə/ *n* Muhammad's flight from Mecca to Medina; Muslim era reckoned from this (AD 622).

heifer /ˈhefə(r)/ *n* young cow that has not yet had a calf.

heigh·ho /ˈheɪˈhəʊ/ *int* used to express disappointment, boredom, etc.

height /hɑɪt/ *n* **1** measurement from bottom to top; distance to the top of sth from a level, esp sea-level: *the ~ of a mountain. What is your ~,* How tall are you? *He is six feet in ~.* **2** high place: *on the mountain ~s.* **3** utmost degree: *the ~ of his ambition; dressed in the ~ of fashion. The storm was at its ~.*

heighten /ˈhɑɪtn/ *vt,vi* [VP6A,2A] make or become high(er); make greater in degree: *~ a person's anger; ~ an effect; her ~ed colour,* the increased colour in her face, e g caused by emotion.

hei·nous /ˈheɪnəs/ *adj* (of crime) odious; atrocious. **~·ly** *adv* **~·ness** *n*

heir /eə(r)/ *n* person with the legal right to receive a title, property, etc when the owner dies: *The eldest son is usually the ~. He is ~ to a large fortune. Who is ~ to the throne?* **ˈ~ apˈparent** *n* (*pl* ~s apparent) ~ whose right cannot be superseded by the birth of a nearer ~. **ˈ~ preˈsumptive** *n* whose right of inheritance may be lost by the birth of a nearer ~. **~ess** /ˈeəres/ *n* female ~.

heir·loom /ˈeəlum/ *n* sth handed down in a family for several generations.

He·jira /hɪˈdʒɑɪərə/ *n* = Hegira.

held /held/ *pt,pp* of hold.

heli·cop·ter /ˈhelɪkoptə(r)/ *n* kind of aircraft with horizontal revolving blades or rotors, able to take off and land in a very small space and remain stationary in the air.

a helicopter

he·lio·graph /ˈhilɪəgrɑf *US:* -græf/ *n* apparatus formerly used for sending signals by reflecting flashes of sunlight. □ *vt* send (a message) by ~.

he·lio·trope /ˈhilɪətrəʊp/ *n* [U] plant with small, sweet-smelling purple flowers; colour of these.

heli·port /ˈhelɪpɔt/ *n* airport for helicopters.

he·lium /ˈhilɪəm/ *n* light, colourless gas (symbol **He**) that does not burn, used in balloons and airships.

hell /hel/ *n* **1** (in some religions) place of punishment after death. **2** place, condition, of great suffering or misery: *suffer ~ on earth; make sb's life a ~. We gave the enemy ~.* **gambling ~,** place where gambling takes place regularly, esp if this causes ruin, misery, etc. **3** (colloq, in exclamations, to express anger, or to intensify a meaning) *H~! What the ~ do you want? He ran like ~,* very fast. *I like him a ~ of a lot. What a ~ of a noise!* ***for the ~ of it,*** for no particular reason. ***ride ~ for leather,*** as quickly as possible. **ˈ~-cat** *n* spiteful or furious woman. **~·ish** /-ɪʃ/ *adj* horrible; devilish. ***be ˈ~-ˈbent on,*** (US sl) recklessly bent in sth, doing sth.

he'll /hil/ = he will, he shall.

Hel·lene /ˈhelin/ *n* subject of modern Greece; person of genuine Greek race in ancient times. **Hel·lenic** /heˈlinɪk *US:* heˈlenɪk/ *adj* of the Greeks, their arts, culture, etc.

hello /heˈləʊ/ *int* = hallo.

helm¹ /helm/ *n* handle (also called *tiller*) or wheel for moving the rudder of a boat or ship: *the man at the ~,* the steersman; *the ~ of state,* (fig) the government of the nation. **~s·man** /-mən/ *n* (*pl* -men) man at the ~.

helm² /helm/ *n* (archaic) helmet.

hel·met /ˈhelmɪt/ *n* protective head-covering worn by soldiers, firemen, miners, motorbike riders, divers (as part of a diving-suit), and some policemen. ⇨ the illus at armour. ⇨ also *sun-~* at sun. **~ed** *adj* wearing, provided with, a ~.

helot /ˈhelət/ *n* one of a class of slaves in ancient Sparta; (fig) member of any social class that is despised and kept in subjection.

help¹ /help/ *n* **1** [U] act of ~ing: *Thank you for your kind ~.* ***be of (some/no/much) ~ (to sb),*** be ~ful: *Can I be of any ~ to you? It wasn't (of) much ~,* didn't ~ much. **2** (*sing* with *indef art*) sb or sth that ~s: *Your advice was a great ~. Far from being a ~ to me, you're a hindrance.* **3** [U] remedy: *There's no ~ for it,* it can't be ~ed. ⇨ help²(3). **4** [C] (orig US) (usu non-resident) girl or woman who ~s with the housework: *a new lady ~; a home ~.* ⇨ home¹(3). *The ~ hasn't come this morning.* **~·ful** /-fl/ *adj* giving ~; *be ~ful to one's friends.* **~·fully** /-flɪ/ *adv* **~·ful·ness** *n* **~·less** *adj* **1** without ~; not receiving ~. **2** unable to ~ oneself; dependent upon others: *a ~less invalid; as ~less as a baby.* **~·less·ly** *adv* **~er** *n* person who ~s. **~·ing** *n* (esp) portion of food served at a meal: *three ~ings of pie; a generous ~ing of pudding.*

help² /help/ *vt,vi* **1** [VP6A,17A,18B,15A,B,2A,C] do part of the work of another person; make it easier for (sb) to do sth or for (sth) to happen; do sth for the benefit of (sb in need): *I can't lift this box alone, please ~ me. I ~ed him (to) find his things.* (The omission of *to* is more usual in US than in GB usage.) *Please ~ me up/down/out, etc with this heavy trunk,* ~ me to carry it up, etc. *Will you ~ me on with my overcoat, please,* ~ me to put it on? *We ~ed the injured man off with his clothes,* ~ed him to get them off. *Tom has to ~ his father, who is too old to work. Would it ~ you to know that…,* if I told you that…. **~ *out,*** give ~ (esp in a crisis). **2** [VP6A,14] ***~ sb/oneself (to sth),*** serve with food, drink, etc: *May I ~ you to some more meat? H~ yourself to the fruit/cigarettes. Here's a spoon to ~ the gravy with.* **3** [VP6A,C] ***can/can't/could(n't) ~ doing sth,*** avoid; refrain; prevent: *Don't tell him more than you can ~,* more than you must. *I can't ~ his being so foolish,* It's not my fault, I can't prevent his foolish behaviour: *I can't ~ thinking he's still alive. She burst out crying; she couldn't ~ herself. I can't ~ my husband having so many dull relations. It can't be ~ed,* is inevitable. **4** ***So ~ me God,*** (in an oath) (since I speak the truth, etc) may God ~ me.

help·mate /ˈhelpmeɪt/, **help·meet** /ˈhelpmit/ *nn* helpful partner, esp a wife or husband.

hel·ter-skel·ter /ˌheltə ˈskeltə(r)/ *adv* in disorderly haste. □ *n* tall slide¹(2) in a fairground, etc.

helve /helv/ *n* handle of a tool, esp an axe.

hem¹ /hem/ *n* border or edge of cloth, esp one on an article of clothing, when turned and sewn down. **ˈhemming-stitch** *n* style of sewing hems on dresses, skirts, etc by joining the turned edge to the length of material using diagonal stitches. **ˈhem·line** *n* (esp) lower edge of a skirt or dress: *lower/raise the hemline,* make a skirt, etc longer/shorter. □ *vt* (-mm-) **1** [VP6A] make a hem on: *hem a handkerchief.* **2** [VP15B] ***hem about/around/in,*** enclose; confine; surround: *hemmed in by the enemy.*

hem² (also **h'm**) /hem, hm/ *int* sound used to indicate doubt or sarcasm, or to call attention. □ *vi* (-mm-) make this sound; hesitate in speech.

he·ma·tite (also **hæ-**) /ˈhemətaɪt/ *n* iron oxide (Fe_2O_3) the main ore of iron.

hemi·sphere /ˈhemɪsfɪə(r)/ *n* half a sphere; half the earth. **the Northern/Southern ~,** north/south of the equator. **the Eastern ~,** Europe, Asia, Africa and Australia. **the Western ~,** N and S America.

hem·lock /ˈhemlok/ *n* plant with finely divided leaves and small, white flowers, from which a poison is made. **ˈ~ spruce** *n* evergreen tree, common in America and Asia, valuable for its timber.

he·mo·glo·bin (also **hæ-**) /ˌhiməˈgləʊbɪn/ *n* [U] colouring matter of the red corpuscles of the blood.

he·mo·philia (also **hæ-**) /ˌhiməˈfɪlɪə/ *n* [U] (usu hereditary) tendency of blood (from a wound, etc) not to clot, so that bleeding continues. **he·mo·phil·iac** (also **hæ-**) /ˌhiməˈfɪlɪæk/ *n* person having ~.

hem·or·rhage (also **hæm-**) /ˈhemərɪdʒ/ *n* [U] bleeding; [C] escape of blood.

hem·or·rhoids (also **hæm-**) /ˈhemərɔɪdz/ *n pl* swelling of a vein or veins, esp at or near the anus; piles.

hemp /hemp/ *n* [U] (kinds of) plant from which coarse fibres are obtained for the manufacture of rope and cloth. **(Indian) ~,** narcotic from the flowering tops, seed and resin of such plants, e g *bhang, cannabis, hashish, marijuana.* **~en** /ˈhempən/ *adj* made of ~; like ~: *a ~en rope.*

hem·stitch /ˈhemstɪtʃ/ *vt, n* (ornament the hem of a handkerchief, dress, skirt, towel, etc with a) decorative stitch made by pulling out some of the threads and tying the cross-threads in groups.

hen /hen/ *n* **1** female of the common domestic fowl. ⇨ cock¹(1). ⇨ the illus at fowl. **ˈhen·bane** *n* (narcotic obtained from a) poisonous plant. **ˈhen-coop** *n* coop for keeping poultry in. **ˈhen-house** *n* (usu wooden) building for poultry. **ˈhen-party** *n* (colloq) party for women only. ⇨ stag party. **ˈhen-pecked** *adj* (of a man) ruled by his wife. **ˈhen-roost** *n* place where fowls roost at night. **2** female (of the bird named): *ˈguinea-hen, ˈpea-hen.*

hence /hens/ *adv* **1** from here; from now: *a week ~,* in a week's time. **2** for this reason. **ˌ~ˈforth** /-ˈfɔθ/, **ˌ~ˈforward** /-ˈfɔwəd/ *advv* from this time on; in future.

hench·man /ˈhentʃmən/ *n* (*pl* -men /-mən/) faithful supporter, esp a political supporter who obeys without question the orders of his leader: *the Dictator and his henchmen.*

henna /ˈhenə/ *n* [U] (plant, kind of Egyptian privet, producing) reddish-brown dye stuff for colouring leather, the finger-nails, the hair, etc. **hen·naed** /ˈhenəd/ *adj* dyed with ~.

hep /hep/ *n* ⇨ hip⁴.

hepa·ti·tis /ˌhepəˈtaɪtɪs/ *n* [U] inflammation of the liver.

hep·ta·gon /ˈheptəgən *US:* -gon/ *n* plane figure with 7 (esp equal) sides.

her /*usu form:* ɜ(r) *strong form:* hɜ(r)/ *pers pron* (as an object, corresponding to *she*): *She's in the garden; I can see her. Give her the book.* □ *poss adj* belonging to her: *Mary's mother is dead but her father is alive. That's her hat, not yours.* **hers** /hɜz/ *poss pron* belonging to her: *Is that his or hers? I've borrowed a book of hers,* one of her books.

her·ald /ˈherld/ *n* **1** (historical) person making public announcements for, and carrying messages from, a ruler. **2** person or thing foretelling the coming of sb or sth: *In England the cuckoo is a ~ of spring.* **3** official who keeps records of families that have coats of arms. **H~s' College,** corporation that records pedigrees and grants coats of arms. **4** (as a newspaper title) messenger. □ *vt* [VP6A] proclaim the approach of. **her·al·dic** /heˈrældɪk/ *adj* of ~s or ~ry. **~ry** *n* [U] science dealing with the coats of arms, descent, and history of old families.

herb /hɜb *US:* ɜb/ *n* low-growing, soft-stemmed plant which dies down at the end of the growing season; plant of this kind whose leaves or seeds, because of their scent or flavour, are used in medicine or for flavouring food, e g sage, mint, dill. **~ beer** *n* drink made from ~s. **~·age** /-ɪdʒ/ *n* [U] ~s collectively; grass and other field plants. **~al** /ˈhɜbl *US:* ˋɜbl/ *adj* of (esp) medicinal ~s: *~al remedies.* **~·al·ist** /ˈhɜblɪst *US:* ˋɜb-/ *n* person who grows or sells ~s for medical use. **her·bivor·ous** /hɜˋbɪvərəs/ *adj* (of animals) feeding on ~age. ⇨ *carnivorous* at **carnivore.**

her·ba·ceous /hɜˋbeɪʃəs/ *adj* (of plants) having stems that are not woody: *a ~ border,* (in a garden) border with plants which come up and flower year after year (not shrubs, annuals, etc).

her·cu·lean /ˈhɜkjʊˋliən/ *adj* having, needing, great powers of body or mind.

herd /hɜd/ *n* **1** number or company of animals, esp cattle, feeding or going about together: *a ~ of cattle/deer/elephants.* **2** (chiefly in compounds) keeper of a ~: *ˋcow~; ˋgoat~.* **3** (derog) *the common/vulgar ~,* the mass of common people; *the ~ instinct,* the instinct to act, feel, think, etc like the mass of people, and to be with the mass. □ *vi,vt* [VP2C,15A,B] (cause to) gather into a ~ or as in a ~; look after a ~: *people who ~ed/were ~ed together like cattle.* **~s·man** /-mən/ *n* (*pl* **-men**) keeper of a ~.

here /hɪə(r)/ *adv* **1** in, at, to this point of place: *Come ~. I live ~. Put the box ~. Look ~.* **2** (with front position, and inversion of the subject and finite *v* if the subject is a *n,* but not if the subject is a *pers pron*): *H~ comes the bus! H~ it comes! H~ are the others! H~ they/we are! H~'s something interesting. H~ you are/it is!* H~ is what you asked for, are looking for, etc according to context. **3** at this point (in a series of events, in a process, etc): *H~ he stopped reading and looked up. H~ the speaker paused to have a drink.* ***H~ goes!*** Now I'm going to make a start, have a go. **4** (after *preps*): *Come over ~,* near to where I am. *Do you live near ~,* near this place? **5** ***~ and there,*** in various places. ***~, there and everywhere,*** in all parts; all round. ***neither ~ nor there,*** (colloq) not to the point; irrelevant. **6** (used after a *n* to call attention, or for emphasis): *My friend ~ was a witness of the accident.* **7** (used when drinking to sb's health, wishing success to an enterprise, etc): *H~'s to the bride and bridegroom!* **~·abouts** /ˈhɪərəˋbaʊts/ *adv* near or about ~. **~·after** /hɪərˋɑftə(r) *US:* -ˋæf-/ *adv, n* (in the) future; the life to come. **~·by** /hɪəˋbɑɪ/ *adv* (legal) by means or by reason of this. **~·in** /ˈhɪərˋɪn/ *adv* (legal) in this. **~of** /hɪərˋov/ *adv* (legal) of or about this. **~·to·(fore)** /ˈhɪətuˋfɔ(r)/ *adv* (legal or archaic) until now; formerly. **~·upon** /ˈhɪərəˋpon/ *adv* (formal) at this point; in consequence of this. **~·with** /ˈhɪəˋwɪð *US:* -wɪθ/ *adv* (comm) with this.

her·edita·ment /ˈherɪˋdɪtəmənt/ *n* (legal) property that can be inherited.

her·edi·tary /hɪˋredɪtrɪ *US:* -terɪ/ *adj* passed on from parent to child, from one generation to following generations: *~ rulers/beliefs/diseases.*

her·ed·ity /hɪˋredətɪ/ *n* [U] tendency of living things to pass their characteristics on to offspring, etc: characteristics, qualities, etc so passed on: *~ factors/genes.*

her·esy /ˈherəsɪ/ *n* (*pl* **-sies**) [C,U] (holding of a) belief or opinion contrary to what is generally accepted, esp in religion: *fall into ~; be guilty of ~; the heresies of the Protestants.* **her·etic** /ˈherətɪk/ *n* person guilty of ~ or supporting a ~; person who holds an unorthodox opinion. **her·eti·cal** /hɪˋretɪkl/ *adj* of ~ of heretics: *heretical beliefs.*

heri·table /ˈherɪtəbl/ *adj* (legal) capable of inheriting or being inherited.

heri·tage /ˈherɪtɪdʒ/ *n* that which has been or may be inherited.

her·maph·ro·dite /hɜˋmæfrədɑɪt/ *n* [C] animal or other creature, e g an earthworm, which has both male and female sexual organs or characteristics.

her·metic /hɜˋmetɪk/ *adj* completely air-tight: *a ~ seal.* **her·meti·cally** /-klɪ/ *adv: ~ally sealed,* sealed so as to keep all the air in or out.

her·mit /ˈhɜmɪt/ *n* person (esp man in early Christian times) living alone. **~·age** /-ɪdʒ/ *n* cell or living-place of a ~ or groups of ~s.

her·nia /ˈhɜnɪə/ *n* [U] rupture, esp one caused by a part of the bowel being pushed through a weak point of the muscle wall of the abdomen.

hero /ˈhɪərəʊ/ *n* (*pl* **-roes** /-rəʊz/) **1** boy or man respected for bravery or noble qualities. **2** chief man in a poem, story, play, etc. **her·oine** /ˈherəʊɪn/ *n* female. **~ism** /ˈherəʊɪzm/ *n* [U] quality of being a ~; courage.

her·oic /hɪˋrəʊɪk/ *adj* **1** of, like, fit for, a hero: *~ deeds/tasks; use ~ remedies,* hazardous remedies but worth trying. **2** of a size larger than life: *a statue of ~ size/on a ~ scale.* **3** of poetry dealing with heroes. **ˈ~ ˋverse,** lines of ten syllables and five stresses, rhyming in pairs. **4** (of language) grand; attempting great things; (hence) **her·oics** *n pl* high-flown or high-sounding talk or sentiments. **he·roi·cally** /-klɪ/ *adv*

her·oin /ˈherəʊɪn/ *n* narcotic drug prepared from morphine, used medically to cause sleep or relieve pain, and used by drug addicts.

heron /ˈherən/ *n* long-legged water-bird living in marshy places. ⇨ the illus at **water.** **~ry** *n* (*pl* **-ries**) place where ~s breed.

Herr /heə(r)/ *n* (*pl* **Herren** /ˈherən/) German equivalent of *Mr;* German gentleman.

her·ring /ˈherɪŋ/ *n* (*pl* often unchanged) seafish, usu swimming in immense shoals, valued as food (fresh, salted, or dried). ⇨ the illus at **fish.** **ˋ~-bone** *n* pattern (like the spine and bones of a ~) used for stitching, designs on cloth, etc. **ˈred ˋ~,** ⇨ **red(3).**

hers /hɜz/ ⇨ **her.**

her·self /*usu form:* ɜˋself; *strong form:* hɜ-/ *reflex, emph pron* **1** (reflex) *She hurt ~. She ought to be ashamed of ~.* ***(all) by ~,*** **(a)** alone. **(b)** without help: *Can she do it by ~ or does she need help?* **2** (emph) *She ~ told me the news. She told me the news ~. I saw Mrs Smith ~,* i e not one of her family, one of her staff, etc. **3** *She's not quite ~ today,* not in her normal state of health or mind. *She has come to ~,* is now in her normal mental state. Cf *She has come to,* has regained consciousness.

hertz /hɜts/ *n* (symbol **Hz**) unit of frequency equal to one cycle per second.

Hertz·ian /hɜtsɪən/ *adj* **~ waves,** electromagnetic waves as used in radio.

he's /ɪz, iz; *strong form:* hiz/ = he is, he has.

hesi·tant /ˈhezɪtənt/ *adj* tending or inclined to hesitate. **~·ly** *adv* **hes·i·tance** /-əns/, **hes·i·tancy** /-ənsɪ/ *nn* state or quality of being ~.

hesi·tate /ˈhezɪteɪt/ *vi* [VP2A,3A,B,4C] show signs of uncertainty or unwillingness in speech or action: *He's still hesitating about joining/about* *whether to join the expedition. He ~s at nothing. I ~ to spend so much money on clothes. He ~d (about) what to do next.* **hesi·tat·ing·ly** *adv*

hesi·ta·tion /ˈhezɪˋteɪʃn/ *n* [U] state of hesitating; [C] instance of hesitating: *She agreed without the slightest ~. I have no ~ in stating that...; There's no room for ~. His doubts and ~s were tiresome.*

Hes·perus /ˋhespərəs/ *n* the evening star.

hes·sian /ˋhesɪən *US:* ˋheʃn/ *n* **1** [U] strong, coarse cloth of hemp or jute; sack-cloth. **2** (19th c) type of high boot.

het·ero·dox /ˋhetərədoks/ *adj* not orthodox. **~y** /-sɪ/ *n* opposite of orthodoxy.

het·ero·gen·eous /ˈhetərəˋdʒinɪəs/ *adj* different; unlike; made up of different kinds: *the ~ population of the USA,* of many different races. ⇨ homogeneous.

het·ero·sex·ual /ˈhetərəˋsekʃʊəl/ *adj* normally sexual; attracted to/by the opposite sex.

het-up /ˈhet ˋʌp/ *adj* excited; over-wrought.

heu·ris·tic /hjʊəˋrɪstɪk/ *adj* of the theory in education that a learner should discover things for himself. **~s** *n* method of solving problems by inductive reasoning, by evaluating past experience and moving by trial and error to a solution.

hew /hju/ *vt,vi* (*pt* **hewed**, *pp* **hewed** or **hewn** /hjun/) [VP6A,15A,B,2A,C] **1** cut (by striking or chopping); aim cutting blows (*at, among*): *hew down a branch. He hewed his enemy to pieces,* e g with his sword. **2** shape by chopping: *hewn timber,* roughly shaped by hewing. **3** make by hard work: *hew one's way through dense jungle,* cut out and beat a path; *hew out a career for oneself.* **hewer** *n* person who hews, esp a man who cuts out coal in a mine: *hewers of wood and drawers of water,* persons doing hard menial work. (⇨ Joshua 9: 21.)

hexa·gon /ˋheksəgən *US:* -gon/ *n* plane figure with 6 (esp equal) sides. **hex·ag·onal** /heksˋægənl/ *adj* six-sided.

hex·am·eter /heksˋæmɪtə(r)/ *n* (kinds of) line of verse (esp Gk or Lat) with six feet.

hey /heɪ/ *int* used to call attention, or to express surprise or interrogation. **ˈHey ˋpresto!** conjuror's phrase used to announce the completion of a trick.

hey-day /ˋheɪ deɪ/ *n* (*sing* only) time of greatest prosperity or power: *in the ~ of youth. The 19th century was the ~ of steam railways.*

hi /hɑɪ/ *int* **1** = hey. **2** (esp US) = hallo.

hi·atus /hɑɪˋeɪtəs/ *n* (*pl* **-ses** /-sɪz/) gap in a series, making it incomplete.

hi·ber·nate /ˋhɑɪbəneɪt/ *vi* [VP2A] (of some animals) pass the whole of the winter in a state like sleep. **hi·ber·na·tion** /ˈhɑɪbəˋneɪʃn/ *n*

Hi·ber·nian /hɑɪˋbɜnɪən/ *adj* of Ireland; Irish.

hi·bis·cus /hɪˋbɪskəs/ *n* [U] cultivated plant or shrub with brightly coloured flowers (chiefly in the tropics). ⇨ the illus at flower.

hic·cup, hic·cough /ˋhɪkʌp/ *vt, n* (have a) sudden stopping of the breath with a cough-like sound; (*pl*) an attack of ~s: *have the ~s.*

hick /hɪk/ *n* (sl; derog) countrymen; yokel.

hick·ory /ˋhɪkərɪ/ *n* (*pl* **-ries**) (hard wood of a) N American tree with edible nuts.

hid, hidden ⇨ hide[1].

hide[1] /hɑɪd/ *vt,vi* (*pt* **hid** /hɪd/, *pp* **hidden** /ˋhɪdn/ or **hid**) **1** [VP6A,14] **~ *(from),*** put or keep (sb, sth, oneself) out of sight; prevent from being seen, found or known: *Quick, ~ yourself! The sun was hidden by the clouds. The future is hidden from us. She tried to ~ her feelings. His words had a hidden meaning.* **2** [VP2A] be or become hidden: *You had better ~. Where is he hiding?* **~-and-seek** /ˈhæɪd n ˋsik/ *n* children's game in which one child ~s and others try to find him (or her). □ *n* (US = *blind*) place where wild animals, birds, etc may be observed, e g by photographers, without alarming them. **ˋ~-out/-away** *nn* (colloq) hiding-place: *a guerrilla ~-out in the mountains.* **hid·ing** *n* [U] (used of persons) ***be in/go into hiding,*** be hidden/~ oneself. ***come out of hiding,*** show oneself. **ˋhiding-place** *n* place where sb or sth is or could be hidden.

hide[2] /hɑɪd/ *n* **1** [C] animal's skin, esp as an article of commerce and manufacture. **2** (colloq) human skin. ***save one's ~,*** save oneself from a beating, from punishment. ***tan sb's ~,*** give him a beating. **hid·ing** *n* [C] beating; thrashing: *give sb/get a good hiding.*

hide·bound /ˋhɑɪdbaʊnd/ *adj* narrow-minded; having, showing, too much respect for rules and traditions.

hid·eous /ˋhɪdɪəs/ *adj* very ugly; filling the mind with horror; frightful: *a ~ face/crime/noise.* **~·ly** *adv*

hie /hɑɪ/ *vi* (archaic, or joc) go quickly (*to*).

hi·er·archy /ˋhɑɪərɑkɪ/ *n* (*pl* **-chies**) [C] organization with grades of authority from lowest to highest: *the ~ of the Civil Service;* (esp) organized priesthood.

hi·ero·glyph /ˋhɑɪərəglɪf/ *n* picture or figure of an object, representing a word, syllable or sound, as used in the writing of the ancient Egyptians and Mexicans; other secret or unintelligible written symbol. **~ic** /ˈhɑɪərəˋglɪfɪk/ *adj* of, written in, ~s. **~·ics** *n* ~s.

hieroglyphics

hi-fi /ˈhɑɪ ˋfɑɪ/ *adj* (colloq abbr of) high fidelity. ⇨ high[1](12).

hig·gledy-pig·gledy /ˈhɪgldɪ ˋpɪgldɪ/ *adj, adv* mixed up; without order.

high[1] /hɑɪ/ *adj* (**-er, -est**) (For combinations of ~ and *nn, participles,* etc with meanings not at once to be identified from the meanings in the definitions, ⇨ 12 below. **1** extending far upwards; measuring (the distance given) from the base to the top. (Note that *tall* is used for human beings and for a few things which have great height in relation to breadth, e g *a tall building/tower*): *There was an aeroplane ~ in the sky. How ~ is Mt Everest?* ***~ and dry,*** **(a)** (of a ship) stranded; aground; out of the water. **(b)** (fig) abandoned; isolated; out of the current of events. ***be/get on one's ~ horse,*** ⇨ horse(1). ***(do sth) with a ~ hand,*** arrogantly (*high-handed(ly)* is preferred). **2** chief; important: *a ~ official; a ~ caste; the ~ altar,* in a church; *the Most H~,* (in the Bible) God; *~ society,* upper classes. ***~ and low,*** all classes of society. **3** (of sounds) at or near the top of the scale; shrill; sharp: *speak in a ~ tone/key.* **4** extreme; tense; great: *~ prices/temperatures; bought at a ~ cost; a ~ wind; in ~ favour; have a ~ opinion of sb; in ~ spirits; ~* (= angry) *words; in ~ latitudes,* near the Poles; *have a ~* (=

joyous) *time;* ~ (= luxurious) *living;* ~ *noon/summer*, at or near its peak. **5** ˋ~ **time,** time when sth should be done at once: *It's* ~ *time you started,* You should start at once. *It's* ~ *time to go,* We must go at once. **6** noble; virtuous: *a woman of* ~ *character;* ~ *aims/ideals; a* ~ *calling,* e g that of a priest, doctor or nurse. **7 H~ Church,** that section of the C of E that gives an important place to the authority of bishops and priests, to ritual and the sacraments. Hence, **H~ Churchman. 8** (of food, esp meat and game) slightly tainted. **9** (colloq) intoxicated. **10** (sl) under the influence of hallucinatory drugs: *The hippies were* ~ *on marijuana.* **11** (as *n*) ~ level: *from (on)* ~, from Heaven. *Shares* (i e on the Stock Exchange) *reached a new* ~ (= the ~est recorded level) *last month.* **12** (compounds) **ˋ~-ball** *n* (US) whisky with soda water or ginger ale, served with ice in a tall glass. **ˋ~·born** *adj* of noble birth. **ˋ~·brow** *n, adj* (person) with tastes and interests considered to be superior (often used contemptuously for *intellectual*): ~ *drama/music.* **ˋ~·chair** *n* one on ~ legs for an infant at table, or a baby's chair with a hinged tray attached to it. **ˈH~ ˋChurch** *n* ⇨ 7 above. **ˈ~-ˋclass** *adj* first-class. **ˈ~ ˋcolour** *n* reddish complexion. **ˈH~ Comˋmissioner** *n* representative of one Commonwealth country in another, equivalent to an ambassador. **ˋH~ Court** *n* supreme court of justice. **ˋ~ day** *n* festival (only in): *~days and holidays.* **ˋ~er-ups** *n pl* (colloq) persons ~er in rank or status. **ˈ~ exˋplosive** *n* very powerful explosive, e g TNT. **ˈ~-faˋlutin'** *adj* (colloq) ridiculously pompous, bombastic or pretentious: ~ *falutin' ideas/language.* **ˈ~-fiˋdelity** *adj* (abbr **hi-fi**) (of radios, records, tapes and equipment for reproducing sound) giving faithful reproduction by the use of a wide range of sound waves. **ˈ~ˋ·flier/·flyer** *n* ambitious person who goes to great extremes to get what he aims at. **ˈ~·ˋflown** *adj* exalted; bombastic and pretentious: *a ~flown style,* e g of writing. **ˈ~·ˋflying** *adj* (fig) (of persons) ambitious. **ˈ~-ˋfrequency** *n* (abbr **h f**) radio frequency between 3 and 30 megacycles per second. **H~ German** *n* literary German; standard spoken German. **ˋ~-grade** *adj* of ~ or superior quality. **ˈ~-ˋhanded** *adj* domineering; using power or authority without consideration for the feelings of others. **ˈ~-ˋhanded·ly** *adv* **ˈ~ ˋhat** *adj, n* snobbish (person). □ *vt* treat (sb) in a snobbish or condescending way. **ˋ~·jack** *vt* (variant spelling of) hijack. **ˋ~ jinks,** ⇨ jinks. **ˋ~ jump** *n* athletic contest for jumping over an adjustable horizontal bar: *enter for/win the* ~ *jump.* ***be for the* ~ *jump,*** (sl) due to be hanged (for murder). **ˈ~-ˋkeyed** *adj* (⇨ 3 above) having a ~ pitch; (fig) easily excited or made nervous. **~·land** /-lənd/ *n* mountainous region; (*pl*) mountainous parts of a country (esp **The H~lands,** those of N W Scotland). **ˈH~land ˋfling** *n* Scottish reel³. **ˋ~·lander** *n* one who lives in the H~ lands; soldier in a (Scottish) H~land regiment. **ˋ~-level** *adj* (attrib only) (of conferences, etc) of persons in ~ position, e g in government, commerce. **ˋ~ life** *n* **(a)** fashionable and luxurious style of living. **(b)** (in W Africa) popular kind of music and dance. **ˋ~·light** *n* (usu *pl*) luminous area on a photograph, picture, etc which shows reflected light; reflection of light on a shiny object; (fig) most conspicuous or prominent part: *the ~lights of the week's events.* □ *vt* give prominence or emphasis to. **ˈH~ ˋMass** *n* (R C Church) ⇨ Mass². **ˈ~-ˋminded** /ˋmaɪndɪd/ *adj* of morally ~ character; having ~ ideals or principles. Hence, **ˈ~-ˋminded·ly** *adv* **ˈ~-ˋminded·ness** *n* **ˈ~-ˋnecked** *adj* (of a dress) with the neckline cut ~. **ˈ~-ˋoctane** *adj* having a ~ octane number. ⇨ **octane. ˈ~-ˋpitched** *adj* **(a)** (of sounds) shrill. **(b)** (of roofs) having a steep slope. **ˈ~-ˋpowered** *adj* having, using, great power: *a ~-powered salesman,* aggressive in selling his goods. **ˈ~-ˋpressure** *n* pressure ~er than normal, esp ~er than atmospheric pressure; (fig) aggressive and persistent: *~-pressure salesmanship.* **ˈ~-ˋpriced** *adj* expensive. **ˈ~ ˋpriest** *n* chief priest. **ˈ~-ˋprincipled** *adj* honourable. **ˋ~-ranking** *adj* (of officers, etc) having ~ rank. **ˈ~ reˋlief** *n* ⇨ relief²(1). **ˋ~-rise** *adj* (attrib only) used of tall buildings with many storeys or levels, reached by lifts (elevators): *~-rise flats.* ⇨ *tower-block* at tower. **ˋ~·road** *n* main road; (fig) most direct way: *Is there a ~road to happiness?* **ˋH~ School** *n* secondary school giving more advanced education than primary or elementary schools. **ˈ~ ˋseas** *n pl* (with *def art*) all parts of the seas and oceans beyond territorial waters. **ˋ~-sounding** *adj* (of style) impressively pretentious. **ˈ~-speed** *adj* (able to be) operated at very fast speeds. **ˈ~-ˋspirited** *adj* having a courageous spirit; lively; (of a horse) frisky. **ˋ~ spot** *n* outstanding feature, memory, event, etc. **ˋ~ street,** (esp in proper names) main street of a town: *There are three banks in the* ~ *street.* **ˈ~ ˋtable** *n* table (on a dais) where senior members (fellows, dons) of a college dine. **ˈ~ ˋtea** *n* (GB) early evening meal (or late tea) in homes where dinner is not eaten in the evening, usu with meat or fish. **ˈ~-ˋtension** *adj* (electr) (of wires) having a ~ voltage. **ˈ~ ˋtide** *n* (time at which the) tide is at its ~est level. **ˋ~ time** *n* ⇨ 5 above. **ˋ~-toned** *adj* socially or intellectually superior: *a ~-toned finishing school for girls.* **ˈ~ ˋtreason** *n* treason against the State or a sovereign. **ˋ~-up** *n* (colloq) person of ~ rank or great importance. **ˈ~ ˋwater** *n* ~ tide. **ˈ~-ˋwater mark** *n* mark showing the ~est reached by the tide (or any body of water); (fig) ~est point of achievement. **ˋ~·way** *n* main public road; main route (by air, sea or land); (fig) easiest or most direct way. **~·way·man** /-mən/ *n* (*pl* -men) (formerly) man (usu on horseback) who robbed travellers on ~ways by using, or threatening to use, violence.

high² /haɪ/ *adv* in or to a ~ degree: *climb* ~; *aim* ~ (liter and fig); *pay* ~, pay a ~ price; *play* ~, play a card of ~ value, e g an ace; *live* ~, on rich, luxurious food and drink. ***fly* ~,** (fig) have great ambitions. ***hold one's head* ~,** proudly. ***run* ~, (a)** (of the sea) have a strong current with a ~ tide. **(b)** (of the feelings) be excited: *Popular feelings/passions ran* ~, were strong. ***search/hunt/look* ~ *and low (for sth),*** look everywhere (for it).

high·ly /ˋhaɪlɪ/ *adv* in or to a high degree: *a* ~ *paid official; a* ~ *amusing film;* ~ (= nobly) *descended; think* ~ *of sb,* have a high opinion of him; *speak* ~ *of sb,* praise him.

high·ness /ˋhaɪnəs/ *n* **1** [U] (opposite of *lowness*) state or quality of being high: *the* ~ *of his character/aims.* **2** title used of and to British and various foreign princes: *His/Her/Your/Royal/Imperial H~.*

hi·jack (also **high·jack**) /ˋhaɪdʒæk/ *vt* [VP6A] **1**

steal goods from, e g a lorry, by stopping it in transit. **2** rob (a vehicle of goods) in this way. **3** use force, or the threat of force, against those in control of (an aircraft or vehicle) in order to achieve certain aims or to reach a desired destination. **~er** *n*

hike /haɪk/ *vi, n* (colloq) (go for a) long walk in the country, taken for pleasure or exercise. **hiker,** one who ~s. ⇨ **hitch-hike.**

hil·ari·ous /hɪˋleərɪəs/ *adj* noisily merry. **~·ly** *adv* **hil·ar·ity** /hɪˋlærətɪ/ *n* [U] noisy merriment; loud laughter.

Hil·ary /ˋhɪlərɪ/ *n* ˋ**~ term,** legal or university term beginning in January.

hill /hɪl/ *n* **1** natural elevation on the earth's surface, lower than a mountain. ˋ**~·side** *n* side of a ~. **2** slope, e g on a road: *The cyclists had to push their machines up the steep ~.* **3** heap of earth: *ˋant-~s; ˋmole-~s.* **~y** *adj* (**-ier, -iest**) having many ~s: *~y country; a ~y road.*

hill-billy /ˋhɪl bɪlɪ/ *n* (*pl* **-lies**) (colloq, often used derog) farmer, farm-worker, etc from the mountains in the S E of the US; (attrib) of these people: *~ music.*

hill·ock /ˋhɪlək/ *n* small hill(**1**).

hilt /hɪlt/ *n* handle of a sword or dagger. ***(up) to the ~,*** completely: *His guilt was proved to the ~. She's in debt up to the ~.*

him /*usu form:* ɪm; *strong form:* hɪm/ *pers pron* used as object form of *he*: *Mr Smith is in town; I saw him yesterday. Give him the money. That's him,* (colloq) That's he.

him·self /*usu form:* ɪmˋself; *strong form:* hɪm-/ *reflex, emph pron* **1** (reflex) *He cut ~. He ought to be ashamed of ~.* ***(all) by ~,*** **(a)** alone. **(b)** without help. **2** (emph) *He ~ says so. He says so ~. Did you see the manager ~?* **3** *He's not quite ~ today,* not in his normal state of health or mind.

hind[1] /haɪnd/ *adj* (of things in pairs, front and back; cf *fore*) at the back: *the ~ legs of a horse.* ˈ**~ ˋquarters** *n pl* ~ legs and loin of the carcass of lamb, mutton, beef, etc. **~·most** /-məʊst/ *adj* farthest behind or back. **~·sight** /-saɪt/ *n* [U] perception of an event after its occurrence.

hind[2] /haɪnd/ *n* female of (esp the red) deer.

hin·der /ˋhɪndə(r)/ *vt* [VP6A,C,15A] obstruct; delay; get in the way of: *Don't ~ me in my work. I was ~ed from getting here earlier. I have much business that has ~ed my answering your letter.*

hin·drance /ˋhɪndrns/ *n* [C] sth or sb that hinders: *You are more of a ~ than a help.*

Hindi /ˋhɪndɪ/ *n, adj* (vernacular language) of N India (one of the official languages).

Hindu /ˈhɪnˋdu *US:* ˋhɪndu/ *n* person, esp of N India, whose religion is Hinduism. □ *adj* of the ~s. **Hin·du·ism** /-ɪzm/ *n* a religion, philosophy and culture characterized by elaborate ritual, an ordained caste system, belief in reincarnation and by the desire for freedom from temporal(**2**) evil.

Hindu·stani /ˈhɪndʊˋstɑnɪ/ *n* language widely used in India (Hindi with an admixture of Urdu and other languages).

hinge /hɪndʒ/ *n* joint on which a lid, door or gate turns or swings; (fig) central principle on which sth depends: *Take the door off its ~s and rehang it.* □ *vt, vi* **1** [VP6A] support, attach with, a ~ or ~s. **2** [VP3A] **~ *(up)on,*** turn or depend on: *Everything ~s (up) on what happens next.*

hint /hɪnt/ *n* [C] slight or indirect indication or suggestion: *She gave him a ~ that she would like him to leave. I know how to take a ~,* quickly realize and do what is suggested. *H~s for housewives,* (e g as the title of an article giving) suggestions that will help housewives. □ *vt, vi* **1** [VP9,6A] **~ *(to sb),*** suggest indirectly: give a ~: *I ~ed that he ought to work harder. He ~ed to me nothing of his intentions.* **2** [VP3A] **~ at,** refer indirectly to: *He ~ed at my imprudence.*

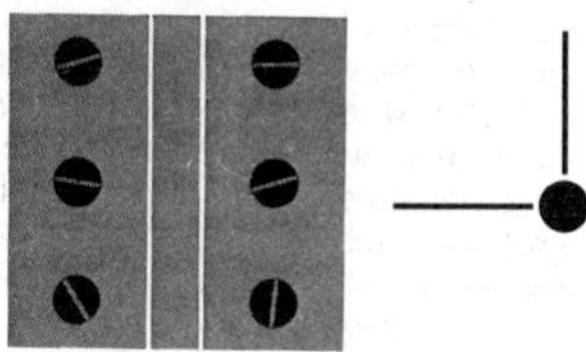
hinges

hin·ter·land /ˋhɪntəlænd/ *n* parts of a country behind the coast or a river's banks.

hip[1] /hɪp/ *n* part on either side where the bone of a person's leg is joined to the trunk: *He stood there with his hands on his hips.* ⇨ the illus at **trunk.** ˋ**hip-bath** *n* small tub in which one can sit immersed up to the hips. ˋ**hip-flask** *n* small flask (for brandy, etc) to be carried in the hip-pocket. ˈ**hip-ˋpocket** *n* pocket (in a pair of trousers) on the hip.

hip[2] /hɪp/ *n* fruit (red when ripe) of the wild rose.

hip[3] /hɪp/ *int* (only in) ˈ***Hip, hip, hurˋrah!*** cry, cheer, of satisfaction or approval.

hip[4] /hɪp/ *adj* (also **hep** /hep/) (sl) aware of, in keeping with, advanced trends.

hip·pie, hippy /ˋhɪpɪ/ *n* (*pl* **-pies**) (late 1960's) person who rejects established social conventions and institutions and expresses his personality by unusual styles of dress, living habits, etc.

hippo /ˋhɪpəʊ/ *n* (*pl* **-pos** /-pəʊz/) (colloq abbr of) hippopotamus.

Hip·po·cratic /ˈhɪpəˋkrætɪk/ *adj* ˈ**~ ˋoath,** oath to observe the medical code of ethical and professional behaviour, sworn by entrants to the profession.

hip·po·drome /ˋhɪpədrəʊm/ *n* place for horse- or chariot-races in ancient Greece and Rome; (modern use) open space or building for circuses or horse-riding displays; (formerly) theatre providing variety(**5**) entertainment.

hip·po·pota·mus /ˈhɪpəˋpɒtəməs/ *n* (*pl* **-ses** /-sɪz/ or **-mi** /maɪ/) large, thick-skinned African river animal.

hip·ster /ˋhɪpstə(r)/ *n* one who is hip(**4**). □ *adj* (attrib) *~ trousers,* held (usu) by a belt at the hips (not at the waist).

hire /ˋhaɪə(r)/ *vt* [VP6A,15B] **~ *(out),*** obtain or allow the use or services of in return for fixed payment: *~ a horse/a concert-hall; ~ out boats; ~d troops* (in olden times, mercenaries); (US) *a ~d girl/woman,* (term formerly used for) a domestic servant (now *lady-help*). Cf *rent a house* and *hire a concert-hall,* i e for a special occasion. □ *n* [U] (money paid for) hiring: *bicycles on ~, 50p an hour; pay for the ~ of a hall; work for ~.* ***(pay for/buy sth) on ~ purchase,*** (abbr *H P*) (buy by a) contract to pay by instalments, and the right to use it after the first payment. **~·ling** /ˋhaɪəlɪŋ/ *n* (derog) person whose services may be ~d.

hir·sute /ˋhɜsjut *US:* -sut/ *adj* hairy; rough; shaggy (e g of a man with untidy long hair and beard).

his /*usu form:* ɪz *strong form:* hɪz/ *adj, pron* /hɪz/

belonging to him: *He hurt his hand. That book is his, not yours. Are you a friend of his?*

hiss /hɪs/ *vi,vt* **1** [VP2A] make the sound /s/, or the noise heard when water falls on a very hot surface: *The snake raised its head and ~ed. The steam escaped with a ~ing sound.* **2** [VP6A,15A,3A] ***~ off, ~ at,*** show disapproval by making this sound: *~ an actor off the stage; ~ (at) a new play.* □ *n* [C] ~ing sound: *The speaker was received with a mixture of applause and ~es.*

hist /hɪst/ *int* (archaic) used to call attention, or to ask for silence (in order to listen for sth).

his·tor·ian /hɪˋstɔrɪən/ *n* writer of history.

his·toric /hɪˋstorɪk *US:* -ˋstɔr-/ *adj* **1** notable or memorable in history; associated with past times: *a(n) ~ spot/event/speech.* ***~ times,*** of which the history is known and recorded (contrasted with *prehistoric times*). **2** (gram) ***the ~ present,*** simple present tense used for events in the past (to make the description more vivid).

his·tori·cal /hɪˋstorɪkl *US:* -ˋstɔr-/ *adj* **1** belonging or pertaining to history (as contrasted with legend and fiction): *~ events and people,* real, not imaginary; *a(n) ~ novel/play/film/painting, etc,* one dealing with real events in history. **2** having to do with history: *~ studies; the ~ method of investigation.* **~ly** /-klɪ/ *adv*

his·tory /ˋhɪstrɪ/ *n* (*pl* -ries) **1** [C] branch of knowledge dealing with past events, political, social, economic, of a country, continent or the world: *a student of ~.* ***make ~,*** do sth which will be recorded in ~. **ˋancient ~,** to A D 476, when the Western Roman Empire was destroyed. **ˋmedieval ~,** to 1453, when Constantinople was taken by the Turks. **ˋmodern ~,** since 1453. **2** [C] orderly description of past events: *a new ~ of Europe.* **3** [C] train of events connected with a person or thing; interesting or eventful past career: *a house with a strange ~; the inner ~ of the Dreyfus affair.* **4 natural ~,** systematic account of natural phenomena.

his·tri·onic /ˈhɪstrɪˋonɪk/ *adj* **1** of drama, the theatre, acting: *~ ability.* **2** theatrical; insincere. **his·tri·on·ics** *n pl* **1** theatrical performances. **2** dramatic or theatrical manners, behaviour, etc, esp when exaggerated to create an effect.

hit /hɪt/ *vt,vi* (-tt-; *pt,pp* hit) **1** [VP6A,15A,12C] give a blow or stroke to; strike (a target, an object aimed at); come against (sth) with force: *hit a man on the head; be hit by a falling stone; hit sb a hard blow; hit the mark/target; hit a ball over the fence. He hit his forehead against the kerb when he fell.* ***hit a man when he's down, hit a man below the belt,*** act contrary to the rules of boxing; (fig) take an unfair advantage. ***hit it, hit the nail on the head,*** guess right; say or do exactly the right thing. ***hit one's fancy,*** (more usu *take one's fancy*) appeal to one's fancy. ***hit it off (with sb/ together),*** agree, get on well: *They hit it off well.* **ˈhit-and-ˋrun** *attrib adj* (of a road accident) in which a pedestrian or vehicle is hit by a vehicle which does not stop; of an aircraft: *a hit-and-run raider.* **2** ***hit sb hard,*** cause him to suffer: *The slump hit his business hard. He was hard hit by his financial losses. He has fallen in love and is hard hit.* **3** [VP6A] go to; find; reach: *hit the right path,* find it during a journey. ***hit the headlines,*** (colloq, of news) be printed prominently in the headlines (because sensational, etc). ***hit the road,*** set out on the road. **4** [VP2C] strike: *Hit hard!* ***hit out (against),*** strike vigorously; (fig) attack strongly: *The Minister hit out against trade union leaders.* **5** [VP3A] ***hit (up)on,*** find by chance or unexpectedly: *hit upon an idea/the right answer/a plan for making money.* **6** [VP15B] ***hit sth/sb off,*** (colloq) describe briefly and accurately (in words); make a quick sketch of. **7** [VP6A] (cricket) score: *He quickly hit 60 runs.* □ *n* **1** blow; stroke: *three hits and five misses; a clever hit.* **2** successful attempt or performance: *hit songs, ˋsong hits,* songs that win wide popularity; *a lucky hit. The new play is quite a hit,* has been welcomed by the public. **ˋhit parade** *n* list of top selling popular records. **3** stroke of sarcasm, etc: *That was a hit at me,* the words were directed against me.

hitch /hɪtʃ/ *vt,vi* **1** [VP6A,15B] ***~ sth up,*** pull up with a quick movement: *~ up one's trousers.* **2** [VP15A,2C] fasten, become fastened, on or to a hook, etc, or with a loop of rope, etc: *~ a horse to a fence; ~ a rope round a bough of a tree. Her dress ~ed on a nail.* **3** [VP6A] ***~ a ride,*** (colloq) ask a driver for a ride. ⇨ **hitch-hike.** □ *n* **1** sudden pull or push. **2** kind of noose or knot used by sailors. **3** temporary stoppage or impediment: *Everything went off without a ~,* quite smoothly, without difficulty: *The blast-off was delayed by a technical ~.*

hitch·hike /ˋhɪtʃhaɪk/ *vi* [VP2A] get a free ride by asking for one (from the driver of a car, lorry, etc). ⇨ **thumb(2). hitch·hiker** *n*

hither /ˋhɪðə(r)/ *adv* (old use) here. **~·to** /ˈhɪðəˋtu/ *adv* until now.

hive /haɪv/ *n* **1** box (of wood, straw, etc) for bees to live in; the bees living in a ~. **2** place full of busy people: *What a ~ of industry!* □ *vt,vi* **1** [VP6A] cause (bees) to go into a ~: *~ a swarm;* (of bees) store (honey) in a ~. **2** [VP2C] enter a ~; live close together as bees do. ***~ off (from),*** (fig) become a separate (and perhaps self-governing) body (as when a colony of bees leaves a ~ and forms a new ~); separate and make independent (a part of an organization): *~ off parts of the nationalized steel industry.*

hives /haɪvz/ *n pl* skin disease with red patches and itching.

h'm /hm/ ⇨ **hem²**.

ho /həʊ/ *int* expressing surprise, admiration, etc.

hoar /hɔ(r)/ *adj* (of hair) grey or white with age; (of a person) having such hair. **ˋ~·frost** *n* [U] white frost; frozen dew on grass, the surface of leaves, roofs, etc.

hoard /ˋhɔd/ *n* carefully saved and guarded store of money, food or other treasured objects; collection of coins, valuable objects, etc dug up, e g one dating from Saxon times in GB: *a miser's ~; a squirrel's ~ of nuts.* □ *vt,vi* [VP6A,15B] ***~ (up),*** save and store: *~ gold; ~ up treasure.* **~er** *n* person who ~s.

hoard·ing /ˋhɔdɪŋ/ *n* (US = *billboard*) (often temporary) fence of boards round waste land, building work, etc, frequently used for posting advertisements.

hoarse /hɔs/ *adj* (of the voice) rough and harsh; (of a person) having a ~ voice: *He shouted himself ~.* **~·ly** *adv* **~·ness** *n*

hoary /ˋhɔrɪ/ *adj* (-ier, -iest) grey or white with age; very old: *the ~ ruins of English abbeys.* **hoari·ness** *n*

hoax /həʊks/ *n* [C] mischievous trick played on sb for a joke. □ *vt* [VP6A,14] deceive (sb) in this way:

~ *sb into believing or doing sth foolish.* **~er** *n*

hob /hob/ *n* flat metal shelf at the side of a fireplace (with a surface level with the top of the grate) where pots and pans can be kept warm or a kettle boiled.

hobble /ˋhobl/ *vi,vt* **1** [VP2A,C] walk as when lame, or as when the feet or legs are impeded: *The old man ~d along with the aid of his stick.* **2** [VP6A] tie two legs of a horse or donkey to prevent it from going far away. □ *n* stumbling or limping way of walking. **ˋ~-skirt** *n* (1910—14) very narrow skirt which caused the wearer to walk with short steps.

hobby /ˋhobɪ/ *n* (*pl* **-bies**) [C] occupation, not one's regular business, for one's leisure time, e g stamp-collecting, growing roses.

hobby·horse /ˋhobɪhɔs/ *n* [C] wooden horse on rockers as a child's toy, or on a merry-go-round; long stick with a horse's head; figure of a horse (in wickerwork) fastened to a dancer (in the morris-dance): *Now he's started on his ~,* (fig) started on his favourite subject.

hob·gob·lin /hobˋgoblɪn/ *n* [C] mischievous imp; ugly and evil spirit.

hob·nail /ˋhobneɪl/ *n* short nail with a heavy head used for the soles of heavy shoes and boots, e g for mountain-climbing. **~ed** *adj* (of boots, etc) set with ~s.

hob·nob /hobˋnob/ *vi* (**-bb-**) [VP2A,C,3A] ~ ***with sb/together,*** have friendly talk, drink (with/together): *Mrs Green, happily ~bing with the great.*

hobo /ˋhəʊbəʊ/ *n* (*pl* **-bos, -boes** /-bəʊz/) (US, sl) unemployed worker who wanders from place to place; vagrant.

Hob·son's choice /ˈhobsnz ˋtʃɔɪs/ *n* ⇨ **choice**.

hock[1] /hok/ *n* middle joint of an animal's hind leg.

hock[2] /hok/ *n* [U] (kinds of) German white wine.

hock[3] /hok/ *vt* (sl) [VP6A] pawn. □ *n* ***in ~,*** pawned.

hockey /ˋhokɪ/ *n* [U] **ˋfield ~,** game played with sticks on a field by two teams of eleven players each and a ball. **ˋice ~,** game played on ice by two teams of six players each wearing skates and with sticks and a rubber disc (a *puck*). **ˋ~ stick,** long curved or angled stick used to hit the ball or puck.

ho·cus-po·cus /ˈhəʊkəs ˋpəʊkəs/ *n* [U] talk, behaviour, designed to draw one's attention away from sth; deception.

hod /hod/ *n* light open box with a long handle used by workmen for carrying bricks, etc on the shoulder.

hoe /həʊ/ *n* tool for loosening the soil, uprooting weeds among growing crops, etc. ⇨ the illus at tool. ***Dutch hoe,*** the kind pushed forward by the user. □ *vt,vi* (*pt,pp* **hoed**) [VP6A,15B,2A] work with a hoe: *hoeing up weeds.*

hog /hog *US:* hɔg/ *n* castrated male pig reared for meat. ⇨ **boar(2), sow**[1]; (fig) greedy, dirty, selfish person. **ˋhog·wash** *n* swill(2); (fig) nonsense; rubbish (esp of sth said or written). ***go the whole hog,*** do sth thoroughly. □ *vt* [VP6A] take more than one's fair share of; take greedily and selfishly. **hog·gish** /-ɪʃ/ *adj* greedy and selfish.

Hog·ma·nay /ˋhogmәneɪ/ *n* (Scotland) New Year's Eve (and its festivities).

hogs·head /ˋhogzhed *US:* ˋhɔg-/ *n* large barrel for beer; liquid measure (52½ gallons in GB or about 238·5 litres, 62 gallons in US or about 234·5 litres).

hoi pol·loi /ˈhɔɪ ˋpolɔɪ *US:* pəˋlɔɪ/ *n* **the ~,** (pej) the masses; the rabble.

hoist /hɔɪst/ *vt* [VP6A,15B] lift with an apparatus of ropes and pulleys or a kind of elevator: *~ a flag/sail; ~ casks and crates aboard; ~ in the boats,* raise them from the water up to the deck. □ *n* apparatus for ~ing: *an ammunition ~* (on a warship); (colloq) push up: *give sb a ~,* e g when he is climbing a wall.

hoity-toity /ˈhɔɪtɪ ˋtɔɪtɪ/ *adj* (colloq) supercilious and haughty. □ *int* used to a ~ person to express disapproval of him or her.

hold[1] /həʊld/ *vt,vi* (*pt,pp* **held** /held) (For uses with *adverbial particles* and *preps,* ⇨ **14** below.) **1** [VP6A,15A,B] have or keep in one's possession, keep fast or steady, in or with the hand(s), arm(s) or other part of the body, e g the teeth, or with a tool: *The girl was ~ing her father's hand. They held hands/held each other's hands. She held me by the sleeve. She was ~ing up an umbrella. He held the knife in his teeth as he climbed the tree.* ***~ the line,*** keep a telephone connection (e g whilst the person at the other end goes away to find sth or sb). ⇨ also **baby, brief**[2]**(1), pistol. 2** [VP6A, 15A,B] restrain; keep back; control: *The police held back the crowd. It took three of us to ~ the madman. Try to ~ the thief until the police arrive. He held his attacker at arm's length. The dam gave way; it was not strong enough to ~ the flood waters.* ***~ one's breath,*** e g from excitement or fear: *The watchers held their breath as the acrobat crossed the tightrope.* ***~ one's hand,*** refrain from, delay, action, e g punishing sb. ***~ one's tongue/peace,*** be quiet. ***There to be no ~ing,*** It is impossible to restrain or control: *There was no ~ing her,* e g because she was so determined or high-spirited. **3** [VP15A,B,2C] keep or maintain sb/sth in a specified position, manner, attitude or relationship: *H~ your head up. H~ your arms up/out. H~ yourself* (= Be still) *for a moment while I take your photograph.* ***~ oneself in readiness (for),*** be prepared (for sth, an

field hockey

ice hockey

emergency). **~ one's sides with laughter,** laugh heartily. **4** [VP6A] maintain a grip of: *This new car ~s the road well/has good road-~ing qualities,* is stable, e g when cornering at speed. **5** [VP6A] support; bear the weight of: *This nail won't ~ such a heavy mirror. Come down—that branch won't ~ you!* **6** [VP6A] be filled by; have the capacity to contain or accommodate: *Will this suitcase ~ all your clothes? This barrel ~s 25 litres. What does the future ~ for us? He ~s* (= has) *strange views on this question.* **~ sth in one's head,** retain, not forget, e g a mass of details, statistics. **(not) ~ water,** (not) be sound, valid, logical: *Your argument doesn't ~ water.* **7** [VP6A,22] keep the interest or attention of: *The speaker held his audience spellbound.* **8** [VP9, 15A,B,22,25] consider; regard; believe; affirm: *~ a man to be a fool/~ that he is foolish; ~ the view that a plan is/~ a plan to be impracticable. The President is not held in great respect. He does not ~ himself responsible for his wife's debts.* **~ sb in high/low esteem,** have a high/low regard for him. **~ sth dear/cheap,** place a high/low value on it: *He ~s his reputation dear.* **9** [VP6A] defend; keep possession of: *They held the fort against all attacks.* **~ the fort,** (fig) be in charge during sb's absence: *Jane had to ~ the fort* (be in charge of the house) *while her mother was in hospital.* **~ one's ground,** stand firm, not retreat: *Our soldiers held their ground bravely.* **~ one's ground/own,** (fig) not give way: *The patient is still ~ing his own,* maintaining his strength. *Mr Green held his own,* e g in a debate, maintained his position (by arguing well). **10** [VP6A] be the legal owner or possessor of: *~ shares/stock.* ⇨ *land~er* at land[1](6), *share~er* at share[1](3), *stock~er* at stock[1](5). **11** [VP6A] occupy; have the position of: *The Social Democrats held office then.* Hence, **'office-~er. 12** [VP6A] have; conduct; cause to take place: *~ a meeting/debate/examination. We ~ a General Election every four or five years. The Motor Show is usually held in October.* **~ court,** (fig) entertain, welcome, admirers: *a film-star ~ing court at London Airport.* ⇨ court[1](2). **13** [VP2A,D] remain unbroken, unchanged, secure, under strain, pressure, etc. ⇨ 5 above: *How long will the anchor ~,* stay fast in the sea bed? *How long will this fine weather ~,* continue? ⇨ break[1](5). *The argument still ~s (good/true),* is still valid. **14** [VP15B,3A,2C,14] (uses with *adverbial particles* and *preps;* for non-idiomatic uses ⇨ 1,2,3 above):

hold sth against sb, allow sth to influence one's opinions adversely: *Don't ~ his criminal convictions against him.*

hold (oneself) aloof, ⇨ aloof.

hold back, hesitate; show unwillingness: *Buyers are ~ing back,* making few or no offers. *When danger came, no one held back.* **~ sb/sth back,** **(a)** ⇨ 2 above. **(b)** hinder the progress of: *His poor education is ~ing him back.* **(c)** keep secret or to oneself: *~ back information.*

hold sb/sth down, **(a)** ⇨ 3 above. **(b)** hinder control; keep down or under: *rulers who ~ the people down,* oppress them. *We must ~* (= keep) *prices down.* **~ a job down,** (colloq) keep it by proving one's capabilities.

hold forth, speak rather pompously, as if in public. **~ sth forth,** (*~ sth out,* below is preferred) offer; propose.

hold sth in, check; restrain: *~ in one's temper; ~ oneself in,* control one's feelings, e g of indignation.

hold off, **(a)** remain at a distance: *The storm held off. Will the rain ~ off until after the picnic?* **(b)** delay action: *H~ off for a minute.* **~ sb/sth off,** keep at a distance: *H~ your dog off! His cold manner ~s* (better *keeps*) *people off,* deters them from trying to be friendly.

hold on, **(a)** stand firm when there is danger, difficulty, etc: *How much longer do they think we can ~ on?* **(b)** (usu imper) stop: *H~ on a minute!* Not so fast! Don't go further in what you're doing. **~ on to,** **(a)** keep one's grips on; not let go: *~ on to one's hat on a windy day. The boy held on to the bush until someone climbed down the cliff to rescue him.* **(b)** not give up the ownership of: *You should ~ on to your oil shares.* **~ sth on,** keep in position: *These bolts and nuts ~ the wheels on.*

hold out, **(a)** maintain resistance; not give way: *How long can we ~ out against these attacks?* **(b)** last: *How long will our food supplies ~ out? I can't ~ out* (= retain my urine) *much longer—I must find a loo.* **~ out for,** refuse compromise: *The workers are still ~ing out for higher wages,* insisting on being granted their demands. **~ out on,** refuse to deal with: *He's still ~ing out on me,* still opposing my wishes, refusing my request. **~ sb/sth out,** **(a)** ⇨ 3 above. **(b)** offer: *The doctors ~ out little hope of recovery.*

hold sth over, defer; postpone; adjourn: *The matter was held over until the next meeting.* **~ sth over sth,** use sth as a threat: *He's ~ing my past record over me.*

hold to sth, **(a)** remain loyal or steadfast to: *He held to his convictions/choice/course of action.* **(b)** keep to: *The ship held to a Southerly course.* **~ sb to sth,** make sb keep, e g a promise: *We must ~ the contractors to their estimates,* not allow them to exceed them. **~ sb (up) to ransom,** demand money by threatening penalties, etc; blackmail: *Those strikers were not ~ing the country (up) to ransom.* ⇨ ransom.

hold together, **(a)** be and continue whole: *The bodywork of this old car hardly ~s together,* is falling apart, e g from rust. **(b)** remain united: *We Tories always ~ together in times of crisis.* **~ sb/sth together,** cause to remain together; united: *The country needs a leader who will ~ the nation together.*

hold sb/sth up, **(a)** ⇨ 1,2 above. **(b)** delay: *They were held up by fog/the immigration authorities.* **(c)** stop by the use or threat of force, for the purpose of robbery: *The travellers were held up by bandits.* Hence, **'~-up** *n*: *a ~-up on the Underground,* e g by a power failure; *a bank ~-up,* e g one by armed robbers. **(d)** put forward as an example: *Don't ~ me up as a model husband.* **~ sb up to derision/scorn/ridicule,** expose him to derision, etc.

hold with sth, approve of: *Do you ~ with nudity on the stage?*

hold[2] /həʊld/ *n* **1** [C,U] act, manner, power of holding. **catch/get/take/lay/seize ~ of sth. let go/lose (one's) ~ of sth**: *He has a great ~* (= influence) *over his younger brother. How long can the Government keep its ~ over the district,* keep the district under control? **2** [C] sth that may be used for holding on to: *The rock face afforded few ~s to climbers.* ⇨ *foothold* at foot[1](8). **3** (boxing and wrestling) (kinds of) grip: *all-in wrestling, with no ~s barred.*

hold³ /həʊld/ *n* part of a ship below deck, where cargo is stored.

hold-all /ˈhəʊld ɔl/ *n* portable bag or case large enough to hold clothes, etc when travelling. ⇨ hold¹(6).

holder /ˈhəʊldə(r)/ *n* person or thing that holds: *a ˈpen-~; a ˈcigarette-~; an ˈoffice-~; a ˈkettle-~* cloth for handling a hot kettle.

hold·ing /ˈhəʊldɪŋ/ *n* sth held or owned; land or the owning of land. **ˈsmall-~s,** small areas of land farmed by the tenant himself. **a ˈ~ company,** one formed to hold the shares of subsidiary companies.

hold-up /ˈhəʊld ʌp/ *n* ⇨ hold¹(14).

hole /həʊl/ *n* **1** opening or hollow place in a solid body: *a ~ in a tooth; roads full of ~s; ~s in the walls and roof of a building, caused by shell fire; wear one's socks into ~s,* wear them until there are ~s. ***make a ~ in,*** use a large amount of: *The hospital bills made a large ~ in his savings.* ***pick ~s in,*** find fault with, e g an argument. ***a square peg in a round ~,*** person not fitted for the position he occupies. **2** (colloq) awkward situation: *I'm in rather a ~. You've put me in a devil of a ~.* **3** animal's burrow: *a mouse's ~; the ~ of a fox;* (fig) small, dark, wretched place; den; hiding-place: *What a wretched little ~ he lives in!* **ˈ~-and-ˈcorner,** (colloq, attrib) secret; underhand: *We don't like these ~-and-corner methods.* **4** (golf) hollow into which the ball must be hit; point scored by a player who gets his ball from one ~ to another with the fewest strokes: *a ˈnine-~ golf course; win the first ~.* □ *vt,vi* **1** [VP6A] make a ~ or ~s in or through: *~ a ship,* e g by striking a rock. **2** [VP6A,15B,2C] get (a ball) into a ~ (in golf, etc): *~ out in one,* get the ball from the tee into the ~ with only one stroke.

holi·day /ˈholədɪ *US:* -deɪ/ *n* **1** day of rest from work: *Sunday is a ~ in Christian countries; Friday is a ~ in Muslim countries.* ⇨ also *bank ~* at bank³(1). **2** (often *pl*) (US = *vacation*) period of rest from work: *the school ~s; the Christmas ~s; take a month's ~ in summer;* (attrib) *ˈ~ camps.* ***on ~,*** having a ~: *Our typist is away on ~ this week.* **ˈ~-maker** *n* person on ~.

holi·ness /ˈhəʊlɪnəs/ *n* **1** being holy or sacred. **2 His/Your H~,** title used of (to) the Pope.

hol·land /ˈholənd/ *n* **1** [U] strong, coarse linen or cotton cloth. **2** (*pl*) spirit made from grain, a kind of gin.

hol·ler /ˈholə(r)/ *vi,vt* (sl) yell (to indicate excitement, etc): *Stop ~ing—nobody's going to hurt you!*

hollo /ˈholəʊ/ *int* (archaic) cry used to call attention. □ *vi,vt* (also **hol·loa**) shout, esp to hounds (during a fox-hunt).

hol·low /ˈholəʊ/ *adj* **1** not solid; with a hole or empty space inside: *a ~ tree; a ~ ball.* **2** (of sounds) as if coming from sth ~: *a ~ voice/groan.* **3** (fig) unreal; false; insincere: *~ sympathy/words/promises; a ~ laugh; ~ joys and pleasures,* not giving true happiness; *a ~ victory,* one without real value. **4** sunken: *~ cheeks; ˈ~-ˈeyed.* **5** (colloq, as *adv*) ***beat sb ~,*** completely. □ *n* hole; ~ place: *a ~ in the ground;* small valley: *a wooded ~,* small valley with trees. □ *vt* [VP6A,15A,B] make a ~ or ~s in; bend into a ~ shape: *river banks ~ed out by rushing water.*

holly /ˈholɪ/ *n* [U] evergreen shrub with hard, shiny, dark-green sharp-pointed leaves and, in winter, red berries.

holly

holly·hock /ˈholɪhok/ *n* [C] tall garden plant with brightly coloured flowers.

Holly·wood /ˈholɪwʊd/ *n* centre of the US film industry: *~ films/stars.*

holm-oak /ˈhəʊm əʊk/ *n* [C] evergreen oak, ilex.

holo·caust /ˈholəkɔst/ *n* [C] large-scale destruction, esp of human lives by fire, etc: *a nuclear ~.*

holo·graph /ˈholəgrɑf *US:* -græf/ *n* document written wholly by the person in whose name it appears.

hol·ster /ˈhəʊlstə(r)/ *n* leather case for a pistol or revolver.

holy /ˈhəʊlɪ/ *adj* (-ier, -iest) **1** of God; associated with God or with religion: *the H~ Bible; H~ Writ,* the Bible; *the H~ Land,* where Jesus lived; the *H~ City,* Jerusalem; *ˈH~ Week,* the week before Easter Sunday; *H~ Communion; the H~ Father,* the Pope; *the H~ Office,* the Inquisition; *~ ground,* land held in religious awe; *~ water,* water blessed by a priest, to be used for purification; *a ~ war,* one (said to be) fought in defence of sth sacred. **2** devoted to religion: *a ~ man; live a ~ life.* **3** ***a ~ terror,*** (sl) formidable person; mischievous, embarrassing child. □ *n* **the ˈH~ of ˈHolies,** **(a)** most sacred inner chamber in a Jewish temple, entered by the High Priest once a year. **(b)** (fig) any sacred place.

holy·stone /ˈhəʊlɪstəʊn/ *n* [U] soft sandstone used for scrubbing wooden decks of ships. □ *vt* scrub with ~.

hom·age /ˈhomɪdʒ/ *n* [U] **1** expression of respect; tribute paid (*to* sb, his merits). ***do/pay ~ (to sb)***: *Many came to do the dead man ~. We pay ~ to the genius of Shakespeare.* **2** (in feudal times) formal and public acknowledgement of loyalty to a lord or ruler.

home¹ /həʊm/ *n* **1** place where one lives, esp with one's family: *He left ~ at the age of 16,* left his parents and began an independent life. *He looks forward to seeing the old ~ again,* e g his birthplace. *He was born in England, but he now looks on Paris as his ~. When I retire I shall make my ~ in the country. He left India for ~,* for his own country. ***at ~,*** **(a)** in the house: *I've left my books at ~. Is there anybody at ~?* **(b)** (football, etc) in the town, etc to which the team belongs: *Is our next match at ~ or away?* Hence **the ˈ~ team,** the team playing at ~. **(c)** expecting and ready to receive visitors at an appointed time: *'Mrs Carr will be at ~, Monday, 1 May, 5p m.'* **an at-ˈ~,** a social function at which guests are expected at a time announced. ***not at ~ (to),*** not receiving visitors: *Mrs Hill is not at ~ to anyone except relatives.* ***be/feel/make oneself at ~,*** as if in one's own house; at one's ease: *The boy did not feel at ~ in such a splendid house.* ***at ~ in,*** familiar with, accustomed to: *Is it difficult to feel at ~ in a foreign language,* to feel easy and confident while using one? ***a ~ from ~,*** a place where one is as happy, comfortable, etc as in one's own ~: *Prison is not usually a ~ from ~.* ***nothing to write ~ about,*** (colloq) nothing remarkable. **2** institution or place (for the care of children, old or sick people, etc): *an 'orphans' ~; a 'nursing ~; ma'ternity ~s.* **3** (often attrib) family or domestic life: *the pleasures of ~; ~ comforts/joys; ~ life.* **'~ 'economics** = housecraft. **'~ 'help** *n* (GB) woman paid (often from public funds) to help persons who are elderly, infirm or ill (and who are without the help of relatives or friends). **4** (= habitat) place where an animal or plant is native or most common: *the ~ of the tiger and the elephant,* e g the jungle; *the ~ of the fur-seal.* **5** (in sport and in various games) goal; place where a player is safe and cannot be caught, put out, etc. **the '~ plate,** (baseball) base at which the batsman stands to bat. ⇨ the illus at baseball. ***a ~ run,*** one made after a hit which enables the batsman to go round all the bases without stopping. **the ~ straight/stretch,** last part of a track(4). **6** (attrib) of the ~; of one's own country (= *domestic, inland,* contrasted with *foreign*): *~ industries/products; the ~ trade/market.* ***one's '~ town,*** town (not necessarily one's birthplace) in which one lives permanently. **the 'H~ 'Counties,** those round London. **the 'H~ Office,** department controlling local government, police, etc in England and Wales, under the minister called *H~ Secretary,* or *Secretary of State for H~ Affairs* (US = *Department of the Interior*). **7** (compounds) **'~-'baked** *adj* (of bread, etc) baked at ~, not bought from a shop. **'~-'brewed** *adj* beer, etc brewed at ~ (contrasted with beer from a brewery). **'~-coming** *n* arrival at ~, coming to one's ~; *~coming weekend,* (US) when alumni or alumnae return to their school, etc. **'~-'cured** *adj* (of food, esp bacon) treated (by smoking, salting, etc) at ~ (contrasted with food cured in factories). **'~-farm** *n* farm that supplies the needs of a large estate or establishment (contrasted with farmland that is rented out). **the '~ front,** the civilians (in a country at war). **'~-'grown** *adj* (of food, etc) produced in the country (contrasted with what is imported). **'H~ 'Guard** *n* (member of the) British citizen army formed in 1940. **~-land** /-lænd/ *n* native land; country from which one's ancestors came. **H~ Rule,** government of a country by its own citizens. **'~-'made** *adj* (of bread, cakes, etc) made at ~ (contrasted with what is bought from shops). **'~-sick** *adj* sad because away from ~; Hence, **'~-sick-ness** *n* **'~-spun** *adj, n* (cloth made of yarn) spun at ~; (fig) (anything) plain and homely. **'~-stead** /-sted/ *n* house with the land and outbuildings round it; farmhouse; (US and some GB territories) land given to a settler on condition that he lives on it and cultivates it. **'~ thrust** *n* attack (with a weapon or in words) that is effective. **'~ 'truth** *n* one that comes ~ to sb. ⇨ home²(2). **'~-work** *n* [U] work which a pupil is required to do **(a)** at ~ in the evening and take to his teacher(s) at school. **(b)** (colloq) preparatory work, e g for a report or discussion. ⇨ *housework* at house¹(7). **~-less** *adj* having no ~. **~-like** *adj* like ~: *a boarding-house with a ~like atmosphere.* **'~-ward** /-wəd/ *adj* going towards ~. **'~-wards** /-wədz/ *adv* towards ~.

home² /həʊm/ *adv* **1** at, in or to one's ~ or country: *Is he ~ yet? I saw him on his way ~. He went ~. Send the children ~. We ought to turn back and get ~,* i e to the starting-point, whether this is or is not one's usual place of residence. **2** to the point aimed at; so as to be in the right place: *drive a nail ~,* strike it so that it is completely in. ***bring sth/come ~ to sb,*** (cause sb to) realize fully: *The foolhardiness of his behaviour was brought/came ~ to him.* ***drive a point/an argument ~,*** cause its full force to be understood.

home·ly /'həʊmlɪ/ *adj* **(-ier, -iest) 1** simple and plain; of the sort used every day: *a ~-looking old lady,* not trying to seem important or dignified; *a ~ meal.* **2** causing one to think of home or feel at home: *a ~ atmosphere.* **3** (US) (of people, their features) not attractive or good-looking. **home·li·ness** *n*

ho·meo·path *n* = homoeopath.

Ho·meric /həʊ'merɪk/ *adj* of, in the style of, Homer /'həʊmə(r)/ (about 10th c B C; Greek poet) or his epics. **~ laughter,** loud, boisterous laughter like that of the gods in Homer's epics.

homey /'həʊmɪ/ *adj* (US colloq) like home; cosy.

homi·cide /'homɪsaɪd/ *n* [U] killing of a human being; [C] person who kills a human being: *H~ is not criminal when committed in self-defence.* **'~ squad,** (US) group of police officers who investigate ~s. ⇨ murder. **homi·cidal** /'homɪ'saɪdl/ *adj* of ~: *a homicidal lunatic; homicidal tendencies.*

hom·ily /'homɪlɪ/ *n* (*pl* **-lies**) [C] sermon; long and tedious moralizing talk. **homi·letic** /'homɪ'letɪk/ *adj* of homilies. **homi·let·ics** *n pl* art of preaching.

hom·ing /'həʊmɪŋ/ *adj* (of pigeons) having the instinct to fly home (when released a long way from home); (of torpedoes, missiles) fitted with electronic devices that enable them to reach a predetermined target: *'~ devices; a '~ 'guidance system.*

hom·iny /'homɪnɪ/ *n* [U] ground maize boiled in water or milk: *~ grits,* (US) biscuits made from ground maize.

homo /'həʊməʊ/ *n* (Lat) man. **'~ 'sapiens** /'sæpɪenz/ modern man regarded as a species.

ho·moeo·pathy (US = **ho·meo-**) /'həʊmɪ'opəθɪ/ *n* [U] treatment of disease by drugs (usu in small doses) that, if given to a healthy person, would produce symptoms like those of the disease. **ho·moeo·path** (US = **ho·meo-**) /'həʊmɪəpæθ/ *n* person who practises ~.

ho·mo·gene·ous /'həʊmə'dʒiːnɪəs/ *adj* (formed of parts) of the same kind. ⇨ heterogeneous. **ho·mo·gene·ity** /'həʊmədʒɪ'niːətɪ/ *n* quality of being ~. **hom·ogen·ize** /hə'modʒɪnaɪz/ *vt* [VP6A] make ~; (esp) make milk more uniform in consistency by breaking down and blending the particles of fat.

homo·graph /'homəgraːf *US:* -græf/ *n* word spelt like another but with a different meaning.

homo·nym /'homənɪm/ *n* word that is the same in form or sound as another but different in meaning, e g *pale, pail.*

homo·phone /'homəfəʊn/ *n* word pronounced like another but different in meaning, spelling or origin, e g *sum/some, new/knew.*

homo·sex·ual /'həʊmə'sekʃʊəl/ *adj* having sexual propensity for persons of one's own sex. □ *n* ~ person. **~·ity** /'həʊmə'sekʃʊ'ælətɪ/ *n*

hone /həʊn/ *n* [C] stone used for sharpening tools (e g old-style razors). □ *vt* [VP6A] sharpen on a ~.

hon·est /'onɪst/ *adj* **1** not telling lies; not cheating or stealing; straight-forward: *an ~ man; ~ in business; give an ~ opinion.* **to be quite ~ about it,** phrase used before a statement that one wishes to be believed. **earn an ~ penny,** earn money fairly. **2** showing, resulting from, an ~ mind: *an ~ face; look ~; an ~ piece of work,* done conscientiously; *~ weight,* not short weight. **make an ~ woman of sb,** (dated use) marry her after having an affair with her. **~·ly** *adv* in an ~ manner; really: *Honestly, that's all the money I have.* **hon·esty** *n* [U] the quality of being ~; freedom from deceit, cheating, etc.

honey /ˈhʌnɪ/ *n* [U] **1** sweet, sticky yellowish substance made by bees from nectar; (fig) sweetness. **ˈ~·bee** *n* ordinary kind of bee that lives in hives. **ˈ~·dew** *n* [U] **(a)** sweet, sticky substance found on the leaves and stems of plants in hot weather. **(b)** tobacco sweetened with molasses. **~·suckle** /ˈhʌnɪsʌkl/ *n* [U] climbing shrub with sweet-smelling tube-shaped yellow or reddish flowers. **2** [C] (*pl* **-neys**) (colloq) sweetheart; darling: *Come here, my ~s,* e g a mother to her children. **~ed** /ˈhʌnɪd/ *adj* sweet as ~: *~ed words.*

honey·comb /ˈhʌnɪkəʊm/ *n* [C,U] (container with) wax structure of six-sided cells made by bees for honey and eggs; (piece of) ornamental work in a ~ pattern. □ *vt* [VP6A] fill with holes, tunnels, etc: *The rock at Gibraltar is ~ed with galleries.*

a honeycomb

honey·moon /ˈhʌnɪmun/ *n* holiday taken by a newly married couple; (fig) period of harmony at the start of an undertaking, etc. □ *vi* spend a ~: *They will ~ in Paris.*

honk /hoŋk/ *n* cry of the wild goose; sound made by (the old style of) motor horn. □ *vi* make a ~.

hon·or·arium /ˌonəˈreərɪəm/ *n* fee offered (but not claimed) for professional services.

hon·or·ary /ˈonṛɪ *US:* ˈonərerɪ/ *adj* **1** (shortened in writing to *Hon*) (of a position) unpaid: *the ~ secretary.* **2** (of a degree, rank) conferred as an honour, without the usual requirements: *an ~ degree/doctorate;* holding an ~ title or position: *an ~ vice-president.*

ho·nor·ific /ˌonəˈrɪfɪk/ *n, adj* (expression) implying respect: *the ~s so frequently used in oriental languages.*

hon·our[1] (US = **honor**) /ˈonə(r)/ *n* **1** [U] great respect; high public regard: *win ~ in war; a ceremony in ~ of those killed in battle; show ~ to one's parents.* **do sb ~, do ~ to sb,** show courtesy to, esteem of: *Twenty heads of state attended the Queen's coronation to do her ~.* **ˈmaid of ˈ~,** lady in attendance upon a queen, princess, etc. **ˈguard of ˈ~,** number of soldiers chosen to escort or welcome a distinguished person as a mark of respect. **2** [U] good personal character; reputation for good behaviour, loyalty, truthfulness, etc. **on one's ~,** on one's reputation for telling the truth. **an affair of ~,** now more a duel fought to settle a question of ~. **be/feel in ~ bound to do sth,** required to do it as a moral duty, but not by law. **give/on one's word of ~,** guarantee to fulfil an obligation, keep a promise, etc. **pay/incur a debt of ~,** one that need not be paid legally, but which one's good name requires one to pay. **put sb on his ~,** trust him, his ~ being lost if he fails to do what is required, breaks a promise, etc. **3** (in polite formulas): *May I have the ~ of your company at dinner? Will you do me the ~ of dining with me this evening?* (formal style) *I have the ~ to inform you that....* **4 Your/His H~,** title of respect used to (of) some judges. **5** (with *indef art*) person or thing bringing credit: *He is an ~ to his school/family.* **6** (*pl*) marks of respect, distinction, etc; titles; civilities. **birthday ~s,** (in GB) list of titles, decorations, etc conferred by the Sovereign on her or his birthday. **New Year H~s,** similar list awarded on 1 Jan. **full military ~s,** ceremonies, marks of respect, paid by soldiers at the burial of a soldier, to distinguished visitors, e g Presidents. **the ~s of war,** privileges granted to a defeated enemy, e g allowing them to march off with their colours. **do the ~s,** (colloq) of the table, house, etc) act as host(ess), guide, etc and do what politeness requires; perform some small ceremony, e g propose a toast. **7** (*pl*) (in universities) (place in) top division of marks in degree examinations; special distinction for extra proficiency. **take an ~s degree, pass with ~s,** obtain a degree requiring some specialization and a high level of attainment: *first/second/third class ~s.* ⇨ **general, pass**[1]**(1)**. **8** (in card games, whist and bridge) cards of highest value, 10, knave, queen, king, ace of trumps.

hon·our[2] (US = **honor**) /ˈonə(r)/ *vt* [VP6A] **1** respect highly, feel honour for; confer honour on: *Fear God and ~ the Queen. I feel highly ~ed by the kind things you say about me. Will you ~ me with a visit?* **2** accept and pay when due: *~ a bill/cheque/draft, etc; ~one's signature,* agree that one has signed a bill, note, etc and pay the money.

hon·our·able (US = **hon·or-**) /ˈonrbl/ *adj* **1** possessing or showing the principles of honour; consistent with honour(**1,2**): *~ conduct; conclude an ~ peace; ~ burial.* **2** (shortened to *Hon*) title given to judges and some other officials, to the children of peers below the rank of Marquis, and (during debates) to members of the House of Commons: *my H~ friend the member for Chester.* **hon·our·ably** /-əblɪ/ *adv*

hooch /hutʃ/ *n* [U] (US sl) alcoholic (esp inferior) liquor, esp whisky.

hood[1] /hʊd/ *n* **1** bag-like covering for the head and neck, often fastened to a cloak so that it can hang down at the back when not in use; (in universities) fold of cloth worn over an academic gown showing by its colour the degree gained by the wearer and the university by which it was conferred. **2** anything like a ~ in shape or use; folding roof over a carriage (for protection against rain or sun), or over an open motor-car; (US) hinged cover over the engine of a motor-car (GB = *bonnet*). □ *vt* (chiefly in *pp*) cover with, or as with, a ~: *a ~ed falcon.*

hood[2] /hʊd/ *n* (US sl) (abbr of) hoodlum.

hood·lum /ˈhudləm/ *n* (sl) gangster; dangerous criminal.

hoo·doo /ˈhudu/ *n* (chiefly US) (person or thing regarded as bringing) bad luck. □ *vt* make unlucky.

hood·wink /ˈhʊdwɪŋk/ *vt* [VP6A,14] deceive; trick; mislead.

hooey /ˈhuɪ/ *n* (US sl) humbug; nonsense.

hoof /huf/ *n* (*pl* ~s or hooves /huvz/) horny part of the foot of a horse, ox or deer: *buy cattle on the* ~, alive. ⇨ the illus at domestic.

hook[1] /hʊk/ *n* **1** curved or bent piece of metal or other material, for catching hold of sth, or for hanging sth on: *a ˈfish-~; a ˈcrochet ~; a ˈclothes-~; ~s and eyes,* for fastening a dress. ***~, line and sinker,*** (from fishing) (fig) entirely; completely. ***be on the ~,*** (colloq) in a position where one has problems, difficult or distressing decisions to make. ***be/get off the ~,*** no longer in such a position. ***sling one's ~,*** ⇨ sling[1] *v.* **~-ˈnosed** *adj* having a nose shaped like a ~ (or like the nose of an eagle). **ˈ~·worm** *n* worm that infests the intestines of men and animals, the male of which has ~-like spines. **2** curved tool for cutting (grain, etc) or for chopping (branches, etc): *a ˈreaping-~; a ˈbill-~.* ***by ~ or by crook,*** by one means or another. **3** (cricket, golf) kind of stroke; (boxing) short blow with the elbow bent: *a left ~.* □ *vt, vi* **1** [VP6A,15A,B,2C] fasten, be fastened, catch with a ~ or ~s: *a dress that ~s/is ~ed at the back; ~ something on/up; ~ a fish; ~ a husband,* (fig) catch a man and marry him. **2** make into the form of a ~: *~ one's finger.* **3** ***~ it,*** (sl) run away. **4** **ˈ~-up** *n* network of broadcasting stations connected to transmit the same programme: *speak over a country-wide ~-up.* **~ed** *adj* **1** ~-shaped: *a ~ed nose;* furnished with hooks. **2** (sl) addicted to; completely committed to: *be/get ~ed on heroin. My aunt is ~ed on package holidays in Spain.*

hookah /ˈhʊkə/ *n* tobacco pipe (also called a *hubble-bubble*) with a long flexible tube through which smoke is drawn through water in a vase and so cooled.

a hookah

hooky /ˈhʊkɪ/ *n* ***play ~,*** (US sl) play truant.

hoo·li·gan /ˈhulɪgən/ *n* one of a gang of disorderly persons making disturbances in the streets or other public places. **~·ism** /-ɪzm/ *n*

hoop[1] /hup/ *n* **1** circular band of wood or metal for a barrel, etc; similar band bowled along the ground as a plaything. **2** round framework of wire, bone, etc formerly used to expand a woman's skirt; hence, *a ˈ~-ˈskirt.* **3** large ring with paper stretched over it through which circus riders and animals jump. ***put sb/go through the ~(s),*** (fig) undergo an ordeal. **4** iron arch used in the game of croquet □ *vt* bind (a cask, etc) with ~s.

hoop[2] /hup/ *vt* utter the cry ~. **ˈ~·ing cough** *n* ⇨ whoop.

hoop-la /ˈhup lɑ/ *n* game in which rings are thrown at small objects which are won if the rings encircle them.

hoo·ray /huˈreɪ/ ⇨ hurrah.

hoot /hut/ *n* **1** cry of an owl. **2** sound made by a motor-car horn, steam-whistle, foghorn, etc. **3** shout or cry expressing disapproval or scorn. ***not care a ~ (two ~s),*** (sl) not care at all. □ *vi, vt* **1** [VP2A,C] make a ~ or ~s: *an owl ~ing in the garden. The crowd ~ed and jeered at the speaker.* **2** [VP6A,15A,B] make ~s at, drive away by doing this: *~ an actor; ~ a speaker down/off/away.* **~er** *n* siren or steam-whistle, esp as a signal for work to start or stop; similar device in a motor-vehicle to attract attention from other motorists, pedestrians, etc.

Hoover /ˈhuvə(r)/ *n* (P) kind of a vacuum cleaner. □ *vt* [VP6A] (colloq) clean (carpets, etc) with a vacuum cleaner.

hooves /huvz/ *pl* of hoof.

hop[1] /hɒp/ *n* [C] tall climbing plant with flowers growing in clusters; (*pl*) ripe cones (seed-vessels) of this plant, dried and used for giving a bitter flavour to beer, etc. **ˈhop-garden/-field** *nn* field for the cultivation of hops. **ˈhop·pole** *n* tall pole to support wires for hop lines. **ˈhop-picker, hop·per** *nn* worker, machine, employed to pick hops. □ *vi* (-pp-) gather hops: *go hopping in Kent.*

hop[2] /hɒp/ *vi, vt* (-pp-) **1** [VP2A,C] (of persons) jump on one foot; (of other living creatures, e g birds, frogs, grasshoppers) jump with both or all feet together: *Sparrows were hopping about on the lawn. He had hurt his left foot and had to hop along.* ***hop it,*** (sl) go away. ***hopping mad,*** (colloq) very angry. **2** [VP6A] cross (a ditch, etc) by hopping. □ *n* **1** the action of hopping. ***on the hop,*** active, restless. ***catch sb on the hop,*** when he is unprepared, off guard. ***keep sb on the hop,*** keep him active, alert. **2** short jump. ***hop, skip/step and jump,*** athletic exercise or contest consisting of these three movements one after the other. **3** (colloq) informal party and dance, with popular music. **4** (flying) one stage in a long-distance flight: *from Berlin to Tokyo in three hops.* **hop-scotch** /ˈhɒpskɒtʃ/ *n* [U] children's game of throwing a stone into numbered squares marked on the ground, and hopping from square to square to collect it.

hope[1] /həʊp/ *n* **1** [C,U] feeling of expectation and desire; feeling of trust and confidence: *There is not much ~ that they are/of their being still alive.* ***hold out some/no/little/not much ~ (of sth),*** give some, etc encouragement or expectation: *The doctors could hold out no ~ of recovery.* ***(be) past/beyond ~,*** without possibility of success, recovery, etc. ***in the ~ of doing sth,*** hoping to do it: *I called in the ~ of finding you at leisure.* ***live in ~(s) of sth,*** have ~(s) of: *I haven't much money now but live in ~. We live in ~s of better times.* ***raise sb's ~s,*** give him encouragement of better fortune, etc: *Don't raise his ~s too much.* **2** [C] person, thing, circumstance, etc on which ~ is based: *He was the ~ of the school. You are my last ~; if you can't help, I'm ruined.* **ˈ~ chest** *n* (US) chest or drawer used by a young woman for storing linen, e g sheets, articles for household use, etc in anticipation of marriage (GB = *bottom drawer*).

hope[2] /həʊp/ *vt, vi* [VP7A,9,2A,3A] expect and desire: *We ~ to see you soon. I ~ you haven't hurt yourself. 'Will it be fine tomorrow?'—'I ~ so.' 'Will it rain tomorrow?'—'I ~ not.' Let's ~ for the best. We've had no news from him but we're still hoping.* ***~ against ~,*** ~ even though there is only a mere possibility.

hope·ful /ˋhəʊpfl/ *adj* **1** having hope: *be/feel ~ about the future; feel ~ of success/that he will succeed.* **2** giving hope; promising: *The future does not seem very ~. He seems quite a ~ pupil,* likely to do well. **3** (as *n*): *a young ~,* boy or girl who seems likely to succeed. **~ly** /-flɪ/ *adv* **~ness** *n*

hope·less /ˋhəʊpləs/ *adj* **1** feeling no hope; giving or promising no hope: *give way to ~ grief; a ~ case; a ~ illness.* **2** incurable: *a ~ idiot.* **~·ly** *adv* **~·ness** *n*

hop·ped-up /hopt ˋʌp/ *adj* (US sl) (GB) souped up, supercharged: *a ~ engine.*

hop·per[1] /ˋhopə(r)/ *n* hop-picker. ⇨ **hop**[1].

hop·per[2] /ˋhopə(r)/ *n* **1** structure like an inverted cone or pyramid through which grain passes to a mill, coal or coke to a furnace, etc; any similar contrivance for feeding materials into a machine, etc. **2** any hopping insect, e g a flea, a young locust; (in Australia) kangaroo.

horde /hɔd/ *n* **1** wandering tribe (of nomads): *a gipsy ~; ~s of Tartars.* **2** (usu contemptuous) crowd; great number: *~s of people.* **3** multitude: *a ~ of locusts.*

hor·izon /həˋraɪzn/ *n* **1** line at which the earth or sea and sky seem to meet: *The sun sank below the ~.* **2** (fig) limit of one's knowledge, experience, thinking, etc. **hori·zon·tal** /ˈhorɪˋzontl *US:* ˈhɔr-/ *adj* parallel to the ~; flat or level: *a ~tal line* ⇨ **vertical**; *~tal bars,* above the floor for gymnastic exercises. □ *n* ~tal line, bar, etc. **~·tally** /-tlɪ/ *adv*

hor·mone /ˋhɔməʊn/ *n* (kinds of) internal secretion that passes into the blood and stimulates the bodily organs; medical preparation made from a secretion of this kind. ˋ**~ cream,** beauty cream used on the skin, containing ~s.

horn /hɔn/ *n* **1** [C] one of the hard, pointed, usu curved, outgrowths on the heads of cattle, deer, and some other animals. ⇨ the illus at **domestic, large.** ⇨ **bull**[1]**(1).** **2** [U] substance of these outgrowths: *a knife with a handle of ~/a ~ handle; a ~ spoon.* ˋ**~-rimmed** *adj* (of spectacles) with the frame made of material that resembles ~. **3** [C] article made from this substance (or a modern substitute): *a* ˋ*powder-~,* for gunpowder in olden times; *a* ˋ*shoe-~; a* ˋ*drinking-~; a ~ of plenty.* ⇨ **cornucopia. 4** (music) wind instrument (not now usu made of ~): *a* ˋ*hunting ~; a French ~* (like a trumpet): *an English ~,* (also, esp GB *cor anglais* /ˈkɔr ˋoŋgleɪ *US:* oŋˋgleɪ/) woodwind instrument like, but larger than, an oboe, lower in pitch; device which makes a sound similar to a ~ as a warning: *a* ˋ*fog-~; a* ˋ*motor-~.* **5** ~-like part, e g on the head of a snail. ˋ**~·bill** *n* bird with a ~like growth on its beak. ***draw in one's ~s,*** (fig) draw back, show less zeal for an undertaking. **6** either of the ends of the crescent moon. ***on the ~s of a dilemma,*** faced with a choice between things that are equally undesirable, etc. □ *vi* (sl, only in) ***~ in (on),*** intrude; join in without being invited. **~ed** *adj* having ~s**(3)**: *~ed cattle; the ~ed owl,* with tufts like ~s. **~·less** *adj* without ~s: *~less cattle.* ˋ**~·like** *adj* **~y** *adj* **(-ier, -iest)** made of ~; hard like ~: *hands ~y from hard work.*

horn·beam /ˋhɔnbim/ *n* tree with hard wood resembling a small beech, often used in hedges.

hor·net /ˋhɔnɪt/ *n* large insect of the wasp family, able to inflict a severe sting. ***stir up a ~'s nest, bring a ~s' nest about one's ears,*** stir up enemies; cause an outburst of angry feeling.

horn·pipe /ˋhɔnpaɪp/ *n* [C] (music for a) lively dance (usu for one person, esp a sailor).

hor·ol·ogy /hɔˋrolədʒɪ/ *n* [U] art of designing and constructing clocks.

hor·oscope /ˋhorəskəʊp *US:* ˋhɔr-/ *n* diagram of, observation of, positions of planets at a certain time, e g a person's birth, for the purpose of forecasting future events; such a forecast.

hor·rible /ˋhorəbl *US:* ˋhɔr-/ *adj* **1** exciting horror: *~ cruelty/crimes.* **2** (colloq) unpleasant: *~ weather.* **hor·ribly** /-əblɪ/ *adv*

hor·rid /ˋhorɪd *US:* ˋhɔrɪd/ *adj* **1** frightful; terrible; **2** (colloq) disagreeable: *~ weather.* **~·ly** *adv* **~ness** *n*

hor·rific /həˋrɪfɪk/ *adj* (colloq) horrifying.

hor·rify /ˋhorəfaɪ *US:* ˋhɔr-/ *vt* (*pt,pp* **-fied**) [VP6A] fill with horror; shock: *We were horrified by what we saw. Don't let the children see such ~ing scenes.*

hor·ror /ˋhorə(r) *US:* ˋhɔr-/ *n* [C,U] (sth that causes a) feeling of extreme fear or dislike: *She recoiled in ~ from the snake. She expressed her ~ of cruelty. To her ~ she saw her husband knocked down by a bus. A good housewife has a ~ of dirt. We have all read about the ~s of modern warfare.* ˈ**chamber of** ˋ**~s,** collection of objects, representations, etc, connected with crime, cruelty, etc. ˋ**~ fiction/comics/films,** in which the subject-matter and treatment are intended to arouse feelings of ~. ˋ**~-struck/ -stricken** *adj* overcome with ~.

hors de com·bat /ˈɔ də ˋkõbɑ/ *pred adj* (F) unable to take further part in fighting because wounded or disabled.

hors d'œuvres /ˈɔ ˋdɜvr *with unsyllabic* r, *US:* ˋdɜv/ *n pl* (colloq = *starters*) dishes of food served at the beginning of a meal as a relish.

horse /hɔs/ *n* **1** four-legged solid-hoofed animal with flowing mane and tail, used from early times to carry loads, for riding, etc. ⇨ the illus at **domestic.** ⇨ **colt**[1]**, filly, foal, mare, stallion.** ***a dark ~,*** (liter, fig) one whose chances of success are not yet known, or have been overlooked. ***a willing ~,*** willing worker. ***a ~ of another colour,*** (fig) quite a different matter. ***back the wrong ~,*** support the loser in a contest. ***be/get on one's high ~,*** insist on being treated with proper respect. ***eat/work like a ~,*** eat a lot, work hard. ***flog a dead ~,*** ⇨ **flog.** ***hold one's ~s,*** hesitate; show restraint. ***look a gift ~ in the mouth,*** accept sth ungratefully esp by examining it critically for faults (because a ~'s teeth indicate its age). ***put the cart before the ~,*** ⇨ **cart.** ***(straight) from the ~'s mouth,*** (of tips, advice, information) from a first-hand source. **2** (collective *sing*) cavalry: *~ and foot,* cavalry and infantry: *light ~,* lightly armed mounted soldiers; *~ artillery,* light artillery with mounted gunners; *the H~ Guards,* ⇨ **guard**[1]**(6).** **3** framework, often with legs, on which sth is supported: *a* ˋ*clothes-~,* on which clothes may be dried in front of a fire; *a* ˋ*vaulting-~,* block used in a gymnasium for vaulting over. **4** (compounds) ˋ**~·back** *n* (only in) ***on ~back,*** on a ~. ˋ**~·box** *n* closed vehicle for taking a ~ by rail, or towing behind a car, etc. ˈ**~-**ˋ**chestnut** *n* large tree with spreading branches and clusters of white or pink blossom;

shiny reddish-brown nut of this tree. **'~-flesh** *n* [U] **(a)** flesh of ~s as food. **(b)** ~s collectively: *He's a good judge of ~flesh.* **'~-fly** *n* (*pl* **-flies**) large insect troublesome to ~s and cattle. **'~-hair** *n* hair from the mane or tail of ~s, formerly used for stuffing sofas, etc. **'~-laugh** *n* loud, coarse laugh. **~-man** /-mən/ *n* (*pl* -men) rider on ~back, esp one who is skilled. **~-man-ship** /-ʃɪp/ *n* [U] art of riding, skill in riding, on ~back. **'~-meat** *n* = ~flesh. **'~-play** *n* rough, noisy fun or play. **'~-pond** *n* pond for watering and washing ~s. **'~-power** *n* (shortened to *h p*) unit for measuring the power of an engine, etc (550 foot-pounds per second). **'~-race** *n* race between ~s with riders. **'~-racing** *n* **'~-radish** *n* [U] (plant with a) hot-tasting root which is ground or scraped to make a sauce (eaten with beef). **'~-sense** *n* ordinary wisdom. **~-shoe** /'hɔʃʃu/ *n* U-shaped metal shoe for a ~; sth of this shape, e g *a ~-shoe table.* **'~-whip** *n, vt* (-pp-) (thrash with a) whip for ~s. **'~-woman** *n* woman who rides on ~back.

horsy /'hɔsɪ/ *adj* concerned with, fond of, horses or horse-racing; showing by dress, conversation, manners, etc familiarity with horses, horseracing, grooms, jockeys, etc.

hor·ta·tive /'hɔtətɪv/ *adj* exhorting; serving to encourage.

hor·ti·cul·ture /'hɔtɪkʌltʃə(r)/ *n* [U] (art of) growing flowers, fruit and vegetables. **hor·ti·cul·tural** /'hɔtɪ'kʌltʃərl/ *adj* of ~: *a horticultural show/ society.* **hor·ti·cul·tur·ist** /'hɔtɪ'kʌltʃərɪst/ *n* person who practises ~.

ho·sanna /həʊ'zænə/ *n* cry of praise and adoration (to God).

hose[1] /həʊz/ *n* [C,U] (length of) flexible tubing (of rubber, canvas or plastic) for directing water on to fires, watering gardens, cleaning streets, etc: *60 feet of plastic ~; plenty of fire ~s in the building.* **'~-pipe** *n* length of ~. □ *vt* [VP6A,15B] ~ ***(down),*** water (a garden, etc) with a ~; wash (a motor-car, etc) by using a ~: *~ (down) the car.*

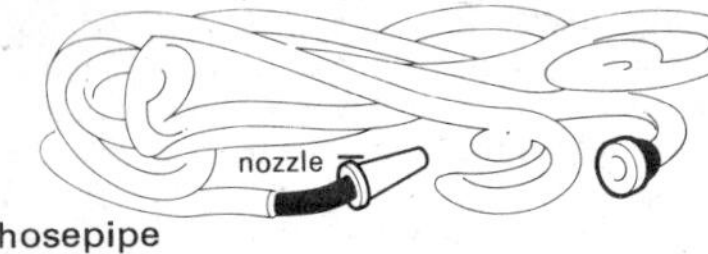

a hosepipe

hose[2] /həʊz/ *n* **1** (collective, as *pl*) (trade name for) stockings and socks: *six pair of ~.* **2** close-fitting garment from the waist to the knees or feet worn by men in former times; tights: *dressed in doublet and ~.* ⇨ the illus at doublet.

ho·sier /'həʊzɪə(r) *US:* -ʒə(r)/ *n* tradesman who sells ~(1) and knitted underwear. **ho·siery** /'həʊzɪərɪ *US:* /'həʊʒərɪ/ *n* [U] goods sold by a hosier.

hos·pice /'hospɪs/ *n* house of rest for travellers, esp one kept by members of a religious order, e g in the Swiss mountains.

hos·pit·able /hə'spɪtəbl/ *adj* giving, liking to give, hospitality: *a ~ man/household.* **hos·pit·ably** /-əblɪ/ *adv*

hos·pi·tal /'hospɪtl/ *n* place where people are treated for, nursed through, their illness or injuries: *He's still in ~. I'm going to the ~ to see my brother. His sister is a ~ nurse.* ***go to ~,*** enter a ~ as a patient. **~-ize** *vt* send to, admit into, ~. **~-iz·ation** /'hospɪtlɑɪ'zeɪʃn *US:* -lɪ'z-/ *n* state of being ~ized.

hos·pi·tal·ity /'hospɪ'tælətɪ/ *n* [U] friendly and generous reception and entertainment of guests, esp in one's own home.

hoss /hos *US:* hɔs/ *n* (colloq) horse.

host[1] /həʊst/ *n* **1** great number (*of*): *He has ~s of friends. We are faced with a ~ of difficulties. He is a ~ in himself,* can do as much as a number of ordinary persons. **2** (old use) army: *Lord of H~s,* Jehovah, God of the Hebrews.

host[2] /həʊst/ *n* **1** person who entertains guests: *As Mr Hill was away, Tom, the eldest son, acted as ~ at the dinner party,* welcomed the guests, etc. (In the *pl* this word may be common gender.) *The Parnwells are such good ~s.* **2** inn-keeper; hotel-keeper. ***reckon without one's ~,*** make calculations, plans, etc without consulting the chief person(s) concerned; overlook possible opposition. **3** (biol) organism which harbours a parasite.

Host /həʊst/ *n* **the ~,** bread eaten at Holy Communion.

hos·tage /'hostɪdʒ/ *n* person (less often, a thing) given or left as a pledge that demands will be satisfied: *take sb ~. The bandits demanded that one of the travellers should stay with them as a ~.* ***give ~s to fortune,*** by an unwise step, take the risk of being harmed in future.

hos·tel /'hostl/ *n* **1** building in which board and lodging are provided (with the support of the authorities concerned) for students, workmen in training, etc: *a 'YMC'A ~.* **'youth ~,** one for young people walking, riding or cycling on holiday tours, used by members of the International Youth H~ Association. **2** (archaic) inn. **~ry** *n* (*pl* **-ries**) (archaic) inn. **~-ler** /'hostlə(r)/ *n* person travelling from ~ to ~, esp youth ~lers.

host·ess /'həʊstɪs/ *n* **1** woman who entertains guests; wife of one's host. **2** woman inn-keeper. **3** **'air ~,** ⇨ air[1](7).

hos·tile /'hostɑɪl *US:* -tl/ *adj* **1** of an enemy: *a ~ army.* **2** feeling or showing enmity (*to*); unfriendly: *a ~ crowd; ~ looks; ~ to reform.* **~-ly** /-llɪ/ *adv*

hos·til·ity /ho'stɪlətɪ/ *n* **1** [U] enmity; ill will: *feelings of ~; feel no ~ towards anyone: show ~ to sb.* **2** (*pl;* **-ties**) (acts of) war: *at the outbreak of hostilities; open/suspend hostilities,* begin/stop fighting.

hot /hot/ *adj* **(-ter, -test) 1** having great heat or a high temperature: *hot weather; hot springs,* springs of water above body temperature; *a hot day; feel hot. I like my food hot. This coffee is too hot to drink.* ***be in/get into hot water,*** in trouble or disgrace (because of foolish behaviour, etc). ***be/get hot under the collar,*** angry, excited, indignant. ***make a place/make it too hot for sb,*** (fig) compel him to leave by rousing hostility against him. **2** producing a burning sensation to the taste: *This curry is too hot. Pepper and mustard are hot.* **3** fiery; eager; intense; violent; impetuous: *get hot over an argument; a man with a hot temper; in the hottest part of the election campaign.* ***be hot on the trail of sb/on sb's tracks,*** near to what is being pursued; close behind. **4** (in hunting, of the scent) fresh and strong. **5** (of music, esp jazz) performed with strong rhythms, improvisation, and syncopated. **6** (sl) (of stolen goods) difficult to dispose of (because of determined efforts made by the police to trace them): *These articles are too hot to* *handle/hold.* **7** (as *adv*) **(a)** recently: *hot off the press.* ⇨ hot news below. **(b)** ***blow hot and cold,*** (fig) be by turns favourable and unfavourable. **(c)** ***give it sb hot,*** punish or scold severely. **8** (special uses with *nn* and *participles*) **ˈhot ˋair** *n* meaningless talk, promises, etc. **hot-air balloon** *n* ⇨ balloon. **ˋhot-bed** *n* bed of earth heated by rotting manure to promote growth of plants; (fig) place favourable to growth, esp of sth evil: *a hotbed of vice/crime.* **ˈhot-ˋblooded** *adj* passionate. **ˈhot cross ˋbun** *n* one with a cross marked on it, eaten on Good Friday. **ˋhot dog** *n* hot sausage served with onions and mustard in a sandwich or bread roll. **ˋhot-foot** *adv* eagerly; in great haste: *follow the enemy hotfoot.* □ *vi* go hastily: *hotfoot it down to the library.* **ˈhot ˋgospeller** *n* (colloq) fervent evangelist preacher. **ˋhot-head** *n* impetuous person. **ˈhot-ˋheaded** *adj* impetuous. **ˋhot-house** *n* heated building, usu made of glass, for growing delicate plants. **ˋhot line** *n* direct line of communication (telephone or teleprinter) between heads of governments, e g between Moscow and Washington. **ˋhot money** *n* short-term funds moved from one financial centre to another by speculators seeking high interest rates and security. ⇨ also 6 above. **hot news** *n* recent (esp sensational) news. **ˋhot pants** *n pl* (GB) brief shorts as worn by some girls and women. **ˋhot-plate** *n* flat surface of a cooking-stove; similar surface (not part of a stove) that can be heated, e g electrically, for cooking, boiling water, etc. **ˈhot poˋtato** *n* (fig, colloq) sth difficult or unpleasant to deal with: *The issue is a political hot potato.* **ˋhot rod** *n* (US sl) supercharged car. **ˋhot seat** *n* (with *def art*) electric chair (for the electrocution of murderers); (fig) position of sb who has to make difficult, often agonizing, decisions, e g of a head of state. **ˋhot spring** *n* naturally heated spring[1](2). **ˈhot ˋstuff** *n* (sl) sb/sth of first-rate quality. **ˈhot-ˋtempered** *adj* easily angered. **ˈhot ˋwater** *n* (colloq) trouble: *be/get into hot water.* **ˈhot-ˋwater-bottle** *n* container (often of rubber) to be filled with hot water for warmth in bed. □ *vt, vi* (-tt-) [VP2C,15B] (colloq) ***hot (sth) up,*** make or become hotter or (fig) more exciting: *Things are hotting up.* **hot·ly** *adv* passionately; excited: *He replied hotly that...; It was a hotly contested match.*

hotch·potch /ˋhotʃpotʃ/ *n* jumble; number of things mixed together without order: *His essay was a* ~ *of other people's ideas.*

ho·tel /həʊˋtel/ *n* (either *a* ~ or *an* ~) building where meals and rooms are provided for travellers. **~·ier** /həʊˋtelɪeɪ *US:* ˈhəʊtelˋjeɪ/ *n* a ~-keeper.

hound /haʊnd/ *n* **1** (kinds of) dog used for hunting and racing: *ˋfox~; ˋblood~; ˋgrey~.* (When not in a compound, ~ usu means *fox~.*) ***follow the ~s, ride to ~s,*** hunt with a pack of ~s. **Master of H~s,** the master of a hunt(3). **2** mean, wretched, contemptible fellow. □ *vt* [VP6A] chase or hunt with, or as with, ~s; harass: *be ~ed by one's creditors,* worried by requests for payment of money owing.

hour /aʊə(r)/ *n* **1** twenty-fourth part of a day; 60 minutes: *hire a horse by the ~; walk for ~s (and ~s); a three ~s' journey; the happiest ~s* (= period) *of my life; work a ˋforty-~ week.* ***at the eleventh ~,*** when almost too late. ***the small ~s,*** the three or four ~s after midnight. **ˋ~·glass** *n* sandglass which runs out in one ~. **ˋ~ hand** *n* small hand on a clock or watch, pointing to the ~. **2** time of day; point or period of time: *1800 hours,* time calculated on a 24-~ basis, i e 6.00pm. *The church clock was striking the ~ as we got home. This clock strikes the ~s and the half-~s, but not the quarters. Please come at an early ~. They disturb me at all ~s of the day and night,* constantly. **3** (*pl*) fixed periods of time, esp for work: *ˋschool ~s. ˋOffice ~s, 9am to 5pm.* ***after ~s,*** after the period of regular business, etc. ***out of ~s,*** outside (before or after) regular ~s (of duty, etc). ***keep good/bad/early/late/regular, etc ~s,*** get up, go to bed, start/stop work, leave/arrive home, etc, early/late, etc. **4** a particular, or the present, point in time: *questions of the ~,* now being discussed; *in the ~ of danger/temptation; in a good/evil ~,* at a lucky/unlucky time.

houri /ˋhʊərɪ/ *n* young and beautiful woman of the Muslim Paradise.

hour·ly /ˋaʊəlɪ/ *adv* **1** every hour; once every hour: *This medicine is to be taken ~.* **2** at any hour: *We're expecting news ~.* □ *adj* **1** done or occurring every hour: *an ~ service of trains; an ~ bus service.* **2** continual: *live in ~ dread of discovery.*

house[1] /haʊs/ (*pl* ~s /ˋhaʊzɪz/) **1** building made for people to live in, usu for one family (or a family and lodgers, etc): *New ~s are going up everywhere. I've bought a ~.* ⇨ home[1](1). ***get on like a ˋ~ on fire,*** (of people) quickly become friendly and jolly together. ***under ~ arrest,*** forbidden (by persons in authority) to leave one's ~ or receive visitors, e g because under suspicion of disloyalty. **2** (usu with a *pref*) building made or used for some particular purpose or occupation: *ˋhen~; ˋcow~; ˋstore~; ˋware~; ˋalms-~; ˋbake~; ˋcustom-~,* etc, ⇨ these entries. **the H~ of God,** church or chapel. ***~ of ill fame,*** (old use) brothel. ***~ of cards,*** one built by a child out of playing cards; (fig) scheme likely to collapse. ***on the ~,*** at the expense of the inn, firm, etc. **3** (building used by an) assembly: *the H~ of Commons/Lords. the H~s of Parliament.* **the H~,** (colloq, GB) **(a)** the Stock Exchange. **(b)** the H~ of Commons or Lords: *enter the H~,* become an MP. **(c)** (US) the H~ of Representatives. **(d)** business firm. **4** [U] ***keep ~,*** manage the affairs of a ~hold. ***keep a good ~,*** provide good food and plenty of comfort. ***keep open ~,*** be ready to welcome guests at any time. ***set/put one's ~ in order,*** put one's affairs straight. **5** household; family line; dynasty: *the H~ of Windsor,* the British Royal family; *an ancient ~; an old trading ~,* business firm. **6** spectators, audience, in a theatre: *make oneself heard in every part of the ~; a full ~,* every seat occupied. *The second ~* (= performance) *starts at 9 o'clock. Is there a doctor in the ~?* ***bring down the ~, bring the ˋ~ down,*** win very great applause and approval. **7** (compounds) **ˋ~ agent** *n* (GB) person who sells or lets ~s for others. ⇨ (US) realtor. **ˋ~·boat** *n* boat fitted up as a place to live in, e g on a river or estuary. **ˋ~·bound** *adj* confined to the ~, e g through ill-health: *Should wives with children be ~bound?* **ˋ~·breaker** *n* **(a)** person who enters another's ~ by day to steal. ⇨ burglar. **(b)** (US = **ˋ~·wrecker**) workman employed to pull down old buildings. **ˋ~·coat** *n* usu cotton or silk coat worn by women in the house during the day. **ˋ~-craft** *n* theory and practice of running a home[1](1).

a hovercraft

ˈ~·**dog** *n* dog trained to guard a ~. ˈ~·**father** *n* man in charge of children in an institution. ˈ~ **flag** *n* flag flown by a firm's ships. ⇨ 5 above. ˈ~·**fly** *n* (*pl* -flies) ⇨ fly¹. ~·**ful** /-fʊl/ *n* as much as a ~ can contain or accommodate. ˈ~·**hold** *n* all persons (family, lodgers, etc) living in a ~: *~hold cavalry/troops*, employed to guard the Sovereign; *~hold duties/expenses.* ˈ~·**hold** ˈ**word**, a commonly used word or name. ˈ~·**holder** *n* person leasing or owning and occupying a ~, not sb living in a hotel, lodgings, etc. ˈ~·**keeper** *n* woman employed to manage the affairs of a ~hold. ˈ~-**lights** *n pl* lights in the auditorium of a theatre, cinema, etc. ˈ~·**maid** *n* female servant in a ~, esp one who cleans rooms, etc. ˈ~**maid's** ˈ**knee**, inflammation of the kneecap due to kneeling. ˈ~-**man** /-mən/ *n* (*pl* -men) (GB) doctor who is an assistant to a physician or surgeon in a hospital (US = *intern*). ˈ~ **martin** *n* common bird which nests in the walls of ~s and cliffs. ˈ~·**master** *n* teacher in charge of a school boarding-~. ˈ~-**mother** *n* woman in charge of children in an institution. ˈ~-**party** *n* party of guests being entertained for several days at a country ~, etc. ˈ~-**proud** *adj* very much concerned with the care of the ~, with the appearance of the furnishings, etc. ˈ~ **physician** *n* one who resides in a hospital. ˈ~·**room** *n* space: *I wouldn't give that table ~room*, would not have it in my ~, would not accept it even as a gift. ˈ~ **sparrow** *n* common grey and brown bird. ˈ~ **surgeon** *n* one who resides in a hospital. ˈ~·**top** *n* (chiefly in) *cry/publish/proclaim sth from the ~tops*, make known to all; declare publicly. ˈ~·**trained** *adj* (of domestic pets) trained not to defecate and urinate inside buildings. ˈ~-**warming** *n* party given to friends by a person who moves into a new ~. ˈ~-**wife** *n* **(a)** woman head of a family, who runs the home, brings up the family, etc. **(b)** /ˈhʌzɪf/ (dated) case for needles and thread. ˈ~·**wife·ly** *adj* of a ~wife(1). ˈ~·**wifery** /-wɪfərɪ/ *n* [U] work of a ~wife. ˈ~·**work** *n* [U] work done in a ~, cleaning, cooking, etc. ⇨ *homework* at home¹(7).

house² /haʊz/ *vt* [VP6A] **1** provide a ~ or shelter for; find room for: *We can ~ you and your friends if the hotels are full.* **2** store (goods, etc): *~ one's old books in the attic.*

hous·ing /ˈhaʊzɪŋ/ *n* **1** [U] accommodation in houses, etc: *More ~ is needed for old people. The ~ in this part of the town is sub-standard. The ~ problem in London gets more serious every year.* ˈ~ **association** *n* non-profitmaking society that buys and provides ~ing. ˈ~ **estate** *n* area of houses planned and built either by a local authority or other organization, to be let or sold.

hove /həʊv/ *pt,pp* of heave.

hovel /ˈhovl *US:* ˈhʌvl/ *n* small house or cottage that is unfit to live in; open-sided shed or outhouse; *a cart ~.*

hover /ˈhovə(r) *US:* ˈhʌvər/ *vi* [VP2A,C] **1** (of birds) remain in the air at one place: *a hawk ~ing overhead/~ing over its prey; a helicopter ~ing over the lawn.* ˈ~·**craft** *n* craft capable of moving over land or water while supported on a cushion of air made by jet engines. **2** (of persons) wait about; remain at or near: (fig) *~ between life and death.*

how /haʊ/ *adv* **1** in what way or manner; by what means: *How is the word spelt? Tell me how to spell the word. How did you escape? Tell me how you escaped.* **2** (in questions and exclamations) to what extent; in what degree: *How old is he? How often do you go there? How many are there? How much do you want? How dirty the house is! How kind you are! How he snores!* i e he snores very loudly. *How well you look!* **3** in what state of health: *How are you? How's your father? How do you do?* (formula used as a conventional greeting, esp when persons are formally introduced; used only with the *pron you.*) **how-d'ye-do** /ˈhaʊ djə ˈdu/ *n* (colloq) awkward state of affairs: *Well, here's a pretty how-d'ye-do!* **4** (introducing an indirect statement) that: *He told me how* (= that) *he had read about it in the newspapers.* **5** used in asking for an opinion, decision, explanation, etc: *How's that?* **(a)** What's the explanation of that? **(b)** What's your opinion of that? e g an object pointed to. **(c)** (in cricket, to the umpire) Is the batsman out or not out? *How so?* Can you prove that it is so? *How about going* (= What do you think about going) *for a walk? How do you find your new job,* Do you like it, etc. ***How come...*** (colloq) Why is it that...: *How come we don't see you more often?* **how·beit** /haʊˈbiɪt/ *conj* (archaic) nevertheless. **how·ever** /haʊˈevə(r)/ *adv* in whatever way or degree: *He will never succeed however hard he tries. We must do something, on however humble a scale.* □ *conj* all the same; nevertheless: *Later, however, he decided to go. He was mistaken, however.*

how·dah /ˈhaʊdɑ/ *n* seat (usu with a canopy) on an elephant's back.

how·it·zer /ˈhaʊɪtsə(r)/ *n* short gun for firing shells at a high angle at short range.

howl /haʊl/ *n* [C] long, loud cry, e g of a wolf; long cry of a person in pain, or of sb expressing scorn, amusement, etc: *~s of derision.* □ *vi,vt* [VP2A,C] utter such cries: *wolves ~ing in the forest. The wind ~ed through the trees. The boy ~ed with laughter.* **2** [VP6A,15A,B] utter ~s at; utter with ~s: *~ defiance at the enemy; ~ down a speaker,* prevent him from being heard. **~er** *n* (colloq) foolish and laughable mistake. **~·ing** *adj* (sl) extreme; glaring: *a ~ing shame.*

hoy·den /ˈhɔɪdn/ *n* boisterous girl. **~·ish** /-ɪʃ/ *adj* of or like a ~.

hub /hʌb/ *n* central part of a wheel from which the spokes radiate, ⇨ the illus at bicycle; (fig) central point of activity or importance: *a hub of industry/commerce. He thinks that Cleethorpes is the hub of the universe.*

hubble-bubble /ˈhʌbl bʌbl/ *n* form of hookah; bubbling noise.

hub·hub /ˈhʌbʌb/ *n* [U] confused noise, e g of many voices; uproar.

hubby /ˈhʌbɪ/ *n* (*pl* -bies) (GB) (colloq) husband.

hu·bris /ˈhjubrɪs/ *n* [U] (Gk) arrogant pride or feeling of security.

hucka·back /ˈhʌkəbæk/ *n* strong, rough, cotton or linen material used for towels, etc.

huckle·berry /ˈhʌklberɪ/ *n* (*pl* **-ries**) (small, dark-blue berry of a) low shrub from N America.

huck·ster /ˈhʌkstə(r)/ *n* hawker. □ *vt,vi* peddle; haggle.

huddle /ˈhʌdl/ *vt,vi* **1** [VP2C] crowd together: *sheep huddling together for warmth.* **2** [VP2C] **~ up (against),** curl or coil up against: *Tom was cold, so he ~d up against his brother in bed.* **3** [VP15B] heap up in a confused mass: *~ things together/up/into sth.* □ *n* number of things or persons close together without order or arrangement: ***be in/go into a ~,*** (colloq, of persons) be, get together to confer.

hue¹ /hju/ *n* [C] (shade of) colour: *the hues of the rainbow; the dark hue of the ocean.* **hued** /hjud/ (in compounds) having the hue(s) indicated: *ˈdark-hued; ˈmany-hued.*

hue² /hju/ *n* (only in) ***hue and cry,*** /ˈhju ən ˈkrɑɪ/ general outcry of alarm (as when a criminal is being pursued, or when there is opposition to sth): *raise a hue and cry against new tax proposals.*

huff¹ /hʌf/ *n* fit of ill temper. ***be in/get into a ~.*** **~ish** /-ɪʃ/, **~y** *adjj* in a ~; taking offence easily. **~·ily** /-əlɪ/ *adv*

huff² /hʌf/ *vi* puff; blow.

hug /hʌg/ *vt* (**-gg-**) [VP6A] **1** put the arms round tightly, esp to show love: *The child was hugging her doll.* **2** cling to: *hug cherished beliefs.* **3** ***hug the shore,*** (of a ship) keep close to it. **4** ***hug oneself (with pleasure/delight) over sth,*** be very pleased with oneself, congratulate oneself □ *n* [C] tight embrace: *She gave her mother a big hug.*

huge /hjudʒ/ *adj* very great. **~·ly** *adv* enormously; very much.

hug·ger-mug·ger /ˈhʌgə mʌgə(r)/ *n, adj, adv* secrecy; secret(ly); confusion; confused(ly).

Hu·gue·not /ˈhjugənot/ *n* (16th and 17th cc) French Protestant.

hula /ˈhulə/ *n* native Hawaiian dance.

hulk /hʌlk/ *n* **1** old ship no longer in use or used only as a storehouse; (formerly) old ship used as a prison. **2** big, clumsy person. **~·ing** *adj* clumsy; awkward: *Get out of my way, you big ~ing creature!*

hull¹ /hʌl/ *n* outer covering of some fruits and seeds, esp the pods of peas and beans. □ *vt* remove the ~s of.

hull² /hʌl/ *n* body or frame of a ship. ⇨ the illus at **barque**. **~ *down*** **(a)** (of a ship almost below the horizon) with only the mast(s), funnel(s), etc, visible. **(b)** (of a tank) with only the turret showing.

hul·la·ba·loo /ˈhʌləbəˈlu/ *n* uproar; disturbance: *What a ~! What's all this ~ about?*

hullo /ˈhʌˈləʊ/ *int* used to call attention, express surprise, and to answer a call, e g on the telephone.

hum /hʌm/ *vi,vt* (**-mm-**) [VP6A,2A,C] **1** make a continuous sound like that made by bees; sing with closed lips: *She was humming a song to herself. The bees were humming in the garden.* **ˈhum·ming·bird** *n* name used of several species, usu small and brightly coloured, that make a humming sound by vibration of the wings. **ˈhumming-top** *n* top that hums when it spins. **2** be in a state of activity: *make things hum; a factory humming with activity.* **3** (sl) smell unpleasantly: *This ham is beginning to hum.* **4** usu ***hum and haw,*** (colloq) make sounds expressing hesitation or doubt. □ *n* humming noise: *the hum of bees/of distant traffic; a hum of voices/conversation from the next room.*

hu·man /ˈhjumən/ *adj* **1** of man or mankind (contrasted with animals, God): *a ~ being; ~ nature; ~ affairs. 'To err is ~, to forgive divine.'* **2** having, showing, the qualities that distinguish man: *His cruelty suggests that he is less than ~.* **~·ly** *adv* (esp) by ~ means; without divine help: *The doctors have done all that is ~ly possible.* **ˈ~-ˈkind** *n* [U] (liter) mankind.

hu·mane /hjuˈmeɪn/ *adj* **1** tender; kind-hearted: *a man of ~ character; a ~ officer.* **~ killer,** instrument for the painless killing of animals. **2** (of branches of study) tending to refinement; polished. ⇨ **humanity(4)**. **~·ly** *adv.*

hu·man·ism /ˈhjumənɪzm/ *n* [U] **1** devotion to human interests; system that is concerned with ethical standards (but not with religions), and with the study of mankind. **2** literary culture (of about the 14th to 16th cc) based on Greek and Roman learning.

hu·man·ist /ˈhjumənɪst/ *n* **1** student of human nature or human affairs (as opposed to theological subjects). **2** believer in humanism. **3** (esp in the 14th or 16th cc) student of Greek and Roman literature and antiquities.

hu·mani·tarian /hjuˈmænɪˈteərɪən/ *adj, n* (of, holding the views of, a) person who works for the welfare of all human beings by reducing suffering, reforming laws about punishment, etc. **~·ism** /-ɪzm/ *n*

hu·man·ity /hjuˈmænətɪ/ *n* [U] **1** the human race; mankind: *crimes against ~.* **2** human nature. **3** quality of being humane(**1**): *treat people and animals with ~.* **4** (*pl*) **the humanities,** the branches of learning concerned with ancient Greek and Latin culture; the Arts subjects, esp literature, history and philosophy.

hu·man·ize /ˈhjumənɑɪz/ *vt,vi* [VP6A,2A] make or become human or humane.

humble /ˈhʌmbl/ *adj* (**-r, -st**) **1** having or showing a modest opinion of oneself, one's position, etc: *He is very ~ towards his superiors.* ***your ~ servant,*** (dated) formula at the end of a formal letter. ***eat ~ pie,*** make an abject apology, humiliate oneself. **2** (of persons) low in rank or position; obscure and unimportant; (of things) poor; mean: *men of ~ birth; a ~ home; a ~ occupation,* e g street-cleaning. □ *vt* [VP6A] make ~; make lower in rank or self-opinion: *~ one's enemies; ~ sb's pride; ~ oneself before God.* **hum·bly** *adv* in a ~ way: *beg most humbly for forgiveness; humbly born,* of ~ parents.

hum·bug /ˈhʌmbʌg/ *n* **1** [C,U] (instance of) dishonest and deceiving behaviour or talk; [C] dishonest, deceitful person. **2** (GB) hard boiled sweet flavoured with peppermint. □ *vt* (**-gg-**) [VP6A,14] deceive or trick (sb *into* or *out of* sth): *Don't try to ~ me!* □ *int* Nonsense!

hum·dinger /ˈhʌmˈdɪŋə(r)/ *n* (US) sth marvellous or extraordinary.

hum·drum /ˈhʌmdrʌm/ *adj* dull; commonplace; monotonous: *live a ~ life; engaged in ~ tasks.*

hu·merus /ˈhjumərəs/ *n* (anat) bone of the upper arm in man. ⇨ the illus at **skeleton**.

hu·mid /ˈhumɪd/ *adj* (esp of air, climate) damp. **~·ify** /hjuˈmɪdɪfɑɪ/ *vt* (*pt,pp* **-fied**) make ~. **~·ity** /hjuˈmɪdətɪ/ *n* [U] (degree of) moisture (in the air).

hu·mili·ate /hjuˈmɪlɪeɪt/ *vt* [VP6A] cause to feel ashamed; put to shame; lower the dignity or self-respect of: *a country that was ~d by defeat; humiliating peace terms.* **hu·mili·ation** /hjuˌmɪlɪˈeɪʃn/ *n* [U] humiliating or being ~d; [C] instance of this: *the humiliation of having to surrender.*

hu·mil·ity /hjuˈmɪlətɪ/ *n* [U] humble condition or state of mind.

hum·ming·bird /ˈhʌmɪŋbɜd/ *n* ⇨ **hum(1).**

hum·mock /ˈhʌmək/ *n* hillock; rising ground in a marsh; hump in an ice-field.

hu·mor·ist /ˈhjumərɪst/ *n* humorous talker or writer; facetious person.

hu·mor·ous /ˈhjumərəs/ *adj* having or showing a sense of humour; funny: *a ~ writer,* e g Mark Twain; *~ remarks.* **~·ly** *adv*

hu·mour (US = **hu·mor**) /ˈhjumə(r)/ *n* **1** [U] (capacity to cause or feel) amusement: *a story full of ~; have no/not much/a good sense of ~.* **2** [U] person's state of mind (esp at a particular time); temper: *in a good/bad ~; not in the ~ for work,* not feeling inclined to work; *in no ~ to trifle. when the ~ takes him,* when he feels so inclined. ***out of ~,*** displeased, in a bad mood. **3** [C] (old use) one of certain liquids in the body, said to determine a person's mental and physical qualities. □ *vt* [VP6A] give way to, gratify: *When a person is ill he may have to be ~ed,* his wishes may have to be granted, even if they are senseless. *Is it wise to always ~ a child,* give it everything it wants?

hump /hʌmp/ *n* **1** round lump, e g on a camel's back or (as a deformity) on a person's back. ⇨ the illus at **large**. **ˈ~·back** *n* (person having a) back with a ~. **ˈ~·backed** *adj* having such a back. **2** ***have/give sb the ~,*** (sl) fit of depression or irritation: *It gives me the ~.* □ *vt* [VP6A,15B] make ~-shaped; gather the shoulders into a ~: *The cat ~ed (up) her back when she saw the dog.*

humph /hʌmpf *or spontaneously as a grunt with lips closed and then puffed open*/ *int* used to show doubt or dissatisfaction.

hu·mus /ˈhjuməs/ *n* [U] earth formed by the decay of vegetable matter (dead leaves, plants).

Hun /hʌn/ *n* member of an Asiatic race which ravaged Europe in the 4th and 5th cc.

hunch /hʌntʃ/ *n* **1** thick piece; hunk; hump. **ˈ~-back(ed),** = **humpback(ed). 2** ***have a ~ that,*** (sl) have a presentiment, rather think, that. □ *vt* [VP6A] arch to form a hump: *sitting at the table with his shoulders ~ed up.*

hun·dred /ˈhʌndrəd/ *n, adj* the number 100, ⇨ App 4: *two ~ and five,* 205; *a few ~ people; ~s of people.* **ˈ~·weight** *n* (often written *cwt*) (in GB) $\frac{1}{20}$ of one ton, 112 lb (in US 100 lb). ⇨ App 5. **ˈ~·fold,** (US) **ˈ~ˈfold** *adv* one ~ times as much or as many. **hun·dredth** /ˈhʌndrədθ/ *n, adj* next after the 99th; one of a ~ equal parts.

hung /hʌŋ/ *pt,pp* of **hang**.

hun·ger /ˈhʌŋgə(r)/ *n* **1** [U] need, desire for food: *die of ~; satisfy one's ~.* ***be/go on (a) ˈ~-strike,*** refuse to take food as a protest, in order to win release, etc. **ˈ~-march** *n* one undertaken, e g by unemployed workers, to call attention to sufferings, etc. Hence, **ˈ~-marcher** *n* **2** (fig) any strong desire: *a ~ for excitement/adventure.* □ *vi* [VP2A,3A,4] ***~ for/to do sth,*** feel, suffer from, ~; have a strong desire: *~ for news.*

hun·gry /ˈhʌŋgrɪ/ *adj* (**-ier, -iest**) feeling, showing signs of, causing, hunger: *be/go ~; The boy had a ~ look. Hay-making is ~ work. The orphan child was ~ for affection.* **hun·grily** /ˈhʌŋgrəlɪ/ *adv*

hunk /hʌŋk/ *n* thick piece cut off: *a ~ of bread/cheese/meat.*

hun·kers /ˈhʌŋkəz/ *n pl* (colloq) haunches, esp ***on one's ~,*** in a squatting position.

hunt¹ /hʌnt/ *n* **1** (*sing* with *def* or *indef art*) act of ~ing: *have a good ~; find sth after a long ~,* search. **2** (esp in GB) group of persons who regularly ~ foxes and stags with horses and hounds; the area in which they do this: *The Quorn H~; a member of the ~.* **ˈ~ ˈball,** ball organized by members of a ~. **~er** *n* **1** person who ~s; *~ers of big game in Africa. The Red Indians used to be clever ~s.* (Note that a person who ~s foxes, etc on horseback or shoots grouse, pheasants, etc in GB is not called a ~er. 'Do you hunt/shoot?' is preferred to 'Are you a ~er?') **2** horse used in fox-hunting. **3** pocket watch with a metal cover protecting the glass face. **~·ing** *n* [U] **1** the act of ~ing; (esp in GB) fox ~ing: *He's fond of ~ing.* **2** (attrib) *a ˈ~ing-man; a ˈ~ing-horn.* **ˈ~ing ground,** (fig) place where one may search for sth with hope of success. **ˈ~ing pink,** shade of pink worn by huntsmen. **~·ress** /ˈhʌntrəs/ *n* (liter) woman who ~s, e g the goddess Diana.

hunt² /hʌnt/ *vi,vt* **1** [VP6A,2A,C] go after (wild animals) for food or sport: *~ big game; go out ~ing. Wolves ~ in packs.* ⇨ *shooting* at **shoot. 2** [VP2A,3A,15B] ***~ down,*** look for, pursue and find; bring to bay: *~ down a criminal/an escaped prisoner.* ***~ for,*** search; try to find: *~ for a lost book.* ***~ high and low,*** search everywhere: *They ~ed high and low for the missing will.* ***~ out,*** (try to) find by searching (sth that has been put away and forgotten): *~ out an old diary/a black tie that hasn't been needed for years.* ***~ up,*** search for (sth hidden or difficult to find): *~ up old records/references/quotations.* **3** [VP6A,15A] drive or chase away: *~ the neighbour's cats out of the garden.* **4** [VP6A] (special uses in GB; foxhunting) follow the hounds through or in (a district): *~ the county;* employ (a horse) in ~ing: *~ one's horse all winter;* act as master or huntsman of (a pack of hounds): *~ the hounds.*

hunts·man /ˈhʌntsmən/ *n* (*pl* **-men**) **1** hunter(1) **2** man in charge of the hounds during a hunt(2).

hurdle /ˈhɜdl/ *n* **1** (GB) movable oblong frame of wood, etc used for making temporary fences, e g for sheep pens. **2** light frame to be jumped over in a *ˈ~-race.* **3** (fig) difficulty to be overcome. □ *vt* [VP15B] ***~ off,*** fence with ~s. **hur·dler** *n* person who makes ~s(1); person who runs in ~-races.

hurdling

hurdy-gurdy /ˈhɜdɪ gɜdɪ/ *n* (*pl* **-dies**) street piano or barrel organ, usu mounted on wheels, played by turning a handle.

hurl /hɜl/ *vt* [VP6A,15A,B] throw violently: *~ a spear at a tiger. They ~ed themselves at/upon th* *enemy and attacked them violently.* □ *n* violent throw.

hurl·ing /ˈhɜlɪŋ/ *n* [U] Irish ball game resembling lacrosse.

hurly-burly /ˈhɜlɪ bɜlɪ/ *n* [U] noisy commotion; uproar.

hur·rah /hʊˋrɑ/ *int* expressing joy, welcome, approval, etc *H~ for the Queen! Hip, hip, ~!* □ *vi* shout ~. cheer.

hur·ri·cane /ˈhʌrɪkən *US:* ˋhɜəkeɪn/ *n* [C] violent windstorm, esp a W Indian cyclone. ˋ**~ lamp/lantern** *nn* kind with the light protected from the wind.

hurry /ˈhʌrɪ *US:* ˋhɜɪ/ *n* [U] eager haste; wish to get sth done quickly; (with neg, or in the interr) need for haste: *Everything was ~ and excitement. Why all this ~? Is there any ~,* need for ~? *Don't start yet—there's no ~,* there's plenty of time. ***in a ~,*** **(a)** impatient; acting, anxious to act, quickly: *He was in a ~ to leave. In his ~ to catch the train, he left his luggage in the taxi.* **(b)** (colloq) soon, willingly: *I shan't ask that rude man to dinner again in a ~.* **(c)** (colloq) easily: *You won't find a better specimen than that in a ~.* □ *vt,vi* (*pt,pp* **-ried**) [VP6A,15A,B,2A,C] (cause to) move or do sth quickly or too quickly: *Don't ~; there's plenty of time. It's no use ~ing her/trying to make her ~. If we ~ the work, it may be spoiled. He picked up his bag and hurried off. More soldiers were hurried to the front line. H~ up!* Make haste. *H~ him up! Make him ~.* **hur·ried** *adj* done, etc in a ~; showing haste: *a hurried meal; write a few hurried lines.* **hur·ried·ly** *adv*

hurt /hɜt/ *vt,vi* (*pt,pp* **hurt**) **1** [VP6A,2A] cause bodily injury or pain to; damage: *He ~ his back when he fell. He was more frightened than ~. Did you ~ yourself? These shoes are too tight; they ~ (me).* **2** pain a person, his feelings: *He was rather ~ by their criticisms. She was ~ to find that no one admired her performance.* **3** [VP2A] suffer injury; come to harm. have a bad effect (on): *It won't ~ to postpone the matter for a few days.* □ *n* [U] (or with *indef art*) harm; injury: *I intended no ~ to his feelings. It was a severe ~ to his pride.* **~·ful** /-fl/ *adj* causing ~: *~ful to the health.*

hurtle /ˈhɜtl/ *vi* [VP2C] (cause to) rush or fly violently: *During the gale chimney-pots and roof-tiles came hurtling down.*

hus·band /ˈhʌzbənd/ *n* man to whom a woman is married. □ *vt* [VP1,6A] use sparingly: *~ one's resources/strength.*

hus·band·man /ˈhʌzbəndmən/ *n* (*pl* **-men** /-mən/) (old use) farmer. **hus·bandry** /ˈhʌzbəndrɪ/ *n* [U] farming; management: *animal husbandry; good/bad husbandry.*

hush /hʌʃ/ *vt,vi* [VP2A,15A,B] make or become silent or quiet: *H~!* Be silent! *She ~ed the baby to sleep.* ***~ sth up,*** prevent it from becoming public knowledge: *She tried unsuccessfully to ~ up the fact that her husband was an ex-convict.* □ *n* [U] silence; stillness: *in the ~ of night.* ˋ**~-money** *n* money paid to ~ sth up (usu sth scandalous or discreditable). ˈ**~-ˋ~** *adj* (colloq) (to be) kept very secret: *a ~-~ affair.*

husk /hʌsk/ *n* (usu *pl*) dry outer covering of seeds, esp of grain, ⇨ the illus at **cereal**: *rice in the ~,* with the ~s not removed; (fig) worthless outside part of anything. □ *vt* remove ~s from.

husky /ˈhʌskɪ/ *adj* (**-ier, -iest**) **1** (dry) like husks. **2** (of a person, his voice) hoarse; with a dry and almost whispering voice: *a ~ voice/cough. You sound ~ this morning.* **3** (colloq) big and strong: *a fine ~ woman, excellent as a farmer's wife.* □ *n* **1** thick-coated dog of N American Eskimos. **2** ~(3) person. **husk·ily** /-əlɪ/ *adv* **huski·ness** *n*

hus·sar /hʊˋzɑ(r)/ *n* soldier of a light cavalry regiment.

hussy /ˈhʌzɪ/ *n* (*pl* **-sies**) worthless woman; ill-mannered girl.

hus·tings /ˈhʌstɪŋz/ *n pl* proceedings (canvassing, speech-making, etc) leading up to a parliamentary election.

hustle /ˈhʌsl/ *vt,vi* [VP6A,15A,B,2A,C] **1** push or jostle roughly; (make sb) act quickly and with energy: *The police ~d the thief into their van. I don't want to ~ you into a decision. Come on, now: ~!* **2** (esp US) (colloq) sell or obtain sth by energetic (esp deceitful) activity. □ *n* (*sing* only) quick and energetic activity: *The railway station was a scene of ~ and bustle.* **hus·tler** *n* person who ~s.

hut /hʌt/ *n* **1** small, roughly made house or shelter: *Alpine huts,* for the use of mountain climbers. **2** temporary wooden building for soldiers. ˋ**hut·ment** *n* encampment of huts. **hut·ted** *adj*: *hutted camps,* with huts, not tents (for troops, etc)

hutch /hʌtʃ/ *n* box or cage with a front of wire netting, esp one used for rabbits.

huzza /hʊˋzɑ/ *int* (archaic) = **hurrah**.

hya·cinth /ˈhaɪəsɪnθ/ *n* plant growing from a bulb; its sweet-smelling flowers. ˋ**water-~,** wild plant that grows in floating masses on rivers, lakes, etc and may hinder navigation.

hy·æna /haɪˋinə/ ⇨ **hyena**.

hy·brid /ˈhaɪbrɪd/ *n, adj* (animal, plant, etc) from parents of different species or varieties: *A mule is a ~ animal. 'Cablegram' is a ~; half the word is Latin and half is Greek.* ˋ**~·ize** /-ɑɪz/ *vt,vi* [VP6A,2A] (cause to) produce ~s; interbreed.

hy·dra /ˈhɑɪdrə/ *n* (Gk myth) great sea serpent with many heads that grew again if cut off.

hy·drangea /hɑɪˋdreɪndʒə/ *n* (sorts of) shrub with large round heads of white, blue or pink flowers.

hy·drant /ˈhɑɪdrənt/ *n* pipe from a water-main (esp in a street) with a nozzle to which a hose can be attached for street-cleaning, putting out fires, etc.

hy·drate /ˈhɑɪdreɪt/ *n* chemical compound of water with another substance. □ *vt,vi* combine with water to make a ~; become a ~.

hy·drau·lic /hɑɪˋdrɔlɪk/ *adj* of water moving through pipes; worked by the pressure of a fluid, esp water: *a ~ lift; ~ brakes,* in which the braking force is transmitted by compressed fluid; hardening under water: *~ cement.* **hy·drau·lics** *n pl* science of using water to produce power.

hy·dro /ˈhɑɪdrəʊ/ *n* (colloq abbr of) hydropathic establishment.

hy·dro·car·bon /ˈhɑɪdrəˋkɑbən/ *n* [C] substance formed of hydrogen and carbon, e g benzene, paraffin, coal gas.

hy·dro·chloric /ˈhɑɪdrəˋklorɪk *US:* -ˋklɔr-/ *adj*: *~ acid,* acid (**HCl**) containing hydrogen and chlorine.

hy·dro·elec·tric /ˈhɑɪdrəʊɪˋlektrɪk/ *adj* of electricity produced by water-power.

hy·dro·foil /ˈhɑɪdrəfɔɪl/ *n* boat equipped with plates or fins which, when the boat is in motion, raise the hull out of the water.

hy·dro·gen /ˈhaɪdrədʒən/ *n* gas (symbol **H**) without colour, taste or smell, that combines with oxygen to form water. **ˈ~ bomb,** ⇨ *fusion bomb* at fusion. **ˈ~ peˈroxide** *n* solution of peroxide of ~, (H_2O_2), used as an antiseptic and bleaching agent.

hy·drop·athy /haɪˈdropəθɪ/ *n* [U] use of water (internally and externally) in the treatment of disease. **hy·dro·pathic** /ˈhaɪdrəˈpæθɪk/ *adj* of ~: *hydropathic establishments* (abbr *hydro*), e g hotels with baths for ~.

hy·dro·pho·bia /ˈhaɪdrəˈfəʊbɪə/ *n* [U] rabies; disease marked by strong contractions of the muscles of the throat and consequent inability to drink water.

hy·dro·plane /ˈhaɪdrəpleɪn/ *n* speedboat; motorboat with a flat bottom, able to skim very fast over the surface; (old name for) seaplane.

hy·dro·pon·ics /ˈhaɪdrəˈponɪks/ *n pl* art of growing plants without soil, in water to which necessary chemical food is supplied.

hy·ena, hy·æna /haɪˈinə/ *n* flesh-eating wild animal, like a wolf, with a laughing cry. ⇨ the illus at large.

hy·giene /ˈhaɪdʒin/ *n* [U] science of, rules for, healthy living; cleanliness. **hy·gienic** /ˈhaɪˈdʒinɪk *US:* ˈhaɪdʒɪˈenɪk/ *adj* of ~; likely to promote health; free from disease germs: *hygienic conditions.* **hy·gieni·cally** /-klɪ/ *adv*

hy·men /ˈhaɪmən/ *n* **1 H~,** Greek god of marriage. **2** (anat) fold of tissue partly closing the vagina of a virgin girl or woman.

hymn /hɪm/ *n* song of praise to God, esp one for use in a religious service. □ *vt* praise (God) in ~s; express (praise) in ~s. **hym·nal** /ˈhɪmnl/ *n* book of ~s.

hy·per·bola /haɪˈpɜbələ/ *n* curve produced when a cone is cut by a plane passing anywhere except through its point.

hy·per·bole /haɪˈpɜbəlɪ/ *n* [U] (use of) exaggerated statement(s) made for effect and not intended to be taken literally; [C] instance of this, e g *waves as high as Everest.*

hy·per·criti·cal /ˈhaɪpəˈkrɪtɪkl/ *adj* too critical, esp of small faults.

hy·per·market /ˈhaɪpəmakɪt/ *n* immense supermarket occupying an extensive area, outside a town, with a large car park, selling all varieties of goods.

hy·phen /ˈhaɪfn/ *n* the mark (-) used to join two words together (as in *Anglo-French*), or between syllables. □ *vt* join (words) with a ~; write (a compound word) with a ~. **~·ate** /-eɪt/ *vt* = ~: *~ated Americans,* e g *German-Americans, Irish-Americans.*

hyp·no·sis /hɪpˈnəʊsɪs/ *n* (*pl* **-ses** /-siz/) state like deep sleep in which a person's acts may be controlled by another person. **hyp·notic** /hɪpˈnotɪk/ *adj* of ~: *in a hypnotic state.* **hyp·not·ism** /ˈhɪpnətɪzm/ *n* [U] (artificial production of) ~. **hyp·not·ize** /ˈhɪpnətaɪz/ *vt* [VP6A] produce ~ in (sb). **hyp·not·ist** /ˈhɪpnətɪst/ *n* person able to produce ~.

hypo /ˈhaɪpəʊ/ *n* (colloq abbr of) hyposulphate of soda ($Na_2S_2O_2$), used in photography as a fixing agent.

hy·po·chon·dria /ˈhaɪpəˈkondrɪə/ *n* [U] state of mental depression either without apparent cause or due to unnecessary anxiety about one's health. **hy·po·chon·driac** /ˈhaɪpəˈkondrɪæk/ *adj* of, affected by, ~. □ *n* suffer from ~.

hy·poc·risy /hɪˈpokrəsɪ/ *n* (*pl* **-sies**) [C,U] (instance of) falsely making oneself appear to be virtuous or good. **hyp·ocrite** /ˈhɪpəkrɪt/ *n* person guilty of ~. **hy·po·criti·cal** /ˈhɪpəˈkrɪtɪkl/ *adj* of ~ or a hypocrite. **hy·po·criti·cally** /-klɪ/ *adv*

hy·po·der·mic /ˈhaɪpəˈdɜmɪk/ *adj* (of drugs, etc) injected beneath the skin: *~ injections; a ~ needle/syringe,* used for giving such injections. ⇨ the illus at syringe. □ *n* ~ injection.

hy·pot·en·use /haɪˈpotənjuz *US:* -tṇus/ *n* side of a right-angled triangle opposite the right angle.

hy·poth·ecate /haɪˈpoθɪkeɪt/ *vt* pledge; mortgage.

hy·poth·esis /ˈhaɪˈpoθəsɪs/ *n* (*pl* **-ses** /-siz/) idea, suggestion, put forward as a starting-point for reasoning or explanation. **hy·po·theti·cal** /ˈhaɪpəˈθetɪkl/ *adj* of, based on, a ~; not based on certain knowledge.

hys·sop /ˈhɪsəp/ *n* strong-smelling plant formerly used in medicine.

hys·teria /hɪˈstɪərɪə/ *n* [U] **1** disturbance of the nervous system, with outbursts of emotion, often uncontrollable. **2** senseless, uncontrolled excitement, e g in a crowd of young people round a popular film star. **hys·teri·cal** /hɪˈsterɪkl/ *adj* caused by, suffering from, ~: *hysterical laughter; hysterical outbursts of fury.* **hys·teri·cally** /-klɪ/ *adv* **hys·ter·ics** /hɪˈsterɪks/ *n pl* attack(s) of ~: *go into hysterics.*

Ii

I[1] i /aɪ/ (*pl* **I's i's** /aɪz/), the ninth letter of the English alphabet; as Roman numeral, = 1, as iii (= 3), IX (= 9). ⇨ App 4.

I[2] /aɪ/ *pers pron* used by a speaker or writer to refer to himself. Cf *me,* object form, and *we, us,* plural forms.

iamb /ˈaɪæm/ *n* = iambus.

iam·bus /aɪˈæmbəs/ *n* (*pl* **-buses** or **-bi** /-baɪ/) metrical foot of one short and one long, or one unaccented and one accented, word or syllable. **iam·bic** /aɪˈæmbɪk/ *adj* of, containing, ~es: *iambic feet,* e g / I cóme / from háunts / of cóot / and férn. □ *n* (*pl*) iambic verse.

ibex /ˈaɪbeks/ *n* wild goat (of the Alps and Pyrenees) with large curved horns.

ibi·dem /ˈɪbɪdem/ *adv* (abbr *ibid*) (Lat) in the same book, chapter, etc (previously quoted).

ibis /ˈaɪbɪs/ *n* large wading bird (like a stork) found in lakes and swamps in warm climates.

ice[1] /aɪs/ *n* **1** [U] frozen water; water made solid by cold: *Is the ice thick enough for skating?* ***break the ice,*** (fig) get people on friendly terms; overcome formality or reserve; take the first steps in a delicate matter. ***cut no ice (with sb),*** have little or no effect or influence (on him). ***keep sth on ice,*** in a refrigerator; (fig) reserve for later use. ***be skating on thin ice,*** (fig) in a dangerous or delicate situation. **dry ice,** ⇨ dry[1](13). **2** [C] frozen sweet of various kinds: *ˋwater-ice; cream ices; two strawberry ices.* ⇨ **ice-cream** below. **3** (compounds) **ˋIce Age** *n* time when much of the N hemisphere was covered with glaciers; glacial period. **ˋice-axe** *n* axe used by mountain climbers for cutting steps in ice. **ˋice·berg** *n* mass of ice (broken off a glacier) moving in the sea; (fig) unemotional person: *his iceberg of a wife.* **ˋice·boat** *n* boat fitted with runners and sails for travelling on a frozen lake or sea. **ˋice·bound** *adj* (of harbours, etc) obstructed by ice. **ˋice·box** *n* box in which ice is used to keep food cool; (US) refrigerator. **ˋice·breaker** *n* ship with strong curved bows used for breaking a passage through ice. **ˋice·cap** *n* permanent covering of ice sloping down on all sides from a high centre. **ˈice-ˋcream** *n* [C,U] (portion of) cream or custard (or various modern substitutes), sweetened, and flavoured and frozen. **ˋice·fall** *n* steep part of a glacier, like a frozen waterfall. **ˋice·field** *n* large expanse of (esp marine) ice in the Polar regions. **ice·floe** /-fləʊ/ *n* large sheet of floating ice. **ˋice-free** *adj* (of a port or harbour) free from ice. ⇨ **icebound** above. **ˋice hockey,** ⇨ **hockey. ˋice·house** *n* building often partly or wholly underground for storing ice in winter for use in summer. **ˋice-lolly** *n* flavoured ice on a stick. **ice-man** /-mæn/ *n* (*pl* **-men**) (US) man who retails and delivers ice (for use in iceboxes, etc). **ˋice·pack** *n* **(a)** stretch of sea covered with broken ice that has drifted into masses. **(b)** bag of broken ice used as an application, e g to the head, for fever. **ˋice-pantomime/-show** *nn* variety entertainment in which the performers are on ice-skates (on a floor of artificial ice). **ˋice·pick** *n* tool for breaking ice. **ˋice·rink** *n* indoor skating-rink with a floor of artificial ice. **ˋice-skate** *n* thin metal runner or blade on a boot for skating on ice. □ *vi* skate on ice. ⇨ the illus at **skate. ˋice-tray** *n* one in a refrigerator, for making cubes of ice.

an iceberg

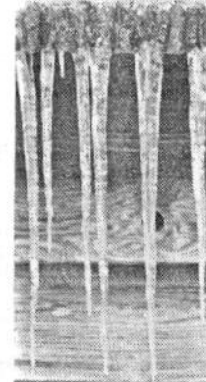
icicles

ice[2] /aɪs/ *vt,vi* **1** [VP6A] make very cold: *ice a bottle of beer; iced water.* **2** [VP2C,15B] ***ice over/up,*** cover, become covered, with a coating of ice: *The pond (was) iced over. The wings of the aircraft had iced up.* **3** [VP6A] cover (a cake) with sugar icing. ⇨ **icing.**

ich·neu·mon /ɪkˋnjumən/ *n* **1** small brown weasel-like animal noted for destroying crocodiles' eggs. **2** (also **ˋ~-fly**) insect which lays its eggs in or on the larva of another insect.

icicle /ˋaɪsɪkl/ *n* pointed piece of ice formed by the freezing of dripping water.

icing /ˋaɪsɪŋ/ *n* [U] **1** mixture of sugar, white of egg, flavouring, etc for covering cake(s). **2** formation of ice on the wings of aircraft.

icon /ˋaɪkon/ *n* (in the Eastern Church) painting or mosaic of a sacred person, itself regarded as sacred.

icons

icono·clast /aɪˋkonəklæst/ *n* person who took part in the movement against the use of images in religious worship in the churches of Eastern Europe in the 8th and 9th cc (also applied to Puritans in England, 17th c); (fig) person who attacks popular beliefs or established customs which he thinks mistaken or unwise.

icy /ˋaɪsɪ/ *adj* (**-ier, -iest**) very cold, like ice: *icy winds;* covered with ice: *icy roads;* (fig) *an icy welcome/manner.* **icily** /ˋaɪsɪlɪ/ *adv* (liter, fig) in an icy manner.

I'd /aɪd/ = *I had* or *I would.*

idea /aɪˋdɪə/ *n* **1** thought; picture in the mind: *This book gives you a good ~ of life in ancient Greece.* **2** plan; scheme; design; purpose: *That man is full of new ~s.* **3** opinion: *You shouldn't force your ~s on other people.* **4** vague belief; fancy; feeling that sth is probable: *I have an ~ that she will be late.* **5** conception: *What ~ can a man who is blind from birth have of colour? Picnicking is not my ~ of pleasure. You can have no ~ (of) how anxious we have been.* ***put ~s into sb's head,*** give him expectations that are not likely to be realized. **6** (in exclamations): *The ~ of such a thing! What an ~!* (used to suggest that what has been suggested is unrealistic, outrageous, etc). **7** way of thinking: *the young ~,* the child's mind.

ideal /aɪˋdɪəl/ *adj* **1** satisfying one's idea of what is perfect: *~ weather for a holiday.* **2** (contrasted with *real*) existing only in the imagination or as an idea; not likely to be achieved: *~ happiness; ~ plans for reforming the world.* □ *n* [C] idea, example, looked upon as perfect: *the high ~s of the Christian religion. She's looking for a husband but hasn't found her ~ yet.* **~ly** /aɪˋdɪəlɪ/ *adv*

ideal·ism /aɪˋdɪəlɪzm/ *n* [U] **1** living according to, being guided by, one's ideals. **2** (in art) (opposite of *realism*) imaginative treatment, showing beauty and perfection even if this means being untrue to facts. **3** (in philosophy) system of thought in which ideas are believed to be the only real things or the only things of which we can know anything. **ideal·ist** /-ɪst/ *n* person who believes in ~. **ideal·istic** /aɪˈdɪəˋlɪstɪk/ *adj* of idealists and ~.

ideal·ize /aɪˋdɪəlaɪz/ *vt* [VP6A] see, think of, as perfect: *Some biographers ~ their subjects.* **ideal·iz·ation** /aɪˈdɪəlaɪˋzeɪʃn *US:* -lɪˋz-/ *n*

idem /ˋɪdem/ *n, adj* (Lat) (by) the same author, etc; the same word, book, authority, etc (already mentioned).

ident·ical /aɪˋdentɪkl/ *adj* **1** the same: *This is the ~ knife with which the murder was committed.* **2** exactly alike; agreeing in every way: *The fingerprints of no two persons are ~. Our views of what should be done are ~. 40 inches is ~ with 3 feet 4 inches.* **3** **ˈ~ ˋtwins,** twins from one single fertilized ovum. **~ly** /-klɪ/ *adv*

ident·ify /ɑɪˋdentɪfɑɪ/ *vt* (*pt,pp* -fied) [VP6A,14] **1** say, show, prove, who or what sb or sth is; establish the identity of: *Could you ~ your umbrella among a hundred others? His accent was difficult to ~.* **2 ~ with,** treat (sth) as identical (with); equate (one thing with another). **3 ~ *oneself* with,** give support to, be associated with: *He refused to ~ himself/become identified with the new political party.* **identi·fi·ca·tion** /ɑɪˈdentɪfɪˋkeɪʃn/ *n* [U] ~ing or being identified: *the identification of persons killed in a road accident,* finding out who they are.

iden·ti·kit /ɑɪˋdentɪkɪt/ *n* composite drawing or photograph of the face of an unidentified person (esp a suspected criminal), from features recalled by those who saw him.

ident·ity /ɑɪˋdentətɪ/ *n* (*pl* -ties) **1** [U] state of being identical; absolute sameness; exact likeness. **2** [C,U] who sb is; what sth is: *There is no clue to the ~ of the thief,* nothing to show who he is. *The cheque will be cashed upon proof of ~. He was arrested because of mistaken ~.* **ˋ~ card/disc/certificate,** card, etc that gives proof of one's ~.

ideo·gram /ˋɪdɪəgræm/, **ideo·graph** /ˋɪdɪəgrɑf *US:* -græf/ *nn* written or printed character that symbolizes the idea of a thing without indicating the sounds that make up the word, e g as used in Chinese writing. **ideo·graphic** /ˈɪdɪəˋgræfɪk/ *adj*

ideograms

ideo·lect /ˋɪdɪəlekt/ *n* the total of a person's language that he knows and uses at any stage of his language development: *Is the word 'psychosis' part of your ~?*

ideol·ogy /ˈɑɪdɪˋolədʒɪ/ *n* (*pl* -gies) **1** [C] manner of thinking, ideas, characteristic of a person, group, etc, esp as forming the basis of an economic or political system: *bourgeois, Marxist and totalitarian ideologies.* **2** [U] unproductive thought. **ideo·logi·cal** /ˈɑɪdɪəˋlodʒɪkl/ *adj* **ideo·logi·cally** /-klɪ/ *adv*

ides /ɑɪdz/ *n pl* (in the calendar of ancient Rome) the 15th of March, May, July, Oct or the 13th of other months.

id est /ˈɪd ˋest/ (abbr *i e*) (Lat) that is to say.

idi·ocy /ˋɪdɪəsɪ/ *n* **1** [U] state of being an idiot; extreme stupidity. **2** [C] (*pl* -cies) extremely stupid act, remark, etc.

id·iom /ˋɪdɪəm/ *n* **1** language of a people or country; specific character of this, e g one peculiar to a country, district, group of people, or to one individual: *the French ~; the ~ of the New England countryside,* i e the kind of English used by country people there; *Shakespeare's ~,* the method of expression peculiar to him. **2** (gram) succession of words whose meaning is not obvious through knowledge of the individual meanings of the constituent words but must be learnt as a whole, e g *give way, in order to, be hard put to it.* **idio·matic** /ˈɪdɪəˋmætɪk/ *adj* **1** in accordance with the ~s of a language, dialect, etc: *speak ~atic English.* **2** full of ~s(2): *an ~atic language.* **idi·om·ati·cally** /ˈɪdɪəˋmætɪklɪ/ *adv*

idio·syn·crasy /ˈɪdɪəˋsɪŋkrəsɪ/ *n* [C] (*pl* -sies) way of thinking or behaving that is peculiar to a person; personal mannerism. **idio·syn·cratic** /ˈɪdɪəsɪŋˋkrætɪk/ *adj*

id·iot /ˋɪdɪət/ *n* **1** person so weak-minded that hs is incapable of rational conduct. **2** (colloq) fool: *'I've left my umbrella in the train. What an ~ I am!'* **idi·otic** /ˈɪdɪˋotɪk/ *adj* stupid. **~i·cally** /-klɪ/ *adv*

idle /ˋɑɪdl/ *adj* (-r, -st) **1** doing no work; not employed; not active or in use; (of time) not spent in doing something: *When men cannot find employment they are ~* (though not necessarily lazy). *During the business depression half the machines in the factory were ~. We spent many ~ hours during the holidays.* **2** (of persons) not willing to work; lazy (which is the commoner word for this sense): *an ~, worthless girl.* **3** useless; worthless: *Don't listen to ~ gossip/tales. It's ~ to expect help from that man.* □ *vi,vt* **1** [VP2A, C] be ~; *Don't ~ (about).* **2** [VP15B] **~ away,** spend in an ~ manner: *Don't ~ away your time.* **3** (of a car engine) run slowly in neutral gear. **idler** /ˋɑɪdlə(r)/ *n* person who ~s. **idly** /ˋɑɪdlɪ/ *adv* **~-ness** *n* state of being ~: *live in ~ness.*

idol /ˋɑɪdl/ *n* **1** image in wood, stone, etc of a god; such an image used as an object of worship; false god. **2** sb or sth greatly loved or admired: *He was an only child, and the ~ of his parents. Don't make an ~ of wealth.* **~·ater** /ɑɪˋdolətə(r)/ *n* **1** worshipper of ~s. **2** devoted admirer (*of...*). **~-atress** /ɑɪˋdolətrəs/ *n* woman ~ater. **~·atrous** /ɑɪˋdolətrəs/ *adj* (of a person) worshipping ~s; of the worship of ~s. **~·atrous·ly** *adv* **~·atry** /ɑɪˋdolətrɪ/ *n* **1** [U] the worship of ~s; excessive devotion to or admiration of (sb or sth). **2** [C] (*pl* -ries) instance of this. **~·ize** /ˋɑɪdl̩ɑɪz/ *vt* [VP6A] make an ~ of; love or admire to excess. **~·iz·ation** /ˈɑɪdl̩ɑɪˋzeɪʃn *US:* -l̩ɪˋz-/ *n* ~izing or being ~ized.

idyll /ˋɪdl *US:* ˋɑɪdl/ *n* short description, usu in verse, of a simple scene or event, esp of country life; scene, etc suitable for this. **idyl·lic** /ɪˋdɪlɪk *US:* ɑɪˋd-/ *adj* suitable for, like, an ~; simple and pleasant.

if /ɪf/ *conj* **1** on the condition that; supposing that: **(a)** (Present or Present Perfect Tense in the *if*-clause, indicating that sth is possible, probable, or likely): *If you ask him, he will help you. If (it is) necessary, I can come at six. If you have finished with that book, take it back to the library.* **(b)** (to indicate that an event is unlikely or improbable; *should* may be used in the *if*-clause): *If anyone should call, please let me know. If it should be necessary, I could come at six.* **(c)** (Note the use of *will* in an *if*-clause, not to show future time, but as part of the polite formula 'Will you, please'): *If you will wait a moment* (= Please wait a moment and) *I'll go and tell the manager that you are here.* **(d)** (Past Tense in the *if*-clause, indicating a condition that cannot be, or is unlikely to be realized, or is one put forward for consideration): *If you were a bird, you could fly. If I asked him/If I were to ask him for a loan, would he agree? If you would lend me £5 until Monday, I should be grateful.* **(e)** (Past Perfect Tense in the *if*-clause, indicating that the condition was not fulfilled, e g because it was an impossible one, or through sb's failure to act): *If they'd started earlier, they would have arrived in time. If they had not started when they did, they wouldn't be here now.* (After some *vv,* e g *think, remember, ask,* the main clause depending upon the condition is usu omitted): *If you think about it,* (you realize that) *there were many bright boys in that class. If you ask me,* (I will tell you) *he's a fool.* **2** (Note that in literary style *if* may be omitted, inversion of subject and *aux v* being used instead, esp *were/had/should*): *Should it* (= If it should) *be necessary...; Were I* (= If I were) *in your place...; Had I* (= If I had) *known earlier....* **3** (When *if* is used meaning 'when' or 'whenever', so that there is no condition, tenses in the main clause and the *if*-clause may be the same): *If you mix yellow and blue you get green. If she wants the steward she rings the bell.* **4** (often preceded by *even*) granting or admitting that: *If I'm mistaken, you're mistaken, too. Even if he did say that, I'm sure he didn't intend to hurt your feelings.* **5** ***(even) if,*** (may mean 'although'): *I'll do it, even if it takes me all the afternoon.* **6** (*if* may replace *whether* in colloq style, to introduce an interrogative clause): *Do you know if Mr Smith is at home? She asked if that was enough.* (*if* should not replace *whether* in cases where there may be ambiguity). Cf *Let me know whether you are coming,* say *'I'm coming'* or *'I'm not coming'. 'Let me know if you are coming,* say *'I'm coming'* or, alternatively, say nothing. **7** ***as if,*** as it would be if. (*It isn't as if* suggests that the contrary of what follows is true): *It isn't as if we were rich,* i e We are *not* rich. *It isn't as if he doesn't know the rules,* i e He *does* know the rules. (*As if* often introduces an exclamation): *As if I would allow it!* i e I would certainly *not* allow it! ⇨ **as**[2]**(11)**. **8** ***if only,*** (often introduces a wish, or indicates an unfulfilled condition, esp in exclamations): *If only he arrives in time! If only she would marry me! If only she had known about it* (but she did not know)! *If only you could/If you could only have seen it.* **9** (*if,* followed by a *v* in the neg, is used in exclamations to indicate dismay, surprise, etc): *Well, if I haven't left my umbrella in the train! And if he didn't try to knock me down!* What do you think he did? He tried to knock me down!

ig·loo /ˋɪglu/ *n* (*pl* ~s) dome-shaped winter hut made of blocks of hard snow, used by the Eskimos.

ig·neous /ˋɪgnɪəs/ *adj* (of rocks) formed by volcanic action.

ig·nis fatuus /ˈɪgnɪs ˋfætʃʊəs/ *n* (*pl* **ignes fatui** /ˈɪgniz ˋfætjuɪ/) **1** = **will-o'-the-wisp**. **2** (colloq) sth misleading.

ig·nite /ɪgˋnaɪt/ *vt,vi* [VP6A,2A] set on fire; take fire. **ig·ni·tion** /ɪgˋnɪʃn/ *n* igniting or being ~d; (in a petrol engine) electrical mechanism for igniting the mixture of explosive gases: *switch on the ignition.*

ig·noble /ɪgˋnəʊbl/ *adj* **1** dishonourable; shameful: *an ~ man/action; an ~ peace.* **2** (old use) of low birth. **ig·nobly** *adv*

ig·nom·ini·ous /ˈɪgnəˋmɪnɪəs/ *adj* bringing contempt, disgrace, shame; dishonourable: *~ behaviour; an ~ defeat.* **~·ly** *adv*

ig·nom·iny /ˋɪgnəmɪnɪ/ *n* **1** [U] public dishonour or shame. **2** [C] (*pl* **-nies**) dishonourable or disgraceful act; [U] dishonourable behaviour.

ig·nor·amus /ˈɪgṇəˋreɪməs/ *n* (*pl* **~es** /-sɪz/) ignorant person.

ig·nor·ance /ˋɪgnərəns/ *n* [U] the state of being ignorant; want of knowledge: *We are in complete ~ of his plans. If he did wrong, it was from/through ~.*

ig·nor·ant /ˋɪgnərnt/ *adj* **1** (of persons) knowing little or nothing; not aware: *He's quite ~—he can't even read. He's not stupid, merely ~. You are not ~ of the reasons for her behaviour. What his plans are I am quite ~ of.* **2** showing ignorance; resulting from ignorance: *an ~ reply; ~ conduct.* **~·ly** *adv*

ig·nore /ɪgˋnɔ(r)/ *vt* [VP6A] take no notice of; refuse to take notice of: *~ rude remarks; be ~d by one's superiors.*

iguana /ɪˋgwɑnə/ *n* large tree-climbing lizard of tropical America. ⇨ the illus at **reptile**.

ikon /ˋɑɪkon/ *n* = **icon**.

ilex /ˋɑɪleks/ *n* holm-oak; (bot) genus of trees including the common holly.

ilk /ɪlk/ *n* (Scot) ***of that ilk,*** (now hum, joc) of the same place, estate, etc.

I'll /ɑɪl/ = *I will* or *I shall*.

ill /ɪl/ *adj* **1** (usu pred) in bad health; sick: *She was ill with anxiety.* ***fall/be taken ill,*** become ill. ⇨ **worse, worst**. **2** (attrib) bad: *ill health; in an ill temper/humour; ill repute; do sb an ill turn; have ill luck; a bird of ill omen.* ***It's an ill wind that blows nobody any good,*** (prov) An affair must be very bad indeed if it does not benefit somebody. ***Ill weeds grow apace,*** (prov) Harmful things grow or spread rapidly. **ˈill-ˋbreeding** *n* bad manners. **ˈill-ˋfavoured** *adj* (of a person) unpleasant to look at; ugly. **ˈill-ˋmannered** *adj* having bad manners; rude. **ˈill-ˋnatured** *adj* bad-tempered. **ˈill-ˋomened** *adj* destined to misfortune. **ˈill-ˋstarred** *adj* born under an evil star; unlucky. **ˈill-ˋtreatment/-ˋusage** *n* [U] cruelty; harsh treatment. **ˈill ˋwill** *n* enmity; unkind feeling. □ *n* **1** [U] evil; injury: *do ill.* **2** [C] misfortune; trouble: *the various ills of life.* □ *adv* badly; imperfectly; unfavourably: *They were ill* (= insufficiently) *provided with ammunition. We could ill* (= not well, not easily) *afford the time and money. It ill becomes you to critize him,* It is not right or proper for you to do so. ***speak ill of sb,*** in an unkind or unfavourable way. ***be/feel ill at ease,*** uncomfortable, embarrassed. **ˈill-adˋvised** *adj* unwise; imprudent. **ˈill-afˋfected (towards)** *adj* not well-disposed; not feeling favour. **ˈill-ˋbred** *adj* badly brought up; rude. **ˈill-disˋposed (towards)** *adj* **(a)** wishing to do harm (to). **(b)** unfavourable (towards a plan, etc). **ˈill-ˋfated** *adj* destined to misfortune; bringing misfortune. **ˈill-gotten ˋgains** *n pl* money gained by evil or unlawful methods. **ˈill-ˋjudged** *adj* done at an unsuitable time; showing poor judgement: *an ill-judged attempt.* **ˈill-ˋtimed** *adj* badly timed; done at a wrong or unsuitable time. **ˈill-ˋtreat/-ˋuse** *vt* treat badly or cruelly.

il·legal /ɪˋligl/ *adj* not legal; contrary to law. **~ly** /-gḷɪ/ *adv* **~·ity** /ˈɪlɪˋgæləti/ *n* [U] being ~; [C] (*pl* **-ties**) ~ act.

il·leg·ible /ɪˋledʒəbl/ *adj* difficult or impossible to read. **il·leg·ibly** /-əblɪ/ *adv* **il·leg·ibil·ity** /ɪˈledʒəˋbɪlətɪ/ *n* [U].

il·legit·imate /ˈɪlɪˋdʒɪtɪmət/ *adj* **1** not authorized by law; contrary to law. **2** born of parents who were not married to each other: *an ~ child; of ~ descent.* **3** (of a conclusion in an argument, etc) not logical; wrongly inferred. □ *n* an ~ person. **~·ly** *adv* **il·legit·imacy** /ˈɪlɪˋdʒɪtɪməsɪ/ *n* [U].

il·lib·eral /ɪˋlɪbrl/ *adj* not befitting a free man; narrow-minded; intolerant; ungenerous; mean. **~ly** /-rlɪ/ *adv* **~·ity** /ˈɪˈlɪbəˋrælətɪ/ *n*

il·licit /ɪˋlɪsɪt/ *adj* unlawful; forbidden: *the ~ sale of opium.* **~·ly** *adv*

il·limit·able /ɪˋlɪmɪtəbl/ *adj* unboundless; without limits: *~ space/ambition.*

il·lit·er·ate /ɪˋlɪtr̩ət/ *adj* with little or no education; unable to read or write; showing such ignorance: *an ~ letter,* one full of spelling and grammatical errors. □ *n* ~ person. **il·lit·er·acy** /ˈɪˋlɪtr̩əsɪ/ *n*

ill·ness /ˋɪlnəs/ *n* **1** [U] state of being ill (contrasted with *health*): *There has been no/not much/a great deal of ~ in the village this winter.* **2** [C] specific kind of, occasion of, ~: *~es of children; a serious ~; one ~ after another.*

il·logi·cal /ɪˋlodʒɪkl/ *adj* without logic; contrary to logic. **~ly** /-klɪ/ *adv* **~·ity** /ɪˈlodʒɪˋkælətɪ/, (rarely **~·ness**) *nn*

il·lume /ɪˋlum/ *vt* (poet) illuminate.

il·lumi·nate /ɪˋlumɪneɪt/ *vt* [VP6A] **1** give light to; throw light on: *a street ~d by oil lamps; poorly ~d rooms.* **2** decorate (streets, etc) with bright lights as a sign of rejoicing. **3** decorate (initial letters in a manuscript) with gold, silver and bright colours (as was the custom in the Middle Ages). **4** make clear, help to explain: *~ a difficult passage in a book.* **il·lumi·na·tion** /ɪˈlumɪˋneɪʃn/ *n* **1** [U] illuminating or being ~d. **2** (usu *pl*) lights, etc, used to ~(**2**) a town for a special occasion. **3** (*pl*) decorations on a manuscript. **il·lu·mine** /ɪˋlumɪn/ *vt* [VP6A] enlighten spiritually; make bright.

il·lu·sion /ɪˋluʒn/ *n* **1** [C] (the seeing of) sth that does not really exist, or of sth as different from the reality; false idea or belief: *an optical ~.* ***be under an ~,*** be deceived by one. ***cherish an ~/the ~ that...,*** like to believe.... ***have no ~s about sb/sth,*** have no false beliefs about him/it. **2** [U] state of mind in which one is deceived in this way. **~·ist** /-ɪst/ *n* person who produces optical ~s on the stage; conjurer.

il·lu·sive /ɪˋlusɪv/, **il·lu·sory** /ɪˋlusərɪ/ *adjj* deceptive; based on illusion.

il·lus·trate /ˋɪləstreɪt/ *vt* [VP6A] **1** explain by examples, pictures, etc. **2** supply a book, article, lecture, etc with pictures, diagrams, etc: *a well-~d textbook.* **il·lus·tra·tor** /-tə(r)/ *n* person who ~s books, etc. **il·lus·tra·tion** /ˈɪləˋstreɪʃn/ *n* **1** [U] illustrating or being ~d: *cite instances in illustration of a theory. Illustration is often more useful than definition for giving the meanings of words.* **2** [C] sth that ~s; picture, diagram, etc. **il·lus·tra·tive** /ˋɪləstrətɪv *US:* ɪˋlʌs-/ *adj* serving to ~, as an explanation or example (*of* sth).

il·lus·tri·ous /ɪˋlʌstrɪəs/ *adj* greatly distinguished; celebrated. **~·ly** *adv*

I'm /ɑɪm/ = *I am.* ⇨ **be**[1].

im·age /ˋɪmɪdʒ/ *n* [C] **1** likeness or copy of the shape of sb or sth, esp one made in wood, stone, etc: *an ~ of the Virgin Mary; graven ~s,* ~s carved in wood, etc and regarded as gods. **2** close likeness; counterpart: *Did man create God in his own ~?* ***be the (very/spitting) ~ (of sth/sb),*** be exactly like it/him. **3** mental picture or idea; concept of sth or sb, e g a politician, political party, commercial firm, product, held by the public: *How can we improve our ~?* **4** simile; metaphor: *speak in ~s,* use figures of speech that bring pictures to the mind. **5** reflection seen in a mirror or through the lens of a camera. □ *vt* [VP6A] **1** make an ~ of, portray. **2** reflect; mirror; symbolize. **~ry** /ˋɪmɪdʒrɪ/ *n* [U] the use of ~s(**4**), or figures of speech, in writing; ~s(**1**) collectively.

im·agin·able /ɪˋmædʒn̩əbl/ *adj* that can be imagined: *We had the greatest difficulty ~ getting here in time.*

im·agin·ary /ɪˋmædʒnrɪ *US:* -dʒn̩erɪ/ *adj* existing only in the mind; unreal.

im·agin·ation /ɪˈmædʒɪˋneɪʃn/ *n* [C,U] **1** power of the mind to imagine: *He hasn't much ~. Novelists use their ~. Children are encouraged to use their ~s.* **2** what is imagined: *You didn't really see a ghost—it was only ~.* **im·agin·ative** /ɪˋmædʒn̩ətɪv *US:* -n̩eɪtɪv/ *adj* of, having, using, ~: *imaginative writers.*

im·ag·ine /ɪˋmædʒɪn/ *vt* [VP6A,C,9,10,16B,19A,C,25] form a picture of in the mind; think of (sth) as probable: *Can you ~ life without electricity and other modern conveniences? I~ yourself (to be) on a desert island. I~ you've been ship-wrecked. I ~ him as a big, tall man. Can you ~ him/yourself becoming famous as an actor? I can't ~ (my) marrying a girl of that sort. Don't ~* (= get the idea) *that I can lend you money every time you need it!*

imam /ɪˋmɑm/ *n* title of various Muslim leaders; prayer leader in a mosque; scholar on Islamic law.

im·bal·ance /ˈɪmˋbæləns/ *n* absence of balance between two totals, e g payments; lack of proportion: *the country's ~ in world payments,* the state that exists when the total sum paid for imports, etc, is unequal to the total received for exports, services, etc; *the increasing ~ between rich and poor countries,* the increasing wealth of some and the increasing poverty of others.

im·be·cile /ˋɪmbəsil *US:* -sl/ *adj* weak-minded; stupid: *~ remarks/conduct.* □ *n* ~ person; fool; **im·be·cil·ity** /ˋɪmbəˋsɪlətɪ/ *n* [U] stupidity; [C] (*pl* **-ties**) stupid act, remark, etc.

im·bed /ɪmˋbed/ *vt* (**-dd-**) = **embed.**

im·bibe /ɪmˋbɑɪb/ *vt* (formal) drink; take in: *~ ideas/knowledge.*

im·bro·glio /ɪmˋbrəʊlɪəʊ/ *n* (*pl* ~s /-z/) complicated (esp political or dramatic) situation.

im·bue /ɪmˋbju/ *vt* (*pt,pp* **-bued**) [VP14] ***~ with,*** (formal) fill, inspire: *~d with patriotism/hatred, etc; politicians ~d with a sense of their own importance.*

imi·tate /ˋɪmɪtəɪt/ *vt* [VP6A] **1** copy the behaviour of; take as an example: *You should ~ great and good men.* **2** mimic (consciously or not): *Parrots ~ human speech.* **3** be like; make a likeness of: *wood painted to ~ marble.* **imi·ta·tor** /-tə(r)/ *n*

imi·ta·tion /ˈɪmɪˋteɪʃn/ *n* **1** [U] imitating: *I~ is the sincerest form of flattery. He sets us a good example for ~. She was pirouetting in ~ of her teacher.* **2** (attrib) not real: *~ leather/jewellery.* **3** [C] sth made or done in ~: *~s of the cries of birds and animals. Beware of ~s.*

imi·tat·ive /ˋɪmɪtətɪv *US:* -teɪtɪv/ *adj* following the model or example of: *the ~ arts,* painting and sculpture; *~ words,* e g *buzz, plop,* the sound of the word being considered similar to the sound it represents; *as ~ as a monkey.*

im·macu·late /ɪˋmækjʊlət/ *adj* **1** pure; faultless: *~ conduct; the I~ Conception,* of the Virgin Mary. **2** right in every detail: *an ~ white suit.* **~·ly** *adv*: *~ly dressed.*

im·ma·nent /ˋɪmənənt/ *adj* ***~ (in),*** (of qualities) present; inherent; (of God) permanently pervading the universe. **im·ma·nence** /-əns/ *n*

im·ma·terial /ˈɪməˋtɪərɪəl/ *adj* ***~ (to),*** **1** unimportant: *~ objections. That's quite ~ to me.* **2** not having physical substance: *as* ~ *as a ghost.*

im·ma·ture /ˈɪməˈtjʊə(r) *US:* -ˈtʊər/ *adj* not yet fully developed: *an* ~ *girl; the* ~ *minds of young children.* **im·ma·tur·ity** /ˈɪməˈtjʊərətɪ *US:* -ˈtʊər-/ *n* [U].

im·measur·able /ɪˈmeʒr̩əbl/ *adj* that cannot be measured.

im·medi·ate /ɪˈmidɪət/ *adj* **1** without anything coming between; nearest: *two objects in* ~ *contact; the* ~ *heir to the throne,* the next in succession, not a remote heir; *my* ~ *neighbours;* ~ *information,* first-hand or direct, not second-hand. **2** occurring, done, at once: *an* ~ *answer; take* ~ *action.* **~·ly** *adv* **1** at once; without delay. **2** directly or closely. □ *conj* as soon as: *You may leave* ~*ly he comes.*

im·mem·or·ial /ˈɪməˈmɔrɪəl/ *adj* (esp) ***from time* ~,** going back beyond the reach of memory: *the* ~ *privileges of the House of Commons.*

im·mense /ɪˈməns/ *adj* very large. **~·ly** *adv* in an ~ degree; (colloq) very much: *They enjoyed themselves* ~*ly.* **im·men·sity** /ɪˈmənsətɪ/ *n* [U] great size; (*pl;* **-ties**) things that are ~.

im·merse /ɪˈmɜs/ *vt* [VP6A,14] **1** put under the surface of (water or other liquid): ~ *one's head in the water.* **2** absorb, involve deeply: *be* ~*d in a book/thought/work/one's business.* **im·mer·sion** /ɪˈmɜʃn *US:* -ʒn/ *n* immersing or being ~d; (esp) baptism by putting the whole body into water. **ˈimmersion heater,** electric water-heater (usu one that is fixed in a hot-water tank).

im·mi·grate /ˈɪmɪgreɪt/ *vi* [VP2A,3A] ~ ***(into),*** come as a settler (into another country), not as a tourist or visitor. **im·mi·grant** /ˈɪmɪgrənt/ *n* person who ~s: *European immigrants in Australia.* **im·mi·gra·tion** /ˈɪmɪˈgreɪʃn/ *n* [U] immigrating; [C] instance of this: *the numerous immigrations into the US.*

im·mi·nent /ˈɪmɪnənt/ *adj* (of events, esp dangers) likely to come or happen soon: *A storm is* ~. *He was faced with* ~ *death.* **~·ly** *adv* **im·mi·nence** /-əns/ *n* [U] the state of being ~.

im·mo·bile /ɪˈməʊbɑɪl *US:* -bil/ *adj* not able to move or be moved; motionless. **im·mo·bi·lize** /ɪˈməʊbl̩ɑɪz/ *vt* [VP6A] make ~; render armed forces, vehicles, etc incapable of being moved; take capital, specie out of circulation. **im·mo·bil·iz·ation** /ɪˈməʊbl̩ɑɪˈzeɪʃn *US:* -l̩ɪˈz-/ *n* **im·mo·bil·ity** /ˈɪməˈbɪlətɪ/ *n* [U] state of being ~.

im·mod·er·ate /ɪˈmodr̩ət/ *adj* excessive; extreme: ~ *eating and drinking.* **~·ly** *adv*

im·mod·est /ɪˈmodɪst/ *adj* **1** lacking in modesty; indecent or indelicate: *an* ~ *dress;* ~ *behaviour.* **2** impudent: ~ *boasts.* **~·ly** *adv* **~y** *n* [U] ~ behaviour; boldness; [C] (*pl* **-ties**) ~ act or remark.

im·mo·late /ˈɪməleɪt/ *vt* (formal) kill as an offering; sacrifice (one thing *to* another). **im·mo·la·tion** /ˈɪməˈleɪʃn/ *n* [U] immolating or being ~d; [C] instance of this.

im·moral /ɪˈmorl *US:* ɪˈmɔrl/ *adj* contrary to morality; wicked and evil: ~ *conduct. You* ~ *old man!* **~ly** /-rl̩ɪ/ *adv* **~·ity** /ˈɪməˈrælətɪ/ *n* [U] ~ conduct: *a life of* ~*ity;* [C] (*pl* **-ties**) ~ act.

im·mor·tal /ɪˈmɔrtl/ *adj* living for ever: *the* ~ *gods;* never forgotten: ~ *poetry/music;* ~ *fame.* □ *n* ~ being; (*pl*) **the ~s,** the gods of ancient Greece and Rome. **~·ity** /ˈɪmɔˈtælətɪ/ *n* [U] endless life or fame. **~·ize** /ɪˈmɔtl̩ɑɪz/ *vt* [VP6A] give endless life or fame to.

im·mov·able /ɪˈmuvəbl/ *adj* **1** that cannot be moved: ~ *property,* e g buildings, land. **2** fixed (*in* purpose, etc). **im·mov·ably** /-əblɪ/ *adv*

im·mune /ɪˈmjun/ *adj* ~ ***(from/against),*** free, secure: ~ *from smallpox as the result of vaccination;* ~ *against attacks.* **im·mun·ity** /ɪˈmjunətɪ/ *n* [U] safety, security (*from* disease, etc); exemption (*from* taxation, etc): *diplomatic immunity.* **im·mu·nize** /ˈɪmjʊnɑɪz/ *vt* make ~ (*against*). **im·mu·niz·ation** /ˈɪmjʊnɑɪˈzeɪʃn *US:* -nɪˈz-/ *n* [U].

im·mure /ɪˈmjʊə(r)/ *vt* [VP6A] (formal) imprison; shut (oneself) up: ~*d in a dungeon;* ~ *oneself in one's study in order to work undisturbed.*

im·mut·able /ɪˈmjutəbl/ *adj* (formal) that cannot be changed. **im·mut·ably** /-əblɪ/ *adv* **im·muta·bil·ity** /ɪˈmjutəˈbɪlətɪ/ *n*

imp /ɪmp/ *n* child of the devil; little devil; (playfully) mischievous child.

im·pact /ˈɪmpækt/ *n* ~ ***(on),*** **1** [C] collision. **2** [U] force exerted by one object when striking against another: *The car body collapses on* ~, when it collides with sth. **3** strong impression or effect: *the* ~ *of new ideas on a backward race of people.* □ *vt* /ɪmˈpækt/ pack, drive or wedge firmly together: *an* ~*ed tooth,* incapable of growing out of the jawbone.

im·pair /ɪmˈpeə(r)/ *vt* [VP6A] weaken; damage: ~ *one's health by overwork.* **~·ment** *n*

im·pala /ɪmˈpɑlə/ *n* (kind of) African antelope.

im·pale /ɪmˈpeɪl/ *vt* [VP6A,15A] pierce through, pin down, with a sharp-pointed stake, spear, etc. **~·ment** *n*

im·pal·pable /ɪmˈpælpəbl/ *adj* that cannot be touched or felt; not easily grasped by the mind.

im·panel /ɪmˈpænl/ = **empanel.**

im·part /ɪmˈpɑt/ *vt* [VP6A,14] ~ ***(to),*** (formal) give, pass on a share of sth, a quality, a secret, news, etc: *I have nothing of interest to* ~ *to you today.*

im·par·tial /ɪmˈpɑʃl/ *adj* fair (in giving judgements, etc); not favouring one more than another. **~ly** *adv* **im·par·tial·ity** /ˈɪmˈpɑʃɪˈælətɪ/ *n* [U] the quality of being ~.

im·pass·able /ɪmˈpɑsəbl *US:* -ˈpæs-/ *adj* (of country roads, etc) impossible to travel through or on: *Alpine passes* ~ *in winter.*

im·passe /ˈæmpɑs *US:* ˈɪmpæs/ *n* blind alley; place, position, from which there is no way out; deadlock.

im·pas·sioned /ɪmˈpæʃnd/ *adj* full of, showing, deep feeling: *an* ~ *speech.*

im·pass·ive /ɪmˈpæsɪv/ *adj* showing no sign of feeling; unmoved. **~·ly** *adv* **~·ness, im·pass·iv·ity** /ˈɪmpæˈsɪvətɪ/ *nn*

im·pa·tient /ɪmˈpeɪʃnt/ *adj* not patient: *The children were* ~ *to start. She is* ~ *of delay. They are growing* ~. **~·ly** *adv* **im·pa·tience** /ɪmˈpeɪʃns/ *n* [U].

im·peach /ɪmˈpitʃ/ *vt* **1** [VP6A] (formal) question, raise doubts about (sb's character, etc): *Do you* ~ *my motives,* suggest that they are dishonourable? **2** [VP14] ~ ***sb for sth/doing sth,*** (legal) accuse sb of wrongdoing; (esp) accuse (sb) of a crime against the State: ~ *a judge for taking bribes;* ~ *sb of a crime.* **~·ment** *n* [U] ~ing or being ~ed; [C] instance of this.

im·pec·cable /ɪmˈpekəbl/ *adj* (formal) faultless; incapable of doing wrong: *an* ~ *character/record.*

im·pe·cuni·ous /ˈɪmpɪˈkjunɪəs/ *adj* (formal)

having little or no money.

im·pede /ɪm`pid/ *vt* [VP6A] get in the way of; hinder: *What ~s your making an early start?*

im·pedi·ment /ɪm`pedɪmənt/ *n* [C] sth that hinders, esp a defect in speech, e g a stammer. **im·pedi·menta** /ɪm'pedɪ`mentə/ *n pl* baggage (esp of an army).

im·pel /ɪm`pel/ *vt* (-ll-) [VP17A,14] drive, force, urge: *He said he had been ~led to crime by poverty. The President's speech ~led the nation to greater efforts.* **~·ler** *n* rotor or rotor blade (of a jet engine).

im·pend /ɪm`pend/ *vi* (chiefly in *pres part*) (formal) be imminent; be about to come or happen: *her ~ing arrival; the ~ing storm; the danger ~ing over us.*

im·pen·etrable /ɪm`penɪtrəbl/ *adj* **~ *(to),*** that cannot be penetrated: *~ forests and swamps; dig down to ~ rock; ~ darkness; men who are ~ to reason.*

im·peni·tent /ɪm`penɪtənt/ *adj* (formal) not penitent. **~·ly** *adv* **im·peni·tence** /-əns/ *n*

im·pera·tive /ɪm`perətɪv/ *adj* **1** urgent; essential; needing immediate attention: *Is it really ~ for them to have such a large army? Is it ~ that they should have/for them to have six cars?* **2** not to be disobeyed; done, given with, authority: *The duke's orders were ~, 'Go at once!', he said, with an ~ gesture.* **3** (gram) form of the *verb* and sentence expressing commands: *the ~ mood.* **~·ly** *adv*

im·per·cep·tible /'ɪmpə`septəbl/ *adj* that cannot be perceived; very slight or gradual. **im·per·cep·tibly** /-əblɪ/ *adv*

im·per·fect /ɪm`pɜfɪkt/ *adj* **1** not perfect or complete. **2** (gram): *~ tenses,* those that denote action in progress but not completed (also called *progressive* or *continuous* tenses). □ *n* ~ tense. **~·ly** *adv* **im·per·fec·tion** /'ɪmpə`fekʃn/ *n* [U] state of being ~; [C] fault: *A woman has to overlook the little ~ions in her husband's character.*

im·perial /ɪm`pɪərɪəl/ *adj* **1** of an empire or its ruler(s): *~ trade; His I~ Majesty.* **2** majestic; august; magnificent: *with ~ generosity.* **3** (of weights and measures) used by law in the United Kingdom: *an ~ pint/gallon.* □ *n* small, pointed beard grown beneath the lower lip. **~ly** /-rɪəlɪ/ *adv*

im·peri·al·ism /ɪm`pɪərɪəl-ɪzm/ *n* belief in the value of colonies; policy of extending a country's empire and influence. **im·per·ial·ist** /-ɪst/ *n* supporter of, believer in, ~. **im·per·ial·is·tic** /ɪm'pɪərɪə`lɪstɪk/ *adj* of ~: *imperialistic views.*

im·peril /ɪm`perl/ *vt* (-ll-, US also -l-) [VP6A] (liter) put or bring into danger.

im·peri·ous /ɪm`pɪərɪəs/ *adj* (formal) **1** commanding; haughty; arrogant: *~ gestures/looks.* **2** urgent; imperative. **~·ly** *adv* **~·ness** *n*

im·per·ish·able /ɪm`perɪʃəbl/ *adj* (formal) that, cannot perish; that will never pass away: *~ fame/glory.*

im·per·ma·nent /ɪm`pɜmənənt/ *adj* (formal) not permanent. **im·per·ma·nence** /-əns/ *n*

im·per·me·able /ɪm`pɜmɪəbl/ *adj* **~ *(to),*** (formal) that cannot be permeated (esp by fluids); impervious.

im·per·sonal /'ɪm`pɜsnl/ *adj* **1** not influenced by personal feeling; not referring to any particular person: *~ remarks; an ~ discussion.* **2** having no existence as a person: *~ forces,* e g those of nature. **3** (of *verbs*) used after 'it' to make general statements such as *'It is raining/freezing'.* **~ly** /-nlɪ/ *adv*

im·per·son·ate /ɪm`pɜsṇeɪt/ *vt* [VP6A] **1** act the part of (in a play, etc); pretend to be (another person). **2** personify. **im·per·son·ation** /ɪm'pɜsn`eɪʃn/ *n* **1** [U] impersonating or being ~d. **2** [C] instance of this: *He gave some clever impersonations of well-known men.*

im·per·ti·nent /ɪm`pɜtɪnənt *US:* -tṇənt/ *adj* **1** not showing proper respect; impudent; saucy: *~ remarks; an ~ boy.* **2** not pertinent; not pertaining to the matter in hand. **~·ly** *adv* **im·per·ti·nence** /-əns/ *n* [U] being ~; [C] ~ act or remark.

im·per·turb·able /'ɪmpə`tɜbəbl/ *adj* (formal) not capable of being excited; calm. **im·per·turb·abil·ity** /'ɪmpə'tɜbə`bɪlətɪ/ *n* [U].

im·per·vi·ous /ɪm`pɜvɪəs/ *adj* **~ *(to),*** **1** (of materials) not allowing (water, etc) to pass through: *Rubber boots are ~ to water.* **2** (fig) not moved or influenced by: *~ to criticism/argument.*

im·pe·tigo /'ɪmpɪ`tɑɪgəʊ/ *n* [U] contagious skin disease.

im·petu·ous /ɪm`petʃʊəs/ *adj* moving quickly or violently; acting, inclined to act, on impulse, energetically but with insufficient thought or care; done or said hastily: *Children are usually more ~ than old people. Your ~ remarks will get you into trouble.* **~·ly** *adv* **im·petu·os·ity** /ɪm'petʃʊ`ɒsətɪ/ *n* [U] quality of being ~; [C] (*pl* -ties) ~ act, remark, etc.

im·pe·tus /`ɪmpɪtəs/ *n* (*pl* -tuses /-təsɪz/) **1** [U] force with which a body moves. **2** [C] impulse; driving force: *The treaty will give an ~ to trade between the two countries.*

im·pi·ety /ɪm`pɑɪətɪ/ *n* (formal) **1** [U] lack of reverence or dutifulness. **2** [C] (*pl* -ties) act, remark, etc that shows lack of reverence or dutifulness.

im·pinge /ɪm`pɪndʒ/ *vi* [VP3A] **~ *(up)on,*** (formal) make an impact. **~·ment** *n*

im·pi·ous /`ɪmpɪəs/ *adj* (formal) not pious; wicked. **~·ly** *adv*

imp·ish /`ɪmpɪʃ/ *adj* of or like an imp; mischievous. **~·ly** *adv* **~·ness** *n*

im·plac·able /ɪm`plækəbl/ *adj* (formal) that cannot be appeased; relentless: *an ~ enemy; ~ hatred, love.*

im·plant /ɪm`plɑnt *US:* -`plænt/ *vt* [VP6A,14] **~ *in,*** fix or put ideas, feelings, etc in: *deeply ~ed hatred; ~ sound principles in the minds of children.*

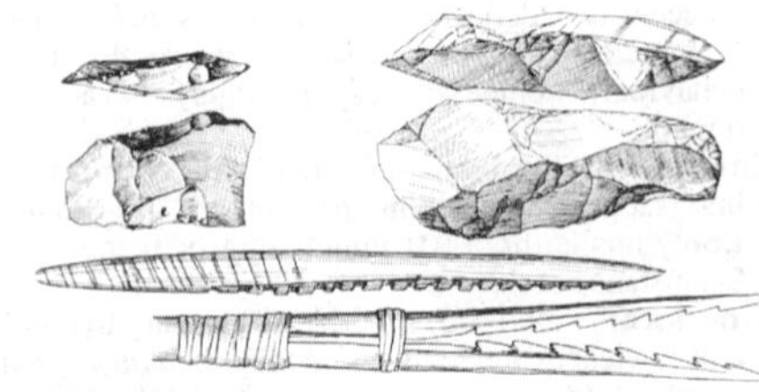

primitive stone implements

im·ple·ment[1] /`ɪmpləmənt/ *n* tool or instrument for working with, ⇨ the illus at **tool**: *farm ~s; stone and bronze ~s made by primitive man.*

im·ple·ment[2] /`ɪmpləment/ *vt* [VP6A] carry an undertaking, agreement, promise into effect: *~ a* *scheme.* **im·ple·men·ta·tion** /ˌɪmpləmen`teɪʃn/ *n*

im·pli·cate /`ɪmplɪkeɪt/ *vt* [VP6A,14] ~ **in,** (formal) show that (sb) has a share (*in* a crime, etc): *~ officials in a bribery scandal.* ⇨ **involve.**

im·pli·ca·tion /ˌɪmplɪ`keɪʃn/ *n* (formal) **1** [U] implicating or being implicated (in a crime, etc). **2** [C] what is implied; sth hinted at or suggested, but not expressed: *What are the ~s of this statement?* What is implied by it?

im·pli·cit /ɪm`plɪsɪt/ *adj* (formal) **1** ~ **(in),** implied though not plainly expressed: *an ~ threat; ~ in the contract.* ⇨ **explicit. 2** unquestioning: *~ belief.* **~·ly** *adv*

im·plore /ɪm`plɔ(r)/ *vt* [VP6A,17A,14] request earnestly: *~ a judge for mercy; ~ a friend to help one; an imploring glance.* **im·plor·ing·ly** *adv*

im·plo·sion /ɪm`pləʊʒn/ *n* bursting inward, collapse, of a vessel, e g an electric light bulb, from external pressure. ⇨ **explosion.**

im·ply /ɪm`plaɪ/ *vt* (*pt,pp* **-plied**) [VP6A,9] give or make a suggestion (*that*); involve the truth (of sth not definitely stated): *an implied rebuke. Silence sometimes implies consent,* failure to say 'No' may be taken to mean 'Yes'. *Are you ~ing that I am not telling the truth?*

im·po·lite /ˌɪmpə`laɪt/ *adj* not polite. **~·ly** *adv* **~·ness** *n*

im·poli·tic /ɪm`polətɪk/ *adj* (formal) not politic; not expedient.

im·pon·der·able /ɪm`pondrəbl/ *adj* (formal) of little or no weight; of which the effect cannot be estimated. □ *n* ~ thing; (esp fig, *pl*) qualities, emotions, etc of which the effect cannot be estimated.

im·port /ɪm`pɔt/ *vt* **1** [VP6A,14] ~ ***(from) (into),*** bring in, introduce, esp goods from a foreign country: *~ wool from Australia.* **2** [VP6A,9] (formal) mean; signify; make known (that): *What does this ~?* What is its significance? **3** be of consequence to: *It ~s us to know whether....* □ *n* /`ɪmpɔt/ **1** (usu *pl*) goods ~ed: *~s of raw cotton; food ~s.* **2** [U] act of ~ing goods. **3** [U] what is implied; meaning: *What is the ~ of his statement?* **4** [U] (formal) importance: *questions of great ~.* **~er** *n* person (usu a merchant) who ~s goods. **im·port·ation** /ˌɪmpɔ`teɪʃn/ *n* [U] act of ~ing (goods); [C] sth ~ed.

im·port·ant /ɪm`pɔtnt/ *adj* **1** of great influence; to be treated seriously; having a great effect: *~ decisions/books, etc.* **2** (of a person) having a position of authority. **~·ly** *adv* **im·port·ance** /-tns/ *n* [U] being ~: *The matter is of great/no/not much/little importance to us. He spoke with an air of importance.*

im·por·tu·nate /ɪm`pɔtʃʊnət/ *adj* (formal) **1** (of persons) making repeated and inconvenient requests: *an ~ beggar.* **2** (of affairs, etc) urgent: *~ demands/claims.* **~·ly** *adv* **im·por·tun·ity** /ˌɪmpə`tjunətɪ *US:* -`tu-/ *n* [U] being ~(1); (*pl;* **-ties**) instance of this.

im·por·tune /ɪm`pɔtʃun/ *vt* [VP6A,9,14,17A] (formal) **1** beg urgently and repeatedly: *She ~d her husband for more money/with requests for money/to give her more money.* **2** (of a prostitute) solicit(**2**).

im·pose /ɪm`pəʊz/ *vt,vi* **1** [VP14] ~ **on,** lay or place a tax, duty, etc on: *New duties were ~d on wines and spirits. I must perform the task that has been ~d upon me.* **2** [VP14] ~ ***(oneself) (on sb),*** force (sth, oneself, one's company on others): *Don't ~ yourself/your company on people who don't want you.* **3** [VP3A] ~ ***upon sth,*** take advantage of: *~ upon sb's good nature.* **im·pos·ing** *adj* making a strong impression because of size, character, appearance: *an imposing old lady; an imposing display of knowledge.* **im·pos·ing·ly** *adv*

im·po·si·tion /ˌɪmpə`zɪʃn/ *n* **1** [U] the act of imposing(**1**): *Everyone grumbled at the ~ of new taxes.* **2** [C] sth imposed; tax, burden, punishment. **3** [C] fraud; trick; overcharge.

im·poss·ible /ɪm`posəbl/ *adj* **1** not possible: *Don't ask me to do the ~.* **2** that cannot be endured: *It's an ~ situation! He's an ~ person.* **im·poss·ibly** /-əblɪ/ *adv* **im·possi·bil·ity** /ɪmˌposə`bɪlətɪ/ *n* [U] state of being ~; [C] (*pl* **-ties**) sth that is ~.

im·post /`ɪmpəʊst/ *n* (old use) tax or duty, e g on imported goods.

im·pos·tor /ɪm`postə(r)/ *n* person pretending to be sb he is not.

im·pos·ture /ɪm`postʃə(r)/ *n* [C] act of deception by an impostor; [U] fraudulent deception: *make a living by lying and ~.*

im·po·tent /`ɪmpətənt/ *adj* lacking sufficient strength (to do sth); unable to act; (of males) wholly lacking in sexual power. **~·ly** *adv* **im·po·tence** /-əns/ *n* [U] state of being ~: *We have reduced the enemy to impotence,* made them quite powerless.

im·pound /ɪm`paʊnd/ *vt* [VP6A] **1** take possession of by law or by authority. **2** (in former times) shut up (cattle that had strayed) in a pound. ⇨ **pound[2].**

im·pov·er·ish /ɪm`povrɪʃ/ *vt* [VP6A] (formal) cause to become poor; take away good qualities: *~ed by doctors' bills; ~ed soil,* e g when crops are grown year after year without the use of fertilizers; *~ed rubber,* rubber that has lost its elasticity. **~·ment** *n*

im·prac·ti·cable /ɪm`præktɪkəbl/ *adj* **1** that cannot be put into practice: *an ~ scheme.* **2** (of routes) impassable; that cannot be used. **im·prac·ti·cably** /-əblɪ/ *adv* **im·prac·ti·ca·bil·ity** /ɪmˌpræktɪkə`bɪlətɪ/, **~·ness** *nn*

im·prac·ti·cal /ɪm`præktɪkl/ *adj* not practical.

im·pre·cate /`ɪmprɪkeɪt/ *vt* [VP14] ~ **on,** (formal) invoke, call down (evil *upon* sb). **im·pre·ca·tion** /ˌɪmprɪ`keɪʃn/ *n* [C] curse.

im·preg·nable /ɪm`pregnəbl/ *adj* that cannot be overcome or taken by force; able to resist all attacks: *an ~ fortress; ~ defences/arguments.* **im·preg·nably** /-əblɪ/ *adv* **im·preg·na·bil·ity** /ɪmˌpregnə`bɪlətɪ/ *n*

im·preg·nate /`ɪmpregneɪt *US:* ɪm`preg-/ *vt* [VP6A,14] ~ **with, 1** make pregnant; fertilize, e g an ovum. **2** fill, saturate: *water ~d with salt.* **3** imbue, fill with feelings, moral qualities, etc.

im·pres·sario /ˌɪmprɪ`sarɪəʊ/ *n* (*pl* **-s** /-z/) manager of an operatic or concert company.

im·press /ɪm`pres/ *vt* [VP6A,14] ~ ***on/with,*** **1** press (one thing on or with another); make (a mark, etc) by doing this: *~ wax with a seal; ~ a seal on wax; ~ a figure/design on sth.* **2** have a strong influence on; fix deeply (on the mind, memory): *His words are strongly ~ed on my memory. The book did not ~ me at all,* I did not think it good, useful, etc. *I ~ed on him the importance of his work. He ~ed me unfavourably,* I formed an unfavourable opinion of him. □ *n* /`ɪmpres/ mark made by stamping a seal, etc on sth.

im·pression /ɪm`preʃn/ *n* **1** [C] mark made by pressing: *the ~ of a seal on wax.* **2** [C] print (of an engraving, etc). **3** [C] (product of) any one printing operation: *a first ~ of 5 000 copies. Seven ~s* (= reprints without resetting; ⇨ **edition**) *of this book have been sold so far.* **4** [C,U] effect produced on the mind or feelings: *It's my ~ that...; The speech made a strong ~ on the House. I'm surprised you got an unfavourable ~ of him. What were your first ~s of London? First ~s are often misleading.* **5** [C] (vague or uncertain) idea, belief: *It's my ~ that he doesn't want to come.* ***be under the ~ that,*** have a vague idea, think, that. **~·ism** /-ɪzm/ *n* method of painting or writing so as to give the general effect without elaborate detail. **~·ist** /-ɪst/ *n* person who uses this method. **~·is·tic** /ɪm'preʃn`ɪstɪk/ *adj* **1** of, characteristic of, ~ism or ~ists. **2** giving only a general ~.

im·pression·able /ɪm`preʃn̩əbl/ *adj* easily influenced: *children who are at the ~ age,* adolescent; *an ~ young lady,* e g one who easily falls in love.

im·press·ive /ɪm`presɪv/ *adj* making a deep impression on the mind and feelings: *an ~ ceremony.* **~·ly** *adv* **~·ness** *n*

im·pri·ma·tur /'ɪmprɪ`meɪtə(r)/ *n* official licence to print (now usu granted by the R C Church); (fig) sanctions approval.

im·print /ɪm`prɪnt/ *vt* [VP14] **~ *sth with/on,*** print; stamp: *~ a letter with a postmark/a postmark on a letter; ideas ~ed on the mind.* □ *n* /`ɪmprɪnt/ [C] that which is ~ed: *the ~ of a foot* (= footprint); *the ~ of suffering on a person's face; a publisher's/printer's ~,* his name, address, etc on the title-page or at the end of the book.

im·prison /ɪm`prɪzn/ *vt* [VP6A] put or keep in prison. **~·ment** *n* [U] ~ing or being ~ed: *sentenced to one year's ~ment.*

im·prob·able /ɪm`probəbl/ *adj* not likely to be true or to happen: *an ~ story/result. Rain is ~.* **im·prob·ably** /-əblɪ/ *adv* **im·prob·abil·ity** /'ɪm'probə`bɪlətɪ/ *n* [U] being ~; [C] (*pl* -ties) sth which is or seems ~: *Don't worry about such improbabilities as floods and earthquakes.*

im·promptu /ɪm`promptju *US:* -tu/ *adj, adv* without preparation: *an ~ speech; speak ~.* □ *n* musical composition that seems to have been improvised.

im·proper /ɪm`propə(r)/ *adj* **1** not suited for the purpose, situation, circumstances, etc: *Laughing and joking are ~ at a funeral.* **2** incorrect: *~ diagnosis of disease.* **3** indecent: *~ stories.* **~·ly** *adv*

im·pro·pri·ety /'ɪmprə`praɪətɪ/ *n* (formal) [U] incorrectness; unsuitability; [C] (*pl* -ties) improper act, remark, etc.

im·prove /ɪm`pruv/ *vt,vi* **1** [VP6A,2A] make or become better: *This is not good enough; I want to ~ it. He came back from his holiday with greatly ~d health. He is improving in health. His health is improving.* [VP3A] **~ *(up)on,*** produce sth better than: *Your complexion is wonderful; don't try to ~ upon nature.* **2** [VP6A] make good use of; turn to account: *~ the occasion.* **~·ment** *n* **1** [U] improving or being ~d: *There is need for ~ment in your handwriting. Little/no/not much ~ment seemed possible.* **2** [C] sth which ~s, which adds to beauty, usefulness, value, etc: *I have noticed a number of ~ments in the town since I was here six years ago. We all hope for an ~ment in the weather. This is an ~ment upon your first attempt.*

im·provi·dent /ɪm`provɪdənt/ *adj* (formal) wasteful; not looking to future needs. **~·ly** *adv* **im·provi·dence** /-əns/ *n*

im·pro·vise /`ɪmprəvaɪz/ *vt,vi* [VP6A,2A] **1** compose music while playing, compose verse while reciting, etc: *If an actor forgets his words, he has to ~. The pianist ~d an accompaniment to the song.* **2** provide, make or do sth quickly, in time of need, using whatever happens to be available: *an ~d meal for unexpected guests; an ~d bed,* e g one made up on a couch. **im·pro·vis·ation** /'ɪmprəvaɪ`zeɪʃn *US:* -vɪ`z-/ *n*

im·prud·ent /ɪm`prudnt/ *adj* rash; indiscreet: *Isn't it ~ of you to marry while your salary is so low?* **~·ly** *adv* **im·prud·ence** /-əns/ *n* [U] being ~; [C] ~ act, remark, etc.

im·pu·dent /`ɪmpjʊdənt/ *adj* shamelessly rude; rudely disrespectful: *What an ~ rascal he is! He was ~ enough to call me a fool.* **~·ly** *adv* **im·pu·dence** /-əns/ *n* [U] being ~; ~ words and actions: *None of your impudence! He had the impudence to thumb his nose at me.*

im·pugn /ɪm`pjun/ *vt* [VP6A] (formal) challenge, express doubt about a statement, act, quality, etc.

im·pulse /`ɪmpʌls/ *n* **1** [C] push or thrust; impetus: *give an ~ to trade/education.* **2** [C] sudden inclination to act without thought about the consequences: *seized with an ~ to do sth; feel an irresistible ~ to jump out of a window,* e g during a fit of insanity. **3** [U] state of mind in which such inclinations occur; tendency to act without reflection: *a man of ~; a woman who acts on ~.* **4** (science) very brief electric signal.

im·pul·sion /ɪm`pʌlʃn/ *n* [U] impelling; driving or being driven forward; [C] impetus; mental impulse.

im·pul·sive /ɪm`pʌlsɪv/ *adj* **1** (of persons, their conduct) acting on impulse; resulting from impulse: *a girl with an ~ nature.* **2** (of a force) tending to impel. **~·ly** *adv* **~·ness** *n*

im·pun·ity /ɪm`pjunətɪ/ *n* [U] freedom from punishment, esp ***with ~,*** without risk of injury or punishment.

im·pure /ɪm`pjʊə(r)/ *adj* not pure: *the ~ air of towns; ~ milk; ~ motives.* **im·pur·ity** /-ətɪ/ *n* [U] state of being ~; [C] (*pl* -ties) ~ thing: *impurities in food.*

im·pute /ɪm`pjut/ *vt* [VP14] **~ *to,*** consider as the act, quality, or outcome of: *They ~d the accident to the driver's carelessness. He was innocent of the crime ~d to him.* **im·pu·ta·tion** /'ɪmpjʊ`teɪʃn/ *n* [U] act of imputing; [C] accusation or suggestion of wrong-doing, etc: *imputations on a person's character.*

in[1] /ɪn/ *adv part* (contrasted with *out*) **1** (used with many *vv,* in obvious meanings, as *come in* (= enter) and meanings that are not obvious, as *give in* (= surrender); ⇨ the *v* entries for these) **2** (used with the *v be*) **(a)** at home: *Is there anyone in? My husband won't be in until six o'clock.* **(b)** arrive: *Is the steamer/train, etc in yet,* Has it arrived? **(c)** (of crops) harvested; brought in from the fields: *The wheat crop/the harvest is safely in.* **(d)** in season; obtainable: *Strawberries are in now. When will oysters be in?* **(e)** in fashion: *Long skirts are in again.* **(f)** elected; in power; in office: *The Democrats are in. The Liberal candidate is in,* has been elected. **(g)** burning: *Is the fire still in?* **(h)**

(cricket, baseball) batting: *Which side is in? He was bowled before he had been in* (= at the wicket) *five minutes.* **3** ***in for,*** **(a)** likely to have or experience (esp sth unpleasant): *I'm afraid we're in for a storm. You're in for an unpleasant surprise.* **(b)** committed to; having agreed to take part in: *I'm in for the competition,* shall be a competitor. *Are you in for the 1 000 metres race?* ***have it in for sb,*** be waiting ready to punish him when a chance occurs. ***be in on,*** (colloq) participate in; have a share in: *I'd like to be in on this scheme.* ***day in, day out; week in, week out; year in, year out,*** day after day, week after week, etc in a monotonous way. ***in and out,*** now in and now out: *He's always in and out of hospital,* is frequently ill and in hospital. ***be well in with sb,*** be on good terms with him (and likely to benefit from his friendship). **4** (preceding a *n*): *an ˋin-patient,* one who lives in a hospital while receiving treatment (contrasted with *ˋout-patient*).

in[2] /ɪn/ *prep* (For the use of *in* with many *nn* and *vv*, ⇨ the *n* and *v* entries, e g *in print, in memory of, fail in an examination*). **1** (of place; ⇨ **at**): *the highest mountain in the world; in Africa; in the east of Asia; in Denmark; in the provinces; in Kent; in London; the village in which he was born; the only shop in the village; islands in the Pacific Ocean; sailing in British waters,* i e on the seas round Britain; *in every quarter of the town; children playing in the street; not a cloud in the sky; swimming in the lake; standing in the corner of the room.* Cf the house *at* the corner; *working in the fields/in coal-mines; a picnic in the woods; a holiday in the country/in the mountains.* Cf *at* the seaside; *a light in the distance; in the background/foreground; lying in bed.* Cf sitting *on* the bed; *sitting in an armchair.* Cf *on* a chair without arms; *in school/church/prison; a ride in a motor-car. He was wounded in the leg. The key is in the lock. There were plants in the window,* i e *on* the window-sill, framed by the window. *What would you do in my place,* if you were situated as I am situated? *I read about it in the newspapers. He had a stick in his hand and a cigar in his mouth. You will find the verse in the second chapter of Genesis.* **2** (of direction): *in this/that direction; in all directions.* **3** (indicating direction of motion or activity) into: *He dipped his pen in the ink. He put his hands in his pockets. Cut the apple in two,* into halves. *Cut/break it in two. Throw it in the fire. They fell in love.* **4** (of time when): *in the 20th c; in 1970; in the reign of Queen Anne; in spring/summer, etc; in my absence; in his youth; in old age; still in her teens; in these/those days; in the morning/afternoon/evening.* Cf *on* Monday morning; *in the daytime; at ten o'clock in the night.* Cf *at* night; *in (the) future; in the past; in the end,* finally; *in time of war; in the hour of victory/death, etc He has met many famous men in his time,* during his lifetime. *She was a famous beauty in her day,* during her best years. *The school was quite small in my time,* when I was there. **5** (of time) in the course of; within the space of: *I shall be back in a short time/in a few days/in a week's time, etc. Can you finish the work in an hour? I'll be ready in a moment.* Cf also *in time.* **6** (indicating inclusion) *seven days in a week; four quarts in a gallon; a man in his thirties,* i e between 29 and 40 years of age; *in the early thirties of this century,* i e between 1930 and 1934 or 1935. *There is 10 per cent for service in the (hotel) bill. He has nothing of the hero in him,* Heroism is not among his characteristics. *He has in him the makings of a good soldier,* has qualities, abilities, etc that will help him to become a good soldier. **7** (indicating ratio): *a slope/gradient of one in five. He paid his creditors 25p in the pound. Not one in ten of the boys could spell well.* **8** (of dress, etc): *dressed/clothed in rags; the man in the top hat; a prince in disguise; the woman in white,* wearing white clothes; *in uniform; in mourning; in brown shoes; in his shirt sleeves,* not wearing a jacket or coat; *a prisoner in irons.* **9** (indicating physical surroundings, circumstances, etc): *go out in the rain; sitting in the sun(shine); standing outside in the cold; sleep in the open; a temperature of 95°F in the shade; lose one's way in the dark; unable to work in this heat; go for a walk in the moonlight.* **10** (indicating state or condition): *in a troubled state; in good order. in poor health; in good repair; in a good humour; in a fever of excitement; in despair; in a rage; in tears; in a hurry; living in luxury; in poverty; in ruins; not in the mood for work; in debt; in love; in doubt; in wonder; in public; in secret; in fun/jest/joke; in earnest.* **11** (indicating form, shape, arrangement): *a novel in three parts; books packed in bundles of ten; men standing about in groups; children sitting in rows; wolves hunting in packs; words in alphabetical order; with her hair in curls/in ringlets; dancing in a ring; cloth hanging in folds.* **12** (indicating the method of expression, the medium, means, material, etc): *speaking/writing in English; a message in code; written in ink/pencil; (printed) in italic type; in two colours; in writing; in a few words; in round numbers,* e g 200 000 for 197 563; *talking in a loud voice; bound in leather; painted in oils; carved in oak; cast in bronze; a statue in marble; payment in cash/in kind.* **13** (indicating degree or extent): *in large/small quantities; in great numbers; in some measure; in part. The enemy appeared in great strength.* ***in all,*** as the total: *We were fifteen in all.* **14** (indicating identity): *You will always have a good friend in me,* I shall always befriend you. *We have lost a first-rate teacher in Hill,* Hill, who has left us, was a first-rate teacher. *The enemy lost 200 in killed and wounded,* 200 of them were killed or wounded. **15** (indicating relation, reference, respect): *in some/all respects; in every way; inferior in physique but superior in intellect; young in years but old in wisdom; weak in the head,* not intelligent; *deficient in courage; a country rich/poor in minerals; blind in the left eye; my equal in strength; ten feet in length/depth/diameter, etc; wanting/lacking in judgement.* **16** (indicating occupation, activity, etc): *He's in the army/in insurance/in the motor business/in the Cabinet/in the Air Ministry. He's in politics,* is a politician. *He was killed in action,* while fighting in war. *How much time do you spend in reading.* **17** (used in numerous prepositional phrases of the pattern *in + n + prep*; ⇨ the *n* entries, e g): *in defence of; in exchange for; in justice to; in memory of; in touch with.* **18** ***in camera,*** (legal) in private, in the judge's private room, not in open court; (colloq) secretly. ***in that,*** since, because: *The higher income tax is harmful in that it may discourage people from trying to earn more.* ***in as/so far as,*** in such measure as; to the extent that: *He is a Russian in so far as he was* *born in Russia, but he became a French citizen in 1920.* ***in itself,*** in its own nature; absolutely; considered apart from other things: *Card playing is not harmful in itself; it is only when combined with wild gambling that it may be harmful.*

in[3] /ɪn/ *n* (only in) **the ins and the outs, (a)** political party in office and political party out of office. **(b)** the different parts; the details and complexities: *know all the ins and outs of a problem.*

-in /ɪn/ *suff* added to another word (usu a *v*) to indicate participation in a group activity, etc. ⇨ the *v* entries, e g *sit-in, teach-in.*

in·abil·ity /ˈɪnəˋbɪlətɪ/ *n* [U] ~ ***(to do sth),*** being unable; lack of power or means.

in·ac·cess·ible /ˈɪnəkˋsesəbl/ *adj* ~ ***(to),*** (formal) not accessible. **in·ac·cessi·bil·ity** /ˈɪnəkˈsesəˋbɪlətɪ/ *n* [U].

in·ac·cur·ate /ˋɪnækjʊrət/ *adj* not accurate. **~·ly** *adv* **in·ac·cur·acy** /-əsɪ/ *n* [U] being ~; [C] (*pl* **-cies**) ~ statement, etc.

in·ac·tion /ˋɪnækʃn/ *n* [U] doing nothing; lack of activity.

in·ac·tive /ɪnˋæktɪv/ *adj* not active. **in·ac·ti·vate** /ɪnˋæktɪveɪt/ *vt* make ~: *inactivate a virus.* **in·ac·tiv·ity** /ˈɪnækˋtɪvətɪ/ *n* [U].

in·ad·equate /ɪnˋædɪkwət/ *adj* ~ ***(for a purpose/to do sth),*** not adequate; insufficient. **~·ly** *adv* **in·ad·equacy** /ɪnˋædɪkwəsɪ/ *n* [U].

in·ad·miss·ible /ˈɪnədˋmɪsəbl/ *adj* that cannot be admitted or allowed: *~ evidence; ~ in evidence.*

in·ad·ver·tent /ˈɪnədˋvɜtnt/ *adj* (formal) not paying or showing proper attention; (of actions) done thoughtlessly or not on purpose. **~·ly** *adv* **in·ad·ver·tence** /-tns/ *n* [U] the quality of being ~; [C] oversight or error which is the result of being ~.

in·alien·able /ɪnˋeɪlɪənəbl/ *adj* (formal) (of rights, etc) that cannot be given away or taken away.

in·ane /ɪˋneɪn/ *adj* silly; senseless: *an ~ remark.* **~·ly** *adv* **in·an·ity** /ɪˋnænətɪ/ *n* [U] being ~; [C] (*pl* **-ties**) ~ remark, act, etc.

in·ani·mate /ɪnˋænɪmət/ *adj* **1** lifeless: *~ rocks and stones.* **2** without animal life: *~ nature,* outside the animal world. **3** spiritless; dull: *~ conversation.*

in·ani·tion /ˈɪnəˋnɪʃn/ *n* [U] emptiness; extreme weakness from lack of food.

in·ap·pli·cable /ɪnˋæplɪkəbl/ *adj* ~ ***(to),*** not applicable.

in·ap·preci·able /ˈɪnəˋpriʃəbl/ *adj* not worth reckoning; too small or slight to be perceived: *an ~ difference.*

in·ap·pro·pri·ate /ˈɪnəˋprəʊprɪət/ *adj* ~ ***to,*** not appropriate or suitable.

in·apt /ɪnˋæpt/ *adj* unskilful; not bearing on the subject: *~ remarks.* **in·ap·ti·tude** /ɪnˋæptɪtjud *US:* -tud/ *n* [U] being ~.

in·ar·ticu·late /ˈɪnɑˋtɪkjʊlət/ *adj* **1** (of speech) not clear or distinct; not well joined together; (of a person) not speaking distinctly; not able to express himself clearly and fluently; not of the nature of speech: *~ rage.* **2** not jointed: *an ~ body,* e g a jelly-fish.

in·as·much as /ˈɪnəzˋmʌtʃ əz/ *adv* since; because.

in·at·ten·tion /ˈɪnəˋtenʃn/ *n* lack of, failure to pay, attention. **in·at·ten·tive** /ˈɪnəˋtentɪv/ *adj* not attentive.

in·aud·ible /ɪnˋɔdəbl/ *adj* that cannot be heard. **in·audi·bil·ity** /ɪnˈɔdəˋbɪlətɪ/ *n*

in·aug·ural /ɪˋnɔgjʊrl/ *adj* of or for an inauguration: *an ~ lecture.* □ *n* ~ address.

in·au·gur·ate /ɪˋnɔgjʊreɪt/ *vt* [VP6A] **1** introduce a new official, professor, etc at a special ceremony: *~ a president.* **2** enter, with public formalities, upon (an undertaking); open an exhibition/a new public building with formalities. **3** be the beginning of: *The invention of the internal combustion engine ~d a new era in travel.* **in·aug·ur·ation** /ɪˈnɔgjʊˋreɪʃn/ *n* inaugurating or being ~d: *the inauguration of the President of the US* (20 Jan).

in·aus·pi·cious /ˈɪnɔˋspɪʃəs/ *adj* not auspicious; not of good omen. **~·ly** *adv*

in·board /ˈɪnˋbɔd/ *adj* within the hull of a ship: *an ~ motor.* ⇨ **outboard.**

in·born /ˈɪnˋbɔn/ *adj* (of a quality) possessed (by a person or animal) at birth; implanted by nature: *a boy with an ~ love of mischief; an ~ talent for art.*

in·bound /ˋɪnbaʊnd/ *adj* (US) in coming; homeward bound.

in·bred /ˈɪnˋbred/ *adj* **1** inborn; innate: *~ courtesy.* **2** bred for several or many generations from ancestors closely related. **in·breed·ing** /ˈɪnˋbridɪŋ/ *n* [U] breeding from closely related ancestors, stocks, etc.

in·cal·cu·lable /ɪnˋkælkjʊləbl/ *adj* **1** too great to be calculated: *This has done ~ harm to our reputation.* **2** that cannot be reckoned beforehand. **3** (of a person, his character, etc) uncertain: *a lady of ~ moods.*

in·can·descent /ˈɪnkænˋdesnt/ *adj* giving out, able to give out, light when heated: *an ~ filament,* e g in an electric-light bulb. **in·can·descence** /-sns/ *n* [U] being or becoming ~.

in·can·ta·tion /ˈɪnkænˋteɪʃn/ *n* [C,U] (the use of) (a form of) words used in magic; charm or spell.

in·ca·pable /ɪnˋkeɪpəbl/ *adj* ~ ***(of),*** not capable: *~ of telling a lie,* too honest to do so. ***drunk and ~,*** helplessly drunk. **in·capa·bil·ity** /ɪnˈkeɪpəˋbɪlətɪ/ *n* [U].

in·ca·paci·tate /ˈɪnkəˋpæsəteɪt/ *vt* [VP6A,14] ~ ***sb (for/from),*** **1** make incapable or unfit: *His poor health ~d him for work/from working.* **2** disqualify.

in·ca·pac·ity /ˈɪnkəˋpæsətɪ/ *n* [U] ~ ***(for sth/doing sth/to do sth),*** inability; powerlessness.

in·car·cer·ate /ɪnˋkɑsəreɪt/ *vt* [VP6A] (formal) imprison. **in·car·cer·ation** /ˈɪnˈkɑsəˋreɪʃn/ *n*

in·car·nate /ɪnˋkɑnət/ *adj* **1** having a body; (esp) in human form: *That prison officer is a devil ~/an ~ fiend.* **2** (of an idea, ideal, etc) appearing in human form: *Liberty ~.* □ *vt* /ɪnˋkɑneɪt/ [VP6A] **1** make ~. **2** put (an idea, etc) into a real or material form. **3** (of a person) be a living form of (a quality): *a wife who ~s all the virtues.*

in·car·na·tion /ˈɪnkɑˋneɪʃn/ *n* **1 the I~,** the taking of bodily form by Jesus. **2** [C] person looked upon as a type of a quality: *She looked the ~ of every desirable quality.*

in·cau·tious /ɪnˋkɔʃəs/ *adj* not cautious; rash. **~·ly** *adv*

in·cen·di·ary /ɪnˋsendɪərɪ *US:* -dɪerɪ/ *n* (*pl* **-ries**) *adj* **1** (person) setting fire to property unlawfully and with an evil purpose; (person) tending to stir up violence: *an ~ speech/newspaper article.* **2** (bomb) causing fire. **in·cen·di·ar·ism** /ɪnˋsendjərɪzm/ *n* [U].

in·cense[1] /ˋɪnsens/ *n* [U] (smoke of a) substance producing a sweet smell when burning.

in·cense[2] /ɪnˋsens/ *vt* [VP6A] make angry: *~d by sb's conduct; ~d at sb's remarks.*

in·cen·tive /ɪn`sentɪv/ *n* ~ ***(to sth/to do sth/to doing sth),*** [C,U] that which incites, rouses or encourages a person: *He hasn't much ~/many ~s to work hard/to hard work.*

in·cep·tion /ɪn`sepʃn/ *n* (formal) start.

in·cer·ti·tude /ɪn`sɜtɪtjud *US:* -tud/ *n* [U] uncertainty.

in·cess·ant /ɪn`sesnt/ *adj* continual; often repeated: *a week of ~ rain.* **~·ly** *adv*

in·cest /`ɪnsest/ *n* [U] sexual intercourse between near relations, e g brother and sister. **in·ces·tuous** /ɪn`sestʃʊəs/ *adj* of ~; guilty of; involving, ~.

inch /ɪntʃ/ *n* **1** measure of length, one-twelfth of a foot: *six ~es of rain in one day.* ⇨ App 5. **2** small amount. ***by ~,*** by degrees. ***by ~es,*** **(a)** only just: *The car missed me by ~es.* **(b)** bit by bit; gradually ~. ***every ~,*** entirely, completely: *He's every ~ a soldier.* ***within an ~ of,*** very near, almost: *He came within an ~ of being struck by a falling tile.* ***not yield an ~,*** not give way at all. □ *vt,vi* [VP15A,B,2C] move by ~es; edge one's way: *~ one's way forward; ~ along a ledge on a cliff.*

in·cho·ate /ɪn`kəʊɪt/ *adj* (formal) just begun; in an underdeveloped, half-formed state. **in·choa·tive** /ɪn`kəʊətɪv/ *adj* expressing the beginning of an action or state: (gram) *inchoative verbs,* e g *get* in *get dark, fall* in *fall ill.*

in·ci·dence /`ɪnsɪdəns/ *n* way in which sth falls or affects things: *the ~ of a disease,* the range or extent of its effect, the number and kind of people who catch it; *the ~ of a tax,* the way it falls to certain people to pay it.

in·ci·dent[1] /`ɪnsɪdənt/ *adj* ~ ***to,*** forming a natural or expected part of; naturally connected with: *the risks ~ to the life of a test pilot; the social obligations ~ to life in the diplomatic service.*

in·ci·dent[2] /`ɪnsɪdənt/ *n* **1** event, esp one of less importance than others: *frontier ~s,* e g disputes between forces on a frontier. **2** happening which attracts general attention. **3** (modern use) happening, e g rebellion, bomb explosion, war, which for various reasons persons in authority do not wish to describe precisely. **4** separate piece of action in a play or poem.

in·ci·den·tal /ˈɪnsɪ`dentl/ *adj* **1** accompanying but not forming a necessary part: *~ music to a play.* **2** small and comparatively unimportant: *~ expenses,* additional to the main expenses. **3** ~ ***to,*** liable to happen or occur: *discomforts ~ to exploration in a wild country.* **~ly** /-tlɪ/ *adv* in an ~ manner; by chance.

in·cin·er·ate /ɪn`sɪnəreɪt/ *vt* [VP6A] burn to ashes. **in·cin·er·ator** /-tə(r)/ *n* furnace, enclosed fireplace, for burning rubbish, etc. **in·cin·er·ation** /ɪnˈsɪnə`reɪʃn/ *n* [U] burning up: *Household and industrial waste disposal—the choice is between tipping and incineration.*

in·cipi·ent /ɪn`sɪpɪənt/ *adj* beginning; in an early stage: *~ decay of the teeth.*

in·cise /ɪn`saɪz/ *vt* [VP6A] make a cut in; engrave. **in·ci·sion** /ɪn`sɪʒn/ *n* [U] cutting (into sth); [C] cut, e g one made in a surgical operation.

in·cis·ive /ɪn`saɪsɪv/ *adj* sharp and cutting; (of a person's mind, remarks) acute; clear-cut: *~ criticism.* **~·ly** *adv*

in·cisor /ɪn`saɪzə(r)/ *n* (in human beings) any one of the eight sharp-edged front cutting teeth, four in the upper and four in the lower jaw. ⇨ the illus at mouth.

in·cite /ɪn`saɪt/ *vt* [VP6A,14,17A] ~ ***sb (to sth/to do sth),*** stir up, rouse: *Insults ~ resentment. The soldier was shot for inciting his comrades to rise against their officers.* **~·ment** *n* [U] inciting or being ~d; [C] instance of this; sth that ~s.

in·civ·il·ity /ˈɪnsɪ`vɪlətɪ/ *n* (formal) [U] impoliteness; [C] (*pl* -ties) impolite act, remark, etc.

in·clem·ent /ɪn`klemənt/ *adj* (formal) (of weather or climate) severe; cold and stormy. **in·clem·ency** /-ənsɪ/ *n* [U] being ~.

in·cli·na·tion /ˈɪnklɪ`neɪʃn/ *n* **1** [C] bending; bowing; slope; slant: *an ~ of the head,* a nod; *an ~ of the body,* a bow; *the ~ of a roof,* its degree of slope. **2** [C,U] ~ ***(to sth/to do sth),*** mental leaning; liking or desire; disposition: *Are you usually ready to sacrifice ~ to duty,* put on one side what you like doing in order to do your duty? *He showed no ~ to leave. She is not free to follow her own ~s, even in the matter of marriage. He has an ~* (= tendency) *to stoutness/to grow fat.*

in·cline[1] /ɪn`klaɪn/ *vt,vi* **1** [VP6A,15A,2A] (cause to) lean, slope or slant; bend (the head, body, oneself) forward or downward: *~ the head in prayer.* **2** [VP17] (liter) dispose; direct: *'I~ our hearts to keep this law.'* **3** [VP17A] (usu passive) direct the mind in a certain direction; cause (sb) to have a tendency or wish (*to do* sth): *The news ~s me/I am ~d to start at once. His letter ~s me to believe that he doesn't want to come. I am ~d to think* (= I have a feeling or idea) *that he is opposed to the plan. He's ~d to be lazy. We can go for a walk if you feel so ~d.* **4** [VP4C] tend; be disposed: *I ~ to believe in his innocence.* **5** [VP3A] ~ ***to/towards sth,*** have a physical or bodily tendency: *He ~s to leanness. She ~s towards melancholia.*

in·cline[2] /`ɪnklaɪn/ *n* slope; sloping surface: *run down a steep ~; an ~ of 1 in 5.* ⇨ gradient.

in·close, in·clos·ure /ɪn`kləʊz, ɪn`kləʊʒə(r)/ = enclose, enclosure.

in·clude /ɪn`klud/ *vt* [VP6A,C,15B] bring in, reckon, as part of the whole: *This atlas contains fifty maps, including six of North America. Price $2.75, postage ~d. Your duties will ~ putting the children to bed.* **in·clu·sion** /ɪn`kluʒn/ *n* [U] including or being ~d.

in·clus·ive /ɪn`klusɪv/ *adj* **1** including: *£10, ~ of interest; from 1 May to 3 June ~,* 1 May and 3 June being included. ⇨ (US) through. **2** including much or all: *~ terms,* (at a hotel, etc) without any extra charges. **~·ly** *adv*

in·cog /ɪn`kog/ *adj, adv* (colloq abbr of) incognito.

in·cog·nito /ˈɪnkog`nitəʊ/ *adj* concealed under a disguised character; with an assumed name: *a king ~.* □ *adv* with one's name, character, etc concealed: *The duke called himself Dick Brown and travelled ~.*

in·co·her·ent /ˈɪnkəʊ`hɪərnt/ *adj* not coherent: *so drunk as to be quite ~.* **~·ly** *adv* **in·co·her·ence** /-əns/ *n*

in·com·bus·tible /ˈɪnkəm`bʌstəbl/ *adj* (formal) that cannot be consumed by fire.

in·come /`ɪnkʌm/ *n* money received during a given period (as salary, receipts from trade, interest from investments, etc): *live within one's ~,* spend less than one receives. **~-tax** /`ɪŋkəm tæks/ *n* tax levied on ~ above a certain level. *Tax was payable on ~ over £450.*

in·com·ing /ˈɪn`kʌmɪŋ/ *adj* coming in: *the ~ tide/tenant.*

in·com·men·sur·ate /ˈɪnkəˋmenʃʊrət/ *adj* **1** not comparable (*to*) in respect of size; not worthy to be measured (*with*): *His abilities are ~ to the task he has been given.* **2** that cannot be compared; having no common measure.

in·com·mode /ˈɪnkəˋməʊd/ *vt* [VP6A] (formal) cause trouble or inconvenience to: *Will it ~ you if I don't pay what I owe you until next year?*

in·com·muni·cado /ˈɪnkəˈmjunɪˋkɑdəʊ/ *adj* (of sb in confinement) not permitted to communicate with persons outside.

in·com·par·able /ɪnˋkomprəbl/ *adj* **~ (to/with),** not to be compared; without equal: *her ~ beauty.*

in·com·pat·ible /ˈɪnkəmˋpætəbl/ *adj* **~ (with),** opposed in character; unable to exist in harmony; inconsistent: *Excessive drinking is ~ with good health. They are sexually ~.* **in·com·pati·bil·ity** /ˈɪnkəmˈpætəˋbɪlətɪ/ *n* [U] being ~: *Incompatibility of temper may cause friction between husband and wife.*

in·com·pe·tent /ɪnˋkompətənt/ *adj* not qualified or able: *~ to teach science/for teaching science/ as a teacher of science.* **~·ly** *adv* **in·com·pe·tence** /-əns/, **in·com·pe·tency** /-ənsɪ/ *nn* [U] being ~.

in·com·plete /ˈɪnkəmˋplit/ *adj* not complete. **~·ly** *adv*

in·com·pre·hen·sible /ˈɪnˈkomprɪˋhensəbl/ *adj* (formal) that cannot be understood. **in·com·pre·hen·si·bil·ity** /ˈɪnˈkomprɪˈhensɪˋbɪlətɪ/ *n* [U].

in·com·pre·hen·sion /ˈɪnˈkomprɪˋhenʃn/ *n* [U] failure to understand.

in·com·press·ible /ˈɪnkəmˋpresəbl/ *adj* (formal) that cannot be compressed; hard and unyielding.

in·con·ceiv·able /ˈɪnkənˋsivəbl/ *adj* that cannot be imagined; (colloq) hard to believe. very remarkable.

in·con·clus·ive /ˈɪnkənˋklusɪv/ *adj* (of evidence, arguments, discussions, actions) not decisive or convincing; not bringing a definite result. **~·ly** *adv*

in·con·gru·ous /ɪnˋkoŋgrʊəs/ *adj* **~ (with),** not in harmony or agreement; out of place. **~·ly** *adv* **in·con·gru·ity** /ˈɪnkoŋˋgruətɪ/ *n* [U] the quality of being ~; [C] (*pl* -ties) sth ~.

in·con·sequent /ɪnˋkonsɪkwənt/ *adj* not following naturally what has been said or done before: *an ~ remark;* (of a person) saying or doing ~ things. **~·ly** *adv* **in·con·sequen·tial** /ˈɪnˈkonsɪˈkwenʃl/ *adj* = ~; (by extension) unimportant.

in·con·sider·able /ˈɪnkənˋsɪdrəbl/ *adj* not worth considering; of small size, value, etc.

in·con·sider·ate /ˈɪnkənˋsɪdrət/ *adj* (of a person, his actions) thoughtless; lacking in regard for the feelings of others; *~ children; ~ remarks.* **~·ly** *adv*

in·con·sist·ent /ˈɪnkənˋsɪstənt/ *adj* **~ (with), 1** not in harmony: *actions that are ~ with one's principles.* **2** contradictory; having parts that do not agree: *His account of what happened was ~.* **~·ly** *adv* **in·con·sist·ency** /-ənsɪ/ *n* [U] the quality of being ~; [C] (*pl* -cies) instance of this.

in·con·sol·able /ˈɪnkənˋsəʊləbl/ *adj* that cannot be consoled: *~ grief. The widow was ~.*

in·con·spicu·ous /ˈɪnkənˋspɪkjʊəs/ *adj* not conspicuous: *The shy girl tried to make herself as ~ as possible,* tried to avoid attention. *She always dresses in ~ colours,* colours that are not striking or obvious. **~·ly** *adv*

in·con·stant /ɪnˋkonstənt/ *adj* (formal) (of persons) changeable in feelings, intentions, purpose, etc: *an ~ lover.* **in·con·stancy** /-ənsɪ/ *n* [U] being ~; [C] instance of this.

in·con·test·able /ˈɪnkənˋtestəbl/ *adj* that cannot be disputed.

in·con·ti·nent /ɪnˋkontɪnənt/ *adj* wanting in self-control or self-restraint; (med) unable to control the bladder, hold in one's urine. **in·con·ti·nence** /-əns/ *n* [U].

in·con·tro·vert·ible /ɪnˈkontrəˋvɜtəbl/ *adj* that cannot be disputed.

in·con·ven·ience /ˈɪnkənˋvinɪəns/ *n* [C,U] (cause or instance of) discomfort or trouble: *I was put to/I suffered great ~. They have been at great ~ in order to help us. Think of the ~s of living in such a small house with a large family.* □ *vt* [VP6A] cause ~ to.

in·con·ven·ient /ˈɪnkənˋvinɪənt/ *adj* causing discomfort, trouble or annoyance. **~·ly** *adv*

in·con·vert·ible /ˈɪnkənˋvɜtəbl/ *adj* that cannot be converted, e g paper money that cannot be exchanged for gold. **in·con·ver·ti·bil·ity** /ˈɪnkənˈvɜtəˋbɪlətɪ/ *n*

in·cor·por·ate[1] /ɪnˋkɔpərət/ *adj* incorporated; formed into, united in, a corporation.

in·cor·por·ate[2] /ɪnˋkɔpəreɪt/ *vt,vi* [VP6A,14,2A, 3A] **~ (into/with),** make, become, united in one body or group; (legal) form into, become, a corporation(2): *Hanover was ~d into Prussia in 1886. He was ~d a member of the college. Your suggestions will be ~d in the plan. The firm ~d with others.* **in·cor·por·ation** /ɪnˈkɔpəˋreɪʃn/ *n* incorporating or being ~d.

in·cor·por·eal /ˈɪnkɔˋpɔrɪəl/ *adj* not composed of matter; having no bodily form.

in·cor·rect /ˈɪnkəˋrekt/ *adj* not correct. **~·ly** *adv* **~·ness** *n*

in·cor·ri·gible /ˈɪnˋkorɪdʒəbl *US:* -ˋkɔr-/ *adj* (of a person, his faults, etc) that cannot be cured or corrected: *an ~ liar; ~ bad habits.*

in·cor·rupt·ible /ˈɪnkəˋrʌptəbl/ *adj* that cannot decay or be destroyed; that cannot be corrupted, esp by being bribed: *as ~ as an English judge.* **in·cor·rupti·bil·ity** /ˈɪnkəˈrʌptəˋbɪlətɪ/ *n*

in·crease[1] /ˋɪnkris/ *n* [U] **~ (in),** increasing; growth; [C] amount by which sth ~s: *I~ in population made emigration necessary. There was a steady ~ in population. Is the consumption of beer still on the ~?*

in·crease[2] /ɪnˋkris/ *vt,vi* [VP6A,2A] make or become greater in size, number, degree, etc: *The population has ~d by 200 000 to 50 000 000. The driver ~d speed. Our difficulties are increasing.* **in·creas·ing·ly** /ɪnˋkrisɪŋlɪ/ *adv* more and more.

in·cred·ible /ɪnˋkredəbl/ *adj* that cannot be believed; (colloq) difficult to believe; surprising. **in·cred·ibly** /-əblɪ/ *adv* **in·credi·bil·ity** /ˈɪnˈkredəˋbɪlətɪ/ *n*

in·credu·lous /ɪnˋkredjʊləs *US:* -dʒʊ-/ *adj* unbelieving; showing disbelief: *~ looks/smiles.* **~·ly** *adv* **in·cred·ul·ity** /ˈɪnkrɪˋdjulətɪ *US:* -ˋdu-/ *n*

in·crement /ˋɪnkrəmənt/ *n* **1** [U] profits; increase: *unearned ~,* increased value of sth, e g land, due not to the owner's labour but to other causes, e g a big demand for land. **2** [C] amount of increase: *'Salary £1 000 per annum, with yearly ~s of £100 to a maximum of £2 500.'*

in·crimi·nate /ɪnˋkrɪmɪneɪt/ *vt* [VP6A] say, be a sign, that (sb) is guilty of wrongdoing: *Don't say anything that may ~ your friends.*

in·crus·ta·tion /ˈɪnkrʌˋsteɪʃn/ *n* [U] encrusting; [C] crust; hard coating.

in·cu·bate /ˋɪnkjʊbeɪt/ *vt,vi* [VP6A,2A] hatch (eggs) by sitting on them or by artificial warmth; sit on eggs. **in·cu·ba·tor** /-tə(r)/ *n* apparatus for hatching eggs by artificial warmth or for rearing small, weak babies (esp those born prematurely). **in·cu·ba·tion** /ˈɪnkjʊˋbeɪʃn/ *n* hatching (of eggs): *artificial incubation*, hatching by artificial warmth.

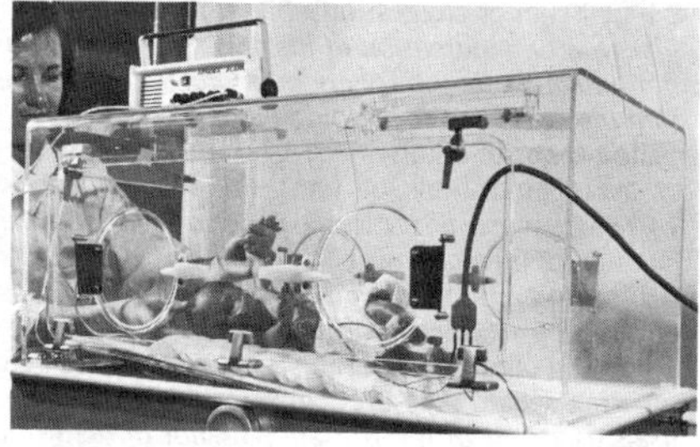

an incubator

in·cu·bus /ˋɪnkjʊbəs/ *n* (*pl* -ses /-sɪz/, -bi /-bɑɪ/) nightmare; evil spirit supposed to lie on a sleeping person and weigh him down; sb or sth, e g a debt, an approaching examination, that oppresses one like a nightmare.

in·cul·cate /ˋɪnkʌlkeɪt *US:* ɪnˋkʌl-/ *vt* [VP6A,14] **~ sth (in sb)** (formal) fix (ideas, etc) firmly by repetition: *~ in young people the duty of loyalty.*

in·cul·pate /ˋɪnkʌlpeɪt *US:* ɪnˋkʌl-/ vt [VP6A] (formal) involve (sb) in a charge or wrongdoing; blame.

in·cum·bent /ɪnˋkʌmbənt/ *adj* **~ upon sb (to do sth),** rest upon him as a duty: *It is ~ upon you to warn the boy of the danger of smoking.* □ *n* person holding a church benefice; rector or vicar. **in·cum·bency** /-ənsɪ/ *n* (*pl* -cies) position of an ~.

in·cur /ɪnˋkɜ(r)/ *vt* (-rr-) [VP6A] bring upon oneself: *~ debts; ~ hatred; ~ great expense.*

in·cur·able /ɪnˋkjʊərəbl/ *adj* that cannot be cured: *~ diseases/habits.* □ *n* person who is ~: *a home for ~s.* **in·cur·ably** /-əblɪ/ *adv*

in·curi·ous /ɪnˋkjʊərɪəs/ *adj* (formal) having no curiosity; not inquisitive; inattentive.

in·cur·sion /ɪnˋkɜʃn *US:* -ˋkɜʒn/ *n* **~ (up)on,** sudden attack or invasion (not usu made for the purpose of permanent occupation): *the Danish ~s on our coasts in early times;* (fig) *~s upon my leisure time.*

in·curved /ˈɪnˋkɜvd/ *adj* curved inwards; bent into a curve.

in·debted /ɪnˋdetɪd/ *adj* **~ to sb,** owing money or gratitude: *I am greatly ~ to you for your help.* **~·ness** *n*

in·de·cent /ɪnˋdisnt/ *adj* **1** (of behaviour, talk, etc) not decent(2); obscene. **2** (colloq) improper: *leave a party in ~ haste,* e g as if to suggest that one is glad to escape from boredom. **~·ly** *adv* **in·de·cency** /-snsɪ/ *n* [U] being ~; [C] (*pl* -cies) act, gesture, expression, etc that is ~.

in·de·cipher·able /ˈɪndɪˋsɑɪfrəbl/ *adj* that cannot be deciphered.

in·de·ci·sion /ˈɪndɪˋsɪʒn/ *n* the state of being unable to decide; hesitation.

in·de·cis·ive /ˈɪndɪˋsɑɪsɪv/ *adj* not decisive: *an ~ battle/answer; ~ evidence;* hesitating; uncertain: *a man with an ~ manner.* **~·ly** *adv*

in·dec·or·ous /ɪnˋdekərəs/ *adj* (formal) in bad taste; not in accordance with good manners. **~·ly** *adv*

in·de·cor·um /ˈɪndɪˋkɔrəm/ *n* [U] lack of decorum; [C] improper proceeding; indecorous act.

in·deed /ɪnˋdid/ *adv* **1** really; as you say; as you may imagine: *I was ~ very glad to hear the news. 'Are you pleased at your son's success?'—'Yes, ~'* (or) *'I~, yes.'* **2** (to intensify) *Thank you very much ~. It was very kind ~ of you to help.* **3** used as a comment to show interest, surprise, irony, etc: *'He spoke to me about you.'—'Oh, ~!'* 'Oh, did he?' *'Who is this woman?'—'Who is she, ~?'* 'That's what we all want to know!'

in·de·fati·gable /ˈɪndɪˋfætɪgəbl/ *adj* (formal) untiring; that cannot be tired out: *~ workers.*

in·de·feas·ible /ˈɪndɪˋfizəbl/ *adj* (formal) that cannot be forfeited or done away with: *~ rights/claims.*

in·de·fens·ible /ˈɪndɪˋfensəbl/ *adj* that cannot be defended, justified or excused.

in·de·fin·able /ˈɪndɪˋfɑɪnəbl/ *adj* that cannot be defined.

in·defi·nite /ɪnˋdefnɪt/ *adj* vague; not clearly defined or stated: *He has rather ~ views on the question. He gave me an ~ answer,* neither 'Yes' nor 'No'. **the ˈ~ ˋarticle,** *a* or *an.* **~·ly** *adv*

in·del·ible /ɪnˋdeləbl/ *adj* (of marks, stains, ink or fig of disgrace) that cannot be rubbed out or removed: *an ~ pencil; ~ shame.* **in·del·ibly** /-əblɪ/ *adv*

in·deli·cate /ɪnˋdelɪkət/ *adj* (of a person, his speech, behaviour, etc) lacking in refinement; immodest: *~ remarks.* **in·deli·cacy** /-kəsɪ/ *n* [U] being ~; [C] (*pl* -cies) ~ act, utterance, etc.

in·dem·nify /ɪnˋdemnɪfɑɪ/ *vt* (*pt,pp* -fied) **1** [VP6A,14] **~ sb (from/against),** (legal, comm) make (sb, oneself) safe: *~ a person against harm/loss.* **2** [VP6A,14] **~ sb (for sth),** pay sb back: *I will ~ you for any expenses you may incur on my behalf.* **in·dem·ni·fi·ca·tion** /ɪnˈdemnɪfɪˋkeɪʃn/ *n* [U] ~ing or being indemnified; [C] sth given or received as compensation or repayment.

in·dem·nity /ɪnˋdemnətɪ/ *n* (*pl* -ties) **1** [U] security against damage or loss; compensation for loss. **2** [C] sth that gives security against damage or loss; sth given or received as compensation, esp a sum of money, or goods, demanded from a country defeated in war.

in·dent /ɪnˋdent/ *vt,vi* **1** [VP6A] break into the edge or surface of (as if with teeth): *an ~ed* (= very irregular) *coastline.* **2** [VP6A] start (a line of print or writing) farther from the margin than the others: *You must ~ the first line of each paragraph.* **3** [VP3A] **~ (on sb) for sth,** order goods by means of an ~. *The firm ~ed for new machinery.* □ *n* /ˋɪndent/ trade order placed in the United Kingdom for goods to be exported; official requisition for stores. **in·den·ta·tion** /ˈɪndenˋteɪʃn/ *n* **1** [U] ~ing or being ~ed. **2** [C] deep recess in a coastline; notch; space left at the beginning of a line of print or writing.

in·den·ture /ɪnˋdentʃə(r)/ *n* agreement of which two copies are made, esp one binding an apprentice to his master. ***take up one's ~s,*** receive them back at the end of the period of training. □ *vt* bind (a person) by ~s (as an apprentice).

in·de·pen·dence /ˈɪndɪˋpendəns/ *n* [U] **~ (from),** the state of being independent: *When a boy leaves* *college and begins to earn money he can live a life of ~. Several of these colonies have claimed and have been given ~ from the mother country.* **ˈI~ Day,** 4 July, celebrated in the US as the anniversary of the day, in 1776, on which the Declaration of I~ (that the American colonies were free and independent of GB) was made.

in·de·pen·dent /ˈɪndɪˋpendənt/ *adj* **1** ~ ***(of),*** not dependent on or controlled by (other persons or things); not relying on others; not needing to work for a living: *If you have a car you are ~ of trains, trams and buses. They went camping, so as to be ~ of inns and hotels; ~ means,* private means. **2** self-governing: *when the colony became ~.* **3** acting or thinking upon one's own lines; free from control; not influenced by others; *an ~ thinker; an ~ witness; ~ proofs/research,* resulting from ~ work, not related to the work of others. □ *n* (esp) M P, candidate, etc who does not belong to a political party: *Vote for the ~s at the next election.* **~·ly** *adv*

in·de·scrib·able /ˈɪndɪˋskraɪbəbl/ *adj* that cannot be described.

in·de·struct·ible /ˈɪndɪˋstrʌktəbl/ *adj* that cannot be destroyed: *~ plastics.*

in·de·ter·mi·nate /ˈɪndɪˋtɜmɪnət/ *adj* not fixed; vague or indefinite: *an ~ vowel,* e g the first sound in *ago;* (maths) *an ~ quantity,* with no fixed value. **in·de·ter·min·able** /ˈɪndɪˋtɜmɪnəbl/ *adj* that cannot be determined, decided or (esp of an industrial dispute) be settled. **in·de·ter·min·ably** /-əblɪ/ *adv* **in·de·ter·min·acy** /-əsɪ/ *n* the state or quality of being ~: *the indeterminacy of small-scale physical events,* the impossibility of determining them in advance.

in·dex /ˋɪndeks/ *n* (*pl* -dexes or, in science, indices /ˋɪndɪsiz/) **1** sth that points to or indicates; sign; pointer (on an instrument) showing measurements: *The increasing sale of luxuries was an ~ of the country's prosperity. The ~ on the scale showed that she was overweight.* **the ˋ~ finger,** the forefinger. **2** list of names, subjects, references, etc in ABC order, at the end of a book, or on cards (*a ˋcard ~*) in a library, etc. **the I~,** list of books not to be read by members of the R C Church without permission. **3 ˋ~ number/figure,** one that indicates the relative level of prices or wages at a particular date compared with the figure 100 (for an earlier period) taken as a standard (as in *the cost of living ~*). **4** (alg) exponent: *In* b^3 *and* x^n, *3 and n are indices.* □ *vt* [VP6A] make an ~ for a book, collection of books, etc; put a word, reference, etc in an ~: *The book is not well ~ed.* **~er** *n* person who prepares an ~.

In·dia /ˋɪndɪə/ *n* **ˋ~ paper** *n* very thin paper, e g for airmail editions of newspapers. **~man** /-mən/ *n* (*pl* -men) (formerly) sailing-ship engaged in the trade with India. **ˈ~-ˋrubber** *n* [C] piece of rubber for rubbing out pencil or ink marks.

In·dian /ˋɪndɪən/ *adj, n* **1** (native) of the Republic of India. **2 Aˈmerican/ˈRed ˋ~,** (one) of the original inhabitants of America. **ˈWest ˋ~,** (native) of the West Indies. **3** (various uses) **ˋ~ club,** bottle-shaped club, for use in gymnastic exercises. **ˋ~ corn,** [U] maize. ***in ~ file,*** in single file, one behind the other. **ˈ~ ˋhemp,** ⇨ hemp. **ˈ~ ˋink,** black ink made in China and Japan (used when writing ideographs with a brush). **ˈ~ ˋred,** (soil of a) yellowish-red colour. **ˈ~ ˋsummer,** period of calm, dry hazy weather in late autumn, esp in the northern part of the US; (fig) revival of the feelings of youth in old age.

in·di·cate /ˋɪndɪkeɪt/ *vt* [VP6A,9,14] point to; point out; make known; be a sign of; show the need of; state briefly: *A sign-post ~d the right road for us to follow. He ~d that the interview was over. The sudden rise in temperature was indicating the use of penicillin. A fresh approach to industrial relations is ~d,* is necessary or advisable. **in·di·ca·tion** /ˈɪndɪˋkeɪʃn/ *n* **1** [U] indicating or being ~d. **2** [C,U] sign or suggestion; that which ~s: *Did he give you any indication of his feelings? There was not much indication/were not many indications that the next few years would be peaceful.*

in·dica·tive /ɪnˋdɪkətɪv/ *adj* **1** (gram) stating a fact or asking questions of fact: *the ~ mood.* **2** ***~ of/that,*** giving indications (of): *Is a high forehead ~ of great mental power?*

in·di·ca·tor /ˋɪndɪkeɪtə(r)/ *n* person, thing, that points out or gives information, e g a pointer, needle, recording apparatus, on a machine, etc showing speed, pressure, etc: *Litmus paper can be used as an ~ of the presence or not of acid in a solution;* (*ˋtraffic-~*) (on a motor-vehicle) flashing light or other device to indicate a change of direction; (*ˋtrain ~*) one in a railway station showing times of arrivals and departures of trains, their platform numbers, etc.

in·di·ces /ˋɪndɪsiz/ *pl* of index.

in·dict /ɪnˋdɑɪt/ *vt* [VP6A,14,16B] (legal) accuse (sb) (*for riot, as a rioter, on a charge of rioting,* etc). **in·dict·able** /-əbl/ *adj* liable to be ~ed; for which one may be ~ed: *~able offences,* that may be tried by jury. **~·ment** *n* [C] written statement that ~s sb: *bring in an ~ment against sb. This is a clear ~ment of government mismanagement.* [U] ~ing or being ~ed.

in·dif·fer·ence /ɪnˋdɪfrns/ *n* [U] the state of being indifferent; absence of interest or feeling: *He treated my request with ~. Success or failure cannot be a matter of ~ to you. His ~ to/toward future needs is unfortunate.*

in·dif·fer·ent /ɪnˋdɪfrnt/ *adj* **1** ~ ***to/towards,*** having no interest in; neither for nor against; not caring for: *How can you be so ~ to the sufferings of these children? The explorers were ~ to the discomforts and dangers of the expedition. We cannot remain ~* (= neutral) *in this dispute. It is quite ~ to me whether you go or stay,* I don't care which you do. **2** commonplace; not of good quality or ability: *an ~ book; a very ~ footballer.* **~·ly** *adv*

in·digen·ous /ɪnˋdɪdʒɪnəs/ *adj* ~ ***(to),*** native (to); native, belonging naturally to: *Kangaroos are ~ to Australia; ~ language,* that of the people regarded as the original inhabitants of an area.

in·di·gent /ˋɪndɪdʒənt/ *adj* (formal) poor. **in·di·gence** /-əns/ *n* [U] poverty.

in·di·gest·ible /ˈɪndɪˋdʒestəbl/ *adj* difficult or impossible to digest.

in·di·ges·tion /ˈɪndɪˋdʒestʃən/ *n* [U] (pain from) difficulty in digesting food: *suffer from ~; have an attack of ~.*

in·dig·nant /ɪnˋdɪgnənt/ *adj* angry and scornful, esp at injustice or because of undeserved blame, etc: *~ at a false accusation; ~ with a cruel man.* **~·ly** *adv*

in·dig·na·tion /ˈɪndɪgˋneɪʃn/ *n* [U] anger caused by injustice, misconduct, etc: *arouse the ~ of the people; to the ~ of all decent people. They felt* *strong ~ against their teachers. An ~ meeting* (= a meeting to express public ~) *will be held this evening.*

in·dig·nity /ɪn`dɪgnətɪ/ *n* [U] rude or unworthy treatment causing shame or loss of respect; [C] (*pl* **-ties**) sth said or done that humiliates a person: *The bandits subjected us to all sorts of indignities.*

in·digo /`ɪndɪgəʊ/ *n* [U] deep blue dye (obtained from plants). **~ blue,** blue-violet.

in·direct /'ɪndɪ`rekt/ *adj* **1** not straight or direct; not going straight to the point: *an ~ road; make an ~ reference to sb,* not mentioning his name although making clear who is referred to; *an ~ answer to a question; ~ lighting,* by reflected light. **2** (of taxes) not paid direct to a tax-collector, but in the form of higher prices for taxed goods: *the ~ taxes on tobacco, wines, etc.* **3 '~ `speech,** (gram) speech as it is reported with the necessary changes of pronouns, tenses, etc, e g *He said he would come.* for *He said 'I will come'.* **'~ `object/`noun, etc,** referring to the person, etc affected by the *v,* e g *him* in *Give him the money.* **4** not directly aimed at: *an ~ result.* **~·ly** *adv* **~-ness** *n*

in·dis·cern·ible /'ɪndɪ`sɜnəbl/ *adj* that cannot be discerned.

in·dis·ci·pline /ɪn`dɪsəplɪn/ *n* [U] absence of discipline.

in·dis·creet /'ɪndɪ`skrit/ *adj* not wary, cautious or careful. **~·ly** *adv* **in·dis·cre·tion** /'ɪndɪ`skreʃn/ *n* [U] ~ conduct; lack of discretion; [C] ~ remark or act; offence against social conventions.

in·dis·crete /'ɪndɪ`skrit/ *adj* not formed of distinct or separate parts.

in·dis·crimi·nate /'ɪndɪ`skrɪmɪnət/ *adj* acting, given, without care or taste: *~ in making friends; give ~ praise; deal out ~ blows,* hit out at anyone, whether an enemy or not. **~·ly** *adv*

in·dis·pens·able /'ɪndɪ`spensəbl/ *adj* **~ *to,*** that cannot be dispensed with; absolutely essential: *Air, food and water are ~ to life.* **in·dis·pen·sa·bil·ity** /'ɪndɪ'spensə`bɪlətɪ/ *n*

in·dis·posed /'ɪndɪ`spəʊzd/ *adj* **1** unwell: *She has a headache and is rather ~.* **2 ~ *for/to do sth,*** not inclined: *He seems ~ to help us.*

in·dis·po·si·tion /'ɪn'dɪspə`zɪʃn/ *n* [C,U] **1** ill health; slight illness. **2 ~ *for/to do sth,*** feeling of unwillingness or disinclination; feeling of aversion.

in·dis·put·able /'ɪndɪ`spjutəbl/ *adj* that cannot be disputed.

in·dis·sol·uble /'ɪndɪ`soljʊbl/ *adj* (formal) that cannot be dissolved or broken up; firm and lasting: *the ~ bonds of friendship between my country and yours. The Roman Catholic Church regards marriage as ~.*

in·dis·tinct /'ɪndɪ`stɪŋkt/ *adj* not distinct: *~ speech; ~ sounds/memories.* **~·ly** *adv* **~·ness** *n*

in·dis·tin·guish·able /'ɪndɪ`stɪŋgwɪʃəbl/ *adj* that cannot be distinguished.

in·dite /ɪn`dɑɪt/ *vt* [VP6A] (formal) put into words; compose: *~ a poem/speech.*

in·di·vid·ual /'ɪndɪ`vɪdʒʊəl/ *adj* **1** (opp of *general*) specially for one person or thing: *A teacher cannot give ~ attention to his pupils if his class is very large.* **2** characteristic of a single person, animal, plant or thing: *an ~ style of speaking/dressing.* □ *n* **1** any one human being (contrasted with *society*): *Are the rights of the ~ more important or less important than the rights of society as a whole?* **2** (colloq) person: *What a scruffy ~ he is!* **~ly** /-dʒʊəlɪ/ *adv* (opp of *collectively*) separately; one by one: *speak to each member of a group ~ly.*

in·di·vid·ual·ism /'ɪndɪ`vɪdʒʊəl-ɪzm/ *n* [U] **1** social theory that favours the free action and complete liberty of belief of individuals (contrasted with the theory favouring the supremacy of the state). **2** feeling or behaviour of a person who puts his own private interests first; egoism. **in·di·vid·ual·ist** /-ɪst/ *n* supporter of ~. **in·di·vid·ual·is·tic** /'ɪndɪ'vɪdʒʊə`lɪstɪk/ *adj* of ~ or its principles.

in·di·vidu·al·ity /'ɪndɪ'vɪdʒʊ`ælətɪ/ *n* (*pl* **-ties**) **1** [U] all the characteristics that belong to an individual and that mark him out from others: *a man of marked ~.* **2** state of separate existence. **3** (usu *pl*) individual tastes, etc.

in·di·vid·ual·ize /'ɪndɪ`vɪdʒʊəlɑɪz/ *vt* [VP6A] **1** give an individual or distinct character to: *Does your style of writing ~ your work?* **2** specify; treat separately and in detail.

in·di·vis·ible /'ɪndɪ`vɪzəbl/ *adj* that cannot be divided.

Indo- /`ɪndəʊ/ *pref* in compounds = Indian. **'~-Chi`nese,** of Indo-China. **'~-'Euro`pean, '~-Ger`manic,** of the family of languages spoken in Europe and parts of western Asia, esp Persia and India. **~·nesian** /'ɪndə`nizɪən *US:* -`niʒn/ *adj* of Indonesia.

in·do·cile /ɪn`dəʊsɑɪl/ *adj* rebellious; unwilling to be guided, helped, etc: *~ young people.*

in·doc·tri·nate /ɪn`doktrɪneɪt/ *vt* [VP6A,14] **~ *sb with,*** fill the mind of (sb) (with particular ideas or beliefs). **in·doc·tri·na·tion** /ɪn'doktrɪ`neɪʃn/ *n* [U].

in·do·lent /`ɪndələnt/ *adj* lazy; inactive. **~·ly** *adv* **in·dol·ence** /-əns/ *n*

in·domi·table /ɪn`domɪtəbl/ *adj* that cannot be subdued or conquered; unyielding: *~ courage; an ~ will.*

in·door /`ɪn`dɔ(r)/ *adj* (attrib only) belonging to, carried on, situated, inside a building: *~ games/photography; an ~ swimming-bath.*

in·doors /`ɪn`dɔz/ *adv* in or into a building: *go/stay ~; kept ~ all week by bad weather.*

in·dorse /ɪn`dɔs/ = endorse.

in·drawn /`ɪn`drɔn/ *adj* drawn in: *an ~ breath.*

in·dubi·table /ɪn`djubɪtəbl *US:* -`du-/ *adj* (formal) that cannot be doubted.

in·duce /ɪn`djus *US:* -`dus/ *vt* **1** [VP17A] **~ *sb to do sth,*** persuade or influence; lead or cause: *What ~d you to do such a thing? We couldn't ~ the old lady to travel by air.* **2** [VP6A,14] bring about: *illness ~d by overwork; ~ magnetism in a piece of iron,* by holding it near a magnet. **~·ment** *n* [C,U] that which ~s; incentive: *He hasn't much ~ment/many ~ments to study English.*

in·duct /ɪn`dʌkt/ *vt* [VP14] install formerly or with ceremony in position or office: *~ a clergyman to a benefice;* admit as a member of.

in·duc·tion /ɪn`dʌkʃn/ *n* **1** inducting or being inducted: *an ~ course,* one designed to provide general knowledge of future activities, requirements, etc. **2** method of reasoning which obtains or discovers general laws from particular facts or examples; production of facts to prove a general statement. ⇨ **deduction. 3** the bringing about of an electric or magnetic state in a body by proximity (without actual contact) of an electrified or magnetized body: *~ coils/motors.* ⇨ **induce(2).**

in·duc·tive /ɪn`dʌktɪv/ *adj* **1** (of reasoning) based on induction(2). **2** of magnetic/electrical induction.

in·due /ɪnˋdju *US:* -ˋdu/ = endue.

in·dulge /ɪnˋdʌldʒ/ *vt,vi* **1** [VP6A] gratify; give way to and satisfy (desires, etc): *It is sometimes necessary to ~ a sick child/the fancies of a sick child.* **2** [VP3A] **~ in,** allow oneself the pleasure of: *He occasionally ~s in the luxury of a good cigar.* **in·dul·gent** /-ənt/ *adj* inclined to ~; *indulgent parents,* parents who ~ their children. **in·dul·gent·ly** *adv*

in·dul·gence /ɪnˋdʌldʒəns/ *n* **1** [U] **~ *(in),*** indulging; the state of being indulged; the habit of gratifying one's own desires, etc: *Constant ~ in bad habits brought about his ruin.* **2** [C] sth in which a person indulges: *One pint of beer a day and an occasional game of billiards are his only ~s.* **3** [U] (in the R C Church) granting of freedom from punishment still due for sin after sacramental absolution; [C] instance of this.

in·dus·trial /ɪnˋdʌstrɪəl/ *adj* of industries: *~ alcohol,* for ~ use; made unfit for drinking; *the ~ areas of England* (contrasted with agriculture, etc); *an ~ dispute,* one between workers and management; *an ~ estate,* area of land planned and used for the building of factories (to be rented to manufacturers); *the ~ revolution,* the changes brought about by mechanical inventions in the 18th and early 19th cc); *an ~ school,* where trades are taught. **~·ism** /-ɪzm/ *n* social system in which large-scale industries have an important part. **~·ist** /-ɪst/ *n* owner of a large-scale ~ undertaking; supporter of ~ism.

in·dus·tri·ous /ɪnˋdʌstrɪəs/ *adj* hard-working; diligent. ⇨ **industry(1). ~·ly** *adv*

in·dus·try /ˋɪndəstrɪ/ *n* (*pl* **-tries**) **1** [U] quality of being hard-working; being always employed usefully: *His success was due to ~ and thrift.* **2** [C,U] (branch of) trade or manufacture (contrasted with distribution and commerce): *the cotton and woollen industries.*

in·dwell·ing /ˈɪnˋdwelɪŋ/ *adj* (formal) living, always present, in the mind or soul.

in·ebri·ate /ɪˋnibrɪeɪt/ *vt* [VP6A] make drunk; intoxicate. □ *n, adj* /ɪˋnibrɪət/ (person who is habitually) drunk: *an institution for ~s.* **in·ebri·ety** /ˈɪnɪˋbrɑɪətɪ/ *n* [U] drunkenness.

in·ed·ible /ɪnˋedəbl/ *adj* (of a kind) not suitable to be eaten.

in·ef·fable /ɪnˋefəbl/ *adj* too great to be described in words: *~ joy/beauty.* **in·ef·fably** /-əblɪ/ *adv*

in·ef·fec·tive /ˈɪnɪˋfektɪv/ *adj* not producing the effect(s) desired; (of a person) inefficient. **~·ly** *adv* **~·ness** *n*

in·ef·fec·tual /ˈɪnɪˋfektʃʊəl/ *adj* without effect; unsuccessful; lacking confidence and unable to get things done: *an ~ teacher/leader.* **~ly** /-tʃʊəlɪ/ *adv*

in·ef·fic·ient /ˈɪnɪˋfɪʃnt/ *adj* (of persons) wasting time, energy, etc in their work or duties: *an ~ management/administration;* (of machines, processes, etc) wasteful; not producing adequate results. **~·ly** *adv* **in·ef·fic·iency** /-ənsɪ/ *n* [U].

in·elas·tic /ˈɪnɪˋlæstɪk/ *adj* not flexible or adaptable; unyielding: *an ~ programme/timetable.*

in·el·egant /ɪnˋelɪgənt/ *adj* not graceful or refined. **~·ly** *adv* **in·el·egance** /-əns/ *n*

in·eli·gible /ɪnˋelɪdʒəbl/ *adj* not eligible; not suitable or qualified: *~ for the position.* **in·eli·gi·bil·ity** /ɪnˈelɪdʒəˋbɪlətɪ/ *n* [U].

in·eluc·table /ˈɪnɪˋlʌktəbl/ *adj* (formal) that cannot be escaped from: *the victim of ~ fate.*

in·ept /ɪˋnept/ *adj* absurd, said or done at the wrong time: *~ remarks.* **~·ly** *adv* **in·ep·ti·tude** /ɪˋneptɪtjud *US:* -tud/ *n* [U] quality of being ~; [C] ~ action, remark, etc.

in·equal·ity /ˈɪnɪˋkwolətɪ/ *n* (*pl* **-ties**) **1** [U] want of, absence of, equality in size, degree, circumstances, etc; [C] instance of this; difference in size, rank, wealth, etc: *Great inequalities in wealth causes social unrest.* **2** (*pl*) (of a surface) irregularity: *the inequalities of the landscape,* the rise and fall of the ground, etc.

in·equi·table /ɪnˋekwɪtəbl/ *adj* (formal) unjust; unfair: *an ~ division of the profits.*

in·equity /ɪnˋekwətɪ/ *n* (*pl* **-ties**) [C,U] (instance of) injustice or unfairness.

in·eradi·cable /ˈɪnɪˋrædɪkəbl/ *adj* that cannot be rooted out; firmly and deeply rooted: *an ~ fault/failing.*

in·ert /ɪˋnɜt/ *adj* **1** without power to move or act: *~ matter.* **2** without active chemical properties: *~ gases.* **3** heavy and slow in (mind or body). **in·er·tia** /ɪˋnɜʃə/ *n* [U] **1** state of being **~(3). 2** property of matter by which it remains in a state of rest or, if it is in motion, continues in the same direction and in a straight line unless it is acted upon by an external force.

in·es·cap·able /ˈɪnɪˋskeɪpəbl/ *adj* not to be escaped from: *We were forced to the ~ conclusion that he was an embezzler.*

in·es·ti·mable /ɪnˋestɪməbl/ *adj* too great, precious, etc to be estimated.

in·evi·table /ɪnˋevɪtəbl/ *adj* **1** that cannot be avoided, that is sure to happen. **2** (colloq) so frequently seen, heard, etc that it is familiar and expected: *a Japanese or an American tourist with his ~ camera.* **in·evi·ta·bil·ity** /ɪnˈevɪtəˋbɪlətɪ/ *n*

in·ex·act /ˈɪnɪgˋzækt/ *adj* not exact. **in·ex·acti·tude** /ˈɪnɪgˋzæktɪtjud *US:* -tud/ *n* [U] being ~; [C] instance of this: *terminological ~itudes,* (joc euphem for) lies.

in·ex·cus·able /ˈɪnɪkˋskjuzəbl/ *adj* that cannot be excused: *~ conduct/delays.*

in·ex·haust·ible /ˈɪnɪgˋzɔstəbl/ *adj* that cannot be exhausted: *My patience is not ~.*

in·exor·able /ɪnˋeksərəbl/ *adj* relentless; unyielding: *~ demands/pressures.* **in·exor·ably** /-əblɪ/ *adv*

in·ex·pedi·ent /ˈɪnɪkˋspidɪənt/ *adj* not expedient. **in·ex·pedi·en·cy** /-ənsɪ/ *n* quality of being ~.

in·ex·pen·sive /ˈɪnɪkˋspensɪv/ *adj* not expensive; low priced. **~·ly** *adv*

in·ex·peri·ence /ˈɪnɪkˋspɪərɪəns/ *n* [U] lack of experience. **in·ex·pe·ri·enced** *adj* lacking experience.

in·ex·pert /ɪnˋekspɜt/ *adj* unskilled. **~·ly** *adv*: *~ advice/guidance.*

in·ex·pi·able /ɪnˋekspɪəbl/ *adj* (of an offence) that cannot be expiated; (of resentment, hatred, etc) that cannot be appeased.

in·ex·plic·able /ˈɪnɪkˋsplɪkəbl/ *adj* that cannot be explained.

in·ex·press·ible /ˈɪnɪkˋspresəbl/ *adj* that cannot be expressed in words: *~ sorrow/anguish.*

in·ex·tin·guish·able /ˈɪnɪkˋstɪŋgwɪʃəbl/ *adj* that cannot be extinguished or quenched: *~ hatred.*

in·ex·tri·cable /ɪnˋekstrɪkəbl/ *adj* that cannot be reduced to order, solved, untied, or escaped from: *~ confusion/difficulties.*

in·fal·lible /ɪnˋfæləbl/ *adj* **1** incapable of making mistakes or doing wrong: *None of us is ~.* **2** never failing: ~ *remedies/cures/methods/tests.* **in·fal·li·bil·ity** /ˌɪnˈfæləˈbɪlətɪ/ *n* complete freedom from the possibility of being in error: *the infallibility of the Pope.*

in·fa·mous /ˈɪnfəməs/ *adj* wicked; shameful; disgraceful: ~ *behaviour; an* ~ *plot/traitor.* **in·famy** /ˈɪnfəmɪ/ *n* **1** [U] being ~; public dishonour: *hold a person up to infamy.* **2** [U] ~ behaviour; [C] (*pl* **-mies**) ~ act.

in·fancy /ˈɪnfənsɪ/ *n* [U] **1** state of being, period when one is, an infant; early childhood; (legal, in GB) minority(**1**), period before one reaches 18. ⇨ **minority. 2** early stage of development or growth: *the* ~ *of a nation; when aviation was still in its* ~.

in·fant /ˈɪnfənt/ *n* **1** child during the first few years of its life; (legal) minor. **2** (attrib) ~ *voices;* ~ *food; an* ˈ~*-school,* part of a primary school for children under 7; ~ *industries,* new, in an early stage.

in·fan·ti·cide /ɪnˈfæntɪsaɪd/ *n* [U] crime of killing an infant; the custom, among some peoples in the past, of killing unwanted new-born children.

in·fan·tile /ˈɪnfəntaɪl/ *adj* characteristic of infants: ~ *diseases/pastimes;* ~ *paralysis,* name formerly used for poliomyelitis. **in·fan·til·ism** /ɪnˈfæntɪlɪzm/ *n* [U] mentally and physically underdeveloped or arrested state.

in·fan·try /ˈɪnfəntrɪ/ *n* (collective *sing*) footsoldiers: *two regiments of* ~*; an* ~ *regiment.* **~man** /-mən/ *n* (*pl* **-men**) soldier in an ~ regiment.

in·fatu·ate /ɪnˈfætʃʊeɪt/ *vt* ***be ~d with/by sb,*** (usu passive) be filled with a wild and foolish love for: *He's* ~*d with that girl.* **in·fatu·ation** /ɪnˌfætʃʊˈeɪʃn/ *n* [U] infatuating or being ~d; [C] instance of this; unreasoning love or passion (*for*).

in·fect /ɪnˈfekt/ *vt* [VP6A] contaminate; give disease, (fig) feelings, ideas, to a person, his body or mind: ~ *a wound;* ~*ed with cholera. Mary's high spirits* ~*ed all the girls in the class.*

in·fec·tion /ɪnˈfekʃn/ *n* **1** [U] infecting or being infected; communication of disease, esp by agency of the atmosphere or water, ⇨ **contagion. 2** [C] disease, (fig) influence, that infects.

in·fec·tious /ɪnˈfekʃəs/ *adj* **1** infecting with disease; (of disease) that can be spread by means of bacteria carried in the atmosphere or in water. ⇨ **contagious. 2** (fig) quickly influencing others; likely to spread to others: ~ *humour.*

in·fer /ɪnˈfɜ(r)/ *vt* (**-rr-**) [VP6A,9,14] ~ ***(from sth) (that...),*** conclude; reach an opinion (from facts or reasoning): *Am I to* ~ *from your remarks that you think I am a liar?* **~·ence** /ˈɪnfərns/ *n* **1** [U] process of ~ring: *by* ~*ence,* as the result of drawing a conclusion. **2** [C] that which is ~red; conclusion: *Is that a fair* ~*ence from his statement?* **~·en·tial** /ˌɪnfəˈrenʃl/ *adj* that may be ~red.

in·ferior /ɪnˈfɪərɪə(r)/ *adj* low(er) in rank, social position, importance, quality, etc: *goods* ~ *to sample; goods of* ~ *workmanship; an* ~ *officer/court of law; make sb feel* ~. □ *n* person who is ~ (in rank, ability, etc). **~·ity** /ɪnˌfɪərɪˈorətɪ *US:* -ˈɔr-/ *n* [U] state of being ~. ˈ**~ity complex,** state of mind in which a person who has a morbid feeling of being ~ to others may try to win recognition for himself by boasting and being aggressive.

in·fer·nal /ɪnˈfɜnl/ *adj* of hell; devilish; abominable: *the* ~ *regions;* ~ *cruelty; an* ~ *machine,* (dated description of a) time-bomb. **~ly** /-nlɪ/ *adv*

in·ferno /ɪnˈfɜnəʊ/ *n* (*pl* **-nos** /nəʊz/) hell; scene of horror, e g a blazing building in which people are trapped.

in·fer·tile /ˌɪnˈfɜtaɪl *US:* -tl/ *adj* not fertile; barren. **in·fer·til·ity** /ˌɪnfəˈtɪlətɪ/ *n*

in·fest /ɪnˈfest/ *vt* [VP6A] (of rats, insects, brigands, etc) be present in large numbers: *warehouses* ~*ed with rats; clothes* ~*ed with vermin/lice.* **in·fes·ta·tion** /ˌɪnfeˈsteɪʃn/ *n* ~ing or being ~ed.

in·fi·del /ˈɪnfɪdl/ *n* **1** person with no belief in a specify religion, esp in what is considered to be the true religion **2** (attrib) unbelieving; of unbelievers: *He showed an* ~ *contempt for sacred places.*

in·fi·del·ity /ˌɪnfɪˈdelətɪ/ *n* (*pl* **-ties**) [C,U] (formal act of) disloyalty or unfaithfulness; adultery: *conjugal* ~, ~ to one's husband or wife.

in·field /ˈɪnfild/ *n* (cricket) (opp *outfield*) part of the ground near the wicket; fieldsmen stationed there; baseball diamond.

in-fight·ing /ˈɪn faɪtɪŋ/ *n* [U] boxing at rather close quarters; (colloq) often ruthless competition between colleagues or rivals (esp in commerce and industry).

in·fil·trate /ˈɪnfɪltreɪt/ *vt,vi* [VP6A,14,2A,3A] ~ ***sth into sth,*** ~ ***into/through,*** (cause to) pass through or into by filtering; (of troops) pass through defences without attracting notice; (of ideas) pass into people's minds. **in·fil·tra·tion** /ˌɪnfɪlˈtreɪʃn/ *n* infiltrating or being ~d; (esp) gradual and unnoticed occupation of land by small groups, e g of soldiers or settlers.

in·fi·nite /ˈɪnfənɪt/ *adj* endless; without limits; that cannot be measured, calculated, or imagined: ~ *space; the* ~ *goodness of God; Such ideas may do* ~ *harm.* **the I~,** God. **~·ly** *adv* in an ~ degree: *Atoms and molecules are* ~*ly small.* **in·fini·tesi·mal** /ˌɪnˌfɪnɪˈtesɪml/ *adj* ~ly small.

in·fini·tive /ɪnˈfɪnətɪv/ *adj, n* (gram) (in English non-finite form of a *v* used with or without *to,* e g let him *go*; allow him *to go.*

in·fini·tude /ɪnˈfɪnɪtjud *US:* -tud/ *n* [U] (formal) the state of being infinite or boundless; boundless number or extent (*of*): *the* ~ *of God's mercy;* [C] infinite number, quantity, or extent: *an* ~ *of small particles.*

in·fin·ity /ɪnˈfɪnətɪ/ *n* [U] infinitude; (maths) infinite quantity (expressed by the symbol ∞).

in·firm /ˌɪnˈfɜm/ *adj* **1** physically weak (esp through age): *walk with* ~ *steps.* **2** mentally or morally weak. ~ ***of purpose,*** not purposeful; undecided. **in·firm·ity** /ˌɪnˈfɜmətɪ/ *n* (*pl* **-ties**) [C,U] (particular form of) weakness: *I~ity often comes with old age. Deafness and failing eyesight are among the* ~*ities of old age.*

in·firm·ary /ɪnˈfɜmərɪ/ *n* (*pl* **-ries**) **1** hospital. **2** (in a school, institution, etc) room used for people who are ill or injured.

in·flame /ɪnˈfleɪm/ *vt,vi* [VP2A,6A] (cause to) become red, angry, overheated: ~*d eyes; an* ~*d boil,* red and angry looking; *speeches that* ~*d popular feeling,* roused people to anger, indignation, etc; ~*d with passion.*

in·flam·mable /ɪnˈflæməbl/ *adj* easily set on fire or (fig) excited: *Aviation Spirit—Highly I~!* ⇨ **inflammable.**

in·flam·ma·tion /ˌɪnfləˈmeɪʃn/ *n* [U] inflamed condition (esp of some part of the body): ~ *of the* *lungs/liver;* [C] instance of this; place on or in the body where there is redness, swelling and pain.

in·flam·ma·tory /ɪnˈflæmətrɪ *US:* -tɔrɪ/ *adj* **1** tending to inflame: ~ *speeches.* **2** of, tending to produce, inflammation(**1**): *an ~ condition of the lungs,* e g as a symptom of pneumonia.

in·flate /ɪnˈfleɪt/ *vt* [VP6A,14] **~ sth (with), 1** fill a tyre, balloon, etc with air or gas; (cause to) swell: (fig) *~d with pride; ~d language,* full of high-sounding words but containing little substance. **2** take action to increase the amount of money in circulation so that prices rise. ⇨ deflate. **in·flat·able** /-əbl/ *adj* that can be ~d: *an inflatable rubber dinghy.* **in·fla·tion** /ɪnˈfleɪʃn/ *n* [U] act of inflating; state of being ~d; (esp) (rise in prices brought about by the) expansion of the supply of bank money, credit, etc. **in·fla·tion·ary** /ɪnˈfleɪʃnrɪ *US:* -nerɪ/ *adj* of, caused by, inflation: *the inflationary spiral,* economic situation in which prices and wages rise in turn as the supply of money is increased.

in·flect /ɪnˈflekt/ *vt* [VP6A] **1** (gram) change the ending or form of (a word) to show its relationship to other words in a sentence. **2** modulate (the voice); bend inwards; curve.

in·flec·tion /ɪnˈflekʃn/ *n* **1** [U] inflecting. **2** [C] inflected form of a word; suffix used to inflect, e g *-ed, -ing.* **3** [U] rise and fall of the voice in speaking. **~al** /-ʃnl/ *adj* of ~: *~al endings/forms,* e g *-ed.*.

in·flex·ible /ɪnˈfleksəbl/ *adj* that cannot be bent or turned; (fig) unbending; not to be turned aside: ~ *courage; an ~ will.* **in·flex·ibly** /-əblɪ/ *adv* **in·flexi·bil·ity** /ˈɪnˈfleksɪˈbɪlətɪ/ *n*

in·flexion /ɪnˈflekʃn/ *n* = inflection.

in·flict /ɪnˈflɪkt/ *vt* [VP6A,14] **~ sth (up)on,** give (a blow, etc); cause to suffer; impose: ~ *a blow/a severe wound upon sb. The judge ~ed the death penalty upon the murderer. I'm sorry to have to ~ myself/my company upon you,* force my company upon you. **in·flic·tion** /ɪnˈflɪkʃn/ *n* [U] ~ing or being ~ed: *the unnecessary ~ion of pain and suffering;* [C] sth ~ed; painful or troublesome experience.

in·flor·escence /ˈɪnfləˈresns/ *n* [U] arrangement of a plant's flowers on the stem; collective flower of a plant; flowering.

in·flow /ˈɪnfləʊ/ *n* [U] flowing in; [C,U] that which flows in; *an ~ of capital/investment; an ~ of 25 litres an hour;* (attrib) *an ~ pipe.*

in·flu·ence /ˈɪnflʊəns/ *n* **~ (up)on, 1** [U] power to affect sb's character, beliefs or actions through example, fear, admiration, etc; [C] person, fact, etc that exercises such power; [U] the exercise of such power: *Many a woman has had a civilizing ~ upon her husband. He's an ~ for good in the town. Heredity and environment are ~s on character. He was under the ~ of alcohol,* had had too much to drink. **2** [U] action of natural forces: *the ~ of the moon (on the tides); the ~ of climate (on vegetation).* **3** [U] power due to wealth, position, etc: *Will you please use your ~ with the manager on my behalf? Will you use your ~ to get me a job?* □ *vt* [VP6A] exert an ~ on; having an effect on: *Can the planets ~ human character, as astrologers claim? Don't be ~d by bad examples.*

in·flu·en·tial /ˈɪnflʊˈenʃl/ *adj* having influence: ~ *politicians; considerations which are ~ in reaching a decision.* **~ly** /-ʃlɪ/ *adv*

in·flu·enza /ˈɪnflʊˈenzə/ *n* [U] infectious disease with fever, muscular pain and catarrh.

in·flux /ˈɪnflʌks/ *n* [U] flowing in; [C] (*pl* **-xes**) constant inflow of large numbers or quantities: *repeated ~es of visitors; an ~ of wealth.*

in·form /ɪnˈfɔm/ *vt,vi* **1** [VP6A,11,14,21] **~ sb (of sth, that...),** give knowledge to: *We were ~ed that two prisoners had escaped. Keep me ~ed of fresh developments. He's a well-~ed man. Have you ~ed them of your intended departure?* **2** [VP3A] **~ against sb,** (legal) bring evidence or an accusation against him (to the police). **3 ~·ant** /-ənt/ *n* person who gives information; native speaker of a language who helps a foreign scholar who is making an analysis of it. **~er** *n* person who ~s(**2**), esp against a criminal or fugitive.

in·for·mal /ˈɪnˈfɔml/ *adj* not formal(**1,2**); irregular; without ceremony or formality: *an ~ visit; ~ dress; ~ conversations between the statesmen of two countries,* no official records being kept. **~ly** /-mlɪ/ *adv* **~·ity** /ˈɪnfɔˈmælətɪ/ *n* [U] being ~; [C] (*pl* **-ties**) ~ act, etc.

in·for·ma·tion /ˈɪnfəˈmeɪʃn/ *n* [U] **~ on/about, 1** informing or being informed. **2** sth told; news or knowledge given: *That's a useful piece/bit of ~. Can you give me any ~ on/about this matter? The ˈ~ bureau may be able to help you.*

in·forma·tive /ɪnˈfɔmətɪv/ *adj* giving information; instructive: *~ books; an ~ talk.* **~·ly** *adv*

in·fra /ˈɪnfrə/ *adv* (Lat) below; farther or later on (in a book, etc): *See ~, p 21,* See p 21 farther on in this book. **ˈ~-ˈdig** *phrase* (colloq abbr of Lat ~ *dignitatem*) beneath one's dignity. **ˈ~-ˈred** *adj* of those invisible rays below the red in the spectrum. **ˈ~·structure** *n* system of airfields, communications, etc forming a basis for defence.

in·frac·tion /ɪnˈfrækʃn/ *n* [U] breaking of a rule, law, etc; [C] instance of this.

in·fre·quent /ɪnˈfrikwənt/ *adj* not frequent; rare. **~·ly** *adv* **in·fre·quency** /ɪnˈfrikwənsɪ/ *n* [U].

in·fringe /ɪnˈfrɪndʒ/ *vt,vi* **1** [VP6A] break (a rule, etc); transgress; violate: *~ a rule/an oath/ a copyright/a patent.* **2** [VP3A] **~ upon,** encroach: *Be careful not to ~ upon the rights of other people.* **~·ment** *n* [U] infringing; [C] ***~ment of,*** instance of this, e g the unlawful use of a trade name or of copyright material.

in·furi·ate /ɪnˈfjʊərɪeɪt/ *vt* [VP6A] fill with fury or rage: *infuriating delays.*

in·fuse /ɪnˈfjuz/ *vt,vi* (formal) **1** [VP14] put, pour (a quality, etc *into*); fill (sb with): *~ fresh courage/new life into soldiers; ~ soldiers with fresh courage.* **2** [VP6A] pour (hot) liquid on (leaves, herbs, etc) to flavour it or to extract its constituents: *~ herbs.* **3** [VP2A] undergo infusion: *Let the herbs ~ for three minutes.*

in·fu·sion /ɪnˈfjuʒn/ *n* **1** [U] infusing or being infused. **2** [C] liquid made by infusing. **3** [U] pouring in; mixing: *the ~ of new blood into old stock,* the use of new breeds to improve old breeds.

in·gath·er·ing /ˈɪŋgæðrɪŋ/ *n* [C] (formal) gathering in; harvest.

in·geni·ous /ɪnˈdʒinɪəs/ *adj* **1** (of a person) clever and skilful (at making or inventing); showing skill, etc: *an ~ mind.* **2** (of things) skilfully made: *an ~ toy/tool.* **~·ly** *adv* **in·gen·uity** /ˈɪndʒɪˈnjuətɪ *US:* -ˈnu-/ *n* [U] cleverness and skill; originality in design.

in·gé·nue /ˈæ̃ʒeɪnju *US:* ˈændʒənu/ *n* (formal) simple, innocent girl, esp as a type in dramas;

actress playing such a part.

in·genu·ous /ɪnˋdʒenjʊəs/ *adj* (formal) frank; open; innocent, natural: *an ~ smile.* **~·ly** *adv* **~·ness** *n*

in·gest /ɪnˋdʒest/ *vt* [VP6A] take in (food, etc) by, or as if by, swallowing.

ingle-nook /ˋɪŋgl nʊk/ *n* chimney-corner (in a wide old-fashioned fireplace) where the fire burns on an open hearth.

in·glori·ous /ɪnˋglɔrɪəs/ *adj* **1** shameful; ignominious. **2** obscure. **~·ly** *adv*

in·go·ing /ˋɪngəʊɪŋ/ *adj* going in: *the ~* (= new) *tenant of a house/flat.*

in·got /ˋɪŋgət/ *n* [C] (usu brick-shaped) lump of metal (esp gold and silver), cast in a mould.

in·graft /ɪnˋgrɑft *US:* -ˋgræft/ *v* = **engraft**.

in·grained /ˈɪnˋgreɪnd/ *adj* **1** (of habits, tendencies, etc) deeply fixed; through: *~ prejudices/honesty.* **2** going deep: *~ dirt.*

in·grati·ate /ɪnˋgreɪʃɪeɪt/ *vt* [VP14] ***~ oneself (with sb),*** bring oneself into favour, esp in order to gain an advantage: *with an ingratiating smile.* **in·grati·at·ing·ly** *adv*

in·grati·tude /ɪnˋgrætɪtjud *US:* -tud/ *n* [U] want of gratitude.

in·gredi·ent /ɪnˋgridɪənt/ *n* [C] one of the parts of a mixture: *the ~s of a cake; the ~s of a man's character,* all those qualities, etc that together form it.

in·gress /ˋɪngrəs/ *n* [U] (formal) going in; (right of) entrance: *a means of ~.* ⇨ **egress**.

in·grow·ing /ˈɪnˋgrəʊɪŋ/ *adj* growing inwards: *an ~ toe-nail,* one growing into the flesh.

in·habit /ɪnˋhæbɪt/ *vt* [VP6A] live in; occupy. **in·hab·it·able** /-əbl/ *adj* that can be lived in. **in·habit·ant** /-ənt/ *n* person living in a place.

in·hale /ɪnˋheɪl/ *vt,vi* [VP6A,2A] draw into the lungs: *~ air/gas/tobacco smoke. I~! Exhale!* Breathe in! Breathe out! **in·haler** *n* device for producing a chemical vapour to make breathing easier.

in·har·moni·ous /ˈɪnhɑˋməʊnɪəs/ *adj* not harmonious.

in·herent /ɪnˋhɪərnt/ *adj* **~ *(in),*** existing as a natural and permanent part or quality of: *Weight is an ~ quality of matter. He has an ~ love of beauty. The power ~ in the office of President must not be abused.*

in·herit /ɪnˋherɪt/ *vt,vi* [VP6A,2A] **1** receive property, a title, etc as heir: *The eldest son will ~ the title.* **2** derive (qualities, etc) from ancestors: *She ~ed her mother's good looks and her father's bad temper.* **in·herit·ance** /-əns/ *n* [U] ~ing: *receive sth by ~ance;* [C] (liter, fig) what is ~ed: *an ~ance of ill-feeling.*

in·hibit /ɪnˋhɪbɪt/ *vt* [VP6A,14] ***~ sb from sth/doing sth,*** hinder, restrain: *~ wrong desires and impulses; an ~ed person,* one who is unable or unwilling to express his feelings. **in·hi·bi·tion** /ˈɪnɪˋbɪʃn/ *n* [U] (psych) restraint on, habitual shrinking from, an action for which there is an impulse or desire; [C] instance of this: *Wine weakens a person's ~ions.* **in·hibi·tory** /ɪnˋhɪbɪtrɪ *US:* -tɔrɪ/ *adj* tending to ~; of an inhibition.

in·hos·pi·table /ˈɪnhoˋspɪtəbl/ *adj* not hospitable; (of a place, coast, etc) not affording shelter: *an ~ coast.*

in·hu·man /ˈɪnˋhjumən/ *adj* cruel; unfeeling: *~ treatment.* **~·ity** /ˈɪnhjuˋmænətɪ/ *n* [U] ~ conduct or behaviour: *man's ~ity to man;* [C] (*pl* **-ties**) ~ act.

in·hu·mane /ˈɪnhjuˋmeɪn/ *adj* not humane; cruel; without pity. **~·ly** *adv*

in·imi·cal /ɪˋnɪmɪkl/ *adj* (formal) unfriendly or harmful: *actions ~ to friendly relations between countries.*

in·imi·table /ɪˋnɪmɪtəbl/ *adj* (formal) too good, clever, etc to be imitated. **in·imi·tably** /-əblɪ/ *adv*

in·iqui·tous /ɪˋnɪkwɪtəs/ *adj* (formal) very wicked or unjust: *an ~ system/regime.* **~·ly** *adv* **in·iquity** /ɪˋnɪkwətɪ/ *n* [U] being ~; [C] (*pl* **-ties**) ~ act.

in·itial /ɪˋnɪʃl/ *adj* of or at the beginning: *the ~ letter of a word; the ~ stages of an undertaking.* □ *n* ~ letter, esp (*pl*) first letters of a person's names, as *GBS* (for *George Bernard Shaw*). □ *vt* (**-ll-**, US also **-l-**) [VP6A] mark, sign, with one's ~s: *~ a note or document.* **~ly** /-ʃlɪ/ *adv* at the beginning.

in·iti·ate /ɪˋnɪʃɪeɪt/ *vt* **1** [VP6A] set (a scheme, etc) working: *~ a plan.* **2** [VP14] ***~ sb into sth,*** admit or introduce sb to membership of (a group, etc). **3** [VP14] ***~ sb into sth,*** give sb elementary instruction, or secret knowledge of: *~ students into the mysteries of interstellar communication.* □ *n, adj* /ɪˋnɪʃɪət/ *n* (person) who has been ~d(**2,3**): *an ~,* member of a secret society. **in·iti·ation** /ɪˈnɪʃɪˋeɪʃn/ *n* [U] initiating or being ~d; being made acquainted with the rules of a society, etc: (attrib) *initiation ceremonies.*

in·iti·at·ive /ɪˋnɪʃətɪv/ *n* **1** [U] first or introductory step or move. ***act/do sth on one's own ~,*** without an order or suggestion from others. ***have the ~,*** be in the position to make the first move, e g in war. ***take the ~ (in doing sth),*** make the first move towards it. **2** [U] capacity to see what needs to be done and enterprise enough to do it: *A statesman must have/show/display ~.* **3** [C] power or right of citizens outside the legislature to put forward proposals for legislation (as in Switzerland).

in·ject /ɪnˋdʒekt/ *vt* [VP6A,14] ***~ sth into sb/sth, ~ sb/sth with sth,*** drive or force a liquid, drug, etc into sth with, or as with, a syringe; fill (sth with a liquid, etc) by ~ing: *~ penicillin into the blood-stream; ~ sb's arm with morphia;* (fig, colloq) *His appointment may ~ some new life into the committee.* **in·jec·tion** /ɪnˋdʒekʃn/ *n* [U] ~ing; [C] instance of this: *five ~ions of glucose; an ~ion in the left buttock;* [C] liquid, etc that is ~ed. ˋ**fuel injection,** method by which liquid fuel is converted to vapour and sprayed into the cylinders of an internal combustion engine.

in·ju·di·cious /ˈɪndʒʊˋdɪʃəs/ *adj* (formal) not well-judged: *~ remarks.* **~·ly** *adv*

in·junc·tion /ɪnˋdʒʌŋkʃn/ *n* [C] authoritative order, esp a written order from a law court, demanding that sth shall or shall not be done (called an *interdict* in Scotland).

in·jure /ˋɪndʒə(r)/ *vt* [VP6A] hurt; damage. **in·jured** *adj* wounded; hurt; wronged; offended: *~d looks; in an ~d voice; the dead and the ~d,* those people killed and hurt (in an accident, etc).

in·juri·ous /ɪnˋdʒʊərɪəs/ *adj* **~ *to,*** (formal) causing, likely to cause, injury; hurtful: *behaviour that is ~ to social order; habits that are ~ to health.*

in·jury /ˋɪndʒərɪ/ *n* (*pl* **-ries**) **1** [U] harm; damage; wrongful treatment: *If you knock a man down with your car, and then call him a fool, you are adding insult to ~.* ***do sb an ~,*** cause sb harm. **2** [C] place (in the body) that is hurt or wounded; act that hurts; insult: *The cyclist suffered severe injuries. This attack was a severe ~ to his reputation.*

in·jus·tice /ˈɪnˋdʒʌstɪs/ *n* [U] lack of justice; [C] unjust act, etc. ***do sb an ~,*** judge him unfairly.

ink /ɪŋk/ *n* [U] (kinds of) coloured liquid used for writing and printing; black liquid ejected by cuttlefish, etc: *written in ink; a pen and ink drawing.* **ˋink-bottle/-pot** *nn* for holding ink. **ˋink-pad** *n* pad for ink used on rubber stamps. **ˋink-stand** *n* stand for one or more ink-bottles, with grooves or a tray for pens, etc. **ˋink-well** *n* ink-pot that fits into a hole in a desk. □ *vt* [VP6A,15B] mark with ink: *ink one's fingers.* ***ink in***: *ink in a drawing,* mark with ink lines previously drawn in pencil. **inky (-ier, -iest)** marked with ink: *inky fingers;* black like ink: *inky darkness.*

ink·ling /ˋɪŋklɪŋ/ *n* [C] ***have/get/give sb some/an ~ (of sth),*** have, get, some idea (of what is going on).

in·laid /ɪnˋleɪd/ *pt,pp* of **inlay**.

in·land /ˋɪnlənd/ *adj* **1** situated in the interior of a country, far from the sea or border: *~ towns; the I~ Sea of Japan,* area of sea almost enclosed by large islands. **2** carried on, obtained, within the limits of a country: *~* (= domestic) *trade.* **the ˌI~ ˋRevenue,** (GB) money obtained by taxation within the country (excluding taxes on imported goods); (colloq) department responsible for collecting these taxes. □ *adv* /ɪnˋlænd/ in or towards the interior.

in-laws /ˋɪn lɔz/ *n pl* (colloq) relatives by marriage: *All my ~ will be visiting us this summer.*

in·lay /ɪnˋleɪ/ *vt* (*pt,pp* **inlaid** /-leɪd/) [VP6A,14] set pieces of (designs in) wood, metal, etc in the surface of another kind of wood, metal, etc so that the resulting surface is smooth and even: *gold inlaid into ivory; ivory inlaid with gold.* □ *n* **1** [U] inlaid work; materials used for this; [C] design, pattern, made by ~ing. **2** [C,U] (dentistry) (method of making a) solid filling of gold, plastic, etc for a cavity in a tooth.

in·let /ˋɪnlet/ *n* **1** strip of water extending into the land from a larger body of water (the sea, a lake), or between islands. **2** sth let in or inserted, e g a piece of material inserted into a garment. **3** (attrib) way in: *~ and outlet channels,* e g in a reservoir.

in loco par·en·tis /ˈɪn ˈləʊkʊ pəˋrentɪs/ (Lat) in the place or position of a parent: *I stood towards him ~.*

in·mate /ˋɪnmeɪt/ *n* one of a number of persons living together, esp in a hospital, prison or other institution.

in mem·oriam /ˈɪn məˋmɔrɪəm/ (Lat) (used in epitaphs, on gravestones) in memory of; as a memorial to.

in·most /ˋɪnməʊst/ *adj* most inward; farthest from the surface; (fig) most private or secret: *my ~ feelings.*

inn /ɪn/ *n* **1** public house where lodgings, drink and meals may be had, usu (today) in the country. ⇨ **hotel**. **ˋinn-keeper** *n* person who keeps an inn. **2** **ˈInn of ˋCourt,** (building of) four law societies in London having the exclusive right of admitting persons to the bar. ⇨ **bar**[1]**(12)**.

in·nards /ˋɪnədz/ *n pl* (colloq) **1** stomach and bowels; entrails. **2** any inner parts.

in·nate /ɪˋneɪt/ *adj* (of a quality, etc) in one's nature possessed from birth: *her ~ courtesy.* **~·ly** *adv*

in·ner /ˋɪnə(r)/ *adj* inside; of the inside: *an ~ room; an ˋ~ tube,* a tube, (to be) filled with air, inside the cover of a pneumatic tyre. **the ˈ~ ˋman,** **(a)** man's soul or mind (contrasted with *body*). **(b)** (joc) the stomach: *satisfy the ~ man.* **~·most** /-məʊst/ *adj* = **inmost**.

in·ning /ˋɪnɪŋ/ *n* **1** (baseball) division of a game in which each team bats. **2** (cricket, always *pl*) time during which a player or team is batting: *Our team made 307 runs in its first ~s. The first batsman had a short ~s.* **3** (fig) period of power, e g of a political party, or of opportunity to show one's ability, period of active life: *have a good ~s,* (colloq) have a long and happy life.

in·no·cent /ˋɪnəsnt/ *adj* **1** ***~ (of),*** not guilty: *~ of the charge/accusation.* **2** harmless: *~ amusements.* **3** knowing nothing of evil or wrong: *as ~ as a new-born babe.* **4** foolishly simple: *Don't be so ~ as to believe everything the politicians say.* □ *n* ~ person, esp a young child. **~·ly** *adv* **in·no·cence** /-sns/ *n* [C] quality or state of being ~.

in·nocu·ous /ɪˋnokjʊəs/ *adj* causing no harm: *~ snakes/drugs.*

in·no·vate /ˋɪnəveɪt/ *vi* [VP2A] make changes; introduce new things. **in·no·va·tor** /-tə(r)/ *n* person who ~s. **in·no·va·tion** /ˈɪnəˋveɪʃn/ *n* [U] innovating; [C] instance of this; sth new that is introduced: *technical innovations in industry.*

in·nu·endo /ˈɪnjʊˋendəʊ/ *n* (*pl* **-does** /-dəʊz/) indirect reference (usu sth unfavourable to a person's reputation): *If you throw out such ~es against the Minister, you'll be sued for libel.*

in·nu·mer·able /ɪˋnjumrəbl *US:* ɪˋnu-/ *adj* too many to be counted.

in·ocu·late /ɪˋnokjʊleɪt/ *vt* [VP6A,14] ***~ sb (against),*** inject a serum or vaccine into (a person or animal) to give (him, it) a mild form of the disease to safeguard him against it: *~ sb against cholera;* (fig) fill the mind with opinions, etc: *~d with evil doctrines.* **in·ocu·la·tion** /ɪˈnokjʊˋleɪʃn/ *n* [U] inoculating or being ~d; [C] instance of this: *have inoculations against cholera and yellow fever.* ⇨ **vaccinate**.

in·of·fen·sive /ˈɪnəˋfensɪv/ *adj* not giving offence; not objectionable: *an ~ remark/person.*

in·op·er·able /ɪnˋoprəbl/ *adj* (of tumours, etc) that cannot be cured by a surgical operation.

in·op·er·at·ive /ɪnˋoprətɪv/ *adj* (of laws, rules, etc) not working or taking effect; invalid.

in·op·por·tune /ˈɪnˋopətʃun *US:* -tun/ *adj* not seasonable(2): *at an ~ time.* **~·ly** *adv*

in·or·di·nate /ɪˋnɔdnət/ *adj* (formal) not properly restrained or controlled; excessive: *~ passions; the ~ demands of the Tax Collector.* **~·ly** *adv*

in·or·ganic /ˈɪnɔˋgænɪk/ *adj* **1** not having an organized physical structure, esp as plants and animals have; not forming part of the substance of living bodies: *~ chemistry. Rocks and metals are ~ substances.* **2** not the result of natural growth: *an ~ form of society.* **in·or·gani·cally** /-klɪ/ *adv*

in·pa·tient /ˋɪn peɪʃnt/ *n* person who lives in hospital while receiving treatment. ⇨ **out-patient**.

in·pour·ing /ˋɪnpɔrɪŋ/ *n, adj* (formal) pouring in: *an ~ of spiritual comfort.*

in·put /ˋɪnpʊt/ *n* ***~ (to),*** what is put in or supplied, e g data for processing in a computer, power supplied to a machine.

in·quest /ˋɪnkwest/ *n* ***~ (on),*** official inquiry to learn facts, esp concerning a death which may not be the result of natural causes.

in·quie·tude /ɪnˋkwaɪətjud *US:* -tud/ *n* [U] (formal) uneasiness of mind; anxiety.

in·quire /ɪn`kwaɪə(r)/ *vt,vi* **1** [VP6A,8,10,14,2A] ask to be told: ~ *a person's name;* ~ *what a person wants/where to stay/how to do sth;* ~ *of sb the reason for sth.* **2** [VP3A] ~ ***about/concerning/upon,*** ask for information about: ~ *about trains to London; I~ within upon everything,* e g as the title of a small encyclopedia. ~ ***after,*** ask about (sb's health, welfare). ~ ***for,*** ask for (goods in a shop), ask to see (sb): ~ *for a book in a shop;* ~ *for the manager.* ~ ***into,*** try to learn the facts about; investigate: *We must* ~ *into the matter.* **in·quirer** *n* person who ~s. **in·quir·ing** *adj* in the habit of asking for information: *an inquiring mind,* showing a desire to learn; *inquiring looks.* **in·quir·ing·ly** *adv*

in·quiry /ɪn`kwaɪərɪ *US:* `ɪnkwaɪərɪ/ *n* (*pl* **-ries**) **1** [U] asking; inquiring: *learn sth by* ~. ***on*** ~, when one has asked. **court of** ~, (mil) one to investigate charges brought against sb. **2** [C] question; investigation: *make inquiries about sb or sth; hold an official* ~ *into sth.*

in·qui·si·tion /ˌɪnkwɪ`zɪʃn/ *n* **1** [U] thorough search or investigation; [C] instance of this, esp a judicial or official inquiry. **2 the I**~, (also called *the Holy Office*) court appointed by the Church of Rome to suppress heresy (esp active in 15th and 16th cc) and to compile the Index(**2**).

in·quisi·tive /ɪn`kwɪzətɪv/ *adj* fond of, showing a fondness for, inquiring into other people's affairs. **~·ly** *adv* **~·ness** *n*

in·quisi·tor /ɪn`kwɪzɪtə(r)/ *n* investigator, esp an officer of the Inquisition(**2**); person appointed by law to make an inquiry. **in·quisi·tor·ial** /ɪnˌkwɪzɪ`tɔrɪəl/ *adj* of or like an ~.

in·road /`ɪnrəʊd/ *n* sudden attack (into a country, etc), esp one made for the purpose of plunder; (fig) sth that encroaches (*upon*): *make* ~*s upon one's leisure time/one's savings.*

in·rush /`ɪnrʌʃ/ *n* rushing in: *an* ~ *of water/tourists.*

in·sane /ɪn`seɪn/ *adj* mad; senseless: *an* ~ *person; an* ~ *asylum,* place where ~ people are cared for, now called a mental hospital or home. **~·ly** *adv* **in·san·ity** /ɪn`sænətɪ/ *n* [U] madness.

in·sani·tary /ɪn`sænɪtrɪ *US:* -terɪ/ *adj* not sanitary: *living under* ~ *conditions.*

in·sa·tiable /ɪn`seɪʃəbl/ *adj* (formal) that cannot be satisfied; very greedy: ~ *appetites; politicians who are* ~ *of power.* **in·sa·tiably** /-ʃəblɪ/ *adv*

in·sa·tiate /ɪn`seɪʃɪət/ *adj* (formal) never satisfied.

in·scribe /ɪn`skraɪb/ *vt* [VP6A,15A] ~ ***on/in/with,*** write (words, one's name, etc in or on); mark (sth with words, etc): ~ *names on a war memorial/one's name in a book;* ~ *a tomb with a name.* **~d stock,** stock of which the names of the holders are recorded in lists or registers. **in·scrip·tion** /ɪn`skrɪpʃn/ *n* [C] sth ~d, esp words cut on a stone, e g a monument, or stamped on a coin or medal.

in·scru·table /ɪn`skrutəbl/ *adj* that cannot be understood or known; mysterious: *the* ~ *ways of Providence; the* ~ *face of the Sphinx.*

in·sect /`ɪnsekt/ *n* sorts of small animal, e g ant, fly, wasp, having six legs and no backbone and a body divided into three parts (head, thorax, abdomen); (incorrect but pop usage) similar tiny, crawling creature, e g spider. ⇨ p448. **`~-powder** *n* powder for killing or driving away ~s. **in·sec·ti·cide** /ɪn`sektɪsaɪd/ *n* preparation used for killing ~s, e g DDT. **in·sec·tivor·ous** /ˌɪnsek`tɪvərəs/ *adj* eating ~s as food: *Swallows are* ~*ivorous.*

in·se·cure /ˌɪnsɪ`kjʊə(r)/ *adj* **1** not safe; not providing good support; not to be relied on: *have an* ~ *hold on sth,* e g when rock-climbing. **2** feeling unsafe; without protection; lacking confidence. **~·ly** *adv* **in·se·cur·ity** /ˌɪnsɪ`kjʊərətɪ/ *n* [U]: *suffer from feelings of insecurity.*

in·semi·nate /ɪn`semɪneɪt/ *vt* [VP6A] implant; introduce (semen into). **in·semi·na·tion** /ɪnˌsemɪ`neɪʃn/ *n* [U] inseminating. **ˈartificial inˌsemi`nation,** the introduction of semen taken, e g from a pedigree animal, into the generative organs of a female animal so that offspring may be produced without sexual union.

in·sen·sate /ɪn`senseɪt/ *adj* (formal) **1** without the power to feel or experience: ~ *rocks.* **2** unfeeling; without sensibility; foolish: ~ *rage/cruelty.*

in·sen·si·bil·ity /ɪnˌsensə`bɪlətɪ/ *n* [U] (formal) lack of mental feeling or emotion; state of being unable to know, recognize, understand or appreciate: ~ *to pain/beauty/art; in a state of* ~, unconscious.

in·sen·sible /ɪn`sensəbl/ *adj* **1** unconscious as the result of injury, illness, etc: *The rock struck her on the head and she was* ~ *for nearly an hour.* **2** ~ ***(of),*** unaware (of): *He seemed to be* ~ *of his danger. I'm not* ~ *how much I owe to your help.* **3** ~ ***to,*** without feeling: *When your hands are frozen they become* ~ *to any feeling,* numb (the usu word). **4** unsympathetic; emotionless; callous. **5** (of changes) too small or gradual to be perceived: *by* ~ *degrees.* **in·sen·sibly** /-əblɪ/ *adv*

in·sen·si·tive /ɪn`sensətɪv/ *adj* ~ ***(to),*** not sensitive (to touch, light, the feelings of other people). **~·ly** *adv* **in·sen·si·tiv·ity** /ˌɪnˌsensə`tɪvətɪ/ *n*

in·sen·tient /ɪn`senʃnt/ *adj* (formal) inanimate; without feeling or awareness.

in·sep·ar·able /ɪn`seprəbl/ *adj* ~ ***(from),*** that cannot be separated: ~ *friends.*

in·sert /ɪn`sɜt/ *vt* [VP6A,15A] put, fit, place (sth *in, into, between,* etc): ~ *a key in a lock/an advertisement in a newspaper/a new paragraph in an essay.* □ *n* /`ɪnsɜt/ sth ~ed, e g in a book. **in·ser·tion** /ɪn`sɜʃn/ *n* [U] ~ing or being ~ed; [C] sth ~ed, e g an announcement or advertisement in a newspaper, a piece of lace, etc ~ed in a dress.

in-ser·vice /`ɪn sɜvɪs/ *attrib adj,* while in service (contrasted with pre-service training, etc): *the* ~ *training of teachers.* Cf *refresher course.*

in·set /`ɪnset/ *n* [C] extra page(s) inserted in a book, etc; small map, diagram, etc within the border of a printed page or of a larger map; piece of material, e g lace, let into a dress. □ *vt* /ˈɪn`set/ put in; insert.

in·shore /ˈɪn`ʃɔ(r)/ *adj, adv* close to the shore: *an* ~ *current;* ~ *fisheries.*

in·side /ɪn`saɪd/ *n* **1** inner side or surface; part(s) within: *the* ~ *of a box; a door bolted on the* ~. ~ ***out,*** with the inner side out: *He put his socks on* ~ *out. The wind blew her umbrella* ~ *out. The burglars turned everything* ~ *out,* put drawers, boxes, etc and their contents into great disorder. *He knows the subject* ~ *out,* knows it thoroughly. **2** part of a road, track, etc on the inner edge of a curve; part of a pavement or footpath farthest from the road. **3** (colloq) stomach and bowels: *a pain in his* ~. □ *adj* (or *n* used attrib) situated on or in, coming from the ~: *the* ~ *pages of a newspaper; an* ~ *seat in a stage-coach.* **ˈ~ `left/`right,** (foot-

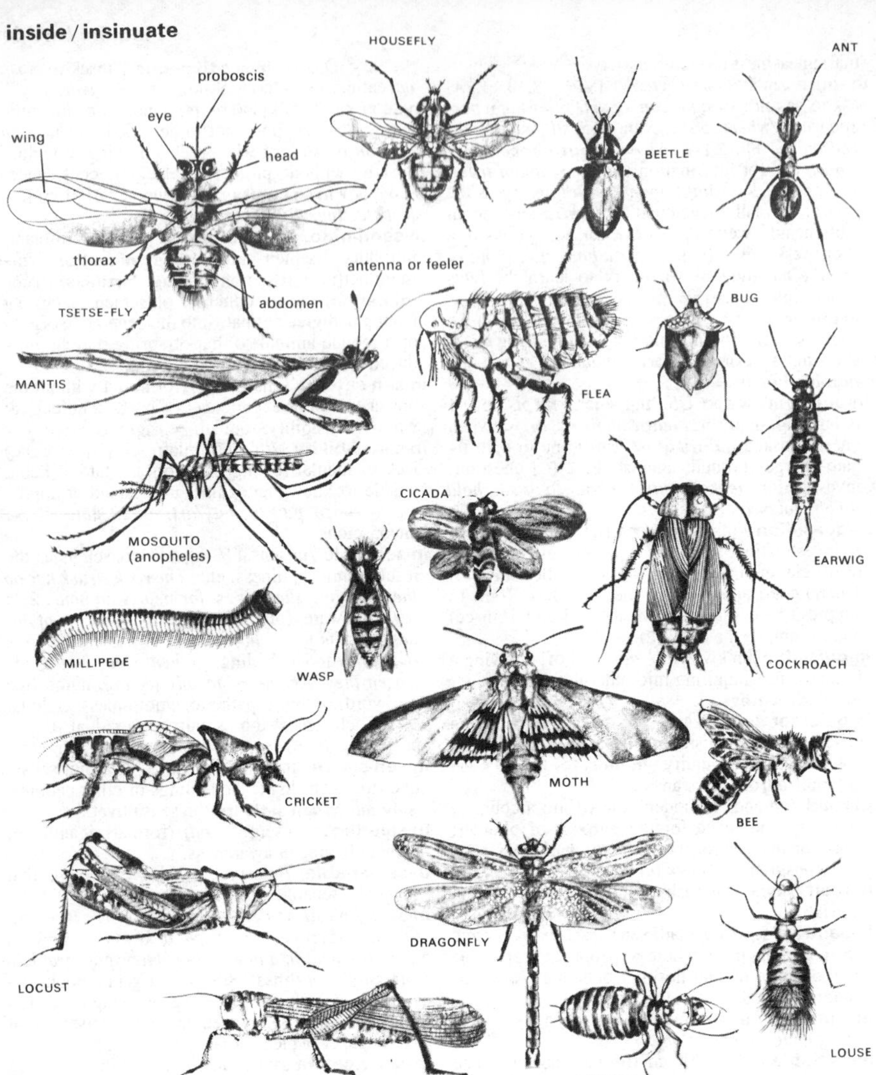

insects

ball, etc) player in the forward (attacking) line immediately to the left/right of the centre-forward. ⇨ the illus at **football**. **the ~ track,** (in racing) track nearest to the inner edge of a curve, giving an advantage to those using it; (fig) a position of advantage. **an ~ job,** (sl) theft committed by, or with the help of, sb employed in a building. □ *adv* **1** on or in the ~: *Is this coat worn with the fur ~ or outside? Look ~. There's nothing ~.* **~ of,** (colloq) in less than: *We can't finish the work ~ of a week.* **2** (GB sl) in prison: *Jones is ~ for three years.* □ *prep* on the inner side of: *Don't let the dog come ~ the house. She was standing just ~ the gate.* **in·sider** *n* person who, because he is a member of some society, organization, etc is in a position to obtain facts and information, or win advantages, that others cannot get for themselves. ⇨ **outsider.**

in·sidi·ous /ɪn`sɪdɪəs/ *adj* doing harm secretly, unseen: *an ~ enemy/disease.* **~·ly** *adv* **~·ness** *n*

in·sight /`ɪnsɑɪt/ *n* **1** [U] **~ *(into sth),*** understanding; power of seeing into sth with the mind; [C] instance of this: *a man of ~; show ~ into human character; a book full of remarkable ~s.* **2** [C] (often sudden) perception, glimpse, or understanding: *When he spoke, she had an unpleasant ~ into what life would be like as his wife.*

in·sig·nia /ɪn`sɪgnɪə/ *n pl* symbols of authority, dignity, or honour, e g the crown and sceptre of a king; (mil) identifying badge of a regiment, etc.

in·sig·nifi·cant /`ɪnsɪg`nɪfɪkənt/ *adj* having little or no value, use, meaning or importance: *~ talk; an ~-looking little man.* **~·ly** *adv* **in·sig·nifi·cance** /-əns/ *n* [U].

in·sin·cere /`ɪnsɪn`sɪə(r)/ *adj* not sincere. **~·ly** *adv* **in·sin·cer·ity** /`ɪnsɪn`serətɪ/ *n* [U].

in·sinu·ate /ɪn`sɪnjʊeɪt/ *vt* **1** [VP6A,14] **~ *sth/ oneself into,*** make a way for (oneself/sth) gently and craftily: ~ *oneself into a person's favour.* ⇨ worm. **2** [VP9] ~ ***(to sb) that,*** suggest unpleasantly and indirectly: ~ *(to sb) that a man is a liar.* **in·sinu·ation** /ɪnˈsɪnjʊˈeɪʃn/ *n* [U] insinuating; [C] sth ~d; indirect suggestion.

in·sipid /ɪnˈsɪpɪd/ *adj* without taste or flavour: ~ *food;* (fig) ~ *conversation; a pretty but* ~ *young lady,* one who is lacking in interest or spirit. **~·ly** *adv* **~·ness** *n* **in·si·pid·ity** /ˈɪnsɪˈpɪdətɪ/ *n* [U].

in·sip·ient /ɪnˈsɪpɪənt/ *adj* foolish. **in·sip·ience** /-əns/ *n* stupidity.

in·sist /ɪnˈsɪst/ *vi, vt* [VP3A,9] **1** ~ ***on/that,*** urge with emphasis, against opposition or disbelief; declare emphatically: ~ *on one's innocence;* ~ *that one is innocent;* ~ *on the importance of being punctual.* **2** [VP3A,9] ~ ***(on/that),*** declare that a purpose cannot be changed; urge in a forcible or emphatic manner: *I ~ed that he should come with us/~ed on his coming with us. I ~ on your being there. 'You must come'—'All right, if you ~.'* **in·sist·ent** /-ənt/ *adj* urgent; compelling attention: *the ~ent demands of the Commander-in-Chief for more troops.* **in·sist·ence** /-əns/ *n* [U] ~ing or being ~ed: *the officer's ~ence on strict obedience.*

in situ /ˈɪn ˈsɪtju/ (Lat) in its (original) place.

in·so·far /ˈɪnsəˈfɑ(r)/ (US) = in so far. ⇨ in²(18).

in·sole /ˈɪnsəʊl/ *n* inner sole of a shoe.

in·so·lent /ˈɪnsələnt/ *adj* ~ ***(to),*** insulting; offensive; contemptuous. **~·ly** *adv* **in·so·lence** /-əns/ *n* [U] being ~.

in·sol·uble /ɪnˈsoljʊbl/ *adj* **1** (of substances) that cannot be dissolved. **2** (of problems, etc) that cannot be solved or explained.

in·sol·vable /ɪnˈsolvəbl/ *adj* = insoluble(2).

in·sol·vent /ɪnˈsolvənt/ *n, adj* (debtor) unable to pay debts; bankrupt. **in·sol·vency** /-ənsɪ/ *n* [U] being ~.

in·som·nia /ɪnˈsomnɪə/ *n* [U] inability to sleep; want of sleep: *ill after weeks of ~.* **in·som·niac** /ɪnˈsomnɪæk/ *n* person suffering from ~.

in·so·much /ˈɪnsəʊˈmʌtʃ/ *adv* to such a degree or extent *(that/as).*

in·souci·ance /ɪnˈsusɪəns/ *n* [U] freedom from care; state of being unconcerned. **in·souci·ant** /-ənt/ *adj*

in·span /ɪnˈspæn/ *vt* (S African) (-nn-) yoke (oxen, etc) to a vehicle; harness (a wagon).

in·spect /ɪnˈspekt/ *vt* [VP6A] examine carefully; visit officially to see that rules are obeyed, that work is done properly, etc. **in·spec·tion** /ɪnˈspekʃn/ *n* **1** [U] ~ing or being ~ed: *On ~ion the notes proved to be forgeries.* **2** [C] instance of this: *carry out ten ~ions a week.*

in·spec·tor /ɪnˈspektə(r)/ *n* **1** official who inspects, e g schools, factories, mines: *ˈI~ of ˈTaxes,* offical who examines returns of income and assesses the tax to be paid. **2** (GB) police officer who is, in rank, below a superintendent and above a sergeant. **~·ate** /ɪnˈspektərət/ *n* body of ~s: *the Ministry of Education ~ate.*

in·spi·ra·tion /ˈɪnspəˈreɪʃn/ *n* **1** [U] influence(s) arousing creative activity in literature, music, art, etc: *Many poets and artists have drawn their ~ from nature.* **2** [C] person or thing that inspires: *His wife was a constant ~ to him.* **3** [C] (colloq) good thought or idea that comes to the mind: *have a sudden ~.* **4** [U] divine guidance held to have been given to those who wrote the Bible.

in·spire /ɪnˈspɑɪə(r)/ *vt* [VP6A,14,17] ~ ***sth (in sb),*** ~ ***sb with sth/to do sth,*** **1** put uplifting thoughts, feelings or aims into: ~ *sb with hope/enthusiasm/confidence;* ~ *confidence in sb. What ~d him to give such a brilliant performance?* **2** fill with creative power: *~d poets/artists; in an ~d moment.* **3** *an ~d article,* (in a newspaper) one secretly suggested or dictated by an influential person who has special information.

in·sta·bil·ity /ˈɪnstəˈbɪlətɪ/ *n* [U] lack of stability (usu of character, moral qualities).

in·stall (US also **in·stal**) /ɪnˈstɔl/ *vt* [VP6A,14] ~ ***sb in,*** **1** place (sb) in a new position of authority with the usual ceremony: ~ *a dean.* **2** place, fix (apparatus) in position for use: ~ *a heating or lighting system.* **3** settle (sb/oneself) in a place: *be comfortably ~ed in a new home. She ~ed herself in her father's favourite chair.* **in·stal·la·tion** /ˈɪnstəˈleɪʃn/ *n* [U] ~ing or being ~ed; [C] sth that is ~ed, esp apparatus: *a heating ~ation.*

in·stal·ment (US also **in·stall·ment**) /ɪnˈstɔlmənt/ *n* [C] **1** any one of the parts in which sth is presented over a period of time: *a story that will appear in ~s,* e g in a periodical. **2** any one of the parts of a payment spread over a period of time: *We're paying for the 'telly' by monthly ~s.* **ˈ~ plan,** (chiefly US) this method of paying for goods (also called, chiefly GB, *hire purchase*).

in·stance /ˈɪnstəns/ *n* [C] **1** example; fact, etc supporting a general truth: *This is only one ~ out of many.* ***for ~,*** by way of example. ***in the first ~,*** firstly. **2** ***at the ~ of,*** at the request of. □ *vt* [VP6A] give as an example.

in·stant¹ /ˈɪnstənt/ *adj* **1** coming or happening at once: *feel ~ relief after taking a dose of medicine. The novel was an ~ success.* **2** urgent: *in ~ need of help.* **3** (comm or official style, in correspondence; usu shortened to *inst*) of the present month: *in reply to your letter of the 9th inst.* **4** (of food preparations) that can be made ready for use quickly and easily: ~ *coffee,* prepared by adding boiling water or milk to a powder. **~·ly** *adv* at once.

in·stant² /ˈɪnstənt/ *n* **1** precise point of time: *Come here this ~!* at once! *He left that ~/on the ~,* immediately. *I sent you the news the ~ (that) I heard it,* as soon as I heard it. **2** moment: *I shall be back in an ~. Help arrived not an ~ too soon.*

in·stan·ta·neous /ˈɪnstənˈteɪnɪəs/ *adj* happening, done in, an instant: *Death was ~,* e g in an accident. **~·ly** *adv*

in·stead /ɪnˈsted/ *adv* **1** as an alternative or substitute: *If Harry is not well enough to go with you, take me ~. The water here is not good, so I'm drinking beer ~.* ~ ***of,*** *prep phrase* in place of; as an alternative to or substitute for (followed by a *n, pron, gerund,* or *prep phrase*): *Shall we have fish ~ of meat today? I will go ~ of you. He has been playing all afternoon ~ of getting on with his work. We'll have tea in the garden ~ of in the house.*

in·step /ˈɪnstep/ *n* upper surface of the human foot between the toes and the ankle; ⇨ the illus at leg; part of a shoe, etc covering this.

in·sti·gate /ˈɪnstɪgeɪt/ *vt* [VP6A,17A] ~ ***sth/sb to do sth,*** incite; goad (sb to do sth); cause (sth) by doing this: ~ *workers to down tools;* ~ *a strike.* **in·sti·ga·tor** /-tə(r)/ *n* **in·sti·ga·tion** /ˈɪnstɪˈgeɪʃn/ *n* instigating or being ~d.

in·stil (US = **in·still**) /ɪnˈstɪl/ *vt* (-ll-) [VP6A,14] ~ ***sth into,*** introduce (ideas, etc) gradually.

instil·la·tion /ˌɪnstɪˈleɪʃn/ *n*

in·stinct /ˈɪnstɪŋkt/ *n* **1** [U] natural tendency to behave in a certain way without reasoning or training: *Birds learn to fly by ~. We often do things by ~.* **2** [C] innate impulse or intuition; instance of ~(1): He seems to have an ~ for always doing and saying the right thing. □ *pred adj* **~ with,** filled with, animated by: *a picture ~ with life; a poem ~ with beauty.* **in·stinc·tive** /ɪnˈstɪŋktɪv/ *adj* based on ~, not coming from training or teaching: *Animals have an ~ive dread of fire.* **in·stinc·tive·ly** *adv*

in·sti·tute¹ /ˈɪnstɪtjut *US:* -tut/ *n* [C] society or organization for a special (usu a social or educational) purpose; its office(s) or building(s).

in·sti·tute² /ˈɪnstɪtjut *US:* -tut/ *vt* **1** [VP6A] establish, get started an inquiry, custom, rule, etc: *~ legal proceedings against sb; ~ an action at law; ~ restrictions on the use of pesticides.* **2** [VP14] ~ **sb to/into,** appoint (sb to, into, a benefice).

in·sti·tu·tion /ˌɪnstɪˈtjuʃn *US:* -ˈtuʃn/ *n* **1** [U] instituting or being instituted: *the ~ of customs/rules, etc; ~ to a benefice.* **2** [C] long-established law, custom or practice, e g a club or society; the habit of going to church on Sunday mornings; a person who has become known to everyone because of long service. **3** (building of) organization with charitable purposes or for social welfare, e g an orphanage, a home for old people. **~al** /-ʃnl/ *adj* of or connected with ~s (esp charitable ~s): *old people in need of ~al care.*

in·struct /ɪnˈstrʌkt/ *vt* **1** [VP6A,15A] teach a school subject, a skill: *~ a class in history; ~ recruits/a class of apprentices.* **2** [VP17A,20,21] give orders or directions to: *~ sb to start early; ~ sb how to do his work.* **3** [VP11,20,21] inform: *I have been ~ed by my agent that you still owe me £50.* **in·struc·tor** /-tə(r)/ *n* person who ~s; trainer. **in·struc·tress** /-trəs/ *n* woman who ~s.

in·struc·tion /ɪnˈstrʌkʃn/ *n* **1** [U] instructing or being instructed: *~ in chemistry; give/receive ~.* **2** (*pl*) directions; orders: *give sb ~s to arrive early; ~s* (= coded commands) *to a computer.* **~al** /-ʃnl/ *adj* educational: *~al films,* e g of industrial processes.

in·struc·tive /ɪnˈstrʌktɪv/ *adj* giving or containing instruction: *~ books.* **~·ly** *adv*

in·stru·ment /ˈɪnstrʊmənt/ *n* [C] **1** implement, apparatus, used in performing an action, esp for delicate or scientific work: *optical ~s,* e g a microscope; *surgical ~s,* e g a scalpel. Cf *tools* used by labourers and craftsmen. **2** apparatus for producing musical sounds, e g a piano or drum. ⇨ the illus at **brass, keyboard, percussion, string. 3** person used by another for his own purposes: *be made the ~ of another's crime.* **4** formal (esp legal) document: *The King signed the ~ of abdication.* **in·stru·men·ta·tion** /ˌɪnstrʊmenˈteɪʃn/ *n* [U] arrangement of music for ~s; the development and manufacture of ~s for scientific use.

in·stru·men·tal /ˌɪnstrʊˈmentl/ *adj* **1** serving as an instrument or means: *be ~ in finding well-paid work for a friend.* **2** of or for musical instruments: *~ music.* **~·ist** /-tlɪst/ *n* player of a musical instrument. **~·ity** /ˌɪnstrʊmenˈtælətɪ/ *n* [U] agency: *by the ~ity of,* by means of.

in·sub·or·di·nate /ˌɪnsəˈbɔdɪnət *US:* -dnət/ *adj* disobedient; rebellious. **in·sub·or·di·na·tion** /ˌɪnsəˌbɔdɪˈneɪʃn *US:* -dnˈeɪʃn/ *n* [U] being ~; [C] instance of this.

in·sub·stan·tial /ˌɪnsəbˈstænʃl/ *adj* **1** not solid or real; lacking substance: *an ~ vision.* **2** without good foundation: *an ~ accusation.*

in·suf·fer·able /ɪnˈsʌfrəbl/ *adj* over-proud; unbearably conceited; unbearable: *~ insolence.*

in·suf·fi·cient /ˌɪnsəˈfɪʃnt/ *adj* not sufficient: *~ evidence/grounds.* **~·ly** *adv* **in·suf·fi·ciency** /-ʃnsɪ/ *n*

in·su·lar /ˈɪnsjʊlə(r) *US:* -səl/ *adj* **1** of an island: *an ~ climate.* **2** of or like islanders; (esp) narrow-minded: *~ habits and prejudices.* **~·ism** /-ɪzm/ *n* **in·su·lar·ity** /ˌɪnsjʊˈlærətɪ *US:* -səˈl-/ *n* [U] state of being ~ (esp 2).

in·su·late /ˈɪnsjʊleɪt *US:* -səl-/ *vt* [VP6A,14] ~ *(from),* **1** cover or separate (sth) with non-conducting materials to prevent loss of heat, prevent passage of electricity, etc: *~ a cooking-stove with asbestos; ˈinsulating tape,* as used for covering joins in flex for electric current. **2** separate (sb or sth (from): *children carefully ~d from harmful experiences;* isolate. **in·su·la·tor** /-tə(r)/ *n* [C] substance, device, for insulating, esp a device of porcelain used for supporting bare electric wires and cables. **in·su·la·tion** /ˌɪnsjʊˈleɪʃn *US:* -səˈl-/ *n* [U] insulating or being ~d; materials used for this.

in·su·lin /ˈɪnsjʊlɪn *US:* -səl-/ *n* [U] substance (a hormone) prepared from the pancreas of sheep, used in the medical treatment of sufferers from diabetes.

in·sult /ɪnˈsʌlt/ *vt* [VP6A] speak or act in a way that hurts or is intended to hurt a person's feelings or dignity. □ *n* /ˈɪnsʌlt/ [C,U] remark or action that ~s. **~·ing** *adj* **~·ing·ly** *adv*

in·super·able /ɪnˈsjuprəbl *US:* -ˈsu-/ *adj* (of difficulties, etc) that cannot be overcome: *~ barriers.*

in·sup·port·able /ˌɪnsəˈpɔtəbl/ *adj* unbearable; that cannot be endured.

in·sur·ance /ɪnˈʃʊərns/ *n* **1** [U] (undertaking, by a company, society, or the State, to provide) safeguard against loss, provision against sickness, death, etc in return for regular payments. **2** [U] payment made to or by such a company, etc: *When her husband died, she received £20 000 ~. He pays out £110 in ~/in ~ premiums every year.* **ˈ~ policy** *n* contract made about ~. **3** [C] ~ policy: *How many ~s have you?* **4** any measure taken as a safeguard against loss, failure, etc: *He's sitting an entrance exam at Leeds University as an ~ against failure at York.*

in·sure /ɪnˈʃʊə(r)/ *vt* [VP6A,14] ~ ***(against),*** make a contract that promises to pay, secures payment of, a sum of money in case of accident, damage, loss, injury, death, etc: *~ one's house against fire; ~ oneself/one's life for £50 000. Insurance companies will ~ ships and their cargoes against loss at sea.* **the ~d,** the person to whom payment will be made. **the ~r,** the person or company undertaking to make payment in case of loss, etc. **the insurant** /ɪnˈʃʊərnt/, (legal) the person who pays the premiums.

in·sur·gent /ɪnˈsɜdʒənt/ *adj* (rarely *pred*) rebellious; in revolt: *~ troops.* □ *n* rebel soldier.

in·sur·mount·able /ˌɪnsəˈmaʊntəbl/ *adj* (of obstacles, etc) that cannot be surmounted or overcome.

in·sur·rec·tion /ˌɪnsəˈrekʃn/ *n* [U] rising of people in open resistance to the government; [C] instance of this.

in·tact /ɪnˈtækt/ *adj* untouched; undamaged; complete: *He lived on the interest and kept his capital* ~.

in·taglio /ɪnˈtɑlɪəʊ/ *n* (*pl* ~**s** /-z/) [U] (I) (process of) carving in depth; [C] (gem with a) figure or design made by cutting into the surface of metal or stone. ⇨ **cameo**.

in·take /ˈɪnteɪk/ *n* **1** [C] place where water, gas, etc is taken into a pipe, channel, etc. **2** [C,U] quantity, number, etc entering or taken in (during a given period): *an annual* ~ *of 100 000 National Service men,* i e for military service. **3** (area of) land reclaimed from a moor, marsh or the sea.

in·tan·gible /ˈɪnˈtændʒəbl/ *adj* that cannot be touched or grasped; (esp) that cannot be grasped by the mind: ~ *ideas;* ~ *assets,* assets (of a business) which cannot be measured, e g a good reputation. **in·tan·gi·bil·ity** /ɪnˈtændʒəˈbɪlətɪ/ *n*

in·te·ger /ˈɪntɪdʒə(r)/ *n* whole number (contrasted with *fractions*): *0, 1, 3 and −3, are* ~*s,* $4\frac{3}{4}$ *is not an* ~.

in·te·gral /ˈɪntɪgrl/ *adj* **1** necessary for completeness: *The arms and legs are* ~ *parts of a human being.* **2** whole; having or containing all parts that are necessary for completeness. **3** (maths) of, denoted by, an integer; made up of integers. ~**ly** /-grl̩ɪ/ *adv*

in·te·grate /ˈɪntɪgreɪt/ *vt* [VP6A] **1** combine (parts) into a whole; complete (sth that is imperfect or incomplete) by adding parts: *an* ~*d personality,* person whose physical, mental and emotional components fit together well (so that his behaviour is normal, etc). **2** join with other social groups or different race(s); deseparate: *The US armed forces are now* ~*d,* black and white soldiers now serve together. **in·te·gra·tion** /ˈɪntɪˈgreɪʃn/ *n* [U] integrating or being ~d: *the integration of Negro children into the school system in the Southern States of America.*

in·teg·rity /ɪnˈtegrətɪ/ *n* [U] **1** quality of being honest and upright in character: *a man of* ~; *commercial* ~. **2** state or condition of being complete: *The old Roman walls may still be seen, but not in their* ~. *Wasn't this Treaty supposed to guarantee our territorial* ~?

in·tegu·ment /ɪnˈtegjʊmənt/ *n* (formal) (usu natural) outer covering, e g skin, a husk, rind or shell.

in·tel·lect /ˈɪntəlekt/ *n* **1** [U] power of the mind to reason (contrasted with feeling and instinct): *I*~ *distinguishes man from the animals. He's a man of* ~. **2** (collective *sing,* or in *pl*) person of good understanding, reasoning power, etc: *the* ~*(s) of the age.*

in·tel·lec·tual /ˈɪntəˈlektʃʊəl/ *adj* **1** of the intellect: ~ *pursuits; the* ~ *faculties.* **2** having or showing good reasoning power; interested in things of the mind (the arts, ideas for their own sake): ~ *people;* ~ *interests/pursuits.* □ *n* [C] ~ person: *a play/book for the* ~*s.* ~**ly** /-tʃʊəlɪ/ *adv*

in·tel·li·gence /ɪnˈtelɪdʒəns/ *n* [U] **1** the power of seeing, learning, understanding and knowing; mental ability: *a boy who shows little* ~. *The children were given an* ~ *test. When the water-pipe burst, she had the* ~ *to turn the water off at the main.* **2** news; information, esp with reference to important events: *have secret* ~ *of the enemy's plans; the I*~ *Department/Service,* e g of an army or navy, collecting and studying information useful in war. **in·tel·li·gent** /-ənt/ *adj* having, showing, ~: *intelligent looking girls/answers to questions.* **in·tel·li·gent·ly** *adv*

in·tel·li·gent·sia /ɪnˈtelɪˈdʒentsɪə/ *n* (usu collective *sing* with *def art*) that part of a community which can be regarded (or which regards itself) as intellectual and capable of serious independent thinking.

in·tel·li·gible /ɪnˈtelɪdʒəbl/ *adj* that can be easily understood; clear to the mind: ~ *speech; an* ~ *explanation.* **in·tel·li·gibly** /-əblɪ/ *adv* **in·tel·li·gi·bil·ity** /ɪnˈtelɪdʒəˈbɪlətɪ/ *n* the quality of being ~.

in·tem·per·ate /ɪnˈtempr̩ət/ *adj* (formal) (of a person or his behaviour) not moderate; showing lack of self-control: ~ *habits,* (esp) habits of excessive drinking. ~**·ly** *adv* **in·tem·per·ance** /-prəns/ *n*

in·tend /ɪnˈtend/ *vt* [VP6A,D,7A,9,14,17A] **1** have in mind as a purpose or plan: *What do you* ~ *to do/*~ *doing today? They* ~ *that this reform shall be carried through this year. We* ~ *them to do it/ that they shall do it. His son is* ~*ed for the medical profession. This book is* ~*ed for you,* is to be given to you. *Is this sketch* ~*ed to be me,* Is it a sketch of me? *Does he* ~ *marriage or is he only flirting with her? Let me introduce you to my* ~*ed,* (sl for 'my future wife'). **2** (old use) mean: *What do you* ~ *by this word?*

in·tense /ɪnˈtens/ *adj* **1** (of qualities) high in degree: ~ *heat.* **2** (of feelings, etc) ardent; violent; (of persons) highly emotional: *an* ~ *young lady.* ~**·ly** *adv*

in·ten·sify /ɪnˈtensɪfɑɪ/ *vt,vi* (*pt,pp* **-fied**) [VP6A,2A] make or become more intense. **in·ten·si·fi·ca·tion** /ɪnˈtensɪfɪˈkeɪʃn/ *n*

in·ten·sity /ɪnˈtensətɪ/ *n* [U] state or quality of being intense; strength or depth (of feeling, etc).

in·ten·sive /ɪnˈtensɪv/ *adj* **1** characterized by, relating to, intensity (as opposed to extent); deep and thorough: *make an* ~ *study of a subject;* ~ *methods of horticulture,* producing large quantities by concentrating labour and care on small areas of land; *an* ~ *bombardment.* **2** (gram) giving force and emphasis: *In 'a bloody difficult book' and 'a terribly hot day', 'bloody' and 'terribly' are used colloquially as* ~ *words.* ~**·ly** *adv*

in·tent[1] /ɪnˈtent/ *adj* **1** (of looks) eager; earnest: *There was an* ~ *look on her face as she watched the game.* **2** ~ ***(up)on sth/doing sth,*** (of persons) with the desires or attentions directed towards: *He was* ~ *on his work/on getting to the office in time.* ~**·ly** *adv* ~**·ness** *n*

intent[2] /ɪnˈtent/ *n* **1** [U] (chiefly legal) purpose; intention: *shoot with* ~ *to kill; with good/evil/ malicious* ~. **2** (*pl*) ***to all*** ~***s and purposes,*** in all essential points.

in·ten·tion /ɪnˈtenʃn/ *n* [C,U] intending; thing intended; aim; purpose: *If I've hurt your feelings, it was quite without* ~. *He hasn't the least* ~ *of coming. He has no* ~ *of marrying yet. Her* ~ *to live abroad is surprising. He went to Paris with the* ~ *of learning French. His* ~*s are good, but he seldom carries them out. Has he made known his* ~*s,* said what he intends to do? **(-)in·ten·tioned** *adj:* ˈ*well-*ˈ~*ed,* having good ~s; ˈ*ill-*ˈ~*ed,* having bad, wrong, etc ~s.

in·ten·tional /ɪnˈtenʃnl/ *adj* intended; done on purpose: *If I hurt your feelings, it was not* ~. ~**·ly** /-ʃnl̩ɪ/ *adv* on purpose.

in·ter /ɪnˈtɜ(r)/ *vt* **(-rr-)** (formal) place (a corpse) in a grave or tomb; bury.

in·ter·act /ˈɪntərˈækt/ *vi* act on each other. **in·ter·ac·tion** /-ˈækʃn/ *n* **in·ter·ac·tive** /-ˈæktɪv/ *adj*

in·ter alia /ˈɪntər ˋeɪlɪə/ (Lat) among other things.

in·ter·breed /ˈɪntəˋbrid/ *vt,vi* (*pt,pp* -bred /-ˋbred/) [VP6A,2A] crossbreed; (of animals of different race or species) breed with each other; produce hybrids.

in·ter·ca·lary /ɪnˋtɜkələrɪ *US:* -lerɪ/ *adj* (of a day or month) added to make the calendar year correspond to the solar year; (of a year) having such an addition.

in·ter·cede /ˈɪntəˋsid/ *vi* [VP3A] ~ ***(with sb) (for...)***, plead (as a peacemaker, or to obtain a favour): ~ *with the father for/on behalf of the daughter.* **in·ter·cession** /ˈɪntəˋseʃn/ *n* [U] interceding; [C] prayer or entreaty (esp for others).

in·ter·cept /ˈɪntəˋsept/ *vt* [VP6A] stop, catch (sb or sth) between starting-point and destination: ~ *a letter/a messenger. Can our fighter-planes ~ the enemy's bombers?* **in·ter·cep·tion** /ˈɪntəˋsepʃn/ *n* **in·ter·cep·tor** /-tə(r)/ *n* sb or sth that ~s, e g a fast fighter-plane.

in·ter·change /ˈɪntəˋtʃeɪndʒ/ *vt* **1** [VP6A] (of two persons, etc) give and receive; make an exchange of: ~ *views/gifts/letters.* **2** [VP6A,2A] put (each of two things) in the other's place. **~·able** /-əbl/ *adj* that can be ~d: *True synonyms are ~able. This machine has ~able parts.* □ *n* /ˋɪntətʃeɪndʒ/ interchanging: *an ~ of views.*

in·ter·col·legi·ate /ˈɪntəkəˋlidʒɪət/ *adj* carried on, etc between colleges: ~ *games/debates.*

in·ter·col·on·ial /ˈɪntəkəˋləʊnɪəl/ *adj* carried on, etc between colonies: ~ *trade.*

in·ter·com /ˋɪntəkom/ *n* (colloq abbr) **the ~,** the system of intercommunication, esp in aircraft.

in·ter·com·mu·nal /ˈɪntəˋkomjʊnl/ *adj* for, shared by, members of two or more communities: ~ *schools in Cyprus,* e g for both Greek- and Turkish-speaking children.

in·ter·com·mu·ni·cate /ˈɪntəkəˋmjunɪkeɪt/ *vi* communicate with one another: *The prisoners ~ by using the Morse code.* **in·ter·com·mu·ni·ca·tion** /ˈɪntəkəˈmjunɪˋkeɪʃn/ *n*

in·ter·com·mu·nion /ˈɪntəkəˋmjunɪən/ *n* mutual communion, esp between different Churches, e g C of E and R C.

in·ter·con·ti·nen·tal /ˈɪntəˈkontɪˋnentl/ *adj* carried on, etc between continents: ~ *ballistic missiles,* that can be fired from one continent to another.

in·ter·course /ˋɪntəkɔs/ *n* [U] **1** social dealings between individuals; exchanges of trade, ideas, etc between persons, societies, nations, etc: *our commercial ~ with S America.* **2 (sexual) ~,** = coitus.

in·ter·de·nomi·na·tional /ˈɪntədɪˈnomɪˋneɪʃnl/ *adj* common to, shared by, different religious denominations, e g Methodist, Baptists, C of E.

in·ter·de·pen·dent /ˈɪntədɪˋpendənt/ *adj* depending on each other. **in·ter·de·pen·dence** /-əns/ *n*

in·ter·dict /ˈɪntəˋdɪkt/ *vt* [VP6A] (formal) prohibit (an action); forbid (the use of sth); (R C Church) exclude from sacraments and church services. □ *n* /ˋɪntədɪkt/ [C] formal or authoritative prohibition, esp (R C Church) an order debarring a person or place from church services, etc: *lay a priest/a town under an ~.*

in·ter·est[1] /ˋɪntrəst/ *n* **1** [U] condition of wanting to know or learn about sth or sb: *feel/take no/not much/a great ~ in politics; events that arouse great ~.* ⇨ **lose. 2** [U] quality that arouses concern or curiosity, that hold's one's attention: *a matter of considerable/not much ~. Suspense adds ~ to a story.* **3** [C] sth with which one concerns oneself: *Her chief ~ seems to be horse-racing. His two great ~s in life are music and painting.* **4** [C] (often *pl*) advantage; profit; well-being: *look after one's own ~s; work in the ~(s) of humanity; travel in Asia in the ~s of a business firm. It is to your ~ to go.* **5** [C] legal right to a share in sth, esp in its profits: *have an ~ in a brewery,* e g by owning shares; *have an ~ in an estate,* a legal claim to part of it; *American ~s in the Caribbean,* e g capital invested in the countries of that area; *He has sold his ~ in the company.* **6** [U] money charged or paid for the use of money: *rate of ~/¼ ~ rate,* payment made by a borrower for a loan, expressed as a percentage, e g 8%; *pay 6 per cent ~ on a loan.* **with ~,** (fig) with increased force: *return a blow/sb's kindness with ~,* give back more than one received. **7** (often *pl*) group of persons engaged in the same trade, etc or having sth in common: *the landed ~,* landowners collectively; *the business ~s,* large business firms collectively; *the brewing ~,* brewers collectively.

in·ter·est[2] /ˋɪntrəst/ *vt* [VP6A,14] **~ sb (in sth),** cause (sb) to give his attention to: *Can I ~ you in this question? He is ~ed in shipping,* **(a)** likes to know and learn about ships. **(b)** has money invested in the shipping industry. **~ed** *adj* **1** having an interest(**6**) in; not impartial: *When manufacturers demand higher tariffs, we may suspect them of having ~ed motives.* **2** showing interest(**1**): *an ~ed look.* **3** taking an interest(**1**) in: *~ed spectators; not ~ed in botany/his work. I shall be ~ed to know what happens.* **~·ing** *adj* holding the attention; arousing interest(**1**): *~ing men/books/conversation.* **~·ing·ly** *adv*

in·ter·fere /ˈɪntəˋfɪə(r)/ *vi* **1** [VP2A,3A] ~ ***(in sth),*** (of persons) break in upon (other person's affairs) without right or invitation; *Please don't ~ in my business. Isn't she an interfering old lady! It's unwise to ~ between husband and wife.* **2** [VP2A,3A] ~ ***(with),*** (of persons) meddle; tamper (with): *Do not ~ with this machine.* **3** [VP3A] ~ ***with,*** (of events, circumstances, etc) come into opposition; hinder or prevent: *Do you ever allow pleasure to ~ with duty?* **in·ter·fer·ence** /ˈɪntəˋfɪərəns/ *n* [U] interfering: *interference from foreign broadcasting stations,* e g when these have a wave-length close to that of the station one wishes to receive; (computers) existence of unwanted signals in a communications circuit.

in·terim /ˋɪntərɪm/ *n* **1** ***in the ~,*** meanwhile; during the time that comes between. **2** (attrib) as an instalment: ~ *dividends,* paid between annual dividends as advance payments; provisional or temporary: *an ~ report,* one that precedes the final report.

in·terior /ɪnˋtɪərɪə(r)/ *adj* **1** situated inside; of the inside. **2** inland; away from the coast. **3** home or domestic (contrasted with *foreign*). □ *n* **1** the inside: (used attrib) ~ *decorators,* those who decorate the inside of a building (with paint, wall-paper, etc). **2** inland areas. **3** (department dealing with the) domestic affairs of a country: (US) *the Department of the I~.* Cf *Home Office* in GB.

in·ter·ject /ˈɪntəˋdʒekt/ *vt* [VP6A] put in suddenly (a remark, etc) between statements, etc made by another. **in·ter·jec·tion** /ˈɪntəˋdʒekʃn/ *n* word or phrase used as an exclamation, e g *Oh! Good! Stone the crows!*

in·ter·lace /ˈɪntəˋleɪs/ *vt,vi* [VP6A,2A,14] ~

(with), join, be joined, by weaving or lacing together, one with another; cross as if woven: *interlacing branches.*

in·ter·lard /ˌɪntəˈlɑd/ *vt* [VP14] ~ ***with,*** (formal) mix writing, speech, etc with foreign phrases, etc: *essays ~ed with quotations from the poets.*

in·ter·leave /ˌɪntəˈliv/ *vt* [VP6A,14] ~ ***with,*** insert (usu blank leaves) between the leaves of (a book, etc): *a diary ~ed with blotting-paper.*

in·ter·line /ˌɪntəˈlɑɪn/ *vt* [VP6A,14] ~ ***with,*** write between the lines of (a document, etc): *a printer's proof ~d with corrections.*

in·ter·linear /ˌɪntəˈlɪnɪə(r)/ *adj* written, printed, between the lines.

in·ter·link /ˌɪntəˈlɪŋk/ *vt,vi* [VP6A,2A] link together.

in·ter·lock /ˌɪntəˈlok/ *vt,vi* [VP6A,2A] lock or join together; clasp firmly together.

in·ter·locu·tor /ˌɪntəˈlokjʊtə(r)/ *n* person taking part in a discussion or dialogue.

in·ter·lo·per /ˈɪntələʊpə(r)/ *n* person who, esp for profit or personal advantage, pushes himself in where he has no right.

in·ter·lude /ˈɪntəlud/ *n* **1** interval between two events or two periods of time of different character: *~s of bright weather.* **2** interval between two acts of a play, two scenes of an opera or between parts of a psalm, church service, etc; music played during such an interval.

in·ter·marry /ˌɪntəˈmærɪ/ *vi* (*pt,pp* -married) [VP2A,3A] ~ ***(with),*** (of tribes, races, etc) become connected by marriage with other tribes, etc. **in·ter·mar·riage** /ˌɪntəˈmærɪdʒ/ *n* [U] marriage between members of different families, tribes, castes, etc.

in·ter·meddle /ˌɪntəˈmedl/ *vi* = meddle (the usu word).

in·ter·medi·ary /ˌɪntəˈmidɪərɪ *US:* -dɪerɪ/ *n* (*pl* -ries), *adj* **1** ~ ***(between),*** (sb or sth) acting as a link between (persons and groups); go-between; mediator. **2** (sth) intermediate.

in·ter·medi·ate /ˌɪntəˈmidɪət/ *adj* situated or coming between in time, space, degree, etc: *at an ~ stage,* e g the cocoon stage of development of a butterfly; *the I~ Examination,* as between Matric and the Degree Examination in some universities; *~ courses, between elementary and advanced; ~-range ballistic missiles.* □ *n* sth that is ~. **~·ly** *adv*

in·ter·ment /ɪnˈtɜmənt/ *n* [U] being buried; [C] instance of this; burial.

in·ter·mezzo /ˌɪntəˈmetsəʊ/ *n* (*pl* -zos /-səʊz/ or -zi /-sɪ/) short musical composition to be played between the acts of a drama or an opera, or one that connects the main divisions of a large musical work such as a symphony.

in·ter·mi·nable /ɪnˈtɜmɪnəbl/ *adj* endless; tedious because too long: *an ~ debate/sermon.* **in·ter·mi·nably** /-əblɪ/ *adv*

in·ter·mingle /ˌɪntəˈmɪŋgl/ *vt,vi* [VP6A,14] ~ ***(with),*** mix together (two things, one with the other); mingle: *The conference delegates ~d over coffee.*

in·ter·mission /ˌɪntəˈmɪʃn/ *n* [C,U] pause; interval: *work from 8a m until 5p m without ~/with a short ~ at noon.*

in·ter·mit·tent /ˌɪntəˈmɪtnt/ *adj* pausing or stopping at intervals; stopping and starting again: *~ fever.* **~·ly** *adv*

in·ter·mix /ˌɪntəˈmɪks/ *vt,vi* = mix (the usu word).

~·ture /-tʃə(r)/ *n*

in·tern[1] /ɪnˈtɜn/ *vt* [VP6A] compel (persons, esp aliens during a war) to live within certain limits or in a special building, camp, etc. **~·ment** *n* [U] ~ing or being ~ed: *ˈ~ment camp.* **~ee** /ˌɪntɜˈni/ *n* person who is ~ed.

in·tern[2] (US also **in·terne**) /ˈɪntɜn/ *n* (US) young doctor who is completing his training by residing in a hospital and acting as an assistant physician or surgeon there. (GB = *house physician/surgeon*).

in·ter·nal /ɪnˈtɜnl/ *adj* **1** of or in the inside: *suffer ~ injuries in an accident; ~ bleeding,* e g in the bowels. ~ ***combustion,*** the process by which power is produced by the explosion of gases or vapours inside a cylinder (as in the engine of a car). **2** domestic; of the home affairs of a country: *~ trade/revenue,* (also *Inland Revenue*). **3** derived from within the thing itself: *~ evidence,* e g of when an old book was written, or of the date of an old manuscript. **~·ly** /-nḷɪ/ *adv*

in·ter·na·tional /ˌɪntəˈnæʃnl/ *adj* existing, carried on, between nations: *~ trade/law/agreements/conferences.* ~ **money order,** one which may be cashed in a country other than the country of origin. □ *n* **the 1st/2nd/3rd I~,** three socialist associations for members of the working classes in all countries, formed in 1864, 1889 and 1919. The Second I~ and the Vienna I~ (formed in 1921) were united in 1923 as the *Labour and Socialist I~.* **~·ism** /-nḷɪzm/ *n* the doctrine that the common interests of nations are greater and more important than their differences. **~·ist** /-nḷɪst/ *n* person who supports and advocates ~ism. **~·ize** /-ʃṇəlɑɪz/ *vt* [VP6A] make ~; bring under the combined control or protection of all or many nations: *Should the Suez and Panama Canals be ~ized?* **~·iz·ation** /ˌɪntəˌnæʃṇḷɑɪˈzeɪʃn *US:* -ḷɪˈz-/ *n* **in·ter·na·tio·nale** /ˌɪntəˌnæʃnˈɑl/ *n* **the ~,** (revolutionary) socialist hymn.

in·terne /ˈɪntɜn/ *n* ⇨ intern[2].

in·ter·necine /ˌɪntəˈnisɑɪn/ *adj* (usu of war) causing destruction to both sides.

in·ternee /ˌɪntɜˈni/ *n* ⇨ intern[1].

in·ter·pel·late /ɪnˈtɜpeleɪt/ *vt* [VP6A] (in some Parliaments, e g the French and Japanese) interrupt the proceedings and demand a statement or explanation from (a Minister). **in·ter·pel·la·tion** /ɪnˌtɜpəˈleɪʃn/ *n* [U] interpellating or being ~d; [C] instance of this.

in·ter·phone /ˈɪntəfəʊn/ *n* (US) = intercom.

in·ter·plan·etary /ˌɪntəˈplænɪtrɪ *US:* -terɪ/ *adj* between planets: *an ~ journey in a spacecraft.*

in·ter·play /ˈɪntəpleɪ/ *n* [U] operation of two things on each other: *the ~ of colours,* their combined effect.

In·ter·pol /ˈɪntəpol/ *n* International Police Commission.

in·ter·po·late /ɪnˈtɜpəleɪt/ *vt* [VP6A] make (sometimes misleading) additions to a book. **in·ter·po·la·tion** /ɪnˌtɜpəˈleɪʃn/ *n* [U] interpolating; [C] sth ~d.

in·ter·pose /ˌɪntəˈpəʊz/ *vt,vi* **1** [VP6A] put forward an objection, a veto, etc as an interference: *Will they ~ their veto yet again?* **2** [VP6A,2A] say (sth) as an interruption; make an interruption. **3** [VP2A,3A,14] ~ ***(oneself) between,*** ~ ***in,*** place oneself, be, between others: *~ between two persons who are quarrelling;* mediate (in a dispute). **in·ter·po·si·tion** /ˌɪntəpəˈzɪʃn/ *n* [U] interposing; [C] sth ~d.

in·ter·pret /ɪn`tɜprɪt/ *vt,vi* **1** [VP6A] show, make clear, the meaning of (either in words or by artistic performance): *~ a difficult passage in a book. Poetry helps to ~ life. The actor ~ed the role of Hamlet very well.* **2** [VP6A,16B] consider to be the meaning of: *We ~ed his silence as a refusal.* **3** [VP2A] act as ~er: *Will you please ~ for me,* translate what is (to be) said? **~er** *n* person who gives an immediate oral translation of words spoken in another language. **in·ter·pre·ta·tion** /ɪn'tɜprɪ`teɪʃn/ *n* [U] interpreting; [C] result of this; explanation or meaning: *The passage may be given several ~ations.*

in·ter·racial /'ɪntə`reɪʃl/ *adj* between, involving, different races.

in·ter·reg·num /'ɪntə`regnəm/ *n* (*pl* ~s, -na /-nə/) period during which a State has no normal or legitimate ruler, esp between the end of a Sovereign's reign and the beginning of his successor's reign; pause or interval.

in·ter·re·late /'ɪntərɪ`leɪt/ *vt,vi* come together in reciprocal relationship: *~d studies,* of separate but related subjects as a united group, e g politics, philosophy and economics.

in·ter·re·la·tion /'ɪntərɪ`leɪʃn/ *n* ~ ***of/between,*** mutual relation. **~·ship** /-ʃɪp/ *n* mutual relationship.

in·ter·ro·gate /ɪn`terəgeɪt/ *vt* [VP6A] put questions to, esp closely or formally: *~ a prisoner.* **in·ter·ro·ga·tor** /-tə(r)/ *n* **in·ter·ro·ga·tion** /ɪn'terə`geɪʃn/ *n* **1** [U] asking questions: *note/mark/point of interrogation,* question mark; the mark (?). **2** [C,U] oral examination; inquiry: *long and tiring interrogations by police officers.*

in·ter·roga·tive /'ɪntə`rogətɪv/ *adj* **1** showing or having the form of a question; of inquiry: *an ~ look/glance; in an ~ tone.* **2** (gram) used in questions: *~ pronouns/adverbs,* e g who, why. □ *n* ~ word, esp a pronoun. **~·ly** *adv*

in·ter·roga·tory /'ɪntə`rogətrɪ *US:* -tɔrɪ/ *adj* of inquiry: *in an ~ tone.*

in·ter·rupt /'ɪntə`rʌpt/ *vt,vi* [VP6A,2A] **1** break the continuity of: *The war ~ed the flow of commerce between the two countries. Traffic was ~ed by floods. Those trees are growing so high that they ~* (= obstruct) *the view.* **2** break in upon (a person speaking or doing sth, his speech, etc): *Don't ~ (me) while I'm busy. Don't ~ the speaker; ask your questions afterwards.* **~er** *n* **in·ter·rup·tion** /'ɪntə`rʌpʃn/ *n* [U] ~ing or being ~ed; [C] instance of this; sth that ~s: *Numerous ~ions have prevented me from finishing the work.*

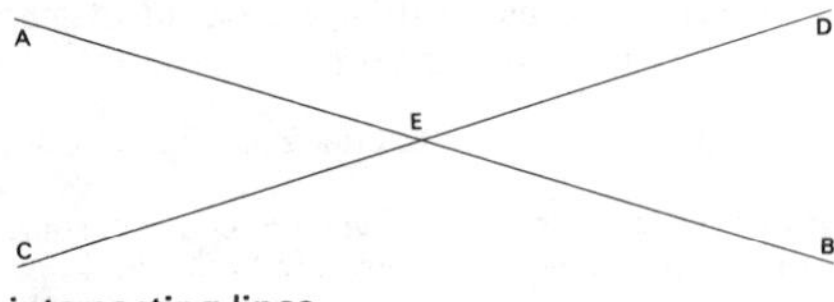

intersecting lines

in·ter·sect /'ɪntə`sekt/ *vt,vi* **1** [VP6A] divide by cutting, passing or lying across. **2** [VP6A,2A] (of lines) cut or cross each other: *The lines AB and CD ~ at E. The line AB ~s the line CD at E.* **in·ter·sec·tion** /'ɪntə`sekʃn/ *n* [U] ~ing or being ~ed; [C] point where two lines, etc ~.

in·ter·sperse /'ɪntə`spɜs/ *vt* [VP14] ~ ***among/between,*** place here and there. ~ ***with,*** diversify: *a speech ~d with witty remarks.*

in·ter·state /'ɪntə`steɪt/ *adj* (US) between States: *~ commerce.*

in·ter·stel·lar /'ɪntə`stelə(r)/ *adj* between the stars: *~ matter,* e g the masses of gas between stars; *~ communications.*

in·ter·stice /ɪn`tɜstɪs/ *n* [C] crack; chink; crevice: *~s* (= very small spaces) *between stones in a heap.*

in·ter·tribal /'ɪntə`traɪbl/ *adj* between tribes: *~ wars.*

in·ter·twine /'ɪntə`twaɪn/ *vt,vi* [VP6A,2A] twine or twist together; become twined or twisted together: *a lattice ~d with vines.*

in·ter·ur·ban /'ɪntər`ɜbən/ *adj* between towns: *~ railways.*

in·ter·val /`ɪntəvl/ *n* **1** time (between two events or two parts of an action); (esp) time between two acts of a play, two parts of a concert, etc: *buses leaving at short ~s,* i e very frequently. **2** space between (two objects or points): *arranged at ~s of ten feet.* **3** (music) difference of pitch between two notes on a given scale.

in·ter·vene /'ɪntə`vin/ *vi* **1** [VP2A] (of events, circumstances) come between (others) in time: *I shall leave on Sunday if nothing ~s.* **2** [VP2A,3A] ~ ***(in),*** (of persons) interfere so as to prevent sth or change the result: *~ in a dispute; ~ between people who are disputing.* **3** [VP2A] (of time) come or be between: *during the years that ~d.* **in·ter·ven·tion** /'ɪntə`venʃn/ *n* [U] intervening (esp 2 above): *armed intervention by one country in the affairs of other countries;* [C] instance of this.

in·ter·view /`ɪntəvju/ *n* [C] meeting with sb for discussion or conference, e g between employers and applicants for posts; meeting (of a reporter, etc) with sb whose views are requested: *The Ambassador refused to give any ~s to journalists or TV men.* □ *vt* [VP6A] (of a reporter, etc) have or obtain an ~ with.

in·ter·weave /'ɪntə`wiv/ *vt* (*pt* -wove /-`wəʊv/, *pp* -woven /-`wəʊvən/) [VP6A,14] ~ ***(with),*** weave together (one with another).

in·tes·tate /ɪn`testeɪt/ *adj* not having made a will before death occurs: *die ~.*

in·tes·tine /ɪn`testɪn/ *n* ⇨ the illus at alimentary. (usu *pl*) lower part of the food canal from below the stomach to the anus: *small/large ~,* parts of this. **in·tes·ti·nal** /ɪn`testɪnl/ *adj* of the ~s: *intestinal disorders.*

in·ti·mate[1] /`ɪntɪmət/ *adj* **1** close and familiar: *~ friends.* ***be/get on ~ terms (with),*** e g when one calls a man 'Jack' instead of 'Mr Hill'. **2** innermost; private and personal: *tell a friend the ~ details of one's life; an ~ diary,* one in which one records experiences, thoughts, emotions, etc usu kept secret. **3** resulting from close study or great familiarity: *an ~ knowledge of Greek philosophy.* □ *n* ~ friend. **~·ly** *adv* **in·ti·macy** /`ɪntɪməsɪ/ *n* (*pl* -cies) **1** [U] the state of being ~; close friendship or relationship; (euphem, esp in newspaper reports of divorce proceedings, for) illicit sexual relations. **2** (*pl*) ~ actions, e g caresses or kisses.

in·ti·mate[2] /`ɪntɪmeɪt/ *vt* [VP6A,9,14] ~ ***sth (to sb),*** ~ ***that,*** make known; show clearly: *~ one's approval of a plan/that one approves of a plan. He ~d to me his intention of leaving early.* **in·ti·ma·tion** /'ɪntɪ`meɪʃn/ *n* [U] intimating; [C] sth ~d; notification; suggestion.

in·timi·date /ɪn`tɪmɪdeɪt/ *vt* [VP6A,14] frighten,

esp in order to force (sb into doing sth): *~ a witness,* e g by threatening him. **in·timi·da·tion** /ɪnˈtɪmɪˈdeɪʃn/ *n* [U] intimidating or being ~d: *surrender to intimidation.*

into /ˈɪntə *strong form:* ˈɪntu/ *prep* **1** (indicating motion or direction to a point within): *Come ~ the house/garden. Throw it ~ the fire. Don't get ~ trouble.* **2** (indicating change of condition, result): *She burst ~ tears. The rain changed ~ snow. He poked the fire ~ a blaze,* poked it so that it blazed up. *Collect them ~ heaps. He frightened her ~ submission.* **3** (maths): *5 ~ 25* (= 25 divided by 5) *goes 5.*

in·tol·er·able /ɪnˈtolr̩əbl/ *adj* that cannot be tolerated or endured: *~ heat/insolence. Is the world becoming an ~ place to live in?* **in·tol·er·ably** /-əblɪ/ *adv*

in·tol·er·ant /ɪnˈtolr̩ənt/ *adj* **~ (of),** not tolerant: *a man who is ~ of opposition.* **~·ly** *adv* **in·tol·er·ance** /-əns/ *n*

in·ton·ation /ˈɪntəˈneɪʃn/ *n* [U] the rise and fall of the pitch of the voice in speaking; this as an element of meaning in language.

in·tone /ɪnˈtəʊn/ *vt,vi* [VP6A,2A] recite a prayer, psalm, etc in a singing tone; speak with a particular tone.

in toto /ɪn ˈtəʊtəʊ/ (Lat) totally; altogether.

in·toxi·cant /ɪnˈtoksɪkənt/ *adj, n* intoxicating (liquor).

in·toxi·cate /ɪnˈtoksɪkeɪt/ *vt* [VP6A] **1** make stupid with, cause to lose self-control as the result of taking, alcoholic drink: *If a man drinks too much whisky, he becomes ~d.* **2** excite greatly, beyond self-control: *be ~d by success; ~d with joy.* **in·toxi·ca·tion** /ɪnˈtoksɪˈkeɪʃn/ *n* [U] being ~d; alcoholic poisoning.

in·trac·table /ˈɪnˈtræktəbl/ *adj* not easily controlled or dealt with; hard to manage: *~ children; an ~ temper.* **in·trac·ta·bil·ity** /ˈɪnˈtræktəˈbɪlətɪ/ *n*

in·tra·mural /ˈɪntrəˈmjʊərl/ *adj* **1** existing, done, within the walls of a town, building, etc: *~ burial,* inside a church instead of in the churchyard. **2** intended for full-time, residential students. ⇨ extramural.

in·tran·si·gent /ɪnˈtrænsɪdʒənt/ *adj* (formal) uncompromising, esp in politics. **in·tran·si·gence** /-əns/ *n*

in·tran·si·tive /ɪnˈtrænsətɪv/ *adj* (of verbs) used without a direct object. **~·ly** *adv*

in·tra-uter·ine /ˈɪntrə ˈjutərɑɪn/ *adj* (med) within the uterus: *an ~ device,* (abbr I U D), loop or coil inserted in the uterus as a contraceptive.

in·tra·venous /ˈɪntrəˈvinəs/ *adj* within a vein or veins: *~ injections,* and so into the blood stream.

in·trench /ɪnˈtrentʃ/ = entrench.

in·trepid /ɪnˈtrepɪd/ *adj* fearless. **~·ly** *adv* **in·trep·id·ity** /ˈɪntrəˈpɪdətɪ/ *n* [U] fearlessness; [C] (*pl* -ties) fearless act.

in·tri·cate /ˈɪntrɪkət/ *adj* complicated; puzzling; difficult to follow or understand: *a novel with an ~ plot; an ~ piece of machinery.* **~·ly** *adv* **in·tri·cacy** /ˈɪntrɪkəsɪ/ *n* (*pl* -cies) [U] the quality of being ~; (*pl*) ~ things, events, etc.

in·trigue /ˈɪntrig/ *vi,vt* **1** [VP2A,3A] **~ (with sb) (against sb),** make and carry out secret plans or plots: *~ with Smith against Robinson.* **2** [VP6A] arouse the interest or curiosity of: *The news ~d all of us.* □ *n* **1** [U] secret plotting. **2** [C] plot; secret plan; secret love affair.

in·trin·sic /ɪnˈtrɪnsɪk/ *adj* (of value, quality) belonging naturally; existing within, not coming from outside: *a man's ~ worth,* e g such qualities as honour and courage, contrasted with *extrinsic* qualities, e g family connections; *the ~ value of a coin,* the value of the metal in it, usu less than its face value. **in·trin·si·cally** /-klɪ/ *adv*

in·tro·duce /ˈɪntrəˈdjus *US:* -ˈdus/ *vt* [VP6A,15A] **1** bring in; bring forward: *~ a Bill before Parliament.* **2** [VP14] **~ (into),** bring (sth) into use or into operation for the first time; cause (sb) to be acquainted with (sth): *~ new ideas into a business. Tobacco was ~d into Europe from America. The teacher ~d his young pupils to the intricacies of Euclid.* **3** [VP6A,14] **~ sb to,** make (persons) known by name (to one another), esp in the usual formal way: *~ two friends. He ~d me to his parents. The chairman ~d the lecturer to the audience.* **4** [VP14] **~ (into),** insert: *~ a tube into a wound; ~ a subject into a conversation.*

in·tro·duc·tion /ˈɪntrəˈdʌkʃn/ *n* **1** [U] introducing or being introduced: *a letter of ~,* one that introduces the bearer to friends of the writer; *foreign words of recent ~,* recently introduced into the language. **2** [C] introducing of persons to one another: *It was necessary to make ~s all round,* to introduce many people to one another. **3** [C] sth that leads up to sth else; the opening paragraph of a letter, essay, speech, etc; explanatory article at or before the beginning of a book. **4** [C] elementary textbook: *'An I~ to Greek Grammar.'*

in·tro·duc·tory /ˈɪntrəˈdʌktərɪ/ *adj* serving to introduce: *an ~ chapter; a few ~ remarks by the chairman.*

in·tro·spect /ˈɪntrəˈspekt/ *vi* [VP2A] (formal) examine one's own thoughts and feelings. **in·tro·spec·tion** /ˈɪntrəˈspekʃn/ *n* [U] ~ing. **in·tro·spec·tive** /-tɪv/ *adj* inclined towards, based on, ~ion.

in·tro·vert /ˈɪntrəˈvɜt/ *vt* [VP6A] turn (the mind, thought) inward upon itself. □ *n* /ˈɪntrəvɜt/ person who habitually does this; one who is more interested in his own thoughts and feelings than in things outside himself. ⇨ extrovert.

in·trude /ɪnˈtrud/ *vt,vi* [VP14,2A,3A] **~ (oneself) upon sb, ~ oneself/sth (upon sth),** force (sth, oneself, upon sb, into a place); enter without invitation: *the thought/suspicion that ~d itself into my mind; ~ oneself into a meeting; ~ upon a person's time/privacy. I hope I'm not intruding.* **in·truder** *n* person or thing that ~s: (attrib) *~r aircraft; ~r patrols,* i e intruding into the enemy's country.

in·tru·sion /ɪnˈtruʒn/ *n* [U] intruding: *guilty of unpardonable ~ upon sb's privacy;* [C] instance of this: *angry at numerous ~s on one's privacy by rude journalists.* **in·tru·sive** /ɪnˈtruzɪv/ *adj* intruding: *the intrusive 'r',* e g the r-sound often heard in *law and order.*

in·trust /ɪnˈtrʌst/ = entrust.

in·tuit /ɪnˈtjuɪt *US:* -ˈtu-/ *vt,vi* [VP2A,6A] sense by intuition.

in·tu·ition /ˈɪntjʊˈɪʃn *US:* -tʊ-/ *n* **1** [U] (power of) the immediate understanding of something without conscious reasoning or study. **2** [C] piece of knowledge gained by this power. **in·tu·itive** /ɪnˈtjuɪtɪv *US:* -ˈtu-/ *adj* of ~: *intuitive knowledge;* possessing ~: *Are women more intuitive than men?* **in·tu·itive·ly** *adv*

in·tu·mescence /ˈɪntjʊˈmesns *US:* -tʊ-/ *n* (med)

process or condition of swelling or expanding.

in·un·date /ˈɪnəndeɪt/ *vt* [VP6A,14] ~ ***with,*** flood; cover (with water) by overflowing; (fig, esp passive) be overwhelmed: *be ~d with requests for help/applications for a post.* **in·un·da·tion** /ˈɪnənˈdeɪʃn/ *n* [U] flooding; [C] instance of this; flood.

in·ure /ɪˈnjʊə(r)/ *vt* [VP14] ~ ***oneself/sb to,*** (usu passive) accustom: *Living in the far North had ~d him to cold. He had become ~d to ridicule.*

in·vade /ɪnˈveɪd/ *vt* [VP6A] **1** enter (a country) with armed forces in order to attack; (fig) crowd into; enter: *a city ~d by tourists; a mind ~d by worry and anxiety.* **2** violate; interfere with: *~ sb's rights.* **in·vader** *n* person or thing that ~s.

in·valid[1] /ɪnˈvælɪd/ *adj* not valid: *~ excuses/claims/arguments; an ~ will/cheque,* e g one without a signature; *declare a marriage ~.* **in·vali·date** /ɪnˈvælɪdeɪt/ *vt* [VP6A] make ~. **in·vali·da·tion** /ɪnˌvælɪˈdeɪʃn/ *n* [U] state of being ~; [C,U] (act of) rendering sth ~: *the invalidation of a passport.* **in·val·id·ity** /ˌɪnvəˈlɪdətɪ/ *n* [U] state of being ~.

in·va·lid[2] /ˈɪnvəlid *US:* -lɪd/ *adj* **1** weak or disabled through illness or injury: *a home of rest for ~ soldiers.* **2** suitable for ~ persons: *an ~ chair,* one with wheels; *an ~ diet.* □ *n* ~ person. □ *vt* [VP15A] (esp of members of the armed forces) remove from active service as an ~; send (*home*) as an ~: *be ~ed home; ~ed out of the army.* **~·ism** /-ɪzm/ *n* chronic ill health.

in·valu·able /ɪnˈvæljʊbl/ *adj* ~ ***(to),*** of value too high to be measured: *Her services are ~ to me.*

in·vari·able /ɪnˈveərɪəbl/ *adj* never changing; unchangeable; constant: *an ~ pressure/temperature.* **in·vari·ably** /-əblɪ/ *adv*

in·va·sion /ɪnˈveɪʒn/ *n* [U] invading or being invaded; [C] instance of this: *an ~ of privacy.*

in·vas·ive /ɪnˈveɪsɪv/ *adj* making invasion; tending to spread.

in·vec·tive /ɪnˈvektɪv/ *n* [U] abusive language; *speeches filled with ~;* (*pl*) curses; violent expressions: *a stream of coarse ~s.*

in·veigh /ɪnˈveɪ/ *vi* [VP3A] ~ ***against sb/sth,*** speak bitterly; attack violently in words.

in·veigle /ɪnˈvigl *US:* ɪnˈveɪgl/ *vt* [VP14] ~ ***sb into doing sth,*** trick by using flattery, deception, etc: *~ sb into investing his money unwisely.*

in·vent /ɪnˈvent/ *vt* [VP6A] **1** create or design (sth not existing before): *When was the steam engine ~ed?* Cf *discover,* find sth existing before, but unknown. **2** make up, think of: *~ a story/an excuse.* **in·ven·tive** /ɪnˈventɪv/ *adj* able to ~: *an ~ive mind; ~ive powers.* **in·ven·tor** /-tə(r)/ *n* person who ~s things.

in·ven·tion /ɪnˈvenʃn/ *n* **1** [U] inventing: *the ~ of the telephone;* capacity for inventing: *Necessity is the mother of ~.* **2** [C] sth invented: *the numerous ~s of Edison; newspapers that are full of ~s,* invented, untrue stories. **3** (archaic) finding; discovery: *the ~ of the Cross.*

in·ven·tory /ˈɪnvəntrɪ *US:* -tɔrɪ/ *n* (*pl* **-ries**) detailed list, e g of household goods, furniture, etc.

in·verse /ɪnˈvɜs/ *adj* inverted; reversed in position, direction or relations: *~ ratio/proportion,* that between two quantities one of which increases proportionately as the other decreases. **~·ly** *adv*

in·vert /ɪnˈvɜt/ *vt* [VP6A] put upside down or in the opposite order, position or arrangement: *~ a glass,* so that it is bottom upwards. **ˌ~ed ˈcommas,** quotation marks (''—'' or '—'). □ *n* [C] /ˈɪnvɜt/ homosexual. **in·ver·sion** /ɪnˈvɜʃn *US:* -ˈvɜʒn/ *n* [U] ~ing or being ~ed; [C] instance of this; sth ~ed.

in·vert·ebrate /ɪnˈvɜtəbreɪt/ *adj* not having a backbone or spinal column, e g insects, worms; (fig) weak-willed. □ *n* ~ animal.

in·vest /ɪnˈvest/ *vt,vi* **1** [VP6A,14] ~ ***(in),*** put (money in): *~ £1 000 in government stock; ~ one's savings in a business enterprise.* **2** [VP3A] ~ ***in,*** (colloq) buy (sth considered useful): *~ in a new hat.* **3** [VP14] ~ ***sb with,*** clothe; endow; decorate; surround (with qualities): *The military governor has been ~ed with full authority. The old ruins were ~ed with romance.* **4** [VP6A] surround a fort, town, etc with armed forces; lay siege to. **~or** /-tə(r)/ *n* person who ~s money. **~·ment** *n* **1** [U] ~ing money: *By careful ~ment of his capital, he obtained a good income.* **2** [C] sum of money that is ~ed; that in which money is ~ed: *an ~ment of £500 in oil shares; wise and profitable ~ments.* **3** [U] act of ~ing a town, fort, etc; blockade. **4** = investiture.

in·ves·ti·gate /ɪnˈvestɪgeɪt/ *vt* [VP6A] examine, inquire into; make a careful study of: *~ a crime/the causes of a railway accident; ~ the market for sales of a product.* **in·ves·ti·ga·tor** /-tə(r)/ *n* person who ~s. **in·ves·ti·ga·tion** /ɪnˈvestɪˈgeɪʃn/ *n* [U] careful and thorough inquiry; [C] instance of this: *The matter is under investigation.*

in·ves·ti·ture /ɪnˈvestɪtʃə(r) *US:* -tʃʊə(r)/ *n* (from invest(3)) ceremony of investing sb *with* an office, rank, power or dignity.

in·vest·ment ⇨ invest.

in·vet·er·ate /ɪnˈvetərət/ *adj* (esp of habits, feelings) deep-rooted; long-established: *an ~ smoker; ~ prejudices.*

in·vi·able /ɪnˈvaɪəbl/ *adj* not viable.

in·vidi·ous /ɪnˈvɪdɪəs/ *adj* likely to cause ill-feeling (because of real or apparent injustice): *make ~ distinctions.* **~·ly** *adv*

in·vigi·late /ɪnˈvɪdʒɪleɪt/ *vi* [VP2A] watch over students during examinations. **in·vigi·la·tor** /-tə(r)/ *n* person who ~s. **in·vigi·la·tion** /ɪnˌvɪdʒɪˈleɪʃn/ *n*

in·vig·or·ate /ɪnˈvɪgəreɪt/ *vt* [VP6A] make vigorous; give strength or courage to: *an invigorating climate/speech.*

in·vin·cible /ɪnˈvɪnsəbl/ *adj* too strong to be overcome or defeated: *an ~ will.* **in·vin·cibly** /-əblɪ/ *adv* **in·vin·ci·bil·ity** /ɪnˌvɪnsəˈbɪlətɪ/ *n* [U].

in·viol·able /ɪnˈvaɪələbl/ *adj* not to be violated, dishonoured or profaned: *an ~ oath/law.*

in·viol·ate /ˈɪnˈvaɪələt/ *adj* kept sacred; held in respect; not violated: *keep an oath/a promise/rule ~; remain ~.*

in·vis·ible /ɪnˈvɪzəbl/ *adj* that cannot be seen: *stars that are ~ to the naked eye; ~ exports/imports,* money that goes out of/comes into a country as interest on capital, payments for shipping services, tourist expenditure, etc; *~ ink,* ink which, when used for writing, can be seen only after treatment by heat, etc; *~ mending,* repair of woven materials, silk stockings, etc by interweaving threads so that the repair is hardly noticeable. **in·vis·ibly** /-əblɪ/ *adv* **in·visi·bil·ity** /ɪnˌvɪzəˈbɪlətɪ/ *n* [U].

in·vite /ɪnˈvaɪt/ *vt* **1** [VP15A,B,17] ask (sb to do sth, come somewhere, etc): *~ a friend to dinner/to one's house. He didn't ~ me in. We are old* *now, and seldom get ~d out.* **2** [VP6A] ask for: *~ questions/opinions/confidences.* **3** [VP6A,17] encourage: *The cool water of the lake ~d us to swim. Don't leave the windows open—it's inviting thieves to enter.* □ *n* /ˈɪnvɑɪt/ (sl) = invitation(2). **in·vit·ing** *adj* tempting; attractive. **in·vit·ing·ly** *adv* in an inviting way: *The doors were invitingly open,* open in a way that ~d people to enter. **in·vi·ta·tion** /ˈɪnvɪˋteɪʃn/ *n* **1** [U] inviting or being ~d: *a letter of invitation; admission by invitation only.* **2** [C] request to come or go somewhere, or do sth: *send out invitations to a dinner party.*

in·vo·ca·tion /ˈɪnvəˋkeɪʃn/ *n* ⇨ invoke.

in·voice /ˈɪnvɔɪs/ *vt, n* [VP6A] (make a) list of goods sold with the price(s) charged: *~ sb for goods.*

in·voke /ɪnˋvəʊk/ *vt* **1** [VP6A] call upon God, the power of the law, etc for help or protection. **2** [VP6A,14] **~ *sth (up)on,*** request earnestly; call down from heaven: *~ vengeance on one's enemies.* **3** [VP6A] summon up (by magic): *~ evil spirits.* **in·vo·ca·tion** /ˈɪnvəˋkeɪʃn/ *n* [U] invoking or being ~d; [C] prayer or appeal that ~s.

in·vol·un·tary /ɪnˋvɒləntrɪ *US:* -terɪ/ *adj* done without intention; done unconsciously: *an ~ movement of fear.* **in·vol·un·tar·ily** /ɪnˋvɒləntrḷɪ *US:* ɪnˈvɒlənˋterḷɪ/ *adv*

in·vo·lute /ˈɪnvəlut/ *adj* complex; intricate; (bot) curled spirally. **in·vo·lu·tion** /ˈɪnvəˋluʃn/ *n* anything internally complex or intricate.

in·volve /ɪnˋvɒlv/ *vt* **1** [VP6A,14] cause (sb or sth) to be caught or mixed up (in trouble, etc); get (sb or sth) into a complicated or difficult condition: *They are deeply ~d in debt. Don't ~ yourself in unnecessary expense.* **2** [VP6A,B] have as a necessary consequence: *To accept the position you offer would ~ my living in London. The war ~d a great increase in the national debt.* **3** (*pp*) complicated in form, etc: *an ~d sentence; Henry James's ~d style.* **~·ment** *n*

in·vul·ner·able /ɪnˋvʌlnrəbl/ *adj* that cannot be wounded or hurt: (fig) *in an ~ position.*

in·ward /ˈɪnwəd/ *adj* **1** situated within; inner: *~ happiness,* i e of the spirit; *one's ~* (i e mental or spiritual) *nature.* **2** turned towards the inside: *an ~ curve.* □ *n pl* (colloq) (often spelt *innards*) /ˈɪnədz/ entrails; bowels. **~·ly** *adv* in mind or spirit: *grieve ~ly,* i e so as not to show one's grief. **~·ness** *n* (person's) inner nature; spiritual quality: *the true ~ness of Christ's teaching.* **~(s)** *adv* towards the inside; into or towards the mind or soul.

in·wrought /ˈɪnˋrɔt/ *adj* (of a fabric) decorated (*with* a pattern, etc); (of a pattern or design) worked or woven (*in* or *on*).

iod·ine /ˈɑɪədin *US:* -dɑɪn/ *n* [U] chemical substance found in seawater and seaweed, widely used as an antiseptic (in the form 'tincture of ~'), in photography and in the manufacture of some dyes.

ion /ˈɑɪən/ *n* electrically charged particle formed by losing or gaining electrons. Such particles make a solution of certain chemicals a conductor of electricity. **ion·ize** /ˈɑɪənɑɪz/ *vt* convert into ions. **ion·iz·ation** /ˈɑɪənɑɪˋzeɪʃn *US:* -nɪˋz-/ *n*

iono·sphere /ɑɪˋɒnəsfɪə(r)/ *n* (also known as the *Heaviside Layer*) set of layers of the earth's atmosphere, which reflect radio waves and cause them to follow the earth's contour.

Ionic /ɑɪˋɒnɪk/ *adj* of the order of Greek architecture having scrolls in the capitals of the columns. ⇨ the illus at column.

iota /ɑɪˋəʊtə/ *n* the Greek letter (ι); infinitesimal part: *not an ~ of truth in the story,* no truth at all.

I O U /ˈɑɪ əʊ ˋju/ *n* (= *I owe you*) signed paper acknowledging that one owes the sum of money stated.

ipse dixit /ˈɪpsɪ ˋdɪksɪt/ (Lat) (= *he himself said it*) dogmatic statement made on sb's unsupported word.

ipso facto /ˈɪpsəʊ ˋfæktəʊ/ *adv phrase* (Lat) by that very fact.

iras·cible /ɪˋræsəbl/ *adj* (formal) easily made angry. **iras·ci·bil·ity** /ɪˈræsəˋbɪlətɪ/ *n* tendency to anger; angry behaviour.

irate /ɑɪˋreɪt/ *adj* (formal) angry. **~·ly** *adv*

ire /ˈɑɪə(r)/ *n* (poet or formal) anger. **ire·ful** /-fl/ *adj* angry.

iri·descent /ˈɪrɪˋdesnt/ *adj* (formal) showing colours like those of the rainbow; changing colour as light falls from different directions. **iri·descence** /-ˋdesns/ *n*

irid·ium /ɪˋrɪdɪəm/ *n* [U] hard, silver-white metal (symbol **Ir**): *an ~ pen point,* point of this metal at the end of the nib of a fountain-pen.

iris /ˈɑɪərɪs/ *n* **1** coloured part round the pupil of the eye. ⇨ the illus at eye. **2** kinds of flowering plant with sword-shaped leaves.

Irish /ˈɑɪərɪʃ/ *adj* of Ireland: *the ~ Free State* (or *Eire* /ˈeərə/), part of Ireland that became independent in 1922. **ˈ~ ˋstew,** one of mutton, boiled with onions and other vegetables. □ *n* the language: *the ~,* ~ people. **~·man** /-mən/ *n* (*pl* -men) **~·woman** /-wʊmən/ *n* (*pl* -women) native of Ireland.

irk /ɜk/ *vt* trouble; annoy (chiefly in): *It irks me to (do that).* **irk·some** /-səm/ *adj* tiresome.

iron[1] /ˈɑɪən *US:* ɑɪərn/ *n* **1** [U] commonest of all metallic elements (symbol **Fe**), used in various forms. ⇨ *cast-~* at cast[1](3), *wrought ~* at wrought: *~ ore; as hard as ~;* (fig) *an ~ will.* ***rule with a rod of ~/with an ~ hand,*** with extreme severity. ***a man of ~,*** a hard, unyielding or merciless man. ***an ~ fist in a velvet glove,*** an appearance of gentleness concealing severity, determination. ***strike while the ~ is hot,*** act while the opportunity is good. **the ˋI~ Age,** prehistoric period, following the Bronze Age, when ~ came into use for tools and weapons. **~ curtain,** (fig) frontier(s) dividing USSR and allied countries from other countries; this as a barrier to information and trade. **~ lung,** apparatus fitted over the whole body, except the head, to provide a person with artificial respiration by the use of mechanical pumps. **~ rations,** store of food for use in an emergency as for troops/explorers. **2** [U] (esp in compounds) tool, etc made of ~: (ˋ*flat-*)~, flat-bottomed implement heated and used for smoothing clothes, etc: ˋ*fire-~s,* poker, tongs, etc used at a fireplace or stove; golf-club with an ~ head; branding tool; (*pl*) fetters: *put sb in ~s,* fasten his wrists and ankles in chains. *have too many ~s in the fire,* too many undertakings needing attention at the same time. **3** (compounds) **ˋ~·clad** *n* (name formerly used for a) warship protected by ~ plates. **ˋ~-foundry** *n* foundry where cast-~ is produced. **ˈ~-ˋgrey** *adj, n* (of) the colour of freshly broken cast-~. **ˋ~·master** *n* (old use) manufacturer of ~ articles. **ˋ~·monger** /-mʌŋgə(r)/ *n* dealer in metal goods. **ˋ~-**

mongery /-mʌŋgrɪ/ *n* business of an ~monger. **ˈ~-mould** *n* discolouration caused by ~ rust or ink. **ˈ~-side** *n* one of Oliver Cromwell's cavalry troopers (17th c); (fig) tough, obstinate man. **ˈ~-ware** /-weə(r)/ *n* [U] goods made of ~; hardware. **ˈ~-work** *n* anything made of ~, e g gratings, rails, railings. **ˈ~-works** *n* (usu with *sing v*) place where ~ is smelted or where heavy ~ goods are made.

iron² /ˈɑɪən *US:* ˈɑɪərn/ *vt,vi* [VP6A,15A,B,2A,C] smooth cloth/clothes with an ~ (a ˈflat-~): *~ a shirt. Do clothes ~ more easily when they are damp? She's been ~ing all afternoon.* **~ out,** remove by ~ing: *~ out wrinkles;* (fig) remove: *~ out misunderstandings/points of disagreement.* **ˈ~ing-board** *n* padded board on which to ~ clothes, etc.

ironic /ɑɪˈronɪk/, **ironi·cal** /ɑɪˈronɪkl/ *adjj* of, using, expressing, irony: *an ~ smile/remark/person.* **ironi·cally** /-klɪ/ *adv*

irony /ˈɑɪərənɪ/ *n* **1** [U] the expression of one's meaning by saying sth which is the direct opposite of one's thoughts, in order to make one's remarks forceful. **2** [C] (*pl* -nies) event, situation, etc which is itself desirable, but which, because of the circumstances, is of little or no value, thus appearing to be directed by evil fate: *the ~ of fate/circumstances. If a poor man inherits a large fortune and dies a month later, one might call it one of life's ironies.*

ir·ra·di·ate /ɪˈreɪdɪeɪt/ *vt* [VP6A] (formal) **1** send rays of light upon; subject to sunlight or ultra-violet rays; (fig) throw light on (a subject). **2** light up: *faces ~d with joy.*

ir·ra·tional /ɪˈræʃnl/ *adj* **1** not endowed with reason: *behave like an ~ animal.* **2** absurd; illogical; *~ fears/behaviour.* **~ly** /-ʃnḷɪ/ *adv*

ir·rec·on·cil·able /ɪˈrekənˈsɑɪləbl/ *adj* (formal) (of persons) that cannot be reconciled; (of ideas, actions) that cannot be brought into harmony.

ir·re·cover·able /ˈɪrɪˈkʌvr̩əbl/ *adj* (formal) that cannot be recovered or remedied: *~ losses.*

ir·re·deem·able /ˈɪrɪˈdiməbl/ *adj* **1** (of paper currency) that cannot be exchanged for coin; (of government annuities) that cannot be terminated by repayment. **2** that cannot be restored, reclaimed, saved: *an ~ loss/misfortune.*

ir·re·den·tist /ˈɪrɪˈdentɪst/ *n* person who advocates the reunion to his own country of territory which has been lost to a foreign government, or which is culturally related to his own country, e g to Italy of Italian-speaking districts. **ir·ri·den·tism** /-ɪzm/ *n*

ir·re·duc·ible /ˈɪrɪˈdjusəbl *US:* -ˈdus-/ *adj* (formal) **1** that cannot be reduced or made smaller: *£250 is the ~ minimum for repairs to the house.* **2** that cannot be brought (*to* a desired condition).

ir·re·fut·able ˈɪrɪˈfjutəbl/ *adj* that cannot be proved false: *an ~ argument/case.*

ir·regu·lar /ɪˈregjʊlə(r)/ *adj* **1** contrary to rules, to what is normal and established: *an ~ proceeding/marriage; be ~ in church attendance,* be absent frequently; *~ troops,* not trained for, or not forming part of, the regular army. **2** uneven; not regular in shape, arrangement, etc: *~ lines and figures; a coast with an ~ outline,* with many bays, inlets, etc. **3** (gram) not inflected in the usual way: *'Child' has an ~ plural.* □ *n* (usu *pl*) member of an ~ military force. **~·ly** *adv* **~·ity** /ˈɪˈregjʊˈlærətɪ/ *n* (*pl* -ties) [U] state or quality of being ~; [C] sth ~: *~ities in behaviour; the ~ities of the earth's surface.*

ir·rel·evant /ɪˈreləvənt/ *adj* ~ **(to),** not to the point; having nothing to do with: *~ remarks/evidence. What you say is ~ to the subject.* **ir·rel·evance** /-əns/, **ir·rel·evancy** /-ənsɪ/ *nn* (*pl* ~s, -cies) [U] state of being ~; [C] ~ remark, question, etc: *Let us ignore these irrelevancies.*

ir·re·li·gious /ˈɪrɪˈlɪdʒəs/ *adj* opposed to, showing no interest in, religion: *~ acts/persons.*

ir·re·medi·able /ˈɪrɪˈmidɪəbl/ *adj* that cannot be remedied: *~ acts/faults.*

ir·re·mov·able /ˈɪrɪˈmuvəbl/ *adj* that cannot be removed (esp from office).

ir·rep·ar·able /ɪˈreprəbl/ *adj* (of a loss, injury, etc) that cannot be put right or restored: *~ harm.*

ir·re·place·able /ˈɪrɪˈpleɪsəbl/ *adj* of which the loss cannot be supplied.

ir·re·press·ible /ˈɪrɪˈpresəbl/ *adj* that cannot be held back or controlled: *a girl with ~ high spirits.*

ir·re·proach·able /ˈɪrɪˈprəʊtʃəbl/ *adj* free from blame or fault: *~ conduct.*

ir·re·sist·ible /ˈɪrɪˈzɪstəbl/ *adj* too strong, convincing, delightful, etc to be resisted: *~ desires/temptations. On this hot day the sea was ~,* We couldn't resist the desire to go to or into the sea.

ir·res·ol·ute /ˈɪˈrezəlut/ *adj* undecided; hesitating. **ir·res·ol·ution** /ˈɪˈrezəˈluʃn/ *n* [U].

ir·re·spec·tive /ˈɪrɪˈspektɪv/ *adj* **~ of,** not paying consideration to; not taking into account: *He rushed forward to help, ~ of the consequences.*

ir·re·spon·sible /ˈɪrɪˈsponsəbl/ *adj* **1** not responsible for conduct, etc; not to be blamed or punished: *an ~ child.* **2** (doing things, done) without a proper sense of responsibility; not trustworthy: *~ teenagers; ~ behaviour.* **ir·re·spon·si·bil·ity** /ˈɪrɪˈsponsəˈbɪlətɪ/ *n*

ir·re·triev·able /ˈɪrɪˈtrivəbl/ *adj* that cannot be retrieved or remedied: *an ~ loss.*

ir·rev·er·ent /ɪˈrevərənt/ *adj* feeling or showing no respect for sacred things. **~·ly** *adv* **ir·rev·er·ence** /-əns/ *n* [U].

ir·re·vers·ible /ˈɪrɪˈvɜsəbl/ *adj* that cannot be reversed or revoked: *an ~ decision.*

ir·revo·cable /ɪˈrevəkəbl/ *adj* final and unalterable; that cannot be revoked: *an ~ decision/judgement; an ~ letter of credit.*

ir·ri·gate /ˈɪrɪgeɪt/ *vt* [VP6A] **1** supply (land, crops) with water (by means of rivers, water-channels, overhead pipes, etc): *~ desert areas and make them fertile.* **2** construct reservoirs, canals, etc for the distribution of water (to fields). **3** wash out (a wound, etc) with a constant flow of liquid. **ir·ri·ga·tion** /ˈɪrɪˈgeɪʃn/ [U] irrigating: (attrib) *an irrigation project; irrigation canals.*

ir·ri·table /ˈɪrɪtəbl/ *adj* easily annoyed or made angry. **ir·ri·tably** /-əblɪ/ *adv* **ir·ri·ta·bil·ity** /ˈɪrɪtəˈbɪlətɪ/ *n*

ir·ri·tant /ˈɪrɪtənt/ *adj* causing irritation. □ *n* ~ substance, e g dust or pepper in the nose; sth that irritates the mind.

ir·ri·tate /ˈɪrɪteɪt/ *vt* [VP6A] **1** make angry or annoyed; excite the temper of: *~d by the delay.* **2** cause discomfort to (part of the body); make sore or inflamed: *The smoke ~d her eyes.* **ir·ri·ta·tion** /ˈɪrɪˈteɪʃn/ *n* [U] irritating or being ~d; [C] instance of this.

ir·rup·tion /ɪˈrʌpʃn/ *n* sudden and violent entry; bursting in.

is ⇨ **be¹**.

isin·glass /ˈɑɪzɪŋglɑs *US:* -glæs/ *n* [U] clear white

jelly made from the air bladders of some freshwater fish, used for making glue, preserving eggs, and in the brewing of beer.

Is·lam /ɪzˋlɑm/ *n* faith, religion, proclaimed by the Prophet Muhammad; all Muslims; all the Muslim world. **~ic** /ɪzˋlæmɪk/ *adj*

is·land /ˋɑɪlənd/ *n* piece of land surrounded by water; sth resembling an ~ because it is detached or isolated: *a ˋtraffic ~*, a raised place in a busy street where people may be safe from traffic. **~er** *n* person born on or living on an ~.

isle /ɑɪl/ *n* island (not much used in prose, except in proper names: *the I~ of Wight; the British I~s.* **is·let** /ˋɑɪlət/ *n* small island.

ism /ˋɪzm/ *n* distinctive doctrine or practice: *behaviourism and all the other isms of the twentieth century.*

isn't ⇨ be[1].

iso·bar /ˋɑɪsəbɑ(r)/ *n* line on a map, esp a weather chart, joining places with the same atmospheric pressure at a particular time.

iso·late /ˋɑɪsəleɪt/ *vt* [VP6A,14] **1** separate, put or keep apart from others: *When a person has an infectious disease, he is usually ~d. Several villages in the north have been ~d by heavy snowfalls.* **2** (chem) separate a substance, germ, etc from its combinations.

iso·la·tion /ˌɑɪsəˋleɪʃn/ *n* [U] isolating or being isolated: *live in ~*, e g as Robinson Crusoe did; *an ˋ~ hospital/ward,* one for persons with infectious diseases. **~·ism** /-ɪzm/ *n* (in international affairs) policy of non-participation in the affairs of other countries. **~·ist** /-ɪst/ *n* supporter of ~ism.

isos·celes /ɑɪˋsosl̩iz/ *adj* (of a triangle) having two sides equal.

iso·therm /ˋɑɪsəθɜm/ *n* line on a map joining places having the same mean temperature.

iso·tope /ˋɑɪsətəʊp/ *n* atom of an element, e g heavy hydrogen, having a nuclear mass different from that of other atoms of the same element although chemically identical: *radio-active ~s*, unstable forms used in medicine and industry.

issue /ˋɪʃu/ *vi,vt* **1** [VP2A,3A] **~ *from,*** come, go, flow, out: *smoke issuing from chimneys; blood issuing from a wound.* **2** [VP6A,14] **~ *sth to sb,* ~ *sb with sth,*** distribute for use or consumption: *~ warm clothing to the troops; ~ them with warm clothing.* **3** [VP6A,14] **~ *(to),*** publish (books, etc); put stamps, banknotes, shares[1](3), etc into circulation. □ *n* **1** [U] outgoing; outflowing: *the point or place of ~*; [C] the act of flowing out; that which flows out: *an ~ of blood from the nose.* **2** [U] putting forth; sending out; publication: *the ~ of a newspaper/a new coinage; buy new stamps on the day of ~*; [C] that which is sent out, etc: *new ~s of banknotes; the most recent ~s of a periodical; an ~ of winter clothing to the troops.* **3** [C] question that arises for discussion: *debate an ~; raise a new ~; argue political ~s.* ***join/take ~ with sb (on/about sth),*** proceed to argue with him (about it). ***the point/matter at ~,*** the point being discussed. **4** [C] result; outcome; consequence: *bring a campaign to a successful ~; await the ~.* **5** [U] (legal) offspring: *die without ~*, i e childless.

isth·mus /ˋɪsməs/ *n* (*pl* **-ses** /-sɪz/) neck of land joining two larger bodies of land: *the I~ of Panama.*

it /ɪt/ *pron* (*pl* **they** /ðeɪ/, **them** /ðem/) **1** (used of lifeless things, of animals (when sex is unknown or unimportant), and of a baby or small child when the sex is unknown or a matter of indifference): *This is my watch; it's a Swiss one. Where's my book?—Have you seen it? Where's the cat?—It's in the garden. She's expecting another baby and hopes it will be a boy.* **2** (used to refer to a group of words which follows, this being the grammatical subject. This may be) **(a)** an infinitive phrase: Is *it* difficult *to learn written Chinese?* **(b)** a construction with *for*, a *(pro)noun*, and a *to*-infinite: *It was* hard *for him to live on his small pension.* **(c)** a gerundial phrase: *It* doesn't seem much use *going on. It's no use your trying to do that.* **(d)** a clause: *It* seems unlikely *that he will catch the train.* I think *it* a pity *that you didn't try harder. It* doesn't matter *whether we start now or later.* Does *it* matter *what you do next?* **3** (used to refer backwards or forwards to identify sb or sth. Note that if the identity of a person is already known, *it* is not used): *'Who's that at the door?'—'It's the postman.'* Cf *Mr Smith is at the door. He wants to see you. 'What was that noise?'—'It was a mouse.'* **4** (used as a formal or meaningless word to supply a subject) **(a)** dealing with the weather, atmospheric conditions, etc: *It is raining/snowing, etc. It's warm/cold/windy, etc. Isn't it a nice day! How dark it is!* **(b)** for time: *It's six o'clock. It is past midnight. It's Monday, the 1st of May. It is three years since I last met you. It's a month to Christmas.* **(c)** for distance: *It's ten miles to Oxford. It's only a short way now.* **(d)** vaguely for the general situation, or for sth that is to be understood from the context: *So it seems. It can't be helped. Whose turn is it next? That's the best/worst of it! Keep at it,* i e at whatever you are doing. *You've got what it takes,* have the qualities, etc needed for this job, situation, etc. *You've had it,* there's nothing more to be had from this situation, experience, etc. *Go it!* Go on with your efforts, etc. *Now you've done it!* i e You've done sth wrong or foolish! *Now you'll catch it!* You'll be reprimanded, punished, etc! *As it happened,...; If it hadn't been for your help,....* **5** (used to bring into prominence one part of a sentence) **(a)** the subject: *It was his work during the weekend that exhausted him.* **(b)** the object of a *v*: *It's the red book that I want, not the green one.* **(c)** the object of a *prep*: *It was John I gave the book to, not Harry.* **(d)** adverbial adjunct: *It was on Sunday that I saw him, not on Saturday.* **its** /ɪts/ *poss adj* of it: *The dog wagged its tail. The child fell and hurt its knee. I don't like this hat; its shape is wrong.* **itself** /ɪtˋself/ *reflex pron*: *The dog got up and stretched itself.* □ *emph pron*: *The thing itself is not valuable, but I want it as a keepsake.* ***by itself,*** **(a)** automatically: *The machine works by itself.* **(b)** alone: *The farmhouse stands by itself in the fields.*

italic /ɪˋtælɪk/ *adj* (of printed letters) sloping: *This is ~ type.* □ *n pl* ~ letters: *in ~s.* **itali·cize** /ɪˋtælɪsɑɪz/ *vt* print in ~s. ⇨ roman.

itch /ɪtʃ/ *n* **1** (with *def* or *indef art*, but rarely *pl*) feeling of irritation on the skin, causing a desire to scratch: *have/suffer from the ~/an ~.* **2** (usu with the *indef art* or a *poss adj*) restless desire or longing: *have an ~ for money; his ~ to go to the South Seas.* □ *vi* **1** [VP2A,4A] have an ~: *scratch where it ~es. Scratch yourself if you ~. Are your mosquito bites still ~ing?* **2** [VP3A] **~ *for,*** (colloq) long for: *The boys were ~ing for the lesson to end.* ***have an ~ing palm,*** be ~ing for money. **~y** *adj* (-ier, -iest): *~y hair/fingers.*

item /ˈaɪtəm/ *n* **1** single article or unit in a list, etc: *the first ~ on the programme; number the ~s in a catalogue; I~, one chair; ~, two carpets, etc.* **2** detail or paragraph (of news): *Are there any interesting ˈnews ~s/~s of news in the paper this morning?* □ *adv* likewise; also (used to introduce successive articles in a list). **~·ize** /-aɪz/ *vt* [VP6A] give, write, every ~ of: *an ~ized account; ~ize a bill.*

it·er·ate /ˈɪtəreɪt/ *vt* [VP6A] say again and again; make (an accusation, etc) repeatedly. **it·er·ation** /ˌɪtəˈreɪʃn/ *n* [U] iterating; [C] sth ~d.

itin·er·ant /aɪˈtɪnərənt/ *adj* travelling from place to place: *~ musicians.*

itin·er·ary /aɪˈtɪnərərɪ *US:* -rerɪ/ *n* [C] (*pl* -ries) plan for, details or records of, a journey; route.

it'll /ˈɪtl/ = *it will.*

it's /ɪts/ = *it is* or *it has.*

its, it·self /ɪts, ɪtˈself/ ⇨ **it.**

I've /aɪv/ = *I have.*

ivory /ˈaɪvr̩ɪ/ *n* [U] white, bone-like substance forming the tusks of elephants, used for ornaments, piano-keys, etc; (attrib) the colour of ~: *an ~ skin/complexion.* **ˌ~ ˈtower,** place of seclusion or retreat from the realities of life.

ivy /ˈaɪvɪ/ *n* [U] climbing, clinging, evergreen plant with dark, shiny (often five-pointed) leaves. **ivied** /ˈaɪvɪd/ *adj* covered with ivy: *ivied walls.*

ivy

Jj

J, j /dʒeɪ/ (*pl* **J's, j's** /dʒeɪz/) the tenth letter of the English alphabet.

jab /dʒæb/ *vt,vi* (-bb-) **1** [VP3A] ***jab at,*** poke or push at sb, sth with force: *jab at sb/sth with a knife. He jabbed at his opponent,* (boxing) aimed a quick blow at him. **2** [VP14] ***jab sth into sth/sb,*** force sth into sth/sb: *He jabbed his elbow into my side.* **3** [VP15B] ***jab sth out,*** force or push out by jabbing: *Be careful! Don't jab my eye out with your umbrella!* □ *n* sudden, rough blow or thrust: *a jab in the arm,* (colloq) an injection or inoculation: *Have you had your smallpox jabs yet?*

jab·ber /ˈdʒæbə(r)/ *vi,vt* **1** [VP2A,C] talk excitedly; talk in what seems to be a rapid and confused manner: *Listen to those children ~ing away!* **2** [VP6A,15B] utter (words, etc) rapidly and indistinctly: *~ (out) one's prayers.* □ *n* [U] ~ing; chatter: *Listen to the ~ of those monkeys.* **~er** *n* person who ~s.

jabot /ˈʒæbəʊ/ *n* [C] ornamental frill on the front of a woman's blouse or a man's shirt.

jack[1] /dʒæk/ *n* **1 J~,** familiar form of the name *John.* **J~ Frost,** frost personified. **ˈJ~ in office,** self-important official who fusses over details. **ˌJ~ of ˈall trades,** person who can turn his hand to anything; workman knowing something of many trades. ***before one can say J~ Robinson,*** very quickly or suddenly. ***J~ is as good as his master,*** the workman is the equal of his employer. **2** (colloq) man. ***every man ~,*** everybody. **3** (usu portable) device for raising heavy weights off the ground, esp one for raising the axle of a car so that a wheel may be changed. **4** (in the game of bowls) small white ball towards which bowls are rolled. **5** ship's flag to show nationality. **the ˌUnion ˈJ~,** of the United Kingdom. ⇨ the illus at **flag. ˈ~ staff** *n* staff on which a ship's flag is flown to show nationality. **6** (in a pack of playing-cards) (also *knave*) court-card between 10 and Queen. **7** (compounds) **ˈ~-in-the-box** *n* toy in the form of a box with sth inside which springs up when the lid is opened. **ˌ~-o'-ˈlantern** *n* will-o'-the-wisp; pumpkin cut to look like a face and used as a lantern (by placing a candle inside) in fun. **ˈ~ rabbit** *n* large hare of Western N America. **~ tar** *n* (old name for a) naval rating; ordinary seaman in the Navy, wearing a jumper and wide-bottomed trousers.

jack[2] /dʒæk/ *vt* [VP6A,15B] ***~ sth up,*** lift with a jack(2): *J~ (up) the car and change the wheel with the punctured tyre.*

jackal /ˈdʒækəl *US:* -kl/ *n* wild dog-like animal.

jack·a·napes /ˈdʒækəneɪps/ *n* **1** conceited person. **2** (often playfully of a child) impudent or mischievous person.

jack·ass /ˈdʒækæs/ *n* male ass; foolish person. **ˌlaughing ˈ~,** (in Australia) Giant Kingfisher.

jack-boot /ˈdʒæk buːt/ *n* large boot coming above the knee (as formerly worn by cavalrymen).

jack·daw /ˈdʒækdɔ/ *n* bird of the crow family (noted for flying off with small bright objects).

jacket /ˈdʒækɪt/ *n* **1** short, sleeved coat. ***dust a person's ~,*** beat him. **2** outer covering round a boiler, tank, pipe, etc to lessen loss of heat, or (*a water ~*) to cool an engine. **3** skin (of a potato): *baked in their ~s.* **4** (also *ˈdust ~*) loose paper cover in which a hardback book is usually issued.

jack·fish /ˈdʒækfɪʃ/ *n* pike.

jack-knife /ˈdʒæk naɪf/ *n* large pocket-knife with a folding blade. □ *n* [VP2A] (esp of an articulated truck) fold and double back like the blade and handle of a ~.

jack plane /ˈdʒæk pleɪn/ *n* plane[2] for rough smoothing of wood.

jack·pot /ˈdʒækpot/ *n* accumulated stakes in various games (esp poker), increasing in value until won. ***hit the ~,*** (by extension) have great success or good fortune.

Jaco·bean /ˌdʒækəˈbɪən/ *adj* of the reign of James I (1603—25) of England: *~ literature/architecture/furniture.*

Jac·obin /ˈdʒækəbɪn/ *n* member of a group of revolutionaries organized in 1789 during the French Revolution. □ *adj* violent; extremely radical. **~·ism** /-ɪzm/ *n* (politics) extreme radicalism.

Jac·obite /ˈdʒækəbaɪt/ *n* supporter of James II (reigned 1685—1688) King of England after his overthrow or of his descendants who claimed the English throne.

jade[1] /dʒeɪd/ *n* [U] hard, usu green stone, carved into ornaments, etc.

jade[2] /dʒeɪd/ *n* **1** tired out or worn-out horse. **2** (either contemptuous or playful) woman: *You* *saucy little ~!* □ *vt* (usu *pp* **jaded**) worn out; overworked: *He looks ~d. He has a ~d* (= dull) *appetite.*

jaffa /ˈdʒæfə/ *n* (P) large oval (often seedless) orange.

jag[1] /dʒæg/ *n* sharp projection, e g of rock. **jaggy** *adj* having ~s.

jag[2] /dʒæg/ *vt* (-gg-) [VP6A] cut or tear in an uneven manner; give an edge like that of a saw to. **jag·ged** /ˈdʒægɪd/ *adj* notched; with rough, uneven edges: *jagged rocks.*

jag·uar /ˈdʒægjʊə(r)/ *n* large, fierce, cat-like meat-eating animal of Central and South America. ⇨ the illus at **cat**.

jail /dʒeɪl/ ⇨ **gaol**.

jakes /dʒeɪks/ *n pl* (with *sing v*) (US) privy.

ja·lopy /dʒəˈlopɪ/ *n* (*pl* **-pies**) (US sl) old, rickety or battered automobile or aircraft.

jam[1] /dʒæm/ *n* [U] fruit boiled with sugar until it is thick, and preserved in jars, pots, tins, etc. ***money for jam,*** (sl) something for nothing; something coming by good luck. **ˈjam-jar/-pot** *nn* one for containing jam. **ˈjam session** *n* impromptu performance by jazz musicians.

jam[2] /dʒæm/ *vt,vi* (-mm-) **1** [VP6A,15A,B,14, 2A,C] crush, be crushed, between two surfaces or masses; squeeze, be squeezed: *a ship jammed in the ice. The logs jammed in the river,* become tightly packed. **2** [VP15B,2A,C] (of parts of a machine, etc) (cause to) become fixed so that movement or action is prevented: *jam the brakes on/jam on the brakes. The brakes jammed and the car skidded badly.* **3** [VP6A,15A,B] push (things) together tightly: *jam one's clothes into a small suitcase. The corridors were jammed by hordes of schoolchildren.* **4** [VP6A] make the reception of a broadcast programme impossible or difficult by broadcasting that deliberately interferes: *jam the enemy's stations during a war.* □ *n* [C] **1** number of things or people crowded together so that movement is difficult or impossible: *ˈtraffic-jams in our big towns; a ˈlog-jam,* on a river, etc. **2** stoppage of a machine due to jamming(2). **3** (sl) awkward position; difficult situation: *be in/get into a jam.*

jamb /dʒæm/ *n* vertical side post of a doorway, window frame, etc; (*pl*) stone sides of a fireplace.

jam·boree /ˈdʒæmbəˈri/ *n* **1** merry meeting. **2** large rally or gathering, esp of Boy Scouts.

jam·pack /ˈdʒæmˈpæk/ *vt* (colloq) crowd to capacity: *a stadium ~ed with spectators.*

jangle /ˈdʒæŋgl/ *vt,vi* [VP6A,2A] (cause to) give out a harsh metallic noise; argue noisily. □ *n* [U] harsh noise.

jani·tor /ˈdʒænɪtə(r)/ *n* **1** doorkeeper. **2** (US) person hired to take care of a building, offices, etc, e g by cleaning, stoking the furnaces.

jan·is·sary /ˈdʒænɪsərɪ *US:* -serɪ/ *n* (*pl* **-ries**) one of a body of Turkish infantry forming, until 1826, the Sultan's bodyguard.

jani·zary /ˈdʒænɪzərɪ *US:* -zerɪ/ *n* (*pl* **-ries**) = **janissary**.

Jan·uary /ˈdʒænjʊərɪ *US:* -jʊerɪ/ *n* the first month of the year.

Ja·nus /ˈdʒeɪnəs/ *n* ancient Italian god, guardian of gates and doors, beginnings and ends, represented with two faces, one on the front and the other on the back of his head.

ja·pan /dʒəˈpæn/ *vt* (-nn-), *n* (cover with) hard, shiny black enamel.

jape /dʒeɪp/ *vi* (archaic) jest. □ *n* jest; joke.

ja·pon·ica /dʒəˈponɪkə/ *n* [U] (sorts of) ornamental variety of pear or quince.

jar[1] /dʒɑ(r)/ *n* [C] **1** (usu harsh) sound or vibration: *We felt a jar when the engine was coupled to the train.* **2** shock; thrill of the nerves; discord: *The fall from his horse gave him a nasty jar. It was an unpleasant jar to my nerves.*

jar[2] /dʒæ(r)/ *n* tall vessel, usu round, with a wide mouth, with or without handle(s), of glass, stone or earthenware; its contents: *a jar of strawberry jam.* **jar·ful** /-fʊl/ *n*

jar[3] /dʒɑ(r)/ *vi,vt* (-rr-) **1** [VP3A] ***jar against/on,*** strike with a harsh unpleasant sound. **2** [VP3A] ***jar on,*** have an unpleasant effect (on): *The way he laughs jars on me/on my ears/on my nerves.* **3** [VP6A] send a shock through (the nerves): *He was badly jarred by the blow. She was jarred by this sad news.* **4** [VP2A,3A] ***jar (with),*** be out of harmony: *His opinions jar with mine. Try to avoid colours that jar when choosing curtains and rugs.* **jar·ring** *adj* causing disharmony; harsh: *a jarring note.* **jar·ring·ly** *adv*

jar·gon /ˈdʒɑgən/ *n* [U] **1** language difficult to understand, because it is a bad form or spoken badly: *Only a mother can understand her baby's ~.* **2** language full of technical or special words: *the ~ of radio technicians/linguists.*

jas·mine /ˈdʒæzmɪn/ *n* [U] kinds of shrub with white or yellow sweet-smelling flowers.

jas·per /ˈdʒæspə(r)/ *n* [U] semi-precious stone, red, yellow or brown.

jaun·dice /ˈdʒɔndɪs/ *n* [U] disease, caused by stoppage of the flow of bile, marked by yellowness of the skin and the whites of the eyes; (fig) state of mind in which one is jealous, spiteful, envious and suspicious. □ *vt* (usu passive) affect with ~: *take a ~d view,* one influenced by jealousy, spite, etc.

jaunt /dʒɔnt/ *n* short journey for pleasure. □ *vi* [VP2A,C] make such a journey. **~·ing-car** *n* light, two-wheeled horse-drawn vehicle with seats back to back, used in Ireland.

jaunty /ˈdʒɔntɪ/ *adj* (-ier, iest) feeling or showing self-confidence and self-satisfaction: *He wore his hat at a ~ angle,* tipped to one side as a sign of high spirits, etc **jaunt·ily** /-əlɪ/ *adv* **jaunti·ness** *n*

jav·elin /ˈdʒævlɪn/ *n* light spear for throwing (usu in sport).

throwing the javelin

jaw /dʒɔ/ *n* **1** *lower/upper jaw,* either of the bone structures containing the teeth; ⇨ the illus at **head**: *Which jaw moves up and down when you talk?* **ˈjaw-bone** *n* one of the bones in which the teeth are set. **ˈjaw-breaker** *n* (colloq) word hard to pronounce. **2** (*pl*) framework of the mouth, including the teeth; (*sing*) lower part of the face: *a man with a strong jaw.* **3** (*pl*) narrow mouth of a valley, channel, etc: (fig) *into/out of the jaws of death,* into/out of great danger. **4** (*pl*) parts of a tool, machine, etc, e g a vice, between which things are gripped or crushed. **5** (colloq) talkativeness: *None of your jaw! Stop/Hold your jaw,* (vulg) Shut up! Be quiet! **6** (colloq) long, dull talk giving moral advice. □ *vi* [VP2A,C,3A] ***jaw (at),*** talk, esp at tedious length; give a moral talk to: *Stop jawing at me!*

jay /dʒeɪ/ *n* (sorts of) noisy European bird with brightly coloured feathers; (fig) impertinent person who chatters too much. **ˋjay-walker** *n* person who walks erratically across or along streets without paying attention to traffic. **ˋjay-walk** *vi* (US) walk in this way.

jazz /dʒæz/ *n* [U] popular music first played by Negro groups in Southern U S A in the early 20th c, characterized by improvisation and strong rhythms, called *traditional* ~; similar music played by large bands for dancing; a later variation much influenced by the *blues* to produce an unhurried emotive style, called *modern* ~: *the* ˋ~ *age;* (attrib) ~ *music; a* ˋ~ *band.* □ *vt* **1** [VP6A] play or arrange in the style of ~: ~ *a song/tune;* dance to ~ music. **2** [VP15B] ~ ***sth up,*** (fig) liven up; put more energy into: ~ *up a party;* ~ *things up a bit.* **jazzy** *adj* (colloq) of or like ~; flashy, showy: ~*y cushions; a* ~*y sports car.*

jeal·ous /ˋdʒeləs/ *adj* **1** feeling or showing fear or ill will because of possible or actual loss of rights or love: *a* ~ *husband;* ~ *looks.* **2** ~ ***(of sb/sth),*** feeling or showing unhappiness because of the better fortune, etc of others: ~ *of sb else's success.* **3** taking watchful care (*of*): ~ *of one's rights; keep a* ~ *eye on sb.* **4** (in the Bible, of God) requiring exclusive loyalty and whole-hearted worship and service. **~·ly** *adv* **jeal·ousy** *n* (*pl* **-sies**) **1** [U] being ~: *a lover's* ~*y.* **2** [C] instance of this; act or utterance that shows ~y: *I'm tired of all these jealousies and quarrels.*

jean /dʒin/ *n* **1** [U] heavy, strong cotton cloth: (attrib) ~ *overalls.* **2** (*pl*) workman's overalls, made of ~; tough (usu denim) trousers similar to overalls worn informally by men, women and children.

jeep /dʒip/ *n* small, light utility motor-vehicle with great freedom of movement, useful on rough ground.

jeer /dʒɪə(r)/ *vi,vt* [VP2A,3A,6A] ~ ***(at sb),*** mock, laugh rudely: ~ *at a defeated enemy;* ~ *(at) the speaker; a* ~*ing crowd.* □ *n* [C] ~ing remark; taunt. **~·ing·ly** *adv*

Je·ho·vah /dʒɪˋhəʊvə/ *n* name of God used in the Old Testament.

je·june /dʒɪˋdʒun/ *adj* (formal) (of writings) dry; uninteresting; unsatisfying to the mind. **~·ly** *adv* **~·ness** *n*

jell /dʒel/ *vi,vt* [VP2A,6A] (colloq) (cause to) become like jelly; take shape: *My ideas are beginning to* ~.

jelly /ˋdʒelɪ/ *n* (*pl* **-lies**) **1** [U] soft, semi-solid food substance made from gelatin; similar substance made of fruit juice and sugar. **2** [C,U] (portion of) this substance prepared in a mould, flavoured and coloured, as a sweet dish. **3** [U] ~-like substance. **ˋ~-fish** *n* ~-like sea animal. ⇨ the illus at **sea**. □ *vt,vi* [VP6A,2A] (cause to) become like ~. **jel·lied** *adj* set in ~; prepared in ~; like ~: *jellied eels.*

jemmy /ˋdʒemɪ/ *n* (*pl* **-mies**) (US = *jimmy*) crowbar, esp as used by burglars for forcing open doors, windows and drawers.

jenny /ˋdʒenɪ/ *n* ⇨ *spinning* ~ at **spin**.

jeop·ard·ize /ˋdʒepədaɪz/ *vt* [VP6A] put in danger. **jeop·ardy** /ˋdʒepədɪ/ *n* [U] danger, usu in the phrase: ***be in jeopardy*** (*of* one's life, etc).

jer·boa /dʒɜˋbəʊə/ *n* small rat-like animal of Asia and the N African deserts with long hind legs and the ability to jump well.

jere·miad /ˌdʒerɪˋmaɪæd/ *n* long, sad and complaining story of troubles, misfortunes, etc.

jerk[1] /dʒɜk/ *n* [C] **1** sudden push, pull, start, stop, twist, lift or throw: *The train stopped with a* ~/*a series of* ~*s.* **2** sudden involuntary twitch of a muscle or muscles. **3** *physical* ~*s,* (colloq) gymastic exercises. □ *vt,vi* [VP6A,15A,B,2C] give a ~ to; move with a ~ or ~s: *He* ~*ed the fish out of the water. The train* ~*ed along/*~*ed to a stop. Don't* ~ *out your words; try to recite more smoothly.* **~y** *adj* (**-ier, -iest**) with ~s; not smooth: *a* ~*y ride in an old bus.* **~·ily** /-əlɪ/ *adv* **~i·ness** *n*

jerk[2] /dʒɜk/ *vt* [VP6A] cure (esp beef) by cutting it into long slices and drying it in the sun.

jer·kin /ˋdʒɜkɪn/ *n* short, close-fitting jacket, usu of leather (as worn by men in olden times). ⇨ the illus at **doublet**.

jerry /ˋdʒerɪ/ *n* (*pl* **-ries**) **1** **ˋ~-builder/-building,** builder/building of houses of poor quality with bad materials. Hence, **ˋ~-built** (houses). **2** **ˋ~-can,** army-style metal container used for carrying extra supplies of water or petrol on long journeys. **3** **J~,** (army sl) German soldier. **4** (sl) chamber-pot.

jer·sey /ˋdʒɜzɪ/ *n* (*pl* **-seys**) **1** [U] (ˋ~*-wool*) soft, fine knitted fabric used for clothes; [C] close-fitting knitted woollen garment with sleeves. **2** **J~,** cow of the breed that originally came from J~, one of the Channel Islands (near the French coast).

jes·sa·mine /ˋdʒesəmɪn/ = **jasmine**.

jest /dʒest/ *n* [C] **1** jokes; sth said or done to cause amusement. ***in*** **~,** as a joke, not in earnest. **2** object of ridicule: *a standing* ~, sth or sb always laughed at. □ *vi* [VP2A,3A] make ~s; act or speak lightly: *Don't* ~ *about serious things. He's not a man to* ~ *with.* **~·ing** *adj* spoken in ~: ~*ing remarks;* fond of ~s: *a* ~*ing fellow.* **~·ing·ly** *adv*

jester /ˋdʒestə(r)/ *n* person who jests, esp (in olden times) a man whose duty it was to make jokes to amuse the court or noble household in which he was employed.

Jesuit /ˋdʒezjʊɪt *US:* ˋdʒeʒʊɪt/ *n* member of the Society of Jesus, a R C order founded in 1534 by Ignatius Loyola /ɪgˈneɪʃəs lɔɪˋəʊlə/ (1491—1556), Spanish priest, taking vows of obedience, poverty and chastity; (as used by opponents of the Society) person who thinks that it may be right to dissemble or prevaricate if this helps to obtain good results. **~i·cal** /ˌdʒezjʊˋɪtɪkl *US:* ˌdʒeʒʊ-/ *adj* of or like the ~s.

Jesus /ˋdʒɪzəs/ *n* the founder of the Christian religion.

jet[1] /dʒet/ *n* [C] **1** fast, strong stream of gas liquid, steam or flame, forced out of a small opening: *The pipe burst and a jet of water shot across the kitchen.* **ˌjet-proˋpulsion (engine),** propulsion of aircraft and spacecraft by engines that suck in air at the front, mix the air with gases, and send out the hot, burnt gases in jets at the back. Hence, **ˌjet ˋaircraft/ˋairliner, ˌjet-ˋfighter, ˌjet-proˋpelled,**

etc. ⇨ the illus at **air**. **the 'jet set**, wealthy persons who often travel by jet aircraft for holidays. **2** (*pl*) (often a brief but repeated) stream of liquid, gas, etc: *He cut his wrist so badly that jets of blood spurted out.* **3** narrow opening from which a jet comes out: *a 'gas-jet.* □ *vi,vt* (**-tt-**) **1** come, send out, in a jet or jets. **2** travel by jet airliner.

jet[2] /dʒet/ *n* [U] hard, black mineral that takes a brilliant polish, used for buttons, ornaments, etc; the colour of this mineral; (attrib) made of jet; (also **ˌjet-'black**) deep, glossy black.

jet·sam /'dʒetsəm/ *n* [U] goods thrown overboard from a ship at sea to lighten it, e g in a storm; such goods washed up on the seashore. **flotsam and ~**, (fig use) persons whose lives have been wrecked: *Sick and starving refugees are the flotsam and ~ of war.*

jet·ti·son /'dʒetɪsn/ *vt* [VP6A] throw (goods) overboard in order to lighten a ship, e g during a storm; abandon, discard (what is unwanted): *~ a ship/an aircraft.*

jetty /'dʒetɪ/ *n* (*pl* **-ties**) structure built out into a body of water as a breakwater or as a landing-place for ships and boats.

Jew /dʒu/ *n* person of the Hebrew race or religion. **Jew·ess** /dʒu'es *US:* 'dʒuɪs/ *n* female Jew. **Jew·ish** /'dʒuɪʃ/ *adj* of the Jews.

jewel /'dʒuḷ/ *n* **1** precious stone, e g a diamond or a ruby; ornament with a ~ or ~s set in it. **2** artificial diamond: *This watch has 15 ~s.* **3** (fig) sth or sb highly valued: *His wife is a ~.* □ *vt* (**-ll-**, US **-l-**) adorn with ~s: (usu in *pp*) *a ~led ring; a ~led watch,* with industrial, not gem diamonds, in the movement. **~·ler**, (US = **~er**) /'dʒuḷə(r)/ *n* trader in ~s; person who sells ~s. **~ry, ~·lery** /'dʒuḷrɪ/ *n* [U] ~s collectively, i e precious stones, ornaments set with ~s, etc.

Jeze·bel /'dʒezəbl *US:* -bel/ *n* (as a term of abuse) shameless, immoral woman.

jib[1] /dʒɪb/ *n* **1** small triangular sail (in front of the mainsail). **ˌjib-'boom** *n* spar to which the lower part of a jib is fastened. ⇨ the illus at **barque**, **sail**. ***the cut of his jib***, his personal appearance. **2** projecting arm of a crane or derrick. ⇨ the illus at **crane**.

jib[2] /dʒɪb/ *vi* (**-bb-**) [VP2A] (of a horse, etc) stop suddenly; refuse to go forwards; (fig) refuse to proceed: *On seeing the gate the horse jibbed.* [VP3A] ***jib at***, (fig) show unwillingness or dislike: *He jibbed at working overtime every day. My small car sometimes jibs at a steep hill.*

jibe /dʒɑɪb/ *vi* = **gibe**.

jiffy /'dʒɪfɪ/ *n* (colloq) moment. ***in a ~***, very soon.

jig[1] /dʒɪg/ *n* [C] **1** (music for a) quick, lively dance. **2** appliance that holds a piece of work and guides the tools that are used on it. □ *vi,vt* (**-gg-**) **1** [VP2A,C] dance a jig. **2** [VP15B,2C] move up and down in a quick, jerky way: *jigging up and down in excitement; jig a baby (up and down) on one's knees.* **'jig·saw** *n* = machine fretsaw. **'jigsaw puzzle** *n* picture, map, etc pasted on thin board or wood and cut in irregularly shaped pieces which are to be fitted together again.

jig·ger /'dʒɪgə(r)/ *n* **1** flea or other parasite that burrows under the skin; (in England) harvest mite. **2** small measure for liquor (esp spirits), as fitted to bottles in bars.

jig·gered /'dʒɪgəd/ *adj* (*pred* only, colloq) **1** amazed: *Well, I'm ~!* **2** exhausted.

jig·gery-po·kery /ˌdʒɪgərɪ 'pəʊkərɪ/ *n* [U] (colloq) hocus-pocus; humbug.

ji·had /dʒɪ'hɑd/ *n* religious war by Muslims against unbelievers.

jilt /dʒɪlt/ *vt* [VP6A] (usu of a woman) give up, send away, a man after giving him encouragement or a promise to marry: *When he lost his job, she ~ed him.* □ *n* woman who ~s a man.

Jim Crow /ˌdʒɪm 'krəʊ/ *n* ⚠ (US) contemptuous name for a Negro: *~ car*, public vehicle set apart for use of Negroes.

ji·miny /'dʒɪmənɪ/ *int* (colloq) exclamation of surprise.

jim-jams /'dʒɪm dʒæmz/ *n pl* (sl) (with *def art*) ***have/get the ~***, be/be made nervous: *He gives me the ~.*

jimmy /'dʒɪmɪ/ *n* (US) = **jemmy**.

jingle /'dʒɪŋgl/ *n* [C] **1** metallic clinking or ringing sound (as of coins, keys or small bells). **2** series of the same or similar sounds in words, esp when designed to attract the attention; jingling verse. □ *vt,vi* **1** [VP6A,15B,2A,C] (cause to) make a light, ringing sound: *He ~d his keys. The money in his pocket ~d.* **2** [VP2A] (of verse) be full of alliterations and rhymes that make it easy to learn and remember.

jingo /'dʒɪŋgəʊ/ *n* (*pl* **-goes** /-gəʊz/) person who combines excessive patriotism with contempt for other countries, esp one who supports a warlike policy. ***By ~!*** (dated sl) exclamation of surprise, pleasure, etc or giving emphasis to a statement. **~·ism** /-ɪzm/ *n* attitude of mind, principles of, ~es. **~·ist** /-ɪst/ *n* **~·is·tic** /ˌdʒɪŋgəʊ'ɪstɪk/ *adj* characteristic of ~es.

jinks /'dʒɪŋks/ *n* [U] (only in) ***high ~***, noisy merrymaking; uncontrolled fun.

jinn /dʒɪn/ *n* = **genie**.

jin·rik·sha (US also **jin·rick·sha**) /ˌdʒɪn'rɪkʃɔ/ *n* = **rickshaw**.

jinx /dʒɪŋks/ *n* (sl) person or thing that brings bad luck. ***put a ~ on sb***, do sth to bring him bad luck.

jit·ney /'dʒɪtnɪ/ *n* (US colloq) **1** (old use) nickel. **2** motor-bus that carries passengers at low fares.

jit·ters /'dʒɪtəz/ *n pl* (sl) extreme nervousness: *have/get/give sb the ~.* **jit·ter-bug** /'dʒɪtə bʌg/ *n* **1** (person who participated in a) lively, popular dance of the 1940's to swing music. **2** (old use) flustered person. **jit·tery** /'dʒɪtərɪ/ *adj* nervous; frightened.

jiu-jitsu /ˌdʒu'dʒɪtsu/ *n* (older, now dated form of) judo.

jive /dʒɑɪv/ *n* (sl) style of popular music with a strong beat; dancing to this. □ *vi* dance to ~ music.

job[1] /dʒob/ *n* **1** piece of work, either to be done, or completed: *Your new Bentley car is a lovely job,* is magnificent. ***on the job***, (colloq) at work; busy. ***be paid by the job***, separately for each job. ***make a good/fine job of sth***, do it well. ***odd jobs***, bits of work not connected with one another. ***an odd-'job man***, one who makes a living by doing any bits of work he is asked to do. **2** ***a good job***, (colloq) a fortunate state of affairs: *He lost his seat in Parliament, and a good job, too!* ***give sb/sth up as a bad job***, (colloq) decide that sb/sth is hopeless. ***make the best of a bad job***, do what one can in spite of difficulties, bad tools, etc. **3** ***be/have a (hard) job doing/to do sth***, be/have a difficult task: *It's a (hard) job for a poor man to keep his wife and children decently dressed. You'll have a job convincing your wife that you* *were really detained at the office.* **4** (colloq) employment; position: *He has a job as a bus-driver. He has lost his job.* ***out of a job,*** unemployed. ***jobs for the boys,*** (sl) positions for one's political supporters, friends, etc. **5** ***a job lot,*** a collection of miscellaneous articles, bought together. **6** (colloq) ***just the job,*** exactly what is wanted. **7** (sl) sth done by intrigue or dishonesty for private profit or advantage: *a put-up job.* ⇨ *put-up* at put[1](11). **8** (sl) criminal act, esp theft: *He got three years for a job he did in Leeds.*

job[2] /dʒɒb/ *vt,vi* **1** [VP2A] ⇨ 1 above; do odd jobs: *a jobbing gardener,* one who works for several employers and is paid by the hour/day: *a jobbing printer,* one who prints leaflets, posters, etc. **2** [VP6A] (on the Stock Exchange) act as a broker; buy, sell (stocks and shares) for others. **3** [VP2A] use a position of trust for private advantage or for the benefit of one's friends; [VP14] *He jobbed his brother into a well-paid post.* **job·ber** *n* **1** dealer in Stock Exchange securities. ⇨ broker. **2** person who jobs(1). **3** person who jobs(3). **job·bery** /ˋdʒɒbərɪ/ *n* [U] jobbing; (esp) use of unfair means to gain private advantage.

Job /dʒəʊb/ *n* (from Job in the Book of Job in the Old Testament) person of great patience: *She would try the patience of Job,* is very difficult to endure, very vexatious. **a Job's comforter,** one who aggravates the distress of the person he is supposed to be comforting.

jockey /ˋdʒɒkɪ/ *n* (*pl* -keys) professional rider in horse-races. ⇨ also disc. **ˋJ~ Club,** club that controls horse-racing in England. □ *vt,vi* [VP15A,3A] trick; cheat: *He ~ed Green out of his job.* ***~ for position,*** (a) (in racing) jostle other riders in order to get a more favourable position. (b) (fig) try by skilful management, by tricky manœuvring, to gain an advantage.

jo·cose /dʒəʊˋkəʊs/ *adj* (formal) humorous; playful. **~·ly** *adv* **~·ness, jo·cos·ity** /dʒəʊˋkɒsətɪ/ *nn* [U].

jocu·lar /ˋdʒɒkjʊlə(r)/ *adj* humorous; given to joking. **~·ly** *adv* **jocu·lar·ity** /ˌdʒɒkjʊˋlærətɪ/ *n* (*pl* -ties) [U] being ~; [C] ~ act or utterance.

joc·und /ˋdʒɒkənd/ *adj* (liter) merry; cheerful. **~·ity** /dʒəʊˋkʌndətɪ/ *n* (*pl* -ties) [U] being ~; [C] ~ act or utterance.

jodh·purs /ˋdʒɒdpəz/ *n pl* long breeches for horse-riding, close-fitting from the knee to the ankle.

jog /dʒɒg/ *vt,vi* (-gg-) **1** [VP6A,15B] give a slight knock or push to; shake with a push or jerk: *The horse jogged its rider up and down. He jogged my elbow,* touched it, e g to attract my attention, to warn me, etc. ***jog sb's memory,*** try to make him remember or recall sth. **2** [VP15B] cause to move unsteadily, in a shaking manner: *The old bus jogged us up and down on the rough mountain road.* **3** [VP2C] ***jog along/on,*** make slow, patient progress: *We jogged along the bad roads. Matters jog along. We must jog on somehow until business conditions improve.* □ *n* [C] **1** slight push, shake or nudge. **2** (also ˋ**jog-trot**) slow walk or trot.

joggle /ˋdʒɒgl/ *vt,vi* [VP6A,2A] shake, move, by or as if by repeated jerks. □ *n* slight shake.

john /dʒɒn/ *n* (US sl) = toilet(4). ⇨ loo.

John Bull /ˌdʒɒn ˋbʊl/ *n* the English nation; typical Englishman.

joie de vivre /ˌʒwɑ də ˋvivr *with unsyllabic* r/ *n* (F) carefree enjoyment of life.

join /dʒɔɪn/ *vt,vi* **1** [VP6A,14,15A,B] ***~ sth to sth, ~ things together/up,*** put together; unite; connect (two points, things) with a line, rope, bridge, etc: *~ one thing to another; ~ two things together; ~ the pieces together; ~ an island to the mainland* (*with a bridge*)*; ~ two persons in marriage,* make them man and wife. *Where does this stream ~ the Danube?* ***~ battle,*** begin fighting. ***~ hands,*** clasp each other's hands; (fig) combine in an enterprise, etc. ***~ forces (with...),*** unite in action; work together. **2** [VP2A,C] come together; unite: *Parallel lines are, by definition, lines that never ~. Which two rivers ~ at Lyons?* **3** [VP6A] become a member of: *~ the army/one's regiment/a club/a band of robbers.* [VP2C] ***join up,*** (colloq) join the army. **4** [VP6A,15A,3A] ***~ (sb) in sth,*** come into the company of; associate with (sb in sth): *I'll ~ you in a few minutes. Will you ~ us in a walk,* come with us? *Why doesn't Tom ~ in the conversation,* Why is he silent? *May I ~ in* (*the game*)? □ *n* place or line where two things are ~ed: *The two pieces were put together so cleverly that the ~ could not be seen.*

joiner /ˋdʒɔɪnə(r)/ *n* skilled workman who makes the inside woodwork of buildings, etc. ⇨ carpenter, cabinet-maker. **join·ery** *n* [U] work of a ~: *learn ~y; lessons in ~y.*

joint[1] /dʒɔɪnt/ *adj* (attrib only) held or done by, belonging to, two or more persons together: *~ efforts/ownership/responsibility; ~ heirs to a legacy; a ~ account,* bank account in the name of more than one person, e g a husband and wife; *a ~-ˋstock company,* a number of persons who carry on a business with capital contributed by all; *during their ~ lives,* (legal) while they are both (or all) living; *settle a trade dispute by ~ consultation,* e g workers and management. **~·ly** *adv*

joint[2] /dʒɔɪnt/ *n* **1** place, line or surface at which two or more things are joined: *the ~s in a suit of armour.* **2** device or structure by which things, e g lengths of pipe, bones, are joined together: *ˋfinger ~s.* ***out of ~,*** (of bones) dislocated; pushed out of position: *He fell and put his knee out of ~.* ***put sb's ˋnose out of ~,*** (fig) take his place in another's affections or favour; upset or humble sb who is a nuisance. **3** limb (shoulder, leg) or other division of an ox, a sheep, etc which a butcher supplies to customers: *a slice off the ~ and two veg,* e g beef and potato and cabbage. **4** (sl) place visited by low-class people for gambling, drinking or drug-taking. **ˋclip ~,** bar, night-club, etc at which extortionate charges are made (often for services not rendered). **5** (sl) cigarette containing a drug such as marijuana.

joint[3] /dʒɔɪnt/ *vt* [VP6A] **1** provide with a joint or joints(2): *a ~ed fishing-rod/doll.* **2** divide at a ~ or into ~s(3).

join·ture /ˋdʒɔɪntʃə(r)/ *n* [C] (legal) property settled on a woman during her marriage, to be used by her after her husband's death.

joist /dʒɔɪst/ *n* one of the parallel pieces of timber (from wall to wall) to which floorboards are fastened; steel beam supporting a floor or ceiling laths.

joke /dʒəʊk/ *n* sth said or done to cause amusement; circumstances that causes amusement. ***have a ~ with sb,*** share one with him. ***make a ~ about sb or sth,*** speak lightly or amusingly about. ***play a ~ on sb,*** cause him to be the victim of a ~. ***a practical ~,*** a trick played on sb in order to make him appear ridiculous. ***It's no ~,***

It's a serious matter. ***the ~ of the village/town, etc,*** the laughing-stock; person, event, etc which causes great amusement. □ *vi* [VP2A,C] make ~s: *He's always joking. I was only joking.* **jok·ing·ly** *adv* in a joking manner.

joker /ˈdʒəʊkə(r)/ *n* **1** person who is fond of making jokes. **2** (sl) fellow. **3** extra playing card (the 53rd) which is used in some games as the highest trump.

jolly /ˈdʒolɪ/ *adj* (-ier, -iest) joyful; gay; merry; slightly drunk. ˌ**J~ ˈRoger,** pirate's black flag (with skull and crossbones). □ *adv* (GB colloq) very: *I'll take ~ good care not to lend him money again.* □ *vt* [VP6A,15A,B] (colloq) keep (sb) in a good humour (esp in order to win his co-operation): *They jollied me along until I agreed to help them.* **jol·li·fi·ca·tion** /ˌdʒolɪfɪˈkeɪʃn/ *n* [U] merry-making; festivity; [C] instance of this. **jol·lity** /ˈdʒolətɪ/ *n* [U] state of being ~.

jolly·boat /ˈdʒolɪbəʊt/ *n* kind of ship's boat.

jolt /dʒəʊlt/ *vt,vi* [VP6A,15A,B,2A,C] give a jerk or jerks to; shake up; (of a vehicle) move along by jerks: *The old bus ~ed us as it went over the stony road. The bus ~ed along.* □ *n* jerk; sudden bump or shake. **~y** *adj* ~ing.

Jo·nah /ˈdʒəʊnə/ *n* person whose presence seems to bring ill luck; person who is sacrificed lest he should bring ill luck.

jon·quil /ˈdʒoŋkwɪl/ *n* kind of narcissus.

joss /dʒos/ *n* (in China) carving in stone, etc, of a god. ˈ**~-house** *n* temple. ˈ**~-stick** *n* stick of incense.

josser /ˈdʒosə(r)/ *n* (GB sl) fool; fellow.

jostle /ˈdʒosl/ *vt,vi* [VP6A,2C] push roughly (against); push: *We were ~d by the crowd. The pickpocket ~d against me in the crowd.*

jot[1] /dʒot/ *n* (usu with *neg*) small amount: *There's not a jot of truth in the story,* no truth at all.

jot[2] /dʒot/ *vt* (-tt-) [VP15B] ***jot sth down,*** make a quick written note of: *The policeman jotted down my name and address.* ˈ**jot·ter** *n* notebook or pad for rough notes. ˈ**jot·tings** *n pl* notes jotted down; memoranda.

joule /dʒul/ *n* (electr) (abbr **J**) unit of energy or work.

jour·nal /ˈdʒɜnl/ *n* **1** daily newspaper; other periodical: *the Ladies' Home J~; the Economic J~.* **2** daily record of news, events, business accounts, etc. **~·ese** /ˌdʒɜnlˈiz/ *n* [U] style of English composition full of clichés, common in some ~s, e g the use of 'prior to interment' for 'before burial'. **~·ism** /-ɪzm/ *n* [U] work of writing for, editing, or publishing ~s. **~·ist** /-ɪst/ *n* person engaged in ~ism. **~·is·tic** /ˌdʒɜnlˈɪstɪk/ *adj* of ~ism; characteristic of ~ism.

jour·ney /ˈdʒɜnɪ/ *n* (*pl* -neys) (distance travelled (esp on land) in) going to a place, esp a distant place: *reach one's ~'s end; go/come/send sb on a ~; make a ~ half-way round the world.* ⇨ **flight**[1]**(2), voyage.** □ *vi* [VP2A,C] travel; make a ~.

jour·ney·man /ˈdʒɜnɪmən/ *n* (*pl* -men /-mən/) skilled workman who works for a master (contrasted with an *apprentice*).

joust /dʒaʊst/ *vi, n* (engage in a) fight on horse-back with lances (as between knights in the Middle Ages).

Jove /dʒəʊv/ *n* Jupiter, esp ***By ~!*** (as an exclamation of surprise, etc).

jov·ial /ˈdʒəʊvɪəl/ *adj* full of fun and good humour; merry: *a ~ fellow; in a ~ mood.* **~ly** /-ɪəlɪ/ *adv* **~·ity** /ˌdʒəʊvɪˈælətɪ/ *n* [U] being ~; good humoured behaviour; (*pl;* -ties) ~ acts or utterances.

jowl /dʒaʊl/ *n* jaw; lower part of the face: *a man with a heavy ~/a heavy-jowled man,* one with heavy jaws, a fold or folds of flesh hanging from the chin. ***cheek by ~,*** ⇨ **cheek(1).**

joy /dʒɔɪ/ *n* **1** [U] deep pleasure; great gladness: *I wish you joy. We heard with joy that she had escaped injury. He has been a good friend to me, both in joy and in sorrow. They danced/jumped for joy,* because they were full of joy. ˈ**joy-bells** *n pl* bells rung to celebrate a happy occasion. ˈ**joy-ride** *n* (sl) ride in a motor-car, esp in one taken for fun and thrills. ˈ**joy-stick** *n* (sl) control lever on an aircraft. **2** [C] sth that gives joy; occasion of great happiness: *the joys and sorrows of life.* □ *vi* (poet) rejoice: *joy in a friend's success.* **joy·ful** /-fl/ *adj* filled with, showing, causing, joy. **joy·fully** /-flɪ/ *adj* **joy·less** *adj* without joy; gloomy; sad. **joy·less·ly** *adv* **joy·ful·ness, joy·less·ness** *nn* **joy·ous** /ˈdʒɔɪəs/ *adj* full of joy. **joy·ous·ly** *adv* **joy·ous·ness** *n*

ju·bi·lant /ˈdʒubɪlənt/ *adj* (formal) triumphant; showing joy. **~·ly** *adv* **ju·bi·la·tion** /ˌdʒubɪˈleɪʃn/ *n* [U] rejoicing; [C] occasion of this.

ju·bi·lee /ˈdʒubɪli/ *n* [C] (celebration of a special anniversary of some event, e g a wedding. ˈ**diamond ~,** 60th anniversary. ˈ**golden ~,** 50th anniversary. ˈ**silver ~,** 25th anniversary.

Ju·da·ism /ˈdʒudeɪɪzm *US:* -dɪɪzm/ *n* the religion of the Jewish people; their culture and social way of life. **Ju·daic** /dʒuˈdeɪɪk/ *adj* of Jews and ~.

Judas /ˈdʒudəs/ *n* (from ~ who betrayed Jesus Christ; ⇨ Mark 3: 19) betrayer; traitor.

jud·der /ˈdʒʌdə(r)/ *vi* shudder violently.

judge[1] /dʒʌdʒ/ *n* **1** (of God) supreme arbiter; public officer with authority to hear and decide cases in a law court: *~-made law,* principles based on ~s' decisions, not statute law; *as grave as a ~.* ⇨ **justice(3,4), magistrate.** **2** person who decides in a contest, competition, dispute, etc: *the ~s at a flower show.* **3** person qualified and able to give opinions on merits and values: *a good ~ of horses. He says the diamonds are not genuine; but then, he's no ~,* does not know much about diamonds. **4** (in Hebrew history) officer given temporary authority as ruler in the period between Joshua and the Kings. **J~s,** the book of the Old Testament recording this period.

judges

judge /dʒʌdʒ/ *vt,vi* (*pres part* judging) **1** [VP6A, 2A] act as a judge(1); hear and try (cases) in a law court: *God will ~ all men.* **2** [VP6A,2A] give a decision (in a competition, etc): *Who is going to ~ the roses at the Flower Show? Will you ~ at the Baby Show next week?* **3** [VP6A,9,10,22,25, 2A,3A] estimate; consider; form an opinion about: *I ~d him to be about 50. I can't ~ whether he was* *right or wrong. I ~d, from his manner, that he was guilty. The committee ~d it better to postpone the meeting. Don't ~ (of) a man by his looks. Judging from what you say, he ought to succeed.*

judge·ment (US, and in GB legal use **judg·ment**) /ˈdʒʌdʒmənt/ *n* **1** [U] judging or being judged: *sit in ~ on a case,* (in a law court); *pass ~ on a prisoner,* give a decision after trial. **the ˈDay of ˋJ~,** (also **ˋJ~ Day, the ˈLast ˋJ~**) the day when God will judge all men. **2** [C] decision of a judge or court: *The ~ was in his favour.* **3** [U] process of judging: *an error of ~. His ~ was at fault.* **4** [U] good sense; ability to judge(2,3): *a man of ~. He showed excellent ~ in choosing a wife.* **5** [C] misfortune considered to be a punishment from God: *Your failure is a ~ on you for being so lazy.* **6** [C,U] opinion: *in my ~; in the ~ of most people.*

ju·di·ca·ture /ˈdʒudɪkətʃə(r)/ *n* **1** [U] administration of justice: *the Supreme Court of J~,* full title of the English Courts of Justice. **2** [C] body of judges.

ju·di·cial /dʒuˋdɪʃl/ *adj* **1** of or by a court of justice; of a judge or of judgement: *the ~ bench,* the judges; *take/bring ~ proceedings against sb,* bring a law case against him: *a ~ separation,* the right to separate from a husband or wife, granted by a judge, usu with arrangements favourable to the wronged person concerning money or children; *~ murder,* legal but unjust sentence of death. **2** critical; impartial: *a man with a ~ mind.* **~ly** /-ʃlɪ/ *adv*

ju·dici·ary /dʒuˋdɪʃərɪ *US:* -ʃierɪ/ *n* (*pl* **-ries**) **1** the judges of a State collectively. **2** the system of law courts in a country.

ju·di·cious /dʒuˋdɪʃəs/ *adj* (formal) showing or having good sense. **~·ly** *adv* **~·ness** *n*

judo /ˈdʒudəʊ/ *n* [U] Japanese art of wrestling and self-defence in which an opponent's own weight and strength are used against him.

jug[1] /dʒʌg/ *n* **1** deep vessel with a handle and lip; the contents of such a vessel: *a ˋmilk-jug; drink a jug of milk.* **2** (sl) prison. **jug·ful** /-fʊl/ *n* (*pl* **jug-fuls**).

jug[2] /dʒʌg/ *vt* (**-gg-**) [VP6A] **1** (usu in *pp*) stew or boil (hare, etc) in a jug or jar: *jugged hare.* **2** (colloq) imprison.

jug·ger·naut /ˈdʒʌgənɔt/ *n* **1** (fig) cause or belief to which persons are sacrificed or to which they sacrifice themselves: *the ~ of war.* **2** (colloq) huge long-distance transport vehicle.

juggle /ˈdʒʌgl/ *vi,vt* **1** [VP2A,3A] **~ *(with),*** do tricks, perform (with balls, plates, etc) to amuse people; play tricks (with facts, figures, etc) to deceive people. **2** [VP6A,16A] play tricks with; deceive: *The manager ~d his figures to make it seem that the company was prosperous.* **jug·gler** *n* person who ~s.

jugu·lar /ˈdʒʌgjʊlə(r)/ *adj* of the neck or throat: *~ veins,* the large veins of the neck, returning blood from the head to the heart.

juice /dʒus/ *n* [C,U] **1** fluid part of fruits, vegetables and meat: *a glass of ˋorange ~; a mixture of ˋfruit ~s.* **2** fluid in organs of the body: *gastric/digestive ~s,* those that help to digest food. **3** (colloq) electricity, petrol or other source of power.

juicy /ˈdʒusɪ/ *adj* (**-ier, -iest**) **1** containing much juice: *~ oranges.* **2** (colloq) interesting (esp because scandalous, etc). **juici·ness** *n*

ju-jitsu /ˈdʒu ˋdʒɪtsu/ *n* Japanese art of self-defence from which judo was developed.

juju /ˈdʒudʒu/ *n* West African charm or fetish; its magic power.

ju·jube /ˈdʒudʒub/ *n* [C] lozenge of gelatin, flavoured and sweetened.

juke-box /ˈdʒuk bɒks/ *n* [C] coin-operated record-player in cafés, amusement arcades, etc.

ju·lep /ˈdʒulɪp/ *n* **1** sweet drink, esp one in which medicine is taken. **2** (US) spirit (e g whisky), mint and ice: *mint ~.*

Jul·ian /ˈdʒulɪən/ *adj* of Julius Caesar: *the ~ calendar,* the calendar introduced by him in Rome in 46 BC.

July /dʒuˋlaɪ/ *n* seventh month of the year.

jumble /ˈdʒʌmbl/ *vi,vt* [VP15B,2C] **~ *(up),*** mix, be mixed, in a confused way: *The untidy girl's toys, books, shoes and clothes were all ~d up together in the cupboard.* □ *n* confused mixture; muddle. **ˋ~-sale** *n* sale of a mixed collection of old or second-hand articles, usu for charity.

jumbo /ˈdʒʌmbəʊ/ *n* (attrib use) unusually large: *~ jets; ~-sized.*

jump[1] /dʒʌmp/ *n* **1** act of jumping; sudden spring from the ground. **the ˋlong/ˋhigh ~,** athletic competitions in which competitors jump over distance/height. **2** sudden movement caused by fear. ***give sb a ~,*** frighten him. **the ~s,** (colloq) form of nervous excitement with uncontrollable bodily movements. **3** sudden rise in amount, price, value, etc: *a ~ in car exports.* **jumpy** *adj* (**-ier, -iest**) excited and nervous. **~i·ness** *n*

jump[2] /dʒʌmp/ *vi,vt* **1** [VP2A,C] move quickly by the sudden use of the muscles of the legs or (of fish) the tail; rise suddenly (from a seat, etc); move quickly (*into* sth): *~ to one's feet; ~ over a fence; ~ up out of one's chair; ~ into a taxi,* enter one quickly; (fig) *~ from one subject to another in a speech.* ***~ down sb's throat,*** answer, interrupt, him violently. **ˈ~ing-ˋoff place,** starting point. **2** [VP6A] pass over by moving in this way: *~ a ditch;* cause (a horse, etc) to move in this way: *~ a horse over a fence.* ***~ the rails/track,*** (of a train, tram, etc) leave the rails suddenly. **3** [VP2A,C] move with a jerk or jerks from excitement, joy, etc; start suddenly: *~ for joy; ~ up and down in excitement. Her heart ~ed when she heard the news.* **4** [VP2A,C] rise suddenly in price: *Gold shares ~ed on the Stock Exchange yesterday.* **5** ***~ at,*** accept eagerly: *~ at an offer.* ***~ to conclusions,*** reach them hastily. ***ˈ~ ˋto it,*** act quickly or promptly. ***~ (up)on,*** attack, reprove severely; scold: *The teacher ~ed on the inattentive pupil.* ***~ on the bandwagon,*** ⇨ band(5). **6** ***~ one's bail,*** fail to surrender to one's bail; abscond. ⇨ bail[1]. ***~ a claim,*** (colloq) take possession of land or mining rights, e g in a new goldfield, to which another person has already established a claim. ***~ the gun,*** start too soon (as from the use of a shot to start a race). ***~ the queue,*** (fig) obtain sth without waiting for one's proper turn. ***~ a train,*** travel illegally by goods train, e g by riding in or under a closed wagon.

jumper /ˈdʒʌmpə(r)/ *n* **1** outer loose-fitting garment worn by women, or, made of cloth, by sailors, pulled on over the head and coming down to the hips; (US) pinafore. **2** person, animal or insect, that jumps.

junc·tion /ˈdʒʌŋkʃn/ *n* **1** [U] joining or being joined; [C] instance of this: *The allied armies hope to effect a ~,* meet and unite. **2** [C] place where roads; railway lines or sections of an electrical circuit meet or diverge.

junc·ture /ˋdʒʌŋktʃə(r)/ *n* [C] (formal) **1** junction(**3**). **2** state of affairs, esp the phrase: ***at this ~,*** at this time, when affairs are/were in this state.

June /dʒun/ *n* sixth month of the year.

jungle /ˋdʒʌŋgl/ *n* **1** (usu with *def art, sing* or *pl*) (land covered with) thickly growing underwood and tangled vegetation: *cut a path through the ~; ~ warfare; ~ birds and animals; ˋ~ fever,* malarial fever. ***the law of the ~,*** (fig) ruthless competition or exploitation. **2** (in compounds) *ˋ~-cat, ˋ~-fowl.* **jun·gly** /ˋdʒʌŋglɪ/ *adj* of, like, from the ~ or its inhabitants.

jun·ior /ˋdʒunɪə(r)/ *n, adj* **1** (person) younger, lower in rank, than another: *a ~ high school; ~ dress sizes. He is my ~ by two years. He is the ~ partner in the firm. Tom Brown, Junior* (or abbr to *Jun, Jnr* or *Jr*), used of a son having the same first name as his father, or the younger of two boys of the same surname in a school, etc. **2** (US schools and colleges) student in his third year (of four).

ju·ni·per /ˋdʒunɪpə(r)/ *n* evergreen shrub with dark berries from which an oil is obtained (*oil of ~*), used in medicine, etc.

junk[1] /dʒʌŋk/ *n* [U] old, discarded things of little or no value: *an attic full of ~; a ~ dealer/shop.*

junk[2] /dʒʌŋk/ *n* [C] flat-bottomed Chinese sailing-vessel.

a junk

junket /ˋdʒʌŋkɪt/ *n* **1** [C,U] (dish of) milk curdled by the addition of acid, often sweetened and flavoured. **2** social gathering for a feast; picnic. □ *vi* take part in a ~(**2**). Hence, **~·ing** *n* feasting; merrymaking.

junkie, junky /ˋdʒʌŋkɪ/ *n* (sl) drug (esp heroin) addict.

Juno·esque /ˈdʒunəʊˋesk/ *adj* (of a woman) having a stately beauty (like the goddess Juno).

junta /ˋdʒʌntə *US:* ˋhʊntə/ *n* (in Spain and Italy) deliberative or administrative council; group of army officers who have seized power by a coup d'état.

junto /ˋdʒʌntəʊ/ *n* (*pl* -tos /-təʊz/) body of men who combine secretly for political purposes; faction; clique.

Jupi·ter /ˋdʒupɪtə(r)/ *n* (ancient Rome) ruler of gods and men; largest planet of the solar system. ⇨ the illus at **planet**.

ju·ridi·cal /dʒʊˋrɪdɪkl/ *adj* of law or legal proceedings.

ju·ris·dic·tion /ˈdʒʊərɪsˋdɪkʃn/ *n* [U] administration of justice; legal authority; right to exercise this; extent of this: *The courts have ~ not only over our own citizens but over foreigners living here. This matter does not come/fall within our ~,* We have no authority to deal with it.

ju·ris·pru·dence /ˈdʒʊərɪsˋprudns/ *n* [U] science and philosophy of human law.

jur·ist /ˋdʒʊərɪst/ *n* expert in law.

juror /ˋdʒʊərə(r)/ *n* member of a jury.

jury /ˋdʒʊərɪ/ *n* (*pl* -ries) [C] **1** body of persons (in US and GB twelve) who swear to give a true decision (*a verdict*) on issues of fact in a case in a court of justice: *trial by ~. The ~ found the prisoner not guilty.* **ˋ~-box** *n* enclosure for a ~ in court. **2** **grand ~,** specially chosen body of 12 to 23 persons who (until 1933) inquired into a charge in order to decide whether there was enough evidence to justify a trial or whether the case should be abandoned. **coroner's ~,** one that decides the cause of a death (if unnatural death, e g suicide or murder, is suspected). **3** body of persons chosen to give a decision or make an award in a competition; (fig) *the ~ of public opinion,* the public, thought of as a ~, deciding a question. **~·man** /-mən/ (*pl* -men) *n*

jury-mast /ˋdʒʊərɪ mɑst *US:* mæst/ *n* temporary mast put up in place of one that is broken or lost overboard.

just[1] /dʒʌst/ *adj* **1** fair; in accordance with what is right: *a ~ man; a ~ sentence; be ~ to a person.* **2** well deserved; fairly earned: *get/receive one's ~ deserts,* be rewarded or punished as one deserves. **3** reasonable; based on reasonable grounds: *a ~ opinion; ~ suspicions.* **~·ly** *adv* **~·ness** *n*

just[2] /dʒʌst/ *adv* **1** used (GB) in the perfect tenses and (US often) with the simple past tense, placed with the *v*, to indicate an immediate past: (GB) *I've ~ had dinner.* (US) *I ~ had dinner.* Cf *I had dinner an hour ago. My son had ~ left school.* **2** (followed by *nn, n phrases* and *clauses*) exactly; precisely: *It's ~ two o'clock. This is ~ what I wanted. That's ~ what I was going to say. J~ my luck! J~ the thing!* **3** **~ as** (*adj*) **as,** (**a**) exactly as: *Leave everything ~ as* (*tidy as*) *you find it. Come ~ as you are,* Do not make any special preparations. *This is ~* (= quite) *as good as the other.* (**b**) (introducing adverbials of time) when: *He arrived ~ as I was about to go out/~ as I was shaving.* (**c**) (introducing clauses of comparison) in the same way as: *J~ as you find it difficult to like Mr Green, so I find it easy to like his wife.* **4** (with *v*) exactly: *~ here/there.* **5** (used to indicate approximation) more or less: *I've had ~ about enough of your impudence,* almost more than I can endure. *Put it ~ over there,* near that place. *It's ~ about tall enough,* will be satisfactory. **6** at this, that very moment: *We're ~ off/going/about to start. His new book is ~ out/~ published.* **~ now,** (**a**) at this moment: *I'm busy ~ now.* (**b**) a short time ago: *Tom came in ~ now—he's probably upstairs.* **7** (often preceded by *only*) barely: *We* (*only*) *~ caught the train,* almost missed it. *Jane ~ managed to pass the exam.* Cf She *almost* failed. *I've ~ enough money to last me till pay-day.* **8** (used in familiar, colloquial style, esp with imperatives, to call attention to sth, sometimes to soften what follows): *J~ listen to him! and note how clever/silly/amusing, etc he is. J~ taste this!* (so that you may judge its quality, say whether it is right, etc). *J~ feel it!* and note how hard, soft, smooth, etc it is! *J~* (= Please) *come here a moment. J~ a moment, please.* Please wait a moment. **9** only; merely: *He's ~ an ordinary man. I've come here ~* (= on purpose) *to see you. Would you walk five miles ~ to see a film?* **10** (colloq) absolutely: *The concert was ~ splendid. 'Did you enjoy yourselves?'—'I should ~ say we did!'* or *Didn't we ~!'* (emph) We had a most enjoyable time.

jus·tice /ˈdʒʌstɪs/ *n* **1** [U] just conduct; the quality of being right and fair: *treat all men with* ~. ***in*** ~ ***to***, in order to be just to. ***do*** ~ ***to***, treat fairly; show that one has a just opinion of, that one realizes the value of: *To do him* ~, *we must admit that his intentions were good. He did* ~ *to the dinner*, showed by eating heartily, that the food was good. ***do oneself*** ~, behave in a way that is worthy of one's abilities: *You're not doing yourself* ~, You could do much better if you tried. **2** [U] the law and its administration: *a court of* ~; ***bring sb to*** ~, arrest, try and sentence sb (a criminal). **3** [C] judge of the Supreme Courts: *the Lord Chief J*~; *the Lords J*~*s; the Chief J*~ *of England; Mr J*~ *Smith*. **4** **ˈJ~ of the ˈPeace,** a magistrate. **Department of J~,** (US) executive department, headed by the Attorney General, supervising internal security, naturalization, immigration, etc.

jus·tici·ary /dʒʌˈstɪʃərɪ *US:* -ʃɪerɪ/ *n* (*pl* -ries) (jurisdiction of a) judge or chief justice: (in Scotland) *the High Court of J*~.

jus·tify /ˈdʒʌstɪfaɪ/ *vt* (*pt,pp* -fied) [VP6A,19C] **1** show that (a person, statement, act, etc) is right, reasonable or proper: *The Prime Minister justified the action of the Government. You can hardly* ~ *such conduct. You'd be hard put to it to* ~ *your behaviour.* **2** be a good reason for: *Your wish to go for a walk does not* ~ *your leaving the baby alone in the house.* **3** adjust (a line of type) to fill a space neatly. **jus·ti·fi·able** /ˈdʒʌstɪˈfaɪəbl/ *adj* that can be justified: *justifiable homicide.* **jus·ti·fi·ably** /-əblɪ/ *adv* **jus·ti·fi·ca·tion** /ˌdʒʌstɪfɪˈkeɪʃn/ *n* [U] **1** sth that justifies: *His justification for stealing was that his children were starving.* **2** the act of ~ing sth. **3** the state of being free from blame: *It can be said in justification for what he had done that....*

jut /dʒʌt/ *vi* (-tt-) [VP2C] ***jut out,*** stand out from; be out of line (from what is around): *The soldier saw a gun jutting out from a bush. The balcony juts out over the garden.*

jute /dʒut/ *n* [U] fibre from the outer skin of certain plants, used for making canvas, rope, etc: *the* ~ *mills of Bangladesh.*

ju·ven·ile /ˈdʒuvənaɪl/ *n* young person. □ *adj* of, characteristic of, suitable for, ~s: ~ *books; a* ~ *appearance; a* ~ *court,* where children are tried; ~ *delinquency,* law-breaking by young people; ~ *delinquent,* young offender: *a* ~ *sense of humour,* e g in an adult.

jux·ta·pose /ˈdʒʌkstəˈpəʊz/ *vt* [VP6A] place side by side. **jux·ta·po·si·tion** /ˈdʒʌkstəpəˈzɪʃn/ *n* [U] placing side by side; the state of being placed side by side.

Kk

K, k /keɪ/ (*pl* K's, k's /keɪz/) the 11th letter of the English alphabet.

Kaf·fir, Kafir /ˈkæfə(r)/ *n* ⚠ (colloq) (offensive term for) African person.

Kaiser /ˈkaɪzə(r)/ *n* Emperor (esp of Germany before 1918).

kake·mono /ˈkækɪˈməʊnəʊ/ *n* Japanese painting in a hanging scroll of silk or paper.

kale, kail /keɪl/ *n* kind of curly-leaved cabbage.

ka·leido·scope /kəˈlaɪdəskəʊp/ *n* [C] **1** tube containing mirrors and small, loose pieces of coloured glass. When the tube is turned, constantly changing patterns are seen through the eye-piece. **2** (fig) frequently changing pattern of bright scenes: *Sunlight and shadow made the landscape a* ~ *of colour.* **ka·leido·scopic** /kəˈlaɪdəˈskopɪk/ *adj* quickly changing.

kal·ends /ˈkælendz/ *n pl* ⇨ calends.

kam·pong /ˈkæmpoŋ/ *n* (in Malaysia) enclosed space; village.

kan·ga·roo /ˈkæŋgəˈru/ *n* Australian marsupial that jumps along on its strong hind legs. The female has a pouch in which its young are carried. ⇨ the illus at large. ~ **court,** one set up without authority by workers, prisoners, etc to try someone whom they consider to have acted against their interests.

kao·lin /ˈkeɪəlɪn/ *n* [U] fine white clay used in making porcelain, etc.

ka·pok /ˈkeɪpok/ *n* [U] soft cotton-like material (from seeds of a tropical tree) used for filling cushions, life-belts, mattresses, etc.

ka·put /kəˈpʊt/ *adj* (*pred* only) (G) (sl) done for; ruined; smashed.

karat /ˈkærət/ = carat.

ka·rate /kəˈrɑtɪ/ *n* [U] Japanese method of unarmed combat using blows made with the sides of the hands, foot, head or elbow.

karma /ˈkɑmə/ *n* (in Buddhism) person's acts in one of his successive existences, looked upon as deciding his fate in his next existence.

kava /ˈkɑvə/ *n* [U] (intoxicating drink made from the roots of a) Polynesian shrub.

kayak /ˈkaɪæk/ *n* Eskimo canoe of light wood covered with sealskins; any rigid, canvas-covered, and decked canoe.

ke·bab /kəˈbæb/ *n* (also **ke·bob** /kəˈbob/) dish of small pieces of meat, seasoned and roasted on skewers.

ked·geree /ˈkedʒəri/ *n* [U] rice cooked with fish, eggs, etc.

keel /kil/ *n* timber or steel structure on which the framework of a ship is built up: *lay down a* ~, start the building of a ship. ***(keep) on an even*** ~, (**a**) (of a ship) without movement to one side or the other. (**b**) (fig) steady; steadily; calm(ly). □ *vt,vi* **1** [VP6A] turn (a ship) over on one side to repair it, clean the ~, etc. **2** [VP15B,2C] ~ ***over,*** capsize; upset.

keen[1] /kin/ *adj* (-er, -est) **1** (of points and edges) sharp: *a knife with a* ~ *edge;* (fig) *a* ~ (= cutting) *wind;* ~ *sarcasm.* **2** (of interest, the feelings) strong; deep: *He has a* ~ *interest in his work.* **3** (of the mind, the senses) active; sensitive; sharp: ~ *sight;* ˈ~-ˈ*sighted; a* ~ *intelligence.* **4** (of persons, their character, etc) eager; anxious to do things: *a* ~ *sportsman. He's very* ~ *to see his birthplace again.* ~ ***on,*** (colloq) interested in, fond of, eager: ~ *on going abroad. Mrs Hill is* ~ *on Tom('s) marrying Stella/*~ *that Tom should marry Stella. Tom is not very* ~ *on Stella,* does not like her much. *I'm not very* ~ *on jazz.* **~·ly** *adv* **~·ness** *n*

keen[2] /kin/ *n* Irish funeral song accompanied by

wailing. □ *vi,vt* utter this song; lament (a person) in this way.

keep[1] /kip/ *vt,vi* (*pt,pp* kept /kept/) (For idiomatic uses with *adverbial particles* and *preps*, ⇨ 18 below. For *keep* and *nn* not given here, ⇨ the *n* entries, e g ~ *pace/step (with) sb*, ~ *time*, ~ *watch*, ~ *good/early hours*.) **1** [VP22,15A] cause sb/sth to remain in a specified state or position: ~ *the children quiet/happy. The cold weather kept us indoors. If your hands are cold*, ~ *them in your pockets. Will they* ~ *me in prison/custody? Extra work kept* (= detained) *me at the office. Will you* ~ *these things safe for me?* **~ an eye on,** (colloq) watch over closely: *Please* ~ *an eye on the baby while I'm in the garden.* **~ sth in mind,** remember it: *Do* ~ *it in mind that we expect a report next week.* **~ track of/tabs on/a tab on,** ⇨ track(1), tab(2). **2** [VP19B] cause a process or state to continue: *Please* ~ *the fire burning. I'm sorry I've kept you waiting.* **~ sb going,** help him to continue in some way: *Will £10* ~ *you going until payday*, cover your expenses? *The doctors manage to* ~ *me going*, help me to remain active. **~ the ball rolling,** ⇨ ball[1]. **~ the pot boiling,** ⇨ pot[1](2). **3** [VP14] **~ sb/sth from doing sth,** prevent, hold back, refrain: *What kept you from joining me?* Often shortened to '*What kept you?*'. *We must* ~ *them from getting to know our plans. We must do something to* ~ *the roof from falling in.* [VP3A] **~ from doing sth,** refrain: *I couldn't* ~ *from laughing.* **4** [VP15B,14] **~ sth (back) from,** **(a)** not let others know about it: *She can* ~ *nothing (back) from her friends.* **(b)** hold back; withhold: *They* ~ *back £3 a month from my salary for National Insurance.* **~ sth to oneself,** **(a)** (often *imper*) not express, e g comments, views, etc: *K~/You may* ~ *your remarks to yourself*, I don't want to hear them. **(b)** refuse to share: *He kept the good news to himself.* **~ one's own counsel,** ⇨ counsel[1](1). **~ a secret,** ⇨ secret. **5** [VP6A] (with an implied complement, e g *inviolate*) pay proper respect to; be faithful to; observe; fulfil: ~ *a promise/a treaty/an appointment/the law.* **~ faith with sb,** ⇨ faith. **6** [VP6A] celebrate: ~ *the Sabbath*, i e ~ it sacred; ~ *Christmas/one's birthday.* **7** [VP6A] guard; protect: ~ *goal*, ⇨ goalkeeper; ~ *wicket*, (cricket) stand behind the wicket to stop or catch the ball, ⇨ wicketkeeper. *May God/the Lord bless and* ~ *you*, i e keep you safe. **8** [VP6A] continue to have; have in one's possession and not give away; not lose; preserve, e g for future use or reference: *You may* ~ *this—I don't want it back. K~ the change*, i e from money offered in payment. *Please* ~ *these things for me while I'm away. We'll* ~ *these for another day.* **~ hold of,** **~ a firm/tight hold on,** not let go: *K~ a tight hold on the horse's reins.* **9** [VP6A,15A,22] support; take care of; provide what is needed for; maintain: *Does he earn enough to* ~ *himself and his family? He has a wife and ten children to* ~, *poor fellow! How many servants do they* ~*? She lives with her parents but earns enough to* ~ *herself in clothes*, to buy her own clothes. *He* ~*s sheep in the Highlands. He* ~*s a mistress in Highgate.* Hence (now dated) *a kept women*, one whose needs are provided by a man whose mistress she is. **10** [VP6A] have habitually on sale or in stock: *'Do you sell batteries for transistor sets?'—'Sorry, but we don't* ~ *them'.* **11** **~ house,** be responsible for the housework, cooking, shopping, etc: *His sister* ~*s house for him.* ⇨ *housekeeper* at house[1](4). **~ open house,** be ready to entertain friends, etc at any time. **12** [VP6A] own or manage, esp for profit: ~ *hens/bees/pigs;* ~ *a shop/an inn.* Hence, **ˈshopkeeper, ˈinnkeeper**. **13** [VP6A] make entries in, records of: ~ *a diary;* ~ *accounts*, records of money paid out and received; ~ *books*, = ~ accounts. Hence, **ˈbook-keeper**. **14** [VP2C,D] continue to be, remain, in a specified condition: *If you've got the 'flu, you'd better go to bed and* ~ *warm. Please* ~ *quiet! I hope you're* ~*ing well. K~ cool!* (fig) Don't get excited! **~ fit,** (do physical exercise to) remain in good health: (attrib) ~*-fit classes.* **15** [VP6A,2C,3A] **~ on/to,** continue in a particular direction; remain in a particular relationship to a place, etc: *We kept (on) our way/course all morning. While that big lorry* ~*s (to) the middle of the road, we can't possibly overtake it. K~ straight on until you get to the church. Traffic in Britain* ~*s (to the) left. K~ left*, as a traffic sign. *He was ill and had to* ~ *(to) his bed/the house for weeks. She couldn't* ~ *her seat*, i e on her horse. **16** [VP2E] continue doing sth; do sth frequently or repeatedly: *K~ smiling!* (Often ~ *(on) doing sth*): *Why does she* ~ *(on) giggling? My shoe lace* ~*s (on) coming undone.* **~ going,** not stop; not give up; continue to function: *This is exhausting work, but I manage to* ~ *going. I'm not sure that the company can* ~ *going*, continue in business. **17** [VP2A] (of food) remain in good condition: *Will this meat* ~ *till tomorrow?* Cf ~ *fresh*, ⇨ 14 above. *This news will* ~, (fig) need not be told now, can be told later. **18** [VP2C,3A,14,15B] (uses with *adverbial particles* and *preps*):

keep at sth, work at it: *K~ at it*, Don't give up! **~ sb at sth,** make him work: *K~ them at it!* Don't let them get lazy!

keep away (from), avoid coming/going near (to): *K~ away from the water's edge.* **~ sb/sth away (from),** prevent from going/coming near: *K~ the child away from the water's edge.*

keep back (from), remain in the rear, at the back. **~ sb back,** restrain sb; prevent sb from advancing. **~ sth back,** ⇨ 4 above.

keep sb down, hold in subjection; oppress: ~ *down subject races.* **~ sth down,** **(a)** control: *He couldn't* ~ *down his anger. This chemical will* ~ *the weeds down.* **(b)** limit: *We must* ~ *down expenses.* **(c)** retain: *He couldn't* ~ *his food down*, had to vomit.

keep in, e g of a coal fire in a grate, continue burning: *Will the fire* ~ *in until we get back?* Cf *go out.* **~ in with sb,** remain on good terms with, continue to be friendly with: *You must* ~ *in with your customers*, retain their good will. **~ sb in,** (esp) detain (a child in school) as a punishment. **~ sth in,** **(a)** see that (a fire) continues to burn; ⇨ ~ in, above: *Shall we* ~ *the fire in or let it out?* **(b)** restrain. *He couldn't* ~ *in his indignation.* Cf *burst out.*

keep off, remain at a distance; not come: *if the rain* ~*s off*, if it doesn't start to rain. **~ off sth,** refrain from: *Please* ~ *off that subject*, say nothing about it. *Do please* ~ *off drugs*, Don't use them. **~ sb/sth off,** hold, cause to remain, at a distance: *They made a big fire to* ~ *wild animals off. K~ your hands off.* Don't touch it, me, etc.

keep on (doing sth), continue; persist: ~ *on (working) although one is tired. Don't* ~ *on ask-*

ing silly questions. Why do the dogs ~ on barking? ⇨ also 16 above. ***~ sth on,*** continue to wear: *~ one's hat on.* ***~ your hair on,*** ⇨ hair(1). ***~ one's shirt on,*** ⇨ shirt(1). ***~ sb on,*** continue to employ: *~ an old employee on,* not dismiss her/him. ***~ on at sb,*** worry with repeated complaints, questions, etc.
keep out (of), remain outside: *Danger! K~ out! K~ out of their quarrels,* Don't get involved in them. ***~ sb/sth out (of),*** prevent from entering: *Shut the window and ~ the cold out. K~ that dog out of my study.*
keep to sth, (a) do what one has agreed to do: *He always ~s to his promises/an agreement/his word.* (b) limit oneself to: *keep to the subject/the point at issue.* ***~ (oneself) to oneself,*** avoid meeting people.
keep sb/sth under, control; repress: *The firemen managed to ~ the fire under,* prevented it from spreading. *That boy needs ~ing under,* needs discipline. ***~ sb under observation,*** ⇨ observation(1).
keep up (with), go forward at the same pace or speed as: *Harry couldn't ~ up with the class,* learn as quickly as his fellow pupils. *I can't ~ up with you,* walk as fast as you. ***~ up with the Joneses,*** compete with them (in the purchase of articles, e g clothes, a car, indicating social status). ***~ sb up,*** delay sb from going to bed: *It's wrong to ~ the children up so late,* They should go to bed. *I don't want to ~ you up; you look sleepy and ready for bed.* ***~ sth up,*** (a) prevent from sinking or getting low: *K~ up your courage/spirits. K~ your chin up!* Cheer up, have courage, etc. (b) observe: *~ up old customs.* (c) continue: *They kept up the attack all day.* (d) maintain in proper condition: *How much does it cost you to ~ up your large house and garden?* ***~ up appearances,*** ⇨ appearance. (e) continue; carry on: *~ up a correspondence with an old friend.* ***~ one's end up,*** ⇨ end[1](1). *Do you still ~ up your Greek,* still read the Greek classics? ***~ it up,*** continue without slackening: *He works far too hard; he'll never be able to ~ it up.*

keep[2] /kip/ *n* **1** [U] (food needed for) support: *The dog doesn't earn his ~,* is not useful enough to be worth the cost of keeping him. **2** [C] tower of a fortress, etc (in olden times): *the castle ~.* **3** ***for ~s,*** (sl) permanently: *Is this mine for ~s?*

keeper /ˋkipə(r)/ *n* **1** guard, e g a person who looks after animals in a zoo. **2** (in compounds) person with special duties: *ˋpark-~; ˋlighthouse-~; game~,* ⇨ game[1](6); *ˋgoal~,* ⇨ goal; person who manages a shop, inn, etc: *ˋshop~; ˋinn~.*

keep·ing /ˋkipɪŋ/ *n* [U] **1** care. ***in safe ~,*** being kept carefully: *The valuables are in safe ~.* **2** (in verbal senses): *the ~ of bees; ˋbee-~.* **3** agreement; harmony. ***in/out of ~ with:*** *His actions are not in ~ with his promises.*

keep·sake /ˋkipseɪk/ *n* sth kept in memory of the giver: *Please have this ring for a ~.*

keg /keg/ *n* small barrel, usu of less than 10 gallons: *a ~ of brandy.*

kelp /kelp/ *n* [U] large kinds of seaweed.

Kelt /kelt/ *n* = Celt.

ken[1] /ken/ *n* [U] (only in) ***beyond/outside my ~,*** (colloq) not within one's range of knowledge.

ken[2] /ken/ *vt* (-nn-) (Scot) [VP6A,9] know.

ken·nel /ˋkenl/ *n* **1** hut to shelter a dog. **2** (establishment for a) pack of hounds; place where dogs are cared for during quarantine. □ *vt,vi* (-ll-, US also -l-) put, keep, in a ~; live in a ~.

kepi /ˋkeɪpɪ/ *n* French military cap with a horizontal peak.

kept /kept/ ⇨ keep[2].

kerb /k3b/ *n* (also *curb*) stone edging to a raised path or pavement. ***ˋ~·stone*** *n* stone forming a part of this.

ker·chief /ˋk3tʃɪf/ *n* [C] square piece of cloth or lace used by women as a head covering.

ker·nel /ˋk3nl/ *n* [C] **1** softer, inner (usu edible) part of a nut or fruit-stone. **2** part of a seed, e g a grain of wheat, within the husk; (fig) central or important part of a subject, problem, etc: *the ~ of the argument.*

kero·sene /ˋkerəsin/ *n* [U] paraffin oil: (attrib) *a ~ lamp.*

kes·trel /ˋkestrl/ *n* kind of small hawk.

ketch /ketʃ/ *n* small two-masted sailing vessel used in coastal trading.

ketch·up /ˋketʃəp/ *n* [U] sauce made from tomato juice, mushrooms, etc.

kettle /ˋketl/ *n* metal vessel with lid, spout and handle, for boiling water. ***a pretty ~ of fish,*** ⇨ fish[1](1).

kettle·drum /ˋketldrʌm/ *n* drum shaped like a hemisphere, made of brass or copper, with parchment stretched over the edge. ⇨ the illus at percussion. ⇨ timpani.

key[1] /ki/ *n* **1** metal instrument for moving the bolt of a lock: *put the key in the lock; turn the key.* ⇨ the illus at bunch. **ˋmaster/ˋskeleton key,** one that will open several locks. **ˋkey-ring** *n* (usu split) ring on which to keep keys. **ˋkey·hole** *n* hole in a lock, door, etc, into which a key fits. **ˋkey money,** extra payment (requested by some house agents, now illegal in GB) before completion of an agreement about renting a house, flat, etc. **2** instrument for winding a clock or a watch by tightening the spring. **3** ***~ (to),*** (fig) sth that provides an answer (to a problem or mystery). **4** set of answers to exercises or problems; translation of sth from a foreign language: *a key for the use of teachers only,* e g to a book of problems in algebra. **5** (also attrib) place which, from its position, gives control of a route or area: *a key position. Gibraltar has been called the key to the Mediterranean.* **6** (attrib) *key industry,* one (e g coal-mining) that is essential to the carrying on of others: *a key man/a man in a key position,* one whose work is essential to the work of others. **7** operating part (lever or button) of a typewriter, piano, organ, flute, etc pressed down by a finger. **ˋkey·board** *n* row of such keys (on a piano, organ, typewriter): (attrib) *keyboard instruments.* **8** (bot) usu one-seeded winged fruit of some trees, e g the ash and elm. **9** (music) scale of notes definitely related to each other and based on a particular note called the *ˋkey-note*: *the key of C major;* (fig) tone or style of thought or expression: *in a minor key,* sadly; *all in the same key,* monotonously, without expression; *speak in a high/low key.* **ˋkey·note** *n* (a) note on which a key is based. (b) (fig) prevailing tone or idea: *The keynote of the Minister's speech was the need for higher productivity.* **key·less** *adj* not having or needing a key.

key[2] /ki/ *vt* [VP15B] ***key up,*** (rare) tune (the strings of a musical instrument by tightening or loosening); (fig) stimulate or raise the standard of (a person, his activity, etc): *The thought of the coming adventure keyed him up to a state of great excitement. The crowd was keyed up for the football match.*

key[3] /ki/ *n* low island or reef, esp off the coasts of Florida, W Indies.

key·stone /ˈki-stəʊn/ *n* [C] stone at the top of an arch locking the others into position; the illus at window; (fig) central principle on which everything depends.

khaki /ˈkɑkɪ/ *n, adj* (cloth, military uniform, of a) dull yellowish-brown.

kha·lif /ˈkeɪlɪf/ *n* = caliph. **~·ate** /ˈkeɪlɪfeɪt/ *n* = caliphate.

khan[1] /kɑn/ *n* title used by some rulers and officials in Central Asia, Afghanistan, etc; (in olden times) title used by supreme rulers of Turkish, Tartar and Mongol tribes.

khan[2] /kɑn/ *n* (in the East) inn built round a courtyard where caravans may rest.

kick[1] /kɪk/ *n* **1** act of ~ing: *give a ~ at the door; give sb a ~ in the arse. The bruise was caused by a ~.* ***more ~s than halfpence,*** more harsh treatment than reward (for what one does). **ˈ~-back** *n* (US sl) percentage payment made to sb who has enabled one to make money. ⇨ rake-off. **ˌ~-ˈstart(er)** *n* lever on a motor-cycle or lawnmower which is ~ed to start the engine. **2** (colloq) thrill of pleasure or excitement: *He gets a good deal of ~/a big ~ out of motor-racing. He gets his ~s by playing football.* ***do sth/live for ~s,*** for thrills; excitement: *I don't expect to win when I bet—I do it for ~s.* **3** [U] resilience; strength: *He has no ~ left in him,* is exhausted. *This cocktail has a lot of ~ in it, is strong.*

kick[2] /kɪk/ *vt, vi* **1** [VP6A,15A,B,2A,C] hit with the foot; move the foot; move sth by doing this; move the foot or feet jerkily: *~ a ball; ~ a man on the shin; ~ a hole in sth,* make one by ~ing. *The baby was ~ing and screaming. This horse ~s,* has the habit of ~ing. ***~ a goal,*** (Rugby football) score a penalty; convert a try. Cf *score a goal* in Association football. ***~ one's heels,*** be idle (as when forced to waste time when waiting for sth/sb). ***~ the bucket,*** (sl) die. **2** [VP2A] (of a gun) recoil when fired: *The old blunderbuss ~s badly.* **3** [VP2A,C,3A,15B] (with *preps* and *advv*) ***~ against/at,*** show annoyance; protest: *He ~ed at/against the treatment he was receiving. If the people are taxed much more they'll begin to ~.* ***~ off,*** (football) start the game; resume after half-time, by making the first ~. Hence, **ˈ~-off** *n*: *~-off at 2.30.* ***~ sth off,*** remove by ~ing: *He ~ed off his slippers.* ***~ sb out***: *The drunken man was ~ed out of the bar.* ***~ over the traces,*** ⇨ trace[3]. ***~ sth up,*** raised by ~ing: *~ up the carpet,* turn up the edge by striking it with the foot. ***~ up a fuss/shindy/row/stink,*** (colloq) cause a disturbance, e g by protesting vigorously. ***~ up one's heels,*** (of a horse) make lively jumps, showing enjoyment of freedom after a period of work; (fig) enjoy oneself. ***~ sb upstairs,*** (fig) get sb out of the way, e g from the House of Commons, by giving him a higher position, e g a peerage, so that he sits in the House of Lords. **~er** *n* horse with the habit of ~ing.

kick·shaw /ˈkɪkʃɔ/ *n* **1** fancy dish in cookery. **2** toy; trifle; thing of little value.

kid[1] /kɪd/ *n* **1** [C] young goat. **2** [U] leather made from skin of this: *kid gloves; a book bound in kid.* **kid gloves** *n pl* gloves made of kid: *handle sb with kid gloves,* deal with him gently, avoiding severe methods; (attrib) *kid-glove methods.* **3** (sl) child; (US sl) young person: *college kids.* **kiddy** *n* (*pl* -dies) (sl) child.

kid[2] /kɪd/ *vt* (-dd-) (sl) hoax: *You're kidding (me)!* Cf You're pulling my leg!

kid·nap /ˈkɪdnæp/ *vt* (GB -pp-, US -p-) steal (a

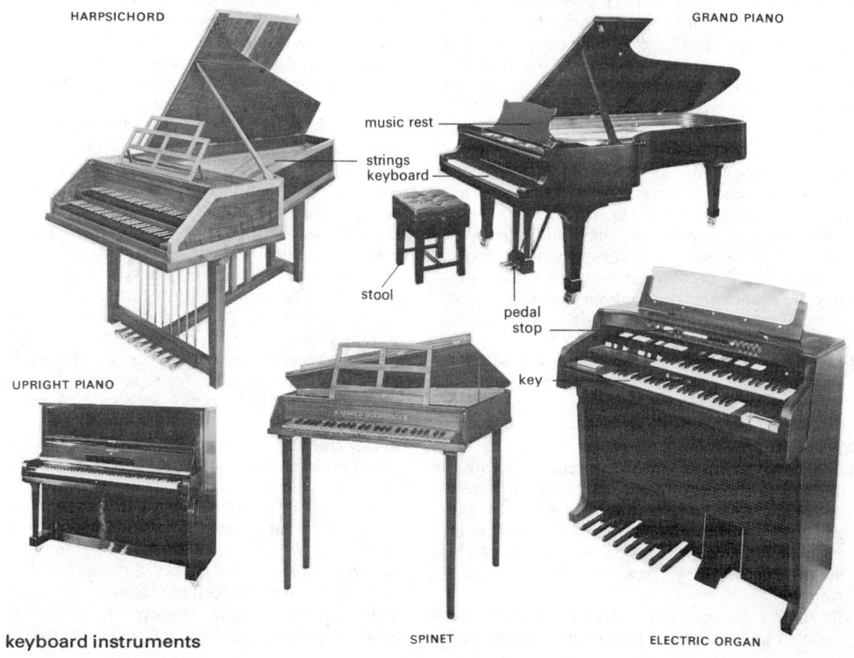

keyboard instruments

child); carry away (sb) by force and unlawfully (esp in order to obtain a ransom. **~·per** *n* person who ~s.

kid·ney /ˋkɪdnɪ/ *n* (*pl* ~s) one of a pair of organs in the abdomen that separate waste liquid (urine) from the blood; ~ of sheep, cattle, etc as food. ˋ~ **machine** *n* one which does the work of diseased ~s by washing the blood and removing waste materials. ˈ~-ˋ**bean** *n* (plant with pod containing) reddish-brown ~-shaped bean (either the dwarf French bean or the runner bean).

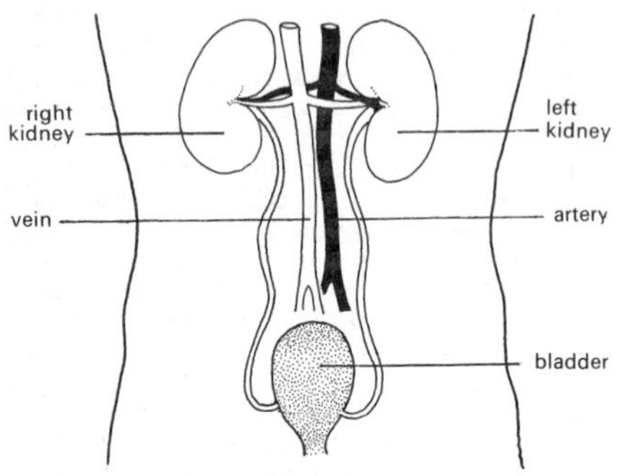

the kidneys and the bladder

kill /kɪl/ *vt, vi* **1** [VP6A,2A] put to death; cause the death of: *~ animals for food. Thou shalt not ~,* (biblical, one of the Ten Commandments). *The troops were shooting to ~,* e g in a riot, shooting with the intention of ~ing, not merely to warn or wound the rioters. *The frost ~ed the flowers.* ***~ sb/sth off,*** [VP15B] get rid of: *The frost ~ed off most of the insect pests.* ***~ time,*** find ways of passing the time without being bored, e g when compelled to wait for sb/sth. ***~ two birds with one stone,*** ⇨ bird. **2** [VP6A] neutralize, make ineffective, by contrast: *The scarlet carpet ~s* (= deadens) *your curtains.* **3** [VP6A] cause the failure or defeat of; veto: *~ a proposal/a Bill in Parliament.* ˋ**~·joy** *n* person who throws gloom over those who are enjoying themselves. **4** [VP6A,2A] overwhelm with admiration; impress deeply: *~ sb with kindness.* ***(be) dressed/got up to ~,*** dressed elaborately, so as to impress people. □ *n* (*sing* only) **1** act of ~ing, esp in hunting. ***be in at the ~,*** be present when sth, e g a fox, is ~ed. **2** (in hunting) number of animals ~ed: *There was a plentiful ~,* many animals were ~ed. **~·ing** *adj* (colloq, dated) amusing: *a ~ing joke;* exhausting: *a ~ing experience.* □ *n* ***make a ~ing,*** be extraordinarily successful. **~·ing·ly** *adv* **~er** *n* one who, that which, ~s; (journalese) murderer.

kiln /ˋkɪln/ *n* [U] furnace or oven for burning, baking or drying, esp ˋ*brick-~,* for baking bricks; ˋ*hop-~,* for drying hops; ˋ*lime-~,* for burning lime.

kilo /ˋkiləʊ/ *n* abbr of kilogram.

kilo- *pref* 1 000, esp in **kilo·cycle** /ˋkɪləsaɪkl/ *n* unit of frequency of vibration, used of wireless waves. **kilo·gram(me)** /ˋkɪləgræm/ *n* 1 000 grammes. **kilo·litre** *n* 1 000 litres. **kilo·metre** (US = **-meter**) /ˋkɪləmitə(r) *US:* kɪˋlomɪtər/ *n* 1 000 metres. **kilo·watt** /ˋkɪləwot/ *n* 1 000 watts. ⇨ App 5.

kilt /kɪlt/ *n* pleated skirt, usu of tartan cloth, from waist to knee, worn as part of male dress in the Scottish Highlands; similar skirt worn by children. **~ed regiments,** regiments of Scottish soldiers wearing ~s.

kilts

kim·ono /kɪˋməʊnəʊ *US:* -nə/ *n* (*pl* ~s) **1** wide-sleeved long flowing gown, characteristic of Japanese traditional costume. ⇨ the illus at sari. **2** style of loose garment worn as a dressing-gown.

kin /kɪn/ *n* (collectively) family; relations: *We are near kin,* are closely related. ***next of kin,*** nearest relation(s).

kind[1] /kaɪnd/ *adj* (-er, -est) having, showing, thoughtfulness, sympathy or love for others: *be ~ to animals. Will you be ~ enough/so ~ as to close the door? It was ~ of you to help us.* ˈ~-ˋ**hearted** *adj* having a ~ heart; sympathetic. **~·ly** *adv* **1** in a ~ manner: *speak ~ly to sb; treat sb ~ly.* **2** (in polite formulas) *Will you ~ly tell me the time?* **3** naturally; easily: *He took ~ly to his new duties. He doesn't take ~ly to being treated as an inferior.* **~·ness** *n* **1** [U] ~ nature; being ~. ***out of ~ness (to sb),*** because of feeling ~ (towards): *He did it all out of ~ness,* not in the hope of reward. **2** [C] ***do sb a ~ness,*** perform a ~ act: *He has done/shown me many ~nesses.*

kind[2] /kaɪnd/ *n* **1** race, natural group, of animals, plants, etc: *manˋkind; ˈhumanˋkind.* **2** class, sort or variety: *apples of several ~s/several ~s of apples; people of this ~,* or (colloq) *these ~ of people. What ~ of tree is this? She's the ~ of woman who likes to help other people. She's not the ~ (of person) to talk scandal.* ***nothing of the ~,*** not at all like it. ***something of the ~,*** sth like the thing in question. ***of a ~,*** **(a)** of the same ~: *two of a ~.* **(b)** (implying contempt) scarcely deserving the name: *They gave us coffee of a ~.* ***a ~ of...,*** used when there is uncertainty: *I had a ~ of suspicion* (= I vaguely suspected) *that he was cheating.* ***~ of,*** (colloq or vulg, sometimes spelt **kinda** /ˋkaɪndə/) *adv* to some extent: *I ~ of thought this would happen.* **3** [U] nature; character: *They differ in degree but not in ~.* **4** ***in ~,*** (of payment) in goods or natural produce, not in money: *benefits in ~,* benefits other than wages or salary received by employees, e g the right to buy articles at cost price; (of repayment, fig) with what was received: *repay insolence in ~,* be insolent in return.

kin·der·gar·ten /ˋkɪndəgɑtn/ *n* school for very young children too young to begin formal education.

kindle /ˋkɪndl/ *vt, vi* [VP6A,2A] **1** (cause to) catch fire or burst into flames or flaming colour: *The sparks ~d the dry wood. This wood is too wet to ~. The setting sun ~d the sky.* **2** rouse, be roused, to a state of strong feeling, interest, etc: *~ the interest of an audience. Her eyes ~d with excitement.* **kind·ling** /ˋkɪndlɪŋ/ *n* [U] (no *pl*) material for lighting a fire, esp light, dry sticks of wood.

kind·ly[1] /ˈkaɪndlɪ/ *adj* (-ier, -iest) friendly: *speak in a ~ tone; give sb ~ advice.*

kind·ly[2] /ˈkaɪndlɪ/ *adv* ⇨ kind[1].

kin·dred /ˈkɪndrəd/ *n* (*sing* only) **1** [U] relationship by birth between persons: *claim ~ with sb.* **2** (with *pl v*) all one's relatives: *Most of his ~ are still living in Ireland.* □ *adj* (attrib only) **1** related; having a common source: *~ languages,* e g English and Dutch; *dew, frost and ~ phenomena; ~ tribes/races.* **2** similar: *~ natures; a ~ spirit,* sb whom one feels to be congenial, sympathetic.

kine /kaɪn/ *n pl* (old form) cows.

kin·ema /ˈkɪnəmə/ *n* (rare) = cinema.

kin·etic /kɪˈnetɪk/ *adj* of, relating to, produced by, motion. **ˌ~ ˈart,** sculptural objects parts of which may be in motion, e g from air currents. **ˌ~ ˈenergy,** energy of a moving body because of its motion. **kin·etics** *n* (*sing v*) science of the relations between the motions of bodies and the forces acting on them.

king /kɪŋ/ *n* **1** male sovereign ruler (esp one whose position is hereditary) of an independent state: *the K~ of Denmark.* ⇨ queen. **K~'s/Queen's Bench,** ⇨ bench. **K~'s/Queen's Counsel,** ⇨ counsel[1](3). ***turn K~'s/Queen's evidence,*** (of one who has shared in a crime) give evidence against accomplices (often in order to escape punishment). **~'s evil,** disease formerly thought to be curable by the touch of a ~. **K~s,** either of two books in the Old Testament, giving the history of the ~s of Israel and Judah. **2** person of great influence: *an ˈoil ~.* **3** principal piece in the game of chess; the illus at chess; (playing-cards) court-card with a picture of a ~: *the ~ of spades.* **4** (advertising, etc) extra large: *ˈ~-size(d) cigarettes.* **5** largest variety of a species; most prominent member of a group, category, etc: *the ~ of beasts,* the lion; *the ~ of the forest,* the oak; *the ~ of terrors,* death; *~ cobra/crab/penguin.* **6** (compounds) **ˈ~·cup** *n* large variety of buttercup; marsh marigold. **ˈ~·fisher** *n* small brightly-coloured bird feeding on fish in rivers, etc. ⇨ the illus at bird. **ˈ~·pin** *n* vertical bolt used as a pivot; (fig) indispensable or essential person or thing. **ˈ~·like, ~·ly** *adjj* of, like, suitable for, a ~; majestic; regal. **~·ship** /-ʃɪp/ *n* state or office of a ~.

King·dom /ˈkɪŋdəm/ *n* **1** country ruled by a king or a queen: *the United K~,* Great Britain and Northern Ireland. **2** the spiritual reign of God: *Thy K~ come,* May the rule of God be established. ***gone to k~ come,*** (colloq) dead, gone to the next world. **3** any one of the three divisions of the natural world: *the animal, vegetable and mineral ~s.* **4** realm or province: *the ~ of thought,* the mind.

kink /kɪŋk/ *n* **1** irregular back-twist in a length of wire, pipe, cord, etc such as may cause a break or obstruction. **2** (fig) mental twist; sth abnormal in a person's way of thinking. □ *vt,vi* make a ~ in; form a ~ or ~s: *This hosepipe ~s easily.* **~y** *adj* (colloq) eccentric; perverted.

kins·folk /ˈkɪnzfəʊk/ *n pl* relations by blood. **kins·man** /-mən/ *n* (*pl* -men) male relative. **kins·woman** *n* (*pl* -women) female relative.

kin·ship /ˈkɪn-ʃɪp/ *n* [U] relationship by blood; similarity in character.

kiosk /ˈkiosk/ *n* **1** small open-fronted structure, esp a round one, for the sale of newspapers, sweets, cigarettes, etc, e g in a park. **2** small booth for a public telephone.

kip /kɪp/ *n* (GB sl) (room or bed in a) house where beds may be rented; sleep. □ *vi* [VP2A,C] go to bed; sleep: *time to kip down.*

kip·per /ˈkɪpə(r)/ *n* salted herring, dried or smoked.

kirk /kɜk/ *n* (Scot) church.

kirsch /kɪəʃ/ *n* [U] colourless brandy made from the juice of wild cherries.

kirtle /ˈkɜtl/ *n* (archaic) woman's gown or outer petticoat; man's tunic.

kis·met /ˈkɪzmet/ *n* [U] destiny; the will of Allah.

kiss /kɪs/ *vt,vi* [VP6A,2A,15A,B] touch with the lips to show affection or as a greeting: *~ the children goodnight. He ~ed her (on the) cheek. She ~ed the child goodbye. She ~ed away the child's tears.* ***~ the book,*** ~ the Bible on taking an oath. ***~ the dust/ground,*** **(a)** give abject submission to a conqueror. **(b)** be killed. ***~ hands/the Queen's hand,*** ~ the sovereign's hand on being appointed to an office (e g as a member of the Cabinet). ***~ the rod,*** accept punishment meekly. □ *n* touch, caress, given with the lips. ***~ of life,*** method of mouth-to-mouth resuscitation, e g for sb rescued from drowning. **~er** *n* (sl) mouth.

kit /kɪt/ *n* **1** (collective) all the equipment (esp clothing) of a soldier, sailor or traveller: *ˈkit inspection,* examination of kit by an officer to see that it is complete, etc. **ˈkit-bag** *n* long canvas bag in which kit is carried. **2** [C] equipment needed by a workman for his trade: *a plumber's kit.* **3** [C,U] outfit or equipment needed for sport or some other special purpose: *ˈshooting/ˈgolfing/ˈskiing kit; a survival kit,* articles to be used by a person in distress, e g an airman who has come down in a desert or jungle. **4** ***ˌdo-it-yourˈself kit,*** collection of parts, e g for a piece of furniture, or a set, to be assembled by the purchaser. □ *vt* (-tt-), ***n kit out/up (with sth),*** fit out, be fitted out, with a kit.

kit·chen /ˈkɪtʃɪn/ *n* room in which meals are cooked or prepared, and for other forms of housework; (in many homes in GB) general purpose rooms, e g where meals are eaten. **ˈ~ unit,** unit combining two or more articles of ~ equipment, e g a sink and a storage cabinet. **ˌ~ ˈsink,** ⇨ sink[1](1). **ˌ~-sink ˈdrama,** drama in GB (late 1950's, early 1960's) portraying working-class family life, showing political, social and educational awareness. **ˌ~ ˈgarden** *n* one for fruit and vegetables. **ˈ~-maid** *n* servant employed in a ~, usu to help the cook. **~·ette** /ˌkɪtʃɪˈnet/ *n* tiny room or alcove used as a ~ (esp in a small flat).

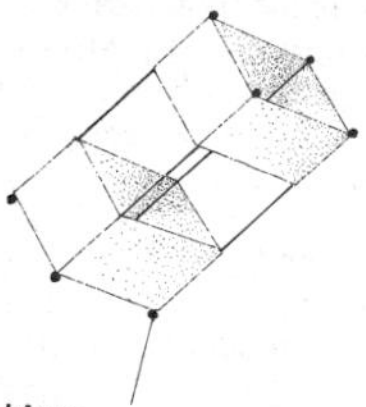

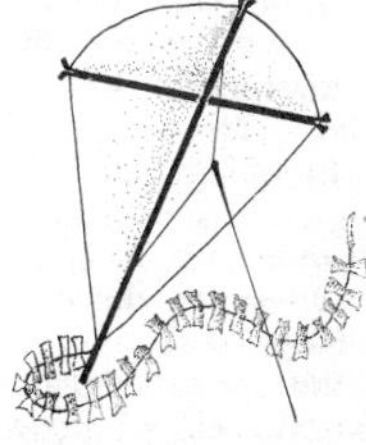

kites

kite /kaɪt/ *n* **1** bird of prey of the hawk family. **2** framework of wood, etc covered with paper or cloth, made to fly in the wind at the end of a long string or wire. ***fly a ~,*** (fig) test possible public reactions by means of hints, rumours, etc. Cf *see which way the wind blows.* **ˈ~-balloon,** sausage-shaped captive balloon for military observation.

kith /kɪθ/ *n* (only in) ~ ***and kin,*** friends and relations.

kit·ten /ˈkɪtn/ *n* young cat. **~·ish** /-ɪʃ/ *adj* like a ~; playful. **kitty** *n* playful name for a ~.

kitty /ˈkɪtɪ/ *n* (in some card games) pool of stakes to be played for; (colloq) any joint pool or fund, e g of savings.

kiwi /ˈkiwi/ *n* New Zealand bird with undeveloped wings; (sl) New Zealander. ⇨ the illus at rare.

klaxon /ˈklæksn/ *n* powerful electric horn for a motor-car.

kleenex /ˈklineks/ *n* (P) tissue paper. ⇨ **tissue(3).**

klep·to·mania /ˈkleptəˈmeɪnɪə/ *n* obsessive wish to steal, not necessarily from poverty. **klep·to·maniac** /-nɪæk/ *n* person with ~.

knack /næk/ *n* (rarely *pl*) cleverness (intuitive or acquired through practice) enabling one to do sth skilfully: *There's a ~ in it,* You have to learn by doing it. *It's quite easy when you have/get the ~ of it.*

knacker /ˈnækə(r)/ *n* **1** person who buys and slaughters useless horses (to sell the meat and hides). **2** person who buys and breaks up old houses, ships, etc for the materials in them. **~'s yard,** place where old metal goods, etc are broken up for scrap.

knap /næp/ *vt* (-pp-) break (flints for roads) with a hammer.

knap·sack /ˈnæpsæk/ *n* [C] canvas or leather bag, strapped to the back and used (by soldiers, travellers) for carrying clothing, food, etc.

knave /neɪv/ *n* **1** (old use) dishonest man; man without honour. **2** (in a pack of playing-cards) (also *jack*) court-card between 10 and Queen: *the ~ of hearts.* **knav·ery** /ˈneɪvərɪ/ *n* [U] dishonesty; [C] (*pl* -ries) dishonest act. **knav·ish** /ˈneɪvɪʃ/ *adj* deceitful: *knavish tricks.* **knav·ish·ly** *adv*

knead /nid/ *vt* [VP6A] **1** make (flour and water) into a firm paste (dough) by working with the hands; do this with wet clay; make (bread, pots) in this way. **2** massage; apply hands to (muscles, etc) as if making dough.

knee /ni/ *n* **1** joint between the thigh and the lower part of the leg in man; the illus at leg; corresponding part in animals: ***be on/go (down) on one's ~s,*** be kneeling/kneel down (to pray, or in submission). ***bring sb to his ~s,*** force him to submit. ***on the ~s/in the lap of the gods,*** (of future events) uncertain. **2** part of a garment covering the ~s: *the ~s of a pair of trousers.* **3** (compounds) **ˈ~-breeches** /brɪtʃɪz/ *n pl* breeches reaching down to or just below the ~s. **ˈ~·cap** *n* **(a)** flat, movable bone forming the front part of the ~-joint. ⇨ the illus at skeleton. **(b)** protective covering for the ~. **ˈ~-ˈdeep** *adj, adv* so deep as to reach the ~s: *The water was ~-deep.* **ˈ~-ˈhigh** *adj, adv* so high as to reach the ~s: *The grass was ~-high*

kneel /nil/ *vi* (*pt,pp* knelt /nelt/) [VP2A,C] ~ ***(down),*** go down on the knees; rest on the knees. *He knelt down to look for a coin he had dropped. Everyone knelt in prayer.*

knell /nel/ *n* (*sing* with *a* or *the*) sound of a bell, esp for a death or at a funeral; (fig) sign of the end or death of sth; *toll the ~; the ~ of her hopes.*

knelt /nelt/ ⇨ kneel.

Knes·set /ˈkneset/ *n* Israeli parliament.

knew /nju *US:* nu/ ⇨ know.

knicker·bock·ers /ˈnɪkəbokəz/ *n pl* loose wide breeches gathered in below the knees.

knick·ers /ˈnɪkəz/ *n pl* **1** (colloq) knickerbockers. **2** (dated use) woman's or girl's undergarment from the waist to the thighs.

knick-knack /ˈnɪk næk/ *n* small ornament, piece of jewellery, article of dress, piece of furniture, etc.

knife /nɑɪf/ *n* (*pl* knives /nɑɪvz/) sharp blade with a handle, used as a cutting instrument or as a weapon: *a ˈtable ~,* used for food at table; *a ˈpocket ~,* one with hinged blade(s). ***get one's ~ into sb,*** have the wish to harm him. ***war to the ~,*** war without mercy; relentless enmity. **ˈ~-edge** *n* cutting edge of the blade of a ~. ***on a ~-edge,*** (of (a person awaiting) an important outcome, result, etc) extremely uncertain. □ *vt* [VP6A] cut or stab with a ~.

knight /nɑɪt/ *n* **1** (in the Middle Ages) man, usu of noble birth, raised to honourable military rank (after serving as a page and squire). **ˈ~-ˈerrant** /ˈerənt/ *n* (*pl* ~s-errant) ~ who went about in search of adventure. **2** (modern use) man on whom a title or honour is conferred (lower than that of baronet) as a reward for services to the State or to a political party. (The title *Sir* is used before Christian name and surname, as *Sir James Hill*). **3** (GB history) ~ *of the shire,* person who represented a shire or county in Parliament. **4** piece in the game of chess, usu made with a horse's head. ⇨ the illus at chess. □ *vt* [VP6A] make (sb) a ~. **~·hood** /-hʊd/ *n* **1** [U] rank, character or dignity of a ~; [C] (after *confer*): *The Queen conferred ~hoods on two bankers.* **2** [U] ~s collectively: *the ~hood of Frane.* **~·ly** *adj* chivalrous; brave and gentle; like a ~: *~ly qualities.*

knit /nɪt/ *vt,vi* (*pt,pp* ~ted or knit; -tt-) [VP6A, 15A,B,2A,C] ~ ***sth (up) (from/into),*** **1** make (an article of clothing, etc) by looping wool, silk, etc yarn on long needles: *~ stockings out of wool: ~ wool into stockings; ~ sth up,* repair it by ~ting. *She often ~s while reading.* **2** unite firmly or closely: *~ broken bones; a closely ~ argument. Mortar is used to ~ bricks together. The two families are ~ together by common interests.* **3** draw together. ~ ***the brows,*** frown. **~·ter** *n* person who ~s; **~·ting** *n* **1** action of one who ~s. **2** material that is being ~ted: *Her ~ting fell from her lap to the floor.* **ˈ~·ting-maching,** machine that ~s. **ˈ~·ting-needle** *n* long slender rod of steel, wood, etc two or more of which are used together in ~ting. **ˈ~·wear** /-weə(r)/ *n* (trade use) ~ted garments.

knives /nɑɪvz/ ⇨ knife.

knob /nob/ *n* [C] **1** round-shaped handle of a door, drawer, walking-stick, etc; (colloq) control, e g of a radio or television set: *turn the ~ clockwise to switch the set on.* **2** round-shaped swelling or mass on the surface of sth, e g a tree trunk. **3** small lump (e g of coal). **~·ker·rie** /ˈnobkerɪ/ *n* short stick with a head that has ~s on it, formerly used as a weapon (by S African tribes). **~·bly** /ˈnoblɪ/ *adj* (-ier, -iest) having ~s(2); *~bly knees.*

knock[1] /nok/ *n* [C] **1** (short, sharp sound of a) blow: *He got a nasty ~ on the head when he fell. I heard a ~ at the door. I knew him by his ~,* because of the way he ~ed (at the door). *The car ~ed against/into the one in front and broke its rear lights.* ~ ***for*** ~, situation in a motoring accident when insurance companies agree to pay only for the damage to the vehicle for which they are liable. **2** sound of ~ing in a petrol engine. ⇨ knock²(3), and anti~. **3** (cricket) innings: *have a good ~.* **4** (sl) criticism; insult; financial loss: *He's taken a bad ~*, suffered a financial reverse. **~er** *n* person or thing that ~s; (esp) hinged metal device on a door for ~ing on it (now often replaced by an electric bell).

knock² /nok/ *vt,vi* **1** [VP6A,15A,B,14,2A,C] hit; strike; cause to be (in a certain state) by hitting; make by hitting: *Someone is ~ing at the door/on the window. Come in—don't ~. He ~ed the bottom out of the box. Let's ~ a hole in the wall. He ~ed* (= struck by accident) *his head on/against the wall. The blow ~ed me flat/senseless.* **~ sb/sth into a cocked hat,** ⇨ cock³(1). **~ the bottom out of an argument,** ⇨ bottom(7). **~ spots off sth/sb,** ⇨ spot(7). **2** [VP6A] (sl) surprise; shock: *What ~s me is his impudence.* **3** [VP2A] (of a petrol engine) make a tapping or thumping noise (because of a defect that prevents the engine from running smoothly): *The engine of this old car is ~ing badly.* ⇨ anti-knock. **4** [VP6A] (sl) criticize unfavourably: *Why must you always ~ British products? You should boost them!* **5** (compounds) **'~-about** *adj* (of a comic performance) = *slapstick.* ⇨ slap; (of clothes) suitable for rough wear. **'~-down** *adj* **(a)** (of prices, e g at an auction) lowest at which goods are to be sold; reserve price. **(b)** (fig, liter) overwhelming; stunning. **'~-'kneed** *adj* having legs curved so that the knees touch when walking. **'~ out** *adj, n* **(a)** (abbr **KO**) (blow) that ~s a boxer out. **(b)** (in a tournament or competition) round for eliminating weaker competitors. **(c)** (person, thing) impressive or attractive: *Isn't she a ~ out!* **(d)** (sl) drug, etc which induces sleep or unconsciousness: *~ out pills.* **6** [VP2C,15B] (uses with *adverbial particles* and *preps*):

knock about, (colloq) lead an unsettled life, travelling and living in various places: *He has ~ed about all over Asia.* **~ *about (with sb),*** (sl) have a (casual) sexual relationship with sb: *She's ~ing about with a married man.* **~ *sb/sth about,*** hit repeatedly, treat roughly: *The ship had been ~ed about by storms.*

knock sth back, (sl) drink: *~ back a pint of beer.*

knock sb down, strike to the ground or floor: *He was ~ed down by a bus. He ~ed his opponent down.* **~ *sth down,*** **(a)** demolish: *These old houses are to be ~ed down.* **(b)** take to pieces to save cost and space in transport: *The machines will be ~ed down before being packed for shipment to Singapore.* Hence, *'~-down furniture, etc,* which can be taken to pieces. **~ *sth down to sb,*** (at an auction sale) sell (to a bidder): *The painting was ~ed down to Smith for £50.* **~ *sth/sb down (to sth),*** (compel sb to) lower a price: *He asked £500 for his car but I managed to ~ him down 10 per cent/~ed his price down to £450.* Hence, *~-down prices.*

knock sth in, strike so that sth goes/is in: *~ in a nail; ~ in the top of a barrel.*

knock off (work), stop work: *It's time to ~ off for tea.* **~ *sb off,*** (sl) murder him; quickly seduce and then abandon her. **~ *sth off,*** **(a)** deduct: *I'll ~ 50p off the price.* **(b)** compose or finish rapidly: *~ off an article/some verses for a magazine.* **(c)** (cricket) score quickly: *~ off the runs needed to win a match.* **(d)** (sl) break into, rob: *~ off a bank.* ***K~ it off!*** (sl) Stop it!

knock on, (Rugby) ~ the ball forward when trying to catch it (a foul). Hence, **'~-on** *n*

knock sb out, **(a)** (boxing) strike (an opponent) so that he cannot rise to his feet for the count. **(b)** (fig) overwhelm; stun: *She was ~ed out by the news.* **~ *sth out,*** **(a)** empty by ~ing: *~ out one's pipe,* i e of ash, etc.

knock (things) together, make roughly or hastily: *~ boards together for a camp table. The bookshelves had obviously been ~ed together,* not made with care. **~ *your/their, etc heads together,*** use force to prevent them from quarrelling, being foolish or stubborn.

knock up, (tennis) practise shots before the start of a match. **~ *sb up,*** **(a)** (GB colloq) waken or rouse sb by ~ing at his door, etc: *Please tell the servant to ~ me up at five o'clock.* **(b)** (GB colloq) make tired; exhaust: *He was ~ed up after the long steep climb.* **(c)** ⚠ (US vulg sl) (of a man) have sexual intercourse with; make pregnant. **~ *sth up,*** **(a)** drive upwards with a blow: *K~ his arm up!* **(b)** arrange, put together quickly: *~ up a meal from whatever there is in the larder; ~ up a shelter for mountain-climbers.* **(c)** score (runs) at cricket. **~ *up copy,*** prepare material for printing (in a newspaper, etc).

knoll /nəʊl/ *n* small hill; mound.

knot /not/ *n* [C] **1** parts of one or more pieces of string, rope, etc, twisted together to make a fastening: *tie a ~ in a rope; tie a rope in a firm ~; make a ~;* (fig) sth that ties together: *the 'marriage-~.* **2** piece of ribbon, etc twisted and tied as an ornament. **3** difficulty; hard problem: ***tie oneself in/up in/into ~s,*** get badly confused about sth. ⇨ Gordian. **4** hard lump in wood where a branch grew out from a bough or trunk; round cross-grained piece caused by this in a board. **'~-hole** *n* hole (in a board) from which such a piece has come out. **5** group of persons or things: *People were standing about in ~s, anxiously waiting for news.* **6** measure of speed for ships: *a vessel of 20 ~s,* able to sail 20 nautical miles an hour. □ *vt,vi* (-tt-) [VP6A,15B,2A] make a ~ or ~s in; tie sth with ~s; form ~s: *~ two ropes together; ~ a parcel firmly; string that ~s easily.* **~ty** *adj* (-ier, -iest) full of ~s: *a ~ty board.* ***a ~ty problem,*** one that is difficult to solve.

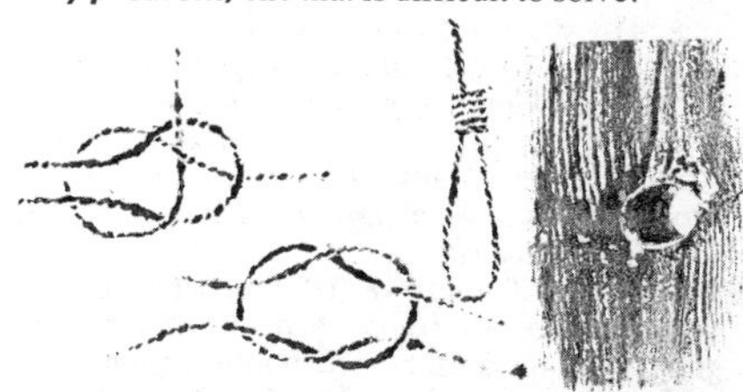

knots a knot-hole

knout /naʊt/ *n* leather whip formerly used in Russia for punishment.

know /nəʊ/ *vt,vi* (*pt* knew /nju *US:* nu/, *pp* known /nəʊn/) **1** [VP6A,8,9,10,17,25,2A] have in the mind as the result of experience or of being informed, or because one has learned: *Every child ~s that two and two make four. He ~s a lot of English. Do you ~ how to play chess? I don't ~ whether he is here or not. I ~ (that) he's an honest man. I ~ him to be honest. I'm not* *guessing—I really* ~. *Oh, yes, I* ~ *all about it. There's no* ~*ing* (= It is impossible to ~) *when we shall meet again.* [VP17A,18B] (past and perfect tenses only): *I have never* ~*n a man (to) die of love, but I have* ~*n a disappointed lover (to) lose weight.* **~ one's business/what's what/the ropes/a thing or two,** have common sense, good judgement, practical experience. **~ better than to do sth,** be wise enough (not to...): *You ought to* ~ *better than to go swimming on such a cold day.* **2** [VP6A] be acquainted with (a person); be able to distinguish (sb) from others: *Do you* ~ *Mr Hill?* Have you met him, talked with him, etc? Cf *You* ~(1) *who Napoleon was. I should like to* ~ *Mr Green,* should like to meet him and be introduced to him. *I* ~ *Mr White by sight but have never spoken to him. I've* ~*n Mrs Grey since I was a child. I was introduced to Miss Wood last week, but I've a bad memory for faces and might not* ~ (= recognize) *her again.* **make oneself ~n to sb,** introduce oneself: *There's your host; you'd better make yourself* ~*n to him.* **be ~n to**: *He's* ~*n to the police,* The police have his name in their records, e g because he has been a criminal. **be ~n as**: *He's* ~*n as* (= has the reputation of being) *a successful architect.* **~ sb from,** distinguish from: *They're twins and it's almost impossible to* ~ *one from the other.* **not ~ sb from Adam,** have no idea who he is. **3** [VP6A] have personal experience of: *He knew poverty and sorrow in his early life. He's* ~*n better days,* has not always been so poor, unfortunate, etc, as he is now. **4** [VP6A] be able to recognize: *He* ~*s a good drama when he sees one. She doesn't* ~ *a swallow from a house-martin.* **5** [VP3A] **~ about/of,** have information concerning; be aware of: *I knew about that last week. I didn't* ~ *about that,* was in ignorance. *I* ~ *of an excellent little restaurant near here. 'Has Smith been ill?'—'Not that I* ~ *of.'* I am not aware of his having been ill. *I don't* ~(2) *the man you mention, but of course I* ~ *of him,* I'm aware of his existence. **6** (compounds) **'~-all** *n* person who ~s, or claims to ~, everything. **'~-how** *n* [U] faculty of ~ing how (to do sth); knowledge of methods; ingenuity (contrasted with theoretical knowledge). □ *n* (only in) ***in the ~,*** (colloq) having information not shared by all or not available to all.

know·ing /ˈnəʊɪŋ/ *adj* cunning; wide-awake; having, showing that one has, intelligence, sharp wits, etc: *a* ~ *fellow;* ~ *looks.* **~·ly** *adv* **1** consciously; intentionally: *He would never* ~*ly do anything to hurt your interests.* **2** in a ~ manner: *look* ~*ly at someone.*

knowl·edge /ˈnolɪdʒ/ *n* [U] **1** understanding: *A baby has no* ~ *of good and evil.* **2** familiarity gained by experience; range of information: *My* ~ *of French is poor. K*~ *of the defeat soon spread. It has come to my* ~ (= I have been informed) *that you have been spreading gossip about me. To the best of my* ~ (= As far as I know) *he is honest and reliable. She married without the* ~ *of her parents.* **~·able** /-əbl/ *adj* (colloq) well-informed; having much ~.

knuckle /ˈnʌkl/ *n* **1** bone at a finger-joint; ⇨ the illus at arm: *give a boy a rap over/on the* ~*s.* **2** (in animals) knee-joint, or part joining leg to foot (esp as food). □ *vi* **~ down to,** (of a task, etc) apply oneself earnestly. **~ under,** submit, yield.

ko·ala /kəʊˈɑlə/ *n* Australian tree-climbing tailless mammal, like a small bear. ⇨ the illus at small.

Ko·dak /ˈkəʊdæk/ *n* [C] (P) hand camera.

kohl /kəʊl/ *n* cosmetic preparation used in the East to darken the eyelids.

kohl·rabi /ˈkəʊlˈrɑbɪ/ *n* [C,U] cabbage with turnip-shaped stem.

kooka·burra /ˈkʊkəbʌrə *US:* -bɜə/ *n* (Australia) large kind of kingfisher (also called *laughing jackass*).

ko·peck /ˈkəʊpek/ *n* = copeck.

kopje, kop·pie /ˈkopɪ/ *n* (in S Africa) small hill.

Ko·ran /kəˈrɑn *US:* kəʊˈræn/ *n* sacred book containing the Prophet Muhammad's oral revelations, written in Arabic. **~ic** *adj*

ko·sher /ˈkəʊʃə(r)/ *n, adj* (food, foodshop) fulfilling the requirements of Jewish dietary law.

kow·tow, ko·tow /ˈkaʊˈtaʊ, ˈkəʊˈtaʊ/ *n* (former Chinese custom) touching of the ground with the forehead (as a sign of respect, submission, etc). □ *vi* **~ (to),** make a ~; show great humility.

kraal /krɑl *US and S Africa:* krɔl/ *n* (in S Africa) fenced-in village of huts; fence for enclosing domestic animals.

Krem·lin /ˈkremlɪn/ *n* citadel of a Russian town, esp that of Moscow; the Government of the Soviet Union.

kris /kris/ *n* (also *creese*) Malayan or Indonesian dagger with a wavy blade.

krona /ˈkrəʊnə/ *n* (*pl* -nor) unit of currency in Sweden.

krone /ˈkrəʊnə/ *n* (*pl* -ner) unit of currency in Denmark and Norway.

ku·dos /ˈkjudos/ *n* [U] (colloq) honour and glory; credit.

kukri /ˈkʊkrɪ/ *n* heavy, curved knife used by Ghurkas.

ku·lak /ˈkulæk/ *n* (in Czarist Russia) rich peasant landowner; (in USSR) disfranchised peasant landowner.

kumis /ˈkumɪs/ *n* fermented liquor made by the Tartars from mare's milk.

küm·mel /ˈkʊml/ *n* [U] herb-flavoured liqueur.

kurus /kuˈruʃ/ *n* unit of currency in Turkey.

kvass /ˈkvæs/ *n* kind of Russian beer.

kwela /ˈkweɪlə/ *n* kind of jazz music using simple instruments, e g a whistle (popular among the Africans in S Africa).

Ll

L, l /el/ (*pl* L's l's /elz/), the 12th letter of the English alphabet; the Roman numeral 50. ⇨ App 4.

la /lɑ/ *n* (music) sixth note of the musical scale.

laa·ger /ˈlɑgə(r)/ *n* camp, defensive encampment, esp inside a circle of carts or wagons; (army use) park for armoured vehicles.

lab /læb/ *n* (colloq abbr of) laboratory.

label /ˈleɪbl/ *n* piece of paper, cloth, metal, wood or other material used for describing what sth is, where it is to go, etc: *plant* ~*s; put* ~*s on one's* *luggage.* □ *vt* (-ll-, US -l-) [VP6A] put a ~ or ~s on: *properly ~led luggage;* (fig) *~ sb as a demagogue,* assign him to this class of persons.

la·bial /ˈleɪbɪəl/ *adj* of the lips; made with the lips: *~ sounds,* e g m, p, b.

labor /ˈleɪbə(r)/ *n* (US) = labour.

lab·ora·tory /ləˈbɒrətrɪ *US:* ˈlæbrətɔrɪ/ *n* (*pl* -ries) room or building used for scientific experiments, research, testing, etc esp in chemistry. ⇨ language.

la·bori·ous /ləˈbɔrɪəs/ *adj* **1** (of work, etc) requiring great effort: *a ~ task.* **2** showing signs of great effort; not fluent or easy: *a ~ style of writing.* **3** (of persons) hard-working. **~·ly** *adv*

la·bour (US = **la·bor**) /ˈleɪbə(r)/ *n* **1** [U] bodily or mental work: *The majority of men earn their living by manual ~.* **ˌhard ˈ~,** work done by criminals (sentenced to penal servitude) as a punishment. **ˈ~-saving** *adj* that reduces the amount of ~ needed: *~-saving devices,* e g washing-machines, vacuum cleaners. **2** [C] task; piece of work. ***a ~ of love,*** task gladly undertaken (e g one for the good of sb one loves). **3** [U] workers as a class (contrasted with the owners of capital, etc): *skilled and unskilled ~; ~ relations,* between ~ and employers. **the ˌMinistry of ˈL~,** (name used until 1970 for) the Government Department in GB responsible for laws regarding ~. **ˈL~ Exchange,** Government agency used by employers for finding workers and by workers for finding jobs. **the ˈL~ Party,** one of the two large political parties in Britain, representing socialist opinion. **ˈL~ leaders,** leaders of this party; trade union officials; **the ˈL~ vote,** of those who support the L~ Party. **Labor Day,** (US) first Monday in September, a legal holiday in honour of the working class. **ˈlabor union,** (US) = trade union. **4** [U] process of childbirth: *a woman in ~.* □ *vi,vt* **1** [VP2A,C, 4A] work; try hard: *~ for the happiness of mankind; ~ at a task; ~ to complete a task; ~ in the cause of peace.* **2** [VP2A,C] move, breathe, slowly and with difficulty: *The ship ~ed through the heavy seas. The old man ~ed up the hillside.* **3** ***~ under,*** [VP3A] be the victim of, suffer because of: *~ under a delusion/difficulty/disadvantage.* **4** [VP6A] work out in detail; treat at great length: *There's no need to ~ the point/argument.* **~ed** *adj* **1** slow and troublesome: *~ed breathing.* **2** not easy or natural; showing too much effort: *a ~ed style of writing.* **~er** *n* man who performs heavy unskilled work: *agricultural ~ers,* farm workers. **~·ite** /-ɑɪt/ *n* member or supporter of the L~ Party.

la·bur·num /ləˈbɜnəm/ *n* small tree with yellow flowers that hang down gracefully and with seeds in long pods.

lab·yr·inth /ˈlæbərɪnθ/ *n* network of winding paths, roads, etc through which it is difficult to find one's way without help; (fig) entangled state of affairs. **lab·yr·in·thine** /ˌlæbəˈrɪnθɑɪn *US:* -θɪn/ *adj*

lac /læk/ = lakh.

lace /leɪs/ *n* **1** [U] delicate, ornamental openwork fabric of threads: *a dress trimmed with ~; a ~ collar.* **gold/silver ~,** braid used for trimming uniforms, e g of diplomats, army officers. **2** [C] string or cord put through small holes in shoes, etc to draw edges together: *a pair of ˈshoe-~s.* □ *vt,vi* [VP6A,15A,B,2A,C] ***~ (up),*** **1** fasten or tighten with ~s(2): *~ (up) one's shoes; a corset that ~s (up) at the side.* **2** [VP14] put (a ~) (*through* holes). **3** [VP3A] ***~ into sb,*** lash him, beat him. **4** [VP14] ***~ with,*** flavour or strengthen (a liquid) (with some kind of spirit): *a glass of milk ~d with rum.*

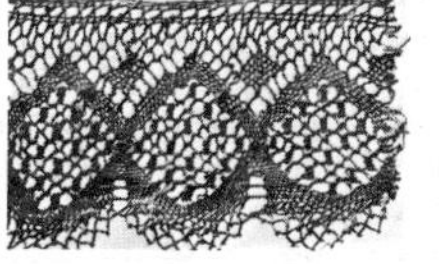
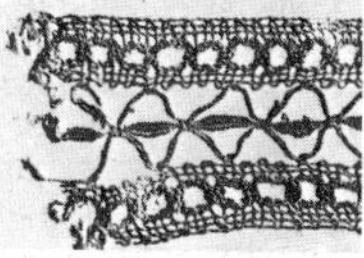

lace

lac·er·ate /ˈlæsəreɪt/ *vt* [VP6A] tear (the flesh; fig the feelings). **lac·er·ation** /ˌlæsəˈreɪʃn/ *n* [U] tearing; [C] tear or injury.

lach·ry·mal /ˈlækrɪml/ *adj* of tears: (esp) *~ glands.* **lach·ry·mose** /ˈlækrɪməʊs/ *adj* tearful; in the habit of weeping.

lack /læk/ *vt,vi* **1** [VP6A,3A] be without; not have; have less than enough of: *~ wisdom. I ~ words with which to express my thanks.* ***be ~ing in sth,*** not have enough of it: *He's ~ing in/He ~s courage.* **2** ***be ~ing,*** be in short supply, not be available: *Money was ~ing* (= There was no money) *for the plan.* **3** [VP3A] ***~ for,*** (formal) need: *They ~ed for nothing,* had everything they wanted. □ *n* [U] want, need, shortage: *The plants died for ~ of water.* **ˈ~-lustre** *adj* (of eyes) dull.

lacka·daisi·cal /ˌlækəˈdeɪzɪkl/ *adj* appearing tired, uninterested, unenthusiastic. **~ly** /-klɪ/ *adv*

lackey /ˈlækɪ/ *n* (*pl* -keys) manservant (usu in livery); (fig) person who is too obsequious, who obeys orders without question, etc.

la·conic /ləˈkɒnɪk/ *adj* using, expressed in, few words: *a ~ person/reply.* **la·coni·cally** /-klɪ/ *adv* **la·coni·cism** /-sɪzm/, **lac·on·ism** /ˈlækənɪzm/ *nn* [U] being ~; [C] instance of this; short; pithy saying.

lac·quer /ˈlækə(r)/ *n* [U] (sorts of) varnish used to give a hard, bright coating to metal (esp brass); kind of varnish used for wooden articles (esp **Japanese ~**); articles coated with this. □ *vt* [VP6A] coat with ~.

lac·quey /ˈlækɪ/ *n* = lackey.

la·crosse /ləˈkrɒs *US:* -ˈkrɔs/ *n* [U] outdoor game, popular in N America, played with a ball which is caught in, carried in, and thrown from, a racket with a net (called a *crosse*).

lac·tic /ˈlæktɪk/ *adj* of milk. **ˌ~ ˈacid,** the acid in sour milk.

la·cuna /ləˈkjunə/ *n* (*pl* -nas, -nae /-nɑɪ/) blank; empty part; missing portion, esp in writing, or in an argument where sth is missing.

lacy /ˈleɪsɪ/ *adj* (-ier, -iest) of or like lace.

lad /læd/ *n* boy; young man.

lad·der /ˈlædə(r)/ *n* **1** two lengths of wood, metal or rope, with crosspieces (called *rungs*), used in climbing up and down walls, a ship's side, etc. **2** (US = *run*) fault in a stocking caused by stitches becoming undone, so that there is a vertical ~-like flaw. **ˈ~-proof** *adj* proof against such flaws. □ *vi* (of stockings, etc) develop ~s: *Have you any tights that won't ~?*

lad·die /ˈlædɪ/ *n* = lad.

lade /leɪd/ *vt* (*pp* laden /ˈleɪdn/) [VP6A] load (which is the usu word).

laden /ˈleɪdn/ *adj* ***~ with,*** weighted or burdened with: *trees ~ with apples; a mind ~ with grief.*

la-di-da /ˈlɑ dɪ ˋdɑ/ *adj* (colloq) pretentious; genteel; affected (esp in pronunciation).

lad·ing /ˋleɪdɪŋ/ *n* [U] cargo; freight. **ˈbill of ˋ~,** list with details of a ship's cargo.

ladle /ˋleɪdl/ *n* large, deep, cup-shaped spoon for dipping out liquids: *a ˋsoup ~.* □ *vt* [VP6A,15B] **~ *out,*** serve with or as from a ~: *~ out soup;* (fig) *~ out honours.*

lady /ˋleɪdɪ/ *n* (*pl* -dies) **1** (corresponding to *gentleman*) woman belonging to the upper classes; woman who has good manners and some claim to social position. **ˈ~-in-ˋwaiting, ˈ~ of the ˋbed-chamber,** ~ attending upon a queen. **2** (used courteously for any) woman of any kind or class, with or without good manners and refinement. **3** (*pl* only) form of address, esp *'Ladies and Gentlemen'.* **4** (attrib) female: *~ doctor/clerk,* (*woman* being preferable); *the ~ help,* the domestic servant. **5 Ladies** (as a *sing n*) women's public lavatory: *Is there a Ladies near here?* **6 L~,** (title in GB) used of and to the wives of some nobles; (prefixed to Christian names) titles used of and to the daughters of some nobles. **7 *My L~,*** term of address used (esp by servants and tradesmen) to holders of the title *Lady* (as in **6** above). **8** (various) **Our ˋL~,** the Virgin Mary. **ˋL~-chapel,** chapel (in a large church) dedicated to the Virgin Mary. **ˋ~-bird** *n* reddish-brown or yellow insect (a small flying beetle) with black spots. **ˋL~ Day,** 25th March, one of the quarter-days. **ˋ~-killer** *n* man with the reputation of being very successful with women. **ˋ~'s-maid** *n* ~'s personal servant, esp in charge of her toilet. **ˋ~'s/ˋladies' man,** man fond of the society of women. **ˋ~-like** *adj* behaving as a ~: befitting a ~; genteel. **ˋ~-ship** /-ʃɪp/ *n* ***Your/Her L~ship,*** used in speaking to or of a titled ~.

lag[1] /læg/ *vi* (-gg-) [VP2A,C] go too slow, not keep up with: *The lame child lagged behind.* □ *n* **ˋtime lag,** period of time by which sth is slower or later.

lag[2] /læg/ *n* (sl) person convicted of crime; (esp) ***an old lag,*** one who has served several sentences of imprisonment.

lag[3] /læg/ *vt* (-gg-) [VP6A,14] ***lag (with),*** encase (waterpipes, cisterns, etc) with material that will not conduct heat or cold, esp do this to prevent freezing of water in pipes, waste of heat, etc. **lagging** *n* material used for this.

la·ger /ˋlɑgə(r)/ *n* [U] sort of light beer; [C] bottle or glass of this.

lag·gard /ˋlægəd/ *n* person who lags behind; person who is lacking in energy, etc.

la·goon /ləˋgun/ *n* (usu shallow) salt-water lake separated from the sea by sandbank(s) or coral reef(s); water enclosed by an atoll. ⇨ the illus at atoll.

laic /ˋleɪɪk/ *adj* of the laity; secular. **lai·cize** /ˋleɪɪsɑɪz/ *vt* [VP6A] free from ecclesiastic control; make, e g priest, a layman.

laid /leɪd/ *pt,pp* of lay[1].

lain /leɪn/ *pp* of lie[2].

lair /leə(r)/ *n* wild animal's resting-place or den.

laird /leəd/ *n* (Scot) landowner.

laissez-faire /ˈleɪseɪ ˋfeə(r)/ *n* [U] (policy of) allowing individual activities (esp in commerce) to be conducted without government control.

laity /ˋleɪətɪ/ *n* (usu with *def art* and a *pl v*) **1** all laymen (i e all those persons not in Holy Orders, those who are not clergy). **2** all those persons outside a particular learned profession (thus, used by a doctor, the word may mean all those not trained for the medical profession).

lake[1] /leɪk/ *n* large area of water enclosed by land. **the ˋL~ District,** part of N W England with many ~s. **the Great Lakes,** ⇨ great. **ˋL~ Poets,** poets who lived in this area, esp Coleridge and Wordsworth. **ˋ~ dwelling,** ⇨ *pile-dwelling* at pile[1].

lake[2] /leɪk/ *n* (often *crimson ~*) dark red colouring material.

lakh /lɑk/ *n* (India and Pakistan) 100 000: *25,87,000,* 25 ~s, 87 thousand rupees. ⇨ crore.

lam /læm/ *vt,vi* (-mm-) (sl) [VP6A] thrash. [VP3A] ***lam into sb,*** attack him, physically or verbally.

lama /lɑmə/ *n* Buddhist priest in Tibet or Mongolia. **lama·sery** /ˋlɑməsərɪ *US:* -serɪ/ *n* (*pl* -ries) monastery of ~s.

lamb /læm/ *n* [C] **1** ⇨ the illus at domestic. young of the sheep; [U] its flesh as food: *a leg of ~; roast ~.* **2** innocent, mild-mannered person; dear person. ***like a ~,*** without resistance or protest. □ *vi* bring forth ~s: *the ~ing season,* when ~s are born. **ˋ~·kin** /-kɪn/ *n* very young ~. **ˋ~·skin** *n* [C] skin of a ~ with the wool on it (as used for coats, gloves, etc); [U] leather made from ~skin.

lam·baste /ˈlæmˋbeɪst/ *vt* (sl) thrash; beat; scold violently.

lam·bent /ˋlæmbənt/ *adj* (liter) (of a flame or light) moving over the surface with soft radiance; (of the eyes, sky) shining softly; (of humour, wit) gently brilliant. **lam·bency** /-ənsɪ/ *n*

lame /leɪm/ *adj* **1** not able to walk normally because of an injury or defect: *~ in the left leg.* ***a ~ duck,*** ⇨ duck[1](1). **2** (of an excuse, argument, etc) unconvincing; unsatisfactory. **3** (of metre) halting. □ *vt* make ~. **~·ly** *adv* **~·ness** *n*

lamé /ˋlɑmeɪ *US:* ˈlɑˋmeɪ/ *n* [U] fabric with metal threads interwoven: *gold/silver ~.*

la·ment /ləˋment/ *vt,vi* [VP6A,3A,2A] ***~ (for/over),*** show, feel, express, great sorrow or regret: *~ the death of a friend; ~ for a friend; ~ (over) one's misfortunes.* □ *n* [C] expression of grief; (music) song or poem expressing grief: *a funeral ~.* **lam·en·table** /ˋlæməntəbl/ *adj* regrettable; to be deplored: *a ~able* (= poor, unsatisfying) *performance of an opera.* **lam·en·tably** /-əblɪ/ *adv* **lam·en·ta·tion** /ˈlæmenˋteɪʃn/ *n* [U] ~ing; [C] ~; expression of grief.

lami·nate /ˋlæmɪneɪt/ *vt,vi* [VP6A,2A] beat or roll (metal) into thin plates; split into layers; manufacturer by placing layer on layer; cover with metal plates: *~d wood/plastics,* of layers one over the other.

Lam·mas /ˋlæməs/ *n* 1st August, formerly a harvest festival in England.

lamp /læmp/ *n* container with oil and wick, used to give light; (in modern times) any apparatus for giving light (from gas, electricity, etc); device for heating. ⇨ *spirit-~* at spirit(11). **ˋ~-black** *n* [U] black colouring matter made from the soot of burning oil, formerly used in making paint and printing-ink. **ˋ~·light** *n* [U] light from a ~: *read by ~light.* **ˋ~·lighter** *n* man who went round the streets to light public ~s (when gas was used). **ˋ~-oil** *n* [U] paraffin oil for ~s. **ˋ~-post** *n* (usu metal) post for a street ~. **ˋ~·shade** *n* globe of glass, screen of silk, parchment, etc placed round or over a lamp.

lam·poon /læm'pun/ *n* [C] piece of satirical writing attacking and ridiculing sb. □ *vt* [VP6A] write a ~ against.

lam·prey /'læmprɪ/ *n* (*pl* -reys) eel-like sea animal.

lance[1] /lɑns *US:* læns/ *n* weapon with a long wooden shaft and a pointed steel head used by a horseman; similar instrument used for spearing fish. **'~-'corporal** *n* lowest grade of non-commissioned officer in the army. ⇨ App 9. **lancer** *n* soldier of a cavalry regiment originally armed with ~s. **lancers** *n* (with *sing v*) (music for a) dance for four or more couples.

lance[2] /lɑns *US:* læns/ *vt* [VP6A] cut open, prick, with a lancet: *~ an abscess.*

lan·cet /'lɑnsɪt *US:* 'læn-/ *n* **1** pointed, two-edged knife used by surgeons. **2** high, narrow, pointed arch or window.

land[1] /lænd/ *n* **1** [U] solid part of the earth's surface (contrasted with *sea, water*): *travel over ~ and sea; come in sight of ~; glad to be on ~/to reach ~/come to ~ again. Are you going by ~ or by sea,* by train, car, etc, or by boat? *a ~ breeze,* one blowing from the land towards the sea (after sunset); *~-based aircraft,* using bases on ~ (contrasted with aircraft based on carriers). ***make ~,*** see, reach the shore. ***see/find out how the '~ lies,*** ⇨ lie[2](4). **2** [U] ground, earth, as used for farming, etc: *working on the ~; '~-workers; rough and stony ~.* **'~ army,** (GB) body of women farm workers in World War II. **3** [U] property in the form of ~: *How far does your ~ extend? Do you own much ~ here?* **'~-agent,** (chiefly GB) person employed to manage an estate; person who buys and sells estates (US = *real estate agent*). **4** (*pl*) estate; area of ~ with the trees, etc on it: *own houses and ~s.* **5** country and its people (liter or emotive in this sense, *country* being the ordinary word): *my native ~; visit distant ~s.* ***the ~ of the living,*** this present existence. **the Promised L~, the L~ of Promise,** Canaan /'keɪnən/, promised by God to the Jews. **6** (compounds, etc) **'~·fall** *n* approach to ~, esp for the first time during a voyage: *a good ~fall,* one that corresponds well to the calculations made by the ship's officers. **'~ forces** *n pl* military forces (not naval). **'~·holder** *n* owner or (more usu) tenant of ~. **'~·lady** *n* (*pl* -ladies) woman who owns a house which she leases to a tenant, or who rents a house, rooms of which she sublets to tenants: *owe one's ~lady a month's rent.* **'~-locked** *adj* (of a bay, harbour, etc) almost or entirely surrounded by ~. **'~·lord** *n* **(a)** person from whom another rents ~ or building(s). **(b)** keeper of an inn, a public house, a boarding-house or lodging-house. **'~-lubber** /lʌbə(r)/ *n* (used by sailors to describe a) person not accustomed to the sea and ships. **'~·mark** *n* [C] **(a)** object that marks the boundary of a piece of ~. **(b)** object, etc easily seen from a distance and helpful to travellers (e g navigating officers of a ship). **(c)** (fig) event, discovery, change, etc that marks a stage or turning-point: *~marks in the history of mankind.* **'~·mine** *n* [C] explosive charge laid in or on the ground or dropped by parachute and exploded by vehicles passing over it. **'~·owner** *n* owner of ~. **'L~-rover** *n* (P) strongly-built motor vehicle for use over rough ground. **'~-slide** *n* [C] **(a)** sliding down of a mass of earth, rock, etc from the side of a cliff, hillside, railway cutting, etc. **(b)** sudden change in political opinion resulting in an overwhelming majority of votes for one side in an election; *a Democratic ~slide,* a great victory for the Democratic party. **'~-slip** *n* = ~slide(a). **'~s·man** /-mən/ *n* (*pl* -men) person who is not a sailor.

land[2] /lænd/ *vt,vi* **1** [VP6A,2A,C] go, come, put, on ~ (from a ship, aircraft, etc): *The passengers ~ed/were ~ed as soon as the ship reached harbour. We ~ed at Bombay. The airliner ~ed safely. The pilot ~ed the airliner safely.* ⇨ also *crash-~* at crash[1] and *soft~* at soft(1). ***~ on one's feet, ~ like a cat,*** (fig) be lucky; escape injury. **2** ***~ sb/oneself in,*** get into (trouble, difficulties, etc): *What a mess you've ~ed us all in!* ***~ up,*** (colloq) arrive; find oneself: *If you go on behaving in this way, you'll ~ up in prison one day. Tom has been away for months, but he'll ~ up one of these days. She ~ed up in a strange city without any money or friends.* **3** [VP6A] (colloq) obtain: *~ a good job/a contract for building a factory.* **4** [VP12C] (sl) strike (a blow): *She ~ed him one in the eye.* **~ed** *adj* **1** consisting of ~: *~ed property.* **2** owning ~: *the ~ed classes/gentry.* **3** (colloq) in difficulties. ⇨ land[2](2). **~-less** *adj* without ~; not owning ~.

lan·dau /'lændɔ/ *n* four-wheeled horse-carriage with a folding roof in two sections.

land·grave /'lændgreɪv/ *n* (hist) title of some German princes.

land·ing /'lændɪŋ/ *n* **1** act of coming or bringing to land: *the ~ of the Pilgrim Fathers in America. The pilot made an emergency ~.* **'~-craft** *n* ship whose bows can be opened up to allow (usu military) vehicles to get ashore without being lifted out. **'~-field/-strip** *n* area of land for aircraft to take off from and land on. **'~-gear** *n* undercarriage and wheels of an aircraft. **'~-net** *n* bag-shaped net on a long handle for landing fish caught with a rod and line. **'~-party** *n* party of armed men who are landed (e g to keep order). **2** (also **'~-place**) place where people and goods may be landed from a boat, etc. **'~-stage** *n* platform (usu floating) on which passengers and goods are landed. **3** platform at the top of a flight of stairs on to which doors may open.

land·scape /'lændskeɪp/ *n* [C] (picture of) inland scenery; [U] branch of art dealing with this. **'~ 'gardening/'architecture** *n* the laying out of grounds and gardens in imitation of natural scenery.

lane /leɪn/ *n* **1** narrow country road, usu between hedges or banks. **2** (usu as part of a proper name) narrow street or alley between buildings: *Drury L~.* **3** passage made or left between lines of persons. **4** route regularly used by ocean steamers or aircraft. **5** marked division of a wide road for the guidance of motorists; line of vehicles within such a division: *the inside/nearside ~; the outside/offside ~; four-~ traffic.* **6** marked course for a competitor in a race (e g on a running track or a swimming pool).

lang·syne /'læŋ'zɑɪn/ *adv, n* (Scot) (in) the old days; (in) past time.

lan·guage /'læŋgwɪdʒ/ *n* **1** [U] human and non-instinctive method of communicating ideas, feelings and desires by means of a system of sound symbols. **2** [C] form of ~ used by a nation or race: *the ~s of Asia; foreign ~s.* ***a dead ~,*** one no longer in spoken use (e g classical Greek). **~ lab-**

oratory, classroom(s) where ~s are taught using tape-recorders, etc. **3** [U] manner of using words: *a person with a great command/flow of ~*, person who is fluent or eloquent. **4** [U] words, phrases, etc used by a profession or class: *technical/legal ~; the ~ of diplomacy.* **5** ***bad ~, strong ~,*** language full of oaths, violent words, etc. **6** system of signs used as ~: *com'puter ~*, ordered system for giving instructions to a computer; *'finger ~*, as used by deaf and dumb persons; *the ~ of flowers; the ~ of algebra.*

lan·guid /ˈlæŋgwɪd/ *adj* lacking in energy; slow-moving. **~·ly** *adv*

lan·guish /ˈlæŋgwɪʃ/ *vi* [VP2A,C] be or become languid; lose health and strength; be unhappy because of a desire (*for* sth): *~ in prison; ~ for love and sympathy. She gave the young man a ~ing look*, one that suggested a desire for love or sympathy.

lan·guor /ˈlæŋgə(r)/ *n* **1** [U] weakness of body (as produced by hard work) or of spirit (as produced by sorrow or an unhappy love affair); lack of life or movement; stillness or heaviness: *the ~ of a summer day.* **2** (often *pl*) soft or tender mood. **~·ous** /-əs/ *adj* **~·ous·ly** *adv*

lan·gur /ˈlæŋˈgʊə(r)/ *n* (kind of) long-tailed monkey.

lank /læŋk/ *adj* **1** (of hair) straight and lying limp or flat. **2** tall and lean.

lanky /ˈlæŋkɪ/ *adj* **(-ier, -iest)** (of a person, his arms or legs) long and lean in an ungraceful way: *a ~, overgrown girl.*

lano·lin /ˈlænəlɪn/ *n* [U] fat extracted from sheep's wool used as the basis of ointments for the skin.

lan·tern /ˈlæntən/ *n* case (usu metal and glass) protecting a light from the wind, etc, outdoors. ⇨ **dark**[2]**(1), magic.** **'~-jawed** *adj* having long and thin jaws so that the face has a hollow look.

lan·yard /ˈlænjəd/ *n* **1** cord (worn by sailors and soldiers) for a whistle or knife. **2** short rope used on a ship for fastening or moving sth.

lap[1] /læp/ *n* front part of a person's legs from the waist to the knees, when sitting, as the place on which a child is nursed or sth held: *The mother had the baby on her lap.* ***be/live in the lap of luxury,*** in fortunate and luxurious circumstances. ***in the lap of the gods,*** ⇨ **knee(1).** **'lap-dog** *n* small pet dog. **'lap-strap** *n* seatbelt, fastened across the lap in an aircraft.

lap[2] /læp/ *vt,vi* **(-pp-)** **1** [VP15B] wrap or fold (cloth, etc) *round* or *in.* **2** [VP6A,2A,C] (cause to) overlap: *Put the slates on the roof so that they lap over.* ⇨ **overlap.** □ *n* **1** amount by which one thing laps over. **2** one circuit round a track or race-course: *Smith overtook the other runners/riders/drivers on the last lap.*

lap[3] /læp/ *vi,vt* **(-pp-)** **1** [VP15B] ***lap up,*** drink by taking up with the tongue, as a cat does: *The cat quickly lapped up all the milk.* **2** (of human beings) take quickly or eagerly: *lap up compliments.* **3** [VP2A,C] (of water) move with a sound like the lapping up of liquid: *waves lapping on the beach; water lapping against the sides of a canoe.* □ *n* **1** act of lapping: *The dog emptied the plate with three laps of the tongue.* **2** [U] sound of lapping: *the lap of the waves against the side of the boat.*

la·pel /ləˈpel/ *n* part of the breast of a coat or jacket folded back and forming a continuation of the collar.

lapi·dary /ˈlæpɪdərɪ *US:* -derɪ/ *adj* cut on stone: *a ~ inscription.* □ *n* person who cuts, polishes or engraves, gems.

lapis la·zuli /ˈlæpɪs ˈlæzjʊlɪ *US:* ˈlæʒəlɪ/ *n* bright blue semi-precious stone; its colour.

lapse /læps/ *n* [C] **1** slight error in speech or behaviour; slip of the memory, tongue or pen. **2** falling away from what is right: *a ~ from virtue; a ~ from true belief/into heresy.* **3** (of time) passing away; interval: *the ~ of time; a long ~ of time.* **4** (legal) ending of a right, etc from failure to use it or ask for its renewal. □ *vi* **1** [VP2A,3A] ***~ from/into,*** fail to keep one's position; fall (from good ways into bad ways): *~ from virtue into vice; ~ into bad habits; a ~d Catholic.* **2** [VP2A] (legal) (of rights and privileges) be lost because not used, claimed or renewed.

lap·wing /ˈlæpwɪŋ/ *n* bird of the plover family; pewit.

lar·board /ˈlɑbɔd/ *n, adj* left side of a ship when looking forward (now always called the *port* side). ⇨ **starboard.**

lar·ceny /ˈlɑsn̩ɪ/ *n* (*pl* **-nies**) [U] stealing; theft; [C] instance of this.

larch /lɑtʃ/ *n* [C] deciduous tree with small cones and light-green leaves; [C] its wood.

lard /lɑd/ *n* [U] fat of pigs prepared for use in cooking. □ *vt* [VP6A] put ~ on; put pieces of bacon into or on (meat, etc) before cooking, in order to add to the flavour. ***~ with,*** (fig, often derog) enrich: *a speech ~ed with boring quotations.*

lar·der /ˈlɑdə(r)/ *n* room or cupboard where meat and other kinds of food are stored.

large /lɑdʒ/ *adj* **(-r, -st)** **1** of considerable size; taking up much space; able to contain much: *A man with a ~ family needs a ~ house. She inherited a ~ fortune.* ***as ~ as life,*** ⇨ **life(10).** (Note that *large* is less colloq than *big* and not so emotive as *great.* 'A great city' is large, but the use of 'great' suggests that it is also important or famous. *Large* is seldom used of persons, but note *~ of limb*, having ~ limbs.) **'~-scale** *adj* **(a)** extensive: *~-scale operations.* **(b)** made or drawn to a ~ scale: *a ~-scale map.* **2** liberal; generous; unprejudiced (chiefly in the following): *a ~ heart*, (hence) *'~-'hearted; '~-'minded*, hence, *'~-'mindedness.* **3** of wide range; not confined or restricted: *give an official ~ powers/discretion; a man with ~ ideas; ~ and small farmers*, men farming on a ~ and a small scale. □ *n* (only in) ***at ~,*** **(a)** at liberty; free: *The escaped prisoner is still at ~.* **(b)** at full length; with details: *to talk/write at ~.* **(c)** in general: *Did the people at ~ approve of the government's policy?* **(d)** at random; without definite aim: *scatter accusations at ~.* □ *adv* boastfully: *talk ~.* ***by and ~,*** ⇨ **by**[1]**(4).** **~·ish** /-ɪʃ/ *adj* rather ~. **~·ly** *adv* **1** to a great extent: *His success was ~ly due to luck.* **2** generously; freely: *He gives ~ly to charity.* **~·ness** *n*

lar·gesse (US also **lar·gess**) /lɑˈdʒes/ *n* (old use) [U] generous giving; money or other things generously given.

largo /ˈlɑgəʊ/ *n* (*pl* **-gos** /-gəʊz/), *adv* (piece of music, movement) in slow time.

lar·iat /ˈlærɪət/ *n* rope for picketing a horse; long rope with a noose; lasso.

lark[1] /lɑk/ *n* (kinds of) small songbird, esp the skylark. ⇨ the illus at **bird.**

lark[2] /lɑk/ *n* [C] bit of fun; frolic: *Boys are fond of*

wild animals 1

having a ~. He did it for a ~, in fun. *What a ~!* How amusing! □ *vi* [VP2A,C] play pranks: *Stop ~ing about and get on with your work.*

lark·spur /ˈlɑkspɜ(r)/ *n* tall garden plant with blue, white or pink flowers.

larn /lɑn/ *vt,vi* (colloq or dial for) learn.

larva /ˈlɑvə/ *n* (*pl* -vae /-vi/) insect in the first stage of its life-history, after coming out of the egg. ⇨ the illus at **butterfly**. **lar·val** /ˈlɑvl/ *adj* of or in the form of a ~.

lar·ynx /ˈlærɪŋks/ *n* upper part of the windpipe where the vocal cords are. ⇨ the illus at **head**. **lar·yn·gi·tis** /ˈlærɪnˋdʒɑɪtɪs/ *n* [U] inflammation of the ~.

las·car /ˈlæskə(r)/ *n* seaman from the East Indies.

las·civ·ious /ləˋsɪvɪəs/ *adj* feeling, causing, expressing, lust. **~·ly** *adv* **~·ness** *n*

laser /ˈleɪzə(r)/ *n* device for generating, amplifying and concentrating light waves into an intense highly directional beam: (attrib) *~ beams.*

lash[1] /læʃ/ *n* **1** part of a whip with which strokes are given; (usu leather) thong; blow or stroke given with a ~: *He was given twenty ~es.* **the ~,** punishment of flogging: *mutinous sailors sentenced to the ~*; (fig) *the ~ of criticism; the ~ of an angry woman's tongue.* **2** = eyelash.

lash[2] /læʃ/ *vt,vi* **1** [VP6A,14,2C] strike violently; make a sudden movement of (a limb, etc): *The rain was ~ing (against) the windows. The tiger ~ed its tail angrily. He ~ed his faint-hearted men with his tongue. He ~ed the horse across the back with his whip.* **2 *~ sb into (a state),*** rouse into: *The speaker ~ed his listeners into a fury.* ***~ out (against/at) sb/sth,*** attack violently (with blows or words): *The horse ~ed out at me,* kicked or tried to kick, me. *The speaker ~ed out against the government.* **3** [VP15A,B] ***~ one thing to another, ~ things together,*** fasten tightly together (with rope, etc). ***~ sth down,*** make it secure with rope, etc. **ˋ~-up** *n* improvised or roughly constructed piece of apparatus.

lash·ing /ˈlæʃɪŋ/ *n* **1** [C] cord or rope used for binding or fastening. **2** [C] whipping or beating. **3** (*pl,* colloq) plenty: *strawberries with ~s of cream; ~s of drink/~s to drink.*

lass /læs/ *n* girl; sweetheart.

las·sie /ˈlæsɪ/ *n* = **lass**.

lassi·tude /ˈlæsɪtjud *US:* -tud/ *n* [U] tiredness; state of being uninterested in things.

lasso /læˋsu/ *n* (*pl* -sos, -soes /-ˋsuz/) long rope with a slipknot, used for catching horses and cattle, esp in America. □ *vt* catch with a ~.

last[1] /lɑst *US:* læst/ *adj* **1** (contrasted with *first*. ⇨ **late**[1].) coming after all others in time or order: *the ~ month of the year; the ~ Sunday in June; the ~ time I saw you; the ~ letters of the alphabet,* i e XYZ; *the two/the ~ two persons to arrive; ~ but not least,* i e coming at the end, but not least in importance; *a ~-minute appeal*, one made just before sth is to be done, decided, etc. ***be on one's ~ legs***, ⇨ leg(2). ***the L~ Day***, ⇨ *Doomsday* at doom[1]. ***the ~ post***, ⇨ post[2]. ***the ~ straw***, ⇨ straw. ***have the ~ word***, ⇨ word. **2** (contrasted with *next*) coming immediately before the present: *~ night/week/month/summer/year; on Tuesday ~; ~ May; in May ~; in/for/during the ~ few days/weeks, etc; this day ~ week*, a week ago. **3** only remaining: *He had spent his ~ dollar. He would share his ~ crust with a beggar. This is our ~ hope. I wouldn't marry you if you were the ~ person on earth.* **4** least likely, suitable, willing, desirable, etc: *She's the ~ woman I want to sit next to at dinner*, I have no wish whatever to do so. *That's the ~ thing I should expect him to do*, it seems most improbable that he will do it. **5** final; leaving nothing more to be said or done: *I've said my ~ word on this question. This is the ~ thing* (= the newest, the most up-to-date, thing) *in labour-saving devices.* □ *adv* **1** (contrasted with *first*) after all others: *I am to speak ~ at the meeting. The horse on which I bet my money came in ~.* **2** (contrasted with *next*) on the ~ occasion before the present time: *When did you ~ get a letter from her? She was quite well when I saw her ~/when I ~ saw her. When were you ~ in London/in London ~?* □ *n* that which comes at the end: *These are the ~ of our apples. James II was the ~ of the Stuart kings. We shall never hear the ~ of this*, People will always talk about it. *I hope we've seen the ~ of her*, that we shall never see her again. ***at (long) ~***, in the end; after (much) delay: *At (long) ~ we reached London. The holidays came at ~.* ***to/till the ~***, until the end; (liter or rhet) until death: *faithful to the ~.* ***breathe one's ~***, (liter) die. **~·ly** *adv* (in making a list) in the ~ place; finally: *L~ly I must explain that....*

last[2] /lɑst *US:* læst/ *vi* [VP2A,B] go on; be enough (for): *We have enough food to ~ (us) three days. How long will the fine weather ~?* **~·ing** *adj* continuing for a long time: *a ~ing peace.*

last[3] /lɑst *US:* læst/ *n* block of wood shaped like a foot for making shoes on. ***stick to one's ~***, not try to do things one cannot do well.

latch /lætʃ/ *n* **1** simple fastening for a door or gate, the bar falling into a catch and being lifted by a small lever. ***on the ~***, fastened with a ~, but not locked. **2** small spring lock for a door opened from outside with a ~key. **ˈ~·key**, key for releasing or turning back a ~. **ˈ~key ˈchildren**, (colloq) those left to look after themselves because both parents go out to work. □ *vt,vi* **1** [VP6A,2A] fasten with a ~: *L~ the doors. This door won't ~ properly.* **2** [VP2C] ***~ on(to)***, (colloq) cling to; get possession of; understand.

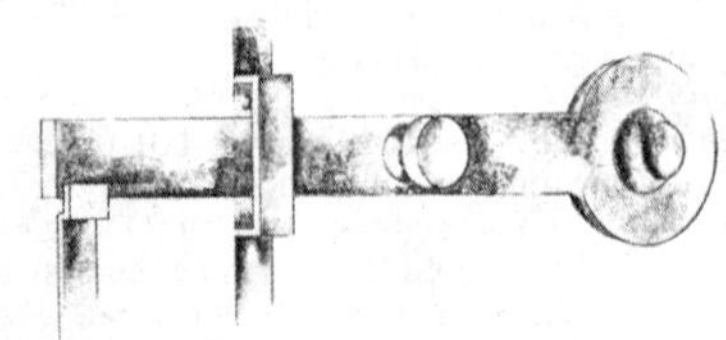

a latch

late[1] /leɪt/ (-r, st. ⇨ last[1], latter.) *adj* **1** (contrasted with *early*) after the right, fixed or usual time: *Am I ~? Don't be ~ for work. The train was ten minutes ~. The crops are ~ this year.* **2** far on in the day or night, in time, in a period or season: *at a ~ hour; in the ~ afternoon; in ~ summer*, e g in Sept; *in the ~ eighties*, e g of the 19th c, in the years just before 1890; *~ Latin*, between classical Latin and the Latin of the Middle Ages; *keep ~ hours*, i e much after the usual times; *~ dinner*, in the evening, contrasted with mid-day dinner. *The ~ edition of this paper appears at 3p m; there's a later one at 5p m; the final edition comes out at 7p m.* **3** recent; that recently was: *the ~ political troubles; the ~st news/fashions; the very ~st improvements; Mr Greene's ~st novel*, the most recently published. Cf *latest* and *last*: *Mr Greene has said that his ~st novel will be his last*, that he will write no more novels. **4** former, recent (and still living): *the ~ prime minister.* **5** former, recent (and not now living): *her ~ husband; the ~ King.* **6** ***of ~***, recently. ***at (the) latest***, before or not later than: *Be here on Monday at (the) latest.*

late[2] /leɪt/ *adv* **1** (contrasted with *early*) after the usual, right, fixed or expected time: *get up/go to bed/arrive home ~; marry ~ in life*, e g at the age of 50; *two years ~r; sit/stay up ~*, not go to bed until a ~ hour; *better ~ than never.* ***~r on***, at a ~r time; afterwards: *a few days ~r on; as we shall see ~r on.* **early and ~**, at all hours: *He's at his desk early and ~.* **sooner or ~r**, some time or other. **2** recently: *I saw him as ~ as/no ~r than yesterday.* **lat·ish** /ˈleɪtɪʃ/ *adj* rather ~.

la·teen /ləˈtin/ *adj* (only in) ~ **sail**, triangular sail on a long yard at an angle of 45° to the mast.

late·ly /ˈleɪtlɪ/ *adv* (usu in neg and interr sentences, or with *only*, or in *as ~ as*) in recent times; recently: *Have you been to the cinema ~? We haven't been there ~.* Cf (in the affirm): *I saw him a few days ago. I was there not long ago. I saw her as ~ as last Sunday. It is only ~ that she has been well enough to go out.*

latent /ˈleɪtnt/ *adj* present but not yet active, developed or visible: *~ bacteria; ~ energy; the ~ image on a photographic film*, not visible until the film is developed: *~ abilities.*

lat·eral /ˈlætrl/ *adj* of, at, from, to, the side(s): *Pinch out the ~ buds to get large chrysanthemum blooms.*

lat·erite /ˈlætəraɪt/ *n* [U] kind of red soil much used for road-making in the tropics.

latex /ˈleɪteks/ *n* [U] milk-white liquid of (esp rubber) plants; emulsion of rubber globules used in paints, etc.

lath /lɑθ *US:* læθ/ *n* (*pl* ~s /lɑðz *US:* /læðz/) long, thin strip of wood, esp as used for plaster walls and ceilings, and for making trellises, Venetian blinds.

lathe /leɪð/ *n* **1** machine for holding and turning pieces of wood or metal while they are being shaped, etc. **2** potter's wheel.

lather /ˈlɑðə(r) *US:* ˈlæð-/ *n* [U] **1** soft mass of white froth from soap and water (as made on a man's face before shaving). **2** frothy sweat on a horse. □ *vt,vi* [VP6A] make ~ on: *~ one's chin before shaving. The horse was badly ~ed.* **2** [VP2A] form ~: *Soap does not ~ in sea-water.* **3** [VP6A] (colloq) whip or beat.

lathi /ˈlætɪ/ *n* long, iron-bound stick used as a weapon (by the police) in India.

Latin /ˈlætɪn *US:* ˈlætn/ *n* language of ancient Rome. □ *adj* of the ~ language; of peoples speaking languages descended from ~. ~ **'America,** countries of S and Central America in which Spanish and Portuguese are spoken. **the ~ Church,** the R C Church. ~ **cross,** ⇨ the illus at cross. **the '~ Quarter,** (in Paris) area on the south bank of the Seine, a centre for students and artists for many centuries. **the ~ races/peoples,** those of Italy, France, Spain, Portugal, etc. **~·ist** /-ɪst/ *n* ~ scholar. **~·ize** /-ɑɪz/ *vt* give a ~ form to (a word); put (sth) into ~.

lati·tude /ˈlætɪtjud *US:* -tud/ *n* **1** [U] distance north or south of the equator measured in degrees. ⇨ the illus at projection. **2** (*pl*) regions or districts: *high/low ~s,* places a long way from/near to the equator; *warm ~s.* **3** [U] (measure of) freedom in action or opinion: *Does your government allow much ~ in political belief,* allow people to hold widely different political beliefs? **4** (photo) time limits within which a film may safely be under- or over-exposed. **lati·tudi·nal** /ˈlætɪtjudɪnl *US:* -ˈtudnl/ *adj* **lati·tudi·nar·ian** /ˈlætɪˈtjudɪˈneərɪən *US:* -ˈtudnˈeər-/ *adj, n* (person who is) tolerant, broad-minded (esp in religious beliefs and dogmas).

la·trine /ləˈtrin/ *n* (in places where there are no sewers, e g camps) pit or trench to receive human urine and excrement.

lat·ter /ˈlætə(r)/ *adj* **1** recent; belonging to the end (of a period): *the ~ half of the year.* **'~-'day** *adj* modern. **2** *the ~,* (contrasted with *the former*) the second of two things or persons already mentioned: *Of these two men the former is dead, but the ~ is still alive.* **~·ly** *adv* of late; nowadays.

lat·tice /ˈlætɪs/ *n* framework of crossed laths or metal strips as a screen, fence or door, or for climbing plants to grow over: (attrib) *a ~ frame/girder/pylon,* made with iron or steel ~-work. **~ window,** one with small square- or diamond-shaped pieces of glass in a framework of lead. ⇨ the illus at window. **lat·ticed** *adj* made in the form of a ~; provided with a ~.

laud /lɔd/ *vt* [VP6A] (rare except in hymns) praise; glorify. **~·able** /-əbl/ *adj* deserving praise. **~ably** /-əblɪ/ *adv*

lauda·num /ˈlɔdn̩əm/ *n* [U] opium prepared for use as a sedative.

lauda·tory /ˈlɔdətərɪ *US:* -tɔrɪ/ *adj* expressing or giving praise.

laugh /lɑf *US:* læf/ *vi, vt* **1** [VP2A,B,C,3A] make sounds and movements of the face and body, showing amusement, joy, contempt, etc: *The jokes made everyone ~.* **~ at, (a)** be amused by: *~ at a joke/a funny story.* **(b)** make fun of; ridicule: *It's unkind to ~ at a person who is in trouble.* **(c)** disregard; treat with indifference: *~ at difficulties.* ***~ in sb's face,*** defy openly, show contempt for. ***~ one's head off,*** ~ heartily. ***~ on the other side of one's face,*** change from joy or triumph to sorrow or regret. ***~ over,*** ~ while discussing, examining, etc: *~ over a letter.* ***~ up one's sleeve,*** be secretly amused. ***He ~s best who ~s last, He who ~s last ~s longest,*** (prov) warning against expressing triumph too soon. **2** [VP15B] ***~ away,*** dismiss (a subject) by ~ing: *~ away sb's fears or doubts,* suggest, by ~ing, that they are without real cause. **~ down,** silence by ~ing scornfully; reject by ~ing: *They ~ed the speaker/the proposal down.* **~ off,** escape from, get rid of, by ~ing: *~ off an embarrassing situation.* **3** [VP22,15A] arrive at a state, obtain a result, by ~ing: *~ oneself silly/helpless; ~ oneself into convulsions; ~ a person out of his depression/out of a foolish belief.* □ *n* [C] sound made in ~ing; act of ~ing: *We've had a good many ~s over his foolishness. They all joined in the ~. "Oh, yes", she answered with a ~.* ***have/get the ~ of sb,*** score off him. ⇨ score[2](4). ***have the last ~,*** have the last ~ of sb. **'belly-~,** ⇨ belly[1](1). **~·able** /-əbl/ *adj* amusing; causing persons to ~: *a ~able mistake.* **~·ably** /-əblɪ/ *adv* **~·ing** *adj* showing happiness, amusement, etc: *~ing faces.* □ *n* laughter: *It's no ~ing matter,* not a suitable occasion for ~ing. **'~ing-gas** *n* nitrous oxide (N_2O) used in dental surgery. **~·ing·ly** *adv* **~·ter** *n* [U] ~ing: *burst into ~ter; roar with ~ter; an outburst of ~ter.*

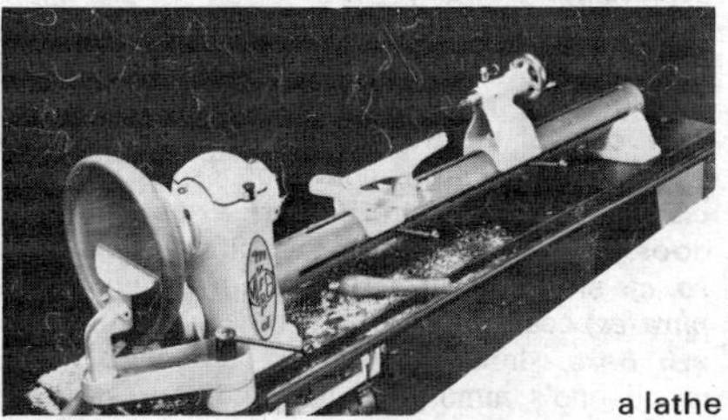

a lathe

launch[1] /lɔntʃ/ *vt, vi* **1** [VP6A] set (a ship, esp one newly built) afloat: *~ a new passenger liner.* **2** [VP6A,15A] ***~ sth (against/at),*** set in motion; send; aim: *~ an attack; ~ threats at an opponent; ~ a missile/spacecraft into outer space.* **'~ing-pad** *n* base or platform from which spacecraft, etc are ~ed. **'~ing-site** *n* place for ~ing-pads. ⇨ the illus at rocket. **3** [VP6A,15A] (fig) get started; set going: *~ a new business enterprise; ~ a man into business.* **4** [VP2C] ***~ out/into, ~ (out) into,*** make or start (on): *~ out into a new argument/debate; ~ into a new subject; ~ out into extravagance.* □ *n* act of ~ing (a ship or spacecraft).

launch[2] /lɔntʃ/ *n* mechanically-propelled passenger-carrying boat (on rivers and lakes, in harbours).

launder /ˈlɔndə(r)/ *vt, vi* [VP6A,2A] wash and press (clothes): *Send these sheets to be ~ed. Will these shirts ~ well?*

laun·der·ette /ˈlɔndəˈret/ *n* laundry at which members of the public may launder their clothes, etc in coin-operated automatic washing-machines and dryers.

laun·dress /ˈlɔndrəs/ *n* woman who earns money by washing and ironing clothes.

laun·dry /ˈlɔndrɪ/ *n* (*pl* -dries) **1** [C] laundering business; place where clothes, sheets, etc, are sent to be laundered. **2** (*sing* with *def art*) clothes (to be) laundered: *Has the ~ come back yet?* **'~·man** /-mæn/ *n* (*pl* -men) man who collects and delivers ~.

laur·eate /ˈlorɪət *US:* ˈlɔr-/ *adj* crowned with a laurel wreath. *n* **the ('Poet) 'L~,** poet officially appointed to the Royal Household in GB. The holder may write poems on great national occasions.

laurel /ˈlorl *US:* ˈlɔrl/ *n* evergreen shrub with smooth, shiny leaves, used by ancient Romans and Greeks as an emblem of victory, success and distinction. ***look to one's ~s,*** beware of losing one's reputation; be on the look out for possible successes among rivals. ***rest on one's ~s,*** be content with one's successes and rest. ***win/gain one's ~s,*** win reputation, honour. **~-led** *adj* crowned with ~.

lav /læv/ *n* (colloq abbr of) lavatory.

lava /ˈlɑvə/ *n* [U] hot liquid material flowing from a volcano: *a stream of ~;* this material when it has cooled and hardened: *ˈ~ beds.* ⇨ pumice.

lava·tory /ˈlævətrɪ *US:* -tɔrɪ/ *n* (*pl* -ries) [C] room for washing the hands and face in; toilet; water-closet.

lave /leɪv/ *vt* (poet) wash; bathe; (of a stream) flow gently past or against.

lav·en·der /ˈlævɪndə(r)/ *n* [U] plant with pale purple sweet-scented flowers; the dried flowers and stalks (sewn up in bags and placed among linen sheets, etc); the colour of ˈ~ **water,** scent distilled from ~.

lav·ish /ˈlævɪʃ/ *adj* **1** ~ ***(of),*** giving or producing freely, liberally or generously: *He is never ~ of praise/in giving money to charity.* **2** ~ ***(in),*** (of what is given) given abundantly; excessive: ~ *praise/expenditure on luxuries.* □ *vt* [VP14] give abundantly and generously: ~ *care on an only child.* **~·ly** *adv*

law /lɔ/ *n* **1** [C] rule made by authority for the proper regulation of a community or society or for correct conduct in life: *When a Bill is passed by Parliament and signed by the Sovereign, it becomes a law.* **ˈlaw-giver** *n* man who gives a code of laws (e g Moses in Hebrew history, Solon in Greek history). **ˈlaw-officer** *n* (esp) Attorney or Solicitor-General. ⇨ regulation, statute. **2** [U] **the law,** the whole body of laws considered collectively: *If a man breaks the law/fails to observe the law he can be punished. Does the law allow me to do this?* ***lay down the law,*** talk authoritatively, as if one were certain of being right. **ˈlaw-abiding** *adj* obeying the law. **ˈlaw-breaker** *n* person who disobeys the law. **3** [U] controlling influence of the laws: *maintain law and order,* see that the laws are respected. *Necessity knows no law,* When sth cannot be avoided, ordinary laws and rules will be ignored or broken. **4** [U] the laws as a system or science; the legal profession: *study law; law students; read law,* study in order to become a lawyer; *follow/go in for the law,* be, prepare to become, a lawyer. ⇨ jurisprudence. **5** (with a defining word) one of the branches of the study of law: *commercial law; the law of nations; international law.* **6** [U] operation of the law (as providing a remedy for wrongs). ***go to law (against sb), have the law on sb,*** (colloq) appeal to the law courts. ***take the law into one's own hands,*** use force to redress a wrong. **ˈlaw court** *n* court of justice. **ˈlaw suit** *n prosecution of a claim in a law court.* **7** [C] rule of action or procedure, esp in an art department or life, or a game: *the laws of perspective/harmony; the laws of cricket.* ***be a law unto oneself,*** disregard rules and conventions; do what one thinks right. **8** (also *law of nature* or *natural law*) factual statement of what always happens in certain circumstances; regularity in nature, e g the order of the seasons: *Newton's law; the laws of motion; the law of supply and demand; the law of self-preservation,* the instinct of men and animals to behave in a way that will save them from danger. **law·ful** /-fl/ *adj* **1** allowed by law; according to law: *lawful acts; the lawful ruler.* **2** (of offspring) legitimate: *the lawful heir.* **law·fully** /-flɪ/ *adv* **law·less** *adj* **1** not in accordance with the law; not conforming to the law; not restrained by law; unruly: *lawless acts: lawless tribes.* **law·less·ly** *adv* **law·less·ness** *n* [U].

lawn[1] /lɔn/ *n* [C] area of grass (turf) kept closely cut and smooth, e g in a private garden or a public park; such an area of grass used for a game: *a ˈcroquet ~; a ˈtennis ~.* **ˈ~-mower** *n* machine for cutting grass on ~s. **ˌ~ ˈtennis** *n* the game of tennis played on an unwalled court, either hard surfaced or turfed. ⇨ the illus at tennis.

lawn[2] /lɔn/ *n* [U] kind of fine linen used for dresses, blouses and esp for a bishop's sleeves.

law·yer /ˈlɔjə(r)/ *n* person who practises law, esp an attorney or solicitor.

lax /læks/ *adj* **1** negligent; inattentive; not strict or severe: *lax discipline/behaviour; lax in morals.* **2** (of the bowels) free in action. **lax·ity** /ˈlæksətɪ/ *n* [U] being lax; [C] (*pl* -ties) instance of being lax. **lax·ly** *adv*

laxa·tive /ˈlæksətɪv/ *n, adj* (medicine, drug) causing the bowels to empty.

lay[1] /leɪ/ *vt,vi* (*pt,pp* laid /leɪd/) For uses with *adverbial particles* and *preps* ⇨ 12 below. **1** [VP6A,15A] put on a surface; put in a certain position, in the proper place for a purpose: *Who will lay the linoleum,* spread it out, fasten it down, etc? *He laid his hand on my shoulder. A new submarine cable was laid between England and Holland. The woodcutter laid his axe to the tree,* began to chop. *A bricklayer is a man who lays bricks.* ***lay a snare/trap/an ambush (for sb/sth),*** prepare one. **2** [VP6A,15B] (of non-material things, and fig uses) place; put. ***lay (one's) hands on sth/sb,*** **(a)** seize; get possession of: *He keeps everything he can lay (his) hands on.* **(b)** do violence to: *How dare you lay hands on me? He laid violent hands on himself,* (dated) tried to commit suicide. **(c)** find: *I have the book somewhere, but can't lay my hands on it just now.* **(d)** (eccles) confirm; ordain (sb) as a deacon or priest by the laying on of hands (as a bishop does) or consecrate (sb) as a bishop (as an archbishop does). Hence, ***laying-on of hands,*** confirmation; consecration. ***lay the blame (for sth) on sb,*** say that he is responsible for what is wrong, etc. ***lay a (heavy) burden on sb,*** cause sb to be responsible for sth likely to be difficult, to cause suffering, etc. ***lay one's hopes on,*** = pin (the more usu word) one's hopes on. ***lay a strict injunction on sb (to do sth),*** give him strict orders (to do it). ***lay great/little store by/on sth,*** value, very much/little. ***lay stress/emphasis/weight on sth,*** treat it as important; emphasize it. ***lay a tax on sth,*** impose one. **3** [VP15A] cause to be in a certain state, condition, or situation. ***lay sb to rest,*** (esp) bury sb: *He was laid to rest in the churchyard.* ***lay sb under a/the necessity/obligation,*** make it necessary or obligatory for him (to do sth): *Your conduct lays me under the necessity of dismissing you. He was laid under an obligation to support the wife he had deserted.* ***lay sb under contribution,*** compel him to contribute money, etc. ***lay sth to sb's charge,*** hold him responsible. ***lay claim to sth,*** ⇨ claim. ***lay sth at sb's door,*** ⇨ door. ***lay one's finger on,*** ⇨ finger. ***lay siege to,*** ⇨ siege. **4** [VP22] (*lay* with *n, adj* or *adv phrases*) cause to be in a specified condition. ***lay sth bare,*** show; reveal: *lay bare one's heart,* reveal one's inmost feelings, etc. ***lay sth flat,***

cause to be flat: *crops laid flat by heavy rainstorms.* **lay sb (fast) by the heels,** (dated formal) capture him; make him helpless (orig used of putting sb in the stocks(**14**)). **lay sb low,** send him to the ground: *I've been laid low* (= kept in bed) *by influenza.* **lay sth open,** (**a**) expose, reveal: *lay open a plot.* (**b**) cut, gash: *lay open one's cheek,* e g by falling and striking it against a rock. **lay oneself open to sth,** render oneself liable to criticism, calumny, etc. **lay sth waste,** ravage, destroy: *a countryside laid waste by invading armies.* **5** [VP6A] cause to be down, settle: *sprinkle water on the roads to lay the dust.* **lay sb's doubts,** get rid of them, ⇨ **allay,** the more usu word. **lay a ghost/spirit,** expel or exorcize it; cause it to stop appearing to people. **6** [VP6A,2A] (of birds and insects) produce: *Are your hens laying yet? How many eggs does this hen lay each week? New laid eggs, 5p each.* **7** [VP15A] (usu passive) set (a story, etc) in time and place: *The scene is laid in Athens, in the third century,* BC. **8** [VP6A] place or arrange (ready for use, etc): *lay the table (for breakfast),* put out plates, knives, etc: *lay the cloth,* spread it on the table ready for a meal; *lay a fire,* put wood, coal, etc in a fireplace, ready for lighting. **9** [VP6A,12C,14] put down (a sum of money) as a wager or stake (on sth of which the result is uncertain); offer as a bet: *They laid a wager on the result of the race. I'll lay you £5 that he won't come. I'll lay* (= make) *you a bet that….* **10** [VP6A,15A] cover; coat: *Lay carpet on the floor/lay the floor with carpet; lay straw over the yard/lay the yard with straw; lay colours on canvas.* ⇨ *lay on* at **12** below. **11** [VP6A] (sl) (of a man) have sexual intercourse with: *He's the sort of boss who likes to lay his typist.* **12** [VP2C,B] (uses with *adverbial particles* and *preps*):

lay about one (with sth), (dated formal) hit out in all directions: *When they rushed at him, Harry laid about him with his big stick.*

lay sth aside, (**a**) save; keep for future use: *lay aside money for one's old age.* (**b**) put down: *He laid his book aside to listen to me.* (**c**) abandon; give up: *lay aside bad habits.*

lay sth back, turn back: *The horse laid back its ears.*

lay sth by, = lay sth aside(**a**).

lay sb/oneself down, place in a lying or recumbent position: *Lay the baby down gently. She laid herself down.* **lay sth down,** (**a**) pay or wager: *How much are you ready to lay down?* (**b**) (begin to) build: *lay down a new ship.* (**c**) convert (land) to pasture: *lay down land in/to/with/under grass.* (**d**) store (wine) in a cellar: *lay down claret and port.* **lay sth down/lay it down that,** establish: *You can't lay down hard and fast rules. It was laid down that all applicants should sit a written examination. These prices have been laid down by the manufacturers.* **lay down one's arms,** put one's weapons down as a sign of surrender. **lay down the law,** say with (or as if with) authority what must be done. **lay down one's life,** sacrifice it: *He laid down his life for his country.* **lay down office,** resign a position of authority.

lay sth in, provide oneself with a stock of: *lay in provisions/stores.*

lay off, (colloq) (**a**) discontinue work or activity; rest: *The doctor told me to lay off for a week.* (**b**) stop doing sth which irritates or annoys: *I hear you've been seeing my sister again—Well, you can just lay off.* **lay sb off,** dismiss temporarily: *lay off workmen,* e g because of a shortage of materials. Hence, **ˈlay-off** *n* period during which men are temporarily dismissed.

lay sth on, (**a**) supply gas, water, electricity to a building: *We can't occupy the new house until gas and water are laid on.* (**b**) (colloq) provide lavishly: *Theatres and concerts were laid on for the distinguished visitors from Poland.* **lay it on (thick/with a trowel),** use exaggerated praise, flattery, etc: *To call him a genius is laying it on a bit too thick!*

lay sth out, (**a**) spread out ready for use or so as to be seen easily: *lay out one's evening clothes; the magnificent scene that was laid out before the climbers when they reached the summit.* (**b**) prepare for burial: *lay out a corpse.* (**c**) spend (money): *lay out one's money carefully.* (**d**) make a plan for; arrange well: *well-laid out streets and avenues; lay out a printed page.* Hence, **ˈlay-out** *n* arrangement, plan, design of a printed page, an advertisement, a book, a factory. **lay oneself out (to do sth),** exert oneself, take pains: (dated) *She laid herself out to make her guests comfortable.*

lay over, (US) (= GB *stop over*) stop at a place during a journey because of a requirement in a schedule. **ˈlay·over** *n* such a stop.

lay sth up, (**a**) save; store: *lay up provisions.* (**b**) ensure by what one does or fails to do that one will have trouble, etc in future: *You're only laying up trouble for yourself.* (**c**) put (a ship) out of commission: *lay a ship up for repairs.* **lay sb up,** (usu passive) force sb to stay in bed: *He's laid up with a broken leg. The flu has laid him up for a few days.*

lay[2] /leɪ/ *n* (chiefly in) *the lay of the land* (*lie* is more usu), the nature or formation of an area of land.

lay[3] /leɪ/ *n* (sl) partner (usu female) in sexual intercourse. ⇨ **lay**[1](**11**).

lay[4] /leɪ/ *n* (liter) minstrel's song. ballad.

lay[5] /leɪ/ *pt* of **lie**[2].

lay[6] /leɪ/ *adj* (attrib only) **1** of, for, done by, persons who are not priests: *a lay brother/sister,* one who wears the dress and has taken the vows of a religious order, but who does manual work and is excused other duties. ⇨ **laity. 2** non-professional; not expert (esp with reference to the law and medicine): *lay opinion,* what non-professional people think. To the lay mind the language of a lawyer seems to be full of jargon. **ˈlay·man** /-mən/ *n* (*pl* **-men**) lay person: *Where the law is concerned I am only a layman,* I have no expert knowledge.

lay·about /ˈleɪəbaʊt/ *n* (GB sl) loafer; person who avoids working for a living.

lay-by /ˈleɪbaɪ/ *n* (older use) railway siding; (modern use, GB) area at the side of a road where vehicles may park without hindering the flow of traffic.

layer /ˈleɪə(r)/ *n* [C] **1** thickness of material (esp one of several) laid or lying on or spread over a surface, or forming one horizontal division: *a ~ of clay.* **ˈ~-cake,** one with horizontal divisions separated by cream, jam, etc. **2** (gardening) shoot of a plant fastened down to take root while still growing from the parent plant. **3** (of hens) *good/bad ~s,* laying eggs in large/small numbers. **4** (betting) *~s and backers,* persons betting against and on a horse, etc. □ *vt* [VP6A] fasten down (a shoot of a plant): *~ carnations.*

lay·ette /leɪˈet/ *n* garments, blankets, etc for a

new-born baby.

lay fig·ure /ˈleɪ ˋfɪgə(r)/ *n* jointed wooden figure of the human body (used by artists for arranging drapery, etc).

lay·man ⇨ lay[6].

lazar /ˈlæzə(r)/ *n* (archaic) poor and diseased person, esp a leper.

laza·retto /ˈlæzəˋretəʊ/ (*pl* -tos /-təʊz/) (also **laza·ret, laza·rette** /ˈlæzəˋret/) *nn* quarantine station.

Laz·arus /ˈlæzərəs/ *n* beggar; (in contrasts) very poor man: *~ and Dives.*

laze /leɪz/ *vi,vt* [VP2A,C,15B] be lazy; pass (time) in idleness: *~ all day; lazing away the afternoon.*

lazy /ˈleɪzɪ/ *adj* (-ier, -iest) unwilling to work; doing little work; suitable for, causing, inducing, inactivity: *a ~ fellow; a ~ afternoon.* ⇨ idle. **ˋ~-bones** *n* ~ person. **lazi·ly** *adv* **lazi·ness** *n*

lea /li/ *n* (poet) stretch of open grass land.

leach /litʃ/ *vt* **1** [VP6A] cause (a liquid) to percolate through some material. **2** [VP15B] ***~ out/away,*** purge (a soluble matter) away or out by the action of a percolating fluid: *the ~ing of the soil,* the washing away, e g by heavy rainfall, of elements in it necessary for plant growth.

lead[1] /led/ *n* **1** [U] soft, heavy, easily melted metal (symbol **Pb**) of a dull bluish-grey colour used for water- and gas-pipes, as a roofing material, and in numerous alloys. **ˋ~-ore,** rock containing ~. **ˈ~ ˋpoisoning** *n* diseased condition caused by taking ~ into the system. **~ shot,** ⇨ shot[1](4). **ˋ~ works** *n sing* place where ~-ore is smelted. **2** [U] (also **ˋblack ~**) graphite; stick of graphite as used in a ~-pencil. **3** [C] lump of ~ fastened to a line marked in fathoms for measuring the depth of the sea from ships. ***cast/heave the ~,*** take soundings. ***swing the ~,*** (sl) evade one's proper share of work by pretending to be ill, using tricks, etc. **4** (*pl*) strips of ~ used to cover a roof; area of (esp horizontal) ~-covered roof; ~ frames for glass, e g in a lattice window. **~ed** *adj* secured with strips of ~: *~ed windows.* **~ed light,** ⇨ light[3](10). **~en** /ˈledn/ *adj* **1** made of ~: *a ~en coffin.* **2** having the colour or appearance of ~: *~en clouds.* **3** dull and heavy like ~: *~en sleep; a ~en heart.*

lead[2] /lid/ *n* **1** (*sing* with *def* or *indef art*) action of guiding or giving an example; direction given by going in front; sth that helps or hints. ***follow sb's ~,*** follow his example. ***give sb a ~,*** encourage him by doing sth first, or by giving a hint towards the solution of a problem. ***take the ~,*** take the leading place, give an example. **2** (with *def art*) first place or position: *have/gain the ~ in a race;* (attrib) *the ~ story,* (journalism, news broadcasting) item of news given the greatest prominence: (with *indef art*) distance by which one leads: *have a ~ of ten feet.* ***take over/lose the ~,*** move to the front/fall behind in a race, in business, etc. **3** [C] cord, leather strap, for leading a dog: *Keep your dog on the ~ in these busy streets.* **4** [C] principal part in a play; actor or actress who plays such a part: *the juvenile ~,* the actor who plays the part of the handsome young hero. **5** [C] artificial watercourse leading to a mill; channel of open water in an ice-field. **6** [C] (electr) conductor conveying current from a source to the place where it is used. **ˋ~-in** *n* **(a)** preliminary remarks, introduction (to). **(b)** wire joining an aerial to a wireless receiver or television set. **7** [C] (in card games) act or right of playing first: *Whose ~ is it?*

lead[3] /lid/ *vt,vi* (*pt,pp* led /led/) **1** [VP6A,15A,B] guide or take, esp by going in front: *Our guide led us through a series of caves. The servant led the visitors in/out/back.* ***~ the way (to),*** go first; show the way. **2** [VP6A,15A,B] conduct (sb) by the hand, by touching him, or by a rope, etc: *~ a blind man; ~ a horse,* by holding the halter and walking at its head. ***~ sb astray,*** (fig) tempt him to do sth wrong. ***~ sb on,*** (fig) entice sb to do more than he intended. ***~ sb by the nose,*** control him completely; make him do everything one wishes him to do. ***~ a woman to the altar,*** marry her. **3** [VP6A,2A] act as chief; direct by example or persuasion; direct the movements of: *~ an army/an expedition/a mutiny; ~ the Conservative Party; ~ the fashion; ~ the choir/the singing. Who's going to ~?* **4** [VP6A,2A,C] have the first place in; go first: *A brass band led the regiment. Which horse is ~ing,* e g in a race? ***~ off,*** start. *Who's going to ~ off? He led off by saying that....* **5** [VP6A,17A,14] guide the actions and opinions of; influence; persuade: *What led you to this conclusion? He is easier led than driven. I am led to believe* (= Certain facts, etc cause me to believe) *that he is disloyal to us. What led you to think so?* **6** [VP2C] be a path, way or road to; (fig) have as a result: *Where does this road ~? Your work seems to be ~ing nowhere,* getting no result. *This led to great confusion.* ***~ up to,*** be a preparation for or an introduction to; direct the conversation towards: *That's just what I was ~ing up to. Chapter One describes the events that led up to the war.* ***All roads ~ to Rome,*** (fig) There are many ways of reaching the same result. **7** [VP6A,12C] (cause sb to) pass, go through, spend (life, etc): *~ a miserable existence; ~ a double life/a Jekyll and Hyde existence.* ***~ sb a (pretty) dance,*** ⇨ dance[1](1). ***~ sb a dog's life,*** make his life wretched. **8** [VP6A,2A] (in card games) put down, as first player (a certain card or kind of card): *~ the two of clubs; ~ trumps.* **9** [VP3A] ***~ with,*** (journalism) have as the main article or news story: *We'll ~ with the dock strike.*

leader /ˈlidə(r)/ *n* **1** person who leads: *the ~ of an army/an expedition/the Labour Party; the ~ of the choir; the ~ of an orchestra* (usu the first violinist). **2** principal counsel in a law court case: *the ~ for the defence.* **3** (GB) leading article (in a newspaper). ⇨ leading below. **4** shoot growing at the end of a stem or principal branch. **5** tendon or sinew. **~·less** *adj* **ˋ~·ship** /-ʃɪp/ *n* [U] being a ~; power of leading; the qualities of a ~.

lead·ing /ˈlidɪŋ/ *adj* chief; most important: *the ~ men of the day; the ~ topics of the hour,* those now being discussed; *the ~ lady,* the actress with the chief part in a play; *L~ Aircraftman,* non-commissioned rank in the R A F. **ˈ~ ˋarticle,** (in a newspaper) one giving editorial opinions on events, policies, etc. **~ case,** (legal) one that establishes a precedent. **ˈ~ ˋlight,** (colloq) prominent person. **ˈ~ ˋquestion,** one that suggests the answer that is hoped for. □ *n* act of ~: **ˋ~-rein** *n* for ~ a horse. **ˋ~-strings** *n pl* straps, etc with which babies were formerly taught to walk: *in ~-strings,* (fig) guided and controlled like a young child.

leaf /lif/ *n* (*pl* leaves /livz/) **1** one of the parts (usu green and flat) growing from the side of a stem or branch or direct from the root of a tree, bush, plant, etc (collectively called *foliage*): *sweep up dead leaves in autumn;* ⇨ the illus at flower, tree; (pop) petal (as in *rose-leaves*). ***in*** ***~,*** with the leaves grown: *The trees will soon be in ~.* ***come into ~,*** grow leaves: *The trees come into ~ in spring.* **ˈ~-bud** *n* one from which leaves, not flowers, develop. **ˈ~-mould** *n* [U] soil composed chiefly of decaying leaves. **2** single sheet of paper forming two pages of a book. ***take a ~ out of sb's book,*** take him as a model. ***turn over a new ~,*** (fig) make a new and better start. **3** hinged or loose part of an extending table (used to make the table larger). **4** [U] very thin sheet of metal, esp of gold or silver: *gold ~.* □ *vi:* *~ through* (a book, etc), turn over the pages quickly; glance through. **~·less** *adj* having no leaves. **~y** *adj* (-ier, -iest) covered with leaves; having leaves; made by leaves: *a ~y shade.*

leaf·let /ˈliflət/ *n* **1** young leaf. **2** printed sheet (unbound but sometimes folded) with announcements, etc esp one for free distribution.

league[1] /lig/ *n* (old) measure of distance (about three miles or 4·8 kms).

league[2] /lig/ *n* [C] **1** agreement made between persons, groups or nations for their common welfare, e g to work for peace; the parties that make such an agreement. **the L~ of Nations,** that formed in 1919 after the First World War, with headquarters at Geneva, dissolved in 1946. ⇨ United Nations. ***in ~ with,*** allied with; having made an agreement with. **2** group of sports clubs or teams playing matches among themselves: *~ football matches.* □ *vt,vi* [VP6A,15A,B,2C] form into, become, a ~: *countries that are ~d together.*

leak /lik/ *n* **1** hole, crack, etc caused by wear, injury, etc through which a liquid, gas, etc may wrongly get in or out: *a ~ in the roof,* allowing rain to enter; *a ~ in the gas-bag of a balloon,* allowing gas to escape; (fig) *a ~ of information; an inspired ~,* of news that is deliberately disclosed. ***spring a leak,*** ⇨ spring[3](6). **2** the liquid, gas, etc that gets out or in. □ *vi,vt* **1** [VP2A,C] (allow to) pass out or in through a ~: *The rain is ~ing in. The ship was ~ing badly.* **2** [VP2A,6A, 14] (of news, secrets, etc) (cause to) become known by chance or with authority: *The news has ~ed out. Who ~ed the news to the press?* **ˈ~·age** /-ɪdʒ/ *n* **1** [U] the process of ~ing: *~age of military secrets.* **2** [C] instance of this; that which ~s in or out; amount that ~s in or out. **~y** *adj* having a ~: *a ~y kettle.*

leal /lil/ *adj* (Scot or liter) loyal.

lean[1] /lin/ *adj* (-er, -est) **1** (of persons and animals) having less than the usual proportion of fat; (of meat) containing little or no fat. **2** not productive; of poor quality: *a ~ harvest; ~ years,* years of scarcity. □ *n* [U] meat with little or no fat. **~-ness** *n*

lean[2] /lin/ *vi,vt* (*pt,pp* ~ed or leant /lent/) **1** [VP2A,C] be or put in a sloping position; *~ backwards; ~ out of a window; trees that ~ over in the wind; the L~ing Tower of Pisa.* ***~ over backward(s) (to do sth),*** (colloq) make too great an effort (to please sb, get a result, etc) **2** [VP2C, 3A] rest in a sloping position for support: *~ on a table; ~ upon one's elbows; ~ on sb's arm.* **3** [VP15A] cause to rest against and be supported by: *~ a ladder against a wall/one's elbows on a table.* **4** [VP3A] ***~ towards,*** have a tendency: *Do some oriental philosophies ~ towards fatalism?* **5** [VP3A] ***~ (up)on,*** depend: *~ on a friend's advice; ~ upon others for guidance.* **~·ing** *n* [C] tendency (of mind *towards* sth): *He has pacifist ~ings/~ings towards pacificism.* **ˈ~-to** *n* building with the rafters of its roof resting against the side of another building: (attrib) *a ~-to greenhouse.*

leap /lip/ *vi,vt* (*pt,pp* leaped /lept/ or leapt /lept/) **1** [VP2A,C,3A] jump (*jump* is the usu word; *leap* is used in liter and rhet style): *He ~t at the opportunity,* seized it eagerly. ***Look before you ~,*** ⇨ look[1](1). **2** [VP6A,15A] (cause to) jump over: *~ a wall; ~ a horse over a fence.* □ *n* [C] jump; sudden upward or forward movement: *a great ~ forward,* (fig) a great advance. ***a ~ in the dark,*** an attempt to do sth the result of which cannot be foreseen. ***by ~s and bounds,*** very rapidly. **ˈ~-frog** *n* game in which players jump with parted legs over others who stand with bent backs. □ *vt* (-gg-) jump over in this way. **ˈ~-year** *n* in which February has 29 days.

learn /lɜn/ *vt,vi* (*pt,pp* ~t /lɜnt/, ~ed) [VP2A, 3A,6A,7A,8,9,10,15A,B] **1** gain knowledge of or skill in, by study, practice or being taught: *~ a foreign language; ~ to swim/how to ride a horse. Has he ~t his lessons? Some boys ~ slowly.* ***~ sth by heart,*** memorize it. **2** be told or informed: *I'm sorry to ~ of his illness/that he's ill. We have not yet ~ed whether he arrived safely.* **3** (vulg or dialect sometimes *larn* /lɑn/) teach: *I'll ~ you* (= punish you and so teach you how unwise it is) *to come into my orchard and steal apples.* **~ed** /ˈlɜnɪd/ *adj* having or showing much knowledge, esp of the humanities: *the ~ed professions,* those needing much knowledge; *~ed men; ~ed books/periodicals/societies; to look ~ed.* **~ed·ly** *adv* **~er** *n* person who is ~ing; beginner: *He hasn't passed his driving test yet; he's only a ~er.* **~·ing** *n* [U] wide knowledge gained by careful study: *a man of great ~ing.*

lease /lis/ *n* [C] contract by which the owner of land or a building (*the lessor*) agrees to let another (*the lessee*) have the use of it for a certain time for a fixed money payment (called *rent*); the rights given under such a contract: *take a farm on a ~ of several years. When does the ~ expire?* **by/on ~**: *We took the land on ~.* ***get/give sb a new ~ of life,*** a better chance of living longer, or of being happier, more active. □ *vt* [VP6A] give, take possession of (land, etc), by ~. **ˈ~-ˈlend** *n* arrangement (1941) by which the President of the US could supply war materials to countries whose defence he considered important. **ˈ~·hold** *n, adj* (land) (to be) held for a term of years on ~. ⇨ *freehold* at free[1](3). **ˈ~·holder** *n* person who holds a ~; lessee.

leash /liʃ/ *n* [C] leather strap or thong for holding or controlling an animal (esp a hound): *hold in ~,* (fig) control. ***strain at the ~,*** (fig) show eagerness to be free, to have an opportunity to do sth.

least /list/ *adj, n* (contrasted with *most;* ⇨ less, little) **1** smallest in size, amount, extent, etc: *A has little, B has less, and C has (the) ~. There isn't the ~ wind today,* no wind at all. *That's the ~ of my anxieties.* ***The ~ said the better,*** The best thing is silence. ***L~ said soonest mended,*** (prov) Talking will only make things worse. **2** (phrases) ***at ~***: *It will cost at ~ five pounds,* five pounds and perhaps more. *He is at ~ as tall as you. You should at ~ have warned her. You can at ~ try.* **(not) in the ~:** *It doesn't matter in the ~. I don't understand in the ~ what this author is trying to say. 'Would you mind holding this box?' 'Not in the ~.'* I do not mind at all. **to say ~ (of it),** without saying more; without exaggeration: *It wasn't a very good dinner, to say the ~ of it.* □ *adv* to the smallest extent: *He works hardest and is being paid ~. This is the ~ useful of the four books.* **~ of all:** *None of you can complain, Charles ~ of all,* Charles has the ~ reason for complaining. *L~ of all would I want to hurt your feelings,* That is sth I would never do. **'~·wise** /-waɪz/ **'~·ways** /-weɪz/ *adv* or at least, or rather.

leather /'leðə(r)/ *n* [U] material made by curing animal skins, used for making shoes, gloves, bags, etc: *~ upholstery,* e g for the seats of a car. **'~-jacket** *n* grub of the crane-fly. **'~·neck** *n* (US, sl) marine. **~y** *adj* like ~: *~y meat,* hard, tough. **'~·'ette** /-'et/ *n* imitation ~.

leave[1] /liv/ *vt,vi* (*pt,pp* **left** /left/) **1** [VP6A,2A, 3A] go away from: *When did you ~ London? It's time for us to ~/time we left.* **~ for,** go away to: *We're leaving for Rome next week.* **2** [VP6A, 15A,2A] go away finally or permanently; no longer live (in a place); cease to belong to a school, society, etc; give up working for (an employer, etc): *When did you ~ school? The secretary has threatened to ~. The boy left home and went to sea. He left medicine for the law,* changed from the medical to the legal profession. *My typist has left me,* has resigned. **be/get nicely left,** (colloq) be tricked, deceived or deserted. **3** [VP15A,B] neglect or fail to take, bring or do sth: *I've left my umbrella in the train. I left my books on the table. He left half his work until the next day.* **~ sb/sth behind,** neglect or forget to bring or take: *The luggage has been left behind! Don't ~ me behind!* **4** [VP15A,B,22,19C,2C,24,25] allow or cause to remain in a certain place or condition: *L~ your hat and coat in the hall. Always ~ things where you can find them again. Did you ~ the doors and windows firmly fastened? Who left that window open? His illness has left him weak. Don't ~ her waiting outside in the rain.* **~ sb/sth alone,** not touch, spoil or interfere with: *L~ the cat alone,* Don't tease it. **~ well alone,** (prov) Don't try to improve what is already satisfactory. **~ off,** stop: *Has the rain left off yet? We left off at the end of Chapter Five.* **~ sth off, (a)** stop: *It's time to ~ off work. Do ~ off biting your nails, Jane!* **(b)** no longer wear: *They left off their woollen underwear when the weather got warm.* **~ sth/sb out,** omit; fail to consider: *~ out a possibility; ~ out a letter,* e g spell *embarrass* with one r instead of two r's. *Don't ~ me out, please!* Don't forget me—I want a share, a place, etc. **~ sth over,** postpone: *That matter can be left over until the committee meets next week.* **~ it at that,** do or say nothing more: *There's nothing we can do; we must leave it at that.* **~ sb to himself/to his own devices,** not try to control or direct his activities: *The children were left very much to themselves during the holidays,* were allowed to do what they liked, without guidance or help. **~ sth unsaid,** not say it: *Some things are better left unsaid,* It is better to remain silent about them. **~ much/a lot/sth/nothing to be desired,** be un/satisfactory: *His behaviour ~s a lot/nothing to be desired,* is very unsatisfactory/is quite satisfactory. **~ go/hold (of sth),** (more usu *let go*) cease holding: *L~ go of my hair, you brute!* **5** [VP6A, 12B,13B,14] (cause to) remain; allow to remain: *Three from seven ~s four* (7 − 3 = 4). *When I've paid all my debts, there'll be nothing left/I'll have nothing left. Have you left anything for me/left me anything?* **To be left until called for,** used as a direction for a letter, package, etc which is to be collected. **6** [VP6A,14,12B,13B] hand over before going away: *Did the postman ~ anything for me?* **~ word (with sb) (for sb),** give a message etc: *Please ~ word (for me) with your secretary if you get news of what happened.* **7** [VP17A,14] entrust; commit; hand over: *I'll ~ the matter in your hands/~ it to you/~ you to attend to the matter. He left his assistant in charge of the shop/left the shop in his assistant's charge.* **8** [VP6A,12B,13B,15A,22] **~ sth (to sb), ~ sb sth,** bequeath by will; have at the time of one's death: *She left all her money to charity. He left me £500. He died leaving nothing but debts. He ~s a widow and two sons. He left her poor. He left a great name behind him,* was famous when he died. **9** [VP15A] pass beyond (a place, etc) so that it is in the direction or relation indicated: *L~ the church on your left and go on up the hill.*

leave[2] /liv/ *n* **1** [U] permission; consent; authority, esp to be absent from duty in the armed forces or government service: *You have my ~ to stay away from the office tomorrow.* **~ of absence,** permission to be absent (esp from mil duty): *The soldier asked for ~ of absence.* **on ~,** absent with permission: *He went home on ~.* **by/with your ~,** with your permission. **(take) French ~,** absence without permission. **2** [C] period of such absence; occasion of being absent from duty, etc: *have only two ~s in six years; a six months' ~.* **3** (*sing* only) departure. **take (one's) ~ (of sb),** say goodbye. Hence, **'~-taking** *n* **take ~ of one's senses,** behave as if mad.

leaven /'levn/ *n* [U] substance, e g yeast, used to make dough rise before it is baked to make bread; (fig) quality or influence spreading in and changing sth □ *vt* [VP6A] add ~ to: act like ~ upon.

leaves /livz/ *pl* of **leaf.**

leav·ings /'livɪŋz/ *n pl* what is left, esp sth unwanted or of little value: *Give the leavings,* e g unwanted food, *to the dog.*

lech·er·ous /'letʃərəs/ *adj* lustful; having, giving way to, strong sexual desires. **lecher** /'letʃə(r)/ *n* ~ man. **lech·ery** /'letʃərɪ/ *n* [U] lust; [C] (*pl* -ries) lustful or lascivious act.

lec·tern /'lektən/ *n* sloping reading-desk as for a Bible in church.

lec·ture /'lektʃə(r)/ *n* [C] **1** talk (to an audience or class) for the purpose of teaching: *give/read a ~; a course of ~s on Greek philosophy; go on a ~ tour.* **2** reproof: *give sb a ~,* scold or reprove him. □ *vi,vt* **1** [VP2A,3A] give a ~ or course of ~s: *~ on modern drama.* **2** [VP6A,14] **~ sb for,** scold, reprove: *The teacher ~d the boys for being lazy.* **lec·turer** *n* person, lower in rank than a professor, who gives ~s, esp at a college or university. **~·ship** /-ʃɪp/ *n* post as a ~r at a university, etc.

led /led/ *pt,pp* of **lead**[3].

ledge /ledʒ/ *n* **1** narrow horizontal shelf coming out from a wall, cliff or other upright surface: *a 'window ~; a ~ for chalk at the bottom of a* *blackboard*. **2** ridge of rocks under water, esp near the shore.

ledger /ˈledʒə(r)/ *n* **1** book in which a business firm's accounts are kept. **2** (music) ˈ~ (or ˈ*leger*) *line*, short line added above or below the stave for outside notes. ⇨ the illus at **notation**.

lee /li/ *n* place giving) protection against wind; (attrib) (of or on the side away from the wind (contrasted with the *windward* or *weather* side): *the lee side of a ship; a* ˈ*lee shore*, on the lee side of one's ship; *a* ˈ*lee tide*, one flowing in the same direction as the wind.

leech /litʃ/ *n* **1** small blood-sucking worm living in wet places of which one kind was formerly used by doctors for bleeding patients: *stick like a* ~, (fig) be very persistent, be difficult to get rid of. **2** (fig) person who sucks profit out of others. **3** (old use) doctor.

leek /lik/ *n* onion-like vegetable with a long, slender white bulb. ⇨ the illus at **vegetable**.

leer /lɪə(r)/ *n* [U] sly, unpleasant look that suggests evil desire or ill will. □ *vi* [VP2A,3A] ~ ***(at sb)***, look with a ~: *~ing at his neighbour's pretty young wife*.

lees /liz/ *n pl* dregs; sediments (of wine, etc); basest part; refuse (as at the bottom of a cask, etc). ***drink/drain to the ~***, (fig) experience the last extremes of suffering, passion, etc.

lee·ward /ˈliwəd (among sailors) /ˈluəd/ *adj, adv* on or to the sheltered side (contrasted with *windward*). □ *n* [U] lee side; sheltered side: *on the ~; steer to ~*.

lee·way /ˈliweɪ/ *n* [U] sideways drift (of a ship) in the direction towards which the wind is blowing. ***make up leeway***, (fig) make up for lost time; get back into position. ***have much leeway to make up***, be behind with one's work.

left[1] *pt,pp* of **leave**.

left[2] /left/ *adj n adv* (opposite of *right*) (of, in, on, the) side of a person's body which is towards the west when he faces north: *Not many people write with the ~ hand. The ~ bank of a river is on your ~ as you face the direction in which it flows. Come and sit on my ~*, i e at my ~ side. *Turn (to the) ~ at the church*. **the L~ (Wing)**, more radical group(s), party or parties, e g socialists, communists: (attrib) *~-wing militants*. ˈ**~-ˈhand** *adj* of, situated on, the ~ side: *a house on the ~-hand side of the street; a ~-hand blow/stroke*. ˈ**~-ˈhanded** *adj* (of a person) using the ~ hand more easily or with more skill than the right. ***a ~-handed compliment***, one that is ambiguous, of doubtful sincerity. ˈ**L~·ist** /-ɪst/ *n* supporter of socialism or radicalism.

leg /leg/ *n* **1** one of the parts of an animal's or a person's body used for walking, esp (of a human body) the part above the foot: *have a leg of mutton for dinner. He lost his right leg in the war*. ***be all legs***, (of a person) be overgrown, lanky and thin. ***off one's legs***, resting: *Poor woman! She's never off her legs*, is always working. ***be on one's legs*** (or joc, ***on one's hind legs***), **(a)** be standing, esp to make a speech. **(b)** (after an illness) be well enough to walk about again. ***be on one's last legs***, fatigued, exhausted: *near one's death or end*. ***feel/find one's legs***, (*feet* is more usu) **(a)** (of a baby) get the power of standing or walking. **(b)** (fig) begin to realize one's powers, abilities, etc; become self-confident. ***find one's sea-legs***, ⇨ **sea(7)**. ***give sb a leg up***, (liter) help him to mount a horse or to climb up sth; (fig) help him in time of need. ***pull sb's leg***, try, for a joke, to make him believe sth that is untrue. Hence, ˈ**leg-pull** [C] and ˈ**leg-pulling** [U] *nn* ***run sb off his legs***, tire him by keeping him constantly busy. ***shake a leg***, (colloq) dance. ***show a leg***, (colloq) get out of bed; (imper) do sth with more effort. ***not have a leg to stand on***, have nothing to support one's opinion, defence, etc. ***stretch one's legs***, go for a walk (esp to take exercise after sitting for a long time). ***take to one's legs***, (*heels* is more usu) run away. ***walk one's*** ˈ***legs off, walk sb off his legs***, tire oneself/him out with walking. **2** that part of a garment that closely covers a leg: *the leg of a stocking; the legs of a pair of trousers*. **3** support of a chair, table, etc: *a stool with three legs; the legs of a bed*. ***on its last legs***, weak and likely to collapse. **4** (cricket) part of the field to the left rear of a right-handed batsman in position (or vice versa): ˈ*leg-stump*, stump nearest to this; *hit a ball to leg*. ⇨ the illus at **cricket**. **5** one section of a journey, esp by air: *the first leg of a round-the-world flight;* one of a series of games in a competition. **-legged** /legd/ *adj* (in compounds) ˈ*long-*ˈ*legged*, having long legs; ˈ*three-*ˈ*legged*, having three legs, e g a stool; *a three-legged race*, for pairs with two legs tied together; ˈ*bare-*ˈ*legged*, having bare legs. **leg·less** *adj* having no legs.

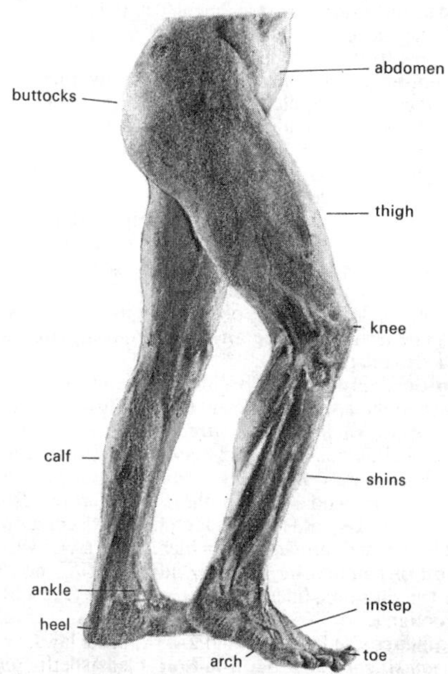

the leg and the foot

leg·acy /ˈlegəsɪ/ *n* (*pl* -cies) [C] **1** money, etc (to be) received by a person under the will of and at the death of another person. **2** (fig) sth handed down from ancestors or predecessors: *a ~ of ill will*.

legal /ˈligl/ *adj* connected with, in accordance with, authorized or required by, the law: *~ affairs; my ~ adviser/representative*, e g a solicitor; *take ~ action (against sb); the ~ fare; ~ tender*, form of money which must be accepted if offered in payment; *a ~ offence*, one against the law, contrasted with an offence against convention; *free ~ aid*, help (from lawyers paid by the State) given to persons unable to pay the usual charges. **~ly** /ˈliɡl̩ɪ/ *adv* **ˈ~·ism** /-ɪzm/ *n* strict adherence to, undue respect for, the law and ~ forms.

legal·ity /liˈɡælətɪ/ *n* [U] the state or quality of being legal: *the ~ of an act.*

legal·ize /ˈliɡl̩ɑɪz/ *vt* [VP6A] make legal: *~ the sale of alcoholic drinks.* **legal·iz·ation** /ˈliɡl̩ɑɪˈzeɪʃn *US:* -l̩ɪˈz-/ *n*

legat /ˈleɡət/ *n* Pope's ambassador to a country.

lega·tee /ˈleɡəˈti/ *n* [C] person who receives a legacy.

leg·ation /lɪˈɡeɪʃn/ *n* [C] (house, offices, etc, of a) diplomatic minister below the rank of ambassador, with those under him, representing his government in a foreign country.

le·gato /lɪˈɡɑtəʊ/ *adv* (musical direction) smoothly, without breaks.

leg·end /ˈledʒənd/ *n* **1** [C] old story handed down from the past, esp one of doubtful truth: *the ~s of King Arthur.* **2** [U] literature of such stories: *heroes who are famous in ~.* **3** [C] inscription on a coin or medal; explanatory words on a map, a picture, etc. **leg·end·ary** /ˈledʒəndrɪ *US:* -derɪ/ *adj* famous, known only, in ~s: *~ary heroes.*

leger /ˈledʒə(r)/ ⇨ **ledger(2).**

leger·de·main /ˈledʒədəˈmeɪn/ *n* [U] juggling; quick and clever performance of tricks with the hands; (fig) deceitful argument.

leg·ging /ˈleɡɪŋ/ *n* (usu *pl*) outer covering, of leather or strong cloth, for the leg up to the knee, or (for small children) for the whole of the leg: *a pair of ~s.*

leggy /ˈleɡɪ/ *adj* having long legs (esp of young children, puppies and colts).

leg·horn /leˈɡɔn *US:* ˈleɡən/ *n* **1** kind of domestic fowl. **2** (also /ˈleɡhɔn/) hat made of the kind of straw imported from Leghorn (also called Livorno), a town in W Italy.

leg·ible /ˈledʒəbl/ *adj* (of handwriting, print) that can be read easily. **leg·ibly** /-əblɪ/ *adv* **legi·bil·ity** /ˈledʒəˈbɪlətɪ/ *n*

legion /ˈlidʒən/ *n* **1** division of several thousand men in the armies of ancient Rome; (fig) any great number: *Their numbers are ~.* **2 British L~,** national association of ex-service men formed in 1921. **(French) Foreign L~,** body of non-French volunteers who serve in the French army, usu overseas. **L~ of Honour,** high French decoration (civilian and military). **3** (in liter or rhet style) vast host or number. **legion·ary** /ˈlɪdʒənərɪ *US:* -nerɪ/ *n* (*pl* -ries) *adj* (member) of a ~, esp the (French) Foreign L~.

legis·late /ˈledʒɪsleɪt/ *vi* [VP2A,3A] make laws: *~ against gambling.* **legis·la·tion** /ˈledʒɪsˈleɪʃn/ *n* [U] making laws; the laws made.

legis·lat·ive /ˈledʒɪslətɪv *US:* -leɪtɪv/ *adj* (of) law-making: *~ assemblies; ~ reforms.*

legis·la·tor /ˈledʒɪsleɪtə(r)/ *n* member of a law-making body.

legis·la·ture /ˈledʒɪsleɪtʃə(r)/ *n* law-making body, e g Parliament in GB.

le·git·imate /lɪˈdʒɪtɪmət/ *adj* **1** lawful, regular: *the ~ king; use public money only for ~ purposes.* **2** reasonable; that can be justified: *a ~ reason for being absent from one's work.* **3** born of persons married to one another; the result of lawful marriage: *a ~ child; of ~ birth.* **4** *the ~ drama,* of the theatre, not cinema or TV. **~·ly** *adv* **le·git·imacy** /lɪˈdʒɪtɪməsɪ/ *n* [U] being ~. **le·git·ima·tize** /lɪˈdʒɪtɪmətɑɪz/ *vt* make ~.

leg·umin·ous /lɪˈɡjumɪnəs/ *adj* of like, the botanical family that includes peas and beans (and other seeds in pods).

lei /ˈleɪi/ *n* garland of flowers worn round the neck (as in Polynesian islands).

lei·sure /ˈleʒə(r) *US:* ˈliʒər/ *n* [U] **1** spare time; time free from work: *have no ~ for sport.* **at ~,** not occupied; when there is ~: *I am seldom at ~.* ***at one's ~,*** when one has free time: *Please look through these papers at your ~.* **2** (attrib): *~ time/hours/clothes.* **~·ly** *adv* without haste or hurry: *work ~ly.* □ *adj* unhurried; deliberate: *~ly movements.* **lei·sured** *adj* having plenty of ~: *the ~d classes.*

lem·ming /ˈlemɪŋ/ *n* small arctic migratory rodent like a field-mouse.

lemon /ˈlemən/ *n* **1** (tree with) pale yellow fruit with acid juice used for drinks and flavouring. ⇨ the illus at **fruit. ˈ~ drop** *n* piece of boiled sugar flavoured with ~. **ˈ~ ˈsquash** *n* drink of ~-juice and water or soda-water. **ˈ~ squeezer** *n* device for pressing juice out of a ~. ⇨ **curd. ~ sole** *n* kind of plaice. **2** (GB sl) silly and plain-looking girl. **~·ade** /ˈleməˈneɪd/ *n* [U] drink made from ~-juice, sugar and water.

lemur /ˈlimə(r)/ *n* (kinds of) nocturnal animal of Madagascar, similar to a monkey but with a fox-like face.

lend /lend/ *vt* (*pt,pp* lent /lent/) **1** [VP6A,12A, 13A,14] ***~ sth to sb, ~ sb sth,*** give (sb) the use of (sth) for a period of time on the understanding that it or its equivalent will be returned: *I will ~ you £100, but I can't ~ money to everyone.* ***~ a hand (with sth),*** help. **ˈ~ing-library,** one from which books may be borrowed. **2** [VP14] contribute: *facts that ~ probability to a theory.* **3** [VP14] help or serve: *Don't ~ yourself to such dishonest schemes. This peaceful garden ~s itself to* (= is favourable for) *meditation.* **~er** *n* person who ~s.

length /leŋθ/ *n* **1** measurement from end to end (space or time): *the ~ of a road/field/stick; a river 300 miles in ~; a room 8 metres in ~ and 6 in breadth; a river navigable for most of its ~; make a stay in Rome for some ~,* for a considerable period of time; *the ~ of time needed for the work.* **at ~, (a)** at last; finally. **(b)** for a long time: *speak at (great) ~.* **(c)** in detail; thoroughly: *treat a subject at ~.* ***(at) full ~,*** with the body stretched out and flat: *lying at full ~ on the grass.* ***keep sb at arm's ~,*** avoid being friendly with him. **2** measurement of a particular thing from end to end: *The car can turn in its own ~. The horse/boat won by a ~,* by its own ~, this being used as a unit of measurement. **3** extent; extreme. ***go to any ~(s),*** do anything necessary to get what one wants. **4** piece of cloth, etc, long enough for a purpose: *a ˈdress ~; a ~ of tubing/pipe.* **~en** /ˈleŋθn/ *vt,vi* [VP6A,2A] make or become longer: *~en a skirt. The days ~en in March.* **ˈ~·wise** /-wɑɪz/, **ˈ~·ways** /-weɪz/ *adv, adj* in the direction from end to end. **~y** *adj* (of speech, writing) very long; too long.

leni·ent /ˈliniənt/ *adj* not severe (esp in punishing people): *~ towards wrongdoers.* **leni·ence** /-əns/, **leni·ency** /-ənsɪ/ *nn* [U] being ~. **~·ly**

adv

len·ity /ˈlenətɪ/ *n* [U] (formal) mercifulness; mercy shown.

lens /lenz/ *n* (*pl* **lenses**) **1** piece of glass or glass-like substance with one or both sides curved, for use in spectacles, cameras, telescopes and other optical instruments. ⇨ the illus at **camera**. **2** (anat) transparent part of the eye, behind the pupil, through which light is refracted. ⇨ the illus at **eye**.

lent /lent/ *pt,pp* of **lend**.

Lent /lent/ *n* (in Christian Churches) period of forty days before Easter, the weekdays of this period being observed by devout persons as a period of fasting and penitence. **~ lily,** daffodil. **ˈ~ term,** university term in which ~ falls. **~en** /ˈlentən/ *adj* of ~: *~en services* (in church).

len·til /ˈlentl/ *n* [C] kind of bean plant; edible seed of this: *~ soup.*

lento /ˈlentəʊ/ *adj, adv* (musical direction) slow(ly).

Leo /ˈliəʊ/ *n* the fifth sign of the zodiac. ⇨ the illus at **zodiac**.

leo·nine /ˈlɪənaɪn/ *adj* of or like a lion.

leop·ard /ˈlepəd/ *n* large African and South Asian flesh-eating animal with a yellowish coat and dark spots. ⇨ the illus at **cat**. **~·ess** /ˈlepəˈdes/ *n* female ~.

leper /ˈlepə(r)/ *n* person suffering from leprosy.

lep·re·chaun /ˈleprəkɔn/ *n* (in Irish folklore) fairy or sprite.

lep·rosy /ˈleprəsɪ/ *n* [U] skin disease that forms silvery scales on the skin, causes local insensibility to pain, etc and the loss of fingers and toes. **lep·rous** /ˈleprəs/ *adj* of, having, ~.

les·bian /ˈlezbɪən/ *n* homosexual woman. **~·ism** /-ɪzm/ *n*

lese maj·esty /ˈleɪz ˈmæʒəsteɪ *US:* ˈliz ˈmædʒəstɪ/ *n* [U] treason; (joc) presumptuous conduct on the part of inferiors.

lesion /ˈliʒn/ *n* [C] harmful change in the tissues of a bodily organ, caused by injury or disease.

less /les/ *adj* (~ is contrasted with *more*. It is an independent comparative, with no real corresponding positive. ⇨ **little, least.**) **1** (used with *nn* that stand for what is measured by amount or quality or degree; *fewer* is preferred before a *pl n* but *less* is used by some educated speakers) not so much; a smaller quantity of: *~ butter.* Cf *fewer eggs; ~ food.* Cf *fewer meals; ~ manpower.* Cf *fewer workers; ~ shipping.* Cf *fewer ships; pay ~ money for the house.* Cf *pay a lower rent; have ~ difficulty with one's work.* Cf *meet with fewer difficulties; ~ size means ~ weight; of ~ value/importance; in/to a ~er degree* (or *a lower degree,* which is preferable). **2** (followed by *than*): *I have ~ money than you.* □ *adv* **1** (modifying *vv*) to a smaller extent; not so much: *Eat ~, drink ~, and sleep more. He was ~ hurt than frightened.* **2** (with *adjj, participles* and *advv*) not so: *Tom is ~ clever than his brother. Try to be ~ impatient. Please behave ~ foolishly.* Note that *not... so* is usu preferred to *less... than,* e g *Try not to be so impatient.* **3 the ~,** as in: *I was the ~ surprised as I had been warned,* My surprise was ~ because.... *The ~ you worry about it the better it will be.* ⇨ **the**[2]. ***any the ~,*** in a lower degree: *I don't think any the ~ of him* (= My opinion of him is not lower) *because of this one failure.* ***no ~,*** as in: *He won no ~ than £50 in the lottery/He won £50, no ~, in the lottery* (expressing surprise at the amount). *Our soldiers fought with no ~ daring than skill,* Their daring equalled their skill. ***even/still ~,*** (as in): *I don't suspect him of robbery, still ~ of robbery with violence.* ***none the ~,*** but for all that; all the same: *Though he cannot leave the house, he is none the ~* (= he is, in spite of that) *busy and active.* □ *n* smaller amount, quantity, time, etc: *in ~ than an hour. I won't sell it for ~ than £50. I want ~ of this and more of that.* Cf *fewer of these and more of those. I expect to see ~ of her* (= to see her ~ often) *in future.* □ *prep* minus; with the deduction of: *£10 a week ~ 50p for National Insurance contribution.*

les·see /leˈsi/ *n* person who holds land, a building, etc on a lease.

les·sen /ˈlesn/ *vt,vi* **1** [VP6A,2A] make or become less: *to ~ the impact/effect of sth.* **2** [VP6A] cause(sth) to appear smaller, less important; belittle: *~ a person's services.*

les·ser /ˈlesə(r)/ *adj* (attrib only) not so great as the other: *choose the ~ evil.*

les·son /ˈlesn/ *n* **1** sth to be learnt or taught; period of time given to learning or teaching: *ˈEnglish ~s; a ~ in music.* **2** (*pl*) children's education in general: *Tom is very fond of his ~s.* **3** sth experienced, esp sth serving as an example or a warning: *Let his fate be a ~ to all of you!* **4** passage from the Bible read aloud during a church service.

les·sor /lesˈɔ(r)/ *n* person who grants a lease.

lest /lest/ *conj* **1** for fear that; in order that... not: *He ran away ~ he should be seen.* **2** (after *fear, be afraid, anxious*) that: *We were afraid ~ he should get here too late.*

let[1] /let/ *vt,vi* (*pt,pp* **let**) (**-tt-**) (For uses with *adverbial particles* and *preps* ⇨ **8** below.) **1** [VP18B] (followed by a *(pro)noun* and an *infinitive* without *to;* rarely used in the passive in this sense) allow to: *Her father will not let her go to the dance. She wants to go to the dance but her father won't let her* (i e let her *go*. The omission of the *infinitive* is frequent when it may be inferred from the context). *Please let me know* (i e inform me) *what happens. Don't let the fire go out.* **2** [VP18B] (used with first and third person *pronouns* to supply an indirect imperative): *Let's start at once, shall we? Don't let's start yet! Let me see*where did I leave my hat? Let us both have a try! Let her do it at once. Let there be no mistake about it,* Don't make any mistake, don't misunderstand me, etc. ***Live and let live,*** ⇨ **live**[2](2). **3** [VP18B] (*let,* in the imperative, may also indicate an assumption. It may also indicate permission, with a suggestion of defiance): *Let A B be equal to C D. Let A B C be an angle of ninety degrees. Let them do their worst! I defy them to do their worst! Let them all come!* **4** [VP18B] (The pattern *let + noun + infinitive,* as in *let the waitress go,* is sometimes replaced by the pattern *let + infinitive + noun,* as in *let drop a hint.* In some cases, e g in *let fly,* the object of *let* is omitted). Note the following: ***let sb/sth be,*** allow to be quiet or unworried: *Let me be,* Don't worry me. *Let the poor dog be,* Don't tease it. ***let drive (at sb/sth),*** aim a blow (at); throw sth (at): *He let drive with his left fist. He let drive at me with a stone.* ***let sb/sth drop,*** allow to drop; (fig) utter (on purpose or by chance). ***let sth fall,*** allow to fall; (fig) allow to be heard: *He let fall a hint of his intentions.* ***let fly (at***

sb/sth), discharge; send out violently; shoot; strike out (at): *He aimed carefully and then let fly* (i e fired) *at the ducks. The angry man let fly a volley of oaths.* ***let sb/sth go,*** release one's hold of: *Don't let go the rope. Let me go! Take your hands off me;* don't hold or keep me. ***let oneself go,*** give way to, no longer hold back, one's feelings, desires, impulses, etc: *He let himself go on the subject.* ***let it go at that,*** say no more about it; dismiss the subject: *I don't agree with all you say but we'll let it go at that.* ***let sth pass,*** overlook; disregard: *It's not a serious error; we can let it pass, I think.* ***let sth slip,*** miss (an opportunity, etc). **5** [VP22] (combined with *adjj*) ***let sb/sth alone,*** allow (sb) to do sth unaided; not interfere with: *Let it alone!* ***Let well alone,*** (prov) Don't try to improve sth that is already satisfactory. ***let alone,*** (colloq) to say nothing of; not to mention: *There were seven people in the car, let alone a pile of luggage and three dogs.* ***let sb/sth loose (on sb),*** allow to be free; (fig) release (one's anger, etc): *Don't let that dog loose.* **6** give the use of (buildings, land) in return for regular money payments: *This house is to be let. The house would let* (= could be let) *easily. She has let her house furnished.* ***let out,*** put out to hire: *He used to let out horses and carriages by the day.* **7** [VP6A] (surgery) ***~ blood,*** cause it to flow. Hence, **'blood-letting** *n* **8** [VP15A,B,2C,14] (uses with *adverbial particles* and *preps*):

let sth down, lower; put or take down: *Please let the window down. This skirt needs letting down,* lengthening by lowering the hem-line. *She let down her hair. That chair has a broken leg, it might let you down,* might not support you. ***let sb down,*** (fig) disappoint; fail to help: *Harry will never let you down,* You can rely upon him to help you always. *I've been badly let down,* placed in a difficult or awkward situation through the failure of others to support me. Hence, **'let-down** *n* feeling of having been let down; disappointment. ***let the side down,*** ⇨ **side**[1]**(10)**.

let sb/sth in/into sth, allow to enter: *Windows let in the light and air. These shoes let (in) water. He let himself in/into the flat with a latch-key,* opened the door using the key. *Who let you into the building?* ***let sth in,*** make (a garment, etc) narrower: *This skirt needs letting in at the waist.* ***let sb in for,*** involve in loss, difficulty, hard work, etc: *He didn't know what a lot of unpaid work he was letting himself in for when he agreed to become secretary of the society.*

let sb into, allow to share (a secret): *She has been let into* (= told) *the secret.* ***let sth into sth,*** put into the surface of: *We must let another window into this wall.*

let sb off, excuse; not compel; not punish; not punish severely: *He was let off with a fine instead of being sent to prison. You have let him off easily,* e g by excusing him from too much work, by punishing him lightly, etc. ***let sth off,*** fire off: *The boys were letting off fireworks.*

let on (that), (colloq) reveal a secret: *He knew where the boy was hiding but he didn't let on,* didn't tell anyone. ***let sb/sth out,*** allow to go (flow, etc) out: *He let the air out of the tyres. Let the water out of the bath-tub.* ***let sth out,*** make (a garment, etc) looser, larger, etc: *He's getting so fat that his trousers need to be let out round the waist.* ⇨ also **6** above. ***let out at,*** aim a violent blow, kick, etc, at; (fig) use violent language: *Be careful! That man has a habit of letting out at people.*

let sb/sth through, allow to pass through: *He got only 40%, so the examiners couldn't possibly let him through.*

let up, become less strong, etc: *Will the rain never let up?* **'let-up** *n* (colloq) cessation; diminution: *There has been no let-up in the rain yet. I've been working ten hours without a let-up.*

let up on sb, (colloq) treat more leniently.

let[2] /let/ *n* (from **let**[1]**(6)**) letting: lease: *I can't get a let for my house,* can find no one willing to rent it from me. **let·ting** *n* [C] property that is let: *a furnished letting,* a furnished house or flat that is let.

let[3] /let/ *vt* (archaic) hinder; obstruct. □ *n* **1** hindrance, esp in the legal phrase: *without let or hindrance.* **2** (tennis) ball which when served, strikes the net before dropping into the opponent's court.

lethal /ˈliθl/ *adj* causing, designed to cause, death: *a ~ dose of poison; ~ weapons; a ~ chamber,* e g in which sick animals may be put to death painlessly.

leth·argy /ˈleθədʒɪ/ *n* [U] (state of) being tired, uninterested; want of energy. **leth·ar·gic** /lɪˈθɑdʒɪk/ *adj* sleepy; lacking in energy; caused by, likely to cause, ~. **leth·ar·gi·cally** /-klɪ/ *adv*

Lethe /ˈliθɪ/ *n* (Gk myth) (river in Hades /ˈheɪdiz/, the Greek underworld, producing) forgetfulness of the past.

let's /lets/ = let us. ⇨ **let**[1]**(2)**.

let·ter /ˈletə(r)/ *n* **1** character or sign representing a sound, of which words in writing are formed: *the 26 ~s of the English alphabet; capital ~s* (A, B, C, etc) *and small ~s* (a, b, c, etc). Cf phonetic *symbol.* **2** written message, request, account of events, etc sent by one person to another: *I have some ~s to write. Inform me by ~ of your plans.* **'~ of 'credit,** ⇨ **credit**[1]**(1)**. **'~-box** *n* (US = *mail box*) **(a)** box (in the street, at a post office) in which ~s are posted; pillar-box. **(b)** box (in a building) for receiving ~s from the post. **'~-card** *n* folded card with a gummed edge for use instead of notepaper and an envelope. **'~-case** *n* pocket-book for holding ~s. **'~-head** *n* (sheet of paper with a) printed name and address, e g of a business firm. **'~-press** *n* contents of an illustrated book other than the pictures; printing from type. **3** (phrases) ***keep the ~ of the law/an agreement,*** carry out the stated conditions without regard to its spirit or true purpose. ***to the ~,*** paying strict attention to every detail: *carry out an order to the ~.* **4** (*pl*) literature and learning: *the profession of ~s; a man of ~s.* **let·tered** /ˈletəd/ *adj* having a good knowledge of books: *a ~ed young man.* **let·ter·ing** /ˈletrɪŋ/ *n* [U] ~s, words, esp with reference to their style and size: *the ~ing on a book cover; poor ~ing on a gravestone.*

let·tuce /ˈletɪs/ *n* [C] ⇨ the illus at **vegetable**. garden plant with crisp green leaves used in salads; [U] these leaves as food.

leu·co·cyte, leu·ko·cyte /ˈlukəsɑɪt/ *n* [C] white blood-cell. **leu·ke·mia** /luˈkimɪə/ *n* disease in which there is excess of ~s with changes in the lymph glands.

Lev·ant /lɪˈvænt/ *n* (*the L~*) Eastern part of the Mediterranean, its countries and islands. **~·ine** /-ɑɪn/ *n, adj* (native) of the ~.

lev·ant /lɪˈvænt/ *vi* abscond; leave (esp without

paying gambling losses).

levee[1] /ˈlevɪ/ *n* (formerly) assembly held by a king or his representative at which men only were received.

levee[2] /ˈlevɪ/ *n* embankment built to protect land from a river in flood: *the ~s along the Mississippi.*

level[1] /ˈlevl/ *adj* **1** having a horizontal surface: *~ ground; make a surface ~.* **~ crossing,** (US = *grade crossing*) place where a road and a railway cross on the same ~. **2** on an equality: *a ~ race,* one in which the competitors keep close together; *draw ~ with the other runners.* **3 have a ~ head,** be steady and well-balanced, able to judge well. Hence, **ˈ~-ˈheaded** *adj* **do one's ~ best,** do all that one can do, do everything possible.

level[2] /ˈlevl/ *n* **1** [C] line or surface parallel with the horizon; such a surface with reference to its height: *1 000 metres above sea ~. The water rose until it was on a ~ with the river banks. Water always finds its own ~.* **2** natural or right position, stage, social standing, etc: *He has found his own ~,* (fig) has found the kind of people with whom he is morally, socially or intellectually equal. *They'll rise to higher ~s* (= advance in civilization, etc) *very quickly.* **3** [U] (group of persons having) equal position or rank: *consultations at cabinet ~,* among members of the cabinet; *top-level talks,* talks between persons in the highest positions (in government, etc). Cf *summit* talks. **ˈO-/ˈA-~ (examination)** [C] ~ of achievement (Ordinary/Advanced) in the school-leaving examination in England and Wales: *a girl with five O-~s and three A-~s.* **4 on the ~,** (colloq) honest(ly); straightforward(ly): *Is he on the ~?* ⇨ crooked(2). **5 ˈspirit ~,** ⇨ spirit(11).

level[3] /ˈlevl/ *vt,vi* (-ll-, US -l-) **1** [VP6A,15A,B] make or become ~ or flat: *~ a building with the ground. Death ~s all men,* makes them equal by ending social distinctions, etc. **~ sth down/up,** make (incomes, marks, standards, surfaces, etc) equal by lowering the higher or raising the lower. **2** [VP6A,14,2C,3A] bring or come into a horizontal plane: *~ a gun at a tiger,* raise it and aim. **~ sth against sb,** put forward (a charge, an accusation, etc). **~ off/out, (a)** cause an aircraft to fly parallel to the earth's surface: *On reaching 1 000 metres, the pilot ~led off.* **(b)** (fig) reach a point in one's career beyond which no further progress is likely: *You're unlikely to get further promotion—we all have to ~ off some time.* **~·ler,** US **~er** /ˈlevḷə(r)/ *n* (esp) person who wishes to abolish social distinctions.

lever /ˈlivə(r) *US:* ˈlevər/ *n* bar or other tool turned on a fulcrum to lift sth or to force sth open, e g a window or drawer; (fig) means by which moral force may be exerted. □ *vt* [VP6A,15B] move (sth *up, along, into/out of position,* etc) with a ~. **~-age** /-ɪdʒ/ *n* [U] action of, power or advantage gained by, using, a ~.

lev·eret /ˈlevərɪt/ *n* young (esp first-year) hare.

lev·ia·than /lɪˈvɑɪəθən/ *n* **1** (in the Bible) sea animal of enormous size. **2** anything of very great size and power.

levi·tate /ˈlevɪteɪt/ *vt,vi* [VP6A,2A] (with reference to powers claimed by spiritualists) (cause to) rise and float in the air in defiance of gravity. **levi·ta·tion** /ˈlevɪˈteɪʃn/ *n*

lev·ity /ˈlevətɪ/ *n* [U] tendency to treat serious matters without respect; lack of seriousness; [C] (*pl* -ties) instance of this.

levy /ˈlevɪ/ *vt,vi* (*pt,pp* levied) **1** [VP6A,14] impose; collect by authority or force: *~ a tax/a fine/a ransom on sb; ~ing an army/troops,* using compulsion to get men as soldiers. **2 ~ war upon/against,** declare, make, war on after ~ing men and supplies. **3** [VP3A] **~ on,** seize by law: *~ on a person's property/estate,* seize this in order to get money for an unpaid debt. □ *n* (*pl* levies) [C] act of ~ing; amount of men, number of men, so obtained. **capital ~,** ⇨ capital(3).

lewd /lud/ *adj* indecent; lustful. **~·ly** *adv* **~·ness** *n*

lexi·cal /ˈleksɪkl/ *adj* (contrasted with *grammatical*) of the vocabulary of a language. **~ly** /-klɪ/ *adv*

lexi·cogra·phy /ˈleksɪˈkogrəfɪ/ *n* [U] dictionary compiling. **lexi·cogra·pher** /ˈleksɪˈkogrəfə(r)/ *n* person who compiles a dictionary.

lexi·con /ˈleksɪkən *US:* -kon/ *n* dictionary (esp of Greek, Latin or Hebrew).

ley /leɪ/ *n* [C] area of land temporarily under grass: *new-sown leys.*

lia·bil·ity /ˈlɑɪəˈbɪlətɪ/ *n* (*pl* -ties) **1** [U] the state of being liable: *~ to pay taxes; ~ for military service,* in a country where there is conscription; *~ to disease; Don't admit ~ for the accident,* e g because of car insurance claims. **ˈlimited ˈ~ company,** ⇨ limit[2]. **2** (*pl*) debts; sums of money that must be paid (contrasted with *assets*). **3** (colloq) handicap: *His wife is more of a ~ at a party than an asset.*

li·able /ˈlɑɪəbl/ *adj* (usu *pred*) **1 ~ for,** responsible according to law: *Is a man ~ for his wife's debts in your country?* **2 be ~ to sth,** be subject to: *If you drive a car to the danger of the public, you make yourself ~ to a heavy fine, or even to imprisonment. He is ~ to seasickness.* **3 be ~ to do sth,** have a tendency to, be likely to: *We are all ~ to make mistakes occasionally.*

li·aison /lɪˈeɪzn *US:* ˈlɪəzon/ *n* **1** [U] (mil) connection; linkage between two separated parts of an army, or two different armies. **ˈ~ officer,** one who keeps two such parts or armies in touch with each other (esp when armies of different countries are fighting and allies); member of a committee, etc acting as a link between the committee and other people. **2** [C] illicit sexual relationship. **li·aise** /lɪˈeɪz/ *vi* (colloq) act as a link (*with, between*).

li·ana /lɪˈɑnə *US:* -ˈænə/ *n* (kinds of) climbing and twining tropical plant.

liar /ˈlɑɪə(r)/ *n* person who tells an untruth or who has told an untruth; person who habitually tells lies.

lib /lɪb/ *n* (colloq abbr for) liberation. **women's lib,** movement (early 1970's) for the liberation of

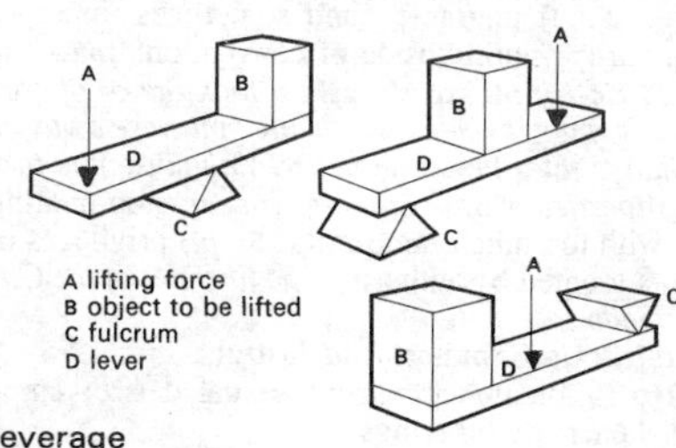

leverage

women from social and economic inequalities.

li·ba·tion /laɪˋbeɪʃn/ *n* [C] **1** (pouring out of an) offering of wine, etc to a god for his munificence: *make a* ~ *to Jupiter.* **2** (colloq) drinking bout.

li·bel /ˋlaɪbl/ *n* **1** [U,C] (the publishing of a) written or printed statement that damages sb's reputation: *sue a newspaper for* ~; *utter/publish a* ~ *against sb.* **2** [C] ~ **on,** (colloq) anything that brings discredit upon or fails to do justice to: *The portrait is a* ~ *on me.* □ *vt* (-ll-, US -l-) [VP6A] publish a ~ against; fail to do full justice to. **~·lous,** US **~·ous** /ˋlaɪbləs/ *adj* containing a ~; in the nature of a ~: *~lous reports;* in the habit of uttering ~s: *a ~lous person/periodical.*

lib·eral /ˋlɪbrl/ *adj* **1** giving or given freely; generous: *a* ~ *giver to charities; a* ~ *supply of food and drink; a* ~ *table,* one with plenty of food and drink. *He is* ~ *of promises but not* ~ *of money,* gives plenty of promises but not much money. **2** open-minded; having, showing, a broad mind, free from prejudice. **3** (of education) directed chiefly towards the broadening of the mind, not specially to professional or technical needs: *the* ~ *arts,* e g philosophy, history, languages. **4** (politics in GB) of the party (dominant until the 1920's), favouring moderate democratic reforms. □ *n* person in favour of progress and reform and opposed to privilege. **L~,** member of the L~ party in GB. **~·ism** /-ɪzm/ *n* [U] ~ views, opinions and principles. **~·ize** /ˋlɪbrlaɪz/ *vt* make ~; free from narrow-mindedness. **~·iz·ation** /ˌlɪbrlaɪˋzeɪʃn *US:* -lɪˋz-/ *n*

lib·er·al·ity /ˌlɪbəˋrælətɪ/ *n* (*pl* **-ties**) **1** [U] generosity; free giving; quality of being broad-minded; freedom from prejudice. **2** (*pl*) instances of generosity: *He has made himself poor by his liberalities.*

lib·er·ate /ˋlɪbəreɪt/ *vt* [VP6A,14] ~ ***(from),*** set free: ~ *slaves;* ~ *the mind from prejudice.* **lib·er·ator** /-tə(r)/ *n* **lib·er·ation** /ˌlɪbəˋreɪʃn/ *n* [U] liberating or being ~d. ⇨ **lib.**

lib·er·tine /ˋlɪbətin/ *n* licentious man. **chartered** ~**,** person whose irregularities and eccentricities of behaviour are tolerated.

lib·erty /ˋlɪbətɪ/ *n* (*pl* **-ties**) **1** [U] state of being free (from captivity, slavery, imprisonment, despotic control, government by others); right or power to decide for oneself what to do, how to live, etc: *They fought to defend their* ~. **at** ~**,** (of a person) free; not imprisoned: *You are now at* ~ *to leave any time,* may do so. ***set sb at*** ~**,** release: *set prisoners/slaves at* ~. ~ ***of conscience,*** freedom to have one's own (esp religious) beliefs without interference. ~ ***of speech,*** freedom to say openly, in public, what one thinks, e g on social and political questions. ~ ***of the press,*** freedom to write and print in periodicals, books, etc whatever one wishes without interference. **2** [U] ungranted and sometimes improper familiarity; setting aside of convention. ***take the*** ~ ***of doing sth/to do sth***: *I took the* ~ *of borrowing your lawn-mower while you were away on holiday.* ***take liberties with***: *You must stop taking liberties with the young woman,* stop treating her with too much familiarity. **3** (*pl*) privileges or rights granted by authority: *the liberties of the City of London.*

li·bid·in·ous /lɪˋbɪdɪnəs/ *adj* lustful.

li·bido /lɪˋbidəʊ/ *n* (psych) sexual desire; emotional energy or cravings.

Libra /ˋlibrə/ *n* the seventh sign of the zodiac (also called 'the scales' or 'the balance'). ⇨ the illus at **zodiac.**

li·brary /ˋlaɪbrɪ *US:* -brerɪ/ *n* (*pl* **-ries**) **1** room or building for a collection of books kept there for reading; the books in such a room or building: *the public* ~, maintained by a town or city council, etc; *a ˋcirculating* ~, one that lends books for profit, members paying a subscription fee; *ˋreference* ~, one in which books may be consulted but not taken away. **2** (attrib) *a ˋ~ book; a ˋ~ edition,* book usu of large size and print and with a strong binding. **3** writing and reading room in a private house. **4** series of books issued by a publisher in uniform binding and connected in some way: *the Home University L~.* **li·brar·ian** /laɪˋbreərɪən/ *n* person in charge of a ~. **li·brar·ian·ship** *n*

li·bretto /lɪˋbretəʊ/ *n* (*pl* **-tos** /-təʊz/ or **-ti** /-ti/) book of words of an opera or musical play. **li·bret·tist** /lɪˋbretɪst/ *n* writer of a ~.

lice /laɪs/ *n pl* of **louse.**

li·cence (US = **li·cense**) /ˋlaɪsns/ *n* **1** [C] (written or printed statement giving) permission from someone in authority to do sth; [U] authorization: *a* ~ *to drive a car/a ˋdriving* ~; *a* ~ *to practise as a doctor; marry by (special)* ~ (contrasted with *banns*); *a* ~ *for the sale of alcoholic drinks.* **ˋon-~,** for the sale of alcoholic drinks to be consumed on the premises. **ˋoff-~,** for the sale of liquor to be taken away. **2** [U] wrong use of freedom; disregard of laws, customs, etc; licentious behaviour: *The* ~ *shown by the troops when they entered enemy territory disgusted everyone.* **poetic** ~**,** freedom from the ordinary rules of language, e g of word order, allowed in verse.

li·cense (also **li·cence**) /ˋlaɪsns/ *vt* [VP6A,17A] give a licence to: *shops ~d to sell tobacco;* ~ *a doctor to practise medicine; a ~d house/~d premises,* where the sale of alcoholic drinks is allowed, e g hotels, restaurants; *a ~d victualler; the ~d quarters,* (in some countries) part of a town where there are ~d brothels. **li·cen·see** /ˌlaɪsnˋsi/ *n* person holding a licence (esp to sell alcohol).

li·cen·tiate /laɪˋsenʃɪət/ *n* person who has a licence or certificate showing that he is competent to practice a profession.

li·cen·tious /laɪˋsenʃəs/ *adj* immoral (esp in sexual matters); not held back by morality. **~·ly** *adv* **~·ness** *n*

li·chee, li·chi /ˋlaɪtʃi/ variant spellings of **lychee.**

li·chen /ˋlaɪkən, ˋlɪtʃən/ *n* [U] dry-looking plant that grows on rocks, walls, tree-trunks, etc, usu green, yellow or grey.

lich·gate, lych·gate /ˋlɪtʃgeɪt/ *n* roofed gateway of a churchyard, where, at a funeral, the coffin used to await the arrival of the clergyman.

licit /ˋlɪsɪt/ *adj* lawful; permitted.

lick /lɪk/ *vt,vi* **1** [VP6A,15A,B,22] pass the tongue over or under: *The cat was ~ing its paws. He ~ed the spoon clean.* ~ ***sb's boots,*** cringe before sb; be abject, servile. ~ ***one's lips,*** show eagerness or satisfaction. ~ ***one's wounds,*** try to recover after a defeat. ~ ***sth off,*** remove by ~ing: *The boy ~ed the jam off his lips.* ~ ***sth up,*** take it up by ~ing: *The cat ~ed up the milk.* ~ ***into shape,*** (fig) make presentable, efficient, properly trained: *The recruits were soon ~ed into shape by the drill sergeants.* ~ ***the dust,*** (rhet) fall to the ground, defeated or killed. **2** [VP6A,15B] (esp of waves, flames) touch lightly: *The flames* ~*ed up the dry grass.* **3** [VP6A] (colloq) overcome; triumph over; give a whipping to: *Well, that* ~*s everything!* That is more surprising than anything I've ever seen or heard! **4** [VP2A] (sl) go; hurry: *He went off as hard as he could* ~. □ *n* **1** act of ~ing with the tongue. ***give sth a* ~ *and a promise,*** a feeble attempt to clean, polish, etc (with a promise of sth more thorough later). **2** (also **ˈsalt-**~) place to which animals go for salt. **3** (sl) ***at a great* ~, *at full* ~,** at a great pace. **~·ing** *n* (colloq) beating; defeat: *Our football team got a* ~*ing yesterday.*

licor·ice /ˈlɪkrɪs/ *n* ⇨ liquorice.

lid /lɪd/ *n* **1** movable cover (hinged or detachable) for an opening, esp at the top of a container: *the lid of a kettle/box; the ˈteapot lid.* **2** eyelid. **~·less** *adj*

lido /ˈlidəʊ/ *n* (*pl* -dos /-dəʊz/) open-air swimming pool.

lie[1] /laɪ/ *vi* (*pt,pp* lied, *pres part* lying), *n* [VP2A] (make a) statement that one knows to be untrue: *tell lies. He lied to me. He's lying. He's telling lies. What a pack of lies!* What a lot of untrue statements! *He lived a lie,* deceived without using words. **white lie,** ⇨ white[1](3). ***give sb the lie,*** accuse him of lying. **ˈlie detector** *n* device which records physiological changes, e g heart beats, rate of breathing, caused by emotional stresses while a person is being questioned.

lie[2] /laɪ/ *vi* (*pt* lay /leɪ/, *pp* lain /leɪn/, *pres part* lying) [VP2A,C,D,3A] **1** be, put oneself, flat on a horizontal surface or in a resting position; be at rest: *lie on one's back/side, lie face downwards. Don't lie in bed all morning! His body lies* (= He is buried) *in the churchyard. He lay on the grass enjoying the sunshine.* ***lie back,*** get into, be in a resting position: *lie back in an armchair.* ***take sth lying down,*** submit to a challenge, an insult without protest. ***lie down under*** (an insult, etc), fail to protest, resist, etc. ***lie in,*** **(a)** stay in bed after one's usual time for getting up. Hence, **ˈlie-ˈin** *n*: *have a nice lie-in on Sunday morning.* **(b)** remain in bed to give birth to a child: *The time had come for her to lie in.* **ˈlying-ˈin hospital** (obs) maternity hospital. ***lie in ambush,*** ⇨ ambush. ***lie low,*** (colloq) ⇨ low[1](12). ***lie up,*** stay in bed or in one's room (from illness, etc). ***lie with,*** (old use, biblical, now usu *sleep with*) have sexual intercourse with. ***Let sleeping dogs lie,*** (prov) Avoid discussing problems that are likely to cause trouble. **ˈlie-abed** /əbed/ *n* lazy person who lies in bed instead of getting up. **2** (of things) be resting flat on sth: *The book lay open on the table. How long has your bicycle been lying out on the wet grass?* **3** be kept, remain, in a certain state or position: *money lying idle in the bank; towns lying in ruins; men who lay* (= were) *in prison for years. The snow lay thick on the ground. The fields lay thickly covered with snow.* ***lie heavy on sth,*** cause discomfort, trouble, distress: *The lobster lay heavy on his stomach. The theft lay heavy on his conscience.* ***lie over,*** be left for action at a future time: *Let the matter lie over until the next committee meeting.* **4** be spread out to view; extend: *The valley lay before us. The coast was undefended and lay open to attack. If you are young, life still lies before you.* ***see/find out how the land lies,*** (fig) learn how matters stand, what the state of affairs is. **5** be situated: *ships lying at anchor. The ship is lying at No 5 berth. The fleet lay off the headland.* ***lie to,*** (of a ship) come almost to a stop, facing the wind. **6** (of abstract things) exist; be in a certain position or manner: *The trouble lies* (= is) *in the engine. The answer to this difficulty lies in not putting too much pressure on the engine. He knows where his interest lies,* where he may win an advantage, make a profit. *I will do everything that lies in* (= that is within) *my power.* ***lie at sb's door,*** be attributable to: *At whose door should the blame/fault/responsibility lie,* Who should we attribute it to? ***lay sth at sb's door,*** ⇨ door(1). ***lie with sb,*** be sb's duty or responsibility: *The solution/burden/proof lies with you. It lies with you* (= It is your duty) *to accept or reject the proposal.* ***as far as in me lies,*** to the best of my power. **7** (legal) be admissible: *The appeal will not lie,* is not according to law, cannot be admitted. □ *n* (*sing* only) the way sth lies. ***the lie of the land,*** the natural features (esp the contours) of an area; (fig) the state of affairs; (golf) the position of a ball when it comes to a stop.

lied /lid/ *n* (*pl* ~er /ˈlidə(r)/) (G) German song or lyric. **ˈ~er-singer,** person who sings ~er.

lief /lif/ *adv* (archaic or liter) willingly: *I would (had) as* ~ *join the Crusade as anything,* would do this more willingly than anything else.

liege /lidʒ/ *adj* (legal) (only in) **ˈ~ lord/sovereign,** (feudal times) ruler, landowner, entitled to receive service and homage. **~·man** /-mən/ *n* (*pl* -men) feudal vassal; faithful follower. □ *n* ~ lord; ~man.

lien /lɪən/ *n* legal claim (*upon* property) until a debt on it is repaid: *A shipping company has a* ~ *upon cargo until the freight is paid.*

lieu /lu/ *n* (only in) ***in* ~ *(of),*** instead (of).

lieu·ten·ant /lefˈtenənt *US:* luˈt-/ *n* **1** army officer below a captain; junior officer in the Navy. ⇨ App 9. **2** (in compounds) officer with the highest rank under: *ˈ~-ˈcolonel; ˈ~-comˈmander; ˈ~-ˈgovernor,* official under a governor-general (as in a British colony, or formerly in a dominion). **3** deputy or substitute; one who acts for a superior. **Lord L~ (of the County),** the Queen's representative in a county. **L~ of the Tower,** i e the Tower of London. **leiu·ten·ancy** /-ənsɪ/ *n* rank, position, of a ~.

life /laɪf/ *n* (*pl* lives /laɪvz/) **1** [U] condition that distinguishes animals and plants from earth, rock, etc: *How did* ~ *begin? Where did* ~ *come from?* **life force,** vital energy thought of as working for the survival of the human race and the individual. **2** [U] living things collectively, in general; plants, animals, people: *Is there any* ~ *on the planet Mars? A naturalist studies animal and plant* ~. **3** [U] state of existence as a human being: *L~ is sweet. The battle was won, but only with great loss of* ~, many were killed. ***bring to* ~,** cause to live; cause to recover from a faint, an illness thought to be fatal, etc. ***come to* ~,** recover consciousness, recover from a faint, etc: *We all thought he was drowned, but after an hour's artificial respiration he came (back) to* ~. ***run for one's* ~*/for dear* ~,** in order, or as if to, save oneself from death. ***a matter of* ~ *or death,*** one on which sb's continued existence depends. ***the kiss of* ~,** ⇨ kiss. ***this* ~,** ~ on earth. ***the other* ~, *future/eternal/everlasting* ~,** conscious existence, the state of existence, after bodily death. ***with all the pleasure in* ~,** with the greatest possible pleasure. **4** [C] state of existence, as an individual living being: *How many lives were lost in the disaster?* ***take sb's ~,*** kill him. ***take one's own ~,*** kill oneself; commit suicide. ***a ~ for a ~,*** phrase used to express the view that murder must be revenged by the killing or execution of the murderer or (in a vendetta) by the killing of a member of his family. ***cannot for the ~ of me,*** however hard I try (= even if my ~ depended on it): *For the ~ of me I couldn't recall her name.* ***Not on your ~!*** (colloq *int*) Quite definitely not. **5** [C] period between birth and death, or between birth and the present, or between the present and death: *He lived all his ~ in London. I have lived here all my ~. The murderer received a ~ sentence/was sentenced to imprisonment for ~. The murderer is doing ~/ was given ~,* (sl) imprisonment for ~. **~ annuity,** one that will be paid for the rest of a person's ~. **'~ cycle,** progression through different stages of development: *the ~ cycle of a frog,* from the egg to the tadpole to the final stage. **~ interest,** (legal) benefit valid (from property, etc) during a person's ~. **~ peer,** member of the House of Lords, whose title is not inherited by his heirs. ***early/late in ~,*** during the early/late part of one's ~: *marry early/late in ~.* ***have the time of one's ~,*** (colloq) enjoy oneself immensely, as never before. **6** [U] human relations; the business, pleasures, social activities, etc, of the world: *Sailors don't earn much money, but they do see ~,* see how people everywhere live. *An air hostess really does see ~. There is not much ~* (e g social activity) *in our small village.* ***true to ~,*** (of a story, drama, etc) giving a true description of how people live. **7** [C,U] (way of) living; career: *Some people have easy lives. Which do you prefer, town ~ or country ~? That's the ~ for me!* That's how I should like to live. **'high ~,** ⇨ high[1](12). **8** [C] written account of sb's ~; biography: *Do you enjoy reading the lives of great men? He has written a new ~ of Newton.* **'~ story,** biography. **9** [U] activity, liveliness, interest: *The children are full of ~,* are active and cheerful. *Put more ~ into your work.* ***the ~ (and soul) of the party,*** person who is the most lively and amusing member of a social gathering. **10** [U] living form or model: *a portrait/picture taken from (the) ~; a '~ drawing; a '~ class,* (in an art school) one in which students draw or paint from living models. ***to the ~,*** with great fidelity or exactness: *draw/ portray/imitate sb to the ~.* ⇨ lifelike below. ***as large as ~,*** **(a)** of natural or ordinary size: *a statue as large as ~.* **(b)** (colloq and in joke) in person; without possibility of doubt or error. **11** [C] fresh start or opportunity after a narrow escape from death, disaster, etc: *The batsman was given a ~,* e g when the fielders missed an easy catch. *They say a cat has nine lives.* **12** [C] period during which sth is active or useful: *the ~ of a steamship/a government.* **13 '~ assurance/insurance,** ⇨ these words. ***expectation of ~, '~ expectancy,*** (insurance) statistically determined number of years that a person at a particular age may expect to live. ***a good/bad ~,*** person who is likely to pass/not to reach this average. **14** (compounds) **'~-belt** *n* belt of cork or other buoyant material to keep a person afloat in water. **'~-blood** *n* [U] blood necessary to ~; (fig) vitalizing influence; sth that gives strength and energy. **'~-boat** *n* **(a)** boat specially built for going to the help of persons in danger at sea along the coast. **(b)** boat carried on a ship for use in case the ship is in danger of sinking, is on fire, etc. **'~-buoy** *n* ~belt in the form of a ring, through which a person puts his head, shoulders and arms. **'~ cycle** *n* ⇨ 5 above. **'~ estate** *n* property that a person enjoys for ~, but cannot dispose of further. **'~-giving** *adj* that strengthens or restores physical or spiritual ~. **'~-guard** *n* **(a)** expert swimmer on duty at dangerous places where people swim. **(b)** (*pl* **'L~ Guards**) cavalry regiment in the British army. **(c)** bodyguard of soldiers. **'~ history** *n* (biol) record of the ~ cycle of an organism. **'~-jacket** *n* one of cork or other buoyant material or that can be inflated. **'~-like** *adj* resembling real ~; looking like the person represented: *a ~like portrait.* **'~-line** *n* rope used for saving ~, e g one attached to a ~buoy, or one fastened along the deck of a ship during a storm, for persons to cling to; diver's line for signalling to the ship from which he is working; (fig) anything on which one's ~ depends; (palmistry) line across the palm of the hand, alleged to show one's length of ~, major events in one's ~, etc. **'~-long** *adj* continuing for a long time; lasting throughout ~. **'~-office** *n* life assurance office or business. **~ peer** *n* ⇨ 5 above. **'~-preserver** *n* **(a)** (GB) short stick with a heavy, weighted end, used as a weapon of defence. **(b)** (US) = ~-jacket. **'~-saver** *n* (esp in Australia) ~guard**(a)**. **'~-size(d)** *adj* (of pictures, statues, etc) having the same size, proportions, etc, as the person represented. **'~-span** *n* (biol) longest period of ~ of an organism known from the study of it. **'~-sup'port system,** equipment in a spacecraft which provides an environment in which astronauts may live. **'~-time** *n* duration of a person's ~. ***the chance of a ~time,*** an opportunity that comes only once. **'~-work** *n* task that occupies one's whole ~ or to which one devotes all one's ~. **~-less** *adj* **1** never having had ~: *~less stones.* **2** having lost ~; dead. **3** dull; not lively: *answer in a ~less manner.* **~-less-ly** *adv* like a living thing. **lifer** /ˈlaɪfə(r)/ *n* **1** (with *adj* prefixed) person who lives a certain kind of ~: *a simple-lifer.* **2** (sl) (one who serves a) sentence of ~ imprisonment.

a life-buoy

a life-jacket

lift /lɪft/ *vt,vi* **1** [VP6A,15A,B] raise to a higher level or position: *~ (up) a table; ~ sth out of a box/a child out of his cot. This box is too heavy for me to ~. This piece of good luck ~ed her spirits.* ***~ up one's eyes (to...),*** look up (at). ***have one's face ~ed,*** have a face-lift; ⇨ face[1](2). ***not ~ a finger,*** ⇨ finger. ***~ up one's voice,*** raise it, cry out. **2** [VP2C] ***~ off,*** (of a rocket, spacecraft) rise from the launching site. Hence, **'~-off** *n*: *We have ~-off.* **3** [VP2A] yield to an attempt to ~: *This window won't ~*, won't go up. **4** [VP2A] (of clouds, fog, etc) rise; pass away: *The mist began to ~.* **5** [VP6A] dig up (root crops); remove (plants, shrubs, etc) from the ground: *~ potatoes.* **6** [VP6A] steal: *~ articles in a supermarket.* Hence, **`shoplifter, `shoplifting,** stealing from shops; take without permission or proper acknowledgement: *Long passages in that textbook have been ~ed from other authors.* **7** [VP6A] end a ban, prohibition, blockade, siege. □ *n* [C] **1** act of ~ing. ***get/give sb a ~,*** **(a)** be offered/offer sb a ride in a car or other vehicle: *Can you give me a ~ to the station?* ⇨ also *air ~* at **air¹(7). (b)** (of a person's spirits) become/make more cheerful, contented: *The big increase in her salary gave her a tremendous ~.* **2** (US = *elevator*) apparatus for taking people up or down to another floor: *take the ~ to the tenth floor.* **`~-boy/-man** /-mæn/ *n* one who operates a ~.

liga·ment /ˈlɪgəmənt/ *n* [C] band of tough, strong tissues that holds two or more bones together in the body.

liga·ture /ˈlɪgətʃə(r)/ *n* [C] **1** bandage, piece of thread, etc used in tying, esp cord used to tie up a bleeding artery. **2** (printing) two or more letters joined e g *f* and *l* joined as ﬂ.

light¹ /laɪt/ *adj* (-er, -est) (opposite of *dark*) **1** (of a place) well provided with light(**1**): *a ~ room. It's beginning to get ~.* **2** pale-coloured: *~ hair; a ~ complexion; ~ blue/green/brown.* **`~-coloured** *adj* having a ~ colour: *a ~-coloured dress; ~-coloured hair.*

light² /laɪt/ *adj* (-er, -est) **1** not heavy; not having much weight (for its size): *as ~ as air/as a feather; a ~ fall of snow; a pair of ~ shoes; a ~ cart or van,* one made for ~ loads and quick movement: *~ clothing,* for summer; *a ~ building/bridge; a ~ railway,* for ~ traffic; *a ~ cruiser,* with ~ armour and guns; *~ horse,* light-armed cavalry: *a `~ brigade,* with ~ equipment and weapons. Hence, **'~-`armed** *adj* **2** gentle; delicate: *give sb a ~ touch on the shoulder; walk with ~ footsteps/movements; have a ~ hand for pastry,* have delicacy of touch that gives good results. Hence, **'~-`handed** *adj* having a ~ hand. **'~-`handed·ly** *adv* **'~-`fingered** *adj* skilful in using the fingers; clever at stealing, e g as a pickpocket. **3** below the correct weight, amount, etc: *a ~ coin; give ~ weight. We're about 50p ~ on the petty cash,* 50p short. **4** (of beer, wines) not very strong; (of food) easily digested; (of meals) small in quantity: *a ~ supper,* (hence) *a ~ eater;* (of sleep) not deep; easily disturbed; (of sleepers) easily waked; (of books, plays, music) primarily for amusement, not for serious entertainment or study: *~ reading/music/comedy; a ~ comedian;* (of soil) easily broken up; (of work) easily done; (of taxes, punishment) not difficult to bear; (of a syllable) not stressed, unemphatic. ***make ~ work of sth,*** do it without much effort. **5** not serious or important: *a ~ attack of illness.* ***make ~ of,*** treat as of no or little importance: *He makes ~ of his illness.* **6** thoughtless; frivolous; jesting: *~ conduct; a man of ~ character,* not troubling much about moral questions. **'~ `minded** /ˈmaɪndɪd/ *adj* frivolous. Hence, **'~ `mindedness** *n* **7** cheerful; free from sorrow: *a ~ heart.* Hence, **'~ `hearted** *adj* **'~ `heartedly** *adv* **'~ `heartedness** *n* **8** without moral discipline; wanton: *a ~ woman.* **9** dizzy, delirious: (chiefly in) **'~ `headed** *adj* **'~ `headedly** *adv* and **'~ `headedness** *n* **10** (compounds) **'~-o'-`love** *n* fickle woman; harlot. **`~-weight** *n, adj* (man or animal) below average weight; (esp, boxing) boxer weighing between 126 and 135 lb or (57 to 61 kg). **`~-heavyweight** *n* (esp) boxer weighing between 160 and 175 lb or (72·5 to 79·3 kg). □ *adv* in a ~ manner: *tread/sleep ~; travel ~,* with little luggage; *get off ~(ly),* (colloq) escape without heavy punishment. **~·ly** *adv* **~·ness** *n*

light³ /laɪt/ *n* (opposite of *darkness*) **1** [U] (and with *indef art* and *adjj*) that which makes things visible: *the ~ of the sun/a lamp/the fire; read by the ~ of a candle; go for a walk by `moon~; bathed in `sun~. We need more ~. The ~* (i e day~) *began to fail,* It began to get dark. ***in a good/bad ~,*** **(a)** so as to be seen well/badly: *The picture has been hung in a bad ~.* **(b)** (fig) so as to make a good/bad impression: *Press reports always make him appear in a bad ~.* ***see the ~,*** **(a)** (liter or rhet) be born. **(b)** be made public. **(c)** realize the truth of sth that one has been obstinate about. **(d)** undergo religious conversion. ***be/stand in sb's ~,*** **(a)** obscure what he is looking at. **(b)** (fig) hamper, hinder (sb's chances of success, progress). ***stand in one's own ~,*** **(a)** so as to obscure one's work, etc. **(b)** act against one's own interests. **`~ year,** (astron) unit of measurement for distances between stars; distance travelled by ~ in one year (about 6 million million miles). **2** [C] source of ~; sth that gives ~, e g a candle or lamp: *`traffic ~s; 'navi`gation ~s. L~s were burning in every room. Turn/switch the ~s on/off. Put that ~ out! All the ~s went out—there was a power failure.* **northern/southern ~s,** ⇨ **aurora. 3** [C] flame; spark; sth used for producing a spark or flame: *Can you give me a ~, please?* e g for a cigarette or pipe. Note that *fire* is not used in this sense. *Strike a ~,* make a ~ by striking a match. ***L~s out,*** (bugle call signalling) the time when ~s are to be turned out. **4** [U] expression of brightness or liveliness in a person's face (esp in the eyes), suggesting happiness or other emotion: *The ~ died out of her eyes,* Her looks changed from happiness to sadness, from liveliness to lack of interest. ***the ~ of one's countenance,*** (biblical) favour, approval. **5** [U] knowledge or information that helps understanding; [C] fact or discovery that explains. ***come/bring sth to ~,*** become/cause sth to be visible or known: *Much new evidence has come to ~/has been brought to ~ in recent years.* ***shed/throw ~/a new ~/on sth,*** make sth clearer, provide new information: *These facts shed (a) new ~ on the matter.* ***by the ~ of nature,*** without the help of revelation or teaching. ***in the ~ of,*** with the help given by or gained from. **6** [C] aspect; way in which sth appears: *I cannot view your conduct in a favourable ~,* cannot approve of it. *I have never looked upon the matter in that ~.* **7** (*pl*) (natural or acquired) abilities; mental powers, esp in ***according to one's ~s,*** to the best of one's abilities. **8** [C] famous person; person (to be) regarded as an example or model: *one of the shining ~s of our age.* **9** [C] window or opening in a wall or roof for the admission of ~ (esp in a roof): *a `sky~;* compartment of glass in the side or roof of a greenhouse or frame (used for ventilation). **leaded ~,** small pane or panel of glass, secured in strips of lead, often coloured, forming part of a larger window. ⇨ also *quarter-~* at quarter(16). **10** (art of painting) part of a picture shown as lighted up: ˈ*high ~s*, the brightest parts; *~ and shade*, contrasts. **11** (compounds) ˈ**~-house** *n* tower or other tall structure containing beacon ~s for warning or guiding ships at sea. ˈ**~-ship** *n* ship moored or anchored and provided with beacon ~s for the same purpose as those in a ~house.

a lighthouse

light[4] /lɑɪt/ *vt,vi* (*pt,pp* lit /lɪt/ or ~ed) (*~ed* is more usu as a *pred adj*, as in *a ~ed candle*). **1** [VP6A] cause to begin burning or to give out ~: *~ a lamp/candle/cigarette; ~ a fire*, put a burning match to the material in a fireplace, etc. **2** [VP6A] provide lights(2) to or for: *Is your flat ~ed by gas or by electricity? Our streets are ~ed/lit by electricity.* **3** [VP15B] *~ sth up*, cause to become bright: *The shops were brilliantly lit up. The burning building lit up the whole district.* **4** [VP2C] *~ up*, **(a)** switch on (electric) ~s; turn on gas-lamps, etc: *It's getting dark—time to ~ up.* Hence, ˈ**~ing-ˈup time** *n* time at which, according to regulations, lamps in the roads and on vehicles must be lit. **(b)** (colloq) begin to smoke a pipe or cigarette: *He struck a match and lit up.* **5** [VP2C] *~ up (with)*, (of a person's face or expression) (cause to) become bright: *Her face lit up with pleasure. A smile lit up her face.* **6** [VP15A] guide with or by a light: *~ a person on his way.*

light[5] /lɑɪt/ *vi* (*pt,pp* lit /lɪt/ or ~ed) [VP3A] *~ (up)on*, come by chance: *~ upon a rare book in a secondhand bookshop.*

lighten[1] /ˈlɑɪtn/ *vt,vi* [VP6A,2A] make or become less heavy; reduce the weight of: *~ a ship's cargo; ~ a ship of her cargo; ~ taxes. Her heart ~ed when she heard the news.*

lighten[2] /ˈlɑɪtn/ *vt,vi* **1** [VP6A] make light or bright: *A solitary candle ~ed the darkness of the cellar.* **2** [VP2A] become light or bright: *The eastern sky ~ed.* **3** [VP2A] send out lightning: *It's thundering and ~ing.*

lighter[1] /ˈlɑɪtə(r)/ *n* [C] **1** device for lighting cigarettes or cigars. **2** (chiefly in compounds) person or thing that lights: ˈ*lamp-~*, man who went round the streets with a ladder to light gas-lamps.

lighter[2] /ˈlɑɪtə(r)/ *n* boat, usu flat-bottomed, used for loading and unloading ships not brought to a wharf, and for carrying goods in a harbour or river: *a tug with a string of ~s behind it.* □ *vt* remove (goods) in a ~. ˈ**~-age** /-ɪdʒ/ *n* fees charged for carrying goods in ~s.

light·ning /ˈlɑɪtnɪŋ/ *n* [U] flash of bright light produced by natural electricity between clouds in the sky or clouds and the ground, with thunder: *struck/killed by ~; like ~, with ~ speed*, very fast; (attrib) *a ~ strike*, a strike, of workers, started without warning. ˈ**~-rod/-conductor** *nn* metal rod fixed on the top of a high building, etc and connected with the earth, to prevent damage by ~. ˈ**~ bug**, (US) firefly.

lights /lɑɪts/ *n pl* lungs of sheep, pigs, bullocks, etc used as food for pet animals.

light·some /ˈlɑɪtsəm/ *adj* **1** graceful. **2** merry; light-hearted; frivolous. **~·ly** *adv* **~·ness** *n*

lig·neous /ˈlɪgnɪəs/ *adj* (of plants) woody. ⇨ herbaceous.

lig·nite /ˈlɪgnɑɪt/ *n* [U] soft, brownish-black coal.

lik·able, like·able /ˈlɑɪkəbl/ *adj* of a kind that is, or deserves to be, liked; pleasing: *He's a very ~ fellow.*

like[1] /lɑɪk/ *adj* ⇨ alike. (used attributively and predicatively) similar; having the same or similar qualities, etc; having a resemblance: *The two girls are very ~. L~* (i e similar) *causes produce ~* (i e similar) *results. He writes well on this and ~ subjects. They are as ~ as two peas. L~ father, ~ son; ~ master, ~ man* (prov) As the one is, so the other will be. ˈ**~-ˈminded** /ˈmɑɪndɪd/ *adj* having the same tastes, aims, etc. □ *adv* **1** (archaic) in the same manner: *'L~ as a father pitieth his children, so the Lord pitieth them that fear him.'* ⇨ Psalm 103: 13. **2** probably: (only in) *~ enough; very ~.* □ *conj* **1** as (common use among those who have not been taught to avoid it; considered incorrect, but found in many good writers): *She can't cook ~ her mother does. Don't think you can learn grammatical rules ~ you learn the multiplication tables.* **3** (non-standard use) as if: *It rained like the skies were falling.* □ *n* **1** ~ person or things; that which is equal or similar to sth else: *That was acting, the ~ of which we shall not see again,* We shall not see acting equally good. *Music, painting and the ~,* and similar branches of the arts. *I never heard the ~ (of it)*, anything so strange, etc according to context. **2** (*pl*, colloq) similar persons, things, etc: *the ~s of us/them. Have you ever seen the ~s of this?* □ *prep* **1** (Often governing a *pron, n*, or *gerund* originally *like to* or *like unto*, this use being now obs or poet) such as; resembling: *What is he ~?* What sort of person is he—in looks, behaviour, etc, according to the situation? *He was wearing a hat rather ~ this one. It looks ~ gold,* has the appearance of gold. *This is nothing ~ as good,* not nearly so good. ***nothing ~***, nothing to equal; nothing to be compared with: *There's nothing ~* (= nothing as good as) *leather. There's nothing ~ walking as a means of keeping fit.* ***something ~***, nearly; about: *The cost will be something ~ five pounds. This is something* ˈ*~ a dinner!* This is a remarkably good or satisfactory dinner! **2** ˈ***feel ~***, be in a state or mood right or suitable for: *Do you feel ~ having a rest? She felt ~ crying. We'll go for a walk if you feel ~ it.* ˈ***look ~***, look as if sb/it might (used to show probability or in likelihood). *He looks ~ winning,* It seems likely that he will

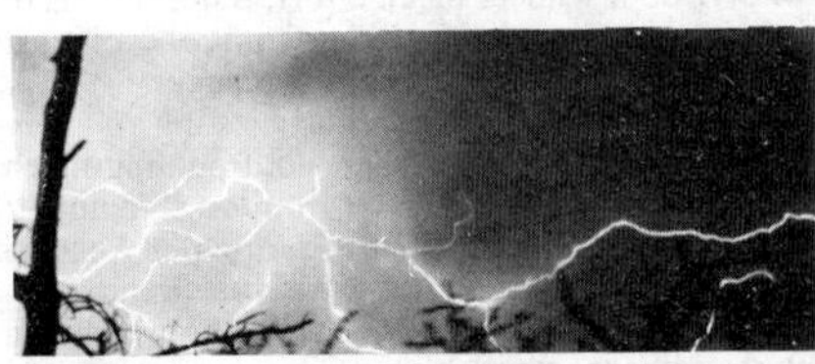

lightning

win. *It looks ~ being a fine day,* Appearances suggest that the day will be fine. *It looks ~ rain.* **3** characteristic of: *That's just ~ him!* He has behaved, spoken, etc just as one would expect! *It's (just) ~ her to think of others before thinking of herself. Isn't that just ~ a woman,* what you might expect from a woman! **4** (originally *~ to;* followed by a *n* or the object form of a *pron*) in the manner of; to the same degree as: *Don't talk ~ that,* in that way. *If I were to behave ~ you...,* in the way you behave.... *If everyone worked ~ me,....* *It fits him ~ a glove,* closely, tightly. *He drinks ~ a fish.* **5** (colloq, sl) ***~ anything,*** as hard, etc as can be expected or imagined: *She works ~ anything when she's interested.* ***~ mad/crazy,*** as if crazy: *He complains ~ mad when things go wrong.* ***~ hell/blazes,*** **(a)** furiously; energetically: *He moans ~ hell when he loses a bet.* **(b)** (as an *int*) of course (not)!: *'But you were there, weren't you?' 'L~ hell, I was!'* I certainly wasn't!

like[2] /laɪk/ *vt,vi* **1** [VP6A,D,7A] be fond of; have a taste for; find satisfactory or agreeable: *Do you ~ fish? I ~ to read in bed but I don't ~ having meals in bed. She ~s him but she doesn't love him. I ~ his impudence!* (ironic, meaning that his impudence is preposterous or amusing). *Well, I ~ that!* (ironic, meaning that what has been said or done is surprising, unexpected, etc). **2** [VP6D,7A] (in *neg* sentences) be unwilling or reluctant: *I didn't ~ to disturb you. I don't ~ troubling her.* **3** [VP6A,7A] (with *should, would*) used to indicate a wish: *I should ~ to go there,* if it were possible, if I were invited, etc. *I shouldn't ~ to do that,* have no wish to do it. *She would ~ a cup of tea, I think. I should ~ to know/to see...,* often ironic, meaning that it would be difficult to explain, show, etc. *They would have ~ed to come....* **4** [VP6A,7A, 17B,2A] prefer; choose; wish: *I ~ people to tell the truth. How do you ~ your tea? I ~* (= prefer) *it rather weak. I ~ this more* (or, colloq *better*) *than that. You wouldn't ~ there to be another war, would you?* ***if you ~,*** used to express consent to a request or suggestion: *I will come if you ~.* **5** [VP6A] suit the health of: *I ~ lobster but it doesn't ~ me,* i e it gives me indigestion. □ *n* (*pl,* only in) **ˈ~es and ˋdis~s,** ⇨ **dislike.**

like·ly /ˈlaɪklɪ/ *adj* (**-ier, -iest**) **1** that seems reasonable or suitable, that seems right for a purpose: *That's a ~ story/excuse* (often used ironically). *This looks a ~ field for mushrooms. What do you think is the likeliest/the most ~ time to find him at home? Which are the most ~ candidates,* those with the best chance of success? **2** to be expected (to...): *He is not ~ to succeed. It's highly* (= very) *~ that he will succeed. An incident ~ to lead to war is reported from X. That is not ~ to happen.* □ *adv* ***most/very ~,*** probably. *I shall very ~ be here again next month.* ***as ~ as not,*** with greater probability: *He will succeed as ~ as not. He'll forget all about it as ~ as not.* **like·li·hood** /-hʊd/ *n* [U] probability: *In all likelihood* (= Very probably), *we shall be away for a week.*

liken /ˈlaɪkən/ *vt* [VP14] ***~ sth to sth,*** point out the likeness of one thing (to another): *~ the heart to a pump.*

like·ness /ˈlaɪknəs/ *n* **1** [U] resemblance; being like: *I can't see much ~ between the two boys.* ***in the ~ of,*** in the form, shape or external appearance of. **2** [C] point of resemblance; instance of being like: *There's a family ~ in all of them.* **3** [C] copy, portrait, picture, photograph: *The portrait is a good ~.*

like·wise /ˈlaɪkwaɪz/ *adv* in the same or a similar way: *Watch him and do ~.* □ *conj* also; moreover.

lik·ing /ˈlaɪkɪŋ/ *n* (with *indef art,* but not *pl*) fondness. ***have a ~ for,*** be fond of. ***to one's ~,*** as one likes it; satisfactory: *Is everything to your ~?*

li·lac /ˈlaɪlək/ *n* **1** shrub with sweet-smelling pale purple or white blossom: *an avenue of ~s, ~ shrubs; a bunch of ~* (*sing* for the blossom). **2** pale purple or pinkish-purple: *a ~ dress.*

Lil·li·pu·tian /ˈlɪlɪˋpjuʃn/ *n* native of Lilliput /ˈlɪlɪpʌt/ (the country described in Swift's *Gulliver's Travels*). □ *adj* very small.

lilt /lɪlt/ *n* [C] (lively song or tune with a) well-marked rhythm or swing. □ *vt,vi* go, sing with a ~: *a ~ing waltz.*

lily /ˈlɪlɪ/ *n* (*pl* **-lies**) (kinds of) plant growing from a bulb, of many sizes, shapes and colours: *ˈ~ of the ˋvalley; ˋwater lilies; ˋEaster lilies; ˋcalla lilies.* **~-livered** /ˈlɪlɪ lɪvəd/ *adj* cowardly. **ˈ~-ˋwhite** *adj* as white as a ~; pure white.

limb /lɪm/ *n* **1** leg, arm or wing (the more usu words): *rest one's tired ~s; be torn ~ from ~ by wolves; escape with life and ~,* without serious injury. **2** bough (of a tree). ***leave sb/be/go out on a ~,*** (colloq) leave sb/be/put oneself in a vulnerable position, e g because separated from supporters. **3** (colloq) *a ~ of the devil/of Satan,* a mischievous child. **-limbed** /lɪmd/ *suff* (in compounds) *ˈlong-/ˈstrong-ˋ~ed,* having long/strong ~s.

lim·ber[1] /ˈlɪmbə(r)/ *n* detachable front part (formerly horse-drawn) of a gun-carriage, consisting of an ammunition box on wheels. □ *vt,vi* [VP15B,2C] ***~ (up),*** fasten (a gun) to a ~.

lim·ber[2] /ˈlɪmbə(r)/ *adj* flexible, pliable. □ *vt,vi* [VP15B,2C] ***~ (oneself) up,*** make oneself (one's muscles) pliant, flexible.

limbo /ˈlɪmbəʊ/ *n* (*pl* **-bos** /-bəʊz/) **1** [U] condition of being forgotten and unwanted. (colloq) *The idea of forming a staff association is in ~* (= has been put to one side) *until the new Manager is appointed.* **2** [C] place for forgotten and unwanted things. **3** (theol) (usu cap L) region for souls of unbaptized infants and pre-Christian righteous persons.

lime[1] /laɪm/ *n* [U] **1** white substance (calcium oxide, **CaO**) obtained by burning limestone, used in making cement and mortar. **ˋquick~,** ~ before water is added. **ˋslaked ~,** ~ after being acted upon by water. **ˋ~-kiln** *n* kiln in which ~stone is burnt. **ˋ~-light** *n* [U] intense white light produced by heating a rod of ~ in a very hot flame, formerly used for lighting the stage in theatres: *fond of the ~light,* fond of publicity. ***in the ~light,*** (fig) receiving great publicity. **ˋ~·stone** *n* [U] (kinds of) rock containing much ~, quarried for industrial use. **2** [U] (**ˋbird-**)**~,** sticky substance made from holly bark for catching small birds. □ *vt* [VP6A] put ~ on (fields, etc) (to control acidity).

lime[2] /laɪm/ *n* (also **ˋ~-tree, linden**) tree with smooth heart-shaped leaves and sweet-smelling yellow blossoms.

lime[3] /laɪm/ *n* (tree with) round juicy fruit like, but more acid than, a lemon. **ˋ~-juice** *n* juice of this fruit used for flavouring, as a drink, and medicinally.

lim·er·ick /ˈlɪmərɪk/ *n* humorous or nonsense poem of five lines.

limey /ˈlaɪmɪ/ *n* (*pl* -meys) (US sl) British seaman.

limit¹ /ˈlɪmɪt/ *n* [C] line or point that may not or cannot be passed; greatest or smallest amount, degree, etc of what is possible; *within the city* ~*s*, boundaries; *within a* ~ *of five miles/a five-mile* ~. *We must set a* ~ *to the expense of the trip*, fix a sum not to be exceeded. *As we grow older we learn the* ~*s of our abilities*, learn what we can do and what we cannot do. *His greed knows no* ~*s. There is a* ~ *to my patience. She reached the* ~ *of her patience.* **within ~s,** in moderation: *I'm willing to help you, within* ~*s.* ***without ~,*** to any extent or degree: *If only the banks would lend money without* ~! ***off ~s,*** (US) = out of bounds, ⇨ bound¹. ***That's the ~,*** (colloq) is as much as (or more than) can be tolerated. ˈ**age** ~ *n* age¹(1) given as a ~ for participation in an activity, etc.

limit² /ˈlɪmɪt/ *vt* [VP6A,14] ***~ sb/sth (to sth),*** put a limit or limits to; be the limit of: *We must* ~ *the expense to what we can afford. I shall* ~ *myself to three aspects of the subject.* **~ed** *pp* small; restricted; narrow: *a* ~*ed edition*, one ~ed to a specified number of copies. *Our accommodation is very* ~*ed. He seems to have only a* ~*ed intelligence.* ˈ**~ed ˈliaˈbility company,** (abbr *Ltd* placed after the name) business company whose members are liable for its debts only to the extent of the capital sum they have provided. ˈ**~ed ˈmonarchy,** one that is restricted by the constitution. ⇨ absolute(2). **~·less** *adj* without ~: *the* ~*less ocean; a dictator whose ambitions were* ~*less.*

limi·ta·tion /ˈlɪmɪˈteɪʃn/ *n* **1** [U] limiting; condition of being limited. **2** [C] condition, fact or circumstance that limits; disability or inability: *He knows his* ~*s*, knows well that in some respects his abilities are limited.

limn /lɪm/ *vt* (old use) paint (a picture); portray (in drawing or in words).

lim·ou·sine /ˈlɪməzin/ *n* car with an enclosed body, the front seats being separated by means of a partition (as in a London taxi). Cf *saloon-car*, with no partition behind the driver.

limp¹ /lɪmp/ *adj* not stiff or firm; lacking strength: *The book is bound in* ~ *cloth; a* ~ *edition of a book. The flowers looked* ~ *in the heat.* **~·ly** *adv* **~·ness** *n*

limp² /lɪmp/ *vt* [VP2A,C] walk lamely or unevenly as when one leg or foot is hurt or stiff: *The wounded soldier* ~*ed off the battlefield. The damaged ship* ~*ed* (= managed with difficulty to get) *back to port.* □ *n* (usu with *indef art*) lame walk: *have/walk with a bad* ~.

lim·pet /ˈlɪmpɪt/ *n* small shellfish that fastens itself tightly to rocks; ⇨ the illus at mollusc; (fig) person who sticks tightly to an office, a position or another person. ˈ~ **mine,** explosive mine (to be) placed in position against the hull of a ship, e g by frogmen.

lim·pid /ˈlɪmpɪd/ *adj* of liquids, the atmosphere, the eyes, (fig or liter and rhet) clear; transparent. **~·ly** *adv* **~·ity** /lɪmˈpɪdətɪ/ *n* [U] quality or state of being ~.

linch·pin /ˈlɪntʃpɪn/ *n* iron pin passed through the end of an axle to keep the wheel in position; (fig) vital part; person who, because of his work, etc, keeps an organization, etc together.

Lin·coln green /ˈlɪŋkən ˈgrin/ *n* bright green cloth as made at Lincoln: *Robin Hood and his men, dressed in* ~.

lin·den /ˈlɪndən/ *n* ⇨ lime².

line¹ /laɪn/ *n* **1** piece or length of thread, string, rope or wire for various purposes: ˈ*fishing-lines;* ˈ*telephone* ~*s. Hang* (*out*) *the clothes on the* ~, (i e *the* ˈ*clothes-*~). *L*~ *fishing is quite different from net-fishing. He's clever with rod and* ~, is a good angler. *The* ~*s* (i e telephone, etc ~s) *are all down as the result of the blizzard. Give me a* ~, *please,* (to the operator of a telephone switchboard) Connect me to the Exchange, please (so that I can dial direct). *L*~ *engaged!* (US *L*~ *busy*) used of a telephone ~ already in use. ***hot ~,*** ⇨ hot¹(8). **party/shared ~,** telephone ~ serving two or more subscribers. **2** [C] long, narrow mark made on a surface: *L*~*s may be straight, crooked or curved. Draw a* ~ *from A to B. In mathematics a* ~ *is defined as having length but not breadth or thickness.* **3** [U] the use of ~s(2) in art, etc: *a* ˈ~ *drawing*, e g with a pen or pencil; ˈ~*-engraving*, done with ~s cut on a surface; *the beauty of* ~ *in the work of Botticelli; translate life into* ~ *and colour*, represent living things by means of ~s and colour. **4** (in games) mark made to limit a court or ground, or special parts of them: *Did the ball cross the* ~? ⇨ lineman. **5** mark like a ~ on the skin of the face; furrow or wrinkle; one of the marks on the palm of the hand: *There were deep* ~*s of care on her face.* **6** (*pl*) contour; outline: *a ship of fine* ~*s*, with a graceful outline; *the severe* ~*s of Norman architecture;* (in shipbuilding) plans, esp of horizontal, vertical and oblique sections. **7** row of persons or things: *a* ~ *of trees/chairs/people waiting to go into a cinema; manufactured goods on the as*ˈ*sembly* ~; *a long* ~ *of low hills. The boys were standing in* (*a*) ~. ***in ~ for,*** next in order for: *He's in* ~ *for promotion.* ***on the ~,*** (of objects exhibited, esp paintings) with the centre about level with the eyes of the viewer. **8** edge, boundary, that divides: *cross the* ~ *into Canada* (i e from US); equator: *cross the* ~. ***draw the ~ (at),*** ⇨ draw²(13). **9** railway; single track of railway ~s: *the* ˈ*up/*ˈ*down* ~, to/from the chief terminus; *the main* ~; *a* ˈ*branch* ~. *Cross the* ~ *by the bridge.* ***reach the end of the ~,*** (fig, of a relationship) reach the point where it breaks down, ends. **10** organized system of transport under one management and giving a regular service: *an* ˈ*air*~; *a new* ˈ*bus* ~; *a* ˈ*steamship* ~. **11** direction; course; track; way of behaviour, dealing with a situation, etc: *the* ~ *of march of an army;* ˈ*communi*ˈ*cation* ~*s. Don't stand in the* ~ *of fire! You'll get shot!* ***choose/follow/take the ~ of least resistance,*** the easiest way of doing things. ***take a firm/hard/strong ~ (over sth),*** deal with a problem, etc resolutely: *Should the government take a stronger* ~ *over inflation? What* ~ *do you intend to take*, How will you approach the problem? ***do sth along/on/sound/correct, etc ~s,*** use good, etc methods: *He is studying the subject on sound* ~*s/on the wrong* ~*s. I shall proceed along/on these* ~*s until further notice. You should keep to your own* ~, be independent of others. ***(be) in/out of ~ (with),*** in agreement/disagreement (with). ***bring sth into ~,*** cause sth to conform. ***come/fall into (with),*** (persuade or cause sb to) accept views, conform, agree. ***toe the ~,*** (fig) submit to discipline, accept the ideas, programme, etc of a (political, etc) party. **the party ~,** the agreed or established policy of a political party: *follow the party ~*, vote, speak, write, etc in accordance with this policy. **12** connected series of persons following one another in time, esp of the same ancestry: *a long ~ of great kings; the last of his ~; trace back one's family ~*, one's ancestry; *a descendant of King David in a direct ~/in the male ~*. **13** row of words on a page of writing or in print: *page 5, ~ 10. 'L~s to a friend on her birthday'*, e g as the title of a poem. ***drop sb a ~,*** (colloq) write to sb: *Drop me a ~ to say how you're getting on.* ***get a ~ on,*** find out about. ***read between the ~s,*** (fig) find more meaning than the words appear to express. **'marriage ~s,** (GB) certificate of marriage. **~s,** *(pl)* **(a)** words of an actor's part: *The leading actor was not sure of his ~s.* **(b)** form of punishment by which a schoolboy is required to write out a specified number of ~s, e g 200 ~s of verse. **14** series of connected military defence posts, trenches, etc: *go into the front ~(s)*, the area nearest to the enemy's ~s; *high-ranking officers well behind the ~s; be successful all along the ~*, at every point. ***go up the ~,*** leave base for the front ~(s). **15** (mil) row of tents, huts, etc in a camp: *inspect the ~s; the 'horse ~s.* **16** (GB army) regular infantry regiments (excluding the Guards and Rifles): *regiments of the ~; a ~ regiment; infantry of the ~;* (US army) regular fighting forces of all classes. **17** (mil) double row (front and rear ranks) of men standing side by side (contrasted with *file* and *column*): *The troops attacked in extended ~. The men formed into ~.* **18** (naval) ***~ abreast,*** (number of parallel ships) abreast of each other. ***~ astern,*** (number of ships) in a ~ one behind the other. ***ship of the ~, ~-of-battle ship,*** (in former times) ship of 74 or more guns; largest type of warship. **19** department of activity; business; occupation: *He's in the 'drapery ~. His ~ is stockbroking/banking. That's not much in my ~*, I don't know much about it, am not much interested in it. **20** class of commercial goods: *a cheap ~ in felt hats; the best-selling ~ in woollen underwear.* **21** *(pl)* conditions of life; one's lot or fate: (biblical style) *My ~s have fallen in pleasant places*, I have been fortunate. ***Hard ~s!*** Bad luck! **22** (sl) ***shoot a ~,*** brag, boast. Hence, **'~-shooting, '~-shooter** *nn* **23** (colloq) ***get/have/give sb a ~ on sth,*** information about.

line[2] /laɪn/ *vt,vi* **1** [VP6A,15B] mark (sth) with lines: *~d paper*, with lines printed on it. *~ in a contour*, on a blank map; *~ sth out on paper*, mark it out with ~s. **2** [VP6A] cover with lines: *a ~d face; a face ~d with anxiety. Pain had ~d her forehead.* **3** [VP2C,15B] ***~ up,*** (cause to) be in a line, get into a line. *The general ~d up his troops. The soldiers quickly ~d up.* ⇨ line-up below. ***~ up (for sth),*** (US) queue for. **4** [VP6A] form, be placed, in a line or lines along: *a road ~d with trees; a road ~d with police. Crowds of people ~d the kerb to see the funeral procession.*

line[3] /laɪn/ *vt* [VP6A,14] ***~ sth with sth,*** ⇨ lining below. **1** provide with an inside covering; add a layer of (usu different) material to the inside of (bags, boxes, articles of clothing): *fur-~d gloves; an overcoat ~d with silk.* **2** (fig) fill (one's purse, pocket, stomach, etc): *He has ~d his purse well*, made a lot of money.

lin·eage /ˈlɪnɪɪdʒ/ *n* [U] family line; ancestry; line of descent: *a man of good ~.*

lin·eal /ˈlɪnɪəl/ *adj* in the direct line of descent (from father to son, etc): *a ~ descendant/heir.* **~·ly** /-ɪəlɪ/ *adv*

lin·ea·ment /ˈlɪnɪəmənt/ *n* (formal) (usu *pl* except after *each* and *every*) line, detail, distinctive feature or characteristic (of the face): *the ~s of a Mongol face.*

lin·ear /ˈlɪnɪə(r)/ *adj* **1** of or in lines: *a ~ design.* **2** of length: *~ measure*, e g feet and inches or metres. ⇨ App 5.

line·man /ˈlaɪnmən/ *n* **1** man who puts up and maintains telegraph and telephone lines. **2** (US) = linesman.

linen /ˈlɪnɪn/ *n* [U] cloth made of flax; articles made from this cloth, esp shirts and collars, bedsheets, tablecloths and table napkins: (attrib) *~ handkerchiefs.* **'~-draper** *n* person who sells ~ and cotton goods. ***wash one's dirty ~ in public,*** discuss family quarrels, unpleasant personal affairs, etc in the presence of other people.

liner /ˈlaɪnə(r)/ *n* **1** ship or aircraft of a line(10) of ships or aircraft: *a fast 'air~; a trans-Atlantic ~.* ⇨ the illus at air, ship. **2 '~ train** (also *'freight ~*), long distance express goods train between industrial centres and seaports, with facilities for fast (un)loading of goods.

lines·man /ˈlaɪnzmən/ *n* (sport) person who helps the umpire or referee by saying whether or where the ball touches or crosses one of the lines.

line-up /ˈlaɪn ʌp/ *n* **1** way in which persons, states, etc are arranged or allied; alignment: *a new ~ of Afro-Asian powers; a ~ of men in an identification parade.* **2** formation of players ready for action (in a game such as baseball or football); ⇨ the illus at football. **3** programme of items (esp for radio or TV): *This evening's ~ includes an interview with the Chairman of British Rail.*

ling[1] /lɪŋ/ *n* [U] (kinds of) heather.

ling[2] /lɪŋ/ *n* long, slender N European seafish (usu salted) for food.

lin·gam /ˈlɪŋgəm/ *n* phallic emblem (as a symbol of Shiva /ˈʃivə/, third god of the Hindu trinity).

lin·ger /ˈlɪŋgə(r)/ *vi* [VP2A,C] be late or slow in going away; stay at or near a place: *~ on after everyone else has left; ~ about/around. The custom ~s on*, is still observed but is now weak. **~·ing** *adj* long; protracted: *a ~ing illness; a ~ing look*, one showing regret, unwillingness to leave or give up sth; *a few ~ing* (= remaining) *doubts.* **~·ing·ly** *adv* **~er** *n* person who ~s.

linge·rie /ˈlɔ̃ʒəri *US:* -reɪ/ *n* [U] (F) (trade name for) women's underclothing.

lingo /ˈlɪŋgəʊ/ *n* (*pl* -goes /-gəʊz/) (hum or contemptuous) language, esp one that one does not know; way of talking, vocabulary, of a special subject or class of people: *the strange ~ used by experts in radio and television.*

lin·gua franca /ˈlɪgwə ˈfræŋkə(r)/ *n* language adopted for local communication over an area in which several languages are spoken, e g Swahili in E Africa.

lin·gual /ˈlɪŋgwl/ *adj* of the tongue, speech or languages, esp in compounds, as **ˌaudio-'~,** (of methods, devices, etc) requiring one to listen and speak: *audio-~ aids*, e g a tape-recorder. **ˌbi'~,** speaking two languages. **ˌmulti-'~,** speaking many languages.

lin·guist /ˈlɪŋgwɪst/ *n* **1** person skilled in foreign languages: *She's a good ~. I'm no ~*, am poor at foreign languages. **2** one who makes a scientific study of language(s).

lin·guis·tic /lɪŋˋgwɪstɪk/ *adj* of (the scientific study of) languages: *the ~ study of literature,* centred on the language. **lin·guis·tics** *n sing* the science of language, e g of its structure, acquisition, relationship to other forms of communication. ˈ**applied** ˋ**~s,** this study put to practical uses, esp in the teaching of languages.

lini·ment /ˋlɪnɪmənt/ *n* [C,U] (kind of) liquid usu made with oil for rubbing on stiff or aching parts of the body.

lin·ing /ˋlaɪnɪŋ/ *n* ⇨ line[3]. **1** [C] layer of material added to the inside of sth: *an overcoat with a fur ~; a jewel-box with a velvet ~.* ***Every cloud has a silver ~,*** (prov) There is sth good in every evil. **2** [U] material used for this purpose.

link[1] /lɪŋk/ *n* **1** one ring or loop of a chain. **2** (usu *pl*) one of a pair of fasteners for the sleeves of a shirt: *ˋcuff-~s.* **3** person or thing that unites or connects two others: *a ~ in a chain of evidence; the ~ between the past and the future.* ***missing ~,*** that which is needed to complete a series; type of animal supposed to have existed between the apes and man. ˋ**~·man** /-mæn/ *n* (*pl* -men) man who holds together items in a programme. **4** measure of length, one hundredth of a chain; 7·92 inches or about 20 centimetres. ⇨ App 5. □ *vt,vi* [VP6A,15A,B,2A,C] join, be joined, with, or as with, a ~ or ~s: *~ things together; ~ one's arm in/through another person's arm; two towns ~ed by a canal; ~ing verbs,* e g *be. Where do they ~ up?* Hence, ˋ**~-up** *n*

link[2] /lɪŋk/ *n* torch formerly used for lighting people along streets. ˋ**~·boy,** ˋ**~·man** /-mæn/ *nn* one formerly employed to carry ~s and guide people through badly lighted streets.

links /lɪŋks/ *n* **1** (*pl v*) grassy land, esp sand-hills, near the sea. **2** (often with *indef art* and *sing v*) golf-course.

lin·net /ˋlɪnɪt/ *n* small brown songbird, common in Europe.

lino /ˋlaɪnəʊ/ *n* [U] abbr for *linoleum.* ˋ**~-cut** *n* [C] design cut in relief on a block of linoleum; print made from this.

lin·oleum /lɪˋnəʊlɪəm/ *n* [U] strong floor-covering of canvas treated with powdered cork and oil.

lino·type /ˋlaɪnəʊtaɪp/ *n* (P) machine (with a keyboard like that of a typewriter) used for setting type, each line of type being cast in the form of a complete bar of metal.

lin·seed /ˋlɪnsid/ *n* [U] seed of flax. ˋ**~-oil** *n* [U] oil pressed from ~, used in making printing-ink, linoleum, etc.

lin·sey-wool·sey /ˈlɪnzɪ ˋwʊlzɪ/ *n* [U] strong, coarse material made from inferior wool woven with cotton.

lint /lɪnt/ *n* [U] linen, with one side scraped so as to be fluffy, used for dressing wounds: (attrib) *a ~ bandage.*

lin·tel /ˋlɪntl/ *n* horizontal piece of wood or stone forming the top of the frame of a door or window. ⇨ the illus at window.

lion /ˋlaɪən/ *n* **1** large, strong, flesh-eating animal found in Africa and S Asia, called 'the King of Beasts' because of its fine appearance and courage. ⇨ the illus at cat. ***the ~'s share,*** the larger or largest part. ˋ**~-hearted** *adj* brave. **2** person whose company is very much desired at social gatherings, e g a famous author or musician. ˋ**~-hunter** *n* person who tries to get ~s as guests at dinner parties, etc. **~·ess** /-es/ *n* female ~. ⇨ the illus at cat. ˋ**~·ize** /-aɪz/ *vt* [VP6A] treat as a ~(2): *The famous explorer was ~ized when he returned home.*

lip /lɪp/ *n* **1** one or other of the fleshy edges of the opening of the mouth: *the lower/upper lip; a man with a cigar between his lips. She refused to open her lips,* wouldn't say anything. ⇨ the illus at mouth. ***bite one's lip,*** show vexation. ***curl one's lip,*** show scorn. ***give/pay ˋlip-service to sth,*** make promises, express regret, admiration etc not sincerely felt. ***hang (up)on sb's lips,*** listen eagerly to every word he says. ***keep a stiff upper lip,*** show no emotion, sign of fear, anxiety, etc. ***lick/smack one's lips,*** show (anticipation of) enjoyment. ˋ**lip-reading** *n* method (taught to deaf people) of understanding speech from lip movements. Hence, ˋ**lip-read** *vt* ˋ**lip·stick** *n* [C,U] (stick of) cosmetic material for reddening the lips: *buy three lipsticks; use too much lipstick.* **2** edge of a hollow vessel or opening: *the lip of a saucer/crater.* **3** [U] (sl) impudence: *None of your lip!* Don't be impudent! **-lipped,** in compounds: ˈ*thick-/ˈdry-ˋlipped,* having thick/dry lips.

liquefy /ˋlɪkwɪfaɪ/ *vt,vi* (*pt,pp* -fied) [VP6A,2A] make or become liquid. **lique·fac·tion** /ˈlɪkwɪˋfækʃn/ *n* making or becoming liquid; being liquified.

li·quescent /lɪˋkwesnt/ *adj* becoming, apt to become, liquid.

li·queur /lɪˋkjʊə(r) *US:* -ˋkɜ/ *n* (kinds of) strong-flavoured alcoholic drink for taking in small quantities: *~ brandy,* of special quality for drinking as a ~; ˋ*~ glass,* very small for ~s.

liquid /ˋlɪkwɪd/ *n* **1** [C,U] substance like water or oil that flows freely and is neither a solid nor a gas: *Air is a fluid but not a ~; water is both a fluid and a ~. You have added too much ~ to the mixture.* **2** the consonants /r/ and /l/. □ *adj* **1** in the form of a ~; not solid or gaseous: *~ food,* soft, easily swallowed, suitable for sick people; *~ mud,* so soft that it can be poured. **~ air,** air reduced to a ~ state by intense cold. **2** clear, bright and moist-looking: *~ eyes,* bright and shining; *a ~ sky.* **3** (of sounds) clear; pure; not guttural: *the ~ notes of a blackbird.* **4** not fixed; easily changed: *~ opinions.* **5** (in finance) easily sold or changed into cash: *~ assets.*

liqui·date /ˋlɪkwɪdeɪt/ *vt,vi* **1** [VP6A] pay or settle (a debt). **2** [VP6A] bring (esp an unsuccessful business company) to an end by dividing up its property to pay debts; [VP2A] (of a company) go through this process. **3** [VP6A] (colloq or newspaper style) get rid of, put an end to; kill: *gangsters who ~ their rivals.* **liqui·da·tion** /ˈlɪkwɪˋdeɪʃn/ *n* [U] liquidating or being ~ed. ***go into liquidation,*** become bankrupt. **liq·ui·da·tor** /-tə(r)/ *n* official who ~s (2).

li·quid·ity /lɪˋkwɪdətɪ/ *n* [U] state of being liquid(5); state of being able to raise funds easily by selling assets.

liquid·ize /ˋlɪkwɪdaɪz/ *vt* [VP6A] crush, e g fruit, vegetables, to a liquid pulp. **liquid·izer** *n* device (usu with an electric motor) for liquidizing fruit, etc.

liquor /ˋlɪkə(r)/ *n* **1** [C,U] (GB) (kind of) alcoholic drink: *under the influence of ~,* partly drunk; *in ~; the worse for ~,* drunk; *malt ~,* beer; *brandy and other spirituous ~s.* **2** (US) distilled alcoholic drinks: ~ *store.* **3** [U] liquid produced by boiling or fermenting a food substance.

liquor·ice (US = **licor·ice**) /ˈlɪkrɪs/ *n* [U] (plant from whose root is obtained a) black substance used in medicine and in sweets.

lira /ˈlɪərə/ *n* (*pl* **lire** /ˈlɪəreɪ/ or **liras**) unit of money in Italy.

lisle /laɪl/ *n* [U] fine, hard-twisted cotton fabric, used for stockings, gloves, etc.

lisp /lɪsp/ *vi,vt* [VP2A,6A,15B] fail to use the sounds /s/ and /z/ correctly, e g by saying /θɪk ˈθtin/ for *sixteen;* say in a ~ing manner: *She ~s. He ~ed (out) his words.* □ *n* lisping way of speaking: *The child has a bad ~.* **~·ing·ly** *adv*

lis·som, lis·some /ˈlɪsəm/ *adj* lithe; quick and graceful in movement. **~·ness** *n*

list[1] /lɪst/ *n* number of names (of persons, items, things, etc) written or printed: *a ˈshopping ~; make a ~ of things one must do; put sb's name on/take his name off the list.* **~ price,** (comm) published or advertised price. **the active ~,** ~ of officers in the armed forces who may be called upon for service. **the free ~, (a)** those goods admitted into a country free of duty. **(b)** those persons who are admitted to a cinema, theatre, concert hall, etc without payment. □ *vt* [VP6A] make a ~ of; put on a ~: *~ all one's engagements; ~ sb's name.*

list[2] /lɪst/ *vi* [VP2A,C] (esp of a ship) lean over to one side, e g because the cargo has shifted: *The ship ~s to starboard.* □ *n* ~ing of a ship: *a bad ~ to port.*

list[3] /lɪst/ *vt,vi* (old use) listen (*to*).

list[4] /lɪst/ *vi* (old use) please; choose: *'The wind bloweth where it ~eth.'*

lis·ten /ˈlɪsn/ *vi* [VP2A,C,3A] **~ (to), 1** try to hear; pay attention: *We ~ed but heard nothing. The boys heard their father's voice but were not ~ing to what he was saying. Please ~ carefully for the telephone while I'm upstairs.* **~ in (to), (a)** listen to a broadcast programme: *Did you ~ in to the Prime Minister yesterday evening?* **(b)** ~ in to a conversation, e g by tapping telephone lines or using an extension telephone receiver. **2** agree to a suggestion, request, etc: *Don't ~ to him; he wants to get you into trouble.* **~er** *n* one who ~s.

list·less /ˈlɪstləs/ *adj* too tired to show interest or do anything. **~·ly** *adv* **~·ness** *n*

lists /lɪsts/ *n pl* (palisades enclosing an) area of ground for fights (in former times) between men on horseback wearing armour and using lances. ***enter the ~,*** (fig) send out, accept, a challenge to a contest.

lit /lɪt/ *pt,pp* of **light**[4]. ***lit up,*** (sl) drunk.

lit·any /ˈlɪtənɪ/ *n* (*pl* -**nies**) form of prayer for use in church services, recited by a priest with responses from the congregation. **the L~,** that in the Book of Common Prayer of the Church of England.

li·tchi /ˈlaɪtʃi/ variant spelling of **lychee**.

liter /ˈlitə(r)/ ⇨ **litre**.

lit·er·acy /ˈlɪtrəsɪ/ *n* [U] ability to read and write.

lit·eral /ˈlɪtrl/ *adj* **1** connected with, expressed in, letters of an alphabet: *a ~ error,* a misprint. **2** corresponding exactly to the original: *a ~ transcript/copy of an old manuscript; a ~ translation.* Cf *free* translation. **3** taking words in their usual and obvious sense, without allegory or metaphor: *I hear nothing in the ~ sense of the word,* (i e of the word 'hear') get no news by hearing people speak (though I may get news from letters, etc). **4** (of a person) prosaic; matter of fact; lacking in imagination: *He has a rather ~ mind.* □ *n* ~ error; misprint. **~ly** /ˈlɪtrəlɪ/ *adv* **1** word for word; strictly: *translate ~ly; carry out orders too ~ly.* **2** (informal use, to intensify meaning) without exaggeration: *The children were ~ly starving.*

lit·er·ary /ˈlɪtrɪ US: ˈlɪtərerɪ/ *adj* of literature or authors: *the ~ profession; a ~ man,* either an author or a man interested in literature; *~ style,* as used in literature contrasted with *colloquial,* etc; *~ property,* the right of an author to fees, royalties, etc coming from his writings. **lit·er·ati** /ˈlɪteˈrɑtɪ/ *n pl* the ~ intelligentsia.

lit·er·ate /ˈlɪtrət/ *adj* **1** able to read and write. **2** cultured; well-read: *He's a remarkably ~ young man.* □ *n* ~ person.

lit·era·ture /ˈlɪtrətʃə(r) US: -tʃʊər/ *n* [U] **1** (the writing or the study of) books, etc valued as works of art (drama, fiction, essays, poetry, biography, contrasted with technical books and journalism). **2** (also with *indef art*) all the writings of a country (*French ~*) or a period (*18th century English ~*); books dealing with a special subject: *travel ~; the ~ of poultry-farming. There is now an extensive ~ dealing with the First World War.* **3** [U] printed material describing or advertising sth, e g pamphlets: *We shall be glad to send you some ~ about our refrigerators/package holidays.*

lithe /laɪð/ *adj* (of a person, a body) bending, twisting or turning easily: *~ movements; make one's muscles ~.*

lith·ogra·phy /lɪˈθɒgrəfɪ/ *n* [U] process of printing from parts of a flat stone or sheet of zinc or aluminium that are prepared to receive a greasy ink. **litho·graph** /ˈlɪθəgrɑf US: -græf/ *n* sth (esp a picture) printed by this process. □ *vt,vi* print by this process. **litho·graphic** /ˈlɪθəˈgræfɪk/ *adj* of ~.

liti·gant /ˈlɪtɪgənt/ *n* person engaged in a lawsuit.

liti·gate /ˈlɪtɪgeɪt/ *vi,vt* **1** [VP2A] go to law; make a claim at a court of law. **2** [VP6A] contest (sth) at a court of law. **liti·ga·tion** /ˈlɪtɪˈgeɪʃn/ *n* [U] litigating; going to law. **lit·igious** /lɪˈtɪdʒəs/ *adj* **1** fond of going to law. **2** that can be disputed at law.

lit·mus /ˈlɪtməs/ *n* blue colouring-matter that is turned red by acid and can then be restored to blue by alkali. **ˈ~-paper,** paper stained with ~ and used as a test for acids and alkalis.

li·totes /ˈlaɪtətiz/ *n* understatement used ironically, esp using a negative to express the contrary, as 'I shan't be sorry when it's over' meaning 'I shall be very glad', or 'It was no easy matter' for 'It was very difficult'.

litre (US = **liter**) /ˈlitə(r)/ *n* unit of capacity in the metric system. 1 ~ = about 1¾ pints. ⇨ **App 5.**

lit·ter[1] /ˈlɪtə(r)/ *n* **1** couch or bed (often with a covering and curtains) in which a person may be carried about, e g on men's shoulders, and as used in ancient Rome. **2** sort of stretcher for carrying a sick or wounded person.

lit·ter[2] /ˈlɪtə(r)/ *n* **1** [U] odds and ends, bits of paper, discarded wrappings, bottles, etc left lying about in a room or public place: *Pick up your ~ after a picnic.* **ˈ~-bin/-basket,** bin, basket, into which to place ~. **ˈ~-lout** *n* (colloq) person who leaves ~ about in public places. **2** (*sing* with *indef art*) state of untidiness that results when things are left lying about instead of being put away: *Her room was in such a ~ that she was ashamed to ask me in.* **3** [U] straw and dung of a farmyard; straw and similar material, e g dry bracken, used as bedding for animals or for protecting plants from frost. **4** [C] all the newly born young ones of an animal: *a ~ of puppies; ten little pigs at a ~.* □ *vt,vi* **1** [VP6A,15A,B,14] ***~ sth (up) with sth,*** make untidy with odds and ends; scatter ~(1): *~ a desk with papers; ~ up one's room.* **2** [VP6A, 15B] ***~ sth down,*** supply (a horse, etc) with straw; make a bed for an animal: *~ down a horse/a stable.* **3** [VP2A] (of animals, esp dogs and pigs) bring forth a ~ of young ones.

little /ˈlɪtl/ *adj* (In senses **1**, **2** and **3** ~ has no real *comp* and *superl*. **Littler** and **littlest** are occasionally used but are better avoided. ⇨ **less** and **least** for senses **4** and **5**.) **1** small, or small in comparison; (as a distinctive epithet) *the ~ finger/toe.* **2** (often preceded by another *adj* with no connotation of smallness, to indicate affection, tenderness, regard, admiration, or the contrary, depending upon the preceding *adj*): *Isn't he a ~ rascal!* (indicating affectionate regard). *What a pretty ~ house! That poor ~ girl!* (indicating sympathy). *What horrid ~ children! She's a nice ~ thing* (indicating tenderness or regard, but possibly patronage, or a feeling of superiority). *Such a dear ~ man* (suggesting benign patronage) *came round and fixed my central heating. He's quite the ~ gentleman!* (suggesting patronage). ***the ~ people/folk,*** (esp in Ireland) fairies; elves. **3** short (in time, distance, stature): *Won't you stay a ~ time with me? Come a ~ way with me.* **4** young: *How are the ~ ones,* the children? *Here come the ~ Smiths,* the Smith children. **5** not much: *He gained ~ advantage from the scheme. I have very ~ time for reading. He knows ~ French and less German.* **6** (with *indef art*) some but not much; a small quantity of: *He knows a ~ Italian. A ~ care would have prevented the accident. Will you have a ~ cake,* a piece or slice of cake? Cf *Will you have a cake,* one of these cakes? *It has caused me not a ~ anxiety,* considerable anxiety. **7** **ˈ~-go** *n* (colloq) first examination for B A degree at Cambridge. □ *adv* **1** not much; hardly at all; only slightly: *He is ~ known. She slept very ~ last night. I see him very ~* (i e rarely) *nowadays. He left ~ more than an hour ago. That is ~ short of* (= is almost) *madness! He is ~ better than* (= is almost as bad as) *a thief.* ***a ~,*** (used *adverbially* meaning) rather; somewhat: *She seemed to be a ~ afraid. This hat is a ~ too large for me. He was not a ~ annoyed,* was considerably annoyed. **2** (with such *vv* as *know, think, imagine, guess, suspect, realize,* and always placed before the *v*) not at all: *They ~ suspect that their plot has been discovered. He ~ knows/L~ does he know that the police are about to arrest him.* **~·ness** *n* the quality of being ~. □ *n* (⇨ **less**, **least**). **1** not much; only a small amount: *You have done very ~ for us,* have not helped us much. *I see very ~ of him,* do not see him often or for long. *The ~ of his work that I have seen seems excellent. I got ~ out of it,* not much advantage or profit. *He did what ~ he could. Every ~ helps.* ***~ by ~,*** gradually; by degrees. ***~ or nothing,*** hardly anything. ***in ~,*** on a small scale. **2** (with *indef art*) a small quantity; something (*a ~* is positive; *~* is negative): *He knows a ~ of everything. A ~ makes some people laugh. Please give me a ~.* ***after/for a ~,*** after/for a short time or distance.

lit·toral /ˈlɪtərl/ *n, adj* (part of a country which is) along the coast.

lit·urgy /ˈlɪtədʒɪ/ *n* (*pl* **-gies**) [C] fixed form of public worship used in a church. **li·turgi·cal** /lɪˈtɜdʒɪkl/ *adj*

liv·able /ˈlɪvəbl/ *adj* (of a house, room, climate, etc) fit to live in; (of life) tolerable. ***~ with,*** (of persons) easy to live with.

live[1] /laɪv/ *adj* (rarely *pred*; ⇨ **living** and **alive** for *pred* uses). **1** having life: *~ fish;* (joc) actual, not pretended: *There's a real ~ burglar under my bed!* **2** burning or glowing: *~ coals/embers;* unexploded: *a ~ shell/cartridge/bomb;* not used: *a ~ match;* charged with electricity: *a ~ rail,* carrying current for trains. ***a ˈ~ wire,*** (fig) a lively energetic person. **3** (of sth broadcast) not recorded in advance (on tape or records): *It was a ~ broadcast, not a recording.* **4** **ˈ~-births,** (contrasted with *still-births*) babies born alive: *the ratio of ~-births to still-births.* **5** full of energy, activity, interest, importance, etc: *a ~ question/issue,* one in which there is great interest. □ *adv* (from **3** above): *The concert will be broadcast ~.*

live[2] /lɪv/ *vi,vt* **1** [VP2A] have existence as a plant or animal; be alive (the more usu words: *He's still alive* is preferable to *He still ~s*). **2** [VP2A,B,C, 4A] continue to be alive; remain alive: *~ to be old/to a great age; ~ to see all one's grandchildren married. She's very ill—the doctors don't think she will ~. Can he ~ through the night?* ***~ on,*** continue to ~; *The old people died but the young people ~d on in the village.* ***~ through,*** experience and survive: *He has ~d through two wars and three revolutions.* ***You/We ~ and learn,*** phrase used when one hears sth new, esp sth surprising. ***~ and let ~,*** be tolerant; ignore the failings of others in order that one's failings may be ignored. **3** [VP3A] ***~ on,*** have as food or diet: *~ on fruit/a milk diet;* depend upon for support, etc: *~ on one's salary/on £1 500 a year/on one's wife's income.* ***~ on one's wits,*** get money by ingenious and irregular methods, not necessarily honest. ***~ on one's name/reputation,*** keep one's position, continue to earn money, because one has been successful in the past. ***~ off the land,*** use its agricultural products for one's food needs. **4** [VP2C,3A] ***~ in/at,*** make one's home; reside: *~ in England; ~ abroad; ~ in lodgings/an hotel. Where do you ~?* ***~ in/out,*** (esp of domestic staff, shop assistants, workers) lodge in/out of the building where one is employed: *Does your cook ~ in or out?* ***~ together,*** live in the same house, etc; (of the two persons of opposite sex) live as if married: *I hear that Jane and Bill are living together.* **5** [VP6A, 2D] (with cognate object) spend, pass, experience: *~ a happy life/a virtuous life; ~ a double life,* act two different parts in life. *He ~d the life of a Christian He ~d and died a bachelor.* **6** [VP2C] conduct oneself; pass one's life in a specified way: *~ honestly/happily; ~ like a saint; ~ to oneself,* in isolation, without trying to make friends; *~ a lie,* express a lie by one's manner of living; *~ well,* have good food, etc. **7** [VP15B] ***~ sth down,*** live in such a way that (past guilt, scandal, foolishness, etc) is forgotten: *He hopes to ~ down the scandal caused by the divorce proceedings.* ***~ up to sth,*** put (one's faith, principles, etc) into practice; reach the standard that may be expected: *It's difficult to ~ up to the principles of the Christian religion. He didn't ~ up to his reputation.* ~

with sth, [VP3A] accept and endure it: *I don't like the noise of these jet aircraft, but I've learnt to ~ with it.* **8** [VP2A] (of things without life) remain in existence; survive: *His memory will always ~*, He will never be forgotten. *No ship could ~ in such a rough sea.* **9** [VP2A] enjoy life intensely: *'I want to ~', she said, 'I don't want to spend my days cooking and cleaning and looking after babies.'* ***~ it up,*** live a life of hectic enjoyment.

live·li·hood /ˈlaɪvlɪhʊd/ *n* means of living; way in which one earns money: *earn/gain one's ~ by teaching; earn an honest ~; deprive a man of his ~.*

live·long /ˈlɪvlɒŋ *US:* ˈlaɪvlɔŋ/ *adj* (only in) ***the ~ day/night,*** the whole length of the day/night (implying, according to context, weariness or delight).

live·ly /ˈlaɪvlɪ/ *adj* (**-ier, -iest**) **1** full of life and spirit; gay and cheerful: *She's as ~ as a kitten. The patient seems a little livelier/a little more ~ this morning. He has a ~ imagination. They had a ~ time,* exciting, perhaps with an element of danger. ***make things ~ for sb,*** make it exciting and perhaps dangerous for him. **2** (of colour) bright; gay. **3** (of non-living things) moving quickly or causing quick movement: *a ~ ball; a ~ (cricket) pitch.* ***look ~,*** move more quickly, show more energy. **4** lifelike; realistic: *a ~ description of a football game; give sb a ~ idea of what happened.* **live·li·ness** *n* [U] state of being ~.

liven /ˈlaɪvn/ *vt,vi* [VP15B,2C] ***~ up,*** make or become lively: *How can we ~ things up? The party is beginning to ~ up.*

liver[1] /ˈlɪvə(r)/ *n* **1** [C] large, reddish-brown organ in the body which secretes bile and purifies the blood. ⇨ the illus at **alimentary**. **2** [U] animal's ~ as food. **~·ish** /-ɪʃ/, **~y** *adjj* (colloq) suffering from ~ trouble; bilious.

liver[2] /ˈlɪvə(r)/ *n* person who lives in a specified way: *an evil/clean/loose ~.*

liver·wurst /ˈlɪvəwɜst/ *n* (US) sausage of chopped liver, popular in sandwiches.

liv·ery /ˈlɪvərɪ/ *n* (*pl* **-ries**) **1** special dress or uniform worn by men servants in a great household (esp of a king or noble) or by members of one of the city companies of London (trade or craft guilds). ***in/out of ~,*** wearing/not wearing such dress or uniform. **ˈ~ company,** one of the London trade guilds that has a distinctive uniform. **2** (fig, poet) dress; covering: *trees in the ~ of spring,* with new green leaves; *birds in their winter ~.* **3 ˈ~ (stable),** stable where horses are kept for their owners, fed and looked after for payment; stable from which horses may be hired. **liv·er·ied** /ˈlɪvərɪd/ *adj* wearing ~(1). **~·man** /-mən/ *n* (*pl* **-men**) **1** member of a ~ company. **2** keeper of, workers in, a ~ stable.

lives /laɪvz/ *pl* of **life**.

live·stock /ˈlaɪvstɒk/ *n* [U] (esp farm) animals kept for use or profit, e g cattle, sheep, pigs.

livid /ˈlɪvɪd/ *adj* of the colour of lead, blue-grey; (of a person or his looks) furiously angry: *~ marks/bruises on the body; ~ with cold/rage.* **~·ly** *adv*

liv·ing[1] /ˈlɪvɪŋ/ *adj* **1** alive, esp now existent: *~ languages. No man ~* (= No man who is now alive) *could do better.* ***within/in ~ memory,*** within the memory of people now alive. **2** (of a likeness) true to life: *He's the ~ image of* (= is exactly like) *his father.* **3** strong; active; lively: *a ~ hope/faith.* ***the ~ theatre,*** the ordinary theatre (contrasted with the cinema, TV, etc). □ *n* **the ~,** (with *pl v*) those now alive: *He's still in the land of the ~.*

liv·ing[2] /ˈlɪvɪŋ/ *n* **1** means of keeping alive, of earning what is needed for life: *earn/gain/get/make a ~ as a car salesman.* **2** [U] manner of life: *good ~,* having good food, etc; *plain ~ and high thinking,* having plain, simple food and leading a philosophic life; *the standard of ~ in the US; the art of ~.* **a ˈ~ ˈwage,** minimum wage for a worker and his family to live on. **ˈ~-room** *n* room for general use during the day (often a general purpose room, used for meals, recreation, etc). **ˈ~-space** *n* area of land considered by a State as necessary for further expansion. **3** (Church of England) benefice.

liz·ard /ˈlɪzəd/ *n* (kinds of) small, creeping, long-tailed four-legged reptile. ⇨ the illus at **reptile**.

llama /ˈlɑmə/ *n* S American animal with a thick woolly coat, used as a beast of burden. ⇨ the illus at **large**.

Lloyd's /lɔɪdz/ *n* society of underwriters in London. **~'s Register,** annual list of ships in various classes. **A1 at ~,** first-rate; excellent.

lo /ləʊ/ *int* (old use) Look! See!

load[1] /ləʊd/ *n* [C] **1** that which is (to be) carried or supported, esp if heavy: (fig) weight of care, responsibility, etc: *a heavy ~ on one's shoulders; a ˈcoach-~ of passengers.* ***take a ~ off sb's mind,*** relieve him of anxiety, etc. ***~s of,*** (e g money) (colloq) a large amount. **ˈ~-line** *n* line painted on a ship's side to show depth at which the ship floats when fully loaded. **2** amount which a cart, etc can take: *a ˈcart-~ of hay; two ˈlorry-~s of coal.* ⇨ also *pay load* at **pay**[1]. **3** amount of work that a dynamo, motor, engine, etc is required to do; amount of current supplied by a generating station or carried by an electric circuit. **ˈ~-shedding** *n* cutting off the supply of current on certain lines when the demand for current is greater than the supply.

load[2] /ləʊd/ *vt,vi* **1** [VP6A,14,15A,B,2A,C] ***~ sth into/on to sth/sb; ~ sth/sb (with sth), ~ sb/sth down (with sth),*** put a ~ in or on: *~ sacks on to a cart/a donkey; ~ a cart with coal; ~ a lot of work on to one's staff; a poor old woman ~ed (down) with her shopping;* (fig) *~ a man with favours/honours; a heart ~ed with sorrow.* ***~ (sth) up,*** fill with goods, materials, etc: *Have you finished ~ing up (the van) yet?* **2** [VP6A,2A] put a cartridge or shell into (a gun) or a length of film into (a camera): *Are you ~ed?* Is there a cartridge in your gun? *L~ quickly!* **3** [VP6A] weight with lead; add extra weight to: *a ~ed cane/stick,* one having lead added to make the cane useful as a weapon; *~ed dice,* so weighted as to fall with a certain face, e g the six, uppermost. ***~ the dice (against sb),*** (fig) do sth that gives one an unfair advantage (over him). ***a ~ed question,*** one that is intended to trap a person into making an admission which may be harmful. **~ed** *adj* (sl) having ~s of money.

load·star, load·stone ⇨ lodestone.

loaf[1] /ləʊf/ *n* (*pl* **loaves** /ləʊvz/) **1** mass of bread cooked as a separate quantity; *a two-pound ~.* ***Half a ~ is better than none/no bread,*** It is better to take what one can get or is offered than to run the risk of having nothing. **2 ˈsugar-~,** [C] cone-shaped mass of sugar, as formerly made and sold. **ˋ~-sugar,** [U] sugar cut into small lumps. **3** [C,U] (quantity of) food shaped and cooked: *(a) meat ~*, made of minced meat, eggs, etc. **4** (sl) ***use one's ~,*** think intelligently; reflect.

loaf[2] /ləʊf/ *vi,vt* [VP2A,C,15A,B] waste time; spend time idly: *out-of-work men ~ing at street corners. Don't ~ about while there's so much work to be done. Don't ~ away your time.* □ *n* (*sing* only) ~ing: *I feel like a ~.* **~er** *n* person who ~s.

loam /ləʊm/ *n* [U] rich soil with some sand or a little clay, and with much decayed vegetable matter in it. **~y** *adj* of or like ~: *~y land.*

loan /ləʊn/ *n* **1** sth lent, esp a sum of money: *government ~s,* sum lent to the government; *domestic and foreign ~s.* **2** [U] lending or being lent. ***have the ~ of sth; have sth on ~ (from sb),*** have it as a borrower: *May I have the ~ of* (*borrow* is more usu) *your bike? I have the book out on ~ from the library.* **ˋ~-collection** *n* number of pictures, etc lent by their owners for exhibition. **ˋ~-office** *n* one for lending money to private borrowers. **ˋ~-word** *n* word taken from another language. □ *vt* [VP6A,14] ***~ sth (to sb),*** lend (which is the more usu word except in formal style).

loath, loth /ləʊθ/ *adj* (*pred* only) ***~ to do sth,*** unwilling. ***nothing ~,*** quite willing.

loathe /ləʊð/ *vt* [VP6A,C] **1** feel disgust for; dislike greatly: *She was seasick, and ~d the smell of greasy food.* **2** (colloq) dislike: *He ~s travelling by air.* **loath·ing** *n* disgust. **loath·ly,** (rare), **loath·some** /-səm/ *adjj* disgusting; causing one to feel shocked: *a loathsome disease.*

loaves /ləʊvz/ *pl* of **loaf**[1].

lob /lɒb/ *vi,vt* (-bb-) [VP6A,15A,2C] strike or send (a ball) in a high arc (in tennis). □ *n* ball bowled underhand at cricket or hit high up into the air at tennis.

lobby /ˋlɒbɪ/ *n* (*pl* **-bies**) **1** porch, entrance-hall, ante-room, corridor: *the ~ of a hotel/theatre.* **2** (in the House of Commons, etc) large hall used for interviews between members and the public; group of people who try to influence members, e g of the House of Commons, the Senate in Washington, D C, to support or oppose proposed legislation. **3 (diˋvision) ~,** (House of Commons) one of two corridors to which members retire when a vote is taken in the House. □ *vt,vi* [VP6A,15A, 2A,C] (try to) influence the members of a law-making body; get (a bill) passed or rejected in this way: *~ a bill through the Senate; the National Union of Farmers ~ing in order to maintain subsidies/~ing for higher subsidies/~ing their MP's.* **ˋ~·ist** /-ɪst/ *n* person who lobbies.

lobe /ləʊb/ *n* **1** lower rounded part of the external ear. ⇨ the illus at **ear**. **2** subdivision of the lungs or the brain. ⇨ the illus at **respiratory**. **lobed** *adj* having ~s.

lob·ster /ˋlɒbstə(r)/ *n* **1** [C] shellfish with eight legs and two claws, bluish-black before and scarlet after being boiled. ⇨ the illus at **crustacean**. **ˋ~-pot** *n* basket in which ~s are trapped. **2** [U] its flesh as food.

lo·cal /ˋləʊkl/ *adj* **1** of, special to, a place or district: *the ~ doctor,* living in the district; *~ customs; a column of ~ news; ~ government; ~ option/veto,* (in some countries) system by which people may decide, by voting, whether they do or do not want sth, e g the sale of alcoholic drink, in their district. ***~ colour,*** details of the scenes and period described in a story, added to make the story more real. **~ time,** time at any place in the world as calculated from the position of the sun: *L~ time changes by one hour for every 15° longitude.* **2** affecting a part, not the whole: *a ~ pain/injury; a ~ anaesthetic.* □ *n* **1** (usu *pl*) inhabitant(s) of a particular district. **2** item of ~ news in a newspaper. **3** (colloq) ~ public house: *pop into the ~ for a pint.* **~ly** /-klɪ/ *adv*

lo·cal·ism /ˋləʊklɪzm/ *n* **1** [U] interest in a district, esp one's own; favouring of what is local; narrowness of ideas that may be the result of this. **2** [C] local idiom, pronunciation, etc.

lo·cale /ləʊˋkɑl/ *n* [C] scene of an event; scene of a novel, etc.

lo·cal·ity /ləʊˋkælətɪ/ *n* (*pl* **-ties**) **1** [C] thing's position; place in which an event occurs; place, district, neighbourhood. **2** [U] faculty of remembering and recognizing places, features of the landscape, etc, esp as a help in finding one's way: *She has a good sense of ~.*

lo·cal·ize /ˋləʊklɑɪz/ *vt* [VP6A] **1** make local, not general; confine within a particular part or area: *There is little hope of localizing the disease.* **2** invest with local characteristics. **lo·cal·iz·ation** /ˈləʊklɑɪˋzeɪʃn *US:* -lɪˋz-/ *n*

lo·cate /ləˋkeɪt *US:* ˋləʊkeɪt/ *vt* [VP6A,15A] **1** discover, show, the locality of: *~ a town on a map.* **2** establish in a place: *a new school to be ~d in the suburbs. Where is the new factory to be ~d?* **3 be ~d,** be situated. **lo·ca·tion** /ləʊˋkeɪʃn/ *n* **1** [U] locating or being ~d. **2** [C] position or place: *suitable locations for new factories.* **3** place, not a film studio, where (part of) a cinema film is photographed. ***on location,*** shooting film in this way. **4** (esp in S Africa) suburb for Africans.

loch /lɒk/ *n* (Scot) **1** long, narrow arm of the sea almost enclosed by land. **2** lake.

lock[1] /lɒk/ *n* portion of hair that naturally hangs or clings together; (*pl*) hair of the head: *my scanty ~s.*

lock[2] /lɒk/ *n* **1** appliance, mechanism, by which a door, gate, lid, etc may be fastened with a bolt that needs a key to work it. ***be/put/keep sth under ~ and key,*** in sth fitted with a ~. **ˋ~·smith** *n* maker and mender of ~s. **2** mechanism by which a gun is fired. ***~, stock and barrel,*** the whole of the thing; completely. **3** enclosed section of a canal or river at a point where the water level changes, for raising or lowering boats by the use of gates fitted with sluices. **ˈ~-ˋgate,** gate on a lock. **ˋ~-keeper** *n* keeper of a canal or river ~, who opens and shuts the gates to allow boats to pass through. **4** [U] condition of being fixed or jammed so that movement is impossible. **ˋ~·jaw** *n* [U] form of disease (tetanus) that causes the jaws to be firmly locked together. **ˋ~·nut** *n* extra nut screwed over another to prevent its turning. **ˋ~-stitch** *n* sewing-machine stitch by which two threads are firmly joined together. ⇨ also *air ~* at **air**[1]**(7)**. **5** (motoring) extent of the turning arc of a steering wheel: *full ~,* with the steering wheel turned (right or left) as far as it will go.

lock[3] /lɒk/ *vt,vi* **1** [VP6A,15A,B] fasten a door, box, etc with a lock. ***~ the stable door after the horse has bolted/has been stolen,*** take precautions when it is too late. ***~ sth away,*** put it away in a ~ed box, drawer, etc; (fig) keep securely:

have a secret safely ~ed (away) in one's breast. **~ sb in,** put sb in a room of which the door is ~ed on the outside. **~ oneself in,** ~ the door(s) so that no one can enter from outside. **~ sb out,** keep him outside, prevent him from entering, by ~ing the gate or door(s) on the inside: *If you don't get back before midnight, you'll be ~ed out.* **'~-out** *n* refusal of employers to allow workmen to enter their place of work until certain conditions are agreed to or demands given up. ⇨ strike[1]. **~ sth/sb up,** (a) make safe by placing in sth that ~s: *L~ up your jewellery before you go away.* (b) shut up a house, etc by ~ing all the doors. (c) put (a person) in a ~ed room, a prison, a mental home, etc. (d) invest (money) in such a way that it cannot easily or quickly be exchanged for cash: *All his capital is ~ed up in land.* **'~-up** *n* place where prisoners may be kept temporarily; (colloq) any prison. □ *adj* (attrib only) that can be ~ed: *a ~-up shop,* one that can be ~ed at night, the shopkeeper sleeping elsewhere; *a ~-up garage,* one, e g at a hotel, with door(s) that can be ~ed. **2** [VP2A] have a ~; become ~ed; be capable of being ~ed: *This trunk doesn't ~,* has no lock or has a lock that does not work. *The door ~s easily.* **3** [VP6A,2A,C] (cause to) become fixed, unable to move: *His jaws were tightly ~ed. He ~ed the wheels of the car to prevent its being stolen. They were ~ed together in a fierce struggle. They were ~ed in each other's arms. The parts ~ into each other,* interlock. **4** [VP2C] **~ on to,** (of a missile, etc) find and automatically follow (a target) by radar.

locker /ˈlɒkə(r)/ *n* **1** small cupboard, esp one of a number used by individuals in a public place, e g for clothes at a swimming-pool or sports ground, for a pupil's books, etc at school. **'~ room,** room for changing one's clothes, e g at a swimming-pool or golf-club. **2** box or compartment in a ship used for clothes, stores, ammunition, etc. ***be in/go to Davy Jones's ~,*** be drowned at sea.

loci /ˈləʊksaɪ/ *pl* of locus.

locket /ˈlɒkɪt/ *n* small (often gold or silver) case for a portrait, a lock of hair, etc, usu worn round the neck on a chain.

loco /ˈləʊkəʊ/ *adj* (sl) mad.

loco·mo·tion /ˌləʊkəˈməʊʃn/ *n* [U] moving, ability to move, from place to place. **loco·mo·tive** /ˈləʊkəˈməʊtɪv/ *adj* of, having, causing, ~. □ *n* self-propelled engine for use on railways: *steam/Diesel/electric ~s.*

locum tenens /ˌləʊkəm ˈtinənz/ *n* (Lat) priest or doctor performing the duties of another who is away, e g on holiday.

lo·cus /ˈləʊkəs/ *n* (*pl* loci /ˈləʊsaɪ/) exact place of sth. **'~ 'classicus** /ˈklæsɪkəs/, best known or most authoritative passage on a subject.

lo·cust /ˈləʊkəst/ *n* **1** (kinds of) migratory African and Asian winged insect which flies in great swarms and destroys crops and vegetables. ⇨ the illus at insect. ⇨ hopper[2](2). **2 '~(-tree),** (kind of) tree, esp *carob* and a N American tree, *false acacia.*

loc·ution /ləˈkjuʃn/ *n* [U] style of speech; way of using words; [C] phrase or idiom.

lode /ləʊd/ *n* vein of metal ore. **'~·star** *n* star by which a ship may be steered; the pole-star; (fig) guiding principle. **'~·stone** *n* magnetized iron-ore.

lodge[1] /lɒdʒ/ *n* **1** small house, esp one at the entrance to the grounds of a large house, occupied by a gatekeeper, gardener or other staff of the estate. **2** country house used in the hunting or shooting season: *a 'hunting ~ in the Highlands;* (US) hut or cabin for temporary use: *a 'skiing ~.* **3** porter's room(s) in the chief gateway or entrance to a college, factory, block of flats, etc. **4** residence of the head of a college at Cambridge. **5** (place of meeting for) members of a branch of a society such as the Freemasons. **6** beaver's lair.

lodge[2] /lɒdʒ/ *vt,vi* **1** [VP6A,15A] supply (sb) with a room or place to sleep in for a time; receive as a guest: *The shipwrecked sailors were ~d in the school.* **2** [VP3A] **~ at/with,** live as a paying guest: *Where are you lodging now? I'm lodging at Mrs P's/with Mr and Mrs X.* **3** [VP3A] **~ in,** enter and become fixed: *The bullet ~d in his jaw.* **4** [VP6A,15A] cause (sth) to enter and become fixed (*in*); put or place (in a particular place): *~ a bullet in a man's brain.* **5** [VP6A,15A] put (money, etc) for safety: *~ one's valuables in the bank while away from home on holiday.* **6** [VP6A,14] **~ sth (with sb) (against sb),** place (a statement, etc) with the proper authorities: *~ a complaint against one's neighbours with the authorities.* **lodger** *n* person paying for rooms, etc in sb's house: *The widow makes a living by taking in lodgers.*

lodg·ing /ˈlɒdʒɪŋ/ *n* (usu *pl*) room or rooms (not in a hotel) rented to live in: *It's cheaper to live in ~s than in a hotel. Where can we find (a) ~ for the night?* **'~-house** *n* house in which ~s are let (usu by the week).

lodge·ment (also **lodgment**) /ˈlɒdʒmənt/ *n* **1** [U] act or process of lodging: *the ~ of a complaint.* ⇨ lodge[2](6). **2** [C] sth that has accumulated or been deposited: *a ~ of dirt in a pipe.* **3** (mil) position gained in enemy territory: *gain a ~ on an enemy-held coast.*

lo·ess /ˈləʊes/ *n* [U] deposit of fine yellowish-grey

a canal lock

soil, found esp in northern China, central U S A and central Europe.

loft[1] /loft *US:* lɔft/ *n* **1** room, place, used for storing things, in the highest part of a house, under the roof; space under the roof of a stable or barn, where hay or straw is stored. **2** gallery in a church or hall: *the ˋorgan-~.*

loft[2] /loft *US:* lɔft/ *vt* [VP6A] (golf, cricket) hit (a ball) high: *~ a ball over the fielders' heads.*

lofty /ˋloftɪ *US:* ˋlɔftɪ/ *adj* (-ier, -iest) **1** (not used of persons) of great height: *a ~ tower/mountain.* **2** (of thoughts, aims, feelings, etc) distinguished; noble: *~ sentiments; a ~ style.* **3** haughty; proud; consciously superior: *a ~ appearance; in a ~ manner.* **loft·ily** /-əlɪ/ *adv* **lofti·ness** *n*

log[1] /log *US:* lɔg/ *n* [C] rough length of tree-trunk that has fallen or been cut down; short piece of this for a fire: *a raft of logs,* floating down a river; *a ˋlog jam,* mass of floating logs tightly mixed together; (US) deadlock. ***like a log,*** unconscious; immovable. ***sleep like a log,*** sleep soundly and with little or no movement. **ˈlog-ˋcabin** *n* cabin with walls and roof made of logs, not boards. **ˋlog-rolling** *n* practice of giving support to others in return for support from them, e g by author-reviewers who praise each other's books. **log·ging** *n* work of cutting down forest trees for timber: *a logging camp.*

log[2] /log *US:* lɔg/ *n* **1** device attached to a knotted line, trailed from a ship, to measure its speed through the water: *sail by the log,* calculate a ship's position by means of information gained from the log. **2** (also **ˋlog-book**) book with a permanent daily record or events during a ship's voyage (esp the weather, ship's position, speed, and distance as recorded by the log); (by extension) any record of performance, e g of a car or aircraft. **3** (colloq) Registration Book (of a motor-vehicle). □ *vt* (-gg-) [VP6A] enter (facts) in the log-book of a ship or aircraft.

log[3] /log *US:* lɔg/ short for logarithm.

lo·gan·berry /ˋləʊgənberɪ/ *n* (*pl* -ries) large dark-red berry from a plant that is a cross between a blackberry and a raspberry.

log·ar·ithm /ˋlogərɪθm *US:* ˋlɔg-/ *n* one of a series of numbers set out in tables which make it possible to work out problems in multiplication and division by adding and subtracting.

log·ger·heads /ˋlogəhedz/ *n* (only in) ***at ~ (with),*** disagreeing or disputing: *He's constantly at ~ with his wife.*

log·gia /ˋlodʒɪə/ *n* (I) open-sided gallery or arcade; part of a house with one side open to the garden.

logic /ˋlodʒɪk/ *n* [U] science, method, of reasoning; (person's) ability to argue and convince: *argue with learning and ~.* **logi·cal** /-kl/ *adj* in accordance with the rules of ~; able to reason correctly: *a ~al mind/argument/conclusion; ~al behaviour.* **logi·cally** /-klɪ/ *adv* **lo·gician** /ləˋdʒɪʃn/ *n* person skilled in ~. **lo·gis·tics** /ləˋdʒɪstɪks/ *n* (with *sing v*) supply, distribution and replacement of materials and personnel, e g for the armed forces.

loin /lɔɪn/ *n* **1** (*pl*) the lower part of the body on both sides of the spine between the ribs and the hip-bones. ⇨ the illus at dog, domestic. ***gird (up) one's ~s,*** (biblical) prepare for a journey; make ready for action. **ˋ~-cloth** *n* piece of cloth covering the middle of the body, folded between the legs, and fastened round the ~s. **2** joint of meat which includes the ~s: *~ of mutton.*

loi·ter /ˋlɔɪtə(r)/ *vi,vt* [VP2A,C,15B] go slowly and stop frequently on the way somewhere; stand about; pass (time) thus: *~ on one's way home; ~ the hours away; ~ over a job.* **~er** *n*

loll /lol/ *vi,vt* [VP2A,C] ***~ about/around,*** rest, sit or stand (*about*) in a lazy way. **2** [VP2C,15B] ***~ out,*** (of the tongue) (allow to) hang: *The dog ~ed its tongue out. The dog's tongue was ~ing out.*

lol·li·pop /ˋlolɪpop/ *n* large sweet of boiled sugar on a stick, held in the hand and sucked: *ˋice-~,* quantity of frozen fruit juice on a stick. **ˋ~ man/woman** (GB colloq) one who carries a pole with a disc marked 'Stop! Children crossing', to conduct children across busy roads, e g outside a school.

lolly /ˋlolɪ/ *n* (*pl* -lies) **1** [C] (colloq) lollipop: *iced lollies.* **2** [U] (sl) money, (esp money easily earned and lavishly spent).

lone /ləʊn/ *adj* (*attrib* only; ⇨ alone and lonely, which are more usu) solitary; without companions; unfrequented. ***play a ~ hand,*** (fig) do sth without the help or support of others, esp sth not very popular.

lone·ly /ˋləʊnlɪ/ *adj* (-ier, -iest) **1** without companions: *a ~ traveller.* **2** sad or melancholy because one lacks companions, sympathy, friendship: *a ~-looking girl; feel ~.* **3** (of places) not often visited; far from inhabited places or towns: *a ~ house; a ~ mountain village.* **lone·li·ness** *n* state of being ~: *suffer from loneliness.*

lone·some /ˋləʊn-səm/ *adj* **1** sad because alone: feel ~; causing a feeling of loneliness: *a ~ journey.* **2** solitary, unfrequented: *a ~ valley.*

long[1] /loŋ *US:* lɔŋ/ *adj* (-er, -est) **1** concerned with extent in space; measuring much from end to end: *How ~ is the River Nile? The new road is twenty miles ~. Your car is ~er than mine. What a lot of men have ~ hair nowadays! What a lot of ~-haired men we see today!* ***put on a ~ face,*** ⇨ face[1](3). **2** in phrases indicating (great) extent. ***have a ~ arm,*** be able to make one's power felt far. ***the ~ arm of the law,*** its far-reaching power. ***make a ~ arm for sth,*** reach out for sth, e g at table. ***it's/as broad as it is ~,*** ⇨ broad[1](9). **3** expressing duration or extent in time: *the ~ vacation,* the summer vacation of law courts and universities. *He was ill for a ~ time. How ~ are the holidays? They're six weeks ~. He won't be ~ (in) making up his mind,* will soon do so. *Don't be too ~ about it,* Do it soon or quickly. **4** (of vowel sounds) taking more time to utter than others: *'Slip' has a short vowel and 'sleep' has a ~ vowel. The 'u' in 'lucre' is ~.* **5** (in phrases concerned with extent in time) **~ bonds,** (fin) which mature in 20 years or more. ***take a ~ cool/hard look at sth,*** consider facts, problems shrewdly and at length. ***take the ~ view,*** consider events, factors, etc a ~ time ahead, rather than the present situation, etc. ***in the ~ run,*** ⇨ run[1](7). ***in the ~ term,*** looking ahead for a ~ time. Hence, **ˈ~-ˋterm,** *attrib adj*: *~-term agreements / contracts / investments.* **6** (compounds) **ˋ~-boat** *n* sailing-ship's largest boat. **ˋ~-bow** *n* bow drawn by hand, equal in length to the height of the archer, used with feathered arrows. ⇨ crossbow. ***draw the ~bow,*** tell exaggerated or invented stories. **ˈ~-ˋdistance** *attrib adj* covering a ~ distance: *~-distance run-*

ners (in sport); *a ~-distance telephone call; a ~-distance lorry driver.* ***a ~ drink,*** large quantity, e g of beer, served in a tall glass (contrasted with a *short drink*, e g neat whisky). ***a ~ dozen,*** thirteen. **ˈ~-hand** *n* [U] ordinary handwriting (contrasted with *shorthand and typing*). **ˈ~-ˈhaired** *adj* **(a)** ⇨ **1** above. **(b)** (of men) intellectual; artistic; young and unconventional. ***a ~ haul,*** ⇨ **haul**. **ˈ~-ˈheaded** *adj* shrewd; having foresight. **the ˈ~ jump,** measured along the ground for distance. ⇨ *high jump* at **high**[1]**(12)**. **~ measure,** ⇨ **App 5**. **~ metre,** stanza of four eight-syllable lines. **~ odds,** (in betting) very uneven, e g 50 to 1. **~-play(ing) ˈdisc/ˈrecord,** (abbr **LP**) playing (at slow speed) for a ~er time than earlier kinds. **ˈ~-range** *attrib adj* of ~ periods of time or ~ distances: *a ~-range weather forecast*, e g for one month ahead; *~-range planning*, for a ~ time ahead, e g ten years; *~-range missiles.* **ˈ~-shore·man** *n* man who works on shore (on wharves, in dockyards) loading and unloading ships. **a ~ shot,** ⇨ **shot**[1]**(2)**. **ˈ~ ˈsighted** *adj* able to see things a great distance away; (fig) prudent; having foresight. **ˈ~-ˈstanding** *adj* of ~ duration: *a ~-standing engagement to do sth*, a promise made a time ago. **~ suit,** ⇨ **suit**[1]**(5)**. **ˈ~ stop,** (cricket) player who fields straight behind the wicket-keeper ⇨ the illus at **cricket**. **~ ton,** 2 240 lb. **ˈ~ waves,** (wireless telegraphy) waves of 1 000 metres or over. **ˈ~-ˈwinded** *adj* (fig) tedious; wearisome because of diffuse: *a ~-winded and boring lecturer.* Hence, **ˈ~-ˈwindedˈness**

long[2] /lɒŋ *US:* lɔŋ/ *n* (*sing* only) **1** ~ time or interval: *I shall see you before ~. The work won't take ~. Shall you be away for ~?* ***at (the) ~est,*** to give the most distant date, etc: *I can wait only three days at ~est,* not after the third day from now. ***the ~ and the short of it,*** all that need be said; the general effect or result. **2** ~ syllable, esp in Latin verse: *four ~s and six shorts.*

long[3] /lɒŋ *US:* lɔŋ/ *adv* **(-er, -est) 1** for a long time: *Stay (for) as ~ as you like. I've ~ been intending to call on you.* **as/so ~ as,** on condition that, provided that: *You may borrow the book so ~ as you keep it clean.* **2** in numerous compounds: **ˈ~-ˈlived** *adj* having a long life; living for a long time: *a ~-lived family.* **ˈ~-drawn-ˈout** *adj* extended; unduly prolonged: *a ~-drawn-out visit from my mother-in-law.* **ˈ~ˈstanding** *adj* that has existed for a long time: *a ~-standing invitation to visit the Browns.* **ˈ~-ˈsuffering** *adj* patient and uncomplaining in spite of trouble, provocation, etc: *his ~-suffering wife.* **3** at a long time (from a point of time): *~ ago/before/after/since. That happened ~ ago.* **4** (with *nn* indicating duration) throughout the specified time: *all day ~*, throughout the whole day; *all my life ~.* **5** ***no/any/much ~er,*** after a certain point of time: *I can't wait any/much ~er. He's no ~er living here.*

long[4] /lɒŋ *US:* lɔŋ/ *vi* [VP3A,4C] ***~ for sth/for sb to do sth,*** desire earnestly; wish for very much: *She ~ed for him to say something. I'm ~ing to see you. The children are ~ing for the holidays.* **~·ing** *n* [C,U] (an) earnest desire: *a ~ing for home.* □ *adj* having or showing an earnest desire: *a ~ing look; with ~ing eyes.* **~·ing·ly** *adv*

lon·gev·ity /lɒnˈdʒevətɪ/ *n* [U] long life.

longi·tude /ˈlɒndʒɪtjud *US:* -tud/ *n* distance east or west (measured in degrees) from a meridian, esp that of Greenwich, in London. ⇨ the illus at **projection**. **longi·tudi·nal** /ˈlɒndʒɪˈtjudɪnl *US:* -ˈtudnl/ *adj* **1** of ~. **2** of or in length. **3** running lengthwise: *longitudinal stripes*, e g in a flag.

long·ways /ˈlɒŋweɪz *US:* ˈlɔŋ-/, **long·wise** /ˈlɒŋwaɪz *US:* ˈlɔŋ-/ *adv* = **lengthways**.

loo /lu/ *n* (esp GB colloq) lavatory.

loo·fah, loofa /ˈlufə/ *n* [C] dried pod of a plant (kind of gourd or pumpkin) used as a sponge.

look[1] /lʊk/ *vi,vt* (*pt,pp* **~ed**) (For uses with *adverbial particles* and *preps* ⇨ **7** below.) **1** [VP2A,C,3A,4A] ***~ (at),*** use one's sight; turn the eyes in some direction; try to see: *~ (up) at the ceiling; ~ (down) at the floor. We ~ed but saw nothing. I happened to be ~ing another way*, in a different direction. *L~ to see whether the road's clear before you cross.* ***to ~ at him/it, etc,*** judging by the outward appearance: *To ~ at her you'd never guess that she was a university teacher.* ***fair/good, etc to ~ at,*** fair, etc in outward appearance. ***L~ before you leap,*** (prov) Avoid acting hastily, without considering the possible consequences. **ˈ~·ing-glass** *n* mirror made of glass. **2** [VP2D,4D] seem to be, have a certain appearance: *~ sad/ill/tired. The town always ~s deserted on Sunday mornings. It ~s very suspicious to me,* I suspect that it is not strictly honest, straightforward, etc. *The girl ~ed puzzled.* ***(not) ~ oneself,*** not have one's normal appearance: *You're not ~ing yourself today*, You're ~ing ill, worried, etc. *He's beginning to ~ himself again*, ~ well again, e g after an illness. ***~ one's age,*** have an appearance that conforms to one's age: *She ~s her age*, seems as old as she in fact is. *You don't ~ your age*, look younger than you are. ***~ one's best,*** appear to the greatest advantage: *She ~s her best in tweeds.* ***~ black (at...),*** ~ angry. ***~ blue,*** appear sad or discontented. ***~ good,*** **(a)** seem attractive, enticing, etc. **(b)** seem to be making satisfactory progress, doing well, etc: *The horse I put my money on ~ed good until the last hundred metres.* ***~ small,*** ~ mean or insignificant: *We made him ~ small*, exposed him as being insignificant. ***L~ alive!*** Get busy! Make haste! ***L~ here!*** often used to call attention to sth; or demand attention. ***L~ sharp!*** Hurry up! ***~ well,*** **(a)** (of persons) be healthy in appearance. **(b)** (of things) be attractive, pleasing, satisfactory: *Does this hat ~ well on me?* **(c)** (of a person wearing sth) ~ attractive: *He ~s well in naval uniform.* **3** ***~ like/as if,*** seem (to be): *It ~s like salt and it is salt. It ~s like* (= threatens to) *rain. It ~s like being* (= promises to be) *a fine day. This ~s to me like a way in. She ~s as if she were about to faint. You ~ as if you slept badly. It doesn't ~ to me as if we shall get there in time.* **4** [VP8] pay attention; learn by seeing: *L~ where you're going! L~ who's here! L~ (and see) whether the postman has been yet.* **5** (= ~ at) ***~ sb/sth in the face,*** face boldly: *~ death/one's enemy in the face.* **6** [VP6A] express by one's appearance: *~ one's thanks (consent).* **7** [VP2C, 3A,15B] (uses with *adverbial particles* and *preps*): ***look about (for sth),*** be on the watch, in search of; examine one's surroundings, the state of affairs, etc: *Are you still ~ing about for a job?* ***~ about one,*** examine one's surroundings; give oneself time to make plans: *We hardly had time to*

~ about us before we had to continue our journey. **look after sb/sth,** **(a)** take care of; watch over; attend to: *Who will ~ after the children while their mother is in hospital? He needs a wife to ~ after him. He's well able to ~ after himself/to ~ after his own interests.* **(b)** follow with the eyes: *They ~ed after the train as it left the station.*
look at sth, (special uses) **(a)** (in neg sentences, usu with *will, would*) refuse; reject: *They wouldn't ~ at my proposal.* **(b)** examine: *We must ~ at the question from all sides. Will you please ~ at the battery of my car? Doctor, will you ~ at my ankle?* **(c)** in polite requests: *Will you please ~ at* (i e read) *this letter?* **good/bad, etc to ~ at,** of good, etc appearance: *The hotel is not much to ~ at,* does not appear to be good.
look away (from sth), turn the eyes away.
look back (on/to sth), (fig) turn one's thoughts to sth in the past. **never ~ back,** make uninterrupted progress.
look down on sb, despise; consider oneself superior to; show false contempt for: *When she married a solicitor, she ~ed down on the office girls she had worked with.* **~ down one's nose at sb,** (colloq) regard with displeasure or contempt.
look for sb/sth, **(a)** search for; try to find: *Are you still ~ing for a job? That foolish fellow is ~ing for trouble,* is behaving in a way that will get him into trouble. **(b)** expect: *It's too soon yet to ~ for results.*
look forward to sth, anticipate (usu with pleasure): *We're ~ing forward to seeing you again.*
look in (on sb), make a short (usu casual) visit; pay a call: *Won't you ~ in (on me) next time you're in town? The doctor will ~ in again this evening.* **get/give sb a ˋ~-in,** (colloq, sport, etc) chance (of winning, etc): *You won't have (get) a ~-in with such strong competition.*
look into sth, **(a)** investigate; examine: *~ into a question.* **(b)** dip into (a book, etc). **(c)** ~ at the inside of, the depths of: *He ~ed into the box/the mirror/her eyes.*
look on, **(a)** be a spectator; watch: *Why don't you play football instead of just ~ing on?* Hence, **ˈ~er-ˋon** *n* person who ~s on. **(b)** read from a book, etc (*with* sb), at the same time: *May I ~ on with you?* **~ on sb as,** regard as. *Do you ~ on him as an authority on the subject?* **~ on sb with,** regard in the way specified: *He seems to ~ on me with distrust.* **~ on to,** (of a place, room, etc) overlook, give a view of: *My bedroom ~s on (to) the garden.*
look out (of sth) (at sth), *He stood at the window and ~ed out (at the view). They were ~ing out of the window.* **~ out on/over,** supply an outlook or view over: *Our hotel room here ~s out on the sea front.* **~ out (for sb/sth),** be prepared (for), be on the watch for: *L~ out!* Be on the watch, be careful! *Will you go to the station and ~ out for Mr Hill?* Hence, **ˋ~-out** *n* **(a)** state of being watchful (*sing* only): *keep a good ~-out; be on the ~-out for bargains.* **(b)** [C] place from which to watch; person who has the duty of watching: (attrib) *a ~-out post; send ~-outs in advance.* **(c)** (*sing* only) prospect; what seems likely to come or happen: *It seems a bad ~-out for their children. That's ˋyour own ~-out,* sth you yourself must be responsible for. **~ sth out (for sb),** select by making an inspection: *~ out some old clothes for poor relations.*
look over sth, **(a)** inspect; examine: *We must ~ over the house before we decide to rent it.* **(b)** pardon; overlook (a fault, etc) (*overlook* is preferred). **~ sth over,** inspect one by one or part by part: *Here's the correspondence; I've ~ed it over.* Hence. **ˋ~-over** *n*: *give something a ~-over,* examine it.
look round, **(a)** (fig) examine possibilities before deciding sth: *Don't make a hurried decision; ~ round well first.* **(b)** turn the head (to see): *When I ~ed round for her, she was leaving the hall.* **~ round sth,** go sight-seeing, etc: *Have we time to ~ round (the town) before lunch?*
look through sth, revise (a lesson, etc); study; examine: *L~ through your notes before the examination. I must ~ through these bills and check them before I pay them.* **~ sth through,** inspect carefully or successively: *He ~ed the proposals through before approving them.*
look to sth, be careful of or about: *The country must ~ to its defences. L~ to your manners, my boy,* Don't be so rude. *L~ to it* (= Take care) *that this does not happen again.* **~ to sb for sth/to do sth,** rely on: *They all ~ to you for help. They're ~ing to you for a solo/to sing to them.* **~ to/towards,** face: *a house ~ing towards the river/to the south.*
look up, **(a)** raise the eyes: *Don't ~ up.* **(b)** improve in price or prosperity: *Business is/Oil shares are ~ing up.* **~ sth up,** search for (a word in a dictionary, facts in a reference book, etc): *Please ~ up a fast train to Leeds,* in a railway guide. **~ sb up,** pay a call on; visit: *Do ~ me up next time you're in London.* **~ up to sb (as...),** respect: *They all ~ up to him as their leader.* **~ sb up and down,** examine him carefully or contemptuously.

look² /lʊk/ *n* [C] **1** act of looking: *Let me have a ~ at your new car.* **2** appearance; what sth suggests when seen: *A ~ of pleasure came to her face. There were angry ~s from the neighbours. The town has a European ~.* **give sth/get a new ~,** a new and more up-to-date appearance: *The High Street has been given a new ~.* **3** (*pl*) person's appearance: *She's beginning to lose her ~s.* her beauty. **~er** *n*: *a ˈgood-ˋ~er,* a good-looking person.

loom¹ /lum/ *n* machine for weaving cloth.

a hand loom

loom² /lum/ *vi* [VP2C,D] appear indistinctly and in a threatening way; (fig) appear great and fill the mind: *The dark outline of another ship ~ed (up) through the fog. The threat of the H-bomb ~ed large in their minds.*

loon[1] /lun/ *n* large diving-bird that lives on fish and has a loud, wild cry.

loon[2] /lun/ *n* (Scot and archaic) foolish, idle, good-for-nothing person.

loony /ˈlunɪ/ *n, adj* (sl) lunatic. **ˈ~-bin** /-bɪn/ *n* (sl) mental home.

loop /lup/ *n* **1** (shape produced by a) curve crossing itself as in the letters *l* and *h* in ordinary handwriting). **2** part of a length of string, wire, ribbon, etc in such a shape, e g as a knot or fastening; curved piece of metal as a handle; (colloq) ~-shaped intra-uterine contraceptive device. **3** (also **ˈ~-line**) railway or telegraph line that separates from the main line, runs in a curve, and then rejoins the main line farther on. **4** circuit in which an aviator, motor-cyclist, etc is for a time travelling in a ~ or in ~s: *The airman looped the ~ five times,* flew the shape of a ~ five times. □ *vt,vi* **1** [VP6A,15B] form or bend into a ~ or ~s; supply with a ~ or ~s: *~ the curtains up/back; ~ things together.* **2** [VP6A,2A] perform a ~(4); make a ~ or ~s.

loop·hole /ˈluphəʊl/ *n* **1** narrow vertical opening in a wall for shooting or looking through, or to admit light and air (as in old forts, stockades, etc). **2** (fig) way of escape from control, esp one provided by careless and inexact wording of a rule: *find a ~ in the law.*

loopy /ˈlupɪ/ *adj* (dated sl) crazy.

loose[1] /lus/ *adj* (-r, -st) **1** free; not held, tied up, fastened, packed, or contained in sth: *Many Englishmen carry their small change* (i e coins) *~ in their trouser pocket, not in a purse. That dog is too dangerous to be left ~.* ***break/get ~,*** escape confinement: *One of the tigers in the zoo has broken/got ~,* has escaped from its cage. ***let sth ~,*** allow it to be free from control: *He let ~ his indignation,* did not control it. **ˈ~ box,** separate compartment in a stable or railway van, in which a horse can move about freely. **ˈ~-ˈleaf** *pred adj* (of a notebook) with leaves that may be detached separately and replaced. **2** not close-fitting; not tight or tense: *a ~ collar; ~-fitting clothes.* **3** moving more freely than is right or usual: *a ~ tooth; ~ bowels,* with a tendency to diarrhoea; *a ~ thread; a ~ window,* one that shakes or rattles in the wind. *There's a screw ~ somewhere,* sth wrong or suspicious. ***have a ˈscrew ~,*** (colloq) be unsound in one's mind. ***have a ~ tongue,*** be in the habit of talking too freely. ***ride with a ~ rein,*** **(a)** allow the horse freedom. **(b)** (fig) manage a person indulgently. ***come ~,*** (of a fastening, etc) come unfastened or insecure. ***work ~,*** (of a bolt, etc) become insecure, no longer tight. **4** not firmly or properly tied: *a ~ knot; a ~ end of rope,* one that is not fastened. ***at a ~ end,*** (fig of a person) having nothing to do. **5** (of talk, behaviour, etc) not sufficiently controlled: *~ conduct; lead a ~ life; a ~* (= immoral) *woman.* ***(be) on the ~,*** (colloq) free from the restraints of morality or discipline; dissipated. ***play fast and ~ (with sb),*** behave dishonestly or in a deceitful manner. **6** not strict; inexact; indefinite; (of translations) not close to the original: *~ thinking; a ~ thinker; a ~* (= badly constructed) *argument.* **7** not compact; not closely packed: *~ soil; cloth with a ~ weave.* **8** (of the human body) not closely knit: *a ~ frame; ~ limbs,* rather awkward, ungainly in appearance; (of bodily actions) careless, bungling or inaccurate: *~ bowling and fielding* (in cricket). **~·ly** *adv* in a ~ manner: *words ~ly employed,* ⇨ 6 above; *rules ~ly enforced.*

loose[2] /lus/ *vt* [VP6A] make free or loose: *Wine ~d his tongue,* made him talk freely (*loosen* is commoner).

loosen /ˈlusn/ *vt,vi* [VP6A,2A,15B] make or become loose or looser: *L~ the screw. The screw has ~ed. This medicine may ~ your cough,* help to get up the phlegm. *I must take some exercise and ~ up my muscles.*

loot /lut/ *n* [U] goods (esp private property) taken away unlawfully and by force, e g by thieves, or by soldiers in time of war. □ *vt,vi* [VP6A,2A] carry off ~ from: *The brutal soldiers ~ed and massacred for three weeks.* **~er** *n*

lop[1] /lɒp/ *vt* (-pp-) [VP6A,15B] ***lop away/off,*** cut off, separate branches, etc from a tree.

lop[2] /lɒp/ *vi* (-pp-) hang down loosely. (chiefly in compounds). **ˈlop-ears** *n pl* drooping ears. **ˈlop-eared** *adj* having lop-ears: *a lop-eared rabbit.* **ˈlop-ˈsided** *adj* with one side lower than the other.

lope /ləʊp/ *vi* [VP2A,C] move along with long, easy steps or strides (as a hare does). □ *n* step or stride of this kind: *The deer went off at an easy ~.*

lo·qua·cious /ləʊˈkweɪʃəs/ *adj* talkative; fond of talking. **~·ly** *adv* **~·ness** *n* **lo·quac·ity** /ləˈkwæsətɪ/ *n* [U] being ~.

lo·quat /ˈləʊkwæt/ *n* [C] (tree, common in China and Japan, with a) yellow or yellowish-red fruit that grows in clusters and has a sharp taste. ⇨ the illus at **fruit**.

lor /lɔ(r)/ *int* (vulg substitute for) Lord! ⇨ **lord(2)**.

lord /lɔd/ *n* **1** supreme male ruler: *our sovereign ~ the King.* **2** **L~,** God; Christ: *the ˈL~'s Day,* Sunday; *the ˈL~'s ˈPrayer,* that given by Jesus to his followers; *the L~'s Supper,* the bread and wine taken at Eucharist; *L~! L~ God! Good L~! L~ knows! L~ bless us (me)!* exclamations of surprise, etc. **3** peer; nobleman: *live/treat sb like a ~,* sumptuously. ***as drunk as a ~,*** excessively drunk. **the House of L~s,** (in GB) the upper division of Parliament, consisting of *the ~s spiritual* (the Archbishops and Bishops) and *the ~s temporal* (hereditary and life peers). **4** (in feudal times) superior. **the ~ of the manor,** man from whom vassals held land and to whom they owed service. **5** (joc, also *~ and master*) husband; great leader of industry: *the ˈcotton ~s.* Cf beer *barons; the ~s of creation,* mankind (contrasted with the animals); (joc) men. **6** person in a position of authority: *the L~s of the Admiralty/Treasury,* the chief members of these Boards; *the First L~ of the Admiralty,* the president of this Board. **7** first word in many official titles: *the L~ Mayor of London; the L~ Chamberlain,* etc. **8** title prefixed to names of peers and barons: *L~ Derby.* Cf *the Earl of Derby.* **9** ***My ~,*** respectful formula for addressing certain noblemen and judges and bishops. □ *vt* (chiefly in) ***~ it over sb,*** rule over like a ~: *'I will not be ~ed over', she said to her husband.* **~·less** *adj* without a ~.

lord·ly /ˈlɔdlɪ/ *adj* (-ier, -iest) **1** haughty; insolent. **2** like, suitable for, a lord; magnificent. **lord·li·ness** *n*

lord·ship /ˈlɔdʃɪp/ *n* **1** [U] ***~ over,*** rule, authority. **2** [C] ***His (Your) L~,*** used when speaking of (to) a lord.

lore /lɔ(r)/ *n* [U] learning or knowledge, esp handed down from past times, or possessed by a class of people: *ˈIrish ~; ˈgypsy ~;* or of a special subject: *'fairy ~/'bird ~/'folk ~.*

lor·gnette /lɔ'njet/ *n* pair of eye-glasses held to the eyes on a long handle.

lorn /lɔn/ *adj* (poet or hum) forlorn; desolate: *a lone, ~ widow.*

lorry /'lorɪ US: 'lɔrɪ/ *n* (*pl* -ries) (US = *truck*) strong wagon (usu long, low, open), formerly horse-drawn, now usu a motor-vehicle, for carrying goods by road.

lose /luz/ *vt,vi* (*pt,pp* lost /lost *US:* lɔst/) **1** [VP6A] no longer have; have taken away from one by accident, carelessness, misfortune, death, etc: *~ one's money; ~ a leg,* e g in a road accident; *~ a lot of money at the races* (by betting); *~ one's balance,* fall over. *He lost two sons in the war,* They were killed. *She lost her husband,* He is dead. *He has lost his job,* has been dismissed. *You're losing your hair,* getting bald. *She has lost her good looks,* is no longer good-looking. *It was so cold that we lost the use of our hands,* could not use them. *He's losing patience,* is becoming impatient. ***~ one's cool,*** (colloq) lose one's composure; be no longer calm or composed. ***~ ground,*** ⇨ ground[1](2). ***~ one's head,*** ⇨ head[1](19). ***~ heart,*** ⇨ heart(2). ***~ one's heart to sb,*** ⇨ heart(2). ***~ interest (in sb/sth),*** cease to be interested in, attracted by. ***~ one's reason/senses,*** become insane or wildly excited. ***~ one's temper,*** become angry. **2** be lost, disappear; die; be dead: *The ship and all its crew were lost. Is letter-writing a lost art,* Has the art of writing (social) letters died, e g because of the use of the telephone? ***be lost to sth,*** be no longer affected by, be insensible to, e g all sense of shame, decency, honour, duty. ***be lost in sth,*** be deeply occupied or filled with, e g thought, wonder, admiration. **3** [VP6A] (contrasted with *find, recover*) be unable to find: *I've lost the keys of my car. The books seem to be lost/to have been lost. She lost her husband in the crowd.* ***~ one's place,*** (in a book, etc) be unable to find the page, paragraph, etc where one stopped reading. ***~ oneself/one's way,*** get lost, be unable to find the right way, road, etc; not know where one is: *The children lost their way in the forest. We lost our way in the dark. I hope the children haven't got lost/lost themselves.* ***~ sight of sth,*** **(a)** overlook; fail to take account of: *We mustn't ~ sight of the fact that....* **(b)** no longer be able to see: *The early navigators disliked losing sight of land. We lost sight of him in the crowd.* ***~ the thread of sth,*** e g an argument, ⇨ thread. ***have lost one's tongue,*** ⇨ tongue(1). ***~ track of sb/sth,*** ⇨ track(1). **4** [VP6A] (contrasted with *catch*) be too late for; fail to hear, see, etc: ~ (more usu *miss*) *one's train/the bus.* ***~ the post,*** get to the post office, etc too late for the collection; ~ (= not hear) *the end of a sentence. What he said was lost in the applause that greeted him.* **5** [VP12C] cause (sb) the loss of: *Such insolence will ~ you your situation. This remark lost him our sympathy.* **6** [VP6A,2A] fail to win, be defeated: *~ a game/a match/a battle/a war/a lawsuit/a prize; ~ a motion,* fail to carry it in a debate. ***a lost cause,*** one that has already been defeated or is sure to be defeated. ***(play) a losing game,*** one in which defeat is likely or certain. **7** [VP6A,15A,3A] ***~ by/in/on sth,*** be or become worse: *You will ~ nothing by waiting,* will not suffer any loss. *Will the publisher ~ by it,* be worse off because of publishing the book? *How much did he lose on the transaction? The story does not ~ in the telling,* is not made less interesting, is perhaps exaggerated. **8** [VP2A,B] (of a watch or clock) go too slowly; fail to keep correct time because of this: *Does your watch gain or ~? My watch ~s two minutes a day.* **9** [VP6A] spend time, opportunity, efforts to no purpose; waste: *There's not a moment to ~. I shall ~ no time in doing it,* shall do it at once. ***be lost upon sb,*** fail to influence or attract the attention of: *My hints were not lost upon him,* They were noted. **10** ***~ oneself in sth,*** (reflex) become engrossed in it: *She lost herself in a book,* became so deeply interested in it that she was unaware of other things. **loser** *n* one who ~s or is defeated: *He's a good/bad ~r,* is cheerful/discontented when he ~s.

loss /los *US:* lɔs/ *n* **1** [U] act or fact or process of losing: *~ of blood; ~ of prestige. L~ of health is more serious than ~ of money. The ~ of his heavyweight title doesn't seem to worry him. The ~ of so many ships worried the Admiral.* **2** [U] (and with *indef art*) failure to keep, maintain or use: *a heavy ~; ~ of opportunities; without (any) ~ of time. There was a temporary ~ of power.* **3** [U] failure to win or obtain: *the ~ of a contract.* **4** [C] that which is lost: *sell sth at a ~; suffer heavy ~es in war,* men killed, wounded, captured; ships and aircraft lost. ⇨ gain[1], profit[1](2). ***a total ~,*** sth from which nothing can be saved: *The ship was wrecked and became a total ~.* **'~-'leader** *n* (comm) article, etc sold at a ~ in order to attract customers to buy other goods. **5** (*sing* only) disadvantage or deprivation: *Such a man is no great ~,* We need not regret losing his services. ***be a dead ~,*** (colloq, of a person) be quite worthless: *We'd better fire Smith—He's a dead ~.* **6** ***(be) at a ~ for sth/to do sth,*** be perplexed, uncertain: *He was at a ~ for words/to know what to say,* did not know how to express himself.

lost /lost *US: lɔst/ pt,pp* of lose.

lot[1] /lot/ *n* (colloq) **1** **the lot,** the whole number or quantity: *That's the lot,* That's all or everything. *Take the (whole) lot. Go away, the whole lot of you/all the lot of you,* (emphat for) 'all of you', 'every one of you'. *She wants a new car, a fridge, and a colour TV—the lot!* **2** ***a lot (of)/lots (and lots) (of),*** a great amount or number (of): *What a lot of time you take to dress! She spends a lot of money on clothes. There were such a lot of people in the shops! I want lots. I saw quite a lot of her* (= saw her often) *when I was in London last month. We don't see a lot of her nowadays.* **3** (used *adverbially*) very much: *He's feeling a lot better today. A lot you care!* (ironic) You don't care at all! Cf *a good deal, a little.*

lot[2] /lot/ *n* **1** (one of a set of objects used in) the making of a selection or decision by methods depending upon chance: *divide property by lot.* ***draw/cast lots,*** e g by taking pieces of paper marked in some way from a box: *They drew lots as to who should begin.* **2** [C] decision or choice resulting from this: *The lot came to/fell upon me.* **3** [C] person's fortune or destiny: *His lot has been a hard one. Such good fortune falls to the lot of few men. It has fallen to my lot to oppose the President in the election.* ***cast/throw in one's lot with sb,*** decide to share the fortunes of. **4** item, or number of items, (to be) sold at an auction sale: *Lot 46, six chairs.* **5** collection of objects of the same kind: *We have received a new lot of hats from the manufacturers.* **6 a bad lot,** (colloq) a bad person. **7** (cinema) studio and surrounding land. **8** plot of land: (esp US) *a `parking lot,* for cars; *a vacant lot,* a building site.

loth /ləʊθ/ *adj* ⇨ loath.

lo·tion /`ləʊʃn/ *n* [C,U] (kind of) medicinal liquid for use on the skin: *a bottle of cleansing ~ for the face; soothing ~s for insect bites.*

lot·tery /`lotərɪ/ *n* (*pl* -ries) [C] **1** arrangement to give prizes to holders of numbered tickets previously bought by them and drawn by lot: (attrib) *`~ tickets.* **2** (fig) sth considered to be as uncertain as the winning of prizes in a ~: *Is marriage a ~?*

lot·to /`lotəʊ/ *n* [U] game of chance; bingo.

lo·tus /`ləʊtəs/ *n* (*pl* -ses /-sɪz/) (not often used in the *pl; `~ blooms* is preferred). **1** (kinds of) water-lily, esp Egyptian and Asiatic kinds. ⇨ the illus at flower. **2** (in old Gk legends) plant represented as bringing about a distaste for an active life. **`~-eater** *n* person who gives himself up to indolent enjoyment.

loud /laʊd/ *adj* (-er, -est) **1** not quiet or soft; easily heard: *~ voices/cries/laughs. The bomb exploded with a ~ noise.* **'~-`speaker** *n* (often shortened to *speaker*) part of a radio receiving apparatus that converts electric impulses into audible sounds. **'~-`hailer** *n* electronic device that enables a voice to be magnified and so be audible at a great distance: *The naval officer called to the trawler by ~-hailer across the water.* **2** (of a person's behaviour; of colours) of the kind that forces itself on the attention. □ *adv* in a ~ manner: *Don't talk so ~. They laughed ~ and long. Speak ~er! Who laughed ~est?* **~·ly** *adv* in a ~ manner: *Someone knocked ~ly at the door. What a ~ly dressed girl!* **~·ness** *n*

lough /lok/ *n* (in Ireland) lake; arm of the sea.

lounge /laʊndʒ/ *vi* [VP2A,C] sit, stand about (leaning against sth) in a lazy way: *idlers lounging at street corners; lounging over a café table.* □ *n* act of lounging: *have a ~.* **2** comfortable sitting-room, esp in a club or hotel. **`~-lizard** *n* (dated sl) professional dance-partner for women at dances in hotel ~s. **3 `~-bar** *n* best bar in a public house, where women guests would normally be taken. ⇨ public bar. **`~-chair** *n* comfortable easy-chair. **`~-suit** *n* man's suit of jacket (waistcoat) and trousers for informal wear. **lounger** *n*

lour, lower /`laʊə(r)/ *vi* [VP2A,3A] **~ *at/(up)on,*** frown; look sullen or threatening; (of the sky, clouds) look dark, as if threatening a storm. **~-ing·ly** *adv*

louse /laʊs/ *n* (*pl* lice /laɪs/) (sorts of) **1** small insect living on the bodies of animals and human beings under dirty conditions; similar insect living on plants. **2** (sl) contemptible person: *He's an absolute ~.*

lousy /`laʊzɪ/ *adj* (-ier, -iest) infested with lice; (colloq) bad: *a ~ dinner;* (sl) well provided (*with*): *He's ~ with money.*

lout /laʊt/ *n* clumsy, ill-mannered man. **`litter-~,** ⇨ litter[2](1). **`~·ish** /-ɪʃ/ *adj* of or like a ~: *~ish behaviour.*

louvre (also **lou·ver**) /`luvə(r)/ *n* arrangement of fixed or moveable slats (in a door or window) for ventilation (like the slats in a Venetian blind). **lou·vered** *adj* having ~s: *a ~ed door.*

lov·able /`lʌvəbl/ *adj* deserving or inspiring love; worthy of love: *a ~ child; a child's ~ ways.*

love[1] /lʌv/ *n* **1** [U] warm, kind feeling; fondness; affectionate and tender devotion: *a mother's ~ for her children; a ~ of learning/adventure; ~ of (one's) country,* patriotism; *show ~ towards one's neighbours.* ***give/send sb one's ~,*** give or send an affectionate greeting. ***play for ~,*** for the pleasure of the game, not for stakes. ***not to be had for ~ or money,*** impossible to get by any means. ***There's no ~ lost between them,*** They dislike each other. ***a labour of ~,*** **(a)** sth that one enjoys doing for its own sake. **(b)** one does for the ~ of sb. ***for the ~ of,*** (in appeals, etc) for the sake of; in the name of: *Put that gun down, for the ~ of God!* **`~-feast** *n* meal taken by early Christians in token of brotherly ~; religious service among Methodists imitating this. **2** [U] warm, kind feeling between two persons of opposite sex; sexual passion or desire; this as a literary subject: *a `~-story; marry for ~, not for money.* ***be in ~ (with sb),*** have ~ and desire (for): *Hero and Leander were in ~. Leander was in ~ with Hero.* ***fall in ~ (with sb),*** come to feel ~ (for); begin to be in ~ (with). ***make ~ (to sb),*** show that one is in ~ with sb; do the things that lovers do, e g kiss, caress, have sexual intercourse: *Jane thinks it's more fun to make ~ than to make the beds. Make ~, not war!* Hence, **`~-making** *n* **`~-affair** *n* instance of being in ~, often with a physical relationship: *a girl who had numerous ~-affairs before her marriage.* **`~-bird** *n* small brightly coloured parrot said to pine away when it loses its mate; (*pl*) (young) lovers very much in ~. **`~-child** *n* (dated) child of unmarried parents. **`~-knot** *n* bow of ribbon, tied in a special way, formerly given or worn as a pledge of ~. **`~-letter** *n* letter between persons in ~ and concerned with their ~. **`~-lorn** /-lɔn/ *adj* unhappy because one's ~ is not returned; pining with ~. **`~-match** *n* marriage made for love's sake, not an arranged marriage. **`~-philtre/-potion** *nn* magic drink supposed to make the person who drinks it fall in ~ with the person from whom it is received. **`~-seat** *n* S-shaped bench with two seats facing in opposite directions. **`~-sick** *adj* languishing because of ~. **`~-song** *n* song about or expressing ~. **`~-story** *n* novel or story of which the main theme is ~. **`~-token** *n* sth given as a symbol of ~. **3** form of address between lovers, husband and wife, or to a child: *Come here, my ~.* **4** (colloq) delightful or lovable person or thing: *Isn't she a little ~? What a ~ of a hat!* **5** woman who is a sweetheart: *She was an old ~ of mine years ago* (*flame* is commoner). **6** personification of ~, i e a Cupid. **7** (in games) no score, nothing, nil: *~ all,* no score for either side; *`~ game,* one in which the loser did not score. **~·less** *adj* unloving; unloved; without ~: *a ~less marriage.*

love[2] /lʌv/ *vt* **1** [VP6A] have strong affection or deep tender feelings for: *~ one's parents/one's country.* **2** [VP6A] worship: *~ God.* **3** [VP6A] have kind feelings towards: *The Bible tells us to ~ all men.* **4** [VP6A,D,7,17B] be very fond of; like; find pleasure in: *~ comfort/mountain-climbing. She ~s to have/~s having a lot of dogs and young men round her. 'Will you come with me?'—'I should ~ to'. I'd ~ you to come with me.*

love·ly /`lʌvlɪ/ *adj* (-ier, -iest) **1** beautiful; attractive; pleasant: *a ~ view; a ~ woman; ~ hair/weather.* **2** (colloq) enjoyable; amusing: *We had a ~ holiday. What a ~ joke! It's ~ and warm here,*

~ because warm. **3** (US) lovable: *Oh, she's a ~ person.* **love·li·ness** *n*

lover /ˋlʌvə(r)/ *n* **1** person who is fond of or devoted to (sth): *a ~ of music/horses/good wine.* **2** (*pl*) man and woman in love: *the happy ~s.* **3** person, esp a man, who deeply admires a woman, esp, now, a man who loves a woman and has a physical relationship with her. **ˋ~-like** *adj* in the manner of a ~.

lov·ing /ˋlʌvɪŋ/ *adj* feeling or showing love: *a ~ friend.* **ˈ~-ˋkindness** *n* tender consideration; mercy and kindness coming from love. **ˋ~-cup** *n* large wine-cup passed round from person to person so that everyone may drink from it. **~·ly** *adv* in a ~ way: *Yours ~ly,* formula at the end of a letter, e g from a child to its parents.

low¹ /ləʊ/ *adj* (**-er, -est**) **1** not high; not extending far upwards: *a low wall/ceiling/shelf; a low range of hills; low-rise housing,* of houses not many storeys high. *The moon was low in the sky. The glass is low,* The mercury in the barometer is low. *He has a low brow,* short distance between the hair and the eyebrows. *She was wearing a dress low in the neck/a ˋlow-necked dress,* one leaving the neck and (part of) the shoulders and breasts visible. **ˈlow-reˋlief,** ⇨ **bas-relief.** **2** below the usual or normal level or intensity: *low-lying land; low pressure,* e g of the atmosphere, of gas or water from the mains; *a low-density housing estate,* with comparatively few houses to the acre. *The rivers were low during the dry summer.* **low gear,** ⇨ **gear(1).** **low tide/water,** time when the tide is out and far from the shore or river bank. **ˈlow-ˋwater mark,** lowest points reached at low tide. ***be in low water,*** (fig) short of money. **3** (of sounds) not loud; not high in pitch: *speak in a low voice; the low notes of a cello. A tenor cannot get so low as a baritone.* **ˈlow-ˋkeyed,** (fig) restrained in style or quality. **ˈlow-ˋpitched,** (music) low in pitch. **4** of or in inferior rank or social class: *all classes of people, high and low; men of low birth; have a low station in life,* e g as a street sweeper. ***be brought low,*** be humbled. **5** commonplace; coarse; vulgar; little civilized: *low manners; low company; low life,* of persons who are vulgar, coarse, etc; *low tastes; I never fell as low as that,* never let my standard of behaviour fall so low; *low cunning,* cunning typical of sb who is mean or morally degraded; *a low-down trick.* **6** feeble; lacking in strength of body or mind: *in a low state of health; feel low/in low spirits,* unhappy, depressed. Hence, **ˈlow-ˋspirited** *adj* **7** of small amount as measured by a scale or by degrees: *a low temperature; a low pulse; low prices/wages/ rates of pay.* **low latitudes,** near the equator. ***have a low opinion of sb/sth,*** think very little of him, his work, etc. ***at lowest,*** at the least possible figure, quantity, etc. **8** (of a supply of anything) ***be/run low,*** be/become nearly exhausted: *Our stock of coal is running low. Food supplies were running low in the besieged town.* **9** (of the position of the tongue when speaking) not raised: *a low vowel,* one, e g the vowel /ɑ/) made with the tongue low in the mouth. **10** not highly developed: *low forms of life.* **11 Low Church,** party in the Church of England giving a low place to the authority of bishops and priests, ecclesiastical organization, ritual, etc. (contrasted with *High Church*). Hence, **Low Churchman,** supporter of this. **12** (phrases) ***bring sb/sth low,*** make low in health, wealth, position, etc. ***lay sb/sth low,*** overthrow. ***lie low,*** (fig) keep quiet or hidden; say nothing and wait: *The escaped prisoners had to lie low for months.* **13** (compounds) **ˈlow-ˋborn** *adj* of humble birth. **ˈlow-ˋbred** *adj* having vulgar manners. **ˋlow·brow** *n, adj* (person) showing little interest in or taste for intellectual things, esp art, music, literature. **lower case,** (in printing) small letters, not capitals. **Lower Chamber/House,** lower branch of a legislative assembly, e g the House of Commons in GB, the House of Representatives in US. **low comedian,** person who acts in **low comedy,** kind of drama bordering on farce, with laughable situations, comic dialogue, etc. **the lower deck,** (in the Navy) the ratings; those who are not officers. **ˋlow-down** *adj* (colloq) caddish; dishonourable: *~-down behaviour/ tricks.* □ *n* ***get/give sb the low-down (on sth/ sb),*** (colloq) the true facts, inside information which is not generally known. **ˋlow·lander** /-ləndə(r)/ *n* person who lives in lowlands, esp (**L~**) one who lives in the Scottish Lowlands. **low·lands** /-ləndz/ *n pl* low level country: *the lowlands of Scotland.* **Low Latin,** late, popular Latin (contrasted with classical Latin). **Low Mass,** celebration of the Eucharist without a choir. **Low Sunday, Low Week,** coming after Easter Day and Easter Week. **ˋlow·er·most** *adj* lowest. **low·ness** *n*

low² /ləʊ/ *adv* (**-er, -est**) in or to a low position; in a low manner; *aim/shoot low; bow low to the Queen; buy low* (= at low prices) *and sell high; play low,* (in gambling) for small sums; *speak low.*

low³ /ləʊ/ *n* sth low; low level or figure: *Several industrial shares reached new lows yesterday,* Their prices went down to a new low price (on the stock market).

low⁴ /ləʊ/ *n* sound made by cows. □ *vt* (of cows) make this characteristic sound.

lower¹ /ˋləʊə(r)/ *vt, vi* **1** [VP6A] let or bring down; cause to be down: *~ the sails/a flag.* **~ away,** (naut) lower a boat, sail, etc. **2** [VP6A,15A,2A] make or become less high: *~ the rent of a house. The stocks ~ed in value. He ~ed his voice to a whisper. We can't ~ the ceiling.* **3** [VP15A] **~ *oneself,*** degrade, disgrace: *He would never ~ himself by taking bribes.* **4** [VP6A] weaken: *Poor diet ~s resistance to illness.*

lower² /ˋlaʊə(r)/ *vi* = **lour.**

low·ly /ˋləʊlɪ/ *adj* (**-ier, -iest**) humble; simple; modest. **low·li·ness** *n*

loyal /ˋlɔɪl/ *adj* true and faithful (*to*): *~ subjects of the Queen; ~ supporters; ~ to one's country.* **ˋ~·ist** /-ɪst/ *n* person who is ~ to his ruler and government, esp one who supports the head of an established government during a revolt: (attrib) *the ~ist army/troops.* **~·ly** /ˋlɔɪlɪ/ *adv* **~·ty** *n* (*pl* **-ties**) **1** [U] being ~; ~ conduct. **2** (*pl*) kinds of attachment: *tribal loyalties.*

loz·enge /ˋlozɪndʒ/ *n* **1** four-sided, diamond-shaped figure. **2** small tablet of flavoured sugar, esp one containing medicine: *cough ~s.*

LSD /ˈel es ˋdi/ *n* odourless, colourless and tasteless semi-synthetic substance causing hallucinations (often referred to as 'acid').

£sd /ˈel es ˋdi/ *n* term used, before British currency was decimalized, for pounds, shillings and pence; (colloq) money: *I'm short of £ s d just now.*

L-plate /ˋel pleɪt/ *n* plate with a large capital L,

fixed to a motor-vehicle being driven by a learner who has not passed his driving test.

lub·ber /ˈlʌbə(r)/ *n* big, clumsy, stupid fellow. ⇨ *land-~* at land[1](6). **~·ly** *adj*

lu·bri·cate /ˈlubrɪkeɪt/ *vt* [VP6A] put oil or grease into (machine parts) to make (them) work easily; (fig) do sth that makes action, etc easier. **lu·bri·cant** /ˈlubrɪkənt/ *n* [U] substance that ~s. **lu·bri·ca·tion** /ˈlubrɪˈkeɪʃn/ *n* lubricating or being ~d.

lu·cent /ˈlusnt/ *adj* shining; translucent.

lu·cerne /luˈsɜn/ *n* [U] (GB) clover-like plant used for feeding animals. (US = *alfalfa*).

lu·cid /ˈlusɪd/ *adj* **1** clear; easy to understand: *a ~ explanation; a ~ literary style; a ~ mind.* **2** mentally sound: *~ intervals,* periods of sanity between periods of insanity. **3** (poet) bright, clear, transparent. **~·ly** *adv* **~·ity** /luˈsɪdətɪ/ *n* [U] quality of being ~.

Luci·fer /ˈlusɪfə(r)/ *n* **1** name of Satan, the chief rebel angel, before his defeat: *as proud as ~.* **2** (the planet Venus as) the morning star.

luck /lʌk/ *n* [U] chance; fortune (good or bad); sth that is considered to come by chance: *have good/bad ~ in one's affairs; have hard ~,* be unfortunate. *As ~ would have it,...* Fortunately,... (or Unfortunately,... according to context). *It was hard ~ on you that...,* used to show sympathy. *He tried his ~ at the gaming tables,* gambled, hoping for success. *What rotten ~! Bad ~!* (used to show sympathy). *Good ~!* (used to encourage, express hopes of good fortune, etc). *Just my ~!* I am unlucky, as usual. *My ~'s in/out,* I am/am not fortunate. *I never have any ~. I had the ~* (= was fortunate enough) *to find him at home.* ***be down on one's ~,*** (colloq) be unfortunate; suffer misfortune. ***be in/out of ~,*** have/not have good fortune. ***for ~,*** to bring good fortune: *keep sth for ~.* ***worse ~,*** (used parenthetically) more's the pity; unfortunately. **~·less** *adj* unfortunate; turning out badly: *a ~less day/attempt.*

lucky /ˈlʌkɪ/ *adj* (-ier, -iest) having, bringing, resulting from, good luck: *a ~ man (guess, escape). It's my ~ day,* one on which I am having good fortune. *You are ~ to be alive after being in that accident.* **ˈ~ ˈdip** *n* tub, etc containing articles of various values for which a person may dip in (taking the chance of getting sth of value) for a payment: *L~ dip, 10p.* **luck·ily** /ˈlʌkḷɪ/ *adv* in a ~ manner; fortunately: *Luckily for me the train was late, so I just caught it.*

lu·cra·tive /ˈlukrətɪv/ *adj* profitable; bringing in money.

lucre /ˈlukə(r)/ *n* [U] (in a bad sense) profit or money-making (as a motive for action): *a man who would do anything for ~.*

Lud·dite /ˈlʌdɑɪt/ *n* member of bands of workers who, in England, 1811—16, destroyed new machinery which, they thought, would cause unemployment.

lu·di·crous /ˈludɪkrəs/ *adj* ridiculous; causing laughter. **~·ly** *adv*

ludo /ˈludəʊ/ *n* simple game played by moving counters on a special board after throwing dice.

luff /lʌf/ *vt, vi* bring the head of a ship in a direction nearer to that of the wind; turn (the helm) so that this happens.

lug[1] /lʌg/ *vt* (-gg-) [VP6A,15A,B] pull or drag roughly and with much effort: *lugging two heavy suitcases up the stairs; lug a handcart along.* □ *n* hard or rough pull.

lug[2] /lʌg/ *n* projecting part (of a metal casting) by which it is kept securely in place.

lug[3] /lʌg/ *n* lugsail.

luge /luʒ/ *n* (F) short toboggan for one person, as used in Switzerland.

lug·gage /ˈlʌgɪdʒ/ *n* [U] bags, trunks, etc and their contents taken on a journey: *six pieces of ~; get one's ~ through the Customs.* (US = *baggage.*) **ˈ~-carrier** *n* metal frame, e g one fixed behind the saddle of a bicycle, for ~. **ˈ~-rack** *n* rack (above the seats) in a railway carriage, coach, etc for ~. **ˈ~-van** *n* van for ~ on a railway train.

lug·ger /ˈlʌgə(r)/ *n* small ship with one or more four-cornered sails set fore and aft.

lug·sail /ˈlʌgseɪl/ *n* four-cornered sail.

lu·gu·bri·ous /luˈgubrɪəs/ *adj* (formal) dismal; mournful. **~·ly** *adv* **~·ness** *n*

luke·warm /ˈlukˈwɔm/ *adj* **1** (of liquids, etc) neither very warm not cold. **2** (fig) not eager either in supporting or opposing: *give only ~ support to a cause; ~ friendship.* **~·ly** *adv* **~·ness** *n*

lull /lʌl/ *vt, vi* [VP6A,15A,2A] make or become quiet or less active: *~ a baby to sleep,* e g by rocking it and singing to it; *~ a person's fears/suspicions. The wind/sea was ~ed. The wind ~ed.* □ *n* [C] interval of quiet; period of lessened activity, etc: *a ~ in the storm/in the conversation.*

lull·aby /ˈlʌləbɑɪ/ *n* (*pl* -bies) song for lulling a baby to sleep; gentle, soft sound, e g made by wind in trees or by the running water of a brook.

lum·bago /lʌmˈbeɪgəʊ/ *n* [U] muscular pain in the lumbar regions.

lum·bar /ˈlʌmbə(r)/ *adj* of the loins: *the ~ regions,* the lower part of the back.

lum·ber[1] /ˈlʌmbə(r)/ *n* [U] **1** roughly prepared wood; wood that has been sawn into planks, boards, etc. **ˈ~·man** /-mæn/, **ˈ~·jack** *nn* man who fells trees; man who saws or transports ~. **ˈ~-mill** *n* saw-mill. **ˈ~·yard** *n* place where ~ is stored. **2** (chiefly GB) useless or unwanted articles stored away or taking up space (e g old furniture, pictures). **ˈ~·room** *n* one in which ~ is stored. □ *vt* [VP6A,15A,B] ***~ sth (up) (with),*** fill with ~; fill space inconveniently: *a room ~ed up with useless articles;* (fig) *a mind that is ~ed (up) with useless bits of information.*

lum·ber[2] /ˈlʌmbə(r)/ *vi* [VP2C] move in a heavy, clumsy, noisy way: *The heavy army tanks ~ed along/by/past. What a big ~ing cart!*

lu·min·ary /ˈlumɪnərɪ *US:* -nerɪ/ *n* (*pl* -ries) **1** star; the sun or moon; any light-giving body in the sky. **2** (fig) person who, because of his learning, is like a shining light; great moral or intellectual leader.

lu·mi·nous /ˈlumɪnəs/ *adj* **1** giving out light; bright: *~ paint,* as used on road signs, clocks and watches, visible in the dark. **2** (fig) clear; easily understood: *a ~ speaker/explanation.* **lu·min·os·ity** /ˈlumɪˈnɒsətɪ/ *n* [U] quality of being ~.

lummy, lumme /ˈlʌmɪ/ *int* indicating surprise.

lump[1] /lʌmp/ *n* [C] **1** hard or compact mass, usu without a regular shape: *a ~ of clay; break a piece of coal into small ~s; a ~ of sugar; ~ sugar,* sugar cut into cubes. ***a ~ sum,*** one payment for a number of separate sums that are owed. ***in the ~,*** added together; taken as a whole. **2** swelling or bump; bruise: *He has a bad ~ on the forehead.* ***have a ~ in the throat,*** a feeling of pressure (as caused by strong emotion). **3** (colloq) heavy, dull person: *Get out of my way, you big fat ~ of a man!*

□ *vt* **1** [VP6A,15B] ~ ***together,*** put together in one ~; include (a number of things) under one heading: *The boys agreed to ~ the expenses of their camping holiday. Can we ~ all these items together under the heading 'incidental expenses'?* **2** [VP2A] form into ~s: *This oatmeal ~s if you don't stir it well.* **~·ish** /-ɪʃ/ *adj* (of a person) thickset; clumsy; stupid. **~y** *adj* (**-ier, -iest**) full of, covered with ~s: *a ~y sauce;* (of the surface of water) cut up by wind into small waves; choppy.

lump[2] /lʌmp/ *vt* (only on) ~ ***it,*** endure, put up with, sth unpleasant or unwanted: *If you don't like it you can ~ it. Well, you'll just have to ~ it!*

lu·nacy /ˈlunəsɪ/ *n* (*pl* **-cies**) **1** [U] madness; state of being a lunatic; mad or foolish behaviour: *It's sheer ~.* **2** (*pl*) mad or very foolish acts.

lu·nar /ˈlunə(r)/ *adj* of the moon: *a ~ month,* average time between successive new moons, about 29½ days; *a ~ module,* detachable section of a spacecraft that orbits the moon and may descend to its surface; *a ~ orbit* (by a spacecraft); *a ~ year,* period of 12 ~ months.

lu·na·tic /ˈlunətɪk/ *n* **1** mental patient (the preferred term). **ˈ~ asylum,** hospital (*mental home* and *mental institution* are the names in present-day use) for the care and treatment of ~s. **2** (attrib) mad; extremely foolish: *a ~ proposal.* **ˌ~ ˈfringe,** minority group with extreme views, or engaged in eccentric activities, e g in drama or literature.

lunch /lʌntʃ/ *n* meal taken in the middle of the day: *They were at ~ when I called.* □ *vi, vt* eat ~; provide ~ for: *He ~ed me well at the Savoy.* **~eon** /ˈlʌntʃən/ *n* (formal word for) ~.

lung /lʌŋ/ *n* **1** either of the two breathing organs in the chest of man and other animals: *the ˈ~ passages/tissues; ~ cancer. That opera singer has good ~s,* produces a great volume of sound. ⇨ the illus at respiratory. **ˈ~-power** *n* power of voice. **2** (fig) open space in or close to a large city.

lunge /lʌndʒ/ *n* sudden forward movement, e g with a sword, or forward movement of the body (e g when aiming a blow). □ *vi* [VP2A,C] make a ~: *He ~d at his opponent/~d out suddenly.*

lu·pin, lu·pine /ˈlupɪn/ *n* garden plant with tall spikes of flowers of various colours.

lurch[1] /lɜtʃ/ *n* (only in) ***leave sb in the ~,*** leave him when he is in difficulties and needing help.

lurch[2] /lɜtʃ/ *n* sudden change of weight to one side; sudden roll or pitch: *The ship gave a ~ to starboard.* □ *vi* [VP2C] move along with a ~ or ~es: *The drunken man ~ed across the street.*

lurcher /ˈlɜtʃə(r)/ *n* dog, a cross between a sheep-dog and a greyhound, used for retrieving game (esp by poachers).

lure /lʊə(r)/ *n* [C] bunch of brightly coloured feathers used to attract and recall a trained hawk; bait or decoy to attract wild animals; (fig) sth that attracts or invites; the attraction or interest that sth has: *the ~ of the sea; the ~s used by a pretty woman to attract men.* □ *vt* [VP6A,15B] attract, tempt: *~ sb away from his duty; be ~d on to destruction.*

lu·rid /ˈlʊərɪd/ *adj* **1** highly coloured, esp suggesting flame and smoke: *a ~ sky/sunset; ~ thunder-clouds.* **2** (fig) sensational; violent and shocking: *~ details of a railway accident; a ~ tale.* **~·ly** *adv* **~·ness** *n*

lurk /lɜk/ *vi* [VP2C] be, keep, out of view, lying in wait or ready to attack: *a suspicious-looking man ~ing in the shadows. Some suspicion still ~ed in his mind.* **ˈ~·ing-place** *n* hiding-place.

luscious /ˈlʌʃəs/ *adj* **1** rich and sweet in taste and smell, attractive: *~ peaches/lips.* **2** (of art, music, writing) very rich in ornament; suggesting sensual delights. **~·ly** *adv* **~·ness** *n*

lush /lʌʃ/ *adj* (esp of grass and vegetation) growing luxuriantly: *~ meadows; a ~ growth of vegetation after the rains;* (fig) luxuriously comfortable. □ *n* (US sl) drunkard.

lust /lʌst/ *n* [U] violent desire to possess sth, esp strong sexual desire (for); passionate enjoyment (*of*): *filled with ~;* [C] instance of this: *a ~ for power/gold; the ~s of the flesh.* □ *vi* [VP3A] have ~ for: *~ for/after gold;* (biblical) *~ after a woman,* have strong sexual desire. **~·ful** /-fl/ *adj* full of ~ **~·fully** /-flɪ/ *adv*

lustre (US = **lus·ter**) /ˈlʌstə(r)/ *n* [U] **1** quality of being bright, esp of a smooth or polished surface; sheen; soft reflected light: *the ~ of pearls.* **2** (fig) glory; distinction: *add ~ to one's name; deeds that shed ~ on an honoured family,* make its reputation more distinguished. **3** (glass pendant of a) chandelier. **lus·trous** /ˈlʌstrəs/ *adj* having ~: *~ pearls; her ~ eyes.*

lusty /ˈlʌstɪ/ *adj* healthy and strong; vigorous: *a ~ girl from the country; ~ cheers.* **ˈ~·ily** /-əlɪ/ *adv*: *work/fight/shout ~ily.*

lute /lut/ *n* stringed musical instrument (14th to 17th cc) associated with poets and poetry. **lu·tan·ist** /ˈlutənɪst/ *n* player of the ~.

Lu·theran /ˈluθərən/ *adj, n* (follower) of Martin Luther; (member) of the Protestant Church of Germany named after Luther.

luxe /lʌks/ = **de luxe.**

lux·ur·iant /ləgˈʒʊərɪənt/ *adj* **1** strong in growth; abundant: *the ~ vegetation of the tropics;* (fig) *a ~ imagination.* **2** (of liter and artistic style) richly ornamented; very elaborate. **~·ly** *adv* **lux·ur·iance** /-əns/ *n* [U] ~ growth.

lux·ur·iate /ləgˈʒʊərɪeɪt/ *vi* [VP3A] ~ ***in,*** take great delight in: *~ in the warm spring sunshine.*

lux·ur·ious /ləgˈʒʊərɪəs/ *adj* **1** supplied with luxuries; very comfortable: *live in ~ surroundings; a ~ hotel.* **2** choice and costly: *~ food.* **3** fond of luxuries; self-indulgent: *~ habits.* **~·ly** *adv*

lux·ury /ˈlʌkʃərɪ/ *n* (*pl* **-ries**) **1** [U] state of life in which one has and uses things that please the senses (good food and drink, clothes, comfort, beautiful surroundings): *live in ~; a life of ~.* **2** (attrib use) *enabling people to live this kind of life: a ~ hotel/ocean liner* (perhaps suggesting ostentation rather than real comfort, etc. ⇨ luxurious. **3** [C] sth not essential but which gives enjoyment and pleasure, esp sth expensive, out of season, etc: *His salary is low and he gets few luxuries.*

lycée /ˈliseɪ *US:* liˈseɪ/ *n* state secondary school in France.

ly·ceum /lɑɪˈsiəm/ *n* literary institution; (building of an) association for organizing lectures, concerts, etc).

ly·chee /ˈlɑɪtʃi/ *n* (also **lichee, litchee, litchi**) fruit-tree, originally from China, widely grown in Bengal; its fruit consisting of a thin brown shell containing a white pulp round a single seed. ⇨ the illus at fruit.

lych·gate /ˈlɪtʃgeɪt/ *n* variant spelling of lichgate.

lye /lɑɪ/ *n* alkali obtained by passing water through wood ashes, used in washing; any alkaline solution or detergent.

ly·ing /ˈlaɪɪŋ/ *pres p* of **lie**[1], **lie**[2].

lymph /lɪmf/ *n* [U] colourless fluid in animal matter, like blood but without colouring matter. **lymphatic** /lɪmˈfætɪk/ *adj* **1** of or carrying ~: *the ~atic vessels,* carrying ~ from the tissues with any waste matter. **2** (of persons) sluggish; slow in thought and action.

lynch /lɪntʃ/ *vt* [VP6A] put to death (usu by hanging) without a lawful trial (sb believed to be guilty of crime). □ *n* ˈ~ **law,** procedure of persons who executed a (supposed) criminal in this way.

lynch·pin /ˈlɪntʃpɪn/ variant spelling of **linchpin.**

lynx /lɪŋks/ *n* short-tailed wild animal of the cat family, noted for its keen sight. ⇨ the illus at **cat.** Hence, ˈ~-ˈ**eyed** *adj* keen-sighted.

lyre /ˈlaɪə(r)/ *n* kind of harp with strings fixed in a U-shaped frame, used by the ancient Greeks. ˈ~-**bird** *n* Australian bird, the male having a long tail, shaped like a ~ when spread out.

lyric /ˈlɪrɪk/ *adj* **1** of, composed for, singing. **2** of poetry written on the theme of love, death, etc. □ *n* [C] ~ poem; (*pl*) verses of a song, e g in a musical play.

lyri·cal /ˈlɪrɪkl/ *adj* **1** = **lyric. 2** full of emotion: enthusiastic: *She became/waxed quite ~ over the new dresses she had brought back from Paris.* **~ly** /-klɪ/ *adv*

ly·sol /ˈlaɪsol *US:* -sɔl/ *n* [U] (P) dark oily, liquid used as an antiseptic and disinfectant.

Mm

M, m /em/ (*pl* **M's, m's** /emz/) the 13th letter of the English alphabet; the Roman numeral 1 000. ⇨ **App 4.**

ma /mɑ/ *n* short for **mamma.**

ma'am /mæm/ *n* (colloq) madam, e g as used in addressing the Queen and other royal ladies and by a servant when addressing her mistress, and pronounced (in GB) /məm/: *'Yes, ma'am'.*

mac /mæk/ *n* (GB colloq, abbr for) **mackintosh.**

ma·cabre /məˈkɑbr *with unsyllabic* r/ *adj* gruesome; suggesting death: (F) *danse ~,* dance of death.

ma·cadam /məˈkædəm/ *n* [U] ~ **road,** road with a surface of several layers of crushed rock or stone, each rolled hard before the next is put down. ˈ~·**ize** /-ɑɪz/ *vt* make or cover with such layers: *~ized roads.*

maca·roni /ˈmækəˈrəʊnɪ/ *n* [U] flour paste made in the form of long tubes (often chopped into short pieces), prepared for eating by being boiled.

maca·roon /ˈmækəˈrun/ *n* [C] small, hard, flat, sweet cake or biscuit made of sugar, white of egg, and crushed almonds or coconut.

ma·caw /məˈkɔ/ *n* large, long-tailed parrot of tropical America.

mace[1] /meɪs/ *n* **1** large, heavy club, usu with a metal head covered with spikes, used as a weapon in the Middle Ages. **2** ceremonial rod or staff (often very much ornamented) carried or placed before an official, e g a Mayor. ˈ~-**bearer** *n* person who carries an official ~.

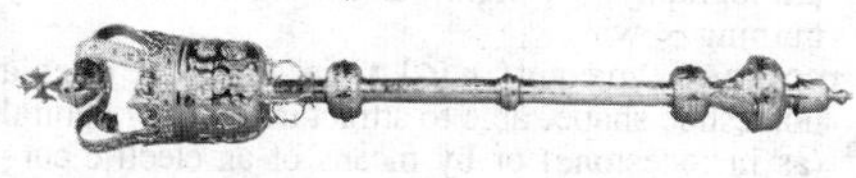

a ceremonial mace

mace[2] /meɪs/ *n* [U] dried outer covering of nutmegs, used as spice.

mac·er·ate /ˈmæsəreɪt/ *vt, vi* [VP6A,2A] make or become soft by soaking in water or caustic potash.

Mach /mɑk/ *n* ˈ~ **number,** ratio of the air speed of an aircraft to the speed of sound: *~ two,* twice the speed of sound.

ma·chete /məˈtʃeɪtɪ *US:* -ˈtʃetɪ/ *n* broad, heavy knife used in Latin America as a tool and weapon.

mach·ia·vel·lian /ˈmækɪəˈvelɪən/ *adj* showing or having no scruples in gaining what is wanted; of or like the ideas set out by Machiavelli /ˈmækɪəˈvelɪ/ (Italian statesman, 1469—1527), who advocated putting expediency above political morality and the use of deceit in statecraft.

machi·na·tion /ˈmækɪˈneɪʃn/ *n* [C,U] evil plotting) or scheme (scheming).

ma·chine /məˈʃin/ *n* [C] **1** appliance or mechanical device with parts working together to apply power, often steam or electric power (*a* ˈ*printing-~*), but also human power (*a* ˈ*sewing-~*). *We live in the ~ age,* the age in which ~s more and more replace hand labour. ˈ~-**gun** *n* gun that fires continuously while the trigger is pressed. ˈ~-ˈ**made** *adj* made by ~ (contrasted with *handmade*). ˈ~ **tool,** tool, mechanically operated, for cutting or shaping materials. **2** persons organized to control a political group: (US) *the Democratic ~.* □ *vt* [VP6A] operate on, make (sth) with, a ~ (esp of sewing and printing). **ma·chin·ist** /məˈʃinɪst/ *n* one who makes, repairs or controls ~ tools; one who works a ~, esp a sewing-~.

ma·chin·ery /məˈʃinrɪ/ *n* [U] **1** moving parts of a machine; machines collectively: *How much new ~ has been installed?* Cf *How many new machines have...?* **2** (*pl* -**ries**) methods, organization (e g of government).

mack·erel /ˈmækrl/ *n* (*pl* unchanged) small seafish used as food.

mack·in·tosh /ˈmækɪntoʃ/ *n* (GB) rainproof coat made of cloth treated with rubber.

mac·ro·biotic /ˈmækrəʊbaɪˈotɪk/ *adj* prolonging life: *~ food,* containing pure vegetable substances grown and prepared without chemical assistance.

mac·ro·cosm /ˈmækrəʊkozm/ *n* the great world or universe; any great whole. ⇨ **microcosm.**

mad /mæd/ *adj* (-**der,** -**dest**) **1** having, resulting from a diseased mind; mentally ill. ***drive/send sb mad,*** cause him to be mad. ***as mad as a March hare/as a hatter,*** (prov) very mad. ˈ**mad·house** *n* (colloq) lunatic asylum. ˈ**mad·man** /-mən/, ˈ**mad·woman** *nn* person who is mad. **2** (colloq) much excited; filled with (unreasonable) enthusiasm: *mad about pop music;* (esp US) angry: *mad with pain. They were mad about/at missing the train. The dog was mad for water,* behaving wildly because it needed water. *Dad was mad with me for spilling the ink. What a mad* (= foolish) *thing to do!* ***be/go mad,*** be/become wildly excited, angry, upset, etc. ***like mad,*** wildly or furiously: *He ran off like mad.* **ˋmad·cap** /-kæp/ *n* person acting recklessly or on impulse. **3** (of a dog, etc) rabid. **mad·ly** *adv* in a mad manner; (colloq) extremely: *madly excited/jealous.* **mad·ness** *n* [U] the state of being mad; mad behaviour: *It would be madness to try to climb the mountain in such a snowstorm.* **mad·den** /ˋmædn/ *vt* [VP6A] make mad; irritate; annoy: *maddening delays.*

madam /ˋmædəm/ *n* **1** respectful form of address to a woman (whether married or unmarried): *Can I help you, ~?* (e g asked by a shop assistant); (used in letters, as *Sir* is used to a man): *Dear M~.* **2** (colloq) woman or girl who likes to order people about: *She's a bit of a ~. Isn't she a little ~!* **3** (colloq) woman who manages a brothel.

Mad·ame /ˋmædəm/ *n* (*pl* **Mesdames** /meɪˋdɑmz/) French title for a married woman; also used before names of married women who are not British or American: *M~ Chang Kai Shek.*

mad·der /ˋmædə(r)/ *n* [U] (red dye obtained from the root of a) herbaceous climbing plant with yellowish flowers.

made /meɪd/ *pt,pp* of **make**[1].

Ma·deira /məˋdɪərə/ *n* white dessert wine from ~ (an island in the Atlantic Ocean). **ˋ~ cake** *n* kind of sponge-cake.

mad·emoi·selle /ˈmædəməˋzel/ *n* (abbr **Mlle**) French title used before the name of a young girl or an unmarried woman.

Ma·donna /məˋdɒnə/ *n* **the ~,** (picture or statue of) Mary, Mother of Jesus Christ. **ˋ~ lily,** kind of pure white lily (as often shown in pictures of the ~).

mad·ri·gal /ˋmædrɪgl/ *n* part-song for several voices without instrumental accompaniment.

Mae·cenas /maɪˋsinəs/ *n* generous patron of literature or art.

mael·strom /ˋmeɪlstrəm/ *n* great whirlpool: (fig) violent or destructive force; whirl of events: *the ~ of war.*

mae·nad /ˋminæd/ *n* priestess of Bacchus, the Greek god of wine; frenzied woman.

maes·tro /ˋmaɪstrəʊ/ *n* (*pl* **maestri** /ˋmaɪstrɪ/) (I) eminent musical composer, teacher, or conductor.

maf·fick /ˋmæfɪk/ *vi* go in for wild public merry-making and rejoicing (e g in war, when there is news of a victory).

Ma·fia /ˋmæfɪə *US:* ˋmɑf-/ *n* secret organization in Sicily, opposed to legal authority and engaged in crime; similar organization on the mainland of Italy and in US.

mag /mæg/ *n* (colloq abbr of) **magazine(3)**: *the colour mags.*

maga·zine /ˈmægəˋzin *US:* ˋmægəzin/ *n* **1** store for arms, ammunition, explosives, etc. **2** chamber for holding cartridges to be fed into the breech of a rifle or gun; place for rolls or cartidges of film in a camera. **3** paper-covered (usu weekly or monthly) periodical, with stories, articles, etc by various writers.

ma·genta /məˋdʒentə/ *adj, n* bright crimson (substance used as a dye).

mag·got /ˋmægət/ *n* larva or grub, esp of a kind of fly (the bluebottle) that lays its eggs in meat, and of the cheese-fly. ***have a ~ in one's head,*** have a strange whim or fancy. **~y** *adj* having ~s: *~y cheese.*

Magi /ˋmeɪdʒaɪ/ *n pl* **the M~,** the three wise men from the East who brought offerings to the infant Jesus.

magic /ˋmædʒɪk/ *n* [U] **1** art of controlling events by the pretended use of supernatural forces; witchcraft; primitive superstitious practices based on a belief in supernatural agencies. ***like/as if by ~,*** in a mysterious manner. **black/white ~,** done with/without the help of devils. **2** art of obtaining mysterious results by tricks: *The conjurer used ~ to produce a rabbit from his hat.* **3** the identification of a symbol with the thing it stands for, as when the wearing of a lion's skin is thought to give the wearer a lion's courage. **4** (fig) mysterious charm; quality produced as if by ~: *the ~ of Shakespeare's poetry/of the woods in autumn.* □ *adj* done by, or as if by, ~; possessing ~; used in ~: *~ arts/words; a ~ touch. The result was ~al.* **~ eye,** (colloq) name used for various electronic devices which control or indicate sth, e g the automatic opening and closing of doors, exact tuning of a radio set. **~ lantern,** apparatus (now a toy) for throwing a magnified image of a picture, etc from a glass slide on to a white screen (*projector* is the name of the modern apparatus). **~ square,** large square divided into smaller squares, each with a number, so that the sum or each row, vertical, horizontal or diagonal is always the same. **magi·cal** /-kl/ *adj* = ~. **magi·cally** /-klɪ/ *adv* **ma·gician** /məˋdʒɪʃn/ *n* person skilled in **~(2)**; wizard.

magis·terial /ˈmædʒɪˋstɪərɪəl/ *adj* of, conducted by, a magistrate; having or showing authority: *~ rank; a ~ manner/opinion.* **~ly** /-ɪəlɪ/ *adv*

magis·trate /ˋmædʒɪstreɪt/ *n* civil officer acting as a judge in the lowest courts (Police Courts); Justice of the Peace. **magis·tracy** /ˋmædʒɪstrəsɪ/ *n* (*pl* **-cies**) position of a ~; (with *def art*) ~s collectively.

mag·nani·mous /mægˋnænɪməs/ *adj* having, showing, generosity. **~·ly** *adv* **mag·na·nim·ity** /ˈmægnəˋnɪmətɪ/ *n* [U] being ~; [C] (*pl* **-ties**) ~ act, etc.

mag·nate /ˋmægneɪt/ *n* wealthy leading man of business or industry; person who has power through wealth or position: *territorial ~s,* influential landowners.

mag·nesia /mægˋniʃə/ *n* [U] white, tasteless powder (carbonate of magnesium, **MgO**) used medicinally and in industry.

mag·nesium /mægˋnizɪəm/ *n* [U] silver-white metal (symbol **Mg**) used in the manufacture of aluminium and other alloys, fireworks and flash photography: *~ light,* bright light obtained by burning ~ wire.

mag·net /ˋmægnɪt/ *n* [C] **1** piece of iron, often a horseshoe shape, able to attract iron, either natural (as in lodestone) or by means of an electric current. **2** (fig) person or thing that attracts. **mag·net·ic** /mægˋnetɪk/ *adj* **1** having the properties of a ~; able to attract, etc: *~ field,* area in all parts of which a ~ force may be detected; *a ~ mine,* sub-

a maggot

marine mine that is detonated when a large mass of iron (e g a ship) approaches it; *a ~ needle*, one that points north and south; *the ~ north*, the point indicated by such a needle; *a ~ smile/personality*, attracting the attention of people. **~ tape,** kind of tape coated with iron oxide used for recording sound and vision. **2** of magnetism. **mag·neti·cally** /-klı/ *adv*

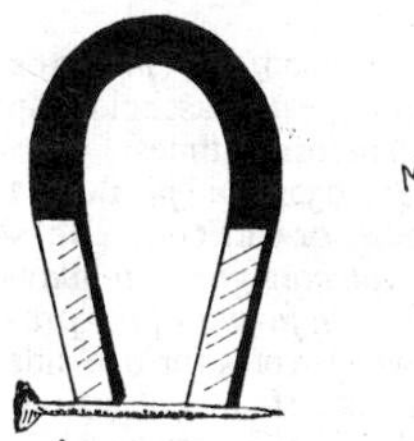

a magnet

a magnifying glass

mag·net·ism /ˋmægnıtızm/ *n* [U] (the science of) magnetic phenomena and properties; (fig) personal charm and attraction.

mag·net·ize /ˋmægnıtɑız/ *vt* [VP6A] give magnetic properties to; (fig) attract as a magnet does, e g by personal charm, moral or intellectual power.

mag·neto /mægˋnitəʊ/ *n* (*pl* **-tos** /-təʊz/) electric apparatus for producing sparks in the ignition system of an internal combustion engine.

Mag·nifi·cat /mægˋnıfıkæt/ *n* hymn of the Virgin Mary in Luke 1: 46—55, one of the hymns (canticles) in the Book of Common Prayer of the Church of England.

mag·nifi·cent /mægˋnıfısnt/ *adj* splendid; remarkable; important-looking: *a ~ house; his ~ generosity*. **~·ly** *adv* **mag·nifi·cence** /-sns/ *n* [U].

mag·nify /ˋmægnıfɑı/ *vt* (*pt,pp* **-fied**) [VP6A] **1** make (sth) appear larger (as with a lens or microscope): *a ˋ~ing glass*, lens for this purpose. **2** exaggerate: *~ dangers*. **3** extol; give praise to (God): *~ the Lord*. **mag·ni·fier** /-fɑıə(r)/ *n* instrument, etc, that magnifies. **mag·ni·fi·ca·tion** /ˈmægnıfıˋkeıʃn/ *n* (esp) power of ~ing, e g of a lens, a pair of binoculars.

mag·nil·oquent /mægˋnıləkwənt/ *adj* (of words, speech) pompous; (of a person) using pompous or high-sounding words. **~·ly** *adv* **mag·nil·oquence** /-əns/ *n*

mag·ni·tude /ˋmægnıtjud *US:* -tud/ *n* size; (degree of) importance; comparative brightness of stars.

mag·no·lia /mægˋnəʊlıə/ *n* tree with large, sweet-smelling wax-like flowers.

mag·num /ˋmægnəm/ *n* (bottle containing) two quarts (of wine or spirit).

mag·num opus /ˈmægnəm ˋəʊpəs/ *n* ⇨ **opus**.

mag·pie /ˋmægpɑı/ *n* noisy black-and-white bird which is attracted by, and often takes away, small, bright objects; (fig) person who chatters very much; (fig) petty thief.

Mag·yar /ˋmægjɑ(r)/ *n* (member, language) of the dominant race of people in Hungary.

Ma·ha·ra·ja(h) /ˈmɑhəˋrɑdʒə/ *n* title of a prince in India, esp a sovereign ruler, one of the indigenous states. **Ma·ha·ra·nee** /ˈmɑhərɑˋni/ *n* wife of a ~; queen or princess with a position like that of a ~.

Ma·hatma /məˋhætmə/ *n* (in India, etc) (title given to) one of a class of persons revered as having great high-mindedness and love of humanity.

mah·jong /ˈmɑˋdʒɔŋ/ *n* Chinese game for four persons played with 136 (or 144) pieces or tiles of wood, bone or ivory.

ma·hog·any /məˋhɔgənı/ *n* (tropical tree with) dark-brown wood much used for furniture.

ma·hout /mɑˋhut/ *n* elephant-driver.

maid /meıd/ *n* **1** (liter) girl. **2** (old use) young, unmarried woman. **old ~,** elderly woman who is considered unlikely to marry. **ˈ~ of ˋhonour,** unmarried woman attending a queen or princess. **3** (usu modern sense) woman servant: *It's the ~'s day off*, (in compounds): *ˋ~servant, ˋhouse~, ˋnurse~*.

mai·dan /ˈmeıˋdɑn/ *n* (in India) open space in a town; parade-ground.

maiden /ˋmeıdn/ *n* (liter) girl; young unmarried woman. □ *adj* (attrib only) **1** of a girl or woman. **~ name,** family name before marriage. **2** first or earliest: *a ship's ~ voyage*. **~ speech,** first speech in Parliament of a new member. **3 ~ (over),** (cricket) one in which no runs are scored. **4** (of a woman) unmarried: *my ~ aunt*. **5** (compounds) **ˋ~·hair** *n* (kinds of) fern with fine stalks and delicate fronds. **ˋ~·head** /-hed/ *n* [U] the hymen; virginity. **ˋ~·hood** /-hʊd/ *n* state of being a ~, period when one is a ~. **ˋ~·like, ~·ly** *adjj* gentle; modest; of or like a ~. □ *adv* (liter) modestly: *She turned her eyes ~ly away from the scene*.

mail[1] /meıl/ *n* [U] body armour of metal rings or plates: *a coat of ~; ˋchain-~*. **~ed** *adj* only in ***the ~ed fist,*** (threat of) armed force.

mail[2] /meıl/ *n* **1** [U] government system of collecting, carrying and delivering letters and parcels: *send a letter by air~; the ˋ~-coach*, (formerly) horse-drawn stage-coach for carrying ~. **ˋ~bag** *n* stout bag in which ~ is carried. **ˋ~·boat** *n* one that transports ~. **ˋ~·box** *n* (US) letter-box. **ˋ~-man** /-mæn/ *n* (*pl* **-men**) (US) postman. **ˈ~ ˋorder,** order for goods to be delivered by post; *a ~-order business*, one in which the buying and selling of goods is conducted by correspondence; *a ~- order catalogue*, one with a price-list of goods. **ˋ~-train,** train that carries ~. **2** [C,U] letters, parcels, etc, sent or delivered by post; the letters, etc, sent, collected or delivered at one time: *Is there ~ this morning? I had a lot of ~ last week. My secretary usually opens the ~. The ship sank and the ~s were lost.* □ *vt* [VP6A] (chiefly US; in GB *post* is more usu) send by ~. **ˋ~ing-card,** (US) postcard. **ˋ~·ing-list** *n* list of names of persons to whom sth, e g announcements of new books from a publisher, is regularly sent: *Please add my name to your ~ing-list*.

maim /meım/ *vt* wound or injure so that some part of the body is useless: *He was seriously ~ed in the war*.

main[1] /meın/ *adj* (attrib only; no *comp* or *superl*) **1** chief; most important: *the ~ thing to remember; the ~ street of a town; the ~ line of a railway; the ~ point of my argument; the ~ current/stream of traffic; the ~ course of a meal*. ***have an eye to the ~ chance,*** ⇨ chance[1](3). **2** exerted to the full. ***do sth by ~ force,*** using one's strength to the utmost. **3** (compounds) **ˋ~ deck** *n* upper deck. **ˋ~·land** /-lænd/ *n* country, continent or land mass, without its lands. **ˋ~·mast** *n* principal mast of a sailing-ship. **ˋ~-spring** *n* **(a)** principal spring of a clock or watch. **(b)** (fig) driving force or motive. **ˈ~·stay** /-steɪ/ *n* rope from the top of the ~mast to the bottom of the foremast; (fig) chief support. **ˈ~·stream** *n* **1** dominant trend, tendency, etc: *the ~stream of political thought.* **2** style of jazz between traditional and modern. **~·ly** *adv* chiefly; for the most part: *The people who came were ~ly country visitors. You are ~ly to blame.*

main² /meɪn/ *n* **1** [C] principal pipe bringing water or gas, principal wire transmitting electric current, from the source of supply into a building (contrasted with pipes from a cistern inside the building, etc); principal sewer to which pipes from a building are connected: *My new house is not yet connected to the ~s. We take our electric current from the ~s.* **ˈ~s set,** radio set to be connected to the ~s for current, not a battery set. **2** ***in the ~,*** for the most part; on the whole. **3** [U] physical force; strength: (only in) *with might and ~.* **4** (poet) sea, esp a wide expanse of sea. **5 the Spanish M~,** that part of the NE coast of S America visited by the early Spanish navigators and the adjoining part of the Caribbean Sea.

main·tain /meɪnˈteɪn/ *vt* **1** [VP6A] keep up; retain; continue: *~ friendly relations (with...); ~ prices,* keep them steady; *~ law and order; ~ a speed of 60 miles an hour. The improvement in his health is being ~ed.* ***~ an open mind on sth,*** be ready to listen to and consider the views of others on a subject. **2** [VP6A] support: *~ a son at the university; neglect to ~ one's family. Can you ~ my daughter* (ie if you marry her) *in the style she has been accustomed to? It's difficult to ~ a family on £15 a week.* **3** [VP6A,9,25] assert as true: *~ one's innocence; ~ that one is innocent of a charge.* **4** [VP6A] keep in good repair or working order: *~ the roads.* **5** [VP6A] defend: *~ one's rights.* **~·able** /-əbl/ *adj* that can be ~ed.

main·ten·ance /ˈmeɪntənəns/ *n* [U] maintaining or being maintained; (esp) what is needed to support life. **ˈ~ order,** (legal) order made by a court of law obliging sb to support sb, eg a husband to support his wife from whom he is separated. **ˈ~ men/gang,** workmen who maintain roads and other public services. **ˈretail ˈprice ˈ~,** practice of maintaining fixed retail prices. ⇨ *cut prices,* at cut¹(9).

mai·son·nette /ˈmeɪzənˈet/ *n* small house; part of a house let or used separately as a self-contained dwelling.

maize /meɪz/ *n* [U] (also called *Indian corn*) sort of grain plant. ⇨ the illus at cereal.

ma·jes·tic /məˈdʒestɪk/ *adj* having, showing, majesty. **ma·jes·ti·cally** /-klɪ/ *adv*

maj·esty /ˈmædʒəstɪ/ *n* (*pl* **-ties**) **1** [U] kingly or queenly appearance, conduct, speech, causing respect; stateliness; royal power. **2** ***His/Her/Your ~; Their/Your Majesties,*** form used when speaking of or to a sovereign ruler or rulers.

ma·jol·ica /məˈdʒɒlɪkə/ *n* [U] (kinds of) Italian ornamented pottery; modern imitations of these, with white or coloured glazes.

ma·jor¹ /ˈmeɪdʒə(r)/ *adj* **1** (contrasted with *minor*) greater or more important: *~ roads; the ~ portion; a ~ operation,* (surgery) one that may be dangerous to the person's life. **~ premise** *n* ⇨ premise. ***~ scale,*** (music) scale having two full tones between the key note and the third note. ***~ suit,*** (cards, bridge) either spades or hearts. **2** (placed after a name) elder or first of two persons of the same name, eg in a school: *Smith ~.* ⇨ minor, senior. □ *vi* [VP3A] ***~ in sth,*** specialize in (a certain subject, at college or university): *Christina ~ed in two subjects at Keele University. Brian ~ed in economics.*

ma·jor² /ˈmeɪdʒə(r)/ *n* army officer between a captain and a colonel. **ˈ~-ˈgeneral** *n* army officer next above a brigadier and under a lieutenant-general. ⇨ App 9.

ma·jor-domo /ˈmeɪdʒə ˈdəʊməʊ/ *n* (*pl* -mos /-məʊz/) head steward in a great household, esp of a prince in Italy or Spain in former times.

ma·jor·ity /məˈdʒɒrətɪ *US:* -ˈdʒɔr-/ *n* (*pl* **-ties**) **1** (*sing* or *pl,v*) greater number or part (*of*): *The ~ of people seem to prefer watching games to playing games. The ~ were/was in favour of the proposal.* **2** [C] number by which votes for one side exceed those for the other side: *He was elected by a large ~/by a ~ of 3 749. The Government's ~ was a small one.* ***be in (the) ~,*** have the ~. **a ~ verdict,** verdict of the ~ (of a jury, etc). **3** legal age of reaching manhood or womanhood: *He will reach his ~ next month.* **4** army rank of major: *obtain one's ~.*

make¹ /meɪk/ *vt,vi* (*pt,pp* made /meɪd/) (For uses with *nn,* ⇨ 25,26 below; for uses with *adjj,* ⇨ 27 below; for uses with *adverbial particles* and *preps,* ⇨ 30 below.) **1** [VP6A,14,12B,13B] ***~ sth from/(out) of sth, ~ sth into sth,*** construct or produce by combining parts or putting materials together; form or shape from material; bring into existence (esp by effort): *~ bricks; ~ bread; ~ a coat; ~* (= manufacture) *paper. She made* (= prepared) *coffee for all of us. I made myself a cup of tea. Cloth is made of cotton, wool, silk and other materials. Wine is made from grapes. We ~ bottles (out) of glass. Glass is made into bottles. God made man.* ***show sb/let sb see what one is made of,*** show sb one's qualities, powers, abilities, etc. ***be as clever as they make 'em,*** be very cunning, shrewd, sly. **2** [VP6A] cause to appear by breaking, tearing, removing material: *~ a hole in the ground/a gap in a hedge.* ***~ a hole/dent in one's savings/reserves/finances,*** reduce them by a considerable amount. **3** [VP6A,16A] enact; establish: *The regulations were made to protect children. Who made this ridiculous rule?* **4** [VP6A] draft; draw up: *Father is making a fresh Will. A treaty has been made with our former enemies. I'll get my solicitor to ~ a deed of transfer.* **5** [VP6A] eat, have (a meal): *We made a good breakfast before leaving. He made a hasty lunch.* **6** [VP6A,13B] *Why ~ a disturbance at this time of night? I don't want to ~ any trouble for you.* **7** [VP16A] (passive only) be meant or intended: *John and Mary seem to have been made for each other,* eg because they get on so well together. *In England we think bacon and eggs were made to be eaten together.* **8** [VP22,24A] cause to be or become: *The news made her happy. He made his meaning clear. He made clear his objections/ made it clear that he objected to the proposal. His actions made him universally respected. He soon made himself understood. Can you easily ~ yourself understood in English? The full story was never made known/public. He couldn't ~ himself/his voice heard above the noise of the traffic.* ***~ oneself useful*** (*about the house/to one's employers, etc*), do sth to help: *Don't stand about doing nothing—~ yourself useful!* ***make it***

worth sb's while (to do sth), pay or reward him: *If you will help me with this job, I'll ~ it worth your while.* ***~ sth good,*** ⇨ good[1](20). **9** [VP6A] earn; win; gain; acquire: *~ £2000 a year; ~ a profit/loss of £100. He first made his name/reputation as a junior Minister. He made a name/reputation for himself at the Bar,* i e as a barrister. *He soon made a fortune on the Stock Exchange.* ***~ a pile/packet,*** (colloq) acquire a great deal of money. ***~ one's living (as/at/by/from),*** have as one's work or livelihood: *He ~s his living by giving piano lessons. Can you ~ a living from freelance journalism? Does he ~ a living at it?* **10** (various uses in card games, e g bridge) **(a)** win (a trick); play to advantage: *He made his Queen of Hearts.* **(b)** (of a card) win a trick: *Your ace and king won't make until you've drawn trumps.* **(c)** win (what one has set out to win): *Little slam bid and made.* **(d)** shuffle, mix (the cards): *Will you ~ the pack? My turn to ~.* **11** [VP6A] score (at cricket): *~ a century in a test match. 50 runs were made in the first hour.* **12** [VP2A] (of the tide) begin to flow or ebb: *The tide is making fast. The ebb was now making,* the ebb tide was flowing. **13** ***~ or break/mar,*** secure either success or be ruined. **a made man,** one whose success has been assured: *Get the Minister's help and you'll be a made man.* **14** [VP18B] compel; force; persuade; cause (sb) to do sth; cause (sth) to happen: *They made me/I was made to repeat the story. Can you ~ this old engine start? The children never behave well and no one ever tries to ~ them* (= ~ them behave well). *What ~s the grass grow? I can't ~ anyone hear,* e g by ringing the door bell, knocking, calling. *His jokes made us all laugh.* ***'~ one's 'blood boil/one's 'hackles rise,*** make one furious. ***'~ sb's 'hair stand on end,*** shock or frighten: *His ghost stories made our hair stand on end.* ***~ sth do, make do with sth,*** manage with it although it may not be really adequate or satisfactory: *You'll have to ~ do with cold meat for dinner. There's not much of it but I'll try to ~ it do.* ***~ do and mend,*** manage without buying new articles, e g clothing, bed linen, household articles, esp by repairing and remaking old ones. ***~ sth go round,*** make it last or be enough: *I don't know how she ~s the money go round.* ***~ believe (that/to be),*** cause people to believe, pretend to oneself: *Let's ~ believe that we're Red Indians. The children made believe that they were/made believe to be shipwrecked on a desert island.* Hence, **'~-believe** *n* [U] pretending; [C] pretence. **15** [VP22,18B,23] represent as; cause to appear as; allege (to be, to do): *Olivier, in the film, ~s Hamlet a figure of tragic indecision. Most of the old Chronicles ~ the king die in 1026,* give 1026 as the date of his death. *In the play the author ~s the villain commit suicide,* describe him as doing this. *You've made my nose too big,* e g in a drawing or painting. **16** [VP6A,25] estimate or reckon (to be); put (a total, etc) at: *What time do you ~ it? What do you ~ the time? How large do you ~ the audience? I ~ the total (to be) about £50. I ~ the distance about 70 miles.* **17** [VP6A] come to, equal; add up to; constitute; amount to (in significance): *Twenty shillings used to ~ one pound. Twelve inches ~ one foot. 5 and 7 is 12 and 3 is 15, and 4 more ~s 19. How many members ~ a quorum? His adventures ~ excellent reading. The play ~s an excellent evening's entertainment.* ***~ (good/much) sense,*** seem to have (plenty of/little) sense: *His arguments have never made much sense.* ***One swallow does not ~ a summer,*** ⇨ swallow[1]. **18** [VP6A] be (in a series); count as: *This ~s the fifth time you've failed this examination. Will you ~ a fourth at bridge?* **19** [VP6A,23B] turn into; turn out to be; prove to be: *If you work hard, you will ~ a good waiter. He will ~ an excellent husband. She will ~ him a good wife,* will be one. *This length of cloth will ~ me a suit,* can be made up into one. **20** [VP6A] (colloq uses) travel, over (a distance); reach, maintain (a speed); be in time for, catch; reach (a place); (US) gain the rank of or place of: *We've made 80 miles since noon. We've made good time,* travelled the distance in good time, i e fast. *The ship was making only nine knots. The disabled cruiser was only just able to ~* (= reach) *port. The train leaves at 7.13; can we ~ it,* reach the station in time? *He's tired out already—he'll never ~ the summit. His new novel has made the best-seller list,* has sold enough copies to be on this list. *He'll never ~* (= win a place on) *the team. Jones made* (= reached the rank of) *sergeant in six months.* **21** [VP23] elect; appoint; nominate; raise to the dignity of: *~ sb King/an earl/a peer. Newton was made President of the Royal Society. He was made General Manager by the directors. We ~ you our spokesman. He made her his wife,* married her. **22** [VP12A,13A] offer, propose, hold out (to sb): *M~ me an offer,* suggest a price! *We made them two or three attractive proposals. The Chairman of British Rail has made a new offer to the men,* e g of a rise in wages during a strike. *I made him a bid for the antique table. I made her a present of the vase.* **23** in the pattern. ***~ + n + of (sth/sb),*** or ***~ sth/sb sth,*** cause sb/sth to be or become what is denoted by the object of ~: *His parents want to ~ a doctor of him,* want him to be educated for the medical profession. *We must ~ an example of him,* e g by punishing him as a warning to others. *Don't ~ a habit of it/~ it a habit,* don't let it become a habit. *Don't ~ a hash/mess/muddle of it,* do the job badly. *He has made a business of politics,* has made politics his chief concern. *Don't ~ an ass/fool of yourself,* behave like an ass. *Don't ~ a practice of cheating at exams. Don't ~ cheating a practice.* ⇨ *n* entries esp in **25** and **26** below for other examples of this pattern. **24** [VP2C] behave as if about to do sth: *He made as if to strike me. He made to reply* (= seemed to be about to do so) *and then became silent.* **25** [VP6A,14] (used with many *nn* where ~ and the *n* together have the same meaning as a *v* related in form to the *n*. ***~ allowances (for),*** ⇨ allowance(3). ***~ an application (to sb) (for sth),*** apply (to sb) (for sth). ***~ arrangements for,*** arrange for. ***~ a decision,*** decide. ***~ a guess (at),*** guess (at). ***~ an impression on,*** impress. ***~ a request (to sb) (for sth),*** request sth (from sb). ***~ a success of (sth),*** succeed in/with. For other phrases of this kind, ⇨ the *n* entries. **26** [VP6A,14] (used with a large number of *nn* in special senses. ⇨ do[2], for *nn* used with *do;* the examples below are a selection only; for definitions ⇨ the entry for the *n* in the example): *~ much* ado *(about); ~* advances *(to); ~* amends *(to sb/for sth); ~ an* attempt; *~ an* appointment; *~ a* bid *(for); ~ the* bed(s); ~ *a* bee-line *(for);* ~ *the* best *of;* ~ *no* bones *about;* ~ *a* break *for it;* ~ *a clean* breast *of;* ~ *a* change; ~ capital *(out) of sth;* ~ *one's* day; ~ *a* deal *(with sb);* ~ demands *(of/on);* ~ *some/little* difference; ~ *an* effort; ~ *an* excuse; ~ eyes *at;* ~ *a* face/faces *(at);* ~ fun *of;* ~ *a* fuss *(of);* ~ game *of;* ~ *a* gesture; ~ *a* go *of sth;* ~ hay *of;* ~ head *or tail of;* ~ *a* hit *(with);* ~ inroads *into;* ~ *a good/poor* job *of;* ~ *a* man *of;* ~ *one's* mark; ~ mischief; ~ mincemeat *of;* ~ *a* mockery *of;* ~ *the* most *of;* ~ *a* mountain *out of a molehill;* ~ much *of;* ~ *a* name *for oneself;* ~ *a* night *of it;* ~ nonsense *of;* ~ *a* pass *at;* ~ *one's* peace *(with);* ~ *great* play *(with);* ~ *a* point *(of);* ~ room *(for);* ~ *a* secret *of;* ~ shift *with;* ~ *a* song *and dance about;* ~ war *(on);* ~ water; ~ *one's* way *in the world;* ~ *heavy* weather *of;* ~ *the* worst *of.* **27** [VP2D] (used with *adjj* in special senses; for definitions ⇨ the entries for the *adj* in the example): ~ *so bold (as to);* ~ *certain (of/that);* ~ *sth fast;* ~ *free with; sth good;* ~ *light of;* ~ *merry;* ~ *sure.* **28** [VP2C,3A] (of arguments, evidence, etc) point; tend: *All the evidence* ~*s* (*points* is more usu) *in the same direction.* **~ against,** (rare) be contrary, unfavourable, prejudicial or harmful to: *These dissipations* ~ *against your chance of success.* **29** (compounds) **ˈ~-believe** *n* ⇨ 14 above. **ˈ~-shift** *n* sth used for a time until sth better is obtainable: *use an empty crate as a* ~*shift for a table/as a* ~*shift table.* **ˈ~-up** *n* ⇨ ~ *up* in **30** below. **(a)** arrangement of type, etc on a printed page. **(b)** character, temperament: *people of that* ~*-up.* **(c)** [C,U] cosmetics, etc as used by actors; result of using these: *What a clever* ~*-up!* **(d)** [U] cosmetics as used on the face: *use too much* ~*-up/the wrong kind of* ~*-up.* **ˈ~-weight** *n* small quantity added to get the weight required; (fig) sth or sb of small value that fills a gap, supplies a deficiency. **30** [VP2C,14,15B,3A] (uses with *adverbial particles* and *preps*):

make after, (dated use) pursue; chase: *She made after him like a mad-woman.*

make at sb, move aggressively towards: *The angry woman made at me with her umbrella.* ⇨ *come at* at come(15).

make away with oneself, commit suicide: *Why did he* ~ *away with himself?* **~ away with sth,** destroy, steal or squander sth.

make for sb/sth, (a) move in the direction of; head for: *The frigate made for the open sea. It's late; we'd better turn and* ~ *for home.* **(b)** charge at, rush towards: *The bull made for me and I had to run. When the interval came everyone made for the bar,* i e to buy drinks. **(c)** contribute to, tend towards: *Does early rising* ~ *for good health? The improved lid of this jar* ~*s for easier opening.*

make sth/sb into sth, change or convert to: *The huts can be made into temporary houses. He wasn't always a bully—you made him into one.*

make sth/sb of, understand, interpret: *What do you* ~ *of it all? What are we to* ~ *of his behaviour? I can* ~ *nothing of all this scribble.*

make off, hurry away (esp in order to escape): *The get-away car made off at top speed.* **~ off with sth,** steal and hurry away: *The cashier made off with the firm's money.*

make sth out, (a) write out; complete or fill in: ~ *out a cheque for £10;* ~ *out a list for the grocer;* ~ *out a document in duplicate.* **(b)** manage to see, read (usu implying difficulty): *We made out a figure in the darkness. The outline of the house could just be made out.* **~ out that.../ ~ sb out to be,** claim; assert; maintain: *He made out that he had been badly treated. He* ~*s himself out to be cleverer than he really is. He's not such a good lawyer as some people* ~ *out,* i e ~ him out to be. **~ sb out,** understand sb's nature: *What a queer fellow he is! I can't* ~ *him out at all.* **~ it out, ~ (it) out if/whether,** understand: *I can't* ~ *out what he wants. I couldn't* ~ *it out. Did they want our help or not? How do you/does he, etc* ~ *that out? How do you/does he reach that conclusion, support that contention?* **~ out (with sb),** progress, get on: *How are things making out? How are you making out with Lucy?* How's your friendship progressing? **~ out a case for/against/that,** argue for/against: *He has made out a strong case for prison reform. A case could be made out that Smith should be released/for Smith's release.*

make sth/sb over, (a) change, transform, convert: *The basement has been made over into a workshop. You can't* ~ *over a personality in one day.* **(b)** transfer the possession or ownership of: *He has made over the whole of his property to the National Trust. How much did he* ~ *over?*

make sth up, (a) complete: *We still need £5 to* ~ *up the sum we asked for. They had to recruit men from Italy to* ~ *up their full complement of labourers.* **(b)** supply; ~ good: *Our losses have to be made up with fresh drafts. There's a good deal of leeway to* ~ *up.* **(c)** invent; compose (esp to deceive): *The whole story is made up. It's all a made-up story. Stop making things up!* **(d)** arrange type, illustrations, etc in columns or pages for printing: *Who is in charge of making up/the* ~*-up of the financial pages?* **(e)** form; compose; constitute: *Are all animal bodies made up of cells? What are the qualities that* ~ *up Hamlet's character? I object to the way the committee is made up/to the make-up of the committee.* **(f)** prepare, e g medicine, a prescription, tonic, by mixing ingredients: *Ask the chemist to* ~ *this up for you.* **(g)** put together; shape: ~ *up a bundle of old clothes for the church bazaar. The grocer was making up the butter into packages of half a kilo. Have you made up Mrs Smith's order yet,* i e collected the items, articles, etc she ordered? **(h)** ~ (material, cloth, etc) into a garment: *Customer's own materials made up. Can you* ~ *up this suit length for me? This material will* ~ *up into two dresses.* **(i)** add fuel to, e g a fire in a fireplace or stove: *The fire needs making up,* needs to have more coal put on it. *If the stove isn't made up, it will go out.* **(j)** prepare (a bed) not at present in use (as for a new hospital patient); prepare (a new makeshift bed, e g on the floor): *You can't go into the ward yet; your bed's still to be made up. They made up a bed on the sofa for the unexpected visitor.* **~ sb/oneself up,** prepare (an actor/oneself) for the stage by applying grease-paint, hair, etc to his/one's face or body; apply cosmetics to the face: *It takes him more than an hour to* ~ *up/do his* ~*-up for the part of Othello. Wipe your tears away and* ~ *up your pretty little face, darling. Isn't she badly made up! Ought she to* ~ *up at the age of twelve?* Hence, **ˈ~-up** *n* **~ up one's/sb's mind,** come/cause sb to come to a decision: *I've made up my mind. My mind's made up. He needs* *someone to ~ up his mind for him.* ***~ up for sth,*** compensate for; outweigh: *Hard work can often ~ up for a lack of intelligence. Do you think her beauty could ~ up for her stupidity?* ***~ up for lost time,*** hurry, work hard, etc after losing time, starting late, etc. ***~ up to sb for sth,*** atone; redress; ~ amends for: *How can we ~ it up to them for what they have suffered?* ***~ up to sb,*** ~ oneself pleasant to sb, to win favours: *He's always making up to influential people. He doesn't welcome being made up to.* ***~ it/this up to sb,*** compensate sb for sth missed or suffered: *I'm sorry you can't come with me to the party—I'll ~ it up to you later,* e g by taking you to another party. ***~ it up (with sb),*** end a quarrel, dispute or misunderstanding: *They quarrel every morning and ~ it up every evening. Why don't you ~ it up with her?*

make[2] /meɪk/ *n* [C,U] **1** way a thing is made; method or style of manufacture: *cars of all ~s; an overcoat of first-class ~. Is this your own ~,* made by you? ***on the ~,*** (sl) concerned with making a profit, gaining sth. **2** (electr) completion of an electric circuit.

maker /ˈmeɪkə(r)/ *n* **1 the/our M~,** the Creator; God. **2** (esp in compounds) person or thing that makes: *ˈdress~.*

mak·ing /ˈmeɪkɪŋ/ *n* **1** ***be the ~ of,*** cause the well-being of; cause to develop well: *The two years he served in the Army were the ~ of him,* made him develop well (physically, etc according to context). **2** ***have the ~s of,*** have the necessary qualities for becoming: *He has in him the ~s of a great man.*

ma·lacca /məˈlækə/ *n* ˈ~ ˈ**cane,** cane walking-stick.

mala·chite /ˈmæləkɑɪt/ *n* [U] green mineral, a kind of stone used for ornaments, decoration, etc.

mal·adjusted /ˈmæləˈdʒʌstɪd/ *adj* badly adjusted; (esp of a person) unable to adapt himself properly to his environment, e g social or occupational. **mal·adjust·ment** *n* condition of being ~.

mal·adroit /ˈmælədrɔɪt/ *adj* not adroit; clumsy; tactless. **~·ly** *adv* **~·ness** *n*

mal·ady /ˈmælədɪ/ *n* (*pl* -**dies**) [C] disease; illness: *a social ~; spiritual maladies.*

mal·aise /mæˈleɪz/ *n* (*sing* with *indef art*) feeling of bodily discomfort, but without clear signs of a particular illness: (fig) *years of ~ in industrial relations.*

mala·prop·ism /ˈmæləprop-ɪzm/ *n* [C] misuse of a word, esp in mistake for one that resembles it, causing amusement, e g *'Come girls, this gentleman will exhort* (for *escort*) *us!*

mal·apro·pos /ˈmælˈæprəˈpəʊ/ *adj, adv* inappropriate(ly); inopportunate(ly).

ma·laria /məˈleərɪə/ *n* [U] kinds of fever conveyed by mosquitoes, which introduce the germs into the blood. **ma·lar·ial** /-ɪəl/ *adj* of ~; having ~: *a ~l patient; a ~l district.*

Ma·lay /məˈleɪ/ *adj, n* (language, member) of the race of people living in the ~ peninsula and islands nearby.

mal·con·tent /ˈmælkəntent/ *adj, n* [C] (person who is) discontented and inclined to rebel.

male /meɪl/ *adj* **1** of the sex that does not give birth to offspring; of or for this sex: *a ˈ~ voice ˈchoir,* of men and/or boys. **2** (of parts of tools, etc) designed for insertion into a bore or socket, the corresponding female part: *a ~ screw.* □ *n* ~ person, animal, etc.

mal·edic·tion /ˈmælɪˈdɪkʃn/ *n* [C] curse; prayer to God that sb or sth may be destroyed, hurt, etc.

mal·efac·tor /ˈmælɪfæktə(r)/ *n* wrongdoer; criminal.

mal·efi·cent /məˈlefɪsnt/ *adj* hurtful (*to*).

mal·evol·ent /məˈlevl̩ənt/ *adj* wishing to do evil or cause suffering to others; spiteful (*to, towards*). **~·ly** *adv* **mal·evol·ence** /-əns/ *n* [U] ill will.

mal·feas·ance /mælˈfizns/ *n* [U] (legal) wrongdoing; [C] illegal act, esp an instance of official misconduct.

mal·for·ma·tion /ˈmælfɔˈmeɪʃn/ *n* [U] state of being badly formed or shaped; [C] badly formed part: *a ~ of the spine.* **mal·formed** /ˈmælˈfɔmd/ *adj* badly formed or shaped.

mal·ice /ˈmælɪs/ *n* [U] ***~ (towards),*** active ill will; desire to harm others: *bear sb no ~; with ~ towards none.* **ma·licious** /məˈlɪʃəs/ *adj* feeling, showing, caused by, ~: *malicious gossip.* **ma·licious·ly** *adv*

ma·lign /məˈlɑɪn/ *adj* (of things) injurious: *exercise a ~ influence.* □ *vt* [VP6A] speak ill of (sb); tell lies about: *~ an innocent person.*

ma·lig·nant /məˈlɪgnənt/ *adj* **1** (of persons, their actions) filled with, showing, a desire to hurt (~ is stronger in meaning than *malicious* and *malevolent*): *~ fairies; ~ glances.* **2** (of diseases) harmful to life; violent: *~ cancer.* **~·ly** *adv* **ma·lig·nancy** /-nənsɪ/ *n* [U] the state of being ~.

ma·lig·nity /məˈlɪgnətɪ/ *n* (*pl* -**ties**) **1** [U] deep-rooted ill will; [C] instance of this; act, remark, etc. caused by such ill will. **2** (of diseases) malignant character.

ma·lin·ger /məˈlɪŋgə(r)/ *vi* [VP2A] pretend to be ill, protract an illness, in order to escape duty or work. **~er** *n* person who ~s.

mal·lard /ˈmælɑd/ *n* kind of wild duck.

mal·leable /ˈmælɪəbl/ *adj* **1** (of metals) that can be hammered or pressed into new shapes. **2** (fig, e g of a person's character) easily trained or adapted. **mal·lea·bil·ity** /ˈmælɪəˈbɪlətɪ/ *n*

mal·let /ˈmælɪt/ *n* **1** hammer with a wooden head, e g for striking the handle of a chisel. **2** long-handled wooden-headed hammer for striking a croquet or polo ball.

mal·low /ˈmæləʊ/ *n* wild plant with hairy stems and leaves and pink, mauve or white flowers; garden varieties of this.

malm·sey /ˈmɑmzɪ/ *n* [U] a sweet wine from Greece, Spain, etc.

mal·nu·tri·tion /ˈmælnjuˈtrɪʃn *US:* -nu-/ *n* [U] condition caused by not getting enough food or (enough of) the right kind(s) of food.

mal·odor·ous /ˈmælˈəʊdərəs/ *adj* (formal) ill-smelling.

mal·prac·tice /ˈmælˈpræktɪs/ *n* (legal) [U] wrongdoing; neglect of duty; [C] instance of this, e g the dishonest use of a position of trust for personal gain.

malt /mɔlt/ *n* [U] grain (usu barley) allowed to sprout, prepared for brewing or distilling: (attrib) *~ liquors,* e g beer, stout. □ *vt,vi* **1** [VP6A] make (grain) into ~; [VP2A] (of grain) come to the condition of ~. **2** [VP6A] prepare with ~: *~ed milk.*

Mal·tese /mɔlˈtiz/ *adj, n* (*pl* unchanged) (language, native) of Malta: **~ cross,** ⇨ the illus at cross.

Mal·thu·sian /mælˈθjuzɪən *US:* -ˈθuʒn/ *adj* (supporter) of the principles of T R Malthus

/ˈmælθəs/, 1766—1834, English economist (who declared that the growth of the world's population would, unless checked, lead to a world shortage of food).

mal·treat /mælˈtrit/ *vt* [VP6A] treat roughly or cruelly. **~·ment** *n* [U] ~ing or being ~ed.

mal·ster /ˈmɔltstə(r)/ *n* person who makes malt.

mal·ver·sa·tion /ˈmælvəˈseɪʃn/ *n* [U] (formal) corrupt administration (*of* public money, etc).

mamba /ˈmæmbə/ *n* black or green poisonous African tree snake. ⇨ the illus at **snake**.

mam(m)a /məˈmɑ *US:* ˈmɑmə/ *n* familiar word for mother.

mam·mal /ˈmæml/ *n* any of the class of animals which feed their young with milk from the breast. ⇨ the illus at **ape, cat, domestic, large, small**.

mam·mon /ˈmæmən/ *n* [U] wealth (regarded as an evil influence). **M~,** the god of greed: *worshippers of M~.*

mam·moth /ˈmæməθ/ *n* large kind of elephant now extinct; (attrib) immense: *~ business enterprises.*

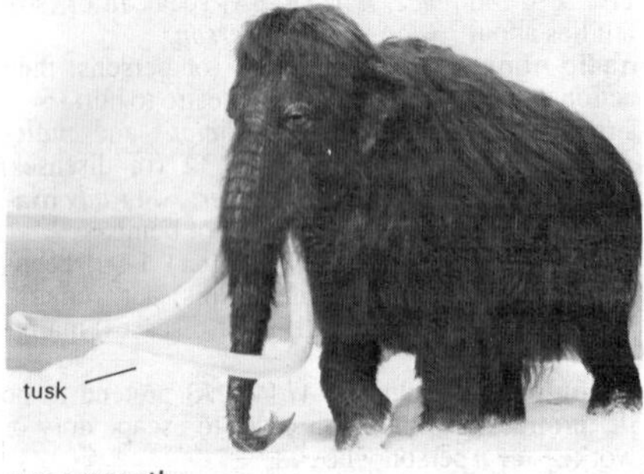

a mammoth

mammy /ˈmæmɪ/ *n* (*pl* -mies) **1** (child's word for) mother. **2** (US) Negro nursemaid for white children.

man[1] /mæn/ *n* (*pl* men /men/) **1** adult male human being. ***one's man of business,*** one's agent or solicitor. ***a man of letters,*** a writer and scholar. ***a man about town,*** one who spends much time in society, in clubs, at parties, theatres, etc. ***a man of the world,*** one with wide experience of business and society. ***the man in the street,*** person looked upon as representing the interests and opinions of ordinary people. ***man and boy,*** from boyhood onwards: *He has worked for the firm for thirty years, man and boy.* ***be one's own man,*** be free to act or do as one pleases; be in full possession of one's senses. ***to a man, to the last man,*** all without exception: *They answered 'Yes' to a man. They were killed to the last man.* **2** human being; person: *All men must die. Growing old is something a man has to accept.* **3** (*sing* only, without any *article*) the human race; all mankind: *Man wants but little here below. Man is mortal.* **4** husband (usu in *man and wife*). **5** male person under the authority of another; manservant or valet: *masters and men,* employers and workers; *officers and men,* e g in the army. **6** piece used in such games as chess. **7** male person having the good qualities associated with men: *Be a man! Play the man!* Be brave! *He's only half a man,* is lacking in spirit, strength, courage. *How can we make a man of him?* **8** (as a vocative, to call attention; used in a lively or impatient way): *Hurry up, man! Nonsense, man!* **9** (with *possessive adjj*): *If you want to sell your car, I'm your man,* I'll make an offer. *If you want a good music teacher, here's your man,* here's someone suitable. **10** (in comb) *ˈclergyman; ˈpostman; ˈfisherman,* etc. **11** (compounds) **ˌman-at-ˈarms** *n* soldier, esp (in the Middle Ages) a mounted soldier with heavy armour and weapons. **ˈman-eater** *n* cannibal; man-eating tiger or shark. **ˈman-handle** *vt* move by physical strength; (sl) handle roughly: *The drunken man was manhandled by the police.* **ˈman·hole** *n* opening (usu with a lid) through which a man may enter (an underground sewer, boiler, tank, etc) for inspection purposes. **ˈman-hour** *n* work done by one man in one hour. **ˌman-of-ˈwar** *n* (old use) armed ship belonging to a country's navy. **ˈman-power** *n* number of men available for military service, industrial needs, etc: *a shortage of manpower in the coal-mines.* **ˈman·servant** *n* male servant. **ˈman-sized** *adj* of a size right for a man; *a man-sized beefsteak.* **ˈman·slaughter** *n* [U] act of killing a human being unlawfully but not wilfully. **ˈman-trap** *n* trap for catching trespassers, poachers, etc.

man[2] /mæn/ *vt* (-nn-) [VP6A] **1** supply with men for service or defence: *man a fort/a ship; man the barricades.*

man·acle /ˈmænəkl/ *n* (usu *pl*) fetter or chain for the hands or feet. □ *vt* [VP6A] fetter with ~s; (fig) restrain.

man·age /ˈmænɪdz/ *vt,vi* **1** [VP6A] control: *~ a horse; ~ a sailing-boat,* handle the sails, etc, properly; *~ a business/household; ~ a naughty child/one's wife; the managing director,* who controls the business operations of a company. *Mrs Hill is a very managing woman,* one who likes to ~ or control other people. **2** [VP2A,C,4A,3A] ***~ (to do sth), ~ with/without,*** succeed; contrive: *I shan't be able to ~ without help. If I can't borrow the money I shall have to ~ without. We can't ~ with these poor tools. In spite of these insults, she ~d to keep her temper.* **3** [VP6A] (colloq, with *can, could, be able to*) make use of; eat: *can you ~ another slice of cake?* **ˈ~·able** /-əbl/ *adj* that can be ~d; easily controlled. **~·abil·ity** /ˈmænɪdʒəˈbɪlətɪ/ *n*

man·age·ment /ˈmænɪdʒmənt/ *n* **1** [U] managing or being managed: *The failure was caused by bad ~. The business is under new ~.* **2** [U] skilful treatment; delicate contrivance (and perhaps trickery): *It needed a good deal of ~ to persuade them to give me the job.* **3** [C,U] (collective) all those concerned in managing an industry, enterprise, etc: *joint consultation between workers and ~. What this department store needs is a stronger ~.*

man·ager /ˈmænɪdʒə(r)/ *n* **1** person who controls a business, a hotel, etc. **2** (usu with an *adj*) one who conducts business, manages household affairs, etc, in a certain way: *My wife is an excellent ~.* **~·ess** /ˈmænɪdʒəˈres/ *n* woman ~(1).

mana·gerial /ˈmænɪˈdʃɪərɪəl/ *adj* of managers: *the ˈ~ class,* people such as managers, directors, etc.

mana·tee /ˈmænəˈti/ *n* large sea mammal with flippers and a broad, flat tail; sea-cow.

man·da·rin /ˈmændərɪn/ *n* **1** (old use) name for high Chinese government official. **2** standard spoken Chinese (as used by educated Chinese in all parts of China). **3** **~ duck,** small Chinese duck with brightly coloured feathers. **4** **~ orange,** tangerine. **5** (often attrib) behaviour and language which seems deliberately remote and difficult: *the ~ prose of some civil servants.*

man·date /ˋmændeɪt/ *n* [C] **1** order from a superior; command given with authority. **2** authority to administer a territory authorized by the League of Nations after the First World War. **3** authority given to representatives by voters, members of a trade union, etc: *the ~ given to us by the electors.* □ *vt* [VP6A] put (a territory) under a ~(2): *the ~d territories.* **man·da·tory** /ˋmændətrɪ *US:* -tɔrɪ/ *adj* of, conveying, a command: *the mandatory power.* □ *n* (also **-tary** /-tərɪ *US:* -terɪ/) person or state to whom a ~ has been given.

man·dible /ˋmændəbl/ *n* **1** jaw, esp the lower jaw in mammals and fishes. **2** either part of a bird's beak. **3** (in insects) either half of the upper pair of jaws, used for biting and seizing.

man·do·lin /ˋmændəlɪn/ *n* musical instrument with 6 or 8 metal strings stretched in pairs on a rounded body.

man·drag·ora /mænˋdrægərə/ *n* [U] poisonous plant used in medical preparations (as an emetic and for causing sleep).

man·drake /ˋmændreɪk/ *n* = mandragora.

man·drill /ˋmæn-drɪl/ *n* large fierce, baboon of western Africa.

mane /meɪn/ *n* [C] long hair on the neck of a horse, lion, etc; (colloq or hum) thick hair on a man's head. ⇨ the illus at **cat, domestic.**

manes /ˋmɑneɪz/ *n pl* (Lat) (among the ancient Romans) spirits of the dead, esp of ancestors worshipped as guardian influences.

ma·neu·ver /məˋnuvə(r)/ *n, v* (US spelling of) manœuvre.

man·ful /ˋmænfl/ *adj* brave; resolute; determined. **~ly** /-flɪ/ *adv*

man·ga·nese /ˌmæŋgəˋniz *US:* ˋmæŋgəniz/ *n* [U] hard, brittle, light-grey metal (symbol **Mn**) used in making steel, glass, etc.

mange /meɪndʒ/ *n* [U] contagious skin disease, esp of dogs and cats. **mangy** /ˋmeɪndʒɪ/ *adj* **1** suffering from ~: *a mangy dog.* **2** squalid; neglected. **mang·ily** /ˋmeɪndʒəlɪ/ *adv*

man·gel-wur·zel /ˋmæŋgl wɜzl/ *n* [C] large round root, a kind of beet, used as cattle food.

manger /ˋmeɪndʒə(r)/ *n* long open box or trough for horses or cattle to feed from. ***dog in the ~,*** ⇨ dog[1](2).

mangle[1] /ˋmæŋgl/ *n* [C] machine with rollers for pressing out water from and for smoothing clothes, etc, that have been washed. □ *vt* [VP6A] put (clothes, etc) through a ~.

mangle[2] /ˋmæŋgl/ *vt* [VP6A] **1** cut up, tear, damage, badly: *He was knocked down by a lorry and badly ~d.* **2** (fig) spoil by making bad mistakes: *~ a piece of music.*

mango /ˋmæŋgəʊ/ *n* (*pl* -goes or -gos /-gəʊz/) ⇨ the illus at **fruit.** (tropical tree bearing) pear-shaped fruit with yellow flesh: *~ chutney,* kind made with unripe (green) ~es.

man·go·steen /ˋmæŋgəˋstin/ *n* (E Indian tree bearing) fruit with thick red rind and white juicy pulp.

man·grove /ˋmæŋgrəʊv/ *n* [C] tropical tree growing in swamps and sending down new roots from its branches.

mangy /ˋmeɪndʒɪ/ ⇨ mange.

Man·hat·tan /mænˋhætn/ *n* (US) cocktail of whisky and vermouth.

man·handle ⇨ man[1](11).

man·hood /ˋmænhʊd/ *n* [U] **1** the state of being a man: *reach ~; ~ suffrage,* giving the vote to male citizens. **2** manly qualities; courage; sexual virility. **3** all the men (collectively, *of* a country): *the ~ of Scotland.*

mania /ˋmeɪnɪə/ *n* **1** [U] violent madness. **2** [C] **~ *(for),*** extreme enthusiasm (*for* sth): *a ~ for collecting china ornaments.* **maniac** /ˋmeɪnɪæk/ *n* raving madman; (fig) extreme enthusiast. **ma·niacal** /məˋnaɪəkl/ *adv* violently mad; (fig) extremely enthusiastic. **ma·niacally** /-klɪ/ *adv*

manic-depressive /ˈmænɪk dɪˋpresɪv/ *adj, n* (person) suffering from alternating periods of excitement and melancholic depression.

mani·cure /ˋmænɪkjʊə(r)/ *n* [U] care of the hands and finger-nails: *have a course in ~;* (with *indef art*) treatment of this kind: *She has a ~ once a week.* □ *vt* [VP6A] give ~ treatment to; cut, clean and polish the finger-nails. **mani·cur·ist** /-ɪst/ *n* person who practises ~ as an occupation.

mani·fest[1] /ˋmænɪfest/ *n* list of a ship's cargo for the use of customs officials.

mani·fest[2] /ˋmænɪfest/ *adj* clear and obvious: *a ~ truth; sth that should be ~ to all of you.* □ *vt* [VP6A] **1** show clearly: *~ the truth of a statement.* **2** give signs of: *She doesn't ~ much desire to marry him.* **3** (reflex) come to light; appear: *No disease ~ed itself during the long voyage. Has the ghost ~ed itself recently?* **mani·fes·ta·tion** /ˈmænɪfeˋsteɪʃn/ *n* [U] ~ing; making clear; [C] act or utterance that ~s. **~·ly** *adv*

mani·festo /ˈmænɪˋfestəʊ/ *n* (*pl* -tos or -toes /-təʊz/) public declaration of principles, policy, purposes, etc by a ruler, political party, etc or of the character, qualifications of a person or group.

mani·fold /ˋmænɪfəʊld/ *adj* having or providing for many uses, copies, etc. □ *vt* [VP6A] (now usu *duplicate*) make a number of copies of (a letter, etc) on a machine. □ *n* pipe or chamber with several openings, for connections, e g for leading gases into or out of cylinders.

mani·kin /ˋmænɪkɪn/ *n* **1** small, undersized man; dwarf. **2** anatomical model of the human body; figure of the human body used by artists, e g for drapery, clothes. **3** = mannequin.

Ma·nilla (US also **Manila**) /məˋnɪlə/ *n* **1 ~ (hemp),** plant fibre used for making ropes, mats, etc. **2 ~ paper,** strong, brown wrapping paper made from ~ hemp. **~ envelopes,** strong variety. **3** cheroot made in ~, the capital of the Philippine Islands.

ma·nipu·late /məˋnɪpjʊleɪt/ *vt* [VP6A] **1** operate, handle, with skill: *~ the gears and levers of a machine.* **2** manage or control (sb or sth) skilfully or craftily, esp by using one's influence or unfair methods: *A clever politician knows how to ~ his supporters/~ public opinion.* **ma·nipu·la·tion** /məˈnɪpjʊˋleɪʃn/ *n* [U] manipulating or being ~d; [C] instance of this: *make a lot of money by clever manipulation of the Stock Market.*

man·kind *n* [U] **1** /ˈmænˋkaɪnd/ the human species. **2** /ˋmænkaɪnd/ the male sex (contrasted with ˋ*womankind*).

man·like /ˋmænlaɪk/ *adj* having the qualities (good or bad) of a man.

man·ly /ˋmænlɪ/ *adj* (-ier, -iest) having the strong qualities expected of a man; (of a woman) having a man's qualities; (of things, qualities, etc) right for a man. **man·li·ness** *n*

manna /ˈmænə/ *n* [U] (in the Bible) food provided by God for the Israelites during their forty years in the desert (⇨ Exod 16); (fig) sth unexpectedly supplied or that gives spiritual refreshment.

man·ne·quin /ˈmænəkɪn/ *n* **1** woman employed to display new clothes for sale by wearing them (*model* is the usual word today). **2** life-size dummy of a human body, used by tailors and in shops and shop-windows for the display of clothes.

man·ner /ˈmænə(r)/ *n* [C] **1** way in which a thing is done or happens: *Do it in this ~.* ***(as) to the ~ born,*** as if knowing how to deal with a situation, practice, custom, etc from birth; naturally fitted for a position, duty, etc. **2** (*sing* only) person's way of behaving towards others: *He has an awkward ~. I don't like his ~.* **3** (*pl*) habits and customs. **4** (*pl*) social behaviour: *good/bad ~s; a comedy of ~s,* theatrical play which is a satire on fashionable society. *He has no ~s at all,* is very badly behaved. *It is bad ~s to stare at people. Aren't you forgetting your ~s, Mary?* (e g to a child who forgets to say 'Thank you' for a present). **5** style in literature or art: *a painting in the ~ of Raphael.* **6** kind, sort: *What ~ of man is he?* ***all ~ of,*** every kind of. ***in a ~,*** in a certain degree; to a certain extent. ***in a ~ of speaking,*** as one might say (used to weaken or qualify what one says). ***by ˋno ~ of means,*** in no circumstances. **~ed** *adj* **1** (in compounds) ***ˋill-/ˋwell-/ˋrough-~ed,*** having bad/good/rough ~s(4). **2** showing mannerisms.

man·ner·ism /ˈmænərɪzm/ *n* [C] peculiarity of behaviour, speech, etc, esp one that is habitual; excessive use of a distinctive manner in art or literature.

man·ner·ly /ˈmænəlɪ/ *adj* having good manners; polite.

man·nish /ˈmænɪʃ/ *adj* **1** (of a woman) like a man. **2** more suitable for a man than for a woman: *a ~ style of dress;* characteristic of a man: *a ~ way to thread a needle.*

ma·nœuvre (US = **ma·neu·ver**) /məˋnuvə(r)/ *n* **1** planned movement (of armed forces); (*pl*) series of such movements, e g as training exercises: *army/fleet ~s; troops on ~s.* **2** movement or plan, made to deceive, or to escape from sb, or to win or do sth: *the despicable ~s of some politicians.* □ *vi,vt* [VP2A,C,6A,15A] (cause to) perform ~s: *The fleet is manœuvring off the east coast. Can we ~ the enemy out of their strong position? She ~d her car into a difficult parking space. Can you ~ me into a good job,* use your influence, etc in order to get a good job for me? *The yachts were manœuvring for position,* moving about to get advantageous positions (in a race). **ma·nœuvr·able** (US = **ma·neu·ver·able**) /-vrəbl/ *adj* that can be ~d. **ma·nœuvr·abil·ity** (US = **-neu·ver-**) /məˌnuvrəˋbɪlətɪ/ *n* **~r** (US = **ma·neu·verer**) *n*

manor /ˈmænə(r)/ *n* (in England) **1** unit of land under the feudal system, part of which was used directly by the lord of the ~ (⇨ lord(4)) and the rest occupied and farmed by tenants who paid rent in crops and service. **2** (modern use) area of land with a principal residence (called the *ˋ~-house*). **ma·nor·ial** /məˋnɔrɪəl/ *adj* of a ~.

man·sard /ˈmænsɑd/ *n* **~ (roof),** roof with a double slope, the lower being steeper than the upper.

manse /mæns/ *n* Presbyterian church minister's house, esp in Scotland.

man·sion /ˈmænʃn/ *n* **1** large and stately house. **the ˋM~-house,** the official residence of the Lord Mayor of London. **2** (*pl*, in proper names) block of flats: *Victoria M~s.*

man·tel /ˈmæntl/ *n* structure of wood, marble, etc above and around a fireplace; (in modern houses, usu *ˋ~piece*) shelf projecting from the wall above a fireplace.

man·tilla /mænˋtɪlə/ *n* large veil or scarf worn by Spanish women to cover the hair and shoulders.

man·tis /ˈmæntɪs/ *n* (kinds of) long-legged insect. ⇨ the illus at **insect**.

mantle[1] /ˈmæntl/ *n* **1** loose, sleeveless cloak; (fig) covering: *hills with a ~ of snow.* **2** lace-like cover fixed round the flame of a gas lamp and becoming incandescent, to provide bright light.

mantle[2] /ˈmæntl/ *vt,vi* **1** [VP6A] cover in, or as in, a mantle: *an ˋivy-~d wall.* **2** [VP6A,2C] (old use, or liter) (of blood) flow into the blood-vessels of; (of the face) flush: *Blushes/Blood ~d (over) her cheeks. Her face ~d with blushes.* (fig) *Dawn ~d in the sky.*

man·ual /ˈmænjʊəl/ *adj* of, done with, the hands: *~ labour; ~ training,* e g in schools, training in carpentry, metal work; *~ exercises,* e g drill in handling a rifle. □ *n* **1** handbook or textbook: *a shorthand ~.* **2** keyboard of an organ, played with the hands. **~ly** /-jʊəlɪ/ *adv*

manu·fac·ture /ˌmænjʊˋfæktʃə(r)/ *vt* [VP6A] **1** make, produce (goods, etc) on a large scale by machinery: *~ shoes/cement; manufacturing industries; ~d goods* (contrasted with raw materials, hand-made goods, etc). **2** invent (a story, an excuse, etc). □ *n* **1** [U] the making or production of goods and materials: *firms engaged in the ~ of plastics; goods of foreign ~.* **2** (*pl*) ~d goods and articles. **manu·fac·turer** *n* person, firm, etc that ~s things.

manu·mit /ˌmænjʊˋmɪt/ *vt* (**-tt-**) (in former times) set (a slave) free. **manu·mission** /ˌmænjʊˋmɪʃn/ *n*

ma·nure /məˋnjʊə(r)/ *n* [U] animal waste, e g from stables, cow barns or other material, natural or artificial, spread over or mixed with the soil to make it fertile. ⇨ *fertilizer,* the usu word for chemical or artificial manure, at **fertilise**. □ *vt* [VP6A] put ~ in or on land/soil.

manu·script /ˈmænjʊskrɪpt/ *n* (shortened to **MS**, *pl* **MSS**) book, etc as first written out or typed: *send a ~ to the printers.* **in ~,** not yet printed: *poems still in ~.*

Manx /mæŋks/ *adj* of the Isle of Man. **ˋ~ cat,** tailless kind of cat. □ *n* ~ language.

many /ˈmenɪ/ *adj, n* (contrasted with *few;* ⇨ **more, most**) **1** (used with *pl nn;* ⇨ **much**; in purely affirm sentences it is often preferable to use *a large number (of), numerous,* or (colloq) *a lot (of), lots (of), plenty (of)*): *Were there ~ people at the meeting? I have some, but not ~. M~ people think so. M~ of them were broken. M~ of us left early. How ~ do you want? How ~ of them were absent? You gave me two too ~. Do you need so ~? He made ten spelling mistakes in as ~ lines,* i e in ten lines. *I have six here and as ~ again* (i e six more) *at home.* ***a great/good ~,*** a large number (of): *I have a good ~ things to do today.* ***one too ~,*** one more than the correct or needed number: *I wish Jane would go away; she's* *one too ~ here,* We don't want her company. *He's had one too ~ again,* is slightly drunk. ***be one too ~ for,*** be more than a match(2) for; get the better of; outwit: *He was one too ~ for you that time.* **the ~,** the masses; the large numbers of ordinary people: *Is it right that the ~ should starve while the few have plenty?* **2 ~ a,** (used with a *sing n;* rather liter, usu replaced by ~ and the *pl n* in ordinary style): *M~ a man* (= M~ men) *would welcome the opportunity. I've been here ~ (and ~) a time. M~'s the time I've...,* I have often.... **ˈ~-ˈsided** *adj* having ~ sides; (fig) having ~ aspects, capabilities, etc: *a ~-sided problem.*

Mao·ism /ˈmaʊɪzm/ *n* political theories and practice of Mao Tse-Tung /ˈmaʊ tseɪ ˈtʊŋ/ born 1893, chairman of the Communist Party in China since 1943. **Mao·ist** /ˈmaʊɪst/ *n* supporter of ~.

Maori /ˈmaʊrɪ/ *n* member, language, of the aboriginal race of New Zealand.

map /mæp/ *n* representation on paper, etc of the earth's surface or a part of it, showing countries, oceans, rivers, mountains, etc; representation of the sky showing positions of the stars, etc. ⇨ the illus at projection. ⇨ chart, plan. ***put sth on the map,*** cause it to be considered important, to be reckoned with. ***off the map,*** (colloq, of a place) inaccessible. **ˈmap-reader** *n* (with an *adj*) person able to get information from maps: *He's a good/poor map-reader.* □ *vt* (-pp-) [VP6A] make a map of; show on a map; [VP15B] ***map out,*** plan, arrange: *map out one's time.*

maple /ˈmeɪpl/ *n* **1** [C] (sorts of) tree of the northern hemisphere, grown for timber and ornament. ⇨ the illus at tree. **ˈ~-sugar/-syrup** *n* sugar/syrup obtained from the sap of one kind of ~. **ˈ~-leaf** *n* emblem of Canada. **2** [U] wood of this tree.

ma·quis /ˈmækɪ *US:* ˈmɑkɪ/ *n* **the ~,** the secret army of French patriots during World War II, fighting in France against the Germans.

mar /mɑ(r)/ *vt* (-rr-) [VP6A] injure; spoil; damage: *Nothing marred the happiness of our outing.* ***make or mar,*** make a great success of or ruin completely.

mara·bou /ˈmærəbu/ *n* large W African stork; tuft of its soft feathers as trimming, e g for a hat.

mar·as·chino /ˈmærəˈʃinəʊ/ *n* (*pl* -nos /-nəʊz/) sweet liqueur made from a small black kind of cherry.

mara·thon /ˈmærəθən *US:* -θon/ *n* **the M~,** long-distance race on foot (about 26 miles (or 41·8 kilometres) at modern sports meetings); (fig) test of endurance.

ma·raud /məˈrɔd/ *vi* [VP2A] go about in search of plunder or prey: *The Roman Empire was attacked by ~ing Goths and Huns.* **~er** *n* person or animal that ~s.

marble /ˈmɑbl/ *n* **1** [U] (sorts of) hard limestone used, when cut and polished, for building and sculpture: (attrib) *a ~ statue/tomb.* **2** (*pl*) works of art in ~; collection of ~ sculptures. **3** small ball of glass, clay or stone used in games played by children; (*pl*) game played with these balls: *a game of ~s.* **4** (attrib) like ~: *a ~ brow,* smooth and white; *a ~ breast,* hard and unsympathizing. **marbled** *adj* stained or printed so as to look like variegated ~: *a book with ~d edges.*

March /mɑtʃ/ *n* the third month of the year: *M~ hare,* ⇨ hare.

march[1] /mɑtʃ/ *vi,vt* **1** [VP2A,B,C] walk as soldiers do, with regular and measured steps: *They have ~ed thirty miles today. They ~ed into the town. Quick ~!* (military command to begin ~ing). *The troops ~ed by/past/in/out/off/away. He ~ed impatiently up and down the station platform.* **~ing orders,** orders for troops to leave for manœuvres, for war, etc. **2** [VP15A,B] cause to ~: *They ~ed the prisoner away. He was ~ed off to prison.*

march[2] /mɑtʃ/ *n* **1** [U] act of marching (by soldiers, etc). ***on the ~,*** marching. ***a line of ~,*** a route followed by troops when ~ing: *Scouts were sent out to discover the enemy's line of ~.* **2** [C] instance of marching; distance travelled: *a ~ of ten miles.* ***a ~ past,*** i e of troops past a saluting point at a review. ***a forced ~,*** one made more quickly than usual, or for a greater distance, in an emergency. ***steal a ~ on sb,*** win a position of advantage by doing sth earlier than expected by him. **3** (*sing* with *def art*) progress; onward movement: *the ~ of events/time.* **4** [C] piece of music for marching to: *military ~es; a dead ~,* one in slow time for a funeral. **~er** *n*

march[3] /mɑtʃ/ *n* (usu *pl*) frontier areas (esp between England and Scotland or Wales), esp land that is in dispute: *riding round the ~es.* □ *vi* (archaic) [VP3A] **~ *upon/with,*** (of countries, estates, etc) border upon; have a common frontier with: *Our territory ~es with theirs.*

mar·chion·ess /ˈmɑʃnˈes/ *n* wife or widow of a marquis; woman who holds in her own right a position equal to that of a marquis.

Mardi gras /ˈmɑdɪ ˈgrɑ/ *n* (F) Shrove Tuesday; last day of carnival before Lent, celebrated in some places with parades and merrymaking.

mare /meə(r)/ *n* female horse or donkey. **a ~'s nest,** a hoax; a discovery that turns out to be false or worthless.

mar·gar·ine /ˈmɑdʒəˈrin *US:* ˈmɑdʒərɪn/ *n* [U] food substance, used like butter, made from animal or vegetable fats.

marge /mɑdʒ/ *n* (colloq abbr for) margarine.

mar·gin /ˈmɑdʒɪn/ *n* [C] **1** blank space round the printed or written matter on a page: *wide/narrow ~s; notes written in the ~.* **2** edge or border: *sit on the ~ of a lake/swimming pool; road ~s.* **3** amount (of time, money, etc) above what is estimated as necessary. **4** condition near the limit or borderline, below or beyond which sth is impossible: *a safety ~. He escaped defeat by a narrow ~.* **5** (comm) difference between cost price and selling price: *an increase of a penny a gallon in the dealer's ~ on the price of petrol.* **~al** /-nl/ *adj* **1** of or in a ~(1): *~al notes.* **2** of a ~(4): *~al land,* land which is not fertile enough for profitable farming except when prices of farm products are high; *a ~al seat/constituency,* one where the M P has been elected by a small majority. *The differences between the employers and the workers are ~al.* **~·ally** /-nlɪ/ *adv*

Mar·grave /ˈmɑgreɪv/ *n* hereditary title of certain princes in the Holy Roman Empire.

mar·guer·ite /ˈmɑgəˈrit/ *n* kinds of daisy, esp the ox-eye daisy with white petals round a yellow centre.

mari·gold /ˈmærɪgəʊld/ *n* (kinds of) plant with orange or yellow flowers.

mari·juana, mari·huana /ˈmærɪˈwɑnə/ *n* (also called *hashish, cannabis, pot*) dried leaves and flowers of Indian hemp smoked in cigarettes (called *reefers* or *joints*) to induce euphoria.

mar·imba /məˋrɪmbə/ *n* musical instrument similar to the xylophone.

ma·rina /məˋrinə/ *n* harbour designed for pleasure boats (small yachts, cabin cruisers, etc) often with hotels, etc.

mari·nade /ˌmærɪˋneɪd/ *n* [U] pickle of wine, vinegar and spice; fish or meat pickled in this. □ *vt* (also **mari·nate** /ˋmærɪneɪt/) steep, make tender, in ~.

mar·ine /məˋrin/ *adj* **1** of, by, found in, produced by, the sea: *~ products; a* ˋ*~ painter*, artist who paints seascapes. **2** of ships, sea-trade, the navy, etc: *~ insurance*, of ships and cargo; *~ stores*, materials and supplies for ships. **a ~ corps,** of soldiers serving on warships and trained for amphibious warfare. □ *n* **1** ˌ**merchant/** ˌ**mercantile** ˋ**~,** all the merchant ships of a country. **2** [C] soldier serving on a warship. ***Tell that to the ~s,*** (used to express disbelief in an impossible story).

mari·ner /ˋmærɪnə(r)/ *n* sailor, esp one who assists in navigating a ship: *a ~'s compass;* (official use) *master ~*, captain of a merchant ship.

mari·on·ette /ˌmærɪəˋnet/ *n* jointed doll or puppet moved by strings on a small stage.

mari·tal /ˋmærɪtl/ *adj* of a husband; of marriage: *~ obligations*, e g providing for one's wife.

mari·time /ˋmærɪtaɪm/ *adj* **1** connected with the sea or navigation: *~ law; the great ~ powers.* **2** situated or found near the sea: *the ~ provinces of the USSR.*

mar·joram /ˋmɑdʒərəm/ *n* [U] sweet-smelling herb used as seasoning in cooking and in medicine.

mark[1] /mɑk/ *n* **1** line, scratch, cut, stain, etc that spoils the appearance of sth: *Who made these dirty ~s on my new book?* **2** noticeable spot on the body by which a person or animal may be recognized: *a horse with a white ~ on its head; a* ˋ*birth~.* **3** visible trace; sign or indication (of a quality, etc): *~s of suffering/old age. Please accept this gift as a ~ of my esteem.* **4** figure, design, line, etc, made as a sign or indication: ˌ*punctuˋation ~s;* ˋ*price-~s*, on goods; ˋ*trade ~s.* **5** numerical or alphabetical symbol, e g $\beta +$, to indicate an award in an examination, or for conduct. ***give sb/get/gain a good/bad, etc ~ (for sth)***: *get 72 ~s out of 100 for geography/full ~s for science. He got the best ~s of his year.* **6** target; sth aimed at. ***be/fall wide of the ~,*** be inaccurate, imprecise: *Your guess/calculation is wide of the ~.* ***hit/miss the ~,*** (fig) succeed/fail in an attempt. ***an easy ~,*** (colloq) person who is easily cheated, persuaded or ridiculed. ***beside the ~,*** irrelevant. **7** [U] distinction; fame: ***make one's ~,*** become distinguished. **8** (*sing* only) standard. ***be up to/below the ~,*** equal to/below the required standard. **9** what is normal. ***not be/feel (quite) up to the ~,*** not in one's usual health. **10** cross made on a document by an illiterate person: *make one's ~. John Doe, his ~*, cross made by John Doe instead of a signature. **11** (athletics) line indicating the starting-point of a race: *On your ~s, get set, go!* (words used by the starter). **12** (with numbers) model or type: *Meteor M~ III*, e g of an aircraft.

mark[2] /mɑk/ *vt* **1** [VP6A,15A,B] ***~ sth on/with sth, ~ sth down/up,*** put or have a ~ on sth by writing, stamping, etc: *~ one's name on one's clothes/~ one's clothes with one's name. All our stock has been ~ed down for the sales,* reduced in prices. *The new tax made it necessary to ~ up all the goods in the shop,* put higher price ~s on them. Hence, ˋ**~-up** *n* amount by which a price is ~ed up: *a 10% ~-up.* ˋ**~·ing-ink** *n* indelible ink for ~ing linen, etc. **2** (passive) have natural ~s or visible signs: *A zebra is ~ed with stripes. His face is ~ed with smallpox,* has the scars of smallpox. *Her face is ~ed with grief.* **3** [VP6A] give ~s(5) to: *~ examination papers; have twenty essays to ~/to be ~ed.* **4** [VP22] indicate sth by putting a ~, e g a tick or a cross, on or against: *~ sth wrong; ~ a pupil absent.* **5** [VP6A,8,10,2A] pay attention (to): *M~ carefully how it is done/how to do it/how he does it.* ***(You) M~ my words,*** Note what I say (and you will find, later, that I am right). **a ~ed man,** one whose conduct is watched with suspicion or enmity. **6** [VP6A] be a distinguishing feature of: *What are the qualities that ~ a great leader?* **7** [VP6A] signal; denote: *His death ~ed the end of an era. There will be ceremonies to ~ the tenth anniversary of the Queen's accession.* **8** ***~ time,*** stamp the feet as when marching but without moving forward; (fig) wait until further progress becomes possible. **9** [VP15B] (uses with *adverbial particles*) ***~ sth off,*** put ~s on (to show boundary lines, measurements, etc). ***~ sth out,*** put lines on sth to indicate limits, etc: *~ out a tennis-court.* ***~ sb out for sth,*** decide in advance that sb will receive sth: *~ sb out for promotion. Peter was ~ed out for a special management course.* **~ed** *adj* clear: readily seen: *a ~ed difference/improvement; a man of ~ed ability.* **~·ed·ly** /ˋmɑkɪdlɪ/ *adv* in a ~ed manner. **~·ing** *n* (esp) pattern of different colours of feathers, skin, etc.

mark[3] /mɑk/ *n* unit of German currency.

marker /ˋmɑkə(r)/ *n* **1** person or tool that marks, esp a person who marks the score at games, e g billiards. **2** sth that marks or indicates, e g a flag or post on a playing field, a post showing distances.

mar·ket[1] /ˋmɑkɪt/ *n* **1** [C] public place (an open space or a building) where people meet to buy and sell goods; time during which such a meeting takes place: *She went to (the) ~ to buy food for the family. There are numerous small ~s in the town. The next ~ is on the 15th.* ***bring one's eggs/hogs to a bad ~/to the wrong ~,*** fail in one's plans, fail because one goes to the wrong people for help. ***go to ~,*** go there for the purpose of shopping. ***go to a bad/good ~,*** be un/successful. ˋ**~-day** *n* fixed day on which a ~ is held. ˌ**~-ˋgarden** *n* one where vegetables are grown for ~s. ˌ**~-ˋgardening** *n* ˋ**~-place/-square** *n* square or open place in a town where a ~ is held. ˋ**~ hall,** (usu large) roofed area for a ~. ˋ**~-town** *n* one where a ~ (esp one for cattle and sheep) is held. **2** trade in a class of goods: *the* ˋ*corn ~; the* ˋ*coffee ~*; state of trade as shown by prices: *a dull/lively ~. The ~ rose/fell/was steady,* Prices rose/fell/did not change much. **~ price,** price for which sth, e g commodities/securities, is sold in the open ~. **3** demand: *There's no/not much/only a poor ~ for these goods.* **4** (*sing* only) buying and selling. ***be on/come on (to) the ~,*** be offered for sale: *This house will probably come on the market next month.* ***be in the ~ for sth,*** be ready to buy sth. ***play the ~,*** speculate (by buying and selling shares, commodities, etc). ***put sth on the ~,*** offer it for sale. **'~ re'search,** study of the reasons why people buy, or do not buy, certain goods, how sales are affected by advertising, etc. **5** [C] area, country, in which goods may be sold: *We must find new ~s for our manufacturers. Which countries are Brazil's best ~s for coffee?* **'Common 'M~,** ⇨ common[1](1).

mar·ket[2] /ˈmɑkɪt/ *vi,vt* **1** [VP2A] buy or sell in a ~: *go ~ing.* **2** [VP6A] take or send to ~; prepare for ~ and offer for sale. **'~·able** /-əbl/ *adj* that can be sold; fit to be sold: *~able products.* **'~·ing** *n* theory and practice of (large-scale) selling.

marks·man /ˈmɑksmən/ *n* (*pl* -men /-mən/) person skilled in aiming at a mark, esp with a rifle. **'~·ship** /-ʃɪp/ *n* skill in shooting.

marl /mɑl/ *n* [U] soil consisting of clay and carbonate of lime, used as a fertilizer.

mar·line·spike /ˈmɑlɪnspaɪk/ *n* pointed iron tool used for separating the strands of a rope which is to be spliced.

mar·ma·lade /ˈmɑməleɪd/ *n* [U] (bitter) jam made from citrus fruit (usu oranges).

mar·mor·eal /ˈmɑˈmɔrɪəl/ *adj* (poet) white, cold or polished, like marble.

mar·mo·set /ˈmɑməzet/ *n* small, tropical American monkey with soft, thick hair and a bushy tail. ⇨ the illus at ape.

mar·mot /ˈmɑmət/ *n* small animal of the squirrel family.

ma·ro·cain /ˈmærəˈkeɪn/ *n* [U] thin, fine dress material of silk or wool.

ma·roon[1] /məˈrun/ *adj, n* brownish-red (colour).

ma·roon[2] /məˈrun/ *n* rocket, esp the kind used as a warning signal.

ma·roon[3] /məˈrun/ *vt* [VP6A] put (sb) on a desert island, uninhabited coast, etc, and abandon him there. □ *n* West Indian Negro; (esp former times) fugitive from slavery.

marque /mɑk/ *n* **1** **'letters of '~,** authority formerly given to private persons to fit out an armed ship and use it to attack, capture, and plunder enemy merchant ships in time of war. **2** = mark[1](12) (esp for cars).

mar·quee /mɑˈki/ *n* large tent (as used for flower shows, garden parties, or for a circus).

mar·quetry /ˈmɑkɪtrɪ/ *n* [U] inlaid work (wood, ivory, etc) used for decorating furniture.

mar·quis, mar·quess /ˈmɑkwɪs/ *n* (GB) nobleman next in rank above an earl and below a duke; (in other countries) nobleman next in rank above a count. ⇨ marchioness.

mar·riage /ˈmærɪdʒ/ *n* **1** [C,U] (instance of a) legal union of a man and woman as husband and wife; state of being married: *A ~ has been arranged between... and.... She has had an offer of ~.* ***give sb*** (esp one's daughter) ***in ~ (to sb),*** to offer her as a wife. ***take sb in ~,*** take as husband or wife. **'~ certificate/licence/settlement,** ⇨ these words. **'~ lines,** (colloq) ~ certificate. **2** (usu *wedding*) ceremony of being married: *Was it a civil or a church ~?* ⇨ civil(1). **'~·able** /-əbl/ *adj* (of a young person) old enough, fit for, ~: *a girl of ~able age.* **~·abil·ity** /ˈmærɪdʒəˈbɪlətɪ/ *n*

mar·ried /ˈmærɪd/ *adj* united in marriage; of marriage: *~ couples; ~ life.*

mar·row /ˈmærəʊ/ *n* **1** [U] soft, fatty substance that fills the hollow parts of bones. ***chilled to the ~,*** cold through and through. **'~·bone** *n* bone containing edible ~. **2** [U] (fig) essence; essential part: *the pith and ~ of his statement.* **3** [C] **('vegetable) ~,** vegetable of the gourd family (US = squash), like a large fat cucumber; [U] this as food, e g stuffed with minced meat: *stuffed ~ for lunch.* ⇨ the illus at vegetable.

marry /ˈmærɪ/ *vt,vi* (*pt,pp* -ried) **1** [VP6A,2A,4A] take as a husband or wife; have a husband or wife: *John is going to ~ Jane. Tom and Alice are going to get married. Mary married a Frenchman. Harry didn't ~ until he was over fifty. She married again six months after the death of her first husband. She married to get away from her tyrannical mother.* **2** [VP6A] (of a priest, a civil official) join as husband or wife: *Which priest is going to ~ them?* **3** [VP6A,15B] give in marriage: *He married both his daughters to rich directors. She has married off all her daughters,* has found husbands for them. **4** obtain by ~ing: *~ money/wealth.*

Mars /mɑz/ *n* **1** (Roman myth) the god of war. **2** (astron) planet fourth in order from the sun. ⇨ the illus at planet.

Mar·sala /mɑˈsɑlə/ *n* [U] sweet white wine originally exported from Marsala, Sicily.

Mar·seil·laise /ˈmɑsəˈleɪz/ *n* French national anthem.

marsh /mɑʃ/ *n* [C,U] (area of) low-lying, wet land: *miles and miles of ~; the Romney ~es.* **'~ gas,** fire-damp; methane. **'~-'mallow** *n* **(a)** shrubby herb that grows near salt ~es. **(b)** soft, spongy sweetmeat. **~y** *adj* (-ier, -iest) of or like a ~.

mar·shal[1] /ˈmɑʃl/ *n* **1** ⇨ App 9. Officer of highest rank: *'Field-'M~,* Army; *'Air-'M~,* Air Force. **2** official responsible for important public events or ceremonies, e g one who accompanies a High Court judge; an officer of the royal household. **3** (US) official with the functions of a sheriff; head of a fire or police department.

mar·shal[2] /ˈmɑʃl/ *vt* (-ll-, US -l-) [VP6A,15A,B] **1** arrange in proper order: *~ facts/military forces.* **'marshalling-yard** *n* railway yard in which goods trains, etc are assembled. **2** guide or lead (sb) with ceremony: *~ persons into the presence of the Queen.*

mar·su·pial /mɑˈsupɪəl/ *adj, n* (animal) of the class of mammals the females of which have a pouch in which to carry their young, which are born before developing completely, e g kangaroos.

mart /mɑt/ *n* **1** (liter) market-place; centre of commerce. **2** auction room.

mar·ten /ˈmɑtɪn/ *n* [C] small animal of the weasel family; [U] its fur.

mar·tial /ˈmɑʃl/ *adj* **1** of, associated with, war: *~ music; ~ bearing.* **'~ 'law,** military government, by which ordinary law is suspended, e g during a rebellion; *declare ~ law; be under ~ law.* **2** brave; fond of fighting: *show a ~ spirit,* show eagerness for war. **~ly** /-ʃlɪ/ *adv*

Mar·tian /ˈmɑʃn/ *n, adj* (hypothetical inhabitant) of the planet Mars.

mar·tin /ˈmɑtɪn *US:* -tn/ *n* **('house-)~,** bird of the swallow family that builds a mud nest on walls, etc.

mar·ti·net /ˈmɑtɪˈnet *US:* -tnˈet/ *n* person who requires and enforces strict discipline.

mar·tini /mɑˈtinɪ/ *n* cocktail made of gin and dry vermouth.

Mar·tin·mas /ˈmɑtɪnməs *US:* -tn-/ *n* St Martin's Day, 11 Nov, a quarter-day in Scotland.

mar·tyr /ˈmɑtə(r)/ *n* person who is put to death or caused to suffer greatly for his religious beliefs or for the sake of a great cause or principle: *the early Christian ~s in Rome. He died a ~ in the cause of science,* lost his life through his efforts to help forward the cause of science. ***make a ~ of oneself,*** sacrifice one's own wishes or advantage (or pretend to do so) in order to get credit or reputation. ***be a ~ to sth,*** suffer greatly from: *He's a ~ to rheumatism.* □ *vt* [VP6A] put to death, cause to suffer, as a ~. **ˈ~·dom** /-dəm/ *n* ~'s suffering or death: *His wife's never-ending complaints made his life one long ~dom.*

mar·vel /ˈmɑvl/ *n* [C] **1** wonderful thing; sth causing great surprise, pleased astonishment: *the ~s of modern science. It's a ~ to me that he escaped unhurt. The doctor's pills worked ~s,* had wonderful results. **2** ***~ of sth,*** wonderful example: *She's a ~ of patience. Your room is a ~ of neatness and order.* □ *vi* (-ll-, US -l-) **1** [VP3A] ***~ (at sth),*** be greatly surprised (at): *~ at sb's boldness.* **2** [VP3B] ***~ that/why, etc,*** wonder: *I ~ that she should agree to marry that man/~ why she should want to marry him.* **~·lous,** (US = **~·ous**) /ˈmɑvləs/ *adj* astonishing; wonderful. **~·lous·ly** (US = **~·ous·ly**) *adv*

Marx·ist /ˈmɑksɪst/ *n* follower of Karl Marx /mɑks/, (1818—83) the German economist and socialist: (attrib) *~ dogma; a ~ position.* **Marx·ism** /ˈmɑksɪzm/ *n* (esp) economic theory that class struggle has been the major force behind historical change, that the dominant class has exploited the masses and that capitalism will inevitably be superseded by socialism and a classless society.

mar·zi·pan /ˈmɑzɪpæn/ *n* [U] thick paste of ground almonds, sugar, etc, made up into small cakes; [C] small cake made of this mixture.

mas·cara /mæˈskɑrə/ *n* [U] cosmetic preparation for darkening the eyelashes.

mas·cot /ˈmæskət/ *n* person, animal or object considered likely to bring good fortune.

mas·cu·line /ˈmæskjʊlɪn/ *adj* **1** of, like, the male sex: *a ~ style; a ~ woman.* **2** of male gender: *'He' and 'him' are ~ pronouns.* **mas·cu·lin·ity** /ˌmæskjʊˈlɪnətɪ/ *n* quality of being ~. ⇨ **feminine.**

ma·ser /ˈmeɪzə(r)/ *n* device for producing or amplifying micro waves.

mash /mæʃ/ *n* [U] **1** grain, bran, etc cooked in water for poultry, cattle or pigs. **2** any substance softened and crushed, e g boiled potatoes beaten and crushed: *a plate of sausage and ~.* **3** mixture of malt and hot water used in brewing. □ *vt* [VP6A] beat or crush into a ~: *~ed turnips.* **~er** *n* cooking utensil for ~ing, e g potatoes.

mashie /ˈmæʃɪ/ *n* golf club with a metal head.

mask[1] /mɑsk *US:* mæsk/ *n* **1** covering for the face, or part of it, e g a piece of silk or velvet for hiding the face at balls; replica of the face carved in wood, ivory, etc; disguise. ***do sth under a/the ~ of friendship,*** while pretending to be a friend. ***throw off one's ~,*** (fig) show one's true character and intentions. **2** (ˈ**gas**)-**~,** breathing apparatus, in some cases for the whole of the head, worn as a protection against poisonous gas, smoke, etc, e g in coalmines, or by a fireman in a burning building. **3** pad of sterile gauze worn over the mouth and nose by doctors and nurses, e g for a surgical operation. **4** replica of the face worn by an actor or actress. **5** likeness of a face made by taking a mould in wax, etc, esp: ˈ**death ~,** one made by taking a mould of the face of a dead person. **6** face or head of a fox.

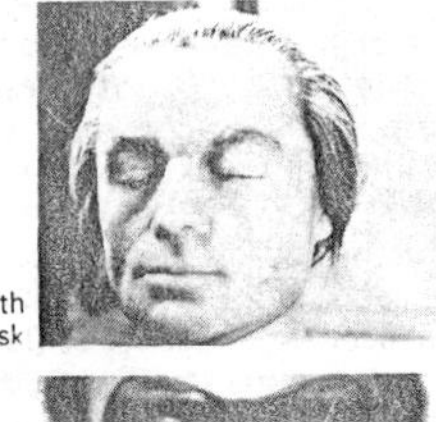

death mask

masks

mask[2] /mɑsk *US:* mæsk/ *vt* [VP6A] **1** cover (the face) with a mask: *a ~ed woman,* one wearing a mask; *a ~ed ball,* one at which masks are worn. **2** conceal: *~ one's enmity under an appearance of friendliness; ~ed guns,* hidden from the enemy.

maso·chism /ˈmæsəkɪzm/ *n* [U] mental disorder which causes a sufferer to get satisfaction (esp sexual pleasure) from (self-inflicted) pain or humiliation. ⇨ **Sadism. maso·chist** /-kɪst/ *n* **maso·chis·tic** /ˌmæsəˈkɪstɪk/ *adj*

ma·son /ˈmeɪsn/ *n* **1** stone-cutter; worker who builds or works with stone. **2** freemason. **~ic** /məˈsonɪk/ *adj* of freemasons. **~ry** /ˈmeɪsnrɪ/ *n* **1** stonework; that part of a building made of stone and mortar. **2** freemasonry.

Mason-Dixon line /ˈmeɪsn ˈdɪksn lɑɪn/ *n* (US) boundary between Pennsylvania and Maryland, dividing the free and the slave States before the Civil War.

masque /mɑsk *US:* mæsk/ *n* drama in verse, often with music, dancing, fine costumes and pageantry, esp as given in castles and great mansions in England during the 16th and 17th cc.

mas·quer·ade /ˌmɑskəˈreɪd *US:* ˌmæsk-/ *n* **1** ball at which masks and other disguises are worn. **2** (fig) false show or pretence. □ *vi* [VP2A,C] ***~ (as),*** appear, be, in disguise: *a prince who ~d as a peasant.*

mass /mæs/ *n* **1** [C] ***~ (of),*** lump, quantity of matter, without regular shape; large number, quantity or heap: *~es of dark clouds in the sky. The azaleas made a ~ of colour in the garden. A ~ of snow and rock broke away and started an avalanche. The poor fellow was a ~ of bruises,* (colloq) was covered with bruises. **2 the ~es,** the proletariat; (manual) workers. ***in the ~,*** in the main; as a whole: *The nation in the ~ was not interested in politics.* **~ meeting,** large meeting, esp of people wishing, or requested, to express their views (protesting against sth, urging that sth be done, etc). **ˌ~ comˌmuniˈcations, ˌ~ ˈmedia,** means (esp newspapers, radio, TV) of imparting information to, influencing the ideas of, enormous numbers of people. **ˌ~ ˌobserˈvation,** study of the social customs of ordinary people. **ˌ~ proˈduction,** manufacture of large numbers of identical articles by standardized processes. Hence, **ˌ~-proˈduce** *vt* **3** [U] (science) quantity of material in a body measured by its resistance to change of motion. ⇨ **size**[1]**(1).** □ *vt,vi* [VP6A,2A] form or collect into a ~: *~ed bands,* number of bands(5) playing together. *Troops are ~ing/are being ~ed on the frontier. The clouds are ~ing.* **~y** *adj* solid; massive.

Mass /mæs/ *n* celebration (esp RC) of the Eucharist: *High/Low ~*, with/without incense, music and considerable ceremony; *go to ~; hear ~. M~es were said for peace in the world.*

mass·acre /ˈmæsəkə(r)/ *n* [C] cruel killing of large numbers of (esp defenceless) people (occasionally used of animals). □ *vt* [VP6A] make a ~ of.

mass·age /ˈmæsɑʒ/ *n* [C,U] (instance of) pressing and rubbing the body, usu with the hands, esp the muscles and joints, in order to lessen pain, stiffness, etc. □ *vt* [VP6A] apply ~ to. **mass·eur** /mæˈsɜ(r)/, **mass·euse** /mæˈsɜz/ *nn* man, woman, who practises ~. ⇨ *physiotherapist* at **physiotherapy.**

massif /mæˈsif/ *n* compact group of mountain heights.

mass·ive /ˈmæsɪv/ *adj* **1** large, heavy and solid: *a ~ monument.* **2** (of the features) heavy-looking: *a ~ forehead.* **3** (fig) substantial; impressive. **~·ly** *adv* **~·ness** *n*

mast[1] /mɑst *US:* mæst/ *n* **1** upright support (of wood or metal) for a ship's sails. ⇨ the illus at **barque, sailing.** ***sail before the ~,*** (now usu *teaching-post*) *in a common seaman* (*with a berth in the forepart of the ship*). **ˈ~-head** *n* highest part of a ~, used as a look-out post. **2** tall pole (for a flag). **3** tall steel structure for aerials of a radio or television transmitter; (also *ˈmooring-~*) tall tower to which an airship may be moored.

mast[2] /mɑst *US:* mæst/ *n* [U] fruit of beech, oak and other forest trees (as food for pigs).

mas·ter[1] /ˈmɑstə(r) *US:* ˈmæs-/ *n* **1** man who has others working for him or under him: *~ and man,* employer and workman (or manservant); (attrib) skilled workman or one in business on his own account: *a ~ carpenter/builder, etc.* ***be one's own ~,*** be free and independent. **2** male head of a household: *the ~ of the house.* ***be ~ in one's own house,*** manage one's affairs without interference from others. **3** captain of a merchant ship: *a ~ mariner; obtain a ~'s certificate,* one that gives the holder the right to be a ship's captain. **4** male owner of a dog, horse, etc. **5** male teacher: *the ˌmatheˈmatics ~; ˈschool~; ˈhouse~,* ⇨ **house**[1](7); male teacher of subjects taught outside school: *a ˈdancing/ˈfencing/ˈriding-~.* **6** ***~ of,*** person who has control or who has (sth) at his disposal: *He is ~ of the situation,* has it under control. *If only I could be ~ of this subject,* come to know it thoroughly. *He has made himself ~ of the language,* has learnt it well, so that he can use it freely. *You cannot be the ~ of your fate,* cannot decide your own destiny. *He is ~ of a large fortune,* can use it as he wishes. **7 the M~,** Jesus Christ. **ˌM~ of ˈArts/ˈScience, etc,** holder of the second university degree. ⇨ **bachelor. 8** (with a boy's name) young Mr: *M~ Charles Smith,* sometimes used when speaking of or to a boy up to about the age of 14. **9** title of the heads of certain colleges: *the M~ of Balliol,* Oxford. **10** great artists, esp **old ~s,** the great painters of the 13th to 17th cc; painting by one of these artists. **11** (attrib) commanding; superior: *the work of a ~ hand,* a superior and skilful artist, etc. *His ~ passion* (= The passion that dominates his thoughts, etc) *is motor-racing.* **ˈ~-mind,** person with superior brains (esp one who plans work to be carried out by others). Hence, **ˈ~-mind** *vt* plan, direct, a scheme: *The whole affair was ~-minded by the publicity department.* **12** as title of various officials. **M~ of the Horse,** official in the royal household. **M~ of foxhounds,** man who controls them. **M~ of Ceremonies,** (abbr **MC**) person who superintends the forms to be observed on various social occasions, e g a public banquet. **13** (compounds) **ˌ~-at-ˈarms** *n* police officer in the Navy and in passenger ships of the merchant service. **ˈ~-key** *n* one that will open many different locks, each also opened by a separate key. **ˈ~-piece** *n* sth made or done with very great skill. **ˈ~·stroke** *n* surpassingly skilful act or piece (of policy, etc).

mas·ter[2] /ˈmɑstə(r) *US:* ˈmæs-/ *vt* [VP6A] become the ~ of; overcome: *~ one's temper/feelings; ~ a foreign language/the saxophone.* **~·less** *adj* having no ~.

mas·ter·ful /ˈmɑstəfl *US:* ˈmæs-/ *adj* fond of controlling others; dominating: *speak in a ~ manner.* **~ly** /-flɪ/ *adv*

mas·ter·ly /ˈmɑstəlɪ *US:* ˈmæs-/ *adj* worthy of a great master; very skilful: *with a few ~ strokes of the brush.*

mas·ter·ship /ˈmɑstəʃɪp *US:* ˈmæs-/ *n* **1** [U] dominion; control. **2** [C] office, duties, of (esp a school)master: *He was offered an assistant-~* (now usu *teaching post*) *in Bolton.*

mas·tery /ˈmɑstərɪ *US:* ˈmæs-/ *n* [U] **1** ***~ (of),*** complete control or knowledge: *his ~ of the violin; get ~ of a wild horse.* **2** ***~ (over),*** supremacy: *Which side will get the ~?*

mas·ti·cate /ˈmæstɪkeɪt/ *vt* [VP6A] chew; soften, grind up (food) with the teeth. **mas·ti·ca·tion** /ˌmæstɪˈkeɪʃn/ *n*

mas·tiff /ˈmæstɪf/ *n* large, strong dog with drooping ears, much used as a watchdog.

mas·to·don /ˈmæstədon/ *n* large extinct elephant-like animal.

mas·toid /ˈmæstɔɪd/ *n* bone at the back of the ear. **~·itis** /ˌmæstɔɪˈdɑɪtɪs/ *n* inflammation of the ~.

mas·tur·bate /ˈmæstəbeɪt/ *vi* procure sexual excitement by manual or other stimulation of the genital organs. **mas·tur·ba·tion** /ˌmæstəˈbeɪʃn/ *n*

mat[1] /mæt/ *n* **1** piece of material (woven or plaited, of straw, rope, rushes, rags, fibre, etc) used for a floor covering, for packing furniture, for sleeping on, or (a *ˈdoormat*) for wiping dirty shoes on. **2** small piece of material placed under vases, ornaments, etc, or (a *ˈtable-mat* of cork, asbestos, etc) under hot dishes on a table (to prevent injury to a varnished surface, etc). **3** anything thickly tangled or twisted together: *a mat of weeds; comb the mats out of a dog's thick hair.* □ *vt,vi* (-tt-) [VP6A] cover or supply with mats; [VP6A,15A,2A,C] (cause to) be or become tangled or knotted: *matted hair.*

mat[2], **matt** (US = **matte**) /mæt/ *adj* (of surfaces, e g paper) dull; not shiny or glossy: *paint that dries with a ~ finish.* ⇨ **gloss**[1](1).

mata·dor /ˈmætədɔ(r)/ *n* man whose task is to kill the bull in the sport of bull-fighting.

match[1] /mætʃ/ *n* short piece of wood, pasteboard, wax taper, etc, with a head made of material that bursts into flame when rubbed on a rough or specially prepared surface (the second kind being called *ˈsafety ~es*): *strike a ~; a box of ~es.* **ˈ~-box** *n* box for holding ~es. **ˈ~·wood** *n* **(a)** wood suitable for making ~es. **(b)** splinters or fragments of wood: *smashed to ~wood,* completely destroyed (esp fig) or broken up.

match[2] /mætʃ/ *n* **1** contest; game: *a `football/ `wrestling ~; a `boxing ~ of twenty rounds.* **'~-`point,** final point needed to win a ~, e g tennis. **2** person able to meet another as his equal in strength, skill, etc: *find/meet one's ~. He is up against more than his ~,* has met sb who is his superior (in skill, etc). *You are no ~ for him,* are not strong, clever, etc enough to compete with him. **3** marriage: *They decided to make a ~ of it,* (of two persons) They decided to marry. **`~-maker** *n* (esp) person who is fond of arranging ~es(3) for others. **4** person considered from the point of view of marriage' *He's a good ~,* is considered satisfactory or desirable as a possible husband. **5** person or thing exactly like, or corresponding to, or combining well with, another: *colours/materials that are a good ~.*

match[3] /mætʃ/ *vt,vi* **1** [VP6A,14] ~ ***sth/sb against/with,*** put in competition: *I'm ready to ~ my strength with/against yours.* **2** [VP6A] be equal to; be, obtain, a match(2) for: *a well-~ed pair,* e g boxers about equal in skill. *No one can ~ him in archery. Can you ~ that story,* tell one that is equally good, amusing, etc? **3** [VP6A,2A] be equal to or corresponding (with) (in quality, colour, design, etc): *The carpets should ~ the curtains. The curtains and carpets should ~. She was wearing a brown dress with hat and gloves to ~.* ⇨ clash(4). **4** [VP6A,12B,13B] find a material, etc that ~es(3) with (another): *Can you ~ (me) this silk?* **5** [VP6A,14] join (one person *with* another) in marriage. **~·less** *adj* unequalled.

matchet /ˈmætʃɪt/ *n* = machete.

match·lock /ˈmætʃlok/ *n* old-fashioned style of musket.

mate[1] /meɪt/ *n* **1** (among working-class men) companion; fellow-workman (often as a form of address): *Where are you going, ~?* ⇨ *class-~* at class, *play~* at play[1](1). **2** ship's officer (not an engineer) below the rank of captain: *the chief ~,* below the captain; *the first/second/third ~.* ⇨ App 9. **3** helper: (in titles) *the cook's/gunner's/ surgeon's ~; a plumber's ~.* **4** one of a pair of birds or animals: *the lioness and her ~.* **5** (colloq) partner in marriage, i e husband or wife: *She has been a faithful ~ to him.*

mate[2] /meɪt/ *vt,vi* [VP6A,14,2A,3A] ~ ***(with),*** (of birds or animals) (cause to) unite for the purpose of having sexual intercourse, producing young: *the `mating season,* spring, when birds make their nests. *The zoo camels have not ~d this year.*

mate[3] /meɪt/ *n, v* (in chess) = checkmate.

maté /ˈmɑteɪ/ *n* (tea made from) dried leaves of a S American evergreen holly shrub.

ma·ter /ˈmeɪtə(r)/ *n* (Lat) (GB schoolboy sl, now dated) mother.

ma·terial[1] /məˈtɪərɪəl/ *adj* **1** (contrasted with *spiritual*) made of, connected with, matter or substance: *the ~ world; a `~ noun,* naming a material, e g stone, wood, wool. **2** of the body; of physical needs: *~ needs,* e g food and warmth; *~ comforts and pleasures; a ~ point of view,* worldly, considering only the things of the senses. **3** (legal) important; essential: *~ evidence/ testimony. The judge warned the witness not to hold back ~ facts,* facts that might influence a decision. ***Is this point ~ to your argument?*** **~ly** /-ɪəlɪ/ *adv* in a ~(3) manner; essentially.

ma·terial[2] /məˈtɪərɪəl/ *n* **1** [C,U] that of which sth is or can be made or with which sth is done: *raw ~s,* not yet used in manufacture; *`dress ~s,* cloth; fabrics from which dresses may be made; *too much ~ for one overcoat; not enough ~ for two overcoats.* **`writing ~s,** pen, ink, paper, etc. **2** [U] (fig) facts, happenings, elements: *~ for a newspaper article; the ~ from which history is made.*

ma·teri·al·ism /məˈtɪərɪəl-ɪzm/ *n* [U] **1** theory, belief, that only material things exist. **2** tendency to value, valuation of, material things (wealth, bodily comforts, etc) too much and spiritual and intellectual things too little. **ma·teri·al·ist** /-ɪst/ *n* believer in ~; person who ignores religion, art, music, etc. **ma·teri·al·is·tic** /məˈtɪərɪəˈlɪstɪk/ *adj* of ~ or materialists. **ma·teri·al·is·ti·cally** /-klɪ/ *adv*

ma·teri·al·ize /məˈtɪərɪəlɑɪz/ *vi* [VP6A,2A] take material form; (cause to) become fact: *Our plans did not ~,* came to nothing, were not carried out. *The boy didn't ~,* (colloq) arrive. **ma·teri·al·iz·ation** /məˈtɪərɪəlɑɪˈzeɪʃn *US:* -lɪˈz-/ *n*

ma·ternal /məˈtɜnl/ *adj* of or like a mother: *~ care/instincts; my ~ grandfather/aunt, etc,* on my mother's side of the family. **~·ly** /-nlɪ/ *adv*

ma·tern·ity /məˈtɜnətɪ/ *n* [U] being a mother: (attrib) *`~ ward/hospital,* for women who are about to become mothers.

matey /ˈmeɪtɪ/ *adj* ~ ***(with),*** (colloq) sociable, familiar, friendly.

mathe·mat·ics /ˈmæθəˈmætɪks/ *n* (*sing* or *pl v*) science of size and numbers (of which arithmetic, algebra, trigonometry and geometry are branches): *His ~ are weak. M~ is his weak subject.* **math·emat·ical** /ˈmæθəˈmætɪkl/ *adj* of ~. **math·emat·ically** /-klɪ/ *adv* **math·ema·tician** /ˈmæθəməˈtɪʃn/ *n* expert in ~.

maths /mæθs/ (US **math** /mæθ/) *n* (colloq abbr of) mathematics.

mati·née /ˈmætɪneɪ *US:* ˈmætnˈeɪ/ *n* [C] afternoon performance at a cinema or theatre: *`~ idol,* much admired actor.

mat·ins /ˈmætɪnʒ *US:* -tnz/ *n pl* service for Morning Prayer in the Church of England; prayers recited at daybreak in the R C Church.

ma·tri·arch /ˈmeɪtrɪɑk/ *n* woman head of a family or tribe. **ma·tri·archy** /-ɑkɪ/ *n* social organization in which mothers are the heads of families. **ma·tri·ar·chal** /ˈmeɪtrɪˈɑkl/ *adj*

ma·tric /məˈtrɪk/ *n* (colloq abbr of) matriculation.

ma·trices /ˈmeɪtrɪsiz/ *pl* of matrix.

mat·ri·cide /ˈmætrɪsɑɪd/ *n* [U] killing of one's own mother; [C] instance of this; [C] person guilty of this.

ma·tricu·late /məˈtrɪkjʊleɪt/ *vt,vi* **1** [VP6A,2A] (allow to) enter a university as a student, usu after passing an examination; admit, be admitted, as a member of a university. **2** [VP2A,C] (formerly) pass an external examination at school exempting one from some of the requirements for most universities (now replaced by GCE). **ma·tricu·la·tion** /məˈtrɪkjʊˈleɪʃn/ *n* **1** [U] matriculating or being ~d; [C] instance of this. **2** [U] (former) examination for this.

mat·ri·mony /ˈmætrɪmənɪ *US:* -məʊnɪ/ *n* [U] state of being married: *unite persons in holy ~.* **mat·ri·mo·nial** /ˈmætrɪˈməʊnɪəl/ *adj* of ~: *solicitors who help people who have matrimonial troubles,* e g persons wanting divorce.

ma·trix /ˈmeɪtrɪks/ *n* (*pl* matrices /ˈmeɪtrɪsiz/, or

-trixes) **1** mould into which hot metal, or other material in a soft or liquid condition, is poured to be shaped, e g in the printing trade, or for making gramophone records. **2** substance in which a mineral, etc is found embedded in the ground.

ma·tron /ˈmeɪtrən/ *n* **1** woman housekeeper in a school or other institution. **2** woman who manages the domestic affairs and nursing staff of a hospital. **3** married woman or widow (often used with a suggestion of dignity and social position): (dress-making) *styles suitable for ~s,* for middle-aged women. **~·ly** *adj* of, like, suitable for, ~s: *~ly duties; a ~ly* (i e dignified) *manner.*

matt /mæt/ *adj* variant spelling of mat².

mat·ted /ˈmætɪd/ *adj* ⇨ mat¹ *v.*

mat·ter¹ /ˈmætə(r)/ *n* **1** [U] substance(s) of which a physical thing is made (contrasted with mind, spirit, etc): *organic/inorganic ~.* **2** material for thought or expression, substance of a book, speech, etc contrasted with the form or style: *The ~ in your essay is good but the style is deplorable.* **3** [U] sth printed or written. **ˈreading ~,** books, periodicals, etc. **ˈpostal ~,** everything sent by post. **ˈprinted ~,** (used on sth sent by post, to show that it goes out at a rate cheaper than for ordinary letters, etc). **4** [C] sth to which attention is given; piece of business; affair: *ˈmoney ~s. This is a ~ I know little about. There are several ~s to be dealt with at the committee meeting. That's a ~ of opinion,* sth about which opinions may differ. ***a ~ of course,*** sth to be expected in the natural course of events. ***as a ~ of fact,*** in reality; although you may not know it or may be surprised. ***for ˈthat ~, for the ~ of that,*** so far as that is concerned. ***in the ~ of,*** as regards, in what concerns: *He is strict in the ~ of discipline.* ***a ˈhanging ~,*** a crime for which the penalty may be death by hanging. ***no ˈlaughing ~,*** sth serious, sth not to be joked about. **5** [U] importance. ***(make/be) no ~,*** (be) of no importance: *If you can't do it, no ~. It's no ~/makes no ~ whether you arrive early or late.* ***no ~ who/what/where, etc,*** whoever (it is), whatever (happens, etc): *Don't trust him, no ~ what* (= whatever) *he says. Don't believe the rumour, no ~ who* (= whoever) *repeats it/no ~ how often you hear it.* **6** (*sing* with *def art*) ***be the ~ (with),*** be wrong (with): *What's the ~ with it?* (colloq) Surely this is all right, isn't it? *Is there anything the ~ with him,* Is he ill, in trouble, etc (according to context)? **7** [U] pus. **8** (*sing* with *indef art*) ***a ~ of,*** about: *a ~ of 20 weeks/10 miles/£50; within a ~ of hours.* **9** (compounds) **ˈ~-of-ˈcourse** *adj* to be expected. **ˈ~-of-ˈfact** *adj* (of a person, his manner) unimaginative; ordinary; keeping to the facts.

mat·ter² /ˈmætə(r)/ *vi* [VP2A,C] (chiefly in interr, neg and conditional sentences) be of importance: *What does it ~? It doesn't ~ much, does it? It hardly ~s at all. It doesn't ~ to me what you do or where you go.*

mat·ting /ˈmætɪŋ/ *n* [U] rough woven material used for floor covering and for packing goods: *coconut-~.*

mat·tins /ˈmætɪnz *US:* -tnz/ *n pl* = matins.

mat·tock /ˈmætək/ *n* tool used for breaking up hard ground, etc, one end of the metal head being at a right angle to the handle. ⇨ the illus at tool.

mat·tress /ˈmætrəs/ *n* [C] long, thick, flat, oblong pad of wool, hair, feathers, foam rubber, etc on which to sleep. **spring ~,** one with coiled wires fitted inside a padded cover of canvas or other frame of strong material.

matu·rate /ˈmætʃʊreɪt/ *vi* [VP2A] become mature. **matu·ra·tion** /ˈmætʃʊˈreɪʃn/ *n* [U] process of becoming mature.

ma·ture /məˈtʃʊə(r) *US:* -ˈtʊər/ *vt,vi* [VP6A,2A] **1** come or bring to full development or to a state ready for use: *His character ~d during these years. These years ~d his character. This wine has not ~d properly.* **2** (of bills) become due. □ *adj* **1** fully grown or developed; ripe with fully developed powers: *persons of ~ years.* **2** careful; perfected: *after ~ deliberation; ~ plans,* based on ~ deliberation. **3** (in comm, of bills) due for payment. **~·ly** *adv* **ma·tur·ity** /məˈtjʊərətɪ/ *n* [U] the state of being ~.

ma·tuti·nal /məˈtjʊtɪnl *US:* -ˈtutnl/ *adj* (formal) of, occurring in, the morning.

maud·lin /ˈmɔdlɪn/ *adj* sentimental or self-pitying in a silly or tearful way: *The drunken man began to get ~.*

maul /mɔl/ *vt* [VP6A,15B] hurt or injure by rough or brutal handling: *~ed by a tiger. Stop ~ing the cat. His latest novel has been ~ed by the critics,* They have written extremely adverse reviews. *Stop ~ing me about!*

maul·stick /ˈmɔlstɪk/ *n* light stick held by a painter to support the hand that holds the brush.

maun·der /ˈmɔndə(r)/ *vi* [VP2A,C] talk in a rambling way; move or act in a listless way.

Maundy Thurs·day /ˈmɔndɪ ˈθɜzdɪ/ *n* Thursday before Easter, commemorating the Last Supper. ⇨ John 13: 14.

mau·so·leum /ˈmɔsəˈlɪəm/ *n* magnificent and monumental tomb.

mauve /məʊv/ *adj, n* bright but delicate pale purple.

mav·er·ick /ˈmævərɪk/ *n* (US) **1** unbranded calf. **2** unorthodox person; person who dissents from the ideas, etc of an organized group: *~ politicians.*

ma·vis /ˈmeɪvɪs/ *n* (poet) song-thrush.

maw /mɔ/ *n* animal's stomach or outlet; (fig) devouring or destructive agency ready to swallow or engulf sth.

mawk·ish /ˈmɔkɪʃ/ *adj* foolishly sentimental. **~·ly** *adv* **~·ness** *n*

maxi /ˈmæksɪ/ *n* (colloq) woman's ankle-length skirt, coat, cloak, etc.

maxim /ˈmæksɪm/ *n* widely accepted rule of conduct or general truth briefly expressed, e g *'Waste not, want not'.*

Maxim /ˈmæksɪm/ *n* (early type of) quick-firing machine-gun.

maxi·mize /ˈmæksɪmɑɪz/ *vt* [VP6A] increase to a maximum: *~ educational opportunities.* **maxi·mi·za·tion** /ˈmæksɪmɑɪˈzeɪʃn *US:* -mɪˈz-/ *n*

maxi·mum /ˈmæksɪməm/ *n* (*pl* -mums or -ma /-mə/) (opp of *minimum*) greatest possible or recorded degree, quantity, etc: *the ~ temperature recorded in London; a ~ and minimum thermometer,* made so as to register ~ and minimum temperatures; *obtain 81 marks out of a ~ of 100. The ~ load for this lorry is one ton.*

may /meɪ/ *anom fin* (*pt* **might** /mɑɪt/) (*neg* may *not,* shortened to **mayn't** /meɪnt/ and *might not* shortened to **mightn't** /ˈmɑɪtnt/) [VP5] **1** (used to indicate possibility or probability; as *might* is used to indicate a future condition, the perfect infinitive *might have* is used for past time): *That may or may not be true. He may have* (= Perhaps he has) *missed his train. This medicine may/might cure your cough. This might have cured your cough,* if you had taken it. *You may walk* (= It is possible to walk) *for miles and miles among the hills without meeting anyone.* **2** (used to indicate permission or request for permission; *might* suggests greater hesitation or diffidence. ⇨ can[2](3)): *May I come in? Might I make a suggestion? Well, if I may say so,.... You may come if you wish.* **3** (used to indicate uncertainty, and asking for information, or expressing wonder): *Well, who may you be? How old may/might she be?* **4** (used to suggest 'There is good reason'): *You may well say so. Well may/might you be surprised! We may as well stay where we are,* It seems reasonable to do so. *You might just as well go as not,* There is just as much to be said in favour of going as there is against. ⇨ well[2](4). **5** (used to express wishes and hopes): *May you both be happy! May they live long! Long may she live to enjoy her good fortune!* **6** (used to express requests): *You might do me a favour,* Please do sth for me. *I think you might at least offer to help.* **7** (in clauses) (used to express purpose, and after *wish, fear, be afraid,* etc): *He died so that others might live. I'll write to him today so that he may know when to expect us. I'm afraid the news may be true.* **may·be** /ˋmeɪbɪ/ *adv* perhaps; possibly. ***as soon as maybe,*** as soon as possible.

May /meɪ/ *n* **1** the fifth month of the year. **ˋMay Day,** 1st of May, celebrated as a spring festival and also a day for socialist and labour demonstrations. **ˋMay Queen,** girl crowned with flowers on May Day. **ˋmay-beetle, ˋmay-bug** *nn* cockchafer. **ˋmay·fly** *n* short-lived insect that appears in May. **ˋmay·pole** *n* flower-decorated pole danced round on May Day. **2** (small *m*) hawthorn blossom.

may·day /ˋmeɪdeɪ/ *n* (wireless telegraphy) (from French *m'aider,* help me) international signal (used by aircraft and ships) of distress: *a ~ call from an airliner.*

May·fair /ˋmeɪfeə(r)/ *n* fashionable district in the West End of London.

may·hem /ˋmeɪhem/ *n* **1** (old use, and US) crime of maiming. **2** state of violent disorder; havoc: *cause/create ~.*

may·on·naise /ˈmeɪəˋneɪz *US:* ˋmeɪəneɪz/ *n* [U] thick dressing of eggs, cream, oil, vinegar, etc used on cold foods, esp salads; dish of food with this dressing: *salmon ~.*

mayor /meə(r) *US:* ˋmeɪə(r)/ *n* head of a municipal corporation of a city or borough. **~·ess** /meəˋres *US:* ˋmeɪərəs/ *n* wife or female relative of a ~, helping in social duties; woman holding the office of ~. **~·alty** /ˋmeərltɪ *US:* ˋmeɪər-/ *n* ~'s (period of) office.

maze /meɪz/ *n* **1** network of lines, paths, etc; labyrinth: *a ~ of narrow alleys.* **2** state of confusion or bewilderment (when faced by a confused mass of facts, etc). ***be in a ~,*** be puzzled, bewildered. **mazed** *adj* bewildered.

ma·zurka /məˋzɜkə/ *n* (piece of music for a) lively Polish dance for four or eight couples.

Mc·Carthy·ism /məˋkɑθɪɪzm/ *n* (US, 1950's after J R McCarthy, 1909—1957, US politician) political policy of accusing persons of disloyalty (esp by saying they were pro-Communist); unscrupulous methods of investigation used for this purpose.

me /mi/ *pron* object form for the pronoun *I*: *He saw me. Give me one. It's me* (now usu for 'It is I').

mead[1] /mid/ *n* [U] alcoholic drink made from fermented honey and water.

mead[2] /mid/ *n* [C] (poet) meadow.

meadow /ˋmedəʊ/ *n* [C,U] (area, field, of) grassland, esp kept for hay.

meagre (US = **mea·ger**) /ˋmigə(r)/ *adj* **1** thin; lacking in flesh: *a ~ face.* **2** insufficient; poor; scanty: *a ~ meal; ~ fare; a ~ attendance at the council meeting.* **~·ly** *adv* **~·ness** *n*

meal[1] /mil/ *n* [C] **1** occasion of eating: *three ~s a day; breakfast, the first ~ of the day.* **ˋ~·time** *n* usual time for taking a ~. **2** food that is eaten: *have a good ~.*

meal[2] /mil/ *n* [U] grain coarsely ground: *ˋoat~; corn ~,* (US) ~ of maize or other grain. Cf *flour* for grain finely ground.

mealie /ˋmilɪ/ *n* (usu *pl*) (S Africa) maize.

mealy /ˋmilɪ/ *adj* (-ier, -iest) of, like, containing, covered with, meal; (of potatoes when boiled) dry and powdery. **ˋ~-bug** *n* insect that infests vines, etc. **ˈ~-ˋmouthed** *adj* too squeamish in the choice of words; tending to avoid plain speaking.

mean[1] /min/ *adj* (-er, -est) **1** poor in appearance; shabby-looking: *a ~ house in a ~ street.* **2** (of behaviour) unworthy; discreditable: *That was a ~ trick! It was ~ of you to eat all the peaches! He took a ~ advantage of me. What a ~ revenge!* **3** (of persons, their character, etc) having or showing a fondness for ~ behaviour: *a ~ rascal. Don't be so ~ to your little brother,* Don't tease him, treat him unkindly, etc. *He's a ˋ~-minded sort of fellow.* **4** of low rank or humble birth: *men of the ~er sort. We dispense justice even to the ~est citizens.* **5** (of the understanding, the natural powers) inferior; poor: *This should be clear even to the ~est intelligence. He is no ~ scholar,* is a good one. **6** lacking in generosity; selfish: *Her husband is rather ~ over money matters.* **7** (colloq) secretly ashamed: *feel rather ~ for not helping more.* **8** (US) nasty; vicious: *He's a really ~ fellow—he likes to see people suffer.* **~·ly** *adv* **~·ness** *n* **~ie, ~y** /ˋminɪ/ *nn* (colloq) ~-minded person: *What a ~ie you are!* ⇨ 3,6 above.

mean[2] /min/ *adj* occupying the middle position between two extremes: *the ~ annual temperature in Malta.* **Greenwich M~ Time,** ⇨ Greenwich. **~ price,** (fin, Stock Exchange) the average between the Stock jobber's buying and selling price; the market price of an investment.

mean[3] /min/ *n* **1** [C] condition, quality, course of action, etc that is halfway between two extremes; (esp) ***the happy/golden ~,*** a moderate course of action. **2** (maths) term between the first and the last of a series: *In 1:3 :: 3:8, the ~ is 3. The ~ of 3, 5 and 7 is 5* (because 3 + 5 + 7 = 15 and 15 ÷ 3 = 5).

mean[4] /min/ *vi* (*pt,pp* meant /ment/) **1** [VP6A] (of words, sentences, etc) signify; import: *A dictionary tries to tell you what words ~. The Latin word 'amo' ~s 'I love'.* **2** [VP6A] be a sign of; be likely to result in: *This new frontier incident probably ~s war. These new orders for our manufacturers will ~ working overtime.* **3** [VP6A,14, 16B,17A] have as a purpose; contemplate; intend; refer to: *What do you ~ by saying that?* What have you in mind? (or if the context allows) How dare you say that? *I wasn't serious—I ~t it/It was ~t as a joke. Do you ~* (= refer to) *Miss Elsie*

Smith or Miss Dora Smith? I didn't ~ you to read the letter. Is this figure ~t to be a 1 or a 7? I'm sorry if I hurt your feelings—I didn't ~ to. I ~ there to be no argument about this, won't allow any argument. *Is this valuable painting ~t for me,* Is the owner thinking of giving it to me? ***~ business,*** (colloq) be in earnest, ready to act (not merely talk). ***~ mischief,*** have in mind sth evil or injurious. **4** [VP7,12A,13A,14,17B] intend; be determined; destine: *He ~s to succeed. He ~s his son to succeed. He ~s you no harm,* does not intend to hurt you. *He ~s no harm to anyone. I ~t this for my son,* intended to give it to him. *He seems obviously ~t for the army/~t to be a soldier,* is the sort of man destined for the army. **5** [VP14] ***~ sth to sb,*** be of importance or value to: *Your friendship ~s a great deal to me,* I value it highly. *£20 ~s a lot to her,* is quite a large sum in her view. *I can't tell you what Mary has ~t to me,* what a difference she has made in my life. *The high cost of living ~s nothing to some people,* They do not worry about it (e g because they are very rich). **6** ***~ well,*** have good intentions (though perhaps not the will or capacity to carry them out): *Of course he ~s well.* ***~ well by sb,*** have kindly intentions towards sb: *We all know that he ~s well by you.* **ˈ~·ing** *n* [C,U] what is ~t or intended: *a word with many distinct ~ings; a passage without much ~ing. He looked at me with ~ing. What's the ~ing of this?* (asked, for example, by sb who thinks he has been badly treated, etc). □ *adj* full of ~ing: *a ~ing look; well ~ing,* having good intentions. **ˈ~·ing·ful** /-fl/ *adj* significant; full of ~ing. **ˈ~·ing·fully** /-flɪ/ *adv* **ˈ~·ing·less** *adj* without ~ing or motive. **ˈ~·ing·ly** *adv* with ~ing.

me·ander /mɪˈændə(r)/ *vi* [VP2A,C] wander here and there; (fig) speak in an aimless way; (of a stream) follow a winding course, flowing slowly and gently. **~·ings** /mɪˈændrɪŋz/ *n pl* winding path, course, etc. **~·ing·ly** /mɪˈændrɪŋlɪ/ *adv*

means[1] /minz/ *n pl* (often treated as a *sing,* as in examples) method, process, by which a result may be obtained: *a ~ to an end,* a way of achieving sth. *There is/are no ~ of learning what is happening. Every ~ has/All possible ~ have been tried. Does the end always justify the ~,* If the aim or purpose is good, may any methods, even if bad, be employed? ***by ~ of,*** through; with the help of: *Thoughts are expressed by ~ of words.* ***by all ~,*** certainly. ***by no ~,*** not at all: *These goods are by no ~ satisfactory.* ***by no manner of ~,*** in no way. ***by some ~ or other,*** somehow or other; if not in one way, then in another. ***by fair ~ or foul,*** by any methods, just or unjust. **ways and ~,** methods, esp of providing money by taxation for government needs.

means[2] /minz/ *n pl* money; wealth; resources: *a man of ~,* a rich man; *a man of your ~,* with the money, etc you have at your disposal; *have private ~,* an income from property, investments, etc (not earned as salary, etc). ***live beyond/within one's ~,*** spend more/less than one's income. **ˈ~ test** *n* inquiry into the ~ of sb seeking help from the State or local authorities (e g if unemployed or too old to work).

meant /ment/ *pt,pp* of **mean**[4].

mean·time /ˈmin-taɪm/ *adv, n* (in the) interval between.

mean·while /ˈminˈwaɪl *US:* -ˈhwaɪl/ *adv* in or during the time between.

measles /ˈmizlz/ *n* (*sing v*) infectious disease, marked by fever and small red sports that cover the whole body.

measly /ˈmizlɪ/ *adj* (colloq) of little value; of poor quality; of small size or amount: *What a ~ birthday present! What a ~ helping of ice-cream!*

measure[1] /ˈmeʒə(r)/ *n* **1** [U] size, quantity, degree, weight, etc as found by a standard or unit. ***give full/short ~,*** give the full (less than the full) amount. ***made to ~,*** (of clothes) specially made for sb after taking ~ments. ***get the ~ of sb,*** (fig) form an estimate of his character, abilities, etc. **2** [C] unit, standard or system used in stating size, quantity, or degree: *liquid/dry ~. An inch is a ~ of length. Twenty ~s of wheat means twenty bushels.* **3** [C] with which to test size, quantity, etc: *a pint ~. A yardstick is a ~; so is a foot-rule. A chain's weakest link is the ~ of its strength. Words cannot always give the ~ of one's feelings,* cannot show the depth or strength of one's feelings. **ˈtape-~,** ⇨ tape. **ˈgreatest ˈcommon ˈ~,** (abbr **GCM**) largest number that will divide each of several given numbers exactly. **4** extent, (esp in) ***beyond ~,*** very great(ly): *Her joy was beyond ~.* ***in some/any ~,*** to some/any extent or degree. ***in great/large ~,*** to a large extent: *Their success was in some ~/in great ~ the result of thorough preparation.* ***set ~s to,*** limit: *set ~s to one's ambitions.* **5** [C] (proposed) law. **6** [C] proceeding; stop: *What ~* (= plan) *do you propose? They took strong ~s* (= acted vigorously) *against dangerous drivers.* **7** [U] verse-rhythm metre; time of a piece of music; [C] (archaic) dance. ***tread a ~ (with sb),*** dance with.

measure[2] /ˈmeʒə(r)/ *vt,vi* **1** [VP6A] find the size, extent, volume, degree, etc of (sth or sb): *~ a piece of ground/the strength of an electric current/the speed of a car; tested for speed over a ~d mile. The tailor ~d me for a suit. Can you ~ accurately?* **2** [VP2B] be (a certain length, etc): *This room ~s 10 metres across.* **3** [VP6A,15A,B] ***~ out/off,*** give a ~d quantity of: *~ out a dose of medicine;* mark out: *~ off 2 metres of cloth.* **4** ***~ one's length,*** fall flat on the ground. ***~ swords against/with sb,*** (fig) try out one's strength against him. ***~ one's strength (with sb),*** try or test it. **meas·ured** *adj* **1** (of language) considered and weighed: *~d words.* **2** in slow and regular rhythm: *with a ~d tread.* **measur·able** /ˈmeʒṛəbl/ *adj* that can be ~d: *We came within measurable distance of* (close to) *success.* **measur·ably** /-əblɪ/ *adv* **~·less** *adj* immeasurable; limitless. **~·ment** *n* **1** [U] measuring: *the metric system of ~ment.* **2** (*pl*) figures about length, breadth, depth, etc: *the ~ments of a room.*

meat /mit/ *n* **1** [U] flesh of animals used as food, excluding fish and birds: *~-eating animals; cold ~,* meat that has been cooked and has then become cold; *chilled/frozen ~,* meat chilled/ frozen in order to keep it in good condition; *fresh ~,* from a recently killed animal. **ˈ~·ball** *n* small ball of minced meat or sausage-meat. **ˈ~-safe** *n* cupboard for storing ~, usu with sides of wire gauze. **~ pie** *n* ~ cooked with a covering of pastry. **a ~ tea,** high tea with some kind of ~ dish included. ⇨ **high**[1]**(12).** **2** (old use) food in general: *~ and drink; say grace before ~,* before eating a meal. *There's not much ~ in this argument,* (fig) nothing substantial. **~·less** *adj* without

~: *~less days during the war.* **~y** *adj* (-ier, -iest) (fig) full of substance; substantial.

Mecca /ˈmekə/ *n* **1** city in Saudi Arabia, birthplace of Muhammad and the spiritual centre of Islam. **2** goal of one's ambitions; place one is anxious to visit: *Stratford-on-Avon, the ~ of tourists in Britain.*

mech·anic /mɪˈkænɪk/ *n* skilled workman, esp one who repairs or adjusts machinery and tools: *a ˈmotor-~.*

mech·an·ical /mɪˈkænɪkl/ *adj* **1** of, connected with, produced by, machines: *~ power/transport/engineering.* **2** (of persons, their actions) like machines; automatic; as if done without thought: *~ movements.* **~ly** /-klɪ/ *adv* in a ~ way: *~ly operated.* ⇨ *manually* at manual.

mech·an·ics /mɪˈkænɪks/ *n* **1** (usu with *sing v*) science of motion and force; science of machinery: *M~ is taught by Mr Hill.* **2** (*pl*) (method of) construction: *the ~ of play-writing.*

mech·an·ism /ˈmekənɪzm/ *n* [C] **1** working parts of a machine collectively; structure or arrangement of parts that work together as the parts of a machine do: *the ~ of the body; the ~ of government.* **2** way in which sth works or is constructed.

mech·an·is·tic /ˈmekəˈnɪstɪk/ *adj*: *the ~ theory,* the theory that all changes in the universe and all living creatures are caused by physical and chemical forces only.

mech·an·ize /ˈmekənaɪz/ *vt* [VP6A] use machines in or for; give a mechanical character to: *~d forces,* e g in the army, using motor transport instead of horses or mules. **mech·an·iz·ation** /ˈmekənaɪˈzeɪʃn *US:* -nɪˈz-/ *n*

medal /ˈmedl/ *n* flat piece of metal, usu shaped like a coin, with words and a design stamped on it, given as an award, for bravery to commemorate sth or for distinction in scholarship. **~·list** (US = **~·ist**) /ˈmedlɪst/ *n* person who has been awarded a ~, e g for distinction in literature, art, sport.

me·dal·lion /mɪˈdælɪən/ *n* large medal; large, flat circular ornamental design, e g on a carpet or on a lace curtain.

meddle /ˈmedl/ *vi* [VP2A,3A] ~ ***in sth,*** busy oneself in sth without being asked to do so: *Don't ~ in my affairs. Don't ~ in politics.* ~ ***(with sth),*** interfere: *Who's been meddling with my papers? You're always meddling.* **meddler** *n* person who ~s. **ˈ~·some** /-səm/ *adj* fond of, in the habit of, meddling.

me·dia /ˈmidɪə/ *n* ⇨ mass(2), medium. **the ~,** (usu with *sing v*) mass communications, e g television, radio, the press.

medi·æval /ˈmedɪˈivl *US:* ˈmid-/ = medieval.

me·dial /ˈmidɪəl/ *adj* **1** situated in the middle. **2** of average size. **~ly** /-ɪəlɪ/ *adv*

me·dian /ˈmidɪən/ *adj* situated in, passing through, the middle. □ *n* ~ point, line, part, etc.

me·di·ate /ˈmidɪeɪt/ *vi,vt* **1** [VP2A,3A] ~ ***(between),*** act as go-between or peacemaker: *~ between two warring countries/between employers and their workers.* **2** [VP6A] bring about by doing this: *~ a settlement/a peace.* **me·dia·tion** /ˈmidɪˈeɪʃn/ *n* [U] mediating: *All offers of mediation by a third party were rejected.* **me·dia·tor** /-tə(r)/ *n* one who ~s.

medic /ˈmedɪk/ *n* (colloq abbr for) medical student.

medi·cal /ˈmedɪkl/ *adj* **1** of the art of medicine (the treatment of disease): *a ˈ~ examination,* to ascertain one's state of health; *a ~ practitioner,* a qualified doctor; *a ˈ~ school; ˈ~ students/knowledge; ~ jurisprudence,* legal knowledge required by a doctor. **2** of the art of medicine (contrasted with *surgery*): *~, not surgical, treatment. The hospital has a ~ ward and a surgical ward.* □ *n* **1** (colloq) ~ student. **2** ~ examination. **~ly** /-klɪ/ *adv*

medic·ament /mɪˈdɪkəmənt/ *n* substance used in medical treatment, internally or externally. ⇨ medicine(2).

Medi·care /ˈmedɪkeə(r)/ *n* [U] (US) government programme providing medical care for old persons.

medi·cate /ˈmedɪkeɪt/ *vt* [VP6A] treat medically; permeate with a medicinal substance: *~d soap/gauze.* **medi·ca·tion** /ˈmedɪˈkeɪʃn/ *n* [U] process of medicating: *mass medication,* e g, the addition of fluorine to public water supplies; the supply of vitamin tablets through the social services.

med·ici·nal /mɪˈdɪsnl/ *adj* having healing or curative properties: *~ preparations for both internal and external use.*

medi·cine /ˈmedsn *US:* ˈmedɪsn/ *n* **1** [U] the art and science of the prevention and cure of disease: *study ~ and surgery; a ˈDoctor of ˈM~.* **2** [C,U] (kind of) substance, esp one taken through the mouth, used in ~: *He's always taking ~s. He takes too much ~. This is a good (kind of) ~ for a cough.* (Note: for remedies not taken through the mouth, ⇨ *injection* at inject, lotion, *medicinal preparation* at medicinal, ointment.) **ˈ~-ball** *n* large, heavy ball thrown and caught for physical exercise. **ˈ~-chest** *n* chest with a selection of useful medicinal preparations. **3** (fig) deserved punishment: ***take one's ~,*** (fig) submit to what is unwelcome and unpleasant. ***get some/a little of one's own ~,*** be given the kind of unwelcome treatment that one has given to others. **4** [U] (among primitive peoples) spell; charm; fetish; magic. **ˈ~-man** /-mæn/ *n* (*pl* -men) witch-doctor.

med·ico /ˈmedɪkəʊ/ *n* (*pl* -cos /-kəʊz/) (colloq, hum) doctor or medical student.

medi·eval (also **medi·æval**) /ˈmedɪˈivl *US:* ˈmid-/ *adj* of the Middle Ages (about A D 1100—1500).

me·di·ocre /ˈmidɪˈəʊkə(r)/ *adj* not very good; neither very good nor very bad; second-rate. **me·di·oc·rity** /ˈmidɪˈokrətɪ/ *n* (*pl* -ties) [U] quality of being ~; [C] person who is ~ (in qualities, abilities, etc): *a Government of mediocrities.*

medi·tate /ˈmedɪteɪt/ *vt,vi* **1** [VP6A] think about; consider: *~ revenge/mischief.* **2** [VP2A,3A] ~ ***(up)on,*** give oneself up to serious thought: *He sat there meditating upon his misfortunes.*

medi·ta·tion /ˈmedɪˈteɪʃn/ *n* **1** [U] meditating: *deep in ~.* **2** [C] instance of this: *'A M~ on a Broomstick'* (treatise by Swift); *'The M~s of Marcus Aurelius'.* **medi·tat·ive** /ˈmedɪtətɪv *US:* -teɪt-/ *adj* of ~; fond of ~. **medi·tat·ive·ly** *adv*

Medi·ter·ra·nean /ˈmedɪtəˈreɪnɪən/ *adj* of, characteristic of, the M~ Sea or the countries, etc bordering this sea: *~ climate.*

me·dium /ˈmidɪəm/ *n* (*pl* ~s or media /ˈmidɪə/) **1** that by which sth is expressed: *Commercial television is a ~ for advertising. Vacant positions can be made known through the ~ of the press,* by putting announcements in newspapers. *Oil paints and water colours are ~s for the creation of works of art.* ⇨ also mass(2). **2** middle quality or degree. **the happy ~,** avoidance of extremes, e g by being neither very lax nor very severe in maintaining discipline. **3** (*pl* often **media**) substance, surroundings, in which sth exists or through which sth moves: *Air is the ~ of sound.* **4** person who acts as a go-between, esp in spiritualism; person who claims to be able to receive messages from the spirits of the dead. □ *adj* coming halfway between; not extreme: *a man of ~ height; a ~-sized firm; ~ waves,* in radio, between long and short; *~ bonds,* maturing in a period between 15 and 20 years; *the ~ income group,* those who have incomes between high and low.

med·lar /ˈmedlə(r)/ *n* (tree with) fruit like a small brown apple, eaten when it begins to decay.

med·ley /ˈmedlɪ/ *n* (*pl* **-leys**) [C] mixture of things or persons of different sorts: *the ~ of races in Hawaii.*

meed /mid/ *n* (poet) deserved portion (*of* praise, etc).

meek /mik/ *adj* (**-er, -est**) mild and patient; unprotesting (the contrary of *self-assertive*): *She's as ~ as a lamb.* **~·ly** *adv* **~·ness** *n*

meer·schaum /ˈmɪəʃəm/ *n* [U] white clay-like substance; [C] tobacco pipe with a bowl made of this.

meet[1] /mit/ *vt,vi* (*pt,pp* **met** /-met/) **1** [VP6A, 2A,C] come face to face with (sb or sth coming from the opposite or a different direction); come together from different points or directions: *~ sb in the street. We met (each other) quite by chance. Goodbye till we ~ again. The two trains ~* (= pass each other) *at Crewe. We write regularly but seldom ~,* see each other. *Can you ~* (= face) *misfortune with a smile? The Debating Society ~s every Friday at 8p m.* **~ with, (a)** experience: *~ with misfortune/an accident/great kindness.* **(b)** come upon by chance: *~ with obstacles; ~ with an old friend at a dinner party.* **2** [VP6A,2A] make the acquaintance of; be introduced to: *I know Mrs Hill by sight, but have never met her/we've never met.* (As a form of introduction) *M~ my wife. Pleased to ~ you.* **3** [VP6A] go to a place and await the arrival of: *Will you ~ your sister at the station? I'll ~ your train. The hotel bus ~s all the trains.* **4** [VP6A] satisfy (a demand, etc): *~ sb's wishes,* do what he wants. *Can you ~ their objections/criticisms,* answer them in a satisfactory way? ***~ the case,*** be adequate, satisfactory: *I'm afraid your proposal hardly ~s the case.* ***~ sb halfway,*** (fig) compromise; give way to some extent in order to satisfy him. ***~ all expenses/bills, etc,*** pay them. **5** [VP6A,2A] come into contact; touch: *Their hands met. His hand met hers. My waistcoat won't ~,* is too small to be buttoned. ***make both ends ~,*** make one's income and one's expenditure equal. **6** ***~ the eye/ear, our eyes/ears,*** be visible/ audible. *There's more to that man than ~s the eye,* (fig) he has qualities, characteristics, etc that are not immediately seen. ***~ sb's eye,*** see that he is looking at one, look back at him: *She was afraid to ~ my eye.*

meet[2] /mit/ *n* **1** (GB) gathering of riders and hounds at a fixed place (for foxhunting). **2** (US) coming together of a number of people for a purpose: *an athˈletic ~; a ˈtrack/ˈswimming ~* (*meeting* is the usu word in GB).

meet[3] /mit/ *adj* (archaic) right; suitable; proper *for/to do/to be done.*

meet·ing /ˈmitɪŋ/ *n* **1** coming together of a number of persons at a certain time and place, esp for discussion: *political ~s. Mr Smith will now address the ~.* **ˈ~-house** *n* building for ~s, esp those held by Quakers. **ˈ~-place** *n* place fixed for a ~. **2** any coming together: *a ˈrace-~; a ˈsports-~. The ~ between Mr Hill and his family was a joyful one. She is shy at a first ~,* when she meets sb for the first time.

mega·cycle /ˈmegəsɑɪkl/ *n* [C] million cycles (of changes of radio current).

mega·death /ˈmegədeθ/ *n* death of one million people (in nuclear war).

mega·lith /ˈmegəlɪθ/ *n* large stone, esp one used as a monument. **mega·lithic** /ˈmegəˈlɪθɪk/ *adj* made of ~s; marked by the use of ~s (esp in very early times).

megaliths

mega·lo·ma·nia /ˈmegələˈmeɪnɪə/ *n* [U] form of madness in which a person has exaggerated ideas of his importance of power, wealth, etc: *The dictator was obviously suffering from ~.* **mega·lo·ma·niac** /-nɪæk/ *n* person suffering from ~.

mega·phone /ˈmegəfəʊn/ *n* [C] horn for speaking through, carrying the voice to a distance.

mega·ton /ˈmegətʌn/ *n* explosive force equal to one million tons of T N T.

me·grim /ˈmigrɪm/ *n* (archaic) **1** migraine. **2** (*pl*) low spirits.

mei·osis /mɑɪˈəʊsɪs/ *n* = **litotes.**

mel·an·cholic /ˈmelənˈkolɪk/ *adj* melancholy; with a tendency to melancholy.

mel·an·choly /ˈmelənkəlɪ *US:* -kolɪ/ *n* [U] sadness; low spirits. □ *adj* sad; low-spirited; causing sadness or low spirits: *~ news; a ~ occasion,* e g a funeral. **mel·an·cholia** /ˈmelənˈkəʊlɪə/ *n* [U] mental illness marked by ~.

mé·lange /ˈmeɪlɔ̃ʒ *US:* meɪˈlɔ̃ʒ/ *n* mixture; medley.

mê·lée /ˈmeleɪ *US:* meɪˈleɪ/ *n* (F) confused struggle; confused crowd of people.

meli·or·ate /ˈmilɪəreɪt/ *vt,vi* [VP6A,2A] make or become better; improve. **meli·or·ation** /ˈmilɪəˈreɪʃn/ *n* process of improving. **meli·or·ism** /ˈmilɪər-ɪzm/ *n* belief that mankind tends to ~, and that conscious human effort may further this tendency.

mel·lif·lu·ous /meˈlɪflʊəs/ *adj* (of a person's voice or words, of music, etc) sweet-sounding; smooth-flowing.

mel·low /ˈmeləʊ/ *adj* (**-er, -est**) **1** soft and sweet in taste; soft, pure and rich in colour or sound: *a ~ wine; the ~ colours of the roofs in Dubrovnik.* **2** made wise and sympathetic by age or experience: *~ judgement.* **3** (colloq) genial; slightly intoxicated. □ *vt,vi* [VP6A,2A] make or become ~. **~·ly** *adv* **~·ness** *n*

mel·odic /məˈlodɪk/ *adj* of melody; melodious.

mel·odi·ous /məˈləʊdɪəs/ *adj* of, producing, melody; sweet-sounding: *the ~ notes of a thrush.* **~·ly** *adv* **~·ness** *n*

melo·drama /ˈmelədrɑmə/ *n* **1** [C] exciting and emotional (often sensational, exaggerated) drama, usu with a happy ending; event or series of events, piece of behaviour or writing, which suggests a stage ~. **2** [U] language, behaviour, suggestive of plays of this kind; such as a branch of dramatic art. **melo·dram·atic** /ˌmelədrəˈmætɪk/ *adj* of, like, suitable for, ~. **melo·dram·ati·cally** /-klɪ/ *adv*

mel·ody /ˈmelədɪ/ *n* (*pl* -dies) **1** [U] sweet music; tunefulness; musical arrangement of words: *a master of* ~. **2** [C] song or tune: *old Irish melodies.* **3** [C] principal part or thread in harmonized music: *The ~ is next taken up by the flutes.*

melon /ˈmelən/ *n* (kinds of) large, juicy round fruit growing on a plant that trails along the ground: *a slice of* ~. ⇨ the illus at fruit.

melt /melt/ *vt,vi* (*pt,pp* ~ed; *pp* as *adj*, of metal molten /ˈməʊltən/) **1** [VP6A,15B,2A,C] (cause to) become liquid through heating: *The ice will ~ when the sun shines on it. The hot sun soon ~ed the ice. It is easy to ~ butter.* **~ away,** become less, disappear, by ~ing: *The snow soon ~ed away when the sun came out. The fog ~ed away. Her money seemed to ~ away in Paris. The crowd quickly ~ed away* (= dispersed) *when the storm broke.* **~ sth down,** ~ (articles of gold and silver) in order to use the metal as raw material. **2** [VP2A,C] (of soft food) dissolve, be softened, easily: *This cake/pear ~s in the mouth.* **3** [VP2A,6A] (of a solid in a liquid) dissolve: *Sugar ~s in tea.* **4** [VP6A,2C] (of a person, heart, feelings) soften, be softened: *Her heart ~ed with pity. Pity ~ed her heart. She ~ed into tears.* **5** [VP2C] fade; go (slowly) away: *One colour ~ed into another,* e g in the sky at sunset. **ˈ~·ing** *adj* (fig) tender; sentimental: *in a ~ing voice/mood.* **ˈ~-ing-point** *n* temperature at which a solid ~s: *Lead has a lower ~ing-point than iron.* **ˈ~ing-pot** *n* **(a)** pot in which metals, etc, are ~ed: *go into the ~ing-pot,* (fig) undergo a revolution. **(b)** place, country, e g US, where immigrants of different races are assimilated.

mem·ber /ˈmembə(r)/ *n* **1** person belonging to a group, society, etc: *a ~ of the university/a club. Every ~ of her family came to her wedding.* **ˌM~ of ˈParliament,** (abbr **M P**) elected representative in the House of Commons. **2** (old use) part of a human or animal body: *The tongue is sometimes called 'the unruly ~'.* **ˈ~·ship** /-ʃɪp/ *n* **1** [U] the state of being a ~ (of a society, etc). **2** number of ~s: *The society has a large ~ship/a ~ship of 80.*

mem·brane /ˈmembreɪn/ *n* [C] soft, thin, pliable skin-like covering or lining, or connecting part, in an animal or vegetable body; [U] tissue of which such coverings, etc, are made. **mem·bra·nous** /ˈmembrənəs/ *adj* of or like ~.

mem·ento /məˈmentəʊ/ *n* (*pl* -tos, -toes /-təʊz/) sth that serves to remind one of a person or event.

memo /ˈmeməʊ/ *n* (*pl* -mos /-məʊz/) short for memorandum.

mem·oir /ˈmemwɑ(r)/ *n* **1** short life-history, esp by someone with first-hand knowledge; biographical notice, e g in a periodical. **2** essay on a learned subject specially studied by the writer. **3** (*pl*) person's written account of his own life or experiences: *the flood of war ~s by generals and politicians.*

mem·or·able /ˈmemṛəbl/ *adj* deserving to be remembered. **mem·or·ably** /-əblɪ/ *adv*

mem·or·an·dum /ˌmeməˈrændəm/ *n* (*pl* -da /-də/ or -dums) (abbr **memo**) **1** note or record for future use: *make a ~ of sth.* **2** informal business communication, usu without a personal signature, on paper headed *M~* (or *memo*). **3** report of an agreement that has been reached but not yet formally drawn up and signed: *M~ and articles of association,* legal document for this.

mem·or·ial /məˈmɔrɪəl/ *n* **1** sth made or done to remind people of an event, person, etc: *a ~ to the dead; a ˈwar ~,* a monument with the names of men killed in wars. **2** (attrib use) serving to keep in mind: *a ~ tablet,* e g in the wall of a church, in memory of someone; *a ~ service.* **ˈM~ Day,** (US) day set aside by law for honouring the memory of members of the armed forces killed in war (30 May in most States). **3** (usu *pl*) historical records or chronicles. **4** (more usu *petition*) written statement of facts, views, etc sent to authorities making a request or protest. **~·ize** /-ɑɪz/ *vt* [VP6A] **1** (more usu *petition*) present a ~(4) to. **2** commemorate (which is the more usu word).

mem·or·ize /ˈmemərɑɪz/ *vt* [VP6A] learn by heart; commit to memory.

mem·ory /ˈmemərɪ/ *n* (*pl* -ries) **1** [U] power of keeping facts in the conscious mind and of being able to call them back at will; preservation of past experience for future use. ***commit sth to ~,*** learn it by heart. ***speak from ~,*** i e without referring to notes, etc. ***to the best of my ~*** (*knowledge* is more usu), as far as I can remember. ***in ~ of sb, to the ~ of sb,*** serving to recall sb, keep him fresh in peoples' minds. **2** [C] this power in an individual (also used, by extension, of the unit of a computer which stores data for future use): *Some people have better memories than others. He has a bad ~ for dates.* **3** [U] period over which the ~ can go back: *beyond/within the ~ of men.* ***within living ~,*** within the years that people now alive can remember. **4** [C] sth that is remembered; sth from the past stored in the ~: *memories of childhood.* **5** [U] reputation after death (esp of saints, great rulers): *the late king/pope, of blessed ~.*

mem·sa·hib /ˈmemsɑb/ *n* (In India) (form of address to a) European woman.

men /men/ *n pl* of man[1](1).

men·ace /ˈmenəs/ *n* [C,U] danger; threat: *a ~ to world peace; in a speech filled with ~. That woman is a ~,* is a nuisance, is troublesome! □ *vt* [VP6A] threaten: *countries ~d by/with war.* **men·ac·ing·ly** *adv* in a threatening manner.

mé·nage /ˈmeɪnɑʒ *US:* meɪˈnɑʒ/ *n* household management; domestic establishment.

men·ag·erie /məˈnædʒərɪ/ *n* collection of wild animals in captivity, esp for a travelling circus.

mend /mend/ *vt,vi* **1** [VP6A] remake, repair, set right (sth broken, worn out, or torn); restore to good condition or working order: *~ shoes/a broken window.* **2** [VP6A,2A] (= *amend*) free from faults or errors: *That won't ~* (= improve) *matters.* ***It's never too late to ~,*** (prov) reform one's way of living. ***~ one's ways,*** ⇨ way(10). **3** [VP2A] regain health; heal: *The patient is ~ing nicely.* **4** [VP6A] *~ one's pace,* quicken it; walk faster; *~ the fire,* (regional use) put more coal on it. □ *n* damage or torn part, that has been ~ed: *The ~s were almost invisible.* **on the ~,** improving in health or condition. **~er** *n* (chiefly in compounds) one who ~s: *ˈroad-~er.* **ˈ~·ing** *n* (esp) work of ~ing (clothes, etc): *a basketful of ~ing,* of clothes, etc, to be ~ed; *invisible ~ing,* ⇨ invisible.

men·da·cious /men'deɪʃəs/ *adj* false; untruthful: ~ *newspaper reports.* **~·ly** *adv* **men·dac·ity** /ˈmen'dæsətɪ/ *n* (formal) [U] untruthfulness; [C] (*pl* -**ties**) untrue statement.

Men·delian /men'dilɪən/ *adj* of the theory of genetics of Mendel /ˈmendl/, 1822—1884, the Austrian biologist.

men·di·cant /ˈmendɪkənt/ *n, adj* (person) getting a living by asking for alms, or as a beggar: ~ *friars.*

men·folk /ˈmenfəʊk/ *n pl* (colloq) men, esp the men of a family: *The ~ have all gone out fishing.*

me·nial /ˈminɪəl/ *adj* **1** suitable for, to be done by, a household servant: *She has to spend too much time on such ~ tasks as washing pots and pans.* **2** (of persons, derog) domestic: *the ~ staff,* the servants. □ *n* (usu derog) ~ servant. **~ly** /-ɪəlɪ/ *adv*

men·in·gi·tis /ˈmenɪn'dʒaɪtɪs/ *n* [U] (serious illness caused by) inflammation of any or all of the membranes enclosing the brain and spinal cord.

meno·pause /ˈmenəpɔz/ *n* final cessation of the menses at the age of about 50 (colloq called *'change of life'*).

men·ses /ˈmensiz/ *n pl* monthly bleeding from the uterus. **men·strual** /ˈmenstrʊəl/ *adj* of the ~. **men·stru·ate** /ˈmenstrʊeɪt/ *vi* discharge the ~. **men·stru·ation** /ˈmenstrʊ'eɪʃn/ *n*

men·sur·ation /ˈmensjʊ'reɪʃn/ *n* process of, mathematical rules for, finding length, area and volume. **men·sur·able** /ˈmensjʊrəbl/ *adj* (rare) measurable.

men·tal /ˈmentl/ *adj* of or in the mind. **~ age,** person's ~ level measured in terms of the average age of children having the same ~ standard. **ˈ~ a'rithmetic,** done in the mind without using written figures or a mechanical device. **ˈ~ de'ficiency,** subnormal development of intellectual powers, preventing a person from learning normally, looking after himself, etc. **'~ home/hospital,** one for ~ patients. **ˈ~ 'illness,** illness of the mind. **'~ patient,** person suffering an illness of the mind. **'~ reservation,** one concerning a statement, oath, etc present in the mind but not spoken in words. **'~ specialist,** doctor who studies ~ illness. **'~ test,** one of which the purpose is to learn about a person's capacities and characteristics. **~ly** /ˈmentḷɪ/ *adv*: *~ly deficient/defective,* suffering from ~ illness; unable to profit from the ordinary kind of school education; *~ly deranged,* mad.

men·tal·ity /men'tælətɪ/ *n* **1** [U] general intellectual character; degree of intellectual power: *persons of average ~.* **2** [C] (*pl* -**ties**) characteristic attitude of mind: *a war ~.*

men·thol /ˈmenθol/ *n* [U] solid white substance obtained from oil of peppermint, used, e g by being rubbed on the skin, to relieve neuralgia, etc and as a flavouring, e g in ~ cigarettes. **men·tho·lated** /ˈmenθəleɪtɪd/ *adj*

men·tion /ˈmenʃn/ *vt* [VP6A,C,9,13A] speak or write sth about; say the name of; refer to: *He ~ed to me that he had seen you. I shall ~ it to him. Did I hear my name ~ed,* Was somebody talking about me? ***not to ~, without ~ing,*** phrases used either to excuse ~ of sth unimportant or to emphasize sth important: *We're too busy to take a long holiday this year, not to ~ the fact that we can't afford it.* ***Don't ~ it,*** phrase used to indicate that thanks, an apology, etc are unnecessary. □ *n* **1** [U] ~ing or naming: *He made no ~ of your request.* **2** [C] brief notice or reference: *a soldier who has received several honourable ~s in dispatches.* **-men·tioned** *adj* (with an *adv* prefixed): *ˈabove-'mentioned, ˈbelow-'mentioned,* referred to above, below.

men·tor /ˈmentɔ(r)/ *n* wise and trusted adviser and helper (of an inexperienced person).

menu /ˈmenju/ *n* bill of fare; list of courses at a meal or of dishes that can be served in a restaurant.

Mephi·stoph·elian /ˈmefɪstə'fɪlɪən/ *adj* of or like Mephistopheles /ˈmefɪ'stofəliz/ (the devil in the Faust legend); fiendish.

mer·can·tile /ˈmɜkəntaɪl/ *adj* of trade, commerce and merchants: ~ *marine,* country's merchant ships and seamen.

Mer·cator's pro·jec·tion /mə'keɪtəz prədʒekʃn/ *n* method of making maps of the world in which meridians and parallels of latitude cross at right angles (so that areas far from the equator are exaggerated in size). ⇨ the illus at **projection**.

mer·cen·ary /ˈmɜsnrɪ *US:* -ṇerɪ/ *adj* working only for money or other reward; inspired by love of money: *~ politicians; act from ~ motives.* □ *n* (*pl* -ries) soldier hired for pay to serve in a foreign army.

mer·cer /ˈmɜsə(r)/ *n* (GB) dealer in woven materials, esp silk and other textiles.

mer·cer·ize /ˈmɜsəraɪz/ *vt* [VP6A] treat (cotton threads) so that they are better able to take dyes and become glossy like silk: *~d cotton.*

mer·chan·dise /ˈmɜtʃəndaɪz/ *n* [U] goods bought and sold; trade goods.

mer·chant /ˈmɜtʃənt/ *n* **1** (usu wholesale) trader, esp one doing business with foreign countries. **2** (chiefly attrib) of overseas trade and the carriage of goods by sea: (attrib) *~ ships; the ~ service/marine,* the ~ ships collectively; *a ~-seaman,* sailor in a ~-ship. **3** (with a *pref*) person trading inside a country in the goods indicated: *a 'coal-~/wine-~.* **4** (GB sl) person who is very fond of (sth) or addicted to (sth): *a speed ~,* person who likes to drive at high speeds. **'~·man** /-mən/ *n* (*pl* -men) ~ ship.

mer·ci·ful /ˈmɜsɪfl/ *adj* ~ ***(to),*** having, showing, feeling mercy (to). **~ly** /-flɪ/ *adv*

mer·ci·less /ˈmɜsɪləs/ *adj* ~ ***(to),*** showing no mercy; pitiless (to). **~·ly** *adv*

mer·cur·ial /mɜ'kjʊərɪəl/ *adj* **1** of, like, caused by, containing, mercury: *~ ointment; ~ poisoning.* **2** (fig) lively; quickwitted: *a ~ temperament.* **3** (of persons) changeable; inconstant.

mer·cury /ˈmɜkjʊrɪ/ *n* [U] (also called *quicksilver*) heavy, silver-coloured metal (symbol **Hg**) usu liquid, as in thermometers and barometers.

Mer·cury /ˈmɜkjʊrɪ/ *n* (astron) planet nearest the sun. ⇨ the illus at **planet**.

mercy /ˈmɜsɪ/ *n* (*pl* -cies) **1** [U] (capacity for) holding oneself back from punishment, or from causing suffering to, sb whom one has the right or power to punish; *They showed little ~ to their enemies. We were given no ~. He threw himself on my ~,* begged me to have ~ on him, not to punish him, etc. *The jury brought in a verdict of guilty, with a recommendation to ~,* asking that the punishment should not be too servere. ***at the ~ of,*** in the power of; without defence against: *The ship was at the ~ of the waves,* was out of control, likely to be wrecked, etc. ***be left to the tender ~/mercies of,*** be exposed to the probably unkind, rough or cruel treatment of. **2** [C] piece of good fortune; sth to be thankful for; relief: *That's a ~! We must be thankful for small mercies. His death was a ~*, e g of sb with a painful and incurable illness. **`~ killing** *n* (colloq for) euthanasia. **3** *M~! M~ on us!* exclamations of surprise or (often pretended) terror.

mere[1] /mɪə(r)/ *adj* not more than: *She's a ~ child. It's a ~/the ~st trifle*, nothing at all important, nothing of any value, etc. *M~ words* (= Words without acts) *won't help.* **~·ly** *adv* only; simply: *I ~ly asked his name. I said it ~ly as a joke.*

mere[2] /mɪə(r)/ *n* pond; small lake.

mer·etri·cious /ˌmerəˈtrɪʃəs/ *adj* attractive on the surface but of little value: *~ jewellery; a ~ style*, superficially attractive. **~·ly** *adv* **~·ness** *n*

merge /mɜdʒ/ *vt,vi* **1** [VP2A,3A,6A,14] (comm) (of business companies) (cause to) become one: *We are merging with the company that supplies components for our cars. The small banks ~d/were ~d into one large organization.* **2** [VP3A] **~ *into*,** fade or change gradually into: *Twilight ~d into darkness. His fear gradually ~d into curiosity to know what was happening.* **merger** *n* [U] merging; [C] instance of this; combining of estates, business companies, etc.

mer·id·ian /məˈrɪdɪən/ *n* **1** (either half of a) circle round the globe, passing through a given place and the north and south poles: *the ~ of Greenwich* (of longitude 0° on British maps). **2** highest point reached by the sun or other star as viewed from a point on the earth's surface; 12 noon. **3** (fig) period of greatest splendour, success, power, etc. **4** (attrib use) of a ~: *~ line/altitude;* (fig) *in his ~ splendour.*

mer·idi·onal /məˈrɪdɪənl/ *adj* of the south; of the south of Europe, esp the south of France.

me·ringue /məˈræŋ/ *n* [U,C] whites of egg and sugar baked and used as a covering over pies, tarts, etc; small cake made of this mixture.

mer·ino /məˈrinəʊ/ *n* (*pl* **-nos** /-məʊz/) **1** (also *`~-sheep*) breed of sheep with long, fine wool. **2** [U] yarn or cloth from this wool; soft wool and cotton material.

merit /ˈmerɪt/ *n* **1** [U] quality or fact of deserving well; worth; excellent: *There isn't much ~ in giving away things you don't value or want. Do men of ~ always win recognition? She was awarded a certificate of ~ for her piano playing.* **2** [C] quality, fact, action, etc, that deserves reward (or, less often, punishment): *We must decide the case on its ~s*, according to the rights and wrongs of the case, without being influenced by personal feelings. ***make a ~ of sth,*** represent it as deserving reward or praise: *Don't make a ~ of being punctual—it's only what we expect of you.* □ *vt* [VP6A] deserve; be worthy of: *~ reward.*

meri·toc·racy /ˌmerɪˈtokrəsɪ/ *n* (*pl* **-cies**) (system of government or control by) persons of high practical or intellectual ability.

meri·tori·ous /ˌmerɪˈtɔrɪəs/ *adj* praiseworthy; deserving reward: *a prize for ~ conduct.* **~·ly** *adv*

mer·maid /ˈmɜmeɪd/ *n* (in children's stories, etc) woman with a fish's tail in place of legs. **merman** /ˈmɜmən/ *n* (*pl* **-men**) *male type.*

merry /ˈmerɪ/ *adj* (**-ier, -iest**) **1** happy; cheerful; bright and gay: *a ~ laugh; wish sb a ~ Christmas.* ***make ~,*** be gay and cheerful; laugh, talk, sing and feast. **`~-making** *n* [U] being joyful and gay. **`~-go-round** *n* revolving machine with horses, cars, etc on which children ride at fun fairs, etc. **2** (old use) pleasant: *the ~ month of May; M~ England.* **mer·rily** /ˈmerəlɪ/ *adv* **merri·ment** /ˈmerɪmənt/ *n*

mé·sal·liance /ˌmeɪzæˈlɪɔns/ *n* marriage with a person of lower social position.

mes·cal /ˈmeskl/ *n* globe-shaped cactus of Mexico; narcotic drug, producing strong hallucinations, extracted from the juice of this cactus. **mes·ca·line** /ˈmeskəlɪn/ *n* Mexican liquor distilled from the juices of the agave plant, producing psychedelic effects.

mes·dames /meɪˈdɑmz/ *n pl* of **madame**.

mes·demoi·selles /ˌmeɪdmwɑˈzelz/ *pl* of **mademoiselle**.

me·seems /mɪˈsimz/ *vi* (old use) it seems to me (*that…*).

mesh /meʃ/ *n* **1** one of the spaces in a net or wire screen: *a net with half-inch ~es;* spaces in other material. ⇨ **micromesh**. **2** (*pl*) network: *the ~es of a spider's web;* (fig) *entangled in the ~es of political intrigue.* **3** (mechanics) ***in ~,*** (of the geared teeth of wheels) engaged, interlocked. ⇨ also **synchromesh**. □ *vt,vi* **1** [VP6A] catch (e g fish) in a net. **2** [VP2A,3A] **~ *(with),*** (of toothed wheels) interlock; be engaged (with others); (fig) harmonize: *Our ways of looking at these problems don't ~.*

mes·mer·ism /ˈmezmərɪzm/ *n* [U] (older name for) hypnotism. **mes·meric** /mezˈmerɪk/ *adj* hypnotic. **mes·mer·ist** /-ɪst/ *n* hypnotist. **mes·mer·ize** /-ɑɪz/ *vt* [VP6A] hypnotize.

me·son /ˈmisən/ *n* (phys) type of subatomic particle with a mass between that of an electron and a proton.

mess[1] /mes/ *n* (with *indef art*, but rarely *pl*) state of confusion, dirt or disorder: *The workmen cleaned up the ~ before they left. Who's going to clear up the ~ made by the cat? You've made a ~ of the job*, have done it very badly. *He has got into another ~*, is in trouble again. *A nice ~ you've made of it*, You've spoilt it! *I've never seen so much ~ and disorder!* □ *vt,vi* **1** [VP6A,15B] **~ *sth up,*** make a ~ of; put into disorder or confusion: *The late arrival of the train ~ed up all our plans.* Hence, **`~-up** *n* (colloq) disorder or confusion: *There's been a bit of a ~-up* (= a misunderstanding, a failure to do what was needed) *about booking seats for that concert.* **2** [VP2C, 15B] **~ *about,*** **(a)** do things with no very definite plan; behave foolishly. **(b)** make a mess or muddle (of sth); treat (sb) roughly or inconsiderately: *Stop ~ing me about!* **~y** *adj* (**-ier, -iest**) dirty; in a state of disorder: *a messy job*, e g one that makes the hands and clothes dirty.

mess[2] /mes/ *n* [C] company of persons taking meals together (esp in the Armed Forces); these meals; the room, etc in which the meals are eaten. **`~-jacket** *n* (uniform) jacket worn at ~. **`~-mate** *n* member of the same ~ (esp a ship's ~ in the Navy). □ *vi* **~ *with sb,* ~ *together,*** eat meals. *The five young men ~ together.* **`~·ing allowance** *n* money allowed (in the Armed Forces) for cost of meals in a ~.

mess·age /ˈmesɪdʒ/ *n* **1** piece of news, or a request, sent to sb: *Radio ~s told us that the ship was sinking. Will you take this ~ to my brother? Got the ~?* (sl) Have you understood? **2** sth announced by a prophet and said to be inspired social or moral; teaching: *the ~ of H G Wells to* *his age.* **mess·en·ger** /ˋmesɪndʒə(r)/ *n* person carrying a ~.

Mess·iah /məˋsaɪə/ *n* person expected by the Jews to come and set them free; the Saviour, Jesus Christ.

Mess·ieurs /meˋsjɜz/ *n pl* (of *monsieur*) gentlemen.

Messrs /ˋmesəz/ *n* (abbr of *Messieurs*) used as the *pl* of *Mr* before a list of men's names: *~ Smith, Brown and Robinson,* and before names of business firms: *~ T Brown & Co.*

mes·suage /ˋmesjʊɪdʒ/ *n* (legal) dwelling-house with the outbuildings and land that go with it.

mes·tizo /meˋstizəʊ/ *n* (*pl* **-zoes** /-zəʊz/) Spanish or Portuguese half-caste, esp with an American Indian as one of the parents.

met /met/ *pt,pp* of **meet**[1].

Met /met/ *n* (abbr of) Meteorological: *get the latest ~ report,* issued by the *ˋMet Office* on the weather.

me·tab·olism /mɪˋtæbəlɪzm/ *n* [U] process by which food is built up into living matter or by which living matter is broken down into simple substances. **meta·bolic** /ˌmetəˋbolɪk/ *adj* of ~.

meta·car·pal /ˌmetəˋkɑpl/ *adj, n* (anat) (of a) bone in the hand. ⇨ the illus at **skeleton**.

metal /ˋmetl/ *n* **1** [C] any of a class of mineral substances such as tin, iron, gold and copper: *a worker in ~s.* **ˋ~-work** *n* artistic work in ~. **ˋ~-worker** *n* one who shapes objects in ~. **2** [U] one of these (as a material *n*): *Is it made of wood or ~?* **3** [U] (**ˋroad-)~,** (GB) broken stone used for making roads or (the beds of) railways. **4** (*pl*) railway-lines: *The train left/jumped the ~s.* **5** = **mettle**. □ *vt* (-ll-; US -l-) [VP6A] repair a road with ~(3): *~led roads; a ~led road surface.*

me·tal·lic /məˋtælɪk/ *adj* of or like metal: *a ~ currency,* i e with metal coins; *~ compounds; ~ sounds,* e g as made by brass objects struck together.

metal·lurgy /mɪˋtælədʒɪ *US:* ˋmetlɜdʒɪ/ *n* [U] art of separating metal from ore, purifying it, and of working in metal. **metal·lur·gist** /-dʒɪst/ *n* expert in ~. **metal·lur·gi·cal** /ˌmetəˋlɜdʒɪkl/ *adv* of ~.

meta·mor·phose /ˌmetəˋmɔfəʊz/ *vt* [VP6A,14] *~ **sth (into),*** change in form, change the nature of (as by sorcery): *Circe ~d the companions of Odysseus into swine.*

meta·mor·pho·sis /ˌmetəˋmɔfəsɪs/ *n* (*pl* **-ses** /-siz/) change of form or character, e g by natural growth or development: *the ~ in the life of an insect,* from the egg, etc; *the social ~ that has occurred in China.*

meta·phor /ˋmetəfɔ(r)/ *n* [C,U] (example of) the use of words to indicate sth different from the literal meaning, as in 'I'll make him *eat* his words' or 'He has a heart *of stone*'. Cf *simile*: 'a heart *like stone*'. **~i·cal** /ˌmetəˋforɪkl *US:* -ˋfɔr-/ *adj* of or like a ~; containing or using ~s. **~i·cally** /-klɪ/ *adv*

meta·phys·ics /ˋmetəfɪzɪks/ *n* (with *sing v*) **1** branch of philosophy dealing with the nature of existence, truth and knowledge: *M~ deals with abstractions. Do we need a new ~?* (Note: on the analogy of French and German, *metaphysic* is sometimes used, meaning 'system of ~). **2** (pop use) speculative philosophy; abstract talk. **meta·phys·ical** /ˌmetəˋfɪzɪkl/ *adj* of ~; based on abstract reasoning.

meta·tar·sal /ˌmetəˋtɑsl/ *adj, n* (anat) (of a) bone in the foot. ⇨ the illus at **skeleton**.

mete /mit/ *vt* [VP15B] *~ **out,*** portion or measure: *~ out rewards/punishments. Justice was ~d out to them.*

me·teor /ˋmitɪə(r)/ *n* [C] small body rushing from outer space into the earth's atmosphere and becoming bright (as a *'shooting star'* or *'falling star'*) as it is burnt up.

me·teoric /ˌmitɪˋorɪk *US:* -ˋɔr-/ *adj* **1** of the atmosphere or of atmospheric conditions; of meteors. **2** (fig) swift and dazzling; brilliant: *a ~ career.*

me·teor·ite /ˋmitɪəraɪt/ *n* [C] fallen meteor; meteoric stone.

me·teor·ol·ogy /ˌmitɪəˋrolədʒɪ/ *n* [U] science of the weather; study of the earth's atmosphere and its changes. **me·teor·ol·ogist** /ˌmitɪəˋrolədʒɪst/ *n* expert in ~. **me·teoro·logi·cal** /ˌmitrəˋlodʒɪkl *US:* ˌmitɪər-/ *adj* of ~: *weather forecasts from the Central Meteorological Office.*

me·ter[1] /ˋmitə(r)/ *n* [C] apparatus which measures, esp one that records the amount of whatever passes through it, or the distance travelled, fare payable, etc: *an ˌelecˋtricity-~; a ˋgas-~; a ˋwater-~; an exˋposure-~,* for measuring the time needed for exposure of photographic film, etc; *a ˋparking-~,* one that measures the time during which a car is (for a fee) parked in a public place; *fares mounting up on the ~,* e g of a taxi-cab.

a meter

a metronome

me·ter[2] /ˋmitə(r)/ *n* (US) = **metre**.

meth·ane /ˋmiθeɪn/ *n* [U] odourless, colourless inflammable gas (**CH_4**) that occurs in coalmines (as fire damp, causing explosions) and (as natural gas, marsh gas) on marshy areas.

me·thinks /mɪˋθɪŋks/ *vi* (*pt* **methought** /mɪˋθɔt/) (old use) it seems to me.

method /ˋmeθəd/ *n* **1** [U] system, orderliness: *He's a man of ~. **There's ~ in his madness,*** His behaviour, etc is not so unreasonable as it seems. **2** [C] way of doing sth: *modern ~s of teaching arithmetic; ~s of payment,* e g cash, cheques, monthly instalments. **~i·cal** /məˋθodɪkl/ *adj* **1** done, carried out, with order or ~: *~ical work.* **2** doing things with ~; having orderly habits: *a ~ical worker.* **~i·cally** /-klɪ/ *adv* **~·ol·ogy** /ˌmeθəˋdolədʒɪ/ *n* [U] science or study of ~, esp in academic subjects.

Meth·od·ism /ˋmeθədɪzm/ *n* teaching, organization and manner of worship in the Christian denomination started by John Wesley. **Meth·od·ist** /-ɪst/ *n, adj* (member) of this denomination. ⇨ **Wesleyan**.

me·thought /mɪˋθɔt/ *pt* of **methinks**.

meths /meθs/ *n pl* (colloq abbr for) **methylated spirits**.

Me·thuse·lah /mɪˋθjuzələ *US:* -ˋθuz-/ *n* (in the Bible) man stated to have lived 969 years; (hence) type of longevity. ⇨ Gen 5: 27.

methyl /ˋmeθl/ *n* ˋ**~ alcohol,** kind of alcohol (also called *wood spirit*) present in many organic compounds. ˋ**~·ated** /-eɪtɪd/ *adj* ˈ**~ated ˋspirit,** [U] form of alcohol (made unfit for drinking) used for lighting and heating.

me·ticu·lous /mɪˋtɪkjʊləs/ *adj* **~ *(in),*** giving, showing, great attention to detail; careful and exact. **~·ly** *adv*

mé·tier /ˋmeɪtɪeɪ *US:* meɪˋtjeɪ/ *n* one's trade, profession or line of business.

metre[1] (US = **me·ter**) /ˋmitə(r)/ *n* unit of length in the metric system. ⇨ App 5.

metre[2] (US = **me·ter**) /ˋmitə(r)/ *n* [U] verse rhythm; [C] particular form of this; fixed arrangement of accented and unaccented syllables.

met·ric /ˋmetrɪk/ *adj* of the metre[1]: **the ˋ~ system,** the decimal measuring system based on the metre as the unit of length, the kilogram as the unit of mass and the litre as the unit of capacity. ⇨ App 5. ˋ**~ ton,** 1 000 kilograms. **met·ri·cize** /ˋmetrɪsaɪz/ *vt* convert to the ~ system.

metri·cal /ˋmetrɪkl/ *adj* **1** of, composed in, metre[2] (contrasted with ordinary prose): *a ~ translation of the Iliad.* **2** connected with measurement: *~ geometry.* **~ly** /-klɪ/ *adv*

metri·ca·tion /ˈmetrɪˋkeɪʃn/ *n* conversion to the metric system.

Metro /ˋmetrəʊ/ *n* the underground railway system in Paris. Cf in London, *Underground* or *tube.*

met·ro·nome /ˋmetrənəʊm/ *n* (music) graduated inverted pendulum for sounding an adjustable number of beats per minute.

me·trop·olis /məˋtropəlɪs/ *n* (*pl* -lises) **1** chief city of a country; capital; (in GB) *the ~,* London. **2** archbishop's see.

metro·poli·tan /ˈmetrəˋpolɪtn/ *adj* **1** of or in a capital city: *the ~ police.* **2** of an ecclesiastical province: *a ~ bishop,* one having authority over the bishops in his province. **3 M~ France,** France itself as distinct from its dependencies overseas. □ *n* **1** person who lives in a metropolis. **2 M~,** ~ bishop.

mettle /ˋmetl/ *n* [U] quality, e g in persons, horses, of endurance and courage: *a man of ~; a horse that is full of ~; try sb's ~,* test his quality. ***be/put sb on his ~,*** rouse him to do his best, put him in a position that tests his ~: *He was put on his ~.* ˋ**~·some** /-səm/ *adj* high-spirited.

mew[1] /mju/ *n* (also *miaow*) sound made by a cat. □ *vi* [VP2A] make this sound: *We heard the mewing of a cat.*

mew[2] /mju/ *vt* [VP6A,15B] ***mew up (in),*** (old use) confine in, or as if in (a cage).

mews /mjuz/ *n* (with *sing v*) (formerly a) square or street of stables behind a residential street; number of stables round an open yard; (modern use) such stables rebuilt for use as garages or converted into flats, etc: *living in a South Kensington ~.*

mezza·nine /ˋmetsənin *US:* ˋmezə-/ *n, adj* (floor) between ground floor and first floor, often in the form of a balcony.

mezzo /ˋmetsəʊ/ *adv* (musical direction) moderately; half: *~ forte,* moderately loud. **~-soprano** /ˈmetsəʊsəˋprɑnəʊ *US:* -ˋpræn-/ *n* (person with, part for a) voice between soprano and contralto.

mezzo·tint /ˋmetsəʊtɪnt/ *n* (print produced by a) method of printing from a metal plate which has a rough surface of small dots scraped and polished to produce areas of light and shade.

mi·aou, mi·aow /miˋaʊ/ *n, vi* = mew[1].

mi·asma /mɪˋæzmə/ *n* unhealthy mist rising from the ground, formerly associated with ague (malaria, etc).

mica /ˋmɑɪkə/ *n* [U] transparent mineral substance easily divided into thin layers, used as an electrical insulator, etc.

mice /mɑɪs/ *n pl* of mouse.

Michael·mas /ˋmɪklməs/ *n* 29 Sept, the feast of St Michael, a quarter-day. ˈ**~ ˋdaisy,** perennial aster flowering in autumn, with blue, white, pink or purple flowers. ˋ**~ term,** autumn term (at Oxford, the Inns of Court).

mickey /ˋmɪkɪ/ *n* ***take the ~ (out of sb),*** (sl) hold sb up to ridicule; mock or tease him.

mickle /ˋmɪkl/ *n* (also *muckle*) large amount: (only in Scot) *Many a little makes a ~.*

microbe /ˋmɑɪkrəʊb/ *n* tiny living creature that can be seen only with the help of a microscope, esp kinds of bacteria causing diseases and fermentation.

micro-biology /ˈmɑɪkrəʊ bɑɪˋolədʒɪ/ *n* study of micro-organisms.

micro·cosm /ˋmɑɪkrəʊkozm/ *n* [C] sth, (esp man, by the ancient philosophers) considered as representing (on a small scale) mankind or the universe; miniature representation (*of* a system, etc). ⇨ macrocosm.

micro·dot /ˋmɑɪkrəʊdot/ *n* photograph reduced to the size of a minute dot: (attrib) a *~ photograph,* one made up of ~s.

mi·cro·elec·tron·ics /ˈmɑɪkrəʊˈelɪkˋtronɪks/ *n pl* (with *sing v*) design, construction and use of devices with extremely small (usu solid state) components.

micro·fiche /ˋmɑɪkrəʊfiʃ/ *n* sheet of microfilm.

micro·film /ˋmɑɪkrəʊfɪlm/ *n* [C,U] (roll, section, of) photographic film for small-scale reproduction of documentary material, etc. □ *vt* [VP6A] photograph in this way: *~ old historical records/bank accounts.*

micro·mesh /ˋmɑɪkrəʊmeʃ/ *adj* **~ *stockings,*** of very small mesh.

mi·crom·eter /mɑɪˋkromɪtə(r)/ *n* device for measuring very small objects.

mi·cron /ˋmɑɪkron/ *n* unit of length (symbol μ) equal to one millionth of a metre.

micro-or·gan·ism /ˈmɑɪkrəʊ ˋɔɡənɪzm/ *n* organism so small as to be visible only under a microscope.

micro·phone /ˋmɑɪkrəfəʊn/ *n* instrument for changing sound waves into electrical waves, as in telephones, radio, etc.

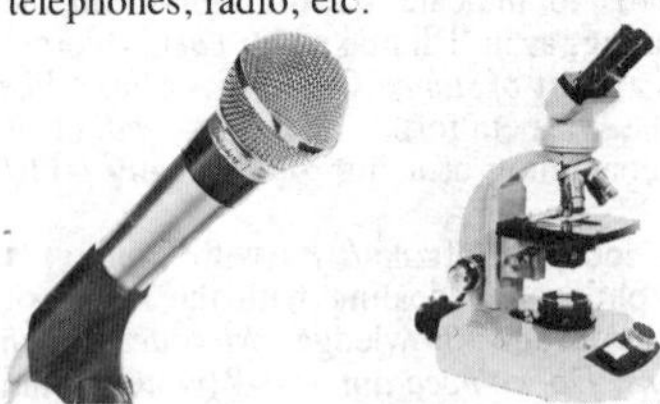

a microphone a microscope

micro·scope /ˋmɑɪkrəskəʊp/ *n* instrument with lenses for making very small near objects appear larger: *examine sth under the ~.* **micro·scopic** /ˈmɑɪkrəˋskopɪk/, **micro·scopi·cally** /-klɪ/ *adjj* of the ~; too small to be visible except under a ~.

micro·wave /ˈmaɪkrəʊweɪv/ *n* very short wave (as used in radio and radar).

mid[1] /mɪd/ *adj* **1** in the middle of; middle: *from mid June to mid August; in mid winter; a collision in mid Channel/in mid air.* **2** (in compounds used attrib): *a midwinter day; mid-morning coffee.* **the 'Mid'west,** (also known as **the Middle West**) that part of the US which is the Mississippi basin as far south as Kansas, Missouri and the Ohio River. **3** (cricket) **'mid-'off, 'mid-'on,** fielder near the bowler on the off, on, side. ⇨ the illus at cricket. **mid·most** /ˈmɪdməʊst/ *adj, adv* (*superl* of mid) (that is) in the very middle.

mid[2] /mɪd/ prep (poet) amid; among.

mid·day /ˈmɪdˈdeɪ/ *n* noon: (attrib) *the ~ meal,* i e lunch or dinner.

mid·den /ˈmɪdn/ *n* heap of dung or rubbish.

middle /ˈmɪdl/ *n* **1** (*sing* with *def art*) point, position or part, which is at an equal distance from two or more points, etc or between beginning and end: *the ~ of a room; in the ~ of the century; in the very ~ of the night; standing in the ~ of the street; a pain in the ~ of the back. They were in the ~ of dinner* (= were having dinner) *when I called. I was in the ~ of reading* (= was busy reading) *when she telephoned.* **'~-of-the-'road,** (attrib) (of policies, etc) avoiding extremes. **2** (colloq) waist: *seize sb round the ~; eighty centimetres round the ~.* **3** (attrib use) in the ~: *the ~ house in the row.* **'~ 'age,** the period of life between youth and old age (the actual figures varying with the age of the person who gives them). Hence, **'~-'aged** *adj* of ~ age: *a ~-aged woman; ~-age(d) spread,* (colloq) corpulence that tends to come with ~ age. **the M~ Ages,** the period (in European history) from about A D 1100 to 1400 (or, in a wider sense, A D 600—1500). **'~ 'class,** class of society between the lower and upper classes (e g shopkeepers, business men, professional workers). Hence, **'~-'class** *adj* of this class: *a ~-class residential area.* ***(take/follow) a ~ course,*** a compromise between two extreme courses (of action). **the ~ distance,** that part of a landscape, scene, painting, etc between the foreground and the background. **the 'M~ 'East,** ⇨ East. **'~ 'finger,** the second. **the M~ Kingdom,** (an old name for) China. **'~·man** /-mæn/ *n* (*pl* -men) any trader through whose hands goods pass between the producer and the consumer. **~ name,** second of two given names, e g *Bernard* in *George Bernard Shaw.* **'~ school,** (in some countries) type of school between elementary school and high school. **the ~ watch,** (on ships) between midnight and 4am. **'~-weight,** (esp) boxer weighing between 147 and 160 lb or (66·6 to 72·5 kg). **the 'M~ 'West,** ⇨ *Midwest* at mid[1](2).

mid·dling /ˈmɪdlɪŋ/ *adj* of middle or medium size, quality, grade, etc: *a town of ~ size. He says he's feeling only ~* (often *fair to ~*), (colloq) in fairly good but not very good health. □ *adv* (colloq) moderately: *~ tall.* □ *n* (usu *pl*) goods of second or inferior quality, esp coarse-ground wheat flour mixed with bran.

middy /ˈmɪdɪ/ *n* (*pl* -dies) (colloq abbr of) midshipman. **'~ blouse,** loose blouse like that worn by naval seamen.

midge /mɪdʒ/ *n* small winged insect like a gnat.

midget /ˈmɪdʒɪt/ *n* extremely small person, e g one exhibited as a curiosity at a circus; (attrib) very small: *a ~ submarine.*

midi·nette /ˈmɪdɪˈnet/ *n* Parisian shop-assistant, esp a milliner's assistant.

mid·land /ˈmɪdlənd/ *n* (often attrib) middle part of a country. **the M~s,** the ~ counties of England.

mid·night /ˈmɪdnaɪt/ *n* **1** 12 o'clock at night: *at/before/after ~.* **2** (attrib) during the middle of the night; at ~: *the ~ hours.* ***burn the ~ oil,*** sit up and work late at night. **the ~ sun,** the sun as seen at ~ in summer within the Arctic or Antarctic Circle.

mid·riff /ˈmɪdrɪf/ *n* **1** (anat) diaphragm. **2** abdomen, belly: (boxing) *a blow on the ~.*

mid·ship·man /ˈmɪdʃɪpmən/ *n* (*pl* -men) non-commissioned officer ranking below a sublieutenant in the Royal Navy; student training to be commissioned as an officer in the US Navy. ⇨ App 9.

mid·ships /ˈmɪdʃɪps/ *adv* = amidships.

midst /mɪdst/ *n* (liter or archaic) middle part: *in/into/from/out of the ~ (of); in our/your/their ~.* □ *prep* (liter or archaic) in the middle of; amidst.

mid·sum·mer /ˈmɪdˈsʌmə(r)/ *n* [U] period about 21 June. **'M~ 'day,** 24 June, a quarter-day. **'~ 'madness,** the height of madness.

mid·way /ˈmɪdˈweɪ/ *adj, adv* ***~ between,*** situated in the middle; halfway.

mid·wife /ˈmɪdwaɪf/ *n* (*pl* midwives /-waɪvz/) woman trained to help women in childbirth. **mid-wifery** /ˈmɪdwɪfrɪ/ *n* [U] profession and work of a ~; obstetrics: *take a course in ~ry.*

mien /min/ *n* (liter) person's appearance or bearing (as showing a mood, etc): *with a sorrowful ~; of pleasing ~; the severity of his ~.*

might[1] /maɪt/ *pt* of may.

might[2] /maɪt/ *n* [U] great power; strength: *work with all one's ~; 'M~ is right', he said,* i e Power to enforce one's will gives one the right to do so. ***by/with ~ and main,*** (by) using physical force.

mighty /ˈmaɪtɪ/ *adj* (-ier, -iest) **1** (liter, biblical) powerful: *a ~ nation.* **2** great; massive: *the ~ ocean.* **3** (colloq) great, esp ***high and ~,*** very proud. □ *adv* (colloq) very: *think oneself ~ clever.* **'might·ily** /-əlɪ/ *adv* greatly; (dated colloq) extremely: *mightily indignant.*

mignon·ette /ˈmɪnjəˈnet/ *n* [U] garden plant with small, sweet-smelling, greenish-white flowers.

mi·graine /ˈmigreɪn/ *n* (= (archaic) *megrim*) severe, frequently recurring, headache (usu on one side only of the head or face).

mi·grant /ˈmaɪgrənt/ *n* one who migrates, esp a bird: *Swallows are migrants.*

mi·grate /maɪˈgreɪt *US:* ˈmaɪgreɪt/ *vi* [VP2A,3A] ***~ (from/to),*** **1** move from one place to another (to live there). **2** (of birds and fishes) come and go with the season; travel regularly from one region to another. **mi·gra·tion** /maɪˈgreɪʃn/ n [U] migrating; [C] instance of this; [C] number of persons, animals, etc migrating together. **mi·gra·tory** /ˈmaɪgrətərɪ *US:* -tɔrɪ/ *adj* having the habit of migrating: *migratory birds.*

mi·kado /mɪˈkɑdəʊ/ *n* (name formerly used outside, but not inside, Japan for) Emperor of Japan.

mike /maɪk/ *n* (colloq abbr for) microphone.

mi·lady /mɪˈleɪdɪ/ *n* (*pl* -dies) (dated term for a) lady of quality. Cf current use of *My Lady* as a form of address.

mi·lage /ˈmaɪlɪdʒ/ *n* = mileage.

milch /mɪltʃ/ *adj* (of domestic mammals) kept for,

giving, milk: *'~ cows.*

mild /maɪld/ *adj* (-er, -est) **1** soft; gentle; not severe: *~ weather; ~ punishments; a ~ answer. I'm the ~est man alive,* No one is gentler, kinder, etc than I am. **2** (of food, drink, tobacco) not sharp or strong in taste or flavour: *~ cheese; a ~ cigar; ~ (ale) and bitter,* ~ and bitter beer mixed. ***draw it ~,*** ⇨ draw²(5). **3** **~ steel,** tough and malleable, with a low percentage of carbon. **~·ly** *adv* in a ~ manner. ***to put it ~ly,*** to say the least of it, to speak without exaggeration. **~·ness** *n*

mil·dew /'mɪldju *US:* -du/ *n* [U] (usu destructive) growth of tiny fungi forming on plants, leather, food, etc in warm and damp conditions: *roses ruined by ~.* □ *vt,vi* [VP6A,2A] affect, become affected, with ~.

mile /maɪl/ *n* measure of distance, 1 760 yards, ⇨ App 5 and ⇨ nautical: *For ~s and ~s there's nothing but desert. It's a 30 ~/a 30 ~s' journey. He ran the ~ in 4 minutes/a 4-minute ~. the metric ~,* (athletics) the 1 500 metres race. *She's feeling ~s better today,* (colloq) very much better. *There's no one within ~s of him as a tennis player,* no one who can rival him. **~·om·eter** /maɪ'lomɪtə(r)/ *n* device (in a motor-vehicle) recording the number of ~s travelled. **'~·stone** *n* (a) stone set up at the side of a road showing distances. (b) (fig) (important) stage or event in history or in human life.

mile·age /'maɪlɪdʒ/ *n* **1** distance travelled, measured in miles: *a used car with a small ~,* one that has not run many miles. **2** allowance for travelling expenses at so much a mile.

miler /'maɪlə(r)/ *n* (colloq) runner specializing in one mile races: *He's our best ~.*

mi·lieu /'milɪɜ *US:* 'milɪ'ɜ *the* ɜ *having no* r *quality/ n* environment; social surroundings.

mili·tant /'mɪlɪtənt/ *adj* ready for fighting; actively engaged in or supporting the use of force: *~ students/workers.* □ *n* ~ person, e g in trade unionism, politics. **mili·tancy** /-ənsɪ/ *n*

mili·tar·ism /'mɪlɪtərɪzm/ *n* [U] belief in, reliance upon, military strength and virtues. **mili·tar·ist** /'mɪlɪtərɪst/ *n* supporter of, believer in ~.

mili·tary /'mɪlɪtrɪ *US:* -terɪ/ *adj* of or for soldiers, an army, war on land: *~ training; in ~ uniform; ~ government; a ~ attaché; called up for two years' ~ service,* to serve as a soldier. □ *n* [U] **the ~,** the soldiers; the army: *The ~ were called in to deal with these civil disorders.*

mili·tate /'mɪlɪteɪt/ *vi* [VP3A] **~ *against,*** (of evidence, facts) have force, operate: *Several factors combined to ~ against the success of our plan.*

mil·itia /mɪ'lɪʃə/ *n* (usu **the ~**) force of civilians trained as soldiers but not part of the regular army; British conscript army formed in 1939. **'~·man** /-mən/ *n* (*pl* -men) member of the ~.

milk¹ /mɪlk/ *n* [U] **1** white liquid produced by female mammals as food for their young, esp that of cows, drunk by human beings and made into butter and cheese: *~ fresh from the cow; tinned ~; be on a ~ diet,* a diet principally of ~; *~ puddings,* e g rice, sago or tapioca baked with ~ in a dish. ***the ~ of human kindness,*** the kindness that should be natural to human beings. ***It's no use crying over spilt ~,*** over a loss or error for which there is no remedy. ***~ and water,*** (fig) feeble discourse or sentiment. **2** (compounds) **'~-bar** *n* bar for the sale of drinks made from ~, ice-cream and other light refreshments. **'~-churn** *n* large vessel fitted with a lid for carrying ~. **'~ loaf,** sweet-tasting white bread. **'~·maid** *n* woman who milks cows and works in a dairy. **'~-man** /-mən/ *n* (*pl* -men) man who sells ~; man who goes from house to house delivering ~. **'~-powder** *n* ~ dehydrated by evaporation. **'~ round** *n* ~man's route from house to house, street to street. **'~·shake** *n* drink of ~ with flavouring mixed into it and stirred up. **'~·sop** /-sop/ *n* man or youth who is lacking in spirit, who is too soft and gentle. **'~-tooth** *n* (*pl* -teeth) one of the first (temporary) teeth in young mammals. **'~-'white** *adj* as white as ~. **3** ~-like juice of some plants and trees, e g the juice inside a coconut. **'~·weed** *n* name used for several kinds of wild plant with a juice like ~. **4** ~-like preparation made from herbs, drugs, etc: *~ of magnesia.*

milk² /mɪlk/ *vt,vi* **1** [VP6A] draw milk from a cow/ewe/goat, or juice, virus, etc, e g from a snake; extract money, information, etc (by guile or dishonesty) from a person or institution. **2** [VP2A] yield milk: *The cows are ~ing well.* **'~ing-machine** *n* apparatus for ~ing cows mechanically.

milky /'mɪlkɪ/ *adj* (-ier, -iest) of or like milk; mixed with milk; (of a liquid) cloudy, not clear. **the 'M~ 'Way,** the broad luminous band of stars encircling the sky; the Galaxy.

mill¹ /mɪl/ *n* **1** (building (*'flour-~*) with) machinery or apparatus for grinding grain into flour (old style, *'water~, 'wind~*). ***go/put sb through the ~,*** (cause to) undergo hard training or experience. ***run-of-the-~,*** ⇨ run¹(10). **'~-dam** *n* dam built across a stream to make water available for a ~. **'~-pond** *n* water retained by a ~-dam, to flow to the ~: *like a ~-pond,* (of the sea) very calm. **'~-race** *n* current of water that turns a ~-wheel. **'~·stone** *n* one of a pair of circular stones between which grain is ground; (fig) heavy burden: *That mortgage has been like a ~stone round my neck. He's between the upper and nether* (= lower) *~stone,* is subject to irresistible pressure. **'~-wheel** *n* wheel (esp a water-wheel) that supplies power to drive a ~. **'~·wright** *n* man who builds and repairs water~s and wind~s. **2** building, factory, workshop, for industry: *a 'cotton/'paper/'silk/'steel-~.* **'~-hand** *n* factory worker. **'~-girl** *n* girl who works in a ~, esp a cotton-~. **3** small machine for grinding: *a 'coffee-~; a 'pepper-~.*

mill² /mɪl/ *vt,vi* **1** [VP6A] put through a machine for grinding; produce by doing this: *~ grain; ~ flour; ~ ore,* crush it; *~ steel,* make it into bars. **2** [VP6A] produce regular markings on the edge of (coin): *silver coins with a ~ed edge.* **3** [VP2C] **~ *about/around,*** (of cattle, crowds of people) move in a confused way; move in a mass.

mill·board /'mɪlbɔd/ *n* [U] stout pasteboard used in binding books.

mil·len·nium /mɪ'lenɪəm/ *n* (*pl* -nia /-nɪə/, -niums) **1** period of 1 000 years. **2** (fig) future time of great happiness and prosperity for everyone. **mil·len·arian** /'mɪlɪ'neərɪən/ *n* person who believes that the ~(2) will come.

mil·le·pede /'mɪlɪpid/ *n* small worm-like creature with very many legs, usu in double pairs at each segment. ⇨ the illus at insect.

mil·ler /'mɪlə(r)/ *n* owner or tenant of a mill, esp the old-fashioned flour-mill worked by wind or water.

mil·let /ˈmɪlɪt/ *n* [U] cereal plant growing 3 to 4 feet high and producing a large crop of small seeds; the seeds (as food).

milli- /mɪlɪ/ *pref* one-thousandth part of: *ˈ~gram; ˈ~metre.* ⇨ App 3.

mil·liard /ˈmɪlɪɑd/ *n* (GB) thousand millions (1 000 000 000) (US = *billion*). ⇨ App 4.

mil·li·bar /ˈmɪlɪbɑ(r)/ *n* unit of atmospheric pressure.

mil·liner /ˈmɪlɪnə(r)/ *n* person who makes and sells women's hats, and sells lace, trimmings, etc for hats. **~y** /-nṛɪ *US:* -nerɪ/ *n* [U] (the business of making and selling) women's hats, with lace, ribbons, etc.

mil·lion /ˈmɪlɪən/ *n, adj* one thousand thousand (1 000 000). (Note: the *pl* is rarely used after a number): *six ~ people.* ***make a ~,*** make a ~ pounds/dollars, etc. **~·aire** /ˈmɪlɪəˈneə(r)/ *n* person who has a ~ dollars, pounds, etc; extremely rich man. **ˈ~·fold** *adv* a ~ times. **mil·lionth** /-lɪənθ/ *n, adj* ⇨ App 4.

mil·li·pede /ˈmɪlɪpid/ = millepede.

mil·ometer /mɑɪˈlomɪtə(r)/ *n* instrument showing the total distance travelled by a motor-vehicle.

mi·lord /mɪˈlɔd/ *n* (F word formerly used for) English lord; wealthy Englishman.

milt /mɪlt/ *n* [U] (soft) roe of male fish; fish sperm.

mime /mɑɪm/ *n* **1** (in ancient Greece and Rome) simple kind of drama in which real persons and events were made fun of and in which mimicry and dancing were important. **2** (in the theatre, etc) use of only facial expressions and gestures to tell a story; actor in such drama. □ *vi, vt* **1** [VP2A] act in a ~. **2** [VP6A] mimic; express by ~(1).

mimeo·graph /ˈmɪmɪəʊgrɑf *US:* -græf/ *n* apparatus for making copies of written or typed material from a stencil. □ *vt* [VP6A] make (copies) with a ~.

mi·metic /mɪˈmetɪk/ *adj* of, given to, imitation or mimicry.

mimic /ˈmɪmɪk/ *attrib adj* imitated or pretended; done in play: *~ warfare,* as in peacetime manœuvres; *~ colouring,* e g of animals, birds and insects that have the colours of their natural surroundings. □ *n* person who is clever at imitating others, esp in order to make fun of their habits, appearance, etc. □ *vt* (*pt,pp* ~ked) [VP6A] **1** ridicule by imitating: *He was ~king his uncle's voice and gestures very cleverly.* **2** (of things) resemble closely: *wood painted to ~ marble.* **ˈ~ry** *n* [U] ~king: *protective ~ry,* the resemblance of birds, animals and insects to their natural surroundings, giving some protection from enemies.

mim·osa /mɪˈməʊzə *US:* -ˈməʊsə/ *n* [U] name of several kinds of shrub, esp the kind with clusters of small, ball-shaped, sweet-smelling yellow flowers.

min·aret /ˈmɪnəˈret/ *n* tall, slender spire, connected with a mosque, from the balconies of which people are called to prayer by a muezzin (or, often today, by loudspeaker). ⇨ the illus at mosque.

mina·tory /ˈmɪnətərɪ *US:* -tɔrɪ/ *adj* threatening.

mince /mɪns/ *vt, vi* **1** [VP6A] cut or chop (meat, etc) into small pieces (with a knife, or a machine with revolving blades, called a *ˈmincing machine* or *mincer*). ***not to ˈ~ matters/one's words,*** to speak plainly or bluntly in condemnation of sth or sb; not take pains to keep within the bounds of politeness. **3** [VP6A] say (words) with an affectation of delicacy; [VP2A] put on fine airs when speaking or walking, trying to appear delicate or refined. □ *n* minced meat. **ˈ~·meat** *n* [U] mixture of currants, raisins, sugar, candied peel, apples, suet, etc cooked and served with a covering of pastry. ***make ~meat of,*** (colloq) destroy a person/an argument, etc. **ˈ~-ˈpie** *n* small round pie containing ~meat. **mincer** *n* device for mincing food. **minc·ing** *adj: take mincing steps; an affected, mincing young girl,* ⇨ 3 above. **minc·ing·ly** *adv*

mind[1] /mɑɪnd/ *n* **1** [U] memory; remembrance: ***bear/keep sth in ~,*** remember sth. ***bring/call sth to ~,*** recall it to the memory. ***go/pass from/out of one's ~,*** be forgotten. ***put sb in ~ of sth,*** remind sb of, cause sb to think of sth. ***Out of sight, out of ~,*** (prov) What is not seen is soon forgotten. **2** [U] (but with indef art or *pl* in some *phrases,* as shown below) what a person thinks or feels; way of thinking; conscious thoughts; feeling, wishing; opinion; intention; purpose: *Nothing was further from his ~,* his intentions. ***absence of ~,*** failure to think of what one is doing. ⇨ *absent-minded* at absent[1]. ***presence of ~,*** ability to act or decide quickly when this is needed. ***out of one's ~/not in one's right ~,*** mad. ***ˈ~ reading,*** (= thought reading) guessing; knowing by intuition what sb is thinking. Hence, **ˈ~-reader** *n* ***be of one ~ (about sth),*** be in agreement; have the same opinion. ***be of the same ~,*** **(a)** (of a number of persons) be in agreement. **(b)** (of one person) be unchanged in an opinion, decision, etc: *Is he still of the same ~?* ***be in two ~s about sth,*** feel doubtful, hesitate, about sth. ***bend one's ~,*** influence the ~ so that it is permanently affected (by beliefs, etc). Hence, **ˈ~-bending** *adj* ***blow one's ~,*** (colloq) (of drugs, extraordinary or sensational sights, sounds, etc) cause mental excitement, state of ecstasy, etc. Hence, **ˈ~-blowing** *adj* ***change one's ~,*** change one's purpose or intention. ***give one's ~ to sth,*** direct one's attention to sth. ***give sb a piece of one's ~,*** ⇨ piece[1](2). ***have a good ~ to do sth,*** be strongly disposed to do sth. ***have half a ~ to do sth,*** be rather inclined to do sth. ***have sth on one's ~,*** be troubled about sth which, one feels, one ought to deal with. ***keep one's ~ on sth,*** continue to pay attention to, not be diverted from: *Keep your ~ on what you're doing.* ***know one's own ~,*** know what one wants, have no doubts: *He never knows his own ~,* often doubts, hesitates, about what to do. ***make up one's ~,*** **(a)** come to a decision; *I've made up my ~ to be a doctor. Have you made up your ~ about what you'll do?* **(b)** reconcile oneself to sth that cannot be changed, etc: *We're no longer a first-class power; we must make up our ~s to that.* ***set one's ~ on sth,*** want very much; be determined to have: *We've set our ~s on a holiday in France.* ***speak one's ~,*** say plainly what one thinks. ***take one's/sb's ~ off sth,*** turn one's/sb's attention away from sth; distract. ***in the ~'s eye,*** in imagination; in memory. ***to one's ~,*** **(a)** according to one's way of thinking: *To my ~, this is just a nonsense.* **(b)** to one's liking. **3** [C,U] (person with) mental ability; intellect: *He has a very good ~. He has one of the great ~s of the age. No two ~s think alike.*

mind[2] /mɑɪnd/ *vt, vi* **1** [VP6A] take care of; attend to: *Who is ~ing the baby? When Mr Green was* *called to the phone, his wife had to ~ the shop,* to attend to the shop. *M~ the step,* Watch out for it. *M~ your head,* (as a warning to stoop, e g at a low doorway). *M~ the dog,* Beware of it. *If you don't ~* (= If you're not careful), *you'll be hurt. M~ (out), there's a bus coming. M~ and do* (colloq, = Be careful to do) *what you're told.* **~ one's P's and Q's,** be careful what one says or does. **'M~ your 'own `business,** Do not interfere in the affairs of others. **~ `you** or **~,** used as an *int* meaning 'Please note': *I have no objection, ~ (you) but I think it unwise.* **2** [VP6A,C,2A] (usu in interr, neg and conditional sentences, and in affirm sentences that answer a question) be troubled by; feel objection to: *He doesn't ~ the cold weather at all. Do you ~ if I smoke? Do you ~ my smoking? Would you ~ opening the window,* Will you please do this? *Would you ~ my opening the window,* Would you object if I did this? *'Do you ~ my leaving this payment until next year?'—'Yes, I do ~',* I object to that. *I shouldn't ~ a glass of iced beer,* I should like one. ***Never ~,*** **(a)** It doesn't matter. **(b)** Don't worry about it. **~er** *n* person whose duty it is to attend to sth or sb; (in compounds) *ma`chine-~er; `baby~er.*

minded /ˈmaɪndɪd/ *adj* **1** (*pred* only) ***~ to do sth,*** disposed or inclined: *He could do it if he were so ~. If she were ~ to help,....* **2** having the kind of mind indicated (by an *adj* or *adv* prefixed): *a `strong-~ man; `high-~ leaders; `evil-~ opponents; com`mercially-~ men.* **3** conscious of the value or importance of (what is indicated by a *n* prefixed): *He has become very `food-~ since his holiday in France,* has become a gourmet.

mind·ful /ˈmaɪndfl/ *adj* (usu *pred*) **~ of,** giving thought and attention to: *~ of one's duties/the nation's welfare.* **~ly** /-flɪ/ *adv* **~·ness** *n*

mind·less /ˈmaɪndləs/ *adj* (usu *pred*) **1 ~ of,** paying no attention to; forgetful of: *~ of danger.* **2** quite lacking in or not requiring intelligence: *~ drudgery; ~ layabouts.* **~·ly** *adv* **~·ness** *n*

mine[1] /maɪn/ *poss pron* of or belonging to me: *Is this book yours or ~? He's an old `friend of ~,* one of my old friends. □ *poss adj* (in poet and biblical style only, before a vowel sound or *h*; sometimes placed after the *n*) my: *~ eyes; ~ heart; O mistress ~; ~ enemy.*

mine[2] /maɪn/ *n* **1** excavation with shafts/galleries, etc made in the earth from which coal, mineral ores, etc, are extracted. ⇨ quarry for stone or slate: *`coal~; `gold~;* (fig) rich or abundant source: *A good encyclopedia/My grandmother is a ~ of information.* **2** (tunnel for) charge of high explosive (as used to destroy enemy fortifications); charge of high explosive buried and exploded, e g electrically, from a distance or laid on or just below the ground, exploded by contact with a vehicle, or a time fuse, etc: *The lorry was destroyed by a buried ~.* **3** (in war at sea) charge of high explosives in a metal case, placed in the sea, exploded on contact, or electrically, or magnetically. **4 `~-detector** *n* electro-magnetic device for finding ~s(2,3). **`~-disposal** *n* the making of ~s harmless (by defusing them, etc): *~-disposal squads.* **`~-field** *n* **(a)** area of land or sea where ~s(2,3) have been laid. **(b)** area of land where there are many ~s(1). **`~-layer** *n* ship or aircraft used for laying ~s at sea. Hence, **`~-laying,** as in *~-laying vessel.* **`~-sweeper** *n* naval vessel (usu a trawler) employed for clearing the sea of ~s. Hence, **`~-sweeping** *n*

mine[3] /maɪn/ *vt,vi* **1** [VP6A,2A,3A] dig (for coal, ores, etc) from the ground; obtain (coal, etc) from mines: *~ (for) coal/gold; ~ the earth for coal. Gold is ~d from deep under ground.* **2** [VP6A] (= *undermine*) make tunnels in the earth under: *~ the enemy's trenches/forts.* **3** [VP6A] lay mines(2,3) in; destroy by means of these: *~ the entrance to a harbour. The cruiser was ~d, and sank in five minutes.* **4** [VP6A] (fig) weaken; undermine (which is the more usu word).

miner /ˈmaɪnə(r)/ *n* **1** man who works in a mine underground: *`coal~s.* **2** soldier trained to dig tunnels and lay mines under enemy trenches, etc.

min·eral /ˈmɪnr̩l/ *n* [C] natural substance (not vegetable or animal) got from the earth by mining, esp one that has a constant chemical composition: *Coal and iron ore are ~s.* □ *adj* of the class of ~s; containing, mixed with, ~s: *~ ores.* **the ~ kingdom,** natural substances of inorganic matter. ⇨ animal and vegetable. **`~ oil,** any oil of ~ origin. **`~ pitch,** asphalt. **`~ water, (a)** water that naturally contains a ~ substance, esp one said to have medicinal value. **(b)** (GB) non-alcoholic drink (usu bottled, often flavoured) containing soda-water. **`~ wool,** inorganic fibrous material (used for insulating, etc).

min·er·al·ogy /ˈmɪnəˈrælədʒɪ/ *n* [U] the study and science of minerals. **min·er·al·ogist** /ˈmɪnə`rælədʒɪst/ *n* student of ~.

min·estrone /ˈmɪnɪˈstrəʊnɪ/ *n* [U] (I) rich soup (of Italian origin) of mixed vegetables, vermicelli and meat broth.

mingle /ˈmɪŋgl/ *vt,vi* [VP6A,14,2A,C] ***~ (with),*** mix: *truth ~d with falsehood; ~ with* (= go about among) *the crowds; two rivers that join and ~ their waters.*

mingy /ˈmɪndʒɪ/ *adj* **(-ier, -iest)** (GB colloq) mean, ungenerous, stingy: *a ~ fellow.*

mini /ˈmɪnɪ/ *pref* of small size, length, etc. ⇨ maxi: *`~bus; `~cab; `~skirt; `~tour.*

minia·ture /ˈmɪnɪtʃə(r) *US:* -tʃʊər/ *n* **1** [C] very small painting of a person, esp one on ivory or vellum; [U] this branch of painting. ***in ~,*** on a small scale. **2** [C] small-scale copy or model of any object. **3** (attrib) on a small scale: *a ~ railway; a ~ camera,* one for 35 mm or sub-standard size of film. **minia·tur·ist** /ˈmɪnɪtʃərɪst/ *n* painter of ~s.

minim /ˈmɪnɪm/ *n* (music) note half the value of a semibreve. ⇨ the illus at notation.

mini·mal /ˈmɪnɪml/ *adj* smallest in amount or degree: *On these cliffs vegetation is ~.*

mini·mize /ˈmɪnɪmaɪz/ *vt* [VP6A] reduce to, estimate at, the smallest possible amount or degree: *~ an accident,* try to reduce its importance, say that it is not serious.

mini·mum /ˈmɪnɪmən/ *n* (*pl* **-ma** /-mə/, **-mums**) least possible or recorded amount, degree, etc (contrasted with *maximum*): *reduce sth to a ~;* (attrib) *the ~ temperature; a maximum and ~ thermometer,* ⇨ maximum; *a ~ wage,* lowest wage that regulations allow to be paid.

min·ing /ˈmaɪnɪŋ/ *n* the process of getting minerals, etc from mines: *a `~ engineer; the `~ industry; open-cast ~,* getting coal, etc that is near the surface, using mechanical shovels, etc.

min·ion /ˈmɪnɪən/ *n* favourite servant; (usu contemptuous) servant who, in order to win favour, obeys a master slavishly: *the ~s of the law,* (derog) police, jailers.

min·is·ter¹ /ˈmɪnɪstə(r)/ *n* **1** person at the head of a Department of State (and often a member of the Cabinet): *the M~ of Employment and Productivity; the Prime M~*. **2** person representing his Government in a foreign country but of lower rank than an ambassador. **3** Christian priest or clergyman, esp one in the Presbyterian and Nonconformist Churches. Cf *priest* for the R C Church, and *vicar, rector, curate* for the Church of England.

min·is·ter² /ˈmɪnɪstə(r)/ *vi* [VP3A] **~ to,** give help or service: *~ to the wants of a sick man; ~ing to her husband's needs,* satisfying them.

min·is·ter·ial /ˌmɪnɪˈstɪərɪəl/ *adj* **1** of a Minister of State, his position, duties, ect: *~ functions/duties*. **2** of or for the Ministry (or Cabinet): *the ~ benches*. **~ly** /-ɪəlɪ/ *adv*

min·is·trant /ˈmɪnɪstrənt/ *adj* administering. □ *n* attendant; supporter or helper.

min·is·tra·tion /ˌmɪnɪˈstreɪʃn/ *n* [U] ministering or serving, e g in performing a religious service; [C] act of this kind: *Thanks to the ~s* (= nursing, services) *of my devoted wife, I was restored to health.*

min·is·try /ˈmɪnɪstrɪ/ *n* (*pl* **-ries**) **1** Department of State under a Minister: *the ˈAir M~; the ˌM~ of ˈFinance*. **2 the ~,** the ministers of religion as a body: *He was intended for the ~,* destined to be a minister, e g by his parents. ***enter the ~,*** become a minister of religion. **3** office, duties, term of service, of a minister.

mini·ver /ˈmɪnɪvə(r)/ *n* [U] ermine fur (as for the ceremonial robes of peers).

mink /mɪŋk/ *n* [C,U] (valuable brown fur skin of a) small stoat-like animal: (attrib) *a ~ coat*.

min·now /ˈmɪnəʊ/ *n* (sorts of) very small freshwater fish.

mi·nor /ˈmaɪnə(r)/ *adj* ⇨ major. **1** smaller, less important: *~ repairs/alteration; a broken leg and ~ injuries*. **2** comparatively unimportant: *the ~ planets; ~ poets; play only a ~ part in the play;* (cards) *a ~ suit,* i e diamonds or clubs. **3** (in schools) second or younger of two boys (esp in the same school): *Smith ~*. **4** (music) *a ~ third,* an interval of three semi-tones; *a ~ key,* in which the scale has a ~ third. ***in a ~ key,*** (fig) in a melancholy or depressed mood. □ *n* (legal) person not yet legally of age.

mi·nor·ity /maɪˈnɒrətɪ *US:* -ˈnɔr-/ *n* (*pl* **-ties**) **1** [U] (legal) the state of being under age (in GB under 18). **2** the smaller number or part, esp of a total of votes; small racial, religious, etc group in a community, nation, etc. ***be in the ~,*** be in the smaller of two groups. *We're in the ~,* More people are against us than with us. *I'm in a ~ of one,* have had support from no one. **a ˈ~ government,** one which has a ~ of the total number of seats in a legislative assembly. **a ˈ~ programme,** (T V, radio) one viewed or listened to by a comparatively small proportion of the total viewers or listeners. **a ˈ~ report,** one made (after an official inquiry or investigation) by the ~, giving views, etc, different from those of the majority.

Mino·taur /ˈmaɪnətɔ(r)/ *n* (Gk myth) monster, half man and half bull, fed with human flesh, kept in the labyrinth in Crete.

min·ster /ˈmɪnstə(r)/ *n* large or important church, esp one that once belonged to a monastery, and now usu named: *York ~*.

min·strel /ˈmɪnstrəl/ *n* **1** (in the Middle Ages) travelling composer, player and singer of songs and ballads. **2** one of a company of public entertainers, often with blackened faces, at fairs, race-meetings and on the seashore at holiday resorts. **~sy** /ˈmɪnstrlsɪ/ *n* [U] the art, songs, etc of ~s(1).

a Minotaur

a centaur

mint¹ /mɪnt/ *n* [U] (sorts of) plant whose leaves are used for flavouring (e g in drinks and in chewing-gum) and in making a sauce: *~ sauce,* chopped-up ~ leaves, in vinegar and sugar, as eaten with lamb.

mint² /mɪnt/ *n* **1** place where coins are made, usu under State authority: *coins fresh from the ~*. **2** ***make/earn a ~ (of money),*** (colloq) a large amount. **3** (attrib, of medals, stamps, prints, books, etc). ***in ~ condition,*** as if new; unsoiled; perfect. □ *vt* [VP6A] **1** make (coin) by stamping metal: *~ coins of 50p*. **2** (fig) invent a word, phrase, etc.

min·uet /ˌmɪnjʊˈet/ *n* [C] (piece of music for a) slow, graceful dance for groups of two couples (dating from the middle of the 17th c).

minus /ˈmaɪnəs/ *adj* ⇨ plus. **1** *the ˈ~ sign,* the sign −. **2** negative: *a ~ quantity,* a quantity less than zero (e g $-2x^2$). ⇨ positive. □ *prep* less; with the deduction of: *7 ~ 3 is 4;* (colloq) without: *He came back from the war ~ a leg.* □ *n* ~ sign or quantity.

min·us·cule /ˈmɪnəskjul/ *adj* tiny; small.

min·ute¹ /ˈmɪnɪt/ *n* **1** the sixtieth part of one hour: *seven ~s to six; arrive ten ~s early*. **ˈ~-gun** *n* one fired at intervals of a ~, e g in days before radio, by a ship in danger of sinking. **ˈ~-hand** *n* hand indicating the ~s on a watch or clock. **ˈ~-man** /-mən/ *n* (*pl* **-men**) (US, period of the revolution) militiaman ready to fight at a minute's notice. ***in a ~,*** soon: *I'll come downstairs in a ~*. ***to the ~,*** exactly: *The train arrived at 5 o'clock to the ~*. ***the ~ (that),*** as soon as: *I'll give him your message the ~ (that) he arrives*. **ˌup-to-the-ˈ~,** (attrib, with hyphens) most recent: *up-to-the-~ information*. **2** the sixtieth part of a degree (in an angle): *37° 30′*, 37 degrees 30 ~s. **3** [C] official record giving authority, advice or making comments: *make a ~ of sth*. **4** (*pl*) summary, records, of what is said and decided at a meeting, esp of a society or committee: *read and confirm the ~s of the last meeting*. **ˈ~-book** *n* book in which ~s are written. □ *vt* [VP6A] record (sth) in the ~s(4); make a record of sth in a memorandum.

mi·nute² /maɪˈnjut *US:* -ˈnut/ *adj* **1** very small: *~ particles of gold dust*. **2** giving small details; careful and exact: *a ~ description; the ~st details*. **~·ly** *adv* **~·ness** *n*

mi·nu·tiæ /maɪˈnjuʃii *US:* mɪˈnuʃii/ *n pl* precise or trivial details.

minx /mɪŋks/ *n* sly, impudent girl.

mir·acle /ˋmɪrəkl/ *n* **1** act or event (sth good or welcome) which does not follow the known laws of nature; remarkable and surprising event: *work/accomplish ~s. Her life was saved by a ~. The doctors said that her recovery was a ~.* ˋ**~ play,** dramatic representation (in the Middle Ages) based on the life of Jesus or the Christian saints. **2** *~ of,* remarkable example or specimen: *It's a ~ of ingenuity.* **mir·acu·lous** /mɪˋrækjʊləs/ *adj* like a ~; contrary to the laws of nature; surprising. **mir·acu·lous·ly** *adv*

mi·rage /ˋmɪrɑʒ *US:* mɪˋrɑʒ/ *n* [C] **1** effect, produced by air conditions, causing sth distant to become visible, esp the illusive appearance of a sheet of water in the desert. **2** (fig) any illusion or hope that cannot be realized.

mire /ˋmɑɪə(r)/ *n* [U] **1** swampy ground; soft, deep mud. **2** ***be in the ~,*** (fig) be in difficulties. ***drag sb/sb's name through the ~,*** bring disgrace on him, expose him to contempt. □ *vt,vi* **1** [VP6A] cover with mud; cause to be fast in deep mud. **2** [VP2A] sink in mud. **3** (fig) [VP6A] involve (sb) in difficulties. **miry** *adj* muddy: *miry roads.*

mir·ror /ˋmɪrə(r)/ *n* **1** polished surface that reflects images, formerly of metal; (modern use) looking-glass: *a ˋdriving ~,* ~ in a motor-car to enable the driver to see what is behind him. ˈ**~ ˋimage,** reflection or copy of sth with the right and left sides reversed. **2** (fig) sth that reflects or gives a likeness: *Pepys's 'Diary' is a ~ of the times he lived in.* □ *vt* [VP6A] reflect as in a ~: *The still water of the lake ~ed the hillside.*

mirth /mɜθ/ *n* [U] being merry, happy and bright; laughter. **~·ful** /-fl/ *adj* full of ~; merry. **~·fully** /-fl̩ɪ/ *adv* **~·less** *adj* without ~: *a ~less laugh.*

mis·ad·ven·ture /ˈmɪsədˋventʃə(r)/ *n* [C,U] (event caused by) bad luck; misfortune. ***death by ~,*** by accident.

mis·ad·vise /ˈmɪsədˋvɑɪz/ *vt* [VP6A] (usu passive) advise wrongly.

mis·al·liance /ˈmɪsəˋlɑɪəns/ *n* unsuitable alliance, esp marriage; mésalliance.

mis·an·thrope /ˋmɪsnθrəʊp/ *n* person who hates mankind; person who avoids society. **mis·an·thropic** /ˈmɪsnˋθropɪk/ *adj* hating or distrusting mankind or human society. **mis·an·thropy** /mɪsˋænθrəpɪ/ *n* [U] hatred of mankind.

mis·apply /ˈmɪsəˋplɑɪ/ *vt* (*pt,pp* -lied) [VP6A] apply wrongly; use for a wrong purpose, e g public funds. **mis·ap·pli·ca·tion** /ˈmɪsˈæplɪˋkeɪʃn/ *n* wrong or unjust use (*of*).

mis·ap·pre·hend /ˈmɪsˈæprɪˋhend/ *vt* [VP6A] misunderstand. **mis·ap·pre·hen·sion** /ˈmɪsˈæprɪˋhenʃn/ *n* ***be/do sth under a misapprehension,*** have, do sth because of, a failure to understand correctly.

mis·ap·pro·pri·ate /ˈmɪsəˋprəʊprɪeɪt/ *vt* [VP6A] take and use wrongly; apply (sb else's money) to a wrong (esp one's own) use: *The treasurer ~d the society's funds.* **mis·ap·pro·pri·ation** /ˈmɪsəˈprəʊprɪˋeɪʃn/ *n*: *misappropriation of public funds.*

mis·be·got·ten /ˈmɪsbɪˋgotn/ *adj* illegitimate; bastard; (colloq, as a term of approbrium): *Who's the author of these ~* (= ill-advised, worthless) *plans?*

mis·be·have /ˈmɪsbɪˋheɪv/ *vt,vi* [VP6A,2A] behave (oneself) improperly. **mis·be·hav·iour** (US = **-ior**) /ˈmɪsbɪˋheɪvɪə(r)/ *n*

mis·be·liever /ˈmɪsbɪˋlivə(r)/ *n* person having, or held to have, false beliefs, e g about religion.

mis·cal·cu·late /ˈmɪsˋkælkjʊleɪt/ *vt,vi* calculate (amounts, etc) wrongly. **mis·cal·cu·la·tion** /ˈmɪsˈkælkjʊˋleɪʃn/ *n*

mis·call /ˈmɪsˋkɔl/ *vt* call by a wrong name: *King Robert, ~ed 'the Just'.*

mis·car·riage /ˋmɪskærɪdʒ/ *n* **1** [U] ***~ of justice,*** failure of a court to administer justice properly; mistake in judgement or in punishment; [C] instance of this. **2** [C] failure to deliver to, or arrive at, the destination: *~ of goods;* [C] instance of this. **3** [U] premature expulsion of a foetus from the womb; [C] instance of this: *have a ~.*

mis·carry /ˈmɪsˋkærɪ/ *vt* (*pt,pp* -ried) [VP2A] **1** (of plans, etc) fail; have a result different from what was hoped for. **2** (of letters, etc) fail to reach the right destination. **3** (of a woman) have a miscarriage(3).

mis·cast /ˈmɪsˋkɑst *US:* -ˋkæst/ *vt* (*pt,pp* miscast) [VP6A] (usu passive) **1** (of an actor) be cast for a role for which he is unfitted: *She was badly ~ as Juliet.* ⇨ **cast**[1](6). **2** (of a play) have the parts badly allocated to the actors and actresses.

mis·cegen·ation /ˈmɪsɪdʒɪˋneɪʃn/ *n* [U] mixture of races, the production of offspring, esp by sexual union of white and non-white peoples.

mis·cel·laneous /ˈmɪsəˋleɪnɪəs/ *adj* of mixed sorts; having various qualities and characteristics: *a ~ collection of goods; Milton's ~ prose works.* **mis·cel·lany** /mɪˋselənɪ *US:* ˋmɪsl̩eɪnɪ/ *n* (*pl* -nies) collection, e g of writings on various subjects by various authors. **mis·cel·lanea** /ˈmɪsəˋleɪnɪə/ *n pl* literary miscellany.

mis·chance /ˈmɪsˋtʃɑns *US:* -ˋtʃæns/ *n* [C,U] (piece of) bad luck: *by ~; through a ~.*

mis·chief /ˋmɪstʃɪf/ *n* **1** [U] injury or damage done by a person or other agent, esp on purpose: *a storm that did much ~ to shipping.* ***do sb a ~,*** hurt him. **2** [U] moral harm or injury: *Such wild speeches may work great ~,* e g may rouse evil passions. ***make ~ (between...),*** cause discord or ill feeling. Hence, ˋ**~-maker,** ˋ**~-making. 3** [U] foolish or thoughtless behaviour likely to cause trouble; not very serious wrongdoing: *Boys are fond of ~,* of playing tricks, etc. *Tell the children to keep out of ~. He's up to ~ again,* planning some piece of ~. *She's always getting into ~.* **4** light-hearted, innocent desire to tease: *Her eyes were full of ~.* **5** [C] person who is fond of ~(4): *Those boys are regular ~s. Where have you hidden my book, you little ~?*

mis·chiev·ous /ˋmɪstʃɪvəs/ *adj* **1** causing mischief; harmful: *a letter/rumour.* **2** filled with, fond of, engaged in, mischief; showing a spirit of mischief: *~ looks/tricks; as ~ as a monkey.* **~·ly** *adv* **~·ness** *n*

mis·con·ceive /ˈmɪskənˋsiv/ *vt,vi* **1** [VP6A] understand wrongly. **2** [VP3A] ***~ of,*** have a wrong conception: *~ of one's duty.* **mis·con·cep·tion** /ˈmɪskənˋsepʃn/ *n* [U] misconceiving; [C] instance of this.

mis·con·duct /mɪsˋkondʌkt/ *n* [U] **1** improper behaviour, e g adultery. **2** bad management. □ *vt* /ˈmɪskənˋdʌkt/ **1** [VP6A,14] ***~ oneself (with sb),*** behave badly; be guilty of adultery (*with...*). **2** [VP6A] manage badly: *~ one's business affairs.*

mis·con·struc·tion /ˈmɪskənˋstrʌkʃn/ *n* [U] false or inaccurate interpretation or understanding; [C] instance of this: *Your words were open to ~.*

mis·con·strue /ˈmɪskənˋstru/ *vt* [VP6A] get a wrong idea of (sb's words, acts, etc): *You have*

~*d my words.*

mis·count /ˈmɪsˋkaʊnt/ *vt,vi* [VP6A,2A] count wrongly. □ *n* [C] wrong count, esp of votes at an election.

mis·cre·ant /ˋmɪskrɪənt/ *n* (dated) scoundrel; villain.

mis·cre·ated /ˈmɪskrɪˋeɪtɪd/ *adj* deformed; (as a word of abuse) monstrous.

mis·date /ˈmɪsˋdeɪt/ *vt* [VP6A] give a wrong date to an event, etc; put a wrong date on a letter, cheque, etc.

mis·deal /ˈmɪsˋdil/ *vt* (*pt,pp* -dealt /-ˋdelt/) [VP6A,2A] deal (playing-cards) wrongly. □ *n* error in dealing cards: *I've got 14 cards; it's a* ~.

mis·deed /mɪsˋdid/ *n* wicked act; crime: *be punished for one's* ~*s.*

mis·de·mean·our (US = **-meanor**) /ˈmɪsdɪˋminə(r)/ *n* (legal) offence less serious than a felony.

mis·di·rect /ˈmɪsdɪˋrekt/ *vt* [VP6A] direct wrongly: ~ *a letter,* by failing to put the full or correct address on it; ~ *one's energies or abilities,* e g by using them for a bad purpose; ~ *a jury,* (of a judge in a law court) give the jury wrong information on a point of law. **mis·di·rec·tion** /ˈmɪsdɪˋrekʃn/ *n*

mis·doing /ˈmɪsˋduɪŋ/ *n* (usu *pl*) misdeed.

mis·doubt /ˈmɪsˋdaʊt/ *vt* (archaic) have doubts or misgivings.

mise en scène /ˈmiz õ ˋsen *US:* ˋseɪn/ *n* scenery and properties of an acted play; (fig) general surroundings of an event.

miser /ˋmaɪzə(r)/ *n* person who loves wealth for its own sake and spends as little as possible. **~·ly** *adj* like a ~; stingy. **~·li·ness** *n*

mis·er·able /ˋmɪzrəbl/ *adj* **1** wretched; very unhappy: ~ *from cold and hunger; the* ~ *lives of the refugees in Europe after the war. He makes her life* ~. **2** causing wretchedness and unhappiness: ~ *weather;* ~ *slums.* **3** poor in quality: *What a* ~ *meal! What a* ~ *pension after fifty years' hard work!* **mis·er·ably** /-əblɪ/ *adv: die miserably; be miserably poor; miserably underpaid.*

mis·ery /ˋmɪzərɪ/ *n* (*pl* -ries) **1** [U] state of being miserable; great suffering (of mind or body): *be in a* ~*/suffer* ~ *from the toothache; living in* ~ *and want,* in wretched conditions and poverty. ***put the animal out of its*** ~, end its sufferings by killing it. **2** (*pl*) painful happenings; great misfortunes: *the miseries of mankind.* **3** (colloq) person who is always miserable and complaining: *I've had enough of your complaints, you little* ~*!*

mis·fire /ˈmɪsˋfaɪə(r)/ *vi* [VP2A] (of a gun) fail to go off; (of a motor-engine) fail to ignite in a cylinder; (colloq of a joke, etc) fall flat; fail to have the intended result. □ *n* such a failure.

mis·fit /ˋmɪsfɪt/ *n* article of clothing which does not fit well the person it is meant for; (fig) person not well suited to his position or his associates.

mis·for·tune /ˈmɪsˋfɔtʃun/ *n* **1** [U] bad luck: *suffer* ~*; companions in* ~. **2** [C] instance of bad luck; unfortunate accident or happening: *He bore his* ~*s bravely.*

mis·give /ˈmɪsˋgɪv/ *vt* (*pt* misgave /-ˋgeɪv/, *pp* misgiven /-ˋgɪvn/) (used impersonally; old use) *My mind/heart* ~*s me,* I am filled with suspicion or foreboding, I feel doubtful, troubled. **mis·giv·ing** /ˈmɪsˋgɪvɪŋ/ *n* [C,U] (feeling of) doubt, suspicion, distrust, etc: *a heart/mind full of misgivings*.

mis·gov·ern /ˈmɪsˋgʌvən/ *vt* [VP6A] govern (the State, etc) badly. **~ment** *n* [U].

mis·guide /ˈmɪsˋgaɪd/ *vt* [VP6A,14] give wrong or misleading information or directions to: *We had been* ~*d into thinking that....* **mis·guided** *adj* foolish and wrong (because of bad or wrong guidance or influence): ~*d conduct/zeal;* ~*d boys.*

mis·handle /ˈmɪsˋhændl/ *vt* deal with roughly, rudely or inefficiently.

mis·hap /ˋmɪshæp/ *n* [C] unlucky accident: *meet with a slight* ~*; arrive home after many* ~*s;* [U] bad luck; accident: *arrive without* ~.

mish·mash /ˋmɪʃmæʃ/ *n* [U] confused mixture; hodge podge.

mis·in·form /ˈmɪsɪnˋfɔm/ *vt* [VP6A] give wrong information to; mislead: *You've been* ~*ed.*

mis·in·ter·pret /ˈmɪsɪnˋtɜprɪt/ *vt* [VP6A] give a wrong interpretation to; make a wrong inference from: *He* ~*ed her silence as giving consent.*

mis·judge /ˈmɪsˋdʒʌdʒ/ *vt,vi* [VP6A,2A] judge or estimate wrongly; form a wrong opinion of: *You have* ~*d my motives. He* ~*d the distance and fell into the stream.*

mis·lay /ˈmɪsˋleɪ/ *vt* (*pt,pp* mislaid /-ˋleɪd/) [VP6A] put (sth) by an oversight where it cannot easily be found: *I've mislaid my passport.*

mis·lead /ˈmɪsˋlid/ *vt* (*pt,pp* misled /-ˋled/) [VP6A] lead wrongly; cause to be or do wrong; give a wrong idea to: *be misled by a guide,* during a journey; *misled by bad companions,* led into evil ways. *You misled me as to your intentions. This information is rather* ~*ing,* gives a wrong impression.

mis·man·age /ˈmɪsˋmænɪdʒ/ *vt* [VP6A] manage badly or wrongly. **~ment** *n*

mis·name /ˈmɪsˋneɪm/ *vt* [VP6A] (usu passive) call by a wrong or improper name.

mis·nomer /ˈmɪsˋnəʊmə(r)/ *n* [C] wrong use of a name or word: *It's a* ~ *to call this place a first-class hotel.*

mis·ogyn·ist /mɪˋsodʒɪnɪst/ *n* hater of women.

mis·place /ˈmɪsˋpleɪs/ *vt* [VP6A] **1** put in a wrong place. **2** (usu passive) give love, affection wrongly or unwisely: ~*d confidence,* given to sb who does not deserve it or who misuses it.

mis·print /ˋmɪsprɪnt/ *n* /ˈmɪsˋprɪnt/ *vt* [VP6A] (make an) error in printing, e g *errors and omissions expected* for *errors and omissions excepted.* □ *n* /ˋmɪsprɪnt/ such an error.

mis·pro·nounce /ˈmɪsprəˋnaʊns/ *vt* [VP6A] pronounce wrongly. **mis·pro·nun·ci·ation** /ˈmɪsprəˈnʌnsɪˋeɪʃn/ *n*

mis·quote /ˈmɪsˋkwəʊt/ *vt* [VP6A] quote wrongly. **mis·quo·ta·tion** /ˈmɪs-kwəʊˋteɪʃn/ *n* [C,U].

mis·read /ˈmɪsˋrid/ *vt* (*pt,pp* misread /-ˋred/) [VP6A] read or interpret wrongly: ~ *one's instructions.*

mis·rep·re·sent /ˈmɪsˈreprɪˋzent/ *vt* represent wrongly; give a false account of: *be grossly* ~*ed by the press.* **mis·rep·re·sen·ta·tion** /ˈmɪsˈreprɪzenˋteɪʃn/ *n* [C,U].

mis·rule /ˈmɪsˋrul/ *n* [U] bad government; lawlessness; confusion.

miss[1] /mɪs/ *n* [C] **1** failure to hit, catch, reach, etc: *ten hits and one* ~. *That was a lucky* ~, a fortunate escape. ***give sth a*** ~, (colloq) omit it, leave it alone: *I'll give the fish course a* ~. ***A*** ~ ***is as good as a mile,*** (prov) A narrow escape is the same in effect as an escape by a wide margin. **2**

(colloq) miscarriage(3).

miss[2] /mɪs/ *n* **1 M~,** title for an unmarried woman or girl who has no other title: *M~ Smith; (pl,* e g of sisters) *the M~ Smiths, the M~es Smith; M~ Italy,* e g as the title of a beauty queen. **2** (small *m,* usu playful or perhaps derog) young girl, schoolgirl: *She's a saucy ~.* **3** (as a vocative, e g by schoolchildren to a woman teacher, also to shopkeepers, etc: *Good morning, ~! Two cups of coffee, ~.* **4** (trade use, *pl*) young girls: *shoes, coats, etc for Junior M~es,* (today, often replaced by *teenagers*).

miss[3] /mɪs/ *vt,vi* (*pt,pp* missed) **1** [VP6A,B,2A] fail to hit, hold, catch, reach, see, etc what it is desired to hit, hold, etc: *fire at a tiger and ~ (it); ~ one's aim; ~ the target. He ~ed his footing,* slipped, e g while climbing on rocks. *He ~ed the 9.30 train* (= was too late for it, did not catch it), *and therefore ~ed* (i e luckily escaped) *the accident. The house is at the next corner; you can't ~ it,* you'll certainly see it. *He ~ed* (= failed to see) *the point of my joke. I ~ed* (= did not hear) *the first part of the speech. We only just ~ed* (= escaped) *having a nasty accident. We ~ed seeing* (= didn't see, failed to see) *that film when it was at the local cinema.* **2** [VP6A] realize, learn, feel regret at, the absence of: *When did you ~ your purse,* realize that you no longer had it? *He's so rich that he wouldn't ~ £100. She'd ~ her husband if he died. Old Smith won't be ~ed,* Nobody will feel regret at his absence, death, retirement, etc. **3** [VP2C] ***~ out (on sth),*** lose an opportunity to benefit from sth, enjoy oneself: *If I don't go to the party, I shall feel that I'm ~ing out. I ~ed out on his offer of a free holiday in Spain.* [VP15B] ***~ sth out,*** omit; fail to put in or say: *The printers have ~ed out a word/line. I shall ~ out the sweet course,* i e at a meal, not take it. *When we sing this hymn, ~ out the second and fourth verses,* don't sing them. **~·ing** *adj* not to be found; not in the place where it ought to be: *a book with two pages ~ing; the dead, wounded and ~ing,* i e soldiers in war; *~ing persons,* persons who cannot be traced. ***the ~ing link.*** ⇨ link[1](1).

mis·sal /ˈmɪsl/ *n* book containing the order of service for Mass in the R C Church; book of prayers and devotions.

mis·shapen /ˌmɪsˈʃeɪpən/ *adj* (esp of the body or a limb) deformed; badly shaped.

mis·sile /ˈmɪsaɪl *US:* ˈmɪsl/ *n* object or weapon that is thrown (e g a stone), shot (e g an arrow) or projected (e g a rocket): **inter-continental ballistic ~,** long-range rocket with a warhead. **guided ~s,** e g from ground to air, for destroying aircraft, guided by electronic devices; (attrib) ˈ**~ sites/bases** *nn pl* for ballistic ~s, etc.

mission /ˈmɪʃn/ *n* **1** (the sending out of a) number of persons entrusted with special work, usu abroad: *a trade ~ to S America; go/come/send sb on a ~ of inquiry; complete one's ~ successfully.* **2** (esp) the sending out of religious teachers (*~aries*) to convert people by preaching, teaching, etc: *Foreign M~s; Home M~s,* i e to preach to people in the home country, esp those not usu interested in religion. **3** place where the work of a ~(2) is carried on; building(s), organization, etc needed for such work; settlement where charitable or medical work is carried on, esp among poor people. **4** ***~ in life,*** that work which a person feels called upon to do by God: *She thinks her ~ in life is to reform juvenile delinquents.* **5** (esp US) special task, assigned to an individual or a unit of the armed forces: *The group has flown twenty ~s.*

mission·ary /ˈmɪʃnrɪ *US:* -ṇerɪ/ *n* (*pl* -ries) person sent to preach his religion, esp among people who are ignorant of it; (attrib) of missions(2) or missionaries: *a ~ meeting,* at which a ~ talks about his work or one held to raise funds; *a ~ box,* in which money is collected for charitable missions.

mis·sis /ˈmɪsɪz/ *n* ⇨ missus.

mis·sive /ˈmɪsɪv/ *n* (used hum for) (esp a long, serious-looking) letter.

mis-spell /ˌmɪs ˈspel/ *vt* (*pt,pp* mis-spelled or mis-spelt /ˈspelt/) [VP6A] spell wrongly. **~·ing** *n*

mis-spend /ˌmɪs ˈspend/ *vt* (*pt,pp* mis-spent /ˈspent/) [VP6A] spend or use wrongly or foolishly (esp *pp*): *a mis-spent youth,* (used of one who spends or has spent his early years only in foolish pleasures).

mis·state /ˌmɪsˈsteɪt/ *vt* [VP6A] state wrongly: *He was careful not to ~ his case.* **~ment** *n*

mis·sus, mis·sis /ˈmɪsɪz/ *n* (GB colloq or sl) **1** (as used by servants) the mistress: *The ~ has gone out.* **2** (used with *the, my, his, your*) wife: *How's the ~? My ~ won't like that.*

missy /ˈmɪsɪ/ *n* (*pl* -sies) (colloq, familiar) young girl; Miss: *Well, ~, what do you want?*

mist /mɪst/ *n* **1** [C,U] (occasion when there is, an area with) water vapour in the air, at or near the earth's surface, less thick than fog and not so light as haze: *Hills hidden/shrouded in ~;* (fig) *lost in the ~s of time;* such vapour condensed on a surface, e g glass, clouding its appearance. **2** [C] filmy appearance before the eyes (caused by tears, etc); (fig) sth that darkens the mind, makes understanding difficult, etc: *see things through a ~.* □ *vi,vt* [VP2C,6A] ***~ (over),*** cover, be covered, with ~: *The scene ~ed over. The mirror ~ed over. Her eyes (were) ~ed with tears.* **~y** *adj* (-ier, iest) **1** with ~: *a ~y evening; ~y weather; a ~y view.* **2** not clear: *have only a ~y idea.* ˈ**~·ily** /-əlɪ/ *adv* ˈ**~i·ness** *n*

mis·take[1] /mɪˈsteɪk/ *n* [C] wrong opinion, idea or act: *spelling ~s. We all make ~s occasionally. There's some ~! There must be some ~!* ***by ~,*** as the result of carelessness, forgetfulness, etc; in error: *I took your umbrella by ~.* ***and no ~,*** (colloq) without any doubt: *It's hot today and no ~!*

mis·take[2] /mɪˈsteɪk/ *vt,vi* (*pt* mistook /mɪˈstʊk/, *pp* mistaken /mɪˈsteɪkn/) **1** [VP6A,10] be wrong, have a wrong idea, about: *~ sb's meaning. We've ~n the house,* come to the wrong house. ***There's no mistaking,*** no possibility of being wrong about: *There's no mistaking what ought to be done.* **2** [VP14] ***~ sb/sth for,*** wrongly suppose that sb or sth is (sb or sth else): *Don Quixote mistook the windmills for giants. She is often ~n for her twin sister.* **3** (older uses) *If I ~ not,* unless I am wrong. *You ~. my dear,* you're wrong. **mistaken** (*pp* as) *adj* **1** in error; wrong in opinion: *a case of ~n identity; ~n ideas.* ***be ~n (about sth),*** be in error: *If I'm not ~n, there's the man we met on the train. Your ~n.* **2** ill-judged: *~n kindness/zeal.* **mis·tak·en·ly** *adv*

mis·ter /ˈmɪstə(r)/ *n* **1** (always written *Mr*) title prefixed to a man's name when he has no other title (*Mr Green*), or to his office (*Mr Secretary*).

2 (used without a person's name; sl, or used by children): *Listen to me, ~. Please, ~, can I have my ball back?*

mis·time /ˈmɪsˋtaɪm/ *vt* (used esp in the *pp*) say or do sth out of season, at an unsuitable time: *a ~d* (= inopportune) *intervention.*

mistle·toe /ˋmɪsltəʊ/ *n* [U] parasitic evergreen plant (growing on fruit and other trees) with small white sticky berries (used in making bird-lime). It is used as a Christmas decoration.

mis·took /mɪˋstʊk/ *pt* of **mistake.**

mis·tral /ˋmɪstrəl/ *n* cold, dry wind blowing from the north through the Rhone valley in France.

mis·trans·late /ˈmɪstrɑnzˋleɪt *US:* -trænz-/ *vt* [VP6A] translate wrongly. **mis·trans·la·tion** /-ˋleɪʃn/ *n* [C,U].

mis·tress /ˋmɪstrəs/ *n* **1** woman at the head of a household or family; woman in authority who gives orders to servants: *Servants willingly obey a kind ~. Is your ~ at home?* ⇨ **master(2). 2** woman school teacher: *the ˋFrench mistress,* teacher of French (but not necessarily a Frenchwoman); *the ˋgames ~,* in charge of games (hockey, etc). **3** woman with a good knowledge or control of sth: *a ~ of needlework. She is ~ of the situation. Venice used to be called the ~ of the Adriatic.* **4** (in stories, plays, etc dealing with periods before the 18th c, and still in Scotland by some people) title equivalent to the modern *Mrs* or *Miss.* **5** (poet) woman loved and courted by a man: *'O ~ mine!'* **6** woman having regular sexual intercourse with one man to whom she is not married. Cf *paramour* (liter) and *concubine* (dated).

mis·trial /ˈmɪsˋtraɪl/ *n* (legal) trial which is made invalid because of some error in the proceedings.

mis·trust /ˈmɪsˋtrʌst/ *vt* [VP6A] feel no confidence in: *~ one's own powers.* □ *n* [U] (or with *in def art*) want of confidence or trust: *She had a strong ~ of anything new and strange.* **~·ful** /-fl/ *adj* suspicious (*of*). **~·fully** /-flɪ/ *adv*

misty /ˋmɪstɪ/ ⇨ **mist.**

mis·un·der·stand /ˈmɪsˈʌndəˋstænd/ *vt* (*pt,pp* **-stood** /-ˋstʊd/ [VP6A] take a wrong meaning from (instructions, messages, etc); form a wrong opinion of (sb or sth): *His intentions were misunderstood. She had always felt misunderstood.* **~·ing** *n* [C,U] failure to understand rightly, esp when this has led or may lead to ill feelings: *~ings between nations that may lead to war; clear up a ~ing.*

mis·use /ˈmɪsˋjuz/ *vt* [VP6A] use wrongly; use for a wrong purpose; treat badly. □ *n* /ˈmɪsˋjus/ [U] using wrongly; [C] instance of this: *the ~ of power.*

mite[1] /maɪt/ *n* **1** very small coin no longer in use. ⇨ **Mark 12: 22**; very small or modest contribution or offering: *offer a ~ of comfort; give one's ~ to a good cause.* **2** tiny object, esp a small child (usu as an object of sympathy): *Poor little ~! What a ~ of a child!*

mite[2] /maɪt/ *n* [C] small parasitic arachnid that may be found in food, e g *ˋcheese ~s,* and may carry disease.

mi·ter /ˋmaɪtə(r)/ *n* (US) = **mitre.**

miti·gate /ˋmɪtɪgeɪt/ *vt* [VP6A] make less severe, violent or painful. ***mitigating circumstances,*** those that may make a mistake, crime, etc seem less serious. **miti·ga·tion** /ˈmɪtɪˋgeɪʃn/ *n* [U].

mitre (US = **mi·ter**) /ˋmaɪtə(r)/ *n* **1** tall head-dress worn by bishops at some ceremonies. ⇨ the illus at **vestment. 2 ˋ~(-joint),** joint whose line of junction bisects the angle between the two bevelled surfaces it joins.

mitt /mɪt/ *n* **1** mitten. **2** baseball glove; (colloq) boxing-glove. **3** (sl) hand; fist.

mit·ten /ˋmɪtn/ *n* **1** kind of glove covering four fingers together and the thumb separately. **2** covering for the back and palm of the hand only, leaving the thumb and fingers bare.

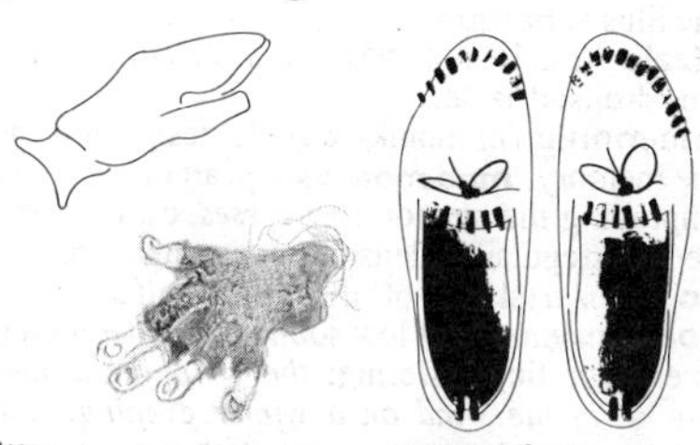

mittens moccasins

mix[1] /mɪks/ *vt,vi* **1** [VP6A,12B,13B,14,2A,C] (of different substances, people, etc) put, bring or come together so that the substances, etc are no longer distinct; make or prepare (sth) by doing this: *mix flour and water. The doctor mixed me a bottle of medicine/mixed a bottle of medicine for me. We can sometimes mix business with pleasure. She was mixing* (= preparing) *a salad. Oil and water don't mix. You can't mix oil with water. Many races are mixed in Hawaii.* **2** [VP2A,3A] ***mix (with),*** (of persons) come or be together in society: *He doesn't mix well,* doesn't get on well with people, esp people of different social classes or different interests. **3** ***be/get mixed up in sth,*** be involved or confused: *Don't get mixed up in politics/mixed up with those politicians,* keep clear of them. *He feels very mixed up* (= confused) *about life,* cannot see clearly what principles, etc to adopt. *I'm sorry for these mixed-up kids,* children who are confused by social problems. *I don't want to be mixed up in the affair,* I don't want to be connected with it in any way. Hence, **ˋmix-up** *n* confused state: *What a mix-up! There's been a bit of a mix-up about who should be invited to the party,* some confusion and mistakes.

mix[2] /mɪks/ *n* (chiefly in trade and comm) ingredients, mixed or to be mixed, for a purpose, e g for plaster, mortar, concrete or kinds of food: *an ice-ˋcream mix; a ˋcake mix,* of flour, egg-powder, sugar, etc to be used in making cakes.

mixed /mɪkst/ *adj* of different sorts: *~ biscuits/pickles; a ~ school,* for boys and girls; *a ~ company,* including people of different classes, tastes, etc. ***have ~ feelings*** (e g sorrow and pleasure) ***about sth.*** **ˈ~ ˋdoubles,** (tennis, etc) with two players, one man and one woman, on each side. **ˈ~ ˋfarming,** e g dairy farming and cereals. **a ˈ~ ˋgrill,** e g liver, kidney and bacon. **a ˈ~ ˋmarriage,** one between persons of different races or religions. **a ˈ~ ˋmetaphor,** two or more metaphors used together, producing a ludicrous effect, e g 'The scourge of tyranny had breathed his last'.

mixer /ˋmɪksə(r)/ *n* **1** person or thing that mixes: *a ceˋment ~; an electric ˋfood-~.* (TV, films) one who combines shots on to one length of film or video-tape. **2** ***be a good ~,*** (colloq) one who is at ease with others on social occasions. ⇨ **mix**[1]**(2).**

mix·ture /ˋmɪkstʃə(r)/ *n* **1** [U] mixing or being mixed. **2** [C] sth made by mixing: *a* ˋ*smoking* ~, made by blending different kinds of tobacco; *a* ˋ*cough* ~, ~ of several medicines. *Air is a* ~, *not a compound, of gases.* ***the ~ as before,*** (colloq) the same procedure, treatment, etc as in the past.

miz·zen, mizen /ˋmɪzn/ *n* **1** ˋ**~(-mast),** mast nearest the stern on a ship with three masts. **2** ˋ**~(-sail),** lowest square sail set on this mast. ⇨ the illus at barque.

mizzle /ˋmɪzl/ *vi* [VP2A] (dial or colloq) rain in fine drops; drizzle.

mne·monic /niˋmonɪk/ *adj* of, designed to help, the memory. **mne·mon·ics** *n pl* art of, system for, improving the memory: ~ *verses,* e g for remembering irregular declensions or conjugations.

mo /məʊ/ *n* (sl abbr of) moment: *half a mo.*

moan /məʊn/ *n* [C] low sound of pain or regret, or one suggesting suffering: *the* ~*s of the wounded; the* ~ *of the wind on a winter evening.* □ *vi,vt* [VP2A,C,15B] utter ~s; say with ~s: ~ (*out*) *a plea for help. What's she* ~*ing* (= complaining) *about now?*

moat /məʊt/ *n* deep, wide ditch filled with water, round a castle, etc as a defence. **~ed** *adj* having a ~: *a* ~*ed manor house.*

mob /mob/ *n* [C] **1** disorderly crowd, rabble, esp one that has gathered for mischief or attack: (attrib) *mob law, mob rule,* imposed or enforced by a mob. **2 the mob,** (formerly) the masses; the common people: *mob oratory,* the kind of speech-making that appeals to the emotions of the masses, not to the intellect. **3** gang of criminals. □ *vt* (-bb-) [VP6A] (of people) crowd round in great numbers, either to attack or to admire: *The pick-pocket was mobbed by angry women. The pop singer was mobbed by teenagers.* **mob·ster** /ˋmobstə(r)/ *n* member of a gang or mob of rowdy persons.

mob·cap /ˋmobkæp/ *n* (18th c) woman's indoor head-dress covering the whole of the hair.

mo·bile /ˋməʊbaɪl *US:* -bl/ *adj* **1** moving, able to be moved, easily and quickly from place to place: ~ *troops/artillery.* **2** easily and often changing: ~ *features,* quickly showing changes of thought and emotion. □ *n* ornamental structure with parts that move in currents of air. **mo·bil·ity** /məʊˋbɪlətɪ/ *n* [U] being ~.

mo·bi·lize /ˋməʊbḷaɪz/ *vt,vi* [VP6A,2A] collect together for service or use, esp in war. **mo·bi·liz·ation** /ˌməʊbḷaɪˋzeɪʃn *US:* -ḷɪˋz-/ *n* mobilizing or being ~d: (attrib) *mobilization orders.*

mob·ster /ˋmobstə(r)/ *n* ⇨ mob.

moc·ca·sin /ˋmokəsɪn/ *n* [U] soft leather made from deerskin; (*pl*) shoes made from this, as worn by N American Indians. ⇨ the illus at mitten.

mo·cha /ˋmokə *US:* ˋməʊkə/ *n* [U] fine quality of coffee, originally shipped from the Arabian port of M~.

mock /mok/ *vt,vi* **1** [VP6A,3A] ***~ sb, ~ at sb,*** make fun (of); ridicule (esp by copying in a funny or contemptuous way): *The naughty boys* ~*ed the blind man. They* ~*ed at my fears.* ˋ**~·ing bird** *n* American bird of the thrush family that mimics the notes of other birds. **2** [VP6A] defy contemptuously: *The heavy steel doors* ~*ed the attempts of the thieves to open the safe.* ˋ**~-up** *n* **(a)** full-scale model, e g of an aircraft, made of wood, showing the appearance of a proposed machine (or any part of it). **(b)** layout of sth to be printed. □ *attrib adj* not real or genuine: *a* ~ *battle;* ~*-turtle soup,* made to imitate turtle soup; ˈ~*-*ˋ*modesty,* pretence of being modest; ˈ~*-he*ˋ*roic,* making fun of heroic style in literature. □ *n* (archaic) derision: usu ***make a ~ of,*** ridicule. **~er** *n* person who ~s. **~·ing·ly** *adv*

mock·ery /ˋmokərɪ/ *n* (*pl* -ries) **1** [U] contemptuous, mocking; ridicule: *hold a person up to* ~. **2** [C] sb or sth that is mocked; occasion when sb or sth is mocked. **3** [C] bad or contemptible example (of sth): *His trial was a* ~ *of justice. He received only the* ~ *of a trial.*

mod /mod/ *adj* (sl) up-to-date and smart (esp in dress). □ *n* **Mod,** (1960's in GB) name used of a young person wearing distinctive modern clothes and devoted to riding on motor-scooters: *Mods and Rockers.*

mo·dal /ˋməʊdl/ *adj* relating to mode or manner (contrasted with substance), or (gram) the mood of a verb: ~ *auxiliaries,* e g *can, may.*

mode /ˋməʊd/ *n* [C] **1** way in which sth is done; way of speaking or behaving: *a* ~ *of life/dressing the hair;* fashion or style: *the latest* ~*s* (of clothes). **2** (music) one of the two chief scale systems in modern music (the major and the minor ~s).

model[1] /ˋmodl/ *n* [C] **1** small-scale reproduction or representation of sth; design to be copied: ~ *of an ocean liner; a clay or wax* ~ *for a statue,* to be copied in stone or metal; (attrib) ~ *aircraft/trains.* **2** person or thing to be copied: *He's a* ~ *of industry. Make yours on the* ~ *of your brother's.* **3** (colloq) person or thing exactly like another: *She's the* ~*/a perfect* ~ *of her mother.* **4** person who poses for sculptors, painters or photographers. **5** person employed to wear clothes, hats, etc so that prospective buyers may see them; mannequin. **6** article of clothing, hat, etc shown publicly by ~s(5): *the latest Paris* ~*s,* clothes, etc from the Paris dressmakers. **7** design or structure of which many copies or reproductions are (to be) made: *the latest* ~*s of Ford cars; a* ˋ*sports* ~, a car designed for fast driving. **8** (attrib) perfect; deserving to be imitated: ~ *behaviour; a* ~ *wife.*

model[2] /ˋmodl/ *vt,vi* (-ll-, US -l-) **1** [VP6A,14, 15A] shape (in some soft substance): ~ *sb's head in clay;* (fig): *delicately* ~*led features.* **2** [VP2A, 6A] practise as a model(4,5): *She earns a living by* ~*ling clothes/hats.* **3** [VP14] ***~ oneself (up)on sb,*** make from a model; take as a copy or example: ~ *oneself* (*up*)*on one's father.* **~(l)er** *n* person who practises ~ling. **~(l)ing** *n* [U] art of making ~s(1); way in which this is done; working as a ~(5): *She did some* ~*ling as a student to earn pocket-money.*

mod·er·ate[1] /ˋmodrət/ *adj* **1** not extreme; limited; having reasonable limits: *He has a* ~ *appetite. Prices in this hotel are strictly* ~, not at all high. *I'd like a* ~*-price room,* e g in a hotel. *We need a* ~*-sized house,* e g with 3 or 4 bedrooms, not 7 or 8. **2** midway; keeping or kept within reasonable limits: *a man of* ~ *opinions; a* ~ *political party; a* ~ *drinker; be* ~ *in one's demands.* □ *n* person who holds ~ opinions, e g in politics. **~·ly** *adv* to a ~ extent: *a* ~*ly large audience.*

mod·er·ate[2] /ˋmodəreɪt/ *vt,vi* [VP6A,2A] **1** make or become less violent or extreme: ~ *one's enthusiasm/demands. The wind is moderating. His wife exercises a moderating influence upon him,* is able to restrain him. **2** act as moderator.

mod·er·ation /ˌmɒdəˈreɪʃn/ *n* **1** [U] quality of being moderate; freedom from excess: *My doctor has advised ~ in eating and drinking.* ***in ~,*** in a moderate manner or degree: *Will alcoholic drinks be harmful taken in ~?* **2** (*pl*) (shortened to *Mods*) first public examination for a degree in classical studies at Oxford. ⇨ *Greats* at **great(12).**

mod·er·ator /ˈmɒdəreɪtə(r)/ *n* **1** Presbyterian minister presiding over a church court. **2** presiding examiner at some university examinations. **3** material in which neutrons are slowed down in an atomic pile.

mod·ern /ˈmɒdn/ *adj* **1** of the present or recent times: *~ history,* e g of Europe, from 1475 onwards; *~ languages,* contrasted with classical Greek and Latin, and, of other languages, near the form now spoken and written; *M~ English,* from the 15th c onwards; *~ inventions and discoveries.* **secondary ˈ~ school,** ⇨ **secondary. 2** new and up-to-date: *~ methods and ideas; a house with all ~ conveniences.* □ *n* person living in ~ times.

mod·ern·ism /ˈmɒdn̩ɪzm/ *n* [U] modern views or methods; [C] instance of these, e g (theology) subordination of tradition or modern thought. **mod·ern·ist** /-ɪst/ *n* believer in, supporter of, ~. **mod·ern·is·tic** /ˌmɒdn̩ˈɪstɪk/ *adj* of ~.

mo·dern·ity /məˈdɜnətɪ/ *n* [U] being modern.

mod·ern·ize /ˈmɒdn̩ɑɪz/ *vt* [VP6A] make suitable for present-day needs; bring up to date: *Ought we to ~ our spelling?* **mod·ern·iz·ation** /ˌmɒdn̩ɑɪˈzeɪʃn *US:* -n̩ɪˈz-/ *n* [U].

mod·est /ˈmɒdɪst/ *adj* **1** having, showing, a not too high opinion of one's merits, abilities, etc: *be ~ about one's achievements; a ~ hero.* **2** moderate; not large in size or amount: *He lives in a ~ little house,* not showy or splendid. *My demands are quite ~. He is ~ in his requirements.* **3** taking, showing, care not to do or say anything impure or improper: *~ in speech, dress and behaviour.* **~·ly** *adv* **mod·esty** /ˈmɒdɪstɪ/ *n* [U] state of being ~ (all senses): *Her ~y prevented her from making her feelings known to him.* ***in all ~y,*** without the least idea of boasting, etc.

modi·cum /ˈmɒdɪkəm/ *n* (*sing* only) small or moderate amount: *achieve success with a ~ of effort; a simple meal with a ~ of wine.*

mod·ify /ˈmɒdɪfɑɪ/ *vt* (*pt,pp* -fied) [VP6A] **1** make changes in; make different: *The industrial revolution modified the whole structure of English society.* **2** make less severe, violent, etc: *You'd better ~ your tone,* e g be less rude. *He won't ~ his demands,* reduce them. **3** (gram) qualify the sense of (a word): *Adjectives ~ nouns.* **modi·fier** /-fɑɪə(r)/ *n* (gram) word that modifies, e g an *adj* or *adv.* **modi·fi·ca·tion** /ˌmɒdɪfɪˈkeɪʃn/ *n* [U] ~ing or being modified; [C] instance of this; change or alteration.

mod·ish /ˈməʊdɪʃ/ *adj* fashionable. **~·ly** *adv*

mo·diste /məʊˈdist/ *n* (formal) milliner; dressmaker.

modu·late /ˈmɒdjʊleɪt *US:* -dʒʊ-/ *vt,vi* **1** [VP6A] regulate; adjust; adapt; (music) make a change in the pitch intensity or key of. **2** [VP2C] ***~ from/to,*** change or pass from one key to another. **3** [VP6A] (radio) vary the frequency, amplitude or other characteristics or waves. ⇨ **modulation.**

modu·la·tion /ˌmɒdjʊˈleɪʃn *US:* -dʒʊˈl-/ *n* **1** [U] process of modulating; state of being modulated; [C] change resulting from this; [U] (music) changing of key; [C] particular change of key. **2** (radio) variation in the amplitude, frequency or phase of a wave so that it is suitable for radio, e g of the human voice to a wave for radio or the telephone.

mod·ule /ˈmɒdjul *US:* -dʒul/ *n* [C] **1** standard or unit of measurement as used in building. **2** standard uniform component used in the structure of a building or in sectional furniture; unit of electronic components as used in the assembly of a computer: *a ˈmemory ~,* unit of components in a mechanical system. **3** independent and self-contained unit of a spacecraft. **comˈmand ~,** for the astronaut in command of the whole space expedition. **ˈlunar ~,** to be separated for a moon landing. **modu·lar** /ˈmɒdjʊlə(r) *US:* -dʒʊ-/ *adj* based on a ~ or unit: *modular design/construction,* based on a ~ which is repeated throughout the design.

modus op·er·andi /ˌməʊdəs ˌɒpəˈrændɪ/ *n* (Lat) method of dealing with a piece of work; method of being operated.

modus vi·vendi /ˌməʊdəs vɪˈvendɪ/ *n* (Lat) way of living; (way of getting a) temporary agreement (while awaiting the final settlement of a dispute, etc.

mo·gul /ˈməʊgl/ *n* very great, rich or important person: *Hollywood ~s.*

mo·hair /ˈməʊheə(r)/ *n* [U] (thread, cloth, made from the) fine, silky hair of the Angora goat.

Mo·ham·medan /məˈhɒmɪdən *US:* məʊˈhæmɪdən/ *n* ⇨ **Muhammad.**

moi·ety /ˈmɔɪətɪ/ *n* (*pl* **-ties**) (esp in legal sense) one of two parts into which sth is divided.

moil /mɔɪl/ *vi* (only in) ***toil and ~,*** work hard.

moist /mɔɪst/ *adj* (esp of surfaces) slightly wet: *eyes ~ with tears; a ~ wind from the sea.* **~en** /ˈmɔɪsn/ *vt,vi* [VP6A,2A] make or become ~: *~en the lips,* e g by licking them; *~en a sponge with water,* e g to stick stamps on envelopes.

mois·ture /ˈmɔɪstʃə(r)/ *n* [U] condensed vapour on a surface; liquid in the form of vapour.

moke /məʊk/ *n* (GB sl) donkey.

mo·lar /ˈməʊlə(r)/ *n, adj* (one) of the teeth used for grinding food. ⇨ the illus at **mouth.**

mo·las·ses /məˈlæsɪz/ *n* (with *sing v*) thick, dark syrup drained from raw sugar during the refining process.

mold, molder, mold·ing, moldy, ⇨ **mould,** etc.

mole[1] /məʊl/ *n* permanent, small dark spot on the human skin.

mole[2] /məʊl/ *n* small, dark-grey fur-covered animal with tiny eyes, living in tunnels (or burrows) which it makes in the ground. ⇨ the illus at **small.** ***blind as a ~,*** seeing badly. **ˈ~-skin** *n* fur of a ~, used for making garments and hats. **ˈ~-hill** *n* pile of earth thrown up by a ~ while burrowing. ***make a mountain out of a ~-hill,*** make a trivial matter seem important.

mole[3] /məʊl/ *n* stone wall built in the sea as a breakwater or causeway. ⇨ the illus at **breakwater.**

mol·ecule /ˈmɒlɪkjul/ *n* smallest unit (usu of a group of atoms) into which a substance could be divided without a change in its chemical nature. **mol·ecu·lar** /məˈlekjʊlə(r)/ *adj* of or related to ~s: *molecular structure.*

mo·lest /məˈlest/ *vt* [VP6A] trouble or annoy intentionally. **mol·es·ta·tion** /ˌməʊləˈsteɪʃn/ *n* [U].

moll /mɒl/ *n* (sl) woman companion of a gangster,

vagrant, etc; prostitute.

mol·lify /ˈmɒlɪfaɪ/ *vt* (*pt,pp* **-fied**) [VP6A] make (a person, his feelings) calmer or quieter: *~ing remarks; ~ sb's anger.* **mol·li·fi·ca·tion** /ˌmɒlɪfɪˈkeɪʃn/ *n* [U].

mol·lusc (US also **mol·lusk**) /ˈmɒləsk/ *n* one of a class of animals with soft bodies (and often hard shells), e g oysters, mussels, cuttlefish, snails, slugs.

molly·coddle /ˈmɒlɪkɒdl/ *n* person who takes too much care of his health, who pampers himself and likes others to pamper him. □ *vt* [VP6A] (often reflex) pamper (sb, oneself).

Mo·loch /ˈməʊlɒk/ *n* (in the O T) god to whom children were sacrificed; (fig) dreadful thing, e g war, that requires great sacrifice of human life.

molt /molt/ ⇨ **moult.**

mol·ten /ˈməʊltən/ *pp* of **melt. 1** (of metals) melted: *~ steel.* **2** made of metal that has been melted and cast: *a ~ image,* e g of a god.

molto /ˈmɒltəʊ *US:* ˈməʊltəʊ/ *adv* (musical direction) very: *~ espressivo,* with much expression.

mo·lyb·denum /məˈlɪbdənəm/ *n* [U] silvery-white brittle metallic element (symbol **Mo**) used in alloys for making high-speed tools.

mo·ment /ˈməʊmənt/ *n* **1** [C] point or very brief period of time: *It was all over in a few ~s. Please wait a ~. Just a ~, please. He'll be here at any ~,* very soon now. *It was done in a ~. He arrived at the last ~,* almost too late. *Study your notes at odd ~s,* whenever you have a few minutes to spare. *I have just this ~/only this ~ heard the news,* heard it only a ~ ago. ***Not for a ~,*** never: *'Have you ever thought of making your own dresses?'—'Not for a ~!'* ***men of the ~,*** men who are important just now. **2** ***the ~,*** (used as a *conj*) as soon as; at the time when: *I started the ~ your letter arrived. The ~ I saw you I knew you were angry with me.* **3** [U] ***of (great, small, little, no, etc) ~,*** of great, small, etc importance: *an affair of great ~; a matter of ~; men of ~.*

mo·men·tary /ˈməʊməntrɪ *US:* -terɪ/ *adj* **1** lasting for, done in, a moment. **2** at every moment: *with a learner at the wheel, and in ~ expectation of an accident.* **mo·men·tar·ily** /ˈməʊmənˈterļɪ *US:* -ˈterəlɪ/ *adv*

mo·men·tous /məˈmentəs/ *adj* important; serious. **~·ly** *adv* **~·ness** *n*

mo·men·tum /məˈmentəm/ *n* [U] **1** (science) quantity of motion of a moving body (the product of its mass and velocity): *Do falling objects gain ~?* **2** (fig, of events) impetus gained by movement: *lose/gain ~.*

mon·arch /ˈmɒnək/ *n* supreme ruler (a king, queen, emperor or empress). **mon·ar·chic** /məˈnɑkɪk/ *adj* of a ~ or a ~y. ⇨ **absolute(2), limited**[2]. **mon·ar·chism** /-ɪzm/ *n* [U] system of government by a single ruler or ~. **mon·ar·chist** /-ɪst/ *n* supporter of ~ism. **mon·archy** /ˈmɒnəkɪ/ *n* [U] government by a ~; [C] (*pl* **-chies**) state ruled by a ~.

mon·as·tery /ˈmɒnəstrɪ *US:* -sterɪ/ *n* (*pl* **-ries**) building in which monks live as a secluded community under religious vows.

mon·as·tic /məˈnæstɪk/ *adj* of monks or monasteries: *~ vows,* i e of poverty, chastity, and obedience; *~ architecture,* of the kind used for monasteries, abbeys, etc. **mon·as·ti·cism** /məˈnæstɪs-ɪzm/ *n* [U] system of living as practised by monks in monasteries.

mon·aural /ˈmɒnˈɔrl/ *adj* for one ear; (with trade abbr *mono*; of sound-reproducing equipment and recordings) not stereophonic.

Mon·day /ˈmʌndɪ/ *n* second day of the week.

mon·et·ary /ˈmʌnɪtrɪ *US:* -terɪ/ *adj* of money or coins: *The ~ unit in the US is the dollar. M~ reform has given the British a decimal coinage.*

money /ˈmʌnɪ/ *n* **1** [U] coins stamped from metal (gold, copper, alloys), printed and accepted when buying and selling, etc: *Do you know any easy ways of making ~?* **be ˈcoining/ˈminting ~,** be getting rich quickly. ***be in the ~,*** (sl) be rich. ***get one's ˈ~'s worth,*** get full value for ~ spent. ***marry ~,*** marry a rich person. ***put ~ into sth,*** invest ~ in an enterprise, etc. ***(pay) ~ down,*** (pay) in cash (contrasted with *credit*). **ˈ~ of acˈcount,** ⇨ **account**[1](2). **ready ~,** cash contrasted with credit, etc). **2** (compounds) **ˈ~-box** *n* closed box into which coins are dropped through a slit, used for savings or for collecting contributions (to charities, etc). **ˈ~-changer** *n* one whose business is to exchange ~ of one country for that of another country. **ˈ~-grubber** *n* person whose chief or only interest in life is making ~. **ˈ~-lender** *n* one whose business is to lend ~ at interest. **the ˈ~-market** *n* the body of bankers, financiers, etc whose operations decide the rates of interest on borrowed capital. **ˈ~-order** *n* official

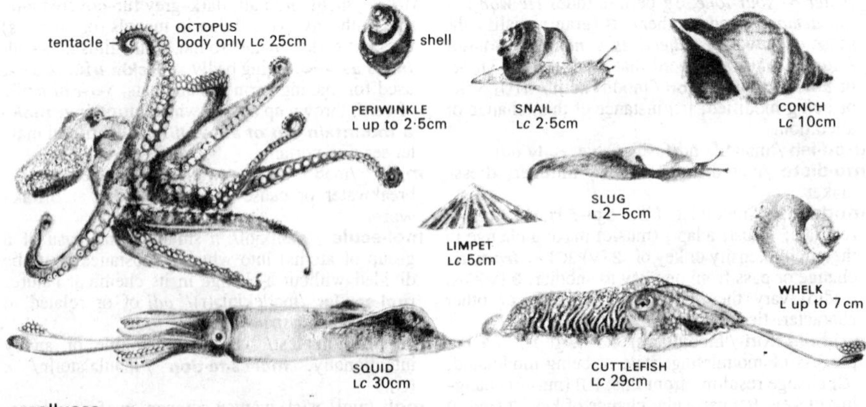

molluscs

a monogram

a monolith

order bought from a post office for ~ to be paid by another post office to a named person. ˋ~-**spinner** *n* (colloq) book, play, etc that makes a lot of ~. **3** (*pl,* moneys legal or archaic) sums of ~: *~s paid in/out; sundry ~s owing to the estate.* **~ed** /ˋmʌnɪd/ *adj* having (much) ~*: a ~ed man: the ~ed classes; the ~ed interest,* the owners of capital. **~less** *adj* having no ~.

mon·ger /ˋmʌŋgə(r)/ *n* (chiefly in compounds) trader, dealer: *ˋiron~; ˋfish~; ˋcoster~; ˋscandal-~.*

mon·gol·ism /ˋmoŋgḷ-ɪzm/ *n* [U] congenital condition in which a child is born with mental deficiency and a flattened broad skull and slanting eyes. **mon·gol** /ˋmoŋgl/ *attrib adj* suffering from ~: *a mongol baby.*

mon·goose /ˋmoŋgus/ *n* (*pl* ~s /-sɪz/) small Indian animal clever at destroying venomous snakes. ⇨ the illus at **small**.

mon·grel /ˋmʌŋgrəl/ *n* **1** dog of mixed breed. **2** any plant or animal of mixed origin; person not of pure race: *We're all ~s if we go back far enough.* □ *attrib adj* of mixed breed, race or origin.

moni·tor /ˋmonɪtə(r)/ *n* **1** pupil given authority over his fellows. **2** (out-of-date) warship with heavy guns for use in coastal waters. **3** person employed to listen to and report on foreign broadcasts; apparatus for testing transmissions by radio, etc or for detecting radio-activity, tracing the flight of missiles, etc. ˋ**~ (screen),** television screen used in a studio to check or select transmissions. □ *vt, vi* act as ~(3).

monk /mʌŋk/ *n* member of a community of men living together under religious vows in a monastery. ˋ**~·ish** /-ɪʃ/ *adj* of or like ~s.

mon·key /ˋmʌŋkɪ/ *n* (*pl* -keys) **1** animals of the group of animals most closely resembling man. ⇨ the illus at **ape**. ***be/get up to ˋ~ business/tricks,*** to mischief. ***have a ~ on one's back,*** (sl) **(a)** be a drug addict; **(b)** bear a grudge. ***get one's ~ up,*** (sl) become angry. ***put sb's ~ up,*** (sl) make him angry. ˋ**~-jacket** *n* short, close-fitting jacket as worn by some sailors. ˋ**~-nut** *n* groundnut. ˋ**~-puzzle** *n* Chile pine-tree. ˋ**~-wrench** *n* wrench (spanner) with a jaw that can be adjusted to various lengths. **2** (playfully) person, esp a child, who is fond of mischief: *You little ~!* **3** (sl) £500 or $500. □ *vi* [VP2C] ***~ about (with),*** play mischievously: *Stop ~ing about with those tools!*

mono /ˋmonəʊ/ ⇨ **monaural** and **App 2**.

mono·chrome /ˋmonəkrəʊm/ *n* painting in (different tints of) one colour. □ *adj* having only one colour.

mon·ocle /ˋmonəkl/ *n* eyeglass for one eye only, kept in position by the muscles round the eye.

mon·og·amy /məˋnogəmɪ/ *n* [U] practice of being married to only one person at a time. ⇨ **polygamy**. **mon·og·amist** /-ɪst/ *n* person who practises ~. **mon·og·amous** /məˋnogəməs/ *adj* having only one wife or husband at a time.

mono·gram /ˋmonəgræm/ *n* two or more letters (esp a person's initials) combined in one design (used on handkerchiefs, notepaper, etc).

mono·graph /ˋmonəgrɑf *US:* -græf/ *n* detailed scientific account, esp a published report on one particular subject.

mono·lith /ˋmonəlɪθ/ *n* single upright block of stone (as a pillar or monument). **~ic** /ˌmonəˋlɪθɪk/ *adj* of or like a ~: *a ~ic monument.*

mono·logue /ˋmonəlog *US:* -lɔg/ *n* scene in a play, etc in which only one person speaks; dramatic composition for a single performer; soliloquy.

mono·mania /ˌmonəʊˋmeɪnɪə/ *n* [U] state of mind, sometimes amounting to madness, caused by the attention being occupied exclusively by one idea or subject; [C] instance of this. ⇨ **paranoia**. **mono·maniac** /ˌmonəʊˋmeɪnɪæk/ *n* sufferer from ~.

mono·plane /ˋmonəpleɪn/ *n* aircraft with one wing on each side of the fuselage.

mon·op·ol·ize /məˋnopəlɑɪz/ *vt* [VP6A] get or keep a monopoly of; control the whole of, so that others cannot share: *Don't let me ~ the conversation.* **mon·op·ol·iz·ation** /məˌnopəlɑɪˋzeɪʃn *US:* -lɪˋz-/ *n*

mon·op·oly /məˋnopəlɪ/ *n* (*pl* -lies) [C] **1** (possession of the) sole right to supply; the supply or service thus controlled. **2** complete possession of trade, talk, etc: *In many countries tobacco is a government ~.* **3** anything over which one person or group has control and which is not or cannot be shared by others. **mon·op·ol·ist** /-lɪst/ *n* person who has a ~. **mon·op·ol·is·tic** /məˌnopəˋlɪstɪk/ *adj*

mono·rail /ˋmonəʊreɪl/ *n* single rail serving as a track for vehicles; railway system for vehicles using such a rail, or for vehicles suspended from a single rail.

mono·syl·lable /ˋmonəsɪləbl/ *n* word of one syllable. **mono·syl·labic** /ˌmonəsɪˋlæbɪk/ *adj* having only one syllable; made up of words of one syllable: *monosyllabic answers,* e g 'Yes' or 'No'.

mono·theism /ˋmonəʊθi-ɪzm/ *n* doctrine that there is only one God (contrasted with *polytheism*). **mono·theist** /ˋmonəʊθi-ɪst/ *n* believer in ~.

mono·tone /ˋmonətəʊn/ *n* (keeping a) level tone in talking or singing; utterance without change of pitch: *speak in a ~.*

mon·ot·onous /məˋnotənəs/ *adj* (uninteresting because) unchanging, without variety: *a ~ voice,* one with little change of pitch; *~ work.* **~·ly** *adv*

mon·ot·ony /məˋnotənɪ/ *n* [U] the state of being monotonous; wearisome absence of variety.

mono·type /ˋmonətɑɪp/ *n* (P) composing machine that casts, sets and assembles type letter by letter.

mon·ox·ide /moˋnoksɑɪd/ *n* [C,U] oxide containing one oxygen atom in the molecule: *carbon ~,* **(CO)**.

Mon·roe /ˋmʌnrəʊ/ *n* ˋ**~ doctrine,** (based on statements by James Monroe, US president (1817—1825) in 1823) the policy of opposing any interference by European powers in N and S America.

mon·sieur /məˋsjɜ(r)/ *n* (F for) Mr, sir, gentleman: *M~ Pompidou; yes, ~.* ⇨ **messieurs**.

Mon·si·gnor /monˋsinjə(r)/ *n* (title given to) certain officials in the R C Church.

mon·soon /mon`sun/ *n* seasonal wind blowing in the Indian Ocean from S W from April to October (*wet* ~) and from N E during the other months (*dry* ~); the rainy season that comes with the wet ~.

mon·ster /`monstə(r)/ *n* **1** abnormally mis-shaped animal or plant; person or thing of extraordinary size, shape or qualities; (in stories) imaginary creature (e g half animal, half bird): *Mermaids, griffins and dragons are ~s. A five-legged dog is a ~.* **2** person who is remarkable for some bad or evil quality: *a ~ of cruelty/ingratitude; the Commissioners of Inland Revenue, those ~s of greed.* **3** (attrib) huge: *a ~ ship.*

mon·strance /`monstrəns/ *n* (in R C Church) glass or crystal vessel in a setting of gold or silver in which the Host is exposed.

mon·strous /`monstrəs/ *adj* **1** of or like a monster; of great size. **2** atrocious; causing horror and disgust: *~ crimes.* **3** (colloq) quite absurd; incredible; scandalous: *It's perfectly ~ that men should be paid more than women for the same job.* **~·ly** *adv* **mon·stros·ity** /mon`strosətɪ/ *n* (*pl* -**ties**) [U] state of being ~; [C] monster; hideous object, building, etc.

mon·tage /`montɑʒ/ *n* (F) [U] selection, cutting and arrangement of photographic film, etc to make a consecutive whole; process of using many pictures, designs, etc sometimes superimposed, to make a composite picture.

month /mʌnθ/ *n* **calendar ~,** any of the twelve parts into which the year is divided; period of time from a day in one ~ to the corresponding day in the next ~ (e g 2 Jan to 2 Feb). **lunar ~,** period in which the moon makes a complete revolution; period of 28 days: *a baby of three ~s: a three-~ old baby. In which ~ were you born? I shall be back this day ~,* four weeks from today. ***a ~ of Sundays,*** a very long time: *Never in a ~ of Sundays!* **~·ly** *adj, adv* done, happening, published, etc, once a ~; valid for one ~: *a ~ly season ticket, e g* for railway travel. □ *n* **1** periodical issued once a ~. **2** (*pl* -**lies**) (colloq, dated use) menses.

monu·ment /`monjʊmənt/ *n* **1** building, column, statue, etc serving to keep alive the memory of a person or event: *a ~ in the church to the late rector.* **the M~,** the column in London that commemorates the Great Fire of London in 1666. **2** **Ancient M~s,** objects, of special historic interest, such as prehistoric fortifications and remains, old buildings and bridges (often preserved by offical bodies). **3** piece of scholarship or research that deserves to be remembered; work of literature or science of lasting value: *a ~ of learning.*

monu·men·tal /'monjʊ`mentl/ *adj* **1** of, serving for, a monument: *a ~ inscription; ~ masons,* e g making tombstones. **2** (of books, studies, etc) of lasting value: *a ~ production,* e g *the Oxford English Dictionary.* **3** (of qualities, buildings, tasks) very great: *~ ignorance.*

moo /mu/ *n* sound made by a cow or ox. □ *vi* (*pt* **mooed**) make the sound moo. **`moo-cow** *n* (child's word for) cow.

mooch /mutʃ/ *vi* [VP2C] **~ *about,*** (colloq) loiter about: *out-of-work men ~ing about (the streets).*

mood[1] /mud/ *n* [C] state of mind or spirits: *in a merry ~; in the ~ for work,* inclined to work; *not in the ~ for serious music. He's a man of ~s,* his ~s change often. **~y** *adj* (-**ier**, -**iest**) **1** having ~s that often change. **2** gloomy; bad-tempered. **`~·ily** /-əlɪ/ *adv* **`~i·ness** *n*

mood[2] /mud/ *n* (gram) one of the groups of forms that a verb may take to show whether things are regarded as certain, possible, doubtful, etc: *the indicative/imperative/subjunctive ~.*

moon[1] /mun/ *n* **1** ⇨ the illus at **phase**. (*sing* with *def art*) the body which moves round the earth once in a month and shines at night by light reflected from the sun; (with *indef art* and *adj*) this body regarded as an object distinct from that visible in other months: *Men have explored the surface of the ~. Is there a ~ tonight? Is it a new ~ or a full ~,* i e with the whole of its disc illuminated? *There was no ~,* It was a night with no ~ visible in the sky. ***cry for the ~,*** yearn for sth impossible. ***promise sb the ~,*** make extravagant promises. **2** (compounds) **`~·beam** *n* ray of ~light. **`~ buggy/rover** *n* vehicle for travelling on the ~. **`~·flower** *n* ox-eye daisy. **`~·light** *n* light of the ~; (often attrib) *go swimming in the ~light/by ~light; a ~light night.* **`~·lit** *adj* lit by the ~: *a ~lit scene/landscape.* **`~·shine** *n* **(a)** light of the ~. **(b)** foolish or idle talk, ideas, etc. **(c)** (US) whisky or other spirits illicitly distilled or smuggled. **`~·stone** *n* semi-precious felspar. **`~·struck** *adj* wild and wandering in the mind (supposedly as the result of the ~'s influence). **3** [C] satellite of other planets: *How many ~s has the planet Jupiter?* **4** [C] (poet) month. ***once in a blue ~,*** (colloq) rarely or never. **~·less** *adj* without a visible ~: *a dark, ~less night.*

moon[2] /mun/ *vi, vt* **1** [VP2C] **~ *about/around,*** move or look listlessly. **2** [VP15B] **~ *away,*** pass (time) listlessly or aimlessly: *~ away the summer holidays.* **~y** *adj* (-**ier**, -**iest**) given to ~ing away the time.

moor[1] /mʊə(r)/ *n* [C,U] (area of) open, uncultivated land, esp if covered with heather (and often, in GB, used for preserving game, esp grouse). **`~·fowl, `~·game** *nn* (*pl* unchanged) red grouse. **`~·cock** *n* male of this. **`~·hen** *n* **(a)** female of this. ⇨ the illus at **water**. **(b)** water-hen. **`~·land** /-lənd/ *n* land consisting of open ~ and covered with heather.

moor[2] /mʊə(r)/ *vt* [VP6A,15A] make (a boat, ship, etc) secure (to land or buoys) by means of cables, etc. **`~·ing-mast** *n* one for ~ing airships. **~·ings** /`mʊərɪŋz/ *n pl* **1** cables, anchors and chains, etc, by which a ship or boat is ~ed. **2** place where a ship is ~ed.

Moor /mʊə(r)/ *n* member of the Muslim peoples of mixed Arab and Berber who now live in N W Africa; one of the Muslim Arabs who invaded Spain in the 8th c: *the conquest of Spain by the ~s.*

Moor·ish /`mʊərɪʃ/ *adj* of the Moors and their culture: *~ palaces in Granada.*

moose /mus/ *n* (*pl* ~ or **~s** /-sɪz/) large sort of deer with coarse fleece and palm-shaped horns, found in the forests of N America, and in northern Europe (where it is called an *elk*).

moot /mut/ *adj* (only in) **~ point/question,** one about which there is uncertainty. □ *vt* [VP6A] raise or bring forward for discussion: *This question has been ~ed again.*

mop[1] /mop/ *n* **1** bundle of coarse strings, cloth, etc fastened to a long handle for cleaning floors, etc; similar material on a short handle for cleaning dishes, etc. **2** mass of thick, untidy hair. □ *vt* (-pp-) **1** [VP6A] clean with a mop: *mop the floor.* **2** [VP6A,15B] wipe up with, or as with, a mop: *mop one's brow,* wipe away sweat, e g with a handkerchief; *mop up a mess.* ***mop up,*** (colloq uses) finish off, make an end of: *mop up arrears of work; mopping-up operations* (in a military campaign, getting rid of defeated remnants of enemy troops). ***mop the floor with sb,*** defeat him completely, e g in a debate.

mop² /mop/ *vi* (-pp-) (archaic or liter; only in) ***mop and mow,*** make grimaces.

mope /məʊp/ *vi* [VP2A,C] pity oneself, give oneself up to sadness or low spirits: *~ (about) in the house all day.* □ *n* **the ~s,** low spirits: *suffer from the ~s; have a fit of the ~s.*

mo·ped /ˈməʊped/ *n* (GB) pedal bicycle fitted with a small petrol engine (under 50 cc).

mo·quette /məˈket *US:* məʊ-/ *n* [U] synthetic fabric used for carpets and soft furnishings.

mo·raine /moˈreɪn *US:* mɔ-/ *n* heap or mass of earth, gravel, rock, etc carried down and deposited by a glacier. ⇨ the illus at mountain.

moral¹ /ˈmorl *US:* ˈmɔrl/ *adj* **1** concerning principles of right and wrong: *~ standards; a ~ question; the ~ sense,* the power of distinguishing right and wrong; *~ law; ~ rights/obligations,* based on ~ law; *~ philosophy,* ethics, the study of right and wrong in human behaviour. **2** good and virtuous: *live a ~ life; a ~ man.* **3** able to understand the difference between right and wrong: *At what age do we become ~ beings?* **4** teaching or illustrating good behaviour: *a ~ book/story/talk.* **5** (contrasted with *physical* or *practical*) connected with the sense of what is right and just: *a ~ victory,* outcome of a struggle in which the weaker side is comforted because it has established the righteousness of its cause. ***give sb ~ support,*** help by saying that he has justice and right on his side. **~ courage,** strength to face contempt or ridicule rather than do wrong. ***a ~ certainty,*** sth so probable that there is little room for doubt. **~ly** /-rlɪ/ *adv* **1** in a manner: *M~ly he is all that can be desired.* **2** according to what is most probable: *The attempt is ~ly bound to fail.*

moral² /ˈmorl *US:* ˈmɔrl/ *n* **1** that which a story, event or experience teaches: *And the ~ of this story is that a young girl should not speak to strange men. You may draw your own ~ from this.* **2** (*pl*) moral habits; standards of behaviour; principles of right and wrong: *a man without ~s; a man of loose ~s; improve the ~s of a country.*

mo·rale /məˈrɑl *US:* -ˈræl/ *n* [U] state of discipline and spirit (in a person, an army, a nation, etc); temper, state of mind, as expressed in action: *The army recovered its ~ and fighting power. The failing ~ of the enemy* (= Their loss of confidence in themselves) *helped to shorten the war.*

mor·al·ist /ˈmorlɪst *US:* ˈmɔr-/ *n* person who points out morals(1); person who practises or teaches morality.

mor·al·is·tic /ˌmorlˈɪstɪk *US:* ˌmɔr-/ *adj* concerned with morals(2).

mor·al·ity /məˈrælətɪ/ *n* (*pl* -ties) **1** [U] (standards, principles, of) good behaviour: *Have standards of international ~ become low in recent years? Is commercial ~ high in your country?* **2** [C] particular system of morals: *Christian ~.* **3** [C] ˈ**~ (play),** form of drama, popular in the 16th c, teaching good behaviour, the chief characters being personifications of virtues and vices.

mor·al·ize /ˈmorlɑɪz *US:* ˈmɔr-/ *vt, vi* **1** [VP2A,3A] ***~ (about/(up)on),*** deal with moral questions; talk or write on questions of duty, right and wrong, etc: *~ upon the failings of the younger generation. Oh, stop your moralizing!* Stop preaching at me! **2** [VP6A] give a moral interpretation of.

mo·rass /məˈræs/ *n* [C] stretch of low, soft, wet land; marsh.

mora·torium /ˌmorəˈtɔrɪəm *US:* ˌmɔ-/ *n* (*pl* -riums or -ria /-rɪə/) [C] legal authorization to delay payment of debts; deferment or delay agreed.

mor·bid /ˈmɔbɪd/ *adj* **1** diseased: *a ~ growth,* e g a cancer or tumour; *~ anatomy,* the study of diseased organs in the body. **2** (of sb's mind or ideas) unhealthy: *a ~ imagination,* one that dwells on horrible or nasty things. **~·ly** *adv* **~·ity** /mɔˈbɪdətɪ/, **~·ness** *nn* state of being ~.

mor·dant /ˈmɔdnt/ *adj* biting; sarcastic: *~ criticism; a ~ wit.*

more /mɔ(r)/ (contrasted with *less* and *fewer;* ⇨ many, most¹, much¹) *adj* (independent comp) greater in number, quantity, quality, degree, size, etc; additional. □ *n* a greater amount, number, etc; an additional amount: *We need ~ men/help, etc. Instead of fewer helpers, we want ~. Have you any ~ paper? Would you like some/a little ~ soup/a little ~ of this soup? What ~ do you want? There are still a few ~. There is hardly any ~. That is ~ than enough. May I have one ~? I should like as many ~,* the same number again. *I hope to see ~ of you,* to see you ~ often. □ *adv* **1** (forming the comparative degree of most *adjj* and *advv* of more than two syllables and of some of two syllables, esp if stressed on the first): *~ beautiful/useful/interesting/serious (than...); ~ easily/quietly/foolishly (than...).* ***and what is ~,*** ~ important, serious, etc (according to context). **2** to a greater extent; in a greater degree: *You need to sleep ~,* i e ~ than you sleep now. *You must attend to your work ~. He was ~ frightened than hurt. He likes summer ~ than autumn.* **3** again: *Once ~, please. I shall not go there any ~,* ever again. *We saw him no ~,* did not see him again. **4** ***~ and ~,*** increasingly: *The story gets ~ and ~ exciting. Life is becoming ~ and ~ expensive.* ***~ or less,*** about: *It's an hour's journey, ~ or less.* **5** (with a *n*, equivalent to an *adj*): *The ~ fool you to believe him,* You are, if you believe him, foolish in a higher degree. *It had ~ the characteristic* (= was ~ characteristic) *of a foolish dream than of a nightmare. The ~'s the pity,* It is, to that extent, a greater pity. ⇨ also the *adv.* ***no ~,*** neither: *A: 'I can't understand this at all.' B: 'No ~ can I.'* ***no ~... than:*** *He's no ~ able to read Chinese than I am,* He is as unable to do so as I am.

mo·rello /məˈreləʊ/ *n* (*pl* -los /-ləʊz/) **~ (cherry),** bitter kind of cherry (used for jam).

more·over /mɔrˈəʊvə(r)/ *adv* further; besides; in addition (to this).

mores /ˈmɔreɪz/ *n pl* (formal) customs, usages, conventions, regarded as essential to a social group.

Mo·resque /mɔˈresk/ *adj* (of style, design, decoration, architecture) Moorish.

mor·ga·natic /ˌmɔgəˈnætɪk/ *adj* **~ marriage,** one between a man of high rank (e g a prince) and a woman of lower rank, who remains in her lower social station, the children having no claim to succeed to the property, titles, etc, of their father.

morgue /mɔg/ *n* **1** building in which bodies of persons found dead are kept until they are identified and claimed by members of their families. ⇨ **mortuary. 2** file (in the office of a newspaper or magazine) with obituary notices of famous people still living (ready for use when they die).

mori·bund /ˈmorɪbənd *US:* ˋmɔrɪbʌnd/ *adj* at the point of death; about to come to an end: *~ civilizations.*

Mor·mon /ˈmɔmən/ *n* member of a religious organization founded in the US in 1830, officially called 'The Church of Jesus Christ of Latter-day Saints'. **~·ism** /-ɪzm/ *n*

morn /mɔn/ *n* (poet) morning.

morn·ing /ˈmɔnɪŋ/ *n* **1** early part of the day between dawn and noon (or, more generally, before the midday meal): *in/during the ~; this ~; yesterday/tomorrow ~; every ~; on Sunday/Monday, etc ~; the ~ of May the 1st; one ~ last week; one summer ~; a few ~s ago; several ~s lately. When he awoke it was ~.* **2** (attrib): *a ~ walk; an early ~ swim.* **ˋ~ coat,** long black coat with the front sloped away. **ˋ~ dress,** as worn on formal occasions in the ~. **ˈM~ ˋPrayer,** service used in the Church of England at ~ service. **the ~ star,** Venus, or other bright star seen about dawn. **the ~ watch,** (at sea) period of duty, 4am to 8am. **ˈ~-ˋglory** *n* climbing plant of the convolvulus family, with flowers that fade by mid-day. **ˋ~-room** *n* sitting-room for the ~. **ˈ~ ˋsickness** *n* (feeling of) nausea early in the morning, often during the first few months of pregnancy.

mo·rocco /məˋrokəʊ/ *n* [U] soft leather made from goatskins.

moron /ˈmɔron/ *n* feeble-minded person (with a mental level not so low as imbeciles or idiots); (colloq) stupid person. **~ic** /məˋronɪk/ *adj*

mo·rose /məˋrəʊs/ *adj* sullen; ill-tempered; unsocial. **~·ly** *adv* **~·ness** *n*

mor·pheme /ˈmɔfim/ *n* (linguistics) smallest meaningful part into which a word can be divided: *'Run-s' contains two ~s and 'un-lucki-ly' contains three.*

Mor·pheus /ˈmɔfɪəs/ *n* (Gk myth) god of dreams and sleep.

mor·phia /ˈmɔfɪə/, **mor·phine** /ˈmɔfin/ *nn* [U] drug, usu in the form of a white powder, made from opium and used for relieving pain.

mor·phol·ogy /mɔˋfolədʒɪ/ *n* [U] **1** branch of biology dealing with the form and structure of animals and plants. **2** (gram) study of the morphemes of a language and of how they are combined to make words. ⇨ **syntax.**

mor·ris dance /ˈmorɪs dɑns *US:* ˋmɔrɪs dæns/ *n* old English folk-dance for men.

mor·row /ˈmorəʊ *US:* ˋmɔr-/ *n* **1** (liter) the next day after the present or after any given day: *Their prospects for the ~ were excellent. What had the ~ in store for them?* **2** (archaic) morning: *Good ~!*

Morse /mɔs/ *n* **ˋ~ (code),** system of dots and dashes or short and long sounds, flashes of light, representing letters of the alphabet and numbers, to be signalled by lamp, radio, etc: *a message in ~; the ~ alphabet.*

mor·sel /ˈmɔsl/ *n* [C] tiny piece (esp of food); mouthful: *I haven't had a ~ of food since I left the house. What a dainty/choice ~!*

mor·tal /ˈmɔtl/ *adj* **1** (contrasted with *immortal*) which must die; which cannot live for ever: *Man is ~,* All men must die. *Here lie the ~ remains of...,* (eg on a tombstone) Here is buried what now remains of the body of.... **2** causing death: *a ~ wound. His injuries proved ~.* **~ sins,** causing spiritual death. **3** lasting until death: *~ hatred.* **~ combat,** only ended by the death of one of the fighters. **~ enemies,** whose enmity will not end until death. **4** accompanying death: *in ~ agony.* **5** (colloq) extreme; very great or long: *in ~ fear; in a ~ hurry.* □ *n* human being; (colloq) *What a thirsty ~* (= person) *you are!* **~ly** /-tlɪ/ *adv* **1** so as to cause death: *~ly wounded.* **2** deeply, seriously: *~ly offended.*

mor·tal·ity /mɔˋtælətɪ/ *n* [U] **1** state of being mortal. **2** number of deaths caused by sth (eg a disaster or disease): *an epidemic with a heavy ~,* a large number of deaths. **3** death-rate: **~ tables,** (insurance) tables showing how long people at various ages may expect to live.

mor·tar[1] /ˈmɔtə(r)/ *n* [U] mixture of lime, sand and water used to hold bricks, stones, etc together in building. **ˋ~-board** *n* **(a)** small, flat board with a short handle on the underside, used for holding a supply of ~ (while laying bricks, etc). **(b)** square cap worn as part of their academic costume by members of a college, etc. □ *vt* [VP6A,15] join (bricks, etc) with ~.

mor·tar[2] /ˈmɔtə(r)/ *n* **1** bowl of hard material in which substances are crushed with a pestle. **2** (mil) muzzle-loading cannon for firing shells at high angles.

mort·gage /ˈmɔgɪdʒ/ *vt* [VP6A,14] give sb a claim on (property) as a security for payment of a debt or loan: *~ a house (to sb for £8 000); land that may be ~d.* □ *n* act of mortgaging; agreement about this: *raise a ~ (on one's house) from a bank. I can buy the house only if a ~ for £8 000 is obtainable. We must pay off the ~ this year.* **be ~d up to the hilt,** have the maximum ~ possible (on property). **mort·gagee** /ˈmɔgɪˋdʒi/ *n* person to whom property is ~d. **mort·gagor** /ˈmɔgɪˋdʒɔ(r) *US:* ˋmɔrgɪdʒər/ *n* person who gives a ~ on his property.

mor·tice /ˈmɔtɪs/ *n* ⇨ **mortise.**

mor·ti·cian /mɔˋtɪʃn/ *n* (US) funeral director; undertaker.

mor·tify /ˈmɔtɪfaɪ/ *vt,vi* (*pt,pp* -fied) **1** [VP6A] cause (sb) to be ashamed, humiliated, or hurt in his feelings: *mortified by sb's rudeness; feel mortified at one's failure to pass an examination; a ~ing defeat.* **2** [VP6A] **~ the flesh,** discipline bodily passions, overcome bodily desires. **3** [VP2A] (of flesh, eg round a wound) decay, be affected with gangrene. **mor·ti·fi·ca·tion** /ˈmɔtɪfɪˋkeɪʃn/ *n* [U] ~ing or being mortified (all senses).

mor·tise, mor·tice /ˈmɔtɪs/ *n* hole (usu rectangular) cut in a piece of wood, etc to receive the end of another piece (the *tenon*); (attrib) **ˋ~ lock,** secure lock which is fitted inside the woodwork (of a door, etc), not screwed on to the surface. □ *vt* [VP15A,B] join or fasten in this way: *~ two beams together; ~ one beam (in)to another.*

mor·tu·ary /ˈmɔtʃʊrɪ *US:* -tʃʊerɪ/ *n* (*pl* -ries) room or building (eg part of a hospital) to which dead bodies are taken to be kept until burial; (attrib) of death or burial: *~ rites.*

mo·saic /məʊˋzeɪɪk/ *n, adj* (form or work of art) in

which designs, pictures, etc are made by fitting together differently coloured bits of stone, etc: *a design in ~; a ~ pavement; newly discovered ~s in an excavated Roman villa; ~ jewellery.*

Mo·saic /məʊˋzeɪɪk/ *adj* of Moses: **the ~ law,** the first five books of the O T.

mo·selle /məʊˋzel/ *n* dry, white wine from the valley of the River M~ (Germany).

Mos·lem /ˋmɒzləm/ *n, adj* (variant of) Muslim.

mosque /mɒsk/ *n* building in which Muslims worship Allah.

a mosque

mos·quito /məˋskiːtəʊ/ *n* (*pl* -toes /-təʊz/) small, flying, blood-sucking insect, esp the sort that spreads malaria. ⇨ the illus at insect. **ˋ~-net** *n* net spread over a bed against ~es. **ˋ~-craft** *n* (collective *pl*) small, armed ships with high speed and able to manœuvre easily.

moss /mɒs *US:* mɔːs/ *n* [U] sorts of small green or yellow plant growing in thick masses on wet surfaces: *~-covered rocks/roofs/tree-trunks.* ***A rolling stone gathers no ~,*** (prov) A person who too frequently changes his occupation or who never settles in one place will not succeed in life. **ˋ~-grown** *adj* covered with growing ~. **~y** *adj* (-ier, -iest) covered with ~; like ~: *~y green.*

most[1] /məʊst/ (contrasted with *least* and *fewest;* ⇨ many, more, much[1]) *adj, n* **1** (independent superl) (the) greatest in number, quantity, degree, etc: *Which is ~, 3, 13 or 30? Which of you has made (the) ~ mistakes? Those who have (the) ~ money are not always the happiest. Do the ~ you can.* ***at (the) ~, at the very ~,*** not more than: *I can pay only £10 at the ~. There were only 30 people at the meeting at the very ~,* There were 30 or fewer. ***make the ~ of,*** use to the best advantage: *We have only a few hours so we must make the ~ of our time. She's not really beautiful, but she makes the ~ of her looks.* ***for the ˋ~ part,*** usually; on the whole: *Japanese T V sets are, for the ~ part, of excellent quality.* **2** (not preceded by *def art* in this sense) the majority of; the greater part of: *M~ boys like outdoor games. M~ people think so. He was ill ~ of the summer.*

most[2] /məʊst/ *adv* **1** (forming the superlative degree of nearly all *adjj* and *advv* of more than one syllable): *the ~ beautiful/interesting/useful, etc; ~ carefully/accurately, etc.* **2** (modifying *vv*, but not to be placed between a *v* and its object): *What is troubling you ~? What ~ pleased me/What pleased me ~ was that....* **3** (intensive; may be preceded by *indef art*) very; exceedingly: *This is a ~ useful book. He was ~ polite to me. Your news is ~ interesting.* **4** (modifying an *adv*) quite: *I shall ~ certainly go.* **5** (dial and US colloq) almost: *M~ everybody has gone home.* **~·ly** *adv* chiefly; almost all; generally: *The medicine was ~ly sugar and water. The village is ~ly of mud houses. We are ~ly out on Sundays,* are not at home on ~ Sundays.

mote /məʊt/ *n* particle (of dust, etc): *~s dancing in a sunbeam;* (fig) *the ~ that is in thy brother's eye,* the fault that he has committed (trifling if compared to one's own fault). ⇨ Matt 7: 3.

mo·tel /məʊˋtel/ *n* motorists' hotel (with rooms or cabins, a parking area, service station, etc).

moth /mɒθ *US:* mɔːθ/ *n* sorts of winged insect flying chiefly at night, attracted by lights. ⇨ the illus at insect. **ˋ~·ball** *n* small ball (of camphor, etc) intended to discourage clothes-~s; (by extension) *in ~-balls,* (of ships, aircraft, etc) laid up; in storage: *After ten years in ~balls the destroyers were sent to be broken up.* **ˋclothes-~** *n* kind which breeds in cloth, fur, etc, its grub feeding on the cloth and making holes. **ˋ~-eaten** *adj* eaten or destroyed by clothes-~s; (fig) antiquated; out-of-date. **ˋ~-proof** *adj* (of fabrics) treated chemically against damage by clothes ~s. □ *vt* make ~-proof: *~-proof carpets.*

mother /ˋmʌðə(r)/ *n* **1** female parent; woman who has adopted a child; woman (often *ˋhousemother*) who is in charge of children in a boarding-school or home[1](2): *She was like a ~ to the poor waifs.* **2** quality or condition that gives rise to sth: *Misgovernment is often the ~ of revolt.* ***Necessity is the ~ of invention,*** (prov). **3** head of a female religious community. **M~ Superior,** head of a convent. **4** (various uses) **the ˋ~ country, (a)** one's native land. **(b)** a country in relation to dominions (e g Great Britain for Canada). **~-in-law** /ˋmʌðr ɪn lɔː/ *n* (*pl* ~s-in-law) ~ of one's wife or one's husband. **ˌ~-of-ˋpearl** *n* [U] hard, smooth, shiny rainbow-coloured material that forms the lining of some shells, esp the pearl-oyster, used for making buttons, ornaments, etc. **~ ship** *n* one from which other ships (e g submarines) get supplies. **~ tongue** *n* one's native language. **~ wit** *n* common sense; the intelligence with which one is born. □ *vt* [VP6A] take care of (as a ~ does); protect or adopt (a child) as one's own. **ˋ~·hood** /-hʊd/ *n* [U] state of being a ~. **~·less** *adj* having no ~. **ˋ~·like** *adj* in the manner of a ~. **~·ly** *adj* having, showing, the tender, kind qualities of a ~. **~·li·ness** *n*

mo·tif /məʊˋtiːf/ *n* [C] theme in music for treatment and development, often one which recurs; main feature in a work of art.

mo·tion /ˋməʊʃn/ *n* **1** [U] (manner of) moving: *If a thing is in ~, it is not at rest.* **put/set sth in ~,** cause it to start moving or working. **~ picture** *n* cinema film. Cf (colloq) *moving pictures, the movies.* ***(time and) ˋ~ study,*** analysis of the movements of workers (in industry, etc) undertaken by experts, who aim at improving efficiency. **2** [C] gesture; particular movement; way of moving the hand, body, etc: *If you watch my ~s carefully you will see how the trick is performed. All her ~s were graceful.* ***go through the ~s,*** (colloq) do sth (that one is expected or required to do) in a perfunctory or insincere manner. **3** [C] proposal to be discussed and voted on at a meeting: *On the ~ of Mr X the committee agreed to...; The ~ was adopted/carried/rejected, etc by a majority of six.* **4** [C] = movement(6). □ *vt,vi* **1** [VP17,15A,B] direct (sb) by a motion or gesture: *~ sb in/away/to a seat. He*

the motor-car

~ed me to enter. **2** [VP3A] ***~ to sb (to do sth),*** indicate by a gesture: *He ~ed to me to come nearer.* **~·less** *adj* not moving; still.

mo·ti·vate /ˋməʊtɪveɪt/ *vt* [VP6A] be the motive of; give a motive or incentive to; act as an incentive. **mo·tiv·ation** /ˈməʊtɪˋveɪʃn/ *n*

mo·tive /ˋməʊtɪv/ *adj* (pred only) causing motion: *~ power/force,* e g steam, electricity. □ *n* [C] **1** that which causes sb to act: *actuated by low and selfish ~s; do sth from ~s of kindness. Hatred was his ~ for attacking me.* **2** = motif. **~·less** *adj* without a ~.

mot·ley /ˋmɒtlɪ/ *adj* **1** of various colours: *a ~ coat,* e g that worn by a jester or fool in olden times. **2** of varied character or various sorts: *a ~ crowd,* e g people of many different occupations, social classes, etc. □ *n* jester's dress: (esp) ***wear the ~,*** play the part of a fool or jester.

mo·tor /ˋməʊtə(r)/ *n* **1** device which imparts or utilizes power (esp electric power) to produce motion, but not used of a steam engine: *fans driven by electric ~s.* **2** (attrib, and in compounds) having, driven by, an internal combustion engine, a diesel engine, etc which generates mechanical power: *ˋ~-vehicles; a ˋ~-car/-bike/-cycle/-boat/-bus/-scooter, etc.* **ˈ~-asˋsisted** *adj* (e g of a pedal bicycle) having an engine to help propulsion. **ˋ~·cade** *n* (US) procession of ~ vehicles. **ˋ~·man** *n* (*pl* -men) man in control of a ~, esp on an electric tram or train. **ˋ~·way** *n* road designed and built especially for fast traffic, with dual carriageways and going over or under other roads. **3** (*car* is more usu) short for *~-car: the ˋ~ trade; the ˋM~ Show.* **4** muscle able to produce movement of a part of the body: *~ nerve,* nerve that excites movements of a muscle or muscles. □ *vi, vt* [VP2A,C] travel by ~-car: *~ from London to Brighton.* **ˋ~·ist** /-ɪst/ *n* person who drives (and usu owns) a car. **ˋ~·ize** /-ɑɪz/ *vt* [VP6A] equip (troops, etc) with ~ transport.

mottle /ˋmɒtl/ *vt* [VP6A] (usu in *pp*) mark with spots or areas of different colours without a regular pattern: *the ~d skin of a snake; linoleum with a ~d finish.*

motto /ˋmɒtəʊ/ *n* (*pl* -toes or -tos /-təʊz/) **1** short sentence or phrase used as a guide or rule of behaviour (e g *'Every man for himself', 'Always merry and bright*). **2** short sentence or phrase written or inscribed on an object (e g a coat of arms) expressing a suitable sentiment; quotation prefixed to a book or chapter.

mou·jik /ˋmuʒɪk/ *n* (esp before the Revolution of 1917) Russian peasant.

mould[1] (US = **mold**) /məʊld/ *n* [C] container, hollow form, into which molten metal or a soft substance is poured to cool into a desired shape; the shape or form given by this container; jelly, pudding, etc made in such a container. ***be cast in one/the same/a different, etc ~,*** (fig) have the same (e g heroic, stubborn, rugged) character. □ *vt* [VP6A,14] ***~ sth (in/from/out of sth),*** sth in, or as in, a ~, from some material: *~ a head out of/in clay;* (fig) guide or control the growth of; influence: *~ a person's character.*

mould[2] (US = **mold**) /məʊld/ *n* woolly or furry growth of fungi appearing upon moist surfaces, e g leather, cheese or on objects left in a moist, warm atmosphere. ⇨ *iron~* at iron[1](3). □ *vi* [VP2A] (US) become covered with ~: *Cheese ~s in warm, wet weather.* **~y** *adj* (-ier, -iest) **1** covered with ~: *~y bread.* **2** stale; smelling of ~. **3** (fig) out-of-date; old-fashioned; (of a person) mean and obstructive; worthless.

mould[3] (US = **mold**) /məʊld/ *n* [U] soft, fine loose earth, esp from decayed vegetable matter, e g *ˋleaf~,* from decayed leaves fallen from trees.

moulder (US = **molder**) /ˋməʊldə(r)/ *vi* [VP2A,C] crumble to dust by natural decay: *the ~ing* *ruins of an old castle; ~ing away in the churchyard,* of a corpse buried there.

mould·ing (US = **mold-**) /ˋməʊldɪŋ/ *n* **1** [U] act of moulding or shaping; way in which sth is shaped. **2** line of ornamental plaster, carved woodwork, etc round a wall or window, or in the cornices of a building, or on a pillar.

moult (US = **molt**) /məʊlt/ *vt,vi* [VP6A,2A] (of birds) lose (feathers) before a new growth; (more rarely, of dogs and cats) lose hair. □ *n* process or time of ~ing.

mound /maʊnd/ *n* [C] mass of piled up earth; small hill: *a ˋburial-~,* of earth over a grave; *~s built for defensive purposes in olden times.*

mount[1] /maʊnt/ *n* (liter except in proper names) mountain, hill: *Christ's sermon on the ~;* (shortened to *Mt* before proper names): *Mt Everest.*

mount[2] /maʊnt/ *vt,vi* **1** [VP6A,2A] go up (a hill, a ladder, etc); get on to (a horse, etc); supply (sb) with a horse; put (sb) on a horse: *He ~ed (his horse) and rode away. The ~ed police were called out to control the crowds.* ***~ the throne,*** become king/queen/emperor, etc. **2** [VP2A,C] ***~ (up),*** become greater in amount: *Our living expenses are ~ing up. Bills soon ~ up at hotels.* **3** (of blood) rise into the cheeks: *A blush ~ed to* (= spread over) *the child's face.* **4** [VP6A] put and fix in position: *~ a gun,* on a gun-carriage; *~ pictures,* fix them with backings, margins, etc; *~ jewels in gold; ~ specimens,* e g on a slide for a microscope; *~ insects,* e g for display or preservation in a museum. **5** (mil uses): *~ an offensive,* take the offensive, attack. ***~ guard (at/over),*** act as a guard or sentinel: *The Household Troops ~ guard at Buckingham Palace.* **6** [VP6A] put (a play) on the stage: *The play was well ~ed,* was provided with good scenery, costumes, etc. **7** (esp of large animals, e g a stallion) get up on (a female animal) in order to copulate. □ *n* [C] that on which a person or thing is or may be ~ed (e g a card for a drawing or photograph, a glass slide for specimens, a horse for riding on, a gun-carriage, the ornamental metal part in which a jewel is fixed).

moun·tain /ˋmaʊntɪn *US:* -ntn/ *n* **1** mass of very high land going up to a peak: *Everest is the highest ~ in the world.* **~ ash,** the rowan tree, with scarlet berries. **~ chain,** series of ~s. **ˋ~ dew,** (colloq) Scotch whisky. **~ range,** series of ~s more or less in a line. **ˋ~ sickness,** illness caused by rarefied air on high ~s. **2** (fig uses) sth immense: *a ~ of debts/difficulties. The waves were ~ high,* very high. **~·eer** /ˈmaʊntɪˋnɪə(r) *US:* -ntnˋɪər/ *n* person who lives among ~s or is skilled at climbing ~s; hence, **~·eer·ing** *n* climbing ~s (as a sport). **~·ous** /ˋmaʊntɪnəs *US:* -ntṇəs/ *adj* having ~s; *~ous country;* huge: *~ous waves.*

moun·te·bank /ˋmaʊntɪbæŋk/ *n* sb who tries to persuade people by clever and humorous talk to buy worthless medicines, etc.

Mountie /ˋmaʊntɪ/ *n* (colloq) member of the Canadian Mounted Police.

mourn /mɔn/ *vi,vt* [VP3A,6A] **~ *(for/over),*** feel or show sorrow or regret: *~ for a dead child; ~ over the child's death;* grieve for: *~ the loss of one's mother.* **~er** *n* person who ~s, esp one who attends a funeral as a relative or friend of the dead person. **~·ful** /-fl/ *adj* sad; sorrowful. **~·fully** /-flɪ/ *adv.*

mourn·ing /ˋmɔnɪŋ/ *n* [U] **1** grief. **2** (the wearing of) black clothes as a sign of grief: *The widow was in deep ~. The Court will go into ~ for three weeks.* **ˋ~-band** *n* band of black crepe worn round the sleeve. **ˋ~-ring** *n* (formerly) worn as a memorial of a dead person.

mouse /maʊs/ *n* (*pl* **mice** /maɪs/) sorts of small rodent (*ˋhouse ~, ˋfield-~, ˋharvest-~*); (fig) shy, timid person. **ˋ~-trap** *n* trap for catching mice: *~-trap cheese,* (hum) unpalatable kind of cheese. □ *vi* (of cats) hunt for, catch, mice: *Our cat ~s well.* **mousy** /ˋmaʊsɪ/ *adj* (**-ier, -iest**) (esp of hair) dull brown; (of a person) timid, shy.

mousse /mus/ *n* [C,U] (dish of) flavoured cream beaten and frozen: *chocolate ~.*

mous·tache (US = **mus-**) /məˋstɑʃ *US:* ˋmʌstæʃ/ *n* [C] hair allowed to grow on the upper lip.

mouth[1] /maʊθ/ *n* (*pl* **~s** /maʊðz/) **1** opening

mountains

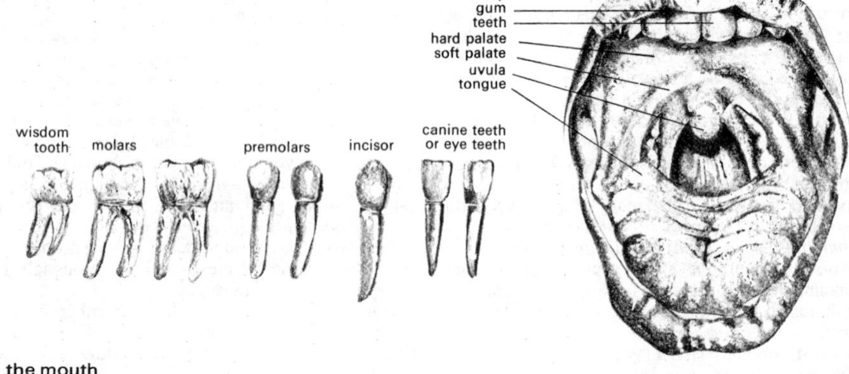

the mouth

through which animals take in food; space behind this containing the teeth, tongue, etc. ⇨ the illus. ***by word of* ~,** (of news, etc) orally (not in writing, etc). ***down in the* ~,** sad, dejected. ***put words into sb's* ~,** **(a)** tell him what to say. **(b)** suggest or claim that he has said something. ***take the words out of sb's* ~,** say what he was about to say; anticipate his words. ***laugh on the wrong side of one's* ~,** lament, be disappointed. ***look a gift-horse in the* ~,** accept sth ungratefully esp by examining it critically for faults. **ˈ~-organ** *n* small musical wind-instrument with metal reeds, played by passing it along the lips; harmonica. **ˈ~-piece** *n* **(a)** that part of a tobacco pipe, a musical instrument, etc placed at or between the lips. **(b)** person, newspaper, etc, that expresses the opinions of others: *Which newspaper is the ~piece of the Socialists?* **2** opening or outlet (of a bag, bottle, tunnel cave, river, etc).

mouth[2] /maʊð/ *vt,vi* [VP6A,2A] **1** speak (words) with too much movement of the jaw; utter pompously: *An actor who ~s his words is a poor actor.* **2** take (food) into the ~; touch with the ~. **~·ful** /-fʊl/ *n* as much as can be put into the ~ comfortably at one time: *swallow sth at a ~ful; have only a ~ful of food.*

mov·able /ˈmuvəbl/ *adj* **1** that can be moved; (of property) that can be taken from place to place (e g furniture, contrasted with land and buildings, called *real* property or estate). ⇨ **portable. 2** varying in date: *Christmas is fixed but Easter is a ~ feast.* □ *n (pl)* personal property; articles that can be removed from the house (contrasted with *fixtures*).

move[1] /muv/ *n* [C] **1** change of place or position, esp of a piece in chess or other games played on boards; player's turn to do this: *Do you know all the ~s in chess? Whose ~ is it?* **2** sth (to be) done to achieve a purpose: *a ~ towards settling the strike. What's our next ~?* **3** ***on the* ~,** moving about: *Our planes reported that large enemy forces were on the ~.* ***make a* ~,** **(a)** ~ to a different place: *Shall we make a ~ now?* **(b)** begin to act: *Unless we make a ~ soon, we shall be in a hopelessly weak position.* ***get a* ~ *on*,** (sl) hurry up.

move[2] /muv/ *vt,vi* **1** [VP6A,15A,B,2A,C] (cause to) change position; put, cause to be, in a different place or attitude; (cause to) be in motion: *M~ your chair nearer to the fire. Lorries were used to ~ the troops to the front. It was calm and not a leaf ~d. It's your turn to ~,* (in chess, etc) to ~ a piece from one square to another. **~ *heaven and earth*,** do one's utmost, use every possible means (*to do* sth). **moving staircase,** = escalator. **2** [VP6A,2C] **~ *house*,** take one's furniture, etc to another house, flat, etc: *We're moving (house) next week.* **~ *in*,** take possession of a new dwelling-place. **~ *out*,** give up a dwelling-place: *We ~d out on Monday and the new tenants ~d in on Tuesday.* **3** [VP2C,15B] **~ *on*,** ~ to another place or position (e g when ordered to do so by a policeman). **~ *sb on*,** cause him to ~ by giving him the order 'M~ on, please'. **~ *along/down/up*,** ~ farther in the direction indicated so as to make space for others. *'M~ along, please', said the bus conductor.* **4** [VP6A,15A] arouse, work on, the feelings of; affect with pity, etc: *be ~d with pity/compassion; be ~d to tears. We were all ~d by her entreaties. The story of their sufferings ~d us deeply. It was a moving sight* (i e ~d the feelings). **5** [VP17A,14] cause to do sth: *Nothing I said ~d him to offer his help. The spirit ~d him to get up and address the meeting,* He felt a desire to do this. *Who was the moving spirit in the enterprise,* Who started it and was most active? **6** [VP6A,9] put forward for discussion and decision (at a meeting): *Mr Chairman, I ~ that the money be used for library books.* ⇨ **motion(3). 7** [VP3A] **~ *for*,** make formal application (*for*): *The noble Lord ~d for papers,* i e in a debate in the House of Lords. **8** [VP2A,C] make progress; go forward: *Time ~s on. The work ~s slowly. Things are not moving as rapidly as we had hoped.* **9** [VP2A,C] take action: *Nobody seems willing to ~ in the matter.* **10** [VP2C] live one's life; pass one's time: *They ~ in the best society.* **11** [VP6A,2A] cause (the bowels) to act, to empty; (of the bowels) be emptied.

move·ment /ˈmuvmənt/ *n* **1** [U] moving or being moved; activity (contrasted with quiet and rest): *He lay there without ~. The novel/play lacks ~,* i e there is not enough action in it. **2** [C] act of changing position, esp a military evolution: *By a series of rapid ~s the general placed his forces in an advantageous position.* **3** [C] moving part of a machine or mechanism or a particular group of such parts: *the ~ of a clock or a watch.* **4** [C] united actions and efforts of a group of people for a special purpose: *the ~ to abolish slavery.* **the 'Labour M~,** organized(2) (manual) workers. **5** [C] (music) principal division of a musical work with a distinctive structure of its own: *the final ~ of the Ninth Symphony.* **6** [C] emptying of the bowels. **7** [U] activity (in a stock market, etc) for some commodity: *not much ~ in oil shares.*

mover /'muvə(r)/ *n* (esp) person who moves(6) a proposal. ***the prime ~,*** the person chiefly responsible for starting sth.

movie /'muvɪ/ *n* (colloq) **1** motion picture: *I'm a ~ addict.* **2 the ~s,** the cinema; the cinema industry: *How often do you go to the ~s?*

mow[1] /məʊ/ *vt* (*pt* **mowed** *pp* **mown** /məʊn/ or **mowed**) **1** [VP6A,2A] cut (grass, etc) with a scythe or a machine (called a *'lawn-mower*): *mow the lawn; new-mown hay; mow a field.* **2** [VP15B] ***mow down,*** cut down like grass; destroy as if by sweeping movements: *Our men were mown down by the enemy's machine-gun fire.* **mower** /'məʊə(r)/ *n* person or machine that mows.

mow[2] /məʊ/ *n* [C] heap of hay, straw, etc; place in a barn where hay, etc is stored.

mow[3] /məʊ/ *vi* ⇨ **mop.**

Mr /'mɪstə(r)/ ⇨ **mister.**

Mrs /'mɪsɪz/ title prefixed to the surname of a married woman who has no title.

much[1] /mʌtʃ/ (*more, most.* ⇨ **little**) *adj, n* (~ is used with *sing nn,* uncountable. Cf *many,* used with *pl nn.* In purely affirm sentences it is often preferable to use *plenty (of), a lot (of), a large quantity (of), a good (great) deal (of). M~* is often used in affirm sentences when it is (a part of) the subject, and when used with *how, too, so,* or *as*): *There isn't ~ food in the house. He never eats ~ breakfast. Did you have ~ difficulty in finding the house? M~ of what you say is true. We have ~ to be thankful for. You have given me too ~.* ***how ~,*** **(a)** what quantity: *How ~ flour* (= What weight) *do you want?* **(b)** what price: *How ~ a kilo is that beef?* ***(not) up to ~,*** (not) worth ~: *I don't think his work is up to ~,* i e it is not good. ***not ~ of a,*** not a good: *He's not ~ of a linguist/scholar, etc. It wasn't ~ of a dinner. I'm not ~ of a cinema-goer,* I seldom go to the cinema. ***this/that ~,*** the quantity, extent, etc indicated: *Can you let me have this ~? I will say this ~ in his favour...,* I will admit in his favour that.... *This ~ is certain, that he will never try to play that trick on us again.* ***be too ~ for,*** be more than a match for, too difficult for; be superior in skill, etc, to: *The school tennis champion was too ~ for me. I couldn't finish that book on relativity; it was too ~ for me.* ***make ~ of,*** **(a)** understand: *I didn't make ~ of that lecture.* **(b)** attach importance to; exaggerate: *We mustn't make too ~ of this incident. He makes (too) ~ of his connections with rich people.* ***not think ~ of,*** have a poor opinion of: *I don't think ~ of my new music teacher.* ***as ~ (as):*** *Give me as ~ again,* the same quantity again. *I thought as ~,* That is what I thought. *You have always helped me and I will always do as ~ for you,* will always help you. *It is as ~ your responsibility as mine,* You and I are equally responsible. *It was as ~ as he could do to* (= He could do no more than) *pay his way. That is as ~ as to say* (= is the same thing as saying) *that I am a liar.* ***(with) not/without so ~ as,*** not even: *He left without so ~ as saying 'Thank you'. He rushed past me with not so ~ as a 'By your leave',* without any apology. He hadn't so ~ as his fare home. ⇨ also *so ~ (many), not so ~ as, so ~ so that, so ~ for,* under **so**[1]**(6).**

much[2] /mʌtʃ/ *adv* **1** (modifying comparatives and superlatives, preceding the *def art*): *He is ~ better today. You must work ~ harder. This is ~* (= by far) *the best. He's ~ the worse for his fall into the canal.* ***~ more/less,*** (used to indicate that what has been stated about sth applies with greater force to the following statement): *It is difficult to understand his books, ~ more his lectures. I didn't even speak to him, ~ less discuss your problems with him.* **2** (modifying passive *participles* and *pred adjj* such as *afraid.* Cf *very,* used to modify passive and *present participles* which are true *adjj* as *very frightened*): *I am very ~ afraid that...; I shall be surprised if he succeeds. I hope you will not be inconvenienced.* **3** (When *much* modifies a *v* phrase, it may occur within the *v* phrase or in end position, but may not occur between this *v* phrase and its object): *It doesn't ~ matter. It doesn't matter very ~. I very ~ enjoyed the concert. I enjoyed it very ~. He doesn't like beef ~.* **4** (in phrases) ***~ as:*** *M~ as I should* (= Although I should ~) *like to go,...; M~ as she disliked the idea* (= Although she ~ disliked the idea),.... ***~ the same,*** about the same: *The patient's condition is ~ the same.* ***~ to,*** greatly to; to my/his, her, etc, great...: *M~ to her surprise/regret, etc.* ***how ~,*** to what extent: *How ~ do you really want to marry the man?* ⇨ **much**[1]. ***too ~,*** too highly: *He thinks too ~ of himself.* ***so ~:*** *Oceans don't so ~ divide the world as unite it,* They serve to unite countries rather than to divide them. **~-ness** *n* (only in the colloq phrase) ***~ of a ~ness,*** ~ the same; almost alike.

mu·ci·lage /'mjusɪlɪdʒ/ *n* [U] kinds of vegetable glue (obtained from plants, seaweed, etc), used as an adhesive.

muck /mʌk/ *n* [U] **1** dung; farmyard manure (the droppings of animals). **'~-heap** *n* heap of farmyard ~. **'~-raker** *n* (usu fig) person who is always looking for scandal, corruption, etc. Hence, **'~-raking** *n* **2** dirt; filth; (colloq) anything disgusting or dirty. ***make a ~ of sth,*** (colloq) make a mess of it; make it dirty; spoil it. □ *vt, vi* **1** [VP6A,15B] ***~ sth up,*** (colloq) make dirty; spoil; make a mess of it; spoil it. **2** [VP2C] ***~ about,*** (GB sl) do useless or unnecessary things; go about, spend time, aimlessly: *'What's he up to?'—'Oh, just ~ing about.'* **3** [VP2C,15B] ***~ out,*** clean out (stables, etc) by removing dung: *She ~s out (the stables) every morning.* **~y** *adj* (**-ier, -iest**) dirty.

muckle /'mʌkl/ *n* ⇨ **mickle.**

mu·cous /'mjukəs/ *adj* of, like, covered with, mucus. **the ~ membrane,** the moist skin that lines the nose, mouth and food canal. **mu·cus** /'mjukəs/ *n* [U] sticky, slimy substance produced by the ~ membrane; similar slimy substance: *Snails and slugs leave a trail of mucus.*

mud /mʌd/ *n* [U] soft, wet earth: *Rain turns dust into mud.* ***throw/fling mud at sb,*** speak evil of him, try to damage his reputation. Hence, **'mud-slinger** *n* ***his/her/your, etc name is mud,*** he/she/you, etc are in disgrace. **'mud-bath** *n* bath in mud of mineral springs (e g as a cure for rheumatism). **'mud flat** *n* muddy land covered by the sea at high tide and not covered at low tide. **'mud-**

guard *n* guard (curved cover) over a wheel (of a bicycle, etc). ⇨ the illus at **bicycle**. □ *vt* [VP6A] make muddy: *You've muddied the carpet.* **muddy** *adj* (-ier, -iest) **1** full of, covered with, mud: *muddy roads/shoes.* **2** mud-coloured; like mud because thick: *a muddy stream; a muddy skin; muddy coffee; muddy* (fig, = confused) *ideas.*

muddle /ˋmʌdl/ *vt,vi* **1** [VP6A,15B] bring into a state of confusion and disorder; make a mess of: *You've ~d the scheme completely. A glass of whisky soon ~s him. Don't ~* (= mix) *things up (together).* **2** [VP2C] ***~ along/on,*** get on in a foolish or helpless way, with no clear purpose or plan: *He's still muddling on/along.* ***~ through,*** reach the end of an undertaking in spite of inefficiency, obstacles of one's own making, etc. □ *n* (usu *sing* with *indef art*) ~d state; confusion of ideas: *Everything was in a ~ and I couldn't find what I wanted. You have made a ~ of it,* mismanaged it, bungled it. **ˋ~-headed** *adj* confused in mind; stupid.

mu·ez·zin /muˋezɪn *US:* mju-/ *n* man who proclaims the hours of prayers from the minaret of a mosque.

muff[1] /mʌf/ *n* covered, usu a cylindrical padded bag of fur, open at both ends, used by a woman to keep the hands warm; similar covering for the foot.

muff[2] /mʌf/ *n* person who is awkward or clumsy, esp in games (e g by failing to catch the ball at cricket). □ *vt* [VP6A] bungle; fail to catch; miss: *~ a ball; ~ an easy catch.*

muf·fin /ˋmʌfɪn/ *n* light, flat, round tea-cake, usu eaten hot with butter. **ˋ~-man** /-mæn/ *n* (*pl* -men) street vendor of ~s.

muffle /ˋmʌfl/ *vt* [VP6A,15B] ***~ (up),*** **1** wrap or cover for warmth or protection: *~ oneself up well; ~ one's throat,* e g by putting a scarf round it; *~d up in a heavy overcoat.* **2** [VP6A] make the sound of sth (e g a bell or a drum) dull by wrapping it up in cloth, etc: *~ the oars of a boat,* to deaden the sound of their touching the water; *~d voices,* e g from persons whose mouths are covered.

muf·fler /ˋmʌflə(r)/ *n* **1** cloth, scarf, worn round the neck for warmth. **2** cloth, etc used to muffle sound: *the ~ in the engine of a motor-vehicle.*

mufti[1] /ˋmʌftɪ/ *n* (usu ***in ~***) plain, ordinary clothes worn by someone (e g an offical, an army officer) who has the right to wear uniform.

mufti[2] /ˋmʌftɪ/ *n* official expounder of Muslim law.

mug[1] /mʌg/ *n* **1** (usu straight-sided) drinking vessel of china or metal with a handle, for use without a saucer; its contents: *a ˋbeer-mug; a mug of milk for the baby.* **2** (sl) face; mouth: *What an ugly mug you have!*

mug[2] /mʌg/ *n* (sl) simpleton; easily deceived person. ***a ˋmug's game,*** sth unlikely to bring profit or reward.

mug[3] /mʌg/ *vt* (-gg-) [VP15B] ***mug sth up,*** (colloq) (try to) become quite familiar with sth on which one is to be tested.

mug[4] /mʌg/ *vt* (-gg-) [VP6A] (sl) attack (sb) violently and rob (e g in a dark street, a lift, an empty corridor, etc). **mug·ger** *n* **mug·ging** *n*

mug·gins /ˋmʌgɪnz/ *n* (sl) fool.

muggy /ˋmʌgɪ/ *adj* (-ier, -iest) (of the weather, a day, etc) damp and warm; close and sticky: *~ days during the rainy season.* **muggi·ness** *n*

mug·wump /ˋmʌgwʌmp/ *n* (US) conceited person; person who has a high opinion of his own importance.

Mu·ham·mad /məˋhæmɪd/ *n* Prophet and Founder of Islam. **~an** /-ən/ *adj* **Mu·ham·ma·dan·ism** /məˋhæmɪdən-ɪzm/ *n* Islam (the preferred name).

mu·jik *n* = moujik.

mu·latto /mjʊˋlætəʊ *US:* məˋl-/ *n* (*pl* -tos, -toes /-təʊz/) person who has one parent of a white race and one Negroid parent.

mul·berry /ˋmʌlbrɪ *US:* -berɪ/ *n* (*pl* -ries) [C] tree with broad, dark-green leaves on which silkworms feed; its fruit (dark purple or white).

mulch /mʌltʃ/ *n* [C] protective covering of peat, spread over the roots of trees and bushes, to retain moisture, smother weeds, etc. □ *vt* cover (ground) with a ~.

mulct /mʌlkt/ *vt* [VP12C,14] punish by means of a fine; take (sth) away from: *~ a man £5; ~ a man in £5; be ~ed of one's money.*

mule[1] /mjul/ *n* **1** animal that is the offspring of an ass and a mare. ***as obstinate/stubborn as a ~,*** very obstinate/stubborn. **2** (colloq) stubborn person. **3** kind of spinning-machine. **mu·le·teer** /ˈmjulɪˋtɪə(r)/ *n* ~-driver. **ˋmul·ish** /-ɪʃ/ *adj* stubborn; obstinate. **ˋmu·lish·ly** *adv* **ˋmu·lish·ness** *n*

mule[2] /mjul/ *n* heelless slipper.

mull[1] /mʌl/ *vt* [VP6A] make (wine, beer) into a hot drink with sugar, spices, etc: *~ed claret.*

mull[2] /mʌl/ *n* (Scot) (in place-names) promontory: *the M~ of Kintyre.*

mull[3] /mʌl/ *vt* [VP15A] ***~ sth over, ~ over sth,*** ponder over it.

mul·lah /ˋmʌlə/ *n* Muslim learned in theology and sacred law.

mul·lein /ˋmʌlɪn/ *n* kinds of plant with leaves covered with grey hairs, and small yellow flowers.

mul·let /ˋmʌlɪt/ *n* kinds of seafish used as food, esp *red ~* and *grey ~.*

mul·li·ga·tawny /ˈmʌlɪgəˋtɔnɪ/ *n* **ˋ~ (soup),** thick, highly seasoned soup with curry powder in it, often with boiled rice added.

mul·lion /ˋmʌlɪən/ *n* vertical stone division between parts of a window. ⇨ the illus at **window**. **~ed** /ˋmʌlɪənd/ *adj* having ~s.

multi- /ˈmʌltɪ/ *pref* having many of (e g *~ coloured,* of many colours; *a ˈ~-ˈmillioˋnaire,* person having 2 or more millions of money); *a ˈ~-ˈstage ˋrocket,* with parts that ignite (and then fall away) in stages; a *ˈ~-ˈracial ˋcountry,* with many races of people.

mul·ti·far·ious ˈmʌltɪˋfeərɪəs/ *adj* many and various: *his ~ duties;* having great variety. **~·ly** *adv*

mul·ti·form /ˋmʌltɪfɔm/ *adj* having many forms or shapes.

mul·ti·lat·eral /ˈmʌltɪˋlætrl/ *adj* involving two or more participants: *~ disarmament,* after agreement between two or more countries; *~ trade,* carried on between many or all countries without the need for pairs of countries to balance payment between themselves.

mul·tiple /ˋmʌltɪpl/ *adj* having many parts or elements: *a man of ~ interests; a ~ shop/store,* one with many branches. Cf *chain store,* the modern term; *a ~-unit train,* made up of several coaches (e g Diesel coaches) each of which can run independently. □ *n* quantity which contains another quantity a number of times without remainder: *28 is a ~ of 7. 30 is a common ~ of 2, 3, 5, 6, 10 and 15.* **least/lowest common ~,**

(abbr **LCM**) least quantity that contains two or more given quantities exactly: *12 is the LCM of 3 and 4.* ⇨ factor(1).

mul·ti·plex /ˈmʌltɪpleks/ *adj* having many parts or forms; of many elements.

mul·ti·pli·ca·tion /ˈmʌltɪplɪˈkeɪʃn/ *n* **1** [U] multiplying or being multiplied: *The symbol × stands for ~.* ˈ**~ table,** list of numbers, usu 1 to 12, showing the results of multiplying by the same number successively. **2** [C] instance of this: *3 × 11 is an easy ~.*

mul·ti·plic·ity /ˈmʌltɪˈplɪsətɪ/ *n* [U] being great in number: *the ~ of small city states into which Hellas was divided; a ~ of duties.*

mul·ti·ply /ˈmʌltɪplaɪ/ *vt, vi* (*pt, pp* -lied) **1** [VP14] ***~ by,*** take (a given quantity or number) a given number of times: *~ 3 by 5. 6 multiplied by 5 is 30,* 6 × 5 = 30. **2** [VP6A] produce a large number of; make greater in number: *~ instances,* produce a larger number of examples. **3** [VP2A] increase in number by procreation: *Rabbits ~ rapidly.*

mul·ti·tude /ˈmʌltɪtjud *US:* -tud/ *n* **1** [C] great number (esp of people gathered together). **2** (with the *def art*) the common people; the masses: *demagogues who appeal to the ~.* **3** [U] greatness of number: *like the stars in ~.* **multi·tud·in·ous** /ˈmultɪˈtjudɪnəs *US:* -ˈtudṇəs/ *adj* very numerous; great in number.

mul·tum in parvo /ˈmʊltəm ɪn ˈpɑvəʊ/ *n* (Lat) much in a small space.

mum[1] /mʌm/ *int, n* Silence! ***Mum's the word!*** Say nothing about this. □ *adj* ***keep mum,*** silent.

mum[2] /mʌm/ *n* (colloq) mother.

mumble /ˈmʌmbl/ *vt, vi* [VP6A,2A,C] **1** say sth, speak one's words, indistinctly: *The old man was mumbling away to himself. Don't ~ your words.* **2** bite or chew as with toothless gums.

mumbo jumbo /ˈmʌmbəʊ ˈdʒʌmbəʊ/ *n* (fig) object of senseless veneration; meaningless or obscure ritual; gibberish.

mum·mer /ˈmʌmə(r)/ *n* actor in an old form of drama without words. **~y** *n* (*pl* -ries) **1** [C] performance by ~s; dumb show. **2** [U] foolish or unnecessary ceremonial (esp religious); [C] instance of this.

mum·mify /ˈmʌmɪfaɪ/ *vt* (*pt, pp* -fied) [VP6A] preserve (a corpse) by embalming; shrivel. **mum·mi·fi·ca·tion** /ˈmʌmɪfɪˈkeɪʃn/ *n*

mummy[1] /ˈmʌmɪ/ *n* (*pl* -mies) body of a human being or animal embalmed for burial; dried-up body preserved from decay (as in early Egypt).

a mummy

mummy[2] /ˈmʌmɪ/ *n* (*pl* -mies) (colloq) mother.

mumps /mʌmps/ *n* (with *sing v*) contagious disease with painful swellings in the neck.

munch /mʌntʃ/ *vt, vi* [VP6A,2A,C] chew with much movement of the jaw: *~ing away at a hard apple; cattle ~ing their fodder.*

mun·dane /ˈmʌndeɪn/ *adj* worldly (contrasted with spiritual or heavenly): *When a man is near death he loses interest in ~ affairs.* **~·ly** *adv*

mu·nici·pal /mjuˈnɪsɪpl/ *adj* of a town or city having self-government: *~ buildings,* e g the town hall, public library; *~ undertakings,* e g the supply of water, tram and bus services; *the ~ debt.* **~ly** /-plɪ/ *adv* **~·ity** /mjuˈnɪsɪˈpælətɪ/ *n* (*pl* -ties) town, city, district, with local self-government; governing body of such a town, etc.

mu·nifi·cent /mjuˈnɪfɪsnt/ *adj* (formal) extremely generous; (of sth given) large in amount or splendid in quality. **~·ly** *adv* **mu·nifi·cence** /-sns/ *n* [U] great generosity.

mu·ni·ments /ˈmjunɪmənts/ *n* (legal) documents kept as evidence of rights or privileges.

mu·ni·tion /mjuˈnɪʃn/ *n* (*pl* except when attrib) military supplies, esp guns, shells, bombs, etc: *The war was lost because of a shortage of ~s/a ~ shortage.* □ *vt* [VP6A] provide with ~s: *~ a fort.*

mural /ˈmjʊərl/ *adj* of, like, on, a wall: *a ~ painting.* □ *n* [C] wall-painting; fresco.

mur·der /ˈmɜdə(r)/ *n* **1** [U] unlawful killing of a human being on purpose; [C] instance of this: *commit ~; be declared guilty of ~; six ~s in one week.* ***M~ will out,*** (prov) cannot be hidden. ⇨ homicide, manslaughter, regicide, etc. **2** [U] unjustifiable sacrifice of life (e g in war): *Nothing could justify the bombing of the town; it was sheer ~.* ***cry blue ~,*** (colloq) shout loudly and in alarm. □ *vt* [VP6A] **1** kill (a human being) unlawfully and on purpose. **2** spoil by lack of skill or knowledge: *~ a piece of music,* play it very badly. *Do you ever ~ the English language?* **~er** *n* person guilty of ~. **~·ess** /-əs/ *n* woman ~er. **~·ous** /ˈmɜdṛəs/ *adj* planning, suggesting, designed for, ~: *a ~ous-looking villain; a ~ous fire from the enemy's guns.* **~·ous·ly** *adv*

murk /mɜk/ *n* [U] darkness; gloom. **~y** *adj* (-ier, -iest) dark; gloomy: *a ~y night;* (of darkness) thick. ˈ**~·ily** /-əlɪ/ *adv*

mur·mur /ˈmɜmə(r)/ *n* **1** low, continuous, indistinct sound, rising and falling very little in pitch: *the ~ of bees in the garden; the ~ of a distant brook/of distant traffic.* **2** softly spoken word(s): *a ~ of conversation from the next room.* **3** subdued expression of feeling: *a ~ of delight. They paid the higher taxes without a ~,* i e without complaining. □ *vi, vt* **1** [VP2A,C] make a ~(1): *a ~ing brook.* **2** [VP2C,3A] ***~ (at/against),*** complain in a ~(3): *~ at injustice; ~ against new taxes.* **3** [VP6A] utter in a low voice: *~ a prayer.*

murphy /ˈmɜfɪ/ *n* (*pl* -phies) (sl) potato.

mur·rain /ˈmʌreɪn *US:* ˈmɜɪn/ *n* **1** [U] infectious disease of cattle. **2** (old use): *A ~ on you!* A plague on you! Curse you!

mus·ca·tel /ˈmʌskəˈtel/ *n* [U] rich, sweet wine made from musk-flavoured kinds of grape.

muscle /ˈmʌsl/ *n* [C,U] (band or bundle of) elastic substance in an animal body that can be tightened or loosened to produce movement: *When you walk you exercise your leg ~s. Physical exercises develop ~. Don't move a ~,* stay perfectly still. ˈ**~-man** /-mæn/ *n* (*pl* -men) man of great muscular development. ˈ**~-bound** *adj* having stiff ~s as the result of over-training or excessive exercise. □ *vi* [VP2C] ***~ ˈin (on),*** (sl) use force to get a share of sth considered advantageous (e g by one group of gangsters in an area dominated by another group).

Mus·covy /ˈmʌskəvɪ/ *n* (old name for) Russia. **Mus·co·vite** /ˈmʌskəvaɪt/ *n* native of ~.

mus·cu·lar /ˈmʌskjʊlə(r)/ *adj* **1** of the muscles: *~ tissue/rheumatism.* **2** having strong muscles.

muse[1] /mjuz/ *n* **1** (Gk myth) any one of the nine goddesses, daughters of Zeus, who protected and encouraged poetry, music, dancing, history and other branches of art and learning. **2 the ~,** poet's genius; spirit that inspires a poet.

muse[2] /mjuz/ *vi* [VP2A,3A] ~ ***over/(up)on,*** think deeply or dreamily, ignoring what is happening around one: *musing over memories of the past.* □ *n* (archaic) fit of obstraction: *in a ~.* **'mus·ing·ly** *adv*

mu·seum /mju'zɪəm/ *n* building in which objects illustrating art, history, science, etc are displayed. **a ~ piece,** fine specimen suitable for a ~; (fig) sth or sb antiquated.

mush /mʌʃ/ *n* [U] soft, thick mixture or mass; (US) boiled corn meal. **~y** *adj* like ~; (colloq) weakly sentimental: *the ~y postcard he sent to his girlfriend from Paris.*

mush·room /'mʌʃrʊm *US:* -rum/ *n* [C] fast-growing fungus of which some kinds can be eaten; ⇨ the illus at **fungi**: (attrib) *the ~* (= rapid) *growth of London suburbs. The ~ cloud* (because of its ~ shape) *of a nuclear explosion.* □ *vi* **1 *go ~ing,*** go out into the fields to gather ~s. **2** [VP2C] spread or grow rapidly: *English language schools are ~ing in Bournemouth.*

mu·sic /'mjuzɪk/ *n* [U] art of making pleasing combinations of sounds in rhythm and harmony; the sounds and composition so made; written or printed signs representing these sounds. the illus at **brass, keyboard, notation, percussion, string. *set/put sth to ~,*** provide words, e g of a poem, with ~; (attrib) *a ~ lesson/teacher.* ***face the ~,*** face one's critics; face difficulties boldly. **'~-box** *n* (US) musical-box, ⇨ below. **'~-hall** *n* (GB) hall or theatre used for variety entertainment (e g songs, acrobatic performances, juggling). ⇨ *concert-hall* at **concert**[1]**(1)**. **'~-stand** *n* light (usu folding) framework for holding sheets of printed music. **'~-stool** *n* seat without a back (usu adjustable in height) used when playing a piano.

mu·si·cal /'mjuzɪkl/ *adj* of, fond of, skilled in, music: *~ instruments,* e g the violin, piano, harp; *She's not at all ~,* does not enjoy or understand music. **'~-box** *n* box with a mechanical device that produces a tune when the box is opened. **'~ 'chairs,** game in which players go round a row of chairs one fewer than the number of players. Each time the music stops, the players sit down and the one left without a chair is eliminated. **'~ 'comedy,** a light, amusing play with songs and dancing. □ *n* [C] **1** musical comedy. **2** cinema film in which music has an essential part. **~ly** /-klɪ/ *adv*

mu·si·cian /mju'zɪʃn/ *n* person skilled in music; composer of music.

musk /mʌsk/ *n* [U] **1** strong-smelling substance produced in glands by male deer, used in the manufacture of perfumes. **'~-deer** *n* small hornless deer of central Asia. **'~-rat** (or *musquash*) *n* large rat-like water animal of N America, valuable for its fur. **2** kinds of plant with musky smell. **'~ melon** *n* sweet juicy kind of melon. **'~-rose** *n* rambling rose with large, sweet-smelling flowers. **~y** *adj* (-ier, -iest) having the smell of ~.

mus·ket /'mʌskɪt/ *n* firearm used by foot-soldiers (16th to 19th cc) now replaced by the rifle. **~·eer** /'mʌskɪ'tɪə(r)/ *n* foot-soldier armed with a ~. **~ry** /'mʌskɪtrɪ/ *n* [U] **1** (science of, instruction in) shooting with rifles. **2** (old use) troops armed with ~s.

Mus·lim /'mʊzlɪm/ *n* one who professes Islam; follower of Muhammad: (attrib) of ~s and Islam: *~ historians/holidays.*

mus·lin /'mʌzlɪn/ *n* [U] thin, fine, cotton cloth, used for dresses, curtains, etc.

mus·quash /'mʌskwoʃ/ *n* (fur of the) musk-rat. ⇨ **musk(1)**.

muss /mʌs/ *n* (US) [U] disorder; [C] muddle. □ *vt* [VP6A,15B] ~ ***(up),*** put into disorder: *Don't ~ up my hair!*

mus·sel /'mʌsl/ *n* (sorts of) mollusc with a black shell in two parts. ⇨ the illus at **bivalve**.

Mus·sul·man /'mʌslmən/ *n* (*pl* -mans) (variant spelling, Persian and Turkish, of) Muslim (the preferred word).

must[1] /mʌst/ *n* [U] grape-juice before fermentation has changed it into wine.

must[2] /*usual form:* məst *strong form:* mʌst/ *aux v, anom fin* (No infinitive, no participles, no inflected forms; *~ not* may be contracted to ~n't /'mʌsnt/.) [VP5] **1** (expressing an immediate or future obligation or necessity; *~ not* expresses a prohibition. Cf the use of *may* to express permission and of *need not* to express non-obligation. Cf the use of *had to* for a past obligation and *shall, will have to* for a future obligation): *You ~ do as you're told. Soldiers ~ obey orders. Cars ~ not be parked in front of the entrance. You ~n't do that. We ~n't be late, ~ we? A: 'M~ you go so soon?' B: 'Yes, I ~'* (or) *'No, I needn't.'* **2** (used to indicate what was necessary or obligatory at a time in the past): *She said she ~ have a new hat for Easter. As he had broken it, he agreed that he ~ buy a new one. On the other side of the wood was a field that he ~* (= had to) *cross.* **3** (with less emphasis on necessity; stressing what is desirable or advisable): *We ~ see what can be done. I ~ ask you not to do that again.* **4** (expressing certainty): *Don't bet on horse-races, you ~ lose* (= will certainly lose) *in the long run.* **5** (expressing strong probability): *You ~ be hungry after your long walk. This ~ be* (= very probably is) *the book you want. You ~ have known* (= Surely you knew) *what she wanted. You ~ be joking!* You can't be serious! **6** (indicating the occurrence of sth unwelcome, sth contrary to what was wanted): *He ~ come and worry her with questions, just when she was busy cooking the dinner!* □ *n* (colloq) sth that ~ be done, seen, heard, etc: *Green's new novel is a ~ for all lovers of crime fiction.*

mus·tache *n* ⇨ **moustache**.

mus·tachio /mə'stɑʃɪəʊ *US:* -'stæʃ-/ *n* (*pl* -ios /-ɪəʊz/) a large (usu long-haired) moustache.

mus·tang /'mʌstæŋ/ *n* small wild or half-wild horse of the American plains.

mus·tard /'mʌstəd/ *n* [U] **1** plant with yellow flowers and seeds (black or white) in long, slender pods. **2** fine, yellow powder made from the seeds of this plant; this powder made into hot-tasting sauce. **'~ gas** *n* kind of liquid poison gas that burns the skin (used in World War I). **'~ plaster** *n* poultice made with ~. ***as keen as ~,*** very keen. ***grain of ~ seed,*** sth very small capable of developing into sth very large. ⇨ **Matt 13: 31**.

mus·ter /'mʌstə(r)/ *n* assembly or gathering of persons, esp for review or inspection. ***pass ~,*** be considered satisfactory; be good enough for the purpose or occasion. □ *vt,vi* [VP6A,15B] ~ ***(up),***

call, collect or gather together: *Go and ~ all the men you can find. They ~ed (up) all their courage.*

musty /ˈmʌstɪ/ *adj* (-ier, -iest) **1** stale; smelling or tasting mouldy: *~ books; a ~ room.* **2** (fig) stale; out-of-date: *a professor with ~ ideas.* **musti·ness** /ˈmʌstɪnəs/ *n*

mu·table /ˈmjutəbl/ *adj* liable to change; likely to change. **mu·ta·bil·ity** /ˌmjutəˈbɪlətɪ/ *n* [U].

mu·ta·tion /mjuˈteɪʃn/ *n* [U] change; alteration; [C] instance of this: *Are ~s in plants caused by cosmic rays?*

mu·ta·tis mu·tan·dis /muˈtatɪs muˈtændɪs/ *adv* (Lat) with necessary alterations or changes (when comparing cases).

mute /mjut/ *adj* **1** silent; making no sound: *staring at me in ~ amazement.* **2** (of a person) dumb; unable to speak. **3** (of a letter in a word) not sounded: *The 'b' in 'dumb' is ~.* □ *n* **1** dumb person. **2** piece of bone or metal used to soften the sounds produced from a stringed instrument; pad placed in the mouth of a wind instrument for the same purpose. □ *vt* [VP6A] deaden or muffle the sound of (esp a musical instrument). **~·ly** *adv*

mu·ti·late /ˈmjutɪleɪt *US:* -tl̩-/ *vt* [VP6A] damage by breaking, tearing or cutting off a necessary part; destroy the use of (a limb, etc). **mu·ti·la·tion** /ˌmjutɪˈleɪʃn *US:* -tl̩ˈeɪʃn/ *n* [U] mutilating or being ~d; [C] injury or loss caused by this.

mu·ti·nous /ˈmjutɪnəs *US:* -tn̩əs/ *adj* guilty of mutiny; rebellious: *~ sailors; ~ behaviour.*

mu·tiny /ˈmjutɪnɪ *US:* -tn̩ɪ/ *n* (*pl* -nies) [U] (esp of soldiers and sailors) open rebellion against lawful authority; [C] instance of this. □ *vi* [VP2A,3A] **~ (against),** be guilty of ~; revolt. **mu·tin·eer** /ˌmjutɪˈnɪə(r) *US:* -tn̩ˈɪə(r)/ *n* person guilty of ~.

mutt /mʌt/ *n* (sl) **1** ignorant blunderer: *You silly ~!* **2** mongrel dog.

mut·ter /ˈmʌtə(r)/ *vt,vi* [VP6A,14,2A,C] speak, say (sth), in a low voice not meant to be heard; grumble in a indistinct voice: *He was ~ing away to himself. Are you ~ing threats at me? We heard thunder ~ing in the distance.* □ *n* ~ed utterance or sound. **~er** *n* person who ~s.

mut·ton /ˈmʌtn/ *n* [U] flesh of fully grown sheep: *a leg/shoulder of ~; roast ~; a ~ chop,* piece of ~ rib. ***as dead as ~,*** quite dead. ***~ dressed as lamb,*** used of an elderly woman dressed in a style suitable for a young woman. **ˈ~-head** *n* (colloq) dull, stupid person.

mu·tual /ˈmjutʃʊəl/ *adj* **1** (of love, friendship, respect, etc) shared; exchanged equally; (of feelings, opinions, etc) held in common with others: *~ suspicion/affection.* **2** each to the other(s): *~ enemies/well-wishers; ~ aid.* **~ funds,** (US) = unit trusts. **a ˌ~ inˈsurance company,** one in which some or all of the profits being divided among the policy-holders. **3** common to two or more persons: *our ~ friend Smith,* i e Smith, a friend of both of us. **~ly** /-ʊəlɪ/ *adv*

muzzle /ˈmʌzl/ *n* **1** nose and mouth of an animal (e g dog or fox); guard of straps or wires placed over this part of an animal's head to prevent it from biting, etc. **2** open end or mouth of a fire-arm: *a ~-loading gun.* **ˈ~-velocity,** speed of a projectile as it leaves the ~. ⇨ **breech.** □ *vt* [VP6A] put a ~ on (a dog, etc); (fig) prevent (a person, society, newspaper, etc) from expressing opinions freely.

muzzy /ˈmʌzɪ/ *adj* (-ier, -iest) **1** confused in mind; spiritless; stupid from drinking. **2** blurred.

my /maɪ/ *poss adj* **1** belonging to me: *Where's my hat? This car is my own.* **2** as a part of a form of address: *Yes, my dear. My dear fellow!* **3** in exclamations: *My goodness! Oh, my!*

my·col·ogy /maɪˈkolədʒɪ/ *n* [U] science or study of fungi.

my·na(h) /ˈmaɪnə/ *n* (kinds of) starling of S E Asia, known for their ability to mimic human speech. ⇨ the illus at rare.

my·el·itis /maɪəˈlaɪtɪs/ *n* (path) inflammation of the spinal cord.

my·opia /maɪˈəʊpɪə/ *n* [U] short-sightedness. **my·opic** /maɪˈopɪk/ *adj* short-sighted.

myr·iad /ˈmɪrɪəd/ *n* [C] **~ (of),** very great number.

myr·mi·don /ˈmɜmɪdən *US:* -don/ *n* (contemptuous or humorous term for a) person who carries out any kind of order without questions: *~s of the law,* e g bailiffs.

myrrh /mɜ(r)/ *n* [U] sweet-smelling, bitter-tasting kind of gum or resin obtained from shrubs, used for making incense and perfumes.

myrtle /ˈmɜtl/ *n* (kinds of) evergreen shrub with shiny leaves and sweet-smelling white flowers.

my·self /maɪˈself/ *pron* (reflex and emphat): *I hurt ~. I can do it (all) by ~,* i e without help. *I tired ~ out. I ~ said so. I said so ~. I'm not ~ today,* am not feeling so well as I usually do.

mys·teri·ous /mɪˈstɪərɪəs/ *adj* full of, suggesting, covered in, mystery: *a ~ crime; a ~-looking parcel.* **~·ly** *adv*

mys·tery /ˈmɪstr̩ɪ/ *n* (*pl* -ries) **1** [C] sth of which the cause or origin is hidden or impossible to understand: *The murder remained an unsolved ~.* **2** [U] condition of being secret or obscure: *The origin of this tribe is lost in ~,* It has been impossible to learn anything about it. **3** (*pl*) secret religious rites and ceremonies (of ancient Greeks, Romans, etc). **4** [C] **ˈ~ (play),** medieval drama based on episodes in the life of Jesus.

mys·tic /ˈmɪstɪk/ *adj* of hidden meaning or spiritual power; causing feelings of awe and wonder: *~ rites and ceremonies; ~ teachings.* □ *n* person who seeks union with God and, through that, realization of truth beyond men's understanding. **mys·ti·cal** /ˈmɪstɪkl/ *adj* = mystic.

mys·ti·cism /ˈmɪstɪs-ɪzm/ *n* [U] beliefs, experiences, of a mystic; teaching and belief that knowledge of God and of real truth may be obtained through meditation or spiritual insight, independently of the mind and the senses.

mys·tify /ˈmɪstɪfaɪ/ *vt* (*pt,pp* -fied) [VP6A] puzzle; bewilder. **mys·ti·fi·ca·tion** /ˌmɪstɪfɪˈkeɪʃn/ *n* [U] ~ing or being mystified; [C] sth that mystifies.

mys·tique /mɪˈstik/ *n* **1** esoteric character of a person, institution, etc caused by mystical devotion and veneration: *the ~ of the monarchy in Great Britain.* **2** incommunicable quality; secret known only to inspired practitioners (of an art, etc).

myth /mɪθ/ *n* **1** [C] story, handed down from olden times, esp concepts or beliefs about the early history of a race, explanations of natural events, such as the seasons. **2** [U] such stories collectively: *famous in ~ and legend.* **3** [C] persons, thing, etc, that is imaginary, fictitious, or invented: *That rich uncle of whom he boasts is only a ~.* **~i·cal** /ˈmɪθɪkl/ *adj* **1** of ~; existing only in ~: *~ical heroes; ~ical literature.* **2** imaginary; fictitious:

~ical wealth/political support/interest in music. **myth·ol·ogy** /mɪˈθɒlədʒɪ/ *n* (*pl* **-gies**) **1** [U] study or science of myths. **2** [U] myths collectively: *Greek* ~; [C] body or collection of myths: *the mythologies of primitive races.* **myth·ol·ogist** /mɪˈθɒlədʒɪst/ *n* student of ~. **mytho·logi·cal** /ˌmɪθəˈlɒdʒɪkl/ *adj* of ~ or myths; unreal.

myxo·ma·to·sis /ˌmɪksəməˈtəʊsɪs/ *n* [U] infectious fatal disease of rabbits.

Nn

N, n /en/ (*pl* **N's, n's** /enz/) the 14th letter of the English alphabet.

nab /næb/ *vt* (**-bb-**) (colloq) catch in wrongdoing; seize: *The thief was nabbed by the police.*

na·bob /ˈneɪbɒb/ *n* (18th c use) wealthy, luxury-loving person, esp one returned to GB from India with a fortune.

na·celle /næˈsel/ *n* outer casing for an engine of an aircraft or airship. ⇨ the illus at **air**.

nacre /ˈneɪkə(r)/ *n* [U] mother-of-pearl. ⇨ **mother(4)**.

na·dir /ˈnædɪə(r) *US:* ˈneid-/ *n* (fig) lowest, weakest, point: *at the ~ of one's hopes.* ⇨ **zenith**.

nag[1] /næg/ *n* (colloq) small horse.

nag[2] /næg/ *vt,vi* (**-gg-**) [VP6A,2A,C,3A] ***nag (at sb)***, find fault with continuously; worry or annoy by scolding: *She nagged (at) him all day long.* **nag·ger** *n*

naiad /ˈnaɪæd/ *n* (*pl* **~s, -des** /-diz/) (Gk myth) water-nymph.

nail /neɪl/ *n* **1** layer of hard substance over the outer tip of a finger (ˈ**finger-~**) or toe (ˈ**toe-~**). ⇨ the illus at **arm, leg**. ***fight tooth and ~***, with all one's strength, making every possible effort to win. ˈ**~·brush** *n* for cleaning the ~s. ˈ**~-file**, small, flat file for shaping the ~s. ˈ**~-scissors** *n* for trimming the ~s. ˈ**~-varnish/-polish** *n* for giving a shiny tint to the ~s. **2** piece of metal, pointed at one end and with a head at the other, (to be) hammered into articles to hold them together, or into a wall, etc to hang sth on. ***(pay) on the ~***, at once. ***hit the (right) ~ on the head***, pick out the real point at issue; give the true explanation. ***(right) on the ~***, on the spot; at once. ***drive a ~ into sb's coffin***, ⇨ **coffin**. ***as hard as ~s***, (of a person) **(a)** in first-rate physical condition. **(b)** (fig) pitiless; unsympathetic. ***right as ~s***, quite right. □ *vt* [VP15A,B] **1** make fast with a ~ or ~s: *~ a lid on a box.* ***~ sb down (to sth)***, make him say clearly what he intends to do. ***~ sth down***, make (e g a carpet, a cover) secure by using nails. ***~ sth up***, make (a door, window, etc) secure with ~s. ***~ one's colours to the mast***, ⇨ **colour[1](8)**. ***~ a lie (to the counter)***, prove that a statement is false. **2** hold fast, keep fixed (a person, sb's attention, etc): *He ~ed me in the hall.*

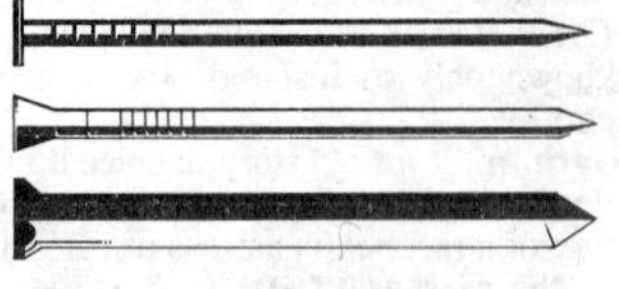

nails

nain·sook /ˈneɪnsʊk/ *n* [U] fine cotton cloth.

naïve, naive /nɑɪˈiv/ *adj* natural and innocent in speech and behaviour (e g because young or inexperienced); amusingly simple: *a ~ girl; ~ remarks.* **~·ly** *adv* **~té, ~ty** /nɑɪˈivteɪ/ *n* [U] artlessness; being ~; [C] ~ remark, etc.

naked /ˈneɪkɪd/ *adj* **1** without clothes on: *as ~ as the day he was born.* **2** without the usual covering: *a ~ sword*, without its sheath; *fight with ~ fists*, without boxing-gloves. *~ trees*, without leaves; *a ~ light*, not protected from the wind by glass, without a lampshade. ***see sth with the ~ eye***, without using a microscope, telescope or other aid to seeing. ***the ~ truth***, not disguised, softened, ornamented. **~·ly** *adv* **~·ness** *n*

namby-pamby /ˈnæmbɪ ˈpæmbɪ/ *adj* (of persons, talk) foolishly sentimental.

name[1] /neɪm/ *n* **1** word(s) by which a person, animal, place, thing, etc is known and spoken to or of: *A person of the ~ of Smith* (= Someone who is called Smith) *wants to see you. He writes under the ~ of Nimrod*, uses Nimrod instead of his real name. *I know the man by ~*, only by hearsay, not by personal acquaintanceship. *The teacher knows all the pupils in his class by ~*, knows them individually. ***in the ~ of***, **(a)** with the authority of: *Stop! in the Queen's ~. In the ~ of the law....* **(b)** in the cause of (used when making an appeal): *In the ~ of common sense, what are you doing?* ***call sb ~s***, call him insulting ~s (e g liar, coward). ***enter/put down one's ~ for***, (a school, college, etc), apply for entry (at a future date). ***not have a penny to one's ~***, be without money. ***lend one's ~ to***, (an enterprise, etc), allow it to be quoted in support or in favour of (the enterprise, etc). ***take sb's ~ in vain***, use a ~ (esp God's) disrespectfully. ˈ**~-day** *n* day of the Saint whose ~ one was given at christening; Saint's Day (in the R C Church). ˈ**~-dropping** *n* the practice of casually mentioning the ~s of important people (as if they were friends) to impress people. Hence, ˈ**~-drop** *v* ˈ**~-part** *n* title-role of a play: *Who will play the ~-part in 'Hamlet'?* ˈ**~·plate** *n* plaque (on the door of a building, room, etc) with the ~ of the occupant. ˈ**~·sake** *n* person or thing with the same ~ as another. **2** (*sing* only) reputation; fame. ***make/win a ~ for oneself***, become well-known. *The firm has a ~ for good workmanship.* **3** famous person: *the great ~s of history.*

name[2] /neɪm/ *vt* **1** [VP6A,14,23] give a ~ to: *They ~d the child John. The child was ~d after its father*, given its father's first (or Christian) ~. *Tasmania was ~d after its discoverer, A J Tasman.* **2** [VP6A] say the ~(s) of: *Can you ~ all the plants and trees in this garden?* **3** make an offer of (price, etc): *N~ your price*, Say what price you want. **4** state (what is desired, etc): *Please ~ the day*, say on what date you will be willing to (e g marry). **5** [VP6A,14] nominate for, appoint to, a position: *Mr X has been ~d for the directorship.*

name·less /ˈneɪmləs/ *adj* **1** not having a name; having an unknown name: *a ~ grave; a well-*

known person who shall be ~, whose name I shall not mention. **2** too bad to be named: *~ vices.* **3** difficult or impossible to name or describe: *a ~ longing/horror.*

name·ly /ˈneɪmlɪ/ *adv* that is to say: *Only one boy was absent, ~ Harry.*

nancy /ˈnænsɪ/ *n, adj* (GB sl) effeminate (man or boy); homosexual.

nan·keen /nænˈkin/ *n* [U] kind of cotton cloth, originally made of naturally yellow cotton.

nanny /ˈnænɪ/ *n* (*pl* **-nies**) nursemaid employed by rich people to look after their babies and young children below school age.

nanny-goat /ˈnænɪ gəʊt/ *n* she-goat. ⇨ **billy-goat.**

nap[1] /næp/ *n* [C] short sleep (esp during the day, not necessarily in bed): *have/take a nap after lunch on a hot day.* □ *vi* (**-pp-**) (rare, except in) ***catch sb napping,*** find him asleep; catch him unawares (in error, etc).

nap[2] /næp/ *n* [U] surface of cloth, felt, etc, made of soft, short hairs or fibres, smoothed and brushed up.

nap[3] /næp/ *n* (GB) name of a card-game.

na·palm /ˈneɪpɑm/ *n* [U] jellied petroleum used in making fire-bombs.

nape /neɪp/ *n* back (of the neck). ⇨ the illus at **head.**

na·pery /ˈneɪpərɪ/ *n* [U] (old use) household linen, esp table linen (tablecloths and napkins).

naph·tha /ˈnæfθə/ *n* [U] kinds of inflammable oil obtained from coaltar and petroleum. **~·lene** /-lin/ *n* [U] strong-smelling substance made from coaltar and petroleum, used in the manufacture of dyes and (in the form of white 'moth balls') to put among clothes.

nap·kin /ˈnæpkɪn/ *n* [C] **1** (**ˈtable**) **~,** piece of cloth used at meals for protecting clothing, for wiping the lips, etc. **ˈ~-ring** *n* ring to hold and distinguish a person's ~. ⇨ **serviette. 2** (US = *diaper*) (*nappy* is more usu) towel folded round a baby's bottom and between its legs, to absorb excreta.

Na·po·leonic /nəˌpəʊlɪˈɒnɪk/ *adj* of or like Napoleon I.

nappy /ˈnæpɪ/ *n* (*pl* **-pies**) (GB colloq) baby's napkin.

nar·ciss·ism /ˈnɑsɪs-ɪzm/ *n* [U] (in psychoanalysis) mental state in which there is self-worship and excessive interest in one's own perfections.

nar·cissus /nɑˈsɪsəs/ *n* (*pl* **-suses** /-səsɪz/ or **-cissi** /-sɪsɑɪ/) sorts of bulb plant (daffodil, jonquil, etc), esp the kind having heavily scented white or yellow flowers in the spring.

nar·cotic /nɑˈkɒtɪk/ *n, adj* (kinds of drug) producing sleep, often blunting the senses and, in large doses, producing complete insensibility: *Opium is a ~ drug. The use of ~s by teenagers is a problem in many countries;* (person) addicted to ~s.

nark[1] /nɑk/ *n* (GB sl) police decoy or spy.

nark[2] /nɑk/ *vt* (GB colloq) annoy: *feel ~ed at unjust criticism.*

nar·rate /nəˈreɪt/ *vt* [VP6A] tell (a story); give an account of: *~ one's adventures.* **nar·rator** /-tə(r)/ *n* person who ~s. **nar·ra·tion** /nəˈreɪʃn/ *n* [U] the telling of a story, etc; [C] story; account of events, etc.

nar·ra·tive /ˈnærətɪv/ *n* **1** [C] story or tale; orderly account of events; [U] (composition that consists of) story-telling. **2** (attrib) in the form of, concerned with, story-telling: *~ literature,* stories and novels; *~ poems; a writer of great ~ power,* able to describe events well.

nar·row /ˈnærəʊ/ *adj* (**-er, -est**) (contrary to *wide*) **1** measuring little across in comparison with length: *a ~ bridge. The road was too ~ for cars to pass. A ~-gauge railway is one with rails less than 4 ft 8 in apart.* **2** small, limited: *a ~ circle of friends; living in ~ circumstances,* in poverty. **3** with a small margin: *a ~ escape from death.* ***a ~ squeak,*** (colloq) sth barely avoided or escaped from; *elected by a ~ majority,* e g when voting is 67 to 64. **4** strict; exact: *a ~ search. What does the word mean in the ~est sense?* **5** limited in outlook; having little sympathy for the ideas, etc, of others. **ˈ~-ˈminded** /ˈmɑɪndɪd/ *adj* not easily seeing or sympathizing with the ideas of others. **ˈ~-ˈminded·ly** *adv* **ˈ~-ˈmindedness** *n* □ *vt,vi* [VP6A,2A] (cause to) become ~. □ *n* (usu *pl*) ~ strait or channel between two larger bodies of water; ~ place in a river or pass. **~·ly** *adv* **1** only just; with little to spare: *He ~ly escaped drowning.* **2** (rare) closely; carefully (the usu words): *Watch that fellow ~ly.* **~·ness** *n*

nar·whal /ˈnɑwl/ *n* Arctic whale with (in the male) a long spiral tusk.

na·sal /ˈneɪzl/ *adj* of, for, in the nose: *~ sounds,* e g /m, n, ŋ/; *~ catarrh; a ~ douche.* □ *n* [C] nasal sound. **~·ize** /ˈneɪzl̩ɑɪz/ *vt* [VP6A] make (a sound) with the air stream, or part of it, passing through the nose.

nascent /ˈnæsnt/ *adj* (formal) coming into existence: beginning to exist.

nas·tur·tium /nəˈstɜʃəm *US:* næ-/ *n* [C] garden plant with red, orange or yellow flowers, round-shaped leaves, and seeds that may be pickled and eaten.

nasty /ˈnɑstɪ *US:* ˈnæ-/ *adj* (**-ier, -iest**) **1** dirty; disgusting; unpleasant; *medicine with a ~ smell and a nastier taste. A hangman's job is a ~ one.* **2** morally dirty and unpleasant: *a man with a ~ mind; ~ stories.* **3** showing ill will and spite: *Don't go near that dog; he has a ~ temper. Was the tax collector ~ when you said you couldn't pay him?* **4** dangerous; threatening: *There was a ~ sea when we got out of the harbour. There was a ~ look in his eye.* **5** causing difficulty or danger; awkward: *That's a ~ corner for a car that's travelling fast.* **nas·tily** /-əlɪ/ *adv* **nas·ti·ness** *n*

na·tal /ˈneɪtl/ *adj* of, from, one's birth.

na·tion /ˈneɪʃn/ *n* [C] large community of people associated with a particular territory usu speaking a single language and usu having a political character or political aspirations: *the ~s of Western Europe; the United N~s Organization,* U N O. ⇨ **state**[1]**(2). ˈ~·wide** *adj* throughout a ~; concerning, expressed by, all citizens.

nation·al /ˈnæʃnl/ *adj* of a or the nation; common to the whole nation; characteristic of a particular nation: *a ~ theatre,* one supported by the State; *~ opposition to a government policy,* expressed by all citizens. **ˈ~ ˈanthem,** song or hymn of a nation (e g 'God Save the Queen' in GB). **the ˈN~ ˈDebt,** total money owed by the State to those who have lent it money. **ˈ~ ˈmonument,** structure, landmark, site of historic interest (often one maintained by the government). **ˈ~ ˈpark,** area of land declared to be public property, for the use and enjoyment of the people. **ˈ~ ˈservice,** period of compulsory service in the armed forces. **ˈN~**

'Socialism, Nazism. **'N~ 'Trust,** (in GB) society founded in 1895 to preserve places of natural beauty or historic interest for the nation. **the 'Grand 'N~,** the chief steeplechase in GB, run in March. □ *n* citizen of a particular nation: *British ~s in Spain. One of a consul's duties is to help his own ~s,* his fellow countrymen. **~ly** /'næʃnḷɪ/ *adv*

nation·al·ism /'næʃnḷ-ɪzm/ *n* [U] **1** strong devotion to one's own nation; patriotic feelings, efforts, principles. **2** movement for political (economic, etc) independence (in a country controlled by another).

nation·al·ist /'næʃnḷ-ɪst/ *n* supporter of nationalism(2): *Scottish ~s,* those who want Scotland to have more self-government. □ *adj* (also **~ic** /'næʃnḷ'ɪstɪk/) favouring, supporting, nationalism: *~(ic) movements in Angola.*

nation·al·ity /'næʃn'ælətɪ/ *n* (*pl* -ties) [C,U] being a member of a nation: *What is your ~? There were men of all nationalities in Geneva.*

nation·al·ize /'næʃnḷaɪz/ *vt* [VP6A] **1** transfer from private to State ownership: *~ the railways/the coalmines/the steel industry.* **2** make (a person) a national: *~d Poles and Greeks in the US.* **3** make into a nation: *The Poles were ~d after the war of 1914—18,* They became an independent nation. **nation·al·iz·ation** /'næʃnḷaɪ'zeɪʃn *US:* -ḷɪ'z/ *n* nationalizing or being ~d: *the nationalization of the railways.*

na·tive /'neɪtɪv/ *n* **1** person born in a place, country, etc and associated with it by birth: *a ~ of London/Wales/India/Kenya.* **2** such a person as distinguished from immigrants, residents, visitors, tourists, etc from other countries, usu when the race to which he belongs is different in culture: *the first meetings between Captain Cook and the ~s* (= the aboriginal inhabitants) *of Australia.* **3** animal or plant natural to and having its origin in a certain area: *The kangaroo is a ~ of Australia.* **4** (GB) oyster reared wholly or partly in British waters, esp in artificial beds: *Whitstable ~s.* □ *adj* associated with the place and circumstances of one's birth: *your ~ land/place.* **2** of ~s(2 above): *~ customs.* **3** (of qualities) belonging to a person by nature, not acquired through training, by education, etc: *~ ability/charm.* **4** *~ to,* (of plants, animals, etc) having their origin in: *plants ~ to America,* e g tobacco, potatoes. *One of the animals ~ to India is the tiger.* **5** (of metals) found in a pure state, uncombined with other substances: *~ gold.*

na·tiv·ity /nə'tɪvətɪ/ *n* (*pl* -ties) birth, esp (**the N~**) of Jesus Christ; picture of the N~ of Christ. **a 'N~ Play,** one about the N~.

nat·ter /'nætə(r)/ *vi* [VP2A,C] (GB colloq) chatter, grumble (esp to oneself): *What's she ~ing (on) about now?*

natty /'nætɪ/ *adj* (-ier, -iest) (colloq) **1** neat; smart and tidy: *new and ~ uniforms for bus conductresses.* **2** quick and skilful. **nat·tily** /-əlɪ/ *adv*

natu·ral /'nætʃərl/ *adj* **1** of, concerned with, produced, by nature: *animals living in their ~ state,* wild, not domesticated; *a country's ~ resources,* its minerals, forests, etc; *land in its ~ state,* not used for industry, farming, etc. **'~ 'forces/phe'nomena,** the forces of nature, such as storms, thunder and lightning. **'~ 'gas,** gas occurring with petroleum deposits, e g North Sea gas. **'~ 'history,** botany and zoology; (formerly) scientific study of all nature. **'~ 'law,** rules for behaviour considered as innate and universal. **'~ phi'losophy,** (name formerly used for) the science of physics, or physics and dynamics. **'~ re'ligion,** religion and ethics based on reason (contrasted with religion from divine revelation). **'~ se'lection,** evolutionary theory that animals and plants survive or become extinct in accordance with their ability to adapt themselves to their environment. **2** of, in agreement with, the nature(4) of a living thing: *~ gifts/abilities.* **3** (of persons) possessing qualities by nature(4); born with qualities or powers: *He's a ~ orator,* makes speeches easily. *She's a ~ linguist,* learns languages easily. *It comes ~ to her.* ⇨ come(9). **4** ordinary; normal; to be expected: *die a ~ death,* not as the result of an accident, violence, etc. *It is ~ for a bird to fly. He was sentenced to prison for the term of his ~ life,* i e until he died. **5** simple; not cultivated or self-conscious: *~ behaviour; speak in a ~ voice,* not affected. *It was a ~ piece of acting,* with no exaggeration. **6** (music) of the normal scale of C; neither sharp nor flat: *B ~.* Cf *B sharp, B flat.* ⇨ the illus at notation. **7** (of offspring) illegitimate: *a ~ child/son/daughter.* □ *n* **1** (music) ~ note; musical note that is not a sharp or a flat; the sign (♮) placed before a note (in printed music) to make it a ~. **2** person born without ordinary intelligence; person feeble-minded from birth. **3** (colloq) ***a ~ for sth,*** person naturally fitted or qualified: *He's a ~ for the job/the part.*

natu·ral·ism /'nætʃrḷ-ɪzm/ *n* [U] **1** adherence to nature in literature and art; drawing and painting things in a way true to nature. **2** (phil) system of thought which rejects the supernatural and divine revelation and holds that natural causes and laws explain all phenomena.

natu·ral·ist /'nætʃrḷ-ɪst/ *n* person who makes a special study of animals or plants.

natu·ral·is·tic /'nætʃrl'ɪstɪk/ *adj* of naturalism: *a ~ painter.* ⇨ abstract[1](1), cubism, surrealism.

natu·ral·ize /'nætʃrḷaɪz/ *vt,vi* **1** [VP6A] give (sb from another country) rights of citizenship: *~ immigrants into the US. Lafcadio Hearn was ~d in Japan,* was made a Japanese subject. **2** [VP6A] take (a word) from one language into another: *English sporting terms have been ~d in many languages.* **3** [VP6A] introduce and acclimatize (an animal or plant) into another country. **4** [VP6A] plant (bulbs, etc) in woodland areas so that the flowers appear to be growing wild or naturally. **5** [VP2A] become ~d. **natu·ral·iz·ation** /'nætʃrlaɪ'zeɪʃn *US:* -lɪ'z-/ *n* [U] naturalizing or being ~d: *naturalization papers,* the documents that prove that a person has been admitted to citizenship of another country.

nat·urally /'nætʃrḷɪ/ *adv* **1** by nature(4): *She's ~ musical.* **2** of course; as might be expected: *'Did you answer her letter?'—'N~!'* **3** without artificial help, special cultivation, etc: *Her hair curls ~. Plants grow ~ in such a good climate.* **4** without artifice: *She speaks and behaves ~.*

na·ture /'neɪtʃə(r)/ *n* **1** [U] the whole universe and every created thing. *Is ~ at its best in spring? Wordsworth and Shelley were ~ poets.* **'~ study,** the study of animals, plants, insects, etc. **'~ worship,** the worship of trees, oceans, the winds. **2** [U] force(s) controlling the phenomena of the physical world: *Man is engaged in a constant* *struggle with* ~. *Miracles are contrary to* ~. ˈ~ **cure,** form of therapy relying upon natural remedies (sunlight, diet, exercise). ***pay the debt of*** ~, ***pay one's debt to*** ~, die. ***in the course of*** ~, according to the ordinary course of things. **3** [U] simple life without civilization; outdoor, animal-like existence: *Some 18th-century writers were in favour of a return to* ~, to the simple and primitive life that people were thought to have led before mankind became civilized. ***be in a state of*** ~, be completely naked (as in a nudist camp). **4** [C,U] qualities and characteristics, physical, mental and spiritual, which naturally belong to a person or thing: *It is the* ~ *of a dog to bark. Cats and dogs have quite different* ~*s. That man is proud by* ~. ˈ**human** ˈ~, the qualities possessed by man (in contrast with animals). **good** ~, unselfishness; willingness and readiness to help; kind-heartedness. Hence, ˈ**good-**/ˈ**ill-**ˈ~**ed,** having a good/ill ~. **5** qualities of non-material things: *Chemists study the* ~ *of gases.* **6** sort; kind: *Things of this* ~ *do not interest me. His request was in the* ~ *of a command,* could not be ignored.

na·tur·ism /ˈneɪtʃərɪzm/ *n* nudism. **na·tur·ist** /-ɪst/ *n* nudist.

naught /nɔt/ *n* nothing (esp in the phrases) ***bring (plans, etc) to*** ~, ruin, defeat. ***care*** ~ ***for,*** have no interest in; consider worthless. ***come to*** ~, fail. ***set at*** ~, (old use) defy.

naughty /ˈnɔtɪ/ *adj* (-ier, -iest) **1** (of children, their behaviour, etc) bad; wrong; disobedient; causing trouble: *a* ~ *child. It was* ~ *of you to pull the cat's tail.* **2** taking pleasure in shocking, intended to shock, people: *a* ~ *novel(ist);* ~ *stories.* **naught·ily** /-əlɪ/ *adv* **naughti·ness** *n*

nausea /ˈnɔsɪə *US:* ˈnɔʃə/ *n* [U] feeling of sickness (e g as caused by bad food) or disgust: *overcome by* ~ *after eating octopus; filled with* ~ *at the sight of cruelty to animals.* **naus·eate** /ˈnɔsɪeɪt *US:* ˈnɔʒ-/ *vt* [VP6A] cause ~: *nauseating food; a nauseating sight.* **naus·eous** /ˈnɔsɪəs *US:* ˈnɔʃəs/ *adj* disgusting; causing ~.

nautch /nɔtʃ/ *n* performance by professional dancing-girls in India, etc. ˈ~**-girl** *n* one of these girls.

nauti·cal /ˈnɔtɪkl/ *adj* of ships, sailors or navigation: ~ *terms,* used by sailors: *a* ~ *almanac,* with information about the sun, moon, tides, etc: *a* ~ *mile,* 1/60 of a degree, 6 080 ft (= 1 852 metres).

nauti·lus /ˈnɔtɪləs *US:* ˈnɔtḷəs/ *n* (*pl* -luses /-ləsɪz/) small sea animal of which the female has a very thin shell.

na·val /ˈneɪvl/ *adj* of a navy; of warships: ~ *officers/battles.*

nave /neɪv/ *n* central part of a church where the people sit. ⇨ the illus at church.

na·vel /ˈneɪvl/ *n* small depression in the middle of the surface of the belly (left by the severance of the umbilical cord). ⇨ the illus at trunk. ˈ~ **orange,** large orange with a ~-like formation in the top.

navi·gable /ˈnævɪgəbl/ *adj* **1** (of rivers, seas, etc) that can be navigated; suitable for ships: *The Rhine is* ~ *from Strasbourg to the sea.* **2** (of ships, etc) that can be steered and sailed: *not in a* ~ *condition.* **navi·ga·bil·ity** /ˌnævɪgəˈbɪlətɪ/ *n*

navi·gate /ˈnævɪgeɪt/ *vt,vi* [VP6A,2A] **1** plot the course, find the position, etc of a ship or aircraft, using charts and instruments. **2** steer (a ship); pilot (an aircraft); (fig) direct: ~ *a Bill through the House of Commons.* **3** sail over (a sea); sail up or down (a river). **navi·gator** /-tə(r)/ *n* **1** person who ~s(1). **2** sailor with skill and experience who has taken part in many voyages; (esp) early explorer: *the Spanish and Portuguese navigators of the 16th c who explored South America.*

navi·ga·tion /ˈnævɪˈgeɪʃn/ *n* [U] **1** the act of navigating. **2** the art or science of navigating. **3** the making of voyages on water or of journeys through the air: *inland* ~, by river and canal. *There has been an increase in* ~ *through the Panama Canal,* more ships have used or are using it.

navvy /ˈnævɪ/ *n* (*pl* -vies) (GB) unskilled workman employed in making roads, railways, canals, etc where digging is necessary.

navy /ˈneɪvɪ/ *n* (*pl* -vies) [C] **1** a country's warships. ˈ~ ˈ**blue,** dark blue as used for naval uniforms. **2** the officers and men of a country's warships: *join the* ~. **3** (old use) fleet, esp of merchant ships.

nay /neɪ/ *adv* (old use) no; (rhet) not only that, but also: *I suspect, nay, I am certain, that he is wrong.*

Nazi /ˈnɑtsɪ/ *n, adj* (member) of the German National Socialist Party founded by Hitler. **Naz·ism** /ˈnɑts-ɪzm/ *n* the ideology of the ~s.

neap /nip/ *n* ˈ~**(-tide),** tide when high water is at its lowest level of the year. ⇨ *spring tide* at spring[1](3).

Ne·an·der·thal /niˈændətɑl/ *adj* ~ **man,** extinct type of man of the stone age.

Nea·poli·tan /nɪəˈpɒlɪtən/ *n, adj* **1** (inhabitant) of Naples. **2** (small *n*) with many flavours and colours: ~ *ice-cream.*

near[1] /nɪə(r)/ *adj* (-er, -est) **1** not far from; close in space or time: *The post office is quite* ~. *Christmas is* ~. *Come* ~*er. Can you tell me the* ~*est* (= shortest) *way to the station? She was* ~ *to tears,* was almost crying. ***the*** ~ ***distance,*** that part of a scene between the foreground and the background. ***a*** ~ ***miss,*** e g of a bomb or shell, not a direct hit, but close enough to the target to cause damage. ***a*** ~ ***thing,*** a narrow escape. ˈ~-ˈ**sighted** *adj* short-sighted; seeing well only when sth, e g a book, is held close to the eyes. **2** close in relation or affection: *a* ~ *relation,* e g a mother, a son or daughter; *friends who are* ~ *and dear to us.* **3** (contrasted with *off*) (of parts of animals and vehicles, or of horses in a team (when on a road, etc) the left side: *the* ~ *foreleg; the* ~ *front wheel of a car.* ˈ~**·side** *n* side ~est the kerb: *the* ~*side lane of traffic.* **4** niggardly (contrasted with *generous*): *He's very* ~ *with his money.* □ *vt,vi* [VP6A,2A] come or draw ~ (to); approach: *The ship was* ~*ing land. He's* ~*ing his end,* is dying. *The road is* ~*ing completion.* ~**·ness** *n*

near[2] /nɪə(r)/ *adv* not far; to or at a short distance in space or time: *We searched far and* ~ (= everywhere) *for the missing child.* **as** ~ **as,** nearly: *As* ~ *as I can guess* (= My ~est or best guess is that) *there were forty people present. He was as* ~ *as could be to* (= only just escaped, narrowly escaped) *being knocked down by the bus.* **as** ~ (= nearly) ***as makes no difference,*** with no difference worth considering: *They're the same height, or as* ~ *as makes no difference.* ~ ***at hand,*** **(a)** within easy reach: *Always have your reference books* ~ *at hand.* **(b)** not far distant in the future: *The examinations are* ~ *at hand.* ~ ***(up)on,*** not far in time from; almost: *It was near* *upon midnight.* **nowhere ~** (and, colloq **not ~**), far from: *The concert hall was nowhere ~ full. She's nowhere ~ as old as her husband.* **~ by,** not far off. Hence, **'~-by** *adj*

near[3] /nɪə(r)/ *prep* (equivalent to *near*[1] with *to*) close to (in space, time, relationship, etc): *Come and sit ~ me. It's convenient living so ~ the station.*

near·ly /'nɪəlɪ/ *adv* **1** almost: *It's ~ one o'clock/~ time to start. I'm ~ ready.* ⇨ hardly, scarcely. **2** closely: *We're ~ related,* are near relations. **3** **not ~,** far from: *I have £20, but that isn't ~ enough for my journey, I shall need much more.*

neat[1] /nit/ *adj* (-er, -est except 5 below) **1** (liking to have everything) tidy; in good order with nothing out of place; done carefully: *~ work; a ~ worker; a ~ desk; ~ writing.* **2** simple and pleasant; in good taste: *a ~ dress.* **3** pleasing in shape and appearance: *a woman with a ~ figure/~ ankles.* **4** cleverly said or done: *a ~ answer/conjuring trick.* **5** (of wines and spirits) unmixed with water; undiluted: *drink one's whisky ~.* **~·ly** *adv* **~·ness** *n*

neat[2] /nit/ *n* (old use; *sing* and collective as *pl*) any animal of the ox kind; (collective) cattle. **'~-herd,** cowherd.

'neath /niθ/ *prep* (poet) beneath.

neb·ula /'nebjʊlə/ *n* (*pl* -lae /-li/) [C] cluster of very distant stars, diffuse mass of gas, seen in the night sky as an indistinct patch of light. **nebu·lar** /-lə(r)/ *adj* of ~s.

nebu·lous /'nebjʊləs/ *adj* cloud-like; hazy; indistinct; vague.

necess·ar·ily /'nesə'serəlɪ/ *adv* as a necessary result; inevitably: *Big men are not ~ strong men.*

necess·ary /'nesəsrɪ *US:* -serɪ/ *adj* which has to be done; which must be; which cannot be done without or escaped from: *Sleep is ~ to health. Is war a ~ evil in this world? Is it ~ for you to be/Is it ~ that you should be so economical?* □ *n* [C] (usu *pl;* -ries) things ~ (for living).

ne·cessi·tate /nɪ'sesɪteɪt/ *vt* [VP6A,D] make necessary: *Your proposal ~s borrowing money. The increase in population ~s a greater food supply.*

ne·cessi·tous /nɪ'sesɪtəs/ *adj* (formal) poor; needy: *in ~ circumstances,* in poverty.

ne·cess·ity /nɪ'sesətɪ/ *n* (*pl* -ties) **1** [U] urgent need; circumstances that compel sb to do sth; natural laws that direct human life and action: *He was driven by ~ to steal food for his starving children. The doctor asked us not to call him during the night except in case of ~,* e g unless the patient's condition changed very much for the worse. ***be under the ~ of...,*** find it necessary to. ***bow to ~,*** do what one is compelled to do. ***make a virtue of ~,*** accept credit without protest; claim credit for doing sth that one cannot help doing. ***of ~,*** as a matter of ~. **2** [C] sth that is necessary: *The necessities of life,* food, clothing and shelter. **3** [C] sth of which the absence or non-occurrence cannot be imagined: *Is it a logical ~ that the cost of living will go up if wages go up?* Can the one be considered possible without the other?

neck /nek/ *n* **1** part of the body that connects the head and the shoulders: *wrap a scarf round one's ~.* ⇨ the illus at head. ***break one's ~,*** be killed as the result of breaking the bones in the ~. ***break one's ~,*** work extremely hard to achieve sth. ⇨ breakneck. ***breathe down sb's ~,*** (colloq) be close behind, almost touching, e g in a race; be watching closely. ***get it in the ~,*** (sl) suffer a severe or a fatal blow; have a painful experience. ***have the ~*** (more usu *nerve*) ***to do sth,*** (sl) be impudent, cheeky enough to do it. ***save one's ~,*** escape hanging; (fig) escape the results of being foolish, etc. ***stick one's ~ out,*** (sl) do or say sth that may bring severe criticism, or result in a painful experience. ***win/lose by a ~,*** (horse-racing) by the length of a horse's ~, and fig. ***~ and crop,*** headlong; altogether; bag and baggage: *throw him out ~ and crop.* ***~ and ~,*** (of horse-racing, and fig) side by side, with no advantage over the other in a race or struggle. ***~ or nothing,*** taking desperate risks; venturing everything. **2** flesh of an animal's ~ as used for food, esp *~ of mutton.* **3** sth like a ~ in shape or position: *the ~ of a bottle; a narrow ~ of land,* e g an isthmus. **4** (compounds) **'~-band** *n* part of a shirt, etc that goes round the ~. **'~-cloth** *n* cravat. **~·er·chief** /'nekətʃif/ *n* (old use) cloth or scarf worn round the ~. **'~-lace** /-ləs/ *n* string of beads, pearls, etc worn round the ~ as an ornament. **'~-let** /-lət/ *n* ornament (e g of beads) for the ~. **'~-line** *n* (of fashions for women's clothes) line of a garment at or near the ~: *This year the ~line is up and the hemline is down.* **'~-tie** *n* (now usu *tie*) band of material worn round the ~ and knotted in front. **'~-wear** /-weə(r)/ *n* [U] (term used by shopkeepers for) collars and ties. □ *vi* (sl) (of young couples of opposite sex) exchange kisses, caresses and hugs: *sitting on park benches petting and ~ing in the dark; a '~ing party,* one at which young couples do this.

nec·ro·mancy /'nekrəmænsɪ/ *n* [U] art or practice of communicating by magic with the dead in order to learn about the future. **nec·ro·man·cer** /-sə(r)/ *n* person who practises ~.

ne·crop·olis /nɪ'kropəlɪs/ *n* (*pl* -lises /-lɪsɪz/) cemetery, esp a large one in an ancient town.

nec·tar /'nektə(r)/ *n* [U] **1** (in old Gk stories) the drink of the gods. ⇨ ambrosia. **2** sweet liquid in flowers, collected by bees; any delicious drink.

nec·tar·ine /'nektərɪn/ *n* kind of peach with thin, smooth skin and firm flesh.

née /neɪ/ *adj* (F) born (put after the name of a married woman and before her father's family name): *Mrs J Smith, née Brown.*

need[1] /nid/ *anom fin* (no *inf,* no participles, *3rd p sing* present tense is need, not *needs; int* and *interr* followed by *inf* without *to;* ~ not contracted to needn't /'nidnt/) [VP5] **1** be obliged; be necessary *N~ you go yet? No, I ~n't. Yes, I must. You ~n't go yet, ~ you? I ~ hardly tell you* (= You must already know or guess) *that....* **2** (followed by a *perfect infinitive,* ~ indicates that although sth may have occurred or been done in the past, it was or may have been unnecessary): *N~ it have happened? We ~n't have hurried,* We hurried but now we see that this was unnecessary. Cf *We didn't ~ to hurry,* We didn't hurry because it was unnecessary. ⇨ need[3](2). **~·ful** /-fl/ *adj* ~ed; necessary: *do what is ~ful.* ***do the ~ful,*** (colloq) provide the money, perform the action, that is required. **~·fully** /-flɪ/ *adv* **~·less** *adj* not ~ed; unnecessary: *~less work/trouble. N~less to say, he kept his promise.* **~·less·ly** *adv*

need[2] /nid/ *n* **1** [U] **~ *(for),*** circumstances in which sth is lacking, or necessary, or requiring some course of action: *There's no ~ (for you) to* *start yet. There's no/not much ~ for anxiety. There's a great ~ for a book on this subject.* **if ~ be,** if necessary. **2** (used in *pl*) requirement; sth felt to be necessary: *He earns enough to satisfy his ~s,* i e to buy food, clothing, etc. *My ~s are few. £10 will meet my immediate ~s.* **'~s test,** = means test (which is more usu). ⇨ means². **3** [U] poverty; misfortune; adversity: *He helped me in my hour of ~.* ***A friend in ~ is a friend indeed,*** (prov) A friend who helps when one is in trouble is a real friend. **~y** *adj* (-ier, -iest) very poor; lacking the necessities of life: *a ~y family; help the poor and ~y.*

need³ /nid/ *vt* **1** [VP6A,E] want; require: *The garden ~s rain. Does he ~ any help? It only ~s good will from both sides. This chapter ~s rewriting/~s to be rewritten.* **2** [VP7] be under a necessity or obligation: *He didn't ~ to be reminded about it. Does he ~ to know? It ~s to be done carefully. He ~s to be kept informed about developments. I agree that they ~ to be told about the arrangement.* **3** [VP6A] deserve; ought to have: *What he ~s is a good whipping!*

needle /'nidl/ *n* **1** small, thin piece of polished steel, pointed at one end and with a small hole at the other end for thread, used in sewing and darning: ***look for a ~ in a haystack,*** (prov) engage in a hopeless search. ***as sharp as a ~,*** quick-witted; observant. **'~-woman** *n* (*pl* -women) woman who sews. **'~-craft, '~-work** *nn* [U] sewing; embroidery. **'pins and '~s,** ⇨ pin¹(1). **2** long, thin piece of polished wood, bone or metal (without an eye), with a pointed end (for knitting) or a hook (for crocheting). **3** thin steel pointer in a compass, showing the magnetic north; similar pointer in a telegraphic instrument. **4** sth which is like a ~(1) in shape, appearance or use (e g the thin, pointed leaves of pine-trees; a sharp, pointed peak or rocky summit; the sharp, hollow end of a syringe used for giving injections). **5** steel stylus used in recording and playing gramophone records. Cf *sapphire* and *diamond styli,* used now for long-playing discs. **6 the ~,** (sl) nervous excitement: *give sb the ~,* provoke or excite him; *get the ~,* be provoked. **7** obelisk: *Cleopatra's ~,* in London. □ *vt* **1** [VP6A,15A] sew, pierce, operate on, with a ~; thread (one's way) between or through things. **2** (colloq) goad, provoke (sb, esp by making cruel comments, etc).

needs /nidz/ *adv* (now used only with *must*) of necessity. ***N~ must when the devil drives,*** (prov) Circumstances may compel us to act in a certain way. (When the *adv* follows *must,* as in 'He must ~', the sense is usu sarcastic, as here): *He must ~ go away just when I want his help, He foolishly or stupidly insisted on going away....*

ne'er /neə(r)/ *adv* (poet) never. **~-do-well** /'neə du wel/ *n* useless or good-for-nothing person.

nef·arious /nɪ'feərɪəs/ *adj* (formal) wicked; unlawful. **~·ly** *adv* **~·ness** *n*

ne·gate /nɪ'geɪt/ *vt* [VP6A] (formal) deny; nullify.

ne·ga·tion /nɪ'geɪʃn/ *n* [U] **1** act of denying (opp of *affirmation*): *Shaking the head is a sign of ~.* **2** absence of any positive or real quality or meaning: *The life of an evil man is a moral ~.*

nega·tive /'negətɪv/ *adj* **1** (of words and answers) indicating *no* or *not* (opp of *affirmative*): *give sb a ~ answer.* **2** (opp of *positive*) expressing the absence of any positive character; that stops, hinders or makes powerless: *~ criticism,* that does not help by building up, making suggestions; *~ praise,* not finding fault; *~ virtue,* doing nothing wrong, but doing nothing good or right, either. **3** (maths) of a number or quantity that has to be subtracted (e g $-x^2y$). **4** of that kind of electricity produced by rubbing wax, vulcanite, etc; of or from the cathode: *the ~ plate in a battery,* from which electrons will flow to the positive plate. **the ~ pole** (made of zinc) *in a cell.* **5** (photo) having lights and shades reversed. □ *n* [C] **1** word or statement that denies: *'No', 'not' and 'neither' are ~s. The answer is in the ~,* is 'No'. **2** (maths) a minus quantity (e g $-5x$). **3** (photo) developed plate or film on which lights and shades are reversed. □ *vt* [VP6A] **1** prove (a theory, etc) to be untrue: *Experiments ~d his theory.* **2** reject; refuse to accept; neutralize (an effect). **~·ly** *adv*

the negative of the photograph on p 819

ne·glect /nɪ'glekt/ *vt* **1** [VP6A] pay no attention to; give no or not enough care to: *~ one's studies/children/health.* **2** [VP7,6C] omit or fail (*to do* sth); leave undone (what one ought to do): *He ~ed to write and say 'Thank you'. Don't ~ writing to your mother.* □ *n* [U] ~ing or being ~ed: *He lost his job because of ~ of duty. The garden was in a state of ~.* **~·ful** /-fl/ *adj* in the habit of ~ing things: *boys who are ~ful of their appearance.* **~·fully** /-flɪ/ *adv* **~·ful·ness** *n*: *He has a tendency to ~fulness.*

nég·ligé, neg·li·gee /'neglɪʒeɪ *US:* 'neglɪ'ʒeɪ/ *n* [C,U] (condition of being in a) loose, free style of informal dress.

neg·li·gence /'neglɪdʒəns/ *n* [U] **1** carelessness; failure to take proper care or precautions: *The accident was due to ~.* **2** neglected condition or appearance: *~ of dress.*

neg·li·gent /'neglɪdʒənt/ *adj* taking too little care, guilty of neglect: *He was ~ in* (= in respect of) *his work. He was ~ of his duties.* **~·ly** *adv*

neg·li·gible /'neglɪdʒəbl/ *adj* that need not be considered; of little or no importance or size: *a ~ quantity.*

ne·go·ti·able /nɪ'gəʊʃəbl/ *adj* **1** that can be negotiated(2): *Is the dispute ~?* **2** that can be changed into cash, or passed from person to person instead of cash: *~ securities/instruments,* e g cheques, promissory notes. **3** (of roads, rivers, etc) that can be passed over or along.

ne·go·ti·ate /nɪ'gəʊʃɪeɪt/ *vi,vt* **1** [VP2A,3A] ***~ (with sb),*** discuss, confer, in order to come to an agreement: *We've decided to ~ with the employers about our wage claims.* **2** [VP6A,14] ***~ sth (with sb),*** arrange by discussion: *~ a sale/a loan/a treaty/peace.* **3** [VP6A] get or give money for (cheques, bonds, etc). **4** [VP6A] get past or over: *This is a difficult corner for a large car to ~. My horse ~d* (i e jumped over) *the fence very well.* **ne·go·ti·ator** /-tə(r)/ *n* one who ~s.

ne·go·ti·ation /nɪˈgəʊʃɪeɪʃn/ *n* [C,U] negotiating: *enter into/ open/ start/ carry on/ resume ~s with sb; be in ~ with sb. Price is a matter of ~.*
Ne·gress /ˈnigrəs/ *n* Negro woman or girl.
Ne·gro /ˈnigrəʊ/ *n* (*pl* **-roes** /-rəʊz/) (cap N to be preferred) member (or, outside Africa, descendant) of one of the black-skinned African races south of the Sahara.
Ne·groid /ˈnigrɔɪd/ *adj* of or akin to Negroes or the Negro race. □ *n* person of a ~ race.
ne·gus /ˈnigəs/ *n* hot, sweetened wine, lemon juice, nutmeg and water.
Ne·gus /ˈnigəs/ *n* (title of the) ruler of Ethiopia.
neigh /neɪ/ *vi, n* (make the) cry of a horse.
neigh·bour (US = **-bor**) /ˈneɪbə(r)/ *n* person living in a house, street, etc near another; person, thing or country that is near(est) another: *We're nextdoor ~s,* Our houses are side by side. *We were ~s at dinner,* We sat together at table. *When the big tree fell, it brought down two of its smaller ~s,* two smaller trees near it. *Britain's nearest ~ is France.* □ *vt,vi* [VP6A,3A] **~ *(upon),*** chiefly in the form ~*ing*) be near to: *~ing countries; in the ~ing village.* **ˈ~·hood** /-hʊd/ *n* **1** (people living in a) district; area near the place, etc referred to: *There's some beautiful scenery in our ~hood. He was liked by the whole ~hood. He wants to live in the ~hood of London.* **2** condition of being near: *The ~hood of this noisy airport is a serious disadvantage. He lost a sum in the ~hood of £500.* **~·ly** *adj* kind; friendly. **~·li·ness** *n* [U] friendly feeling, help, that is expected from ~s.
nei·ther /ˈnaɪðə(r) *US:* ˈnið-/ *adj, pron* (used with a *sing n* or *pron*; cf *either*) not one nor the other (of two): *N~ statement is true. N~ (one) is satisfactory. I like ~ of them. I can agree in ~ case. In ~ case can I agree.* □ *adv* (and *conj*) **1 ~... *nor.*** *He ~ knows nor cares what happened. It's ~ pleasant to eat nor good for you. N~ you nor I could do it. The cats have not been fed: ~ has the dog* (or, colloq) *N~ the cats nor the dog have been fed.* **2** (after a negative *if*-clause, etc): *If you don't go, ~ shall I. As he won't help you, ~ will I. I haven't been to the Exhibition; ~ do I* (= and I do not) *intend to go. A: 'I don't like it'—B: 'N~ do I'* Cf *Nor do I. No more do I.*
Nelly /ˈnelɪ/ *n* (only in) ***not on your ~,*** (sl) not on your life!
nem con /ˈnem ˈkon/ *adv* (abbr Lat) unanimously; without any objection being raised: *The resolution was carried ~.*
nem·esis /ˈneməsɪs/ *n* (*pl* **-eses** /-əsiz/) (formal) **1** deserved fate; just punishment for wrong-doing. **2 N~,** goddess of vengeance.
neo- /ˈniəʊ/ *pref* new; modern.
neo-col·onial·ism /ˈniəʊ kəˈləʊnɪəlɪzm/ *n* control by powerful countries of former colonies, or less developed countries by economic pressure.
neo·lithic /ˈniəˈlɪθɪk/ *adj* of the new or later stone age: *~ man.*
neol·ogism /niˈolədʒɪzm/ *n* [U] coining or using of new words; [C] new-coined word.
neon /ˈnion/ *n* [U] colourless gas forming a very small proportion of the earth's atmosphere. **ˈ~ light** *n* coloured light produced when an electric current passes through this gas in a low-pressure bulb or tube. **ˈ~ sign** *n* advertisement, etc in which ~ light is used.
neo·phyte /ˈniəfaɪt/ *n* person who has newly been converted to some belief or religion; (in the RC Church) one who has recently become a priest or entered a monastery.
nephew /ˈnevju *US:* ˈnefju/ *n* son of one's brother or sister.
neph·ri·tis /nɪˈfraɪtɪs/ *n* [U] inflammation of the kidneys.
neo·plasm /ˈniəʊplæzm/ *n* (path) tumor.
ne plus ultra /ˈni ˈplʌs ˈʌltrə/ *n* (Lat) farthest point attained or attainable; highest point, culmination (*of*).
nep·ot·ism /ˈnepətɪzm/ *n* [U] the giving of special favour (esp employment) by a person in high position to his relatives.
Nep·tune /ˈneptjun *US:* -tun/ *n* **1** (God of) the sea. **2** one of the farthest planets of the solar system. ⇨ the illus at **planet**.
ne·reid /ˈnɪərɪɪd/ *n* (Gk myth) sea-nymph.
nerve /nɜv/ *n* **1** [C] fibre or bundle of fibres carrying feelings and impulses between the brain and all parts of the body. **ˈ~-cell** *n* cell that conducts impulses. **ˈ~-centre** *n* group of closely connected ~-cells. **2** (*pl*) condition of being easily excited, worried, irritated: *He is suffering from ~s,* quickly and easily becomes excited, frightened, etc. *That man doesn't know what ~s are,* is never worried, upset, etc by events. *He has ~s of iron,* is never upset, etc. ***get on one's ~s,*** worry or annoy: *That noise gets on my ~s.* **war of ~s,** campaign in which an attempt is made to weaken an opponent by destroying his morale. **ˈ~-racking** *adj* inflicting strain on the ~s. **3** [U] quality of being bold, self-reliant, etc: *A test pilot needs plenty of ~. What a ~!* What cheek! ***have the ~ to do sth,*** **(a)** have the necessary courage, self-reliance: *have ~ enough to drive a racing car.* **(b)** (colloq) be impudent enough: *He had the ~ to suggest that I was cheating.* ***have a ~,*** (colloq) be self-assured or audacious: *He's got a ~, going to work dressed like that!* ***lose/regain one's ~,*** lose/recover one's courage and self-assurance. **4** [C] (old use) sinew, tendon. ***strain every ~ to do sth,*** make great efforts. **5** (bot) rib, esp mid-rib, of a leaf. □ *vt* [VP6A,14,16A] **~ *oneself for sth/to do sth,*** summon up one's strength (physical or moral): *~ oneself for a task; ~ oneself ready to face troubles.* **~·less** *adj* from ~(4) lacking in vigour or spirit; without energy: *The knife fell from his ~less hand.* **~·less·ly** *adv*
nerv·ous /ˈnɜvəs/ *adj* **1** of the nerves(1): *the ~ system of the human body.* **a ˈ~ ˈbreakdown,** neurasthenia. **2** having or showing nerves(2): *Are you ~ in the dark? What's she so ~ about?* **3** having strong sinews; vigorous: *full of ~ energy; a ~ style of writing.* **~·ly** *adv* **~·ness** *n*
nervy /ˈnɜvɪ/ *adj* **1** (GB colloq) suffering from nervous strain. **2** (sl) impudent.
nes·cience /ˈnesɪəns/ *n* [U] (formal) absence of knowledge. **nes·cient** /-ənt/ *adj* without knowledge.
ness /nes/ *n* (usu in place names) promontory; headland.
nest /nest/ *n* **1** place made or chosen by a bird for its eggs. ***feather one's ~,*** ⇨ feather[2](1). ***foul one's own ~,*** abuse(2) one's own family, home, etc. **ˈ~-egg** *n* (fig) sum of money saved for future use. **2** place in which certain living things have and keep their young: *a ˈwasp's ~; a ˈturtle's ~.* **3** comfortable place: *make oneself a ~ of cushions.* **4** number of like things (esp boxes, tables) fitting one inside another. **5** (fig) shelter;

hiding-place; secluded retreat: *a ~ of crime/vice/pirates; machine-gun ~s,* where they are hidden from direct view. □ *vi* [VP2A,C] **1** make and use a ~: *The swallows are ~ing in the woodshed.* **2 go ~ing,** search for the ~s of wild birds and take the eggs.

nestle /ˋnesl/ *vt,vi* **1** [VP2C] **~ (down),** settle comfortably and warmly: *~ down among the cushions; ~ down in bed.* **2** [VP2C] **~ up (against/to),** press oneself lovingly to: *The child was nestling closely/~d up to her mother.* **3** [VP15A] cradle: *She ~d the baby in her arms.*

nest·ling /ˋnestlɪŋ/ *n* [C] bird too young to leave the nest.

Nes·tor /ˋnestə(r)/ *n* wise, old counsellor (from the name of one of the Greeks at Troy, in Homer's *Iliad*).

net[1] /net/ *n* [U] open-work material of knotted string, hair, wire, etc; [C] such material made up for a special purpose: *a mosˋquito-net,* for use over a bed; *ˋfishing-nets; ˋtennis nets; ˋhair-nets* (used by women to keep the hair in place); (fig) moral or mental snare. **ˋnet·ball** *n* girls' game in which a ball has to be thrown so that it falls through a net fastened to a ring on the top of a post. **the nets,** (cricket) wickets set up inside a net for practice: *have an hour at the nets.* **ˋnet·work** *n* **(a)** complex system of lines that cross: *a network of railways/canals.* **(b)** connected system: *An intelligence/spy network. A world communications network,* e g for radio and TV, using satellites. □ *vt* (-tt-) [VP6A] **1** catch (fish, animals, etc) with or in a net. **2** cover (e g fruit trees) with a net or nets: *net strawberries/current bushes,* against birds. **3** put nets in place in: *net a river.*

net[2]**, nett** /net/ *adj* remaining when nothing more is to be taken away: *net price,* off which discount is not to be allowed; *net profit,* when working expenses have been deducted; *net weight,* of the contents only, excluding the weight of packing, the container, etc. □ *vt* (-tt-) gain as a net profit: *He netted £5 from the deal.*

nether /ˋneðə(r)/ *adj* **1** (archaic) lower: *the ~ regions/world,* the world of the dead; hell. **2** (joking style) *~ garments,* trousers. **~·most** /-məʊst/ *adj*

Neth·er·lander /ˋneðəlændə(r)/ *n* native of the Netherlands (Holland).

nett ⇨ net[2].

net·ting /ˋnetɪŋ/ *n* [U] **1** making or using nets. **2** netted string, thread or wire: *five yards of wire ~; windows screened with ~.*

nettle /ˋnetl/ *n* [C] common wild plant which has on its leaves hairs that sting and redden the skin when touched. **ˋ~·rash** *n* eruption on the skin with red patches like those caused by ~s. □ *vt* [VP6A] sting (oneself) with ~s; (fig) make rather angry; annoy: *She looked ~d by my remarks.*

net·work ⇨ net[1].

neu·ral /ˋnjʊərl *US:* ˋnʊə-/ *adj* of the nerves. **~·gia** /njʊˋrældʒə *US:* nʊ-/ *n* [U] sharp, jumping pain in the nerves, esp of the face and head. **~·gic** /-dʒɪk/ *adj*

neur·as·thenia /ˌnjʊərəsˋθiniə *US:* ˌnʊr-/ *n* [U] exhausted condition of the nervous system; low state of health, general weakness, accompanying this condition. **neur·as·thenic** /-nɪk/ *adj* suffering from, related to, ~. □ *n* person suffering from ~.

neur·itis /njʊˋraɪtɪs *US:* nʊ-/ *n* [U] inflammation of a nerve or nerves.

neur·ol·ogy /njʊəˋrolədʒɪ *US:* nʊ-/ *n* [U] branch of medical science that is concerned with nerves. **neu·rol·ogist** /njʊəˋrolədʒɪst *US:* nʊ-/ *n* expert in ~.

neur·osis /njʊˋrəʊsɪs *US:* nʊ-/ *n* (*pl* -oses /-əʊsɪz/) functional derangement caused by disorders of the nervous system or by something in the subconscious mind. **neur·otic** /njʊˋrotɪk *US:* nʊ-/ *adj* **1** (of a person) suffering from a ~; of abnormal sensitivity; easily excited. **2** (of a drug) affecting the nervous system. □ *n* neurotic person or drug.

neu·ter /ˋnjutə(r) *US:* ˋnu-/ *adj* **1** (gram; of gender) neither feminine nor masculine. **2** (of plants) without male or female parts. **3** (of insects, e g worker ants) sexually undeveloped; sterile. □ *n* **1** ~ noun or gender. **2** sexually undeveloped insect; castrated animal: *My cat is an enormous ginger ~.* □ *vt* castrate: *a ~ed tomcat.*

neu·tral /ˋnjutrl *US:* ˋnu-/ *adj* **1** helping neither side in a war or quarrel: *~ nations; be/remain ~.* **2** of a country that remains ~ in war: *~ territory/ships.* **3** having no definite characteristics; not clearly one (colour, etc) or another: *~ tints.* **4** (chem) neither acid nor alkaline. **5** (of gear mechanism) of the position in which no power is transmitted: *leave a car in ~ gear.* □ *n* ~ person, country, etc; ~ position of gears: *slip the gears into ~.* **~·ity** /njuˋtrælətɪ *US:* nu-/ *n* [U] state of being ~, esp in war: *armed ~ity,* readiness to fight if attacked, but remaining ~ unless or until this happens. **~·ize** /-ɑɪz/ *vt* [VP6A] **1** make ~; declare by agreement that (a place) shall be treated as ~ in war; exempt or exclude from hostilities: *~ize the Dardanelles.* **2** take away the effect or special quality of, by means of sth with an opposite effect or quality: *~ize a poison.* **~·iz·ation** /ˌnjutrəlɑɪˋzeɪʃn *US:* -lɪˋz-/ *n*

neu·tron /ˋnjutron *US:* ˋnu-/ *n* particle carrying no electric charge, of about the same mass as a proton, and forming part of the nucleus of an atom.

never /ˋnevə(r)/ *adv* **1** at no time; on no occasion: *She ~ goes to the cinema. He has ~ been abroad. They say that he ~ told a lie. I'm tired of listening to your ~-ending complaints.* (Front position for emphasis): *N~ in all my life have I heard such nonsense!* (modifying *again* and *before*): *I shall ~ again stay at that hotel. Such a display has ~ before been seen/has ~ been seen before.* **2** (used as an emphatic substitute for *not*): *That will ~ do,* won't do at all. *I ~ slept a wink all night. He ~ so much as smiled,* didn't smile even once. **3** (phrases) ***Well, I ~ (did)!*** expressing surprise. ***N~ mind!*** Don't worry! Don't trouble about it. **4 the ˈN~ ˋN~ (Land),** the outback, esp north Queensland (Australia). **5** (sl) ***on the ˈ~ˋ~,*** on the hire-purchase system: *buy sth on the ~~.* **~-more** /ˈnevəˋmɔ(r)/ *adv* ~ again.

never·the·less /ˈnevəðəˋles/ *adv, conj* however; in spite of that; still: *There was no news; ~, she went on hoping.*

new /nju *US:* nu/ *adj* (-er, -est) **1** not existing before; seen, heard of, introduced, for the first time; of recent origin, growth, manufacture, etc: *a new school/idea/film/novel/invention; new potatoes,* lifted from the soil early in the season; *new clothes/furniture; new* (= freshly baked) *bread; the newest* (= latest) *fashions; new members of Parliament,* elected to Parliament for the first time. **new look,** ⇨ look[2](2). **the New Testa-**

ment, (abbr NT) the second part of the Bible. **2** already in existence, but only now seen, discovered, etc: *learn new words in a foreign language; discover a new star.* **the New World,** N and S America. **3** ***new to,*** unfamiliar with; not yet accustomed to: *I am new to this town. They are still new to the work/trade.* ***new from,*** freshly or recently arrived from: *an office boy new from school; a person new from the provinces.* **4** (with *def art*) later, modern, having a different character. ***the new poor/rich,*** those people recently made poor/rich by social changes, etc. **the new woman,** (as used in the first half of the 20th c) woman having or claiming independence, social freedom, etc. **a new deal,** ⇨ **deal**[4]**(1)**. **5** beginning again. **a new moon,** seen as a thin crescent. ***lead a new life,*** give up old habits, etc. ***wish sb a Happy New Year,*** i e on **New Year's Day,** 1 Jan, or **New Year's Eve,** 31 Dec. □ *adv* (preceding, joined or hyphened to, the word it qualifies) recently: *a newborn baby; new-laid eggs; new-fallen snow; new-made graves.* **ˋnew-comer** *n* person who has recently arrived in a place. **ˈnew-ˋfangled** *adj* newly come into use or fashion (and, for this reason, disliked by some): *new-fangled ideas about education.* **new·ly** *adv* **1** recently: *a newly married couple; her newly awakened curiosity.* **ˋnewly-weds** *n pl* newly married couple(s). **2** in a new, different way: *newly arranged furniture.* **new·ness** *n*

newel /ˋnjuḷ *US:* ˋnuḷ/ *n* centre pillar of a winding stair; post supporting a hand-rail at the top, bottom or turn of a staircase.

new-fangled /ˈnju ˋfæŋgld *US:* ˈnu/ *adj* ⇨ **new.**

New·found·land /ˈnjufəndˋlænd *US:* ˈnu-/ *n* large breed of spaniel, originally from ~, a large island in Canada, noted for its intelligence and swimming powers.

New·mar·ket /ˋnjumɑkɪt *US:* ˋnu-/ *n* English town noted for horse-races; kind of card-game.

news /njuz *US:* nuz/ *n* (*pl* in form but used only in *sing* constructions) new or fresh information; report(s) of what has most recently happened: *What's the latest ~?* (T V and radio): *Here is the ~. Here are the ~ headlines. Here is a ~ summary/a summary of the ~. Here are some interesting items/pieces/bits of ~. That's no ~ to me,* I already know that. *Miss White is in the ~,* is being written about in the papers. *The ~ that the enemy were near alarmed the citizens. Have you any ~ of* (= concerning) *where your brother is staying?* ***No ~ is good ~,*** (prov) If there were bad ~ we should hear it. **ˋ~·agent** *n* shopkeeper who sells ~papers, periodicals, etc. **ˋ~ agency** *n* agency that collects ~ and sells it to the press. **ˋ~·boy** *n* boy who sells ~papers in the streets. **ˋ~·cast** *n* broadcast of ~. **ˋ~·caster** *n* **ˋ~ cinema/theatre,** cinema showing ~reels, cartoons, and other short films. **ˋ~·dealer,** (US) = ~agent. **ˋ~·letter** *n* letter or circular sent out to members of a society, etc. **ˋ~·monger** /-mʌŋgə(r)/ *n* person who gossips. **ˋ~·paper** /ˋnjuspeɪpə(r) *US:* ˋnu-/ *n* printed publication, usu issued every day, with ~, advertisements, etc. **ˋ~·print** *n* [U] paper for printing ~papers on. **ˋ~·reel** *n* cinema film of recent events. **ˋ~·room** *n* room (in a library, etc) where ~papers and other periodicals may be read. **ˋ~·sheet** *n* simple form of ~paper. **ˋ~·stand** *n* stall for the sale of ~papers, etc. **ˋ~·vendor** *n* seller of ~papers. **ˋ~-worthy** *adj* sufficiently interesting for reporting, e g in a newspaper. **~·less** *adj* without ~. **~y** *adj* (colloq) full of ~ or gossip: *a ~y letter.*

newt /njut *US:* nut/ *n* (kinds of) small lizard-like animal which spends most of its time in the water. ⇨ the illus at **amphibians.**

New·to·nian /njuˋtəʊnɪən *US:* nu-/ *adj* related to Sir Izaac Newton /ˋnjutn *US:* ˋnu-/, 1642—1727, English scientist and philosopher, and his theories, esp his law of gravity. □ *n* follower of Newton and his system.

next /nekst/ *adj, n* **1** coming immediately after, in order or space: *What's the ~ thing to do? Take the ~ turning to the right. Miss Green was the ~ (person) to arrive. Which is the town ~ to London in size?* ***the ~ best (thing),*** that which is chosen or accepted if the first choice fails: *There are no tickets left for the Circus: the ~ best thing is the Zoo.* ***~ to nothing,*** scarcely anything; almost nothing: *No wonder she's ill! She eats ~ to nothing.* ***~ door,*** the ~ house: *He lives ~ door (to me). The people ~ door are very noisy. We are ~-door neighbours.* ***~ door to,*** (fig) almost; not far from: *Such ideas are ~ door to madness.* ***next of kin,*** ⇨ **kin. 2** (of time; *def art* needed if the reference is to a time that is future in relation to a time already mentioned): *I shall go there ~ Friday/week/year. We shall be in France by this time ~ week. He will spend the first week of his holiday in France and the ~ (week) in Italy. We arrived in Turin on a Monday; the ~ day we left for Rome. That summer was very wet; the ~ summer was even wetter. Is he coming this weekend* (i e the coming weekend) *or ~ weekend* (i e the following weekend)? □ *adv* **1** after this/that; then: *What are you going to do ~? When I ~ saw her she was dressed in green.* ***come ~,*** follow: *What comes ~,* what's the ~ thing (to do, etc). **2** used to express surprise or wonder: *What will he be saying ~? A new motor-car! What ~?* □ *prep* (older use; elliptical use of the *adj*; = *~ to*): *May I bring my chair ~ yours? He doesn't like wearing wool ~ his skin.*

nexus /ˋneksəs/ *n* (*pl* **-suses** /-səsɪz/) connection; bond; connected series.

nib /nɪb/ *n* split pen-point (to be) inserted in a pen-holder.

nibble /ˋnɪbl/ *vt,vi* [VP6A,2A,3A] ***~ (at),*** **1** take tiny bites: *fish nibbling (at) the bait.* **2** (fig) show some inclination to accept (an offer), agree to (a suggestion, etc), but without being definite. □ *n* [C] act of nibbling: *I felt a ~ at the bait.*

nib·lick /ˋnɪblɪk/ *n* golf-club with a large, round, heavy head, used esp for playing balls out of bunkers.

nice /nɑɪs/ *adj* (**-r, -st**) **1** (contrary to *nasty*) pleasant; agreeable; kind; friendly; fine: *a ~ day; ~ weather; a ~ little girl; ~ to the taste/the feel, etc; medicine that is not ~ to take.* ***~ and..., ~*** because...: *~ and warm by the fire; ~ and cool in the woods.* **2** needing care and exactness; sensitive; subtle: *a ~ point of law,* one that may be difficult to decide; *~* (= delicate) *shades of meaning.* **3** (ironic) difficult; bad: *You've got us into a ~ mess.* **4** fussy; having or showing delicate tastes: *speaking with a ~* (= affected) *accent.* **5** punctilious; scrupulous: *He's not so ~ in his business methods.* **~·ly** *adv* **1** in a ~ manner. **2** (colloq) very well; all right: *That will suit me ~ly. The patient is doing ~ly,* is making good progress. **~·ness** *n*

nicety /ˋnɑɪsətɪ/ *n* (*pl* -ties) **1** [U] accuracy; exactness: *~ of judgement; a point of great ~*, one needing most careful and exact consideration. **2** [C] delicate distinction: *the niceties of criticism.* ***to a ~,*** exactly right: *He judged the distance to a ~.*

niche /nɪtʃ/ *n* [C] **1** (usu shallow) recess (often with a shelf) in a wall, e g for a statue or ornament: *He has a ~ in the temple of fame,* His achievements are not forgotten. **2** (fig) suitable or fitting position: *He found the right ~ for himself,* a place where he could do what he wanted to do, comfortably and happily.

nick[1] /nɪk/ *n* **1** small V-shaped cut (made in sth), e g as a record. **2** ***in the ~ of time,*** only just in time; at the critical or opportune time. **3** ***in the ~,*** (sl) in prison. □ *vt* make a ~ in: *~ one's chin,* while shaving; cut a notch in.

nick[2] /nɪk/ *n* (sl) (only in) ***in good/poor ~,*** in good health or condition: *feeling in very good ~. The house is in pretty poor ~.*

Nick /nɪk/ *n* short for *Nicholas.* **Old N~,** the devil.

nickel /ˋnɪkl/ *n* **1** [U] hard, silver-white metal (symbol **Ni**) used in the form of ~-plating and in alloys (*'~-ˋsteel, '~-ˋsilver*). **2** coin used in the US, value 5 cents. □ *vt* (-ll-, US = -l-) coat with ~.

nick·nack /ˋnɪknæk/ *n* = knick-knack.

nick·name /ˋnɪkneɪm/ *n* name given in addition to or altered from or used instead of the real name (e g *Fatty* for a fat boy: *Shorty,* humorously, for a very tall man). □ *vt* [VP6A,23] give a ~ to: *They ~d him Hurry.*

nic·otine /ˋnɪkətin/ *n* [U] poisonous, oily substance in tobacco-leaves: *~-stained fingers; cigarettes with a low ~ content.*

niece /nis/ *n* daughter of one's brother(-in-law) or sister(-in-law).

niff /nɪf/ *n* (GB sl, dial) (unpleasant) smell. **~y** *adj* (sl) having a bad smell.

nifty /ˋnɪftɪ/ *adj* (sl) **1** smart; stylish. **2** having an unpleasant smell. **3** quick, efficient: *Look ~!* (more usu *Look nippy!*)

nig·gard /ˋnɪgəd/ *n* mean, stingy person. **~·ly** *adj* giving, given, unwillingly, in small amounts; miserly: *~ly contributions.* **~·li·ness** *n*

nig·ger /ˋnɪgə(r)/ *n* ⚠ (impolite and offensive word for) Negro.

niggle /ˋnɪgl/ *vi* give too much time or attention to unimportant details; complain about trivial matters. **nig·gling** *adj* trifling; lacking in boldness of effect.

nigh /nɑɪ/ *adv, prep* (-er, -est) (archaic and poet) near (to).

night /nɑɪt/ *n* [C] **1** dark hours between sunset and sunrise or twilight and dawn: *in/during the ~; on Sunday ~; on the ~ of Friday, the 13th of June; a late-~ show at the cinema,* one given much later than the usual shows. *He stayed three ~s with us,* slept at our house three ~s. *Can you stay over ~,* spend the ~ with us? *What a dirty ~ it has been,* how stormy, rainy, etc the ~ has been! *It's the cook's ~ off,* the evening when she is not expected to be on duty. ***~ after ~,*** for many ~s in succession. ***all ~ (long),*** throughout the whole ~. ***~ and day,*** continuously: *travel ~ and day for a week.* ***at ~,*** when ~ comes; during the ~: *6 o'clock at ~,* 6 p m. ***by ~,*** during the ~: *travel by ~.* ***o' ~s*** /ə ˋnɑɪts/ (old use) by or at ~. ***get/have/take a ~ off,*** a ~ free from work usually done at ~. ***have a good/bad ~,*** sleep well/badly. ***have a ~ out,*** spend an evening and ~ in pleasure, e g by having dinner out, followed by a visit to the cinema. ***make a ~ of it,*** spend all ~ in pleasure-making, esp at a party. ***turn ~ into day,*** do at ~ what is usu done during the day. ***work ~s,*** work on ~ shift: *My husband's working ~s this week.* ⇨ shift[1](2). **2** (compounds) **ˋ~-bell** *n* bell (e g on the street door, at a doctor's house) to be used at ~. **ˋ~-bird** *n* **(a)** bird (e g an owl) which is active at ~. **(b)** person (usu disreputable) who goes about at ~. **ˋ~-cap** *n* **(a)** cap (formerly) worn in bed. **(b)** (usu alcoholic) drink taken before going to bed. **ˋ~-club** *n* club open until the early hours of the morning to members for dancing, supper, entertainment, etc. **ˋ~-dress** *n* long, loose garment worn by a woman or child in bed. **ˋ~-fall** *n* [U] the coming of ~; evening. **ˋ~-gown** *n* = ~dress. **ˋ~ie, ˋ~y** *n* (colloq) = ~dress. **ˋ~-jar** *n* ~-flying bird that resembles a swift. **ˋ~ life,** entertainment, e g cabaret, ~clubs, available in a town late at ~: *the ~ life of London.* **ˋ~-light** *n* light (e g a short, thick candle, or a small electric bulb) kept burning in a bedroom at ~ (esp for a small child or an invalid). **ˋ~-line** *n* line left in a river, lake, etc with baited hooks, to catch fish by ~. **ˋ~-long** *adj* lasting the whole ~. **ˋ~-mare** /-meə(r)/ *n* [C] **(a)** terrible, frightening dream. **(b)** haunting fear; sth dreaded; memory of a horrible experience: *Travelling on those bad mountain roads was a ~mare.* **ˋ~-porter** *n* hotel porter on duty during the ~. **ˋ~ safe** *n* facility or opening like a letter-box in a wall of a bank, so that valuables, money, etc may be deposited after banking hours. **ˋ~ school** *n* one that gives lessons to persons who are unable to attend classes during the day. **ˋ~-shade** *n* [U] name of various wild plants with poisonous berries. **ˋ~ shift,** ⇨ shift[1](2). **ˋ~-shirt** *n* boy's or man's long shirt for sleeping in. **ˋ~-soil** *n* contents of earth-closets and cess-pools, removed during the ~. **ˋ~ stop** *n,* **ˋ~-stop** *vi* (of airliners on long journeys) stop for a ~ at an airport, etc: *These flying-boats ~-stop/make ~ stops at Cairo and Kampala.* **ˋ~-time** *n* time of darkness: *in the ~-time,* by ~. **ˋ~-walker** *n* person who walks the streets at ~. **'~-ˋwatch** *n* (person or group of persons keeping) watch by ~. ***in the ~-watches,*** during the wakeful, restless, or anxious periods of ~. **'~-ˋwatchman** /-mən/ *n* (*pl* -men) man employed to keep watch (e g in a factory) at ~. **ˋ~-work** *n* work that is done, or must be done, by ~. **~·ly** *adj, adv* (taking place, happening, existing) in the ~ or every ~: *~ly performances; a film show twice ~ly; do something ~ly.*

night·in·gale /ˋnɑɪtɪŋgeɪl *US:* -tŋg-/ *n* small, reddish-brown migratory bird that sings sweetly by night as well as by day. ⇨ the illus at bird.

ni·hil·ism /ˋnɑɪhɪl-ɪzm/ *n* [U] teachings of an extreme revolutionary party in Russia (19 c) which considered the existing order of government to deserve destruction; total rejection of current political institutions and religious and moral beliefs. **ni·hil·ist** /-ɪst/ *n* believer in ~. **ni·hil·is·tic** /ˋnɑɪ-hɪˋlɪstɪk/ *adj* relating to ~.

nil /nɪl/ *n* nothing: *The result of the game was 3—0* (read 'three-nil' or 'three-nothing').

Ni·lotic /nɑɪˋlotɪk/ *adj* of the Nile, the Nile region, or its inhabitants.

nimble /ˈnɪmbl/ *adj* **1** quick-moving: *as ~ as a goat.* **2** (of the mind) sharp; quick to understand. **nim·bly** /ˈnɪmblɪ/ *adv* **~·ness** *n*

nim·bus /ˈnɪmbəs/ *n* (*pl* -buses /-bəsɪz/, -bi /-baɪ/) **1** bright disc round or over the head of a saint (in a painting, etc). **2** rain-cloud.

nim·iny-pim·iny /ˈnɪmɪnɪ ˈpɪmɪnɪ/ *adj* affected; mincing; prim.

Nim·rod /ˈnɪmrod/ *n* great hunter. ⇨ Gen 10: 8,9.

nin·com·poop /ˈnɪŋkəmpup/ *n* foolish, weak-minded person.

nine /naɪn/ *n, adj* the number 9, ⇨ App 4. **nine-pence** /ˈnaɪmpəns *US:* -npens/ *n* **nine·penny** /ˈnaɪmpənɪ *US:* -npenɪ/ *adj* ***a ~-days' wonder,*** sth that attracts attention for a few days and is then forgotten. ***dressed up to the ~s,*** (colloq) dressed very elaborately or extravagantly. ***~ times out of ten,*** very often. **~·teen** /ˈnaɪnˈtin/ *n, adj* the number 19. ***(talk) ~teen to the dozen,*** (talk) continually. **~·teenth** /ˈnaɪnˈtinθ/ *n, adj* the next after the 18th; one of 19 equal parts. **~·ti·eth** /ˈnaɪntɪəθ/ *n, adj* the next after the 89th; one of 90 equal parts. **~ty** /ˈnaɪntɪ/ *n, adj* the number 90. ***~ty-~ times out of a hundred,*** almost always. **the ~ties,** between 89 and 100, e g of a person's age, or of the years -90 to -99 of a century (esp the 19th c), or the temperature (in the Fahrenheit scale). **ˈ~·fold** /-fəʊld/ *adj, adv* ~ times as many or much. **ninth** /naɪnθ/ *n, adj* the next after the 8th; one of 9 equal parts.

nine·pins /ˈnaɪnpɪnz/ *n pl* (with *sing v*) **1** game in which a ball is rolled along the floor at nine bottle-shaped pieces of wood. ⇨ tenpins. **2** (*sing*) one of these pins. ***go down like a ninepin,*** fall heavily.

ninny /ˈnɪnɪ/ *n* (*pl*-nies) fool; simpleton.

Niobe /ˈnaɪəbɪ/ *n* (Gk myth) woman who was changed into a stone fountain while weeping for her children who had been killed; woman who weeps and cannot be comforted.

nip[1] /nɪp/ *vt,vi* (-pp-) **1** [VP6A,15A,B] pinch; press hard (e g between finger and thumb, or with the claws, as a crab does, or with the teeth, as a dog or horse might do): *A crab nipped my toe while I was swimming. He nipped his finger in the door,* i e between the door and the door-post. *The gardener was nipping off* (= pinching out) *the side shoots from his chrysanthemums;* (sewing) alter the size slightly: *The dress fits me now that I've nipped in the sides a little,* reduced the width by altering the seams. **2** [VP6A,15A] (of frost, wind, etc) stop the growth of; damage. ***nip sth in the bud,*** stop its development. **3** [VP2A] perform the action of biting or pinching. **4** (colloq) [VP2C] hurry: *nip along. He nipped in* (= got in quickly) *just in front of me. I'll nip on ahead and open the door.* □ *n* [C] **1** sharp pinch or bite: *a cold nip in the air,* a feeling of frost. **2** small drink (esp of) spirits): *a nip of brandy.* **ˈnip·ping** *adj* (of the air or wind) sharp; biting cold. ⇨ nippy(1).

nip·per /ˈnɪpə(r)/ *n* **1** (*pl;* colloq) pincers, forceps or other tool for gripping. **2** crustacean's claw. **3** (GB colloq) small child.

nipple /ˈnɪpl/ *n* **1** part of the breast through which a baby gets its mother's milk; similar small projection on the breast of a human male. Cf *teat* for other mammals. **2** (more usu *teat*) rubber mouth-piece of a baby's feeding bottle. **3** sth shaped like a ~: *greasing ~s,* through which grease is injected.

Nip·pon·ese /ˈnɪpəˈniz/ *adj* of Nippon /ˈnɪpon/ (= Japan).

nippy /ˈnɪpɪ/ *adj* (-ier, -iest) (colloq) (from *nip*[1]) **1** (GB) biting cold. **2** nimble. ***look ~,*** be quick.

nir·vana /nɪəˈvɑnə/ *n* (in Buddhism) state in which individuality becomes extinct by being absorbed into the supreme spirit.

nisi /ˈnaɪsaɪ/ *conj* (Lat, legal) unless. **ˈdecree ˈ~,** decree (of divorce, etc) valid unless cause is shown for rescinding it before the time when it is made absolute.

Nis·sen hut /ˈnɪsn hʌt/ *n* prefabricated semicircular hut of sheets of corrugated iron, erected over a concrete floor.

nit[1] /nɪt/ *n* egg of a louse or other parasitic insect (e g as found in the hair of persons who seldom wash).

nit[2] /nɪt/ *n* = nitwit.

ni·ter /ˈnaɪtər/ ⇨ nitre.

ni·trate /ˈnaɪtreɪt/ *n* salt formed by the chemical reaction of nitric acid with an alkali, esp *potassium ~* and *sodium ~,* used as fertilizers. (Used in *pl* for 'kinds of ~').

nitre (US = **niter**) /ˈnaɪtə(r)/ *n* [U] potassium or sodium nitrate (also called *saltpetre*).

ni·tric /ˈnaɪtrɪk/ *adj* of, containing, nitrogen. **ˈ~ ˈacid, (HNO_3),** clear colourless, powerful acid that eats into and destroys most substances.

ni·tro·chalk /ˈnaɪtrəʊˈtʃɔk/ *n* [U] fertilizer used in spring to encourage growth of grass.

ni·tro·gen /ˈnæɪtrədʒən/ *n* [U] gas (symbol **N**) without colour, taste or smell, forming about four-fifths of the atmosphere.

ni·tro·glycer·ine, -glycerin /ˈnaɪtrəʊˈglɪsəˈrin *US:* -ˈglɪsərɪn/ *n* [U] powerful explosive made by adding glycerine to a mixture of nitric and sulphuric acids.

ni·trous /ˈnaɪtrəs/ *adj* of, like, nitre. **ˈ~ ˈoxide,** gas (**N_2O**) (also called *laughing-gas*) sometimes used by dental surgeons to make a person unconscious while having a tooth or teeth pulled out.

nit·wit /ˈnɪtwɪt/ *n* (colloq) person with very little intelligence. Hence, **~·ted** /ˈnɪtˈwɪtɪd/ *adj* unintelligent.

nix /nɪks/ *n* (sl) nothing.

no /nəʊ/ *adj* **1** not one; not any: *She had no umbrella. The poor boy had no money for books. No words can describe the scene. There was no end to our troubles,* They were endless. ***no end of,*** (colloq) a large number or quantity of; very great: *He spends no end of money on clothes. We had no end of a good time,* a very enjoyable time. (Note that *no* precedes numerals and *other*): *No one man could have done it,* No man could have done it by himself. *No two men think alike. No other man could do the work.* **2** (implying the opposite of the following word): *He's no friend of mine. The task is no easy one. This nightclub is no place for a young and innocent girl. Miss Green is no beauty,* is not at all beautiful. ***It's no go,*** (colloq) can't be done, won't succeed. **3** (in the pattern: *there + to be + no + gerund*): *There's no saying* (= It is impossible to say) *what he'll be doing next. There's no denying* (= We cannot deny) *that....* **4** (in elliptical constructions): *No smoking* (= Smoking is not allowed). *No surrender! It's raining hard and no mistake,* and there can be no doubt about it. **5** (phrases) ***be no good/use,*** useless: *It's no good crying over spilt* *milk.* ***be no wonder (that),*** not surprising (that). ***by `no means,*** ⇨ means[1]. ***in `no time,*** very soon, very quickly. **'no-`ball,** unlawfully delivered ball in cricket. **'no-`go,** (colloq) impossible to do (successfully). **'no-`go area,** (colloq) (usu urban) area barricaded to prevent the police or security force from entering. **`no-man's-land,** (in war) ground between the fronts of two opposing armies. **`no-one, `no one,** *pron* = nobody. □ *adv* **1** (used with comparatives): *We went no farther than* (= only as far as) *the bridge. I hope you're feeling no worse this morning. I have no more money.* **2** (phrases) ***no more... than,*** ⇨ more(5). ***no such,*** ⇨ such. **3** ***whether or no,*** = whether or not: *Whether or no you like it, you've got to do it.* □ *particle* **1** (opposite of 'Yes'): *Is it Monday today? No, it isn't. Isn't it Monday today? No, it isn't. Aren't you busy? No, I'm not.* **2** (used with *not* or *nor* to emphasize a negative): *I've not found better hotels anywhere; no, not in Switzerland. One man couldn't lift it; no, nor half a dozen.* **3** (as a *n* substitute): *The noes* /nəʊz/ *have it,* Those voting 'no' are in the majority.

Noah's ark /'nəʊəz `ɑk/ *n* model of the ark in which Noah and his family were saved from the Flood, with small animal and human figures. ⇨ Gen 5:9.

nob[1] /nob/ *n* (sl) head.

nob[2] /nob/ *n* (sl) member of the upper classes; person of high rank.

nobble /`nobl/ *vt* (GB sl) [VP6A] **1** tamper with (a race-horse) to lessen its chance of winning. **2** (colloq) get the attention of (in order to gain an advantage, etc); get sth dishonestly or by devious means.

Nobel Prize /nəʊ'bel `prɑɪz/ *n* any of the prizes awarded each year by the Nobel Foundation for outstanding achievements in literature, science and the promotion of world peace (after A B Nobel /nəʊ`bel/, 1833—1896, Swedish inventor of dynamite who established the awards).

no·bil·ity /nəʊ`bɪlətɪ/ *n* [U] **1** quality of being noble; noble character, mind, birth, rank. **2** (usu with *def art*) the nobles as a class: *a member of the ~; marry into the ~.*

noble /`nəʊbl/ *adj* **1** having, showing, high character and qualities: *a ~ leader; ~ sentiments; a ~ mind.* Hence, **'~ `minded** /`mɑɪndɪd/ *adj* **'~-`minded·ness** *n* **2** of high rank, title or birth: *a man of ~ rank/birth.* **3** splendid; that excites admiration: *a building planned on a ~ scale; a ~ horse; ~ metals,* e g gold, silver, platinum, that do not easily tarnish in air or water. □ *n* **1** person of ~ birth. **`~·man** /-mən/ *n* (*pl* -men) (GB) peer; person of parallel rank in other countries. **2** obsolete English gold coin. **nobly** /`nəʊblɪ/ *adv* in a ~ manner; splendidly.

no·blesse /nəʊ`bles/ *n* (F) class of nobles. **'~ o`blige** /ə`bliʒ/ (prov) privilege entails responsibility.

no·body /`nəʊbədɪ/ *pron* (*pl* -dies) **1** not anybody; no person: *We saw ~ we knew. He said he would marry me or ~. N~ could find their luggage* (colloq for *his or her luggage*). *N~ else* (= No other person) *offered to help.* **2** (used in the *sing* with the *indef art,* and in the *pl*) unimportant or unimpressive person: *Don't marry a ~ like James.*

noc·tam·bu·list /nok`tæmbjʊlɪst/ *n* sleepwalker.

noc·tur·nal /nok`tɜnl/ *adj* of, in or done, active, or happening in, the night: *a man of ~ habits; ~ birds,* e g owls.

noc·turne /`noktɜn/ *n* [C] **1** (art) nightscene. **2** soft, dreamy piece of music.

nod /nod/ *vi,vt* (-dd-) **1** [VP2A,3A,4A] bow (the head) slightly and quickly as a sign of agreement or as a familiar greeting: *He nodded to me as he passed. He nodded to show that he understood.* ***have a nodding acquaintance with,*** ⇨ acquaintance. **2** [VP2A,2C] let the head fall forward when sleepy or falling asleep; make a mistake as if asleep or half asleep: *She sat nodding by the fire. She often nods off* (= falls asleep) *during the afternoon. The teacher caught one of her pupils nodding,* falling asleep, or so sleepy as to make mistakes. *Homer sometimes nods,* (prov) Even the greatest may make a small mistake. **3** [VP6A,12A,13A] indicate by nodding: *He nodded approval. He nodded me a welcome/nodded a welcome to Mary.* □ *n* **1** nodding of the head: *He gave me a nod as he passed.* **2** ***the Land of Nod,*** sleep. **3** ***on the ~,*** (US sl) on credit.

noddle /`nodl/ *n* (colloq) head.

node /nəʊd/ *n* [C] point on the stem of a plant where a leaf or bud grows out.

nod·ule /`nodjul *US:* `nodʒul/ *n* small rounded lump; small knob or swelling. **nod·u·lar** /-lə(r)/, **nod·u·lat·ed** /-leɪtɪd/ *adj* having ~s.

Noel /nəʊ`el/ *n* Christmas.

nog·gin /`nogɪn/ *n* small measure, usu ¼ pint, of liquor.

no·how /`nəʊhɑʊ/ *adv* (colloq) **1** in no way; not at all. **2** out of order; out of sorts: *feel/look ~.*

noise /nɔɪz/ *n* [C,U] loud and unpleasant sound, esp when confused and undesired: *the ~ of jet aircraft; Don't make so much ~/such a loud ~! What's that ~? What are those strange ~s? It made a ~ like a train.* ***make a ~ (about sth),*** talk or complain in order to get attention. ***make a ~ in the world,*** become famous, be much talked about. **a big ~,** (sl) important person. □ *vt* ***~ sth abroad,*** make public: *It was ~d abroad that he had been arrested.* **~·less** *adj* making little or no ~: *with ~less footsteps.* **~·less·ly** *adv* **~·less·ness** *n*

noi·some /`nɔɪsəm/ *adj* offensive; (esp, of smell) disgusting.

noisy /`nɔɪzɪ/ *adj* (-ier, -iest) **1** making, accompanied by, much noise: *~ children; ~ games.* **2** full of noise: *a ~ classroom.* **nois·ily** /-əlɪ/ *adv* **noisi·ness** *n*

no·mad /`nəʊmæd/ *n* member of a tribe that wanders from place to place, with no fixed home. **~ic** /nəʊ`mædɪk/ *adj* of ~s: *a ~ic society.*

nom de plume /'nom də `plum/ *n* (*pl* noms de plume) (F) pen-name.

no·men·cla·ture /`nəʊmənkleɪtʃə(r)/ *n* [C] (formal) system of naming: *botanical ~; the ~ of chemistry.*

nom·inal /`nomɪnl/ *adj* **1** existing, etc, in name or word only, not in fact: *the ~ ruler of the country; the ~ value of the shares.* **2** inconsiderable: *a ~ sum; a ~ rent,* one very much below the actual value of the property. **3** (gram) of a noun or nouns. **4** of, bearing, a name: *a ~ list; ~ shares.* **~ly** /-nlɪ/ *adv*

nomi·nate /`nomɪneɪt/ *vt* [VP6A,14,23] **1** ***~ sb (for),*** put forward for election to a position: *~ a man for the Presidency; ~ Mr X for Mayor.* **2** ***~ sb (to),*** appoint to office: *a committee of five ~d* *members and eight elected members.* **nomi·nee** /ˌnɒmɪˈni/ *n* person who is ~d for an office or appointment.

nomi·na·tion /ˌnɒmɪˈneɪʃn/ *n* **1** [U] nominating; [C] instance of this: *How many ~s have there been* (= How many persons have been nominated) *so far?* **2** [U] right of nominating sb for an office or position.

nomi·na·tive /ˈnɒmnətɪv/ *adj, n* (of the) form of a word when it is the grammatical subject; *the ~ case,* e g the pronoun *we.*

nomi·nee /ˌnɒmɪˈni/ *n* ⇨ nominate.

non- /ˌnɒn/ *pref* who or which is not, does not, etc:

non-aˈlignment *n* principle or practice of not joining either of the two large groups of world powers.

ˌnon-agˈgression *n* not attacking; not starting hostilities: *a ˌnon-agˈgression pact.*

ˌnon-ˈcombatant *n* person (esp in the armed forces, e g a surgeon or chaplain) who does not take part in the fighting.

ˌnon-comˈmissioned *adj* (esp of army officers such as sergeants and corporals) not holding commissions(4) ⇨ App 9.

ˌnon-comˈmittal *adj* not committing oneself to a definite course or to either side (in a dispute, etc): *give a non-committal answer.*

ˌnon-comˈpliance *n* refusal to comply (with an order, etc).

ˌnon-conˈductor *n* substance that does not conduct heat or electric current.

ˌnon-conˈformist *n* person, esp a Protestant, who does not conform to the ritual, etc, of an established Church; (in England) member of a sect that has separated from the Church of England. **ˌnon-conˈformity** *n* (beliefs and practices of) nonconformists as a body; failure to conform.

ˌnon-conˈtentious *adj* not likely to cause contention.

ˌnon-deˈlivery *n* failure to deliver (goods).

ˌnon-esˈsential *adj* that is not essential.

ˌnon-eˈvent *n* planned event which turns out to be unworthy of what it was declared to be.

ˌnon-ˈfiction *n* [U] prose books other than novels, stories, plays which deal with fictitious events and persons.

ˌnon-ˈflammable *adj* (in official use, contrary to *inflammable*) having no tendency to burst into flames.

ˌnon-ˌinterˈference, ˌnon-ˌinterˈvention *nn* principle or practice, esp in international affairs, of keeping out of other people's disputes.

ˌnon-ˈmember *n* person who is not a member (of a club, etc). **ˌnon-ˈmembership** *n*

ˌnon-ˈmoral *adj* that cannot be considered or judged as either moral or immoral.

ˌnon-obˈservance *n* failure to observe (a rule, etc).

ˌnon-ˈpayment *n* failure or neglect to pay (a debt, etc).

ˌnon-ˈresident *adj* who does not reside in: *a non-resident priest,* not living where he performs his duties. □ *n* person not staying at a hotel, etc: *Meals served to non-residents.*

ˌnon-ˈskid *adj* (of tyres) designed to prevent or reduce the risk of skidding.

ˌnon-ˈsmoker *n* person who does not smoke tobacco; place, e g a train compartment, where smoking is forbidden.

ˌnon-ˈstarter *n* horse which, although entered for a race, does not run; (fig) person who has no chance of success in sth he undertakes to do.

ˌnon-ˈstick *adj* (e g of a pan) made so that food, etc will not stick to its surface.

ˌnon-ˈstop *adj, adv* without a stop: *a non-stop train from London to Brighton; fly non-stop from New York to Paris.*

ˌnon-ˈU *adj* ⇨ App 2.

ˌnon-ˈunion *adj* not belonging to a trade union; not observing trade union rules: *non-union labour.*

ˌnon-ˈviolence *n* policy of rejecting violent means (but using peaceful protest, etc) to gain a political or social objective.

non·age /ˈnəʊnɪdʒ/ *n* [U] state of being under age, a minor.

nona·gen·arian /ˌnɒnəgəˈneərɪən/ *n, adj* (person who is) between 89 and 100 years old.

nonce /nɒns/ *n* (old use, or liter; only in) ***for the ~,*** for the present time only. **ˈ~-word** *n* word coined for one occasion.

non·cha·lant /ˈnɒnʃələnt/ *adj* not having, not showing, interest or enthusiasm. **~·ly** *adv* **non·cha·lance** /-ləns/ *n* [U] indifference; unconcern.

non com·pos men·tis /ˌnɒn ˌkɒmpəs ˈmentɪs/ (Lat) (legal) not legally responsible because not of sound mind.

non·de·script /ˈnɒndɪskrɪpt/ *n, adj* (person or thing) not easily classed, not having a definite character.

none /nʌn/ *pron* **1** not any, not one: *I wanted some string but there was ~ in the house. N~ of this money is mine. 'Is there any coal left?' 'No, ~ at all.' There are faults from which ~ of us* (= not one of us, or not any of us) *is/are free. N~ of them has/have come back yet. He is aware, ~ better than he* (i e no one is better aware than he), *that....* **~ *the less,*** nevertheless. **~ *but,*** only: *They chose none but the best.* **~ *other than*:** *The new arrival was ~ other than the President* (emph for *the President himself*). **2** (in constructions equal to an imperative): *N~ of that!* Stop that! *N~ of your impudence!* Don't be impudent! **3** (separated from its *n,* in liter or rhet style): *They looked down on the plain, but village there was ~. Sounds there were ~* (= There were no sounds) *except the murmur of the bees.* □ *adv* by no means; in no degree; not at all: *I hope you're ~ the worse for that fall from your horse. I'm afraid I'm ~ the wiser for your explanation. The salary they pay me is ~ too high.* ***There are ~ so deaf as those who won't hear,*** (prov) who refuse to hear.

non·en·tity /nɒnˈentətɪ/ *n* (*pl* -ties) [C] **1** unimportant person. **2** thing that does not really exist or that exists only in the imagination.

none·such, non·such /ˈnʌnsʌtʃ, ˈnɒn-/ *n* person or thing without equal.

non·pareil /ˈnɒn pəˈreɪl *US:* -ˈrel/ *adj, n* (formal) unique or unrivalled (person or thing).

non·plus /nɒnˈplʌs/ *vt* (-ss-, US -s-) [VP6A] (usu passive) surprise or puzzle (sb) so much that he does not know what to do or say: *I was completely ~sed when she said 'No' to my proposal of marriage.*

non·sense /ˈnɒnsns *US:* -sens/ *n* (with or without the *indef art* but not usu *pl*) meaningless words; foolish talk, ideas, behaviour: *N~! I don't believe a word of it. I want no more of your ~. What a ~!*

non·sen·si·cal /nɒnˈsensɪkl/ *adj* not making

sense: *nonsensical remarks.*

non-such ⇨ nonesuch.

non sequi·tur /'non `sekwɪtə(r)/ *n* (Lat) (logic) conclusion which does not follow from the premises; paradoxical result.

noodle[1] /`nudl/ *n* fool.

noodle[2] /`nudl/ *n* (usu *pl*) type of paste of flour and water or flour and eggs prepared in long, narrow strips and used in soups, with a sauce, etc.

nook /nʊk/ *n* out-of-the-way place; inside corner: *search every ~ and cranny,* everywhere.

noon /nun/ *n* midday; 12 o'clock in the middle of the day; *at ~; the ~ gun.* **`~·day** /-deɪ/, **`~·tide** /-taɪd/ *nn* = ~.

no-one, no one /`nəʊ wʌn/ *pron* = nobody(1).

noose /nus/ *n* loop of rope (with a running knot) that becomes tighter when the rope is pulled: *the hangman's ~.* ***put one's head in the ~,*** (fig) allow oneself to be caught. □ *vt* catch with a ~; make a ~ on a cord, rope, etc.

nope /nəʊp/ *int* (sl) No!

nor /nɔ(r)/ *conj* **1** (after *neither* or *not*) and not: *I have neither time nor money for nightclubs. Not a flower nor even a blade of grass will grow in this desert.* **2** and... not: *He can't do it; nor can I, nor can you, nor can anybody. Nor was this all,* And this was not all. *Nor will I* (= And I will not) *deny that....*

nor'- /'nɔ(r)/ *pref* ⇨ north.

Nor·dic /`nɔdɪk/ *n, adj* (member) of the race or type marked by tall stature, blond hair, and blue eyes, esp in Scandinavia.

Nor·folk /`nɔfək/ *n* English county. **~ jacket,** man's loose-fitting jacket with a waistband.

norm /nɔm/ *n* **1** standard; pattern; type (as representative of a group when judging other examples). **2** (in some industries, etc) amount of work required or expected in a working day: *set the workers a ~; fulfil one's ~.*

nor·mal /`nɔml/ *adj* in agreement with what is representative, usual, or regular: *the ~ temperature of the human body.* **`~ school,** (in some countries, not in GB) one for the training of teachers (usu in elementary grades). □ *n* (*sing* only) usual state, level, etc. ***above/below ~,*** **~ly** /`nɔmḷɪ/ *adv* **~·ity** /nɔ`mæləti/, **~cy** /`nɔmlsɪ/ *nn* [U] the state of being ~. **~·ize** /`nɔmḷaɪz/ *vt* make ~. **~·iz·ation** /'nɔmḷaɪ`zeɪʃn *US:* -lɪ`z-/ *n*

Nor·man /`nɔmən/ *n* inhabitant or native of Normandy; descendant of the mixed Scandinavian and Frankish race established there in the 9th c. □ *adj* of the ~s, esp those who conquered England in the 11th c: *the ~ Conquest; ~ architecture.*

nor·ma·tive /`nɔmətɪv/ *adj* setting a standard: *a ~, prescriptive grammar of the English language.*

Norse /nɔs/ *n* the Norwegian language. □ *adj* of Norway.

north /nɔθ/ *n* **1** one of the four cardinal points of the compass, lying to the left of a person facing the sunrise; ⇨ the illus at compass; part of any country lying farther in this direction than other parts: *the ~ of England; cold winds from the ~.* **2** (attrib) situated in, living in, pertaining to, coming from, the ~: *the N~ Star,* the pole-star; *the ~ pole; N~ Britain,* Scotland; *N~ Wales; a ~ wind; a ~ light,* from the ~, as usu desired by artists in studios; *the `N~ Country,* ~ part of England or Great Britain; *a 'N~ `countryman* /-mən/ a native of the ~ of England. □ *adv* to or towards the ~: *sailing ~.* **'~·`east, '~·`west** (abbr NE, NW) *nn, advv* (sometimes, esp naut, **nor'-east** /'nɔr `ist/, **nor'-west** /'nɔ `west/) (regions) midway between ~ and east, ~ and west. **the 'N~-west `Passage,** the sea route from the Atlantic to the Pacific along the ~ coast of Canada and Alaska. **'~-~·`east, '~-~·`west** (abbr NNE, NNW) *nn, adjj, advv* (sometimes, esp naut, **nor'-nor'-east** /'nɔ nɔr `ist/, **nor'-nor'-west** /'nɔ nɔ `west/) (regions) midway between ~ and ~east, ~west. **'~·`easter** *n* strong wind, storm, or gale, from the ~east. **'~-`easter·ly** *adj* (of wind) blowing from the ~east; (of direction) towards the ~ east. **'~·`wester** *n* strong wind from the ~west. **'~·`wester·ly** *adj* (of wind) from the ~west; (of direction) towards the ~west. **'~·`eastern** /-`istən/ *adj* of, from, situated in, the ~east. **'~·`western** /-`westən/ *adj* of, from, situated in the ~west. **`N~·man** /-mən/ *n* (*pl* -men) Norseman or Viking; native of Scandinavia in olden times. **~·wards** /`nɔθwədz/ *adv* towards the ~.

north·er·ly /`nɔðəlɪ/ *adj, adv* (of winds) from the north; towards the north; in or to the north.

north·ern /`nɔðən/ *adj* in or of the north: *the ~ hemisphere.* **the ~ lights,** streamers and bands of light appearing in the sky; the aurora borealis. **~er** /`nɔðənə(r)/ *n* person born in or living in the ~ regions of a country. **`~·most** /-məʊst/ *adj* lying farthest north.

Nor·we·gian /nɔ`widʒən/ *n, adj* (native, language) of Norway.

nose[1] /nəʊz/ *n* **1** part of the face above the mouth, through which breath passes, and serving as the organ of smell; ⇨ the illus at head; *hit a man on the ~* (note *def art*). ***bite/snap sb's ~*** (*head* is more usu) ***off,*** answer him sharply and angrily. ***count/tell ~s,*** (*heads* is more usu) count the number of persons (esp supporters, when voting to decide sth). ***cut off one's ~ to spite one's face,*** damage one's own interests in a fit of bad temper. ***follow one's ~,*** go straight forward; be guided by instinct. ***keep a person's ~ to the grindstone,*** make him work hard without rest. ***lead sb by the ~,*** ⇨ lead[3](2). ***look down one's ~ at sb,*** treat haughtily. ***pay through the ~,*** pay an excessive price. ***poke/stick one's ~ into,*** (sb else's business), intrude; ask questions without being asked to do so. ***put sb's ~ out of joint,*** ⇨ joint[1](1). ***turn one's ~ up at,*** show disdain for. ***as plain as the ~ on one's face,*** obvious; easily seen. ***(right) under one's very ~,*** (a) directly in front of one. (b) in one's presence, and regardless of one's disapproval. **2** sense of smell: *a dog with a good ~;* (fig) *a reporter with a ~ for news/scandal/a story.* **3** sth like a ~ in shape or position, e g the open end of a pipe, bellows or retort; the most forward part of the fuselage of an aircraft. **4** (compounds) **`~·bag** *n* bag for food (oats, etc) fastened on a horse's head. **`~·bleed** *n* bleeding from the ~. **`~·cone** *n* most forward section of a rocket or guided missile, usu separable. ⇨ the illus at capsule. **`~·dive** *n* sharp vertical descent made by an aircraft. □ *vi* (of an aircraft) come down steeply with the ~ pointing to earth. **`~-flute** *n* musical instrument blown with the ~, as used in some Asian countries. **`~·gay** *n* bunch of cut (esp sweet-scented) flowers. **`~·ring** *n* ring fixed in the ~ of a bull, etc, for leading it. **`~-wheel,** the front landing-wheel under the fuselage of an aircraft. **-nosed** *suff* (in compounds) having the kind of ~ indicated: *red-~d; long-~d.*

nose[2] /nəʊz/ *vt,vi* **1** [VP15A] go forward carefully, push (one's way): *The ship ~d its way slowly through the ice.* **2** [VP15B] ***~ sth out,*** discover by smelling: *The dog ~d out a rat. That man will ~ out a scandal anywhere.* **3** [VP2C,3A] ***~ about (for sth),*** smell, (fig) pry or search for. ***~ into sth,*** pry into: *a man who is always nosing into other people's affairs.*

nosey, nosy /ˈnəʊzɪ/ *adj* (-ier, -iest), *n* (sl) inquisitive (person). ˈ~ **parker** *n* (colloq) inquisitive person.

nosh /noʃ/ *n* [U] (sl) food. ˈ~**-up** *n* a good meal. □ *vi* (colloq) eat.

nos·tal·gia /noˈstældʒə/ *n* [U] home-sickness; wistful longing for sth one has known in the past. **nos·tal·gic** /noˈstældʒɪk/ *adj* of, feeling or causing, ~. **nos·tal·gi·cally** /-klɪ/ *adv*

nos·tril /ˈnostrɪl/ *n* either of the two external openings into the nose. ⇨ the illus at **head**.

nos·trum /ˈnostrəm/ *n* [C] (usu contemptuous) medicine, etc, prepared by the person who recommends it; quack remedy; scheme for political or social reform (called a ~ by its opponents).

not /not/ *adv* **1** (used to make a finite *v* negative; in modern English only with the 24 anom finites listed in the Introduction under 'Anomalous Verbs'; often contracted to **-n't** /-nt/, as in *hasn't* /ˈhæznt/, *needn't* /ˈnidnt/.) **2** (used with non-finite *vv*): *He warned me not to be late. You were wrong in not making a protest.* **3** (used after certain *vv*, esp *think, suppose, believe, expect, fear, fancy, trust, hope, seem, appear,* and the phrase *be afraid* equivalent to a *that*-clause): *'Can you come next week?'—'I'm afraid not.'* I'm afraid that I cannot come. *'Will it rain this afternoon?'—'I hope not'.* **4** (used elliptically, in phrases.) ***as likely as not,*** probably: *He'll be at home now, as likely as not.* ***as soon as not,*** ⇨ **soon(5)**. ***not at all,*** /ˈnot əˈtɔl/ used as a polite response to thanks, enquiries after sb's health, etc: *'Thank you very much'. 'Are you tired?'—'Not at all.'* Not in the least. ***not that,*** it is not suggested that: *If he ever said so—not that I ever heard him say so—he told a lie.* ***not but what,*** nevertheless; although: *I can't do it; not but what a younger man might be able to do it.* **5** (in understatements): *not a few,* = many; *not seldom,* = often; *not without reason,* = with good reason; *not once or twice,* = often; *not half,* (sl) exceedingly; *in the not-so-distant* (= recent) *past.*

nota bene /ˈnəʊtə ˈbeneɪ/ *v imper* (Lat) (abbr **N B, n b** /ˈen ˈbi/) observe carefully.

no·table /ˈnəʊtəbl/ *adj* deserving to be noticed; remarkable: *~ events/speakers/artists.* □ *n* eminent person. **no·tably** /ˈnəʊtəblɪ/ *adv* **nota·bil·ity** /ˈnəʊtəˈbɪlətɪ/ *n* (*pl* -**ties**) **1** [U] the condition of being ~. **2** [C] ~ person.

no·tary /ˈnəʊtərɪ/ *n* (*pl* -**ries**) (often ˈ~ ˈ**public**) official with authority to perform certain kinds of legal transactions, esp to record that he has witnessed the signing of legal documents.

no·ta·tion /nəʊˈteɪʃn/ *n* **1** [C] system of signs or symbols representing numbers, amounts, musical notes, etc. **2** [U] representing of numbers, etc by such signs or symbols.

notch /notʃ/ *n* V-shaped cut (*in* or *on* sth); (US) narrow pass through mountains; defile[2]. □ *vt* **1** [VP6A] make or cut a ~ or ~es in or on, e g a stick, as a way of keeping count. **2** [VP15B] ***~ up,*** (colloq) achieve; score: *~ up a new record.*

note[1] /nəʊt/ *n* **1** short record (of facts, etc) made to help the memory: *He spoke for an hour without a ~/without ~s.* ˈ~**·book** *n* book in which to write ~s. **2** short letter: *a ~ of thanks; an exchange of ~s between two governments.* ˈ~**-paper** *n* [U] paper for (esp private) correspondence. **3** short comment on or explanation of a word or passage in a book, etc: *a new edition of 'Hamlet', with copious ~s.* ⇨ *footnote* at **foot**[1]**(8)**. **4** observation (not necessarily written): *He was comparing ~s with a friend,* exchanging views, comparing experiences, etc. **5** written or printed promise to pay money: *ˈbank~s; a £5 ~; a promissory ~.* ˈ~**-case** *n* wallet**(1)**. **6** single sound of a certain pitch and duration: *the blackbird's merry ~*; sign used to represent such a sound in manuscript or printed music ⇨ the illus at **notation**; any one of the keys of a piano, organ, etc. ***sound a ~ of warning (against sth),*** warn against sth. ***strike the right ~,*** (fig) speak in such a way that one wins the approval or sympathy of one's listeners. ***strike/sound a false ~,*** (fig) do or say sth that causes one to lose sympathy or approval. **7** quality (esp of voice) indicating the nature of sth (usu *sing* with the *indef art*): *There was a ~ of self-satisfaction in his speech.* **8** sign or mark used in writing and printing: *a ~ of excla-*

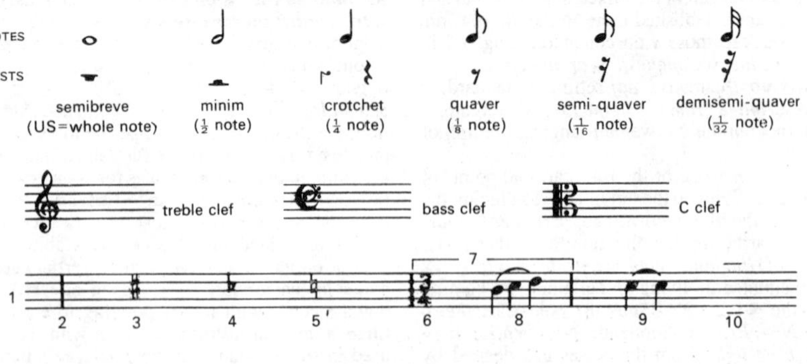

musical notation

mation (!) or interrogation (?). **9** [U] distinction; importance: *a family of* ~. **10** [U] notice; attention: *worthy of* ~. *Take* ~ *of what he says,* pay attention to it.

note[2] /nəʊt/ *vt* **1** [VP6A,8,9,10] notice; pay attention to: *Please* ~ *my words.* *N*~ *how to do it/how I did it. She* ~*d that his hands were dirty.* **2** [VP6A,15B] ***~ sth down,*** make a ~ of; write down in order to remember: *The policeman* ~*d down every word I said.* **noted** *adj* celebrated (*for, as*): *a town* ~*d for its pottery/*~*d as a health resort.* **ˈ~·worthy** *adj* deserving to be ~d; remarkable.

noth·ing /ˈnʌθɪŋ/ *n* **1** (with *adj, inf,* etc, following) not anything: *There's* ~ *interesting in the newspaper. He's had* ~ *to eat yet. N*~ *(that) I could say had any influence on her. N*~ *ever pleases her. He has* ~ *in him,* has no good qualities, etc. *He's five foot* ~, exactly five foot tall. *There's little or* ~ *wrong with him,* very little wrong. *There's* ~ *like leather* (= N~ is as good as leather) *for shoes.* **2** (phrases) ***be ~ to,*** **(a)** be a matter of indifference to: *She's* ~ *to him,* He is indifferent to, uninterested in, her. **(b)** be as ~ if compared: *My losses are* ~ *to yours.* ***come to ~,*** fail; be without result. ***go for ~,*** be without reward, result, value: *Six months' hard work all gone for* ~. ***have ~ to do with,*** **(a)** avoid; have no dealings with: *I advise you to have* ~ *to do with that man.* **(b)** not to be the business or concern of: *This has* ~ *to do with you.* ***make ~ of,*** be unable to understand. ***mean ~ to,*** **(a)** have no meaning for: *These technical words mean* ~ *to me.* **(b)** be sth or sb that sb has no concern or interest in: *He used to like Jane but she means* ~ *to him now.* ***to say ~ of,*** not to mention: *He had his wife and seven children with him in the car, to say* ~ *of* (= as well as) *two dogs, a cat and a parrot.* ***think ~ of,*** consider as ordinary, usual or unremarkable: *He thinks* ~ *of a twenty-mile walk/of asking me to lend him £20.* ***think ~ ˈof it,*** friendly reply to sb who offers thanks, an apology, etc: *'You didn't mind my using your typewriter?'—'Of course not! Think* ~ *of it!* ***for ~,*** **(a)** free; without payment. **(b)** without a reward or result; to no purpose: *It was not for* ~ *that he spent three years studying the subject.* ***next to ~,*** ⇨ next. ***~ but,*** merely: *N*~ *but doubts can prevent you from succeeding;* only: *N*~ *but a miracle can save him.* ***There's ~ ˈfor it but to…,*** The only thing we can do is to…. ***N~ doing!*** (colloq) expression used to indicate refusal of a request, etc. □ *adv* not at all; in no way: *The house is* ~ *near as large as I expected. His new book is* ~ *like as good as his earlier books.* **~·ness** *n* [U] being ~; the state of non-existence: *pass into* ~*ness.*

no·tice /ˈnəʊtɪs/ *n* **1** [C] (written or printed) news of sth about to happen or sth that has happened: *put up a* ~; ~*s of births, deaths and marriages in the newspapers; church* ~*s,* of church activities, etc, often put up on a church door. **ˈ~-board** *n* one provided for ~s to be affixed to. **2** [U] warning, intimation (of what will happen): *give a member of staff a month's* ~, tell him that he must leave one's employment at the end of one month; (of a tenant) *receive two months'* ~ *to quit,* to vacate a house, etc; *give one's employer* ~ *that one intends to leave. The cook left without* ~, without giving any warning. ***(do sth) at short ~,*** with little warning, little time for preparation, etc. **3** [U] attention. ***be beneath one's ~,*** be sth one should ignore: *Their insults should be beneath your* ~. ***bring sth to sb's ~,*** call sb's attention to sth. ***come to sb's ~,*** have one's attention called to sth: *It has come to my* ~ *that…,* I have learnt that…. ***sit up and take ~,*** (of sb who is ill, etc) show signs of recovery from illness. ***make sb sit up and take ~,*** make sb keenly aware of events: *This new process should make our competitors sit up and take* ~. ***take no ~ (of sth),*** pay no attention to sth: *Take no* ~ *of what they're saying about you.* **4** [C] short particulars of a new book, play, etc in a periodical. □ *vt,vi* **1** [VP6A,8,9,10, 18,19,2A] take ~ (of); observe: *I didn't* ~ *you. I* ~*d that he left early. I wasn't noticing. Did you* ~ *him pause? Did you* ~ *his hand shaking? He was too proud to* ~ *me.* **2** [VP6A] say or write sth about (a book, play, etc). **~·able** /-əbl/ *adj* easily seen or ~d. **~·ably** /-əblɪ/ *adv*

no·ti·fi·able /ˈnəʊtɪˈfaɪəbl/ *adj* that must be notified (esp of certain diseases that must be notified to public health authorities).

no·tify /ˈnəʊtɪfaɪ/ *vt* (*pt,pp* -fied) [VP6A,14,11] ***~ sb of sth/that, ~ sth to sb,*** give notice of; report: ~ *the police of a loss;* ~ *a loss to the police;* ~ *a birth;* ~ *the authorities that….* **no·ti·fi·ca·tion** /ˌnəʊtɪfɪˈkeɪʃn/ *n* [U] ~ing; [C] instance of this (e g to the authorities, of births, deaths, cases of infectious disease).

no·tion /ˈnəʊʃn/ *n* [C] **1** idea; opinion: *I have no* ~ *of what he means. Your head is full of silly* ~*s. He has a* ~ *that I'm cheating him.* **2** (*pl*) (US) small miscellaneous goods. ⇨ novelty(3). **~al** /-nl/ *adj* **1** (of knowledge, etc) speculative; not based on experiment or demonstration. **2** nominal; token.

no·tori·ous /nəʊˈtɔrɪəs/ *adj* widely known (esp for sth bad): *a* ~ *criminal;* ~ *for his goings-on;* ~ *as a rake.* **~·ly** *adv* **no·tor·iety** /ˌnəʊtəˈraɪətɪ/ *n* [U] state of being ~.

not·with·stand·ing /ˌnɒtwɪðˈstændɪŋ/ *prep* in spite of. □ *adv* nevertheless; all the same. □ *conj* although.

nou·gat /ˈnugɑ *US:* ˈnugət/ *n* sort of hard sweet made of sugar, nuts, etc.

nought /nɔt/ *n* nothing; the figure 0: *point* ~ *one,* i e ·01. ***bring sb/sth to ~,*** ruin; baffle. ***come to ~,*** be ruined; fail. ***set sb at ~,*** defy. **~s and crosses,** game played by writing ~s (zero signs) and crosses on lines of vertical and horizontal squares.

noun /naʊn/ *n* (gram) word (not a *pron*) which can function as the subject or object of a *v*, or the object of a *prep;* word which is marked *n* in this dictionary.

nour·ish /ˈnʌrɪʃ *US:* ˈnɜ-/ *vt* [VP6A] **1** keep (sb) alive and well with food; make well and strong; improve (land) with manure, etc: ~*ing food;* ~ *the soil.* **2** have or encourage (feelings): ~ *feelings of hatred;* ~ *hope in one's heart.* **~·ment** *n* [U] food.

nous /naʊs/ *n* [U] (Gk) **1** (phil) divine reason. **2** (GB colloq) common sense; gumption.

nou·veau riche /ˈnuvəʊ ˈriʃ/ *n* (usu in *pl* **nouveaux riches**, pronunciation unchanged) (F) person who has recently become rich, esp one who is ostentatious.

nova /ˈnəʊvə/ *n* (*pl* -vas, -vae /-vɪ/) (astron) star that suddenly increases its brilliance for a variable period.

novel[1] /ˋnovl/ *adj* strange; of a kind not previously known: ~ *ideas.*

novel[2] /ˋnovl/ *n* story in prose, long enough to fill one or more volumes, about either imaginary or historical people: *the ~s of Dickens.* **ˈ~ˋette** /-ˋet/ *n* short ~. **ˋ~·ist** /-ɪst/ *n* writer of ~s.

nov·elty /ˋnovltɪ/ *n* (*pl* **-ties**) **1** [U] newness; strangeness; quality of being novel: *The ~ of his surroundings soon wore off,* He become accustomed to them. **2** [C] previously unknown thing, idea, etc; sth strange or unfamiliar. **3** (*pl*) miscellaneous manufactured goods of low cost, e g toys, small ornaments.

No·vem·ber /nəʊˋvembə(r)/ *n* the eleventh month of the year, with thirty days.

nov·ice /ˋnovɪs/ *n* person who is still learning and who is without experience, esp a person who is to become a monk or a nun. **no·vi·ci·ate, no·vi·ti·ate** /nəʊˋvɪʃɪət/ *nn* novice; period of being a ~.

now /nɑʊ/ *adv* **1** at the present time; in the present circumstances: *Where are you now living/living now? Now is the best time to visit Devon. I cannot now* (i e in the circumstances, after what has happened, etc) *ever believe you again.* **2** (used after a *prep*): *He will be in London by now. Up to/till/until now we have been lucky. From now onwards I shall be stricter.* **3** (phrases) ***(every) now and then/again,*** occasionally; from time to time: *We go to the opera now and then.* ***now... now; now... then,*** at one time, at another time: *What mixed weather, now fine, now showery!* **4** at once; immediately: *Do it now. Now or never!* ***just now,*** ⇨ just[2](6). **5** (used without reference to time, to indicate the mood of the speaker, to explain, warn, comfort, etc): *Now what happened was this* (explanatory). *Now stop quarrelling and listen to me* (entreaty or reproof). *No nonsense, now!* (warning). ***now, now; now then,*** (used at the beginning of a sentence, often as a protest or warning, or simply to call attention): *Now then, what mischief are you up to?* □ *conj* as a consequence of the fact (that): *Now* (*that*) *you mention it, I do remember. Now* (*that*) *you're grown up, you must stop this childish behaviour.*

now·adays /ˋnɑʊədeɪz/ *adj* at the present time (and often used in contrasts between present day manners, customs, etc, and those of past times): *N~ children don't expect to have to amuse themselves.*

no·where /ˋnəʊweə(r) *US:* -hweər/ *adv* not anywhere: *The boy was ~ to be found. Such methods will get you ~,* will not produce results. *£50 is ~ near enough,* not nearly enough. ***be/come in ~,*** fail to win or get a place (in a competition).

no·wise /ˋnəʊwɑɪz/ *adv* (old use) not at all; in no way.

noxious /ˋnokʃəs/ *adj* harmful: ~ *gases.* **~·ly** *adv* **~·ness** *n*

nozzle /ˋnozl/ *n* metal end of a hose or bellows, through which a stream of liquid or air is directed. ⇨ the illus at hose-pipe.

nuance /ˋnjuəns *US:* nuˋæns/ *n* [C] delicate difference in or of shade of meaning, opinion, colour, etc.

nub /nʌb/ *n* **1** small lump or knob (e g of coal). **2** (colloq, fig) gist or point (of a story, affair).

nu·bile /ˋnjubɑɪl *US:* ˋnubl/ *adj* (of girls) marriageable; old enough to marry.

nu·cleic /njuˋkleɪɪk *US:* nu-/ *adj* ~ **acid,** member of two complex compounds occurring in all living cells.

nu·clear /ˋnjuklɪə(r) *US:* ˋnu-/ *adj* of a nucleus, esp of heavy atoms, with release of energy: ~ *energy,* obtained by ~ fission; *a ~ power station; ~-powered submarines; ~ bombs/missiles; ~ disarmament,* the renunciation of ~ weapons.

nu·cleus /ˋnjuklɪəs *US:* ˋnu-/ *n* (*pl* nuclei /-klɪɑɪ/) central part, round which other parts are grouped or round which other things collect; (esp) central part of an atom, consisting of protons and neutrons.

nude /njud *US:* nud/ *adj* naked. □ *n* [C] ~ human figure (esp in art). ***in the ~,*** unclothed: *pose in the ~ for an artist.* **nu·dist** /-ɪst/ *n* person who believes that exposure of the naked body to sun and air is good for the health. **ˋnudist camp/colony,** place where nudists practise their beliefs. **nu·dism** /-ɪzm/ *n* the practice of going ~. **nu·dity** /ˋnjudətɪ *US:* ˋnu-/ *n* nakedness.

nudge /nʌdʒ/ *vt* [VP6A] touch or push slightly with the elbow in order to draw sb's attention privately. □ *n* push given in this way.

nu·ga·tory /ˋnjugətərɪ *US:* ˋnugətɔrɪ/ *adj* (formal) trifling; worthless; not valid.

nug·get /ˋnʌgɪt/ *n* lump of metal, esp gold, as found in the earth.

nui·sance /ˋnjusns *US:* ˋnu-/ *n* [C] thing, person, act, etc that causes trouble or offence: *The mosquitoes are a ~. What a ~ that child is! Commit no ~,* (as a public notice) **(a)** Do not urinate here. **(b)** Do not leave rubbish or litter here.

null /nʌl/ *adj* of no effect or force. ***~ and void,*** (legal) without legal effect; invalid. **nul·lify** /ˋnʌlɪfɑɪ/ *vt* (*pt,pp* **-fied**) [VP6A] make ~ and void. **nul·li·fi·ca·tion** /ˈnʌlɪfɪˋkeɪʃn/ *n* **nul·lity** /ˋnʌlətɪ/ *n* being ~; invalidity: *nullity of marriage; a ˋnullity suit,* one that asks for nullity of marriage.

nul·lah /ˋnʌlə/ *n* (in India, etc) watercourse; ravine.

numb /nʌm/ *adj* without ability to feel or move: *fingers ~ with cold.* □ *vt* [VP6A] make ~; deaden: *~ed with grief.* **~·ly** *adv* **~·ness** *n*

num·ber /ˋnʌmbə(r)/ *n* **1** *3, 13, 33 and 103 are ~s.* ⇨ App 4. **2** quantity or amount: *a large ~ of people. N~s of people* (= Very many people) *came from all parts of the country to see the exhibition. The ~ of books missing from the library is large. A ~ of books* (= Some books) *are missing from the library.* ***His/Your, etc ~ is up,*** (colloq) He is/You are, etc ruined, going to die, to pay a penalty, etc. ***in ~:*** *They were fifteen in ~,* There were fifteen of them. ***to the ~ of,*** mounting to. ***without ~,*** too many to be counted. ***times without ~,*** very often; so often that counting is impossible. **ˋ~-plate** *n* plate showing the index-mark and number of motor-vehicles, the ~ of a house, etc. ⇨ the illus at motor. **3** (usu shortened to **No,** for *numero,* meaning *in ~,* with *pl* **Nos,** before a figure): *Room No 145,* e g in a hotel; *living at No 4,* house number four. **No 10 (Downing Street),** official residence of the British Prime Minister. ***look after/take care of ~ one,*** (colloq) look after oneself and one's own interests. **4** one issue of a periodical, esp for one day, week, etc: *the current ~ of 'Punch'; back ~s* (= earlier issues) *of 'Nature'. That man is a back ~,* (fig) is out of date or old-fashioned. **5** part of an opera indicated by a ~; dance, song, etc for the stage. **6** (gram) variations in the forms of *nn, vv,* etc according to whether only one or more than one is to be indicated: *Man/men, does/do and I/we illustrate grammatical ~ in English.* **7** (*pl*) numerical superiority: *The enemy won by ~s/by force of ~s.* **8** (*pl*) (old use) verses; metre: *in mournful ~s.* **9** (*pl*) arithmetic: *He's not good at ~s.* **10 N~s,** the fourth book of the Old Testament. ⇨ App 10. □ *vt* [VP6A,14] **1** give a ~ to: *Let's ~ them from 1 to 10.* **2** amount to; add up to: *We ~ed 20 in all.* **3** [VP14] ***~ sb/sth among,*** include; place: *~ sb among one's friends.* **4** (passive) be restricted in ~: *His days are ~ed,* He has not long to live. **5** [VP2C] ***~ (off),*** (mil) call out one's ~ in a rank of soldiers: *The company ~ed off from the right.*

nu·mer·able /ˈnjumərəbl *US:* ˈnu-/ *adj* that can be numbered or counted.

nu·meral /ˈnjumərl *US:* ˈnu-/ *n, adj* (word, figure or sign) standing for a number; of number. **Arabic ~s,** 1, 2, 3, etc. **Roman ~s,** I, II, III, etc. ⇨ App 4.

nu·mer·ate /ˈnjumərət *US:* ˈnu-/ *adj* (of a person) having a good basic competence in mathematics and science. ⇨ literate. **nu·mer·acy** /ˈnjumərəsɪ *US:* ˈnu-/ *n*

nu·mer·ation /ˌnjuməˈreɪʃn *US:* ˌnu-/ *n* method or process of numbering or calculating; expression in words of numbers written in figures.

nu·mer·ator /ˈnjuməreɪtə(r) *US:* ˈnu-/ *n* number above the line in a vulgar fraction, e g 3 in $\frac{3}{4}$. ⇨ denominator.

nu·meri·cal /njuˈmerɪkl *US:* nu-/ *adj* of, in, denoting, numbers: *~ symbols.* **~ly** /-klɪ/ *adv*: *The enemy were ~ly superior.*

nu·mer·ous /ˈnjumərəs *US:* ˈnu-/ *adj* great in number; very many: *her ~ friends.*

nu·min·ous /ˈnjumɪnəs *US:* ˈnu-/ *adj* awe-inspiring; divine.

nu·mis·mat·ics /ˌnjumɪzˈmætɪks *US:* ˌnu-/ *n* (with *sing v*) the study of coins, coinage and medals. **nu·mis·ma·tist** /njuˈmɪzmətɪst *US:* nu-/ *n* expert in ~; collector of coins and medals.

num·skull /ˈnʌmskʌl/ *n* stupid person.

nun /nʌn/ *n* woman who, after taking religious vows, lives, with other women, in a convent, a secluded life in the service of God. **nun·nery** /ˈnʌnərɪ/ *n* (*pl* -ries) house of nuns; convent. ⇨ monk, monastery.

nun·cio /ˈnʌnsɪəʊ/ *n* (*pl* -cios) ambassador or representative of the Pope in a foreign country.

nup·tial /ˈnʌpʃl/ *adj* of marriage or weddings: *~ happiness; the ~ day.* **nup·tials** *n pl* wedding.

nurse[1] /nɜs/ *n* **1** (**ˈ~-)maid,** woman or girl employed to look after babies and small children. ⇨ nanny. **2** (**ˈwet-)~,** woman employed to suckle the infant of another. **3** [U] nursing or being nursed: *put a child to ~.* **4** person, usu trained, who cares for people who are ill or injured: *hospital ~s; Red Cross ~s; male ~s,* e g in a mental home for men. **5** country, college, institution, etc which protects or encourages a certain quality: *England, the ~ of liberty.*

nurse[2] /nɜs/ *vt* [VP6A] **1** take charge of and look after (persons who are ill, injured, etc) (but not used as in the sense of nurse[1](1)): (gerund) *the nursing profession; take up nursing as a career. Careful nursing will be needed.* **ˈnursing-home** *n* building, usu privately owned and smaller than a hospital, where persons who are ill may be cared for, operated on, etc. **2** feed (a baby) at the breast; suckle. **3** hold (a baby, a child, a pet dog) on the knees; clasp caressingly. **4** give special care to: *~ young plants.* ⇨ nursery(2); *~ a constituency,* keep in touch with the voters (to obtain or retain their support). ***~ a cold,*** stay at home, keep warm, in order to cure it. **5** have in the mind, think about a great deal: *~ feelings of revenge.*

nurs·ery /ˈnɜsrɪ/ *n* (*pl* -ries) **1** room (in a house, passenger liner, etc) for the special use of small children. **ˈday ~,** (**a**) room (in a wealthy home) where small children play, have their meals, etc. (**b**) building where mothers who go out to work may leave babies and young children. **ˈ~-governess,** woman who is both a nurse(1) and a governess. **ˈ~ rhymes,** poems or songs (usu traditional) for young children. **ˈ~ school,** for children of 2 to 5; pre-primary school. **~ slopes,** (skiing) slopes suitable for learners. **2** place where young plants and trees are raised (for transplanting later, and usu for sale). **ˈ~·man** /-mən/ *n* (*pl* -men) man who owns a ~(2).

nurse·ling, nurs·ling /ˈnɜslɪŋ/ *n* infant, esp in relation to its nurse.

nur·ture /ˈnɜtʃə(r)/ *n* [U] (formal) care, training; education (of children). □ *vt* bring up; give ~ to: *a delicately ~d girl.*

nut /nʌt/ *n* **1** fruit consisting of a hard shell enclosing a kernel that can be eaten. ***a hard nut to crack,*** a problem difficult to solve. **ˈnut-brown** *adj* (e g of ale) coloured like ripe hazel-nuts. **ˌnut-ˈbutter** *n* butter substitute made from nuts (e g *peanut butter*). **ˈnut-crackers** *n pl* device for cracking nuts open. **ˈnut·shell** *n* hard outside covering of a nut. ***(put sth) in a nutshell,*** (fig) in the fewest possible words; in the smallest possible space. **2** small piece of metal with a threaded hole for screwing on to a bolt. ⇨ the illus at bolt. **3** (sl) head (of a human being). ***off one's nut,*** (sl) insane. **ˈnut house** *n* (sl) mental hospital. **4** (*pl*) small lumps of coal. **5** (dated sl) dandified young man. □ *vi* (-tt-) ***go nutting,*** look for, gather nuts (e g hazel-nuts in the woods and hedges).

nut·meg /ˈnʌtmeg/ *n* **1** [C] hard, small, round, sweet-smelling seed of an E Indian evergreen. **2** [U] this seed grated to powder, used as a flavouring.

nu·tria /ˈnjutrɪə *US:* ˈnu-/ *n* skin or fur of the small S American rodent called coypu.

nu·tri·ent /ˈnjutrɪənt *US:* ˈnu-/ *adj* (formal) serving as or providing nourishment.

nu·tri·ment /ˈnjutrɪmənt *US:* ˈnu-/ *n* (formal) nourishing food.

nu·tri·tion /njuˈtrɪʃn *US:* nu-/ *n* (formal) [U] the process of supplying and receiving nourishment; the science of food values: *the care and ~ of children.*

nu·tri·tious /njuˈtrɪʃəs *US:* nu-/ *adj* (formal) nourishing; having high value as food.

nu·tri·tive /ˈnjutrɪtɪv *US:* ˈnu-/ *adj* (formal) serving as food; of nutrition.

nuts /nʌts/ *adj* (sl) crazy; insane. ***be ~ about/over sb/sth,*** be in love with, infatuated with.

nutty /ˈnʌtɪ/ *adj* (-ier, -iest) **1** tasting like nuts. **2** (sl) mad; crazy. **3** containing, made up of, nuts(4): *~ slack coal.*

nuzzle /ˈnʌzl/ *vt,vi* **1** [VP6A] press the nose against: *The horse ~d my shoulder.* **2** [VP2C] ***~ up (against/to),*** rub or push with the nose: *The horse ~d up against my shoulder.*

ny·lon /ˈnɑɪlon/ *n* **1** [U] (P) synthetic fibre used for hosiery, rope, brushes, etc: *~ stockings/blouses, etc.* **2** (*pl*) ~ stockings.

nymph /nɪmf/ *n* **1** (in old Gk and Roman stories) one of the lesser goddesses, living in rivers, trees, hills, etc; (liter) beautiful young woman. **2** pupa; chrysalis.

nym·phet /nɪmˋfet/ *n* (colloq) young girl looked upon as sexually desirable.

nym·pho /ˋnɪmfəʊ/ *n* (*pl* -phos /-fəʊz/) (colloq abbr of) nymphomaniac.

nym·pho·mania /ˈnɪmfəˋmeɪnɪə/ *n* [U] abnormal sexual desire in women. **nym·pho·maniac** /-ˋmeɪnɪæk/ *n, adj* (woman) suffering from ~.

Oo

O, o /əʊ/ (*pl* O's, o's /əʊz/) the 15th letter of the English alphabet; O-shaped sign or mark; (in quoting telephone numbers) 6033, 'six oh double three'. ⇨ App 4.

O, oh /əʊ/ *int* cry of surprise, fear, pain, sudden pleasure, etc.

o' /ə/ (abbr of) *of*, as in *o'clock, man-o'-war.*

oaf /əʊf/ *n* (*pl* ~s or, rarely oaves /əʊvz/) awkward lout. **ˋoaf·ish** /-ɪʃ/ *adj* roughly behaved; loutish.

oak /əʊk/ *n* [C] sorts of large tree with tough, hard wood, common in many parts of the world. ⇨ the illus at tree; [U] the wood of this tree: *a forest of oak(s)/oak-trees; an oak door; oak panels.* **ˋoak-apple** *n* growth on an oak leaf or stem caused by an insect. **the Oaks,** name of a classic horse-race, run at Epsom, near London. **oaken** /ˋəʊkən/ *adj* made of oak.

oa·kum /ˋəʊkəm/ *n* [U] loose fibre or threads obtained by picking old ropes, used for filling up spaces between the boards of a ship.

oar /ɔ(r)/ *n* pole with a flat blade, pulled by hand against a pin, rowlock or other support on the side of a boat, in order to propel the boat through the water. ***pull a good oar,*** be a good oarsman. ***put/shove one's oar in,*** (colloq) interfere. ***rest on one's oars,*** stop working for a time. **oars·man** /ˋɔzmən/ *n* (*pl* -men), **ˋoars·woman** *n* (*pl* -women) rower. Hence, **ˋoars·man·ship** /-mənʃɪp/ *n*

oasis /əʊˋeɪsɪs/ *n* (*pl* -ses /-siz/) fertile place, with water and trees, in a desert; (fig) experience, place, etc which is pleasant in the midst of what is dull, unpleasant, etc.

oast /əʊst/ *n* kiln for drying hops. **ˋ~-house** *n* building containing an ~.

oat /əʊt/ *n* (usu *pl*) **1** (grain from a) hardy cereal plant grown in cool climates as food (*oats* for horses, *oatmeal* for human beings). ⇨ the illus at cereal. ***feel one's oats,*** (colloq) feel gay, lively, ready for activity, active. ***sow one's wild oats,*** lead a life of pleasure and gaiety while young before settling down seriously. **ˋoat·cake** *n* (esp in Scot and N England) thin, unleavened cake made of oatmeal. **ˋoat·meal** *n* meal made from oats, used in porridge and oatcakes. **2** (with *sing v*) oatmeal porridge: *Is Scotch ~s on the menu?*

oath /əʊθ/ *n* (*pl* ~s /əʊðz/) **1** solemn undertaking with God's help to do sth; solemn declaration that sth is true. ***be on ~,*** (legal) having sworn to tell the truth: *The judge reminded the witness that he was still under ~.* ***put sb under ~,*** (legal) require sb to swear an ~. ***swear/take an ~,*** promise solemnly to give (one's loyalty, allegiance, etc). ***on one's ~,*** (non-legal) used to emphasize that one is telling the truth: *I didn't say anything to him about you, on my ~.* **2** wrongful use of God's name or of sacred words to express strong feeling; swear-word; piece of profanity.

ob·bli·gato /ˈoblɪˋgatəʊ/ *n* (*pl* -tos /-təʊz/), *adj* (music) (accompanying part) forming an integral part of the composition.

ob·du·rate /ˋobdjʊərət *US:* -dər-/ *adj* (formal) stubborn; impenitent. **~·ly** *adv* **ob·du·racy** /ˋobdjʊərəsɪ *US:* -dər-/ *n* [U].

obedi·ent /əˋbidɪənt/ *adj* doing, willing to do, what one is told to do: *~ children.* ***your ~ servant,*** formula used at the end of letters of an official or public nature. **~·ly** *adv* **obedi·ence** /-əns/ *n* [U] being ~: *Soldiers act in obedience to the orders of their superior officers.*

obeis·ance /əʊˋbeɪsns/ *n* [C] (formal) deep bow (of respect or homage): *do/pay ~ to a ruler,* show respectful homage or submission.

ob·elisk /ˋobəlɪsk/ *n* tall, pointed, tapering, four-sided stone pillar, set up as a monument or landmark.

obese /əʊˋbis/ *adj* (of persons) very fat. **obes·ity** /əʊˋbisətɪ/ *n* [U] being ~.

obey /əˋbeɪ/ *vt, vi* [VP6A,2A] do what one is told to do; carry out (a command): *~ an officer; ~ orders.*

ob·fus·cate /ˋobfʌskeɪt/ *vt* [VP6A] (formal) darken or obscure (the mind); bewilder.

obi /ˋəʊbɪ/ *n* (*pl* obis) (Japanese) broad sash (often ornamental) fastened round the waist so that there is a large bow.

obiter dic·tum /ˈəʊbɪtə ˋdɪktəm/ *n* (*pl* dicta /ˋdɪktə/) (Lat) incidental remark or statement.

obitu·ary /əˋbɪtʃʊərɪ *US:* -tʃuerɪ/ *n* (*pl* -ries) printed notice of sb's death, often with a short account of his life; (attrib) *~ notices,* e g in a newspaper.

ob·ject¹ /ˋobdʒɪkt/ *n* **1** sth that can be seen or touched; material thing: *Tell me the names of the ~s in this room.* **ˋ~ lesson, (a)** one (to be) taught or learnt from an example, or from specimens, etc placed before or shown to the learner. **(b)** practical illustration of some principle, often given or used as a warning. **ˋ~ glass/lens** *n* = objective *n*(2). **2** person or thing to which action or feeling or thought is directed; thing aimed at; end; purpose: *an ~ of pity/admiration,* sb or sth pitied/admired; *with no ~ in life; work with the ~ of earning fame; fail/succeed in one's ~.* ***no ~,*** no hindrance; not important: *money/time/distance, etc no ~,* (in advertisements, e g for jobs) the person answering may make his own terms about money, time, etc. **3** person or thing of strange appearance, esp if ridiculous, pitiful or contemptible: *What an ~ you look in that old hat!* **4** (gram) *n* or *n* equivalent (e g a clause) towards which the action of the *v* is directed, or to which a preposition indicates some relation, as in (direct object) 'He took *the money*' or 'He took *what he wanted*' or (indirect ~) 'I gave *him* the money' or (prepositional ~) 'I gave the money to *the treasurer*'.

ob·ject[2] /əbˋdʒekt/ *vi, vt* **1** [VP2A,3A] ***~ (to),*** say that one is not in favour of sth; be opposed (to); make a protest against: *I ~ to all this noise/to being treated like a child. He stood up and ~ed in strong language.* **2** [VP9] ***~ (against sb) that,*** give as a reason against: *I ~ (against him) that he is too young for the position.* **ob·jec·tor** /-tə(r)/ *n* person who ~s. **conscientious ~or**, ⇨ **conscientious**.

ob·jec·tion /əbˋdʒekʃn/ *n* **1** [C,U] statement or feeling of dislike, disapproval or opposition: *He has a strong ~ to getting up early. He took ~ to what I said. O~s to the plan will be listened to sympathetically.* **2** [C] that which is objected to; drawback; defect. **~·able** /-əbl/ *adj* likely to be objected to; unpleasant: *an ~able smell; ~able remarks.* **~·ably** /-əblı/ *adv*

ob·jec·tive /əbˋdʒektıv/ *adj* **1** (in philosophy) having existence outside the mind; real. ⇨ **subjective**. **2** (of persons, writings, pictures) uninfluenced by thought or feeling; dealing with outward things, actual facts, etc uninfluenced by personal feelings or opinions. **3** (gram) of the object(**4**): *the ~ case*, in Latin and other inflected languages. □ *n* **1** object aimed at; purpose; (esp mil) point to which armed forces are moving to capture it: *All our ~s were won.* **2** lens of a microscope or telescope closest to the object being looked at. **~·ly** *adv* in an ~(**2**) manner. **ob·jec·tiv·ity** /ˈobdʒekˋtıvətı/ *n* state of being ~; impartial judgement; ability to free oneself from personal prejudice.

ob·jur·gate /ˋobdʒɜgeıt/ *vt* [VP6A] scold; rebuke. **ob·jur·ga·tion** /ˈobdʒɜˋgeıʃn/ *n* [C,U] scolding; rebuke.

ob·late /ˈoˋbleıt/ *adj* (geom) flattened at the poles: *The earth is an ~ sphere.*

ob·la·tion /əˋbleıʃn/ *n* [C] offering made to God or a god.

ob·li·gate /ˋoblıgeıt/ *vt* [VP17] ***~ sb to do sth,*** bind (a person, esp legally) (usu passive): *He felt ~d to help.*

ob·li·ga·tion /ˈoblıˋgeıʃn/ *n* [C] promise, duty or condition that indicates what action ought to be taken (e g the power of the law, duty, a sense of what is right): *the ~s of good citizenship/of conscience; fulfil/repay an ~*, e g by returning hospitality that one has received. ***be/place sb under an ~,*** be/make sb indebted to another.

ob·li·ga·tory /əˋblıgətrı *US:* -tɔrı/ *adj* that is required by law, rule or custom: *Is attendance at school ~ or optional in that country? It is ~ on café owners to take precautions against fire.*

ob·lige /əˋblaıdʒ/ *vt* **1** [VP17] ***~ sb to do sth,*** require, bind (sb) by a promise, oath, etc: *The law ~s parents to send their children to school.* **2** [VP17] (esp in passive) ***be ~d to do sth,*** compel: *They were ~d to sell their house in order to pay their debts.* ⇨ **have**[3](**1**). **3** [VP6A,14] do sth for sb as a favour or in answer to a request: *Please ~ me by closing the door. Can you ~ me with…*, lend or give me…? *I'm much ~d to you,* I'm grateful for what you've done. **oblig·ing** *adj* willing to help: *obliging neighbours.* **oblig·ing·ly** *adv*

ob·lique /əˋblik/ *adj* sloping; slanting: *an ~ angle*, any angle that is not a right angle (i e not 90°). **~·ly** *adv* **ob·li·quity** /əˋblıkwətı/ *n* (*pl* -ties) **1** [U] state of being ~. **2** [C,U] (instance of) moral perversity.

ob·lit·er·ate /əˋblıtəreıt/ *vt* [VP6A] rub or blot out; remove all signs of; destroy. **ob·lit·er·ation** /əˈblıtəˋreıʃn/ *n* [U].

ob·liv·ion /əˋblıvıən/ *n* [U] state of being quite forgotten: *sink/fall into ~.*

ob·livi·ous /əˋblıvıəs/ *adj* ***~ of,*** unaware, having no memory: *~ of one's surroundings/of what was taking place.*

ob·long /ˋobloŋ/ *n, adj* (figure) having four straight sides and angles at 90°, longer than it is wide.

ob·loquy /ˋobləkwı/ *n* [U] public shame or reproach; abuse; discredit.

ob·nox·ious /əbˋnokʃəs/ *adj* nasty; very disagreeable (*to*). **~·ly** *adv* **~·ness** *n*

oboe /ˋəʊbəʊ/ *n* woodwind instrument of treble pitch with a double-reed mouthpiece. ⇨ the illus at **brass**. **ˋobo·ist** /-ıst/ *n* player of the ~.

ob·scene /əbˋsin/ *adj* (of words, thoughts, books, pictures, etc) morally disgusting; offensive; likely to corrupt and deprave (esp by regarding or describing sex indecently). **~·ly** *adv* **ob·scen·ity** /əbˋsenətı/ *n* (*pl* -ties) [U] being ~; ~ language, etc; [C] instance of this.

ob·scure /əbˋskjʊə(r)/ *adj* **1** dark; hidden; not clearly seen or understood: *an ~ view/corner. Is the meaning still ~ to you?* **2** not well known: *an ~ village/poet.* □ *vt* [VP6A] make ~: *The moon was ~d by clouds. Mist ~d the view.* **~·ly** *adv* **ob·scur·ity** /əbˋskjʊərətı/ *n* (*pl* -ties) **1** [U] state of being ~: *content to live in obscurity.* **2** [C] sth that is ~ or indistinct: *an essay full of obscurities.*

ob·sequies /ˋobsıkwız/ *n pl* funeral ceremonies.

ob·sequi·ous /əbˋsikwıəs/ *adj* ***~ (to/towards),*** too eager to obey or serve; showing excessive respect (esp from hope of reward or advantage): *~ to the Manager.* **~·ly** *adv* **~·ness** *n*

ob·serv·able /əbˋzɜvəbl/ *adj* that can be seen or noticed; deserving to be observed. **ob·serv·ably** /-əblı/ *adv*

ob·serv·ance /əbˋzɜvəns/ *n* **1** [U] the keeping or observing(**2**) of a law, custom, festival, etc: *the ˈLord's ˈDay Obˋservance Society,* i e for seeing that proper respect is paid to Sunday; *the ~ of the Queen's birthday.* **2** [C] act performed as part of a ceremony, or as a sign of respect or worship.

ob·serv·ant /əbˋzɜvənt/ *adj* **1** quick at noticing things: *an ~ boy.* **2** careful to observe(**2**) laws, customs, etc: *~ of the rules.* **~·ly** *adv*

ob·ser·va·tion /ˈobzəˋveıʃn/ *n* **1** [U] observing or being observed: *~ of natural phenomena; escape ~.* ***be/come under ~,*** be observed. ***keep sb under ~,*** watch him carefully (e g a suspected criminal by the police; a hospital patient by the medical staff). **ˋ~ balloon,** (mil) captive balloon from which movements of the enemy may be observed. **ˋ~ car,** (in a railway train) one with wide windows through which to watch the scenery, etc. **ˋ~ post,** (mil) post as near to the enemy's lines as possible, from which reports of the enemy's movements may be obtained. **2** [U] power of taking notice: *a man of little ~.* **3** [U] (usu *pl*) collected and recorded information: *Has he published his ~s on bird life in the Antarctic yet?* **4** ***take an ~,*** take the altitude of the sun or other heavenly body in order to find the latitude and longitude of one's position.

ob·serv·atory /əbˋzɜvətrı *US:* -tɔrı/ *n* (*pl* -ries) building from which natural phenomena (e g the sun and the stars, volcanic activity, marine life) may be observed. ⇨ p 588.

an observatory

ob·serve /əbˋzɜv/ *vt,vi* **1** [VP6A,8,9,10,25,2A, and 18,9, passive] see and notice; watch carefully: *~ the behaviour of birds. The accused man was ~d to enter the bank/trying to force the lock of the door. I have never ~d him do otherwise. He ~d that it had turned cloudy. He ~s keenly but says little.* **2** [VP6A] pay attention to (rules, etc); celebrate (festivals, birthdays, anniversaries, etc): *Do they ~ Christmas Day in that country?* **3** [VP6A,9] say by way of comment: *He ~d that we should probably have rain.* **ob·server** *n* **1** one who ~s(1): *an ~r of nature.* **2** one who observes(2): *an ~r of the Sabbath.* **3** person who attends a conference, etc to listen but who does not otherwise take part. **ob·serv·ing** *adj* quick to notice. **ob·serv·ing·ly** *adv*

ob·sess /əbˋses/ *vt* [VP6A] (usu passive) (of a fear, a fixed or false idea) occupy the mind of; continually distress: *~ed by fear of unemployment.* **ob·session** /əbˋseʃn/ *n* **1** [U] state of being ~ed. **2** [C] sth that ~es; fixed idea that occupies one's mind. **ob·sess·ive** /əbˋsesɪv/ *adj* of or like an obsession.

ob·sid·ian /əbˋsɪdɪən/ *n* dark volcanic rock like the glass of which some bottles are made.

ob·sol·escent /ˌobsəˋlesnt/ *adj* becoming out of date; passing out of use. **ob·sol·escence** /-ˋlesns/ *n* [U] being ~.

ob·sol·ete /ˋobsəlit/ *adj* no longer used; out of date.

ob·stacle /ˋobstəkl/ *n* sth in the way that stops progress or makes it difficult: *~s to world peace.* **ˋ~ race,** one in which ~s, natural or artificial, e g ditches, hedges, have to be crossed.

ob·stet·ric /əbˋstetrɪk/, **ob·stet·ri·cal** /-kl/ *adj* of obstetrics: *the ~ ward* (in a hospital). **ob·stet·rics** *n pl* branch of medicine and surgery connected with childbirth, its antecedents and sequels. **ob·ste·trician** /ˌobstɪˋtrɪʃn/ *n* expert in obstetrics.

ob·sti·nate /ˋobstɪnət/ *adj* **1** not easily giving way to argument or persuasion: *~ children; ~ in disposition.* **2** not easily overcome: *~ resistance; an ~ disease.* **~·ly** *adv* **ob·sti·nacy** /-nəsɪ/ *n* [U] being ~; stubbornness.

ob·strep·er·ous /əbˋstrepərəs/ *adj* unruly; noisily resisting control: *~ behaviour/children.* **~·ly** *adv* **~·ness** *n*

ob·struct /əbˋstrʌkt/ *vt* [VP6A] **1** be, get, put, sth in the way of; block up (a road, passage, etc): *The mountain roads were ~ed by falls of rock. Trees ~ed the view.* **2** make (the development, etc of sth) difficult: *~ the progress of a Bill through the House of Commons.*

ob·struc·tion /əbˋstrʌkʃn/ *n* **1** [U] obstructing or being obstructed: *The Opposition adopted a policy of ~.* **2** sth that obstructs: *~s on the road,* e g trees blown down in a gale. **~·ism** /-ɪzm/ *n* systematic ~ of plans, legislation, etc. **~·ist** /-ɪst/ *n*

ob·struc·tive /əbˋstrʌktɪv/ *adj* causing, likely or intended to cause, obstruction: *a policy ~ to our plans.* **~·ly** *adv*

ob·tain /əbˋteɪn/ *vt,vi* **1** [VP6A] get; secure for oneself; buy; have lent or granted to oneself: *~ what one wants. Where can I ~ the book?* **2** [VP2A] (of rules, customs) be established or in use: *The custom still ~s in some districts.* **~·able** /-əbl/ *adj* that can be ~ed.

ob·trude /əbˋtrud/ *vt,vi* [VP14,2A] ***~ (upon),*** push (oneself, one's opinions, etc) forward, esp when unwanted. **ob·trus·ive** /əbˋtrusɪv/ *adj* inclined to ~. **ob·trus·ive·ly** *adv*

ob·tuse /əbˋtjus *US:* -ˋtus/ *adj* **1** blunt. **2** (of an angle) between 90° and 180°. ⇨ the illus at **angle**. **3** slow in understanding; stupid. **~·ly** *adv* **~·ness** *n*

ob·verse /ˋobvɜs/ *n* side of a coin or medal having on it the head or principal design. ⇨ **reverse**; face of anything intended to be presented; counterpart; (attrib) *the ~ side.*

ob·vi·ate /ˋobvɪeɪt/ *vt* [VP6A] get rid of, clear away, anticipate (dangers, difficulties, etc).

ob·vi·ous /ˋobvɪəs/ *adj* easily seen or understood; clear; plain. **~·ly** *adv* **~·ness** *n*

oca·rina /ˌokəˋrinə/ *n* small, egg-shaped musical wind-instrument (with holes for the finger-tips) made of porcelain, plastic or metal.

oc·ca·sion /əˋkeɪʒn/ *n* **1** [C] time at which a particular event takes place; right time (*for* sth): *on this/that ~...; on the present/last ~...; on one ~,* once; *on rare ~s. I have met Mr White on several ~s. This is not an ~* (= a suitable time) *for laughter. He has had few ~s to speak French.* ***on ~,*** now and then; whenever the need arises. ***rise to the ~,*** show that one is equal to what needs to be done. ***take this/that ~ to say sth,*** avail oneself of the opportunity. **2** [U] reason; cause; need: *I've had no ~ to visit him recently. You have no ~ to be angry.* **3** [C] immediate, subsidiary or incidental cause of sth: *The real causes of the strike are not clear, but the ~ was the dismissal of two workmen.* **4** (*pl*) (old use) affairs; business: *going about their lawful ~s.* □ *vt* [VP6A,12A,13A] be the cause of: *The boy's behaviour ~ed his parents much anxiety.*

oc·ca·sional /əˋkeɪʒnl/ *adj* **1** happening, coming, seen, etc from time to time, but not regularly: *He pays me ~ visits. There will be ~ showers during the day.* **2** used or meant for a special event, time, purpose, etc: *~ verses,* e g written to celebrate an anniversary. **~ly** /-nlɪ/ *adv* now and then; at times.

oc·ci·dent /ˋoksɪdənt/ *n* **the ~,** (liter) the West (Europe and America), contrasted with the Orient. **Oc·ci·den·tal** /ˌoksɪˋdentl/ *n, adj* (native) of the ~ or a country in the ~.

oc·cult /oˋkʌlt *US:* əˋkʌlt/ *adj* **1** hidden; secret; only for those with more than ordinary knowledge: *the ~,* that which is ~. **2** supernatural, magical: *~ sciences,* e g astrology.

oc·cu·pant /ˋokjʊpənt/ *n* person who occupies a house, room or position; person in actual possession of land, etc. **oc·cu·pancy** /-pənsɪ/ *n* act, fact, period of occupying a house, land, etc by being in possession.

oc·cu·pa·tion /ˌokjʊˈpeɪʃn/ *n* **1** [U] act of occupying(**1**); taking and holding possession of: *the ~ of a house by a family; an army of ~,* one that occupies conquered territory until peace is made. **2** [U] period during which land, a building, etc is occupied. **3** [C] business, trade, etc; that which occupies one's time, either permanently or as a hobby, etc: *useful ~s for long winter evenings.* **~al** /-nl/ *adj* arising from, connected with, a person's ~. **ˌ~al ˈhazards,** risks that arise from a person's ~ (e g explosions in coalmines). **ˌ~al ˈtherapy,** treatment of illness, etc by activity in creative or productive employment.

oc·cu·pier /ˈokjʊpaɪə(r)/ *n* occupant; person in (esp temporary or subordinate) possession of land or a building (contrasted with the owner or tenant).

oc·cupy /ˈokjʊpaɪ/ *vt* (*pt,pp* **-pied**) [VP6A] **1** live in, be in possession of (a house, farm, etc). **2** take and keep possession of (towns, countries, etc, in war): *~ the enemy's capital.* **3** take up, fill (space, time, attention, the mind): *The dinner and speeches occupied three hours. Many anxieties ~ my mind. He is occupied in translating/occupied with a translation of a French novel. He occupied himself with solving some algebra problems.* **4** hold, fill: *Mr H occupies an important position in the Department of the Environment.*

oc·cur /əˈkɜ(r)/ *vi* (**-rr-**) **1** [VP2A] take place; happen: *Don't let this ~ again. When did the accident ~?* **2** [VP3A] **~ to,** come into (sb's mind): *An idea has ~red to me. Did it ever ~ to you that...,* Did you ever have the idea that...? **3** [VP2C] exist; be found: *Misprints ~ on every page.*

oc·cur·rence /əˈkʌrns *US:* əˈkɜns/ *n* **1** [C] happening; event: *an everyday ~; an unfortunate ~.* **2** [U] fact or process of occurring: *of frequent/rare ~,* happening frequently/rarely.

ocean /ˈəʊʃn/ *n* **1** the great body of water that surrounds the land masses of the earth: *an ~ voyage. ~-going ships,* (contrasted with *coastal* ships). **2** one of the main divisions of this: *the Atlantic/Pacific, etc O~.* **the ~ lanes,** the routes regularly used by steamers. **3** (colloq) great number or quantity: *~s of time/money.* **oceanic** /ˌəʊʃɪˈænɪk/ *adj* of, like, living in, the ~.

ochre (US also **ocher**) /ˈəʊkə(r)/ *n* [U] sorts of earth used for making pigments varying from light yellow to brown; pale yellowish-brown colour.

o'clock /əˈklok/ *particle* (= of the clock) used in asking and telling the time (to specify an hour): *He left at five ~/between five and six ~.* ⇨ App 4.

oc·ta·gon /ˈoktəgən *US:* -gon/ *n* plane figure with eight sides and angles. **oc·tag·onal** /okˈtægənl/ *adj* eight-sided.

oc·tane /ˈokteɪn/ *n* paraffin hydro-carbon: *high ~,* (of fuels used in internal-combustion engines) having good anti-knock properties; *ˈ~ rating,* measure of these properties, esp of petrol. ⇨ knock²(3).

oc·tave /ˈoktɪv/ *n* **1** (music) the note that is six whole tones above or below a given note; the interval of five whole tones and two semi-tones; note and its ~ sounded together. **2** (poetry) first eight lines of a sonnet; stanza of eight lines.

oc·tavo /okˈteɪvəʊ/ *n* (abbr *8vo, oct; pl* -vos /-vəʊz/) (size of a) book or page produced by folding sheets of paper three times or into eight leaves.

oc·tet, oc·tette /okˈtet/ *n* **1** (piece of music for) eight singers or players. **2** = octave(**2**).

Oc·to·ber /okˈtəʊbə(r)/ *n* the tenth month of the year, with 31 days.

oc·to·gen·arian /ˌoktədʒɪˈneərɪən/ *n, adj* (person) of an age from 80 to 89.

oc·to·pus /ˈoktəpəs/ *n* (*pl* **-puses** /-pəsɪz/) sea animal with a soft body and eight arms (*tentacles*) provided with suckers. ⇨ the illus at mollusc.

oc·to·roon /ˌoktəˈrun/ *n* offspring of a quadroon and a white person; person with one-eighth Negro blood.

oc·troi /ˈoktrwa *US:* okˈtrwa/ *n* [C] duty levied (in some European countries) on goods brought into a town; place where, officials by whom, the levy is collected.

ocu·lar /ˈokjʊlə(r)/ *adj* of, for, by, the eyes; of seeing: *~ proof/demonstration.*

ocu·list /ˈokjʊlɪst/ *n* specialist in diseases of the eye.

oda·lisque /ˈəʊdəlɪsk/ *n* Eastern female slave or concubine, e g in a seraglio in olden times.

odd /od/ *adj* **1** (of numbers) not even; not exactly divisible by two: *1, 3, 5 and 7 are odd numbers.* **2** of one of a pair when the other is missing: *an odd shoe/boot/glove.* **3** of one or more of a set or series when not with the rest: *two odd volumes of an encyclopædia; an odd player,* (in a game) an extra player above the number actually needed. ***odd man out,*** (**a**) person or thing left when the others have been arranged in pairs. (**b**) (colloq) person who stands aloof from, or cannot fit himself into, the society, community, etc, of which he is a member. **4** with a little extra: *five ˈhundred odd,* a number greater than 500; *ˈthirty-odd years,* between 30 and 40; *twelve ˈpounds odd,* £12 and some pence extra. **5** not regular, habitual, or fixed; occasional: *make a living by doing odd jobs; weed the garden at odd times/moments,* at various and irregular times. **6** (**-er, -est**) strange; peculiar: *He's an odd/odd-looking old man. How odd!* **odd·ly** *adv* in an odd manner: *oddly enough,* strange to say.

odd·ity /ˈodətɪ/ *n* (*pl* **-ties**) **1** [U] quality of being odd(**6**); strangeness: *~ of behaviour/dress.* **2** [C] queer act, thing or person: *He's something of an ~,* is unusual in some ways.

odd·ment /ˈodmənt/ *n* [C] **1** remnant; sth left over; old piece: *The chair was sold as an ~ at the end of the auction.* **2** (*pl*) odd pieces. ⇨ *odds and ends* at odds(**5**).

odds /odz/ *n pl* **1** the chances in favour of or against sth happening: *The ~ are against us,* We are unlikely to succeed. *The ~ are in your favour,* You are likely to succeed. *The ~ are that...,* It is probable that...; *They were fighting against heavy ~.* ***It makes no ~,*** makes no difference, will not influence the outcome. ***What's*** (colloq, with *sing v*) ***the ~?*** What does it matter? ***give/receive ~,*** give/receive an equalizing allowance (e g a number of strokes in golf, when a player is known to be stronger or weaker than another). **2** things that are not even; inequalities: *make ~ even.* **3** (betting) difference in amount between the money staked on a chance and the money that will be paid if the chance is successful: *~ of ten to one.* **fixed ~,** (e g football pools) with a promise to pay agreed odds, e g 100—1, regardless of the number of punters, gamblers. **lay ~ of,** offer ~ of: *I'll lay*

~ *of three to one that....* **long ~,** e g 20 to 1. **short ~,** e g 3 to 1. **'~-'on,** better than even (chance). **4** ***be at ~ (with sb) (over sth),*** be quarrelling or disagreeing (with) (*on* a question). **5 ~ and ends,** small articles, bits and pieces, of various sorts and usu of small value.

ode /əʊd/ *n* poem, usu in irregular metre and expressing noble feelings, often in celebration of some special event.

odi·ous /ˈəʊdɪəs/ *adj* hateful; repulsive. **~·ly** *adv*

odium /ˈəʊdɪəm/ *n* [U] general or widespread hatred; strong feeling against sth: *behaviour that exposed him to ~.*

odor·ifer·ous /ˌəʊdəˈrɪfərəs/ *adj* (formal) fragrant.

odor·ous /ˈəʊdərəs/ *adj* (chiefly poet) fragrant.

odour (US = **odor**) /ˈəʊdə(r)/ *n* **1** [C] smell; pleasant or unpleasant. **2** [U] reputation; approval; favour. ***be in good/bad ~ (with sb),*** enjoy/not enjoy his favour or approval. **~·less** *adj*

od·ys·sey /ˈɒdɪsɪ/ *n* long, adventurous journey or series of adventures (from the voyage of Odysseus after the siege of Troy, in Homer's epic).

œcu·meni·cal /ˌikjuˈmenɪkl/ *adj* = **ecumenical.**

Oedipus complex /ˈidɪpəs kɒmpleks *US:* ˈed-/ *n* (psych) unconscious love of a son (usu arising when very young) for his mother, with jealousy of, hatred for, his father.

o'er /ɔ(r)/ *adv, prep* (poet) over.

œsoph·agus /iˈsɒfəgəs/ *n* = **esophagus.**

of /*usual form:* əv *strong form:* ɒv/ *prep* **1** (indicating separation in space or time): *five miles south of Leeds; within a hundred yards of the station; within a year of his death; five minutes/a quarter of* (= before) *two,* (US; GB = 'five minutes/a quarter *to* two.' **2** (indicating origin, authorship): *a man of humble origin; of royal descent; a man who comes of good stock; the works of Shakespeare; the Iliad of Homer.* **3** (indicating cause): *die of grief/hunger, etc; do sth of necessity/of one's own choice/of one's own accord; sick/proud/ashamed/afraid/glad/tired, etc of sth or sb; taste/smell, etc of sth; because of; for fear of. The explosion couldn't have happened of itself,* i e without an external cause. **4** (indicating relief, deprivation, riddance): *cure sb of a disease/a bad habit, etc; rid a warehouse of rats; be/get rid of sth or sb; rob sb of his money; relieve sb of anxiety; clear oneself of an accusation; destitute of sense; trees bare of leaves; free of customs duty; independent of help; short of money.* **5** (indicating material or substance): *a table of wood; a house of stone; a dress of silk; made of steel and concrete; built of brick.* **6** (forming *adj* phrases; descriptive genitive): *goods of our own manufacture; tomatoes of my own growing,* that I have grown myself; *a girl of ten years,* a girl ten years old, a ten-year-old girl; *a man of foreign appearance; a man of genius; a man of ability,* an able man; *a woman of no importance,* an unimportant woman; *the vice of drunkenness,* the vice that is drunkenness; *a coat of many colours,* a many-coloured coat; *the city of Dublin; the Isle of Wight.* **7** (in the pattern 'noun[1] *of* noun[2]' = noun[2] that is noun[1]): *They live in a palace of a house,* a house that is a palace, a palatial house. *He has the devil of a temper,* a devilish temper. *Where's that fool of an assistant,* that foolish assistant? *What a mountain of a wave,* a mountainous wave! *She's a fine figure of a woman,* a woman with a fine figure. *Where's your scamp of a husband,* your rascally husband? **8** (objective genitive): *a maker of pots,* a man who makes pots; *the love of study; the writing of a letter; loss of power/appetite; great eaters of fish,* people who eat much fish; *the fear of God,* i e felt by men towards God. **9** (subjective genitive): *the love of God,* God's love for mankind. ⇨ **8** above, *the fear of God; the love of a mother,* a mother's love, the love that a mother has for her children. Cf *his love of* (i e for) *his mother.* **10** (indicating connection, reference or relation): *the cause of the accident; the result of the debate; a topic of conversation; the first day of June; the manners of the present day; those of the middle classes; the master of the house; the wall of the garden,* the garden wall; *the leg of the table,* the table leg; *the opposite of what I intended; Doctor of Medicine; Master of Arts; think well of sb; admitting/allowing of no doubt; accused/ suspected/ convicted of a crime; speaking/ talking/ dreaming of sth; sure/ certain/confident/fond/guilty/innocent, etc of sth; hard of hearing,* deaf; *blind of* (= in respect of) *one eye; at thirty years of age. What of* (= about) *the risk? Well, what of it?* **11** (indicating partition, inclusion, measure): **(a)** *a sheet of paper; a roll of cloth; a pint of milk; a ton of coal; 3 acres of land; 2 yards of cloth; some of that cake; one/a few/all of us; a lot/a great deal/not much of this stuff; no more of that. The car won't hold the six of us.* **(b)** (after superlatives): *He is the most dangerous of enemies. You have had the best of teachers,* the best of those teachers who were available. **(c)** (= out of): *It surprises me that you, of all men, should be so foolish. On this day of all days.* **(d)** (intensive): *the song of songs; the Holy of Holies,* best deserving the name. **(e)** (old use): *to drink deep of flattery. Hast thou not eaten of the tree of knowledge?* **12** (in the pattern *n* + *of* +) **(a)** from among the number of: *a friend of mine; no business of yours; reading a volume of Ruskin's,* a book, one of a number of which Ruskin was the author; *a painting of the king's,* one of a number belonging to the king. Cf *a portrait of the king,* a painting to show the king's appearance. **(b)** (used when the *n* is modified by a demonstrative or other word that cannot be combined with a possessive): *that long nose of his; this essay of Green's; that foolish young wife of yours; that queer-looking hat of hers.* **13** (in the pattern *adj* + *of* + *pron/n*): How kind of you to help! It was good of your brother to come. **14** (indicating time): *What do you do of a Sunday,* on Sundays? *He sometimes comes in of an evening,* in the evenings. *In days of old/of yore,* in the past; *of late,* recently; *of late years,* during recent years. **15** by: *beloved of all; tempted of the Devil; forsaken of God and men.*

off[1] /ɒf *US:* ɔf/ *adj* **1** (contrasted with *near*) (of horses, vehicles) on the right-hand side: *the off front wheel; the off hind leg of a horse; the off horse* (of a pair). **2** (remotely) possible or likely. ***on the off chance,*** ⇨ **chance**[1]**(2). 3** inactive; dull: *the ˈoff season,* ⇨ **season.**

off[2] /ɒf *US:* ɔf/ *adverbial particle* (For special uses with *off* as an *adverbial particle* such as *go off: turn sth off* ⇨ the *v* entries.) **1** (indicating distance in space or time) departure, removal, separation at or to a distance; away: *The town is five miles off. We're still some way off,* from our destination. *The holidays are not far off. Why don't you have that long beard off,* cut off, shaved off? *He's off to London. It's time I was off/I must be off now,* I must leave now. *We're off/Off we go!* We've started/We're starting! *They're off!* (in racing) The race has started! *Off with him!* Take him away! *Off with his head!* Cut his head off! **2** (contrasted with *on*) indicating the ending of sth arranged, planned, etc: *Their engagement* (i e to marry) *is off/broken off*, ended. *The miners' strike is off*, will not now take place. **3** (contrasted with *on*) disconnected; no longer available: *The water/gas/electricity is off. Are the brakes off? The central heating is off. That dish is off*, (in a restaurant) no more of that dish is available (even though it is on the menu). **4** indicating absence or freedom from work or duty: *I think I'll take the afternoon off*, not do my usual work, etc. *The manager gave the staff a day off*, a day's holiday. *You mustn't take time off* (= stay away from work) *just because you want to see a football match.* **5** (of food) no longer fresh: *This meat/fish is/has gone slightly off*, is beginning to smell or taste rather bad. **6** (in a theatre) behind or at the side(s) of the stage: *Noises off*, e g as a stage direction in a printed play. **7** (phrases) ***on and off/off and on***, from time to time; now and again; irregularly: *It rained on and off all day.* ***better/ worse off***, ⇨ better²(1), worse *adv*(1). ***badly/ comfortably/well off***, ⇨ these adverbs. ***right/ straight off***, at once; immediately.

off³ /of *US:* ɔf/ *prep* **1** not on; down from; away from: *fall off a ladder/a tree/a horse. The rain ran off the roof. The ball rolled off the table. Keep off the grass. Cut another slice off the loaf. Can you take something off* (i e reduce) *the price?* **2** (of a road or street) extending or branching from: *a narrow lane off the main road; a street off the Strand*, branching from the street called the Strand. **3** at some distance from: *a house off the main road;* a short distance seaward of: *an island off the Cornish coast; a ship anchored off the harbour entrance. The battle was fought off Cape Trafalger.* **4** (colloq) feeling averse to; not taking or indulging in: *I'm off my food*, have little or no appetite, don't enjoy it. *She's off smoking/drugs*, does not smoke/take drugs any more. **5** (phrases) ***(look) off colour***, ⇨ colour¹(2). ***off duty***, ⇨ duty. ***(go) off one's head***, ⇨ head¹(19). ***off the map***, (colloq, of a place) remote from populated areas, difficult to reach; (sl) no longer existing; unimportant. ***(wander) off the point***, ⇨ point¹(9). ***off side***, (football, etc), ⇨ offside.

off⁴ /of *US:* ɔf/ *pref* (used in numerous compounds) ⇨ the entries below.

of·fal /ˋofl *US:* ˋɔfl/ *n* [U] those parts, e g heart, head, kidneys, which are considered less valuable than the flesh when an animal is cut up for food.

off-beat /ˈof ˋbit *US:* ˈɔf/ *adj* (colloq) unusual; unconventional: *an* ~ *boutique.*

off-Broad·way /ˈof ˋbrɔdweɪ *US:* ˈɔf/ *adj* situated outside the Broadway district (N Y City); (of theatres and theatrical activities in this area) experimental and done cheaply (contrasted with the large theatres on Broadway).

of·fence (US = **of·fense**) /əˋfens/ *n* **1** [C] ***an ~ against***, crime, sin, breaking of a rule: *an* ~ *against God and man; an* ~ *against the law/ against good manners; be charged with a serious* ~. **2** [U] the hurting of sb's feelings; condition of being hurt in one's feelings. ***give/cause ~ (to sb); take ~ (at sth)***: *He is quick to take* ~, is easily offended. ***No ~!*** (phrase used to say) I did not intend to hurt your feelings. **3** [U] attacking: *weapons of* ~. *They say that the most effective defence is* ~. **4** [C] that which annoys the senses or makes sb angry: *That cess-pool is an* ~ *to the neighbourhood.* **~·less** *adj* without ~; not giving ~.

off-day /ˋof deɪ *US:* ˋɔf/ *n* (colloq) day when one is unlucky, when one does things badly, clumsily, etc: *I'm afraid this is one of my* ~*s.*

of·fend /əˋfend/ *vi,vt* **1** [VP3A] ***~ against***, do wrong; commit an offence: ~ *against good manners/the law/traditions, etc.* **2** [VP6A] hurt the feelings of; give offence to: *I'm sorry if I've* ~*ed you. He was* ~*ed at/by my remarks. She was* ~*ed by/with her husband.* **3** [VP6A] displease; annoy: *sounds that* ~ *the ear; ugly buildings that* ~ *the eye.* **~er** *n* person who ~s, esp by breaking a law; *first* ~*ers*, found guilty for the first time and not usu treated severely; *an old* ~*er*, one who has often been found guilty.

of·fense /əˋfens/ ⇨ offence.

of·fen·sive /əˋfensɪv/ *adj* **1** causing offence to the mind or senses; disagreeable: *fish with an* ~ *smell;* ~ *language; language that is* ~ *to polite people.* **2** used for, connected with, attacking: ~ *weapons/wars.* ⇨ defensive. □ *n* attacking; an attitude of attack. ***go into/take the ~***, go into attack. ***a peace ~***, (modern jargon) sustained effort the declared aim of which is to lessen the risk of war. **~·ly** *adv* **~·ness** *n*

of·fer /ˋofə(r) *US:* ˋɔf-/ *vt,vi* **1** [VP6A,7A,12A, 13A,14] ***~ sth to sb; ~ sb sth; ~ sth for***, hold out, put forward, to be accepted or refused; say what one is willing to pay, give or exchange: *They* ~*ed a reward for the return of the jewels that had been lost. I have been* ~*ed a job in Chile. He* ~*ed to help me. He* ~*ed me his help. We* ~*ed him the house for £9 000/*~*ed him £9 000 for the house.* ***~ battle***, give the enemy an opportunity of fighting. ***~ one's hand***, hold it out (to shake hands). ***~ one's hand (in marriage)***, make a proposal of marriage to a woman. **2** [VP6A,12A,13A,15B] ***~ sth to sb; ~ sth up***, present (to God): ~ *prayers to God;* ~ *up a sacrifice.* **3** [VP6A,7A,14] ***~ (to)***, attempt; give signs of: ~ *no resistance to the enemy.* **4** [VP2A] occur; arise: *Take the first opportunity that* ~*s*, that there is. ***as occasion ~s***, when there is an opportunity. □ *n* [C] statement ~ing to do sth or give sth; that which is ~ed: *an* ~ *of help; your kind* ~ *to help; an* ~ *of marriage*, a proposal. *I've had an* ~ *of £9 000 for the house. Make me an* ~. ***be open to an ~***, be willing to consider a price to be named by a buyer. ***(goods) on ~***, for sale at a certain price. **~·ing** /ˋofrɪŋ *US:* ˋɔf-/ *n* **1** [U] act of ~ing: *the* ~*ing of bribes.* **2** [C] sth ~ed or presented, esp the money collected during a church service: *a* ˋ*peace* ~*ing*, sth ~ed in the hope of restoring friendship after a quarrel, etc.

of·fer·tory /ˋofətrɪ *US:* -tɔrɪ/ *n* (*pl* -ries) [C] money collected in church during, or at the end of, a service.

off-hand /ˈof ˋhænd *US:* ˈɔf/ *adj* **1** without previous thought or preparation; extempore: ~ *remarks.* **2** (of behaviour, etc) casual; curt: *in an* ~ *way.* □ *adv* without previous thought: *I can't say* ~. **ˈoff-ˋhanded(ly)** *adj, adv* = ~.

of·fice /ˋofɪs *US:* ˋɔf-/ *n* [C] **1** (often *pl*) room(s) used as a place of business, for clerical work: *a lawyer's* ~; *working in an* ~, in business, e g as a clerk or typist; *our London* ~, our branch in London; (US = surgery). **ˋbooking ~,** ⇨ book²(2). **ˋbox-~,** ⇨ box¹(2). **ˋ~-block,** (usu large) building containing ~s (often of more than one company or firm). **ˋ~-boy** *n* boy employed to do less important duties in an ~. **2** (buildings of a) government department, including the staff, their work and duties: *the ˋForeign O~; the O~ of Works,* (formerly attending to the repair, furnishing, etc of government-owned buildings). **3** the work which it is sb's duty to do, esp in a public position of trust and authority: *enter upon/leave/accept/resign ~,* esp of positions in the government service. *Which party will be in ~ after the next general election? The Liberals have been out of ~ for a long time now.* **ˋ~-bearer** *n* person who holds an ~. **4** duty: *the ~ of host/chairman.* **5** (*pl*) attentions, services, help: *through the good ~s* (= kind help) *of a friend; perform the last ~s for...,* conduct the burial service of.... **Divine O~,** certain forms of worship in the Roman Catholic and Episcopal Churches. **6** (*pl*) rooms in a building other than the living-rooms and bedrooms (e g the rooms where domestic work is carried on, cellars, etc): *two reception rooms, three bedrooms and the usual ~s.*

of·fi·cer /ˋofɪsə(r) *US:* ˋɔf-/ *n* **1** person appointed to command others in the armed forces, in merchant ships, aircraft, the police force, etc usu wearing special uniform with indications of rank: *~s and men; ~s and crew.* **2** person with a position of authority or trust, engaged in active duties, e g in the government: *executive/clerical ~s,* in the civil service; *a customs ~; ~s of state,* ministers in the government; *the ~s of the Debating Society,* i e the President, Secretary, Treasurer; *the Medical O~ of Health; ˋWelfare O~s.* **3** form of address to a policeman.

of·fi·cial /əˋfɪʃl/ *adj* **1** of a position of trust or authority; said, done, etc with authority: *~ responsibilities/records, in his ~ uniform; ~ statements. The news is not ~.* **2** characteristic of, suitable for, persons holding office: *written in ~ style.* □ *n* person holding public office (e g in national or local government): *government ~s.* **~ly** /-ʃlɪ/ *adv* in an ~ manner; with ~ authority. **~·dom** /-dəm/ *n* ~s collectively; the ways of doing business of (government) ~s. **~ese** /əˈfɪʃlˋiz/ *n* [U] language characteristic of the writing of some government ~s (considered to be too formal or obscure). ⇨ *journalese* at journal.

of·fici·ate /əˋfɪʃɪeɪt/ *vi* [VP2A,C,3A] **~ *as/at,*** perform the duties of an office or position: *~ as chairman; ~ as host at a dinner party; ~ at a marriage ceremony,* (of a priest) perform the ceremony.

of·fi·cious /əˋfɪʃəs/ *adj* too eager or ready to help, offer advice, use authority, etc. **~·ly** *adv* **~·ness** *n*

off·ing /ˋofɪŋ *US:* ˋɔf-/ *n* part of the sea distant from the point of observation but visible: *a steamer in the ~;* (fig) *a quarrel in the ~,* one that appears likely to break out.

off·ish /ˋofɪʃ *US:* ˋɔf-/ *adj* (colloq) inclined to aloofness; distant in manner. ⇨ *stand-offish* at stand²(11).

off-li·cence /ˋof laɪsns *US:* ˋɔf/ *n* (GB) licence to sell beer and other alcoholic drinks for consumption off the premises; shop, part of a public house, where such drinks may be bought and taken away.

off-peak /ˋof pik *US:* ˋɔf/ *attrib adj* ⇨ peak¹(4).

off-print /ˋof prɪnt *US:* ˋɔf/ *n* [C] separate printed copy of an article in part of a larger publication.

off-put·ting /ˈof ˋpʊtɪŋ *US:* ˈɔf/ *adj* (colloq) disconcerting. ⇨ *put off* at put¹(11).

off-scour·ings /ˋof skaʊərɪŋz *US:* ˋɔf/ *n pl* refuse; dregs: (usu fig) *the ~s of humanity.*

off·set /ˋofset *US:* ˋɔf-/ *vt* (-tt-) [VP6A,14] balance, compensate for: *He has to ~ his small salary by living economically.* □ *n* **1** (also **~ process**) method of printing in which the ink is transferred from a plate to a rubber surface and then on to paper. **2** = offshoot.

off·shoot /ˋofʃut *US:* ˋɔf-/ *n* [C] stem or branch growing from a main stem (liter or fig): *an ~ of a plant/a mountain range/a family.*

off-shore /ˈof ˋʃɔ(r) *US:* ˈɔf/ *adj* **1** in a direction away from the shore or land: *~ breezes.* **2** at a short way out to sea: *~ islands/fisheries.* **3 ~ purchases,** (US) goods purchased by the US for countries in receipt of economic or military aid, but which do not come from the US directly, e g aluminium shipped from Canada to Europe.

off·side /of ˋsaɪd *US:* ɔf/ *attrib adj, adv* (football, hockey) (of a player) in a position on the field in relation to the ball which is debarred by the rules: *~ play; the ~ rule.*

off·spring /ˋofsprɪŋ *US:* ˋɔf-/ *n* (*pl* unchanged) child; children; young of animals: *He is the ~ of a scientific genius and a ballet dancer. Their ~ are all slightly mad.*

off-street /ˋof strit *US:* ˋɔf/ *attrib adj* not on the main streets: *~ parking,* of motor-vehicles; *~ (un)loading,* e g of lorries at the rear entrances of buildings.

off-white /ˈof ˋwaɪt *US:* ˈɔf ˋhwaɪt/ *adj* not pure white, but with a pale greyish or yellowish tinge.

oft /oft *US:* ɔft/ *adv* (in poetry) often: *an oft-told tale; many a time and oft,* very often. **ˋoft-times** *adv* (archaic) often.

of·ten /ˋofn *US:* ˋɔfn/ *adv of frequency* (usu occupying mid-position (i e with the *v*); may occupy front-position or end-position for emphasis (esp when modified by *very* or *quite*), or for contrast; comp and sup either *~er, ~est,* or *more ~, most ~.*) **1** many times; in a large proportion of the instances: *We ~ go there. We have ~ been there. We've been there quite ~. It very ~ rains here in April.* **2** (in phrases) ***how ~***: *How ~ do the buses run?* ***as ~ as,*** each time that: *As ~ as I tried to get an answer from him he made some excuse and avoided giving me the information. I wanted.* ***as ~ as not, more ~ than not,*** very frequently: *During foggy weather the trains are late more ~ than not.* ***every so ~,*** from time to time. ***once too ~,*** once more than is wise, safe, etc: *He exceeded the speed limit once too ~ and was fined £10.*

ogle /ˋəʊgl/ *vi,vt* [VP2A,6A] **~ *(at),*** look meaningly at; make eyes at (suggesting love or longing): *ogling all the pretty girls.*

ogre /ˋəʊgə(r)/ *n* [C] (in fables) cruel man-eating giant. **ogress** /ˋəʊgres/ *n* female ~. **ˋogre·ish** /-ɪʃ/ *adj* like an ~.

oh /əʊ/ *int* exclamation of surprise, fear, etc.

ohm /əʊm/ *n* [C] unit of electrical resistance (symbol Ω).

oho /əʊˋhəʊ/ *int* exclamation of surprise or triumph.

oil /ɔɪl/ *n* [C,U] **1** (sorts of) (usu easily burning) liquid which does not mix with water, obtained from animals (e g *whale-oil*), plants (*coconut oil, 'olive-`oil, oil of peppermint, essential oils*), or found in rock underground (*mineral oil, petroleum*): *cod-liver oil; salad oil; hair oil.* **2** (phrases) ***burn the midnight oil,*** sit up late at night to study, etc. ***paint in oils,*** paint with oil-colours (⇨ below). ***pour oil on the flame(s),*** make anger more intense, make a quarrel more bitter, etc. ***pour oil on troubled waters,*** act or speak in such a way as to end quarrelling, bitterness, etc. ***smell of the midnight oil,*** bear marks of study (as if done late at night by the light of an oil-lamp). ***strike oil,*** find petroleum in the ground by sinking a shaft, etc; (fig) become very prosperous or successful. **3** (compounds) **`oil-bearing** *adj* (e g rock strata) containing mineral oil. **`oil-burner** *n* engine, ship, heater, etc that uses oil as fuel. **`oil-cake** *n* [U] cattle food made from seeds after the oil has been pressed out. **`oil-can** *n* can with a long nozzle, used for oiling machinery. **`oil·cloth** *n* [U] cotton material waterproofed and used as a covering for shelves, etc. **`oil-colours** *n pl* paints made by mixing colouring matter in oil. **`oil-field** *n* area where petroleum is found. **`oil-fired** *adj* (e g of a furnace) burning oil as fuel: *oil-fired central heating.* **`oil·man** *n* one who sells oil and oil-colours. **`oil-palm** *n* tropical palm tree yielding oil. **`oil-painting** *n* [U] art of painting in oil-colours; [C] picture painted in oil-colours. **`oil-paper** *n* paper made transparent and waterproof by being treated with oil. **`oil-rig** *n* structure for drilling (e g in the sea-bed) for oil. **`oil-silk** *n* silk cloth treated with oil to make it air-tight and water-tight, used for making raincoats, etc. **`oil-skin** *n* [C,U] (coat etc, made of) cloth treated with oil to make it waterproof; (*pl*) suit of clothes made of this material, as worn by sailors, etc. **`oil-slick,** ⇨ slick. **`oil-tanker** *n* ship, large vehicle, for carrying oil (esp petroleum). **`oil-well** *n* well from which petroleum is obtained. □ *vt* [VP6A] put oil on or into (e g to make a machine run smoothly: *oil a lock/bicycle; oil the wheels/works,* (fig) make things go smoothly by being tactful; *oil* (more usu *grease*) *sb's palm,* give him a bribe. **oiled** *adj* (usu *well-oiled*) (sl) intoxicated.

an oil-tanker

oiler /`ɔɪlə(r)/ *n* **1** ship built for carrying oil; oil-tanker. **2** oil-can for oiling machinery. **3** person who oils machinery, e g in the engine-room of a steamer.

oily /`ɔɪlɪ/ *adj* (-ier, -iest) **1** of or like oil: *an ~ liquid.* **2** covered or soaked with oil: *~ fingers.* **3** (of speech or manner) too smooth; fawning; trying by fawning to win favour. **`oil·ily** /-əlɪ/ *adv* **`oili·ness** *n* ⇨ oleaginous.

oint·ment /`ɔɪntmənt/ *n* [C,U] (sorts of) medicinal paste made from oil or fat and used on the skin (to heal injuries or roughness, or as a cosmetic).

okapi /əʊ`kɑpɪ/ *n* rare forest ruminant animal of the Congo region in Africa.

okay /'əʊ`keɪ/ (abbr **OK**) *adj, adv* (colloq) all right; correct; approved. □ *vt* [VP6A] (colloq) agree to; approve of. □ *n* (colloq) agreement; sanction: *Have they given you their OK?*

okra /`əʊkrə/ *n* (tropical and semi-tropical plant with) edible green seed pods used as a vegetable.

old /əʊld/ *adj* (-er, -est) ⇨ also elder[1], eldest. **1** (with a period of time, and with *how*) of age: *He's forty years old. At fifteen years old he left home to become a sailor. How old are you? He is old enough to know better. Ought a seven-year-old child to be able to read?* **2** (contrasted with *young*) having lived a long time; no longer young or middle-aged: *Old people cannot be so active as young people. He's far too old for a young girl like you to marry. What will he do when he grows/is/gets old?* **the old,** old people. **old and young** (or) **young and old,** everyone. **old age,** the latter part of life. **old age pension,** (now *retirement pension*) pension paid by the State to old persons. Hence, **old age pensioner** *n* (now *senior citizen*). **the old man,** (colloq) **(a)** one's husband or father. **(b)** (among sailors) the captain of a ship. **the old woman,** (colloq) one's wife. **'old-`womanish** *adj* (of men) fussy and timid. **an old maid,** ⇨ maid. **'old-`maidish** *adj* (ironic, of a man) precise, tidy, fidgety (as old maids are said to be). **3** (contrasted with *new, modern, up to date*) belonging to past times; having been in existence or use for a long time: *old customs/families/civilizations; old houses/clothes.* ***one of the old school,*** conservative; old-fashioned. **'old-`clothesman** *n* dealer in clothes that have been discarded as no longer good enough, or as too small, too old-fashioned, etc. **the Old World,** Europe, Asia and Africa. **'old-`fashioned** *adj* **(a)** out of date: *old-fashioned styles/clothes.* **(b)** keeping to old ways, ideas, customs, etc: *an old-fashioned aunt; an old-fashioned child,* one who behaves like a much older person. **(c)** (of glances) reproving: *She gave him an old-fashioned look.* □ *n* (US) kind of cocktail made with whiskey. **'old-`fog(e)yish** *adj* (of a man) old-fashioned; behind the times. **old hat,** (colloq) out of date. **`old-time** *adj* belonging to, typical of, past times: *old-time dances.* **`old-world** *adj* belonging to, typical of, past times; not modern: *an old-world cottage/garden.* **4** long known or familiar: *an old friend of mine,* one who has been a friend for a long time (but not necessarily old in years). **Old Glory,** used by Americans of the flag of the US. **5** former; previous (but not necessarily old in years): *I prefer old houses to these modern ones.* **old boy,** former member of the school in question. Hence, *Old Etonian,* etc old boy of Eton College; *Old `Boys' Day,* academic anniversary attended by old boys. Cf US *Homecoming Weekend.* **the old country,** one's mother country (used esp when one has left it to settle elsewhere). **the/one's old school,** the school one attended as a boy/girl. **the/one's old school tie,** **(a)** tie worn by former pupils. **(b)** feeling of solidarity, wish to give mutual help, among former pupils of the same school or similar types of school. **6** having much experience or practice: *a man who is old in diplomacy.* **the old guard,** long-standing faithful supporters. **old offender,** person who has often been convicted of crime. **an old hand (at sth),** person with long experience. **old-`timer** *n* person who has for many years lived in a place, been associated with (a club, occupation, etc). ***come the old soldier (over sb),*** (colloq) claim, because of long experience, to have superior knowledge or ability. **7** (colloq) used in addressing persons, and with names (and nicknames) giving intimacy, or in joking style: *'Good old John!' 'Listen, old man.' 'Hullo, old thing!'* ***the old one, the old gentleman, old Harry/ Nick/Scratch,*** the devil. **8** (sl) used as an intensifier: *We're having a high old time,* a very good time. *Any old thing* (= Anything whatever) *will do.* □ *n* the past: *in days of old; the men of old.* **`old·ish** /-ɪʃ/ *adj* rather old.

olden /`əʊldn/ *adj* (archaic, liter) of a former age: *in ~ times/days.*

old·ster /`əʊldstə(r)/ *n* (colloq) old person (the word is used chiefly as an antithesis to *youngster*): *Some of us ~s have more energy than the youngsters.*

oleagi·nous /'əʊlɪ`ædʒɪnəs/ *adj* having properties of oil; producing oil; fatty; greasy.

olean·der /'əʊlɪ`ændə(r)/ *n* [C] evergreen shrub with tough leaves and red, pink or white flowers growing in clusters.

oleo·graph /`əʊlɪəgrɑf *US:* -græf/ *n* picture printed in oils.

oleo·mar·gar·ine /'əʊlɪəʊ'mɑdʒə`rin *US:* -`mɑdʒərɪn/ *n* [U] fatty substance extracted from beef fat and used with other substances in margarine.

ol·fac·tory /ol`fæktərɪ/ *adj* concerned with smelling: *the ~ nerves.*

oli·garchy /`olɪgɑkɪ/ *n* (*pl* -chies) [C,U] (country with) government by a small group of all-powerful persons; such a group. **oli·garch** /`olɪgɑk/ *n* member of an ~.

ol·ive /`olɪv/ *n* **1** **`~(-tree),** (evergreen tree common in S Europe bearing a) small oval fruit with a hard stone-like seed and a bitter taste, yellowish-green when unripe and bluish-black when ripe; used for pickling, to be eaten as a relish, and for oil, **('~-`oil),** which is used for cooking, dressing salads, etc. **2** leaf, branch or wreath of ~ as an emblem of peace. ***hold out the `~-branch,*** show that one is ready to discuss peace-making. □ *adj* the colour of the unripe fruit, yellowish-green or yellowish-brown.

Olym·piad /ə`lɪmpɪæd/ *n* period of four years between celebrations of the Olympic Games.

Olym·pian /ə`lɪmpɪən/ *adj* (of manners, etc) magnificent; god-like: *~ calm.* □ *n* one of the greater gods of ancient Greece; person with god-like qualities.

Olym·pic /ə`lɪmpɪk/ *adj* of or at Olympia. **the ~ Games, (a)** the contests held at Olympia in Greece in ancient times. **(b)** the international athletic competitions held in modern times every four years in a different country.

om·buds·man /`ombʊdzmæn/ *n* **the O~,** (in GB officially called *Parliamentary Commissioner*) experienced person having authority to inquire into and pronounce upon grievances of citizens (against the executive branch of Government).

omega /`əʊmɪgə *US:* əʊ`megə/ *n* the last letter (Ω) of the Greek alphabet. ⇨ App. 4; final development. ***Alpha and O~,*** the beginning and the end.

om·elet, om·elette /`omlət/ *n* [C] eggs beaten together and fried, often flavoured with cheese or containing herbs, etc or (*sweet ~*) jam, sugar.

omen /`əʊmen/ *n* [C,U] (thing, happening, regarded as a) sign of sth good or warning of evil fortune: *an ~ of success; an event of good/bad ~.* □ *vt* [VP6A] be an ~ of.

om·in·ous /`omɪnəs/ *adj* of bad omen; threatening: *an ~ silence; ~ of disaster.* **~·ly** *adv*

omission /ə`mɪʃn/ *n* **1** [U] act of omitting, leaving out or undone: *sins of ~,* leaving undone those things that ought to be done. **2** [C] sth that is omitted.

omit /ə`mɪt/ *vt* (-tt-) **1** [VP7A,6B] ***~ to do/doing sth,*** fail: *~ to do/~ doing a piece of work.* **2** [VP6A] fail to include; leave out: *This chapter may be ~ted.*

om·ni·bus /`omnɪbəs/ *n* (*pl* -buses /-bəsɪz/) **1** (former name for a) bus; (in names): *The 'Midland `O~ Co.* **2** (attrib) for, including, many purposes: *an ~ volume,* a large book in which a number of books, e g by the same author, are reprinted.

om·nip·otence /om`nɪpətəns/ *n* [U] infinite power: *the ~ of God.* **om·nip·otent** /-ənt/ *adj* having infinite power: *the O~,* God.

om·niscience /om`nɪʃns/ *n* [U] (formal) infinite knowledge. **om·niscient** /-ʃnt/ *adj* having infinite knowledge.

om·niv·or·ous /om`nɪvərəs/ *adj* (formal) eating all kinds of food; (fig) reading all kinds of books, etc: *an ~ reader.*

on[1] /on/ *adverbial particle* (For special uses with *on* as an *adverbial particle* such as *go on, go on sth,* ⇨ the *v*entries.) **1** (expressing the idea of progress, advance, continued activity; ⇨ *v*entries for special uses): *Come on! They hurried on. I will follow on,* come after you. *He's getting on in years,* growing old. *The war still went on,* did not end. *How can you work on* (= continue working) *so long without a rest? On with the show!* Let the show begin! Let the show continue! ***and so on,*** and other things of the same kind; et cetera. ***later on,*** at, during, a later time. ***on and on,*** without stopping: *We walked on and on.* **2** (corresponding in meaning to on[2](1): *On with your coat,* Put it on. *Your hat is not on straight. He had nothing on,* was naked. *Has he got his spectacles on?* Is he wearing them? **3** (contrasted with off[2](3)) **(a)** in action; in use; functioning; flowing, running, etc: *The lights were all full on,* giving their maximum light. *Someone has left the bathroom tap on,* running. *I can smell gas—is one of the taps on,* is gas escaping from one of them? *Be sure the hand-brake is on before you leave the car. The performance is on,* has begun. **(b)** available or procurable when or if needed: *Is the water on yet?* Is a supply available from the mains? *The strike of postal workers is still on,* has not ended yet. **4** (combined with *be* and *have* in various meanings): *What's on?* What's the programme? What's happening? *What's on* (= What films are being shown) *at the local cinema this week? There's nothing on tomorrow, is there,* e g no meeting I ought to attend, no engagement I ought to carry out? *Have you anything on this evening,* any engagements, plans, etc? **5** towards: *a ship broadside on to the dock gates,* with its side facing towards the gates; *end on,* i e with the end forward.

on[2] /on/ *prep* **1** supported by; fastened or attached to; covering or forming part of (a surface); lying against; in contact with: *a carpet on the floor; the jug on the table; pictures on the wall; the words (written) on the blackboard; flies on the ceiling; a blister on the sole of my foot; put a roof on the shed; sit on the grass; floating on the water; write on paper; hang sth on a peg/a nail; stick a stamp* *on the envelope; live on the Continent.* Cf live *in* Europe; *have a hat on one's head/a ring on one's finger; carry a coat on/over one's arm; be/go on board a ship; have lunch on the train; continued on page five.* Cf *in* a book, magazine, etc. *Have you a match/any money on you,* i e in your pockets, etc? **2** (indicating time) **(a)** *on Sunday(s); on the 1st of May; on the evening of May the first.* Cf *in* the evening; *on New Year's Day/Eve; on a sunny day in July;* ⇨ one[1](4); *on a cold, wet day like this; on that day; on this occasion.* **(b)** at the time of: *on the death of his parents,* when they died; *on my arrival home; payable on demand; on (my) asking for information.* **(c)** *on time, on the minute,* i e punctually. **3** about; concerning: *speak/lecture/write on international affairs; a lecture on Shakespeare; be keen/bent/determined/set on sth/on doing sth.* **4** (indicating membership): *He is on the committee/the jury/the staff. He's on 'The Daily Telegraph',* is a member of the staff of this newspaper. **5** (indicating direction): towards: *marching on the enemy's capital; turn one's back on sb; smile/frown on sb; draw a knife on sb,* i e to attack him; *a ship drifting on(to) the rocks; hit sb on the head,* (note: not *his* head); *give sb a box/blow on the ear.* **6** (expressing the basis, ground or reason for sth): *on this/that/no account; a story based on fact; have sth on good authority; act on your lawyer's advice; arrested on a charge of theft; retire on a pension; on penalty of death; on an average; swear sth on the Bible; be on one's oath/one's honour.* **7** (indicating a charge or imposition): *put a tax on tobacco; charge interest on money; place a strain on the economy.* **8** (indicating proximity) close to; against: *Henley-on-Thames; a town on the coast; a house on the main road; a village on the frontier; on both sides of the river; on my right/left; just on* (= almost) *2 o'clock; just on a year ago; just on £10.* **9** (followed by a *n,* or *adj* an activity, action, manner, state): *on business,* engaged in business; *on holiday; on tour,* touring; *go on an errand; on the way; on the sly,* in a sly manner; *buy sth on the cheap,* (colloq) at a low price; *on his best behaviour,* behaving very well; *be on the look-out for sb,* watching for him; *on fire,* burning; *on sale; on loan.* **10** added to: *suffer disaster on disaster,* pile insult on insult.

once /wʌns/ *adv* **1** (usu end position) for one time, on one occasion, only: *I have been there* ~. *This clock needs winding* ~ *a week. He goes to see his parents in Wales* ~ *(in) every six months. We go to the cinema* ~ *a week/a fortnight,* every week/every two weeks. ***~ more,*** again; another time. ***~ or twice, ~ and again, ~ in a while,*** now and again; occasionally; a few times. ***(for) this ~, (just) for ~,*** on this one occasion only, as an exception. ***~ and for all,*** ⇨ all[5](5). ***~ in a blue moon,*** ⇨ blue[1]. **2** (often mid position) at some indefinite time in the past; formerly. **(a)** *He* ~ *lived in Persia. This novel was* ~ *very popular but nobody reads it today.* **(b)** (in story-telling style): *O~ upon a time there was a giant with two heads. There* ~ *lived a king who had twelve beautiful daughters.* **3** (in negative, conditional or indefinite clauses) ever; at all; even for one time: *He didn't ~/He never ~ offered to help. O~* (= If you ~, As soon as) *you understand this rule, you will have no further difficulty.* **4 at ~, (a)** without delay; immediately: *I'm leaving for Rome at ~. Come here at ~!* **(b)** at the same time: *Don't all speak at ~! I can't do two things at ~. The book is at ~ interesting and instructive.* ***all at ~,*** suddenly: *All at ~ I saw a rabbit dart across the road.* ***get/give sb/sth the ~-over,*** (colloq) have/give sb/sth a rapid inspection or examination.

on·com·ing /ˈonˋkʌmɪŋ/ *adj* advancing; approaching: *the ~ shift, the shift (of workers) coming on duty (in a factory): ~ traffic.* □ *n* approach: *the ~ of winter.*

one[1] /wʌn/ *numeral adj, pron* **1 (a)** as in the series: *one pen, two pencils and three books;* as in: *one from twenty leaves nineteen; one is enough; one o'clock;* as in: *ˈtwenty-ˋone, ˈthirty-ˋone,* etc (= old use *one and twenty,* etc). **(b)** as in: *one hundred, one thousand, one million; one half, one third,* etc. Except in formal, precise or legal style, *a year and a half* or *eighteen months* is preferred to *one and a half years; a million and a half* to *one and a half millions; a pound of tea* to *one pound of tea.* **(c)** as in: *one and six,* one shilling and sixpence (of GB currency before decimalization); *one pound ten,* one pound and ten pence or (formerly) ten shillings. **2** (with *pl* ones) the symbol or figure 1: *a row of ones,* i e 1 1 1 1. **3** as in: *Book One, Chapter One,* the first book, the first chapter. **4** as in: *one day/morning/afternoon/evening/night,* (similar in function to the *indef art,* but with the difference that the *prep 'on'* is used before the *indef art.* ⇨ on[2](1). Cf *one summer evening* and *on a summer evening; one morning in June* and *on a June morning*). **5** (*One* is used to indicate a contrast (expressed or implied) with *the other,* or *another,* or *other(s)*): *The two girls are so much alike that it is difficult for strangers to tell (the) one from the other. He did not know which to admire more, the one's courage or the other's determination. Well, that's one way of doing it, but there are other and better ways. I, for one, don't like the idea,* suggesting 'and there may be others who do not like it'. ***for one thing,*** for one reason (out of several or many): *I can't help you. For one thing, I've no money.* **6** (always stressed; used for emphasis): *There's only ˋone way to do it. That's the ˋone thing needed. No one of you could lift it,* i e two or more of you would be needed. *They went forward as one man,* i e all together, in a body. **7** (before a family name, with or without a title; ⇨ a[2](9); a certain: *I heard the news from one (Mr) Smith,* (dated formal) from a certain person named Smith. (Note that if *one* is replaced by the *indef art* a title must be used: *A Mr Smith has called to see you*). **8** (as *adj*) the same: *They all went off in one direction.* ***be at one (with sb),*** be in agreement. *I'm at one with you on this subject/We are at one on this subject,* Our opinions are the same. ***It's all one,*** It's all the same, it makes no difference: *It's all one to me whether you go or don't go.* ***one and the same,*** (emph for) the same: *One and the same idea occurred to each of them.* ***become one, be made one,*** be united; be married. **9** (phrases) ***one and all,*** everyone. ***in one,*** combined: *He is President, Chairman and Secretary in one.* ***one or two,*** a few: *I shall be away only one or two days.* ***by ones and twos,*** one or two at a time: *People began to leave the meeting by ones and twos.* ***be one up (on sb),*** have an advantage over him, be one step ahead of him. Hence, **ˈone-ˋup-man-**

ship /-mənʃɪp/ *n* technique of being one up. **'number `one,** (colloq) oneself; one's own interests: *He's always thinking of 'number one'*, of himself, his own welfare. **10** (with an *of adjunct*) a single person or thing of the sort indicated or supplied (with *some, any, several*, etc. for the *pl;* ⇨ **a²(3)** and **one²(1)**): *One of my friends* (*pl some* of my friends) *arrived late. If one of them* (*pl any* of them) *should need help...; I borrowed one of your books* (= a book of yours; *pl some* of your books) *last week.* (Note the use of *his, her, herself* and *himself* in these examples): *One of the boys/girls lost his/her hat. One of the girls/boys has hurt herself/himself.* **one... one's,** ⇨ **one⁴**. **11** (compounds) **'one-`armed** *adj* having only one arm. **'one-armed `bandit** *n* coin-operated gambling machine. **'one-`eyed** *adj* having only one eye. **'one-`horse** *adj* **(a)** drawn or worked by a single horse. **(b)** (fig, sl) poorly equipped: *a one-horse town*, a small provincial town with few attractions, etc. **'one-i`dea'd** *adj* possessed by a single idea. **'one-`sided** *adj* having one side only; occurring on one side only; partial; unfair; prejudiced: *a one-sided argument; a one-sided account of a quarrel.* **`one-step** *n* kind of foxtrot. **`one-time** *adj* former: *a one-time politician.* **`one-track** *attrib adj* having only one track: (esp) *a one-track mind*, dominated by one interest, subject, etc. **'one-way `street** *n* street in which traffic may proceed in one direction only.

one² /wʌn/ *indef pron* (used in place of a preceding or following *n* standing for a member of a class) **1** (with an *of*-adjunct, indicating inclusion; equivalent to *among;* ⇨ **a²(3)**; no corresponding *pl* word): *Mr Smith is not one of* (= not numbered or included among) *my customers.* Cf for *pl*: *Mr Green and Mr Smith are not customers of mine. This problem is one of great difficulty* (*pl*: *These problems are of great difficulty*). *We have always treated her as one* (= as a member) *of the family* (*pl*: *We have always treated them as members of the family*). *One of my friends was ill* (*pl*: *Some of my friends were ill.* ⇨ **one¹(10)**. **2** (Cf *one* and *it*. *One* replaces a *n* modified by the *indef art* or a *pl n* modified by *some* or *any*. *It* replaces a *n* made definite in some way, e g a *n* modified by *the, this, that*): *I haven't a pen. Can you lend me one? I haven't any stamps. Will you please give me one?* Cf *I'd like to look at that atlas. May I borrow it? Where's the railway timetable? Have you seen it?* **3** (the *pron 'one', pl 'ones'*, is used, in colloq style, equivalent to *that, those*): *I drew my chair nearer to the one* (= to that) *on which Mary was sitting. It's in that drawer—the one* (= that) *with the key in the lock. The children who do best in examinations are not always the ones* (= those) *with the best brains.* **4** (when the *pron 'one'* is used after the *def art*, or after an *adj* (or a *n* used as an *adj*), it may be called a 'prop-word'. As an *adj* cannot stand alone for one or more members of a class, *one* is used to support or 'prop up' the *adj*, as in): *a better one; that one; my old ones. Your plan is a good one on paper. There's a right answer and a wrong one. Yours may be the right answer and mine the wrong one. The chance was too good a one to let pass. He keeps his postage-stamps—he has some very rare ones—in a fire-proof safe.* **5** (The 'prop-word' *one* is not used after a possessive (e g *your, Mary's*) unless there is also an *adj* It is not used after *own*): *This is my hat and that is my brother's.* Not: *my brother's one. Tom's exercise book is neater than John's.* Not: *John's one. Do you rent the house or is it your own?* (With an *adj*): *My cheap camera seems to be just as good as John's expensive one. Your old suit looks as smart as your brother's new one.* **6** (In formal or written style it is preferable to avoid the use of the 'prop-word' *one*, esp when there are two *adjj* indicating a contrast. The *n* is placed after only one of the *adjj*): *If we compare British with American universities* (better than: *If we compare British universities with American ones*).... *Don't praise the younger child in the presence of the elder. I put my right arm through Mary's left. At home Hanako prefers Japanese to European-style clothes. What the teacher said seemed to go in at one ear and out at the other.* **7** (*One* is used after *this* and *that*, but is better avoided, in liter style, after *these* and *those*): *Will you have this (one) or that (one)? Will you have these or those?* (With an *adj, 'one'* is, of course, necessary): *Will you have this green one/these green ones or that blue one/those blue ones?* **8** (The 'prop-word' *one* is used with *which*, esp to distinguish *sing* from *pl*): *Here are some books on European history. Which one(s) do you want?*

one³ /wʌn/ *pers pron* **1** (used, always with a qualifying word or phrase, for a particular person or creature): *the `Holy One*, God; *the `Evil One*, Satan, the Devil; *the absent one*, e g the absent member of the family; *the little ones*, the children; *a nest with five young ones*, young birds; *my sweet one*, as a term of endearment. **2** (used, in liter style, with a following *adj*, phrase or clause): *He lay there like one dead*, as if he were dead. *He worked like one possessed*, like a man possessed by a spirit. *He was one* (= the sort of person) *who never troubled about his personal comfort. He's not one to be* (= not a man who is) *easily frightened.* **3 one another,** (used like *each other*, to indicate mutual action or relation; may be the object of a *v* or a *prep;* possessive form is *one another's*): *They don't like one another. They have quarrelled and no longer speak to one another. They were fighting with cudgels, trying to break one another's heads.*

one⁴ /wʌn/ *impers pron* (standing for any person, including the speaker or writer. Cf French *on*, German *man*. Possessive, *one's*, reflexive, *oneself.* ⇨ **one¹(10)**): *One cannot always find time for reading. If one wants a thing done well, one had best do it oneself. One doesn't like to have one's word doubted.* (In colloq style it is more usual to employ *you, we, people*): *We live and learn. You never can tell. What's a chap/a fellow to do in such a situation?* (In US usage, *one* may be followed by *he, him, his, himself* instead of by *one, one's, oneself*): *One does not like to have his word doubted.*

on·er·ous /ˈɒnərəs/ *adj* needing effort; burdensome (*to*): *~ duties.* **~·ly** *adv*

one·self /wʌnˈself/ *reflex, emphat pron* one's own self: *wash/dress oneself. One should not live for oneself alone.*

onion /ˈʌnɪən/ *n* [C] **1** vegetable plant with a round bulb of many concentric coats, a strong smell and flavour, used in cooking and to pickle; ⇨ the illus at **vegetable**: *spring-~s; Spanish ~s;* [U] this plant as food: *too much ~ in the salad; the ~-domed churches of Austria*, having ~-shaped domes. ***know one's ~s,*** (sl) be clever (because experienced). **2** (sl) head. ***off his ~,*** (sl) mentally unbalanced.

on·looker /ˋonlʊkə(r)/ *n* person who looks on at sth happening. ***The ~ sees most of the game,*** (prov) The spectator is in a better position to judge than those who are taking part.

only[1] /ˋəʊnlɪ/ *adj* **1** (with a *sing n*) that is the one specimen of its class; single: *Smith was the ~ person able to do it. Harry is an ~ child,* has no brothers or sisters. *Her ~ answer was a shrug.* **2** (with a *pl n*) that are all the specimens or examples: *We were the ~ people wearing hats.* **3** best; most or best worth consideration: *He's the ~ man for the position. She says holidays abroad are the ~ thing these days.*

only[2] /ˋəʊnlɪ/ *adv* solely; and no one, nothing, more. **1** (modifying a single word, and placed, in written or formal style, close to the word it modifies; in speech the stress-pattern may indicate this, so that *only* may have various positions): *I ˈ~ saw ˋMary,* I saw Mary and no one else (= written style, *I saw ~ Mary*). Cf *I ˈ~ ˋsaw Mary,* I saw her but didn't speak to her. *O~ the teachers are allowed to use this room. O~ five men were seriously hurt in the accident. We've ~ half an hour to wait now. Ladies ~,* e g on a compartment in a railway carriage. *We can ~ guess* (= We cannot be certain about) *what happened.* **2** ***~ too,*** (with an *adj* or *pp*) very: *I shall be ~ too pleased to get home. The news was ~ too true,* was really true, and not, as might be hoped or expected, untrue. ***if ~,*** expressing a wish or assumption. ⇨ **if(8)**.

only[3] /ˋəʊnlɪ/ *conj* but then; it must, however, be added that: *The book is likely to be useful, ~ it's rather expensive. He's always ready to promise help, ~ he never keeps his promises.* ***~ that,*** with the exception that; were it not that: *He would probably do well in the examination, ~ that he gets rather nervous.*

ono·mato·pœia /əˈnomətəˋpɪə *US:* ˈonəˈmætəˋpɪə/ *n* [U] formation of words in imitation of the sounds associated with the thing concerned (as *cuckoo* for the bird that utters this cry).

on·rush /ˋonrʌʃ/ *n* strong, onward rush or flow.

on·set /ˋonset/ *n* attack; vigorous start: *at the first ~; the ~ of a disease.*

on·shore /ˋonʃɔ(r)/ *adj, adv* toward the shore.

on·slaught /ˋonslɔt/ *n* [C] furious attack (*on*).

onto /ˋontə *strong form:* ˋontu/ *prep* = on to; upon. ⇨ **on**[1].

on·tol·ogy /onˋtolədʒɪ/ *n* [U] department of metaphysics concerned with the properties of existence; the essence of things.

onus /ˋəʊnəs/ *n* (*sing* only) responsibility for, burden of, doing sth: *The ~ of proof rests with you,* It is for you to supply proof.

on·ward /ˋonwəd/ *adj, adv* forward: *an ~ march/movement.* □ *adv* (also **~s**) towards the front; forward: *move ~(s).*

onyx /ˋonɪks/ *n* [U] (sorts of) quartz in layers of different colours; used for ornaments, cameos, etc.

oodles /ˋudlz/ *n pl* (sl) ***~ of,*** great amounts or sums: *~ of money.*

oof /uf/ *n* [U] (sl) money.

oomph /ʊmf/ *n* (sl) energy; sex-appeal.

ooze /uz/ *n* [U] soft liquid mud, esp on a riverbed, the bottom of a pond, lake, etc. □ *vi,vt* **1** [VP2C] (of moisture, thick liquids) pass slowly through small openings: *Blood was still oozing from the wound.* (fig) *Their courage was oozing away.* **2** [VP6A] pass out; emit: *He was oozing sweat.* **oozy** *adj* of or like ~; slimy.

opac·ity /əʊˋpæsətɪ/ *n* [U] (quality of) being opaque.

opal /ˋəʊpl/ *n* semi-precious stone in which changes of colour are seen, often used as a gem. **opal·escent** /ˈəʊpəˋlesnt/ *adj* like an ~.

opaque /əʊˋpeɪk/ *adj* not allowing light to pass through; that cannot be seen through; dull. **~·ly** *adv* **~·ness** *n*

op art /ˋop ɑt/ *n* form of modern abstract art using geometrical patterns which produce optical illusions of movement.

open[1] /ˋəʊpən/ *adj* **1** not closed; allowing (things, persons) to go in, out, through: *sleep with ~ windows; leave the door ~.* **~ vowel,** one made with the roof of the mouth and the tongue fairly wide apart, e g /e, æ, o/ **ˈ~-ˋeyed** *adj* with ~ eyes; watchful; surprised. **ˈ~-ˋmouthed** /ˋmaʊðd/ *adj* **(a)** showing greed (for food, etc). **(b)** showing great surprise or stupidity. **ˋ~-work** *n* [U] pattern (in metal, lace, etc) with spaces: *~-work lace; ~-work stockings.* **2** not enclosed, fenced in, barred or blocked: *the ~ country,* land affording wide views, without forests, etc. **the ~ sea,** not a bay or harbour, not closed in by land. **an ~ river,** not barred by ice, mudbanks, etc. **~ water,** navigable, free from ice. **an ~ prison,** one with fewer restrictions than usual, esp one where prisoners with good records come and go freely to work outside. **3** not covered in or over: *an ~ boat,* one without a deck; *an ~ carriage/car,* with no roof, or a roof that is folded back; *an ~ drain/sewer,* in the form of a ditch, not in pipes under the ground: *an ~ sandwich,* single slice of bread with meat, etc on top; *in the ˈ~ ˋair,* out of doors. **ˋ~-air** *attrib adj* taking place out of doors; fond of life in the ~ air: *an ˈ~-air ˋschool; ˈ~-air ˋtreatment of diseases,* e g consumption. **4** spread out; unfolded: *The flowers were all ~. The book lay ~ on the table. His mind was/His thoughts were an ~ book,* It was easy to read his thoughts. ***with ~ hands,*** generously. Hence, **ˈ~-ˋhanded** *adj* generous; giving freely. **ˈ~-ˋhearted** *adj* sincere; frank. ***with ~ arms,*** with affection or enthusiasm. **~ order,** (of troops), with wider space than usual between ranks. **5** public; free to all; not limited to any special persons, but for anyone to enter: *an ~ competition / championship/ scholarship; tried in ~ court,* of a law case, the public being freely admitted to hear the trial. *The position is still ~,* No one has yet been chosen to fill it. **the ~ door,** policy of free trade or freedom from tariffs; admission of foreign traders. **~ shop,** workshop, factory, etc where members and non-members of trade unions work on equal terms. ⇨ *closed shop* at **close**[3]**(2)**. ***keep ~ house,*** offer hospitality to all comers. **6** not settled or decided: *leave a matter ~.* **ˈ~-ˋended** *adj* (of a discussion, a subject for debate, etc) having a variety of possible solutions; on which no decision or agreement is reached, expected or required. **an ~ question,** with no decision, answer. **an ~ verdict,** jury's verdict of the fact and cause of a death, but not saying whether it is natural, accidental, suicide or murder. ***have/keep an ~ mind (on sth),*** be ready to consider sth further, to listen to new evidence, agreements, etc.

Hence, ˈ~-ˋ**minded** *adj* unprejudiced. **7** ready for business or for the admission of the public: *Are the shops ~ yet? Doors ~ at 7.00p m,* e g of a theatre. **8** known to all; not secret or disguised; frank: *an ~ quarrel/scandal; an ~ character/ countenance; Let me be quite ~* (= frank) *with you.* **an ~ letter,** one that is addressed to an individual or group but sent to and published in a periodical, usu in protest against sth. **9** unprotected; unguarded; vulnerable. ***be/lay oneself ~ to sth,*** behave so that one is vulnerable to sth: *Don't lay yourself ~ to ridicule/ attack.* **an ~ town/city,** (formerly) one without fortifications; (modern use) one which, its inhabitants declare, will not be defended if attacked, e g Paris, Rome, in World War II. **10** not settled, finished or closed: *keep one's account ~ at a bank; be ~ to an offer,* willing to consider one. **11** (phrases) ˋ**~-cast** *adj* surface: *~-cast coal; ~-cast mining,* from strata near the earth's surface (contrasted with production from deep mines). **an ~ cheque,** one that is not crossed and which may be cashed at the bank on which it is drawn. **the** ˋ**~ season,** (fishing and shooting) when there are no restrictions. ⇨ close[1](12). **an ~ secret,** sth supposed to be a secret but in fact known to all people. **an ~ town,** (US) one in which gambling, drinking saloons, etc are allowed without restrictions, e g *Las Vegas.* **the O~ University,** (GB) university (founded in 1971) whose students live at home and get tuition by correspondence, textbooks and special radio and TV programmes. **~ weather, an ~ winter,** free from severe frost and snow, so that it is possible to get about. □ *n* **the ~,** the ~ air. ⇨ 3 above. ***come out into the ~,*** (fig) come into public view; make one's ideas, plans, etc, known. **~·ly** *adv* without secrecy; frankly; publicly: *speak ~ly; go ~ly into a place,* e g where one might be expected to go secretly. **~·ness** *n* [U].

open[2] /ˋəʊpən/ *vt,vi* **1** [VP6A,14,16A] make ~ or cause to be ~; unfasten: *~ a box. He ~ed the door for me to come in/to let me in.* ***~ one's eyes,*** express surprise. ***~ (sb's) eyes to sth,*** cause him to realize sth, e g how he has been deceived. **2** [VP6A,15A,B] cut or make an ~ing in or a passage through: *~ a mine/a well; ~ a new road through a forest; O~ up!* command to ~ a door, etc. ***~ sth up,*** make ~; make accessible; make possible the development of: *~ up a wound/a mine/undeveloped land/a new territory to trade.* **3** [VP6A,15A,B] spread out; unfold: *~ one's hand/a book/a newspaper/a parcel; ~ out a folding map.* ***~ one's mind/heart to sb,*** make known one's ideas/feelings. **4** [VP6A] start: *~ an account,* e g at a bank, shop; *~ a debate/a public meeting.* ***~ the bidding,*** make the first bid (at an auction, at auction bridge). ***~ fire (at/on),*** start shooting. **5** [VP6A] declare, indicate, that business, etc may now start: *~ a shop; ~ Parliament.* **6** [VP2A,C] become ~; be ~ed; allow of being ~ed: *The flowers are ~ing. This shop does not ~ on Sundays. The door ~ed and a man came in. Does this door ~ inwards or outwards? The two rooms ~ into one another,* have a door between them. *This door ~s on to the garden.* **7** [VP3A] ***~ with,*** start: *The story ~s with a murder.* **8** [VP2A,C] become visible: *The view ~ed (out) before our eyes.* **~er** *n* person or thing that ~s: (chiefly in compounds) ˋ*pew-~er;* ˋ*tin-~er;* ˋ*bottle-~er.* ˋ**eye-opener,** ⇨ eye[1](3).

open·ing /ˋəʊpnɪŋ/ *n* **1** open space; way in or out: *an ~ in a hedge.* **2** beginning: *the ~ of a book/ speech.* **the ~ night,** e g on which a new play/ film is performed/shown for the first time, and to which dramatic critics are invited. **~ time,** e g at which public houses open and begin to serve drinks. **3** process of becoming open: *watch the ~ of a flower.* **4** position (in a business firm) which is open or vacant; opportunity: *an ~ in an advertising agency.* □ *adj* first: *his ~ remarks.*

op·era /ˋoprə/ *n* **1** [C] dramatic composition with music, in which the words are sung. **comic ~,** with spoken dialogue and a happy ending. **grand ~,** with no spoken dialogue. **light ~,** with a humorous subject. **2** [U] dramatic works of this kind as entertainment: *fond of ~; the ~ season.* ˋ**~-cloak** *n* lady's cloak for wearing with evening dress. ˋ**~-glasses** *n pl* small binoculars for use in a theatre. ˋ**~-hat** *n* man's tall, black silk hat, made so that it folds flat. ˋ**~-house** *n* theatre for performances of ~s. **op·er·atic** /ˈopəˋrætɪk/ *adj* of or for an ~: *~tic music/singers.*

op·er·ate /ˋopəreɪt/ *vt,vi* **1** [VP6A,2A,C,4A] (cause to) work, be in action, have an effect; manage: *~ a machine; machinery that ~s night and day. The company ~s three factories and a coal-mine. The lift was not operating properly. The lift is ~d by electricity. This new law ~s* (= produces an effect) *to our advantage. Several causes ~d to bring on the war.* **2** [VP2A,3A] ***~ (on sb) (for sth),*** perform a surgical operation: *The doctors decided to ~ at once.* ˋ**operating-table/-theatre** *n* for use in surgical operations. **3** [VP2A,C] (of an army) carry out various movements: *operating on a large scale.* **4** [VP2A,C] (of a stockbroker) buy and sell, esp in order to influence prices. **op·er·able** /ˋopərəbl/ *adj* that can be treated by means of a surgical operation.

op·er·ation /ˈopəˋreɪʃn/ *n* **1** [U] working; way in which sth works. ***be in/bring sth into/come into ~,*** be/cause to be/become effective: *When does the plan come into ~? Is this rule in ~ yet?* **2** [C] piece of work; sth (to be) done: *begin ~s; the ~s of nature,* changes brought about by natural forces. **3** (usu *pl;* colloq abbr **ops**) movements of troops, ships, aircraft, etc in warfare or during manœuvres. ˋ**~s/**ˋ**ops room,** from which ~s are controlled; (*sing*) in code names for military campaigns (*O~ Overlord*) and, by extension, for planned campaigns in industry, commerce, etc: *building/banking ~s; ~s research,* to promote greater efficiency in industry. **4** [C] ***an ~ (on sb) (for sth),*** act performed by a surgeon on any part of the body, esp by cutting to take away or deal with a diseased part: *an ~ for appendicitis.* **5** (maths) addition, subtraction, multiplication, division, etc. **~al** /-nl/ *adj* **1** of, for, used in, ~s. **~al costs/expenditure,** needed for operating (machines, aircraft, etc). **~al research,** into the best ways of using, improving, etc new weapons, machinery, etc. **2** ready for use: *When will the newly designed airliner be ~al?*

op·er·at·ive /ˋoprətɪv *US:* -reɪt-/ *adj* **1** operating; having an effect: *This law became ~ on 1 May.* **2** **~ words,** those having legal effect in a deed, etc; (loosely) most significant words. **3** of surgical operations: *~ treatment.* □ *n* worker; mechanic: *cotton ~s.*

op·er·ator /ˋopəreɪtə(r)/ *n* **1** person who operates

or works sth: *telephone/wireless telegraphy ~s; private ~s in civil aviation,* privately owned companies (contrasted with state-owned corporations). **2** (sl) confident, efficient man (in business, love affairs, etc): *He's a smooth/slick ~.*

op·er·etta /ˈopəˋretə/ *n* one-act, or short, light musical comedy.

oph·thal·mia /ofˋθælmɪə/ *n* [U] inflammation of the eye. **oph·thal·mic** /-mɪk/ *adj* of the eyes; afflicted with ~. **oph·thal·mo·scope** /ofˋθælməskəʊp/ *n* instrument with a mirror (having a hole in the centre) through which the eye may be examined.

opi·ate /ˋəʊpɪət/ *n* [C] drug containing opium, used to relieve pain or to help sb to sleep.

opine /əˋpɑɪn/ *vt* [VP9] **~ *that,*** (formal) have or express the opinion.

opin·ion /əˋpɪnɪən/ *n* **1** [C] belief or judgement not founded on complete knowledge: *political ~s. What's your ~* (= view) *of the new President? Those are my ~s about the affair.* ***in my, your, etc ~; in the ~ of sb,*** it is my, your, etc view that...: *In my ~/In the ~ of most people, the scheme is unsound.* ***act up to one's ~,*** act according to them. ***be of the ~ that...,*** feel, believe, that.... ***have a good/bad/high/low ~ of sb/sth,*** think well/badly, etc of. **2** [U] views, beliefs, of a group: *O~ is shifting in favour of stiffer penalties for armed robbery.* **public ~,** what the majority of people think: *Public ~ is against the proposed change.* **~ poll,** ⇨ poll[1](2). **3** [C] professional estimate or advice: *get a lawyer's ~ on the question. You had better have another ~ before you let that man take out all your teeth.* **~-ated** /-eɪtɪd/, **~·at·ive** /-ətɪv *US:* -eɪtɪv/ *adjj* obstinate in one's ~s; dogmatic.

opium /ˋəʊpɪəm/ *n* [U] substance prepared from poppy seeds, used to relieve pain, cause sleep, and as a narcotic drug. **ˋ~-den** *n* place where ~ smokers can obtain and use this drug.

opos·sum /əˋposəm/ (also **possum** /ˋposəm/) *n* kinds of small American animal that lives in trees.

op·po·nent /əˋpəʊnənt/ *n* person against whom one fights, struggles, plays games, or argues.

op·por·tune /ˋopətjun *US:* -tun/ *adj* **1** (of time) suitable, favourable; good for a purpose: *arrive at a most ~ moment.* **2** (of an action or event) done, coming, at a favourable time: *an ~ remark/speech.* **~·ly** *adv*

op·por·tun·ism /ˈopəˋtjun-ɪzm *US:* -ˋtun-/ *n* [U] being guided by what seems possible, or by circumstances, in determining policy; preferring what can be done to what should be done. **op·por·tun·ist** /-ɪst/ *n* person who acts on this principle; person who is more anxious to gain an advantage for himself than to consider whether he is trying to get it fairly.

op·por·tun·ity /ˈopəˋtjunətɪ *US:* -ˋtun-/ *n* (*pl* -ties) [C,U] **~ *(for sth/of doing sth/to do sth),*** favourable time or chance: *to make/find/get an ~; have few opportunities of meeting interesting people; have no/little/not much ~ for hearing good music. I had no ~ to discuss the matter with her. The ~ for the reformers to do this came in 1972.*

op·pose /əˋpəʊz/ *vt* **1** [VP6A] set oneself, fight, against (sb or sth): *~ the Government; ~ a scheme. I am very much ~d to your going abroad,* I am against the plan. **2** [VP14] put forward as a contrast or opposite; set up against: *~ your will against mine/your views to mine; ~ a vigorous resistance to the enemy.* ***as ~d to,*** in contrast with.

op·po·site /ˋopəzɪt/ *adj* **1 ~ *(to),*** facing; front to front or back to back (with): *the house ~ (to) mine; on the ~ side of the road.* **2** entirely different; contrary: *in the ~ direction.* **3** similarly placed elsewhere. **one's ~ number,** person or thing occupying the same or a similar position in another group, etc: *The British Foreign Minister is in Washington discussing problems with his ~ number.* □ *n* word or thing that is ~: *Black and white are ~s. I thought quite the ~.*

op·po·si·tion /ˈopəˋzɪʃn/ *n* **1** [U] the state of being opposite or opposed: *The Socialist Party was in ~,* formed the O~. ⇨ 2 below. *We found ourselves in ~ to our friends on this question.* **2** (*sing*) MP's of the political party or parties opposing the Government: *Her Majesty's O~; the leader of the O~; the O~ benches. We need a stronger O~.* **3** [U] resistance: *Our forces met with strong ~ all along the front.*

op·press /əˋpres/ *vt* [VP6A] **1** rule unjustly or cruelly; keep down by unjust or cruel government. **2** (fig) weigh heavily on; cause to feel troubled, uncomfortable: *~ed with anxiety/with a foreboding of misfortune; feel ~ed with the heat.* **~or** /-sə(r)/ *n* person who ~es; cruel or unjust ruler. **op·pression** /əˋpreʃn/ *n* **1** [U] the condition of being ~ed: *a feeling of ~ion.* **2** [U] ~ing or being ~ed: *victims of ~ion;* [C] instance of this; cruel or unjust act. **op·press·ive** /əˋpresɪv/ *adj* **1** unjust: *~ive laws/rules.* **2** hard to endure; overpowering: *~ive weather/heat/taxes.* **op·press·ive·ly** *adv*

op·pro·bri·ous /əˋprəʊbrɪəs/ *adj* (formal) (of words, etc) showing scorn or reproach; abusive. **~·ly** *adv* **op·pro·brium** /-brɪəm/ *n* (formal) [U] scorn; disgrace; public shame.

op·pugn /əˋpjun/ *vt* [VP6A] call in question; be contrary to.

opt /opt/ *vi* **1** [VP3A] ***opt for sth,*** exercise a choice; decide: *Fewer students are opting for science courses nowadays.* **2** ***opt out of,*** choose to take no part in: *young people who have opted out of society,* chosen not to be conventional members of society, e g by becoming hippies.

op·tat·ive /ˋoptətɪv/ *adj, n* (of) verbal form expressing desire: *~ mood,* e g in Greek, but not in English.

op·tic /ˋoptɪk/ *adj* of the eye or the sense of sight: *the ~ nerve,* from the eye to the brain. ⇨ the illus at eye. **op·tics** *n* (with *sing v*) science of light and the laws of light.

op·tical /ˋoptɪkl/ *adj* **1** of the sense of sight. **an ~ illusion,** sth by which the eye is deceived: *A mirage is an ~ illusion.* **2** for looking through; to help eyesight: *~ instruments,* e g microscopes, telescopes; *~ glass,* the kind used for ~ instruments. **op·ti·cally** /-klɪ/ *adv*

op·ti·cian /opˋtɪʃn/ *n* person who makes or supplies optical instruments, esp lenses and spectacles.

op·ti·mism /ˋoptɪmɪzm/ *n* [U] belief that in the end good will triumph over evil; tendency to look upon the bright side of things; confidence in success. **op·ti·mist** /-mɪst/ *n* person who is always hopeful and looks upon the bright side of things, who believes that all things happen for the best. **op·ti·mis·tic** /ˈoptɪˋmɪstɪk/ *adj* expecting the best; confident: *an optimistic view of events.* **op·ti·mis·ti·cally** /-klɪ/ *adv*

op·ti·mum /ˈɒptɪməm/ *n* (attrib) best or most favourable: *the ~ temperature for the growth of plants.*

op·tion /ˈɒpʃn/ *n* **1** [U] right or power of choosing. ***have no/little, etc ~,*** have little/no, etc choice: *I haven't much ~ in the matter,* cannot choose. *I had no ~,* was forced to act as I did. *He was given six months' imprisonment without the ~ of a fine.* **local ~,** right of people (in some towns, districts) to decide, by voting, whether or not to have or allow sth, e g the sale of alcoholic liqour. **2** [C] thing that is or may be chosen: *None of the ~s is satisfactory.* ***leave one's ~s open,*** not commit oneself. **3** [C] (comm) right to buy or sell sth at a certain price within a certain period of time: *have an ~ on a piece of land.* **ˈ~al** /-nl/ *adj* which may be chosen or not as one wishes; not compulsory: *~al subjects at school.* **~·ally** /ˈɒpʃnlɪ/ *adv*

opu·lence /ˈɒpjʊləns/ *n* [U] (formal) wealth; abundance. **opu·lent** /-ənt/ *adj* rich; wealthy; luxuriant: *~ vegetation.* **op·u·lent·ly** *adv*

opus /ˈəʊpəs/ *n* (*pl* opera /ˈɒpərə/, rarely used) separate musical composition (abbr **op,** used in citing a composition by number, as *Beethoven, Op 112*). **ˈmagnum ˈ~,** great literary undertaking, completed or in course of being written.

or /ɔ(r)/ *conj* **1** (introducing an alternative): *Is it green or blue? Are you coming or not?* ***either... or,*** ⇨ either. ***whether... or.*** *I don't care whether he stays or goes.* ***or else,*** otherwise; if not: *Hurry up or (else) you'll be late. Pay up, or else!* (as a threat). **2** (introducing all but the first of a series): *I'd like it to be black, (or) white or grey.* **3** (introducing a word that explains, or means the same as, another): *an English pound, or one hundred new pence; a dugout, or a canoe made by hollowing out a tree trunk; geology, or the science of the earth's crust.* **4** ***or so,*** (often equivalent to *about*) suggesting vagueness or uncertainty: *I'd like twenty or so.* ***or somebody/something/somewhere***: *I put it in the cupboard or somewhere,* i e somewhere, perhaps in the cupboard. ***somebody/something/somewhere or other,*** (colloq) (expressing uncertainty about who it was).

or·acle /ˈɒrəkl *US:* ˈɔr-/ *n* **1** (in ancient Greece) (answer given at) place where questions about the future were asked of the gods; priest(ess) giving the answers: *consult the ~.* **2** person considered able to give reliable guidance. **oracu·lar** /əˈrækjʊlə(r)/ *adj* of or like an ~; with a hidden meaning: *oracular utterances.*

oral /ˈɔrl/ *adj* **1** using the spoken, not the written, word: *an ~ examination.* **2** (anat) of, by, for, the mouth: *~ contraceptives,* ⇨ pill(2). □ *n* (colloq) ~ examination. **~ly** /ˈɔrlɪ/ *adv* by spoken words; by the mouth: *not to be taken ~ly,* (e g of medical preparations) not to be swallowed; for external use only.

or·ange /ˈɒrɪndʒ *US:* ˈɔr-/ *n, adj* [C] (evergreen tree with a) round, thick-skinned juicy fruit, green and usu changing to a colour between yellow and red; [U] usu colour of this fully-ripened fruit; ⇨ the illus at fruit. **~·ade** /ˈɒrɪndʒˈeɪd *US:* ˈɔr-/ *n* [U] drink made of ~ juice.

Or·ange·man /ˈɒrɪndʒmæn *US:* ˈɔr-/ *n* (*pl* -men) member of a Protestant political society in Ulster, Northern Ireland.

orang-outang /ɔˈræŋ uˈtæŋ *US:* əˈræŋ əˈtæŋ/ (also **-utan, -outan** /-ˈtæn/) *n* large, long-armed ape of Borneo and Sumatra. ⇨ the illus at ape.

orate /ɔˈreɪt/ *vi* [VP2A] speak publicly.

ora·tion /ɔˈreɪʃn/ *n* **1** [C] formal speech made on a public occasion: *a funeral ~.* **2** [U] (gram) way of speaking: *direct / indirect ~,* direct / reported speech.

ora·tor /ˈɒrətə(r) *US:* ˈɔr-/ *n* person who makes speeches (esp a good speaker). **~i·cal** /ˈɒrəˈtɒrɪkl *US:* ˈɔrəˈtɔr-/ *adj* of speech-making and ~s: *~ical phrases/gestures; an ~ical contest.*

ora·torio /ˈɒrəˈtɔrɪəʊ *US:* ˈɔr-/ *n* (*pl* -rios) [C] musical composition for solo voices, chorus and orchestra, usu with a biblical subject: *the ~s of Handel;* [U] musical compositions of this kind collectively: *Do you like ~?*

ora·tory[1] /ˈɒrətrɪ *US:* ˈɔrətɔrɪ/ *n* (*pl* -ries) [C] small chapel for private worship or prayer.

ora·tory[2] /ˈɒrətrɪ *US:* ˈɔrətɔrɪ/ *n* [U] (art of) making speeches; rhetoric.

orb /ɔb/ *n* globe, esp the sun, moon or one of the stars; jewelled globe with a cross on top, part of a sovereign's regalia. ⇨ the illus at regalia.

or·bit /ˈɔbɪt/ *n* path followed by a heavenly body, e g a planet, the moon, or a man-made object, e g a spacecraft, round another body: *the earth's ~ round the sun. How many satellites have been put in ~ round the earth?* □ *vt,vi* [VP6A,2A,C] put into, (cause to) move, in ~: *When was the first man-made satellite ~ed? How many spacecraft have orbited the moon?* **~al** /ˈɔbɪtl/ *adj* of an ~: *a spacecraft's ~al distance from the earth; ~ velocity,* minimal velocity needed to place sth in ~.

or·chard /ˈɔtʃəd/ *n* [C] piece of ground (usu enclosed) with fruit-trees: *apple-~s.*

or·ches·tra /ˈɔkɪstrə/ *n* **1** band of persons playing musical instruments (including stringed instruments) together: *a ˈdance ~; a ˈsymphony ~.* ⇨ *brass band* at brass(3). **2** **~ (pit),** place in a theatre for an ~. **~ stalls,** front seats on the floor of a theatre. **3** semicircular space in front of the stage of a theatre in ancient Greece, where the chorus sang and danced. **or·ches·tral** /ɔˈkestrl/ *adj* of, for, by, an ~: *orchestral instruments/performances.*

or·ches·trate /ˈɔkɪstreɪt/ *vt* [VP6A] compose, arrange, score, for orchestral performances. **or·ches·tra·tion** /ˈɔkɪˈstreɪʃn/ *n*

or·chid /ˈɔkɪd/ (also **or·chis** /ˈɔkɪs/) *n* [C] sorts of plant of which the English wild kinds (usu *orchis*) have tuberous roots, and the tropical kinds (usu *orchid*) have flowers of brilliant colours and fantastic shapes. ⇨ the illus at flower.

or·dain /ɔˈdeɪn/ *vt* **1** [VP6A,23] make (sb) a priest or minister: *He was ~ed priest.* **2** [VP9] **~ *that,*** (of God, law, authority) decide; give orders (that); destine: *God has ~ed that all men shall die.*

or·deal /ɔˈdil/ *n* **1** [U] (in former times) method of deciding sb's guilt or innocence by requiring him to pass a physical test, such as passing through fire unharmed or fighting his accuser: *trial by ~; ~ by fire; ~ by battle.* **2** [C] any severe test of character or endurance: *pass through terrible ~s.*

or·der[1] /ˈɔdə(r)/ *n* **1** [U] way in which things are placed in relation to one another: *names in alphabetical ~; in chronological ~,* i e according to dates. ***in ~ of,*** arranged according to: *in ~ of size/merit/importance, etc.* **2** [U] condition in which everything is carefully arranged; working condition. ***(not) in ~,*** (not) as it should be: *Is your passport in ~*, Has it all the necessary entries to satisfy the authorities? *He put/left his affairs/accounts/papers in ~ before going into hospital for the operation. Get your ideas into some kind of ~ before beginning to write.* ***in good ~,*** without any confusion: *The troops retired in good ~*, Their retreat was orderly, disciplined. ***in good/bad/running/working ~,*** (esp of machines) working well/badly/smoothly, etc: *The engine has been tuned and is now in perfect running ~.* ***out of ~,*** (of a machine, a bodily organ) not functioning properly: *The lift/phone is out of ~. My stomach is out of ~.* **3** [U] (condition brought about by) good and firm government, obedience to law, rules, authority: *The army restored law and ~. It is the business of the police to keep ~. Some teachers find it difficult to keep ~ in their classes/to keep their classes in ~.* ⇨ disorder. **4** [U] rules usual at a public meeting; rules accepted, e g in Parliament, committee meetings, by members and enforced by a president, chairman, or other officer. ***call (sb) to ~,*** (of the Speaker in the House of Commons, the chairman of a meeting, etc) request (a member, etc) to obey the rules, the usual procedures. ***be in ~ to do sth,*** be according to the rules, etc: *Is it in ~ to interrupt?* ***on a point of ~,*** on a point (= question) of procedure. ***O~! O~!*** (used to call attention to a departure from the usual rules of debates or procedures). **~ of the day,** programme of business to be discussed. **ˋ~-paper** *n* written or printed ~ of the day. **standing ~s,** ⇨ standing *adj*(1). **5** [C] command given with authority: *Soldiers must obey ~s. He gave ~s for the work to be started/that the work should be started at once.* ***be under ~s (to do sth),*** have received ~s: *He is under ~s to leave for Finland next week.* ***by ~ of,*** according to directions given by proper authority of: *by ~ of the Governor.* ***under the ~s of,*** commanded by. ***under starters' ~s,*** ⇨ start[2] *n*(2). **6** [C] request to supply goods; the goods (to be) supplied: *an ~ for two tons of coal; give a tradesman an ~ for goods; fill an ~*, supply the goods asked for. *The butcher has called for ~s*, to ask what is wanted. ***on ~,*** requested but not yet supplied. ***made to ~,*** made according to the customer's special requirements or instructions. ⇨ *ready-made* at ready(4). **a large/tall ~,** (colloq) sth difficult to do or supply. **ˋ~-book** *n* one in which a tradesman, commercial traveller, manufacturer, etc writes down ~s for goods: *The company has full ~-books*, orders for large quantities of goods. **ˋ~-form** *n* printed form with blank spaces to be filled in by the customer. **7** [C] written direction (esp to a bank or post office) to pay money, or giving authority to do sth: *an ~ on the Midland Bank; a postal ~ for thirty new pence; an ~ to view*, e g from an estate-agent to inspect a house that is for sale. **8** [U] purpose, intention. ***in ~ to do sth,*** with the purpose of doing sth, with a view to doing sth: *in ~ (for you) to see clearly.* ***in ~ that,*** with the intention that; so that: *in ~ that he may/might/shall/should arrive in time.* **9** [C] rank or class in society: *the ~ of knights/baronets; the lower ~s*, name formerly used for those who were called 'the common people', i e peasants, labourers, etc. **10** [C] group of people belonging to or appointed to a special class (as an honour or reward): *the O~ of Merit/of the Bath/the Golden Kite, etc;* badge, sign, etc worn by members of such an ~: *wearing all his ~s and decorations.* **11** (*pl*) authority given by a bishop to perform church duties. ***be in/take (holy) ~s,*** be/become a priest. **12** [C] class of persons on whom holy ~s have been conferred: *the O~ of Deacons/Priests/Bishops.* **13** [C] group of persons living under religious rules, esp a brotherhood of monks: *the monastic ~s; the ~ of Templars.* **14** [C] method of treating architectural forms, esp of columns (pillars) and capitals, esp the classical ~s (*Doric, Ionic, Corinthian*, etc). ⇨ the illus at column. **15** (biol) [C] highest division under *class* in the grouping of animals, plants, etc: *The rose and the bean families belong to the same ~.* **16** [C] kind; sort: *intellectual ability of a high ~.* **17** arrangement of military forces: *advance in review ~*, on parade; *advance in extended ~*, in battle. ***advance in open/close ~,*** with wide/with only slight spaces between the men, etc.

or·der[2] /ˋɔdə(r)/ *vt* **1** [VP6A,9,12B,13B,15A,B,17] give an order(5,6,7) *to* (sb) or *for* sth: *The doctor ~ed me to (stay in) bed. The disobedient boy was ~ed out of the room. The chairman ~ed silence. The regiment was ~ed to the front. The judge ~ed that the prisoner should be remanded. The doctor has ~ed me absolute quiet. She ~ed herself two dozen oysters and a pint of stout. I've ~ed lunch for 1.30. The regiment was ~ed up (to the front).* **~ sb about,** keep on giving orders to him. **2** [VP6A,15A] arrange; direct: *~ one's life according to strict rules.* **~·ing** *n* (from 2 above) arrangement.

or·der·ly /ˋɔdəlɪ/ *adj* **1** well arranged; in good order; tidy: *an ~ room/desk;* methodically inclined: *a man with an ~ mind.* **2** well behaved; obedient to discipline: *an ~ crowd.* **3** (army use, attrib only) concerned with carrying out orders: *the ~ officer*, the officer on duty for the day; *the ˋ~ room*, room in barracks where the clerical work is done. □ *n* (*pl* -lies) (army) officer's messenger; attendant in a military hospital; *medical ~*, in a hospital. **or·der·li·ness** *n*

or·di·nal /ˋɔdɪnl *US:* -dnl/ *n, adj* [C] (number) showing order or position in a series. **~ numbers,** e g *first, second, third.* ⇨ cardinal, App 4.

or·di·nance /ˋɔdṇəns/ *n* [C] order, rule, statute, made by authority or decree: *the ~s of the City Council.*

or·di·nand /ˈɔdɪˋnænd *US:* ˋɔdṇænd/ *n* candidate for ordination.

or·di·nary /ˋɔdnrɪ *US:* ˋɔdṇerɪ/ *adj* normal; usual; average: *an ~ day's work; in ~ dress.* ***in an ~ way,*** *if the circumstances were ~ or usual.* ***in the ~ way,*** in the usual or customary way. **~ seaman,** (abbr **O S**) one who has not yet received the rank of *able seaman* (abbr *A B*). ⇨ App 9. ***in ~,*** by permanent appointment, not temporary or extraordinary: *physician in ~ to Her Majesty.* **or·di·nar·ily** /ˋɔdnrlɪ *US:* ˋɔdṇerlɪ/ *adv* in an ~ way: *behave quite ordinarily.*

or·di·na·tion /ˈɔdɪˋneɪʃn *US:* -dnˋeɪʃn/ *n* [U] ceremony of ordaining (a priest or minister); [C] instance of this.

ord·nance /ˋɔdnəns/ *n* [U] artillery; munitions. **the Army O~ Department/Corps,** (US = **O~ Corps**) that which is responsible for military supplies. **O~ Survey,** (the preparation of) accurate and detailed maps of GB and Ireland.

or·dure /ˋɔdjʊə(r) *US:* -dʒər/ *n* [U] excrement; dung; filth.

ore /ɔ(r)/ *n* [C,U] (kinds of) rock, earth, mineral, etc from which metal can be mined or extracted: *iron ore; a district rich in ores.*

or·gan /ˋɔgən/ *n* **1** any part of an animal body or plant serving an essential purpose: *the ~s of speech,* the tongue, teeth, lips, etc; *the ˋnasal ~,* the nose; *the reproductive ~s; the ~s of generation.* ⇨ the illus at alimentary, ear, eye, reproduce. **2** means of getting work done; organization: *Parliament is the chief ~ of government.* **3** means for making known what people think: *~s of public opinion,* newspapers, radios, TV, etc. **5** musical instrument from which sounds are produced by air forced through pipes, played by keys pressed with the fingers and pedals pressed with the feet (in US also called a **ˋpipe-~**). ⇨ the illus at church. **ˋreed/Aˋmerican ~,** harmonium (with reeds instead of pipes). **ˋ~-blower** *n* person who works the bellows of an ~. **ˋ~-grinder** *n* person who plays a barrel-~. ⇨ barrel. **ˋ~-loft** *n* gallery (in some churches, etc) where the ~ is placed. **ˋ~·ist** /-ɪst/ *n* person who plays an ~(5).

or·gan·die (US also **-dy**) /ɔˋgændɪ/ *n* [U] kind of fine translucent muslin.

or·ganic /ɔˋgænɪk/ *adj* **1** of an organ or organs of the body: *~ diseases,* affecting the structure of these organs, not only their functions. **2** (opp *inorganic*) having bodily organs: *~ life.* **~ chemistry,** dealing with the products of animal and vegetable bodies, e g the carbon and hydrogen compounds. **3** made of related parts; arranged as a system: *an ~* (i e organized) *whole; an ~* (i e structural) *part.* **or·gani·cally** /-klɪ/ *adv*

or·gan·ism /ˋɔgən-ɪzm/ *n* [C] living being with parts which work together; individual animal or plant; any system with parts dependent upon each other: *the social ~.*

or·gan·iz·ation /ˈɔgənaɪˋzeɪʃn *US:* -nɪˋz-/ *n* **1** [U] act of organizing; condition of being organized: *He is engaged in the ~ of a new club. An army without ~ would be useless.* **2** [C] organized body of persons; organized system: *The human body has a very complex ~.*

or·gan·ize /ˋɔgənaɪz/ *vt* [VP6A] **1** put into working order; arrange in a system; make preparations for: *~ an army/a government/a political party/an expedition to the South Pole/one's work/oneself.* **2** (of workers, etc) form into, join, a trade union. **or·gan·ized** *adj* **1** furnished with organs; made into a living organism: *highly ~d forms of life.* **2** (of workers, etc) in a trade union. **or·gan·izer** *n* person who ~s things.

or·gasm /ˋɔgæzm/ *n* [C] violent (esp erotic) excitement; the climax of sexual excitement during intercourse.

or·gi·as·tic /ˈɔdʒɪˋæstɪk/ *adj* of the nature of an orgy; frenzied.

orgy /ˋɔdʒɪ/ *n* [C] (*pl* **orgies**) **1** occasion of wild merry-making; (*pl*) drunken or licentious revels. **2** (colloq) succession of innocent, pleasant activities: *an ~ of parties/concerts/spending.*

oriel /ˋɔrɪəl/ *n* **1** part of a room projecting from an upper storey and supported from the ground or on corbels and having a window in it. **2** **ˋ~ (window),** window of an ~.

orient[1] /ˋɔrɪənt/ *n* **the O~,** (poetical name for) countries east of the Mediterranean, esp the Far East. □ *adj* (poet) Eastern; (of the sun) rising: *the ~ sun.*

orient[2] /ˋɔrɪənt/ *vt* (US) = orientate.

orien·tal /ˈɔrɪˋentl/ *adj* of the Orient: *~ civilization/art/rugs.* □ *n* **O~,** inhabitant of the Orient, esp China and Japan. **~·ist** /-ɪst/ *n* person who studies the languages, arts, etc of ~ countries.

orien·tate /ˋɔrɪənteɪt/ *vt* [VP6A] (US = *orient*) **1** place (a building, etc) so as to face east; build (a church) with the chancel end due east. **2** place or exactly determine the position of (sth) with regard to the points of the compass; (fig) bring into clearly understood relations: *~ oneself,* make oneself familiar with a situation, determine how one stands in relation to one's surroundings, etc. **orien·ta·tion** /ˈɔrɪənˋteɪʃn/ *n* [U] orientating or being ~d.

ori·fice /ˋɔrəfɪs *US:* ˋɔr-/ *n* outer opening; mouth (of a cave, etc).

ori·gin /ˋɔrədʒɪn *US:* ˋɔrədʒɪn/ *n* [C,U] starting-point: *the ~ of a quarrel; the ~(s) of civilization; a man of humble ~,* parentage; *words of Latin ~.*

orig·inal /əˋrɪdʒnl/ *adj* **1** first or earliest: *the ~ inhabitants of the country: The ~ plan was better than the plan we followed.* **~ sin,** ⇨ sin. **2** newly formed or created; not copied or imitated: *~ ideas; an ~ design.* **3** able to produce new ideas, etc: *an ~ thinker/writer; an ~ mind.* □ *n* **1** [C] that from which sth is copied: *This is a copy; the ~ is in the Prado in Madrid.* **2** (*sing* with *def art*) language in which sth was first composed: *read Homer in the ~,* in ancient Greek; *study Don Quixote in the ~,* in Spanish. **3** [C] eccentric person. **~ly** /-nlɪ/ *adv* **1** in an ~ manner: *speak/think/write ~ly.* **2** from or in the beginning: *The school was ~ly quite small.* **~·ity** /əˈrɪdʒəˋnælətɪ/ *n* [U] state or quality of being ~: *work that lacks ~ity,* is copied or imitated.

orig·inate /əˋrɪdʒɪneɪt/ *vi,vt* **1** [VP2C,3A] ***~ from/in sth; ~ from/with sb,*** have as a cause or beginning: *The quarrel ~d in rivalry between two tribes. With whom did the scheme ~?* **2** [VP6A] be the author or creator of: *~ a new style of dancing.* **orig·in·ator** /-tə(r)/ *n*

ori·ole /ˋɔrɪəʊl/ *n* **(golden) ~,** kinds of bird with black and yellow feathers.

ori·son /ˋɔrɪzn *US:* ˋɔr-/ *n* [C] (archaic) prayer.

or·lop /ˋɔlop/ *n* **ˋ~ (deck),** lowest deck of a ship with three or more decks.

or·molu /ˋɔməlu/ *n* (article made of, or decorated with) gilded bronze or a gold-coloured alloy of copper, zinc and tin: *an ~ clock.*

or·na·ment /ˋɔnəmənt/ *n* **1** [U] adorning or being adorned; that which is added for decoration: *add sth by way of ~; an altar rich in ~.* **2** [C] sth designed or used to add beauty to sth else: *a shelf crowded with ~,* e g small vases, statuettes, pieces of china. **3** [C] person, act, quality, etc that adds beauty, charm, etc: *He is an ~ to his profession.* □ *vt* /ˋɔnəment/ [VP6A,14] be an ~ to; make beautiful: *~ a dress with lace.* **or·na·men·tal** /ˈɔnəˋmentl/ *adj* of or for ~. **or·na·men·ta·tion** /ˈɔnəmenˋteɪʃn/ *n* [U] ~ing or being ~ed; that which ~s: *a church with no ~ation.*

or·nate /ɔˋneɪt/ *adj* richly ornamented; (of liter style) full of flowery language; not simple in style or vocabulary. **~·ly** *adv* **~·ness** *n*

or·nery /ˋɔnərɪ/ *adj* (US colloq) ill-tempered; perverse and stubborn.

or·ni·thol·ogy /ˈɔnɪˋθɒlədʒɪ/ *n* [U] scientific study of birds. **or·ni·thol·ogist** /-dʒɪst/ *n* expert in ~.

or·ni·tho·logi·cal /ˌɔnɪθəˈlodʒɪkl/ *adj*

oro·tund /ˈɔrəʊtʌnd/ *adj* (formal) **1** imposing; dignified. **2** pompous; pretentious.

or·phan /ˈɔfən/ *n* person (esp a child) who has lost one or both of its parents by death: (attrib) *an ~ child.* □ *vt* [VP6A] cause to be an ~: ~ed by war. **ˈ~·age** /-ɪdʒ/ *n* charitable home for ~s.

or·ris·root /ˈorɪsrut *US:* ˈɔr-/ *n* violet scented root of some kinds of iris, used in perfumes and cosmetics.

or·tho·dox /ˈɔθədoks/ *adj* (having opinions, beliefs, etc which are) generally accepted or approved: *an ~ member of the Church; ~ beliefs; ~ behaviour.* ⇨ heterodox. **the O~ Church,** the Eastern or Greek Church, recognizing the Patriarch of Istanbul (Constantinople) as its head, and the national churches of Russia, Rumania, etc. **~y** /ˈɔθədoksɪ/ *n* (*pl* **-xies**) [U] being ~; [C] ~ belief, character, practice.

or·thogra·phy /ɔˈθogrəfɪ/ *n* [U] (system of) spelling; correct or conventional spelling. **or·tho·graphic** /ˈɔθəˈgræfɪk/ *adj*

or·tho·paedic (also **-pedic**) /ˈɔθəˈpidɪk/ *adj* of the curing of deformities and diseases of bones: *~ surgery.* **or·tho·paed·ics** (also **-ped·ics**) *n* (with *sing v*) branch of surgery dealing with bone deformities and diseases.

or·to·lan /ˈɔtələn/ *n* small wild bird valued as a table delicacy.

oryx /ˈɔrɪks/ *n* African antelope with long, straight or arching horns.

Os·car /ˈoskə(r)/ *n* the annual US award for what is judged to be a great achievement in cinema: *be nominated for/win an ~.*

os·cil·late /ˈosɪleɪt/ *vi,vt* **1** [VP2A] swing backwards and forwards as the pendulum of a clock does; (fig) waver or change between extremes of opinion, etc. **2** [VP6A] cause to swing to and fro. **3** (electr, of current) undergo high frequency alternations; (of radio receivers) radiate electromagnetic waves; experience interference (in reception) from this. **ˈoscillating current,** current whose direction is periodically reversed. **os·ci·la·tion** /ˈosɪˈleɪʃn/ *n* oscillating or being ~d; [C] one swing of a pendulum or other object or of an electric charge. **os·cil·lator** /-tə(r)/ *n* (esp) device for producing electric oscillations (e g for radio telegraphy).

os·cillo·graph /əˈsɪləgrɑf *US:* -græf/ *n* (electr) instrument for recording oscillations.

os·cillo·scope /əˈsɪləskəʊp/ *n* (electr) instrument which shows on the screen of a cathode ray tube (like a T V screen) variations of current as a wavy line on a graph.

osier /ˈəʊzɪə(r) *US:* ˈəʊʒə(r)/ *n* [C] kind of willow-tree, the twigs of which are used in basket-work.

os·prey /ˈosprei *US:* -prɪ/ *n* (*pl* ~s) large kind of hawk that preys on fish.

osseous /ˈosɪəs/ *adj* consisting of bone; having a bony skeleton.

oss·ify /ˈosɪfɑɪ/ *vt,vi* (*pt,pp* -fied) [VP6A,2A] (formal) make or become hard like bone; change into bone; (fig) make or become rigid, unprogressive. **ossi·fi·ca·tion** /ˈosɪfɪˈkeɪʃn/ *n* ~ing or being ossified; that part of a structure that is ossified.

os·ten·sible /ˈostensəbl/ *adj* (of reasons, etc) put forward in an attempt to hide the real reason; apparent. **os·ten·sibly** /-əblɪ/ *adv*

os·ten·ta·tion /ˈostenˈteɪʃn/ *n* [U] display (of wealth, learning, skill, etc) to obtain admiration or envy: *the ~ of the newly rich.*

os·ten·ta·tious /ˈostenˈteɪʃəs/ *adj* fond of showing, ostentation: *~ jewellery; in an ~ manner.* **~·ly** *adv*

os·te·opathy /ˈostɪˈopəθɪ/ *n* [U] treatment of certain diseases by manipulation of the bones and muscles. **os·teo·path** /ˈostɪəpæθ/ *n* person who practises ~.

os·tler /ˈoslə(r)/ *n* stableman (man who looks after horses) at an inn.

os·tra·cize /ˈostrəsɑɪz/ *vt* [VP6A] **1** shut out from society: refuse to meet, talk to, etc: *People who hold very unorthodox opinions are sometimes ~d.* **2** (in ancient Greece) banish by popular vote for ten or five years. **os·tra·cism** /-ɪzm/ *n* [U] ostracizing or being ~d.

os·trich /ˈostrɪtʃ/ *n* (*pl* **~es** /-rɪdʒɪz/) fast-running bird, the largest in existence, unable to fly, bred for its valuable tail feathers; ⇨ the illus at rare; *have the digestion of an ~,* be able to digest almost anything.

other /ˈʌðə(r)/ *adj, pron* (person or thing) not already named or implied. **1 the ~,** (*sing*) the second of two: *The twins are so much alike that people find it difficult to know (the) one from the ~. One of them is mine; the ~ is my sister's. The post office is on the ~ side of the street.* ***on the ~ hand,*** used (sometimes, but not always, after *on the one hand*) to introduce sth in contrast to an earlier statement, etc: *It's cheap, but on the ~ hand the quality is poor.* **2 the ~s,** (*pl*) when the reference is to two or more: *Six of them are mine; the ~s are John's. Where are the ~ boys?* **3** (with the *indef art,* written and printed as one word, **an~** /əˈnʌðə(r)/) an additional (one); a different one. ⇨ another. *Will you have an~ cup of tea? I won't say an~ word about it. I don't like this one; can you show me an~?* (The *pl* of *an~* is some/any ~s or *some/any more*): *I don't like these. Have you any ~s/any more? Please let me see some ~s/some more.* **4** (when one member of a group is compared with any ~ member of the group, *other* is usu used): *Green is far better as a bowler than any ~ member of the team.* **5** (phrases) ***each ~,*** ⇨ each(4). ***every ~,*** **(a)** all the ~s: *John is stupid; every ~ boy in the class knows the answer.* **(b)** alternate: *Write only on every ~ line.* ***one an~,*** ⇨ one[3](3). ***one after the ~, one after an~,*** in succession, not together. ***…or ~,*** used to suggest absence of certainty or precision: *I shall be coming again some day or ~,* one of these days. *I'll get there somehow or ~,* by one means if not by an~. *Someone or ~* (= Some unknown person) *has left the gate open.* ***~ things being equal,*** if conditions are/were the same or alike except for the point in question: *O~ things being equal, Alice would marry Jim, not Tom, but Jim is poor and Tom is rich.* ***the ~ day,*** a few days ago. **6** different: *I do not wish her ~ than she is. The question must be decided by quite ~ considerations.* **~·worldly** /ˈʌðəˈwɜldlɪ/ *adj* concerned with, thinking of, another world/sth mystic rather than with this world. □ *adv* (= *otherwise*) in a different way: *I could not do it ~ than hurriedly.*

other·wise /ˈʌðəwɑɪz/ *adv* **1** in another or different way: *You evidently think ~. He should have been working but he was ~ engaged,* but he was doing sth different. **2** in other or different respects; in different conditions: *The rent is high, but ~ the house is satisfactory.* □ *conj* if not; or else: *Do* *what you've been told; ~ you will be punished.*

oti·ose /ˈəʊʃɪəʊs/ *adj* (formal) serving no practical purpose; not required; functionless.

ot·ter /ˈotə(r)/ *n* [C] fur-covered, fish-eating aquatic animal with four webbed feet and a flat tail; [U] its fur. ⇨ the illus at **small**.

ot·to·man /ˈotəmən/ *n* long cushioned seat without back or arms, often used as a box, e g for storing bedding.

ou·bli·ette /ˈublɪˈet/ *n* secret dungeon (underground prison) with an entrance only by a trapdoor in the roof.

ouch /aʊtʃ/ *int* used to express sudden pain.

ought /ɔt/ *anom fin* (defective; no infinitive, no particles, no inflected forms; *ought not* is contracted to **oughtn't** /ˈɔtnt/. For past time, *ought* is used with a perfect infinitive; in reported speech, the perfect infinitive is not always necessary.) **1** (indicating duty or obligation; synonymous with one sense of *should*): *You ~ to start at once. Such things ~ not to be allowed, ~ they? 'O~ I to go'—'Yes, I think you ~ (to)'. You ~ to have done that earlier. I told him (that) he ~ to do it,* i e now, or in future. *I told him (that) he ~ to have done it,* i e in the past. **2** (indicating what is advisable, desirable or right): *There ~ to be more buses during the rush hours. You ~* (i e I advise you) *to see that new film at the Odeon. Coffee ~ to be drunk while it is hot. Your brother ~ to have been a doctor,* He would probably have been a good doctor. **3** (indicating probability): *If he started at nine, he ~ to be here now. That ~ to be enough fish for three people, I think. Harry ~ to win the race.*

ouija /ˈwidʒə/ *n* **ˈ~(-board),** board lettered with the alphabet, and with other signs, used in seances to obtain messages said to come from the spirits of the dead.

ounce /aʊns/ *n* (abbr **oz**) unit of weight, one sixteenth of a pound avoirdupois or one twelfth of a pound troy. ⇨ App 5.

our /*usual form:* ɑ(r) *strong form:* aʊə(r)/ *adj* of or belonging to us, that we are concerned with, etc: *We have done our share.* **Our Father,** God. **Our Lady,** the Virgin Mary.

ours /ˈaʊəz/ *pron, pred adj* (the one or ones) belonging to us: *This house is ~. Don't stay at their house; stay at ~. O~ is larger than theirs. Let me show you some of ~. This dog of ~ never wins any prizes. The land became ~ by purchase.*

our·selves /ɑˈselvz/ *reflex, emph pron* **1** (reflex): *It's no use worrying ~ about that. We shall give ~ the pleasure of visiting you soon.* **2** (emph) *We ~ have often made that mistake/We've often made that mistake ~. We'd better go and see the house (for) ~,* not be content to rely upon what others say. ***(all) by ~,*** **(a)** without help. **(b)** alone, without company: *Come in; we're all by ~,* there are no visitors, etc.

oust /aʊst/ *vt* [VP6A,14] ***~ sb (from),*** drive or push (sb) out (from his employment, position, etc): *~ a rival from office.*

out /aʊt/ *adverbial particle* (For special uses in combination with *vv,* ⇨ the *v* entries. Specimens only are given here.) **1** away from, not in or at, a place, the usual or normal condition, etc: *go out; run out; walk out; take sb out; order sb out; find one's way out; lock sb out; throw sth out. Out you go!* Go out! *Out with it!* Bring it out! Say it! **2** (with *be,* various meanings): *Mrs White is out,* not at home. *The manager is out,* not in the office. *The dockers are out again,* on strike. *The book I wanted was out,* i e had been borrowed; was not in the library. *The tide is out,* low. *The ship was four days out from Lisbon,* had sailed from Lisbon four days earlier. *The Socialist party was out,* out of office; not in power. *Short skirts are out,* not fashionable. ***be out and about,*** (of a person who has been in bed through illness or injury) able to get up, go outdoors, etc. **3** (in various phrases to indicate absence from home): *We don't go out much. Let's have an evening out,* e g at a cinema or discotheque, or having dinner at a restaurant, etc. *The cleaner has her meals with us but sleeps out,* i e not in our house. *We're dining out this evening. It's the au pair's day out,* her free day, when she is not required to work. **4** (with *advv* and *adv* phrases, to emphasize the idea of distance): *He lives out in the country. My brother is out in Australia. He lived out East for many years. The Fishing boats are all out at sea. What are you doing out there?* **5** (indicating liberation from confinement or restraint; into the open; exposed; discovered): *The secret is out,* discovered, known. *The apple blossom is out,* open. *The sun is out,* not hidden by cloud. *The floods are out,* spreading over the land. *His new book is out,* published. *Is your daughter out yet,* introduced to society, taking part with grown-ups in social affairs? *There's a warrant out* (i e issued) *against him. Out with it!* Tell the news! Explain it! etc, according to context. *It's the best game out,* the best ever invented. **6** (indicating exhaustion, extinction): *The fire/gas/candle, etc is out,* not burning. *The fire has burnt out. The lease/copyright is out,* has reached the end of its term. *The warships steamed towards the enemy with all lights out. Put that cigarette out! The wind blew the candles out. The candle blew out.* **7** (to or at an end; completely): *I'm tired out. He'll be here before the week is out. Let her have her sleep out,* have all the sleep she needs. ***cry one's eyes out,*** continue crying until this brings relief. ***have it out with sb,*** ⇨ have[4](9). (Used with many *vv,* as): *hear sb out, work out a problem, supplies running out; fight it out,* settle the dispute by fighting. ***out and out,*** thorough(ly); surpassing(ly): *He's a scoundrel out and out/an out-and-out scoundrel.* ***out and away,*** by far: *I was out and away the handsomest man in the room.* **8** (indicating error): *I'm out in my calculations/reckoning. We're ten pounds out in our accounts. You're not far out,* not much in error; almost right. *Your guess was a long way out,* badly in error. *You've put me out,* distracted me, upset the thread of my ideas, etc. *My watch is five minutes out* (more usu five minutes *slow* or *fast*). **9** (indicating clearness or loudness): *call/cry/shout out; say sth out loud,* in a loud voice: *speak out,* clearly, or without hesitation; *bring out* (= make clearer) *the meaning of a paragraph by paraphrasing it; tell sb sth straight out, right out,* without keeping anything back, without ambiguity. **10** (in phrases) ***be out for,*** be engaged in seeking, interested in obtaining: *I'm not out for compliments. He's out for your blood,* anxious to attack you. ***out to + inf,*** trying or hoping to: *I'm not out* (= It is not my aim) *to reform the world. The firm is out to capture the Canadian market.* ***all out,*** exerting the maximum power or effort: *His new car does 80 miles an hour when it's going* *all out. What is needed is an all-out effort.* **11** (cricket) (of a batsman) no longer batting; having been bowled, caught, etc: *The captain was out for three. Kent all out, 137,* innings ended for 137 runs. **12 *out of,*** *prep* (contrasted with *in* and *into.* ⇨ the *n* and *v* entries for special uses, e g *out of date* at date[1](3), *out of the way* at way(2).) **(a)** (of place): *Fish cannot live out of water. Mr Green is out of town this week. This plant is not found out of* (= is found only in) *a small area in Central Asia.* **(b)** (of movement): *He walked out of the shop. He jumped out of bed. We pulled the cart out of the ditch.* **(c)** (indicating motive or cause): *It was done out of mischief/spite. They helped us out of pity/kindness. She asked only out of curiosity.* **(d)** from among: *Choose one out of these ten. It happens in nine cases out of ten. This is only one instance out of several.* **(e)** by the use of; from: *The hut was made out of old planks. She made a hat out of bits of old material. Can good ever come out of evil?* **(f)** without: *out of breath,* breathless; *out of work,* unemployed; *out of patience; (born) out of wedlock,* of unmarried parents. *We're out of tea/petrol,* We have no tea/petrol left. This book is out of stock, There are no copies left in the shop. **(g)** (indicating condition): *out of fashion; out of control; out of order; out of danger.* ⇨ the *n* entries. **(h)** (indicating origin or source): *a scene out of a play; drink out of a cup/a bottle; copy sth out of a book; steps cut out of the solid rock; paid for out of the housekeeping money; a dog and a cat eating out of the same dish.* **(i)** (indicating result): *talk sb out of doing sth,* talk to him with the result that he does not do it; *reason sb out of his fears; cheat sb out of his money;* (colloq) *be done* (= cheated) *out of sth; frighten sb out of his wits.* **(j)** (at a certain distance from): *The ship struck a mine ten miles out of Hull.* ***out of it,*** **(a)** not invited to be a member of a party, etc; sad for this reason: *She felt out of it as she watched the others set out on the picnic.* **(b)** not concerned with, not involved in, sth: *It's a dishonest scheme and I'm glad to be out of it.* **13** (used as *n*) ***the ins and outs,*** **(a)** those in office and those out of office; the Government and the Opposition. **(b)** the details (of procedure, etc). □ *vt* (sl or colloq) eject by force.

out·back /ˋɑʊtbæk/ *adj, n* (e g in Australia) (of) the more remote and sparsely populated areas.

out·bal·ance /ɑʊtˋbæləns/ *vt* [VP6A] weigh down; outweigh.

out·bid /ɑʊtˋbɪd/ *vt* (-dd-) [VP6A] go beyond in bidding; bid higher than (another person) at an auction, etc.

out·board /ˋɑʊtbɔd/ *attrib adj* placed on or near the outside of a ship or boat. **an ∼ motor,** detachable engine that is mounted at the stern, outside the boat.

out·bound /ˋɑʊtbɑʊnd/ *adj* (of a ship) outward bound; going away from a home port.

out·brave /ɑʊtˋbreɪv/ *vt* [VP6A] defy: *∼ the storm.*

out·break /ˋɑʊtbreɪk/ *n* [C] breaking out: *an ∼ of anger/fever/hostilities.*

out·build·ing /ˋɑʊtbɪldɪŋ/ *n* building, e g a shed or stable, separate from the main building: *a ten-roomed farmhouse, with useful ∼s.*

out·burst /ˋɑʊtbɜst/ *n* [C] bursting out (of steam, energy, laughter, anger, etc).

out·cast /ˋɑʊtkɑst *US:* -kæst/ *n, adj* (person or animal) driven out from home or society; homeless and friendless.

out·caste /ˋɑʊtkɑst *US:* -kæst/ *n, adj* (e g in India) (person) having lost, or been expelled from, or not belonging to, a caste.

out·class /ɑʊtˋklɑs *US:* -ˋklæs/ *vt* [VP6A] be much better than; surpass: *He was ∼ed from the start of the race,* His competitors were much better.

out·come /ˋɑʊtkʌm/ *n* [C] effect or result of an event, or of circumstances.

out·crop /ˋɑʊtkrop/ *n* [C] that part of a layer or vein (of rock, etc) which can be seen above the surface of the ground.

out·cry /ˋɑʊtkrɑɪ/ *n* (*pl* -cries) **1** [C] loud shout or scream (of fear, alarm, etc). **2** [C,U] public protest (*against* sth).

out·dated /ɑʊˋdeɪtɪd/ *adj* made out of date (by the passing of time).

out·dis·tance /ɑʊtˋdɪstəns/ *vt* [VP6A] travel faster than, and leave behind: *Tom ∼d all his competitors in the mile race.*

out·do /ɑʊtˋdu/ *vt* (*3rd person sing pres t* -does /-ˋdʌz/, *pt* -did /-ˋdɪd/, *pp* -done /ˋdʌn/) [VP6A] do more or better than: *Not to be outdone* (i e not wanting to let someone do better than he himself had done), *he tried again.*

out·door /ɑʊtˋdɔ(r)/ *attrib adj* done, existing, used, outside a house or building: *leading an ∼ life,* e g of a person fond of open-air games and sport; *∼ dress/clothes,* worn outside the house; *∼ sports;* Cf *indoor games; ∼ relief;* Cf *outrelief.*

out·doors /ɑʊtˋdɔz/ *adv* in the open air; outside: *It's cold ∼. In hot countries it's possible to sleep ∼. Farm workers spend most of their time ∼.*

outer /ˋɑʊtə(r)/ *adj* of or for the outside. ⇨ inner; farther from the middle or inside: *∼ garments.* ⇨ underwear; *the ∼ suburbs; journeys to ∼ space,* e g to the planet Mars; *the ∼ man,* his personal appearance, dress, etc. **ˋ∼·most** /-məʊst/ *adj* farthest from the inside or centre.

out·face /ɑʊtˋfeɪs/ *vt* [VP6A] face boldly; stare at (sb) until he turns his eyes away; cause (sb) to be out of countenance.

out·fall /ˋɑʊtfɔl/ *n* place where water falls or flows out (of a lake, river, etc); outlet; river mouth.

out·field /ˋɑʊtfild/ *n* (usu *sing* with the *def art*) (cricket and baseball) part of the field farthest from the batsmen; the fielders there. **∼er** *n*

out·fight /ˋɑʊtfɑɪt/ *vt* [VP6A] fight better than: *The champion outfought his opponent.*

out·fit /ɑʊtˋfɪt/ *n* [C] all the clothing or articles needed for a purpose: *a camping ∼,* tent, etc; *a boy's ∼ for school; a carpenter's ∼,* his tools, etc. □ *vt* (-tt-) fit out (chiefly in the *pp* ∼ted). **∼ter** *n* shopkeeper selling clothes: *a gentlemen's ∼ter,* tradesman selling men's clothes.

out·flank /ɑʊtˋflæŋk/ *vt* [VP6A] go or pass round the flank of (the enemy): *an ∼ing movement.*

out·flow /ˋɑʊtfləʊ/ *n* [C] flowing out: *an ∼ of water/bad language; the ∼ of gold bullion.*

out·fox /ɑʊtˋfoks/ *vt* [VP6A] get the better of by being cunning.

out·gen·eral /ɑʊtˋdʒenrl/ *vt* (-ll-) [VP6A] defeat by superior skill on the part of one's general(s).

out·go /ˋɑʊtgəʊ/ *n* (*pl* -goes /-gəʊz/) (opp of *income*) that which goes out or is paid out; expenditure.

out·go·ing /ˋɑʊtgəʊɪŋ/ *adj* (attrib only) going out; leaving: *the ∼ tenant,* the one who is giving up the house, etc; *an ∼ ship/tide.* **out·go·ings** *n pl* expenditure; outlay.

out·grow /ɑʊtˋgrəʊ/ *vt* (*pt* -grew /-ˋgru/, *pp* -grown /-ˋgrəʊn/) [VP6A] grow too large or too tall for, e g one's clothes; grow faster or taller than, e g one's brother; leave behind, as one grows older (bad habits, childish interests, opinions, etc): *~ one's strength*, grow too quickly (during childhood), so that the health suffers.

out·growth /ˋɑʊtgrəʊθ/ *n* [C] **1** natural development or product. **2** that which grows out of sth; offshoot: *an ~ on a tree.*

out·herod (also **~-Herod**) /ɑʊtˋherəd/ *vt* [VP6A] be more cruel, violent, etc then King Herod (King of the Jews when Jesus was born).

out·house /ˋɑʊthɑʊs/ *n* (*pl* -houses /-hɑʊzɪz/) small building adjoining the main building (e g a shed, barn, or stable); (US) outdoor lavatory.

out·ing /ˋɑʊtɪŋ/ *n* [C] **1** holiday away from home; pleasure trip: *go for an ~; an ~ to the seaside.* **2** practice row, e g by a racing crew; practice gallop (by a race-horse).

out·land·ish /ɑʊtˋlændɪʃ/ *adj* looking or sounding odd, strange or foreign: *~ dress/behaviour/ideas.* **~·ly** *adv* **~·ness** *n*

out·last /ɑʊtˋlɑst *US:* -ˋlæst/ *vt* [VP6A] last or live longer than.

out·law /ˋɑʊtlɔ/ *n* (in olden times) person punished by being placed outside the protection of the law; criminal. □ *vt* [VP6A] make (sb) an ~; drive out from society. **~ry** /ˋɑʊtlɔrɪ/ *n* [U] being an ~; being ~ed.

out·lay /ˋɑʊtleɪ/ *n* [U] **~ *(on)*,** spending; laying out money; [C] sum of money that is spent: *a large ~ on/for scientific research.*

out·let /ˋɑʊtlet/ *n* **~ *(for)*,** **1** way out for water, steam, etc: *an ~ for water; the ~ of a lake.* **2** (fig) means of or occasion for releasing (one's feelings, energies, etc): *Boys need an ~ for their energies.*

out·line /ˋɑʊtlɑɪn/ *n* [C] **1** line(s) showing shape or boundary: *an ~ map of Great Britain; draw sth in ~.* **2** statement of the chief facts, points, etc: *an ~ for an essay/a lecture; An O~ of European History,* title of a book with a summary of the chief events, etc. □ *vt* [VP6A] draw in ~; give an ~ of: *~ Napoleon's Russian campaign.*

out·live /ɑʊtˋlɪv/ *vt* [VP6A] **1** live longer than: *~ one's wife.* **2** live until sth is forgotten: *~ a disgrace.*

out·look /ˋɑʊtlʊk/ *n* **1** view on which one looks out: *a pleasant ~ over the valley; an ~ on to roofs and chimneys.* **2** what seems likely to happen: *a bright ~ for trade;* (weather forecast): *further ~, dry and sunny.* **3** person's way of looking at sth: *a man with a narrow ~ on life.*

out·lying /ˋɑʊtlɑɪɪŋ/ *adj* far from the centre: *~ villages, with poor communications.*

out·man·œuvre (US = **-ma·neu·ver**) /ɑʊtməˋnuvə(r)/ *vt* [VP6A] overcome, get the better of, by being superior in manœuvring.

out·march /ɑʊtˋmɑtʃ/ *vt* [VP6A] surpass by marching faster or longer.

out·match /ɑʊtˋmætʃ/ *vt* [VP6A] be more than a match for; excel: *be ~ed in skill and endurance.*

out·moded /ɑʊtˋməʊdɪd/ *adj* out of fashion.

out·most /ˋɑʊtməʊst/ *adj* = outermost.

out·num·ber /ɑʊtˋnʌmbə(r)/ *vt* [VP6A] be greater in number than.

out-of-date /ˈɑʊt əv ˋdeɪt/ *adj* (hyphens when *attrib*) = out of date. ⇨ **date**[1](3).

out-of-door /ˈɑʊt əv ˋdɔ(r)/ *attrib adj* = out-door.

out-of-doors /ˈɑʊt əv ˋdɔz/ *adv* = outdoors.

out-of-the-way /ˈɑʊt əv ðə ˋweɪ/ *adj* **1** remote; secluded: *an ~ cottage.* **2** not commonly known: *~ items of knowledge.*

out·patient /ˋɑʊtpeɪʃnt/ *n* person visiting a hospital for treatment but not lodged there.

out·play /ɑʊtˋpleɪ/ *vt* [VP6A] play better than: *The English team was ~ed by the Brazilians.*

out·point /ɑʊtˋpɔɪnt/ *vt* [VP6A] (in boxing, etc) score more points than; defeat on points: *The British champion was ~ed by the Mexican.*

out·port) /ˋɑʊtpɔt/ *n* port or harbour away from a central custom-house or centre of trade.

out·post /ˋɑʊtpəʊst/ *n* **1** (soldiers in an) observation post at a distance from the main body of troops. **2** any distant settlement: *an ~ of the Roman Empire.*

out·pour·ing /ˋɑʊtpɔrɪŋ/ *n* [C] pouring out; (usu *pl*) expression of feeling: *~s of the heart.*

out·put /ˋɑʊtpʊt/ *n* **1** quantity of goods, etc, produced: *the ~ of a gold mine/a factory; the literary ~ of the year,* the books, etc published. **2** power, energy, etc produced; information produced from a computer. ⇨ **input.**

out·rage /ˋɑʊt-reɪdʒ/ *n* [U,C] **1** (act of) extreme violence or cruelty: *never safe from ~; ~s committed by a drunken mob; The use of H-bombs would be an ~ against humanity?* **2** act that shocks public opinion: *an ~ upon decency.* □ *vt* [VP6A] treat violently; be guilty of an ~ upon; violate; ravish; assault sexually: *~ public opinion; ~ one's sense of justice; ~ all decency.*

out·rage·ous /ɑʊtˋreɪdʒəs/ *adj* shocking; very cruel, shameless, immoral: *~ behaviour; an ~ price/remark.* **~·ly** *adv*

out·range /ɑʊtˋreɪndʒ/ *vt* [VP6A] have a greater range than: *Our guns were ~d by those of the enemy's cruisers.*

out·rank /ɑʊtˋræŋk/ *vt* [VP6A] rank higher than.

outré /ˋutreɪ *US:* uˋtreɪ/ *adj* outside the bounds of what is conventionally correct; contrary to what is decorous: *~ behaviour.*

out·re·lief /ˋɑʊtrɪlif/ *n* [U] (in GB, before modern social services were introduced) outdoor relief; help given by the authorities (Relieving Officers) to poor people living in their own homes (not in institutions).

out·ride /ɑʊtˋrɑɪd/ *vt* (*pt* -rode /-ˋrəʊd/, *pp* -ridden /-ˋrɪdn/) [VP6A] ride better or faster than: *~ one's pursuers.*

out·rider /ˋɑʊt-rɑɪdə(r)/ *n* servant on horseback, or policeman on a motor-cycle, accompanying a vehicle, as an attendant or guard.

out·rig·ger /ˋɑʊt-rɪgə(r)/ *n* (boating) beam, spar or structure projecting from or over the side of a boat for various purposes (e g for the rowlock in a racing shell, or to give stability to a canoe or yacht). **out·rigged** /ˋɑʊt-rɪgd/ *adj* (of a boat) having an ~ or ~s.

out·right /ˋɑʊt-rɑɪt/ *adj* **1** thorough; positive: *an ~ denial; ~ wickedness; an ~ manner,* i e thoroughly frank. **2** clear; unmistakable: *On the voting for secretary, Smith was the ~ winner.* □ *adv* **1** openly, with nothing held back: *tell a man ~ what one thinks of his behaviour.* **2** completely; at one time; *buy a house ~,* i e not by instalments; *be killed ~ by a blow.*

out·rival /ɑʊtˋrɑɪvl/ *vt* (-ll-, US also -l-) [VP6A] be or do better than (sb) as a rival.

out·run /aʊtˋrʌn/ *vt* (*pt* -ran /-ˋræn/, *pp* -run; -nn-) [VP6A] run faster or better than; go beyond: *His ambition outran his ability,* He was ambitious to do more than he was able to do.

out·run·ner /ˋaʊt-rʌnə(r)/ *n* **1** (in former times) servant running beside a carriage. **2** leading dog acting as a guide to a team of dogs pulling a sledge.

out·sail /aʊtˋseɪl/ *vt* [VP6A] sail faster than.

out·set /ˋaʊtset/ *n* start (chiefly in) ***at/from the ~,*** the beginning: *at the ~ of his career.*

out·shine /aʊtˋʃaɪn/ *vt* (*pt,pp* -shone /-ˋʃɒn/) [VP6A] shine more brightly than.

out·side /aʊtˋsaɪd/ *n* (contrasted with *inside*) **1** the other side or surface; the outer part(s): *The ~ of the house needs painting. Don't judge a thing from the ~,* from the external appearance. **2** ***at the (very) ~,*** at the most; at the highest reckoning: *There were only fifty people there at the ~,* certainly not more than fifty. *He earns £1 500 a year at the ~.* □ *adj* (or attrib use of *n*) **1** of or on, nearer, the ~: *~ repairs,* i e to the ~ of a building; *~ measurements,* e g of a box; *an ~ broadcast,* from a place ~ the studios. **2** greatest possible or probable: *an ~ estimate.* **3** not connected with or included in a group, organization, etc: *We shall need ~ help* (= extra workers) *for this job. She doesn't like meeting the ~ world,* people not belonging to the close circle of her family and friends. □ *adv* on or to the ~: *The house is painted green ~. The car is waiting ~.* □ *prep* **1** at or on the outer side of: *~ the house; a ship moored ~ the harbour.* **2** beyond the limits of: *We cannot go ~ the evidence. He has no occupation ~ his office work.*

out·sider /aʊtˋsaɪdə(r)/ *n* **1** person who is not, or who is not considered to be, a member of a group, society, etc; (colloq) ill-mannered person not socially acceptable. **2** (racing) horse that is thought to have little chance of winning a race.

out·size /aʊtˋsaɪz/ *adj* (esp of articles of clothing, etc) larger than the usual size.

out·skirts /ˋaʊtskɜts/ *n pl* borders or outlying parts (esp of a town): *on the ~ of Lille.*

out·smart /aʊtˋsmɑt/ *vt* [VP6A] (colloq) be smarter (= cleverer, more cunning) than.

out·span /aʊtˋspæn/ *vi,vt* (-nn-) [VP6A,2A] (S Africa) unyoke; unharness.

out·spoken /aʊtˋspəʊkən/ *adj* saying freely what one thinks; frank: *~ comments; be ~ in one's remarks.* **~·ly** *adv* **~·ness** *n*

out·spread /aʊtˋspred/ *adj* spread or stretched out: *with ˈ~ ˋarms; with arms ~.*

out·stand·ing /aʊtˋstændɪŋ/ *adj* **1** in a position to be easily noticed; attracting notice: *the ~ features of the landscape; an ~ landmark. The boy who won the scholarship was quite ~.* **2** (of problem, work, payments, etc) still to be attended to: *~ debts/liabilities; a good deal of work still ~.* **3** /ˋaʊstændɪŋ/ sticking out: *a boy with big, ~ ears.* **~·ly** *adv*

out·station /ˋaʊtsteɪʃn/ *n* remote cattle or sheep station in Australia.

out·stay /aʊtˋsteɪ/ *vt* [VP6A] stay longer than: *~ the other guests.* ***~ one's welcome,*** stay until one is no longer a welcome guest.

out·stretched /aʊtˋstretʃt/ *adj* stretched or spread out: *with ~ arms; lie ~ on the grass.*

out·strip /aʊtˋstrɪp/ *vt* (-pp-) [VP6A] do better than; pass (sb) in a race, etc: *The hare was ~ped by the tortoise.*

out·vie /aʊtˋvaɪ/ *vt* [VP6A] do better than in competition.

out·vote /aʊtˋvəʊt/ *vt* [VP6A] win, obtain, more votes than.

out·ward /ˋaʊtwəd/ *adj* **1** of or on the outside: *the ~ appearance of things; the ~ man* (contrasted with the spiritual nature, the soul). **2** going out: *during the ~ voyage.* □ *adv* (also **out·wards**) towards the outside; away from home or the centre: *The two ends must be bent ~s. The ship is ~ bound,* sailing away from its home port. **~·ly** *adv* on the surface; apparently: *Though badly frightened she appeared ~ly calm.*

out·wear /aʊtˋweə(r)/ *vt* (*pt* -wore /-ˋwɔ(r)/ *pp* -worn /-ˋwɔn/) [VP6A] **1** last longer than: *Well-made leather shoes will ~ two pairs of these cheap rubber shoes.* **2** wear out; use up; exhaust (esp in the *pp* when attrib): *outworn quotations,* used so often that they no longer strike the listener or reader; *outworn* (= out-of-date) *practices in industry.*

out·weigh /aʊtˋweɪ/ *vt* [VP6A] be greater in weight, value or importance than: *Do the disadvantages ~ the advantages?*

out·wit /aʊtˋwɪt/ *vt* (-tt-) [VP6A] get the better of by being cleverer or more cunning than: *The thief ~ted the police and got away with his loot.*

out·work /ˋaʊtwɜk/ *n* part of a military defence system away from the centre: *the ~s of a castle.*

out·wore /aʊtˋwɔ(r)/, **out·worn** /aʊtˋwɔn/ ⇨ outwear.

ouzel /ˋuzl/ *n* kinds of small bird of the thrush family.

ouzo /ˋuzəʊ/ *n* [U] aniseed-flavoured Greek liqueur, drunk with water.

ova /ˋəʊvə/ *n pl* of ovum.

oval /ˋəʊvl/ *n, adj* (plane figure or outline that is) egg-shaped; shaped like an ellipse.

ovary /ˋəʊvərɪ/ *n* (*pl* -ries) either of the two reproductive organs in which ova are produced in female animals; seed-vessel in a plant. ⇨ ovum and the illus at flower, reproduce.

ova·tion /əʊˋveɪʃn/ *n* [C] enthusiastic expression of welcome or approval: *The leader was given a standing ~,* The audience stood to clap, etc.

oven /ˋʌvn/ *n* **1** enclosed box-like space which is heated for cooking food: *Bread is baked in an ~.* **2** small furnace or kiln used in chemistry, etc. **ˋ~·ware** /-weə(r)/ *n* heat-proof dishes for use in an ~: *~ware pottery.*

over¹ /ˋəʊvə(r)/ *adv* (⇨ the *v* entries for special combinations, e g *give over.* Some examples are given here.) **1** (indicating movement from an upright position, from one side to the other side, or so that a different side is seen, etc): *He fell ~ on the ice. Don't knock that vase ~. A slight push would send it ~. He gave me a push and ~ I went,* I fell. *Turn the patient ~ on his face and rub his back. Turn ~ the page. It rolled ~ and ~,* made a series of revolutions. *He turned ~ in bed.* **2** (indicating motion upwards and outwards): *The milk boiled ~. He was boiling ~ with rage.* **3** from beginning to end; through: *I'll look the papers ~,* look or read through them. *You should think it ~,* consider the matter carefully. **4** (indicating repetition): *Count them ~,* again. ***~ again:*** *He did the work so badly that I had to do it all ~ again myself.* ***~ and ~ again,*** repeatedly; many times: *I've warned you ~ and ~ again not to do that.* **5**

across (a street, an open space, a distance, etc): *Take these letters ~ to the post office. Let me row you ~ to the other side of the lake. Ask him ~. He's ~ in/has gone ~ to France. Come ~ and see me some time. Some wild geese have just flown ~.* **~ against,** (a) opposite to. (b) in contrast with. **6** remaining; not used after part has been taken or used: *Seven into thirty goes four times and two ~. If there's any meat (left) ~, give it to the dog. I've paid all my debts and have £15 ~.* **7** in addition; in excess; more: *children of fourteen and ~; 10 metres and a bit ~.* **8** ended; finished; done with: *The meeting will be ~ before we arrive if we don't hurry. The storm is ~. His sufferings will soon be ~. It's all ~ with him,* He's ruined, sure to die soon, etc, according to context. **9** more than is right, usual, wise, etc: *~(-)anxious; ~(-)polite. If she grieves ~ much, she may fall ill. He's not ~ strong,* not so strong as is desirable. *He hasn't done it ~ well,* He has done it rather badly. ⇨ over- below. **10** (indicating transference or change from one person, party, etc to another): *He has gone ~ to the enemy,* joined them. *He made his business ~ to his son,* made his son the owner. *Hand that weapon ~ to me. O~! O~ to you!* (in radio telegraphy, etc) It is now your turn to speak. **11** on the whole surface; in all parts: *He was aching all ~. This pianist is famous all the world ~. Your clothes are all ~ dust/are dusty all ~. Paint the old name ~,* cover it with paint. *That's Smith all ~,* It's characteristic of him, what he might be expected to do.

over[2] /ˈəʊvə(r)/ *prep* **1** resting on the surface of and covering, partly or completely (not, in this sense, replaceable by *above*): *He spread his handkerchief ~ his face to keep the flies off. Spread a cloth ~ the table. Tie a piece of paper firmly ~ the top of the jar. I knocked the man's hat ~ his eyes,* so that he couldn't see. **2** at or to a level higher than, but not touching (in this sense often replaceable by *above*): *Attendants held a large umbrella ~/above the chief's head. The sky is ~/above our heads. These telegraph wires ~ the streets are ugly. The balcony juts out ~ the street. There was a lamp ~ the table.* **3** (indicating superiority in rank, authority, etc): *He reigns ~ a great empire. He has jurisdiction ~ three provinces. These people need a firm ruler ~ them. He has no command ~ himself/~ his passions. Mr White is ~ me in the office.* **4** in or across every part of: *Snow is falling ~ the north of England. He is famous all ~ the world.* ⇨ over[1](11). *He has travelled all ~ Europe.* **5** from one side to the other of: to or at the other side of: *He escaped ~ the frontier. She spoke to me ~ her shoulder. Look ~ the hedge. We heard voices from ~ the fence. Who lives in that house ~ the way,* on the opposite side of the road or street? **6** (of time): *Can you stay ~ Sunday,* until Monday? **7** so as to be ~ and on the other side of: *climb ~ a wall; jump ~ a brook.* **8** (opp *under*) more than: *He spoke for ~ an hour. He stayed in London (for) ~ a month. She is ~ 40 inches round the waist. The river is ~ fifty miles long. He's ~ fifty.* **~ and above,** besides; in addition to: *The waiters get good tips ~ and above their wages.* **9** in connection with; while engaged in; concerning: *He went to sleep ~ his work,* while doing it. *How long will he be ~ it?* How long will it take him to do it, get there, etc? *We had a pleasant chat ~ a cup of tea,* while drinking tea. *We all laughed ~ the affair.*

over[3] /ˈəʊvə(r)/ *n* (cricket) number of balls bowled in succession by each bowler in turn.

over- /ˈəʊvə(r)/ *pref* too (much): *ˈ~-poˈlite; ˈ~-ˈtired; ˈ~-ˈheated.* (Note: compounds not entered below have two stresses, as in the examples above). The meanings of the *adjj* below may be obtained by putting *too* in place of *over.*

ˈ~-aˈbundant	**ˈ~-exˈcited**
ˈ~-ˈactive	**ˈ~-faˈmiliar**
ˈ~-amˈbitious	**ˈ~-ˈfond**
ˈ~-ˈanxious	**ˈ~-ˈfull**
ˈ~-ˈbold	**ˈ~-ˈgenerous**
ˈ~-ˈbusy	**ˈ~-ˈgreedy**
ˈ~-ˈcareful	**ˈ~-ˈhasty**
ˈ~-ˈcautious	**ˈ~-ˈjealous**
ˈ~-ˈconfident	**ˈ~-ˈmodest**
ˈ~-ˈcredulous	**ˈ~-ˈnervous**
ˈ~-ˈcritical	**ˈ~-ˈproud**
ˈ~-ˈcurious	**ˈ~-ˈripe**
ˈ~-ˈdelicate	**ˈ~-ˈsensitive**
ˈ~-ˈeager	**ˈ~-ˈserious**
ˈ~-eˈmotional	**ˈ~-susˈpicious**
ˈ~-enˈthusiˈastic	**ˈ~-ˈzealous**

The meanings of the *nn* below may be obtained by putting *too much* in place of *over.*

ˈ~-aˈbundance	**ˈ~-inˈdulgence**
ˈ~-anˈxiety	**ˈ~-ˈpayment**
ˈ~-ˈconfidence	**ˈ~-ˈpopuˈlation**
ˈ~-creˈdulity	**ˈ~-proˈduction**
ˈ~-exˈertion	**ˈ~-ˈstrain**
ˈ~-exˈposure	**ˈ~-ˈvaluˈation**

The meaning of the *vv* below may be obtained by putting *too much* after the *v* in place of *over.*

ˈ~-ˈburden	**ˈ~-ˈheat**
ˈ~-ˈcook	**ˈ~-inˈdulge**
ˈ~-ˈeat	**ˈ~-ˈpraise**
ˈ~-ˈemphasize	**ˈ~-proˈduce**
ˈ~-ˈestimate	**ˈ~-ˈsimplify**
ˈ~-exˈert	**ˈ~-ˈstrain**
ˈ~-exˈpose	**ˈ~-ˈvalue**

over·act /ˈəʊvərˈækt/ *vi,vt* [VP2A,6A] act in an exaggerated way: *~ing (in) his part.*

over·all[1] /ˈəʊvərˈɔl/ *adj* including everything; containing all: *the ~ measurements of a room; coal burnt at an ~ efficiency of only 18 per cent.*

over·all[2] /ˈəʊvərɔl/ *n* **1** loose-fitting garment that covers other garments (e g as worn by housewives, or small children during play). **2** (*pl*) loose-fitting trousers, usu with the front extended above the waist and of heavy, strong material, worn over other clothes to protect them from dirt, etc.

over·arch /ˈəʊvərˈɑtʃ/ *vt,vi* [VP6A,2A] form an arch (over): *Trees ~ed the road.*

over·arm /ˈəʊvərɑm/ *n, adv* (sport, e g cricket) with the arm swung over the shoulder: *~ bowling; an ~ bowler.*

over·awe /ˈəʊvərˈɔ/ *vt* [VP6A] awe completely; awe through great respect, etc: *~ sb into submission.*

over·bal·ance /ˈəʊvəˈbæləns/ *vt,vi* **1** [VP6A,2A] (cause to) lose balance; fall over: *He ~d and fell into the water. Don't ~ the canoe.* **2** [VP6A] outweigh: *The gains ~ the losses.*

over·bear /ˈəʊvəˈbeə(r)/ *vt* (*pt* -bore /-ˈbɔ(r)/, *pp* -borne /-ˈbɔn/) [VP6A] overcome (by forcible arguments, strong force, or authority): *My objections were overborne in the argument.* **~·ing** *adj* masterful; forcing others to one's will: *an ~ing* *manner.* **~·ing·ly** *adv*

over·bid /ˈəʊvəˋbɪd/ *vt,vi* (*pt,pp* -bid; -dd-) **1** [VP6A] (at an auction) bid higher than (another person). **2** [VP6A,2A] bid more than the value of (sth offered for sale). **3** (bridge) make a higher bid than (one's partner) or than one's hand is worth. □ *n* act of ~ding.

over·blown /ˈəʊvəˋbləʊn/ *adj* (of flowers) too fully open; past their best.

over·board /ˋəʊvəbɔd/ *adv* over the side of a ship or boat into the water: *fall/jump ~; throw sb ~,* (fig) get rid of him, stop supporting him, etc.

over·bore /ˈəʊvəˋbɔ(r)/, **over·borne** /ˈəʊvəˋbɔn/ ⇨ overbear.

over·bur·den /ˈəʊvəˋbɜdn/ *n* surface soil, etc which must be moved away to get at coal, etc underneath. □ *vt* [VP6A] burden too heavily: *~ed with grief.*

over·call /ˈəʊvəˋkɔl/ *vt,vi* = overbid(3).

over·capi·tal·ize /ˈəʊvəˋkæpɪtl̩ɑɪz/ *vt* fix or estimate the capital of (a company) too high. **over·cap·i·tal·iz·ation** /ˈəʊvəˈkæpɪtl̩ɑɪˋzeɪʃn *US:* -l̩ɪˋz-/ *n*

over·cast /ˈəʊvəˋkɑst *US:* -ˋkæst/ *adj* (of the sky) darkened (as) by clouds; (fig) gloomy; sad. □ *n* cloud-covered sky: *Breaks in the ~ will give sunny periods* (weather forecasting).

over·charge /ˈəʊvəˋtʃɑdʒ/ *vt,vi* **1** [VP6A,2A] charge (sb) too high a price: *We were ~d for the eggs. That grocer never ~s.* **2** [VP6A] fill or load too heavily: *~ a gun; ~ an electric circuit.* □ *n* /ˋəʊvətʃɑdʒ/ [C] charge that is too high or great, e g of electric current, explosive or for a purchase, etc.

over·cloud /ˈəʊvəˋklɑʊd/ *vt,vi* [VP6A,2A] cover, become covered, with clouds or shadows; (fig) make or become gloomy.

over·coat /ˋəʊvəkəʊt/ *n* long coat worn out of doors over ordinary clothes in cold weather.

over·come /ˈəʊvəˋkʌm/ *vt* (*pt* -came /-ˋkeɪm/, *pp* -come) [VP6A] **1** get the better of; be too strong for: *~ the enemy; ~ a bad habit; ~ temptation.* **2** make weak: *be ~ by fatigue/emotion/liquor/fumes.*

over·crop /ˈəʊvəˋkrɒp/ *vt* (-pp-) [VP6A] take too many crops from (land) (so that it loses fertility).

over·crowd /ˈəʊvəˋkrɑʊd/ *vt* [VP6A] crowd too much: *~ed buses and trains; the ~ing of large cities.*

over·do /ˈəʊvəˋdu/ *vt* (*pt* -did /-ˋdɪd/, *pp* -done /-ˋdʌn/) [VP6A] **1** do too much; exaggerate; overact: *The comic scenes in the play were overdone. He overdid his part in the play.* **~ it,** **(a)** work, etc too hard: *You should work hard, but don't ~ it and make yourself ill.* **(b)** exaggerate; go too far in order to achieve one's object: *He showed sympathy for us, but didn't he rather ~ it?* **2** cook too much: *overdone beef.*

over·draft /ˋəʊvədrɑft *US:* -dræft/ *n* amount of money by which a bank account is overdrawn.

over·draw /ˈəʊvəˋdrɔ/ *vt,vi* (*pt* -drew /-ˋdru/, *pp* -drawn /-ˋdrɔn/) [VP6A,2A] **1** draw a cheque for a sum in excess of (one's credit balance in a bank): *an ~n account.* **2** exaggerate: *The characters in this novel are rather ~n,* are not true to life.

over·dress /ˈəʊvəˋdres/ *vt,vi* [VP6A,2A] dress (oneself, etc) too richly or more showily than good taste requires.

over·drive /ˋəʊvədrɑɪv/ *n* mechanism fitted into the normal gear-box of a motor vehicle to reduce the power output while maintaining the driving speed.

over·due /ˈəʊvəˋdju *US:* -ˋdu/ *adj* beyond the time fixed (for arrival, payment, etc): *The train is ~,* is late. *These bills are all ~,* ought to have been paid before now; *The baby is two weeks ~,* still not born two weeks after the expected date of birth.

over·flow /ˈəʊvəˋfləʊ/ *vt,vi* (*pt,pp* ~ed) **1** [VP6A,2A] flow over; flow over the edges or limits; flood; spread beyond the ordinary or usual area: *The river ~ed its banks. The lake is ~ing. The crowds were so big that they ~ed the barriers.* **2** [VP3A] **~ with,** be more than filled: *a heart ~ing with gratitude; a friend ~ing with kindness.* □ *n* /ˋəʊvəfləʊ/ [C] flowing over of liquid; flood; that which flows over or is too much for the space, area, etc available: *new suburbs for the ~ of population; an ~ meeting,* one held for those unable to find room in the hall, etc where the principal meeting is held.

over·grown /ˈəʊvəˋgrəʊn/ *adj* **1** having grown too fast: *an ~ boy.* **2** covered with sth that has grown over: *a garden ~ with weeds; walls ~ with ivy.*

over·growth /ˋəʊvəgrəʊθ/ *n* **1** that which has grown over: *an ~ of weeds.* **2** growth that is too fast or excessive: *weakness due to ~.*

over·hand /ˋəʊvəhænd/ *adj* (cricket, etc) = overarm; (in swimming) with the hand and arm raised out of the water: *the ~ stroke.*

over·hang /ˈəʊvəˋhæŋ/ *vt,vi* (*pt,pp* -hung /-ˋhʌŋ/) [VP6A,2A] **1** hang over; be over, project over, like a shelf: *The cliffs ~ the stream. The ledge ~s several feet.* **2** threaten; be likely to come: *~ing dangers.* □ *n* /ˋəʊvəhæŋ/ part that ~s: *the ~ of a roof/cliff.*

over·haul /ˈəʊvəˋhɔl/ *vt* [VP6A] **1** examine thoroughly in order to learn about the condition of: *have the engine of a car ~ed;* (colloq) *go to one's doctor to be ~ed,* physically examined. **2** overtake; catch up with: *The fast cruiser soon ~ed the old cargo boat.* □ *n* /ˋəʊvəhɔl/ [C] examination for the purpose of repairing, cleaning, etc.

over·head /ˈəʊvəˋhed/ *adv* above one's head; in the sky: *the people in the room ~; the stars ~.* □ *adj* /ˋəʊvəhed/ **1** raised above the ground: *~ wires/cables; an ~ railway,* built at a level higher than that of the streets. **2** (business): *~ expenses/charges* (or, *n pl,* **~s**), those expenses, etc needed for carrying on a business, e g rent, advertising, salaries, light, heating, not manufacturing costs.

over·hear /ˈəʊvəˋhɪə(r)/ *vt* (*pt,pp* -heard /-ˋhɜd/) [VP6A,18,19] hear without the knowledge of the speaker(s); hear what one is not intended to hear; hear by chance.

over·joyed /ˈəʊvəˋdʒɔɪd/ *adj* greatly delighted (*at* one's success, etc).

over·kill /ˋəʊvəkɪl/ *n* nuclear capacity greatly exceeding what is needed to exterminate the enemy.

over·land *adj* /ˋəʊvəlænd/, *adv* /ˈəʊvəˋlænd/ across the land (contrasted with the sea): *the ~ route used by Marco Polo; travel ~.*

over·lap /ˈəʊvəˋlæp/ *vt,vi* (-pp-) [VP6A,2A] **1** partly cover by extending beyond one edge: *tiles that ~ one another; ~ping shingles; ~ping boards.* **2** (fig) partly coincide; involve duplication: *His duties/authority and mine ~. His visit and mine ~ped.* □ *n* /ˋəʊvəlæp/ [C] ~ping part; [U] fact or process of ~ping.

over·lay /ˈəʊvəˋleɪ/ *vt* (*pt,pp* -laid /-ˋleɪd/) put a coating over the surface of: *wood overlaid with gold.* □ *n* /ˈəʊvəleɪ/ thing laid over sth; small tablecloth.

over·leaf /ˈəʊvəˈlif/ *adv* on the other side of the leaf (of a book, etc).

over·leap /ˈəʊvəˈlip/ *vt* (*pt,pp* ~ed or -leapt /-ˈlept/) [VP6A] leap over; (fig) go too far, attempt too much: *Ambition often ~s itself.*

over·load /ˈəʊvəˈləʊd/ *vt* [VP6A] put too great a load on; (electr) put too great a change into.

over·look /ˈəʊvəˈlʊk/ *vt* [VP6A] **1** have a view of from above: *From my study window I ~ the bay and the headlands. Our garden is ~ed from the neighbours' windows,* They can look down on to our garden from their windows. **2** fail to see or notice; pay no attention to: *~ a printer's error. His services have been ~ed by his employers,* They have not properly rewarded him. **3** pass over without punishing: *~ a fault.* **4** superintend; supervise.

over·lord /ˈəʊvəlɔd/ *n* (in feudal times) nobleman in relation to his vassals; superior from whom men held land and to whom they owed service.

over·ly /ˈəʊvəlɪ/ *adv* to an excessive degree: *~ cautious.* Cf *overcautious.*

over·man·tel /ˈəʊvəmæntl/ *n* structure (wood or stone, carved or decorated) over a mantlepiece.

over·mas·ter /ˈəʊvəmɑstə(r) *US:* -mæs-/ *vt* [VP6A] overcome, overpower: *an ~ing passion,* a passion so strong that it is difficult to subdue it.

over·much /ˈəʊvəˈmʌtʃ/ *adj, adv* too great(ly): *give children ~ homework; an author who has been praised ~.*

over·night /ˈəʊvəˈnɑɪt/ *adv* **1** on the night before: *get everything ready for the journey ~; make preparations ~.* **2** for, during, the night: *stay ~ at a friend's house,* sleep there for the night; *The situation changed ~.* □ *adj* during or for the night: *an ~ journey; an ~ stop at Rome.*

over·pass /ˈəʊvəpɑs *US:* -pæs/ *n* bridge or road that carries a road over a highway or motorway. ⇨ **flyover, underpass.**

over·pay /ˈəʊvəˈpeɪ/ *vt* (*pt,pp* -paid /-ˈpeɪd/) [VP6A,14] pay too much or too highly: *Has Jack been overpaid for his work?*

over·play /ˈəʊvəˈpleɪ/ *vt* ***~ one's hand,*** (gaming, cards) take risks that are not justified (by over-estimating one's own strength).

over·plus /ˈəʊvəplʌs/ *n* [C] amount which is surplus or in excess.

over·power /ˈəʊvəˈpɑʊə(r)/ *vt* [VP6A] overcome; be too strong for; defeat by greater strength or numbers: *The criminals were easily ~ed by the police. He was ~ed by the heat.* **~·ing** *adj* too strong; very powerful: *an ~ing stink; ~ing grief.*

over·print /ˈəʊvəˈprɪnt/ *vt* [VP6A] print additional matter on (an already printed surface, e g of postage stamps).

over·rate /ˈəʊvəˈreɪt/ *vt* [VP6A] put too high a value on: *~ sb's abilities; an ~d book.*

over·reach /ˈəʊvəˈritʃ/ *vt* [VP6A] **1** get the better of (by trickery). **2** ***~ oneself,*** fail in one's object, damage one's own interests, by being too ambitious.

over·ride /ˈəʊvəˈrɑɪd/ *vt* (*pt* -rode /-ˈrəʊd/, *pp* -ridden /-ˈrɪdn/) [VP6A] prevail over (sb's opinions, decisions, wishes, claims, etc): *They overrode my wishes,* set them aside without consideration.

over·rule /ˈəʊvəˈrul/ *vt* [VP6A] decide against (esp by using one's higher authority): *~ a claim or objection. The judge ~d the previous decision. We were ~d by the majority.*

over·run /ˈəʊvəˈrʌn/ *vt* (*pt* -ran /-ˈræn/, *pp* -run) [VP6A] **1** spread over and occupy or injure: *a country ~ by enemy troops; warehouses ~ with rats; a garden ~ with weeds.* **2** go beyond (a limit): *speakers who ~ the time allowed them. The broadcast overran the allotted time.*

over·sea /ˈəʊvəˈsi/ *adj* (at, to, from, for, places) across the sea: *~(s) trade; an ~(s) broadcast programme.* **over·seas** *adv: go/live ~s,* across the sea; abroad.

over·see /ˈəʊvəˈsi/ *vt* (*pt* -saw /-ˈsɔ/, *pp* -seen /-ˈsin/) [VP6A] look after, control (work, workmen). **over·seer** /ˈəʊvəsɪə(r)/ *n* foreman; person whose duty it is to take charge of work and see that it is properly done.

over·sexed /ˈəʊvəˈsekst/ *adj* having sexual desire in excess of what is normal; obsessed by sex.

over·shadow /ˈəʊvəˈʃædəʊ/ *vt* [VP6A] throw a shade over; (fig) render less conspicuous; cause to seem less important.

over·shoe /ˈəʊvəʃu/ *n* [C] rubber shoe worn over an ordinary one for protection against wet and mud. ⇨ **galosh.**

over·shoot /ˈəʊvəˈʃut/ *vt* (*pt,pp* -shot /-ˈʃot/) [VP6A] shoot over or beyond (a mark); (liter, fig) go too far: *The aircraft overshot the runway.*

over·shot /ˈəʊvəˈʃot/ *adj* **~ wheel,** water wheel driven by the pressure of water falling on to it from above.

over·side /ˈəʊvəsɑɪd/ *adv* over the side (of a ship, etc): *discharge cargo ~,* e g into lighters, not on to the quay.

over·sight /ˈəʊvəsɑɪt/ *n* **1** [U] failure to notice sth; [C] instance of this: *Through an unfortunate ~ your letter was left unanswered.* **2** [U] watchful care: *under the ~ of a nurse.*

over·skirt /ˈəʊvəskɜt/ *n* one worn over a skirt.

over·sleep /ˈəʊvəˈslip/ *vi* (*pt,pp* -slept /-ˈslept/) [VP2A] sleep too long; continue sleeping after the proper time for waking: *He overslept and was late for work.*

over·spill /ˈəʊvəspɪl/ *n* spreading into surrounding areas (esp) excess population: *build new towns for London's ~.*

over·state /ˈəʊvəˈsteɪt/ *vt* [VP6A] express or state too strongly; state more than is true about: *Don't ~ your case.* **~·ment** /ˈəʊvəsteɪtmənt/ *n* [U] exaggeration; [C] exaggerated statement.

over·stay /ˈəʊvəˈsteɪ/ *vt* [VP6A] stay too long. ***~ one's welcome,*** stay until one is no longer a welcome guest.

over·step /ˈəʊvəˈstep/ *vt* (-pp-) [VP6A] go beyond: *~ one's authority.*

over·stock /ˈəʊvəˈstok/ *vt* [VP6A] supply with too large a stock: *~ a farm with cattle,* with more cattle than there is food or space for.

over·strung /ˈəʊvəˈstrʌŋ/ *adj* **1** (of a person, his nerves) intensely strained; easily excited; too sensitive. **2** (of a piano) with strings crossing obliquely to save space.

over·stuffed /ˈəʊvəˈstʌft/ *adj* (of seats, etc) made soft and comfortable by very thick padding.

over·sub·scribed /ˈəʊvəsəbˈskrɑɪbd/ *adj* (fin) (of an issue of shares, etc) with applications in excess of what is offered.

overt /ˈəʊvɜt *US:* əʊˈvɜt/ *adj* done or shown openly, publicly: *~ hostility.* **~·ly** *adv*

over·take /ˌəʊvəˈteɪk/ *vt* (*pt* -**took** /-ˈtʊk/, *pp* -**taken** /-teɪkən/) [VP6A] **1** come or catch up with; outstrip: *~ other cars on the road; ~ arrears of work.* **2** (of storms, troubles, etc) come upon (sb) suddenly, by surprise: *be ~n by/with fear/surprise, etc; be ~n by a storm.*

over·tax /ˌəʊvəˈtæks/ *vt* [VP6A] tax too heavily; put too heavy a burden or strain on: *~ one's strength/sb's patience.*

over·throw /ˌəʊvəˈθrəʊ/ *vt* (*pt* -**threw** /-ˈθru/, *pp* -**thrown** /-ˈθrəʊn/) [VP6A] defeat; put an end to; cause to fall or fail: *~ the government.* □ *n* /ˈəʊvəθrəʊ/ ruin; defeat; fall.

over·time /ˈəʊvətɑɪm/ *n* [U], *adv* (time spent at work) after the usual hours: *working ~; be paid extra for ~; be on ~,* i e working *~; ~ pay.*

over·tone /ˈəʊvətəʊn/ *n* (music) higher note more faintly heard than the main note produced from a string, pipe, etc; (*pl*) (fig) implications.

over·top /ˌəʊvəˈtɒp/ *vt* (-pp-) [VP6A] be higher than; rise above: *~ped by the new skyscraper.*

over·trump /ˌəʊvəˈtrʌmp/ *vt* [VP6A] (whist, bridge) play a higher trump than.

over·ture /ˈəʊvətʃə(r)/ *n* **1** (often pl) approach made (*to* sb) with the aim of starting discussions: *peace ~s; make ~s to sb.* **2** musical composition played as an introduction to an opera, or as a separate item at a concert.

over·turn /ˌəʊvəˈtɜn/ *vt,vi* [VP6A,2A] (cause to) turn over; upset: *He ~ed the boat. The boat ~ed.*

over·ween·ing /ˌəʊvəˈwinɪŋ/ *adj* having, marked by, excessive self-confidence or conceit: *~ ambition/vanity.*

over·weight /ˈəʊvəweɪt/ *n* excess of weight above what is usual or legal: *Shopkeepers rarely give ~.* □ *adj* /ˌəʊvəˈweɪt/ exceeding the weight allowed or normal: *an ~ bag; If your luggage is ~ you'll have to pay extra. She's as ~ as the women in the paintings of Rubens.* **~ed** /ˌəʊvəˈweɪtɪd/ *part adj* carrying too much weight: *~ed with packages.*

over·whelm /ˌəʊvəˈwelm *US:* -ˈhwelm/ *vt* [VP6A] weigh down; submerge, cover completely by flowing over or pouring down on; crush; destroy; cause to feel confused or embarrassed: *be ~ed by the enemy/by superior forces; an ~ing victory; ~ing sorrow; be ~ed by a flood; be ~ed with brief/gratitude.*

over·work /ˌəʊvəˈwɜk/ *vt,vi* [VP6A,2A] (cause to) work too hard or too long: *~ oneself; ~ a horse. It's foolish to ~.* □ *n* /ˈəʊvəwɜk/ [U] working too much or too long: *ill through ~.*

over·wrought /ˌəʊvəˈrɔt/ *adj* tired out by too much work or excitement; in a state of nervous illness.

ovi·duct /ˈəʊvɪdʌkt/ *n* (also called *Fallopian tube*) either of two tubes through which ova pass from the ovary to the uterus. ⇨ the illus at reproduce.

ovip·ar·ous /əʊˈvɪpərəs/ *adj* producing young from eggs which hatch outside the body.

ovoid /ˈəʊvɔɪd/ *adj, n* egg-shaped (object).

ovum /ˈəʊvəm/ *n* (*pl* ova /ˈəʊvə/) female germ or sex cell in animals, capable of developing into a new individual when fertilized by male sperm.

owe /əʊ/ *vt,vi* **1** [VP6A,12A,13A,2A,3A] ***owe sb sth; owe sth to sb; owe for,*** be in debt to (sb) (for sth): *He owes his father £50. He owes £50 to his father. I have paid all that was owing. He still owes for the goods he had last month.* **2** [VP12A,13A] be under an obligation to, feel the necessity of gratitude to: *We owe a great deal to our parents and teachers. I owe it to you that I am still alive.* **3** [VP12A,13A] be bound to give as a duty: *owe reverence and obedience to the Pope.* **4** [VP14] ***owe sth to sth,*** be indebted to as the source of: *He owes his success to good luck more than to ability. To whom do we owe the discovery of penicillin?*

ow·ing /ˈəʊɪŋ/ *adj* still to be paid: *large sums still ~.* **~ to** *prep* because of; on account of: *O~ to the rain they could not come.*

owl /ɑʊl/ *n* night-flying bird that lives on small birds and animals, e g mice. ⇨ the illus at prey. **ow·let** /ˈɑʊlət/ *n* young owl. **owl·ish** /ˈɑʊlɪʃ/ *adj* of or like an owl; looking, or trying to look, solemn and wise. **owl·ish·ly** *adv*

own[1] /əʊn/ *adj, pron* **1** (used with possessives, either attributively or predicatively, to give emphasis to the idea of personal possession, to the peculiar or individual character of sth): *I saw it with my own eyes. It was her own idea. This is my own house/This house is my own,* belongs to me, is not rented. *This fruit has a flavour all its own,* is not to be compared to the flavour of any other fruit. *May I have it for my very own,* Are you willing to let me be the sole owner, so that I need not share it? *My time is my own,* I can spend it as I wish. *For reasons of his own* (= For particular reasons, reasons perhaps only known to him), *he refused to join the club.* ***(be) on one's own,*** **(a)** alone: *I'm (all) on my own today. She lives on her own,* alone, not with family or friends. **(b)** independently of an employer: *He's (working) on his own. He can be left to work on his own, without supervision.* **(c)** outstanding; excellent: *For craftsmanship, Smith is on his own,* has no equal. ***own brother/sister,*** with both parents the same, not a half-brother/sister. ***be one's own man/master,*** be independent; be self-employed. ***come into one's own,*** receive what rightly belongs to one, the credit, fame, etc that one deserves: *Along unpaved and rutted tracks, this sturdy car really comes into its own,* shows what it is capable of. ***get one's own back,*** have one's revenge. ***hold one's own (against sb/sth),*** **(a)** maintain one's position against attack; not be defeated. **(b)** not lose strength: *The patient is holding her own.* **2** (used to indicate the idea of personal activity; done or produced by and for oneself): *She makes all her own clothes. I can cook my own meals. It's unwise to try to be your own lawyer.*

own[2] /əʊn/ *vt,vi* **1** [VP6A] possess; have as property; *This house is mine; I own it. Who owns this land,* To whom does it belong? **2** [VP6A,9,2C,3A] agree; confess; recognize: *own that a claim is justified; own to having told a lie; own one's faults; own oneself (to be) defeated; own the force of an argument. The man refused to own the child,* would not admit that he was its father. *I must own myself no* (= confess that I am not a) *supporter of reform.* ***own up (to sth),*** confess fully and frankly.

owner /ˈəʊnə(r)/ *n* person who owns sth: *Who's the ~ of this house?* **ˈ~-ˈdriver** *n* motorist who drives a car which he owns. **ˈ~-ˈoccupier** *n* one who owns the house he lives in. **ˈ~-ˈoccupied** *adj* (of a house, etc) lived in by the ~ (not rented to sb else). **~·less** *adj* without an ~; not known to belong to anyone: *~less dogs.* **ˈ~·ship** /-ʃɪp/ *n* state of being an ~; right of possessing: *land of uncertain ~ship.*

ox /oks/ *n* (*pl* oxen /ˋoksn/) **1** general name for domestic cattle. ⇨ bull¹(1), bullock, cow¹(1) and the illus at domestic. **2** (esp) fully grown castrated bullock, used as a draught animal. **ˋox-cart** *n* cart drawn by oxen. **ˋox-eye** *n* name (often used *attrib*) of several kinds of plants (daisies, wild chrysanthemums, etc). **ˈox-ˋeyed** *adj* with large, round eyes like those of an ox. **ˋox-tail** *n* tail of ox, much used for soup, etc.

Ox·bridge /ˋoksbrɪdʒ/ *n* (invented name for) Oxford and/or Cambridge (contrasted with *Redbrick,* used for newer provincial universities in GB).

Ox·ford /ˋoksfəd/ *n* (university city in England) ~ **bags,** style of baggy, wide-bottomed trousers. **The ~ Group,** recent religious movement that stresses public confession of one's faults and asking God for direct guidance. **The ~ Movement,** 19th c movement advocating the revival of Catholicism within the Anglican Church. **~ mixture,** dark, grey (cloth). **~ shoes,** low shoes lacing over the instep.

ox·ide /ˋoksaɪd/ *n* [C,U] compound of oxygen: *iron ~; ~ of tin.* **oxi·dize** /ˋoksɪdaɪz/ *vt,vi* [VP6A,2A] (cause to) combine with oxygen; make or become rusty. **oxi·diz·ation** /ˈoksɪdaɪˋzeɪʃn *US:* -dɪˋz-/ *n*

Ox·on·ian /okˋsəʊnɪən/ *n, adj* (member) of the University of Oxford.

oxy·acety·lene /ˈoksɪəˋsetəlin/ *adj, n* (of a) mixture of oxygen and acetylene: *~ torch/blowpipe,* tool burning ~; *~ welding,* by means of a hot flame of ~.

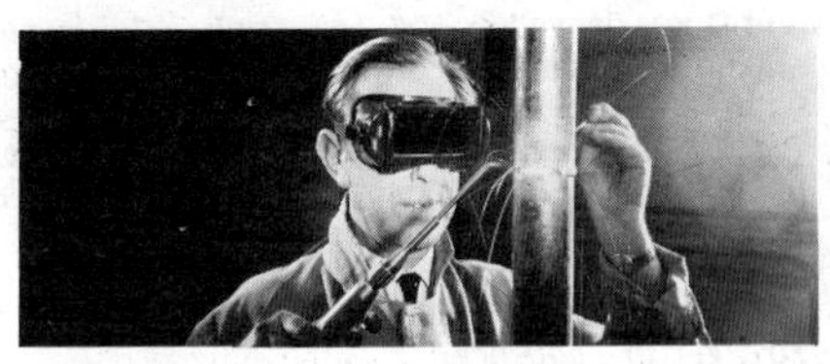

oxyacetylene welding

oxy·gen /ˋoksɪdʒən/ *n* [U] chemical element (symbol **O**), gas without colour, taste, or smell, present in the air and necessary to the existence of all forms of life. **ˋ~ mask,** mask placed over the nose and mouth to supply ~, e g in an aircraft at a great altitude. **ˋ~ tent,** small tent or canopy placed over a patient who needs an extra supply of ~. **ˋ~·ate** /-eɪt/, **ˋ~·ize** /-aɪz/ *vt* supply, treat, or mix, with ~.

oyez /əʊˋjez/ (also **oyes** /əʊˋjes/) *int* cry meaning 'Listen', repeated three times by a town-crier, or (in a law court) by an usher to demand silence and attention.

oy·ster /ˋɔɪstə(r)/ *n* kinds of shellfish much used as food, usu eaten uncooked. ⇨ the illus at bivalve. **ˋ~-bar** *n* counter (in a restaurant, etc) where ~s are served. **ˋ~-bed, ˋ~-bank** *nn* part of the sea-bottom where ~s breed or are bred. **ˋ~-catcher** *n* wading seabird.

ozone /ˋəʊzəʊn/ *n* [U] form of oxygen with a sharp and refreshing smell; (fig) exhilarating influence; (pop use) pure refreshing air as at the seaside.

Pp

P, p /pi/ (*pl* P's, p's /piz/) the 16th letter of the English alphabet. ***mind one's P's and Q's,*** be careful not to offend against propriety.

pa /pɑ/ *n* (colloq) short for *papa.*

pabu·lum /ˋpæbjʊləm/ *n* [U] (liter) food (usu fig): *mental ~,* food for thought.

pace /peɪs/ *n* [C] **1** (distance covered by the foot in a) single step in walking or running. **2** rate of walking or running, or (fig) progress. ***go at a good ~,*** go fast. ***go the ~,*** **(a)** go at great speed. **(b)** (fig) spend money freely (esp on pleasure or in dissipated ways). ***keep ~ (with sb),*** (liter, fig) go forward at the same rate: *He finds it hard to keep ~ with all the developments in nuclear physics.* ***set the ~ (for sb),*** set a speed for sb. **ˋ~-maker** *n* **(a)** (also **ˋ~-setter**) rider, runner, etc who sets the ~ for another in a race. **(b)** electronic device (with radio active core) to correct weak or irregular heart beats. **3** (esp of horses) way of walking, running, etc. ***put a person through his ~s,*** test his abilities, etc. □ *vi,vt* **1** [VP2A,C] walk with slow or regular steps: *~ up and down;* (of a horse) amble; go at an easy, unhurried ~. **2** [VP6A] move across in this way: *~ a room; pacing the station platform.* **3** [VP6A,15B] *~* ***off/out,*** measure by taking ~s: *~ off a distance of 30 metres; ~ out a room.* **4** [VP6A] set the ~ for (a rider or runner in a race).

pachy·derm /ˋpækɪdəm/ *n* (kinds of) thick-skinned, four-footed animal, e g an elephant.

pa·cific /pəˋsɪfɪk/ *adj* peaceful; making or loving peace. **pa·cifi·cally** /-klɪ/ *adv*

paci·fi·ca·tion /ˈpæsɪfɪˋkeɪʃn/ *n* [U] making or becoming peaceful; bringing about a state of peace.

paci·fism /ˋpæsɪf-ɪzm/ *n* [U] principle that war should and could be abolished. **paci·fist** /-ɪst/ *n* believer in ~.

pac·ify /ˋpæsɪfaɪ/ *vt* (*pt,pp* -fied) [VP6A] calm and quieten; end violence in.

pack¹ /pæk/ *n* **1** bundle of things tied or wrapped up together for carrying; (US =) packet: *a ~ of cigarettes.* **ˋ~-horse, ˋ~-animal** *nn* one used for carrying ~s. **ˋ~·man** /-mən/ *n* (*pl* -men) (old use) pedlar. **ˋ~-saddle** *n* one with straps for supporting ~s. **ˋ~-thread** *n* [U] strong thread for sewing or tying up ~s or canvas bags. **2** number of dogs kept for hunting (*a ~ of hounds*) or of wild animals that go about together: *Wolves hunt in ~s.* **3** (usu contemptuous) number of things or persons: *a ~ of thieves/liars/lies.* **4** complete set (usu 52) of playing-cards. **5** (Rugby football) a side's forwards. **6 ˋ~-ice,** mass of large pieces of floating ice in the sea. **7** quantity of fish, meat, fruit, etc packed in a season: *this year's ~ of salmon.* ⇨ pack²(5).

pack² /pæk/ *vt,vi* [VP6A,14,15A,B,2A,C] put things, put (things), into a box, bundle, bag, etc;

fill (a bag, box, etc) with things; get ready for a journey by doing this: ~ *clothes into a trunk; ~ a trunk with clothes. Have you ~ed (up) your things? You must begin ~ing at once. These books ~ easily,* It is easy to ~ them. *Her husband takes a ~ed lunch* (e g sandwiches, etc ~ed into a box or other container) *to work every day.* **~ up,** (colloq) put one's tools, etc away; stop working: *It's time to ~ up. One of the aircraft's engines ~ed up,* (sl) failed. **~ it in,** (sl) give up doing sth; end it. **2** [VP14,3D] **~ into,** crush or crowd together (into a place or period of time): *~ing people into an already overcrowded bus; crowds ~ing into the cinemas on a wet day. She managed to ~ a lot of sightseeing into the short time she had in London.* **3** [VP6A,15A] put soft material into or round (sth) to keep it safe, or to prevent loss or leakage: *glass ~ed in straw; ~ a leaking joint.* **4 ~ sb off; send sb ~ing,** send him away quickly and unceremoniously (because he is troublesome, etc): *I wish you'd ~ yourself off,* go away. **5** [VP6A] prepare and put (meat, fruit, etc) in tins for preservation. ⇨ pack[1](7). **6** [VP6A] choose (the members of a committee, etc) so that their decisions are likely to be in one's favour. **~er** *n* person or machine that ~s; (esp, usu *pl*) person who ~s meat, fruit, etc for market.

pack·age /ˈpækɪdʒ/ *n* [C] parcel, bale, bundle of things, packed together. **~ deal/offer,** (colloq) number of proposals put forward for discussion or acceptance. ˌ**~ ˈtour,** (colloq) holiday tour with every detail arranged in advance by travel agents and sold at a fixed price. □ *vt* place in a ~; make a ~ of.

packet /ˈpækɪt/ *n* **1** small parcel or bundle: *a ~ of letters; a postal ~; a ~ of 20 cigarettes.* **2 ˈ~(-boat),** mailboat. **3** (sl) considerable sum of money: *make/cost a ~.* **4** (army sl) trouble of some sort: *catch/stop/get a ~,* (esp) be severely wounded.

pack·ing /ˈpækɪŋ/ *n* [U] process of packing (goods); materials used in packing(3), e g for closing a leaking joint. **ˈ~-case** *n* one of rough boards in which goods, e g bicycles, are packed for shipment. **ˈ~-needle** *n* large needle used for sewing up canvas packages, etc.

pact /pækt/ *n* compact; agreement: *the P~ of Locarno; a new Peace P~.*

pad[1] /pæd/ *n* **1** mass of, container filled with, soft material, used to prevent damage, give comfort or improve the shape of sth. **2** guard for the leg or other parts of the body (in cricket and other games). ⇨ the illus at cricket. **3** number of sheets of writing-paper fastened together along one edge. **4** (also **ˈinking-pad**) absorbent material (usu in an oblong box) used for inking rubber stamps. **5** soft, fleshy underpart of the foot (of a dog, fox, etc). **6** (usu **ˈlaunching-pad**) platform from which missiles are launched into outer space. ⇨ the illus at rocket. **7** (sl) bed; room to sleep in; apartment. □ *vt* (-dd-) **1** [VP6A] put pads(1) in or on (to prevent injury, to give comfort, or to fill out hollow spaces, etc): *a jacket with padded shoulders,* e g to make the wearer seem more manly: *a padded cell,* one with padded walls (in a mental home). **2** [VP6A,15B] ***pad sth out,*** make (a sentence, essay, book, etc) longer by using unnecessary material: *an essay padded out with numerous quotations.* **pad·ding** /ˈpædɪŋ/ *n* [U] material used for making pads(1) or for padding(*v*, 2).

pad[2] /pæd/ *vi,vt* (-dd-) [VP2A,C] travel on foot: *padding along;* [VP6A] tramp (the roads) on foot: *He lost all his money and had to pad it home.*

paddle[1] /ˈpædl/ *n* **1** short oar with a broad blade at one or (*double* ~) at both ends, used (without a rowlock) to propel a canoe through the water. **2** (in rowing) act or period of propelling a boat with light, easy strokes. **3 ˈ~-box** *n* wooden covering for the upper part of a ~-wheel. **ˈ~-steamer** *n* steam vessel propelled by ~-wheels. **ˈ~-wheel** *n* one of a pair of wheels, each with boards round the circumference which press backwards against the water and propel a ~-steamer. **4** ~-shaped instrument (e g one used for beating, stirring or mixing things). □ *vt,vi* [VP6A,2A] send (a canoe) through the water by using a ~ or ~s; row with light, easy strokes. **~ one's own canoe,** (prov) depend on oneself alone.

paddle[2] /ˈpædl/ *vi* [VP2A] walk with bare feet in shallow water (as children do at the seaside): *a paddling pool,* shallow pool (e g in a public park) where children ~. □ *n* act or period of paddling.

pad·dock /ˈpædək/ *n* **1** small grass field, esp one used for exercising horses. **2** (at a race-course) enclosed area of grassland where horses are assembled and paraded before a race.

paddy[1] /ˈpædɪ/ *n* [U] rice that is still growing; rice in the husk. **ˈ~-field** *n* rice-field.

paddy[2] /ˈpædɪ/ *n* (*pl* **-dies**) (colloq) rage; fit of bad temper: *She's in one of her paddies,* one of the fits of bad temper to which she is subject.

Paddy /ˈpædɪ/ *n* (nickname for an) Irishman. **ˈ~-wagon,** (US sl) police van for taking persons suspected of crime into custody.

pad·lock /ˈpædlɒk/ *n* lock of the kind shown here. □ *vt* [VP6A] fasten with a ~: *The gate was ~ed.*

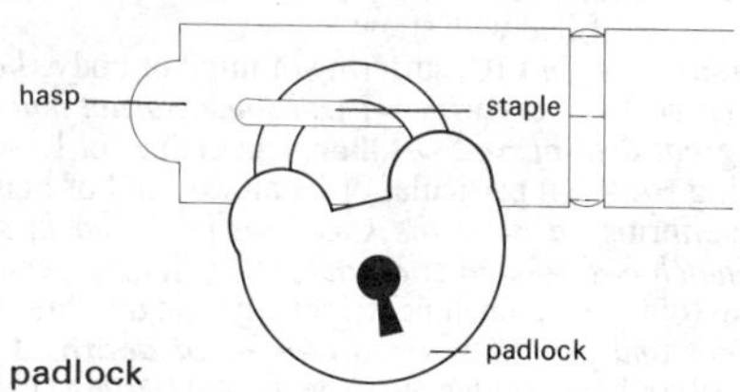

a padlock

padre /ˈpɑdreɪ/ *n* (army and navy colloq) chaplain; (GB colloq) priest; parson.

paean, pean /ˈpiən/ *n* song of thanksgiving, praise or triumph.

paed·er·asty /ˈpedəræstɪ/ *n* ⇨ pederasty.

paedi·at·rics /ˈpidɪˈætrɪks/ ⇨ pediatrics.

pae·ony /ˈpiənɪ/ *n* ⇨ peony.

pa·gan /ˈpeɪgən/ *n, adj* (person who is) not a believer in any of the chief religions of the world; (colloq) any person with no religious beliefs: *They've brought up their children as ~s.* **ˈ~·ism** /-ɪzm/ *n* beliefs, practices, of ~s.

page[1] /peɪdʒ/ *n* one side of a leaf of paper in a book, periodical, etc; entire leaf of a book, etc: *Several ~s have been torn out.* □ *vt* number the ~s of.

page[2] /peɪdʒ/ *n* **1** (also **ˈ~ boy**) boy servant, usu in uniform, in a hotel, club, etc. **2** (in the Middle Ages) boy in training for knighthood and living in a knight's household. **3** boy acting as a personal attendant of a person of high rank. □ *vt* [VP6A] (of a page(1)) go through the public rooms of a hotel, club, etc calling sb's name: *paging Mr Hall.*

pag·eant /ˈpædʒənt/ *n* **1** public entertainment, usu outdoors, in which historical events are acted in the costume of the period. **2** public celebration, esp one in which there is a procession of persons in fine costumes (e g a coronation). **~ry** /ˈpædʒəntrɪ/ *n* [U] rich and splendid display.

pagi·na·tion /ˈpædʒɪˈneɪʃn/ *n* (figures used for the) numbering of the pages of a book.

pa·goda /pəˈgəʊdə/ *n* (in India, Ceylon, Burma, China, Japan, etc) religious building, typically a sacred tower of pyramidal form (Hindu temple), or of several storeys (Buddhist tower).

pagodas

pah /pɑ/ *int* expressing disgust.

paid /peɪd/ ⇨ pay².

pail /peɪl/ *n* vessel, usu round and open, of metal or wood, for carrying liquid: *a ~ of milk.* **ˈ~·ful** /-fʊl/ *n* as much as a ~ holds.

pail·lasse, pail·liasse /ˈpælɪæs *US:* ˈpælɪˈæs/ *nn* mattress filled with straw.

pain /peɪn/ *n* **1** [U] suffering of mind or body: *be in (great) ~; cry with ~; feel some/no/not much/a great deal of ~.* **ˈ~-killer** *n* medicine for lessening ~. **2** [C] particular or localized kind of bodily suffering: *a ~ in the knee; ~s in the back; stomach ~s.* ***a ~ in the neck,*** (sl) irritating person. **3** (old use) punishment; penalty: (legal phrases): *~s and penalties.* ***on/under ~ of death,*** at the risk of being sentenced to death. □ *vt* [VP6A] cause ~ to: *Doesn't your laziness ~ your parents? My foot is still ~ing me.* **~ed** *adj* distressed: *She looked ~ed when I refused to help. She had a ~ed look.* **ˈ~·ful** /-fl/ *adj* causing ~: *This duty is ~ful to me.* **ˈ~·fully** /-flɪ/ *adv* **~·less** *adj* without ~; causing no ~: *~less extractions,* (of teeth). **~-less·ly** *adv*

pains /peɪnz/ *n pl* trouble; effort: *work hard and get very little for all one's ~.* ***be at ~ to do sth,*** make a great effort, work hard, to do it. ***spare no ~,*** do everything possible. ***take (great) ~ (over sth/to do sth),*** take great trouble: *take great ~ to please one's employer.* **ˈ~·taking** *adj* careful; industrious.

paint /peɪnt/ *n* **1** [U] solid colouring matter (to be) mixed with oil or other liquid and used to give colour to a surface: *give the doors two coats of ~.* **2** [U] material used to colour the face. **3** (*pl*) collection of tubes or cakes of colouring materials. **ˈ~-box** *n* box with such a collection. **ˈ~-brush** *n* brush for applying ~. □ *vt,vi* **1** [VP6A,22] coat with paint: *~ a door; ~ the gate green.* ***~ the town red,*** (colloq) go out and have a lively, exciting time esp when celebrating sth. **2** [VP6A, 15A,B,2A,C] make a picture (of) with paint: *~ flowers/a landscape; ~ in oils/in water-colours.* ***~ sth in,*** add to a picture: *~ in the foreground.* ***~ sth out,*** cover up or hide by using paint. **3** [VP6A] (fig) describe vividly in words. ***not so black as one is ~ed,*** not so bad as one is represented to be. **~er** *n* **1** person who ~s pictures; artist. **2** workman who ~s woodwork, buildings, ships, etc. **~·ing** *n* [U] using paint; occupation of a ~er; [C] ~ed picture.

painter¹ /ˈpeɪntə(r)/ *n* ⇨ paint.

painter² /ˈpeɪntə(r)/ *n* rope fastened to the bow of a boat by which it may be tied to a ship, pier, etc. ***cut the ~,*** **(a)** set (a boat, etc) adrift. **(b)** (fig) (e g of a colony) effect a separation. become independent.

pair /peə(r)/ *n* **1** two things of the same kind (to be) used together: *a ~ of shoes/gloves; two ~(s) of stockings.* **2** single article with two parts always joined: *a ~ of trousers/braces/scissors/tongs.* **3** two persons closely associated, e g an engaged or married couple: *the happy ~,* e g two newly married persons. ***in ~s,*** in twos. **4** two animals of opposite sex; two horses harnessed together. **5** (in Parliament) two persons of opposite political parties who absent themselves from a division by mutual agreement; one member willing to do this: *The member for Lewisham couldn't find a ~.* □ *vt,vi* [VP6A,15B,2A,C] form a ~ or ~s; join in ~s; two; go off in ~s; (Parliament) make a ~(5).

pais·ley /ˈpeɪzlɪ/ *n* (soft wool fabric with) curved patterns in soft bright colours: *a ~ shawl.*

pa·ja·mas /pəˈdʒɑməz/ *n pl* ⇨ pyjamas.

pal /pæl/ *n* (colloq) comrade; friend. *vi* (-ll-) ***pal up (with sb),*** become friendly. **pally** /ˈpælɪ/ *adj* (colloq) friendly.

pal·ace /ˈpælɪs/ *n* **1** official residence of a sovereign, archbishop or bishop; any large and splendid house; large, splendid building for entertainment. **2 the ~,** influential persons at the ~ of a sovereign ruler. **~ revolution,** overthrow of sb in a position of great power, e g a President, by high-ranking colleagues or close subordinates.

pala·din /ˈpælədɪn/ *n* any of the twelve Peers of the court of Emperor Charlemagne /ˈʃɑləmeɪn/ A D 742—814; knight errant; notable champion.

palæo- /ˈpælɪəʊ- *US:* ˈpeɪlɪəʊ-/ *pref* (in compounds, etc) = paleo-.

palan·quin, palan·keen /ˈpælənˈkin/ *nn* covered litter for one person, carried on poles by two or more men, as formerly used in India and other Eastern countries.

pal·at·able /ˈpælətəbl/ *adj* agreeable to the taste or (fig) to the mind.

pala·tal /ˈpælətl/ *n, adj* (sound) made by placing the tongue against or near (usu the hard) palate (e g /j, ʒ, ʃ, dʒ/); of the palate.

pal·ate /ˈpælət/ *n* **1** roof of the mouth: *the hard/soft ~,* its front/back part. **ˈcleft ˈ~,** ⇨ cleave¹(3). **2** sense of taste: *have a good ~ for wines.*

pa·la·tial /pəˈleɪʃl/ *adj* of or like a palace; magnificent: *a ~ residence.*

pa·lat·in·ate /pəˈlætɪnət *US:* -tṇət/ *n* territory ruled over by an earl or count having some royal privileges.

pal·aver /pəˈlɑvə(r) *US:* -ˈlæv-/ *n* [C] talk or conference, esp one between traders or explorers and the people of the country; [U] idle talk; [U] (colloq) bother. □ *vi* [VP2A] talk idly for a long time.

pale[1] /peɪl/ *adj* (-r, -st) **1** (of a person's face) having little colour; bloodless: *He turned ~ at the news. You're looking ~ today.* **ˋ~-face** *n* name said to have been used by N American Indians for a European white person. **2** (of colours) not bright; faintly coloured: *~ blue.* □ *vi* [VP2A,C] grow ~; lose colour. ***~ before/by the side of,*** (fig) be far outdone by; appear weak when seen with. **~·ly** /ˋpeɪllɪ/ *adv* **~·ness** *n*

pale[2] /peɪl/ *n* pointed piece of wood used for fences; stake. ⇨ paling.

pale[3] /peɪl/ *n* (hist) area around Dublin (in Ireland) controlled by the English. Now, only in: ***beyond/outside the ~,*** socially unacceptable or unreasonable: *His remarks put him quite outside the ~.*

paleo·lithic (also **palæo-**) /ˈpælɪəʊˋlɪθɪk *US:* ˈpeɪl-/ *adj* of the period marked by the use of primitive stone implements.

pale·on·tol·ogy (also **palæ-**) /ˈpælɪonˋtolədʒɪ *US:* ˈpeɪl-/ *n* [U] study of fossils as a guide to the history of life on earth. **pale·on·tol·ogist** (also **palæ-**) /-ədʒɪst/ *n*

a palette

a paling

pal·ette /ˋpælɪt/ *n* board (with a hole for the thumb) on which an artist mixes his colours. **ˋ~-knife** *n* thin steel blade with a handle, used (by artists) for mixing (and sometimes spreading) oil colours, by potters for moulding clay and in cookery.

pal·frey /ˋpɔlfrɪ/ *n* (*pl* -freys) (old use, and in poetry) saddle-horse for riding, esp one for a woman.

pal·imp·sest /ˋpælɪmpsest/ *n* [C] piece of parchment or other writing material from which the original writing has been erased to make room for new writing, esp as a source for lost works of the remote past.

pal·in·drome /ˋpælɪndrəʊm/ *n* word, verse, etc that reads the same backwards as forwards, e g *madam.*

pal·ing /ˋpeɪlɪŋ/ *n* fence made of pales[2].

pali·sade /ˈpælɪˋseɪd/ *n* **1** fence of strong, pointed wooden stakes (e g as used to defend a building in former times). **2** (*pl*) (US) line of high, steep cliffs (esp along a river). □ *vt* [VP6A] enclose or fortify with a ~(1).

pal·ish /ˋpeɪlɪʃ/ *adj* somewhat pale.

pall[1] /pɔl/ *n* **1** heavy cloth spread over a coffin. **ˋ~-bearer** *n* person who walks alongside a coffin at a funeral. **2** (fig) any dark, heavy covering: *a ~ of smoke.*

pall[2] /pɔl/ *vi* [VP2A,3A] ***~ (upon),*** become distasteful or boring because done, used, etc for too long a time: *pleasures that ~ after a time; a long lecture that ~ed upon most of the listeners.*

pal·let /ˋpælɪt/ *n* **1** straw-filled mattress for sleeping on. **2** large tray or platform for moving loads (by means of slings, etc), e g from a lorry into a train or on to a ship, and so save handling of separate items.

pal·li·asse /ˋpælɪæs *US:* ˈpælɪˋæs/ *n* = paillasse.

pal·li·ate /ˋpælɪeɪt/ *vt* [VP6A] (formal) lessen the severity of (pain, disease); excuse the seriousness of (a crime, etc). **pal·li·ation** /ˈpælɪˋeɪʃn/ *n* [U] the act of palliating; the state of being ~d; [C] that which ~s; excuse. **pal·li·ative** /ˋpælɪətɪv/ *n, adj* (sth) serving to ~.

pal·lid /ˋpælɪd/ *adj* pale; ill looking. **~·ly** *adv* **~·ness** *n*

pal·lor /ˋpælə(r)/ *n* [U] paleness, esp of the face.

pally ⇨ pal.

palm[1] /pɑm/ *n* inner surface of the hand between the wrist and the fingers. ⇨ the illus at arm. ***grease/oil sb's ~,*** give him a bribe. ***have an itching ~,*** be always ready to receive a bribe. □ *vt* [VP6A,15B] hide (a coin, card, etc) in the hand when performing a trick. ***~ sth off (upon sb),*** get him to accept it by fraud, misrepresentation, etc.

palm[2] /pɑm/ *n* **1** sorts of tree growing in warm climates, with no branches and a mass of large wide leaves at the top: *the ˋdate-~. the ˋcoconut ~.* **ˋ~-oil** *n* oil obtained from the nuts of a W African ~. **ˋ~ wine,** alcoholic drink made from the fermented sap from ~s. **ˈP~-ˋSunday,** the Sunday before Easter. **2** leaf of a ~ as a symbol of victory. ***bear/carry off the ~,*** be victorious. ***yield the ~ (to sb),*** admit defeat (by sb). **~y** *adj* (-ier, -iest) flourishing; prosperous: *in my ~y days.* **~er** *n* (formerly) pilgrim returning from the Holy Land with a ~-leaf; intinerant monk under a vow of poverty.

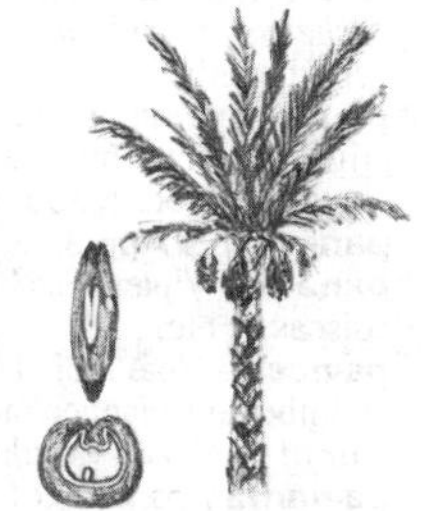

palms

palm·ist /ˋpɑmɪst/ *n* person who claims to tell a person's future by examining the lines on his palm. **palm·is·try** /ˋpɑmɪstrɪ/ *n* art of doing this.

pal·metto /pælˋmetəʊ/ *n* (*pl* -tos or -toes /-təʊz/) kinds of small palm with fan-shaped leaves, common in the West Indies and the S E coast of the US.

pal·pable /ˋpælpəbl/ *adj* that can be felt or touched; clear to the mind: *a ~ error.* **pal·pably** /-əblɪ/ *adv*

pal·pi·tate /ˋpælpɪteɪt/ *vi* [VP2A,C] (of the heart) beat rapidly and irregularly; (of a person, his body) tremble (with terror, etc). **pal·pi·ta·tion** /ˈpælpɪˋteɪʃn/ *n* palpitating of the heart (from disease, great efforts, etc).

palsy /ˋpɔlzɪ/ *n* [U] paralysis: *suffering from cerebral ~.* ⇨ spastic. □ *vt* paralyse.

pal·ter /ˋpɔltə(r)/ *vi* [VP3A] ***~ with,*** be insincere when dealing with; trifle with: *Don't ~ with the question,* do treat it seriously.

pal·try /ˋpɔltrɪ/ *adj* (-ier, -iest) worthless; of no

importance; contemptible.

pam·pas /ˈpæmpəs *US:* -əz/ *n pl* extensive, treeless plains of S America. Cf *prairie* in N America and *savannah* in tropical America and W Africa. **ˈ~-grass** *n* [U] tall grass with sharp-edged blades and a silvery plume-like flower.

pam·per /ˈpæmpə(r)/ *vt* [VP6A] indulge too much; be unduly kind to: *a ~ed poodle. She sometimes ~s herself and has a day in bed.*

pamph·let /ˈpæmflət/ *n* [C] small paper-covered book, esp on a question of current interest. **~·eer** /ˈpæmfləˈtɪə(r)/ *n* writer of ~s.

pan[1] /pæn/ *n* **1** flat dish, usu shallow and without a cover, used for cooking and other domestic purposes. **ˈpan·cake** *n* **(a)** batter cooked on both sides until brown and (usu) eaten hot. **ˈPancake Day,** Shrove Tuesday. **(b) pancake landing,** emergency landing in which the aircraft drops flat to the ground. **(c)** cosmetic face-powder pressed into a flat cake, used without a foundation cream. **2** receptacle with various uses: *the pan* (= bowl) *of a lavatory; a ˈbedpan,* ⇨ bed[1](6). **3** (natural or artificial) depression in the ground: *a ˈsalt-pan,* where salt water is evaporated. **4 ˈbrain-pan,** upper part of the skull, enclosing the brain. **5** either of the dishes on a pair of scales. ⇨ the illus at balance. **6** open dish for washing gravel, etc to separate gold ore or other metals. **7** (in flintlock guns) cavity in the lock that holds the gunpowder. ***a flash in the pan,*** ⇨ flash[1](1). **8 (ˈhard-)pan,** hard subsoil. **9** (sl) face. □ *vt,vi* (-nn-) **1** [VP15B, 3A,2C] ***pan sth off/out,*** wash (gold-bearing gravel, etc) in a pan. ***pan for (gold),*** wash gravel, etc for (gold). ***~ out,*** **(a)** yield gold. **(b)** (fig) succeed; turn out: *How did things pan out? The scheme panned out well.* **2** [VP6A] (colloq) criticize harshly.

pan[2] /pæn/ *vi,vt* (cinema and TV) turn a camera right or left to follow a moving object or get a panoramic effect. ⇨ zoom(2).

pan- *pref* ⇨ App 3.

pana·cea /ˈpænəˈsɪə/ *n* remedy for all troubles, diseases, etc.

pa·nache /pæˈnæʃ *US:* pə-/ *n* [U] confidence, flamboyant manner, an air of ease: *There was an air of ~ about everything he did.*

pa·nama /ˈpænəˈmɑ *US:* ˈpænəmɑ/ *n* **~ (hat),** hat made from fine pliant straw-like material from the leaves of a plant of S and Central America.

pana·tella /ˈpænəˈtelə/ *n* [C] long slender cigar.

pan·chro·matic /ˈpænkrəˈmætɪk/ *adj* (photo) equally sensitive to all colours: *~ film.*

pan·creas /ˈpæŋkrɪəs/ *n* [C] gland near the stomach, discharging a juice which helps digestion. ⇨ the illus at alimentary. **pan·cre·atic** /ˈpæŋkrɪˈætɪk/ *adj* of the ~.

panda /ˈpændə/ *n* bear-like mammal of Tibet, with black legs and a black and white body. ⇨ the illus at bear. **ˈP~ car** *n* (GB) police patrol car. **ˈP~ crossing** *n* (GB) road crossing controlled by flashing lights, operated by pedestrians who press a button on a post.

pan·demic /pænˈdemɪk/ *n, adj* (disease) prevalent over the whole of a country or continent.

pan·de·mo·nium /ˈpændɪˈməʊnɪəm/ *n* [C,U] (scene of) wild and noisy disorder.

pan·der /ˈpændə(r)/ *vi* [VP3A] **~ *to,*** **1** give help or encouragement (to sb, to his base passions and desires): *newspapers that ~ to the public interest in crime; ~ to low tastes.* **2** act as a go-between (*to* sb's lust, sexual desires). ⇨ procure(3), the more usu word now. □ *n* person who ~s(2).

pane /peɪn/ *n* single sheet of glass in (a division of) a window. ⇨ the illus at window.

pan·egyric /ˈpænɪˈdʒɪrɪk/ *n* [C] speech, piece of writing, praising a person or event.

panel /ˈpænl/ *n* **1** separate part of the surface of a door, wall, ceiling, etc usu raised above or sunk below the surrounding area. **2** piece of material of a different kind or colour inserted in a dress. **3** board or other surface for controls and instruments: *ˈinstrument ~,* of an aircraft or motor-vehicle; *conˈtrol ~,* on a radio or TV set. **4** list of names, e g of men who may be summoned to serve on a jury, or of doctors who (in GB) have agreed to attend persons under the National Health Service. **a ˈ~ doctor,** one who is registered on the official list as a doctor of the National Health Service. ***be on the ~,*** have one's name registered with a ~ doctor. **5** group of speakers, esp one chosen to speak, answer questions, take part in a game, before an audience, e g of listeners to a broadcast: (attrib) *a ˈ~ discussion/game.* **6** long, narrow size of photograph. □ *vt* (-ll-, US -l-) furnish or decorate with ~s(1,2): *a ~led room/wall/wainscot.* **~·ling** *n* [U] series of ~s on a wall, etc.

pang /pæŋ/ *n* sharp, sudden feeling of pain, remorse, etc.

panga /ˈpæŋgə/ *n* large chopping knife used by African workers.

pan·handle /ˈpænhændl/ *n* (US) narrow strip of land projecting from a larger area so that, on a map, it appears like the handle of a pan. □ *vi* (US colloq) beg, esp on the streets.

panic /ˈpænɪk/ *n* [C,U] **1** unreasoning, uncontrolled, quickly spreading fear: *There is always danger of (a) ~ when a cinema catches fire.* **ˈ~-stricken** *adj* terrified; overcome by ~. *The crowd was ~-stricken,* filled with ~. **2** (attrib) unreasoning: *~ fear.* □ *vi* (-ck-) be affected with ~: *Don't ~! There's no danger!* **pan·icky** /ˈpænɪkɪ/ *adj* (colloq) easily affected by ~; in a state of ~.

pan·jan·drum /pænˈdʒændrəm/ *n* name applied jokingly to an exalted personage or to a pompous official.

pan·nier /ˈpænɪə(r)/ *n* **1** one of a pair of baskets placed across the back of a horse or ass; one of a pair of bags on either side of the back of a (motor-)bike. **2** part of a skirt looped up round the hips.

panniers

pan·ni·kin /ˈpænɪkɪn/ *n* (GB) small metal cup; its contents.

pan·oply /ˈpænəplɪ/ *n* (*pl* -lies) complete suit of armour. Hence, **pan·oplied** /ˈpænəplɪd/ *adj* provided with a ~.

pan·op·tic /pæn`optɪk/ *adj* giving a complete view, e g by diagram, illustration, of sth.

pan·or·ama /ˈpænəˋrɑmə *US:* -ˋræmə/ *n* wide, uninterrupted view; constantly changing scene: *the ~ of London life.* **pan·or·amic** /ˈpænəˋræmɪk/ *adj*

pan-pipes /ˋpæn pɑɪps/ *n pl* musical instrument made of a series of reeds or pipes, played by blowing across the open ends.

pansy /ˋpænzɪ/ *n* (*pl* -**sies**) **1** flowering herbaceous plant. **2** (colloq) effeminate young man; homosexual.

pant /pænt/ *vi,vt* **1** [VP2A,C] take short, quick breaths; gasp; throb: *The dog ~ed along behind its master's horse.* **2** [VP6A,15B] say while ~ing: *He ~ed out his message.* **3** [VP3A] ***~ for,*** (old use) have a strong wish for. □ *n* short, quick breath; gasp; throb. **~·ing·ly** *adv*

pan·ta·loon /ˈpæntəˋlun/ *n* **1** (in pantomime) foolish character upon whom the clown plays tricks. **2** (*pl*) (now hum, or US) = pants.

pan·tech·ni·con /pænˋteknɪkən/ *n* (GB) large van for removing furniture.

pan·the·ism /ˋpænθɪɪzm/ *n* [U] belief that God is in everything and that everything is God; belief in and worship of all gods. **pan·the·ist** /-ɪst/ *n* **pan·the·is·tic** /ˈpænθɪˋɪstɪk/ *adj* of ~.

pan·theon /ˋpænθɪən *US:* -θɪon/ *n* temple dedicated to all the gods: *the P~ in Rome;* all the gods of a nation collectively: *the (ancient) Egyptian ~;* building in which the illustrious dead are buried or have memorials.

pan·ther /ˋpænθə(r)/ *n* leopard; (US) puma. ⇨ the illus at **cat**.

pan·ties /ˋpæntɪz/ *n pl* (colloq) pants worn by children; (woman's or girl's) close-fitting short knickers.

pan·tile /ˋpæntɑɪl/ *n* curved roof tile: (attrib) *a ~ roof.*

panto /ˋpæntəʊ/ *n* (colloq abbr of) pantomime.

pan·to·graph /ˋpæntəgrɑf *US:* -græf/ *n* device for copying a plan, etc on a different scale.

pan·to·mime /ˋpæntəmɑɪm/ *n* **1** [C,U] (example of a) kind of English drama based on a fairy tale or traditional story, with music, dancing and clowning. **2** [C] acting without words.

pan·try /ˋpæntrɪ/ *n* (*pl* -**ries**) **1** room (in a large house, hotel, ship, etc) in which silver, glass, table-linen, etc are kept. **ˋ~·man** /-mən/ *n* (*pl* -**men**) butler or his assistant. **2** larder; room (in a house) in which food is kept.

pants /pænts/ *n pl* **1** trousers; (in trade use) long tight-fitting drawers(2). **2** *ˋhot-~,* brief shorts (as worn by women and girls, 1971—2).

panty-hose /ˋpæntɪ həʊz/ *n* = **tights**.

pan·zer /ˋpæntsə(r)/ *attrib adj* (G) armoured: *~ divisions/troops.*

pap /pæp/ *n* [U] soft or semi-liquid food for very young children, invalids.

papa /pəˋpɑ *US:* ˋpɑpə/ *n* (child's word for) father.

pa·pacy /ˋpeɪpəsɪ/ *n* (*pl* -**cies**) position of, authority of, the Pope; system of government by Popes. **pa·pal** /ˋpeɪpl/ *adj* of the Pope or the ~.

pa(w)·paw /pəˋpɔ *US:* ˋpɔpɔ/ *n* **1** tropical tree with a straight trunk like that of a palm; its large edible fruit with a yellow pulp inside (also called *papaya*). ⇨ the illus at **fruit**. **2** small N American evergreen tree with small fleshy edible fruit (also called *custard apple*).

pa·per /ˋpeɪpə(r)/ *n* **1** [U] substance manufactured from wood fibre, rags, etc in the form of sheets, used for writing, printing, drawing, wrapping, packing, etc: *a sheet of ~; a ~ bag.* ***(be) good on ~,*** (be) good when judged from written or printed evidence, e g plans, proposals, diplomas, testimonials: *a good scheme on ~* (but not yet tested). *This applicant looks good on ~,* has good ~ qualifications. ***put pen to ~,*** (dated for) begin to write, e g a letter. **ˋ~-backed** *adj* (of books) bound in paper covers. Hence, **ˋ~·back** *n* such a book and such a form: *Has the book appeared in ~back?* **ˋ~-chase** *n* ⇨ *hare and hounds* at **hare**. **ˋ~-clip** *n* ⇨ **clip**[1](1). **ˋ~-hanger** *n* man whose trade is to paste ~ on the walls of rooms. **ˋ~-knife** *n* one for cutting open the leaves of books, opening envelopes, etc. **ˋ~-mill** *n* one where ~ is made. **ˈ~ ˋtiger** *n* person, group of persons, etc which seems to be, but is not, powerful. **ˋ~-weight** *n* weight placed on loose ~s to prevent them from being blown away. **ˋ~-work,** written work (in an office, etc, e g filling in forms, correspondence, contrasted with practical affairs, dealing with people): *He's good at ~-work.* **2** [C] (**ˋnews-**)~: *today's ~s; the evening ~s.* **3** [U] **ˋ~ (money),** banknotes, etc used as currency. **4** (*pl*) documents showing who sb is, what authority he has, etc: *send in one's ~s,* (mil) resign. **5** [C] set of printed examination questions on a given subject: *The biology ~ was difficult.* **6** [C] essay, esp one to be read to a learned society: *a ~ on currency reform.* □ *vt* [VP6A,15B] paste ~ on (walls, etc): *~ the dining-room;* cover with ~. ***~ over the cracks,*** (fig) cover up, conceal, faults, etc. ***~ the house,*** issue free tickets for a theatre, etc (to give the impression of success).

pa·pier-mâché /ˈpæpɪeɪ ˋmæʃeɪ *US:* ˈpeɪpər məˋʃeɪ/ *n* [U] paper pulped and used as a plastic material for making trays, boxes, etc.

pa·pist /ˋpeɪpɪst/ *n* (unfriendly word, as used by some Protestants, for a) member of the Roman Catholic Church.

pa·poose /pəˋpus *US:* pæˋpus/ *n* (word used by Indians of N America for a) baby; framed bag (like a rucksack) for carrying a young baby on sb's back.

pa·pis·ti·cal /pəˋpɪstɪkl/ *adj* popish; of the Church of Rome.

pap·rika /ˋpæprɪkə *US:* pəˋprikə/ *n* [U] sweet red pepper used in cooking. ⇨ the illus at **vegetable**.

pa·py·rus /pəˋpɑɪərəs/ *n* **1** [U] (kind of paper made in ancient Egypt from) tall water plant or reed. **2** [C] (*pl* **papyri** /pəˋpɑɪərɑɪ/) manuscript written on this paper.

par[1] /pɑ(r)/ *n* [U] average or normal amount, degree, value, etc. ***above/below/at par,*** (of shares, bonds, etc), above/below/at the original price or face value. **par value,** nominal or face value of a share. **par of exchange,** normal rate of exchange between two currencies, e g the £ and the US $. ***on a par (with),*** equal (to). ***not feeling quite up to par,*** (colloq) not so well as usual. **2** (golf) number of strokes considered necessary for a scratch player to complete a hole or course.

par[2] /pɑ(r)/ ⇨ **parr**.

par·able /ˋpærəbl/ *n* simple story designed to teach a moral lesson: *speak in ~s. Jesus taught in ~s.* **para·boli·cal** /ˈpærəˋbolɪkl/ *adj* of, expressed in, ~s.

par·ab·ola /pəˋræbələ/ *n* plane curve formed by

cutting a cone on a plane parallel to its side, so that the two arms get farther away from one another. **para·bolic** /ˌpærəˈbɒlɪk/ *adj* of, like, a ~.

para·chute /ˈpærəʃut/ *n* apparatus used for a jump from an aircraft or for dropping supplies, etc: (attrib) ˈ~ *troops/flares/mines.* □ *vt,vi* [VP2A,C, 6A,15A,B] drop, descend, from an aircraft by means of a ~: *men ~d behind the enemy lines.* **para·chut·ist** /-ɪst/ *n* person who jumps with a ~.

par·ade /pəˈreɪd/ *vt,vi* **1** [VP6A,2A] (of troops) (cause to) gather together for drilling, inspection, etc; march in procession. **2** [VP6A] make a display of; try to attract attention to: *~ one's abilities.* □ *n* **1** [U] parading of troops: *be on ~*; [C] instance of this: *a church ~.* **2** [C] ˈ**~-ground,** area of ground on which ~s are held. **3** [C] display or exhibition: *a* ˈ*mannequin ~,* e g showing new styles in dress. ***make a ~ of one's virtues,*** try to impress people by showing them. **4** public promenade; wide, often ornamented pathway, esp on a seafront.

para·digm /ˈpærədaɪm/ *n* example or pattern of the declension of a noun, the conjugation of a verb, etc.

para·dise /ˈpærədaɪs/ *n* **1** the Garden of Eden, home of Adam and Eve. ˈ**bird of** ˈ**~,** bird (of New Guinea) with beautiful feathers. **2** Heaven. **3** (with *indef art*) any place of perfect happiness; [U] condition of perfect happiness. **a fool's ~,** ⇨ fool[1](1). **para·dis·iac** /ˌpærəˈdɪsɪæk/, **para·disia·cal** /ˌpærədɪˈsaɪəkl/ *adjj* of or like ~: *Adam and Eve in their paradisiac state,* in their pristine innocence.

para·dox /ˈpærədɒks/ *n* [C] statement that seems to say sth opposite to common sense or the truth, but which may contain a truth (e g 'More haste, less speed'). **~i·cal** /ˌpærəˈdɒksɪkl/ *adj* **~i·cally** /-klɪ/ *adv*

par·af·fin /ˈpærəfɪn/ *n* [U] **1** ˈ**~ (oil),** (GB) oil obtained from petroleum, coal, etc used as a fuel (in lamps, heating and cooking-stoves). (US = *kerosene*). **2 ~ (wax),** wax-like substance used for making candles. **3 (**ˈ**liquid)** ˈ**~,** odourless, tasteless form of ~ used as a laxative.

para·gon /ˈpærəgən *US:* -gɒn/ *n* model of excellence; apparently perfect person or thing: *I make no claim to be a ~ of virtue.*

para·graph /ˈpærəgrɑf *US:* -græf/ *n* [C] **1** division (usu a group of several sentences dealing with one main idea) of a piece of writing, started on a new line (and usu inset); the mark (¶) used to show where a new ~ is to begin, and as a mark of reference. **2** small item of news in a newspaper. □ *vt* divide into ~s.

para·keet /ˈpærəkit/ *n* small, long-tailed parrot of various kinds. ⇨ the illus at rare.

par·al·lel /ˈpærəlel/ *adj* (of lines) continuing at the same distance from one another; (of one line) having this relation (*to* or *with* another): *a road running ~ to/with the railway; in a ~ direction (with...).* ˈ**~** ˈ**bars,** pair of ~ bars on posts for gymnastic exercises. □ *n* [C] **1 ~ of latitude,** line on a map ~ to, and passing through all places the same distance north or south of, the equator. ***in ~,*** (of the components of an electrical circuit) with the supply of current taken to each component independently, not in series). ⇨ series. **2** person, event, etc precisely similar: *a brilliant career without (a) ~ in modern times.* **3** comparison: *draw a ~ between....* □ *vt* (-l- or (GB) -ll-) [VP6A] **1** quote, produce or mention sth ~ or comparable. **2** be ~ to: *His experiences ~ mine in many instances. The street ~s the railway.* ˈ**~-ism** /-ɪzm/ *n (liter or fig) being ~.* **~o·gram** /ˌpærəˈleləgræm/ *n* four-sided plane figure whose opposite sides are ~. ⇨ the illus at quadrilateral.

par·al·ysis /pəˈræləsɪs/ *n* [U] loss of feeling or power to move in any or every part of the body; (fig) state of utter powerlessness. **para·lyt·ic** /ˌpærəˈlɪtɪk/ *n, adj* **1** (person) suffering from ~: *a paralytic stroke;* (fig) helpless: *paralytic laughter.* **2** (person who is) very drunk. **para·lyse,** (US = **-lyze**) /ˈpærəlaɪz/ *vt* [VP6A] **1** affect with ~. **2** make helpless: *paralysed with fear.*

para·mili·tary /ˌpærəˈmɪlɪtrɪ *US:* -terɪ/ *adj* having a status or function ancillary to that of regular military forces: *~ formations.*

para·mount /ˈpærəmaʊnt/ *adj* (formal) supreme, superior in power: *~ chiefs;* pre-eminent: *of ~ importance;* superior. **~cy** /-tsɪ/ *n*

para·mour /ˈpærəmʊə(r)/ *n* (archaic) illicit partner of a married man or woman.

para·noia /ˌpærəˈnɔɪə/ *n* [U] mental disorder (usu incurable), marked by fixed delusions, e g of persecution or grandeur. **para·noiac** /ˌpærəˈnɔɪæk/ *n, adj* (person) suffering from ~.

para·pet /ˈpærəpɪt/ *n* **1** (usu low) protective wall at the edge of a flat roof, side of a bridge, etc. **2** defensive bank of earth, stone, etc along the front edge of a trench (in war).

para·pher·nalia /ˌpærəfəˈneɪlɪə/ *n* [U] numerous small possessions, tools, instruments, etc esp concerning sb's hobby or technical work.

para·phrase /ˈpærəfreɪz/ *vt* [VP6A], *n* (give a) restatement of the meaning of (a piece of writing) in other words.

para·ple·gia /ˌpærəˈplidʒə/ *n* [U] (path) paralysis of the lower part of the body, including both legs, caused by injury to the spinal cord. **para·plegic** /ˌpærəˈplidʒɪk/ *n, adj* (person) suffering from ~.

paras /ˈpærəz/ *n pl* (colloq abbr of) paratroopers.

para·site /ˈpærəsaɪt/ *n* **1** animal (e g *louse, hookworm*) or plant (e g *mistletoe*) living on or in another and getting its food from it. **2** person supported by another and giving him nothing in return. **para·sitic** /ˌpærəˈsɪtɪk/, **para·siti·cal** /ˌpærəˈsɪtɪkl/ *adjj* caused by, living as, a ~.

para·sol /ˈpærəsɒl *US:* -sɔl/ *n* umbrella used to give shade from the sun.

para·troops /ˈpærətrups/ *n pl* troops trained for being dropped by parachute. **para·trooper** /ˈpærətrupə(r)/ *n* one of these.

para·typhoid /ˌpærəˈtaɪfɔɪd/ *n* [U] kind of fever in some ways like typhoid but milder and caused by a different bacterium.

par·boil /ˈpɑbɔɪl/ *vt* [VP6A] boil (food) until partially cooked; (fig) make uncomfortably hot.

par·cel /ˈpɑsl/ *n* [C] **1** thing or things wrapped and tied up for carrying, sending by post, etc: *She left the shop with an armful of ~s.* ˈ**~ post** *n* system, method, etc of carrying ~s by post. **2** (old use) part, esp in: ***part and ~ of,*** an essential part of. ***a ~ of land,*** an area of land (esp part of an estate). □ *vt* (-ll-, US also -l-) [VP6A,15B] ***~ out,*** divide into portions. ***~ up,*** make (books, etc) into a ~.

parch /pɑtʃ/ *vt* [VP6A] **1** (of heat, the sun, etc) make hot and dry: *the ~ed deserts of N Africa.* **2** dry or roast by heating: *~ed peas.*

parch·ment /ˈpɑtʃmənt/ *n* **1** [C,U] (manuscript on) writing material prepared from the skin of a sheep or goat. **2** [U] kind of paper resembling ~.

par·don /ˈpɑdn/ *n* **1** [U] forgiveness: *ask for ~*; [C] instance of this. **2** indulgence; forbearance. ***beg sb's ~,*** excuse oneself, e g for disagreeing with what sb says, or apologize, e g for not hearing or understanding what sb says. **3** (Church use) indulgence(**3**). □ *vt* [VP6A,12B,13B] **~ *sb for sth; ~ sb sth,*** forgive; excuse; overlook: *~ sb for doing wrong; ~ sb an offence. P~ me for/P~ my contradicting you.* **~·able** /ˈpɑdn̩əbl/ *adj* that can be ~ed. **~·ably** /-əblɪ/ *adv* (formal) in a way that can be ~ed: *She was ~ably proud of her wonderful cooking.* **~er** *n* (in the Middle Ages) person who had been licensed to sell papal indulgences(**3**).

pare /peə(r)/ *vt* [VP6A,15B] cut away the outer part, edge or skin of: *~ one's (finger-)nails; ~ the claws of an animal; ~* (= peel) *an apple;* (fig) *~ down* (= reduce) *one's expenses.* **par·ings** /ˈpeərɪŋz/ *n pl* that which is ~d off: *ˈnail-parings.*

par·egoric /ˌpærɪˈgɒrɪk *US:* -ˈgɔr-/ *n* [U] soothing medicine containing opium and flavoured with aniseed.

par·ent /ˈpeərnt/ *n* father or mother; ancestor: *our first ~s,* Adam and Eve; *the ~ birds; the ~ plant.* **~ company,** (comm) one that controls another, e g by owning more than half its shares or because of the composition of its Board of Directors. **ˈ~-age** /-ɪdʒ/ *n* [U] fatherhood or motherhood; origin; birth: *of unknown ~age,* having unknown parents. **~al** /pəˈrentl/ *adj* of a ~: *~al anxieties; children who lack ~al care.* **~·ally** /-tl̩ɪ/ *adv*

par·enth·esis /pəˈrenθəsɪs/ *n* (*pl* **-eses** /-əsiz/) sentence within another sentence, marked off by commas, dashes or brackets; (*sing* or *pl*) *round brackets ( ) for this: in ~; in parentheses.* **par·en·thetic** /ˌpærənˈθetɪk/, **par·en·theti·cal** /-ɪkl/ *adjj* of, relating to, used as, a ~. **par·en·theti·cally** /-klɪ/ *adv*

par ex·cel·lence /ˌpɑr ˈeksəlɔ̃s *US:* ˌeksəˈlɔ̃s/ *adv* (F) by virtue of special excellence; in the highest degree.

pa·riah /ˈpærɪə *US:* pəˈrɑɪə/ *n* (India) person of low caste or of no caste; (fig) social outcast. **ˈ~-dog** *n* (India) ownerless dog of mixed breed.

pari-mu·tuel /ˌpærɪ ˈmjutjʊel *US:* ˈmjutʃʊəl/ *n* (F) form of betting (on races) in which the winners divide the stakes of the losers, less a percentage for management expenses.

pari passu /ˌpærɪ ˈpɑsu/ *adv* (Lat) simultaneously and equally; at an equal rate of progress.

par·ish /ˈpærɪʃ/ *n* division of a county with its own church and priest; (*civil ~,* GB) division of a county for local government: *the ~ church; the ~ council; the ~ register,* book with records of christenings, marriages and burials. **~ clerk,** official with various duties connected with the ~ church. **ˌ~-ˈpump,** (used attrib) of local interest only, e g of villagers gossiping round the ~ pump: *~-pump affairs/politics.* ***go on the ~,*** ⇨ go[1](28). **~ioner** /pəˈrɪʃn̩ə(r)/ *n* inhabitant of a ~.

Pa·ris·ian /pəˈrɪzɪən *US:* -ɪʒn/ *n, adj* (native, inhabitant) of Paris.

par·ity /ˈpærətɪ/ *n* [U] equality; being equal; being at par: *Should teachers in secondary schools and teachers in primary schools receive ~ of esteem and ~ of pay? The two currencies have now reached ~,* are at par. **ˌ~ of exˈchange,** rates of exchange officially determined by Governments.

park /pɑk/ *n* **1** public garden or public recreation ground in a town. **a ˈball ~,** (US) playing field. **2** area of grassland (usu with trees) round a large country house or mansion. **3** (**ˈcar-)~,** place where motor-vehicles may be left for a time. **4** **ˌnational ˈ~,** area of natural beauty, e g mountains, forests, lakes, set apart by the State for public enjoyment, and where industrial and urban development is forbidden or limited. **5** place used by the military for artillery, stores, etc. □ *vt,vi* **1** [VP6A,2A] put or place (a motor-vehicle) for a time, unattended: *Where can we ~ (the car)?* **2** [VP6A,15A] (colloq) put (sth or sb) somewhere: *Where can I ~ my luggage? P~ yourself in that chair while I make you a cup of tea.*

parka /ˈpɑkə/ *n* (US) waterproof jacket with a hood attached (as worn for skiing, mountain-climbing, etc). (GB = *anorak*).

parking /ˈpɑkɪŋ/ *n* [U] (area for the) ~ of motor-vehicles: *No ~ between 9am and 6pm.* **ˈ~ lot,** (US) area for the ~ of motor-vehicles. **ˈ~ meter,** coin-operated meter beside which a vehicle may be parked in a public place, e g a street. **ˈ~ orbit,** temporary orbit for a spacecraft.

Park·in·son's dis·ease /ˈpɑkɪnsns dɪziz/ *n* (path) chronic progressive disease of old people, with muscular tremors, muscular rigidity and general weakness.

parky /ˈpɑkɪ/ *adj* (sl) (of the air, weather) chilly.

par·lance /ˈpɑləns/ *n* ***in common ~,*** in the way of speaking commonly used.

par·ley /ˈpɑlɪ/ *n* (*pl* **-leys**) [C] conference, esp between leaders of two opposed forces. □ *vi* [VP2A,3A] **~ *(with sb),*** discuss terms, hold a conference.

par·lia·ment /ˈpɑləmənt/ *n* (in countries with representative government) supreme law-making council or assembly, esp of GB, formed of the House of Commons and the House of Lords: *enter P~; ˌMembers ofˈP~; summon/adjourn P~; P~ sits/rises; open P~,* (of the Sovereign) declare it open with traditional ceremonial. **par·lia·men·tarian** /ˌpɑləmənˈteərɪən/ *n* person skilled in the rules and procedures of ~, who is a good debater, etc. **par·lia·men·tary** /ˌpɑləˈmentrɪ/ *adj* of ~: *~ary debates; ~ary language,* polite, civil, as required in ~ary debates.

par·lour (US = **-lor**) /ˈpɑlə(r)/ *n* **1** ordinary sitting-room for the family in a private house (now more usu called sitting-room or living-room). **ˈ~ games,** games played in the home (competitions, guessing, etc). **ˈ~-maid** *n* (not US) maid who waits at table. **2** private sitting-room at an inn; room for the reception of visitors: *the Mayor's ~,* in a town hall, etc. **3** (esp US) room for customers and clients: *a ˈbeauty ~; a ˈhairdresser's ~.* **ˈ~-car** *n* (US) car with individual reserved seats.

par·lous /ˈpɑləs/ *adj* (archaic) perilous.

Par·me·san /ˌpɑmɪˈzæn/ *n* kind of cheese made at Parma and elsewhere in N Italy.

par·ochial /pəˈrəʊkɪəl/ *adj* of a parish; (fig) limited, narrow: *a ~ outlook/mind/point of view.* **~ly** /-kɪəlɪ/ *adv* **~·ism** /-ɪzm/ *n*

par·ody /ˈpærədɪ/ *n* (*pl* **-dies**) **1** [C,U] (piece of) writing intended to amuse by imitating the style of writing used by sb else. **2** [C] weak imitation. □ *vt* [VP6A] make a ~ of: *~ an author/a poem.* **par·odist** /-ɪst/ *n* person who writes parodies.

pa·role /pəˈrəʊl/ *n* [U] prisoner's solemn promise, on being given certain privileges, that he will not try to escape. ***on ~,*** liberated after making such a promise. ***break one's ~,*** (try to) escape while on ~. □ *vt* [VP6A] set (a prisoner) free on ~.

paro·quet /ˈpærəkit/ *n* = parakeet.

par·ox·ysm /ˈpærəksɪzm/ *n* [C] sudden attack or outburst (of pain, anger, laughter, etc).

par·quet /ˈpɑkeɪ *US:* pɑrˋkeɪ/ *n* flooring of wooden blocks fitted together to make a pattern.

parr, par /pɑ(r)/ *n* young salmon.

par·ri·cide /ˈpærɪsɑɪd/ *n* [C,U] (person guilty of the) murder of one's father or near relation.

par·ro·ket, par·ro·quet /ˈpærəket/ *n* (variants of) *parakeet.*

par·rot /ˈpærət/ *n* **1** sorts of bird with a hooked bill and (usu) brightly coloured feathers. Some kinds can be trained to imitate human speech. ⇨ the illus at rare. **ˋ~ fever,** = psittacosis. **2** person who repeats, often without understanding, what others say.

parry /ˈpærɪ/ *vt* (*pt,pp* -ried) [VP6A] turn aside (a blow); (fig) evade (a question). □ *n* [C] act of ~ing, esp in fencing and boxing.

parse /pɑz *US:* pɑrs/ *vt* [VP6A] describe (a word) grammatically; point out how the words of a sentence are related.

Par·see /pɑˋsi/ *n* supporter of a religious system in India, the members being descended from Persians who settled in India in the 8th c.

par·si·mony /ˈpɑsɪmənɪ *US:* -məʊnɪ/ *n* [U] (formal) (usu as a bad quality) excessive carefulness in using money or (fig) immaterial things. **par·si·moni·ous** /ˈpɑsɪˋməʊnɪəs/ *adj* too economical; miserly.

pars·ley /ˈpɑslɪ/ *n* [U] garden plant with crinkled green leaves, used in seasoning and sauces and for garnishing food.

pars·nip /ˈpɑsnɪp/ *n* [C] long, white or pale-yellow root, cooked as a vegetable.

par·son /ˈpɑsn/ *n* parish priest; (colloq) any clergyman. **~'s nose,** (colloq) rump of a cooked fowl. **ˋ~·age** /-ɪdʒ/ *n* ~'s house; vicarage.

part[1] /pɑt/ *n* [C] **1** (often *sing* without *indef art*) some but not all of a thing or a number of things; something less than the whole: *We spent (a) ~ of our holiday in France/in a ~ of the country we had never visited before. P~s of the book are interesting. The greater ~ of what you heard is only rumour.* ***for the most ~,*** in most cases; mostly. ***in ~,*** in some degree. **ˈ~-ˋowner** *n* person who owns sth in common with others. **ˈ~-ˋtime** *adj, adv* for only a ~ of the working day or week: *be employed ~-time; ~-time teaching,* e g two days a week. Hence, **ˈpart-ˋtimer** *n* **2** (*pl*) region; district: *in these/those ~s.* **3** any one of a number of equal divisions: *A minute is the sixtieth ~ of an hour.* **4** person's share in some activity; his duty or responsibility; what an actor in a play, film, etc says and does: *a man with a ~ in a play/in a conference. He spoke/acted his ~ very well. Do the actors all know their ~s? I had only a small ~ in these events.* ***play a (big/small) ~ (in sth),*** be concerned in sth, make a contribution: *He had an important ~ to play in ensuring the success of the scheme.* ***take ~ (in),*** have a share (in); help: *Are you going to take ~ in the discussion,* Do you intend to speak? **5** side in a dispute, transaction, agreement, mutual arrangement, etc. ***take sb's ~; take the ~ of sb,*** support sb: *He always takes his brother's ~.* ***for ˋmy ~,*** as far as I am concerned: *For my ~ I am quite happy about the division of the money.* ***on ˋmy/ˋhis/ˋyour, etc ~; on the ~ of (Mr A, etc),*** proceeding from, done by, me/him/you/Mr A, etc: *There was no objection on his ~/on the ~ of the owner of the land,* He did not object. *The agreement has been kept on my ~ but not on his. An indiscretion on the ~ of his wife nearly ruined him.* **6** ***take sth in good ~,*** not be offended at it. **7** division of a book; each issue of a work published in instalments: *a new encyclopaedia to be issued in monthly ~s.* **8** essential piece or section of sth. **(spare) ~,** extra piece, etc to be used when needed, when sth breaks or wears: *When can I get a ~ for my pump?* **9** (music) each of the melodies that make up a harmony; the melody for a particular voice or instrument: *orchestra ~s; sing in three ~s.* **ˋ~-singing, ˋ~-song** *n* singing, song, with three or more voice ~s. **10** (gram) **ˈ~ of ˋspeech,** one of the classes of words, e g *noun, verb, adjective.* **11** (archaic) (*pl*) abilities: *a man of ~s.* □ *adv* in ~; partly: *made ~ of iron and ~ of wood.*

part[2] /pɑt/ *vt,vi* **1** [VP6A,2A,D] (cause to) separate or divide: *The policemen ~ed the crowd. We tried to ~ the two fighters. Let us ~ friends,* leave each other with no feeling of enmity. *The crowd ~ed and let us through.* ***~ company (with),*** **(a)** end a relationship. **(b)** leave and travel in a different direction. **(c)** disagree: *On that question I am afraid I must ~ company with you.* **2** [VP3A] ***~ with,*** give up, give away: *He hates to ~ with his money,* doesn't like to spend it or give it away. **3** [VP6A] ***~ one's hair,*** make a dividing line by combing the hair in opposite ways. **~·ing** *n* **1** [C] line where the hair is combed in opposite ways. **2** [C,U] departure; leave-taking: (attrib) *his ~ing injunctions,* those given on taking leave. ***at the ~ing of the ways,*** at the point where the road divides or forks; (fig) when one has to choose between courses of action. **~·ly** *adv* in ~; to some extent.

par·take /pɑˋteɪk/ *vi,vt* (*pt* -took /-ˋtʊk/, *pp* -taken /-ˋteɪkən/) **1** [VP6A,2A,3A] ***~ of/in sth (with sb),*** take a share in: *They partook (of) our triumph. They were partaking of our simple meal.* **2** [VP3A] ***~ of,*** have some of (the nature or characteristics of): *His manner ~s of insolence.*

par·terre /pɑˋteə(r)/ *n* **1** (in a garden) level space with lawns and flower-beds. **2** (in a theatre) part of the auditorium behind the orchestra.

par·theno·gen·esis /ˈpɑθɪnəʊˋdʒenɪsɪs/ *n* [U] reproduction of offspring without fertilization by sexual union.

Par·thian /ˈpɑθɪən/ *adj* of Parthia /ˈpɑθɪə/, ancient country of N E Iran conquered by the Persians in A D 226. **~ shot/shaft,** (fig) sth said or done as a final reply, argument, etc at the moment of parting.

par·tial /ˈpɑʃl/ *adj* **1** forming only a part; not complete: *a ~ success; a ~ eclipse of the sun.* **2** ***~ (towards),*** showing too much favour to one person or side: *examiners who are ~ towards pretty women students.* **3** ***~ to,*** having a liking for: *~ to French cuisine.* **~ly** /ˈpɑʃlɪ/ *adv* **1** partly; not completely. **2** in a ~(2) manner. **~·ity** /ˈpɑʃɪˋælətɪ/ *n* **1** [U] being ~(2) in treatment of people, etc; bias; favouritism. **2** ***~ity for,*** [C] fondness: *a ~ity for moonlight walks.*

par·tici·pate /pɑˋtɪsɪpeɪt/ *vi* [VP2A,3A] ***~ (in),*** **1** have a share, take part (in): *~ in sb's suffering/in* *a plot.* **par·tici·pant** /pɑˈtɪsɪpənt/ *n* person who ~s (*in* sth). **par·tici·pa·tion** /pɑˈtɪsɪˈpeɪʃn/ *n* [U] act of participating.

par·ti·ciple /ˈpɑtəspl *US:* -sɪpl/ *n* (verbal *adj* qualifying *nn* but retaining some properties of a *v*): *'Hurrying' and 'hurried' are the present and past ~s of 'hurry'.* **par·ti·cip·ial** /ˈpɑtɪˈsɪpɪəl/ *adj* of a ~: *a participial adjective,* e g 'loving' in 'a loving mother'.

par·ticle /ˈpɑtɪkl/ *n* **1** very small bit: *~s of dust;* smallest possible quantity: *She hasn't a ~ of sense.* **2** (gram) minor part of speech, e g an article (*a, an, the*), a *prep* or *adv* (*up, in, out*), a conjunction (*or*), an affix (*un-, in-, -ness, -ly*).

parti-col·oured, (US = **-col·ored**) /ˈpɑtɪ kʌləd/ *adj* differently coloured in different parts.

par·ticu·lar /pəˈtɪkjʊlə(r)/ *adj* **1** relating to one as distinct from others: *in this ~ case.* **2** special; worth notice; outstanding: *for no ~ reason. He took ~ trouble to get it right.* ***in ~,*** especially: *I remember one of them in ~.* **3** very exact; scrupulous: *a full and ~ account of what we saw.* **4** ***~ (about/over),*** hard to satisfy; fastidious: *She's ~ about what she wears. He's too ~ over what he will eat and drink.* □ *n* detail. ***go into ~s,*** give details. **~·ly** *adv* in a ~ manner: *His good humour was ~ly noticeable. I ~ly mentioned that point.* **~·ity** /pəˈtɪkjʊˈlærətɪ/ *n* [U] exactness; attention to detail. **~·ize** /-ɑɪz/ *vt, vi* [VP6A,2A] name specially or one by one.

part·ing /ˈpɑtɪŋ/ ⇨ part[2].

par·ti·san /ˈpɑtɪˈzæn *US:* ˈpɑrtɪzn/ *n* **1** person devoted to a party, group or cause. **2** (esp) member of an armed resistance movement in a country occupied by enemy forces: *~ troops.* □ *adj* uncritically devoted to a cause: *His loyalties are too ~.* ˈ**~·ship** /-ʃɪp/ *n*

par·ti·tion /pɑˈtɪʃn/ *n* **1** [U] division into parts: *the ~ of India in 1947.* **2** [C] that which divides, esp a thin wall between rooms, etc. **3** [C] part formed by dividing; section. □ *vt* [VP6A,15B] ***~ (sth off),*** divide into sections, etc separate by means of a ~(2).

par·ti·tive /ˈpɑtɪtɪv/ *n, adj* (word) denoting part of a collective whole: *'Some' and 'any' are ~s.*

part·ner /ˈpɑtnə(r)/ *n* **1** person who takes part with another or others in some activity, esp one of the owners ot a business: *~s in crime; profits shared equally among all the ~s; active ~,* one taking part in the affairs of the business. **sleeping ~,** ⇨ sleep[2](3). **2** one of two persons dancing together, playing tennis, cards, etc together; husband or wife. □ *vt* [VP6A,15A] be a ~ to; bring (people) together as ~s. ˈ**~·ship** /-ʃɪp/ *n* [C] state of being a ~; [C] joint business: *enter into ~ship* (*with* sb); *be in ~ship.*

par·took /pɑˈtʊk/ ⇨ partake.

par·tridge /ˈpɑ-trɪdʒ/ *n* [C] sorts of bird of the same family as the pheasant; [U] its flesh as food; ⇨ the illus at fowl.

par·tur·ation /ˈpɑtjʊˈrɪʃn *US:* -tʃʊ-/ *n* [U] childbirth.

party /ˈpɑtɪ/ *n* (*pl* **-ties**) **1** [C] group of persons united in policy and opinion, in support of a cause, esp in politics: *the Conservative, Liberal and Socialist parties.* **2** [U] (esp attrib use) government based on political parties: *the ˈ~ system; ~ politics,* politics of and within a ~, e g manœuvres designed to win influence or power; *Our best men put public interest before ~.* ***follow the line,*** ⇨ line[1](11). **the ~ machine,** ⇨ machine(2). ˈ**~-ˈspirit,** enthusiasm for, devotion to, a (political) ~. Hence, ˈ**~-ˈspirited** *adj* **3** one of the persons or sides in a legal agreement or dispute. ˈ**~-ˈwall,** one that divides two properties and is the joint responsibility of the owners of these properties. **a ~ line,** ⇨ line[1](1). **4** group of persons travelling or working together, or on duty together: *a ˈfiring-~,* of soldiers, at a military funeral or execution. **5** gathering of persons, by invitation, for pleasure: *a ˈdinner/ˈbirthday ~; give a ~,* arrange one and be the host(ess); (attrib) *a ~ dress.* ***lack the ~ spirit,*** be without enthusiasm for a ~. ***make up a ~,*** join together to form a ~. **6** person taking part in and approving of or being aware of what is going on: *a ~ to a conspiracy; an innocent ~.* **7** (hum) person: *Who's the old ~ in blue,* the old person dressed in blue? **8** ˈ**~-coloured,** ⇨ parti-coloured.

par·venu /ˈpɑvənju *US:* -nu/ *n* person who has suddenly reached higher economic or social status from a lower status.

pas·chal /ˈpæskl/ *adj* **1** of the Jewish Passover. **2** of Easter: *enjoy ~ lamb in Rome,* lamb killed and eaten at Easter.

pasha /ˈpɑʃə *US:* ˈpæʃə/ *n* former title of honour placed after the name of a Turkish officer of high rank or the governor of a province.

pass[1] /pɑs *US:* pæs/ *n* **1** success in an examination, esp (in university degree examinations) success in satisfying the examiners but without distinction or honours[1](7): *get a ~; a ˈ~ degree.* **2** (*sing* only) ***reach/come to such a/to a fine/ sad/pretty ~,*** reach such a state or condition: *Things have come to a sad/a fine ~ that....* **3** ***bring to ~,*** accomplish, carry out. ***come to ~,*** happen: *How exactly did that come to ~?* **4** (paper, ticket, etc giving) permission or authority to travel, enter a building, occupy a seat in a cinema, etc: *a free ~,* ticket giving free travel on the railways, etc. *All ~es to be shown at the barrier,* e g in a station. *No admittance without a ~.* ⇨ ~-book below. **5** act of kicking, throwing, or hitting the ball from one player to another player (of the same team): *a clever ~ to the forward.* **6** movement of the hand over or in front of sth (as in conjuring or juggling, or in mesmerism). **7** forward movement, blow (in fencing, etc). ***make a ~ at (a woman),*** (sl) make (possibly unwelcome) amorous advances. **8** narrow way over or through mountains; such a way viewed as the entrance to a country; ⇨ the illus at mountain. ***hold the ~,*** (fig) defend a cause. ***sell the ~,*** (fig) betray a cause; yield up a position. **9** (card games) act of passing. ⇨ pass[2](15). **10** (compounds) ˈ**~·book** *n* **(a)** book supplied by a bank to a customer with records of his account. **(b)** (S Africa) booklet, document, allowing a person to be in a certain area. ˈ**~·key** *n* private key to a gate, etc; key which opens a number of locks; master key. ˈ**~·word** *n* secret word or phrase which enables a person to be recognized as a friend by sentries: *give/demand the ~word.*

pass[2] /pɑs *US:* pæs/ *vi, vt* (*pp* **~ed**, or, as *adj* past) (For special uses with *advv* and *preps,* ⇨ 19 below.) **1** [VP2A,C] move towards and beyond, proceed (*along, through, down, etc*): *~ through a village. Please let me ~. The road was too narrow for cars to ~. The two ships ~ed each other during the night. I bowed to her and ~ed on. He ~ed* *by/behind/in front of me. They ~ed by,* went past. Hence, **'~er-'by** *n* (*pl* **passers-by**) person who ~es sb or sth: *The purse was picked up by a ~er-by.* **2** [VP6A] leave (a person, place, object, etc) on one side or behind as one goes forward: *Turn right after ~ing the Post Office. I ~ed Miss Green in the street.* **3** [VP6A] go through, across, over or between: *The ship ~ed the channel. No complaints ~ed her lips.* **4** [VP2A] (of time) go by; be spent: *Six months ~ed and still we had no news of them. The time ~ed pleasantly.* **5** [VP6A] spend (time): *How shall we ~ the evening? What can we do to ~ the time?* **6** [VP3A] **~ *(from...) (into...),*** change from one state of things to another; change into another state of things: *Water ~es from a liquid to a solid state when it freezes. When water boils it ~es into steam.* **7** [VP6A, 15B,12A,13A] give by handing: *Please ~ (me) the butter. The letter was ~ed on/round to all the members of the family. The note was ~ed round the table. Read this and ~ it on to your neighbour.* **8** [VP6A] utter: *~ a remark,* say sth. **~ *the time of day with sb,*** engage them in light conversation. **9** [VP6A,2A,C] (cause to) circulate: *He was imprisoned for ~ing forged banknotes. These South African coins won't ~* (= be accepted) *in England. He ~es under the name of Mr Green,* is known and accepted as Mr Green. **10** [VP6A,2A] examine and accept; be examined and accepted: *Parliament ~ed the Bill. The Bill ~ed and became law. The examiners ~ed most of the candidates. The candidates ~ed (the examination). Will the play ~ the censor? We have to ~ the Customs before we leave.* **11** [VP2A,C] take place; be said or done (between persons): *Did you see/hear what was ~ing? Tell me everything that ~ed between you.* **12** [VP6A] be beyond the range of: *a story that ~es belief. It ~es my comprehension.* **13** [VP14] **~ *(on sb/sth),*** give (an opinion, judgement, sentence on sth or sb): *~ sentence on an accused man. I can't ~ an opinion on your work without seeing it.* ***pass one's word/oath,*** give a pledge or promise. **14** [VP2A] be accepted without rebuke or blame; go unnoticed or unreproved: *His rude remarks ~ed without comment. I don't like it, but I'll let it ~,* will not make objections, etc. *Such conduct may ~ in certain circles but cannot be tolerated here.* **~ muster,** ⇨ muster. **15** [VP2A] (card games) let one's turn go by without playing a card or making a bid. **16** [VP15A] move; cause to go: *He ~ed his hand across his forehead/his fingers through his hair. I ~ed a rope round the barrel. Will you please ~ your eye* (= glance) *over this note.* **~ *water,*** urinate. **17** (in football, hockey, etc) kick, hand or hit (the ball) to a player of one's own side. **18** [VP6A,15A] cause (troops) to go by: *~ troops in review.* **19** [VP2C,15B] (special uses with *adverbial particles* and *preps*):

pass away, (euphem) die: *He ~ed away peacefully.*

pass sb/sth by, pay no attention to; disregard: *I can't ~ the matter by without a protest.*

pass for sb/sth, be accepted as: *In this small village, he ~ed for a learned man. Do I speak French well enough to ~ for a Frenchman? She's fair-skinned enough to ~ for a white.*

pass in/into, gain admission to: *He ~ed into Sandhurst* (Royal Military College) *twenty-fifth.*

pass off, **(a)** (of events) take place, be carried through: *The meeting of the strikers ~ed off quietly.* **(b)** (of pain, a crisis) end: *Has your toothache ~ed off yet?* **~ *sth off,*** turn attention from: *~ off an awkward situation.* **~ *sth/sb off as,*** represent falsely to be: *He tried to ~ himself off as a qualified doctor.*

pass on, (euphem) die: *I'm grieved to learn that your dear mother has ~ed on.* **~ *sth on,*** hand or give it (to sb else, to others).

pass out, (colloq) faint; lose consciousness. **~ *out (of),*** leave college, etc having ~ed one's examinations. Hence, **'~ing-'out (ceremony/parade),** esp for cadets who have completed their training.

pass sb over, overlook; fail to notice: *They ~ed me over* (e g failed to promote me) *in favour of young Hill.*

pass through, experience.

pass sth up, (colloq) neglect it; not take advantage of sth: *~ up an opportunity.*

pass·able /'pɑsəbl *US:* 'pæs-/ *adj* **1** (of roads, etc) that can be passed over or crossed: *Are the Alpine roads ~ yet?* **2** that can be accepted as fairly good but not excellent: *a ~ knowledge of German.* **pass·ably** /-əblɪ/ *adv*

pass·age /'pæsɪdʒ/ *n* **1** [U] passing; act of going past, through or across; right to go through: *the ~ of time.* **a bird of ~. (a)** migratory bird. **(b)** person who passes through a place without staying there long. **2** [C] voyage; journey from point to point by sea or air: *book one's ~ to New York.* ***work one's ~,*** ⇨ work[2](4). **3** [C] way through: *force a ~ through a crowd; the long ~s,* the bronchial tubes. **4** [C] **'~-(way),** corridor in a building: *She has to keep her bicycle in the ~.* **5** [C] short extract from a speech or piece of writing, quoted or considered separately. **6** passing of a Bill so that it becomes law. **7** (*pl*) what passes between two persons in conversation: *have angry ~s with an opponent during a debate.* **8 '~ of 'arms,** (liter, fig) combat; dispute.

pass·book *n* ⇨ pass[1](10).

passé /'pɑseɪ *US:* pæ'seɪ/ *adj* (fem **passée**) past his/her/its best; no longer current; (esp, of a woman) past the period of greatest beauty.

pass·en·ger /'pæsndʒə(r)/ *n* **1** person being conveyed by bus, taxi, tram, train, ship, aircraft, etc. **2** (colloq) member of a team, crew, etc who does no effective work.

passe·par·tout /'pæspɑ'tu/ *n* kind of adhesive tape used e g as a mounting for a picture, etc (to form a frame).

passer-by /'pɑsə 'baɪ *US:* 'pæsər/ ⇨ pass[2](1).

pas·sim /'pæsɪm/ *adv* (Lat) (of allusions, phrases, etc to be found in a book or author) frequently; in every part: *This occurs in Spenser ~.*

pas·sing /'pɑsɪŋ *US:* 'pæs-/ *adj* going by; not lasting: *the ~ years.* □ *adv* (old use) very: *~ rich.* □ *n* the act of going by: *the ~ of the old year,* i e on New Year's Eve.

passion /'pæʃn/ *n* **1** [U] strong feeling or enthusiasm, esp of love, hate or anger: *be filled with ~* (i e love) *for sb; choking with ~,* i e anger or hate. **2** (with *indef art*) outburst of strong feeling: *fly into a ~,* become very angry; *be in a ~;* **3 the P~,** the suffering and death of Jesus. **'P~ 'Sunday,** the fifth Sunday in Lent. **'P~ Week,** the week between P~ Sunday and Palm Sunday. **'P~ play,** drama dealing with the P~. **'~-flower** *n* kinds of (usu climbing) plants with flowers that are thought to resemble the crown of thorns placed on the head of Jesus. `~ **fruit,** edible fruit of the ~-flower. **~·less** *adj*

passion·ate /`pæʃṇət/ *adj* easily moved by passion; filled with, showing, passion; *a ~ nature; ~ language.* **~·ly** *adv* in a ~ manner: *She is ~ly fond of tennis.*

pass·ive /`pæsɪv/ *adj* **1** acted upon but not acting; not offering active resistance: *In spite of my efforts the boy remained ~,* showed no signs of interest, activity, etc; *~ obedience.* '~ **re`sistance,** resistance that takes the form of not obeying orders, the law, etc but without active measures of opposition; '*~ re`sisters,* persons who practise this. **2 the ~ (voice),** (gram) the form in italic type in the sentence 'The letter *was written* yesterday.' □ *n* ~ voice. **~·ly** *adv* **~·ness** *n* **pass·iv·ity** /pæ`sɪvətɪ/ *n* [U] the state or quality of being ~.

pass·key ⇨ pass[1](10).

Pass·over /`pɑsəʊvə(r) *US:* `pæs-/ *n* Jewish religious festival commemorating the liberation of the Jews from slavery in Egypt. ⇨ Exod 12.

pass·port /`pɑspɔt *US:* `pæs-/ *n* government document to be carried by a traveller abroad, giving personal particulars; (fig) sth that enables one to win or obtain sth: *Is flattery a ~ to success with that teacher?*

pass·word ⇨ pass[1](10).

past[1] /pɑst *US:* pæst/ *adj* (Cf *passed, pp* of pass) of the time before the present; gone by in time: *for the ~ few days/weeks, etc; during the ~ week; in times ~; for a long time ~; ~ generations; the ~ tense; a ~ participle,* e g *passed, taken, gone.* **~ master,** one who has a thorough mastery (*of* or *in* a subject). □ *n* **1** (with *def art*) ~ time: *We cannot change the ~. Memories of the ~ filled her mind.* **2** person's ~ life or experiences, esp when these are not reputable: *We know nothing of his ~. She's a woman with a ~.*

past[2] /pɑst *US:* pæst/ *prep* **1** beyond in time; after: *half ~ two; ten (minutes) ~ six; buses every twenty minutes ~ the hour,* i e at 1.20, 2.20, 3.20, etc; *stay out until ~ 11 o'clock; an old man ~ seventy; a woman ~ middle age.* **2** beyond in space; up to and farther than: *He walked ~ the house. He hurried ~ me without stopping to speak. The driver took the bus ~ the traffic signal.* **3** beyond the limits, power or range of: *The old man is ~ work,* too old, weak, etc to work. *She's ~ child-bearing,* too old to bear a child. *The pain was almost ~ bearing,* too severe to be endured. *He's ~ praying for,* There's no hope of cure, improvement, etc. *She's ~ caring what happens,* has reached the stage of complete indifference, is quite resigned to ill fortune, etc. ***be/get ~ it,*** (colloq) be no longer able to do the things one could formerly do: *My gardener is over seventy-five and I'm afraid he's getting past it.* ***would not put sth ~ sb,*** consider him capable of doing sth disreputable, unusual, etc: *You may say that he is honest but I wouldn't put it ~ him to run off with the money.* □ *adv* (in the sense of 2 above: *walk/march/go/run/hurry ~.*

pasta /`pæstə/ *n* (I) (dish of food prepared from a dough of) flour, eggs and water mixed and dried, e g macaroni, spaghetti, ravioli.

paste /peɪst/ *n* [U] **1** soft mixture of flour, fat, etc for making pastry. **2** preparation of foodstuffs, cut up and pounded to a soft, moist mass: *`anchovy ~; `fish-~.* **3** mixture of flour and water used for sticking things together, esp paper on walls and boards: *a bottle of ~.* `**~·board** *n* [U] stiff board-like material made by pasting sheets of paper together; cardboard. **4** substance (a glass-like material) used in making artificial diamonds, etc □ *vi* **1** [VP6A,15A,B] stick with ~(3). ***~ sth down,*** fasten down with ~. ***~ sth up,*** **(a)** fasten with ~ to a surface: *~ up a notice.* **(b)** seal or cover using ~: *~ up cracks with paper.* **(c)** fasten sheets or strips of paper on larger sheets, e g to design pages for a magazine, book, etc. Hence, `**~-up** *n* **2** [VP6A] (colloq) thrash; beat. Hence, **past·ing** *n* (colloq) severe beating: *Get/Give sb a pasting.*

pas·tel /`pæstl *US:* pæ`stel/ *n* **1** (picture drawn with) coloured chalk made into crayons. **2** (attrib) *~ shades,* soft, light, delicate shades of colour.

pas·tern /`pæstən/ *n* part of a horse's foot between the fetlock and the hoof. ⇨ the illus at domestic.

pas·teur·ize /`pæstʃəraɪz/ *vt* [VP6A] rid (milk, etc) of disease-producing bacteria by using the heating method of Louis Pasteur /`pæstɜ(r)/, 1822—1895, French chemist. **pas·teur·iz·ation** /'pæstʃəraɪ`zeɪʃn *US:* -rɪ`z-/ *n*

pas·tiche /pæ`stiʃ/ *n* [C] literary or other work of art composed in the style of another author, etc; musical composition made up from various sources.

pas·tille /`pæstɪl *US:* pæ`stil/ *n* [C] small flavoured tablet to be sucked, e g one containing medicine for the throat.

pas·time /`pɑs-taɪm *US:* `pæs-/ *n* [C] anything done to pass time pleasantly; game: *Flirting was her favourite ~.*

pas·tor /`pɑstə(r) *US:* `pæs-/ *n* minister(3), esp of a nonconformist church.

pas·toral /`pɑstərl *US:* `pæs-/ *adj* **1** of shepherds and country life: *~ poetry.* **2** of a pastor; (esp) of a bishop: *a ~ letter,* one to the members of a bishop's diocese; *~ staff,* bishop's emblem, like a shepherd's crook, carried by or before bishops ceremonially. **3** of (duties towards) a priest's or a minister's flock: *~ care/responsibilities.* □ *n* ~ poem, play, letter, etc.

pas·tor·ate /`pɑstərət *US:* `pæs-/ *n* **1** office of a pastor; time during which he holds it. **2** body of pastors.

pas·try /`peɪstrɪ/ *n* (*pl* -ries) **1** [U] paste of flour, fat, etc baked in an oven; pie-crust. **2** [C] article of food made wholly or partly of this, e g a pie or tart; [U] such articles collectively: *eat less ~.* `**~-cook** *n* person who makes ~, esp for public sale.

pas·ture /`pɑstʃə(r) *US:* `pæs-/ *n* [U] grassland for cattle; grass on such land. ⇨ meadow; [C] piece of land of this kind. □ *vt, vi* **1** [VP6A] (of persons) put (cattle, sheep, etc) to graze: *~ one's sheep on the village common;* (of cattle, etc) eat down grassland. **2** [VP2A] graze. **pas·tur·age** /-ɪdʒ/ *n* [U] (right to graze cattle on) ~ land.

pasty[1] /`peɪstɪ/ *adj* (-ier, -iest) like paste(1): *a ~ complexion,* white and unhealthy.

pasty[2] /`pæstɪ/ *n* (*pl* -ties) pie of meat, jam, etc enclosed in paste and baked without a dish: *a Cornish ~.*

pat[1] /pæt/ *adv* at the right moment; at once and without hesitation: *The answer came pat. He had his excuse pat.* ***stand pat,*** stick to one's decision; refuse to change.

pat[2] /pæt/ *vt, vi* (-tt-) **1** [VP6A,15A] tap gently with the open hand or with sth flat: *pat a dog; pat a ball,* so that it bounces up and down. ***pat sb/***

oneself on the back, (fig) express approval, congratulate, etc. **2** [VP2A] carry out the action of patting. □ *n* [C] **1** tap with the open hand, e g as a caress or to show sympathy. **2** small mass of sth, esp butter, formed by patting. **3** light sound made by striking sth with a flat object.

patch[1] /pætʃ/ *n* **1** small piece of material put on over a hole or a damaged or worn place: *a coat with ~es on the elbows; a ~ on the inner tube of a tyre.* **'~-'pocket** *n* one made by sewing a piece of cloth on to the outside of a garment. **2** piece of plaster put over a cut or wound. **3** pad worn to protect an injured eye. **4** small, irregular, differently coloured part of a surface: *a dog with a white ~ on its neck.* **5** small area (of ground, esp for garden vegetables): *the cabbage ~*; small area of anything: *~es of fog; small ~es of blue in a cloudy sky.* **6** small (usu black), round piece of silk or plaster worn by women on the face in the 17th and 18th cc (intended to show up the beauty of the skin). **7** ***not a ~ on,*** not nearly so good as. **8** ***hit/strike/be going through a bad ~,*** a period of bad luck, difficulty, unhappiness. **'~-work** *n* **1** piece of material made up of bits of cloth of various sizes, shapes and colours: (attrib) *a ~ work quilt.* **2** (fig) piece of work made up of odds and ends.

patch[2] /pætʃ/ *vt* [VP6A] **1** put a patch on; (of material) serve as a patch for. **2** [VP15B] ***~ up,*** repair; make roughly ready for use: *an old, ~ed-up motor-cycle;* (fig) *~ up a quarrel,* settle it for a time. **~y** *adj* **(-ier, -iest)** made up of ~es; not regular or uniform; or uneven quality: *~y work/knowledge. The fog was ~y.* **'~-ily** /-əlɪ/ *adv* **~i-ness** *n*

patch·ouli /'pætʃʊlɪ/ *n* [U] (perfume derived from an) Asiatic plant.

pate /'peɪt/ *n* (colloq in mod Eng) head: *a bald ~.* Hence, **-pated** *suff* as in *'curly-'~d,* having a head of curly hair.

pâté /'pæteɪ *US:* pɑ'teɪ/ *n* **1** pie; patty. **2** paste. **~ de foie gras** /'pæteɪ də fwɑ 'grɑ/, (F) (patty of) goose-liver paste.

pa·tella /pə'telə/ *n* (anat) kneecap.

pat·ent[1] /'peɪtnt *US:* 'pætnt/ *adj* **1** evident, easily seen: *It was ~ to everyone that he disliked the idea.* **2 'letters '~** /'pætnt/, government authority to manufacture sth invented and protect it from imitation. **3** protected by letters ~: *~ medicines,* made by one firm or person only. **4 ~ leather,** leather with a hard, smooth, shiny surface. **5** (colloq) original; peculiar to one person only; ingenious; well-contrived: *a ~ device.* **~-ly** *adv* clearly; obviously.

pat·ent[2] /'peɪtnt *US:* 'pætnt/ *n* [C] **1** (privilege granted by) letters patent: *take out a ~ to protect a new invention.* **P~** (usu /'pætnt/) **Office,** government department which issues ~s. **2** that which is protected by letters ~; invention or process. □ *vt* [VP6A] obtain a ~ for (an invention or process). **~ee** /'peɪtn'ti *US:* 'pætn-/ *n* person to whom a ~ is issued.

pa·ter /'peɪtə(r)/ *n* (schoolboy sl) father.

pater fa·mil·ias /'peɪtə fə'mɪlɪæs *US:* 'pæt-/ *n* (hum) father or head of a family.

pa·ter·nal /pə'tɜnl/ *adj* **1** of or like a father: *~ care.* **2** related through the father: *my ~ grandfather.* **~ly** /-nlɪ/ *adv* **~-ism** /-ɪzm/ *n* (practice of) governing or controlling people in a ~ way (providing for their needs but giving them no responsibility).

pa·ter·nity /pə'tɜnətɪ/ *n* [U] **1** fatherhood; being a father; origin on the father's side: *~ unknown.* **2** (fig) source; authorship.

pater·nos·ter /'pætə'nɒstə(r)/ *n* (Lat for 'Our Father') **1** (recital of) the Lord's Prayer. **2** place in a rosary(2) at which the Lord's Prayer is repeated. **3** lift(2) with a series of doorless cars(3) moving on a continuous belt so that passengers can step on or off at each floor.

path /pɑθ *US:* pæθ/ *n* (*pl* ~s /pɑðz *US:* pæðz/) **1** **'~-(way),** way made (across fields, through woods, etc) by people walking: *Keep to the ~ or you may lose your way.* **'~-finder** *n* explorer; sb sent on ahead to find a route, etc; pioneer. **2** track specially made for foot or cycle racing (usu *cinder track*). **3** **('foot)-~,** track specially made for pedestrians along the side of a road. Cf *pavement,* along the side of a street. **4** line along which sth or sb moves: *the moon's ~ round the earth; the 'flight ~ of a spacecraft; the ~ of a tornado.* **~-less** *adj* having no ~s; ~less jungles.

pa·thetic /pə'θetɪk/ *adj* **1** sad; pitiful: *a ~ sight; ~ ignorance.* **2** of the emotions. **the ~ fallacy,** the error of imaginatively endowing inanimate objects with life, human feelings, etc. **pa·theti·cally** /-klɪ/ *adv*

pa·thol·ogy /pə'θɒlədʒɪ/ *n* [U] science of diseases. **path·ol·ogist** /pə'θɒlədʒɪst/ *n* student of, expert in, ~. **path·o·logi·cal** /'pæθə'lɒdʒɪkl/ *adj* of ~; of the nature of disease. **path·o·logi·cally** /-klɪ/ *adv*

pa·thos /'peɪθɒs/ *n* [U] quality in speech, writing, etc which arouses a feeling of pity, sympathy or tenderness.

pa·tience /'peɪʃns/ *n* [U] **1** (power of) enduring trouble, suffering, inconvenience, without complaining; ability to wait for results, to deal with problems calmly and without haste: *I haven't the ~ to hear your complaints again. She has no ~ with people who are always grumbling,* cannot endure them. ***be out of ~ (with),*** be unable to endure further. **the ~ of Job,** endless ~: *His behaviour would try* (= test) *the ~ of Job.* ⇨ Job. **2** (GB) kind of card game, usu for one player (US = *solitaire*).

pa·tient /'peɪʃnt/ *adj* having, showing, patience: *be ~ with a child; be ~ of insults,* endure them with patience. □ *n* [C] person who has received, is receiving, or is on a doctor's list for, medical treatment: *an old ~ of mine. The Smiths are ~s of mine.* **~-ly** *adv*

pat·ina /'pætɪnə/ *n* (usu) green, glossy surface formed on old bronze or copper; glossiness of old woodwork, etc.

patio /'pætɪəʊ/ *n* (*pl* ~s) **1** courtyard, open to the sky, within the walls of a Spanish or Spanish American house. **2** (modern use) paved area near a house, used for recreation.

pa·tis·serie /pə'tisərɪ/ *n* (F) shop, bakery, specializing in (French) pastry and cakes.

pat·ois /'pætwɑ/ *n* dialect of the common people of a district, differing from the standard language of the country.

pa·trial /'peɪtrɪəl/ *n* person who has qualifications which give him the right to be considered legally a British citizen, e g an Asian in E Africa who has a British passport.

patri·arch /'peɪtrɪɑk *US:* 'pæt-/ *n* **1** venerable old man. **2** male head of a family or tribe. **3** bishop among the early Christians; (in the RC Church) high-ranking bishop; (in Eastern Churches) bishop of highest honour: *the P~ of Antioch/Jerusalem.* **~al** /ˈpeɪtrɪˈɑkl *US:* ˈpæt-/ *adj* of or like a ~. **ˈ~·ate** /-eɪt/ *n* position, see, residence, of a Church ~.

pa·tri·cian /pəˈtrɪʃn/ *n, adj* (person) of noble birth (esp in ancient Rome); aristocrat(ic).

pat·ri·cide /ˈpætrɪsɑɪd/ *n* [U] killing of one's own father; [C] instance of this; [C] person guilty of this.

pat·ri·mony /ˈpætrɪmənɪ *US:* -məʊnɪ/ *n* (*pl* -nies) [C] property inherited from one's father or ancestors; endowment of a church, etc. **pat·ri·mo·nial** /ˈpætrɪˈməʊnɪəl/ *adj* of a ~.

pa·triot /ˈpeɪtrɪət *US:* ˈpæt-/ *n* person who loves and is ready to defend his country. **ˈ~·ism** /-ɪzm/ *n* [U] the feelings and qualities of a ~. **~ic** /ˈpeɪtrɪˈotɪk *US:* ˈpæt-/ *adj* having, showing, the qualities of a ~. **~i·cally** /-klɪ/ *adv*

pa·trol /pəˈtrəʊl/ *vt,vi* (-ll-) [VP6A,2A] go round (a camp, town, the streets, roads, etc) to see that all is well, to look out (for wrongdoers, persons in need of help, the enemy, etc). □ *n* **1** [U] the act of ~ling: *soldiers on ~; maintain a constant sea and air ~,* e g looking for submarines during a war; (attrib) *a police ˈ~ car,* e g on a motorway. **2** [C] person(s), ship(s) or aircraft on ~ duties: *We were helped by an AA* (= Automobile Association) *~(man)*, scout. **3** (US) **ˈ~ wagon** *n* one used by the police for conveying prisoners or persons who have been arrested. **~·man** /-mən/ (*pl* -men) policeman who ~s an area.

pa·tron /ˈpeɪtrən/ *n* **1** person who gives encouragement, moral or financial support, to a person, cause, the arts, etc: *Modern artists have difficulty in finding wealthy ~s.* **ˈ~ ˈsaint,** saint regarded as the special protector (*of* a church, town, travellers, etc). **2** regular customer at a shop. **ˈ~·ess** /-ɪs/ *n* woman ~.

pa·tron·age /ˈpætrənɪdʒ/ *n* [C] **1** support, encouragement, given by a patron: *with/under the ~ of the Duke of X.* **2** right of appointing sb to a benefice or office, to grant privileges, etc: *He's an influential man, with a great deal of ~ in his hands.* **3** customer's support (to a shopkeeper, etc): *take away one's ~ because of poor service.* **4** patronizing manner. ⇨ patronize(2).

pa·tron·ize /ˈpætrənɑɪz *US:* ˈpeɪt-/ *vt* [VP6A] **1** act as patron towards: *~ a young musician/a dressmaker.* **2** treat (sb whom one is helping, talking to, etc) as if he were an inferior person; be condescending towards. **pat·ron·iz·ing** *adj* **pat·ron·iz·ing·ly** *adv*

pat·ro·nymic /ˈpætrəˈnɪmɪk/ *n, adj* (name) derived from that of a father or ancestor, e g *Robertson.*

pat·ten /ˈpætn/ *n* clog, wooden shoe, mounted on a metal framework to keep the wearer's foot above the mud.

pat·ter[1] /ˈpætə(r)/ *n* [U] **1** kind of talk used by a particular class of people: *thieves' ~; the ~ of an auctioneer.* **2** rapid talk of a conjuror or comedian; rapid speech introduced into a song (*a ˈ~ song*). □ *vt,vi* [VP6A] recite, say, repeat (prayers, etc) very quickly or in a mechanical way; [VP2A] talk fast or glibly.

pat·ter[2] /ˈpætə(r)/ *n* [U] sound of quick, light taps or footsteps: *the ~ of rain on a roof; the ~ of footsteps.* □ *vi* [VP2A,C] make this sound: *rain ~ing on the window-panes.*

pat·tern /ˈpætn/ *n* [C] **1** excellent example; sb or sth serving as a model: *She's a ~ of all the virtues.* (attrib) *He has a ~* (*model* is the usu word) *wife.* **2** sth serving as a model, esp shape of a garment, cut out in paper, used as a guide in dressmaking, etc; model from which sth is to be cast and from which a mould is made (in a foundry, etc): *ˈ~-maker; ˈ~-shop,* in a foundry. **3** sample, esp a small piece of cloth: *a bunch of ~s from the tailor.* **4** ornamental design, e g on a carpet, on wallpaper, curtain material: *a ~ of roses; geometrical ~s.* **5** way in which sth happens, develops, is arranged, etc: *new ~s of family life,* e g when married women, instead of keeping house, go out to work and add to the family income. □ *vt* **1** [VP14] **~ sth/oneself upon/after,** model: *a dress ~ed upon a Paris model. He ~s himself upon his father.* **2** decorate with a ~.

patty /ˈpætɪ/ *n* (*pl* -ties) little pie or pasty: *oyster patties.* **ˈ~-pan** *n* pan for baking a ~ in.

pau·city /ˈpɔsətɪ/ *n* [U] (formal) smallness of number or quantity.

Paul /pɔl/ *n* **rob Peter to pay ~,** ⇨ Peter. **ˈ~ Pry,** an inquisitive person.

paunch /pɔntʃ/ *n* belly, esp if fat: *a ~ like that of Falstaff. He was getting quite a ~,* getting wide round the waist. **~y** *adj* having a large ~. **~i·ness** *n*

pau·per /ˈpɔpə(r)/ *n* person with no means of livelihood, esp one who is supported by charity. **ˈ~·ism** /-ɪzm/ *n* [U] state of being a ~; existence of ~s: *abolish ~ism.* **ˈ~·ize** /-ɑɪz/ *vt* [VP6A] bring to the state of being a ~. **~·iz·ation** /ˈpɔpərɑɪˈzeɪʃn *US:* -rɪˈz-/ *n*

pause /pɔz/ *n* **1** short interval or stop (while doing or saying sth): *during a ~ in the conversation; a ~ to take breath.* **give ~ to,** cause (a person) to hesitate, to stop and think. **2** (music) sign (𝄐 or 𝄑) over or under a note or rest to show that it is to be prolonged. □ *vi* [VP2A,4A] make a ~: *~ to look round.*

pave /peɪv/ *vt* [VP6A] put flat stones, bricks, etc on (a path, etc): *a path ~d with brick;* (fig) *a career ~d with* (= full of) *good intentions.* **ˈpaving-stone** *n* slab of stone for paving. **~ the way for,** make conditions easy or ready for.

pave·ment /ˈpeɪvmənt/ *n* **1** (GB) paved way at the side of a street for people on foot (US = *sidewalk*). **ˈ~ artist,** one who draws pictures on a ~ with coloured chalks (to get money from passers-by). **ˈcrazy ˈ~,** ⇨ crazy(4). **2** (US) hard surface for streets, roads, etc.

pa·vil·ion /pəˈvɪlɪən/ *n* **1** building on a sports ground for the use of players, spectators, etc. **2** ornamental building for concerts, dancing, etc. **3** large tents, e g as used for a flower exhibition.

paw /pɔ/ *n* animal's foot that has claws or nails (contrasted with *hoof*): *a dog's paw;* (colloq, hum) hand. ⇨ the illus at dog. □ *vt* [VP6A,15B] **1** (of animals) feel or scratch with the paw(s); (of a horse) strike (the ground) with a hoof. **2** (of persons) touch with the hands, awkwardly, rudely or with improper familiarity: *No girl likes being pawed* (*about*) *by men.*

pawky /ˈpɔkɪ/ *adj* (Scot) sly; arch: *~ humour.* **pawk·ily** /ˈpɔkəlɪ/ *adv*

pawl /pɔl/ *n* **1** lever with a catch for the teeth of a ratchet wheel or rod, to prevent slipping or movement in the opposite direction. **2** short bar used to prevent a capstan or windlass from recoiling.

pawn[1] /pɔn/ *n* least valuable piece in the game of chess; person made use of by others for their own advantage. ⇨ the illus at **chess**.

pawn[2] /pɔn/ *vt* [VP6A] **1** deposit (clothing, jewellery, etc) as a pledge for money borrowed: *The medical student* ~*ed his microscope to pay his rent.* **2** (fig) pledge: ~ *one's life/honour.* □ *n* [U] state of being ~ed: *My watch is in* ~. **'~-broker** *n* person licensed to lend money at interest on the security of goods left with him. **'~-shop** *n* ~broker's place of business. **'~-ticket** *n* ~broker's receipt for goods pledged with him.

paw·paw /pə'pɔ *US:* 'pɔpɔ/ *n* = papaw.

pax /pæks/ *n* **1** (schoolboy sl) Peace! i e Let's stop quarrelling! **2** (in phrases) **Pax Romana** /'pæks rəʊ'mɑnə/, peace enforced on states in the ancient Roman Empire.

pay[1] /peɪ/ *n* [U] money paid for regular work or services, esp in the armed forces (*Pay* is used instead of *wages* and *salary* in the Navy, Army and Air Force): *draw one's pay; get an increase in pay.* ***in the pay of,*** employed by (often with a suggestion of dishonour, e g *in the pay of the enemy.* **'pay-day** *n* **(a)** day on which wages, salaries, etc are (to be) paid. **(b)** day (on the Stock Exchange) on which transfer of stock has to be paid for. **'pay-dirt** *n* (US) earth in which there is ore of a grade high enough to make mining profitable. **'pay load** *n* that part of the load (of a ship, aircraft, etc) for which payment is received, e g passengers and cargo, but not fuel. **'pay·master** *n* official responsible for paying troops, workers, etc. **'pay·master 'general,** officer at the head of a department of the Treasury. **'pay-off** *n* (colloq) (time of) full and final settlement of accounts or of final retribution or revenge. **'pay-packet** *n* envelope or packet containing pay. **'pay-phone/-station** *n* (US) coin-operated telephone call-box. **'pay-roll/-sheet** *nn* **(a)** list of persons to be paid and the amounts due to each. **(b)** total amount of wages, salaries, etc to be paid to them. **'pay-slip** *n* slip of paper included in a pay-packet, showing how pay has been calculated, deductions for tax, etc.

pay[2] /peɪ/ *vt,vi* (*pt,pp* paid /peɪd/ (For special uses with *adverbial particles* and *preps,* ⇨ 6 below.) **1** [VP6A,12B,13B,14,3A] ***pay sb/pay sb for sth/pay sb sth; pay sth (to sb) (for sth),*** give (sb) money for goods, services, etc: *You must pay me what you owe. Have you paid the tradesmen this month? I paid you the money last week. He paid £600 to a dealer for that car. I pay £5 a week for her music lessons.* **2** [VP2A,14,12B,13B] give (sb) reward or recompense: *He says that sheep farming doesn't pay,* that it isn't profitable. *He has been amply paid for his trouble. They say it pays to advertise.* **3** [VP6A] settle (debts, etc): *Have you paid all your debts yet? He has paid his dues/subscriptions/taxes.* ***put 'paid' to sth,*** (colloq) settle; end it so that it gives no more trouble. **4** [VP6A,12A,13A] ***pay (sb/sth), pay sth (to sb),*** give, e g attention, respect, etc to sb: *Please pay more attention to your work. He has called to pay* (= offer) *his respects. He seldom pays his wife any compliments,* seldom compliments her. *I look forward to paying you a visit* (= visiting you) *next week.* **5** (phrases) ***pay one's way,*** not get into debt. ***pay through the nose,*** ⇨ **nose**[1]**(1)**. **'pay-as-you-'earn,** (abbr **PAYE**), method of collecting income tax (in GB) by requiring employers to deduct it from earnings. **pay·able** /'peɪəbl/ *adj* which must or may be paid. **payee** /peɪ'i/ *n* person to whom sth is (to be) paid. **payer** *n* person who pays or who is to pay. **6** [VP15B,3A] (special uses with *adverbial particles* and *preps*):

pay sth back, return (money, etc) that has been borrowed. ***pay sb back/out (for sth),*** punish him; have one's revenge: *I've paid him out for the trick he played on me.*

pay for, **(a)** ⇨ **1** above. **(b)** suffer pain or punishment for: *He'll have to pay for this foolish behaviour.*

pay in/into, deposit (money) with a bank, to one's own or another's account: *Please pay this sum into my/my wife's account.*

pay sb off, **(a)** pay sb his wages and discharge him. **(b)** pay in full and be free from obligation: *pay off one's creditors; pay off the crew of a ship.* ⇨ *pay-off* at **pay**[1].

pay sth out, **(a)** give money, e g in settlement of expenses: *When you move into a new house you really have to start paying out (money).* **(b)** (naut) allow (rope) to run out freely through the hands; slacken (rope) so that it runs freely.

pay up, pay in full what is owing: *If you don't pay up, I'll take you to court,* take legal action against you.

pay·ment /'peɪmənt/ *n* **1** [U] paying or being paid: *demand prompt* ~; *a cheque in* ~ *for services rendered.* **2** [C] sum of money (to be) paid: *£50 cash down and ten monthly* ~*s of £5.* **3** [C,U] (fig) reward; punishment.

pay·nim /'peɪnɪm/ *n* (archaic) pagan; heaven; (esp during the Crusades to the Holy Land) Saracen.

pea /pi/ *n* [C] ⇨ the illus at **vegetable**. plant with seeds in pods, used for food: *duck and green peas.* ***as like as two peas (in a pod),*** exactly alike. **'pea-flour** *n* [U] meal made from dried peas. **'pea-green** *adj, n* bright light-green colour of young peas. **'pea-fowl, 'pea-chick, 'pea-hen,** ⇨ **peacock**. **'pea-shooter** *n* (toy) tube from which dried peas are shot by blowing through the tube. **'pea-'soup** *n* thick soup made from dried peas. **'pea-'souper** *n* (colloq) thick yellow fog.

peace /pis/ *n* [U] (not used in *pl*, but see examples for use of *indef art*) **1** state of freedom from war: *be at* ~ *with neighbouring countries. After a brief* ~ (= a brief period of ~) *war broke out again.* ***make* ~ *(with),*** bring about ~ (with). **2** (often **P**~) treaty of ~: *P~/A P~ was signed between the two countries.* **3** freedom from civil disorder. ***break the* ~,** cause civil disorder, rioting, etc. ***keep the* ~,** obey the laws and refrain from disorder and strife. ***a breach of the* ~,** a disturbance or riot. ***the King's/Queen's* ~,** the general ~ of the country, as secured by law. **a Justice of the P~,** (abbr **JP**) a magistrate. **4** rest; quiet; calm: *the* ~ *of the countryside;* ~ *of mind.* ***at* ~ *(with),*** in a state of friendship or harmony: *He's never at* ~ *with himself,* is always restless. ***in* ~,** peacefully: live in ~ with one's neighbours. ***hold one's* ~,** keep silence; stop talking or arguing. ***make one's* ~ *(with sb),*** settle a quarrel. **'~-maker** *n* person who restores friendly relations. **'~-offering** *n* sth offered to show that one is willing to make ~.

peace·able /'pisəbl/ *adj* not quarrelsome; free from fighting or uproar. **peace·ably** /-əblɪ/ *adv*

peace·ful /ˈpisfl/ *adj* **1** loving peace: *~ nations.* **2** calm; quiet: *a ~ evening; a ~ death.* **~ly** /-fḷɪ/ *adv* **~·ness** *n*

peach[1] /pitʃ/ *n* **1** (tree with) juicy, round fruit with delicate yellowish-red skin and a rough stone-like seed; ⇨ the illus at fruit; yellowish-red. **2** (sl) person or thing greatly admired, e g a very attractive girl: *Isn't she/it a ~!*

peach[2] /pitʃ/ *vi* (now schoolboy sl) turn informer: *~ against/upon an accomplice.*

pea·cock /ˈpikok *with* i *as short as in 'peak'*/ *n* large male bird noted for its fine tail feathers. ⇨ the illus at rare. **ˈ~-ˈblue** *adj, n* bright blue (colour). **ˈpea-chick** *n* young pea-fowl. **ˈpea-fowl** *n* ~ or pea-hen. **ˈpea-hen** *n* female of the ~.

pea-jacket /ˈpi dʒækɪt/ *n* short double-breasted overcoat of thick woollen cloth, as worn by sailors.

peak[1] /pik/ *n* **1** pointed top, esp of a mountain ⇨ the illus at mountain; point, e g of a beard. **ˈP~ District,** area in Derbyshire, England having many ~s. **2** pointed front part of a cap; projecting brim (to shade the eyes). **3** narrow part of a ship's hold at the bow (*ˈfore~*) or stern (*ˈafter~*). **4** highest point in a record of figures that fluctuate: *~ hours of traffic,* times when the traffic is heaviest; *industry's ~ hours,* when consumption of electric current, etc is highest: *off-~ periods,* when traffic, consumption of current, etc is light: *off-~ flights to Rome,* during the less busy times, e g during hours of darkness. **peaked** *adj* having a ~: *~ed cap/roof.*

peak[2] /pik/ *vi* waste away: (in Shakespeare) *~ and pine.* **peaked** *pp* sharp-featured; thin, pale and weak-looking. **peaky** *adj* = peaked.

peal /pil/ *n* [C] **1** loud ringing of a bell or of a set of bells with different notes; changes rung upon a set of bells; set of bells tuned to each other. **2** loud echoing noise: *a ~ of thunder; ~s of laughter.* □ *vi, vt* **1** [VP2A,C] sound forth in a ~; ring out loudly. **2** [VP6A] cause to ring or sound loudly.

pea·nut /ˈpinʌt/ *n* groundnut. **ˈ~ ˈbutter,** paste of roasted ground ~s. **ˈ~ ˈoil,** oil pressed from ~s, used in cooking, etc.

pear /peə(r)/ *n* [C] (tree with) sweet, juicy fruit, usu tapering towards the stalk. ⇨ the illus at fruit.

pearl /pɜl/ *n* **1** silvery-white or bluish-white spherical formation found inside the shells of some oysters, valued as a gem: *a necklace of ~s; a ~ necklace.* **ˈ~-diver** *n* one who dives for ~-oysters. **ˈ~-fishery** *n* place where ~-oysters are fished up. **ˈ~-oyster** *n* kind in which ~s are found. **2** = mother-of-~: *~ buttons.* ⇨ mother(4). **3** small round fragment of various substances. **ˈ~-ˈbarley/-ˈsago** *nn* barley/sago rubbed into small ~-like grains. **4** sth that looks like a ~, e g a dew-drop; sb or sth very precious: *She's a ~ among women.* ***cast ~s before swine,*** (prov) offer sth valuable or beautiful to those who cannot appreciate it. □ *vi* fish for ~s: *go ~ing.* **~y** *adj* of, like, ornamented with, ~s. **P~y King/Queen,** costermonger wearing pearlies. **pearl·ies** *n pl* (the now festive) dress of some London costermongers, ornamented with many mother-of-~ buttons; (GB sl) teeth.

pear·main /ˈpeəmeɪn/ *n* variety of apple.

peas·ant /ˈpeznt/ *n* (not current in GB, Australia, Canada, New Zealand, US) countryman working on the land, either for wages or on a very small farm which he either rents or owns: (attrib) *~ labour.* ⇨ for GB, *smallholder,* at small and, for US, *sharecropper* at share[1](1). **~ry** /ˈpezntrɪ/ *n* (usu with *def art*) the ~s of a country; ~s as a class.

pease /piz/ *n* peas, (obs except in) **~-pudding.**

peat /pit/ *n* [U] plant material partly decomposed by the action of water, found in bogs, used in horticulture, and as a fuel: *a bag/bale of ~; a ˈ~-bog,* a marshy place where ~ is found; *a ~ fire,* one on which cut pieces of ~ are burnt as fuel. **peaty** *adj* of, like, smelling of, ~.

pebble /ˈpebl/ *n* small stone made smooth and round by being rolled in water, e g in a stream or on the seashore. **peb·bly** /ˈpebḷɪ/ *adj* covered with ~s: *a pebbly beach.*

pe·can /pɪˈkæn *US:* pɪˈkɑn/ *n* [C] (nut of a) kind of hickory tree growing in the Mississippi region of the U S A.

pec·cable /ˈpekəbl/ *adj* (formal) liable to sin.

pecca·dillo /ˌpekəˈdɪləʊ/ *n* (*pl* -loes or -los /-ləʊz/ small weakness in a person's character; small sin or fault.

pec·cary /ˈpekərɪ/ *n* (*pl* -ries) kind of wild pig found in America.

peck[1] /pek/ *n* measure of capacity for dry goods (= 2 gallons or approx 9 litres); *a ~ of beans;* (fig) a lot: *a ~ of troubles.*

peck[2] /pek/ *vi, vt* **1** [VP2A,C,3A,6A] (try to) strike with the beak: *hens ~ing at the corn; cocks ~ing (at) the hens;* (colloq) *~ at one's food,* (of a person) eat only small bits of food; eat without appetite. **ˈ~·ing order,** order (within a flock of poultry) in which each bird submits to ~ing and domination by stronger birds and itself ~s and dominates weaker birds; any similar arrangement in a group of human beings: *Poor Tom! He's at the bottom of the ~ing order,* is dominated by all the members of his group. **2** [VP6A] get or make by striking with the beak; *~ corn. The hens ~ed a hole in the sack.* **3** (colloq) kiss (sb's cheek, e g one's wife's) hurriedly from habit or a sense of duty rather than from affection. □ *n* **1** stroke with the beak; mark made by this. **2** (colloq) hurried, unemotional kiss. **~er** *n* (GB sl) human nose; (fig) courage; spirits. ***keep your ~er up,*** stay cheerful; don't let your spirits droop. **ˈ~·ish** /-ɪʃ/ *adj* (colloq) hungry.

pec·tin /ˈpektɪn/ *n* [U] (chem) compound similar to sugar, formed in fruits by ripening process and by heating, e g when fruit is made into jam. **pec·tic** /ˈpektɪk/ *adj* of ~; producing ~: *pectic acid.*

pec·toral /ˈpektərl/ *adj* **1** of, for, good for, diseases of, the chest or breast. *a ~ muscle/fin.* **2** worn on the chest or breast: *a ~ cross,* as worn by a bishop.

pecu·late /ˈpekjʊleɪt/ *vi, vt* embezzle. **pecu·la·tion** /ˌpekjʊˈleɪʃn/ *n* [U] peculating; [C] instance of this.

pe·cu·liar /pɪˈkjulɪə(r)/ *adj* **1** ~ ***(to),*** belonging exclusively; used, adopted, practised, only by: *customs ~ to these tribes; a style ~ to the 18th century; God's ~ people,* i e the Jews, who considered themselves God's elect people. **2** strange; unusual; odd. **3** particular; special: *a matter of ~ interest.* **~·ly** *adv* in a ~ manner: *~ly annoying,* more than usually annoying. **~·ity** /pɪˌkjulɪˈærətɪ/ *n* (*pl* -ties) **1** [U] the quality of being ~. **2** [C] sth distinctive or characteristic. **3** [C] sth odd or strange: *~ities of speech/dress/behaviour.*

pe·cuni·ary /pɪˈkjunɪərɪ *US:* -ɪerɪ/ *adj* (formal) of

money: ~ *aid; work without ~ reward.*

peda·gogue (US also **-gog**) /ˋpedəgog/ *n* schoolmaster; pedantic teacher. **peda·gogy** /ˋpedəgodʒɪ/ *n* [U] science of teaching. **peda·gog·ic** /ˈpedəˋgodʒɪk/, **peda·gogi·cal** /-ɪkl/ *adjj* of pedagogy.

pedal[1] /ˋpedl/ *n* lever (e g on a bicycle, sewing-machine, organ or piano) worked by the foot or feet; ⇨ the illus at **bicycle, keyboard**: (attrib) ~ *cyclists;* ~ *boats,* propelled by the use of ~s □ *vi,vt* (-ll-, US also -l-) [VP2A,C,6A] use a ~ or ~s (for playing an organ, riding a bicycle, etc); move or work by the use of a ~ or ~s: *The boy ~led away on his tricycle.*

pedal[2] /ˋpedl/ *adj* (zool) of the foot or feet.

ped·ant /ˋpednt/ *n* person who lays too much stress on book-learning, technical knowledge, rules and adherence to rules. **~ry** /ˋpedntrɪ/ *n* [U] tiresome and unnecessary display of learning; too much insistence upon formal rules; [C] instance of this. **pe·dan·tic** /pɪˋdæntɪk/ *adj* of or like a ~. **pe·danti·cally** /-klɪ/ *adv*

peddle /ˋpedl/ *vi,vt* **1** [VP2A] be a pedlar; go from house to house trying to sell small articles. **2** [VP6A] deal out in small quantities: *She loves to ~ gossip round the village.* **ped·dler** *n* = pedlar. **ped·dling** *adj* petty; trivial: *peddling details.*

ped·er·asty /ˋpedəræstɪ/ *n* sexual relations between a man and a boy. **ped·er·ast** *n* man who practices ~.

ped·estal /ˋpedɪstl/ *n* base of a column; base for a statue or other work of art; each of the two supports of a knee-hole writing-desk. Hence, ˋ~ *desk.* ***knock sb off his ~,*** show that he is no longer highly regarded. ***set sb on a ~,*** make him an object of high regard.

pe·des·trian /pɪˋdestrɪən/ *n* person walking in a street, etc: *~s killed in traffic accidents;* (attrib) **~ crossing,** street crossing specially marked, where ~s have priority over traffic. **~ precinct,** ⇨ **precinct.** □ *adj* **1** connected with walking. **2** (of writing, a person's way of making speeches, etc) prosaic; dull; uninspired. **~·ize** /-aɪz/ *vt* (colloq) convert (streets, etc) for the use of ~s only: *~ized shopping-centres.*

pedi·at·rics /ˈpidɪˋætrɪks/ *n* (with *sing v*) branch of medicine concerned with children and their illness. **pedia·tric·ian** /ˈpidɪəˋtrɪʃn/ *n* physician who specializes in ~.

pedi·cab /ˋpedɪkæb/ *n* (in some Asian countries) tricycle with one seat for the man in charge and a seat behind for two passengers, used as a form of public transport.

pedi·cure /ˋpedɪkjʊə(r)/ *n* treatment of the feet, toe-nails, corns, bunions, etc.

pedi·gree /ˋpedɪgri/ *n* **1** [C] line of ancestors: *proud of their long ~s;* [U] ancestry, esp ancient descent. **2** (attrib) having a line of descent that has been recorded: *~ cattle; a ~ poodle.*

pedi·ment /ˋpedɪmənt/ *n* (in Gk architecture) triangular part over the front of a building; similar part over the portico of a building in other styles of architecture. ⇨ the illus at **column.**

ped·lar, ped·dler /ˋpedlə(r)/ *n* person who goes from house to house peddling small articles.

ped·ometer /pɪˋdomɪtə(r)/ *n* device which measures the number of steps taken by a walker, and the approximate distance he walks.

pee /pi/ *vi, n* (colloq) (pass) urine: *Do you want to pee? I must have/go for a pee.*

peek /pik/ *vi* **~ at,** peep at. □ *n* quick look: *have a quick ~ over the fence.*

peek-a-boo /ˈpik ə ˋbu/ *n* game for amusing a small child, in which one covers and then uncovers the face, repeatedly, saying '~!' as one does this.

peel /pil/ *vt,vi* **1** [VP6A,15B] take the skin off (fruit, etc): *~ a banana; ~ potatoes.* **2** [VP2A,C] come off in strips or flakes: *These potatoes ~ easily,* the skin comes off them easily. *The wall-paper is ~ing off. After a day in the hot sun my skin began to ~/my face ~ed. The bark of plane-trees ~s off regularly. It was so hot that we all ~ed off* (= undressed) *and jumped into the lake.* □ *n* [U] skin of fruit, some vegetables, young shoots, etc: *candied ~,* ⇨ **candy. ~er** *n* (in compounds) device used for ~ing, e g potatoes. **~·ings** *n pl* parts ~ed off (esp of potatoes).

peeler /ˋpilə(r)/ *n* (out of date sl for) policeman.

peep[1] /pip/ *n* **1** short, quick look, often one taken secretly or inquisitively; incomplete view: *have a ~ at sb through the window.* **ˋ~-hole** *n* small opening in a wall, partition, etc through which one can have a ~. **ˋ~-show** *n* exhibition of small pictures to be seen through a magnifying lens in a small opening. **2** the first light (of day): *~ of day,* dawn. □ *vi* [VP2A,C] **1 ~ *(at),*** take a ~ (at); look slyly or cautiously: *~ through a keyhole at sth; neighbours ~ing at us from behind curtains.* **ˈ~ing ˋTom,** name used of a prurient person who spies on persons who think they are alone; voyeur. **2** come slowly or partly into view: *The moon ~ed out from behind the clouds.* **~er** *n* **1** person who ~s. **2** (sl) eye.

peep[2] /pip/ *n* [C] weak, shrill sound made by mice, young birds, etc □ *vi* make this sound.

pee·pul, pi·pal /ˋpipəl/ *n* large Indian fig-tree.

peer[1] /pɪə(r)/ *n* **1** equal in rank, merit or quality: *It will not be very easy to find his ~.* **2** (in GB) member of one of the degrees of nobility, e g duke, marquis, earl, viscount, baron. **3 ~ of the realm,** person with the right to sit in the House of Lords. **ˋlife ~,** one elected to the House of Lords for life only (contrasted with a **ˋhereditary ~**). **~ess** /ˋpɪəres/ *n* woman ~; wife of a ~(3). **~·less** *adj* without a ~(1); without equal.

peer[2] /pɪə(r)/ *vi* [VP2A,3A] **~ *at/into,*** look closely, as if unable to see well: *~ into dark corners; ~ing at her over his spectacles.*

peer·age /ˋpɪərɪdʒ/ *n* **1** the whole body of peers; rank of peer(3). ***raise sb to the ~,*** elect sb to the ~. **2** book containing a list of peers with their ancestry.

peeve /piv/ *vt* (colloq) vex; annoy. **peeved** *adj* (colloq) annoyed.

pee·vish /ˋpivɪʃ/ *adj* irritable. **~·ly** *adv* **~·ness** *n*

pee·wit /ˋpiwɪt/ = **pewit.**

peg[1] /peg/ *n* **1** wooden or metal pin or bolt, usu pointed at one end, used to fasten parts of woodwork together. ***a square peg in a round hole,*** a person unsuited to the position he fills. **2** pin driven into the ground to hold a rope (*a ˋtent-peg*), or fastened to a wall or door (*ˋhat and ˋcoat pegs*), or to mark a position or boundary. ***(buy sth) off the peg,*** (colloq) (buy clothes) ready-made (as if off a peg in a shop). **3 ˋclothes-peg,** device for holding laundered clothes in place on a line. **4** (fig) theme, pretext or excuse: *a peg on which to hang a sermon.* **5** wooden screw for tightening or loosening the string of a violin, etc. ***ˈtake sb ˋdown a peg (or two),*** humble him. **6**

(GB) drink, esp of whisky or brandy with soda-water. **7** piece of wood for stopping the vent of a cask, etc. **8** (colloq) wooden leg.

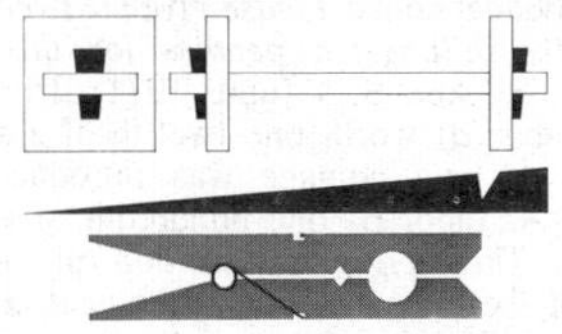
pegs

peg[2] /peg/ *vt,vi* (-gg-) **1** [VP6A,15B] fasten with pegs: *peg a tent down.* ***peg sb down,*** (fig) make him keep to a certain line of action, restrict him to the rules, etc. **2** [VP15B] ***peg sth out,*** mark by means of pegs fixed in the ground: *peg out a claim,* mark the boundaries by means of pegs, show (a score, esp at cribbage) by means of pegs. ***level pegging,*** (often fig) making progress at the same rate. **3** [VP6A,15B] (comm) keep (prices, etc) steady by buying and selling (stocks) freely at fixed prices; keep (wages) steady: *wage-pegging efforts that failed.* **4** [VP2C] ***peg away at,*** keep on working at. ***peg out,*** (colloq) die.

pei·gnoir /ˋpeɪnwɑ(r)/ *n* (archaic) woman's loose robe worn while dressing the hair or as a bath-robe.

pe·jor·at·ive /pɪˋdʒorətɪv *US:* -ˋdʒɔr-/ *adj* (abbr *pej* used in this dictionary) depreciatory; disparaging; deteriorating in use or meaning. **~·ly** *adv*

peke /pik/ *n* short for *pekinese (dog).*

pe·kin·ese /ˈpikɪˋniz/ *n* small Chinese dog with long, silky hair. ⇨ the illus at dog.

pe·koe /ˋpikəʊ/ *n* high grade of black tea.

pelf /pelf/ *n* [U] (usu contemptuous use) money.

peli·can /ˋpelɪkən/ *n* large water-bird with a large bill under which hangs a pouch for storing food. ⇨ the illus at water.

pe·lisse /peˋlis/ *n* (archaic) child's or woman's outdoor garment.

pel·let /ˋpelɪt/ *n* **1** small ball of sth soft, e g wet paper, bread, made, for example, by rolling between the fingers. **2** slug of small shot, e g as used from an air gun. **3** pill.

pell-mell /ˈpel ˋmel/ *adv* in a hurrying, disorderly manner.

pel·lu·cid /peˋlusɪd/ *adj* (liter, fig) very clear. **~·ly** *adv*

pel·met /ˋpelmɪt/ *n* valance or ornamental strip above a window or door to conceal a curtain rod.

pe·lota /pəˋləʊtə/ *n* [U] ball game popular in Spain, Latin America and the Phillippines, the players using a long basket strapped to the wrist to hit the ball against a wall.

pelt[1] /pelt/ *n* animal's skin with the fur or hair on it.

pelt[2] /pelt/ *vt,vi* **1** [VP6A,14] ***~ sth at sb; ~ sb with sth,*** attack by throwing things at: *~ sb with stones/snowballs/mud.* **2** [VP2C] (of rain, etc) beat down; fall heavily: *It was ~ing with rain. The rain was ~ing down. The hail was ~ing against the roof.* □ *n* ~ing. ***at full ~,*** (running) as fast as possible.

pel·vis /ˋpelvɪs/ *n* (*pl* pelves /ˋpelviz/) (anat) bony frame within the hip-bones and the lower part of the backbone, holding the kidneys, rectum, bladder, etc. ⇨ the illus at skeleton. **pel·vic** /ˋpelvɪk/ *adj* of the ~.

pem·mi·can /ˋpemɪkən/ *n* [U] dried lean meat beaten and mixed into cakes (as by N American Indians).

pen[1] /pen/ *n* **1** (formerly) quill-feather, pointed and split at the end, for writing with ink; (today) instrument with a pointed piece of split metal (ˋ*pen-nib*) fixed into a holder (ˋ*pen-holder*) of wood or other material. ⇨ also *ball(point)-pen* at ball[1](1) and *fountain-pen* at fountain. **2** (style of) writing: *make a living with one's pen.* **3** **ˈpen-and-ˋink,** (attrib) drawn with these: *a pen-and-ink sketch.* **ˋpen-friend** *n* person (e g in another country) with whom one has a friendship through exchanges of letters. **ˋpen·knife** *n* small folding knife, usu carried in the pocket. **pen·man·ship** /ˋpenmənʃɪp/ *n* art or style of handwriting. **ˋpen-name** *n* name used by a writer instead of his real name. **ˋpen-pusher** *n* (colloq) clerk. □ *vt* (-nn-) write (a letter, etc).

pen[2] /pen/ *n* **1** small enclosure for cattle, sheep, poultry, etc or other purposes. **2** **(ˋplay)-pen,** portable enclosure for a very small child to play in safety. **3** bomb-proof shelter for submarines. □ *vt* (-nn-) [VP15A,B] ***pen up/in,*** shut up in, or as in, a pen.

penal /ˋpinl/ *adj* connected with punishment: *~ laws; a ~ offence,* one for which there is legal punishment. **ˈ~ ˋservitude,** imprisonment with hard labour. **ˋ~ settlement/colony,** one used as a place of punishment. **~ly** /ˋpinl̩ɪ/ *adv*

pe·nal·ize /ˋpinl̩ɑɪz/ *vt* **1** [VP6A] make (sth) penal; declare to be punishable by law. **2** [VP14] ***~ sb (for sth),*** place at a disadvantage; give a penalty(2) to (a player, competitor, etc). **pe·nal·iz·ation** /ˈpinl̩ɑɪˋzeɪʃn *US:* -l̩ɪˋz-/ *n*

pen·alty /ˋpenltɪ/ *n* (*pl* -ties) **1** [U] punishment for wrongdoing, for failure to obey rules or keep an agreement; [C] what is imposed (imprisonment, payment of a fine, etc) as punishment; (fig) suffering which a wrongdoer brings upon himself or others: *Spitting forbidden: ~ £5. The ~* (e g in a business agreement) *for non-performance of contract is heavy.* **ˋ~ clause,** (comm) clause in a contract requiring payment for breaking it. ***on/under ~ of (death, etc),*** with (death, etc) as the ~: *forbidden under ~ of death.* **2** (in sport, competitions, etc) disadvantage to which a player or team must submit for breaking a rule. **ˋ~ area,** (football) part of the ground in front of the goal where a breach of the rules by defenders gives the opposing team the right to a free kick (*a ˋ~ kick*) at the goal: *The referee awarded a ~.* ⇨ the illus at football. **3** handicap imposed upon a player or team for winning a previous contest.

pen·ance /ˋpenəns/ *n* [U] punishment which one imposes upon oneself to show repentance, e g upon the advice of a priest. ***do ~ (for sth),*** perform an act of ~ (for sth).

pence /pens/ *n* ⇨ penny.

pen·chant /ˋpõʃõ *US:* ˋpentʃənt/ *n* taste, liking, inclination (*for*).

pen·cil /ˋpensl/ *n* instrument for drawing or writing with, esp of graphite or coloured chalk enclosed in wood or fixed in a metal holder; stick of cosmetic material: *an ˋeyebrow ~.* □ *vt* (-ll-, US also -l-) [VP6A] write, draw, mark, with a ~: *~led eyebrows.*

pen·dant /ˋpendənt/ *n* **1** ornament which hangs down, esp one attached to a necklet, bracelet, lustre attached to a chandelier, etc. **2** (naut) pennant.

pen·dent /ˈpendənt/ *adj* (formal) **1** hanging; overhanging: ~ *rocks.* **2** = pending.

pend·ing /ˈpendɪŋ/ *adj* waiting to be decided or settled: *The lawsuit was then* ~. □ *prep* **1** during: ~ *these discussions.* **2** until: ~ *his acceptance of the offer.*

pen·du·lous /ˈpendjʊləs *US:* -dʒʊləs/ *adj* (formal) hanging down loosely so as to swing freely: *the* ~ *nests of the weaver birds.*

pen·du·lum /ˈpendjʊləm *US:* -dʒʊləm/ *n* weighted rod hung from a fixed point so that it swings freely, esp one to regulate the movement of a clock. ***the swing of the*** ~, (fig) the movement of public opinion from one extreme to the other.

pen·etrable /ˈpenɪtrəbl/ *adj* (formal) that can be penetrated. **pen·etra·bil·ity** /ˌpenɪtrəˈbɪlətɪ/ *n*

pen·etrate /ˈpenɪtreɪt/ *vt, vi* **1** [VP6A] make a way into or through; (fig) see into or through; [VP3A] make a way (*into* or *through*): *The cat's sharp claws* ~*d my skin. The mist* ~*d (into) the room. He* ~*d their designs. Our eyes could not* ~ *the darkness. We soon* ~*d his disguise,* saw through it, knew who he really was. **2** ***be*** ~***d with,*** be inbued with: *be* ~*d with a desire for mystical experiences.* **pen·etrat·ing** *adj* **1** (of a person, his mind) able to see and understand quickly and deeply. **2** (voices, cries, etc) piercing; loud and clear. **pen·etrat·ing·ly** *adv*

pen·etra·tion /ˌpenɪˈtreɪʃn/ *n* **1** penetrating: *peaceful* ~, acquiring influence, control, etc without the use of force, e g by trade, supplying a country with capital. **2** mental quickness; ability to grasp ideas.

pen-friend /ˈpen frend/ ⇨ pen[1](3).

pen·etra·tive /ˈpenɪtreɪtɪv/ *adj* able to penetrate; intelligent.

pen·guin /ˈpengwɪn/ *n* seabird of the Antarctic with wings used for swimming. ⇨ the illus at water.

peni·cil·lin /ˌpenɪˈsɪlɪn/ *n* [U] antibiotic drug that, by changing the chemical environment of germs, prevents them from surviving or multiplying.

pen·in·sula /pəˈnɪnsjʊlə *US:* -nsələ/ *n* area of land, e g Italy, almost surrounded by water and connected to the mainland by an isthmus. **pen·in·su·lar** /-lə(r)/ *adj* of or like a ~.

pe·nis /ˈpinɪs/ *n* organ of copulation of a male animal.

peni·tence /ˈpenɪtəns/ *n* [C] ~ ***(for),*** sorrow and regret (for wrongdoing, sin).

peni·tent /ˈpenɪtənt/ *adj* feeling regret; showing regret or remorse. ~**·ly** *adv*

peni·ten·tial /ˌpenɪˈtenʃl/ *adj* of penitence or penance. ~**·ly** /-ʃlɪ/ *adv*

peni·ten·tiary /ˌpenɪˈtenʃərɪ/ *n* (*pl* -ries) prison for persons guilty of serious crimes, esp one in which reform of the prisoners is the main aim. □ *adj* of reformatory treatment.

pen-name /ˈpen neɪm/ ⇨ pen[1](3).

pen·nant /ˈpenənt/ *n* flag (usu long and narrow) used on a ship for signalling, identification, etc.

pen·ni·less /ˈpenɪləs/ *adj* without any money: *I'm* ~ *until pay-day.*

pen·non /ˈpenən/ *n* **1** long, narrow (usu triangular) flag, as used by a knight on his lance, by soldiers in lancer regiments, and on ships, e g in signalling. **2** (US) flag of this shape as a school banner, with the school's name or initials on it.

penn'orth /ˈpenəθ/ *n* = *pennyworth;* ⇨ penny(5).

penny /ˈpenɪ/ *n* (*pl* pence /pens/ when combined with numbers, as in *ˈsixpence, ˈtenpence, ˈeighteen-pence; pl* pennies /ˈpenɪz/ when used of individual coins: *Please give me twelve pennies for this shilling/ten pennies for this tenpence piece.*) ⇨ App 5. **1** (until 1971) British bronze coin (abbr **d**) worth one-twelfth of a shilling. **2** (since decimal coinage was introduced, 1971) **(new)** ~ (abbr **p**) one hundredth of an English pound: *These cigarettes are 30p /pi/ a packet.* **3** coin of the US and Canada, the cent. **4** (phrases, all pre-1971 in origin) ***(cost) a pretty*** ~, a good sum of money. ***in for a*** ~, ***in for a pound,*** sth that one has begun must be finished, whatever the cost may be. ~***-wise and pound foolish,*** careful in small matters and wasteful in large matters. ***turn an honest*** ~, earn a little money honestly. **5** (compounds) ˌ~ ˈ**dreadful,** (colloq) cheap popular literature. ˈ~ **pincher,** (colloq) miser. ˈ~ **pinching** *adj* ˈ~**-weight** *n* 24 grains, one-twentieth of an ounce Troy. ⇨ App 5. ˌ~ ˈ**whistle,** simple cheap wind instrument. ˈ~**-worth** (also **penn'orth** /ˈpenəθ/) *n* as much as can be bought for a ~: *a good/bad* ~*worth,* a good/bad bargain. **6** (from the use of pennies in coin-operated machines, locks on doors, etc). ***spend a*** ~, (colloq) visit a WC. ***the*** ~ ***dropped,*** the desired result was achieved, the meaning of a remark, etc was understood.

pe·nol·ogy /piˈnolədʒɪ/ *n* [U] study of the problems of legal punishment and prison management.

pen·sion[1] /ˈpenʃn/ *n* [C] regular payment made by the State to sb old (*Reˈtirement P*~, formerly *oldˈage* ~), disabled (e g *ˈwar* ~) or widowed, or by a former employer to an employee after long service: *retire on a* ~. ***draw one's*** ~, obtain it: *go to the Post Office to draw one's* ~. □ *vt* [VP6A, 15B] ~ ***sb off,*** grant or pay a ~ to: dismiss or allow to retire with a ~. ˈ~**·able** /-əbl/ *adj* (of services, posts, age, work, etc) entitling one to a ~. ~**er** *n* person who is receiving a ~.

pen·sion[2] /ˈpõsɪõ/ *n* boarding-house at which fixed rates are charged (by the week or month). ***en*** ~ /õ ˈpõsɪõ/, as a boarder.

pen·sive /ˈpensɪv/ *adj* deep in thought; seriously thoughtful: ~ *looks; looking* ~. ~**·ly** *adv* ~**·ness** *n*

pen·stock /ˈpen-stok/ *n* flood-gate; sluice.

pen·ta·gon /ˈpentəgən *US:* -gon/ *n* plane figure with five sides and five angles. **the P**~, building in Arlington, Virginia, headquarters of the US Armed Forces. **pen·tag·onal** /penˈtægənl/ *adj*

pen·tam·eter /penˈtæmɪtə(r)/ *n* (in English verse) line of five iambic feet.

Pen·ta·teuch /ˈpentətjuk/ *n* the first five books of the Bible.

pen·tath·lon /penˈtæθlən/ *n* (modern Olympic Games) contest in which each competitor takes part in five events (running, horseback riding, swimming, fencing and shooting with a pistol).

Pente·cost /ˈpentɪkost *US:* -kɔst/ *n* **1** Jewish harvest festival, fifty days after the Passover. **2** (esp US) Whitsunday, the seventh Sunday after Easter.

pent·house /ˈpenthaʊs/ *n* **1** sloping roof supported against a wall, esp one for a shelter or shed. **2** (orig US) apartment or flat built on the roof of a tall building.

pent-up /ˈpent ʌp/ *adj* repressed: ~ *feelings/fury.*

pen·ul·ti·mate /penˈʌltɪmət/ *n, adj* (word, syllable, event, etc which is) last but one.

pen·um·bra /pɪnˋʌmbrə/ *n* partly shaded region around the shadow of an opaque body (esp round the total shadow of the moon or earth in eclipse).

pen·uri·ous /pɪˋnjʊərɪəs/ *adj* (formal) poor; grudging; stingy: *a man who is ~ in his habits.* **~·ly** *adv* **~·ness** *n* **pen·ury** /ˋpenjʊrɪ/ *n* (formal) [U] poverty: *living in penury; reduced to penury.*

peon /ˋpiən/ *n* **1** (in Latin America) unskilled farm worker, esp one who is not wholly free. **2** (in India and Pakistan) office messenger; orderly. **ˋ~·age** /-ɪdʒ/ *n* [U] system of employing ~s(**1**); (legal) use of indebtedness to compel sb to work.

peony /ˋpiənɪ/ *n* (*pl* **-nies**) [C] garden plant with large round pink, red or white flowers.

people /ˋpipl/ *n* (**1** to **5** below collective, never *pl* in form but used with a *pl v*. Note that for one human being, it is preferable to use *man, woman, boy, girl* and not *person*, which, although useful in definitions, may be derogatory or formal). **1** persons in general: *streets crowded with ~. Some ~ are very inquisitive.* **2** those persons belonging to a place, or forming a social class: *The ~ in the village like the new doctor. Some ~ spend a lot of money on clothes.* **3** all the persons forming a State: *government of the ~, by the ~, for the ~; the P~'s Republic of China,* (official name). **4** those persons who are not nobles, not high in rank, position, etc. **5** (colloq) one's near relations: *You must come home with me and meet my ~, darling.* **6** (with *sing v* and in *pl*) race, tribe, nation: *the ~s of Asia; a brave and intelligent ~.* □ *vt* [VP6A] fill with ~; put ~ in: *a thickly ~d district.*

pep /pep/ *n* [U] (sl) vigour; spirit. **ˋpep pill,** one that stimulates the nervous system (usu one containing amphetamine). **ˋpep talk,** one intended to fill the listener(s) with spirit and energy. □ *vt* (-pp-) (usu) ***pep up,*** give energy to; liven up.

pep·per /ˋpepə(r)/ *n* **1** [U] hot-tasting powder made from the dried berries of certain plants, used to season food. **ˈ~-and-ˋsalt** *n* (colour of) cloth of dark and light wools woven together, with small dark and light dots. **ˋ~·corn** *n* the dried, black berry of the plant; (fig) a nominal rent. **ˋ~·pot/-box** *nn* small container with a perforated top from which ~ is sprinkled on food. **ˋ~-mill** *n* container in which ~corns are ground to powder and sprinkled on food. **ˋ~·mint** *n* **(a)** [U] kind of mint grown for its essential oil, used in medicine and confectionery. **(b)** [C] sweet of boiled sugar flavoured with ~mint. **2** (garden plant with a) red or green seed-pod (e g capsicum) which is used as a vegetable: *stuffed ~s.* □ *vt* [VP6A] **1** put ~ on (food). **2** pelt (sb) (with stones, shot, questions, etc). **~y** *adj* tasting of ~; (fig) hot-tempered: *a ~y old colonel.*

pep·sin /ˋpepsɪn/ *n* [U] liquid (an enzyme) produced in the stomach for helping to digest food. **pep·tic** /ˋpeptɪk/ *adj* digestive; of digestion or the digestive system: *a peptic ulcer.*

per /pɜ(r)/ *prep* **1** for each: *per annum* /ˋænəm/, for each year; *per diem* /ˋdiem/, for each day; *per pound; 15 rounds of ammunition per man; interest at 6 per cent,* (6%); *30 miles per gallon,* (abbr **m p g**). **2** by means of: *per post.*

per·ad·ven·ture /ˈperədˋventʃə(r) *US:* ˈpɜəd-/ *adv* (archaic) **1** perhaps. **2** (after *if* and *lest*) (old use) by chance: *If ~ you fail.* □ *n* (archaic) chance: *beyond* (*a*) *~,* beyond all doubt.

per·am·bu·late /pəˋræmbjʊleɪt/ *vi,vt* [VP6A,2A] walk through or over; walk up and down. **per·am·bu·la·tion** /pəˈræmbjʊˋleɪʃn/ *n*

per·am·bu·la·tor /pəˋræmbjʊleɪtə(r)/ *n* (common colloq abbr **pram**) four-wheeled carriage, pushed by hand, for a baby; baby-carriage (the usu word in US).

per·ceive /pəˋsiv/ *vt* [VP6A,9,10,18,19,25] (formal) become aware of, esp through the eyes or the mind: *On entering his house, we at once ~d him to be/~d that he was a man of taste.* **per·ceiv·able** /-əbl/ *adj*

per·cen·tage /pəˋsentɪdʒ/ *n* **1** rate or number per cent (= for each hundred). **2** proportion: *What ~ of his income is paid in income tax?*

per·cep·tible /pəˋseptəbl/ *adj* (formal) that can be perceived. **per·cep·tibly** /-əblɪ/ *adv* **per·cep·ti·bil·ity** /pəˈseptəˋbɪlətɪ/ *n*

per·cep·tion /pəˋsepʃn/ *n* [U] (formal) process by which we become aware of changes (through the senses of sight, hearing, etc); act or power of perceiving.

per·cep·tive /pəˋseptɪv/ *adj* (formal) having, connected with, perception; able to perceive; discerning. **~·ly** *adv*

perch[1] /pɜtʃ/ *n* kinds of freshwater fish with spiny fins, used as food.

perch[2] /pɜtʃ/ *n* **1** bird's resting-place, e g a branch; bar or rod provided, e g in a bird-cage, a hen-roost, for this purpose. **2** (colloq) high position occupied by a person; elevated and secure position: *come off your ~,* (colloq) stop being so superior (in manner, etc); *knock sb off his ~,* stop sb being too confident and superior. **3** (also *pole, rod*) measure of length, esp for land, $5\frac{1}{2}$ yds; *square ~,* $30\frac{1}{4}$ sq yds. ⇨ App 5. □ *vi,vt* **1** [VP2C] alight: *The birds ~ed upon the television aerial.* **2** [VP2C] (of a person) take up a position (usu on sth high): *~ed on stools at the bar.* **3** (chiefly in *pp*) (of buildings) be situated (on sth high): *a castle ~ed on a rock.*

per·chance /pəˋtʃɑns *US:* -ˋtʃæns/ *adv* (archaic) by chance; possibly.

per·cipi·ent /pəˋsɪpɪənt/ *adj* (formal) perceiving (quickly and keenly).

per·co·late /ˋpɜkəleɪt/ *vi,vt* [VP6A,2A,3A] **~ *(through),*** (of liquid) (cause to) pass slowly; filter: *Water ~s through sand. Has the water ~d through the coffee yet? We can make coffee by percolating boiling water through coffee. I'll ~ some coffee.* **per·co·lator** /-tə(r)/ *n* (esp) kind of coffee pot in which boiling water ~s through coffee (in a container near the top).

per·cussion /pəˋkʌʃn/ *n* the striking together of two (usu hard) objects; sound or shock produced by this. **the ˋ~ (section),** musical instruments played by ~, ⇨ p 632. **ˋ~ cap,** ⇨cap *n*(4). **~·ist** /-ɪst/ *n* player of ~ instruments.

per·di·tion /pəˋdɪʃn/ *n* [U] (formal) complete ruin; everlasting damnation.

per·egri·na·tion /ˈperəgrɪˋneɪʃn/ *n* [U] (formal) travelling; [C] journey.

per·emp·tory /pəˋremptərɪ *US:* ˋperəmptɔrɪ/ *adj* (formal) (of commands) not to be disobeyed or questioned; (of a person, his manner) (too) commanding; insisting upon obedience. **a ~ writ,** (legal) one that compels a defendant to appear in court. **per·emp·torily** /-trɪlɪ *US:* -tɔrḷɪ/ *adv*

per·en·nial /pəˋrenɪəl/ *adj* **1** continuing throughout the whole year. **2** lasting forever or for a very long time: *of ~ interest; the ~ philosophy.* **3** (of plants) living for more than two years. □ *n* ~

plant: *hardy*(1) ~s. **~ly** /-nɪəlɪ/ *adv*

per·fect[1] /ˈpɜfɪkt/ *adj* **1** complete with everything needed. **2** without fault; excellent: *a ~ wife.* **3** exact; accurate: *a ~ circle.* **4** having reached the highest point in training, skill, etc: *~ in the performance of one's duties.* **5** (gram) **the ~ tenses,** those composed of finites of *have* and a *pp*, e g 'He *has/had/will have written* the letter.' (present, past, future ~). **6** (attrib only) complete; utter unqualified: *a ~ stranger/fool; ~ nonsense.* **~·ly** *adv* quite; quite well; completely: *~ly happy/ satisfied.*

per·fect[2] /pəˈfekt/ *vt* [VP6A] make ~: *~ oneself in a foreign language.* **~·ible** /-əbl/ *adj* that can be ~ed. **~i·bil·ity** /pəˌfektəˈbɪlətɪ/ *n*

per·fec·tion /pəˈfekʃn/ *n* [U] **1** perfecting or being perfected: *busy with the ~ of detail.* **2** perfect quality or example: *It was the very ~ of beauty.* **3** best possible state; highest point attainable: *bring something to ~.* **4** (with *pl*) accomplishment(3). **~·ist** /-ɪst/ *n* **1** person who believes that moral ~ may be attained, that it is possible to live without sinning. **2** (colloq) person who is satisfied with nothing less than what he thinks to be perfect.

per·fer·vid /ˈpɜˈfɜvɪd/ *adj* (formal) extremely zealous or eager.

per·fidi·ous /pəˈfɪdɪəs/ *adj* (formal) treacherous; faithless (*to*). **~·ly** *adv* **~·ness** *n* **per·fidy** /ˈpɜfɪdɪ/ *n* [U] treachery; breaking of faith; [C] (*pl* -dies) instance of this.

per·for·ate /ˈpɜfəreɪt/ *vt, vi* [VP6A] make a hole or holes in; make rows of tiny holes (in paper) so that part may be torn off easily: *a ~d sheet of postage stamps; a ~ed ulcer.* **per·for·ation** /ˌpɜfəˈreɪʃn/ *n* **1** perforating or being ~d. **2** [C] series of small holes made in paper, etc e g as between postage stamps.

per·force /pəˈfɔs/ *adv* of necessity.

per·form /pəˈfɔm/ *vt, vi* **1** [VP6A] do (a piece of work, sth one is ordered to do, sth one has promised to do): *~ a task.* **2** [VP6A,2A] act (a play); play (music); sing, do tricks, etc before an audience: *~ 'Hamlet'; ~ skilfully on the flute. The seals ~ed well at the circus. Do you enjoy seeing ~ing animals?* **~er** *n* one who ~s, esp at a concert or other entertainment.

per·form·ance /pəˈfɔməns/ *n* **1** [U] performing: *faithful in the ~ of his duties.* **2** [C] notable action; achievement: *His innings of 150 was a fine ~. Are you satisfied with the ~ of your new car?* **3** [C] performing of a play at the theatre; public exhibition; concert: *two ~s a day; tickets for the afternoon ~. What a ~!* (derog) What shocking behaviour!

per·fume /ˈpɜfjum/ *n* [C,U] (kinds of prepared liquid with) sweet smell, esp from an essence of flowers. □ *vt* /pəˈfjum/ [VP6A] give a ~ to; put ~ on. **per·fumer** *n* person who makes and sells ~s.

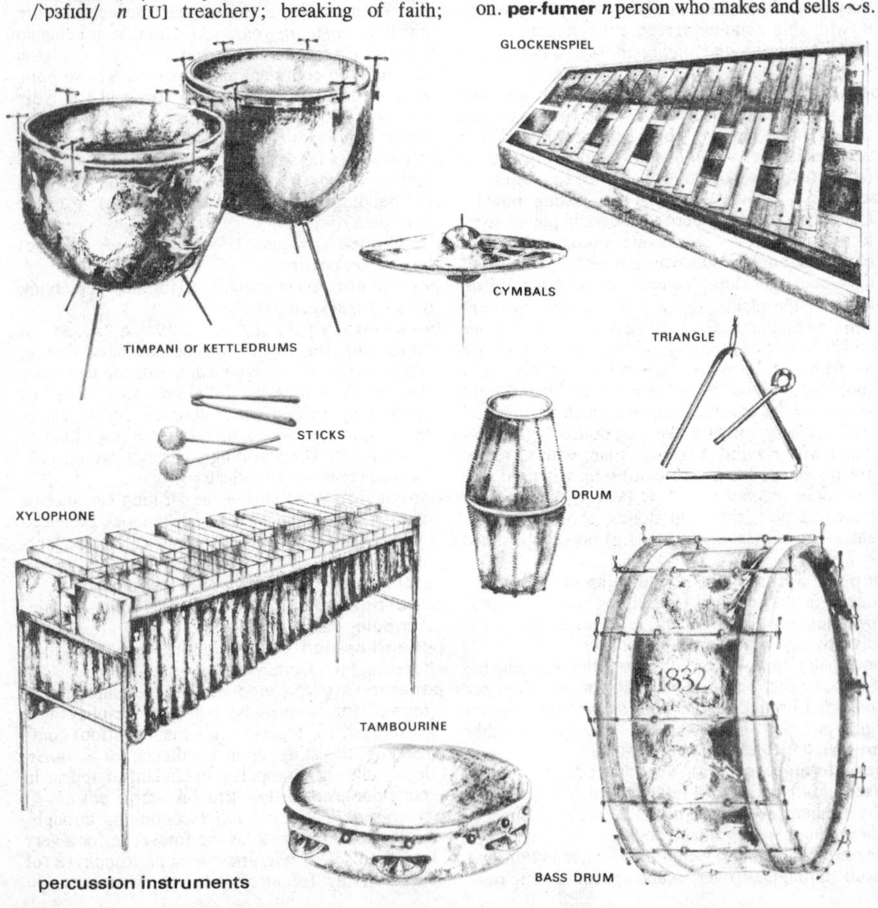

percussion instruments

per·func·tory /pəˈfʌŋktərɪ/ *adj* **1** done as a duty or routine but without care or interest: *a ~ inspection.* **2** (of persons) doing things in this way. **per·func·torily** /-trɪlɪ *US:* -tɔrlɪ/ *adv*

per·gola /ˈpɜgələ/ *n* structure of posts (forming an arbour, or over a garden path) for climbing plants.

per·haps /pəˈhæps/ *adv* possibly; it may be.

peri /ˈpɪərɪ/ *n* (in Persian myth) beautiful girl or woman; fairy; elf.

peri·gee /ˈperɪdʒi/ *n* point in an orbit of a planet or spacecraft at which it is closest to the earth.

peri·helion /ˌperɪˈhilɪən/ *n* point in a planet's orbit at which it is nearest to the sun.

peril /ˈperl/ *n* **1** [U] serious danger: *in ~ of one's life; do sth at one's ~,* at one's own risk. **2** [C] sth that causes danger: *the ~s of the ocean,* storm, shipwreck, etc. □ *vt* (-ll-, US also -l-) (liter, poet) (= *imperil,* which is more usu) put or bring into danger. **~·ous** /ˈperləs/ *adj* dangerous; full of risk. **~·ous·ly** *adv*

per·imeter /pəˈrɪmɪtə(r)/ *n* [C] (length of the) outer boundary of a closed figure, a military position, an airfield, etc.

period /ˈpɪərɪəd/ *n* [C] **1** length or portion of time marked off by events that recur, e g hours, days, months and years, fixed by events in nature: *20 teaching ~s a week; a lesson ~ of 45 minutes.* **2** portion of time in the life of a person, a nation, a stage of civilization, etc; division of geological time: *the ~ of the French Revolution. The actors will wear costumes of the ~/~ costumes,* i e of the time when the events of the play took place. *The house is 18th century and has ~ furniture,* i e of the same century. **3** full pause at the end of a sentence; full stop (.) marking this in writing and print: *put a ~ to sth,* bring it to an end. **4** (gram) complete sentence or statement, usu complex; (*pl*) rhetorical or flowery language. **5** time during which a disease runs its course; stage in the course of a disease: *the ~ of incubation,* the time during which it is latent. **6** (astron) time taken to complete one revolution. **7** occurrence of menstruation.

peri·odic /ˌpɪərɪˈodɪk/ *adj* occurring or appearing at regular intervals: *~ attacks of malaria; the ~ revolution of a heavenly body.* **ˈ~ ˈtable,** (chem) tabular arrangement of the elements according to their atomic weights. **peri·od·ical** /-kl/ *adj* = ~. □ *n* magazine or other publication which appears at regular intervals, e g monthly, quarterly. **peri·od·ically** /-klɪ/ *adv*

peri·pa·tetic /ˌperɪpəˈtetɪk/ *adj* going about from place to place; wandering: *the ~ religious teachers of India.*

pe·riph·ery /pəˈrɪfərɪ/ *n* (*pl* -ries) external boundary or surface. **pe·riph·eral** /-ərl/ *adj* of, on, forming, a ~.

pe·riph·ra·sis /pəˈrɪfrəsɪs/ *n* (*pl* -ses /-siz/) *roundabout way of speaking; circumlocution; (gram) using an auxiliary word in place of an inflected form.* **peri·phras·tic** /ˌperɪˈfræstɪk/ *adj* of ~, e g *'It does work'* for *'It works', 'the word of God'* for *'God's word'.*

peri·scope /ˈperɪskəʊp/ *n* instrument with mirrors and lenses arranged to reflect a view down a tube, etc so that the viewer may get a view as from a level above that of his eyes; used in submarines, trenches, etc.

per·ish /ˈperɪʃ/ *vi,vt* **1** (liter or journalism) [VP2A,C] be destroyed, come to an end, die: *Hundreds of people ~ed in the earthquake. I shall do it or ~ in the attempt.* **P~ the thought!** (liter) May even the thought (e g of a possible disaster) die! **2** (of cold or exposure; usu passive) reduce to distress or inefficiency: *We were ~ed with cold/hunger.* **3** [VP6A,2A] (cause to) lose natural qualities; decay: *The rubber belt on this machine has ~ed,* has lost its elasticity. *Oil on your car tyres will ~ them.* **~·able** /-əbl/ *adj* (esp of food) quickly or easily going bad. **~·ables** *n pl* (esp) goods that go bad if delayed in transit, e g fish, fresh fruit. **~er** *n* (sl) person who is unpleasant and disliked; naughty child: *Be off at once, you little ~er!*

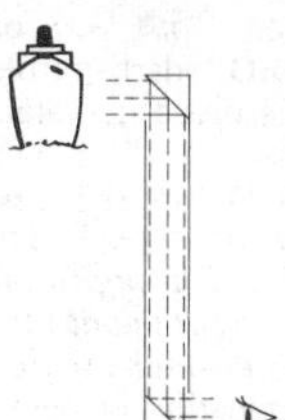
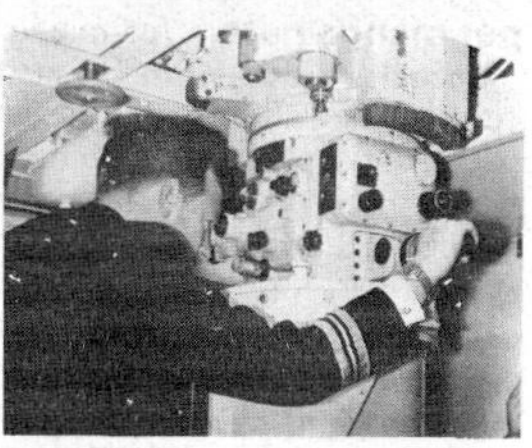

a submarine periscope

peri·style /ˈperɪstaɪl/ *n* row of columns surrounding a temple, court, etc; space surrounded.

per·ito·ni·tis /ˌperɪtəˈnaɪtɪs/ *n* [U] inflammation of the membrane lining the walls of the abdomen.

peri·wig /ˈperɪwɪg/ *n* = **wig.**

peri·winkle[1] /ˈperɪwɪŋkl/ *n* [U] creeping, evergreen plant with light-blue flowers.

peri·winkle[2] /ˈperɪwɪŋkl/ *n* [C] edible sea-snail with a spiral shell. ⇨ the illus at **mollusc.**

per·jure /ˈpɜdʒə(r)/ *vt* [VP6A] (reflex) **~ oneself,** knowingly make a false statement after taking an oath to tell the truth. **per·jurer** /ˈpɜdʒərə(r)/ *n* person who has ~d himself. **per·jury** /ˈpɜdʒərɪ/ *n* [U] act of perjuring oneself; [C] (*pl* -ries) wilful false statement.

perk[1] /pɜk/ *vi,vt* **1** [VP2C] **~ up,** (of a person) become lively and active (after depression, illness, etc). **2** [VP15B] **~ sb/sth up,** smarten; show interest, liveliness: *~ oneself up. The horse ~ed up its head,* lifted its head as a sign of interest. **~y** *adj* (-ier, -iest) **1** lively; showing interest or confidence. **2** self-assertive; impudent. **ˈ~·ily** /-əlɪ/ *adv* **~i·ness** *n*

perk[2] /pɜk/ *vi,vt* (colloq) percolate: *Is the coffee(-pot) ~ing yet? We ~ed some coffee.*

perk[3] /pɜk/ *n* (colloq; usu *pl*) perquisite: *an executive's salary with the usual ~s.*

perm /pɜm/ *n* (colloq abbr for) **1** permanent wave: *go to the hairdresser's for a ~.* **2** permutation (in football pools) □ *vt* give a ~ to.

per·ma·frost /ˈpɜməfrost *US:* -frɔst/ *n* permanently frozen subsoil (in the polar regions).

per·ma·nence /ˈpɜmənəns/ *n* [U] state of being permanent. **per·ma·nency** /-nənsɪ/ *n* (*pl* -cies) **1** [U] = permanence. **2** permanent thing, person or position: *Is your new job a permanency or merely temporary?*

per·ma·nent /ˈpɜmənənt/ *adj* not expected to change; going on for a long time; intended to last: *my ~ address; a ~ position in the Civil Service.* ⇨ **temporary. the ~ way,** finished railway track. **a ~ (wave),** style of hairdressing in which artificial waves or curls are put in the hair so that they last several months. **~·ly** *adv*

per·manga·nate /pə`mæŋgəneɪt/ *n* **'~ of `potash, 'potassium `~, ($KMnO_4$)** dark-purple crystalline salt which is used, dissolved in water, as an antiseptic and disinfectant.

per·meate /`pɜmɪeɪt/ *vt, vi* [VP6A,3A] ~ ***(through/among),*** pass, flow or spread into every part of: *water permeating (through) the soil; new ideas that have ~d (through/among) the people. The smell of cooking ~d through the flat.* **per·meation** /'pɜmɪ`eɪʃn/ *n* permeating or being ~d. **per·meable** /`pɜmɪəbl/ *adj* that can be ~d by fluids; porous. **per·mea·bil·ity** /'pɜmɪə`bɪlətɪ/ *n*

per·miss·ible /pə`mɪsəbl/ *adj* that may be permitted. **per·mis·sibly** /-əblɪ/ *adv*

per·mission /pə`mɪʃn/ *n* [U] act of allowing or permitting; consent: *with your ~,* if you will allow me; *give sb ~ to do sth. You have my ~ to leave. By whose ~ did you enter these gardens?*

per·miss·ive /pə`mɪsɪv/ *adj* giving permission: *~ legislation,* that gives powers to do sth but does not order that it shall be done. **the '~ so`ciety,** (in GB, 1967 onwards) term used for social changes, including greater sexual freedom, homosexual law reform, abolition of censorship in the theatre, frank discussion of hitherto taboo subjects, increased drug-taking, etc. **~·ness** *n*

per·mit /pə`mɪt/ *vt, vi* (-tt-) **1** [VP6A,C,17] allow: *weather ~ting. Smoking not ~ted in this cinema. Circumstances do not ~ me to help you/do not ~ my helping you.* **2** [VP3A] ***~ of,*** (formal) admit of: *The situation does not ~ of any delay,* There must be no delay. □ *n* /`pɜmɪt/ [C] written authority to go somewhere, do sth, etc: *You won't get into the atomic research station without a ~.*

per·mu·ta·tion /'pɜmjʊ`teɪʃn/ *n* [C] (maths) change in the order of a set of things arranged in a group; any one such arrangement: *The ~s of x, y and z are xyz, xzy, yxz, yzx, zxy, zyx.*

per·mute /pə`mjut/ *vt* [VP6A] change the order of.

per·ni·cious /pə`nɪʃəs/ *adj* ~ ***(to),*** harmful, injurious: *~ habits; ~ to the welfare of society; ~ anaemia,* a severe kind, often fatal. **~·ly** *adv* **~·ness** *n*

per·nick·ety /pə`nɪkətɪ/ *adj* (colloq) fussy; worrying about trifles.

per·or·ation /'perə`reɪʃn/ *n* (formal) last part of a speech; summing up.

per·ox·ide /pə`roksaɪd/ *n* (esp) *~ of hydrogen,* (H_2O_2) colourless liquid used as an antiseptic and to bleach hair. ***a ~ blonde,*** woman with hair bleached with ~.

per·pen·dicu·lar /'pɜpən`dɪkjʊlə(r)/ *adj* **1** at an angle of 90° (*to* another line or surface). **2** upright; crossing the horizontal at an angle of 90°: (archit; often **P~**) of the style of English Gothic architecture of the 14th and 15th cc, marked by vertical lines in the tracery of its windows. □ *n* [C] ~ line; [U] ~ position: *The wall is a little out of the ~.* **~·ly** *adv*

per·pe·trate /`pɜpɪtreɪt/ *vt* [VP6A] commit (a crime, an error); be guilty of (sth wrong or sth considered outrageous): *~ a crime/a blunder/a frightful pun.* **per·pe·tra·tor** /-tə(r)/ *n* **per·pe·tra·tion** /'pɜpɪ`treɪʃn/ *n*

per·pet·ual /pə`petʃʊəl/ *adj* **1** never-ending; going on for a long time or without stopping. **'~ `motion,** the motion of a machine, if such could be invented, which would go on for ever without a continuing source of energy. **2** continual; often repeated: *She's tired of their ~ chatter.* **~ly** /-ʃʊəlɪ/ *adv*

per·petu·ate /pə`petʃʊeɪt/ *vt* [VP6A] preserve from being forgotten or from going out of use: *~ the memory of a great statesman by erecting a statue of him.* **per·petu·ation** /pə'petʃʊ`eɪʃn/ *n*

per·petu·ity /'pɜpɪ`tjuətɪ *US:* -`tu-/ *n* (*pl* -ties) **1** [U] state of being perpetual. ***in ~,*** for ever. **2** [C] (legal) perpetual annuity or possession.

per·plex /pə`pleks/ *vt* [VP6A,14] **1** puzzle; bewilder: *~ sb with questions.* **2** make more complex or intricate. *Don't ~ the issue.* **per·plexed** *adj* puzzled; complicated. **~·ed·ly** /-ɪdlɪ/ *adv* **~·ity** /-ətɪ/ *n* (*pl* -ties) **1** [U] ~ed condition; mental difficulty caused by doubt: *He looked at us in ~ity.* **2** [C] perplexing thing; cause of bewilderment.

per·qui·site /`pɜkwɪzɪt/ *n* [C] profit, allowance, etc given or looked upon as one's right, in addition to regular wages or salary: *The salesman's ~s include the use of his firm's car out of business hours. Politics in Britain used to be the ~ of the great landowners.* ⇨ **perk**[3].

perry /`perɪ/ *n* [U] drink made from the fermented juice of pears. ⇨ **cider**.

per·se·cute /`pɜsɪkjut/ *vt* **1** [VP6A] punish, treat cruelly, esp because of religious beliefs. **2** allow no peace to; worry: *~ a man with questions.* **per·se·cu·tor** /-tə(r)/ *n* **per·se·cu·tion** /'pɜsɪ`kjuʃn/ *n* **1** [U] persecuting or being ~d: *suffer persecution for one's religious beliefs.* **2** [C] instance of this (in history, etc): *the numerous persecutions of the Jews.*

per·se·vere /'pɜsɪ`vɪə(r)/ *vi* [VP2A,3A] ~ ***(at/in/with),*** keep on steadily, continue (esp sth difficult or tiring): *~ in one's studies.* **per·se·ver·ing** *adj* **per·se·ver·ing·ly** *adv* **per·se·ver·ance** /-rns/ *n* [U] constant effort to achieve something; steadfastness.

Per·sian /`pɜʃn *US:* `pɜʒn/ *n, adj* (inhabitant) of Persia or Iran; language of the people of Persia (now Iran): *~ carpets; ~ cats,* with long, silky hair.

per·si·flage /`pɜsɪflɑʒ/ *n* [U] banter; light, good-humoured teasing.

per·sim·mon /pə`sɪmən/ *n* (tree bearing) soft yellow fruit which becomes sweet, when completely ripe, esp when softened by frost.

per·sist /pə`sɪst/ *vi* **1** [VP3A] ~ ***in sth/in doing sth,*** refuse, in spite of argument, opposition, failure, etc to make any change in (what one is doing, one's beliefs, etc): *She ~s in wearing that old-fashioned hat.* ***~ with,*** continue to work hard at. **2** [VP2A] continue to exist: *The fog is likely to ~ in most areas.* **~·ence** /-əns/ *n* [U] ~ing or being ~ent: *The ~ence of a high temperature in the patient puzzled the doctor.* **~·ent** /-ənt/ *adj* ~ing; continuing; occurring again and again: *~ent attacks of malaria.* **~·ent·ly** *adv*

per·son /`pɜsn/ *n* **1** man, woman (which are usu to be preferred, as is *people* for *persons;* ~ is often derog except when official or impersonal): *Who is this ~? There's a young ~* (usu = woman) *to see you. Any ~* (= Anyone) *leaving litter in the park will be prosecuted.* **~-to-~ call,** (of a telephone call) made (via the operator) to a particular ~ and charged for only from the time that ~ answers the phone. **2** living body of a human being. ***in ~,*** physically present: *I shall be present at the meeting in ~,* I shall be there myself (instead of sending sb to represent me). *Will you apply for the* *position by letter or in* ~. *She found a good friend in the* ~ *of her landlady,* Her landlady became a good friend to her. *Offences against the* ~ (e g assaults, bodily attacks) *are punished severely.* **3** (gram) each of three classes of personal pronouns: *the first* ~ (I, we), *the second* ~ (you) *and the third* ~ (he, she, it, they).

per·sona /pɜˋsəʊnə/ *n* (psych) role that a person assumes to show his conscious intentions to himself and others. **ˈ~ ˋgrata** /ˋgrɑtə/, (Lat) person who is acceptable, esp a diplomat who is acceptable to a foreign government. **ˈ~ ˈnon ˋgrata** /ˈnon ˋgrɑtə/, one who is not acceptable in this way.

per·son·able /ˋpɜsn̩əbl/ *adj* good-looking; handsome.

per·son·age /ˋpɜsn̩ɪdʒ/ *n* (important) person; person of distinction.

per·sonal /ˋpɜsnl/ *adj* **1** private; individual; of a particular person: *My* ~ *affairs/needs/opinions; your* ~ *rights. I have something* ~ *to discuss with you,* either my own or your intimate affairs. **ˋ~ column,** (in a newspaper, etc) column in which private messages or advertisements appear. **2** done or made by a person himself: *a* ~ *interview. The Prime Minister made a* ~ *appearance at the meeting,* appeared in ~ instead of sending one of his colleagues. **3** done or made for a particular person: *provide a* ~ *service for sb; give sb one's* ~ *attention. He did me a* ~ *favour,* one directed to me and by him. **ˈ~ asˋsistant,** one who helps an official, etc in an office, government department, etc usu doing more than a secretary, e g by making travel arrangements, interviewing people. **4** of the body: *P~ cleanliness is important to health as well as to appearance.* **5** of the nature of a human being: *Do you believe in a* ~ *God?* **6** of or about a person in a critical or hostile way: *I object to such highly* ~ *remarks. Let's not be too* ~. **7 ˈ~ ˋproperty/eˋstate,** (legal) temporal or movable property, not land. ⇨ *real estate* at real[1](2). **8** (gram) **~ pronoun,** of the three persons(3): *I, we, you, he, she, it, they.* □ *n* [C] short newspaper item about a particular person. **~ly** /-nl̩ɪ/ *adv* **1** in one's own person, not through an agent: *He conducted me ~ly through the mansion. She likes ~ly conducted tours,* holiday tours with a courier or guide who accompanies those making the tour. **2** speaking for oneself; for one's own part: *P~ly I see no objection to your joining us.*

per·son·al·ity /ˈpɜsəˋnælətɪ/ *n* (*pl* **-ties**) **1** [U] state of being a person; existence as an individual: *respect the* ~ *of a child.* **2** [C,U] qualities that make up a person's character: *a man with little* ~; *a woman with a strong* ~. *They both have striking personalties.* **3** [C] (mod use) person, esp one who is well known in certain circles (though perhaps quite unknown in other circles): *personalities of the stage and screen; a T V* ~, sb known to television viewers. **ˋ~ cult,** practice of giving fervent admiration, devotion, etc to a ~, esp a political leader, e g as to Stalin in the USSR. **4** (*pl*) impolite remarks about sb's looks, habits, etc: *indulge in personalities,* utter such remarks.

per·son·al·ize /ˋpɜsnl̩ɑɪz/ *vt* [VP6A] **1** personify. **2** have (sth) printed with one's address (*~d stationery*) or monogrammed with one's initials (*~d shirts, handkerchiefs*).

per·son·alty /ˋpɜsnltɪ/ *n* [U] (legal) personal estate.

per·son·ate /ˋpɜsəneɪt/ *vt* [VP6A] **1** play the part of (a character in a drama). **2** = impersonate (the more usu word). **per·son·ation** /ˈpɜsəˋneɪʃn/ *n*

per·son·ify /pəˋsonɪfɑɪ/ *vt* (*pt,pp* **-fied**) [VP6A] **1** regard or represent (sth) as a person: ~ *the sun and moon,* by using 'he' and 'she'. **2** be an example of (a quality): *That man personifies avarice/is avarice personified.* **per·soni·fi·ca·tion** /pəˈsonɪfɪˋkeɪʃn/ *n* **1** [U] ~ing or being personified; [C] instance of this. **2** (usu *sing* with *def art*) striking example of a quality: *He's the personification of selfishness.*

per·son·nel /ˈpɜsnˋel/ *n* (*sing* or *pl v*) staff; persons employed in any work, esp public undertakings and the armed forces: *There were five airline* ~ *on the plane that crashed. naval* ~; *a ˋ~ officer/manager,* one employed to deal with relationships between individual employees, their problems, grievances, etc. *Please report to* ~, the ~ department or manager.

per·spec·tive /pəˋspektɪv/ *n* **1** [U] the art of drawing solid objects on a flat surface so as to give the right impression of their relative height, width, depth, distance, etc; [C] drawing so made. ***in/out of* ~,** drawn/not drawn according to the rules of ~. **2** [U] apparent relation between different aspects of a problem: ***in the/its right/wrong* ~,** in the right/wrong relationship; with/without exaggeration or neglect of any aspects: *You must get the story in (its right)* ~. *He sees things in their right* ~. **3** [C] (liter, fig) view; prospect: *a* ~ *of the nation's history; a distorted* ~ *of the man's true intentions.*

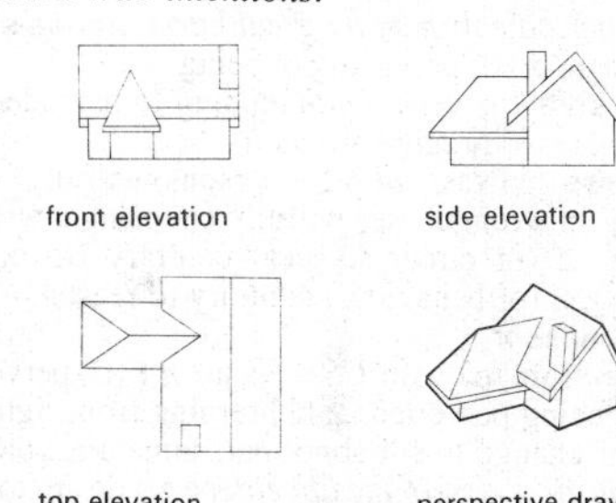

perspective and elevation

per·spex /ˋpɜspeks/ *n* [U] (P) tough unsplinterable plastic material used as a substitute for glass (e g in the windscreens of cars).

per·spi·ca·cious /ˈpɜspɪˋkeɪʃəs/ *adj* (formal) quick to judge and understand. **per·spi·cac·ity** /ˈpɜspɪˋkæsətɪ/ *n* [U].

per·spicu·ous /pəˋspɪkjʊəs/ *adj* (formal) expressed clearly; expressing things clearly. **~ly** *adv* **~·ness** *n* **per·spi·cu·ity** /ˈpɜspɪˋkjuətɪ/ *n*

per·spire /pəˋspɑɪə(r)/ *vi* [VP2A] sweat. **per·spir·ation** /ˈpɜspəˋreɪʃn/ *n* [U] sweat; sweating.

per·suade /pəˋsweɪd/ *vt* **1** [VP11,14] ***~ sb that; ~ sb of sth,*** convince (sb): *How can I* ~ *you of my sincerity/that I am sincere?* **2** [VP17A] cause (sb) by reasoning (to do sth): *We ~d him/He was ~d to try again.* **3** [VP14] ***~ sb into/out of doing sth,*** cause sb to do/stop doing sth, etc; thinking. Can you ~ her out of her foolish plans? **per·suad·able** /-əbl/ *adj*

per·sua·sion /pəˋsweɪʒn/ *n* **1** [U] persuading or being persuaded; power of persuading. **2** [U] conviction; belief (the usu word): *It is my ~ that....* **3** [C] group or set holding a particular belief: *men of various (religious) ~s.*

per·sua·sive /pə`sweɪsɪv/ *adj* able to persuade; convincing: *She has a ~ manner.* **~·ly** *adv* **~-ness** *n*

pert /pɜt/ *adj* **1** saucy; not showing proper respect: *a ~ child/answer.* **2** (US) lively; sprightly. **~·ly** *adv* **~·ness** *n*

per·tain /pə`teɪn/ *vi* [VP3A] **~ to,** (formal) belong as a part or accessory; have reference; be appropriate: *the enthusiasm ~ing to youth; the mansion and the lands ~ing to it.*

per·ti·na·cious /ˌpɜtɪ`neɪʃəs *US:* -tn̩`eɪʃəs/ *adj* (formal) not easily giving up (what has been started); determined. **~·ly** *adv* **per·ti·nac·ity** /ˌpɜtɪ`næsətɪ *US:* -tn̩`æ-/ *n* [U].

per·ti·nent /`pɜtɪnənt *US:* -tn̩ənt/ *adj* **~ (to),** (formal) referring directly: *remarks not ~ to the subject under discussion; a ~ reply.* **~·ly** *adv* **per·ti·nence** /-əns/ *n* [U].

per·turb /pə`tɜb/ *vt* [VP6A] (formal) trouble; make anxious: *~ing rumours; a man who is never ~ed.* **per·tur·ba·tion** /ˌpɜtə`beɪʃn/ *n* [U] ~ing or being ~ed.

pe·ruke /pə`ruk/ *n* long wig.

pe·ruse /pə`ruz/ *vt* [VP6A] (formal) read carefully. **pe·rusal** /pə`ruzl/ *n* [C,U] act of reading carefully.

Peru·vian /pə`ruvɪən/ *adj* of Peru: *~ bark,* of the cinchona tree, the source of quinine. □ *n* native of Peru.

per·vade /pə`veɪd/ *vt* [VP6A] spread through every part of: *The subversive ideas that ~ all these periodicals may do great harm.* **per·va·sion** /pə`veɪʒn/ *n* [U] pervading or being ~d.

per·va·sive /pə`veɪsɪv/ *adj* tending to pervade: *~ influences.* **~·ly** *adv* **~·ness** *n*

per·verse /pə`vɜs/ *adj* **1** (of persons) wilfully continuing in wrongdoing; wilfully choosing a wrong course. **2** (of circumstances) contrary (to one's wishes). **3** (of behaviour) contrary to reason. **~·ly** *adv* **~·ness** *n*

per·ver·sion /pə`vɜʃn *US:* -`vɜʒn/ *n* **1** [U] perverting or being perverted. **2** [C] turning from right to wrong; change to sth abnormal, unnatural, etc: *a ~ of justice; a ~ of the appetite,* e g a desire to eat grass, as Nebuchadnezzar had; *sexual ~s.*

per·ver·sity /pə`vɜsətɪ/ *n* (*pl* **-ties**) [U] being perverse; [C] perverse act.

per·vert /pə`vɜt/ *vt* [VP6A] **1** turn (sth) to a wrong use. **2** cause (a person, his mind) to turn away from right behaviour, beliefs, etc: *~ (the mind of) a child. Did Socrates really ~ the youth of Athens? Do pornographic books ~ those who read them?* □ *n* /`pɜvɜt/ ~ed person; person whose behaviour deviates from what is normal, e g in sexual practices.

pe·seta /pə`seɪtə/ *n* unit of currency in Spain.

pesky /`peskɪ/ *adj* (colloq) troublesome; annoying.

peso /`peɪsəʊ/ *n* unit of currency in many Latin American countries and the Philippines.

pes·sary /`pesərɪ/ *n* (*pl* **-ries**) (med) any of various devices placed and left to dissolve in the vagina.

pessi·mism /`pesɪm-ɪzm/ *n* [U] tendency to believe that the worst thing is most likely to happen, that everything is essentially evil. **pes·si·mist** /-ɪst/ *n* person subject to ~. **pes·si·mis·tic** /ˌpesɪ`mɪstɪk/ *adj* **pessi·mis·ti·cally** /-klɪ/ *adv*

pest /pest/ *n* [C] **1** troublesome or destructive thing, animal, etc; (colloq) child who is a nuisance: *garden ~s,* e g insects, mice, snails; *`~ control,* the use of various methods to get rid of ~s. **2** (old use) pestilence. **`~-house** *n* (formerly) hospital for plague or other infectious diseases. **pes·ti·cide** /`pestɪsaɪd/ *n* substance used to destroy ~s.

pes·ter /`pestə(r)/ *vt* [VP6A,17,14] **~ sb with sth/for sth/to do sth,** annoy; trouble: *be ~ed with flies/with requests for help; ~ sb for money; ~ sb to help.*

pes·tif·er·ous /pe`stɪfərəs/ *adj* causing disease; morally dangerous.

pes·ti·lence /`pestɪləns/ *n* [C,U] (any kind of) fatal epidemic disease, esp bubonic plague. **pes·ti·lent** /-ənt/, **pes·ti·len·tial** /ˌpestɪ`lenʃl/ *adjj* **1** like a ~; carrying infection. **2** (colloq) extremely annoying or objectionable: *These pestilential flies/children give me no peace.*

pestle /`pesl/ *n* stick with a thick end used in a mortar for pounding or crushing things. □ *vt* crush in (or as in) a mortar.

pet[1] /pet/ *n* **1** (often attrib) animal, etc kept as a companion, treated with care and affection, e g a cat or a dog: *a `pet shop,* one where pets, e g dogs, canaries, tortoises are sold. **2** person treated as a favourite: *Mary is the teacher's pet.* **3** sb specially loved or lovable: *make a pet of a child. She's a perfect pet,* (colloq) has very winning ways, is very lovable. **pet aversion,** sth or sb most disliked: *Cowboy films are her pet aversion.* **`pet-name.** name other than the real name, used affectionately. □ *vt* (**-tt-**) fondle; treat with affection; kiss and caress: *silly women petting their poodles.*

pet[2] /pet/ *n* fit of ill temper, esp about sth trifling: *in one of her pets.*

petal /`petl/ *n* one of the leaf-like divisions of a flower: *`rose ~s.* ⇨ the illus at **flower. pet·al·led** (US **pet·aled**) /`petld/ *adj* having ~s.

pe·tard /pe`tɑd/ *n* kind of bomb used in former times to break down doors, gates, walls, etc. ***hoist with one's own ~,*** (prov) caught or injured by what one intended as a snare for others.

peter /`pitə(r)/ *vi* **~ out,** (of supplies, ect) come gradually to an end.

Peter /`pitə(r)/ *n* **rob ~ to pay Paul,** take from one to give to another. **ˈblue `peter,** blue flag with a white square, flown by a ship before leaving port.

pe·ter·sham /`pitəʃəm/ *n* [C] (in the 19th c) heavy overcoat of thick woollen material; [U] cloth used for this.

pe·tite /pə`tit/ *adj* (of a woman) small, slender, neat and dainty.

pe·ti·tion /pɪ`tɪʃn/ *n* [C] **1** prayer; earnest request; appeal (esp a written document signed by a large number of people). **2** formal application made to a court of law. □ *vt,vi* **1** [VP6A,17,11,14] ***~ sb (for sth/to do sth/that...),*** make a ~ to, e g the authorities: *~ Parliament to redress grievances.* **2** [VP3A] **~ for,** ask earnestly or humbly: *~ for a retrial.* **~er** *n* one who ~s, esp the plaintiff in a divorce suit.

pet·rel /`petrl/ *n* long-winged black and white seabird. ⇨ the illus at **water. stormy ~,** (fig) person whose coming causes, e g social or industrial unrest.

pet·rify /`petrɪfaɪ/ *vt,vi* (*pt,pp* **-fied**) [VP6A,2A] (cause to) change into stone; (fig) take away power to think, feel, act, etc (through terror, surprise, etc): *petrified with terror.* **pet·ri·fac·tion** /ˌpetrɪˈfækʃn/ *n* ~ing or being petrified; petrified substance.

petro- *pref* **~-chemical** *n* chemical substance derived from petroleum or natural gas.

pet·rol /ˈpetrl/ *n* [U] refined petroleum used as a fuel in internal combustion engines (US = *gasoline*): *fill up with ~; stop at the next ˈ~ station; the ˈ~ tank.*

pe·tro·leum /pɪˈtrəʊlɪəm/ *n* [U] mineral oil (vegetable in origin, from forests in prehistoric times) found underground and obtained from wells; used in various forms (petrol, paraffin, etc) for lighting, heating and driving machines. ˌ**~ ˈjelly** *n* [U] semi-solid substance obtained from ~, used as a lubricant and in ointments.

pe·trol·ogy /pɪˈtrolədʒɪ/ *n* [U] the study of rocks.

pet·ti·coat /ˈpetɪkəʊt/ *n* woman's under-skirt. **~ government,** rule by, authority of, women over men.

pet·ti·fog·ging /ˈpetɪfogɪŋ/ *adj* (of persons) worrying about small and unimportant details; (of methods) unnecessarily concerned with small matters.

pet·tish /ˈpetɪʃ/ *adj* **1** (of a person) having short and often repeated fits of ill temper, like a spoiled child. **2** (of remarks, acts) said or done in a fit of ill temper. **~·ly** *adv* **~·ness** *n*

petty /ˈpetɪ/ *adj* **(-ier, -iest) 1** small; unimportant: *~ troubles/details; ~ regulations enforced by ~ officials.* **2** on a small scale: *~ farmers/shopkeepers.* **3** having or showing a narrow mind; mean: *~ spite.* **4 ~ cash,** (business) money for or from small payments. **~ larceny,** theft of articles of little value. **~ officer,** naval officer below commissioned rank. **pet·tily** /ˈpetəlɪ/ *adv* **pet·ti·ness** *n*

petu·lant /ˈpetjʊlənt *US:* -tʃʊ-/ *adj* unreasonably impatient or irritable. **~·ly** *adv* **petu·lance** /-əns/ *n* [U].

pe·tu·nia /pɪˈtjunɪə *US:* -ˈtu-/ *n* [C] garden plant with funnel-shaped flowers of various colours.

pew /pju/ *n* bench with a back, usu fixed to the floor, in a church: *empty pews at morning service;* (colloq) seat. **ˈpew-opener** *n* person who conducted persons to their seats when, in former times, family pews were enclosed and had doors.

pe·wit, pee·wit /ˈpiwɪt/ *n* lapwing; kind of mountain plover, named after its cry.

pew·ter /ˈpjutə(r)/ *n* [U] grey alloy of lead and tin; kitchen vessels made of this: *a good collection of ~;* (attrib) *~ mugs/dishes.*

pe·yote /peɪˈəʊtɪ/ *n* Mexican cactus from which is derived a drug (*mescaline*) which causes hallucinations.

pfen·nig /ˈfenɪg/ *n* German copper coin, one hundredth of a mark.

phae·ton /ˈfeɪtn *US:* ˈfeɪətən/ *n* (in former times) light, four-wheeled open carriage, usu drawn by a pair of horses.

phago·cyte /ˈfægəsaɪt/ *n* sort of leucocyte (blood-cell) capable of guarding the system against infection by absorbing microbes.

phal·anx /ˈfælæŋks/ *n* (*pl* **~es** or **phalanges** /fəˈlændʒiz/) **1** (in ancient Greece) body of soldiers in close formation for fighting. **2** number of persons banded together for a common purpose. **3** (anat) bone in a finger or toe. ⇨ the illus at **skeleton.**

phal·lus /ˈfæləs/ *n* image of the penis, as a symbol of generative power. **phal·lic** /ˈfælɪk/ *adj* of a ~: *phallic symbols/emblems.*

phan·tasm /ˈfæntæzm/ *n* phantom. **phan·tas·mal** /fænˈtæzml/ *adj* of or like a ~. **phan·tas·ma·goria** /ˌfæntæzməˈgorɪə/ *n* changing group of images, real or imagined figures, etc e g as seen in a dream.

phan·tasy /ˈfæntəsɪ/ *n* = **fantasy.**

phan·tom /ˈfæntəm/ *n* [C] ghost; sth without reality, as seen in a dream or vision: (attrib) *~ ships.*

Phar·aoh /ˈfeərəʊ/ *n* title of the kings of ancient Egypt.

Phari·see /ˈfærɪsi/ *n* member of an ancient Jewish sect known for strict obedience to written laws and for pretensions to sanctity; (small **p**) hypocritical self-righteous person. **phari·saic** /ˌfærɪˈseɪɪk/, **phari·sai·cal** /-kl/ *adjj* of or like a ~ or the ~s.

phar·ma·ceuti·cal /ˌfɑməˈsjutɪkl *US:* -ˈsu-/ *adj* of, engaged in, pharmacy; of medicinal drugs: *the ~ industry.*

phar·ma·cist /ˈfɑməsɪst/ *n* person skilled in preparing medicines. ⇨ **chemist, druggist.**

phar·ma·col·ogy /ˌfɑməˈkolədʒɪ/ *n* [U] science of pharmacy. **phar·ma·col·ogist** /-ədʒɪst/ *n* expert in, student of, ~.

phar·ma·co·poeia /ˌfɑməkəˈpiə/ *n* (officially published) book with list of medicinal preparations and directions for their use.

phar·macy /ˈfɑməsɪ/ *n* (*pl* **-cies**) **1** [U] preparation and dispensing of medicines and drugs. **2** [C] dispensary; (part of a) shop where medical goods are sold. (US = *drug-store*).

pharos /ˈfeəros/ *n* lighthouse; beacon for sailors.

phar·ynx /ˈfærɪŋks/ *n* cavity (with the muscles, etc that enclose it) at the back of the mouth, where the passages to the nose, mouth and larynx begin. ⇨ the illus at **head. phar·yn·gi·tis** /ˌfærɪnˈdʒɑɪtɪs/ *n* inflammation of the mucous membrane of the ~.

phase /feɪz/ *n* [C] **1** stage of development: *a ~ of history; the critical ~ of an illness; enter upon a new ~ of one's career.* **2** (of the moon) amount of bright surface visible from the earth (new moon, full moon, etc). □ *vt* [VP6A,15B] plan, carry out, by ~s: *a well-~d withdrawal,* one made by stages. **~ *in*,** introduce, one stage at a time. **~ *out*,** withdraw, one stage at a time.

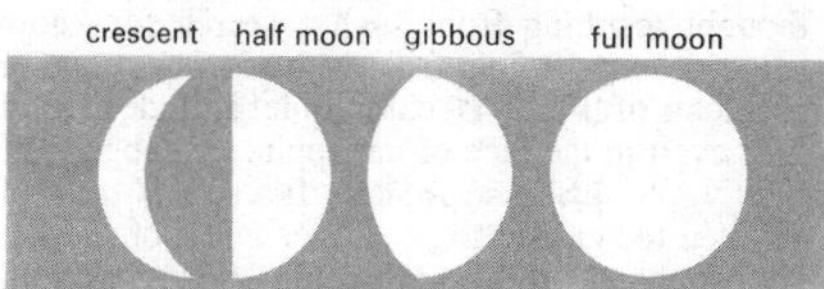

the phases of the moon

pheas·ant /ˈfeznt/ *n* [C] long-tailed game bird; [U] its flesh as food. ⇨ the illus at **fowl.**

pheno·bar·bi·tone /ˌfinəʊˈbɑbɪtəʊn/ *n* drug used to calm the nerves and induce sleep.

phenol /ˈfinol/ *n* (comm, science) carbolic acid (as used in disinfectants).

phe·nom·enal /fɪˈnomɪnl/ *adj* **1** perceptible to the senses. **2** concerned with phenomena. **3** prodigious; extraordinary. **~ly** /-nḷɪ/ *adv*

phe·nom·enon /fɪˈnomɪnən *US:* -non/ *n* (*pl* **-ena** /-nə/) **1** thing that appears to or is perceived by the senses: *the phenomena of nature.* **2** remarkable or unusual person, thing, happening, etc.

phew /fju *or a less precise puffing noise*/ *int* natural cry indicating astonishment, impatience, discomfort, disgust, etc according to context.

phi /fɑɪ/ *n* Greek letter corresponding to English *ph* (f). ⇨ App 4.

phial /ˈfɑɪəl/ *n* small bottle, esp one for liquid medicine; vial.

phil·an·der /fɪˈlændə(r)/ *vi* [VP2A] (of a man) be in the habit of making love without serious intentions. **~er** *n* person who does this. ⇨ **flirt**.

phil·an·thropy /fɪˈlænθrəpɪ/ *n* [U] love of mankind; practical sympathy and benevolence. **phil·an·thro·pist** /-ɪst/ *n* person who helps others, esp those who are poor or in trouble. **phil·an·thropic** /ˈfɪlənˈθropɪk/ *adj* of ~; benevolent; kind and helpful: *philanthropic institutions,* e g for blind people or orphans. **phil·an·thropi·cally** /-klɪ/ *adv*

phil·at·ely /fɪˈlætəlɪ/ *n* postage-stamp collecting. **phil·at·el·ist** /-ɪst/ *n* person who collects postage-stamps; person with expert knowledge of them.

phil·har·monic /ˈfɪləˈmonɪk/ *adj* fond of, devoted to, music: *the ~ society.*

phil·hel·lene /fɪlˈhelin/ *n, adj* (person) loving or friendly to the Greeks. **phil·hel·lenic** /ˈfɪlheˈlinɪk/ *adj*

Phi·lis·tine /ˈfɪlɪstɑɪn *US:* -stin/ *n* **1** (Biblical) one of the warlike people in Palestine who were the enemies of the Israelites. **2** (mod use; small *p*) uncultured person; person whose interests are material and commonplace: (attrib) *~ neighbours.*

phil·ol·ogy /fɪˈlolədʒɪ/ *n* [U] study of the development of language, or of particular languages. ⇨ **linguistics**. **phil·ol·ogist** /fɪˈlolədʒɪst/ *n* student of, expert in, ~. **philo·logi·cal** /ˈfɪləˈlodʒɪkl/ *adj* of ~.

phil·os·opher /fɪˈlosəfə(r)/ *n* **1** person studying or teaching philosophy, or having a system of philosophy **2** person whose mind is untroubled by passions and hardships; person who lets reason govern his life. **~'s stone,** substance which, alchemists believed, could change any metal into gold; elixir.

phil·os·ophy /fɪˈlosəfɪ/ *n* (*pl* -**phies**) **1** [U] the search for knowledge, esp the nature and meaning of existence. **moral ~,** the study of the principles underlying the actions and behaviour of men. **natural ~,** (old use) physics. **2** [C] system of thought resulting from such a search for knowledge: *a man without a ~,* with no views upon the problems of life. **3** [U] calm, quiet attitude towards life, even in the face of unhappiness, danger, difficulty, etc. **philo·sophi·cal** /ˈfɪləˈsofɪkl/ *adj* **1** of, devoted to, guided by, ~. **2** resigned; of or like a philosopher(2) **philo·sophi·cally** /-klɪ/ *adv* **phil·os·ophize** *vi* [VP2A] think or argue like a philosopher; discuss, speculate about, a theory in ~.

philtre (US = **phil·ter**) /ˈfɪltə(r)/ [C] love-potion.

phiz /fɪz/ *n* (colloq) (expression of the) face.

phleb·itis /flɪˈbɑɪtɪs/ *n* inflammation of a vein.

phlegm /flem/ *n* [U] **1** thick, semi-fluid substance forming on the skin of the throat and in the nose, and brought up by coughing. **2** quality of being slow to act, or to feel and show emotion or interest. **phleg·matic** /flegˈmætɪk/ *adj* having the quality of ~(2): *Not all English people are ~atic.* **phleg·mat·i·cally** /-klɪ/ *adv*

phlox /floks/ *n* [U] kinds of garden plant with clusters of flowers in various colours.

pho·bia /ˈfəʊbɪə/ *n* morbid or pathological fear and dislike; aversion.

phoe·nix /ˈfinɪks/ *n* mythical bird which, after living hundreds of years in the Arabian desert, burnt itself on a funeral pile and rose from the ashes young again, to live for another cycle.

phone[1] /fəʊn/ *n, vt, vi* (colloq abbr for) telephone. **ˈ~·booth** *n* telephone kiosk; call-box.

phone[2] /fəʊn/ *n* (linguistics) single speech-sound (vowel or consonant).

pho·neme /ˈfəʊnim/ *n* [C] (linguistics) unit of the system of word-distinguishing sounds of a language as represented ideally by single letters of the alphabet: *English can be said to have twenty-four consonant ~s.* **pho·nemic** /fəˈnimɪk/ *adj* (of transcriptions) providing one symbol for each ~ of the language transcribed (as with the pronunciations in this dictionary). **pho·nem·ics** *n* (esp US) study and description of the phonemic systems of languages.

pho·netic /fəˈnetɪk/ *adj* **1** concerned with the sounds of human speech. **2** (of transcriptions) providing not only a symbol for each phoneme of the language transcribed but with additional symbols for differences between variations of the same phoneme in different situations, e g English 'light' and 'dark' /l/. **3** (of a language) having a system of spelling that approximates closely to the sounds represented by the letters used: *Spanish spelling is ~.* **pho·net·ics** *n* (with *sing v*) study and science of speech sounds, their production, and the signs used to represent them. **pho·neti·cally** /-klɪ/ *adv* **pho·neti·cian** /ˈfəʊnɪˈtɪʃn/ *n* expert in ~s.

pho·ney, phony /ˈfəʊnɪ/ *adj* (sl) sham; unreal; not genuine. □ *n* ~ person: *He's a complete ~.*

pho·nic /ˈfonɪk/ *adj* of sound; of vocal sounds. **pho·nics** *n* (with *sing v*) the use of elementary phonetics in the teaching of reading.

pho·no·graph /ˈfəʊnəgrɑf *US:* -græf/ *n* (US) record-player.

pho·nol·ogy /fəˈnolədʒɪ/ *n* [U] (linguistics) scientific study of the organization of speech sounds (including phonemes), esp in particular languages. **pho·no·logi·cal** /ˈfəʊnəˈlodʒɪkl/ *adj*

phooey /ˈfuɪ/ *int* exclamation of contempt, disbelief or disappointment.

phos·gene /ˈfozdʒin/ *n* [U] colourless gas ($COCl_2$), used as a poison gas and in industry.

phos·phate /ˈfosfeɪt/ *n* any salt of phosphoric acid, esp one of the numerous artificial fertilizers containing or composed of various salts of this kind, used widely in agriculture.

phos·pho·rescence /ˈfosfəˈresns/ *n* [U] the giving out of light without burning, or by gentle burning without heat that can be felt. **phos·pho·rescent** /-snt/ *adj* giving out light without burning.

phos·phorus /ˈfosfərəs/ *n* [U] yellowish, non-metallic, poisonous wax-like element (symbol **P**) which catches fire easily and gives out a faint light in the dark; red, non-poisonous form used in the manufacture of safety matches. **phos·phoric** /fosˈforɪk *US:* -ˈfɔr-/, **phos·phor·ous** /ˈfosfərəs/ *adjj* relating to or containing ~.

photo /ˈfəʊtəʊ/ *n* (*pl* -**tos** /-təʊz/) (colloq abbr for) photograph.

photo- /ˈfəʊtəʊ/ *pref* light. **ˈ~·copy** *vt, n* [VP6A] (make a) copy of (a document, etc) by a photographic method. Hence, **ˈ~·copier** *n* **ˈ~·eˈlectric** *adj*: *~-electric cell,* cell or device which emits an electric current when light falls on it, used for many purposes, e g to measure light for photography, to cause a door to open when someone approaches it, to count objects passing before it. '~ 'finish *n* (horse-racing) finish so close that only a photograph of the horses as they pass the winning-post can decide the winner. '~·'**genic** /-'dʒenɪk/ *adj* suitable for being photographed; photographing well or effectively. '~·'**sensitize** *vt* make (sth) sensitive to light.

pho·to·graph /'fəʊtəgrɑf *US:* -græf/ *n* [C] picture recorded by means of the chemical action of light on a specially prepared glass plate or film in a camera, transferred to specially prepared paper. □ *vt* **1** [VP6A] take a ~ of. **2** ~ ***well/badly,*** come out well/badly when ~ed. **photographer** /fə'tɒgrəfə(r)/ *n* person who takes ~s: *amateur and professional ~ers.* Cf *camera man,* for cinema and TV. **pho·togra·phy** /fə'tɒgrəfɪ/ *n* [U] art or process of taking ~s. **pho·to·graphic** /'fəʊtə'græfɪk/ *adj* of, related to, used in, taking ~s: *photographic apparatus/goods/periodicals, etc.* **photo·graphi·cally** /-klɪ/ *adv*

pho·to·gra·vure /'fəʊtəgrə'vjʊə(r)/ *n* [U] process of producing a picture on a metal plate from a photographic negative so that the plate can be used in printing; [C] picture printed from such a plate.

pho·to·li·thogra·phy /'fəʊtəʊ'lɪ'θɒgrəfɪ/ *n* [U] process of reproducing on plates (stone or zinc) by means of photography.

pho·to·meter /fəʊ'tɒmɪtə(r)/ *n* device for measuring the intensity of light.

pho·to·stat /'fəʊtəstæt/ *n* (P) apparatus for producing direct facsimile reproductions of documents, drawings, etc; reproduction so made: *a ~ of a business letter.* □ *v* make ~s. **~ic** /'fəʊtə'stætɪk/ *adj*

phrase /freɪz/ *n* [C] **1** group of words (often without a finite *v*) forming part of a sentence, e g *in the garden. in order to.* '**~-book** *n* one containing and explaining (or giving equivalents of in another language) ~s of a language: *an English-Polish ~-book.* **2** striking, clever way of saying sth. **3** (music) short, independent passage forming part of a longer passage. □ *vt* [VP6A] express in words: *a neatly ~d compliment.* **phrasal** /'freɪzl/ *adj* in the form of a ~: *phrasal verbs,* e g *go in for, fall over, blow up.* **phras·eol·ogy** /'freɪzɪ'ɒlədʒɪ/ *n* [U] choice of words; wording.

phren·etic /frə'netɪk/ *adj* (formal) frenzied; frantic; fanatic.

phren·ol·ogy /frə'nɒlədʒɪ/ *n* [U] the judging of a person's character, capabilities, etc from an examination of the shape of his skull. **phren·ol·ogist** /-ɪst/ *n* person who practises ~.

phthi·sis /'θɑɪsɪs/ *n* [C] tuberculosis of the lungs.

phut /fʌt/ *n* sound made by (esp) a hollow rubber object bursting. □ *adv* ***go ~,*** (colloq) collapse; break down; (fig) come to nothing: *His holiday plans have all gone ~.*

physic /'fɪzɪk/ *n* **1** (old use) medicine: *take a good dose of ~.* **2** (*pl*) ⇨ physics. □ *vt* (-ck-) [VP6A] (colloq) dose with medicine.

physi·cal /'fɪzɪkl/ *adj* **1** of material (contrasted with moral and spiritual) things: *the ~ world/universe; ~ force.* **2** of the body; bodily: *~ exercise,* e g walking, playing football; *~ education.* **3** of the laws of nature: *It's a ~ impossibility to be in two places at once.* **4** of the natural features of the world: *~ geography,* of the earth's structure. **~ly** /-klɪ/ *adv*

phys·ician /fɪ'zɪʃn/ *n* doctor of medicine and surgery; person licensed to practice medicine (but not surgery).

physi·cist /'fɪzɪsɪst/ *n* expert on physics.

phys·ics /'fɪzɪks/ *n* (with *sing v*) group of sciences dealing with matter and energy (e g heat, light, sound), but usu excluding chemistry and biology: *P~ is taught by Professor Molecule.*

physi·og·nomy /'fɪzɪ'ɒnəmɪ *US:* -'ɒgnəʊmɪ/ *n* (*pl* -mies) [C,U] (art of judging character from the features of) the face; general features of a country.

physi·ol·ogy /'fɪzɪ'ɒlədʒɪ/ *n* [U] science of the normal functions of living things, esp animals. **physi·ol·ogist** /-ɪst/ *n* expert in, student of, ~. **physio·logi·cal** /'fɪzɪə'lɒdʒɪkl/ *adj*

physio·ther·apy /'fɪzɪəʊ'θerəpɪ/ *n* [U] treatment of disease by means of exercise, massage, the use of light, heat, electricity and other natural forces. **physio·thera·pist** /-pɪst/ *n* person trained to give such treatment.

phy·sique /fɪ'zik/ *n* [U] structure and development of the body: *a man of strong ~.*

pi /pɑɪ/ *n* the Greek letter p (π), esp as (maths) a symbol of the ratio of the circumference of a circle to its diameter (i e 3·14159). ⇨ App 2.

pi·ano[1] /pɪ'ɑnəʊ/ *adv* (music) softly. **pia·nis·simo** /pɪə'nɪsɪməʊ/ *adv* very softly.

pi·ano[2] /pɪ'ænəʊ/ *n* (*pl* -nos /-nəʊz/) musical instrument in which stretched metal strings are struck by hammers operated by keys. ⇨ the illus at keyboard. **cottage ~,** small upright ~. **grand ~, ~** with horizontal strings. **upright ~,** one with vertical strings. '**~-player** *n* device for playing a ~ mechanically. **pia·nist** /'pɪənɪst/ *n* person who plays the ~. **piano·forte** /pɪ'ænəʊ'fɔtɪ *US:* pɪ'ænəfɔrt/ *n* (full name, now formal, for) ~. **pia·nola** /pɪə'nəʊlə/ *n* (P) ~ incorporating a ~-player.

pi·astre (US = **pi·as·ter**) /pɪ'æstə(r)/ *n* unit of currency in some countries in the Middle East.

pi·azza /pɪ'ætsə/ *n* **1** public square or market-place, esp in an Italian town. **2** (US) veranda.

pi·broch /'pibrɒk/ *n* piece of martial music for the bagpipes.

pica /'pɑɪkə/ *n* printer's unit for the size of type (the largest normally used for books).

pica·dor /'pɪkədɔ(r)/ *n* man (mounted on a horse) who uses a lance to incite and weaken bulls in the sport of bull-fighting.

pic·ar·esque /'pɪkə'resk/ *adj* (of a style of fiction) treating of the adventures of rogues and vagabonds.

pic·ca·lilli /'pɪkə'lɪlɪ/ *n* [U] kind of hot-tasting pickle made of chopped vegetables, spices in mustard, vinegar, etc.

pic·ca·ninny /'pɪkə'nɪnɪ/ *n* (*pl* -nies) (old use) small child, esp a Negro baby.

pic·colo /'pɪkələʊ/ *n* (*pl* -los /-ləʊz/) small flute producing notes an octave higher than those of the ordinary flute. ⇨ the illus at brass.

pick[1] /pɪk/ *n* picking; selection. ***the ~ of,*** the best part of: *the ~ of the bunch,* the best of all of them.

pick[2] /pɪk/ *n* **1** '**~(-axe),** heavy tool with an iron head having two pointed ends, used for breaking up hard surfaces (e g roads, brickwork). ⇨ the illus at tool. **2** small, sharp-pointed instrument: *an 'ice-~; a 'tooth~.*

pick[3] /pɪk/ *vt,vi* (For special uses with *adverbial particles* and *preps,* ⇨ 7 below.) **1** [VP6A] take up, remove, pull away, with the fingers: ~ *flowers,* gather flowers; ~ *fruit,* take fruit from the bush or tree; ~ *a thread from one's coat;* ~ *one's nose,* remove bits of dried mucus from the nostrils. ~ ***sb's brains,*** get ideas and information from sb. ~ ***sb's pocket,*** steel sth from it. Hence, '~**-pocket** *n* person who ~s pockets. ~ ***and steal,*** pilfer. **2** [VP6A] tear or separate; use a pointed instrument to clean, etc: ~ *rags,* tear them to small pieces; ~ *one's teeth,* get bits of food from the spaces between them, etc by using a pointed stick of wood (*a* '*toothpick*); ~ *a lock,* use a pointed tool, a piece of wire, etc to unlock it without a key; ~ *a bone,* get all the meat from it. ***have a bone to*** ~ ***with sb,*** ⇨ bone(1). **3** [VP6A] choose; select: ~ *only the best;* ~ *one's words,* choose those words that express one's meaning best, that will not cause offence, etc (according to context); ~ *one's way/steps along a muddy road;* ~ *sides,* choose players for the two teams in a game (of football, cricket, etc) or competition; ~ *the winning horse/*~ *the winner,* make a successful guess at the winner (before the race). ~ ***a quarrel with sb,*** bring about a quarrel intentionally. **4** [VP6A] make by ~ing: ~ *holes in sth.* ~ ***holes in an argument,*** (fig) find its weak points. **5** [VP6A] (of birds) take up (grain, etc) in the bill; peck; (of persons) eat (food, etc) in small amounts; [VP3A] ~ ***at,*** eat without interest or appetite: *She only* ~*ed at her food.* **6** (US) pluck (the strings of): ~ *a banjo/the strings of a banjo.* **7** [VP3A,15B] (special uses with *adverbial particles* and *preps*):

pick at sb, (colloq) nag at; find fault with: *Why are you always* ~*ing at the poor child?*

pick sth off, take or pluck off. ~ ***sb off,*** shoot (persons), one by one with deliberate aim: *A sniper behind the bushes* ~*ed off three of our men.*

pick on sb, single out, esp for sth unpleasant: *Why should you* ~ *on me to do the chores?*

pick sb/sth out, **(a)** choose. **(b)** distinguish from surrounding persons, objects, etc: ~ *out one's friends in a crowd.* ~ ***sth out,*** **(a)** make out, see, (the meaning of a passage, etc) by careful study. **(b)** play (a tune) by ear on a piano, etc. **(c)** relieve (one colour, the ground colour) with touches of a different colour: *green panels* ~*ed out with brown.*

pick sth over, examine and make a selection from: ~ *over a basket of strawberries,* e g to throw out any that are bad.

pick sth up, **(a)** break up (ground) with a pick-axe. **(b)** take hold of and lift: ~ *up one's hat/parcels, etc.* **(c)** gain; acquire: ~ *up a foreign language,* learn it without taking lessons or studying: ~ *up a livelihood by selling things from door to door;* ~ *up bits of information;* ~ *up a bargain at an auction sale. The locomotive* ~*s up current from a third rail.* **(d)** succeed in seeing or hearing (by means of apparatus): *enemy planes* ~*ed up by our searchlights/radar installations, etc.* **(e)** recover; regain: *You'll soon* ~ *up health when you get to the seaside.* ~ ***sb up,*** **(a)** make the acquaintance of casually: *a girl he* ~*ed up on the street.* **(b)** take (persons) along with one: *He stopped the car to* ~ *up a young girl who was hitch-hiking across Europe. The escaped prisoner was* ~*ed up* (= seen and arrested) *by the police at Hull.* ~ ***oneself up,*** raise (oneself) after a fall: *She slipped and fell, but quickly* ~*ed herself up.* ~ ***up health,*** recover health; improve: *He's beginning to* ~ *up now.* ~ ***up speed,*** gain speed. ~ ***up with sb,*** make acquaintance with: *Where did you* ~ *up that queer fellow?* '~**-up** *n* (*pl* ~**-ups**) **(a)** that part of a record-player that holds the stylus (corresponding to the sound-box of the older kind of gramophone; the tone-arm of a record-player. **(b)** small general-purpose van or truck, open and with low sides, (e g as used by builders, farmers, etc, for carrying merchandise). **(c)** (sl) person whose acquaintance is made casually. **(d)** acceleration: *an engine/car with a good* ~*-up.* ~**-me-up** /'pɪk mɪ ʌp/ *n* sth, e g a drink, that gives new strength and cheerfulness.

picka·back /'pɪkəbæk/ *adv* (e g of the way a child is carried) on the shoulders or back like a bundle.

picker /'pɪkə(r)/ *n* person or thing that picks (chiefly in compounds): '*hop-*~*s;* '*rag-*~*s.*

pick·erel /'pɪkərl/ *n* young pike.

picket /'pɪkɪt/ *n* **1** pointed stake, etc set upright in the ground (as part of a fence, or to tether a horse to). **2** small group of men on police duty, or sent out to watch the enemy. **3** worker, or group of workers, stationed at the gates of a factory, dockyard, etc during a strike, to try to persuade others not to go to work: *a* '~ *line,* line of ~s, e g outside a factory. □ *vt,vi* [VP6A,2A] **1** put ~s(1) round; tether (a horse) to a ~(1). **2** place ~s(2) in or round; station (men) as ~s. **3** place ~s(3) at: ~ *a factory;* act as a ~(3).

pick·ing /'pɪkɪŋ/ *n* **1** [U] act of picketing. ~ ***and stealing,*** pilfering; petty theft. **2** (*pl*) odds and ends left over from which profits may be made; these profits; profits made from pilfering or (perhaps dishonest) appropriation of trifles.

pickle /'pɪkl/ *n* **1** [U] salt water, vinegar, etc for keeping meat, vegetables, etc, in good condition. ***have a rod in*** ~ ***for sb,*** ⇨ rod. **2** (usu *pl*) vegetables kept in ~: *onion* ~*s.* **3** ***in a sad/sorry/nice*** ~, in a sad, etc plight. **4** (colloq) mischievous child: *Stop that, you little* ~*!* □ *vt* [VP6A] **1** preserve in ~: ~*d onions/walnuts.* **2** (*pp* ~**ed**) (sl) intoxicated.

pic·nic /'pɪknɪk/ *n* **1** pleasure trip on which food is carried to be eaten outdoors: *have/go for a* ~; (attrib) *a* '~ *hamper,* one for holding food, dishes, etc. **2** (colloq) sth easy and enjoyable: *It's no* ~, is not an easy job. □ *vi* (**-ck-**) take part in a ~: ~ *in the woods.* **pic·nicker** *n* person who ~s.

pic·ric /'pɪkrɪk/ *adj* ~ **acid,** acid used in dyeing, explosives and antiseptics.

pic·tor·ial /pɪk'tɔrɪəl/ *adj* of, having, represented in, pictures: *a* ~ *record of the wedding.* □ *n* periodical of which pictures are the main feature.

pic·ture /'pɪktʃə(r)/ *n* **1** painting, drawing, sketch, of sth, esp as a work of art. '~**-book** *n* book consisting mainly of ~s, esp one for children. '~**-card** *n* (in playing cards) court-card; one with a king, queen or knave on it. '~**-gallery** *n* room or building in which ~s are exhibited. '~ **hat,** woman's hat with a very wide brim. **2** beautiful scene, object, person, etc. **3** type or embodiment. ***be the*** ~ ***of health,*** appear to have it in a high degree. **4** (fig) account or description that enables sb to see in his mind an event, etc. ***be/put sb in the*** ~, be/cause sb to be well informed, aware of all the facts of a situation. **5** film (to be) shown in a cinema. **the** ~**s,** the cinema: *We don't often go to the* ~*s.* **6** what is seen on a television screen: *a set free from* ~ *distortion.* □ *vt* **1** [VP6A] make a ~

of: paint. **2** [VP14] **~ sth to oneself,** imagine: *He ~d to himself the family sitting out on the lawn.*

pic·tur·esque /ˌpɪktʃəˈresk/ *adj* **1** having the quality of being like, or of being fit to be, the subject of a painting: *a ~ village.* **2** quaint; vivid; graphic: *~ language.* **3** (of a person, his character) striking; original. **~·ly** *adv* **~·ness** *n*

piddle /ˈpɪdl/ *vi, n* (colloq) (pass) urine.

pid·dling /ˈpɪdlɪŋ/ *adj* trifling; insignificant: *~ jobs.*

pidgin /ˈpɪdʒɪn/ *n* any of several languages resulting from contact between European traders and local peoples, e g in West Africa and the Far East, containing elements of the local language(s) and English, French or Dutch, still used for internal communication. **2** (only in) ***(not) one's ~,*** (colloq) not one's job or concern: *Don't ask me; that's your ~.*

pie /paɪ/ *n* [C,U] meat or fruit covered with paste and baked in a deep dish: *fruit pies; a meat pie; eat too much pie.* ⇨ flan, tart[2]. ***have a finger in the/every pie,*** be concerned in the matter (esp in an officious way). ***as easy as pie,*** (sl) very easy. ***pie in the sky,*** happiness in Heaven; unrealistic hopes. **ˈpie-crust** *n* baked paste of a pie.

pie·bald /ˈpaɪbɔld/ *adj* (of a horse) having white and dark patches of irregular shape.

piece[1] /pis/ *n* **1** part or bit of a solid substance (complete in itself, but broken, separated or made from a larger portion): *a ~ of paper/wood/glass/chalk. Will you have another ~* (= slice) *of cake? This ~ of string is too short.* ***(be) in ~s,*** broken; dismantled: *The vase is in ~s.* ***break (sth) to ~s,*** be in ~s as the result of an accident: *The teapot fell and was broken to ~s.* ***come/take (sth) to ~s,*** divide (sth) into the parts which make it up: *Does this machine come/take to ~s?* ***go (all) to ~s,*** (colloq) (of a person) break up physically, mentally or morally: *Poor Paul! He's gone (all) to ~s.* ***a ~ of cake,*** (sl) sth very easy. ***~ by ~,*** one at a time. ***of a ~ (with sth),*** (fig) of the same character (as); consistent (with); in keeping (with). **2** separate instance or example: *a ~ of news/luck/advice/information, etc;* single article: *a ~ of furniture.* ***give sb a ~ of one's mind,*** tell him candidly what one thinks of him. ***say one's ~,*** say what one has to say, sth one has learnt to say, e g a poem to be recited. **3** standard length or quantity in which goods are prepared for distribution: *a ~ of wallpaper* (usu 12 yds); *a ~ of cloth; sold only by the ~.* **ˈ~-goods** *n pl* textile fabrics (esp cotton and silk) made in standard lengths. **4** single composition (in art, music, etc): *a fine ~ of work/music/poetry; a dramatic ~.* **5** single thing out of a set: *a dinner service of 50 ~s;* one of the wooden, metal, etc objects moved on a board in such games as chess. **6** coin: *a ten-pence ~; a five cent ~; a ~ of eight,* an old Spanish silver coin. **7** gun: *a fixed-~,* field-gun; *a ˈfowling-~,* for shooting game. **8** (fixed or agreed) amount of work (to be) done: *pay a workman by the ~,* according to the work produced (not by the time taken). Hence, **ˈ~-work** *n* ⇨ *time-work* at time[1](13). **9** (in compounds) (player of a) musical instrument: *a six-~ pop group.*

piece[2] /pis/ *vt* [VP6A,15A,B] ***~ (together),*** put (parts, etc together); make by joining or adding (pieces) together: *~ together odds and ends of cloth; ~ a quilt,* make one by putting ~s together; *~ one thing to another.* **~ sth out,** make (a story, theory, etc) complete by connecting the parts.

piece·meal /ˈpismil/ *adv* piece by piece; part at a time: *work done ~.* □ *adj* coming, done, etc piece by piece.

pied /paɪd/ *adj* of mixed colours, of black and white, e g of birds.

pied-à-terre /pɪˈed ɑ ˈteə(r)/ *n* (F) extra room(s) or house which one keeps for use when needed: *He lives in the country, and has a ~ in London.*

pier /pɪə(r)/ *n* **1** structure of wood, iron, etc built out into the sea as a landing-stage; similar structure for walking on for pleasure (often with a pavilion, restaurant, etc). **2** pillar supporting a span of a bridge, etc. **3** brickwork between windows or other openings. **ˈ~-glass** *n* large, long mirror in which one can see the whole of oneself.

a pier

pierce /pɪəs/ *vt,vi* **1** [VP6A] (of sharp-pointed instruments) go into or through; make (a hole) by doing this: *The arrow ~d his shoulder. She had her ears ~d in order to be able to wear earrings.* **2** [VP6A] (fig, of cold, pain, sounds, etc) force a way into or through; affect deeply: *Her shrieks ~d the air. A ray of light ~d the darkness.* **3** [VP2C] penetrate (*through, into,* etc): *Our forces ~d through the enemy's lines.* **~·ing** *adj* (esp of cold, voices) sharp; penetrating: *a piercing wind.* **~·ing·ly** *adv: a piercingly cold wind.*

pier·rot /ˈpɪərəʊ/ *n* **1** character in French pantomime. **2** member of a group of entertainers (esp at seaside resorts), dressed in loose white clothes and with a whitened face.

pietà /ˈpierˈtɑ/ *n* (I) painting or sculpture of the Virgin Mary holding the dead body of Jesus in her lap.

piety /ˈpaɪətɪ/ *n* **1** [U] devotion to God and good works; being pious. **filial ~,** correct behaviour towards a parent. **2** [C] (*pl* -ties) act, etc that shows ~.

piffle /ˈpɪfl/ *n* [U] (colloq) nonsense. □ *vt* talk ~.

pif·fling /ˈpɪflɪŋ/ *adj* trivial; worthless.

pig /pɪg/ *n* **1** [C] domestic and wild animal, ⇨ the illus at domestic. ⇨ boar, hog, sow[1], swine; [U] its flesh (esp *roast pig*) as meat. ⇨ bacon, ham, pork. ***bring one's pigs to the wrong market,*** fail in an undertaking (to sell sth). ***buy a pig in a poke,*** buy sth without seeing it or knowing its value. ***pigs might fly,*** wonders might happen. **ˈpig·boat** *n* (US sl) submarine. **ˈpig-headed** *adj* stubborn. **ˈpig-ˈheadedly** *adv* **ˈpig-ˈheadedness** *n* **ˈpig·skin** *n* [U] (leather made of a) pig's skin; (sl) saddle. **ˈpig-sticking** *n* the sport of hunting wild boars with spears. **ˈpig·sty** /-staɪ/ *n* **(a)** small building for pigs. **(b)** dirty hovel. **ˈpig-tail** *n* plait of hair hanging down over the back of the neck and shoulders. **ˈpig·wash, ˈpig·swill** *nn* waste food (from a brewery or kitchen) given to pigs as food. **2** (colloq) dirty, greedy or ill-mannered person. ***make a pig of oneself,*** eat or drink to excess. **3** (**ˈpig-iron**) oblong mass of iron extracted from ore and shaped in a mould. **4** (sl) policeman. □ *vi* (-gg-) ***pig it, pig together,*** live or herd together in dirty conditions. **'pig·gish** /-ɪʃ/ *adj* like a pig; dirty, greedy. **pig·gish·ly** *adv* **pig·gish·ness** *n* **pig·gery** /ˈpɪgərɪ/ *n* (*pl* -ries) pig-breeding establishment; pig-farm. **piggy** /ˈpɪgɪ/ *n* (*pl* -gies) little pig. □ *adj* (colloq) greedy. **'pig·gyback,** (US) = (GB) pickaback. **'piggy bank** *n* model (of a pig) with a slot for coins, used by a child for saving coin money.

pigeon /ˈpɪdʒən/ *n* **1** bird, wild or tame, of the dove family: *'carrier-~, 'homing-~,* kind trained to carry messages or bred for sport. ⇨ the illus at bird. **'~-breasted** *adj* (of a human being) having a bulging, convex chest. **'~-'toed** *adj* having the toes turned inwards. **'~-hole** *n* one of a number of small open boxes (e g above a desk) for keeping papers in. □ *vt* put (papers, etc) in a ~hole and ignore or forget them; postpone consideration of: *The scheme was ~holed.* **2 clay ~,** disc thrown up into the air as a mark for shooting. **3** simpleton; easily deceived person. **4 ('stool-) ~,** ⇨stool.

pig-iron /ˈpɪg aɪən/ *n* ⇨ pig(3).

pig·let /ˈpɪglət/ *n* young pigs.

pig·ment /ˈpɪgmənt/ *n* **1** [U] colouring matter for making dyes, paint, etc; [C] particular substance used for this. **2** [U] the natural colouring matter in the skin, hair, etc of living beings. **pig·men·ta·tion** /ˌpɪgmenˈteɪʃn/ *n* colouring of tissues by ~.

pigmy /ˈpɪgmɪ/ *n* = pygmy.

pi·jaw /ˈpaɪdʒɔ/ *n* (sl) (from *pious* and *jaw*) talk on religion or morals.

pike[1] /paɪk/ *n* long wooden shaft with a spearhead, formerly used by soldiers fighting on foot. **'~-staff** *n* wooden shaft of a ~. ***as plain as a ~staff,*** quite plain; easy to see or understand.

pike[2] /paɪk/ *n* large, fierce, freshwater fish.

pike[3] /paɪk/ *n* **1** turnpike road. **2** toll-bar; toll.

pike[4] /paɪk/ *n* (dialect, N of England) peaked top of a hill: *Langdale P~.*

pi·laf(f) /pɪˈlæf *US:* -ˈlɑf/ ⇨ pilau.

pi·las·ter /pɪˈlæstə(r)/ *n* rectangular column, esp an ornamental one that projects from a wall into which it is set.

pi·lau /pɪˈlaʊ/ (also **pi·laf(f)** /pɪˈlæf *US:* -ˈlɑf/) *n* oriental dish of steamed rice with meat, etc.

pil·chard /ˈpɪltʃəd/ *n* small sea-fish resembling the herring.

pile[1] /paɪl/ *n* [C] heavy beam of timber, steel, concrete, etc driven into the ground, esp under water, as a foundation for a building, a support for a bridge, etc. **'~-driver** *n* machine for driving ~s into the ground. **'~-dwelling** *n* house resting on ~s, esp at the side of a lake. □ *vt* [VP6A] supply with ~s.

pile[2] /paɪl/ *n* **1** number of things lying one upon another: *a ~ of books.* **2 'funeral ~,** heap of wood, etc on which a corpse is burnt. **3** (colloq) large amount of money. ***make a/one's ~,*** earn a lot of money. **4** large high building or group of buildings. **5** dry battery for producing electric current. **atomic ~,** apparatus for the controlled release of atomic energy; nuclear reactor.

pile[3] /paɪl/ *vt,vi* **1** [VP6A,15A,B] make into a ~; put on or in a ~: *~ logs; ~ up dishes on a table; ~ a table with dishes; ~ more coal on (the fire)....* **~ arms,** place (usu four) rifles together with butts on the ground and muzzles touching. ***~ it on,*** (colloq) exaggerate. ***~ on the agony,*** (colloq) make a description of a painful event more agonizing than is necessary. **2** [VP2C] **~ up, (a)** accumulate: *My work keeps piling up,* There is more and more work for me to do. **(b)** (of a number of vehicles) crash into each other, forming a ~. Hence, **'~-up** *n*: *another bad ~-up on the motorway during thick fog.* **3 *~ into/out of sth,*** enter/leave in a disorderly way: *They all ~d into/out of the car/cinema.*

pile[4] /paɪl/ *n* [U] soft, thick, hair-like surface of velvet, some carpets, etc.

piles /paɪlz/ *n* [U] hemorrhoids.

pil·fer /ˈpɪlfə(r)/ *vt,vi* [VP6A,2A] steal, esp in small quantities: *~ed during transit by rail.* **~er** *n* **'~·age** /-ɪdʒ/ *n* [U] act of ~ing; loss by ~ing.

pil·grim /ˈpɪlgrɪm/ *n* person who travels to a sacred place as an act of religious devotion: *~s to Mecca; the Canterbury ~s,* in England, during the Middle Ages. **the P~ Fathers,** English Puritans who went to America in 1620 and founded the colony of Plymouth, Massachusetts. **'~·age** /-ɪdʒ/ *n* journey of a ~: *go on a ~age to Benares.*

pill /pɪl/ *n* **1** small ball or tablet of medicine for swallowing whole. ***a bitter ~ (to swallow),*** ⇨ bitter. ***sugar/sweeten the ~,*** make sth disagreeable seem less so. **'~·box** *n* **(a)** small cylindrical box for holding ~s. **(b)** (army use) small (often partly underground) concrete fort. **2** (usu **the ~**) oral contraceptive. ***be/go on the ~,*** *be taking/start to take such ~s regularly.*

pil·lage /ˈpɪlɪdʒ/ *n, vt* plunder, esp in war. **pil·lager** /-ɪdʒə(r)/ *n* one who ~s.

pil·lar /ˈpɪlə(r)/ *n* **1** upright column, of stone, wood, metal, etc as a support or ornament. ⇨ the illus at column. ***(driven) from ~ to post,*** (fig) (driven) from one resource to another, to and fro. **2** (fig) **~ of,** strong supporter: *a ~ of the establishment.* **3 '~-box** *n* cylindrical container (in GB, scarlet) about 5 feet high, standing in a public place, in which letters are posted: *a ~-box hat,* cylindrical in shape. **4** sth in the shape of a ~, e g a column of fire, smoke, cloud or, in a coalmine, of coal left to support the roof.

pil·lion /ˈpɪlɪən/ *n* seat for a second rider behind the rider of a horse; saddle for a passenger behind the driver of a motor-bike: *riding ~; the ~ passenger.*

pil·lory /ˈpɪlərɪ/ *n* (*pl* -ries) wooden framework in which the head and hands of wrongdoers were, in olden times, secured whilst they were ridiculed by passers-by as a punishment. □ *vt* [VP6A] put in the ~; (fig) expose to ridicule.

pil·low /ˈpɪləʊ/ *n* soft cushion for the head, esp when lying in bed. **'~-case/-slip** *n* washable cover for a ~. **'~-fight,** child's game of fighting with ~s. □ *vt* [VP6A] rest, support, on or as on a ~; serve as a ~ for.

pi·lot /ˈpaɪlət/ *n* **1** person trained and licensed to take ships into or out of a harbour, along a river, through a canal, etc. ***drop the ~,*** (fig) dismiss a trusted adviser. **2** person trained to operate the controls of an aircraft. **P~ Officer,** lowest commissioned rank in the Air Force. ⇨ App 9. **3** (attrib) experimental; used to test how sth on a larger scale will work, etc how it may be improved: *a '~ census/survey/scheme; a '~ plant,* for a manufacturing process; *a '~ tunnel.* **4** (compounds) **'~-boat** *n* one which takes ~s to ships. **'~-cloth** *n* blue woollen cloth used for overcoats, etc. **'~-engine** *n* railway engine that goes in advance (e g to check for safety). '~-fish *n* small fish which often swims in company with larger fish, e g sharks, or sometimes ships. '~-light/-burner *n* small flame in a gas cooker or lamp, kept burning continuously, which lights large burners, etc when the gas is turned on. □ *vt* [VP6A,15A] act as a ~ to: *~ ships through the Panama Canal.*

pi·mento /pɪ'mentəʊ/ *n* (*pl* -tos /-təʊz/) **1** [U] dried aromatic berries of a West Indian tree, also called *Jamaica pepper* and *all-spice*. **2** [C] tree that produces the berries.

pimp /pɪmp/ *n* pander(2). □ *vt* ~ ***(for sb)***, act as a ~.

pim·per·nel /'pɪmpənel/ *n* small annual plant growing wild in wheatfields and on waste land, with scarlet, blue or white flowers.

pimple /'pɪmpl/ *n* small, hard, inflamed spot on the skin. **pim·pled** *adj* having ~s. **pim·ply** /'pɪmplɪ/ *adj* (-ier, -iest) having ~s: *a pimply boy/ face.*

pin[1] /pɪn/ *n* **1** short, thin piece of stiff wire with a sharp point and a round head, used for fastening together parts of a dress, papers, etc. ***don't care a pin,*** don't care at all. ***neat as a new pin,*** very neat. ***pins and needles,*** tingling sensation in a part of the body caused by blood flowing again when its circulation has been checked for a time. **2** similar piece of wire with an ornamental head for special purposes: *a 'tie-pin; a 'hat-pin.* **'safety-pin,** pin bent with a guard at one end to protect the point at the other end. **3** peg of wood or metal for various purposes. ⇨ *drawing-pin* at drawing, *hairpin* at hair(2), ninepins, *rolling-pin* at roll[2](11); each of the pegs round which the strings of a musical instrument are fastened. **'pin-table** *n* table game (often as a gambling device) played with a small ball which has to be guided into one of several numbered holes on a sloping board covered with upright pins. **'pin-ball** *n* game played on a pin-table. **4** (*pl*) (sl) legs: *He's quick on his ~s.* **5** (compounds) **'pin·cushion** *n* pad into which (a dressmaker's) pins are stuck. **'pin·head** *n* (colloq) very stupid person. **'pin-money** *n* [U] money allowance to, or money earned by, a woman for dress, small personal necessities, etc. **'pin-point** *n* sth very small; (attrib of targets) requiring accurate and precise bombing or shelling. □ *vt* find, hit, such a target with the required accuracy: *Our planes pin-pointed the target.* **'pin-prick** *n* (fig) small act, remark, etc causing annoyance. **'pin-stripe,** (of dress material) with many very narrow stripes.

pin[2] /pɪn/ *vt* (-nn-) [VP15A,B] **1** fasten (things *together, up, to* sth, etc) with a pin or pins: *pin papers together; pin up a notice,* e g with drawing-pins on a notice-board. ***pin sth on sb,*** make him appear responsible; place the blame for sth on sb. ***pin one's hopes on sb,*** have strong hope that he will help; rely on him unquestioningly. **'pin-up** *n* picture of a favourite or much admired person, esp of a pretty woman, pinned up on a wall: (attrib) *a 'pin-up girl.* **2** make unable to move: *He was pinned under the wreckage/the wrecked car. He pinned his assailant against the wall,* held him there and prevented him from moving. *The troops were pinned down by accurate fire,* were unable to advance or withdraw. ***pin sb down,*** (fig) get him to commit himself, to state his intentions, etc: *He's a difficult man to pin down.* ***pin sb down to sth,*** get him to agree to keep, e g a promise, an agreement.

pina·fore /'pɪnəfɔ(r)/ *n* loose article of clothing worn over a dress to keep it clean.

pince-nez /'pæ̃s neɪ *US:* 'pæns/ *n* pair of spectacles with a spring to clip the nose (instead of a frame that fits round the ears).

pin·cers /'pɪnsəz/ *n pl* (also **a pair of ~s**) **1** instrument for gripping things, pulling nails out of wood, etc. ⇨ the illus at tool. **'pincer movement,** (mil) attack by two converging forces. **2** pincer-shaped claws of certain shellfish. ⇨ the illus at crustacean.

pinch /pɪntʃ/ *vt,vi* **1** [VP6A,15A,B] take in a tight grip between the thumb and finger; have in a tight grip between two hard things which are pressed together: *He ~ed the boy's cheek. He ~ed the top of the plants off/~ed out the side shoots. I ~ed my finger in the doorway.* **2** [VP6A,2A] be too tight; hurt by being too tight: *These shoes ~ (me).* ***(see, etc) where the shoe ~es,*** (fig) where the difficulty or hardship lies.
3 *be ~ed with cold/poverty,* suffer from cold, etc. ***be ~ed for money,*** be short of money. **4** [VP6A] (colloq) steal; take without permission: *Who's ~ed my dictionary?* **5** [VP2A] be niggardly; be very mean; live sparingly or economically: *parents who have to ~ and scrape in order to save money for a child's clothes.* **6** (sl) (of the police) take into custody; arrest: *You'll be ~ed if you're not careful.* □ *n* **1** act of ~ing; painful squeeze: *He gave her a spiteful ~.* **2** (fig) stress: *feel the ~ of poverty.* **3** amount which can be taken up with the thumb and finger: *a ~ of salt/snuff; take sth with a ~ of salt,* ⇨ salt. **4** ***at a ~, if it comes to the ~,*** if there is need and if there is no other way: *We can get six people round the table at a ~.*

pinch·beck /'pɪntʃbek/ *n* alloy of copper and zinc, simulating gold, used in cheap jewellery, etc. □ *adj* sham.

pine[1] /paɪn/ *n* [C] kinds of evergreen tree with needle-shaped leaves (**'~-needles**) and cones (**'~-cones**); [U] the wood of this tree. ⇨ the illus at tree.

pine[2] /paɪn/ *vi* **1** [VP2A,C] waste away through sorrow or illness: *pining from hunger.* **2** [VP3A, 4C] ~ ***for sth;*** ~ ***to do sth,*** have a strong desire: *exiles pining for home/to return home.*

pin·eal /'paɪnɪəl/ *adj* shaped like a pine-cone: *~ gland,* gland in the brain.

pine·apple /'paɪnæpl/ *n* [C] (tropical plant with) sweet, juicy fruit; [U] this as food: *~ juice; tinned ~.* ⇨ the illus at tree.

ping /pɪŋ/ *n* short, sharp, ringing sound as of elastic being stretched and released or a rifle bullet in the air or striking a hard substance. □ *vi* make this sound.

ping·pong /'pɪŋpoŋ/ *n* table-tennis.

pin·head /'pɪnhed/ ⇨ pin[1](5).

pin·ion[1] /'pɪnɪən/ *n* **1** bird's wing, esp the outer joint; flight-feather of a bird. **2** (poet) wing: *an eagle's ~s.* □ *vt* [VP6A] **1** cut off a ~ of (a wing or bird) to hamper flight. **2** [VP15A,B] ~ ***(to/ together),*** bind the arms of (a person); bind (sb's) arms; bind (sb) fast (to sth).

pin·ion[2] /'pɪnɪən/ *n* small cog-wheel with teeth fitting into those of a larger cog-wheel. ⇨ the illus at gear.

pink[1] /pɪŋk/ *n* **1** pale red colour of various kinds (*rose ~, salmon ~*). ~ **gin,** portion of gin with angostura. **2** garden plant with sweet-smelling white, ~, crimson or variegated flowers. **3** ***in the ~ (of health),*** (colloq) very well. □ *adj* **1** of pale red colour. **2** (colloq) inclined to be left wing in politics. ⇨ red. **ˋ~·ish** /-ɪʃ/ *adj* rather ~.

pink[2] /pɪŋk/ *vt* **1** [VP6A] pierce with a sword. **2** [VP15B] **~ *(out),*** decorate (leather, cloth) with small holes, etc. **ˋ~·ing scissors/shears** *n pl* sewing scissors with serrated edges, used to prevent edges of cloth from fraying.

pink[3] /pɪŋk/ *vi* (of an internal-combustion engine) make high-pitched explosive sounds; knock(3).

pin-money /ˋpɪn mʌnɪ/ *n* ⇨ pin[1](5).

pin·nace /ˋpɪnɪs/ *n* warship's boat with (usu) eight oarsmen; ship's boat driven by steam or petrol.

pin·nacle /ˋpɪnəkl/ *n* **1** tall, pointed ornament built on to a roof or buttress. ⇨ the illus at church. **2** high, slender mountain peak. **3** (fig) highest point: *at the ~ of his fame.* □ *vt* set (as) on a ~; supply with ~s.

pin·nate /ˋpɪneɪt/ *adj* (bot) (of a leaf) formed of small leaves on opposite sides of a stem.

pinny /ˋpɪnɪ/ *n* (*pl* -nies) (child's name for a) pinafore.

pin-point /ˋpɪn pɔɪnt/ ⇨ pin[1](5).

pin-prick /ˋpɪn prɪk/ ⇨ pin[1](5).

pin-stripe /ˋpɪn straɪp/ ⇨ pin[1](5).

pint /paɪnt/ *n* unit of measure for liquids and certain dry goods, one-eighth of a gallon or about ·57 of a litre: *a ~ of milk/beer/lentils.* ⇨ App 5.

pin-up /ˋpɪn ʌp/ ⇨ pin[2](1).

pion·eer /ˈpaɪəˋnɪə(r)/ *n* **1** person who goes into a new or undeveloped country to settle or work there; first student of a new branch of study, etc; explorer. **2** (mil) one of an advance party of soldiers (e g clearing or making roads). □ *vi,vt* [VP2A] act as a ~; [VP6A] open up (a way, etc); show (new methods, etc) to others.

pious /ˋpaɪəs/ *adj* **1** having, showing, deep devotion to religion. **2** (old use) dutiful to parents. **~·ly** *adv*

pip[1] /pɪp/ *n* seed, esp of a lemon, orange, apple or pear. ⇨ the illus at fruit.

pip[2] /pɪp/ *n* **the pip,** disease of poultry; (sl) fit of depression. ***have/get/give sb the pip***: *That man gives me the pip.*

pip[3] /pɪp/ *n* note of a time-signal on the telephone or radio: *The last of the six pips gives the time to the second.*

pip[4] /pɪp/ *n* **1** each spot on playing-cards, dice and dominoes. **2** (GB colloq) star (1 to 3 according to rank) on an army officer's shoulder-strap.

pip[5] /pɪp/ *vt* (-pp-) [VP6A] (GB colloq) hit with a gunshot.

pi·pal /ˋpipəl/ ⇨ peepul.

pipe[1] /paɪp/ *n* **1** tube through which liquids or gases can flow: *ˋwater-~s; ˋgas-~s; ˋdrain~s.* **ˋ~·line** *n* (esp) line of connected ~s, often underground, for conveying petroleum to distant places. ***in the ~line,*** (mod use, of any kind of goods or proposals) on the way; about to be delivered in a schedule, list, etc to receive attention. **2** musical wind-instrument (a single tube with holes stopped by the fingers); each of the tubes from which sound is produced in an organ; (*pl*) *ˋbag~s.* **3** (sound of the) whistle used by a boatswain. **4** song or note of a bird. **5** tubular organ in the body: *ˋwind~.* **6 (toˋbacco) ~,** tube with a bowl, used for smoking tobacco; quantity of tobacco held in the bowl: *smoke a ~. Give me a ~ of tobacco, please.* ***Put that in your ~ and smoke it,*** (colloq) That is sth for you to reflect upon and accept if you can. **ˋ~-clay** *n* [U] fine, white clay used for making (now old-fashioned) tobacco ~s, and (by soldiers) for whitening leather belts and other pieces of equipment. **ˋ~-dream** *n* plan, idea, etc that is fantastic and impracticable. **ˋ~-rack** *n* rack for tobacco ~s. **7** cask for wine (equal to about 105 gallons). **ˋ~·ful** /-fʊl/ *n* as much as a ~(6) holds.

pipe[2] /paɪp/ *vi,vt* **1** [VP6A,15A] convey (water, etc) through pipes: *~ water into a house.* **2** [VP6A,2A] play (a tune) on a pipe; whistle; utter or sing in a thin, treble voice. [VP2C] **~ *up,*** (colloq) begin to play, sing or speak. **~ *down,*** be less noisy or cocksure. **3** [VP15A] (naut) summon (sailors) by blowing a boatswain's pipe: *~ all hands on deck;* lead or welcome (sb) by the sound of a boatswain's pipe: *~ the captain on board.* **4** [VP6A] trim (a dress), ornament (a cake, etc) with piping. ⇨ piping(2).

pipe·line /ˋpaɪplaɪn/ *n* ⇨ pipe[1](1).

piper /ˋpaɪpə(r)/ *n* one who plays on a pipe, esp a player of the bagpipes. ***pay the ~ (and call the tune),*** bear the cost of an undertaking (and have control of what is done).

pip·ette /pɪˋpet/ *n* slender tube for transferring small quantities of liquid, esp in chemistry.

pip·ing /ˋpaɪpɪŋ/ *n* [U] **1** length of pipes(1), esp for water and drains: *ten feet of lead ~.* **2** narrow cord-like material used to ornament the edges of some garments; cord-like lines of icing-sugar used to decorate cakes, etc. **3** action of playing on a pipe; sound produced from a pipe. □ *adj* like the sound from a pipe(2): *a ~ voice; the ~ times of peace,* times when there is peaceful music instead of martial music. □ *adv* **~ *hot,*** (of liquids, food) hissing or steaming hot.

pip·pin /ˋpɪpɪn/ *n* kinds of apple.

pip·squeak /ˋpɪpskwik/ *n* (sl) insignificant or contemptible person or thing: *What a little ~ you are!*

pi·quant /ˋpikənt/ *adj* pleasantly sharp to the taste: *a ~ sauce;* (fig) pleasantly exciting to the mind: *a ~ bit of gossip.* **~·ly** *adv* **pi·quancy** /-ənsɪ/ *n* the quality of being ~.

pique /pik/ *vt* [VP6A] **1** hurt the pride or self-respect of. **2** stir (the curiosity); stir the curiosity of (sb). **3 ~ *oneself on sth,*** pride oneself on; feel proud about: *He ~d himself on being punctual.* □ *n* [U] feeling one has when one's curiosity is unsatisfied; resentment: *go away in a fit of ~; take a ~ against sb.*

pi·qué /ˋpikeɪ *US:* pɪˋkeɪ/ *n* [U] stiff cotton fabric.

pi·quet /pɪˋket/ *n* card game for two players with a pack of 32 cards.

pi·ranha /pɪˋrɑnjə/ *n* (kinds of) tropical American freshwater fish, noted for attacking and eating live animals.

pi·rate /ˋpaɪərət/ *n* **1** sea-robber; sea-robber's ship. **2** person who infringes another's copyright, who broadcasts without a licence, usurps trading rights, etc. □ *vt* [VP6A] use, reproduce (a book, a recording, another's work, etc) without authority and for one's own profit. **pi·rati·cal** /ˈpaɪəˋrætɪkl/ *adj* of, in the manner of, a ~. **pi·rati·cally** /-klɪ/ *adv* **pi·racy** /ˋpaɪərəsɪ/ *n* (*pl* -cies) [U] robbery by ~s; pirating of books, etc; [C] instance of either of these.

pir·ou·ette /ˈpɪrʊˋet/ *n* [C] ballet-dancer's rapid turn on the ball of the foot or on the point of the toe. □ *vi* dance a ~ or ~s.

pis al·ler /ˈpiz ˋæleɪ *US:* ˈpiz æˋleɪ/ *n* (F) the last resort; course of action taken because there seems to be nothing better.

pis·ca·tor·ial /ˈpɪskəˋtɔrɪəl/ *adj* of fishing; addicted to fishing.

Pis·ces /ˋpɑɪsiz/ *n* twelfth sign of the zodiac (also called *the fish*). ⇨ the illus at zodiac.

pish /pɪʃ/ *int* exclamation of contempt or impatience.

piss /pɪs/ *vt,vi* ⚠ (not in polite use) pass urine; discharge (blood) with urine; wet with urine: *~ the bed; P~ off!* (vulg) Go away! **~ed** *adj* (vulg) very drunk. □ *n* urine.

pis·ta·chio /pɪˋstɑtʃɪəʊ *US:* -ˋstæʃɪəʊ/ *n* (*pl* -chios /-ʃɪəʊz/) (tree yielding) nut with a green edible kernel; colour of this kernel.

pis·til /ˋpɪstl/ *n* seed-producing part of a flower. ⇨ the illus at flower.

pis·tol /ˋpɪstl/ *n* [C] small firearm held and fired in one hand. ***hold a ~ to sb's head,*** try, by using threats, to make him do what one wants.

pis·ton /ˋpɪstn/ *n* round plate or short cylinder of wood or metal, fitting closely inside another cylinder or tube in which it moves up and down or backwards and forwards, used in engines, pumps, etc to impart or receive motion by means of a rod, called a ˋ*~-rod.* **ˋ~ engined,** (of aircraft) having engines with ~s (contrasted with jet engines). **ˋ~ ring** *n* split metal ring used in a ~ to make a gas-tight joint.

pit¹ /pɪt/ *n* **1** hole in the earth, usu with steep sides, esp one from which material is dug out (*a ˋchalk-pit; a ˋclay-pit; a ˋcoal-pit*) or for industrial purposes (*a ˋsaw-pit; a ˋtan-pit*). **ˋpit·head** *n* entrance of a coalmine: *pithead baths.* **ˋpit·man** /-mən/ *n* (*pl* -men) collier; worker in a coal-pit. **ˋpit pony** *n* pony kept underground in coalmines. **ˋpit-prop** *n* prop used to support the roof of a gallery in a pit. **2** covered hole as a trap for wild animals, etc. **ˋpit·fall** *n* covered pit as a trap for animals; (more usu, fig) unsuspected snare or danger. **3** hollow in an animal or plant body, esp *the ~ of the stomach,* the depression in the belly between the ribs. ⇨ also *armpit* at arm¹(1). **4** scar left on the body after smallpox. **5** (GB, not US) seats on the ground floor of a theatre behind the stalls; people occupying these seats. **6** (US) part of the floor of an exchange used for a special commodity *the ˋwheat-pit.* **7 the pit,** (rhet, biblical) hell. **8** hole in the floor (of a garage, workshop) from which the underside of a motor-vehicle can be examined and repaired; place at which cars stop (at race-courses) for fuel, new tyres, etc. **9** = cockpit. □ *vt* [VP6A] mark with pits(4) or with hollows in the ground: *a face pitted with smallpox; the surface of the moon, pitted with craters.*

pit² /pɪt/ *n* (US) hard, stone-like seed (of such fruits as cherries, plums, peaches, dates) □ *vt* (-tt-) (US) remove pits from.

pit-a-pat /ˈpɪt ə ˋpæt/ *adv* with quick beating, with the sound of light, quick taps or steps: *Her heart/feet went ~.*

pitch¹ /pɪtʃ/ *n* **1** place where sb (esp a street trader) usu does business, where a street entertainer usu performs. ***queer sb's ~,*** upset his plans; thwart him. **2** (cricket) part of the ground between the wickets; point at which the ball strikes the ground; manner in which the ball is delivered in bowling; (baseball) manner or act of pitching the ball. **3** act of pitching or throwing anything; distance to which sth is thrown. **4** (music and speech) degree of highness or lowness: *the ~ of a voice.* **5** degree: *at the lowest ~ of his (ill) fortune. Excitement rose to fever ~.* **6** amount of slope (esp of a roof). **7** (of a ship) process of pitching(5).

pitch² /pɪtʃ/ *n* [U] black substance made from coal-tar, turpentine or petroleum, sticky and semi-liquid when hot, hard when cold, used to fill cracks or spaces, e g between planks forming a floor or ship's deck, make roofs waterproof, etc. ***as dark/black as ~,*** quite dark. **ˈ~-ˋblack/-ˋdark** *adjj* quite black or dark. **ˋ~-blende** *n* [U] black, shining mineral ore (oxide of uranium) yielding radium. **ˋ~ pine** *n* specially resinous kinds of pine-tree or its wood.

pitch³ /pɪtʃ/ *vt,vi* **1** [VP6A] set up, erect (a tent, camp); [VP2A] set up one's tent or camp. **2** [VP6A,15A,B] throw (a ball, etc); throw (sb or sth *out, aside,* etc), esp with impatience or energetic dislike: *Let's ~ the drunkard out. The men were ~ing hay,* lifting it, e g into a wagon, with forks. **ˋ~·fork** *n* long-handled fork with sharp prongs for lifting hay, etc. □ *vt* lift or move with a fork; (fig) thrust (a person) forcibly (*into* a position, etc). **3** [VP15A] (music) set in a certain key: *~ a tune too high/in a lower key. This song is ~ed too low for me.* **4** [VP2C,15A,B] (cause to) fall heavily forwards or outwards: *He ~ed on his head. The carriage overturned and the passengers were ~ed out.* **5** [VP2A,C] (of a ship) move up and down as the bows rise and fall. ⇨ roll²(6). **6 *~ in,*** set to work with energy. ***~ into,*** (a) attack violently: *They ~ed into him.* (b) get busy with: *We ~ed into the work. The hungry boy ~ed into the meat-pie,* began to eat it. ***~ upon,*** select by chance; light or pick upon: *~ upon the most suitable man for the job.* **7 *~ed battle,*** one that is fought with troops arranged in prepared positions, not a casual encounter. **8** [VP15B,22] (cricket) (cause the ball to) strike the ground near or around the wicket: *~ the ball short; ~ the balls up a bit;* (baseball) throw (the ball) to the batter. ***~ wickets,*** fix the stumps in the ground with the bails in place. **9** (sl) tell (a yarn, a story). **10 ˈ~-and-ˋtoss** *n* game of skill and chance in which coins are ~ed at a mark.

pitcher¹ /ˋpɪtʃə(r)/ *n* large (usu earthenware) vessel with a handle and lip for holding liquids; large jug.

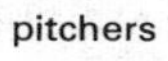

pitchers

pitcher² /ˋpɪtʃə(r)/ *n* (baseball) player who throws the ball. ⇨ the illus at baseball.

pit·eous /ˋpɪtɪəs/ *adj* arousing pity. **~·ly** *adv*

pit·fall /ˋpɪtfɔl/ ⇨ pit¹(2).

pith /pɪθ/ *n* [U] **1** soft substance that fills the stems of some plants (e g reeds); similar substance lining the rind of oranges, etc. **ˋ~ hat/helmet,** light sun hat made of dried ~. **2** spinal cord. **3** (fig) essential part: *the ~ of his argument/speech, etc.* **4** vigour; force. **~y** *adj* (-ier, -iest) **1** of, like, full of, ~. **2** forcible; full of meaning: *~y sayings.* **`~ily** /-əlɪ/ *adv*

piti·able /ˈpɪtɪəbl/ *adj* exciting pity; deserving only contempt: *a ~ attempt.* **piti·ably** /-əblɪ/ *adv*

piti·ful /ˈpɪtɪfl/ *adj* **1** feeling pity; compassionate. **2** causing pity: *a ~ sight.* **3** arousing contempt. **~ly** /-flɪ/ *adv*

piti·less /ˈpɪtɪləs/ *adj* showing no pity. **~·ly** *adv*

pi·ton /ˈpitɔ̃ *US:* ˈpiton/ *n* metal spike driven into rock, with a hole for rope, used as a hold in mountain climbing.

pit·tance /ˈpɪtns/ *n* low, insufficient payment or allowance (for work, etc): *work all day and every day for a mere ~.*

pitter-patter /ˈpɪtə pætə(r)/ *n* patter: *the ~ of rain on the roof.*

pi·tu·itary /pɪˈtjuɪtərɪ *US:* -ˈtuəterɪ/ *adj* **`~ gland,** small ductless gland at the base of the brain, secreting hormones that influence growth, etc. □ *n* ~ gland.

pity /ˈpɪtɪ/ *n* (*pl* -ties) **1** [U] feeling of sorrow for the troubles, sufferings, etc of another person: *be filled with/feel ~ for sb.* ***have/take ~ on sb,*** help sb in trouble, etc. ***for ~'s sake,*** (used as a form of entreaty): *For ~'s sake try to stop this persecution.* ***out of ~,*** because of a feeling of ~: *give a beggar a few coins out of ~.* **2** (with *indef art*, but not in *pl* except as below) (event which gives) cause for regret or sorrow: *What a ~* (= How unfortunate) *(that) you can't come with us! It's a ~ (that) he can't swim. The ~ is that...,* The thing to be regretted is that.... *It's a thousand pities that,* is most unfortunate that.... □ *vt* (*pt,pp* -tied) [VP6A] feel genuine ~ for; feel contemptuous ~ for: *He is much to be pitied. I ~ you if you think that you deserve to be helped.* **~·ing** *adv* expressing ~. **~·ing·ly** *adv*

pivot /ˈpɪvət/ *n* **1** central pin or point on which sth turns; ⇨ the illus at balance; (fig) sth on which an argument or discussion depends. **2** (mil) man or unit on whom a body of troops turns or wheels when changing front or direction. □ *vt,vi* **1** [VP3A] ***~ on,*** turn as on a ~. **2** [VP6A] place on a ~; supply with a ~. **~al** /-tl/ *adj* of, forming, a ~; (fig) of great importance because other things depend upon it.

pixi·lated /ˈpɪksɪleɪtɪd/ *adj* (dial) slightly crazy.

pixy, pixie /ˈpɪksɪ/ *n* (*pl* -xies) small elf or fairy.

pizza /ˈpitsə/ *n* (I) dish of food made by baking a layer of dough covered with a mixture of tomatoes, cheese, etc.

piz·zi·cato /ˌpɪtsɪˈkɑtəʊ/ *adj, adv* (I) (music) (played) by plucking the strings (of a violin, etc) instead of using the bow.

plac·ard /ˈplækɑd/ *n* written or printed announcement (to be) publicly displayed; poster. □ *vt* [VP6A] put ~s on (walls, etc); make known by means of ~s.

pla·cate /pləˈkeɪt *US:* ˈpleɪkeɪt/ *vt* [VP6A] soothe; pacify.

place[1] /pleɪs/ *n* **1** particular part of space occupied by sb or sth: *I can't be in two ~s at once.* **2** city, town, village, etc: *go to ~s and see things,* travel as a tourist. ***`go ~s,*** (colloq) enjoy increasing success. **3** building or area of land used for some particular purpose that is specified: *a ~ of worship,* a church, etc; *~s of amusement,* theatres, discotheques, cinemas, etc; *a `market-~; a ~ of business.* **4** particular ~ on a surface: *a sore ~ on my neck.* **5** passage, part, in a book, etc: *I've lost my ~,* can't find the ~ where I stopped reading. *Use a book-mark to keep your ~ instead of turning down the corner of the leaf.* **6** rank or station (in society, etc): *You must keep him in his ~,* not allow him to treat you as an equal, with too much familiarity. *Fifty years ago servants had to know their ~,* regard themselves as of inferior rank. **7** (in a race) position among those competitors who are winners: *Whose horse got the first ~? I shall back* (= bet some money on) *the favourite for a ~,* i e to be one of the first three past the winning-post. Hence, **`~-bet** *n* **8** (maths) position of a figure in a series as indicating its value in decimal or other notation: *calculated to five ~s of decimals/to five decimal ~s,* e g 6·57132. **9** single step or stage in an argument, etc: *in the first/second, etc ~.* **10** proper or natural position: *A tidy person likes to have a ~ for everything and everything in its ~. Please take your ~s,* e g ready for a dance. *Go back to your ~,* e g your seat. *There's always a ~ for you at my dinner-table,* You will always be a welcome guest. ***in ~,*** **(a)** in the right or proper ~: *I like to have everything in ~.* **(b)** (fig) suitable; appropriate: *The proposal is not quite in ~.* ***out of ~,*** **(a)** not in the right or proper place. **(b)** (fig) unsuitable; inappropriate: *Your remarks were rather out of ~.* ***in ~ of,*** instead of. ***give ~,*** yield. ***give ~ to,*** be succeeded by. ***make ~ for,*** **(a)** make room (which is more usu word) for. **(b)** yield precedence to. **(c)** be superseded by. ***put sb in his (proper) ~; put oneself in sb's/sb else's ~,*** ⇨ put[1](2). ***take the ~ of,*** be substituted for: *Who will take the ~ of Mr X/take Mr X's ~? Plastics have taken the ~ of many conventional materials.* ***take ~,*** happen. ***pride of ~,*** position of superiority. **11** office, employment, esp a government appointment; duties of an office-holder: *It's your ~ to see that the junior members of the staff do not arrive late. He will get a ~ in the Oxford boat,* will be chosen to be a member of the crew. **`~-men, `~-seekers,** men looking for favoured positions, e g in government. **12** country-house of some size, with the land round it; (colloq) house or other residence, e g a flat: *He has a nice little ~ in the country. Come round to my ~ one evening.* **13** (in proper names) alternative name for *Street, Square,* etc in a town: *St James's P~.* **14** **`~-kick** *n* (Rugby football) kick made when the ball is previously placed for that purpose on the ground.

place[2] /pleɪs/ *vt* [VP6A,15A,B] **1** put (sth) in a certain place; arrange (things) in their proper places: *P~ them in the right order.* **2** appoint (sb) to a post; put in office or authority: *He was ~d in command of the Second Army.* **3** put, invest (money): *~ £500 in Saving Bonds; ~ £100 to sb's credit in the bank.* **4** put (an order for goods, etc) with a business firm: *~ an order for books with W H Smith & Sons.* **5** dispose of (goods) to a customer: *How can we ~ all this surplus stock?* **6** have, fix, repose: *~ confidence in a leader.* **7** recognize or estimate (sb) by connecting him with past experience; fully identify: *I know that man's face, but I can't ~ him. He's a difficult man to ~.* **8** (racing) state the position of runners (in a race), contestants (in an athletic contest). ***be ~d,*** be among the first three: *The Duke's horse wasn't ~d.*

pla·cebo /plə`sibəʊ/ *n* (*pl* -bos, -boes /-bəʊz/) sth not containing medicine given to humour, not to cure, a patient.

pla·centa /plə`sentə/ *n* (zool) organ lining the womb during pregnancy, by which the foetus is nourished. It is expelled with the foetus and the umbilical cord following birth. ⇨ the illus at reproduce.

pla·cid /`plæsɪd/ *adj* calm; untroubled; (of a person) not easily irritated. **~·ly** *adv* **~·ity** /plə`sɪdətɪ/ *n* [U].

placket /`plækɪt/ *n* opening in a woman's skirt to make it easier to put on and take off; pocket inside this.

plage /plɑʒ/ *n* (F) sea beach (esp at a fashionable seaside resort).

pla·giar·ize /`pleɪdʒəraɪz/ *vt* [VP6A] take and use (e g in an essay) sb else's ideas, words, etc as if they were one's own. **pla·giar·ism** /-ɪzm/ *n* [U] plagiarizing; [C] instance of this. **pla·giar·ist** /-ɪst/ *n* person who ~s.

plague /pleɪg/ *n* **1** pestilence: *bubonic ~*. **`~-spot** *n* **(a)** spot on the skin characteristic of ~. **(b)** district infected with ~. **(c)** centre, source or symptom of moral evil. **2** cause of trouble, annoyance or disaster: *a ~ of locusts/flies. What a ~ that boy is!* What a nuisance he is! *P~ on it!* (dated) (used as an imprecation, or to express annoyance.) □ *vt* [VP6A,14] **~ *(with)*,** annoy (esp with repeated requests or questions). **plaguy** /`pleɪgɪ/ *adj* (colloq) annoying. **pla·guily** *adv* annoyingly; provokingly.

plaice /pleɪs/ *n* edible flatfish. ⇨ the illus at fish.

plaid /plæd/ *n* **1** [C] long piece of woollen cloth worn over the shoulders by Scottish Highlanders. **3** [U] cloth, usu with a chequered or tartan pattern, used for this article of dress.

plain¹ /pleɪn/ *adj* (-er, -est) **1** easy to see, hear or understand: *~ English; in ~ speech; ~ language,* (of telegrams, etc) not in code; *The meaning is quite ~*. **~ `sailing,** (fig) course of action that is simple and free from difficulties: *After we engaged a guide, everything was ~ sailing.* **2** simple; ordinary; without luxury or ornament: *a ~ blue dress,* of blue material without a design on it, or without trimmings, etc: *in ~ clothes,* (esp of policemen) in ordinary clothes, not in uniform; *~ food/cooking; a ~ cook,* one who can prepare ~ meals. **3** (of persons, their thoughts, actions, etc) straightforward; frank: *in ~ words,* frankly; *~ dealing,* honesty, sincerity. ***to be ~ with you,*** to speak openly. **'~-`spoken** *adj* frank in speech. **4** (of a person's appearance) not pretty or handsome: *It's a pity his wife is so ~*. **5 `~-song/-chant** *n* music for a number of voices in unison, used in the Anglican and Roman Catholic Church services. □ *adv* clearly: *learn to speak ~*. **~·ly** *adv*: *It was ~ly visible.* **~·ness** *n*

plain² /pleɪn/ *n* area of level country: *the wide ~s of Canada.* **`~s·man** /-zmən/ *n* (*pl* -men) inhabitant of a ~.

plain³ /pleɪn/ *n* simple stitch in knitting. ⇨ purl¹. □ *vt, vi* knit this stitch.

plaint /pleɪnt/ *n* **1** (legal) charge; accusation. **2** (poet) complaint; lamentation.

plain·tiff /`pleɪntɪf/ *n* person who brings an action at law. ⇨ defendant.

plain·tive /`pleɪntɪv/ *adj* sounding sad; sorrowful. **~·ly** *adv* **~·ness** *n*

plait /plæt/ *vt* [VP6A] weave or twist (three or more lengths of hair, straw, etc) under and over one another into one rope-like length. □ *n* sth made by ~ing: *wearing her hair in a ~*.

plan /plæn/ *n* **1** outline drawing (of or for a building) showing the relative size, positions, etc of the parts, esp as if seen from above: *~s for a new school.* ⇨ elevation(5) and the illus at perspective. **2** diagram (of the parts of a machine). **3** diagram showing how a garden, park, town or other area of land has been, or is to be, laid out. Cf *map* for a large area of land. **4** arrangement for doing or using sth, considered in advance: *make ~s for the holidays; a ~ to encourage thrift; a five-year ~,* e g for a country's economic and industrial development. ***go according to ~,*** happen as planned. □ *vt* (-nn-) **1** [VP6A] make a ~ of or for: *~ a house/garden.* **2** [VP7A] **~ *to do sth,*** make ~s: *We're ~ning to visit Europe this summer.* **3** [VP6A,15B] consider and arrange in advance: *~ (out) a military campaign.* **a ~ned economy,** economic system ~ned by government authorities. **~·ner** *n* one who makes ~s. **~·less** *adj* without a ~.

plan·chette /plɔ̃`ʃet *US:* plæn`ʃet/ *n* small board supported by two castors, with a vertical pencil said to trace marks on paper at spiritualistic seances without conscious direction by hand.

plane¹ /pleɪn/ *n* **`~(-tree),** one of several kinds of tree with spreading branches, broad leaves and thin bark, which comes off in flakes.

plane² /pleɪn/ *n* tool for trimming the surface of wood by taking shavings from it. ⇨ the illus at tool. □ *vt, vi* [VP2A,15B,2A,D] use a ~; make smooth with a ~. ***~ away/down, remove irregularities with a ~:*** *~ sth smooth.*

plane³ /pleɪn/ *n* **1** flat or level surface; surface such that the straight line joining any points on it is touching it at all points; imaginary surface of this kind; (attrib) **'~ ge`ometry,** geometry of figures on a ~. **'~ `sailing,** the art of determining a ship's position on the theory that the ship is moving on a ~. ⇨ *plain sailing* at plain¹(1). **2** wing or supporting surface of an aeroplane; (colloq, abbr for) aeroplane: *take the next ~ for São Paulo.* **3** (fig) level or stage (*of* development, etc): *on the same ~ as a savage; on a higher social ~*. □ *vi* **~ *(down)*,** (of aeroplanes) travel, glide.

planet /`plænɪt/ *n* one of the heavenly bodies (e g *Mars, Venus*) which move round a star such as the sun and is illuminated by it. **plan·et·ary** /`plænɪtrɪ *US:* -terɪ/ *adj* relating to, moving like, a ~. **plan·et·ar·ium** /'plænɪ`teərɪəm/ *n* (building with a) device for representing the movements of the stars and ~s by projecting spots of light on the inner surface of a large dome that represents the sky.

plan·gent /`plændʒənt/ *adj* (formal) (of sounds) resounding; vibrating.

plank /plæŋk/ *n* **1** long, flat piece of timber, 2 to 6 inches thick, 9 or more inches wide; board. **`~-bed** *n* one of boards, without mattresses. ***walk the ~,*** ⇨ walk²(4). **2** basic principle in a political platform. □ *vt* **1** [VP6A] furnish with ~s; cover (a floor, etc) with ~s. **2** [VP15B] **~ *sth down,*** (colloq) put down (esp money); pay at once. **`~·ing** *n* [U] ~s put down to form a floor.

plank·ton /`plæŋktn/ *n* [U] the (chiefly microscopic) forms of organic life that drift in or float on the water of the oceans, lakes, rivers, etc.

plant¹ /plɑnt *US:* plænt/ *n* **1** living organism

which is not an animal, esp the kind smaller than trees and shrubs: *garden ~s; a tobacco ~.* **`~-louse** *n* kinds of insect pest that attack ~s, esp aphis. **2** apparatus, fixtures, machinery, etc used in an industrial or manufacturing process: *We get our tractors and bulldozers from a ~-hire firm. The farm has its own lighting ~,* e g a generator for producing electric current. **3** (US) factory; buildings and equipment of an institution. **4** (sl) planned swindle; hoax; person who joins a gang of criminals to get evidence against them.

plant[2] /plɑnt *US:* plænt/ *vt* [VP6A,15A,B] **1** put ~s, bushes, trees, etc in (a garden, etc): *~ a garden with rose-bushes; set up a monument and ~ it round with trees/~ trees round it.* **2** put (plants, trees, etc) in the ground to grow; (fig) cause (an idea) to take root in sb's mind: *~ (out) strawberry runners/pansies.* ⇨ **sow**[2]. **3** place firmly in position; take up a position or attitude: *He ~ed his feet firmly on the ground. He ~ed himself in front of the fire. He ~ed his feet wide apart.* **4** establish, found (a community, colony, etc); settle (a person) in a place as a colonist, etc. **5** deliver (a blow, etc) with deliberate aim: *~ a blow on sb's ear.* **6** (sl) hide (esp in order to deceive sb, to cause an innocent person to seem guilty, etc): *~ stolen goods on sb.* **~er** *n* **1** person who grows crops on a plantation: *`tea-~ers; `rubber-~ers.* **2** machine for ~ing: *po`tato-~er.*

plan·tain[1] /ˋplæntɪn/ *n* tree-like tropical plant bearing fruit similar to that of the banana-palm; its fruit. ⇨ the illus at **vegetable**.

plan·tain[2] /ˋplæntɪn/ *n* common wild plant with broad leaves and seeds much used for cage-birds.

plan·ta·tion /plænˋteɪʃn/ *n* **1** area of land planted with trees: *~s of fir and pine.* **2** large estate on which tea, cotton, sugar, tobacco or other commercial crop is cultivated: *`~ songs,* songs sung by Negroes who formerly worked as slaves on cotton ~s in N America.

plaque /plɑk *US:* plæk/ *n* flat metal or porcelain plate fixed on a wall as an ornament or memorial.

plash /plæʃ/ *n* (*sing* only) light splashing sound: *the ~ of oars in water.* □ *vt,vi* [VP6A,2A] strike the surface of (water) gently; splash.

plasm /plæzm/ *n* genetic material of a cell.

plasma /ˋplæzmə/ *n* **`blood ~,** clear, yellowish fluid in which the blood-cells are carried.

plas·ter /plɑstə(r) *US:* ˋplæs-/ *n* **1** [U] soft mixture of lime, sand, water, etc used for coating walls and ceilings. **'~ of `Paris,** white paste made from gypsum, that becomes very hard when dry, used for making moulds, etc. **`~ cast, (a)** mould made with gauze and ~ of Paris to hold a broken or dislocated bone in place. **(b)** mould (e g for a small statue) made of ~ of Paris. **`~·board** *n* board made of gypsum and thick paper or cardboard, used for inside walls and ceilings instead of plastering. **2** [C] piece of fabric spread with a medicinal substance, for application to part of the body, to relieve pain, cover a wound, etc. **3 (`sticking-)~,** material treated with some substance so that it will stick to the skin; used for covering a slight cut, holding a bandage in position, etc. □ *vt* [VP6A,14] **1** cover (a wall, etc) with ~(1); put a ~(2) on (the body). **2 *~ sth with sth; ~ sth on sth,*** cover thickly: *hair ~ed with oil; an old suitcase ~ed with hotel labels.* **~ed** *adj* (colloq) drunk. **~er** *n* workman who ~s walls and ceilings.

plas·tic /ˋplæstɪk/ *adj* **1** (of materials) easily shaped or moulded: *Clay is a ~ substance; (of goods) made of such materials, esp synthetic resinous substances: ~ raincoats/curtains.* **'~ ex`plosive,** kind that is easily moulded around the object it is to destroy. **'~-`bomb,** one made of such explosive. **2** of the art of modelling: *the ~ arts.* **'~ `surgery,** for the restoration of deformed or diseased parts of the body (by grafting skin, etc). **3** (fig) easily influenced or changed: *the ~ mind of a child.* □ *n* [C] ~ substance. **plas·tics** *n pl* (with *sing v*) (science of) ~ substances, esp synthetic resinous substances, moulded under pressure while heated, or drawn into filaments for use in textiles. **~·ity** /plæˋstɪsətɪ/ *n* [U] state or quality of being ~.

plas·ti·cine /ˋplæstɪsin/ *n* [U] (P) plastic substance resembling clay but remaining soft for a long time, used for modelling in schools.

plate[1] /pleɪt/ *n* **1** [C] shallow, usu circular, almost flat dish, made (usu) of earthenware or china, from which food is served or eaten: *a dinner/soup/dessert ~*; contents of this: *a ~ of beef and vegetables.* **`~-rack** *n* rack in which ~s are kept or placed to drain after being washed. ***hand/give sb sth on a ~,*** (colloq) give, allow sb to have, sth

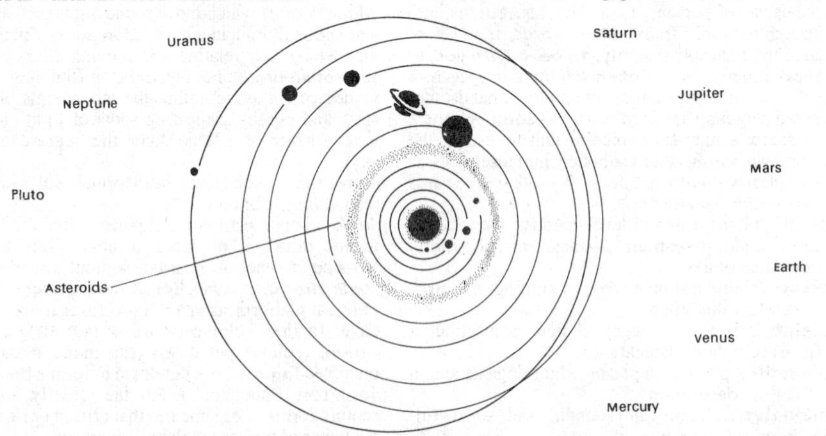

the planets of our solar system

without his having to make any effort. **2** [C] similar vessel or dish (usu of metal) used for collection of money in churches: *put only a dime in the* ~. **3** [U] (collective) gold or silver articles, e g spoons, dishes, bowls, for use at meals: *a fine piece of* ~, one of these articles. ⇨ plate²(2). **'~-powder** *n* powder for cleaning and polishing ~. **4** [C] flat, thin sheet of metal, glass, etc e g steel ~s for building ships: *'boiler ~s.* **'~-'glass** *n* [U] thick and very clear glass in sheets for windows, mirrors, etc. **5** [C] sheet of glass coated with sensitive film for photography: *'whole-~, 'half-~, 'quarter-~,* the usual sizes. **6** [C] oblong piece of metal (usu brass) with a person's name, etc on it, fixed to the door or gate (as used by doctors, solicitors and other professional persons). **7** sheet of metal, plastic, rubber, etc from which the pages of a book are printed; book illustration (usu photographic) printed separately from the text. **8** **'dental ~,** (also called a *denture*) thin piece of plastic material, moulded to the shape of the gums, with artificial teeth attached to it. **9** [C] silver or gold cup as a prize for a horse-race; the race. **10** (in baseball) (also **home ~**) home base of the batting side. **'~·ful** /-fʊl/ *n* amount that a ~ holds.

plate² /pleɪt/ *vt* [VP6A,14] **1** cover (esp a ship) with metal plates(**4**). **2** cover (another metal) with gold, silver, copper or tin: *gold-~d dishes; silver-~d spoons.*

pla·teau /'plætəʊ *US:* plæ'təʊ/ *n* (*pl* **-teaus** or **teaux** /-təʊz/) expanse of level land high above sea-level. ⇨ the illus at mountain.

plate·layer /'pleɪtleɪə(r)/ *n* workman who lays and repairs railway tracks.

plat·form /'plætfɔm/ *n* **1** flat surface built at a higher level than the track in a railway station, used by travellers: *Which ~ does the Bournemouth train leave from?* **2** flat structure raised above floor-level for speakers in a hall or in the open air, teachers in a classroom, etc; space at the entrance of a bus or tram (for the conductor). **3** programme of a political party, esp as stated before an election.

plat·ing /'pleɪtɪŋ/ *n* (esp) thin coating of gold, silver, etc. ⇨ plate²(2).

plati·num /'plætn̩əm/ *n* [U] grey untarnishable metal (symbol **Pt**) used for jewellery and alloyed with other metals for use in industry. **'~ 'blonde,** (colloq) woman with silvery-white hair (but not used of a hair that has turned white with age).

plati·tude /plætɪtjud *US:* -tud/ *n* **1** [C] statement that is obviously true, esp one often heard before, but uttered as if it were new. **2** [U] commonplaceness; quality of being trite. **plati·tudi·nous** /'plætɪ'tjudɪnəs *US:* -'tudn̩əs/ *adj* commonplace: *platitudinous remarks.*

Pla·tonic /plə'tonɪk/ *adj* of Plato /'pleɪtəʊ/ (about 428–347 BC) the Greek philosopher, or his teachings: ~ *love/friendship,* between two people without a desire for physical love.

pla·toon /plə'tun/ *n* body of soldiers, subdivision of a company, acting as a unit and commanded by a lieutenant.

plat·ter /'plætə(r)/ *n* **1** (US) large, shallow dish for serving food, esp meat and fish. **2** (archaic in GB) flat dish, often of wood.

platy·pus /'plætɪpəs/ *n* (*pl* **-puses** /-pəsɪz/) **'duck·billed '~,** small Australian animal which suckles its young but lays eggs (called *duckbill* because it has a bill like that of a duck). ⇨ the illus at small.

plau·dit /'plɔdɪt/ *n* (usu *pl*) cry, clapping or other sign of approval: *gratified at the ~s of the audience.*

plaus·ible /'plɔzəbl/ *adj* **1** seeming to be right or reasonable: *a ~ excuse/explanation.* **2** (of persons) clever at producing ~ arguments, etc: *a ~ rogue.* **plaus·ibly** /-əblɪ/ *adv* **plausi·bil·ity** /'plɔzə'bɪlətɪ/ *n* [U] state of being ~; [C] (*pl* **-ties**) ~ excuse, argument, etc.

play¹ /pleɪ/ *n* **1** [U] (what is done for) amusement; recreation: *The children are at ~,* engaged in playing. *What I said was only in ~,* not intended to be taken seriously. ***a ~ on words,*** pun. **'child's-~,** sth simple and easy. **'~-box** *n* box to hold toys. **'~-boy** *n* (mod use) rich young man chiefly interested in enjoying himself. **'~-fellow/-mate** *nn* companion in ~. **'~-mate** *n* friend one ~s with. **'~-group** *n* = ~-school. **'~·ground** *n* piece of ground used for ~, e g one at a school or in a public park. Cf *playing-field* below. **'~-pen** *n* portable enclosure in which a baby or small child may be left to ~. **'~·room** *n* one in a house for children to ~ in. **'~-school** *n* one for infants under four years old. **'~-suit** *n* loose garment(s) to be worn (e g by young children) while playing. **'~·thing** *n* toy; (fig) sb treated as a mere toy. **'~-time** *n* period for ~. **2** [U] the playing of a game; manner of playing: *There was a lot of rough ~ in the football match yesterday. That was pretty ~/a pretty bit of ~!* ***in/out of ~,*** (of the ball in football, cricket, etc) in/not in a position where the rules of the game allow it to be played. **fair ~,** (fig) justice, equal conditions and treatment for all: *I will see fair ~,* that both sides are treated justly. **foul ~,** ~ contrary to the rules; (fig) treachery; violence: *Do the police suspect foul ~?* **3** (*sing* only) turn or move in a game (e g chess): *It's your ~,* You are to make the next move. **4** [U] gaming; gambling: *lose £50 in one evening's ~; high ~,* i e for high stakes. **5** [C] drama for the stage: *the ~s of Shakespeare. Let's go to a ~* (= theatre) *this evening.* ***as good as a ~,*** amusing, interesting. **'~-actor** *n* (old use) actor. **'~-acting** *n* performance of ~s; (fig) pretence. **'~·bill** *n* bill announcing the performance of a ~. **'~·goer** /-gəʊə(r)/ *n* person who often goes to the theatre. **'~·house** *n* theatre. **'~·wright** *n* dramatist. **6** [U] light, quick, fitful movement: *the ~ of sunlight upon water.* **7** [U] (space for) free and easy movement; scope for activity: *allow full ~ to one's curiosity; give free ~ to one's fancy/emotions; a knot with too much ~,* one that is not tight enough. *Give the rope more ~,* keep it less taut. **8** [U] activity; operation: *the ~ of forces.* ***be in full ~/come into ~,*** begin to operate or be active. ***bring sth into ~,*** make use of it; bring it into action.

play² /pleɪ/ *vt,vi* (*pt,pp* ~ed /pleɪd/) (For special uses with *adverbial particles* and *preps,* ⇨ 15 below.) **1** [VP2A,B,C] (contrasted with *work*) have fun; do things to pass the time pleasantly, as children do: *The children are ~ing in the park. Let's go out and ~.* **~ with,** amuse oneself with: *~ with the kitten.* **2** [VP3A,6A] ***~ (at doing sth),*** pretend, for fun, to be sth or do sth: *Let's ~ (at being) pirates. The children were ~ing at keeping shop.* **3** [VP6A,14,12C] practice; execute: *~ a joke/trick/prank on sb. He has played me a mean* *trick.* **4** [VP6A,2A,C,3A] (be able to) take part in a game, e g of cricket, football, golf, cards: *Do you ~ cricket? He ~s (football) for Stoke/England. On Saturday France ~s (Rugby) against Wales/ ~s Wales at Rugby. They were ~ing bridge. Will you ~ me at chess? He went on ~ing* (= gambling) *until he had lost everything.* **5** [VP2C] ***~ (as/at),*** fill a particular position in a team: *I've never ~ed (as/at) centre-forward before. Who's ~ing in goal/as goal-keeper?* [VP6A,15A,16B] ***~ sb (as/at),*** include in a team: *I think we should ~ Smith in the next match. Who shall we ~ as goal-keeper?* **6** [VP15A,B] (cricket, football, etc) strike (the ball) in a specified manner: *~ the ball to mid-on; ~ (the ball) on to one's own wicket* (and so put oneself out). *In soccer only the goal-keeper may ~ the ball with his hands.* ***~ ball (with),*** (fig, colloq) be ready to act in partnership; co-operate: *The French President refused to ~ ball,* e g to co-operate with the leader of another country. [VP2C] (cricket, of the ground) be in good, poor, etc condition for ~ing: *The pitch is ~ing well/badly.* **7** [VP6A] move (a piece) in chess: *~ a pawn;* take (a playing-card) from one's hand (in whist, bridge, etc) and lay it down face upwards when one's turn comes: *~ one's ace of hearts/a trump.* ***~ one's cards well/badly,*** (fig) make good/bad use of opportunities. **8** ***~ fair,*** fairly; in accordance with the rules. ***~ hard,*** (of a player) ~ vigorously. ***~ the ball, not the man,*** kick the ball, not one's opponent. ***~ the game,*** observe the rules of the game; (fig) be fair and honest; observe the code of honour. **9** [VP6A,2A,12B,13B] perform on (a musical instrument), perform (a musical composition): *~ the piano/flute/violin, etc; ~ a Beethoven sonata. Won't you please ~ me some Chopin/~ some Chopin for me? He was ~ing an old tune on his guitar. He ~ed some good pop music at the party,* i e on discs or tapes. [VP15B] ***~ sth back,*** reproduce (music, speech, etc) from a tape or disc after it has been recorded: *The discussion was recorded on tape and then ~ed back.* Hence, **'~-back** *n* **(a)** the device on a tape-recorder which ~s back recorded material. **(b)** occasion when this is done. ***~ second fiddle (to sb),*** ⇨ fiddle. ***~ sth by ear/at sight,*** ⇨ ear[1](2), *at/on sight* at sight[1](2). ***~ it cool,*** ⇨ cool[1](5). **10** [VP6A,2A] perform (a drama on the stage); act (a part in a drama); (of a drama) be performed: *~ 'Twelfth Night'; ~ Shylock; the National Theatre, where 'Hamlet' is now ~ing,* = being ~ed. ***~ the fool,*** act foolishly. ***~ the man,*** act like a man; be manly. ***~ a (big, small) part (in sth),*** ⇨ part[1](3). **11** [VP2A,C,15A] move about in a light or capricious manner; direct (light) (*on, over, along,* etc sth): *sunlight ~ing on the water. They ~ed coloured lights over the dance floor. A smile ~ed on her lips. His fancy ~ed round the idea of proposing to Mary. They ~ed searchlights on the clouds/along the road.* **12** [VP2A,6A,15A] operate continuously; discharge in a steady stream: *The fountains in the park ~ on Sundays. The firemen ~ed their hoses on the burning building.* **13** [VP14,3A] ***~ (sth) (up)on,*** fire: *We ~ed our guns on the enemy's lines. Their guns ~ed on the fort.* **14** ***~ a fish,*** (when angling with a rod and line) allow a fish to exhaust itself by pulling against the line. **15** [VP2C,3A,15B] (special uses with *adverbial particles* and *preps*):

play at sth, **(a)** ⇨ 2,5 above. **(b)** engage in sth in a trivial or half-hearted way, or merely for pleasure: *Go for him properly—you're only ~ing at boxing!*

play sth back, ⇨ 9 above.

play down to sb, deliberately talk to or behave towards sb so that they do not feel inferior in order to win support or favour. ***~ sth down,*** deliberately minimize its importance.

play (the congregation) in/into, ~ music, e g on the organ, while people are entering a church.

play into (the palms of) sb's hands/the hands of sb, act so as to give him an advantage or benefit: *My opponent ~ed into my hands.*

play one person off against another, oppose him against another, esp for one's own advantage; stimulate rivalry between them. ***~ (sth) off,*** ~ (e g a football) match that was drawn: *~ off a draw/tie. Leeds and Liverpool ~ off (their tie) tomorrow.* Hence, **'~-off** *n* such a match.

play upon sth, try to rouse or make use of (sb's feelings, incredulity, etc): *He tried to ~ on her sympathies.* ***~ upon words,*** make puns.

play sth out, ~ it to the end (usu fig): *The long struggle between the strikers and their employers is not yet ~ed out.* ***be ~ed out,*** be exhausted of energy or usefulness; be out of date: *His horse was ~ed out when the day's hunting was over. Is that theory ~ed out,* no longer worth considering?

play up, **(a)** (esp in the *imper*) (sport) ~ vigorously, energetically. **(b)** (colloq) behave mischievously: *Don't let the children ~ up.* ***~ sth up,*** give excessive importance to: *Don't let him ~ up his illness,* e g by making it an excuse for doing nothing. ***~ sb up,*** (colloq) give trouble to: *This wretched sciatica has been ~ing me up again.* ***~ up to sb,*** **(a)** act in a drama so as to support another actor. **(b)** (colloq) flatter (to win favour for oneself): *He always ~s up to his political bosses.*

play with sb, **(a)** ⇨ 1 above. **(b)** trifle with; consider lightly: *It's wrong for a man to ~ with a woman's affections. He's ~ing with the idea of emigrating to Canada.*

player /ˈpleɪə(r)/ *n* **1** one who plays a game; (cricket, formerly, in GB) one who played cricket professionally, not as an amateur: *Gentlemen v P~s.* **2** actor. **3** person who plays a musical instrument; mechanical device for producing musical sounds: *a 'record-~.* **'~-piano** *n* piano fitted with a mechanism which enables the piano to be played automatically.

play·ful /ˈpleɪfl/ *adj* full of fun; in a mood for play; not serious: *as ~ as a kitten; a ~ manner.* **~ly** /-fḷɪ/ *adv* **~·ness** *n*

play·ing /ˈpleɪɪŋ/ *n* **'~-card,** ⇨ card[1](3). **'~-field** *n* field for such games as football and cricket; field for children's games.

play·let /ˈpleɪlət/ *n* short dramatic piece.

plaza /ˈplɑzə *US:* ˈplæzə/ *n* market-place; open square (esp in a Spanish town).

plea /pli/ *n* [C] **1** (legal) statement made by or for a person charged in a law court. **2** request: *~s for mercy.* **3** reason or excuse offered for wrongdoing or failure to do sth, etc: *on the ~ of ill health.*

pleach /plitʃ/ *vt* [VP6A] interlace: *~ed hedges,* made by intertwining growing branches.

plead /plid/ *vt,vi* (*pt,pp* ~ed, or, US pled, /pled/) **1** [VP3A] (legal) ***~ for/against sb,*** address a court of law as an advocate on behalf of either the plaintiff or the defendent. ***~ guilty/not guilty,*** admit/deny that one is guilty: *'How do you*

~?'—'*Not guilty, my Lord*'. **2** [VP6A] (legal) (of a lawyer) present the case of (to a court of law); put forward as a plea: *You should get a lawyer to ~ your case. Her Counsel ~ed insanity,* declared that his client was insane, and therefore not legally responsible for her actions. **3** [VP3A] ***~ (with sb) (for sth/to do sth),*** ask earnestly: *~ (with sb) for mercy. He ~ed with his boy to be less trouble to his mother.* **4** [VP6A] offer as an explanation or excuse: *The thief ~ed poverty. She ~ed ignorance of the law.* **5** [VP6A] argue in favour of; advance reasons for (a cause, etc): *~ the cause of the Senior Citizens.* **~·ing** *n* (legal; *pl*) formal (usu written) statements, replies to accusations, etc, made by the parties in a legal action. **~·ing·ly** *adv*

pleas·ance /ˈplezns/ *n* [C] pleasure-ground, esp a garden with trees, fountains, etc attached to a mansion.

pleas·ant /ˈpleznt/ *adj* giving pleasure; agreeable; friendly: *a ~ afternoon/taste/wine/surprise/companion; make oneself ~ to visitors; ~ to the taste.* **~·ly** *adv* **~·ness** *n* [U].

pleas·an·try /ˈplezntrɪ/ *n* (*pl* -ries) **1** [U] being jocular; humour. **2** [C] humorous or joking remark: *The girls smiled dutifully at the headmistress's pleasantries.*

please /pliz/ *vi,vt* **1** (imper) (abbr of *if you ~*) (used as a polite form of request): *Come in, ~. P~ come in. Two coffees, ~. P~ don't do that.* **2** [VP6A] give satisfaction to; be agreeable to: *That will ~ you. It's difficult to ~ everybody. Are you ~d with your new clothes? We're very ~d to see you here. I shall be ~d to come.* ***P~ yourself,*** Do as you like. **3** [VP2A] think fit; choose: *I shall do as I ~. Take as many as you ~. You may do as you ~.* **4** ***if you ~,*** (used with the ironical implication that nothing could be more reasonable): *'And now, if you ~, I'm to get nothing for all my work!'* ***~ God,*** if it be pleasing to God: *War may be abolished one day, ~ God.* **pleased** *adj* glad; feeling or showing satisfaction: *He looked ~d with himself. I'm very (much) ~d with what he has done.* **pleas·ing** *adj* affording pleasure (*to*); agreeable. **pleas·ing·ly** *adv*

pleas·ure /ˈpleʒə(r)/ *n* **1** [U] feeling of being happy or satisfied: *It gave me much ~ to hear of your success. Is this a ~-seeking age? Has he gone abroad for ~ or on business? May we have the ~ of your company for lunch? 'Will you join us?'—'Thank you, with ~'. His life is given to ~,* to sensuous enjoyments. ***take (no/great, etc) ~ in sth,*** experience (no, etc) enjoyment: *Some boys take great ~ in teasing their little sisters.* **ˈ~-boat/-craft** *n* one used for ~ only. **ˈ~-ground** *n* amusement park; recreation ground. **2** [U] will; desire: *We await your ~. We needn't consult his ~. You may go or stay at your ~,* as you wish. **3** [C] thing that gives happiness: *the ~s of friendship.* **pleas·ur·able** /ˈpleʒərəbl/ *adj* giving ~. **pleas·ur·ably** /-əblɪ/ *adv*

pleat /plit/ *n* fold made by doubling cloth on itself. □ *vt* [VP6A] make ~s in: *a ~ed skirt.*

pleb /pleb/ *n* (colloq abbr for) plebeian.

pleb·eian /plɪˈbiən/ *n, adj* (person who is) of the lower social classes (originally in ancient Rome); coarse; ignoble.

plebi·scite /ˈplebɪsɪt *US:* -saɪt/ *n* [C] (decision made upon a political question by) the votes of all qualified citizens.

plec·trum /ˈplektrəm/ *n* small piece of metal, bone or ivory attached to the finger for plucking the strings of some stringed instruments, e g the mandolin, guitar.

pled /pled/ ⇨ plead.

pledge /pledʒ/ *n* **1** [C] sth left with sb to be kept by him until the giver has done sth which he is under an obligation to do; article left with a pawnbroker. **2** [U] state of being left with sb on these conditions: *goods lying in ~; put/hold sth in ~; take sth out of ~.* **3** [C] sth given as a sign of love, approval, etc: *a ~ of friendship;* (fig) *the ~ of their youthful love,* of their child. **4** [U] agreement; promise: *under ~ of secrecy.* ***take/sign the ~,*** (esp) make a written promise to abstain from alcoholic drink. □ *vt* [VP6A] **1** give as security; put in pawn. **2** give; engage; make an undertaking (to do sth): *be ~d to secrecy; ~ one's word/honour.* **3** drink the health of: *~ the bride and bridegroom.*

ple·nary /ˈplinərɪ/ *adj* **1** (of powers, authority) unlimited; absolute. **2** (of meetings) attended by all who have a right to attend: *a ~ session.* **plen·ar·ily** /ˈplinərəlɪ/ *adv*

pleni·po·ten·tiary /ˌplenɪpəˈtenʃərɪ/ *n* (*pl* -ries), *adj* (person, e g a representative, an ambassador) having full power to act, make decisions, etc (on behalf of his government, etc).

pleni·tude /ˈplenɪtjud *US:* -tud/ *n* (*sing* only) (formal) fullness; abundance: *in the ~ of his powers.*

plen·teous /ˈplentɪəs/ *adj* (chiefly poet) plentiful. **~·ly** *adv*

plen·ti·ful /ˈplentɪfl/ *adj* in large quantities or numbers; abundant. **~ly** /-flɪ/ *adv*

plenty /ˈplentɪ/ *n* [U] ***~ (of),*** as much as or more than is needed or desired; a large number or quantity: *There are ~ of eggs in the house. There's ~ more (of it). We must get to the station in ~ of time. Six will be ~,* as many as I need. *I've had ~, thank you.* **in ~**: *There was food and drink in ~.* □ *adv* (colloq) quite: *It's ~ big enough.*

pleo·nasm /ˈplɪənæzm/ *n* [C,U] (instance of the) use of more words than are needed to express the meaning, e g each of the *two* twins; divide sth into *four* quarters.

pleth·ora /ˈpleθərə/ *n* (formal) **1** unhealthy repletion; over-abundance. **2** (med) unhealthy condition of the body marked by an excess of red corpuscles in the blood.

pleur·isy /ˈplʊərɪsɪ/ *n* [U] serious illness with inflammation of the delicate membrane of the thorax and the lungs, marked by pain in the chest or sides.

plexus /ˈpleksəs/ *n* (*pl* ~es /-səsɪz/ or ~) (anat) network of fibres or vessels in the body: *the solar ~,* in the abdomen.

pli·able /ˈplɑɪəbl/ *adj* easily bent, shaped or twisted; (of the mind) easily influenced; open to suggestions. **pli·abil·ity** /ˌplɑɪəˈbɪlətɪ/ *n* [U].

pli·ant /ˈplɑɪənt/ *adj* pliable. **~·ly** *adv* **pli·ancy** /ˈplɑɪənsɪ/ *n*

pli·ers /ˈplɑɪəz/ *n pl* (also **a pair of ~**) kind of pincers with long, flat jaws, used for holding, bending, twisting or cutting wire, etc. ⇨ the illus at tool.

plight[1] /plɑɪt/ *n* serious and difficult condition: *His affairs were in a terrible ~. What a ~ you are in!*

plight[2] /plɑɪt/ *vt* [VP6A] **1** pledge, promise: *one's ~ed word.* **2** *~ one's troth; ~ oneself,* (archaic) engage oneself to be married: (archaic) ~*ed lovers*.

Plim·soll[1] /ˋplɪmsl/ *n* ˋ~ **line/mark,** line on the hull of a ship to mark how far it may legally go down in the water when loaded.

plim·solls[2] /ˋplɪmslz/ *n pl* rubber-soled canvas shoes (US = *sneakers*).

plinth /plɪnθ/ *n* square base or block on which a column or statue stands. ⇨ the illus at column.

plod /plɒd/ *vi, vt* (-dd-) [VP2C] continue walking, working, etc slowly but without resting: ~ *on one's way;* ~ *away at a dull task.* **~·der** *n* person who ~s; slow but earnest person. **~·ding** *adj* **~·ding·ly** *adv*

plonk[1] /plɒŋk/ *n* sound of sth dropping (esp into liquid). □ *adv* with a ~. □ *vi* ~ ***(down),*** drop sth with a ~ing sound: ~ *the fish down on the table.*

plonk[2] /plɒŋk/ *n* [U] (sl) cheap wine.

plop /plɒp/ *n* [C] sound (as) of a small smooth object dropping into water without a splash. □ *adv* with a ~. □ *vi* (-pp-) make a ~; fall with a ~.

plo·sive /ˋpləʊsɪv/ *n, adj* (phonetics) (consonant sound) with a complete closing of the air passage followed by an audible release of the air compressed behind the closure, e g /p/ in *top*.

plot[1] /plɒt/ *n* piece of ground (usu small): *a building ~; a ~ of vegetables.* □ *vt, vi* (-tt-) **1** make a plan, map or diagram of; mark (the position of sth) on a diagram by connecting points on a graph: ~ *a temperature curve;* ~ *aircraft movements by radar.* **2** [VP15B] ~ ***(out),*** divide into ~s.

plot[2] /plɒt/ *n* [C] **1** secret plan (good or bad); conspiracy: *a ~ to overthrow the government.* **2** plan or outline (of the events of a story, esp of a novel or drama). □ *vt, vi* (-tt-) [VP2A,3A,4,6A,8,10] make secret plans; form, take part in, a ~: ~ *with sb against the government.* **~·ter** *n* person who ~s; conspirator.

plough (US = **plow**) /plaʊ/ *n* **1** implement for cutting furrows in soil and turning it up, drawn by animals or (more usually) a tractor. ***put one's hand to the ~,*** (fig) undertake a task. ˋ**~·boy** *n* boy who leads the horses that pull a ~. ˋ**~·man** /-mən/ *n* (*pl* -men) man who guides a ~. ˋ**~·share** *n* broad blade of a ~. **2** kinds of implement resembling a ~. ˋ**snow·~** *n* one for clearing away snow from roads and railways. **3** [U] ploughed land: *100 acres of ~.* **4 the P~,** (astron) the group of stars called *Charles's Wain, the Dipper* or *the Great Bear.* □ *vt, vi* **1** [VP6A,15B] ~ ***(back),*** break up (land) with a ~; ~ *a field;* (fig) ~ *back the profits of a business,* reinvest them. ~ ***a lonely furrow,*** (fig) work without help or support. ~ ***the sand,*** do useless work. **2** [VP3A] ~ ***through,*** force a way through; advance laboriously: *a ship ~ing through the heavy waves; ~ (one's way) through the mud; ~ through a dull textbook.* **3** [VP6A] (sl) reject (a candidate) in an examination: *The examiners ~ed half the candidates.*

plover /ˋplʌvə(r)/ *n* sorts of long-legged, short-tailed land bird that frequents marshy ground near the sea, esp (in England) the golden ~, the green ~, and the lapwing or peewit.

plow /plaʊ/ (US) = plough.

ploy /plɔɪ/ *n* [C] employment; frolic; undertaking; (colloq) sth said or done, e g in a game, to win an advantage over one's opponent.

pluck /plʌk/ *vt, vi* **1** [VP6A] pull the feathers off (a hen, goose, etc): *Has this goose been ~ed?* **2**

a plough

[VP6A] pick (flowers, fruit, etc); [VP15B] ~ ***out/up,*** pull (weeds, etc, up or out). **3** [VP3A] ~ ***at,*** snatch at; take hold of and pull: *The child was ~ing at its mother's skirt.* **4** ~ ***up courage,*** summon one's courage; overcome one's fears. **5** [VP6A] (sl) = plough(3). **6** [VP6A] (sl) swindle (esp a young or inexperienced person, e g in gambling). □ *n* **1** [U] courage; spirit: *a boy with plenty of ~.* **2** [U] that which is ~ed out, esp the heart, liver and lungs of an animal that has been killed. **3** [C] short, sharp pull. **~y** *adj* (-ier, -iest) brave; having ~(1). **~·ily** /-əlɪ/ *adv*

plug /plʌg/ *n* **1** piece of wood, metal, etc used to stop up a hole (e g in a barrel, wash-basin, cistern, etc). **2** hydrant. **3** device for making a connection with a supply of electric current: *a three-/two-pin ~; put the ~ in the socket/outlet.* ⇨ also *sparking-~* at spark[1]. **4** cake of pressed or twisted tobacco; piece of this cut off for chewing. **5** (sl) piece of favourable publicity (e g in a radio or TV programme) for commercial product. ⇨ 5 below. □ *vt, vi* (-gg-) **1** [VP6A,15B] ~ ***(up),*** stop or fill (up) with a ~: ~ *a leak.* **2** [VP2C] (colloq) ~ ***away at,*** work hard at. **3** [VP2C,15B] ~ ***(sth) in,*** make a connection with a ~(3): ~ *in the TV set.* **4** [VP6A] (US, sl) hit; shoot. **5** [VP6A] (sl) cause (sth) to be widely known by giving repeated publicity: ~ *a new song,* e g on radio or TV.

plum /plʌm/ *n* **1** (tree having) soft round, smooth-skinned fruit with a stone-like seed. ⇨ the illus at fruit. **2** ˈ~ ˋ**cake,** kind containing dried raisins, currants, etc. ˈ~ ˋ**duff,** boiled pudding containing dried raisins, currants, etc. ˈ**~-ˋpudding,** rich boiled pudding containing dried fruits and spices, part of traditional Christmas fare. **2** (colloq) sth considered good and desirable, esp a well-paid position.

plum·age /ˋplumɪdʒ/ *n* [U] bird's feathers: *tropical birds in their brightly coloured ~.*

plumb /plʌm/ *n* ball or piece of lead tied to the end of a cord or rope (**a** ˋ**~-line**) for finding the depth of water or testing whether a wall is vertical. ***out of ~,*** not vertical. □ *adv* **1** exactly. **2** (US, colloq) quite: ~ *crazy.* □ *vt* [VP6A] (fig) get to the root of: ~ *the depths of a mystery.*

plum·bago[1] /plʌmˋbeɪgəʊ/ *n* [U] black substance, graphite, used for pencils, etc and mixed with clay for making crucibles.

plum·bago[2] /plʌmˋbeɪgəʊ/ *n* (*pl* -gos /-gəʊz/) blue-flowered plant.

plumber /ˋplʌmə(r)/ *n* workman who fits and repairs pipes. **plumb·ing** /ˋplʌmɪŋ/ *n* [U] **1** the work of a ~. **2** the pipes, water-tanks, cisterns, etc in a building: *The plumbing is out of order.*

plume /plum/ *n* feather, esp a large one used as a decoration; ornament of feathers; sth suggesting a feather by its shape: *a ~ of smoke/steam.* ***in borrowed ~s,*** (fig) in fine garments displayed as one's own but borrowed from someone. □ *vt* [VP6A] (of a bird) smooth (its feathers); preen (itself, its wings). ***~ oneself (on sth),*** (fig) congratulate oneself.

plum·met /ˈplʌmɪt/ *n* (weight attached to a) plumb-line; weight attached to a fishing-line to keep the float upright. □ *vi* (-tt-) [VP2A] fall, plunge, steeply: *Share prices have ~ted.*

plummy /ˈplʌmɪ/ *adj* (-ier, -iest) (colloq) good; desirable: *~ jobs;* affected, snobbish: *a ~ voice.*

plump[1] /plʌmp/ *adj* (esp of an animal, a person, parts of the body) rounded; fat in a pleasant-looking way: *a baby with ~ cheeks.* □ *vt,vi* [VP6A,2A,15B,2C] ***~ out/up,*** make or become rounded: *His cheeks are beginning to ~ up/out. She ~ed up the pillows.*

plump[2] /plʌmp/ *vi,vt* **1** [VP2C,15B] ***~ (sb/oneself/sth) down,*** (cause to) fall or drop, suddenly and heavily: *~ (oneself) down in a chair; ~ down a heavy bag.* **2** [VP3A] ***~ for,*** vote for, choose, with confidence: *~ for the Liberal candidate.* □ *n* abrupt, heavy fall. □ *adv* **1** suddenly, abruptly: *fall ~ into the hole.* **2** bluntly: *I told him ~ that….* □ *adj* unqualified; direct: *give sb a ~ 'No' for an answer.*

plun·der /ˈplʌndə(r)/ *vt,vi* [VP6A,14,2A] rob (people), esp during war or civil disorder; take goods from (places) by force: *~ a palace of its treasures; ~ the citizens of a conquered town.* □ *n* [U] ~ing; goods taken: *live by ~; wagon-loads of ~.* **~er** *n*

plunge /plʌndʒ/ *vt,vi* **1** [VP6A,14,2A,C] ***~ (into),*** put (sth), or go suddenly and with force, into: *~ one's hand into cold water/a hole; ~ a country into war; ~ a room into darkness,* e g by cutting off the current; *~ into a swimming-pool; ~ into an argument; be ~d into grief.* **2** [VP2A,C] (of a horse) move forward and downward quickly; (of a ship) thrust its bows into the water; (sl) gamble deeply; run into debt. □ *n* act of plunging (e g from a diving-board into water); violent thrust or other movement. ***take the ~,*** (fig) take a critical step; do sth decisive. **plunger** *n* (esp) part of a mechanism that moves with a plunging motion, e g the piston of a pump; suction device for clearing a blocked pipe.

plunk /plʌŋk/ = **plonk**[1].

plu·per·fect /ˈpluˈpɜfɪkt/ *n, adj* (gram) (tense) expressing action completed before some past time stated or implied (and in English conveyed by *had* and a *pp*, as in 'As he *had* not *received* my letter, he did not come').

plu·ral /ˈplʊərl/ *n, adj* (form of word) used with reference to more than one: 'The ~ of *child* is *children*'. *a ~ society,* one with more than one race, e g Kenya, with Africans, Asians and Europeans. **~ voter,** person who has a vote in more than one constituency.

plu·ral·ism /ˈplʊərḷ-ɪzm/ *n* [U] the holding of more than one office, esp in the church, at one time. **plu·ral·ist** /-ɪst/ *n*

plu·ral·ity /plʊəˈrælətɪ/ *n* (*pl* -ties) **1** [U] state of being plural; [C] large number; majority (*of* votes, etc). **2** [U] holding of more than one office at a time; [C] benefice, office, held with another benefice, etc.

plus /plʌs/ *prep* with the addition of: *Two ~ five is seven,* 2 + 5 = 7. **ˌ~-ˈfours** *n pl* wide, loose knickerbockers. **the 11 + (examination),** examination (at the age of 11 + some months) by which the kind of state secondary education suitable for a particular child is sometimes decided. □ *adj*: *a ~ quantity,* one greater than zero. ⇨ **minus.** □ *n* the sign +. ⇨ **App 4.**

plush /plʌʃ/ *n* [U] kind of silk or cotton cloth with a soft nap. □ *adj* (also **~y** (-ier, -iest)) (sl) smart; sumptuous: *a ~(y) restaurant.*

Pluto /ˈplutəʊ/ *n* (astron) planet farthest from the sun. ⇨ the illus at **planet.**

plu·toc·racy /pluˈtokrəsɪ/ *n* (*pl* -cies) [C,U] (government by a) rich and powerful class. **plu·to·crat** /ˈplutəkræt/ *n* person who is powerful because of his wealth. **plu·to·cratic** /ˌplutəˈkrætɪk/ *adj* of ~ or a plutocrat.

plu·to·nium /pluˈtəʊnɪəm/ *n* [U] (artificially produced) radioactive element (symbol **Pu**) derived from uranium, used in nuclear reactors and weapons.

ply[1] /plaɪ/ *n* [C] **1** layer of wood or thickness of cloth: *three-ply wood,* made by sticking together three layers with the grain of each at a right angle to that of the next. **ˈply·wood** *n* [U] board(s) made by gluing together thin layers of wood. **2** one strand in wool, rope, etc: *four-ply wool for knitting socks.*

ply[2] /plaɪ/ *vt,vi* (*pt,pp* **plied,** *pres part* **plying**) **1** [VP6A] (formal) work with (an instrument): *ply one's needle,* work busily with it. **2** [VP2C] (of ships, buses, etc) go regularly to and fro: *ships that ply between Glasgow and New York; ferry-boats plying across the Channel.* **3** ***ply a trade,*** work at it. ***ply sb with sth,*** keep him constantly supplied with (food and drink), attack him constantly with (questions, arguments, etc).

pneu·matic /njuˈmætɪk *US:* nu-/ *adj* worked or driven by compressed air: *~ drills;* filled with compressed air: *~ tyres.* **pneu·mati·cally** /-klɪ/ *adv*

pneu·monia /njuˈməʊnɪə *US:* nu-/ *n* [U] serious illness with inflammation of one or both lungs.

po /pəʊ/ *n* (word used by children for a) chamber-pot.

poach[1] /pəʊtʃ/ *vt* [VP6A] cook (an egg) by cracking the shell and dropping the contents into boiling water; simmer (e g fish) in liquid (e g wine).

poach[2] /pəʊtʃ/ *vt,vi* [VP6A,2A,3A] ***~ on/for,*** **1** (go on sb else's property and) take (hares, pheasants, salmon, etc) illegally: *~ hares; ~ for salmon; go out ~ing; ~ on a neighbour's land.* **2** (fig) be active in some kind of work that properly belongs to another (or that he considers to be his preserve): *Don't ~ on my preserves.* **~er** *n*

pock /pok/ *n* spot on the skin caused by smallpox. **ˈ~-marked,** with marks left after smallpox. **pocked** *adj* ***be ~ed with,*** have holes or depressions in: *The moon's surface is ~ed with small craters.*

pocket /ˈpokɪt/ *n* **1** small bag sewn into and forming part of an article of clothing, for carrying things in: *trouser/waistcoat, etc ~.* ***pick sb's ~,*** steal from sb's ~. ***put one's pride in one's ~,*** do sth that would normally make one feel mortified. ***put one's hand in one's ~,*** be ready to spend or give money. **ˈ~-book** *n* **(a)** notebook. **(b)** leather case for paper money (now more usu called *wallet*). **(c)** (US) woman's purse or handbag. **ˌ~-ˈhandkerchief** *n* one to be carried in the ~; (attrib) of small size: *a ~-handkerchief lawn.*

ˋ~-knife n small knife with one or more folding blades. ˋ~-money n money for small needs, esp money given to children. 2 money resources; money: *He will suffer in his ~*, will lose financially. ***in/out of ~,*** having gained/lost money as the result of doing sth: *He was a few dollars out of ~ as a result of the transaction.* **out-of-~ expenses,** actual outlay incurred; what one has actually spent. 3 bag, hollow, cavity, e g a string pouch at the corner of a billiard or pool table; a small cavity in the ground or in rock, containing gold or ore; a partial vacuum in the atmosphere (*an ˋair-~*) affecting the flight of an aircraft; cavity of air (*an ˋair-~*) in a mine[2](1), e g when a shaft is flooded; (an isolated area occupied by) enemy forces: *enemy ~s; ~s of resistance; ~s* (= isolated areas) of unemployment in the Midlands. 4 (attrib) of a size suitable for a ~: *a ~ guide/dictionary; edition; a ~-size camera.* ˋ~-ful /-fʊl/ n amount which a ~ holds. □ vt [VP6A] 1 put into one's ~: *He ~ed the money.* ***~ an insult,*** endure it without protest. ***~ one's pride,*** suppress or hide one's feelings of mortification. 2 appropriate for oneself (usu but not necessarily dishonestly): *He ~ed half the profits. He was given £5 for expenses, but ~ed most of it.* 3 send (a ball) into a ~ on a billiard or pool table.

pod /pod/ n [C] long seed-vessel of various plants, esp peas and beans. ⇨ the illus at vegetable. □ *vt, vi* (-dd-) 1 [VP6A] take (peas, etc) out of pods. 2 [VP2A,C] ***~ (up),*** form pods: *The peas are podding (up) well.*

podgy /ˋpodʒɪ/ *adj* (-ier, -iest) (of a person) short and fat.

podi·atry /pəˋdɑɪətrɪ/ n [U] (US) = chiropody.

po·dium /ˋpəʊdɪəm/ n platform, e g for the conductor of an orchestra; a lecturer, etc.

poem /ˋpəʊɪm/ n [C] piece of creative writing in verse form, esp one expressing deep feeling or noble thought in beautiful language, composed with the desire to communicate an experience; piece of prose writing in elevated style: *a prose ~*.

po·esy /ˋpəʊɪzɪ/ n [U] (archaic) poetry.

poet /ˋpəʊɪt/ n writer of poems. ˈ~ ˋ**laureate,** ⇨ laureate. ˋ**poet·ess** /-es/ n woman ~.

po·etic /pəʊˋetɪk/ *adj* of poets and poetry: *in ~ form; ~ genius; the ~al works of Keats.* ˈ~ ˋ**justice,** ideal justice, with proper distribution of rewards and punishments. ˈ~ ˋ**licence,** ⇨ licence. **po·eti·cally** /-klɪ/ *adv*

po·etry /ˋpəʊɪtrɪ/ n [U] 1 the art of a poet; poems. 2 quality that produces feelings as produced by poems: *the ~ of motion,* e g in ballet or some kinds of athletics.

po·grom /ˋpogrəm *US:* pəˋgrom/ n [C] organized persecution or killing and plunder (of a group or class of people).

poign·ant /ˋpɔɪnjənt/ *adj* distressing to the feelings; deeply moving; keen: *~ sorrow/regret/memories.* **~·ly** *adv* **poign·ancy** /-ənsɪ/ n [U] state or quality of being ~.

poin·set·tia /pɔɪnˋsetɪə/ n tropical plant with small, greenish-yellow flowers surrounded by large scarlet leaves.

point[1] /pɔɪnt/ n 1 [C] sharp tip (of a pin, pencil, knife, etc). ***not to put too fine a ~ on it,*** to speak bluntly, to tell the plain truth. 2 [C] tapering end; tip: *the ~ of the jaw,* e g as the place for a knockout in boxing; headland or promontory; piece of land that stretches out into the sea, a lake, etc: *a ~ of land; Battery P~,* New York Bay. 3 dot made by or as with the ~ of a pen, etc: *a decimal ~; four ~ six* (4·6); *a full ~,* a full stop, the sign (.) 4 [C] real or imaginary mark of position, in space or time: *a ~ of departure; a ˋturning-~ in my career.* ***at this ~,*** at this place or moment. ***the ~ of no return,*** ⇨ return[1](1). **a ˈ~-to-ˋ~ race,** a race (by persons riding horses) across country, from one ~ to another (these being recognized by certain landmarks). **a ~ of view,** position from which sth is viewed; (fig) way of looking at a question. ⇨ angle[1](2) (US). ˋ**~-duty** n duty of a policeman stationed at a particular ~ to control traffic. ***be at the ~ of death,*** be dying. ***be on the ~ of doing sth,*** be about to do sth. ***if/when it comes to the ~.*** if/when the moment for action or decision comes: *When it came to the ~, he refused to help.* 5 (printing) unit of measurement for type: *6-~ is small and 18-~ is large. Is this sentence printed in 8-~?* 6 [C] mark on a scale; unit of measuring; degree: *the ˋboiling-~ of water; the ˋmelting-~ of lead. The cost of living went up several ~s last month,* e g from 105 to 110, with 100 as a standard fixed earlier. *Oil shares rose several ~s* (i e on the Stock Exchange) *yesterday.* ***Possession is nine ~s*** (= nine-tenths) ***of the law,*** is strong evidence in favour of the person in possession of sth. 7 [C] unit of scoring in some games and sports, in measuring the quality, etc of exhibits in a show: *score twenty ~s.* ***give sb ~s, give ~s to sb,*** be able to offer him advantages and still win: *He can give me ~s at golf,* give me odds; is a better player. ***score a ~ off/against sb,*** ⇨ score[2](3). ***win/be beaten on ~s,*** (boxing) win/be beaten by the ~s awarded, there being no knockout. 8 [C] **(cardinal) ~,** one of the thirty-two marks on the circumference of a compass; one of the divisions (11° 15′) between two consecutive marks; (from the N) N, N by E, NNE, NE by N, ENE, etc. ⇨ the illus at compass. 9 [C] chief idea of sth said, done or planned; single item, detail or particular: *There are ~s on which we've agreed to differ. Let me explain the theory ~ by ~. What was the first ~ in his argument?* ***carry/gain one's ~,*** persuade sb to agree to one's objective. ***come to/get to/reach the ~,*** give the essential fact or part of what one is trying to say, ignoring what is irrelevant. ***get/see/miss the ~ of sth,*** see/fail to see what sb is trying to make clear, etc: *I don't quite get the ~. She missed the ~ of the story/joke.* ***make one's ~,*** win acceptance for an argument, establish what one is proposing. ***make a ~ of doing sth,*** regard or treat it as important or necessary. ***stretch a ~,*** go beyond what is normally allowable on a question of principle, etc: *Can't you stretch a ~ in my favour?* ***take sb's ~,*** (during a discussion) understand, appreciate what sb is proposing, etc. ***(wander) off/away from the ~,*** say sth not relevant to what is being discussed. ***What's the ~?*** Why bother? (It's irrelevant.) ***a case in ~,*** one connected with the subject being discussed: *Let me give you a case in ~,* an example that illustrates my argument. ***in ~ of fact,*** in reality; indeed. ***a ~ of honour/conscience,*** sth of great importance to one's honour/conscience. ***on a ~ of order,*** ⇨ order[1](4). 10 [U] ***no/not much ~ in doing sth,*** no good reason, little reason, for doing it: *There's very little ~ in protesting,* It won't help much. 11 [C] marked quality; characteristic: *What are her best ~s as a secretary? He has many good ~s and few bad ~s. Singing is not my best ~,* I don't sing well. **12** (GB) socket or outlet for electric current. **13** (*pl*) tapering movable rails by which a train can move from one track to another. **'~s·man** /-mən/ *n* (*pl* -men) worker in charge of ~s on a railway, to keep them in order, see that they are moved as needed, etc. **14** [U] effectiveness; urgency: *His remarks lack ~.* **15** (of a dog; ⇨ point[2](6)) act of ~ing: *make/come to a ~.* **16** (in former times) lace for attaching hose to a doublet, for lacing a bodice, etc

point[2] /pɔɪnt/ *vt,vi* **1** [VP2A,3A] ~ ***(to),*** direct attention to; show the position or direction of; be a sign of: *The needle of a compass ~s to the north. He ~ed to the door. It's rude to ~. Both the hour hand and the minute hand ~ed to twelve,* It was noon. All the evidence ~s to his guilt. **2** [VP14] ~ ***sth at/towards,*** aim or direct (at, towards): *~ a gun at sb; ~ a telescope at a deer on the hillside; ~ing his forefinger at me reprovingly.* **3** [VP15B] ~ ***sth out,*** show; call or direct attention to: *~ out a mistake; ~ out to sb the folly of his conduct. Can you ~ (me) out the man you suspect? He ~ed out the finest pictures to me. I must ~ out that delay is unwise.* **4** [VP6A] make a point on (a pencil); give force to (advice, a moral). **5** [VP6A] fill in the joints of (brickwork, etc) with mortar or cement, using a trowel to smooth the material. **6** (of a dog) take up a position with the body steady and the head ~ing in the direction of game. ⇨ pointer(3). **~ed** *adj* **1** (fig) directed definitely against a person or his behaviour: *a ~ed reproof. Jack was showing ~ed attentions to the glamorous film star.* **2** (of wit) incisive. **~·ed·ly** *adv*

point-blank /ˌpɔɪnt ˈblæŋk/ *adj* **1** (of a shot) aimed, fired, at very close range: *fired at ~ range.* **2** (fig, of sth said) in a manner that leaves no room for doubt: *a ~ refusal.* □ *adv* in a ~ manner: *fire ~ at sb; ask sb ~ whether he intends to help; refuse ~ to help.*

point-duty /ˈpɔɪnt djutɪ *US:* dutɪ/ ⇨ point[1](4).

pointer /ˈpɔɪntə(r)/ *n* **1** stick used to point to things on a map, etc. **2** indicator on a dial or balance. **3** large, short-haired hunting dog trained to stand still with its nose pointing in the direction of game it scents.

point·less /ˈpɔɪntləs/ *adj* **1** (fig) with little or no sense, aim or purpose: *It seemed ~ to go on until they were certain of being on the right road.* **2** without points scored: *a ~ draw.* **~·ly** *adv*

points·man /ˈpɔɪntsmən/ ⇨ point[1](13).

poise /pɔɪz/ *vt,vi* **1** [VP2C] be or keep balanced: *~d in mid-air/on the brink.* **2** [VP6A,15A] balance; support in a particular place or manner: *He ~d himself on his toes. Note the way he ~s his head.* □ *n* **1** [U] balance, equilibrium; [C] way in which one carries oneself, holds one's head, etc. **2** [U] quiet self-confidence; self-possession.

poi·son /ˈpɔɪzn/ *n* [C,U] **1** substance causing death or harm if absorbed by a living thing (animal or plant): *'rat-~; ~ for killing weeds on gravel paths; commit suicide by taking ~.* **'~-'gas** *n* deadly gas used in warfare. **'~-'ivy** *n* N American shrub or vine which causes painful spots if brought into contact with a person's skin. **'~ pen,** person who writes anonymous letters full of malice, slander, etc. **'~ 'pen letter,** letter of this kind. **2** (fig) evil principle, teaching, etc considered harmful to society. □ *vt* [VP6A] **1** give ~ to; put ~ on or in; kill with ~; infect: *~ a cat; ~ the wells; a ~ed hand,* inflamed because of an infected cut, etc. **2** injure morally: *~ a person's mind against sb; an experience which ~ed his whole life,* which spoilt or ruined his life. **~er** *n* (esp) person who murders by means of ~. **~·ous** /ˈpɔɪzn̩əs/ *adj* **1** acting as ~; causing death or injury if taken into the system: *~ous plants.* **2** morally injurious: *a ~ous play/novel/doctrine; a man with a ~ous tongue,* one who spreads evil reports, wicked scandal, etc. **~·ous·ly** *adv*

poke[1] /pəʊk/ *vt,vi* **1** [VP6A,15A,B] push sharply, jab (with a stick, one's finger, etc): *~ a man in the ribs,* nudge him in a friendly way: *~ the fire,* move the coals, to make the fire burn up. **2** [VP15A] put, move (sth) in a given direction, with a sharp push: *Don't ~ your umbrella through the bars of the lion's cage. She ~d a toffee into my mouth. Don't let your boy ~ his head out of the (train) window—it's dangerous!* ~ ***fun at sb,*** ridicule him. ~ ***one's nose into sth,*** (colloq) interfere in (sb's business, affairs). **3** [VP2C] ~ ***(about),*** search, feel about: *He was poking (about) at the rubbish. Who's that poking about in the attic?* **4** [VP6A,15A] make (a hole) by poking: *~ a hole in a paper screen.* □ *n* act of poking; nudge: *give the fire a ~; give sb a ~ in the ribs.*

poke[2] /pəʊk/ *n* sack (now dial, except in) ***buy a pig in a ~,*** ⇨ pig(1).

poke-bonnet /ˈpəʊk ˈbɒnɪt/ *n* bonnet (esp as worn by the Salvation Army women) with a broad projecting brim.

poker[1] /ˈpəʊkə(r)/ *n* strong metal rod or bar for stirring or breaking up the coal in the fire.

poker[2] /ˈpəʊkə(r)/ *n* [U] card game for two or more persons in which the players bet on the value of the cards they hold. **'~-face** *n* (colloq) (person with a) face that betrays no emotion.

poky /ˈpəʊkɪ/ *adj* (-ier, -iest) (of a place) small; limited in space: *a ~ little room.*

po·lar /ˈpəʊlə(r)/ *adj* **1** of or near the North or South Pole: *the ~ circles,* the Arctic and Antarctic Circles. **the ~ bear,** the white kind living in the north ~ regions. ⇨ the illus at bear. **2** directly opposite. **~·ity** /pəˈlærətɪ/ *n* possession of two contrasted or opposite qualities, principles or tendencies.

po·lar·ize /ˈpəʊləraɪz/ *vt* [VP6A] cause to concentrate about two opposite, conflicting or contrasting positions. **po·lar·iz·ation** /ˌpəʊləraɪˈzeɪʃn *US:* -rɪˈz-/ *n* act of polarizing; state of being ~d.

po·lar·oid /ˈpəʊlərɔɪd/ *n* [U] thin transparent film used in sun-glasses, car windows, etc to lessen sun glare; (P): *P~ camera,* one able to produce positive prints within seconds after the picture has been taken.

pole[1] /pəʊl/ *n* **1** either of the two ends of the earth's axis: *the North P~; the South P~.* **2** (*magnetic ~*), point near the North P~ or South P~ to which the compass needle points. **3** *North P~, South P~,* (astron) two points in the celestial sphere about which the stars appear to turn. **'~-star** *n* the North Star or **Polaris** /pəʊˈlɑrɪs/, almost coinciding with the true north of the celestial sphere. **4** either of the two ends of a magnet or the terminal points of an electric battery: *the negative/positive ~.* **5** (fig) each of two opposed principles, etc. ***be ~s apart,*** be widely separated: *The employers and the trade union leaders are* *still ~s apart,* are far from reaching an agreement or compromise, e g about wages.

pole[2] /pəʊl/ *n* **1** long, slender, rounded piece of wood or metal, esp as a support for a tent, telegraph wires, etc or for flying a flag. ***under bare ~s,*** (naut) with all sails furled. ***up the ~,*** (sl) **(a)** in a difficulty. **(b)** slightly mad; eccentric. ˋ**~-jumping** *n* (athletic contest) jumping with the help of a long ~ held in the hands. ˋ**~-vault** *n* jump of this kind over a bar which can be raised or lowered. **2** measure of length (also called *rod* or *perch*), 5½ yds or about 5 metres.

Pole /pəʊl/ *n* native of Poland.

pole-axe, pole-ax /ˋpəʊl æks/ *n* **1** (hist) axe for use in war, with a long handle. **2** butcher's implement for slaughtering cattle. □ *vt* [VP6A] strike down with a ~.

pole·cat /ˋpəʊlkæt/ *n* small, dark-brown, fur-covered animal of the weasel family which gives off an unpleasant smell, native of Europe.

pol·emic /pəˋlemɪk/ *n* [C] (formal) dispute; argument; (*pl*) art or practice of carrying on arguments, esp in theology. □ *adj* of ~s. **pol·emi·cally** /-klɪ/ *adv*

po·lice /pəˋlis/ *n* (collective *n,* always *sing* in form, used with *pl v*) department of government, body of men, concerned with the keeping of public order: *the ~,* the members of this body; *Several hundred ~ were on duty at the demonstration. Extra ~ are needed here. The town has an efficient* ˋ*~ force. The ~ have not made any arrests.* **~·man** /-mən/ *n* (*pl* -men) member of the ~ force. ˋ**~ constable** *n* ~man of ordinary rank. ˋ**~-court** *n* court in which minor offences, charged by the ~, can be dealt with by a magistrate. ˋ**~ dog** *n* dog trained to track or attack suspected criminals. ˋ**~-magistrate** *n* one who presides in a ~-court. ˋ**~-office** *n* headquarters of the ~ in a city or town. ˋ**~-officer** *n* ~man. ˋ**~ State** *n* one controlled by political ~, usu a totalitarian state. ˋ**~-station** *n* office of a local ~ force: *The drunken driver was taken to the ~-station.* ˋ**~ woman** *n* (*pl* -women) woman constable. □ *vt* [VP6A] keep order in (a place) with ~ or as with ~; control: *United Nations forces ~d the Gaza strip for a long period.*

pol·icy[1] /ˋpoləsɪ/ *n* (*pl* -cies) **1** [C] plan of action, statement of aims and ideals, esp one made by a government, political party, business company, etc: *foreign ~; Is honesty the best ~?* **2** [U] wise, sensible conduct; art of government.

pol·icy[2] /ˋpoləsɪ/ *n* written statement of the terms of a contract of insurance: *a* ˋ*fire-insurance ~; a* ˋ*~-holder.*

po·lio /ˋpəʊlɪəʊ/ *n* [U] (colloq abbr for) poliomyelitis: ˋ*~ victims;* ˈ*anti-*ˋ*~ injections.* **~·myel·itis** /ˈpəʊlɪəʊˈmaɪəˋlaɪtɪs/ *n* [U] infectious, virus-caused disease with inflammation of the grey matter of the spinal cord, often resulting in physical disablement; formerly called 'infantile paralysis'.

polish /ˋpolɪʃ/ *vt,vi* **1** [VP6A,15B,2A] make or become smooth and shiny by rubbing (with or without a chemical substance): *~ furniture/shoes; ~ sth up. This wood won't ~.* **2** [VP6A] (usu in *pp*) improve in behaviour, intellectual interests, etc; make refined or elegant: *a ~ed gentleman.* **3** [VP15B] ***~ sth off,*** finish quickly: *~ off a large plateful of pie; ~ off arrears of correspondence.* □ *n* **1** [U] (surface, etc obtained by) ~ing: *shoes/tables with a good ~.* **2** substance used for ~ing: ˋ*shoe/*ˋ*furniture/*ˋ*floor ~; a tin of metal ~.* **3** (fig) refinement; elegance. **~er** *n* workman skilled in ~ing wood or metal.

Pol·ish /ˋpəʊlɪʃ/ *adj* of Poland or the Poles. □ *n* language of the Poles.

pol·it·buro /pəˋlɪtbjʊərəʊ/ *n* (*pl* -ros /-rəʊz/) chief executive committee of a political (esp the Communist) party.

pol·ite /pəˋlaɪt/ *adj* **1** having, showing the possession of, good manners and consideration for other people: *a ~ boy; a ~ remark.* **2** refined: *~ society; ~ literature.* **~·ly** *adv* **~·ness** *n*

poli·tic /ˋpolətɪk/ *adj* **1** (of persons) acting or judging wisely; prudent. **2** (of actions) well judged; prudent: *follow a ~ course; make a ~ retreat.* **3 the ˈbody** ˋ**~,** the state as an organized group of citizens.

pol·iti·cal /pəˋlɪtɪkl/ *adj* **1** of the State; of government; of public affairs in general: *~ liberties; for ~ reasons.* ˈ**~ a**ˋ**sylum,** protection given by a Government to sb who has left his own country for ~ reasons: *a sailor who deserted his ship and asked for ~ asylum.* ˈ**~ e**ˋ**conomy,** = economics. ˈ**~ ge**ˋ**ography,** dealing with boundaries, communications, etc. Cf *physical* and *economic* geography. ˈ**~** ˋ**prisoner,** one who is imprisoned because he opposes the (system of) government. **2** of politics: *a ~ crisis.* **~ly** /-klɪ/ *adv*

poli·ti·cian /ˈpoləˋtɪʃn/ *n* person taking part in politics or much interested in politics; (in a bad sense) person who follows politics as a career, regardless of principle: *party ~s. Is your leader a ~ or a statesman?*

poli·tics /ˋpolətɪks/ *n pl* (with *sing* or *pl v*) the science or art of government; political views, affairs, questions, etc: *party ~; local ~. P~ sometimes have/has an unfortunate influence on character. 'P~ is much more difficult than physics', said Einstein.*

pol·ity /ˋpolətɪ/ *n* (*pl* -ties) [U] form or process of government. [C] society as an organized State.

polka /ˋpolkə *US:* ˋpəʊlkə/ *n* [C] (piece of music, of E European origin, for a) lively kind of dance. ˋ**~ dots,** regular pattern of large dots on cloth: (attrib) *a ~-dot scarf.*

poll[1] /pəʊl/ *n* **1** voting at an election; list of voters; counting of the votes; place where voting takes place: *a light/heavy ~,* voting by a small/large proportion of the voters; *awaiting the result of the ~; go to the ~s* (= ~ing-booths), vote; *exclude people from the ~; be successful at the ~; head the ~,* have the largest number of votes; *declare the ~,* announce the result. **2** survey of public opinion by putting questions to a representative selection of persons: *a public opinion ~; the Gallup ~.* ⇨ *straw vote* at **straw**. **3** (old use) head: (hum) *a grey ~,* a grey-haired person. ˋ**~-tax** *n* tax levied on every person in a community.

poll[2] /pəʊl/ *vt,vi* **1** [VP2A,C] vote at an election; [VP6A] receive (a certain number of) votes; take the votes of electors in (a constituency): *Mr Hill ~ed over 3 000 votes. The constituency was ~ed thoroughly.* ˋ**~·ing-booth/-station** *nn* place where voters go to record votes. ˋ**~·ing-day** *n* day appointed for a ~. **2** [VP6A] cut off the top of (the horns of cattle): *~ed cattle;* cut off the top of (a tree) (= **pollard**).

poll[3] /pol/ *n* (also ˋ*~parrot*) conventional name for a parrot.

pol·lard /ˋpoləd/ *vt* [VP6A] cut off the top of (a

tree) so that a thick head of new branches grows out. □ *n* ~ed tree.

pol·len /ˈpɒlən/ *n* [U] fine powder (usu yellow) formed on flowers which fertilizes other flowers when carried to them by the wind, insects, etc. ˈ~ **count,** figure of the ~ in the atmosphere in a given volume of air during 24 hours, from deposits on slides, as a guide to possible attacks of hay fever, etc.

pol·lin·ate /ˈpɒlɪneɪt/ *vt* [VP6A] make fertile with pollen. **pol·li·na·tion** /ˌpɒlɪˈneɪʃn/ *n* [U].

poll·ster /ˈpəʊlstə(r)/ *n* person who conducts public opinion polls.

pol·lute /pəˈluːt/ *vt* [VP6A] make dirty; destroy the purity or sanctity of: *rivers ~d with filthy waste from factories; ~d water,* unfit to drink. **pol·lu·tant** /-ənt/ *n* anything that ~s, e g exhaust fumes from motor-vehicles. **pol·lu·tion** /pəˈluːʃn/ *n* polluting or being ~d; that which ~s.

polo /ˈpəʊləʊ/ *n* [U] ball game played on horseback with mallets. ˈ**water-~** *n* game played by swimmers with a large ball. ˈ**~-neck,** (attrib) having a (usu thick) rolled collar: *~-neck sweaters.*

pol·on·aise /ˌpɒləˈneɪz/ *n* (piece of music for a) slow processional dance of Polish origin.

po·lony /pəˈləʊnɪ/ *n* [U] sausage of partly cooked pork.

pol·ter·geist /ˈpɒltəgaɪst/ *n* [C] (in folklore, etc) noisy, mischievous spirit.

pol·troon /pɒlˈtruːn/ *n* coward. **~·ery** /-ərɪ/ *n* cowardice.

poly /ˈpɒlɪ/ *n* (colloq abbr for) polytechnic.

poly·an·dry /ˈpɒlɪændrɪ/ *n* [U] custom of having more than one husband at the same time. **poly·an·drous** /ˌpɒlɪˈændrəs/ *adj* **1** of, practising, ~. **2** (bot) (of plants) having numerous stamens.

poly·an·thus /ˌpɒlɪˈænθəs/ *n* (*pl* -thuses /-θəsɪz/ for individual plants) kinds of cultivated primrose with several flowers on one stalk.

pol·ygamy /pəˈlɪgəmɪ/ *n* [U] custom of having more than one wife at the same time. **pol·yga·mist** /-ɪst/ *n* man who practises ~. **pol·yga·mous** /pəˈlɪgəməs/ *adj* of, practising, ~.

poly·glot /ˈpɒlɪglɒt/ *adj* knowing, using, written in, many languages. □ *n* ~ person or book.

poly·gon /ˈpɒlɪgən *US:* -gɒn/ *n* plane figure with many (usu five or more) straight sides.

poly·mor·phous /ˌpɒlɪˈmɔːfəs/, (also **poly·mor·phic** /-fɪk/) *adj* having, passing through many stages (of development, growth, etc).

polyp /ˈpɒlɪp/ *n* (zool) very simple form of animal life found in water; polypus.

pol·yph·ony /pəˈlɪfənɪ/ *n* (music) counterpoint. **poly·phonic** /ˌpɒlɪˈfɒnɪk/ *adj* (music) contrapuntal.

poly·pus /ˈpɒlɪpəs/ *n* (*pl* -puses /-pəsɪz/, -pi /-paɪ/) (path) kinds of tumour (e g in the nose) usu with many stems like tentacles, extending down into the tissue.

poly·syl·lable /ˈpɒlɪsɪləbl/ *n* word of several (usu more than three) syllables. **poly·syl·labic** /ˌpɒlɪsɪˈlæbɪk/ *adj*

poly·tech·nic /ˌpɒlɪˈteknɪk/ *n* institution for advanced full-time and part-time education, esp of scientific and technical subjects: *Manchester P~.*

poly·theism /ˈpɒlɪθiːɪzm/ *n* belief in, worship of, more than one god. **poly·theis·tic** /ˌpɒlɪθiːˈɪstɪk/ *adj*

poly·thene /ˈpɒlɪθiːn/ *n* [U] plastic material widely used for waterproof packaging, insulation, etc.

pom /pɒm/ *n* (abbr) = pommy.

po·made /pəˈmɑːd *US:* pəʊˈmeɪd/ *n* [U] perfumed ointment for use on the hair. □ *vt* put ~ on.

pom·egran·ate /ˈpɒmɪgrænət/ *n* (tree with) thick-skinned round fruit which, when ripe, has a reddish centre full of seeds.

pom·elo /ˈpɒmɪləʊ/ *n* (*pl* -los /-ləʊz/) kind of large grapefruit; shaddock.

pom·mel /ˈpʌml/ *n* **1** the rounded part of a saddle which sticks up at the front. ⇨ the illus at harness. **2** rounded knob on the hilt of a sword. □ *vt* (-ll-, US also -l-) = pummel.

pommy /ˈpɒmɪ/ *n* (*pl* -mies) (sl) British immigrant in Australia or New Zealand.

pomp /pɒmp/ *n* [U] splendid display, magnificence, esp at a public event: *the ~ and ceremony of the State Opening of Parliament.*

pom·pon /ˈpɔ̃pɔ̃ *US:* ˈpɒmpɒn/ *n* ornamental tuft or bunch of feathers, silk, ribbon, etc worn on a hat or dress or shoes; ball of wool worn on a soldier's cap.

pom·pous /ˈpɒmpəs/ *adj* full of, showing, self-importance: *a ~ official; ~ language,* full of high-sounding words. **pom·pos·ity** /pɒmˈpɒsətɪ/ *n* [U] being ~; [C] (*pl* -ties) instance of this.

ponce /pɒns/ *n* man who cohabits with a prostitute and lives on her earnings.

pon·cho /ˈpɒntʃəʊ/ *n* (*pl* -chos /-ʃəʊz/) large piece of cloth with a slit in the middle for the head, worn as a cloak; similar garment in waterproof material used by hikers, cyclists, etc.

pond /pɒnd/ *n* small area of still water, esp one used or made as a drinking place for cattle.

pon·der /ˈpɒndə(r)/ *vt, vi* [VP6A,2A,8,10,3A] ~ ***(over),*** consider; think over: *We ~ed many things. He ~ed over the incident.*

pon·der·able /ˈpɒndr̩əbl/ *adj* that can be weighed or measured. □ *n* (*pl*) events, conditions, etc that can be taken into account and estimated.

pon·der·ous /ˈpɒndərəs/ *adj* **1** heavy; bulky; unwieldy: *~ movements,* e g of a heavy man. **2** (of style) dull; laboured. **~·ly** *adv*

pone /pəʊn/ *n* (also ˈ**corn ~**) maize bread, esp as made by N American Indians.

pon·gee /pɒnˈdʒiː/ *n* [U] kind of soft silk cloth, usu unbleached so that it has the natural colour (brownish yellow).

pon·iard /ˈpɒnjəd/ *n* dagger.

pon·tiff /ˈpɒntɪf/ *n* **1** the Pope. **2** (old use) bishop; high priest; chief priest.

pon·tifi·cal /pɒnˈtɪfɪkl/ *adj* **1** of or relating to the Pope; papal. **2** authoritative (in a pompous way). □ *n pl* vestments and insignia used by bishops and cardinals at some church functions and ceremonies.

pon·tifi·cate /pɒnˈtɪfɪkeɪt/ *n* office of a pontiff, esp of the Pope; period of this. □ *vi* [VP2A] assume airs of infallibility.

pon·toon[1] /pɒnˈtuːn/ *n* **1** flat-bottomed boat; one of a number of such boats, or a floating hollow metal structure, supporting a roadway over a river: *a ~ bridge.* ⇨ the illus at bridge. **2** either of two boat-shaped supports that enable a flying-boat to come down on, and take off from, water.

pon·toon[2] /pɒnˈtuːn/ *n* kind of card game.

pony /ˈpəʊnɪ/ *n* (*pl* -nies) **1** horse of small breed, used by children for riding. ˈ**~-tail** *n* style of girls' hairdressing which became popular in the

1950's with long hair tied in a bunch at the back of the head. **`~-trekking** *n* the making of a journey for pleasure by young people riding on ponies. **2** (GB sl) £25. **3** (US sl) = crib²(2).

poodle /`pudl/ *n* kind of dog with thick curling hair, often clipped and shaved into fantastic patterns.

poof /pʊf/ *n* = pouf(2).

pooh /pu/ *int* expressing impatience or contempt or a bad smell.

pooh-pooh /'pu `pu/ *vt* [VP6A] treat (an idea, etc) with contempt.

pool¹ /pul/ *n* **1** small area of still water; esp one naturally formed: *After the rainstorm there were ~s on the roads.* **2** quantity of water or other liquid lying on a surface: *The corpse was lying in a ~ of blood.* **3** (**`swimming-**)**~,** large open-air tank of water to swim in. **4** part of a river where the water is quiet and deep.

pool² /pul/ *n* **1** (gambling) total of money staked by a number of gamblers. **the `football ~s,** organized gambling on the results of football matches: *hoping to win a fortune on the ~s.* **2** arrangement by business firms to share business and divide profits, to avoid competition and agree on prices. **3** common fund, supply or service, provided by or shares among many: *a `typing ~,* arrangement by which many persons share the services of typists instead of each having the services of his or her own typist. **4** (US) (GB = *snooker*) game for several players played on a billiard-table with six pockets: *to shoot* (= play) *~.* **`~-room** *n* place, room, in which the game of ~ is played. □ *vt* [VP6A] share in common; put (money, resources, etc) together for the use of all who contribute: *They ~ed their savings and bought a used car.*

poop /pup/ *n* (raised deck at the) stern of a ship. ⇨ the illus at **barque**.

poor /pʊə(r)/ *adj* (**-er, -est**) **1** having little money; not having and not able to get the necessaries of life. **the ~** *n pl* ~ people. **`~-box** *n* (in a church) box in which money may be placed to be given to the ~. **`~-house** *n* (formerly) building where ~ people were maintained at the public expense. **`~ law** *n* group of laws relating to the relief and care of the ~ (now replaced by Social Security Services). **`~-rate** *n* (formerly) rate (= local tax) for the relief of the ~. **'~ `white,** (in southern US) one of a pauperized class of white farmers and farm labourers. **2** deserving or needing help or sympathy: *The ~ little puppy had been abandoned.* **3** (often hum or ironic) humble; of little value: *in my ~ opinion.* **4** small in quantity: *a ~ supply of well-qualified science teachers; a country ~ in minerals.* **5** low in quality: *~ soil; ~ food; in ~ health.* **6** lacking in spirit: *What a ~ creature he is!* **'~-`spirited** *adj* lacking in courage; timid.

poor·ly /`pʊəlɪ/ *pred adj* (colloq) unwell: *He's rather ~ this morning.* □ *adv* **1** in a poor manner; badly; with little success: *~ lighted streets; ~ dressed.* **2 ~ off,** having very little money: *She's been ~ off since her husband died.*

poor·ness /`pʊənəs/ *n* lack of some desirable quality or element (note that *poverty* is usu for being poor(**1**)): *the ~ of the soil.*

pop¹ /pop/ *n* **1** short, sharp, explosive sound: *the pop of a cork.* **2** (sl) bottled drink with gas in it: *ginger pop,* ginger beer; *a bottle of pop.* **3** (sl) ***in pop,*** in pawn. □ *adv* with the sound of popping: *I heard it go pop. Pop went the cork!*

pop² /pop/ *n* (US abbr for) poppa.

pop³ /pop/ *adj* (colloq abbr for) popular: *`pop music; `pop singers; `pop groups,* (singers and players) (esp) those whose records sell in large numbers and who are most popular on radio, TV and in discotheques. **`pop art,** the depiction of scenes of everyday life, using comic strips, commercial technique, etc. **`pop concert,** of popular music. **`pop festival,** large, usu outdoor, gathering of people to hear pop singers and musicians. □ *n* (colloq) [U] pop music, pop art, etc; [C] pop song: *top of the pops,* disc, etc which (calculated by sales) is most popular during a given period of time.

pop⁴ /pop/ *vt,vi* (**-pp-**) **1** [VP6A,15B,2C] (cause to) make a sharp, quick sound (as when a cork comes out of a bottle): *Champagne corks were popping (away) on all sides.* **`pop-gun** *n* child's toy gun which fires a cork with a popping sound. **2** [VP15A,B,2A,C] (uses with *adverbial particles* and *preps*) ***pop across to,*** ⇨ pop over below. ***pop in/out,*** (cause to) go or come in/out quickly (giving the idea of rapid or unexpected movement or activity): *He popped his head in at the door. Pop in and see me some time. The neighbours' children are always popping in and out,* are very frequent visitors. ***pop sth into sth,*** quickly put it there: *She popped the gin bottle into the cupboard as the vicar entered the room.* ***pop off,*** (**a**) go away. (**b**) (sl) die: *I don't intend to pop off yet.* ***pop out of:*** *His eyes almost popped out in surprise.* ***pop over/across to,*** make a quick, short visit to: *She has just popped over/across to the grocer's.* **`pop-eyed** *adj* having eyes wide open (with surprise, etc). ***pop the question,*** (sl) propose marriage. **3** (sl) [VP2C] shoot: *They were popping away at the wood-pigeons.* **4** (sl) pawn: *I'll pop my watch and take you to the cinema.* **5** (US) parch (maize) until it bursts open and puffs out. **`pop·corn** *n* maize treated in this way.

pope /pəʊp/ *n* Bishop of Rome. **P~,** Bishop of Rome as head of the Roman Catholic Church. **pop·ery** /`pəʊpərɪ/ *n* (in hostile use) Roman Catholicism; papal system. **pop·ish** /`pəʊpɪʃ/ *adj* (in hostile use) of popery. **pop·ish·ly** *adv*

pop·in·jay /`popɪndʒeɪ/ *n* conceited person, esp one who is vain about clothes.

pop·lar /`poplə(r)/ *n* [C] tall, straight, fast-growing tree; [U] its wood.

pop·lin /`poplɪn/ *n* [U] (formerly) cloth of silk and wool with a ribbed surface; (now, usu) kind of strong, shiny cotton cloth used for shirts, etc.

poppa /`popə/ *n* (US) = papa.

pop·pet /`popɪt/ *n* (GB) used as a term of endearment (usu to a child): *Isn't she a ~? And how's my little ~ this morning?*

poppy /`popɪ/ *n* (*pl* **-pies**) sorts of plant, wild and cultivated, with large flowers, esp red, and a milky juice: *`opium ~,* kind from which opium is obtained.

poppy·cock /`popɪkok/ *n* [U] (sl) nonsense.

popu·lace /`popjʊləs/ *n* (formal) the common people; the general public; the masses.

popu·lar /`popjʊlə(r)/ *adj* **1** of or for the people: *~ government,* by the elected majority of all those who have votes. **'~ `front,** (in politics) coalition of parties opposed to reaction and fascism. **2** suited to the tastes, needs, educational level, etc of the general public: ~ *science; meals at* ~ (= low) *prices.* **3** liked and admired: *a* ~ *hero;* ~ *film stars; a man who is* ~ *with his neighbours.* ⇨ pop[3]. **~·ly** *adv*

popu·lar·ity /ˈpɒpjʊˋlærətɪ/ *n* [U] quality of being popular(3): *win* ~*; the* ~ *of baseball in Japan.*

popu·lar·ize /ˋpɒpjʊləraɪz/ *vt* [VP6A] make popular: ~ *a new method of teaching spelling.* **popu·lar·iz·ation** /ˈpɒpjʊləraɪˋzeɪʃn *US:* -rɪˋz-/ *n*

popu·late /ˋpɒpjʊleɪt/ *vt* [VP6A] supply with people; inhabit; form the population of: *thinly* ~*d; the densely* ~*d parts of India.*

popu·la·tion /pɒpjʊˋleɪʃn/ *n* (number of) people living in a place, country, etc or a special section of them: *a fall/rise in* ~*; the* ~ *of London; the working-class* ~*.*

popu·lism /ˋpɒpjʊl-ɪzm/ *n* (US) (also called *People's Party*) government or politics based on an appeal to popular sentiments or fears. **popu·list** /-ɪst/ *n* supporter of this party.

popu·lous /ˋpɒpjʊləs/ *adj* thickly populated.

por·ce·lain /ˋpɔsl̩ɪn/ *n* [U] (articles, e g cups and plates, made of a) fine china with a coating of translucent material called *glaze.*

porch /pɔtʃ/ *n* **1** built-out roofed doorway or entrance to a building. **2** (US, also) veranda.

por·cine /ˋpɔsaɪn/ *adj* of or like swine.

por·cu·pine /ˋpɔkjʊpaɪn/ *n* small rat-like animal covered with spines that the animal can stick out if attacked.

pore[1] /pɔ(r)/ *n* tiny opening (esp in the skin of an animal body) through which fluids (e g sweat) may pass: *He was sweating at every* ~*.*

pore[2] /pɔ(r)/ *vi* [VP3A] ***~ over sth,*** study it with close attention: ~ *over a letter/book.* ***~ upon sth,*** give one's close attention to it: ~ *upon a problem.*

pork /pɔk/ *n* [U] flesh (usu fresh, not salted or cured) used as food: *a leg of* ~*; a* ~ *chop; roast* ~*.* ⇨ bacon, ham(1). **ˋ~-butcher** *n* one who kills pigs for sale as food, makes ~ sausages, ~ pies, etc. **ˈ~ ˋpie** *n* minced ~, highly seasoned, in a container of pie-crust. **ˋ~-barrel** *n* (US, sl) money from State or Federal taxes, etc spent to confer local benefits for political reasons. **~er** *n* pig raised for food, esp one fattened for killing.

porn /pɔn/ *n* (colloq abbr of) pornography. **ˋ~ shop** *n* shop where pornographic books, etc are sold.

por·nogra·phy /pɔˋnɒgrəfɪ/ *n* [U] treatment of obscene subjects, esp sexual perversions, in writing, pictures, etc; such writings, etc. **por·nogra·pher** /pɔˋnɒgrəfə(r)/ *n* **por·no·graphic** /ˈpɔnəˋgræfɪk/ *adj*

po·rous /ˋpɔrəs/ *adj* **1** full of pores. **2** allowing liquid to pass through: *Sandy soil is* ~*.* **~·ness, po·ros·ity** /pɔˋrɒsətɪ/ *nn* quality or condition of being ~.

por·phyry /ˋpɔfɪrɪ/ *n* [U] hard, red kind of rock with red and white crystals bedded in it, polished and made into ornaments.

por·poise /ˋpɔpəs/ *n* sea animal rather like a dolphin or small whale. ⇨ the illus at sea.

por·ridge /ˋpɒrɪdʒ *US:* ˋpɔr-/ *n* [U] soft food made by boiling oatmeal in water or milk: *a bowl/plate of* ~*.*

por·rin·ger /ˋpɒrɪndʒə(r) *US:* ˋpɔr-/ *n* small bowl with a handle (for a child) from which porridge, soup, etc is eaten.

port[1] /pɔt/ *n* **1** harbour: *a naval* ~*; reach* ~*.* **2** town or city with a harbour, esp one where customs officers are stationed: *a free* ~, one open for the merchandise of all countries to load and unload in; one where there is exemption of duties for imports or exports. ***any ~ in a storm,*** in time of difficulty help or safety may be sought anywhere. **3** (fig) refuge: ~ *after stormy seas,* rest after struggles.

port[2] /pɔt/ *n* (naut) opening in the side of a ship for entrance, or for loading and unloading cargo; ~hole(b). **ˋ~·hole** *n* **(a)** opening in a ship's side for admission of light and air. **(b)** small glass window in the side of a ship or aircraft.

port[3] /pɔt/ *n* (naut) left-hand side of a ship or aircraft as one faces forward: *put the helm to* ~*;* (attrib) *on the* ~ *bow/quarter.* ⇨ starboard; ⇨ the illus at ship. □ *vt* [VP6A] turn (the ship's helm) to ~.

port[4] /pɔt/ *n* [U] strong (usu sweet) dark-red wine of Portugal.

port[5] /pɔt/ *n* ***at the ~,*** (mil) position of a rifle on porting arms. □ *vt* carry (a rifle or other weapon) diagonally across and close to the body ready for inspection by an officer: *P~ arms!* command for this to be done.

port·able /ˋpɔtəbl/ *adj* that can be carried about; not fixed: ~ *radios/typewriters.* **port·abil·ity** /ˈpɔtəˋbɪlətɪ/ *n* being ~: *The portability of my tape-recorder is exaggerated.*

port·age /ˋpɔtɪdʒ/ *n* [C,U] (cost of) carrying goods, esp when (e g in forest country in Canada) goods have to be carried overland between two rivers or parts of a river; place where this is done.

por·tal /ˋpɔtl/ *n* doorway, esp an imposing one of a large building.

port·cul·lis /ˈpɔtˋkʌlɪs/ *n* iron grating that could be raised or lowered to protect the gateway of a castle.

porte-cochere /ˈpɔt kəˋʃeə(r)/ *n* gateway at the entrance to a building to give shelter to persons entering or leaving cars, etc.

por·tend /pɔˋtend/ *vt* [VP6A] (formal) be a sign or warning of (a future event, etc): *This* ~*s war.*

por·tent /ˋpɔtent/ *n* thing, esp sth marvellous or mysterious, that portends sth; omen. **por·ten·tous** /pɔˋtentəs/ *adj* **1** ominous; threatening. **2** marvellous; extraordinary. **por·ten·tous·ly** *adv*

por·ter[1] /ˋpɔtə(r)/ *n* **1** person whose work is to carry luggage, etc at railway stations, airports, hotels, etc. **2** person carrying a load on his back or head (usu in country where there are no roads for motor-vehicles). **3** (US) attendant in a sleeping-car or parlour-car on a train. **ˋ~·age** /-ɪdʒ/ *n* [U] (the charge for) carrying of luggage, etc by a ~.

por·ter[2] /ˋpɔtə(r)/ *n* doorkeeper (at a hotel, public building, etc): *The hotel* ~ *will call a taxi for you; gatekeeper* (*US* = *doorman*). **~'s lodge,** ⇨ lodge[1](3).

por·ter[3] /ˋpɔtə(r)/ *n* [U] dark-brown bitter beer.

por·ter·house /ˋpɔtəhaʊs/ *n* **~ (steak),** choice cut of beefsteak.

port·folio /pɔtˋfəʊlɪəʊ/ *n* (*pl* -lios /lɪəʊz/) **1** flat case (usu leather) for keeping loose papers, documents, drawings, etc. **2** position and duties of a minister of state: *He resigned his* ~*. Mr X is minister without* ~, not in charge of any particular department. **3** list of securities and investments (stocks, shares, etc) owned by an individual, a bank, etc.

port·hole *n* ⇨ port[2].

a portico

port·ico /ˈpɔtɪkəʊ/ *n* (*pl* -coes or -cos /kəʊz/) roof supported by columns, esp at the entrance of a building.

port·ière /ˈpɔtɪˈeə(r)/ *n* (F) heavy curtain hung over a door(way).

por·tion /ˈpɔʃn/ *n* **1** part, esp a share, (to be) given when sth is distributed: (of a railway ticket) *this ~ to be given up;* (of a railway train) *the through ~ for Liverpool,* the coaches for Liverpool (passengers in which will not need to change trains); *a marriage ~,* dowry. **2** quantity of any kind of food served in a restaurant: *a generous ~ of roast duck.* **3** (*sing*) one's lot or fate: *Brief life is here our ~.* □ *vt* **1** [VP15B] ***~ sth out (among/ between),*** divide into ~s, share. **2** [VP14] ***~ sth to sb,*** provide a ~ of (sth to sb).

Port·land /ˈpɔtlənd/ *n* **~ stone,** yellowish-white limestone (quarried near ~, Dorset), used for building. **~ cement,** cement used for concrete that resembles ~ stone in colour.

port·ly /ˈpɔtlɪ/ *adj* (usu of elderly persons) stout; round and fat: *a ~ city councillor.*

port·man·teau /pɔtˈmæntəʊ/ *n* (*pl* -teaus or -teaux /-təʊz/) oblong, square-shouldered leather case for clothes, opening on a hinge into two equal parts. **~ word,** one made by using two or more words and combining their meanings, e g *shamateur* (from *sham* and *amateur*).

por·trait /ˈpɔtrɪt/ *n* **1** painted picture, drawings, photograph, of a person or animal. **2** vivid description in words. **ˈ~·ist** /-ɪst/ *n* maker of ~s. **ˈpor·trait·ure** /-tʃə(r) *US:* -tʃʊə(r)/ *n* [U] art of making ~s; ~.

por·tray /pɔˈtreɪ/ *vt* [VP6A] **1** make a picture of. **2** describe vividly in words. **3** act the part of (in a play). **~al** /pɔˈtreɪl/ *n* [U] ~ing; [C] description.

pose /pəʊz/ *vt,vi* **1** [VP6A] put (sb) in a desired position before making a portrait, taking a photograph, etc: *The artist ~d his model carefully. All the subjects are well ~d.* **2** [VP2A,3A] ***~ for,*** take up a position (for a portrait, etc): *Are you willing to ~ for me?* **3** [VP6A] put forward for discussion; create; give rise to: *The increase in student numbers ~s many problems for the universities.* **4** [VP2C] ***~ as,*** set oneself up as, claim to be: *~ as an expert on old coins.* **5** [VP2A] behave in an affected way hoping to impress people: *She's always posing,* is never natural in her behaviour. □ *n* **1** position taken up for a portrait, photograph, etc: *a striking and unusual ~.* **2** attitude, unnatural way of behaving, intended to impress people; affectation: *That rich man's socialism is a mere ~.* **poser** *n* awkward or difficult question.

po·seur /pəʊˈzɜ(r)/ (fem) **poseuse** /pəʊˈzɜz/ *n* person who ~s(5); affected person.

posh /pɒʃ/ *adj* (colloq) smart; first-class: *a ~ hotel; ~ clothes; her ~ friends.* □ *vt* [VP15B] ***~ up,*** (colloq) make ~: *We must ~ ourselves up for the party.*

po·si·tion /pəˈzɪʃn/ *n* **1** [C] place where sth or sb is or stands, esp in relation to others: *fix a ship's ~,* e g by observation of the sun or stars; *secure a ~ where one will get a good view of the procession; storm the enemy's ~s,* the places they occupy. ***in/out of ~,*** ~ in/not in the right place. **2** [U] state of being advantageously placed (in war or any kind of struggle): *They were manœuvring for ~.* **3** [C] way in which sb or sth is placed; attitude or posture: *sit/lie in a comfortable ~.* **4** [C] person's place or rank in relation to others, in employment, in society, etc: *a pupil's ~ in class; a high/low ~ in society;* [U] social standing: *people of ~,* i e of the middle and upper classes. **5** [C] job; employment: *get a ~ as a governess; apply for the ~ of assistant manager.* **6** [C] condition; circumstances: *placed in an awkward ~. I regret I am not in a ~* (= am unable) *to help you.* **7** [C] attitude; opinion: *What's your ~ on this problem?* □ *vt* [VP6A] place (sth or sb) in ~; determine the ~ of.

posi·tive /ˈpɒzətɪv/ *adj* **1** definite; sure; leaving no room for doubt: *give a man ~ orders/instructions; ~ knowledge.* **2** (of persons) quite certain, esp about opinions: *Are you ~ (that) it was after midnight? Can you be ~ about what you saw?* **3** practical and constructive; that definitely helps: *a ~ suggestion; ~ help; ~ criticism.* **4** (colloq) downright; out and out: *That man is a ~ fool/nuisance. It's a ~ crime to drink and drive.* **5** (maths) greater than zero: *the ~ sign* (+). **6** (of electricity) of the sort produced by rubbing glass with silk; of the sort caused by deficiency of electrons. **~ pole,** anode: *a ~ charge.* **7** (photo) showing light and shadows as in nature, not reversed (as in a negative). **8** (gram, of *adjj* and *advv*) of the simple form, not the comparative or superlative. □ *n* ~ degree, adjective, quantity, etc; photograph printed from a (negative) plate or film. **~·ly** *adv* definitely; certainly. **~·ness** *n* confidence.

posi·tiv·ism /ˈpɒzətɪv-ɪzm/ *n* philosophical system of Auguste Comte /kõt *US:* kɔ̃t/, 1798—1857, French philosopher, based on observable phenomena and positive facts rather than speculation. **logical ~,** modern (20th c) development of this philosophy mainly concerned with linguistic analysis and verification of empirical statements by observation. **posi·tiv·ist** /-ɪst/ *n*

posse /ˈpɒsɪ/ *n* (chiefly US) body of constables or other men having authority who can be summoned by a sheriff to help him in maintaining order, etc.

pos·sess /pəˈzes/ *vt* [VP6A] **1** own, have; *~ nothing; lose all that one ~es.* **2** keep control over: *~ one's soul in patience,* be patient. ⇨ *self-~ed* at self-. **3** ***~ oneself of,*** (old use) become the owner of. ***be ~ed of,*** have: *He is ~ed of great natural ability.* **4** ***be ~ed,*** be mad, be controlled by an evil spirit: *She is surely ~ed. He fought like one ~ed,* like a person having a devil inside him. **5** occupy (the mind); dominate: *What ~ed you to do that?* What influenced or dominated your mind and caused you to do that? *He is ~ed with the idea that someone is persecuting him.* **~or** /-sə(r)/ *n* owner; person who ~es sth.

pos·session /pəˈzeʃn/ *n* **1** [U] possessing; ownership: *come into ~ of a large estate; get ~ of sth,* succeed in getting ~ of it. *The players fought* *for/won ~ of the ball. Who is in ~ of the property? The information in my ~ is strictly confidential. You can't take ~ of the house* (= move into it) *until all the papers have been signed. Is the woman in full ~ of her senses?* Is she quite sane? **2** [C] (often *pl*) sth possessed; property: *lose all one's ~s; a man of great ~s. Most of Britain's ~s overseas* (= her former colonies, etc) *are now independent countries.*

pos·sess·ive /pəˋzesɪv/ *adj* **1** of possession or ownership: *He has a ~ manner,* seems to assert claims, e g to the attention of people. *She has a ~ nature,* is eager to acquire things or wants the whole of (someone's) love or attention. **2** (gram) showing possession: *the ~ case,* e g *Tom's, the boy's, the boys'; ~ pronouns,* e g *yours, his.* **~·ly** *adv*

pos·set /ˋposɪt/ *n* drink of warm milk with ale or wine and spices in it, formerly much used as a remedy for colds.

possi·bil·ity /ˌposəˋbɪlətɪ/ *n* (*pl* -ties) **1** [U] state of being possible; (degree of) likelihood: *Is there any/much ~ of your getting to London this week? I admit the ~ of your being right. Help is still within the bounds of ~.* **2** [C] sth that is possible: *I see great possibilities in this scheme,* It can have great success in many ways. *Don't neglect the ~ that his train has been delayed/the ~ of an accident.*

poss·ible /ˋposəbl/ *adj* **1** that can be done; that can exist or happen: *Come as quickly as ~. Frost is ~, though not probable, even at the end of May. Are you insured against all ~ risks?* **2** that is reasonable or satisfactory: *a ~ answer to a problem,* one that may be accepted, though not, perhaps, the best. *He is the only ~ man for the position.* □ *n* ~ person or thing: *A trial game was arranged between ~s and probables.* **poss·ibly** /-əblɪ/ *adv* **1** in accordance with what is ~: *I will come as soon as I possibly can. Can you possibly lend me £5?* **2** perhaps: *'Will they put your salary up?'—'Possibly.'*

pos·sum /ˋposəm/ *n* (colloq abbr of) opossum. ***play ~,*** pretend to be asleep, unaware, etc so as to deceive sb (from the ~'s habit of feigning death when attacked).

post[1] /pəʊst/ *n* [C] **1** place where a soldier is on watch; place of duty: *The sentries are all at their ~s.* **2** place occupied by soldiers, esp a frontier fort; the soldiers there. ⇨ **outpost. 3** trading station, esp one in a country where law and order are not yet firmly established: *trading ~s in northern Canada a hundred years ago.* **4** position or appointment; job: *get a better ~; be given a ~ as general manager.* □ *vt* [VP6A, 15A] **1** put at a ~(1): *~ sentries at the gates of the camp.* **2** send to a ~(1,2): *~ an officer to a unit. I hope you will be ~ed to my battalion.*

post[2] /pəʊst/ *n* (mil) bugle-call sounded at sunset: (esp) **the first/last ~.** (The last ~ is also sounded at military funerals.)

post[3] /pəʊst/ *n* **1** (formerly) one of a number of men placed with horses at intervals, the duty of each being to ride with letters, etc to the next stage; letter-carrier; mail-cart. **ˋ~-horse** *n* horse kept (in former times) at inns, etc for the use of men carrying letters, etc and for other travellers. **ˈ~-ˋchaise** *n* (hist) travelling carriage hired from stage to stage or drawn by ~-horses hired from stage to stage. **2** (GB) (US = *mail*) (formerly) government transport and delivery of letters, parcels, etc; one collection of letters, parcels, etc; one delivery or distribution of letters, etc; (since 1969) public corporation set up to perform these duties, responsible to the Ministry of Posts and Telecommunications. **3** box (into which letters are dropped for collection) or ~ office. ⇨ below: *take letters to the ~; miss/catch the ~,* be too late/in time for one of the regular clearances of letters. *Has the ~ come yet?* Has there been a delivery of letters, etc? *I will send you the book by ~. Please reply by return of ~,* by the next ~ (from your town, etc to mine). **ˋ~·bag** *n* = mailbag. **ˋ~·box,** pillar box; mail box; **ˋ~·card** *n* card of regulation size carried by ~ at a lower rate than a letter. **ˋ~·code,** (US = *zipcode*) group of letters and numbers, e g W1X 4AH, used to make the sorting and delivery of mail easier (by use of a computer). **ˈ~-ˋfree** *adj, adv* carried free of charge by ~, or with postage prepaid; (of a price) including the charge for postage. **ˋ~·man** /-mən/ *n* (*pl* -men) man employed to deliver letters, etc (US = *mailman*). **ˋ~·mark** *n* official mark stamped on letters, cancelling postage stamp(s) and giving the place, date, and time of collection, □ *vt* mark (an envelope, etc) with this. **ˋ~·master, ˋ~·mistress** *nn* official in charge of a ~ office. **ˋ~ office** *n* office, building, etc where ~al business is carried on, together with the business of telegraphs and telephones, payment of state pensions, etc. **ˋ~ office box** *n* numbered box in a ~ office for ~ addressed to an individual or company. **ˈ~-ˋpaid** *adj, adv* with postage already paid.

post[4] /pəʊst/ *vt, vi* **1** [VP6A] (US = *mail*) put (letters, etc) into a pillar-box or take (them) to a post office to be forwarded. **2** [VP3A] (old use) travel by stages, using relays of horses: *~ from London to Bristol;* travel with haste; hurry. ⇨ **post**[3]**(1). ˈ~-ˋhaste** *adv* in great haste. **3** [VP6A, 15B] ***~ up,*** (book-keeping) write items in (a ledger); transfer (items) from a day-book to a ledger: *~ (up) export sales; ~ up a ledger.* ***keep sb ~ed,*** (fig) keep him supplied with news.

post[5] /pəʊst/ *adv* in post-haste. ⇨ **post**[4]**(2).**

post[6] /pəʊst/ *n* upright piece of wood, metal, etc supporting or marking sth: *ˋgate~s; the ˋstarting/ˋwinning-~,* marking the starting and finishing points in a race; *ˋbed~s* (in the old-fashioned kind of bed which had curtains round it); *ˋlamp-~s,* poles in towns, etc with electric lamps for street-lighting. □ *vt* [VP6A, 15A,B] **1** display publicly in a public place by means of a paper, placard, etc: *P~ no bills* (warning that notices, advertisements, etc, must not be pasted on the wall, etc). *The announcement was ~ed up on the wall of the town hall.* **2** cover with bills, placards, etc: *~ a wall (over) with placards.* **3** make known by means of a ~ed notice: *a ship ~ed as missing.*

post- /pəʊst/ *pref* after; later than: *ˋ~-war; ˋ~-nuptial.*

post·age /ˋpəʊstɪdʒ/ *n* [U] payment for the carrying of letters, etc: *What is the ~ for an air-letter?* **ˋ~ stamp** *n* stamp (to be) stuck on letters, etc with a specified value, showing the amount of ~ paid.

postal /ˋpəʊstl/ *adj* of the **post**[3]**(2)**: *ˋ~ rates; ˋ~ workers; a ~ vote,* e g of members of a trade union, sent by post to decide a ballot; *~ union,*

union of governments of most countries for the regulation of international postal business. '~ **order,** ⇨ order[1](7).

post·date /ˌpəʊstˈdeɪt/ *vt* [VP6A] **1** put (on a letter, cheque, etc) a date later than the date of writing. **2** give to (an event) a date later than its actual date.

poster /ˈpəʊstə(r)/ *n* **1** placard displayed in a public place (announcing or advertising sth); large printed picture, e g of a pop star. **2** (ˈ**bill-**)~, person who posts bills or placards on walls, hoardings, etc.

poste res·tante /ˌpəʊst ˈrestɒ̃t *US:* reˈstænt/ *n* post office department to whose care letters may be addressed, to be kept until called for.

pos·terior /poˈstɪərɪə(r)/ *adj* **1** ~ ***(to),*** later in time or order. ⇨ **prior**[1]. **2** placed behind; at his back. □ *n* (hum) buttocks: *kick his* ~.

pos·ter·ity /poˈsterətɪ/ *n* [U] **1** person's descendants (his children, their children, etc). **2** future generations: *plant trees for the benefit of* ~.

pos·tern /ˈpostən/ *n* side way or entrance; (esp, in former times) concealed entrance to a castle or fortress: (attrib) ~ *door/gate.*

post ex·change /ˈpəʊst ɪkˈstʃeɪndʒ/ *n* (abbr **PX**) (US) store at a military base where personnel and their families may buy services and tax-free goods.

post·gradu·ate /ˌpəʊst ˈgrædʒʊət/ *adj* (of studies, etc) done after taking a first academic degree. □ *n* person engaged in ~ studies.

post·hum·ous /ˈpostʃʊməs/ *adj* **1** (of a child) born after the death of its father. **2** coming or happening after death: ~ *fame; a* ~ *novel,* published after the author's death; *the* ~ *award of a Victoria Cross.* ~**·ly** *adv*

pos·til·ion (also **pos·til·lion**) /poˈstɪlɪən/ *n* man riding on one of the two or more horses pulling a carriage or coach.

post·mas·ter /ˈpəʊstmɑstə(r) *US:* -mæs-/ *n* ˌ**P**~ ˈ**General,** (GB, until 1969) the Minister at the head of the Post Office Department. ⇨ **post**[3](2).

post mer·id·iem /ˌpəʊst məˈrɪdɪəm/ *adv* (*abbr* **p m**) after midday.

post-mor·tem /ˌpəʊst ˈmɔtəm/ *n, adj* **1** (medical examination) made after death: *A* ~ *showed that the man had been poisoned.* **2** (colloq) review of an event, etc in the past.

post·pone /pəˈspəʊn/ *vt* [VP6A] put off until another time: ~ *a meeting;* ~ *sending an answer to a request.* ~**·ment** *n* [U] postponing; [C] instance of this: *after numerous* ~*ments.*

post·pran·dial /ˌpəʊstˈprændɪəl/ *adj* (usu hum) after dinner: ~ *oratory.*

post·script /ˈpəʊsskrɪpt/ *n* **1** (abbr **PS**) sentence(s) added (*to* a letter) after the signature. **2** talk following a news broadcast.

pos·tu·lant /ˈpostjʊlənt *US:* -tʃʊ-/ *n* candidate, esp for admission to a religious order. ⇨ **novice.**

pos·tu·late /ˈpostjʊleɪt *US:* -tʃʊ-/ *vt* [VP6A] demand, put forward, take for granted, as a necessary fact, as a basis for reasoning. □ *n* sth ~d; sth that may be considered axiomatic: *the* ~*s of Euclidean geometry,* e g the possibility of drawing a straight line between any two points.

pos·ture /ˈpostʃə(r)/ *n* **1** [C] attitude of, way of holding, the body: *The artist asked his model to take a reclining* ~. *Good* ~ *helps you to keep well.* **2** [U] state or condition: *in the present* ~ *of public affairs.* **3** frame of mind; attitude: *Will the Government alter its* ~ *over aid to the railways?* □ *vt, vi* **1** [VP6A] put or arrange in a ~: ~ *a model.* **2** [VP2A] adopt a vain, pretentious ~: *The vain girl was posturing before a tall mirror.* **pos·tur·ing** *n* (from the *v*(2)) *All this posturing must stop!*

posy /ˈpəʊzɪ/ *n* (*pl* **-sies**) small bunch of cut flowers.

pot[1] /pot/ *n* **1** round vessel of earthenware, metal or glass, for holding liquids or solids, for cooking things in, etc; contents of such a vessel: *a* ˈ*jam-pot; eat a whole pot of jam; a* ˈ*teapot; a* ˈ*coffee-pot; a* ˈ*flower-pot; a* ˈ*chamber-pot.* ⇨ the *nn* forming the first element of such compounds. **2** (phrases and provs) ***go to pot,*** (sl) be ruined or destroyed. ***keep the pot boiling,*** earn enough money to buy one's food, etc; keep sth, e g a children's game, going briskly. ***take pot luck,*** whatever is available (without choice); whatever is being prepared for a meal: *Come home with me and take pot luck.* ***the pot calling the kettle black,*** the accuser having the same fault as the accused. **3** (colloq) large sum: *make a pot/pots of money.* **4 a big pot,** (colloq) an important person. **5** (colloq) prize in an athletic contest, esp a silver cup: *all the pots he won when he was young.* **6** (compounds) ˈ**pot-belly** *n* (person with a) large, prominent belly. ˌ**pot-**ˈ**bellied** *adj* (of a person) having a pot-belly; (of a stove) having a rounded container in which fuel, e g wood, burns. ˈ**pot-boiler** *n* book, picture, etc produced merely to bring in money. ˈ**pot-bound** *adj* (of a plant) having roots that have filled its pot. ˈ**pot-boy,** ˈ**pot-man** /-mən/ (*pl* **-men**) *nn* one who helps in a public house by filling pots with beer, etc. ˈ**pot hat** *n* (sl) bowler hat. ˈ**pot-herb** *n* plant, etc whose leaves or stems, or whose roots or tubers, are used in cooking. ˈ**pot-hole** *n* **(a)** hole in a road made by rain and traffic. **(b)** deep cylindrical hole worn in rock (e g in limestone caves) by water. ˈ**pot-holer** *n* person who explores pot-holes in caves. ˈ**pot-hook** *n* **(a)** hook, often S-shaped, which can be raised or lowered on a metal bar, for holding pots, etc over a fireplace. **(b)** curved or wavy stroke made by children when learning to write their letters. ˈ**pot-house** *n* (old use) low-class public house; ale-house: *pot-house manners,* vulgar manners. ˈ**pot-hunter** *n* **(a)** sportsman who shoots anything he comes across, thinking only of food for the pot or profit. **(b)** person who takes part in contests merely for the sake of the prizes. ⇨ **5** above. **pot roast** *n* beef, etc browned in a pot and cooked slowly with very little water. ˈ**pot-shot** *n* shot aimed at a bird or animal that is near, so that careful aim is not needed. ˈ**pot-trained** *adj* (of a small child) trained to use a chamber pot. **7** (sl) marijuana. ˈ**pot-head** (sl) habitual marijuana user.

pot[2] /pot/ *vt, vi* **(-tt-) 1** [VP6A] put (meat, fish paste, etc) in a pot to preserve it: *potted shrimps/ham.* **2** [VP6A,15B] ***pot (up),*** plant in a flower-pot: *pot (up) chrysanthemum cuttings.* **3** [VP6A] kill with a pot-shot: *pot a rabbit;* [VP3A] ***pot (at),*** (= shoot at) *a hare.* **4** (billiards) drive a ball into a pocket. **5** (colloq) put (a baby) on a chamber-pot.

pot·able /ˈpəʊtəbl/ *adj* fit to drink.

pot·ash /ˈpotæʃ/ *n* [U] common name for various potassium salts, used in the manufacture of fertilizers, soap, and various chemicals.

po·tass·ium /pəˈtæsɪəm/ *n* [U] soft, shining, white metallic element (symbol **K**), vital to all living matter, occurring in the form of mineral salts and in rocks.

po·ta·tion /pəʊˋteɪʃn/ *n* (usu *pl*) drink, esp of alcoholic liquor: *Liberal ~s left him far from sober.*

po·tato /pəˋteɪtəʊ/ *n* (*pl* -toes /-təʊz/) plant with rounded tubers eaten as a vegetable; one of the tuber; the illus at **vegetable**: *baked ~es; mashed ~(es); ~ soup; (US) ~ chips* (GB = *crisps*); **'sweet ˋ~,** tropical plant with long tuberous roots used for food. **ˋ~ beetle,** beetle that destroys the leaves of ~ plants.

po·teen /poˋtin/ *n* [U] Irish whisky from an illicit still.

po·tent /ˋpəʊtnt/ *adj* (of reasons, charms, drugs, remedies) powerful. **~·ly** *adv* **po·tency** /-nsɪ/ *n*

po·ten·tate /ˋpəʊtnteɪt/ *n* powerful person; monarch; ruler.

po·ten·tial /pəˋtenʃl/ *adj* **1** that can or may come into existence or action: *~ wealth/resources; ~ energy* (waiting to be released); *the ~ sales of a new book.* **2 ~ mood,** (gram) indicating possibility. □ *n* **1** [C] that which is ~; possibility; [U] what sb or sth is capable of: *He hasn't realized his full ~ yet.* **2** (gram) ~ mood. **3** (electr) electro-motive force expressed in volts: *a current of high ~.* **~ly** /-ʃlɪ/ *adv a ~ly rich country,* e g one with rich but undeveloped natural resources. **~·ity** /pə-ˌtenʃɪˋælətɪ/ *n* (*pl* -ties) power or quality which is ~, and needs development; latent capacity: *a situation/a country with great potentialities.*

pother /ˋpoðə(r)/ *n* trouble; commotion.

po·tion /ˋpəʊʃn/ *n* [C] dose of liquid medicine or poison, or of sth used in magic: *a ˋlove ~.*

pot-pourri /ˌpəʊ ˋpʊərɪ *US:* pəˋri/ *n* **1** mixture of dried rose-petals and spices, kept in a jar for its perfume. **2** musical or literary medley.

pot·sherd /ˋpot-ʃɜd/ *n* broken piece of pottery (esp in archaeology).

pot·tage /ˋpotɪdʒ/ *n* (old use) thick soup.

pot·ted /ˋpotɪd/ *adj* **1** ⇨ pot². **2** (of a book, etc) inadequately summarized: *a ~ version of a classical novel.*

pot·ter¹ /ˋpotə(r)/ (US = **put·ter** /ˋpʌtə(r)/) *vi,vt* [VP2A,C] **~ *about,*** **1** work with little energy; move about from one little job to another: *~ing about in the garden.* **2** waste (time) in ~ing: *~ away a whole afternoon.* **~er** *n* person who ~s.

pot·ter² /ˋpotə(r)/ *n* maker of pots. **~'s wheel,** horizontal revolving disc on which pots are shaped. **pot·tery** *n* (*pl* -ries) [U] earthenware; pots; [C] ~'s workshop. **the Potteries,** district in Staffordshire, England where ~y is the chief industry.

a potter's wheel

potty¹ /ˋpotɪ/ *adj* (-ier, -iest) (GB colloq) **1** petty; unimportant; insignificant: *~ little details/jobs.* **2 ~ *(about sb/sth),*** (of a person) foolish, crazy: *She's quite ~,* mad; *He's ~ about his new girl friend.*

potty² /ˋpotɪ/ *n* (*pl* -ties) child's chamber-pot.

pouch /paʊtʃ/ *n* **1** small bag carried in the pocket (*a ˋtobacco-~*) or fastened to the belt (a soldier's *ˌammuˋnition-~*). **2** bag-like formation, e g that in which a female kangaroo carries her young. **3** puffy area of skin, e g under the eyes of a sick or old person. □ *vt* **1** [VP6A] put into a ~. **2** [VP6A] make (part of a dress, etc) like a ~; [VP2A] hang like a ~.

pouf, pouffe /puf/ *n* **1** large, thick cushion used as a seat. **2** /pʊf/ (sl) male homosexual.

poul·terer /ˋpəʊltərə(r)/ *n* (GB) dealer in poultry and game, e g hares.

poul·tice /ˋpəʊltɪs/ *n* [C] soft heated mass of e g linseed, mustard, spread on a cloth, and put on the skin to relieve pain, etc. □ *vt* [VP6A] put a ~ on.

poul·try /ˋpəʊltrɪ/ *n* (collective *n*) **1** hens, ducks, geese, etc (with *pl v*): *The ~ are being fed.* **2** these considered as food (with *sing v*): *P~ is expensive this Christmas.*

pounce /paʊns/ *vi* [VP3A] **~ *on/at,*** make a sudden attack or downward swoop on: *The hawk ~d on its prey. The tiger ~d savagely on the goat.* (fig) *He ~d at* (= seized) *the first opportunity to inform against his colleague.* □ *n* such an attack.

pound¹ /paʊns/ *n* **1** unit of weight, 16 ounces avoirdupois, 12 ounces troy. ⇨ App 5. **2** British unit of money. ⇨ App 5. *five ~s,* written £5; *a five-~ note,* banknote for £5. ***penny wise ~ foolish; in for a penny in for a ~,*** ⇨ penny. **3** monetary unit of various other countries, esp former British dependences, and Israel.

pound² /paʊnd/ *n* **1** enclosed area in a village where, in olden times, cattle that had strayed were kept until claimed by their owners. **2** (mod use) place where stray dogs and cats, and motor-vehicles left in unauthorized places, are kept until claimed.

pound³ /paʊnd/ *vt,vi* [VP6A,15A,2C,3A] **~ *(away) (at/on),*** **1** strike heavily and repeatedly; thump: *Our heavy guns ~ed (away at) the walls of the fort. Who is ~ing (on) the piano? Someone was ~ing at the door with a heavy stick. I could hear feet ~ing on the stairs. She could feel her heart ~ing as she finished the 100 metres race.* **2** crush to powder; break to pieces: *~ crystals in a mortar; a ship ~ing/being ~ed to pieces on the rocks.* **3** [VP2C] ride, run, walk, heavily: *He ~ed along the road.*

pound·age /ˋpaʊndɪdʒ/ *n* commission or fee of so much, e g 5p per pound sterling (£1) or payment of so much per pound weight (1 lb).

pounder /ˋpaʊndə(r)/ *n* (usu in compounds) sth weighing so many pounds: *a three-~,* e g a fish weighing 3 lb; gun that fires a shot of so many pounds: *an eighteen-~.*

pour /pɔ(r)/ *vt,vi* **1** [VP6A,12B,13B,15A,B,14] cause (a liquid or a substance that flows like a liquid) to flow in a continuous stream: *P~ yourself another cup of tea. Please ~ a cup of tea for me, too. He ~ed the coffee out of the saucepan into the jug.* (fig) *He ~ed out his tale of misfortunes. The Underground stations ~ thousands of workers in to the streets between 8 and 9.30 each morning.* **~ *cold water on,*** discourage (a person, his zeal or enthusiasm). **~ *oil on troubled waters,*** try to calm a disturbance or quarrel with soothing words. **2** [VP2C] flow in a continuous stream; come freely (*out/off, etc*): *The sweat was ~ing off him. Tourists ~ into London during the* *summer months. The crowds were ~ing out of the football ground. Letters of complaint ~ed in.* **3** (of rain) come down heavily: *The rain ~ed down. It was a ~ing wet day.* ***It never rains but it ~s,*** a saying used when (usu unwelcome) things come or events happen in quick succession.

pout /paʊt/ *vt,vi* [VP6A,2A] (as a sign of displeasure) push out (the lips). □ *n* such a pushing out of the lips. **~·ing·ly** *adv* sulkily.

pov·erty /ˈpɒvətɪ/ *n* [U] state of being poor: *live in ~; fall into ~; an essay which shows ~ of ideas.* ˋ**~-stricken** *adj* affected by ~: *~-striken homes.*

pow·der /ˈpaʊdə(r)/ *n* **1** [C,U] (kind of) substance that has been crushed, rubbed or worn to dust; special kind of this, e g for use on the skin (*a tin of ˋtalcum-~*), or as a medicine (*take a ~ every morning*), for cleaning things (*ˋsoap-~, ˋbleaching-~*), or for cooking (*ˋbaking-~*). ˋ**~-puff** *n* soft, pad used for applying ~ to the skin. ˋ**~-room** *n* ladies' cloakroom in an hotel, restaurant, cinema, etc with wash-basins and lavatories. **2** = gun~, ⇨ gun: *not worth ~ and shot,* not worth shooting or trying for. ˋ**~-magazine** *n* place where gun~ is stored. ˋ**~-flask/-horn** *n* (in olden times) for carrying gun~. □ *vt,vi* **1** [VP6A] put ~ on (the face, etc). **2** [VP2A] use face-powder. **pow·dered** *adj* reduced to ~; dehydrated: *~ed milk/eggs.* **pow·dery** *adj* of, like, covered with, ~: *~y snow; a ~y nose.*

power /ˈpaʊə(r)/ *n* **1** [U] (in living things, persons) ability to do or act: *It is not within/It is beyond/outside my ~ to help you,* I am unable, or am not in a position, to do so. *This animal, the chameleon, has the ~ of changing its colour. I will do everything in my ~ to help.* **2** (*pl*) faculty of the body or mind: *His ~s are failing,* He is becoming weak. *You are taxing your ~s too much. He's a man of great intellectual ~s.* **3** [U] strength; force: *the ~ of a blow.* ***More ~ to your elbow!*** (phrase used to encourage sb). **4** [U] energy of force that can be used to do work: *ˋwater ~; eˋlectric ~.* ˋ**horse~,** ⇨ horse. (attrib) *ˋ~-lathe/-loom/-mill,* operated by mechanical ~, not by hand labour. ˋ**~-boat,** one with an engine; motorboat (esp one used for racing; or towing water-skiers). ˋ**~-dive** *vt, n* (put an aircraft into a) steep dive with the engines working. ˋ**~-house/-station,** building where electric ~ is generated for distribution. ˋ**~-point,** socket on a wall, etc for a plug to connect an electric circuit. **5** [U] right; control; authority: *the ~ of the law; the ~ of Congress; have a person in one's ~,* be able to do what one wishes with him; *have ~ over sb; Spain at the height of her ~; fall into sb's ~.* ***in ~,*** (of a ministry or political party) in office. **~ politics,** diplomacy backed by force. **6** [C] right possessed by, or granted to, a person or group of persons: *Are the ~s of the Prime Minister defined by law? The President has exceeded his ~s,* has done more than he has authority to do. **7** [C] person or organization having great authority or influence: *Is the press a great ~ in your country?* Are the newspapers influential, etc? ***the ~s that be,*** (hum) those who are in authority. **8** [C] State having great authority and influence in international affairs. **the Great P~s,** the largest and strongest States. **9** [C] (maths) result obtained by multiplying a number or quantity by itself a certain number of times: *the second, third, fourth, etc ~ of x* (= x^2, x^3, x^4, *etc*); *the fourth ~ of 3* (= 3 × 3 × 3 × 3 = 81). **10** [U] capacity to magnify: *the ~ of a lens; a telescope of high ~.* **11** (colloq) large number or amount: *This stout does me a ~ of good.* **12** god or goddess: (old use, in exclamations): *Merciful ~s! Preserve us from the ~s of darkness.* **pow·ered** *adj* having, able to exert or produce, mechanical energy: *a new aircraft ~ed by Rolls Royce engines; a high-~ed car;* (fig) *a high-~ed salesman,* one with great ~s of persuasion.

power·ful /ˈpaʊəfl/ *adj* having or producing great power: *a ~ blow/enemy; a ~ remedy for constipation.* **~ly** /-flɪ/ *adv*

power·less /ˈpaʊəlɪs/ *adj* without power; unable (*to do* sth): *render sb ~; be ~ to resist.* **~·ly** *adv*

pow·wow /ˈpaʊwaʊ/ *n* conference of N American Indians; (hum) any other kind of conference. □ *vi* hold a conference (*about* sth).

pox /pɒks/ *n* (colloq, usu **the ~**) syphilis: *catch/give sb the pox.*

prac·ti·cable /ˈpræktɪkəbl/ *adj* that can be done or used or put into practice: *methods that are not ~; a mountain pass that is ~ only in summer.* **prac·ti·cably** /-əblɪ/ *adv* **prac·ti·ca·bil·ity** /ˌpræktɪkəˋbɪlətɪ/ *n*

prac·ti·cal /ˈpræktɪkl/ *adj* **1** concerned with practice (opp to *theory*): *overcome the ~ difficulties of a scheme; a suggestion/proposal with little ~ value; a ~ joke,* ⇨ joke. **2** (of persons, their character, etc) clever at doing and making things; preferring activity and action to theorizing: *a ~ young wife; ideas that appeal to ~ minds.* **3** useful; doing well what it is intended to do: *Your invention is ingenious, but not very ~.* **~ly** /-klɪ/ *adv* **1** in a ~ manner. **2** almost; so to speak: *We've had ~ly no fine weather this month. He says he is ~ly ruined.* **~·ity** /ˌpræktɪˋkælətɪ/ *n* (*pl* **-ties**): *Let's get down to ~ities,* to considering ~ proposals.

prac·tice /ˈpræktɪs/ *n* **1** [U] performance; the doing of sth (contrasted with *theory*): *put a plan into ~,* carry it out, do what has been planned. *The idea would never work in ~,* may seem good theoretically, but would be useless if carried out. **2** [C] way of doing sth that is common or habitual; sth done regularly: *the ~ of closing shops on Sundays; Christian/Protestant/Catholic ~s,* ceremonies or observances; *an aperitif before dinner, as is my usual ~.* ***make a ~ of (sth),*** do it habitually: *boys who make a ~ of cheating at examinations.* **3** [U] frequent or systematic repetition, repeated exercise, in doing sth (esp an art or craft): *Piano-playing needs a lot of ~. That is a stroke,* e g in golf, *that needs a lot of ~. It takes years of ~ to acquire the skill of an expert;* (attrib) *Let's have a ~ game.* ***in/out of ~,*** having/not having given enough time recently to ~: *Please don't ask me to play the piano for you: I'm out of ~.* **4** [U] work of a doctor or lawyer: *retire from ~; no longer in ~*; [C] (collective) (number of) persons who regularly consult a doctor or lawyer: *a doctor with a large ~; sell one's ~,* sell (to another doctor) the connection one has (of regular patients): *a doctor in general ~;* ⇨ practitioner. **5** ***sharp ~,*** [U] not strictly honest or legal ways of doing business; (*pl*) (old use) illegal or immoral schemes or contrivances.

prac·ti·cian /prækˋtɪʃn/ *n* = practitioner.

prac·tise (US = **-tice**) /ˈpræktɪs/ *vt* [VP6A,C, 2A,B] **1** do sth repeatedly or regularly in order to become skilful: ~ *the piano;* ~ *making a new vowel sound;* ~ *two hours every day.* **2** make a habit of: ~ *early rising.* **~ what one preaches,** make a habit of doing what one advises others to do. **3** exercise or follow (a profession, etc): ~ *medicine/the law,* work as a doctor/lawyer. **4** [VP3A,4A] **~ (up)on; ~ to do sth,** (old use) take advantage of (sb's incredulity, etc); set oneself: ~ *to deceive.* **prac·tised** (US = **-ticed**) *adj* skilled; having had much practice.

prac·ti·tioner /præk`tɪʃn̩ə(r)/ *n* **1** one who practices a skill or art. **2** professional man, esp in medicine and the law. **a 'general `~,** doctor who is qualified in both medicine and minor surgery (also called *a family doctor,* who sees patients either in his surgery or in their homes).

prae·sid·ium /prɪ`sɪdɪəm/ *n* = presidium.

prae·tor (also **pre·tor**) /`pritə(r)/ *n* annually elected magistrate in ancient Rome. **prae·tor·ian** /prɪ`tɔrɪən/ *adj* of, having the rank of, a ~; of the bodyguard of a Roman commander or Emperor.

prag·matic /præg`mætɪk/ *adj* **1** concerned with practical results and values; treating things in a matter-of-fact or practical way. **2** dogmatic; conceited. **prag·mati·cally** /-klɪ/ *adv*

prag·ma·tism /`prægmət-ɪzm/ *n* [U] **1** (phil) belief or theory that the truth or value of a conception or assertion depends upon its practical bearing upon human interests. **2** dogmatism; officiousness; pedantry. **prag·ma·tist** /-tɪst/ *n* believer in ~(1).

prairie /`preərɪ/ *n* wide area of level land with grass but no trees, esp in N America. ⇨ pampas, savanna.

praise /preɪz/ *vt* [VP6A] **1** speak with approval of; say that one admires: ~ *a man for his courage. Our guests* ~*d the meal as the best they had had for years.* **2** give honour and glory to (God). □ *n* **1** [U] act of praising: *His heroism is worthy of great* ~*/is beyond* (= too great to be) ~. *The leader spoke in* ~ *of the man who had given his life for the cause.* **2** (*pl*) **sing sb/one's own ~s,** ~ enthusiastically. **3** [U] worship; glory: *P~ be to God. P~ be!* Thank goodness! **`~worthy** /-wɜðɪ/ *adj* deserving ~. **`~·worth·ily** /-əlɪ/ *adv* **`~·worthi·ness** *n*

pram /præm/ *n* (GB) (short for, and the usu word for) perambulator.

prance /prɑns *US:* præns/ *vi* [VP2A,C] **~ (about), 1** (of a horse) move forwards jerkily, by raising the forelegs and springing from the hind legs. **2** (fig) move, carry oneself, in an arrogant manner; dance or jump happily and gaily. □ *n* prancing movement.

prank[1] /præŋk/ *n* [C] playful or mischievous trick: *play* ~*s on sb.*

prank[2] /præŋk/ *vt* [VP15A,B] (old use, or liter) adorn; ornament: *fields* ~*ed with flowers;* ~ *oneself out.*

prate /preɪt/ *vi* [VP2A,C] **~ about,** talk (foolishly); talk too much: *a silly young fellow prating about a subject of which he knows nothing.*

prattle /`prætl/ *vi* [VP2A,C] (of a child) talk in a simple, artless way; (of adults) talk in a childish, simple way. □ *n* [U] such talk. **prat·tler** /`prætlə(r)/ *n* one who ~s.

prawn /prɔn/ *n* [C] edible shellfish like a large shrimp: *a dish of curried* ~*s.* □ *vi* fish for ~s: *go* ~*ing.*

pray /preɪ/ *vt,vi* **1** [VP2A,3A] **~ (to God) (for sth),** commune with God; offer thanks, make requests known: ~ *to God for help. They knelt down and* ~*ed. The farmers are* ~*ing for rain. He's past* ~*ing for,* There now seems to be little hope for his recovery, e g from illness, or from some fault, etc. **2** [VP17,14,11] **~ sb for sth/to do sth,** (liter, rhet) ask sb as a favour: *I* ~ *you to think again. We* ~ *you to show mercy. We* ~ *you that the prisoner may be set free.* **3** (formal request equivalent to) please: *P~ don't speak so loud.*

prayer /preə(r)/ *n* **1** [U] act of praying to God: *He knelt down in* ~. **2** [U] form of church worship: *Morning/Evening P~.* **2** [C] form of words used in praying: *the Lord's P~.* ⇨ lord; request or petition (spoken or unspoken) to God: *say one's* ~*s; family* ~*s; a* ~ *for rain.* **`~-book** *n* book containing ~s for use in church services, etc. **the P~ Book,** (also called *Book of Common P~*) the one used in Church of England services. **`~-meeting** *n* meeting at which those present offer up ~s to God in turn. **`~-rug/-mat** *n* small rug used by Muslims to kneel on when they pray. **`~-wheel** *n* revolving cylinder inscribed with or containing ~s, used by the Buddhists of Tibet.

pre- /pri/ *pref* before; beforehand: *pre-war; a pre-amplifier; pre-natal; pre-arrange.* ⇨ App 3.

preach /pritʃ/ *vt,vi* **1** [VP6A,2A,B,C] deliver (a sermon); make known (a religious doctrine, etc); give a talk (esp in church) about religion or morals: ~ *the gospel;* ~ *Buddhism;* ~ *against covetousness;* ~ *for two hours.* **2** [VP3A,12A,13A] give moral advice (*to*): *the headmaster* ~*ing to his boys. Don't* ~ *me a sermon about being lazy now, please.* **3** [VP6A] urge; recommend (as right or desirable): *The Dictator* ~*ed war as a means of making the country great.* **~er** *n* one who ~es (esp sermons). **`~·ify** /-ɪfɑɪ/ *vi* (*pt,pp* -fied) ~, esp (2); moralize in a tedious way.

pre·amble /pri`æmbl/ *n* introduction or preliminary statement (esp to a formal document).

pre·arrange /'priə`reɪndʒ/ *vt* arrange in advance. **~·ment** *n*

preb·end /`prebənd/ *n* part of the revenue of a cathedral or a collegiate church granted as a stipend to a canon or member of the chapter. **preb·en·dary** /`prebəndərɪ *US:* -derɪ/ *n* (*pl* -ries) one who receives a ~.

pre·cari·ous /prɪ`keərɪəs/ *adj* (formal) uncertain; unsafe; depending upon chance: *make a* ~ *living as an author.* **~·ly** *adv*

pre·cast /'pri`kɑst *US:* -`kæst/ *adj* (of concrete) cast into blocks ready for use in building.

pre·cau·tion /prɪ`kɔʃn/ *n* [U] care taken in advance to avoid a risk; [C] instance of this: *take an umbrella as a* ~*; take* ~*s against fire; insure one's house as a measure of* ~. **~·ary** /'prɪ`kɔʃn̩ərɪ *US:* -ʃn̩erɪ/ *adj* for the sake of ~.

pre·cede /prɪ`sid/ *vt,vi* [VP6A,2A] come or go before (in time, place or order): *the calm that* ~*d the storm; the Mayor,* ~*d by the mace-bearer; in the preceding paragraph/the paragraph that* ~*s.* **pre·ced·ing** *adj* existing or coming before.

pre·ced·ence /`presɪdəns/ *n* (formal) [U] (right to a) priority, or to a senior place. **have/take ~ (over)**: *questions which take* ~ *over all others,* which must be considered first.

pre·ced·ent /`presɪdənt/ *n* (formal) [C] earlier happening, decision, etc taken as an example or rule for what comes later. **set/create/establish a ~ (for sth)**: *Is there a* ~ *for what you want me to*

do? ~**ed** *adj* having, supported by, a ~.
pre·cen·tor /prɪˈsentə(r)/ *n* (in English cathedrals) member of the clergy in general control of the singing.
pre·cept /ˈprisept/ *n* **1** [U] moral instruction: *Example is better than* ~. **2** [C] rule or guide, esp for behaviour.
pre·cep·tor /prɪˈseptə(r)/ *n* (formal) teacher; instructor.
pre·cession /prɪˈseʃn/ *n* ~ ***of the equinoxes,*** change by which the equinoxes occur earlier in each successive year.
pre·cinct /ˈprisɪŋkt/ *n* [C] **1** space enclosed by outer walls or boundaries, esp of a cathedral or church: *within the sacred* ~*s.* **2** (US) subdivision of a county or city or ward: *an eˈlection* ~; *a poˈlice* ~. **3** (*pl*) neighbourhood or environs (of a town). **4** boundary: *within the city* ~*s.* **5** (mod use; town-planning) area of which the use is in some way restricted. **a pedestrian** ~, where vehicles are not allowed. **a ˈshopping** ~, for shops only.
pre·ci·os·ity /ˈpreʃɪˈosətɪ/ *n* [U] over-refinement; being precious(**4**); [C] (*pl* **-ties**) instance of this.
precious /ˈpreʃəs/ *adj* **1** of great value and beauty: *the* ~ *metals,* gold, platinum; ~ *stones,* diamonds, rubies, etc. **2** highly valued; dear: *Her children are very* ~ *to her.* **3** (colloq) (as in intensive) complete: *He's a* ~ *rascal. It cost a* ~ *sight more than I could afford,* very much more. **4** (of language, workmanship, etc) over-refined; affected. □ *adv* (colloq) very: *I have* ~ *little* (= hardly any) *money left.* ~**·ly** *adv* ~**·ness** *n*
preci·pice /ˈpresəpɪs/ *n* perpendicular or very steep face of a rock, cliff or mountain.
pre·cipi·tate /prəˈsɪpɪteɪt/ *vt* [VP6A,14] **1** throw or send (sb or sth) violently down from a height. ~ ***sb/sth into sth,*** thrust violently into (a condition): ~ *the country into war.* **2** cause (an event) to happen suddenly, quickly, or in haste: ~ *a crisis; events that* ~*d his ruin.* **3** (chem) separate (solid matter) from a solution. **4** condense (vapour) into drops which fall as rain, dew, etc. □ *n* that which is ~d as solid matter, rainfall, etc. □ *adj* /prəˈsɪpɪtət/ violently hurried; hasty; (doing things, done) without enough thought. ~**·ly** *adv*
pre·cipi·ta·tion /prəˈsɪpɪˈteɪʃn/ *n* **1** (esp) fall of rain, sleet, snow or hail: amount of this: *the annual* ~ *in the Lake District; a heavy* ~. **2** [U] being violently hurried or headlong: *act with* ~, without enough thought or consideration of the consequences. **3** act of precipitating.
pre·cipi·tous /prəˈsɪpɪtəs/ *adj* (formal) like a precipice; very steep. ~**·ly** *adv*
pré·cis /ˈpreɪsi *US:* preɪˈsi/ *n* (*pl* unchanged in spelling but with usual change in pronunciation to /-iz/) restatement in shortened form of the chief ideas, points, etc of a speech or piece of writing. □ *vt* make a ~ of.
pre·cise /prɪˈsaɪs/ *adj* **1** exact; correctly and clearly stated; free from error: ~ *measurements;* ~ *orders; at the* ~ *moment when I lifted the receiver.* **2** taking care to be exact, not to make errors: *a very* ~ *man;* too careful, fussy, about details: *prim and* ~ *in his manner.* ~**·ly** *adv* **1** in a ~ manner; exactly: *state the facts* ~*ly; at 2 o'clock* ~*ly.* **2** (as a response, agreeing with sb) quite so. ~**·ness** *n*
pre·ci·sion /prɪˈsɪʒn/ *n* [U] accuracy; freedom from error: (attrib) ~ *instruments/tools,* those, used in technical work, that are very precise (for measuring, etc); ~ *bombing.*
pre·clude /prɪˈklud/ *vt* [VP6A,C,14] ~ ***sb from doing sth,*** prevent; make impossible: ~ *all doubts/misunderstanding.* **pre·clu·sion** /prɪˈkluʒn/ *n*
pre·co·cious /prɪˈkəʊʃəs/ *adj* **1** (of a person) having developed certain faculties earlier than is normal: *a* ~ *child,* e g one who reads well at the age of three. **2** (of actions, knowledge, etc) marked by such development. ~**·ly** *adv* ~**·ness** *n* **pre·coc·ity** /prɪˈkosətɪ/ *n* = ~ness.
pre·cog·ni·tion /ˈprikogˈnɪʃn/ *n* (formal) knowledge of sth before it occurs.
pre·con·ceive /ˈprikənˈsiv/ *vt* [VP6A] form (ideas, opinions) in advance (before getting knowledge or experience): *visit a foreign country with* ~*d ideas.* **pre·con·cep·tion** /ˈprikənˈsepʃn/ *n* [C] ~d idea.
pre·con·certed /ˈprikənˈsɜtɪd/ *adj* (formal) agreed in advance: *following* ~*ed plans.*
pre·con·di·tion /ˈprikənˈdɪʃn/ *n* = prerequisite.
pre·cur·sor /ˈpriˈkɜsə(r)/ *n* [C] (formal) person or thing coming before, as a sign of what is to follow. **pre·cur·sory** /-sərɪ/ *adj* preliminary; anticipating.
preda·tory /ˈpredətərɪ *US:* -tɔrɪ/ *adj* (formal) **1** of plundering and robbery: ~ *tribesmen/habits;* ~ *incursions,* raids made for plunder. **2** (of animals) preying upon others. **pred·ator** /-tə(r)/ *n* ~ animal.
pre·de·cease /ˈpridɪˈsis/ *vt* (legal) die before (another person).
pre·de·cessor /ˈpridɪsesə(r) *US:* ˈpredɪ-/ *n* **1** former holder of any office or position: *Mr Green's* ~ *in office.* **2** thing to which another has succeeded: *Is the new proposal any better than its* ~*?*
pre·des·ti·nate /priˈdestɪneɪt/ *adj* foreordained by God; fated. □ *vt* (theol) = predestine.
pre·des·ti·na·tion /ˈpriˈdestɪˈneɪʃn/ *n* **1** theory or doctrine that God has decreed from eternity that part of mankind shall have eternal life and part eternal punishment. **2** destiny; doctrine that God has decreed everything that comes to pass.
pre·des·tine /priˈdestɪn/ *vt* **1** [VP17,14] (often passive) ~ ***sb to sth/to do sth,*** (of God, fate) decide, ordain, beforehand; cause (sb) to behave, etc in a certain way. **2** [VP17] ~ ***sb to do sth,*** decide or make inevitable: *Everything took place as if he was* ~*d to succeed. These events were clearly* ~*d (to happen).*
pre·de·ter·mine /ˈpridɪˈtɜmɪn/ *vt* (formal) **1** [VP6A] decide in advance: *The social class into which a child is born often seems to* ~ *his later career.* **2** [VP17] ~ ***sb to do sth,*** persuade or impel sb in advance to do sth: *Did an unhappy childhood* ~ *him to behave as he did?* **pre·de·ter·mi·na·tion** /ˈpridɪˈtɜmɪˈneɪʃn/ *n*
pre·dica·ment /prɪˈdɪkəmənt/ *n* trying or unpleasant situation from which escape seems difficult: *be in an awkward* ~.
predi·cate[1] /ˈpredɪkət/ *n* (gram) part of a statement which says sth about the subject, e g 'is short' in 'Life is short'.
predi·cate[2] /ˈpredɪkeɪt/ *vt* (formal) **1** [VP6A,17,9] declare to be true or real: ~ *of a motive that it is good;* ~ *a motive to be good.* **2** [VP6A] make necessary as a consequence: *These policies were* ~*d by Britain's decision to join the Common Market.*
predi·cat·ive /prɪˈdɪkətɪv *US:* ˈpredɪkeɪt-/ *adj*

(gram, of an *adj* or *n*, opposed to *attrib*) forming part or the whole of the predicate. ~ **adjective,** one used in the predicate, e g *asleep, alive.*

pre·dict /prɪˈdɪkt/ *vt* [VP6A,9,10] ~ ***sth/that sth,*** say, tell in advance: ~ *a good harvest;* ~ *that there will be an earthquake.* **pre·dic·tion** /prɪˈdɪkʃn/ *n* [U] ~ing; [C] sth ~ed; prophecy. **~·able** /-əbl/ *adj* that can be ~ed. **~or** /-tə(r)/ *n* instrument or device that ~s, e g one used in war to determine when to open anti-aircraft fire. **~a·bil·ity** /prɪˌdɪktəˈbɪlətɪ/ *n*

pre·di·gest /pri daɪˈdʒest/ *vt* treat (food) so that it is easily digested: *~ed food for babies.*

pre·di·lec·tion /ˌpridɪˈlekʃn *US:* ˌpredḷˈek-/ *n* [C] ***a ~ for,*** special liking, mental preference.

pre·dis·pose /ˌpridɪˈspəʊz/ *vt* [VP14,17] ~ ***sb to sth/to do sth,*** (formal) cause (sb) to be inclined or liable before the event: *His early training ~d him to a life of adventure/to travel widely. I find myself ~d in his favour,* inclined to favour him.

pre·dis·posi·tion /ˌpriˌdɪspəˈzɪʃn/ *n* [C] ~ ***to sth/to do sth,*** state of mind or body favourable to: *a ~ to arthritis; a ~ to find fault.*

pre·domi·nant /prɪˈdɒmɪnənt/ *adj* ~ ***(over),*** (formal) having more power or influence than others; prevailing, conspicuous: *The ~ feature of his character was pride.* **~·ly** *adv* in a ~ manner: *a ~ly brown-eyed race.* **pre·domi·nance** /-əns/ *n* [U] superiority in strength, numbers, etc; state of being predominant.

pre·domi·nate /prɪˈdɒmɪneɪt/ *vi* [VP2A,3A] ~ ***(over),*** (formal) have or exert control (over); be superior in numbers, strength, influence, etc: *a forest in which oak-trees ~.*

pre-emi·nent /pri ˈemɪnənt/ *adj* excelling others; best of all: ~ *above all his rivals.* **~·ly** *adv* **pre-emi·nence** /-əns/ *n* [U].

pre-empt /pri ˈempt/ *vt* [VP6A] (formal) **1** obtain by pre-emption. **2** (US) occupy (public land) so as to have the right of pre-emption. **pre-emp·tion** /pri ˈempʃn/ *n* [U] (formal) purchase by one person, etc before others are offered the chance to buy; right to purchase in this way; the obtaining of sth in advance. **pre-emp·tive** /-tɪv/ *adj* relating to pre-emption: *a ~ bid,* (in auction bridge) one intended to be high enough to prevent further bidding; *a ~ air strike,* e g by bombing, one against forces considered likely to attack.

preen /prin/ *vt* **1** [VP6A] (of a bird) smooth (itself, its feathers) with its beak. **2** [VP6A,14] (of a person) tidy (oneself). ~ ***oneself on,*** (fig) pride oneself (on); show self-satisfaction.

pre-exist /ˌpri ɪgˈzɪst/ *vi* [VP2A] exist beforehand; live a life before this life. **~·ence** /-əns/ *n* life of the soul before entering its present body or this world. **~·ent** /-ənt/ *adj* existing in a former life or previously.

pre·fab /ˈprifæb *US:* ˌpriˈfæb/ *n* [C] (abbr of a) pre-fabricated house (of the kind erected in GB after World War II).

pre·fab·ri·cate /priˈfæbrɪkeɪt/ *vt* [VP6A] manufacture the parts, e g roofs, walls, fitments; of a building, a ship, etc before they are put together on the site, in the yards, etc: *~d houses; a ~d school.* **pre·fab·ri·ca·tion** /ˌpriˌfæbrɪˈkeɪʃn/ *n*

pref·ace /ˈprefɪs/ *n* [C] author's explanatory remarks at the beginning of a book; preliminary part of a speech: *write a ~ to a book.* □ *vt* [VP14] ~ ***sth with sth/by doing sth,*** provide with a ~; begin (a talk, etc, with...): *The headmaster ~d his remarks with some sharp raps on the table.* **prefa·tory** /ˈprefətərɪ *US:* -tɔrɪ/ *adj* of or in the nature of a ~: *after a few prefatory remarks.*

prefect /ˈprifekt/ *n* **1** (in ancient Rome) title of various civil and military officers; governor. **2** (in France) title of the chief administrative officer of a department; head of the Paris police. **3** (in some English schools) one of a number of senior pupils given responsibility, e g for keeping order.

pre·fec·ture /ˈprifektjʊə(r) *US:* -tʃər/ *n* **1** administrative area in some countries, e g France, Japan. ⇨ **county** (in GB). **2** (in France) place or office where a prefect(2) works; his official residence. **3** position of a prefect(1); period of office. **pre·fec·tural** /priˈfektʃərl/ *adj* of a ~: *the prefectural offices.*

pre·fer /prɪˈfɜ(r)/ *vt* (-rr-) **1** [VP6A,D,7A,9,14,17] choose rather; like better: *Which would you ~, tea or coffee? I ~ walking to cycling. He ~s to write his letters rather than dictate them. I'd ~ to wait until evening. I should ~ you not to go/that you did not go there alone.* **2** [VP6A,14] ~ ***a charge/charges (against sb),*** put forward, submit: ~ *a charge against a motorist,* i e accuse him of sth. **3** [VP6A,14] ~ ***sb (to),*** appoint (sb) (to a higher position). **~·able** /ˈprefṛəbl/ *adj* (not used with *more*) ~ ***(to),*** superior; to be ~red. **~·ably** /-əblɪ/ *adv*

pref·er·ence /ˈprefṛəns/ *n* **1** [C,U] act of preferring: *have a ~ for French novels. I should choose this in ~ to any other.* **2** [C] that which is preferred: *What are your ~s?* **3** [U] the favouring of one person, country, etc more than another (in business relations, etc esp by admitting imports at a lower import duty); [C] instance of this: *give sb ~ (over others).* **4** ˈ**P~ Stock,** stock on which dividend payments must be made before profits are distributed to holders of Ordinary Stock.

pref·er·en·tial /ˌprefəˈrenʃl/ *adj* of, giving, receiving, preference; (e g of import duties, etc) favouring particular countries: *get ~ treatment.*

pre·fer·ment /prɪˈfɜmənt/ *n* [U] act of preferring(3); promotion or advancement: ~ *to a benefice.*

pre·fig·ure /priˈfɪgə(r) *US:* -gjər/ *vt* (formal) **1** [VP6A] represent beforehand; show (what is coming). **2** [VP6A,9,10] imagine, picture to oneself, beforehand.

pre·fix /ˈprifɪks/ *n* **1** (abbr *pref* in this dictionary) word or syllable, e g *pre-, co-,* placed in front of a word to add to or change its meaning. ⇨ App **3. 2** word used before a person's name, e g Mr, Dr. □ *vt* /priˈfɪks/ [VP6A,14] ~ ***sth (to sth),*** add a ~ to or in front of; add at the beginning: ~ *a new paragraph to Chapter Ten.*

preg·nant /ˈpregnənt/ *adj* **1** (of a woman or female animal) having in the uterus offspring in a stage of development before birth. **2** (of words, actions) significant; full of promise. ~ ***with,*** filled with: *words ~ with meaning;* certain or likely to have: *political events ~ with consequences.* **preg·nancy** /-nənsɪ/ *n* [U] the state of being ~; (fig) fullness; depth; significance; [C] instance of being ~: *She's had six pregnancies in six years, poor dear!*

pre·hen·sile /priˈhensaɪl/ *adj* (of a foot or tail, e g a monkey's) able to seize and hold.

pre·his·toric /ˌprihɪˈstɒrɪk *US:* -tɔrɪk/, **-tori·cal** /-kl/ *adjj* of the time before recorded history. **pre·his·tory** /priˈhɪstṛɪ/ *n*

pre·judge /ˈpriˋdʒʌdʒ/ *vt* [VP6A] make up one's mind about a person, cause, action, etc before hearing the evidence, making a proper inquiry, etc. **~·ment** *n*

preju·dice /ˋpredʒədɪs/ *n* **1** [U] opinion, like or dislike, formed before one has adequate knowledge or experience; [C] instance of this: *have a ~ against/in favour of modern jazz; listen to new poems without ~; racial ~,* against members of other races. **2** [U] (legal) injury that may or does arise from some action or judgement: *to the ~ of sb's rights,* with (possible) injury to them. ***without ~ (to),*** without injury to any existing right or claim. □ *vt* [VP6A,15A] ***~ sb against/in favour of sb/sth,*** **1** cause sb to have a ~(1). **2** injure or weaken (sb's interests, etc): *He ~d his claim by asking too much.* **preju·di·cial** /ˈpredʒʊˋdɪʃl/ *adj* ***~ (to),*** causing ~ or injury.

prel·acy /ˋpreləsɪ/ *n* (*pl* -cies) **1** office, rank, see, of a prelate. **2 the ~,** the whole body of prelates.

prel·ate /ˋprelət/ *n* bishop or other churchman of equal or higher rank.

pre·lim /prɪˋlɪm/ *n* (colloq abbr for) **(a)** preliminary examination; (*pl*) first year examinations in some subjects at Oxford. **(b)** pages (with title, contents, etc) preceding the actual text (in a book).

pre·limi·nary /prɪˋlɪmɪnərɪ *US:* -nerɪ/ *adj* coming first and preparing for what follows: *a ~ examination; after a few ~ remarks.* □ *n* (*pl* -ries) (usu *pl*) ~ actions, measures, etc: *the usual preliminaries to a Geneva conference,* e g the wrangling about procedures and agenda.

prel·ude /ˋpreljud/ *n* [C] ***~ to,*** action, event, etc that serves as an introduction to (another); (music) introductory movement (to a fugue or as part of a suite). □ *vt* [VP6A] serve as, be, a ~ to.

pre·mari·tal /ˈpriˋmærɪtl/ *adj* before marriage.

pre·ma·ture /ˋpremətʃə(r) *US:* ˋpriməṭʊər/ *adj* done, happening, doing sth, before the right or usual time: *~ decay of the teeth; ~ birth; a ~ baby,* (colloq *prem*) one born at less than 38 weeks of pregnancy. **~·ly** *adv*

pre·medi·tate /priˋmedɪteɪt/ *vt* [VP6A] consider, plan, (sth) in advance: *a ~d murder.* **pre·medi·ta·tion** /ˈpriˈmedɪˋteɪʃn/ *n* [U].

pre·mier /ˋpremɪə(r) *US:* ˋprim-/ *adj* first in position, importance, etc. □ *n* prime minister; head of the government. **ˋ~·ship** /-ʃɪp/ *n*

pre·miére /ˋpremɪeə(r) *US:* prɪˋmɪər/ *n* first performance of a play or (ˋ*film-~*) first public showing of a cinema film.

prem·ise, prem·iss /ˋpremɪs/ *n* **1** statement on which reasoning is based. **2** each of the two first parts of a syllogism: *the major ~,* e g 'Boys like fruit.; *the minor ~,* e g 'You are a boy', the conclusion being 'Therefore you like fruit.' **3** (*pl*) house or building with its outbuildings, land, etc: *business ~s,* the building(s), offices, etc where a business is carried on; *to be consumed on the ~s,* e g of alcoholic drinks in a public house or hotel which has no 'off-licence'. **4** (*pl*) details of property, names of persons, etc in the first part of a legal agreement. □ *vt* [VP6A,9] make a statement (*that*) or a statement of (fact) by way of introduction.

pre·mium /ˋprimɪəm/ *n* (*pl* ~s) **1** amount or instalment paid for an insurance policy. **2** reward; bonus: *a ~ for good conduct.* **P~ bond,** (GB) government bond that offer the chance of prizes (in a draw) instead of the more usual interest[1](6). ***put a ~ on sth,*** make it advantageous for sb (to behave in a certain way, to do sth): *Does high taxation put a ~ on business dishonesty?* **3** addition to ordinary charges, wages, rent, etc; bonus: *He had to pay the agent a ~ before he could rent the house,* an extra sum above the rent. **4** fee (to be) paid by a pupil to a professional man, e g an accountant or architect, for instruction and training. **5** (of stocks and shares) the amount above par value: *The shares are selling at a ~.* **at a ~,** (fig) highly valued or esteemed.

pre·mon·ition /ˈpreməˋnɪʃn/ *n* [C] feeling of uneasiness considered as a warning (of approaching danger, etc): *have a ~ of failure.* **pre·moni·tory** /prɪˋmonɪtərɪ *US:* -tɔrɪ/ *adj*

pre·natal /priˋneɪtl/ *adj* preceding birth.

pren·tice /ˋprentɪs/ *n* (old use, short for *apprentice* in the phrase): *try his ~ hand,* make an unskilled or novice's attempt.

pre·oc·cu·pa·tion /ˈpriˈokjʊˋpeɪʃn/ *n* [U] state of mind in which sth takes up all a person's thoughts; [C] the subject, etc that takes up all his thoughts: *His greatest ~ was how to find money for a holiday in Europe.*

pre·oc·cupy /priˋokjʊpaɪ/ *vt* (*pt,pp* -pied) [VP6A] take all the attention of (sb, his mind) so that attention is not given to other matters: *preoccupied by family troubles; preoccupied with thoughts of the coming holidays.*

pre·or·dain /ˈpriɔˋdeɪn/ *vt* [VP6A,9] degree or determine in advance.

prep /prep/ *n* (schoolboy slang for) **(a)** preparation(3). **(b)** preparatory (school).

pre·pack·aged /pri ˋpækɪdʒd/, **pre·packed** /priˋpækt/ *adjj* (of products) wrapped, packed, before being supplied to shops, etc where they are to be sold.

prep·ara·tion /ˈprepəˋreɪʃn/ *n* **1** [U] preparing or being prepared: *The meal is in ~. We're getting things together in ~ for the journey. Don't try to do it without ~.* **2** [C] (usu *pl*) things done to get ready for sth: *~s for war; make ~s for a voyage.* **3** [U] (colloq abbr *prep*) (time given to) preparing lessons, or writing exercises, after normal school hours (esp at GB public or grammar schools): *two hours' prep; do one's French prep; after/before ~.* ⇨ homework. **4** [C] kind of medicine, food, etc specially prepared: *pharmaceutical ~s.*

pre·para·tory /prɪˋpærətərɪ *US:* -tɔrɪ/ *adj* introductory; needed for preparing: *~ measures/training.* **~ to,** in readiness for; before. **ˋ~ school,** (esp in England) private school where pupils are prepared for entry to a higher school (esp a public school); (US) (usu private) school where pupils are prepared for college.

pre·pare /prɪˋpeə(r)/ *vt,vi* **1** [VP6A,7,14,3A] ***~ (for),*** get or make ready: *~ a meal/one's lessons/a sermon; ~ pupils for an examination,* coach them; *~ for an attack,* get ready to repel an attack; *~ to attack,* get ready to make an attack; *be ~d for anything to happen.* **2 be ~d to,** be able and willing to: *We are ~d to supply the goods you ask for.* **pre·pared·ness** /prɪˋpeərɪdnəs/ *n* [U] being ~d: *Everything was in a state of ~dness.*

pre·pay /ˈpriˋpeɪ/ *vt* (*pt,pp* -paid /-ˋpeɪd/) [VP6A] pay in advance: *send a telegram with reply prepaid.*

pre·pon·der·ant /prɪˋpondərənt/ *adj* (formal) greater in weight, number, strength, etc. **~·ly** *adv*

pre·pon·der·ance /-əns/ *n*

pre·pon·der·ate /prɪˋpondəreɪt/ *vi* [VP2A,C] (formal) be greater in weight, number, strength, influence, etc: *reasons that ~ over other considerations.*

prep·osi·tion /ˈprepəˋzɪʃn/ *n* word or group of words (e g *in, from, to, out of, on behalf of*) often placed before a *n* or *pron* to indicate place, direction, source, method, etc. **~al** /-ʃn̩l/ *adj* of, containing, a ~. **~al phrase, (a)** phrase made up of a group of words, e g *in front of, on top of.* **(b)** ~ and the *n* following it, e g *in the night; on the beach.*

pre·pos·sess /ˈpripəˋzes/ *vt* [VP6A,15A] (formal) give (a person) a feeling (about sth), usu favourable; fill (a person *with* or *by* an idea, a feeling): *I was ~ed by his appearance and manners,* They made a favourable impression upon me. **~·ing** *adj* attractive; making a good impression: *a girl of ~ing appearance.* **pre·pos·session** /ˈpripəˋzeʃn/ *n* [C] favourable feeling experienced in advance.

pre·pos·ter·ous /prɪˋpostərəs/ *adj* completely contrary to reason or sense; absurd. **~·ly** *adv*

pre·puce /ˋpripjus/ *n* (anat) foreskin.

pre·re·cord /ˈpririˋkɔd/ *vt* [VP6A] record, e g a radio or TV programme, in advance on tape or discs.

pre·requi·site /ˈpriˋrekwɪzɪt/ *n, adj* (thing) required as a condition for sth else: *Three passes at 'A' level are a ~ for university entrance/are ~ for university entrance.*

pre·roga·tive /prɪˋrogətɪv/ *n* [C] special right(s) or privilege(s), esp of a ruler: *the ~ of pardon,* e g to pardon a condemned criminal. **the Royal P~,** (GB) the (theoretical) right of the sovereign to act independently of Parliament.

pre·sage /ˋpresɪdʒ/ *n* (formal) [C] presentiment; sign looked upon as a warning. □ *vt* /prɪˋseɪdʒ/ [VP6A] foretell; be a sign of: *The clouds ~ a storm.*

pres·by·ter /ˋprezbɪtə(r)/ *n* elder (person in authority) in some Protestant churches, esp the Presbyterian Church.

Pres·by·terian /ˈprezbɪˋtɪərɪən/ *adj* **~ Church,** one governed by elders, all of equal rank. ⇨ **Episcopal,** governed by bishops (England since 1972, united with the Congregational Church to form the United Reformed Church). □ *n* member of the ~ Church. **~·ism** /-ɪzm/ *n* the ~ system of church government; the beliefs of ~s.

pres·by·tery /ˋprezbɪtərɪ *US:* -terɪ/ *n* (*pl* **-ries**) [C] **1** (in a church) eastern part of the chancel beyond the choir; sanctuary. **2** (regional) administrative court of the Presbyterian Church. **3** residence of a Roman Catholic parish priest.

pre·sci·ent /ˋpreʃɪənt/ *adj* (formal) knowing about, able to see into, the future. **~·ly** *adv* **pre·sci·ence** /-əns/ *n*

pre·scribe /prɪˋskraɪb/ *vt, vi* **1** [VP6A,14] **~ *(sth for sth),*** advise or order the use of: *~d textbooks,* books which pupils are required to use. *The doctor ~d a long rest. What do you ~ for this illness?* **2** [VP6A,8,10,21,2A,3A] say, with authority, what course of action is to be followed: *penalties ~d by the law. Complete the ~d form.*

pre·script /ˋpriskrɪpt/ *n* ordinance; command.

pre·scrip·tion /prɪˋskrɪpʃn/ *n* [U] act of prescribing; [C] that which is prescribed; (esp) doctor's written order or direction for the making up and use of a medicine; the medicine itself: *~ charges,* (in GB) charges made under National Health Service requirements for ~s.

pre·scrip·tive /prɪˋskrɪptɪv/ *adj* giving orders or directions; prescribed by custom: *a ~ grammar of the English language,* one telling the reader how he ought to use the language. ⇨ **descriptive.**

pres·ence /ˋprezns/ *n* [U] **1** being present in a place, etc: *in the ~ of his friends,* with his friends there. *Your ~ is requested at the annual general meeting,* Please be there. *He was calm in the ~ of danger.* ***~ of mind,*** ⇨ **mind**[1]**(2). 2** bearing; person's way of carrying himself: *a man of noble ~.*

pres·ent[1] /ˋpreznt/ *adj* **1** being in the place in question: *The Smiths, and other people ~* (= who were ~); *Were you ~ at the ceremony?* ***~ company excepted,*** (colloq) used to show that one's remarks do not apply to anyone who is ~. ⇨ **absent**[1]**(1). 2** being discussed or dealt with; now being considered: *in the ~ case,* this case. **3** existing now: *the ~ government.* **4 *~ to,*** felt, remembered by; *~ to the mind/imagination.* **5** (archaic) ready at hand: *'a very ~ help in trouble'.* ⇨ **Ps 46: 1.** □ *n* **1 the ~,** the ~ time, the time now passing: *the past, the ~, and the future;* (gram) *the ~ tense.* ***at ~,*** now: *We don't need any more at ~.* ***for the ~,*** for the time being, as far as the ~ is concerned: *That will be enough for the ~.* **2** (legal) *by these ~s,* by this document.

pres·ent[2] /ˋpreznt/ *n* gift: *ˋbirthday ~s; I'm buying it for a ~* (= as a gift), *so please wrap it up nicely.* ***make sb a ~ of sth,*** give sb sth; *I'll make you a ~ of my old car.*

pre·sent[3] /prɪˋzent/ *vt* **1** [VP14,15A] give; offer; put forward; submit. ***~ sth to sb; ~ sb with sth,*** give: *~ the village with a bus-shelter/~ a bus-shelter to the village; the clock that was ~ed to me when I retired; ~ a petition to the Governor; ~ a cheque at the bank,* i e for payment; *~ one's compliments/greetings, etc to sb,* (polite phrases). [VP13A] (archaic) (Shakespeare): *'I thrice ~ed him a kingly crown.'* **2** [VP6A,15A] introduce (sb, esp to a Sovereign): *be ~ed at Court.* **3** [VP15A] (reflex) appear; attend: *~ oneself at a friend's house; ~ oneself for trial/for examination.* **4** [VP6A] show; reveal: *He ~ed a bold front to the world,* showed that he was facing his difficulties, etc bravely. *This case ~s some interesting features. A good opportunity has ~ed itself for doing what you suggested.* **5** [VP6A] (of a theatrical manager or company) produce (a play): cause (an actor) to take part in a play: *The Mermaid Company will ~ 'Hamlet' next week/will ~ Tom Hill as Brutus in 'Julius Caesar'.* **6** [VP14] ***~ sth at sb,*** aim (a weapon at...); hold out a weapon in position for aiming: *The intruder ~ed a pistol at me.* **7** [VP6A] hold (a rifle, etc) vertically in front of the body as a salute, etc. ***P~ arms!*** (the order to do this). **8** [VP14] ***~ sb to ~,*** recommend (a clergyman) to a bishop for appointment (to a benefice). □ *n* position of a weapon in a salute: *at the ~,* with the weapon held in a perpendicular position.

pre·sent·able /prɪˋzentəbl/ *adj* fit to appear, be shown, in public: *Is this old suit still ~? Is the girl he wants to marry ~,* the sort of girl he can introduce to his friends and family? **pre·sent·ably** /-əblɪ/ *adv*

pres·en·ta·tion /ˈpreznˋteɪʃn *US:* ˈprizen-/ *n* [U] presenting or being presented; [C] sth presented: *the ~ of a new play; a ~ copy,* a book given as a present, esp by the author. *The cheque is payable on* ~, i e at the bank.

pre·sen·ti·ment /prɪˋzentɪmənt/ *n* [C] (formal) vague feeling that sth (esp unpleasant or undesirable) is about to happen.

pres·ent·ly /ˋprezntlɪ/ *adv* **1** soon: *I'll be with you* ~. **2** (US) at the present time: *The Secretary of State is* ~ *in Africa.*

pres·er·va·tion /ˌprezəˋveɪʃn/ *n* [U] **1** act of preserving: *the* ~ *of food/one's health; the* ~ *of peace; the* ~ *of wild life.* **2** condition of sth preserved: *old paintings in an excellent state of* ~.

pre·serv·ative /prɪˋzɜvətɪv/ *n, adj* (substance) used for preserving: *fresh cream free from* ~*s*, with no substances added to preserve the cream.

pre·serve /prɪˋzɜv/ *vt* [VP6A,14] ~ ***(from),*** **1** keep safe from harm or danger: *social activities preserving old people from the loneliness of old age; God* ~ *us all!* **2** keep from decay, risk of going bad, etc (by pickling, making into jam, etc): ~ *fruit/eggs, etc.* **3** keep from loss; retain (qualities, etc): ~ *one's eyesight; a well-*~*d old man*, one who shows few signs of the usual weaknesses of old age. **4** care for and protect land, rivers, lakes, etc with the animals, birds and fish, esp to prevent these from being taken by poachers: *The fishing in this stream is strictly* ~*d.* **5** keep alive (sb's name or memory); keep extant: *Few of his early poems are* ~*d.* □ *n* **1** (usu *pl*) jam. **2** woods, streams, etc where animals, birds and fish are ~d: *a* ˋ*game* ~. ***poach on another's*** ~, (fig) take a share in activities, interests, etc looked upon as associated especially with sb else. **pre·serv·able** /-əbl/ *adj* that can be ~d. **pre·server** *n* person or thing that ~s.

pre·side /prɪˋzaɪd/ *vi* [VP2A,C,3A] ~ ***at,*** be chairman: *The Prime Minister* ~*s at meetings of the Cabinet.* ~ ***over,*** be the head or director of: *The city council is* ~*d over by the mayor.*

presi·dency /ˋprezɪdənsɪ/ *n* (*pl* **-cies**) **1 the** ~, the office of president. **2** term of office as a president: *during the* ~ *of Lincoln.*

presi·dent /ˋprezɪdənt/ *n* **1** elected head of the government in the US and other modern republics. **2** head of some government departments (*P*~ *of the Board of Trade*), of some business companies, colleges, societies, etc. **presi·den·tial** /ˌprezɪˋdenʃl/ *adj* of a ~ or his duties: *the* ~*ial election; the* ~*ial year*, (in US) the year of the ~ial elections.

pre·sid·ium /prɪˋsɪdɪəm/ *n* standing committee in various Communist systems and organizations.

press[1] /pres/ *n* **1** act of pressing: *a* ~ *of the hand; give sth a light* ~. ˋ**~-up** *n* (*pl* ~-ups) exercise in which one stretches out face down on the floor, the arms being straightened and bent by ~ing against the floor with the palms of one's hands to raise and lower one's body. **2** machine or apparatus for pressing: *a* ˋ*wine-*~*; a* ˋ*cider-*~*; keep one's (tennis) racket in a* ~*; a hydraulic* ~. **3** (usu *sing* with *def art*) **the** ~, printed periodicals; the newspapers generally; journalists: *The book was favourably noticed by the* ~*/had a good* ~, was favourably reviewed by the literary critics. *There was a* ~ *campaign against him,* He was attacked in the newspapers. *The liberty/freedom of the* ~ (= The right of newspapers to report events, express opinions, etc freely) *is a feature of democratic countries.* ˋ**~-agent** *n* person employed by a theatre, actor, musician, etc to arrange for publicity in the newspapers. Hence, ˋ**~-agency** *n* ˋ**~-box** *n* place reserved for reporters at a football or cricket match, etc. ˋ**~ conference** *n* one of newspaper reporters, convened by a minister, government official, etc who talks about policy, achievements, etc. ˋ**~-cutting/-clipping** *nn* paragraph, article, etc cut out from a newspaper or other periodical. ˋ**~-gallery** *n* gallery reserved for reporters, esp in the House of Commons. ˋ**~-lord** *n* powerful newspaper proprietor. ˋ**~-photographer** *n* newspaper photographer. **4** business for printing (and sometimes publishing) books or periodicals; (also ˋ**printing-~**) machine for printing: *in the* ~, being printed; *send a manuscript to the* ~, send it to be printed; *go to* ~, start printing; *correct the* ~, correct errors in printing, be a proof-reader. **5** crowd: *lost in the* ~*; fight one's way through the* ~. **6** pressure: *the* ~ *of modern life; because of the* ~ *of business.* **7** cupboard with shelves for clothes, books, etc usu in a recess in a wall. ˋ**~-mark** *n* mark or number in a book showing its place in a library shelf. **8** (naut) ~ *of sail/canvas*, as much sail as the wind will allow.

press[2] /pres/ *vt,vi* **1** [VP6A,15B] push steadily against: ~ *the trigger of a gun;* ~ *(down) the accelerator pedal* (of a car); ~ *the button,* e g of an electric bell. **2** [VP6A,15B,22] use force or weight to get sth smooth or flat, to get sth into a smaller space, to get juice out of fruit, etc: ~ *a suit/skirt, etc,* with an iron, to remove creases, etc; ~ *grapes,* when making wine; ~ *the juice out of an orange;* ~*ed beef,* beef that has been boiled and pressed into shape for packing in tin boxes. **3** [VP6A,15A,B] keep close to and attack; bear heavily on: ~ *the enemy hard,* attack with determination; ~ *(home) an attack,* carry it out with determination; ~ *a point* (in an argument, debate) *home,* (fig) obtain support, agreement, etc by a determined, articulate, speech; *be hard* ~*ed,* be under determined attack. **4** ~ ***for,*** make repeated requests for; demand urgently: ~ *for an inquiry into a question.* **5 be ~ed for,** have barely enough of: ~*ed for time/money, space.* **6** [VP2C] push, crowd, with weight or force: *crowds* ~*ing against the barriers/*~*ing round the royal visitors.* **7** [VP3A,14,17] ~ ***(sb) for sth/do do sth,*** urge; insist on: ~ *(sb) for an answer;* ~ *sb to do sth;* ~ *sb for a debt/to pay a debt. He did not need much* ~*ing. They are* ~*ing for a decision to be made.* ~ ***sth (up)on sb,*** insist that sb takes it: *He* ~*ed the money on me,* insisted on my accepting it. *Don't* ~ *your opinions upon her,* don't insist that she should accept them. **8** [VP2A] demand action or attention: *The matter is* ~*ing,* is urgent. **9** ***Time*** ~***es,*** There is no time to lose. **10** [VP6A,15A] squeeze (sb's hand, arm, etc) as a sign of affection or sympathy; draw (sb) to oneself in an embrace: *He* ~*ed her to his side.* **11** [VP2C] ~ ***(down) (up)on sb,*** weigh; oppress: *His responsibilities* ~ *heavily upon him. The new taxes* ~*ed down heavily on the people.* **12** [VP2C] ~ ***on (forward) (with sth),*** hurry, continue in a determined way: ~ *on with one's work. It was getting dark, so the travellers* ~*ed on (forward).* **~ing** *n* one of many identical discs/records made from the same matrix: *make and sell 10 000* ~*ings of a symphony.* □ *adj* **1** urgent; requiring immediate attention: ~*ing business.* **2** (of persons, their requests, etc) insistent: *a* ~*ing invitation; as you* *are so ~ing.* **~·ing·ly** *adv*

press[3] /pres/ *vt* [VP15A] **1** (in former times) force (a man) to serve in the navy or army. **ˋ~-gang** *n* body of men formerly employed to ~ men. **2** take (sth) for puplic use; requisition. ***~ into service,*** make use of because of urgent need: *Even my thirty-year-old car was ~ed into service to take voters to the polling-station.*

press·ure /ˋpreʃə(r)/ *n* [C,U] pressing; (the amount of) force exerted continuously on or against sth by sth which touches it: *a ~ of 6 lb to the square inch; see that the tyre ~ is right; atmospheric ~, the ~ of the atmosphere,* the ~ of weight of air, as measured by a barometer. **ˋblood-~** *n* tension of the blood-vessels. **ˋ~ cabin** *n* cabin (in an aircraft) that is pressurized. **ˋ~-cooker** *n* airtight container for cooking quickly with steam under ~. **ˋ~-gauge** *n* apparatus or device for measuring the ~ of a liquid or gas at a given point. **2** compelling force or influence: *He pleaded ~ of work/family ~s and resigned his place on the committee.* ***be/come under ~,*** feel/be caused to feel strongly compelled (to act): *He's under strong ~ to vote with the government on this issue. He always works best under ~,* when he has to. ***bring ~ to bear on sb (to do sth), put ~ on sb/put sb under ~ (to do sth),*** use force or influence on sb. **ˋ~ group,** organized group, e g an association of manufacturers such as brewers, a farmers' union; which tries to exert influence or lobby for the benefit of its members. **3** sth that oppresses or weighs down: *the ~ of taxation; under the ~ of poverty/necessity.* **4** ***(at) high ~,*** with great energy and speed: *work at high ~; a high-~ salesman.*

press·ur·ized /ˋpreʃəraɪzd/ *adj* (of an aircraft, a submarine, etc) constructed so that its internal air-pressure can be controlled and made normal.

presti·digi·ta·tor /ˈprestɪˋdɪdʒɪteɪtə(r)/ *n* juggler; conjuror. **pres·ti·digi·ta·tion** /ˈprestɪˈdɪdʒɪˋteɪʃn/ *n*

pres·tige /preˋstiʒ/ *n* [U] **1** respect that results from the good reputation (of a person, nation, etc); power or influence coming from this: *behaviour that would mean loss of ~.* **2** distinction, glamour, that comes from achievements, success, possessions, etc: (attrib) *the ~ value of living in a fashionable district/of owning a Rolls-Royce.* **pres·tig·ious** /preˋstɪdʒəs/ *adj* bringing ~.

pres·tis·simo /preˋstɪsɪməʊ/ *adj, adv* (I; music) very quick(ly); as quickly as possible.

presto /ˋprestəʊ/ *adj, adv* quick(ly). ***Hey ~!*** words used by a conjuror when performing a trick.

pre·stressed /ˈpriˋstrest/ *adj* (of concrete) strengthened by being compressed.

pre·sum·able /prɪˋzjuməbl *US:* -ˋzu-/ *adj* that may be presumed. **pre·sum·ably** /-əblɪ/ *adv*

pre·sume /prɪˋzjum *US:* -ˋzum/ *vt,vi* **1** [VP6A,9, 25] take for granted; suppose (to be true): *In Britain an accused man is ~d (to be) innocent until he is proved guilty. Let us ~ that...; Dr Livingstone, I ~.* **2** [VP7] venture; take the liberty: *I won't ~ to disturb you. May I ~ to advise you?* **3** [VP3A] ***~ upon sth,*** (formal) make a wrong use of, take an unfair advantage of: *~ upon sb's good nature,* take advantage of it by asking for help, etc; *~ upon a short acquaintance,* treat sb familiarly even though one has known him for only a short time. **pre·sum·ing** *adj* having, showing, a tendency to ~, to take liberties.

pre·sump·tion /prɪˋzʌmpʃn/ *n* **1** [C] sth presumed(1); sth which seems likely although there is no proof: *on the false ~ that the firm was bankrupt; the ~ that he was drowned.* **2** [U] arrogance; behaviour that is too bold: *If you will excuse my ~, I should like to contradict what you have just said.*

pre·sump·tive /prɪˋzʌmptɪv/ *adj* based on presumption(1): *~ evidence; the ~ heir/the heir ~,* person who is heir (to the throne, etc) until sb with a stronger claim is born. **~·ly** *adv*

pre·sump·tu·ous /prɪˋzʌmptʃʊəs/ *adj* (formal) (of behaviour, etc) too bold or self-confident. **~·ly** *adv*

pre·sup·pose /ˈprisəˋpəʊz/ *vt* [VP6A,9] **1** assume beforehand. **2** imply; require as a condition: *Sound sleep ~s a mind at ease.* **pre·sup·po·si·tion** /ˈpriˈsʌpəˋzɪʃn/ *n* [C] sth ~d; [U] presupposing.

pre·tence (US = **-tense**) /prɪˋtens/ *n* **1** [U] pretending; make-believe: *do sth under the ~ of friendship/religion/patriotism. It's all ~.* **2** [C] pretext or excuse; false claim or reason: *He calls for the night porter on the slightest ~. It is only a ~ of friendship.* ***false ~s,*** (legal) acts intended to deceive: *obtain money by/on/under false ~s.* **3** [C] claim (to merit, etc); [U] ostentation: *a man without ~.*

pre·tend /prɪˋtend/ *vt,vi* **1** [VP7,9] make oneself appear (to be sth, to be doing sth), either in play or to deceive others: *~ to be asleep; boys ~ing that they are pirates. Let's ~ we are cowboys. They ~ed not to see us.* **2** [VP6A] say falsely that one has (as an excuse or reason, or to avoid danger, difficulty, etc): *~ sickness. He ~ed ignorance hoping to avoid being fined for breaking the law.* **3** [VP3A] ***~ to,*** put forward a claim to: *There are not many persons who ~ to an exact knowledge of the subject. Surely he does not ~ to intelligence! The young man ~ed to the throne,* claimed it (falsely). **~·ed·ly** *adv* **~er** *n* person whose claim (to a throne, a title, etc) is disputed.

pre·tense /prɪˋtens/ ⇨ pretence.

pre·ten·sion /prɪˋtenʃn/ *n* **1** [C] (often *pl*) (statement of a) claim: *He makes no ~s to expert knowledge of the subject. Has he any ~s to being considered a scholar? She has some social ~s,* claims some place in high society. **2** [U] being pretentious.

pre·ten·tious /prɪˋtenʃəs/ *adj* claiming (without justification) great merit or importance: *a ~ author/book/speech; use ~ language.* **~·ly** *adv* **~·ness** *n*

pret·er·ite (also **-erit**) /ˋpretərɪt/ *n, adj* **~ (tense),** (gram) (tense) expressing a past or completed action or state.

pre·ter·natu·ral /ˈpritəˋnætʃərl/ *adj* out of the regular course of things; not normal or usual. **~·ly** *adv*: *~ly solemn.*

pre·text /ˋpritekst/ *n* [C] false reason (*for* an action, etc): *On/Under the ~ of asking for my advice, he called and borrowed £10 from me. Can we find a ~ for refusal/refusing the invitation?*

pre·tor /ˋpritə(r)/ *n* ⇨ praetor.

pret·tify /ˋprɪtɪfaɪ/ *vt* (*pt,pp* -fied) [VP6A] make pretty, esp in an insipid way.

pretty /ˋprɪtɪ/ *adj* (-ier, -iest) **1** pleasing and attractive without being beautiful or magnificent; *a ~ girl/garden/picture/piece of music. Go and make yourself ~,* tidy yourself, make up your face, etc. '~-~ *adj* (colloq) superficially ~ or charming. **2** fine; good: *a ~ wit; A ~ mess you've made of it!* (ironic) *You're a ~ sort of fellow.* **3** (colloq) considerable in amount or extent. ***a ~ penny,*** quite a lot: *It will cost you a ~ penny.* ***come to a ~ pass,*** ⇨ pass[1](2). ***a '~ kettle of fish,*** ⇨ fish[1](1). □ *adv* fairly, moderately: *The situation seems ~ hopeless. It's ~ cold outdoors today.* ***~ much,*** very nearly: *The result of the ballot is ~ much what we expected.* ***~ nearly,*** almost: *The car is new, or ~ nearly so,* almost new. ***~ well,*** almost: *We've ~ well finished the work.* ***sitting ~,*** (colloq) well off; favourably placed for future developments, etc. □ *n* (*pl* **-ties**) *my ~,* my ~ one (used of a child). **pret·tily** /'prɪtəlɪ/ *adv* in a ~ or charming manner: *behave prettily.* **pret·ti·ness** *n*

pret·zel /'pretsl/ *n* (G) crisp, salt-flavoured biscuit, made in the shape of a knot or stick, eaten with beer.

pre·vail /prɪ'veɪl/ *vi* **1** [VP2A,3A] ***~ (over/against),*** gain victory (over); fight successfully (against): *Truth will ~. We ~ed over our enemies.* **2** [VP2A] be widespread; be generally seen, done, etc: *the conditions now ~ing in Africa. The use of opium still ~s in the south.* **3** [VP3A] ***~ (up)on sb to do sth,*** persuade (to do): *~ upon a friend to lend you £10.* **~·ing** *adj* most frequent or usual: *the ~ing winds/fashions in dress.*

preva·lent /'prevələnt/ *adj* (formal) common, seen or done everywhere (at the time in question): *the ~ fashions; the ~ opinion on the proposed reforms. Is malaria still ~ in that country?* **preva·lence** /-əns/ *n* [U] being ~: *I'm shocked at the prevalence of bribary among these officials.*

pre·vari·cate /prɪ'værɪkeɪt/ *vi* [VP2A] (formal) make untrue or partly untrue statements; try to evade telling the (whole) truth. **pre·vari·ca·tion** /prɪˌværɪ'keɪʃn/ *n* [U] prevaricating; [C] instance of this.

pre·vent /prɪ'vent/ *vt* **1** [VP6A,14] ***~ sb from doing sth; ~ sth (from happening),*** stop or hinder: *Who can ~ us from getting married/~ our getting married now that you are of age? Your prompt action ~ed a serious accident.* **2** (old use) go before as a guide: *'P~ us, O Lord, in all our doings'.* **~·able** /-əbl/ *adj* that can be ~ed.

pre·ven·tion /prɪ'venʃn/ *n* [U] act of preventing: *the Society for the P~ of Cruelty to Animals. P~ is better than cure.*

pre·ven·tive /prɪ'ventɪv/ *adj* serving or designed to prevent; precautionary. ***~ custody,*** imprisonment of sb considered unlikely to be reformed, so that he may not commit further crimes. ***~ detention,*** detention without trial because a person is thought likely to commit crime or (in some countries) oppose the government. ***~ medicine,*** research into means of warding off disease, illness, e g hygiene, working conditions. ***~ officer,*** customs officer whose duty is to prevent smuggling. **pre·vent·ative** /prɪ'ventətɪv/ *n* medicine to prevent or ward off a disease.

pre·view /'privju/ *n* [C] view of a film, play, etc before it is shown to the general public. □ *vt* have/give a ~ of.

pre·vi·ous /'privɪəs/ *adj* **1** coming earlier in time or order: *on a ~ occasion; ~ convictions,* convictions for earlier offences, taken into account by a judge when passing sentence upon sb convicted of a further offence. *I regret that a ~ engagement prevents me from accepting your kind invitation.* **2** too hasty: *Aren't you rather ~ in supposing that I will marry you?* **3** ***~ to,*** before. **~·ly** *adv*

pre·vi·sion /ˌpri'vɪʒn/ *n* [U] foresight; [C] instance of this: *have a ~ of danger.*

prey /preɪ/ *n* (*sing* only) animal, bird, etc hunted for food: *The eagle was devouring its ~.* ***be/fall a ~ to,*** **(a)** be seized, caught by: *The zebra fell a ~ to the lion.* **(b)** be greatly troubled by: *be a ~ to anxiety and fears.* **'beast/bird of '~,** one that kills and eats others, e g tigers, eagles. □ *vi* [VP3A] ***~ (up)on,*** **1** take, hunt, as ~(1): *hawks ~ing on small birds.* **2** steal from; plunder: *Our coasts were ~ed upon by Viking pirates.* **3** (of fears, etc) trouble greatly: *anxieties/losses that ~ upon my mind.*

price /prɑɪs/ *n* **1** [C] sum of money for which sth is (to be) sold or bought; that which must be done, given or experienced to obtain or keep sth: *What ~ are you asking? P~s are going up/going down/rising/falling. I won't buy it at that ~. He sold the house at a good ~. Loss of independence was a high ~ to pay for peace.* ***at a ~,*** at a fairly high price: *There's fresh asparagus in the shops—at a price!* ***Every man has his ~,*** can be bribed. ***put a ~ on sb's head,*** offer a reward for his capture (dead or alive). **the 'asking ~,** (for a house, etc) price stated by the vendor: *accept an offer of £200 below the asking ~.* **'~-control** *n* control or fixing of ~s by authorities, manufacturers, etc. Hence, **'~-controlled** *adj*: *~-controlled articles.* **'~-list** *n* list of current ~s of goods for sale. **'list-~** *n* ~ recommended by the manufacturer, etc but not always compulsory. **2** [U] value; worth: *a pearl of great ~.* ***beyond/above/without ~,*** so valuable that buying is impossible. **3** [C] (betting) odds. **the 'starting ~,** odds offered by bookmakers as the race is about to start. ***What ~...?*** (colloq, sl) **(a)** What is the chance of.... **(b)** sneer at the failure of sth: *What ~ collective security now?* □ *vt* **1** [VP6A] fix, ask about, the ~ of sth; mark (goods) with a ~: *All our goods are clearly ~d.* **2** ***~ oneself/one's goods out of the market,*** (of manufacturers, producers) fix ~s so high that sales decline or stop. **pricey** /'prɑɪsɪ/ *adj* (sl) expensive. **~·less** *adj* **1** too valuable to be ~d: *~less paintings.* **2** (sl) absurd: *a ~less old fellow;* very amusing: *a ~less joke.*

prick[1] /prɪk/ *n* **1** small mark or hole caused by the act of pricking: *~s made by a needle.* **2** pain caused by pricking: *I can still feel the ~. He feels the ~ of conscience/remorse,* mental uneasiness. **'pin-~,** (fig) sth small that irritates. **3** (old use) goad for oxen. ***kick against the ~s,*** (fig) hurt oneself by useless resistance. **4** ⚠ (vulg) penis; (vulg) term of abuse: *He's a stupid ~!*

prick[2] /prɪk/ *vt, vi* **1** [VP6A] make a hole or a mark in (sth) with a sharp point: *~ a toy balloon; ~ a blister,* on the skin; *~ holes in paper.* **2** [VP6A] hurt, cause pain to, with a sharp point or points: *~ one's finger with/on a needle. The thorns on these roses ~ed my fingers.* (fig) *His conscience ~ed him.* **3** [VP2A] feel sharp pain: *My fingers ~.* **4** [VP15B] ***~ sth out/off,*** put (seedlings) in the earth (in holes made with a pointed stick, etc): *~ out young cabbage plants.* **6** [VP15B] ***~ up one's ears,*** (esp of dogs, horses) raise the ears; (fig, of persons) pay sharp attention to sth being said. **~er** *n* person who, thing which, ~s; instrument for piercing holes, e g a bradawl. **~·ing** *n* act of

birds 3

~ing; ~ing sensation.

prickle /ˈprɪkl/ *n* [C] (usu small) pointed growth on the stem, etc of a plant, or on the skin of some animals, e g hedgehogs; thorn. □ *vt,vi* give or have a pricking sensation. **prick·ly** /ˈprɪklɪ/ *adj* **1** covered with ~s. **ˈprickly pear,** cactus covered with ~s and having pear-shaped fruit. **2 prickly heat,** inflammation of the sweat glands, marked by a pricking sensation, common in the tropics during the hot-weather season. **3** (colloq) easily irritated or angered: *You're a bit ~ today.*

pride /praɪd/ *n* **1** [U] feeling of satisfaction arising from what one has done, or from persons, things, etc one is concerned with: *look with ~ at one's garden.* ***take a ~/no/little ~ in,*** have some/no/little ~ about: *take (a) great ~ in one's achievements/in the success of one's children.* ***~ of place,*** a position of superiority. **2** [U] (also **proper ~**) self-respect: knowledge of one's worth and character: *He has no ~. His ~ prevents him from doing anything dishonourable. Don't say anything that may wound his ~.* **false ~,** mistaken feeling of this kind; vanity. **3** [U] object of ~(1): *a girl who is her mother's ~ and joy.* **4** [U] too high an opinion of oneself, one's position, possessions, etc; arrogance: *the sin of ~; be puffed up with ~.* ***P~ goes before a fall,*** (prov) ⇨ *go before* at **go**[1](28). **5** (*sing* with *def art*) prime; flower: *in the full ~ of youth.* **6** [C] group: (esp) *a ~ of lions/peacocks.* □ *vt* (reflex) ***~ oneself upon sth,*** take ~ in; be pleased and satisfied about: *He ~s himself upon his skill as a pianist.*

prie-dieu /ˈpri djɜ/ *n* small piece of furniture at which to kneel when praying to God.

priest /prist/ *n* **1** clergyman of a Christian Church, esp one who is between a deacon and a bishop in the Church of England or Roman Catholic Church. ⇨ the illus at **vestment**. *Clergyman* is usu in the C of E, except in official use. ⇨ **minister** for Methodist, Baptist, etc Churches. **ˈ~-ridden** *adj* ruled by, under the subjection of, ~s. **2** (of non-Christian religions) person trained to perform special acts of religion, to serve the deity, give advice, etc. **~·ess** /priˈstes *US:* ˈpristɪs/ *n* woman ~(2). **ˈ~·craft** *n* [U] ambitious or worldly policy of ~s. **ˈ~·hood** /-hʊd/ *n* the whole body of ~s of a Church: *the Irish ~hood.* **~·ly, ˈ~·like** *adjj* of or for a ~; like a ~.

prig /prɪg/ *n* [C] smug, self-satisfied, self-righteous person. **~·gish** /-ɪʃ/ *adj* behaving like, typical of, a ~; full of self-satisfaction. **~·gish·ly** *adv* **~·gish·ness** *n*

prim /prɪm/ *adj* (**-mer, -mest**) neat; formal: *a ~ garden;* (of persons, their manner, speech, etc) disliking, showing a dislike of, anything rough, rude, improper: *a very ~ and proper old gentleman.* □ *vt* (**-mm-**) put (the face, lips) into a ~ expression. **~·ly** *adv* **~·ness** *n*

prima /ˈprimə/ *adj* (I) first. **ˈ~ ˈballeˈrina** /ˈbæləˈrinə/, leading woman performer in ballet. **ˈ~ ˈdonna** /ˈdonə/, leading woman singer in opera.

pri·macy /ˈpraɪməsɪ/ *n* (*pl* **-cies**) **1** pre-eminence. **2** position of an archbishop.

pri·mae·val /praɪˈmivl/ *adj* ⇨ **primeval**.

prima facie /ˈpraɪmə ˈfeɪʃɪ/ *adv, adj* (Lat) (based) on the first impression: *have ~ a good case.* **~ evidence,** (legal) sufficient to prove something (unless refuted).

pri·mal /ˈpraɪml/ *adj* (formal) primeval; chief; first in importance.

pri·mary /ˈpraɪmərɪ *US:* -merɪ/ *adj* **1** leading in time, order or development: *of ~ (= chief) importance; a ˈ~ school,* (GB) for junior pupils (5 to 11 years); *~ rocks,* of the lowest series of strata; *the ~ meaning of a word,* the earliest and original meaning. **2 ~ colours,** red, blue and yellow, from which all other colours can be obtained by mixing two or more. □ *n* (*pl* **-ries**) (US) meeting of electors to name candidates for a coming election. **pri·mar·ily** /ˈpraɪmrlɪ *US:* praɪˈmerlɪ/ *adv* in the first place; essentially.

pri·mate[1] /ˈpraɪmeɪt/ *n* archbishop.

pri·mate[2] /ˈpraɪmeɪt/ *n* one of the highest order of mammals (including men, apes, monkeys and lemurs).

prime[1] /praɪm/ *adj* **1** chief; most important: *his ~ motive.* **the P~ Minister,** head of the Government. **2** excellent; first-rate: *~ (cuts of) beef.* **3** fundamental; primary. **~ cost,** cost of production not including overhead charges, margin for profit, etc. **~ meridian,** the zero meridian, that of Greenwich. **~ mover,** primary source of motive power, e g wind, water. **~ number,** one which cannot be divided exactly except by itself and the number 1 (e g 7, 17, 41).

prime[2] /praɪm/ *n* **1** state of highest perfection; the best part: *in the ~ of youth; in the ~ of life. When is a man in his ~? He is past his ~.* **2** first or earliest part: *the ~ of the year,* spring. **3** church service at 6a m or sunrise.

prime[3] /praɪm/ *vt* [VP6A] **1** get ready for use or action: *~ a gun,* (the old-fashioned kind) put in gunpowder, etc; *~ a pump,* wet it, pour in water, to get it started. ***~ the pump,*** (fig) put money into an inactive industry, etc or into the economy, to stimulate it to growth. **2** supply with facts, etc: *The witness had been ~d by a lawyer. The Socialist candidate had been well ~d with facts by Party headquarters.* **3** (colloq) fill (a person) with food or drink: *well ~d with liquor.* **4** cover (a surface) with the first coat of paint, oil, varnish, etc.

primer[1] /ˈpraɪmə(r)/ *n* first school textbook: *a Latin ~.*

primer[2] /ˈpraɪmə(r)/ *n* [C] **1** small quantity of explosive, contained in a cap or cylinder, for igniting the powder in a cartridge, bomb, etc. ⇨ the illus at **cartridge**. **2** priming (of paint).

pri·meval (also **-mae·val**) /praɪˈmivl/ *adj* **1** of the earliest time in the world's history. **2** very ancient: *~ forests,* natural forests in which no trees have ever been felled.

prim·ing /ˈpraɪmɪŋ/ *n* **1** gunpowder used to fire the charge of a gun, bomb, mine, etc. **2** mixture used by painters for a first coat.

primi·tive /ˈprɪmətɪv/ *adj* **1** of the earliest times; of an early stage of social development: *~ man; ~ culture.* **2** simple; old-fashioned; having undergone little development: *~ weapons,* e g bows and arrows, spears. □ *n* painter or sculptor of the period before the Renaissance; example of his work. **~·ly** *adv* **~·ness** *n*

pri·mo·geni·ture /ˈpraɪməʊˈdʒenɪtʃə(r) *US:* -tʃʊər/ *n* fact of being the firstborn of the children of the same parents. **right of ~,** (legal) system by which all real estate passes on from a father to the eldest son.

pri·mor·dial /praɪˈmɔdɪəl/ *adj* in existence at or from the beginning; primeval.

primp /prɪmp/ *vt* = **prink**.

prim·rose /ˈprɪmrəʊz/ *n* [C] common wild plant with pale yellow flowers; the flower; its colour: *the ~ way/path,* (fig) the pursuit of reckless pleasure.

prim·ula /ˈprɪmjʊlə/ *n* kinds of perennial herbaceous plants with flowers of various colours and sizes (including the primrose and polyanthus).

pri·mus /ˈpraɪməs/ *n* (*pl* **-muses** /-məsɪz/) (P) kind of cooking stove that burns vaporized oil.

prince /prɪns/ *n* **1** ruler, esp of a small state. **2** male member of a royal family, esp (in GB) a son or grandson of the Sovereign. **3 the ~ of darkness,** Satan. **the P~ of Peace,** Jesus. **P~ Consort,** husband of a reigning queen. **ˈ~·dom** /-dəm/ *n* rank or dignity of, area ruled by, a ~**(1)**. **~·ly** *adj* **(-ier, -iest)** (worthy) of a ~; splendid; generous: *a ~ly gift.* **prin·cess** /prɪnˈses/ *n* wife of a ~; daughter or granddaughter of a sovereign: (attrib) *Princess Anne.*

prin·ci·pal /ˈprɪnsəpl/ *adj* highest in order of importance: *the ~ rivers of Europe; the ~ food of the people of Java.* **~ boy,** person (traditionally, in GB, an actress, not an actor) who takes the leading part in a pantomime. □ *n* **1** title of some heads of colleges and of some other organizations. **2** person for whom another acts as agent in business: *I must consult my ~.* **3** main girder or rafter in a roof. **4** (fin) money lent, put into a business, etc on which interest is payable. **5** (legal) person directly responsible for a crime (distinguished from an abetter or accessory). **~ly** /-plɪ/ *adv* for the most part; chiefly.

prin·ci·pal·ity /ˈprɪnsəˈpælətɪ/ *n* (*pl* **-ties**) country ruled by a prince. **the P~,** Wales.

prin·ciple /ˈprɪnsəpl/ *n* [C] **1** basic truth; general law of cause and effect: *the (first) ~s of geometry/political economy/navigation.* **2** guiding rule for behaviour: *moral ~s; ~s of conduct; live up to one's ~s;* (collective *sing*) *a man of high ~.* ***in ~,*** (contrasted with *in detail*) in general. ***on ~,*** from conviction, from a settled moral motive: *He refused on ~ to understate his income for taxation purposes.* **3** general law shown in the working of a machine, etc: *These machines work on the same ~.* **prin·cipled** *adj* (in compounds) following, having, the kind of ~**(2)** indicated: *a most high-~d woman, unhappily married to a low-~d man.* ⇨ **unprincipled**.

prink /prɪŋk/ *vt* ***~ oneself up,*** make oneself look smart or spruce.

print[1] /prɪnt/ *n* **1** [U] mark(s), letters, etc in printed form: *clear ~; in large/small ~.* ***in ~,*** (of a book) printed and on sale. ***out of ~,*** (of a book) no more printed copies available from the publisher. ***rush into ~,*** (of an author) hasten to publish sth he has written. **2** [C] (usu in compounds) mark left on a surface preserving the form left by the pressure of sth: *ˈfinger-~s; ˈfoot-~s.* **3** [U] printed cotton fabric: (attrib) *a ~ dress.* **4** [C] picture, design, etc made by ~ing from a block, plate, etc: *old Japanese ~s;* photograph ~ed from a negative. **ˈblue-~,** ⇨ **blue**[2]**(7)**. **ˈ~-seller** *n* man who sells engravings, etchings, etc. **ˈ~-shop** *n* shop of a ~-seller. **5** [C] (now chiefly US) ~ed publication, esp a newspaper.

print[2] /prɪnt/ *vt,vi* **1** [VP6A] make marks on (paper), etc by pressing it with inked type, etc; make books/pictures, etc in this way; (of a publisher, an editor, an author) cause to be ~ed: *~ 6 000 copies of a novel. Do you intend to ~ your lectures/have your lectures ~ed?* (fig) *The incidents ~ed themselves on her memory.* **ˈ~ed matter/papers,** (as on envelopes, wrappers, etc) circulars, prospectuses, etc to be charged for postage, at a reduced rate. **ˈ~-out** *n* the ~ed output of a computer. **2** [VP6A] shape (one's letters), write (words), in imitation of ~ed characters (instead of ordinary handwriting). **3** [VP6A, 15B]

~ (off), make (a photograph) on paper, etc from a negative film or plate: *How many copies shall I ~ (off) for you from this negative?* **4** [VP2A] (of a plate or film) produce a picture; be produced as the result of ~ing(3): *This film/plate/picture hasn't ~ed very well.* **5** [VP6A] mark (a textile fabric) with a coloured design. **'~·able** /-əbl/ *adj* that can be ~ed, or ~ed from; fit to be ~ed. **~er** *n* workman who ~s books, etc; owner of a ~ing business. **'~·ing** *n* (in verbal senses): **'~ing-ink,** kind of ink used for ~ing books, etc. **'~ing-machine, '~ing-press** *nn* machine for ~ing books, etc. **'~ing office** *n* place where ~ing is done.

prior[1] /'praɪə(r)/ *adj* **~ (to),** earlier in time, order or importance: *have a ~ claim to sth.* **~ to,** *prep* before: *The house was sold ~ to auction,* before the day of the auction; *~ to any discussion of this matter.*

prior[2] /'praɪə(r)/ *n* head of a religious order or house; (in an abbey) next below an abbot. **~ess** /'praɪərəs/ *n* woman ~. **~y** /'praɪərɪ/ *n* (*pl* -ries) religious house governed by a ~ or ~ess.

pri·or·ity /praɪ'ɒrətɪ *US:* -'ɔr-/ *n* (*pl* **-ties**) **1** [U] being prior; right to have or do sth before others: *I have ~ over you in my claim. The proceeds of the sale,* e g of the property of a bankrupt, *will be distributed according to ~.* **2** [C] claim to consideration; high place among competing claims: *Road building is a first ~* (or, colloq, *a top ~*). *The Government gave ~ to housing after the War.*

prise /praɪz/ *vt* = **prize**[3].

prism /prɪzm/ *n* **1** solid figure with similar, equal and parallel ends, and with sides which are parallelograms. **2** body of this form, usu triangular and made of glass, which breaks up white light into the colours of the rainbow.

pris·matic /prɪz'mætɪk/ *adj* **1** like, having the shape of, a prism. **2** (of colours) brilliant and varied.

prison /'prɪzn/ *n* [C] building in which wrongdoers are kept locked up; place where a person is shut up against his will; [U] confinement in such a building: *escape/be released from ~; be in/go to/send sb to ~,* **'~-breaking** *n* the illegal act of escaping from ~. **~er** *n* person kept in ~ for crime or until tried in a law court; person, animal or bird kept in confinement: *a bird kept ~er in a cage.* **'~er of 'war,** person captured in war and (usu) kept in a camp for the duration of the war.

pris·tine /'prɪstin/ *adj* (formal) primitive; of early times; unchanged by later developments: *Who would want to get back to the ~ simplicity of Anglo-Saxon days?*

prithee /'prɪðɪ/ *int* (archaic) I pray thee; please: *P~, keep silent. Tell me, ~,....*

priv·acy /'prɪvəsɪ *US:* 'praɪv-/ *n* [U] **1** state of being away from others, alone and undisturbed: *the invasion of ~ by the press and TV. I should hate to live in a household where ~ was impossible. I don't want my ~ disturbed.* **2** secrecy (opp to *publicity*): *They were married in strict ~.*

pri·vate /'praɪvɪt/ *adj* **1** (opp of *public*) of, for the use of, concerning, one person or group of persons, not people in general: *a ~ letter,* about personal matters; *~ theatricals,* for the family and friends; *for ~ reasons,* not to be explained to everybody; *~ means,* income not earned as a salary, etc but coming from personal property, investments, etc; *at my ~ house,* at the place where I live (contrasted with my shop, office, etc). **'~ ac'count,** bank account opened by and drawn on by one person: *My wife and I have a joint account, and in addition we each have a ~ account.* **~ school,** one at which fees are paid (contrasted with a school financially helped by the State, etc). **'~ 'enterprise,** the management of industry, etc by ~ individuals, companies, etc (contrasted with State ownership or control). **2** secret; kept secret; *a letter marked 'P~'; have ~ information about sth. That is for your ~ ears,* is to be considered as secret, is confidential. **~ parts,** external sex organs. **3** having no official position; not holding any public office: *do sth in one's ~ capacity,* not as an official, etc; *his ~ life,* the life he leads away from business or public affairs. ***retire into ~ life,*** retire after a public career. **a ~ member (of the House of Commons),** one who is not a member of the Government. **4 a ~ (soldier),** an ordinary soldier without rank: *P~ Dodd.* □ *n* **1** ~ soldier. **2 *in ~,*** ~ly, not in public, **~·ly** *adv*

pri·va·teer /ˌpraɪvɪ'tɪə(r)/ *n* (formerly) armed vessel under private ownership, allowed to attack enemy shipping in time of war; commander or member of the crew of such a vessel.

pri·va·tion /praɪ'veɪʃn/ *n* **1** [U,C] lack of the necessaries of life; destitution: *fall ill through ~; suffering many ~s.* **2** [C] state of being deprived of sth (not necessarily sth essential): *He found it a great ~ not being allowed to smoke in prison.*

privet /'prɪvɪt/ *n* [U] evergreen shrub, bearing small white flowers, much used for garden hedges: *clipping the ~ hedges.*

pri·vi·lege /'prɪvḷɪdʒ/ *n* **1** [C] right or advantage available only to a person, class or rank, or the holder of a certain position, etc: *the ~s of birth,* e g that come because one is born into a wealthy family. **2** [C] special favour or benefit: *grant sb the ~ of fishing in a privately owned trout stream. It was a ~ to hear her sing.* **3** [C,U] right to do or say things without risk of punishment, etc (as when Members of Parliament may say things in the House which might result in a libel case if said outside Parliament). **privi·leged** *adj* having, granted, a ~ or ~s. **the ~d classes,** those who enjoy the advantages of the best education, of wealth, and secure social position. **'under-'~d,**

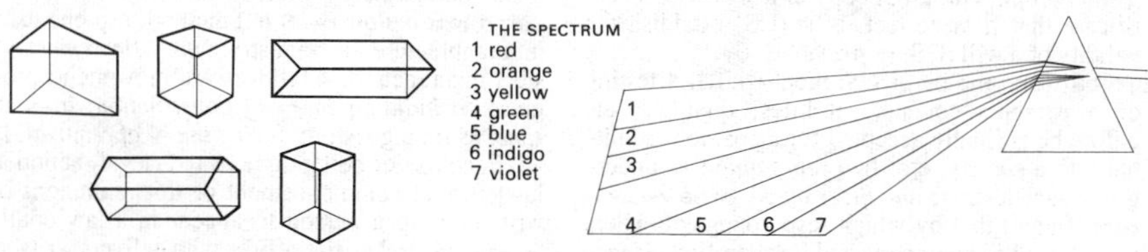

prisms

(mod use) suffering from poverty.

privy /ˈprɪvɪ/ *adj* **1** (old use, except legal) secret; private. **~ to,** having secret knowledge of: *charged with having been ~ to the plot against the prince.* **2 the ˈP~ ˋCouncil,** committee of persons appointed by the Sovereign, advising on some State affairs, but membership now being chiefly a personal dignity. **ˈP~ Councillor/Counsellor,** member of the P~ Council. **P~ Purse,** allowance of money from the public revenue for the Sovereign's private expenses. **P~ Seal,** State seal affixed to documents of minor importance. □ *n* (*pl* -vies) (old use) earth closet or latrine. **priv·ily** *adv* privately; secretly.

prize[1] /prɑɪz/ *n* **1** sth (to be) awarded to one who succeeds in a competition, lottery, etc: *be awarded a ~ for good conduct; draw a ~-winning ticket in a lottery; carry off most of the ~s at the village flower show; win first ~ on the pools; consolation ~s,* given to console those who do not win the good ~s; *~ cattle,* cattle that have been awarded ~s; *a ~ scholarship,* one awarded as a ~. **2** (fig) anything struggled for or worth struggling for: *the ~s of life.* **3 ˋ~-fight** *n* boxing match for money. Hence **ˋ~-fighter, ˋ~-fighting** *nn* **ˋ~-ring** *n* the enclosed area (now usu a square) in which boxing-matches are fought; the sport of ~-fighting. **4 ˋ~-man** /-mən/ *n* (*pl* -men) winner of a ~ (usu with the name of the ~ or scholarship prefixed). □ *vt* value highly: *my most ~d possessions.*

prize[2] /prɑɪz/ *n* [C] sth, esp a ship or its cargo, captured at sea during a war. **ˋ~-money** *n* money realized by the sale of a ~ (and divided up among those who captured it).

prize[3] (also **prise**) /prɑɪz/ *vt* [VP15A,B] use force to get sth, e g a box, lid, *open/up/off.*

pro- /ˈprəʊ/ *pref* supporting; favouring: *pro-British;* acting for: *pro-consul; pro-vice-chancellor.* ⇨ App 3.

pro /prəʊ/ *n* (*pl* pros) (colloq) (short for) professional (player): *a golf pro.*

pro and con /ˈprəʊ ən ˋkon/ *adv* for and against: *argue the matter ~.* □ *n* **the pros and cons,** the arguments for and against.

prob·abil·ity /ˈprobəˋbɪlətɪ/ *n* (*pl* -ties) **1** [U] quality of being probable. ***in all ~,*** most probably. **2** [U] likelihood: *There is no/little/not much ~ of his succeeding/that he will succeed.* **3** [C] (most) probable event or outcome: *What are the probabilities?*

prob·able /ˋprobəbl/ *adj* likely to happen or to prove true or correct: *the ~ result; a ~ winner. Rain is possible but not ~ before evening. It seems ~ that....* □ *n* person who will most likely be chosen, e g for a team, or do sth; ~ candidate, winner, etc. **prob·ably** /-əblɪ/ *adj*

pro·bate /ˋprəʊbeɪt/ *n* **1** [U] the official process of proving the validity of a will: *take out ~ of a will; grant ~ of a will.* **2** [C] copy of a will with a certificate that it is correct. □ *vt* (US) establish the validity of a will (GB = *prove*).

pro·ba·tion /prəˋbeɪʃn *US:* prəʊ-/ *n* [U] **1** testing of a person's conduct, abilities, qualities, etc before he is finally accepted for a position, admitted into a society, etc: *two years on ~,* i e undergoing such testing; *an officer on ~.* **2 the ˋ~ system,** (legal) that by which (esp young) offenders are allowed to go unpunished for their first offence while they continue to live without further breaking of the law: *three years' ~ under suspended sentence of one year's imprisonment.* **ˋ~ officer,** one who watches over the behaviour of offenders who are on ~. **~·ary** /prəˋbeɪʃn̩ərɪ *US:* prəʊˋbeɪʃn̩erɪ/ *adj* relating to ~. **~er** *n* **1** hospital nurse receiving training and still on ~(1). **2** wrongdoer who has been released on ~(2).

probe /prəʊb/ *n* **1** slender instrument with a blunt end, used by doctors for learning about the depth and direction of a wound, etc. **2** (journalism) investigation (*into* a scandal, etc). □ *vt* [VP6A] **1** examine with a ~. **2** investigate or examine thoroughly (sb's thought, the causes of sth).

prob·ity /ˋprəʊbətɪ/ *n* [U] (formal) uprightness of character; integrity.

prob·lem /ˋprobləm/ *n* [C] question to be solved or decided, esp sth difficult: *mathematical ~s; the ~s of youth;* (attrib) *a ˋ~ play/novel,* one dealing with a social or moral ~; *a ˋ~ picture,* one in which the artist's intention is obscure. **a ˋ~ child,** one whose behaviour offers a difficult ~ to his parents, teachers, etc. **~·atic** /ˈprobləˋmætɪk/ *adj* (esp of a result) doubtful; that cannot be seen or foretold. **~·ati·cally** /-klɪ/ *adv*

pro·bos·cis /prəˋbosɪs/ (*pl* -cises /-sɪsiz/) *n* **1** elephant's trunk. **2** elongated part of the mouth of some insects.

pro·cedure /prəˋsidʒə(r)/ *n* [C,U] (the regular) order of doing things, esp legal and political: *the usual ~ at committee meetings; stop arguing about (questions of) ~ and get down to business.* **pro·cedural** /prəˋsidʒərl/ *adj* of ~.

pro·ceed /prəˋsid/ *vi* [VP2A,3A,4] ***~ to sth/to do sth; ~ with sth,*** **1** go forward; continue, go on: *Let us ~ to business/to the next item on the agenda. He ~ed to inform me that.... Please ~ with your work. They ~ed* (more usu *went*) *from London to Leeds.* **2** [VP3A] ***~ from,*** come, arise from: *famine, plague and other evils that ~ from war.* **3** [VP3A] ***~ against sb,*** take legal action. **4** [VP3A] ***~ to,*** go on from a lower university degree: *~ to the degree of M A.*

pro·ceed·ing /prəˋsidɪŋ/ *n* **1** [U] course of action; (way of) behaving: *What is our best way of ~?* **2** [C] sth done; piece of conduct: *What he did was a rather high-handed ~. The ~s at the meeting were rather disorderly. There have been suspicious ~s in committee meetings.* **3** (*pl*) ***take/start legal ~s (against sb),*** take legal action. **4** (*pl*) records (of the activities of a society, etc); minutes: *the P~s of the Kent Archaeological Society.*

pro·ceeds /ˋprəʊsidz/ *n pl* financial results, profits, of an undertaking: *hold a bazaar and give the ~ to local charities.*

pro·cess[1] /ˋprəʊses *US:* ˋproses/ *n* **1** [C] connected series of actions, changes, etc esp such as are involuntary or unconscious: *the ~es of digestion, reproduction and growth.* **2** [C] series of operations deliberately undertaken: *Unloading the cargo was a slow ~.* **3** [C] method, esp one used in manufacture or industry: *the ˋBessemer ~,* steel manufacture. **4** [U] forward movement; progress: *a building in ~ of construction; in ~ of time,* as time goes on; *during the ~ of removal.* ***in ~,*** in course of being done. **5** [C] (legal) action at law; formal commencement of this; summons or writ ordering a person to appear in a law court. **ˋ~-server** *n* sheriff's officer who delivers writs. □ *vt* [VP6A] treat (material) in order to preserve it: ~

leather; put (esp food) through a special ~(3): *~ed cheese;* (photo) ~ *film,* develop it, etc; (computers) ~ *tape/information,* put it through the system in order to obtain the required information.

pro·cess² /prəˋses/ *vi* walk in or as if in procession.

pro·cession /prəˋseʃn/ *n* [C] number of persons, vehicles, etc moving forward and following each other in an orderly way: *a ˋfuneral ~;* [U] act of moving forward in this way: *walking in ~ through the streets.* **~al** /-nl/ *adj* of, for, used in, ~s: *a ~al chant,* sung by persons taking part in a religious ~.

pro·claim /prəˋkleɪm/ *vt* [VP6A,9,23,25] **1** make known publicly or officially: ~ (= declare) *war/peace; ~ a public holiday; ~ a republic; ~ a man (to be) a traitor/~ that he is a traitor. He ~ed Anne his heir.* **2** reveal, show: *His accent ~ed him a Scot/that he was a Scot.* **proc·la·ma·tion** /ˈprokləˋmeɪʃn/ *n* [U] act of ~ing: *by public proclamation;* [C] that which is ~ed: *issue/make a proclamation.*

pro·cliv·ity /prəʊˋklɪvətɪ/ *n* (*pl* -ties) [C] ~ ***(to/towards sth/to do sth),*** (formal) tendency, inclination.

pro·con·sul /ˈprəʊˋkonsl/ *n* (in ancient Rome) governor of a Roman province; (rhet, mod times) governor of a colony or dominion. **pro·con·su·lar** /ˈprəʊˋkonsjʊlə(r) *US:* -səl-/ *adj* **pro·con·su·late** /-lət/ *n* position of a ~; his term of office.

pro·cras·ti·nate /prəʊˋkræstɪneɪt/ *vi* [VP2A] (formal) delay action; keep on putting off: *He ~d until it was too late.* **pro·cras·ti·na·tion** /prəʊˈkræstɪˋneɪʃn/ *n* [U]: *Procrastination is the thief of time,* (prov).

pro·create /ˋprəʊkrɪeɪt/ *vt* [VP6A] beget, generate (offspring). **pro·cre·ation** /ˈprəʊkrɪˋeɪʃn/ *n*

proc·tor /ˋproktə(r)/ *n* **1** (at Oxford and Cambridge) university official with various duties, including the maintenance of discipline among students. **2 Queen's/King's P~,** offical whose duty is to watch the parties in certain kinds of legal cases, e g divorce, and to intervene if there are irregularities, e g collusion or suppression of facts.

procu·ra·tor /ˋprokjʊreɪtə(r)/ *n* **1** agent, esp one who has a power of attorney. **2 ~ fiscal,** public prosecutor of a district in Scotland.

pro·cure /prəˋkjʊə(r)/ *vt* [VP6A,12B,13B] **1** obtain, esp with care or effort: *Can you ~ me some specimens? The book is out of print and difficult to ~.* **2** (old use) bring about; cause: *~ sb's death by poison.* **3** solicit for a prostitute or one's own sexual desires. **pro·cur·able** /-əbl/ *adj* obtainable. **~·ment** *n* procuring: *the ~ment of military supplies.* **pro·curer** *n* (esp) pander. **pro·cur·ess** /-rɪs/ *n* woman ~r.

prod /prod/ *vt,vi* (-dd-) [VP6A,3A] ~ ***(at),*** push or poke with sth pointed; (fig) urge (to action): *The cruel boys were ~ding (at) the bear through the bars of the cage.* □ *n* poke or thrust: *She gave the man a ~ with her umbrella.*

prodi·gal /ˋprodɪgl/ *adj* ~ ***(of),*** wasteful; spending or using too much: *a ~ administration,* spending public funds too freely; *the ~ son,* wasteful and improvident man (in one of the parables of Jesus). *Nature is ~ of her gifts.* **~·ly** /-glɪ/ *adv* in a ~ manner: *a man who gives ~ly to charities.* **~·ity** /ˈprodɪˋgælətɪ/ *n* [U] (in a good sense) being ~: *the ~ity of the sea,* i e in supplying fish; (in a bad sense) extravagance; wasteful spending.

pro·di·gious /prəˋdɪdʒəs/ *adj* enormous; surprisingly great; wonderful: *a ~ sum of money.* **~·ly** *adv*

prod·igy /ˋprodɪdʒɪ/ *n* (*pl* -gies) sth wonderful because it seems to be contrary to the laws of nature; person who has unusual or remarkable abilities or who is a remarkable example of sth: *a ~ of learning; prodigies of nature.* **infant ~,** extremely talented child, e g one who plays the piano well at six.

pro·duce /prəˋdjus *US:* -ˋdus/ *vt,vi* [VP6A,2A] **1** put or bring forward to be looked at or examined: *~ proofs of a statement; ~ one's railway ticket when asked to do so. The conjuror ~d a rabbit from his hat.* **2** manufacture; make; grow; create: *~ woollen goods; fields which ~ heavy crops. We must ~ more food for ourselves and import less. This artist ~s very little.* **3** give birth to; lay (eggs). **4** cause; bring about: *success ~d by hard work and enthusiasm; a film that ~d a sensation.* **5** (maths) make (a line) longer (*to* a point). **6** bring before the public: *~ a new play,* organize it and put it on the stage; *a well-~d book,* one that is well printed, bound, etc. □ *n* /ˋprodjus *US:* -dus/ [U] that which is ~d, esp by farming: *garden/farm/agricultural ~.*

pro·ducer /prəˋdjusə(r) *US:* -ˋdu-/ *n* **1** person who produces goods (contrasted with the *consumer*). **2** person responsible for presenting a play in the theatre or for the production of a film (apart from the directing of the actors); person in charge of a broadcast programme (radio or TV). ⇨ **director. 3** ˋ**~ gas,** gas obtained by passing air through red-hot carbon or air and steam through hot coal or coke.

prod·uct /ˋprodʌkt/ *n* [C] **1** sth produced (by nature or by man): *ˋfarm ~s; the chief ~s of Scotland; the ~s of genius,* e g great works of art. **2** (maths) quantity obtained by multiplication; (chem) substance obtained by chemical reaction.

pro·duc·tion /prəˋdʌkʃn/ *n* **1** [U] process of producing: *the ~ of crops/manufactured goods, etc.* ˈ**mass ~,** ⇨ **mass. 2** [U] quantity produced: *increase ~ by using better methods and tools; a fall/increase in ~.* **3** [C] thing produced: *epic ~s at the cinema; his early ~s as a writer,* his first novels, plays, etc.

pro·duc·tive /prəˋdʌktɪv/ *adj* **1** able to produce; fertile: *~ land.* **2 ~ of,** tending to produce; resulting in: *~ of happiness; discussions that seem to be ~ only of quarrels.* **3** producing things of economic value: *~ labour.* **~·ly** *adv*

pro·duc·tiv·ity /ˈprodʌkˋtɪvətɪ/ *n* [U] being productive; power of being productive: *increase ~,* increase efficiency and the rate at which goods are produced; *a ~ bonus for workers; a ˋ~ agreement,* (as part of a wage settlement) better pay and conditions for an increased output.

pro·fane /prəˋfeɪn *US:* prəʊ-/ *adj* **1** (contrasted with *sacred, holy*) worldly: *~ literature,* (opp *biblical*). **2** having or showing contempt for God and sacred things: *~ language/words/practices; a ~ man.* □ *vt* [VP6A] treat (sacred or holy places, things) with contempt, without proper reverence: *~ the name of God.* **~·ly** *adv* **~·ness** *n* **profa·na·tion** /ˈprofəˋneɪʃn/ *n* [C,U] instance of profaning. **pro·fan·ity** /prəˋfænətɪ *US:* prəʊ-/ *n* (*pl* -ties) **1** [U] ~ conduct or speech; use of ~ language. **2** (*pl*) ~ phrases, utterances: *A string of* *profanities came from his lips.*

pro·fess /prəˋfes/ *vt,vi* **1** [VP6A] declare that one has (beliefs, likes, ignorance, interests, etc): *He ~es a distaste for modern music. He ~ed a great interest in my welfare.* **2** [VP6A] affirm one's faith in, allegiance to, (a religion, Christ): *~ Islam.* **3** [VP6A] (formal) have as one's profession or business: *~ law/medicine;* teach as a professor: *~ history/modern languages.* **4** [VP6A,7,9,25] claim; represent oneself: *I don't ~ to be an expert on that subject. He ~ed himself satisfied. She ~ed that she could do nothing unaided.* **~ed** *adj* **1** self-acknowledged; *a ~ed Christian.* **2** falsely claiming to be: *a ~ed friend.* **3** having taken religious vows: *a ~ed nun.* **~·ed·ly** *adv* according to one's own claims or admissions: *He is ~edly a Communist.*

pro·fession /prəˋfeʃn/ *n* [C] **1** occupation, esp one requiring advanced education and special training, e g the law, architecture, medicine, the Church, sometimes called *the learned ~s. He is a lawyer by ~.* **2** *~ of,* statement or declaration of belief, feeling, etc: *~s of faith/loyalty. She does not believe in his ~s of passionate love.* **3 the ~,** the body of persons engaged in a particular ~(1).

pro·fessional /prəˋfeʃnl/ *adj* **1** of a profession(1): *~ skill; ~ etiquette,* the special conventions, forms of politeness, etc associated with a certain profession; *~ men,* e g doctors, lawyers. **2** doing or practising sth as a full-time occupation or for payment or to make a living (opp of *amateur*): *~ football; ~ tennis-players; a ~ politician.* □ *n* (contrasted with *amateur*) **1** (often abbr to *pro*) person who teaches or engages in some kind of sport for money. **2** person who does sth for payment that others do (without payment) for pleasure: *~ musicians.* ***turn ~,*** become a ~. **~ly** /-nḷɪ/ *adv* in a ~ manner or capacity. **~·ism** /-ɪzm/ *n* **1** mark or qualities of a profession(1). **2** the practice of employing ~s to play games.

pro·fessor /prəˋfesə(r)/ *n* **1** university teacher of the highest grade, holding a chair of some branch of learning; (in US, also) teacher or instructor. **2** title assumed by instructors of various subjects: *P~ Pate, the renowned phrenologist.* **3** one who makes a public profession(2): *a ~ of pacifism/Catholicism.* **prof·ess·orial** /ˈprofɪˋsɔrɪəl/ *adj* relating to a ~: *his ~ial duties.* **~·ship** /-ʃɪp/ *n* ~'s post at a university: *be appointed to a ~ship.*

prof·fer /ˋprofə(r)/ *vt* [VP6A,7] offer. □ *n* offer.

pro·fi·cient /prəˋfɪʃnt/ *adj* ***~ (in),*** skilled; expert. **~·ly** *adv* **pro·fi·ciency** /-nsɪ/ *n* ***proficiency (in),*** [U] being ~: *a certificate of proficiency in English.*

pro·file /ˋprəʊfaɪl/ *n* **1** side view, esp of the head: *a portrait drawn/cut out in ~.* **2** edge or outline of sth seen against a background. **3** brief biography, as given in an article in a periodical or a broadcast talk. □ *vt* draw, show, in ~: *a line of hills ~d against the night sky.*

profit[1] /ˋprofɪt/ *n* **1** [U] advantage or good obtained from sth: *gain ~ from one's studies; study sth to one's ~.* **2** [C,U] money gained in business, etc: *make a ~ of ten pence on every article sold; sell sth at a ~; do sth for ~.* ***~ and loss account,*** (book-keeping) one that shows the trading ~ or loss for a definite period. **ˋ~-margin** *n* difference between cost of purchase or production and selling price. **ˋ~-sharing** *n* the sharing of ~s between employers and employees: *start a ~-sharing scheme.* **~·less** *adj* **~·less·ly** *adv*

profit[2] /ˋprofɪt/ *vt,vi* **1** [VP3A] ***~ from/by,*** (of persons) be benefited or helped: *Have you ~ed by the experience? I have ~ed by your advice.* **2** [VP6A,13A] (old use) (of things) be of advantage to: *What can it ~ him? It ~ed him nothing.*

prof·it·able /ˋprofɪtəbl/ *adj* bringing profit; beneficial: *~ investments; a deal that was ~ to all of us.* **prof·it·ably** /-əblɪ/ *adv*

profi·teer /ˈprofɪˋtɪə(r)/ *vi* [VP2A] make large profits, esp by taking advantage of times of difficulty or scarcity, e g in war. □ *n* person who does this.

prof·li·gate /ˋproflɪgət/ *adj* **1** (of a person, his behaviour) shamelessly immoral. **2** (of the spending of money) reckless; very extravagant: *~ of one's inheritance.* □ *n* ~(1) person. **prof·li·gacy** /ˋproflɪgəsɪ/ *n* [U] being ~.

pro forma /prəʊ ˋfɔmə/ (Lat) as a matter of form. **~ invoice,** one that notifies the value of goods dispatched but does not ask for payment.

pro·found /prəˋfaʊnd/ *adj* **1** deep: *a ~ sleep/sigh/bow; take a ~ interest in sth; listen with ~ interest.* **2** needing, showing, having, great knowledge: *~ books/authors/thinkers; a man of ~ learning.* **3** needing much thought or study to understand: *~ mysteries.* **~·ly** *adv* in a ~ manner: *~ly* (= deeply) *grateful/disturbing.* **pro·fun·dity** /prəˋfʌndətɪ/ *n* (*pl* **-ties**) [U] depth: *the profundity of his knowledge;* [C] (chiefly in non-material senses) that which is deep or obstruse; (*pl*) depths of thought or meaning.

pro·fuse /prəˋfjus/ *adj* **1** very plentiful or abundant: *~ gratitude.* **2** *~ in,* lavish or extravagant: *He was ~ in his apologies,* apologized almost to excess. **~·ly** *adv* **~·ness** *n* **pro·fu·sion** /prəˋfjuʒn/ *n* [U] abundance; great supply: *roses growing in ~; make promises in ~.*

prog /prog/ *n* (sl) = proctor(1). □ *vt* (sl) charge (a student) with an offence.

pro·geni·tor /prəʊˋdʒenɪtə(r)/ *n* (formal) ancestor (of a person, animal or plant); (fig) political or intellectual predecessor.

progeny /ˋprodʒɪnɪ/ *n* (*pl* **-nies**) (formal) (collective *sing*) offspring; descendants, children.

prog·no·sis /progˋnəʊsɪs/ *n* (*pl* **-noses** /-nəʊsiz/) (med) forecast of the probable course of a disease or illness. ⇨ **diagnosis.**

prog·nos·tic /progˋnostɪk/ *adj* (formal) predictive (*of*). □ *n* pre-indication (*of*): *a ~ of failure.*

prog·nos·ti·cate /progˋnostɪkeɪt/ *vt* [VP6A,9] (formal) foretell: predict: *~ trouble.* **prog·nos·ti·ca·tion** /ˈprogˈnostɪˋkeɪʃn/ *n* [U] prognosticating; [C] sth which ~s.

pro·gramme (also **-gram**) /ˋprəʊgræm/ *n* **1** list of items, events, etc, e g for a concert, or to be broadcast for radio or T V, or for a sports meeting; list of names of singers at a pop concert, actors in a play, singers in an opera, etc; (at a dance) list of dances, (formerly) card at a dance for partners' names; *ˋ~ music,* music designed, in sound, to suggest to the listener a known story, picture, etc; *ˋ~ note,* short account, e g of a musical work, a performer, etc. **2** plan of what is to be done: *a political ~. What's the ~ for tomorrow? What are we/you going to do?* **3** coded collection of information, data, etc fed into an electronic computer. □ *vt* [VP6A] make a ~ of or for; supply (a computer) with a ~; plan. **~d course,** (education) one in which the material to be learnt is presented (in books or a machine) in small, carefully graded amounts. **~d learning,** self-instruction using such courses. **pro·gram·mer** *n* person who prepares a computer ~.

prog·ress /ˈprəʊgres *US:* ˈprog-/ *n* **1** [U] forward movement; advance; development: *making fast ~; make ~ in one's studies; ~ in civilization. An inquiry is now in ~*, being made. *The patient is making good ~*, is improving. **2** [C] (old use) state journey: *a royal ~ through Cornwall.* □ *vi* /prəˈgres/ [VP2A,C] make progress: *The work is ~ing steadily. She is ~ing in her studies.*

pro·gression /prəˈgreʃn/ *n* **1** [U] progress; moving forward: *modes of ~*, e g crawling, walking. **2** (maths) ⇨ **arithmetic, geometry.**

pro·gress·ive /prəˈgresɪv/ *adj* **1** making continuous forward movement. **2** increasing by regular degrees or advancing in successive stages: *~ education/schools; ~ taxation*, with an increase of the rate of tax as the incomes increase: *~ cancer*, becoming steadily worse. **3** undergoing improvement; getting better, e g in civilization; supporting or favouring progress: *a ~ policy; a ~ political party.* **4** (mod use) contemporary: *~ music.* □ *n* person supporting a ~ policy. **~·ly** *adv* **~·ness** *n*

pro·hibit /prəˈhɪbɪt *US:* prəʊ-/ *vt* [VP6A,14] **~ sb (from doing sth),** forbid (esp by rules or regulations); say that sth must not be done, that sb must not do sth: *Smoking strictly ~ed. Tourist-class passengers are ~ed from using the promenade deck.*

pro·hib·ition /ˌprəʊɪˈbɪʃn/ *n* **1** [U] prohibiting; (esp) prohibiting by law the making or sale of alcoholic drinks (esp, US, the period 1920—33): *the ~ law(s); in favour of/opposed to ~.* **2** [C] edict or order that forbids: *a ~ against the use of contaminated water.* **~·ist** /-ɪst/ *n* person who favours the ~ of sth, esp the sale of alcoholic drink.

pro·hibi·tive /prəˈhɪbətɪv *US:* prəʊ-/ *adj* tending to, intended to, prevent the use or abuse or purchase of sth: *a ~ tax; books published at ~ prices.*

pro·hibi·tory /prəˈhɪbɪtərɪ *US:* prəʊˈhɪbɪtɔrɪ/ *adj* designed to prohibit sth: *~ laws.*

pro·ject[1] /ˈprodʒekt/ *n* [C] (plan for a) scheme or undertaking: *a ~ to establish a new national park; form/carry out/fail in a ~.*

pro·ject[2] /prəˈdʒekt/ *vt,vi* **1** [VP6A] make plans for: *~ a new dam/waterworks.* **2** [VP6A,14] **~ sth on(to) sth,** cause a shadow, an outline, a picture from a film, slide, etc to fall on a surface, etc: *~ a picture on a screen; ~ a beam of light on to sth.* **3** [VP14] **~ sth onto sb,** attribute unconsciously (usu unpleasant feelings such as guilt, inferiority) to other people (often as a means of self-justification or self-defence: *She always ~s her own neuroses onto her colleagues*, describes them as suffering from them. **4** [VP6A] make known the characteristics of: *Do the B B C External Services adequately ~ Great Britain*, give listeners right ideas about British life, etc? **5** [VP6A,15A] throw; hurl: *an apparatus to ~ missiles into space.* **6** [VP6A] represent (a solid thing) on a plane surface by drawing straight lines through every point of it from a centre; make (a map) in this way. **6** [VP2A,C] stick out; stand out beyond the surface nearby: *~ing eyebrows; a balcony that ~s over the street.*

pro·jec·tile /prəˈdʒektaɪl *US:* -tl/ *n* sth (to be) shot

map projection

Lines of Latitude run parallel to the Equator

Lines of Longitude run vertically from Pole to Pole

CONICAL PROJECTION

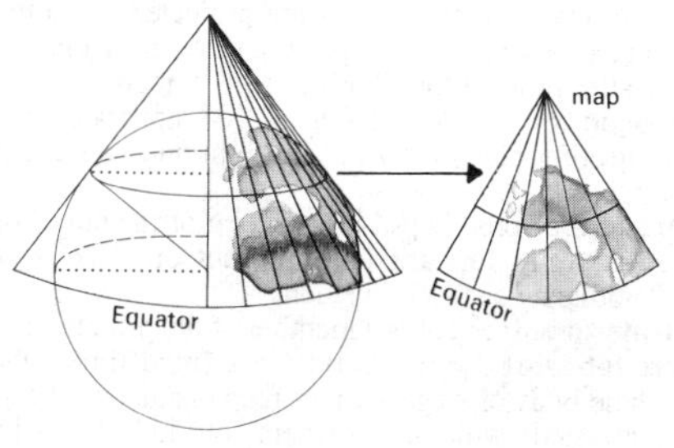

MERCATOR'S PROJECTION

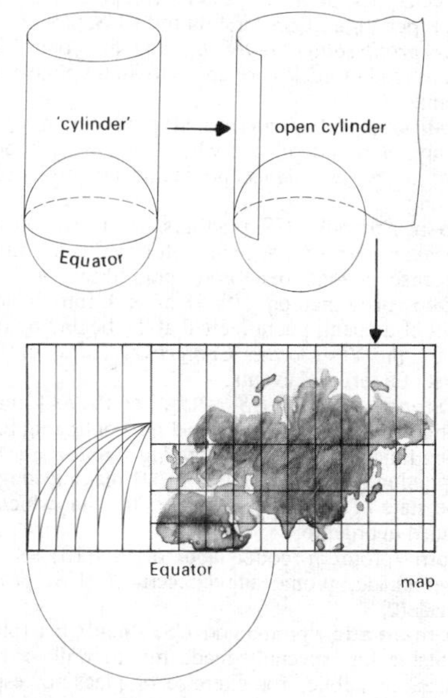

ZENITHAL PROJECTION

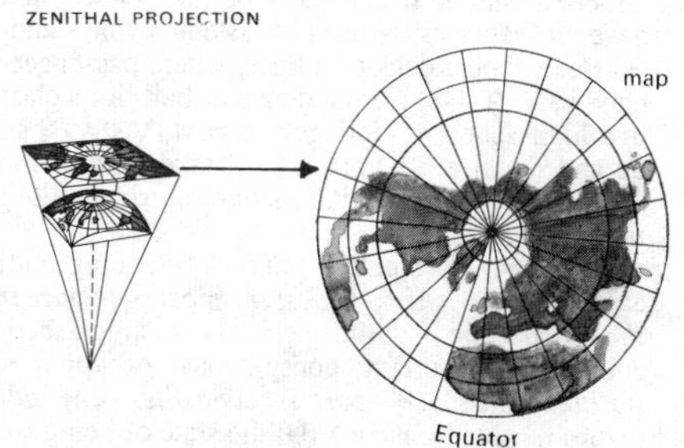

forward, esp from a gun; self-propelling missile, e g a rocket. □ *adj* able to send sth, or be sent, forward through air, water, etc: *a ~ missile/torpedo.*

pro·jec·tion /prəˋdʒekʃn/ *n* [C] the act of projecting (all senses); [C] sth that projects or has been projected; prominence. ⇨ p 679. **ˋ~ room,** (in a room from which pictures are projected on to the screen. **~·ist** /-ɪst/ *n* person who, in a cinema theatre, projects the films on to the screen.

pro·jec·tor /prəˋdʒektə(r)/ *n* [C] apparatus for projecting pictures by rays of light on to a screen: *a ˋcinema/ˆslide ~.*

pro·lapse /prəʊˋlæps/ *vi* (med, e g of the bowel or uterus) slip forward or down out of place. □ *n* /ˆprəʊlæps/ such a movement.

prole /prəʊl/ *n* (colloq) member of the proletariat.

pro·let·ariat /ˈprəʊlɪˋteərɪət/ *n* **1** (mod times) the whole body of wage-earners (esp manual workers) contrasted with the owners of industry (the bourgeoisie): *the dictatorship of the ~,* as a Communist aim or ideal. **2** (in ancient Rome) the lowest class of the community. **pro·let·arian** /-ɪən/ *n, adj* (member) of the ~.

pro·lif·er·ate /prəˋlɪfəreɪt *US:* prəʊ-/ *vi,vt* **1** [VP2A] grow, reproduce, by rapid multiplication of cells, new parts, etc. **2** [VP6A] reproduce (cells, etc). **pro·lif·er·ation** /prəˈlɪfəˋreɪʃn *US:* prəʊ-/ *n: a non-proliferation treaty,* e g one for controlling the spread of nuclear weapons to States not having them.

pro·lific /prəˋlɪfɪk/ *adj* (formal) producing much or many: *a ~ author,* one who writes many books, etc; *as ~ as rabbits,* producing numerous offspring.

pro·lix /ˆprəʊlɪks *US:* prəʊˋlɪks/ *adj* (formal) (of a speaker, writer, speech, etc) tedious; tiring because too long. **pro·lix·ity** /prəʊˋlɪksətɪ/ *n*

pro·logue /ˆprəʊlog *US:* -lɔg/ *n* **1** introductory part of a poem; poem recited at the beginning of a play: *the 'P~' to the 'Canterbury Tales'.* **2** (fig) first of a series of events.

pro·long /prəˋloŋ *US:* -ˋlɔŋ/ *vt* [VP6A] make longer: *~ a visit/a line.* **~ed** *adj* continuing for a long time: *after ~ed questioning.* **pro·lon·ga·tion** /ˈprəʊloŋˋgeɪʃn *US:* -lɔŋ-/ *n* [U] making longer; the state of being made longer; [C] that which is added in order to ~.

prom /prom/ *n* (colloq abbr of) **1** (GB) seaside promenade; promenade concert. **2** (US) promenade(2).

prom·en·ade /ˈproməˋnɑd *US:* -ˋneɪd/ *n* **1** (place suitable for, specially made for, a) walk or ride taken in public, for exercise or pleasure, esp a broad road along the water-front at a seaside resort, or a part of a theatre where people may walk about during the intervals, etc; (attrib) **ˋ~ concert,** one at which parts of the concert hall have no seats and are used by listeners who stand. **ˋ~ deck,** upper deck of a liner, where passengers may walk. **2** (US) formal dance or ball (for a class in a high-school or college). □ *vi,vt* [VP2A,C] go up and down a ~; [VP6A,15A] take (sb) up and down a ~: *~ one's children/one's husband along the sea-front.*

promi·nent /ˆprominənt/ *adj* **1** standing out; easily seen: *~ cheek-bones; the most ~ feature in the landscape.* **2** (of persons) distinguished; eminent. **3** important; conspicuous: *occupy a ~ position; play a ~ part in civic life.* **~·ly** *adv* **promi·nence** /-əns/ *n* **1** [U] the state of being ~. ***bring sth/come into prominence,*** (cause to) become ~. **2** [C] ~ part or place: *a ~ in the middle of a plain.*

pro·mis·cu·ous /prəˋmɪskjʊəs/ *adj* **1** confused and disorderly; unsorted: *in a ~ heap.* **2** indiscriminate; casual: *~ friendships,* made without careful choice; *~ sexual intercourse.* **~·ly** *adv* **prom·is·cu·ity** /ˈpromɪˋskjuətɪ/ *n* (state of) being ~; confusion caused by being ~.

prom·ise[1] /ˆpromɪs/ *n* **1** [C] written or spoken undertaking to do, or not to do, sth, give sth, etc: *~s of help; make/give/keep/carry out/break a ~; under a ~ of secrecy.* **2** [C] that which one undertakes to do, etc: *I claim your ~,* require you to do what you said you would do. **3** [C] (sth that gives) hope of success or good results: *boys who don't show much ~,* do not seem likely to succeed: *a writer of ~; the land of ~.*

prom·ise[2] /ˆpromɪs/ *vt,vi* **1** [VP6A,7A,9,11,12A,13A,17B] make a promise(1) to: *They ~d an immediate reply. He ~d (me) to be here/that he would be here at 6 o'clock. I ~d myself a quiet weekend. 'Will you come?'—'Yes, I ~'.* **the P~d Land,** the land of promise: **(a)** the fertile country ~d to the Israelites by God; Canaan. **(b)** any state of future happiness. **2** [VP6A,2A] give cause for expecting: *The clouds ~ rain. It ~s to be warm this afternoon.* **~ well,** show signs of success. **prom·is·ing** *adj* full of promise(3); seeming likely to succeed, have good results, etc.

prom·iss·ory /ˆpromɪsərɪ *US:* -sɔrɪ/ *adj* conveying a promise. **ˋ~ note,** signed promise to pay a stated sum of money to a specified person or to bearer on a specified date or on demand.

prom·on·tory /ˆpromǝntrɪ *US:* -tɔrɪ/ *n* [C] (*pl* **-ries**) headland; high point of land standing out from the coast-line.

pro·mote /prəˋməʊt/ *vt* **1** [VP6A,14] give (sb) higher position or rank: *He was ~d sergeant/to sergeant/to the rank of sergeant.* **2** [VP6A] help to organize and start; help the progress of; help to found or organize: *~ a new business company; ~ a bill in Parliament; try to ~ good feelings (between...).* **pro·mo·ter** *n* (esp) person who ~s new trading companies, professional sports, etc.

pro·mo·tion /prəˋməʊʃn/ *n* **1** [U] promoting or being promoted; *win/gain ~. Ought ~ to go by seniority or by merit and abilities?* **2** [C] instance of promoting or being promoted: *He resigned from the firm because ~s were few and far between.* **3** encouragement by publicity, etc: *the ~ of a new commercial product/a new book; sales ~,* advertising, publicising one's products.

prompt[1] /prompt/ *adj* acting, done, sent, given, without delay: *a ~ reply; ~ payment; men who are ~ to volunteer; at 6p m ~* (= ~ly). **~·ly** *adv* **~·ness** *n*

prompt[2] /prompt/ *vt* **1** [VP6A,17A] be the reason causing (sb to do sth): *He was ~ed by patriotism. What ~ed him to be so generous?* **2** [VP6A] follow the text of a play and give (an actor) his cue. □ *n* action of ~ing (an actor); the cue: *wait for a ~.* **ˋ~-box** *n* place where the ~er sits. **ˋ~-copy** *n* text of a play, used by a ~er. **~er** *n* person who ~s actors.

promp·ti·tude /ˆpromptɪtjud *US:* -tud/ *n* [U] promptness; readiness to act.

prom·ul·gate /ˆpromlgeɪt/ *vt* [VP6A] **1** make public, announce officially (a decree, a new law, etc).

2 spread widely beliefs, knowledge. **prom·ul·ga·tion** /ˈpromlˋgeɪʃn/ *n* [U].

prone /prəʊn/ *adj* **1** (stretched out, lying) face downwards; prostrate: *in a ~ position; fall ~.* **2** **~ to,** liable, inclined: *~ to accidents/error/anger/idleness/superstition* (and other generally undesirable things). *Some people seem to be ˋaccident ~, ~* to accidents. **~·ness** *n*

prong /proŋ *US:* prɔŋ/ *n* each one of the long, pointed parts of a fork. **~ed** *adj* (in compounds) having the kind or number of ~s indicated: *a ˈthree-~ed ˋfork; a ˈthree-~ed atˋtack,* (mil) one made by three attacking forces.

pro·nomi·nal /prəʊˋnomɪnl/ *adj* of (the nature of) a pronoun.

pro·noun /ˋprəʊnaʊn/ *n* word used in place of a *n* or *n phrase,* e g *he, it, hers, me, them.*

pro·nounce /prəˋnaʊns/ *vt,vi* **1** [VP6A,17,9,25] declare, announce (esp formally, solemnly or officially): *The doctors ~d him to be/~d that he was out of danger. Has judgement been ~d yet?* **2** [VP9,25] declare as one's opinion: *The wine was tasted and ~d excellent. He ~d himself in favour of the plan.* **3** [VP3A] **~ *for/against sb,*** (legal) pass judgement (in a law court). **~ *(up)on,*** give one's opinion on, e g a proposal. **4** [VP6A,2A] utter, make the sound of (a word, etc): *He ~s badly. How do you ~ p-h-l-e-g-m? The 'b' in 'debt' is not ~d.* **~·able** /-əbl/ *adj* (of sounds, words) that can be ~d. **pro·nounced** *adj* definite; strongly marked: *a man of ~d opinions.* **~·ment** *n* [C] formal statement or declaration.

pronto /ˋprontəʊ/ *adv* (sl) quickly; at once.

pro·nun·cia·mento /prəˈnʌnsɪəˋmentəʊ/ *n* (*pl* -tos /-təʊz/) manifesto or proclamation, e g made by insurrectionists in a Spanish-speaking country.

pro·nun·ci·ation /prəˈnʌnsɪˋeɪʃn/ *n* **1** [U] way in which a language is spoken: *lessons in ~; study the ~ of English.* **2** [U] person's way of speaking a language, or words of a language: *His ~ is improving.* **3** [C] way in which a word is pronounced: *Which of these three ~s do you recommend?*

proof[1] /pruf/ *n* **1** [U] evidence (in general), or [C] a particular piece of evidence, that is sufficient to show, or helps to show, that sth is a fact: *We shall require ~(s) of that statement. Is there any ~ that the accused man was at the scene of the crime? They gave him a gold watch as (a) ~ of their regard. Can you give ~ of your nationality/~ that you are British?* **2** [U] demonstrating; testing of whether sth is true, a fact, etc: *Is life on the planet Mars capable of ~? He produced documents in ~ of his claim.* **3** [C] test, trial, examination: *put sth to the ~,* test it. *It has stood the ~,* has passed the test. ***The ~ of the pudding is in the eating,*** (prov) The real test is practical, not theoretical. **4** [C] trial copy of sth printed or engraved, for approval before other copies are printed: *pass the ~s for press,* approve them, agree that printing may be begun. **ˋ~-reader** *n* person employed to read and correct ~s. **5** [U] standard of strength of distilled alcoholic liquors: *This rum is 30 per cent below ~.* **~ spirit,** alcoholic mixture which is up to standard.

proof[2] /pruf/ *adj* **~ *(against),*** giving safety or protection; able to resist or withstand: *~ against bullets; ˋbullet-~; ˋwater~; ˋsound~; ˋsplinter-~;* (fig) *~ against temptation.* **ˋfool-~** *adj* (colloq) incapable of failure; involving no risk. □ *vt* [VP6A] make (sth) ~ (esp make a fabric water~).

prop[1] /prop/ *n* **1** support used to keep sth up: *ˋpit-~s,* supporting the roof in a coalmine; *a ˋclothes-~,* holding up a line on which laundered clothes are drying. **2** person who supports sth or sb: *He is the ~ of his parents in their old age* □ *vt* (-pp-) [VP6A,15A,B,22] **~ *sth up,*** support; keep in position: *Use this box to ~ the door open. The nurse ~ped her patient (up) on the pillows. I ~ped the ladder against the wall.* (fig) *He can't always expect his colleagues to ~ him up.*

prop[2] /prop/ *n* (colloq abbr of) propeller. ⇨ turboprop.

prop[3] /prop/ *n* (colloq abbr of) (stage) property: *Who's in charge of the ~s?* ⇨ property(5).

propa·ganda /ˈpropəˋgændə/ *n* [U] **1** (means of, measures for the) spreading of information, doctrines, ideas, etc: *~ by government departments for public health, better driving, etc; political ~;* (attrib) *~ plays/films.* **2** association or organization (for...). **3** *the Congregation/College of the P~,* a committee of RC cardinals in charge of foreign missions. **propa·gan·dist** /-dɪst/ *n* member or agent of a ~(2). **propa·gan·dize** /-daɪz/ *vi* engage in ~.

propa·gate /ˋpropəgeɪt/ *vt,vi* (formal) **1** [VP6A] increase the number of (plants, animals, diseases) by natural process from the parent stock: *~ plants by taking cuttings. Trees ~ themselves by seeds.* **2** [VP6A] spread more widely: *~ news/knowledge.* **2** [VP6A] transmit; extend the operation of: *vibrations ~d through rock.* **4** [VP2A] (of animals and plants) reproduce; multiply. **propa·ga·tor** /-tə(r)/ *n* **propa·ga·tion** /ˈpropəˋgeɪʃn/ *n* [U] propagating: *the propagation of disease by insects/of plants by cuttings; the Society for the Propagation of the Gospel.*

pro·pane /ˋprəʊpeɪn/ *n* [U] colourless gas (C_3H_8) (in natural gas and petroleum) used as a fuel.

pro·pel /prəˋpel/ *vt* (-ll-) [VP6A,15A] drive forward: *mechanically ~led vehicles; a boat ~led by oars; a ~ling pencil,* with lead that is ~led forward as the outer case is turned. **~·lant, ~·lent** /-ənt/ *adj, n* ~ling (agent); explosive substance that ~s a bullet from a fire-arm; fuel that burns to ~ a rocket, etc. **~·ler** *n* two or more spiral blades, fixed to a revolving shaft, for driving a ship or aircraft.

pro·pen·sity /prəˋpensətɪ/ *n* [C] (*pl* -ties) **~ *to/towards sth/to do sth/for doing sth,*** natural tendency: *a ~ to exaggerate; a ~ for getting into debt.*

proper /ˋpropə(r)/ *adj* **1** right, correct, fitting, suitable: *clothes ~ for such an occasion; not a ~ time for merrymaking. Are you doing it the ~ way? Is this the ~ tool for the job? We must do the ~ thing by him,* treat him in the right way, be fair or loyal to him. **2** in conformity with, paying regard to, the conventions of society; respectable: *~ behaviour. He's not at all a ~ person for a young girl to know. That's not at all a ~ thing to do in the public park.* **3** **~ *to,*** (formal) belonging especially; relating distinctively: *the books ~ to this subject; the psalms ~ to this Sunday.* **4** (old use) own: *I made it with my ~ hands/my own ~ hands.* **5** **~ *noun/name,*** (gram) name used for an individual person, town, etc e g *Mary, Prague.* **6** **~ *fraction,*** (e g $\frac{1}{2}$, $\frac{3}{4}$) one in which the number above the line is smaller than that below the line. **7** (placed after the *n*) strictly so called; genuine:

architecture ~, excluding, for example, the question of water-supply, electric current, etc. **8** (colloq) great; thorough: *We're in a* ~ *mess. He gave his wife a* ~ *licking,* beat her thoroughly. **~·ly** *adv* **1** in a ~ manner: *behave* ~*ly. Do it* ~*ly or not at all. He is not* ~*ly* (= strictly) *speaking a chemist.* **2** (colloq) thoroughly: *The American boxer was* ~*ly beaten by the new world champion.*

prop·erty /ˈprɒpətɪ/ *n* (*pl* -ties) **1** [U] (collectively) things owned; possessions: *Don't interfere with these tools—they're not your* ~. ***a man of*** ***~,*** a wealthy man. **common ~,** known to, possessed by, many people. **personal ~,** movable belongings. **real ~,** land, buildings. **2** [C] estate; (area of land or land and buildings): *He has a small* ~ (i e land and a house) *in Kent.* **3** [U] ownership; the fact of owning or being owned: *There is no* ~ *in the seashore,* it cannot be privately owned. *P*~ *has its obligations,* e g if you own farmland, etc, you have the duty of keeping it free from weeds, etc. **4** [C] special quality that belongs to sth: *the chemical properties of iron; herbs with healing properties.* **5** (theatre) (abbr *prop*) article of dress or furniture or other thing (except scenery) used on the stage in the performance of a play. **ˈ~-man/-master,** (also *ˈpropsman/-master*), *n* man in charge of stage properties. **prop·er·tied** /ˈprɒpətɪd/ *adj* owning ~, esp land: *the propertied classes,* the landowners.

proph·ecy /ˈprɒfɪsɪ/ *n* (*pl* -cies) **1** [U] power of telling what will happen in the future: *have the gift of* ~. **2** [C] statement that tells what will happen: *His* ~ *was fulfilled.*

proph·esy /ˈprɒfɪsaɪ/ *vt,vi* (*pt,pp* -sied) **1** [VP6A,9,10] foretell; say (what will happen in the future): ~ *war/that war will break out.* **2** [VP2A, C] speak as a prophet: *He prophesied of strange things to come. Does he ever* ~ *right?*

prophet /ˈprɒfɪt/ *n* **1** person who teaches religion and claims that his teaching comes to him directly from God: *the* ~ *Isaiah; Muhammad, the P*~ *of Islam.* **the P~s,** the prophetical books of the Old Testament. **2** pioneer of a new theory, cause, etc; advocate: *William Morris, one of the early* ~*s of socialism.* **3** person who tells, or claims to tell, what will happen in the future: *I'm not a good weather-*~. **ˈ~·ess** /-es *US:* -ɪs/ *n* woman ~.

pro·phetic /prəˈfetɪk/ *adj* of a prophet or prophecy; containing a prophecy: *accomplishments which were* ~ *of her future greatness.* **pro·pheti·cally** /-klɪ/ *adv*

pro·phy·lac·tic /ˈprɒfɪˈlæktɪk/ *n, adj* [C] (substance, treatment) serving or tending to protect from diseases such as malaria. **pro·phy·lax·is** /-ˈlæksɪs/ *n* [U] preventive treatment of disease.

pro·pin·quity /prəˈpɪŋkwətɪ/ *n* [U] (formal) nearness (in time, place, relationship); similarity (of ideas).

pro·pi·ti·ate /prəˈpɪʃɪeɪt/ *vt* [VP6A] (formal) pacify; do sth to take away the anger of; win the favour or support of; *offer a sacrifice to* ~ *the gods.* **pro·pi·ti·ation** /prəˈpɪʃɪˈeɪʃn/ *n* [U] propitiating; atoning. **pro·pi·ti·atory** /prəˈpɪʃətərɪ *US:* -tɔrɪ/ *adj* serving to, intended to, ~: *With a propitiatory smile he offered her a large bunch of roses.*

pro·pi·tious /prəˈpɪʃəs/ *adj* ***~ to sb/for sth,*** favourable; well-disposed: ~ *omens; weather that was* ~ *for our enterprise.* **~·ly** *adv*

pro·por·tion /prəˈpɔʃn/ *n* **1** [U] relation of one thing to another in quantity, size, etc; relation of a part to the whole: *The* ~ *of imports to exports* (= The excess of imports over exports) *is worrying the government.* **in ~ to,** relative to: *wide in* ~ *to the height; payment in* ~ *to work done, not in* ~ *to the time taken to do it. Imports will be allowed in* ~ *to exports.* ***get/be sth out of ~ (to),*** (make sth) bear no relation (to): *His earnings are out of all* ~ *to his skill and ability,* He earns much more than is right for his skill and ability. *When you're angry, you may get things out of* ~, have an exaggerated or distorted view of things. **2** (often *pl*) the correct relation of parts or of the sizes of the several parts: *a room of good* ~*s. The two windows are in admirable* ~. **3** (*pl*) size; measurements: *a ship of majestic* ~*s; build up an export trade of substantial* ~*s.* **4** [C] part; share: *You have not done your* ~ *of the work.* **5** (maths) equality of relationship between two sets of numbers; statement that two ratios are equal (e g 4 is to 8 as 6 is to 12. $\frac{5}{8}$ and $\frac{10}{16}$ are in ~). □ *vt* [VP6A,14] put into ~ or right relationship: *Do you* ~ *your expenditure to your income? What a well-*~*ed room!* **~·able** /-ʃn̩əbl/ *adj* = ~al.

pro·por·tional /prəˈpɔʃnl/ *adj* ~ ***(to),*** (formal) in proper proportion; corresponding in degree or amount: *payment* ~ *to the work done; compensation* ~ *to his injuries.* **ˈ~ ˈrepresenˈtation,** ⇨ *representation* at represent[1]. **~ly** /-nl̩ɪ/ *adv*

pro·por·tion·ate /prəˈpɔʃn̩ət/ *adj* (formal) = proportional. **~·ly** *adv*

pro·po·sal /prəˈpəʊzl/ *n* **1** [U] proposing. **2** [C] sth proposed; plan or scheme: *a* ~ *for peace;* ~*s for increasing trade between two countries.* **3** offer (esp of marriage): *a girl who had five* ~*s in one week.*

pro·pose /prəˈpəʊz/ *vt,vi* **1** [VP6A,D,7A,9] offer or put forward for consideration, as a suggestion, plan or purpose: *I* ~ *starting early/an early start/to start early/that we should start early. We* ~ *leaving at noon. The motion was* ~*d by Mr X and seconded by Mr Y.* ***~ a toast/sb's health,*** ask persons to drink sb's health or happiness. **2** [VP6A,2A] ***~ (marriage) (to sb),*** offer marriage. **3** [VP14] ***~ sb (for sth),*** put forward (sb's name) for an office/for membership of a club/etc: *I* ~ *Mr Smith for chairman. Will you please* ~ *me for your club?* **pro·poser** *n*

prop·osi·tion /ˈprɒpəˈzɪʃn/ *n* [C] **1** statement; assertion: *a* ~ *so clear that it needs no explanation.* **2** question or problem (with or without the answer or solution): *a* ~ *in Euclid; Tunnelling under the English Channel is a big* ~. **3** (colloq) matter to be dealt with, esp sth immoral, illegal, e g an indecent suggestion made to a girl. ***a tough ~,*** (colloq) sb or sth difficult to deal with. □ *vt* (sl) make a ~(3) to: *She was* ~*ed by her boss.*

pro·pound /prəˈpaʊnd/ *vt* [VP6A] (formal) put forward or offer for consideration or solution: ~ *a theory/a riddle.*

pro·pri·etary /prəˈpraɪətərɪ *US:* -terɪ/ *adj* **1** (abbr (P) used in this dictionary) owned or controlled by sb; held as property: ~ *medicine,* patented; ~ *rights; a* ~ *name,* e g Kodak for cameras and films. **2** of a proprietor or owner: *He walked round his estate with* ~ *solicitude.*

pro·pri·etor /prəˈpraɪətə(r)/ *n* owner, esp of a hotel, store, land or patent: *the* ~*s of the hotel/this patent medicine.* **pro·pri·e·tress** /prəˈpraɪətrəs/ *n* woman ~.

pro·pri·ety /prəˈpraɪətɪ/ *n* (*pl* -ties) (formal) **1** [U] state of being correct in behaviour and morals: *a breach of ~; (pl)* details of correct social behaviour: *observe the proprieties; offend against the proprieties.* **2** [U] reasonableness; fitness: *I question the ~ of granting such a request,* doubt whether it is right to do so.

pro·pul·sion /prəˋpʌlʃn/ *n* [U] propelling force. **jet ~,** by means of jet engines. **pro·pul·sive** /prəˋpʌlsɪv/ *adj* propelling; serving to propel.

pro rata /ˈprəʊ ˋrɑtə/ *adv* (Lat) in proportion; according to the share, etc of each.

pro·rogue /prəʊˋrəʊg/ *vt* [VP6A] bring (a session of Parliament) to an end without dissolving it (so that unfinished business may be taken up again in the next session). **pro·ro·ga·tion** /ˈprəʊrəˋgeɪʃn/ *n*

pro·saic /prəˋzeɪɪk/ *adj* dull; uninteresting; commonplace: *a lively woman with a ~ husband; the ~ life of the ordinary housewife.* **pro·sai·cally** /-klɪ/ *adv*

pro·scenium /prəˋsinɪəm/ *n* (in a theatre) that part of the stage between the curtain and the orchestra; an enclosing arch.

pro·scribe /prəʊˋskrɑɪb/ *vt* [VP6A] **1** (old use) publicly put (a person) out of the protection of the law. **2** denounce (a person, practice, etc) as dangerous. **pro·scrip·tion** /prəˋskrɪpʃn *US:* prəʊ-/ *n* [U] proscribing or being ~d; [C] instance of this.

prose /prəʊz/ *n* [U] language not in verse form: (attrib) *the ~ writers of the 19th century.* ⇨ poetry.

pros·ecute /ˋprɒsɪkjut/ *vt* **1** [VP6A] (formal) continue with: *~ a war/one's studies/an inquiry.* **2** [VP6A,14] ***~ sb (for sth),*** start legal proceedings against: *~d for exceeding the speed limit. Trespassers will be ~d.* **pros·ecu·tor** /ˋprɒsɪkjutə(r)/ *n* person who ~s(2). **ˈPublic ˋProsecutor,** person who ~s on behalf of the State.

pros·ecu·tion /ˈprɒsɪˋkjuʃn/ *n* **1** [U] act of prosecuting(1): *In the ~ of his duties he had to interview people of all classes.* **2** [U] prosecuting or being prosecuted(2): *make oneself liable to ~;* [C] instance of this: *start a ~ against sb; the Director of Public P~s.* **3** (collective) person who prosecutes(2), together with his advisers: *the case for the ~.* ⇨ defence(3).

pros·elyte /ˋprɒsəlɑɪt/ *n* person who has been converted from his religious, political or other opinions or beliefs to different ones. **pros·elyt·ize** /ˋprɒsḷɪtɑɪz/ *vt,vi* [VP6A,2A] make, try to make, converts to a religion or cause; make a ~ of (sb).

pros·ody /ˋprɒsədɪ/ *n* [U] science of verse rhythms or metres; (of a language) rhythm, pause, tempo, stress and pitch features.

pros·pect[1] /ˋprɒspekt/ *n* **1** [C] wide view over land or sea or (fig) before the mind, in the imagination. **2** *(pl)* sth expected, hoped for, looked forward to: *The ~s for the wine harvest are poor this year. The manager held out bright ~s to me if I would accept the position.* **3** [U] expectation; hope: *I see no/little/not much ~ of his recovery. Is there no ~ of your visiting us soon? He is out of work and has nothing in ~* (= no expectation of finding work) *at present.* **4** [C] possible customer or client; sb from whom one hopes to gain something: *He's a good/bad ~.*

pros·pect[2] /prəˋspekt *US:* ˋprɒspekt/ *vi* [VP2A, 3A] ***~ (for),*** search (for): *~ing for gold.* **pros·pec·tor** /-tə(r)/ *n* person who explores a region looking for gold or other valuable ores, etc.

pros·pec·tive /prəˋspektɪv/ *adj* hoped for; looked forward to; which or who is one day to be: *~ advantages/wealth; a ~ buyer; my ~ bride; the ~ Labour candidate.*

pro·spec·tus /prəˋspektəs/ *n (pl* **-tuses** /-təsɪz/) printed account giving details of and advertising sth, e g a privately-owned school, a new business enterprise, a book about to be published.

pros·per /ˋprɒspə(r)/ *vi,vt* **1** [VP2A] succeed; do well: *The business ~ed. Is your son ~ing?* **2** [VP6A] (of God) cause to ~: *May God ~ you!*

pros·per·ity /prɒˋsperətɪ/ *n* [U] state of being successful; good fortune: *a life of happiness and ~; live in ~; The ~ of this industry depends upon a full order book.*

pros·per·ous /ˋprɒspərəs/ *adj* successful; flourishing: *a ~ business; ~ years.* **~·ly** *adv*

pros·tate /ˋprɒsteɪt/ *n* **~ (gland),** (anat) gland in male mammals at the neck of the bladder; inflammation of this: *He had a ~ (operation) last year.*

pros·ti·tute /ˋprɒstɪtjut *US:* -tut/ *n* person who offers herself/himself for sexual intercourse for payment. □ *vt* **1** [VP6A] (reflex) make a ~ of (oneself). **2** [VP6A] put to wrong or unworthy uses: *~ one's energies/abilities; ~ one's honour,* lose it for money basely gained. **pros·ti·tu·tion** /ˈprɒstɪˋtjuʃn *US:* -ˋtuʃn/ *n* [U] practice of prostituting oneself, one's talents, etc.

pros·trate /ˋprɒstreɪt/ *adj* **1** lying stretched out on the ground, usu face downward, e g because exhausted, or to show submission, deep respect. **2** (fig) overcome (with grief, etc); conquered; overthrown. □ *vt* /prɒˋstreɪt *US:* ˋprɒstreɪt/ **1** [VP6A] cause to be ~: *trees ~d by the gale.* **2** [VP6A] (reflex) make (oneself) ~: *The wretched slaves ~d themselves before their master.* **3** (usu passive) overcome; render helpless: *Several of the competitors were ~d by the heat. She is ~d with grief.* **pros·tra·tion** /prɒˋstreɪʃn/ *n* **1** [U] state of extreme physical weakness; complete exhaustion: *Two of the runners in the Marathon race collapsed and were carried off in a state of prostration.* **2** [C] act of bowing or lying face downwards to show submission or humility.

prosy /ˋprəʊzɪ/ *adj* **(-ier, -iest)** (of authors, speakers, books, speeches, style, etc) dull; tedious; unimaginative. **pro·sily** /-əlɪ/ *adv* **prosi·ness** *n*

pro·tag·on·ist /prəʊˋtægənɪst/ *n* (formal) chief person in a drama; (by extension) chief person in a story or factual event.

pro·tean /ˋprəʊtɪən/ *adj* versatile; easily and quickly changing (like Proteus /ˋprəʊtɪəs/, the Greek sea-god who took various shapes).

pro·tect /prəˋtekt/ *vt* [VP6A,14] ***~ sb/sth from/against,*** **1** keep safe (from danger, enemies; against attack); guard: *well ~ed from the cold/against the weather.* **2** guard (home industry) against competition by taxing imports.

pro·tec·tion /prəˋtekʃn/ *n* [U] **1** protecting or being protected: *travel under the ~ of a number of soldiers. These tender plants need ~ against the weather.* **ˋ~ (money),** money demanded by or paid to, gangsters for ~ against acts of violence, etc. **2** [U] system of protecting home industry against foreign competition. **3** [C] person or thing that protects: *wearing a heavy overcoat as a ~ against the cold.* **~·ism** /-ɪzm/ *n* [U] system of giving ~(2) to home industry. **~·ist** /-ɪst/ *n* supporter of, believer in, ~ism.

pro·tec·tive /prəˋtektɪv/ *adj* **1** giving protection: *a ~ covering; a ~ tariff,* i e on imported goods; ~

sheath, ⇨ sheath(2). '~ **'clothing,** clothes that safeguard the wearer against such risks as burns, contamination and radiation. '~ **'colouring,** i e of animals, birds, insects, causing them to be seen with difficulty in their natural surroundings, thus protecting them from their enemies. '~ **'foods,** foods that safeguard health, e g kinds with a good supply of essential vitamins. **2** ~ ***(towards),*** (of persons) with a wish to protect: *A mother naturally feels ~ towards her children.* **~·ly** *adv*

pro·tec·tor /prəˈtektə(r)/ *n* **1** person who protects; sth made or designed to give protection. **2** (GB hist) **the P~,** official title of Oliver and Richard Cromwell.

pro·tec·tor·ate /prəˈtektərət/ *n* **1** country under the protection of one of the great powers. **2 the P~,** period (1653—59) of rule of Oliver and Richard Cromwell.

pro·tégé (fem **-gée**) /ˈprotɪʒeɪ *US:* ˈprəʊtɪˈʒeɪ/ *n* person to whom another gives protection and help (usu over a long period).

pro·tein /ˈprəʊtin/ *n* [C] body-building substance essential to good health, in such foods as milk, eggs, meat.

pro tem·pore /ˈprəʊ ˈtempərɪ/ *adv* (Lat) (often shortened to **pro tem**) for the time being; for the present only: *I'm in charge of the office pro tem.*

pro·test[1] /ˈpreəʊtest/ *n* **1** [C,U] statement of disapproval or objection: *make/lodge/enter a ~ (against sth). The Government's policy gave rise to vigorous ~s. He paid the tax demand under ~,* unwillingly and after declaring that what he was doing was not right or just. *He gave way without ~,* without making any objection. **2** (attrib) expressing ~: *a ˈ~ movement; a ˈ~ march,* e g by persons objecting to official policy.

pro·test[2] /prəˈtest/ *vt,vi* **1** [VP6A,9] affirm strongly; assert against opposition: *He ~ed that he had never been near the scene of the crime. He ~ed his innocence,* asserted his innocence by ~ing. **2** [VP2A,3A] ~ ***(against),*** raise an objection, say sth (*against*): *I ~ against being called an old fool. The children ~ed loudly* (= cried out in disapproval) *when they were told to go to bed early.* **~er** *n* **~·ing·ly** *adv*

Prot·es·tant /ˈprotɪstənt/ *n, adj* (member) of any of the Christian bodies that separated from the Church of Rome at the time of the Reformation (16th c), or their later branches. **~·ism** /-ɪzm/ *n* [U] systems, beliefs, teaching, etc of the ~s; P~s as a body.

prot·esta·tion /ˈprotɪˈsteɪʃn/ *n* [C] (formal) solemn declaration: *~s of innocence/friendship.*

pro·to·col /ˈprəʊtəkol/ *n* **1** [C] first or original draft of an agreement (esp between States), signed by those making it, in preparation for a treaty. **2** [U] code of behaviour; etiquette as practised on diplomatic occasions: *Were the seating arrangements for the dinner party according to ~,* Were rules of precedence, etc properly observed?

pro·ton /ˈprəʊton/ *n* positively charged particle forming part of an atomic nucleus. ⇨ electron.

pro·to·plasm /ˈprəʊtəplæzm/ *n* [C] colourless, jelly-like substance which is the material basis of life in animals and plants.

pro·to·type /ˈprəʊtətɑɪp/ *n* [C] first or original example, e g of an aircraft, from which others have been or will be copied or developed.

pro·to·zoa /ˈprəʊtəˈzəʊə/ *n pl* (division of the animal kingdom consisting of) animals of the simplest type formed of a single cell (and usu microscopic).

pro·tract /prəˈtrækt *US:* prəʊ-/ *vt* [VP6A] prolong; lengthen the time taken by: *a ~ed visit/argument.* **pro·trac·tion** /prəˈtrækʃn *US:* prəʊ-/ *n* lengthening out.

pro·trac·tor /prəˈtræktə(r) *US:* prəʊ-/ *n* instrument, usu in the form of a semicircle, and graduated (0° to 180°), for measuring and drawing angles.

pro·trude /prəˈtrud *US:* prəʊ-/ *vi,vt* [VP2A,6A] (cause to) stick out or project: *a shelf that ~s from a wall; protruding eyes/teeth.* **pro·tru·sion** /prəˈtruʒn *US:* prəʊ-/ *n* [U] protruding; [C] sth that ~s. **pro·trus·ive** /prəˈtrusɪv *US:* prəʊ-/ *adj* protruding.

pro·tu·ber·ant /prəˈtjubərənt *US:* prəʊˈtu-/ *adj* (formal) curving or swelling outwards; bulging. **pro·tu·ber·ance** /-əns/ *n* [U] being ~; [C] sth that is ~; bulge or swelling.

proud /prɑʊd/ *adj* (-er, -est) **1** (in a good sense) having or showing a proper pride or dignity: *~ of their success/of being so successful; ~ to belong/that they belonged to such a fine regiment.* **2** (in a bad sense) arrogant; having or showing too much pride: *He was too ~ to join our party.* **3** arousing justifiable pride; of which one is or may be properly ~; splendid; imposing: *soldiers in ~ array. It was a ~ day for the school when its team won the championship. His rose garden was a ~ sight.* **4** ~ ***flesh,*** overgrown flesh round a healing wound. **5** (compounds) **ˈhouse-~,** of one's house, of the care with which it is looked after, cleaned, etc. **ˈpurse-~,** arrogant because of one's wealth. **6** (*adv* use; colloq) ***do sb ~,*** honour greatly, entertain splendidly. **~·ly** *adv* in a ~ manner; splendidly.

prove /pruv/ *vt,vi* (*pp* ~d, or, as below, **1,** ~n /ˈpruvn/) **1** [VP6A,9,14,25] supply proof of; show beyond doubt to be true: *~ sb's guilt/that he is guilty. His guilt was clearly ~d. I shall ~ to you that the witness is quite unreliable. Can you ~ it to me?* ***The exception ~s the rule,*** shows that the rule is valid in most cases. ***not ~n,*** (in a criminal trial in Scotland) jury's decision that as the charge cannot be ~d, the accused may be released (although not, perhaps, innocent). **2** [VP6A] establish the genuineness of: *~ a will;* test the quality or accuracy of: *~ a man's worth.* **3** [VP25] ~ ***(oneself) to be,*** be seen or found in the end (to be): *The new typist ~d (to be) useless. He ~d (himself) to be a coward.* **4** [VP4D] be found to be: *Our wood supply ~d (to be) insufficient. Let's hope the new typist won't ~ as inefficient as her predecessor.* **prov·able** /-əbl/ *adj* that can be ~d.

prov·enance /ˈprovənəns/ *n* [U] (place of) origin: *antique furniture of doubtful ~,* e g that may not be genuinely antique.

prov·en·der /ˈprovɪndə(r)/ *n* [U] food, e g hay, oats, for horses and cattle; (colloq) food of any kind.

prov·erb /ˈprovɜb/ *n* **1** popular short saying, with words of advice or warning, e g 'It takes two to make a quarrel'. **2 P~s, the Book of P~s,** one of the books of the Old Testament. **3** sb or sth so well known that it has become notorious: *He is a ~ for meanness. His meanness is a ~.* **prov·erb·ial** /prəˈvɜbɪəl/ *adj* widely known and talked about; admitted by everyone: *His stupidity is ~ial.* **prov·erbi·ally** /-əlɪ/ *adv*: *He is ~ially stupid.*

pro·vide /prəˈvaɪd/ *vi,vt* **1** [VP3A] **~ for sb/sth,** make ready, do what is necessary: *He has a large family to ~ for. We must ~ for the entertainment of our visitors,* get in supplies of food, etc. *He died without providing for his widow,* leaving nothing for her to live on. **~ against sth,** take steps to guard against: *Have you ~d against a coal shortage next winter?* **2** [VP14] **~ sth for sb; ~ sb with sth,** give, supply (what is needed, esp what a person needs in order to live): *~ one's children with food and clothes; ~ food and clothes for one's family. I am already ~d with all I need.* **3** [VP9] stipulate: *A clause in the agreement ~s that the tenant shall bear the cost of all repairs to the building.*

pro·vided /prəˈvaɪdɪd/ *conj* on condition (that). **pro·vid·ing** *conj* (colloq) = ~: *I will go providing* (= ~ that) *my expenses are paid.* **pro·vider** *n* person who provides.

provi·dence /ˈprɒvɪdəns/ *n* **1** [U] (old use) thrift; being provident or prudent (about future needs, etc). **2 P~,** God; God's care for human beings and all He has created; (small *p*) particular instance of this care: *the mysterious working of divine ~. A special ~ preserved him from the tragic fate of his companions.*

provi·dent /ˈprɒvɪdənt/ *adj* (careful in) providing for future needs or events, esp in old age: *Our firm has a ~ fund for the staff.* **~·ly** *adv*

provi·den·tial /ˈprɒvɪˈdenʃl/ *adj* of, by, through, coming from, Providence(2): *a ~ escape.* **~·ly** /-ʃlɪ/ *adv*

prov·ince /ˈprɒvɪns/ *n* **1** large administrative division of a country. **2 the ~s,** all the country outside the capital: *people from the ~s visiting London. The pop group is now touring the ~s.* **3** district under an archbishop. **4** area of learning or knowledge; department of activity: *That is outside my ~,* not sth with which I can or need deal. *Doesn't your question fall outside the ~ of science?*

prov·in·cial /prəˈvɪnʃl/ *adj* **1** of a province(1): *~ taxes; ~ government.* **2** of the provinces(2): *~ roads.* **3** narrow in outlook; having, typical of, the speech, manners, views, etc of a person living in the provinces (esp in former times when communications were poor): *a ~ accent.* □ *n* person from the provinces; countrified person. **~ly** /-ʃlɪ/ *adv* **~·ism** /-ɪzm/ *n* [C] example of ~ manners, speech, behaviour, etc; [U] attachment to one's province and its customs, etc rather than to one's country.

pro·vi·sion /prəˈvɪʒn/ *n* **1** [U] providing, preparation (esp for future needs): *the ~* (= supply) *of water and gas to domestic consumers; make ~ for one's old age,* e g by saving money; *make ~ against sth,* guard against it. **2** [C] amount (*of* sth) provided: *issue a ~ of meat to the troops.* **3** (*pl*) food; food supplies: *lay in a store of ~s;* (attrib, *sing*) *a ~ merchant,* a grocer; *a wholesale ~ business.* **4** [C] condition in a legal document, e g a clause in a will: *if there is no ~ to the contrary.* □ *vt* [VP6A] supply with ~s(3) and stores: *~ a ship for a voyage to the Antarctic.*

pro·vi·sional /prəˈvɪʒnl/ *adj* of the present time only, and to be changed or replaced later: *a ~ government/contract, etc.* **~ly** /-nlɪ/ *adv*

pro·viso /prəˈvaɪzəʊ/ *n* (*pl* -sos, US also -soes /-zəʊz/) (clause containing a) limitation, esp in a legal document: *with the ~ that,* on condition that; *subject to this ~,* with this limitation. **pro·vi·sory** /prəˈvaɪzərɪ/ *adj* depending upon a ~.

provo·ca·tion /ˈprɒvəˈkeɪʃn/ *n* **1** [U] provoking or being provoked: *wilful ~ of public disorder; do sth under ~,* when provoked: *She flares up at/on the slightest ~,* Very little things make her anger break out. **2** [C] sth that provokes or annoys.

pro·voca·tive /prəˈvɒkətɪv/ *adj* causing, likely to cause, anger, argument, interest, etc: *~ remarks; a ~ dress.* **~·ly** *adv*

pro·voke /prəˈvəʊk/ *vt* **1** [VP6A] make angry; vex: *He was ~d beyond endurance. If you ~ the dog, it will attack you.* **2** [VP6A] cause; arouse: *~ laughter/a smile/a riot.* **3** [VP17,14] **~ sb to do sth/into doing sth,** cause or compel them: *His impudence ~d her into slapping his face. He was ~d to answer rudely.* **pro·vok·ing** *adj* annoying: *How provoking of them to be so late!* **pro·vok·ing·ly** *adv*

pro·vost /ˈprɒvəst *US:* ˈprəʊ-/ *n* **1** title of some heads of colleges at Oxford, etc: *the P~ of Oriel.* **2** (in Scotland) head of a municipal corporation or burgh (= mayor). **3 ~ marshal** /prəˈvəʊ ˈmɑʃl *US:* ˈprəʊvəʊ/, head of the military police.

prow /praʊ/ *n* pointed front of a ship or boat. ⇨ the illus at barque.

prow·ess /ˈpraʊɪs/ *n* [U] bravery; valour; unusual skill or ability.

prowl /praʊl/ *vi,vt* **1** [VP2A,C] go about cautiously looking for a chance to get food (as wild animals do), or to steal, etc. **2** [VP6A] go about (*the streets*) in this way. □ *n* **be on the ~,** ~ing. ˈ**~ car,** (US) ⇨ *squad car* at squad. **~er** *n* animal or person that ~s.

prox /prɒks/ ⇨ proximo.

proxi·mate /ˈprɒksɪmət/ *adj* (formal) nearest, before or after.

prox·im·ity /prɒkˈsɪmətɪ/ *n* [U] nearness: *in* (*close*) *~ to,* (very) near to (which is usu preferable); *a ~ fuse,* one that explodes the shell to which it is fitted when near the target, e g an enemy aircraft.

prox·imo /ˈprɒksɪməʊ/ *adj* (abbr **prox**) (comm or official style, better avoided) of next month: *on the 22nd prox.*

proxy /ˈprɒksɪ/ *n* (*pl* **-xies**) [C] (document giving) [U] authority to represent or act for another (esp in voting at an election); [C] person given a ~: *vote by ~; make one's wife one's ~.*

prude /prud/ *n* person of extreme or exaggerated propriety (often affected) in behaviour or speech. **pru·dery** /ˈprudərɪ/ *n* (*pl* **-ries**) [U] extreme propriety; [C] prudish act or remark. **prud·ish** /ˈprudɪʃ/ *adj* of or like a ~; excessively modest; easily shocked. **pru·dish·ly** *adv*

pru·dent /ˈprudnt/ *adj* careful; acting only after careful thought or planning: *a ~ housekeeper.* **~·ly** *adv* **pru·dence** /-dns/ *n* [U] being ~; careful forethought.

pru·den·tial /pruˈdenʃl/ *adj* relating to, marked by, prudence (often used in names of insurance companies).

prune[1] /prun/ *n* dried plum: *stewed ~s and custard.*

prune[2] /prun/ *vt* [VP6A,14,15B] **~ sth from sth; ~ sth off sth; ~ sth away,** cut away parts of (trees, bushes, etc) in order to control growth or shape; (fig) take out unnecessary parts from: *~ the rose-bushes; ~ away unwanted growth; ~ an essay of superfluous matter; ~ away unnecessary* *adjectives.* **prun·ing** *n* **ˈpruning-knife/-hook/-saw/-scissors/-shears,** kinds of tool used for pruning. **pruners** *n pl* pruning-scissors.

pru·ri·ent /ˈprʊərɪənt/ *adj* having, showing, an excessive and unhealthy interest in matters of sex. **~·ly** *adv* **pru·ri·ence** /-əns/, **pru·ri·ency** /-ənsɪ/ *nn* state of being ~.

Prus·sian /ˈprʌʃn/ *n, adj* (inhabitant, native) of Prussia. **~ blue,** deep blue colour.

prus·sic /ˈprʌsɪk/ *adj* ˈ**~ ˈacid,** violent and deadly poison.

pry[1] /praɪ/ *vi* (*pt,pp* pried /praɪd/) [VP2A,3A] ***pry into,*** inquire too curiously (into other people's affairs); [VP2C] ***pry about,*** look or peer (about) inquisitively. **pry·ing·ly** *adv*

pry[2] /praɪ/ *vt* [VP22,14] (= *prize*[3]) get (sth *open*) (e g with a lever); lift (sth *up*); (fig) *pry a secret out of sb.*

psalm /sɑm/ *n* sacred song or hymn, esp **(the P~s)** those in the Bible. **ˈ~·ist** /-ɪst/ *n* person who writes ~s, esp **the P~ist,** David, said to be the author of ~s in the Bible. **~·ody** /ˈsɑmədɪ/ *n* (*pl* -dies) **1** [U] practice or art of singing ~s. **2** [C] arrangement of ~s for singing; book of ~s with their musical settings. **psal·ter** /ˈsɔltə(r)/ *n* Book of P~s; copy of the P~s, esp one designed for use in public worship.

psal·tery /ˈsɔltərɪ/ *n* (*pl* -ries) musical instrument (ancient and medieval times) with strings over a sound-board, played by plucking the strings.

pse·phol·ogy /seˈfolədʒɪ *US:* si-/ *n* scientific study of election trends, e g by means of opinion polls. **pse·phol·ogist** /-ɪst/ *n*

pseudo- /ˈsjudəʊ *US:* ˈsu-/ *pref* false; spurious: *~-scientific.* ⇨ App 3.

pseudo /sjudəʊ *US:* ˈsu-/ *adj* (colloq) fake; insincere: *I've always found him very ~.* □ *n* sham person.

pseu·do·nym /ˈsjudənɪm *US:* ˈsudṇɪm/ *n* name taken, esp by an author, instead of his real name. **pseud·ony·mous** /sjuˈdonɪməs *US:* su-/ *adj* writing, written, under an assumed name.

pshaw /pfə *or similar 'burst' of noise/ int* exclamation to indicate contempt or impatience.

psit·ta·co·sis /ˈsɪtəˈkəʊsɪs/ *n* [U] (also called *ˈparrot fever*) contagious virus disease of parrots and related birds, producing fever and other complications (as in influenza).

psyche /ˈsɑɪkɪ/ *n* **1** human soul or spirit. **2** human mind; mentality.

psyche·delic /ˈsɑɪkɪˈdelɪk/ *adj* **1** (of drugs) mind-expanding; mind-changing; of, causing, hallucinations, ecstasy, terror, etc: *Mescalin and LSD are ~ drugs.* **2** (of visual and sound effects) acting on the mind like ~ drugs: *~ music.*

psy·chia·try /sɑɪˈkɑɪətrɪ *US:* sɪ-/ *n* [U] the study and treatment of mental illness. **psy·chia·trist** /-ɪst/ *n* expert in ~; alienist. **psy·chi·atric** /ˈsɑɪkɪˈætrɪk/ *adj* of ~: *a psychiatric clinic.*

psy·chic[1] /ˈsɑɪkɪk/ *n* [C] person apparently, or claiming to be, responsive to occult powers; (pop term for a) medium(4).

psy·chic[2] /ˈsɑɪkɪk/, **psy·chi·cal** /ˈsɑɪkɪkl/ *adjj* **1** of the soul or mind. **1** of phenomena and conditions which appear to be outside physical or natural laws: *~ research,* the study and investigation of supernormal phenomena, e g telepathy, second sight.

psy·cho-an·aly·sis /ˈsɑɪkəʊ əˈnæləsɪs/ *n* [U] **1** method of healing mental illnesses by tracing them, through interviews, to events in the patient's early life, and bringing those events to light. **2** body of doctrine based on this method concerned with the investigation and treatment of emotional disturbances. **psy·cho-anal·yst** /ˈsɑɪkəʊ ˈænəlɪst/ *n* person who practises ~. **psy·cho-an·a·lytic(al)** /ˈsɑɪkəʊ ˈænəˈlɪtɪk(l)/ *adj* relating to ~. **psy·cho-an·al·yse** (US = **-lyze**) /ˈsɑɪkəʊ ˈænəlɑɪz/ *vt* treat (sb) by ~.

psy·chol·ogy /sɑɪˈkolədʒɪ/ *n* [U] **1** science, study, of the mind and its processes: *abnormal/animal/child/industrial ~,* branches of this science. **2** (pop, unscientific, use) mental nature, processes, etc of a person: *She understands her husband's ~ very well.* **psy·chol·ogist** /-ɪst/ *n* student of, expert in, ~. **psy·cho·logi·cal** /ˈsɑɪkəˈlodʒɪkl/ *adj* **1** of ~; of the mind: *psychological warfare,* waged by trying to influence people's ideas and beliefs. **2** (pop, unscientific use) *the psychological moment,* the most appropriate time; the time when one is most likely to achieve the desired end. **psy·cho·logi·cally** /-klɪ/ *adv*

psy·cho·path /ˈsɑɪkəʊpæθ/ *n* person suffering from severe emotional derangement, esp one who is aggressive and antisocial. **~ic** /ˈsɑɪkəʊˈpæθɪk/ *adj* of, suffering from, emotional or mental disorder.

psy·cho·sis /sɑɪˈkəʊsɪs/ *n* (*pl* -choses /-ˈkəʊsiz/) abnormal or diseased mental state.

psy·cho·therapy /ˈsɑɪkəʊˈθerəpɪ/ *n* [U] treatment by psychological methods of mental, emotional and nervous disorders.

ptar·mi·gan /ˈtɑmɪgən/ *n* bird of the grouse family with black or grey feathers in summer and white in winter.

ptero·dac·tyl /ˈterəˈdæktɪl/ *n* extinct flying reptile.

pto·maine /ˈtəʊmeɪn/ *n* (sorts of) poison which is found in decaying food: *ill with ~ poisoning.*

pub /pʌb/ *n* (abbr for) public house: *go round to the pub for a drink.* **ˈpub crawl,** ⇨ crawl *n*(1).

pu·berty /ˈpjubətɪ/ *n* [U] stage at which a person becomes physically able to become a parent; maturing of the sexual functions: *reach the age of ~.*

pu·bic /ˈpjubɪk/ *adj* of the lower part of the abdomen: *~ hair.*

pub·lic /ˈpʌblɪk/ *adj* (opp of *private*) **1** of, for, connected with, owned by, done for or done by, known to, people in general: *a ~ library/park; a matter of ~ knowledge,* sth known to everyone; *enter ~ life,* engage in the affairs or service of the people, e g in government; *~ secondary schools,* government-controlled schools providing free education (but ⇨ ~ school below). **ˈ~-adˈdress system** *n* (abbr *PA system*) system of microphones and loud speakers for broadcasting in ~ areas. **ˈ~ asˈsistance,** (GB) help that may be given to people with low incomes from ~ funds (the Social Security Services). **ˈ~ ˈbar,** one in a hotel, ~ house, etc for all sections of the community. **ˈ~ ˈcorpoˈration,** (legal) corporation providing services for the public, e g in GB *the British Broadcasting Corporation, the BBC.* **ˈ~ ˈenemy,** person thought to be a danger to the ~, to the whole community. **ˈ~ ˈhouse** *n* (GB) (formal) house (not a club, hotel, etc) licensed to sell alcoholic drinks to be consumed on the premises but not offering accommodation. **ˈ~ ˈnuisance,** (legal) illegal act harmful to people in general rather than to an individual; (colloq) sb who is a nuisance to a community. '~ **o'pinion poll,** ⇨ poll[1](2). '~ **'ownership,** ownership by the State, e g of the railways. '**P~ 'Prosecutor,** ⇨ *prosecutor* at prosecute. '~ **re'lations** *n pl* (esp) relations between a government department or authority, business organization, etc with the general ~, usu through the distribution of information. '~ **re'lations officer,** person employed in ~ relations. '~ **school,** (a) (GB) school for older fee-paying pupils, usu a boarding school, supported partly by endowments and managed by a board of governors. (b) (US and Scot) school providing free education, supported by ~ funds. '~ **'spirit,** readiness to do things that are for the good of the community. Hence, '**~-'spirited** *adj* '~ **trustee,** ⇨ trustee. '~ **'transport,** transport systems (road and rail) owned by ~ corporations, e g city and town authorities: *travel by ~ transport,* contrasted with privately owned systems, one's own car, etc. '~ **u'tilities,** organizations which supply services and commodities, e g water, gas, electricity, transport, communications, to the general ~. ***go ~,*** (of a business organization) offer shares for purchase (on the Stock Exchange) by the ~: *Rolls-Royce, after its bankruptcy in 1971, went ~ in 1972.* □ *n* **1 the ~,** members of the community in general: *the British ~. The ~ are not admitted. The ~ is/are requested not to leave litter in the park.* ***in ~,*** openly, not in private. **2** particular section of the community: *the theatre-going ~; the reading ~; a book that will appeal to a large ~,* to many readers. **~·ly** /-klɪ/ *adv*

pub·li·can /ˈpʌblɪkən/ *n* **1** (GB) keeper of a public house. **2** (in Roman times and in the NT) tax-gatherer.

pub·li·ca·tion /ˌpʌblɪˈkeɪʃn/ *n* **1** [U] act of making known to the public, of publishing sth: *the ~ of a report; date of ~.* **2** [C] sth published, e g a book or a periodical.

pub·li·cist /ˈpʌblɪsɪst/ *n* newspaper man who writes on current topics of public interest, e g a political journalist.

pub·lic·ity /pʌbˈlɪsətɪ/ *n* [U] **1** the state of being known to, seen by, everyone: *an actress who seeks/avoids ~; royal personages who live their lives in the full blaze of ~.* **2** (business of) providing information to win public interest: *give a new book/play, etc. wide ~; conduct a '~ campaign.* '~ **agent,** person employed to keep the name of a person, e g an actor, or product constantly before the public.

pub·li·cize /ˈpʌblɪsaɪz/ *vt* [VP6A] give publicity to; bring to the attention of the public.

pub·lish /ˈpʌblɪʃ/ *vt* [VP6A] **1** have (a book, periodical, etc) printed and announce that it is for sale. **2** make known to the public: *~ the news; ~ the banns of marriage,* announce formally in a church the names of persons shortly to be married. **~er** *n* person whose business is the ~ing of books.

puce /pjus/ *n* [U] purple-brown.

puck[1] /pʌk/ *n* (in folklore) mischievous sprite or goblin. '**~·ish** /-ɪʃ/ *adj* mischievous: *a ~ish smile.* **~·ish·ly** *adv*

puck[2] /pʌk/ *n* hard rubber disc used instead of a ball in ice-hockey.

pucka /ˈpʌkə/ ⇨ pukka.

pucker /ˈpʌkə(r)/ *vt,vi* [VP6A,15B,2A,C] **~ up,** draw or come together into small folds or wrinkles: *~ up one's brows/lips. This coat ~s (up) at the shoulders.* □ *n* wrinkle.

pud /pʊd/ *n* [U] (colloq) pudding.

pud·den /ˈpʊdn/ *n* (colloq) (only in) '**~-head** *n* slow, stupid person.

pudding /ˈpʊdɪŋ/ *n* **1** [C,U] (dish of) food, usu a soft, sweet mixture, served as part of a meal, generally eaten after the meat course: *milk ~s,* of some kind of grain, e g rice, cooked with milk and flavourings, '**~-face,** large fat face. **2** kind of sausage. '**black ~,** intestine of pig stuffed with oatmeal, blood, etc. **3** sth like a ~ in appearance. **4** '~ **stone,** rock composed of rounded pebbles in a kind of stone like concrete.

puddle /ˈpʌdl/ *n* **1** [C] small, dirty pool of rain-water, esp on a road. **2** [U] wet clay and sand mixed to a paste, used as a watertight covering for embankments, etc. □ *vt* **1** mix (wet clay and sand) into a thick paste. **2** stir (molten iron) to produce wrought iron by expelling carbon. **pud·dler** /ˈpʌdl̩ə(r)/ *n* worker who ~s clay, etc or molten iron.

pu·denda /pjuˈdendə/ *n pl* external genital organs, esp of the female.

pudgy /ˈpʌdʒɪ/ *adj* (-ier, -iest) short, thick and fat: *~ fingers.*

pueblo /ˈpwebləʊ/ *n* (*pl* -los /-ləʊz/) communal village dwelling of adobe and stone, as built by American Indians in Mexico and the south-western US.

puer·ile /ˈpjʊəraɪl *US:* -rl/ *adj* trivial; suitable only for a child: *ask ~ questions.* **puer·il·ity** /ˌpjʊəˈrɪlətɪ/ *n* [U] childishness; foolishness; [C] childish or foolish act, idea, utterance, etc.

pu·er·peral /pjuˈɜpərl/ *adj* of, due to, childbirth: *~ fever.*

puff[1] /pʌf/ *n* [C] **1** (sound of a) short, quick sending out of breath, air, etc; amount of steam, smoke, etc sent out at one time: *~s from a steam-engine; have a ~ at a pipe; be out of ~,* (colloq) short of breath (because of exertion). **2** ('**pow·der-)~,** piece or ball of soft material, for putting powder on the skin. '**~-box** *n* box containing powder and a powder-~. **3** round, soft mass of material used on an article of dress as an ornament: *~ sleeves,* swelling out like balloons; *gather a dress into ~s.* **4 ~ pastry,** light, flaky pastry. **5** quantity of ~ pastry filled with jam, whipped cream, etc: *jam ~s.* **6** review of a book, play, etc, praising it extravagantly. **7** '**~-adder** *n* poisonous African viper which inflates the upper part of its body when excited. '**~-ball** *n* kind of fungus shaped like a ball which when ripe breaks open and sends out ~s of dust-like spores. **puffy** *adj* (-ier, -iest) short of breath; easily made short of breath (by running, climbing, etc); swollen: *a red face, ~y under the eyes.* **~i·ness** *n* state of being ~y.

puff[2] /pʌf/ *vi,vt* **1** [VP2A,C] move along with puffs(1); breathe quickly (as after running); (of smoke, steam, etc) come out in puffs: *The old steam-engine ~ed out of the station. He was ~ing hard when he jumped on to the bus. He was ~ing (away) at his cigar. Smoke ~ed up from the crater of the volcano.* **2** [VP15A,B] send out in puffs: *He ~ed smoke into my face. He managed to ~ out a few words. He was rather ~ed* (= out of breath) *after running to the bus stop.* ***~ed up,*** filled with pride; conceited. **3** [VP15B] ***~ sth out,*** (a) blow out: *He ~ed out the candle.* (b) cause to swell with air: *He ~ed out his chest with pride.* **4**

[VP6A] praise (a book, etc) in an advertisement or review, esp in an exaggerated way.

puf·fin /ˋpʌfɪn/ *n* N Atlantic seabird with a large bill. ⇨ the illus at water.

pug[1] /pʌg/ *n* (also **ˋpug-dog**) small breed of pug-nosed dog. **ˋpug-nose(d)** *adj, n* (with a) short, squat or snub nose.

pug[2] /pʌg/ *n* (Anglo-Indian) animal's footprint: *the pugs of a tiger.*

pu·gil·ist /ˋpjudʒɪl-ɪzt/ *n* (formal) boxer. **pu·gil·ism** /-ɪzm/ *n* boxing. **pu·gil·is·tic** /ˈpjudʒɪˋlɪstɪk/ *adj* of ~s or pugilism.

pug·na·cious /pʌgˋneɪʃəs/ *adj* (formal) fond of, in the habit of, fighting. **~·ly** *adv* **pug·nac·ity** /pʌgˋnæsətɪ/ *n* [U].

puis·sant /ˋpjuɪsnt/ *adj* (archaic) having great power or influence. **puis·sance** /-sns/ *n* strength.

puke /pjuk/ *vi, vt* vomit.

pukka, pucka /ˋpʌkə/ (Anglo-Indian) genuine; authentic; superior.

pul·chri·tude /ˋpʌlkrɪtjud *US:* -tud/ *n* (formal) physical beauty. **pul·chri·tudi·nous** /ˈpʌlkrɪˋtjudɪnəs *US:* -ˋtudṇəs/ *adj*

pule /pjul/ *vi* [VP2A] e g of a baby, cry feebly; whimper.

pull[1] /pʊl/ *n* **1** [C] act of pulling: *give a ~ at a rope. He took a ~ at the bottle,* drank from it. *We went for a short ~* (= row) *on the lake.* **2** [U] force or effort: *It was a long ~* (= a long, hard climb) *to the top of the mountain.* **3** [C,U] (colloq) power to get help or attention through influence, e g with people in high positions: *He has a strong ~/a great deal of ~ with the Managing Director.* **4** handle, etc which is to be pulled: *a ˋbell-~* (old-fashioned kind now replaced by a button to be pressed); *a ˋbeer-~,* for draught beer from a barrel (more usu *pump*). **5** (printing) proof: single impression.

pull[2] /pʊl/ *vt,vi* (For special uses with *adverbial particles* and *preps,* ⇨ 7 below.) **1** [VP6A,15A, B,22,2A] (contrasted with *push*) use force upon (sth or sb) so as to draw towards or after one, or in the direction indicated: *The horse was ~ing a heavy cart. How many coaches can that engine ~? Would you rather push the barrow or ~ it? The baby was ~ing its father's beard. P~ your chair up to the table. She ~ed her tights/gloves on/off. He ~ed my ears/~ed me by the ears. I'm going to the dentist to have a bad tooth ~ed out. Stop ~ing, please!* **~ sth to pieces,** use force to separate its parts or to break it up into parts; (fig) criticize severely by pointing out the weak points or faults: *He ~ed my proposals/theory to pieces.* **2** [VP6A,15A,B,2A,C] move (a boat) by ~ing an oar or a pair of oars; (of a boat) be rowed (by): *Now, all ~ together, please! The men/boat ~ed for the shore. The boat ~s eight oars,* has eight oarsmen. *He ~s a good oar,* rows well. **~ together,** (fig) work together; co-operate. **~ one's weight,** **(a)** use one's weight effectively when rowing. **(b)** exert oneself so as to do a fair share of the work: *Is Smith ~ing his weight?* **3** [VP3A] **~ at/on sth,** **(a)** give a tug: *~ at/on a rope.* **(b)** draw or suck: *~ing at his pipe,* drawing in breath and smoke through his (tobacco) pipe; *~ at a bottle,* have a drink from one. ⇨ pull[1](1). **4** **~ a fast one,** deceive sb. **~ a muscle,** strain it. **~ a proof,** take an impression (from type); print a proof. For other uses with *nn,* ⇨ the *n* entries, e g **~ a face/faces; ~ sb's leg; ~ one's punches; ~ strings; ~ wires; ~ the wool over sb's eyes.** **5** (in games, sport) (golf) mis-hit (the ball) to the left. Cf *slice*(4); (cricket) strike (the ball) forward and to the left of the wicket, by striking across the ball's path; (horse-racing) pull in the reins (of a horse) to prevent it from winning. **6** (sl) raid; rob: *~ a bank;* steal: *~ a few thousand quid.* **7** [VP15B,2C] (special uses with *adverbial particles* and *preps*):

pull sb/sth about, ~ in different directions; treat roughly.

pull sth apart, tear or ~ into its parts.

pull sth down, destroy or demolish, e g an old building.

pull sb down, (of illness, etc) weaken; lower the spirits of: *An attack of influenza soon ~s you down.*

pull in, **(a)** (of a train) enter a station: *The express from Rome ~ed in on time.* **(b)** (of a motor-vehicle or boat) move in towards: *The boat ~ed in to the bank/shore. The lorry driver ~ed in to the side of the road.* Hence, **ˋ~-in** *n* ⇨ ~-up below. **~ sb in,** **(a)** attract, draw: *The new play at the National Theatre is ~ing in large audiences.* **(b)** (colloq, of the police) detain; arrest: *He was ~ed in for questioning/loitering.* **~ sth in,** **(a)** (colloq) earn: *How much money is he ~ing in, do you think?* **~ oneself in,** draw in the stomach muscles (so as to be upright, less flabby).

pull sth off, **(a)** drive a motor-vehicle into a lay-by or hard shoulder. Hence, **ˋ~-off** *n* (US) = lay-by. **(b)** succeed in a plan, in winning sth: *~ off a good speculation; ~ off some good things at the races,* make successful bets.

pull out, **(a)** move or row out: *The boat ~ed out into midstream. The driver of the car ~ed out from behind the lorry.* **(b)** detach, e g from a periodical: (attrib) *a ˋ~-out supplement,* part of a magazine, etc which can be ~ed out and kept separately. Hence, **ˋ~-out** *n* **~ out of,** leave: *The train ~ed out of Euston right on time.* **~ (sb) out (of),** leave a place or situation which is too difficult to manage: *Troops are being ~ed out/are ~ing out of these troubled areas.* Hence, **ˋ~-out** *n: The ~-out was planned to spread over a month.*

pull (sth) over, (cause a vehicle, boat, etc to) move or steer to one side, e g to let another vehicle or boat pass: *P~ (your car) over and let me pass!*

pull (sb) round, (help to) recover from illness, weakness, a faint, etc: *You'll soon ~ round here in the country. Have this brandy; it will ~ you round.*

pull through, **(a)** = ~ round(a). **(b)** succeed in avoiding difficulties, dangers, etc; avoid failure. **~ sb through,** **(a)** help to recover from illness, etc: *The doctors ~ed me through.* **(b)** help to avoid failure, help to pass an examination, etc: *David's tutor did what he could to ~ him through.* **ˋ~-through** *n* oily rag attached to a cord, ~ed through the barrel of a rifle, etc to clean it.

pull together, ⇨ 2 above. **~ oneself together,** get control of oneself, of one's feelings, etc.

pull (sth) up, bring or come to a stop: *The driver ~ed up when he came to the traffic lights. He ~ed up his car at the entrance.* Hence, **ˋ~-up** *n* place (a café, etc) at which to ~ up: *'Good ~-up for lorry-drivers',* e g as a sign outside a roadside cafe. **~ sb up,** check; reprimand: *He was ~ed up by the chairman.* **~ up to/with sb/sth,** improve

one's relative position (in a race, etc): *The favourite soon ~ed up with the other horses.*
pul·let /ˈpʊlɪt/ *n* young hen, esp at the time she begins to lay eggs.
pul·ley /ˈpʊlɪ/ *n* (*pl* -leys) grooved wheel(s) for ropes or chains, used for lifting things. **ˈ~-block** *n* wooden block in which a ~ is fixed.
Pull·man /ˈpʊlmən/ *n* **1** (also **ˈ~ car**) sleeping-car on a railway train. **2** railway carriage arranged with comfortable chairs and refreshment service.
pull·over /ˈpʊləʊvə(r)/ *n* knitted garment pulled on over the head.
pul·lu·late /ˈpʌljʊleɪt/ *vi* breed, multiply, rapidly; swarm.
pul·mon·ary /ˈpʌlmənərɪ *US:* -nerɪ/ *adj* of, in, connected with, the lungs: *~ diseases; the ~ arteries,* conveying blood to the lungs.
pulp /pʌlp/ *n* [U] **1** soft, fleshy part of fruit: *ˈapple ~.* **2** soft mass of other material, esp of wood fibre as used for making paper: *reduce to (a) ~,* destroy the shape of by beating up and making soft; *~ magazines/literature,* (term applied disparagingly to) cheap, popular periodicals, etc. *His arm was caught in the machinery and crushed to a ~.* □ *vt, vi* [VP6A,2A] make into, become like, ~; remove ~ from: *~ old books.* **pulpy** *adj* (-ier, -iest) like or consisting of ~.
pul·pit /ˈpʊlpɪt/ *n* (usu small) raised and enclosed structure in a church, used by a clergyman, esp when preaching. **the ~,** the clergy.
pul·que /ˈpulkeɪ/ *n* [U] fermented milky drink made in Mexico from some kinds of agave.
pul·sar /ˈpʌlsɑ(r)/ *n* star (in a Galaxy) detected by pulsating radio signals only.
pul·sate /pʌlˈseɪt *US:* ˈpʌlseɪt/ *vt, vi* **1** [VP2A] beat or throb; expand and contract rhythmically; vibrate; quiver. **2** [VP6A] cause to vibrate; agitate; **pul·sa·tion** /pʌlˈseɪʃn/ *n* **1** [C] single beat or throb; heartbeat. **2** [U] pulsating; throbbing.
pulse¹ /pʌls/ *n* **1** the regular beat of the arteries, e g as felt at the wrist, as the blood is pumped through them by the heart: *The patient has a weak/strong/low/irregular ~.* ***feel/sb's ~,*** feel the artery at the wrist and count the number of beats per minute. **2** (fig) throb or thrill of life or emotion: *an event that stirred my ~s,* roused my emotion, excited me. □ *vi* [VP2C] beat; throb; *the life pulsing through a great city; news that sent the blood pulsing through his veins.*
pulse² /pʌls/ *n* [U] (collective *sing,* sometimes with *pl v*) seeds growing in pods, e g peas, beans and lentils, used as food.
pul·ver·ize /ˈpʌlvəraɪz/ *vt, vi* **1** [VP6A] grind to powder; smash completely; (fig): *~ an opponent's arguments.* **2** [VP2A] become powder or dust.
puma /ˈpjumə/ *n* large brown American animal of the cat family (also called a *cougar* and *mountain lion*). ⇨ the illus at **cat**.
pum·ice /ˈpʌmɪs/ *n* [U] **ˈ~(-stone),** light, porous stone (lava) used for cleaning and polishing.
pum·mel /ˈpʌml/ *vt* (-ll-, US also -l-) [VP6A,15B] beat repeatedly with the fists: *give sb a good ~ling.*
pump¹ /pʌmp/ *n* machine or device for forcing liquid, gas or air into, out of or through sth, e g water from a well, petrol from a storage tank, air into a tyre, oil through a pipe-line; the illus at **bicycle**: *the village ~,* (in olden days, often one that supplied a village with water). ⇨ also *parish-pump* at **parish**; *a row of ˈpetrol ~s; a ˈbicycle ~.* **ˈ~-room** *n* (in a watering-place or spa) room where medicinal water is dispensed. □ *vt, vi* **1** [VP6A,15A,B,22] force, e g water, etc *out/up/into/through* sth, by using a ~: *~ water up/out; ~ a well dry,* ~ until there is no water left in the well; *~ air into a tyre; ~ up the tyres;* (fig) *~ information out of sb; ~ facts into the heads of dull pupils; a ˈ~ing station,* e g on a pipe-line carrying petroleum. **2** [VP2A,C] use a ~: *He was ~ing away.*
pump² /pʌmp/ *n* kind of light shoe of soft, shiny leather, worn for dancing; (US) woman's low-heeled shoe with a fastening.
pum·per·nickel /ˈpʌmpə-nɪkl/ *n* [U] wholemeal rye bread.
pump·kin /ˈpʌmpkɪn/ *n* (plant, a trailing vine, with a) large, round orange-yellow fruit with many seeds in it, used as a vegetable and (US) as a filling for pies.
pun /pʌn/ *n* [C] humorous use of words which sound the same or of two meanings of the same word, e g 'A cannonball took off his legs, so he laid down his *arms.*' □ *vi* (-nn-) [VP2A,3A] make a pun or puns (on/upon a word).
punch¹ /pʌntʃ/ *n* **1** tool or machine for cutting holes in leather, metal, paper, etc; tool for forcing nails beneath a surface, or bolts out of holes. **2** tool for stamping designs on surfaces. □ *vt* **1** [VP6A] make a hole (in sth) with a ~: *~ holes in a sheet of metal; ~ a train-ticket; ~ed cards,* as used in filing systems or computers; *~d (paper) tape,* used by computer programmers. **2** [VP15B] ***~ sth in/out,*** drive sth in or out with a ~.
punch² /pʌntʃ/ *n* [U] drink made of wine or spirits mixed with hot water, sugar, lemons, spice, etc: *rum ~.* **ˈ~-bowl** *n* bowl in which ~ is mixed.
punch³ /pʌntʃ/ *vt* [VP6A,15A] strike hard with the fist: *~ a man on the chin. He has a face I'd like to ~.* □ *n* **1** [C] blow given with the fist: *give sb a ~ on the nose; a boxer with a strong ~,* the ability to deliver strong ~es. ***pull one's ~es,*** attack less vigorously than is able to. **ˈ~-ball, ˈ~ing-ball** *nn* inflated or stuffed ball hung up and ~ed with the fists for exercise. **ˌ~-ˈdrunk** *adj* (in boxing) dazed by ~es received in a fight; (fig) confused. **ˈ~ line** *n* climax of a story (where the point is made, where laughter comes). **ˈ~-up** *n* (colloq) fight with the fists: *The quarrel ended in a ~-up.* **2** [U] (fig) energy: *a speech with plenty of ~ in it.*
Punch /pʌntʃ/ *n* grotesque hump-backed figure in the traditional puppet-show called P~ and Judy. ***as pleased/proud as P~,*** greatly pleased/very proud.
punc·tilio /pʌŋkˈtɪlɪəʊ/ *n* (*pl* -lios /-lɪəʊz/) **1** [C] particular point of good conduct, ceremony, honour. **2** [U,C] formality; (point of) etiquette (esp when it is not really important): *stand upon ~s,* insist too much upon protocol(2).
punc·tili·ous /pʌŋkˈtɪlɪəs/ *adj* (formal) very careful to carry out correctly details of conduct and ceremony; careful in performing duties: *as ~ as a Spaniard.* **~·ly** *adv* **~·ness** *n*
punc·tual /ˈpʌŋktʃʊəl/ *adj* neither early nor late; coming, doing sth, at the time fixed: *be ~ for the lecture/in the payment of one's rent.* **~ly** /-ʊəlɪ/ *adv* in a ~ manner: *The train arrived ~ly.* **~·ity** /ˌpʌŋktʃʊˈælətɪ/ *n* [U] being ~.
punc·tu·ate /ˈpʌŋktʃʊeɪt/ *vt* **1** [VP6A] put stops, commas, etc, e g . , ; : ? ! , into a piece of writing.

2 [VP15A] interrupt from time to time: *a speech ~d with cheers; ~ one's remarks with thumps on the table.* **punc·tu·ation** /ˈpʌŋktʃʊˈeɪʃn/ *n* [U] punctuating; art or practice of punctuating.

punc·ture /ˈpʌŋtʃə(r)/ *n* [C] small hole made by sth sharp, esp one made accidentally in a pneumatic tyre. □ *vt,vi* **1** [VP6A] make a ~ in: *~ an abscess/a motor-car tyre;* (fig) deflate: *She likes to ~ her husband's ego,* lessen his self-conceit. **2** [VP2A] experience a ~: *Two of my tyres ~ed while I was on that stony road.*

pun·dit /ˈpʌndɪt/ *n* very learned Hindu; authority on a subject; (hum) learned teacher; pedant.

pun·gent /ˈpʌndʒənt/ *adj* (of smells, tastes; fig of remarks) sharp; biting; stinging: *a ~ sauce; ~ remarks/satire/criticism.* **~·ly** *adv* **pun·gency** /-nsɪ/ *n* [U] ~ quality.

Pu·nic /ˈpjunɪk/ *adj* of ancient Carthage and its people. **the ~ Wars,** the wars between Rome and Carthage. **~ faith,** treachery.

pun·ish /ˈpʌnɪʃ/ *vt* [VP6A,14] ***~ sb (for sth),*** **1** cause (sb) suffering or discomfort for wrongdoing; cause suffering or discomfort to sb (for wrongdoing): *~ a man with/by a fine. How would you ~ lying/~ persons who tell lies?* **2** treat roughly; knock about: *The champion ~ed his opponent severely,* (boxing) gave him severe blows. *Chappell ~ed the bowling,* (cricket) scored freely (from poor or weak bowling). **3** (colloq) make heavy inroads on: *~ the cold beef/the cider cask.* **ˈ~·able** /-əbl/ *adj* that can be ~ed (by law). **~·ment** *n* [U] ~ing or being ~ed: *Does the ~ment fit the crime?* [C] penalty inflicted for wrongdoing: *make the ~ment fit the crime; inflict severe ~ments on criminals.*

pu·ni·tive /ˈpjunɪtɪv/ *adj* (intended for) punishing: *a ~ expedition,* a military expedition with the purpose of punishing rebels, etc.

punk /pʌŋk/ *n* **1** [U] (US) partly decayed wood; rotten wood used as tinder. **2** (colloq) worthless stuff; rubbish: *He talked a lot of ~.* **3** [C] (sl) worthless person. **4** (attrib; sl) worthless; rotten: *It was an absolutely ~ party.*

punka, pun·kah /ˈpʌŋkə/ *n* (formerly in India) large piece of cloth on a frame, kept moving by means of a cord and pulley, used to keep the air in movement (as an electric fan does).

pun·net /ˈpʌnɪt/ *n* small basket, made of very thin wood, plastic, etc esp as a measure for fruit: *strawberries, 20p a ~.*

pun·ster /ˈpʌnstə(r)/ *n* person who has the habit of making puns.

punt[1] /pʌnt/ *n* flat-bottomed, shallow boat with square ends, moved by pushing the end of a long pole against the river-bed. □ *vt,vi* [VP6A,2A] move (a ~) in this way; carry (sb or sth) in a ~; go in a ~. **punter** *n*

punt[2] /pʌnt/ *vt* [VP6A] kick (a football) after it has dropped from the hands and before it reaches the ground. □ *n* such a kick.

punt[3] /pʌnt/ *vi* [VP2A] (in some card-games) lay a stake against the bank; bet on a horse, etc. **~er** *n* person who ~s or bets.

puny /ˈpjunɪ/ *adj* (-ier, -iest) small and weak: *What a ~ little creature! My ~ efforts are not worth much.* **pun·ily** /ˈpjunəlɪ/ *adv*

pup /pʌp/ *n* **1** young dog; puppy. ***sell a man a pup,*** (colloq) swindle him, esp by selling him sth which, he is made to believe, may have greatly increased value in the future; young of some other animals, e g the seal. **2** conceited young man.

pupa /ˈpjupə/ *n* (*pl* **pupas,** or **pupae** /-pi/) chrysalis. ⇨ the illus at **butterfly.**

pu·pil[1] /ˈpjupl/ *n* young person who is learning in school or from a private teacher.

pu·pil[2] /ˈpjupl/ *n* (anat) circular opening in the centre of the iris of the eye, regulating the passage of light. ⇨ the illus at **eye.**

pup·pet /ˈpʌpɪt/ *n* **1** doll, small figure of an animal, etc with jointed limbs moved by wires or strings, used in plays or shows called ˈ*~-plays/-shows;* marionette; (ˈ*glove-~*) doll of which the body can be put on the hand like a glove, the arms and head being moved by the fingers of the operator. **2** person, group of persons, whose acts are completely controlled by another: (attrib) *a ~ government/State.*

puppets

puppy /ˈpʌpɪ/ *n* (*pl* -pies) **1** young dog: *~ love,* first love affair(s); ˈ*~ fat,* the kind of fat that boys and girls sometimes have before adolescence. **2** conceited young man.

pur·blind /ˈpɜblaɪnd/ *adj* partly or nearly blind; (fig) stupid.

pur·chase[1] /ˈpɜtʃəs/ *n* **1** [U] buying: ˈ*~-money,* price (to be) paid. ˈ**~ tax** *n* (US = *sales tax*) tax on the retail price of goods, collected by the retailer and paid by him to the Government (GB since 1973 replaced by value-added tax.) ⇨ **value(3). 2** [C] sth bought: *He filled the car with his ~s. I have some ~s to make.* **3** (*sing* only) firm hold or grip (for pulling or raising sth, or to prevent sth from slipping: *get a/any/some ~ on sth.* **4** [U] value or worth, esp as reckoned in annual yield or return: *sold at thirty years' ~,* (of land, etc) sold for the equivalent of thirty years' rent. *His life is not worth a day's ~,* He is on the point of death.

pur·chase[2] /ˈpɜtʃəs/ *vt* [VP6A] buy (which is much more usu): *a dearly ~d victory,* e g a battle in which many lives are lost. **pur·chas·able** /-əbl/ *adj* that can be ~d. **pur·chaser** *n* buyer.

pur·dah /ˈpɜdə/ *n* [U] (esp in Muslim communities) curtain for, convention of, keeping women from the sight of strangers, esp men: *live/be in ~.*

pure /pjʊə(r)/ *adj* (-r, -st except 5,6 below) **1** unmixed with any other substance, etc: *~ water/milk/gold; ~ air,* free from smoke, fumes, etc. **2** of unmixed race: *~ blood; a ~ Negro; a ~bred* (= *thoroughbred* which is more usu) *Alsation dog.* **3** clean; without evil or sin: *~ in body and mind; ~ thoughts; the ~ in heart.* **4** (of sounds) clear and distinct: *a ~ note.* **5** dealing with, studied for the sake of, theory only (not *applied*): *~ mathematics/science.* **6** mere; nothing but: *~ mischief; a ~ waste of time; spread unkind gossip out of ~ malice.* ...**~ and simple,** nothing but...: *laziness ~ and simple,* sheer laziness. **~·ly** *adv* (esp) entirely; completely; merely: *~ly by accident; a ~ly formal request.* **~·ness** *n* = purity (which is more usu).

pu·rée /ˈpjʊəreɪ *US:* pjʊəˈreɪ/ *n* soup of vegetables, etc boiled to a pulp and pressed through a sieve; fruit similarly treated.

pur·ga·tion /pɜˈgeɪʃn/ *n* [U] (formal) **1** purging or purification from sin. **2** purging of the bowels.

pur·ga·tive /ˈpɜgətɪv/ *n, adj* (substance) having the power to purge or cleanse the bowels.

pur·ga·tory /ˈpɜgətrɪ *US:* -tɔrɪ/ *n* (*pl* -**ries**) **1** (esp in R C doctrine) condition after death in which the soul requires to be purified by temporary suffering; place where souls are so purified. **2** any place or temporary suffering or expiation. **pur·ga·torial** /ˌpɜgəˈtɔrɪəl/ *adj* of ~.

purge /pɜdʒ/ *vt* [VP6A,14,15A,B] ***~ sb (of/from sth); ~ sth (away) (from sb),*** **1** make clean or free (of physical or moral impurity): *be ~d of/from sin; ~ away one's sins.* **2** empty (the bowels) of waste matter by means of medicine. **3** clear (oneself, a person, of a charge, of suspicion); (legal) atone for (an offence, etc) by submission. ***~ one's contempt,*** do what is right after showing contempt for a judge or court of law. **4** rid (a political party, etc) of members who are considered undesirable. □ *n* [C] **1** purging, clearing out or away: *the political ~s that followed the counter-revolution.* **2** medicine used for purging(2).

pu·rify /ˈpjʊərɪfɑɪ/ *vt* (*pt,pp* -**fied**) [VP6A,14] ***~ sth (of),*** make pure; cleanse: *an air-~ing plant* (e g for providing pure air in a factory). **pu·ri·fi·ca·tion** /ˌpjʊərɪfɪˈkeɪʃn/ *n* [U] ~ing, e g as a religious ceremony.

pu·rist /ˈpjʊərɪst/ *n* person who pays great attention to the correct use of words, grammar, style, etc.

puri·tan /ˈpjʊərɪtən/ *n* **1 P~,** (16th and 17th cc, in England) member of a division of the Protestant Church which wanted simpler forms of church ceremony. **2** person who is strict in morals and religion, who looks upon some kinds of fun and pleasure as sinful: *Don't marry a ~.* □ *adj* of or like a P~ or a ~. **~·ism** /-ɪzm/ *n* practices and beliefs of the P~s. **puri·tani·cal** /ˌpjʊərɪˈtænɪkl/ *adj* very strict and severe, like a ~. **puri·tani·cally** /-klɪ/ *adv*

pu·rity /ˈpjʊərətɪ/ *n* [U] state or quality of being pure.

purl[1] /pɜl/ *n* (knitting) inverted stitch, which produces a ribbed appearance (the opp of *plain*). □ *vt,vi* invert (stitches); invert stitches of (sth being knitted).

purl[2] /pɜl/ *vi* (of a small stream) flow with a murmuring sound. □ *n* this sound.

pur·lieus /ˈpɜljuz/ *n pl* outskirts; outlying parts: *the ~ of the camp.*

pur·loin /pɜˈlɔɪn/ *vt* [VP6A] (formal) steal.

purple /ˈpɜpl/ *n, adj* (colour) of red and blue mixed together: *a ~ sunset; become ~ with rage.* **the ~,** the ~ robes of a Roman emperor or a cardinal. ***born in the ~,*** a member of a royal family. ***raise sb to the ~,*** make him a cardinal. ˌ**~ ˈheart** *n* **(a)** (GB) heart-shaped tablet containing amphetamine, used as a stimulant. **(b)** (US *P~ H~*) medal awarded to a soldier wounded in battle. **pur·plish** /ˈpɜplɪʃ/ *adj* somewhat ~.

pur·port /ˈpɜpət *US:* -pɔrt/ *n* (formal) general meaning or intention of sth said or written; likely explanation of a person's actions: *the ~ of what he said.* □ *vt* /ˈpɜpət *US:* -ˈpɔrt/ **1** [VP6A,9] seem to mean: *The statement ~s that....* **2** [VP7] claim: *The book ~s to be an original work but is really a compilation.*

pur·pose /ˈpɜpəs/ *n* **1** that which one means to do, get, be, etc; plan; design; intention: *For what ~(s)* (*Why* is more usu) *do you want to go to Canada? I wouldn't go to London for/with the mere ~ of buying a new tie. This van is used for various ~s. This is a novel with a ~,* one written to explain or defend a doctrine, etc not merely to amuse. ˌ**~-ˈbuilt** *adj* made to serve a particular function. **2** [U] determination; power of forming plans and keeping to them: *weak of ~; wanting in ~.* **3** (phrases) ***on ~,*** by intention, not by chance: *You sometimes hurt yourself by accident but you don't hurt yourself on ~. He has left the book here on ~ for you to read. He came here on ~ to borrow money from you. She sometimes does things on ~ just to annoy me.* ***of set ~,*** deliberately; designedly; not by accident. ***to the ~,*** useful for one's ~; relevant: *The reply was so little to the ~ that it was not worth our consideration.* ***to little/no/some ~,*** with little/no/some result or effect. ***serve/answer one's ~,*** be satisfactory; do what is required. □ *vt* [VP6A,D,7,9] have as one's ~: *They ~ a further attempt/~ to make/~ making a further attempt.* ˈ**~·ful** /-fl/ *adj* having a conscious ~; full of meaning. ˈ**~·fully** /-flɪ/ *adv* **~·less** *adj* lacking ~; having no object in view. **~·less·ly** *adv* on ~; intentionally. **pur·pos·ive** /ˈpɜpəsɪv/ *adj* having, serving, done with, a ~: *purposive movements;* (of a person, his conduct) having, showing, ~ and determination.

purr /pɜ(r)/ *vi,vt* **1** [VP2A,C] (of a cat) make a low, continuous vibrating sound expressing pleasure; (of a car engine) make a vibrating sound; (fig, of a person) indicate contentment by using a pleasant tone: *Mrs Black ~ed with delight on receiving the invitation to dine with the duchess.* **2** [VP6A] express (contentment, etc) thus: *She ~ed her approval of the suggestion.* □ *n* ~ing sound.

purse /pɜs/ *n* **1** small bag, usu of leather, for money (originally closed by drawing strings together, now usu closed with a clasp): *That big car is beyond my ~,* costs more than I can afford. ˈ**~-proud** *adj* ⇨ **proud(5).** ***hold the ~-strings,*** have control of expenditure. ***tighten/loosen the ~-strings,*** reduce/increase expenditure; be economical/generous. **2** money; funds. **the privy ~,** ⇨ **privy. the public ~,** the national treasury. **3** sum of money collected or offered as a prize, gift, etc: *make up a ~; give/put up a ~,* e g for the winner of a boxing match. **4** (US) = handbag. □ *vt* [VP6A,15B] ***~ (up), ~ (up) the lips,*** draw the lips together in tiny folds or wrinkles.

purser /ˈpɜsə(r)/ *n* officer responsible for a ship's accounts and stores, esp in a passenger liner.

pur·su·ance /pəˈsjuəns *US:* -ˈsu-/ *n* ***in ~ of,*** (formal) in the carrying out of or the performance of (one's duties, a plan, etc). **pur·su·ant** /-ənt/ *adj* ***pursuant to,*** (formal) in accordance with; in agreement with: *pursuant to your instructions.*

pur·sue /pəˈsju *US:* -ˈsu/ *vt* [VP6A] **1** go after in order to catch up with, capture or kill: *~ a robber/a bear; make sure that you are not being ~d.* **2** (fig) (of consequences, penalties, etc) persistently attend: *His record as a criminal ~d him wherever he went. He has been ~d by misfortune.* **3** go on with; work at: *~ one's studies after leaving school.* **4** have as an aim or purpose: ~

pleasure. **pur·suer** *n* person who ~s(1).

pur·suit /pəˈsjut *US:* -ˈsut/ *n* **1** [U] ***(in)*** **~ *(of),*** act of pursuing: *a dog in ~ of rabbits; a fox with the hounds in hot ~; in his ~ of happiness;* (attrib) *a ~ plane,* one that pursues and fights enemy planes. **2** [C] sth at which one works or to which one gives one's time: *engaged in scientific/literary ~s.*

pursy[1] /ˈpɜsɪ/ *adj* (old use) (of a person) fat and short-winded.

pursy[2] /ˈpɜsɪ/ *adj* (old use) puckered: *~ eyes.* ⇨ purse, *v.*

puru·lent /ˈpjʊərələnt/ *adj* of, containing, discharging, pus. **puru·lence** /-əns/ *n*

pur·vey /pɜˈveɪ/ *vt,vi* **1** [VP6A,14] (formal) provide, supply (food, as a trader): *A butcher ~s meat to his customers.* **2** [VP3A] **~ *for,*** supply provisions for: *a firm that ~s for the Navy.* **~or** /-ə(r)/ *n* person whose business is to supply provisions on a large scale, e g for the Army or Navy, for large public dinners. **~·ance** /-əns/ *n*

pur·view /ˈpɜvju/ *n* (formal) range or operation or activity; scope; extent: *These are questions that lie outside/that do not come within the ~ of our inquiry.*

pus /pʌs/ *n* [U] thick yellowish-white liquid formed in and coming out from a poisoned place in the body: *It is unwise to squeeze a boil to force the pus out.*

push[1] /pʊʃ/ *n* **1** [C] act of pushing: *Give the door a hard ~. He opened the gate with/at one ~.* **2** [C] vigorous effort: *We must make a ~ to finish the job this week. The enemy made a ~* (= an attack in force) *on the western front.* **3 *get the ~,*** be dismissed (from one's employment, etc). ***give sb the ~,*** (sl) (of an employee) dismiss him. **4** [U] determination to make one's way in life, to attract attention, etc: *He hasn't enough ~ to succeed as a salesman.* **5 *at a ~,*** if compelled by need or circumstances: *We can sleep seven or eight people in the house at a ~.* ***if/when/until it comes to the ~,*** if/when/until one is compelled by need or circumstances, when an effort is needed: *He seemed a satisfactory man until it came to the ~; then he failed us.*

push[2] /pʊʃ/ *vt,vi* (For special uses with *adverbial particles* and *preps,* ⇨ 9 below.) **1** [VP6A,15A,B,22,2A,C] (contrasted with *pull*) use force on (sth/sb) to cause forward movement; exert pressure against: *Please ~ the table nearer to the wall. If you'll ~ the car, I'll steer it. You can pull a rope, but you can't ~ it! We had to ~ our way* (= go forward by ~ing) *through the crowd. Stop ~ing at the back! He ~ed the door open. The rude fellow ~ed past me.* **2** [VP6A] persuade others to recognize, e g claims, or buy, e g goods: *Unless you ~ your claims you'll get no satisfaction. You must ~ your wares if you want better sales. Haven't you a friend who can ~ you,* use his influence to help you? **~ *oneself,*** show energy, etc to win recognition: *You'll never get anywhere if you don't ~ yourself.* ⇨ also *~ oneself forward* in 9 below. **3** [VP6A] sell (illicit drugs) by acting as a link between large suppliers and the drug addicts. ⇨ pusher below. **4** [VP14] **~ *sb for sth,*** press sb hard (to get sth): *We're ~ing them for payment/an answer to our request.* ***be ~ed for sth,*** have difficulty in finding: *I'm rather ~ed for money/time just now.* **5** [VP14,17] **~ *sb/oneself to sth/to do sth,*** drive or urge: *Tony had to ~ himself to go on doing such dull work. She'll ~ him to the verge of suicide.* **6** [VP6A] press: *~ a button,* e g to ring a bell; *~-button warfare,* war in which missiles, e g with atomic war-heads, are fired by pressing buttons. **7 *be ~ing thirty/forty, etc,*** (colloq) be nearing the age indicated: *She wouldn't like you to think so, but she's ~ing thirty.* **8** (compounds) **ˈ~-bike** *n* one that is worked by pedalling (not a *moped* or *motor-bike*). **ˈ~-cart** *n* small cart ~ed by a man. **ˈ~·chair** *n* carriage for a child, like a chair on wheels (used when a child is old enough to sit up). **~er** *n* **1** person who ~es himself/herself forward: *Isn't she a ~er!* (said of someone who takes every opportunity of gaining an advantage for herself). **2** (sl) pedlar of illicit drugs. **ˈ~·ful** /-fl/, **~·ing** *adjj* having a tendency to ~ oneself: *He's too ~ing with strangers,* tries too much to force himself upon their attention. ⇨ 3 above. **9** [VP15A,B,3A] (special uses with *adverbial particles* and *preps*):

push along, (colloq) leave sb/a place: *I'm afraid it's time I was ~ing along,* time for me to go.

push sb around, (colloq) bully him; order him about: *I'm not going to be ~ed around by you or anybody!*

push forward/on (to), go on resolutely with a journey, one's work, etc: *It's getting dark; we must ~ on to our destination. We must ~ on with our work,* hurry and finish it. **~ *oneself forward,*** ambitiously draw attention to oneself, e g at work, in society: *He never ~es himself forward,* is modest, doesn't try to attract attention.

push off, (colloq) leave; go away: *Tell that rude fellow to ~ off! It's time we ~ed off.* **~ *(sth) off,*** (of sb in a boat) ~ against the bank, etc, e g with an oar or pole, to get the boat into the stream, etc.

push (sth) out, (of a boat, etc) = ~ off.

push sb/sth over, cause to fall; overturn: *Don't ~ me over! Several children were ~ed over in the stampede.* **ˈ~-over** *n* (sl) sth very easy to do; person who is easily overcome or controlled.

push sb through (sth), enable sb (esp sb needing help) to succeed in sth: *~ a weak student through an exam.* **~ *sth through,*** bring sth to the final stage by special efforts: *~ legislation through,* get it passed. *We must ~ the matter through.*

push sth up, force, e g prices, to rise. **~ *up the daisies,*** (colloq) be buried in a grave.

pu·sil·lani·mous /ˈpjusɪˈlænɪməs/ *adj* (formal) timid; easily frightened. **pu·sil·la·nim·ity** /ˈpjusɪləˈnɪmətɪ/ *n* [U].

puss /pʊs/ *n* **1** cat; word used to call a cat. **2** (colloq) girl: *She's a sly ~.* **pussy** /ˈpʊsɪ/ *n* (*pl* -sies) (also **ˈpussy-cat**) (child's word for a) cat; any soft furry thing, esp hazel catkins (called **ˈpussy-willows**). **ˈpussy·foot** *vi* [VP2A,C] (colloq) move about in a quiet, stealthy way (as a cat does): *Was that you pussyfooting about in the corridor last night?*

pus·tule /ˈpʌstjul *US:* -tʃul/ *n* (med) pimple or blister, esp one filled with pus.

put[1] /pʊt/ *vi,vt* (*pt,pp* put, *pres part* -tt-) (For special uses with *adverbial particles* and *preps,* ⇨ 11 below.) **1** [VP6A,15A] move (sth) so as to be in a certain place or position: *He put the book on the table. He put his hands in(to) his pockets. He put the corpse down the well. Did you put milk in my tea? It's time to put the baby to bed. I will put* (= harness) *the horse to the cart. Can you put* (= take, e g in a ferry boat) *me across the river? Will* *you please put* (= sew) *a patch on these trousers? He put* (= fastened) *a new handle to the knife. He put his horse at the fence,* tried to make the horse jump over it. *He put* (= pushed) *a knife into me/between my ribs. I'll put a bullet through your head,* kill you. *They've put a satellite into orbit round Mars. They've put men on the moon. He put* (= pushed) *his fist through the window,* broke it by doing this. *He put his pen through the word,* struck the word out. ***put pen to paper,*** start writing. ***put one's foot in it,*** ⇨ foot[1](1). **2** [VP15A] cause (sb/oneself) to be in some relationship, e g as an employee, client, with sb. ***put oneself/sth in(to) sb's hands,*** let him deal with one's problems, etc: *I put myself entirely in your hands. I shall put the matter into the hands of my solicitors.* ***put sb in his (proper) place,*** make him humble. ***put oneself in sb's/sb else's position,*** imagine oneself in his position: *How would you feel (about the matter)?—Just put yourself in my/her position!* ***put sb out to service,*** (formerly) find employment (for one's child) as a domestic servant. ***put sb to a trade,*** find a trade for (usu a son). **3** [VP14] make sb bear (the particular nervous or moral strain indicated). ***put the blame on sb***: *Don't put all the blame on me.* ***put pressure on sb (to do sth)***: *They're putting great pressure on him* (= pressing him hard) *to resign.* ***put (a) strain on sb/sth,*** make him/it suffer from hard work or use: *All this work is putting (a) great strain on him.* **4** [VP15A] affect the progress of. ***put an end/a stop to sth,*** end or abolish it. ***put an end to one's life,*** commit suicide. ***put the brake(s) on sth,*** (fig, colloq) slow it down. **5** [VP15A] cause to pass into or suffer the emotional, physical etc state indicated by the phrase that follows. ***put sb to the blush,*** cause him to blush. ***put oneself to death,*** commit suicide. ***put sb to death,*** kill him. ***put sb at his ease,*** cause him to feel relaxed, free from anxiety, etc. ***put sb to (great) expense,*** cause him to spend a lot. ***put sb to (great) inconvenience,*** cause him inconvenience. ***put sb to the indignity of doing sth,*** cause him to do sth involving loss of dignity. ***put sb in mind of sb/sth,*** recall or remind him of sb/sth. ***put sb/sth out of his/its misery,*** relieve him/it of anxiety, pain, etc; kill (e g an animal in pain). ***put sb on (his) oath,*** make sb swear on oath; bind him to tell the truth. ***put sb to the question,*** ⇨ question[1](4). ***put sb/sth to the test,*** test him/it. ***put sb in the wrong,*** cause him to appear to be wrong. **6** [VP22] cause sb/sth to become (what is indicated by the *adj*): *That picture on the wall is crooked—I must put it straight.* ***put sth right***, correct it: *A short note put the matter right,* ended any misunderstanding. ***put sb right/straight,*** correct an error he has made; give him correct information: *We had taken a wrong turning, but a policeman put us right,* told us which way to go. **7** [VP15A] write; indicate; mark: *put a tick against a name/a price on an article/one's signature to a will.* **8** [VP15A] ***put sth (to sb); put it to sb (that),*** submit; propound; express: *put a proposal to the Board of Directors; put a question to the vote/a resolution to the meeting; I put it to you that...,* invite you to agree with me that.... *You have put the case very clearly. Put it* (= submit the matter) *to her so as not to offend her. How can I put it,* express it? *How would you put* (= express, translate) *this in Danish? That can all be put in a few words; put a question to sb.* ***put the question,*** ⇨ question[1](2). **9** [VP15A] set a value (on); estimate. ***put a price/value/valuation on sth,*** state or estimate the value: *The experts refused to put a price on the Rubens painting. What value do you put on her advice?* ***put sth at (a figure),*** say that, e g sb's age, sth's value, weight, is: *I would put her age at about sixty. I put her fur coat at £200.* **10** [VP6A] throw with an upward and outward movement of the arm. ***put the shot,*** ⇨ shot[1](3). Hence, **'shot-put** *n* this as an event at an athletic meeting. **11** [VP15B,2C,14] (special uses with *adverbial particles* and *preps*):

put (a ship) about, (cause to) change direction: *The captain put the ship about.* ***put oneself about,*** (chiefly Scots) trouble, distress, oneself: *He was very much put about by these false allegations.* ***put sth about,*** spread, e g rumours: *Don't believe all these stories that are being put about.*

put sth across (to sb), **(a)** communicate sth successfully: *a teacher who quickly puts his ideas across to his students.* **(b)** (colloq) make a success of: *Put a business deal across* (more usu *through*). ***put sth across sb,*** deceive; trick: *You can't put that across me,* make me believe or accept it.

put sth aside, **(a)** lay down: *put aside one's book; put one's work aside.* **(b)** save: *He has put aside a good sum of money.* **(c)** disregard; ignore: *Put aside for a moment the fact that the man's been in prison.*

put sth away, **(a)** put in the usual place of storage, e g a drawer, box: *Put your books/toys away.* **(b)** save: *put money away for one's old age.* **(c)** (colloq) eat or drink (to excess): *How can that boy put away so much pie and ice-cream?* **(d)** give up; renounce: *He's had to put away all ideas of becoming a concert pianist.* ***put sb away,*** **(a)** (archaic, biblical) divorce (one's wife). **(b)** (colloq) put into confinement, e g in a mental home: *He acted so strangely that he had to be put away.* **(c)** (colloq, of pets) put to death (because of age, illness): *The dog was so old and weak that it had to be put away.*

put back, (naut) return: *The ship/We put back to harbour.* ***put sth back,*** **(a)** replace: *Put the reference books back on the shelf when you've finished with them.* **(b)** move backwards: *That clock is fast; I'd better put it back five minutes,* move the minute hand back. **(c)** (fig) check the advance of, cause delay to: *put back the efforts of the reformers. The strike at the car factory put back production badly.*

put sth by, save for future use: *Has she any money put by?*

put (sth) down, **(a)** land: *He put down (his glider) in a field.* **(b)** set or place down: *Put down that gun!* **(c)** press down: *When you get on the motorway, you can really put your foot down,* press the accelerator pedal down. ***put one's foot down,*** ⇨ foot[1](1). **(d)** place in storage: *put down eggs,* e g by packing in isinglass. *He has put down a good supply of port and claret.* **(e)** suppress by force or authority: *put down a rebellion; put down gambling and prostitution.* **(f)** write down; make a note of: *Here's my address—put it down before you forget it.* ***put sb down,*** **(a)** allow to alight: *The bus stopped to put down passengers.* **(b)** snub; reduce to silence: *put down hecklers at a political meeting.* **(c)** make humble: (biblical) *put down the* *mighty from their seats.* **put sb down as,** consider that sb is: *They put me down as a fool.* **put sb down for,** write his name on a list as willing to give, e g to a charity or other fund: *You can put me down for £5;* put sb's name down as an applicant, participant, etc: *They put him down for Eton/the school football team.* **put sth down to sth, (a)** charge to an account: *Put the shoes down to my account. You can put the cost of the petrol down to business expenses.* **(b)** attribute to: *The cholera outbreak was put down to bad drinking water. Can we put it down to his ignorance?*

put sth forth, (formal) **(a)** exert: *You must put forth all your strength.* **(b)** send out: *The trees are putting forth new leaves.*

put sth forward, (a) advance; put before people for consideration: *put forward a new theory.* **(b)** move on: *put forward the hands of a clock,* e g when it is stopped or slow. **put sb forward,** propose: *put oneself/a friend forward as a candidate.*

put in, exclaim (often as an interruption): *'But what about us?' he put in.* **put in/into,** (naut) (of a boat, its crew) enter: *The boat put in at Malta/put into Malta for repairs.* **put in for sth,** apply formally for: *put in for the position of manager.* **put in for leave,** request permission to be absent from duty, work, etc. **put sth in, (a)** cause to be in: *He put his head in at the window.* **(b)** submit; present formally: *put in a claim for damages; put in a document* (in a law case); *put in a plea of not guilty.* **(c)** manage to strike or utter: *put in a blow.* **put in a good word for sb,** say sth on his behalf, to help him. **(d)** do, perform: *put in an hour's work before breakfast; put in an hour's piano practice.* **(e)** pass (time): *There's still an hour to put in before the pubs open.* **put sb in, (a)** give duties to: *put in a caretaker/bailiff.* **(b)** elect to office: *Which party will be put in at the next general election?* **put sb in mind of sb/sth,** ⇨ 5 above. ⇨ the *n* entries for **put in an appearance; put the boot in; put one's oar in. put sth in/into sth,** devote; give: *put a lot of work into improving one's French.* **put sb in for sth,** recommend sb for promotion, an award, etc: *The commanding officer is putting Sergeant Green in for the Victoria Cross.*

put off, (of a boat or crew) leave: *We put off from the pier.* **put sth off, (a)** postpone: *put off a meeting; put off going to the dentist.* **(b)** (usu of non-material things, *take off* being usual for clothes) get rid of: *You must put off your doubts and fears.* **put sb off (sth), (a)** put to a later date an arrangement, etc: *We shall have to put the Smiths off till next week.* **(b)** make excuses and try to avoid, e g sth one has promised to do, a duty: *He tried to put me off with vague promises. I won't be put off with such flimsy excuses,* won't accept them. **(c)** hinder or dissuade: *put a man off his game,* e g distract him when he is about to strike the ball at golf. *The mere smell of garlic put him off his supper,* caused him not to want supper. Hence, **'put-off** *n* evasion; postponement.

put sth on, (a) (contrasted with *take off*) clothe oneself with: *put one's hat/shoes, etc on.* **(b)** assume; pretend to have: *put on an air of innocence. Her modesty is all put on,* she's only pretending to be modest, e g about her ability or skill. **(c)** increase; add to: *put on more steam/pressure; put on speed.* **(d)** add to: *He's putting on weight/flesh,* is getting heavier/fatter. *This policy will put pounds on the cost of living,* make it much higher. *Boycott and Edrich put on sixty runs,* (cricket) added sixty to the score. **(e)** arrange for; make available: *put on extra trains during the rush hours; put a play on,* arrange for it to be shown at a theatre. **(f)** advance: *put the clock on one hour,* move the hands forward, e g for Summer Time. **put sb on,** (colloq) deceive them: *He's not really interested; he's putting you on.* Hence, **'put-on** *n*: *What a put-on!* **put it on,** (colloq) **(a)** exaggerate a show of feeling; pretend to be more important, etc than is justified or warranted; talk or behave in a pretentious way. **(b)** overcharge: *Some of the hotels put it on during the holiday season.* **put sb on to bowl,** tell him to do this: *The captain put me on to bowl.* **put money on sb/sth,** stake (horse-racing, etc): *I've put a pound on the favourite.*

put out (from), (naut) (of a boat or crew) move out, leave, e g from harbour. **put sth out, (a)** extinguish; cause to stop burning: *put out the lights/the candle/the gas/the gas-fire. The fireman soon put the fire out.* **(b)** cause to be out of joint; dislocate: *She fell off a horse and put her shoulder out.* **(c)** give (sth) to be done off the premises: *All repairs are done on the premises and not put out. We put out the washing,* send it to a laundry instead of having it done at home. **(d)** lend (money) at interest: *He has £1 000 put out at 5 per cent.* **(e)** produce: *The firm puts out 1 000 bales of cotton sheeting every week.* ⇨ output. **(f)** issue; broadcast: *The Health Department has put out a warning about dangerous drugs.* **put one's hand out,** hold it out in welcome, for caning as a punishment, etc. **put one's tongue out,** show it, e g for a doctor, or at sb, as a rude act. **put sb out, (a)** disconcert; cause to be confused or worried: *The least thing puts him out,* he is easily upset. *She was very much put out by your rudeness.* **(b)** inconvenience: *Would it put you out to lend me £5 until Friday? He was very much put out by the late arrival of his guests.* **put sb out (of),** expel; drive out: *Don't get drunk—you'll be put out!* e g of the bar.

put over, (naut) (of a boat or crew) move over: *put over to the other side of the harbour.* **put sth over to sb,** (colloq) = put sth across to sb.

put sth through, carry it out: *put through a business deal.* **put sb/sth through,** connect (by telephone): *Please put me/this call through to the Manager.* **put sb through sth,** cause him to undergo, e g an ordeal, a test: *The police put him through a severe examination. The trainees were put through an assault course.* **put a person through his paces,** ⇨ pace *n* (3). **put sb through it,** (colloq) test or examine him thoroughly, e g by giving him a medical examination, or by inflicting suffering on him to get a confession.

put sth to sb, ⇨ 8 above. **be hard put to it to do sth,** find difficulty in doing sth: *I'd be hard put to it to say exactly why I disliked him. He was hard put to it to satisfy his creditors.*

put sth together, construct (a whole) by combining parts: *It's easier to take a machine to pieces than to put it together again. I must put my thoughts/ideas together before I go on the platform,* collect my ideas, etc before I give my address, speech, etc. **put our/your/their heads together,** consult one another. **put two and two**

together, ⇨ two.

put up (at), obtain lodging and food: *put up at an inn for the night.* ***put up (for sth),*** offer oneself for election: *Are you going to put up for Finchley again,* i e as a prospective member of Parliament? ***put sth up,*** **(a)** raise; hold up: *put up one's hands,* e g over one's head, as a sign that one is ready to surrender, or with fists clenched, ready to fight; *put up a flag/a sail. She hasn't started to put her hair up yet,* (of long hair) wear it coiled on the head instead of letting it fall over the neck and shoulders. **(b)** build, erect: *put up a shed/a tent.* **(c)** publish (banns); place so as to be seen: *put up a notice.* **(d)** raise, increase: *put up the rent by 50p (a week).* **(e)** pack (in parcels, boxes, etc): *herrings put up in barrels; solutions put up in capsules. The hotel will put us up some sandwiches,* prepare and pack some for us. **(f)** offer, make: *put up a stout resistance/a good fight.* **(g)** supply (a sum of money for an undertaking): *I will supply the skill and knowledge if you will put up the £2 000 capital.* **(h)** (old use) sheathe (a sword); pack away: *The deck chairs have been put up for the winter.* **(i)** cause (wild birds or animals) to leave shelter or cover: *put up a partridge.* ***put sb's back up,*** ⇨ back[1](1). ***put sth up for auction/sale,*** offer it to be auctioned/sold: *Has the house been put up for auction?* ***put up a prayer (for sth),*** offer a prayer. **a put-up job,** sth done in order to give a false impression, to swindle sb, etc. ***put sb up,*** provide lodging and food (for): *We can put you up for the weekend.* ***put sb up (for sth),*** propose, nominate sb for a position: *She was put up for the position of secretary,* e g of a society; *put sb up for a club.* ***put sb up to sth,*** **(a)** inform him of it, instruct him in it: *Please put the new office-boy up to his duties.* **(b)** suggest sth to sb, esp urge him to do sth mischievous or wrong: *Who put you up to all these tricks?* ***put up with sb/sth,*** endure without protest; bear patiently: *There are many inconveniences that have to be put up with when you are camping.*

put[2] /pʌt/ *n, vi,vt* = putt.

pu·ta·tive /ˈpjutətɪv/ *adj* commonly reputed to be: *his ~ father.*

pu·trefy /ˈpjutrɪfaɪ/ *vt,vi* (*pt,pp* -fied) [VP6A,2A] (cause to) become putrid. **pu·tre·fac·tion** /ˌpjutrɪˈfækʃn/ *n* ~ing; sth which has putrefied.

pu·tres·cent /pjuˈtresnt/ *adj* becoming putrid; in the process of rotting. **pu·tres·cence** /-sns/ *n*

pu·trid /ˈpjutrɪd/ *adj* **1** having become rotten; decomposed and ill-smelling: *~ fish.* **2** (sl) very distasteful or unpleasant: *~ weather.* **~·ity** /pjuˈtrɪdətɪ/ *n* [U] decomposed matter; ~ state.

putsch /pʊtʃ/ *n* (G) revolutionary attempt; insurrection.

putt /pʌt/ *vi,vt* [VP2A,6A] strike (a golf-ball) gently with a club so that it rolls across the ground towards or into a hole: *spend an hour practising ~ing.* **ˈ~·ing-green** *n* smooth area of lawn around a hole. **ˈ~·ing-iron** *n* club for ~ing. □ *n* stroke as described above.

put·tee /ˈpʌtɪ/ *n* long band of cloth wound round the leg from ankle to knee, for protection and support.

put·ter /ˈpʌtə(r)/ *vt,vi* = **potter**.

putty /ˈpʌtɪ/ *n* [U] soft paste of white powder and oil used for fixing glass in window frames, etc. □ *vt* (*pt,pp* -tied) [VP6A,15B] fill or make fast with ~: *~ up a hole.*

puzzle /ˈpʌzl/ *n* [C] **1** question or problem difficult to understand or answer. **2** problem (e g *a ˈcrossword-~*) or toy (e g *a ˈjigsaw-~*) designed to test a person's knowledge, skill, patience or temper. **3** (*sing* only) state of bewilderment or perplexity: *be in a ~ about sth.* □ *vt,vi* **1** [VP6A] cause (sb) to be perplexed; make hard thought necessary: *This letter ~s me. He was ~d what to do next/how to answer the letter. He ~d his brains* (= thought hard) *to find the answer.* **2** [VP3A] ***~ over sth,*** think deeply about it. **3** [VP15B] ***~ sth out,*** (try to) find the answer or solution by hard thought. **~·ment** *n* state of being ~d. **puzz·ler** *n* puzzling question: *ask sb a few ~rs. That's a real ~r!*

pygmy, pigmy /ˈpɪgmɪ/ *n* (*pl* -mies) **1 the Pygmies,** dwarf race in Equatorial Africa. **2** very small person; dwarf; person of intellectual inferiority. **3** (attrib) very small.

py·ja·mas (US = **pa·ja·mas**) /pəˈdʒɑməz *US:* -ˈdʒæm-/ *n pl* **1** (also **a pair of ~**) loose-fitting jacket and trousers for sleeping in (*sing* when attrib): *pyˈjama tops/jacket/bottoms/trousers.* **2** loose trousers tied round the waist, worn by Muslims of both sexes in India and Pakistan.

py·lon /ˈpaɪlən *US:* ˈpaɪlɒn/ *n* **1** tower (steel framework) for carrying overhead high-voltage electric cables. **2** gateway to an ancient Egyptian temple; tall structure erected as a support, boundary or decoration.

pylons

py·or·rhoea (also **-rhea**) /ˌpaɪəˈrɪə/ *n* [U] inflammation of the gums causing them to shrink, with loosening of the teeth.

pyra·mid /ˈpɪrəmɪd/ *n* structure with a triangular or square base and sloping sides meeting at a point, esp one of those built of stone in ancient Egypt; pile of objects in the shape of a ~. **~ selling,** (comm) method of selling goods whereby distributors pay a premium for the right to sell a company's goods and then sell part of that right to other distributors.

pyre /ˈpaɪə(r)/ *n* large pile of wood for burning, esp a funeral pile for a corpse.

py·rites /ˌpaɪəˈraɪtiz *US:* pɪˈr-/ *n* [U] **copper ~,** sulphide of copper and iron. **iron ~,** either of two sulphides of iron, gold in colour.

pyro·tech·nics /ˌpaɪərəʊˈteknɪks/ *n pl* art of making or using fireworks; public display of fireworks; (fig, often ironic) brilliant display of oratory, wit, etc. **py·ro·tech·nic** *adj* of ~.

Pyr·rhic /ˈpɪrɪk/ *adj* ***a ~ victory,*** one gained at too great a cost.

py·thon /ˈpaɪθən/ *n* large snake that kills its prey by twisting itself round it and crushing it. ⇨ the illus at snake.

pyx, pix /pɪks/ *n* (eccles) vessel in which consecrated bread used at Communion is kept.

Qq

Q, q /kju/ (*pl* Q's, q's /kjuz/) the seventeenth letter of the English alphabet. ***mind one's P's and Q's,*** ⇨ P,p. ***on the q t,*** ⇨ quiet(5).

qua /kweɪ/ *conj* (Lat) as; in the character or capacity of.

quack[1] /kwæk/ *vi, n* [VP2A] (make the) cry of a duck. **ˈ~-~** *n* (child's name for a) duck.

quack[2] /kwæk/ *n* person dishonestly claiming to have knowledge and skill (esp in medicine); (attrib) of, used by, sold by, such persons: *a ~ doctor; ~ remedies.* **ˈ~·ery** /-ərɪ/ *n* [U] methods, practices, etc of ~s; (*pl;* -ries) instances of the use of such methods, etc.

quad /kwod/ *n* (colloq abbr of) **1** quadrangle. **2** quadruplet: *one of the ~s* (more usu than *quadruplet*).

quad·rangle /ˈkwo-dræŋgl/ *n* **1** plane figure with four sides, esp a square or a rectangle. **2** (abbr *quad*) space in the form of a ~, wholly or nearly surrounded by buildings, esp in a college, e g at Oxford. Cf *court* at Cambridge. **quad·ran·gu·lar** /kwoˈdræŋgjʊlə(r)/ *adj* in the form of a ~.

Quad·ra·gesima /ˌkwodrəˈdʒesɪmə/ *n* first Sunday in Lent.

quad·rant /ˈkwo-drənt/ *n* **1** fourth part of a circle or its circumference. ⇨ the illus at circle. **2** graduated strip of metal, etc shaped like a quarter-circle, for use in measuring angles (of altitude) in astronomy and navigation.

quad·ratic /kwoˈdrætɪk/ *adj* (maths) **~ equation,** one in which the second and no higher power of an unknown quantity is used, e g $x^2 + 2x - 8 = 0$.

quad·ri·lat·eral /ˌkwo-drɪˈlætrl/ *adj, n* four-sided (plane figure).

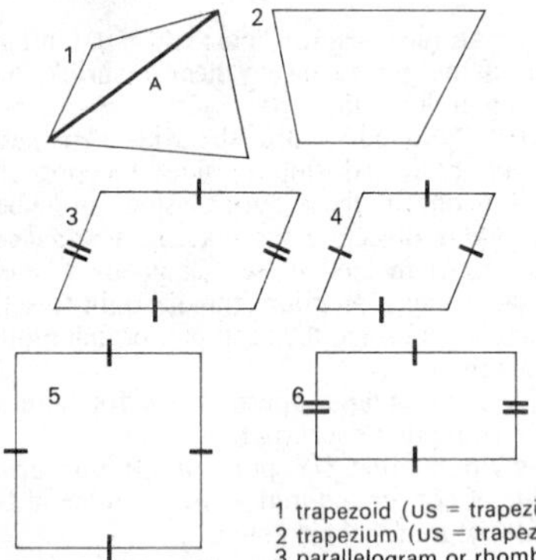

1 trapezoid (US = trapezium)
2 trapezium (US = trapezoid)
3 parallelogram or rhomboid
4 rhomb or rhombus
5 square
6 rectangle
A diagonal

quadrilaterals

qua·drille /kwəˈdrɪl *US:* kwo-/ *n* [C] (music for an) old-fashioned square dance for four couples.

quad·ril·lion /kwoˈdrɪlɪən/ *n* **1** (GB) fourth power of one million (1 followed by 24 ciphers). **2** (US and F) fifth power of one thousand (1 followed by 15 ciphers). ⇨ App 4.

quad·roon /kwoˈdrun/ *n* person of quarter-Negro blood.

quad·ru·ped /ˈkwo-drʊped/ *n* four-footed animal.

quad·ru·ple /ˈkwo-drupl *US:* kwoˈdrupl/ *adj* **1** made up of four parts. **2** agreed to by four persons, parties, etc: *a ~ alliance,* of four Powers. □ *n* number or amount four times as great as another: *20 is the ~ of 5.* □ *vt,vi* [VP6A,2A] multiply by 4: *He has ~d his income/His income has ~d in the last four years.*

quad·ru·plet /ˈkwo-druplɪt *US:* kwoˈdrup-/ *n* (common abbr *quad*) one of four babies at a birth (usu *pl*: *one of the ~s,* not *a ~*).

quad·ru·pli·cate /kwoˈdruplɪkət/ *adj* four times repeated or copied. □ *n* ***in ~,*** in four exactly similar examples or copies. □ *vt* /kwoˈdruplɪkeɪt/ [VP6A] make four specimens of.

quaff /kwof *US:* kwæf/ *vt,vi* [VP6A,15B,2A] (liter) drink deeply: *~ (off) a glass of wine.*

quagga /ˈkwægə/ *n* (now extinct) S African quadruped related to the ass and the zebra.

quag·mire /ˈkwægmɑɪə(r)/ *n* [C] area of soft, wet land; bog; marsh.

Quai d'Or·say /ˌkeɪ dɔˈseɪ/ *n* (F) (used for) French Foreign Office; French foreign policy.

quail[1] /kweɪl/ *n* small bird, similar to a partridge, valued as food: (unchanged in the collective *pl*) *shoot ~ and duck.* ⇨ the illus at fowl.

quail[2] /kweɪl/ *vi* [VP2A,3A] ***~ (at/before),*** feel or show fear; *His heart ~ed. He ~ed at the prospect before him. His eyes ~ed before her angry looks.*

quaint /kweɪnt/ *adj* (-er, -est) attractive or pleasing because unusual or old-fashioned; whimsical; *American visitors to England admire our ~ villages/customs.* **~·ly** *adv* **~·ness** *n*

quake /kweɪk/ *vi* [VP2A,C] **1** (of the earth) shake: *The ground ~d under his feet.* **2** (of persons) tremble; *quaking with fear/cold.* □ *n* (colloq abbr for) earthquake.

Quaker /ˈkweɪkə(r)/ *n* (not used by the members of this Society) member of the Society of Friends, a Christian group that holds informal meetings instead of formal church services and is opposed to the use of violence or resort to war under any circumstances.

quali·fi·ca·tion /ˌkwolɪfɪˈkeɪʃn/ *n* **1** [U] act of qualifying, modifying or limiting; [C] sth which modifies, restricts or limits: *You can accept his statement without ~/with certain ~s.* **2** [C] training, test, etc that qualifies(1) a person; degree, diploma, etc awarded at the end of such training: *a doctor's ~s.*

qual·ify /ˈkwolɪfɑɪ/ *vt,vi* (*pt,pp* -fied) **1** [VP2C, 6A,14,17,16B] ***~ sb (for sth/to do sth/as sth),*** be equipped, equip (sb) by training: *He's qualified/His training qualifies him as a teacher of English/for this post. He's not qualified to teach French. A qualifying examination* (= one at which candidates must reach certain standards for a profession, etc) *will be held next week.* **2** [VP17,4,3A] ***~ (sb) to do sth, ~ for sth:*** *He's the manager's son but that does not ~ him to criticize my work. Do you ~ for the vote/to vote?* **3** [VP6A] limit; make less inclusive, less general: *The statement 'Boys are lazy' needs to be qualified,* e g by saying 'Some boys' or 'Many boys'. **4**

[VP6A] (gram) limit the meaning of; name the qualities of: *Adjectives* ~ *nouns.* **5** [VP16B] **~ sb as,** describe: ~ *a man as an ambitious self-seeker.* **quali·fied** /-faɪd/ *adj* **1** having the necessary qualifications: *a qualified doctor.* **2** limited: *give a scheme one's qualified approval.* **quali·fier** /-faɪə(r)/ *n* (gram) ~ing word, e g an adjective or adverb.

quali·tat·ive /ˈkwɒlɪtətɪv *US:* -teɪt-/ *adj* relating to quality: ~ *analysis.* ⇨ **quantitative.**

qual·ity /ˈkwɒlətɪ/ *n* (*pl* **-ties**) **1** [C,U] (degree, esp high degree, of) goodness or worth: *goods of first-rate* ~. *Poor* ~ *goods won't sell easily. We aim at* ~ *rather than quantity,* aim to produce superior goods, not large quantities. *We manufacture goods in various qualities. He is a man with many good qualities. Give us a taste of your* ~, Show us what accomplishments you have. **2** [C] sth that is special in or that distinguishes a person or thing: *One* ~ *of pine-wood is that it can be sawn easily. He has the* ~ *of inspiring confidence.* **3** [U] (archaic) high social position: *a lady of* ~; *Several of the* ~ *were present.*

qualm /kwɑm/ *n* [C] **1** feeling of doubt (esp about whether one is doing or has done right); misgiving: *He felt no* ~*s about borrowing money from friends.* **2** temporary feeling of sickness in the stomach: ~*s which spoilt his appetite during the first few days of the voyage.*

quan·dary /ˈkwɒndərɪ/ *n* [C] (*pl* **-ries**) state of doubt or perplexity: *be in a* ~ *about what to do next.*

quan·ti·tat·ive /ˈkwɒntɪtətɪv *US:* -teɪt-/ *adj* relating to quantity: ~ *analysis.* ⇨ **qualitative.**

quan·tity /ˈkwɒntətɪ/ *n* (*pl* **-ties**) **1** [U] the property of things which can be measured, e g size, weight, number: *I prefer quality to* ~. *Mathematics is the science of pure* ~. **2** [C] amount, sum or number: *There's only a small* ~ (i e not much or not many) *left. What* ~ *do you want?* **3** (often *pl*) large amount or number; *We've had quantities of rain this summer. He buys things in* ~*/in large quantities.* **4 *an unknown* ~,** (maths) symbol (usu *x*) representing an unknown ~ in an equation; (fig) person or thing whose action, ability etc cannot be foreseen. **~ surveyor,** expert who estimates quantities of materials needed in building, their cost, etc. **bill of ~,** one prepared by a ~ surveyor.

quan·tum /ˈkwɒntəm/ *n* (*pl* **quanta** /-tə/) amount required or desired. ˈ**~ theory,** (phys) the hypothesis that in radiation the energy of electrons is discharged not continuously but in certain fixed amounts (or *quanta*).

quar·an·tine /ˈkwɒrəntin *US:* ˈkwɔr-/ *n* [U] (period of) separation from others until it is known that there is no danger of spreading disease: *be in* ~ *for a week; be out of* ~; (attrib) of the system of ~: *the* ~ *regulations; the* ~ *service. How long will my dog be kept in* ~*?* □ *vt* [VP6A] put in ~: ~*d because of yellow fever.*

quar·rel /ˈkwɒrl *US:* ˈkwɔrl/ *n* [C] **1** angry argument; violent disagreement: *have a* ~ *with sb about sth. They made up their* ~, ended it and became friendly. *He's always fighting other people's* ~*s,* helping them, e g to get social justice. **2** cause for being angry; reason for protest or complaint: *I have no* ~ *with/against him.* ***pick a* ~ *(with sb),*** find or invent some occasion or excuse for disagreement, etc. □ *vi* (-ll-, US also -l-) **1** [VP2A,C,3A] ~ ***(with sb) (about sth),*** have, take part in, a ~: *The thieves* ~*led with one another about how to divide the loot.* **2** [VP3A] ~ ***with,*** disagree with; refuse to accept; complain about. *It's not the fact of examinations I'm* ~*ling with; it's the way they're conducted.* ˈ**~·some** /-səm/ *adj* quick-tempered; fond of ~s.

quarry[1] /ˈkwɒrɪ *US:* ˈkwɔrɪ/ *n* (*pl* **-ries**) (usu *sing*) animal, bird, etc which is hunted; anything eagerly pursued.

quarry[2] /ˈkwɒrɪ *US:* ˈkwɔrɪ/ *n* [C] (*pl* **-ries**) place (not underground like a mine) where stone, slate, etc is obtained (for building, road-making, etc). □ *vt,vi* **1** [VP6A,15A,B] get from a ~: ~ *limestones;* ~ *(out) a block of marble;* (fig) search for (facts, etc) in old books, records, etc. **2** [VP2A,C] engage in work of this kind: ~ *in old manuscripts.* ˈ**~·man** /-mən/ *n* (*pl* **-men**) man who works in a ~.

quart /kwɔt/ *n* measure of capacity equal to two pints or about 1·14 litre. ⇨ **App 5**: *drink a* ~ *of beer.* ***put a* ~ *into a pint pot,*** make the less contain the greater; attempt the impossible.

quar·ter /ˈkwɔtə(r)/ *n* **1** fourth part ($\frac{1}{4}$); one of four equal or corresponding parts: *a* ~ *of a mile; a mile and a* ~; *a* ~ *of an hour,* 15 minutes; *an hour and a* ~; *the first* ~ *of this century,* i e 1901—25. *We've come a* ~ *of the distance now. Divide the apples into* ~*s.* ***a bad* ~ *of an hour,*** a short but unpleasant experience (e g in a dentist's chair). **the ~,** (colloq) race of a ~ of a mile, 440 yds. **2** point of time 15 minutes before or after any hour: *a* ~ *to* (US = *of*) *two; a* ~ *past six. It isn't the* ~ *yet. This clock strikes the hours, the half-hours, and the* ~*s.* **3** three months, esp as a period for which rent and other payments are made: *owe several* ~*s' rent; pay one's rent at the end of each* ~. ˈ**~-day** *n* first day of a legal ~ of the year, on which rents and other three-monthly accounts are paid (in England, 25 Mar, Lady Day; 24 June, Midsummer; 29 Sept, Michaelmas; 25 Dec, Christmas). ˈ**~ sessions,** ⇨ *court of* ~ *sessions* at **court**[1]**(1)**. **4** (US) 25 cents; a ~ of a dollar. **5** joint of meat including a leg: *a* ~ *of beef;* also used of the living animal (usu in compounds, as ˈ*fore-*~*s;* ˈ*hind-*~*s*). **6** direction; district; source of supply. help, information, etc: *men running from all* ~*s/from every* ~; *travel in every* ~ *of the globe,* everywhere. *From what* ~ *does the wind blow? As his father was penniless, he could expect no help from that* ~. *The suggestion did not find favour in the highest* ~*s,* was not welcomed by those at the head of affairs. **7** division of a town, esp one of a special class of people, etc: *the Chinese* ~ *of San Francisco; the manufacturing/residential* ~. **8** one-fourth of a lunar month; the moon's phase at the end of the first or third week; *the moon at the first* ~*/in its last* ~. **9** (*pl*) lodgings; place to stay in: *We found excellent* ~*s at a small inn. I took up* ~*s with a friend. All troops are to return to* ~*s at once,* return to barracks. *The Roman army went into winter* ~*s.* ⇨ **headquarters. 10 *at close* ~*s,*** narrow or limited living space: close together. **married ~s,** houses in or near barracks where members of the armed forces live with their families. **11** post assumed for duty by sailors on a ship, esp for fighting: *Officers and men at once took up their* ~*s.* **12** [U] ***ask for/give* ~,** mercy to an enemy; life granted to a defeated enemy who is willing to surrender: *No* ~ *was asked for and none given,* There were no prisoners. **13** after part of a ship's side: *on the port/starboard* ~. ˋ~**-deck** *n* part of the upper deck between the stern and the aftermast of a warship, reserved for officers; officers of a warship or navy. ⇨ *lower deck* at **low**[1]**(13), forecastle. 14** (GB) fourth part of a hundredweight, 28 lb; (US) 25 lb; grain-measure of eight bushels. ⇨ App 5. **15** one of the four parts of a shield used in armorial bearings. **16** (compounds) ˈ~-ˋ**final** *n* (sport) one of four competitions or matches, the winners of which play in the semi-finals. ˋ~**-light** *n* triangular section at the front or back window of a car, opened to admit air. ˋ~**-master** *n* **(a)** (army) (abbr **QM**) officer in charge of the stores, etc of a battalion. **(b)** (navy) petty officer in charge of steering the ship, signals, etc. ˈ~**-master-ˋgeneral** *n* (abbr **QMG**) staff officer in charge of supplies for a whole army. ˋ~**-plate** *n* photographic plate 3¼ inches × 4½ inches; photograph made from it. ˋ~**-staff** *n* strong pole, 6 to 8 ft long, formerly used as a weapon and in a rough kind of fencing. □ *vt* **1** [VP6A] divide into ~s: ~ *an apple;* (in former times) divide (a traitor's body) into ~s: *condemned to be hanged, drawn* (= disembowelled) *and* ~*ed.* **2** [VP6A,15A] find lodgings for (troops); place (troops) in lodgings: ~ *troops on the villagers.* ~**·ing** *n* method of arranging two or more coats of arms, to show alliances with or descent from various families; coat of arms resulting from this.

quar·ter·ly /ˋkwɔtəlɪ/ *adj, adv* (happening) once in each three months: ~ *payments/subscriptions; to be paid* ~. □ *n* (*pl* **-lies**) periodical published ~.

quar·tern /ˋkwɔtən/ *n* **1** one-fourth of a pint; gill. **2** ˋ~**(-loaf)**, a loaf of bread weighing 4 lb.

quar·tet, quar·tette /kwɔˋtet/ *n* (piece of music for) four players or singers: *a string* ~, for (usu) two violins, viola and cello; *a piano* ~, for piano and three stringed instruments.

quarto /ˋkwɔtəʊ/ *n* (*pl* **-tos** /-təʊz/) (also written **4to**) size given by folding a sheet of paper twice (making four leaves or eight pages); book made of sheets so folded (usu about 9 by 12 in): *the first* ~ *of 'Hamlet'.*

quartz /ˋkwɔts/ *n* [U] sorts of hard mineral (esp crystallized silica), including agate and other semi-precious stones: *a* ˋ~ *clock,* one of very great accuracy, with ~ oscillators.

quash /kwɒʃ/ *vt* [VP6A] put an end to, annul, reject as not valid (by legal procedure): ~ *a verdict/decision.*

quasi- /ˋkweɪsɑɪ/ *pref* (with a *n* or *adj*) half; seeming(ly): *a* ~*-official position.* ⇨ App 3.

quas·sia /ˋkwɒʃə/ *n* [U] (bitter drug used medicinally and obtained from the) wood or bark of a S American tree; the tree.

quat·er·cen·ten·ary /ˈkwætəsenˋtinərɪ *US:* ˈkwɒtərˋsentn̩erɪ/ *n* 400th anniversary: *the* ~ *celebrations in 1964 of Shakespeare's birth.*

quat·rain /ˋkwɒtreɪn/ *n* verse of four lines, usu rhyming *a b a b.*

quat·tro·cento /ˈkwætrəʊˋtʃentəʊ/ *n* (I) the 15th century as a period of Italian art and literature.

qua·ver /ˋkweɪvə(r)/ *vt,vi* **1** [VP2A] (of the voice or a sound) shake; tremble: *in a* ~*ing voice; in a voice that* ~*ed.* **2** [VP6A,15B] say or sing in a shaking voice: *She* ~*ed (out/forth) her little song.* □ *n* [C] **1** ~ing sound. **2** musical note with one-half the time value of a crotchet. ⇨ the illus at **notation**.

quay /ki/ *n* solid, stationary landing-place usu built of stone or iron, alongside which ships can be tied up for loading and unloading.

quean /kwin/ *n* (archaic) impudent or ill-behaved girl; hussy.

queasy /ˋkwizɪ/ *adj* (**-ier, -iest**) **1** (of food) causing a feeling of sickness in the stomach. **2** (of the stomach) easily upset. **3** (of a person) easily made sick; feeling sick. **4** (fig, of a person or his conscience) over-scrupulous, tender or delicate. **queas·ily** /-əlɪ/ *adv* **queasi·ness** *n*

queen /kwin/ *n* **1** woman ruler in her own right: *the Q*~ *of England; Q*~ *Elizabeth* II. **2** wife of a king: *King William* III *and Q*~ *Mary* II. **3** ~ *dowager,* widow of a king. ~ **mother,** ~ dowager who is the mother of a reigning Sovereign. **4** woman regarded as first of a group: *the* ~ *of the May;* ˋ*May Q*~, girl chosen as ~ in old-time May Day ceremonies; town or place regarded as occupying a leading position: *Venice, the* ~ *of the Adriatic.* ˋ**beauty** ~**,** winner of a beauty contest. **5** ~ **ant/bee/wasp,** fertile, egg-producing ant/bee, etc. **6** (chess) most powerful piece for attack or defence; ⇨ the illus at **chess;** (cards) one with the picture of a ~: *the* ~ *of spades/hearts.* **7** (GB sl) (elderly) male homosexual. □ *vt* ~ ***it over sb,*** act like a ~; assume the leadership. ~**·ly** *adj* like a ~; fit for a ~; majestic; generous: ~*ly robes; her* ~*ly duties.*

queer /kwɪə(r)/ *adj* **1** strange; unusual: *a* ~ *way of talking.* **2** causing doubt or suspicion: *a* ~ *character;* ~ *noises in the attic.* **3** (colloq) unwell; faint: *feel very* ~. **4** (sl, of a man) homosexual. **5** ***in*** ˋ***Q***~ ***street,*** (GB sl) in debt; in trouble. □ *n* homosexual. □ *vt* [VP6A] (sl) put out of order; cause to go wrong, esp ~ ***sb's pitch,*** ⇨ **pitch**[1]**(1)**. ~**·ly** *adv* ~**·ness** *n*

quell /kwel/ *vt* [VP6A] (poet and rhet) suppress, subdue (a rebellion, rebels, opposition).

quench /kwentʃ/ *vt* [VP6A] **1** put out (flames, fire). **2** satisfy (thirst). **3** put an end to (hope). **4** cool in water: ~ *steel.* ~**·less** *adj* that cannot be, or is never, ~ed: *a* ~*less flame.*

quern /kwɜn/ *n* mill for grinding corn by hand; small hand-mill for pepper, etc.

queru·lous /ˋkwerjələs/ *adj* full of complaints; fretful: *in a* ~ *tone.* ~**·ly** *adv* ~**·ness** *n*

query /ˋkwɪərɪ/ *n* [C] (*pl* **-ries**) **1** question, esp one raising a doubt about the truth of sth: *raise a* ~. **2** the mark (?) put against sth, e g in the margin of a document, as a sign of doubt. □ *vt* **1** [VP10] ~ ***whether/if,*** inquire: *I* ~ *whether his word can be relied on.* **2** [VP6A] express doubt about: ~ *a person's instructions.* **3** [VP6A] put the mark (?) against.

quest /kwest/ *n* [C] **1** search or pursuit: *the* ~ *for gold.* **in** ~ **of,** (old or liter use) seeking for, trying to find: *He went off in* ~ *of food.* **2** (old use) *coroner's* ~, coroner's inquest. □ *vt* [VP3A] ~ ***for,*** (esp of dogs) look for; (formal) go about in ~ of: ~*ing for further evidence.*

ques·tion[1] /ˋkwestʃən/ *n* **1** sentence which by word-order, use of interrogative words (*who, why,* etc) or intonation, requests information, an answer, etc: *ask a lot of* ~*s; put a* ~ *to sb.* ˋ~**-mark** *n* the mark (?). ˋ~**-master** *n* (in panel games) chairman. ˋ~ **time,** (in the House of Commons) period of time during which ministers answer ~s put to them by members. **2** sth about which there is discussion; sth which needs to be decided; inquiry; problem; affair: *a difficult/vexed ~; economic ~s. Success is only a ~ of time,* will certainly come sooner or later. *The ~ is...,* What we want to know, what we must decide, is.... *That's not the ~,* not the matter being discussed. **in ~,** being talked about: *Where's the man in ~?* **out of the ~,** impossible; not to be discussed at all: *We can't go out in this weather; it's out of the ~.* **be some/no, etc ~ of,** some/no, etc discussion of: *There was no ~ of my being invited to become Chairman,* that was not discussed or proposed. **beg the ~,** ⇨ beg(2). **come into ~,** be discussed, become of practical importance: *If sending me in a spacecraft to the moon ever comes into ~, I shall refuse without hesitation.* **Q~!** (at a public meeting) used to warn a speaker that he is not keeping to the subject being discussed, or (less correctly) to express doubt about the truth of sth he has said. **put the ~,** (at a meeting) ask those present to record their votes for or against the proposal. **3** [U] (the putting forward of) doubt, objection: *There is no ~ about/some ~ as to his honesty. There is no ~ but that he will* (= He will undoubtedly) *succeed.* **beyond (all)/without ~,** certain(ly); without doubt. *His integrity is beyond all ~. Without ~, he's the best man for the job.* **call sth in ~,** raise objections to, express doubt about, it: *No one has ever called my honesty in ~. His conduct was called in ~.* **4** (archaic) torture (as a means of obtaining confession): *put a man to the ~.*

ques·tion[2] /ˈkwestʃən/ *vt* **1** [VP6A] ask a ~ or ~s of; examine: *He was ~ed by the police. They ~ed the Conservative candidate on his views.* **2** [VP6A,10] ~ ***(whether/if),*** express or feel doubt about: *~ sb's veracity; ~ the value/importance of compulsory games as school. I ~ whether his proposal will be approved.* **ˈ~·able** /-əbl/ *adj* which may be ~ed(2): *a ~able assertion.* **ˈ~·ably** /-əblɪ/ *adv* **~er** *n* person who ~s(1). **~·ing·ly** *adv* in a ~ing manner.

ques·tion·naire /ˌkwestʃəˈneə(r)/ *n* list of (usu printed) questions to be answered by a group of people, esp to get facts or information, or for a survey.

quet·zal /ˈkwetsl *US:* ketˈsæl/ *n* beautiful bird of Central America; monetary unit of Guatemala.

queue /kju/ *n* **1** line of people waiting for their turn (e g to enter a cinema, get on a bus, buy sth): *form a ~; stand in a ~.* **jump the ~,** ⇨ jump[2](6). **2** line of vehicles waiting to proceed: *a ~ of cars held up by the traffic lights.* **3** plait of hair hanging down over the back of the neck (e g part of a wig, as worn by men in Europe in former times). □ *vi* ~ ***(up) (for),*** get into, be in, a ~: *~ up for a bus; ~ up to buy tickets for the pop festival.*

quibble /ˈkwɪbl/ *n* [C] evasion of the main point of an argument, attempt to escape giving an honest answer, by using a secondary or doubtful meaning of a word or phrase. □ *vi* ~ ***(over),*** use ~s; argue about small points or differences: *~ over trivialities.* **quib·bler** *n* **quib·bling** *adj*

quick /kwɪk/ *adj* (-er, -est) **1** moving fast; able to move fast and do things in a short time; done in a short time: *a ~ train/worker; walking at a ~ pace; have a ~ meal; find ~ ways of doing sth/getting somewhere. Be ~ about it!* Hurry up! *Try to be a little ~er. She's as ~ as lightning. The flashes of lightning came in ~ succession,* at very short intervals of time; *We just have time for a ~ one,* (usu = a ~ (alcoholic) drink). ***(in)*** **~ time,** (at) the ordinary rate of marching for soldiers (about four miles an hour). **~ march** *int* (command to) begin marching in ~ time. **ˈ~·step** *n* quick ballroom dancing step: *The next dance will be a ~step.* **ˈ~-ˈchange** *attrib adj* (of an actor, etc) ~ly changing his appearance, costume, etc to play another part: *a ~-ˈchange artist.* **ˈ~-freeze** *vt* freeze (food) very ~ly so as to keep the natural flavours unchanged: *~-frozen foods.* **ˈ~-ˈlunch bar/counter** *n* self-service one at which meals are served very ~ly. **2** lively; bright; active; prompt: *~ to understand; a ~ ear for music; ~ to make up one's mind/to seize an opportunity; ~ at figures; a ~* (= intelligent) *child; not very ~,* (colloq, of a child) rather dull or stupid; *a ~ temper,* one that is soon aroused. **ˈ~-ˈeared/-ˈeyed/-ˈsighted/-ˈtempered/-ˈwitted** *adjj* having ~ ears/eyes/sight, etc. **3** (old use) living. **the ~ and the dead.** □ *n* [U] tender or sensitive flesh below the skin, esp the nails: *bite one's nails to the ~.* **cut/touch sb to the ~,** hurt his feelings deeply. □ *adv* (-er, -est) (common in colloq use for *quickly,* always placed after the *v*). **1** *You're walking too ~ for me. Can't you run ~er? He wants to get rich ~. I don't know any get-rich-~ methods.* **2** (in compounds, for *~ly*) a ~-firing gun. **~·ly** *adv* **~·ness** *n*

quicken /ˈkwɪkən/ *vt,vi* [VP6A,2A] **1** make or become quick(er): *We ~ed our pace. Our pace ~ed.* **2** make or become more lively, vigorous or active: *Good literature ~s the imagination. His pulse ~ed. The child ~ed in her womb,* She felt its movement for the first time.

quickie /ˈkwɪkɪ/ *n* (colloq) sth made or done very quickly, e g a cheap film made or used to fill up a programme.

quick·lime /ˈkwɪklaɪm/ *n* unslaked lime. ⇨ lime[1](1).

quick·sand /ˈkwɪksænd/ *n* [C] (area of) loose, wet, deep sand which sucks down men, animals, vehicles, etc that try to cross it.

quick·set /ˈkwɪkset/ *adj* (of hedges) formed of living plants, esp hawthorn, set in the ground to grow.

quick·sil·ver /ˈkwɪksɪlvə(r)/ *n* [U] mercury.

quick·step /ˈkwɪkstep/ *n* ⇨ quick(1).

quid[1] /kwɪd/ *n* lump of chewing tobacco.

quid[2] /kwɪd/ *n* (GB, sl; *pl* unchanged) pound: *earning twenty quid* (= £20) *a week.*

quid pro quo /ˈkwɪd prəʊ ˈkwəʊ/ *n* (Lat) sth given or returned as the equivalent of sth else.

qui·esc·ent /kwaɪˈesnt/ *adj* at rest; motionless; passive. **~·ly** *adv* **qui·esc·ence** /-sns/ *n*

quiet /ˈkwaɪət/ *adj* (-er, -est) **1** with little or no movement or sound: *a ~ sea; a ~ evening; ~ footsteps.* **2** free from excitement, trouble, anxiety: *live a ~ life in the country; have a ~ mind; ~ times.* **3** gentle; not rough (in disposition, etc): *~ children; a ~ old lady.* **4** (of colours) not bright. **5** not open or revealed: *harbouring ~ resentment.* **keep sth ~,** keep it secret. **on the ~,** (or, sl, **on the q t** /ˈkju ˈti/), secretly: *have a drink on the ~; tell sb sth on the ~,* in confidence. □ *n* [U] state of being ~ (all senses): *in the ~ of the night; have an hour's ~,* an hour free from activity, disturbance, etc; *live in peace and ~; a period of ~ after an election,* free from all the activity, etc that usu accompanies an election. □

vt,vi (more usu **quieten** /ˋkwɑɪətn/) [VP6A,15B, 2C] make or become ~: ~*(en) a fretful child;* ~*(en) sb's fears/suspicions. The city* ~*ed/*~*ened down after the political disturbances.* **~·ly** *adv* **~·ness** *n*

quiet·ism /ˋkwɑɪət-ɪzm/ *n* [U] (as a form of religious mysticism) the abandoning of all desire, with a passive acceptance of whatever comes. **quiet·ist** /-ɪst/ *n* person who follows this principle.

quiet·ude /ˋkwɑɪətjud *US:* -tud/ *n* stillness; tranquillity.

qui·etus /kwɑɪˋitəs/ *n* (old use) release from life; extinction: *give sb his* ~, put an end to his life.

quiff /kwɪf/ *n* lock of hair brushed up above the forehead.

quill /kwɪl/ *n* **1** ˋ**~(-feather),** large wing or tail feather; (hollow stem of) such a feather as formerly used for writing with: *a* ~ *pen.* **2** long, sharp, stiff spine of a porcupine.

quilt /kwɪlt/ *n* thick bed-covering of two layers of cloth padded with soft material kept in place by cross lines of stitches. ⇨ **duvet.** □ *vt* make in the form of a ~, i e with soft material between layers of cloth: *a* ~*ed dressing-gown.*

quin /kwɪn/ *n* (colloq) one of five children at a birth. (abbr for, and more usu than, *quintuplet*).

quince /kwɪns/ *n* (tree with) hard, acid, pear-shaped fruit, deep yellow when ripe, used in jams and jellies.

quin·cen·ten·ary /ˌkwɪnsənˋtinərɪ *US:* -ˋsentṇerɪ/ *adj, n* (of the) 500th anniversary.

quin·ine /kwɪˋnin *US:* ˋkwɑɪnɑɪn/ *n* [U] bitter liquid made from the bark of a tree and used as a medicine for fevers.

Quin·qua·ges·ima /ˌkwɪŋkwəˋdʒesɪmə/ *n* the Sunday before Lent.

quinsy /ˋkwɪnzɪ/ *n* [U] inflammation of the throat with discharge of pus from the tonsils.

quin·tal /ˋkwɪntl/ *n* unit of weight, 100 or 112 lb or 100 kilograms.

quin·tes·sence /kwɪnˋtesns/ *n* perfect example: *the* ~ *of virtue/politeness.*

quin·tet, quin·tette /kwɪnˋtet/ *n* (piece of music for) group of five players or singers. *piano* ~, string quartet and piano. *string* ~, string quartet and an additional cello or viola. *wind* ~, bassoon, clarinet, flute, horn and oboe.

quin·tu·plet /ˋkwɪntjuplɪts *US:* kwɪnˋtuplɪts/ *n* (common abbr *quin*) one of five children at a birth. (*Two of the* ~*s* is commoner than *two* ~*s*).

quip /kwɪp/ *n* clever, witty or sarcastic remark or saying; quibble. □ *vi* (-pp-) make ~s.

quire /ˋkwɑɪə(r)/ *n* twenty-four sheets of writing-paper: *buy/sell paper by the* ~*/in* ~*s.*

Quiri·nal /ˋkwɪrɪnl/ *n* (used for the) Italian Government (esp as contrasted with the Vatican).

quirk /kwɜk/ *n* **1** quip; quibble. **2** trick of action or behaviour.

quis·ling /ˋkwɪzlɪŋ/ *n* person who co-operates with the authorities of an enemy country who are occupying his country.

quit¹ /kwɪt/ *pred adj* free, clear: *We are well* ~ *of him,* fortunate to be rid of him.

quit² /kwɪt/ *vt* (-tt-, US also -t-; *pt* ~ted or ~) **1** [VP6A,2A] go away from; leave: *I* ~*ted him in disgust. We've had notice to* ~, a warning that we must give up the house we rent. *I've given my secretary notice to* ~, told her that she must leave my service. **2** [VP6A,D] stop: ~ *work when the siren sounds;* ~ *grumbling. Q*~ *that!* Stop doing that! **3** (old use; reflex) acquit: *They* ~*ted themselves like heroes.* **quit·ter** *n* (colloq) person who does not finish what he has started, esp sth undertaken as a duty.

quite /kwɑɪt/ *adv* **1** completely; altogether: *He has* ~ *recovered from his illness. I* ~ *agree/understand. She was* ~ *alone. See that your watch is* ~ (= exactly) *right. That man is not* ~ *acceptable. It was* ~ (= at least) *six weeks ago. That's* ~ *another* (i e a completely different) *story.* ~ ***the thing,*** (colloq) what is considered correct, fashionable, etc: *These Italian dress materials are* ~ *the thing this summer.* **2** to a certain extent; more or less; in some degree: (preceding articles and *adjj*) ~ *a good player. It's* ~ *warm today. He was* ~ *polite, but he wasn't ready to help me. She* ~ *likes him, but not enough to marry him.* **3** really; truly: *They are both* ~ *young. She's* ~ *a beauty. I believe they're* ~ *happy together.* **4** (used to indicate agreement, understanding, polite acquiescence): A: *'It's a difficult situation'.* B: *'Q*~ *(so)!'* A: *'I'm so sorry; I'm afraid I sat on your hat'.* B: *'Oh, that's* ~ *all right'.*

quits /kwɪts/ *pred adj* ***be*** **~ *(with sb),*** be on even terms (by repaying a debt of money, punishment, etc): *We're* ~ *now. I'll be* ~ *with him,* will have my revenge. ***call it*** **~,** agree that things are even, that a dispute or quarrel may cease. ***double or*** **~,** ⇨ **double³(1).**

quit·tance /ˋkwɪtns/ *n* (document giving) release from an obligation or debt.

quiver¹ /ˋkwɪvə(r)/ *n* archer's sheath for carrying arrows.

quiver² /ˋkwɪvə(r)/ *vt,vi* [VP6A,2A] (cause to) tremble slightly or vibrate: *a* ~*ing leaf. The moth* ~*ed its wings.* □ *n* ~ing sound or movement.

qui vive /ˌki ˋviv/ *n* (only in) ***on the*** **~,** on the alert; watchful.

quix·otic /kwɪkˋsotɪk/ *adj* generous, unselfish, imaginative, in a way that disregards one's own welfare. **quix·oti·cally** /-klɪ/ *adv*

quiz /kwɪz/ *vt* (-zz-) [VP6A] **1** ask questions of, as a test of knowledge. **2** (old use) make fun of; tease. **3** (in former times) stare at impudently or curiously through an eye-glass. □ *n* **1** (modern use) general knowledge test; (broadcasting) game in which members of a panel undergo such a test. ˋ**~-master,** = question-master. **2** (older use, e g in the novels of Jane Austen) amused, supercilious look.

quiz·zi·cal /ˋkwɪzɪkl/ *adj* **1** comical; causing amusement. **2** teasing: *a* ~ *smile.* **~ly** /-klɪ/ *adv*

quod /kwod/ *n* (GB sl) prison.

quoin /kɔɪn/ *n* exterior angle in the brickwork or stonework of a building; cornerstone.

quoit /kɔɪt *US:* kwɔɪt/ *n* ring (of metal, rubber, rope) to be thrown at a peg so as to encircle it; (*pl*) this game (as often played on the deck of a ship).

quon·dam /ˋkwondæm/ *attrib adj* (old use) that once was but is not now: *a* ~ *friend.*

Quonset /ˋkwonsɪt/ *n* ˋ**~ (hut),** (US) (P) large prefabricated hut, usu of corrugated iron, semicircular at each end and with a rounded roof, similar to, but much larger than, a Nissen hut.

quorum /ˋkwɔrəm/ *n* (*pl* ~s) number of persons who must, by the rules, be present at a meeting (of a committee, etc) before its proceedings can have authority: have/form a ~.

quota /ˋkwəʊtə/ *n* limited share, amount or number, esp a quantity of goods allowed to be manufactured, sold, etc or number, e g of immigrants allowed to enter a country: *The village was unable to raise its ~ of men for the army. The ~ of immigrants for this year has already been filled.*

quo·ta·tion /kwəʊˋteɪʃn/ *n* **1** [U] quoting(**1**). **2** [C] sth quoted(**1**): *~s from Shakespeare.* **ˋ~ marks,** the marks (" " or ' ') enclosing words quoted. **3** [C] statement of the current price of an article, etc: *the latest ~s from the Stock Exchange.* **4** [C] estimate of the cost of a piece of work: *Can you give me a ~ for building a garage?*

quote /kwəʊt/ *vt* **1** [VP6A,14] **~ *(from),*** repeat, write (words used by another); repeat or write words (from a book, an author, etc): *~ a verse from the Bible; ~ the Bible. Is Shakespeare the author most frequently ~d from? He is ~d as having said that there will be an election this autumn.* **2** [VP6A,13] give (a reference, etc) to support a statement: *Can you ~ (me) a recent instance?* **3** [VP6A] name, mention (a price): *This is the best price I can ~ you. The shares are ~d on the Stock Exchange at 80p.* **quot·able** /-əbl/ *adj* that can be, or deserves to be, ~d. **quo·ta·bil·ity** /ˌkwəʊtəˋbɪlətɪ/ *n* [U].

quoth /kwəʊθ/ *vt* (1st and 3rd person *sing, pt* only) said: *~ I/he/she. 'Q~ the raven, "Nevermore!"'*

quo·tid·ian /kwəʊˋtɪdɪən/ *adj* (of fevers) recurring every day.

quo·tient /ˋkwəʊʃnt/ *n* (maths) number obtained by dividing one number by another.

Rr

R, r /ɑ(r)/ (*pl* **R's, r's** /ɑz/) the eighteenth letter of the English alphabet. **the three R's,** reading, (w)riting and (a)rithmetic as the basis of an elementary education.

rabbi /ˋræbɑɪ/ *n* teacher of the Jewish law; (title of a) spiritual leader of a Jewish congregation. **rab·bini·cal** /rəˋbɪnɪkl/ *adj* of ~s, their learning, writings, etc.

rab·bit /ˋræbɪt/ *n* **1** small burrowing animal of the hare family, brownish-grey in its natural state, black or white or bluish-grey in domestic varieties. the illus at small. **ˋ~-hole/-burrow** *nn* hole in which wild ~s live. **ˋ~-hutch** *n* wooden cage for domestic ~s. **ˋ~-punch** *n* punch on the back of the neck. **ˋ~-warren** *n* area of land full of ~-burrows; area of narrow, winding streets or rooms and passages. **ˌWelsh ˋ~,** = rarebit. **2** (colloq) poor performer at any game, esp tennis. □ *vt* (-tt-) hunt ~s: *go ~ting.*

rabble /ˋræbl/ *n* **1** disorderly crowd; mob. **ˋ~-rousing** *adj* inciting, designed to rouse, the passions of the mob: *~-rousing speeches/speakers.* **2 the ~,** (contemptuous) the lower classes of the populace.

Rab·elais·ian /ˌræbəˋleɪzɪən *US:* -eɪʒn/ *adj* of or like the writings, marked by coarse humour and satire, of Rabelais /ˋræbəleɪ/, 1490—1553, French writer.

rabid /ˋræbɪd/ *adj* **1** affected with rabies; mad. **2** furious; fanatical; violent: *~ hate; a ~ Socialist/Conservative,* one with extreme views, forcefully expressed.

ra·bies /ˋreɪbiz/ *n* [U] infectious disease causing madness in wolves, dogs and other animals; hydrophobia.

rac·coon = racoon.

race[1] /reɪs/ *n* [C] **1** contest or competition in speed, e g in running, swimming or to see who can finish a piece of work, or get to a certain place, first: *a ˋhorse-~; a ˋboat-~; a half-ˋmile ~; run a ~ with sb; a ~ for a train,* an effort to catch it. ***a ~ against time,*** an effort to do sth before a certain time or possible event. **ˋ~-card** *n* programme of a ~-meeting with a list of ~s and names of horses. **ˋ~-course** *n* ground where horse-~s are run. **ˋ~-horse** *n* horse specially bred for running ~s. **ˋ~-meeting** *n* occasion when a number of horse-~s are held on a certain ~-course on a certain day, or a number of successive days: *the Epsom ~-meeting.* **the ~s,** ~-meeting. **2** strong, fast current of water in the sea, a river, etc: *a ˋmill-~,* the channel carrying water to the wheel of a water-mill. **3** (liter) course of the sun or moon, or (fig) of life: *His ~ is nearly run,* He is near the end of his life. □ *vi,vt* **1** [VP2A,C,4A] **~ *(with/against sb),*** compete in speed, have a ~; move at full speed: *~ along; ~ over the course; boys racing home from school; ~ to see what is happening; ~ against time; ~ with sb for a prize. I'll ~ you home,* (colloq) ~ against you to get home first. **2** [VP2A,6A] own or train horses for racing and take part in ~-meetings; cause (a horse) to compete in ~s: *He ~s at all the big meetings. Are you going to ~ your horse at Newmarket next week?* **3** [VP6A,15A] cause (sth or sb) to move at full speed: *He ~d me to the station in his car. The Government ~d the bill through the House,* pushed it through the House of Commons at great speed. *Don't ~ your engine,* cause the engine to run very fast when it is not doing any work. [VP2A] *Don't let the engine ~.* **rac·ing** *n* [U] (esp) the hobby, sport or profession of running horses or motor-cars in races: *a ˋracing man; keep a racing stable; a ˋracing car/yacht,* designed for racing. **racer** *n* horse, car, etc designed for racing.

race[2] /reɪs/ *n* **1** [C,U] any of several subdivisions of mankind sharing certain physical characteristics, esp colour of skin, colour and type of hair, shape of eyes and nose: *the ˋNegroid ~; the Cauˋcasian/ˋwhite ~; people of mixed ~; people of the same ~ but different culture.* **2** [C] (used loosely for) group of people having a common culture, history and/or language: *the ˌAngloˋSaxon ~; the ˋGerman ~.* **3** (attrib) of, between, ~s(**1,2**): *Can ~ relations be improved by legislation?* **4** [U] ancestry: descent; a man of ancient and noble ~. **5** [C] main division of any living creatures: *the human ~,* mankind; *the ˋfeathered ~,* (joc) birds; *the ˋfinny ~,* (joc) fish.

ra·ceme /reɪˋsim/ *n* (bot) flower cluster with the separate flowers on short equal stalks springing from a main central stem, the lowest flowers opening first.

racial /ˋreɪʃl/ *adj* relating to ⇨ race[2](**1,2**): *~ con-*

flict/hatred/pride; ~ minorities; ~ discrimination. **~ly** /-ʃlɪ/ *adv* **~·ism** /-ɪzm/ *n* [U] tendency to ~ conflict; antagonism between different races; belief that one's own race is superior. **~·ist** /-ɪst/ *n* person who supports, stirs up, ~ism.

rac·ily, raci·ness ⇨ racy.

rac·ism /ˈreɪs-ɪsm/ *n* racialism. **rac·ist** /-ɪst/ *n* = racialist.

rack[1] /ræk/ *n* **1** wooden or metal framework for holding food (esp hay) for animals (in a stable or in the fields). **2** framework with bars, pegs, etc for holding things, hanging things on, etc: *a ˈplate-~; a ˈhat-~; a ˈtool-~.* **3** shelf over the seats of a railway-carriage, air-liner, bus, etc for light luggage: *a ˈluggage-~.* **4** rod, bar or rail with teeth or cogs into which the teeth on a wheel (or pinion) fit (as used on special railways up a steep hillside). **ˈ~-railway** *n* one with a third rail with cogs between the two rails on which the wheels of trains are supported.

rack[2] /ræk/ *n* (usu *the rack*) instrument of torture consisting of a frame with rollers to which a person's wrists and ankles were tied so that his joints were stretched when the rollers were turned. ***on the ~,*** undergoing severe suffering (physical or mental. □ *vt* [VP6A,15A] **1** torture by placing on the ~; (of a disease or of mental agony) inflict torture on: *~ed with pain; a ~ing headache; ~ed with a bad cough; ~ed by remorse.* **2** ***~ one's brains (for),*** make great mental efforts (for, in order to find, an answer, method, etc). **3** oppress (tenants) with excessive rent. Hence, **ˈ~-rent** *n* exorbitant rent.

rack[3] /ræk/ *n* [U] **1** (liter) drifting cloud.

rack[4] /ræk/ *n* (only in) ***go to ~ and ruin.*** fall into a ruined state.

racket[1] /ˈrækɪt/ *n* **1** (*sing* only, with *indef art* or [U]) uproar, loud noise: *What a ~! The drunken men in the street kicked up no end of a ~,* were very noisy and boisterous. **2** [U] (time of) great social activity, hurry and bustle: *the ~ of modern life. I can't stand the ~ of the London season,* all the cocktail and dinner parties, social engagements, etc. *He has gone on/is on the ~ again,* having a gay (perhaps dissipated) time. **3** [C] (orig US; colloq) dishonest way of getting money (by deceiving or threatening people, selling worthless goods, etc): *be in on a ~,* have a share in it, be one of those who make money from it. **4** [C] ordeal or trying experience. ***stand the ~,*** **(a)** come successfully through a test (of sth). **(b)** accept, be responsible for, the consequences (of sth); take the blame, pay the costs. □ *vi* [VP2A,C] lead a gay social life: *She's still ~ing about.* ⇨ 2 above. **~·eer** /ˌrækɪˈtɪə(r)/ *n* person who is engaged in a ~(3). **~·eer·ing** *n* [U] the actions of ~eers. **rackety** *adj*: *lead a ~y life,* be always engaged in social activities, etc. ⇨ 2 above.

racket[2], **rac·quet** /ˈrækɪt/ *n* **1** light bat used for hitting the ball in tennis, badminton, etc. ⇨ the illus at badminton, tennis. **2** (*pl*) ball-game for two or four players in a court with four walls.

rac·on·teur /ˌrækonˈtɜ(r)/ *n* person who tells anecdotes or stories with skill and wit: *a good ~.*

ra·coon, rac·coon /rəˈkun *US:* ræ-/ *n* small, flesh-eating animal of N America with a bushy, ringed tail; (US) its fur.

rac·quet = racket[2].

racy /ˈreɪsɪ/ *adj* (-ier, -iest) **1** (of speech or writing) vivid; spirited; vigorous: *a ~ style.* **2** having strongly marked qualities: *a ~ flavour; ~ of the soil,* showing traces of origin; lively and stimulating. **rac·ily** /-əlɪ/ *adv* **raci·ness** *n*

radar /ˈreɪdɑ(r)/ *n* [U] (the use of) apparatus that indicates on a screen (by means of radio echoes) solid objects that come within its range, used (e g by pilots of ships, aircraft or spacecraft) in fog or darkness and which gives information about their position, movement, speed, etc: *follow the flight of an aircraft by ~;* (attrib) *ˈ~ installation; on the ˈ~ screen.*

radial /ˈreɪdɪəl/ *adj* relating to a ray, rays or a radius; (of spokes in a bicycle wheel, etc) from a centre; arranged like rays or radii. □ *n* **~ (tyre),** tyre designed (by having the material inside the tyre wrapped in a direction ~ to the hub of the wheel) to give more grip on road surfaces, esp when cornering or when roads are wet. **~ly** /-ɪəlɪ/ *adv*

radi·ant /ˈreɪdɪənt/ *adj* **1** sending out rays of light; shining: *the ~ sun.* **2** (of a person, his looks, eyes) bright; showing joy or love: *a ~ face; the ~ figures in the paintings of Renoir.* **3** (in physics) transmitted by radiation: *~ heat/energy.* **~·ly** *adv* **radi·ance** /-əns/ *n* [U] ~ quality.

radi·ate /ˈreɪdɪeɪt/ *vt,vi* **1** [VP6A] send out rays of (light or heat): *a stove that ~s warmth;* (fig) spread abroad, send out: *a woman who ~s happiness; an orator who ~s enthusiasm for the cause he supports.* **2** [VP2A,3A] **~ from,** come or go out in rays; show: *heat that ~s from a stove/a fireplace; the happiness that ~s from her eyes.* **3** [VP2A,3A] spread out like radii: *the avenues that ~ from the Arc de Triomphe in Paris.*

radi·ation /ˌreɪdɪˈeɪʃn/ *n* **1** [U] radiating; the sending out of energy, heat, etc in rays. **ˈ~ sickness,** illness caused by gamma rays or rays from radioactive dust (as from nuclear weapons). **2** [C] sth radiated: *~s emitted by an X-ray apparatus.*

radi·ator /ˈreɪdɪeɪtə(r)/ *n* [C] **1** apparatus for radiating heat, esp heat from steam or hot water supplied through pipes or from electric current. **2** device for cooling the cylinders of the engine of a motor-vehicle: *This car has a fan-cooled ~.*

rad·ical /ˈrædɪkl/ *adj* **1** of or from the root or base; fundamental: *~ (= thorough and complete) reforms; make ~ changes in a scheme.* **2** (politics) favouring fundamental reforms; advanced in opinions and policies: *a member of the R~ Party.* **3** (maths) relating to the root of a number or quantity: *the ~ sign* (√). □ *n* **1** person with ~(2) opinions; member of the R~ Party. **2** (maths) the ~ sign; a quantity expressed as the root of another. **~ly** /-klɪ/ *adv* **~·ism** /-ɪzm/ *n* beliefs and policies of ~s.

rad·icle /ˈrædɪkl/ *n* embryo root (e g of a pea or bean).

radii /ˈreɪdɪaɪ/ ⇨ radius.

radio /ˈreɪdɪəʊ/ *n* (*pl* -dios /-dɪəʊz/) **1** [U] (communication by) ~ telegraphy or telephony: *send a message by ~.* **2** [U] broadcasting by this means: *hear something on the ~; talk over the ~;* (attrib) *the ~ programme.* **3** [C] **ˈ~(-set),** apparatus, e g on ships, aircraft, for transmitting and receiving ~ messages or (as in the home) for receiving sound broadcast programmes: *a portable ~; the latest types of ~s/~-sets.* **4** **ˈ~ beacon,** station for transmitting signals to help aircraft pilots. **ˈ~ beam,** beam of ~ signals from a ~ beacon. **ˈ~ frequency,** frequency between 10 kilocycles per second to 300 000 megacycles per second. ˋ~ **link,** (sound broadcasting) programme in which speakers in widely separated towns are linked by the same ~ programme.

radio- /ˈreɪdɪəʊ/ *pref* of rays or radium. ˈ~ ˋ**ac·tive** *adj* (of such metals as radium and uranium) having atoms that break up and, in so doing, send out rays in the form of electrically charged particles capable of penetrating opaque bodies and of producing electrical effects: *~active carbon; ~active dust,* dust (e g as carried by winds) from explosions of nuclear bombs, etc; *~active waste,* waste material from nuclear power stations, etc. ˈ**~·acˋtivity** *n* ˋ**~·graph** *n* X-ray photograph. ˈ**radi·ˋogra·phy** *n* production of X-ray photographs. ˈ**radi·ˋogra·pher** *n* person trained to take ~graphs. ˈ**~·ˋiso·tope** *n* ~active form of an element, used in medicine, industry, etc to study the path and speed of substances through bodies and objects. ˈ**~-loˋcation** *n* radar. ˋ**~-gram** *n* **(a)** (abbr of): ~-gramophone. **(b)** X-ray photograph. ˈ**~-ˋgramophone** *n* combined ~ receiver and record-player. ˈ**~ ˋtelescope** *n* apparatus that detects stars by means of ~ waves from outer space and tracks spacecraft. ˈ**~-ˋtherapy** *n* [U] treatment of disease by means of X-rays or other forms of radiation, e g of heat. ˈ**~-ˋtherapist** *n*

a radio telescope

rad·ish /ˋrædɪʃ/ *n* salad plant with a white or red edible root.

radium /ˋreɪdɪəm/ *n* [U] radioactive metallic element (symbol **Ra**) used in the treatment of some diseases, e g cancer.

radius /ˋreɪdɪəs/ *n* (*pl* -dii /-dɪɑɪ/) **1** (length of a) straight line from the centre of a circle or sphere to any point on the circumference or surface. ⇨ the illus at circle. **2** circular area measured by its ~: *The police searched all the fields and woods within a ~ of two miles.* **3** (anat) outer of the two bones in the forearm. ⇨ the illus at skeleton.

raf·fia /ˋræfɪə/ *n* [U] fibre from the leaf-stalks of a kind of palm-tree, used for making baskets, hats, mats, etc.

raff·ish /ˋræfɪʃ/ *adj* disreputable; dissipated: *a ~ young man; with a ~ air.* **~·ly** *adv*

raffle /ˋræfl/ *n* [C] sale of an article by a lottery, often for a charitable purpose: *buy ˋ~ tickets/tickets for a ~.* □ *vt* [VP6A,15B] **~ *sth (off),*** sell in a ~: *~ (off) a motor-scooter.*

raft /rɑft *US:* ræft/ *n* **1** number of tree trunks fastened together to be floated down a river. **2** (ˋ**life-**)**~,** flat, floating structure of rough timber, barrels, etc as a substitute for a boat or for the use of swimmers: *The sailors got away from the wrecked ship on a ~.* □ *vt,vi* **1** [VP6A,15A,B] carry on a ~; cross (a stream) on a ~. **2** [VP2C] go on a ~: *~ down the stream.* **~er, rafts·man** /-mən/ (*pl* -men) *nn* man who ~s timber.

rafter /ˋrɑftə(r) *US:* ˋræf-/ *n* one of the sloping beams of the framework on which the tiles or slates of a roof are supported. **raft·ered** *adj* provided with ~s: *a ~ed roof,* (esp) one of which the ~s are visible from beneath, e g in a hall that has no ceiling.

rag[1] /ræg/ *n* [C] **1** odd bit of cloth: *a rag to polish the car with.* **2** piece of old and torn cloth; (*pl*) old and torn clothes: *dressed in rags; My coat was worn to rags.* **the ˋrag trade,** (sl) the business of making and selling women's clothes. ˋ**glad rags,** ⇨ glad. **3** scrap; irregular piece: *There wasn't a rag of evidence against me. The meat was cooked to rags,* cooked so that it had fallen to pieces. ˋ**rag-bag** *n* **(a)** bag in which scraps of fabric are stored. **(b)** motley collection; confused mass. **(c)** (sl) untidily dressed person. **4** (*pl*) old, waste pieces of cloth from which a good quality of paper (ˋ*rag paper*) is made. **5** (used contemptuously for a) newspaper: *Why do you read that worthless rag?*

rag[2] /ræg/ *vt* (-gg-) [VP6A] (colloq) tease; play practical jokes on; be noisy and boisterous. □ *n* (colloq) rough, noisy disturbance; carnival with side-shows, a procession of amusing floats[1](3), etc, e g as held by college students. ˋ**rag-day,** day (usu annually) on which students hold a rag, and often collect money for charity.

raga·muf·fin /ˋrægəmʌfɪn/ *n* dirty, disreputable person, esp a small boy dressed in rags.

rage /reɪdʒ/ *n* **1** [C,U] (outburst of) furious anger; violence: *livid with ~; the ~ of the sea,* its violence during a storm. ***be in/fly into a ~,*** be, become, violently angry. **2** [C] **~ *(for),*** strong desire: *He has a ~ for collecting butterflies.* **3 *be (all) the ~,*** (colloq) sth for which there is a widespread but temporary enthusiasm; sth very fashionable: *The new dance at the discotheque is all the ~. These white handbags from Italy are (all) the ~ this summer.* □ *vi* **1** [VP2A,C] be violently angry; (of storms, etc) be violent: *He ~d and fumed against me for not letting him have his own way. The storm ~d all day. The wind ~d round the house. Pestilence ~d throughout the town.* **2** (reflex): *The storm ~d itself out,* at last ceased to ~.

rag·ged /ˋrægɪd/ *adj* **1** (with clothes) badly torn or in rags: *a ~ coat; a ~ old man.* **2** having rough or irregular edges or outlines or surfaces: *a dog with a ~ coat of hair; a sleeve with ~ edges/which is ~ at the cuff; ~ rocks; ~ clouds driven by the gale.* **3** (of work, etc) imperfect; lacking smoothness or uniformity: *a ~ performance,* e g of a theatrical rôle, a piece of music: *~ rhymes; row a ~ stroke,* i e with the oars not all entering the water smoothly and together. **~·ly** *adv* **~·ness** *n*

rag·lan /ˋræglən/ *n* (usu attrib) sweater or coat without shoulder seams (so that the seams for the sleeves go up from the armpit to the neckline).

ra·gout /ˋrægu *US:* ræˋgu/ *n* (dish of) meat and vegetable stew.

rag·tag /ˋrægtæg/ *n* (usu) ˈ***~ and ˋbobtail,*** the riff-raff; disreputable people.

rag·time /ˋrægtɑɪm/ *n* [U] **1** (1920's) popular music and dance of US Negro origin, the accent of the melody falling just before the regular beat of the accompaniment. **2** (attrib) farcical; comic: *a ~ army.*

rah /rɑ/ *int* hurrah (as used, in US) in cheers at a sports meeting, etc: *Rah, rah, rah!*

raid /reɪd/ *n* **1** surprise attack made by troops, ship(s) or aircraft: *make a ~ upon the enemy's camp; killed in an ˋair-~* (attack by aircraft). **2** sudden visit by police to make arrests: *a ~ on a gambling-den.* **3** sudden attack or inroad for the purpose of taking money: *a ~ on a bank by armed men; a ~ on the bank's reserves,* when they are to be used by the directors for expansion, etc. □ *vt,vi* [VP6A,2A] make a ~ on or into; carry out a ~: *Boys have been ~ing my orchard,* visiting it to steal fruit. **~er** *n* person, ship, aircraft, etc that makes a ~.

rail[1] /reɪl/ *n* **1** horizontal or sloping bar or rod or continuous series of bars or rods, of wood or metal, as part of a fence, as a protection against contact or falling over: *wooden ~s round a field; metal ~s round a monument; build a ~ fence. He was leaning on the ship's ~, looking over the water. One of the horses was forced to the ~s,* (in a horse-race) pressed so close to the ~s of the race-course that it was at a disadvantage. **2** similar bar or rod placed for things to hang on: *a ˋtowel-~,* e g at the side of a wash-basin. **3** steel bar or continuous line of such bars, laid on the ground as one side of a track for trains or trams: *send goods by ~,* by ~way; *a ~ strike,* of railway workers. ***off the ~s,*** (of a train) off the track; (fig) out of order, out of control; disorganized; (colloq) eccentric; neurotic; mad. **ˋ~-road** *n* (US) = ~way. □ *vt* (colloq) [VP15A,B] rush (sb or sth) unfairly (*to, into, through, etc*): *~road a bill through Congress.* **ˋ~-way** *n* **(a)** road or track laid with ~s on which trains run: *build a new ~way.* **(b)** system of such tracks, with the locomotives, cars, wagons, etc and the organization controlling the system: *work on the ~way. The ~ways in many countries are owned by the State.* **(c)** (attrib) *ˋ~way station/ bridge/ carriage/ engineer/ contractors/transport, etc.* **ˋ~-car** *n* single coach or car, with its own motive power, used on a ~way. **ˋ~-head** *n* farthest point reached by a ~way under construction. □ *vt* [VP6A,15B] ***~ off/in,*** put ~s(1) round; shut (in, off) separate, by means of ~s(1): *~ off a piece of ground; fields that are ~ed off from the road.* **~-ing** *n* [C] (often *pl*) fence made with ~s, e g as a protection at the side of a series of steps.

rail[2] /reɪl/ *vi* [VP2A,3A] ***~ (at/against),*** find fault; utter reproaches: *It's no use your ~ing at fate.* **~-ing** *n* [U] act of finding fault, complaining, protesting, etc: (*pl*) utterances of this kind.

rail·lery /ˈreɪlərɪ/ *n* [U] good-humoured teasing; [C] (*pl* -ries) instance of this.

rai·ment /ˈreɪmənt/ *n* [U] (liter) clothing.

rain[1] /reɪn/ *n* **1** [U] condensed moisture of the atmosphere falling in separate drops; fall of such drops: *It looks like ~,* as if there will be a fall of ~. *Don't go out in the ~. Come in out of the ~. The farmers want ~.* ***~ or shine,*** whether the weather is wet or sunny. **~-bow** /ˈreɪnbəʊ/ *n* arch containing the colours of the spectrum, formed in the sky opposite the sun when ~ is falling or when the sun shines on mist or spray. **ˋ~-bow trout,** food fish with reddish bands and black spots. **ˋ~-coat** *n* light coat of waterproof or tightly-woven material. **ˋ~-drop** *n* single drop of ~. **ˋ~-fall** *n* amount of ~ falling within a given area in a given time, (e g measured in cm of depth per annum). **ˋ~ forest,** hot, wet forest in tropical areas, where ~fall is heavy and there is no dry season. **ˋ~-gauge** *n* instrument for measuring ~fall. **ˋ~-proof** *adj* able to keep ~ out. **ˋ~-water** *n* water that has fallen as ~ and has been collected as ~ (contrasted with *well-water*, etc); soft water. **2** (with *indef art* and an *adj*) fall or shower of ~: *There was a heavy ~ last night.* **the ~s,** the season in tropical countries when there is heavy and continuous ~. **3** (usu *sing* with *indef art*) descent of sth that comes like ~: *a ~ of arrows/ bullets; a ~ of ashes,* e g from a volcano; (fig) *a ~ of congratulations.*

rain[2] /reɪn/ *vi,vt* **1** (impers): *It was ~ing, ~* was falling. *It has ~ed itself out,* has stopped ~ing. ***It never ~s but it pours,*** (prov) Things, usu unwelcome, do not come singly but in numbers, e g if one disaster happens, another will follow. **2** [VP2C] fall in a stream: *Tears ~ed down her cheeks. Misfortunes have ~ed heavily upon the old man.* **3** [VP14] ***~ sth (up) on,*** send or come down on: *He ~ed blows/Blows ~ed on the door. The people ~ed gifts upon the heroes returning from the war.* **~-less** *adj*

rainy /ˈreɪnɪ/ *adj* (-ier, -iest) having much rain: *~ weather; a ~ day/climate; the ˋ~ season.* ***save/ provide/put away/keep sth for a ~ day,*** save (esp money) for a time when one may need it.

raise /reɪz/ *vt* [VP6A,15A,B] **1** lift up; move from a low(er) to a high(er) level; cause to rise: *~ a sunken ship to the surface of the sea; ~ one's hat to sb,* as a sign of respect; *~ one's glass to one's lips; ~ prices; ~* (= build, erect) *a monument.* ***~ one's glass to sb,*** drink his health. ***~ one's hand to sb,*** move as if to give him a blow. ***~ sb's hopes,*** make him more hopeful. ***~ a man to the peerage,*** make him a peer. ***~ the temperature,*** **(a)** make a place warmer. **(b)** (fig) increase tension, e g by losing one's temper. ***~ one's voice,*** speak more loudly or in a higher tone: *voices ~d in anger.* **2** cause to be upright: *~ a man from his knees; ~ the standard of revolt.* ***~ sb from the dead,*** restore him to life. **3** cause to rise or appear: *~ a cloud of dust; ~ the spirits of the dead; shoes that ~ blisters on my feet; a story that might ~ a blush on a young girl's cheeks; a long, hot walk that ~d a good thirst,* caused the walker to be thirsty. ***~ a dust/commotion,*** (fig) cause a disturbance. ***~ a laugh,*** do sth to cause laughter. ***~ Cain/hell/the devil/the roof,*** (sl) cause an uproar; start a big row or disturbance. **4** bring up for discussion or attention: *~ a new point/a question/a protest/an objection.* **5** grow or produce (crops); breed (sheep, etc); rear, bring up (a family). **6** get or bring together; manage to get: *~ an army; ~ a loan; ~ money for a new undertaking; ~ funds for a holiday,* e g by pawning one's jewels. **7** ***~ a siege/blockage,*** end it. ***~ an embargo,*** remove it. **8** ***~ land,*** (naut) come in sight of (land that appears to rise above the horizon): *The ship ~d land the next morning.* □ *n* (esp US, cf GB, *rise*) increase in salary, etc. **raiser** *n* (in compounds) one who, that which, ~s (in various senses): *ˋcattle-raisers; ˋcurtain-raiser,* short introductory play; *ˋfire-raisers,* arsonists.

raisin /ˈreɪzn/ *n* [C] dried sweet grape, as used in cakes, etc.

raison d'être /ˈreɪzõ ˋdeətr *with unsyllabic* r *US:* ˈreɪzəʊn ˋdetrə/ *n* (F) reason for, purpose of, a thing's existence.

raj /rɑdʒ/ *n* sovereignty: *the ending of the British raj in India.*

ra·jah /ˈrɑdʒə/ *n* Indian prince; Malayan chief.

rake[1] /reɪk/ *n* **1** long-handled tool with prongs used for drawing together straw, dead leaves, etc or for smoothing soil or gravel; ⇨ the illus at **tool**; similar kinds of tool on wheels, drawn by a horse or tractor. **2** implement used by a croupier for drawing in money or chips at a gaming-table. □ *vt,vi* **1** [VP6A,22] use a ~ (on); make smooth with a ~: *~ garden paths; ~ the soil smooth for a seedbed.* **2** [VP6A,15A,B,14] get (sth *together, up, out, etc*) with or as with a ~: *~ together dead leaves; ~ out a fire,* get the ashes or cinders out from the bottom of a grate, etc; *~ up hay; ~ the dead leaves off the lawn.* **~ sth in,** (fig) earn, make, much money: *The firm is very successful —they're raking it in/raking in the money.* **ˈ~-off** *n* (sl) (usu suggesting dishonesty) commission; share of profits: *If I put this bit of business in your way, I expect a ~-off.* **~ sth up,** (esp) bring to people's knowledge (sth forgotten, esp sth which it is better not to recall to memory): *~ up old quarrels/accusations/slanders/grievances. Don't ~ up the past.* **3** [VP6A,15A,B,2C,3A] ***~ over/through sth,*** search for facts, etc: *~ through old manuscripts for information; ~ one's memory; ~ about among old documents.* **4** [VP6A,15A] fire with guns at, from end to end: *~ a ship; ~ a trench with machine-gun fire.*

rake[2] /reɪk/ *n* dissolute man.

rake[3] /reɪk/ *vi,vt* [VP2A,6A] (of a ship, or its bow or stern) project beyond the keel; (of the funnel, masts) (cause to) slope towards the stern; (of the stage of a theatre) slope down (towards the audience. □ *n* degree of slope: *the ~ of a ship's masts/of the stage of a theatre.*

rak·ish[1] /ˈreɪkɪʃ/ *adj* **1** of or like a rake[2]; dissolute: *a ~ appearance.* **2** jaunty: *set one's hat at a ~ angle* (from *rake*[3]). **~·ly** *adv* in a ~ manner: *with his hat tilted ~ly.* **~·ness** *n*

rak·ish[2] /ˈreɪkɪʃ/ *adj* (of a ship) looking as if built for speed (and therefore, in olden times, suggesting that she might be a pirate ship).

ral·len·tando /ˌrælənˈtændəʊ/ *n, adj* (musical direction) gradually slower.

rally[1] /ˈrælɪ/ *vt,vi* (*pt,pp* **-lied**) [VP6A,15A,2A,C] **1** (cause to) come together, esp after defeat or confusion, or in the face of threats or danger, to make new efforts: *The troops rallied round their leader. The leader rallied his men. My supporters are ~ing round me again. They rallied to the support of the Prime Minister.* **2** give new strength to; (cause to) recover health, strength, firmness: *~ one's strength/spirits; ~ from an illness. The boy rallied his wits. The market rallied,* e g of the Stock Exchange, prices stopped dropping and became firm. □ *n* [C] (*pl* **-lies**) **1** act or process of ~ing; coming together after being dispersed; recovery of strength; improvement during illness. **2** (tennis) exchange of several strokes before a point is scored. **3** gathering or assembly, esp to encourage fresh effort: *a poˈlitical ~: a ˈpeace ~,* one to urge the necessity of ending or avoiding war. **4** meeting of a number of car drivers or motor-cyclists, often of a special kind (e g cars of pre-1920 manufacture, or fast sports cars), for a competition, test of reliability, etc.

rally[2] /ˈrælɪ/ *vt* (*pt,pp* **-lied**) [VP6A] tease; chaff good-humouredly.

ram /ræm/ *n* **1** uncastrated male sheep. **2** one of various implements or devices for striking or pushing with great force, e g the falling weight of a pile-driving machine; form of water-pump in which a heavy fall of water is used to force a smaller quantity to a higher level. **3** ⇨ *battering-ram* at **batter**[1]. **4** metal projection on a warship's bow for piercing the side of an enemy ship. □ *vt* (**-mm-**) **1** [VP6A,15A,B] strike and push heavily: *ram down the soil,* e g when building roads or embankments; *ram piles into a river bed; ram a charge home/into a gun;* (colloq) *ram one's clothes into a suitcase.* ***ram sth down a person's throat,*** (fig) say sth repeatedly so as to impress it upon sb, get him to learn it or recognize its truth. **2** [VP6A] (of a ship) strike with a ram(**4**): *ram and sink a submarine.* **3** **ˈram jet** *n* jet engine in which the air is rammed or forced through the engine and compressed by the speed of flight. **ˈram·rod** *n* iron rod for ramming the charge into old (muzzle-loading) guns.

Rama·dan /ˌræməˈdɑn *US:* -ˈdæn/ *n* ninth month of the Muslim year, when Muslims fast between sunrise and sunset.

ramble /ˈræmbl/ *vi* [VP2A,C] **1** walk for pleasure, with no special destination; (fig) wander in one's talk, not keeping to the subject. **2** (of plants) grow with long shoots that trail or straggle. □ *n* rambling walk: *go for a country ~.* **ram·bler** *n* person or thing that ~s: (attrib) *~r roses.* **ram·bling** *adj* **1** (esp of buildings, streets, towns), extending in various directions irregularly, as if built without planning. **2** (of a speech, essay, etc) disconnected.

ram·bunc·tious /ræmˈbʌŋkʃəs/ *adj* boisterous.

ram·ify /ˈræmɪfaɪ/ *vi,vt* (*pt,pp* **-fied**) [VP2A,6A] form or produce branches; make or become a network: *a ramified system.* **rami·fi·ca·tion** /ˌræmɪfɪˈkeɪʃn/ *n* [C] subdivision of sth complex or like a network: *the widespread ramifications of trade/a plot/an argument.*

ram·jet ⇨ **ram(3).**

ramp[1] /ræmp/ *n* sloping way from one level to another, e g instead of, or in addition to, stairs or steps in a hospital, so that beds can be wheeled from one floor to another, or, at a kerb in a many-storeyed garage, so that cars can be driven up and down. change of level during road repairs; in olden times, a sloping bank of earth in military fortifications.

ramp[2] /ræmp/ *n* (GB, sl) dishonest attempt to obtain an exorbitant price: *the furnished flat ~ in London,* the excessively high rents demanded for them. *The whole thing's a ~,* It's a scandalous attempt to extort money.

ramp[3] /ræmp/ *vt* [VP2C] ***~ about,*** (now usu joc) storm, rage or rush: *How much longer are those boys going to ~ about in the garden?* □ *n* = **rampage.**

ram·page /ˈræmpeɪdʒ/ *vi* [VP2A] rush about in excitement or rage. □ *n* ***be/go on the ~,*** be/go rampaging. **ram·pa·geous** /ræmˈpeɪdʒəs/ *adj* excited and noisy.

ram·pant /ˈræmpənt/ *adj* **1** (of plants, etc) rank; luxuriant: *Rich soil makes some plants too ~,* causes them to spread too thickly, to have too much foliage, etc. **2** (of diseases, social evils, etc) unchecked; beyond control: *Heresy was ~ among them.* **3** (of animals, esp of a lion in heraldry) on the hind legs. **~·ly** *adv*

ram·part /ˈræmpɑt/ *n* [C] **1** wide bank of earth, often with a wall, built to defend a fort or other defensive work. **2** (fig) defence; protection.

ram·rod /ˈræmrod/ ⇨ ram(3).

ram·shackle /ˈræmʃækl/ *adj* almost collapsing; nearly at breaking-point: *a ~ house; a ~ old bus; their ~ empire.*

ran /ræn/ *pt* of run².

ranch /rɑntʃ *US:* ræntʃ/ *n* (in N America) large farm, esp one with extensive lands for cattle, but also for fruit, chickens, etc. **ˈ~ house,** (US) rectangular bungalow type of house. **ˈ~ wagon,** (US) = station wagon. **~er** *n* person who owns, manages or works on, a ~.

ran·cid /ˈrænsɪd/ *adj* with the smell or taste of stale, decaying fat or butter; (of fat) having gone bad; ill smelling: *This butter smells ~/has grown ~.*

ran·cour (US = **-cor**) /ˈræŋkə(r)/ *n* [U] deep and long-lasting feeling of bitterness; spitefulness: *full of ~ (against sb).* **ran·cor·ous** /ˈræŋkərəs/ *adj*

rand /rænd/ *n* monetary unit of the Republic of S Africa, divided into 100 cents.

ran·dom /ˈrændəm/ *n* **1** ***at ~,*** without aim or purpose: *shooting/dropping bombs at ~; hit out at ~.* **2** (attrib) done, made, taken, at ~: *~ remarks; a ~ sample/selection; ~ sampling.*

randy /ˈrændɪ/ *adj* (-ier, -iest) **1** (Scot) boisterous; aggressively noisy. **2** full of sexual lust.

ranee, rani /rɑˈni/ *n* Hindu queen or princess; wife of a rajah.

rang /ræŋ/ *pt* of ring².

range¹ /reɪndʒ/ *n* [C] **1** row, line or series of things: *a magnificent ~ of mountains; a ˈmountain-~; a long ~ of cliffs.* **2** area of ground with targets for shooting at: *a ˈrifle-~*; area in which rockets and missiles are fired. **3** distance to which a gun will shoot or to which a shell, etc can be fired: *at a ~ of five miles; in/within/out of/beyond ~*; distance between a gun, etc and the target: *fire at short/long ~.* **ˈ~-finder** *n* **(a)** instrument for finding the distance of sth to be fired at. **(b)** device fitted in some cameras for measuring distances. **4** distance at which one can see or hear, or to which sound will carry. **5** extent; distance between limits: *the annual ~ of temperature,* e g from −10°C to 40°C; *a long-~ weather forecast,* for a long period; *a narrow ~ of prices; cotton fabrics in a wide ~ of colours; the ~ of her voice,* i e between her top and bottom notes; (fig) *a subject that is outside my ~,* one that I have not studied; *a wide ~ of interests.* **6** (US) area of grazing or hunting ground. **7** area over which plants are found growing or in which animals are found living: *What is the ~ of the nightingale in this country?* **8** cooking-stove, usu with ovens, a boiler, and a surface with openings or hot-plates for pans, kettles, etc: *a ˈkitchen ~.*

range² /reɪndʒ/ *vt,vi* **1** [VP6A,15A] place or arrange in a row or rows; put, take one's place, in a specified situation, order, class or group: *The general ~d his men along the river bank. They were ~d against us/among the rebels. The spectators ~d themselves along the route of the procession.* **2** [VP2C,3A,6A] ***~ through/over,*** go, move, wander: *animals ranging through the forests; ~ over the hills; ~ the seas/hills, etc;* (fig) *researches that ~d over a wide field; a speaker who ~d far and wide,* spoke on many topics; *a wide-ranging discussion.* **3** [VP2C] extend, run in a line: *a boundary that ~s north and south/from A to B.* **4** [VP2C] vary between limits: *prices ranging from £7 to £10/between £7 and £10.* **5** (of guns, projectiles) carry: *This gun ~s over six miles,* can fire to this distance.

ranger /ˈreɪndʒə(r)/ *n* **1** (N America) forest guard. **2** one of a body of mounted troops employed as police (e g in thinly populated areas). **3** (US) commando. **4** (GB) keeper of a royal park, who sees that the forest laws are observed.

rani /rɑˈni/ ⇨ ranee.

rank¹ /ræŋk/ *n* **1** [C] line of persons or things: *a ˈcab-~. Take the taxi at the head of the ~,* the first one in the line. **2** number of soldiers placed side by side (on parade, usu in three lines, called the *front, centre* and the *rear ~s*). ***keep/break ~,*** remain/fail to remain in line. **3 the ~s; the ~ and file; other ~s,** ordinary soldiers, i e privates and corporals, contrasted with officers. ***be reduced to the ~s,*** (of a non-commissioned officer, e g a sergeant) made an ordinary private soldier (as a punishment). ***pull ~ on sb,*** use one's superior position to gain an advantage over them. ***rise from the ~s,*** (of an ordinary soldier) be given a commission as an officer. **4** [C,U] position in a scale, distinct grade in the armed forces; category or class: *promoted to the ~ of captain; above/below a major in ~; officers of high ~; hold the ~ of colonel; officers and other ~s,* ⇨ 3 above; *persons of high ~,* of high social position; *people of all ~s and classes; be in the ~s of the unemployed; a painter of the first ~; a second-~* (more usu *second-rate*) *dancer.* □ *vt,vi* **1** [VP6A, 15A,16B] put or arrange in a ~ or ~s; put in a class: *Where/How do you ~ Addison as an essayist? Would you ~ him among the world's great statesmen?* **2** [VP3A] have a place: *Does he ~ among/with the failures? A major ~s above a captain. Will my shares ~ for the next dividend?* **3** (US) *the ~ing officer,* the officer of highest ~ present.

rank² /ræŋk/ *adj* **1** (of plants, etc) growing too luxuriantly, with too much leaf: *~ grass; roses that grow ~*; (of land) choked with weeds or likely to produce a lot of weeds: *~ soil; a field that is ~ with nettles and thistles.* **2** smelling or tasting bad; offensive: *~ tobacco.* **3** unmistakably bad; possessing a bad quality to an extreme degree: *a ~ traitor; ~ injustice. These fungi are ~ poison.* **~·ly** *adv* **~·ness** *n*

ranker /ˈræŋkə(r)/ *n* commissioned officer who has risen from the ranks. ⇨ rank¹(3).

rankle /ˈræŋkl/ *vi* [VP2A] continue to be a painful or bitter memory: *The insult ~d in his mind.*

ran·sack /ˈrænsæk *US:* rænˈsæk/ *vt* [VP6A,14, 16A] ***~ sth for/to...,*** **1** search (a place) thoroughly (for sth): *~ a drawer; ~ a dictionary to find just the right word.* **2** rob; plunder: *The house had been ~ed of all that was worth anything.*

ran·som /ˈrænsəm/ *n* [U] freeing of a captive on payment; [C] sum of money, etc, paid for this. ***hold a man to ~,*** keep him as a captive and ask for ~. ***worth a king's ~,*** a very large sum of money. □ *vt* [VP6A] obtain the freedom of (sb), set (sb) free, in exchange for ~: *~ a kidnapped diplomat.*

rant /rænt/ *vi,vt* [VP2A,6A] use extravagant, boasting language; say or recite (sth) noisily and theatrically: *an actor who ~s his part.* □ *n* piece of ~ing talk. **~er** *n* person who ~s.

rap[1] /ræp/ *n* [C] **1** (sound of a) light, quick blow: *give sb a rap on the knuckles,* (liter, or fig for a reproof); *I heard a rap on the door.* **2** (colloq) blame; consequences. ***take the rap (for sth),*** be reproved or reprimanded (esp when innocent). □ *vt,vi* (-pp-) [VP6A,15B,2A,C] **1** give a rap to; make the sound of a rap: *rap (on) the table; rap (at) the door.* **2 *rap sth out,*** **(a)** say sth suddenly or sharply: *rap out an oath.* **(b)** (of spirits at a seance) express by means of raps: *rap out a message.*

rap[2] /ræp/ *n* obsolete valueless coin: (chiefly in) ***not care/give a rap,*** not care at all.

ra·pa·cious /rəˋpeɪʃəs/ *adj* (formal) greedy (esp for money). **~·ly** *adv* **ra·pac·ity** /rəˋpæsətɪ/ *n* [U] greed; avarice.

rape[1] /reɪp/ *n* [U] plant grown as food for sheep and pigs; plant grown for the oil obtained from its seeds.

rape[2] /reɪp/ *vt* [VP6A] **1** seize and carry off by force. **2** commit the crime of forcing sexual intercourse on (a woman or girl). □ *n* act of raping. **rap·ist** /ˋreɪpɪst/ *n*

rapid /ˋræpɪd/ *adj* **1** quick; moving, occurring with great speed: *a ~ decline in sales; a ~ pulse/river/worker;* (of action) done quickly; *~-fire questions,* in ~ succession. **2** (of a slope) steep; descending steeply. □ *n* (usu *pl*) part of a river where a steep slope causes the water to flow fast. **~·ly** *adv* **rap·id·ity** /rəˋpɪdətɪ/ *n* [U].

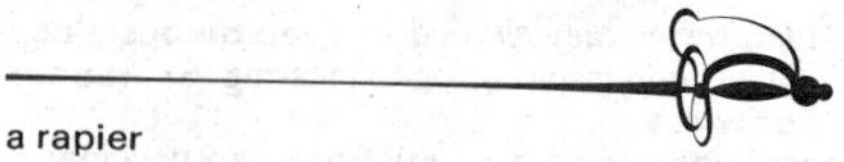

a rapier

rapier /ˋreɪpɪə(r)/ *n* light sword used for thrusting in duels and the sport of fencing: (attrib) *a ˋ~-thrust,* (fig) a delicate or witty retort.

rap·ine /ˋræpaɪn *US:* ˋræpɪn/ *n* (liter or rhet) [U] plundering.

rap·port /ræˋpɔ *US:* -ˋpɔrt/ *n* [U] ***be in ~ (with),*** (or as in French, ***en ~*** /ɔ̃/) in close relationship or sympathy (with).

rap·proche·ment /ræˋprɔʃmɔ̃ *US:* ˌræprəʊʃˋmɔ̃/ *n* [C] coming together again (of persons, parties, States) in friendly relations; renewal of friendship.

rap·scal·lion /ræpˋskælɪən/ *n* (old use) rascal; rogue.

rapt /ræpt/ *adj* so deep in thought, so carried away by feelings, that one is unaware of other things; enraptured: *listening to the orchestra with ~ attention; ~ in contemplation of the scenery; ~ in a book.*

rap·ture /ˋræptʃə(r)/ *n* **1** [U] state of being rapt; ecstatic delight: *gazing with ~ at the face of the girl he loved.* **2** (*pl*) ***be in/go into/be sent into/~s (over/about),*** be/become extremely happy, full of joy and enthusiasm: *She went into ~s over*

PARROT
KIWI
PARAKEET
EMU
PEACOCK
feather
TOUCAN
OSTRICH
MYNAH
beak
COCKATOO

birds 4

the dresses they showed her. **rap·tur·ous** /ˋræptʃərəs/ *adj* inspiring or expressing ~. **rap·tur·ous·ly** *adv*

rare[1] /reə(r)/ *adj* (**-r, -st**) **1** unusual; uncommon; not often happening, seen, etc: *a ~ occurrence; a ~ book,* one of which few copies are obtainable. *It is very ~ for her to arrive late.* **2** (colloq) unusually good: *We had a ~ time/~ fun.* **3** (of a substance, esp the atmosphere) thin; not dense: *the ~ air of the mountains in the Himalayas.* **~·ly** *adv* **1** seldom. **2** uncommonly. **~·ness** *n*

rare[2] /reə(r)/ *adj* (of meat) underdone; cooked so that the redness and juices are retained: *rare steak.*

rare·bit /ˋreəbɪt/ *n* [C] (= colloq *Welsh rabbit*) melted or toasted cheese on toasted bread.

rarefy /ˋreərɪfaɪ/ *vt,vi* (*pt,pp* **-fied**) [VP6A,2A] make or become less dense; purify; refine: *the rarefied air of the mountain tops.*

rar·ing /ˋreərɪŋ/ *adj* (colloq) full of eagerness: *They're ~ to go.*

rar·ity /ˋreərətɪ/ *n* (*pl* **-ties**) **1** [U] rareness. **2** [C] sth rare, uncommon or unusual; sth valued because rare: *Rain is a ~ in Upper Egypt.*

ras·cal /ˋrɑskl *US:* ˋræskl/ *n* **1** dishonest person. **2** (playfully) mischievous person (esp a child), fond of playing tricks. **~ly** /-klɪ/ *adj* of or like a ~; mean; dishonest: *a ~ly trick.*

rash[1] /ræʃ/ *n* (breaking out of, patch of) tiny red spots on the skin: *a* ˋ*heat-~;* ˋ*nettle-~;* (fig) *a ~ of new red brick bungalows on a country road. If a ~ appears, the child may have (the) measles.*

rash[2] /ræʃ/ *adj* too hasty; overbold; done, doing things, without enough thought of the consequences: *a ~ act/statement; a ~ young man.* **~ly** *adv* **~·ness** *n*

rasher /ˋræʃə(r)/ *n* slice of bacon or ham (to be) fried: *eat three ~s and two fried eggs for breakfast.*

rasp /rɑsp *US:* ræsp/ *n* [C] metal tool like a coarse file with a surface or surfaces having sharp points, used for scraping; rough, grating sound produced by this tool. □ *vt,vi* **1** [VP6A,15A,B,22] ***~ sth away/off,*** scrape with a ~; scrape. **2** [VP6A] (fig) grate upon, have an irritating effect upon: *~ sb's feelings/nerves.* **3** [VP15B] ***~ out,*** utter in a way that grates or sounds like the noise of a ~: *~ out orders/insults.* **4** [VP2A,C] make a harsh, grating sound: *a learner ~ing (away) on his violin; a ~ing voice.* **~·ing·ly** *adv*

rasp·berry /ˋrɑzbrɪ *US:* ˋræzberɪ/ *n* (*pl* **-ries**) **1** bush with small, sweet yellow or red berries, wild or cultivated: (attrib) *~ jam/canes;* one of these berries. **2** (sl) contemptuous noise made with the tongue and lips or by wind passing out of the anus, or a gesture indicating dislike, derision or disapproval. ***get/give or blow sb a ~.***

rat /ræt/ *n* **1** animal like, but larger than, a mouse; ☞ the illus at small; person who deserts a cause that he thinks is about to fail (from the belief that rats desert a ship that will sink or be wrecked). ***smell a rat,*** suspect that sth wrong is being done. ***(look) like a drowned rat,*** wet and miserable; soaked to the skin. **the** ˋ**rat race,** ceaseless and undignified competition for success in one's career, social status, etc as among office workers, etc. **2** (fig) cowardly traitor, a strike-breaker. ˋ**rat-fink** *n* (US colloq) particularly unpleasant rat(2). **Rats!** (sl, as an exclamation) Nonsense! I don't believe a word of it! □ *vt* (**-tt-**) **1** hunt rats: *go ratting.* **2** [VP2A,3A] ***~ (on sb),*** break a promise, withdraw from an undertaking. **rat·ter** *n* man, dog or cat that catches rats: *Are terriers good ratters?* **rat·ty** *adj* (**-ier, -iest**) (colloq) irritable; snappish.

rat·able, rat·abil·ity ☞ **rateable, rateability.**

rat·an /ræˋtæn/ ☞ **rattan.**

rat-a-tat-tat /ˈræt ə ˈtæt ˋtæt/ ☞ **rat-tat.**

ratch /rætʃ/ *n* = ratchet-wheel.

ratch·et /ˋrætʃɪt/ *n* toothed wheel provided with a catch (*pawl*) that prevents the wheel from slipping back and allows it to move in only one direction.

rate[1] /reɪt/ *n* **1** [C] standard or reckoning, obtained by bringing two numbers or amounts into relationship: *walk at the ~ of 3 miles an hour; a train travelling at the (a) ~ of 50 miles an hour; an aircraft with a good ~ of climb; at a great/fearful, etc ~,* at great speed; *buy things at the ~ of 55p a hundred. What is the letter postage ~ to foreign countries?* ˋ**birth/**ˋ**marriage/**ˋ**death, etc ~,** the number of births, etc in relationship to a period of time and a number of people: *a death-~ of 2·3 per 1000 (per year).* ***~ of exchange,*** relationship between two currencies (e g US dollars and F francs). **the** ˋ**discount ~, the** ˋ**bank ~,** the officially announced percentage at which a country's central bank is prepared to discount Bills. **2** (phrases) ***at*** ˋ***this/***ˋ***that ~,*** if this/that is true, if we may assume that this/that is the case; if this/that state of affairs continues. ***at any ~*** /ə ˋtenɪ reɪt/, in any case; whatever happens. **3** (GB) tax on property (land and buildings), paid to local authorities for local purposes: *an extra penny on the ~s for the public library,* i e a charge of one penny on each pound of the assessment. **the ~s,** these payments collectively; *~s and taxes,* payments to local authorities and taxes levied by the national government. ˋ**~-payer** *n* person liable to have ~s exacted from him. ☞ also *water-~* at **water**[1]**(7).** **4** (with ordinal numbers): class or grade: *first ~,* excellent; *second ~,* fairly good; *third ~,* (rather) poor; (attrib, with a hyphen): *a first-~ teacher.* Hence, *first-*ˋ*rater,* ˈ*second-*ˋ*rater, etc.*

rate[2] /reɪt/ *vt,vi* **1** [VP6A,15A,16B] judge or estimate the value or qualities of: *What do you ~ his fortune at? He was a man whom all his friends ~d as kind and hospitable. Do you ~* (= consider) *Mr X among your friends?* **2** [VP6A,14] ***~ sth (at),*** (GB) value (property) for the purpose of assessing rates(2) on: *My property was ~d at £100 per annum. Should private houses be more heavily ~d than factories?* **3** (naut) place in a certain class in a ship's books or records: *He was ~d as a midshipman.*

rate[3] /reɪt/ *vt,vi* [6A,2A] scold, berate: *~ sb soundly.* **rat·ing** *n* scolding: *give sb a good rating.*

rat·able (also **rate·able**) /ˋreɪtəbl/ *adj* liable to payment of municipal rates: *~ property; the ~ value of a house,* its value as assessed for the levying of rates. **rat·abil·ity** (also **rate·abil·ity**) /ˈreɪtəˋbɪlətɪ/ *n*

rather /ˋrɑðə(r)/ *US:* ˋræ-/ *adv* **1** more willingly; by preference or choice (usu ***would/had ~***; also with inversion: ***~ than... would***): *I would ~ you came tomorrow than today. She would ~ have the small one than the large one. Wouldn't you ~ be liked than feared? He resigned ~ than take part in such a dishonest transaction. A: 'Will you join us in a game of cards?'—B: 'Thank you, but I'd ~ not.' R~ than refuse to help you, I'd borrow money from my bank.* **2** more truly, accurately or precisely: *He arrived very late last night or ~ in the early hours this morning.* **3** (to be distinguished from *fairly*[2]) in a certain degree or measure; more (so) than not; somewhat; **(a)** (with *adjj*, preceding or following the *indef art*, following the *def art*): *a ~ surprising result/~ a surprising result; the ~ tall boy in the corner.* **(b)** (with comparatives): *My brother is ~ better today. This hat is ~ more expensive than that.* **(c)** (with *too*): *This book is ~ too difficult for the juniors and ~ too easy for the seniors.* Note that *fairly* cannot be used with comparatives and *too*. **(d)** (with *nn*): *It's ~ a pity, ~* regrettable. *She's ~ a dear, ~* lovable. *£50 is ~ a lot to pay for a dress, isn't it?* **(e)** (with *vv* and *pp*): *I ~ think you may be mistaken. The rain ~ spoiled our holiday. We were all ~ exhausted when we got to the top of the mountain.* **(f)** (with *advv*): *You've done ~ well/~ better than I had expected.* **4** (colloq; GB /ˈrɑˋðɜ(r)/) (in answers) most certainly.

rat·ify /ˋrætɪfaɪ/ *vt* (*pt,pp* **-fied**) [VP6A] confirm (an agreement) by signature or other formality. **rati·fi·ca·tion** /ˈrætɪfɪˋkeɪʃn/ *n* ~ing or being ratified.

rat·ing /ˋreɪtɪŋ/ *n* **1** [C] act of valuing property for the purpose of assessing rates. ⇨ **rate**[2](2); amount or sum fixed as the municipal rate. **2** [C] class, classification, e g of yachts by tonnage, motor-cars by engine capacity or horse-power; popularity of radio or TV programmes as estimated by asking a selected group. **3** (navy) person's position or class as recorded in the ship's books; non-commissioned sailor: *officers and ~s.*

ra·tio /ˋreɪʃɪəʊ/ *n* (*pl* **-tios** /-ʃɪəʊz/) [C] relation between two amounts determined by the number of times one contains the other: *The ~s of 1 to 5 and 20 to 100 are the same.*

rati·oc·in·ation /ˈrætɪˈɒsɪˋneɪʃn *US:* ˈræʃɪ-/ *n* [U] the process of methodical reasoning, esp by the use of syllogisms.

ration /ˋræʃn/ *n* fixed quantity, esp of food, allowed to one person; (*pl*) fixed allowance served out to, e g members of the armed forces: *go and draw ~s;* ˋ~ **card/book,** one that entitles the holder to ~s, e g for a civilian when there is a food shortage during or immediately after a war. ***be on short ~s,*** be allowed or able to have less than the usual quantity of food. ***an iron ~,*** a quantity of concentrated food carried for use in case of emergency, e g by soldiers, explorers. □ *vt* **1** [VP6A] limit (sb) to a fixed ~. **2** [VP6A,15B] limit (food, water, etc): *We'll have to ~ the water. He ~ed out* (= distributed ~s of) *the bread.*

ra·tional /ˋræʃnl/ *adj* **1** of reason or reasoning. **2** able to reason; having the faculty of reasoning. **3** sensible; that can be tested by reasoning: *~ conduct/explanations.* **~ly** /-ʃnlɪ/ *adv* **~·ity** /ˈræʃnˋælətɪ/ *n* quality of being ~; reasonableness.

ration·ale /ˈræʃəˋnɑl/ *n* fundamental reason, logical basis (of sth).

ration·al·ism /ˋræʃnl-ɪzm/ *n* [U] the practice of treating reason as the ultimate authority in religion as in other subjects of study. **ration·al·ist** /-ɪst/ *n* person who accepts reason as the ultimate authority in religion, ethics, etc. **ration·al·is·tic** /ˈræʃnl-ˋɪstɪk/ *adj* of ~ or rationalists.

ration·al·ize /ˋræʃnlaɪz/ *vt* **1** [VP6A] bring into conformity with reason; treat or explain in a rational manner: *~ one's fears/behaviour.* **2** [VP6A] reorganize (an industry, etc) so as to lessen or get rid of waste (in time, labour, materials, etc). **ration·al·iz·ation** /ˈræʃnlaɪˋzeɪʃn *US:* -lɪˋz-/ *n*

rat·lin, rat·line /ˋrætlɪn/ (usu *pl*) small rope fixed across the shrouds of a ship (like a rung on a ladder) used as a step by a sailor climbing up or down.

rat·tan, ratan /ræˋtæn/ *n* **1** [C] (East Indian palm-tree with a) cane-like stem. **2** [C] walking-stick or cane made from a ~ stem. **3** [U] ~ stems (collectively), as used for building, basketwork, furniture, etc: *a chair with a ~ seat.*

rat-tat /ræ ˋtæt/ (also **rat-a-tat-tat** /ˈræt ə ˈtæt ˋtæt/) *n* sound of a rapping or knocking, esp on a door.

rattle /ˋrætl/ *vt,vi* **1** [VP6A,15A,2A,C] (cause to) make short, sharp sounds quickly, one after the other: *The wind ~d the windows. The windows were rattling in the wind. The hailstones ~d on the tin roof. The old bus ~d along over the stony road.* (fig) *The wind caused the old man's bones to ~.* **2** [VP15B] **~ *sth off,*** talk, say or repeat (sth) quickly and in a thoughtless or lively way: *The boy ~d off the poem he had learnt.* [VP2C] **~ *away*:** *The child ~d away merrily.* □ *n* **1** [U] rattling sound: *the ~ of bottles from a milkman's van; the ~ of hail on the window-panes.* **2** [C] baby's toy for producing a rattling sound; similar device whirled (e g by spectators at a football match) to make a noisy clatter. **3** [U] lively flow of talk; chatter. **4** [C] series of horny rings in a ~snake's tail. ˋ**~·snake** *n* poisonous American snake that makes a rattling noise with its tail. ⇨ the illus at snake. **5** (ˋ**death-**)**~,** rattling sound sometimes produced in the throat immediately before death. **6** ˋ**~-brain,** ˋ**~-pate** *nn* person with an empty head; silly chatterer. Hence, ˋ**~-brained,** ˋ**~-pated** *adjj* **rat·tler** /ˋrætlə(r)/ *n* **1** person or thing that ~s, esp a ~snake. **2** (colloq, dated) very good specimen of sth. **rat·tling** /ˋrætlɪŋ/ *adj* (sl) quick(-moving); first-rate; excellent: *travelling at a rattling rate; a rattling breeze; have a rattling* (= enjoyable) *time. adv* (sl) very: *a rattling good speech.*

ratty ⇨ rat.

rau·cous /ˋrɔkəs/ *adj* (of sounds) harsh; rough; hoarse: *the ~ cries of the crows; a ~ voice; ~ laughter.* **~·ly** *adv*

rav·age /ˋrævɪdʒ/ *vt,vi* [VP6A] **1** destroy; damage badly: *forests ~d by fire; a face ~d by disease,* e g covered with marks after smallpox. **2** (of armies, etc) rob, plunder, with violence: *They had ~d the countryside* □ *n* **1** [U] destruction; devastation. **2** (*pl*) ***~s of,*** destructive effects: *the ~s of time,* e g on a woman's looks; *the ~s of torrential rains.*

rave /reɪv/ *vi* **1** [VP2A,C,3A] **~ *(at/against/about sth),*** talk wildly, violently, angrily: *The patient* (e g someone with a high fever) *began to ~. When he was accused of stealing he ~d wildly against me.* [VP22] (reflex): *He ~d himself hoarse.* **2** (of the sea, wind, etc) roar; rage. [VP15B] (reflex): *The storm ~d itself out,* ended. **3** [VP3A] **~ *about sb/sth,*** talk or act with (often) excessive enthusiasm: *She ~d about the food she had had in France.* □ *n* **1** (colloq, often attrib) enthusiastic praise: *a ~ review,* e g of a book; *~ notices.* **2** (sl) wild, exciting party, dance, outing, etc. **3** (sl) great enthusiasm: *be in a ~ about sb.*

raver *n* (colloq) sb who ~s(3). **rav·ing** *adj* talking wildly: *a raving lunatic.* □ *adv* to the point of talking wildly: *You're raving mad!* **rav·ings** *n pl* foolish or wild talk: *the ravings of a madman.*

ravel /ˈrævl/ *vt,vi* (-ll-, US also -l-) **1** [VP2A,C] (of knitted or woven things) separate into threads; become untwisted; fray: *Bind the edge of the rug so that it won't ~.* **2** [VP6A] cause (threads, hair, etc) to be twisted together, knotted, etc; (fig) make confused. **3** [VP6A,15B] ***~ (out),*** disentangle: *~ (out) a rope's end.*

raven /ˈreɪvn/ *n* **1** large, black bird like a crow, popularly regarded as a bird of ill omen. **2** (attrib) glossy, shining black: *~ locks,* black hair.

rav·en·ing /ˈrævn̩ɪŋ/ *adj* fierce; savage; crazy for food: *a ~ wolf.*

rav·en·ous /ˈrævn̩əs/ *adj* **1** very hungry. **2** greedy: *a ~ appetite; ~ hunger; ~ for power.* **~·ly** *adv* hungrily; greedily: *eat ~ly.*

ra·vine /rəˈvin/ *n* deep, narrow valley.

ravi·oli /ˈrævɪˈəʊlɪ/ *n* (I) dish of small cases of pasta containing chopped meat, etc usu served with a sauce.

rav·ish /ˈrævɪʃ/ *vt* [VP6A] **1** fill with delight; enchant: *a ~ing view; ~ed by the view; ~ed with her beauty.* **~·ing·ly** *adv* **~·ment** *n* ~ing or being ~ed. **2** (archaic or poet) seize and carry off: *~ed from the world by death.* **3** (archaic) rape (a woman or girl).

raw /rɔ/ *adj* **1** uncooked: *raw meat; eat oysters raw.* **2** in the natural state, not manufactured or prepared for use: *raw hides,* not yet tanned; *raw sugar,* not yet refined; *the raw materials of industry,* e g coal, ores; *raw spirit,* undiluted alcohol. ***in the raw,*** unrefined; in the natural state; (fig) naked. **ˈraw·hide** *adj* made of untanned hide: *rawhide boots.* **3** (of persons) untrained; unskilled; inexperienced: *raw recruits,* for the army, etc. **4** (of the weather) damp and cold: *a raw February morning; raw winds.* **5** (of wounds) unhealed; bloody; (of a place on the flesh) with the skin rubbed off; sore and painful. **ˈraw-ˈboned** *adj* having little flesh on the bones: *a raw-boned horse.* **6** artistically crude: *His literary style is still rather raw.* **7** (colloq) harsh; unjust; (esp) ***a raw deal,*** harsh or cruel treatment. □ *n* raw place on the skin, esp on a horse's skin. ***touch sb on the raw,*** (fig) wound a person's feelings, wound him on the question, topic, etc on which he is most sensitive.

ray¹ /reɪ/ *n* [C] **1** line, beam, of radiant light, heat, energy: *the rays of the sun; ˈX-rays; ˈheat-rays;* (fig) *a ray of hope.* **2** any one of a number of lines coming out from a centre. □ *vi,vt* send out or come out in rays.

ray² /reɪ/ *n* kinds of large sea-fish with a broad, flat body, e g *skate.*

rayon /ˈreɪɒn/ *n* [U] silk-like material made from cellulose: (attrib) *~ shirts.*

raze, rase /reɪz/ *vt* [VP6A] destroy (towns, buildings) completely, esp by making them level with the ground: *a city ~d by an earthquake.*

razor /ˈreɪzə(r)/ *n* instrument with a sharp blade or cutters (some electrically driven) used for shaving hair from the skin. **ˈsafety ~,** kind in which a thin blade is fitted between metal guards. **ˈ~-back** *n* kind of whale. **ˈ~-backed** *adj* having a thin, sharp back: *a ~-backed pig.* **ˈ~-ˈedge** *n* sharp line of division; critical situation. □ *vt* (rare, except in *pp*): *a well-~ed chin, well shaved.*

razzle /ˈræzl/ *n* (also **ˈ~-ˈdazzle**) ***be/go on the ~,*** (sl) be on a spree. ⇨ spree.

re¹ /ri/ *prep* (in legal style) in the matter of; concerning.

re² /reɪ/ *n* second note in the musical octave.

re- /ri-/ *pref* **1** again: *reappear, refloat, replay.* **2** in a different way: *rearrange.* ⇨ App 3.

reach /ritʃ/ *vt,vi* **1** [VP2C,3C,15B] ***~ out (for),*** stretch out: *He ~ed out his hand for the knife, but it was too far away. He ~ed (out) for the dictionary.* **2** [VP6A,15B,12B,13B] stretch out the hand for and take (sth); get and give (sth) to: *Can you ~ that book for your brother? Please ~ me that book. He ~ed down the atlas from the top shelf.* **3** [VP6A] get to, go as far as: *~ London; ~ the end of the chapter. Can you ~ the branch with those red apples? Not a sound ~ed our ears.* **4** [VP2C] extend; go; pass: *My land ~es as far as the river. The speaker's voice did not ~ to the back of the hall.* ***as far as the eye can ~,*** to the horizon. **5** **ˈ~-me-downs** *n pl* (sl) ready-made garments; second-hand clothes. □ *n* **1** (*sing* only) act of ~ing or stretching out (a hand, etc): *get sth by a long ~.* **2** [U] extent to which a hand, etc can be ~ed out, a movement carried out or one's mental powers extended or used: *This boxer has a long ~.* ***within/out of/beyond ~:*** *I like to have my reference books within my ~/within easy ~,* so near that I can get them quickly and easily. *Put that bottle of weed-killer out of the children's ~/out of ~ of the children. The hotel is within easy ~ of the waterfront. The village is within ~ of London. He was beyond ~ of human aid,* No one could do anything to help him. **3** [C] continuous extent, esp of a river or canal, that can be seen between two bends or locks. ⇨ lock²(3): *one of the most beautiful ~es of the Thames.*

re·act /rɪˈækt/ *vi* **1** [VP2A,3A] ***~ (up)on,*** have an effect (on the person or thing acting): *Applause ~s upon a speaker,* e g has the effect of giving him confidence. **2** [VP3A] ***~ to,*** respond; behave differently, be changed, as the result of being acted upon: *An orator ~s to applause. Do children ~ to kind treatment by becoming more self-confident?* **3** [VP3A] ***~ against,*** respond to sth with a feeling: *Will the people one day ~ against the political system that oppresses them?* **4** [VP3A] ***~ on,*** (chem) (of one substance applied to another) have an effect: *How do acids ~ on metals?*

re·ac·tion /rɪˈækʃn/ *n* [C,U] **1** action or state resulting from, in response to, sth, esp a return to an earlier condition after a period of the opposite condition: *action and ~. After these days of excitement there was a ~,* e g a period when life seemed dull. *Higher wages affect costs of production and then comes the ~ of costs on prices. Is it true that there is a healthy ~* (e g a pleasant glow) *after a cold bath?* **2** retrograde tendency, esp in

razors

politics; opposition to progress: *The forces of ~ made reform difficult.* **3** responsive feeling: *What was his ~ to your proposal?* **4** (science) action set up by one substance in another; change within the nucleus of an atom. **~·ary** /rɪˈækʃnrɪ *US:* –ŋerɪ/ *n* (*pl* **-ries**), *adj* (person) opposing progress or reform.

re·ac·tor /rɪˈæktə(r)/ *n* **nuclear ~,** apparatus for the controlled production of nuclear energy; atomic pile.

read /rid/ *vt,vi* (*pt,pp* read /red/) **1** [VP6A,2A] (used in the simple tenses or with *can/be able*) look at and (be able to) understand (sth written or printed): *Can you ~ Chinese characters/French/a musical score? A motorist must be able to ~ traffic signs. Can the child ~ the time/the clock yet? I can't ~ your shorthand notes. The boy can neither ~ nor write.* **2** [VP6A,12A,13B,15B,2A,C] (simple or continuous tenses) reproduce mentally or vocally the words of (an author, book, etc): *R~ the letter aloud, please. She was ~ing the letter silently/to herself. She was ~ing a story to the children. Mr Hay always ~s his sermons,* preaches them by ~ing. *I haven't enough time to ~/for ~ing. He ~ the letter through six times. Please ~ me the letter. She ~ out the letter to all of us. The old man ~ me a lesson/~ me a severe lecture,* reproved me. *The play was ~* (i e each actor ~ his part aloud) *before the cast went on the stage.* **3** [VP6A,15A,B] study (a subject, esp at a university): *He's ~ing physics/~ing for a degree in physics/~ing for a physics degree at Cambridge. He's ~ing for the Bar,* studying law in order to become a barrister. *You had better ~ the subject up,* make a special study of it. **4** [VP6A] interpret mentally; learn the significance of: *~ a riddle/dream; ~ sb's thoughts. The gipsy offered to ~ my hand/palm,* tell me about myself and the future by examining the lines on the palm of my hand. **5** [VP2C] give a certain impression; seem (good, etc) when ~: *The play ~s better than it acts,* is better for ~ing than for performance on the stage. **6** [VP16B] assume, find implications in (what is read, etc): *Silence mustn't always be ~ as consent,* We must not always assume that a person means 'Yes' when no answer is given to a request, etc. **~ *into,*** add more than is justified: *You have ~ into her letter more sympathy than she probably feels.* **~ *between the lines,*** look for or discover meanings that are not actually expressed. **7** [VP2B] (of instruments) indicate: *What does the thermometer ~?* **8** [VP15A] bring into a specified state by ~ing: *She ~ herself to sleep.* **9** (*pp* with an *adv*) having knowledge gained from books, etc: *a well-~ man; deeply ~ in the classics.* □ *n* period of time given to ~ing: *have a good ~ in the train; have a quiet ~.* **~·able** /ˈridəbl/ *adj* **1** that is easy or pleasant to ~. **2** that can be ~. ⇨ **legible**, the more usu word. **~·abil·ity** /ˌridəˈbɪlətɪ/ *n*

re-ad·dress /ˌri əˈdres/ *vt* [VP6A] change the address on (a letter, etc).

reader /ˈridə(r)/ *n* **1** person who reads, esp one who spends much time in reading; (*publisher's ~*) person employed to read manuscripts offered for publication and say whether they are good, etc; printer's proof-corrector; (*lay ~*) person appointed to read aloud parts of a service in church. **2** (GB) university teacher of a rank immediately below a professor: *R~ in English Literature* **3** textbook for reading in class; book with selections for reading by students of a language: *a Latin R~.* **4** person who can interpret what is hidden or obscure, esp *a ˈmind/ˈthought-~.* **ˈ~·ship** /-ʃɪp/ *n* **1** position of a ~(2). **2** (of a periodical) number of persons who read it (which may be larger than its circulation).

read·ily, readi·ness ⇨ ready.

read·ing /ˈridɪŋ/ *n* **1** [U] act of one who reads. **ˈ~ desk,** lectern. **ˈ~-glasses** *n* glasses for ~ (contrasted with glasses for long-distance use). **ˈ~-lamp** *n* shaded table-lamp used to read by. **ˈ~-room** *n* room (e g in a club or public library) set apart for ~. **2** [U] knowledge, esp of books: *a man of wide ~.* **3** [C] way in which sth is interpreted or understood: *my solicitor's ~ of this clause in the agreement,* what he says it means. **4** [C] figure of measurement, etc as shown on a dial, scale, etc: *The ~s on my thermometer last month were well above the average.* **5** [C] variant reading of a text that occurs in copying or printing from time to time: *The ~ of the First Folio is the true one.* **6** [C] entertainment in which sth is read to an audience: passage so read: *R~s from Dickens.* **ˈplay-~,** recital of the text of a play by a group. **7** [C] (in Parliament) one of the three stages through which a Bill must pass before it is ready for royal assent.

re·ad·just /ˈriəˈdʒʌst/ *vt* [VP6A,3A,15A] **~ *(to),*** adjust again: *It's sometimes difficult to ~ (oneself) to life in England after working abroad.* **~·ment** *n* ~ing or being ~ed; [C] instance of this.

ready /ˈredɪ/ *adj* (**-ier, -iest**) **1** (*pred* only) **~ *(for sth/to do sth),*** in the condition needed for use; in the condition for doing sth; willing: *~ for work; get ~ for a journey; be ~ to start. He's always ~ to help his friends.* ***make* ~,** prepare. **2** quick; prompt: *Don't be so ~ to find fault. He always has a ~ answer. You are too ~ with excuses. He has a ~ wit.* **3** within reach; easily procured: *keep a revolver ~,* near at hand. **~ *money,*** money in the form of coins or notes, which can be used for payment at the time when goods are bought (contrasted with *credit*). **ˌ~ ˈreckoner,** book of answers to various common calculations needed in business, etc. **4** (*adv* use, with *pp*) prepared beforehand: *buy food ~ cooked.* **ˌ~-ˈmade** *adj* **(a)** ~ to wear or use: *~-made clothes,* made in standard sizes, not to measurements of customers. **(b)** (fig) not original; of standard pattern, etc: *come to a subject with ~-made ideas.* □ *n* (only in) ***at the* ~,** (of a rifle) in the position for aiming and firing. **read·ily** *adv* **1** without showing hesitation or unwillingness. **2** without difficulty. **readi·ness** /ˈredɪnəs/ *n* [U] **1** ***in readiness (for),*** in a ready or prepared state: *have everything in readiness for an early start.* **2** willingness: *a surprising readiness to accept the proposal.* **3** promptness; quickness: *readiness of wit.*

re·af·firm /ˈriəˈfɜm/ *vt* [VP6A,9] affirm again; repeat an affirmation with reaffirm: *~ one's loyalty.*

re·af·for·est /ˈri əˈfɒrɪst *US:* -ˈfɔr-/, (US = **re·for·est** /ˈriˈfɒrɪst *US:* -ˈfɔr-/) *vt* replant (an area of land) with forest trees. **re·af·for·est·ation** /ˈri əˈfɒrɪˈsteɪʃn *US:* -ˈfɔr-/, (US = **re·for·est·ation** /ˈriˈfɒrɪˈsteɪʃn *US:* -ˈfɔr-/) *n*

re·agent /riˈeɪdʒənt/ *n* [C] (chem) substance used to detect the presence of another by reaction; reactive substance or force.

real[1] /rɪəl/ *adj* **1** existing in fact; not imagined or supposed; not made up or artificial: *Is this ~ gold or pinchbeck? Is this ~ silk or rayon? Was it a ~ man you saw or a ghost? The doctors could not effect a ~* (= genuine, complete) *cure. Things that happen in ~ life are sometimes stranger than things that occur in fiction. Who is the ~ manager of the business? Tell me the ~* (= true) *reason for your absence from work.* **2** **'~ estate,** (legal) immovable property consisting of land, any natural resources, and buildings (contrasted with *personal estate*). **3** (colloq as *adv*) really, very: *We had a ~ good time;* (US) *I'm ~ sorry.* **~ly** /ˈrɪəlɪ/ *adv* **1** in fact; without doubt; truly: *What do you ~ly think about it? It was ~ly not my fault. I'm ~ly sorry.* **2** (as an expression of interest, surprise, mild protest, doubt, etc according to context): *'We're going to Mexico next month.'—'Oh, ~ly!'* (or) *'Not ~ly?' R~ly, you ought not to knock your wife about like that!*

real² /reɪˈɑl/ *n* [C] silver coin and unit of currency formerly used in Spain and in Spanish-speaking countries.

real·ism /ˈrɪəl-ɪzm/ *n* [U] **1** (in art and literature) showing of real life, facts, etc in a true way, omitting nothing that is ugly or painful, and idealizing nothing. **2** behaviour based on the facing of facts and disregard of sentiment and convention. **3** (phil) theory that matter has real existence apart from our mental perception of it. ⇨ **idealism. real·ist** /-ɪst/ *n* person who believes in ~ in art, philosophy, social problems, etc; person who believes himself to be without illusions. **real·is·tic** /ˈrɪəˈlɪstɪk/ *adj* **1** marked by, relating to, ~ in philosophy or art. **2** practical; not moved by sentiment: *realistic politics.* **real·is·ti·cally** /-klɪ/ *adv*

re·al·ity /rɪˈælətɪ/ *n* (*pl* **-ties**) **1** [U] the quality of being real; real existence; that which underlies appearance: *belief in the ~ of miracles; the search after God and ~.* ***bring sb back to ~,*** get him to stop dreaming, being sentimental, etc. ***in ~,*** really, in actual fact. **2** [C] sth real; sth actually seen or experienced: *the grim realities of war,* contrasted with romantic ideas, etc. **3** [U] (in art, etc) truth; lifelike resemblance to the original: *The T V broadcast described what was happening with extraordinary ~.*

real·ize /ˈrɪəlɑɪz/ *vt* **1** [VP6A,9,10] be fully conscious of; understand: *Does he ~ his error yet/~ that you must have help?* **2** [VP6A] convert (a hope, plan, etc) into a fact: *~ one's hopes/ambitions.* **3** [VP6A] exchange (property, business shares, etc) for money: *Can these shares/bonds, etc, be ~d at short notice?* **4** [VP6A] ***~ (on),*** (of property, etc) obtain as a price for or as a profit: *The furniture ~d a high price at the sale. How much did you ~ on the paintings you sent to the sale?* **real·iz·able** /-əbl/ *adj* that can be ~d. **real·iz·ation** /ˈrɪəlɑɪˈzeɪʃn *US:* -lɪˈz-/ *n* [U] realizing (of a plan, one's ambitions or hopes); act of exchanging property for money.

realm /relm/ *n* **1** (poet, rhet or legal use) kingdom: *the defence of the R~; a Peer of the R~.* **2** region (fig): *the ~ of the imagination; in the ~s of fancy.*

Re·al·tor /ˈrɪəltə(r)/ *n* (US) person engaged in real estate business who is a member of the National Association of Real Estate Boards and subscribes to its standards of ethical conduct (GB = *estate agent*).

re·alty /ˈrɪəltɪ/ *n* (*pl* **-ties**) (legal) real estate.

ream /rim/ *n* measure for paper, 480 (or US 500) sheets or 20 quires; (colloq, *pl*) great quantity (of writing): *She has written ~s of verse.*

re·ani·mate /riˈænɪmeɪt/ *vt* [VP6A] fill with new strength, courage or energy.

reap /rip/ *vt,vi* [VP6A,2A] cut (grain, etc); gather in a crop of grain from (a field, etc): *~ a field of barley; ~ the corn;* (fig) *~ the reward of virtue; ~ where one has not sown,* profit from work done by others. ***(sow the wind and) ~ the whirlwind,*** suffer for one's foolish conduct. **'~ing-hook** *n* sickle. **~er** *n* **1** person who ~s. **2** ~ing-machine for cutting grain (and in some cases binding it into sheaves).

re·appear /ˈriəˈpɪə(r)/ *vi* [VP2A] appear again (esp after disappearing). **~·ance** /-rəns/ *n*

re·apprais·al /ˈriəˈpreɪzl/ *n* new examination and judgement: *a ~ of our relations with China.*

rear¹ /rɪə(r)/ *n* **1** back part: *The kitchen is in the ~ of the house. The garage is at the ~ of* (US *in the ~ of*) *the house.* **2** (attrib) in or at the ~: *the ~ wheels/lamps,* of a car, etc; *leave the bus by the ~ entrance; a ~-view mirror,* driving mirror (in a motor-vehicle) for seeing out of the back window. **3** last part of any army, fleet, etc: *attack the enemy in the ~.* ***bring up the ~,*** come/be last. **4** **'~-'admiral** /ˈrɪər ˈædmrl/ *n* naval officer below a vice-admiral. **'~·guard** *n* body of soldiers given the duty of guarding the ~ of an army. ***a ~guard action,*** fight between an army in retreat and the enemy. **~·most** /ˈrɪəməʊst/ *adj* farthest back. **~·ward** /ˈrɪəwəd/ *n*: *to ~ward of,* some distance behind; *in the ~ward,* at the back. **~·wards** /ˈrɪəwədz/ *adv* towards the ~.

rear² /rɪə(r)/ *vt,vi* **1** [VP6A] cause or help to grow; bring up: *~ poultry/cattle; ~ a family* (US usu *raise a family*). **2** [VP2A,C] (esp of a horse) rise on the hind legs. **3** [VP6A,15B] raise; lift up: *The snake ~ed its head. The horse ~ed itself up.* **4** [VP6A] set up: *~ a monument.*

re·arm /riˈɑm/ *vt,vi* [VP6A,2A] supply (an army, etc) with weapons again, or with weapons of new types, etc. **re·arma·ment** /riˈɑməmənt/ *n*

rea·son¹ /ˈrizn/ *n* **1** [C,U] (fact put forward or serving as) cause of or justification for sth: *There is ~ to believe that he is dishonest. Is there any ~ why you should not help? He complains with ~* (= rightly) *that he has been punished unfairly. Give me your ~s for doing it. My ~ is that the cost will be too high. The ~ why he's late is that/because there was a breakdown on the railway.* ***by ~ of,*** because of: *He was excused by ~ of his age.* **2** [U] power of the mind to understand, form opinions, etc: *Only man has ~.* ***lose one's ~,*** go mad: *The poor old fellow has lost his ~.* **3** [U] what is right or practicable; common sense; sensible conduct: *He's not amenable to ~.* ***bring sb to ~,*** persuade him to give up foolish activities, useless resistance, etc. ***do anything (with)in ~,*** anything sensible or reasonable: *I'm willing to do anything (with)in ~.* ***listen to/hear ~,*** allow oneself to be persuaded; pay attention to commonsense, advice, etc. ***lose all ~,*** become irrational, illogical. ***without rhyme or ~,*** ⇨ **rhyme(1).** ***It stands to ~ (that),*** is obvious to sensible people; most people will agree.... **~·less** *adj* lacking ~.

rea·son² /ˈrizn/ *vi,vt* **1** [VP2A] make use of one's reason(2); exercise the power of thought: *Man's ability to ~ makes him different from the animals.* **2** [VP3A] ***~ with sb,*** argue in order to convince him: *She ~ed with me for an hour about the folly* *of my plans.* **3** [VP9] ~ ***(that),*** say by way of argument: *He ~ed that if we started at dawn, we could arrive before noon.* **4** [VP6A] express logically or in the form of an argument: *a well-~ed statement/manifesto.* ***~ sth out,*** find an answer by considering successive arguments, etc: *~ out the answer to a question.* **5** [VP14] ***~ sb into/out of sth,*** persuade by argument to do/not to do sth: *~ a person out of his fears,* show him that his fears are groundless; *~ sb out of a false belief; ~ sb into a sensible course of action.* **~·ing** *n* [U] process of reaching conclusions by using one's reason: *He surpasses most of us in power of ~ing,* is better at drawing conclusions from facts, etc. *There's no ~ing with that woman,* She won't listen to reason.

rea·son·able /ˋriznəbl/ *adj* **1** having ordinary common sense; able to reason; acting, done, in accordance with reason; willing to listen to reason: *You're not very ~ if you expect a child to understand sarcasm. Is the accused guilty beyond ~ doubt?* **2** moderate; neither more or less than seems right or acceptable: *a ~ price/offer.* **3** fair; just; not absurd: *a ~ excuse; be ~ in one's demands.* **~·ness** *n* **rea·son·ably** /-əblɪ/ *adv*

re·as·sure /ˈriəˋʃʊə(r)/ *vt* [VP6A] remove the fears or doubts of: *She felt ~d after the bank had told her that her investments were safe.* **re·as·sur·ance** /-rns/ *n* [U] **re·as·sur·ing·ly** *adv*

re·bar·ba·tive /rɪˋbɑbətɪv/ *adj* (formal) stern; repellent.

re·bate /ˋribeɪt/ *n* [C] sum of money by which a debt, tax, etc may be reduced; discount: *There is a ~ of £1.50 if the account is settled before 31 Dec.*

rebel[1] /ˋrebl/ *n* **1** person who takes up arms against, or refuses allegiance to, the established government; person who resists authority or control: *a ~ in the home,* e g a child who resists the authority of its parents. **2** (attrib) relating to ~s; of the nature of a rebellion: *the ~ forces.*

re·bel[2] /rɪˋbel/ *vi* (-ll-) [VP2A,3A] ~ ***(against),*** **1** take up arms to fight (against the government). **2** show resistance; protest strongly: *The children ~led against having to do three hours' homework each evening. Such treatment would make anyone ~.*

re·bel·lion /rɪˋbelɪən/ *n* [U] ~ ***(against),*** rebelling, esp against a government: *rise in ~;* [C] instance of this: *five ~s in two years; a ~ against the dictator.*

re·bel·li·ous /rɪˋbelɪəs/ *adj* **1** acting like a rebel; taking part in a rebellion: *~ subjects; ~ behaviour.* **2** not easily controlled: *a child with a ~ temper.* **~·ly** *adv* **~·ness** *n*

re·bind /ˈriˋbaɪnd/ *vt* (*pt,pp* -bound /-ˋbaʊnd/) [VP6A] put a new binding on (a book, etc).

re·birth /ˈriˋbɜθ/ *n* **1** spiritual change, e g by conversion or englightenment, causing a person to lead a new kind of life. **2** revival: *the ~ of learning.*

re·born /ˈriˋbɔn/ *adj* (fig) born again, i e spiritually.

re·bound /ˋribaʊnd/ *vi* [VP2A,3A] **1** ~ ***(from),*** spring or bounce back after hitting sth: *The ball ~ed from the wall into the lily pond.* **2** ~ ***(up)on,*** (fig) come back upon the agent; happen as the consequence of one's own action: *The evil you do may ~ upon yourselves.* ***on the ~,*** **(a)** while bouncing back: *hit a ball on the ~.* **(b)** (fig) while still reacting to depression or disappointment: *She quarrelled with Paul and then married Peter on the ~.* **3** ⇨ rebind.

re·buff /rɪˋbʌf/ *n* [C] ***meet with/suffer a ~ (from sb),*** unkind or contemptuous refusal of, or show of indifference to (an offer of or request for help, friendship, etc); snub. □ *vt* [VP6A] give a ~ to.

re·build /ˈriˋbɪld/ *vt* (*pt,pp* -built /-ˋbɪlt/) [VP6A] build or put together again: *a rebuilt typewriter.*

re·buke /rɪˋbjuk/ *vt* [VP6A,14] ~ ***sb (for sth),*** reprove, speak severely to (officially or otherwise): *~ a subordinate for being impudent.* □ *n* [C] reproof: *administer ~s to sb.* **re·buk·ing·ly** *adv*

re·bus /ˋribəs/ *n* puzzle in which a word or phrase has to be guessed from pictures or diagrams that suggest the syllables that make it.

re·but /rɪˋbʌt/ *vt* (-tt-) [VP6A] prove (a charge, piece of evidence, etc) to be false; refute. **~·tal** /-tl/ *n* act of ~ting; evidence that ~s a charge, etc.

re·cal·ci·trant /rɪˋkælsɪtrənt/ *adj* disobedient; resisting authority or discipline. **re·cal·ci·trance** /-əns/, **re·cal·ci·trancy** /-ənsɪ/ *nn* [U] being ~.

re·call /rɪˋkɔl/ *vt* **1** [VP6A,14] ~ ***sb (from/to),*** summon back: *~ an ambassador (from his post/ to his own country.* **2** [VP6A,D,8,9,10] bring back to the mind; recollect: *I don't ~ his name/face/ meeting him/where I met him. Can you ~ your schooldays?* **3** [VP6A] take back; revoke (an order, a decision). □ *n* **1** summons to return; (esp) summons to an ambassador to return to his own country: *letters of ~.* **2** [U] ability to remember: *a man gifted with instant ~;* possibility of recalling. ***beyond/past ~,*** that cannot be brought back or revoked. **3** [C] signal, e g a bugle call, to troops, etc to return: *sound the ~.*

re·cant /rɪˋkænt/ *vt,vi* [VP6A,2A] give up (an opinion, a belief); take back (a statement) as being false: *The torturers could not make the man ~,* give up his beliefs, e g religious or political. **re·can·ta·tion** /ˈrikænˋteɪʃn/ *n* [U] ~ing; [C] instance of this; statement disavowing former beliefs.

re·cap[1] /ˋrikæp/ *vt,vi, n* (colloq abbr of) recapitulate, recapitulation.

re·cap[2] /ˈriˋkæp/ *vt* (-pp-) (US) retread (a tyre).

re·cap·itu·late /ˈrikəˋpɪtʃʊleɪt/ *vt,vi* [VP6A,2A] repeat, go through again, the chief points of (sth that has been said, discussed, argued about, etc). **re·cap·itu·la·tion** /ˈrikəˈpɪtʃʊˋleɪʃn/ *n* [U] recapitulating; [C] instance of this.

re·cap·ture /riˋkæptʃə(r)/ *vt* [VP6A] **1** capture again. **2** recall: *try to ~ the past.*

re·cast /ˈriˋkɑst *US:* -ˋkæst/ *vt* [VP6A] **1** cast or fashion anew: *~ a gun/a bell; ~* (= rewrite) *a sentence/paragraph/chapter.* **2** change the cast of a play, i e find different actors or give actors different parts.

recce /ˋrekɪ/ *n* (mil; colloq abbr of) reconnaissance.

re·cede /rɪˋsid/ *vi* [VP2A,3A] **1** (appear to) go back from the observer or from an earlier position: *As the tide ~d we were able to explore the rocky pools on the beach. As our ship steamed out to sea the coast slowly ~d.* **2** slope away from the front or from the observer: *a receding chin/forehead.* **3** withdraw (*from* an opinion, etc). **4** decline in character or value: *receding prices.*

re·ceipt /rɪˋsit/ *n* **1** [U] receiving or being received: *on ~ of the news. I am in ~ of your letter of the*

3rd, (pompous for) I have received.... **2** (*pl*) money received (in a business, etc contrasted with *expenditure*). **3** [C] written statement that sth (money or goods) has been received: *get a ~ for money spent; sign a ~; a `~ book*, one with forms and counterfoils for writing out ~s. **4** [C] = recipe. **5** (archaic) place where money is officially received, esp ***at the ~ of custom,*** the custom-house. □ *vt* [VP6A] write out and sign or stamp a ~(3): *~ a hotel bill*, put 'Paid' or 'Received with thanks' on it.

re·ceiv·able /rɪ`sivəbl/ *adj* **1** that can be received; fit to be received. **2** (comm; of bills, accounts, etc) on which money is to be received. ***bills ~,*** contrasted with *bills payable*.

re·ceive /rɪ`siv/ *vt,vi* [VP6A,2A] **1** accept, take, get (sth offered, sent, etc): *When did you ~ the letter/news/telegram, etc? He ~d a good education. We ~d nothing but insults. You will ~ a warm welcome when you come to England. He was caught receiving* (i e taking possession of stolen property) *soon after his release from prison.* **re`ceiving-set** *n* radio receiver. **2** allow to enter; (formally) see, welcome or entertain (friends, guests, etc): *The hotel is now open to ~ guests. He was ~d into the Church*, admitted as a member. *Lady Snooks ~s on Monday afternoons*, is at home to her friends and acquaintances then. **re·ceived** *adj* (old use) widely accepted as correct: *the ~d version/text; the ~d view/opinion.*

re·ceiver /rɪ`sivə(r)/ *n* **1** person who receives, esp who knowingly receives stolen goods. **2** **(Official) R~,** official appointed to take charge of the property and affairs of a bankrupt, or to administer property in dispute. **3** part of an apparatus for receiving sth, e g that part of a telephone that is held to the ear; apparatus for receiving broadcast signals: *a `radio-~.* **~·ship** /-ʃɪp/ *n* office of a ~(2); his period of office.

re·cent /`risnt/ *adj* (having existed, been made, happened) not long before; begun not long ago: *~ news; a ~ event; within ~ memory. Ours is a ~ acquaintance*, We have been acquainted for only a short time. **~·ly** *adv* lately; not long ago: *until quite ~ly.*

re·cep·tacle /rɪ`septəkl/ *n* container or holder in which things may be put away or out of sight.

re·cep·tion /rɪ`sepʃn/ *n* **1** [U] receiving or being received: *prepare rooms for the ~ of guests; `~ area/camp/centre*, one where persons, e g evacuees, refugees, are received and accommodated: *a `~ committee. The house has two ~ rooms* (rooms for the ~ of guests, but this usu means living-rooms), *a kitchen, and three bedrooms.* **`~-desk,** (in a hotel) counter where guests are received, where they ask for rooms, etc. **`~ clerk,** (US) person at a ~-deck, who attends to inquiries from guests. **2** [C] occasion on which guests are received; formal party or welcome: *Mrs X holds a ~ every Monday. There was a ~ after the wedding ceremony.* **3** [C] welcome or greeting of a specified kind; demonstration of feeling toward sb or sth: *The new book had a favourable ~*, was welcomed by the critics, the public, etc. *The President's ~ was all that he could desire.* **4** [U] receiving of radio, etc signals; degree of efficiency of this: *Is radio ~ good in your district? R~ of TV programmes is unsatisfactory here.* **~·ist** /-ɪst/ *n* person employed in a hotel, or by a hairdresser, dentist or other professional person, to receive clients.

re·cep·tive /rɪ`septɪv/ *adj* quick or ready to receive suggestions, new ideas, etc: *a ~ mind; ~ to new ideas.* **~·ly** *adv* **re·cep·tiv·ity** /ˈrisep`tɪvətɪ/ *n*

re·cess /rɪ`ses *US:* `rises/ *n* **1** (US = *vacation*) period of time when work or business is stopped, e g when Parliament, the law courts, are not in session. **2** part of a room where the wall is set back from the main part; alcove or niche: *a ~ with a writing-desk and a chair in it.* **3** secret place; place difficult of access: *the dark ~es of a cave; a mountain ~*; (fig) *in the innermost ~es of the heart/mind.* □ *vt* [VP6A] **1** place in a ~; set back: *~ a wall.* **2** provide with ~es.

re·cession /rɪ`seʃn/ *n* **1** [U] withdrawal; act of receding. **2** [C] slackening of business and industrial activity: *Did the ~ in the States cause a lot of unemployment?*

re·cessional /rɪ`seʃnl/ *n* **~ (hymn),** hymn sung while the clergy and choir withdraw after a church service. □ *adj* **1** of a recession: *`~ music.* **2** relating to a Parliamentary recess.

re·cess·ive /rɪ`sesɪv/ *adj* **1** having a tendency to recede or go back. **2** (biol) exhibiting weak characteristics (the stronger ones are called *dominant*) which are passed on by means of genes to later generations, e g blue eyes and blond hair.

ré·chauffé /reɪ`ʃəʊfeɪ *US:* ˈreɪʃəʊ`feɪ/ *n* dish of food warmed up again; rehash.

re·cher·ché /rə`ʃeəʃeɪ/ *adj* (esp of meals) devised with care; choice; (of words) selected with care; too studied or far-fetched.

re·cidi·vist /rɪ`sɪdəvɪst/ *n* person who habitually relapses into crime; one who apparently cannot be cured of criminal tendencies; persistent offender. **re·cidi·vism** /-ɪzm/ *n*

recipe /`resəpɪ/ *n* [C] direction for preparing (a cake, a dish of food, a medical remedy) or for getting (any result): *a ~ for a fruit cake. Have you a ~ for happiness?*

re·cipi·ent /rɪ`sɪpɪənt/ *n* person who receives sth.

re·cip·ro·cal /rɪ`sɪprəkl/ *adj* **1** given and received in return; mutual: *~ affection/help.* **2** corresponding, but the other way round: *a ~ mistake*, e g I thought he was a waiter and he thought I was a guest, but I was a waiter and he was a guest. **3** (gram) **~ pronouns,** those expressing mutual action or relation, e g *each other, one another.* **~·ly** /-klɪ/ *adv*

re·cip·ro·cate /rɪ`sɪprəkeɪt/ *vt,vi* [VP6A,2A] **1** give in return; give and receive, each to and from each: *I ~ your good wishes. He ~d by wishing her a pleasant journey.* **2** (of parts of a machine) (cause to) move backwards and forwards in a straight line (e g the piston of an engine): *a reciprocating engine/saw.* ⇨ **rotatory. re·cip·ro·ca·tion** /rɪˈsɪprə`keɪʃn/ *n* [U].

reci·proc·ity /ˈresɪ`prosətɪ/ *n* [U] principle or practice of give and take, of making mutual concessions; the granting of privileges in return for similar privileges: *~ in trade* (*between two countries*).

re·cital /rɪ`saɪtl/ *n* [C] **1** detailed account of a number of connected events, etc: *We were bored by the long ~ of his adventures.* **2** performance of music by a soloist or small group, or of the works of one composer: *a pi`ano ~; a ~ of Hugo Wolf songs.*

reci·ta·tion /ˈresɪ`teɪʃn/ *n* **1** [U] the act of reciting(2): *the ~ of his grievances.* **2** [U] public delivery of passages of prose or poetry learnt by heart; [C] instance of this: *a `Dickens ~*, of dramatic extracts from the novels. **3** [C] piece of poetry or prose (to be) learnt by heart and recited: *a book of ~s.* **4** (US) [U] repetition of a prepared lesson by a pupil to his teacher; [C] instance of this.

reci·ta·tive /ˌresɪtəˋtiv/ *n* **1** [U] style of music between singing and talking, many words being spoken or sung on the same note, used for the narrative and dialogue parts of some operas. **2** [C] passage (in an opera or oratorio) (to be) rendered thus.

re·cite /rɪˋsɑɪt/ *vt, vi* [VP6A,15A,2A] **1** say (esp poems) aloud from memory: *The mayor ~d to the Queen a long and tedious speech of welcome. The little girl refused to ~ at the party.* **2** give a list of, tell one by one (names, facts, etc): *~ one's grievances; ~ the names of all the capital cities of Europe.*

reck /rek/ *vi, vt* (old use; poet or rhet; in *neg* and *interr* sentences, or with *little*) care about; head; take account *of*: *They ~ed little of hardship.*

reck·less /ˋrekləs/ *adj* rash; not thinking of the consequences: *a ~ spender; ~ of danger/the consequences; fined £10 for ~* (= dangerous) *driving.* **~·ly** *adv* **~·ness** *n*

reckon /ˋrekən/ *vt, vi* **1** [VP6A,15B,2A] calculate; find out (the quantity, number, cost, etc) by working with numbers: *~ the cost of a holiday. Hire charges are ~ed from the date of delivery. The child can't ~ yet.* ***~ sth in,*** include, take into account, when ~ing: *Did you ~ in the cost of a taxi across London?* ***~ sth up,*** find the total of: *~ up the bill.* ***~ without one's host,*** ⇨ host²(2). **2** ***~ with sb,*** **(a)** deal with; settle accounts with: *When the fighting is over, we'll ~ with the enemy's sympathizers.* **(b)** take into account; consider: *He is certainly a man to be ~ed with,* a man who cannot be ignored, who may be a serious competitor, opponent, etc (according to context). **3** ***~ (up)on sb/sth,*** depend on, base one's hopes on: *I ~ on your help. The proprietors of the Casino ~ on human foolishness and greed,* can depend, for making profit, on the foolishness and greed of those who gamble. *He's the sort of man you can ~ on in a crisis.* **4** [VP9,16B,25] ***~ sb/sth as/to be; ~ that,*** be of the opinion, suppose; consider: *One-fourth of the country is ~ed as unproductive. She was ~ed the most handsome woman at Court. Do you still ~ him among/as one of your friends? I ~ he is rather too old to marry again.* **5** (US colloq) assume: *I ~ we'll go next week.* **~er** /ˋreknə(r)/ *n* person or thing that counts. **ready ~er,** ⇨ ready. **~·ing** /ˋreknɪŋ/ *n* (esp) **1** [C] (old use) (totalled) account of items to be paid for, e g at a hotel or restaurant: *pay the ~ing. There'll be a heavy ~ing to pay if he continues this wild life,* He will have to suffer for it. ***day of ~ing,*** time when sth must be atoned for. **2** [U] calculation, e g of a ship's position by observation of the sun, stars, etc. ***dead ~ing,*** method of calculating the position of a ship or aircraft from a known earlier position, and later course and distance, when observations of the sun, etc are impossible. ***out in one's ~ing,*** mistaken in one's calculations.

re·claim /rɪˋkleɪm/ *vt* [VP6A] **1** bring back (waste land, etc) to a useful condition, a state of cultivation, etc. **2** reform (a person): *~ a man from error/vice; a ~ed drunkard.* **3** demand that sth be given back. **rec·la·ma·tion** /ˌrekləˋmeɪʃn/ *n* [U].

re·cline /rɪˋklɑɪn/ *vi, vt* [VP2A,C,15A] place oneself, be, in a position of rest; put (one's arms, etc) in a resting position; lie back or down: *~ on a couch; ~ one's arms on the table; a reˋclining chair,* one with a back that tilts.

re·cluse /rɪˋklus/ *n* person who lives alone and avoids other people: *live the life of a ~,* live like a hermit, avoiding meeting people.

rec·og·ni·tion /ˌrekəgˋnɪʃn/ *n* [U] recognizing or being recognized: *~ signals; aircraft ~. He was given a cheque for £25 in ~ of his services. R~ of the new State is unlikely,* It is unlikely that diplomatic relations will be established with it. ***alter/change beyond/out of (all) ~,*** change so much that ~ is impossible: *The town has changed out of all ~ since I was there ten years ago.*

re·cog·ni·zance /rɪˋkognɪzns/ *n* [C] (legal) **1** bond by which a person is bound to appear before a court of law at a certain time, or to observe certain conditions, and to forfeit a certain sum if he fails to do so. ***enter into ~s,*** sign such a bond. **2** sum of money (to be) paid as surety for observing such a bond.

rec·og·nize /ˋrekəgnɑɪz/ *vt* **1** [VP6A,16A] know, (be able to) identify again (sb or sth) that one has seen, heard, etc before: *~ a tune/an old acquaintance.* **2** [VP6A] be willing to accept (sb or sth) as what he or it claims to be or has been in the past: *refuse to ~ a new government/~ sb as lawful heir. The Browns no longer ~ the Smiths,* do not accept them as acquaintances or friends. **3** [VP6A,9] be prepared to admit; be aware: *He ~d that he was not qualified for the post/~d his lack of qualifications.* **4** [VP6A,9,25] acknowledge: *Everyone ~d him to be the greatest living authority on ancient Roman coins. His services to the State were ~d,* e g he was made a knight. **rec·og·niz·able** /-əbl/ *adj* that can be ~d. **rec·og·niz·ably** /-əblɪ/ *adv*

re·coil /rɪˋkɔɪl/ **1** [VP2A,3A] ***~ (from),*** draw or jump back; shrink: *~ from doing sth* (in fear, horror, disgust, etc). **2** [VP2A] (of a gun) kick back (when fired). **3** [VP3A] ***~ (up)on,*** (fig) rebound; react: *His meanness ~ed upon his own head. Revenge may ~ upon the person who takes it.* □ *n* act of ~ing.

rec·ol·lect /ˌrekəˋlekt/ *vt, vi* [VP6A,D,8,10,9,2A] call back to the mind; succeed in remembering: *~ childhood days; ~ hearing Chaliapin; ~ how to do sth/how sth was done. As far as I ~,....*

rec·ol·lec·tion /ˌrekəˋlekʃn/ *n* **1** [U] act or power of recollecting: *scenes which arise in quiet ~ of the past; to the best of my ~,* so far as I can recollect; if I remember aright. **2** [U] time over which the memory goes back: *Such a problem has never arisen within my ~.* **3** [C] sth recollected; that which is remembered: *The old letters brought many ~s to my mind.*

rec·om·mend /ˌrekəˋmend/ *vt* **1** [VP6A,14,12A,13A,16A] ***~ sth (to sb) (for sth); ~ sb sth; ~ sb (for sth/as sth),*** speak favourably of; say that one thinks sth is good (for a purpose) or that sb is fitted (for a post, etc as...): *I can ~ this soap. He has been ~ed for first class honours. What would you ~ for getting ink stains from my blouse? Can you ~ me a good novel? Can you ~ Miss Hill as a good typist?* **2** [VP17,6D] ***~ sb to do sth,*** suggest as wise or suitable; advise: *I have been ~ed to try* *these pills for sea-sickness. I ~ you not to disobey your officers. Do you ~ raising the school-leaving age?* **3** [VP6A,14] **~ sb (to sb),** (of a quality, etc) cause to be or appear pleasing, satisfactory; make acceptable: *Behaviour of that sort will not ~ you.* **4** [VP14] commend (the more usu word): *~ oneself/one's soul to God; ~ a child to sb's care.* **rec·om·men·da·tion** /ˌrekəmenˈdeɪʃn/ *n* **1** [U] ~ing; *speak in ~ation of sb or sth; buy sth on the ~ation of a friend,* because he has ~ed it. **2** [C] statement that ~s sb or sth: *My bank manager has sent me a list of ~ations,* e g names of stocks which he ~s me to buy. *The jury brought in a verdict of guilty, with a ~ to mercy.* **3** [C] sth which causes a person to be well thought of: *Is a sweet disposition a ~ation in a wife?*

rec·om·pense /ˈrekəmpens/ *vt* [VP6A,14] **~ sb (for sth),** reward or punish; make payment to: *~ sb for his trouble; ~ good with evil; ~ sb for a loss.* □ *n* [C,U] reward; payment; satisfaction given for injury: *receive a ~ for one's services; work hard without ~; in ~ for your help.*

rec·on·cile /ˈrekənsaɪl/ *vt* **1** [VP6A,14] **~ sb with sb,** cause (persons) to become friends after they have quarrelled: *We became ~d. He refused to become ~d with his brother.* **2** [VP6A] settle, arrange (a quarrel, difference of opinion, etc). **3** [VP6A,14] **~ (with) sth,** bring into harmony with; cause to agree with: *How can this decision be ~d with justice? I can't ~ what you say with the facts of the case.* **4** [VP14] **~ oneself to sth; be ~d to sth,** overcome one's objections to; resign oneself to: *You must ~ yourself to a life of hardship and poverty.* **rec·on·cil·able** /-əbl/ *adj* **rec·on·cili·ation** /ˌrekənˌsɪlɪˈeɪʃn/ *n* [U] reconciling or being ~d; [C] instance of this: *bring about a reconciliation between friends who have quarrelled.*

rec·on·dite /ˈrekəndaɪt/ *adj* **1** (of subjects of knowledge) out of the way; little known; abstruse: *~ studies.* **2** (of an author) having ~ knowledge.

re·con·di·tion /ˌrikənˈdɪʃn/ *vt* [VP6A] put into good condition again: *a car with a ~ed engine.*

re·con·nais·sance /rɪˈkɒnɪsns/ *n* **1** [U] act of reconnoitring: *~ in force,* made with sufficient troops to resist any enemy forces that may be encountered. **2** [C] instance of reconnoitring; survey, made by troops or a group of scouting vessels or aircraft, of an enemy's position or whereabouts; (fig) survey of any kind of work before it is started: *make a ~ of the work to be done.*

re·con·noitre (US = **-ter**) /ˌrekəˈnɔɪtə(r)/ *vt,vi* [VP6A,2A] go to or near (a place or area occupied by enemy forces) to learn about their position, strength, etc: *~ the ground.*

re·con·struct /ˌrikənˈstrʌkt/ *vt* [VP6A] **1** construct again. **2** build up a complete structure or description of (sth of which one has only a few parts or only partial evidence): *~ a ruined abbey. The detective tried to ~ the crime,* picture to himself how it had been committed. **re·con·struc·tion** /ˌrikənˈstrʌkʃn/ *n*

rec·ord[1] /ˈrekɔd *US:* ˈrekərd/ *n* **1** [C] written account of facts, events, etc: *a ~ of school attendances/of road accidents; the (ˌPublic) ˈR~ Office,* one in London where public documents with accounts of events, official acts, etc written down at the time they occur, are stored. **2** [U] state of being ~ed or preserved in writing, esp as authentic evidence of sth: *a matter of ~,* sth that is established as fact by being ~ed. ***be/go/put sb on ~***: *It is on ~ that the summer was the wettest for 50 years. I don't want to go on ~/dont want you to put me on ~ as saying that I think the Prime Minister a fool.* **off the ~,** (colloq) not for publication or for recording: *What the President said at his press conference was off the ~,* not to be repeated by the newspaper men there, and not to be used in their reports or articles. **3** [C] facts known about the past of sb or sth: *He has an honourable ~ of service/a good ~. I can bear ~ to his previous good conduct,* can confirm that his conduct was good. *Your ~ is in your favour,* What we know about your past is favourable to you. *That airline has a bad ~,* e g has had many accidents to its aircraft. **4** [C] sth that provides evidence or information: *Our museums are full of ~s of past history. R~s of ancient civilizations are still being excavated.* **5** [C] disc on which sound has been registered; what is ~ed on such a disc: *ˈgramophone ~s.* ⇨ recording. **ˈ~-player** *n* instrument for reproducing sound from discs (often one connected to an external loud-speaker). **6** [C] limit, score, point, attainment, mark, etc (high or low), not reached before; (esp in sport) the best yet done: *Which country holds the ~ for speed on water,* i e the highest speed for hydroplanes or motor-boats? *Two ~s fell during the sports meeting at Oslo last week.* (attrib) *Hill made a ~ score in the match against Kent,* (cricket) scored a total that was a ~. *There was a ~ rice crop in Thailand that year.* ***break/beat the ~,*** do better than has been done before. Hence, **ˈ~-breaking** *adj*

re·cord[2] /rɪˈkɔd/ *vt* [VP6A] **1** set down in writing for reference; preserve for use, by writing or in other ways, e g on a disc, magnetic tape, videotape, film, etc: *This volume ~s the history of the regiment. The programme was ~ed.* Cf *a 'live' broadcast. The tape-recorder has ~ed his voice and the camera has ~ed his features.* **ˈ~ing angel,** angel who, it is said, ~s men's good and bad actions. **2** (of an instrument) mark or indicate on a scale: *The thermometer ~ed 40°C.*

re·corder /rɪˈkɔdə(r)/ *n* **1** magistrate with criminal and civil jurisdiction who presides over quarter sessions in a borough or city. **2** apparatus that records. **ˈtape-~,** one that records sound on magnetic tape. **ˌvideo ˈtape-~,** one that records vision and sound on magnetic tape. **3** wooden musical instrument resembling a flute. ⇨ the illus at brass.

re·cord·ing /rɪˈkɔdɪŋ/ *n* (esp in sound or TV broadcasting, and for record-players, etc) programme, piece of music, etc registered on a disc, magnetic tape, film, etc for reproduction: *It wasn't a 'live' performance but a B B C ~. I have a good ~ of this opera on three long-playing discs.*

re·count[1] /rɪˈkaʊnt/ *vt* [VP6A] give an account of; tell: *He ~ed to them the story of his adventures in Mexico.*

re-count[2] /ˌri ˈkaʊnt/ *vt* [VP6A] count again: *~ the votes.* □ *n* /ˈri kaʊnt/ another count: *One of the candidates demanded a ~.*

re·coup /rɪˈkup/ *vt* [VP6A,14] compensate (sb, oneself, *for* a loss, etc); make up for: *~ one's losses; ~ oneself for one's losses.*

re·course /rɪˈkɔs/ *n* [U] **1** ***have ~ to,*** turn to for help; seek help from: *I don't advise you to have ~ to the money-lenders.* **2** sth turned to for help:

Your only ~ is legal action against them.

re·cover[1] /rɪˋkʌvə(r)/ *vt,vi* **1** [VP6A] get back (sth lost, etc); get back the use of: *~ what was lost; ~ consciousness* (after fainting); *~ one's sight/hearing. I am ~ing my strength,* getting well (after an illness). *We soon ~ed lost time. They have ~ed their losses.* **2** [VP2A,3A] *~* ***from,*** become well; get back to a former position of prosperity, state of health, mental condition, etc: *He is slowly ~ing from his illness. I doubt whether he will ~. I haven't yet ~ed from my astonishment. Has the country ~ed from the effects of the war yet?* **3** [VP6A] regain control of oneself; become calm or normal: *He almost fell, but quickly ~ed (himself). He ~ed his balance/composure.* **~·able** /-əbl/ *adj* that can be ~ed(1): *Is the deposit I've paid ~able?* **re·cov·ery** *n* [U] ~ing or being ~ed: *make a quick ~y,* get well again quickly or quickly regain one's position after losing for a time in a game, athletic match, etc. *~y from influenza; the ~y of a lost article,* getting it back again.

re-cover[2] /ˈri ˋkʌvə(r)/ *vt* [VP6A] supply with a new cover: *This umbrella/quilt needs to be ~ed.*

rec·re·ant /ˋrekrɪənt/ *adj, n* (liter) cowardly, unfaithful or traitorous (person): *a ~ knight.*

rec·re·ation /ˈrekrɪˋeɪʃn/ *n* [C,U] (form of) play or amusement; refreshment of body and mind; sth that pleasantly occupies one's time after work is done: *walk and climb mountains for ~. Is gardening a ~ or a form of hard work? Flirting can be an innocent ~, perhaps.* ˋ**~ ground,** land, e g in a public park, set aside for games, etc. **~al** /-nl/ *adj* of ~: *provide more ~al facilities,* e g sports grounds, swimming pools.

re·crimi·na·tion /rɪˈkrɪmɪˋneɪʃn/ *n* [C] accusation made in return for one already made; counter-charge: *indulge in ~s;* [U] act of retorting an accusation. **re·crimi·nate** *vi* [VP2A,3A] *~* ***(against sb),*** accuse (sb) in return. **re·crimi·na·tory** /rɪˋkrɪmɪnətərɪ *US:* -tɔrɪ/ *adj* of ~.

re·cru·des·ence /ˈrikrʊˋdesns/ *n* (of disease, violence, etc) new outburst; breaking out again: *a ~ of civil disorder; the ~ of influenza.*

re·cruit /rɪˋkrut/ *n* new member of a society, group, etc esp a soldier in the early days of his training: *gain a few ~s to one's party,* e g in politics; *~s being drilled on the parade ground.* □ *vt,vi* **1** [VP6A] get ~s for; enlist (persons) as ~s (for the army, a cause, etc): *a ˋ~ing officer; ~ a new political party from the middle classes. Were men for the Navy ~ed from men on merchant ships?* **2** [VP6A] get a sufficient quantity or store of; bring back to what is usual or normal: *~ supplies; ~ one's health/strength;* [VP2A] *go to the seaside after an illness to ~,* to recover or recuperate (the more usu words). **~·ment** *n*

rec·tal /ˋrektəl/ *adj* of the rectum.

rec·tangle /ˋrek-tæŋl/ *n* [C] plane four-sided figure with four right angles, esp one with adjacent sides unequal. ⇨ the illus at quadrilateral. **rec·tangu·lar** /rekˋtæŋgjʊlə(r)/ *adj* in the shape of a ~.

rec·tify /ˋrektɪfɑɪ/ *vt* (*pt,pp* -fied) [VP6A] **1** put right; take out mistakes from: *~ abuses; mistakes that cannot be rectified.* **2** purify or refine by repeated distillation or other process: *rectified spirits.* **rec·ti·fier** *n* person or thing that rectifies; (electr) device which converts alternating current to direct current. **rec·tifi·ca·tion** /ˈrektɪfɪˋkeɪʃn/ *n* [U] ~ing or being rectified: *the rectification of errors/alcohol;* [C] instance of this; sth that has been rectified.

rec·ti·lin·ear /ˈrektɪˋlɪnɪə(r)/ *adj* in or forming a straight line; bounded by, characterized by, straight lines.

rec·ti·tude /ˋrektɪtjud *US:* -tud/ *n* [U] honesty; upright or straightforward behaviour.

rec·tor /ˋrektə(r)/ *n* **1** (C of E) clergy man in charge of a parish the tithes of which were not withdrawn, e g to a monastery or university, at or after the time when the English Church separated from the Church of Rome. ⇨ vicar. **2** head of certain universities, colleges, schools or religious institutions: *the Lord R~ of St Andrews,* the chief elective officer of this university (in Scotland). **rec·tory** /ˋrektərɪ/ *n* (*pl* -ries) ~'s residence.

rec·tum /ˋrektəm/ *n* (anat) lower and final part of the large intestine. ⇨ the illus at alimentary.

re·cum·bent /rɪˋkʌmbənt/ *adj* (esp of a person) lying down: *a ~ figure on a tomb,* statue or carving in a ~ position.

re·cu·per·ate /rɪˋkjupəreɪt/ *vt,vi* [VP6A,2A] make or become strong again after illness, exhaustion or loss: *~ one's health; go to the seaside to ~.* **re·cu·per·ation** /rɪˈkjupəˋreɪʃn/ *n* recuperating. **re·cu·per·at·ive** /rɪˋkjupərətɪv *US:* -reɪtɪv/ *adj* helping, relating to, recuperation.

re·cur /rɪˋk3(r)/ *vi* (-rr-) **1** [VP2A] come, happen, again; be repeated: *a problem which ~s periodically; ~ring decimals,* figures in decimal fractions that ~ in the same order, as 3·999... (written 3·9̇), 4·014014... (written 4·0̇14̇). **2** [VP3A] *~* ***to,*** go back (to sth) in words or thought: *~ring to what you said yesterday; if I may ~ to your idea.* **3** [VP3A] *~* ***to,*** (of ideas, events etc) come back: *My first meeting with her often ~s to my memory.* **re·cur·rence** /rɪˋkʌrns *US:* /-ˋk3əns/ *n* [C,U] ~ring; repetition: *Let there be no ~rence of this error. The frequent ~rence of these headaches made her life miserable.* **re·cur·rent** /-ənt/ *adj* (of events, fevers etc) ~ring frequently or regularly: *allow £35 a month for ~rent expenses,* e g rent, lighting and heating.

re·curve /riˋk3v/ *vt,vi* curve or bend backwards or downwards.

recu·sant /ˋrekjʊznt/ *n, adj* (person) refusing to submit to authority or to comply with regulations, esp (hist) a Roman Catholic who refused to attend Church of England services. **recu·sancy** /-znsɪ/ *n* [U].

re·cycle /ˈriˋsɑɪkl/ *vt* [VP6A] treat (substances already used for industry, etc) so that further use is possible: *~ old newspapers, by de-inking and pulping them.*

red /red/ *adj* (-der, -dest) **1** of the colour of fresh blood, rubies, human lips, the tongue, maple leaves in autumn, post-office pillar boxes in GB; of shades varying from crimson to bright brown (as of iron rust): *red with anger/embarrassment,* flushed in the face; *with red hands,* with hands stained with blood; *with red eyes,* eyes red with weeping. ˈ**~** ˋ**carpet,** one laid out for the reception of an important visitor: *give a visiting notable a red carpet reception.* ***paint the town red,*** go on a spree and indulge in noisy, rough behaviour. ***see red,*** lose control of oneself through anger, or indignation. **2** Russian; Soviet; Communist: *The Red Army/Air Force.* **3** (various uses in compounds, etc): ˋ**red·breast** *n* (also *robin redbreast*) bird called the robin. **ˋRed·brick** *n* (attrib) (name applied to the larger civic universities founded near the end of the 19th c (contrasted chiefly with Oxford and Cambridge—known as *Oxbridge*). **ˋred·cap** *n* (GB) member of the military police; (US) railroad porter. **ˋred·coat** *n* (old name for) British soldier. **ˈRed ˋCrescent** *n* (emblem of an) organization in Muslim countries corresponding to the Red Cross. **ˈRed ˋCross** *n* (emblem of the) international organization concerned with the relief of suffering caused by natural disasters, etc and for helping the sick and wounded and those taken prisoner in war. **red deer** *n* kind of deer native to the forests of Europe and Asia. **ˈred ˋensign** (or colloq, **ˈred ˋduster**) *n* red flag with the Union Jack in one corner, used by British merchant ships. **ˈred ˋflag** *n* **(a)** flag used a a symbol of danger (e g on railways, by workers on the roads). **(b)** symbol of revolution. **(c)** (*the Red Flag*) revolutionary song. ***(catch sb) ˈred-ˋhanded*** *adj* in the act of committing a crime. **ˋred hat** *n* cardinal's hat. **ˋred·head** *n* person having red hair. **ˈred ˋherring** *n* smoke-cured herring: *neither fish, flesh, nor good red herring*; of a doubtful or ambiguous nature, which cannot be defined; *draw a red herring across the trail*, introduce irrelevant matter to distract attention from the subject being discussed. **ˈred-ˋhot** *adj* (fig) highly excited, furious: *red-hot enthusiasm*. **ˈRed ˋIndian** *n* N American Indian. **ˈred ˋlead** *n* pigment made from red oxide of lead. **ˈred-ˋletter day,** day with red letter(s) in the calendar, e g a saint's day or a festival; (fig) memorable because of some joyful occurrence. **ˈred ˋlight** *n* **(a)** danger signal on railways, etc: 'stop' signal on roads: *see the red light*, realize the nearness of danger or disaster. **(b)** *red-light district*, part of a town where there are brothels. **ˋred meat** *n* beef and mutton (contrasted with *white* meat, i e veal, pork, poultry). **ˈred ˋpepper,** red fruit of the capsicum plant. **red rag** *n* sth (usu *like a red rag to a bull*) that excites a person's anger or passion. **ˋred·skin** *n* (old name for) Red Indian. **the Red Star,** symbol of the USSR and other Communist States. **red tape** *n* excessive use of formalities in public business; too much attention to rules and regulations: *red tape in government offices*. **ˋred·wing** *n* name used of kinds of thrush and other birds with red wing-feathers. **ˋred·wood** *n* name used of kinds of tree with reddish wood, esp an evergreen Californian tree, some of which are of great height. □ *n* **1** [C,U] (shade of) red colour: *too much red in the painting; the reds and browns of the woods in autumn*, the red and brown shades of the leaves. **2** red clothes: *dressed in red*. **3** person favouring or supporting Communism or the Soviet system. **4** debtor side of business accounts. ***be/get into the red,*** have/get liabilities that exceed assets. ***be/get out of the red,*** reach the position when one is no longer in the red.

red·den /ˋredn/ *vt,vi* [VP6A,2A] make or become red; blush.

red·dish /ˋredɪʃ/ *adj* rather red.

re·deem /rɪˋdim/ *vt* [VP6A,14] ~ ***(from),*** **1** get (sth) back by payment or by doing sth: *~ a pawned watch/a mortgage; ~ one's honour.* **2** perform (a promise or obligation). **3** set free by payment; rescue: *~ a slave/prisoner;* (by Jesus) make free from sin: *~ed from vice by the saving grace of Jesus.* **4** compensate; make amends for: *his ~ing feature*, the feature or quality that balances his faults, etc. *The acting barely ~s the play*, The play is poor and the acting not very good. **~·able** /-əbl/ *adj* that can be ~ed. **(the) Re·dee·mer** *n* Jesus Christ.

re·demp·tion /rɪˋdempʃn/ *n* [U] redeeming or being redeemed; *the ~ of a promise;* deliverance or rescue (esp from evil ways): *past/beyond ~*, too bad to be redeemed; *in the year of our ~ 1960*, i e by the sacrifice of Jesus.

re·demp·tive /rɪˋdemptɪv/ *adj* serving to redeem; relating to redemption.

re·de·ploy /ˈridɪˋplɔɪ/ *vt* [VP6A] (of troops, workers in industry, etc) withdraw and rearrange so as to use more efficiently. **~·ment** *n*: *the ~ment of labour.*

re·dif·fu·sion /ˈridɪˋfjuʒn/ *n* system of using broadcast programmes (sound and television) in public places (e g cinemas).

re·do /ˈriˋdu/ *vt* (*pt* -did /-ˋdɪd/, *pp* -done /-ˋdʌn/) [VP6A] do again: *We must have the walls redone*, repapered, recoloured, etc according to context.

redo·lent /ˋredələnt/ *adj* ~ ***of,*** (formal) having a strong smell, esp one that is reminiscent of sth: *bed sheets ~ of lavender;* (fig) *a town ~ of age and romance.* **redo·lence** /-əns/ *n*

re·double /rɪˋdʌbl/ *vt,vi* [VP6A,2A] **1** make or become greater or stronger: *They ~d their efforts. Her zeal ~d.* **2** (bridge) double again a bid already doubled by an opponent.

re·doubt /rɪˋdaʊt/ *n* [C] strong point in a system of fortifications: *attack and capture a ~.*

re·doubt·able /rɪˋdaʊtəbl/ *adj* (liter) to be feared; formidable: *those ~ ladies, the Daughters of the American Revolution.*

re·dound /rɪˋdaʊnd/ *vi* [VP3A] ~ ***to,*** (formal) contribute greatly in the end; promote: *Your success will ~ to the fame of the college. It ~s to your honour.*

re·dress /rɪˋdres/ *vt* [VP6A] **1** set (a wrong) right again; make up for, do sth that compensates for (a wrong): *You should confess and ~ your errors.* **2** ~ ***the balance,*** make things equal again. □ *n* [U] act of ~ing or correcting (abuses, etc); sth that ~es: *seek ~; go to a lawyer to get legal ~.*

re·duce /rɪˋdjus *US:* -ˋdus/ *vt,vi* [VP6A,14] **1** make less; make smaller in size, number, degree, price, etc: *~ speed/pressure/costs, etc; ~ one's expenses; ~ one's weight. He is ~d almost to a skeleton*, has become very thin. [VP2A,B] (colloq): *She has been reducing for the last few weeks*, has been dieting (or trying other methods) in order to ~ her weight. **2** bring or get to a certain condition, way of living, etc: *~ a class of noisy children to order; ~ sb to silence*, cause him to stop talking; *~ sth to order; ~ the rebels to submission; ~ a sergeant to the ranks. They were ~d to begging or starving*, They became so poor that they had either to beg or go hungry. *He was ~d to the necessity of selling his books. His objections have been ~d to writing*, written down. *They are living in ~d circumstances*, in (comparative) poverty. **3** change (to another form): *~ an equation/argument/statement to its simplest form; ~ a sum to shillings and pence*, e g, before decimalization, £10 10s 6d = 210s 6d; *~ water by electrolysis*, separate it into oxygen and hydrogen; ~ (*sth*) *to an absurdity*, make, e g a scheme or argument, appear absurd by removing whatever hides its real nature; ~ *wood logs to pulp.* **re·duc·ible** /-əbl/ *adj* that can be ~d.

re·duc·tio ad ab·surdum /rɪˈdʌktɪəʊ ˈæd əb-ˈsɜdəm/ (Lat) the disproof of a prosposition by showing that its conclusion can be only absurd.

re·duc·tion /rɪˈdʌkʃn/ *n* **1** [U] reducing or being reduced; [C] instance of this: *a ~ in/of numbers; great ~s in prices; price ~s.* **2** [C] copy, on a smaller scale, of a picture, map, etc.

re·dun·dant /rɪˈdʌndənt/ *adj* superfluous; not needed: *a paragraph without a ~ word; ~ labour,* unneeded or surplus workers. *With the decreasing demand for coal many thousands of miners may become ~.* **re·dun·dance** /-əns/, **re·dun·dancy** /-ənsɪ/ *nn* [U] being ~: *redundancy among clerks caused by the increasing use of computers;* [C] (*pl* -cies) instance of this: *more redundancies in the docks.* **reˈdundancy pay,** money paid by an employer to a ~ worker, the sum depending upon age and length of service.

re·dupli·cate /rɪˈdjuplɪkeɪt *US:* -ˈdu-/ *vt* [VP6A] double; repeat. **re·dupli·ca·tion** /rɪˈdjuplɪˈkeɪʃn *US:* -ˈdu-/ *n*

re-echo /ri ˈekəʊ/ *vi, vt* [VP6A,2A] echo again and again. □ *n* (*pl* -oes /-əʊz/) echo of an echo.

reed /rid/ *n* [C] **1** (tall, firm stem or stalk of) kinds of coarse, firm-stemmed, jointed grasses growing in or near water; [U] (collective) mass of such grasses growing together; (*pl*) dried stalks used for thatching. ***a broken ~,*** (fig) an unreliable person or thing. **2** (in some wind-instruments, e g the oboe, bassoon, clarinet and in some organ-pipes) strip of metal, etc that vibrates to produce sound. **the ~s,** ~ instruments of this sort. **reedy** *adj* **1** abounding in ~s(1). **2** (of sounds, voices) shrill; piping.

reef¹ /rif/ *n* that part of a sail which can be rolled up or folded so as to reduce its area: *take in a ~,* shorten sail; (fig) go forward more cautiously. **ˈ~-knot** *n* ordinary double knot (US = *square knot*). □ *vt* [VP6A] reduce the area of (a sail) by rolling up or folding a part.

reef² /rif/ *n* ridge of rock, shingle etc just below or above the surface of the sea: *wrecked on a coral ~.*

reefer /ˈrifə(r)/ *n* **1** close-fitting double-breasted jacket of thick cloth, as worn by sailors. **2** (sl) kind of cigarette containing marijuana.

reek /rik/ *n* [U] **1** strong, bad smell: *the ~ of stale tobacco smoke.* **2** (liter and Scot use) thick smoke or vapour: *the ~ of a peat fire.* □ *vi* **1** [VP3A] ~ ***of,*** smell unpleasantly of: He ~s of whisky/garlic. The room ~ed of stale cigar smoke. **2** ~ ***with,*** be covered (with sweat, blood, etc); show signs or traces of: *a horse ~ing with sweat; a murderer whose hands still ~ed with blood.*

reel¹ /ril/ *n* **1** cylinder, roller or similar device on which cotton, thread, wire, photographic film, magnetic tape, hose (for water, etc), a fishing line, is wound. ***(straight) off the ~,*** (colloq) without a hitch or pause, in rapid succession. **2** (cinema) length of positive film rolled on one ~; *a six-~ film,* a complete film on six ~s. ⇨ **spool.** □ *vt* [VP6A,15A,B] roll or wind (thread, a fishing line etc) on to, or with the help of, a ~; take (sth) *off:* ~ *in the log line;* ~ *up a fish;* ~ *the silk thread off cocoons.* ~ ***sth off,*** tell, say or repeat sth without pause or apparent effort: ~ *off the verses of a long poem;* ~ *off a list of names.*

reel² /ril/ *vi* [VP2A,C] **1** be shaken (physically or mentally) by a blow, a shock, rough treatment, etc: *His mind ~ed when he heard the news.* **2** walk or stand unsteadily, moving from side to side; sway: *He ~ed like a drunken man. He went ~ing down the road.* **3** seem to sway; appear to move or shake: *The street ~ed before his eyes.*

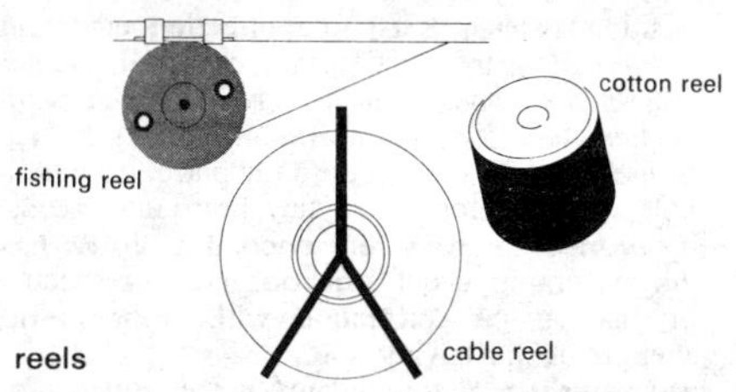

reel³ /ril/ *n* [C] (music for a) lively Scottish dance, usu for two couples.

re-en·try /ˈri ˈentrɪ/ *n* (*pl* -ries) act of re-entering; return of a spacecraft into the earth's atmosphere.

reeve /riv/ *n* **1** (hist) chief magistrate of a town or district. **2** (Canada) president of a village or town council.

re·face /ˈriˈfeɪs/ *vt* put a new surface on.

re·fec·tion /rɪˈfekʃn/ *n* (formal) [U] refreshment in the form of food and drink; [C] light meal; collation.

re·fec·tory /rɪˈfektərɪ/ *n* (*pl* -ries) dining-hall (in a monastery, convent or college).

re·fer /rɪˈfɜ(r)/ *vt, vi* (-rr-) **1** [VP14,15B] ~ ***sb/sth to,*** send, take, hand over (to, back to, sb or sth) to be dealt with, decided etc: *The dispute was ~red to the United Nations. I was ~red to the Manager/to the Inquiry Office. The question was ~red back,* was deferred. **2** [VP3A] ~ ***to,*** (of a speaker, what is said, etc) speak of, allude to; apply to: *When I said that some people are stupid I wasn't ~ring to you. Don't ~ to this matter again, please. What I have to say ~s to all of you. Does that remark ~ to me?* **3** [VP3A] ~ ***to,*** turn to, go to, for information, etc: *The speaker often ~red to his notes.* **4** [VP14] ~ ***sth to sth,*** credit, attribute (the more usu words): *He ~red his success to the good teaching he'd had. The discovery of gunpowder is usually ~red to China.* **ref·er·able** /rɪˈfɜrəbl/ *adj* that can be ~red(5): *Lung cancer is ~able to excessive smoking of cigarettes.*

ref·eree /ˈrefəˈri/ *n* **1** person to whom disputes, e g in industry, between workers and employers, are referred for decision. **2** (in football, boxing, etc) person who controls matches, judges points in dispute, etc. ⇨ **umpire.** □ *vt, vi* [VP6A,2A] act as ~: ~ *a football match.*

ref·er·ence /ˈrefrns/ *n* **1** [C,U] (instance of) referring: *You should make ~ to a dictionary. The book is full of ~s to places that I know well.* **ˈ~ book,** one that is not read through but consulted for information, e g a dictionary or encyclopaedia. **ˈ~ library,** one containing ~ books, to be consulted there but not to be taken away. ***terms of ~,*** (of a commission, etc) scope or range given to an authority: *Is this question outside our terms of ~,* one that we are not required to investigate? **2** [C] (person willing to make a) statement about a person's character or abilities: *The clerk has excellent ~s from former employers. The shop will open a credit account for you if you supply a banker's ~,* a note from your bank stating that your financial position is sound. **3** [C] note, direction, etc telling where certain information may be found: *He dislikes history books that are crowded with ~s to earlier authorities.* '~ **marks,** marks, e g *, †, ‡, §, used to refer the reader to the place, e g a footnote, where information may be found. '**cross-'reference,** ⇨ cross-reference. **4** [U] ***in/with ~ to,*** concerning; about. ***without ~ to,*** irrespective of; having no connection with. **ref·er·en·tial** /ˌrefəˈrenʃl/ *adj* having ~ to.

ref·er·en·dum /ˌrefəˈrendəm/ *n* (*pl* -dums, -da /-də/) [C] the referring of a political question to a direct vote of the electorate.

re·fill /ˌriˈfɪl/ *vt* fill again. □ *n* /ˈrifɪl/ that which is used to ~; a container: *two ~s for a ballpoint pen.*

re·fine /rɪˈfɑɪn/ *vt, vi* **1** [VP6A,2A] free from other substances; make or become pure: *~ sugar/oil/ores.* **2** [VP6A] cause to become more cultured, polished in manners; get rid of what is coarse or vulgar: *~ a language; ~d language/manners/speech/taste.* **3** ***~ upon,*** improve by giving great attention to details: *~ upon one's methods.*

re·fine·ment /rɪˈfɑɪnmənt/ *n* **1** [U] refining or being refined. **2** [U] purity of feeling, taste, language, etc; delicacy of manners: *a lady of ~; lack of ~,* i e vulgarity; *aim at acquiring ~.* **3** [C] ingenious or remarkable example of such purity of tastes, etc; delicate or clever development of sth: *~s of meaning/cruelty; all the ~s of the age.*

re·finer /rɪˈfɑɪnə(r)/ *n* **1** person whose business is to refine sth: *sugar ~s.* **2** machine for refining metals, sugar, etc. **~y** /-nṛɪ/ *n* place, building, etc where sth is refined: *a 'sugar ~y; an 'oil ~y.*

re·fit /ˌriˈfɪt/ *vt, vi* (-tt-) [VP6A] make (a ship, etc) ready for use again by renewing or repairing parts; [VP2A] (of a ship) be made fit for further voyages: *The ship put into Cardiff to ~.* □ *n* /ˈrifɪt/ refitting.

re·fla·tion /riˈfleɪʃn/ *n* [U] inflation of currency after a deflation, to restore the system to its previous condition.

re·flate /rɪˈfleɪt/ *vt* [VP6A] restore to a previous economic or currency state: *plans to ~ the economy.*

re·flect /rɪˈflekt/ *vt, vi* **1** [VP6A] (of a surface) throw back (light, heat, sound); (of a mirror) send back an image of: *The sunlight was ~ed from the water. Look at the trees ~ed in the lake. The moon shines with ~ed light. The sight of my face ~ed in the mirror never pleases me.* '**~·ing telescope,** one in which the image is ~ed in a mirror and magnified. **2** [VP6A] express; show the nature of: *Her sad looks ~ed the thoughts passing through her mind. Does the literature of a nation ~ its manners and morals?* **3** [VP14] ***~ sth upon sb,*** (of actions, results) bring (credit or discredit upon): *The results ~ the greatest credit upon all concerned. Such behaviour can only ~ discredit on you.* **4** [VP3A] ***~ (up)on,*** bring discredit (up)on: hurt the good reputation of: *I do not wish to ~ (up)on your sincerity,* suggest that you are not sincere. *Your rude behaviour ~s only (up)on yourself,* You are the only person whose reputation is hurt by it. **5** [VP2A,3A,9,8,10] consider; think on: *I must ~ (up)on what answer to give/how to answer that question. He ~ed how difficult it would be to escape.*

re·flec·tion (GB also **re·flexion**) /rɪˈflekʃn/ *nn* **1** [U] reflecting or being reflected: *the ~ of heat.* **2** [C] sth reflected, esp an image reflected in a mirror or in still water: *see one's ~ in a mirror; the ~ of trees in (the water of) a lake.* **3** [U] thought; (re)consideration: *lost in ~; do sth without sufficient ~.* ***on ~,*** after reconsidering the matter. **4** [C] expression of a thought in speech or writing; idea arising in the mind: *~s on the pleasures of being idle.* **5** [C] expression of blame: *I intended no ~ on your character,* did not want to suggest that you are blameworthy. *How dare you cast ~s on my motives?* **6** [C] sth that brings discredit: *This is a ~ upon your honour.*

re·flec·tive /rɪˈflektɪv/ *adj* thoughtful; in the habit of reflection(5). **~·ly** *adv*

re·flec·tor /rɪˈflektə(r)/ *n* sth that reflects heat, light or sound, esp a piece of glass or metal for reflecting light, etc in a required direction; the illus at bicycle: '~ *studs,* (GB) studs inserted in a road surface to help drivers by reflecting light from headlamps (= colloq *cat's eyes*).

re·flex /ˈrifleks/ *adj* **1** '**~ action,** action that is independent of the will, being an involuntary response to a stimulation of the nerves, e g shivering, sneezing. **2** '**~ camera,** hand camera in which, by means of a mirror, the reflected image of the object or scene to be photographed can be seen and focused up to the moment of exposure. □ *n* ~ action.

re·flexion /rɪˈflekʃn/ *n* = **reflection.**

re·flex·ive /rɪˈfleksɪv/ *n, adj* (word or form) showing that the agent's action is upon himself. **~ verb,** e g He *cut* himself. **~ pronoun,** e g *myself, themselves.*

re·float /riˈfləʊt/ *vt, vi* [VP6A,2A] cause (sth) to float again after it has gone aground, been sunk, etc; float again.

re·flux /ˈriflʌks/ *n* flowing back; ebb: *flux and ~.*

re·foot /ˌriˈfʊt/ *vt* knit a new foot on (a worn out sock, etc).

re·for·est /riˈforɪst *US:* -ˈfɔr-/ *vt* ⇨ **reafforest. re·for·es·ta·tion** /riˌforɪˈsteɪʃn *US:* -ˌfɔr-/ *n*

re·form[1] /rɪˈfɔm/ *vt, vi* [VP6A,2A] make or become better by removing or putting right what is bad or wrong: *~ a sinner/one's character/the world; ~ oneself; a ~ed man,* one who has given up his bad ways and is now living a good life. □ *n* **1** [U] ~ing; removal of vices, imperfections, etc: *agitate for social or political ~; the Re'form Bill of 1832,* (GB) that which extended the franchise and improved parliamentary representation. **2** [C] instance of ~; change made in order to remove imperfections: *a ~ in teaching methods.* **~er** *n* person actively engaged in advocating or carrying our ~s.

re-form[2] /ˌri ˈfɔm/ *vt, vi* form again; (of soldiers) get into ranks, etc again. **re-for·ma·tion** /ˌri fɔˈmeɪʃn/ *n*

ref·or·ma·tion /ˌrefəˈmeɪʃn/ *n* **1** [U] reforming[1] or being reformed[1]; [C] radical change for the better in social, political or religious affairs. **2 the R~,** the 16th-century movement for reform of the Roman Catholic Church, resulting in the establishment of the Reformed or Protestant Churches.

re·forma·tory /rɪˈfɔmətrɪ *US:* -tɔrɪ/ *adj* tending or intending to produce reform. □ *n* (*pl* -ties) (formerly) school or institution for reforming young offenders against the law by means of special training, mental, moral and physical (usu, in GB, called an *approved school* or *community house*).

re·fract /rɪˈfrækt/ *vt* [VP6A] cause (a ray of light)

to bend aside where it enters, e g water, glass, obliquely: *Light is ~ed when it passes through a prism.* **re·frac·tion** /rɪˈfrækʃn/ *n* ~ing or being ~ed.

re·frac·tory /rɪˈfræktərɪ/ *adj* **1** resisting control, discipline, etc; wilful: *as ~ as a mule;* (of diseases) not yielding to treatment. **2** (of substances, esp metals) hard to melt, fuse or work.

re·frain[1] /rɪˈfreɪn/ *n* [C] lines of a song which are repeated, esp at the end of each verse: *Will you all join in singing the ~, please?*

re·frain[2] /rɪˈfreɪn/ *vi* [VP2A,3A] ***~ (from),*** hold oneself back: *Please ~ from spitting in public places. Let's hope they will ~ from hostile action.*

re·fresh /rɪˈfreʃ/ *vt* [VP6A] **1** give new strength to; make fresh: *~ oneself with a cup of tea/a warm bath.* **2** ***~ one's memory,*** call things back to the memory by referring to notes, etc. **3** take sth to eat or drink: *They stopped at a pub to ~ themselves. They felt much ~ed.* **~·ing** *adj* **1** strengthening; giving rest and relief: *a ~ing breeze/sleep.* **2** welcome and interesting because rare or unexpected: *~ing innocence,* e g of children to older, sophisticated persons. **~·ing·ly** *adv*

re·fresher /rɪˈfreʃə(r)/ *n* **1** extra fee paid to counsel[1](3) while a case is proceeding in the law courts. **2** (colloq) drink. **3** (attrib) ˈ**~ course,** course providing instructions, e g to teachers already in service, on modern methods, newer professional techniques, etc.

re·fresh·ment /rɪˈfreʃmənt/ *n* **1** [U] refreshing or being refreshed: *feel ~ of mind and body.* **2** [U] (often *pl*) that which refreshes, esp food and drink: *order some light ~(s),* snacks; ˈ*~ room,* one where one can buy food and drink, e g at a railway station. *R~s were provided during the interval.*

re·frig·er·ate /rɪˈfrɪdʒəreɪt/ *vt* [VP6A] make cool or cold; keep (food) in good condition by making and keeping it cold. **re·frig·er·ant** /-ənt/ *n, adj* (substance) serving to ~, e g *carbon dioxide.* **re·frig·er·ator** /rɪˈfrɪdʒəreɪtə(r)/ *n* [C] (common colloq abbr *fridge*) cabinet or room in which food is kept cold. **re·frig·er·ation** /rɪˌfrɪdʒəˈreɪʃn/ *n* (esp) the cooling or freezing of food in order to preserve it: *the refrigeration industry.*

reft /reft/ *pp* = bereft.

re·fuel /ˈriˈfjuļ/ *vt* [VP6A,2A] supply with, take on, a fresh quantity of fuel: *The plane came down to ~.*

ref·uge /ˈrefjudʒ/ *n* [C,U] (place giving) shelter or protection from trouble, danger, pursuit, etc: *seek ~ from the floods; take ~ in the cellar;* (fig) *take ~ in silence,* e g to avoid answering impertinent questions. *Books are a ~ of the lonely.* **refu·gee** /ˈrefjʊˈdʒi *US:* ˈrefjʊdʒi/ *n* person who has been forced to flee from danger, e g from floods, war, political persecution: (attrib) ˈ*refuˈgee camps.*

re·ful·gent /rɪˈfʌldʒent/ *adj* shining; brilliant. **re·ful·gence** /-əns/ *n* [U].

re·fund /rɪˈfʌnd/ *vt* [VP6A] pay back (money to sb): *~ the cost of postage.* □ *n* /ˈrifʌnd/ [C,U] repayment: *obtain a ~ of a deposit.*

re·fur·bish /ˈriˈfɜbɪʃ/ *vt* [VP6A] made clean or bright again; make (as if) like new.

re·fusal /rɪˈfjuzl/ *n* **1** [U] act of refusing; [C] instance of this: *the ~ of an invitation; his ~ to do what I asked.* **2** (with *def art*) right of deciding whether to accept or refuse sth before it is offered to others: *If you ever decide to sell your car, please give me (the) first ~.*

ref·use[1] /ˈrefjus/ *n* [U] waste or worthless material: *a* ˈ*~ dump,* e g place where town ~ (collected from houses, etc) is dumped. ˈ**~-collector** *n* dustman.

re·fuse[2] /rɪˈfjuz/ *vt,vi* [VP6A,7,12C,2A] say 'no' to (a request or offer); show unwillingness to accept (sth offered), to do (sth that one is asked to do): *~ a gift; ~ one's consent; ~ to help. They ~d me permission. I was ~d admittance.*

re·fute /rɪˈfjut/ *vt* [VP6A] prove (statements, opinions, etc) to be wrong or mistaken; prove (sb) wrong in his opinions: *~ an argument/an opponent.* **re·fut·able** /ˈrefjʊtəbl *US:* rɪˈfju-/ *adj* that can be ~d. **refu·ta·tion** /ˈrefjʊˈteɪʃn/ *n* [U] refuting; [C] counter-argument.

re·gain /rɪˈgeɪn/ *vt* [VP6A] **1** get possession of again: *~ consciousness; ~ one's freedom.* **2** get back to (a place or position): *~ one's footing,* recover one's balance after slipping or falling.

re·gal /ˈrigl/ *adj* of, for, fit for, by, a monarch; royal: *~ dignity/splendour/power.* **~·ly** /-glɪ/ *adv*

re·gale /rɪˈgeɪl/ *vt* [VP6A,14] ***~ oneself/sb (with/on sth),*** give pleasure or delight to: *~ oneself with a cigar; regaling themselves and their friends on caviar and champagne.*

re·galia /rɪˈgeɪlɪə/ *n pl* [C] (often with a *sing v*) **1** emblems (crown, orb, sceptre, etc) of royalty, as used at coronations. **2** emblems or decorations of an order(**10**), e g of the freemasons.

regalia

re·gard[1] /rɪˈgɑd/ *n* **1** (liter or old use) long, steady or significant look: *He turned his ~ on the accused man. His ~ was fixed on the horizon.* **2** [U] point attended to; relation. ***in*** ˈ***this ~,*** in respect of (= regarding) this point. ***in/with ~ to,*** with respect to; concerning. **3** [U] attention; concern; consideration: *You'll get into trouble if you continue to behave without ~ to decency. He has very little ~ for the feelings of others. More ~ must be paid to safety on the roads.* **4** [U] esteem; consideration; respect: *hold sb in high/low ~; have a high/low ~ for sb's judgement.* **5** (*pl*) kindly thoughts and wishes: *Please give my kind ~s to your brother,* (at the end of a letter) *with kind ~s, yours sincerely,....* **~·ful** /-fl/ *adj* ***~ful (of),*** full of ~(3): *Be more ~ful of your own interests.* **~·less** *adj* ***~less of,*** paying no attention to: *~less of the consequences; ~less of expense.*

re·gard[2] /rɪˈgɑd/ *vt* **1** [VP6A] (liter or old use) look closely at. **2** [VP16B] ***~ sb/sth as,*** consider: *~ sb as a hero; ~ sth as a crime. He's ~ed as the best dentist in town.* **3** [VP14] ***~ sb/sth (with),*** look upon mentally: *I ~ his behaviour with suspicion/horror. How is he ~ed locally? He is ~ed with disfavour/unfavourably.* **4** [VP6A] pay attention to: (chiefly neg and interr): *He seldom ~s my* *advice. Why do you so seldom ~ my wishes?* **5** [VP6A] concern: *This does not ~* (*concern* is much more usu) *me at all,* has nothing to do with me. ***as ~s; ~ing,*** with reference to; about.

re·gatta /rɪˋgætə/ *n* meeting for boat races (rowing boats or yachts).

re·gency /ˋridʒənsɪ/ *n* (*pl* **-cies**) the office of a regent; regent's period of office: *the R~,* (in GB) the period 1810—20.

re·gen·er·ate /rɪˋdʒenəreɪt/ *vt,vi* [VP6A,2A] **1** reform spiritually; raise morally. **2** give new strength or life to; restore lost qualities to. **3** grow again. □ *adj* /rɪˋdʒenərət/ spiritually reborn: *a ~ society.* **re·gen·er·ation** /rɪˈdʒenəˋreɪʃn/ *n* [U] being ~d.

re·gent /ˋridʒənt/ *n* **1** person appointed to perform the duties of a ruler who is too young, old, ill, etc or who is absent. **2** (US) member of a governing board (e g of a State university). □ *adj* (following the *n*) performing the duties of a ~: *the Prince R~.*

Reg·gae /ˋregeɪ/ *n* [U] West Indian popular music and dance with strong rhythms.

regi·cide /ˋredʒɪsɑɪd/ *n* [U] crime of killing a king; [C] person who kills, or takes part in the killing of, a king.

ré·gime, re·gime /reɪˋʒim/ *n* [C] **1** method or system of government or of administration; prevailing system of things: *under the old ~,* before the changes were made, etc (according to context). **2** = **regimen(2)**.

regi·men /ˋredʒɪmən/ *n* [C] **1** (old use) = **régime(1)**. **2** set of rules for diet, exercise, etc for promoting one's health and physical well-being.

regi·ment /ˋredʒɪmənt/ *n* [C] **1** (cavalry and artillery) unit divided into squadrons or batteries and commanded by a colonel; (GB infantry) organization usu based on a city or county, with special traditions and dress, represented in the field by battalions: *the 1st battalion of the Manchester R~.* **2** *~* ***of,*** large number: *whole ~s of starlings.* **3** [U] (old use) government. □ *vt* [VP6A] organize; discipline: *~ the workers of a country.* **regi·men·ta·tion** /ˈredʒɪmenˋteɪʃn/ *n* [U] subjection to control; strict political discipline (as in a police state).

regi·men·tal /ˈredʒɪˋmentl/ *adj* of a regiment: *the ~ tie,* in the colours of the regiment. □ *n* (*pl*) dress worn by the men of a regiment; military uniform: *in full ~s,* in full dress.

Re·gina /rɪˋdʒɑɪnə/ *n* (abbr **R**) reigning queen: (used in signatures to proclamations) *Elizabeth ~;* (legal) (used in titles of lawsuits): *~* v *Hay,* the Crown against Hay.

re·gion /ˋridʒən/ *n* [C] area or division with or without definite boundaries or characteristics: *the ˋArctic ~s; the forest ~; the lower ~s,* hell; (fig) *the ~ of metaphysics;* (med) *the abˋdominal ~.* **~al** /-nl/ *adj* of a ~: *the ~al wines of France; a ~al geography.* **~·ally** /-nlɪ/ *adv*

reg·is·ter[1] /ˋredʒɪstə(r)/ *n* [C] **1** (book containing a) record or list: *a parish ~,* one with records of baptisms, marriages and funerals; *Lloyd's ~,* of shipping; *the R~ of voters, the Parliamentary R~,* of persons qualified to vote at elections. **2** range of the human voice or of a musical instrument; part of this range: *the ˋupper/ˋmiddle ~; the lower ~ of the clarinet.* **3** mechanical device for indicating and recording speed, force, numbers, etc. **cash ~,** as used for recording cash payments in shops, etc. **4** adjustable metal plate or grating for widening or narrowing the size of an opening and so regulating the passage of air, etc through it: *a hot-air ~,* one controlling the flow of hot air, e g in a building heated from a basement furnace. **5** = **registry**. **6** (linguistic) vocabulary, grammar, etc used by speakers in particular circumstances or contexts, e g legal, public oratory, the family.

reg·is·ter[2] /ˋredʒɪstə(r)/ *vt,vi* [VP6A,2A] **1** make a written and formal record of, in a list: *~ one's car/the birth of a child/a new trade-mark; a State R~ed Nurse,* one who is officially ~ed. I am a foreigner here; must I ~ (myself) with the police? **2** put or get sb's name, one's own name, on a register, e g at a hotel, or, if abroad, at one's consulate. **3** (of instruments) indicate; record: *The thermometer ~ed only two degrees above freezing-point.* **4** (of sb's face) show (emotion, etc): *Her face ~ed surprise.* **5** send (a letter or parcel) by special post, paying an extra charge which ensures compensation if it is lost: *It's wise to ~ letters containing banknotes.*

reg·is·trar /ˈredʒɪˋstrɑ(r)/ *n* person whose duty is to keep records or registers, e g for a town council or a university.

reg·is·tra·tion /ˈredʒɪˋstreɪʃn/ *n* **1** [U] registering; recording: *~ of letters/luggage; ~ of students for an examination/an academic course; the ˋ~ number* (e g of a car). **2** [C] entry; record of facts.

reg·is·try /ˋredʒɪstrɪ/ *n* (*pl* **-tries**) **1** (sometimes *register*) place where registers are kept: *a ship's port of ~; married at a ˋ~ office,* before a registrar (without a religious ceremony). **2** [U] = registration.

Re·gius /ˋridʒɪəs/ *adj*: *~ professor* (*of Greek, etc*), holder of a university chair (at Oxford or Cambridge) instituted by King Henry VIII, or of a later chair with the same prerogatives; (Scot) title given to sb holding a professorship founded by the Crown.

reg·nant /ˋregnənt/ *adj* reigning: *Queen ~,* one who is ruling in her own right and not as a consort.

re·gress /rɪˋgres/ *vi* [VP2A] return to an earlier or more primitive form or state. **re·gression** /rɪˋgreʃn/ *n* ~ing. **re·gress·ive** *adj* tending to ~.

re·gret[1] /rɪˋgret/ *n* **1** [U] feeling of sadness at the loss of sth, or of annoyance or disappointment because sth has or has not been done: *express ~ at not being able to help; hear with ~ that a friend is ill. Much to my ~ I am unable to accept your kind invitation.* **2** (*pl*) (in polite expressions of refusal, etc): *Please accept my ~s at having to refuse. He refused with many ~s/with much ~. I have no ~s,* do not feel sorry (about what I did, etc). **~·ful** /-fl/ *adj* sad; sorry; **~·fully** /-flɪ/ *adv* sadly; with ~.

re·gret[2] /rɪˋgret/ *vt* (-tt-) [VP6A,D,7,9] **1** be sorry for the loss of; wish to have again: *~ lost opportunities. He died ~ted by all.* **2** feel sorry for; be sorry (*to say, etc; that…*): *I ~ being unable to help/~ that I cannot help. I ~ to say that…. It is to be ~ted that…,* is a pity that…. *I ~ my child's ignorance.* **~·table** /-əbl/ *adj* to be ~ted: *~table failures.* **~·tably** /-əblɪ/ *adv*: *a ~tably small attendance at the lecture.*

re·group /ˈriˋgrup/ *vt,vi* [VP6A,2A] form again into groups; form into new groups.

reg·ular /ˋregjʊlə(r)/ *adj* **1** evenly arranged; symmetrical; systematic: *~ teeth; ~ features,* e g of the face; *a ~ figure; a ~ nomenclature.* **2** coming, happening, done, again and again at even intervals: *a man with ~ habits,* doing the same things at the same times every day; *keep ~ hours,* e g leaving and returning home, getting up and going to bed, at the same times every day; *~ breathing; have a ~ pulse; walking up and down with ~ steps. He has no ~ work,* no continuous occupation. **3** properly qualified; recognized; trained; full-time or professional: *~ soldiers,* not volunteers or militia; *the ~ army,* made up of ~ soldiers. **4** conforming to a standard of etiquette; in agreement with what is considered correct procedure or behaviour: *Ought you to go and talk to her without a ~ introduction? I doubt whether your procedure would be considered ~ by the Embassy people.* **5** (gram, of *vv, nn,* etc) having normal inflections: *The verb 'go' is not ~.* **6** (old use, and in the Church) bound by, living under, religious rule (opp of *secular*): *the ~ clergy,* e g monks in Roman Catholic countries, but not parish priests. **7** (colloq) thorough; complete: *He's a ~ hero/rascal.* **8** (US) ordinary; normal: *Do you want king size cigarettes or ~ size?* **9** (colloq) likeable; good: *He's a ~ guy.* □ *n* **1** soldier of the ~ army. **2** (colloq) ~ customer or client, e g at a hairdresser's or a pub. **~·ly** *adv* in a ~ manner; at ~ intervals or times: *a garden ~ly laid out; as ~ly as clockwork.* **~·ity** /ˈregjʊˋlærətɪ/ *n* [U] state of being ~: *win a prize for ~ity of attendance at school.*

regu·lar·ize /ˋregjʊləraɪz/ *vt* [VP6A] make lawful or correct: *~ the proceedings.* **regu·lar·iz·ation** /ˈregjʊləraɪˋzeɪʃn *US:* -rɪˋz-/ *n*

regu·late /ˋregjʊleɪt/ *vt* [VP6A] **1** control systematically; cause to obey a rule or standard: *~ one's conduct/expenditure; ~ the traffic. Accidents happen even in the best ~d families.* **2** adjust (an apparatus, mechanism) to get the desired result: *~ a clock; ~ the speed of a machine.* **regu·la·tor** /-tə(r)/ *n* person or thing that ~s, e g a device that ~s a mechanical movement, esp in a clock.

regu·la·tion /ˈregjʊˋleɪʃn/ *n* **1** [U] regulating or being regulated: *the ~ of affairs/of a clock.* **2** [C] rule; order; authoritative direction: *ˋsafety ~s,* e g in factories; *ˋtraffic ~s,* made by the police for drivers of vehicles; *contrary to ~s; Queen's/King's ~s,* those governing the conduct of the armed forces. **3** (attrib) as required by rules; correct: *~ dress/uniform; application forms of the ~ size.*

re·gur·gi·tate /riˋgɜdʒɪteɪt/ *vi,vt* [VP6A,2A] (of liquid, etc) gush back; bring (swallowed food) up again to the mouth.

re·ha·bili·tate /ˈriəˋbɪlɪteɪt/ *vt* [VP6A] **1** restore (e g old buildings) to a good condition. **2** restore (sb) to former rank, position or reputation: *He has been ~d in public esteem.* **3** bring back (sb who is physically disabled or delinquent) to a normal life by special treatment. **re·ha·bili·ta·tion** /ˈriəˈbɪlɪˋteɪʃn/ *n* rehabilitating: *a rehabilitation centre,* place where persons are ~d(**3**).

re·hash /riˋhæʃ/ *vt* take (e g old literary material) and use again in a new form: *~ last term's lectures for the coming term.* □ *n* /ˋrihæʃ/ [C] ~ed material.

re·hear /ˈriˋhɪə(r)/ *vt* [VP6A] hear, consider again (a case, plea etc in a law court). **re·hear·ing** *n* instance of this.

re·hearse /rɪˋhɜs/ *vt,vi* [VP6A,2A] **1** practise (a play, music, programme, etc) for public performance: *~ the parts in a play; ~ an opera.* **2** say over again; give an account of: *~ the events of the day; ~ one's grievances.* **re·hearsal** /-sl/ *n* **1** [U] rehearsing: *put a play into rehearsal.* **2** [C] trial performance of a play or other entertainment: *a ˋdress rehearsal,* one in which the actors wear the costumes and use the props as for public performances.

re·house /ˈriˋhaʊz/ *vt* [VP6A] provide with a new house (esp in place of one officially condemned): *The people in these slums will have to be ~d.*

Reich /raɪk/ *n* the German Commonwealth as a whole. **the First R~,** the Holy Roman Empire, 9th c to 1806. **the Second R~,** 1871—1918. **the Third R~,** the Nazi regime, 1933—45.

reign /reɪn/ *n* [C] (period of) sovereignty, rule; dominance: *during five successive ~s; in the ~ of King Alfred; the ~ of law/reason; the R~ of Terror,* (in France, 1793—94, during the Revolution). □ *vi* [VP2A,3A] ***~ (over),*** **1** hold office as a monarch: *The king ~ed but he did not rule or govern. He ~ed over the country for ten years.* **2** be influential; prevail: *the ~ing beauty,* woman acknowledged to be most beautiful for the time in question. *Silence ~ed everywhere.*

re·im·burse /ˈriɪmˋbɜs/ *vt* [VP6A,12A,13A] ***~ sth (to sb); ~ sb sth,*** pay back (sb who has spent money, the money spent): *We must ~ him the costs of the journey. You will be ~d (for) your expenses.* **~·ment** *n* [C,U] repayment (of expenses).

rein /reɪn/ *n* (often *pl* in the same sense as the *sing*) long, narrow strap fastened to the bit of a bridle for controlling a horse. ⇨ the illus at **harness**. ***assume/drop the ~s of government,*** enter upon (give up) office. ***draw ~,*** pull up; go slower (liter and fig). ***give free ~/the ~s to sb/sth,*** allow freedom to: *give a horse the ~s; give the ~(s) to one's imagination,* allow it great freedom. ***hold/take the ~s,*** have/take control; (fig) *hold the ~s of government.* ***keep a tight ~ on sb/sth,*** be firm with; allow little freedom to. □ *vt* [VP6A,15B] control with, or as with, ~s: *~ in a horse,* restrain it; check it; *~ up/back a horse,* pull it up or back with the ~s.

re·in·car·nate /ˈriɪnˋkɑneɪt/ *vt* give a new body to (a soul). □ *adj* /ˈriɪnˋkɑnət/ born again in a new body. **re·in·car·na·tion** /ˈriɪnˈkɑˋneɪʃn/ *n* [U] religious doctrine that the soul enters, after death, into another (human or animal) body; [C] instance of this; new body inhabited by the soul.

rein·deer /ˋreɪndɪə(r)/ *n* (*pl* unchanged) kind of large deer with branched antlers, used in Lapland for transport and kept in herds for its milk, flesh and hide. ⇨ the illus at **large**.

re·in·force /ˈriɪnˋfɔs/ *vt* [VP6A] make stronger by adding or supplying more men or material; increase the size, thickness, of sth so that it supports more weight, etc: *~ an army/a fleet; ~ a garment,* by adding an extra thickness of cloth in places; *~ a bridge.* **~d concrete,** concrete strengthened with steel bars or metal netting embedded in it. **~·ment** *n* [U] reinforcing or being ~d; (esp *pl*) that which ~s; (esp) men, ships, etc sent to ~.

re·in·state /ˈriɪnˋsteɪt/ *vt* [VP6A,14] ***~ sb (in),*** replace (sb) (in a former position or condition): *~ sb in his former office.* **~·ment** *n*

re·in·sure /ˈriɪnˋʃʊə(r)/ *vt* [VP6A] insure again (esp

of an underwriter who relieves himself of some or all of a risk by taking out an insurance with another underwriter or insurance company. **re·in·sur·ance** /-rns/ *n*

re·is·sue /ˈriˋɪʃu/ *vt* [VP6A] issue again after temporary discontinuance: ~ *stamps/books.* □ *n* sth ~d, esp a reprint of a book with a change of format or price. Cf *new edition,* in which changes are made in the text.

re·iter·ate /riˋɪtəreɪt/ *vt* [VP6A] say or do again several times: ~ *a command.* **re·iter·ation** /ˈriˌɪtəˋreɪʃn/ *n* [U] act of reiterating; [C] instance of this; repetition.

re·ject[1] /ˋridʒekt/ *n* sth ~ed: *export ~s,* articles made for export but ~ed because of a flaw or imperfection. **re·jec·tion** /rɪˋdʒekʃn/ *n* [U] ~ing or being ~ed; [C] instance of this; sth ~ed: *ˋ~ion slip,* printed or written note from an editor or publisher ~ing a proffered article, M S etc.

re·ject[2] /rɪˋdʒekt/ *vt* [VP6A] **1** put aside, throw away, as not good enough to be kept: ~ *fruit that is over-ripe.* **2** refuse to accept: ~ *an offer of help;* ~ *a heart transplant,* (of the body) fail to adapt to the new heart; *a ~ed suitor. The army doctors ~ed him,* would not accept him as medically fit.

re·jig /ˈriˋdʒɪg/ *vt* (-gg-) [VP6A] supply (a factory, etc) with new mechanical equipment.

re·joice /rɪˋdʒɔɪs/ *vt,vi* **1** [VP6A] make glad; cause to be happy: *The boy's success ~d his mother's heart.* **2** [VP2A,C,3B,4C] feel great joy; show signs of great happiness: ~ *over a victory;* ~ *at sb's success. I ~ to hear that you are well again/ ~ that you have recovered so quickly. He ~s in the name of Bloggs,* allegedly humorous for 'His name is Bloggs'. Note: in colloq style 'be glad' and 'be pleased' are commoner than 'rejoice'. **re·joic·ing** *n* [U] happiness; joy; (*pl*) celebrations; merry-making.

re·join[1] /rɪˋdʒɔɪn/ *vt,vi* [VP6A,2A] answer; reply; (legal) answer a charge or plea. **~·der** /-də(r)/ *n* [C] what is said in reply; retort.

re·join[2] /ˈriˋdʒɔɪn/ *vt* [VP6A] join the company of again; ~ *one's regiment/ship.*

re-join[3] /ˈri ˋdʒɔɪn/ *vt* [VP6A] join (together) again.

re·ju·ven·ate /riˋdʒuvəneɪt/ *vt,vi* [VP6A,2A] make or become young or vigorous again in nature or appearance. **re·ju·ven·ation** /rɪˈdʒuvəˋneɪʃn/ *n*

re·kindle /riˋkɪndl/ *vt,vi* [VP6A,2A] kindle again: ~ *a fire. Our hopes ~d.*

re·laid /ˈriˋleɪd/ ⇨ relay[2].

re·lapse /rɪˋlæps/ *vi* [VP2A,3A] ~ ***(into),*** fall back again (into bad ways, error, heresy, illness, silence etc): *He ~d into heresy and was burnt at the stake.* □ *n* [C] falling back, esp after recovering from illness: *The patient has had a ~.*

re·late /rɪˋleɪt/ *vt,vi* **1** [VP6A,14] (formal) tell (a story, etc to sb); give an account of (facts, adventures etc): *He ~d to his wife some amusing stories about his employer. Strange to ~, I once met Smith in Katmandu.* **2** [VP14] connect in thought or meaning: *It is difficult to ~ these results with/to any known cause.* **3** [VP3A] ~ ***to,*** have reference (to): *She is a girl who notices nothing except what ~s to herself.* **4 *be ~d (to),*** be connected by family (to): *I am not ~d to him in any way. He and I are not ~d. She says she is ~d to the royal family.*

re·la·tion /rɪˋleɪʃn/ *n* **1** [U] the act of relating(**1,2**), narrating or telling: *the ~ of his adventures;* [C] that which is narrated; tale or narrative. **2** [U] (= ~ship) connection; what there is between one thing, person, idea, etc and another or others: *the ~ between mother and child/between weather and the crops. The effort and expense needed for this project bore no ~/were out of all ~ to the results,* were not proportional to the results. ***in/with ~ to,*** as regards; concerning. **3** (usu *pl*) dealings; affairs; what one person, group, country etc, has to do with another: *have business ~s with a firm in Stockholm; the friendly ~s between my country and yours; diplomatic ~s.* **(public reˋlations) officer,** ⇨ **public,** *adj*(**1**). *I have broken off all ~s with that fellow,* I have nothing to do with him now. **4** [U] kinship (now usu *~ship*): [C] kinsman or kinswoman; relative(**2**): *He's a near ~ of mine. She's a ~ by marriage. All his poor ~s came to spend their holidays at his home.* **~·ship** /-ʃɪp/ *n* **1** ~(**2**): *He admitted his affair with Susan could never develop into a lasting ~ship.* **2** [U] (= ~(**4**)) condition of belonging to the same family; being connected by birth or marriage. **3** [C] instance of being related; particular connection or ~ (*between/to/with*).

rela·tive /ˋrelətɪv/ *adj* **1** comparative: *the ~ advantages of two methods/of gas and electricity for heating. They are living in ~ comfort,* i e compared with other people or with themselves at an earlier time. **2** ~ ***to,*** referring to; having a connection with: *the facts ~ to this problem; the papers ~ to the case.* **3** (gram) ~ **adverb** (e g *where* in 'the place where the accident occurred'). ~ **clause,** one joined by a ~ *pron* or *adv* to the antecedent of the ~ word. ~ **pronoun** (e g *whom* in 'the man whom we saw'). □ *n* [C] **1** ~ word, esp a ~ pronoun. **2** person to whom one is related (e g an uncle or aunt, a cousin, a nephew or niece). **~·ly** *adv* comparatively; in proportion to: *In spite of her dull husband she is ~ly happy. The matter is unimportant, ~ly speaking,* if we think of this matter in proportion to other matters.

rela·tiv·ity /ˈreləˋtɪvətɪ/ *n* [U] (esp) Einstein's theory of the universe, based on the principle that measures of space and time are relative.

re·lax /rɪˋlæks/ *vt,vi* **1** [VP6A] cause or allow to become less tight, stiff, strict or rigid: ~ *one's grip/hold on sth;* ~ *the muscles;* ~ *discipline; a ~ed throat,* a form of sore throat; *a ~ing climate,* (opp of *bracing*) one that causes an inclination to feel sluggish, lacking in energy. **2** [VP2A,C] become less tense, rigid, energetic, strict: *His severity ~ed. His face ~ed in a smile. Let's stop working and ~ for an hour. He's feeling ~ed now,* free from nervous anxiety, disturbing tensions, etc. **~·ation** /ˈrilækˋseɪʃn/ *n* **1** [U] ~ing or being ~ed: *~ation of the muscles.* **2** [U] recreation; [C] sth done for recreation: *Fishing and mountain-climbing are his favourite ~ations.*

re·lay[1] /ˋrileɪ/ *n* [C] **1** supply of fresh horses to take the place of tired horses; gang or group of men, supply of material, similarly used: *working in/by ~s.* **ˋ~ race** *n* one between two teams, each member of the team running one section of the total distance. **2** (telegraphy, broadcasting) device which receives messages, radio programmes, etc and transmits them with greater strength, thus increasing the distance over which they are carried. **ˋ~ station,** place from which radio programmes are broadcast after being received from another station. **3** (short for) ~ race; ~ed broadcast programme. □ *vt* /rɪˈleɪ/ (*pt,pp* ~**ed**) send out (a broadcast programme received from another station).

re·lay[2] /ˈriˈleɪ/ *vt* (*pt,pp* -**laid** /-ˈleɪd/) lay (a cable, carpet, etc) again.

re·lease /rɪˈlis/ *vt* [VP6A,14] ~ ***sb/sth from,*** **1** allow to go; set free; unfasten: *~ one's hold of sth; ~ a man from prison/from a promise; ~ a bomb* (*from an aircraft*), allow it to fall; *~ a monk from his vows; ~ sb from his suffering; ~ the handbrake* (*of a car*). **2** allow (news) to be known or published; allow (a film) to be exhibited or (goods) to be placed on sale: *recently ~d films/discs.* **3** (legal) give up or surrender (a right, debt, property) to another. □ *n* **1** [U] releasing or being ~d; [C] instance of this: *obtain* (*a*) *~ from an obligation; an order for sb's ~ from prison; the ~ of a film for public exhibition; a ˈpress ~,* i e to the newspapers; *a feeling of ~,* i e of freedom; *the newest ~es,* e g films/discs; *on general ~,* (of cinema films) available for seeing at the usual network of local cinemas. **2** [C] handle, lever, catch, etc that ~s part of a machine: *the ˈcarriage ~* (on a typewriter); (attrib) *ˈ~ gear; the ˈ~ button/knob.*

rel·egate /ˈreləgeɪt/ *vt* [VP14] ~ ***sth/sb to,*** delegate. **2** dismiss to a lower position or condition: *He ~d his wife to the position of a mere housekeeper.* (League football) *Will our team be ~d to the second division?* **rel·ega·tion** /ˈreləˈgeɪʃn/ *n* [U].

re·lent /rɪˈlent/ *vi* [VP2A] become less severe; give up unkind or cruel intentions: *At last mother ~ed and allowed the children to stay up and watch TV.* **~·less** *adj* without pity: *~less persecution.* **~·less·ly** *adv*

rel·evant /ˈreləvənt/ *adj* ~ ***(to),*** connected with what is being discussed: *have all the ~ documents ready; supply the facts ~ to the case.* **~·ly** *adv* **rel·evance** /-ns/, **rel·evancy** /-nsɪ/ *nn*

re·li·able /rɪˈlɑɪəbl/ *adj* that may be relied or depended upon: *~ tools/assistants/information/ witnesses.* **re·li·ably** /-əblɪ/ *adv* **re·lia·bil·ity** /rɪˈlɑɪəˈbɪlətɪ/ *n* [U] state or quality of being ~.

re·li·ance /rɪˈlɑɪəns/ *n* **1** [U] trust; confidence: *Do you place much ~* (*up*)*on your doctor? There is little ~ to be placed on his promises.* **2** person or thing depended upon. **re·li·ant** /-ənt/ *adj* having ~; trusting.

relic /ˈrelɪk/ *n* [C] **1** part of the body, dress, etc of a saint or sth that belonged to him or was connected with him, kept after his death, as an object of reverence, and in some cases said to have miraculous powers. **2** sth that has survived from the past and that serves to keep memories alive: *a ~ of early civilization,* e g a stone implement; *~s of superstition.* **3** (*pl*) person's dead body or bones; what has survived destruction or decay.

re·lict /ˈrelɪkt/ *n* (archaic) widow: *Alice, ~ of Arthur Williams.*

re·lief[1] /rɪˈlif/ *n* [U] (used with the *indef art* as in examples, but not normally in the *pl*) **1** lessening or ending or removal of pain, distress, anxiety, etc: *The doctor's treatment gave/brought some/ not much ~. A doctor's task is to work for the ~ of suffering. She heaved a sigh of ~ when she was told that the child's life was not in danger. To my great ~ the difficulties were all overcome. It was a great ~ to find the children safe.* **2** that which brings ~(**1**); help given to those in need; food, clothes, money, etc for persons in trouble: *send ~ to people made homeless by floods; provide ~ for refugees; a ˈ~ fund; ˈ~ works,* employment provided (on road-building, etc) for people in distress because of business depression, etc: *a ~ road,* alternative road for one that has heavy traffic. **3** (formerly, in GB, before the Poor Law was replaced by later legislation) help given to poor people: *indoor ~,* given to people in a workhouse; *outdoor ~,* given to people living in their homes. **4** sth that makes a change from monotony or that relaxes tension: *We crossed wide stretches of moorland without ~,* with no change of scenery. *Shakespeare introduced comic scenes into his tragedies by way of ~.* **5** ~ ***(of),*** reinforcement of a beseiged town; raising (of a siege): *The general hastened to the ~ of the fortress.* **6** (replacing of a person, persons, on duty by a) person or persons appointed to go on duty: *on duty from 8a m to 8p m with only two hours' ~; happy to know that the ~ is on the way;* (attrib) *a ˈ~ driver.*

re·lief[2] /rɪˈlif/ *n* ⇨ **bas-~**. **1** [U] method of carving or moulding in which a design stands out from a flat surface: *a profile of Julius Caesar in ~; in high/low ~,* with the background cut out to a deep/shallow degree. **2** [C] design or carving made in this way. **3** [U] (in drawing, etc) appearance of being done in ~ by the use of shading, colour, etc. **ˈ~ map,** one showing hills, valleys, etc by shading or other means, not only by contour lines. **4** [U] vividness; distinctness of outline (liter and fig). ***be/stand out in ~ against,*** be in contrast to: *The hills stood out in sharp ~ against the morning sky. His behaviour stood out in strong ~ against his declared principles.*

re·lieve /rɪˈliv/ *vt* [VP6A] **1** give or bring relief[1] to; lessen or remove (pain or distress): *We were ~d to hear that you had arrived safely. The fund is for relieving distress among the flood victims.* ***~ one's feelings,*** provide an outlet for them (e g by shedding tears, or by using strong language, behaving violently). ***~ oneself,*** empty the bladder or bowels. **reˈlieving officer,** parish official who used to care for the poor. ⇨ **relief**[1]**(3)**. **2** take one's turn on duty: *~ the guard/the watch/a sentry. You will be ~d at noon.* ⇨ **relief**[1]**(6)**. **3** ***~ sb of sth,*** **(a)** take it from him: *Let me ~ you of your suitcase,* carry it for you (which is more usu). **(b)** (joc) steal from: *The thief ~d him of his watch.* **(c)** dismiss from: *He was ~d of his post.* **4** bring into relief[2]; make (sth) stand out more clearly (*against* a dark background, etc).

re·lig·ion /rɪˈlɪdʒən/ *n* **1** [U] belief in the existence of a supernatural ruling power, the creator and controller of the universe, who has given to man a spiritual nature which continues to exist after the death of the body. **2** [C] one of the various systems of faith and worship based on such belief: *the great ~s of the world,* e g Christianity, Islam, Buddhism. **3** [U] life as lived under the rules of a monastic order: *Her name in ~ is Sister Mary,* This is her name as a nun. **4** matter of conscience; sth that one considers oneself bound to do: *She makes a ~ of keeping her house clean and tidy.*

re·lig·ious /rɪˈlɪdʒəs/ *adj* **1** of religion. **2** (of a person) devout; God-fearing. **3** of a monastic order: *a ~ house,* a monastery or convent. **4** scrupulous; conscientious: *do one's work with ~ care/ exactitude.* □ *n* (with *indef art*) person bound by monastic vows; monk or nun; (*pl*, unchanged in form) *the/some/several* ~, persons bound by monastic vows. **~·ly** *adv*

re·line /ˈriˈlɑɪn/ *vt* put a new lining in, e g a garment.

re·lin·quish /rɪˋlɪŋkwɪʃ/ *vt* **1** [VP6A] give up: ~ *a hope/a habit/a belief.* ***~ one's hold of/over sb/sth,*** give up control. **2** [VP14] ***~ sth (to sb),*** surrender: ~ *one's rights/shares to a partner.*

reli·quary /ˋrelɪkwərɪ *US:* -kwerɪ/ *n* (*pl* -ries) box, casket, or other receptacle for a relic or relics.

rel·ish /ˋrelɪʃ/ *n* **1** [C,U] (sth used to give, or which has, a) special flavour or attractive quality: *Hunger is the best* ~ *for food. Yorkshire* ~ *is a kind of sauce. Olives and sardines are* ~*es. Some pastimes lose their* ~ *when one grows old.* **2** [U] liking (*for*); zest: *I have no further* ~ *for active pursuits now that I am 90.* □ *vt* [VP6A,D] enjoy; get pleasure out of: *I would* ~ *a lobster and a bottle of Chablis. She won't* ~ *having to get up before dawn to catch that train.*

re·live /ˈriˋlɪv/ *vt* live through, undergo, again: *That was an experience I should not like to* ~.

re·lo·cate /ˈriləʊˋkeɪt *US:* ˈriˋləʊkeɪt/ *vt,vi* establish, become established, in a new place or area. **re·lo·ca·tion** /ˈriləʊˋkeɪʃn/ *n* [U] putting in, moving to, a new place or area: *the relocation of industry; the relocation of population;* compulsory evacuation of persons from military areas during a war, with resettlement in a new area.

re·luc·tant /rɪˋlʌktənt/ *adj* ***~ (to do sth),*** (slow to act because) unwilling or disinclined to manage; ~ *helpers. He seemed* ~ *to join us.* **~·ly** *adv* **re·luc·tance** /-əns/ *n* [U].

rely /rɪˋlɑɪ/ *vi* (*pt,pp* -lied) [VP3A] ***~ (up)on,*** depend upon with confidence, look to for help: *He can always be relied upon for help. You may* ~ *upon my early arrival. You may* ~ *upon it that he will be early.*

re·main /rɪˋmeɪn/ *vi* **1** [VP2A] be still present after a part has gone or has been away: *After the fire, very little* ~*ed of my house. If you take 3 from 8, 5* ~*s. Much* ~*s to be settled.* **2** [VP2A,B,C,4A] continue in some place or condition; continue to be: *How many weeks shall you* ~ (= stay) *here? Let things* ~ *as they are. He* ~*ed silent. I shall* ~ (*stay* is more usu) *to see the end of the game. Man* ~*ed a hunter for thousands of years,* i e before beginning to cultivate crops, etc.

re·main·der /rɪˋmeɪndə(r)/ *n* that which remains; persons or things that are left over: *Twenty people came in and the* ~ (= the rest, the others) *stayed outside.*

re·mains /rɪˋmeɪnz/ *n pl* **1** what is left: *the* ~*s of a meal; the* ~*s* (= ruins) *of an old abbey/of ancient Rome.* **2** dead body; corpse: *His mortal* ~*s are buried in the churchyard.*

re·make /ˈriˋmeɪk/ *vt* (*pt,pp* -made /-ˋmeɪd/) make again. □ *n* /ˋrimeɪk/ sth made again: *a* ~ *of a film.*

re·mand /rɪˋmɑnd *US:* -ˋmænd/ *vt* [VP6A] send (an accused person) back (from a court of law) into custody so that more evidence may be obtained: ~*ed for a week.* □ *n* [U] ~ing or being ~ed: *detention on* ~. ˋ**~ home,** institution to which law-breaking children and adolescents are sent while inquiries are being made, or until the courts have decided their future treatment.

re·mark /rɪˋmɑk/ *vt,vi* **1** [VP6A,9,10] notice; see: *Did you* ~ *the similarity between them?* **2** [VP6A,9] say (*that*): *He* ~*ed that he would be absent the next day. 'I thought it was curious', he* ~*ed.* **3** [VP3A] ***~ (up)on,*** say sth by way of comment. *It would be rude to* ~ *upon her appearance.* □ *n* **1** [U] notice; looking at: *There was nothing worthy of* ~ *at the Flower Show.* **2** [C] comment; sth said: *pass rude* ~*s about sb; make a few* ~*s,* give a short talk. **~·able** /-əbl/ *adj* out of the ordinary; deserving or attracting attention: *a* ~*able event; a boy who is* ~*able for his stupidity.* **~·ably** /-əblɪ/ *adv*

re·marry /ˈriˋmærɪ/ *vt,vi* (*pt,pp* -ried) marry again. **re·mar·riage** /ˈriˋmærɪdʒ/ *n*

rem·edy /ˋremədɪ/ *n* [C,U] (*pl* -dies) ***~ (for),*** cure (for a disease, evil, etc), method of, sth used for, putting right sth that is wrong: *a good* ~ *for colds. The* ~ *seems to be worse than the disease. Your only* ~ (= way to get redress) *is to go to law. The evil is past/beyond* ~, cannot be cured. □ *vt* [VP6A] put right; provide a ~ for (evils, defects): *Your faults of pronunciation can be remedied.* **re·medial** /rɪˋmidɪəl/ *adj* providing, or intended to provide, a ~: *remedial measures; remedial education/classes,* e g for children suffering disadvantages. **re·medi·able** /rɪˋmidɪəbl/ *adj* that can be remedied.

re·mem·ber /rɪˋmembə(r)/ *vt,vi* **1** [VP6A,D,7,8, 9,10,14,16A] have or keep in the memory; call back to mind the memory of: *I can't* ~ *his name. I* ~*ed* (= did not forget) *to post your letters. I* ~ *posting your letters* (= have the memory of that act in my mind). *I* ~ *having heard you speak on that subject. Do you* ~ *where you put the key? I* ~ *her* (= picture her in my mind) *as a slim young girl. Please don't* ~ *this unfortunate affair against me,* don't bear it in mind and, for that reason, be unfriendly to me. *'Have you ever met my brother-?'—'Not that I* ~*.'* I don't ~ having met him. **2** [VP6A] make a present to: *Please* ~ *the waiter,* don't forget to tip him. *I hope you'll* ~ *me in your will,* leave me sth. **3** [VP14] ***~ sb to sb,*** convey greetings: *Please* ~ *me to your brother.*

re·mem·brance /rɪˋmembrns/ *n* **1** [U] remembering or being remembered; memory: *to the best of my* ~*; have no* ~ *of sth; a service in* ~ *of those killed in the war.* **R~ Day,** (GB) Nov 11th, or the preceding Sunday, on which those killed in the two World Wars are commemorated. **2** [C] sth given or kept in memory of sb or sth: *He sent us a small* ~ *of his visit.* **3** (*pl*) regards; greetings (⇨ regard[1](5)): *Give my kind* ~*s to your parents.*

re·mili·tar·ize /ˈriˋmɪlɪtərɑɪz/ *vt* [VP6A] provide, occupy, again with armed forces and military equipment. **re·mili·tar·iz·ation** /ˈriˈmɪlɪtərɑɪˋzeɪʃn *US:* -rɪˋz-/ *n*

re·mind /rɪˋmɑɪnd/ *vt* [VP11,14,17,20,21] ***~ sb (to do sth/that; ~ sb of sth/sb,*** cause (sb) to remember (to do sth, etc); cause (sb) to think (of sth): *Please* ~ *me to answer that letter. Travellers are* ~*ed that inoculation against yellow fever is advisable. He* ~*s me of his brother. This* ~*s me of what we did together during our holidays. That* ~*s me,...,* What you have just said ~s me..., I've just remembered..., etc. **~er** *n* sth (e g a letter) that helps sb to remember sth: *He hasn't paid me that money yet—I must send him a* ~*er,* i e a letter to ~ him about it.

remi·nisce /ˈremɪˋnɪs/ *vi* [VP2A,3A] ***~ (about),*** think or talk about past events and experiences.

remi·nis·cence /ˈremɪˋnɪsns/ *n* ~ ***(of),*** **1** [U] reminiscing; recalling of past experiences. **2** (*pl*) remembered experiences; narrative, spoken or written, of what sb remembers: *~s of my days in the Navy. The scene awakened ~s of my youth.* **3** sth that is suggestive (*of* sth else): *There is a ~ of his father in the way he walks.*

remi·nis·cent /ˈremɪˋnɪsnt/ *adj* ~ ***(of),*** **1** reminding one of; suggestive of. **2** recalling past experiences: *become ~.* **~·ly** *adv*

re·miss /rɪˋmɪs/ *adj* ~ ***in,*** careless of duty: *You have been ~ in your duties.* ~ ***of,*** negligent, lax: *That was very ~ of you.* **~·ness** *n* [U].

re·mission /rɪˋmɪʃn/ *n* **1** [U] pardon or forgiveness (of sins, by God). **2** [U] freeing (from debt, punishment, etc): *~ of a claim;* [C] instance of this: ~ (from a prison sentence) *for good conduct; No ~s of examination fees are allowed.* **3** [U] lessening or weakening (of pain, efforts, etc): *~ of a fever.*

re·mit /rɪˋmɪt/ *vt, vi* (-tt-) **1** [VP6A] (of God) forgive (sins). **2** [VP6A] excuse (sb) payment (of a debt, a punishment): *The taxes have been ~ted. Your fees cannot be ~ted.* **3** [VP12A,13A,2C] send (money, etc) by post: *When can you ~ me the money? Kindly ~ by cheque,* send a cheque for the sum owing. **4** [VP6A] make or become less: *~ one's efforts.* **5** [VP14] ~ ***sth to sb,*** take or send (a question to be decided) (to some authority): *The matter has been ~ted to a higher tribunal.* **~·tance** /-tns/ *n* [U] the ~ting, of money; [C] sum of money sent.

re·mit·tent /rɪˋmɪtnt/ *adj* (esp of a fever) that abates in severity at intervals.

rem·nant /ˋremnənt/ *n* [C] **1** small part that remains: *~s of a banquet; ~s of former glory.* **2** (esp) length of cloth offered at a reduced price after the greater part has been sold: *a ~ sale.*

re·mon·strance /rɪˋmonstrəns/ *n* [U] remonstrating (*with*); [C] protest (*against*).

re·mon·strate /ˈremənstreɪt/ *vi* [VP2A,3A] ~ ***with sb (about sth/that),*** make a protest; argue in protest: *~ with sb about his foolish behaviour; ~ against cruelty to children.*

re·morse /rɪˋmɔs/ *n* [U] **1** ~ ***(for),*** deep, bitter regret for wrongdoing: *feel/be filled with ~ for one's failure to help sb; in a fit of ~.* **2** compunction: *without ~,* merciless(ly). **~·ful** /-fl/ *adj* feeling ~. **~·fully** /-fḷɪ/ *adv* **~·less** *adj* without ~. **~·less·ly** *adv*

re·mote /rɪˋməʊt/ *adj* (-r, -st) ~ ***(from),*** **1** far away in space or time: *in the ~st parts of Asia; live in a house ~ from any town or village; in the ~ past/future.* ~ **control,** control of apparatus, e g in an aircraft, a rocket, from a distance by means of radio signals. **2** widely separated (in feeling, interests, etc *from*): *Some of your statements are rather ~ from the subject we are discussing.* **3** distant in manner; aloof. **4** (esp in the superl) slight: *a ~ possibility; have not the ~st idea of what sth means.* **~·ly** *adv* in a ~ manner: *Smith and I are ~ly related.* **~·ness** *n*

re·mount[1] /ˈriˋmaʊnt/ *vt, vi* [VP6A,2A] get on (a horse, bicycle, etc) again; go up (a ladder, hill, etc) again.

re·mount[2] /ˈriˋmaʊnt/ *vt* [VP6A] **1** supply (a man, a regiment) with a fresh horse or horses. **2** put (a photograph, etc) on a new mount. □ *n* /ˋrimaʊnt/ fresh horse; supply of fresh horses.

re·move[1] /rɪˋmuv/ *vt, vi* **1** [VP6A,14] ~ ***sb/sth from,*** take off or away from the place occupied; take to another place: *~ one's hat/coat; ~ one's hand from sb's shoulder; ~ the cloth from the table; ~ a boy from school,* e g because of ill health. **2** [VP6A] get rid of: *~ doubts/fears. What do you advise for removing grease/ink stains, etc from clothes?* **3** [VP6A] dismiss: *~ a man from office; ~ a Civil Servant.* **4** [VP2A,C] go to live in another place (move is more usu): *We're removing into the country next week/removing from London to the country.* **5** **~d from,** distant or remote from: *a dialect equally ~d from French and Spanish; an explanation far ~d from the truth.* **6** **~d,** (of cousins) different by a generation: *first cousin once ~d,* first cousin's child. **re·mov·able** /-əbl/ *adj* that can be ~d (esp of a magistrate or other official who can be ~d from office at any time). **re·mover** *n* **1** (esp) person who follows the business of moving furniture when people ~(4). **2** (in compounds) sth that ~s(2): *superfluous ˋhair ~r.* **re·moval** /-vl/ *n* [U] act of removing: *the removal of furniture;* (attrib) *a reˋmoval van* (for furniture); *the removal of dissatisfaction;* [C] instance of removal.

re·move[2] /rɪˋmuv/ *n* **1** (at some schools in GB) promotion to a higher form at school: *get one's ~;* certain form or division at school. **2** stage or degree: *only a few ~s from....*

re·mun·er·ate /rɪˋmjunəreɪt/ *vt* [VP6A,14] ~ ***sb (for sth),*** pay (sb) (for work or services); reward. **re·mun·er·ation** /rɪˋmjunəˋreɪʃn/ *n* [U] payment; reward. **re·mun·er·ative** /rɪˋmjunṛətɪv *US:* -nəreɪtɪv/ *adj* profitable.

re·nais·sance /rɪˋneɪsns *US:* ˋrenəsɑns/ *n* **1** **the R~,** (period of) revival of art and literature in Europe in the 14th, 15th and 16th cc, based on ancient Greek learning; (attrib) *~ art.* **2** [C] any similar revival.

re·nal /ˋrinl/ *adj* of or in the (region of the) kidneys: *~ artery.*

re·name /riˋneɪm/ *vt* [VP6A] give a new name to; name again.

re·nas·cence /rɪˋnæsns/ *n* = renaissance(2). **re·nas·cent** /-snt/ *adj* springing up anew; reviving; being reborn.

rend /rend/ *vt* (*pt,pp* rent /rent/) [VP6A,14,15A] (liter) **1** pull or divide forcibly; penetrate: *a country rent (in two) by civil war. Loud cries rent the air.* **2** tear or pull (*off, away*) violently: *Children were rent from their mothers' arms by the brutal soldiers.*

ren·der /ˋrendə(r)/ *vt* **1** [VP6A,14,12A,13A,15A,B] ~ ***sth (to sb),*** give in return or exchange, or as sth due: *~ thanks to God; ~ good for evil; ~ help to those in need; ~ a service to sb/~ sb a service; ~ up* (= surrender) *a fort to the enemy; a reward for services ~ed.* **2** [VP6A] present; offer; send in (an account for payment): *an account ~ed,* previously presented but not yet paid. *You will have to ~ an account of your expenditure.* **3** [VP22] cause to be (in some condition): *~ed helpless by an accident.* **4** [VP6A,14] give a performance of (e g a drama, a character in a drama); express in another language: *The piano solo was well ~ed. Othello was ~ed rather poorly. There are many English idioms that cannot be ~ed into other languages.* **5** [VP6A,15B] ~ ***sth (down),*** melt and make clear: *~ down fat/lard.* **~·ing** /ˋrendṛɪŋ/ *n* [C] way of performing, playing, translating, sth. ⇨ 4 above: *her ~ing of Chopin; clever ~ings of Racine.*

ren·dez·vous /ˈrondɪvu/ *n* (*pl*, unchanged) [C] **1** (place decided upon for a) meeting at a time agreed upon. **2** place where people often meet: *This café is a ~ for writers and artists.* □ *vi* meet at a ~: *We'll ~ at the pub in that village on the other side of the lake.*

ren·di·tion /renˈdɪʃn/ *n* [C] interpretation or rendering (*of* a song, etc).

ren·egade /ˈrenəgeɪd/ *n* [C] person who changes his religious beliefs, esp from Christianity; person who deserts his political party; traitor: (attrib) *a ~ priest.* □ *vi* turn ~.

re·nege, re·negue /rɪˈnig/ *vi* **1** (in card games) revoke(2). **2** [VP3A] ~ ***on,*** (colloq) fail to keep (one's word).

re·new /rɪˈnju *US:* -ˈnu/ *vt* [VP6A] **1** make (as good as) new; put new life and vigour into; restore to the original condition: *~ one's youth; with ~ed enthusiasm.* **2** get, make, say or give, again: *~ a lease/contract; ~ one's subscription to a periodical; ~ an attack; ~ one's complaints.* **3** replace (with the same sort of thing, etc): *We must ~ our supplies of coal. Snakes cast off and ~ their skins.* **~·able** /-əbl/ *adj* that can be ~ed. **~·al** /-ˈnjul̩ *US:* -ˈnul̩/ *n* [U] ~ing or being ~ed: *delighted at the ~al of negotiations; urban ~al,* e g slum clearance for the provision of better housing. [C] sth ~ed.

ren·net /ˈrenɪt/ *n* [U] preparation used in curdling milk for making cheese, etc.

re·nounce /rɪˈnaʊns/ *vt* [VP6A] **1** declare formally that one will no longer have anything to do with, that one no longer recognizes (sb or sth having a claim to one's care, affection, etc): *~ one's faith/religion; ~ the world,* give up meeting people socially, begin to lead the life of a hermit, etc. **2** consent formally to give up (a claim, right, possession): *~ one's claim to the throne/a peerage.* **3** disown; refuse to recognize: *He ~d his sons because they were criminals.*

reno·vate /ˈrenəveɪt/ *vt* [VP6A] restore, e g old buildings, oil paintings, to good or strong condition. **reno·va·tor** /-tə(r)/ **reno·va·tion** /ˈrenəˈveɪʃn/ *n* [U] renovating; (*pl*) instances of this: *costly renovations of old college buildings at Oxford.*

re·nown /rɪˈnaʊn/ *n* [U] fame: *win ~; a man of high ~.* **re·nowned** *adj* famous; celebrated: *~ed as a portrait painter; ~ed for his skill.*

rent[1] /rent/ *n* [C,U] regular payment for the use of land, a building, a room or rooms, machinery, etc; sum of money paid in this way: *owe three weeks' ~ for one's house; have a house free of ~; pay a heavy/high ~ for farming land; collect the ~s.* **ˈ~-collector** *n* person who goes from house to house to collect ~s for the owner(s). **ˈ~-ˈfree** *adj, adv: a ~-free house,* for which no ~ is charged to the tenant; *occupy a house ~-free.* **ˈ~-rebate** *n* rebate, based on earnings and the amount of ~ payable, given by a local government authority on ~ paid, esp by council tenants. **ˈ~-roll** *n* **(a)** register of a person's land and buildings with the ~s due from them. **(b)** total income from ~s. □ *vt,vi* **1** [VP6A] occupy or use (land, buildings, etc) for ~; allow (land, buildings, etc) to be used or occupied in return for ~: *We don't own our house, we ~ it from Mr Gay. Mr Hill ~s this land to us at £50 a year.* **2** [VP2A,C] be ~ed: *The building ~s at £150 a year.* **~·able** /-əbl/ *adj* that may be ~ed; able to yield a ~. **~·al** /ˈrentl/ *n* [C] amount of ~ paid or received; income from ~s. **~·er** *n* (esp) person in the film industry who ~s films.

rent[2] /rent/ *n* [C] **1** torn place in cloth, etc: split: *a ~ in the fabric of the balloon.* **2** (fig) division or split (in a political party, etc).

rent[3] /rent/ *pt,pp* of **rend**.

rent·ier /ˈrõtɪeɪ/ *n* person whose income comes from investments and/or rents from property.

re·nunci·ation /rɪˈnʌnsɪˈeɪʃn/ *n* [U] renouncing, self-denial.

re·open /riˈəʊpən/ *vt,vi* [VP6A,2A] open again after closing or being closed: *~ a shop; ~ a discussion. School ~s on Monday.*

re·or·gan·ize /riˈɔgənaɪz/ *vt,vi* organize again or in a new way.

re·orien·tate /riˈɔrɪənteɪt/ (also **re·orient** /riˈɔrɪənt/) *vt,vi* orient(ate) again or anew.

rep[1], **repp** /rep/, **reps** /reps/ *n* [U] textile fabric used in upholstery.

rep[2] /rep/ *n* (sl abbr of *reprobate*) person of loose character: *You old rep!*

rep[3] /rep/ *n* (colloq abbr of) repertory company or theatre: *act in rep.*

re·pair[1] /rɪˈpeə(r)/ *vt* [VP6A] **1** restore (sth worn or damaged) to good condition: *~ the roads/a puncture/a watch/a shirt.* **2** put right again: *~ an error.* □ *n* **1** [U] ~ing or being ~ed: *road under ~.* **2** (*sing* or *pl* but not with *indef art*) work or process of ~ing: *The shop will be closed during ~s. The ~s needed before we can occupy the house will be considerable.* **3** [U] relative condition for using or being used: *The machine is in a bad state of ~/in good ~.* **~·able** /-əbl/ *adj* that can be ~ed. **~·er** *n* one who ~s things: *boot and shoe ~ers.*

re·pair[2] /rɪˈpeə(r)/ *vi* [VP3A] ~ ***to,*** (formal) (esp go frequently, go in large numbers to): *~ to the seaside resorts for the summer.*

rep·ar·able /ˈreprəbl/ *adj* (of a loss, etc) that can be made good.

rep·ar·ation /ˈrepəˈreɪʃn/ *n* [U] act of compensating for loss or damage; (*pl*) compensation for war damages, demanded from a defeated enemy.

rep·ar·tee /ˈrepɑˈti/ *n* [C] witty, clever retort; [U] the making of such retorts: *He's good at ~.*

re·past /rɪˈpɑst *US:* -ˈpæst/ *n* (formal) meal: *The guests partook of a luxurious ~ in the banqueting hall.*

re·pat·ri·ate /riˈpætrɪeɪt *US:* -ˈpeɪt-/ *vt* [VP6A] send or bring (sb) back to his own country: *~ refugees after a war.* □ *n* ~d person. **re·pat·ri·ation** /ˈriˈpætrɪˈeɪʃn *US:* -ˈpeɪt-/ *n*

re·pay /rɪˈpeɪ/ *vt,vi* (*pt,pp* -paid /-ˈpeɪd/) **1** [VP6A] pay back (money): *If you'll lend me 75p, I'll ~ you next week.* **2** [VP6A,14] ~ ***sth;*** ~ ***sb for sth,*** give in return: *~ sb's kindness; ~ sb for his kindness. I have been repaid (for the help I gave) only with ingratitude.* **3** [VP2A] give equal favour (or justice) in return: *God will ~,* e g will punish injustice. **~·able** /-əbl/ *adj* that can or must be repaid. **~·ment** *n* [U] ~ing; [C] instance of this: *bonds due for ~ment.*

re·peal /rɪˈpil/ *vt* [VP6A] revoke, annul (a law, etc) □ *n* ~ing.

re·peat /rɪˈpit/ *vt,vi* **1** [VP6A,9] say or do again: *~ word/a mistake. I ~ that I cannot undertake the task. Don't ~ yourself,* say or do the same thing more than once (usu without being aware of doing so). *Does history ~ itself,* Do similar events or situations recur? '~**ing watch/rifle,** ⇨ repeater below. **2** [VP6A] say (what sb else has said or what one learnt by heart): *You must not ~ what I've told you; it's very confidential. She ~ed the poem beautifully. His language won't bear ~ing,* e g contained too many curses, swear words, etc. **3** [VP6A] (of food) continue to be tasted after being eaten: *Do you find that onions ~?* **4** [VP2A] (of numbers, e g decimals) recur: *The last two figures ~.* **5** [VP6A] (comm) supply a further consignment of: *We regret that we cannot ~ this article.* □ *n* **1** [C] ~ing (e g of an item in a programme) of a performance: *a ~ performance; a ~ order,* (comm) an order for a further consignment of goods similar to an earlier one. *There will be a ~* (= another broadcast) *of this talk on Friday.* **2** (music) mark indicating a passage intended to be repeated. **~·ed·ly** *adv* again and again. **~er** *n* **1** revolver or rifle which can be fired a number of times without being reloaded (now usu a (*semi-*)*automatic* or *self-loading rifle*). **2** (old-fashioned kind of) clock that will strike the last quarter again if required.

re·pel /rɪˈpel/ *vt* (-ll-) [VP6A] **1** drive back or away; refuse to accept: *~ the enemy/temptation; ~ a young man's advances,* discourage him. **2** cause a feeling of dislike in: *His long, rough beard ~led her.* **~·lent** /-ənt/ *adj* tending to ~; unattractive; uninviting: *~lent work/food. His manner is rather ~lent.* □ *n* [U] sth that ~s, esp a preparation that ~s insects: *Smear some of this mosquito ~lent on your legs.*

re·pent /rɪˈpent/ *vi,vt* **1** [VP2A,3A,6A,D] ~ ***(of),*** think with regret or sorrow of; be full of regret; wish one had not done (sth): *He ~ed of what he had done. Don't you ~ (of) having wasted your money so foolishly? He has bitterly ~ed his folly. Have you nothing to ~ of?* **2** (old use; reflex with *me, him*): *I ~ed me full sore. He hath ~ed him of his sins.* **~·ance** /-əns/ *n* [U] regret for wrongdoing: *show ~ance (for sth).* **~·ant** /-ənt/ *adj* feeling or showing ~ance: *a ~ant sinner; ~ant of his folly; the righteous and the ~ant.* **~·ant·ly** *adv*

re·per·cussion /ˈripəˈkʌʃn/ *n* **1** [U] springing back; driving or throwing back; [C] sth thrown or driven back; echoing sound: *the ~ of the waves from the rocks.* **2** [C] (usu *pl*) far-reaching and indirect effect (of an event, etc): *The assassination of the President was followed by ~s throughout the whole country.*

rep·er·toire /ˈrepətwɑ(r)/ *n* [C] all the plays, songs, pieces, etc which a company, actor, musician, etc, is prepared to perform, etc: *She has a large ~ of songs.*

rep·er·tory /ˈrepətərɪ *US:* -tɔrɪ/ *n* (*pl* -ries) [C] **1** = repertoire. '~ **company/theatre,** (common abbr *rep*) one in which the actors/plays are changed regularly (instead of having long runs as in most London theatres). **2** store or collection, esp of facts, information, etc: *My father is a ~ of useful information.*

rep·eti·tion /ˈrepəˈtɪʃn/ *n* **1** [U] repeating or being repeated; [C] instance of this: *after numerous ~s.* **2** [C] further recurrence: *Let there be no ~ of this,* Don't do it again. **3** [C] piece (of poetry, etc) set to be learnt by heart and repeated. **rep·eti·tious** /ˈrepəˈtɪʃəs/, **re·peti·tive** /rɪˈpetətɪv/ *adjj* characterized by ~: *the repetitive work typical of modern industry.*

re·pine /rɪˈpɑɪn/ *vi* [VP2A,3A] ~ ***(at),*** be discontented with: *~ at misfortune.* ~ ***against,*** fret against: *~ against Providence.*

re·place /rɪˈpleɪs/ *vt* [VP6A,15A] **1** put back in its place: *~ a dictionary on the shelf; ~ the receiver,* i e after telephoning. **2** [VP6A] take the place of: *Have buses ~d trams in your town? Can anything ~ a mother's love and care?* **3** [VP14] ~ ***sth by/with,*** supply as a substitute for: *~ coal by/with oil.* **~·able** /-əbl/ *adj* that can be ~d. **~·ment** *n* [U] replacing or being ~d: *the ~ment of worn-out parts;* [C] sb or sth that ~s: *get a ~ment* (i e sb to do one's work) *while one is away on holiday.*

re·play /ˈriˈpleɪ/ *vt* [VP6A] play (e g a football match that was drawn) again. □ *n* /ˈripleɪ/ [C] ~ed match; ~ing of a disc, etc.

re·plen·ish /rɪˈplenɪʃ/ *vt* [VP6A,14] fill up (sth) again; get a new supply of or for: *I must ~ my wardrobe.* **~·ment** *n*

re·plete /rɪˈplit/ *adj* ~ ***(with),*** (formal) filled with; holding as much as possible: *~ with food; feeling ~; a home ~ with every modern convenience.* **re·ple·tion** /rɪˈpliʃn/ *n* [U] (formal) state of being ~: *Is it wrong to eat to repletion?*

rep·lica /ˈreplɪkə/ *n* [C] exact copy (esp one made by an artist of one of his own pictures): *make a ~ of a painting.*

re·ply /rɪˈplɑɪ/ *vi,vt* (*pt,pp* -plied) [VP2A,6A,9,14] ~ ***(to),*** give as an answer to, in words or action: *He failed to ~ (to my question). 'Certainly, sir', he replied. He replied that I could please myself. The enemy replied to our fire,* fired in return. *Mr Gee rose to ~ for* (= on behalf of) *the guests.* □ *n* act of ~ing; what is replied: *He made no ~. What did he say in ~?* '~-'**paid,** (of a telegram, letter, etc) with the cost of the ~ prepaid by the sender.

re·point /riˈpɔɪnt/ *vt* [VP6A] point (brickwork, etc) again. ⇨ point²(5).

re·port¹ /rɪˈpɔt/ *n* **1** [C] account of, statement about, sth heard, seen, done, etc: *~s on the state of the roads,* e g from an automobile association; *the annual ~ of a business company; the chairman's ~,* ⇨ *chairman* at chair; '*law ~s,* i e of trials, etc, in the law courts; *a school ~,* e g by teachers about a pupil, with his examination marks, etc; *newspaper ~s.* **2** [U] common talk; rumour; [C] piece of gossip: *R~ has it that...,* People are saying that.... *We have only ~(s)* (i e no reliable news) *to go on. Don't listen to idle ~s.* **3** [U] (formal) repute; way a person or thing is spoken about: *of good/evil ~.* **4** [C] sound of an explosion: *the ~ of a gun. It went off with a loud ~.*

re·port² /rɪˈpɔt/ *vt,vi* **1** [VP6A,D,9,25] give an account of (sth seen, heard, done, etc); give as news: *The discovery of a new planet has been ~ed. It is ~ed that another earth satellite has been put into orbit. They ~ed the enemy to be ten miles away. He ~ed having met only a cyclist.* ~ ***progress,*** state what has been done so far: *move to ~ progress,* (in the House of Commons) propose that debate be discontinued. **2** [VP6A] take down (e g in shorthand) the words of speeches, etc for newspapers, etc: *~ a speech/a Parliamentary debate; ~ for 'The Times',* be a correspondent on its staff. **~ed speech,** = indirect speech. ⇨ indirect. **3** [VP24] ~ ***(up)on,*** give news or information concerning: *~ upon a matter.* **4** [VP3A,14,15A] ~ ***(oneself) (to sb/sth) (for sth),*** go (somewhere), and announce that one has come, that one is ready for work, duty, etc: *~ for duty at the office; ~ to the Manager. The officer was told to ~ (himself) to headquarters.* **5** [VP6A,14] ***~ (to sb) (for sth),*** make a complaint against sb (to authorities): *~ an official for insolence. I shall have to ~ your unpunctuality.* **~·age** /-ɪdʒ/ *n* [U] (typical style of) ~ing events for newspapers. **~er** *n* person who ~s for a newspaper, for radio or TV.

re·pose[1] /rɪˋpəʊz/ *vt* [VP14] ***~ sth in sth/sb,*** place (trust, confidence, etc) in: *Don't ~ too much confidence in that man/in his honesty/his promises, etc.*

re·pose[2] /rɪˋpəʊz/ *vt,vi* (formal) **1** [VP6A,15A, 2A,C] rest; give rest or support to: *a girl reposing in a hammock; ~ one's head on a cushion; ~ oneself. Below this stone ~ the mortal remains of....* **2** [VP3A] ***~ on,*** be based or supported on. □ *n* [U] (formal) **1** rest; sleep: *earn a night's ~; disturb sb's ~. Her face is beautiful in ~.* **2** peaceful, restful or quiet behaviour or appearance: *His attitude lacked ~,* ease of manner. **~·ful** /-fl/ *adj* calm; quiet.

re·posi·tory /rɪˋpɒzɪtrɪ *US:* -tɔrɪ/ *n* [C] (*pl* -ries) place where things are or may be stored: *The drawers in my desk are repositories for all sorts of useless papers. The old professor was a ~ of out-of-the-way knowledge.*

re·pot /riˋpɒt/ *vt* transfer (~ plant) from one pot to another (usu larger) pot.

rep·re·hend /ˈreprɪˋhend/ *vt* [VP6A] rebuke, reprove: *~ sb's conduct.* **rep·re·hen·sible** /ˈreprɪˋhensəbl/ *adj* deserving to be ~ed.

rep·re·sent[1] /ˈreprɪˋzent/ *vt* **1** [VP6A] be, give, make, a picture, sign, symbol or example of: *Phonetic symbols ~ sounds. This painting ~s a hunting scene. The new ambassador ~s the best traditions of his country.* **2** [VP16A,25] declare to be; describe (*as*): *He ~ed himself as an expert. I am not what you have ~ed me to be.* **3** [VP6A,9, 14] ***~ sth (to sb),*** explain; make clear: *Let me try to ~ my ideas to you in another way (in different terms).* **4** [VP6A,14] ***~ sth (to sb),*** convey, express: *They ~ed their grievances to the Governor. I will ~ to him the risks he is running. He ~ed to the magistrates that the offender was only a child.* **5** [VP6A] act or speak for; be MP for; be agent for: *members* (ie MP's) *~ing Welsh constituencies. Many countries were ~ed by their ambassadors at the birthday celebrations* (ie of Shakespeare's birthday anniversary) *at Stratford-on-Avon. Our firm is ~ed in India and Pakistan by Mr Hall.* **6** [VP6A] act (a play, etc), play the part of, on the stage. **rep·re·sen·ta·tion** /ˈreprɪzenˋteɪʃn/ *n* **1** [U] ~ing or being ~ed; [C] that which is ~ed: *no taxation without ~ation,* ie citizens should not be taxed without being ~ed (in Parliament, etc); *an unusual ~ation of 'Hamlet'.* **proportional ~ation,** an electoral system designed so that minority parties, etc are ~ed (in a legislative assembly) in proportion to their strength. **2** [C] (esp) polite protest or remonstrance: *make ~ations to the Inspector of Taxes about an excessive assessment.*

re·pre·sent[1] /ˈripriˋzent/ *vt* submit again: *Your cheque has been returned; please ~ it when you have funds in your account.*

rep·re·sen·ta·tive /ˈreprɪˋzentətɪv/ *adj* **1** serving to portray or show; serving as an example of a class or group; containing examples of a number of classes or groups: *manuscripts ~ of monastic life; a ~ collection of domestic utensils of the Middle Ages.* **2** consisting of elected deputies; based on representation by such elected deputies: *~ government/institutions.* □ *n* [C] **1** example; typical specimen (*of* a group or class). **2** person elected or appointed to represent or act for others: *send a ~ to a conference; sole ~s of the XYZ Petrol Company in Cardiff; ~s of the press,* newspaper reporters; *our ~ (= MP) in the House of Commons.* **the House of R~s,** the lower house of the US Congress or of a state legislature.

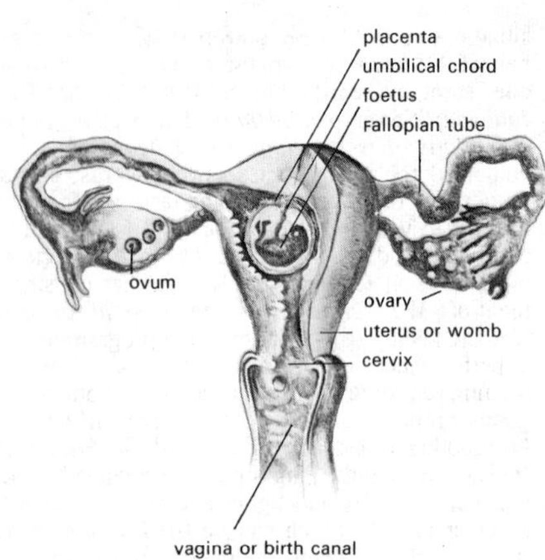

the female reproductive organs

re·press /rɪˋpres/ *vt* [VP6A] keep or put down or under; prevent from finding an outlet: *~ a revolt; ~ sedition; ~ a sneeze; ~ an impulse; ~ed emotions.* **~ed** *adj* suffering from repression. ⇨ the def below marked 'psych': *a terribly ~ed man.* **re·pression** /rɪˋpreʃn/ *n* [U] ~ing or being ~ed; [U] (psych) forcing out of the mind, into the unconscious, of impulses and desires, esp those in conflict with accepted standards of conduct, often resulting in abnormal behaviour; [C] impulse or instinct ~ed in this way. **re·pres·sive** /rɪˋpresɪv/ *adj* serving or tending to ~: *~ive legislation. The ~ive measures taken by the Governor were condemned in Parliament.*

re·prieve /rɪˋpriv/ *vt* [VP6A] postpone or delay punishment (esp the execution of sb condemned to death); (fig) give relief for a short time (from danger, trouble, etc). □ *n* [C] (order giving authority for) postponement or remission of punishment (esp by death): (fig) delay or respite: *grant (sb) a ~.*

re·pri·mand /ˈreprɪˋmɑnd *US:* -ˋmænd/ *vt* [VP6A] rebuke (sb) severely and officially (for a fault, etc). □ *n* /ˋreprɪmɑnd *US:* -mænd/ [C] official rebuke.

re·print /riˋprɪnt/ *vt* [VP6A] print again; print a new impression of: *The book is ~ing,* being ~ed. □ *n* /ˋriprɪnt/ [C] new impression of sth printed (usu without alterations). ⇨ **edition.**

re·prisal /rɪˋprɑɪzl/ *n* **1** [U] paying back injury with injury: *do sth by way of ~.* **2** (*pl*) acts of retaliation, esp of one country on another during a war.

re·proach /rɪˋprəʊtʃ/ *vt* [VP6A,14] ***~ sb (for/with sth),*** find fault with (sb, usu with a feeling of sorrow, or suggesting the need for sorrow): *~ one's*

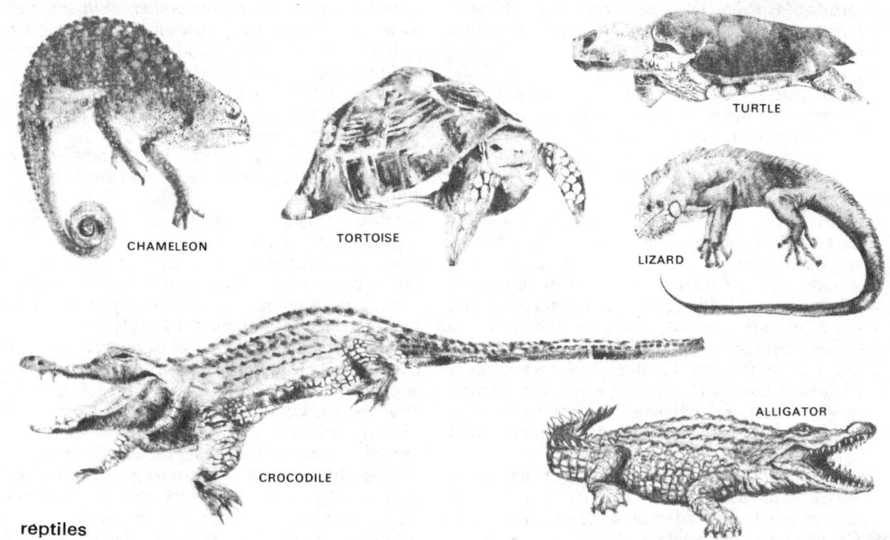

reptiles

wife with extravagance/for being late with the dinner. We have nothing to ~ ourselves with, have done nothing we need regret. □ *n* **1** [U] ~ing: *a term/look of ~.* **2** [C] instance of ~ing; word, phrase, etc that ~es: *She heaped ~es upon her sister.* **3** [U] state of disgrace or discredit: *bring ~ upon oneself.* ***above/beyond ~,*** perfect, blameless. **4** [C] sth that brings disgrace or discredit (*to*): *slums that are a ~ to the city council.* **~·ful** /-fl/ *adj* full of ~; expressing ~: *a ~ful look.* **~·fully** /-flɪ/ *adv*

rep·ro·bate /ˋreprəbeɪt/ *vt* [VP6A] express or feel strong disapproval of. □ *n* depraved person; person with no respect for moral behaviour. **rep·ro·ba·tion** /ˈreprəˋbeɪʃn/ *n* [U].

re·pro·duce /ˈriprəˋdjus *US:* -ˋdus/ *vt, vi* **1** [VP6A] cause to be seen, heard, etc again: *~ music from magnetic tape. This record/record-player ~s every sound perfectly. The artist has ~d your features very well in this portrait.* **2** [VP6A,2A] bring forth as offspring; bring about a natural increase: *~ one's kind; plants that ~ by spores,* e g ferns. **3** [VP6A] grow anew (a part that is lost, etc): *Can lizards ~ their tails? Human beings cannot ~ lost limbs.* **re·pro·ducer** *n* one who, that which, ~s. **re·pro·duc·ible** /-əbl/ *adj* that can be ~d. **re·pro·duc·tion** /ˈriprəˋdʌkʃn/ *n* [U] process of reproducing; [C] sth ~d; copy of sth, esp a work of art. **re·pro·duc·tive** /ˈriprəˋdʌktɪv/ *adj* reproducing; for, relating to, reproduction: *reproductive organs.*

re·proof[1] /rɪˋpruf/ *n* **1** [U] blame; finding fault: *a glance of ~; conduct deserving of ~.* **2** [C] expression of blame or disapproval: *administer sharp ~s to a naughty boy.*

re·proof[2] /ˈriˋpruf/ *vt* [VP6A] make (a coat, etc) waterproof again.

re·prove /rɪˋpruv/ *vt* [VP6A,14] ***~ sb (for sth),*** find fault with; say sharp words to: *The priest ~d the people for not attending church services.* **re·prov·ing·ly** *adv*

rep·tile /ˋreptɑɪl *US:* -tl/ *n* cold-blooded egg-laying animal that creeps or crawls, e g *a lizard, tortoise, crocodile, snake.* ⇨ the illus here and at snake. **rep·til·ian** /repˋtɪlɪən/ *adj* of, or like a ~. □ *n* ~.

re·pub·lic /rɪˋpʌblɪk/ *n* **1** (country with a) system of government in which the elected representatives of the people are supreme, with a non-hereditary head (the President), and (usu) a non-hereditary privileged class or classes: (in France) *the First R~,* 1789—1804; *the Second R~,* 1848—1852; *the Third R~,* 1871—1940; *the Fourth R~,* 1947—58; *the Fifth R~,* from 1958; *a secular ~,* e g Turkey; *an Islamic ~,* e g Pakistan; *a constitutional ~,* e g the US. **2** any society in which the members have equal rights and privileges: *the ~ of letters,* literary men as a class.

re·pub·li·can /rɪˋpʌblɪkən/ *adj* of, relating to, supporting the principles of, a republic. □ *n* **1** person who favours ~ government. **2 R~,** member of one of the two main political parties in the US (the other is *Democrat*). **~·ism** /-ɪzm/ *n* [U] (adherence to) ~ principles.

re·pudi·ate /rɪˋpjudɪeɪt/ *vt* [VP6A] **1** disown; say that one will have nothing more to do with: *~ an old friend/a wicked son.* **2** refuse to accept or acknowledge: *~ the authorship of an article,* declare that one did not write it. **3** refuse to pay (an obligation or debt). **re·pudi·ation** /rɪˈpjudɪˋeɪʃn/ *n*

re·pug·nant /rɪˋpʌgnənt/ *adj* ***~ (to),*** distasteful; causing a feeling of dislike or opposition: *I find his views/proposals ~. All food was ~ to me during my illness.* **re·pug·nance** /-nəns/ *n* [U] strong dislike or distaste: *a great repugnance to accept charity; the repugnance she has to writing letters.*

re·pulse /rɪˋpʌls/ *vt* [VP6A] **1** repel; drive back (the enemy); resist (an attack) successfully. **2** (not replaceable by *repel*) refuse to accept (sb's help, friendly offers, etc); discourage (a person) by unfriendly treatment. □ *n* repulsing or being ~d. **re·pul·sion** /rɪˋpʌlʃn/ *n* [U] **1** feeling of dislike or distaste: *feel repulsion for sb.* **2** (phys) (opp of *attraction*) tendency of bodies to repel each other.

re·pul·sive /rɪˋpʌlsɪv/ *adj* **1** causing a feeling of disgust: *a ~ sight; a ~-looking beggar.* **2** (phys) repelling; exercising repulsion(2): *~ forces.* **~·ly** *adv* in a ~ manner: *~ly ugly.*

repu·table /ˈrepjʊtəbl/ *adj* respected: of good repute: ~ *occupations; a ~ wine merchant.* **repu·tably** /-əblɪ/ *adv*

repu·ta·tion /ˈrepjʊˈteɪʃn/ *n* [U] (used with *indef art* as in examples) the general opinion about the character, qualities, etc of sb or sth: *a man of high ~; have a good ~ as a doctor; have a ~ for courage; make a ~ for oneself; have the ~ of being a miser.* ***live up to one's ~,*** live in the way that people expect (because of one's ~).

re·pute /rɪˈpjut/ *vt* [VP25] **1** (usu *passive*) ***be ~d as/to be,*** be generally considered or reported (to be), be thought of as: *He is ~ed (to be) very wealthy. He is ~d (as/to be) the best surgeon in Paris. He is well/ill/highly ~d,* thought or spoken of. **2** (old use) consider: *Men ~ him (to be) a scholar.* **3** (*pp*) (as *adj*) generally considered to be (but with some element of doubt): *the ~d father of the child; his ~d learning.* □ *n* [U] **1** reputation (good or bad): *know a man by ~; be held in high ~; be in bad ~ with sb.* **2** good reputation: *wines of ~; a doctor of ~.* **re·put·ed·ly** *adv*

re·quest /rɪˈkwest/ *n* **1** [U] asking or being asked: *We came at your ~/at the ~ of Mr X. Buses stop here by ~,* if signalled to do so. *This is a ~ stop. Catalogues of our books will be sent on ~.* **2** [C] expression of desire for sth: *repeated ~s for help; make a ~ for quiet; your ~ that I should lecture on Pakistan.* **3** [C] thing asked for: *You shall have your ~. All my ~s were granted.* **4** [U] state of being in demand, sought after. ***in ~,*** often asked for. □ *vt* [VP6A,9,17] ***~ sth (from/of sb); ~ sb to do sth,*** make a ~: *Visitors are ~ed not to touch the exhibits,* as a notice in a museum, etc. *All I ~ of you is that you should be early. I ~ed him to use/~ed that he should use his influence on my behalf.*

requiem /ˈrekwɪəm/ *n* [C] (musical setting for a) special mass for the repose of the souls of the dead.

re·quire /rɪˈkwaɪə(r)/ *vt* **1** [VP6A,D,9] need; depend on for success, fulfilment, etc: *We ~ extra help. Does this machine ~ much attention? The situation there ~s that I should be present.* **2** [VP6A,17,14] (formal) order; demand; insist upon as a right or by authority: *Students are ~d to take three papers in English literature. What do you ~ of me? They ~d that I should arrive at 8 a m. I have done all that is ~d by law. These books are ~d reading,* must be read, e g for an examination. **~·ment** *n* sth ~d or needed: *fulfil the ~ments of the law; meet sb's ~ments,* do what he wants done.

requi·site /ˈrekwɪzɪt/ *n, adj* ***~ (for),*** (thing) needed or required by circumstances or for success: *We supply every ~ for travel/all travelling ~s. They lack the ~ capital for expanding their business.*

requi·si·tion /ˈrekwɪˈzɪʃn/ *n* [U] act of requiring or demanding; [C] formal and usu written demand (*for* sth or *that* sth should be done): *a ~ for supplies,* e g by army authorities during a war; *make a ~ on the citizens for stores. The hotel bus was in constant ~* (= was needed all the time) *for bringing visitors from, and taking them back to, the railway station.* □ *vt* [VP6A,14] make a ~ for: *~ food for the troops; ~ sb's services; ~ a town for lorries/horses,* e g during a war.

re·quite /rɪˈkwaɪt/ *vt* [VP6A,14] ***~ sth/sb (with sth),*** (formal) **1** repay; give in return: *~ kindness with ingratitude; ~ an obligation. Will she ever ~ my love?* **2** take vengeance on. **re·qui·tal** /-tl/ *n* [U] repayment: *receive food and lodging in requital for/of one's services; make full requital.*

rere·dos /ˈrɪədos *US:* ˈrerədos/ *n* (*pl* -doses /-dosɪz/) [C] ornamental screen covering the wall at the back of a church altar.

re·run /ˈrirʌn/ *n* (cinema and TV) reshowing of a film or recorded programme. □ *vt* (-nn-) show a film, etc again.

re·scind /rɪˈsɪnd/ *vt* [VP6A] (legal) repeal, annul, cancel (a law, contract, etc).

re·script /ˈriskrɪpt/ *n* [C] **1** official announcement, esp an edict or decree issued by a ruler or government. **2** decision made by a Pope (esp in reply to a question on matters of law or morality).

res·cue /ˈreskju/ *vt* [VP6A,14] ***~ sb from sth/sb,*** deliver, make safe (from danger, etc); set free: *~ a child from drowning; ~ a man from bandits/from captivity; ~ a drunkard,* persuade him to give up drinking; *~ sb's name from oblivion,* prevent his name from being quite forgotten. □ *n* [U] rescuing or being ~d. ***come/go to the ~/to sb's ~,*** help them; [C] instance of this: *three ~s from drowning in one afternoon.* **res·cuer** *n*

re·search /rɪˈsɜtʃ *US:* ˈrisɜtʃ/ *n* [U] (and with *indef art,* and in *pl,* but not usu with *many* or numerals) investigation undertaken in order to discover new facts, get additional information, etc: *be engaged in ~; busy with ~ work; carry out a ~/~es into the causes of cancer. His ~es have been successful. R~ students usually supplement their income by teaching. R~ workers are examining the problem.* □ *vi* [VP2A,3A] ***~ (into),*** (a problem, etc). **~er** *n*

re·seat /ˈriˈsit/ *vt* [VP2A] **1** supply with a new seat: *~ an old pair of trousers/a cane chair.* **2** sit on a seat again: *She stood up and then ~ed herself more comfortably.*

re·sem·blance /rɪˈzembləns/ *n* **1** [U] likeness; similarity: *There's very little ~ between them.* **2** [C] point or degree of likeness or similarity: *The boys show great ~s. Are they twins?*

re·semble /rɪˈzembl/ *vt* [VP6A] be like; be similar to: *She ~s her mother. They ~ each other in shape but not in colour.*

re·sent /rɪˈzent/ *vt* [VP6A,D] feel bitter, indignant or angry at: *~ criticism. Does he ~ my being here?* **~·ful** /-fl/ *adj* feeling or showing ~ment; inclined to ~. **~·fully** /-flɪ/ *adv* **~·ment** *n* [U]. feeling that one has when insulted, ignored, injured, etc: *bear/feel no ~ment against anyone; walk away in ~ment.*

res·er·va·tion /ˈrezəˈveɪʃn/ *n* **1** [U] keeping or holding back; failure or refusal to express sth that is in one's mind; [C] that which is kept or held back: *accept sth without ~,* wholeheartedly, completely; *accept a plan with ~s,* with limiting conditions; *the central ~ of a motorway,* land dividing the two carriageways. **2** [C] (US) area of land reserved for a special purpose: *the Indian ~s,* land for the exclusive use of the Indians. ⇨ reserve[1](5). **3** [C] (esp US) arrangement to keep sth for sb, e g a seat in a train, a passage on a steamer or airliner, a room in a hotel: *My travel agents have made all the ~s for my journey.* ⇨ book[2](2), for GB usages. **4** *R~ of the Sacrament,* practice of keeping back part of the bread used in the Eucharist for later use, e g at the home of a sick person.

re·serve[1] /rɪˋzɜv/ *n* **1** [C] sth that is being or has been stored for later use: *a ~ of food; the bank's ~s,* i e of money; *the company's ~s,* its undivided profits; *the ˋgold ~,* i e to cover the issue of notes; (attrib) *a ˋ~ fund; his ~ strength.* **2** (mil, *sing* or *pl*) military forces kept back for use when needed. **3 the R~,** forces outside the regular Navy, Army and Air Force, liable to be called out if needed. **4** [U] ***in ~,*** kept back unused, but available if needed: *have/hold a little money in ~.* **5** [C] place or area reserved for some special use or purpose: *a ˋgame ~,* e g in Africa, for the preservation of wild animals; *a ˋforest ~.* **6** [C,U] (instance of) limitation or restriction; condition that limits or restricts: *We accept your statement without ~,* believe it completely. *He has put a ~ price on his house,* has fixed a price less than which will not be accepted. *He has placed a ~ on the painting,* i e a ~ price. **7** [U] self-control in speech and behaviour; keeping silent or saying little; not showing one's feelings: *~ of manner; break through sb's ~,* get him to talk and be sociable. **re·serv·ist** /rɪˋzɜvɪst/ *n* soldier or sailor belonging to the Army or Navy R~. ⇨ 3 above.

re·serve[2] /rɪˋzɜv/ *vt* [VP6A,14] **1** store, keep back, for a later occasion: *R~ your strength for the climb. The judge ~d his judgement,* deferred announcing it until a future time. **2** keep for the special use of, or for a special purpose: *The first three rows of the hall are ~d for special guests.* **3** secure possession of, or the right to use, e g by advance payment: *~ rooms at a hotel. All seats ~d,* i e the seats (in a theatre, concert hall, etc) can be obtained only by booking them in advance. *All rights ~d,* (legal) secured or kept (for the owners of property, etc). **4** set apart, destine: *A great future is ~d for you.* **re·served** *adj* (of a person, his character) slow to reveal feelings or opinions; uncommunicative: *He is too ~d to be popular.* **re·serv·ed·ly** /rɪˋzɜvɪdlɪ/ *adv*

res·er·voir /ˋrezəvwɑ(r)/ *n* [C] **1** place (often an artificial lake) where water is stored, e g for supplying a town; anything for holding a liquid: *the ~ of a fountain-pen/an oil lamp.* **2** (fig) supply (of facts, knowledge, etc).

re·set /ˈriˋset/ *vt* (*pt,pp* **reset**; **-tt-**) [VP6A] **1** sharpen again: *~ a saw.* **2** place in position again: *~ a diamond in a ring; ~ a broken bone.* **3** (of a book, etc) set the type again. ⇨ **set**[2]**(9)**.

re·settle /riˋsetl/ *vt,vi* [VP6A,2A] (esp of refugees) (help to) settle again in a new country: *~ European refugees in Canada.* **~·ment** *n*

re·shuffle /riˋʃʌfl/ *vt* [VP6A] shuffle again: *~ the cards.* □ *n* shuffling again: *a Cabinet ~,* a redistribution of Cabinet posts among the same persons.

re·side /rɪˋzɑɪd/ *vi* **1** [VP2C,3A] ***~ (in/at),*** live (the more usu word), have one's home: *~ abroad; ~ at 10 Railway Terrace.* **2** [VP3A] ***~ in,*** (of power, rights, etc) be the property of, be present in: *The supreme authority ~s in the President.*

resi·dence /ˋrezɪdns/ *n* **1** [U] residing: *take up one's ~ in a new house,* go and live in it. ***in ~,*** **(a)** (of an official, etc) living in the house officially provided for him. **(b)** (of members of a university) residing in a college or other part of a university: *The undergraduates are not yet in ~.* **2** place where one resides; house (esp a large or dignified one): (as used by house-agents) *town and country ~s; this desirable family ~ for sale.*

resi·dency /ˋrezɪdənsɪ/ *n* [C] (*pl* **-cies**) official residence of a British political representative or Resident. ⇨ **resident(2)**.

resi·dent /ˋrezɪdənt/ *adj* residing: *the ~ population of the town* (contrasted with visitors, tourists, etc); *a ~ tutor,* one who lives in the household as a member of the family; *a ~ physician,* one who lives in the hospital, etc where he works. □ *n* **1** person who resides in a place (contrasted with a visitor). **2 R~,** official sent to another country or State to act as adviser to the administration, etc.

resi·den·tial /ˈrezɪˋdenʃl/ *adj* **1** of residence: *the ~ qualifications for voters,* i e requiring that they should reside in the constituency. **2** of, with, private houses: *a ~ suburb; ~ parts of the town* (contrasted with business or industrial parts).

re·sid·ual /rɪˋzɪdjʊəl *US:* -dʒʊ-/ *adj* remaining; of, forming, a residue.

re·sidu·ary /rɪˋzɪdjʊərɪ *US:* -dʒʊerɪ/ *adj* of a residue; (legal) relating to the residue of an estate: *the ~ legatee,* the person to whom the residue of an estate is left.

resi·due /ˋrezɪdju *US:* -du/ *n* [C] that which remains after a part is taken or used; (legal) that part of an estate which is left after all particular bequests, debts, etc have been settled.

re·sign /rɪˋzɑɪn/ *vt,vi* **1** [VP6A,2A,3A] ***~ (from),*** give up (a post, claim, etc): *~ one's job; ~ one's position as secretary of the club; ~ from the Cabinet. The Minister of Education has ~ed.* **2** [VP14] ***~ sb/oneself to sb/sth,*** hand over: *I ~ my children to your care/myself to your guidance.* **3** [VP14] ***~ oneself to sth/be ~ed to sth,*** be ready to accept or endure uncomplainingly: *be ~ed to one's fate. We must ~ ourselves to doing without domestic help.* **~ed** *adj* having or showing patient acceptance of sth: *with a ~ed look.* **~·ed·ly** /-ɪdlɪ/ *adv* in a ~ed manner.

res·ig·na·tion /ˈrezɪgˋneɪʃn/ *n* **1** [U] resigning(**1**); [C] instance of this; letter (to one's employers, superior, etc) stating this: *offer/send in/hand in one's ~.* **2** [U] state of being resigned to conditions, etc; uncomplaining acceptance or endurance: *accept failure with ~.*

re·sil·ience /rɪˋzɪlɪəns/, **re·sil·iency** /-nsɪ/ *nn* [U] quality or property of quickly recovering the original shape or condition after being pulled, pressed, crushed, etc: *the ~ of rubber;* (fig) power of recuperating quickly; buoyancy: *the ~ of the human body.* **re·sil·ient** /-nt/ *adj* having or showing ~; (of persons) buoyant in disposition.

resin /ˋrezɪn *US:* ˋrezn/ *n* [C,U] sticky substance that flows out from most plants when cut or injured, esp from fir and pine trees, hardening in air, used in making varnish, lacquer, etc; kind of similar substance (plastics) made chemically, widely used in industry. ⇨ **rosin**. **~·ated** /ˋrezɪneɪtɪd *US:* -zn̩-/ *adj* flavoured, permeated with ~. **~·ous** /ˋrezɪnəs *US:* ˋrezn̩əs/ *adj* of or like ~.

re·sist /rɪˋzɪst/ *vt,vi* [VP6A,D,2A] **1** oppose; use force against in order to prevent the advance of: *~ the enemy/an attack/authority/the police. He could ~ no longer.* **2** be undamaged or unaffected by: *a kind of glass dish that ~s heat,* that does not break or crack in a hot oven. **3** try not to yield to; keep oneself back from: *~ temptation. She can't ~ chocolates. She couldn't ~ making jokes about his baldness.* **~er** *n* person who ~s: *passive ~ers.* **~·less** *adj* that cannot be ~ed; inevitable:

a ~less impulse.

re·sis·tance /rɪˋzɪstəns/ *n* **1** [U] (power of) resisting: *break down the enemy's ~; make/offer no/not much ~ to the enemy's advance; drug ~; passive ~,* ⇨ passive. **ˋ~ movement,** (in an enemy-occupied country) effort made by groups of unconquered people to resist the invaders. **2** [U] opposing force: *An aircraft has to overcome the ~ of the air.* ***line of least ~,*** direction in which a force meets least opposition; (fig) easiest way or method. **3** [C,U] antagonism; desire to oppose: *ˋsales ~,* unwillingness of the public to buy goods offered for sale. *A good advertisement should not arouse ~(s) in the public.*

re·sis·tant /rɪˋzɪstənt/ *adj* offering resistance: *insects that have become ~ to DDT; ~ strains of mosquitoes.*

re·sis·tor /rɪˋzɪstə(r)/ *n* device to provide resistance in an electric circuit.

re·sole /ˈriˋsəʊl/ *vt* [VP6A] put a new sole on (a shoe).

res·ol·ute /ˋrezəlut/ *adj* fixed in determination or purpose; firm: *a ~ man; ~ for peace.* **~·ly** *adv* **~·ness** *n*

res·ol·ution /ˈrezəˋluʃn/ *n* **1** [U] quality of being resolute; fixity or boldness of determination: *show great/not much ~; a man who lacks ~.* **2** [C] sth that is resolved(1); formal expression of opinion by a legislative body or a public meeting; proposal for this: *pass/carry/adopt/reject a ~ (for/against/in favour of/that...).* **3** [C] resolve; sth one makes up one's mind to do: *make good ~s; her ~ never to marry; a New Year ~* (sth one resolves to do in a new year, e g to give up smoking). **4** [U] resolving, solution (of a doubt, question, discord, etc). ⇨ **resolve(3)**. **5** process of separating into constituents: *the ~ of white light into the colours of the spectrum.*

re·solve /rɪˋzolv/ *vt,vi* **1** [VP7,9,3A] ***~ that/(up)on sth/to do sth,*** decide; determine: *He ~d that nothing should hold him back/~d to be held back by nothing. He ~d (up)on making an early start. He ~d to succeed.* **2** [VP9] (of a committee, public meeting, legislative body) pass by formal vote the decision (*that*): *The House of Commons ~d that.... R~d, that this meeting is in favour of.../opposed to.../views with alarm..., etc.* **3** [VP6A] put an end to (doubts, difficulties, etc) by supplying an answer. **4** [VP6A,14] ***~ sth into,*** break up, separate (into parts); convert, be converted: *~ a problem into its elements. The House of Commons ~d itself into a committee. A powerful telescope can ~ a nebula into stars.* □ *n* **1** [C] sth that has been determined on; mental resolution(3): *make a ~ to do sth; keep one's ~.* **2** (liter) resolution(1): *deeds of high ~.* **re·solv·able** /-əbl/ *adj* that may be ~d.

res·on·ant /ˋrezənənt/ *adj* **1** (of sound) resounding; continuing to resound: *~ notes; a deep, ~ voice.* **2** (of rooms, etc) tending to prolong sounds by vibration: *~ walls which echo and re-echo sound; a ~ hall.* **3** (of places) resounding: *Alpine valleys ~ with the sound of church bells.* **res·on·ance** /-əns/ *n* [U] quality of being ~. **res·on·ate** /ˋrezəneɪt/ *vt,vi* produce or show resonance **res·ona·tor** /-tə(r)/ *n* appliance or system for increasing sound by resonance.

re·sort /rɪˋzɔt/ *vi* [VP3A] ***~ to,*** **1** make use of for help or to gain one's purpose, etc: *If other means fail, we shall ~ to force. I'm sorry you have ~ed to deception.* **2** frequently visit: *The police watched the cafés to which the wanted man was known to ~.* □ *n* **1** [U] recourse; ~ing(1): *Can we do it without ~ to compulsion/force?* ***in the last ~; as a last ~,*** when all else has failed, as a last means of finding help or relief. **2** sb or sth that is ~ed(1) to: *An old taxi was the only ~ left.* **3** [C] place ~ed(2) to: *ˋseaside/ˋsummer/ˋhealth ~s.*

re·sound /rɪˋzaʊnd/ *vi,vt* **1** [VP2A,3A,14] ***~ with, ~ sth (through sth),*** (of a voice, instrument, sound) echo and re-echo; fill a place with sound; send back (sound); (of a place) ring or echo: *The organ ~ed. The hall ~ed with cries of dissent.* **2** [VP2C] (fig of fame, an event) be much talked of; spread far and wide: *His success ~ed through all Asia. The film was a ~ing success.* **~·ing·ly** *adv*

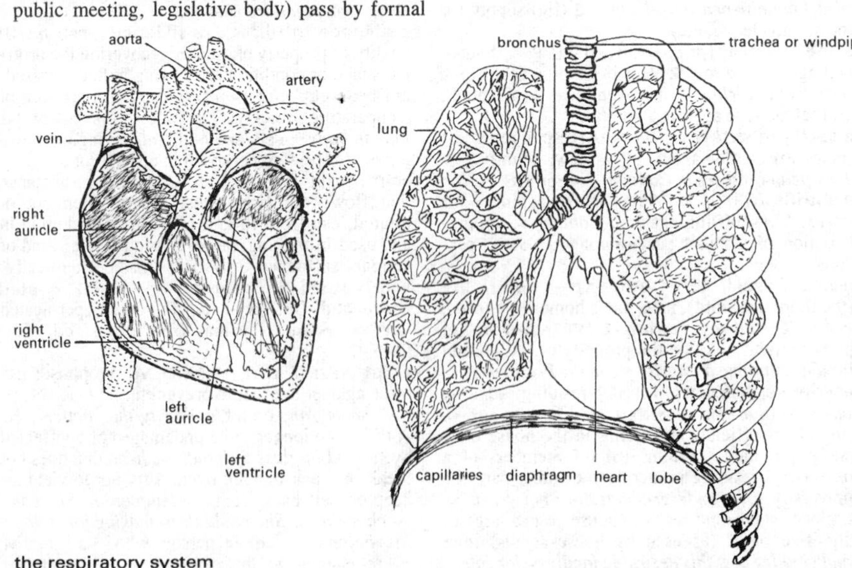

the respiratory system

re·source /rɪˋsɔs *US:* ˋrisɔrs/ *n* **1** (*pl*) wealth, supplies of goods, raw materials, etc which a person, country, etc has or can use: *Our ~s in men and ammunition were inadequate for the defence of the town. We must exploit the natural ~s of our country,* its mineral wealth, potential water power, the productivity of the soil, etc. *I am at the end of my ~s,* have nothing left to use. *We must make the most of our ~s,* use what we have to the best advantage. **2** [C] sth which helps in doing sth, that can be turned to for support, help, consolation: *He has no inner ~s of character/no inner reserves to fall back on. Leave him to his own ~s,* Leave him to amuse himself, find his own way of passing the time. **3** [U] skill in finding ~s(2); quick wit: *a man of ~.* **~·ful** /-fl/ *adj* good or quick at finding ~s(2). **~·fully** /-flɪ/ *adv*

re·spect[1] /rɪˋspekt/ *n* **1** [U] honour; high opinion or regard; esteem for a person or quality: *The prime minister is held in the greatest ~. Children should show ~ for their teachers. He has no ~ for his promises,* does not think it necessary to keep them. **2** [U] consideration; attention: *We must have ~ for/pay ~ to the needs of the general reader,* think about his requirements or preferences. **3** [U] reference; relation. ***with ~ to,*** concerning. ***without ~ to,*** paying no attention to, leaving out of the question. **4** [C] detail; particular aspect. ***in ~ of,*** as regards: *Your essay is admirable in ~ of style but unsatisfactory in other ~s.* ***in some/any/no, etc ~s,*** with regard to some aspect(s), detail(s): *They resemble one another in some/all/no/a few ~s.* **5** (*pl*) regards; polite greetings: *Give him my ~s. My father sends you his ~s.* ***pay one's ~s to sb,*** visit, etc sb as a sign of ~ for him.

re·spect[2] /rɪˋspekt/ *vt* [VP6A] have ~ for; treat with consideration; avoid interfering with or interrupting: *He is ~ed by everyone. We must ~ his wishes. I ~ your opinions. I wish people would ~ my (desire for) privacy. Do you ~ the laws of your country?* ***~ oneself,*** have proper ~ for one's own character and conduct: *If you don't ~ yourself, how can you expect others to ~ you?* **~er** *n* (only in) ***no ~er of persons,*** person or thing paying little or no attention to wealth, social rank, etc: *Death is no ~er of persons.* **~·ing** *prep* relating to; concerned with: *legislation ~ing property.*

re·spect·able /rɪˋspektəbl/ *adj* **1** deserving respect; estimable: *do sth from ~ motives.* **2** (of persons) of good character and fair social position; having the qualities associated with such social position; (of clothes, appearance, behaviour, etc) suitable for such persons: *She is poor but quite ~. He's a man of ~ appearance. They belong to the ~ middle classes. Are these clothes ~ enough for the Smiths' garden party? It is not considered ~ in this country to pick one's teeth in public.* **3** (ironic use) (of behaviour, appearances, etc) conventional; likely to satisfy conventional people: *Need we worry quite so much about being ~?* **4** of some size, merit, importance, etc: *He has quite ~ talents. There was a ~ attendance at church this morning. He earns a ~ income.* **re·spect·ably** /-əblɪ/ *adv* in a ~ manner: *Go and get respectably dressed.* **re·spect·abil·ity** /rɪˌspektəˋbɪlətɪ/ *n* (*pl* -ties) **1** [U] quality of being socially ~(2,3) **2** (*pl*) social conventions: *maintain the respectabilities (of life).*

re·spect·ful /rɪˋspektfl/ *adj* ~ ***(to),*** showing respect: *They stood at a ~ distance from the President.* **~ly** /-flɪ/ *adv* (dated use; at the close of a letter to a much senior person) *I remain, yours ~ly,....*

re·spect·ive /rɪˋspektɪv/ *adj* for, belonging to, each of those in question: *The three men were given work according to their ~ abilities. The party ended and we all went off to our ~ rooms,* each of us went to his or her own room. **~·ly** *adv* separately or in turn, and in the order mentioned: *Training colleges for men and women are to be built at Leeds and Hull ~ly,* i e for men at Leeds and for women at Hull.

res·pir·ation /ˌrespəˋreɪʃn/ *n* [U] breathing; [C] single act of breathing, i e breathing in and breathing out.

res·pir·ator /ˋrespəreɪtə(r)/ *n* [C] apparatus for breathing through, e g by aviators at high altitudes to warm the air inhaled; by firemen, to filter the air of smoke and fumes.

re·spire /rɪˋspaɪə(r)/ *vi* [VP2A] breathe; breathe in and out. **res·pir·at·ory** /rɪˋspɪrətrɪ *US:* ˋrespɪrətɔrɪ/ *adj* of breathing: *the respiratory organs; respiratory diseases,* e g bronchitis, asthma.

res·pite /ˋrespaɪt *US:* ˋrespɪt/ *n* [C] **1** ~ ***(from),*** time of relief or rest (from toil, suffering, anything unpleasant): *work without (a) ~.* **2** postponement or delay permitted in the suffering of a penalty or the discharge of an obligation; reprieve. □ *vt* [VP6A] give a ~ to: *~ a murderer.*

re·splen·dent /rɪˋsplendənt/ *adj* very bright; splendid: *~ in court dress.* **~·ly** *adv* **re·splen·dence** /-əns/, **re·splen·dency** /-ənsɪ/ *nn* [U].

re·spond /rɪˋspond/ *vi* **1** [VP2A,3C] ~ ***(to),*** answer: *~ to a speech of welcome;* (of people at a church service) make the usual answers or responses to the priest. **2** [VP2C] act in answer to, or because of, the action of another: *When Tom insulted Mr Green, he ~ed with a kick.* **3** [VP3A] ~ ***(to),*** react (to); be affected (by): *~ to kindness. The illness quickly ~ed to treatment. The plane ~s well to the controls.*

re·spon·dent /rɪˋspondənt/ *n* (legal) defendant (esp in a divorce case).

re·sponse /rɪˋspons/ *n* **1** [C] answer: *My letter of inquiry brought no ~. She made no ~. In ~ to your inquiry....* **2** [C] (in a church service) part of the liturgy said or sung by the congregation alternately with the priest. **3** [C,U] reaction: *My appeal to her pity met with no ~.*

re·spon·si·bil·ity /rɪˌsponsəˋbɪlətɪ/ *n* (*pl* -ties) **1** [U] being responsible; being accountable: *You did it on your own ~,* without being told or ordered to do it. *You have a post of great ~. I will lend you my camera if you will assume full ~ for it,* pay me the cost of any damage or loss. **2** [C] sth for which a person is responsible; duty: *the heavy responsibilities of the prime minister.*

re·spon·sible /rɪˋsponsəbl/ *adj* **1** ~ ***(to sb) (for sb/sth),*** (of a person) legally or morally liable for carrying out a duty, for the care of sth or sb, in a position where one may be blamed for loss, failure, etc: *The pilot of an airliner is ~ for the safety of the passengers. You are ~ to the Manager for the petty cash.* ~ **government,** one which is answerable to the electors for its actions. **2** ~ ***(for sth),*** involving the obligation to make decisions for others and bear the blame for their mistakes: *The President has a ~ position. I've* *made you ~ and you must decide what to do. Isn't he too young for such a ~ job?* **3** trustworthy; to be relied upon: *Give the task to a ~ man.* **4 *be ~ for sth,*** be the cause or source of: *Bad workmanship was ~ for the collapse of the block of flats. Who's ~ for this mess in the kitchen?* **re·spon·sibly** /-əblɪ/ *adv*

re·spon·sions /rɪˋsponʃnz/ *n pl* first of three examinations for an Oxford B A degree.

re·spon·sive /rɪˋsponsɪv/ *adj* **1** answering: *a ~ gesture; ~ sympathy.* **2 *~ (to),*** answering easily or quickly: *a ~ nature; ~ to affection/treatment.* **~·ly** *adv*

rest[1] /rest/ *n* **1** [U] condition of being free from activity, movement, disturbance; quiet; sleep: *R~ is necessary after hard work. She had a good night's ~,* sleep. *We had several ~s/stops for ~ on the way up the mountain. Sunday is a day of ~ for many people. Let's stop and take/have a ~.* ***at ~,*** **(a)** still; not troubled; free from movement or agitation. **(b)** dead. ***be laid to ~,*** be buried. ***come to ~,*** (of a moving body) stop moving. ***set sb's mind/fears at ~,*** calm him; relieve him of doubt, anxiety, etc. **ˋ~-cure** *n* course of treatment for persons suffering from nervous disorders. **ˋ~-day** *n* day spent in ~. **ˋ~-house** *n* house or bungalow for the use of travellers (esp in areas where there are no hotels). **ˋ~ room,** (US) public lavatory; cloak-room. **2** [C] that on which sth is supported: *a ~ for a billiard cue/a telescope; an ˋarm-~; a ˋneck-~.* **3** [C] (music) (sign marking an) interval of silence. **4** [C] lodging-house or institution provided for workers, etc: *a seamen's ~*; (attrib) place where people may recuperate from illness, etc: *a ˋ~ home/centre.* **~·ful** /-fl/ *adj* quiet; peaceful; giving ~ or a feeling of ~: *a ~ful scene; colours that are ~ful to the eyes.* **~-fully** /-flɪ/ *adv* **~·ful·ness** *n* **~·less** *adj* never still or quiet; unable to rest: *the ~less waves; spend a ~less night. The audience was growing ~less,* showing signs of impatience, wishing to leave, etc. **~·less·ly** *adv* **~·less·ness** *n*

rest[2] /rest/ *n* (always) **the ~. 1** what remains; the remainder: *Take what you want and throw the ~ away. Her hat was red, like the ~ of her clothes.* ***and (all) the ~ (of it),*** and everything else that might be mentioned. ***for the ~,*** as regards other matters. **2** (with *pl v*) the others: *John and I are going to play tennis; what are the ~ of you going to do?*

rest[3] /rest/ *vi,vt* **1** [VP2A,B,C] be still or quiet; be free from activity, movement, disturbance, etc: *We ~ed (for) an hour after lunch. He ~s* (= is buried) *in the churchyard. His last ~ing-place* (his place of burial) *is on the hillside there. He will not ~* (= will have no peace of mind) *until he knows the truth. The matter cannot ~ here,* We must investigate it further. *We shall let this field ~ for a year,* let it lie fallow. **2** [VP6A] give rest or relief to: *He stopped to ~ his horse. These dark glasses ~ my eyes. May God ~ his soul,* give repose to his soul. **3** [VP14,3A] ***~ (sth) (up)on/against,*** (cause to) be supported (on or against sth): *She ~ed her elbows/Her elbows were ~ing on the table. R~ the ladder against the wall. The roof ~s upon eight columns.* ***~ on one's oars,*** **(a)** stop rowing for a time. **(b)** (fig) have a period of rest after any kind of work or effort. **4** [VP14, 3A] ***~ (sth) (up)on,*** lie, spread out, depend or rely (on); (of sight, etc) fall (on), be steadily directed (on): *A shadow ~ed on his face. Look at those clouds ~ing upon the mountain top. Her eyes/gaze ~ed on me. She let her glance ~ on me.*

rest[4] /rest/ *vi* **1** [VP2D] continue to be in a specified state: *You may ~ assured that everything possible will be done. The affair ~s* (remains, the usu word) *a mystery.* **2** [VP3A] ***~ with,*** be left in the hands or charge of: *It ~s with you to decide,* It is your responsibility. **3** [VP3A] ***~ (up)on,*** depend, rely: *His fame ~s upon his plays more than upon his novels.*

re·state /ˈriˋsteɪt/ *vt* [VP6A] state again or in a different way. **~·ment** *n*

res·taur·ant /ˋrestrõ *US:* -tərənt/ *n* place where meals can be bought and eaten. **res·taura·teur** /ˈrestərəˋtɜ(r)/, **res·taur·an·teur** /ˈrestrõˋtɜ(r) *US:* -tərən-/ *n* manager of a ~.

res·ti·tu·tion /ˈrestɪˋtjuʃn *US:* -ˋtu-/ *n* [U] **1** restoring (of sth stolen, etc) to its owner: *make ~ of sth to sb; ~ of property.* **2** = reparation.

res·tive /ˋrestɪv/ *adj* **1** (of a horse or other animal) refusing to move forward; moving backwards or sideways. **2** (of a person) reluctant to be controlled or disciplined. **~·ly** *adv* **~·ness** *n*

re·stock /ˈriˋstok/ *vt* [VP6A] put fresh stock into: *~ a lake with trout.*

res·to·ra·tion /ˈrestəˋreɪʃn/ *n* **1** [U] restoring or being restored: *~ to health and strength; ~ of stolen property.* **2 the R~,** (the period of) the re-establishment of the monarchy in England in 1660, when Charles II became king: *R~ poetry/comedy.* **3** [C] model representing the supposed original form of an extinct animal, ruined building, etc; building formerly ruined and now rebuilt: *The castle is a mere ~,* i e there is very little of the original left. *Closed during ~s,* i e while rebuilding is in progress.

re·stora·tive /rɪˋstɔrətɪv/ *adj* tending to restore health and strength. □ *n* [C,U] ~ food, medicine, etc.

re·store /rɪˋstɔ(r)/ *vt* [VP6A,14] ***~ sth (to),*** **1** give back: *~ stolen property/borrowed books.* **2** bring back into use; reintroduce: *~ old customs.* **3** make well or normal again; bring back (to a former condition): *quite ~d to health; feel completely ~d. Public order was quickly ~d after the attempted revolution. Law and order have been ~d.* **4** repair; rebuild as before; reconstruct (sth) so that it is like the original: *~ a ruined abbey/an extinct kind of animal; ~ a text,* try to make it as it was originally by supplying missing words and phrases, getting rid of errors made by copyists, etc. **5** place in or bring back to the former position, etc: *~ an employee to his old post/an officer to his command.* **re·storer** *n* one who, that which, ~s, e g an expert who cleans old oil paintings: *ˋhair-~r,* preparation that, it is claimed, will ~ hair to a bald head.

re·strain /rɪˋstreɪn/ *vt* [VP6A,14] ***~ sb/sth (from),*** hold back; keep under control; prevent (sb or sth from doing sth): *~ a child from (doing) mischief; ~ one's anger; ~ one's mirth.* **~ed** *adj* (esp) not emotional or wild; kept under control emotional or wild; kept under control. **re·straint** /-ˋstreɪnt/ *n* **1** [U] ~ing or being ~ed: *submit to ~t; break loose from all ~t.* ***be put under ~t,*** (esp of a mentally ill person) be placed in a mental home. ***without ~t,*** freely; without control. **2** [U] (in art, literature, etc) avoidance of excess or exaggeration. **3** [C] that which ~s; check; controlling influence: *the ~ts of poverty.*

re·strict /rɪˋstrɪkt/ *vt* [VP6A,14] **~ *sb/sth (to sth),*** limit; keep within limits: *Discussion at the meeting was ~ed to the agenda. We are ~ed to 30 miles an hour in built-up areas. The trees ~ our vision. Is the consumption of alcohol ~ed by law in your country?* **re·stric·tion** /rɪˋstrɪkʃn/ *n* **1** [U] ~ing or being ~ed: *~ion of expenditure.* **2** [C] instance of this; sth that ~s: *place ~ions on foreign trade/on the sale of alcohol; currency ~ions,* e g on the sums that a person may use for foreign travel. **re·strict·ive** /rɪˋstrɪktɪv/ *adj* ~ing; tending to ~: *~ive practices* (*in industry*), practices that hinder the most effective use of labour, technical resources, etc and tend to damage productive efficiency. **re·strict·ive·ly** *adv*

re·sult /rɪˋzʌlt/ *vi* **1** [VP2A,3A] **~ *(from),*** come about, happen, as a natural consequence: *Any damage ~ing from negligence must be paid for by the borrower.* **2** [VP3A] **~ *in,*** bring about; have as a consequence: *Their diplomacy ~ed in war.* **3** end in a specified manner: *Their efforts ~ed badly.* □ *n* **1** [C,U] that which is produced by an activity or cause; outcome; effect: *work without* (*much*) *~; obtain good ~s; announce the ~s of a competition,* the names of prize-winners, etc; *ˋfootball ~s,* the scores. *His limp is the ~ of a car accident last year.* **2** [C] sth found by calculation; answer (to a mathematical problem, etc). **~·ant** /-ənt/ *adj* coming as a ~, esp as the total outcome of forces or tendencies from different directions. □ *n* [C] product or outcome (*of* sth).

re·sume /rɪˋzjum *US:* -ˋzum/ *vt* **1** [VP6A,D] go on after stopping for a time: *~ one's work/a story; ~ the thread of one's discourse,* take up an interrupted discourse. **2** [VP6A] take or occupy again: *~ one's seat.*

ré·sumé /ˋrezʊmeɪ *US:* ˌrezʊˋmeɪ/ *n* [C] summary; abstract (of sth).

re·sump·tion /rɪˋzʌmpʃn/ *n* [U] resuming; [C] instance of this.

re·sur·face /ˌriˋsɜfɪs/ *vt,vi* **1** [VP6A] put a new surface on (a road, etc). **2** [VP2A] (of a submarine) come to the surface again.

re·sur·gent /rɪˋsɜdʒənt/ *adj* reviving, coming back to activity, vigour, etc (after defeat, destruction, etc): *~ nationalism; ~ hopes.* **re·sur·gence** /-əns/ *n*

res·ur·rect /ˌrezəˋrekt/ *vt,vi* **1** [VP6A] bring back into use; revive the practice of: *~ an old word/custom.* **2** [VP6A] take from the grave; (colloq) dig up: *My dog ~ed an old bone in the garden.* **3** [VP6A,2A] (rare) bring or come back to life again.

res·ur·rec·tion /ˌrezəˋrekʃn/ *n* [U] **1 the R~, (a)** the rising of Jesus from the tomb; anniversary of this. **(b)** the rising of all the dead on the Last Day. **2** revival from disuse, inactivity, etc: *the ~ of hope.*

re·sus·ci·tate /rɪˋsʌsɪteɪt/ *vt,vi* [VP2A,6A] bring or come back to consciousness: *~ a person who has been nearly drowned.* **re·sus·ci·ta·tion** /rɪˌsʌsɪˋteɪʃn/ *n* [U].

ret /ret/ *vt* (-tt-) [VP6A] soften (flax, hemp, etc) by soaking or exposing to moisture: *Coconut shells are buried in wet sea-sand in order to ret the coir fibre.*

re·tail /ˋriteɪl/ *n* [C] sale of goods (usu in small quantities) to the general public, not for resale: *sell goods* (*by*) *~;* (attrib) *~ dealers/prices; the ˋ~ department.* ⇨ wholesale. □ *adv* by ~: *Do you buy wholesale or ~?* □ *vt,vi* **1** [VP6A,3A] **~ *(at),*** sell (goods) by ~; (of goods) be sold ~: *an article that is ~ed at/that ~s at seventy pence.* **2** [VP6A] repeat (what one has heard, esp gossip) bit by bit or to several persons in turn: *~ a slander.* **~er** *n* tradesman who sells by ~.

re·tain /rɪˋteɪn/ *vt* [VP6A] **1** keep; continue to have or hold; keep in place: *This vessel won't ~ water. This dyke was built to ~ the flood waters. The ~ing wall* (i e one built to support and confine a mass of earth or water) *collapsed. He is 90 but still ~s the use of all his faculties. She ~s a clear memory of her schooldays.* **2** get the services of (esp a barrister) by payment (*a ~ing fee*). **~er** *n* **1** (legal) fee paid to ~ the services of, e g a barrister. **2** (old use) servant of sb of high rank: *the duke and his ~ers;* (later use) *an old family ~er,* servant, e g a butler or cook, who has served with a family for many years.

re·take /ˌriˋteɪk/ *vt* (*pt* -took /-ˋtʊk/, *pp* -taken /-ˋteɪkn/) [VP6A] take, capture, photograph, again. □ *n* /ˋriteɪk/ (esp, cinema, TV) rephotographed scene.

re·tali·ate /rɪˋtælɪeɪt/ *vi* [VP2A,3A] **~ *against/upon,*** return the same sort of ill treatment that one has received: *~ upon one's enemy. He ~d by kicking the other fellow on the ankle. If we raise our import duties on their goods, they may ~ against us.* **re·tali·ation** /rɪˌtælɪˋeɪʃn/ *n* [U] retaliating: *in retaliation for.* **re·tali·at·ive** /rɪˋtælɪətɪv *US:* -ɪeɪt-/, **re·tali·at·ory** /rɪˋtælɪətrɪ *US:* -tɔrɪ/ *adjj* returning ill treatment for ill treatment; of or for retaliation: *retaliatory measures.*

re·tard /rɪˋtɑd/ *vt* [VP6A] check; hinder: *~ progress/development; a mentally ~ed child,* one whose mental or emotional development has been checked. **re·tar·da·tion** /ˌritɑˋdeɪʃn/ *n*

retch /retʃ/ *vi* [VP2A] make (involuntarily) the sound and physical movements of vomiting but without bringing up anything from the stomach.

re·tell /ˌriˋtel/ *vt* (*pt,pp* -told /-ˋtold/) [VP6A] tell again; tell in a different way or in a different language: *old Greek tales retold for children.*

re·ten·tion /rɪˋtenʃn/ *n* [U] retaining or being retained: *suffering from ~ of urine,* inability to pass it out from the bladder.

re·ten·tive /rɪˋtentɪv/ *adj* having the power of retaining(1) things: *a memory that is ~ of details; a ~ soil,* one that retains water, does not dry out quickly. **~·ly** *adv* **~·ness** *n*

re·tex·ture /ˌriˋtekstʃə(r)/ *vt* [VP6A] treat (garments, blankets, etc) with chemicals, etc so that the texture is renovated. □ *n* such treatment: *These garments have been given a ~.*

re·think /ˌriˋθɪŋk/ *vt,vi* (*pt,pp* -thought /-ˋθɔt/) [VP2A,6A] think about again; reconsider: *They will have to ~ their policy towards China. A good deal of ~ing is needed on this question.* □ *n* /ˋriθɪŋk/ (colloq) thinking again: *If that's your decision, you'd better have a ~.*

reti·cent /ˋretɪsnt/ *adj* in the habit of saying little; not saying all that is known or felt; reserved: *She was ~ about/on what Tom had said to her.* **~·ly** *adv* **reti·cence** /-sns/ *n* [U] being ~; [C] instance of this: *His reticences are often more revealing than what he says.*

re·ticu·late /rɪˋtɪkjʊleɪt/ *vt,vi* [VP6A,2A] divide, be divided, in fact or in appearance into a network of small squares or intersecting lines. □ *adj*

/rɪˈtɪkjʊlət/ covered with such a network. **re·ticu·la·tion** /rɪˈtɪkjʊˈleɪʃn/ *n* (often *pl*) net-like mark or structure.

reti·cule /ˈretɪkjul/ *n* small handbag (formerly made of netted fabric) carried by a woman (for a handkerchief and other small articles).

ret·ina /ˈretɪnə *US:* ˈretṇə/ *n* (*pl* -nas or -nae /-ni/) [C] layer of membrane at the back of the eyeball, sensitive to light. ⇨ the illus at eye.

reti·nue /ˈretɪnju *US:* ˈretṇu/ *n* [C] number of persons (servants, officers, etc) travelling with a person of high rank.

re·tire /rɪˈtɑɪə(r)/ *vi,vt* **1** [VP2A,3A] ~ ***(from) (to),*** withdraw; go away: *He* ~*d to his cabin. The batsman* ~*d hurt,* left the pitch and went back to the pavilion, because hurt. *The ladies* ~*d* (= left the dining-room), *and the men went on drinking and smoking.* **2** ~ ***(to bed),*** (formal for) go to bed: *My wife usually* ~*s at 10 o'clock.* **3** [VP2A,C] (of an army) withdraw; go back: *Our forces* ~*d to prepared positions.* Cf *The enemy retreated.* **4** [VP2A,C] give up one's work, position, business, etc: *He will* ~ *on a pension at 65.* **5** [VP6A] cause (sb) to ~(3,4): ~ *the head clerk.* **6** ~ *from the world,* enter a monastery or become a hermit; become a recluse. ~ ***into oneself,*** become unsociable because one is wrapped up in one's own thoughts. □ *n* signal to troops to ~: *sound the* ~, i e on the bugle. **re·tired** *adj* **1** having ~d(4): *a* ~*d civil servant; the* ˈ~*d list,* of officers (of the Army, etc) who have ~d; ˈ~*d pay,* pension. **2** secluded; quiet: *a* ~*d valley; live a* ~*d life in a small village.* **re·tir·ing** *adj* (of persons, their way of life, etc) inclined to avoid society; reserved: *a girl of a retiring disposition.* □ *n*: *reach retiring age; a retiring allowance,* one given to a person when he ~s(4). ~**·ment** *n* **1** [U] retiring or being ~d; seclusion: ~*ment from the world,* e g in a convent. **2** [U] condition of being ~d: *be/live in* ~*ment.* ***go into*** ~***ment,*** retire (esp 4 and 6 above). **3** [C] instance of retiring or being ~d: *There have been several* ~*ments in my office recently.* ˈ~**ment pension,** = old-age pension. ⇨ pension.

re·tool /ˈriˈtul/ *vt* [VP6A] equip (a factory, etc) with new machine tools.

re·tort[1] /rɪˈtɔt/ *n* [C] **1** vessel with a long narrow neck turned downwards, used for distilling liquids. **2** receptacle used in the purification of mercury, and in the making of gas.

re·tort[2] /rɪˈtɔt/ *vt,vi* **1** [VP6A,9] answer back quickly, wittily or angrily (esp to an accusation or challenge): *'It's entirely your fault,' he* ~*ed.* **2** [VP14] (formal, rare) get equal with sb by returning (what has been received) in kind: ~ *insult for insult;* ~ *an argument against sb;* ~ *an affront upon sb.* □ *n* [U] ~ing: *say sth in* ~; [C] ~ing answer: *make an insolent* ~.

re·touch /ˈriˈtʌtʃ/ *vt* [VP6A] improve (a photograph, painting, etc) by a few touches of a brush, etc.

re·trace /riˈtreɪs/ *vt* [VP6A] **1** go back over or along: ~ *one's steps.* **2** go over (past actions, etc) in the mind.

re·tract /rɪˈtrækt/ *vt,vi* **1** [VP6A,2A] take back or withdraw (a statement, offer, opinion, etc); take back a statement: *The prisoner of war* ~*ed his parole. Even when confronted with proof the accused man refused to* ~, would not acknowledge the error of what he had said. **2** [VP6A,2A] draw in or back; move back or in; be capable of doing this: *A cat can* ~ *its claws and a snail its horns. A cat's claws can* ~. ~**·able** /-əbl/ *adj* that can be ~ed: *a* ~*able undercarriage,* (in an aircraft) wheels, etc which can be drawn up into the body of the aircraft during flight. **re·trac·tile** /rɪˈtræktɑɪl *US:* -təl/ *adj* that can be drawn in: *the retractile claws of a cat.* **re·trac·tion** /rɪˈtrækʃn/ *n* [U] ~ing; [C] instance of this.

re·tread /ˈriˈtred/ *vt* (*pt,pp* ~ed) furnish (an old tyre) with a new tread. ⇨ tread, *n*(3). □ *n* /ˈritred/ tyre that has been ~ed (US = *recap*).

re·treat /rɪˈtrit/ *vi* **1** [VP2A,C] ~ ***(from) (to),*** (esp of an army) go back; withdraw: *force the enemy to* ~; ~ *on* (i e towards) *the capital.* **2** recede (which is more usu): *a* ~*ing forehead.* □ *n* **1** [U] act of ~ing: *The army was in full* ~. *We made good our* ~, ~ed safely. **2** [U] signal for ~ing: *sound the* ~, e g on a drum or bugle. **3** [C] instance of ~ing: *after many advances and* ~*s.* ***beat a (hasty)*** ~, (fig) withdraw from, abandon, an undertaking. **4** [C,U] (place for a) period of quiet and rest: *a quiet country* ~. ***go into*** ~, e g temporary retirement for religious exercises.

re·trench /rɪˈtrentʃ/ *vt,vi* [VP6A,2A] cut down (expenses); make economies: *We must* ~ *this year in order to have a good holiday next year.* ~**·ment** *n* [U] ~ing; [C] instance of this.

re·trial /ˈriˈtrɑɪl/ *n* act of trying again in a law court; new trial.

ret·ri·bu·tion /ˈretrɪˈbjuʃn/ *n* [U] deserved punishment: *R*~ *for loose living does not always come in this life. There will be a day of* ~. **re·tri·bu·tive** /rɪˈtrɪbjʊtɪv/ *adj* coming as ~; inflicted or coming as a penalty for wrongdoing.

re·trieve /rɪˈtriv/ *vt,vi* **1** [VP6A] get possession of again: ~ *a lost piece of luggage.* **2** [VP6A] put or set right; make amends for: ~ *an error/a loss/disaster/defeat.* **3** [VP6A,14] ~ ***sth (from),*** rescue from; restore to a flourishing state: ~ *sb from ruin;* ~ *one's honour/fortunes;* ~ *oneself.* **4** [VP6A,2A] (of specially trained dogs) find and bring in (killed or wounded birds, etc). **re·triev·able** /-əbl/ *adj* **re·trieval** /-vl/ *n* [U] **1** act of retrieving: *the retrieval of one's fortunes.* **2** possibility of recovery: *beyond/past retrieval.* **re·triever** *n* breed of dog used for retrieving(4).

retro·ac·tive /ˈretrəʊˈæktɪv/ *adj* (of laws, etc) = retrospective(2). ~**·ly** *adv*

retro·grade /ˈretrəgreɪd/ *adj* **1** directed backwards: ~ *motion.* **2** deteriorating; likely to cause worse conditions: *a* ~ *policy.* □ *vi* [VP2A] decline; revert; grow worse.

retro·gress /ˈretrəˈgres/ *vi* [VP2A] go or move backwards.

retro·gression /ˈretrəˈgreʃn/ *n* return to a less advanced state; decline. **retro·gress·ive** /ˈretrəˈgresɪv/ *adj* returning, tending to return, to a less advanced state; becoming worse.

retro·rocket /ˈretrəʊrokɪt/ *n* jet engine fired to slow down or alter the course of a missile, spacecraft, etc.

retro·spect /ˈretrəspekt/ *n* [U] view of past events. ***in*** ~, looking back at past events, etc. **retro·spec·tion** /ˈretrəˈspekʃn/ *n* [U] action of looking back at past events, scenes, etc; [C] instance of this: *indulge in dreamy* ~*ions.* **retro·spec·tive** /ˈretrəˈspektɪv/ *adj* **1** relating to retrospection; looking back on past events, etc. **2** (of laws, payments, etc) applying to the past; not restricted to the future: *~ive legislation; a ~ive* (= back-dated) *wage increase.* **retro·spec·tive·ly** *adv*

re·troussé /rəˋtruseɪ *US:* ˈretrʊˋseɪ/ *adj* (of a nose) turned up at the end.

ret·ro·ver·sion /ˈretrəʊˋvɜʃn *US* -ˋvɜʒn/ *n* state of being turned backwards; turning or tilting backward.

ret·sina /retˋsinə *US:* ˋretsɪnə/ *n* [U] resinated Greek wine.

re·turn[1] /rɪˋtɜn/ *n* **1** [C,U] ~ing or being ~ed; coming, going, giving, sending, putting, back: *a ~ home; on my ~*, when I got/get back; *a poor ~ for kindness*, (e g) ungrateful behaviour; *the ~ of spring; have a ~ of the symptoms* (of an illness). ***by ~***, by the next post out: *Please send a reply by ~.* ***in ~ (for)***, as repayment (for). ***Many happy ~s of the day***, phrase used as a greeting on sb's birthday. ***on sale or ~***, (of goods in commerce) supplied (to retailers) on the understanding that they may be ~ed to the wholesaler or manufacturer if not sold. ***point of no ~***, (on a long voyage, flight across an ocean, etc) point at which fuel supplies, etc are insufficient for a ~ to the starting-point, so that continuation of the voyage, etc is essential; (fig) stage of negotiations at which no further progress seems possible. **2** (attrib) involving going back or coming back, etc: *the ~ voyage.* **~ fare**, needed for the journey back. **~ half**, the half of a ~ ticket for the journey back. **~ match**, one played between teams which have already played one match. **ˋ~ ticket**, one giving a traveller the right to go to a place and back to his starting-point (*two-way ticket* in US). **ˈday-ˋ~**, a ~ ticket available only for the day of issue: *Two cheap day-~s to London, please.* **3** (often *pl*) profit on an investment or undertaking: *get a good ~ on an investment; small profits and quick ~s*, motto for shops that rely on large sales and quick turnover. **4** [C] official report or statement, esp one that is compiled by order: *make one's ~ of income* (to the Inspector of Taxes for purposes of income tax); *the Board of Trade ~s*, statistics about exports and imports, etc; *the eˋlection ~s*, figures of the voting at an election.

re·turn[2] /rɪˋtɜn/ *vi,vt* **1** [VP2A,C,3A,4A] ***~ (to) (from)***, come or go back: *~ home; ~ to London; ~ from a journey; ~ to Paris from London. He ~ed to ask me about something. I shall ~ to this point later in my lecture.* **2** [VP2A,3A] ***~ to***, pass or go back to a former state: *He has ~ed to his old habits. After death animal bodies ~* (= change) *to dust.* **3** [VP6A] (rare) reply; retort: *'Not this time', he ~ed.* **4** [VP6A,12A,13A] give, put, send, pay, carry, back: *When will you ~ (me) the book I lent you? In case of non-delivery, ~ to (the) sender*, often written on letters sent by post. *All books are to be ~ed to the library before Friday. He ~ed the blow* (i e hit back) *smartly. She ~ed the compliment*, said sth pleasant after a compliment had been paid to her. ***~ thanks***, express thanks, esp by saying grace before a meal, or in response to a toast. **~ed empties**, empty bottles, crates, etc ~ed to the sender for re-use. **5** [VP6A, 16A] (of a constituency) send (sb) as representative to Parliament. **~ing officer** *n* official in charge of a Parliamentary election and announcing the name of the person elected. **6** [VP6A,15A] state or describe officially, esp in answer to a demand: *~ the details of one's income* (for taxation purposes); *liabilities ~ed at £2 000. The prisoner was ~ed guilty. The jury ~ed a verdict of guilty.* **7** [VP6A] give as a profit: *an investment that ~s a good interest.* **~·able** /-əbl/ *adj* that can be, or is to be, ~ed.

re·un·ion /ˈriˋjunɪən/ *n* [U] reuniting or being reunited; [C] (esp) meeting of old friends, former colleagues, etc after separation: *a family ~ at Christmas.*

re·unite /ˈrijuˋnaɪt/ *vt,vi* [VP6A,2A] bring or come together again: *~d after long years of separation.*

rev /rev/ *vt,vi* (-vv-) [VP15B,2C] ***rev up***, (colloq) increase the speed of revolutions in (an internal-combustion engine): *Don't rev up (the engine) so hard.* □ *n* revolution: *You're driving at maximum revs.*

re·value /riˋvælju/ *vt* [VP6A] value again or anew. **re·valu·ation** /ˈriˈvæljʊˋeɪʃn/ *n* revaluing: *revaluation of the currency.*

re·vamp /ˈriˋvæmp/ *vt* [VP6A] put a new upper on (a boot or shoe); (colloq) patch up; reconstruct; renew: *~ an old comedy; ~ agriculture in a backward country*, try to improve it.

re·veal /rɪˋvil/ *vt* [VP6A,14] **1** allow or cause to be seen; display: *These new fashions ~ more than a modest woman will approve of.* **2** make known: *~ a secret. One day the truth about these events will be ~ed. The doctor did not ~ to him his hopeless condition. Research has ~ed him* (= shown that he was) *a monster of iniquity.* ***~ed religion***, religion believed to be taught to mankind directly by God.

re·veille /rɪˋvælɪ *US:* ˋrevəlɪ/ *n* (in the armed forces) bugle signal to men to get up in the morning: *sound the ~.*

revel /ˋrevl/ *vi* (-ll-; US also -l-) **1** [VP2A,B,C, 15B] make merry; have a gay, lively time: *They ~led until dawn. They ~led away the time.* **2** [VP3A] ***~ in***, take great delight in: *~ in one's freedom; people who ~ in gossip.* □ *n* [C,U] (occasion of) merrymaking; joyous festivity: *Our ~s now are ended.* **~·ler**, (US = **~er**) /ˋrevl̩ə(r)/ *n* person who ~s.

rev·el·ation /ˈrevəˋleɪʃn/ *n* **1** [U] revealing; making known of sth secret or hidden; [C] that which is revealed, esp sth that causes surprise: *truths which man knows only by ~*, i e from God. *It was a ~ to John when Mary said she had married him only for his money.* **2 R~**, the last book of the New Testament, called *The R~ of St John the Divine*, or (less correctly) *R~s.*

rev·elry /ˋrevlrɪ/ *n* [U] (or *pl*; -ries) noisy, joyous festivity and merrymaking: *when the ~/revelries ended.*

re·venge /rɪˋvendʒ/ *vt* **1** [VP6A] do sth to get satisfaction for (an offence, etc to oneself or another): *~ an injustice/insult; ~ one's friend*, inflict injury (deliberately) on the person who injured one's friend. **2** ***be ~d on sb, ~ oneself on sb***, get satisfaction by deliberately inflicting injury in return for injury inflicted on oneself. ⇨ avenge. □ *n* [U] **1** deliberate infliction of injury upon the person(s) from whom injury has been received: *thirsting for ~; nurse thoughts of ~.* ***take ~ on sb (for sth), have/get one's ~ (on sb) (for sth); do sth in/out of ~ (for sth).*** **2** [U] vindictiveness. **3** (in sport) opportunity given for reversing an earlier result by a return match, etc. ***get/give sb his ~.*** **~·ful** /-fl/ *adj* feeling or showing a desire for ~. **~·fully** /-fl̩ɪ/ *adv*

rev·enue /ˈrevn̩ju *US:* -n̩u/ *n* **1** [U] income, esp the total annual income of the State; government department which collects money for public funds: *a* ˈ~ *officer,* a customs and excise officer; *a* ˈ~ *cutter,* boat used to detect and prevent smuggling. **Inland R~,** income from taxation, etc. ˈ~ **tax,** one designed to produce ~ (contrasted with taxes designed to protect a country's trade and commerce). **2** (*pl*) separate items of ~ put together: *the ~s of the City Council.*

re·ver·ber·ate /rɪˈvɜbəreɪt/ *vt,vi* [VP6A,2A] (esp of sound) send or throw back, be sent back, again and again: *The roar of the train ~d/was ~d in the tunnel. His voice ~d from the walls of the cave.* **re·ver·ber·ant** /-ənt/ *adj* resounding **re·ver·ber·ation** /rɪˈvɜbəˈreɪʃn/ *n* [U] reverberating or being ~d; (*pl*) echoes; repercussions.

re·vere /rɪˈvɪə(r)/ *vt* [VP6A] have deep respect for; regard as sacred, with great respect: *~ virtue; my ~d grandfather.*

rev·er·ence /ˈrevərəns/ *n* **1** [U] deep respect; feeling of wonder and awe. ***hold sb/sth in ~; have/show ~ for sb/sth***: *a bishop who was held in ~ by all; regard sb with ~.* **2** [C] (old use) gesture showing deep respect; curtesy or obeisance. **3** [C] (old use, or in Ireland; in England now vulg or hum) as a title for a priest: *his ~ the Bishop.* □ *vt* [VP6A] treat with ~.

rev·er·end /ˈrevərənd/ *adj* **1** deserving to be treated with respect (because of age, character, etc). **2 the R~,** (usu shortened in writing to *the Rev*), used as a title of a clergyman: *the Rev John Smith* or *the Rev J Smith* (but not *the Rev Smith*); *the Very R~ K Hill* (of a dean); *the Right R~ the Bishop of Barchester; the Most R~ Archbishop of York; the R~ Father O'Higgins* (of a R C priest). **R~ Mother,** Mother Superior of a convent. □ *n* (usu *pl*) clergyman: *a crowd of ~s and right ~s at the Lambeth Conference.*

rev·er·ent /ˈrevərənt/ *adj* feeling or showing reverence. **~·ly** *adv*

rev·er·en·tial /ˌrevəˈrenʃl/ *adj* caused or marked by reverence. **~ly** /-ʃl̩ɪ/ *adv*

rev·erie /ˈrevərɪ/ *n* **1** [C,U] (instance of, occasion of a) condition of being lost in dreamy, pleasant thoughts: *lost in ~; indulge in ~s about the future.* **2** [C] piece of dreamy instrumental music.

re·vers /rɪˈvɪə(r)/ *n* (*pl* ~) turned-back edge of a coat, etc showing the reverse side, as on a lapel.

re·ver·sal /rɪˈvɜsl/ *n* **1** [U] reversing or being reversed: *the ~ of the seasons in the two hemispheres.* **2** [C] instance of this: *a ~ of procedure.*

re·verse[1] /rɪˈvɜs/ *adj* ~ ***(to),*** contrary or opposite in character or order; inverted: *the ~ side of a length of cloth; the ~ side of a coin or disc.* ***in ~ order,*** from the end to the start, or in the opposite order; in the ~ direction. **~·ly** *adv*

re·verse[2] /rɪˈvɜs/ *n* **1** [U] (with *def art*) opposite; contrary: *do the ~ of what one is expected to do. Your remarks were the ~ of polite,* were impolite. **2** [C] ⇨ reverse[1](1). (sth on the) reverse side (of a coin, medal, disc, etc): *On the ~ of this 50p coin there is a design showing a lion wearing a crown.* **3** mechanism or device that reverses: *Most typewriters have an automatic ribbon ~. Most cars have three forward gears and (a) ~. Put the car into ~.* **4** [C] defeat; change to bad fortune: *Our forces have suffered a slight ~. These financial ~s will prevent my taking a holiday.*

re·verse[3] /rɪˈvɜs/ *vt,vi* [VP6A] turn (sth) the other way round or up or inside out: *~ a procedure; ~ one's policy.* ***a ~d charge,*** charge for a telephone call (to be) paid by the person to whom the call is made instead of by the person who makes it. ***~ arms,*** (mil) hold the rifle with the muzzle pointing down (as at military funerals). **2** [VP6A,2A] (cause to) go in the opposite direction: *~ one's car into the garage* (*back* is the more usu word). *She ~s well,* e g of a dancer in a waltz as she begins to revolve in the opposite direction. **3** [VP6A] change the order or position of: *Their positions are now ~d; A is poor and B is rich.* **4** [VP6A] revoke, annul: *~ the decision of a lower court; ~ a decree.* **re·vers·ible** /-əbl/ *adj* that can be ~d, e g of cloth, either side of which can be used on the outside. **re·versi·bil·ity** /rɪˈvɜsəˈbɪlətɪ/ *n*

re·ver·sion /rɪˈvɜʃn *US:* -ˈvɜʒn/ *n* ⇨ revert.

re·vert /rɪˈvɜt/ *vi* [VP2A,3A] ~ ***(to),*** **1** return (to a former state, condition, topic, etc): *The fields have ~ed to moorland,* have gone out of cultivation, etc. *R~ing to your original statement, I think.... Garden plants sometimes ~ to type,* go back to the wild kind from which they were developed. *Mental patients sometimes ~,* i e to their condition before treatment started. **2** (legal) (of property, rights, etc) return at some named time or under certain conditions (*to* the original owner, the State, etc): *property which ~s to the Crown. If he dies without an heir, his property will ~ to the state.* **~·ible** /-əbl/ *adj* that may ~. **re·ver·sion** /rɪˈvɜʃn *US:* -ɜʒn/ *n* **1** [U] ~ing (of property, etc). ⇨ 2 above. **2** [C] right to possess property in certain circumstances; land, property, etc to which one has such a right; **3** [U] ~ing(1): *reversion of plants, etc* (i e to ancestral types). **re·ver·sion·ary** /rɪˈvɜʃnrɪ *US:* -ɜʒn̩erɪ/ *adj* of reversion(2).

re·vet·ment /rɪˈvetmənt/ *n* retaining wall; facing of masonry, concrete, etc on an embankment, etc.

re·view /rɪˈvju/ *vt,vi* **1** [VP6A] consider or examine again; go over again in the mind: *~ the past; ~ last week's lesson.* **2** [VP6A] inspect formally (troops, a fleet, etc). **3** [VP6A,2A,C] write an account of (new books, etc) for newspapers and other periodicals: *His new novel has been favourably ~ed. Mr Hay ~s for 'The Spectator'.* □ *n* **1** [U] act of ~ing(1): *pass one's life in ~,* think about the events of one's life, one by one. ***come under ~,*** be considered or examined; [C] instance of such ~ing: *a ~ of the year's sporting events.* **2** [C] inspection of military, naval, etc forces: *hold a ~.* **3** [C] article that critically examines a new book, etc: *write ~s for the monthly magazines; a ~ copy of a book,* one presented by the publishers to the editor of a periodical for ~. **4** [C] periodical with articles on current events, ~s of new books, etc. **~er** *n* person who writes ~s (of books, etc).

re·vile /rɪˈvaɪl/ *vt,vi* [VP6A,3A] ~ ***at/against,*** swear at; call bad names; use abusive language: *~ at/against corruption; ~ one's persecutors.*

re·vise /rɪˈvaɪz/ *vt* [VP6A] reconsider; read carefully through, esp in order to correct and improve: *~ one's estimates; ~ one's opinions of sb. She's revising her notes for the exams,* going through them in readiness. **the R~d Version,** the Version of the Bible made in 1870—84 as a Revision of the translation published in 1611, known as the Authorized Version. □ *n* [C] (printing) proof-sheet in which errors marked in an earlier proof have been corrected. **re·viser** *n* person who ~s. **re·vision** /rɪˈvɪʒn/ *n* [U] revising or being ~d; [C] instance of this: *after two revisions;* [C] that which has been ~d; corrected version. **re·vision·ist** /rɪˋvɪʒn̩ɪst/ *n* person who supports a review of the fundamental tenets of a political ideology. **re·vision·ism** /-ɪzm/ *n*

re·vital·ize /riˋvaɪtl̩aɪz/ *vt* put new life into; restore vitality. **re·vital·iz·ation** /ˈriˈvaɪtl̩aɪˋzeɪʃn *US:* -l̩ɪˋz-/ *n*

re·vival /rɪˋvaɪvl/ *n* **1** [U] reviving or being revived; bringing or coming back into use or knowledge; [C] instance of this: *the ~ of an old custom; a ~ of a play by Fletcher; a ~ of trade; the R~ of Learning,* the Renaissance. **2** [C] (series of meetings intended to produce an) increase of interest in religion: *a religious ~; ~ meetings.* **~·ist** /-vl̩ɪst/ *n* person who organizes or conducts ~ meetings.

re·vive /rɪˋvaɪv/ *vi,vt* [VP6A,2A] **1** come or bring back to consciousness, strength, health or an earlier state: *~ a person who has fainted; ~ an old play,* produce it for the theatre after many years. *The flowers will ~ in water. Our hopes ~d.* **2** come or bring into use again: *customs which ~/are ~d.*

re·viv·ify /riˋvɪvɪfaɪ/ *vt* (*pt,pp* **-fied**) restore to animation; give new life or liveliness to.

revo·cable /ˈrevəkəbl/ *adj* that can be revoked.

revo·ca·tion /ˈrevəˋkeɪʃn/ *n* [U] revoking or being revoked; [C] instance of this.

re·voke /rɪˋvəʊk/ *vt,vi* **1** [VP6A] repeal; cancel; withdraw (a decree, consent, permission, etc): *~ an order/a driving licence.* **2** [VP2A] (of a player at such card games as whist and bridge) fail to follow suit (i e not play a card of the same suit as that led by another player although he could do so). □ *n* failure of this kind.

re·volt /rɪˋvəʊlt/ *vi,vt* **1** [VP2A,3A] **~ *(against),*** rise in rebellion: *The people ~ed against their rulers.* **2** [VP3A] **~ *against/at/from,*** be filled with disgust or horror: *Human nature ~s at/from/against such a crime. This is a doctrine from which sensitive persons must ~.* **3** [VP6A] fill with disgust or horror: *scenes that ~ed all who saw them.* □ *n* [U] act of ~ing; state of having ~ed(1): *a period of ~; break out in ~; stir the people to ~;* [C] instance of this; rebellion or rising: *~s against authority.*

re·volt·ing /rɪˋvəʊltɪŋ/ *adj* disgusting: *~ behaviour; ~ to our ideas of morality.* **~·ly** *adv* in a way that disgusts: *a ~ly dirty child.*

rev·ol·ution /ˈrevəˋluʃn/ *n* **1** [C] act of revolving or journeying round: *the ~ of the earth round the sun;* [C] complete turn of a wheel, etc: *sixty-five ~s* (or, colloq *revs*) *a minute.* **2** [C,U] (instance of) complete change (in conditions, ways of doing things, esp in methods of government when caused by the overthrow of one system by force): *the French R~* (in 1789); *prefer evolution to ~ in politics; ~s in our ideas of time and space; ~s in our ways of travelling,* e g as the result of travel by air. **~·ary** /-nrɪ *US:* -n̩erɪ/ *adj* of a ~(2); bringing, causing, favouring, great (and perhaps violent) changes: *~ary ideas; a ~ary society; imprisoned for advocating ~ary principles.* □ *n* supporter of a (political) ~. **~·ize** /-n̩aɪz/ *vt* [VP6A] **1** fill with ~ary principles. **2** make a complete change in; cause to be entirely different: *The use of atomic energy will ~ize the lives of coming generations.*

re·volve /rɪˋvolv/ *vt,vi* **1** [VP6A,2A,3A] **~ *(about/around),*** (cause to) go round in a circle: *A wheel ~s about/round its axis. The earth ~s round/about the sun. The life of the home ~s around the mother, is centered on her. This theatre has a revolving stage.* **2** [VP6A] turn over in the mind; think about all sides of (a problem, etc): *~ a problem in one's mind.*

re·volver /rɪˋvolvə(r)/ *n* pistol with a revolving mechanism that makes it possible to fire it a number of times without reloading.

re·vue /rɪˋvju/ *n* [C] theatrical entertainment which consists of a medley of dialogue, dance and song, usu holding up current events, fashions, etc, to satire; [U] this form of entertainment: *to appear/perform in ~.*

re·vul·sion /rɪˋvʌlʃn/ *n* [U] (often with *indef art*) **1** sudden and complete change of feeling: *There was a ~ of public feeling in favour of the accused woman.* **2 ~ *(against/from),*** feeling of reaction.

re·ward /rɪˋwɔd/ *n* **1** [U] recompense for service or merit: *work without hope of ~; the ~ of virtue; get very little in ~ for one's hard work.* **2** [C] that which is offered, given or obtained in return for work or services, or the restoration of lost or stolen property, the capture of a criminal, etc: *offer a ~ of £10 for information about a stolen necklace. The financial ~s of teaching are not among its attractions.* □ *vt* [VP6A,14] **~ *sb (for sth),*** give a ~ to (sb for sth): *~ a man for his honesty. Is that how you ~ me for my help?*

re·wire /ˈriˋwaɪə(r)/ *vt* provide, e g a building with new wiring (for electric current).

re·word /ˈriˋwɜd/ *vt* [VP6A] express again in different words: *If we ~ the telegram we can save one-third of the cost.*

re·write /ˈriˋraɪt/ *vt* [VP6A] write again in a different style, etc. (attrib, US colloq) *a ˋ~ man,* one employed to ~ articles, books, etc in a form suitable for publication. □ *n* sth rewritten.

rex /reks/ *n* (abbr **R**) reigning king (used as *Regina* is used).

rhap·sody /ˈræpsədɪ/ *n* [C] (*pl* **-dies**) **1** enthusiastic expression of delight (in speech, poetry, etc): *Everyone went into rhapsodies over Helen's wedding dress.* **2** (music) composition in irregular form: *Liszt's Hungarian Rhapsodies.* **rhap·so·dize** /ˈræpsədaɪz/ *vi* [VP2A,3A] ***rhapsodize (about/over/on),*** talk or write with great enthusiasm.

rhea /rɪə/ *n* three-toed ostrich of S America.

Rhen·ish /ˈrenɪʃ/ *adj* (old use) of the River Rhine and the districts on its banks. □ *n* ~ wine (now usu *Rhine wine* or *hock*).

rheo·stat /ˈriəstæt/ *n* instrument for regulating the strength of an electric current by means of different resistances in the circuit, e g as in the volume control of a radio receiver.

rhe·sus /ˈrisəs/ *n* small monkey with a short tail, common in N India, used in biological experiments. ⇨ the illus at ape.

rhet·oric /ˈretərɪk/ *n* [U] **1** (art of) using words impressively in speech and writing. **2** language with much display and ornamentation (often with the implication of insincerity and exaggeration): *the ~ of the politicians.*

rhe·tori·cal /rɪˋtorɪkl *US:* -ˋtɔr-/ *adj* in, using, a style designed to impress or persuade; artificial or exaggerated in language: *a remarkable ~ effort.* **a ~ *question,*** one asked for the sake of effect, to impress people, no answer being needed or expected. **~ly** /-klɪ/ *adv*

rhet·or·ician /ˌretəˈrɪʃn/ *n* person skilled in rhetoric or fond of rhetorical language.

rheum /rum/ *n* [U] (old use) watery discharge from the nose or eyes.

rheu·matic /ruˈmætɪk/ *adj* relating to, causing, caused by, rheumatism; suffering from, liable to have, rheumatism: *~ joints; ~ fever,* serious form of rheumatism, chiefly in children. □ *n* **1** person who suffers from rheumatism. **2** (*pl* colloq) ~ pains.

rheu·ma·tism /ˈrumətɪzm/ *n* [U] (kinds of) painful disease with stiffness and inflammation of the muscles and joints.

rheu·ma·toid /ˈrumətɔɪd/ *adj* of rheumatism: *~ arthritis,* chronic form of arthritis.

rhinal /ˈraɪnl/ *adj* of the nose or nostrils.

Rhine /raɪn/ *n* German river: ˈ*~ wine,* kinds of (esp white) wine from ~ vineyards. ˈ**~·stone** *n* kind of rock-crystal; paste gem made in imitation of a diamond.

rhino /ˈraɪnəʊ/ *n* (*pl* **-nos** /-nəʊz/) (colloq abbr of) rhinoceros.

rhi·noc·eros /raɪˈnosərəs/ *n* (*pl* **-oses** /-əsɪz/ or, collectively, ~) thick-skinned, heavily built animal of Africa and Asia with one or two horns on the snout. ⇨ the illus at **large**.

rhi·zome /ˈraɪzəʊm/ *n* [C] thick, horizontal stem of some plants, e g iris, on or just below the ground, from which new roots grow.

rho·do·den·dron /ˌrəʊdəˈdendrən/ *n* [C] kinds of evergreen shrub with large flowers growing in clusters.

rhomb /rom/, **rhom·bus** /ˈrombəs/ *nn* four-sided figure with equal sides, and angles which are not right angles (e g diamond or lozenge shape). ⇨ the illus at **quadrilateral**. **rhom·boid** /ˈrombɔɪd/ *adj* of the shape of a ~. □ *n* rhombus with only its opposite sides equal. ⇨ the illus at **quadrilateral**.

rhu·barb /ˈrubɑb/ *n* [U] **1** (garden plant with) thick, juicy stalks which are cooked and eaten like fruit. **2** (colloq) noisy talk of many speakers; confused discussion.

rhyme (US also **rime**) /raɪm/ *n* **1** [U] sameness of sound of the endings of two or more words at the ends of lines of verse, e g *say, day, play; measure, pleasure; puff, rough.* ***without ~ or reason,*** without meaning; nonsensical(ly). **2** [C] ***~ (for/to),*** word which provides a ~: *Is there a ~ to/for 'hiccups'?* **3** [C] verse or verses with ~. ˈ**nursery ~,** verse for small children. **4** [U] the employment of ~: *The story should be told in ~,* in verse with ~s. □ *vt,vi* **1** [VP6A] put together to form a ~: *Can we ~ 'hiccups' with 'pick-ups'?* **2** [VP2A, 3A] ***~ with,*** (of words or lines of verse) be in ~: *'Piebald' doesn't ~ with 'ribald'.* **rhyming slang,** e g 'trouble and strife' for 'wife'. **3** [VP2A] write verse(s) with ~. **rhymed** *adj* having ~s: *~d verse.* **~·ster** /ˈraɪmstə(r)/ *n* (usu contemptuous) person who writes ~s or verses.

rhythm /ˈrɪðm/ *n* **1** [U] regular succession of weak and strong stresses, accents, sounds or movements (in speech, music, dancing, etc); regular recurrence of events, processes, etc: *the ~ of the tides,* their regular rise and fall. **2** [C] particular kind of such regular succession or recurrence. **rhyth·mic** /ˈrɪðmɪk/, **rhyth·mi·cal** /ˈrɪðmɪkl/ *adjj* marked by ~; having ~: *the ~ical tread of marching soldiers.*

rib /rɪb/ *n* [C] **1** any one of the 12 pairs of curved bones extending from the backbone round the chest to the front of the body in man ⇨ the illus at **skeleton**; corresponding bone in an animal. ***dig/poke sb in the ribs,*** poke him to draw his attention (good-naturedly) to sth or to show enjoyment of a joke. **2** (of various things like ribs) vein of a leaf; mark left on sand on the sea-shore by waves; (in a wooden boat) one of the curved pieces of timber to which planks are secured; raised line in a piece of knitting; long, narrow, raised ridge on cloth; hinged rod of an umbrella-frame. □ *vt* (**-bb-**) [VP6A] **1** supply with, mark off in, ribs: *ribbed cloth,* having rib-like marks. **2** (US, colloq or sl) tease.

rib·ald /ˈrɪbɪd/ *adj* (of a person) using indecent or irreverent language or humour; (of language, laughter, etc) coarse; mocking: *~ jests/songs.* □ *n* person who uses ~ language. **~ry** /-drɪ/ *n* [U] ~ language; coarse jesting.

rib·and /ˈrɪbənd/ *n* (old use) ribbon.

rib·bon /ˈrɪbən/ *n* **1** [C,U] (piece or length of) silk or other material woven in a long, narrow strip or band, used for ornamenting, for tying things, etc: *Her hair was tied up with a ~. She had a ~ in her hair. Typewriter ~s may be all black or black and red.* **2** [C] piece of ~ of a special design, colour, etc worn to indicate membership of an order, as a symbol of a military decoration (when medals are not worn). **3** [C] long, narrow strip: *His clothes were hanging in ~s,* were torn or worn to strips. *The sheets were torn to ~s in the machinery.* **4** (*pl*) (old use) driving-reins (for a horse-drawn carriage, etc): *take the ~s,* drive. **5** (attrib) ˈ**~-deˈvelopment** *n* (the building of) long lines of houses along main roads leading out of a large town (considered to spoil the countryside).

ri·bo·fla·vin /ˌraɪbəʊˈfleɪvɪn/ *n* [U] growth-producing factor in the vitamin B_2 complex, found in meat, milk, some vegetables and produced synthetically.

rice /raɪs/ *n* [U] (plant with) pearl-white grain used as a staple food everywhere: *polished ~,* with the husks removed; *brown ~,* unpolished ~; *ground ~,* ~ ground to a fine powder. ⇨ the illus at **cereal**. ˈ**~-paper** *n* kind of thin paper used by Chinese artists for painting on; edible kind used in cooking and for packing cakes, sweets, etc.

rich /rɪtʃ/ *adj* (**-er, -est**) **1** having much money or property: *the ~ and the poor,* ~ people and poor people. **2** (of clothes, jewels, furniture, etc) costly; splendid; luxurious. **3** ***~ in,*** producing or having much or many; abundant: *~ in minerals; an art gallery ~ in paintings by the Dutch masters.* **4** (of food) containing a large proportion of fat, oil, butter, eggs, etc: *a ~ fruit cake; a ~ diet.* **5** (of colours, sounds, etc) full; deep; mellow; strong: *the colours of the begonias; ~ tones; the ~ voice of the baritone.* **6** (colloq) highly entertaining; giving opportunities for humour: *a ~ joke; a ~ incident. That's ~!* (often ironic). **~·ly** *adv* **1** in a ~ manner: *~ly dressed.* **2** (esp) ***~ly deserved,*** thoroughly; fully: *He ~ly deserved the punishment he received.* **~·ness** *n* [U] quality or state of being ~ (but not usu in sense of **1** above).

riches /ˈrɪtʃɪz/ *n pl* wealth; being rich: *the enjoyment of ~; amass great ~.*

rick[1] /rɪk/ *n* [C] mass of hay, straw, corn, etc regularly built up (and usu thatched or otherwise covered to protect it from the rain). □ *vt* [VP6A] make (hay, etc) into a ~.

rick[2] /rɪk/ = wrick.

rick·ets /ˈrɪkɪts/ *n* (with *sing* or *pl v*) disease of childhood, marked by softening and malformation of the bones, caused by deficiency of vitamin D as found in fresh food, e g milk, butter.

rick·ety /ˈrɪkɪtɪ/ *adj* weak, esp in the joints; likely to break and collapse: *~ furniture; a ~ old cab.*

rick·shaw /ˈrɪkʃɔ/ *n* two-wheeled carriage for one or two passengers, pulled by a man.

rico·chet /ˈrɪkəʃeɪ *US:* ˌrɪkəˈʃeɪ/ *n* [U] jumping or skipping movement (of a stone, bullet, etc) after hitting the ground, a solid substance or the surface of water; [C] hit made by sth after such a jumping or skipping movement. □ *vi,vt* (-t- or -tt-) [VP6A,2A] (of a shot, etc) (cause to) rebound, skip or bound off: *The bullet ~ed.*

rid /rɪd/ *vt* (*pt* ridded or, more usu, rid, *pp* rid) [VP14] ***rid sb/sth of sb/sth,*** make free: *rid oneself of debt/lice; rid a country of bandits/a house of mice.* ***be/get rid of,*** be/become free of. *We were glad to be rid of our overcoats. These articles are difficult to get rid of,* e g of articles in a shop, difficult to sell. *How can we get rid of this unwelcome visitor,* How can we manage to make him leave?

rid·dance /ˈrɪdns/ *n* [U] (usu in ***good ~***) clearing away; state of being rid of sth unwanted or undesirable: *Their departure was a good ~,* it brought satisfaction because we wanted to be rid of them.

rid·den /ˈrɪdn/ *pp* of ride[2]. (esp in compounds) oppressed or dominated by: *ˈpriest-~; poˈlice-~.*

riddle[1] /ˈrɪdl/ *n* [C] **1** puzzling question, statement or description, intended to make a person use his wits: *ask sb a ~; know the answer to a ~.* **2** puzzling person, thing, situation, etc: *the ~ of the universe.* □ *vt* ***~ me this,*** solve this ~ (as a challenge).

riddle[2] /ˈrɪdl/ *n* [C] coarse sieve (for stones, earth, gravel, cinders etc). □ *vt* **1** [VP6A] pass (soil, ashes, corn etc) through a ~; agitate (a grate, e g in a stove) in order to force ashes, small cinders, etc, through. **2** [VP6A,14] ***~ sb/sth (with),*** make many holes in (sth), e g by firing bullets into it: *~ a ship with shot; ~ a man with bullets; ~ an argument,* refute it by bringing many facts, etc against it.

ride[1] /raɪd/ *n* [C] **1** period of riding; journey on horseback, on a bicycle, etc or in a public conveyance. Cf *go for a drive* in a privately owned car, etc: *go for a ~ before breakfast. 'Give me a ~ on your shoulders, Daddy.' It's a fivepenny ~ on a bus.* ***take sb for a ~,*** (colloq) deceive, swindle or humiliate him. **2** road or track (usu unpaved), esp one through a wood or forest for the use of persons on horseback and not normally used by vehicles.

ride[2] /raɪd/ *vi,vt* (*pt* rode /rəʊd/, *pp* ridden /ˈrɪdn/) **1** [VP2A,B,C,4A] sit on a horse, etc and be carried along; sit on a bicycle, etc and cause it to go forward: *He jumped on his horse and rode off/away. He was riding fast. He rode over to see me yesterday. Some women ~ astride and some ~ side-saddle.* ⇨ side[1](14). ***~ for a fall,*** ride recklessly; (fig) act in such a way that failure or disaster is probable. **2** [VP6A] sit on and control: *~ a horse/pony/bicycle.* **3** [VP2A,C,4A] be in, and be carried in, a cart, bus or other vehicle: *~ in a bus; ~ in/on a cart.* **4** [VP6A] compete in, on horseback, etc: *~ a race.* **5** [VP2C,3A] ***~ on,*** sit or go or be on sth, esp astride, as if on a horse: *The boy was riding on his father's shoulders.* **6** [VP15A] allow (sb) to ~(5): *Shall I ~ you on my shoulders/knees?* **7** [VP2A] go out regularly on horseback (as a pastime, for exercise, etc): *I've given up riding.* ***~ to hounds,*** go fox-hunting. **8** [VP6A] go through or over on horseback, etc: *~ the prairies/the desert.* **9** [VP2B] (of a jockey or other person) weigh when ready for riding: *He ~s 9 stone, 6 pounds.* **10** [VP2D] (of ground, etc) be in a specified condition for riding on (usu on horseback): *The heavy rain made the course ~ soft. The ground rode hard after the frost.* **11** [VP6A, 2C] float on: *a ship riding the waves;* float on water: *a ship riding at anchor;* be supported by: *an albatross riding (on) the wind. The moon was riding high,* appeared high as if floating. ***~ out a storm,*** (of a ship) come safely through it; (fig) come safely through trouble, attack, controversy, etc. ***let sth ~,*** (colloq) take no action on it; leave things to take their natural course. **12** ***~ sb down,*** (a) chase (on horseback) and catch up with. (b) direct one's horse at sb so as to let the horse knock him down: *~ down a fugitive.* **13** [VP2C] ***~ up,*** e g of an article of clothing, shift or move upwards, out of place. **14** (*pp*) **ridden,** tyrannized, dominated: *ridden by fears/prejudices; ˈpest-ridden.*

rider /ˈraɪdə(r)/ *n* **1** person who rides, esp one who rides a horse: *Miss White is no ~.* ⇨ also *diˈspatch-~* at dispatch[1](2). **2** additional observation following a statement, verdict, etc: *The jury added a ~ to their verdict recommending mercy.* **~·less** *adj* without a ~: *a ~less horse careering round the race-course.*

ridge /rɪdʒ/ *n* [C] **1** raised line where two sloping surfaces meet: *the ~ of a roof.* **ˈ~-pole** *n* horizontal pole of a long tent. **ˈ~-tile** *n* tile for the ~ of a roof. **2** long, narrow stretch of high land along the tops of a line of hills; long mountain range or watershed. **3** (in ploughed land) raised part between two furrows. □ *vt* [VP6A] make into, cover with, ~s.

ridi·cule /ˈrɪdɪkjul/ *n* [U] holding or being held up as a laughing-stock; being made fun of; derision: *pour ~ on a scheme; an object of ~.* ***hold a man up to ~,*** make fun of him. ***lay oneself open to ~,*** behave so that people are likely to make fun of one. *vt* [VP6A] make fun of; cause (sb or sth) to appear foolish: *Why do you ~ my proposal?*

rid·icu·lous /rɪˈdɪkjʊləs/ *adj* deserving to be laughed at; absurd: *You look ~ in that old hat. What a ~ idea!* **~·ly** *adv*

rid·ing[1] /ˈraɪdɪŋ/ *n* [U] (from ride[2]) **ˈ~-breeches** *n pl* used for riding on horseback. **ˈ~-habit** *n* woman's long skirt and tight-fitting coat (worn when riding a horse). **ˈ~-light/-lamp** *n* light in the rigging of a ship which is at anchor. **ˈ~-master** *n* man who teaches horse-~. **ˈ~-school** *n* one for teaching and practising horse-~.

rid·ing[2] /ˈraɪdɪŋ/ *n* (GB until 1974) one of the three administrative divisions of Yorkshire: *the North/East/West R~.* (since 1974 replaced by *Humberside* and *North/South/West Yorkshire.*)

Ries·ling /ˈrislɪŋ/ *n* dry, white wine similar to Rhine wines.

rife /raɪf/ *adj* (*pred* only) **1** wide-spread; common: *Is superstition still ~ in the country?* **2** ***~ with,*** full of: *The country was ~ with rumours of war.*

riff /rɪf/ *n* repeated phrase in jazz or pop music.

riffle /ˈrɪfl/ *vt, vi* **1** [VP6A] shuffle playing cards by holding part of the pack in each hand and releasing the edges so that they fall haphazardly into one pack again. **2** [VP6A] turn over (the pages of a book, periodical, etc) quickly. [VP3A] **~ *through sth,*** shuffle (a pack of cards); turn over quickly or casually (the pages of a newspaper, a periodical, etc).

riff-raff /ˈrɪf ræf/ *n* **the ~,** ill-behaved people of the lowest class; the rabble; disreputable persons: *Is it only the ~ who leave litter about in the parks?*

rifle¹ /ˈraɪfl/ *vt* [VP6A] cut spiral grooves in (a gun, its barrel or bore). □ *n* gun with a long ~d barrel, to be fired from the shoulder; large gun with such spiral grooves. (*pl*) units of sharpshooters: *the Royal Irish R~s.* **ˈ~-range** *n* **(a)** place where men practise shooting with ~s. **(b)** distance that a ~-bullet will carry: *within/out of ~-range.* **ˈ~-shot** *n* **(a)** = ~-range(b). **(b)** good marksman with a ~. **~-man** /-mən/ *n* (*pl* -men) soldier of a ~ regiment.

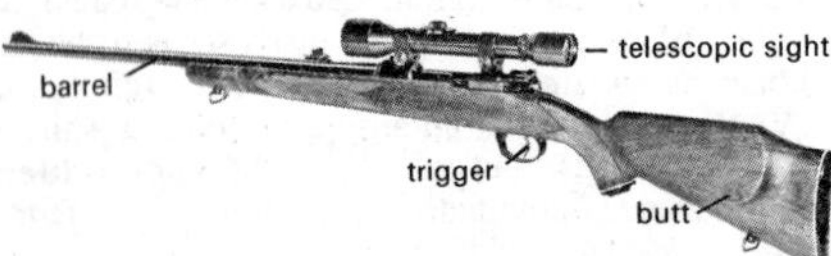

a rifle

rifle² /ˈraɪfl/ *vt* [VP6A] search thoroughly in order to steal from: *The thief ~d every drawer in the room/~d the drawers of their contents.*

rift /rɪft/ *n* [C] **1** split or crack: *a ~ in the clouds.* **ˈ~-valley** *n* steep-sided valley caused by subsidence of the earth's crust. **2** (fig) dissension (e g between two friends or friendly groups, parties, etc.

rig¹ /rɪg/ *vt, vi* (-gg-) **1** [VP6A,14,2A,C] supply (a ship) with masts, spars, rigging, sails, etc; (of a ship) be supplied with these things; prepare for sea in this way: *rig a ship with new sails. The schooner is rigging for another voyage.* **2** [VP15B] ***rig sb out (with sth),*** **(a)** provide with necessary clothes, equipment, etc. **(b)** (colloq) dress up: *She was rigged out in her best. He rigged himself out as a sailor (a tramp).* **ˈrig-out** *n* (colloq) person's clothes, etc: *What a queer rig-out!* ***rig sth up,*** **(a)** assemble or adjust parts (of an aircraft, etc). **(b)** make, put together, quickly or with any materials that may be available: *The climbers rigged up a shelter for the night on a narrow ledge. They rigged up some scaffolding for the workmen.* **(c)** = rig sth out. □ *n* [C] **1** way in which a ship's masts, sails, etc, are arranged: *the fore-and-aft rig of a schooner.* **2** equipment put together for a special purpose: *an ˈoil-rig/ˈdrilling-rig,* ⇨ oil; *a ˈtest-rig,* on which motor-vehicles are tested for fitness. **3** (colloq) style of dress; person's general appearance resulting from his clothing: *Excuse my being in working rig; I've been cleaning out the cellar.* **rig·ging** *n* [U] all the ropes, etc which support a ship's masts and sails. **rig·ger** *n* person who rigs ships, etc; (esp) one whose work is to assemble and adjust the parts of aircraft.

rig² /rɪg/ *vt* (-gg-) [VP6A] manage or control fraudulently for private profit: *rig the market,* cause prices (of stocks, shares, etc) to go up (or down) by trickery.

right¹ /raɪt/ *adj* (contrasted with *wrong*) **1** (of conduct, etc) just; morally good; required by law or duty: *Always do what is ~ and honourable. It seems only ~ to tell you that.... You were quite ~ to refuse. You were ~ in deciding not to go/were ~ in your decision.* **2** true; correct; satisfactory: *What's the ~ time? Your account of what happened is not quite ~. Your opinions are quite ~/are ~ enough. Have you got the ~* (= exact) *fare?* ***get sth ~,*** understand sth clearly, so that there is no error or misunderstanding: *Now let's get this ~ before we pass on to the next point.* ***put/set sth ~,*** restore to order, good health, a good condition, etc: *put a watch ~,* i e to the correct time. *It is not your business to put me ~,* to correct my errors. *This medicine will soon put you ~.* ***R~ you are!/R~ oh!*** (colloq or sl) used to indicate agreement to an order, request, proposal, etc. ***All ~!*** used to indicate agreement, approval, etc. **ˌ~-ˈminded** *adj* having opinions or principles based on what is ~: *All ~-minded people will agree with me when I say....* **3** most suitable; best in view of the circumstances, etc; preferable: *Are we on the ~ road? Which is the ~ way to Lydd? He is the ~ man for the job. Which is the ~ side* (i e the side meant to be seen or used) *of this cloth? Have you got it the ~ side up? He's still on the ~ side of fifty,* is still under 50 years old. ***get on the ~ side of sb,*** win his favour. **4** in good or normal condition; sound; sane: *Do you feel all ~?* ***not (quite) ~ in the/one's head,*** (colloq) not sane; foolish. ***not in one's ~ mind,*** in an abnormal mental state. ***~ as rain/as a trivet,*** (colloq) perfectly sound or healthy. **5** straight (archaic except in): *a ~ line, ~ lined.* **6** (of an angle) of 90° (i e neither acute nor obtuse): *at ~ angles/at a ~ angle.* ⇨ the illus at angle. **ˈ~-angled** *adj* having a ~ angle: *a ~-angled triangle.* **~·ly** *adv* justly; justifiably; correctly; truly: *act ~ly. R~ly or wrongly, I think the man should not be punished. She has been sacked, and ~ly so. Am I ~ly informed?* **~·ness** *n*

right² /raɪt/ *adv* **1** straight; directly: *Put it ~ in the middle. The wind was ~ in our faces.* ***~ away,*** at once, without any delay. ***~ now,*** (orig US) at this very moment. ***~ off,*** (colloq, US), = ~ away. **2** all the way (to/round, etc); completely (*off/out, etc*): *Go ~ to the end of this winding road, and then turn left. He slipped ~ to the bottom of the icy slope. There's a veranda ~ round the building. The pear was rotten ~ through. The prisoner got ~ away. He turned ~ round.* **3** justly; correctly, satisfactorily; properly: *if I remember ~.* Cf *if I am ~ly informed. Have I guessed ~ or wrong? Nothing seems to go ~ with him,* Everything he does is a failure. ***It serves him ~,*** It is what he deserves, he has been ~ly punished, etc. **4** (old or dial use) to the full; very: *We were ~ glad to hear that.... He knew ~ well that....* **ˈ~-down** *adj, adv* (dial; more usu *downright*) thorough(ly): *He's a ~-down scoundrel. You ought to be ~-down sorry. He's ~-down clever.* **5** (in certain titles) very: *The R~ Honourable...; the R~ Reverend the Bishop of....*

right³ /raɪt/ *n* **1** [U] that which is right¹(1), good, just, honourable, true, etc: *know the difference between ~ and wrong. May God defend the ~.* ***be in the ~,*** have justice and truth on one's side. **2** [U] proper authority or claim; the state of being justly entitled to sth. [C] sth to which one has a just claim; sth one may do or have by law: *He has a*

~/no ~/not much ~ to do that. *What gives you the ~ to say that?* **by ~(s),** if justice were done; justly; correctly: *The property is not mine by ~(s).* **by ~ of,** because of: *The Normans ruled England by ~ of conquest.* **in one's own ~,** because of a personal claim, qualification, etc not depending upon another person: *She's a peeress in her own ~,* i e not only by marriage. **~ of way,** (a) ~ of the general public to use a path, road, etc esp a ~ which has existed from ancient times through land that is privately owned: *Is there a ~ of way across these fields?* (b) (in road traffic) ~ to use the carriageway before others; precedence: *It's my ~ of way, so that lorry must stop or slow down until I've passed it.* **women's ~s,** (esp) of equality with men (in political, economic, social, etc affairs). ⇨ lib. **assert/stand on one's ~s,** say what one's ~s are and declare that they will not be surrendered. **3** (*pl*) true state: **set/put things to ~s,** put them in order. ⇨ right[1](2). *What are the ~s and wrongs of the case,* the true facts?

right[4] /rɑɪt/ *vt* [VP6A] put, bring or come back, into the right or an upright condition; make sth right again: *The ship ~ed herself after the big wave had passed. That fault will ~ itself,* will be corrected without help. *The driver quickly ~ed the car after it skidded.* **~ the helm,** put it amidships, i e neither to port nor to starboard.

right[5] /rɑɪt/ *adj* (contrasted with *left*) of the side of the body which is toward the east when a person faces north: *my ~ hand/leg. In Great Britain traffic keeps to the left, not the ~, side of the road. The ~ bank of a river is on the ~ side as you look towards its mouth.* **one's ~ hand/arm,** (fig) one's most reliable helper. **~ hand,** the better and more useful hand: *put one's ~ hand to the work,* work with a will. **ˋ~-hand** *adj* (to be) placed on the ~ hand: *a ~-hand glove.* **ˈ~-ˋhanded** *adj* **(a)** (of a person) using the ~ hand more, or with more ease, than the left. **(b)** (of a blow, etc) given with the ~ hand. **ˈ~-ˋhander** *n* **(a)** ~-handed person. **(b)** ~-handed blow. **ˈ~-ˋturn** *n* turn into a position at ~ angles (90°) with the original one. **ˈ~-about ˋturn/ˋface,** ~ turn continued until one is faced in the opposite direction. **send sb to the ~about,** send him away unceremoniously; dismiss him. □ *adv* to the ~ hand or side: *He looked neither ~ nor left. Eyes ~!* as a military command. *He owes money ~ and left,* owes money everywhere. *The crowd divided ~ and left.* □ *n* [U] **1** side or direction on one's ~ hand: *Take the first turning to the ~. Our troops attacked the enemy's ~,* ~ wing or flank. **2** (politics; usu **R~**) conservative or reactionary party or parties: *members of the R~.* **~·ist** /-ɪst/ *n* member of a ~ wing political party. □ *adj* of such a party: *~ist sympathizers.*

right·eous /ˋrɑɪtʃəs/ *adj* **1** doing what is morally right; obeying the law: *the ~ and the wicked,* good and bad people. **2** morally justifiable: *~ anger.* **~·ly** *adv* **~·ness** *n*

right·ful /ˋrɑɪtfl/ *adj* **1** according to law and justice: *the ~ king; the ~ owner of the land.* **2** (of actions, etc) fair; justifiable. **~ly** /-flɪ/ *adv* **~·ness** *n*

rigid /ˋrɪdʒɪd/ *adj* **1** stiff; unbending; that cannot be bent: *a ~ support for a tent; a ~ airship,* one with a ~ framework. **2** firm; strict; not changing; not to be changed: *a ~ disciplinarian; practise ~ economy.* **~·ly** *adv* **ri·gid·ity** /rɪˋdʒɪdətɪ/ *n* [U] **1** stiffness; inflexibility: *the ~ity of his religious beliefs.* **2** strictness; sternness.

rig·ma·role /ˋrɪgmərəʊl/ *n* [C] long, wandering story or statement that does not mean much; incoherent account or description.

rigor mor·tis /ˈrɑɪgɔ ˋmɔtɪs *US:* ˈrɪgər/ *n* (Lat) the stiffening of the muscles after death.

rig·or·ous /ˋrɪgərəs/ *adj* **1** stern; strict; severe: *~ discipline; a ~ search for dutiable goods.* **2** harsh; severe: *a ~ climate.* **~·ly** *adv*

rig·our (US = **rigor**) /ˋrɪgə(r)/ *n* **1** [U] sternness; strictness; strict enforcement (of rules, etc): *punish sb with the utmost ~ of the law.* **2** (often *pl*) severe conditions: *the ~s of prison life; the ~(s) of the winter in Canada,* the severe climatic conditions.

rile /rɑɪl/ *vt* [VP6A] (colloq) annoy; rouse anger in: *It ~d him that no one would believe his story.*

rill /rɪl/ *n* small stream; rivulet.

rim /rɪm/ *n* [C] circular edge of the framework of a wheel, on which the tyre is fitted; border (of steel, gold, etc) round the lenses of spectacles (hence *rimless spectacles,* having lenses without rims); edge, border or margin of sth circular: *the rim of a cup/bowl;* frame of a sieve. **ˈred-ˋrimmed** *adj* (of eyes) having red rims, e g from weeping. □ *vt* (-mm-) [VP6A] provide with a rim; be a rim for.

rime[1] /rɑɪm/ *n* (liter) hoarfrost. ⇨ hoar. □ *vt* [VP6A] cover with or as with ~.

rime[2] /rɑɪm/ *n* = rhyme.

rind /rɑɪnd/ *n* [U] hard, outside skin or covering (of some fruits, e g melons, or of bacon and cheese); [C] piece or strip of this skin; tough covering of one fruit.

rin·der·pest /ˋrɪndəpest/ *n* [U] contagious virus disease of cattle.

ring[1] /rɪŋ/ *n* [C] **1** circular band (often of gold or platinum, and set with a gem or gems) worn round a finger as an ornament, or as a token: *an enˋgagement ~; a ˋwedding ~;* similar band for other parts of the body: *an ˋear~, a ˋnose-~.* **ˋ~-finger** *n* third of the left hand. **2** circular band of any kind of material, e g metal, wood, ivory: *a ˋnapkin ~; a ˋkey-~,* one of split metal, for carrying keys on. **ˋ~-mail/-armour** *nn* = chain-armour. ⇨ chain(4). **3** circle: *a ~ of light round the moon; the ~s of a tree,* seen in concentric circles of wood when the trunk is cut across, showing the tree's age; *puff out ˋsmoke-~s* (of cigarette smoke). The men were standing in a ~. **make/run ~s round sb,** move, do things, much faster than he does. **4** combination of persons (traders, politicians, etc) working together for their own advantage, e g to get control of a market, to keep prices up or down, to control policy: *a ~ of dealers at a public auction.* **5** (ˋ**circus-)~,** circular enclosure or space for circus-riding. **ˋ~-master** *n* man who directs performances in a circus-~. **6** space for the showing of cattle, dogs, etc (at farming exhibitions, etc). **7** betting at race meetings: **the ~,** book-makers collectively. ⇨ book[1](8). **8 the ˋprize-~,** ⇨ prize[1](3). **9** (compounds) **ˋ~-leader** *n* person who leads others in a rising against authority. **ˋ~-road** *n* road round, and through the outskirts of, a large town, for the use of through traffic and designed to avoid congestion in the centre. Cf *by-pass,* a new road specially constructed. **ˋ~·worm** *n* [U] contagious disease of the skin, esp of children, in round, red patches. **ˈ~·side** *n* place near to the ring of a circus, prize-fight, etc: *have a ~side seat,* be favourably placed for seeing an event, etc. □ *vt,vi* (*pt,pp* ~ed) **1** [VP6A,15B] surround: *~ed about with enemies; ~ cattle,* hem them into one place. **2** [VP6A] put a ~ in the nose of (a bull, etc) or on the leg of (a bird, e g a homing pigeon). **3** [VP6A] (in games) toss or throw a ring or a horseshoe round, e g a mark, peg, etc; make a ring round (sth), e g with a pencil, or by shooting holes round a target. **4** [VP2A] (of a hunted fox) take a circular course.

ring[2] /rɪŋ/ *vt,vi* (*pt* rang /ræŋ/, *pp* rung /rʌŋ/) **1** [VP2A,B,C] give out a clear, musical sound as when metal vibrates: *How long has that telephone (bell) been ~ing? Start work when the bell ~s. A shot rang out,* The noise of a shot was heard. **2** [VP2D] produce a certain effect when heard: *His words rang hollow,* what he said seemed insincere. *His voice rang true. The coin rang true/false,* seemed, when tested by being thrown down, to be genuine/counterfeit. **3** [VP2A,3A] ***~ (for sb/sth),*** cause a bell to sound, as a summons, warning, etc: *She rang for the porter. She rang for the tea things to be cleared away. Did you ~, sir? Someone is ~ing at the door,* ~ing for admittance or attention. *The cyclist didn't ~.* **4** [VP6A] cause sth, esp a bell, to ~: *~ the church bells; ~ the bell for the steward; ~ a coin,* test its genuineness by throwing it down on sth and listening to the sound. ***~ a bell,*** (colloq) bring sth vaguely back to mind: *Ah! That ~s a bell!* ***~ the bell,*** (colloq) be successful in sth (from the use of a bell in machines that test strength or skill). **5** [VP3A] ***~ (with sth),*** resound; re-echo: *The children's playground rang with happy shouts. The village rang with the praises of the brave boy.* **6** [VP2C] linger in one's hearing or memory: *His last words are still ~ing in my ears.* **7** [VP2A,3A] (of the ears) be filled with a ringing or humming sound: *My ears are still ~ing.* **8** ***~ sb (up),*** get into communication with sb by telephone: *I'll ~ you (up) this evening.* (US = *call sb (up)*.) ***~ off,*** end a telephone conversation. **9** [VP6A] (of a chime of bells) announce (the hour, etc); strike the hours: *The church bell ~s the hours, but not the quarters.* **10** [VP6A,15B] give a signal by ~ing a bell, etc: *~ the knell of sth,* announce its end or downfall; *~ an alarm,* give one by ~ing bells. ***~ the curtain up/down,*** (in a theatre) give the signal for it to be raised/lowered. **11** [VP6A] sound (a peal, etc with a ~ or bells). ***~ the changes (on),*** (of church bells) ring the bells in the different orders which are possible; (fig) put or arrange things, do things, in as many different ways as possible: *Our parson ~s the changes on the same few sermons.* **12** [VP15A] announce or celebrate the beginning or end of sth by ~ing bells. ***~ out the Old (year) and ~ in the New.*** □ *n* **1** (*sing* only) resonant sound produced by a bell or piece of metal when it is struck: *This coin has a good ~.* **2** (*sing* only) loud and clear sound: *the ~ of happy voices. There was a ~ of sincerity in his promise.* **3** [C] act of ~ing; sound of a bell: *There was a ~ at the door. I'll give you a ~ this evening,* will ~ you up (by telephone). *Two ~s for the chambermaid and three ~s for the porter,* e g, formerly, in a hotel bedroom. **~er** *n* bell-ringer.

ring·let /ˈrɪŋlət/ *n* [C] small curl of hair: *She arranged her hair in ~s.*

rink /rɪŋk/ *n* [C] specially prepared sheet of ice for skating or hockey, or floor for roller-skating.

rinse /rɪns/ *vt* [VP6A,15A,B] ***~ sth out of sth, ~ sth out,*** **1** wash with clean water in order to remove unwanted substances, etc: *~ soap out of the clothes; ~ the clothes,* to get soapy water out; *~ (out) the teapot; ~ the tea-leaves out of the pot; ~ (out) the mouth,* e g while being treated by a dentist. **2** ***~ sth down,*** help (food) down with a drink: *R~ it down with a glass of beer.* □ *n* **1** act of rinsing: *Give your hair a good ~ after you've had your shampoo.* **2** solution for tinting the hair: *the blue ~ used by some elderly women.*

riot /ˈraɪət/ *n* **1** [C] violent outburst of lawlessness by the people in a district: *put down a ~ by force. R~s during the election were dealt with by the police.* **the ˈR~ Act,** act dealing with the prevention of ~s and the breaking up of disorderly crowds. ***read the R~ Act,*** **(a)** read part of this Act officially to disorderly persons after which, if they do not disperse, they can be arrested for felony. **(b)** (joc, e g of parents) give a warning that noisy and unruly behaviour must stop. **2** [U] noisy, uncontrolled behaviour (not lawless), e g by students making merry. ***run ~,*** throw off all discipline; (of plants) be out of control by growing fast and luxuriantly. **3** (*sing* only, with *indef art*) profusion; luxuriance: *The flower-beds in the park were a ~ of colour.* **4** (*sing* only) unrestrained indulgence in or display of sth: *a ~ of emotion.* **5** (colloq) occasion of wild enthusiasm (as indicating great success): *His latest play was a ~ when it was produced in New York.* □ *vi* [VP2A,B,C] **1** take part in a ~(**1,2**): *They were ~ing all night after the Boat Race.* **2** [VP3A] ***~ in,*** indulge or revel (in): *The tyrant ~ed in cruelty.* **~er** *n* person who ~s. **~·ous** /-əs/ *adj* likely to cause a ~; unruly; disorderly; running wild: *a ~ous assembly; charged with ~ous behaviour.* **~·ous·ly** *adv*

rip[1] /rɪp/ *vt,vi* (-pp-) **1** [VP6A,15A,B,22] pull, tear or cut (sth) quickly and with force (to get it off, out, open, etc): *rip open a letter; rip the cover off; rip the seams of a garment; rip a piece of cloth in two;* make a long cut or tear in: *rip a tyre,* e g on a rocky road. *My poor cat had its ear ripped open by a dog.* **ˈrip-cord** *n* cord which, when pulled during a descent, releases a parachute from its pack; cord pulled to release gas from a balloon. **2** [VP6A] saw (wood, etc) with the grain. **ˈrip-saw** *n* saw used for this. **3** [VP2A] (of material) tear; be ripped. **4** [VP2A,C] go forward, rush along. ***Let her/it rip,*** (colloq) (of a boat, car, machine, etc) allow it to go at its maximum speed. ***let things rip,*** cease to exercise control; let things take their natural course. □ *n* [C] torn place; long cut: *The rips in my tent were made by the horns of that angry bull.*

rip[2] /rɪp/ *n* **1** (colloq) loose-living, dissolute person: *He's becoming an old rip.* **2** worthless horse.

rip[3] /rɪp/ *n* stretch of rough water in the sea or an estuary.

ri·par·ian /raɪˈpeərɪən/ *adj* of, on, the bank(s) of a river or lake: *~ rights,* e g to catch fish in the river; *~ property.*

ripe /raɪp/ *adj* (-r, -st) **1** (of fruit, grain, etc) ready to be gathered and used: *~ fruit; cherries not ~ enough to eat; ~ corn; ~ lips,* red and soft like ~ fruit. **2** matured and ready to be eaten or drunk: *~ cheese/wine.* **3** fully developed: *~ judgement/*

scholarship; a person of ~ age, a mature and experienced person; *a person of ~(r)* years, past the stage of youth. **4 ~ for,** ready, fit, prepared: *~ for mischief/revolt; land that is ~ for development,* e g for building houses or factories. **~·ly** *adv* **~·ness** *n*

ripen /ˈraɪpən/ *vt,vi* [VP6A,2A] make or become ripe.

ri·poste /rɪˈpəʊst/ *n* **1** quick return thrust in fencing (after parrying). **2** quick, sharp reply or retort. □ *vi* deliver a ~.

rip·ping /ˈrɪpɪŋ/ *adj* (GB; schoolchildren's sl, now dated) splendid; enjoyable: *having a ~ time; (adv) a ~ good time.* **~·ly** *adv*

ripple /ˈrɪpl/ *n* [C] (sound of) small movement(s) on the surface of water, etc, e g made by a gentle wind, or of the rise and fall of voices or laughter: *A long ~ of laughter passed through the audience.* □ *vt,vi* [VP6A,2A] (cause to) move in ~s; (cause to) rise and fall gently: *The wheat ~d in the breeze. The breeze ~d the corn-fields. The tide ~d the sand,* caused a wavy surface on the sand.

rip-tide /ˈrɪp taɪd/ *n* tide causing strong currents and rough water.

rise[1] /raɪz/ *n* **1** small hill; upward slope: *a ~ in the ground; a cottage situated on a ~.* **2** upward progress; increase (in value, temperature, etc): *a ~ in prices/social position, etc; have a ~ in wages* (US *= raise*); *the ~ and fall of the tide.* **3** (liter) coming up (of the sun, etc): *at ~ of sun/day,* (more usu *sunrise*). **4** movement of fish to the surface of water: *not a sign of a ~. I fished two hours without getting a ~.* ***get/take a/the ~ out of sb,*** cause him to show petulance or weakness (often by good-natured teasing). **5** origin; start: *The river has/takes its ~ among the hills.* ***give ~ to,*** be the cause of; suggest: *Such conduct might give ~ to misunderstandings.* **riser** *n* **1** *an early/late ~r,* person who gets up early/late. **2** vertical part of a step, connecting two treads of a staircase.

rise[2] /raɪz/ *vi* (*pt* **rose** /rəʊz/, *pp* **risen** /ˈrɪzn/) [VP2A,B,C,3A,4A] **1** (of the sun, moon, stars) appear above the horizon: *The sun ~s in the East. Has the moon ~n yet?* ⇨ **set**[2](1). **2** get up from a lying, sitting or kneeling position: *He rose to welcome me. The wounded man fell and was too weak to ~. The horse rose on its hind legs. On rising from table...,* leaving the table at the end of the meal.... *Parliament will ~ on Thursday next,* cease to sit for business, start the recess. *The House rose at 10p m,* ended its discussions, etc. **3** get out of bed; get up (which is commoner): *He ~s very early.* **4** come to life (*again, from the dead*): *Jesus Christ rose* (*again*) *from the dead. Christ is ~n* (as an Easter greeting). *He looks as though he had ~n from the grave.* **5** go, come, up or higher; reach a high(er) level or position: *The smoke from our fire rose straight up in the still air. The river/flood, etc has ~n two feet. His voice rose in anger/excitement, etc,* became high, shrill. *Sugar has ~n a penny a pound. Prices continue to ~. The mercury/barometer/glass is rising. The bread won't ~,* The dough will not swell with the yeast. *New office blocks are rising in our town.* **ˈhigh-~** (*flats, office-blocks,* etc), having many storeys. ⇨ *skyscraper* at **sky(1)**. ***the rising generation,*** young people who are growing up. ***rising twelve,*** etc, (of a person's age) nearing the age of twelve. **6** develop greater intensity or energy: *The wind is rising. His colour rose,* He became flushed. **7** come to the surface: *The fish were rising,* coming to the surface for food. *They say a drowning man ~s three times. Bubbles rose from the bottom of the lake.* **8** become or be visible above the surroundings: *A range of hills rose on our left.* **9** reach a higher position in society; make progress (in one's profession, etc): *~ in the world; ~ to greatness; ~ from the ranks,* i e to be an officer; *a rising young politician/lawyer.* **10** develop powers equal to. ***~ to the occasion,*** prove oneself able to deal with an unexpected problem, a difficult task, etc. **11** slope upwards: *rising ground.* **12** have as a starting-point: *Where does the Nile ~? The quarrel rose from a mere trifle.* **13** ***~ against,*** rebel (against the government, etc). **ris·ing** *n* (esp) armed outbreak; rebellion.

ris·ible /ˈrɪzəbl/ *adj* of laughing and laughter; inclined to laugh: *the ~ faculty.* **risi·bil·ity** /ˈrɪzəˈbɪlətɪ/ *n* [U] disposition to laugh; (*pl;* **-ties**) (old use) the ~ faculties.

risk /rɪsk/ *n* **1** [C,U] (instance of) possibility or chance of meeting danger, suffering loss, injury, etc: *There's no/not much ~ of your catching cold if you wrap up well.* ***run/take ~s/a ~,*** put oneself in a position where there is ~: *She's too sensible to take ~s when she's driving. To succeed in business one must be prepared to take ~s.* ***run/take the ~ of doing sth,*** do sth which may involve ~: *We'll take the ~ of being late. He was ready to run the ~ of being taken prisoner by the enemy.* ***at the ~ of/at ~ to,*** with the possibility of loss, etc: *He was determined to get there even at the ~ of his life.* ***at ~,*** threatened by uncertainties (such as failure, loss, etc): *Is the Government's income policy seriously at ~?* ***at one's own ~,*** accepting responsibility, agreeing to make no claims, for loss, injury, etc. ***at owner's ~,*** (of goods sent by rail, etc) the owner to bear any loss there may be. **2** [C] (insurance) amount for which sb or sth is insured; the person or thing insured. *He's a good/poor ~.* ⇨ also *security ~* at **security**. □ *vt* **1** [VP6A] expose to ~; *~ one's health/fortune/neck* (i e life), *etc.* **2** [VP6A,D] take the chances of: *~ failure. We must ~ getting caught in a storm.* **risky** *adj* (**-ier, -iest**) **1** full of ~: *a ~y undertaking.* **2** = risqué. **~·ily** /-əlɪ/ *adv* **~i·ness** *n*

ri·sotto /rɪˈzotəʊ/ *n* [C] dish of rice cooked with butter, cheese, onions, etc.

ris·qué /ˈriskeɪ *US:* rɪˈskeɪ/ *adj* (of a story, remark, situation in a drama, etc) likely to offend against propriety; on the borderline of indecency.

ris·sole /ˈrɪsəʊl/ *n* [C] small ball of minced meat, fish, etc mixed with potato, eggs, breadcrumbs, etc and fried.

rite /raɪt/ *n* [C] act or ceremony (esp in religious services): *ˈburial ~s; ~s of baptism; inˈitiˈation ~s. He died after receiving the ~s of the church,* the Holy Sacrament.

rit·ual /ˈrɪtʃʊəl/ *n* [U] all the rites or forms connected with a ceremony; way of conducting a religious service: *the ~ of the Catholic Church;* [C] particular form of ~; any procedure regularly followed, as if it were a ~: *He went through the ~ of cutting and lighting his cigar slowly and carefully.* (*pl*) ceremonial observances. □ *adj* of religious rites; done as a rite: *~ laws; the ~ dances of an African tribe.* **~·ism** /-ɪzm/ *n* [U] fondness for, insistence upon, ~; study of ~. **~·ist** /-ɪst/ *n* person who has expert knowledge of ~ practices and religious rites; person who supports strict observance of ~. **~·is·tic** /ˈrɪtʃʊəˋlɪstɪk/ *adj* relating to ~ism and ~ists.

ritzy /ˈrɪtsɪ/ *adj* (sl) luxurious; elegant.

ri·val /ˋrɑɪvl/ *n* person who competes with another (because he wants the same thing, or to be or do better than the other): *ˋbusiness ~s; ~s in love;* (attrib) *~ business firms.* □ *vt* (-ll-, US also -l-) be a ~ of; claim to be (almost) as good as: *Cricket cannot ~ football in excitement.* **~ry** /ˋrɑɪvlrɪ/ *n* [C,U] (*pl* -ries) (instance of) being ~s; competition: *enter into ~ry with other shops; friendly ~ry between two schools,* e g to see which can get more scholarships to the universities; *the rivalries between political parties.*

rive /rɑɪv/ *vt,vi* (*pt* ~d, *pp* riven /ˋrɪvn/) [VP6A, 15A,B] break or tear away violently; split: *~ off a branch; trees riven by lightning;* (fig) *a heart riven by grief.*

river /ˋrɪvə(r)/ *n* [C] **1** natural stream of water flowing in a channel to the sea or to a lake, etc or joining another ~: *the R~ Thames.* ***sell sb down the ~,*** (fig) betray him. **2** (attrib) **ˋ~-basin** *n* area drained by a ~ and its tributaries. **ˋ~-bed** *n* ground over which a ~ flows in its channel **ˋ~-side** *n* ground along a ~ bank: *a ~side villa.* **3** great flow: *a ~ of lava; ~s of blood,* great bloodshed (in war).

rivet /ˋrɪvɪt/ *n* [C] metal pin or bolt for fastening metal plates (e g in a ship's sides), the plain end being hammered flat to prevent slipping. □ *vt* [VP6A,15A,B] **1** fasten with a ~ or ~s; flatten (the end of a bolt) to make it secure. **2** fix or concentrate (one's eyes, attention) on: *He ~ed his eyes on the scene.* **3** take up, secure (attention, etc): *The scene ~ed our attention.*

Rivi·era /ˈrɪvɪˋeərə/ *n* **the ~,** stretch of the Mediterranean coast (of France and Italy), used as a holiday resort; similar stretch of coast elsewhere: *the Cornish ~,* in Cornwall, England.

rivu·let /ˋrɪvjʊlət/ *n* small stream.

roach[1] /rəʊtʃ/ *n* (*pl* unchanged) fresh-water fish of the carp family.

roach[2] /rəʊtʃ/ *n* (*pl* ~es) (colloq) = **cockroach**.

road /rəʊd/ *n* [C] **1** specially prepared way, publicly or privately owned, between places for the use of pedestrians, riders, vehicles, etc: *main and subsidiary ~s;* (attrib) *ˋ~ junctions; a ˋ~ map of Great Britain* (Cf a *street* map of London); *ˋ~ accidents; a campaign for ~ safety,* for preventing ~ accidents. *How long were you on the ~,* How long did your journey take? *ˋR~ works in progress,* ~s under construction or repair. ***on the ~,*** travelling (e g as a commercial traveller or a vagrant). ***take the ~,*** start a journey. ***take to the ~,*** become a tramp; (old use, e g 18th c) become a highwayman. ***rules of the ~,*** custom which regulates the side to be taken by vehicles, ships, etc when meeting or passing each other. **2** (compounds) **ˋ~-bed** *n* foundation of rock, stones, etc on which the surface of a ~ is laid. **ˋ~-block** *n* barricade built across a ~ to stop or slow down traffic (e g by police to catch an escaped prisoner or by military authorities during a period of political disturbances). **ˋ~-book** *n* book describing the ~s of a country, with itineraries (for tourists, etc). **ˋ~ fund,** (GB) fund (from taxation of vehicles, petrol, etc) for construction and maintenance of ~s. **ˋ~ fund licence,** licence to use a motor-vehicle on public ~s. **ˋ~-hog** *n* motorist who is reckless and inconsiderate of others. **ˋ~-house** *n* building(s) on a main ~, often one with facilities for meals, dancing, a swimming-pool, etc used by people who travel by car. **ˋ~·man** /-mæn/, **ˋ~·mender** *nn* man who repairs ~s. **ˋ~-metal** *n* stone used for making and repairing ~s. **ˋ~-sense** *n* capacity for intelligent behaviour on ~s, e g the avoidance of accidents: *Harry/Harry's dog has no ~ sense.* **ˋ~·side** *n* bordering of a ~: (attrib) *~side flowers/inns.* **ˋ~·way** *n* (usu with *def art*) central part used by wheeled traffic (contrasted with the footpath, etc): *Dogs should be kept off the ~way.* **ˋ~·worthy** *adj* (of a motor-vehicle, etc) fit for use on the ~s. **3** one's way or route: *You're in the/my ~,* in my way, obstructing me. **4** ***~ to,*** way of getting: *Is excessive drinking the ~ to ruin? There's no royal ~ to learning,* no easy way, no way without working hard. **5** (in proper names) **(a)** (with *def art*) name of a ~ leading to the town, etc named: *the Oxford R~,* leading to Oxford; *the Great West R~,* from London to the West of England. **(b)** (without *def art,* usu abbr to **Rd**) street of buildings: *35 York Rd, London, S W.* **6** (usu *pl*) stretch of water near the shore in which ships can ride at anchor: *anchored in the ~s.* **7** (US) = railway. **~·less** *adj* having no ~s. **ˋ~·stead** /-sted/ *n* = road(6).

road·ster /ˋrəʊdstə(r)/ *n* [C] (dated) open motor-car, usu for two persons.

roam /rəʊm/ *vi,vt* [VP2A,C,6A] walk or travel without any definite aim or destination over or through (a country, etc): *go ~ing; ~ about the world; ~ the seas; settle down after years of ~ing.*

roan[1] /rəʊn/ *adj* (of animals) with a coat of a mixed colour, esp brown with white or grey hairs in it. □ *n* ~ horse or cow.

roan[2] /rəʊn/ *n* [U] soft sheepskin leather sometimes used for binding books.

roar /rɔ(r)/ *n* [C] loud, deep sound as of a lion, of thunder, of a person in pain, etc: *the ~s of a tiger; the ~ of the sea/of waves breaking on the rocks; the ~ of London's traffic; with a ~ of rage; ~s of laughter; set the table/room in a ~,* cause everyone to laugh loudly. □ *vt,vi* **1** [VP2A,C,3A] make such loud, deep sounds: *lions ~ing in the distance. Several lorries ~ed past; ~ with laughter/pain/rage; ~ for mercy.* **2** [VP6A,15A] ***~ sth out,*** say, sing, loudly: *~ out an order; ~ out a drinking song.* **3** [VP22,15A] *~ oneself hoarse,* make oneself hoarse by ~ing. ***~ sb down,*** ~ in order to drown the words of a speaker so that he has to give up. **~·ing** *adj* **1** noisy; rough. **2** stormy: *a ~ing night; the ~ing forties,* part of the Atlantic between 40° and 50° N latitude, often very stormy. **3** brisk; healthy: *do a ~ing trade; be in ~ing health.* □ *adv* extremely: *~ing drunk.*

roast /rəʊst/ *vt,vi* [VP6A,2A] (of meat, potatoes, etc) cook, be cooked, in a hot oven, or over or in front of a hot fire, e g on a turnspit, the meat, etc being basted periodically with the fat and juices that come out: *~ a joint. The meat was ~ing in the oven. You've made a fire fit to ~ an ox,* a very large, hot fire. **2** heat, be heated: *~ coffee-beans.* **3** expose for warmth to heat of some kind: *~ oneself in front of the fire; lie in the sun and ~.* □ *attrib adj* that has been ~ed: *~ beef/pork.* □ *n* **1** [C] joint of ~ed meat; [U] slices from such a joint:

cold ~ *on Monday.* **2** operation of ~ing: *give sth a good* ~. **~er** *n* kind of oven for ~ing; apparatus for ~ing coffee-beans; article of food, e g a chicken, sucking pig, suitable for ~ing. **~·ing** *n* (from the dated use of ~ meaning criticize harshly) ***give sb a good ~ing,*** (fig) scold or ridicule him harshly.

rob /rob/ *vt* (-bb-) [VP6A,14] ***rob sb (of sth),*** **1** deprive (sb) of his property; take property from (a place) unlawfully (and often by force): *I was robbed of my watch.* Cf I had my watch *stolen. The bank was robbed last night. The village boys rob my orchard.* Cf They *steal* apples from my orchard. **2** deprive a person of (what is due to him, etc): *be robbed of the rewards of one's labour.* **rob·ber** *n* person who robs; thief. **rob·bery** /ˈrobərɪ/ *n* [C,U] (*pl* **-ries**) (instance of) robbing: *robbery with violence; three robberies in one week.* ***ˈdaylight ˋrobbery,*** (colloq) charging of excessive prices: *20p for a cup of coffee is daylight robbery!*

robe /rəʊb/ *n* [C] **1** long, loose outer garment: *a ˋbath*~; (US) dressing-gown. **2** (often *pl*) long, loose garment worn as a sign of rank or office: *the ˈCoroˋnation* ~*s,* of a king or queen; *magistrates/judges in their black* ~*s.* □ *vt* [VP6A,14] put a ~ or ~s on: *professors* ~*d in their bright-coloured gowns;* ~*d in the scarlet of a cardinal.*

robin /ˈrobɪn/ *n* **1** small, brownish bird with red breast-feathers (also called **ˈ~ ˋredbreast**). ⇨ the illus at bird. **2** (name given to kinds of) small bird outside the British Isles (e g the American ~, a redbreasted thrush). **ˈR~ ˋGoodfellow** *n* type of mischievous but good-natured goblin or elf in English folklore (also called *Puck*).

ro·bot /ˈrəʊbot/ *n* [C] mechanism made to act like a man; machine-like person.

ro·bust /rəʊˋbʌst/ *adj* vigorous; healthy: *a* ~ *young man; a* ~ *appetite.* **~·ly** *adv* **~·ness** *n*

roc /rok/ *n* gigantic bird of Eastern tales.

rock¹ /rok/ *n* **1** [U] solid stony part of the earth's crust: *a house built upon* ~. ⇨ *bed rock* at bed¹(4). **2** [C,U] mass of ~ standing out from the earth's surface or from the sea. ***as firm/solid as a ~,*** immovable; (fig) (of persons) sound; dependable. ***on the ~s,*** (of a ship) wrecked on ~s; (fig, of a person) very short of money; (of a marriage) likely to end in divorce or separation. ***see ~s ahead,*** see danger of shipwreck (or fig, any kind of danger). **the R~ of Ages**, Jesus Christ. **3** [C] large, detached stone or boulder: ~*s rolling down the side of a mountain;* (US) = stone¹(2). **4** [U] (GB) kind of hard, sticky sweet, usu made in long cylindrical pieces: *a stick of* ~*; almond* ~. **5** ***on the ~s,*** (US) (of whisky, etc) served on ice-cubes without water. **6** (compounds) **ˈ~-ˋbottom** *n* [U] lowest point: *Prices have reached* ~*-bottom;* (attrib) ~*-bottom prices.* **ˋ~-cake** *n* [C] small cake or bun with a hard, rough surface. **ˋ~-climbing** *n* the climbing of masses of ~ on mountain-sides (with the help of ropes, etc). **ˋ~-crystal** *n* pure natural transparent quartz. **ˋ~-garden** *n* artificial or natural bank or mound with ~s and stones and ~-plants growing among them. **ˋ~-plant** *n* kinds of plant found growing among ~s, esp on mountains and cultivated in ~-gardens, etc. **ˈ~-ˋsalmon** *n* (trade name for) dogfish. **ˋ~-salt** *n* common salt as found in mines in crystal form. **~·ery** /ˈrokərɪ/ *n* [C] (*pl* **-ries**) = ~-garden.

rock² /rok/ *vt,vi* [VP6A,15A,2A] (cause to) sway or swing backwards and forwards, or from side to side: ~ *a baby to sleep;* ~ *a baby in its cradle. The town was* ~*ed by an earthquake. He sat* ~*ing (himself) in his chair. Our boat was* ~*ed by/was* ~*ed on the waves.* **~ *the boat,*** (fig) do sth that upsets the smooth progress of an undertaking, etc. **ˋ~·ing-chair** *n* one fitted with rockers on which it rests. **ˋ~·ing-horse** *n* wooden horse with rockers for a child to ride on. **~er** *n* **1** one of the curved pieces of wood on which a ~ing-chair or ~ing-horse rests. **2** (US) ~ing-chair. **3** (GB, 1960's) member of a teenage gang, wearing leather jackets and riding motor-bikes. **4** ***off one's ~er,*** (sl) crazy; out of one's mind.

rock³ /rok/ *n* (also **~-'n-roll**) highly rhythmic popular music for dancing, played on electric guitars. □ *vi* dance to this music.

rock-'n-roll /ˈrok ən ˋrəʊl/ *n* ⇨ rock³.

rocket /ˈrokɪt/ *n* **1** [C] tube-shaped case filled with fast-burning material, which launches itself into the air (as a firework, as a signal of distress, or as a self-propelled projectile or missile; also used to launch an aircraft or spacecraft or, attached to an aircraft, to give it higher speed and range): ~ *propulsion;* ~*-propelled.* ⇨ also retro~. **ˋ~-base** *n* military base for ~ missiles. **ˋ~-range** *n* area used for experiments with missiles propelled by ~s. **2** (colloq) severe scolding: *get/give sb a* ~. □ *vi* [VP2A] go up fast like a ~: (colloq) *Prices* ~*ed after the war.* **~ry** /-trɪ/ *n* [U] (art or science of) using ~s for projectiles, space missiles, etc.

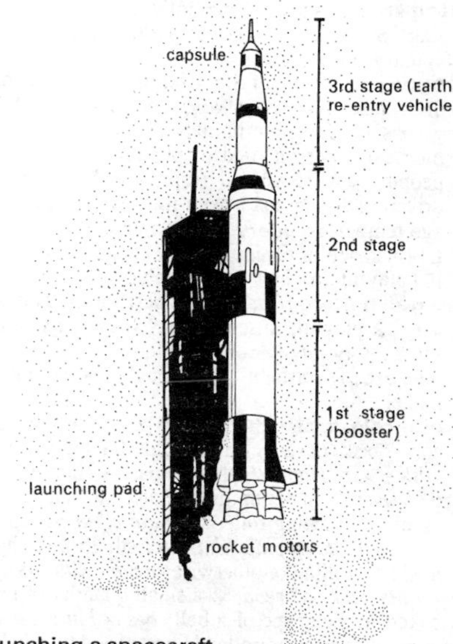

launching a spacecraft

rocky /ˈrokɪ/ *adj* (**-ier, -iest**) **1** of rock, full of or abounding in rocks; hard like rock: *a* ~ *road;* ~ *soil.* **2** (colloq) shaky; unsteady: *The table is rather* ~. *His business is very* ~.

ro·coco /rəˋkəʊkəʊ/ *adj* (of furniture, architecture, etc) with much elaborate ornament (with scrolls, foliage, etc) as in France and Italy in the late 17th and 18th cc.

rod /rod/ *n* **1** thin, straight piece of wood or metal:

ˋcurtain-rods; a ˋfishing-rod; fishing with rod and line. **2** stick used for punishing. ***make a rod for one's own back,*** prepare trouble for oneself. ***spare the rod and spoil the child,*** (prov) A child who is not punished will become undisciplined and unruly. ***have a rod in pickle for sb,*** be saving up severe punishment for him when the opportunity comes. **3** (US, sl) revolver. **4** measure of length equal to 5½ yds or 5·03 metres (also called *pole* or *perch*). **5** metal bar; shaft, etc: *ˋpiston-rods.*

rode /rəʊd/ *pt* of ride².

ro·dent /ˈrəʊdnt/ *n* animal, e g *a rat, rabbit, squirrel* or *beaver,* which gnaws things with its strong teeth specially adapted for this purpose.

ro·deo /rəʊˋdeɪəʊ *US:* ˋrəʊdɪəʊ/ *n* (*pl* -deos /-dɪəʊz/) [C] **1** (on the plains of the western US) rounding up of cattle. **2** contest of skill in lassoing cattle, riding untamed horses, etc.

rodo·mon·tade /ˈrəʊdəmonˋtɑd/ *n* [U] (formal) boastful, bragging talk.

roe¹ /rəʊ/ *n* [C,U] (mass of) eggs or sperm in a fish: *salted cod's-roe for Friday's supper.*

roe² /rəʊ/ *n* (*pl* roes or, collectively, roe) small kind of European and Asiatic deer. **ˋroe·buck** *n* male roe.

Roent·gen /ˈrontjən *US:* ˋrentgən/ ⇨ X-rays.

ro·ga·tion /rəʊˋgeɪʃn/ *n* (usu *pl*) litany of the saints chanted on the three days before Ascension Day: *R~ week,* the week including these days; *R~ Sunday,* the Sunday before Ascension Day.

roger /ˈrodʒə(r)/ *int* (in radio communication) message heard and understood.

Rog·er /ˈrodʒə(r)/ *n* **the jolly ~,** pirates' black flag. ***Sir ~ de Coverley*** /sɜ ˈrodʒə də ˋkʌvəlɪ/, country-dance and tune.

rogue /rəʊg/ *n* [C] **1** (old use) vagabond. **2** scoundrel; rascal. **~'s gallery,** collection of photographs of known criminals. **3** (playfully or humorously) person fond of playing tricks, teasing people. **4** wild animal (esp **ˈ~-ˋelephant**) one driven or living apart from the herd and of a savage temper. **ro·guery** /ˈrəʊgərɪ/ *n* (*pl* -ries) **1** [C, U] (instance or example of the) conduct of a ~. **2** [U] playful mischief; (*pl*) mischievous acts.

ro·guish /ˈrəʊgɪʃ/ *adj* **1** dishonest; of the nature of a ~. **2** playful; mischievous: *~ eyes; as ~ as a kitten.* **~·ly** *adv* **~·ness** *n*

roist·erer /ˈrɔɪstərə(r)/ *n* rough, noisy merry-maker.

role, rôle /rəʊl/ *n* [C] actor's part in a play; person's task or duty in an undertaking: *play the ˋtitle-~ in 'Hamlet',* play the part of Hamlet.

roll¹ /rəʊl/ *n* **1** sth made into the shape of a cylinder by being rolled: *a ~ of cloth/newsprint/carpet/photographic film, etc;* sth in this shape, made by rolling or otherwise: *a man with ~s of fat on his neck; a bread ~,* a small quantity of bread baked in the shape of a ball; *~s of butter; a sausage ~,* a sausage rolled in pastry and then baked. **ˈ~-top ˋdesk** *n* desk with a flexible cover that slides back into a compartment at the top. **2** turned-back edge: *a ˈ~-ˋcollar,* large collar made by turning back the edge of the material. **3** rolling movement: *The slow, steady ~ of the ship made us sick. He walks with a nautical ~,* like a sailor. *The young foal was enjoying a ~ on the grass.* **4** official list or record, esp of names. ***call the ~,*** read the names (to check who is present and who absent). Hence, **ˋ~-call** *n* calling of names. **ˈ~ of ˋhonour,** list of those who have died for their country in war. ***strike off the ~s,*** take (a solicitor's name) off the list of those who have the right to practise, e g when a solicitor has been proved guilty of dishonesty. **5** rolling sound: *the distant ~ of thunder/drums.*

roll² /rəʊl/ *vt,vi* (For special uses with *adverbial particles* and *preps,* ⇨ 11 below.) **1** [VP6A,15A, B,2A,C] (cause to) move along on wheels or by turning over and over: *The man ~ed the barrel into the yard. Rocks and stones were ~ing down the hillside. The coin fell and ~ed under the table. The bicycle hit me and sent me ~ing/~ed me over. A big coach ~ed up to* (= stopped at) *the inn. The child was ~ing a hoop. He ~ed* (= wrapped by turning over) *himself* (*up*) *in the blanket.* **2** [VP6A,12B,13B] cause to revolve between two surfaces; make (sth) by doing this; make into the shape of a ball or a cylinder: *Please ~ me a cigarette/~ a cigarette for me. R~ the string/wool into a ball. R~ up the carpet/that map on the wall. He ~ed up* (= furled) *his umbrella.* **3** [VP2C] come or go in some direction: *The clouds ~ed away as the sun rose higher. The years ~ed on/by,* passed. *The tears were ~ing* (= flowing) *down her cheeks.* **4** [VP2A,C] turn about in various directions: *a porpoise ~ing in the water.* **5** [VP6A,15B,22] make or become flat, level or smooth by pressing with a ~ing cylinder of wood, metal, etc or by passing between two such cylinders: *~ a lawn/a road surface; ~ sth flat. This dough ~s well,* is of the sort that one can ~ easily. **~ sth out,** flatten it by ~ing: *~ out pastry.* ⇨ ~ing-pin in 10 below. **~ed gold,** thin coating of gold on the surface of another metal, applied by ~ing. **6** [VP2A,B,C] (cause to) sway or move from side to side; walk with a side-to-side movement: *The ship was ~ing heavily. We ~ed and pitched for two days after leaving Lisbon. Some sailors have a ~ing gait. The drunken man ~ed up to me.* **7** [VP2A] (of surfaces) have long slopes that rise and fall: *miles and miles of ~ing country; a ~ing plain.* **8** [VP2A,C] move with a rise and fall; be carried with rise-and-fall motion: *The waves ~ed in to the beach.* **9** [VP2A,C,6A, 15A,B] make, utter, be uttered with, long, deep, vibrating or echoing sounds: *The thunder ~ed in the distance. The drums ~ed. He ~ed out his words/song, etc.* **~ one's r's,** utter them with the tongue making a rapid succession of taps against the palate. **10** [VP2A,C,14] (of the eyes) (cause to) move from side to side, change direction: *His eyes ~ed strangely at me. Don't ~ your eyes at me, woman!* **~·ing** *n* (compounds) **ˋ~-ing-mill** *n* mill where metal is ~ed out into sheets, bars, etc. **ˋ~-ing-pin** *n* cylinder of wood, glass, etc usu about a foot long, for ~ing out dough, etc. **ˋ~-ing-stock** *n* railway's coaches, wagons, etc; all the stock that is on wheels. **11** [VP2C,15B] (special uses with *adverbial particles* and *preps*):

roll sth back, turn or force back, e g enemy forces.

roll in, come, arrive, in large numbers or quantities: *Offers of help are ~ing in.* ***be ˋ~ing in,*** **(a)** have large quantities of: *He's ~ing in money.* **(b)** be living in: *~ing in luxury.*

roll on, **(a)** be capable of being put on by ~ing. **(b)** (of time) pass steadily: *Time ~ed on.* **(c)** (of time, chiefly *imper*) come soon: *R~ on the day when I retire from this dull work!* ***~ sth on,*** put on by ~ing over a part of the body: *She ~ed her stockings on.* ˋ~-**on** *n* (woman's) elastic foundation garment ~ed on to the hips.

roll up, arrive; join a group: *Two or three latecomers ~ed up.* ***R~ up! R~ up!,*** used as an invitation to join others, e g possible customers at a street stall. ***~ sth up,*** (mil) drive the flank of (an enemy line) back and round.

roller /ˋrəʊlə(r)/ *n* [C] **1** cylinder-shaped object of wood, metal, rubber, etc, usu part of a machine, for pressing, smoothing, crushing, printing, etc: *a* ˋ*garden-~,* for use on a lawn; *the ~s of a mangle,* (between which articles are passed to press out water); *a* ˋ*road-~,* used for making roads even by crushing rock, etc. **2** cylinder of wood, metal, etc placed beneath an object to make movement easy, or round which sth may be rolled easily: *a* ˋ*~-blind,* on which a window blind (US = *shade*) is rolled; *a* ˋ*~-towel,* an endless towel on a ~. ˋ**~-skates** *n pl* pair of skates, with small wheels for use on a smooth surface. **3** ˋ**~ bandage,** long surgical bandage rolled up for convenience before being applied to a limb, etc. **4** long, swelling wave.

rol·lick·ing /ˋrolɪkɪŋ/ *adj* noisy, jolly and gay: *have a ~ time.*

roly-poly /ˈrəʊlɪ ˋpəʊlɪ/ *n* **1** (GB) (also *~ pudding)* pudding made of paste spread with jam, etc formed into a roll and boiled. **2** (colloq) short, plump child.

Ro·maic /rəʊˋmeɪɪk/ *adj, n* (of, in) modern vernacular Greek (more usu called *demotic*).

Ro·man /ˋrəʊmən/ *adj* **1** of Rome, esp ancient Rome: *the ~ Empire.* **2** (small *r*) *~ numerals,* ⇨ App 4. *~ letters/type,* the plain, upright kind, not italic. **3 R~,** of the Rome of the Popes, esp = Roman Catholic: *the ~ rite* (contrasted with *Protestant*). □ *n* **1** citizen of ancient Rome; (*pl*) Christians of ancient Rome: *the Epistle to the ~s* (in the New Testament). **2** Roman Catholic.

ro·mance /rəˋmæns/ *n* **1** [C] story or novel of adventure; love story, esp one in which the events are quite unlike real life; [U] class of literature consisting of such stories. **2 R~,** medieval story, usu in verse, relating the adventures of some hero of chivalry. **3** [C] real experience, esp a love-affair, considered to be remarkable or worth description: *My first meeting with her was quite a ~.* **4** [U] mental tendency which welcomes stories of the marvellous, etc; the qualities characteristic of stories of life and adventure: *travel abroad in search of ~. There was an air of ~ about the old inn.* **5** [C,U] exaggerated description; picturesque falsehood. □ *vi* [VP2A] (more usu *romanticize*) exaggerate by adding interesting or attractive details when telling a story, recounting events, etc.

Ro·mance /rəˋmæns/ *adj* **~ languages,** French, Italian, Spanish, Portuguese, Rumanian and others developed from Latin.

Ro·man·esque /ˈrəʊməˋnesk/ *n* [U] style of architecture, with round arches and thick walls (in Europe between the classical and the Gothic periods).

ro·man·tic /rəˋmæntɪk/ *adj* **1** (of persons) having ideas, feelings, etc remote from experience and real life given to romance(**1,4**); visionary: *a ~ girl.* **2** of, like, suggesting, romance: *~ scenes/adventures/tales/situations; a ~ old castle.* **3** (in art, literature and music) marked by feeling rather than by intellect; preferring grandeur, passion, informal beauty, to order and proportion (opp of *classic* and *classical*): *the ~ poets,* e g Shelley, Keats. □ *n* **1** person with ~(**3**) ideals. **2** (*pl*) ~ ideas; extravagantly visionary feelings, expressions, etc. **ro·man·ti·cally** /-klɪ/ *adv* **ro·man·ti·cism** /-tɪsɪzm/ *n* [U] ~ tendency in literature, art and music (contrasted with *realism* and *classicism*); ~ spirit; quality of allowing full play to the imagination. **ro·man·ti·cist** /-tɪsɪst/ *n* follower of romanticism in literature or art, e g Wordsworth. **ro·man·ti·cize** /-tɪsaɪz/ *vt,vi* [VP6A,2A] treat in a ~ way; make ~; use a ~ style in writing, etc; be ~.

Rom·any /ˋromənɪ/ *n* (*pl* -nies) **1** [C] gipsy. **2** [U] language of the gipsies. □ *adj* gipsy.

Rom·ish /ˋrəʊmɪʃ/ *adj* (usu disparaging) of the Roman Catholic Church.

romp /romp/ *vi* [VP2A,C] **1** (esp of children) play about, esp running, jumping and being rather rough. **2** win, succeed, quickly or without apparent effort: (in a horse-race) *The favourite ~ed home,* won easily. *John just ~s through his examinations,* passes them easily. □ *n* [C] child fond of ~ing; period of ~ing: *have a ~; a game of ~s.* **~er** *n* (*sing* or *pl*) loose-fitting garment worn by a child: *a pair of ~ers; a* ˋ*~er suit.*

ron·deau /ˋrondəʊ/, **ron·del** /ˋrondl/ *nn* poem of thirteen or ten lines with two rhymes throughout and the opening words used twice as a refrain.

rondo /ˋrondəʊ/ *n* (*pl* -dos /-dəʊz/) piece of music in which the principal theme returns from time to time.

Ro·neo /ˋrəʊnɪəʊ/ *n* (P) machine that duplicates letters, circulars, etc. □ *vt* duplicate on a ~ machine.

Rönt·gen /ˋrontjən *US:* ˋrentgən/ **~ rays** *n pl* = X-rays.

rood /rud/ *n* **1** (old use) ˋ**~(-tree)** cross on which Jesus was put to death. **2** crucifix, esp one raised on the middle of a wooden or stone carved screen (*a* ˋ*~-screen*) separating the nave and choir of a church. **3** (GB) measure of land, one-fourth of an acre.

roof /ruf/ *n* **1** top covering of a building, tent, bus, car, etc: *How can you live under the same ~ as that woman,* in the same building? ***raise the ~,*** (colloq) create an uproar; make a great noise (indoors). ˋ**~-garden** *n* garden on the flat ~ of a building. ˋ**~-tree** *n* ridge-pole of a ~. **2** (fig) *the ~ of heaven,* the sky: *the ~ of the world,* a high mountain range; *the ~ of the mouth,* the palate. □ *vt* (*pp* ~ed /ruft/) [VP6A,15A,B] supply with a ~; be a ~ for: *a shed ~ed over with strips of bark.* **~·less** *adj* having no ~; (fig, of persons) homeless; lacking shelter. **~·ing** *n* (also ˋ*~ing material*) material used for ~s (e g slates, shingles).

rook[1] /rʊk/ *n* large black bird like a crow. **~·ery** /-ərɪ/ *n* (*pl* -ries) **1** place (a group of trees) where many ~s have their nests; colony of ~s. **2** colony of penguins or seals.

rook[2] /rʊk/ *n* person who makes money by cheating at dice and cards, playing with inexperienced gamblers. □ *vt* [VP6A] win money from (sb) at cards, etc by cheating; swindle; charge (a customer) a ridiculously high price.

rook[3] /rʊk/ *n* chess piece (also called a *castle*). ⇨ the illus at **chess**.

rookie /ˋrʊkɪ/ *n* (US army sl) new recruit.

room /rʊm *US:* rum/ *n* **1** [C] part of a house or other buildings enclosed by walls or partitions, floor and ceiling. **-roomed** /rʊmd *US:* rumd/ *adj*: *a six-∼ed house*, having six ∼s. **2** (*pl*) set of ∼s occupied by a person or family; apartments: *Come and see me in my ∼s one evening*. ˈ**∼-mate** *n* one of two or more persons sharing a ∼ or apartment. **3** [U] **∼ *(for sb/sth/to do sth)*,** space that is or might be occupied, or that is enough for a purpose: *Is there ∼ for me in the car? This table takes up too much ∼. There was ∼ in the bus to stand but not to sit. Standing ∼ only!* e g in a bus, theatre. *Can you make ∼ on that shelf for some more books? There's no ∼ for doubt.* **4** [U] scope; opportunity: *There's ∼ for improvement in your work*, It is not as good as it could be. □ *vi* [VP2C] (US) lodge; occupy a ∼ or ∼s: *He's ∼ing with my friend Smith.* ˈ**∼ing house,** (US) building where a number of independent ∼s can be rented (usu without service). **∼er** *n* (US) person who lives in a rented ∼ in sb else's house; lodger. **∼ful** /-fʊl/ *n* amount (of furniture, etc), number of persons, that fills a ∼. **roomy** *adj* (-ier, -iest) having plenty of space: *a ∼y cabin; a ∼y raincoat,* one that is loose-fitting. **∼ily** /-əlɪ/ *adv*

roost /rust/ *n* [C] branch, pole, etc on which a bird rests, esp one for hens to sleep or rest on; hen-house, or that part of it, where fowls rest at night: *at ∼*, on a ∼. *Curses come home to ∼*, (prov) take effect upon the one who utters them. ***rule the ∼,*** be the leader or master. □ *vi* [VP2A] (of birds or, occasionally, persons) settle down for the night's sleep.

rooster /ˈrustə(r)/ *n* domestic cock.

root[1] /rut/ *n* [C] **1** that part of a plant, tree, etc which is normally in the soil and which takes water and food from it: *pull up a plant by the ∼s. He has no ∼s in society,* (fig) is not settled, does not belong to any particular group or place. ***pull up one's ∼s,*** (fig) move from a settled home, job, etc to start a new life elsewhere. ***put down new ∼s,*** (fig) establish oneself in another place after leaving a place where one has been established. ***take/strike ∼,*** **(a)** (e g of a cutting) send out a ∼ or ∼s; begin to grow. **(b)** (fig) become established. ***∼ and branch,*** (fig) thoroughly; completely: *These evil practices must be destroyed ∼ and branch.* **2** (*pl*) (also ˈ**∼-crop**) plant with a ∼ that is used as papers **∼ beer,** (US) non-alcoholic drink made from the ∼s of various plants. **3** that part of a hair, tooth, the tongue, a finger-nail, etc that is like a ∼ in position, function, etc. **4** (fig) that from which sth grows; basis; source; essential substance; *the ∼ of the trouble. Is money the ∼ of all evil?* ***get at/to the ∼ of sth,*** tackle it at its source; (attrib) ***the ∼ cause,*** the fundamental cause. **5** (gram) (also *base form*) form of a word on which other forms of that word are said to be based: *'Walk' is the ∼ of 'walks', 'walked', 'walking', and 'walker'.* **6** quantity which, when multiplied by itself a certain number of times, produces another quantity: *4 is the square ∼ of 16, the cube ∼ of 64, the fourth ∼ of 256* ($\sqrt[4]{256} = 4$).

root[2] /rut/ *vt,vi* **1** [VP6A,2A] (of plants, cuttings, etc) (cause to) send out ∼s and begin to grow: *∼ chrysanthemum cuttings in sand and peat. Some cuttings ∼ easily.* **2** [VP6A,15A] cause to stand fixed and unmoving: *Fear ∼ed him to the ground. He stood there ∼ed to the spot.* **3** (of ideas, principles, etc) establish firmly (chiefly in *pp*): *She has a ∼ed objection to cold baths. Her affection for him is deeply ∼ed.* **4 *∼ sth out,*** get rid of, exterminate (an evil, etc). ***∼ sth up,*** dig or pull up with the ∼s. **∼less** *adj* having no ∼s; (of a person) without ∼s in society. ⇨ root[1](1).

root[3] /rut/ *vi,vt* **1** [VP2C,15B] ***∼ about (for),*** (of pigs) turn up the ground with the snout in search of food; (of persons) search for; turn things over when searching: *∼ing about among piles of papers for a missing document.* ***∼ sth out,*** find by searching: *I managed to ∼ out a copy of the document.* **2** [VP2A,3A] ***∼ (for),*** (US sl) cheer: *∼ing for the college baseball team.*

rootle /ˈrutl/ *vi* [VP2C] ***∼ about for,*** (of pigs, etc) dig about (with the snout) for food, etc.

rope /rəʊp/ *n* **1** [C,U] (piece or length of) thick strong cord or wire cable made by twisting finer cords or wires together: *tie sb's arms behind his back with (a) ∼. The climbers were on the ∼,* fastened together with a ∼ (while climbing on a difficult and dangerous surface). **the ∼,** noose for hanging a condemned person. **the ∼s,** those that enclose the prize-ring or other place used for sport or games. ***know/learn/show sb the ∼s,*** the conditions, the rules, the procedure (in some sphere of action). ***give sb (plenty of) ∼,*** freedom of action. ***Give sb enough ∼ and he'll hang himself,*** (prov) Let a fool follow his own devices and he will come to ruin. **2** (compounds) ˈ**∼-dancer** *n* performer on a tight-∼. ˈ**∼-ˈladder** *n* ladder made of two long ∼s connected by rungs of ∼. ˈ**∼-walk/-yard** *n* long piece of ground or long, low shed where ∼ is made. ˈ**∼-walker** *n* = ∼-dancer. ˈ**∼-way** *n* means of carrying goods in buckets, etc suspended from overhead steel cables: (attrib) ˈ*∼way buckets.* ˈ**∼-yarn** *n* [U] material (esp when unpicked) of which ∼s are made. **3** [C] number of things twisted, strung or threaded together: *a ∼ of onions.* □ *vt* [VP15A,B] **1** fasten or bind with ∼: *∼ a man to a tree; ∼ climbers together,* connect them at intervals with a ∼ for safety. **2 *∼ sth off,*** enclose or mark off with a ∼: *Part of the field was ∼d off.* **3 *∼ sb in,*** persuade him to help in some activity. **ropey** /ˈrəʊpɪ/ *adj* (sl) very inferior in quality.

Roque·fort /ˈrokfɔ(r) *US:* ˈrəʊkfərt/ *n* [U] kind of French cheese made of goats' and ewes' milk.

ro·sary /ˈrəʊzərɪ/ *n* (*pl* -ries) **1** form of prayer used in the R C Church; book containing this. **2** string of beads for keeping count of these prayers; such beads used by a person of another religion. **3** rose-garden.

rose[1] /rəʊz/ *pt* ⇨ rise[2].

rose[2] /rəʊz/ *n* **1** (shrub or bush with prickles or thorns on its stems and bearing a) beautiful and usu sweet-smelling flower (red, pink, white, cream, yellow); one of various flowering plants: *the* ˈ*rock-∼;* ˈ*Christmas ∼.* ⇨ the illus at flower. ***a bed of ∼s,*** a pleasant, easy condition of life. ***not all ∼s,*** not perfect; having some discomfort and disadvantages. ***no ∼ without a thorn,*** complete, unalloyed happiness cannot be found. ***gather life's ∼s,*** seek the pleasures of life. **2** [U] pinkish-red colour. ***see things through ∼-coloured/-tinted spectacles,*** see them as bright and cheerful. **3** (of various things thought to resemble a ∼ in shape) **(a)** sprinkling nozzle of a watering can or hose: *Use a fine-∼d can* (one fitted with such a nozzle) *for watering seedlings.* **(b)**

bunch of ribbons; rosette. (c) ~-shaped conventional design, the national emblem of England (as the shamrock is used for Ireland). 4 (compounds) '**~-bed** *n* bed in which ~ bushes are grown. '**~-bud** *n* bud of a ~; (attrib) *a ~bud mouth,* having this shape. '**~-leaf** *n* petal from a ~ flower. '**~-'red** *adj* red as a ~. '**~-water** *n* perfume made from ~s. '**~ window** *n* ornamental circular window (usu in a church, esp one with a pattern of small sections radiating from the centre). ⇨ the illus at window. '**~-wood** *n* [U] hard, dark red wood obtained from several varieties of tropical tree (so named for their fragrance): *a ~wood piano.*

ro·seate /'rəʊzɪət/ *adj* rose-coloured; pinkish-red.

rose·mary /'rəʊzmərɪ *US:* -merɪ/ *n* [U] evergreen shrub with fragrant leaves used in making perfumes and for flavouring food.

ro·sette /rəʊ'zet/ *n* [C] small rose-shaped badge or ornament, e g of silk or ribbon; carved rose on stonework.

rosin /'rozɪn *US:* 'rozn/ *n* [U] resin, esp in solid form, as used on the strings of violins, etc and on the bow with which violins are played. □ *vt* [VP6A] rub with ~.

ros·ter /'rostə(r)/ *n* list of names of persons showing duties to be performed by each in turn.

ros·trum /'rostrəm/ *n* (*pl* -trums or -tra /-trə/) platform or pulpit for public speaking.

rosy /'rəʊzɪ/ *adj* (-ier, -iest) of the colour of red roses: ~ *cheeks,* indicating good health; ~ (fig, = bright, cheerful) *prospects.*

rot /rot/ *vi,vt* (-tt-) **1** [VP2A,C] decay by processes of nature: *A fallen tree soon rots. The shed had fallen in, and the wood was rotting away. One of the branches had rotted off,* decayed and broken off. **2** [VP2A,C] (fig, of a society, etc) gradually perish from lack of vigour or activity; (of prisoners, etc) waste away: *left to rot in a deep dungeon.* **3** [VP6A] cause to decay or become useless: *Oil and grease will rot the rubber of your tyres.* **rot-gut** *n* [U] strong alcoholic liquor, esp inferior spirit, that is harmful to the stomach. **4** [VP2A] (sl) (in progressive tenses) talk nonsense. □ *n* [U] **1** decay; rotting; condition of being bad: *a tree affected by rot. Rot has set in,* decay has begun. *We have dry rot in the floor.* ⇨ dry[1](13). **2** (usu **the rot**) liver disease of sheep. '**foot-rot,** foot disease of sheep. **3** ('**tommy-**)'**rot,** (sl) nonsense; foolishness; rubbish: *Don't talk rot! His speech was all rot.* **4** (cricket, war, etc) succession of failures: *A rot set in. How can we stop the rot?*

rota /'rəʊtə/ *n* (GB) list of persons who are to do things in turn; list of duties to be performed in turn.

ro·tary /'rəʊtərɪ/ *adj* **1** (of motion) moving round a central point. **2** (of an engine) worked by ~ motion: a ~ printing machine/press, that prints from curved metal plates on to a continuous roll of paper. **3** '**R~ Club,** (branch of an) international association of professional and business men in a town for the purpose of rendering services to the community. □ *n* (US) = roundabout(2). **Ro·tarian** /rəʊ'teərɪən/ *n* member of a R~ Club.

ro·tate /rəʊ'teɪt *US:* 'rəʊteɪt/ *vi,vt* [VP6A,2A] (cause to) move round a central point; (cause to) take turns or come in succession: ~ *crops,* ⇨ rotation(2). *The office of Chairman ~s.*

ro·ta·tion /rəʊ'teɪʃn/ *n* **1** [U] rotating or being rotated: *the ~ of the earth;* [C] complete turning: *five ~s an hour.* **2** [C,U] the regular coming round of things or events in succession: '*crop-~, ~ of crops,* varying the crops grown each year on the same land to avoid exhausting the soil. ***in ~,*** in turn; in regular succession.

ro·ta·tory /'rəʊtətərɪ *US:* -tɔrɪ/ *adj* relating to, causing, moving in, rotation: *~ movement.*

rote /rəʊt/ *n* (only in) ***by ~,*** by heart, from memory without thinking: *do/say/know/learn sth by ~.*

ro·tis·se·rie /rəʊ'tɪsərɪ/ *n* cooking device with a rotating spit on which meat, etc is roasted; shop or restaurant providing food cooked in this way.

roto·gra·vure /'rəʊtəʊgrə'vjʊə(r)/ *n* **1** [U] process of printing from an engraved copper cylinder on which illustrations, etc have been etched. **2** [C] illustration, etc printed by this process.

ro·tor /'rəʊtə(r)/ *n* [C] assembly of horizontally rotating blades of a helicopter propellor.

rot·ten /'rotn/ *adj* **1** decayed; having gone bad: ~ *eggs. The sails were ~ and so were the ropes.* **2** (sl) disagreeable; very unpleasant or undesirable: *What ~ luck! I'm feeling ~ today,* unwell, tired, bored, etc. **~·ly** *adv* **~·ness** *n*

rot·ter /'rotə(r)/ *n* (sl) worthless, objectionable person.

ro·tund /rəʊ'tʌnd/ *adj* **1** (of a person, his face) round and plump; (of the voice) full-sounding; rich and deep. **2** (of speech, liter style) grandiloquent. **~·ly** *adv* **~·ity** /-ətɪ/ *n* [U] state of being ~.

ro·tunda /rəʊ'tʌndə/ *n* round building, esp one with a domed roof.

rouble, ruble /'rubl/ *n* unit of currency in the U S S R (100 kopecks).

roué /'rueɪ *US:* ru'eɪ/ *n* loose-living man; rake[2].

rouge /ruʒ/ *n* [U] fine red powder or other cosmetic substance for colouring the cheeks; powder for cleaning silver plate. □ *vt,vi* [VP6A,2A] use ~ on (the face); use ~.

rough[1] /rʌf/ *adj* (-er, -est) **1** (of surfaces) not level, smooth or polished; (of roads) of irregular surface, not easy to walk or ride on: ~ *paper; a fruit with a ~ skin; ~ hair,* not brushed smooth; *cloth that is ~ to the touch.* **2** not calm or gentle; moving or acting violently: *~ children; ~ behaviour; a ~* (= stormy) *sea; have a ~ crossing from Dover to Calais. Keep away from the ~ quarter of the town,* the part where disorderly and violent people live. *This suitcase has had some ~ handling,* has been treated violently, thrown about, etc. *He has a ~ tongue,* a habit of speaking rudely or sharply. ***be ~ on sb,*** be unpleasant or unlucky for: *It's rather ~ on her, having to live with her mother-in-law.* ***give sb the ~ side of one's tongue,*** He spoke to me rudely and/or severely. ***give sb/have a ~ time,*** (cause sb to) experience hardship, to be treated severely, etc (according to context). '**~ house,** (colloq) noisy quarrelling with exchange of blows, etc. **~ luck,** worse luck than is deserved. **3** made or done without attention to detail, esp as a first attempt: *a ~ sketch/translation;* lacking refinement, delicacy or finish; *a ~ draft,* e g of a letter; *~ accommodation at a small country inn; lead a ~ life away from civilization.* ***a ~ diamond,*** (fig) an uneducated or uncouth person, lacking social graces (but perhaps good-natured). ***~ and ready,*** good enough for ordinary purposes, occasions, etc; not particularly efficient, etc: *~ and ready methods.* **4** (of sounds) harsh; discordant: *a ~ voice.* **5** (compounds) **'~-and-'tumble** *adj, n* disorderly and violent (fight or struggle). **'~-neck** *n* (US colloq) rowdy person; hooligan. **'~-rider** *n* person who is expert at breaking in untamed horses. **~·ly** *adv* in a ~ manner: *treat sb ~ly; a ~ly made table,* not finely finished; *at a cost of ~ly* (= approximately) *£5. ~ly speaking,* with no claim to accuracy. **~·ness** *n* quality or state of being ~.

rough[2] /rʌf/ *adv* **1** in a rough manner: *play ~,* be (rather) violent (in games, etc); *treat sb ~.* ***cut up ~,*** (colloq) become angry. ***live ~,*** live in the open (as a vagrant may do). ***sleep ~,*** (of homeless persons) sleep out of doors or wherever there is some shelter, e g under a bridge, in the open air. **2** (compounds) **'~-cast** *n* coarse plaster containing gravel or pebbles for the surfaces of outside walls. □ *vt* coat (a wall) with this mixture. **'~-dry** *vt* dry (laundered clothes) without ironing them. **'~-hewn** *adj* shaped or carved out ~ly: *a ~-hewn statue.* **'~-shod** *adj* (of a horse) having shoes with the heads of the nails projecting to prevent slipping. ***ride ~shod over sb,*** treat him harshly, inconsiderately or contemptuously. **'~-'spoken** *adj* addicted to, using, unrefined or harsh language.

rough[3] /rʌf/ *n* **1** [U] rough state; rough ground; rough surface; unpleasantness; hardship. ***take the ~ with the smooth,*** (fig) accept what is unpleasant with what is pleasant. **2** [U] **the ~,** unfinished state: *I've seen his new statue only in the ~.* ***in ~,*** (e g of sth written) as a rough draft. **3** [U] **the ~,** (golf) part of a course (not the fairway or a green) where the ground is uneven and the grass uncut: *lose one's ball in the ~.* **4** man or boy ready for lawless violence; hooligan: *He was set on by a gang of ~s who knocked him down and took all his money.*

rough[4] /rʌf/ *vt* **1** [VP6A,15B] ***~ sth (up),*** make untidy or uneven: *Don't ~ (up) my hair, dear.* ***~ sb up,*** (sl) treat him roughly, with physical violence: *He was ~ed up by hooligans.* ~ (more usu *rub*) ***sb up the wrong way,*** ⇨ rub(3). **2** [VP15B] ***~ sth in,*** make a first rough sketch of; sketch in outline. **3** ***~ it,*** live without the usual comforts and conveniences of life: *The explorers had to ~ it when they got into the jungle.*

rough·age /'rʌfɪdʒ/ *n* [U] coarse, rough foodstuff, esp bran of cereals, supplying bulk, not nourishment, and taken to stimulate bowel movements.

roughen /'rʌfn/ *vt, vi* make or become rough.

rou·lette /ru'let/ *n* [U] gambling game in which a small ball falls by chance into one of the compartments of a revolving wheel or disc. **Russian ~,** stunt in which a person holds to his head a revolver of which only one (unknown) chamber contains a bullet in and then pulls the trigger.

round[1] /raʊnd/ *adj* **1** shaped like a circle or a ball: *a ~ plate/window/table; a ~-table conference,* at which there is no position of importance at the head of the table, everyone being apparently of equal importance; *~ cheeks/arms/limbs,* plump and curved. **a '~ game,** one in which there are no teams or partners and in which the number of players is not fixed. **the R~ Table,** the order of knighthood founded by King Arthur. **2** done with, involving, a circular motion (as in) ***a ~ trip/tour/voyage.*** *a ~-'trip ticket,* (US) = (GB) a return ticket, one with a return to the starting-point. **a '~ dance,** one in which the dancers form a circle, with revolving movements. **~ robin,** petition with signatures in a circle to conceal the order in which they were written. **3** entire; continuous; full: *a ~ dozen/score,* that number and not less; *a good, ~ sum,* a considerable sum. ***in ~ figures/numbers,*** given in 10's, 100's, 1 000's, etc; not troubling about smaller denominations; (hence) roughly correct. **4** (various uses, now rather dated) *at a ~ pace/trot,* vigorous; *a ~ oath,* unmistakably an oath; *a ~ voice,* full-toned and mellow; *scold sb in good, ~ terms,* outspokenly; *a ~ unvarnished tale,* the plain truth. **5** (compounds) **'~-arm** *adj, adv* (cricket) with the arm swung ~ at the height of the shoulder: *~-arm bowling; bowl ~-arm.* **'~-'backed** *adj* having the back curved or humped. **'~-'eyed** *adj* with the eyes wide open: *starting/listening in ~-eyed wonder.* **'~-hand** *n* [U] **(a)** style of handwriting with the letters well rounded and clearly written. **(b)** = ~-arm (bowling). **'R~-head** *n* member of the Parliament side in the Civil War in the 17th c in England, so called from his close-cut hair. **'~-house** *n* **(a)** cabin or set of cabins on the after part of the quarter deck (of old sailing ships). **(b)** building (with a turn-table in the middle) where locomotives are or have been stored and repaired. **(c)** (in former times) place where people were locked up as prisoners. **'~-shot** *n* cannon ball (contrasted with a shell). **'~-'shouldered** *adj* having the shoulders bent forward. **~·ish** /-ɪʃ/ *adj* rather ~. **~·ly** *adv* in a thorough-going way; pointedly: *tell a woman ~ly that she is not wanted; be ~ly cursed.* **~·ness** *n*

round[2] /raʊnd/ *adv part* (For special uses with *vv,* ⇨ the *v* entries. Specimens only are given here.) **1** in a circle or curve to face the opposite way: *Turn your chair ~ and face me.* **2** with a return to the starting-point: *The hour hand of a clock goes right ~ in twelve hours. Christmas will soon be ~ again. I shall be glad when spring comes ~ again.* ***~ and ~,*** with repeated revolutions. ***all ~, right ~,*** completely ~: *We walked right ~ the lake.* ***all the year ~,*** at all seasons of the year. **3** in circumference: *Her waist is only twenty-four inches ~.* **4** (so as to be) in a circle: *A crowd soon gathered ~. The garden has a high wall all ~.* **5** from one (place, point, person, etc) to another: *Please hand these papers ~,* i e distribute them. *The news was soon passed ~. Tea was served/handed ~.* ***go ~,*** supply everybody: *Have we enough food to go ~? Will the meat go ~,* i e be enough for everybody? ***look ~,*** visit and look at: *Let's go into the town and look ~/have a look ~,* i e see the places of interest, etc. ***taking it all ~,*** considering the matter from all points of view. **6** by a longer way or route; not by the direct route: *If you can't jump over the stream, you'll have to go ~ by the bridge. The taxi-driver brought us a long way ~.* **7** to a place where sb is or will be: *Come ~ and see me this evening. The Whites have asked me to go ~ this evening,* i e to visit them. **8** in the neighbourhood: *all the country ~; everybody for a mile ~; in all the villages ~ about.*

round[3] /raʊnd/ *n* **1** sth round; a slice made by a complete cut across the end of a loaf: *two ~s* (= sandwiches) *of ham and one of beef; a ~ of toast; the ~s* (= ~ rungs) *of a ladder.* **2** [U] (sculpture) solid form, enabling an object to be viewed from all sides (contrasted with *relief*). ***in the ~,*** (arts) made so that it can be viewed from all sides: *a* *statue in the ~.* **theatre in the ~,** with the audience on (nearly) all sides of the stage. **3** regular series or succession or distribution: *the daily ~,* the ordinary occupations of the day; *the earth's yearly ~,* the cycle of the four seasons; *the doctor's ~ of visits* (to the homes of his patients); *a ~ of pleasures/gaiety,* a succession of parties, gay events, etc; *the postman's ~,* the route he takes to deliver letters. **go the ~s, make one's ~s,** make one's usual visits, esp of inspection: *The night watchman makes his ~s every hour.* **go the ~ of,** be passed on (to): *The news quickly went the ~ of the village.* **4** (in games, contests, etc) one stage: *a boxing-match of ten ~s; knocked out in the third ~; the semi-final ~ of the League Championship; the sixth ~ of the FA Cup,* the quarter-finals of this soccer contest; *have a ~ of cards; a ~ of golf,* to all the 9 or 18 holes of the course. **5** allowance of sth distributed or measured out; one of a set or series: *pay for a ~ of drinks,* drinks for every member of the company; *another ~ of wage claims,* by trade unions for higher wages for their members; *~ after ~ of cheers,* successive bursts of cheering; *have only three ~s of ammunition left,* enough to fire three times. **6** song for several persons or groups, the second singing the first line while the first is singing the second line, etc. **7** dance in which the dancers move in a circle.

round[4] /raʊnd/ *prep* **1** (expressing movement) in a path that passes on all sides of and comes back to the starting-point: *The earth moves ~ the sun. Drake sailed ~ the world.* **(sleep/work) ~ the clock,** all day and all night. **~-the-clock,** (attrib) kept up continuously for 24 hours: *~-the-clock dancing.* **2** (expressing movement) in a path changing direction, from one side to another side of: *walk/follow sb ~ a corner.* **~ the bend,** (sl) mad. **3** (expressing position) so as to be on all sides of: *They were sitting ~ the table. He had a scarf ~ his neck.* **4** in various or all directions: *He looked ~ the room. Shall I show you ~ the house,* i e take you to the various rooms, etc? **5** to or at various points away from the centre: *The captain stationed his fielders ~ the pitch. We haven't time to go ~* (= to visit) *the museums and art galleries.* **6** (fig) approximate(ly): *Come ~ about 2 o'clock. He's ready to pay somewhere ~ £1 000 for a car.*

round[5] /raʊnd/ *vt,vi* **1** [VP6A] make or become round: *~ the lips,* e g when making the sound /u/; *stones ~ed by the action of water.* **2** [VP6A] go round: *~ a corner.* **3** [VP15B,2C,3A] **~ sth off,** bring it to a satisfactory conclusion, add a suitable finish: *~ off a sentence; ~ off one's career by being made a Minister.* **~ out,** (cause to) become round: *Her figure is beginning to ~ out.* **~ sb/sth up,** drive, bring or collect, together: *The courier ~ed up the tourists and hurried them back into the coach.* **~ up (a figure/price),** bring it to a whole number: *The price had been ~ed up from £647.50 to £650. The cowboy ~ed up the cattle.* Hence, **ˈ~-up** *n* a driving or bringing together: *a ~-up of criminals* (by police); *a ~-up of cattle.* **~ upon sb,** turn on him and attack him (in words or action).

round·about /ˈraʊndəbaʊt/ *adj* not going or coming by, or using, the shortest or most direct route: *I heard the news in a ~ way. We came by a ~ route. What a ~ way of doing things!* □ *n* [C] **1** (= *merry-go-round*) revolving circular platform with wooden horses, etc on which children ride for fun (at fairs, etc). ***You lose on the swings what you make on the ~s,*** (prov) have losses and profits which are about equal. **2** circular enclosure at a road junction causing traffic to go round instead of directly across (US = *traffic circle* or *rotary*).

roun·del /ˈraʊndl/ *n* small disc, esp a decorative medallion; small circular panel (e g as used on military aircraft to indicate the country they belong to).

roun·de·lay /ˈraʊndɪleɪ/ *n* short, simple song with a refrain.

roun·ders /ˈraʊndəz/ *n pl* game for two teams, played with bat and ball, the players running through a number of bases arranged in a square, said to be similar to baseball.

Round·head /ˈraʊndhed/ ⇨ round[1](5).

rounds·man /ˈraʊndzmən/ *n* (*pl* **-men**) tradesman or his employee going round to ask for orders and deliver goods.

rouse /raʊz/ *vt,vi* **1** [VP6A] wake up: *I was ~ed by the ringing of a bell.* **2** [VP6A,15A] **~ sb (from sth/to sth),** cause (sb) to be more active, interested, etc (from inactivity, lack of confidence, etc): *~ sb/oneself to action; ~ sb from indolence; demagogues who try to ~ the masses; ~d to anger by insults; rousing cheers; a rousing sermon. He's a terrible man when he's ~d,* when his passions have been stirred. **3** [VP2A] (= ~ oneself) wake; become active.

rout[1] /raʊt/ *n* **1** utter defeat and disorderly retreat: *The defeat became a ~.* **put to ~,** defeat completely. **2** (old use) large festive gathering of people; large evening party or reception. **3** (old use, or legal) disorderly, noisy crowd. □ *vt* [VP6A] defeat completely; put to ~: *~ the enemy.*

rout[2] /raʊt/ *vt* [VP15B] **~ sb out (of),** get or fetch him up, out of bed, etc: *We were ~ed out of our cabins before breakfast for passport examination.*

route /rut/ *n* **1** way taken or planned from one place to another: *The climbers tried to find a new ~ to the top of the mountain. He flew from Europe to Tokyo by the ~ across the Pole.* **en ~** /ˈɒ ˈrut/, on the way. **2** [U] (mil) **column of ~,** marching formation. **ˈ~-march,** one made by soldiers in training. □ *vt* plan a ~ for; send by a specified ~: *We were ~d by way of Dover.*

rou·tine /ruˈtin/ *n* [C,U] fixed and regular way of doing things: *business ~; a question of ~; the ~* (= usual, ordinary) *procedure; my ~ duties,* those performed regularly, as if by rule.

rove /rəʊv/ *vi,vt* **1** [VP2C,6A] roam (the more usu word); wander: *~ over sea and land; ~ the moors.* **a roving commission,** duties that take one from one place to another frequently. **2** [VP2A] (of the eyes, one's affections) be directed first one way, then another. **rover** *n* **1** wanderer. **2** (old use) **ˈsea-rover,** pirate. **3** senior boy scout.

row[1] /rəʊ/ *n* [C] number of persons or things in a line: *a row of books/houses/desks; plant out a row of young cabbages; sitting in a row/in rows; a front-row seat,* e g in a theatre. ***a hard row to hoe,*** a difficult task.

row[2] /rəʊ/ *vt,vi* [VP6A,2A,B,C,15A,B] propel (a boat) by using oars; carry or take (sb or sth) in a boat with oars; be an oarsman in a boat: *Can you row (a boat)? Shall I row you up/down/across the river? They rowed forty (strokes) to the minute.*

He rows No 5 (= has this position) *in the Oxford crew. Let's row a race. The crew were rowed out* (= exhausted by rowing) *at the end of the race.* **'row-boat** *n* = rowing boat. □ *n* journey or outing in a boat moved by oars; period of this; distance rowed: *go for a row; a long and tiring row.* **row·ing** *n* (compounds) **'row·ing-boat** *n* one moved by the use of oars. **'row·ing-club** *n* one for persons who row. **rower** *n* person who rows a boat.

a rowing-boat

row³ /raʊ/ *n* **1** [U] uproar; noisy disturbance: *How can I study with all this row going on outside my windows? Hold your row!* (sl) Be quiet! **2** [C] noisy or violent argument or quarrel: *have a row with the neighbours. That man is always ready for a row,* he has a quarrelsome nature. ***make/kick up a row,*** start a noisy quarrel or scene. **3** [C] instance of being in trouble, scolded, etc: *get into a row for being late at the office.* □ *vt,vi* **1** [VP6A] scold; reprimand. **2** [VP2A,3A] ***row (with),*** quarrel noisily with: *He's always rowing with his neighbours.*

rowan /'rəʊən *US:* 'raʊən/ *n* ('~-)**tree,** small tree of the rose family, also called mountain ash; (also '**~-berry**) one of the scarlet berries of this tree.

rowdy /'raʊdɪ/ *adj* (-**ier,** -**iest**) rough and noisy: *The ~ element in the audience continually interrupted the speaker. There were ~ scenes at the elections.* □ *n* (*pl* -**dies**) ~ person. **row·dily** /-əlɪ/ *adv* **row·di·ness** *n* [U] **~·ism** /-ɪzm/ *n* [U] ~ behaviour.

rowel /'raʊl̩/ *n* [C] revolving disc with sharp teeth at the end of a spur.

row·lock /'rolək *US:* 'rəʊlok/ *n* [C] pivot for an oar or scull on the side (gunwale) of a boat (US = *oarlock*).

royal /'rɔɪl̩/ *adj* of, like, suitable for, supported by, belonging to the family of, a king or queen: *His R~ Highness; the ~ family; the R~ Society; the R~ Navy/Air Force; a ~ welcome,* one fit for a king, etc; splendid. **R~ Commission,** one officially appointed to hold an enquiry and issue a report. **~ly** /'rɔɪəlɪ/ *adv* in a ~ or splendid manner: *We were ~ly entertained.* **~·ist** /'rɔɪəlɪst/ *n* supporter of a king or queen or of ~ government; supporter of the ~ side in a civil war.

roy·alty /'rɔɪl̩tɪ/ *n* (*pl* -**ties**) **1** [U] royal persons: *The play was performed in the presence of ~. The hotel has been patronized by ~.* **2** [U] position, rank, dignity, power, etc of a royal person. **3** [C] payment of money by a mining or oil company to the owner of the land: *oil royalties;* sum (to be) paid to the owner of a copyright or patent: *a ~ of 10 per cent of the price of the book on all copies sold.*

rub¹ /rʌb/ *n* **1** period of rubbing: *give the spoons/table, etc a good rub/rub-up/rub-down.* **2** (esp in the phrase ***'There's the rub'***) difficulty; point at which doubt or difficulty arises.

rub² /rʌb/ *vt,vi* (-**bb**-) (For special uses with *adverbial particles* and *preps,* ⇨ **3** below.) **1** [VP6A,15A,22] move (one thing) backwards and forwards on the surface of (another); make (sth *clean, dry,* etc) by doing this: *He was rubbing his hands together. Rub this oil on your skin. He rubbed his hands with the soap. You've rubbed your coat against some wet paint. The dog rubbed itself/its head against my legs. Rub the surface dry.* ***rub shoulders with,*** meet and mix with (people). **2** [VP2A,C] come into, or be in, contact with, by a sliding or up and down movement: *What is the wheel rubbing on/against? The door rubs on the floor—the hinge must have dropped a little.* **3** [VP2C,15B] (special uses with *adverbial particles* and *preps*):

rub along, (colloq) (of a person) manage to exist, pass one's time, without too much difficulty. ***rub along with sb/together,*** (of two or more persons) live without quarrelling, etc: *I manage to rub along with her. We manage to rub along together.*

rub sb/oneself/a horse down, rub thoroughly, vigorously, e g with a towel, to make dry and clean: *He rubbed himself down after his bath.* ***rub sth down,*** make sth smooth or level by rubbing: *Rub the walls down well before applying new paint.* Hence, **'rub-down** *n*: *Give the horse/the walls a good rub-down.*

rub sth in/into sth, (**a**) force (ointment, etc) into sth, e g the skin, by rubbing: *Rub the ointment well in/into the skin.* (**b**) force (a lesson, a humiliating or unpleasant fact) into sb's mind: *The moral needs to be well rubbed in.* ***rub it in,*** (esp) remind sb repeatedly of a fault, failure, etc: *I know I behaved foolishly but you needn't rub it in.*

rub sth off, remove sth (from a surface) by rubbing: *How did you rub the skin off your knees? The nap of this cloth has been rubbed off.*

rub sth out, remove (marks, writing, etc) by rubbing: *rub out a word/pencil marks/mistakes. The stains won't rub out,* can't be rubbed out. ***rub sb out,*** (US sl) murder him.

rub sth up, (**a**) polish by rubbing: *rub up the silver spoons.* (**b**) (fig, more usu *brush up*) freshen one's knowledge of: *rub up one's Latin/biology.* Hence, **'rub-up** *n* ***rub sb (up) the right/wrong way,*** placate/irritate him.

rub-a-dub /ˌrʌb ə 'dʌb/ *n* [U] sound made by beating a drum.

rub·ber¹ /'rʌbə(r)/ *n* **1** [U] tough elastic substance made from the milky liquid that flows from certain trees when the bark is cut, used for making tyres, tennis balls, etc: (attrib) *'~ trees; the '~ plantations of Malaysia; ~ bands,* elastic bands for keeping things together; *a ~ stamp.* **ˌ~-'stamp** *vt* (colloq) approve or endorse (a proposal, etc) without giving it proper consideration. **'~-neck** *n* (colloq) tourist or sightseer (of the kind who constantly turns his head to see as much as possible). □ *vi* look at sights in this way. **2** [C] piece of ~ material for rubbing out pencil marks, etc: *a pencil with a ~ at one end.* **3** (*pl*) overshoes (galoshes) made of ~. **4** [C] person or thing that rubs, e g a part of a machine that applies friction. □ *vt* [VP6A] cover or coat with ~. **~·ize** /-aɪz/ *vt* [VP6A] cover or treat with ~.

rub·ber² /'rʌbə(r)/ *n* [C] (in such card games as whist and bridge) **1** three successive games between the same sides or persons: *Let's play* *another* ~. **2** the winning of two games out of three; the third game when each side has won one: *game and* ~, (We have won) the third game and (therefore) the ~.

rub·bing /ˈrʌbɪŋ/ *n* impression of sth, e g a brass over a grave, by rubbing paper laid over it with wax, chalk or charcoal.

rub·bish /ˈrʌbɪʃ/ *n* [U] **1** waste material; that which is, or is to be, thrown away as worthless; refuse. **2** nonsense; worthless ideas: *This book is all* ~. **3** (as an exclamation) Nonsense! **rub·bishy** *adj* worthless.

rubble /ˈrʌbl/ *n* [U] bits of broken stone, rock or brickwork: *buildings reduced to* ~ *by bombing; build roads with a foundation of* ~.

Ru·bi·con /ˈrubɪkən *US:* -kon/ *n* (river in Italy) ***pass/cross the*** **~,** commit oneself to an enterprise from which one cannot turn back.

ru·bi·cund /ˈrubɪkənd/ *adj* (of a persons's face or complexion) ruddy; high-coloured.

ruble /ˈrubl/ *n* = rouble.

ru·bric /ˈrubrɪk/ *n* [C] title or heading printed in red or special type, esp a direction given in a Prayer Book.

ruby /ˈrubɪ/ *n* [C] (*pl* -bies /-bɪz/) red jewel. □ *adj, n* deep red (colour).

ruck[1] /rʌk/ *n* **the ~, the common ~,** ordinary commonplace things or persons: *He was ambitious to get out of the* ~, to escape from being thought of as ordinary, commonplace, etc.

ruck[2] /rʌk/ *n* [C] irregular fold or crease (esp in cloth). □ *vi, vt* [VP2A,C,6A,15B] be pulled into ~s; make into ~s: *The (bed) sheets have* ~*ed up.*

ruck·sack /ˈrʌksæk/ *n* [C] canvas bag strapped on the back from the shoulders, used by people on a walking holiday, etc.

ruc·tions /ˈrʌkʃnz/ *n pl* angry words or protests; noisy argument: *There'll be* ~ *if you don't do what you're told.*

rud·der /ˈrʌdə(r)/ *n* [C] **1** flat, broad piece of wood or metal hinged vertically at the stern of a boat or ship for steering. **2** similar structure on an aircraft. ⇨ the illus at air.

ruddle /ˈrʌdl/ *n* [U] red ochre, esp the kind used for marking ownership of sheep. □ *vt* put ~ on sheep.

ruddy /ˈrʌdɪ/ *adj* (-ier, -iest) **1** (of the face) red, as showing good health: ~ *cheeks; in* ~ *health,* having ~ cheeks indicating good health. **2** red or reddish: *a* ~ *glow in the sky.* **3** (euphem for) bloody(3): *What the* ~ *hell are you doing?*

rude /rud/ *adj* (-r, -st) **1** (of a person, his speech, behaviour) impolite; not showing respect or consideration: *It's* ~ *to interrupt/to point at people. What a* ~ *reply! Would it be* ~ *to ask when you are likely to leave,* e g to a guest who stays too long? *Don't be* ~ *to your teacher.* **2** startling; violent; rough: *get a* ~ *shock.* ***a*** **~ *awakening,*** a sudden realization of sth unpleasant. **3** primitive; without refinement: *our* ~ *forefathers.* **4** roughly made; simple: *a* ~ *wooden plough; the* ~ *ornaments made by the Saxons.* **5** vigorous: *in* ~ *health.* **6** in the natural state; crude, raw (the more usu words): ~ *ore/produce; cotton in its* ~ *state.* **~·ly** *adv* in a ~ manner: *a* ~*ly* (i e in a primitive manner) *fashioned craft; be* ~*ly awakened.* ⇨ 2 above. **~·ness** *n* [U].

ru·di·ment /ˈrudɪmənt/ *n* **1** (*pl*) first steps or stages (of an art or science): *learn the* ~*s of chemistry/grammar.* **2** earliest form on which a later development is or might have developed; imperfectly developed part: *Certain types reveal the* ~ *of a thumb. A new-born chicken has only the* ~*s of wings.* **ru·di·men·tary** /ˈrudɪˈmentrɪ/ *adj* **1** elementary: *a* ~*ary knowledge of mechanics.* **2** undeveloped; existing in an imperfect or undeveloped form.

rue[1] /ru/ *n* [U] small evergreen plant with bitter-tasting leaves formerly used in medicine.

rue[2] /ru/ *vt* [VP6A] (dated or liter) repent of; think of with sadness or regret: *You'll live to rue it,* will one day regret it. *You'll rue the day when….* **rue·ful** /ˈru-fl/ *adj* showing, feeling, expressing regret: *a rueful smile.* **rue·fully** /ˈru-flɪ/ *adv*

ruff[1] /rʌf/ *n* **1** ring of differently coloured or marked feathers round a bird's neck, or of hair round an animal's neck. **2** wide, stiff frill worn as a collar in the 16th c. ⇨ the illus at doublet.

ruff[2] /rʌf/ *vi, vt* trump (in a card game). □ *n* act of trumping.

ruf·fian /ˈrʌfɪən/ *n* violent, cruel man. **~·ly** *adj* like a ~; lawless. **~·ism** /-ɪzm/ *n* [U] rough, brutal conduct.

ruffle /ˈrʌfl/ *vt, vi* **1** [VP6A,15B] ~ ***(up),*** disturb the peace, calm or smoothness of: *The bird* ~*d up its feathers. A sudden breeze* ~*d the surface of the lake. Who's been ruffling your hair? Anne is easily* ~*d,* easily annoyed, put out of temper. **2** [VP2A] become ~d: *You* ~ *too easily.* □ *n* [C] **1** strip of material gathered into folds; frill used to ornament a garment at the wrist, neck or breast. **2** ruffling or being ~d(1).

rug /rʌg/ *n* **1** floor mat of thick material (usu smaller than a carpet): = *a* ˈ*hearth-rug.* **2** thick, usu woollen, covering or wrap: *a* ˈ*travelling-rug* (for putting round one's knees in a car, etc).

Rugby /ˈrʌgbɪ/ *n* ~ **(football),** (GB) kind of football using an oval-shaped ball which may be handled: ~ *League,* form of ~ with thirteen players and allowing professionalism; ~ *Union,* with fifteen players and having amateur teams only.

rug·ged /ˈrʌgɪd/ *adj* **1** rough; uneven; rocky: *a* ~ *coast;* ~ *country.* **2** having furrows or wrinkles: *a* ~ *face;* ~ *features.* **3** rough, but kindly and honest: *a* ~ *old peasant;* ~ *manners.* **~·ly** *adv* **~·ness** *n*

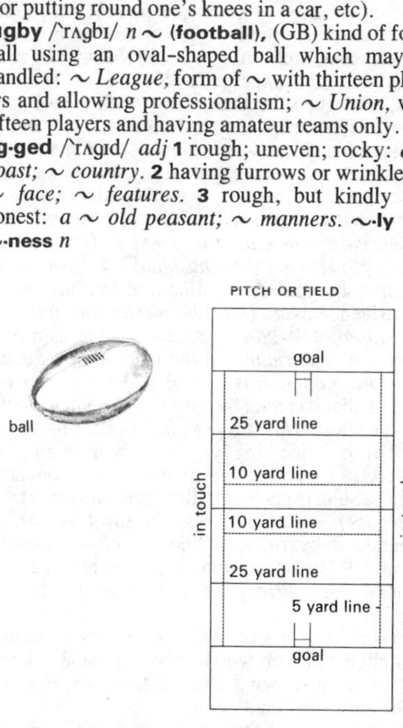

PITCH OR FIELD
ball
goal
25 yard line
10 yard line
in touch
10 yard line
in touch
25 yard line
5 yard line
goal

Rugby football (rugger)

rug·ger /ˈrʌɡə(r)/ *n* [U] (colloq) Rugby football.

ruin /ˈruɪn/ *n* **1** [U] destruction; overthrow; serious damage: *the ~ of her hopes; the impulse that led to my ~; brought to ~ by gambling and drink.* **2** [U] state of being decayed, destroyed, collapsed: *The castle has fallen into ~.* ***go to rack and ~,*** ⇨ rack[4]. [C] sth which has decayed, been destroyed, etc: *The building is in ~s. The abbey is now a ~.* **3** (*sing* only) cause of ~: *Gambling was his ~* (= was the ~ of him). □ *vt* [VP6A] cause the ~ of: *You will ~ your prospects if you continue to be so foolish. The storm ~ed the crops. He's bankrupt and ~ed,* has lost all his money, property, etc. **~·ation** /ˌruɪˈneɪʃn/ *n* [U] being ~ed; bringing to ~: *These late frosts mean ~ation to the fruit farmers.* **~·ous** /-əs/ *adj* **1** causing ~: *~ous expenditure/folly.* **2** in ~s: *live in a ~ous old house.* **~·ous·ly** *adv*

rule /rul/ *n* **1** [C] law or custom which guides or controls behaviour or action; decision made by an organization, etc about what must or must not be done: *obey the ~s of the game. There is a ~ that.... It's against the ~s to handle the ball in soccer.* ***~(s) of the road,*** ⇨ road(1). ***by/according to ~,*** according to ~s and regulations: *He does everything by ~,* never uses his own judgement. ***work to ~,*** pay exaggerated attention (deliberately) to ~s and regulations and so slow down output: *Instead of coming out on strike, the men decided to work to ~.* **ˈ~ book,** book (issued to workers) containing such ~s and regulations. ***~ of thumb,*** ⇨ thumb. **2** [C] sth that is the usual practice; habit: *My ~ is to get up at seven and have breakfast at eight. Rainy weather is the ~ here during April. He makes it a ~ to do an hour's work in the garden every day. She makes a ~ of going for a walk every afternoon.* ***as a ~,*** usually; more often than not. **3** [U] government; authority: *the ~ of the people; countries that were once under French ~. The ~ of law; mob ~,* state that exists when a mob takes over. **4** [C] strip of wood, metal, etc, used to measure: *a ˈfoot-~; a ˈslide-~.* □ *vi,vt* **1** [VP2A, B,6A,3A] ~ ***(over),*** govern; have authority (over): *King Charles I ~d (England) for eleven years without a parliament. An emperor is a monarch who ~s over an empire. Is it true that Mrs Winkle ~s her husband?* **2** (usu in the *passive*) be guided or influenced by; have power or influence over: *Don't be ~d by your passions/by hatred.* **3** [VP6A,9,15A,B,25] give as a decision: *The chairman ~d the motion out of order/that the motion was out of order.* ***~ sth out,*** declare that it cannot be considered, that it is out of the question: *That's a possibility that can't be ~d out,* It is something we must bear in mind. **4** [VP6A,15A,B] make (a line or lines) on paper (with a ruler); make parallel lines on (paper): *~d notepaper; ~ a line across the sheet.* ***~ sth off,*** separate it by ruling a line: *~ off a column of figures.* **5** [VP2C] (comm, of prices) have a certain general level: *Prices ~d high,* were, for the most part, high.

ruler /ˈrulə(r)/ *n* **1** person who rules or governs. **2** straight length of wood, plastic, metal, etc usu flat, used in drawing straight lines, or, if graduated, for measuring.

rul·ing /ˈrulɪŋ/ *adj* that rules; pre-dominating; prevalent; *his ruling passion,* that which governs his actions. □ *n* [C] (esp) decision made by sb in authority, e g a judge.

rum[1] /rʌm/ *n* [U] alcoholic drink made from sugar-cane juice; (US) (any kind of) alcoholic liquor. **ˈrum-runner** *n* person or ship engaged in the illegal importation of alcoholic liquor.

rum[2] /rʌm/ *n* [U] *adj* (**rummer, rummest**) (colloq) queer; odd: *What a rum fellow he is!* **rummy** *adj* = rum[2].

rumba /ˈrʌmbə/ *n* [C] (music for a) ballroom dance that originated among Cuban Negroes.

rumble /ˈrʌmbl/ *vi,vt* **1** [VP2A,C] make a deep, heavy, continuous sound: *thunder/gun-fire rumbling in the distance;* move with such a sound: *heavy carts rumbling along the street;* (of the bowels) make sounds as gas moves through them. **2** [VP15B] utter, say, in a deep voice: *~ out/forth a few comments/remarks.* □ *n* **1** [U] deep, heavy, continuous sound: *the ~ of thunder.* **2** [C] place at the back of a carriage where a person could sit, luggage be carried, etc; (= dickey-seat; US, also *ˈ~-seat*) extra, open seat at the back of an (old-fashioned) automobile.

rum·bus·tious /rʌmˈbʌstʃəs/ *adj* boisterous.

ru·mi·nant /ˈrumɪnənt/ *n, adj* (animal) which chews the cud, e g cows, deer.

ru·mi·nate /ˈrumɪneɪt/ *vi* [VP2A,B,C] meditate; turn over in the mind: *~ over/about/on recent events;* (of animals) chew the cud. **ru·mi·na·tive** /ˈrumɪnətɪv/ *adj* inclined to meditate. **ru·mi·na·tion** /ˌrumɪˈneɪʃn/ *n* [U].

rum·mage /ˈrʌmɪdʒ/ *vi,vt* **1** [VP2A,B,C] turn things over, move things about, while looking for sth: *~ in a desk drawer; ~ about among old papers.* **2** [VP6A,15B] search thoroughly: *~ a ship,* e g by Customs officers who suspect that there is contraband. □ *n* [U] **1** search (esp of a ship by Customs officers). **2** things found by rummaging; miscellaneous old clothes, old stock, etc. **ˈ~ sale,** = jumble (the more usu word) sale.

rummy[1] /ˈrʌmɪ/ *adj* ⇨ rum[2].

rummy[2] /ˈrʌmɪ/ *n* [U] simple game played with two packs of cards.

ru·mour (US = **ru·mor**) /ˈrumə(r)/ *n* [U] general talk, gossip, hearsay, [C] (statement, report, story) which cannot be verified and is of doubtful accuracy: *R~ has it/There is a ~ that there will be a General Election in the autumn. All sorts of ~s are going round. There is a ~ of the Loch Ness monster having been seen/a ~ that the... has been seen.* **ˈ~-monger** *n* person who spreads ~s. □ *vt* (usu passive) report by way of ~: *It is ~ed that.... He is ~ed to have escaped to Dublin.*

rump /rʌmp/ *n* [C] **1** animal's buttocks; tail-end of a bird; (joc, of a human being) bottom. **ˌ~-ˈsteak** *n* beefsteak cut from near the ~. **2** contemptible remnant of a parliament or similar body.

rumple /ˈrʌmpl/ *vt* [VP6A] crease; crumple; make rough: *Don't play too violently or you'll ~ your dresses. I've just done my hair, so please don't ~ it.*

rum·pus /ˈrʌmpəs/ *n* (*sing* only; colloq) disturbance; noise; uproar: *have a ~ with sb. What's all this ~ about?* ***kick up/make a ~,*** cause a ~.

run[1] /rʌn/ *n* **1** act of running on foot: *go for a short run across the fields;* (in fox-hunting) period of chasing a fox. ***at a run,*** running: *He started off at a run but soon tired and began to walk.* ***on the run,*** **(a)** in flight: *He's on the run from the police. We have the enemy on the run,* they are running away. **(b)** continuously active and moving about:

She's always on the run. I've been on the run ever since I got up. ***get/give sb a (good) run for his money,*** **(a)** obtain (sth) in return for his efforts, expenditure. **(b)** provide him with strong competition. *We must give him a good run for his money.* **2** [C] excursion or visit: *a run to Paris; have a run in the country,* e g by car; outing or journey in a car, train, etc: *How many hours' run is Leeds from London by train? Can we have a trial run in the new car?* **3** [C] distance travelled by a ship in a specified time: *make bets on the day's run,* on the distance travelled in 24 hours. **4** route taken by vehicles, ships, etc: *The boat was taken off its usual run.* **5** quick fall: *Prices/The temperature came down with a run.* **6** series of performances: *The play had a long run/a run of six months.* **7** period; succession: *a run of bad luck,* a series of misfortunes. ***a run on a bank,*** a demand by many customers together for immediate repayment. ***in the long run,*** ultimately: *It pays in the long run to buy goods of high quality.* **8** (usu large, enclosed) space for domestic animals, fowls, etc: *a `chicken-run; a `sheep-run,* area of pasture for sheep. **9** (cricket and baseball) unit of scoring, made by running over a certain course. **10** common, average or ordinary type or class: *the common run of mankind,* ordinary, average people; *an hotel out of the common run,* different from, and better than, the kind one usually finds. **'run-of-the-`mill,** ordinary; average. **11** (colloq) permission to make free use (of). ***get/give sb the run of sth,*** the permission to use it: *I have the run of his library.* **12** way in which things tend to move; general direction or trend: *The run of events is rather puzzling. The run of the cards* (= the cards that were dealt to me during the evening) *favoured me.* **13** (music) series of notes sung or played quickly and in the order of the scale. **14** shoal of fish in motion: *a run of salmon,* e g on their way upstream.

run[2] /rʌn/ *vi,vt* (*pt* ran /ræn/, *pp* run; -nn-) (For special uses and *adverbial particles* and *preps,* ⇨ 26 below; for special uses of *running, part adj,* ⇨ running.) **1** [VP2A,B,C,E,4A] (of men and animals) move with quick steps, faster than when walking: *run three miles; run fast; run (out) to see what's happening; run upstairs. She came running to meet me. She ran to meet us. We ran to his aid/ran to help him. The dog was running behind its master.* ⇨ run after in 26 below. *Don't run across the road until you're sure it's safe.* ***take a running jump,*** run up to the point where one starts a jump; (sl, imper) go away, you are being foolish, etc. **2** [VP2A,B,C] escape or avoid by going away; take to flight: *As soon as we appeared the boys ran off. Run for your lives!* ***run for it,*** avoid sth, e g getting wet in a storm, by running. ***cut and run,*** (sl) escape by taking to flight. ***a running fight,*** a fight between a retreating ship/fleet, etc and those in pursuit. **3** [VP2A,B,C] practice running for exercise or as a sport; compete in races on foot: *He used to run when he was at college. Is he running in the 100 metres? Is your horse likely to run in the Derby?* ***also ran,*** **(a)** used of a horse not among the first three past the winning post: *Hyperion also ran.* **(b)** (as a *n*) person or animal unsuccessful in a race or other form of competition. **4** [VP3A] ***~ for,*** (esp US) compete for (an elected office). Cf *stand for,* the more usu GB usage: *run for President/for mayor.* **5** [VP6A,15A] cause to compete (in a race); present or nominate (for an office): *run two horses in the Derby. How many candidates is the Liberal Party running in the General Election?* **6** [VP2D,15A] (cause to) reach a certain condition or place as the result of running: *He ran second in the race.* ***run oneself out (of breath),*** ⇨ run out in 26 below. ***run sb clean off his feet/legs,*** (colloq) keep him going until he is exhausted. ***run oneself/sb into the ground,*** exhaust oneself/sb by hard work or exercise. **7** [VP6A] make one's way quickly to the end of, or through or over (sth). ***run its course,*** develop in the usual or normal way: *The disease ran its course.* ***run a race,*** take part in one. ***run the rapids,*** (of a boat, men in a boat) move rapidly over or through them. ⇨ shoot[2](4), the more usu word. ***run the streets,*** (of children) spend time playing (esp without supervision) in the streets. **8** [VP6A] expose oneself to: be open to. ***run the chance/danger of sth***: *You run the chance of being suspected of theft.* ***run risks/a risk/the risk of sth,*** ⇨ risk. **9** [VP15A] chase; compete with. ***run sb/sth to earth,*** pursue until caught or found: *run a fox to earth,* chase it until it goes to its earth; (fig) *run a quotation to earth,* find, after searching, where it occurs. ***run sb/sth close/hard,*** be almost equal to, as good as, in merit, etc: *We run our competitors close for price and quality. It was a close run thing,* (of competition, etc) The result was very close. **10** [VP2A,C] (of ships, etc) sail or steer; (of fish) swim: *The ship was running before the wind. Our ship ran aground/on the rocks/ashore. We ran into port for supplies. The two ships ran foul of each other,* collided. *The salmon are running,* swimming upstream from the sea. **11** [VP2C] go forward with a sliding, smooth or continuous motion; advance on, or as if on, wheels: *Trams run on rails; buses don't run on rails. Sledges run well over frozen snow. The train ran past the signal.* **12** [VP2A,C] be in action; work freely; be in working order: *Don't leave the engine of your car running. The sewing-machine doesn't run properly. The works have ceased running,* The factory has closed, is no longer producing goods. *His life has run smoothly up to now.* **13** [VP2A,C] (of public conveyances, e g buses, ferry-boats) ply; journey to and fro: *The buses run every ten minutes. The 9.05 train is not running today. There are frequent trains running between London and Brighton.* **14** [VP6A] organize; manage; cause to be in operation: *run a business/a theatre/a bus company; run extra trains during the rush hours. Can I run* (= operate) *my electric sewing-machine off the light circuit? I can't afford to run a car* (= own and use one) *on my small salary. Who runs his house for him now that his wife has divorced him? Mr Green is run by his secretary,* She is the dominant personality and tells him what to do, etc. ***run the show,*** (colloq) be boss in an undertaking; have control. **15** [VP6A,15A,B] convey; transport: *I'll run you up to town/run you back home,* drive you there in my car. ***run errands/messages (for sb),*** make journeys to do things, carry messages, etc. ***run arms,*** convey them into a country unlawfully. ***run liquor/contraband,*** smuggle it into a country; get it past the coastguards secretly. **16** [VP14, 15A] cause to move quickly (in a certain direction or into a certain place): *run a car into a garage; run one's fingers/a comb through one's hair; run* *one's eyes over a page; run one's fingers over the keys of a piano.* **17** [VP2C] (of thoughts, feelings, etc, eyes, exciting news, etc) pass or move briefly or quickly: *The thought kept running through my head. Mary's eyes ran critically over her friend's new dress. The pain ran up my arm. A shiver ran down his spine. The news ran like wildfire. A whisper ran through the crowd. A cheer ran down the ranks of spectators as the Queen drove past.* **18** [VP15A] cause (sth) to penetrate (intentionally or by accident) or come into contact with; penetrate or pierce (sb/sth) with sth: *run a sword through a man/run a man through with a sword; run a splinter into one's finger; run one's head against a glass door in a dark corridor. The drunken driver ran his car into a tree.* **19** [VP2A,B,C] (of liquids, grain, sand, etc) flow, drip; (of surfaces) be wet (with); (of colours, e g dyes) flow and spread: *Rivers run into the sea. The tears ran down my cheeks. Who has left the tap/water running? The tide was running strong. The beggar's legs were covered with running sores. Your nose is running, dear—use your hanky,* i e wipe your nose clean. *Water was running all over the bathroom floor. The floor was running with water. Will the colours run if the dress is washed?* **20** [VP6A,15A,B] cause (a liquid, molten metal, etc) to flow: *Run some hot water into the bowl. Run the water off,* (= let it flow out) *when you've had your bath. The molten metal was run into a mould.* **21** [VP2D] become; pass into (a specified condition): *The rivers are running dry,* ceasing to flow. *Supplies are running short/low. I have run short of money. Feelings/Passions ran high,* became stormy or violent. *My blood ran cold,* I was filled with horror. ***run riot,*** **(a)** behave in a wild and lawless way. **(b)** (of plants, etc) grow unchecked. ***run wild,*** be without control, restraint, discipline, etc: *The garden is running wild. She lets her children run wild.* ***run a temperature,*** (colloq) become feverish. **22** [VP2A,B,C] extend; have a certain course or order; be continued or continuous; *shelves running round the walls; a scar that runs across his left cheek; a road that runs across the plain; a fence running round the paddock. It happened several days running,* several days in succession. *He hit the target seven times running. The play ran (for) six months,* was kept on the stage, was performed, during this period of time. *The lease of my house has only a year to run.* ***a running commentary,*** account of an event as it occurs by a broadcaster: *a running commentary of a football match.* **ˈrunning costs,** continuous costs for producing goods, etc (as opposed to costs of original manufacture. **23** [VP2C,D] have a tendency or common characteristic; have as an average price or level: *This author runs to sentiment. Feeble-mindedness runs in the family. Our apples run rather small this year. Prices for fruit are running high this season.* **24** [VP2A] be told or written: *So the story ran,* that is what was told or said. *The story runs that...,* It is said that.... *The agreement runs in these words. I forget how the next verse runs,* how the words or notes follow one another. **25** [VP2A] (of woven or knitted material) become unwoven or unravelled; drop stitches through several rows: *Nylon tights sometimes run.* ⇨ **ladder**, the more usu word with reference to stockings. **26** [VP2C,3A,15B] (special uses with *adverbial particles* and *preps*):

run across sb/sth, meet or find by chance; *I ran across my old friend Hill in Paris last week.*

run after sb/sth, **(a)** try to catch: *The dog was running after a rabbit.* **(b)** seek the society of; go after in order to get the attention of: *She runs after every good-looking man in the village.*

run against sb, compete with him by running in a race; (esp US) compete with him for (an elected office).

run along, (colloq) go away, be off: *Now, children, run along!*

run away, leave: *Don't run away—I want your advice. The boy ran away and went to sea,* left home and became a sailor. ***run away with sb,*** **(a)** elope with: *The butler ran away with the duke's daughter.* **(b)** go at a speed too high for control: *Don't let your horse/car run away with you.* **(c)** destroy the self-control of: *Don't let your temper run away with you.* ***run away with sth,*** **(a)** use up: *This new scheme will run away with a lot of the ratepayers' money.* **(b)** carry off; steal: *The maid ran away with the duchess's jewels.* **(c)** get a clear win over: *The girl from Peru ran away with the first set,* e g in a tennis tournament. ***run away with the idea/notion that,*** assume too hastily that sth is the case: *Don't run away with the idea that I can lend you money every time you need help.*

run back over sth, review past events, etc: *run back over the past. I'll run back over the procedure again.* ***run sth back,*** rewind (film, tape, etc) (after it has been looked at, listened to).

run down, **(a)** (of a clock or other mechanism worked by weights) stop because it needs winding up. **(b)** (of a battery) become weak or exhausted: *The battery is/has run down; it needs recharging.* ***(be/feel/look) run down,*** (of a person, his health) exhausted or weak from overwork, mental strain, etc. ***run sb/sth down,*** knock down or collide with: *The liner ran down a fishing-boat during the dense fog. The cyclist was run down by a big lorry.* ***run sb down,*** **(a)** say unkind things about; disparage: *That man doesn't like me; he's always running me down.* **(b)** pursue and overtake: *run down an escaped prisoner.* ***run sth down,*** allow to become less active or occupied: *run down the ship's boilers; run down a naval dockyard,* do less work and employ fewer workers. Hence, **ˈrun-down** *n* reduction: *the run-down of the coal industry.*

run for sth, **(a)** ⇨ 2 above. **(b)** ⇨ 4 above.

run in, pay a short informal visit (esp by car): *I'll run in and see you this evening.* ***run sb in,*** (colloq of the police) arrest and take to a police station: *The drunken man was run in for creating a public disturbance.* ***run sth in,*** bring (new machinery, esp the engine of a car) into good condition by running it carefully for a time or distance: *He's still running in his new car and doesn't exceed thirty miles an hour.*

run into sb, meet unexpectedly: *run into an old friend at a race-meeting.* ***run into sth,*** **(a)** collide with: *The bus got out of control and ran into a wall.* **(b)** fall into: *run into debt/danger/difficulties.* **(c)** reach (a level or figure): *a book that has run into six editions. His income runs into five figures,* is now ten thousand (pounds, dollars, etc) or more. ***run sb into sth,*** cause (sb) to fall into (a certain state): *My wife never runs me into debt/unnecessary expense.* ***run sth into sth,***

cause (sth) to be in collision: *run one's car into a wall.*
run off with sb/sth, go away with; steal and take away: *His daughter has run off with a married man. The treasurer has run off with all the funds.* ***run sth off,*** **(a)** cause to flow away: *run off the water from a tank,* empty the tank. **(b)** write or recite fluently, e g a list of names: *run off an article for the local (news)paper.* **(c)** print; produce: *run off a hundred copies on the duplicating machine.* **(d)** decide (a race) after a tie, or trial heats; cause to be run or played: *run off a heat. When will the race be run off?* Hence, **ˈrun-off** *n* deciding race, etc after a dead heat or tie. ⇨ **dead.** ***run off sb (like water off a duck's back),*** have no effect on: *Her scoldings ran off him like water off a duck's back.*
run on, **(a)** talk continuously: *He will run on for an hour if you don't stop him. How that woman's tongue does run on!* **(b)** elapse: *Time ran on.* **(c)** (of a disease) continue its course. ***run (sth) on,*** **(a)** (of written letters of the alphabet) join, be joined, together: *When children are learning to write, they should let the letters run on, not write them separately. They should run the letters on.* ***run on sth,*** be concerned with: *Our talk ran on recent events in India.* ***run (up)on sth,*** ⇨ below.
run out, **(a)** go out: *The tide is running out.* **(b)** (of a period of time) come to an end: *When does the lease of the house run out?* **(c)** (of stocks, supplies) come to an end, be exhausted; (of persons) become short of (supplies, etc): *Our provisions are running out. We're running out of provisions. Her patience is running out. The sands are running out,* (with reference to the sand in an hourglass) the time allowed to us (before something unwelcome comes) is coming to an end. **(d)** jut out; project: *a pier running out into the sea.* ***run (sth) out,*** (of rope) pass out; he passed out: *The rope ran out smoothly. The sailor ran the rope out neatly.* ***be run out,*** (cricket, of a batsman) have his innings ended because, while trying to make a run, he fails to reach his ground before the wicket-keeper or one of the fielders returns the ball and removes the bails or stump(s). *Smith was run out before he had scored.* ***run oneself out (of breath),*** exhaust oneself: *He's completely run out.* ***run out on sb,*** (sl) abandon, desert: *Poor Jane! Her husband has run out on her.*
run over, **(a)** (of a vessel or its contents) overflow. **(b)** pay a short or quick visit to: *run over to a neighbour's house to borrow sth.* ***run over sth,*** **(a)** review; recapitulate: *Let's run over our parts again,* e g when learning and rehearsing parts in a play. **(b)** read through quickly: *He ran (his eyes) over his notes before starting his lecture.* ***run over sb/run sb over,*** (of a vehicle) (knock down and) pass over (sb or sth lying on the ground): *The bus ran over his legs. He was run over and had to be taken to hospital.*
run round, = run over(b): *run round to a neighbour's house to borrow sth.*
run sth through sth, draw a line, one's pen, through sth.
run sb through, pierce with a sword, bayonet, etc: *He was run through and through.*
run through sth, **(a)** use up (a fortune, etc) esp by foolish or reckless spending: *He soon ran through the money he won on the Pools.* **(b)** examine quickly; deal with in rapid succession: *run through one's mail during breakfast.*
run to sth, **(a)** reach (an amount, number, etc): *That will run to a pretty penny,* will cost a lot of money. **(b)** have money for; (of money) be enough for: *We can't/Our funds won't run to a holiday abroad this year. I can't run to that,* can't afford it. **(c)** extend to: *His new novel has already run to great length/run to three impressions.* ***run to fat,*** (of persons) tend to put on too much fat. ***run to ruin,*** fall into ruin. ***run to seed,*** (of plants) tend to develop chiefly seed instead of new growth of leaves, etc. ***run to waste,*** (e g of water) be wasted.
run up, (cricket; of a bowler) gather speed by running, before releasing the ball; (of athletes in some field events) gather speed before jumping, throwing a javelin, etc. Hence, **ˈrun-up** *n* **(a)** (length or manner of a) bowler's or athlete's approach: *a long/short run-up.* **(b)** period leading up (to sth): *the run-up to the General Election,* the period when candidates are busy seeking support, etc. ***run sth up,*** **(a)** raise; hoist: *run up a flag on the mast.* **(b)** erect, make or construct quickly or in an unsubstantial way: *run up a dress/a garden shed.* **(c)** add up (a column of figures). **(d)** cause to grow quickly in amount: *run up a big bill at a hotel; run up the bidding at an auction,* force others to bid higher, force up prices. ***run up against, sth,*** meet by chance or unexpectedly: *run up against difficulties.* ***run up to,*** amount, extend to (a figure): *Prices ran up to £5 a ton.* ***run (up)on sth,*** **(a)** (of thoughts, etc) be concerned with: *That boy's thoughts are always running on food. His thoughts were running upon the past.* **(b)** (of a ship) strike: *The ship ran upon the rocks.*

rune /run/ *n* any letter of an old alphabet used in N Europe, esp of the Scandinavians and Anglo-Saxons (from A D 200); similar mark of a mysterious or magic sort. **runic** /ˈrunɪk/ *adj* of ~s; written in, inscribed with, ~s.

rung[1] /rʌŋ/ *n* [C] **1** crosspiece forming a step in a ladder: (fig) *start on the lowest/reach the highest ~ (of the ladder),* (fig) a particular level in society, one's employment, etc. **2** crosspiece joining the legs of a chair to strengthen it.

rung[2] /rʌŋ/ *pp* of **ring**[2].

run·nel /ˈrʌnl/ *n* **1** brook. **2** open gutter (for rainwater) at a roadside, etc.

run·ner /ˈrʌnə(r)/ *n* **1** person, animal, etc that runs: *How many ~s were there in the Derby?* **ˈ~-ˈup** *n* person or team taking the second place in a competition. **2** messenger, scout, collector, etc: *Bow Street ~,* (old use) police-officer. **3** (in compounds) smuggler: *ˈgun-~s; ˈrum-~s.* **bloˈckade-~,** person who tries to get through the forces that are blockading a port, etc. **4** part on which sth slides or moves along: *the ~s of a sledge.* **5** long piece of cloth (for a sideboard, etc); long piece of carpet, e g for stairs. **6** stem coming from a strawberry plant and taking root; kinds of twining bean-plant, esp *ˈscarlet ~s:* (attrib) *~ beans.*

run·ning /ˈrʌnɪŋ/ *n* [U] **1** act of a person or animal that runs, esp in racing. ***make the ~,*** set the pace (liter and fig). ***take up the ~,*** take the lead. ***in/out of the ~,*** (of competitors) having some/no chance of winning. **2** **ˈ~-board** *n* (now old-fashioned) footboard on either side of a car. **ˈ~ mate, (a)** horse used to set the pace for another horse in a race. **(b)** candidate for the lesser of two associated political offices, e g for the Vice-Presidency of the US. □ *adj* **1** done, made, carried on, while or immediately after running: *a ~ kick/jump/fight.* ⇨ run²(1,2). **2** continuous; uninterrupted: *a ~ fire of questions,* coming in a continuous stream; *a ~ hand,* (of handwriting) with the letters joined. ***a ~ commentary,*** ⇨ run²(22). **3** (after a *pl n*) in succession: *win three times ~.* **4** (of water) flowing; coming from a mains supply: *All bedrooms in this hotel have hot and cold ~ water,* coming when taps are turned. **5** (of sores, etc) with liquid or pus coming out. **6** *a ˋ~ knot,* one that slips along a rope and so makes the noose larger or smaller. ⇨ the illus at knot.

runny /ˈrʌnɪ/ *adj* (-ier, -iest) (colloq) semi-liquid; tending to run(18) or flow: *a ~ nose. The jam is rather ~; you'd better boil it again.*

runt /rʌnt/ *n* (colloq) undersized or stunted plant, animal (esp the smallest of a litter); or person.

run·way /ˈrʌnweɪ/ *n* **1** specially prepared surface along which aircraft take off and land. **2** way made for rolling felled trees and logs down a hill-side.

ru·pee /ruˋpi/ *n* [C] monetary unit of India, Pakistan, Sri Lanka, Nepal, Mauritius, etc.

ru·piah /ruˋpiə/ *n* monetary unit of Indonesia.

rup·ture /ˈrʌptʃə(r)/ *n* **1** [U] breaking apart or bursting; [C] instance of this. **2** [C,U] (instance of) ending of friendly relations. **3** [C] swelling in the abdomen caused by the breaking of some organ or tissue through the wall of its retaining cavity. ⇨ hernia. □ *vt, vi* [VP6A,2A] break or burst, e g a blood-vessel or membrane; end (a connection, etc).

ru·ral /ˈrʊərl/ *adj* in, of, characteristic of, suitable for, the countryside (opp of *urban*): *~ scenery; live in ~ seclusion.*

Ru·ri·tan·ian /ˈrʊərɪˋteɪnɪən/ *adj* (of a State, its politics) full of plots and intrigues (as in a melodramatic story about an imaginary country called Ruritania).

ruse /ruz/ *n* [C] deceitful way of doing sth, getting sth, etc; trick; stratagem.

rush¹ /rʌʃ/ *n* **1** [U] rapid, headlong movement; sudden swift advance; [C] instance of this: *I don't like the ~ of city life. He was swept away by the ~ of the current and drowned. Why all this ~,* this hurry and excitement? *There were several ~es to the refreshment tent during the afternoon. There was the usual Easter ~,* i e of traffic to the holiday resorts, etc. **ˋgold ~,** ⇨ gold. **2** [C] sudden demand: *a ~ for raincoats,* e g when there is heavy rain; sudden or intense activity: *the Christmas ~,* the period before Christmas when crowds of people go shopping. **the ˋ~-hour,** when crowds of people are travelling to or from work in a large town: (attrib) *We were caught in the ~-hour traffic.* **3** (cinema, often *pl*) first print of a film before cutting and editing.

rush² /rʌʃ/ *n* [C] (tall stem of one of numerous varieties of) marsh plant with slender leafless stems containing pith, often dried and used for making seats or chairs, for weaving into baskets, etc, and, in olden times, for strewing floors. **ˋ~-light** *n* kind of candle made by dipping the pith of a ~ into tallow. **rushy** *adj* full of, abounding with, ~es: *a ~y ditch.*

rush³ /rʌʃ/ *vi, vt* **1** [VP6A,15A,B,2A,C,4A] (cause to) go or come, do sth, with violence or speed: *The children ~ed out of the school gates. They ~ed (out) to see the procession. The bull ~ed at me. They ~ed more troops to the front.* ***~ to conclusions,*** form them hastily. ***~ into print,*** publish sth without proper care, consideration, etc. ***~ sth through,*** do sth at high speed: *The order for furniture was ~ed through* (= The goods were packed and sent off) *in two days. The new Bill was ~ed through Parliament.* **2** [VP6A] capture by a sudden attack; get through, over, into, etc by pressing eagerly or violently forward: *~ the enemy's trenches; ~ the gates of the football ground. The panic-stricken passengers tried to ~ the boats,* force their way into them quickly. **3** [VP6A,15A] force into hasty action: *I must think things over, so don't ~ me.* ***~ sb off his feet,*** succeed in forcing him into hasty action with no time for thought; exhaust him. **4** ***~ (for sth),*** (sl) charge an exorbitant price: *How much did they ~ you for this?*

rusk /rʌsk/ *n* [C] piece of bread baked hard and crisp; kind of crisp biscuit: *ˋteething ~s.*

rus·set /ˈrʌsɪt/ *n* **1** [U] yellowish or reddish brown. **2** [C] kind of rough-skinned ~-coloured apple. □ *adj* of the colour of ~.

Rus·sian /ˈrʌʃn/ *adj* of or from Russia. **R~ roulette,** ⇨ roulette. □ *n* **1** native of Russia. **2** the principal language of the Soviet Union.

rust /rʌst/ *n* [U] **1** reddish-brown coating formed on iron by the action of water and air; similar coating on other metals: *~-covered machinery; rub the ~ off sth.* **2** (plant-disease with ~-coloured spots caused by) kinds of fungus; mildew; blight. □ *vt, vi* [VP6A,2A,C] (cause to) become covered with ~; (fig) become poor in quality because not used: *Don't leave the lawn-mower out in the garden to ~. It's better to wear out than to ~ out,* to become worn through use than to lose value by ~ing. **~·less** *adj* that does not ~: *~less steel,* used for stainless cutlery, etc. **rusty** *adj* (-ier, -iest) **1** covered with ~: *~y needles.* **2** in need of being polished or revised: *My German is rather ~y,* hasn't been used for a long time and needs to be practised. **3** (of black cloth) discoloured by age; dingy or shabby. **4** (of persons) behind the times; out of practice. **~i·ness** *n* [U].

rus·tic /ˈrʌstɪk/ *adj* **1** (in a good sense) characteristic of country people; simple; unaffected: *~ simplicity.* **2** rough; unrefined: *~ speech/manners,* contrasted with the speech, etc of smart, city people. **3** of rough workmanship: *a ~ bench/bridge,* made or rough, unplaned timber and untrimmed branches. □ *n* countryman; peasant. **~·ity** /rʌˋstɪsətɪ/ *n* [U] being ~ in appearance or character.

rus·ti·cate /ˈrʌstɪkeɪt/ *vi, vt* **1** [VP2A] lead a rural life. **2** [VP6A] (GB) send (a student) temporarily away from the university as a punishment.

rustle /ˈrʌsl/ *vi, vt* **1** [VP2A,C] make a gentle, light sound (like dry leaves blown by the wind, or of silk clothes in motion); move along making such a sound: *Did you hear something rustling through the undergrowth?* **2** [VP6A] cause to make this sound: *I wish people wouldn't ~ their programmes while the orchestra is playing.* **3** [VP6A] (US, colloq) steal (cattle or horses). **4** [VP15B] ***~ sth up,*** get together, provide: *~ up some food for an unexpected guest.* □ *n* [U] gentle light sound as of dry leaves blown by the wind, of silk clothes, etc: *the ~ of paper.* **rust·ler** /ˈrʌslə(r)/ *n* (US, colloq) cattle thief. **rust·ling** /ˈrʌslɪŋ/ *n* [U] sound made by sth that ~s: *the rustling of dry leaves/of* *sweet wrappings;* (*pl*) repetitions of such sounds. *mysterious rustlings at night.*

rut[1] /rʌt/ *n* [C] **1** line or track made by wheel(s) in soft ground. **2** (fig) way of doing sth, behaving, living, etc that has become established. ***be in/get into a rut,*** a fixed (and boring) way of living so that it becomes difficult to change; *lift sb out of the rut.* □ *vt* (-tt-) (usu in *pp*) mark with ruts: *a deeply rutted road.*

rut[2] /rʌt/ *n* [U] periodic sexual excitement of male animals, esp deer. □ *vi* (-tt-) be affected with this: *the rutting season.*

ruth·less /ˋruθləs/ *adj* cruel; without pity; showing no mercy. **~·ly** *adv* **~·ness** *n*

rye /rɑɪ/ *n* [U] **1** (plant with) grain used for making flour, and as a food for cattle. ⇨ the illus at cereal. **ˋrye-bread** *n* black bread made with flour from rye. **2** kind of whisky made from rye.

Ss

S, s /es/ (*pl* S's, s's /ˋesɪz/) the nineteenth letter of the English alphabet.

sab·ba·tarian /ˌsæbəˋteərɪən/ *n* Christian who advocates strict observance of Sunday (e g by opposing the opening of places of entertainment, the playing of games, etc on Sundays). □ *adj* of the principles of ~s.

Sab·bath /ˋsæbəθ/ *n* day of rest, Saturday for Jews, Sunday for Christians: *break the ~*, work or play on the ~; *keep the ~*, spend it in worship of God and in rest.

sab·bati·cal /səˋbætɪkl/ *adj* of or like the Sabbath: *After this uproar there came a ~ calm.* **~ year,** year of freedom from routine duties given to some university teachers to enable them to travel or undertake special studies.

sa·ber /ˋseɪbə(r)/ ⇨ sabre.

sable /ˋseɪbl/ *n* [C] small animal valued for its beautiful dark fur; [U] fur of this animal: *a ~ coat/stole.* □ *adj* (liter) black; gloomy.

sa·bot /ˋsæbəʊ *US:* sæˋbəʊ/ *n* [C] shoe hollowed out of a single piece of wood, e g as worn by French peasants; wooden-soled shoe with a band of leather across the instep.

sab·otage /ˋsæbətɑʒ/ *n* [U] the wilful damaging of machinery, materials, etc or the hindering of an opponent's activity, during an industrial or political dispute, or during war. □ *vt* [VP6A] perform an act of ~ against. **sab·oteur** /ˌsæbəˋtɜ(r)/ *n* person who commits ~.

sabre (US = **sa·ber**) /ˋseɪbə(r)/ *n* heavy cavalry sword with a curved blade. **ˋ~-rattling** *adj* warlike. **ˋ~-toothed** *adj* having (usu two) ~-like teeth: *a ~-toothed tiger* (now extinct). □ *n* the threatening of war. □ *vt* strike with a ~.

sac /sæk/ *n* bag-like membrane enclosing a cavity in an animal or plant. ⇨ the illus at flower.

sac·char·in /ˋsækərɪn/ *n* [U] very sweet substance made from coaltar, used in place of sugar. **sac·char·ine** /-rin/ *adj* resembling sugar; very sweet; too sweet.

sac·er·do·tal /ˌsæsəˋdəʊtl/ *adj* connected with priests. **~·ism** /-ɪzm/ *n* [U] system of government in which priests (claiming to be mediators between God and mankind) have a great part or exercise great power.

sachet /ˋsæʃeɪ *US:* sæˋʃeɪ/ **1** [C] small perfumed bag. **2** [C,U] (packet of) sweet-smelling dried lavender or other substance for laying among clothes, etc. **3** [C] small, usu plastic bag: *a ~ of shampoo.*

sack[1] /sæk/ *n* **1** (quantity held by a) large bag of strong material (e g coarse flax, hemp, stiffened paper) for storing and carrying heavy goods, e g cement, coal, flour, potatoes: *coal £1 a ~; two ~s of potatoes.* **ˋ~-race** *n* one between competitors each of whom has his legs tied into a sack and moves by short jumps. **ˋ~·cloth** *n* [U] coarse material made of flax or hemp. ***~cloth and ashes,*** **(a)** regret for wrongdoing; penitence. **(b)** mourning. **2** short loose dress. **~·ing** *n* = ~cloth.

sack[2] /sæk/ *n* (*sing* with *def art*) ***give sb/get the ~,*** (colloq) dismiss sb/be dismissed from employment: *He got the ~ for petty thieving.* □ *vt* [VP6A] dismiss from employment.

sack[3] /sæk/ *vt* [VP6A] (of a victorious army) plunder violently (a captured city, etc). □ *n* (usu *sing* with *def art*) ~ing of a captured town, etc: *The citizens lost everything they had during the ~ of the town.*

sack[4] /sæk/ *n* (sl) bed. ***hit the ~,*** go to bed.

sack[5] /sæk/ *n* [U] (old name for) kinds of white wine imported from Spain and the Canaries: *sherry ~; Canary ~.*

sack·but /ˋsækbʌt/ *n* medieval musical wind instrument with a slide like that of a trombone.

sac·ra·ment /ˋsækrəmənt/ *n* [C] solemn religious ceremony in the Christian Church, e g Baptism, Confirmation, Matrimony, believed to be accompanied by great spiritual benefits; (esp) **the Blessed/Holy S~,** Holy Communion, the Eucharist. **sac·ra·men·tal** /ˌsækrəˋmentl/ *adj* of, connected with, ~s: *~al wine.*

sacred /ˋseɪkrəd/ *adj* **1** of God; connected with religion: *a ~ building*, e g a church, mosque, synagogue or temple; *~ music*, for use in religious services; *~ writings*, e g the Koran, the Bible; *~ to the memory of...*, phrase seen on tombstones and memorials to the dead. **2** solemn: *a ~ promise; hold a promise ~; regard sth as a ~ duty.* **3** (to be) treated with great respect or reverence: *In India the cow is a ~ animal. Nothing is ~ to these wild youths,* They respect nothing. **~ cow,** (colloq) sth to be regarded with reverence, and as immune from reasonable criticism. **~·ly** *adv* **~·ness** *n*

sac·ri·fice /ˋsækrɪfɑɪs/ *n* **1** [U] the offering of sth precious to a god; [C] instance of this; [C] the thing offered: *the ~ of an ox to Jupiter; kill a sheep as a ~.* **2** [C,U] the giving up of sth of great value to oneself for a special purpose, or to benefit sb else; [C] sth given up in this way: *He gave his life as a ~ for his country,* e g of a soldier killed in war. *Parents often make ~s* (e g go without things) *in order to educate their children. Is the ~ of one's health to money-making worth while?* **3** sale of sth at a loss or at less than its real value: *He had to sell his house at a ~ in order to pay his gambling debts.* □ *vt,vi* [VP6A,14,3A] ***~ (sth)***

***(to),* 1** make a ~(1): *~ a slave to the gods; ~ to idols.* **2** give up as a ~(2,3): *He ~d his life to save the drowning child. Do you approve of sacrificing comfort to appearance,* e g by wearing formal clothes during hot weather? *She has ~d herself/ her life/her pleasures and pastimes to her husband's interests and welfare.* **sac·ri·fi·cial** /ˈsækrɪˈfɪʃl/ *adj* of or like a ~.

sac·ri·lege /ˈsækrɪlɪdʒ/ *n* [U] disrespectful treatment of, injury to, what should be sacred: *It would be ~ to steal a crucifix from a church altar.* **sac·ri·legious** /ˈsækrɪˈlɪdʒəs/ *adj*

sa·cring bell /ˈseɪkrɪŋ bell/ *n* small bell rung at the Elevation (when the bread and wine is lifted) during Mass.

sac·ris·tan /ˈsækrɪstən/ *n* sexton (which is the usu word in C of E usage).

sac·risty /ˈsækrɪstɪ/ *n* (*pl* -ties) room in a church where vestments and articles used in church worship are kept (*vestry* is the usu word in C of E usage).

sac·ro·sanct /ˈsækrəʊsæŋkt/ *adj* (to be) protected from all harm, because sacred or holy; (fig, often ironic) not to be violated: *He regards his privileges as ~.*

sad /sæd/ *adj* **(sadder, saddest) 1** unhappy; causing unhappy feelings: *John is sad because his dog has died. It was a sad day for Mary when her mother died. Why is he looking so sad?* **2** (of colours) dull. **3** (of pastry, bread) heavy; paste-like because not cooked enough. **4** shameful; deplorably bad: *She's a sad slut.* **sad·ly** *adv* **sad·ness** *n* **sad·den** /ˈsædn/ *vt,vi* [VP6A,2A] make or become sad.

saddle /ˈsædl/ *n* **1** leather seat for a rider on a horse, donkey or bicycle; part of a horse's back on which the seat is placed; ⇨ the illus at **bicycle, harness**. ***in the ~,*** on horseback; (fig) in a position of control or power. **ˈ~-bag** *n* **(a)** one of a pair of bags laid over the back of a horse or donkey. **(b)** small bag hung behind a bicycle ~. **ˈ~-sore** *adj* (of a rider) having sores caused by chafing from the ~. **~ of mutton/venison,** joint of meat from the back of the animal, together with part of the backbone and ribs. **2** line or ridge of high land rising at each end to a high point. ⇨ the illus at **mountain**. □ *vt* **1** [VP6A] put a ~ on (a horse). **2** [VP14] ***~ sb with sth,*** put a heavy responsibility on; put (a burden, etc, on sb): *be ~d with a wife and ten children; ~ sb with heavy tasks.* **sad·dler** /ˈsædlə(r)/ *n* maker of ~s and leather goods for horses. **sad·dlery** /ˈsædlərɪ/ *n* [U] goods made by a saddler; [C] (*pl* -ries) saddler's business.

sadhu /ˈsɑdu/ *n* Hindu holy man who leads an ascetic life.

sa·dism /ˈseɪd-ɪzm/ *n* [C] **1** kind of sexual perversion marked by getting pleasure from cruelty to other persons of either sex. **2** (loosely) (delight in) excessive cruelty. **sa·dist** /-ɪst/ *n* person guilty of ~. **sa·dis·tic** /səˈdɪstɪk/ *adj* of ~.

sa·fari /səˈfɑrɪ/ *n* [C,U] hunting expedition, overland journey, esp in E and Central Africa: *on ~; return from ~;* (by extension) organized tour (for people on holiday) to game reserves, etc.

safe[1] /seɪf/ *adj* **(-r, -st) 1 *~ (from),*** free from, protected from, danger: *~ from attack.* **2** unhurt and undamaged. ***~ and sound,*** secure and unharmed: *return ~ and sound from a dangerous expedition.* **3** not causing or likely to cause harm or danger: *Is 120 kilometres an hour ~ on this wide road? Is your dog ~? Are these toys ~ for small children?* **4** (of a place, etc) giving security: *Keep it in a ~ place. Is this beach ~ for bathing? Is the bathing ~ here? Is this a ~ seat for the Tories,* Is it certain that the Tory candidate will be elected? **5** cautious; not taking risks: *a ~ statesman. They appointed a ~ man as Headmaster.* ***be on the ˈ~ side,*** take more precautions than may be necessary: *Although the sun was shining he took his raincoat and umbrella to be on the ~ side.* **6** certain (to do, be, become): *Mr Hill is ~ to win the seat,* will certainly be elected. **7** (compounds) **ˈ~-ˈconduct** *n* (document giving the) right to visit or pass through a district without the risk of being arrested or harmed (esp in time of war). **ˈ~-deposit** (US = **ˈ~-deˈposit**) *n* building containing strong-rooms and safes which persons may rent separately for storing valuables. **ˈ~-guard (against)** *n* condition, circumstance, etc that tends to prevent harm, give protection. □ *vt* [VP6A,14] protect, guard. **ˈ~-ˈkeeping** *n* [U] care; custody: *Leave your jewels in the bank for ~-keeping while you are on holiday.* **~·ly** *adv* **~·ness** *n*: *a feeling of ~ness* (*safety* is more usu).

safe[2] /seɪf/ *n* **1** fireproof and burglar-proof box in which money and other valuables are kept. **2** cool, airy cupboard in which food is kept to protect it from flies, etc: *a ˈmeat-~.*

safety /ˈseɪftɪ/ *n* [U] **1** being safe; freedom from danger: *do nothing that might endanger the ~ of other people; seek ~ in flight; ensure sb's ~; play for ~,* avoid taking risks in a game (or fig). ***S~ First,*** motto used to warn that ~ is important. ***road ~,*** ~ from traffic dangers. **2** (compounds) **ˈ~-belt,** = seat-belt. **ˈ~-bolt/-catch/-lock,** device that gives ~ against a possible danger (e g to prevent a gun from being fired by accident or a door being opened without the proper key). **ˈ~-curtain** *n* fireproof curtain that can be lowered between the stage and auditorium of a theatre. **ˈ~ glass** *n* glass that does not shatter or splinter. **ˈ~-lamp** *n* miner's lamp in which the flame is protected so as not to ignite dangerous gases. **ˈ~-match** *n* one that lights only when rubbed on a special surface (on the side of the box). **ˈ~-pin** *n* one with a guard for the point. **ˈ~-razor** *n* razor with a guard to prevent the blade from cutting the skin. **ˈ~-valve** *n* **(a)** valve which releases pressure (in a steam boiler, etc) when it becomes too great. **(b)** (fig) way of releasing feelings of anger, excitement, etc harmlessly: *sit on the ~-valve,* follow a policy of repression.

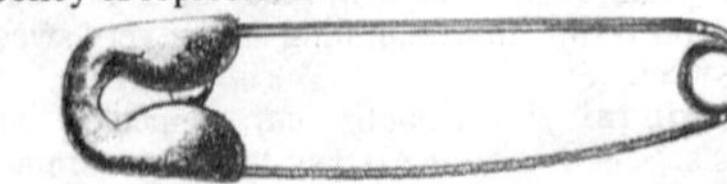

a safety pin

saf·fron /ˈsæfrən/ *n* orange colouring obtained from flowers of the autumn crocus, used as a dye and for flavouring; colour of this, bright orange-yellow.

sag /sæg/ *vi* **(-gg-)** [VP2A] **1** sink or curve down in the middle under weight or pressure: *a sagging roof. Prices are sagging,* falling. **2** hang down unevenly; hang sideways: *His cheeks are beginning to sag.* □ *n* [C] (degree of) sagging: *There is a bad sag in the seat of this chair.*

saga /ˈsɑgə/ *n* [C] **1** old story of heroic deeds, esp of Icelandic or Norwegian heroes. **2** (mod use) long narrative, e g a number of connected books (esp novels) about a family, social group, etc: *the Forsyte S~.* **3** (colloq) tale of an eventful experience: *Have you heard the ~ of my holiday up the Amazon?*

sa·gacious /səˈgeɪʃəs/ *adj* showing good judgement, common sense or (of animals) intelligence. **~·ly** *adv*

sa·gac·ity /səˈgæsətɪ/ *n* [U] sound judgement; wisdom of a practical kind: *S~, unlike cleverness, may increase with age.*

sage[1] /seɪdʒ/ *n* wise man; man who is believed to be wise. □ *adj* wise; having the wisdom of experience; (often ironic) wise-looking. **~·ly** *adv*

sage[2] /seɪdʒ/ *n* [U] herb with dull greyish-green leaves, used to flavour food: *~ and onions,* stuffing used for a goose, duck, etc. **ˈ~-ˈgreen** *n, adj* the colour of ~ leaves.

Sag·it·tarius /ˈsædʒɪˈteərɪəs/ *n* ninth sign of the zodiac. ⇨ the illus at zodiac.

sago /ˈseɪgəʊ/ *n* [U] starchy food, in the form of hard, white grains, from the pith of certain palm-trees (ˈ*~ palms*).

sa·hib /sɑb/ *n* (Anglo-Indian) sir, gentleman. *ˈRaja ~; ˈColonel ~; ˈRobinson ~.*

said /sed/ *pt,pp* of say.

sail[1] /seɪl/ *n* **1** [C,U] sheet of canvas spread to catch the wind and move a boat or ship forward: *hoist/lower the ~s; in full ~,* with all the ~s spread or set. ***under ~,*** (moving) with ~s spread. ***set ~ (from/to/for),*** begin a voyage. ***take in ~,*** reduce the area of sails spread; (fig) become less ambitious or active. ***take the wind out of sb's ~s,*** ⇨ wind[1](1). **ˈ~-cloth** *n* [U] canvas for ~s. **2** [C] set of boards attached to the arm of a windmill to catch the wind. **3** (*pl* unchanged) ship: *a fleet of twenty ~. There wasn't a ~ in sight. S~ ho!* (cry announcing that a ship is in sight). **4** (rarely *pl*) voyage or excursion on water for pleasure: *go for a ~;* voyage of a specified duration: *How many days' ~ is it from Hull to Oslo?* **ˈ~·plane** *n* aircraft that uses air currents and thermals instead of engines. Cf *glider,* towed behind a powered aircraft.

sail[2] /seɪl/ *vi,vt* **1** [VP2A,B,C] move forward across the sea, a lake, etc by using ~s or engine-power, move forward (in sport) across ice or a sandy beach, by means of a sail or sails: *~ up/along the coast; ~ into harbour; go ~ing.* ***~ close/near to the wind,*** **(a)** (naut) sail near to the direction in which the wind is blowing. **(b)** (fig) nearly, but not quite, break a law or offend against a moral principle. **ˈ~·ing-boat/-ship/-vessel,** *n* boat, etc moved by sails. **2** [VP2A,C,3A] ***~ for/from/to,*** (of a ship or persons on board) begin a voyage; travel on water by use of sails or engines: *When does the ship ~? He has ~ed for New York. Here is a list of ~ings* (= ships that ~, with dates) *from London. The captain has received his ~ing orders,* instructions concerning the voyage. **3** [VP6A] voyage across or on: *~ the sea/the Pacific.* **4** [VP6A,2A] (be able to) control (a boat): *He ~s his own yacht. Do you ~?* **ˈ~ing-master** *n* officer who navigates a yacht. **5** [VP2C] move smoothly like a ship with sails: *The moon/clouds ~ed across the sky. The airship ~ed slowly over the city. The duchess ~ed into the room,* entered in a stately manner. **6** ***~ in,*** begin sth with energy and confidence. ***~ into sb,*** scold; attack.

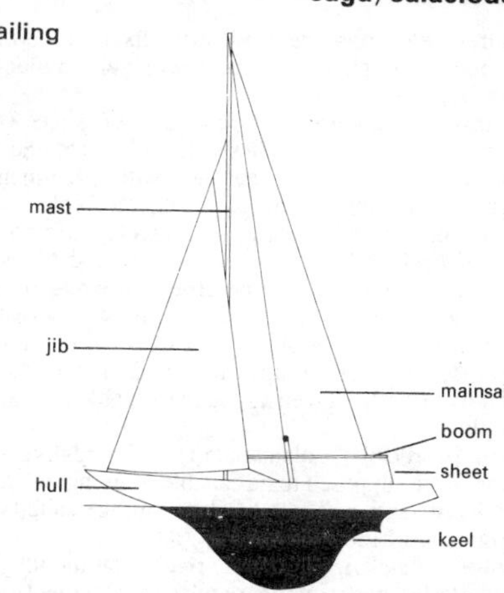

sailor /ˈseɪlə(r)/ *n* **1** seaman; member of a ship's crew. **ˈ~ hat/blouse/suit,** hat, etc e g to be worn by a child, made in imitation of the kind worn by a ~. **2** *a good/bad ~,* person seldom/often seasick in rough weather. **~·ly** *adj* smart; capable.

saint /seɪnt *GB weak form immediately before names* snt/ *n* **1** holy person. **2** person who, having died, is among the blessed in Heaven. **3** (abbr **St**) person who has been declared by the Church to have won by holy living on earth a place in Heaven and veneration on earth. **4** unselfish or patient person: *What a ~ my wife is!* **5** **ˈ~'s-day** *n* Church festival in memory of a ~. **St ˈAndrew's Day,** 30th November (patron ~ of Scotland). **St ˈDavid's Day,** 1st March (patron ~ of Wales). **St ˈGeorge's Day,** 23rd April (patron ~ of England). **St ˈPatrick's Day,** 17th March (patron ~ of Ireland). **St ˈValentine's Day,** ⇨ Valentine. **6 St Bernard** /snt ˈbɜnəd *US:* ˈseɪnt bərˈnɑrd/ *n* large, powerful breed of dog, originally bred by monks in the Swiss Alps, trained to rescue travellers lost in snowstorms. **St Vitus's** /ˈvɑɪtəsɪz/ **ˈdance** *n* nervous disorder with convulsive, involuntary movements. **~ed** *adj* declared to be, regarded as, a ~. **ˈ~·hood** /-hʊd/ *n* [U] **~·like, ~·ly** *adjj* very holy or good; like a ~; of a ~: *a ~ly expression on his face.* **~·li·ness** *n* [U] holiness of life; condition of being ~ly.

saith /seθ/ old form of *says,* ⇨ say.

sake /seɪk/ *n* ***for the ~ of sb/sth; for ˈmy/ˈyour/the ˈcountry's, etc ~,*** for the welfare or benefit of; because of an interest in or desire for: *do sth for the ~ of one's family. I'll help you for your sister's ~,* because I want to save your sister trouble, help her, etc. *We must be patient for the ~ of peace. He argues for the ~ of arguing,* only because he likes arguing. ***for God's/goodness'/pity's/mercy's, etc ~,*** used to make an imperative request emphatic.

saké /ˈsɑkɪ/ *n* [U] Japanese fermented liquor made from rice.

sa·laam /səˈlɑm/ *n* **1** Muslim greeting (from an Arabic word) meaning 'Peace'. **2** [C] low bow. □ *vi* make a low bow (to sb).

sal·able, sale·able /ˈseɪləbl/ *adj* fit for sale; likely to find buyers.

sa·lacious /səˈleɪʃəs/ *adj* (of speech, books, pictures, etc) obscene; indecent; likely to arouse impure thoughts. **~·ly** *adv* **~·ness** *n* **sa·lac·ity** /sə`læsətɪ/ *n*

salad /`sæləd/ *n* **1** [C,U] (cold dish of) sliced (and usu uncooked) vegetables such as lettuce, endive, cucumber, tomatoes, seasoned with oil, vinegar, etc eaten with, or including, cheese, cold meat, fish, etc: *prepare/mix a ~; a chicken/lobster ~; cold beef and ~.* **`~-days** *n pl* period of inexperienced youth. **`~-dressing** *n* mixture of oil, vinegar, cream, etc used with ~. **`~-oil** *n* superior quality of olive oil. **2 fruit ~,** mixture of fruits, sliced or cut up, eaten cold. **3** [U] lettuce, endive or other green vegetable suitable for eating raw.

sala·man·der /`sæləmændə(r)/ *n* lizard-like animal once supposed to be capable of living in fire.

sa·lami /sə`lɑmɪ/ *n* [U] Italian sausage salted and flavoured with garlic.

sal·ary /`sælərɪ/ *n* [C] (*pl* **-ries**) (usu monthly or quarterly) payment for regular employment on a yearly basis: *a ~ of £2000 per annum.* Cf *a weekly wage.* **sal·ar·ied** *adj* receiving a ~; (of employment) paid for by means of a ~; *the salaried classes; salaried posts.*

sale /seɪl/ *n* **1** [U] exchange of goods or property for money; act of selling sth: *The ~ of his old home made him sad.* ***for ~,*** intended to be sold (usu by or on behalf of the owners): *Is the house for ~? I shall put these goods up for ~,* announce that they may be bought. ***on ~,*** (of goods in shops, etc) offered for purchase. ***on ~ or return,*** (of goods sent to a retailer) either to be sold or, if unsold or unsatisfactory, to be returned. **'bill of `~,** (comm) document which transfers the title(3) of personal chattels, etc to another person although the goods remain with the person making the transfer (used as a method of borrowing money). **2** [C] instance of selling sth: *I haven't made a ~ all week. He finds a ready ~ for the strawberries he grows. His strawberries find a ready ~,* He quickly finds buyers. *S~s are up/down this month,* more/fewer goods have been sold. **`~s clerk,** (US) shop assistant. **`~s department,** that part of a business company that is concerned with selling goods (contrasted with manufacture, dispatch, etc). **`~s resistance,** reluctance of the public to buy goods. **`~s talk,** (colloq **`~s chat**), talk (to a prospective customer) to boost the ~s of goods. **`~s tax,** tax payable on the sum received for articles sold by retail. **3** [C] the offering of goods at low prices for a period (to get rid of old stock, etc): *the winter/summer ~s; buy goods at the ~s; `~ price,* low price at a ~. **4** occasion when goods, property, etc are put up for ~ by auction: *for ~ to the highest bidder; get bargains by attending ~s.* **`~-room,** room where goods, etc are sold by public auction. **5 ~ of work,** ~ of articles (e g clothing) made by members of a church, etc for charity. ⇨ jumble. **`~s·man** /-mən/, **`~s·woman** /-wʊmən/ *nn* person selling goods in a shop or (on behalf of wholesalers) to shopkeepers. **`~s·man·ship** /-mənʃɪp/ *n* [U] skill in selling goods. **~·able** /-əbl/ *adj* = salable.

sa·li·ent /`seɪlɪənt/ *adj* **1** outstanding; prominent; easily noticed; *the ~ points of a speech. Honesty is his most ~ characteristic.* **2** (of an angle) pointing outwards. □ *n* ~ angle; forward wedge driven into the enemy's battle front.

sa·lif·er·ous /sə`lɪfərəs/ *adj* (of liquids, etc) containing salt.

sal·ify /`sælɪfaɪ/ *vt* (*pt, pp* **-fied**) form, convert into, saturate with salt.

sa·line /`seɪlaɪn *US:* -lin/ *adj* containing salt; salty: *a ~ solution,* e g as used for gargling; *~ springs.* □ *n* **1** [U] solution of salt and water. **2** [C] ~ lake, marsh, well, spring, etc. **sa·lin·ity** /sə`lɪnətɪ/ *n* [U] quality of being ~.

sali·nom·eter /'sælə`nomətə(r)/ *n* (chem) instrument for measuring the amount of salt contained in a liquid.

sal·iva /sə`laɪvə/ *n* [U] the natural liquid present in the mouth; spittle. **sali·vary** /`sælɪvərɪ *US:* -verɪ/ *adj* of or producing ~: *the `~ry glands.* ⇨ the illus at alimentary. **sali·vate** /`sælɪveɪt/ *vi* secrete too much ~.

sal·low /`sæləʊ/ *adj* (**-er, -est**) (of the human skin or complexion) of an unhealthy yellow colour. □ *vt,vi* make or become ~: *a face ~ed by years of residence in the tropics.*

sally /`sælɪ/ *n* (*pl* **-lies**) [C] **1** sudden breaking out by soldiers who are surrounded by the enemy: *make a successful ~.* **2** lively, witty remark, esp one that is a good-humoured attack on sb or sth. □ *vi* [VP2A,C] **1** make a ~(1): *~ out against the besiegers.* **2 ~ *out/forth,*** go out on a journey or for a walk.

salmon /`sæmən/ *n* [C] (*pl* unchanged) large fish, valued for food and the sport of catching it with rod and line; [U] its flesh as food; the colour of its flesh, orange-pink. **~ trout,** (kinds of) fish like ~, esp (kinds of) trout.

salon /`sælõ *US:* `sælɔ̃/ *n* **1** assembly, as a regular event, of notable persons at the house of a lady of fashion (esp in Paris); reception room used for this purpose. **2 the S~,** annual exhibition of pictures by living artists in a French town. **3** establishment offering services connected with fashion, etc: *a `beauty-~.*

sa·loon /sə`lun/ *n* **1** room for social use in a ship, hotel, etc: *the ship's `dining-~.* **`~ bar,** where drinks are served in a public house or inn. **2** public room or rooms for a specified purpose: *a `billiards/`dancing ~.* **3** (US) place where alcoholic drinks may be bought and drunk (GB = *pub*); bar. **4** (**`~-)car,** (GB) motor-car with wholly enclosed seating space for 4—7 passengers (US = *sedan*).

sal·sify /`sælsɪfaɪ/ *n* [U] (plant with a) long, fleshy root cooked as a vegetable.

salt /sɔlt/ *n* **1** [U] (often *common ~*) white substance obtained from mines, present in sea-water and obtained from it by evaporation, used to flavour and preserve food; sodium chloride (**NaCl**): *too much ~ in the soup; `table ~,* powdered for convenient use at table. ***not/hardly worth one's ~,*** not deserving one's pay. ***take (a statement, etc) with a grain/pinch of ~,*** feel some doubt whether it is altogether true. ***the ~ of the earth,*** the finest citizens; persons with very high qualities. **2** (chem) chemical compound of a metal and an acid. **3** *a ~, an old ~,* an experienced sailor. **4** (*pl*) medicine used to empty the bowels: *take a dose of (Epsom) ~s.* ⇨ also *smelling ~s* at smell[2](4). **5** (fig) sth that gives flavour or zest: *Adventure is the ~ of life to some men.* **6** (compounds) **`~-cellar** *n* small open container for ~ at table. **`~-lick** *n* place where animals come together to lick earth with ~ in it. **`~-pan** *n* depression (natural or artificial) near the sea where ~ is obtained by evaporation of sea-water. **'~-**

ˋ**water,** of the sea: *~-water fish.* ˋ**~-works** *n pl* place where ~ is manufactured (e g from brine pumped up from a mine). □ *vt* [VP6A] put ~ on or in (food) to season it; [VP6A,15B] ***~ sth (down),*** preserve (food) with ~: *~ (down) cod; ~ed meat.* ***~ sth away,*** (colloq) put money away for the future: *He's got quite a bit ~ed away.* □ *adj* **1** (opp of *fresh*) containing, tasting of, preserved with, ~: *~ butter; ~ water.* **2** (of land) impregnated with ~: *~ marshes; the* ˋ*~ flats of Utah.* **salty** *adj* (-ier, -iest) containing, tasting of, ~. **~i·ness** *n*

salt·petre (US = **-peter**) /sɔltˋpitə(r)/ *n* salty white powder (potassium nitrate, nitre) used in making gunpowder, for preserving food and as medicine.

sa·lu·bri·ous /səˋlubrɪəs/ *adj* (esp of climate) health-giving: *the ~ air of Switzerland.* **sa·lu·brity** /səˋlubrətɪ/ *n*

salu·tary /ˋsæljʊtrɪ *US:* -terɪ/ *adj* having a good effect (on body or mind): *~ exercise/advice.*

salu·ta·tion /ˈsæljʊˋteɪʃn/ *n* [C,U] (act or expression of) greeting or goodwill (e g a bow or a kiss): *He raised his hat in ~*; (in a letter, etc) introductory phrase, e g *Dear Sir.*

sa·lute /səˋlut/ *n* **1** sth done to welcome sb or to show respect or honour, esp (e g in the armed forces) the raising of the hand to the forehead, the firing of guns, the lowering and raising of a flag: *give a ~; fire a ~ of ten guns; stand at the ~,* stand with the right hand raised to the forehead. ***take the ~,*** acknowledge the ~s of a body of soldiers who march past and give ~s. **2** friendly greeting such as a bow, raising of the hat (by a man). □ *vt,vi* [VP6A,2A] greet; give a ~ (to): *The soldier ~d smartly.*

sal·vage /ˋsælvɪdʒ/ *n* [U] **1** the saving of property from loss (by fire or other disaster, e g a wrecked ship): *a* ˋ*~ company,* one whose business is to bring wrecked ships to port, raise valuables from a ship that has sunk, etc; *a* ˋ*~ tug,* for towing a disabled ship to port. **2** property so saved. **3** payment given to those who save property. **4** (saving of) waste material that can be used again after being processed: *collect old newspapers and magazines for ~.* □ *vt* [VP6A] save from loss, fire, wreck, etc.

sal·va·tion /sælˋveɪʃn/ *n* [U] **1** the act of saving, the state of having been saved, from sin and its consequences. ˈ**S~** ˋ**Army,** religious and missionary organization on a semi-military model for the revival of religion among the masses and for helping the poor everywhere. **2** that which saves sb from loss, disaster, etc: *Government loans have been the ~ of several shaky business companies.* ***work out one's own ~,*** find, by one's own efforts, how to save oneself.

salve[1] /sɑv *US:* sæv/ *n* **1** [C,U] (kinds of) oily medicinal substance used on wounds, sores or burns: ˋ*lip-~.* **2** (fig) sth that comforts wounded feelings or soothes an uneasy conscience. □ *vt* [VP6A] soothe; put a ~ on; be a ~ to: *~ one's conscience by giving stolen money to charity.*

salve[2] /sælv/ *vt* [VP6A] salvage.

sal·ver /ˋsælvə(r)/ *n* tray, usu of silver or other metal, on which servants hand letters, cards, refreshments, etc.

sal·via /ˋsælvɪə/ *n* garden plant with bright red flowers.

salvo /ˋsælvəʊ/ *n* (*pl* -vos, -voes /-vəʊz/) **1** the firing of a number of guns together as a salute. **2** round of applause.

sal vol·atile /ˈsæl vəˋlætəlɪ/ *n* [U] solution of ammonium carbonate (smelling salts) used medically when a person feels faint or becomes unconscious.

Sa·mari·tan /səˋmærɪtən/ *n* (usu) **Good ~,** person who pities and gives practical help to persons in trouble. ⇨ Luke 10: 33.

samba /ˋsæmbə/ *n* (ballroom dance modified in Brazil from an) African dance.

same /seɪm/ *adj, pron* (always with the *def art* except as noted in **6** below) **1** identical; unchanged; not different: *He is the ~ age as his wife. We have lived in the ~ house for fifty years. We are all going the ~ way.* **2** ***the ~... that; the ~... as***: *He uses the ~ books that you do/the ~ books as you.* ⇨ **as**[2]**(13)**. **3** (with a relative clause introduced by *that, where, who,* etc. *As* replaces *that* if the *v* is omitted): *Put the book back in the ~ place where you found it. Our eggs are sold the ~ day that/as they come in. The price is the ~ as before the war. Are these the ~ people (whom) we saw here last week?* **4** (as *pron*) the same thing: *We must all say the ~. I would do the ~ again.* ***be all/just the ~ to,*** make no difference to; be a matter of indifference to: *You can do it now or leave it till later; it's all the ~ to me.* **5** (in phrases) ***come/amount to the ~ thing,*** have the ~ result, meaning, etc: *You may pay in cash or cheque; it comes to the ~ thing.* ***the very ~,*** (emph): *You've made the very ~ mistake again!* ***one and the ~,*** absolutely the ~: *Jekyll and Hyde were one and the ~ person.* **at the ~ time,** **(a)** together: *Don't all speak at the ~ time. She was laughing and crying at the ~ time.* **(b)** (introducing a fact, etc that is to be borne in mind) yet; still; nevertheless: *At the ~ time you must not forget that....* **6** (with *this, that, these, those*) already thought of, mentioned or referred to: *I felt unwell on the Monday and did not go to the office. On that ~ day, the office was wrecked by a bomb.* **7** (as *pron,* often without the *def art;* dated comm use only): *To dry-cleaning suit, 70p; to repairing ~, 45p.* □ *adv* in the ~ way: *Old people do not feel the ~ about these things as the younger generation.* ***all the ~,*** nevertheless: *He's not very intelligent, but I like him all the ~.* **~·ness** *n* [U] the condition of being the ~, of being uninteresting through lack of variety.

samo·var /ˋsæməvɑ(r)/ *n* metal urn with an interior tube, used in Russia for boiling water for tea.

a samovar

sam·pan /ˋsæmpæn/ *n* small, flat-bottomed boat used along the coasts and rivers of China. ⇨ p768.

sample /ˋsɑmpl *US:* ˋsæmpl/ *n* [C] specimen; one of a number, part of a whole, taken to show what

a sampan

the rest is like (esp as offered by a dealer in goods sold by weight or measure). ***up to ~,*** (of goods) equal in quality to the ~ offered. □ *vt* [VP6A] take a ~ or ~s of; test a part of: *spend an hour at the vintner's, sampling* (= making a random sampling of) *his wines*.

sam·pler /ˈsɑmplə(r) *US:* ˈsæm-/ *n* piece of cloth embroidered by a girl to show her skill in needlework, formerly often displayed on a wall.

sam·urai /ˈsæmʊraɪ/ *n* **1 the ~,** the military caste in feudal Japan. **2** member of this caste.

sana·tor·ium /ˌsænəˈtɔrɪəm/ *n* establishment for the treatment of people with weak lungs or for convalescent people.

sanc·tify /ˈsæŋktɪfaɪ/ *vt* (*pt,pp* -**fied**) [VP6A] make holy; set apart as sacred. **sanc·ti·fi·ca·tion** /ˌsæŋktɪfɪˈkeɪʃn/ *n*

sanc·ti·moni·ous /ˌsæŋktɪˈməʊnɪəs/ *adj* making a show of sanctity. **~·ly** *adv*

sanc·tion /ˈsæŋkʃn/ *n* **1** [U] right or permission given by authority to do sth: *a book that was translated without the ~ of the author and publisher.* **2** [U] approval, encouragement (of behaviour etc), by general custom or tradition. **3** [C] penalty intended to maintain or restore respect for law or authority, esp as adopted by several States together against a country violating international law: *apply ~s against an aggressor country.* **4** [C] reason for obeying a rule, etc: *The best moral ~ is that of conscience; the worst ~ is the fear of punishment.* □ *vt* [VP6A] give a ~ to; agree to: *Would you ~ flogging as a punishment for crimes of violence?*

sanc·tity /ˈsæŋktətɪ/ *n* (*pl* -**ties**) **1** [U] holiness; sacredness; saintliness: *violate the ~ of an oath.* **2** (*pl*) sacred obligations, feelings, etc: *the sanctities of the home.*

sanc·tu·ary /ˈsæŋktʃʊərɪ *US:* -ʊerɪ/ *n* (*pl* -**ries**) **1** [C] holy or sacred place, esp a church, temple or mosque. **2** sacred place (e g the altar of a church) where, in former times, a person running away from the law or his creditors was secure, by Church law, against arrest or violence; place of refuge: *Great Britain has always been a ~ of political refugees from many parts of the world.* **3** area where by law it is forbidden to kill birds, rob their nests, etc to shoot animals, etc: *a ˈbird-~.* **4** [U] (right of offering such) freedom from arrest: *to seek/be offered ~.*

sanc·tum /ˈsæŋktəm/ *n* **1** holy place. **2** (colloq) person's private room or study.

sand /sænd/ *n* **1** [U] (mass of) finely crushed rock as seen on the sea-shore, in river-beds, deserts, etc: *mix ~ and cement.* **2** (often *pl*) expanse of ~ (on the sea-shore or a desert): *children playing on the ~(s).* **3** (*pl*) ***The ~s are running out,*** (with reference to the ~ running through an hour-glass, etc) There is not much time left; time is passing. **4** (compounds) **ˈ~-bag** *n* bag filled with ~ used as a defence (in war, against rising flood-water, etc). **ˈ~·bank** *n* bank or shoal of ~ in a river or the sea. **ˈ~-bar** *n* bank of ~ at the mouth of a river or harbour. **ˈ~-blast** *vt* [VP6A] send a jet of ~ against sth, e g stonework, to clean it, or against metal or glass to cut or make a design on it. **ˈ~·boy** *n* (now used only in) ***as happy as a ~boy,*** very happy. **ˈ~ dune** *n* ridge of drifted ~. **ˈ~-fly** *n* (*pl* -**flies**) kind of midge common on sea-shores. **ˈ~-glass** *n* glass with two bulbs containing enough ~ to take a definite time, e g five minutes, one hour, in passing from one bulb to the other. **ˈ~·paper** *n* [U] strong paper with ~ glued to it, used for rubbing rough surfaces smooth. □ *vt* [VP6A] make smooth with ~paper. **ˈ~·piper** *n* small bird living in wet, sandy places near streams. ⇨ the illus at **water**. **ˈ~-pit** *n* unroofed enclosure filled with ~, for children to play in. **ˈ~-shoes** *n pl* canvas shoes with rubber or hemp soles for wearing on sandy sea-shores. **ˈ~·stone** *n* rock formed of compressed ~. **ˈ~-storm** *n* storm in a sandy desert with clouds of ~ raised by the wind. □ *vt* [VP6A] cover, sprinkle or scrub with ~. **sandy** *adj* (-**ier**, -**iest**) **1** covered with or consisting of ~: *a ~y bottom,* e g of part of the sea. **2** (of hair, etc) yellowish-red. □ *n* (colloq) nickname given to a person with yellowish-red hair. **~i·ness** *n*

san·dal /ˈsændl/ *n* kind of shoe made of a sole with straps to hold it on the foot. **~·led** /ˈsændld/ *adj* wearing ~s.

san·dal·wood /ˈsændlwʊd/ *n* [U] hard, sweet-smelling wood used for making fans, caskets, etc.

sand·wich /ˈsænwɪdʒ *US:* -wɪtʃ/ *n* [C] two slices of bread with meat, etc between: *ham/chicken/cheese, etc ~es.* **ˈ~·man** /-mæn/ *n* (*pl* -**men**) man who walks about the streets with two advertisement boards, one hanging over his chest and the other over his back. **ˈ~-board** *n* one of such boards. **ˈ~ course,** course of theoretical study, e g at a polytechnic, between periods of practical work in industry. □ *vt* [VP6A,14] put (one thing or person) between two others, esp when there is little space: *I was ~ed between two very stout men on the bus.*

sane /seɪn/ *adj* (-**r**, -**st**) **1** healthy in mind; not mad. **2** sensible; balanced: *a ~ policy; ~ views/judgement.* **~·ly** *adv*

sang /sæŋ/ *pt* of **sing**.

sang froid /ˈsɒŋ ˈfrwɑ/ *n* [U] (F) calmness in face of danger or in an emergency; composure.

san·gui·nary /ˈsæŋgwɪnərɪ *US:* -nerɪ/ *adj* (formal) **1** with much bloodshed: *a ~ battle.* **2** fond of bloodshed; delighting in cruel acts: *a ~ ruler.* **3** ~ *language,* full of swear-words (because 'bloody' is a common swear-word).

san·guine /ˈsæŋgwɪn/ *adj* (formal) **1** hopeful; optimistic: *~ of success; ~ that we shall succeed.* **2** having a red complexion.

sani·tarium /ˌsænɪˈteərɪəm/ *n* (US) sanatorium; health resort.

sani·tary /ˈsænɪtrɪ *US:* -terɪ/ *adj* **1** clean; free from dirt which might cause disease: *~ conditions; poor ~ arrangements in a camp.* **2** of, concerned with, the protection of health: *a ˈ~ inspector,* official whose duty it is to see that regulations for the protection of health are obeyed; *ˈ~ towel/*

napkin, absorbent pad used during menstruation.

sani·ta·tion /'sænɪ`teɪʃn/ *n* [U] arrangements to protect public health, esp for the efficient disposal of sewage.

san·ity /`sænətɪ/ *n* [U] **1** health of mind. **2** soundness of judgement.

sank /sæŋk/ *pt* of sink².

sans /sænz/ *prep* (with ref to Shakespeare, *As You Like It*) without: *S~ teeth, ~ eyes, ~ taste, ~ everything.*

San·skrit /`sænskrɪt/ *n* the ancient language of India; the literary language of Hinduism.

Santa Claus /'sæntə `klɔz *US:* `sæntə klɔz/ *n* person who, small children are told, puts toys in their stockings by night at Christmas.

sap¹ /sæp/ *vt* (-pp-) [VP6A] weaken; drain away the life and strength of: *sapped by disease/an unhealthy climate.*

sap² /sæp/ *n* [C] tunnel or covered trench made to get nearer to the enemy (e g in a military strongpoint or, formerly, a beseiged town). **`sap-head** *n* end of a sap nearest to the enemy. □ *vt, vi* (-pp-) [VP6A,2A] make a sap or saps; weaken (a wall, etc) by digging under it; (fig) destroy or weaken (sb's faith, confidence, etc). **sap·per** *n* soldier engaged in making saps or (mod use) in engineering, e g road and bridge building.

sap³ /sæp/ *n* (sl) simpleton; silly fellow: *You poor sap!*

sap⁴ /sæp/ *n* [U] **1** liquid in a plant, carrying food to all parts: *The sap is beginning to rise in the maple-trees.* **sap·wood** /`sæpwʊd/ *n* soft, outer layers of wood. **2** (fig) (anything that provides) vigour or energy. **sap·less** *adj* without sap; dry; lacking vigour. **sap·ling** /`sæplɪŋ/ *n* young tree; (fig) young man. **sappy** *adj* (-ier, -iest) full of sap; young and vigorous.

sa·pi·ent /`seɪpɪənt/ *adj* wise. **~·ly** *adv* **sa·pi·ence** /-əns/ *n* (often ironic) wisdom.

Sap·phic /`sæfɪk/ *adj* of the Greek lesbian poetess Sappho. **~ verse/stanza/ode,** (pros) with three lines that rhyme and one short line.

sap·phire /`sæfɑɪə(r)/ *n* **1** [C] clear, bright blue jewel. **2** [U] bright blue colour.

sara·band /`særəbænd/ *n* [C] (piece of music for a) stately old Spanish dance.

Sara·cen /`særəsn/ *n* (name used by later Greeks and Romans for) Arab or Muslim of the time of the Crusades.

sar·casm /`sɑkæzm/ *n* [U] (use of) bitter remarks intended to wound the feelings; [C] such a remark; taunt that is ironically worded. **sar·cas·tic** /sɑ`kæstɪk/ *adj* of, using, ~. **sar·cas·ti·cally** /-klɪ/ *adv*

sar·copha·gus /sɑ`kofəgəs/ *n* (*pl* -gi /-gɑɪ/, -guses /-gəsɪz/) stone coffin (esp as used in ancient times).

sar·dine /sɑ`din/ *n* small fish (a young pilchard), usu preserved and tinned in oil or tomato sauce. ***packed like ~s,*** closely crowded together.

sar·donic /sɑ`donɪk/ *adj* mocking; scornful: *a ~ smile/laugh/expression.* **sar·doni·cally** /-klɪ/ *adv*

sari /`sɑrɪ/ *n* (*pl* ~s) length of cotton or silk cloth draped round the body, worn by Hindu women.

sa·rong /sə`roŋ *US:* -`rɔŋ/ *n* long strip of cotton or silk material worn round the middle of the body, tucked round the waist, the national garment of Malays.

sar·sa·pa·rilla /'sɑspə`rɪlə/ *n* [U] (tonic drink made from the roots of a) tropical American plant.

a sari

a sarong

a kimono

sar·tor·ial /sɑ`tɔrɪəl/ *adj* concerned with (the making of) men's clothes: *~ elegance.*

sash¹ /sæʃ/ *n* [C] long strip of cloth worn round the waist or over one shoulder for ornament or as part of a uniform.

sash² /sæʃ/ *n* **`~ window,** one with a frame that slides up and down (instead of opening outwards like a casement). **`~-cord/-line** *n* strong cord (with a weight at one end) running over a pulley to keep the window balanced in any desired position.

sas·sa·fras /`sæsəfræs/ *n* small American tree of the laurel family; its bark, used medicinally.

sat /sæt/ *pt,pp* of sit.

Satan /`seɪtn/ *n* the Evil One, the Devil: *S~ never reproves sinners.* **~ic** /sə`tænɪk *US:* seɪ-/ *adj* **1** of ~: *His ~ic Majesty,* (hum) Satan. **2** (small **s**) wicked; evil.

satchel /`sætʃl/ *n* small bag for carrying light articles, esp school-books.

sate /seɪt/ *vt* [VP6A] = satiate.

sa·teen /sə`tin/ *n* [U] shiny cotton fabric woven like satin.

sat·el·lite /`sætəlɑɪt/ *n* **1** comparatively small body moving in orbit round a planet; moon; artificial object, e g a spacecraft put in orbit round a celestial body: *com'muni`cations ~,* for relaying back to the earth telephone messages, radio and TV signals. **2** (fig, often attrib) person, state, depending upon and taking the lead from another. **`~ town,** one built to take the excess population of another.

sati·able /`seɪʃəbl/ *adj* that can be fully satisfied.

sati·ate /`seɪʃɪeɪt/ *vt* [VP6A] satisfy fully; cloy; weary (oneself) with too much: *be ~d with food/pleasure.*

sat·iety /sə`tɑɪətɪ/ *n* [U] condition or feeling of being satiated: *indulge in pleasure to/the point of ~.*

satin /`sætɪn *US:* `sætn/ *n* [U] silk material smooth and shiny on one side: (attrib) *~ dresses/ribbons.* □ *adj* smooth like ~.

sat·in·wood /`sætɪnwʊd *US:* `sætn-/ *n* [U] smooth, hard wood of a tropical tree, much used for furniture.

sat·ire /`sætɑɪə(r)/ *n* **1** [U] form of writing holding up a person or society to ridicule or showing the foolishness or wickedness of an idea, customs, etc. **2** [C] piece of writing that does this; sth that exposes false pretensions: *Are our lives sometimes a ~ upon our religious beliefs?* **sa·tiri·cal** /sə`tɪrɪkl/ *adj* containing, fond of using, ~; mocking. **sa·tiri·cally** /-klɪ/ *adv* **sat·ir·ist** /`sætərɪst/ *n* person who writes ~s. **sat·ir·ize** /`sætərɑɪz/ *vt* [VP6A] attack with ~(s); describe satirically.

sat·is·fac·tion /'sætɪs`fækʃn/ *n* **1** [U] the state of being satisfied, pleased or contented; act of satisfying: *feel ~ at having one's ability recognized; have the ~ of being successful in life; pass an examination to one's own ~ and to the ~ of one's friends: the ~ of one's hopes/desires/ambitions.* **2** (with *indef art,* but rarely *pl*) sth that satisfies: *Your success will be a great ~ to your parents. It is a ~ to know that he is well again.* **3** [U] (opportunity of getting) revenge or compensation for an injury or insult: *give sb/demand/obtain ~. The angry man demanded ~ but the other refused it,* would neither apologize nor fight.

sat·is·fac·tory /ˌsætɪsˋfæktṛɪ/ *adj* giving pleasure or satisfaction; satisfying a need or desire; good enough for a purpose: *The result of the experiment was ~. We want ~ reasons for your failure to help.* **sat·is·fac·tor·ily** /-tṛəlɪ/ *adv* in a ~ manner: *The patient is getting on satisfactorily.*

sat·isfy /ˋsætɪsfaɪ/ *vt,vi* (*pt,pp* -fied) **1** [VP6A,2A] make contented; give (sb) what he wants or needs: *Nothing satisfies him; he's always complaining. Riches do not always ~.* ***~ the examiners,*** just reach the lowest standard needed for passing. **2** [VP6A,2A] be enough for (one's needs); be equal to (what one hopes for or desires): *~ one's hunger.* **3** [VP6A,11,14] convince; make free from doubt: *He satisfied me that he could do the work well. Have you satisfied yourself of the truth of the report?* **~·ing** *adj* giving satisfaction: *a ~ing meal.* **~·ing·ly** *adv*

sa·trap /ˋsætrəp *US:* ˋseɪtræp/ *n* governor of a province in the ancient Persian empire.

satu·rate /ˋsætʃəreɪt/ *vt* [VP6A,14] **1** make thoroughly wet; soak with moisture; cause to take in as much as possible of sth: *We were caught in the rain and came home ~d. They lay on the beach and were ~d with sunshine. He is ~d with Greek history.* **2** be unable to take any more: *The market for used cars is ~d.* **3** (chem) cause (one substance) to absorb the greatest possible amount of another: *a ~d solution of salt.* **satu·ra·tion** /ˌsætʃəˋreɪʃn/ *n* [U] state of being ~d. **saturation bombing,** bombing so that everything in the target area is totally destroyed. **ˈsatuˋration point,** the stage at which, if more of one substance is added to another, they will not unite completely: *The saturation point of a hot liquid is higher than that of a cold one,* e g more sugar can be dissolved in hot tea than in cold tea.

Sat·ur·day /ˋsætədɪ/ *n* the seventh and last day of the week.

Sat·urn /ˋsætən/ *n* **1** (astron) large planet encircled by rings. ⇨ the illus at planet. **2** (myth) ancient Roman god of agriculture.

sat·ur·na·lia /ˌsætəˋneɪlɪə/ *n pl* **1 S~,** yearly festival of the god Saturn, held in ancient Rome in December, a time of wild merry-making. **2** (small *s;* often with *indef art*) time of wild revelry or disorder.

sat·ur·nine /ˋsætənaɪn/ *adj* gloomy.

satyr /ˋsætə(r)/ *n* **1** (Gk and Roman myth) god of the woods, half man and half animal. **2** man with uncontrolled sexual desires. **sa·tyric** /səˋtɪrɪk/ *adj* of or like ~s.

sauce /sɔs/ *n* **1** [C,U] (kind of) liquid or semi-liquid preparation served with some kinds of food to give a relish or flavour; *spaghetti and tomato ~; Christmas pudding and brandy ~.* **ˋ~-boat** *n* vessel in which ~ is served at table. **2** [U] (colloq) impudence (usu amusing rather than annoying): *None of your ~!* Don't be impertinent. *What ~!* How impudent! □ *vt* [VP6A] (colloq) be impudent to: *How dare you ~ your mother?* **saucy** *adj* (-ier, -iest) **1** impudent. **2** (colloq) smart-looking: *a saucy little hat.* **sauc·ily** *adv* **sauci·ness** *n*

sauce·pan /ˋsɔspən *US:* -pæn/ *n* deep metal cooking pot, usu round and with a lid and a handle.

saucer /ˋsɔsə(r)/ *n* **1** small curved dish on which a cup stands. **ˋ~-eyed** *adj* with large, round, wide-opened eyes, e g as the result of surprise. **ˈflying ˋ~,** ⇨ flying. **2** ~-shaped disc (also called a *dish*) of a radio telescope. **3** depression in the ground.

sauer·kraut /ˋsaʊəkraʊt/ *n* [U] (G) cabbage cut up, salted and allowed to ferment until sour.

sauna /ˋsaʊnə/ *n* steam bath(house) as in Finland.

saun·ter /ˋsɔntə(r)/ *vi* [VP2A,C] walk in a leisurely way: *~ along Oxford Street window-shopping.* □ *n* quiet, unhurried walk or pace: *come at a ~.* **~er** *n* person who ~s.

saur·ian /ˋsɔrɪən/ *n, adj* (one) of the order of lizards including crocodiles, lizards and some extinct species.

saus·age /ˋsosɪdʒ *US:* ˋsɔs-/ *n* [U] chopped up meat, etc flavoured and stuffed into a casing or tube of thin skin; some kinds sliced and eaten raw, others cooked and eaten hot; [C] one section of such a tube. **ˋ~-dog,** (GB colloq) dachshund. **ˋ~-meat** *n* meat minced for making ~s. **ˈ~-ˋroll** *n* ~ in a covering of pastry.

sauté /ˋsəʊteɪ *US:* səʊˋteɪ/ *adj* (F) (of food) quickly fried in a little fat: *~ potatoes.* □ *vt* fry food in this way.

sav·age /ˋsævɪdʒ/ *adj* **1** in a primitive or uncivilized state: *~ people/tribes/countries.* **2** fierce; cruel: *a ~ dog; make a ~ attack on sb; ~ criticism.* **3** (colloq) very angry. □ *n* ~ person, esp a member of a primitive tribe living by hunting and fishing. □ *vt* [VP6A] attack, bite, trample on: *The man was badly ~d by his mare.* **~·ly** *adv* **~·ness** *n* **~ry** /ˋsævɪdʒrɪ/ *n* [U] the state of being ~; ~ behaviour: *living in ~ry; treat conquered enemies with great ~ry.*

sa·vanna, sa·van·nah /səˋvænə/ *n* [C] treeless plain, e g in tropical America and parts of W Africa. Cf *prairie,* N America, and *pampas,* S America.

sa·vant /ˋsævõ *US:* sæˋvɑnt/ *n* man of great learning.

save[1] /seɪv/ *vt,vi* **1** [VP6A,14] ***~ sb/sth (from),*** make or keep safe (from loss, injury, etc): *~ sb from drowning; ~ sb's life; ~ a person from himself,* from the results of his own foolishness. ***~ one's bacon,*** ⇨ bacon. ***~ one's face,*** ⇨ face[1](4). ***~ one's skin,*** avoid, often by cowardice, the risk of loss, injury, etc. ***~ the situation*** deal successfully with a situation which seems hopeless. **2** [VP6A,15B,14,2A,C] ***~ sth/~ up (for sth),*** keep for future use: *~ (up) money for a holiday; ~ part of one's salary each month; ~ some of the meat for tomorrow; ~ for one's old age. He has never ~d,* never put money by the for future. *He is saving himself/saving his strength for the heavy work he'll have to do this afternoon.* ***~ for a rainy day,*** ⇨ rainy. **3** [VP6A,D,12B,13B] ***~ sb sth,*** make unnecessary; relieve (sb) from the need of using: *If you walk to the office every morning, you'll ~ spending money on bus fares. That will ~ you 50 pence a week. That will ~ us a lot of trouble. We've been ~d a lot of expense by* *doing the work ourselves. Do you use modern labour-saving devices in your home?* **4** [VP6A, 14,2A] (in the Christian religion) set free from the power of (or the eternal punishment for) sin: *Jesus Christ came into the world to ~ sinners.* **5** [VP6A] make a reservation concerning (sth): *a saving clause,* one that stipulates an exemption, etc. □ *n* (in football, etc) act of preventing the scoring of a goal: *Banks made a brilliant ~.* **saver** *n* person who ~s: *a ~r of souls,* e g a priest; means of saving: *This device is a useful ˈtime-~r. Some machines are ~rs of labour.* **sav·ing** *adj* (esp) that redeems or compensates. **saving grace,** good quality that redeems a person whose other qualities are not all good: *He has the saving grace of humour.* □ *n* **1** way of saving; amount ~d; *a useful saving of time and money.* **2** (*pl*) money ~d up: *keep one's savings in the Post Office.* **ˈsavings account** *n* (with a bank) on which interest is paid. **ˈsavings-bank** *n* bank which holds, and gives interest on, small savings.

save[2] /seɪv/, **sav·ing** /ˈseɪvɪŋ/ *preps* except: *all save him; saving your presence,* (an old-fashioned apology) without meaning to annoy you. *We know nothing about him save that he was in the army during the war.*

sav·eloy /ˈsævəlɔɪ/ *n* [C] kind of highly-seasoned pork sausage.

sav·iour (US = **-ior**) /ˈseɪvɪə(r)/ *n* person who rescues or saves sb from danger: *The S~, Our S~,* Jesus Christ.

savoir-faire /ˈsævwɑ ˈfeə(r)/ *n* [U] (F) social tact; knowledge of how to behave in any situation.

sa·vory /ˈseɪvərɪ/ *n* [U] herb of the mint family used in cooking.

sa·vour (US = **-vor**) /ˈseɪvə(r)/ *n* [C,U] **~ of,** taste or flavour (of sth); suggestion (of a quality): *soup with a ~ of garlic. His political views have a ~ of fanaticism.* □ *vt,vi* **1** [VP6A] (archaic or liter) appreciate the taste or flavour of: *He ~ed the wine.* **2** [VP3A] **~ of,** suggest the presence: *Such a proposal ~s of impertinence.*

sa·voury (US = **-vory**) /ˈseɪvərɪ/ *adj* having an appetizing taste or smell; (of food dishes) having a salt or sharp, not a sweet, taste: *a ~ omelette.* □ *n* [C] (*pl* -ries) ~ dish, esp one taken at the start or end of a meal.

sa·voy /səˈvɔɪ/ *n* [C,U] (kind of) winter cabbage with wrinkled leaves.

savvy /ˈsævɪ/ *v* (sl) know, understand: *No ~,* I do not know/understand. □ *n* [U] wits; understanding: *Where's your ~?*

saw[1] /sɔ/ *pt* of **see**[1].

saw[2] /sɔ/ *n* [C] (kinds of) tool with a sharp-toothed edge, for cutting wood, metal, stone, etc worked by hand or mechanically. **ˈsaw·dust** *n* [U] tiny bits of wood falling off when wood is being sawn. **ˈsaw-horse** *n* frame of wood for supporting wood that is being sawn. **ˈsaw-mill** *n* mill with power-operated saws. □ *vt,vi* (*pt* sawed, *pp* sawn /sɔn/ and (US) sawed) **1** [VP6A,15A,B, 2A] cut with a saw; make (boards, etc) with a saw; use a saw: *saw wood; saw a log into planks; saw a log in two.* ***saw sth off,*** cut off with a saw: *saw a branch off a tree; a sawn-off shotgun,* one with (most of) the barrel sawn off (as used by criminals for ease of concealment and carrying). ***saw sth up,*** cut into pieces with a saw: *sawn timber,* timber that has been sawn into planks (contrasted with logs). **2** [VP2A,C,6A] move backward and forward: *sawing at his fiddle,* using his bow as if it were a saw. **3** [VP2A] capable of being sawn: *This wood saws easily.* **saw·yer** /ˈsɔjə(r)/ *n* man whose work is sawing wood.

saw[3] /sɔ/ *n* [C] proverbial saying.

sax /sæks/ *n* (colloq abbr of) saxophone.

sax·horn /ˈsækshɔn/ *n* musical instrument made of brass, like a bugle, made in various sizes.

saxi·frage /ˈsæksɪfrɪdʒ/ *n* [U] kinds of Alpine or rock plant with white, yellow or red flowers.

Saxon /ˈsæksn/ *n, adj* (member, language) of a people once living in NW Germany, some of whom conquered and settled in Britain in the 5th and 6th cc.

saxo·phone /ˈsæksəfəʊn/ *n* (colloq abbr *sax*) musical wind instrument with a reed in the mouthpiece and keys for the fingers, made of brass. ⇨ the illus at **brass**. **sax·ophon·ist** /sækˈsofənɪst *US:* ˈsæksəfəʊnɪst/ *n* ~ player.

say /seɪ/ *vt,vi* (*3rd pers, pres t* **says** /sez/, *pt,pp* **said** /sed/) [VP6A,14,9,10] **1** utter; make (a specified word or remark); use one's voice to produce (words, sentences): *Be polite and say 'Please' and 'Thank you'. Did you say anything? He said that his friend's name was Smith. Everyone was saying what a handsome couple they made. Everyone said how well I was looking. I've something to say to you,* to tell you. *I wouldn't say no to a glass of beer,* would accept one willingly. *The boy was saying his lessons,* repeating them to his teacher. *You may well say so,* you are right. *So you say* (implying that the speaker may be mistaken). ***go without saying,*** be obvious: *It goes without saying that country life is healthier than town life.* ***have nothing/anything to say for oneself,*** i e in one's own defence: *Well, what have you to say for yourself,* What can you say to explain or defend your conduct? ***say the word,*** express agreement: *You've only to say the word* (e g say 'Yes') *and the car's yours,* i e I will let you have it. ***say a good word for sb/sth,*** commend; praise: *He hasn't a good word to say for anybody.* ***say one's say,*** finish what one has to say: *Have you said your say yet?* ***that is to say,*** in other words: *three weeks tomorrow, that's to say, the 10th of May.* ***What do you say (to sth/doing sth)?*** What do you think (to...): *What do you say to a walk/to going round to my mother's?* ***I say,*** exclamation used to draw attention, open a conversation or express surprise. ***They say, It's said,*** forms used to introduce reports, rumours, etc: *They say/It's said that he's a miser.* **2** (also [VP10] esp neg and interr) suppose; estimate; form and give an opinion concerning: *There is no saying when this war will end. And so say all of us,* that is the opinion of all of us. *You may learn to play the violin in, let's say, three years.* □ *n* (only in the following) ***have/say one's say,*** express one's opinion; state one's views: *Let him have his say.* ***have a/no/not much, etc say in the matter,*** have some/no/not much right or opportunity to share in a discussion, decision, express one's opinions, etc: *He didn't have much say in deciding where they should spend their holidays.* **say·ing** /ˈseɪɪŋ/ *n* remark commonly made; well-known phrase, proverb, etc: *'More haste, less speed', as the saying goes.*

scab /skæb/ *n* **1** [C] dry crust formed over a wound or sore. **2** [U] (= *scabies*) skin disease (esp of sheep). **3** [C] (colloq) workman who refuses to join a strike, or his trade union, or who takes a striker's place; blackleg. **scabby** *adj* covered with scabs(1).

scab·bard /ˈskæbəd/ *n* sheath for the blade of a sword, dagger or bayonet. ⇨ the illus at sword.

sca·bies /ˈskeɪbiz/ *n* [U] kind of skin disease causing itching.

(sca bi ous /ˈskeɪbɪəs/ *n* kinds of wild and cultivated plant with delicately coloured flowers.

scab·rous /ˈskeɪbrəs *US:* ˈskæb-/ *adj* **1** (of animals, plants, etc) having a rough surface. **2** (of subjects) difficult to write delicately about. **3** indelicate; salacious: *a ~ novel.*

scaf·fold /ˈskæfld/ *n* [C] **1** structure put up for workmen and materials around a building which is being erected or repaired. **2** platform on which criminals are executed: *go to the ~,* be executed. **~·ing** *n* [U] (materials for a) ~(1) (e g poles and planks, or, *tubular ~ing,* metal tubes to be bolted together).

scal·awag /ˈskæləwæg/ *n* = scallywag.

scald /skɔld/ *vt* [VP6A] **1** burn with hot liquid or steam: *~ one's hand with hot fat. He was ~ed to death when the boiler exploded.* **~ing tears,** tears of deep and bitter grief. **2** clean (dishes, etc) with boiling water or steam. **3** heat (milk) almost to boiling-point. □ *n* injury to the skin from hot liquid or steam: *an ointment for burns and ~s.*

scale[1] /skeɪl/ *n* **1** [C] one of the thin overlapping plates of hard material that cover the skin of many fish and reptiles: *scrape the ~s off a herring.* ⇨ the illus at fish. **2** [C] scale-like outer piece on an organic or other object, e g a flake of skin that loosens and comes off the body in some diseases; a flake of rust on iron. ***remove the ~s from sb's eyes,*** (fig) enable sb who has been deceived to realize the true state of affairs. **3** [U] chalky deposit inside boilers, kettles, waterpipes, etc (from the lime in hard water); deposit of tartar on teeth. □ *vt,vi* **1** [VP6A,15A,B] cut or scrape ~s from (e g fish) (but *descale* a boiler or kettle). **2** [VP2C] **~ off,** come off in flakes: *paint/plaster scaling off a wall.* **scaly** *adj* covered with ~ or ~s; coming off in ~s: *a kettle scaly with rust.*

scale[2] /skeɪl/ *n* [C] **1** series of marks at regular intervals for the purpose of measuring (as on a ruler or a thermometer): *This ruler has one ~ in centimetres and another in inches.* **2** ruler or other tool or instrument marked in this way. **3** system of units for measuring: *the ˈdecimal ~.* **4** arrangement in steps or degrees: *a ~ of wages; a person who is high in the social ~; sink in the ~,* fall to a lower level. **sliding ~,** ⇨ slide[2](4). **5** proportion between the size of sth and the map, diagram, etc which represents it: *a map on the ~ of ten kilometres to the centimetre; drawn to ~,* with a uniform reduction or enlargement. **6** relative size, extent, etc: *They are preparing for war on a large ~.* **7** (music) series of tones arranged in order of pitch, esp a series of eight starting on a keynote: *the ~ of F,* beginning with F as the keynote; *practise ~s on the piano.* □ *vt* **1** [VP6A] make a copy or representation of, according to a certain ~: *~ a map/building.* **2** **~ up/down,** increase/decrease by a certain proportion: *All wages/marks were ~d up to 10 per cent.*

scale[3] /skeɪl/ *n* [C] **1** one of the two pans on a balance; (*pl,* or **pair of ~s**) simple balance or instrument for weighing. ⇨ the illus at balance. ***hold the ~s even,*** judge fairly (between). ***turn the ~(s),*** decide the result of sth which is in doubt: *The arrival or reinforcements turned the ~(s) in our favour.* ***turn the ~(s) at,*** (colloq) weigh: *The jockey turned the ~(s) at 80 lb.* **2** any machine for weighing: *bathroom ~s,* for measuring one's weight. □ *vi* [VP2B] weigh: *~ 10 lb.*

scale[4] /skeɪl/ *vt* [VP6A] climb up (a wall, cliff, etc). **ˈscaling-ladder** *n* one used for scaling high walls, e g of fortified town in former times.

scal·lop /ˈskɒləp/ *n* **1** kind of bivalve mollusc with a shell divided into grooves. ⇨ the illus at bivalve. **ˈ~-shell** *n* one half of this shell, used as a utensil in which a savoury dish is cooked and served. **2** (*pl*) ornamental edging of ~-shaped projections cut in pastry, cloth, etc. □ *vt* [VP6A] **1** cook (e g oysters) in a ~-shell. **2** decorate the edge of (sth) with ~s.

scally·wag /ˈskælɪwæg/, (US = **scala·wag** /ˈskæləwæg/) *n* (hum) scamp; rascal.

scalp /skælp/ *n* [C] skin and hair of the head, excluding the face; this skin, etc from an enemy's head as a trophy of victory (by some Indians of N America in olden times). ***out for ~s,*** (fig) making efforts to win trophies of victory over opponents. □ *vt* [VP6A] cut the ~ off.

scal·pel /ˈskælpəl/ *n* small, light knife used by surgeons.

scamp[1] /skæmp/ *n* (often used playfully) rascal; worthless person.

scamp[2] /skæmp/ *vt* [VP6A] do (work, etc), make sth, carelessly, hastily or without interest.

scam·per /ˈskæmpə(r)/ *vi* [VP2A,C] (esp of small animals, e g mice, rabbits, when frightened, or of children and dogs at play) run quickly. □ *n* short, quick run: *take the dog for a ~.*

scampi /ˈskæmpɪ/ *n pl* (with *sing v*) large prawns.

scan /skæn/ *vt,vi* (-nn-) **1** [VP6A] look at attentively; run the eyes over every part of: *The shipwrecked sailor ~ned the horizon anxiously every morning.* **2** [VP6A] (mod use) glance at quickly but not very thoroughly: *He ~ned the newspaper while having his breakfast.* **3** [VP6A] test the metre of (a line of verse) by noting the division into feet, as in:

Néver | séek to | téll thy | lóve
Lóve that | néver | tóld can | bé.

4 [VP2A] (of verse) fit a metrical pattern; be composed so that it can be ~ned: *This line does not/will not ~. The verses ~ well.* **5** [VP6A] (T V) resolve (a picture) into its elements of light and shade for transmission; (radar) traverse an area with electronic beams in search of sth. **scan·sion** /ˈskænʃn/ *n* [U] the ~ning of verse; the way verse ~s.

scan·dal /ˈskændl/ *n* **1** [C,U] (action, piece of behaviour, etc that causes a) general feeling of indignation; [C] shameful or disgraceful action: *There have been grave ~s on the Stock Exchange. It is a ~ that the accused man was declared innocent. If she leaves her husband she will certainly create a ~ in the village.* **2** [U] harmful gossip; careless or unkind talk which damages sb's reputation: *Don't talk/listen to ~. Most of us enjoy a bit of ~.* **ˈ~·monger** /-mʌŋgə(r)/ *n* person who spreads ~s. **~·monger·ing** /-mʌŋgrɪŋ/ *n* [U] the spreading of ~s. **~·ize** /ˈskændḷaɪz/ *vt* [VP6A] shock; offend the moral feelings or the ideas of etiquette of: *~ize the neighbours by sunbathing on the lawn in the nude.* **~·ous** /ˈskændḷəs/ *adj* **1** disgraceful; shocking. **2** (of reports, rumours) containing ~. **3** (of persons) fond of spreading ~. **~·ous·ly** *adv*

Scan·di·na·vian /ˈskændɪˋneɪvɪən/ *n, adj* (native) of Scandinavia (Denmark, Norway, Sweden, Iceland).

scan·sion /ˋskænʃn/ ⇨ **scan**.

scant /skænt/ *adj* (having) hardly enough: *~ of breath; pay ~ attention to sb's advice.* □ *vt* [VP6A] skimp; make ~; cut down: *Don't ~ the butter when you make a cake.* **scanty** *adj* (-ier, -iest) (opp of *ample*) small in size or amount; barely large enough: *a ~y rice crop; a ~y bathing dress.* **~·ily** /-əlɪ/ *adv* in a ~y manner: *~ily dressed.* **~i·ness** *n*

scant·ling /ˋskæntlɪŋ/ *n* small beam or piece of timber; board not more than 5 inches wide.

scape·goat /ˋskeɪpgəʊt/ *n* person blamed or punished for the mistake(s) or wrong-doing of another or others.

scape·grace /ˋskeɪpgreɪs/ *n* (dated) (often used playfully) good-for-nothing person who constantly gets into trouble: *Her ~ husband. You young ~!*

scap·ula /ˋskæpjʊlə/ *n* (anat) shoulder-blade. ⇨ the illus at **skeleton**.

scar /skɑ(r)/ *n* mark remaining on the surface (of skin, furniture, etc) as the result of injury or damage: *a long ~ across his cheek;* (fig) *grief that left a ~ (on the heart).* □ *vt,vi* (-rr-) **1** [VP6A] mark with a ~ or ~s: *a face ~red by smallpox; the war-~red towns of Vietnam.* **2** [VP2C] heal over (with a ~); form ~s: *The cut on his forehead ~red over.*

scarab /ˋskærəb/ *n* kinds of beetle, esp one regarded as sacred in ancient Egypt; carving in the shape of a ~ (as an ornament or charm).

scarce /skeəs/ *adj* **1** (opp of *plentiful*) not available in sufficient quantity; not equal to the demand: *Eggs are ~ and dear this month.* **2** rare; seldom met with: *a ~ book.* ***make oneself ~,*** (colloq) keep out of the way, go away. **scarc·ity** /ˋskeəsətɪ/ *n* [U] state of being ~; smallness of supply compared with demand: *The scarcity of fruit was caused by the drought.* [C] (*pl* **-ties**) instance or occasion of scarcity.

scarce·ly /ˋskeəslɪ/ *adv* barely; not quite; almost not: *There were ~ a hundred people present. I ~ know him. He is so uneducated that he can ~ write his name. S~ had he entered the room when the phone rang.*

scare /skeə(r)/ *vt,vi* [VP6A,15A,B,2A] frighten; become frightened: *He was ~d by the thunder. They were ~d at the strange noise. The dogs ~d the thief away. He ~s easily/is easily ~d.* ***~ sb stiff,*** (colloq) alarm sb, make sb nervous: *He's ~d stiff of women.* ***~ sb out of his wits,*** make him extremely frightened: *The sound of footsteps outside ~d her out of her wits.* □ *n* [C] feeling of alarm; state of widespread fear: *The news caused a war ~,* a fear that war might break out. *You did give me a ~,* did frighten me. **ˋ~·crow** *n* figure of a man dressed in old clothes, set up to ~ birds away from crops. **ˋ~ headline** *n* sensational newspaper headline in heavy black print. **ˋ~-monger** /-mʌŋgə(r)/ *n* person who spreads alarming news and starts a ~. **scary** /ˋskeərɪ/ *adj* (colloq) causing fear: *This dark room's a bit scary.*

scarf /skɑf/ *n* (*pl* **~s** /skɑfs/ or **scarves** /skɑvz/) long strip of material (silk, wool, etc) worn over the shoulders, round the neck or (by women) over the hair. **ˋ~-pin** *n* ornamental pin worn on a ~.

scar·ify /ˋskærəfɑɪ/ *vt* (*pt,pp* **-fied**) [VP6A] **1** (in surgery) make small cuts in, cut off skin, from. **2** (fig) hurt by severe criticism. **3** loosen (the surface of the soil or a road) by using an agricultural tool or a machine with prongs.

scar·let /ˋskɑlət/ *n, adj* bright red: *the ~ pillar-boxes in Great Britain.* **ˌ~ ˋfever,** infectious disease with ~ marks on the skin. **ˌ~ ˋhat,** cardinal's hat. **ˌ~ ˋrunner,** ~-flowered kind of bean plant. **ˌ~ ˋwoman,** (old use) whore.

scarp /skɑp/ *n* steep slope; escarpment.

scat /skæt/ *int* (sl) Go away!

scath·ing /ˋskeɪðɪŋ/ *adj* (of criticism, ridicule, etc) severe; harsh: *a ~ retort; a ~ review of a new book.* **~·ly** *adv*

scat·ter /ˋskætə(r)/ *vt,vi* **1** [VP6A,15A,B,2A,C] send, go, in different directions: *The police ~ed the crowd. The crowd ~ed.* **2** [VP6A,15A] throw or put in various directions, or here and there: *~ seed; ~ gravel on an icy road.* **ˋ~-brain** *n* person who cannot keep his thoughts on one subject for long. Hence, **ˋ~-brained** *adj* □ *n* that which is ~ed; sprinkling: *a ~ of hailstones.* **~ed** (*pp* as an) *adj* lying in different directions; not situated together; wide apart: *a few ~ed fishing villages; a thinly ~ed population.*

scatty /ˋskætɪ/ *adj* (-ier, -iest) (colloq) mad: *That man would drive any woman ~!*

scav·en·ger /ˋskævɪndʒə(r)/ *n* **1** animal or bird, e g a vulture, that lives on decaying flesh. **2** (now *dustman* or *refuse-collector*) person paid to take away dirt and rubbish from streets, buildings, etc. **scav·enge** /skævɪndʒ/ *vt, vi* act as a ~.

scen·ario /sɪˋnɑrɪəʊ *US:* -ˋnær-/ *n* (*pl* **-rios** /-rɪəʊz/) written outline of a play, an opera, a film, with details of the scenes, etc. **scen·arist** /sɪˋnɑrɪst *US:* -ˋnær-/ *n* writer of ~s.

scene /sin/ *n* [C] **1** place of an actual or imagined event: *the ~ of a great battle. The ~ of the novel is laid in Scotland.* **2** description of an incident, or of part of a person's life; incident in real life suitable for such a description: *'S~s of Clerical Life',* tales by George Eliot. *There were distressing ~s when the earthquake occurred.* **3** (incident characterized by an) emotional outburst: *She made a ~/ We had a ~ when I scolded her.* **4** view; sth seen; sth spread out to view (indoors or outdoors, in a town or in the country, with or without action; cf *scenery*, which is used of natural features on land): *The boats in the harbour make a beautiful ~. They went abroad for a change of ~.* **5** (abbr **Sc**) one of the parts, shorter than an act, into which some plays and operas are divided; episode within such a part: *'Macbeth', Act II, Sc 1: the ˋduel ~ in 'Hamlet'.* **6** place represented on the stage of a theatre; the painted background, woodwork, canvas, etc representing such a place: *The first ~ of 'Hamlet' is the walk of a castle. The ~s are changed during the intervals.* ***behind the ~s,*** **(a)** out of sight of the audience; behind the stage. **(b)** (fig, of a person) influencing events secretly; having private or secret information and influence. ***come on the ~,*** (usu fig) appear. **ˋ~-painter** *n* (theatre) person who paints scenery(2). **ˋ~-shifter** *n* (theatre) person who changes the ~s. **7** (colloq) area of what is currently fashionable or notable: *the ˌenterˋtainment ~ in the West End of London; the ˋdrug ~ in our big cities.* ***be on the***

~, (colloq) be present in such ~s (with popular and fashionable people). ***make the ~ (with sb),*** take part in sth of this kind, be seen in company with (people who are in such a ~).

scen·ery /ˋsinərɪ/ *n* [U] **1** general natural features of a district, e g mountains, plains, valleys, forests: *mountain ~; stop to admire the ~.* Cf *town scenes.* **2** the furnishings, painted canvas, woodwork, etc used on the stage of a theatre.

scenic /ˋsinɪk/ *adj* of scenery: *the ~ splendours of the Rocky Mountains; a ~ highway across the Alps; ~ effects,* e g in a film. **sceni·cally** /-klɪ/ *adv*

scent /sent/ *n* **1** [U] smell, esp of sth pleasant coming from or belonging to sth: *the ~ of new-mown hay; a rose that has no ~;* [C] particular kind of smell: *~s of lavender and rosemary.* **2** [U] (usu liquid) preparation distilled from flowers, etc; perfume: *a bottle of ~; a ˋ~-bottle. She uses too much ~ on her hair.* **3** (usu *sing*) smell left by an animal; the track of an animal: *follow up/lose/recover the ~. The ~ was strong/poor/hot/cold,* easy/difficult, etc for the hounds. ***on the ~,*** having, following, a clue. ***off the ~,*** having, following, no clue or the wrong clue. ***put/throw sb off the ~,*** (fig) mislead him by giving false information. ***on a wrong/false ~,*** on one that is deceptive; on mistaken lines. **4** [U] sense of smell (in dogs): *hunt by ~.* □ *vt* [VP6A] **1** learn the presence of by smell: *The dog ~ed a rat.* **2** begin to suspect the presence or existence of: *~ a crime; ~ treachery/trouble.* **3** put ~ on; make fragrant: *~ a handkerchief; roses that ~ the air.* **~·less** *adj* having no ~: *~less flowers.*

scep·ter /ˋseptə(r)/ *n* = sceptre.

scep·tic (US = **skep·tik**) /ˋskeptɪk/ *n* person who doubts the truth of a particular claim, theory, etc; person who doubts the truth of the Christian religion or of all religions. **scep·ti·cal** (US = **skep-**) /-kl/ *adj* inclined not to believe; in the habit of questioning the truth of claims, statements, etc. **scep·ti·cally** (US = **skep-**) /-klɪ/ *adv*

scep·ti·cism (US = **skep-**) /ˋskeptɪsɪzm/ *n* [U] doubting state of mind; ~al attitude of mind.

sceptre (US = **scep·ter**) /ˋseptə(r)/ *n* rod or staff carried by a ruler as a sign of power or authority. **scep·tred** (US = **-tered**) *adj* having a ~.

sched·ule /ˋʃedjul *US:* ˋskedʒl/ *n* [C] list or statement of details, esp of times for doing things; programme or timetable for work: *a production ~,* e g in a factory; *a full ~,* a busy programme. ***on/behind ~,*** on/not on time: *The train arrived on ~,* on time, punctually. ***(according) to ~,*** as planned. □ *vt* [VP6A,14] make a ~ of; put in a ~; (esp US) enter in a list of arrangements: *~d services,* (e g of aircraft) flying according to announced time-tables. Cf *charter flights. The President is ~d to make a speech tomorrow. His arrival is ~d for Thursday.*

sche·matic /skiˋmætɪk/ *adj* of the nature of a scheme or plan; (shown) in a diagram or chart. **sche·mati·cally** /-klɪ/ *adv*

scheme /skim/ *n* [C] **1** arrangement; ordered system: *a ˋcolour ~,* e g for a room, so that colours of walls, rugs, curtains, etc are in harmony. **2** plan or design (for work or activity): *a ~ for manufacturing paper from straw; a ~* (= syllabus) *for the term's work.* **3** secret and dishonest plan: *a ~ to defraud a widow.* □ *vi,vt* **1** [VP2A,3A,4A] ***~ for sth/to do sth,*** make a (esp dishonest) ~ or ~s: *He ~d to keep his rivals in ignorance of his plans. They ~d for the overthrow of the government.* **2** [VP6A] make plans for (esp sth dishonest); *a scheming* (= crafty) *young man.* **schemer** *n* person who ~s or intrigues.

scherzo /ˋskeətsəʊ/ *n* (*pl* -zos /-səʊz/) (I; music) lively, vigorous passage in music.

schism /ˋsɪzm/ *n* [U] (offence of causing the) division of an organization (esp a Church) into two or more groups, usu through difference of opinion; [C] instance of such separation. **schis·matic** /sɪzˋmætɪk/ *adj* tending to or inclined to ~; guilty of ~.

schist /ʃɪst/ *n* kinds of rock which splits easily into thin plates.

schizo·phrenia /ˌskɪtsəʊˋfrinɪə/ *n* type of mental disorder (colloq *split personality*) marked by lack of association between the intellectual processes and actions. **schizo·phrenic** /ˌskɪtsəʊˋfrenɪk/ *adj* of ~. □ *n* (colloq abbr *schizo* /ˋskɪtsəʊ/) person suffering from ~.

schmal(t)z /ʃmɔlts/ *n* (colloq) sickly sentimentality. **schmal(t)zy** *adj*

schnapps /ʃnæps/ *n* [U] spirit resembling Holland gin.

schnit·zel /ˋʃnɪtsl/ *n* veal cutlet covered with breadcrumbs and fried in butter.

schnor·kel /ˋsnɔkl/ *n* = snorkel.

scholar /ˋskolə(r)/ *n* **1** (dated use) boy or girl at school. **2** student who, after a competitive examination or other means of selection, is awarded money or other help so that he may attend school or college, or pursue further education: *a Rhodes ~; British Council ~s.* **3** person with much knowledge (usu of a particular subject, and esp one who gives careful attention to evidence, method, etc). *Professor X, the famous Greek ~.* **4** (a common use among uneducated persons) person able to read and write: *I'm not much of a ~.* **~·ly** *adj* having or showing much learning; of suitable, or right for a ~(3); fond of learning: *a ~ly translation; a ~ly young woman.*

schol·ar·ship /ˋskoləʃɪp/ *n* **1** [U] learning or knowledge obtained by study; proper concern for scholarly methods. **2** [C] payment of money, e g a yearly grant to a scholar(2) so that he may continue his studies: *win a ~ to the university.*

schol·as·tic /skəˋlæstɪk/ *adj* **1** of schools and education: *the ˋ~ profession,* that of teaching; *a ˋ~ post,* a position as a teacher; *a ˋ~ agency,* private one that finds positions for teachers and teachers for schools. **2** connected with the learning of the Middle Ages, esp when men argued over small points of dogma. **schol·as·ti·cism** /skəˋlæstɪsɪzm/ *n* [U] the system of philosophy taught in the universities in the Middle Ages.

school[1] /skul/ *n* **1** [C] institution for educating children: *primary and secondary ~s; evening ~s; Sunday ~s; ~ doctors,* medical officers responsible for the health of school children; (US) college, university. **ˋ~-board** *n* (in England, 1870—1902) local education authority responsible for providing and maintaining ~s (called *ˋboard-~s*) for free elementary education. **ˋ~-book** *n* book used in ~s; textbook. **ˋ~·boy** *n* boy at ~: (attrib) *~boy slang.* **ˋ~-days** *n pl* time of being at ~: *look back upon one's ~-days.* **ˋ~·fellow** *n* member, past or present, of the same ~. **ˋ~·girl** *n* girl at ~. **ˋ~·house** *n* building of a ~ esp a small one in a village. Cf *the ˋ~ house,* the headmaster's house or residence. '~-ma'am/-marm /-mɑm/ *n* (colloq) ~mistress. '~-man /-mən/ *n* (*pl* -men) teacher in a European university in the Middle Ages; theologian dealing with religious teachings by the use of Aristotle's logic. '~-master/-mistress *n* teacher (esp in a private school or old-fashioned grammar school. '~-mate *n* = ~fellow. '~-time *n* lesson time either at ~ or at home. **2** (not with the articles) process of being educated in a ~: '~ *age,* between the ages of starting and finishing ~; ~-'*leaving age,* age at which children leave ~; *the ~-leaving age has been raised to 16. Is he old enough for ~/to go to ~? He left ~ when he was fifteen. My boys are still at ~.* **3** (no article) time when teaching is given; lessons: *S~ begins at 9 a m. There will be no ~* (= no lessons) *tomorrow. Will you come for a walk after ~?* **4** (with *def art*) all the pupils in a ~: *The whole ~ hopes that its football team will win the match.* **5** department or division of a university for the study of a particular subject: *The S~ of African and Oriental Studies,* in the University of London; *the 'Law/'Medical S~; the S~ of Dentistry;* (GB) branch of study for which separate examinations are given in a university: *the 'History ~*; hall in which these examinations are held; (*pl*) these examinations: *in the S~s,* at Oxford. **6** (fig) circumstances or occupation that provides discipline or instruction: *the hard ~ of experience/adversity.* **7** (*pl*) **the ~s,** medieval universities, their professors, teaching, and arguments. ⇨ also *~man* in **1** above. **8** [C] group of persons who are followers or imitators of an artist, a philosopher, etc, or of persons having the same principles or characteristics: *the Dutch/Venetian, etc ~ of painting; the Hegelian ~,* of philosophers; *a nobleman of the old ~,* who retains the traditions, manners, etc of olden times. □ *vt* [VP6A,15A] train; control; discipline: *~ a horse; ~ one's temper; ~ oneself to patience; ~ed by adversity.* ~·ing *n* [U] education: *He had very little ~ing. Who is paying for her ~ing?*

school² /skul/ *n* [C] large number (*of* fish) swimming together; shoal.

schoo·ner /'skunə(r)/ *n* **1** kind of sailing-ship with two or more masts and fore and aft sails. **2** tall drinking-glass.

schot·tische /ʃo'tiʃ/ *n* (music for a) kind of polka.

schwa /ʃwɑ/ *n* the symbol /ə/ used in phonetic notation for 'obscure', i e central vowels, or diphthong elements as in /ə'gəʊ/ for *ago.*

sci·atic /sɑɪ'ætɪk/ *adj* of the hip: *the ~ nerve,* nerve extending through the hip and thigh. **sci·atica** /sɑɪ'ætɪkə/ *n* [U] neuralgia of the ~ nerve.

science /'sɑɪəns/ *n* **1** [U] knowledge arranged in an orderly manner, esp knowledge obtained by observation and testing of facts; pursuit of such knowledge. *S~ is an exact discipline.* **2** [C,U] branch of such knowledge. **the 'natural ~s,** e g botany, zoology. **the 'physical ~s,** e g physics, chemistry. **social ~(s),** e g psychology, politics. **the ap'plied ~s,** e g engineering: *study ~/the ~s at school; be on the ~ side.* ⇨ art¹(2). ,~ **'fic·tion,** fiction dealing with recent or imagined scientific discoveries and advances (usu fantasies). **3** [U] expert's skill (opp of strength): *In judo ~ is more important than strength.* **scien·tist** /'sɑɪəntɪst/ *n* person expert in one or more of the natural or physical ~s.

scien·tific /,sɑɪən'tɪfɪk/ *adj* **1** of, for, connected with, used in, science; guided by the rules of science: *~ methods; ~ farming; ~ instruments.* **2** having, using, needing, skill or expert knowledge: *a ~ boxer.* **scien·tifi·cally** /-klɪ/ *adv*

scimi·tar /'sɪmɪtə(r)/ *n* short, curved, single-edged sword as formerly used by Persians, Arabs and Turks.

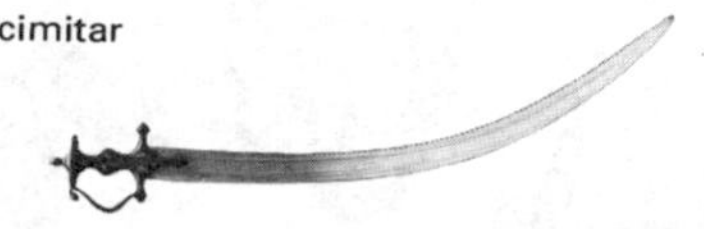
a scimitar

scin·tilla /sɪn'tɪlə/ *n* [C] spark; atom; shred; iota: *not a ~ of truth in the story; not a ~ of evidence,* none at all.

scin·til·late /'sɪntɪleɪt *US:* -tḷeɪt/ *vi* [VP2A] sparkle; be brilliant: *scintillating with wit.* **scin·til·la·tion** /,sɪntɪ'leɪʃn/ *n*

scion /'sɑɪən/ *n* **1** young member of (esp an old or a noble) family. **2** shoot of a plant, esp one cut for grafting or planting.

scis·sors /'sɪzəz/ *n pl* (often **a pair of ~s**) cutting instrument with two blades which cut as they come together: *Where are my ~?* ***~ and paste,*** phrase used to describe the compilation of articles and books out of cuttings from others: *This article's a ~ and paste job.*

scler·osis /sklə'rəʊsɪs/ *n* [U] diseased condition in which soft tissue (e g walls of the arteries) hardens.

scoff¹ /skof *US:* skɔf/ *vi* [VP2A,3A] ***~ (at),*** speak contemptuously, mock (at): *~ at dangers; ~ at religion.* □ *n* **1** taunt; ~ing remark. **2** object of ridicule; laughing-stock: *He was the ~ of the town.* **~er** *n* person who ~s. **~·ing·ly** *adv*

scoff² /skof *US:* skɔf/ *vt* (sl) eat greedily: *Who has ~ed all the pastries?* □ *n* **1** act of ~ing: *have a good ~.* **2** [U] food: *Where's all the ~ gone?*

scold /skəʊld/ *vt,vi* **1** [VP2A,14] ***~ sb (for sth),*** blame with angry words; find fault noisily (e g a bad-tempered woman to her daily help, a weak mother with a wilful child): *~ a child for being lazy.* **2** [VP2A,C] speak angrily or complainingly: *She's always ~ing.* □ *n* woman who ~s. **~·ing** *n* [C] severe rebuke: *get/give sb a ~ing for being late.*

scol·lop /'skoləp/ *n, vt* = scallop.

sconce /skons/ *n* bracket fixed to a wall for a candle (or, today, any other form of light).

scone /skon *US:* skəʊn/ *n* [C] soft, flat cake of barley meal or wheat flour baked quickly.

scoop /skup/ *n* [C] **1** (sorts of) deep, shovel-like, short-handled tool for taking up and moving quantities of grain, flour, sugar, etc; long-handled, ladle-shaped tool for dipping out liquid. **2** motion of, or as of, using a ~: *at one ~,* in one single movement of a ~: (fig) *He won £50 at one ~.* **3** (colloq) piece of news obtained and published by one newspaper before its competitors; (comm) large profit made by anticipating competitors. □ *vt* **1** [VP15B] ***~ sth out/up,*** lift with, or as with, a ~. **2** [VP6A,15B] make (a hole, groove, etc) with, or as with, a ~: *~ out a hole in the sand.* **3** [VP6A] (colloq) get (news, a profit, etc) as a ~(3). **~·ful** /-fʊl/ *n* as much as a ~ holds.

scoot /skut/ *vi* (either imper or inf) (colloq, hum) run away quickly: *S~! Tell him to ~.* ⇨ scram.

scooter /'skutə(r)/ *n* **1** ('**motor-~**) motor-bike

with a low seat, as shown here. **2** child's toy, an L-shaped vehicle with small wheels, one foot being used to steer it and the other to move it by pushing against the ground.

scooters

scope /skəʊp/ *n* [U] **1** opportunity; outlet: *work that gives ~ for one's abilities.* **2** range of action or observation: *Ought politics to be within the ~ of a trade union's activities? Economics is a subject beyond the ~ of a child's mind.*

scor·bu·tic /skɔˋbjutɪk/ *adj* of, affected with, scurvy.

scorch /skɔtʃ/ *vt,vi* **1** [VP6A] burn or discolour the surface of (sth) by dry heat; cause to dry up or wither: *The long, hot summer ~ed the grass. You ~ed my shirt when you ironed it.* **ˈ~ed ˋearth policy,** policy of burning crops, and destroying buildings, etc that might be useful to enemy forces occupying a district. **2** [VP2A] become discoloured, etc with heat. **3** [VP2A,C] (colloq, of cyclists, motorists, etc) travel at very high speed. □ *n* [C] **1** mark on the surface of sth (esp cloth) made by dry heat. **2** (colloq) period of riding or driving at high speed. **~er** *n* sth or sb that ~es: *Yesterday was a ~er,* a very hot day. *Isn't he a ~er,* Doesn't he drive fast! **~·ing** *adj* very hot. □ *adv*: *~ing hot,* extremely hot.

score[1] /skɔ(r)/ *n* [C] **1** cut, scratch or notch made on a surface: *~s on rock,* e g made during the Ice Age; *~s on a slave's back* (made by whipping). **2** (from the old custom of chalking lines on a board in inns, to record what a customer owed for drinks, etc) account or record of money owing: *run up a ~,* get into debt. ***pay/settle/wipe off old ~s,*** (fig) get even with sb for past offences; have one's revenge: *I have some old ~s to settle with that fellow.* **3** (record of) points, goals, runs, etc made by a player or team in sport: *The ~ in the tennis final was 6—4, 3—6, 7—5. The half-time ~* (e g football) *was 2—1.* ***keep the ~,*** keep a record of the ~ as it is made. **ˋ~-board/-book/-card,** one on which the ~ (e g cricket) is recorded (during play). **4** reason; account: ***on the ~ of,*** on account of, in consideration of: *rejected on the ~* (*grounds* is more usu) *of ill health.* ***on more ~s than one,*** for more than one reason. ***on that ~,*** as far as that point is concerned: *You need have no anxiety on that ~.* **5** copy of orchestral, etc music showing what each instrument is to play, each voice to sing: *follow the ~ while listening to music.* **6** twenty; set of twenty: *a ~ of people; three ~ and ten,* 70, the normal length of human life according to the Bible. *I've been there ~s of times,* very often. **7** (sl) remark or act by which a person gains an advantage for himself in an argument, etc: *a politician who is clever at making ~s off hecklers at public meetings,* clever at making them appear foolish. ⇨ score[2](4).

score[2] /skɔ(r)/ *vt,vi* **1** [VP6A,15A,B] mark with cuts, scratches, lines, etc: *The mountain side is ~d by torrents,* shows where torrents of water have washed away soil, etc. *Don't ~ the floor by pushing heavy furniture about. The composition was ~d with corrections in red ink.* **~ out,** draw a line or lines through: *Three words had been ~d out.* ⇨ score[1](1). **2** [VP6A,2A,15B] ***~ (up),*** make or keep a record (esp for games): *~ up runs,* in cricket. *Who's going to ~?* **3** [VP6A,2A] make as points in a game: *~ a goal; ~ a century,* 100 runs at cricket; *a batsman who failed to ~,* who made no runs; *~ no tricks,* i e whist or bridge. ***~ an advantage/a success,*** win one; have good fortune. ***~ a point (over sb),*** = ~ off sb(4). **4** [VP3A] ***~ off sb,*** (colloq) humiliate him; defeat him in an argument; make a clever retort to sth he says. **5** [VP15B] ***~ sth up (against sb),*** enter as a record: *That remark will be ~d up against you,* will be remembered (and, perhaps, be revenged). **6** [VP6A] orchestrate; write instrumental or vocal parts for a musical composition: *~d for violin, viola and cello.* ⇨ score[1](5). **scorer** *n* **1** person who keeps a record of points, goals, runs, etc ~d in a game. **2** player who ~s runs, goals, etc.

sco·ria /ˋskɔrɪə/ *n* [U] rough fragments of lava, etc.

scorn /skɔn/ *n* [U] **1** contempt; feeling that sb or sth deserves no respect: *be filled with ~ for a proposal; dismiss a suggestion with ~.* ***laugh sb/sth to ~,*** treat with contemptuous laughter. **2** object of contempt: *He was the ~ of the village.* □ *vt* [VP6A,D,7A] feel or show contempt for; refuse (to do sth as being unworthy): *We ~ a liar. He ~ed my advice. She ~s lying/telling lies/to tell a lie.* **~·ful** /-fl/ *adj* showing or feeling ~; *a ~ful smile; ~ful of material things.* **~·fully** /-fḷɪ/ *adv*

Scor·pio /ˋskɔpɪəʊ/ *n* eighth sign of the zodiac. ⇨ the illus at zodiac.

scor·pion /ˋskɔpɪən/ *n* small animal of the spider group with a poisonous sting in its long, jointed tail. ⇨ the illus at arachnid.

scot /skot/ *n* (only in) ***pay ~ and lot,*** share financial burdens. ***go/get off/escape ˈ~-ˋfree,*** unharmed, unpunished.

Scot /skot/ *n* native of Scotland.

Scotch /skotʃ/ *adj* of Scotland or its people: *~ whisky,* the kind distilled in Scotland. **ˈ~ ˋterrier,** small, rough-haired, short-legged kind of terrier. □ *n* **1** *the ~,* people of Scotland. **2** [U] ~ whisky. **ˋ~·man** /-mən/, **ˋ~·woman** *nn* = Scotsman, Scotswoman (which are the preferred terms).

scotch /skotʃ/ *vt* [VP6A] (old use) wound without killing: *~ a snake.*

Scot·land Yard /ˈskotlənd ˋjɑd/ *n* (now *ˋNew S~ Y~*) (used for) the London police; headquarters of the Criminal Investigation Department: *They called in ~,* asked for the help of this Department.

Scots /skots/ *n, adj* ⇨ Scot. **ˋ~·man** /-mən/, **ˋ~·woman** /-wʊmən/ *nn* natives of Scotland.

Scot·tish /ˋskotɪʃ/ *adj* = Scotch.

scoun·drel /ˋskaʊndrl/ *n* wicked person with no principles or scruples; villain; rascal. **~ly** /-rḷɪ/ of or like a ~.

scour[1] /ˋskaʊə(r)/ *vt,vi* **1** [VP6A,15A,B] make (a dirty surface) clean or bright by friction: *~ the pots and pans; ~ out a saucepan,* clean the inside (with a ~er); *~ the tiles,* e g with a scrubbing brush and soap. **2** [VP6A,15B] ***~ sth away/off,*** get rid of (rust, marks, etc) by rubbing or with a strong jet of water: *~ the rust off.* **3** [VP6A,15A] clear out (a channel, etc) by flowing over or through it: *The torrent ~ed a channel down the hillside.* □ *n* act of ~ing: *give a dirty saucepan a good ~.* **~er** *n* (esp) pad of stiff nylon or wire for ~ing pots and pans.

scour[2] /ˈskaʊə(r)/ *vt,vi* [VP6A] go rapidly into every part of (a place) looking for: *~ the woods. The police ~ed London for the thief.* **2** [VP2C] ***~ about after/for sb/sth,*** go quickly in search or pursuit of.

scourge /skɜdʒ/ *n* **1** (old use) whip for flogging persons. **2** (usual mod use, fig) cause of suffering; person regarded as an instrument of vengeance or punishment, e g a barbarian conqueror such as Attila: *After the ~ of war came the ~ of disease.* □ *vt* [VP6A] **1** (old use) use a ~ on. **2** (fig) cause suffering to.

scout[1] /skaʊt/ *n* **1** person (not a spy), ship or small, fast aircraft, sent out to get information of the enemy's movements, strength, etc. **2 Boy S~,** member of an organization intended to develop character and teach self-reliance, discipline and public spirit. Cf *Girl Guides* (US = *Girl S~s*). ***a good ~,*** a likeable fellow. **ˈ~·master** *n* officer who leads a troop of Boy S~s. **3** patrol-man on the roads, helping motorists who are members of the Automobile Association or Royal Automobile Club. **4** person employed to look out for talented performers (in sport, the theatre, etc) and recruit them for his employer(s): *a ˈtalent ~.* **5** (at Oxford) college servant. □ *vi* [VP2C] ***~ about/around (for sb/sth),*** go about as a ~(1,4): *~ about/around for...,* go about looking for....

scout[2] /skaʊt/ *vt* [VP6A] dismiss (an idea, suggestion, etc) as worthless or ridiculous.

scow /skaʊ/ *n* large flat-bottomed boat used for carrying sand, rock, rubbish, etc.

scowl /skaʊl/ *n* [C] bad-tempered look (on the face). □ *vi* [VP2A,3A] ***~ (at),*** look in a bad-tempered way: *The prisoner ~ed at the judge.*

scrabble[1] /ˈskræbl/ *n* [U] (P) game in which words are built up on a board (marked with squares) from letters printed on counters or blocks.

scrabble[2] /ˈskræbl/ *vi* **1** [VP2A] scrawl, scribble. **2** [VP2C] ***~ about (for sth),*** grope about to find or collect sth: *~ about for sth dropped under the table.* □ *n* act of scrabbling.

scrag /skræg/ *n* **1** lean, skinny person or animal. **2** **ˈ~(-ˈend),** bony part of a sheep's neck, used for making soup and stews. □ *vt* (-gg-) **1** (colloq) wring the neck of (sb). **2** put to death by strangling; twist the neck of. **scraggy** *adj* (-ier, -iest) thin and bony: *a long, ~gy neck.*

scram /skræm/ *vi* (either *imper* or *inf*) (sl) Be off! Run!: *I told him to ~.*

scramble /ˈskræmbl/ *vi,vt* **1** [VP2A,C,4A] climb, clamber or crawl (over steep or rough ground): *~ up the side of a cliff/over a rocky hillside.* **2** [VP3A,4A] ***~ for/to get sth,*** struggle with others to get sth, or as much or as many as possible of sth, from competitors: *The players ~d for/~d to get possession of the ball. The children ~d for the coins that were thrown to them.* **3** [VP6A] cook (eggs) by beating them and then heating them in a saucepan with butter and milk. **4** [VP6A] make a message sent by telephone, etc unintelligible (by changing the wave frequency) without a special receiver. □ *n* [C] **1** climb, walk, motor-bike competition or trial, over or through obstacles, rough ground, etc. **2** rough struggle: *There was a ~ for the best seats.* **scram·bler** /ˈskræmblə(r)/ *n* device for scrambling telephone messages. ⇨ **4** above.

scrap[1] /skræp/ *n* **1** [C] small (usu unwanted) piece: *~s of paper/broken porcelain;* (fig) small amount: *not a ~ of evidence to support the charge; not even a ~ of comfort in the news.* **2** [U] waste or unwanted articles, esp those of value only for the material they contain: *A man comes round regularly collecting ~; he offers good prices for ˈ~-iron* (articles made of iron, to be melted down for re-use). **ˈ~-heap** *n* pile of waste or unwanted material or articles. ***throw sth/sb on the ~-heap,*** discard sth, dismiss sb, as no longer wanted. **3** (*pl*) odds and ends; bits of uneaten food: *Give the ~s to the dog.* **4** [C] picture or paragraph cut out from a periodical, etc for a collection. **ˈ~-book** *n* book of blank pages on which to paste these. □ *vt* (-pp-) [VP6A] throw away as useless or worn-out: *You ought to ~ that old bicycle and buy a new one.* **~py** *adj* (-ier, -iest) made up of bits or ~s; not complete or properly arranged. **~·ily** /-əlɪ/ *adv* **~i·ness** *n*

scrap[2] /skræp/ *n* (colloq) fight, quarrel, esp one that is not planned or premeditated: *He had a bit of a ~ with his brother.* □ *vi* (-pp-) fight; quarrel: *Tell those boys to stop ~ping.*

scrape /skreɪp/ *vt,vi* **1** [VP6A,14,15A,B,22] ***~ sth (from/off sth); ~ sth away/off,*** make clean, smooth or level by drawing or pushing the hard edge of a tool, or sth rough, along the surface; remove (mud, grease, paint, etc) in this way: *~ out a sticky saucepan; ~ the rust off sth; ~ paint from a door; ~ a dish clean. The ship's bottom needs to be ~d,* e g in order to remove barnacles. **2** [VP6A,14] ***~ sth (from/off sth),*** injure or damage by harsh rubbing, etc: *The boy fell and ~d his knee/~d the skin off his knee. He ~d the side of his car/~d the paintwork of his car.* **3** [VP6A,15B] ***~ sth (out),*** make by scraping: *~ (out) a hole.* **4** [VP2C,3A] go, get, pass along, touching or almost touching: *~ along a wall; branches that ~ against the window panes.* ***~ along,*** (fig) manage to live in spite of difficulties. ***~ through (sth),*** only just pass: *The boy just ~d through (his exams).* ***bow and ~,*** (liter) bow awkwardly while drawing one foot along the floor; (fig) behave with exaggerated respect. **5** [VP6A, 15B] ***~ sth/sb together,*** obtain by being careful, or with effort: *We managed to ~ together an audience of fifty people/enough money for a short holiday.* ***~ (up) an acquaintance with sb,*** force one's acquaintance upon sb; push oneself into a person's company in order to get acquainted with him. ***~ a living,*** with difficulty make enough money for a living. □ *n* **1** act or sound of scraping: *the ~ of sb's pen on paper/of the teacher's fingernail on the blackboard.* **2** place that is ~d: *a bad ~ on the elbow,* e g as the result of a fall. **3** awkward situation resulting from foolish or thoughtless behaviour: *That boy is always getting into ~s. Don't expect me to get you out of your ~s.* **scraper** *n* tool used for scraping, e g for scraping mud from one's shoes at the entrance to a building, or for scraping paint from woodwork. **scrap·ing** *n* (esp *pl*) small bits produced by scraping: *scrapings from the bottom of the barrel.*

scrappy /ˈskræpɪ/ *adj* ⇨ **scrap**[1].

scratch /skrætʃ/ *vt,vi* **1** [VP6A,2A] make lines on or in a surface with sth pointed or sharp, e g fingernails, claws: *The cat ~ed me. Does your cat ~? Who has ~ed the paint?* ***~ the surface,*** (fig) deal with a subject without being thorough, without getting deeply into it: *The lecturer merely ~ed the surface of the subject.* **2** [VP6A] get (oneself, a part of the body) ~ed by accident: *He ~ed his hands badly while pruning the rose-bushes.* **3** [VP15B] **~ sth/sb out,** draw a line or lines through a word or words, a name, etc: *~ out Smith/his name from the list. The essay contained a lot of scratched-out words/ˈ~ings-ˋout.* **4** [VP6A,2A] withdraw (a horse, a candidate, oneself) from a competition; take out (the name of a horse, a candidate) from a list of entries for a race or competition: *The horse was ~ed,* its name was withdrawn. *I hope you're not going to ~* (= withdraw, decline) *at the last moment.* **5** [VP6A, 2A] scrape or rub (the skin), esp to relieve itching: *~ mosquito bites. Stop ~ing (yourself).* **~ one's head,** show signs of being perplexed. **If you'll ~ my back, I'll ~ yours,** (fig) If you'll help, flatter, etc me, I'll do the same for you. **6** [VP6A,15B] **~ sth (out),** make by ~ing: *~ (out) a hole.* **7** [VP6A] write hurriedly; scribble: *~ a few lines to a friend.* **ˋ~-pad** *n* scribbling pad. **8** [VP2A] make a scraping noise: *This pen ~es.* **9** [VP2C,15B] **~ about (for sth); ~ sth up,** tear or dig with the claws, fingernails, etc in search of sth: *The chickens were ~ing about in the yard. The dog ~ed up a bone.* **10** [VP15B] scrape(**5**): *~ up/together a few pounds.* □ *n* **1** [C] mark, cut, injury, sound, made by ~ing(**1**): *Her hands were covered with ~es after she had pruned her rose-bushes. It's only a ~,* a very slight injury. *He escaped without a ~,* quite unhurt. **a ~ of the pen,** a few words quickly and easily written; a signature. **2** (*sing* only) act or period of ~ing(**5**): *The dog enjoys having a good ~.* **3** (*sing* only; no article) starting line for a race. **start from ~,** start from this line; (fig) start without being allowed any advantage(s); (fig) begin (sth) without preparation. **be/come/bring sb up to ~,** (fig) be ready/get sb ready to do what is expected or required: *Will your teachers manage to bring you up to ~ before you take the examination,* get you ready for it? **4** (attrib) (sport) without a handicap: *~ players.* **ˋ~-race** *n* one in which all competitors start from ~, on equal terms. **5** (attrib) collected by chance; brought together, done, made, with whatever is available: *a ~ crew/team; a ~ dinner,* prepared from what happens to be in the house. **scratchy** *adj* (-ier, -iest) **1** (of writing, drawings) done carelessly or unskilfully. **2** (of a pen) making a ~ing noise.

scrawl /skrɔl/ *vi,vt* [VP6A,2A,C] write or draw quickly or carelessly; make meaningless or illegible marks: *Who has ~ed all over this wall? He ~ed a few words on a postcard to his wife.* □ *n* **1** [C] piece of bad writing; hurried note of letter. **2** (*sing* only) shapeless, untidy handwriting: *What a ~! His signature was an illegible ~.*

scrawny /ˋskrɔnɪ/ *adj* (-ier, iest) bony, scraggy: *the ~ neck of a turkey.*

scream /skrim/ *vi,vt* **1** [VP2A,C,6A,15A,B,22] (of human beings, birds, animals) give a loud, sharp cry or cries of, or as of, fear or pain; cry (sth) in a loud shrill voice: *She ~ed in anger. The baby has been ~ing for an hour. This parrot ~s but does not talk. The child ~ed itself red in the face. She ~ed out that there was a burglar under the bed. We all ~ed with laughter,* laughed noisily. **~ one's head off,** ~ very loudly (and for a long time). **2** [VP2A,C] (of the wind, machines, etc) make a loud, shrill noise: *The wind ~ed through the trees.* □ *n* [C] **1** loud, shrill, piercing cry or noise: *the ~ of a peacock; ~s of pain/laughter.* **2** (colloq) sb or sth that causes ~s of laughter: *He/It was a perfect ~.* **~·ing·ly** *adv* (esp): *~ingly funny,* so funny as to cause ~s of laughter.

scree /skri/ *n* [C,U] (part of a mountain-side covered with) small loose stones which slide down when trodden on. ⇨ the illus at **mountain**.

screech /skritʃ/ *vi,vt* [VP2A,C,6A,15A,B] **1** make a harsh, piercing sound: *jet planes ~ing over the house-tops. The brakes ~ed as the car stopped.* **2** scream in anger or pain; cry out in high tones: monkeys ~ing in the trees. *She ~es out her top notes instead of singing them.* □ *n* [C] ~ing cry or noise: *the ~ of tyres,* e g when a car is cornering fast. **ˋ~-owl** *n* kind of owl that ~es instead of hooting.

screed /skrid/ *n* [C] long (and usu uninteresting) letter; long monotonous speech.

screen /skrin/ *n* [C] (often movable) upright framework (some made so as to fold), used to hide sb or sth from view, or to protect from draughts or from too much heat, light, etc. **2** (in a church) structure of wood or stone separating (but not completely) the main part of the church and the altar, or the nave of a cathedral and the choir. **3** anything that is or can be used to give shelter or protection from observation, the weather, etc: *a ~ of trees,* hiding a house from the road; *a ˋsmoke-~,* used in war to hide ships, etc from the enemy; *a ~ of cavalry,* sent forward to prevent close observation of the main body of troops; a ~ of indifference, an appearance of indifference that hides interest. **4** white or silver surface on to which slides, film transparencies, cinema films, TV pictures, etc are projected; surface upon which an image is seen on a cathode ray tube. Hence, (attrib) *a ~ play; ~ actors/stars; a ˋ~ test,* test of a person's suitability for acting in films. **5** frame with fine wire netting (*ˋwindow ~, ˋdoor ~*) to keep out flies, mosquitoes, etc. **6** large sieve or riddle used for separating coal, gravel, etc into different sizes. **7** (cricket) one of two large movable erections of white wood or canvas placed near the boundary line to help batsmen to see the ball. □ *vt,vi* **1** [VP6A,14,15A,B] shelter, hide, protect from view, with a ~: *The trees ~ our house from public view. One corner of the room was ~ed off. You should ~ the lens of your camera from direct sunlight. We have ~ed our house* (i e doors and windows) *against mosquitoes.* **2** [VP6A,14] (fig) protect from blame, discovery, punishment: *I'm not willing to ~ your faults/~ you from blame.* **3** [VP6A] separate (coal, etc) into different sizes by passing through a ~(**6**): *~ed coal,* from which dust has been removed. **4** [VP6A] investigate (sb's) past history, e g the political antecedents of a refugee or displaced person, sb applying for a position in government service, in order to judge his loyalty, dependability, etc; examine (sb) to judge his qualifications for a post, etc. **5** [VP6A] show (an object, a scene) on a ~(**4**); make a cinema film of. [VP2C] **~ well/badly,** (of a stage play, an actor, etc) be suitable/unsuitable for filming.

screw /skru/ *n* **1** metal peg with slotted head and a spiral groove cut round its length, driven into wood, metal, etc by twisting under pressure, for fastening and holding things together. ***a ~ loose,*** (fig) sth wrong or out of order: *There's a ~ loose somewhere. He has a ~ loose,* is a little stupid. **ˈ~-driver** *n* tool for turning ~s. ⇨ the illus at tool. **ˈ~-ˈtopped** *adj* (of jars, etc) having a top or lid with a spiral groove, put on or taken off by twisting. **ˈ~-ball** *adj; n* (US, sl) crazy (person). **2** sth that is turned like a screw and is used for exerting pressure, tightening, etc. ***put the ~(s) on sb; give (sb) another turn of the ~,*** use one's power, a threat of force, etc to force him to do sth. **ˈthumb~** *n* ⇨ thumb. **3** action of turning; turn: *This isn't tight enough yet; give it another ~.* **4** **ˈ~(-propeller)** propeller of a ship: *a twin-~ steamer.* **(ˈair)~,** propeller of an aircraft. **5** [C,U] (in games, e g billiards) spin given to a ball to make it curve or change direction. **6** small, twisted piece of paper and its contents: *a ~ of tea/tobacco.* **7** (colloq) miser. **8** (GB, sl) amount of salary or wages: *He's paid a good ~.* **9** (GB, sl) (= *turnkey*) prison warder. **10** ⚠ act of or partner in sexual intercourse. □ *vt,vi* **1** [VP6A,15A,B] fasten or tighten with a ~ or ~s: *~ a lock on a door; ~ down the lid of a coffin; ~ up a door,* so that it cannot be opened. ***have one's head ~ed on (the right way),*** be sensible, have good judgement. **2** [VP6A,15A,B] twist round; make tight, tense or more efficient: *~ a lid on/off a jar; ~ one's head round,* in order to look over one's shoulder; *~ up one's face/features/eyes,* contract the muscles, e g when going out into bright sunshine from a dark room. ***~ up one's courage,*** overcome one's fears. **3** [VP6A,15A,B] exert pressure on; force (out of): *~ water out of a sponge/more taxes out of the people.* **4** (sl) ***be ~ed,*** be drunk. **5** [VP6A] ⚠ have sexual intercourse with. **screwy** *adj* (GB colloq) eccentric; crazy; (US colloq) ludicrously odd; absurd.

thread

types of head

screws

scribble /ˈskrɪbl/ *vt,vi* [VP6A,2A] write hastily or carelessly; make meaningless marks on paper, etc. **ˈscribbling-block** *n* pad of cheap paper making notes. □ *n* [U] hasty, careless handwriting; [C] sth ~d. **scrib·bler** /ˈskrɪblə(r)/ *n* person who ~s; (colloq) inferior author.

scribe /skraɪb/ *n* **1** professional letter-writer; person who, before the invention of printing, made copies of writings, e g in monasteries. **2** (among the Jews in olden times) maker and keeper of records; teacher of Jewish law (at the time of Jesus Christ).

scrim·mage /ˈskrɪmɪdʒ/ *n* **1** [C] confused struggle or fight. **2** (US football) the play that takes place when two teams are lined up for the players to begin or resume play. **3** = scrum(mage). □ *vi,vt* engage in a ~(**1**); put (the ball) in a ~.

scrimp /skrɪmp/ *vt,vi* = skimp (which is more usu).

scrim·shank /ˈskrɪmʃæŋk/ *vi* (GB army sl) try to avoid duties. **~er** *n*

scrip /skrɪp/ *n* **1** [C] document, the possession of which entitles the holder to a formal certificate for ownership of stock in a business company, etc on completion of formalities; [U] such documents collectively. **2** [U] paper currency for temporary or emergency use (e g issued by armed forces in a country they have occupied in war).

script /skrɪpt/ *n* **1** [U] (opp of *print*) handwriting; printed cursive characters in imitation of handwriting. **2** [C] (short for) manuscript or typescript (esp of an actor's part in a play, a talk, discussion, drama, etc to be broadcast, etc). **ˈ~-writer** *n* person who writes ~s for broadcast programmes. **~ed** *adj* read from a ~: *Un~ed discussions are usually livelier than ~ed discussions,* e g in a broadcast programme.

scrip·ture /ˈskrɪptʃə(r)/ *n* **1 The (Holy) S~s,** the Bible; (attrib) taken from, relating to, the Bible: *a ˈ~ lesson.* **2** sacred book of a religion other than Christianity. **scrip·tural** /ˈskrɪptʃərl/ *adj* based on the Bible.

scriv·ener /ˈskrɪvn̩ə(r)/ *n* (old use) clerk; person who wrote letters for illiterate people and copied and drafted documents.

scrof·ula /ˈskrofjʊlə/ *n* [U] tuberculous disease in which there are swellings of the lymphatic glands. **scrofu·lous** /ˈskrofjʊləs/ *adj*

a scroll

scroll /skrəʊl/ *n* **1** roll of paper or parchment for writing on; ancient book written on a ~. **2** ornamental design cut in stone; flourish in writing, suggesting by its curves a ~ of parchment.

Scrooge /ˈskrudʒ/ *n* mean-spirited miser.

scro·tum /ˈskrəʊtəm/ *n* pouch of skin enclosing the testicles in mammals.

scrounge /skraʊndʒ/ *vi,vt* [VP2A,6A] (colloq) get what one wants by taking it without permission or by trickery. **scrounger** *n* person who ~s.

scrub[1] /skrʌb/ *n* **1** [U] (land covered with) trees and bushes of poor quality; stunted forest growth: (attrib) *ˈ~-pine, ˈ~-oak,* dwarf or stunted kinds. **2** [C] anything below the usual size: *You wretched little ~ of a man!* **~by** *adj* (-ier, -iest) **1** small, stunted; mean. **2** rough and bristly: *a ~by chin.*

scrub[2] /skrʌb/ *vt,vi* (-bb-) [VP6A,15B,22,2A,C] clean by rubbing hard, esp with a stiff brush, soap and water: *~ the floor; ~ out a pan; ~ the walls clean;* cancel; ignore: *~ (out) an order.* **ˈ~-bing-brush** *n* stiff brush for ~bing floors, etc. □ *n* act of ~bing: *The floor needs a good ~.*

scruff /skrʌf/ *n* (only in) ***the ~ of the neck,*** the back of the neck, the nape, when used for grasping or lifting: *seize/take an animal by the ~ of the neck.*

scruffy /ˈskrʌfɪ/ *adj* (-ier, -iest) (colloq) dirty, untended and untidy looking.

scrum /skrʌm/ *n* (abbr of) scrummage. **scrum half,** the half-back who puts the ball into the ~.

scrum·mage /ˈskrʌmɪdʒ/ *n* the play in Rugby football when the forwards of both sides pack together with their heads down while the ball is thrown into the middle of them and they then try to kick the ball back to their own team; all those forwards when such play occurs.

scrump·tious /ˈskrʌmpʃəs/ *adj* (colloq, chiefly of food) delightful: *~ food.*

scrunch /skrʌnʃ/ *n, vt* = crunch(2).

scruple /ˈskrupl/ *n* **1** [C] weight-unit of 20 grains. **2** [C,U] (hesitation caused by) uneasiness of conscience: *Have you no ~s about borrowing things without permission? I can't agree to do that until you remove my ~s,* prove that there is nothing wrong, immoral, etc about it. *He will tell lies without ~.* □ *vi* [VP4C] ***~ to do sth,*** hesitate owing to ~s: (usu neg) *He doesn't ~ to tell a lie if he thinks it useful.*

scru·pu·lous /ˈskrupjʊləs/ *adj* careful to do nothing morally wrong; paying great attention to small points (esp of conscience): *He is not over-~ in his business dealings. A solicitor must act with ~ honesty.* **~·ly** *adv* in a ~ manner: *~ly exact/careful.*

scru·ti·neer /ˈskrutɪˈnɪə(r) *US:* -tn̩ˈɪər/ *n* official who examines ballot papers to see that they are not filled in irregularly.

scru·ti·nize /ˈskrutɪnɑɪz *US:* -tn̩ɑɪz/ *vt* [VP6A] make a detailed examination of.

scru·tiny /ˈskrutɪnɪ *US:* -tn̩ɪ/ *n* (*pl* -nies) **1** [U] thorough and detailed examination; [C] instance of this. **2** [C] official examination of votes, esp a recount of votes at an election when the result of the first count is very close: *demand a ~.*

scud /skʌd/ *vi* (-dd-) [VP2A,C] go straight and fast, with smooth motion: *The clouds ~ded across the sky. The yacht was ~ding along before the wind.* □ *n* [C] act of ~ding; [U] vapoury clouds driven by the wind.

scuff /skʌf/ *vi,vt* **1** [VP2A,C] walk without properly lifting the feet from the ground; shuffle. **2** [VP6A,15A,B] wear out or injure (shoes, etc) by walking in this way: *~ one's shoes.*

scuffle /ˈskʌfl/ *vi* [VP2A,C], *n* (take part in a) rough, confused fight or struggle: *There was a ~ between the police and some young hooligans.*

scull /skʌl/ *n* **1** one of a pair of oars used together by a single rower, one in each hand. **2** oar worked at the stern of a boat with twisting strokes. □ *vt,vi* [VP6A,2A] propel (a boat) with a ~; row (a boat) with ~s; use a ~ or ~s. **~er** *n* person who ~s.

scul·lery /ˈskʌlərɪ/ *n* (*pl* -ries) room usu in a large house next to the kitchen, where dishes, pots, etc are washed up. **ˈ~-maid** *n* servant who helps the cook by washing up dishes, etc.

scul·lion /ˈskʌlɪən/ *n* (archaic) boy or man who did rough work in the kitchen of a mansion or castle in olden times.

sculpt /skʌlpt/ *vt,vi* = sculpture.

sculp·tor /ˈskʌlptə(r)/ *n* artist who sculptures. **sculp·tress** /ˈskʌlptrəs/ *n* woman ~.

sculp·ture /ˈskʌlptʃə(r)/ *n* **1** [U] art of making representations in stone, wood, metal, etc by carving or modelling. **2** [C,U] (piece of) such work. □ *vt,vi* **1** [VP6A] represent in ~; decorate with ~: *~ a statue out of stone; ~d columns.* **2** [VP2A] be a sculptor; do ~. **sculp·tural** /ˈskʌlptʃərl/ *adj* of, like, connected with, ~: *the sculptural arts.*

scum /skʌm/ *n* [U] **1** froth which forms on the surface of some boiling liquids; dirt on the surface of a pond or other area of still water. **2** ***the ~ of,*** (fig) the worst, or seemingly worthless, part (of the population, etc). **~my** *adj* of, like, having or containing, ~.

scup·per /ˈskʌpə(r)/ *n* opening in a ship's side to allow water to run off the deck. *vt* sink a ship deliberately; (colloq, usu passive) ruin; disable: *We're ~ed!*

scurf /skɜf/ *n* [U] small bits of dead skin, esp on the scalp, loosened as new skin grows; dandruff: *monkeys searching each other's fur for ~.* **scurfy** *adj* having, covered with, ~.

scur·ri·lous /ˈskʌrɪləs *US:* ˈskɜl̩əs/ *adj* using, full of, violent and taunting words of abuse: *~ attacks upon the Prime Minister.* **scur·ril·ity** /skəˈrɪlətɪ/ *n* [U] ~ language; (*pl;* -ties) ~ remarks: *indulge in scurrilities.*

scurry /ˈskʌrɪ *US:* ˈskɜɪ/ *vi* (*pt,pp* -ried) [VP2A,C,3A] ***~ about/for/through,*** run with short, quick steps; hurry: *The rain sent everyone ~ing for shelter. Don't ~ through your work.* □ *n* **1** [U] act or sound of ~ing; anxious or excited bustle and movement: *the ~ and scramble of town life. There was a ~ towards the refreshments.* **2** [C] ***~ (of),*** windy shower (of snow); cloud (of dust).

scurvy /ˈskɜvɪ/ *n* [U] diseased state of the blood caused (esp among sailors in former times) by eating too much salt meat and not enough fresh vegetables and fruit. □ *adj* dishonourable, contemptuous: *That was a ~ trick to play on an old lady. You ~ knave!* **scurv·ily** /-əlɪ/ *adv*

scut /skʌt/ *n* [C] short, erect tail, esp of a rabbit, hare or deer.

scutch·eon /ˈskʌtʃən/ *n* = escutcheon.

scuttle[1] /ˈskʌtl/ *n* (**ˈcoal-)~,** container for a supply of coal at the fireside.

scuttle[2] /ˈskʌtl/ *vi* [VP2A,C] ***~ off/away,*** scurry. □ *n* hurried flight or departure; cowardly avoidance of, or running away from, difficulties and dangers: *The Opposition leader accused the Government of a policy of ~.*

scuttle[3] /ˈskʌtl/ *n* small opening with a lid, in a ship's side or on deck or in a roof or wall. □ *vt* [VP6A] cut holes in, open valves in, a ship's sides or bottom to sink it: *The captain ~d his ship to avoid its being captured by the enemy.*

Scylla /ˈsɪlə/ *n* (myth) (six-headed monster living on) a dangerous rock opposite a whirlpool (called *Charybdis*) (in the Strait of Messina, S Italy). ***between ~ and Charybdis,*** between two great dangers.

scythe /sɑɪð/ *n* tool with a slightly curved blade on a long wooden pole with two short handles, for cutting long grass, grain, etc. □ *vt* [VP6A,15A] cut with a ~.

scything

sea /si/ *n* **1** (*sing* with *def art*) expanse of salt water that covers most of the earth's surface and encloses its continents, etc; any part of this (in contrast to areas of fresh water and dry land): *Ships sail on the sea. Fish swim in the sea. The sea covers nearly three-fourths of the world's sur-*

face. Let's go for a swim in the sea. **follow the sea,** be a sailor. **on the sea,** on the coast: *Brighton is on the sea.* **2** (in the *pl*) same sense as **1** above: (esp) ***beyond/over the sea(s),*** abroad; to or in countries separated by the sea (note that *overseas* is more usu). ***the high seas,*** parts which are not near the land, esp outside the territorial limits over which the nearest country has or claims jurisdiction. ***the freedom of the seas,*** the right to carry on sea-trade without interference. **3** (in proper names) particular area of sea which is smaller than an ocean: *the Caspian Sea; the Sea of Galilee; the Inland Sea of Japan.* **the Seven Seas,** (liter or poet name for seven oceans) the Arctic, the Antarctic, the N and S Pacific, the N and S Atlantic and the Indian Oceans: *He has sailed the Seven Seas.* **4** (in various phrases without articles) ***at sea,*** away from, out of sight of, the land: *He was buried at sea.* ***all/completely at sea.*** (fig) puzzled; at a loss: *He was all at sea when he began his new job.* ***by sea,*** in a ship: *travel by sea and land.* ***go to sea,*** become a sailor. ***put to sea,*** leave port or land. **5** (with *indef art,* or in *pl*) local state of the sea; swell of the ocean; big wave or billow: *There was a heavy sea,* large waves. *The ship was struck by a heavy sea,* a large wave. *The seas were mountains high. The boat shipped a green sea,* was flooded by a large wave of green sea-water. ***half seas over,*** having drunk too much; intoxicated. **6** large quantity or expanse (*of*): *a sea of up-turned faces,* e g crowds of people looking upwards; *a sea of flame.* **7** (attrib and in compounds): **ˈsea ˋair** *n* air at the seaside, considered to be good for health: *enjoy the sea air.* **ˋsea-anemone** *n* ⇨ the illus at anemone. **ˋsea-animal** *n* animal inhabiting the sea, e g fish, mammals, molluscs, etc. **ˋsea-bathing** *n* bathing in the sea. **ˋsea·bed** *n* floor of the sea. **ˋsea-bird** *n* any of several species of bird which live close to the sea, i e on cliffs, islands, etc. ⇨ the illus at water. **ˋsea-board** *n* coast region; line of coast. **ˋsea-boat** *n* ship with the sea-going qualities specified: *a good/bad sea-boat,* one that sails well/badly. **ˋsea-borne** *adj* (of trade) carried in ships: *sea-borne commerce/goods.* **ˋsea-breeze** *n* breeze blowing landward from the sea, esp during the day in alternation with a land-breeze at night. Cf *a ˈsea ˋbreeze,* two stresses, any kind of breeze at sea. **ˋsea-coal** *n* (formerly used of) coal brought from Newcastle to London by sea (opp of *charcoal*). **ˋsea-cow** *n* name used of several kinds of warm-blooded creatures living in the sea and feeding their young with milk. **ˋsea-dog** *n* **(a)** old sailor, esp the captains of English ships during the reign of Elizabeth I. **(b)** dogfish. **(c)** seal. **ˋsea·faring** /-feərɪŋ/ *adj* of work or voyages on the sea: *a ˋseafaring man,* a sailor. **ˋsea fog** *n* fog along the coast, caused by difference between land and sea temperatures.

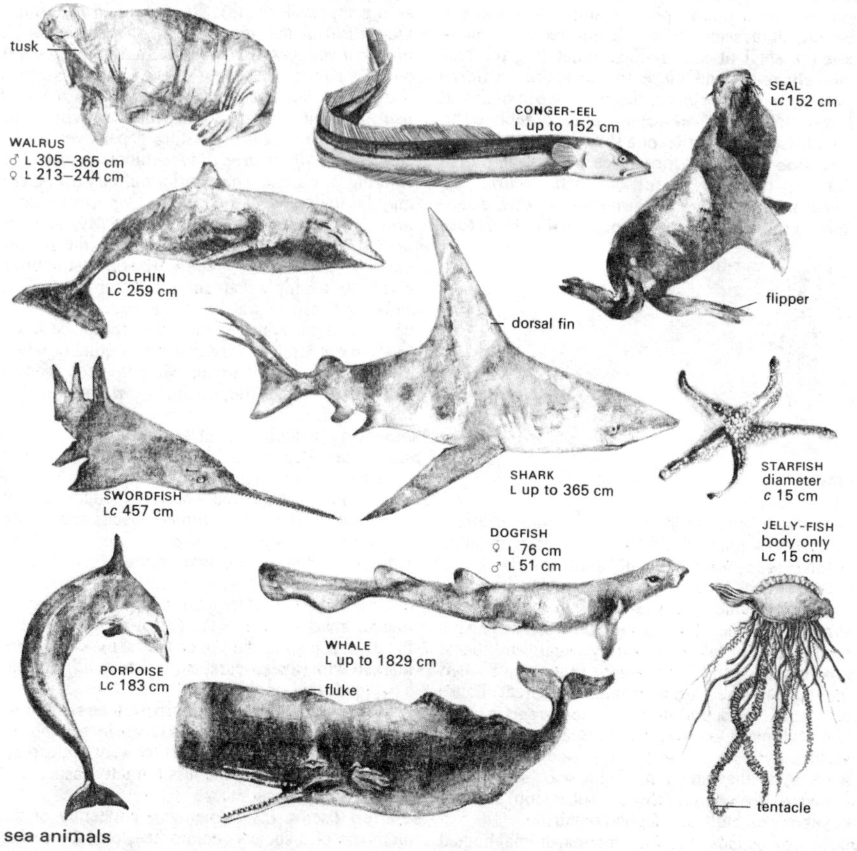

sea animals

ˋsea·food *n* edible fish or shellfish from the sea: *a ˋseafood restaurant; a seafood cocktail.* **ˋsea-front** *n* part of a town facing the sea: *The best hotels are on the sea-front.* **ˋsea-girt** *adj* (poet) surrounded by the sea. **ˋsea-god** *n* god living in or having power over the sea, e g *Neptune.* **ˋsea-going** *adj* (of ships) built for crossing the sea, not for coastal voyages only; (of a person) seafaring. **ˈsea-ˋgreen** *adj, n* bluish-green as of the sea. **ˋsea·gull** *n* common sea-bird with long wings. **ˋsea-horse** *n* small fish. **ˈsea-island ˋcotton** *n* fine quality of long-stapled cotton. **ˋsea·kale** *n* plant whose young white shoots are used as a vegetable. **ˋsea-legs** *n pl* ability to walk on the deck of a rolling ship: *get/find one's sea-legs.* **ˋsea-level** *n* level of sea half-way between high and low tide as the basis for measuring height of land and depth of sea: *100 metres above/below sea level.* **ˋsea-lion** *n* large seal of the N Pacific Ocean. **ˋSea Lord** *n* one of four naval members of the Board of Admiralty (London). **ˋsea·man** /-mən/ *n* (*pl* -men) **(a)** (in the Navy) rating, not an officer. **(b)** person expert in nautical matters. Hence, **ˋsea·man·like** /-mənlaɪk/ *adj* **ˋsea·man·ship** /-mənʃɪp/ *n* skill in managing a boat or ship. **ˋsea mile** *n* nautical mile. **ˋsea·plane** *n* aircraft constructed so that it can come down on and rise from water. **ˋsea·port** *n* town with a harbour used by sea-going ships. **ˋsea-power** *n* ability to control and use the seas (by means of naval strength). **ˋsea-rover** *n* pirate; pirate's ship. **ˋsea·scape** *n* picture of a scene at sea. ⇨ landscape. **ˋsea-shell** *n* shell of any mollusc inhabiting the sea. **ˋsea·shore** *n* land close to the shore: *children playing on the seashore;* (legal) between high and low-water marks. **ˋsea·sick** *adj* sick, inclined to vomit, from the motion of a ship. **ˋsea·sick·ness** *n* **ˋsea·side** *n* (often attrib) place, town, etc by the sea, esp a holiday resort: *go to the seaside for one's summer holidays; own a house by the seaside; a seaside town.* **ˋsea-snake** *n* (kinds of) (usu venomous) snake living in the sea. **ˋsea-urchin** *n* small sea-animal with a shell covered with sharp points. **ˈsea-ˋwall** *n* wall built to check the encroachment of the sea on the land. **ˋsea-water** *n* water from the sea. **ˋsea·way** *n* **(a)** progress of a ship through the water. **(b)** inland waterway, e g a river, series of lakes, joined by canals and locks, used by sea-going ships: *the St Lawrence S~way* (connecting the Atlantic and the Great Lakes between Canada and the US). **ˋsea·weed** *n* [C,U] kinds of plant growing in the sea, esp on rocks washed by the sea. **ˋsea·ward** /-wəd/ *adj* towards the sea; in the direction of the sea. **ˋsea·wards** /-wədz/ *adv* **ˋsea·worthy** *adj* (of a ship) fit for a voyage; well built and in good repair.

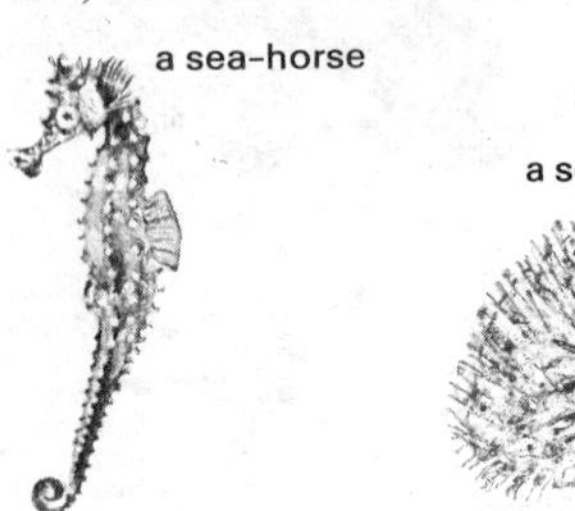

a sea-horse

a sea-urchin

seal[1] /sil/ *n* kinds of fish-eating sea-animal hunted for its oil and skin and the fur of some species. ⇨ the illus above. **ˋ~·skin** *n* skin of a fur-seal; garment made of this. □ *vi* [VP2A] hunt ~s: *go ~ing; a ~ing expedition.* **~er** *n* person or ship engaged in hunting ~s.

seals

seal[2] /sil/ *n* **1** piece of wax, lead, etc stamped with a design, attached to a document or show that it is genuine, or to a letter, packet, box, bottle, door, etc to guard against its being opened by unauthorized persons. ***given under my hand and ~,*** (legal) signed and sealed by me. ***under ~ of secrecy,*** (fig) what has been said must be kept secret because secrecy has been stipulated or is obligatory. **2** sth used instead of a ~(1), e g a paper disc stuck to, or an impression stamped on, a document. **3** piece of metal, etc on which is a design and which is used to stamp the ~ on wax, etc. **ˋ~-ring,** finger-ring with a ~ (often with the design cut on a gem). **4 *~ of,*** (fig) act, event, etc regarded as a confirmation or guarantee (of sth) or giving approval (of sth): *By visiting Drake's ship, Queen Elizabeth* I *put/set the ~ of approval on his piratical voyages.* □ *vt* [VP6A,15A,B] **1** put a ~(1) on: *~ a letter;* fasten or close tightly: *~ up a drawer so that it cannot be opened; ~ a jar of fruit,* make it air-tight so that the fruit will keep; *~ up a window,* e g by pasting paper over all the crevices; *~ off an area of land,* block all means of entering it, e g one where, after military use, there may be unexploded shells, etc. *Our special canning process ~s the flavour in.* ***His/My, etc lips are ~ed,*** He/I, etc must not speak; the matter must be kept secret. ***~ed orders,*** instructions given to a ship's captain (or other person in authority), esp in wartime, in a ~ed envelope to be opened only at a certain time or place. **ˋ~-ing-wax** *n* kind of wax that melts quickly when heated and quickly hardens when cooled, used to ~ letters, etc. **2** settle; decide: *~ a bargain; His fate is ~ed.*

seal·skin /ˋsilskɪn/ ⇨ seal[1].

Sealy·ham /ˋsilɪəm *US:* -lɪhæm/ *n* kind of terrier with a long body and short legs.

seam /sim/ *n* [C] **1** line where two edges, esp of cloth or leather, are turned back and sewn together: *searching for fleas in the ~s of his trousers.* **2** line where two edges, e g of boards forming a ship's deck, meet. **3** layer of coal, etc between layers of other materials, e g rock, clay. **4** line or mark like a ~(1) (e g a wrinkle on the face). □ *vt* (esp in the *pp,* of the face) ***~ed with,*** marked with (lines, scars, etc). **~·less** *adj* without a ~; made in a single piece.

seam·stress /ˋsimstrəs/, **semp·stress** /ˋsempstrəs/ *nn* woman who makes a living by sewing.

seamy /ˋsimɪ/ *adj* (-ier, -iest) (chiefly fig, esp in) ***the ˋ~ side (of life),*** the less attractive aspects of life; poverty, crime, etc.

sé·ance /ˋseɪɔ̃s *US:* ˋseɪæns/ *n* **1** meeting of the members of a society, committee, etc. **2** meeting for the study of spiritualistic phenomena, e g communicating with the spirits of the dead through a medium.

sear[1] /sɪə(r)/ *vt* [VP6A] **1** burn or scorch the surface of, esp with a heated iron; cauterize. '**~-ing-iron** *n* one used for cauterizing. **2** (fig) make (sb's heart, conscience, etc) hard and without feeling: *His soul had been ~ed by injustice.*

sear[2], **sere** /sɪə(r)/ *adj* (liter) dried up; withered (esp of flowers, leaves).

search /sɜtʃ/ *vt,vi* **1** [VP6A,14,15A,B,2A,3A] **~ *(sb/sth) (for sb/sth)*; ~ *sb/sth out*,** examine, look carefully at, through, or into (in order to find sth or sb): *~ a criminal to see what he has in his pockets. He ~ed and ~ed through all the drawers for the missing papers. I've ~ed my memory but can't remember that man's name. Do you spend much time ~ing through dictionaries for words that are not included?* **~ *out*,** look for: *~ out an old friend.* ***~ one's heart/conscience*,** examine carefully one's own beliefs and conduct. ***S~ me!*** (colloq) I have no idea, no knowledge (of what you are asking about)! **2** [VP6A] (liter) go deeply into; go into every part of: *The cold wind ~ed the streets.* □ *n* [C,U] act of ~ing: *go in ~ of a missing child; a ~ for a missing aircraft; make a ~ for contraband.* ***right of ~*,** right of the warships of a country at war to stop and examine a neutral ship (for contraband, etc). '**~-light** *n* powerful light with a beam that can be turned in any direction, as used for discovering enemy movements, etc in war. '**~-party** *n* number of persons looking for sb or sth that is lost. '**~-warrant** *n* official authority to enter and ~ a building (e g for stolen property). **3** (legal) investigation (e g by lawyers, from local authorities) into possible reasons (e g planned demolition) why one should not buy land or property. **~er** *n* person who ~es. **~-ing** *adj* (of a look) taking in all details; (of a test, etc) thorough. **~-ing-ly** *adv*

sea-son /'sizn/ *n* [C] **1** one of the divisions of the year according to the weather, e g spring, summer, etc; the *'dry ~, the 'rainy ~.* **2** period suitable or normal for sth, or closely associated with sth: *the 'football ~; the 'nesting ~,* when birds build nests and lay eggs; *the 'dead ~, the 'off ~,* (in hotels at holiday resorts, etc) the time when there are very few guests; *the 'holiday/'tourist ~; the 'London ~,* early summer, when there is great activity (e g Ascot races, Wimbledon tennis) in fashionable society; *Christmas, the ~ of goodwill.* ***the ~'s greetings*,** (as written on a Christmas card). ***in/out of ~*,** to be had/not to be had at ordinary prices: *Oysters/Strawberries are out of ~ now. Hotel charges are lower out of ~.* ***in ~ and out of ~*,** at all times. **close/the open ~,** ⇨ close[1](12), open[1](11). ***a word in ~*,** advice at a time when it is likely to be useful. **3** (old use) ***for a ~*,** for a short time: *You should stop work and rest for a ~.* **4** (colloq abbr for) '**~-ticket** *n* **(a)** one that gives the owner the right to travel between places over a specified route as often as he wishes during a stated period of time: *a three-month ~(-ticket).* Cf US *commutation ticket.* **(b)** ticket that gives the owner the right to attend a place of amusement, etc, e g a concert hall, as often as he wishes (for the concerts, etc specified on the ticket) during a certain period. □ *vt,vi* **1** [VP6A, 2A] make or become suitable for use; cause to be acclimatized, etc: *Has this wood been well ~ed, dried and hardened? The soldiers were not yet ~ed to the rigorous climate.* **2** [VP6A,14] flavour (food) (with salt, pepper, etc): *mutton ~ed with garlic; highly ~ed dishes;* (fig) *conversation ~ed with wit.* **3** [VP6A] (liter) soften; moderate: *'when mercy ~s justice',* ⇨ Mer of Ven, Act IV, Sc 1. **~-ing** *n* [C,U] sth used to ~ food: *There's not enough ~ing in the sausage. Salt and pepper are ~ings.*

sea-son-able /'siznəbl/ *adj* **1** (of the weather) of the kind to be expected at the time of year. **2** (of help, advice, gifts, etc) coming at the right time; opportune.

sea-sonal /'siznl/ *adj* dependent upon a particular season; changing with the seasons: *~ occupations,* e g fruit-picking; *a ~ trade,* e g the selling of Christmas cards. **~ly** /-nl̩ɪ/ *adv*

seat /sit/ *n* **1** sth used or made for sitting on, e g a chair, box, bench, the floor: *There are no more chairs; you'll have to use that box for a ~. The back ~ of the car is wide enough for three persons.* ***keep one's ~*,** remain in one's ~: *There's no danger—keep your ~s, please,* i e don't panic. ***lose one's ~*,** have one's ~ taken by someone else. ⇨ 4 below. ***take a ~*,** sit: *Won't you take a ~?* ***take one's ~*,** sit down in one's place, e g in a hall or theatre. ***take a back seat*,** ⇨ back[4](2). '**~-belt** *n* safety strap fastened to the sides of a ~ in a passenger vehicle or aircraft. **2** that part of a chair, stool, bench, etc on which one sits (contrasted with the back, legs, etc): *a 'chair-~.* **3** part of the body (the buttocks) on which one sits; part of a garment covering this: *hold a boy up by the ~ of his pants.* **4** place in which one has a right to sit: *I have four ~s for 'Swan Lake' at Covent Garden. Mr Smith has a ~ in the House of Commons,* is a member. ***take one's ~*,** assume one's membership (in the House of Commons). ***win a ~/lose one's ~*,** win/be defeated in a Parliamentary election. **5** place where sth is, or where sth is carried on: *In the US, Washington is the ~ of government and New York City is the chief ~ of commerce. A university is a ~ of learning.* **6** **'country-'~,** large house in the country, usu the centre of a large estate: *He is rich enough to own a country ~ as well as a large house in London.* **7** manner of sitting, esp on a horse: *That rider has a good ~,* rides his horse well. □ *vt* [VP6A] **1** ***~ oneself, be ~ed*,** sit down: *Please be ~ed, gentlemen.* **2** have ~s for: *a hall that ~s 500. Are the ~ing arrangements* (= the arrangements for providing and placing ~s) *in the lecture theatre satisfactory?* '**~-ing-room** *n* [U] seats: *We have ~ing-room for thirty pupils in this classroom.* **3** (usu **re~**) repair the ~ or bottom of: *~ a chair/an old pair of trousers.*

seca-teurs /'sekətɜz/ *n pl* pair of clippers used by gardeners for pruning bushes, etc.

se-cede /sɪ'sid/ *vi* [VP2A,3A] **~ *(from)*,** (of a group) withdraw (from membership of a state, federation, organization, etc).

se-cession /sɪ'seʃn/ *n* [U] seceding; [C] instance of this (as in the US when eleven Southern States withdrew from the Federal Union in 1810—11). **~-ist** /-ʃn̩ɪst/ *n* supporter of ~.

se-clude /sɪ'klud/ *vt* [VP6A,14,15A] **~ *sb/oneself (from)*,** keep (a person, oneself) apart from the company of others: *~ oneself from society; keep women ~d in the harem.* **se-cluded** *adj* (esp of a place) quiet; solitary. **se-clu-sion**

/sɪˈkluʒn/ *n* [U] secluding or being ~d; ~d place; retirement: *live in seclusion; in the seclusion of one's own home.*

sec·ond[1] /ˈsekənd/ *adj* **1** next after the first (in place, time, order, importance, etc): *February is the ~ month of the year. Tom is the ~ son—he has an elder brother. Osaka is the ~ city/the ~ largest city in Japan.* **ˈ~-ˈbest** *adj* next after the best: *my ~-best suit.* □ *n, adv: I won't accept/put up with ~-best; come off ~-best,* get the worst of it. **ˈ~-ˈclass** *adj, n* **(a)** (of the) class next after the first: *a ~-class hotel; ~-class compartments,* in a railway carriage, etc; *~-class mail,* sent at a cheaper rate. **(b)** class below the first in examination results: *take a ~-class in law.* **(c)** (regarded or treated as) inferior: *~-class citizens.* □ *adv: go/travel ~-class.* **~ floor** *n* the one above the first (in GB two floors, in US one floor, above the ground: (attrib) *a ~-floor apartment).* **ˈ~-ˈhand** *adj* **(a)** previously owned by someone else: *~-hand furniture/books.* Cf *used* cars. **(b)** (of news, knowledge) obtained from others, not based on personal observation, etc: *get news ~-hand.* **~ lieutenant** *n* lowest commissioned rank in the Army. ⇨ App 9. **ˈ~-ˈrate** *adj* not of the best quality; inferior: *a man with ~-rate brains.* Hence, **ˈ~-ˈrater** *n* person with ~-rate intelligence or abilities: *a Cabinet made up mainly of ~-raters.* **ˈ~ ˈsight** *n* power to see future events, or events happening at a distance, as if present. Hence, **ˈ~-ˈsighted** *adj* having this power. **ˈ~ ˈteeth** *n* those which grow after a child's first teeth are out. **ˈ~ ˈwind,** ⇨ wind[1](3). ***~ to none,*** surpassed by no other. ***in the ~ place...,*** secondly.... **2** additional; extra: *You will need a ~ pair of shoes.* **3 ˈS~ Advent/Coming,** the return of Jesus Christ at the Last Judgement. **ˈ~ ˈballot,** a method used in some elections by which, if the winner of the first ballot receives less than half the votes cast, a new ballot is taken, in which only he and the next candidate are voted for. **ˈ~ ˈchamber** *n* upper house in a legislature: *The House of Lords is the ~ chamber of Parliament in Great Britain.* **ˈ~ ˈnature** *n* acquired tendency that has become instinctive: *Habit is ~ nature.* **ˈ~ thoughts,** opinion or resolution reached after reconsideration: *On ~ thoughts I will accept the offer. I'm having ~ thoughts* (= am not so sure) *about buying that house.* **4** of the same kind as one that has gone before; subordinate: *This fellow seems to think he's a ~ Napoleon!* **ˈ~ ˈchildhood** *n* old age when accompanied by weakening of the mental powers. **ˈ~ ˈcousin** *n* child of a first cousin of either of one's parents. ***play ~ fiddle (to sb),*** be of only secondary importance (to sb else). □ *adv* in the ~ place; ~ in order or in importance: *The English swimmer came (in) ~.* **~·ly** *adv* in the next place; furthermore.

sec·ond[2] /ˈsekənd/ *n* **1** person or thing that comes next to the first: *the ~ of May; George the S~,* King George II. ***get a ~,*** get a ~ class in an examination for honours. **2** another person or thing besides the person or thing previously mentioned: *You are the ~ to ask me that question.* **3** (*pl*) goods below the best in quality, esp coarse flour. **4** person chosen by the principal in a duel to support him; supporter of a boxer in a boxing-match.

sec·ond[3] /ˈsekənd/ *n* **1** sixtieth part of a minute or a degree (indicated by the mark ″): *The winner's time was 1 minute and 5 ~s. 1° 6′ 10″ means one degree, six minutes, and ten ~s.* **ˈ~-hand** *n* extra hand in some watches and clocks recording ~s. ⇨ also *second-hand* at **second**[1](1). **2** moment; short time: *I shall be ready in a ~ or two/in a few ~s.*

se·cond[4] /ˈsekənd/ *vt* [VP6A] **1** support (esp in a duel or a boxing-match). **2** (of a member of a debating body) rise or speak formally in support of a motion to show that the proposer is not the only person in favour of it: *Mr Smith proposed, and Mr Green ~ed, a vote of thanks to the lecturer.* **~er** *n* person who ~s a proposal at a meeting.

se·cond[5] /sɪˈkond *US:* ˈsekənd/ *vt* [VP6A,15A] (official GB use, esp mil) take (sb) from his ordinary duty and give him special duty: *Captain Smith was ~ed for service on the General's staff.* **~·ment** *n* ~ing or being ~ed.

sec·ond·ary /ˈsekəndrɪ *US:* -derɪ/ *adj* coming after, less important than, what is first or chief: *~ education/schools,* for children over eleven; *a ~ stress,* e g on the first syllable of 'sacrificial' /ˌsækrɪˈfɪʃl/. **sec·ond·ar·ily** /-drɪlɪ *US:* -derḷɪ/ *adv*

se·crecy /ˈsikrəsɪ/ *n* [U] keeping of secrets; ability to keep secrets; habit of keeping secrets; state of being kept secret: *rely on sb's ~; prepare sth in ~,* secretly; *do sth with great ~.* ***swear/bind sb to ~,*** make him promise to keep sth secret.

se·cret /ˈsikrət/ *adj* **1** (to be) kept from the knowledge or view of others; of which others have no knowledge: *a ~ marriage; keep sth ~ from one's family. He escaped through a ~ door.* **the ˈ~ ˈservice,** government department concerned with espionage and counter-espionage. **ˈ~ ˈagent** *n* member of this department (called a 'spy' if he works for a foreign government and 'secret agent' if he works for one's own government). **2** (of places) secluded; quiet. **3** (of persons) secretive (the more usu word). □ *n* **1** [C] sth ~. ***keep a ~,*** not tell anyone else: *Can you keep a ~?* ***in the ~,*** among those who are allowed to know it: *Is your brother in the ~?* ***let sb into a/the ~,*** share it. ***(be) an open ~,*** (of sth which is said to be ~) be (in fact) widely known. **2** [C] hidden cause; explanation, way of doing or getting sth, that is not known to some or most people: *What is the ~ of his success?* **3** [U] secrecy: *I was told about it in ~.* **4** [C] mystery; sth hard to learn about or understand: *the ~s of nature.* **~·ly** *adv*

sec·re·tariat(e) /ˌsekrəˈteərɪæt/ *n* staff of secretaries of a large organization: *get a position on the ~ of UNO in New York.*

sec·re·tary /ˈsekrətrɪ *US:* -rəterɪ/ *n* (*pl* **-ries**) **1** employee in an office, who deals with correspondence, keeps records, makes arrangements and appointments for a particular member of the staff (and often called *private ~*). **2** official who has charge of the correspondence, records, and other business affairs of a society, club or other organization: *honorary ~,* (abbr *hon sec*) unpaid ~ of a society, etc which is not conducted for profit. **3** (GB) **S~ of State,** minister in charge of a Government office: *the S~ of State for Foreign and Commonwealth Affairs/Home Affairs/Scotland/Defence, etc.* (US) *S~ of State,* chief and foreign minister; *S~ of the Treasury,* head of the Treasury Department. **Permanent S~,** senior official in the Civil Service. **ˈS~-ˈGeneral,** principal executive office (e g of UNO). **sec·re·tar·ial** /ˌsekrəˈteərɪəl/ *adj* of (the work of) secretaries: *ˌsecreˈtarial duties/training/colleges.*

se·crete /sɪˋkrit/ *vt* [VP6A] **1** produce by secretion(1). **2** put or keep in a secret place. **se·cre·tion** /sɪˋkriʃn/ *n* **1** [U] process by which certain substances in a plant or animal body are separated (from sap, blood, etc) for use, or as waste matter; [C] substance so produced, e g *saliva, bile.* **2** act of secreting: *the secretion of stolen goods.*

se·cret·ive /ˋsikrətɪv/ *adj* having the habit of keeping things secret; tending to hide one's thoughts, feelings, intentions, etc. **~·ly** *adv* **~·ness** *n*

sect /sekt/ *n* [C] group of people united by (esp religious) beliefs or opinions that differ from these more generally accepted.

sec·tarian /sekˋteərɪən/ *n, adj* (member, supporter) of a sect or sects: *~ jealousies,* e g between one sect and another; *~ politics,* in which the advantage of a sect is considered more important than the public welfare. **~·ism** /-ɪzm/ *n* [U] tendency to split up into sects, work in the interest of sects, etc.

sec·tion /ˋsekʃn/ *n* [C] **1** part cut off; slice; one of the parts into which sth may be divided: *the ~s of an orange.* **2** one of a number of parts which can be put together to make a structure: *fit together the ~s of a complete prefabricated building.* **3** subdivision of an organized body of persons (*the ˋPostal S~*), or of a piece of writing (often indicated by the *ˋ~-mark* §, as § 21), or of a town, county, country or community: *ˌresiˋdential/ˋshopping ~s* (*area* is more usu). **4** view or representation of sth seen as if cut straight through; thin slice of sth, e g tissue, suitable for examination under a microscope. **~al** /-ʃnl/ *adj* **1** made or supplied in ~s(2): *a ~al fishing-rod; ~al furniture.* **2** of a ~ of ~s of a community, etc: *~al interests,* the different and often conflicting interests of various ~s of a community; *~al jealousies.* **~·al·ism** /-ʃnlɪzm/ *n* [U] devotion to ~al interests instead of to those of the community as a whole.

sec·tor /ˋsektə(r)/ *n* [C] **1** part of a circle lying between two straight lines drawn from the centre to the circumference. ⇨ the illus at **circle**. **2** one of the areas into which a battle area is divided for the purpose of controlling operations. **3** branch (of industry, etc): *the public and private ~s of industry,* those parts publicly owned and those privately owned.

secu·lar /ˋsekjʊlə(r)/ *adj* **1** worldly or material, not religious or spiritual: *~ education; ~ art/music; the ~ power,* the State contrasted with the Church. **2** living outside monasteries: *the ~ clergy,* parish priests, etc. **~·ism** /-ɪzm/ *n* [U] the view that morality and education should not be based on religion. **~·ist** /-ɪst/ *n* believer in, supporter of, ~ism. **~·ize** /-ɑɪz/ *vt* [VP6A] make ~: *~ize church/property/courts; a ~ized Sunday,* e g when professional sporting events are permitted.

se·cure /sɪˋkjʊə(r)/ *adj* **1** free from anxiety: *feel ~ about/as to one's future.* **2** certain; guaranteed: *Our victory is ~. He has a ~ position as a university lecturer.* **3** unlikely to involve risk; firm: *Don't go higher up the cliff unless you find ~ footholds. Are you sure the doors and windows are ~? Is that ladder ~?* **4** *~ (from, against),* safe: *Are we ~ from interruption/attack, etc?* □ *vt* **1** make fast: *~ all the doors and windows before leaving the house.* **2** [VP6A,14] *~ sth (against/from),* make ~: *By strengthening the embankments they ~d the village against/from floods.* **3** [VP6A,12B,13B] succeed in getting (sth for which there is a great demand): *Can you ~ me two good seats for the concert? She has ~d a good cook.* **~·ly** *adv*

Se·curi·cor /sɪˋkjʊərɪkɔ(r)/ *n* (P) commercial organization for the secure transportation of money and other valuables (e g to and from banks, offices), for guarding property, etc: *ˋ~ van,* one used for this purpose.

se·cur·ity /sɪˋkjʊərətɪ/ *n* (*pl* **-ties**) **1** [C,U] (sth that provides) safety, freedom from danger or anxiety: *children who lack the ~ of parental care; cross the street in ~ at a pedestrian crossing. Is there any ~ from/against H-bombs?* **the Seˋcurity Council,** the permanent peace-keeping organ of the United Nations (five permanent and ten elected members). *ˋ~ police/forces,* those police officers, etc, whose duty it is to protect important persons, e g the Sovereign, a President, a Prime Minister, and to see that secret agents of foreign powers do not operate successfully. **ˋ~ risk,** a person who, because of his political affiliations, etc may be a danger to the State. **2** [C,U] sth valuable, e g a life-insurance policy, given as a pledge for the repayment of a loan or the fulfilment of a promise or undertaking: *lend money on ~; give sth as (a) ~.* **3** [C] document, certificate, etc showing ownership of property (esp bonds, stocks and shares): *government securities,* for money lent to a government.

se·dan /sɪˋdæn/ *n* **1** **ˈ~(-ˋchair),** enclosed seat for one person, carried on poles by two men, used in the 17th and 18th cc. **2** saloon car for four or more persons.

a sedan-chair

se·date /sɪˋdeɪt/ *adj* (of a person, his behaviour) calm; serious; grave. **~·ly** *adv* **~·ness** *n*

se·da·tion /sɪˋdeɪʃn/ *n* [U] treatment by sedatives; condition resulting from this: *The patient is under ~.*

seda·tive /ˋsedətɪv/ *n, adj* (medicine, drug) tending to calm the nerves and reduce stress: *After taking a ~ she was able to get to sleep. Tobacco has a ~ effect on some people.* ⇨ *tranquillizer* at **tranquil**.

sed·en·tary /ˋsedntrɪ *US:* -terɪ/ *adj* (of work) done sitting down (at a desk, etc); (of persons) spending much of their time seated: *lead a ~ life.*

sedge /sedʒ/ *n* [U] forms of grasslike plant growing in marshes or near wet places. **sedgy** *adj* covered or bordered with ~.

sedi·ment /ˋsedɪmənt/ *n* [U] matter (e g sand, dirt, gravel) that settles to the bottom of a liquid, e g mud left on fields after a river has been in flood over them. **sedi·men·tary** /ˈsedɪˋmentrɪ/ *adj* of the nature of ~; formed from ~: *~ary rocks,* e g slate, sandstone, limestone.

se·di·tion /sɪˋdɪʃn/ *n* [U] words or actions intended

to make people rebel against authority, disobey the government, etc: *incitement to ~.* **se·di·tious** /sɪˋdɪʃəs/ *adj* of the nature of ~: *seditious speeches/writings.*

se·duce /sɪˋdjus *US:* -ˋdus/ *vt* [VP6A,14] ~ ***sb (from/into sth),*** **1** persuade (sb) to do wrong; tempt (sb) into crime or sin: ~ *a man from his duty; ~d by the offer of money into betraying one's country.* **2** by charm, knowledge of the world, etc persuade sb less experienced to have sexual intercourse: *How many women did Don Juan ~? Potiphar's wife tried to ~ young Joseph.* **se·ducer** *n* person who ~s, esp **(2)**.

se·duc·tion /sɪˋdʌkʃn/ *n* **1** [U] seducing or being seduced; [C] instance of this. **2** sth very attractive and charming; sth likely to lead a person astray (but often with no implication of immorality): *surrender to the ~s of country life.* **se·duc·tive** /sɪˋdʌktɪv/ *adj* alluring; captivating: *seductive smiles; a seductive offer.* **se·duc·tive·ly** *adv*

sedu·lous /ˋsedjʊləs *US:* ˋsedʒʊləs/ *adj* persevering; done with perseverance: *He paid her ~ attention,* was persevering in his attempt to please her. **~·ly** *adv*

see[1] /si/ *vi,vt* (*pt* saw /sɔ/, *pp* seen /sin/) (For special uses with *adverbial particles* and *preps,* ⇨ 11 below.) **1** [VP2A,B,C,4A] (often with *can, could;* not usu in the progressive tenses) have or use the power of sight: *If you shut your eyes you can't see. It was getting dark and I couldn't see to read. On a clear day we can see (for) miles and miles from this hill-top. Move aside, please: I can't see through you! He'll never be able to see again.* ***seeing is believing,*** (prov) What we ourselves see is the most satisfactory evidence. ***be ˋseeing things,*** have hallucinations, i e see things that are not there or that do not exist, as a drunken man may: *You're seeing things—there's nobody there!* **2** [VP6A,8,9,10,18,19B,24A] (often with *can, could,* esp when an effort of perception is needed; not in the progressive tenses) be aware of by using the power of sight: *Can/Do you see that ship on the horizon? I looked out but saw nothing. I saw him put the key in the lock, turn it and open the door. The suspected man was seen to enter the building. I saw two men struggling for the knife. He was seen running away from the scene of the crime. Have you ever seen a man hanged? I saw that the box was empty. If you watch carefully you will see how to do it/how I do it/how it is done.* ***see the back of sb,*** get rid of him; see him for the last time: *That fellow's a nuisance; I shall be glad to see the back of him.* ***see the last of sb/sth,*** have done with; see for the last time: *I shall be glad to see the last of this job,* get to the end of it. ***see the sights,*** visit notable places, etc as a sightseer. ***see stars,*** have dancing lights before the eyes, e g as the result of a blow on the head. ***see visions,*** be a seer. ***see one's way (clear) to doing sth,*** see how to manage to do it, feel disposed to doing it: *He didn't see his way to lending me the money I needed.* **3** [VP6A,2A] (in the *imper*) look (at): *See, here he comes! See page 4.* **4** [VP6A,9,10,2A] (not in the progressive tenses) understand; learn by search or inquiry or reflection: *He didn't see the joke/the point of the story. We saw that the plan was unwise. Do you see what I mean? As far as I can see...,* to the best of my understanding. *I think I'll be able to help, but I'll have to see,* wait until I know more. *Go and see if/whether the postman has been yet.* ***see for oneself,*** find out in order to be convinced or satisfied: *If you don't believe me, go and see for yourself!* ***not see the use/good/fun/advantage of doing sth,*** feel doubt about whether it is useful, etc to do it. ***you see,*** (used parenthetically) **(a)** as you no doubt know or understand. **(b)** as I must now tell you or explain to you. ***seeing that,*** in view of the fact that; considering. **5** [VP9] learn from the newspaper or other printed sources: *I see that the Prime Minister has been in Wales.* **6** [VP6A] have knowledge or experience of; have (sth) presented to one's attention: *This coat of mine has seen hard wear,* i e has been worn for a long time. *He has seen a good deal in his long life. I never saw such rudeness.* ***will never see*** *40/50/****etc again,*** is already past that age. ***have seen the day/time when...,*** used to call attention to a past state of affairs: *He had seen the day when there were no cars on the roads,* was living before there were cars. ***have seen better days,*** have now declined, lost former prosperity, etc. ***see service in sth, have seen (good) service,*** ⇨ service(2). **7** [VP15A,6A] give an interview to; visit; receive a call from: *Can I see you on business? You ought to see a doctor about that cough. She's too ill to see anyone at present. The manager can see you for five minutes.* Note: The progressive tenses are used for this sense: *I'm seeing my solicitor this afternoon. I shall be seeing them tomorrow.* ***Be ˋseeing you/ˋSee you ˋsoon,*** (colloq) used as an equivalent for 'Goodbye!' when leaving a friend. **8** [VP18A,15A,24A] allow to; look on without protest or action: *You can't see people starve without trying to help them, can you? You wouldn't see me left here all alone?* **9** [VP9] attend to; take care; make provision: *See that the windows and doors are fastened.* ***see sb damned/in hell first,*** used to express an absolute refusal to do what one is asked, etc. **10** [VP16B,19A] call up a picture of; imagine: *He saw himself as the saviour of his country. I can't see myself allowing people to cheat me.* **11** (special uses with *adverbial particles* and *preps*):

see about sth, deal with: *He promised to see about the matter.* ***see sb about sth,*** consult sb, take advice (on sth): *I must see a builder about the tiles that fell off the roof last night.*

see sb across sth, guide, conduct, help sb across (a road, etc): *That man's blind—I'd better see him across the street.*

see sb back/home, accompany sb: *May I see you home? Tom's had too much to drink—we'd better see him back/home.*

see sb off, go to a railway station, an airport, the docks, etc with sb about to start on a journey: *I was seen off by many of my friends.* ***see sb off sth,*** go with him until he is at the door, outside, etc: *I don't want this fellow here; please see him off the premises,* get rid of him.

see sb out, accompany sb until he is out of a building: *My secretary will see you out.*

see over sth, visit and examine or inspect carefully: *see over a house that one wishes to buy or rent.*

see to sth, attend to sth: *This machine is out of order; get a mechanic to see to it. Will you see to the arrangements for the next meeting of the committee?*

see through sb/sth, not be deceived by: *I see*

through your little game, am aware of the trick you are trying to play on me. *We all saw through him,* knew what kind of man he really was. ***see sb through (sth),*** give him support, encouragement, until the end: *You'll have a difficult time, but I'll see you safely through.* **ˈsee sth ˋthrough,** not give up an undertaking until the end is reached: *He said that whatever happened he would see the struggle through.*

see[2] /si/ *n* district under a bishop; bishop's position, office, jurisdiction: *the See of Canterbury; the Holy See, the See of Rome,* the Papacy.

seed /sid/ *n* (*pl* ~s or ~, unchanged) **1** flowering plant's element of life, from which another plant can grow: *a packet of* ~*(s).* ⇨ the illus at **flower, fruit.** *Sow the* ~ *in May or June. Its* ~*s are/Its* ~ *is very small.* ***run/go to*** ~**,** stop flowering as ~ is produced; (fig) become careless of one's appearance and clothes. **ˋ~-bed** *n* bed of fine soil in which to sow ~. **ˋ~-cake** *n* cake containing ~s, e g carraway, as a flavouring. **ˋ~-corn** *n* grain kept for ~. **ˋ~s·man** /-mən/ *n* (*pl* -men) dealer in ~s. **ˋ~-time** *n* sowing season. **2** (old use) offspring: *the* ~ *of Abraham,* the Hebrews. **3** cause, origin (*of* a tendency, development, etc): *sow the* ~*s of virtue in young children.* **4** semen. **5 ˋ~-potato** *n* potato kept and allowed to sprout before being planted. **ˋ~-pearls** *n pl* small pearls. **6** (sport) ~ed player: *England's No. 1* ~ (in a championship). ⇨ 4 below. □ *vi, vt* **1** [VP2A] (of a plant) produce ~ when full grown; let ~ fall. **2** [VP6A] sow with ~: ~ *a field with wheat; a newly-*~*ed lawn.* **3** [VP6A] remove ~ from: ~ *raisins.* **4** [VP6A] (esp in tennis) separate those players well tested and known to be stronger from the weaker players (in order to have good matches later in a tournament): ~*ed players.* **~·less** *adj* having no ~: ~*less raisins.* **~·ling** /ˋsidlɪŋ/ *n* young plant newly grown from a ~.

seedy /ˋsidɪ/ *adj* (-ier, -iest) **1** full of seed: *as* ~ *as a dried fig.* **2** shabby-looking; in worn clothes: *a* ~ *boarding-house; a* ~*-looking person.* **3** (colloq) unwell: *feel* ~. **seed·ily** /-əlɪ/ *adv* **seedi·ness** *n*

seek /sik/ *vt* (*pt,pp* **sought** /sɔt/) **1** [VP2A,15A] look for; try to find: ~ *shelter from the rain;* ~ *safety in flight. The reason is not far to* ~, is found near at hand, quickly found. *Are you* ~*ing a quarrel,* trying to start one? *He is going to Canada to* ~ *his fortune,* to try to become rich. **2** [VP6A] ask for: *I will* ~ *my doctor's advice.* **3** [VP7A] (dated) try; attempt: *They sought to kill him.* **4** [VP3A] ~ ***for,*** try to win: *unsought-for fame,* fame which came without being looked for. ***(much) sought after,*** (much) in demand.

seem /sim/ *vi* [VP4D,E] have or give the impression or appearance of being or doing; appear to be: *Things far off* ~ *(to be) small. What* ~*s easy to some people* ~*s difficult to others. There* ~ *to be no objections to the proposal. He* ~*s to think so. I shall act as* ~*s best* (= *as it* ~*s best to me*). *The book* ~*s (to be) quite interesting. The child* ~*s to be asleep. It* ~*s that no one knew what had happened. I can't* ~ (= I ~ unable) *to get out of that bad habit. It would* ~ *that...,* (a cautious way of saying 'It ~s that...'). *'I've been out in the rain'—'So it* ~*s',* i e from your wet clothes it appears that you've been out in the rain. **~·ing** *adj* apparent but perhaps not real or genuine: *In spite of his* ~*ing friendship he gave me no help.* **~·ing·ly** *adv* in appearance; apparently.

seem·ly /ˋsimlɪ/ *adj* (-ier, -iest) **1** (of behaviour) proper or correct (for the occasion or circumstances): *It isn't* ~ *to praise oneself.* **2** decent; decorous: *Strip-tease is not a* ~ *occupation for any girl.* **seem·li·ness** *n*

seen /sin/ *pp* of **see**[1]

seep /sip/ *vi* [VP2C] (of liquids) ooze out or through; trickle: *water* ~*ing through the roof of the tunnel.* **~·age** /ˋsipɪdʒ/ *n* [U] slow leaking through.

seer /sɪə(r)/ *n* person claiming to see into the future; prophet.

seer·sucker /ˋsɪəsʌkə(r)/ *n* [U] thin fabric with a striped pattern and a crinkled surface: *a* ~ *tablecloth.*

see·saw /ˋsi-sɔ/ *n* [C,U] (game played on a) long plank with a person astride each end which can rise and fall alternately; up-and-down or to-and-fro motion: *play at* ~. □ *vi* play at ~; move up and down or to and fro; (fig) vacillate: ~ *between two opinions.*

seethe /sið/ *vi,vt* **1** [VP2A,3A] ~ ***(with),*** boil, bubble over; be crowded, agitated (esp fig): ~ *with anger; a country seething with discontent; streets seething with people.* **2** [VP6A,2A] (old use) cook by boiling.

seg·ment /ˋsegmənt/ *n* [C] **1** part cut off or marked off by a line: *a* ~ *of a circle.* **2** division or section: *a* ~ *of an organe.* ⇨ the illus at **fruit.** □ *vt,vi* /segˋment/ divide, become divided, into ~s. **seg·men·ta·tion** /ˈsegmənˋteɪʃn/ *n* division into ~s.

seg·re·gate /ˋsegrɪgeɪt/ *vt* [VP6A] put apart from the rest; isolate: ~ *the sexes;* ~ *people with infectious diseases.* **seg·re·ga·tion** /ˈsegrɪˋgeɪʃn/ *n* segregating or being ~d: *a policy of racial segregation.* ⇨ *integration* at **integrate.**

seign·ior /ˋseɪnjə(r) *US:* ˋsinjər/ *n* feudal lord; landowner in feudal times.

seine /seɪn/ *n* [C] large fishing-net which hangs like a curtain, with floats along the top edge and sinkers (weights) along the bottom edge, used to encircle fish, and usu hauled ashore. □ *vt,vi* fish, catch (fish), with a ~.

seis·mic /ˋsɑɪzmɪk/ *adj* of earthquakes. **seis·mo·graph** /ˋsɑɪzməgrɑf *US:* -græf/ *n* instrument which records the strength, duration and distance away of earthquakes. **seis·mol·ogy** /sɑɪzˋmolədʒɪ/ *n* [U] science of earthquakes. **seis·mol·ogist** /sɑɪzˋmolədʒɪst/ *n*

seize /siz/ *vt,vi* **1** [VP6A,15A] take possession of (property, etc) by law: ~ *sb's goods for payment of debt.* **2** [VP6A,15A] take hold of, suddenly and violently: ~ *a thief by the collar.* **3** [VP6A,3A] ~ ***(up)on,*** see clearly and use: ~ *(upon) an idea/a chance/an opportunity.* **4** [VP2A,C] ~ ***(up),*** (of moving parts of machinery) become stuck or jammed, e g because of too much heat or friction.

seiz·ure /ˋsiʒə(r)/ *n* **1** [U] act of seizing or taking possession of by force or the authority of the law; [C] instance of this: *seizure of contraband by Customs officers.* **2** [C] sudden attack of apoplexy; heart attack.

sel·dom /ˋseldəm/ *adv* (usu placed with the *v*) not often; rarely: *I have* ~ *seen such large apples. She* ~ *goes out. She goes out very* ~. *His wife* ~, *if ever, has a holiday. He* ~ *or never gives his wife a present.*

se·lect /sɪˋlekt/ *vt* [VP6A,15A,16] choose (as being

the most suitable, etc): ~ *a book/a Christmas present for a child. Who has been ~ed to lead the delegation?* □ *adj* **1** carefully chosen: ~ *passages from Milton.* **2** (of a school, society, etc) of or for carefully chosen persons, not for all: *a ~ club; shown to a ~ audience; a ~ school for children of the upper classes.* ~ **committee,** (in the House of Commons) small committee appointed for a special investigation. **se·lec·tor** /-tə(r)/ *n* one who, that which, ~s, e g a member of a committee ~ing a national sports team, etc.

se·lec·tion /sɪˈlekʃn/ *n* **1** [U] choosing: ˈ~ **committee,** one appointed to select, e g new teachers for a school. **natural ~,** (Darwin's theory of) the process in nature by which certain plants and animals flourish and multiply while others are less suited to their surroundings and die out. **2** [C] collection or group of selected things or examples; number of things from which to select: *~s from 18th-century English poetry. That shop has a good ~ of hats.*

se·lec·tive /sɪˈlektɪv/ *adj* having the power to select; characterized by selection: ~ *service,* (US) selection, for compulsory military service, of men with certain requirements, abilities, etc. **~·ly** *adv* **sel·ec·tiv·ity** /sɪˌlekˈtɪvətɪ/ *n* [U] (esp) power (of a radio) to receive broadcasts from one station without interference from other stations.

se·le·nium /sɪˈlɪnɪəm/ *n* non-metallic element (symbol **Se**) whose power to conduct electric current increases with the intensity of the light reaching it. ~ **cell,** one containing a strip of ~, used in photo-electric devices, e g the exposure meter of a camera.

self /self/ *n* (*pl* **selves** /selvz/) **1** [U] person's nature, special qualities; one's own personality: *one's better/worse ~; one's former ~,* one's nobler nature/base nature; oneself as one formerly was. **2** one's own interests or pleasure: *analysis of the ~; the conscious ~. She has no thought of ~,* thinks only of the interests, welfare, etc of others. **3** (comm, dated style): *your good ~/selves,* you (*sing* and *pl*); *pay to ~,* (on a cheque) pay to the person whose signature appears on it. **4** (vulg or joc) myself, yourself, himself, etc: *I want a room for ~ and wife. Let us drink a toast to our noble selves.*

self- /self/ *pref* short for *itself, myself, himself, oneself,* etc: ˈ~-ˈ*taught,* taught by oneself; ˈ~-ˈ*governing colonies,* colonies that govern themselves. ˈ**~-aˈbasement** *n* [U] humiliation of oneself. ˈ**~-abˈsorbed** *adj* having one's attention taken up by one's own interests, thoughts, etc; unaware of other person. ˈ**~-aˈbuse** *n* masturbation. ˈ**~-ˈacting** *adj* automatic. ˈ**~-adˈdressed** *adj* addressed to oneself: *I enclose a stamped ~-addressed envelope.* ˈ**~-ˈactivating** *adj* (e g of an explosive device) made so as to activate itself without external control. ˈ**~-apˈpointed** *adj* chosen or declared by oneself; unsanctioned (and perhaps unqualified): *a ~-appointed arbiter/expert.* ˈ**~-asˈsertion** *n* [U] the putting forward of one's own claims in a determined manner; the putting forward of oneself in an effort to be noticed by everyone. ˈ**~-asˈsertive** *adj* ˈ**~-asˈsurance** *n* confidence in oneself. ˈ**~-asˈsured** *adj* ˈ**~-ˈcentred** *adj* interested chiefly in oneself and one's own affairs. ˈ**~-colˈlected** *adj* (of persons) having or showing presence of mind and composure; calm. ˈ**~-ˈcoloured** *adj* of the same colour all over. ˈ**~-comˈmand** *n* [U] power of controlling one's feelings. ˈ**~-comˈplacency** *n* [U] state of being too easily pleased with oneself. ˈ**~-conˈfessed** *adj* on one's own testimony: *a ~-confessed thief.* ˈ**~-ˈconfidence** *n* belief in one's own abilities. ˈ**~-ˈconfident** *adj* ˈ**~-ˈconscious** *adj* aware of one's own existence, thoughts and actions; (colloq) shy; embarrassed. ˈ**~-ˈconsciousness** *n* ˈ**~-conˈtained** *adj* **(a)** (of a person) not impulsive or communicative. **(b)** (esp of a flat) complete in itself (not sharing the kitchen, bathroom, etc with occupants of other flats) and (usu) with its own private entrance. ˈ**~-conˈtrol** *n* [U] control of one's own feelings, behaviour, etc: *exercise ~-control; lose one's ~-control.* ˈ**~-deˈfence** *n* [U] defence of one's own body, property, rights, etc: *kill sb in ~-defence,* while defending oneself against attack; *the art of ~-defence,* boxing. ˈ**~-deˈnial** *n* [U] going without things one would like to have in order to help others: *practise ~-denial to help the children.* ˈ**~-deˈnying** *adj* ˈ**~-deˌtermiˈnation** *n* **(a)** (in politics) decision, made by a people having the characteristics of a nation, whether they shall be independent or (continue to) be part of another state: *the right of all peoples to ~-determination.* **(b)** the making of one's own decisions; the guidance, by the individual, of his own conduct. ˈ**~-ˈeducated** *adj* educated without much help from schools or teachers. ˈ**~-efˈfacing** *adj* keeping oneself in the background; not trying to get attention. ˈ**~-emˈployed** *adj* working, e g as a shopkeeper, a jobbing gardener, without an employer. ˈ**~-eˈsteem** *n* good opinion of oneself; (sometimes) conceit; *injure one's ~-esteem,* lower one's opinion of oneself. ˈ**~-ˈevident** *adj* clear without proof or more evidence. ˈ**~-exˌamiˈnation** *n* examining one's own behaviour, motives, moods, etc. ˈ**~-exˈplanatory** *adj* clear without (further) explanation. ˈ**~-ˈhelp** *n* use of one's own powers to achieve success, etc. ˈ**~-imˈportant** *adj* pompous; having too high an opinion of oneself. ˈ**~-imˈportance** *n* ˈ**~-imˈposed** *adj* (of a duty, task, etc) imposed on oneself. ˈ**~-inˈdulgent** *adj* giving way too easily to desires for one's own comfort, pleasures, etc. ˈ**~-inˈdulgence** *n* ˈ**~-ˈinterest** *n* one's own interests and personal advantage. ˈ**~-ˈlocking** *adj* locking automatically when closed. ˈ**~-ˈmade** *adj* having succeeded by one's own efforts, esp after beginning life without money, education or influence. ˈ**~-oˈpinionated** *adj* over-certain that one's own opinions are correct; having strong opinions not firmly based. ˈ**~-ˈpity** *n* (exaggerated) pity for oneself. ˈ**~-posˈsessed** *adj* calm, cool, confident: *a ~-possessed young woman.* ˈ**~-posˈsession** *n* coolness; composure: *lose/regain one's ~-possession.* ˈ**~-ˌpreserˈvation** *n* keeping oneself from harm or destruction: *the instinct of ~-preservation.* ˈ**~-ˈraising** *adj* (of flour) not needing the addition of baking-powder (when bread, etc is being made). ˈ**~-reˈliant** *adj* having or showing confidence in one's own powers, judgement, etc. ˈ**~-reˈliance** *n* ˈ**~-reˈspect** *n* feeling that one is behaving and thinking in ways that will not cause one to be ashamed of oneself: *lose all ~-respect.* ˈ**~-reˈspecting** *adj* having ~-respect: *No ~-respecting man could agree to do such a thing.* ˈ**~-ˈrighteous** *adj* convinced of one's own goodness and that one is better than

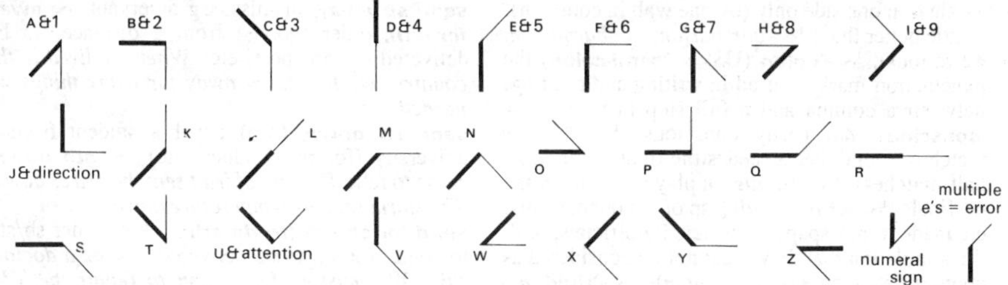

semaphore

others. '~-`**rule** *n* = ~-government. '~-`**sacrifice** *n* the giving up of one's own interests and wishes for the sake of other people. '~-`**sacrificing** *adj* '~-`**same** *adj* very same; identical: *Tom and I reached Paris on the ~-same day.* '~-`**sealing** *adj* (of a fuel tank, pneumatic tyre, etc) having a substance (e g soft rubber) that automatically seals a puncture made in it. '~-`**seeker** *n* person who is too much concerned with gaining advantages for himself. '~-`**seeking** *n, adj* '~-`**service** **(a)** (of a canteen, restaurant), one at which persons collect their own food and drink from counters and carry it to tables. **(b)** (of a shop) one at which customers collect what they want from counters or shelves and pay as they leave. **(c)** (of a garage) one at which customers fill their cars with petrol and then go and pay the charge at a counter. '~-`**sown** *adj* (of plants) coming from seed that has dropped from the plant (not sown by a gardener). '~-`**starter** *n* device (usu electric) for starting an engine, e g of a motor-vehicle, without use of a crank-handle. '~-`**styled** *adj* using a name, title, etc which one has given oneself and to which one has no right: *The ~-styled 'Dr' Smith had never been awarded a degree of any kind.* '~-**suf`ficient** *adj* **(a)** needing no help from others: *The country has now become ~-sufficient in woollen goods,* no longer has to import them. **(b)** over-confident. '~-**suf`ficiency** *n* '~-**suf`ficing** *adj* = ~-sufficient: *a ~-sufficing economic unit.* '~-**sup`porting** *adj* (of a person) earning enough money to keep oneself: *now that my children are ~-supporting;* (of a business, etc) paying its way; not needing a subsidy. '~-`**will** *n* wilfulness; determined to do as one wishes and not be guided by others. '~-`**willed** *adj* obstinate; refusing advice or guidance. '~-`**winding** *adj* (of a watch) winding itself automatically (from movements of the wrist, etc).

self·ish /`selfɪʃ/ *adj* chiefly thinking of and interested in one's own needs and welfare; without care for others: *act from ~ motives.* **~·ly** *adv* **~-ness** *n*

sell /sel/ *vt,vi* (*pt,pp* sold /səʊld/) **1** [VP6A,12A, 13A,15B] ~ ***sth (to sb);*** ~ ***sb sth,*** give in exchange for money: *~ books; ~ sth by auction; ~ sth at a good price; ~ oranges at fivepence each; ~ a man into slavery. I'll ~ it to you for £5. Will you ~ me your bicycle?* ~ ***sth off,*** ~ (a stock of goods) cheaply. ~ ***sth out,*** **(a)** ~ part or all of one's share in a business: *He sold out his share of the business and retired.* **(b)** ~ all of one's stock of sth: *We are sold out of small sizes. The book you ask for is sold out,* There are no copies left. `~-**out** *n* **(a)** event, e g a concert, for which all tickets are sold. **(b)** (colloq) betrayal. ~ ***sb up,*** ~ (a person's goods and property) for payment of debt: *I went bankrupt and was sold up.* ~ ***(sb) short,*** ⇨ short²(3). **2** [VP6A] keep stocks for sale; be a dealer in: *Do you ~ needles? This little shop ~s a wide variety of goods.* `~-**ing price,** price to be paid by the customer; cash price. Cf *cost* price. **3** [VP2A,C] (of goods) be sold; find buyers: *Tennis balls ~ best in summer. His new novel is ~ing well. These articles ~ at 20p apiece. Your house ought to ~ for at least £9000.* **4** [VP6A] cause to be sold: *It is not the low prices but their quality which ~s our goods.* **5** (fig uses): *~ one's life dearly,* kill or wound a number of one's attackers before being killed. ~ ***oneself,*** **(a)** present oneself to others in a convincing way (e g when applying for a job). **(b)** do sth dishonourable for money or reward. ~ ***the pass,*** (prov) do sth that weakens one's country or side; be a traitor. **6** (usu passive) cheat; disappoint by failure to keep an agreement, etc: *I've been sold! Sold again!* I've been tricked, let down, etc! **7** ***be sold on sth,*** (US colloq) accept it, believe that it is good, etc: *Are they sold on the idea of profit-sharing?* □ *n* (colloq, from **6** above) disappointment: *What a ~!* **~er** *n* **1** person who ~s: *a `book~er.* **a ~ers' market,** (comm) situation when goods are scarce and money plentiful, so that ~ers are favoured. **2** sth that is sold. '**best-**`**~er** *n* ⇨ best²(2).

sel·vage, sel·vedge /`selvɪdʒ/ *n* edge of cloth woven so that threads do not unravel.

selves /selvz/ *pl* of self.

sem·an·tic /sɪ`mæntɪk/ *adj* relating to meaning in language; of ~s. **se·man·tics** *n* (with *sing v*) branch of linguistics concerned with studying the meanings of words and sentences.

sema·phore /`seməfɔ(r)/ *n* [U] **1** system for sending signals by using arms on a post or flags held in the hands, with various positions for the letters of the alphabet: *send a message by ~.* **2** mechanical device with red and green lights on mechanically moved arms, used for signalling on railways. □ *vt,vi* [VP6A,2A] send (messages) by ~(**1**).

sem·blance /`sembləns/ *n* [C] likeness; appearance: *put on a ~ of gaiety.*

se·men /`simən/ *n* [U] fertilizing sperm-bearing fluid of male animals. **se·minal** /`semɪnl/ *adj* of seed or semen or reproduction; embryonic; (fig) able to originate: *seminal ideas.*

sem·es·ter /sɪ`mestə(r)/ *n* (esp in Germany and US) each of the two divisions of an academic year. Cf *term* in GB.

semi- /semɪ/ *prep* **1** half of: `~-**circle** *n* ⇨ the illus at circle. '~-`**circular** *adj* (having the shape of a) half a circle; `~-**breve,** `~-**quaver,** half a breve, half a quaver. ⇨ the illus at notation. `~-**tone** *n* half a tone in a musical scale, the smallest interval in normal Western music. **2** on one of two sides. '~-**de`tached** *adj* (of a house) joined to another on one side only (by one wall in common). **3** little better than: '~-bar`*barian*; '~`*barbarism*. **4** (various). '~-`**colon** (US = `**semi·colon**) the punctuation mark (;) used in writing and printing, between a comma and a full stop in value. '~-`**conscious** *adj* partly conscious. '~-`**final** *n* match or round that precedes the final (e g in football matches). '~-`**finalist** *n* player, team, in the ~-finals. '~-**of`ficial** *adj* (esp of announcements, etc made to newspaper reporters by officials, with the stipulation that they must not be considered as coming from an official source). '~-`**rigid** *adj* (esp of airships) having a rigid keel attached to a flexible gas-bag. '~-`**tropical** *adj* of regions near but not in the tropics. `~-**vowel** *n* (letter representing a) sound with a vowel quality but a consonant function (e g /w, j/). **5** occurring, published, etc twice in (a year, etc): '~-`*annual*; *a* '~-`*weekly*.

semi·nal /`semɪnl/ ⇨ semen.

sem·inar /`semɪnɑ(r)/ *n* class of students in a university, or at a summer school, etc studying a problem and meeting for discussion with a tutor or professor.

sem·inary /`semɪnərɪ *US:* -nerɪ/ *n* (*pl* -ries) **1** Roman Catholic training college for priests. **2** (formerly used as a pretentious name for a) place of education: *a ~ for young ladies.* **semin·ar·ist** /`semɪnərɪst/ *n* man trained in a ~(1).

Sem·ite /`simɑɪt/ *n, adj* (member) of any of the group of races that includes the Hebrews and Arabs and formerly the Phoenicians and Assyrians. **Se·mitic** /sɪ`mɪtɪk/ *adj* of the ~s or their languages: *a Semitic race.*

semo·lina /'semə`linə/ *n* [U] hard grains of wheat meal, used for pasta, and in milk puddings, etc.

semp·stress /`sempstrəs/ ⇨ seamstress.

sen·ate /`senət/ *n* [C] **1** (in ancient Rome) highest council of state. **2** (in modern times) Upper House (usu the smaller) of the legislative assembly in various countries, e g France, US. **3** governing council of some universities. **sena·tor** /`senətə(r)/ *n* member of ~(1,2). **sena·torial** /'senə`tɔrɪəl/ *adj* of a ~ or senator: *senatorial rank/powers; a senatorial district,* (US) one entitled to elect a senator.

send /send/ *vt,vi* (*pt,pp* sent) (For special uses with *adverbial particles* and *preps,* ⇨ 5 below.) **1** [VP12A,13A,6A,15A] ~ ***sb/sth,*** ~ ***sth to sb,*** cause sb or sth to go or be carried without going oneself: ~ *a telegram;* ~ *a message to sb/*~ *sb a message. The children were sent to bed. John was sent to school with an older child.* ⇨ take. **2** [VP19B] use force to cause sb/sth to move sharply or rapidly: *The earthquake sent the china and glass crashing to the ground. Mind how you go—you nearly sent me flying,* i e you nearly knocked me over. ~ ***sb packing/about his business,*** (colloq) dismiss him unceremoniously: *His incompetent typist was sent packing. I'll ~ that fellow about his business—he's no use to anybody!* ⇨ bring. **3** [VP22,6A] cause to become: *This noise is ~ing me crazy. This music/This gorgeous girl really ~s me,* (sl) excites me intensely, rouses me to ecstasy. **4** (old use, of God, Providence): *Heaven ~ that he arrives safely,* may God grant this. *'S~ her victorious'* (in the British national anthem) May God grant that the Sovereign may be victorious. **5** [VP15B,2C, 3A] (special use with *adverbial particles* and *preps*):

send sb away, dismiss, e g a servant. ~ ***away for sth,*** order (goods) from a distance, to be delivered by rail, post, etc: *When we lived in the country, we had to ~ away for many things we needed.*

send sb down, (esp) expel a student from a university (for misconduct, etc). ~ ***sth down,*** cause to fall: *The glut of fruit sent the prices down. The storm sent the temperature down.*

send for sb/sth (to do sth), ask or order sb/sth to come, for sth to be delivered: ~ *for a doctor/taxi. We must ~ for a man to repair the TV. Please keep these things until I ~ for them.*

send sth forth, (formal) produce, issue: ~ *forth leaves.*

send sth in (for sth, e g a competition, exhibition): ~ *in one's name for a contest;* ~ *in two oil paintings;* ~ *in a report for consideration.* ~ ***one's name/card in,*** cause one's name to be made known, e g when paying a formal call.

send sb off, (more usu *see sb off*) go with sb to the place from which he will start a journey: *Many of his friends went to the airport to ~ him off.* Hence, `~-**off** *n*: *He was given a good ~-off.* ~ ***sth off,*** dispatch: *Please see that these parcels are sent off at once.*

send sth on, **(a)** ~ it in advance. **(b)** (of letters) readdress and repost: *I asked my wife to ~ all my letters on while I was away from home.*

send sth out, **(a)** give out: *The sun ~s out light and warmth.* **(b)** produce: *The trees ~ out new leaves in spring.*

send sb/sth up, parody; show that sb/sth is ridiculous or false. Hence, `~-**up** *n* mocking imitation or parody. ~ ***sth up,*** cause to rise: *The heavy demand for beef sent the price up.*

sender /`sendə(r)/ *n* person or thing that sends: *If lost, return to ~* (e g on a letter).

se·nescent /sə`nesnt/ *adj* showing signs of old age: *I may be ~, but I'm not yet senile.* **se·nescence** /-sns/ *n* [U].

sen·eschal /`senɪʃl/ *n* (in the Middle Ages) important official (steward or major-domo) in the castle of a noble.

se·nile /`sinɑɪl/ *adj* suffering from bodily or mental weakness because of old age: caused by old age: ~ *decay.* **sen·il·ity** /sɪ`nɪlətɪ/ *n* [U] weakness (of body or mind) in old age.

sen·ior /`sinɪə(r)/ *adj* (opp of *junior*) **1** ~ ***(to),*** older in years; higher in rank, authority, etc: *He is ten years ~ to me. Smith is the ~ partner in* (= the head of) *the firm.* '~ `**citizen,** (euphem for) person over the age of retirement; old age pensioner. **2** (after a person's name, esp when a father and his son have the same Christian name): *John Brown (Sen).* ⇨ major. □ *n* **1** ~ person: *He is my ~ by ten years. The ~s* (= members of the ~ class) *defeated the juniors by 3—1.* **2** (US) student in his/her fourth year at high school or college. ~**·ity** /'sinɪ`ɔrətɪ *US:* -`ɔr-/ *n* [U] condition of being ~ (in age, rank, etc): *Should promotion be through merit or through ~ity? Remember the precedence due to ~ity.*

senna /`senə/ *n* [U] dried leaves of the cassia plant, used as a laxative.

se·ñor /se`njɔ(r)/ *n* (*pl* señores /se`njɔreɪz/) used of or to a Spanish man; Mr; sir. (**S~** when prefixed to a name.) **se·ñora** /sɪ`njɔrə/ *n* used of or to a Spanish woman; Mrs; Madam; madam. **se·ñorita** /'senjə`ritə/ *n* used of or to an unmarried woman or girl; Miss.

sen·sa·tion /sen'seɪʃn/ *n* **1** [C,U] ability to feel; feeling: *lose all ~ in one's legs; have a ~ of warmth/dizziness/falling.* **2** [C,U] (instance of, sth that causes, a) quick and excited reaction: *Our popular newspapers deal largely in ~. The news created a great ~.* **~al** /-nl/ *adj* **1** causing a ~(2): *a ~al murder.* **2** (of newspapers, etc) presenting news in a manner designed to cause ~(2): *a ~al writer/newspaper.* **~·ally** /-nl̩ɪ/ *adv* **~·al·ism** /-nl̩-ɪzm/ *n* [U] the deliberate rousing of ~(2): *the ~alism of the cinema; avoid ~alism during an election campaign.* **~·al·ist** /-nl̩ɪst/ *n*

sense /sens/ *n* **1** any one of the special powers of the body by which a person is conscious of things (i e sight, hearing, smell, taste and touch): *be in the enjoyment of all one's ~s; have a keen ~ of hearing.* **'~-organ** *n* part of the body, e g the ear or eye, concerned in producing sensation. **'sixth '~,** ⇨ **six. 2** (*pl*) normal state of mind (as when a person has the five ~s of **1** above): *in one's (right) ~s,* sane; *out of one's ~s,* insane; *frighten sb out of his ~s,* frighten him so that he behaves in an excited way. ***bring sb to his ~s,*** cause him to give up behaving foolishly or wildly. ***come to one's ~s,*** stop behaving like a fool or madman. ***take leave of one's ~s,*** become mad; start behaving irrationally. **3** (with *indef art* or *poss* but not *pl*) **~ of,** appreciation or understanding of the value or worth (of): *a ~ of humour; my ~ of duty; the moral ~; a ~ of locality/direction,* i e recognition of places, landmarks, directions, etc. **4** (not in *pl*) **~ of,** consciousness: *have no ~ of shame; a ~ of one's own importance/responsibility.* **5** [U] power of judging; judgement; practical wisdom: *Haven't you ~ enough to come in out of the rain? There's a lot of ~ in what he says. There's no ~ in doing that,* It's pointless. *What's the ~ of doing that? Now you're talking ~.* ⇨ also *common ~* at common[1](2). **6** [C] meaning: *a word with several ~s. In what ~ are you using the word? The ~ of the word is not clear.* ***in a ~,*** if the statement, etc is taken in a particular way: *What you say is true in a ~.* ***make ~,*** have a meaning that can be understood: *It just doesn't make ~,* means nothing. ***make ~ of sth,*** find a meaning in it: *Can you make ~ of what this author says?* ***in the strict/ literal/ figurative/ full/ best/ proper, etc ~,*** interpreting (the statement, etc) strictly/literally, etc. **7** [U] general feeling or opinion among a number of people: *take the ~ of a public meeting,* ask questions in order to learn the general sentiment or opinion. □ *vt* [VP6A,9] feel; be vaguely aware of; realize: *He ~d that his proposals were unwelcome.*

sense·less /'sensləs/ *adj* **1** foolish: *a ~ idea. What a ~ fellow he is!* **2** unconscious: *fall ~ to the ground.* **~·ly** *adv* **~·ness** *n*

sen·si·bil·ity /'sensə'bɪlətɪ/ *n* (*pl* -ties) **1** [U] power of feeling, esp delicate emotional impressions susceptibility: *the ~ of an artist or poet; ~ to kindness.* **2** (*pl*) susceptibility in various directions (of what is right, in good taste, due to a person, etc): *Her sensibilities are quickly wounded.*

sen·sible /'sensəbl/ *adj* **1** having or showing good sense(5); reasonable; practical: *a ~ woman; ~ shoes for mountain climbing; ~ clothing,* functional, not merely for appearance or ornament; *~ ideas. That was ~ of you.* **2 ~ of,** (old use) aware of: *He is ~ of the danger of his position.* **3** that can be perceived by the senses(1): *a ~ fall in the temperature; ~ phenomena.* **sen·sibly** /-əblɪ/ *adv* in a ~ way: *sensibly dressed for hot weather.*

sen·si·tive /'sensətɪv/ *adj* **~ (to), 1** quickly or easily receiving impressions: *The eyes are ~ to light. A ~ skin is easily hurt by too much sunshine. A ~ nerve in the gum can cause great pain.* **2** easily hurt in the spirit; easily offended: *Children are usually ~ to blame. An author must not be too ~ to criticism. He is very ~ about his ugly appearance.* **3** (of instruments, and institutions thought of as measuring things) able to record small changes: *~ thermometers/scales. The Stock Exchange is ~ to political disturbances.* **4** (of photographic film, paper, etc) affected by light. **~·ly** *adv* **sen·si·tiv·ity** /'sensə'tɪvətɪ/ *n* [U] quality, degree, of being ~: *The dentist gave her an injection to reduce the sensitivity of the nerves.*

sen·si·tize /'sensətaɪz/ *vt* [VP6A] make (film, paper, etc) ~ to light (for use in photography).

sen·sory /'sensərɪ/ *adj* of the senses(1) or sensation: *~ organs/nerves.*

sen·sual /'senʃʊəl/ *adj* of, given up to, the pleasures of the senses; self-indulgent in regard to food and drink and sexual enjoyment: *~ enjoyment; a ~ life; ~ lips,* giving the impression that a person is ~. **~·ism** /-ɪzm/ *n* = ~ity. **~·ist** /-ɪst/ *n* ~ person. **~·ity** /'senʃʊ'ælətɪ/ *n* [U] love of, indulgence in, ~ pleasures, esp of the body.

sen·su·ous /'senʃʊəs/ *adj* affecting, noticed by, appealing to, the senses(1): *~ music/painting.* (Note that ~ is free of the implied censure in *sensual*). **~·ly** *adv* **~·ness** *n*

sent /sent/ *pt,pp* of send.

sen·tence /'sentəns/ *n* [C] **1** (statement by a judge, etc, of) punishment: *pass ~ (on sb),* declare what the punishment is to be; *under ~ of death. The ~ of the court was three years' imprisonment.* **2** (gram) the largest grammatical unit, consisting of phrases and/or clauses, used to express a statement, question, command, etc. □ *vt* [VP6A,14,17] state that (sb) is to have a certain punishment: *~ a thief to six months' imprisonment. He had been ~d to pay a fine of £10.*

sen·ten·tious /sen'tenʃəs/ *adj* **1** (old use) in the habit of saying or writing things in a short and witty manner. **2** (mod use) having, putting on, an air of wisdom; dull and moralizing: *a ~ speaker/ speech.* **~·ly** *adv*

sen·ti·ent /'senʃənt/ *adj* having, able to have, feeling; experiencing sensation.

sen·ti·ment /'sentɪmənt/ *n* **1** [C] mental feeling, the total of what one thinks and feels on a subject; [U] such feelings collectively as an influence: *The ~ of pity is made up of the feeling of sympathy and of a desire to help and protect. A statesman should be animated by lofty ~s. Should reason be guided by ~? What are your ~s towards my sister,* Do you love her or is it sth less than love? **2** [U] (tendency to be moved by) (display of) tender feeling (contrasted with reason): *There's no place for ~ in business.* **3** expression of feeling; opinions or point of view: *The ambassador explained the ~s of his government on the question.*

sen·ti·men·tal /'sentɪ'mentl/ *adj* **1** having to do with the feelings; emotional: *do sth for ~ reasons; have a ~ attachment to one's birthplace. The bracelet had only ~ value,* e g because it belonged to one's mother. **2** (of things) tending to arouse, expressing (often excessive) feelings: *~ music; ~ novelettes;* (of persons) having such excessive feelings: *She's far too ~ about her cats.* **~ly** /-tḷɪ/ *adv* **~ist** *n* person who is ~(1). **~ity** /ˈsen-tɪmenˋtælətɪ/ *n* [U] the quality of being weakly or foolishly ~. **~ize** /-tḷɑɪz/ *vt, vi* [VP6A,2A] (cause to) become ~(2).

sen·ti·nel /ˋsentɪnl/ *n* = sentry (now the usu word): *stand ~ (over)*, (liter) keep guard (over).

sen·try /ˋsentrɪ/ *n* (*pl* **-ries**) soldier posted to keep watch and guard. **ˋ~-box** *n* hut or cabin for a ~. **ˋ~-go** *n* duty of pacing up and down as a ~: *be on ~-go.*

se·pal /ˋsepl/ *n* one of the divisions of the calyx of a flower. ⇨ the illus at **flower**.

sep·ar·able /ˋseprəbl/ *adj* that can be separated. **sep·ar·ably** /-əblɪ/ *adv* **sep·ar·abil·ity** /ˈseprə-ˋbɪlətɪ/ *n*

sep·ar·ate¹ /ˋseprət/ *adj* **1** divided; not joined or united: *Cut it into three ~ parts.* **2** forming a unit which is distinct and which exists apart: *The children sleep in ~ beds,* Each of them has his own bed. *Mr Green and his wife are living ~* (= apart) *now. Keep these ~ from those.* □ *n* (trade use, *pl*) ~ garments which may be worn in a variety of combinations, e g jerseys, blouses and skirts. **~ly** *adv* in a ~ manner: *Tie them up ~ly.*

sep·ar·ate² /ˋsepəreɪt/ *vt, vi* **1** [VP6A,14,15B] **~ from,** make, be, ~ from: *S~ the good ones from the bad. England is ~d from France by the Channel.* **~ sth (up) into,** divide into: *The land was ~d (up) into small fields.* **2** [VP2A] (of a number of people) go in different ways: *We talked until midnight and then ~d.* **sep·ar·at·ist** /ˋseprətɪst/ *n* (opp of *unionist*) member of a group which wants (esp political or ecclesiastical) separation. **sep·ar·ator** /ˋsepəreɪtə(r)/ *n* (esp) device for separating cream from milk.

sep·ar·ation /ˈsepəˋreɪʃn/ *n* **1** [U] (state of) being separated or separate; act of separating: *S~ from his friends made him sad.* **ˋ~ allowance,** regular allowance of money to a woman who is living apart from her husband, esp one made by a soldier or sailor and augmented by the Government, e g during a war. **judicial ~,** (commonly called *legal ~*) arrangement (ordered by a court of law) which does not end a marriage, but which requires married persons no longer to live together. ⇨ **divorce¹(1)**. **2** [C] instance of, period of, separation: *after a ~ of five years; ~s of husbands and wives in time of war.*

se·pia /ˋsipɪə/ *n* [U] dark brown (ink or paint): *a ˋ~-drawing,* one done in ~.

se·poy /ˋsipɔɪ/ *n* Indian soldier in the British-Indian army before 1947.

sep·sis /ˋsepsɪs/ *n* [U] putrefaction; contamination from a festering wound.

Sep·tem·ber /sepˋtembə(r)/ *n* the ninth month of the year.

sep·tet /sepˋtet/ *n* (musical composition for a) group of seven voices or instruments.

sep·tic /ˋseptɪk/ *adj* of sepsis; causing, caused by, infection (with disease germs): *~ poisoning. A dirty wound may become ~,* affected by bacteria. **~ tank,** one in which sewage is disposed of by bacterial activity.

sep·ti·cemia /ˈseptɪˋsimɪə/ *n* blood-poisoning.

sep·tua·gen·arian /ˈseptjʊədʒɪˋneərɪən *US:* -tʃʊ-/ *n* person 70 to 79 years old.

Sep·tua·gesima /ˈseptjʊəˋdʒesɪmə *US:* -tʃʊ-/ *n* third Sunday before Lent.

Sep·tua·gint /ˋseptjʊədʒɪnt *US:* -tʃʊ-/ *n* Greek version of the Old Testament and the Apocrypha made about 270 B C.

sep·ulchre (US = **-ul·cher**) /ˋseplkə(r)/ *n* [C] tomb, esp one cut in rock or built of stone. **the Holy S~,** that in which Jesus Christ was laid. **whited ~** *n* hypocrite. ⇨ **Matt. 23: 27. sep·ul·chral** /sɪˋpʌlkrl/ *adj* **1** of a ~; of burial. **2** deep and gloomy; suggestive of burial: *sepulchral looks; in a sepulchral voice.*

sep·ul·ture /ˋsepltʃʊə(r)/ *n* [U] burying; putting in the tomb or grave.

se·quel /ˋsikwl/ *n* [C] **1** that which follows or arises out of (an earlier happening): *Famine has often been the ~ of war. Her action had an unfortunate ~.* ***in the ~,*** later on; as things developed afterwards. **2** story, film, etc with the same character of an earlier one.

se·quence /ˋsikwəns/ *n* [U] succession; [C] connected line of events, ideas, etc: *deal with events in historical ~; the ~ of events,* the order in which they occur; *a ~ of bad harvests; a ~ of clubs* (in playing cards), three or more next to each other in value, e g Ace, King, Queen, or 10, 9, 8. ***~ of tenses,*** (gram) principles according to which the tenses of subordinate clauses are suited to the tenses of principal clauses. **se·quent** /-əns/ *adj* following in order or time; resulting. **se·quen·tial** /sɪˋkwenʃl/ *adj* following in order of time or place; following as a result.

se·ques·ter /sɪˋkwestə(r)/ *vt* [VP6A] **1** keep (sb) away or apart from other people; withdraw to a quiet place: *~ oneself from the world; lead a ~ed life.* **2** (legal) = sequestrate. **se·ques·tered** *adj* (of places) quiet; secluded.

se·ques·trate /sɪˋkwestreɪt/ *vt* [VP6A] **1** (legal) take temporary possession of (a debtor's property, estate, etc) until debts are paid or other claims met. **2** confiscate. **se·ques·tra·tion** /ˈsikwə-ˋstreɪʃn/ *n*

se·quin /ˋsikwɪn/ *n* **1** tiny metal disc of silver, jet, etc sewn on to a dress, etc as an ornament. **2** gold coin once used in Venice.

se·quoia /sɪˋkwɔɪə/ *n* large evergreen tree (the *redwood*) of great height (in California).

se·ra·glio /sɪˋrɑlɪəʊ/ *n* (*pl* **-glios** /-lɪəʊz/) harem; (in Turkey, former times) ruler's walled palace with government offices, etc.

ser·aph /ˋserəf/ *n* (*pl* **~s** or **-phim** /-fɪm/) angel. **~ic** /sɪˋræfɪk/ *adj* angelic; happy and beautiful as a ~.

sere /sɪə(r)/ = **sear²**.

ser·en·ade /ˈserəˋneɪd/ *n* (piece of) music (to be) sung or played outdoors at night. □ *vt* [VP6A] sing or play a ~ to (sb).

ser·en·dip·ity /ˈserənˋdɪpətɪ/ *n* [U] faculty of making fortunate and unexpected discoveries by chance.

ser·ene /sɪˋrin/ *adj* clear and calm; tranquil: *a ~ sky; a ~ look; a ~ smile.* **~ly** *adv* **ser·en·ity** /sɪˋrenətɪ/ *n* [U].

serf /s3f/ *n* (in olden times) person who was not allowed to leave the land on which he worked; (fig) person treated almost like a slave; drudge. **~dom** /-dəm/ *n* [U] **1** social and economic system in which land was cultivated by ~s. **2** ~'s condition of life.

serge /s3dʒ/ *n* [U] hard-wearing woollen cloth: (attrib) *a blue ~ suit.*

ser·geant /ˈsɑdʒənt/ *n* **1** non-commissioned army officer above a corporal and below a ~-major. ˈ**~-ˈmajor** *n* warrant officer, between commissioned and non-commissioned army officer. ⇨ App 9. **2** police-officer with rank below that of an inspector.

serial /ˈsɪərɪəl/ *adj* **1** of, in or forming a series: *the* ˈ*~ number of a banknote or cheque.* **2** (of a story, etc) appearing in parts (in a periodical on radio, TV, etc): *An exciting new ~ story will begin in our next week's issue.* □ *n* ~ play, story, etc. **seri·ally** /-ɪəlɪ/ *adv* **~·ize** /-lɑɪz/ *vt* [VP6A] publish or produce in ~ form.

seri·atim /ˈsɪərɪˈeɪtɪm/ *adv* (Lat) point by point; taking subjects, etc after one another in order: *deal with arguments ~.*

seri·cul·ture /ˈserɪkʌltʃə(r)/ *n* (breeding of silk-worms for) the production of silk. **seri·cul·tural** /ˈserɪˈkʌltʃərl/ *adj* **ser·i·cul·tur·ist** /-tʃərɪst/ *n*

series /ˈsɪəriz/ *n* (*pl* unchanged) number of things, events, etc each of which is related in some way to the others, esp to the one before it: *a ~ of stamps/coins,* e g of different values, but issued at one time; *a ~ of brilliant statesmen; a ~ of good harvests; a* ˈ*Television ~,* a number of programmes, each complete in itself, linked by cast, theme, etc. ***in ~,*** in an orderly arrangement; (of the components of an electrical circuit) with the supply of current fed directly through each component. ⇨ *in parallel* at **parallel**.

serio·comic /ˈsɪərɪəʊˈkomɪk/ *adj* serious in intention but appearing to be comic (or vice versa); having both serious and comic elements.

seri·ous /ˈsɪərɪəs/ *adj* **1** solemn; thoughtful; not given to pleasure-seeking: *a ~ mind/appearance/face; look ~.* **2** important because of possible danger: *a ~ illness/mistake. The international situation looks ~.* **3** in earnest; sincere: *a ~ worker. Please be ~ about your work.* **~·ly** *adv* in a ~ manner: *speak ~ly to sb; be ~ly ill.* **~·ness** *n* state of being ~: *the ~ness of the country's financial affairs.* ***in all ~ness,*** very ~ly; not at all in a light-hearted way: *I tell you this in all ~ness.*

ser·jeant /ˈsɑdʒənt/ *n* ˈ**S~-at-ˈarms,** official with ceremonial duties or who keeps order in a court, legislature, etc.

ser·mon /ˈsɜmən/ *n* [C] spoken or written address on a religious or moral subject; esp one given from a pulpit in a church; serious talk reproving a person for his faults, etc. **~·ize** /-ɑɪz/ *vt,vi* [VP6A, 2A] preach or talk seriously to: *Stop ~izing,* lecturing to me on my faults, etc!

serous /ˈsɪərəs/ *adj* of or like serum.

ser·pent /ˈsɜpənt/ *n* snake (which is the more usu word); (fig) sly, treacherous person: *the old S~,* the Devil.

ser·pen·tine /ˈsɜpəntɑɪn *US:* -tin/ *adj* twisting and curving like a snake: *the ~ course of the river.*

ser·rated /seˈreɪtɪd *US:* ˈsereɪtɪd/ *adj* having notches on the edge like a saw; having a toothed edge: *~ leaves.*

ser·ried /ˈserɪd/ *adj* (of lines or ranks of persons) close together, shoulder to shoulder: *in ~ ranks.*

serum /ˈsɪərəm/ *n* **1** [U] watery fluid in animal bodies; thin, transparent part of blood. **2** (dose of) such a fluid taken from the blood of an animal which has been made immune to a disease, used for inoculations.

ser·vant /ˈsɜvənt/ *n* **1** **(domestic) ~,** person who works in a household for wages, food and lodging: *keep a ~; have a large staff of ~s; engage/dismiss a ~; the ~s' hall,* room used by the ~s in a big household; *a* ˈ*~-girl.* **2** **public ~,** person who works for the public, e g a police officer, member of the Fire Service. ˈ**civil** ˈ**~,** government employee, member of the civil service. ***your humble ~,*** form sometimes used preceding the signature in an official letter. **3** person devoted to sb or sth: *a ~ of Jesus Christ,* e g a Christian priest. **4** sth useful that should be treated as a means but not as an end: *Fire is a good ~ but a bad master.*

serve /sɜv/ *vt,vi* **1** [VP6A,15A,2A,C] be a servant to (sb); work for (sb): *She ~d the family well for ten years. He ~s as gardener and also as chauffeur.* **2** [VP6A,15A,2A,B,3A] perform duties (for): *~ one's country,* e g in Parliament; *~ a year in the Army. S~ God and honour the Queen. Can I ~ you in any way,* Is there anything I can do for you? ***~ on sth,*** be a member of: *~ on a committee.* ***~ under sb,*** be in the armed forces under the command of: *My great-grandfather ~d under Nelson.* ***~ two masters,*** (fig) be divided in one's loyalty, or between two opposite principles. **3** [VP6A,2A,14,15B] ***~ sth (to sb), ~ sb (with sth), ~ sth (out),*** attend to (customers in a shop, etc); supply (with goods and services); place (food, etc) on the table for a meal; give (food, etc) to people at a meal: *There was no one in the shop to ~ me. We are well ~d with gas/electricity, etc in this town. Rations were ~d (out) to the troops. Roast pork is often ~d with apple sauce. Dinner is ~d,* is ready. *S~ the coffee in the next room, please.* **4** [VP6A,2A,C,4A] ***~ sb (for/as sth),*** be satisfactory for a need or purpose; *This box will ~ for a seat. It isn't very good but it will ~ me. That excuse will not ~ you/That will not ~ you as an excuse,* will not be accepted. *This accident ~s to show the foolishness of not being prepared.* ***~ sb's needs/purpose(s),*** meet one's requirements: *The house will ~ his needs admirably.* ***as occasion ~s,*** when there is a suitable or convenient occasion or opportunity. **5** [VP15A,B] act towards, treat (sb in a certain way): *They have ~d me shamefully,* behaved very badly towards me. *I hope I shall never be ~d such a trick again,* have such a trick played on me. ***It ~s him right,*** His failure, misfortune, etc is deserved; he does not merit sympathy. ***~ sb out (for sth),*** pay him out (the more usu phrase); make him suffer (for what he has done). **6** [VP6A] *~ one's time, ~ one's apprenticeship,* pass the usual or normal number of years (learning a trade, etc); go through one's term of office. **7** [VP6A] ***~ a sentence, ~ time,*** undergo a period of imprisonment. *He has ~d five years of his sentence.* **8** [VP6A,14] (legal) deliver (a summons, etc) to the person named in it. ***~ a summons/writ/warrant on sb; ~ sb with a writ.*** **9** [VP6A,2A] (tennis, etc) put the ball into play by striking it to an opponent: *~ a ball; ~ well/badly.* **10** [VP6A] of a male animal, e g a bull or boar, copulate with. **11** [VP2A] help a priest at Mass. □ *n* (tennis, etc) first stroke; turn for striking and putting the ball into play: *Whose ~ is it?* **server** *n* **1** person who ~s, e g one who helps a priest at Mass or a tennis-player. **2** tray for dishes; salver. **3** ˈ*salad-servers,* fork and spoon for serving salad. **serv·ing** *n* quantity of food (to be) served to one person: *This recipe will be enough for four servings.*

ser·vice /ˋsɜvɪs/ *n* **1** [U] being a servant; position as a servant. ***be in/go into ~***: *She was in ~* (= employed as a domestic servant) *before her marriage. She will go out to/go into ~*, become a domestic servant. *Miss White has been in our ~ for five years.* **2** [C] department or branch of public work, government employment, etc: *the Civil S~; the ˈDiploˋmatic S~; the fighting ~s*, the Navy, Army, Air Force; *~ men and women*, members of the fighting ~s. ***on active ~***, performing duties required by membership of the fighting ~s in time of war. ***see ~ in sth***, serve (in the armed forces): *He saw ~ in both World Wars. He has seen ~ in many parts of the world.* ***have seen (good) ~***, have served one well: *These old climbing-boots have seen good ~ on my numerous holidays in the Alps.* **ˋ~ dress**, semi-formal khaki uniform worn by officers. **~ rifle**, kind used in the ~s. **3** [C] sth done to help or benefit another or others: *His ~s to the State have been immense. Do you need the ~s of a doctor/lawyer?* ***do sb a ~, help him***: *She did me a great ~ by collecting the children from school.* **4** [U] benefit, use, advantage: *Can I be of ~ to you*, help you in any way? *I am at your ~*, ready to help you. *My car is at your ~*, ready for you to use when you want to. **5** [C] system or arrangement that supplies public needs, esp for communications: *a ˋbus/ˋtrain ~; the ˋtelephone ~; a good ˋpostal ~.* **ˋ~ road**, minor road, off a main road, giving access to houses, etc. **6** [C] form of worship and prayer to God: *three ~s every Sunday; attend morning/evening ~; ˋmarriage/ˋburial/comˋmunion ~. Divine ~ is held daily in this Church.* **7** [C] complete set of plates, dishes, etc for use at table: *a ˋtea/ˋdinner ~ of 50 pieces.* **8** [U] serving of food and drink (in hotels, etc); work done by domestic servants, hotel staff, etc: *The food is good at this hotel, but the ~ is poor. I added 10 per cent to the bill for ~*, e g a bill at a restaurant, instead of giving a tip. *Do you make a ˋ~ charge at this hotel*, e g add 10%? **ˋ~ flat**, one (usu furnished) of which the rent includes a charge for ~. **9** [U] expert help or advice given by manufacturers or their agents after the sale of an article: *send the car in for ~ every 3 000 miles*, e g for greasing, checking of brakes, etc; (attrib) *ˋ~ department.* **ˋ~ station** *n* petrol station which also offers general servicing facilities. **10** (legal) serving of a writ, summons, etc. **11** (tennis, etc) act of serving the ball; manner of doing this; person's turn to serve: *Her ~ is weak. Whose ~ is it?* □ *vt* [VP6A] maintain or repair (a car, radio, machine, etc) after sale (⇨ 9 above): *have the car ~d regularly.* **~·able** /-əbl/ *adj* **1** suited for ordinary wear and use; strong and durable: *~able clothes for schoolchildren.* **2** of use; capable of giving good service.

ser·vi·ette /ˈsɜvɪˋet/ *n* [C] table napkin: *I prefer a linen napkin to a paper ~.*

ser·vile /ˋsɜvaɪl *US:* -vl/ *adj* **1** of or like slaves: *a ~ class*, (in olden times) of workers who did rough labour; *a ~ revolt*, (in ancient Rome, etc) a rebellion of slaves. **2** characteristic of a slave; suggesting the attitude of a slave; lacking in the spirit of independence: *~ flattery; ~ to public opinion*, paying excessive attention to it. **~ly** /-aɪllɪ/ **ser·vil·ity** /sɜˋvɪlətɪ/ *n* [U] ~ behaviour or attitude.

ser·vi·tor /ˋsɜvɪtə(r)/ *n* (old use) manservant; attendant.

ser·vi·tude /ˋsɜvɪtjud *US:* -tud/ *n* [U] condition of being forced to work for others and having no freedom. ⇨ penal.

servo- /sɜvəʊ/ *pref* auxiliary (esp in machinery): *ˈ~-asˋsisted brakes*, e g in a large car; *ˈ~-ˋmechanism*, one that supplies power to a machine to make its operation easier.

ses·ame /ˋsesəmɪ/ *n* **1** plant with seeds used in various ways as food and giving an oil used in salads. **2** ***Open ~!*** magic words used, in one of the Arabian Nights stories, to cause a door to open; hence, easy way of securing access to what is usu inaccessible.

sesqui·ped·alian /ˈseskwɪpɪˋdeɪlɪən/ *adj* having many syllables.

session /ˋseʃn/ *n* [C] **1** (meeting of a) law court, law-making body, etc; time occupied by discussions at such a meeting: *the autumn ~* (= sitting) *of Parliament; have a long ~; go into secret ~.* **petty ~s**, courts held by justices of the peace to hear certain offences without a jury; *Court of S~*, supreme civil court of Scotland. **2** (Scot and US) university term. **3** single, uninterrupted meeting for other purposes: *a reˋcording ~*, period of time during which material is recorded (on discs or tapes, e g for broadcasts).

set[1] /set/ *n* **1** [C] number of things of the same kind, that belong together because they are similar or complementary to each other: *a set of golf-clubs; a ˋtea-set and ˋdinner-set*, (= *service* (7), the more usu word); *a new set of false teeth; a ˋdressing-table set/a ˋtoilet set*, number of porcelain (silver, tortoise-shell, etc) articles as found on a dressing-table. **2** [C] number of persons who associate, or who have similar or identical tastes and interests: *the ˋracing/ˋliterary/ˋgolfing set; the ˋsmart set*, those who consider themselves leaders in society; *the ˋfast set*, those who gamble, etc; *the ˋjet set*, rich pleasure loving people, flying from one holiday resort to another. **3** radio receiving apparatus: *an ˈall-ˋmains set; a transistor set.* **4** (not *pl*) direction (of current, wind, etc); tendency (of opinion): *the set of the tide.* **5** (not *pl*) position or angle; posture: *I recognize him by the set of his head/shoulders.* **6** way in which a garment conforms to the shape of the body: *I don't like the set of this coat*, the way it fits (or doesn't fit). ⇨ set[2](14). **7** (*sing* only; poet) sunset: *at set of sun.* **8** (tennis, etc) group of games counting as a unit to the side that wins more than half the games in it. **9** the act of pointing at game (birds, animals) by a setter. ⇨ set[2](15). ***make a dead set at***, **(a)** combine to attack vigorously, by argument or ridicule. **(b)** (dated) (of a person) try to win the attention and affection of (another person to whom one is attracted). **10** [C] granite paving stone (as used for road surfaces). **11** [C] built-up scenery on the stage of a theatre or in a studio or outdoors for a moving picture: *everyone to be on the set by 7 a m.* **12** [C] young plant, cutting, bulb, etc ready to be planted: *get the onion sets in.* **13** badger's burrow. **14** setting of the hair: *shampoo and set, £1.50.* ⇨ set[2](9).

set[2] /set/ *vt,vi* (-tt-, *pt,pp* set) (For special uses with *adverbial particles* and *preps*, ⇨ 19 below.) **1** [VP2A] (of the sun, moon, stars) go down below the horizon: *It will be cooler when the sun has/is set. His star has set*, (fig) The time of his power, greatness, etc is over. **2** [VP14] ***set sth to sth,*** move or place sth so that it is near to or touching sth else: *set a glass to one's lips* (*one's lips to a glass*); *set one's hand/seal to a document*, sign/seal it; *set spurs to one's horse*, urge it on; *set the axe to*, cut down (a tree), (fig) start to destroy (sth); *set pen to paper*, begin to write. ***set fire/a match/(a) light to sth,*** cause it to begin burning; ***set one's shoulder to the wheel,*** ⇨ shoulder. **3** [VP22,16A] cause (sb/sth) to be in, or reach, a specified state or relation. ***set sb/sth at defiance,*** defy the law/the court/the judge. ***set sb at his ease,*** make him feel free from embarrassment, feel comfortable, etc. ***set sb/sth on his/its feet,*** **(a)** help him to get to his feet after a fall. **(b)** help sb/sth to gain strength, financial stability, etc: *Foreign aid set the country on its feet after the war.* ***set sth on fire,*** (= set fire to sth) cause it to begin burning. ***ˈnot/ˌnever ˈset the ˋThames on fire,*** not/never do anything wonderful, extraordinary: *He'll never set the Thames on fire.* ***set sb free/at liberty,*** free (prisoners, etc). ***set people at loggerheads/variance,*** cause them to argue and dispute. ***set sth in order,*** arrange, organize (one's papers, affairs, etc) properly. ***ˈset one's (ˌown) ˋhouse in order,*** (fig) order one's own affairs, one's own life (before criticizing others). ***set sb's mind at ease/rest,*** set sb's doubts/fears/mind at rest, help him to be free from worry, free him from anxiety. ***set sb's teeth on edge,*** jar his nerves: *That noise sets my teeth on edge.* ***set sb right,*** **(a)** correct his errors; put him on the right road. **(b)** cause him to feel well and fit again. ***set sth right/to rights,*** correct, remedy (faults, grievances). ***set sb on his way,*** (old use) go part of the way with him (when he starts out on foot). ***be all set (for sth/to do sth),*** be quite ready (for the start of a race, etc). **4** [VP19B] cause sb/sth to begin to do sth: *It's time we set the machinery going*, start operations. *What has set the dog barking? The news set me thinking. My jokes set the whole company laughing. 'Blow, bugles, blow, set the wild echoes flying!'* **5** [VP6A,15A] (usu with an *adv* or *adv phrase;* ⇨ 19 below for combinations of *set* and *adverbial particles* with special meanings) put, place, lay, stand: *She set the dishes on the table. We set food and drink before the travellers. He set the stake in the ground.* **6** [VP6A,14,12C] put forward as (material to be dealt with as a task, a pattern, etc): *The teacher set the boys a difficult problem*, gave them one to be solved. *She set her secretary various tasks. I have set myself a difficult task. Who will set the papers for the examination*, draw up the examination questions? *What books have been set for the Cambridge Certificate next year*, What books are to be studied? Hence, **ˈset ˋbook,** book on which examinations are to be given. ***set (sb) an example/a good example,*** offer a good standard for others to follow: *You should set the younger boys a good example.* ***set the fashion,*** start a fashion to be copied by others. ***set the pace,*** fix it by leading (in a race, etc); (fig) fix a standard for an activity, style of living, etc: *The Joneses set the pace and their neighbours try to keep up with them.* ***set the stroke,*** (rowing) fix the number of strokes per minute. **7** [VP17A] ***set (sb/oneself) to do sth,*** give sth (to sb/oneself) as a task: *He set the farm labourer to chop wood. I set myself to study the problem. I've set myself* (= have resolved) *to finish the job by the end of May.* ***ˈSet a ˈthief to ˋcatch a thief,*** (prov) get a thief to do this (as being more likely to succeed). **8** [VP6A,15A] (with various grammatical objects, the *nn* in alphabetical order) ***set one's cap at sb,*** ⇨ cap(5). ***set eyes on sb,*** see him: *I hope I never set eyes on that fellow again.* ***set one's face against sth,*** steadfastly oppose sth. ***set one's heart/hopes/mind on sth,*** be filled with strong desire for, determination to get; direct one's hopes towards: *The boy has set his heart on becoming an engineer.* ***set a price on sth,*** declare what it will be sold for. ***set a price on sb's head,*** offer a specified reward to anyone who kills him. ***set much/great/little/no store by sth,*** value sth highly/little/not at all. **9** [VP6A,15A] put in a certain state or condition for a particular purpose: *set a (broken) bone*, bring the parts together so that they may unite. ***set a butterfly,*** arrange it with wings outspread (in a glass case) as a specimen. ***set a clock/watch,*** put the hands to the correct time (or, for an alarm clock, to sound at the desired time): *set one's watch by the time-signal on the radio.* ***set eggs,*** place them (to be hatched) under a hen, etc in a nest. ***set one's hair,*** arrange it (when damp) so that when it is dried, it is waved: *She's having her hair set for this evening's party.* ***set a hen,*** place it over eggs (to hatch them). ***set a saw,*** sharpen the teeth with a file and put them (alternately) at the right outward angle. ***set the scene,*** describe a place and the people taking part in an activity, e g in a play, novel or sporting event: *Our commentator will now set the scene in the stadium. The scene is now set for the tragedy*, Events leading up to the tragedy have taken place and the tragedy will follow. *The scene is now set for a direct confrontation between the major powers..* ***set sail (from/to/for),*** begin a voyage. ***set the table,*** lay it ready with plates, cutlery, etc: *She set the table for five people.* ***set one's teeth,*** clench them; (fig) become determined and inflexible (against some course of action, etc). ***set a trap (for sth/sb),*** **(a)** adjust one to catch a mouse, rat, etc. **(b)** do sth to discover a dishonest person, etc: *set a trap to catch a thief/for a boy who cheats.* ***set (up) type,*** arrange it ready for printing sth. **10** [VP6A,14] ***set sth in sth/set sth with sth,*** put, fix, one thing firmly in another: *set a diamond in gold; a crown set with jewels; a gold ring set with gems; a heavy lathe set* (= embedded) *in concrete; glass panes set in lead*, i e strips of lead, as in old lattice windows. *The tops of the walls were set with broken glass*, i e to discourage persons from climbing over them. *The sky seemed to be set with diamonds*, the stars looked like diamonds. **11** [VP2A,C] (of tides, currents) move or flow along; gather force; (fig) show or feel a tendency: *A strong current sets through the channel. The current sets in towards the shore. The wind sets from the west. The tide has set in his favour*, (fig) He is winning public support and approval. *Public opinion is setting against the proposal.* **12** [VP6A,14] ***set sth (to sth):*** *set (words, a poem, etc) to music*, provide with music, usu composed for the purpose; *set new words to an old tune.* **13** [VP6A,2A] (of plants, fruit trees, their blossom) form or develop fruit as the result of fertilization: *The apple-blossom hasn't/The apples haven't set well this year. This liquid, if sprayed on the flowers, helps to set the* *tomatoes.* **14** [VP2C] (of a garment) adapt itself to the shape of the body; sit (which is the more usu word): *A well-tailored jacket ought to set well. That dress sets rather badly.* **15** [VP2A,C] (of a sporting dog) stop and stand with the muzzle pointing, to indicate presence of game; (of dancers) take positions facing partners: *set to partners.* **16** [VP6A,2A] (cause to) become firm, solid, rigid (from a liquid or soft state): *Some kinds of concrete set more quickly than others. The jelly is/has not set yet. Heat sets eggs and cold sets jellies.* **17** [VP6A,2A] (rare) (cause to) develop into definite lines and shapes, become mature: *His body has/is set*, is fully developed. *Too much exercise may set a boy's muscles prematurely. His character has/is set*, is no longer pliant, is already formed. **18** (*pp*) **(a)** unmoving, fixed: *a set smile/look/purpose.* **(b)** pre-arranged; *at a set time; set lunches 75p*, (e g at a café, there being no choice of dishes); *a set piece*, a large and elaborate firework set on a platform or scaffold, (attrib) *a set-piece attack*, i e carefully planned in advance. **(c)** unchanging: *set in one's ways*, having fixed habits; *a man of set opinions*, unable or unwilling to change them. **(d)** regular; not extempore: *set phrases; a set speech; set forms of prayers.* **(e)** ***set fair,*** (of the weather) fine and with no signs of change. **19** [VP15A,2C, 3A] (special uses with *adverbial particles* and *preps*):

set about sth, start, take steps towards: *I must set about my packing*, begin to pack my clothes, etc. *I don't know how to set about this job*, how to make a start on it. ***set about sb,*** (colloq) attack: *They set about each other fiercely*, began to exchange blows. ***set sth about,*** spread (rumours, etc): *Who set* (*put* is more usu) *it about that he is resigning?*

set sb against sb, cause him to compete with, struggle against, sb. ***set one thing against another,*** regard it as compensating for, balancing, another.

set sth apart/aside, **(a)** put on one side for future use. **(b)** disregard: *Let's set aside my personal feelings.* **(c)** (legal) reject: *set a claim aside.*

set sth back, **(a)** move back: *set back the hands of a clock. The horse set back its ears.* **(b)** be placed away, at a distance, from: *The house is well set back from the road.* ***set sb/sth back,*** **(a)** hinder or reverse the progress of: *All our efforts at reform have been set back.* Hence, **ˈset-back** *n* (*pl* **set-backs**) check to progress or development: *meet with many set-backs; have a set-back in one's career/business.* **(b)** (sl) cost: *That dinner party set me back £20.*

set sth down, **(a)** put down: *set down a load.* **(b)** write down on paper. ***set sb down,*** (of a vehicle, its driver) allow (a passenger) to get down or out: *The bus stopped to set down an old lady. I'll set you down at the corner of your street.* ***set sb/oneself down as,*** (*put* is more usu) explain or describe as: *How should I set myself down in the hotel register—as a journalist or as an author? We must set him down as either a knave or a fool.*

set sth down to sth, (*put* is more usu), attribute sth to, say that sth is the result of: *set one's success down to hard work.*

set forth, **(a)** begin a journey (*set out* is more usu). ***set sth forth,*** (formal) make known; declare: *set forth one's political views. Is this condition set forth* (= included) *in the agreement?*

set in, **(a)** start and seem likely to continue: *The rainy season has set in. It set in to rain. Go to your dentist before decay of the teeth sets in.* **(b)** (of tides, winds; ⇨ **11** above) begin to flow: *The tide is setting in*, flowing towards the shore.

set off, start (a journey, race, etc): *They've set off on a journey round the world.* ***set sth off,*** **(a)** explode a mine, firework, etc. **(b)** make more striking by comparison: *A large hat sometimes set off a pretty face. This gold frame sets off your oil painting very well.* **(c)** balance; compensate: *set off gains against losses.* **(d)** mark off: *set off a clause by a comma.* ***set sb off (doing sth),*** cause to start (doing sth): *Don't set him off talking on his pet subjects or he'll go on all evening.*

set on, (formal) go forward; advance to the attack. ***set on sb,*** attack: *She had been set on by a savage dog.*

set out, begin (a journey, venture): *They set out at dawn. He set out with the best intentions.* ***set out to do sth,*** have sth as an aim or intention: *He set out to break the record for the Channel swim/ to make his first million in five years.* ***set sth out,*** **(a)** declare; make known: *set out one's reasons (for sth).* **(b)** show; put on display: *The women set out their chickens and ducks on the market stalls. He sets out his ideas clearly in this essay.* **(c)** plant out: *Set the young wallflower plants out one foot apart.*

set sb over sb, put him in control/command.

set to, **(a)** begin doing sth: *The engineers set to and repaired the bridge. They were all hungry and at once set to*, began eating. **(b)** (with *pl* subject) begin to fight, struggle, quarrel, etc. Hence, **ˌset-ˈto** *n*: *The women had a regular set-to*, e g pulling each other about by the hair.

set sth up, **(a)** place sth in position: *set up a post/statue/an altar to Jupiter.* **(b)** establish (an institution, business, argument, etc): *set up a tribunal. What defence did his counsel set up in the trial?* **ˈset-up** *n* (colloq) arrangement of an organization: *What's the set-up here?* How's your business, etc organized? **(c)** cause: *I wonder what has set up this irritation in my throat/this rash on my face?* **(d)** utter loudly; *set up a yell.* **(e)** make ready for printing: *set up type/a book.* ***set sb up,*** restore after illness: *Her holiday in the country has set her up again.* ***set (oneself) up as,*** **(a)** go into business as: *He has set (himself) up as a bookseller.* **(b)** have pretensions to being: *I've never set myself up as a scholar.* ***set sb up (as sth),*** get sb started or established, e g by supplying capital: *set up one's son in business. His father set him up as a bookseller.* ***set up house,*** start living in one, e g after being in lodgings. ***set up house with sb/ together,*** (of two persons) begin living together (as husband and wife). ***be well set up,*** **(a)** (rare) have a body well developed by exercises, etc: *He has a well set up figure. What a well set up young woman!* **(b)** be well provided with: *be well set up with clothes/reading matter.*

be set upon sth, be determined to be, get, etc: *That boy is set upon being a test pilot.*

set-square /ˈset skweər/ *n* [C] triangular plate of wood, plastic, metal, etc with angles of 90°, 60° and 30° (or 90°, 45°, 45°), used for drawing lines at these angles.

sett /set/ *n* = **set**[1](10).

set·tee /seˈti/ *n* [C] long, soft seat like a sofa, with sides and back, for two or more persons.

set·ter /ˈsetə(r)/ *n* **1** (breeds of) long-haired dog trained to stand motionless on scenting game. ⇨ set[1](9). **2** (in compounds) person who, thing which, sets (various meanings): *a ˋbone-∼; a ˋtype-∼.*

set·ting /ˈsetɪŋ/ *n* [C] **1** framework in which sth is fixed or fastened: *the ∼ of a jewel;* (by extension) surroundings, environment: *a beautiful natural ∼ for a pageant,* e g the grounds of an old castle. **2** music composed for a poem, etc. ⇨ set[2](12). **3** descent (of the sun, moon, etc) below the horizon.

settle[1] /ˈsetl/ *n* [C] (as in old houses) long, wooden seat with a high back and arms, the seat often being the lid of a chest.

settle[2] /ˈsetl/ *vt, vi* (For special uses with *adverbial particles* and *preps,* ⇨ 10 below.) **1** [VP2C,6A] make one's home in (permanently, as a colonist); establish colonists in: *The Dutch ∼d in South Africa. By whom was Canada ∼d?* **2** [VP2C] make one's home in; live in (not as a colonist): *∼ in London/in Canada/in the country.* **3** [VP2A, 3A] ∼ ***(on sth),*** come to rest (on); stay for some time (on): *The bird ∼d on a branch. The dust ∼d on everything. The cold has ∼d on my chest.* **4** [VP6A,15A] cause (sb) to become used to, or comfortable in, a new position or posture (after a period of restless movement or activity: *The nurse ∼d her patient for the night,* made him/her comfortable, gave him/her medicine, etc. *Then the nurse ∼d herself in an armchair in the next room. The girl ∼d her feet in the stirrups,* e g of her pony. **5** [VP6A,2C] make or become calm, untroubled, composed: *The thunderstorm will perhaps ∼ the weather. We want a period of ∼d weather for the harvest. Wait until the excitement has ∼d. Things are settling into shape,* becoming orderly, normal. *Take one of these tranquillizers*it will ∼ your nerves.* **6** [VP6A,7,8,10] make an agreement about; decide; determine: *That ∼s the matter. It's time you ∼d the dispute/argument. Nothing is ∼d yet. You ought to ∼ your affairs* (e g by making your Will) *before you go into hospital for that lung operation. The lawsuit was ∼d amicably/out of court/between the parties,* a decision was reached by the parties themselves (and their lawyers) instead of by the court. *What have you ∼d to do about it? Have they ∼d where to go/where they'll spend their holiday.* **7** [VP6A,2A,C] pay: *∼ a bill. Will you ∼ for all of us,* pay what is owing for all of us, e g at a restaurant? **8** [VP6A,2A] (of dust, etc in the air, particles of solid substances in a liquid, etc) (cause to) sink; (of a liquid) become clear as solid particles sink: *We need a shower to ∼ the dust. A beaten egg, they say, will ∼ coffee. The dregs settled and the coffee was clear.* **9** [VP2A,C] (of the ground, the foundation of a building, etc) sink gradually to a lower level: *The road-bed ∼d. The ship was settling/settling down by the stern,* tending to sink. **10** [VP2C,14,15B,2A] (special uses with *adverbial particles* and *preps*):

settle down, sit or lie comfortably (after a period of movement or activity): *He ∼d down in his armchair to read a new novel.* ***∼ (sb) down,*** make or become calm and peaceful: *Wait until the children have ∼d down before you start your lesson. The chairman tried to ∼ the audience down,* get them to stop talking, etc. ***∼ (down) to sth,*** overcome distractions, etc and give one's attention to one's work: *It's terrible—I can't ∼ (down) to anything today,* am too restless to do my work, etc. ***∼ down (to sth),*** become established (in a new way of life, new work, etc): *∼ down well in a new career/job.* ***∼ down to married life; marry and ∼ down,*** live the regular routine life said to be typical of married persons.

settle for sth, accept, although not altogether satisfactory: *I'd hoped to get £200 for my old car but had to ∼ for £180.*

settle (sb) in, (help sb to) move into a new house, flat, job, etc and put things in order: *We haven't ∼d in yet. You must come and see our new house when we're/we've ∼d in.*

settle sth (up)on sb, (legal) give sb (property, etc) for use during his/her lifetime: *∼ part of one's estate on one's son; ∼ an annuity on an old servant.* ⇨ settlement(2). ***∼ (up)on sth,*** decide to take: *Which of the hats have you ∼d on? We must ∼ on a time and place to meet.*

settle (up) (with sb), pay what one owes to sb: *I shall ∼ (up) with you at the end of the month. I've already settled up with the waiter,* paid for our meal. *Now to ∼ with you!* Now I'll deal with you (according to context, pay, fight with you, get rid of you, etc). ***ˈhave an acˋcount to ∼ with sb,*** (colloq) have some unpleasant business, a quarrel, etc to discuss.

settled /ˈsetld/ *adj* **1** fixed; unchanging; permanent: *∼ weather; a man of ∼ convictions; ∼ melancholy.* **2** (written on a paid bill) payment is acknowledged.

settle·ment /ˈsetlmənt/ *n* **1** [U] the act of settling (a dispute, debt, etc); [C] instance of this: *The terms of ∼ seem just. We hope for a lasting ∼ of all these troubles. The strikers have reached a ∼ with the employers. I enclose a cheque in ∼ of your account.* **2** [C] (statement of) property settled(10) on sb: *a ˋmarriage ∼,* one made by a man in favour of his wife. **3** [U] process of settling people in a colony; [C] new colony; group of colonists: *empty lands awaiting ∼; Dutch and English ∼s in North America in the 17th c; former penal ∼s in Australia.* **4** [C] group of persons engaged in social welfare work, e g in a slum district: *(welfare) ∼s in the East End of London.*

set·tler /ˈsetlə(r)/ *n* colonist; person who has settled in a newly developing country: *early ∼s in New Zealand.*

seven /ˈsevn/ *n, adj* (⇨ App 4) the number 7. **ˋ∼·fold** /-fəʊld/ *adj, adv* ∼ times as much or as many; ∼ times as great. **sev·enth** /ˈsevnθ/ *n, adj* ***in the ∼th heaven,*** extremely happy. **the S∼th Day,** Saturday, the Sabbath of the Jews, and in Quaker speech. **sev·enth·ly** *adv* in the 7th place. **∼·teen** /ˈsevnˋtin/ *n, adj* the number 17. **∼-teenth** /ˈsevnˋtinθ/ *n, adj* 17th; next after 16, one of ∼teen parts. **∼ty** /ˈsevntɪ/ *n, adj* the number 70. ***in the seventies,*** **(a)** (of a person's age) between 69 and 80. **(b)** (of a period) the years from 70 to 79 inclusive in a century. **(c)** (of temperature) between 70°F and 79°F. **∼·ti·eth** /ˈsevntɪəθ/ *n, adj*

sever /ˈsevə(r)/ *vt, vi* **1** [VP6A,15A] cut: *∼ a rope; ∼ the head of a sheep from the body;* (fig) break off: *∼ one's connections with sb.* **2** [VP2A] break: *The rope ∼ed under the strain.* **∼·ance** /ˈsevṛəns/ *n* [U] severing or being ∼ed: *the severance of diplomatic relations/of communications.*

sev·eral /ˈsevrl/ *adj* **1** three or more; some but not many: *You will need ∼ more. I've read it ∼*

times. **2** separate; individual: *They went their ~ ways,* Each went his own way. □ *pron* a few; some: *S~ of us decided to walk home.* **~ly** /ˈsevrl̩ɪ/ *adv* separately.

se·vere /səˈvɪə(r)/ *adj* **1** stern, strict: *~ looks; be ~ with one's children; be too ~ on a pupil.* **2** (of the weather, attacks of disease, etc) rigorous; violent: *a ~ storm; ~ pain; a ~ attack of toothache.* **3** making great demands on skill, ability, patience and other qualities: *~ competition. The pace was too ~ to be kept up for long.* **4** (of style, etc) simple; without ornament. **~·ly** *adv* **se·ver·ity** /səˈverətɪ/ *n* (*pl* **-ties**) **1** [U] quality of being ~: *punish sb with severity; acts of severity; the severity* (= extreme cold) *of the winter in Canada.* **2** (*pl*) ~ treatment or experiences: *the severities of the winter campaign.*

sew /səʊ/ *vt,vi* (*pt* **sewed**, *pp* **sewn** /səʊn/ or **sewed**) [VP6A,15B,2A,B,C] work with a needle and thread; fasten with stitches; make (a garment) by stitching: *sew a button on; sew a dress. The garment is ˈhand-ˈsewn/sewn by hand. She has been sewing all evening.* **sew sth up, (a)** join (at the edges) with stitches: *The corpse was sewn up in a sack and thrown into the river.* **(b)** (colloq) arrange; complete: *All the details of the project are sewn up. The deal is sewn up.* **sewer** /ˈsəʊə(r)/ *n* **sew·ing** *n* [U] work (clothes, etc) being sewn. **ˈsewing-machine** *n* machine for sewing.

reel of cotton
thread
tension adjustment
needle
foot
template

a sewing-machine

sew·age /ˈsjuɪdʒ *US:* ˈsu-/ *n* [U] foul liquid material, waste organic matter, etc carried off in sewers; the disposal of ~. **ˈ~-farm/works** *nn* place where ~ is treated and disposed of.

sewer[1] /ˈsjuə(r) *US:* ˈsu-/ *n* [C] underground channel (pipeline, or construction of brick, concrete, etc) to carry off sewage and rainwater to centres (sewage-farms) for treatment, or to a natural waterway for disposal. **ˈ~-gas** *n* bad-smelling gas formed in ~s. **ˈ~-rat** *n* brown rat commonly found in ~s. **~·age** /-ɪdʒ/ *n* system of ~s; drains.

sewer[2] /ˈsəʊə(r)/ *n* ⇨ **sew**.

sewn /səʊn/ *pp* of sew.

sex /seks/ *n* **1** being male or female: *What is its sex? Help them all, without distinction of race, age or sex.* **2** males or females as a group: *the ˈfair sex,* women; *the ˈsterner sex,* men. **3** [U] differences between males and females; consciousness of these differences: *ˈsex antagonisms; the ˈsex instinct; ˈsex appeal,* attractiveness of a person of one sex to the other. **4** [U] sexual activity and everything connected with it: *a film/novel with too much sex in it. Sex and sin are not interchangeable words.* **5** sexual intercourse: *have sex with sb.* **sex·less** *adj* neither male nor female. **sexy** *adj* **(-ier, -iest)** of or about sex; sexually attractive.

sex·ist /ˈseksɪst/ *n, adj* (person who is) derisive of the female sex and expressive of masculine superiority: *~ words,* (e g *chick, baby, doll*), used to mean a girl or woman.

sexa·gen·arian /ˌseksədʒɪˈneərɪən/ *n, adj* (person) between 59 and 70 years of age.

Sexa·gesima /ˌseksəˈdʒesɪmə/ *n* second Sunday before Lent.

using a sextant

sex·tant /ˈsekstənt/ *n* instrument used for measuring the altitude of the sun, etc (in order to determine a ship's position, etc).

sex·tet, sex·tette /seksˈtet/ *n* [C] (piece of music for) six voices, instruments or players in combination.

sex·ton /ˈsekstən/ *n* man who takes care of a church buildings, digs graves in the churchyard, rings the church bell, etc.

sex·ual /ˈsekʃʊəl/ *adj* of sex or the sexes: *~ intercourse* = **coitus. ~·ity** /ˌsekʃʊˈælətɪ/ *n* [U] sex characteristics; over-development of sex impulses.

shabby /ˈʃæbɪ/ *adj* **(-ier, -iest) 1** in bad repair or condition; much worn; poorly dressed: *wearing a ~ hat. You look rather ~ in those clothes.* **ˌ~-genˈteel** *adj* having evidence of former gentility but now ~; trying to keep up appearances. **2** (of behaviour) mean; unfair: *a ~ excuse; play a ~ trick on sb.* **shab·bily** /ˈʃæbəlɪ/ *adv* **shab·bi·ness** *n*

shack /ʃæk/ *n* [C] small, roughly built shed, hut or house (usu of wood). □ *vi* ~ ***up with sb/together,*** (sl) (esp of a man and woman unmarried) live together.

shackle /ˈʃækl/ *n* [C] one of a pair of iron rings joined by a chain for fastening a prisoner's wrists or ankles; (*pl*) fetters; (fig) sth that prevents freedom of action: *the ~s of convention.* □ *vt* [VP6A] put ~s on; prevent from acting freely.

shad /ʃæd/ *n* (*pl* unchanged) large edible fish of the N Atlantic coast of N America.

shad·dock /ˈʃædək/ *n* (tropical tree with a) large edible fruit related to the grapefruit (also called *pomelo*).

shade /ʃeɪd/ *n* **1** [U; with *adj, v* and *indef art*] comparative darkness caused by the cutting off of direct rays of light; (fig) comparative obscurity: *a temperature of 35°C in the ~. Keep in the ~; it's cooler. The trees give a pleasant ~.* ***put sb/sth in(to) the ~,*** cause to appear small, unimportant, etc, by contrast: *You are so clever and brilliant that my poor efforts are put into the ~.* **ˈ~-tree** *n* (esp US) tree planted to give ~. **2** [U] darker part(s) of a picture, etc; reproduction of the darker part of a picture: *There is not enough light and ~ in your drawing.* **3** [C] degree or depth of colour: *dress materials in several ~s of blue.* **4** [C] degree of difference: *a word with many ~s of meaning.*

She is a ~ better today. **5** sth that shuts out light or lessens its brilliance: *an 'eye-~; a 'lamp-~; a 'window-~.* ⇨ blind[3]. (*pl*) (colloq) sunglasses. **6** (*pl;* liter) darkness: *the ~s of evening.* **7** [C] unreal or unsubstantial thing; soul after death. **the ~s,** the abode of spirits; the Greek underworld. □ *vt,vi* **1** [VP6A,15A] keep direct rays of light from: *He ~d his eyes with his hands.* **2** [VP6A] screen (a light, lamp, etc) to reduce brightness. **3** [VP6A] darken with parallel pencil lines, etc (parts of a drawing, etc), to give the appearance of light and ~. **4** [VP2C] change by degrees: *scarlet shading off into pink; a colour that ~s from blue into green.* **shad·ing** *n* **1** [U] use of black, etc to give light and shade to a drawing. **2** [C] slight difference or variation.

shadow /'ʃædəʊ/ *n* **1** [C] area of shade, dark shape, thrown on the ground, a wall, floor, etc by sth which cuts off the direct rays of light: *The earth's ~ sometimes falls on the moon.* ***be afraid of one's own ~,*** be very timid. ***Coming events cast their ~s before them,*** give warning of their coming. **2** [U] area of shade of indefinite shape or extent: *Her face was in deep ~.* **3** [C] sth unsubstantial or unreal: *catch at ~s, run after a ~,* try to get hold of sth unreal. *He is only the ~ of his former self,* is very thin and weak. ***worn to a ~,*** (of a person) weakened, exhausted. **'~-boxing,** sparring against an imaginary opponent (for practice). **4** (*pl*) partial darkness: *the ~s of evening.* **5** [C] dark patch or area: *have ~s under/round the eyes,* such areas thought to be caused by lack of sleep, illness, etc. **6** (*sing* only) slightest trace: *without/beyond a ~ of doubt.* **7** (attrib) ready for use or activity when the time comes: *a '~ factory,* one planned so that it can be changed over from production of peace-time goods to munitions of war, etc. ***a ~ cabinet,*** one to be formed from leaders of the Parliamentary Opposition, i e those who might hold office in the event of a shift of power at a general election. **8** person's inseparable attendant or companion. □ *vt* [VP6A] **1** darken; overspread with ~. **2** keep a secret watch on; follow closely and watch all the movements of: *The suspected spy was ~ed by detectives.* **shad·owy** *adj* **1** having ~ of shade: *cool, ~y woods.* **2** like a ~; indistinct: *a ~y outline.*

shady /'ʃeɪdɪ/ *adj* (-ier, -iest) **1** giving shade from sunlight; situated in shade: *the ~ side of the street.* **2** of doubtful honesty: *a ~ transaction/financier; a ~-looking customer,* (colloq) person who appears to be a rogue. *Politics has its ~ side.*

shaft /ʃɑft *US:* ʃæft/ *n* [C] **1** (long, slender stem of an) arrow or spear; (fig) *~s of envy/ridicule,* expressions of envy, etc. **2** long handle of an axe or other tool. **3** one of the pair of bars (wooden poles) between which a horse is harnessed to pull a cart, etc. **4** main part of a column (between the base and the capital). ⇨ the illus at column. **5** long, narrow space, usu vertical, e g for descending into a coalmine, for a lift in a building, or for ventilation. **6** bar or rod joining parts of a machine, or transmitting power. **7** ray (of light); bolt (of lightning).

shag /ʃæg/ *n* [U] coarse kind of cut tobacco.

shaggy /'ʃægɪ/ *adj* (-ier, -iest) **1** (of hair) rough, coarse and untidy. **2** covered with rough, coarse hair: *a ~ dog; ~ eyebrows.* **shag·gily** /'ʃægəlɪ/ *adv* **shag·gi·ness** *n*

sha·green /ʃə'grin/ *n* [U] kind of leather with a rough surface, untanned.

shah /ʃɑ/ *n* (title of a) ruler of Iran.

shaikh /ʃeɪk/, **shaikh·dom** /'ʃeɪkdəm/ ⇨ sheik(h).

shake /ʃeɪk/ *vt,vi* (*pt* shook /ʃʊk/, *pp* shaken /'ʃeɪkən/) **1** [VP6A,15A,B,2A,C] (cause to) move from side to side, up and down etc: *~ a rug; ~ a man by the shoulder; ~ the dice* (in a box, etc before throwing them on to a table): *~ one's head (at sb),* to indicate 'No', or doubt, disapproval, etc; *~ one's finger at sb,* to indicate disapproval or as a warning; *~ one's fist at sb,* to show defiance; *His sides were shaking with laughter. He was shaking with cold. He was shaking in his shoes,* trembling with fear. *The earth shook under us,* e g in an earthquake. ***~ hands (with sb),*** ⇨ hand[1](1). **2** [VP6A] shock; trouble; weaken: *~ sb's faith/courage. They were badly ~n by the news. The firm's credit has been badly ~n.* **4** [VP2A,C] (of sb's voice) tremble; become weak or faltering: *Her voice shook with emotion.* **3** [VP14, 15B,C] (special uses with *adverbial particles* and *preps*): ***~ down,*** get into harmony, become adjusted to, a new environment, new conditions, etc: *The new teaching staff is shaking down nicely,* The members are getting used to their duties, to one another, etc; *The new liner has sailed on a '~-down cruise,* one during which any troubles, e g in the machinery, may be detected and put right. **'~-down** *n* improvised or makeshift bed, e g of blankets on the floor. ***~ sth from/out of sth,*** get from/out of by shaking: *~ apples from a tree; ~ sand out of one's shoes.* ***~ sb off,*** free oneself from: *The thief ran fast and soon shook off his pursuers.* ***~ sth off,*** get rid of: *~ off a cold/a fit of depression.* ***~ out,*** (mil) spread; disperse: *The troops were ordered to ~ out when crossing open country.* ***~ sth out,*** spread so as to be out by shaking: *~ out a sail/tablecloth.* **'~-out** *n* process or act of making workers redundant: *a new ~-out in the shipbuilding industry.* ***~ sth up,*** (a) mix well by shaking: *~ up a bottle of medicine.* (b) restore sth to shape by shaking: *~ up a cushion.* ***~ sb up,*** restore from apathy or lethargy: *Some of these managers need shaking up—they're asleep on the job.* Hence, **'~-up** *n*: *We need a good ~-up in our club—the officers are getting very slack.* □ *n* [C] **1** shaking or being ~n: *a ~ of the head,* to indicate 'No'; *give sth a good ~.* **2** (colloq) moment: *in two ~s; in half a ~,* almost at once. **3** (*pl*) ***no great ~s,*** (sl) not very good or efficient. **4** **'egg-~, 'milk-~,** etc, glass of milk and egg or milk alone, flavoured and ~n up. **shak·ing** *n* = shake: *give sth a good shaking,* shake it well; *get a shaking,* be ~n. **shaker** *n* one who, that which, ~s; container in which or from which sth is ~n: *a 'cocktail-~r; a 'flour-~r.*

Shake·spear·ian /ʃeɪk'spɪərɪən/ *adj* (in the style) of Shakespeare /'ʃeɪkspɪə(r)/, 1564–1616. ⇨ App 8.

shaky /'ʃeɪkɪ/ *adj* (-ier, -iest) **1** (of a person, his movements, etc) weak; unsteady: *~ hands; speak in a ~ voice; be ~ on one's legs; feel very ~.* **2** unsafe; unreliable: *a ~ table. My French is rather ~.* **shak·ily** /-əlɪ/ *adv* **shaki·ness** *n*

shale /ʃeɪl/ *n* [U] soft rock that splits easily into layers. **'~-oil** *n* oil obtained from bituminous ~.

shall /*usu form:* ʃl *strong form:* ʃæl/ *anom fin* (*shall not* is often shortened to shan't /ʃɑnt *US:*

ʃænt/; with *thou* the old form shalt /ʃælt/ occurred; *pt* form should /ʃʊd *weak form:* ʃəd/; *should not* is often shortened to shouldn't /ˈʃʊdnt/) **1** (used as an *aux v* to express the future tense, used with the first person, affirm and interr, and second person, interr only. Note that *will* is often used for *shall* in colloq style. *I'll* and *We'll* being used for *I/We shall.*): *We ~ arrive tomorrow. S~ we be back in time? He said I was not to go, but I certainly ~.* (The use of *should* in place of ~ indicates either future in the past, or a conditional statement, with an *if*-clause expressed or understood): *I told him that I should see him the next day. I should have bought it if I had had enough money.* **2** (used with the second and third persons to form a future or conditional statement expressing the speaker's will or intention; with stress on ~, *should,* this expresses obligation or compulsion; without special stress on ~, *should,* it expresses a promise or a threat): *You say you will not do it, but I say you ~ do it. He says he won't go, but I say he ~. You ~ not catch me so easily next time. If you work well, you ~ have higher wages.* **3** (used with all persons to form statements or questions expressing the ideas of duty, command, obligation, conditional duty, and (in the *neg*) prohibition): *S~ I* (= Do you want me to) *open the window? S~ the boy* (= Do you want the boy to) *wait?* (Note that *Will I/he* is not used here, but that *'Would you like us/him to',* is the usu equivalent.) *I asked the man whether the boy should wait. You ~ not have it; it's mine! You should* (= ought to) *have been more careful. He shouldn't* (= oughtn't to) *do things like that.* **4** (used with all persons in clauses expressing purpose, equivalent, to *may* or *might,* thus forming a subjunctive equivalent): *I lent him the book so that he should study the subject.* **5** (used with all persons as a subjunctive equivalent): *I'm anxious that it ~/should be done at once. It is surprising that he should be so foolish.* **6** (in reported speech) ~, *should* are used when reporting the first person to other persons (e g *He said: 'I ~ do it'—he said he should do it,* but *will, would* are now commoner), or when reporting from other persons to the first person (e g *He said to me: 'You will succeed'—he told me that I should succeed*). **7** (*should* is used after *how, why,* and (occasionally) other interrogative words): *How should I know? Why should you/he think that?* **8** (*should* is used to express probability or expectation): *They should be there by now, I think,* i e I expect they are there; they are probably there.

shallop /ˈʃæləp/ *n* [C] light, open boat.

shal·lot /ʃəˈlot/ *n* sort of small onion with cloves like, but not so strong-tasting as, those of garlic.

shal·low /ˈʃæləʊ/ *adj* of little depth: *~ water; a ~ saucer/dish;* (fig) not earnest, sound or serious: *a ~ argument; ~ talk.* □ *n* (often *pl*) ~ place in a river or in the sea; shoal. □ *vi* become ~.

sha·lom /ʃæˈlom/ *int* (Hebrew word) (used as a greeting and on parting) Peace!

shalt /ʃælt/ ⇨ shall.

sham /ʃæm/ *vi,vt* (-mm-) [VP2A,D,6A] pretend to be; simulate: *He ~med dead/death. He's only ~ming.* □ *n* **1** person who ~s: sth intended to deceive: *His love was a mere ~; what he really wanted was her money. He's a ~,* an impostor. **2** [U] pretence: *What he says is all ~.* □ *adj* false; pretended: *~ piety; a ~ battle* (as in military training); ˈ~-ˌ*Tudor,* imitating the Tudor style of architecture.

shamble /ˈʃæmbl/ *vi* [VP2A,C] walk unsteadily as if unable to lift the feet properly: *The old man ~d up to me.* □ *n* shambling walk.

shambles /ˈʃæmblz/ *n* (*sing* construction) **1** scene of bloodshed: *The place became a ~.* **2** (loose use) scene of muddle or confusion (with no implication of bloodshed); devastated place: *His flat is a complete ~. He made a ~ of the task,* failed completely.

shame /ʃeɪm/ *n* [U] **1** distressed feeling, loss of self-respect, caused by wrong, dishonourable or foolish behaviour, failure, etc (of oneself, one's family, etc): *feel ~ at having told a lie/at failing in an examination; hang one's head for ~. To my ~, I must confess that....* ˈ**~·faced** *adj* showing ~; looking distressed through ~. Hence, ˈ**~-faced·ly** /ˈʃeɪmfeɪstlɪ/ *adv* ˈ**~-making** *adj* (colloq) causing a feeling of ~. **2** capacity for experiencing ~: *He has no ~/is quite without ~/is lost to ~.* ***For ~!*** an appeal to sb not to disregard this feeling (used as a reproof to sb who does wrong and does not show ~). **3** [U] dishonour. ***bring ~ on sb/oneself,*** dishonour sb/myself. ***cry ~ on sb,*** say that he is disgraceful, ought to be ashamed of himself. ***put sb to ~,*** disgrace him (e g by showing superior qualities). ***S~ on you!*** You should be ashamed of yourself! **4** (with *indef art,* but not *pl*) sth unworthy; sth that causes ~; sth or sb that is wrong or regrettable: *What a ~ to deceive the girl! It's a ~ to take the money for doing such easy work. He's a ~ to his family.* □ *vt* **1** [VP6A] cause ~ to; cause sb to feel ~; bring disgrace on: *~ one's family.* **2** [VP14] ***~ sb into/out of doing sth,*** frighten or force (sb to do/not to do sth) by ~: *~ a man into apologizing.* **~·ful** /-fl/ *adj* causing or bringing ~: *~ful conduct.* **~·fully** /-flɪ/ *adv* **~·less** *adj* without ~; immodest: *The ~less hussy had nothing on.* **~-less·ly** *adv* **~·less·ness** *n*

shammy /ˈʃæmɪ/ *n* ˈ**~ (leather),** ⇨ chamois.

sham·poo /ʃæmˈpu/ *n* [C,U] (special soap, liquid, powder, etc for a) washing of the hair: *give sb a ~; a ~ and set.* □ *vt* wash (the hair of the head).

sham·rock /ˈʃæmrok/ *n* clover-like plant with (usu) three leaves on each stem (serving as the national emblem of Ireland).

shandy /ˈʃændɪ/ *n* [U] (also ˈ~ ˈ*gaff* /ˈgæf/) mixed drink of beer and ginger-beer or lemonade.

shang·hai /ʃæŋˈhaɪ/ *vt* (sl) make (a man) unconscious (with drink or drugs) and then carry him off to be a seaman on an outgoing ship.

shank /ʃæŋk/ *n* **1** leg, esp the part between the knee and the ankle; shin-bone. ***go on ~s's mare/pony,*** (prov) on one's own legs (not riding a horse, etc). **2** straight, slender part of an anchor, key, spoon, etc; smooth part of the stem of a screw.

shan't /ʃɑnt *US:* ʃænt/ = shall not.

shan·tung /ʃænˈtʌŋ/ *n* [U] kind of heavy silk, usu undyed.

shanty[1] /ˈʃæntɪ/ *n* [C] (*pl* -ties) poorly made hut, shed or cabin. ˈ**~-town** *n* slum area of a town, or on the outskirts of a town, consisting of huts or shanties.

shanty[2] /ˈʃæntɪ/ *n* (*pl* -ties) = chanty.

shape[1] /ʃeɪp/ *n* **1** [C,U] outer form; total effect produced by the outlines of sth: *There were clouds of different ~s. The garden is in the ~ of a* *square/oblong/crescent. What's the* ~ *of his nose? That hat hasn't much* ~*/has a queer* ~. **get/put sth into** ~**,** give definite form to: arrange in an orderly way: *get/put one's ideas into* ~. **give** ~ **to,** express (clearly): *He has some difficulty in giving* ~ *to his ideas.* **knock sth into/ out of** ~**,** put sth into/out of the right ~. **take** ~**,** become definite in form or outline: *The new building is beginning to take* ~, One begins to see what the final ~ will be. **take** ~ **in,** find expression in: *His intentions took* ~ *in action,* were realized in action. **in** ~**,** in form, outline or appearance: *What a fat fellow! He's like a barrel in* ~*! He looks like a devil/monster in human* ~. **2** sort, description: *I've had no proposals from him in any* ~ *or form,* none of any sort. **3** condition: *Her affairs are in good* ~, are satisfactory. *Ali is in good* ~ *for his forthcoming fight,* is physically fit. **4** [C] sth indistinctly seen; vague form; apparition: *Two* ~*s could be discerned in the darkness. A huge* ~ *loomed up through the fog.* **5** [C] pattern or mould on which sth is given ~, e g a block on which hats are made.

shape² /ʃeɪp/ *vt,vi* **1** [VP6A,15A] give a shape or form to: ~ *a pot on a wheel;* ~ *clay into an urn,* on a potter's wheel or lathe; ~ (= direct) *one's course for home; (pp)* ~*d like a pear,* having the shape of a pear. **2** [VP2A,C] take shape; give signs of future shape or development: *Our plans are shaping well,* giving promise of success. *The boy is shaping satisfactorily,* making good progress. **~·less** *adj* **~·less·ly** *adv* **~·less·ness** *n*

shape·ly /ˈʃeɪplɪ/ *adj* **(-ier, -iest)** (esp of a person's form, or of limbs) well-formed; having a pleasing shape: *a* ~ *pair of legs.*

shard /ʃɑd/ *n* (old use, but still used by gardeners and archaeologists for a) piece of broken earthenware, e g one placed over the hole in a flower-pot.

share¹ /ʃeə(r)/ *n* **1** [C] part or division which sb has in, receives from, or gives to, a stock held by several or many persons, or which he contributes to a fund, expenses, etc: *Please let me take a* ~ *in the expenses,* pay sth towards them. *We shall all have a* ~ *in the profits.* **go** ~**s (with sb) (in sth),** divide (profits, costs, etc) with others; become part owner (with others); pay (a part of an expense): *Let me go* ~*s with you in the taxi fare.* **ˈ~-cropper** *n* (in some countries, not in GB) tenant farmer who pays a ~ of his crop as rent to the owner of the land. **2** [U] part taken or received by sb in an action, undertaking, etc, e g of responsibility, blame: *What* ~ *had he in their success? You must take your* ~ *of the blame. You're not taking much* ~ *in the conversation,* are saying little. **3** [C] one of the equal parts into which the capital of a company is divided, entitling the holder of the ~ to a proportion of the profits: *hold 500* ~*s in a shipping company; £1* ~*s are now worth £1.75.* **ˈordinary** ~**,** on which dividends are paid according to profits after payments on preference ~s. **ˈpreference** ~**,** one on which a fixed dividend is guaranteed before payments are made on others. **ˈ~ certificate,** document proving ownership of ~s. **ˈ~-holder** *n* owner of (business) ~s. **ˈ~ index** *n* number used to show how ~ prices have fluctuated, based on prices of ~s selected for this purpose: *The Financial Times* ~ *index went up/down five points yesterday.* □ *vt,vi* **1** [VP6A,14,15B] ~ **sth (out) (among/ between),** give a ~ of to others; divide and distribute: ~ *(out) £100 among five men,* e g by giving them £20 each; ~ *the sweets between you.* ~ **sth with sb,** give part to sb else: *He would* ~ *his last pound with me.* **ˈ~-out** *n* distribution. **2** [VP6A] ~ **(with),** have or use (with); have in common: *He hated having to* ~ *the hotel bedroom with a stranger.* **3** [VP6A,3A] ~ **(in) sth,** have a ~: *I will* ~ *(in) the cost with you. She* ~*s (in) my troubles as well as (in) my joys.* ~ **and** ~ **alike,** have equal ~s with others in the use, enjoyment, expense, etc of sth.

share² /ʃeə(r)/ *n* blade of a plough.

shark /ʃɑk/ *n* **1** sea-fish, some kinds of which are large and dangerous to bathers, etc. ⇨ the illus at sea. **ˈ~-skin** *n* textile fabric with a smooth and shiny surface, used for outer clothing: *a* ~*-skin jacket/suit.* **2** (sl) swindler; usurer.

sharp /ʃɑp/ *adj* **(-er, -est) 1** with a fine cutting edge; not blunt: *a* ~ *knife;* with a fine point, able to make holes: *a* ~ *pin/needle.* **2** well-defined; clear-cut; distinct: *a* ~ *outline; a* ~ *image,* (in photography) one with clear contrasts between light and shade. **3** (of curves, slopes, bends) abrupt; changing direction quickly: *a* ~ *bend in the road; a* ~ *turn to the left;* ˈ~-ˈ*featured,* (of a person) having angular features. **4** (of sounds) shrill; piercing: *a* ~ *cry of distress.* **5** quickly aware of things; acute: ~ *eyes/ears; a* ~ *intelligence; a* ~ *sense of smell; keep a* ~ *look-out; a* ~ *child;* ~ *at arithmetic.* **ˈ~-shooter** *n* man skilled at shooting with a rifle, placed where accurate shooting (in war) is required. Hence, **ˈ~-ˈeyed/-ˈsighted/-ˈwitted** *adjj* **6** (of feelings, taste) producing a physical sensation like cutting or pricking: *a* ~ *pain; a* ~ *flavour; a* ~ *frost.* **7** harsh; severe: ~ *words; a* ~ *rebuke; a* ~ *tongue,* of a person who speaks sarcastically, bitterly. **8** quick; brisk; lively: *go for a* ~ *walk; a* ~ *struggle/contest. That was* ~ *work,* was finished or done quickly and energetically. **9** quick to take advantage; unscrupulous: *a* ~ *lawyer. He was too* ~ *for me,* He got the better of me by being unscrupulous. ~ **practice,** business dealings that are not altogether honest. **10** (music) above the normal pitch; (of a note) raised half a tone in pitch: *C* ~, ⇨ flat²(6). ⇨ the illus at notation. □ *n* (music) ~ note; the symbol # used to indicate a ~ note. □ *adv* **1** punctually: *at seven (o'clock)* ~. **2** suddenly; abruptly: *turn* ~ *to the left.* **3** (music) above the true pitch: *sing* ~. **4 look** ~**,** waste no time; hurry. **5** **ˈ~-set** *adj* hungry. **~en** /ˈʃɑpən/ *vt,vi* [VP6A,2A] make or become ~: ~*en a pencil. My razor needs* ~*ening. The walk has* ~*ened my appetite.* **~·ener** /ˈʃɑpnə(r)/ *n* sth that ~ens: *a* ˈ*pencil-*~*ener; a* ˈ*knife-*~*ener.* **~er** *n* swindler, esp **(ˈcard-~er)** person who makes a living by cheating at cards. **~·ly** *adv* **~·ness** *n*

shat·ter /ˈʃætə(r)/ *vt,vi* [VP6A,2A] break suddenly and violently into small pieces: *The explosion* ~*ed every window in the building. Our hopes were* ~*ed. What a nerve-*~*ing noise!* e g that of pneumatic drills or jet engines.

shave /ʃeɪv/ *vt,vi* (*pt,pp* ~d or, chiefly as *adj,* ~n /ˈʃeɪvn/) **1** [VP6A,2A,15B] cut (hair) off the chin, etc with a razor: *Do you* ~ *yourself or go to the barber's? He has* ~*d off his beard. He doesn't* ~ *every day.* **ˈshaving-brush** *n* brush for spreading lather over the face before shaving. **2** [VP15B] ~ **sth off,** pare off (a thin layer, etc). **3** [VP6A,15A] pass very close to, almost but not touching: *The* *bus just* ~*d me by an inch.* **4** **~n** (*pp* as *adj*) **'clean-'~n, 'well-'~n,** having been ~d clean, well. □ *n* [C] **1** shaving (of the face): *A sharp razor gives a good* ~. *How much does a* ~ *cost?* **2** close approach without touching. (only in) ***a close/narrow*** **~,** a narrow escape from injury, danger, etc. **shaver** *n* **1** (**'dry-)shaver,** razor with an electric motor, operated from the mains or by a battery. **2** (joc, usu *young shaver*) lad, youngster. **shav·ings** *n pl* thin parings of wood ~d off (esp with a plane): *The floor of the carpenter's shop was covered with shavings.*

Shav·ian /'ʃeɪvɪən/ *adj, n* (in the manner) (devotee) of G B Shaw /ʃɔ/, 1856—1950, Irish dramatist and critic.

shawl /ʃɔl/ *n* [C] large (usu square or oblong) piece of material worn about the shoulders or head of a woman, or wrapped round a baby.

shay /ʃeɪ/ *n* **1** (old use, or, today, colloq and hum) chaise. **2** (US colloq) light, horse-drawn carriage with two wheels and one seat.

she /ʃi/ *pron* (⇨ her) **1** female person, etc already referred to or implied: *My sister says she is going for a walk.* **2** (*pref*) female: *a 'she-goat/-ass, etc; This cat's a she, not a he.*

sheaf /ʃif/ *n* (*pl* sheaves /ʃivz/) **1** bundle of corn, barley, etc stalks tied together after reaping. **2** bundle of papers, arrows, etc laid lengthwise and tied together.

shear /ʃɪə(r)/ *vt* (*pt*, ~ed, *pp* shorn /ʃɔn/ or ~ed) [VP6A] cut the wool off (a sheep) with shears; (fig) strip bare of; deprive of: *They'll be* ~*ing* (*the sheep*) *next week.* **shorn of,** having lost completely: *The gambler came home shorn of his money.*

shears /ʃɪəz/ *n pl* (also ***a pair of*** **~**) large cutting instrument shaped like scissors, used for shearing sheep, cutting cloth, etc. ⇨ the illus at tool.

sheath /ʃiθ/ *n* (*pl* ~s /ʃiðz/) **1** cover for the blade of a weapon or tool: *Put the dagger back in its* ~. **'~-knife** *n* knife with a fixed blade, that fits into a ~. **2** ~-like cover (of tissue, skin, etc) fitting over part of an animal or plant (e g the *'wing-*~ of some insects). **(protective) ~,** contraceptive device used on the penis. **3** (attrib; dressmaking) close-fitting: *a* ~ *corset/gown.*

sheathe /ʃið/ *vt* [VP6A] **1** put into a sheath: ~ *the sword*, stop fighting. **2** protect with a casing or covering: ~ *a ship's bottom with copper.* **sheath·ing** *n* protective layer of boards, metal plates, etc e g on parts of a building, the underpart of a ship's hull.

sheaves /ʃivz/ ⇨ sheaf.

she·bang /ʃə'bæŋ/ *n* (US sl, usu *the whole* ~) collection of facts or things; situation, organization.

she·been /ʃə'bin/ *n* unlicensed public house (esp in Ireland.

shed[1] /ʃed/ *n* building, roughly made structure, used for storing things (*'tool-*~, *'wood-*~, *'coal-*~, *etc*), for sheltering animals (*'cattle-*~), vehicles, etc (*'engine-*~, *'bicycle-*~).

shed[2] /ʃed/ *vt* (*pt,pp* ~; -dd-) [VP6A] **1** let (leaves, etc) fall; let come off: *Trees* ~ *their leaves and flowers* ~ *their petals. Some kinds of deer* ~ *their horns.* **~ *blood,*** **(a)** be wounded or killed: ~ *one's blood for one's country.* **(b)** cause the blood of others to flow: *The wicked ruler* ~ *rivers of blood.* Hence, **'blood-~** *n* **~ *tears,*** weep. **2** throw or take off; get rid of: *People on the beach began to* ~ *their clothes as it got hotter and hotter.* **3** spread or send out: *a fire that* ~*s warmth; a woman who* ~*s happiness around; a lamp that* ~*s a soft light.* **~ *light on,*** (fig) make clear to the mind. **4** **'load-~ding,** ⇨ load[1](3).

she'd /ʃid/ = *she had* or *she would.*

sheen /ʃin/ *n* [U] brightness; shiny quality: *the* ~ *of silk. That girl's hair has a* ~ *like gold.*

sheep /ʃip/ *n* (*pl* unchanged) grass-eating animal kept for its flesh as food (mutton) and its wool. ⇨ the illus at domestic. ⇨ ewe, lamb and ram. ***separate the* ~ *from the goats,*** good and bad persons. ⇨ Matt 25: 33. ***cast/make* ~*'s eyes at,*** look at in an amorous but foolish way. ***a wolf in* ~*'s clothing,*** a wicked man who pretends to be good. **'black '~,** ⇨ black(4). ***as well be hanged for a* ~ *as a lamb,*** commit a big crime rather than a small one if the punishment is the same. **'~-dog** *n* dog trained to help a shepherd to look after ~. **'~-fold** *n* enclosure for ~. **'~-run** *n* tract of land (esp in Australia) on which ~ are pastured. **'~-skin** *n* **(a)** rug of a ~'s skin with the wool on it; garment made of two or more such skins. **(b)** leather of ~'s skin used in book-binding, etc. **(c)** parchment made from such skin; (esp US) diploma written on such parchment. **'~·ish** /-ɪʃ/ *adj* **1** awkwardly self-conscious: *a* ~*ish-looking boy.* **2** (feeling) foolish or embarrassed by consciousness of a fault. **~·ish·ly** *adv* **~·ish·ness** *n*

sheer[1] /ʃɪə(r)/ *adj* **1** complete; thorough; absolute: ~ *nonsense; a* ~ *waste of time; by* ~ *chance.* **2** (of textiles, etc) finely woven and almost transparent: *stockings of* ~ *nylon.* **3** without a slope; (almost) perpendicular; *a* ~ *drop of 50 feet; a* ~ *rock.* □ *adv* straight up or down; *a cliff that rises* ~ *from the beach. He fell 500 feet* ~.

sheer[2] /ʃɪə(r)/ *vi* [VP2C] **1** **~ *away/off,*** (esp of a ship) deviate from course. **2** **~ *off,*** (colloq) go away (from sb one dislikes, sb by whom one had been offended).

sheet[1] /ʃit/ *n* [C] **1** large rectangular piece of linen or cotton cloth, as used in pairs for sleeping between: *put clean* ~*s on the bed.* **2** broad, flat piece (of some thin material): *a* ~ *of glass/tin/wrapping-paper/note-paper, etc;* ~ *copper/iron, etc,* rolled or hammered into thin ~s; ~ *music*, published in ~s, not in book form. *The book is in* ~*s*, i e in ~s of paper ready for binding. **3** wide expanse (of water, ice, snow, flame, etc): *The rain came down in* ~*s*, very heavily. **'~-lightning** *n* lightning that comes in sheet-like flashes of diffused brightness (not in zigzags, etc). **~·ing** *n* [U] material used for making ~s(1).

sheet[2] /ʃit/ *n* cord fastened at the lower corner of a sail to hold it and control the angle at which it is set. ⇨ the illus at sail. **'~-anchor** *n* (usu fig) sth on which one depends for security as a final resort when other things have failed.

sheik(h) /ʃeɪk *US:* ʃik/ *n* Arab chieftain; head of an Arab village, tribe, etc. **~·dom** /-dəm/ *n*

shekel /'ʃekl/ *n* ancient silver coin used by the Jews; (*pl*) money, riches.

shel·drake /'ʃel-dreɪk/ *n* (kinds of) fish-eating wild duck with brightly coloured feathers.

shelf /ʃelf/ *n* (*pl* shelves /ʃelvz/) **1** flat, rectangular piece of wood, metal, glass or other material, fastened at right angles to a wall or in a cupboard, bookcase, cabinet, etc. ***on the* ~, (a)** put aside as done with, e g of a person too old to continue working. **(b)** (colloq, of a woman) unmarried and considered as being unlikely to be asked to marry. **2** ~-like projection of rock on a cliff face, etc (as used by rock-climbers).

shell /ʃel/ *n* [C] **1** hard outer covering of bird's eggs, nuts (e g walnuts, coconuts), some seeds (e g peas) and fruits, and of some animals (e g oysters, lobsters, snails) or parts of them. ⇨ the illus at mollusc. ***go/retire into/come out of one's ~,*** become/cease to be shy, reserved, uncommunicative. **ˋ~-fish** *n* kinds of molluscs (oysters, etc) and crustaceans (crabs, shrimps, etc) having ~s. **2** walls, outer structure, of an unfinished building, ship, etc or of one of which the contents have been destroyed (e g by fire): *Only the ~ of the factory was left when the fire had been extinguished.* **3** (US = *cartridge*) metal case filled with explosive, to be fired from a large gun. Cf *cartridge* for rifles, shot-guns. **ˋ~-proof** *adj* so thickly or strongly built that a ~ cannot pierce it. **ˋ~-shock** *n* nervous or mental disorder caused by the noise and blast of bursting ~s. **4** light racing-boat propelled by oarsmen. □ *vt,vi* **1** [VP6A] take out of a ~(1) (cf US *shuck*): *It's as easy as ~ing peas,* is very easy. *These peas ~ easily,* = are easily ~ed. **2** [VP6A] fire ~s(3) at: *~ the enemy's trenches.* **3** ***~ out,*** [VP15B,2C] (colloq) pay up (money, a required sum): *I shall be expected to ~ out (the money) for the party.*

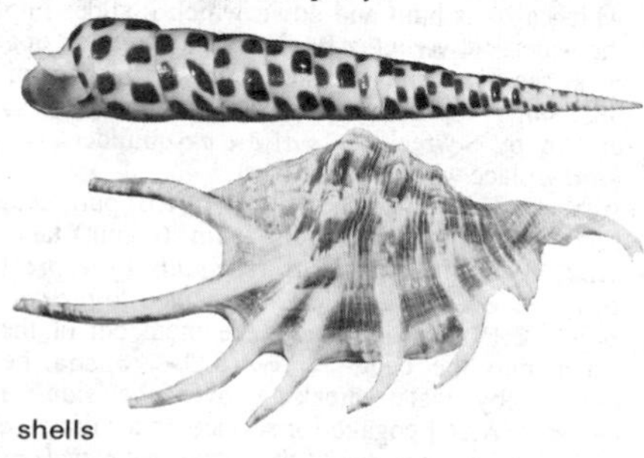

shells

she'll /ʃil/ = *she will, she shall.*

shel·lac /ʃəˋlæk/ *n* [U] resinous substance in the form of thin sheets used in making varnish and (formerly) gramophone records. □ *vt* varnish with ~.

shel·ter /ˋʃeltə(r)/ *n* **1** [U] condition of being kept safe, e g from rain, danger: *take ~ from the rain,* e g under a tree; *get under ~,* e g when bombs are dropping during an air raid. **2** [C] sth that gives safety or protection, esp a hut, etc built to keep off wind and rain: *a ˋbus ~,* in which people wait for buses; *a taxi-drivers' ~,* one where they wait until called by phone, etc; *an ˋair-raid ~.* □ *vt,vi* **1** [VP6A,14] ***~ sb/sth from,*** give ~ to; protect: *trees that ~ a house from cold winds; ~* (= hide, protect) *an escaped prisoner; dig trenches to ~ the men from gunfire; ~ sb from blame; ~ed trades,* those which (like building and inland transport) are not exposed to foreign competition. **2** [VP2A,C] take ~: *~ from the rain; ~ under the trees.*

shelve[1] /ʃelv/ *vt* [VP6A] **1** put (books, etc) on a shelf. **2** (fig, of problems, plans, etc) postpone dealing with; defer consideration of. **3** cease to employ (a person).

shelve[2] /ʃelv/ *vi* [VP2A,C] (of land) slope gently: *The shore ~s down to the sea.*

shelves /ʃelvz/ *pl* of shelf.

shep·herd /ˋʃepəd/ *n* man who takes care of sheep. **the Good S~,** Jesus Christ. **~'s pie,** [U] minced meat baked under mashed potatoes. **~'s plaid,** small black and white check pattern in cloth. □ *vt* [VP6A,15A] take care of; guide or direct (people) like sheep: *The passengers were ~ed across the tarmac to the airliner.* **ˋ~·ess** /-es/ *n* woman ~ (esp as idealized in pastoral poetry).

Shera·ton /ˋʃerətən/ *n* [U] 18th-century style of furniture (in GB): (attrib) *~ chairs.*

sher·bet /ˋʃɜbət/ *n* [C,U] (glass of) cooling drink of sweetened fruit juices, sometimes effervescent (made from powder); (US) water-ice.

sher·iff /ˋʃerɪf/ *n* **1** (usu **High S~**) chief officer of the Crown in counties and certain cities, with legal and ceremonial duties. **2** (US) chief law-enforcing officer of a county.

sherry /ˋʃerɪ/ *n* [U] yellow or brown wine of S Spain; similar kinds of wine from S Africa, Cyprus, etc.

Shet·land /ˋʃetlənd/ *n* (also **the ~s**) group of islands N N E of Scotland. **~ pony,** small, hardy breed. **~ wool,** soft, fine kind spun in the S~s.

shew /ʃəʊ/ ⇨ show.

shib·bol·eth /ˋʃɪbəleθ/ *n* [C] old-fashioned and now generally abandoned expression, custom, etc which was at one time considered to be essential: *the outworn ~s of the past.*

shied /ʃɑɪd/ ⇨ shy[2], shy[3]. **shield** /ʃild/ *n* [C] **1** ⇨ the illus at armour. piece of armous (metal, leather, wood) carried on the arm, to protect the body when fighting; representation of a ~, e g carved on a stone gateway, showing a person's coat of arms. ⇨ arms. **2** (fig) person or thing that protects. **3** (in machinery, etc) protective plate or screen; sth designed to keep out dust, wind, etc. (US *wind~* = GB *windscreen.*) □ *vt* [VP6A,15A] protect; keep safe; save (sb) from punishment or suffering: *~ one's eyes with one's hand; ~ a friend from censure.*

shift[1] /ʃɪft/ *n* **1** change of place or character; substitution of one thing for another: *a ~ in emphasis,* placing the emphasis differently. **2** [C] group of workmen who start work as another group finishes; period for which such a group works: *on the day/night ~; an eight-hour ~; working in ~s.* **3** dodge, trick, scheme, way of evading a difficulty, of getting sth: *resort to dubious ~s in order to get some money. As a last desperate ~, he pawned his wife's wedding ring.* ***make ~ (with sth/to do sth),*** manage or contrive, be able somehow or other: *We must make ~ with the money we have. He must make ~ without help.* ⇨ *make~* at make[1](29). **4** woman's narrow dress without a waistline; (old use) chemise. **5** (motoring) mechanism for gear change: *Do you prefer a manual ~ or automatic no-pedal control?* **~·less** *adj* without ability to find ways of doing things; unable to get on in life.

shift[2] /ʃɪft/ *vt,vi* **1** [VP6A,14,15A,2A,C] ***~ sth (from/to),*** change position or direction; transfer: *~ a burden from one shoulder to the other; ~ the blame (on) to sb else. Will you help me to ~ the furniture about/round, please? The wind has ~ed to the north. The cargo has ~ed,* has been shaken out of place by the movement of the ship. *Don't try to ~ the responsibility on to me.* ***~ one's ground,*** take up a new position, approach the subject in a different way, during an argument. **2** (motoring) change (gears): *~ into second/third gear.* **3** *~ for oneself,* manage as best one can (to make a livelihood, get sth done) without help: *When their father died the children had to ~ for themselves.* **shifty** *adj* (-ier, -iest) untrustworthy; deceitful; not straightforward: *a ~y customer; ~y behaviour; ~y eyes.* **~·ily** /-əlɪ/ *adv* **~i·ness** *n*

shil·ling /ˈʃɪlɪŋ/ *n* **1** (until 1971) British coin with the value of twelve pennies, one-twentieth of a pound: *a ˋ~'s-worth,* as much or as many as a ~ will buy. ⇨ App 4. **2** basic monetary unit of Kenya, Uganda and Tanzania, equal to 100 cents.

shilly-shally /ˈʃɪlɪ ˈʃælɪ/ *vi* [VP2A] be unable to make up one's mind; be undecided. □ *n* [U] indecision.

shim·mer /ˈʃɪmə(r)/ *vi* [VP2A,C], *n* [U] (shine with a) wavering soft or faint light: *moonlight ~ing on the lake; the ~ of pearls.*

shin /ʃɪn/ *n* front part of the leg below the knee. ⇨ the illus at **leg**. **ˋ~-guard** *n* pad worn on the ~ when playing football. **ˋ~-bone** *n* tibia. ⇨ the illus at **skeleton**. □ *vi* (-nn-) *~ up,* climb up (using arms and legs to grip sth): *~ up a tree.*

shin·dig /ˈʃɪndɪg/ *n* (sl) **1** lively and noisy party. **2** (= *shindy*) brawl.

shindy /ˈʃɪndɪ/ *n* [C] (*pl* -dies) (colloq) brawl; noisy disturbance: *kick up a ~.*

shine /ʃɑɪn/ *vi,vt* (*pt,pp* **shone** /ʃɒn *US:* ʃəʊn/ but ⇨ 2 below) **1** [VP2A,C] give out or reflect light; be bright (liter or fig); excel in some way: *The moon is shining. The sun shone out,* suddenly began to ~ (as clouds moved). *His face shone with excitement. He does not ~ in conversation,* is not a good talker. *I don't ~ at tennis.* **2** [VP6A] (colloq, and with *pp* **~d**) polish (which is more usu); make bright: *~ shoes. Have you ~d your shoes/the brass?* □ *n* **1** (*sing* only) polish; brightness: *Give your shoes a good ~. How can I take the ~ out of the seat of my trousers?* **2** [U] ***come rain or ~,*** whatever the weather may be; (fig) whatever may happen. **shiny** *adj* (-ier, -iest) polished; rubbed bright: *a shiny coat,* one with the nap rubbed off (so that the surface ~s).

shingle[1] /ˈʃɪŋgl/ *n* [U] small, rounded pebbles on the seashore. **shin·gly** /ˈʃɪŋglɪ/ *adj* of ~: *I prefer a sandy beach to a shingly beach.*

shingle[2] /ˈʃɪŋgl/ *n* [C] **1** small, flat square or oblong piece of wood used (like tiles and slates) on roofs, spires and walls. **2** (US colloq) small, wooden signboard (used by lawyers, dentists, etc): *put up one's ~,* set up for the first time, e g as a doctor. □ *vt* cover (a roof, etc) with ~s: *a ~d church spire.*

shingle[3] /ˈʃɪŋgl/ *vt* [VP6A] cut (a woman's hair) so that it is short at the back like a man's but longer at the sides. □ *n* this kind of haircut.

shingles /ˈʃɪŋglz/ *n* (with *sing v*) skin disease forming a band of inflamed spots (often round the waist).

ship[1] /ʃɪp/ *n* **1** sea-going vessel of considerable size: *a ˋsailing-~; a ˋmerchant-~; a ˋwar~,* etc; *take ~,* go on board a ~; the ~'s company, the entire crew; *the ~'s articles,* the terms on which seamen are engaged; *the ~'s papers,* the documents showing ownership, nationality, nature of the cargo, etc. ***when my ~ comes in/home,*** when I have made my fortune. ***on ˋ~-board,*** on board ~. **2** (colloq) spacecraft; (US colloq) aircraft. **3** (compounds) **ˋ~-breaker** *n* contractor who buys and breaks up old ~s (for scrap). **ˋ~-broker** *n* agent of a shipping company who does a ~'s business in port; one who buys, sells and charters ~s; agent for marine insurance. **ˋ~-builder** *n* one whose business is building ~s. Hence, **ˋ~-building** *n*: *ˋ~building yard,* = ~yard. **ˋ~('s) biscuit,** hard, coarse biscuit used, in former times, during long voyages. **ˋ~-canal** *n* canal large enough for sea-going vessels. **ˋ~'s-chandler** *n* one who deals in equipment for ~s. **ˋ~·load** *n* as much cargo, or as many passengers, as a ~ can carry. **ˋ~·mate** *n* fellow sailor; person belonging to the same ~ as another: *Harry and I were ~mates in 1962.* **ˋ~·owner** *n* person who owns a ~ or ~s, or shares in a shipping company. **ˋ~·shape** *adj* tidy; in good order. □ *adv* in a ~shape manner. **ˋ~-way** *n* sloping structure on which a ~ is built and down which it slides into the water. **ˋ~·wreck** *n* [U] loss or destruction of a ~ at sea by storm, collision, etc; [C] instance of this: *suffer ~wreck.* □ *vi* causes to suffer ~wreck; destroy by ~wreck. **ˋ~·wright** *n* ~ builder. **ˋ~-yard** *n* place where ~s are built.

ship[2] /ʃɪp/ *vt,vi* (-pp-) **1** [VP6A,15A,B] put, take, send, in a ship: *~ gold to India;* (comm) take, send, by train, road, etc: *~ goods by express train.* *~ off,* send: *~ off young men to the colonies.* **2** [VP6A] *~ oars,* take them out of the water into the boat. ***~ water, ~ a sea,*** be flooded by water breaking over the side. **3** [VP6A,15A,2C] engage for service on a ship: *~ a crew for a voyage round the world. He ~ped* (= took service) *as a steward on an Atlantic liner.* **~·ment** *n* [U] putting of goods, etc on a ship; [C] quantity of goods ~ped. **~·per** *n* person who arranges for goods to be ~ped. **~·ping** *n* [U] all the ships of a country, part, etc. **ˋ~·ping-agent** *n* shipowner's representative at a port. **ˋ~-ping-office** *n* ~ping-agent's office; office where seamen are engaged.

shire /ʃɑɪə(r)/ *n* [C] county (now chiefly used as a suffix in the names of certain counties, and usu pronounced /-ʃə(r)/): *Hampshire, Yorkshire.* ⇨ App 6. **the ~s,** certain midland counties of England and parts of these well known for fox-hunting. **ˋ~ horse,** powerful breed of horse used for pulling carts and wagons.

shirk /ʃɜk/ *vt,vi* [VP6A,D,2A] avoid, try to escape

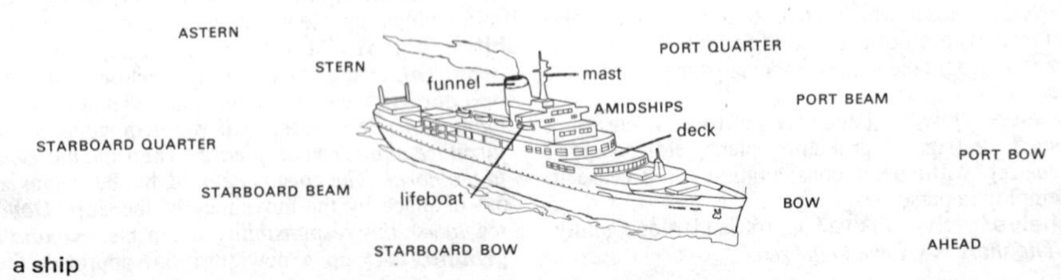

a ship

(doing sth, responsibility, duty, etc): ~ *going to the office;* ~ *school. He's* ~*ing.* **~er** *n*

shirt /ʃɜt/ *n* **1** man's loose-fitting garment for the upper part of the body (of cotton, linen, silk, etc) usu worn under a jacket, with long sleeves or (ˋ*sports* ~) half sleeves. ***in one's* ˋ*~-sleeves,*** not wearing a jacket or coat. ***keep one's ~ on,*** (sl) keep one's temper. ***put one's ~ on*** (a horse, etc), bet all one has on. **ˋ~-front** *n* usu stiffened and starched breast of a white ~. **2** (esp US; also ˋ~-*waister*) woman's plain blouse (worn with a skirt). **~·ing** *n* material for making ~s. **shirty** *adj* (-ier, -iest) (sl) ill-tempered.

shish kebab /ˈʃɪʃ kəˋbæb *US:* ˋʃɪʃ kəˋbæb/ *n* dish of pieces of meat roasted (and served) on skewers.

shit /ʃɪt/ (⚠, not in polite use) *n* [U] **1** excrement. **2** (sl) hashish. **3** (contemptuous for a) person: *You big ~!* □ *vi* (-tt-) empty the bowels of excrement. ***~ on sb,*** (vulg sl) report on him, esp to the police. □ *int* ⚠ (vulg) Bother! Rubbish!

shiver[1] /ˋʃɪvə(r)/ *vi* [VP2A,C] tremble, esp from cold or fear: *~ing all over with cold; ~ing like a leaf.* □ *n* **1** trembling that cannot be controlled: *The sight sent cold ~s down my back. A ~ ran down her back.* **2** (*pl*) ***get/have/give sb the ~s,*** (colloq) get/give sb ~ing movements, a feeling of fear or horror. **~y** *adj* inclined to ~; having or causing a feeling of cold, fear, horror.

shiver[2] /ˋʃɪvə(r)/ *n* (usu *pl*) one of the many small pieces into which sth is broken: *break sth to ~s; burst into ~s.* □ *vt,vi* [VP15A,2C] break into ~s.

shoal[1] /ʃəʊl/ *n* [C] great number of fish swimming together; great number (of people, things): *a ~ of herring; swimming in ~s.* □ *vi* (of fish) form ~s.

shoal[2] /ʃəʊl/ *n* [C] shallow place in the sea, esp where there are sandbanks; (*pl;* fig) hidden dangers. □ *vi* [VP2A] become shallow(er).

shock[1] /ʃok/ *n* **1** [C] violent blow or shaking (e g as caused by a collision or explosion): *the ~ of a fall; earthquake ~s.* **ˋ~ absorber** *n* kinds of device fitted to motor-vehicles, aircraft, etc to lessen ~s and add to the cushioning effects of tyres, springs, etc. **ˋ~ tactics,** use of massed forces to attack (in war). **ˋ~ troops,** troops specially trained for violent assaults. **ˋ~-brigade, ˋ~-workers,** (esp in USSR) body of workers engaged in specially arduous work. **ˋ~ wave,** region of intensely high air pressure caused by an atomic explosion or an aircraft moving at supersonic speed. **2** [C] effect caused by the passage of an electric current through the body: *If you touch that live wire you'll get a ~.* **3** [C] sudden and violent disturbance of the feelings or the nervous system (caused by bad news, severe injury, etc); [U] condition caused by such a disturbance: *The news of her mother's death was a terrible ~ to her. The stock market quickly recovered from the ~ of the election results. It gave me quite a ~ to learn that he had married again. She died of ~ following an operation on the brain.* ⇨ *shell-~* at shell(3). **ˋ~ treatment/therapy,** treatment of (esp mental) disorder by using electric ~s or drugs on the nervous system. □ *vt* [VP6A] cause ~(3) to; fill with surprised disgust, horror, etc: *I was ~ed at the news of her death. He was ~ed to hear his daughter swearing. I'm not easily ~ed, but that book really is obscene.* **~er** *n* **1** person who ~s: *He's a ~er,* a ~ingly bad person. **2** sth that ~s, e g a sensational novel; bad specimen of sth. **~·ing** *adj* **1** very bad or wrong: *~ing behaviour.* **2** causing ~(3): *~ing news,* e g of a flood that causes great loss of life. **3** (colloq) bad: *a ~ing dinner; ~ing handwriting.* □ *adv* (colloq, as an intensive) very: *a ~ing bad cold.* **~·ing·ly** *adv* **1** badly: *You're playing ~ingly.* **2** extremely: *How ~ingly expensive!*

shock[2] /ʃok/ *n* number of sheaves of grain placed together and supporting each other in a field to dry during harvest.

shock[3] /ʃok/ *n* (usu *a ~ of hair*) rough, untidy mass of hair (on sb's head). **ˈ~-ˋheaded** *adj* having such hair.

shod /ʃod/ ⇨ shoe *v.*

shoddy /ˋʃodɪ/ *adj* (-ier, -iest) of poor quality; made to seem better than it is: *~ cloth; a ~ piece of work.* □ *n* [U] (cloth of poor quality, made from) fibre from old cloth, etc.

shoe /ʃu/ *n* **1** (often *a pair of ~s*) outer covering for the foot, esp one which does not reach above the ankle. ⇨ boot: *put on/take off one's ~s.* ***be in/put oneself in another man's ~s,*** occupy, imagine oneself to be in, his position; be in his plight: *I wouldn't be in your ~s for a thousand pounds.* ***know where the ~ pinches,*** understand from one's own experience all about hardships, etc. **2** (compounds) **ˋ~·black** *n* boy or man who polishes ~s of passers-by. **ˋ~·horn** *n* device with a curved blade for getting the heel easily into a ~. **ˋ~·lace** *n* cord for fastening the edges of a shoe's uppers. **ˋ~·string** *n* (US) = ~lace. ***do sth on a ~string,*** do sth (e g start a business) on a very small amount of capital. **ˋ~-leather** *n* leather suitable for making ~s. **ˋ~·maker** *n* person who makes ~s and boots. **ˋ~·making** *n* [U] trade of a ~maker. **3** **(horse-)~** /ˋhɔʃʃu/, metal band nailed to the hoof of a horse: *His horse cast/threw a ~,* lost one. **4** part of a brake that presses against the wheel or drum (of a bicycle, motor-vehicle, etc); any object like a ~ in appearance or use. □ *vt* (*pt,pp* shod /ʃod/) fit with ~s: *well shod for wet weather,* having good ~s able to keep out the wet; *an iron-shod stick,* one with an iron ferrule at the end.

sho·gun /ˋʃəʊgun *US:* -gʌn/ *n* (until 1867) hereditary commander-in-chief of the Japanese army.

shone /ʃon *US:* ʃəʊn/ *pt,pp* of shine.

shoo /ʃu/ *int* cry used for driving away birds, etc. □ *vt* (*pt,pp* ~ed) [VP15B] ***~ sth/sb away/off,*** drive away by making this cry.

shook /ʃʊk/ *pt* of shake.

shoot[1] /ʃut/ *n* [C] **1** new, young growth on a plant or bush: *train the new ~s of a vine.* **2** = chute(1,2). **3** party of people shooting for sport; area of land over which birds, etc are shot: *rent a ~ for the season.*

shoot[2] /ʃut/ *vi,vt* (*pt, pp* shot /ʃot/) **1** [VP2C, 15A,B] move, come, go, send, suddenly or quickly (*out, in, up, forth,* etc): *The snake's tongue shot out. The snake shot its tongue out. Flames were ~ing up from the burning house. The meteor shot across the sky. The horse stumbled and the rider was shot over its head. As the car hit the tree the occupants were shot out. At the half-way mark, Hill shot ahead,* (in a race) came on quickly and passed his competitors. *They shot angry glances at us. Rents have shot up,* (= risen suddenly) *in the last few months. Ben is ~ing up fast,* quickly growing tall. *She shot an angry look at him/shot him an angry look.* ***~ a bolt,*** send a bolt (of a door, etc) into (or out of) its fastening.

~ ***one's bolt,*** do all that one can do. ~ ***dice,*** throw dice. ~ ***rubbish,*** let it slide from a cart, etc (on to a heap or dump). **'~ing 'star,** meteor which burns up as it passes into and through the earth's atmosphere. **2** [VP2A,C] (of plants, bushes) sprout; send out new twigs or branches from a stem: *Rose bushes ~ again after being cut back.* **3** [VP2A,C] (of pain) pass with a stabbing sensation suddenly and swiftly: *The pain shot up his arm. I have a ~ing pain in my left leg.* **4** [VP6A] (of boats) move, be moved, rapidly over, through, etc: *~ the rapids; ~ the bridge,* pass under it rapidly with the current. **5** [VP6A,15A,B,2A,C,4A] aim and fire with a gun or revolver; aim with a bow and send an arrow at; hit with a shell, bullet, arrow, etc; wound or kill (a person, animal, etc) by doing this: *They were ~ing at a target. He ~s well. He shot an arrow from his bow. Can you/Does your gun ~ straight? The soldier was shot* (= executed by ~ing) *for desertion. The police did not ~ to kill,* They used their weapons only to frighten the people (e g by firing over their heads). *He's in Africa ~ing lions. He neither rides, ~s nor fishes,* does not take part in these country sports. *He fell like a shot rabbit,* like a rabbit that had been shot. ~ ***away,*** (more usu *fire away*) continue ~ing. ~ ***sth away,*** (more usu *fire sth away*) get rid of by ~ing: *~ away all one's ammunition.* ~ ***sth down,*** bring to the ground by ~ing: *The bomber was shot down in flames.* ~ ***sth off,*** sever by ~ing: *He had his arm shot off.* ~ ***a covert/an estate, etc,*** ~ the game in it. ~ ***a place up,*** (US sl) terrorize (a town, district, etc) by going through it and shooting at random, firing at houses, etc. **'~ing-box** *n* house used by sportsmen in the ~ing season (e g one on moorlands). **'~ing-brake** *n* (former times) large horse-drawn open carriage used by sportsmen (for carrying equipment, game that was shot, etc); (in modern times, occasionally used for) estate car. **'~ing-gallery** *n* place where ~ing at targets is practised with pistols or airguns. **'~ing-range** *n* ground with butts for rifle practice. **'~ing-stick,** stick with a spiked end (to be pushed into the ground) and a handle which unfolds to form a seat. **'~ing-war** *n* war in which there is ~ing (contrasted with a 'cold war' or a 'war of nerves'). **6** [VP6A,2A] (cinema) photograph (a scene): *a ~ing script,* one to be used while a film is being shot (giving the order in which scenes are photographed, etc). **7** [VP2A] (football, hockey, etc) (chiefly imper) make a shot at scoring a goal. **8** ~ ***a line,*** (sl) ⇨ line[1](22). **~ing** *n* [U] (esp) (right of) ~ing (game) over an area of land: *sell the ~ing on an estate.* ⇨ also **6** above.

shooter /'ʃuːtə(r)/ *n* (in compounds) shooting implement: *a 'pea-~: a 'six-~,* revolver firing six shots without reloading.

shop /ʃɒp/ *n* **1** (US = *store*) building or part of a building where goods are shown and sold retail: *a butcher's/chemist's ~; a 'fruit-~.* ***come/go to the wrong ~,*** (colloq) to the wrong place/person (for help, information, etc). ***keep ~,*** be on duty (e g in a small ~): *Mr Green got a friend to keep ~ for him while he went to his wife's funeral.* ***keep a ~,*** be a shopkeeper, own and manage a ~. ***set up ~,*** set up in business as a retail trader. **'~-assistant** *n* employee in a ~. **'~-bell** *n* bell (on a ~ door) which rings when a customer enters, warning the ~-keeper (of a small ~ only). **'~-girl/-boy** *n* young ~-assistant. **'~-front** *n* frontage of a ~ with its window display, etc. **~ hours** *n pl* hours during which a ~ is, or may legally be, open for business. **'~-keeper** *n* owner of (usu a small) ~. **'~-lifter** *n* person who steals things from ~s while pretending to be a customer. Hence, **'~-lifting** *n* **'~-soiled/-worn** *adjj* damaged or dirty as the result of being put on view or handled in a ~. **'~-walker** *n* person who directs customers (in a large ~ or department store) to the right counters, departments, etc. **'~'window** *n* window used for the display of wares, etc. ***put all one's goods in the ~-window,*** (fig) make a display of all one's knowledge, ability, etc and have nothing in reserve (used of a superficial person). **2** [U] one's profession, trade, business, things connected with it. ***talk ~,*** talk about one's work, profession, etc: *Do school-teachers everywhere talk ~.* ***shut up ~,*** (colloq) stop doing sth (not necessarily connected with buying and selling). **3** ***all over the ~,*** (sl) **(a)** in disorder, scattered in confusion; *My belongings are all over the ~.* **(b)** in every direction: *I've looked for it all over the ~.* **4** (= *work~*) place where manufacturing or repairing is done: *an 'engi'neering-~; a ma'chine-~; the men on the ~ floor,* the workers (contrasted with the management). **'~-'steward** *n* member of a local branch committee of a trade union, chosen by his fellow workers to represent them. ***closed ~,*** system of compulsory membership of trade unions or other professional associations. □ *vi* (-pp-) [VP2A,C] **1** go to ~s to buy things (usu *go ~ping*). ~ ***around,*** (colloq) visit various ~s, markets, etc to obtain the best value for one's money, etc. **2** ~ ***on sb,*** inform against, esp to the police. **~ping** *n* [U] *do one's ~ping; a '~ping street,* one with many ~s; *a '~ping bag/basket,* in which to carry purchases. **'~ping centre,** part of a town where there are ~s, markets, etc close together and often where cars are not allowed. **'window-~ping** *n* visiting a ~ping centre, street, etc to look at the displays in the ~windows. **~per** *n* person who is ~ping: *crowds of Christmas ~pers.*

shore[1] /ʃɔ(r)/ *n* [C] stretch of land bordering on the sea or a large body of water: *a house on the ~(s) of Lake Geneva; go on ~* (from a ship).

shore[2] /ʃɔ(r)/ *n* [C] wooden support set against a wall, tree, etc to keep it up; prop set against the side of a ship while it is being built or repaired out of the water. □ *vt* ~ ***sth up,*** support, prop up (with a wooden beam, etc).

shore[3] /ʃɔ(r)/, **shorn** /ʃɔn/ ⇨ shear.

short[1] /ʃɔt/ *adj* (-er, -est) **1** (opp of *long*) measuring little from end to end in space or time; (opp of *tall*) below the average height: *a ~ stick; a ~ way off,* not far away; *a ~ man; ~ grass; a ~ holiday; a ~ time ago. You've cut my hair very ~. She walked with ~, quick steps. The coat is a little ~ in the sleeves. The days are getting ~er now that autumn is here.* ***a ~ ball,*** (cricket) not bowled on a correct length. **'~ cut,** way of getting somewhere, doing sth, etc (thought to be) quicker than the usual or ordinary way: *They took a ~ cut across the fields instead of going by the road.* **'~ 'circuit** *n* accidental fault in wiring enabling an electric current to flow without going through the resistance of the complete circuit. **'~-'circuit** *vt, vi* cause, make or take a ~ circuit in; cut off current from (sth) in this way; (fig) shorten or simplify (a procedure, etc): *The system has ~-circuited.* ˈ~ **list,** list of candidates (for a position, etc) that has been reduced to a small number from which a final selection is to be made. Hence, ˈ~**-list** *vt: the candidates who have been ~-listed,* whose names have been put on a ~ list (perhaps for interviews). ˈ~-ˈ**lived** /ˈlɪvd *US:* ˈlaɪvd/ *adj* lasting for a ~ time; brief: *a ~-lived triumph.* ~**-range,** (a) (of plans, etc) designed for a limited period of time. (b) (of missiles, etc) with a comparatively limited range[1](3). ***have a ~ temper,*** be lacking in self-control, so that one quickly or easily becomes angry; hence, ˈ~-ˈ**tempered** *adj* ˈ~-ˈ**term** *attrib adj* limited to, due to be repaid in, a ~ period of time: *~-term loans.* **2** not reaching the usual, stated or required (amount, distance, weight, etc): *The shopkeeper was fined for giving ~ weight/ measure. The factory is/The workmen are on ~ time,* working fewer hours per day, or days per week, than usual. *These goods are in ~ supply,* The supply is not equal to the demand (*scarce* is more usu.) ⇨ also commons(2). *You've given me ~ change,* less than the correct change. Hence, ˈ~-ˈ**change** *vt* cheat (sb) by giving less than the correct change. ***be ~ of,*** (a) not have enough of: *~ of money/time.* (b) be distant from: *The car broke down when we were still five miles ~ of our destination.* ***little/nothing ~ of,*** nothing/little less than: *Our escape was little ~ of miraculous,* was almost a miracle. ˈ~**-coming** *n* (usu *pl*) failure (to reach a required standard, to develop properly, to do one's duty). ~ **drink** *n* [C] (or, colloq **a** ~) whisky, gin, etc in comparatively small glasses or small portions at a time (contrasted with a long drink such as a glass of beer). ~ **sight,** inability to see clearly things that are distant, or (fig) to see into the future. Hence, ˈ~-ˈ**sighted** *adj: The Government's policy is ~-sighted,* does not take into account future needs, developments, etc. ~ ***of breath,*** panting, e g after running fast. ˈ~-ˈ**winded** *adj* easily and quickly becoming breathless after exertion; unable to run for long. ***make ~ work of,*** deal with, dispose of, eat or drink, quickly. ˈ~-ˈ**handed** *adj* having not enough workmen or helpers. **3** (in comm) maturing early; to be paid or met soon: *a ~ bill/paper; ~ date,* early date for maturing of a bill, bond, etc. Hence, ˈ~-ˈ**dated** *adj* ˈ~ ˈ**bond,** one which matures within a period of five years. ~**-term capital,** capital raised for short periods. **4** (of a person) saying very little, or saying much in few words; (of what he says, his manner of speaking) expressed in few words; curt; abrupt: *He/His answer was ~ and to the point. He was very ~ with me.* ***for ~,*** as a ~er form; for brevity's sake: *Benjamin,* called *'Ben' for ~.* ***in ~,*** in a few words; to sum up briefly (after a long description, etc). ***the long and the ~ of it,*** all that can or need be said. **5** (of cake, pastry) easily breaking or crumbling. ˈ~ ˈ**pastry,** made with much butter or fat. ˈ~**·bread/-cake** *nn* easily crumbled dry cake made with flour, sugar and much butter. **6** (of vowels or syllables) taking the less of two recognized durations; *the ~ vowel in 'pull' and the long vowel in 'pool'.* **7** (other compounds and special uses). ˈ~**·fall** *n* deficit. ˈ~-**hand** *n* [U] system of rapid writing using special signs; stenography. ***by a ~ head,*** (a) (racing) by a distance of less than the length of a horse's head: *Fly-by-Night won by a ~ head.* (b) (fig) by only a little. ˈ~**·horn** *n* [C] name of a breed of cattle with ~ curved horns. ~ **leg/slip,** (cricket) ⇨ the illus at cricket. ~ **wave,** (radio telegraphy) having a wave-length of from 10 to 100 metres. ~**·ly** *adv* **1** soon; in a ~ time; *~ly after(wards); ~ly before noon. He is ~ly to leave for Mexico.* **2** briefly; in a few words. **3** sharply; curtly: *answer rather ~ly.* ~**·ness** *n*

short[2] /ʃɔt/ *adv* **1** abruptly; suddenly: *stop ~; pull up ~; bring sb up ~,* check him abruptly; *take sb up ~,* interrupt him abruptly. ~ ***of,*** leaving out of question; except: *They would commit every crime ~ of murder.* **2** before the natural or expected time. ***come/fall ~ of,*** be insufficient, inadequate, disappointing (expectations, etc): *The box-office receipts fell ~ of the manager's expectations.* ***cut sth/sb ~,*** (a) interrupt; bring to an end before the usual or natural time: *The chairman had to cut ~ the proceedings.* (b) make ~(er). ***go ~ (of),*** do without; deprive oneself (of): *I don't want you to go ~* (of money, etc) *in order to lend me what I need.* ***run ~ (of),*** reach the end: *Our supplies ran ~. We're running ~ of paraffin.* ***be taken ~,*** (colloq) have a sudden motion of the bowels necessitating a hurried visit to the lavatory. **3** ***sell ~,*** (comm) sell for future delivery (stocks, shares, commodities, etc that one does not own) in the expectation of being able to buy more cheaply before the date agreed upon for delivery. ***sell sb ~,*** betray, cheat, belittle, them.

short·age /ˈʃɔtɪdʒ/ *n* [C,U] amount of) deficiency; condition of not having enough: *ˈfood ~s; a ~ of rice; owing to ~ of staff; a ~ of 50 tons.* ⇨ glut, *n*

shorten /ˈʃɔtn/ *vt,vi* [VP6A,2A] make or become shorter: *The days are beginning to ~,* e g in autumn. *The captain ordered his men to ~ sail,* reduce the area of sail spread to the wind. ~**·ing** /ˈʃɔtnɪŋ/ *n* [U] fat used for making pastry light and flaky. ⇨ short[1](5).

shorts /ʃɔts/ *n pl* short trousers extending to or above the knees, as worn by children, by adults for games, and as informal wear (on the beach, etc).

shot[1] /ʃot/ *n* **1** [C] (sound of the) firing of a gun, etc: *hear ~s in the distance; the first ~s in the campaign,* the start of the attack. *At each ~ he got nearer to the centre of the target.* ***(do sth) like a ~,*** at once; without hesitation. ***off like a ~,*** off at great speed. **2** [C] attempt to hit sth, hitting of sth; attempt to do sth, answer a question, etc; throw, stroke, hit, etc in certain games: *Good ~, Sir! That remark was a ~ at me,* was aimed at me. ***a ~ in the dark,*** a wild or random guess. ***have a ~ (at sth),*** try to do sth: *Have a ~ at solving the problem. The striker had a ~ at goal,* tried to score. *Let me have a ~ at it. He made several lucky ~s at the examination questions.* ***a long ~,*** an attempt to solve a problem, etc with little evidence, few facts to go on: *It's a long ~ but I think John must have known about the murder.* ***not by a long ~,*** not even if circumstances were most favourable. **3** [C] that which is fired from a gun, esp (formerly stone, later metal) non-explosive projectile for old-fashioned cannon. ⇨ shell(3); heavy iron ball thrown in athletic competition called the ˈ*~-put: putting the ~.* **4** ***lead ~,*** [U] quantity of tiny balls (or pellets) of lead contained in the cartridge of a sporting gun (instead of a single bullet), used against birds and small animals. ⇨ the illus at cartridge. ˈ~**-gun** *n* sporting gun with a smooth bore firing cartridges containing ~. **'~-tower** *n* tower in which ~ is made from molten lead poured through a sieve at the top and falling into water. **5** [C] person who shoots, with reference to his skill: *He's a first-class/good/poor, etc ~.* **6** [C] photograph, or one of a series of photographs, taken with a cine-camera: *The exterior ~s were taken in Bermuda.* **'long ~,** (opp of *close-up*) taken with a long distance between the camera and the subject. **7** (esp US) injection from a hypodermic needle (of a drug): *have a ~ in the arm.* ***have/get/give sb a ~ in the arm,*** **(a)** have/give sb an injection. **(b)** have/give sb/sth that revives or restores, e g the economy. **8 a 'big ~,** (sl) an important person, esp a conceited one.

shot[2] /ʃot/ *n* share of a reckoning or of expense: *pay one's ~.*

should /ʃʊd *weak form* ʃəd/ *v* ⇨ shall.

shoul·der /'ʃəʊldə(r)/ *n* **1** that part of the body of a human being or animal where an arm or foreleg is joined to the trunk, (⇨ the illus at trunk), or where the wing of a bird joins its neck; curve from this point to the neck: *This coat is narrow across the ~s. He has one ~ a little higher than the other.* ***~ to ~,*** side by side and touching; (fig) united. ***give sb the cold ~,*** ⇨ cold[1](1). ***put one's ~ to the wheel,*** work energetically at a task. ***stand head and ~s above*** (others), be considerably taller (or, fig, mentally or morally better) than. ***straight from the ~,*** (fig, of criticism, rebukes, etc) frankly put. **'~-blade** *n* either of the flat bones of the upper back, behind and below the neck. ⇨ the illus at skeleton. **'~-strap** *n* **(a)** narrow strap on the ~ of a military uniform (with badges of rank, etc) **(b)** ribbon which passes over a woman's ~ and supports a garment. **'~-flash** *n* strip of material on the ~ of a military uniform, with a coloured patch as the distinguishing emblem of a division, etc. **2** (*pl*) part of the back between the two ~s(1): give a child a ride on one's ~s; shift the blame to other ~s, let others take the blame. ***have broad ~s,*** be able to bear much weight or (fig) responsibility. **3** ~-like part of a bottle, tool, mountain, etc. **hard ~,** hard surface at the side of a roadway (esp a motorway). □ *vt* **1** [VP6A] take on the ~(s) (liter and fig): *~ a burden/a task/the responsibility for sth/one's son's debts.* ***~ arms,*** (mil) move the rifle to an upright position in front of the right ~. **2** [VP15A] push with the ~; make (one's way) thus: *~ people aside; be ~ed to one side; ~ one's way through a crowd.*

shout /ʃaʊt/ *n* [C] loud call or cry: *~s of joy; a ~ of alarm. They greeted him with ~s of 'Long live the President'.* □ *vi,vt* **1** [VP2A,B,C,4B,22] speak or cry out in a loud voice: *Don't ~ at me! He ~ed to attract attention. He ~ed with pain. He ~ed himself hoarse.* **2** [VP6A,15A,3A] say in a loud voice: *~ (out) one's orders. They ~ed their disapproval,* expressed it by ~ing. *He ~ed to me/~ed for me to come. 'Go back!' he ~ed.* ***~ sb down,*** ~ to prevent sb from being heard: *The crowd ~ed the speaker down.* **~·ing** *n* [U] ~s: ***It's all over but/bar the ~ing,*** The struggle, fight, etc is over and the praise, cheers, etc will follow.

shove /ʃʌv/ *vt,vi* [VP6A,15A,B,2A,C] (colloq) push (usu heavily): *~ a boat into the water. Stop shoving!* ***~ off,*** **(a)** start from the shore in a boat (by pushing the shore, etc). **(b)** (sl) leave (a place): *I'm sick of this place; let's ~ off.* □ *n* [C] vigorous push: *Give it a ~.* **'~-'ha'penny** /'ʃʌv 'heɪpnɪ/ *n* = shovel-board.

shovel /'ʃʌvl/ *n* [C] spade-like tool, used for moving coal, sand, snow, etc; ⇨ the illus at tool; large device used for the same purpose, mechanically operated from a crane in a vehicle. □ *vt* (-ll-, US -l-) **1** [VP6A,15A,B] lift, move, with a ~: *~ up coal; ~ the snow away from the garden path.* **2** [VP6A,15A] clear or clean with a ~: *~ a path through the snow.* **~·ful** /-fʊl/ *n* as much as a ~ will hold.

shovel-board /'ʃʌvl bɔd/ *n* game in which discs or coins are pushed along a board to a mark.

show[1] /ʃəʊ/ *n* **1** [U] showing (chiefly in): *by (a) ~ of hands,* (voting) by the raising of hands for or against (a proposal). **2** [C] collection of things publicly displayed, esp for competition, or as a public entertainment: *a 'flower/'horse/'cattle ~; the 'motor ~,* = exhibition; *the Lord Mayor's ~,* a procession through the City of London when a new Lord Mayor is installed; *a travelling ~,* e g of circus animals. ***on ~,*** exhibited. **3** [C] (colloq) natural display; sth to be seen: *a fine ~ of blossom in the Kent orchards.* **4** [C] (colloq) kind of public entertainment, e g circus, theatre, radio, TV, etc: *Have you seen any good ~s lately?* **'~-business, '~-biz** /bɪz/ (colloq) *nn* the public entertainment business. **5** [C] (sl) performance (not theatrical, etc): *put up a good ~,* do sth creditably; *a poor ~,* sth done badly. ***steal the ~,*** attract all the attention: *Good ~!* used to express approval of sth done well. **6** [C] (colloq) organization; undertaking; business; something that is happening: *Who's running/bossing this ~,* Who controls or manages it? ***give the (whole) '~ away,*** let people know what is being done or planned: *I wish she wouldn't talk and give the ~ away.* **7** (*sing* only; dated colloq use) opportunity of doing sth, defending oneself, etc: *Give the man a fair ~. He had no ~ at all.* **8** outward appearance; impression: *a claim with some ~ of justice; with a ~ of reason. He didn't offer even a ~ of resistance.* **9** [U] pomp; display; ostentation: *a house furnished for ~, not comfort. They're fond of ~.* **10** (compounds) **'~-boat** *n* river steam-boat on which theatrical performances were given (esp on the Mississippi, US) **'~-case** *n* case with glass sides and (or) top, for showing and protecting articles in a shop, museum, etc. **'~-down** *n* (sl) full and frank declaration of one's strength, intentions, etc: *call for a ~-down,* ask (opponents, rivals, etc) for such a declaration; *if it comes to a ~-down,* if such a declaration is (or has to be) made. **'~-girl** *n* girl who sings or dances (or is merely decorative) in a musical play, revue, etc. **'~-jumping** *n* display of skill in riding horses over fences, barriers, etc. **'~·man** /-mən/ *n* (*pl* -men) **(a)** organizer of public entertainments (esp circuses). **(b)** person (esp in public life) who uses publicity, etc to attract attention to himself: *Some politicians are great ~men and very little else.* **'~·man·ship** /-mənʃɪp/ *n* art of attracting, ability to attract, public attention, e g to what one is trying to sell. **'~-place** *n* one that tourists go to see: *old palaces, castles and other ~-places.* **'~-room/-window** *n* one in which goods are kept for display, inspection, etc. **showy** *adj* (-ier, -iest) likely to attract attention; (often contemptuous) (too much) decorated or ornamented; (too) brightly coloured: *~y flowers,* e g some kinds of dahlia; *a ~y dress; the ~y patriotism of persons hoping for titles.* **~·ily** /-əlɪ/ *adv* **~i·ness** *n*

show² (occ **shew**) /ʃəʊ/ *vt,vi* (*pt* ~ed, *pp* ~n /ʃəʊn/, rarely ~ed) **1** [VP6A,12A,13A,15A] **~ sth (to sb), ~ sb sth,** bring before the sight: *You must ~ your ticket at the barrier. What films are they ~ing at the local cinema this week? He won several prizes for the roses he ~ed,* exhibited. *He ~ed me his pictures. He has ~n them to all his friends.* **2** [VP6A] allow to be seen: *That frock ~s your petticoat,* is too short to cover it. *A dark suit will not ~ the dirt. My shoes are ~ing signs of wear.* **3** [VP2A,C] be visible or noticeable: *Your panties are ~ing, Jane. Does the mark of the wound still ~? The pink of the apple-blossom is beginning to ~. His fear ~ed in his eyes.* **4** [VP6A] **~ itself,** be visible: *His annoyance ~ed itself in his looks.* **~ oneself,** be present (at a meeting, etc): *Ought we to ~ ourselves at Madame L's reception?* **~ one's face,** appear before people: *He's ashamed to ~ his face at the club.* **~ fight,** give signs of being ready to fight. **~ one's hand/cards,** (fig) make known one's intentions or plans. **~ a leg,** (colloq) get out of bed (orig of sailors, out of a hammock). **~ one's teeth,** (fig) look angry. **have nothing to ~ for it/sth,** have nothing that is evidence of what one has achieved or tried to achieve. **5** [VP6A,14, 12A,13A] give; grant: *~ mercy on sb. He ~ed me great kindness.* **6** [VP6A,25] give evidence or proof of having or being: *He ~s no sign of intelligence. She ~ed great courage. His new book ~s him to be a first-rate novelist.* **7** [VP15A,B] **~ sb in/into; ~ sb out of,** direct conduct sb into/out of a place: *Please ~ this gentleman out. We were ~n into the living-room.* **~ sb over sth,** take sb round a place: *The guide ~ed us over the old castle.* **~ sb the door,** require him to leave and go with him to the door to see that he does so. **8** [VP6A,9,10,20,21,25] make clear; cause (sb) to understand; prove: *He ~ed me how to do it/how he had done it. He ~ed his annoyance/that he was annoyed/how annoyed he was. That ~s how little you know. We have ~n the falsity of the story/that the story is false/the story to be false.* **~ sb the way,** explain which way to go; (fig) set an example. **9** [VP2C,15B] **~ sb/sth off,** display (sth) to advantage: *a swim-suit that ~s off her figure well; mothers who like to ~ off their daughters,* display their daughter's good looks, abilities, accomplishments, etc. **~ off,** make a display of one's wealth, learning, abilities, etc in order to impress people: *a man who is always ~ing off.* Hence, **'~-off** *n* person who ~s off: *He's a dreadful ~-off,* is always trying to show his abilities, etc. **~ sb/sth up,** make the truth about (sb or sth dishonest, disreputable, etc) known: *~ up a fraud/a rogue/an impostor.* **~ up, (a)** be conspicuous, easily visible: *Her wrinkles ~ed up in the strong sunlight.* **(b)** [VP2A] (colloq) put in an appearance; be present (*at*): *Three of those we invited to the party didn't ~ up.* **~·ing** *n* (usu *sing*) (act of) displaying or pointing out; appearance: *a firm with a poor financial ~ing,* whose financial accounts do not appear to be good. **on his/your, etc own ~ing,** by his/your, etc own admission.

shower /'ʃaʊə(r)/ *n* [C] **1** brief fall of rain, sleet or hail; sudden sprinkle of water: *be caught in a ~; a ~ of spray.* **'~(-bath)** *n* (taking of a bath by using a) device by which water comes down in a ~ through a plate with numerous small holes: *have a ~(-bath) every morning.* **2** large number of things arriving together: *a ~ of blows/stones/blessings/insults; sparks falling in a ~/in ~s.* **3** (US) party at which presents are given to a woman about to become a bride. □ *vt,vi* **2** [VP14] **~ sb/sth with/upon,** send or give, in a ~: *They ~ed honours upon the hero/~ed the hero with honours. Questions were ~ed upon the new arrival.* **2** [VP2C] fall in a ~: *Good wishes ~ed (down) upon the bridegroom.* **~y** *adj* (of the weather) with frequent ~s.

shown /ʃəʊn/ *pp* of **show²**.

shrank /ʃræŋk/ *pt* of **shrink**.

shrap·nel /'ʃræpnl/ *n* [U] fragments of shell or bullets packed inside a shell which is designed to explode and scatter these contents over a wide area: *hit by (a piece of) ~.*

shred /ʃred/ *n* [C] strip or piece scraped, torn or broken off sth; fragment: (fig) *not a ~ of truth in what she says; not a ~ of evidence against me.* **tear to ~s,** (liter and fig) destroy: *They have torn her reputation to ~s.* □ *vt* (**-dd-**) [VP6A] tear or scrape into ~s.

shrew /ʃru/ *n* **1** bad-tempered, scolding woman. **2** **'~(-mouse),** small mouse-like animal that feeds on insects. **~·ish** /-ɪʃ/ *adj* scolding; sharp-tongued. **~·ish·ly** *adv* **~·ish·ness** *n*

shrewd /ʃrud/ *adj* (**-er, -est**) **1** having, showing, sound judgement and common sense: *~ business men; ~ arguments.* **2** astute; discriminating: *make a ~ guess,* one likely to be correct; *a ~ blow/thrust,* one carefully made and likely to be effective. **~·ly** *adv* **~·ness** *n*

shriek /ʃrik/ *vi,vt* **1** [VP2A,C] shrill scream. **2** [VP6A,15B] utter in a screaming voice: *~ out a warning; ~ with laughter.* □ *n* [C] scream: *~s of girlish laughter; the ~* (= whistle) *of a railway engine.*

shrift /ʃrɪft/ *n* [U] **1** (old use) confession (of sins) to a priest; confession and absolution. **2** (modern survival) **get/give sb short ~,** little time between condemnation and punishment: *They gave us/We got short ~,* (fig) treated us curtly, gave us brief attention.

shrike /ʃraɪk/ *n* (kinds of) bird (also called *'butcher-bird*) with a strong, hooked bill and the habit of fastening its prey (small birds and insects) on thorns.

shrill /ʃrɪl/ *adj* (of sounds, voices, etc) sharp; piercing; high-pitched: *~ cries; a ~ voice/whistle.* **shrilly** /'ʃrɪlɪ/ *adv* **~·ness** *n*

shrimp /ʃrɪmp/ *n* [C] small marine shellfish used for food; ⇨ the illus at **crustacean**; (hum) very small person. □ *vi* catch ~s: (usu) *go ~ing.*

shrine /ʃraɪn/ *n* [C] **1** tomb or casket containing holy relics; altar or chapel of special associations or hallowed by some memory. **2** building or place associated with sth or sb deeply respected or venerated: *a Shinto ~,* in Japan; *worship at the ~ of Mammon,* give excessive devotion to wealth and money-making. □ *vt* = enshrine (the usu word).

shrink /ʃrɪŋk/ *vi,vt* (*pt* **shrank** /ʃræŋk/, or **shrunk** /ʃrʌŋk/, *pp* **shrunk**, or, as *adj* **shrunken** /'ʃrʌŋkən/) **1** [VP6A,2A] make or become less, smaller (esp of cloth through wetting): *Will this soap ~ woollen clothes? They will ~ in the wash. How* *your gums have shrunk since your teeth were extracted!* **2** [VP2A,3A] **~ *from/back,*** move back, show unwillingness to do sth (from shame, dislike, etc): *A shy man ~s from meeting strangers. She shrank back from the horrifying spectacle.* **ˋ~·age** /-ɪdʒ/ *n* [U] process of ~ing; degree of ~ing: *Make it a little longer, and allow for ~age. The ~age in our export trade/in the value of our currency is serious.*

shrive /ʃraɪv/ *vt* (*pt* ~d or **shrove** /ʃrəʊv/, *pp* ~d or **shriven** /ˋʃrɪvn/) [VP6A] (old use, of a priest) hear the confession of a penitent sinner and absolve him from the spiritual consequences of his sin(s).

shrivel /ˋʃrɪvl/ *vt,vi* (-ll-, US also -l-) [VP6A, 15B,2A,C] **~ *(up),*** (cause to) become dried or curled (through heat, frost, dryness or old age): *The heat ~led up the leaves/the leather. He has a ~led face,* with the skin wrinkled.

shriven /ˋʃrɪvn/ ⇨ **shrive.**

shroud /ʃraʊd/ *n* [C] **1** (also called ˋ*winding-sheet*) cloth or sheet (to be) wrapped round a corpse: *You'll have no pockets in your ~.* **2** sth which covers and hides: *a ~ of mist.* **3** (*pl*) ropes supporting a ship's masts; ⇨ the illus at **barque**; ropes linking a parachute and the harness which is strapped to the parachutist. □ *vt* [VP6A,15A] **1** wrap (a corpse) in a ~. **2** cover; hide: *~ed in darkness/mist; a crime ~ed in mystery.*

shrove /ʃrəʊv/ ⇨ **shrive.**

Shrove Tues·day /ˈʃrəʊv ˋtjuzdɪ *US:* ˋtuz-/ *n* day before the beginning of Lent, on which, and on preceding days (**Shrove·tide**) it was formerly the custom to be shriven.

shrub /ʃrʌb/ *n* [C] plant with woody stem, lower than a tree, and (usu) with several separate stems from the root. **~·bery** /ˋʃrʌbərɪ/ *n* (*pl* -ries) place, e g part of a garden, planted with ~s.

shrug /ʃrʌg/ *vt* (-gg-) [VP6A,15B] lift (the shoulders) slightly (to show indifference, doubt, etc). **~ *sth off,*** dismiss it as not deserving attention, as sth trivial. □ *n* [C] such a movement: *with a ~ of the shoulders/a ~ of despair.*

shrunk(en) /ʃrʌŋk, ˋʃrʌŋkən/ ⇨ **shrink.**

shuck /ʃʌk/ *n* (US) husk; pod; outer covering. **S~s** *int* (US) Nonsense! Rubbish! □ *vt* [VP6A] remove the ~s from: *~ peanuts/maize.*

shud·der /ˋʃʌdə(r)/ *vi* [VP2A,C,4C] shake convulsively; tremble with fear or disgust: *~ with cold/horror; ~ at the sight of blood. The ship ~ed as she struck the rocks. He ~ed to think of it.* □ *n* [C] uncontrollable shaking: *a ~ passed over her. It gives me the ~s,* (colloq) terrifies me. **~·ing·ly** *adv*

shuffle /ˋʃʌfl/ *vi,vt* **1** [VP2A,C,6A] walk without raising the feet properly. **~ *one's feet,*** slide or drag them on the ground when walking, or when standing or sitting. **2** [VP6A,15A,B,2A] slide or move (playing-cards, etc) one over the other to change their relative positions: *~ the dominoes. He ~d the papers together in a drawer.* **3** [VP2C, 15B] do sth in a careless way; slip (sth *off, on*) casually: *~ through one's work; ~ one's clothes on/off;* (fig) *~ off responsibility upon others,* get rid of it by passing it to others. **4** [VP2A] keep shifting one's position; be unstraightforward; try to avoid giving a certain answer, etc: *Don't ~; give a clear answer.* □ *n* [C] **1** shuffling movement; shuffling dance: ˈ*soft-shoe* ˋ*~*; shuffling of cards: *Give the cards a good ~.* **2** general change of relative positions: *a ~ of the Cabinet; a Cabinet ~,* giving members different portfolios. **3** piece of dishonesty; misleading statement or action. **shuf·fler** *n* one who ~s.

shun /ʃʌn/ *vt* (-nn-) [VP6A,D] keep away from; avoid: *~ temptation/publicity/society.*

'shun /ʃʌn/ *int* short for *Attention!* (as a word of command).

shunt /ʃʌnt/ *vt,vi* **1** [VP6A,15B] send (railway wagons, coaches, etc) from one track to another, esp to keep a track clear for important traffic: *~ a train on to a siding.* **2** [VP2A] (of a train) be ~ed to a siding. **3** [VP6A,15A] (colloq) postpone or evade discussion of (sth): *She ~ed the conversation on to less morbid topics.* **4** [VP6A,15A] (fig) lay aside (a project); leave (sb) unoccupied, or inactive. **~er** *n* (esp) railway employee who ~s wagons, etc.

shush /ʃʊʃ/ *vi,vt* hush; call for silence by saying 'Shush!'

shut /ʃʌt/ *vt,vi* (*pt,pp* **shut**; -tt-) (For special uses with *adverbial particles* and *preps,* ⇨ 5 below.) **1** [VP6A,15A] move (a door, one's lips, etc) into position to stop an opening: *~ the doors and windows; ~ a drawer; ~ one's mouth. He ~ his ears to all appeals for help,* refused to listen to them. *He ~ his eyes to* (= deliberately refused to notice) *her faults. Why have you ~ the door upon further negotiations,* refused to consider them? *They ~ the door against her/on her/in her face,* refused to receive or admit her. **ˋ~-eye** *n* (colloq) nap; sleep: *It's time for half an hour's ~-eye.* **2** [VP2A] become closed; admit of being closed: *The window ~s easily. The door won't ~.* **3** [VP6A] bring the folding parts of (sth) together: *~* (= *close,* the more usu word) *a book/a clasp-knife.* **4** [VP15A] catch or pinch by shutting sth: *~ one's fingers/dress, etc in the door,* i e between the door and the door-post. **5** [VP2C,15B] (special uses with *adverbial particles* and *preps*):

shut (sth) down, (of a factory, etc) stop working; end activity: *The workshop has ~ down and the workers are unemployed. They've ~ down their factory.* Hence, **ˋ~-down** *n* (temporary or permanent) closing of a factory, etc.

shut sb in, confine or enclose: *We're ~ in by hills here,* surrounded by hills which make access difficult and which prevent us from seeing far. *They ~ the boy in the cellar,* kept him there as a prisoner.

shut sth off, stop the supply or flow of, e g gas, steam, water.

shut sb/sth out, keep out; exclude; block: *~ out immigrants/competitive goods. Don't ~ me out,* Don't close the door(s) so that I must stay out. *These trees ~ out the view.*

shut sth up, **(a)** close and secure all the doors and windows: *~ up a house before going away for a holiday. It's time to ~ up shop,* close the shop and stop doing business. **(b)** put away for safety: *~ up one's jewels in the safe.* **~ *(sb) up,*** (cause sb to) stop talking: *Tell him to ~ up. Can't you ~ him up?*

shut·ter /ˋʃʌtə(r)/ *n* [C] **1** movable cover (wooden panel or iron plate, hinged or separate and detachable) for a window, to keep out light or thieves: *The shop-front is fitted with rolling ~s.* ***put up the ~s,*** stop doing business (for the day, or permanently). **2** device that opens to admit light through the lens of a camera. □ *vt* [VP6A] provide with ~s; put up the ~s of.

shuttle /ˈʃʌtl/ *n* **1** (in a loom) cigar-shaped instrument with two pointed ends by which thread of weft is carried between threads of warp; (in a sewing-machine) sliding holder which carries the lower thread to meet the upper thread to make a stitch. **2** (compounds) ˋ**~-cock** *n* round-based cork with feathers in it, struck to and fro across a net in the games of battledore and ~cock and badminton. ⇨ the illus at badminton. ˋ**~ service,** service (of trains, buses, etc) to and fro between places not far apart. □ *vt, vi* [VP6A,15A,2C] (cause to) move backwards and forwards, to and fro, like a ~.

shy[1] /ʃaɪ/ *adj* (-er, -est) **1** (of persons) self-conscious and uncomfortable in the presence of others; (of behaviour, etc) showing this: *He's not at all shy with women. She gave him a shy look/smile.* **2** (of animals, birds, fish, etc) easily frightened; unwilling to be seen. **3** ***shy of,*** chary of; hesitating about: *They're shy of speaking to one another. Don't be shy of telling me what you want.* ***fight shy of,*** ⇨ fight[2](1). **shy·ly** *adv* **shy·ness** *n*

shy[2] /ʃaɪ/ *vi* (*pt,pp* shied /ʃaɪd/) [VP2A,3] ***shy (at sth),*** (of a horse) turn aside from in fear or alarm: *The horse was shying at a white object in the hedge.*

shy[3] /ʃaɪ/ *vt* (*pt,pp* shied /ʃaɪd/) (colloq) [VP6A, 15A] throw: *shying stones at a bottle.* □ *n* (*pl* shies /ʃaɪz/) throw: *fivepence a shy,* e g throwing balls at coconuts at a fair; (colloq) any kind of attempt: *have a shy at a task/an examination.*

shy·ster /ˈʃaɪstə(r) *with* aɪ *as in 'ice'*/ *n* (US, colloq) person without professional honour, esp an unscrupulous lawyer.

Sia·mese /ˌsaɪəˈmiz/ *adj* of Siam (Thailand). **~ twins,** two persons joined together from birth. ˋ**~ (cat),** oriental breed of cat with blue eyes and short-haired coat of cream, fawn or light grey hair. □ *n* native of Siam; language of Siam (Thai).

Si·berian /saɪˈbɪərɪən/ *adj* of, coming from, Siberia.

sibi·lant /ˈsɪbələnt/ *adj* having, making, a whistling kind of sound. □ *n* sound such as one of the six English sounds /s, z, ʃ, ʒ, tʃ, dʒ/.

sib·ling /ˈsɪblɪŋ/ *n* one of two or more persons having the same parents; brother or sister.

sibyl /ˈsɪbl/ *n* one of several women in ancient times who, it was believed, could see the future and who gave out messages from the gods; (hence, contemptuous or hum) fortune-teller; prophetess. **~·line** /ˈsɪbḷaɪn/ *adj* uttered by, characteristic of, a ~.

sic[1] /sɪk/ *adv* (Lat) thus (placed in brackets to indicate that the preceding word statement, etc is correctly quoted, etc even though this seems unlikely or is clearly incorrect).

sic[2] /sɪk/ *vt* (US) = sick[2].

Si·cil·ian /sɪˈsɪlɪən/ *n, adj* (native) of Sicily.

sick[1] /sɪk/ *adj* **1** (*pred* only): *be ~,* throw up food from the stomach; *feel ~,* feel that one is about to do this; *ˋsea~ on the first day of the voyage.* **2** unwell; ill (in GB *ill* and *unwell* are more usu; in US *sick* is normal usage): *He has been ~ for six weeks.* (*Sick* is used in GB predicatively in a few cases, archaic, biblical or colloq style and attributively in ordinary style, esp in mil use): *He's a ~ man. He was ~ of a fever* (old or biblical use). *He was ~ at heart,* sad, disappointed. ***fall ~,*** become ill. ***go/report ~,*** (mil use) report to the doctor for medical treatment. **the ~,** (*pl*) those who are ill. ˋ**~-bay** *n* **(a)** (Navy) part of a ship for those who are ill. **(b)** medical centre, e g on a university campus, etc. ˋ**~-bed** *n* bed of a sick person. ˋ**~-benefit** *n* ⇨ sickness. ˋ**~-berth** *n* = *~-bay*(a). ˈ**~-ˋheadache** *n* bilious headache. ˋ**~-leave** *n* permission to be away from duty or work because of illness: *on ~-leave.* ˋ**~-list** *n* list of those who are ill (in a regiment, on a warship, etc): *only three men on the ~-list* (used also, by extension, of persons in civilian life). ˋ**~-parade** *n* (mil) parade of those who are reporting ~. ˋ**~-pay** *n* pay to an employee who is absent because ill. ˋ**~-room** *n* room occupied by, or kept ready for, sb who is ill. **3** ***~ (and tired) of; ~ to death of,*** (colloq) tired of, disgusted with: *I'm ~ of being blamed for everything that goes wrong.* **4** ***~ at/about,*** (colloq) unhappy, filled with regret: *~ at failing to pass the examination.* **5** ***~ for,*** filled with a longing for: *~ for home/old scenes.* **6** (mod use) morbid; perverted; basically sad: *~ humour/jokes.* □ *vt* ***~ sth up,*** (colloq) vomit; throw up from the stomach.

sick[2] (US = **sic**) /sɪk/ *vt* (usu imper to a dog) set upon: *S~ him!* e g as a command to a dog to worry and shake a rat.

sicken /ˈsɪkən/ *vi, vt* **1** [VP2A,3A] ***~ (for sth),*** be in the first stages of (an illness): *The child is ~ing for something.* **2** [VP6A] cause to feel disgusted: *Cruelty ~s most of us. Their business methods ~ me.* **3** [VP3A,4C] ***~ at sth/to see sth,*** feel sick to see: *They ~ed at the sight of so much slaughter/~ed to see so many people slaughtered.* **4** ***~ of sth,*** become tired of, disgusted with: *He ~ed of trying to bring about reforms.* **~·ing** /ˈsɪkṇɪŋ/ *adj* disgusting; unpleasant: *~ing smells.* **~·ing·ly** *adv*

sick·ish /ˈsɪkɪʃ/ *adj* somewhat sick or sickening: *feel ~; a ~ smell.*

sickle /ˈsɪkl/ *n* [C] short-handled tool with a curved blade for cutting grass, grain, etc. ⇨ the illus at tool.

sick·ly /ˈsɪklɪ/ *adj* (-ier, -iest) **1** frequently ill; often in poor health: *a ~ child.* **2** having the appearance of sickness or ill health; pale: *These plants are/look rather ~.* **3** weak; faint; suggesting unhappiness: *a ~ smile.* **4** causing, or likely to cause, a feeling of sickness or distaste: *a ~ smell/taste; ~ sentiments.*

sick·ness /ˈsɪknəs/ *n* **1** [U] illness; ill health: *Is there much ~ in the village now? They were absent because of ~.* ˋ**~ benefit,** (State) insurance payment to sb absent from work through illness. **2** [C,U] (an) illness or disease: *suffering from ˋmountain ~/ˋsea-~/ˋair-~.* **3** [U] inclination to vomit; vomiting.

side[1] /saɪd/ *n* [C] (except 13 below) **1** one of the flat or fairly flat surfaces of a solid object: *the six ~s of a cube.* **2** one of the surfaces which is not the top or the bottom: *A box has a top, a bottom, and four ~s.* **3** one of the surfaces which is not the top, bottom, front or back: (attrib) *the ~ entrance of the house* (contrasted with the *front* or *back* entrance). **4** (maths) one of the lines bounding a plane figure such as a rectangle or triangle. **5** either of the two surfaces of a thin, flat object or of material such as paper, cloth, anything manufactured in sheets: *Write on one ~ of the paper only. Which is the right ~ of the cloth,* the ~ intended to be seen? **6** inner or outer surface of sth vertical, sloping, round or curved: *the ~ of a mountain; put one's socks on the wrong ~ out* (= inside out, the usu phrase); *prehistoric paintings on the ~s* (= walls) *of a cave.* **7** one of the two halves of a person on his left or right, esp from armpit to hip: *wounded in the left ~. Come and sit by/at my ~.* ***~ by ~,*** close together, for mutual support. ***split/burst one's ~s (laughing/with laughter),*** laugh heartily. Hence, **`~-splitting** *adj* causing hearty laughter. ***by the ~ of; by his/her, etc ~,*** close to and compared with: *She looks small by the ~ of her companion.* **8** one of the two halves of an animal from foreleg to hindleg, esp as part of a carcass: *a ~ of beef/bacon.* **9** part of an object, area, space, etc away from, at a distance from, a central line real or imaginary: *the left/right/shady/sunny ~ of the street; the east ~ of the town; the debit/credit ~ of an account. He crossed to the far/the other ~ of the room.* ***on/from all ~s; on/from every ~,*** in/from all directions; everywhere. ***take sb on one ~,*** aside, apart, e g to speak to him in confidence. ***on the right/wrong ~ of*** (*fifty*, etc), below/above (50 years of age, etc). ***(do sth) on the ~,*** **(a)** as a ~line. ⇨ **sideline** below. **(b)** secretly, discreetly: *He lived with his wife but saw his mistress on the ~.* ***put sth on one ~,*** **(a)** put it aside, apart. **(b)** postpone dealing with it. **10** one of two groups or parties of people who are opposed (in games, politics, war, etc) or who uphold beliefs, opinions, etc against the other: *be on the winning/losing ~; faults on both ~s; to pick* (= choose) *~s. The school has a strong ~,* e g a good football team. ***be on sb's ~,*** be a supporter: *Whose ~ are you on, anyway?* = Aren't you supposed to be supporting me? *Both countries claimed that God was on their ~,* e g in a war. ***let the ~ down,*** give an inferior performance and disappoint one's colleagues, team-mates, etc. ***take ~s (with),*** support (sb, a party) in a dispute. ⇨ side[2]. ***off/on ~,*** (football, hockey) in a position (for receiving or playing the ball) that is/is not contrary to the rules. **11** aspect or view that is not complete; aspect different from or opposed to other aspects: *look on the dark/bright/gloomy, etc ~ of things/life, etc; study all ~s of a question; a man with many ~s to his character. There are two ~s to the story,* two aspects. ***on the `high/`low, etc ~,*** rather high/low, etc: *Prices offered for fat cattle were on the high ~.* **12** line of descent through a parent: *a cousin on my father's ~.* **13** [U] (colloq) ***have no/be without ~,*** make no pretence, assumption, of being superior or important. ***put on ~,*** claim to be, behave as if one is, superior. **14** (compounds, etc) **`~-arms** *n pl* swords or bayonets, worn at the left ~ by soldiers. **`~-board** *n* table, usu with drawers and cupboards, placed against the wall of a dining-room. **`~-burns/-boards** *n pl* ~-whiskers. **`~-car** *n* small one-wheeled car fastened to the ~ of a motorbike. **`~-chapel** *n* one in the aisle or at one ~ of a church. **`~-dish** *n* extra dish or course at a meal. **`~-drum** *n* small, double-sided drum, hung at the drummer's ~ (in a military band). **`~ effect,** secondary or indirect effect, e g an undesirable effect of a drug used for a specific purpose. **`~-face** *adv* in profile: *photograph sb ~-face.* **`~-glance** *n* look to or from one ~. **`~ issue** *n* question of less importance (in relation to the main one). **`~-light** *n* light from or at the ~; (fig) incidental illumination, e g of a person's character, of a problem, etc. **`~-line** *n* class of goods sold in addition to the chief class of goods; occupation which is not one's main work. **`~-lines** *n pl* (space immediately outside) lines bounding a football pitch, tennis-court, etc at the ~s. ***on the ~-lines,*** (fig) merely as a spectator, not taking part. **`~-long** *adj, adv* (directed) to or from one ~: *look ~long at sb; a ~long glance.* **`~-road** *n* minor road branching off a main road. **`~-saddle** *n* woman's saddle, made so that both feet may be on the same ~ of the horse. □ *adv* on a ~-saddle: *Not all women ride ~-saddle.* **`~-show** *n* **(a)** small show at a fair or exhibition. **(b)** activity of small importance in relation to the main activity. **`~-slip** *n* **(a)** (motoring) skid. **(b)** (flying) movement to one ~ instead of forward. □ *vi* (-pp-) make a ~-slip. **`~s·man** /-zmən/ *n* (*pl* -men) church office-bearer (who shows worshippers to seats, takes up the collection, etc). **`~-step** *n* step taken to one ~ (e g to avoid a blow in boxing). □ *vt,vi* (-pp-) [VP6A] avoid (a blow, etc) by stepping to one ~; evade (a question); [VP2A] step to one ~. **`~-stroke** *n* (kinds of) stroke used in swimming in which one ~ is above and the other below the water. **`~-track** *n* railway siding; branch road. □ *vi* [VP6A] turn (a train) into a siding; (fig) turn (a person) from his purpose; postpone consideration of (a proposal, etc). **`~-view** *n* view obtained from the ~. **`~-walk** *n* (chiefly US; GB = *pavement*) path at the ~ of a street for persons on foot. **`~-whiskers** *n pl* on the ~s of the face down to, but excluding, the chin. ⇨ **beard.** **-sided** /saɪdɪd/ *suff* having a specified number of ~s: *a `five-~d figure.* **~·wards** /-wədz/, **~ways** /-weɪz/ *advv* to, towards, from, the ~; with the ~ or edge first: *look ~ways at sb; walk/carry sth ~ways through a narrow opening;* (attrib) directed to one ~.

side[2] /saɪd/ *vi* [VP3A] ***~ with,*** take part, be on the same side (as sb in an argument or quarrel): *It is safer to ~ with the stronger party.*

sid·ereal /saɪ`dɪərɪəl/ *adj* of the stars and their measurements: *~ time,* measured by the stars; *the ~ year,* 365 days, 6 hours, 10 minutes.

sid·ing /`saɪdɪŋ/ *n* [C] short railway track to and from which trains may be shunted.

sidle /`saɪdl/ *vi* [VP2C] ***~ away from/up to sb,*** move away from/up to sb in a shy or nervous way: *The little girl ~d up to me.*

siege /siːdʒ/ *n* [C,U] (period of) operations of armed forces who surround and blockade a town or fortress in order to capture it: *a ~ of 50 days. Before the ~ ended, the citizens were almost starving.* ***lay ~ to (a town, etc),*** surround and blockade it. ***raise a ~,*** end it by forcing the enemy's forces to withdraw. **`~ artillery/guns,** big guns used in ~s (too heavy, in former times, for use in the field).

si·enna /sɪ`enə/ *n* [U] kind of earth used as a colouring matter: *burnt ~,* reddish-brown; *raw ~,* brownish-yellow.

si·erra /sɪ`erə/ *n* [C] long mountain chain with sharp slopes and edges (esp in Spain and S America).

si·esta /sɪ`estə/ *n* [C] period of rest or sleep taken in the early afternoons, as is customary in hot countries.

sieve /sɪv/ *n* [C] utensil with wire network or gauze for separating finer grains, etc from coarse grains, etc or solids from liquids. ***have a head/memory like a ~,*** be incapable of remembering anything. □ *vt* [VP6A] put through, sift with, a ~.

sift /sɪft/ *vt,vi* **1** [VP6A,15A] put, separate by putting, through a sieve: *~ the cinders; ~ (out) ashes from the cinders/the wheat from the chaff.* **2** [VP6A,15A] shake through a sieve: *~ flour; ~ sugar on to a cake.* **3** [VP6A] (fig) examine carefully: *~ the evidence.* **4** [VP2C] fall, pass, come through, as from a sieve. **~er** *n* small sieve-like utensil, chiefly used in cooking: *a ˋflour-~er.*

sigh /saɪ/ *vi,vt* **1** [VP2A] take a deep breath that can be heard (indicating sadness, tiredness, relief, etc); (of the wind) make a sound like ~ing. **2** [VP3A] ***~ for sth,*** feel a longing (for): *~ for the country/for the good old times to return.* **3** [VP6A,15B] express, utter, with ~s: *~ out a prayer.* □ *n* [C] act of ~ing; sound of ~ing: *utter/leave a ~; with a ~ of relief.*

sight[1] /saɪt/ *n* **1** [U] power of seeing: *lose one's ~,* become blind; *have long/short* or *near ~,* be able to see things well only at long/short range; *have good/poor ~* (= eyesight). ***know sb by ~,*** know him by appearance only, not as an acquaintance. ***second ~,*** ⇨ second[1](1). **2** [U, but occ with *indef art*] seeing or being seen: *Their first ~ of land came after three days at sea.* ***catch ~ of; have/get a ~ of,*** begin to see; succeed in seeing: *If ever I catch ~ of those boys in my orchard again, I'll have their blood.* ***keep ~ of; keep sb/sth in ~,*** remain near enough to see or watch. ***lose ~ of,*** see no longer; fail to pay further attention to; forget about: *I've lost ~ of Smith. We must not lose ~ of the fact that....* ***at/on ~,*** as soon as (sb or sth) is seen: *play music at ~,* from printed music without previous study or practice; *a draft payable at ~/a ˋ~ draft,* to be paid at once when presented. *The sentry had orders to shoot at/on ~,* as soon as he saw any suspicious person, etc. ***at first ~,*** when first seen; without study, examination, etc: *At first ~ the problem seemed insoluble. He fell in love with her at first ~.* ***at (the) ~ of,*** on seeing: *At ~ of the police officers the men ran off. They all laughed at the ~ of old Green dancing with a girl of sixteen.* **3** [U] range of seeing; distance within which seeing is possible: *in/within/out of (one's) ~,* (of objects, etc) visible/invisible; *The train was still in ~/was not yet out of ~. Victory was not yet in ~.* ***in/within/out of ~ of sth,*** (of the viewer) where sth can/cannot be seen: *We are not yet within ~ of land,* can't see it. *We are now within ~ of the end of this wearisome task,* can look forward to reaching the end. ***come into/go out of ~,*** come near enough/go too far away to be visible. ***keep out of ~,*** stay where one cannot be seen. ***keep out of my/his, etc ~,*** where I/he, etc cannot see you. **4** [U] opinion; way of looking at sth: *Do what is right in your own ~. All men are equal in the ~ of God.* **5** [C] sth seen or to be seen, esp sth remarkable; (*pl*) noteworthy buildings, places, features, etc of a place or district: *The Grand Canyon is one of the ~s of the world. Our tulips are a wonderful ~ this year/are a ~ to see. Come and see the ~s of London.* Hence, **ˋ~-seeing** *n* going about to see places, etc. **ˋ~·seer** /-siə(r)/ *n* person who goes to see the ~s. ***a ~ for sore eyes,*** person or thing one enjoys seeing; sb or sth very welcome. **6** (*sing* with *indef art*) (colloq) person or thing that excites ridicule or unfavourable comment: *What a ~ she looks in that old dress! What a ~ you are! She ˋdoes look a ~!* **7** [C] device that helps to aim or observe when using a rifle, telescope, etc: *the ~s of a rifle;* aim or observation taken with such a device: *take a careful ~ before firing; take a ~ with a compass/quadrant; take a ~ at the sun,* e g to determine a ship's position. **8** (*sing* with *indef art;* dial) great quantity: *It cost him a ~ of money/trouble. He's a ~* (adverbial, = very much) *too clever to be caught by the police.* ***not by a ˋlong ~,*** not nearly. **-~ed** *suff* (with *adjj*) having the kind of ~(1) indicated: *ˋweak-/ˋlong-/ˊfar-~ed.*

sight[2] /saɪt/ *vt* [VP6A] **1** get sight of, esp by coming near: *After many months at sea, Columbus ~ed land.* **2** observe (a star, etc) by using sights(7); adjust the sights(7) of a gun; furnish (a gun, etc) with sights: *a ˋ~ing shot,* one to get the range. **~·ing** *n* occasion on which sth is ~ed: *new ~ings of the Loch Ness monster.*

sight·less /ˈsaɪtləs/ *adj* blind.

sight·ly /ˈsaɪtlɪ/ *adj* (dated) pleasing to the eye; of pleasant appearance.

sign[1] /saɪn/ *n* [C] **1** mark, object, symbol, used to represent sth: *mathematical ~s,* e g +, −, ×, ÷. **2** word or words, design, etc, on a board or plate to give a warning, or to direct sb towards sth: *ˋtraffic ~s,* e g for a speed limit, a bend in the road. **ˋ~·post** *n* post at or near crossroads with names of places on each road (and often distances). □ *vt* provide with ~posts: *The road is well ~-posted.* **3** sth that gives evidence, points to the existence or likelihood of sth: *the ~s of suffering on his face. Are dark clouds a ~ of rain? Violence is a ~ of weakness or fear, not a ~ of strength or confidence.* ***~ and countersign,*** secret sentences, etc by which friends can be distinguished from enemies or from those who do not share a secret. **4** movement of the hand, head, etc used with or instead of words; signal: *a ˋ~-language,* one used by deaf and dumb persons; *the ~ of the cross,* a movement with the hand outlining a cross, as a blessing, or with a prayer. **5** **ˋ~(-board),** device (often painted on a board) displayed by traders and shopkeepers (*ˋshop-~s*), and (usu *ˋinn-~*) by many inns to advertise their business: *at the ~ of the Red Lion,* at the inn of this name. **ˋ~-painter** *n* person who paints ~boards.

sign[2] /saɪn/ *vt,vi* **1** [VP6A,15B] write one's name on (a letter, document, etc) to show that one is the writer or that one accepts or agrees with the contents: *~ a letter/a Will and Testament/a cheque; ~ one's name,* write it for this purpose. ***~ sth away,*** give up (rights, property, etc) by ~ing one's name. ***~ sb on/up,*** (of an employer, etc) ~ an agreement about employment: *The firm ~ed on fifty more workers last week. The manager,* i e of a football team, *has ~ed up some new players.* **2** [VP2A,C] write one's name on a document, etc: *Please ~ on the dotted line.* ***~ on/up,*** (of a worker, etc), ~ an agreement about employment; ~ a register to record arrival at work, etc. ⇨ *clock in* at clock[1], *v* (2): *The seaman ~ed on for a voyage to Valparaiso and back.* **3** [VP2C,3A] make known (to sb) an order or request by making signs(4): *The policeman ~ed (for) them to stop. He ~ed to me to be quiet.* **4** [VP2C] ***~ on/off,*** (radio) indicate the beginning/end of a broadcast (e g by means of a few bars of a tune (or by other sound effects) that are associated with the broadcasters who use it). ⇨ **signature(2).**

sig·nal[1] /ˈsɪgnl/ *n* [C] **1** (making of a) movement, (showing of a) light, (sending of a) message, device used, to give a warning, an order or information, esp to sb at a distance; order, warning, etc, conveyed in this way: *ˈtraffic ~s,* for cars, etc in the streets; *ˈhand ~s,* made with the hand by the driver of a motor-vehicle to show which way it will turn, etc; *give the ~ for a retreat. A red light is usually a ~ of danger. A train must not pass a ~ that is at danger.* **ˈ~-box** *n* building on a railway from which ~s and movements of trains are controlled. **ˈ~·man** /-mən/ *n* (*pl* -men) person who operates ~s on a railway; man who sends and receives ~s (in the army and navy). **ˈ~ gun** *n* one fired as a ~ in case of distress, e g on a wrecked ship. **2** event which is the immediate cause of general activity, etc: *The arrival of the President was the ~ for an outburst of cheering.* **3** electronic impulse in radio, TV, etc; sound or TV image, transmitted or received: *an area with a poor/excellent TV signal.* □ *vt,vi* (-ll-, US, -l-) [VP6A,9,17,2A,C] make a ~ or ~s to; send by ~; make use of ~(s): *~ a message; ~ (to) the commanding officer (that...); ~ (to) the waiter to bring the menu; ~ that one is about to turn left. Sailors ~ with flags by day and with lights at night.* **~·ler** (US = **~er**) /ˈsɪgnələ(r)/ *n* person who ~s, esp a soldier (cf Navy, **ˈ~·man**) specially trained in sending and receiving messages.

sig·nal[2] /ˈsɪgnl/ *attrib adj* remarkable; outstanding: *a ~ victory/success/achievement.* **~ly** /-nlɪ/ *adv* in a ~ manner: *fail ~ly.*

sig·nal·ize /ˈsɪgnəlaɪz/ *vt* [VP6A] make (an event) noteworthy or conspicuous.

sig·na·tory /ˈsɪgnətrɪ *US:* -tɔrɪ/ *n* [C] (*pl* **-ries**) (person, country, etc) that has signed an agreement; *the signatories to the Treaty;* (attrib) *the ~ powers.*

sig·na·ture /ˈsɪgnətʃə(r)/ *n* [C] **1** person's name signed by himself: *put one's ~ to a letter; send letters in to the manager for ~,* for him to sign. **2** **ˈ~ tune,** tune (a few bars of a piece of music) identifying a broadcasting station or a particular programme or performer. **ˈkey ~,** (music) indication of a (change of) key.

sig·net /ˈsɪgnɪt/ *n* [C] private seal used with or instead of a signature. **ˈ~-ring,** finger ring with a ~ set in it. **Writer to the S~,** Scottish law officer.

sig·nifi·cance /sɪgˈnɪfɪkəns/ *n* [U] meaning; importance; *understand the ~ of a remark; a matter/speech of great/little ~; a look of deep ~.*

sig·nifi·cant /sɪgˈnɪfɪkənt/ *adj* having a special or suggestive meaning; important: *a ~ speech. Few things are more ~ of a man's interests than the books on his shelves.* **~·ly** *adv*

sig·nifi·ca·tion /ˌsɪgnɪfɪˈkeɪʃn/ *n* [C] (intended) meaning (of a word, etc).

sig·nifi·cat·ive /sɪgˈnɪfɪkətɪv *US:* -keɪtɪv/ *adj* offering presumptive evidence (*of*).

sig·nify /ˈsɪgnɪfaɪ/ *vt,vi* (*pt,pp* -fied) **1** [VP6A,9,15A] make known (one's views, intentions, purpose, etc); be a sign of; mean: *He signified his agreement/that he agreed by nodding. His wife signified her approval. Does a high forehead ~ intelligence? What does this phrase ~?* **2** [VP2A,C] matter; be of importance: *It doesn't ~. It signifies much/little.*

signor /ˈsinjɔ(r)/, **si·gnora** /sɪˈnjɔrə/, **si·gnor·ina** /ˌsɪnjɔˈrinə/ *nn* **S~,** titles used of or to Italians corresponding to Mr, Mrs and Miss or (with a small *s*) gentleman, Sir, Madam and young lady.

Sikh /sik/ *n* member of a monotheistic Hindu sect founded in the 16th c in the Punjab.

si·lage /ˈsaɪlɪdʒ/ *n* [U] green cattle fodder stored in a silo without drying.

si·lence /ˈsaɪləns/ *n* [U] **1** condition of being quiet or silent; absence of sound: *the ~ of night/of the grave.* **2** condition of not speaking, answering (questions, spoken or written), or making comments, etc; (with *indef art*) period (of saying nothing): *Your ~ on recent events surprises me. There was a short ~ and then uproar broke out.* ***S~ gives consent,*** (prov) If nothing is said in answer to a proposal or suggestion we may suppose that it is agreed to. ***reduce sb to ~,*** (esp) refute his arguments so that he has to stop talking. ***in ~,*** silently: *listen to sb in ~. We should not pass over this disgraceful affair in ~,* We ought to protest, etc. □ *vt* [VP6A] make (sb or sth) silent; cause to be quiet(er): *~ a baby's crying; ~ one's critics/the enemy's guns.* **si·lencer** *n* device that reduces the noise made by the exhaust of a petrol engine, the report of a gun, etc.

si·lent /ˈsaɪlənt/ *adj* **1** making no or little sound; still; not accompanied by any sound: *a ~ prayer; with ~ footsteps; the ~ running of a Rolls Royce car; a ~ film,* without a sound track. **2** saying little or nothing; giving no answer, views, etc: *Do you know when to keep ~,* say nothing, keep a secret? *You'd better be ~ about what happened. Her husband is the strong, ~ type.* **ˈ~ partner,** (US) = sleeping partner. ⇨ **sleep**[2]**(1).** **3** written but not pronounced: *a ~ letter,* e g *b* in *doubt, w* in *wrong.* **~·ly** *adv*

sil·hou·ette /ˌsɪluˈet/ *n* picture in solid black showing only the outline; ⇨ the illus at **hansom**; outline of sb or sth seen against a light background: *see sth in ~.* □ *vt* (usu passive) show, exhibit, in ~: *~d against the eastern sky at dawn.*

sil·ica /ˈsɪlɪkə/ *n* [U] silicon dioxide (**SiO**$_2$), occurring as ~ sand (used in glass-making) and in quartz, and as the principal constituent of sandstone and other rocks.

sili·cate /ˈsɪlɪkeɪt/ *n* [U] one of a great number of compounds containing silica: *~ of soda.*

sili·con /ˈsɪlɪkən/ *n* [U] non-metallic element (symbol **Si**) found combined with oxygen in quartz, sandstone, etc.

sili·cone /ˈsɪlɪkəʊn/ *n* [U] (kinds of) complex organic compounds used in paints, varnish and lubricants.

sili·co·sis /ˌsɪlɪˈkəʊsɪs/ *n* [U] disease caused by breathing in quartz dust (e g in a coalmine).

silk /sɪlk/ *n* **1** [U] fine, soft thread from the cocoons of certain insects; material made from this; (attrib) made of this: *raw ~; ~ stockings; a ~ hat,* a top hat. **ˈ~·screen (printing),** method of printing by forcing the colour(s) through a stencil of ~ or other finely woven material. **ˈ~·worm** *n* caterpillar that spins ~ to form a cocoon. **2** (*pl*) garments of ~: *dressed in ~s and satins,* wearing rich clothes. **3** [C] (in England) Queen's/King's Counsel (abbr **Q C, K C**). ⇨ **counsel**[1]**(3).** ***take ~,*** become a Q C/K C.

silken /ˈsɪlkən/ *adj* **1** soft and smooth; soft and shining: *a ~ voice; ~ hair.* **2** (old use, or liter) made of silk: ~ *dresses.*

silky /ˋsɪlkɪ/ *adj* (-ier, -iest) soft, shiny, smooth, like silk: *a* ~ (= suave) *manner; a* ~ *voice.* **silki·ness** *n*

sill /sɪl/ *n* [C] flat shelf or block of wood or stone at the base of a window (or rarely, doorway): *a vase of flowers on the ˋwindow-sill.* ⇨ the illus at window.

sil·la·bub (US = **syl-**) /ˋsɪləbʌb/ *n* [C,U] soft, sweet dish of food made of cream or milk mixed with wine into curd, etc.

silly /ˋsɪlɪ/ *adj* (-ier, -iest) foolish; weak-minded: *say* ~ *things; a* ~ *little boy. Don't be* ~*! How* ~ *of you to do that!* □ *n* (*pl* -lies) (chiefly used to or by children) ~ person: *Go away, you little sillies! Don't be a* ~*!* **sil·li·ness** *n*

silo /ˋsaɪləʊ/ *n* (*pl* -los /-ləʊz/) [C] airtight structure (either a tall cylindrical tower or a pit) in which green food (*silage*) is stored for farm animals.

silt /sɪlt/ *n* [U] sand, mud, etc carried by moving water (and left at the mouth of a river, in a harbour, etc). □ *vt,vi* [VP2C,15B] ***~ (sth) up,*** (cause to) become stopped with ~: *The harbour has* ~*ed up. The sand has* ~*ed up the mouth of the river.*

sil·van /ˋsɪlvən/ = sylvan.

sil·ver /ˋsɪlvə(r)/ *n* [U] **1** shining white metal (symbol **Ag**) used for ornaments, coins, utensils, etc: *ˋtable* ~, spoons, forks, teapots, dishes, etc. **~ plate,** metal articles coated with ~. ***be born with a ~ ˋspoon in one's mouth,*** (prov) be destined to have great wealth. **2** ~ coins: *£20 in notes and £5 in* ~*; a handful of* ~*; a* ~ *collection,* to which ~ coins are to be given. *Have you any* ~ *on you?* **3** ~ vessels, dishes, articles, e g candlesticks, trays: *have all one's* ~ *taken by burglars; sell one's* ~ *to pay the mortgage interest.* **4** (attrib) the colour of ~: *the* ~ *moon;* (of sounds) soft and clear: *He has a* ~ *tongue/is* ˌ~-ˋ*tongued,* is eloquent. **~ grey,** lustrous grey. **the ~ screen,** cinema screen. **5** (in art and literature) second best: *the* ~ *age,* ⇨ golden(2). **6** (compounds) ˌ~ ˋ**birch** *n* common white birch with ~-coloured bark. ˋ**~-fish** *n* (kinds of) small wingless insect that damages book bindings, clothes, etc. **~ paper,** (colloq) thin, light foil made of tin or aluminium (as used for packing cigarettes, etc). ˋ**~-side** *n* best side of a round of beef. ˋ**~·smith** *n* manufacturer of ~ articles; merchant who sells these. ˌ**~ ˋwedding** *n* 25th anniversary. □ *vt,vi* **1** [VP6A] coat with ~ or with sth that looks like ~; make (sth) bright like ~: *The years have* ~*ed her hair.* **2** [VP2A] become white or ~ colour. *Her hair had* ~*ed.* **sil·very** *adj* like ~: *the* ~*y notes of a temple bell.*

sil·vern /ˋsɪlvən/ *adj* (archaic) silver: *Speech is* ~ *but silence is golden,* it is better to be silent than to speak.

sim·ian /ˋsɪmɪən/ *adj, n* (of, like, a) monkey or ape.

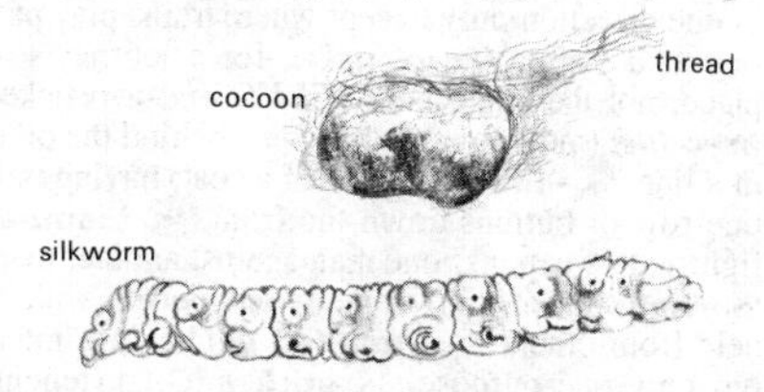

a silkworm

simi·lar /ˋsɪmḷə(r)/ *adj* ~ ***(to),*** like; of the same sort: *My wife and I have* ~ *tastes in music. Gold is* ~ *in colour to brass.* **~·ly** *adv* **~·ity** /ˌsɪməˋlærətɪ/ *n* [U] likeness; state of being ~; [C] (*pl* -ties) point or respect in which there is likeness: *points of* ~*ity between the two men. Are there any* ~*ities between Goethe and Byron?*

sim·ile /ˋsɪmḷɪ/ *n* [C,U] (use of) comparison of one thing to another, e g He is as brave as a lion. Childhood is like a swiftly passing dream: *He uses interesting* ~*s. His style is rich in* ~.

sim·ili·tude /sɪˋmɪlɪtjud *US:* -tud/ *n* **1** [U] resemblance (in general details but not in everything). **2** [C] comparison; simile: *talk in* ~*s.*

simi·tar /ˋsɪmɪtə(r)/ *n* = scimitar.

sim·mer /ˋsɪmə(r)/ *vi,vt* **1** [VP2A,B,6A,15A] be, keep (sth), almost at boiling-point: *Let the soup* ~ *for a few minutes. S*~ *the stew for an hour.* **2** [VP2C] be filled with (anger, etc), which is only just kept under control: ~ *with rage/laughter/annoyance.* **~ down,** (fig) become calm (after being angry or excited). □ *n* (*sing* only) ***keep sth at a ~/on the ~,*** ~ing.

sim·ony /ˋsɪmənɪ/ *n* [U] (in former times) offence of accepting or offering money for a position in the Church.

si·moom /sɪˋmum/, **si·moon** /sɪˋmun/ *n* hot, dry, dust-laden wind blowing in a straight track in the Sahara and the deserts of Arabia.

simp /sɪmp/ *n* (colloq abbr of) simpleton.

sim·per /ˋsɪmpə(r)/ *vi* [VP2A], *n* (give a) silly, self-conscious smile. **~·ing·ly** /ˋsɪmprɪŋlɪ/ *adv*

simple /ˋsɪmpl/ *adj* (-r, -st) **1** unmixed; not divided into parts; having only a small number of parts: *a* ~ *substance; a* ~ *machine; a* ~ *sentence,* one without subordinate clauses. **~ interest,** on capital only, not on accumulated interest. ⇨ compound[1](3). **2** plain; not much decorated or ornamented: ~ *food/cooking; a* ~ *style of architecture; the* ~ *life,* a way of living without luxuries, servants or artificial pastimes, or in the country, contrasted with cities. **3** not highly developed: ~ *forms of life.* **4** easily done or understood; not causing trouble: *written in* ~ *English; a* ~ *task.* **5** innocent; straight-forward: *behave in a pleasant and* ~ *way; as* ~ *as a child;* ~ *folk; a* ~ *peasant.* ˌ**~-ˋhearted** *adj* frank. **6** inexperienced; easily deceived: *Are you* ~ *enough to believe everything your newspapers tell you? I'm not so* ~ *as to suppose you like me. She's a* ~ *soul,* innocent of guile. ˌ**~-ˋminded** *adj* ingenuous, unsophisticated. **7** with nothing added; absolute: *a* ~ *fact.* ***pure and ~,*** (colloq) absolute(ly), unquestionably: *It's a case of kill or be killed, pure and* ~. □ *n* [C] (old use) herb used medicinally. **sim·ply** /ˋsɪmplɪ/ *adv* **1** in a ~(2) manner: *live simply; dress simply; simply dressed.* **2** completely; absolutely: *His pronunciation is simply terrible,* is very bad indeed. *She looks simply lovely.* **3** only; merely; nothing more nor less than: *He is simply a workman. You must believe me simply on my word,* with nothing more than my assertion, without proof or evidence. *It is simply a matter of working hard.*

simple·ton /ˋsɪmpltən/ *n* foolish, weak-minded person, esp one who is easily deceived.

sim·plic·ity /sɪmˋplɪsətɪ/ *n* [U] the state of being simple: *the* ~ *of the problem; speak with* ~. *A small child often has a look of* ~. ***be ~ itself,*** (colloq) be extremely easy.

sim·plify /ˈsɪmplɪfaɪ/ *vt* (*pt,pp* -fied) [VP6A] make simple; make easy to do or understand: *a simplified reader/text. That will* ~ *my task.* **sim·pli·fi·ca·tion** /ˈsɪmplɪfɪˈkeɪʃn/ *n* [U] act or process of ~ing; [C] instance of ~ing; sth simplified.

sim·ply /ˈsɪmplɪ/ *adv* ⇨ simple.

simu·lac·rum /ˈsɪmjʊˈleɪkrəm/ *n* (*pl* -cra /-krə/) sth made in the likeness of a person or object; shadowy likeness that deceives.

simu·late /ˈsɪmjʊleɪt/ *vt* [VP6A] **1** pretend to be; pretend to have or feel: ~*d innocence/enthusiasm.* **2** counterfeit: *insects that* ~ *dead leaves.* **simu·la·tion** /ˈsɪmjʊˈleɪʃn/ *n* [U] pretence; imitation. **simu·la·tor** /-tə(r)/ *n* (esp) apparatus designed to provide (for testing purposes) conditions (e g non-gravity, for simulating weightlessness) like those which are encountered in real operations.

sim·ul·ta·neous /ˈsɪmlˈteɪnɪəs *US:* ˈsaɪm-/ *adj* ~ ***(with),*** happening or done at the same time as. **~·ly** *adv* **~·ness, sim·ul·tane·ity** /ˈsɪmltəˈniətɪ *US:* ˈsaɪm-/ *nn*

sin /sɪn/ *n* **1** [U] breaking of God's laws; behaviour that is against the principles of morality. ⇨ crime; [C] instance of this; immoral act such as telling a lie, stealing, adultery: *confess one's sins to a priest; ask for one's sins to be forgiven.* ***live in sin,*** (dated or hum use) (esp of a man and woman who are not husband and wife) live together as if married. **oˈriginal sin,** proneness to commit sin which, some Christians believe, is part of our inheritance. **ˈdeadly/ˈmortal sin,** one that is fatal to salvation of the soul. ***the seven deadly sins,*** pride, covetousness, lust, anger, gluttony, envy, sloth. **2** [C] (colloq) offence against convention; sth considered contrary to common sense: *It's a sin to give the children so much homework. It's a sin to stay indoors on such a fine day.* □ *vi* (-nn-) [VP2A,3A] ***sin (against),*** commit sin; do wrong: *We are all liable to sin. Is it sinning against society to have lots of children?* **sin·ful** /-fl/ *adj* wrong; wicked. **sin·ful·ness** *n* **sin·less** *adj* free from sin; innocent. **sin·less·ness** *n* **sin·ner** /ˈsɪnə(r)/ *n* person who sins/has sinned.

since /sɪns/ *adv* **1** (with the perfect tenses) after a date, event, etc in the past: before the present time; between some time in the past and the present time, or the time referred to: *The town was/had been destroyed by an earthquake ten years ago/earlier and has/had* ~ *been rebuilt. He left home in 1970 and has not been heard of* ~*/has not* ~ *been heard of.* ***ever*** ~*,* throughout the whole of a period of time referred to and up to the present: *He went to Turkey in 1956 and has lived there ever* ~. **2** (with the simple tenses) ago (which is to be preferred): *He did it many years* ~*. How long* ~ *is/was it?* □ *prep* (with perfect tenses in the main clause) after; during a period of time after: *S*~ *last seeing you I have been ill. She hasn't/hadn't been home* ~ *her marriage.* □ *conj* **1** (with perfect tense in the main clause) from the past time when: *Where have you been* ~ *I last saw you?* (with the simple present tense in the main clause): *How long is it* ~ *you were in London? It is just a week* ~ *we arrived here.* **2** seeing that; as: *S*~ *we've no money, we can't buy it.*

sin·cere /sɪnˈsɪə(r)/ *adj* **1** (of feelings, behaviour) genuine; not pretended: *It is my* ~ *belief that.... Are they* ~ *in their wish to disarm?* **2** (of persons) straightforward; not in the habit of expressing feelings that are pretended. **~·ly** *adv* in a ~ manner. ***yours ~ly,*** commonly used before a signature at the end of a letter to a friend or acquaintance. **sin·cer·ity** /sɪnˈserətɪ/ *n* [U] the quality of being ~; honesty: *speaking in all sincerity,* very ~ly and honestly.

sin·ecure /ˈsaɪnɪkjʊə(r)/ *n* [C] position for which one receives credit or payment but which does not entail work or responsibility.

sine die /ˈsaɪnɪ ˈdaɪɪ/ *adv* (Lat) without a date fixed: *adjourn a meeting* ~, indefinitely.

sine qua non /ˈsɪneɪ kwɑ ˈnəʊn/ *n* (Lat) condition or qualification that cannot be done without; essential condition.

sinew /ˈsɪnju/ *n* [C] **1** tendon (strong cord) joining a muscle to a bone. **2** (*pl*) muscles; energy; physical strength; (fig) means of acquiring strength: *the* ~*s of war,* money (with which to buy supplies). **sin·ewy** *adj* tough; having strong ~s: ~*y arms;* (fig) vigorous; having or showing nervous strength.

sing /sɪŋ/ *vi,vt* (*pt* sang /sæŋ/, *pp* sung /sʌŋ/) **1** [VP2A,C,3A,6A,12B,13B,15A] make musical sounds with the voice, utter words one after the other to a tune: *She* ~*s well. The birds were* ~*ing. He was* ~*ing a French song. He was* ~*ing to the guitar/to a piano accompaniment. She sang the baby to sleep. You're not* ~*ing in tune. You're* ~*ing out of tune. Will you* ~ *me a song/* ~ *a song for me?* ~ ***another tune,*** behave or speak in a different way, e g with less confidence or presumption. ~ ***small,*** (colloq) speak or behave humbly (after being reproved, etc). **2** [VP2A,C] make a humming, buzzing or ringing sound: *The kettle was* ~*ing (away) on the cooker. My ears are* ~*ing,* are affected with buzzing sounds. **3** [VP6A,3A] ~ ***(of) sth,*** celebrate in verse: ~ *(of) sb's exploits. 'Arms and the man I* ~*'.* ~ ***sb's praises,*** praise him with enthusiasm. **4** ~ ***out (for),*** shout (for). ~ ***sth out,*** shout sth: ~ *out an order.* ~ ***up,*** ~ with more force, ~ more loudly: *S*~ *up, girls, and let's hear you.* **~er** *n* person who ~s, esp one who does this in public. **~·ing** *n* (esp) art of the ~er: *teach* ~*ing; my* ˈ~*ing-master; take* ˈ~*ing lessons.* **~·able** /-əbl/ *adj* that can be sung: *Some of this modern music is not* ~*able.* **ˈ~·song** *n* ⇨ separate entry below.

singe /sɪndʒ/ *vt,vi* (*pres part* singeing) **1** [VP6A] burn off the tips or ends (esp of hair, as may be done at the hair-dresser's): *have one's hair cut and* ~*d.* **2** [VP6A] blacken the surface of by burning; burn slightly: *If the iron is too hot you'll* ~ *that nightdress. She was busy* ~*ing the poultry,* burning the downy feathers off the birds (after they had been killed). **3** [VP2A] become ~d or scorched. □ *n* slight burn or scorch (on cloth, etc).

single /ˈsɪŋgl/ *adj* **1** one only; one and no more: *a* ~ *track,* (on a railway) one line only, with traffic in one direction only except where trains may pass (e g at a station); *a* ~ *ticket,* for a journey to a place, not there and back. Cf US *one-way* ticket. ***in ~ file,*** (moving, standing) one behind the other in a line. **ˈ~-ˈbreasted** *adj* (of a coat) having only one row of buttons down the front. **ˈ~ ˈcombat,** fight with weapons, one man against another man. **ˈ~-ˈhanded** *adj, adv* done by one person without help from others. **ˈ~-ˈminded** *adj* having, intent on, only one purpose. **ˈ~·stick** *n* [C,U] (fencing with a) stick about the length of a sword. **2** not married: ~ *men and women; remain ~; the ~ state/life,* that of an unmarried person. **3** for the use of, used for, done by, one person: *a ~ bed; reserve* (at a hotel) *two ~ rooms and one double room.* **4** (bot) having only one set of petals. ⇨ double¹(5): *a ~ tulip.* □ *n* [C] **1** (tennis and golf) game with one person on each side: *play a ~; the men's/women's ~s at Wimbledon;* (cricket) hit for which one run is scored; run a quick ~; (baseball) base hit. **2** (short for a) ~ ticket: *two second-class ~s to Leeds.* □ *vt* [VP15B] ***~ sb/sth out,*** select from others (for special attention, etc): *Why have you ~d out this incident for adverse comment?* **sing·ly** /ˋsɪŋglɪ/ *adv* one by one; by oneself. **~·ness** *n* [U] quality of being ~. ***~ness of purpose,*** complete devotion to one purpose only.

sin·glet /ˋsɪŋglət/ *n* (GB) sleeveless garment worn for games or under a shirt; vest.

single·ton /ˋsɪŋltən/ *n* [C] (in card games) single card of any suit held in one hand (of 13 cards): *a ~ in hearts.*

sing·song /ˋsɪŋsoŋ/ *n* **1** meeting of friends to sing songs together; impromptu vocal concert: *have a ~ round the camp fire.* **2** ***in a ~,*** in a rising and falling way of monotonous regularity: (attrib) ***in a ~ voice/manner.***

sin·gu·lar /ˋsɪŋgjʊlə(r)/ *adj* **1** (dated use) uncommon; strange: *Isn't it unwise to make yourself so ~ in your dress,* to be so unconventional? **2** outstanding: *a man of ~ courage and honesty.* **3** (gram) of the form used in speaking or writing of one person or thing. □ *n* the ~ number: *What is the ~ of children?* **~·ly** *adv* outstanding; strangely; peculiarly. **~·ity** /ˈsɪŋgjʊˋlærətɪ/ *n* (*pl* -ties) [U] strangeness; [C] sth unusual or strange. **ˋ~·ize** /-ɑɪz/ *vt* make ~(1).

Sin·ha·lese, Sin·gha·lese /ˈsɪnhəˋliz, ˈsɪŋhəˋliz/ *adj* of the larger of the communities in Sri Lanka and their language. ⇨ Tamil. □ *n* member, language, of this community.

sin·is·ter /ˋsɪnɪstə(r)/ *adj* **1** suggesting evil or the likelihood of coming misfortune: *a ~ beginning.* **2** showing ill will: *a ~ face; ~ looks.* **3** (in heraldry) on the left side of the shield (regarded from the bearer's point of view). ***bar ~,*** mark on a shield showing illegitimate descent.

sink¹ /sɪŋk/ *n* [C] **1** fixed basin (of stone, porcelain, steel, etc) with a drain for taking off water, usu under water taps in a kitchen or scullery, used for washing dishes, cleaning vegetables, etc: *She complains that she spends half her life at the kitchen-~,* seldom gets away from dull domestic work. **2** cesspool. **3** (fig) place where evil people and evil practices collect: *That part of the town is a ~ of iniquity.*

sink² /sɪŋk/ *vi,vt* (*pt* sank /sæŋk/, *pp* sunk /sʌŋk/, and, as *adj,* sunken /ˋsʌŋkən/) **1** [VP2A, C] go down, esp below the horizon or the surface of water or other liquid or a soft substance, e g mud: *The sun was ~ing in the west. Wood does not ~ in water, it floats. The ship sank,* went to the bottom. ***~ or swim,*** phrase used of running great risks when the alternatives are complete loss or failure and safety or success. **2** [VP2A,C] slope downwards; become lower or weaker: *The foundations have sunk. The ground ~s to the sea. The soldier sank to the ground badly wounded.* (fig) *His heart sank at the thought of failure.* **3** [VP6A, 15A] make by digging: *~ a well;* place (sth) in a hole made by digging: *~ a post one foot deep in the ground.* **4** [VP2C] ***~ in/into,*** (of liquids, and fig) go down deep: *The rain sank into the dry ground. Let this warning ~ into your mind. The lesson hasn't sunk in,* (fig) has not been learnt or fully understood. **5** [VP2C] ***~ in/into/to,*** come to a lower level or state (physical or moral): *~ into a deep sleep; ~ into vice; ~ into insignificance; ~ in the estimation of one's friends. He was sunk in thought/despair. He is ~ing fast,* will soon die. *The old man has sunken cheeks. His cheeks have sunk in. His voice sank to a whisper.* **6** [VP6A, 15A] cause or allow to ~: *~ a ship. He sank* (= lowered) *his voice to a whisper. Let us ~ our differences* (= put them out of our thoughts, forget them), *and work together.* **7** [VP6A,14] invest (money), esp so that it is not easy to withdraw it: *He has sunk half his fortune in a new business undertaking.* **ˋ~·ing fund,** invested cash available for use when needed later on. **ˋ~·able** /-əbl/ *adj* that can be sunk.

sinker /ˋsɪŋkə(r)/ *n* [C] (esp) lead weight attached to a fishing line or net to keep it under the water. ***hook, line and ~,*** ⇨ hook(1).

sink·ing /ˋsɪŋkɪŋ/ *n* (*gerund*) (esp) *a ˋ~ feeling,* feeling in the stomach caused by fear or hunger. **ˋ~-fund** *n* money from revenue put aside by a government, business company, etc for gradual repayment of a debt.

Sinn Fein /ˈʃɪn ˋfeɪn/ *n* political movement and organization founded in Ireland in 1905 for independent republican government.

Si·nol·ogy /sɑɪˋnolədʒɪ/ *n* [U] knowledge, study, of the Chinese language, Chinese literature, art, etc. **Si·nol·ogist** /-dʒɪst/ *n* expert in ~.

sinu·ous /ˋsɪnjʊəs/ *adj* winding; full of curves and twists. **sinu·os·ity** /ˈsɪnjʊˋosətɪ/ *n* [U] being ~; [C] (*pl* -ties) curve or twist.

sinus /ˋsɑɪnəs/ *n* (*pl* ~es) [C] hollow in a bone, esp one of several air-filled cavities in the bones of the skull, communicating with the nostrils. ⇨ the illus at skeleton.

Sioux /su/ *n* member of a N American Indian tribe.

sip /sɪp/ *vt,vi* (-pp-) [VP6A,15B,2A] drink, taking a very small quantity at a time: *sip (up) one's coffee.* □ *n* [C] (quantity taken in a) sipping: *drink brandy in sips, not gulps.*

si·phon /ˋsɑɪfən/ *n* [C] **1** bent or curved tube, pipe, etc so arranged (like an inverted U) that liquid will flow up through it and then down. **2** bottle from which soda-water can be forced out by the pressure of gas in it. □ *vt,vi* [VP15B] ***~ sth off/out,*** draw (liquid) out or off through or as if through a ~: *Who has ~ed off all the petrol from the tank of my car?*

sir /sɜ(r)/ *n* **1** polite form used in addressing a man to whom one wishes to show respect: *Yes, sir. Dinner is served, sir. Sir, it is my duty to inform you that....* **2** used in letters: *My dear Sir; Dear Sir; Dear Sirs.* **3** prefix (usu unstressed) to the name of a knight or baronet: *Sir ˈWinston ˋChurchill.*

sir·dar /ˋsɜdɑ(r)/ *n* (in some Asian countries; formerly in Egypt) officer or leader of high, esp military, rank.

sire /sɑɪə(r)/ *n* **1** (old use) father or male ancestor. **2** (old use) title of respect used when addressing a king or emperor. **3** male parent of an animal: *race-horses with pedigree ~s.* □ *vt* [VP6A] (esp of horses) be the ~ of: *a Derby winner ~d by Pegasus.*

si·ren /ˈsaɪərən/ *n* **1** (Gk myth) one of a number of winged women whose songs charmed sailors and caused their destruction; (hence) woman who attracts and is dangerous to men. **2** ship's whistle for sending warnings and signals; device for producing a loud shrill noise (as a warning, etc): *an ˈair-raid ~; an ambulance/a fire-engine racing along with its ~s wailing.*

sir·loin /ˈsɜlɔɪn/ *n* [C,U] best part of loin of beef.

sir·occo /sɪˈrokəʊ/ *n* (*pl* -cos /-kəʊz/) [C] hot, moist wind reaching Italy from Africa.

sir·rah /ˈsɪrə/ *n* (contemptuous; old use) fellow.

sirup /ˈsɪrəp/ = syrup.

si·sal /ˈsɑɪsl/ *n* [U] plant (⇨ agave) with fleshy leaves which provide strong fibre used for making rope: (attrib) *~ grass/fibre/rope.*

sissy /ˈsɪsɪ/ *n* (colloq; = cissy) effeminate boy or man. **sis·si·fied** /ˈsɪsɪfɑɪd/ *adj* effeminate.

sis·ter /ˈsɪstə(r)/ *n* **1** daughter of the same parents as oneself or another person: *my/your/his ~.* **ˈhalf-~** *n* related by one parent only. ⇨ also *step-~* at step-. **ˈ~-in-law** *n* (*pl* ~s-in-law) ~ of one's wife or husband; wife of one's brother. **2** person who behaves towards one as a ~: *She was a ~ to him.* **3** (GB) senior hospital nurse. **4** member of certain religious orders; nun: *S~s of Mercy,* a nursing sisterhood. **5** (attrib) of the same design or type: *~ ships.* **~·ly** *adj* of or like a ~: *~ly love; a ~ly kiss.* **~·hood** /-hʊd/ *n* [C] society of women who devote themselves to charitable works, nursing, etc or live together in a religious order.

sit /sɪt/ *vi,vt* (*pt,pp* sat /sæt/, -tt-) (For special uses with *adverbial particles* and *preps,* ⇨ 8 below.) **1** [VP2A,C] take or be in a position in which the body is upright and supported by the buttocks (resting on the ground or on a seat): *sit on a chair/on the floor/in an armchair/at a table or desk/on a horse, etc. The child is not big enough to sit at table yet.* ***sit to an artist,*** sit for one's portrait by him. ***sit for an examination,*** take one. ***sit for one's portrait,*** have one's portrait painted while before an artist. ***sit tight,*** **(a)** remain firmly in one's place, esp in the saddle. **(b)** (colloq) stick firmly to one's purpose, opinions, etc. ***sit for (a borough, etc),*** represent it in Parliament. Hence, ***the sitting member,*** the candidate (at a general election) who held the seat before the dissolution of Parliament. **2** [VP6A] cause to sit; place in a sitting position: *He lifted the child and sat* (= seated) *her at a little table.* (old use, reflex): *Sit you down,* be seated. **3** [VP2A] (of Parliament, a law court, a committee, etc) hold meetings: *The House of Commons was still sitting at 3 a m.* **4** [VP6A] keep one's seat on (a horse, etc): *She sits her horse well. He couldn't sit his mule.* **5** [VP2A,C] (of birds) perch: *sitting on a branch.* **ˌsitting ˈduck,** an easy target or victim. **ˌsitting ˈtenant,** one who is actually in occupation (of a house, flat, etc, contrasted with a prospective tenant): *greedy owners who want to get rid of sitting tenants and then charge higher rates to new tenants.* **6** [VP2A] (of domestic fowls) remain on the nest in order to hatch eggs: *That hen wants to sit.* **7** [VP2C] (of clothes) suit, fit, hang: *That dress sits well/loosely, etc on her. The coat sits badly across the shoulders. His new dignity sits well on him,* (fig) suits him well. **8** [VP2C,3A,15B] (special uses with *adverbial particles* and *preps*):

sit back, **(a)** settle oneself comfortably back, e g in a chair. **(b)** (fig) take one's ease (after strenuous activity, etc); take no action.

sit down, **(a)** take a seat: *Please sit down, all of you.* ***a sit down strike,*** strike by workers who refuse to leave the factory, etc until their demands are considered or satisfied. ***sit down under (insults, etc),*** suffer without protest or complaint.

sit in, (of workers, students, etc) demonstrate by occupying a building (or part of it) and staying there until their grievances are considered or until they themselves are ejected: *There are reports of students sitting in at several universities.* Hence, **ˈsit-in** *n* such a demonstration. ***sit in on sth,*** attend (a discussion, etc) as an observer, not as a participant.

sit on sth, **(a)** be a member of (a jury, committee, etc). **(b)** (colloq) neglect to deal with: *They've been sitting on my application for a month.*

sit out, sit outdoors: *It's hot indoors—let's sit out in the garden, shall we?* ***sit sth out,*** **(a)** stay to the end of (a performance, etc): *sit out a play.* **(b)** take no part in (esp a particular dance): *I think I'll sit out the next dance.*

sit up, not go to bed (until later than the usual time): *I shall be late getting back, so please don't sit up for me. The nurse sat up with her patient all night. Ought children to sit up late looking at T V programmes?* ***sit (sb) up,*** (cause to) take an upright position after lying flat or sitting badly: *The patient is well enough to sit up in bed now. Just sit me up a little,* help me to sit up. ***sit up straight!*** Don't lean back! Don't sprawl! ***make sb sit up (and take notice),*** (colloq) alarm or frighten him; rouse him from lethargy to activity.

sit (up)on sth, (of a jury, etc) inquire into, investigate (a case). ***sit (up)on sb,*** (colloq) repress; snub: *That impudent fellow needs to be sat on.*

si·tar /ˈsitɑ(r) *US:* sɪˈtɑ(r)/ *n* Hindu stringed musical instrument. ⇨ the illus at string.

site /sɑɪt/ *n* [C] place where sth was, is, or is to be: *built on the ~ of an old fort; a ~ for a new school; deliver materials to a ˈbuilding ~.* □ *vi* [VP6A] locate; place: *Where have they decided to ~ the new factory?*

sit·ter /ˈsɪtə(r)/ *n* **1** person who is sitting for a portrait. **2** hen that sits(**5**): *a good/poor ~.* **3** bird or animal that is sitting and therefore easy to shoot; (hence) easy shot; sth easily done. **4** ⇨ *baby-~* at baby.

sit·ting /ˈsɪtɪŋ/ *n* **1** time during which a court of law, Parliament, etc is ~ continuously: *during a long ~.* **2** period of time during which one is engaged continuously in a particular occupation: *finish reading a book at one ~.* **3** act of ~ for a portrait: *The artist wants you to give him six ~s,* sit for him six times. **4** occasion of ~ (for a meal, etc): *In the dining-room of this hotel 100 people can be served at one ~,* i e at the same time, together. **5** collection of eggs on which a hen sits. **6** **ˈ~-room** *n* room for general use (contrasted with a dining-room, bedroom, etc).

situ·ated /ˈsɪtʃʊeɪtɪd/ *pred adj* **1** (of a town, building, etc) placed: *The village is ~ in a valley.* **2** (of a person) in (certain) circumstances: *Having six children and no income, the widow was badly ~. I'm awkwardly ~ just now,* in difficult circumstances.

situ·ation /ˌsɪtʃʊˈeɪʃn/ *n* [C] **1** position (of a town, building, etc). **2** condition, state of affairs, esp at a

ice-skating

certain time: *be in an embarrassing ~*. **3** work, employment, e g in domestic service: *S~s vacant, S~s wanted*, headings of newspaper notices of employment offered and asked for; *be in/out of a ~*, be employed/unemployed.

six /sɪks/ *n adj* the number 6, ⇨ App 4. ***six of one and half a dozen of the other,*** very little difference between the one and the other. ***in sixes,*** in groups of six at a time. ***at sixes and sevens,*** in confusion. **ˌsix-ˈfooter** *n* (colloq) person six feet in height; thing six feet long. **ˈsix·pence** *n* **(a)** GB coin (not part of the new decimal currency, but still in circulation) value (formerly) six pennies, or (since 1971) 2½p: *Can you give me two sixpences for this shilling/fivepence piece?* **(b)** the sum of six pennies, either *6p* or *6d*. ⇨ App 5. *This magazine is not worth sixpence.* **ˈsix·penny** *adj* costing *6d* or *6p*: *There are no sixpenny ice-creams in this cinema.* **six-shooter** /ˈsɪkʃ ʃutə(r)/ *n* revolver with six chambers. **ˈsix·fold** /-fəʊld/ *adj, adv* six times as much or as many; six times as great. **six·teen** /sɪkˈstin/ *n, adj* the number 16. **six·teenth** /sikˈstinθ/ *n, adj* **sixth** /sɪksθ/ *n, adj* **ˈsixth form,** (in secondary schools, GB) form (= class) for pupils being prepared for A-level examinations. ⇨ level²(3). **ˈsixth-former** *n* pupil in this form. **ˌsixth ˈsense,** power to be aware of things independently of the five senses; intuition. **sixth·ly** *adv* **six·ti·eth** /ˈsɪkstɪəθ/ *n, adj* **sixty** /ˈsɪkstɪ/ *n, adj* the number 60: *in the sixties*, between 59 and 70 years of age; the years between 59 and 70 of a century.

size¹ /sɑɪz/ *n* **1** [U] degree of largeness or smallness: *a building of vast ~; about the ~ of* (= about as large as) *a duck's egg; of some ~*, fairly large. *They're both of a ~*, are the same ~. ***That's about the ~ of it,*** (colloq) That's a fair account of the affair, situation, etc. **2** [C] one of the standard and (usu) numbered classes in which articles of clothing, etc are made: *~ five shoes; three ~s too large; all ~s of gloves. I take ~ ten.* □ *vt* [VP6A] **1** arrange in ~s or according to ~. [VP15B] ***~ sb/sth up,*** (colloq) form a judgement or opinion of. **-sized** /-sɑɪzd/ *suff* (in compounds) having a certain ~: *medium-sized.* **ˈsiz(e)·able** /-əbl/ *adj* fairly large.

size² /sɑɪz/ *n* [U] sticky substance used to glaze textiles, paper, plaster, etc. □ *vt* [VP6A] stiffen or treat with ~.

sizzle /ˈsɪzl/ *vi* [VP6A], *n* (colloq) (make the) hissing sound as of sth cooking in fat: *sausages sizzling in the pan;* (fig) *a sizzling hot day.*

skate¹ /skeɪt/ *n* one of a pair of sharp-edged steel blades to be fastened to a boot for moving smoothly over ice. ⇨ the illus at hockey. ⇨ also *roller-~s* at roller(2). □ *vi* [VP2A,C] move on ~s: *~ over/round a difficulty (a delicate problem)*, make only passing and cautious reference to it. ***~ on thin ice,*** talk about a subject that needs great tact. **ˈskat·ing** *n* **ˈskat·ing-rink** *n* specially prepared surface for skating. **skater** *n* person who ~s.

skate² /skeɪt/ *n* large, flat, long-tailed sea-fish, valued as food.

ske·daddle /skɪˈdædl/ *vi* [VP2A] (GB, colloq, usu imper) run away.

skeet /skit/ *n* (kind of) clay-pigeon shooting. ⇨ pigeon(2).

skein /skeɪn/ *n* [C] length of silk or wool yarn or thread coiled loosely into a bundle.

skel·eton /ˈskelɪtn/ *n* [C] **1** bony framework of an animal body; bones of an animal body in the same relative positions as in life; hard framework of woody fibre containing a vegetable body: ⇨ the illus on p 820. ***reduced to a~,*** (of an animal, a human being) very thin as the result of hunger, illness, etc. ***the ~ in the cupboard, the family ~,*** sth of which a family is ashamed and which it tries to keep secret. **2** framework of a building, organization, plan, theory, etc; outline to which details are to be added: *the steel ~ of a new building.* **3** (attrib) **ˈ~ key,** one that will open a number of different locks. **a ~ staff/crew/service, etc,** one reduced to the smallest possible number needed for maintenance.

skep /skep/ *n* (kinds of) wicker basket; straw or wicker bee-hive.

skep·tic /ˈskeptɪk/ ⇨ sceptic.

sketch /sketʃ/ *n* [C] **1** rough, quickly made drawing: *make a ~ of a harbour.* **ˈ~-book/-block** *nn* book or pad of sheets of drawing-paper for making ~es on. **ˈ~-map** *n* one with outlines but little detail. **2** short account or description; rough draft or general outline, without details: *He gave me a ~ of his plans for the expedition.* **3** short, humorous play or piece of writing. **4** (colloq) = sight¹(6). □ *vt, vi* **1** [VP6A] make a ~ of; [VP15B] ***~ sth out,*** give a rough plan of; indicate without detail: *~ out proposals for a new road.* **2** [VP2A] practise the art of making ~es: *My sister often goes into the country to ~.* **~er** *n* person who ~es(2). **sketchy** *adj* (-ier, -iest) **1** done roughly and without detail or care. **2** incomplete: *He has a rather ~y knowledge of geography.* **~·ily** /-əlɪ/ *adv* **~i·ness** *n*

skew /skju/ *adj* twisted or turned to one side; not straight. **ˈ~-eyed** *adj* (colloq) squinting. ***on the ˈ~(-ˈwhiff),*** (colloq) askew.

skewer /ˈskjuə(r)/ *n* pointed stick of wood or metal for holding meat together while cooking. □ *vt* [VP6A] fasten with, or as with, a ~.

ski /ski/ *n* (*pl* ski or skis) one of a pair of long,

skiing

narrow strips of wood, strapped under the feet for moving over snow: *a pair of ski(s); bind on one's ski(s).* **'ski-bob** *n* bicycle frame fitted with skis in place of wheels. **'ski-jump** *n* jump made after getting up speed on a downward slope. **'ski-lift** *n* ropeway for carrying skiers up a mountain side. **'ski-plane** *n* aircraft fitted with skis instead of wheels, to enable it to land on an expanse of snow. □ *vi* (*pt,pp* **ski'd**, *pres part* **skiing**) move over snow on ski(s): *go skiing at the New Year; go in for skiing.* **skier** /'skiə(r)/ *n* person using ski(s).

skid /skɪd/ *n* [C] **1** piece of wood or metal fixed under the wheel of a cart, etc to prevent it from turning, and in this way check the speed when going downhill. **2** log, plank, etc used to make a track over which heavy objects may be dragged or rolled. **'~ row** /rəʊ/ *n* (US) slum area where vagrants live. **3** slipping movement, often sideways, of the wheels of a car, etc on a slippery or icy road, or caused by excessive speed while turning a corner: *How would you get out of/correct a ~?* **'~-pan** *n* surface specially prepared to cause ~s, used for practice in controlling vehicles which ~. ***put the ~s under sb,*** (sl) do sth to make him hurry. □ *vi* (-dd-) [VP2A] (of a car, etc) move or slip sideways, etc; have a ~(2).

skies /skaɪz/ *pl* of **sky**.

skiff /skɪf/ *n* small, light boat, esp one rowed or sculled by a single person.

skiffle /'skɪfl/ *n* [U] mixture of jazz and folksong, with improvised instruments and a singer who usu has a guitar or a banjo. **'~-group,** group of such players.

skil·ful (US = **skill·ful**) /'skɪlfl/ *adj* having or showing skill: *He's not very ~ with his/at using chopsticks.* **~ly** /-flɪ/ *adv*

skill /skɪl/ *n* [U] ability to do sth expertly and well; [C] particular kind of ~: *Learning a foreign language is a question of learning new ~s, or a question of acquiring new knowledge.* **~ed** *adj* **1** trained; experienced; having ~; *~ed workmen; ~ed in doing sth.* **2** needing ~: *~ed work.*

skil·let /'skɪlɪt/ *n* **1** small metal cooking-pot with a long handle and (usu) feet. **2** (US) frying-pan.

skilly /'skɪlɪ/ *n* [U] thin broth or soup (usu oatmeal and water flavoured with meat), as served formerly in prisons and workhouses.

skim /skɪm/ *vt,vi* (-mm-) **1** [VP6A,15B,14] remove floating matter from (the surface of a liquid): *~ milk;* remove (cream, scum, etc) from the surface of a liquid: *~ the cream from the milk; ~ off the grease/from soup.* **'~·med-milk** *n* milk from which the cream has been ~med. **2** [VP2C, 15A] move lightly over (a surface), not touching, or only lightly or occasionally touching (it): *The swallows were ~ming (over) the water/~med along the ground.* **3** [VP6A,3A] ***~ (through) sth,*** read quickly, noting only the chief points: *~ (through) a newspaper/catalogue, etc.* **~·mer** *n* **1** utensil with a perforated bowl for ~ming liquids. **2** long-winged water-bird.

skimp /skɪmp/ *vt,vi* [VP6A,2A] supply, use, less than enough of what is needed: *~ the butter when making cakes/the material when making a dress. They are so poor that they have to ~.* **skimpy** *adj* (-ier, -iest) **1** giving, using, less than enough. **2** (of a dress, etc) made with insufficient material; too small; too tight. **~·ily** /-əlɪ/ *adv*: *a ~ily made dress.*

skin /skɪn/ *n* **1** [U] elastic substance forming the outer covering of the body of a person or animal: *We all got wet to the ~,* thoroughly wet (e g in heavy rain). ***~ and bone,*** very thin: *He's only ~ and bone.* ***by the ~ of one's teeth,*** by a narrow margin; narrowly. ***get under one's ~,*** (fig) cause irritation or anger; infatuate one. ***have a thin/thick ~,*** (fig) be (in)sensitive; be easily hurt (not easily hurt) by unkindness, criticism, rebuke,

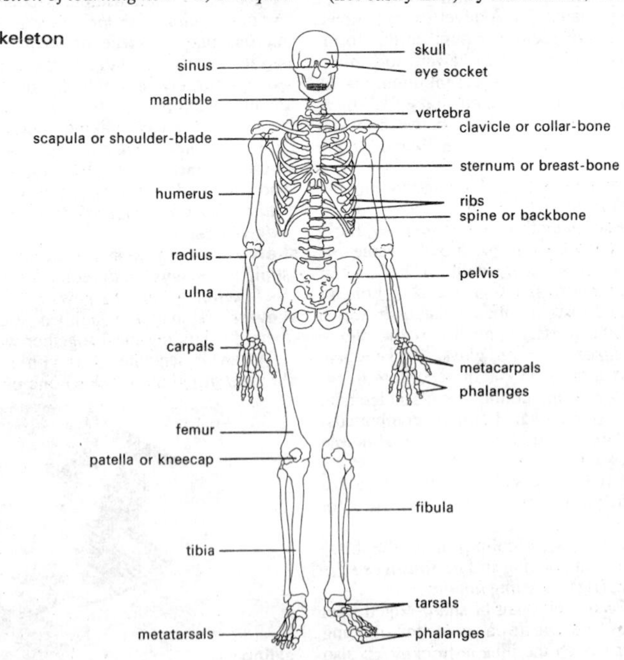

etc. Hence, **'thin/-'thick-`~ned** *adjj* ***save one's ~,*** avoid being hurt, etc; escape safely. **`~-diving** *n* form of sport in which a person dives into and swims under the water without a diving-suit, with goggles to protect the eyes and a snorkel or aqualung to help breathing. **'~-`deep** *adj* (of beauty, feelings, etc) only on the surface; not deep or lasting. **`~-flint** *n* miser. **`~ game** *n* fraudulent gambling game; swindle. **`~-graft** *n* surgical process of grafting ~ from one part of a person's body (or from another person's body) on to a part which has been damaged, e g by burning. **`skin-head** *n* (GB 1969—73) member of a group of young men and girls with closely-cut hair and distinctive dress, addicted to violence in public places. **'~-`tight,** (of a garment) fitting closely to the body. **2** [C] animal ~ with or without the hair or fur; hide; pelt: *`rabbit-~s.* **3** [C] vessel for storing or carrying liquid, made of the whole ~ of an animal: *`wine-~s.* **4** [C,U] outer covering of a fruit, or plant: *slip on a ba`nana ~; `grape ~s.* ⇨ the illus at **fruit**. Cf *peel* for potatoes, apples, etc; the *bark* of a tree. **5** thin layer that forms on boiled milk: *the ~ on a milk pudding.* □ *vt,vi* (-nn-) **1** [VP6A] take the ~ off: *~ a rabbit.* ***keep one's eyes ~ned,*** (colloq) be alert, watchful. **2** [VP6A,14] (colloq) swindle; fleece: *He was ~ned of all his money by confidence tricksters.* **3** [VP2C] ***~ over,*** become covered with ~: *The wound ~ned over.* **~ny** *adj* (-ier, -iest) with little flesh; (colloq) mean; miserly. ⇨ **skinflint** above.

skint /skɪnt/ *adj* (GB sl) without money; penniless.

skip[1] /skɪp/ *vi,vt* (-pp-) **1** [VP2A,C] jump lightly and quickly: *~ over an obstacle/over a brook/out of the way of a bus. The lambs were ~ping about in the fields,* jumping about, gambolling. **2** [VP2A] jump over a rope which is turned over the head and under the feet as one jumps. **`~-ping-rope** *n* length of rope (usu with two wooden handles) used in the children's game of ~ping. **3** [VP2C] go from one place (or, fig, subject) to another quickly or casually: *~ over/across to Paris for the weekend. He ~ped off* (= left) *without saying anything to any of us. He ~ped from one subject to another.* **4** [VP6A,2A] make omissions, go from one part (of a book, etc) to another without reading, paying attention, etc: *He ~ped the dull parts of the book. We'll ~ the next chapter. Do you read without ~ping?* □ *n* [C] ~ping movement: *a hop, a ~ and a jump.*

skip[2] /skɪp/ *n* cage or bucket in which men or materials are raised and lowered in mines and quarries; large metal container for carrying away builders' refuse, etc.

skip·per /`skɪpə(r)/ *n* captain, esp of a small merchant ship or fishing-boat; (colloq) captain of a team in games such as football and cricket.

skirl /skɜl/ *n* shrill, piercing sound: *the ~ of the bagpipes.*

skir·mish /`skɜmɪʃ/ *n* [C] (often unpremeditated) fight between small parts of armies or fleets; (hence) short argument or contest of wit, etc. □ *vi* [VP2A,C] engage in a ~. **~er** *n* one who ~es, esp a member of a force sent out from the main body of troops to hide its movements, or to learn about the movement of the enemy.

skirt /skɜt/ *n* **1** woman's garment that hangs from the waist. **2** part of a dress or other garment (e g a long coat or shirt) that hangs below the waist. **3** (*pl*) (= outskirts) border; extreme parts: *on the ~s of the town.* **4** (vulg sl, often *a piece of ~*) girl or woman. □ *vt,vi* [VP6A,2C] be on, pass along, the edge of: *Our road ~ed the forest. Our path ~ed along the moor.* **`~-ing-board** *n* strip or line of boards fixed round the walls of a room close to the floor.

skit /skɪt/ *n* [C] short piece of humorous writing, short play, mimicking and making fun of sth or sb: *a ~ on Wagner/on 'Macbeth'.*

skit·tish /`skɪtɪʃ/ *adj* (of horses) excitable; lively; difficult to control; (of women) frivolous; coy; fickle: *She's a ~ little thing,* is lively and coquettish, fond of flirting, etc. **~·ly** *adv* **~·ness** *n*

skittle /`skɪtl/ *n* (*pl,* ~s with *sing v*) game in which a ball is bowled along an alley. **(`~-ally)** with the purpose of knocking down a number of bottle-shaped pieces of wood (called **~s** or **`~-pins**). ⇨ **ninepins, tenpins.** ***beer and ~s,*** amusement; fun: *Life is not all beer and ~s.* □ *vt* [VP15B] ***~ out,*** (cricket) dismiss easily: *The whole side was ~d out for 100 runs.*

skivvy /`skɪvɪ/ *n* (*pl* -vies) (GB sl) (pej) servant girl (esp one who is required to do all sorts of work).

skua /`skjuə/ *n* large kind of seagull.

skulk /skʌlk/ *vi* [VP2A,C] hide, move secretly, through cowardice, or to avoid work or duty, or with an evil purpose. **~er** *n*

skull /skʌl/ *n* bony framework of the head. ⇨ the illus at **skeleton**: *have a thick ~,* be stupid. **'~ and `cross-bones,** picture of a ~ and two thigh-bones crossed below it (as an emblem of death, and formerly used on a flag by pirates). **`~-cap** *n* close-fitting (often velvet) cap worn indoors by old or bald men, by Popes and cardinals. **-skulled** *suff* (with *adj* prefixed): *'thick-`~ed,* having a thick ~.

skull·dug·gery /skʌl`dʌgərɪ/ *n* (US) clever deception; trickery.

skunk /skʌŋk/ *n* **1** small, bush-tailed N American animal able to send out a strong evil smell as a defence when attacked; [U] its fur. **2** detestable or contemptible person.

sky /skɑɪ/ *n* (*pl* **skies**) **1** (usu *sing* with *def art;* with *indef art* when modified by an *adj;* often *pl* in the same sense) the space we look up to from the earth, where we see the sun, moon and stars: *under the open sky,* out of doors; *a clear, blue sky; a starry sky.* ***praise/extol/laud sb to the skies,*** praise him very highly. **'sky-`blue** *adj, n* (of) the bright blue colour of the sky on a cloudless day. **'sky-`high** *adv* so as to reach the sky; as high as the sky: *When the bomb exploded, the bridge was blown sky-high.* **`sky·light** *n* window in a sloping roof. **`sky·line** *n* outline of hills, buildings, etc, defined against the sky: *the skyline of New York.* **`sky·lark** *n* small bird that sings as it flies up into the sky. □ *vi* = lark[1]. **`sky pilot** *n* (sl) parson (esp, among sailors, a chaplain on a warship). **`sky-rocket** *vi* (of prices) soar; go up steeply. **`sky-scraper** *n* very tall building. **`sky-writing** *n* (making of) smoke-trails forming legible words in the sky (by aircraft for advertising purposes). **2** (often *pl*) climate: *the sunny skies of southern Italy.* □ *vt* hit (a cricket ball) high up. **sky·ward(s)** /`skɑɪwəd(z)/ *adj, adv* toward(s) the sky; upward(s).

slab /slæb/ *n* thick flat (usu square or rectangular) piece of stone, wood or other solid substance:

skyscrapers

paved with ~*s of stone; a* ~ *of cheese/cooking chocolate; a mortuary* ~.

slack[1] /slæk/ *adj* **1** giving little care or attention to one's work; having or showing little energy: *Don't get* ~ *at your work. She feels* ~ (= lacking in energy) *this morning.* **2** dull; inactive; with not much work to be done or business being done: *Trade/Business is* ~ *this week. There is only a* ~ *demand for S African mining shares.* **3** loose, not tight: *a* ~ *rope.* ***keep a* ~ *rein on sth,*** control sth negligently, (fig) govern carelessly. **4** slow-moving; sluggish: *periods of* ~ *water,* when the tide is neither ebbing nor flowing. □ *vi* [VP2A,C] **1** ~ ***(off),*** be lazy or careless in one's work: *Don't* ~ *off in your studies.* **2** ~ ***up,*** reduce speed: *S*~ *up before you reach the cross-roads.* **3** ~ ***off/away,*** make loose (a rope, etc). ~**er** *n* (colloq) lazy person; person who avoids his proper share of work. ~**·ly** *adv* ~**·ness** *n*

slack[2] /slæk/ *n* **1** **the** ~, that part of a rope, etc that hangs loosely. ***take up the*** ~, pull a rope so that it is taut; (fig) regulate industry so that it is active and productive. **2** (*pl*) loose-fitting trousers, not part of a suit, e g as informal wear for men or women. **3** [U] coal dust.

slacken /ˈslækən/ *vt,vi* [VP6A,2A] **1** make or become slower, less active, etc: ~ *speed. The ship's speed* ~*ed. The gale is* ~*ing a little.* **2** make or become loose(r): ~ *the reins.* ***S*~ *away/off!*** e g as an order to loosen ropes.

slag /slæg/ *n* [U] waste matter remaining when metal has been extracted from ore. ˈ~**-heap** *n* hill of ~ (dumped from a mine).

slain /sleɪn/ *pp* of slay.

slake /sleɪk/ *vt* [VP6A] **1** satisfy or make less strong (thirst, desire for revenge). **2** change the chemical nature of (lime) by adding water.

sla·lom /ˈslɑləm/ *n* ski-race along a zigzag course marked out by poles with flags.

slam /slæm/ *vt,vi* (-mm-) **1** [VP6A,15A,B,22] shut violently and noisily: ~ *the door (to);* ~ *the window shut;* ~ *the door in sb's face.* **2** [VP2A,C] be shut violently: *The door* ~*med (to).* **3** [VP15A,B] put, throw or knock with force: *She* ~*med the box down on the table. The batsman* ~*med the ball into the grand-stand.* □ *n* **1** noise of sth being ~med: *the* ~ *of a car door.* **2** (in whist, bridge) **a grand** ~, taking of 13 tricks. **a small** ~, taking of 12 tricks.

slan·der /ˈslɑndə(r) *US:* ˈslæn-/ *n* [C,U] (offence of making a) false statement that damages a person's reputation: *bring a* ~ *action against sb,* charge him with ~ in a court of law. □ *vt* [VP6A] utter ~ about (sb). ~**er** *n* ~**·ous** /-əs/ *adj* uttering or containing ~.

slang /slæŋ/ *n* [U] (abbr *sl* used in this dictionary) words, phrases, meanings of words, etc commonly used in talk but not suitable for good writing or formal occasions, esp the kind used by and typical of a class of persons: *army* ~; *schoolboy* ~; (attrib) ~ *words and expressions. The use of out-of-date* ~ *is sometimes a feature of foreigners' English.* □ *vt* [VP6A] use violent language to: abuse: *Stop* ~*ing me.* ***a* ~*ing match,*** a long exchange of insults and accusations. I won't take part in a ~ing match. ~**y** *adj* (-ier, -iest) using, in the nature of, ~. ~**·ily** /-əlɪ/ *adv* ~**i·ness** *n*

slant /slɑnt *US:* slænt/ *vi,vt* **1** [VP2A,C,6A] slope: *His handwriting* ~*s from right to left.* **2** [VP6A] ~ ***the news,*** present it so that it is seen from, and supports, a particular point of view, e g of the writer's newspaper or government. □ *n* **1** [C] slope. ***on a/the*** ~, in a sloping position. **2** (colloq) point of view (sometimes prejudiced or biased) when considering sth: *get a new* ~ *on the political situation.* ~**·ing·ly,** ~**·wise** /-waɪz/ *advv* in a ~ing position or direction.

slap /slæp/ *vt* (-pp-) **1** [VP6A,15A] strike with the palm of the hand; smack: *She* ~*ped his face,* ~*ped him on the face. I don't like being* ~*ped on the back as a greeting.* **2** [VP15B] ~ ***sth down,*** put sth down with a ~ping noise: *He* ~*ped the book down on the table.* □ *n* [C] quick blow with the palm of the hand or with sth flat. ***get/give sb a* ~ *in the face,*** (fig) a rebuff or snub. □ *adv* straight; directly; full: *The car ran* ~ *into the wall.* ˈ~-ˈ**bang** *adv* violently; headlong. ˈ~**·dash** *adj, adv* impetuous(ly), vehement(ly): *a* ~*dash worker; do one's work* ~*dash/in a* ~*dash manner.* ˈ~**-happy** *adj* impetuous, carefree. ˈ~**·stick** *n* [U] low comedy of the roughest kind; fun arising from violence: (attrib) ~*stick comedy.* ˈ~**-up** *adj* (sl) first-class; extremely good: *be treated to a* ~*-up dinner at a* ~*-up restaurant.*

slash /slæʃ/ *vt,vi* **1** [VP6A,2C] make a cut or cuts in (or at sth) with sweeping strokes; strike with a whip: *His face had been* ~*ed with a razor-blade. Don't* ~ *your horse in that cruel way. He* ~*ed at the tall weeds with his stick.* **2** [VP6A] condemn vigorously and outspokenly: *a* ~*ing attack on the government's policy;* ~ *a new book/play,* criticize it adversely. **3** [VP6A] (colloq) cut, reduce drastically: ~ *prices/taxes/salaries.* **4** (usu passive) make long, narrow gashes in (for ornament, etc): ~*ed sleeves,* the lining or other material being seen through the ~es. □ *n* **1** act of ~ing; long cut or gash. **2** (vulg sl) act of urinating.

slat /slæt/ *n* long, thin narrow piece of wood, metal or plastic material, e g as in Venetian blinds or louvred doors. ~**·ted** *adj* made with, having ~s.

slate /sleɪt/ *n* **1** [U] kind of blue-grey stone that splits easily into thin, flat layers; [C] one of these layers, square or oblong, used for roofs: *hit on the head by a falling* ~; *a* ~*-covered roof;* ˈ~*-coloured,* blue-grey; *a* ~ *quarry.* **2** [C] sheet of ~ in a wooden frame for writing on (as formerly used by school-children). ***a clean*** ~, (fig) a good record: *start with a clean* ~, (fig) make a new start with past errors, enmities, etc, forgotten. ˈ~**-club** *n* (GB) club collecting small weekly contributions of money, usu saved until Christmas when the total is distributed to members. ˈ~-ˈ**pencil** *n* thin rod of soft ~, used for writing on ~s(2). □ *vt* **1** [VP6A] cover (a roof, etc) with ~s. **2** (US, colloq) propose (sb) for an office, a position, etc: (newspaper headline) *Green* ~*d for the*

Presidency. **3** [VP6A] (colloq) criticize severely (esp in a newspaper notice of a book, play, etc). **slaty** *adj* of or like ~; containing ~: *slaty coal.* **slat·ing** *n* adverse criticism: *give sb a sound slating.*

slat·tern /ˈslætən/ *n* dirty, untidily dressed woman. **~·ly** *adj* (of women) dirty and untidy. **~·li·ness** *n*

slaugh·ter /ˈslɔtə(r)/ *n* [U] **1** killing of animals (esp for food). **ˈ~-house** *n* place where animals are butchered for food. **2** killing of many people at once; massacre: *the ~ on the roads,* the killing of people in road accidents. □ *vt* [VP6A] kill (animals, people) in large numbers. **~er** *n*

Slav /slɑv/ *n* member of a race spread over most of Eastern Europe, including Russians, Poles, Bulgarians, etc. □ *adj* of the ~s.

slave /sleɪv/ *n* **1** person who is the property of another and bound to serve him. **ˈ~-driver** *n* overseer of ~s at work; person who makes those who are under him work very hard. **ˈ~ ship** *n* ship used in the ~-trade. **ˈ~ States** *n pl* southern States of N America in which there was slavery before the Civil War. **ˈ~-trade/-traffic** *n* capturing, transportation, buying and selling, of ~s. **2** person compelled to work very hard for someone else: *You mustn't make a ~ of your au pair girl.* **3** sb completely in the power of, under the control of, an impulse, habit, etc: *~s of fashion,* e g persons who feel compelled to dress in the latest fashions; *a ~ to duty/passion/convention/drink.* □ *vi* [VP2A,B,C] **~ (away) (at sth),** work hard: *Poor Jane! She's been slaving away (cooking) over a hot stove for three hours!* **slaver** *n* ˈ~-trader; ˈ~ ship. **slav·ery** /ˈsleɪvərɪ/ *n* [U] **1** condition of being a ~: *sold into ~ry.* **2** custom of having ~s: *men who worked for the abolition of ~ry.* **3** hard or badly paid work. **slav·ish** /ˈsleɪvɪʃ/ *adj* characteristic of, fit for, a ~: *a slavish imitation,* an exact copy showing no originality. **slav·ish·ly** *adv*

slaver /ˈslævə(r)/ *vi* [VP2A,C] let spit run from the mouth (*over* sth) □ *n* [U] spit; saliva.

slavey /ˈsleɪvɪ/ *n* (*pl* -veys) (sl) young servant girl (esp in a boarding-house).

Slav·onic /sləˈvɒnɪk/ *adj* of the Slavs or their languages.

slaw /slɔ/ *n* [U] (often **ˈcole-~**) sliced cabbage, raw or cooked, served with a dressing.

slay /sleɪ/ *vt* (*pt* **slew** /slu/, *pp* **slain** /sleɪn/) [VP6A] (liter, or hum) kill, murder. **~er** *n* (journalism) murderer.

sleazy /ˈslizɪ/ *adj* (-ier, -iest) (colloq) uncared-for, dirty, untidy: *a ~ lodging house.*

sled /sled/, **sledge** /sledʒ/ *nn* vehicle with runners (long, narrow strips of wood or metal) instead of wheels, used on snow, larger types being pulled by horses or dogs and smaller types used in sport for travelling downhill at speed. □ *vi,vt* (-dd-) travel or carry by ~: *go sledging.*

sledge /sledʒ/ *n* **ˈ~(-hammer),** heavy hammer with a long handle, used for driving posts into the ground, and by blacksmiths.

sleek /slik/ *adj* (of hair, an animal's fur, etc) soft, smooth and glossy; (of a person) having such hair: *as ~ as a cat,* (fig) having smooth manners (perhaps over-anxious to please). □ *vt* [VP6A] make ~: *~ a cat's fur.* **~·ly** *adv* **~·ness** *n*

sleep[1] /slip/ *n* **1** [U] condition of the body and mind such as recurs regularly every night, in which the eyes are closed and the muscles, nervous system, etc are relaxed: *How many hours' ~ do you need? He didn't get much ~. Do you ever talk in your ~?* **2** (with *indef art*) period of ~: *have a short/good/restful, etc ~; a ~ of three hours.* **have one's ~ out,** continue ~ing until one wakes up naturally: *Don't wake her up—let her have her ~ out.* **3** (phrases) **get to ~,** manage to fall asleep, succeed in passing into the condition of ~: *I couldn't get to ~ last night.* **go to ~,** fall asleep. **put sb to ~,** cause him to fall asleep. **ˈ~-walker** *n* person who walks while asleep.

sleep[2] /slip/ *vi,vt* (*pp,pt* **slept** /slept/) **1** [VP2A, B,C] rest in the condition of ~, be or fall asleep: *We go to bed to ~. He ~s well/badly. She slept (for) eight hours.* **~ like a top/log,** very soundly. **~ round the clock; ~ the clock round,** ~ for twelve hours continuously. **ˈ~·ing partner,** (US = *silent partner*) person who provides a share of the capital of a business but does not share in the management. **2** [VP2C,15B,3A] (with *adverbial particles* and *preps*) **~ around,** (colloq) be promiscuous. **~ in/out,** ~ at/outside one's place of employment: *Does the housekeeper ~ in?* **~ sth off,** recover from sth by ~ing: *~ off a bad headache/a hangover.* **~ on,** continue to sleep: *Don't wake him up—let him ~ on for another hour.* **~ on sth,** (often **~ on it**), leave the answer, solution, to a problem, etc to the next day. **~ through sth,** not be woken up by (a noise, the alarm-clock, etc). **~ with sb,** (euphem for) have sexual intercourse with. **3** [VP6A] provide beds for: *This hotel ~s 300 guests.* **~·ing** (*n—gerund*) (in compounds) **ˈ~·ing-bag** *n* warmly lined and waterproof bag in which to ~ when out of doors (e g on holiday) or in a tent. **ˈ~·ing-car** *n* railway coach fitted with beds or berths. **ˈ~·ing-draught/-pill** *n* one that contains a drug to help sb to ~. **ˈ~·ing-sickness** *n* [U] disease caused by the tsetse-fly; it results in weakening of the mental powers and (usu) death. **~er** *n* **1** person who ~s: (with *adjj*) *a heavy/light ~er,* one whom it is hard/easy to wake up; *a good/bad ~er.* **2** (US = *tie*) heavy beam of wood (or similarly shaped piece of other material) on a railway track, etc supporting the rails. **3** (bed or berth in a) ~ing-car on a train. **~·less** *adj* without ~: *pass a ~less night.* **~·less·ly** *adv* **~·less·ness** *n*

sleepy /ˈslipɪ/ *adj* (-ier, -iest) **1** needing, ready for, sleep: *feel/look ~.* **ˈ~-head** *n* (esp as a form of address to a) ~ or inattentive person. **2** (of places, etc) quiet; inactive: *a ~ little village.* **3** (of some kinds of fruit) over-ripe: *~ pears/bananas,* soft and brown inside. **sleep·ily** /-əlɪ/ *adv* **sleepiness** *n*

sleet /slit/ *n* [U] falling snow or hail mixed with rain: *squalls of ~.* □ *vi* [VP2A] *It was ~ing,* S~ was falling. **sleety** *adj*

sleeve /sliv/ *n* **1** part of a garment that covers all or part of the arm: *roll up the ~s of one's shirt/one's ˈshirt-~s.* **have sth up one's ~,** have an idea, plan, etc which one keeps secret for future use. **laugh up one's ~,** be secretly amused. **wear one's heart on one's ~,** allow one's feelings (of love for sb) to be seen; fail to show proper reserve. **2** stiff envelope for a disc of recorded sound, often with notes on the composer, player(s), etc. **3** wind-sock. ⇨ **wind**[1]**(8)**. **-sleeved** *suff*: ˈ*short/*ˈ*loose-~d.* **~·less** *adj* without ~s.

sleigh /sleɪ/ *n* sledge, esp one drawn by a horse:

go for a ˋ~*-ride/a ride in a* ~. □ *vi,vt* [VP2A,6A] travel in a ~; carry (goods) by ~.

sleight /slaɪt/ *n* (usu in) ~ ***of hand,*** great skill in using the hand(s) in performing tricks, juggling, etc.

slen·der /ˋslendə(r)/ *adj* **1** small in width or circumference compared with height or length: ~ *fingers; a* ~ *waist; a wineglass with a* ~ *stem.* **2** (of persons) slim; not stout: *a* ~ *girl,* slight and graceful; *a woman with a* ~ *figure.* **3** slight; scanty; inadequate: *a* ~ *income;* ~ *means/hopes.* **~·ly** *adv* **~·ness** *n* ˋ**~·ize** /-aɪz/ *vt,vi* [VP6A] (US) make, cause to appear, become, ~(2).

slept /slept/ *pt,pp* of sleep.

sleuth(-hound) /ˋsluθ (haʊnd)/ *n* **1** bloodhound; dog that follows a scent. **2** (colloq, **sleuth**) detective.

slew[1] /slu/ *pt* of slay.

slew[2] (US = **slue**) /slu/ *vi,vt* [VP2C,15B] ~ ***(sth) round,*** force or turn round in a new direction: *The crane* ~*ed round. The driver* ~*ed his crane round.*

slice /slaɪs/ *n* [C] **1** thin, wide, flat piece cut off sth, esp bread or meat: *S*~*s of cold beef between* ~*s of bread make good sandwiches.* **2** part, share or price: *a* ~ *of good luck. Smith took too large a* ~ *of the credit for our success.* **3** utensil with a wide, flat blade for cutting, serving or lifting (e g cooked fish, fried eggs). **4** (in games such as golf, bad stroke that causes the ball to go spinning off in a direction different from that desired, i e to the right of a right-handed player). □ *vt,vi* **1** [VP6A, 15A,B,22] cut into ~s: ~ *(up) a loaf. S*~ *the beef thin. The butcher* ~*d off a thick steak.* **2** [VP6A] (golf): ~ *the ball,* strike with a ~(4).

slick /slɪk/ *adj* (colloq) **1** smooth; slippery: *The roads were* ~ *with wet mud.* **2** carried through smoothly and efficiently, perhaps with some trickery: *a* ~ *business deal;* (of a person) doing things in a ~ way: *a* ~ *salesman.* □ *n* [C] ˋ**oil** ~**,** film of thick oil covering an area of the sea, etc (e g from an oil-tanker after a collision). □ *adv* directly, completely: *hit a man* ~ *on the jaw.* **~er** *n* (US colloq) **1** long, loose, waterproof coat. **2** ~ person. ⇨ 2 above: *city* ~*ers.*

slide[1] /slaɪd/ *n* **1** act of sliding(1); smooth stretch of ice, hard snow, etc on which to slide: *have a* ~ *on the ice.* **2** smooth slope down which persons or things can slide (e g for felled timber down a mountain slope, or a wooden or metal slope made for children to play on). **3** picture, diagram, etc on photographic film (and usu mounted in a frame); (formerly) such a picture on a glass plate, to be slid into a projector and shown on a screen. **4** glass plate on which is placed sth to be examined under a microscope. **5** part of a machine, etc that slides (e g the U-shaped part of a trombone). **6** (ˋ**land**)~**,** ⇨ land[1](6). **7** (ˋ**hair**)-~**,** ⇨ hair(2).

slide[2] /slaɪd/ *vi,vt* (*pt,pp* slid /slɪd/) **1** [VP2A,C, 6A,15A] (cause to) move smoothly over, slip along, a polished surface: *children sliding on the ice. The book slid* (= slipped, which is more usu) *off my knee. Let's* ~ *down this grassy slope. The drawers of this desk* ~ *in and out easily. S*~ *the drawer into its place.* ~ ***over sth,*** pass over (a delicate subject, etc) quickly; barely touch upon it. ***let things*** ~**,** not trouble about them, be negligent. **2** [VP3A] ~ ***into,*** pass gradually, without being fully aware, into (a condition, etc): ~ *into dishonesty/bad habits.* **3** [VP2A,15A] (cause to) move quickly, or so as to avoid observation: *The thief slid behind the curtains. She slid a coin into his hand.* **4** (compounds) ˋ**~-rule** *n* device of two rulers with logarithmic scales, one of which ~s in a groove, used for rapid calculations. **slid·ing door** *n* one that is pulled across an opening (instead of turning on hinges). **slid·ing scale** *n* scale by which one thing, e g wages, goes up or down in relation to changes in sth else, e g the cost of living. **slid·ing seat** *n* seat on runners, esp in a racing boat, to lengthen the stroke of the rower or sculler.

slight[1] /slaɪt/ *adj* **1** slim; slender; frail-looking: *a* ~ *figure; supported by a* ~ *framework.* **2** small; not serious or important: *a* ~ *error; a* ~ *headache; do sth without the* ~*est difficulty,* with no difficulty at all. *She takes offence at the* ~*est thing,* is very easily offended. *You didn't embarrass me in the* ~*est,* at all. **~·ly** *adv* **1** slenderly: *a* ~*ly built boy.* **2** to a ~ degree; somewhat: *The patient is* ~*ly better today. I know her* ~*ly.* **~·ness** *n*

slight[2] /slaɪt/ *vt* [VP6A] treat without proper respect or courtesy; neglect in a marked manner: *She felt* ~*ed because no one spoke to her.* □ *n* [C] marked failure to show respect or courtesy: *put a* ~ *on sb; suffer* ~*s.* **~·ing·ly** *adv*

slim /slɪm/ *adj* (**-mer, -mest**) **1** slender: *a* ~*-waisted girl.* **2** (colloq) small; insufficient: ~ *hopes/chances of success; condemned upon the* ~*mest (of) evidence.* □ *vi* (**-mm-**) eat less, diet, take exercise, etc with the object of reducing one's weight and becoming ~(1): ~*ming exercises.* **~·ly** *adv* **~·ness** *n*

slime /slaɪm/ *n* [U] **1** soft, nasty, thick, sticky mud. **2** sticky substance from snails, etc: *a trail of* ~. **slimy** /ˋslaɪmɪ/ *adj* (**-ier, -iest**) of, like, covered with, ~; hard to hold because slippery with ~; (fig) disgustingly dishonest, flattering, obsequious, etc: *I hate that slimy(-tongued) coward.*

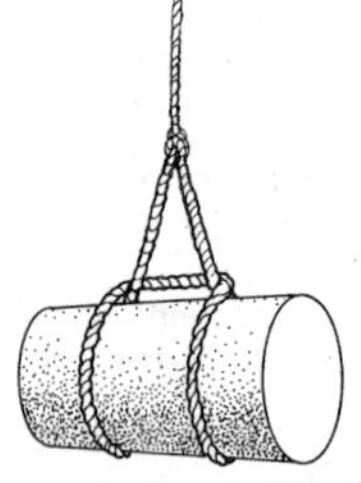

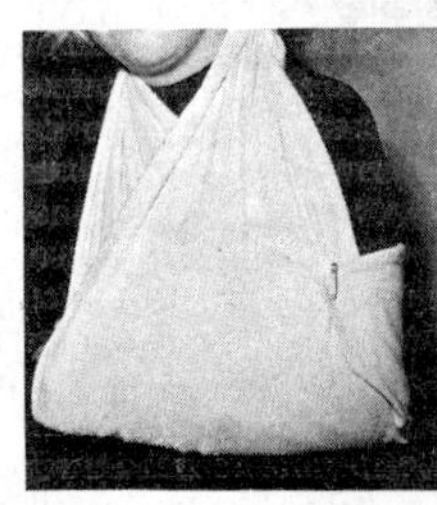

slings

sling[1] /slɪŋ/ *n* [C] **1** band of material, length of rope, chain, etc looped round an object, e g a barrel, a broken arm, to support or lift it. **2** strip of leather used (held in the hand in a loop) to throw stones to a distance. **3** act of throwing. □ *vt,vi* (*pt,pp* slung /slʌŋ/) **1** [VP6A,15A,B] throw with force: *naughty boys* ~*ing stones at street lamps.* ~ ***one's hook,*** (sl) (usu *imper* or *int*) go away: *Tell him to* ~ *his hook.* ~ ***mud at sb,*** (fig) abuse him. ~ ***sb out,*** throw sb out; expel him by force. **2** [VP6A,15A,B] support (sth) so that it can swing, be lifted, etc: ~ *a hammock between two tree-trunks;* ~ *(up) a barrel; with his rifle slung over his shoulder.* **~er** /ˋslɪŋə(r)/ *n* person armed with a ~(2). **'mud-~er,** ⇨ ~ *mud at sb* above.

sling² /slɪŋ/ *n* drink made of gin, rum, etc sweetened with fruit juices (esp lime).

slink /slɪŋk/ *vi* (*pt,pp* **slunk** /slʌŋk/) [VP2C] go or move (*off, away, in, out, by*) in a secret, guilty or sneaking manner.

slip¹ /slɪp/ *n* [C] **1** act of slipping; false step; slight error caused by carelessness or inattention: *make a ~*. ***a ~ of the tongue/pen,*** error in speaking/writing. ***give sb the ~; give the ~ to sb,*** escape from, get away from (one's pursuers, etc). ***There's many a ~ 'twixt (the) cup and (the) lip,*** (prov) Something may easily go wrong before a plan is fully carried out. **2** (**'pillow-~**) loose cover for a pillow; loose sleeveless garment worn under a dress; (**'gym-~**) girl's garment for gymnastic exercises; (*pl,* **'bathing-~s**) men's drawers worn for swimming (now usu called *swimming-/bathing-trunks*). **3** narrow strip of paper; printer's proof on such a strip. **4** cutting (short length of stem) taken from a plant for planting or grafting (to grow a new plant, etc). **5** young, slender person: *a* (*mere*) *~ of a boy/girl,* a slim boy/girl. **6** (usu *pl;* also **'~-way**) sloping way (of stone or timber) down to the water, on which ships are built, or pulled up out of the water for repairs: *The ship is still on the ~s.* **7** (*pl*) (more usu *wings*) parts of the stage of a theatre from which the scenery is pushed on, and where actors stand before going on to the stage: *watch a performance from the ~s.* **8** (cricket) one of the fielders: *first/second/leg ~;* (*pl*) part of the ground where these fielders stand. ⇨ the illus at **cricket. 9** [U] semi-fluid clay for coating earthenware or making patterns on it. **10** (compounds) **'~-carriage/-coach** *nn* one at the end of a train which can be detached without stopping the train. **'~-cover** *n* detachable cover for a piece of furniture. ⇨ 2 above. **'~-knot** *n* **(a)** knot which slips along the cord round which it is made to tighten or loosen the loop. **(b)** knot which can be undone by a pull. **'~-over** *n* knitted garment to be slipped on (over a shirt, etc). **'~-road** *n* road for joining or leaving a motorway (US = *access-road*); minor or local by-pass road. **'~-stream** *n* stream of air from the propeller or jet engine of an aircraft. **'~-up** *n* (colloq) ⇨ **slip²(5)**. **'~-way** *n* ⇨ 6 above.

slip² /slɪp/ *vi,vt* (**-pp-**) **1** [VP2A,C] lose one's balance; fall or almost fall as the result of this: *He ~ped on the icy road and broke his leg.* **2** [VP2A,C] go or move quietly or quickly, esp without attracting attention: *She ~ped away/out/past without being seen. The years ~ped by.* **3** [VP2A,C] move, get away, escape, fall, by being difficult to hold, or by not being held firmly: *The fish ~ped out of my hand. The blanket ~ped off the bed.* ***let sth ~,*** **(a)** allow sth to fall from one's hands, escape, or be neglected: *Don't let the opportunity ~.* **(b)** accidentally reveal (a secret, etc). *The knife ~ped and cut my hand.* ***~ through one's fingers,*** (liter, fig) fail to grasp, keep a hold on. ***~ one's mind,*** (of a name, address, message, etc) be forgotten (because one is in a hurry, busy, etc). **4** [VP15A,B,2C] put, pull on or push off, with a quick, easy movement: *~ a coat on/off; ~ into/out of a dress; ~ a coin into the waiter's hand.* **5** [VP2C] allow (small mistakes, etc) to enter, esp by carelessness: *errors that have ~ped into the text;* make a small error. ***~ up,*** (colloq) make a mistake. Hence, **'~-up** *n* **6** [VP2C] move smoothly and effortlessly; go with a gliding motion: *The ship ~ped through the water.* **7** [VP6A] get free from; let go from restraint: *~ greyhounds from the leash; ~ anchor,* detach a ship from the anchor; (of a cow) *~ her calf,* give birth to it prematurely; *~ a stitch,* (knitting) move a stitch from one needle to the other without knitting it. *The dog ~ped its collar,* got out of it. *The point ~ped my attention.*

slip·per /ˈslɪpə(r)/ *n* loose-fitting light shoe worn in the house. **~ed** *adj* wearing ~s.

slip·pery /ˈslɪpərɪ/ *adj* (**-ier, iest**) **1** (of a surface) smooth, wet, polished, etc so that it is difficult to hold, to stand on, or to move on: *~ roads; ~ under foot;* (fig) (of a subject) needing care: *We're on ~ ground when dealing with this subject.* ***be on a ~ slope,*** (fig) on a course of action which may lead to failure or disgrace. **2** (fig, of persons) unreliable; unscrupulous: *a ~ customer,* a rogue. *He's as ~ as an eel,* is untrustworthy, difficult to manage. **slip·peri·ness** *n*

slippy /ˈslɪpɪ/ *adj* (colloq) **1** slippery. **2** (dated) quick: *Be ~ about it! Look ~!*

slip·shod /ˈslɪpʃod/ *adj* slovenly; careless: *a ~ piece of work; a ~ style.*

slit /slɪt/ *n* [C] long, narrow cut, tear or opening: *the ~ of a letter-box* (through which letters are put); *a ' ~ trench,* a narrow trench made for one soldier or one group of soldiers. □ *vt* (*pt,pp* **slit; -tt-**) **1** [VP6A,15A,22] make a ~ in; open (by ~ting): *~ a man's throat; ~ an envelope open; ~ cloth into strips/a sheet of leather into thongs.* **2** [VP2A,C] be cut or torn lengthwise: *The shirt has ~ down the back.*

slither /ˈslɪðə(r)/ *vi* [VP2A,C] slide or slip unsteadily: *~ down an ice-covered slope.* **~y** *adj* slippery.

sliver /ˈslɪvə(r)/ *n* [C] small, thin strip of wood; splinter; thin piece pared off a large piece: *a ~ of cheese.* □ *vt,vi* [VP6A,2A] break off as a ~; break into ~s; splinter.

slob·ber /ˈslobə(r)/ *vi,vt* **1** [VP2A,3A] let saliva run from the mouth (as a baby does). ***~ over sb,*** show excessive and maudlin love or admiration for (e g by giving wet kisses). **2** [VP6A] make wet with saliva: *The baby has ~ed its bib.* □ *n* [U] saliva running from the mouth; maudlin talk, etc.

sloe /sləʊ/ *n* [C] small, bluish-black wild plum, fruit of the blackthorn; the blackthorn bush. **ˌ~-'gin** *n* liqueur made from ~s steeped in gin.

slog /slog/ *vi,vt* (**-gg-**) [VP6A,2C] hit hard and wildly, esp in boxing and cricket; walk or work hard and steadily: *~ (at) the ball; ~ing away at one's work; ~ing along the road.* **~·ger** *n* person who ~s, e g at cricket; dogged worker.

slo·gan /ˈsləʊgən/ *n* [C] striking and easily remembered phrase used to advertise sth, or to make clear the aim(s) of a group, organization, campaign, etc: *political ~s.*

sloop /slup/ *n* **1** small one-masted sailing-ship with fore-and-aft rig. **2** (mod use) small warship used for anti-submarine escort duty.

slop¹ /slop/ *vi,vt* (**-pp-**) **1** [VP2A,C] (of liquids) spill over the edge: *The tea ~ped (over) into the saucer.* **2** ***~ over sb,*** = slobber over sb. **3** [VP6A,15A] cause to spill: *~ beer over the counter of a pub;* splash. **4** ***~ out,*** empty ~s(1): *The wretched men in prison have to ~ out every morning.* **5** [VP6A,15A] make a mess with: ~

paint all over the floor. **6** [VP2C] splash: *Why do some children love ~ping about in puddles?* □ *n* (*pl*) **1** dirty waste water from the kitchen or from bedrooms (where there are no basins with running water and drains); (*pl*) urine, excrement (in pails, as in a prison cell). **'~-basin** *n* basin into which dregs from teacups are emptied at table. **'~-pail** *n* one in which bedroom ~s are removed. **2** liquid food, e g milk, soup, esp for people who are ill; swill (for pigs).

slop² /slop/ *n* (esp as supplied to sailors in the Navy, usu *pl*) cheap, ready-made clothing; bedding. **'~-shop** *n* shop where ~s are sold.

slope /sləʊp/ *n* **1** [C,U] slanting line; position or direction at an angle, less than 90°, to the earth's surface or to another flat surface: *the ~ of a roof; a slight/steep ~; a ~ up/down; a hill with a ~ of 1 in 5.* **2** area of rising or falling ground: *'mountain ~s; 'ski ~s.* **3** position of a (soldier with his) rifle on the shoulder: *with his rifle at the ~.* □ *vi,vt* **1** [VP2A,C] have a ~; slant: *Our garden ~s (down) to the river. Does your handwriting ~ forward or backward?* **2** [VP6A] cause to ~. ***~ arms,*** (mil) place and hold the rifle in a sloping position on the left shoulder. **3** [VP2C] (colloq) ***~ off,*** (also *do a ~*), go off or away (to evade sb, or escape doing sth). **slop·ing·ly** *adv*

sloppy /'slopɪ/ *adj* (-ier, -iest) **1** wet or dirty with rain, etc; full of puddles; (of a table, etc) wet with slops: *The melting snow made the roads ~.* **2** (of food) consisting of slops. ⇨ **slop¹** *n*(2). **3** (colloq) unsystematic; not done with care and thoroughness: *a ~ piece of work.* **4** (colloq) foolishly sentimental; weakly emotional: *~ sentiment; ~ talk about girl-friends and boy-friends.* **slop·pily** /-əlɪ/ *adv* in a ~ manner: *sloppily* (= carelessly) *dressed.* **slop·pi·ness** *n*

slosh /sloʃ/ *vt,vi* **1** [VP6A,15A] (sl) hit: *~ sb on the chin.* **2** [VP3A] ***~ about,*** flounder about in slush or mud. **3** [VP15B] ***~ sth about,*** throw water or other liquid or semi-liquid substance about.

slot /slot/ *n* [C] **1** narrow opening through which sth is to be put; slit for a coin in a machine (**'~-machine** or *vending-machine*) that automatically delivers sth, e g tickets, cigarettes, packets of sweets. **2** slit, groove or channel into which sth fits or along which sth slides. **3** (colloq) right or suitable place for sth (in a broadcast programme, scheme, etc): *find a ~ for a talk on bee-keeping.* □ *vt* (-tt-) [VP6A,15A] provide with ~s; make a ~ or ~s in: *~ a song recital into a radio programme; ~ 30 000 graduates a year into jobs,* find jobs for them.

sloth /sləʊθ/ *n* **1** [U] laziness; idleness. **2** [C] S American mammal which lives in the branches of trees and moves very slowly. **~·ful** /-fl/ *adj* inactive; lazy.

slouch /slaʊtʃ/ *vi* [VP2A,C] stand, sit or move, in a lazy, tired way: *louts who ~ about at street corners all day.* □ *n* ~ing attitude or way of walking: *walk with a ~.* **'~-'hat** *n* soft hat with a turned-down brim. **~·ing·ly** *adv*

slough¹ /slaʊ *in US topography:* slu/ *n* [C] swamp; marsh.

slough² /slʌf/ *n* [C] cast-off skin of a snake; any dead part of an animal dropped off at regular periods. □ *vt,vi* [VP6A,15A,2A] ***~ (sth) (off),*** put, come or throw off: *~ (off) bad habits; a snake that has ~ed its skin.*

sloven /'slʌvn/ *n* person who is untidy, dirty, careless or slipshod in his appearance, dress, habits, etc. **~·ly** *adj* of or like a ~: *a ~ly appearance; ~ in his dress.* **~·li·ness** *n*

slow¹ /sləʊ/ *adj* (-er, -est) **1** not quick; taking a long time: *a ~ runner; a ~ train,* e g one that stops at all or almost all stations, contrasted with an express train; *a ~ journey.* **2** at less than the usual rate or speed. ***a ~ march,*** e g at a military funeral. ***in ~ motion,*** (of a cinema film) with the number of exposures per second greatly increased (so that when the film is shown at normal rate the action appears to be ~); Hence, *a ~-motion film.* **3** not quick to learn; dull: *a ~ child;* not acting immediately; acting only after a time; *~ poison. He is ~ to anger/~ to make up his mind/~ of speech/~ at accounts/not ~ to defend himself.* **'~·coach** *n* person who is ~ in action, or who is dull, or who has out-of-date ideas. **4** (usu *pred;* of watches and clocks) showing a time behind the correct time (e g 1.55 when it is 2.00): *That clock is five minutes ~.* **5** not sufficiently interesting or lively: *We thought the party/the entertainment was rather ~.* **6** (of a surface) of such a nature that what moves over it (esp a ball) tends to do so at a reduced speed: *a ~ running track/cricket pitch/billiard table.* **~·ly** *adv* **~·ness** *n*

slow² /sləʊ/ *adv* (-er, -est) (Note that *slowly* may precede the finite *v* as in 'He slowly walked up the path', or follow, as in 'He walked slowly up the path', or have front position, as in 'Slowly he walked up the path', whereas ~ follows the *v*, except when used with *how*, or in participial compounds as in **2** below.) **1** at a low speed; slowly: *Tell the driver to go ~er. How ~/How slowly the time passes! S~ astern!* (a command to go astern slowly). ***go ~,*** **(a)** (of workers in a factory, etc) work slowly as a protest, or in order to get attention to demands, etc. Hence, **'go-'slow** *n* **(b)** be less active: *You ought to go ~ until you feel really well again.* **2** (compounds) *'~-'going/-'moving/-'spoken,* going/moving/speaking slowly.

slow³ /sləʊ/ *vi,vt* [VP3C,15B] (cause to) go at a slower speed: *S~ up/down before you reach the crossroads. You should ~ up a bit* (= stop working so hard) *if you want to avoid a breakdown. All this conversation ~s down the action of the play.* **'~-down** *n* (esp) intentional decrease of industrial production by labour or management.

slow-worm /'sləʊ wɜm/ *n* small, limbless non-poisonous reptile.

sludge /slʌdʒ/ *n* [U] **1** thick, greasy mud; slush. **2** sewage. **3** thick, dirty oil or grease.

slue /slu/ ⇨ **slew²**.

slug¹ /slʌg/ *n* slow-moving creature like a snail but without a shell, a garden pest destructive to seedlings and plants. ⇨ the illus at **mollusc**.

slug² /slʌg/ *n* **1** bullet of irregular shape. **2** strip of metal with a line of type along one edge.

slug³ /slʌg/ *vt,vi* (-gg-) (US) = **slog**.

slug·gard /'slʌgəd/ *n* lazy, slow-moving person.

slug·gish /'slʌgɪʃ/ *adj* inactive; slow-moving: *a ~ river/pulse/liver.* **~·ly** *adv* **~·ness** *n*

sluice /slus/ *n* [C] **1** **'~(-gate/-valve),** apparatus, contrivance, for regulating the level of water by controlling the flow into or out of (a canal, lake, etc): *open the ~-gates of the reservoir.* **2** **'~(-way),** artificial water channel, e g one made by gold-miners for rinsing gold from sand and dirt. **3** flow of water above, through or below a floodgate. □ *vt, vi* **1** [VP6A] send a stream of water over; wash with a stream of water: *~ ore*, to separate it from gravel, etc. **2** [VP6A] wash or flood with water from a ~. **2** [VP3A] ***~ out***, (of water) rush out as from a ~.

slum /slʌm/ *n* **1** court, alley or street of dirty, crowded houses: *live in a ~*. **2 the ~s**, part(s) of a town where there are such streets and alleys; *back-to-back ~s*, streets of houses built closely together; *a '~-ˋclearance campaign*, effort to abolish ~s and rehouse the people living in them. □ *vi* (-mm-) **1** visit the ~s to give charitable aid to the people in them: *go ~ming*. **2** (colloq) live very cheaply: *They've been ~ming for years*. **~my** *adj* of ~s: *a ~my part of the town*.

slum·ber /ˋslʌmbə(r)/ *vi, vt* (liter and rhet) **1** [VP2A] sleep, esp sleep peacefully or comfortably. **2** [VP15B] pass (time) in ~: *~ away a hot afternoon*. □ *n* (often *pl*) sleep: *fall into a troubled ~; disturb sb's ~(s)*. **~er** *n* one who ~s. **~·ous** /-əs/ *adj* sleepy.

slump /slʌmp/ *vi* **1** [VP2A,C] drop or fall heavily: *Tired from his walk, he ~ed into a chair. The bullet entered his chest and he ~ed down to the floor*. **2** [VP2A] (of prices, trade, business activity) fall steeply or suddenly. □ *n* [C] general drop in prices, trade activity, etc; business depression.

slung /slʌŋ/ *pt, pp* of **sling**.

slunk /slʌŋk/ *pt, pp* of **slink**.

slur /slɜ(r)/ *vt, vi* (-rr-) **1** [VP6A] join (sounds, letters, words) so that they are indistinct; (music) sing or play legato. **2** [VP3A] ***~ over sth***, deal quickly with in an attempt to conceal: *He ~red over the dead man's faults and spoke chiefly of his virtues*. □ *n* [C] **1** reproach; suggestion of wrongdoing: *cast a ~ on sb's reputation; keep one's reputation free from (all) ~s*. **2** act of ~ring sounds. **3** (music) the mark ⌒ or ⌣ used to show that two or more notes are to be sung to one syllable or performed legato. ⇨ the illus at **notation**.

slurry /ˋslʌrɪ *US:* ˋslɜɪ/ *n* [U] thin semi-liquid mixture of cement, clay, mud, etc.

slush /slʌʃ/ *n* [U] soft, melting snow; soft mud; (fig) foolish sentiment. **slushy** *adj*

slut /slʌt/ *n* slovenly woman; slattern. **~·tish** /-ɪʃ/ *adj*

sly /slɑɪ/ *adj* (-er, -est) **1** deceitful; keeping or doing things secretly; seeming to have, suggesting, secret knowledge: *a sly look*. ***a sly dog***, person who is secretive about the gay life he leads, etc. ***on the sly***, secretly. **2** playful, mischievous. **sly·ly** *adv* **sly·ness** *n*

smack[1] /smæk/ *n* [C] **1** (sound of a) blow given with the open hand on sth with a flat surface; sound of the lips parted suddenly or of a whip: *with a ~ of the lips*, with this sound (suggesting enjoyment of food or drink); *give sb a ~ on the lips*, a loud kiss. *I heard the ~* (= crack) *of a whip*. **2** slap, blow: *give the ball a hard ~*, hit it hard (e g in cricket). ***get a ~ in the eye***, (colloq) experience a setback; suffer a sharp disappointment. ***have a ~ at sth***, (colloq) have a try to do it. □ *vt* [VP6A] **1** strike with the open hand: *~ a naughty child*. **2 *~ one's lips***, part the lips with a ~ing sound to show pleasure (at food or drink, or in anticipation of other sensual pleasures). □ *adv* in a sudden and violent way: *run ~ into a brick wall; hit sb ~ in the eye*. **~er** *n* (colloq) **1** loud kiss. **2** pound (£) or dollar. **~·ing** *n* act or occasion of hitting with the palm of the hand: *The child needs a good ~ing*.

smack[2] /smæk/ *n* small sailing-boat for fishing.

smack[3] /smæk/ *vi* [VP3A], *n* ***~ of***, (have a) slight flavour or suggestion (of): *opinions that ~ of heresy; medicine that ~s of sulphur; have a ~ of obstinacy in one's character*.

small /smɔl/ *adj* (-er, -est) (opp of *large*) **1** not large in degree, size, etc: *~ animals; a ~ town/room/audience/sum of money, etc; a ~ pony*, Cf *a nice little pony*, 'little' being preferred when there are emotive implications; *~ children*, Cf *charming/nice/naughty, etc little children*. **2** not doing things on a large scale: *~ farmers/business men/shopkeepers*. **3** unimportant, trifling. ***be thankful for ~ mercies***, for trifling pieces of good fortune. **ˋ~ talk**, about everyday and unimportant social matters. **4** (attrib only) *a ~ eater*, person who eats ~ quantities of food. **5** morally mean; ungenerous: *Only a ~ man/a man with a ~ mind would behave so badly*. Hence, **'~-ˋminded** *adj* **6** of low social position; humble: *great and ~*, all classes of people. **7 *in a ~ way***, modestly, unpretentiously: *He has contributed to scientific progress in a ~ way. They live in quite a ~ way*, simply and without social ambitions. **8** little or no: *have ~ cause for gratitude. He failed, and ~ wonder*, It is not surprising. **9** (compounds and special uses) **ˋ~-arms** *n pl* weapons light enough to be carried in the hand by a single soldier, e g rifles, revolvers. **~ beer** *n* (archaic) light beer: *think no ~ beer of oneself*, be conceited; *be ~ beer*, be unimportant. **~ change** *n* **(a)** coins of ~ denominations: *Can you give me ~ change for this note*. **(b)** (fig) trivial remarks; light conversation. **ˋ~ fry** *n* ⇨ **fry**[2]. **ˋ~·holding** *n* (in GB) piece of land under fifty acres in extent let or sold to sb for cultivation. **ˋ~·holder** *n* person owning or renting a ~holding. **the ~ hours** *n pl* ⇨ **hour(1)**. **~ letters** *n pl* not capitals. **ˋ~·pox** *n* [U] serious contagious disease which leaves permanent marks on the skin. **ˋ~·time** *adj* (colloq) of minor importance; third-rate. ***the still, ~ voice***, the voice of conscience. ***on the ˋ~ side***, somewhat too small. ***look/feel ~***, be humiliated. □ *adv* ***sing ~***, ⇨ **sing(1)**. □ *n* **1** (with *def art*) slenderest part: *the ~ of the back*. **2** (*pl*, colloq) ~ articles of clothing (for laundering). **~·ness** *n*

smarmy /ˋsmɑmɪ/ *adj* (GB, colloq) ingratiating; trying to win favour by flattery, etc.

smart[1] /smɑt/ *adj* (-er, -est) **1** bright; new-looking; clean; well-dressed: *a ~ hat/suit/car. You look very ~. Go and make yourself ~ before we call on the Joneses*. **2** fashionable; conspicuous in society: *the ˋ~ set; ~ people*. **3** clever; skilful; having a good, quick brain; showing ingenuity: *a ~ student/officer; a ~ retort/saying; ~ dealing*, clever and intelligent, but perhaps dishonest. **4** quick; brisk: *go for a ~ walk; start out at a ~ pace*. ***Look ~!*** Hurry! **5** severe: *~ punishment; a ~ rebuke; a ~ box on the ear*. **~·ly** *adv* **~·ness** *n* **~en** /ˋsmɑtn/ *vt, vi* [VP6A,15B,2C] ***~en (oneself) up***, make or become ~(1,4): *~en oneself up to receive visitors. She has ~ened up since I met her last*.

smart[2] /smɑt/ *vt* [VP2A,C,3A] feel or cause a sharp pain (of body or mind): *The smoke made my eyes ~. Iodine ~s when it is put on a cut. He was ~ing under an injustice/under his father's rebukes. She was ~ing with vexation*. ***~ for***, suffer the consequences of, be paid out for: *He will*

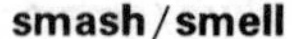

GUINEA PIG Lc 17 cm
BADGER Lc 91 cm
RABBIT Lc 40 cm
ARMADILLO Lc 76 cm
SQUIRREL Lc 25 cm
MOLE Lc 12 cm
BEAVER Lc 73 cm
BAT Lc 5 cm
FOX Lc 104 cm
RAT Lc 20 cm
KOALA Lc 60 cm
MONGOOSE Lc 45 cm
HEDGEHOG Lc 17 cm
DUCKBILLED PLATYPUS Lc 51 cm
OTTER Lc 76 cm

wild animals 2

make you ~ for this impudence. □ *n* [U] sharp pain, bodily or mental: *The ~ of his wound kept him awake.*

smash /smæʃ/ *vt,vi* **1** [VP6A,15A,B,22,2A,C] break, be broken, violently into small pieces: *~ a window. The drunken man ~ed up all the furniture. The firemen ~ed in/down the doors. Don't ~ the door open; I have a key!* **'~-and-'grab raid,** one in which a thief ~es a shop-window, e g a jeweller's, and grabs valuables from behind it. **2** [VP2A,C] rush, force a way, violently (*into, through, etc*): *The car ~ed into a wall.* **3** [VP6A] deal a heavy blow to; defeat: *give sb a ~ing blow; ~ the enemy; ~ a record,* (in sport, etc) set up a far better record. **4** [VP6A] (tennis) hit (a ball) downwards over the net with a hard, overhand stroke. **5** [VP2A] (of a business firm) go bankrupt. □ *n* [C] ~ing; breaking to pieces. **'~(-up),** violent collision: *The teapot fell with an awful ~. He fell and hit his head an awful ~ on the kerbstone. There has been a terrible ~(-up) on the railway. When the banks failed, many businesses were ruined in the ~ that followed.* **go ~,** be ruined. **2** (tennis) stroke in which the ball is brought swiftly down. **3 a (~) hit,** (colloq) sth (esp a new play, song, film, etc) which is at once very successful. □ *adv* with a ~: *go/run ~ into a wall.* **~er** *n* **(a)** violent blow. **(b)** sth or sb considered to be remarkably fine: *That girl's a ~er!* **~ing** *adj* (schoolboy sl) excellent; overwhelmingly fine.

smat·ter·ing /'smætrɪŋ/ *n* (usu *sing* with *indef art*) slight knowledge (*of* a subject).

smear /smɪə(r)/ *vt,vi* **1** [VP14] **~ *sth on/over/with,*** cover or mark with sth oily or sticky; spread (sth oily, etc) on: *~ one's hands with grease; ~ grease on one's hands; hands ~ed with blood.* **2** [VP6A] make dirty, greasy marks on; (fig) defame or sully (sb's reputation). ***a '~(ing) campaign,*** one that aims at damaging sb's reputation (by spreading rumours, etc). **3** [VP6A] blot; obscure the outline of: *~ a word.* **4** [VP2A] become ~ed. □ *n* [C] stain; mark made by ~ing: *a ~ of paint; ~s of blood on the wall.* **'~-word** *n* word (e g *communist* in US) suitable for ~ing (sb's reputation).

smell[1] /smel/ *n* **1** [U] that one of the five senses special to the nose: *Taste and ~ are closely connected. S~ is more acute in dogs than in men.* **2** [C,U] that which is noticed by means of the nose; quality that affects this sense: *What a nice/horrible/unusual ~! There's a ~ of cooking. I like the ~ of thyme.* **3** (without an *adj*) bad or unpleasant quality that affects the nose: *What a ~!* **4** (usu *sing* with *indef art*) act of breathing in through the nose to get the ~**(2)** of sth: *Have/Take a ~ of this egg and tell me whether it's good.*

smell[2] /smel/ *vt,vi* (*pt,pp* **smelt** /smelt/) **1** [VP6A] (not in the progressive tenses; often with *can, could*) be aware of through the sense of smell: *Can/Do you ~ anything unusual? The camels smelt the water a mile off. I can ~ something burning/cooking.* ***~ a rat,*** ⇨ rat. **2** [VP6A,15B,2A,C] (with progressive tenses possible) use one's sense of smell in order to learn sth; inhale the odour of: *S~ this and tell me what it is. The dog was ~ing (at) the lamp-post.* ***~ round/about,*** go here and there ~ing, to get information (liter and fig). ***~ sth out,*** discover, hunt out, by means of the sense of smell or (fig) by intuition. **3** [VP2A] (not in the progressive tenses) have the sense of smell: *Do/Can fishes ~?* **4** [VP2A,D,3A] ***~ (of sth),*** give out a smell (of the kind specified by an *adj* or *adv*); suggest or recall the smell (of): *The flowers ~ sweet. The dinner ~s good. The lamb ~s of garlic. Your breath ~s of brandy.* (Note that if there is no *adj*, the suggestion is usu sth unpleasant): *Fish soon ~s in summer if it is not kept on ice. His breath ~s.* ***~ of the lamp,*** seem to have been composed late at night, with much hard work. **'~ing-salts** *n pl* sharp-smelling substances to be sniffed as a cure for faintness, etc; sal volatile. **'~ing-bottle** *n* one containing ~ing-salts. **smelly** *adj* (-ier, -iest) (colloq) having a bad ~.

smelt¹ /smelt/ *vt* [VP6A] melt (ore); separate (metal) from ore by doing this: *a copper-~ing works.*

smelt² /smelt/ *n* small fish valued as food.

smelt³ *pp,pt* of smell².

smi·lax /'smaılæks/ *n* [U] kind of plant with trailing vines much used in decoration.

smile /smaıl/ *n* [C] pleased, happy, amused or other expression on the face, with (usu a parting of the lips and) loosening of the face muscles: *There was a pleasant/ironical/amused, etc ~ on her face. He was all ~s,* looked very happy. *His face was wreathed in ~s.* □ *vi,vt* **1** [VP2A,B,4B,3A] give a ~ or ~s; show pleasure, amusement, sympathy, contempt, irony, etc by this means: *He never ~s. What are you smiling at? Fortune has not always ~d upon* (= favoured) *me. He ~d to see her so happy.* **2** [VP6A] express by means of a ~: *Father ~d his approval. She ~d her thanks.* **3** [VP6A] give the kind of ~ indicated: *~ a bitter ~.* **smil·ing·ly** *adv* with a ~ or ~s.

smirch /smɜtʃ/ *vt* [VP6A] make dirty; (fig) dishonour. □ *n* [C] (fig) blot or stain.

smirk /smɜk/ *vi* [VP2A], *n* (give a) silly, self-satisfied smile.

smite /smaıt/ *vt,vi* (*pt* smote /sməʊt/, *pp* smitten /'smıtn/) (archaic, or, in mod use, hum or liter) **1** [VP6A] strike; hit hard: *He smote the ball into the grandstand. The sound of an explosion smote our ears. His conscience smote him,* he was conscience-stricken. *He was smitten with remorse/smitten with that pretty girl.* **2** [VP6A] defeat utterly: *God will ~ our enemies.* **3** [VP2A, C] strike; come forcibly: *his knees smote together. A strange sound smote upon our ears.*

smith /smıθ/ *n* worker in iron or other metals: *'black~.* ⇨ gold, silver, tin. **smithy** /'smıðı/ *n* black~'s workshop.

smith·er·eens /'smıðə'rinz/ *n pl* small fragments: *smash sth to/into ~.*

smit·ten /'smıtn/ ⇨ smite.

smock /smok/ *n* loose garment (with smocking on it) like an overall. **~·ing** *n* [U] kind of ornamentation on a garment made by gathering the cloth tightly with stitches.

smog /smog/ *n* [U] mixture of fog and smoke, exhaust fumes from motor-vehicles, etc.

smoke¹ /sməʊk/ *n* **1** [U] visible vapour with particles of carbon, etc coming from a burning substance: *~ pouring from factory chimneys; 'ciga'rette/ci'gar ~.* ***end up in ~,*** come to, end in, nothing. ***go up in ~,*** be burnt up; (fig) be without result, leave nothing solid or worth while behind. ***There is no ~ without fire,*** (prov) ⇨ fire¹(1). **'~-bomb** *n* one that sends out clouds of ~ (used to conceal military operations, etc). **'~-dried** *adj* (of ham, certain kinds of fish, etc) dried and cured in wood ~. **'~-screen** *n* clouds of ~ made to hide military or naval operations; (fig) explanation, etc designed to mislead people about one's real intentions, etc. **'~-stack** *n* **(a)** outlet for ~ and steam from a steamship (and, US, from a steam locomotive). **(b)** tall chimney. **2** [C] act of smoking tobacco: *stop working and have a ~*; (colloq) cigar or cigarette: *pass the ~s round.* **~·less** *adj* **1** that burns without ~: *~less fuel.* **2** free from ~: *a ~less zone,* where ~ is prohibited; *the ~less atmosphere of the countryside.* **smoky** *adj* (-ier, -iest) **1** giving out much ~; full of ~: *smoky chimneys/fires; the smoky atmosphere of an industrial town.* **2** like ~ in smell, taste or appearance.

smoke² /sməʊk/ *vi,vt* **1** [VP2A] give out smoke, or sth thought to resemble smoke, e g visible vapour or steam: *a smoking volcano. That oil-lamp ~s badly.* **2** [VP2A] (of a fire or fireplace) send out smoke into the room (instead of up the chimney): *This fireplace ~s badly.* **3** [VP2A,6A] draw in and let out the smoke of burning tobacco or other substance: *~ a pipe/cigar, etc. Do you ~? If you ~ opium, give it up.* **4** [VP22] bring (*oneself*) into a specific state by smoking tobacco: *He ~d himself sick.* **5** [VP2A,C] (of pipes, cigars, etc, with passive force): *This pipe ~s well,* is satisfactory when ~d. *A good cigar will ~* (= can be ~d) *for at least half an hour.* **6** [VP6A] dry and preserve (meat, fish) with smoke (from wood fires): *~d ham/salmon.* **7** [VP6A] stain, darken, dry, with smoke: *a ~d ceiling; a sheet of ~d glass,* e g through which to look at the sun. **8** [VP6A,15B] send smoke on to (plants, insects); force *out* with smoke. ***~ sth out,*** force to leave by smoking: *~ the plants in a greenhouse,* to kill insects; *~ out snakes from a hole.* **smok·ing** *n* [U] (*gerund,* in compounds) **'smoking-carriage/-car/-compartment** *nn* one for smokers on a railway train. **'smoking-mixture** *n* blend of tobaccos for smoking in pipes. **'smoking-room** *n* room (in a hotel, etc) where smoking is permitted. **smoker** *n* **1** person who habitually ~s tobacco. **2** smoking-carriage on a train. **3** in formal entertainment (at a club, etc) where men sing together, tell (often improper) stories, etc.

smol·der /'smoldə(r)/ ⇨ smoulder.

smooth¹ /smuð/ *adj* (-er, -est) **1** having a surface like that of glass; free from roughness: *~ paper/skin; a ~ road; a ~ sheet of ice; ~ to the touch; a ~ sea,* calm, free from waves; *make things ~ for sb,* (fig) remove difficulties. *The way is now ~.* ***take the rough with the ~,*** take things (both the ups and downs of life) as they come. **'~-bore** *adj* (of a gun) having no rifling in the barrel. **'~-'faced** *adj* (fig) friendly but hypocritical. **2** (of movement) free from shaking, bumping, etc: *a ~*

ride in a good car; a ~ flight in a jet airliner; a ~ crossing, e g from England to France. **3** (of a liquid mixture) free from lumps; well beaten or mixed: *a ~ paste.* **4** free from harshness of sound or taste; flowing easily: *~ verse; a ~ voice; ~ claret/whisky.* **5** (of a person, his manner) flattering, polite, unruffled, conciliatory: *a ~ temper; ~ manners; a ~ face,* often used to suggest hypocrisy. Hence, **'~'faced/-'spoken/-'tongued** *adjj* (all having a suggestion of insincerity). □ *vt,vi* **1** [VP6A,15B] ***~ sth (down/out/away/over),*** make ~: *~ down one's dress; ~ away/over obstacles/difficulties/perplexities, etc,* get rid of them. ***~ sb's path,*** (fig) make progress easier. **2** [VP2C] become ~ or quiet: *The sea has ~ed down.* **3** (compounds) **'~-ing-iron** *n* (*iron* is now used) flat-iron used (heated) to ~ linen, clothes, etc. **'~-ing-plane** *n* small plane for finishing the planing of wood. □ *n* act of ~ing: *give one's hair a ~.* **~·ly** *adv* in a ~ manner: *a ~ly running engine. Things are not going very ~ly,* there are troubles, obstacles, interruptions, etc. **~·ness** *n*

smor·gas·bord (Swedish = **smör·gäs·bord**) /'smɔgəsbɔd/ *n* [U] meal with a variety of dishes served from a buffet.

smote /sməʊt/ *pt* of **smite**.

smother /'smʌðə(r)/ *vt* **1** [VP6A] cause the death of, by stopping the breath of or by keeping air from; kill by suffocation. **2** [VP6A] put out (a fire); keep (a fire) down (so that it burns slowly) by covering *with* ashes, sand, etc. **3** [VP14] ***~ sth (with),*** cover, wrap up, overwhelm with: *~ a grave with flowers/a child with kisses/one's wife with kindness; be ~ed with/in dust by passing cars.* **4** [VP6A,15B] suppress; hold back: *~ a yawn/one's anger/feelings of resentment; ~ up a scandal,* try to conceal it. □ *n* (usu *sing* with *indef art*) cloud of dust, smoke, steam, spray, etc.

smoul·der (US = **smol-**) /'sməʊldə(r)/ *vi* [VP2A,C] burn slowly without flame; (fig, of feelings, etc) exist, operate, unseen, undetected, suppressed, etc: *~ing discontent/ hatred/ rebellion.* □ *n* [U] ~ing burning: *The ~ became a blaze.*

smudge /smʌdʒ/ *n* [C] **1** dirty mark; blotted or blurred mark: *You've got a ~ on your cheek. Wash you hands or you'll make ~s on the writing-paper.* **2** (chiefly US) outdoor fire with thick smoke made to keep away insects. □ *vt,vi* **1** [VP6A] make a ~ or ~s on; make a ~ on (when writing a letter or word). **2** [VP2A] (of ink, paint, etc) become blurred or smeared: *Ink ~s easily.*

smug /smʌg/ *adj* (-gg-) self-satisfied; having, showing, a character that is satisfied although without ambition, imagination, broadmindedness: *a ~ smile; a life of ~ respectability; ~ optimism; ~ young men.* **~·ly** *adv* **~·ness** *n*

smuggle /'smʌgl/ *vt* [VP6A,14,15A,B] **1** get (goods) secretly and illegally (*into, out of,* a country, *through* the customs, *across* a frontier): *~ Swiss watches into England.* **2** take (sth or sb) secretly and in defiance of rules and regulations: *~ a letter into a prison.* **smug·gler** /'smʌglə(r)/ *n*

smut /smʌt/ *n* **1** [C] (mark or stain made by a) bit of soot, dirt, etc. **2** [U] disease of corn (wheat, etc) that causes the ears to turn black. **3** [U] indecent or obscene words, stories: *Don't talk ~.* □ *vt* (-tt-) [VP6A] mark with ~s(1). **~ty** *adj* (-ier, -iest) **1** dirty with ~s. **2** containing ~(3): *~ty stories.* **~·tily** /-əlɪ/ *adv* **~·ti·ness** *n*

snack /snæk/ *n* light usu hurriedly eaten meal. **'~-bar/-counter** *nn* bar/counter/where ~s may be eaten.

snaffle[1] /'snæfl/ *n* **'~(-bit)** horse's bit without a curb.

snaffle[2] /'snæfl/ *vt* [VP6A] (GB sl) take without permission; pinch(**4**).

snag /snæg/ *n* [C] **1** rough or sharp object, root of a tree, hidden rock, which may be a source of danger. **2** (colloq) hidden, unknown or unexpected difficulty or obstacle: *strike/come upon a ~. There's a ~ in it somewhere.*

snail /sneɪl/ *n* kinds of small, soft animal, most of them with a spiral shell. ⇨ the illus at **mollusc**. ***at a '~'s pace,*** very slowly.

snake /sneɪk/ *n* kinds of long, legless, crawling reptile, some of which are poisonous; (fig) (often *~ in the grass*) treacherous person who pretends to be a friend. ***see ~s,*** have hallucinations. **'~-charmer** *n* person who can control ~s with music. □ *vi* [VP2C] move in twists and glides: *The road ~s through the mountains.* **snaky** *adj* of or like a ~; (fig) venomous, ungrateful, treacherous.

snap /snæp/ *vt,vi* (-pp-) **1** [VP6A,15B,2A,3A] ***~ (at) sth,*** (try to) snatch with the teeth: *The dog ~ped at my leg. The fish ~ped at the bait. They ~ped at the offer,* (fig) offered eagerly to accept it. ***~ sth up,*** buy eagerly: *The cheapest articles*

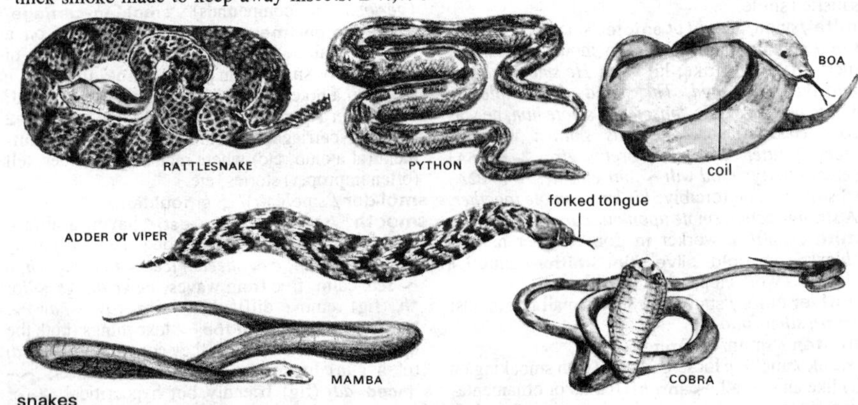

snakes

were quickly ~*ped up.* **2** [VP6A,14,15A,B,22, 2A,C] break with a sharp crack; open or close with, make a sudden, sharp sound; say (sth), speak, sharply: *He stretched the rubber band till it* ~*ped. The rope* ~*ped. He* ~*ped down the lid of the box. He* ~*ped his whip. Her whip* ~*ped down on the pony's back. The sergeant* ~*ped out his orders.* **~ *at sb,*** speak to sb sharply: *Stop* ~*ping at me.* **~ *one's finger at sb/in sb's face,*** make a cracking noise by flicking a finger audibly against the thumb (usu to show contempt). **~ *sb's nose/ head off,*** speak angrily to; interrupt rudely or impatiently. **3** [VP6A] take a ~shot (⇨ 8 below) of. **4** (sl) **~ *(in)to it,*** start moving, get going, quickly. **~ *out of it,*** get out of a mood, habit, etc. □ *n* **1** [C] act or sound of ~ping: *The dog made an unsuccessful* ~ *at the meat. The lid shut with a* ~. *The oar broke with a* ~. *S*~ *went the oar,* (adverbial use) It broke with a ~ping noise. **2** [C] **cold ~,** sudden, short period of cold weather. **3** [U] (colloq) energy, dash, vigour, liveliness: *Put some* ~ *into it.* ⇨ snappy below. **4** [C] kinds of small, crisp cake: (usu in compounds) *'ginger-*~*s.* **5** [C] (usu in compounds) catch, device for fastening things, closed by pressing: *'*~*-fasteners,* used on dresses, gloves, etc. (US *snaps* = press-studs). **6** = ~shot ⇨ 8 below. **7** (attrib) done quickly and with little or no warning: *a* ~ *election; take a* ~ *vote; a* ~ *division,* in the House of Commons. **8** (compounds, etc) **'~-dragon** *n* [C] (= antirrhinum) kinds of plant with flowers that are like bags and can be made to open (like lips) when pressed. **'~-shot** *n* quickly taken photograph with a hand camera (and usu by an amateur). **~py** *adj* (-ier, -iest) bright; lively: ***Make it ~py! Look ~py!*** (colloq) Be quick about it! **~·pish** /-ɪʃ/ *adj* inclined to ~, to be ill-tempered or irritable. **~·pish·ly** *adv* **~·pish·ness** *n*

snare /sneə(r)/ *n* [C] **1** trap, esp one with a noose, for catching small animals and birds. **2** (fig) sth that tempts one to expose oneself to defeat, disgrace, loss, etc: *His promises are a* ~ *and a delusion.* □ *vt* [VP6A] catch in a ~: ~ *a rabbit.*

snarl[1] /snɑl/ *vi,vt* [VP2A,3A] **~ *(at),*** (of dogs) show the teeth and growl (at); (of persons) speak in a harsh voice. □ *n* act or sound of ~ing: *answer with a* ~.

snarl[2] /snɑl/ *n* tangle; confused state: *the traffic* ~*s in a big town.* □ *vt,vi* [VP6A,15B,2A,C,3A] (cause to) become jammed: *The traffic* (*was*) ~*ed up.* Hence, **'~-up** *n*

snatch /snætʃ/ *vt,vi* [VP6A,2A,15A,B] **1** put out the hand suddenly and take: *He* ~*ed the letter from me/*~*ed the letter out of my hand. It's rude to* ~. *He* ~*ed at* (i e tried to seize) *the letter but was not quick enough. He* ~*ed up his gun and fired.* **2** get quickly or when a chance occurs: ~ *an hour's sleep/a meal;* ~ *a kiss.* □ *n* [C] **1** act of ~ing; sudden attempt to get sth by stretching out the hand: *make a* ~ *at sth;* (attrib) *a* ~ *decision,* one that is ~ed(2). **2** short outburst or period: *short* ~*es of verse; overhear* ~*es of conversation; work in* ~*s,* not continuously. **~er** *n*

sneak /snik/ *vi,vt* **1** [VP2A,3A] **~ *(on sb),*** go quietly and furtively (*in, out, away, back, past,* etc). **2** [VP2A] (schoolboy sl) tell tales; go to the teacher and tell him about the faults, wrongdoing, etc of others. **3** [VP6A] (schoolboy sl) steal. □ *n* (colloq) **1** cowardly, treacherous person. **'~-thief** *n* petty thief; person who steals things from open doors and windows. **2** (schoolboy sl) boy or girl who ~s(2). **~·ing** *adj* furtive: *have a* ~*ing respect/sympathy, etc for sb,* respect, etc which is not shown openly; *a* ~*ing suspicion,* a vague, puzzling one. **~·ing·ly** *adv* **sneaky** *adj* = ~ing. **~·ers** *n pl* (chiefly US) (also *a pair of* ~*ers*) shoes soled with rope, rubber or some other substance; tennis shoes.

sneer /snɪə(r)/ *vi* [VP2A,3A] **~ *(at),*** show contempt by means of a derisive smile; utter contemptuous words: ~ *at religion.* □ *n* ~ing look, smile, word or utterance: *You should ignore their* ~*s at your efforts.* **~·ing·ly** *adv*

sneeze /sniz/ *n* [C] sudden, uncontrollable outburst of air through the nose and mouth: *Coughs and* ~*s spread diseases.* □ *vi* [VP2A] make a ~: *Use a handkerchief when you* ~. ***not to be ~d at,*** (colloq) not to be despised; passable: *A prize of £50 in the lottery is not to be* ~*d at.*

snick /snɪk/ *vt,vi, n* **1** (make a) small cut in sth. **2** (cricket) (make a) slight deflection of the ball with the bat: ~ *a ball through the slips.*

snicker /ˈsnɪkə(r)/ *vi, n* whinny; snigger.

snide /snɑɪd/ *adj* sneering; slyly critical: ~ *remarks.*

sniff /snɪf/ *vi,vt* **1** [VP2A] draw air in through the nose so that there is a sound: *They all had colds and were* ~*ing and sneezing.* **2** [VP2A,3A] **~ *(at),*** ~(1) to show disapproval or contempt: *The offer* (e g to sell a good car for £300) *is not to be* ~*ed at.* **3** [VP2A,3A,15B] **~ *at sth;* ~ *sth up,*** draw in through the nose as one breathes: ~ *the sea-air;* ~ (*at*) *a bottle of smelling-salts;* ~ (*at*) *a rose; a preparation* (e g for catarrh) *to be* ~*ed up through the nostrils. The dog was* ~*ing* (*at*) *the lamp-post.* □ *n* [C] act or sound of ~ing; breath (of air, etc): *get a* ~ *of sea air. One* ~ *of this stuff is enough to kill you.* **sniffy** *adj* (colloq) **1** contemptuous. **2** (of sth that should have no smell) ill smelling.

sniffle /ˈsnɪfl/ *vi* = snuffle.

snif·ter /ˈsnɪftə(r)/ *n* (sl) small portion of strong alcoholic drink.

snig·ger /ˈsnɪgə(r)/ *n* [C] half-suppressed laugh (esp at sth improper, or in a cynical manner). □ *vi* [VP2A,C] **~ *(at/over),*** laugh in this way.

snip /snɪp/ *vt,vi* (-pp-) [VP6A,15B,3A] **~ *(at) sth;* ~ *sth off,*** cut with scissors or shears, esp in short, quick strokes: ~ *off the ends;* ~ *a hole in sth;* ~ *cloth/paper.* □ *n* **1** cut made by ~ping; sth ~ped off. **2** (colloq) profitable bargain: *Only 50p! It's a* ~! **~·ping** *n* small piece of material ~ped off a larger piece.

snipe[1] /snɑɪp/ *n* (*pl* unchanged) bird which frequents marshes with a long bill. ⇨ the illus at water.

snipe[2] /snɑɪp/ *vi,vt* [VP2A,3A] **~ *(at),*** fire shots (at) from a hiding-place, usu at long range; [VP6A] kill or hit thus. **sniper** *n* person who ~s.

snip·pet /ˈsnɪpɪt/ *n* small piece cut off; (*pl*) bits (of information, news, etc).

snitch /snɪtʃ/ *vt,vi* **1** [VP6A] (sl) steal (usu sth of little or no value). **2** [VP2A,3A] **~ *(on sb),*** sneak, inform (on sb).

snivel /ˈsnɪvl/ *vi* (GB -ll-; US -l-) [VP2A] cry from pretended grief, sorrow or fear; complain in a miserable, whining way: *a harassed woman with six* ~*ling children.* **~·ler** (US = **~er**) *n* person who ~s.

snob /snob/ *n* person who pays too much respect to social position or wealth, or who despises persons who are of lower social position: '~ *appeal,* power to attract the interest of ~s. **~·bish** /-ɪʃ/ *adj* of or like a ~. **~·bish·ly** *adv* **~·bish·ness, ~·bery** /'snobərɪ/ *nn* [U] state, quality, of being ~bish; (*pl*) ~bish acts or utterances.

snood /snud/ *n* ornamental net worn by a woman to keep her hair in position.

snook /snuk/ *n* (only in) ***cock a ~ (at sb),*** show impudent contempt by placing the thumb to the nose and spreading out the fingers towards him.

snooker /'snukə(r)/ *n* game (a variety of *pool*) played with 15 red balls and six balls of other colours on a billiard-table. ***be ~ed,*** (colloq) be placed in a difficult position.

snoop /snup/ *vi* [VP3A,2C] ~ ***into,*** pry into matters one is not properly concerned with. ~ ***around,*** look for the breaking of rules, etc. **~er** *n* person who ~s.

snooty /'snutɪ/ *adj* (**-ier, -iest**) (colloq) supercilious; snobbish. **snoot·ily** /-əlɪ/ *adv*

snooze /snuz/ *vi* [VP2A], *n* (colloq) (take a) short sleep (esp in the daytime): *have a ~ after lunch.*

snore /snɔ(r)/ *vi* [VP2A,C] breathe roughly and noisily while sleeping: *How frightful to have a husband who ~s!* □ *n* sound of snoring: *His ~s woke me up.* **snorer** *n* person who ~s.

snor·kel, schnor·kel /'snɔkl, 'ʃn-/ *n* tube that enables a submarine to take in air while submerged; device for enabling a swimmer to take in air while under water. ⇨ the illus at **frogman**.

snort /snɔt/ *vi,vt* **1** [VP2A,C] force air violently out through the nose; do this to show impatience, contempt, etc: ~ *with rage* (*at* sb or sth); (colloq) indicate amusement with a burst of loud laughter. **2** [VP6A,15B] express by ~ing: ~ *defiance at sb;* ~ *out a reply. 'Never!', he ~ed.* □ *n* **1** act or sound of ~ing: *give a ~ of contempt.* **2** snorkel (of a submarine). **snorty** *adj* (colloq) ill-tempered. **~er** *n* (colloq) **1** sb or sth that is violent or outstanding in some way: *This problem is a real ~er,* very difficult. **2** strong gale.

snot /snot/ *n* [U] (vulg) mucus of the nose. **~ty** *adj* (vulg) **1** running with, wet with, ~. **2** (esp in) **'~-nosed,** superior; snooty: *You ~-nosed little bastard!* □ *n* (naval sl) midshipman.

snout[1] /snaʊt/ *n* nose (and sometimes the mouth or jaws) of an animal (esp a pig); ⇨ the illus at **domestic, fish;** pointed front of sth, thought to be like a ~.

snout[2] /snaʊt/ *n* (prison sl) [U] tobacco; [C] cigarette.

snow[1] /snəʊ/ *n* **1** [U] frozen vapour falling from the sky in soft, white flakes; mass of such flakes on the ground, etc: *a heavy fall of ~; roads deep in ~;* (*pl*) falls or accumulation of ~: (liter) *Where are the ~s of last year?* **2** (compounds) **'~·ball** *n* **(a)** mass of ~ pressed into a hard ball for throwing in play. **(b)** sth that increases quickly in size as it moves forward. □ *vt,vi* **(a)** throw ~balls (at). **(b)** grow quickly in size, importance, etc: *Opposition to the war ~balled.* **'~-berry** *n* garden shrub with white berries. **'~·blind** *adj* (temporarily) unable to see because the eyes are tired by the glare of the sun on ~. Hence, **'~-blind·ness** *n* **'~·bound** *adj* unable to travel because of heavy falls of ~. **'~-capped/-clad/-covered** *adjj* covered with ~: *~-capped mountains; ~-covered roofs.* **'~·drift** *n* bank of ~ heaped up by the wind: *The train ran into a ~drift.* **'~·drop** *n* bulb plant with small white flowers at the end of winter or in early spring. ⇨ the illus at **flower**. **'~·fall** *n* (esp) amount of ~ that falls on one occasion or in a period of time, e g one winter, one year. **'~-field** *n* permanent wide expanse of ~, e g on high mountains. **'~·flake** *n* one of the feather-like collections of small crystals in which ~ falls. **'~-line** *n* level (in feet or metres) above which ~ lies permanently at any place: *climb above the ~-line.* **'~·man** /-mæn/ *n* (*pl* **-men**) figure of a man made of ~ by children for amusement. **'~-plough** (US **'~-plow**) *n* device for pushing ~ from roads and railways. **'~-shoes** *n pl* frames with leather straps for walking on deep ~ without sinking in. **'~·storm** *n* heavy fall of ~, esp when accompanied by strong wind. **'~-'white** *adj* as white as ~.

snow[2] /snəʊ/ *vi,vt* **1** [VP2A,B] (of snow) come down from the sky: *It ~ed all day.* **2** [VP2C] ~ ***in,*** come in large numbers or quantities: *Gifts and messages ~ed in on her birthday.* **3** ***be ~ed in/up,*** be prevented by heavy snow from going out. ***be ~ed under (with),*** (fig) be overwhelmed: *~ed under with work/with invitations to dinner parties.* **snowy** *adj* (**-ier, -iest**) **1** covered with snow: *~y roofs.* **2** characterized by snow: *~y weather.* **3** as white or fresh as newly fallen snow: *a ~y tablecloth.*

snub[1] /snʌb/ *vt* (**-bb-**) [VP6A] treat (esp a younger or less senior person) with cold behaviour or contempt; reject (an offer) in this way: *be/get ~bed by a civil servant.* □ *n* [C] ~bing words or behaviour: *suffer a ~.*

snub[2] /snʌb/ *adj* (only in) **a ~ nose,** short, stumpy, turned up; hence, **'~-nosed** *adj*

snuff[1] /snʌf/ *n* [U] powdered tobacco to be taken up into the nose by sniffing: *take a pinch of ~.* ***up to ~,*** (colloq) **(a)** shrewd; not childishly innocent. **(b)** in normal health. **'~-box** *n* box for ~. **'~-colour(ed)** *adj, n* (of) dark yellowish-brown.

snuff[2] /snʌf/ *vi, n* = **sniff**.

snuff[3] /snʌf/ *vt,vi* **1** [VP6A,15B] cut or pinch off the burnt black end of the wick of (a candle). ~ ***sth out,*** put out, extinguish (the light of a candle, fig a rebellion): *His hopes were nearly ~ed out.* **2** [VP2C] ~ ***out,*** (colloq) die: *You mustn't ~ out yet.* **~·ers** *n pl* scissors with a kind of box to catch the burnt wick of candles when they are ~ed.

snuffle /'snʌfl/ *vi* [VP2A] make sniffing sounds; breathe noisily (as when the nose is partly stopped up while one has catarrh). □ *n* act or sound of snuffing: *speak in a sanctimonious ~,* nasally, as an affectation said to have been characteristic of some puritans and dissenters.

snug /snʌg/ *adj* (**-gg-**) **1** sheltered from wind and cold; warm and comfortable: ~ *and cosy by the fireside;* ~ *in bed; a ~ woollen vest.* **2** neat and tidy; rightly or conveniently placed or arranged: *a ~ cabin,* on a ship. **3** good enough for modest needs: *a ~ little income.* **4** closely fitting: *a ~ jacket;* (as an *adv*) *a ~-fitting coat.* □ *n* = snuggery. **~·ly** *adv* **~·ness** *n*

snug·gery /'snʌgərɪ/ *n* (*pl* **-ries**) snug place, esp a private room planned for comfort.

snuggle /'snʌgl/ *vi,vt* **1** [VP2C] lie or get (close to sb) for warmth, comfort or affection: *The child ~d up to its mother/~d into its mother's arms. The children ~d up (together) in bed. She ~d down in bed,* made herself comfortable. **2** [VP14]

~ sb to sb, draw close (to one): *She ~d the child close to her.*

so[1] /səʊ/ *adv of degree* to such an extent. **1** (in the pattern: *not + so + adj* or *adv + as*): *It is not so big as I thought it would be. We didn't expect him to stay so long,* as, in fact, he did stay. *He was not so much angry as disappointed.* **2** (in the pattern: *so + adj + as + to + inf*): *Would you be so kind as to help me,* i e will you please help me? *He is not so stupid as to do that.* **3** (in the pattern: *so + adj* or *adv + that*): *He was so ill that we had to send for a doctor. There were so many that we didn't know where to put them all. He was so angry that he couldn't speak.* (Colloq: *He couldn't speak, he was so angry*). **4** (If the *adj modifies a sing n,* the *indef art* is placed between the *adj* and the *n.* It is often better to use *such*): *He is not so clever a boy* (= such a clever boy) *as his brother.* **5** (used, colloq style, with exclamatory emphasis for *very.* ˋ*Ever so* is colloq): *I'm so glad to see you! It was so kind of you! There was so much to do! That's ever so much better!* **6** (in phrases) **so far,** up to this/that time, point or extent: *Now that we've come so far, we may as well go all the way. Everything is in order so far. So far as I know,* i e to the extent that I know,.... **So far, so good,** Up to this point all is satisfactory. **so far from,** instead of; quite contrary to: *So far from being a help, he was a hindrance.* **so long as,** on condition that; provided that: *You may borrow the book so long as you keep it clean.* ˋ**so much/many,** an unspecified quantity/number: *So much butter, so much sugar, so many eggs,.... Twelve dinners, at so much a head.* **not so much as**: He didn't so *much as* (= didn't even) *ask me to sit down. He is not so much unintelligent as uneducated,* i e he lacks education, not intelligence. ⇨ much[1]. **so much** (nonsense, etc), all, merely: *What you have written is so much nonsense.* ˋ**so much for,** that is all that need be said, done, etc, about: *So much for the first stage of our journey.* **so ˋmuch so that,** to such an extent that: *He is rich—so much so that he does not know what he is worth.*

so[2] /səʊ/ *adv of manner* **1** in this (that) way; thus: *So, and so only, can it be done. Stand just so. So it was* (= That is how) *I became a sailor. As X is to Y, so Y is to Z. As you treat me, so I shall treat you.* **2** (in phrases) ˋ**so-called,** called or named thus but perhaps wrongly or doubtfully: *Your so-called friends won't help you in your troubles.* **so that,** **(a)** in order that: *Speak clearly, so that they may understand you.* **(b)** with the result that: *Nothing more was heard of him, so that people thought that he was dead.* **so... that,** **(a)** with the intent that: *We have so arranged matters that one of us is always on duty.* **(b)** with the result that; in a way that: *It so happened that I couldn't attend the meeting.* **so as to,** in order to; in such a way that: *Don't let your television blare so as to disturb your neighbours. I will have everything ready so as not to keep you waiting.* **3** (used as a substitute for a word, phrase or situation): *I told you so!* That is what I told you! *I could scarcely believe it, but it was so,* i e that was the state of affairs, etc. *So I believe/hope/suppose, etc.* **4** (used to express agreement, in the pattern: *so + pron + aux v*): *A: 'It was cold yesterday.' B: 'So it was.' A: 'Tomorrow will be Friday.' B: 'So it will.' A: 'We have all worked hard.' B: 'So we have.'* **5** (used meaning 'also' in the pattern: *so + aux v + (pro)n*): *You are young and so am I,* i e I also am young. *Tom speaks French and so does his brother. A: 'I went to the cinema yesterday.' B: 'Oh, did you? So did I.'* **6** (various uses) **or so** (unstressed), about: *He must be forty or so,* about forty years old. *It will be warmer in another month or so,* in about a month from now. **and (so forth and) so on,** and other things of the same kind, etc. **just so,** **(a)** used to express agreement. **(b)** neat and tidy: *Eric likes everything to be just so.* **so to say/speak,** used as an apology for an unusual use of a word or phrase, an exaggeration, etc. ˋ**so-so,** ⇨ this entry. **so-and-so** /ˋsəʊ n səʊ/, person not needing to be named: *Don't worry about what old so-and-so says. He's an old so-and-so* (i e used to avoid using a derogatory noun).

so[3] /səʊ/ *conj* **1** therefore; that is why: *The shops were closed so I couldn't get any. She asked me to go, so I went. They cost a lot of money, so use them carefully.* **2** (exclamatory) *So you're back again! So you've lost your job, have you? So you're not coming! So there you are!*

soak /səʊk/ *vt,vi* **1** [VP2A] become wet through by being in liquid or by absorbing liquid: *The clothes are ~ing in soapy water.* **2** [VP6A,14A] **~ sth (in sth),** cause sth to absorb as much liquid as possible: *~ dirty clothes in water/bread in milk. S~ the cloth in the dye for one hour.* **3** [VP15A,B] **~ sth up,** absorb; take in (liquid): *Blotting-paper ~s up ink.* **~ oneself in sth,** (fig) absorb: *~ oneself in the atmosphere of a place.* **4** [VP6A, 15B] (of rain, etc) **~ sb (through),** make very wet: *We all got ~ed (through).* **be ~ed to the skin,** get wet right through one's clothes. **5** [VP3A] **~ through sth,** penetrate; enter and pass through: *The rain had ~ed through the roof/his overcoat.* **6** [VP6A] (sl) extract money from by charging or taxing very heavily: *Are you in favour of ~ing the rich?* **7** [VP2A] (colloq) drink alcohol excessively (and habitually). □ *n* **1** act of ~ing: *Give the sheets a good ~.* **in ~,** being ~ed: *The sheets are in ~.* **2** (sl, usu **old ~**) person greatly addicted to alcoholic drink. **~er** *n* **1** (colloq) heavy fall of rain: *What a ~er!* **2** (sl) drunkard.

soap /səʊp/ *n* [U] substance made of fat or oil and an alkali, used for washing and cleaning: *a bar/cake of ~; ˋ~-flakes; ˋ~-powder; use plenty of ~ and water.* ˋ**soft ~,** ⇨ soft(15). ˋ**~-box** *n* improvised stand for an orator (in a street, park, etc): *~-box oratory,* of the kind heard from demagogues. ˋ**~-bubble** *n* filmy ball of ~y water with changing colours, full of air. ˋ**~-opera** *n* (US) (radio) serial drama dealing with domestic problems, etc in a sentimental or melodramatic way. ˋ**~-suds** *n pl* frothy lather of ~ and water. □ *vt* **1** [VP6A,15B] apply ~ to; rub with ~: *~ oneself down.* **2** [VP6A] (colloq) flatter; try to please. **soapy** *adj* (-ier, -iest) **1** of or like ~: *This bread has a ~y taste.* **2** (fig) over-anxious to please: *He has a ~y voice/manner.*

soar /sɔ(r)/ *vi* [VP2A,C] fly or go up high in the air; hover in the air without flapping of wings; rise: *~ like an eagle; a ~ing flight,* e g in a sail-plane: *a cathedral nave that ~s up to the vaulted roof; the ~ing spire of Salisbury cathedral. Prices ~ed when war broke out.*

sob /sɒb/ *vi,vt* (-bb-) **1** [VP2A,C] draw in the breath sharply and irregulary from sorrow or pain, esp while crying; [VP15A,B]: *She sobbed her* *heart out,* sobbed bitterly. *She sobbed herself to sleep.* **2** [VP15B] ***sob sth out,*** tell while doing this: *She sobbed out the story of her son's death in a traffic accident.* □ *n* [C] act or sound of sobbing: *The child's sobs gradually died down.* **ˈsob-stuff** *n* [U] (colloq) the sort of writing, film, etc which is full of pathos and sentiment. **sob·bing·ly** *adv*

so·ber /ˈsəʊbə(r)/ *adj* **1** self-controlled; temperate; serious in thought, etc; calm: *be in ~ earnest; make a ~ estimate of what is possible; exercise a ~ judgement; be ~-minded,* serious; *~ colours,* not bright; *in ~ fact,* in fact (contrasted with what is fancied or imagined). **ˈ~-sides** *n* (dated colloq) serious and sedate person. **2** avoiding drunkenness; not drunk: *Does he ever go to bed ~?* □ *vt,vi* [VP6A,15B,2C] **1** ***~ (sb) down,*** make or become: *The bad news ~ed all of us. I wish those noisy children would ~ down,* become less excited, etc. **2** ***~ (sb) up,*** make or become ~(2): *Put him to bed until he ~s up. Throw a pail of water over him—that'll ~ him up.* **~·ly** *adv* **so·bri·ety** /səˈbraɪətɪ/ *n* [U] quality or condition of being ~.

so·bri·quet /ˈsəʊbrɪkeɪ/ *n* [C] nickname.

soc·cer /ˈsokə(r)/ *n* [U] (colloq) (as contrasted with Rugby football for) Association football.

so·ciable /ˈsəʊʃəbl/ *adj* fond of the company of others; friendly; showing friendliness. **so·ciably** /-əblɪ/ *adv* **so·cia·bil·ity** /ˈsəʊʃəˈbɪlətɪ/ *n* [U].

so·cial /ˈsəʊʃl/ *adj* **1** living in groups, not separately: *~ ants/wasps. Man is a ~ animal.* **2** of people living in communities; of relations between persons and communities: *~ customs/reforms/welfare;* ˈ~ ˈ*welfare workers,* persons who work for the betterment of ~ conditions (esp among the families of manual workers). **ˈS~ ˈDemocrat,** (in politics) person who wishes society to move, by peaceful changes, to a system of socialism. **ˈ~ seˈcurity,** government provisions for helping people who are unemployed, ill, disabled, etc: *The family is on ~ security,* receiving such help. **3** of or in society: *one's ~ equals,* persons of the same class as oneself in society; *~ advancement,* improvement of one's position in society; *~ climbers,* persons trying to obtain ~ advancement. **4** for companionship: *a ˈ~ club; spend a ~ evening,* in the company of friends. **5** = sociable. □ *n* ~ gathering, e g one organized by a club or church. **~ly** /-ʃlɪ/ *adv*

so·cial·ism /ˈsəʊʃlɪzm/ *n* [U] (also *S~*) philosophical, political and economic theory that land, transport, the chief industries, natural resources, e g coal, waterpower, etc, should be owned and managed by the State, or by public bodies, and wealth equally distributed. **so·cial·ist** *n* supporter of, believer in ~: *a Socialist Party,* political party which advocates and works for ~. □ *adj* of, tending towards, ~. **so·cial·ize** /-aɪz/ *vt* [VP6A] make socialistic; govern on socialist principles. **socialized medicine,** (US) the provision of free medical services by the Government. **so·cial·iz·ation** /ˈsəʊʃlaɪˈzeɪʃn *US:* -lɪˈz-/ *n*

so·cial·ite /ˈsəʊʃlaɪt/ *n* (US colloq) person prominent in fashionable society.

so·ciety /səˈsaɪətɪ/ *n* (*pl* **-ties**) **1** [U] social way of living; customs, etc of a civilized community; system whereby people live together in organized communities: *a danger to ~,* person, idea, etc that endangers the bodily or moral welfare of the members of a community; *pests of ~,* persons who prey on the community and contribute nothing to its welfare. **2** [C] social community: *modern industrial societies;* certain grouping of humanity, e g Western Christendom, the people of Islam. **3** [U] company; companionship: *spend an evening in the ~ of one's friends.* **4** [U] people of fashion or distinction in a place, district, country, etc; the upper classes: *leaders of ~; high* (i e the most wealthy, influential, etc) *~; the customs of polite ~;* (attrib) *a ˈ~ man/woman; ~ weddings,* of fashionable persons; *~ gossip/news,* as printed in newspapers, etc. **5** [C] organization of persons formed with a purpose; club; association: *the school deˈbating ~; a co-ˈoperative ~; the S~ of Friends.*

so·ci·ol·ogy /ˈsəʊsɪˈolədʒɪ/ *n* [U] science of the nature and growth of society and social behaviour. **so·ci·ol·ogist** /-dʒɪst/ *n* student of, expert in ~. **so·cio·logi·cal** /ˈsəʊsɪəˈlodʒɪkl/ *adj* of ~. **so·cio·logi·cally** /-klɪ/ *adv*

sock[1] /sok/ *n* **1** short stocking not reaching the knee. **2** loose sole used inside a shoe. ⇨ *wind-~* at wind[1](8).

sock[2] /sok/ *n* (sl) blow given with the fist or sth thrown: *Give him a ~ on the jaw!* Hit him hard! □ *vt* [VP6A,15A] (sl) give (sb) such a blow: *S~ him on the jaw! S~ a brick at him! S~ it to him!* □ *adv* (sl) plump, right: (*hit sb*) *~ in the eye.*

socket /ˈsokɪt/ *n* natural or artificial hollow into which sth fits or in which sth turns: *the ˈeye-~s; a ~ for an electric light bulb/a candle.*

So·cratic /səˈkrætɪk *US:* səʊ-/ *adj* characteristic of Socrates /ˈsokrətiz/, the Greek philosopher (died 339 BC): *the ~ method,* procedure by question and answer.

sod[1] /sod/ *n* [U] upper layer of grassland including the grass with its roots and earth; [C] square or oblong piece of this pared off; turf.

sod[2] /sod/ *n* ⚠ (esp as a vulg term of abuse) sodomite (used in annoyance and sudden anger) = blast!: *You sod!* □ *vi* ⚠ ***Sod it!*** Blast! ***Sod off!*** Go away!

soda /ˈsəʊdə/ *n* [U] common chemical substance used in soap-making, glass manufacture, etc: *ˈwashing-~* (sodium carbonate, Na_2CO_3), used for softening water, etc; *ˈbaking-~* (sodium bicarbonate, $NaHCO_3$), used in cooking. **ˈ~-biscuit/-cracker** *n* biscuit from dough containing baking ~ and sour milk. **ˈ~-fountain** *n* counter, bar, from which ~-water, ices, etc are served. **ˈ~ pop** (US colloq) soft drink of ~-water, flavoured sometimes with ice-cream. **ˈ~-water** *n* water charged with carbon dioxide gas to make it bubble.

sod·den /ˈsodn/ *adj* **1** soaked through: *clothes ~ with rain.* **2** (of bread, etc) heavy and dough-like; moist or sticky because undercooked. **3** (often *ˈdrink-~*) stupid through too much drinking of alcoholic liquor.

so·dium /ˈsəʊdɪəm/ *n* [U] silver-white metal (symbol **Na**) occurring naturally only in compounds: *~ chloride,* (**NaCl**) common salt. ⇨ soda.

sod·omy /ˈsodəmɪ/ *n* [U] anal sexual intercourse, esp between males. **sod·om·ite** /ˈsodəmaɪt/ *n* person practising ~.

so·ever /səʊˈevə(r)/ *suff* used with *relative pronouns, advv* and *adjj*: *ˈhow~, ˈwho~,* etc.

sofa /ˈsəʊfə/ *n* long seat with raised ends and back, on which several persons can sit or one person can lie.

soft /soft *US:* sɔft/ *adj* (**-er, -est**) **1** (opp of *hard*) changing shape easily when pressed; not resisting pressure; *~ soil/ground/mud. Warm butter is ~. She likes a ~ pillow and a hard mattress.* ***a ~ landing,*** (e g of a spacecraft on the moon) one that avoids damage or destruction. Hence, **ˈ~-ˈland** *vi* land in this way. **2** (of surfaces) smooth and delicate: *as ~ as velvet; ~ fur; ~ furnishings,* curtains, hangings, etc; *~ goods,* textiles. **3** (of light, colours) opp of glaring; restful to the eyes: *lampshades that give a ~ light.* **4** (of sounds) subdued; not loud: *~ music; ~ murmurs/whispers; in a ~ voice.* **5** (of outlines) indistinct. **6** (of answers, words, etc) mild; gentle; intended to please: *a ~ answer; have a ~ tongue.* **7** (of the air, weather) mild: *a ~ breeze/wind; ~ weather.* **8** (of water) free from mineral salts and therefore good for washing: *as ~ as rainwater.* **9** (orig US): *~ drinks,* cold, sweet and non-alcoholic, e g fruit juices or drinks often charged with gas. **10** (of certain sounds): *C is ~ in 'city' and hard in 'cat'. G is ~ in 'gin' and hard in 'get'* **11** easy: *have a ~ job,* (sl) an easy, well-paid job; business deal with easily earned money. **12** feeble; lacking in strength and determination: *muscles that have got ~ though lack of exercise. Are the young people of this period getting ~?* **13** sympathetic; considerate: *have a ~ heart.* ***have a ~ spot for sb,*** a liking or fondness for him. **14** (colloq) barmy: *He's not as ~ as he looks. He's gone ~. Jack is ~* (= sentimentally silly) *about Anne.* **15** (various uses; compounds) **ˈ~-ˈboiled** *adj* (of eggs) boiled so that the egg is ~. **~ coal** *n coal that burns with yellow, smoky flames.* **ˈ~ ˈcurrency** *n* one that is not convertible to gold, or into certain other currencies which are more in demand. **~ drug** *n* one, e g marijuana, which is mildly habit-forming (as opposed to a *hard* drug, e g heroin, which is addictive). **ˈ~-ˈfooted** *adj* (of a person) moving with quiet, gentle steps. **ˈ~-ˈheaded** *adj* idiotic; foolish. **ˈ~-ˈhearted** *adj* sympathetic; kind. **~ option** *n* alternative which is thought to involve little work. **ˈ~ ˈpalate** *n* back part of the roof of the mouth. **ˈ~-ˈpedal** *vi,vt* play (music, the piano) with the ~ pedal down; (fig) make (a statement, etc) less definite or confident. ***the ~er sex,*** the female sex. **ˈ~ soap** *n* semi-liquid soap made with potash; (fig) flattery. **ˈ~-ˈsoap** *vt* flatter. **ˈ~-solder** *n* kinds of solder used for easily fusible metal. **ˈ~-ˈsolder** *vt* solder with these soft kinds. **ˈ~-ˈspoken** *adj* having a gentle voice; saying pleasant, friendly things. **ˈ~·ware** *n* data, programmes, etc not forming parts of a computer but used for its operation. ⇨ *hardware* at **hard**[1](9). **ˈ~-ˈwitted** *adj* foolish. **ˈ~·wood** *n* [C,U] (kinds of) easily sawn wood such as pine and other coniferous trees. **ˈ~·ish** /-ɪʃ/ *adj* somewhat ~. **~·ly** *adv* **~·ness** *n* **ˈ~y** *n* stupid person; feeble person.

sof·ten /ˈsofn *US:* ˈsɔfn/ *vt,vi* [VP6A,2A] make or become soft: *curtains that ~ the light; people who are ~ed by luxurious living.* **~ sb up,** weaken (enemy positions) by shelling, bombing, etc; make (persons) unable or less able to resist (attack, salesmanship, etc). **~er** *n* [C] sth used to ~, esp a chemical substance (or apparatus using this) for ~ing hard water.

soggy /ˈsogɪ/ *adj* (**-ier, -iest**) (esp of ground) heavy with water. **sog·gi·ness** *n*

Soho /ˈsəʊhəʊ/ *n* district in the West End of London associated with foreign restaurants and grocery shops and noted for its night clubs.

soi·gné /ˈswɑnjeɪ *US:* swɑˈnjeɪ/ *adj* (F) (fem **-née**) (of a woman's way of dressing, etc) carefully finished or arranged, with attention to detail.

soil /sɔɪl/ *n* [C,U] **1** ground; earth, esp the upper layer of earth in which plants, trees, etc grow: *good/poor/alluvial/sandy, etc ~; clay ~s.* **ˈ~-pipe** *n* pipe from a W C pan to the drains. **2** *one's native ~,* one's native country; *a man of the ~,* one who works on the land (and is devoted to it). □ *vt,vi* **1** [VP6A] make dirty: *~ed linen/underwear, etc,* that has been used and is to be laundered. *He refused to ~ his hands,* refused to do dirty work. **2** [VP2A,C] admit of being ~ed: *material that ~s easily,* is easily ~ed.

soi·rée /ˈswɑreɪ *US:* ˈswɑˈreɪ/ *n* social gathering in the evening, esp for music, conversation, etc, and often to help the aims of a society(**5**).

so·journ /ˈsodʒən *US:* səʊˈdʒən/ *vi* [VP2C], *n* (liter) (make a) stay (*with* sb, *at* or *in*) for a time. **~er** *n*

Sol /sol/ *n* (hum) (often *old Sol*) the sun.

sol·ace /ˈsolɪs/ *n* [C,U] (that which gives) comfort or relief (when one is in trouble or pain): *The invalid found ~ in music.* □ *vt* [VP6A,15A] give ~ to: *The unhappy man ~d himself with whisky.*

so·lar /ˈsəʊlə(r)/ *adj* of the sun. **a ~ cell,** device (as used in satellites) which converts the energy of sunlight into electric energy. **the ˈ~ system,** the sun and the planets which revolve round it. **ˈ~ ˈplexus** /ˈpleksəs/ *n* complex of nerves at the pit of the stomach. **the ~ year,** time occupied by the earth to complete one revolution round the sun, about 365 days, 5 hours, 48 minutes and 46 seconds.

so·larium /səʊˈleərɪəm/ *n* (*pl* **-ria** /-rɪə/) place enclosed with glass for enjoyment of the sun's rays, esp one for the medical use of sunlight.

sold /səʊld/ *pt,pp* of **sell.**

sol·der /ˈsoldə(r) *US:* ˈsodər/ *n* [U] easily melted alloy used, when melted, to join harder metals, wires, etc. □ *vt* [VP6A,15A,B] join with ~. **ˈ~-ing-iron** *n* tool used for this work.

sol·dier /ˈsəʊldʒə(r)/ *n* **1** member of an army: *three ~s, two sailors and one civilian. The children were playing at ~s.* **private ~,** one who is not a commissioned or non-commissioned officer. ***a ~ of fortune,*** man who will take service under any State or person who will hire him; mercenary. **2** military commander of the kind specified by an adj: *He was no/a great/a poor/a fine ~.* □ *vi* [VP2A] serve as a ~: (chiefly in) *go/enjoy ~ing; be tired of ~ing.* **~ on,** continue bravely with one's work, etc in the face of difficulties. **~·ly, ˈ~-like** *adjj* like a ~; smart; brave. **~y** *n* (*sing* only, *collective n*) ~s of a specified character: *the undisciplined ~y; brutal, licentious ~y.*

sole[1] /səʊl/ *n* flat sea-fish with a delicate flavour.

sole[2] /səʊl/ *n* under surface of a human foot, or of a sock, shoe, etc. □ *vt* [VP6A] put a ~ on (a shoe, etc): *send a pair of shoes to be ~d and heeled.* **-soled** *suff* (with *n* or *adj* prefixed) *ˈrubber-~d boots; ˈthin-~d shoes.*

sole[3] /səʊl/ *adj* **1** one and only; single: *the ~ cause of the accident.* **2** restricted to one person, company, etc: *We have the ~ right of selling the article.* **~·ly** *adv* alone; only: *~ly responsible; ~ly because of you.*

sol·ecism /ˈsolɪsɪzm/ *n* [C] error in the use of language; offence against good manners; mistake in etiquette.

sol·emn /ˈsoləm/ *adj* **1** performed with religious or other ceremony; causing deep thought or respect: *a ~ silence as the coffin was carried out of the church; a ~ duty; ~ music; a ~ oath,* grave and important. **2** serious-looking; grave: *~ faces; look as ~ as a judge.* **~·ly** *adv* **~·ness** *n*

sol·em·nity /səˈlemnətɪ/ *n* (*pl* -ties) **1** [U] seriousness; gravity. **2** [U] (but also *pl*) solemn ceremony: *The Queen was crowned with all ~/with all the proper solemnities.*

sol·em·nize /ˈsoləmnɑɪz/ *vt* [VP6A] perform (a religious ceremony, esp a wedding) with the usual rites; make solemn. **sol·em·niz·ation** /ˌsoləmnɑɪˈzeɪʃn *US:* -nɪˈz-/ *n* [U].

sol-fa /ˌsol ˈfɑ *US:* ˌsəʊl/ *n* system of syllables each representing a musical note.

sol·icit /səˈlɪsɪt/ *vt,vi* **1** [VP6A,14] **~ *sb (for sth),*** ask (for) earnestly: make requests (for): *Both the candidates ~ed my vote. The tradesmen are all ~ing us for our custom,* asking us to deal with them. **2** [VP6A,2A] (of a prostitute) make an immoral sexual offer (to), esp in a public place: *a £5 fine for ~ing.* **sol·ici·ta·tion** /səˌlɪsɪˈteɪʃn/ *n* [U] ~ing; [C] instance or occasion of this.

sol·ici·tor /səˈlɪsɪtə(r)/ *n* **1** (GB) lawyer who prepares legal documents, e g wills, sale of land or buildings, advises clients on legal matters, and speaks on their behalf in lower courts. ⇨ **barrister. Soˈlicitor-ˈGeneral,** one of the principal law officers in the British Government, advising on legal matters. **2** (US) person who solicits trade, support, etc; canvasser (e g for votes).

sol·ici·tous /səˈlɪsɪtəs/ *adj* **~ *(for/about/to do sth),*** anxious, concerned about (sb's welfare, etc) or to help/serve sb: *~ to please; ~ for her comfort.* **~·ly** *adv* **sol·ici·tude** /səˈlɪsɪtjud *US:* -tud/ *n* [U] being ~; concern or anxiety: *my deep solicitude for your welfare.*

solid /ˈsolɪd/ *adj* **1** not in the form of a liquid or gas: *~ fuels,* e g coal, wood, *~-fuelled rockets. When water freezes and becomes ~, we call it ice.* **ˌ~-ˈstate** *adj* (of electronic devices) totally transistorized, i e without valves: *a ~-state amplifier.* **2** compact; substantial; heavy: *a man with good ~ flesh on him; ~ food, not slops.* **3** without holes or spaces; not hollow: *a ~ sphere.* **4** of strong or firm material or construction; able to support weight or resist pressure: *~ buildings/furniture; build on ~ foundations; a man of ~ build; on ~ ground; steps cut in the ~ rock.* **5** that can be depended on: *~ arguments; a ~* (= financially sound) *business firm; a man of ~ character.* **6** alike all through; of the same substance throughout: *made of ~ gold.* **7** unanimous; undivided: *We are ~ for peace. The miners are ~ on this issue. There was a ~ vote in favour of the proposal.* **8** continuous; without a break: *wait for a ~ hour; sleep ten ~ hours/ten hours ~.* **9** (maths) having length, breadth and thickness: *a ~ figure,* e g a cube; *~ geometry,* of ~, not plane, figure. □ *n* [C] **1** body or substance which is ~, not a liquid or a gas. **2** (geom) figure of three dimensions. **~·ly** *adv* **sol·id·ity** /səˈlɪdətɪ/, **~·ness** *nn* [U] quality of being ~: *the ~ity of a building/argument, etc.*

soli·dar·ity /ˌsolɪˈdærətɪ/ *n* [U] unity resulting from common interests or feelings: *national ~ in the face of danger.*

sol·id·ify /səˈlɪdɪfɑɪ/ *vt,vi* (*pt,pp* -fied) [VP6A,2A] make or become solid, hard or firm. **sol·idi·fi·ca·tion** /səˌlɪdɪfɪˈkeɪʃn/ *n*

sol·il·oquy /səˈlɪləkwɪ/ *n* (*pl* -quies) [C,U] (instance of) speaking one's thoughts aloud; (in drama) speech in which a character speaks his thoughts without addressing a listener. **sol·il·oquize** /səˈlɪləkwɑɪz/ *vi* [VP2A] talk to oneself; think aloud.

sol·ip·sism /ˈsolɪpsɪzm/ *n* (metaphysics) theory that one can have knowledge only of the self.

soli·taire /ˌsolɪˈteə(r) *US:* ˈsolɪteə(r)/ *n* **1** (ornament such as an earring having a) single gem or jewel. **2** (also called *patience*) kinds of card-game for one player.

soli·tary /ˈsolɪtrɪ *US:* -terɪ/ *adj* **1** (living) alone; without companions; lonely: *a ~ life; a ~ walk.* **~ confinement,** prison punishment by which a person is isolated in a separate cell. (As a *n*: *in ~,* in ~ confinement.) **2** only one: *not a ~ one/instance.* **3** seldom visited: *a ~ valley.* **soli·tar·ily** /ˈsolɪtrɪlɪ *US:* ˌsolɪˈterlɪ/ *adv*

soli·tude /ˈsolɪtjud *US:* -tud/ *n* **1** [U] being without companions; solitary state: *live in ~; not fond of ~.* **2** [C] lonely place: *spend six months in the ~s of the Antarctic.*

solo /ˈsəʊləʊ/ *n* (*pl* -los /-ləʊz/) **1** piece of music (to be) performed by one person: *a violin/piano ~.* **2** any performance by one person; (as *adv*) *fly ~;* (attrib) *his first ~ flight.* **3** [U] kind of whist in which one player opposes others. **ˈ~·ist** /-ɪst/ *n* person who gives a ~**(1)**.

So·lon /ˈsəʊlon/ *n* (the name of an Athenian law-giver, hence) wise legislator.

sol·stice /ˈsolstɪs/ *n* [C] either time (*summer ~,* about 21 June; *winter ~,* about 22 Dec) at which the sun is farthest N or S of the equator.

sol·uble /ˈsoljʊbl/ *adj* **~ *(in),*** that can be dissolved; (= solvable) that can be solved or explained. **solu·bil·ity** /ˌsoljʊˈbɪlətɪ/ *n*

sol·ution /səˈluʃn/ *n* **1** [C] answer (*to* a question, etc); way of dealing with a difficulty: *Recourse to arms is not the best ~ to a quarrel between two countries. Might economy be the ~ to/of your financial troubles?* **2** [U] process of finding an answer or explanation: *problems that defy ~,* cannot be solved. **3** [U] process of dissolving a solid or a gas in liquid: *the ~ of sugar in tea.* **4** [C,U] liquid that results from this process: *a ~ of salt in water.*

solve /solv/ *vt* [VP6A] find the answer to (a problem, etc): *~ a crossword puzzle/an equation*: find a way out of a difficulty, etc. **solv·able** /-əbl/ *adj* that can be ~d or explained.

sol·vent /ˈsolvənt/ *adj* **1** of the power of dissolving or forming a solution: *the ~ action of water.* **2** having money enough to meet one's debts. □ *n* [C] substance (usu a liquid) able to dissolve another substance (usu specified): *grease ~,* e g petrol. **sol·vency** /-nsɪ/ *n* [U] being ~**(2)**.

sombre (US = **som·ber**) /ˈsombə(r)/ *adj* dark-coloured; gloomy; dismal: *a ~ January day; ~ clothes; a ~ picture of the future of mankind.* **~·ly** *adv* **~·ness** *n*

som·brero /somˈbreərəʊ/ *n* (*pl* -ros /-rəʊz/) broad-brimmed hat (as worn in Latin American countries).

some[1] /sʌm *weak form* sm *used only in the adjectival sense consisting of an undefined amount or number of*/ *adj* **1** (used in affirm sentences; usually replaced by *any* in interr and neg sentences, in conditional clauses, and in sentences where doubt or negation is implied. *S*~ and *any* are used with material *nn* to indicate an amount or quantity that is either unknown or not given, with abstract *nn* to indicate a certain degree, and with *pl* common *nn* to indicate a certain number (three or more). *S*~ and *any* are *pl* equivalents of the numeral article *a*(*n*) (⇨ **a**[2]), of numeral *one*, and the *indef pron* '*one*'): *Please give me ~ milk.* Cf *Have you any sugar? We haven't any tea. There are ~ children outside.* Cf *There is a child outside. They haven't any children. Are there any stamps in that drawer? I wonder whether Mr Black has any flowers in his garden. I doubt whether there are any flowers in Mr Green's garden. I don't like a garden without any flowers in it. There are scarcely/hardly any flowers in this garden. S~* (= ~ people) *say that....* **2** (*S*~ is used in sentences that are interr in form if the speaker expects, or wishes to suggest, an affirm answer): *Aren't there ~ stamps in that drawer?* Cf *There are ~ stamps in that drawer, aren't there? Didn't he give you ~ money?* Cf *He gave you ~ money, didn't he?* (*S*~ is used in sentences that are interr in form if these sentences are really invitations or requests: *Will you have ~ cake?* Cf *Please have ~ cake. Will you please buy me ~ stamps when you go out?* Cf *Please buy me ~ stamps.*) **3** (After *if*, introducing a supposition, either *some* or *any* may be used): *If we had ~/any money, we could buy it. If we find ~/any, we'll share them with you.* **4** (*S*~ and *any* are used with *more*): *Give me ~ more* /sə ˈmɔ(r)/. *Do you want any more? I haven't any more. Won't you have ~ more?* **5** (*S*~ (always /sʌm/) is often contrasted with *the rest, other*(*s*), and *all*): *S~ children learn languages easily* (*and others with difficulty*). *All work is not dull; ~ work is pleasant.* **6** (*S*~ (always /sʌm/) is used before *sing* common *nn* to indicate that the person, place, object, etc is unknown, or when the speaker does not wish to be specific. The words *or other* are often added): *He's living at ~ place in East Africa. I've read that story before in ~ book or other. S~ man at the door is asking to see you.* **7** (*S*~ (always /sʌm/) is used adverbially, meaning *about* or *approximately*, before numbers and before *few*): *That was ~ twenty years ago. There were ~ fifteen people there. I waited ~ few minutes.* **8** (*S*~ (always stressed) is used with *nn* meaning 'a considerable quantity or number of'): *I shall be away for ˋ~ time,* a fairly long time. *Mr Green spoke at ˋ~* (= considerable) *length. We went ˋ~* (= several) *miles out of our way. The railway station is at ˋ~ distance* (= quite a long way) *from the village.* **9** (*S*~ (stressed) is also used with *nn* to suggest 'to a certain extent'): *That is ˋ~ help* (i e It helps to a certain extent) *towards understanding the problem.*

some[2] /sʌm/ *pron*: *S*~ as a *pron* is used in the same ways as ~, *adj*, 1,2 and 3. *S~ of* and *any of* are equivalent to *a few of, a little of, part of*: *S~ of these books are quite useful. I don't want any of these (books). I don't want any of this (paper). I agree with ~* (= part) *of what you say. Scotland has ~ of the finest scenery in the world.* □ *adv* ⇨ **some**[1](7).

some·body /ˈsʌmbədɪ/, **some·one** /ˈsʌmwʌn/ *pron* **1** some person; replaced by *anybody* in *interr, neg,* etc sentences: *There's ~ at the door. Is there anyone at home? That must be ~ from the Department of Education.* **2** (often with the *indef art;* also in the *pl*) a person of some importance: *If you had studied harder at college you might have become (a) ~. He's nobody here in town but I suppose he's a ~ in his own village.*

some·how /ˈsʌmhəʊ/ *adv* **1** in some way (or other); by one means or another: *We must find money for the rent ~ (or other). We shall get there ~.* **2** for some (vague) reason (or other): *She never liked me, ~. S~ I don't trust that man.*

some·one /ˈsʌmwʌn/ *n* = **somebody**.

some·place /ˈsʌmpleɪs/ *adv* (US informal) somewhere: *I've left my bag ~. He lives ~ between Baltimore and Washington.*

som·er·sault /ˈsʌməsɔlt/ *n* [C] leap or fall in which one turns heels over head before landing on one's feet: *turn/throw a ~.* □ *vi* [VP2A] turn a ~.

some·thing /ˈsʌmθɪŋ/ *pron* **1** some thing, object, event, etc (of an indefinite nature); replaced by *anything* in *interr, neg,* etc sentences: *There's ~ on the floor. Is there anything in that box? I want ~ to eat. There's ~* (= some truth, some point) *in what he says. It's ~* (= some satisfaction, some comfort) *to be home again without an accident. He is ~* (= has some position or other) *in the Department of the Environment.* **2 or ~,** indicates absence of precise information: *Mr Green is a shopkeeper or ~,* is engaged in trade of some kind. *I hear he has broken an arm or ~,* met with some sort of accident and has broken a limb, etc. *He struck a match too near the petrol tank or ~,* or did something equally foolish and dangerous. **3 ~ of,** used to indicate an indefinite degree: *The soldier found himself ~ of a hero* (= was greeted as a hero to some extent) *when he returned to his village. He's ~ of a liar,* (= is not wholly truthful), *don't you think? I'm ~ of a carpenter,* I have some ability as a carpenter. □ *adv* **~ like, (a)** rather like; having some resemblance to: *The airship was shaped ~ like a cigar.* **(b)** approximately: *He left ~ like ten thousand,* i e died leaving about £10 000. **(c)** (colloq) *Now that's ~ like it,* (used to denote satisfaction).

some·time /ˈsʌmtaɪm/ *adv* **1** at some time: *I saw him ~ in May. It was ~ last summer. I will speak to him about it ~. I hope you will come ~ soon.* (Do not confuse with *some time* meaning 'for some period of time', as in: I have been waiting some time). **2** former(ly): *The Rev Thomas Atkins, ~ priest of this parish; Mr X, ~ fellow of Trinity College.*

some·times /ˈsʌmtaɪmz/ *adv* at some times; now and then; from time to time: *I ~ have letters from him. I have ~ had letters from him. S~ we go to the cinema and at other times we go for a walk.* (When ~ is used in a contrasting statement, or when it is repeated, it may follow the *v*): *She likes ~ the one and ~ the other. He says ~ the one thing and at other times the exact opposite.*

some·way /ˈsʌmweɪ/ *adv* (US, informal) = **somehow**.

some·what /ˈsʌmwɒt *US:* -hwɒt/ *adv* **1** rather; in some degree: *I was ~ surprised/disappointed, etc. He answered ~ hastily. We've arrived ~ late, I'm afraid.* **2 ~ of,** rather: *He was ~ of a liar. I found it ~ of a difficulty.*

some·where /ˈsʌmweə(r) *US:* -hweər/ *adv* (in *interr, neg,* etc sentences replaced by *anywhere*) in, at, to, some place: *It must be ~ near here. Is it* *anywhere near here? I didn't go anywhere yesterday. He lost it ~ between his office and the station. You will find the text ~ in the Bible.*

som·nam·bu·lism /somˋnæmbjʊlɪzm/ *n* [U] sleep-walking. **som·nam·bu·list** /-ɪst/ *n* sleep-walker.

som·nol·ent /ˋsomnələnt/ *adj* sleepy; almost asleep; causing sleep. **~·ly** *adv* **som·nol·ence** /-əns/ *n* [U] sleepiness.

son /sʌn/ *n* **1** male child of a parent. ***the Son of God, the Son of Man,*** Jesus Christ. ***the sons of men,*** mankind. **ˋson-in-law** *n* (*pl* sons-in-law) husband of one's daughter. **2** (used as a form of address, e g by an older man to a young man, a confessor to a penitent): *my son.* **3** ***a son of,*** person having the qualities, etc indicated: *sons of freedom,* those who have inherited freedom from their ancestors; *a son of the soil,* one whose father worked on the land and who follows his father's occupation.

so·nar /ˋsəʊnɑ(r)/ *n* device or system for detecting and locating objects submerged in water by means of reflected sound waves.

so·nata /səˋnɑtə/ *n* (*pl* -tas /-təz/) musical composition for one instrument (e g the piano), or two (e g piano and violin), normally with three or four movements.

song /soŋ *US:* sɔŋ/ *n* **1** [U] singing; music for the voice: *burst into ~; the ~* (= musical cry) *of the birds.* **ˋ~·bird** *n* bird (e g blackbird, thrush) noted for its ~. **2** [U] poetry; verse: *renowned in ~.* **3** [C] short poem or number of verses set to music and intended to be sung: *a marching ~; popular ~s.* **ˋ~-book** *n* collection of ~s (with both words and music). ***buy sth for a ~/an old ~; go for a ~,*** buy sth/be sold for a mere trifle. ***nothing to make a ~ and dance about,*** (colloq) of little or no importance. **~·ster** /-stə(r)/ *n* singer; ~bird. **~·stress** /-strəs/ *n* female singer.

sonic /ˋsonɪk/ *adj* relating to sound, sound-waves or the speed of sound: *a ~ bang/boom,* noise made when an aircraft exceeds the speed of sound; *the ~ barrier,* ⇨ *sound barrier* at sound²(3). ⇨ super~, ultra~.

son·net /ˋsonɪt/ *n* kind of poem containing 14 lines, each of 10 syllables, and with a formal pattern of rhymes. **~·eer** /ˌsonɪˋtɪə(r)/ *n* (usu derog) writer of ~s.

sonny /ˋsʌnɪ/ *n* (*pl* -nies) familiar form of address to a young boy.

son·or·ous /səˋnɔrəs/ *adj* **1** having a full, deep sound: *a ~ voice; the ~ note of the temple bell.* **2** (of language, words, etc) making a deep impression; imposing: *~ titles; a ~ style of writing.* **~·ly** *adv* **son·or·ity** /səˋnorətɪ *US:* -ˋnɔr-/ *n*

sonsy /ˋsonsɪ/ *adj* (Scot) *a ~ lass,* a plump, merry, cheerful girl.

soon /sun/ *adv* **1** not long after the present time or the time in question; in a short time. (*S~* may occupy mid-position with the *v*, or, esp if modified by *too, very* or *quite,* end position): *We shall ~ be home. We shall be home quite ~ now. He'll be here very ~. It will ~ be five years since we came to live in London.* ***~ after,*** a short time after: *He arrived ~ after three.* (The opposite of *~ after* is *a little before.*) **2** early: *How ~ can you be ready? Must you leave so ~? We reached the station half an hour too ~. He will be here ~er than you expect.* **3** ***as/so ~ as,*** at the moment that; when; not later than: *He started as ~ as he received the news. I'll tell him the news as ~ as I see him. We didn't arrive so/as ~ as we had hoped.* ***no ~er... than,*** immediately when or after: *He had no ~er/No ~er had he arrived home than he was asked to start on another journey. No ~er said than done,* i e done immediately. **4** (in double comparative constructions): *The ~er you begin the ~er you'll finish. The ~er the better.* ***~er or later,*** one day whether ~ or (much) later. **5** (suggesting comparison) ***(just) as ~,*** with equal readiness or willingness: *I would (just) as ~ stay at home/as go for a walk.* ***~er than,*** rather than: *He would ~er resign than take part in such dishonest business deals. S~er than marry that man, she would earn her living as a waitress.* ***as ~ as not,*** more willingly: *I'd go there as ~ as not.*

soot /sʊt/ *n* [U] black powder in smoke, or left by smoke on surfaces: *sweep the ~ out of the chimney.* **sooty** *adj* black with ~; black like ~. □ *vt* cover with ~.

sooth /suθ/ *n* (old or liter use) truth. ***in ~,*** truly. **ˋ~·sayer** /-seɪə(r)/ *n* fortune-teller.

soothe /suð/ *vt* [VP6A] **1** make (a person, his nerves, passions) quiet or calm: *~ a crying baby; ~ sb's anger; a soothing voice.* **2** make (pains, aches) less sharp or severe: *~ an aching tooth; a soothing lotion for the skin,* e g against sunburn. **sooth·ing·ly** *adv*

sop /sop/ *n* [C] **1** piece of bread, etc soaked in milk, soup, etc. **2** ***a sop to sb,*** sth offered to prevent trouble or to give temporary satisfaction: (*throw*) *a sop to Cerberus* /ˋsəbərəs/, (do) sth to pacify or bribe a troublesome person. □ *vt* (-pp-) [VP6A,15B] soak (bread, etc in broth, etc). ***sop sth up,*** take up liquid, etc: *Sop up the water with this towel.* **sop·ping** *adj* soaking wet: *sopping clothes.* □ *adv* thoroughly: *sopping wet.*

soph·ism /ˋsof-ɪzm/ *n* [C,U] false reasoning (argument) intended to deceive.

soph·ist /ˋsof-ɪst/ *n* person who uses clever but misleading arguments.

soph·is·ti·cated /səˋfɪstɪkeɪtɪd/ *adj* **1** having learnt the ways of the world and having lost natural simplicity; showing this: *a ~ girl; a girl with ~ tastes.* **2** complex; with the latest improvements and refinements: *~ modern weapons; ~ devices used in spacecraft.* **3** (of mental activity) refined; complex; subtle: *a ~ discussion/argument.* **soph·is·ti·ca·tion** /səˌfɪstɪˋkeɪʃn/ *n*

soph·is·try /ˋsofɪstrɪ/ *n* [U] use of sophisms; [C] (*pl* -tries) instance of this.

sopho·more /ˋsofəmɔ(r)/ *n* (US) person in his second year at a four-year college, etc.

sop·or·ific /ˌsopəˋrɪfɪk/ *n, adj* (substance, drink, etc) producing sleep.

sop·ping /ˋsopɪŋ/ *adj* ⇨ sop.

soppy /ˋsopɪ/ *adj* (-ier, -iest) **1** very wet. **1** (colloq) foolishly sentimental.

so·prano /səˋprɑnəʊ *US:* -ˋpræn-/ *n* (*pl* -nos /-nəʊz/), *adj* (person having the) highest singing voice of women and girls and boys.

sorbet /ˋsɔbɪt/ *n* = sherbet.

sor·cerer /ˋsɔsərə(r)/ *n* man who practises magic with the help of evil spirits. **sor·cer·ess** /ˋsɔsərəs/ *n* woman ~. **sor·cery** *n* (*pl* -ries) [U] witchcraft; (*pl*) evil acts done by a ~.

sor·did /ˋsɔdid/ *adj* **1** (of conditions) wretched; shabby; comfortless: *a ~ slum; living in ~ poverty.* **2** (of persons, behaviour, etc) contemptible; prompted by self-interest or meanness. **~·ly** *adv* **~·ness** *n*

sore /sɔ(r)/ *adj* **1** (of a part of the body) tender and painful; hurting when touched or used: *a ~ knee/throat.* ***like a bear with a ~ head,*** ill tempered, grumpy. ***a sight for ~ eyes,*** sb or sth welcome, pleasant. **2** filled with sorrow; sad: *a ~ heart.* **3** causing sorrow or annoyance. ***a ~ point/subject,*** one that hurts the feelings when talked about. **4** irritated; aggrieved: *feel ~ about not being invited to the party.* **5** (old use; also adverbial) grievous(ly); severe(ly): *in ~ distress; in ~ need of help; ~ oppressed.* □ *n* [C] **1** ~ place on the body (where the skin or flesh is injured): *a beggar displaying his ~s.* **2** (fig) ~ subject; painful memory: *Let's not recall old ~s.* **~·ly** *adv* **1** severely: *~ly tempted/afflicted.* **2** greatly: *More financial help is ~ly needed.* **~·ness** *n*

sor·ghum /ˈsɔgəm/ *n* [U] kinds of millet; kind of Chinese sugar-cane.

sor·or·ity /səˈrɒrətɪ *US:* -ˈrɔr-/ *n* (*pl* **-ties**) (US) women's social club in a college or university.

sor·rel[1] /ˈsɒrl *US:* ˈsɔrl/ *n* kinds of herb with sour-tasting leaves used in cooking.

sor·rel /ˈsɒrl *US:* ˈsɔrl/ *adj, n* (of a) reddish-brown colour; horse of this colour.

sor·row /ˈsɒrəʊ/ *n* [C,U] (cause of) grief or sadness; regret: *express ~ for having done wrong; to my great ~; to the ~ of all who were present; in ~ and in joy,* when we are sad and also when we are happy. *His ~s had turned his hair white.* ***more in ~ than in anger,*** with more regret than anger for what was done, etc. ***the Man of S~s,*** Jesus. □ *vi* [VP2A,C] feel ~ (*at/for/over* sth): *~ing over her child's death.* **~·ful** /-fl/ *adj* feeling, showing, causing, ~. **~·fully** /-flɪ/ *adv*

sorry /ˈsɒrɪ/ *adj* **1** (*pred* only) feeling regret or sadness: *We're ~ to hear of your father's death. I should be ~ for you to think* (= if you should think) *that I dislike you. I'd be ~, if you thought I disliked you.* ***be/feel ~ (about/for sth),*** feel regret or repentance: *Aren't you ~ for/about what you've done? If you'll say you're ~* (= that you repent), *we'll forget the incident.* ***be/feel ~ for sb,*** **(a)** feel sympathy: *I feel ~ for anyone who has to drive in weather like this.* **(b)** feel pity or mild contempt: *I'm ~ for you, but you've been rather foolish, haven't you? If he doesn't realize that he must make sacrifices, I'm ~ for him.* **2** (used to express mild regret or an apology): *'Can you lend me a pound?'—'S~, but I can't.'* **3** (attrib) (**-ier, -iest**) pitiful: *in a ~ state;* worthless; shabby: *a ~ excuse.*

sort[1] /sɔt/ *n* [C] **1** group or class of persons or things which are alike in some way: *Pop music is the ~ she likes most. What ~ of people does he think we are? We can't approve of this ~ of thing/these ~ of things/things of this ~.* ***of a ~, of ~s,*** used (colloq) to suggest that what is referred to does not fully deserve the name: *They served coffee of a ~/coffee of ~s/a ~ of coffee.* ***~ of,*** (colloq) rather; to some extent: *I sort of thought* (= had a vague idea) *this would happen.* ⇨ *kind of* at **kind**[2]**(2)**. **2** ***after a ~, in a ~,*** to a certain extent. **3** ***a good ~,*** (esp) a person who is likable, who has good qualities. **4** ***out of ~s,*** (colloq) feeling unwell, out of spirits.

sort[2] /sɔt/ *vt,vi* **1** [VP6A,15B] ***~ sth (out),*** arrange in groups; separate things of one sort from things of other sorts: *The boy was ~ing/~ing out/over the foreign stamps he had collected. We must ~ out the good apples from the bad.* ***~ sth out,*** (colloq) put in good order; solve: *I'll leave you to ~ that out,* find a solution. *Let's leave that pair to ~ themselves out,* clear up their problems, misunderstandings, etc. **2** ***~ well/ill with,*** (liter) be in/out of harmony with: *His heroic death ~ed well with his character.* **~er** *n* (esp) post-office worker who ~s letters.

sor·tie /ˈsɔtɪ/ *n* [C] **1** attack made by besieged soldiers on their besiegers. **2** flight made by one aircraft during military operations: *The four planes each made two ~s yesterday.*

SOS /ˈes əʊ ˈes/ *n* **1** message for help (sent by radio, etc) from a ship, aircraft, etc when in danger. Cf *mayday call.* **2** urgent call for help, e g a broadcast to find relatives of a person seriously ill.

so-so /ˈsəʊ səʊ/ *pred adj, adv* (colloq) not very good: *'How are you feeling today?'—'Oh, only so-so.'*

sot /sɒt/ *n* habitual drunkard, esp one whose mind has become dulled. **sot·tish** /ˈsɒtɪʃ/ *adj* habitually drinking too much and, for this reason, dull or stupid. **sot·tish·ly** *adv* **sot·tish·ness** *n*

sotto voce /ˈsɒtəʊ ˈvəʊtʃɪ/ *adv* (I) in a low voice, aside.

sou /su/ *n* French coin of low value (a five-centime piece): *He hasn't a sou,* is penniless.

sou·brette /suˈbret/ *n* maidservant (usu pert, coquettish, fond of intrigue) in a comedy for the theatre; actress taking such a part.

sou·bri·quet /ˈsubrɪkeɪ/ *n* = **sobriquet**.

souf·flé /ˈsufleɪ *US:* suˈfleɪ/ *n* [C] (F) dish of eggs, milk, etc beaten to a froth, flavoured (with cheese, etc) and baked.

sough /sʌf *US:* saʊ/ *vi* [VP2A], *n* (make a) murmuring or whispering sound (as of wind in trees).

sought /sɔt/ *pt,pp* of **seek**.

soul /səʊl/ *n* [C] **1** non-material part of a human body, believed to exist for ever: *believe in the immortality of the ~; commend one's ~ to God,* (when at the point of death). *He eats hardly enough to keep body and ~ together,* to keep him alive. *That man has no ~,* is unfeeling, selfish. *She has a ~ above material pleasures.* **2** (often without *indef art*) emotional and intellectual energy: *He put his heart and ~ into the work.* **3** ***the life and ~ of the party,*** (person looked upon as the) animating part (of sth). **4** person regarded as the pattern or personification of some virtue or quality: *He is the ~ of honour/discretion.* **5** departed spirit: *'All ˈS~s' Day,* 2 Nov. **6** person: *There wasn't a ~ to be seen,* No one was in sight. *The ship sank with 200 ~s.* **7** (expressing familiarity, pity, etc according to context): *He's a cheery ~,* a cheerful man. *Be a good ~ and lend me a dollar. She's lost all her money, poor ~.* **8** (US colloq) all those qualities that enable a person to be in harmony with himself and others, used esp by Afro-Americans and expressed through their music and dancing; (attrib) **ˈ~ brother/sister,** fellow Afro-American. **ˈ~ music,** their modern popular blues with strong rhythm for dancing. **9** (compounds) **ˈ~-destroying** *adj* killing the ~ or spirit: *~-destroying work.* **ˈ~-stirring** *adj* exciting, etc. **~ful** /-fl/ *adj* having, affecting, showing, deep feeling: *~ful eyes/music/glances.* **~-fully** /-flɪ/ *adv* **~·less** *adj* with out higher or deeper feelings. **~·less·ly** *adv*

sound[1] /saʊnd/ *adj* **1** healthy; in good condition; not hurt, injured or decayed: *~ fruit/teeth; have a ~ constitution.* ***a ~ mind in a ~ body,*** good mental and physical health. ***~ in wind and limb,*** (colloq) physically fit. **2** dependable; based on reason; prudent: *a ~ argument/policy; ~ advice; a ~ business firm. Is he ~ on national defence?* Are his views, etc reasonable, well-founded? **3** capable, careful: *a ~ tennis player.* **4** thorough; complete: *have a ~ sleep; be a ~ sleeper; give sb a ~ thrashing.* □ *adv* ~ly: *be ~ asleep. You will sleep the ~er for a day in the fresh air.* **~·ly** *adv* in a ~ manner: *sleep ~ly; be ~ly beaten at tennis.* **~·ness** *n*

sound[2] /saʊnd/ *n* [C,U] **1** that which is or can be heard: *within ~ of the guns,* near enough to hear them; *ˋvowel ~s,* e g /u, ʌ, ə/ *and ˋconsonant ~s,* e g /p, b, ʃ, ʒ/. *We heard the ~ of voices.* **2** (*sing* only) mental impression produced by sth stated (or read): *The news has a sinister ~,* seems to be sinister. *I don't like the ~ of it.* **3** (compounds, etc) **ˈ~ ˋarchives** *n pl* recordings on disc or magnetic tape of broadcasts considered to deserve being kept for future use: *the BBC ~ archives.* **ˋ~ barrier** *n* point at which an aircraft's speed equals that of ~-waves, causing sonic booms: *break the ~ barrier,* exceed the speed of sound. **ˋ~-box** *n* part of an old-fashioned gramophone containing a diaphragm and into which the needle that moves over a record is fixed (corresponding to the pick-up of an electrical reproducer). **ˋ~ effects** *n pl* sounds (recorded on discs, magnetic tape, film, etc) for use in broadcasts, in making films, etc or produced when needed (in a studio, etc). **ˋ~-film** *n* cinema film with dialogue, music, etc recorded on it. **ˋ~·proof** *adj* that ~(s) cannot pass through or into: *a ~proof studio.* Hence, **ˋ~·proofed,** made ~proof. **ˋ~-recording,** (contrasted with *video-recording*) of sth recorded in ~ only. **ˋ~-track** *n* (music, etc on a) track or band at the side of a cinema film which has the recording ~. **ˋ~-wave** *n* vibrations made in the air or other medium by which ~ is carried. **~·less** *adj* **~·less·ly** *adv*

sound[3] /saʊnd/ *vt,vi* **1** [VP6A] produce sound from; make (sth) produce sound: *~ a trumpet.* **2** [VP6A] utter: *~ a note of alarm/danger.* **3** [VP6A] pronounce: *Don't ~ the 'h' in 'hour' or the 'b' in 'dumb'.* **4** [VP6A] give notice of: *~ the alarm,* e g by ringing a bell; *~ the retreat,* by blowing a bugle. **5** [VP2A] give forth sound: *The trumpet ~ed. This black key* (e g on the piano) *won't ~,* No sound is produced when the key is struck. **6** [VP6A] test, examine (the wheels of a railway carriage, etc by striking them; a person's lungs by tapping the chest). **7** [VP2C] give an impression when heard (often fig): *How sweet the music ~s! It ~s to me as if there's a tap running somewhere,* I think I can hear water running from a tap. *His explanation ~s all right,* seems reasonable enough. *Her excuse ~s very hollow,* is unconvincing. **8** **ˋ~·ing-board** *n* canopy placed over a pulpit to direct the ~ of the preacher's voice towards his listeners; board placed over a platform, stage, etc with a similar purpose.

sound[4] /saʊnd/ *vt,vi* **1** [VP6A,2A] test the depth of (the sea, etc) by letting down a weighted line (called a *ˋ~ing-line* or *~ing apparatus*); find the depth of water in a ship's hold (with a *ˋ~ing-rod*); get records of temperature, pressure, etc in (the upper atmosphere) (by sending up instruments in a *ˋ~ing-balloon*). **2** [VP6A,15A,B] ***~ sb (out) (about/on sth),*** try (esp cautiously or in a reserved manner) to learn sb's views, sentiments, etc: *I will ~ the manager about/on the question of holidays. Have you ~ed him out yet,* tried to learn his views? **~·ings** *n pl* **1** measurements obtained by ~ing(**1**). **2** place or area near enough to the shore to make it possible to ~(**1**): *We are in ~ings/have come into ~ings.*

sound[5] /saʊnd/ *n* [C] narrow passage of water joining two larger areas of water; strait: *Puget S~.*

soup[1] /sup/ *n* [U] liquid food made by cooking meat, vegetables, etc in water: *chicken/pea/tomato ~.* ***in the ~,*** (colloq) in trouble. **ˋ~-kitchen** *n* public establishment for supplying ~ to persons who are poor, or after a calamity such as an earthquake or flood.

soup[2] /sup/ *vt* [VP15B] ***~ sth up,*** (sl) fit (a motor-vehicle, its engine) with a supercharger (to increase the power output, and so its speed): *a ~ed-up car.*

soup·çon /ˋsupsõ *US:* supˋsɔ̃/ *n* (F) (usu *a ~ of*) trace: *a ~ of garlic in the salad/of malice in his remarks.*

sour /saʊə(r)/ *adj* **1** having a sharp taste (like that of vinegar, a lemon or an unripe plum, apple, etc). ***~ grapes*** ⇨ grape. **2** having a taste of fermentation: *~ milk; a ~ smell,* i e of sth that has fermented. **3** (fig) bad-tempered; sharp-tongued: *made ~ by disappointments. What a ~ face she has!* □ *vt,vi* [VP6A,2A] turn or become ~ (liter, fig): *The hot weather has ~ed the milk. Her temper has ~ed. The old man has been ~ed by poverty.* **~·ly** *adv* **~·ness** *n*

source /sɔs/ *n* [C] **1** starting-point of a river: *the ~s of the Nile. Where does the Rhine have its ~?* **2** place from which sth comes or is got: *The news comes from a reliable ~. Is that well the ~ of infection for these cases of typhoid?* **3** (*pl*) original documents, etc serving as material for a study, e g of sb's life, a period of history: (attrib) *~ materials.*

souse /saʊs/ *vt* [VP6A] **1** throw into water; throw water on. **2** put (fish, etc) into salted water, vinegar, etc to preserve it: *~d herrings.* **3 soused** (*pp*) (sl) drunk.

sou·tane /suˋtɑn/ *n* (F) (in the RC Church) priest's cassock.

south /saʊθ/ *n* **1** one of the four cardinal points of the compass, on the right of a person facing the sunrise; ⇨ the illus at **compass**; part of any place, country, etc lying farther in this direction than other parts: *the ~ of London/England. Mexico is to the ~ of the US.* **2** (attrib) situated in, living in, pertaining to, coming from, the ~: *S~ Wales; S~ America; the S~ Pacific; a room with a ~ aspect,* with windows facing ~; *grow roses on a ~ wall; the S~ Pole.* □ *adv* to or towards the ~: *The ship was sailing due ~.* **ˈ~·ˋeast, ˈ~-ˋwest** (abbr **SE, SW**), *nn, adjj, advv* (sometimes, esp naut, **sou'-east** /ˈsaʊ ˋist/, **sou'-west** /ˈsaʊ ˋwest/) (regions) midway between ~ and east, ~ and west. **ˈ~-~·ˋeast, ˈ~-~·ˋwest** (abbr **SSE, SSW**) *nn, adjj, advv* (sometimes, esp naut, **ˈsou'-sou'-ˋeast, ˈsou'-sou'-ˋwest**) (regions) midway between ~ and ~east, ~west. **ˈ~-ˋeaster** *n* [C] strong wind blowing from the ~east. **ˈ~·ˋeaster·ly** *adj* (of wind) from the ~east; (of direction) towards the ~east. **ˈ~·ˋwester, sou'-**

wester /ˈsaʊ ˋwestə(r)/ *n* **(a)** strong ~west wind. **(b)** (always *sou'wester*) waterproof (usu oilskin) hat with a wide flap at the back to protect the neck. **ˈ~ˋwester·ly** *adj* (of wind) from the ~west; (of direction) towards the ~west. **ˈ~ˋeastern** /-ˋistən/ *adj* of, from, situated in, the ~east. **ˈ~ˋwestern** /-ˋwestən/ *adj* of, from, situated in the ~west. **~·ward(s)** /ˋsaθwədz/ *adv* towards the ~.

south·er·ly /ˋsʌðəlɪ/ *adj, adv* **1** (of winds) blowing from the south. **2** towards the south: *The plane flew off in a ~ direction.*

south·ern /ˋsʌðən/ *adj* in or of the south: *~ Europe; the S~ States of the USA; S~ women* (often, in US, meaning) women from these S~ States. **~er** *n* person from the ~ part of the country, esp from the S~ States (US). **ˋ~·most** /-məʊst/ *adj* farthest south.

sou·venir /ˈsuvəˈnɪə(r) *US:* ˋsuvənɪər/ *n* [C] sth taken, bought or received as a gift, and kept as a reminder of a person, place or event.

sou'·wester /ˈsaʊwestə(r)/ ⇨ **south(2)**.

sov·er·eign /ˋsovrɪn/ *adj* **1** (of power) highest; without limit; (of a nation, state, ruler) having ~ power: *become a ~ state,* fully self-governing and independent in foreign affairs. **2** excellent; effective: *Is there a ~ remedy for leprosy?* □ *n* **1** ~ ruler, e g a king, queen or emperor. **2** British gold coin not now in circulation (face value one pound). **~ty** /ˋsovrəntɪ/ *n* [U] ~ power.

so·viet /ˋsəʊvɪət/ *n* [C] one of the councils of workers, etc in any part of the USSR (the Union of S~ Socialist Republics); any of the higher groups to which these councils give authority, forming part of the system of government (*the Supreme S~*) of the whole of the USSR: *S~ Russia; the S~ Union.* **ˋ~·ize** /-ɑɪz/ *vt* convert to the ~ system of government.

sow[1] /saʊ/ *n* fully grown female pig. ⇨ **boar, hog, swine.**

sow[2] /səʊ/ *vt,vi* (*pt* **sowed,** *pp* **sown** /səʊn/ or **sowed**) [VP6A,15A,2A] put (seed) on or in the ground or in soil (in pots, seed-boxes, etc); plant (land *with* seed): *sow grass; sow a plot of land with grass;* (fig) *sow the seeds of hatred. It's too soon to sow yet.* **sower** *n* one who sows.

sox /soks/ *n pl* (trade use) *pl* of *sock.*

soy /sɔɪ/ *n* (also **ˋsoy-bean**) plant grown as food and for the oil obtained from its seeds. **soy sauce,** sauce made by fermenting soy beans in brine.

soz·zled /ˋsozld/ *adj* (GB, sl) very drunk.

spa /spɑ/ *n* (place where there is a) spring of mineral water having medicinal properties.

space /speɪs/ *n* **1** [U] that in which all objects exist and move: *The universe exists in ~. Travel through ~ to other planets interests many people today.* **ˋ~-capsule, ˋ~·craft, ˋ~-helmet, ˋ~-rocket, ˋ~·ship, ˋ~-suit/-vehicle** *nn* of the kind needed for travel beyond the earth's atmosphere. ⇨ the illus at **capsule, rocket. ˈ~-ˋtime** *n* (also known as 'the fourth dimension') fusion of time and the three dimensions of ~, as a concept much used in modern physics and philosophy. **2** [C,U] interval or distance between two or more objects: *the ~s between printed words; separated by a ~ of ten feet; put as much ~ as possible between the lines; leave a blank ~ for sth to be added.* **ˋ~-bar** *n* bar in a typewriter, tapped to make ~s between words. **3** [C,U] area or volume: *open ~s,* (esp) land, in or near a town, not built on. *Clear a ~ on the platform for the speakers.* **ˋ~-heater** *n* heating apparatus (electric, or oil-burning) designed to warm a room by radiation or convection. **4** [U] limited or unoccupied place or area; room(**3**): *There isn't enough ~ in this classroom for thirty desks. Have you enough ~ to work in?* **5** (*sing* only) period of time: *a ~ of three years.* □ *vt* [VP6A,15B] ***~ sth out,*** set out with regular ~s between: *~ out the posts three feet apart; ~ out the type more; ~* (= spread) *out payments* (e g for a house) *over twenty years: a well-~d family,* one in which children are born at planned intervals of time. **ˈsingle-/ˈdouble-ˋspacing,** the arrangement of typed material with single/double ~s between the lines.

spacious /ˋspeɪʃəs/ *adj* having much space; roomy. **~·ly** *adv* **~·ness** *n*

spade /speɪd/ *n* **1** tool for digging. ⇨ the illus at **tool. ˋ~-work** *n* (fig) hard work (to be) done at the start of an undertaking. ***call a ~ a ~,*** speak plainly. **2** (one of a) suit of playing-cards: *the five of ~s.* ⇨ the illus at **card.** □ *vt* [VP6A,15B] ***~ sth (up),*** dig (up) with a ~. **ˋ~·ful** /-fʊl/ *n* amount that is taken up by a ~.

spa·ghetti /spəˋgetɪ/ *n* [U] Italian pasta of narrow long rods, cooked by boiling.

spake /speɪk/ (old or poet) *pt* of **speak.**

spam /spæm/ *n* [U] (P) chopped or minced ham, spiced, cooked and usu eaten cold.

span /spæn/ *n* [C] **1** distance (about 9 inches or 23 cm) between the tips of a persons's thumb and little finger when stretched out. **2** distance or part between the supports of an arch: *The bridge crosses the river in a single ~. The arch has a ~ of 60 metres.* **3** length in time, from beginning to end: *the ~ of life; for a short ~ of time.* **4** (S Africa) pair of horses or mules; yoke of oxen. **5 ~ roof** *n* one with two inclined roofs (contrasted with a lean-to roof): (attrib) *a ~-roof greenhouse.* □ *vt* (**-nn-**) [VP6A] **1** extend across (from side to side): *The Thames is ~ned by many bridges. His life ~ned almost the whole of the 19th c.* **2** measure by ~s(**1**).

spangle /ˋspæŋgl/ *n* [C] tiny disc of shining metal, esp one of many, as used for ornament on a dress, etc. □ *vt* (esp in *pp*) cover with, or as with, ~s. **the ˈStar-S~d ˋBanner,** the national flag of the US.

Span·iard /ˋspænɪəd/ *n* native of Spain.

span·iel /ˋspænɪəl/ *n* sorts of dog with short legs, long, silky hair and large, drooping ears.

Span·ish /ˋspænɪʃ/ *adj* of Spain; of the Spaniards, or their language. **~ onion,** mild flavoured, yellow-skinned variety. **the S~ Main,** (in history) the NE coast of S America and the Caribbean Sea, near this coast. □ *n* the ~ language.

spank /spæŋk/ *vt,vi* **1** [VP6A] punish (a child) by slapping on the buttocks with the open hand or a slipper, etc. **2** [VP2C] ***~ (along),*** (esp of a horse or a ship) move along at a good pace. **~·ing** *n* slapping on the buttocks: *give a child a ~ing.* □ *adj* (dated colloq) first-rate; excellent: *have a ~ing time; a ~ing* (= strong) *breeze.* □ *adj* (old use) strikingly: *What a ~ing fine woman!*

span·ner /ˋspænə(r)/ *n* (US = *wrench*) tool for gripping and turning nuts on screws, bolts, etc. ⇨ the illus at **tool. *throw a ~ in(to) the works,*** sabotage a scheme, etc.

spar[1] /spɑ(r)/ *n* strong wooden or metal, pole used as a mast, yard, boom, etc.

spar[2] /spɑ(r)/ *vi* (-rr-) [VP2A,C] make the motions of attack and defence with the fists (as in boxing); (fig) dispute or argue. **ˋ~-ring-match** *n* demonstration boxing match; (fig) dispute or argument. **ˋ~-ring-partner** *n* man with whom a boxer ~s as part of his training.

spar[3] /spɑ(r)/ *n* kinds of non-metallic mineral, easily cleavable.

spare[1] /speə(r)/ *adj* **1** additional to what is usually needed or used; in reserve for use when needed; (of time) leisure; unoccupied: *I have no/very little ~ time/money,* no time/money that I cannot use. *Surely you carry a ~ wheel in the back of your car? We have no ~ room* (= extra bedroom, e g for a guest) *in our house.* **~ part,** part to replace a broken or worn-out part of a machine, etc. **2** (of persons) thin; lean: *a tall, ~ man; a ~ figure; ~ of build* **3** (attrib only) small in quantity: *a ~ meal; on a ~ diet.* **ˋ~-rib,** rib of pork with most of the meat cut off. □ *n* [C] ~ part (for a machine, etc). **~·ly** *adv* in a ~(2,3) manner: *~ly built.* **~-ness** *n*

spare[2] /speə(r)/ *vt,vi* **1** [VP6A,12A,13A] refrain from hurting, damaging or destroying; show mercy to: *~ sb's life, ~ sb his life,* not kill him or have him killed. *We may meet again if we are ~d,* if our lives are ~d by Providence. *He doesn't ~ himself,* is severe with himself, does not refrain from making great demands upon himself (his energies, time, etc). ***~ sb's feelings,*** avoid hurting his feelings. ***S~ the rod and spoil the child,*** (prov) If you refrain from punishing the child, you will spoil its character. **2** [VP12B,13B,6A] ***~ sth (for sb/sth), ~ sb sth,*** afford to give (time, money, etc) to sb, or for a purpose: *Can you ~ me a few litres of petrol? Can you ~ one of them for me? Can you ~ me a few minutes (of your time)? I can't ~ the time for a holiday at present. We have enough and to ~,* more than we need. **3** [VP6A] use in small quantities, rarely or in a saving manner. ***No expense(s)/pains ~ed,*** with no economy in money or effort: *I'm going to redecorate the house, no expense ~d.* **spar·ing** *adj* ***sparing of,*** economical, frugal, careful (of): *You should be more sparing of your energy.* **spar·ing·ly** *adv*

spark[1] /spɑk/ *n* [C] tiny glowing bit thrown off from a burning substance or still present in ashes, etc or produced by striking flint or hard metal and stone together; flash of light produced by the breaking of an electric current; (fig) sign of life, energy, etc; flash of wit: *The firework burst into a shower of ~s. He hasn't a ~ of generosity in him.* □ *vt,vi* [VP2A,15B] give out ~s. ***~ sth off,*** (fig) lead to; be the immediate cause of: *His statement ~ed off a quarrel between them.* **ˋ~(·ing)-plug** *n* device for firing the gas in a petrol engine by means of an electric ~.

spark[2] /spɑk/ *n* gay and elegant young fellow.

sparkle /ˋspɑkl/ *vi* [VP2A,C] send out flashes of light; gleam: *Her diamonds ~d in the bright light. Her eyes ~d with excitement.* □ *n* spark; glitter; gleam. **spark·ler** /ˋspɑklə(r)/ *n* sth that ~s, e g a kind of firework; (sl, esp among criminals, often *pl*) diamond. **spark·ling** /ˋspɑklɪŋ/ *adj* (of wines) giving out tiny bubbles of carbonic acid gas when the bottle is opened. ⇨ **still**[1](2).

spar·row /ˋspærəʊ/ *n* small brownish-grey bird common in many parts of the world, esp *the ˋhouse-~,* European kind found around buildings. ⇨ the illus at **bird**.

sparse /spɑs/ *adj* **1** thinly scattered: *a ~ population.* **2** not dense, thick or crowded: *a ~ beard.* **~·ly** *adv*: *a ~ly furnished room,* one with little furniture. **~·ness, spar·sity** /ˋspɑsətɪ/ *nn* [U].

Spar·tan /ˋspɑtn/ *n, adj* (person) caring little for the ordinary comforts of life, unafraid of pain and hardship; (of living conditions) hard because very simple: *live a ~ life: in ~ simplicity.*

spasm /ˋspæzm/ *n* [C] **1** sudden and involuntary tightening of a muscle or muscles: *asthma ~s.* **2** sudden, convulsive movement: *in a ~ of pain/excitement/grief; a ~ of coughing.* **3** sudden burst (of energy).

spas·modic /spæzˋmɒdɪk/ *adj* **1** taking place, done, at irregular intervals. **2** caused by, affected by, spasms: *~ asthma.* **spas·modi·cally** /-klɪ/ *adv*

spas·tic /ˋspæstɪk/ *n, adj* (person) suffering from cerebral palsy, physically disabled because of faulty links between the brain and motor nerves, causing spasmodic movements through difficulty in controlling voluntary muscles.

spat[1] /spæt/ *n* ***~s; a pair of ~s,*** cloth cover (formerly) worn over the upper part of a shoe and round the ankle.

spat[2] /spæt/ *pt,pp* of **spit**.

spat[3] /spæt/ *vi,vt* (-tt-), *n* (US) (have a) slight quarrel; (give a) light slap (to).

spat[4] /spæt/ *n* spawn of oysters. □ *vi* (-tt-) (of oysters) spawn.

spatch·cock /ˋspætʃkɒk/ *n* fowl killed and cooked at once. □ *vt* [VP14] (colloq) insert (words) *(in/into)*: *He ~ed into his speech a curious passage about....*

spate /speɪt/ *n* **1** strong current of water at abnormally high level (in a river): *After the storm the rivers were all in ~.* **2** sudden rush of business, etc: *a ~ of orders; a ~ of new books for review.*

spa·tial /ˋspeɪʃl/ *adj* of, in relation to, existing in, space. **~·ly** /-ʃḷɪ/ *adv*

spat·ter /ˋspætə(r)/ *vt,vi* **1** [VP6A,14] ***~ sth (on/over sth), ~ sth (with sth),*** splash, scatter, in drips: *~ grease on one's clothes/~ one's clothes with grease. As the bus went by it ~ed us with mud.* **2** [VP2C] fall or spread out in drops: *We heard the rain ~ing down on the tin roof of the hut.* □ *n* [C] sprinkling; shower: *a ~ of rain/bullets.*

spat·ula /ˋspætjʊlə *US:* ˋspætʃʊlə/ *n* tool with a wide, flat, flexible blade used for mixing or spreading various substances.

spavin /ˋspævɪn/ *n* [U] disease of horses in which a bony swelling forms at the hock, causing lameness. **spav·ined** *adj* affected with ~.

spawn /spɔn/ *n* [U] **1** eggs of fish and certain water animals, e g frogs. ⇨ the illus at **amphibian**. **2** threadlike matter from which mushrooms and other fungi grow. □ *vt,vi* [VP6A,2A] lay or produce in great numbers: *departments which ~ committees and sub-committees.*

speak /spik/ *vi,vt* (*pt* **spoke** /spəʊk/, old use **spake** /speɪk/, *pp* **spoken** /ˋspəʊkən/) **1** [VP2A, C] make use of language in an ordinary, not a singing, voice: *Please ~ more slowly.* **2** [VP2B, C,3A] ***~ (to sb) (about sth),*** (rarely) ***~ (with sb)***: *I was ~ing to him about plans for the holidays.* ***~ for sb,*** **(a)** state the views, wishes, etc of; act as spokesman for. **(b)** give evidence on behalf of. ***~ for oneself,*** **(a)** express one's views, etc in one's own way. **(b)** (usu *imper*) not presume to ~ for others. ***~ to sb,*** admonish: *Your secretary was late again this morning—you'd better ~ to her about it.* ***~ to sth,*** ~ in confirmation of or in reference to: *Is there anyone here who can ~ to his having been at the scene of the crime,* who can say that he was there? *You must ~ to the subject,* not wander away from it. ***nothing to ~ of,*** nothing worth mentioning; not much. ***~ out/up,*** **(a)** ~ loud(er). **(b)** give one's opinions, etc without hesitation or fear. ***not be on ~ing terms with sb,*** **(a)** not know him well enough to ~ to him. **(b)** no longer ~ to him because one has quarrelled with him. ***so to ~,*** as one might say; if I may use this expression, etc. **'~ing-trumpet** *n* (now replaced by *hearing-aids*) trumpet-shaped device held to the ear by a deaf person to help him to hear. **'~ing-tube** *n* tube that carries the voice from one place to another, e g from a ship's bridge to the engine-room. **3** [VP2C,15A] give evidence (of), convey ideas (not necessarily in words): *Actions ~ louder than words. The portrait ~s/is a ~ing likeness,* is excellent, tells us well what the sitter was like. ***~ volumes for,*** be strong evidence of: *This evidence ~s volumes for his probity.* ***~ well for,*** be evidence in favour of. **4** [VP6A] know and be able to use (a language): *He ~s several languages. Is English spoken here?* **5** [VP2A,B] address an audience; make a speech: *He spoke for forty minutes. Are you good at ~ing in public?* **6** [VP6A] make known; utter: *~ the truth.* ***~ one's mind,*** express one's views frankly or bluntly. **7** (in the pattern, *adv* (in *-ly*) and *pres part*): *strictly/roughly/generally, etc ~ing,* using the word(s) in a strict/rough/general, etc sense. **8** [VP6A] (naut) hail and exchange information with (by flag signals, etc): *~ a passing ship.* **9** [VP2A] (of a gun, musical instrument, etc) make sounds. **10** **'~-easy** *n* illicit liquor shop (esp in the US during the period of prohibition). **~er** *n* **1** person who makes speeches (in the manner indicated): *He's a good/poor, etc ~er.* **2** (short for) *loud-~er.* **3 the S~er,** presiding officer of the House of Commons and other legislative assemblies. **'~er·ship** /-ʃɪp/ *n* office of the S~er; period of office of a S~er.

spear /spɪə(r)/ *n* weapon with a metal point on a long shaft, used in hunting, or (formerly) by men fighting on foot. □ *vt* [VP6A] pierce, wound, make (a hole) in, with a ~. **'~-head** *n* (usu fig) individual or group chosen to lead an attack. □ *vt* act as ~-head for: *armoured vehicles that ~-head the offensive.*

spear·mint /'spɪəmɪnt/ *n* aromatic variety of mint used for flavouring; chewing-gum flavoured with this.

spec /spek/ *n* (colloq abbr of) speculation: *Those mining shares turned out a good ~,* proved profitable. ***on ~,*** as a speculation; as a guess.

special /'speʃl/ *adj* **1** of a particular or certain sort; not common, usual or general; of or for a certain person, thing or purpose: *He did it for her as a ~ favour. What are your ~ interests? Newspapers send ~ correspondents to places where important events take place. On holidays the railways put on ~ trains,* run extra trains for ~ purposes. **~ constable,** man enrolled to help the ordinary police in time of need. **~ delivery,** delivery of mail (a letter, package, etc) by a ~ messenger instead of by the usual postal services. **~ licence,** licence which allows a marriage to take place at a time or place other than those legally authorized. **2** exceptional in amount, degree, etc: *Why should we give you ~ treatment? You've taken no ~ trouble with your work for us.* □ *n* ~ constable, ~ train, ~ edition of a newspaper, etc. **~ly** /-ʃlɪ/ *adv* particularly: *I came here ~ly* (= on purpose) *to see you.* **~·ist** /-ʃlɪst/ *n* person who is an expert in a ~ branch of work or study, esp medicine: *an 'eye ~ist; a ~ist in plastic surgery.*

spe·ci·al·ity /ˌspeʃɪ'ælətɪ/ *n* [C] (*pl* **-ties**) **1** special quality or characteristic of sb or sth. **2** (also **spe·cialty** /'speʃltɪ/ (*pl* **-ties**)) special pursuit, activity, product, operation, etc; thing to which a person (firm, etc) gives special attention or for which a place is well known: *Embroidery is her ~. Wood-carvings are a ~ of this village.*

spe·cial·ize /'speʃlaɪz/ *vi,vt* **1** [VP2A,3A] ***~ (in sth),*** be or become a specialist; give special or particular attention to: *~ in oriental history. After his first degree he wishes to ~.* **2** (usu *pp*) adapt for a particular purpose: *a hospital with ~d wards,* (cf *general wards*); *~d knowledge,* (cf *general knowledge*). **spe·cial·iz·ation** /ˌspeʃlaɪ'zeɪʃn *US:* -lɪ'z-/ *n*

spe·cialty /'speʃltɪ/ *n* (*pl* **-ties**) ⇨ **speciality(2).**

specie /'spiʃi/ *n* [U] (store of, consignment of) money in the form of coins: *~ payments; payment in ~.*

spe·cies /'spiʃiz/ *n* (*pl* unchanged) **1** group having some common characteristics (division of a genus) able to breed with each other but not with other groups: *the human ~,* mankind. **2** sort: *Blackmail is a ~ of crime hated by all decent folk.*

spe·ci·fic /spə'sɪfɪk/ *adj* **1** detailed and precise: *~ orders. What are your ~ aims?* **2** relating to one particular thing, etc, not general: *The money is to be used for a ~ purpose.* **~ gravity,** mass of any substance relative to that of an equal volume of water. **~ name,** (biol) distinguishing name of the species. **~ remedy,** one for a particular disease. □ *n* [C] ~ remedy: *Quinine is a ~ for malaria.* **spe·cifi·cally** /-klɪ/ *adv* in a ~ manner: *You were ~ally warned by your doctor not to eat lobster.*

spec·ifi·ca·tion /ˌspesɪfɪ'keɪʃn/ *n* **1** [U] specifying. **2** (often *pl*) details, instructions, etc for the design, materials, of sth to be made or done: *~s for (building) a garage; the technical ~s of a new car.*

spec·ify /'spesɪfaɪ/ *vt* (*pt,pp* **-fied**) [VP6A] name definitely; include in the specifications: *The contract specifies red tiles, not slates, for the roof.*

speci·men /'spesɪmən/ *n* [C] **1** one as an example of a class: *~s of rocks and ores.* **2** part taken to represent the whole: *a publisher's catalogue with ~ pages of books.* **3** sth to be tested, etc for definite or special purposes: *supply a ~ of one's urine.* **4** (colloq) unusual thing or person regarded with contempt or amusement: *What a queer ~ (of humanity) he is!*

spe·cious /'spiʃəs/ *adj* seeming right or true, but not really so: *a ~ argument/person.* **~·ly** *adv* **~·ness** *n*

speck /spek/ *n* [C] small spot or particle (of dirt, etc) stain; discoloured spot on fruit (showing rottenness); dot: *Do you ever seem to see ~s in front of your eyes? The ship was a mere ~ on the horizon.* **~ed** *adj* marked with ~s: *~ed apples.* **~·less** *adj*

speckle /'spekl/ *n* [C] small mark or spot, esp one

of many, distinct in colour, on the skin, feathers, etc. **speckled** *adj* marked with ~s: *a ~d hen; ~d plumage.*

specs /speks/ *n pl* (colloq) spectacles(3): *Where are my ~?*

spec·tacle /ˈspektəkl/ *n* [C] **1** public display, procession, etc, esp one with ceremony: *The ceremonial opening of Parliament was a fine ~.* **2** sth seen; sth taking place before the eyes, esp sth fine, remarkable or noteworthy: *The sunrise as seen from the top of the mountain was a tremendous ~. The poor drunken man was a sad ~. Don't make a ~ of yourself,* don't draw attention to yourself by dressing, behaving, etc ridiculously. **3** ***~s; a pair of ~s,*** pair of lenses in a frame, resting on the nose and ears, to help the eyesight (or to protect the eyes from bright sunlight) (*glasses* is the more usu name). ***see everything through rose-coloured ~s,*** take a cheerful, optimistic view of things. **spec·tacled** *adj* wearing ~s.

spec·tacu·lar /spekˈtækjʊlə(r)/ *adj* making a fine spectacle(1,2); attracting public attention: *a ~ display of fireworks.* **~·ly** *adv*

spec·ta·tor /spekˈteɪtə(r) *US:* ˈspekteɪtər/ *n* onlooker (esp at a show or game): *~ sports,* those which draw crowds of ~s, e g football.

spectre (US = **spec·ter**) /ˈspektə(r)/ *n* [C] ghost; haunting fear of future trouble. **spec·tral** /ˈspektrəl/ *adj* **1** of or like a ~. **2** of spectra or the spectrum: *spectral colours.*

spec·tro·scope /ˈspektrəskəʊp/ *n* instrument for producing and examining the spectra of a ray of light. **spec·tro·scopic** /ˈspektrəˈskopɪk/ *adj* of, by means of, a ~: *spectroscopic analysis.*

spec·trum /ˈspektrəm/ *n* (*pl* -tra /-trə/) image of a band of colours (as seen in a rainbow and usu described as red, orange, yellow, green, blue, indigo and violet) formed by a ray of light which has passed through a prism; (fig) wide range or sequence: *the whole ~ of recent philosophical enquiry.*

specu·late /ˈspekjʊleɪt/ *vi* [VP2A,C] **1** consider, form opinions (without having complete knowledge); guess: *~ about/upon the future of the human race; ~ as to what sort of man one will marry.* **2** buy and sell goods, stocks and shares, etc with risk of loss and hope of profit through changes in their market value: *~ in oil shares/wheat.* **specu·la·tor** /-tə(r)/ *n* person who ~s(2).

specu·la·tion /ˈspekjʊˈleɪʃn/ *n* **1** [U] speculating(1); meditation; [C] opinion reached by this means; guess. **2** [U] speculating(2): *~ in rice;* [C] transaction, business deal, of this kind: *make some bad ~s; buy mining shares as a ~.*

specu·lat·ive /ˈspekjʊlətɪv *US* -leɪtɪv/ *adj* **1** concerned with speculation(1): *~ philosophy.* **2** concerned with speculation(2): *~ purchase of grain; ~ housing,* the building of houses as a speculation(2). **~·ly** *adv*

sped /sped/ *pt,pp* of speed.

speech /spitʃ/ *n* **1** [U] power, act, manner, of speaking: *Man is the only animal that has the faculty of ~. Our thoughts are expressed by ~. They say that ~ is silver but silence is golden. His indistinct ~ made it impossible to understand him.* **~ therapy,** remedial treatment for defective speech, e g for stuttering. **2** [C] talk or address given in public: *make a ~ on/about the Common Market to a receptive audience.* **ˈ~-day** *n* annual school celebration with ~es and distribution of certificates and prizes. **~·less** *adj* **1** unable to speak, esp because of deep feeling: *~less with surprise. Anger left him ~less.* **2** that causes a person to be unable to speak: *~less rage.* **~·less·ly** *adv* **~·ify** /ˈspitʃɪfaɪ/ *vi* (*pt,pp* -fied) make ~es; talk as if making ~es (usu implying that this is done unnecessarily or badly): *town councillors ~ifying at the unveiling of a statue/at a welcome to the Queen.*

speed /spid/ *n* **1** [U] swiftness; rapidity of movement. ***More haste, less ~,*** (prov) Too much haste may result in delay. **2** [C,U] rate of motion or moving: *travelling at full/top ~; at a ~ of thirty miles an hour. It's dangerous to corner at ~,* to go round corners (in a car) at a high ~. **3** (sl) cocaine; any amphetamine used to produce euphoria. **4** (compounds) **ˈ~-boat** *n* motor-boat designed for high ~s. **ˈ~-cop** *n* (sl) police motorcyclist who checks the ~ of motorists. **ˈ~-indicator** *n* = ~ometer. ⇨ below. **ˈ~-limit** *n* ~ which must not be exceeded, e g in a built-up area. **ˈ~ merchant,** (sl) person who drives a car or motor-bike extremely fast. **ˈ~·way** *n* **(a)** track, for fast driving and racing, esp by motor-bikes. **(b)** (US) road for fast traffic; express way. □ *vt,vi* (*pt,pp* **sped**) **1** [VP2A,C] move along, go quickly: *cars ~ing past the school. He sped down the street.* **2** [VP6A,14] cause to move or go quickly: *~ an arrow from the bow.* **3** (archaic) give success to: *God ~ you,* May God make you prosper. **4** [VP15B,2C] (*pt,pp* ~ed) **~ *(sth) up,*** increase the ~ (of). *They have ~ed up production/the train service. He ~ed up the engine. The train soon ~ed up.* Hence, **ˈ~-up** *n* ~ing up the rate of production, etc. **~·ing** *n* (of motorists) travelling at an illegal or dangerous ~: *fined £10 for ~ing.* **~·om·eter** /spiˈdomɪtə(r)/ *n* instrument showing the ~ of a motor-vehicle, etc. **speedy** *adj* (-ier, -iest) quick; coming, done, without delay: *wish sb a ~y recovery from illness.*

a speed-boat

speed·well /ˈspidwel/ *n* kinds of small, wild plant with bright blue flowers.

spelae·ol·ogy (also **spele-**) /ˈspilɪˈolədʒɪ/ *n* [U] the explanation and scientific study of caves. **spelae·ol·ogist** (also **spele-**) /-dʒɪst/ *n* student of ~.

spell[1] /spel/ *n* [C] **1** words used as a charm, supposed to have magic power: *cast a ~ over sb; put a ~ on sb; be under/lay sb under a ~.* **ˈ~·bound** /-baʊnd/ *adj* with the attention held by, or as by, a ~: *The speaker held his audience ~bound.* **ˈ~-binder** /-baɪndə(r)/ *n* speaker who can hold audiences ~bound. **2** attraction, fascination, exercised by a person, occupation, etc: *under the ~ of her beauty; the mysterious ~ of the music of Delius.*

spell[2] /spel/ *n* **1** period of time: *a long ~ of warm* *weather; a cold* ~ *in January; rest for a (short)* ~. **2** period of activity or duty, esp one at which two or more persons take turns: *take* ~*s at the wheel,* e g of two persons making a long journey by car. □ *vt* ~ ***sb (at sth),*** take turns with sb: *Will you* ~ *me at rowing the boat?*

spell[3] /spel/ *vt,vi* (*pt,pp* ~ed /speld/ or spelt /spelt/) **1** [VP6A] name or write the letters of (a word): *How do you* ~ *your name?* **'~ing pronunciation,** one suggested by the written form of the word (e g /ˈnefju/ instead of /ˈnevju/ for nephew). **2** [VP6A] (of letters) form when put together in a particular order: *C-A-T* ~*s cat.* **3** [VP15B] ~ ***sth out,*** **(a)** make out (words, writing) laboriously, slowly: *It took the boy an hour to* ~ *out a page of German.* **(b)** make clear and easy to understand; explain in detail: *My request seems simple enough—do you want me to* ~ *it out for you?* **4** [VP6A] have as a consequence: *Does laziness always* ~ *failure?* **5** [VP2A,6A] place the letters of words in the correct or accepted order: *These children can't* ~. *Why don't you learn to* ~ *my name (correctly)?* **~er** *n* person who ~s: *a good/poor* ~*er.* **~ing** *n* [C] way a word is spelt: *Which is the better* ~*ing: Tokio or Tokyo? Do you use English or American* ~*ing(s)?*

spelt[1] ⇨ spell[3].

spelt[2] /spelt/ *n* [U] kind of wheat giving very fine flour, grown in the mountains of Germany and Switzerland.

spend /spend/ *vt,vi* (*pt,pp* spent /spent/) **1** [VP6A,14,2A] ~ ***money (on sth),*** pay out (money) for goods, services, etc: ~ *all one's money;* ~ *too much money on clothes;* ~ *£10 a week. He's always* ~*ing.* **'~-thrift** *n* person who ~s money extravagantly. **2** [VP6A,14] use up; consume: ~ *a lot of care/time on sth/in doing sth;* ~ *all one's energies. They went on firing until all their ammunition was spent.* **3** [VP6A] pass: ~ *a weekend in London/one's spare time in gardening. How do you* ~ *your leisure?* **~er** *n* person who ~s money (usu in the way indicated by the *adj*): *an extravagant* ~*er.* **spent** (*pp* as *adj*) exhausted; used up: *a spent runner/swimmer/horse; a spent cartridge/bullet,* one that has been fired and is now useless.

sperm /spɜm/ *n* [U] fertilizing fluid of a male animal. **'~-whale** *n* whale producing spermaceti. **sper·mato·zoa** /ˌspɜmətəˈzəʊə/ *n pl* reproductive cells in ~ (fusing with ova to produce new offspring).

sper·ma·ceti /ˌspɜməˈsetɪ/ *n* [U] white, waxy, fatty substance contained in solution in the heads of sperm-whales, used for ointments, candles, etc.

spew /spju/ *vt,vi* [VP6A,15B,2A] vomit.

sphag·num /ˈsfægnəm/ *n* (*pl* ~s) kinds of moss growing in peat and bogs, used in packing and medicinally.

sphere /sfɪə(r)/ *n* **1** form of a globe; star; planet; (liter) the heavens, the sky. ***music of the*** ~***s,*** (myth) music produced by the movement of heavenly bodies, inaudible to mortals. **2** globe representing the earth or the apparent heavens. **3** person's interests, activities, surroundings, etc: *a woman who is distinguished in many* ~*s,* e g in literary and artistic circles, in the political world. *Your proposal that I should write a novel lies outside the* ~ *of my activities.* **4** range, extent: *a* ~ *of influence,* area over which a country claims certain rights or is recognized as having them. **spheri·cal** /ˈsferɪkl/ *adj* shaped like a ~. **sphe·roid** ˈsfɪərɔɪd/ *n* body that is almost spherical.

sphinx /sfɪŋks/ *n* stone statue (*the S*~) in Egypt with a lion's body and a woman's head; person who keeps his thoughts and intentions secret; enigmatic person.

a pyramid and the Sphinx

spice /spɑɪs/ *n* **1** [C,U] sorts of substance, e g ginger, nutmeg, cinnamon, cloves, used to flavour food: *a dealer in* ~ (collective); *mixed* ~*(s); too much* ~ *in the cake.* **2** [U] (and with *indef art*) (fig) interesting flavour, suggestion, or trace (of): *a story that lacks* ~. *She has a* ~ *of malice in her character.* □ *vt* [VP6A] add flavour to (sth) with ~, or as with ~: ~*d with humour.* **spicy** *adj* (-ier, -iest) of, flavoured with, ~; (fig) exciting or interesting because somewhat improper: *spicy details of the film star's love life.* **spic·ily** /-əlɪ/ *adv* **spici·ness** *n*

spick /spɪk/ *adj* (only in) ~ ***and span,*** bright, clean and tidy.

spi·der /ˈspɑɪdə(r)/ *n* sorts of creature with eight legs, many species of which spin webs for the capture of insects as food. ⇨ the illus at arachnid. **~y** *adj* (esp of handwriting) with long, thin strokes.

spied /spɑɪd/ *pt,pp* of spy.

spiel /ʃpil/ *vi,vt* (sl) talk, say (sth) glibly and at length. □ *n* long voluble talk (usu intended to persuade sb).

spigot /ˈspɪgət/ *n* **1** (usu wooden) plug or peg which can be used to stop the hole of a cask or barrel. **2** valve for controlling the flow of water or other liquid from a tank, barrel, etc.

spike /spɑɪk/ *n* **1** sharp point; pointed piece of metal, e g on iron railings or on running-shoes. ~ **heel,** (also *stiletto heel*) thin, pointed heel on a (woman's) shoe. **2** ear of grain, e g barley; long, pointed cluster of flowers on a single stem: ~*s of lavender.* □ *vt* [VP6A] **1** put ~s (on shoes, etc): ~*d running-shoes.* **2** pierce or injure with a ~; (of cannon in former times) make useless by driving a ~ into the opening where the powder was fired. Hence, ~ ***sb's guns,*** spoil his plans. **spiky** *adj* (-ier, -iest) having ~s or sharp points; (fig, of persons) difficult to manage because unwilling to yield.

spike·nard /ˈspɑɪknɑd/ *n* [U] (costly ointment formerly made from a) tall, perennial, sweet-smelling plant.

spill[1] /spɪl/ *vt,vi* (*pt,pp* spilt /spɪlt/ or ~ed) **1** [VP6A,2A,C] (of liquid or powder) (allow to) run over the side of the container: *Who has spilt/*~*ed the milk? The ink has spilt on the desk.* ~ ***the beans,*** ⇨ bean. ~ ***blood,*** be guilty of wounding or killing sb. **2** [VP6A] (of a horse, carriage, etc) upset; cause (the rider, passenger, etc) to fall: *His horse spilt him. The horse shied and we were all spilt* (= thrown out of the carriage, etc) *into the ditch.* □ *n* fall from a horse, out of a carriage, etc:

have a nasty ~. ˋ**~·over** *n* (often attrib) (of population) excess: *new towns for London's ~over (population)*. ˋ**~·way** *n* passage for surplus water from a reservoir, river, etc.

spill[2] /spɪl/ *n* [C] thin strip of wood, rolled or twisted strip of paper, used to light candles, tobacco in a pipe, etc.

spilt /spɪlt/ ⇨ spill[1].

a spinning-wheel

spin /spɪn/ *vt, vi* (*pt* spun /spʌn/ or span /spæn/, *pp* spun; -nn-) **1** [VP6A,14,2A] form (thread) by twisting wool, cotton, silk, etc; draw out and twist (wool, cotton, etc) into threads; make (yarn) in this way; engage in the occupation of ~ning thread: *~ning wool/thread/yarn.* ˋ**~·ning jenny** *n* early kind of machine for ~ning more than one thread at a time. ˋ**~·ning-wheel** *n* simple household machine for ~ning thread continuously on a spindle turned by a large wheel, usu worked by a treadle. **2** [VP6A] form by means of threads: *spiders ~ning their webs; silkworms ~ning cocoons.* **3** [VP6A,15B] (fig) produce, compose (a narrative). ***~ a yarn,*** tell a story: *The old sailor loves to ~ yarns about his life at sea.* ***~ sth out,*** make it last as long as possible: *~ out the time by talking; economize in order to make one's money ~ out until next pay-day.* **4** [VP6A] cause (sth) to go round and round: *~ a top,* ⇨ top[3]; *~ a coin,* send it up in the air, revolving as it goes up, to decide sth (by 'heads or tails'): *~ the ball,* (in cricket, tennis). ˈ**~-ˋdrier** *n* device that uses centrifugal force to dry what is placed in it (e g laundered clothes). ˈ**~-ˋdry** *vt* (*pt, pp* dried) dry in a ~-drier. ˋ**~-off** *n* incidental benefit or product (from a larger enterprise, or from research for such an enterprise). **5** [VP2A,C] move round rapidly: *The top was ~ning merrily. The collision sent the car ~ning across the roadway. The blow sent him ~ning to the wall. The carriage was ~ning along* (= moving along) *at a good speed.* **6 spun** (*pp*) *spun glass,* glass made into threads (by being spun when heated); *spun silk,* cheap material of short-fibred and waste silk, often mixed with cotton. □ *n* **1** [U] turning or ~ning motion, esp as given to the ball in some games, e g cricket, baseball: *The pitcher gave (a) ~ to the ball.* **2** short ride in a motor-car; ride on a bicycle, etc; *have/go for a ~.* **3** fast ~ning movement of an aircraft during a diving descent: *get into/out of a ~.* ***in a flat ~,*** in a panic.

spin·ach /ˋspɪnɪdʒ *US:* -ɪtʃ/ *n* [U] common garden plant with green leaves, cooked and eaten as a vegetable.

spi·nal /ˋspaɪnl/ *adj* of or to the spine: *the ~ column,* the backbone; *the ~ cord,* nerve-fibres in the spine: *a* ˋ*~ injury.*

spindle /ˋspɪndl/ *n* **1** (in spinning) thin rod for twisting and winding thread by hand. ⇨ the illus at spin. **2** bar or pin which turns round, or on which sth turns (e g an axle or a shaft). ˋ**~-legged/-shanked** *adjj* having long, thin legs. ˋ**~-shanks** *n* person with such legs. ˋ**~-berry/-tree** *n* small tree with hard wood and deep-pink berries used for ~s. **spin·dly** /ˋspɪndlɪ/ *adj* long and thin; too tall and thin.

spin·drift /ˋspɪndrɪft/ *n* [U] foam or spray blown along the surface of the sea.

spine /spaɪn/ *n* **1** backbone. ⇨ the illus at skeleton. **2** one of the sharp needle-like parts on some plants, e g a cactus, and animals, e g a porcupine. **3** part of a book's cover that is visible when it is in a row on a shelf, usu with the book's title on it. **~·less** *adj* having no ~(1); (fig) without power to make decisions; timid. **spiny** *adj* (-ier, -iest) having ~s(2).

spinet /spɪˋnet *US:* ˋspɪnɪt/ *n* old type of keyboard instrument like a harpsichord. ⇨ the illus at keyboard.

spin·na·ker /ˋspɪnəkə(r)/ *n* large triangular sail carried on the main-mast of a racing yacht on the side opposite the mainsail when running before the wind.

spin·ney /ˋspɪnɪ/ *n* (*pl* -neys) thicket; small wood with thick undergrowth, esp (in England) one used for sheltering game[1](6).

spin·ster /ˋspɪnstə(r)/ *n* (usu offical or legal use) unmarried woman; woman who remains single after the conventional age for marrying. ˋ**~·hood** /-hʊd/ *n* the state of being a ~.

spi·ral /ˋspaɪərl/ *adj, n* (in the form of an) advancing or ascending continuous curve winding round a central point: *A barber's pole usually has a ~ stripe on it. A snail's shell is ~. The rocket went up in a ~. A ~ nebula is a group of stars that has the appearance of a ~.* ⇨ also *inflationary ~* at inflate. □ *vi* (-ll-, US also -l-) [VP2A,C] move in a ~: *The smoke ~led up. Prices are still ~ling.*

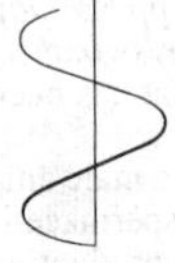
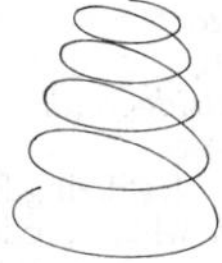

spirals

spire /ˋspaɪə(r)/ *n* pointed structure like a tall cone or pyramid rising above a tower (esp of a church). ⇨ the illus at church.

spirit /ˋspɪrɪt/ *n* **1** [C,U] soul; immaterial, intellectual or moral part of man: *He was vexed in ~,* inwardly. *I shall be with you in (the) ~,* My thoughts will be with you even though I am not with you in the flesh. *The ~ is willing but the flesh is weak,* One is willing to do sth, but physically unable to do it. **2** the soul thought of as separate from the body; disembodied soul: *the abode of ~s,* where the ~s of the dead are; *believe in ~s; raise a ~.* ˋ**~-rapper** *n* person who claims to receive messages from the dead by means of raps on a table. **3** [C] sprite; elf; goblin. **4** [U] life and consciousness not associated with a body; disembodied soul: *God is pure ~.* **5** [C] (always with an *adj*) person considered from the intellectual, moral or emotional point of view: *What a noble/generous, etc ~ he is! He was one of the leading*

~s of the Reform Movement. **6** [U] quality of courage, vigour, liveliness: *Put a little more ~ into your work. You haven't the ~ of a mouse.* **7** (*sing* only) mental or moral attitude: *in a ~ of mischief. Whether it was unwise or not depends upon the ~ in which it was done.* **8** [U] real meaning or purpose underlying a law, etc (contrasted with the apparent meaning of the words, etc): *obey the ~, not the letter, of the law. Have you followed out the ~ of his instructions?* **9** (*pl*) state of mind (as being happy, hopeful, etc or the opposite): *in high ~s,* cheerful; *in poor/low ~s, out of ~s,* depressed, unhappy. *Have a glass of brandy to keep up your ~s.* **10** (*sing* only) influence or tendency that rouses or causes development: *The wind of change is blowing through East Asia and we cannot resist the ~ of the times.* **11** [U] industrial alcohol. **'~-lamp/-stove** *n* one in which ~ is burned. **'~-level** *n* glass tube partly filled with water or alcohol, with a bubble of air which, when centred, shows that a surface is horizontal. **12** (*pl*) solution in alcohol: *~s of camphor/turpentine; ~(s) of salt,* hydrochloric acid. **13** (usu *pl*) strong alcoholic drinks (e g whisky, brandy, gin, rum): *a glass of ~s and water. She drinks no ~ but vodka.* □ *vt* [VP15B] ***~ sb/sth away/off,*** take sb/sth rapidly, secretly or mysteriously: *She has disappeared as completely as if she had been ~ed away to another planet.* **~ed** /'spɪrɪtɪd/ *adj* **1** full of ~(6); lively; courageous: *a ~ed attack/defence/reply; a ~ed horse; a ~ed conversation.* **2** (in compounds) having the kind of spirits(9) indicated: *'high-/'low-/poor-'~ed,* etc. **~·less** *adj* without ~(6); not having or showing energy or courage; depressed.

spiri·tual /'spɪrɪtʃʊəl/ *adj* **1** of the spirit(1) or soul; of religion, not of material things; of, from, God; *concerned about one's ~ welfare.* **2** of spirits(2); supernatural. **3** caring much for things of the spirit(1). **4** of the church; *lords ~,* (GB) bishops and archbishops in the House of Lords. □ *n* [C] *Negro ~,* religious song as sung by Negroes in the US. **~ly** /-tʃʊlɪ/ *adv* **~·ity** /'spɪrɪtʃʊ'ælətɪ/ *n* [U] ~ quality; devotion to ~ things.

spiri·tu·al·ism /'spɪrɪtʃʊlɪzm/ *n* [U] belief in the possibility of receiving messages from the spirits of the dead; practice of attempting to do this. **spiri·tu·al·ist** /-ɪst/ *n* believer in ~. **spiri·tu·al·is·tic** /'spɪrɪtʃʊ'lɪstɪk/ *adj* of ~ or spiritualists.

spiri·tu·al·ize /'spɪrɪtʃʊlaɪz/ *vt* [VP6A] make pure or spiritual. **spiri·tu·al·iz·ation** /'spɪrɪtʃʊlaɪ'zeɪʃn *US:* -lɪ'z-/ *n* [U].

spiri·tu·elle /'spɪrɪtju'el/ *adj* (of women) showing, marked by, refinement, grace and wit.

spiri·tu·ous /'spɪrɪtjʊəs *US:* -tʃʊəs/ *adj* (of liquids) containing alcohol: *~ liquors,* distilled liquors such as whisky, not (usu) fermented liquors such as beer.

spirt /spɜt/ *vi* [VP2C,2A], *n* = **spurt**.

spit[1] /spɪt/ *n* **1** long thin metal spike to which meat, etc is secured for roasting. **2** small, narrow point of land running out into a body of water. □ *vt* (-pp-) put a ~ through (a chicken, piece of meat, etc); pierce with the point of a sword, spear, etc.

spit[2] /spɪt/ *vt,vi* (*pt,pp* spat /spæt/; -tt-) **1** [VP2A,C,3A] ***~ at/(up)on sb/sth,*** send liquid (saliva) out from the mouth; do this as a sign of contempt or hatred: *If you ~ in a London bus you may be fined £5. He spat in the man's face/spat at him. The cat spat* (= made an angry or hostile ~ting noise) *at the dog.* **2** [VP6A,15B] ***~ sth (out),*** send out from the mouth; (fig) utter angrily or sharply: *The baby spat out the nasty pill. After the tooth had been extracted the boy spat a lot of blood. She spat (out) curses at me.* ***~ it out,*** (colloq) say what you have to say, quickly. **3** [VP2A,6A] (of a fire, candle, gun, etc) throw out; make the noise of ~ting: *The engine was ~ting. The guns were ~ting fire.* **'~·fire** *n* hot-tempered person. **4** [VP2A] (of rain or snow) fall lightly: *It's not raining heavily, only ~ting.* □ *n* **1** [U] spittle (the more usu word). **2** act of ~ting. ***~ and polish,*** the cleaning and polishing of equipment (by soldiers, etc). **3** ***the dead ~ of; the ~ and image of*** /'spɪt n 'ɪmɪdʒ/, ***the ~ting image of,*** exact counterpart or likeness of; *He's the dead ~/the ~ting image of his father.* **4** frothy secretion of some insects (seen on plants, etc).

spit[3] /spɪt/ *n* spade's depth: *Dig the patch two ~(s) deep.*

spite /spaɪt/ *n* **1** [U] ill will; desire to cause pain or damage: *do sth out of/from ~.* **2** (with *indef art*) grudge: *have a ~ against sb; do sth to satisfy a private ~.* **3** (*prep* phrase) ***in ~ of,*** not to be prevented by; notwithstanding: *They went out in ~ of the rain. In ~ of all his efforts he failed.* □ *vt* [VP6A] injure or annoy because of ~: *The neighbours let their radio blare every afternoon just to ~ us.* **~·ful** /-fl/ *adj* having, showing, ~. **~·fully** /-flɪ/ *adv* **~·ful·ness** *n*

spittle /'spɪtl/ *n* [U] liquid of the mouth; saliva; spit(4).

spit·toon /spɪ'tun/ *n* pot or other container to spit into.

spiv /spɪv/ *n* (GB sl) person not in regular employment but who makes money by dubious business methods, e g on the black market in wartime, and who goes about smartly dressed and having a good time.

splash /splæʃ/ *vt,vi* **1** [VP6A,15B,14] ***~ sth about on/over sth, ~ sth/sb with sth,*** cause (a liquid) to fly about in drops; make (sb or sth) wet: *~ water on/over the floor; ~ the floor with water; ~ water about. The children love to ~ water over one another.* **2** [VP2A] (of a liquid) fly about and fall in drops: *fountains ~ing in the park. This tap is a bad one—it ~es.* **3** [VP2C] move, fall, so that there is ~ing: *We ~ed (our way) across the stream/into the lake, etc. Look at that fish ~ing about in the river. The spacecraft ~ed down in the Pacific.* Hence, **'~-down** *n* landing of a spacecraft in the sea. **4** ***~ one's money about,*** (sl) spend it freely in order to impress people. □ *n* [C] **1** (sound, spot, mark, made by) ~ing: *He jumped into the swimming pool with a ~. There are some ~es of mud on your trousers.* **2** patch of colour: *Her dog is brown with white ~es.* **3** (colloq) small quantity of soda-water: *a whisky and ~.* **4** ***make a ~,*** (colloq, fig) attract attention by making a display of (esp) one's wealth.

splay /spleɪ/ *vt,vi* make opposite sides (of an opening) diverge; cause to slant or slope: *a ~ed window,* e g one in a very thick wall, so that the opening in the wall is wider on one side than the other; (of an opening) be constructed in this way. *The plumber ~ed the end of the pipe before fitting it over the next section.* □ *n* sloping side of a window opening, etc. □ *adj* (esp of feet) broad, flat and turned outwards. **'~-foot** *n* Hence, **'~-footed,** having ~ feet.

spleen /splin/ *n* **1** [C] bodily organ in the abdomen which causes changes in the blood. ⇨ the illus at **alimentary**. **2** [U] lowness of spirits; bad temper: *in a fit of ~; vent one's ~ on sb.*

splen·did /ˈsplendɪd/ *adj* **1** magnificent: *a ~ sunset/house/victory; ~ jewellery.* **2** (colloq) very satisfactory; excellent: *a ~ dinner/idea.* **~·ly** *adv*

splen·dif·er·ous /splenˈdɪfərəs/ *adj* (colloq, often hum or ironic) splendid.

splen·dour (US = **-dor**) /ˈsplendə(r)/ *n* **1** [U] magnificence; brightness; *the ~ of the royal jewels.* **2** (sometimes *pl*) grandeur, glory.

sple·netic /splɪˈnetɪk/ *adj* ill-tempered; peevish.

splice /splɑɪs/ *vt* [VP6A] **1** join (two ends of rope) by weaving the strands of one into the strands of the other; join (two pieces of wood, magnetic tape, film) by fastening them at the ends. **2** ***get ~d,*** (sl) get married. □ *n* joint made by splicing. **splicer** *n* device for joining two pieces of paper or magnetic tape, film, etc.

splint /splɪnt/ *n* strip of wood, etc bound to an arm, leg, etc to keep a broken bone in the right position: *put an arm/a limb in ~s.*

splin·ter /ˈsplɪntə(r)/ *n* sharp-pointed or sharp-edged bit of hard material (wood, metal, glass, etc) split, torn or broken off a larger piece: *get a ~ into one's finger.* **a ˈ~ group/party,** (in politics) group of persons who have broken off from their party. **ˈ~-proof** *adj* (e g of glass) giving protection against ~s, e g of broken glass, or from a bomb. □ *vt,vi* [VP2C,15B] **~ *(off),*** break into ~s; come off as a ~. **~y** *adj* apt to ~; full of ~s; like ~s.

split /splɪt/ *vt,vi* (*pt,pp* **split**; -tt-) **1** [VP6A,14, 2A,C] **~ *sth (into),*** break, cause to break, be broken, into two or more parts, esp from end to end along the line of natural division: *~ting logs. Some kinds of wood ~ easily. Only a skilled workman can ~ slate into layers.* **2** [VP2D,22] **~ *(open),*** break open by bursting: *His coat has ~ at the seams.* **3** [VP6A,15A,B,2A,C] **~ *(sth) (up) (into),*** (cause to) break into parts; divide: *~ the atom; ~ (up) a compound into its parts. The party ~ up into small groups. Let's ~,* (mod colloq) leave (a party, etc). *Let's ~ the cost of the dinner party,* share it. **~ *the difference,*** (when making a bargain) compromise (on the price, cost, etc). ***a ~ting headache,*** so severe that it feels that one's head may crack. **~ *hairs,*** make very fine distinctions (in an argument, etc). Hence, **ˈhair-~ting** *adj* **~ *an infinitive,*** place an adverb between *to* and the infinitive (as in '*to quickly read a book*'). **~ level** *adj* (of houses, housing) in which adjoining rooms are in a level midway between successive storeys of other parts. **a ~ mind/personality,** ⇨ **schizophrenia**: *He has a ~ personality* (as in *Jekyll and Hyde*). **~ peas,** dried peas ~ into halves. **a ~ ring,** one split along its length, as used for keeping keys on. **a ~ second,** a brief instant of time. **~ *one's sides (with laughter),*** laugh with movements of the sides. Hence, **ˈside-~ting** *adj.* **4** [VP2A,3A] **~ *(on sb),*** (sl) give away the secret of (usu an accomplice); give information about him (to his disadvantage. □ *n* [C] **1** splitting; crack or tear made by splitting: *a ~ in a bag. Will you sew up this ~ in the seat of my trousers, please?* **2** separation or division resulting from splitting: *a ~ in the Labour Party.* **3** (colloq) half-bottle of soda water, etc. **4 the ~s,** acrobat's feat of sinking to the floor by extending the legs laterally with the trunk upright: *do the ~s.*

splosh /splɒʃ/ *vt* = **splash(4)**.

splotch /splɒtʃ/, **splodge** /splɒdʒ/ *nn* [C] daub or smear (of ink, dirt, etc); irregular patch (of colour, light, etc).

splurge /splɜdʒ/ *vi, n* (colloq) (make a) noisy display or effort (intended to attract attention); show off.

splut·ter /ˈsplʌtə(r)/ *vi,vt* **1** [VP2A,C] speak quickly and confusedly (from excitement, etc). **2** [VP6A,15B] **~ *sth (out),*** say quickly, confusedly, indistinctly; *~ out a few words/a threat.* **3** [VP2A] sound; sputter(1): *The swimmers dived and came ~ing to the surface.* □ *n* [U] ~ing sound.

Spode /spəʊd/ *n* [U] type of English porcelain.

spoil /spɔɪl/ *vt,vi* (*pt,pp* ~t or ~ed) **1** [VP6A] make useless or unsatisfactory: *fruit ~t by insects; holidays ~t by bad weather; ~t ballot papers,* made invalid because the voters have not marked them as required by regulations. *Don't ~ your appetite by eating sweets just before dinner.* **ˈ~-sport** *n* person who does things that interfere with the enjoyment of other people. **2** [VP6A] harm the character or temperament of by wrong upbringing or lack of discipline: *parents who ~ their children; a ~t child of fortune,* e g a person whose life has always been easy. **3** [VP6A] pay great attention to the comfort and wishes of: *He likes having a wife who ~s him.* **4** [VP2A] (of food, etc) become bad, unfit for use: *Some kinds of food soon ~.* **5 be ~ing for** (*a fight,* etc), be eager for. **6** [VP6A,14] **~ *sb (of sth),*** (old use, or liter; *pt,pp* always ~ed, never ~t) plunder, rob by force or stealth: *financiers who ~ed* (= despoiled) *widows of their money.* □ *n* **1** (either [U] or *pl*, not with numerals) stolen goods; plunder: *The thieves divided up the ~(s).* **2** (*pl*) profits, profitable positions, gained from political power: *the ~s of office; the ˈ~s system,* (in some countries) system by which positions in the public service (their salaries and other advantages) are given to supporters of the political party which wins power. **3** [U] earth, unwanted material, etc thrown or brought up in excavating, draining, etc.

spoke[1] /spəʊk/ *n* **1** any one of the bars or wire rods connecting the hub (centre) of a wheel with the rim (outer edge). ⇨ the illus at **bicycle**. ***put a ~ in sb's wheel,*** hinder him; prevent him from carrying out his plans. **2** rung of a ladder.

spoke[2], **spoken** /spəʊk, spəʊkən/ ⇨ **speak**.

spokes·man /ˈspəʊksmən/ *n* (*pl* -men) person speaking, chosen to speak, on behalf of a group.

spo·li·ation /ˈspəʊlɪˈeɪʃn/ *n* [U] plunder, esp of neutral merchant ships by countries at war.

spon·dee /ˈspɒndi/ *n* metrical foot of two long or stressed syllables, used in poetry to vary other metres. **spon·daic** /spɒnˈdeɪɪk/ *adj*

sponge /spʌndʒ/ *n* **1** [C] kinds of simple sea animal; its light structures of elastic material full of holes and able to absorb water easily; one of these, or sth of similar texture (e g porous rubber), used for washing, cleaning, etc. ***pass the ~ over,*** wipe out, agree to forget (an offence, etc). ***throw up/in the ~,*** admit defeat or failure. **2** piece of absorbent material, e g gauze, used in surgery; mop used in cleaning the bore of a gun, etc. **3** **ˈ~-cake** *n* soft, light yellow cake made of eggs, sugar and flour. □ *vt,vi* **1** [VP6A,15B] **~ *sth***

(out), wash, wipe or clean with a ~: *~ a wound/ a child's face; ~ out a memory,* wipe it out, end it. **2** [VP15B] ***~ sth up,*** take up (liquid) with a ~: *~ up the mess.* **3** [VP3A] ***~ (up)on sb,*** (colloq) live at his expense, get money from him, without giving, or intending to give, anything in return: *~ (up)on one's friends;* [VP6A,14] ***~ sth (from sb),*** get by sponging: *~ a dinner; ~ a fiver* (= £5) *from an old acquaintance.* **sponger** *n* person who ~s(3). **spongy** *adj* (-ier, -iest) soft, porous and elastic like a ~: *spongy, moss-covered land.* **spongi·ness** *n*

spon·sor /ˈsponsə(r)/ *n* **1** person (e g a godfather) making himself responsible for another. **2** person who first puts forward or guarantees a proposal; person, firm, etc paying for a commercial radio or TV programme (usu in return for advertising of products). □ *vt* [VP6A] act as a ~ for.

spon·ta·neous /sponˈteɪnɪəs/ *adj* done, happening, from natural impulse, not caused or suggested by sth or sb outside: *He made a ~ offer of help. Nothing he says is ~—he thinks carefully before he speaks.* **~ combustion,** burning caused by chemical changes, etc inside the material, not by the application of fire from outside. **~·ly** *adv* **~-ness, spon·ta·neity** /ˌspontəˈniətɪ/ *nn*

spoof /spuf/ *vt, n* (sl) hoax; humbug; swindle: *You've been ~ed,* You've been 'had', hoaxed.

spook /spuk/ *n* (hum) ghost. **~y** *adj* (-ier, -iest) of, suggesting, ~s: *a ~y* (= haunted) *house.*

spool /spul/ *n* reel (for thread, wire, photographic film, typewriter ribbon, paper or magnetic tape, etc). ⇨ the illus at tape.

spoon[1] /spun/ *n* utensil with a shallow bowl on a handle, used for stirring, serving and taking up food; named according to use, as: *desˈsert-/ˈsoup-/ˈtable/ˈtea/ˈegg-~.* ***be born with a silver ~ in one's mouth,*** ⇨ silver(1). **ˈ~-feed** *vt* **(a)** feed (a baby, etc) from a ~. **(b)** (fig) give (sb) excessive help or teaching: *Some teachers ~-feed their pupils.* □ *vt* [VP15B] ***~ sth up/out,*** take with a ~: *~ up one's soup; ~ out the peas,* serve them. **ˈ~·ful** /-fʊl/ *n* (*pl* **~fuls**) as much as a ~ can hold.

spoon[2] /spun/ *vi* [VP2A] (hum) behave in a way that shows that one is in love: *young couples ~ing on park seats.* **~y** *adj: be ~y on sb.*

spoon·er·ism /ˈspunərɪzm/ *n* [C] confusion of two or more words by wrong placing of the initial sounds, e g *well-boiled icicle* for *well-oiled bicycle.*

spoor /spɔ(r)/ *n* [C] track or trail of a wild animal, enabling it to be followed.

spor·adic /spəˈrædɪk/ *adj* occurring, seen, only here and there or occasionally: *~ raids/firing.* **spor·adi·cally** /-klɪ/ *adv*

spore /spɔ(r)/ *n* [C] germ, single cell, by which a flowerless plant (e g moss, a fern) reproduces itself.

spor·ran /ˈsporən/ *n* pouch, usu fur-covered, worn by Scottish Highlanders in front of the kilt. ⇨ the illus as kilt.

sport /spɔt/ *n* **1** [U] amusement, fun: *say sth in ~,* not seriously; *make ~ of sb,* make him seem ridiculous; *be the ~ of Fortune,* be treated by Fortune as a plaything. **2** [U] activity engaged in, esp outdoors, for amusement and exercise; ⇨ the illus at base, cricket, football, Rugby, tennis; [C] particular form of such activity: *fond of/devoted to ~; country ~s,* e g hunting, fishing, shooting, horse-racing; *athletic ~s,* e g running, jumping; *ˈ~s coverage/reporting on TV.* **3** (*pl*) meeting for athletic contests: *the school ~s; inter-university ~s.* **4** (compounds, etc) **ˈ~s-car** *n* small motor-car designed for high speeds. **ˈ~s-coat/-jacket,** loose-fitting coat. **ˈ~s-editor** *n* newspaper editor responsible for reports of ~s and games. **ˈ~s·man** /-mən/ *n* (*pl* -men) **(a)** person who takes part in, is fond of, ~. **(b)** (also ~) person who plays fairly, who is willing to take risks, and is not down-hearted if he loses: *He's a good ~. Come, be a ~.* Hence, **ˈ~s·man·ship** /-ʃɪp/ *n* **ˈ~s·man·like** *adj* **5** (colloq) = ~sman: *be ~smanlike,* be a good fellow. **6** [C] plant or animal that deviates in a striking way from the normal type. □ *vi,vt* **1** [VP2C] play about, amuse oneself: *seals ~ing about in the water.* **2** [VP6A] (colloq) have or wear for proud display: *~ a moustache/a diamond ring/a flower in the buttonhole of one's jacket.* **~·ing** *adj* **1** connected with ~, interested in ~: *a ~ing man; a ~ing parson,* e g in former times, one very fond of fox-hunting. **2** willing to take a risk of losing; involving a risk of losing: *make sb a ~ing offer; give sb a ~ing chance. It's very ~ing of you to give me such an advantage.* **~·ing·ly** *adv*

sport·ive /ˈspɔtɪv/ *adj* playful; merry. **~·ly** *adv* **~·ness** *n*

spot /spot/ *n* **1** small (esp round) mark different in colour from what it is on: *white dress material with red ~s. Which has ~s, the leopard or the tiger?* **2** dirty mark or stain: *~s of mud on your boots.* **3** small, red place, blemish, on the skin: *This ointment won't clear your face of ~s.* **4** (fig) moral blemish: *There isn't a ~ an her reputation.* **5** drop: *Did you feel a few ~s of rain?* **6** particular place or area: *the (very) ~ where he was murdered.* **TV/radio ~,** place in a TV/radio programme for an item or a commercial advertisement. ⇨ slot(3). **7** (phrases) **a ~ check,** a quickly-made investigation, esp one made suddenly and without warning. **a tender ~,** (fig) a subject on which a person's feelings are easily hurt. ***in a ~,*** (colloq) in a difficult situation. ***knock ~s off sb,*** easily surpass, do better than, him. ***on the ~,*** **(a)** at the place where one is needed: *The police were on the ~ within a few minutes of hearing about the crime.* **(b)** then and there; immediately: *He fell dead on the ~. The bullet struck his head and he was killed on the ~.* **(c)** (sl) in trouble. Cf 'on the carpet'. ***the person on the ~,*** the man at the place in question (who, presumably, is acquainted with local conditions, happenings, etc and able to deal with them): *Let's leave the decision to the man/the men/the people on the ~.* ***put sb on the ~,*** **(a)** place sb in danger or difficulty: *You've put me on the ~ here: I can't answer your question.* **(b)** (of gangsters) decide to kill (e g a rival gangster). ***find/put one's finger on sb's weak ~,*** find/locate the point (of character, etc) where he is most open to attack. **8** (comm) **~ cash,** payment on delivery of goods. **~ prices,** prices quoted for such payment. **9** (GB colloq) small quantity of anything: *I need a ~ of brandy. What about doing a ~ of work? He's having a ~ of bother with his brother,* a quarrel. □ *vt,vi* (-tt-) **1** [VP6A,2A] mark, become marked, with ~s: *a table ~ted with ink; material that ~s easily,* easily becomes ~ted. **2** [VP6A] pick out, recognize, see (one person or thing out of many):

~ *a friend in a crowd;* ~ *the winner in a race,* pick out the winner before the start. **3** [VP2A] (colloq) rain slightly: *It's beginning to* ~/*is* ~*ting with rain.* **~·ted** *adj* marked with ~s, e g of such animals as the leopard and panther, and of birds with ~s of different colour on their plumage, of textile material with ~s. **'~·ted 'fever** *n* form of meningitis; form of typhus. **~·less** *adj* free from ~s; clean: *a* ~*less kitchen/reputation.* **~·less·ly** *adv*: ~*lessly clean.* **~ty** *adj* (-ier, -iest) **1** marked with ~s (esp on the skin): *a* ~*ty complexion; windows that are* ~*ty with fly marks.* **2** of varying quality: *a* ~*ty piece of work,* done unevenly. **~·ter** *n* person who ~s(2), e g *'aircraft-*~*ter,* person who, e g during a war, looks for and identifies different types of aircraft; *'train-*~*ter,* (usu) schoolboy who looks for and notes different types of railway-engines.

spot·light /'spɒtlaɪt/ *n* [C] (projector or lamp used for sending a) strong light directed on to a particular place or person, e g on the stage of a theatre: *He likes to be in the/to hold the* ~, (fig) be the centre of attention. □ *vt* [VP6A] direct a ~ on to.

spouse /spaʊz *US:* spaʊs/ *n* (legal or archaic) husband or wife.

spout /spaʊt/ *n* [C] **1** pipe or lip through or from which liquid pours, e g for carrying rain-water from a roof, or tea from a teapot. **2** stream of liquid coming out with great force. ⇨ *water-*~ at **water**[1](7). **3** *up the* ~, (sl) **(a)** in pawn. **(b)** in difficulties, broken, etc according to context. **(c)** pregnant. □ *vt,vi* **1** [VP2A,C,6A] (of liquid) come or send out with great force: *water* ~*ing (out) from a broken water-main; blood* ~*ing from a severed artery; a broken pipe* ~*ing water. The whales were* ~*ing,* sending up jets of water. **2** [VP2A,6A] (colloq) speak, recite (verses, etc) pompously: ~*ing Latin verses.*

sprain /spreɪn/ *vt* [VP6A] injure (a joint, e g in the wrist or ankle) by twisting violently so that there is pain and swelling: ~ *one's wrist; suffering from a* ~*ed ankle.* □ *n* [C] injury so caused.

sprang /spræŋ/ *pt* of **spring**[3].

sprat /spræt/ *n* small European sea-fish used as food.

sprawl /sprɔl/ *vi* **1** [VP2A,C] sit or lie with the arms and legs loosely spread out; fall so that one lies in this way: ~*ing on the sofa; be sent* ~*ing in the mud.* **2** (of plants, handwriting, fig of large towns) spread out loosely and irregularly over much space: *suburbs that* ~ *out into the countryside.* □ *n* ~ing position or movement; widespread untidy area, esp of buildings: *London's suburban* ~.

spray[1] /spreɪ/ *n* small branch of a tree or plant, esp a graceful one with leaves and flowers as an ornament; artificial ornament in a similar form: *a* ~ *of diamonds.*

spray[2] /spreɪ/ *n* **1** [U] liquid sent through the air in tiny drops (by the wind, or through an apparatus): *'sea-*~, ~ blown from waves; *the* ~ *of a waterfall.* **2** [C,U] kinds of liquid preparation, e g a perfume, disinfectant or insecticide, to be applied in the form of ~ through an atomizer or other apparatus. **3** [C] atomizer, etc used for applying such a liquid. **'~-gun** *n* apparatus using pressure to spread cellulose, paint, varnish, etc over surfaces. □ *vt* [VP6A,14] **~ *sth/sb (with sth),* ~ *sth (on sth/sb),*** scatter ~ on: ~ *mosquitoes/fruit-trees;* ~ *the enemy with bullets.* **~er** *n* **1** person who ~s. **2** apparatus for ~ing.

spread /spred/ *vt,vi* (*pt,pp* ~) **1** [VP6A,14,15B] ***~ sth on/over sth; ~ sth with sth; ~ (sth) out,*** extend the surface or width of sth by unfolding or unrolling it; cover (sth) by doing this: ~ *a cloth on a table/a table with a cloth;* ~ *out a map;* ~ *(out) one's arms. The bird* ~ *its wings.* **2** [VP14,15B] ***~ sth on sth, ~ sth with sth,*** put (a substance) on a surface and extend its area by flattening, etc; cover (a surface) by doing this: ~ *butter on bread/a slice of bread with butter.* ***~ the table,*** place dishes, glasses, food, etc on it ready for a meal. **3** [VP6A,15A,B,2A,C] (cause to) become more widely extended or distributed: ~ *knowledge. Flies* ~ *disease. The water* ~ *over the floor. The rumour quickly* ~ *through the village. The fire* ~ *from the factory to the houses near by.* ***~ oneself,*** **(a)** occupy much space, e g by lying with the limbs extended. **(b)** talk or write at length (on a subject). **(c)** let oneself go, e g by being generous in hospitality. **4** [VP2A,B,C] show an extended surface: *a desert* ~*ing for hundreds of miles.* **5** [VP6A,15B] extend in time: *a course of studies* ~ *over three years; instalments/payments* ~ *over twelve months.* **6** **'~·eagle** *n* figure of an eagle with the legs and wings extended (as seen on coins). □ *vt* (reflex) take up a lying position with arms and legs extended to form a cross: *sunbathers* ~*eagled on the grass/sands.* **'~-over** *n* arrangement in an industry by which hours of work are adjusted to special needs. □ *n* (rarely *pl*) **1** extent; breadth: *the* ~ *of a bird's wings.* **2** extension; spreading(3): *the* ~ *of disease/knowledge/education.* **3** (colloq) table ~ with good things to eat and drink: *What a* ~*!* **4** sth that is ~(1) (usu in compounds) *a 'bed*~, a cover ~ over the bed-clothes. *He's developing (a) middle-age* ~, (colloq) is getting big round the waist (as some persons do in middle age). **5** name used for various kinds of paste (to be) ~ on bread, etc. **~er** *n* one who, that which, ~s, e g a *'flame-*~*er* in an oil-stove; an implement used for ~ing paste, etc on bread.

spree /spri/ *n* lively frolic: *have a* ~, have a lively, merry time. ***be on the ~, go out on a ~,*** be having, go out to enjoy, a ~. **a 'spending/'buying ~,** an occasion of (extravagant or unusual) spending of money.

sprig /sprɪg/ *n* **1** small twig (*of* a plant or bush) with leaves, etc: *a* ~ *of mistletoe for Christmas.* **2** (usu contemptuous) youth: *a* ~ *of the nobility.* **~·ged** *adj* ornamented with designs of ~s: ~ged muslin.

spright·ly /'spraɪtlɪ/ *adj* (-ier, -iest) lively; brisk. **spright·li·ness** *n*

spring[1] /sprɪŋ/ *n* **1** act of springing or jumping up. **2** (place where there is) water coming up from the ground: *'hot-*~*; 'mineral-*~*; a hot-'*~ *resort;* (attrib) ~ *water.* **3** device of twisted, bent or coiled metal or wire which tends to return to its shape or position when pulled or pushed or pressed: *the* ~*s of a motor-car; the* ~ *of a watch.* **'~-'balance** *n* device that measures weight by the tension of a ~. **'~-board** *n* board to give a ~ing motion to sb jumping from it. **'~-gun** *n* one that goes off when a trespasser comes against a wire which is attached to the trigger. **'~-'mattress** *n* one containing spiral ~s in a rigid frame. **~ tide** *n* (two words; ⇨ ~*tide,* ~*time* at **spring**[2]) tide with the greatest rise or fall, occurring shortly after new and full moon in each month; ⇨ *neap-tide* at neap. **4** [U] elastic quality: *rubber bands that have lost their ~. The old man's muscles have lost their ~.* **5** (often *pl*) cause or origin: *the ~s of human conduct.* **~·less** *adj* without ~s(3): *a ~less cart.* **~y** *adj* (-ier, -iest) (of movement or substances) elastic; that springs: *walk with a youthful ~y step.*

spring² /sprɪŋ/ *n* season of the year in which vegetation begins; season between winter and summer (in GB from about 21 March to 22 June): *in (the) ~;* (attrib) *~ flowers/weather.* **ˈ~·time** (also, poet **ˈ~·tide**) *nn* season of ~. **ˈ~-ˈclean** *vt* clean (a house, a room) thoroughly. Hence, **ˈ~-ˈcleaning** *n* **ˈ~·like** *adj*: *~like weather.*

spring³ /sprɪŋ/ *vi,vt* (*pt* sprang /spræŋ/, *pp* sprung /sprʌŋ/) **1** [VP2C] jump suddenly from the ground; move suddenly (*up, down, out,* etc) from rest, concealment, etc: *He sprang to his feet/sprang out of bed/sprang forward to help me/sprang up from his seat. The branch sprang back and hit me in the face.* **2** [VP2C] **~ *(up),*** appear; grow up quickly from the ground or from a stem: *A breeze has sprung up. Weeds were ~ing up everywhere. The wheat is beginning to ~ up.* (fig) *A suspicion/doubt sprang up in her mind.* **3** [VP3A] **~ *from,*** arise or come from: *He is sprung from royal blood,* is of royal ancestry. *Where have you sprung from,* suddenly and unexpectedly appeared from? **4** [VP14] **~ *sth on sb,*** bring forward suddenly: *~ a surprise on sb; ~ a new theory/proposal on sb.* **5** [VP6A] cause to operate by means of a mechanism: *~ a mine,* cause it to explode; *~ a trap,* cause it to go off. **6** [VP6A,2A] (of wood) (cause to) warp, split, crack: *My cricket bat has sprung. I have sprung my tennis racket.* **~ *a leak,*** (of a ship) crack or burst so that water enters.

spring·bok /ˈsprɪŋbok/ *n* small S. African gazelle.

sprinkle /ˈsprɪŋkl/ *vt* [VP6A,14] **~ *(sth on sth/ sth with sth),*** direct, throw, a shower of (sth) on to (a surface): *~ water on a dusty path; ~ a dusty path with water; ~ the floor with sand.* **sprink·ler** /ˈsprɪŋklə(r)/ *n* (esp) apparatus or device for sprinkling water (e g on to a lawn) or (permanently installed in buildings) for fighting fire. **sprink·ling** *n* small quantity or number here and there: *There was a sprinkling of young people in the congregation.*

sprint /sprɪnt/ *vi* [VP2A,C] run a short distance at full speed: *He ~ed past his competitors just before reaching the tape.* □ *n* such a run; (esp) burst of speed at the end of a race. **~er** *n*

sprit /sprɪt/ *n* small spar reaching from a mast to the upper outer corner of a sail. ⇨ the illus at barque. **ˈ~·sail** *n* sail extended by a ~.

sprite /sprɑɪt/ *n* fairy; elf.

sprocket /ˈsprokɪt/ *n* each of several teeth on a wheel connecting with the links of a chain or holes in a movie film, paper or magnetic tape. **ˈ~-wheel** *n* such a wheel, e g as on a bicycle.

sprout /sprɑʊt/ *vi,vt* **1** [VP2A,C] **~ *(up),*** put out leaves; begin to grow: *Peter has really ~ed up in the past year.* **2** [VP6A] cause to grow: *The continuous wet weather has ~ed the barley,* e g after it has been cut and left in the field. **3** [VP6A] develop, produce: *When do deer first ~ horns? Tom has ~ed a moustache.* □ *n* [C] shoot, newly ~ed part, of a plant. ⇨ Brussels ~s.

spruce¹ /sprus/ *adj* neat and smart in dress and appearance. □ *vt,vi* [VP6A,15B,2C] **~ *sb/oneself (up),*** make oneself ~: *Go and ~ yourself up. They were all ~d up for the party.* **~·ly** *adv* **~·ness** *n*

spruce² /sprus/ *n* **~ (fir),** kinds of fir-tree grown in plantations for its wood, used for making paper.

sprung /sprʌŋ/ *pp* of spring³.

spry /sprɑɪ/ *adj* (-er, -est) lively; nimble: *still ~ at eighty.* ***look ~,*** be quick.

spud /spʌd/ *n* [C] **1** (colloq) potato. **2** short spade with a narrow blade for digging or cutting up weeds.

spue /spju/ *vt,vi* = spew.

spume /spjum/ *n* [U] foam; froth.

spun /spʌn/ *pp* of spin.

spunk /spʌŋk/ *n* [U] (colloq) courage; mettle; spirit: *Have no ~; a boy with plenty of ~.* **~y** *adj* having ~.

spur /spɜ(r)/ *n* **1** one of a pair of sharp-toothed wheels, worn on the heels of a rider's boots and used to make the horse go faster. ***win one's ~s,*** (hist) gain knighthood; (fig) win honour and reputation. **2** (fig) sth that urges a person on to greater activity: *the ~ of poverty.* ***act on the ~ of the moment,*** on a sudden impulse. **3** sharp, hard projection on a cock's leg. ⇨ the illus at bird. **4** ridge extending from a mountain or hill. □ *vt,vi* (-rr-) **1** [VP6A,15B] **~ *sb/sth (on),*** urge on with, or as with, ~s: *It's foolish to ~ on a willing horse. He was ~red on by ambition.* **2** [VP2C] ride fast or hard: *The rider ~red on/forward to his destination.*

spu·ri·ous /ˈspjʊərɪəs/ *adj* false; not genuine: *~ coins.* **~·ly** *adv* **~·ness** *n*

spurn /spɜn/ *vt* [VP6A] reject or refuse contemptuously; have nothing to do with (an offer, a person or his advances).

spurt /spɜt/ *vi* **1** [VP2C] **~ *(out) (from),*** (of liquids, flame, etc) come out in a sudden burst: *Blood ~ed (out) from the wound.* **2** [VP2A] make a sudden, short and violent effort, esp in a race or other contest: *The runner ~ed as he approached the winning-post.* □ *n* [C] sudden bursting forth; sudden burst of energy: *~s of water/flame/ energy; a ~ of anger; put on a ~* (= increase speed) *towards the end of a race.*

sput·nik /ˈspʊtnɪk/ *n* artificial unmanned satellite put into space by means of rocket propulsion (esp the first, launched from the Soviet Union in 1957).

sput·ter /ˈspʌtə(r)/ *vi,vt* **1** [VP2A,C] make a series of spitting sounds: *The sausages were ~ing in the frying-pan.* **~ *out,*** stop burning after making spitting sounds: *The candle ~ed out.* **2** = splutter(1,2).

spu·tum /ˈspjutəm/ *n* [U] saliva; matter coughed up from the throat (esp as indicating the nature of an illness).

spy /spɑɪ/ *n* (*pl* spies) **1** person who tries to get secret information, esp about the military affairs of other countries (called a 'secret agent' if he is employed by one's own government and a 'spy' if he is working for other countries). **2** person who keeps a secret watch on the movements of others: *police spies,* persons employed by the police to watch suspected criminals; *industrial spies,* employed to learn trade secrets, etc. □ *vi,vt* **1** [VP2A,C,3A] ***spy (up)on/into sth, spy sth out,*** act as a spy (up)on, watch secretly: *spy (up)on the enemy's movements; spy out the land; spy into other people's affairs.* **2** [VP6A,19A] observe; see;

discover: *I spy someone coming up the garden path. You are quick at spying her faults.* **ˈspy-glass** *n* small telescope. **ˈspy-hole** *n* peep-hole.

squab /skwob/ *n* **1** young bird, esp an unfledged pigeon: *~ pie*, pigeon pie. **2** (comm) soft seat or cushion, esp as a seat in a car.

squabble /ˈskwobl/ *vi* [VP2C] engage in a petty or noisy quarrel: *Tom was squabbling with his sister about who should use the bicycle.* □ *n* [C] noisy quarrel about sth trivial.

squad /skwod/ *n* small group of persons, e g of soldiers, working or being trained together: *Scotland Yard's flying ~*, number of special police cars and men always ready for prompt action, e g on reports of burglaries, etc. **ˈ~ car,** (US) police patrol car.

squad·ron /ˈskwodrən/ *n* **1** sub-unit of a cavalry, armoured or engineer regiment (120—200 men). **2** number of warships or military aircraft forming a unit. **ˈ~-leader** *n* R A F rank. ⇨ App 9.

squalid /ˈskwolɪd/ *adj* dirty, mean, uncared for: *living in ~ conditions/houses.* **~·ly** *adv*

squall /skwɔl/ *n* [C] **1** loud cry of pain or fear (esp from a baby or child). **2** sudden violent wind, often with rain or snow: *look out for ~s*, (often fig) be on one's guard against danger or trouble. □ *vi* [VP2A] utter ~s(1): *~ing babies. The boy ~s as soon as he sees the dentist.* **~y** *adv* having, marked by, ~s(2): *a ~y April day.*

squalor /ˈskwolə(r)/ *n* [U] squalid state: *born in ~; the ~ of the slums.*

squan·der /ˈskwondə(r)/ *vt* [VP6A] waste (time, money). **ˈ~·mania** /-meɪnɪə/ *n* [U] (as used by critics of official spending) craze for extravagant spending of money.

square[1] /skweə(r)/ *adj* **1** having the shape of a square(1): *a ~ table.* ***a ~ peg in a round hole,*** ⇨ peg[1](1). **ˈ~ dance/game,** one in which the dancers/players face inwards from four sides. **2** having or forming (exactly or approx) a right angle: *~ corners; ~ brackets* (thus [ ]); *a ~ jaw/chin*, with angular, not curved, outlines. **ˈ~-ˈbuilt** *adj* (of a person) of comparatively broad shape. **ˈ~-ˈrigged** *adj* (of a sailing ship) having the principal sails set at right angles to the mast. Cf *fore-and-aft.* **ˈ~-ˈshouldered** *adj* with the shoulders at right angles to the neck, not sloping. **ˈ~-toed** *adj* (of shoes) having a ~ toe-cap; (fig, of persons) formal; prim. **ˈ~-ˈtoes** *n* formal or prim person. **3** level or parallel (*with*); balanced; settled: *get one's accounts ~*, settled. ***be (all) ~,*** **(a)** (golf) have equal scores: *all ~ at the ninth hole.* **(b)** neither in debt to the other: *Let's call it all ~, shall we?* ***get ~ with sb,*** settle accounts; (fig) have one's revenge on him. **4** connected with a number multiplied by itself: *a ~ metre*, an area equal to that of a ~ surface which has sides of one metre: *nine ~ cm. The ~ root of* x^4 *is* x^2*/of 9 is 3. A carpet 6 metres ~ has an area of 36 ~ metres.* **~ measure,** expressed in ~ feet, metres, etc. **5** thorough; uncompromising: *meet with a ~ refusal.* **a ~ meal,** one that is satisfactory because there is plenty of good food. **6** fair, honest: *~ dealings*, in business; *play a ~ game*, in sport. ***(get/give sb) a ~ deal,*** a fair bargain, equality of opportunity. **7 ~ leg,** ⇨ the illus at cricket. □ *adv* **1** in a ~(2) manner: *stand/sit ~; hit a man ~ on the jaw.* **2** ***fair and ~,*** in a ~(6) manner. **~·ly** *adv* **1** so as to form a right angle. **2** fairly; honestly: *act ~ly* **3** directly opposite: *He faced me ~ly across the table.* **~·ness** *n*

square[2] /skweə(r)/ *n* [C] **1** plane figure with four equal sides and four right angles (□). ⇨ the illus at quadrilateral. ***back to ~ one,*** (from the use of ~s on board games, played by throwing dice, and with penalties for certain numbered ~s) back to the starting-point and forced to start again. **2** anything having the shape of a ~. **3** four-sided open area, e g in a town, used as a garden or for recreation, or one enclosed by streets and buildings: *listening to the band playing in the ~*, e g in any town in Mexico. **ˈbarrack ~** *n* such an open space in a military barracks. **ˈ~-bashing** (sl) military drill (esp marching, etc). **4** buildings and streets surrounding a ~(4): *He lives at No 95 Russell S~.* **5** block of buildings bounded by four streets; distance along one side of such a block (*block* being more usu, esp US). **6** result when a number or quantity is multiplied by itself: *The ~ of 7 is 49. What is the ~ of* x^2*?* **7** L-shaped or (**ˈT-~**) T-shaped instrument for drawing or testing right angles. ***out of ~,*** not at right angles. **8** ***on the ~,*** fair(ly), honest(ly): *Can we trust them to act on the ~? Is their business on the ~?* **9** body of infantry drawn up in a ~ form. **10 ˈword ~,** number of words arranged so that they read alike forwards and downwards. **11** (sl) person (considered to be) out of touch with new ideas, styles, etc: *I'm not even a ~, I'm a 'cube'!* I'm rigidly conventional and old-fashioned.

square[3] /skweə(r)/ *vt,vi* **1** [VP6A] make square; give a square shape to: ***~ the circle,*** attempt sth that is impossible. **2** [VP6A] cause one line or side to make a right angle with another: *~ timber*, give it rectangular edges. **3** [VP6A] make straight or level: *~ one's shoulders.* **4** [VP6A] multiply a number by itself; get the square(6) of a number: *Three ~ed is nine.* **5** [VP6A,15B] ***~ sth off,*** mark (off) in squares. **6** [VP2C,15B] ***~ (up) (with sb),*** settle, balance (accounts): *~ accounts with sb*, settle one's debts; (fig) have one's revenge on him. *It's time I ~ed up with you/time we ~ed up*, settled our accounts. **7** [VP6A] bribe; get the (dishonest) connivance of: *All the officials had to be ~ed before they would do anything for us. He has been ~ed to hold his tongue.* **8** [VP14,3A] ***~ (sth) with,*** make or be consistent: *You should ~ your practice with your principles. It would be convenient if the facts ~ed with the theory, but they do not.* **9** [VP2C] ***~ up to sb,*** take up the attitude of a boxer (ready to begin fighting).

squash[1] /skwoʃ/ *vt,vi* **1** [VP6A,15A,B,22] crush; press flat or into a small space: *~ too many people into a bus. Don't sit on my hat; you'll ~ it flat.* **2** [VP2A] become ~ed or pressed out of shape: *Soft fruits ~ easily.* **3** [VP2C] squeeze or crowd: *Don't all try to ~ into the lift together. They ~ed through the gate into the football ground.* **4** [VP6A] (colloq) silence (sb) with a crushing retort; snub. *He was/felt completely ~ed.* **5** [VP6A] (colloq) subdue (a rebellion). □ *n* (rarely *pl*) **1** crowd of persons ~ed together: *There was a frightful ~ at the gate.* **2** (sound of) sth ~ing or being ~ed: *The ripe tomato hit the speaker in the face with a ~.* **3** (now rare, **ˈ~-ˈhat**), hat made of soft felt. **4** [C,U] drink (cold, usu bottled) made from fruit juice: *ˈorange/ˈlemon ~.* **5 ˈ~(-rackets),** game played with rackets and a rubber ball in a walled court. **~y** *adj* easily ~ed; soft and wet.

squash[2] /skwoʃ/ *n* (*pl* unchanged) kinds of gourd,

like a pumpkin, eaten as a vegetable.

squat /skwot/ *vi* (-tt-) **1** [VP2A,C] sit on one's heels, or on the ground with the legs drawn up under or close to the body; [VP6A,15B] put (oneself) in this position: *The old man* ~*ted in front of the fire. He* ~*ted (himself) down.* **2** [VP2A,C] (of animals) crouch with the body close to the ground. **3** [VP2A,C] (colloq) sit: *Find somewhere to* ~. **4** [VP2A] settle on land without permission, esp publicly owned and unoccupied land (in order to acquire ownership); occupy empty (usu deserted, derelict) buildings without authority. □ *adj* short and thick: *a* ~ *man;* dumpy: *a* ~ *teapot.* **~·ter** *n* **1** person who ~s(4); (in Australia) sheep-farmer. **2** person who takes unauthorized possession of unoccupied premises.

squaw /skwɔ/ *n* N American Indian woman or wife.

squawk /skwɔk/ *vi* [VP2A,C], *n* (chiefly of birds) (utter a) loud, harsh cry, as when hurt or frightened; (colloq) (make a) loud complaint; (sl) betray: *The old man* ~*ed (to the police).* **~er** *n*

squeak /skwik/ *n* [C] **1** short, shrill cry, e g made by a mouse, or similar sound, e g from an unoiled hinge. **2** ***a narrow*** **~,** a narrow escape from danger or failure. □ *vi,vt* **1** [VP2A] make a ~: *These new shoes* ~. **2** [VP6A,15B] **~ *sth (out),*** utter in a ~ing voice: ~ *out a few frightened words.* **3** [VP2A] (colloq) become an informer. **~er** *n* (colloq) informer. **~y** *adj* (-ier, -iest) ~ing: *a* ~*y floor; in a* ~*y voice.*

squeal /skwil/ *n* [C] shrill cry or sound, longer and louder than a squeak, often indicating terror or pain: *the* ~ *of brakes,* e g on lorries. □ *vi,vt* **1** [VP2A,C] make a ~: *The pigs were* ~*ing. He* ~*ed like a pig.* **2** [VP6A,15B] utter with a ~; say in a ~ing voice. **3** [VP2A,C] (colloq) become an informer. **~er** *n* **1** animal that ~s. **2** informer.

squeam·ish /ˈskwimɪʃ/ *adj* **1** having a delicate stomach and easily made sick; feeling sick. **2** easily disgusted or offended; too modest, scrupulous or proper. **~·ly** *adv* **~·ness** *n*

squee·gee /ˈskwiˋdʒi *US:* ˋskwidʒi/ *n* implement with a rubber edge, fastened to a long handle, used for pushing water, etc off a smooth surface; similar implement with a short rubber roller for pressing water from photographic prints. □ *vt* [VP6A] use a ~ on.

squeeze /skwiz/ *vt,vi* **1** [VP6A,15A,22] press on from the opposite side or from all sides; change the shape, size, etc of sth by doing this: ~ *sb's hand;* ~ *a sponge;* ~ *a lemon dry;* ~ *one's fingers,* e g by catching them in a doorway; ~ *paste into a ball.* **2** [VP6A,14,15A,B] **~ *sth (from/out of),*** get (water, juice, etc) out of sth by pressing hard; ~ *(the juice out of) a lemon;* ~ *the water out.* **3** [VP15A,B,2C] force (sb, oneself) into or through a narrow passage or small space: ~ *(one's way) into a crowded bus;* ~ *(oneself) through a gap in a hedge:* ~ *(one's way) through a crowd. Can you* ~ *in,* e g into a crowded lift? **4** [VP15B] **~ *sth out of,*** get by extortion, entreaty, etc: ~ *more money out of the public,* e g by increasing taxes; *blackmailers who* ~ *the last penny out of their victims.* **5** [VP2A] yield to pressure: *Sponges* ~ *easily.* □ *n* [C] **1** act of squeezing; condition of being ~d; sth obtained by squeezing: *give sb a hug and a* ~; *a* ˋ~ *bottle,* plastic container that ejects the contents, e g scent, liquid detergent, when ~d. *It was a tight* ~, we were ~d tightly, e g in a crowd. *Add a* ~ *of lemon to your drink.* ⇨ also credit[1](3). **2** **a close/narrow/tight ~,** a narrow escape. **3** [U] (colloq) policy of high taxation, high interest rates, etc aimed at deflation; [U] money obtained by squeezing(4): *My cook in Hong Kong always expected a certain amount of* ~ *from the money he spent in the food market,* e g by taking 10 per cent commission. **squeezer** *n* one who, that which, ~s, e g a device for squeezing out juice: *a* ˋ*lemon-*~*r.*

squelch /skweltʃ/ *vi,vt* [VP2A,C] make a sucking sound as when feet are lifted from stiff, sticky mud: *cows* ~*ing through the mud. The water* ~*ed in my boots.* □ *n* ~ing sound; act of ~ing.

squib /skwɪb/ *n* **1** small firework of the kind thrown by hand, one that first hisses and then explodes. **2** short satirical attack on sb, spoken or (more usu) written.

squid /skwɪd/ *n* kind of cuttle-fish with ten arms round the mouth (smaller kinds used as bait). ⇨ the illus at mollusc.

squiffy /ˈskwɪfɪ/ *adj* (sl) slightly drunk.

squiggle /ˈskwɪgl/ *n* small twisty line or scrawl: *Is this* ~ *supposed to be his signature?* **squig·gly** /ˈskwɪglɪ/ *adj*

squint /skwɪnt/ *vi* **1** [VP2A] have eyes that do not turn together but look in different directions at once; be cross-eyed. **2** [VP3A] **~ *at/through,*** look at sideways or with half-shut eyes or through a narrow opening. □ *n* **1** ~ing position of the eyeballs: *a man with a* ~. ˋ**~-eyed** *adj* having a ~; cross-eyed; (fig) malignant; disapproving. **2** (colloq) look or glance: *Let me have a* ~ *at it.*

squire /ˈskwaɪə(r)/ *n* **1** (in England) chief landowner in a country parish. **2** (in olden times) young man who was a knight's attendant until he himself became a knight. **3** (often hum) man who escorts a woman; man who is attentive to women and frequents their company. **4** (US) justice of the peace or local judge. □ *vt* [VP6A,15A] (of a man) attend upon, escort (a woman). ˋ**~·ar·chy** /-ɑkɪ/ *n* (*pl* -chies) (in England) great landowners (before 1832); these men as a class.

squirm /skwɜm/ *vi* [VP2A,C] twist the body, wriggle (from discomfort, shame or embarrassment). □ *n* ~ing movement.

squir·rel /ˈskwɪrl *US:* skwɜl/ *n* (kinds of) small, tree-climbing, bushy-tailed animal with red or grey fur. ⇨ the illus at small.

squirt /skwɜt/ *vt,vi* [VP6A,15A,B,2A,C] (of liquid, powder) force out, be forced out, in a thin stream or jet: ~ *soda-water into a glass. The water* ~*ed all over me.* □ *n* **1** thin stream or jet (of liquid, powder, etc). **2** sth from which liquid, etc can be ~ed, e g a syringe, as a child's toy. **3** (colloq, as a term of abuse) insignificant but self-assertive person; nasty little nobody.

stab /stæb/ *vt,vi* (-bb-) **1** [VP6A,15A,3A] pierce or wound with a sharp-pointed weapon or instrument; push (a knife, etc) into (sb); aim a blow (at sb) with such a weapon: ~ *a man in the back;* ~ *sb to the heart. His conscience* ~*bed him,* (fig) caused him to feel regret. **2** [VP2A] produce a sensation of being ~bed: ~*bing pains in the back.* □ *n* [C] **1** ~bing blow; pain inflicted by this. ***a* ~ *in the back,*** (fig) a treacherous attack, e g on sb's reputation. **2** (colloq) try, attempt (= colloq 'go' or 'shot'): *Let me have a* ~ *at it,* try to do it. **~·ber** *n*

stable[1] /ˈsteɪbl/ *adj* firm; fixed; not likely to move or change: *What we need is a ~ Government. He needs a ~ job.* **sta·bil·ity** /stəˋbɪlətɪ/ *n* [U] quality of being ~. **sta·bil·ize** /ˋsteɪbḷɑɪz/ ~ *vt* [VP6A] make ~: *stabilize prices and wages.* **sta·bi·lizer** *n* person or thing that stabilizes; (esp) device to keep a ship or aircraft steady, free from rolling or pitching. **sta·bil·iz·ation** /ˈsteɪbḷɑɪˋzeɪʃn *US:* -ḷɪˋz-/ *n* making or becoming ~.

stable[2] /ˋsteɪbl/ *n* building in which horses are lodged and fed; number of horses (esp race-horses) belonging to one particular owner and kept in one set of ~s. **ˋ~-boy/-man** *nn* boy/man employed in a ~. **ˋ~-companion** *n* horse of the same ~. □ *vt* put, keep, in a ~: *Where did you ~ your horse?* **stab·ling** /ˋsteɪbḷɪŋ/ *n* [U] accommodation for horses: *The house has stabling for 20 horses.*

stac·cato /stəˋkɑtəʊ/ *adj, adv* (musical direction) (to be played) with each successive note clear and detached.

stack /stæk/ *n* [C] **1** circular or rectangular pile of hay, straw, grain, etc usu with a sloping, thatched top, for storage in the open. **2** group of rifles arranged in the form of a pyramid; pile or heap (of books, papers, wood, etc); (colloq) large amount: *I have ~s of work waiting to be done.* **3** (brick-work or stonework enclosing a) number of chimneys. ⇨ *smoke-~* at smoke[1](1). **4** rack with shelves for books (in a library or bookshop). **5** number of aircraft circling at different heights while waiting for instructions to land. □ *vt* **1** [VP6A,15B] ~ ***(up),*** make into a ~ or ~s; pile up: *~ hay/wood; ~ up the dishes on the draining-board.* **2** (US) ~ *the cards,* arrange (playing-)cards unfairly; *have the cards ~ed against one,* be at a great disadvantage. **3** [VP6A] arrange aircraft in a ~(5).

sta·dium /ˋsteɪdɪəm/ *n* enclosed area of land for games, athletic competitions, etc, usu with stands for spectators: *build a new ~ for the Olympic Games.*

an Olympic stadium

staff /stɑf *US:* stæf/ *n* **1** strong stick used as a support when walking or climbing, or as a weapon: (now usu fig) *the ~ of life,* bread. *He is the ~ of my old age,* e g a son who supports his old father. **2** such a ~ as a sign of office or authority: *a pastoral ~,* e g an ornamental one carried by or before a bishop, etc. **3** pole serving as a support: *a ˋflag~.* **4** group of assistants working together under a manager or head: *the headmaster and his ~,* i e the teachers; *ˋoffice-~; be on the ~. A large ~* (collective *n, sing v*) *of domestic servants was usual in England in the 19th c. The school ~* (= Members of the ~, *pl v*) *are expected to supervise school meals.* **ˋ~-office,** (in a business company) office concerned with the personal welfare, etc of the employees. **5** group of senior army officers engaged in planning and organization: *the General S~;* (attrib) *ˋ~ officers.* **6** (music) (*pl* staves /ˋsteɪvz/) set of five parallel lines on or between which notes are placed to indicate their pitch. ⇨ the illus at notation. □ *vt* [VP6A] provide with, act as, a ~(4): *~ a new school; a well-~ed hotel/hospital; an under-~ed office.*

stag /stæg/ *n* **1** male deer. **ˋ~ party** *n* (colloq) party for men only (e g one for a man about to get married). **2** person who buys newly issued stocks and shares hoping that prices will rise and enable him to sell at a profit.

stage /steɪdʒ/ *n* **1** (in a theatre) raised platform or structure of boards on which the actors appear. **2** **the ~,** theatrical work; the profession of acting in theatres. ***be/go on the ~,*** be/become an actor or actress. **ˋ~-craft** *n* [U] skill or experience in writing or directing plays. **ˋ~ direction** *n* printed direction in a play to actors about their positions, movements, etc. **ˈ~ ˋdoor** *n* entrance at the back of a theatre, used by actors and workmen. **ˋ~ fright** *n* [U] nervousness felt when facing an audience. **ˈ~ ˋmanager** *n* person who superintends the production of a play, supervises the rehearsals, etc. **ˋ~-struck** *adj* having a strong desire to become an actor or actress. **ˈ~-ˋwhisper** *n* whisper that is meant to be overheard. **3** (fig) scene of action; place where events occur. **4** point, period or step in development: *at an early ~ in our history. The baby has reached the ˋtalking ~,* is learning to talk. **5** any of two or more successive periods on the journey of a rocket vehicle when one part has been jettisoned: *a multi-~ rocket.* **6** journey, distance, between two stopping-places along a road or route; such a stopping-place: *travel by easy ~s,* for only a short distance at a time. **ˋ~(-coach)** *n* (hist) horse-drawn public vehicle carrying passengers (and often mail) along a regular route. **ˋfare-~** *n* section along the route of a bus or tram for which there is a fixed fare. **7** structure with tiers or shelves, e g for plants. ⇨ also staging below, and *landing-~* at landing. □ *vt,vi* **1** [VP6A] put on the ~(1); put before the public: *~ 'Hamlet';* (fig) arrange to take place dramatically. ***~ a come-back,*** come back (to a sport, e g to the boxing ring) from retirement or after having failed. **2** [VP2C] ~ *well/badly,* (of a drama) be well/badly suited for the theatre.

stager /ˋsteɪdʒə(r)/ *n* (only in) **an old ~,** a person of long experience; an old hand. ⇨ hand[1](6).

stag·ger /ˋstægə(r)/ *vi,vt* **1** [VP2A,C] walk or move unsteadily (from weakness, a heavy burden, drunkenness, etc): *The man ~ed along/to his feet/across the room/from side to side of the road.* **2** [VP6A] (of a blow or shock) cause to walk or move unsteadily; (of news, etc) shock deeply; cause worry or confusion to: *receive a ~ing blow. I was ~ed to hear/on hearing/when I heard that the firm was bankrupt.* **3** [VP6A] arrange (times of events) so that they do not all occur together: *~ office hours,* so that employees are not all using buses, trains, etc, at the same time; *~ the annual holidays.* □ *n* **1** (*sing*) ~ing movement. **2 the ~s,** giddiness; nervous disease of cattle and horses, marked by ~ing. **~er** *n*

stag·ing /ˋsteɪdʒɪŋ/ *n* **1** [C,U] stage(6); (platform or working area on) scaffolding for men on constructional work, e g building. **2** [U] (method of) presenting a play on the stage of a theatre.

stag·nant /ˋstægnənt/ *adj* **1** (of water) without current or tide; still and stale: *water lying ~ in* *ponds and ditches.* **2** (fig) unchanging; inactive: *Business was ~ last week.* **stag·nancy** /-nənsɪ/ *n*

stag·nate /stæg`neɪt *US:* `stægneɪt/ *vi* [VP2A] be stagnant; (fig) be or become dull or sluggish through disuse, inactivity, etc. **stag·na·tion** /stæg`neɪʃn/ *n* [U].

stagy /`steɪdʒɪ/ *adj* theatrical in style, manner or appearance. **stag·ily** /-əlɪ/ *adv* **stagi·ness** *n*

staid /steɪd/ *adj* (of persons, their appearance, behaviour, etc) conservative, quiet and serious. **~·ly** *adv* **~·ness** *n*

stain /steɪn/ *vt,vi* **1** [VP6A] (of liquids, other substances) change the colour of; make coloured patches or dirty marks on: *fingers ~ed with nicotine; blood-~ed hands; a tablecloth ~ed with gravy;* (fig) *a guilt-~ed reputation.* **2** [VP6A,22] colour (wood, fabrics, etc) with a substance that penetrates the material: *He ~ed the wood brown. The scientist ~ed his specimen before examining it under the microscope.* **~ed glass,** glass made by mixing into it transparent colours during the process of manufacture: *~ed glass windows in a church.* **3** [VP2A] (of material) become discoloured or soiled: *Does this material ~ easily?* □ *n* **1** [U] liquid used for ~ing wood, etc. **2** [C] ~ed place; dirty mark or patch of colour: *`ink-/`blood-~s;* (fig) *a ~ on one's reputation; without a ~ on your character.* **~·less** *adj* **1** without a ~: *a ~less reputation.* **2** (esp of a kind of steel alloy) that resists rust and corrosion: *~less steel cutlery.*

stair /steə(r)/ *n* [C] (any one of a) series of fixed steps leading from one floor of a building to another. ⇨ **downstairs, upstairs.** *The child was sitting on the bottom ~. She always runs up/down the ~s. I passed her on the ~s.* ***below ~s,*** in the basement of a house (in large houses, formerly the part used by servants): *Their affairs were being discussed below ~s,* by the servants. ***a flight of ~s,*** a set of ~s in a continuous line, or from one landing, e g halfway between two floors, to another. ***at the foot/head of the ~s,*** at the bottom/top of a flight of ~s. **`~-carpet** *n* strip of carpet for laying on ~s. **`~-rod** *n* rod for keeping a ~-carpet in the angle between two steps. **`~-case** *n* series of ~s (often with banisters) inside a building: *Many old Edinburgh houses have spiral ~cases,* i e winding round a central pillar. **`~-way** *n* = ~case.

stake /steɪk/ *n* [C] **1** strong, pointed length of wood or metal (to be) driven into the ground as a post (e g for a fence) or as a support for sth, e g plants, young trees. **2** post, as used in olden times, to which a person was tied before being burnt to death as a punishment (for heresy): *condemned to the ~; suffer at the ~.* ***go to the ~,*** be burned at the ~; (fig) suffer the consequences of an ill-advised action. **3** sum of money risked on the unknown result of a future event, e g a horse-race; interest or concern (*in* sth); sum of money invested in an enterprise: *He has a ~ in the country,* is concerned in its welfare, is interested in its prosperity, etc (e g because he is a landowner). ***at ~,*** to be won or lost; risked, depending, upon the result of sth: (fig) *His reputation/His life itself was at ~.* **`~-holder** *n* person with whom ~s are deposited until the result is known. **4** (*pl*) money to be contended for, esp in a horse-race; such a race: *the trial ~s at Newmarket.* □ *vt* **1** [VP6A] support with a ~: *~ newly planted trees.* **2** [VP6A,10B] ***~ sth (out/off),*** mark (an area) with ~s: *~ out a claim* (to land in a new country, etc; also fig). **3** [VP6A,14] ***~ sth on sth,*** risk (money, one's hopes, etc): *~ £5 on the favourite,* e g in a horse-race. *I'd ~ my all/my life on it,* am very confident about it.

stal·ac·tite /`stæləktaɪt *US:* stə`læk-/ *n* [C] pencil-shaped or cone-shaped formation of lime hanging from the roof of a cave as water drips from it. **stal·ag·mite** /`stæləgmaɪt *US:* stə`læg-/ *n* [C] similarly shaped growth mounting upwards from the floor of a cave as water containing lime drips from the roof.

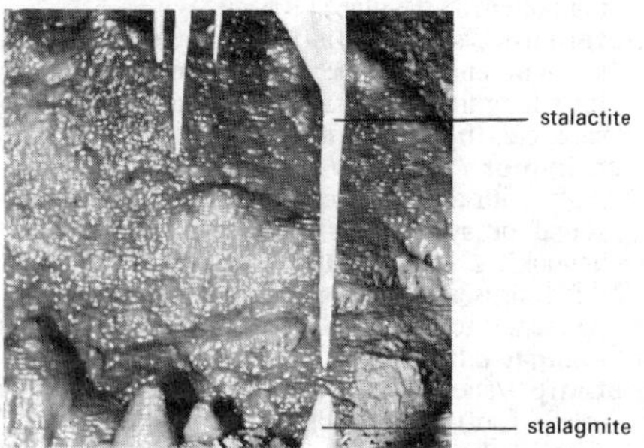

stale /steɪl/ *adj* **1** (of food) dry and unappetizing because not fresh: *~ bread.* **2** uninteresting because heard before: *~ news/jokes.* **3** (of athletes, pianists, etc) no longer able to perform really well because of too much playing, training, practice, etc: *become ~.* □ *vi* [VP2A] become ~: *Are there any kinds of pleasure that never ~?* **~·ness** *n*

stale·mate /`steɪlmeɪt/ *n* [C,U] **1** position of the pieces in chess from which no further move is possible. **2** (fig) any stage of a dispute at which further action by either side seems to be impossible. □ *vt* [VP6A] (chess) reduce a player to a ~; (fig) bring to a standstill.

stalk[1] /stɔk/ *n* [C] non-woody part of a plant that supports a flower or flowers, a leaf or leaves, or a fruit or fruits; stem.

stalk[2] /stɔk/ *vt,vi* **1** [VP2C,6A] walk with slow, stiff strides, esp in a proud, self-important or grim way: *~ out of the room; ~ along (the road). Famine ~ed (through) the land.* **2** [VP6A] move quietly and cautiously towards (wild animals, etc) in order to get near: *~ deer.* **`~·ing-horse** *n* horse behind which a hunter hides; (more usu, fig) pretext; means of hiding one's real intentions. **~er** *n* person who ~s animals: *a `deer-~er.*

stall /stɔl/ *n* **1** compartment for one animal in a stable or cattle shed. **`~-fed** *adj* fattened in a ~, not in the fields. **2** small, open-fronted shop; table, etc used by a trader in a market, on a street, in a railway-station, etc: *a `book-/`flower-/`coffee-~.* **3** (usu *pl*) (not US) seat in the part of a theatre nearest to the stage. **4** fixed seat (usu enclosed at sides and back, often in carved wood) for the special use of a clergyman (usu in the choir or chancel): *canon's/dean's ~.* **5** (**`finger-)~,** ⇨ **finger.** **6** condition of an aircraft when its speed has decreased to the point at which it no longer answers to the controls. □ *vt,vi* **1** [VP6A] place or keep (an animal) in a ~**(1)**, esp for fattening: *~ed oxen.* **2** [VP2A] (e g of an internal combustion engine) fail to keep going through insufficient power or speed; (of a driver) cause an engine to stop from such a cause. **3** [VP6A,2A] (of an aircraft) cause to be, become, out of control through loss of speed. **4** [VP2A] avoid giving a clear answer to a question (in order to get more time): *~ for time; ~ off creditors; Quit ~ing!*

stal·lion /ˈstælɪən/ *n* uncastrated fully grown male horse, esp one used for breeding.

stal·wart /ˈstɔlwət/ *adj* tall and muscular; solidly built; firm and resolved: *~ supporters.* □ *n* loyal supporter of a political party, etc.

sta·men /ˈsteɪmən/ *n* male part of a flower, bearing pollen. ⇨ the illus at **flower**.

stam·ina /ˈstæmɪnə/ *n* [U] vigour, energy, moral strength, enabling a person or animal to work hard for a long time, to survive a serious illness, exposure, etc; (fig) mental toughness.

stam·mer /ˈstæmə(r)/ *vi,vt* **1** [VP2A] speak haltingly with a tendency to repeat rapidly the same sound or syllable, as in 'G-g-give me that b-b-book'. **2** [VP6A,15B] ***~ sth (out),*** say sth in this confused or halting way: *~ out a request.* □ *n* (tendency to) ~ing talk. **~er** *n* person who ~s. **~·ing·ly** *adv*

stamp[1] /stæmp/ *vt,vi* **1** [VP6A,3A,2C,22,15B] put (one's foot) down with force (on sth): *~ one's foot; ~ the ground; ~ on a spider;* move (about, etc) doing this: *~ about/out of the room; ~ upstairs;* flatten by doing this: *~ the ground flat.* ***~ sth out,*** crush, destroy, end: *~ out a fire in the grass/a rebellion/an epidemic disease.* **ˈ~-ing-ground** *n* **(a)** place where specified animals, e g elephants, may usually be found. **(b)** place where specified people often gather: *Soho, the ~ing-ground in London of those who enjoy exotic food and entertainment.* **2** [VP6A,14] ***~ sth on sth, ~ sth with sth,*** print (a design, lettering, the date, etc) on paper, cloth or other surface: *~ one's name and address on an envelope/~ an envelope with one's name and address: a manufacturer's goods ~ed with his trademark. The girl forgot to ~ my library books,* ~ the date on which they were taken out (or should be returned). **3** [VP6A] put a postage ~ on (a letter, etc), an insurance ~ on (a card): *I enclose a ~ed and addressed envelope for your reply. Your insurance card is insufficiently ~ed.* **4** [VP6A,15B] ***~ sth (out),*** give shape to sth (e g pieces of metal) with a die or cutter. **5** [VP6A,15A] (fig uses) impress: *He ~ed his authority/personality on the game,* e g of a great footballer. [VP16B] mark out: *These actions ~ him as a man of high principles.*

stamp[2] /stæmp/ *n* **1** act of stamping with the foot: *a ~ of impatience.* **2** that with which a mark or design is made on a surface: *a rubber ~,* one on which a design, words, etc are cut (used for printing dates, signatures, addresses, etc). **3** design, word(s), etc made by stamping on a surface. **4** **(ˈpostage-)~,** piece of printed paper (usu with perforated edges) stuck on letters, etc to show the postage, insurance dues, etc paid, or the duty paid on legal documents. **ˈ~-album** *n* one in which a collector of postage-~s keeps his specimens. **ˈ~-collector** *n* person who collects ~s. **ˈ~-dealer** *n* person who buys and sells ~s for collectors. **ˈ~-duty** *n* tax imposed on certain kinds of legal documents. **5** (usu *sing*) characteristic mark or quality: *He bears the ~ of genius. Her face bears the ~ of suffering.* **6** (usu *sing*) kind; class: *men of that ~.*

stam·pede /stæmˈpid/ *n* [C] sudden rush of frightened people or animals. □ *vi,vt* **1** [VP2A,6A] take part in a ~; cause to do this. **2** [VP14] ***~ sb into sth/doing sth,*** hustle or frighten sb into rash action: *Don't be ~d into buying the house.*

stance /stæns/ *n* (golf, cricket) position taken for a stroke; person's intellectual attitude.

stanch /stɑntʃ *US:* stæntʃ/ = **staunch**.

stan·chion /ˈstɑntʃən *US:* ˈstæn-/ *n* upright post for supporting sth (e g bars for confining cattle in stalls).

stand[1] /stænd/ *n* **1** stopping of motion or progress: *come/be brought to a ~* (or, more usu *~still*), stop, be stopped. **2** ***make a ~,*** be ready to resist or fight: *make a ~ against the enemy; make a ~ for one's principles.* **3** position taken up: *He took his ~ near the window.* ***take one's ~,*** declare one's position, opinion, etc. *I take my ~ upon sound precedents,* use these to support my claim, etc. **4** small article of furniture, support, etc on or in which things may be placed: *a ˈmusic-/ˈhat-/umˈbrella-~.* ⇨ also *hand~* at **hand**[1](16), *ink~* at **ink**, *wash-~* at **wash-**. **5** structure from which things are sold: *a ˈnews~;* area, structure(s), for the exhibition of goods, etc: *the British ~ at the Hanover Fair.* **6** place where vehicles may stand in line in a street, etc while waiting for passengers: *a ˈcab-~; a ~ for six taxis.* **7** structure, usu sloping, where people may stand or sit to watch races, sports-meetings, etc: *the ˈgrand~.* **8** halt made by a theatrical company when touring the country. ***a one-night ~,*** with a performance on one evening only; (fig) a rendezvous that will not be repeated. **9** (US) witness-box (in a law court): *take the ~.* **10** growing crop in a certain area: *a good ~ of wheat/timber.* **11** (compounds) **ˈ~-pipe** *n* vertical pipe (connected with a water-main and used as a hydrant). **ˈ~-point** *n* point of view: *from the ~point of the consumer.* **ˈ~·still** *n* stop; halt. ***be at/come to/bring sth to a ~still.*** (attrib) *a ~still agreement,* one that agrees to no change, e g in wage rates or hours of work.

stand[2] /stænd/ *vi,vt* (*pt,pp* **stood** /stʊd/) (For special uses with *adverbial particles* and *preps,* ⇨ 11 below.) **1** [VP2A,B,C,4A] have, take, keep, an upright position; balance, support, the body on the feet: *He was too weak to ~. A chair will not ~ on two legs. We had to ~ all the way back in the bus. Standing room only,* all seats are occupied, e g in a bus or cinema. *His hair stood on end,* i e with terror. *He ~s six foot two,* is of this height when ~ing. *Don't ~ there arguing about it. He stood looking over my shoulder. S~ still while I take your photograph. S~ and deliver!* (command given by a highwayman) Stop and give me your valuables, etc! **2** [VP2A,C,4A] ***~ (up),*** rise to the feet: *S~ up, please. Everyone stood (up) when the Queen entered. We stood (up) to see better.* **3** [VP2A,C] remain without change: *Let the words ~,* don't alter them or take them out. *The agreement must ~,* cannot be altered or cancelled. *The house has stood two hundred years and will ~ another century.* ***~ firm/fast,*** not give way, retreat, change one's views, etc. **4** [VP2C] be in a certain condition or situation: *The emergency services ~* (= are) *ready to help if called on. The matter ~s thus,* this is the state of affairs. *As affairs now ~...,* As they are at present.... *He ~s* (= is) *in need of help. Who ~s* (= is) *first on the* *list? Will you* ~ (= be) *godmother to the child? He stood convicted of treachery. I* ~ *corrected,* accept the correction of my views, etc. *He* ~*s alone among his colleagues,* None of them equals him in ability, etc. ~ ***clear (of sth),*** move away: *S*~ *clear of the gates,* e g as a warning when they are about to be closed. ~ ***easy/at ease,*** ⇨ easy, ease. **5** ***It*** ~***s to reason (that)***..., I am certainly right in saying that... and others are obstinately foolish if they say that (often prefacing a statement of doubtful validity). **6** [VP2C] have a certain place; be situated: *These dishes* ~ *on the top shelf. A tall poplar tree once stood there. The house* ~*s on the hill. Where does Tom* ~ *in class,* What is his position (in order of ability, etc)? **7** [VP15A] cause to be placed in an upright position. *S*~ *the ladder against the wall. S*~ *the bottle on the table. If you're naughty again, you'll be stood* (= made to ~) *in the corner. S*~ *the empty barrels on the floor. Don't* ~ *this tin of petrol near the fire. The traitor was stood up against the wall and shot.* **8** [VP6A,D] endure; bear: *He can't* ~ *hot weather. She says she will* ~ *no nonsense,* not put up with foolish behaviour. *I can't* ~ *that woman,* strongly dislike her. *She can't* ~ *being kept waiting.* ~ ***one's ground,*** maintain one's position, e g in battle; (fig) not give way in an argument. ~ ***(one's) trial,*** be tried (in a court of law). **9** [VP6A,12A] ~ ***sb sth,*** provide at one's expense: ~ *sb a good dinner;* ~ *drinks all round,* pay for drinks for everyone. *Will he* ~ *us champagne?* ~ ***treat,*** pay the costs of entertaining sb or others. **10** (phrases) ~ ***a (good/poor, etc) chance,*** (of success, etc) have a (good/poor, etc) prospect (of success, etc). ~ ***sb in good stead,*** ⇨ stead. ~ ***on ceremony,*** ⇨ ceremony. ***It*** ~***s to reason that,*** ⇨ reason[1](3). ~ ***to win/gain/lose sth,*** be in a position where one is likely to win, etc: *What do we* ~ *to gain by the treaty?* **11** [VP2C,3,15B] (special uses with *adverbial particles* and *preps*):

stand aside, **(a)** be inactive, do nothing: *He's a man who never* ~*s aside when there's something that needs doing.* **(b)** move to one side: ~ *aside to let someone pass.* **(c)** withdraw one's name (as a candidate): ~ *aside in favour of a better man.*

stand at, be at a certain level (on a scale, etc): *The appeal fund* ~*s at £10 000. The temperature stood at 30°C.*

stand back, **(a)** move back: *The policeman ordered us to* ~ *back.* **(b)** be situated away from: *The house* ~*s back from the road.*

stand by, **(a)** be a bystander; look on without doing anything: *How can you* ~ *by and see such cruelty?* **(b)** be ready for action: *The troops are* ~*ing by.* ~ ***by sb,*** support, side with, sb; show oneself to be a good friend: *I'll* ~ *by you whatever happens.* ~ ***by sth,*** be faithful to (a promise, one's word, etc). Hence, **'~·by** *n* **(a)** state of readiness: *The troops are on 24-hour* ~*by,* ready to move at 24 hours' notice. **(b)** sb or sth that one may depend upon: (attrib) *a* ~*by generator,* one for use in an emergency, e g for use when electric current from the mains is cut off. *Aspirin is a good* ~*by for headaches.*

stand down, retire from a witness-box or similar position; (of a candidate) withdraw (in favour of sb else).

stand for sth, **(a)** represent: *PO* ~*s for Post Office or postal order. We admire Christianity and all it* ~*s for.* **(b)** support, contend for: ~ *for racial tolerance.* **(c)** (GB) be a candidate for: ~ *for Parliament.* **(d)** (colloq; ⇨ 8 above) tolerate: *She says she's not going to* ~ *for her own children disobeying her.*

stand in (with sb), take a share in: *Let me* ~ *in with you if it's expensive.* ~ ***in (for sb),*** take the place of, e g a principal actor or actress until filming begins. Hence, **'~-in** *n* person who does this.

stand off, remain at a distance; move away. ~ ***sb off,*** dispense with the services of, e g workers, temporarily. **,~-'off·ish** *adj* reserved; cold and distant in behaviour. Hence, **,~-'off·ish·ly** *adv* **,~-'off·ish·ness** *n*

stand out, **(a)** be easily seen above or among others: *Does your work* ~ *out from that of others,* Is it obviously better? ⇨ outstanding. ~ ***out a mile,*** be extremely obvious. **(b)** continue to resist: *The troops stood out against the enemy until their ammunition was exhausted.*

stand over, be postponed: *Let the matter* ~ *over until the next meeting.* ~ ***over sb,*** supervise, watch closely: *Unless I* ~ *over him he makes all sorts of foolish mistakes.*

stand to, (mil) take up positions to resist possible attack: *The company (was) stood to for half an hour.* Hence, **'~-to** *n* army signal to be on the alert.

stand up, ⇨ 2 above. **'~-up** *adj* **(a)** (of collars) upright (opp of *turn-down*). **(b)** (of a meal) eaten while ~ing: *a* ~*-up buffet.* **(c)** (of a fight) violent and hard-hitting. ~ ***sb up,*** (colloq) not keep a rendezvous: *First she agreed to come out with me, then she stood me up.* ~ ***up for sb,*** support; take the part of; defend. ~ ***up to sth,*** (of materials) remain in good condition after long or hard use, etc: *metals that* ~ *up well to high temperatures.* ~ ***(well) with sb,*** be on (good) terms with, be (well) thought of: *How do you* ~ *with your boss? He* ~*s well with his bank manager* (and may, therefore, get an overdraft without difficulty).

stan·dard /ˈstændəd/ *n* **1** distinctive flag, esp one to which loyalty is given or asked: *the royal* ~, e g as flown to show that the Queen is in residence; *raise the* ~ *of revolt,* (fig) begin a struggle and call for support. **'~-bearer** *n* person who carries a ~; (fig) prominent leader in a cause. **2** (often attrib) sth used as a test or measure for weights, lengths, qualities or for the required degree of excellence: *the* ~ *yard/pound, etc;* ~ *weights and measures; the* ~ *of height required for recruits to the police force; set a high* ~ *for candidates in an examination; conform to the* ~*s of society,* live and behave as society expects; *a high* ~ *of living,* one with plenty of material comforts, etc; *a high moral* ~; ~ *authors,* accepted as good. ***be up to/below*** ~, be equal to, not so good as, is normal, required, etc: *Their work is not up to* ~. ~ **time,** time officially adopted for a country or part of it. **3** (former) grade of classification in primary schools (now usu *class*): *boys in S*~ *One.* **4** **monetary** ~, proportion of weight of fine metal and alloy in gold and silver coin: *the 'gold* ~, system by which the value of money is based on that of gold. **5** (often attrib) upright support; pole or column: *a '*~ *lamp,* on a tall support with its base on the floor; a vertical water- or gas-pipe. **6** tree or shrub that has been grafted on an upright stem (contrasted with a bush, climbing plant): ~ *roses.*

stan·dard·ize /ˈstændədaɪz/ *vt* [VP6A] make of one size, shape, quality, etc according to fixed standards: *The parts of motor-vehicles are usually ~d. S~d products are usually cheaper than hand-made articles.* **stan·dard·iz·ation** /ˌstændədaɪˈzeɪʃn *US:* -dɪˈz-/ *n* [U]: *Standardization of use of hyphens in compounds is a difficult problem.*

stand·ing /ˈstændɪŋ/ *n* **1** [U] duration: *a debt/dispute of long ~.* **2** [C,U] position or reputation; (if there is no *adj*) established position: *men of (high) ~; a member in full ~.* □ *adj* **1** established and permanent; ready for use: *a ~ army; a ~ committee,* a permanent one that meets regularly; *a ~ order for newspapers and periodicals,* to be delivered regularly; *a ~ order to a bank,* customer's order for payments that recur regularly, e g rent, rates. *a ~ joke,* sth that regularly causes amusement. **~ orders,** (*pl*) rules and regulations which remain in force until repealed by the proper authorities; *a ~ing reproach.* **2** *~ corn,* not yet cut (harvested); *a ~ jump,* made without a preliminary run.

stank /stæŋk/ *pt* of stink.

stanza /ˈstænzə/ *n* [C] group of rhymed lines forming a division in some forms of poem.

staple[1] /ˈsteɪpl/ *n* U-shaped metal bar with pointed ends hammered or pressed into a surface, to hold sth, e g flexible wire for electric current, in position; ⇨ the illus at padlock; hoop-shaped bar hammered into wood, etc for the point of a hook or hasp; piece of wire for fastening sheets of paper together (as in some periodicals). □ *vt* [VP6A] fasten or fit with a ~. **ˈsta·pling-machine** *n* one used for fastening sheets of paper together with ~s. **sta·pler** /ˈsteɪplə(r)/ *n* small hand-operated device for fastening papers together.

staple[2] /ˈsteɪpl/ *n* **1** [C] chief sort of article or goods produced or traded in: *Cotton is one of the ~s of Egypt.* **2** chief material or element (*of* sth): *The weather forms the ~ of their conversation.* **3** [U] fibre of cotton, wool, etc (as determining its quality): *cotton of short/fine, etc ~; long-~ cotton.* **4** (attrib) forming the ~(2): *Is coffee still the ~ product of Brazil? Rice is the ~ food in many Asian countries.*

star /stɑ(r)/ *n* **1** any one of the bodies seen in the sky at night as distant points of light. **fixed ~** *n* one which is not a planet. **shooting ~** *n* ⇨ shoot[2](1). **ˈ~·fish** *n* ~-shaped sea animal. ⇨ the illus at sea. **ˈ~·light** *n* [U] light from the ~s: *walk home by ~light;* (attrib) *a ~light night.* **ˈ~·lit** *adj* lighted by the ~s: *a ~lit scene.* **2** figure or design with points round it, suggesting a ~ by its shape; an asterick (*): *a five-~ hotel,* given five ~s (in guide-books, etc) to show its grading; badge of rank (worn by officers on the shoulder-strap). ***see ~s,*** seem to see flashes of lights, e g as the result of a blow in the eye(s). **the ˈS~-Spangled ˈBanner,** (**a**) the national flag of the US. (**b**) the national anthem of the US. **3** planet or heavenly body regarded as influencing a person's fortune, etc: *born under a lucky ~. What do the ~s foretell? You may thank your lucky ~s you were not killed in that accident.* **ˈ~-gazer** *n* (hum) astrologer or astronomer. **4** person famous as a singer, actor, actress, etc: *the ~s of stage and screen; ˈfilm~s; an all-~ cast,* in which leading players are all ~s; *the ~ turn,* the principal item in an entertainment or performance. □ *vi,vt* (-rr-) **1** [VP6A] mark or decorate with, or as with, a ~ or ~s, e g an asterisk to direct attention to sth; *a lawn ~red with daisies.* **2** [VP3A,14] ***~ (sb) in,*** be a ~(4) (*in* a play, film, etc); present (sb) as a ~(4): *She is to ~/to be ~red in a new film.* **ˈ~·dom** /-dəm/ *n* status of being a ~(4). **ˈ~·let** /-lət/ *n* young actress on the way to ~dom. **~·less** *adj* with no ~s to be seen: *a ~less sky/night.* **~ry** /ˈstɑrɪ/ *adj* lighted by, shining like, ~s: *a ~ry night; ~ry eyes.* **ˈ~ry-ˈeyed** *adj* (colloq) visionary but impractical: *~ry-eyed reformers.*

star·board /ˈstɑbəd/ *n* right side of a ship or aircraft from the point of view of a person looking forward. ⇨ port: *alter course to ~; on the ~ bow.* ⇨ the illus at ship. □ *vt*: *~ the helm,* turn the helm to ~.

starch /stɑtʃ/ *n* [U] **1** white, tasteless food substance, plentiful in potatoes, grain, etc. **2** this substance prepared in powered form and used for stiffening cotton clothes, etc; (fig) stiffness of manner; formality. □ *vt* [VP6A] make, e g shirt collars, stiff with ~; (fig, in *pp*) *a ~ed manner.* **~y** *adj* of or like ~; containing ~: *~y foods.*

stare /steə(r)/ *vi,vt* **1** [VP2A,B,C,3A] ***~ (at),*** look fixedly; (of eyes) be wide open: *Do you like being ~d at? She was staring into the distance. They all ~d with astonishment. He gazed at the scene with staring eyes.* ***make sb ~,*** surprise him. **2** [VP15B] ***~ sb out (of countenance),*** until he becomes nervous, etc. ***~ sb out/down,*** ~ at him longer than he is able to ~ at you. ***~ one in the face,*** (**a**) ~ at sb's face. (**b**) be right in front of one: *The book I was looking for was staring me in the face. Defeat was staring them in the face,* was clearly inevitable. □ *n* staring look: *give sb a rude ~; with a ~ of horror/astonishment; with a vacant ~,* suggesting an empty mind; *with a glassy ~,* suggesting indifference. **star·ing** *adj* (of colours, etc) too bright or conspicuous: *His tie was a staring red.* □ *adv* (only in) ***stark staring mad,*** completely mad.

stark /stɑk/ *adj* **1** stiff, esp in death. **2** complete; downright: *~ madness/folly.* □ *adv* completely: *~ naked.*

star·ling /ˈstɑlɪŋ/ *n* common European bird (with black, brown-spotted plumage) which nests near buildings and is a good mimic.

starry /ˈstɑrɪ/ ⇨ star.

start[1] /stɑt/ *n* [C] **1** beginning of a journey, activity, etc: *make an early ~; the ~ of a race; after several false ~s; from ~ to finish.* **2** (with *much,* with *def* or *indef art,* but not *pl*) amount of time or distance by which one person starts in front of competitors; advantageous position: *The small boys were given a ~ of ten yards. They didn't give me much/any ~. He got the ~ of* (= gained an advantage over) *his rivals. He got a good ~* (= a position of advantage) *in life/business.* **3** sudden movement of surprise, fear, etc: *He sat up with a ~. The news gave me a ~,* surprised me. ***by fits and ~s,*** ⇨ fit[3](3).

start[2] /stɑt/ *vi,vt* (Note: *begin* may replace *start* only as in 2 below) **1** [VP2A,C] ***~ (out),*** leave; set out: *We must ~ (out) early. We ~ed at six. At last the bus ~ed.* **2** [VP6A,D,7] begin: *~ work. It ~ed raining. It's ~ing to rain. Have you ~ed working yet?* **3** [VP6A,3A] ***~ (on) sth,*** make a beginning: *~ (on) one's journey home. Have you ~ed on your next book yet,* begun to read (or write) it? **4** [VP2A,C] make a sudden movement (from pain, surprise, fear, etc) or change of position: *He ~ed up from his seat. He ~ed at the sound of my voice.* **5** [VP2C] move, rise, spring, suddenly: *Tears ~ed to her eyes,* suddenly came to her eyes. *His eyes nearly ~ed out of his head,* suddenly opened wide (in surprise, etc). **6** [VP2A,C,6A] (of timbers) (cause to) spring out of position; make or become loose: *The ship has ~ed at the seams. The planks have ~ed. The damp has ~ed the timbers.* **7** [VP6A,15A,19A] set going; originate, bring into existence; cause or enable to begin: *This news ~ed me thinking. The smoke ~ed her coughing. He decided to ~ a newspaper. A rich uncle ~ed him in business,* helped him, e g by supplying capital. *She has ~ed a baby,* (colloq) become pregnant. **8** [VP3C] (with *adverbial particles*) ***~ back,*** begin to return: *It's time we ~ed back.* ***~ in (on sth/to do sth),*** (colloq) begin to do it: *Poor Jane! She's ~ed in on a huge pile of ironing.* ***~ off,*** begin to move: *The horse ~ed off at a steady trot.* ***~ out (to do sth),*** (colloq) begin; take the first steps: *~ out to write a novel.* ***~ up,*** **(a)** ⇨ **1** above. **(b)** come into existence suddenly or unexpectedly: *Many difficulties have ~ed up.* ***~ sth up,*** put (an engine, etc) in motion: *We couldn't ~ up the car.* **9** ***to ~ with,*** **(a)** in the first place: *To ~ with, we haven't enough money, and secondly we haven't enough time.* **(b)** at the beginning: *We had only six members to ~ with.* **10** **ˈ~·ing gate** *n* barrier where horses ~ a race, raised when the time comes for them to ~. **ˈ~·ing-point** *n* place at which a start is made. **ˈ~·ing-post,** place from which competitors ~ in a race. **ˈ~·ing-prices** *n pl* (in horse-racing) the odds just before the start of a race. **~er** *n* **1** person, horse, etc that takes part in a race: *There were only five ~ers in the last race.* **2** person who gives the signal for a race to ~. ***under ~er's orders,*** (of horses, athletes, etc lined up for a race) awaiting the starter's order or signal to ~ the race. **3** device for causing an engine to ~ working; ignition. ⇨ *self-~er* at **self-**. **4** (colloq) first course of a meal.

startle /ˈstɑtl/ *vt* [VP6A,15A] give a shock of surprise to; cause to move or jump: *~d out of one's sleep; ~d out of one's wits,* suffered a sudden great shock. She was ~d to see him looking so ill. What startling news!

starve /stɑv/ *vi,vt* **1** [VP6A,15A,2A,C] (cause to) suffer or die from hunger: *~ to death. The silly man said he would ~ rather than beg for food. They tried to ~ the garrison into surrender/~ them out,* force them to surrender by preventing them from getting supplies of food. ***be ~d of/~ for,*** (fig) long for, be in great need of: *The motherless children were ~ed of/were starving for affection.* **2** (colloq) feel hungry: *What's for dinner? We're simply starving (for food).* **star·va·tion** /stɑˈveɪʃn/ *n* [U] suffering or death caused by lack of food; *die of starvation; starvation wages,* too low to buy adequate supplies of food; *be on a starvation diet,* a diet that is inadequate for health. **~·ling** /ˈstɑvlɪŋ/ *n* starving or ill-fed person or animal.

state[1] /steɪt/ *n* **1** (*sing* only) condition in which sth or sb is (in circumstances, appearance, mind, health, etc): *The house was in a dirty ~. These buildings are in a bad ~ of repair,* need to be repaired. *She's in a poor ~ of health. What a ~ he's in!* How anxious, dirty, untidy, etc he is, according to context. *Now don't get into a ~,* (colloq) Don't get excited or anxious! ***~ of play,*** **(a)** (cricket) score. **(b)** (fig) how parties in dispute stand in relation to one another (as likely to win or lose). **2** (often **S~**) organized political community with its apparatus of government; territory in which this exists; such a community forming part of a federal republic: *Railways in Great Britain belong to the S~. A nation is something organic or natural, but a S~ is conventional. How many S~s are there in the United States of America? The President's 'Message to the Union' is not addressed to individual S~s but to the Union as a whole/to the nation.* ⇨ also *police ~, totalitarian ~* at **police, totalitarian. 3** (attrib) of, for, concerned with, the S~**(2)**: *~ documents/records/archives; the ˈS~ Department,* (US) of Foreign Affairs. **S~·house,** building in which a S~ Legislature sits. *A S~ Legislature,* e g that of the S~ of Madras in India. Cf *the National Assembly* for the whole of India. **S~(s') rights,** (US) all rights which are not delegated to the Federal Government in Washington. **~'s evidence,** (US) evidence for the state in criminal cases. Cf *King's-/Queen's* evidence in GB. *S~ forests,* belonging to the S~, not privately owned; *bring industries under S~ control; S~ socialism,* policy of ~ control of industry, etc. **4** [U] civil government: *Church and S~; S~ schools,* contrasted with Church schools. **5** [U] rank; dignity: *persons in every ~ of life. He lived in a style scarcely befitting his ~.* **6** [U] pomp; ceremonial formality: *The President was received in ~. The Queen was in her robes of ~.* **7** (attrib) of or for ceremony and formality: *the ~ coach,* e g as used by the Queen on ceremonial occasions; *the ~ apartments at the palace; a ~ call,* (colloq) formal visit. **8** ***lie in ~,*** be placed on view in a public place before burial. **9** **ˈ~·room** *n* private cabin (or sleeping-compartment) on a steamer (and, in US, in a railway-carriage). **~·ly** *adj* (**-ier, -iest**) impressive; dignified: *a ~ly dowager; the ~ly homes of England,* those of the nobility, etc; *with ~ly grace.* **~·li·ness** *n* **ˈ~·craft** *n* [U] = ~smanship. ⇨ below. **~·less** *adj* (of a person) not recognized as a citizen or national of any country: *~less persons,* e g some political refugees.

state[2] /steɪt/ *vt* [VP6A,9] express in words, esp carefully, fully and clearly: *~ one's views. I have seen it ~d that.... He ~d positively that he had never seen the accused man.* **stated** *adj* made known; announced: *at ~d times/intervals.* **~-ment** *n* **1** [U] expression in words: *Clearness of ~ment is more important than beauty of language.* **2** [C] stating of facts, views, a problem, etc; report: *issue a ~ment; a ˈbank ~ment; make a ~ment (in court),* give a formal account in a law court setting out the cause of a legal action or its defence. *My tradesmen send me monthly ~ments of the money I owe them.*

states·man /ˈsteɪtsmən/ *n* (*pl* **-men**) person taking an important part in the management of State affairs; disinterested political leader. **ˈ~·like** *adj* gifted with, showing, wisdom and a broad-minded outlook in public affairs. **ˈ~·ship** /-ʃɪp/ *n* [U] skill and wisdom in managing public affairs.

static /ˈstætɪk/ *adj* at rest; in a state of balance: *~ water,* not flowing (e g water in a tank, needing to be pumped); *~ electricity,* as accumulated on an insulated body. **stat·ics** *n* [U] (*pl* used as *sing*) **1** branch of knowledge dealing with bodies remaining at rest or with forces which balance one another. **2** (radio, TV) = atmospherics.

sta·tion /ˈsteɪʃn/ *n* [C] **1** place, building, etc where a service is organized and provided: *a ˋbus/ poˋlice/ˆbroadcasting/ˆradar/ˆfire-~.* **2** position, or relative position, to be taken up or maintained by sb/sth: *One of the cruisers was out of ~,* not in its correct position relative to other ships. **3** stopping-place for railway trains; the buildings, offices, etc, connected with it: *a ˋgoods ~,* one for merchandise. **ˋ~-master** *n* man in charge of a railway ~. **4** social position, rank: *people in all ~s of life.* **5** (Australia) (usu extensive) sheep or cattle ranch. **6** military or naval base; those living there. **7 S~s of the Cross,** fourteen crosses, usu with images of the sufferings and death of Jesus, for religious devotions, set up in a church or along a path. **8 ˋ~-wagon** *n* estate car. ⇨ **estate(5).** □ *vt* [VP6A,15A] put (sb, oneself, a military or naval force, etc) at or in a certain place: *The detective ~ed himself among the bushes,* hid there. *HMS Tiger has been ~ed at Hong Kong for the last two years.*

sta·tion·ary /ˆsteɪʃnrɪ *US:* -ṇerɪ/ *adj* **1** not intended to be moved from place to place: *a ~ crane/engine.* ⇨ **mobile(1).** **2** not moving or changing: *remain ~; collide with a ~ van.*

sta·tioner /ˆsteɪʃṇə(r)/ *n* dealer in ~y. **~y** /ˆsteɪʃnrɪ *US:* -ṇerɪ/ *n* [U] writing materials, etc: *the ˋS~y Office,* (abbr *HMSO*) department which publishes and distributes government papers, books, etc.

stat·is·tics /stəˋtɪstɪks/ *n* **1** (with *pl v*) collection of information shown in numbers: *S~ suggest that the population of this country will be doubled in ten years' time.* **vital ~,** ⇨ **vital.** **2** (with *sing v*) the science of ~. **stat·is·ti·cal** /stəˋtɪstɪkl/ *adj* of ~: *statistical tables/experts.* **stat·is·ti·cally** /-klɪ/ *adv* **stat·is·ti·cian** /ˌstætɪˋstɪʃn/ *n* person who is expert in ~.

statu·ary /ˆstætʃʊərɪ *US:* -ʊerɪ/ *adj* of or for statues: *~ marble.* □ *n* sculpture; statues.

statue /ˆstætʃu/ *n* figure of a person, animal, etc in wood, stone, bronze, etc, usu of life size or more than life size. **statu·ette** /ˌstætʃʊˋet/ *n* small ~. **statu·esque** /ˌstætʃʊˋesk/ *adj* like a ~ in having clear-cut outlines, in being motionless, etc.

stat·ure /ˆstætʃə(r)/ *n* [U] (person's) natural bodily height: *short of ~;* (fig) mental or moral quality; calibre.

status /ˆsteɪtəs/ *n* [U] person's legal, social or professional position in relation to others: *have no official ~,* no official rank, e g in the Civil Service. *Many young people desire ~* (= an established social position) *and security.* **ˋ~ symbol,** sth which the ownership of is thought to be evidence of social rank, wealth, etc, e g a better car than one's neighbours, a yacht, a colour TV.

status quo (ante) /ˌsteɪtəs ˋkwəʊ (ˆæntɪ)/ (Lat) as it was before a recent change or as it is now.

stat·ute /ˆstætʃut/ *n* [C] (written) law passed by Parliament or other law-making body. **~ law** *n* all the ~s (contrasted with *case-law* and *common law*). ⇨ **common[1](1).** **ˋ~-book** *n* book(s) containing the ~ law. **statu·tory** /ˆstætʃʊtrɪ *US:* -tɔrɪ/ *adj* fixed, done, required, by ~: *statutory control of prices and incomes.*

staunch[1] /stɔntʃ/ (US also **stanch** /stɑntʃ *US:* stæntʃ/) *vt* [VP6A] stop the flow of (esp blood); check the flow of blood from (a wound).

staunch[2] /stɔntʃ/ *adj* (of a friend, supporter, etc) trustworthy; loyal; firm. **~·ly** *adv* **~·ness** *n*

stave[1] /steɪv/ *n* **1** one of the curved pieces of wood used for the side of a barrel or tub. **2** (music) = staff(6). **3** stanza; verse.

stave[2] /steɪv/ *vt,vi* (*pt,pp* ~d or **stove** /stəʊv/) **1** [VP15B] **~ *sth in,*** break, smash, make a hole in: *The side of the yacht was ~d in by the collision.* [VP3A] **~ *in,*** become or get broken or smashed: *The boat ~d in when it struck the rocks.* **2** [VP15B] **~ *sth off,*** keep off, delay (danger, disaster, bankruptcy, etc).

stay[1] /steɪ/ *vi,vt* **1** [VP2A,B,C,4A] be, remain, in a place or condition: *~ in the house/at home/in bed; ~* (= be a guest) *at a hotel/with friends. I'm too busy to/I can't ~,* must leave now. *I can only ~ a few minutes. I ~ed to see what would happen.* **~ *for/to sth,*** remain for: *Won't you ~ for/ to supper?* **~ *in,*** **(a)** not go outdoors: *The doctor advised me to ~ in for a few days.* **(b)** remain in school after hours: *The teacher made the boy ~ in and do his exercises again.* **~ *out,*** **(a)** remain outdoors: *Tell the children they mustn't ~ out after dark.* **(b)** remain on strike: *The miners ~ed out for several weeks.* **~ *up,*** not go to bed: *I ~ed up reading until midnight. I'll be late home, but please don't ~ up for me.* ***come to ~,*** (colloq) become, or seem likely to be, permanent: *This craze men have for shoulder-length hair—has it come to ~?* **ˋ~-at-home** *n* person who seldom goes anywhere; unadventurous person. **2** [VP2C] continue in a certain state: *~ single,* not marry. *That fellow never ~s sober for long,* frequently gets drunk. **~ *put,*** (colloq) remain where placed: *I wish this curler would ~ put instead of falling out every time.* **3** [VP6A] stop, delay, postpone, check: *~ the progress of a disease; ~ one's hand,* refrain from doing sth; *~* (= delay) *judgement/ proceedings.* **4** [VP2A,6A] be able to continue (work, etc); show endurance: *The horse lacks ˋ~ing power.* **~ *the course,*** be able to continue to the end of the race, (fig) the struggle, etc. **5** (usu in *imper,* old use) pause: *S~! You've forgotten one thing.* **6** [VP6A] satisfy for a time: *have a sandwich to ~ one's hunger.* □ *n* **1** period of ~ing: *make a short ~ in Karachi; a fortnight's ~ with my rich uncle.* **2** (legal) delay; postponement. ***a ~ of execution,*** that an order of the court need not be carried out for the time being. **~er** *n* person or animal able to ~(3): *The horse that won the race is a good ~er.*

stay[2] /steɪ/ *n* [C] **1** rope or wire supporting a mast, pole, etc. ⇨ the illus at **barque.** **2** (fig) support: *the ~ of his old age,* person who helped him, e g by giving him a home, looking after him. **3** (*pl*) (old-fashioned name for) kind of corset reinforced with strips of stiff material (bone or plastic). □ *vt* [VP6A,15B] **~ *(up),*** support by means of a wire, rope or prop.

stead /sted/ *n* [U] ***in sb's ~,*** in his place; instead of him. ***stand sb in good ~,*** be useful or helpful to him in time of need: *This knowledge has stood him in good ~.*

stead·fast /ˆstedfɑst *US:* -fæst/ *adj* firm and unchanging; keeping firm (*to*): *a ~ gaze; ~ in adversity; be ~ to one's principles.* **~·ly** *adv* **~·ness** *n*

steady /ˆstedɪ/ *adj* (-ier, -iest) **1** firmly fixed or supported; balanced; not likely to fall over: *make a table ~,* e g by repairing a leg; *on a ~ founda-*

tion; not very ~ on one's legs, e g of sb after a long illness. **2** regular in movement, speed, direction, etc: *a ~ wind/speed/rate of progress/improvement.* **3** regular in behaviour, habits, etc: *a ~ young man; a ~ worker.* **4** constant, unchanging: *a ~ faith/purpose.* **5** (in exclamations) *Keep her ~!* (naut) Keep the ship on her course unchanged. *S~ (on)!* (colloq, used as a warning) Control yourself! □ *adv* = steadily. ***go ~,*** (colloq) go about regularly with sb of the opposite sex, though not yet engaged to marry: *Are Tony and Jane going ~?* □ *n* (sl) regular boy-friend or girl-friend. □ *vt,vi* [VP6A,2A] make or become ~; keep ~: *~ a boat/table-leg; ~ oneself by holding on to the rail,* e g on the deck of a ship that is rolling. *Prices are ~ing.* **stead·ily** /ˈstedḷɪ/ *adv* in a ~ manner: *work steadily. His health is getting steadily worse.* **steadi·ness** *n*

steak /steɪk/ *n* [C,U] (thick slice of) meat or fish for frying, grilling, stewing, etc: *2 lb of ˈrumpˋ~; two ˈcod-ˋ~s.*

steal /stil/ *vt,vi* (*pt* **stole** /stəʊl/, *pp* **stolen** /ˈstəʊlən/) **1** [VP6A,14,2A] ***~ sth (from sb),*** take (sb else's property) secretly, without right, unlawfully: *Someone has stolen my watch. I have had my watch stolen.* Cf I have been *robbed of* my watch. *It is wrong to ~.* **2** [VP6A,15A] obtain by surprise or a trick: *~ a kiss from sb; ~ a glance at sb in the mirror.* ***~ a march on sb,*** do sth before him and so gain an advantage. **3** [VP2C] move, come, go (*in, out, away, etc*) secretly and quietly: *He stole into the room. A tear stole down her cheek. The morning light was ~ing through the shutters.*

stealth /stelθ/ *n* [U] (only used in) ***by ~,*** secretly and quietly: *do good by ~.* **~y** *adj* (**-ier, -iest**) doing things, done, quietly and secretly: *~y footsteps.* **~·ily** /-əlɪ/ *adv*

steam /stim/ *n* [U] **1** gas or vapour into which boiling water changes; power obtained from ~: *~-covered windows; a building heated by ~. The ship was able to proceed under her own ~,* using her own engines and not needing to be towed. ***Full ~ ahead!*** order to go forward at full speed. ***get up/raise ~,*** provide ~ at a higher pressure in the boilers, etc: *The stokers got up ~.* **2** (fig uses; colloq) energy. ***get up ~,*** collect one's energy; become excited or angry. ***let off ~,*** release surplus energy or emotion; become less excited. ***run out of ~,*** become exhausted: *Is there a danger of the housing programme running out of ~,* losing its impetus? ***under one's own ~,*** without help from others. **3** (compounds) **ˋ~·boat** *n* vessel propelled by ~. **ˈ~-ˋboiler** *n* vessel in which ~ is generated (to work an engine). **~ brake/hammer/whistle/winch, etc** *nn* worked by ~. **ˈ~-ˋcoal** *n* coal used for heating in ~-boilers. **ˋ~-engine** *n* locomotive or stationary engine worked or driven by pressure of ~. **ˈ~-ˋheat** *n* heat given out by ~ from radiators, pipes, etc. □ *vt: ~-heated buildings,* kept warm by ~-heat. **ˈ~ ˋradio** *n* (colloq) sound broadcasting (contrasted with TV). **ˋ~-roller** *n* heavy, slow-moving locomotive with wide wheels used in roadmaking. □ *vt* crush as with a ~-roller: *~-roller all opposition.* **ˋ~·ship** *n* ship driven by ~. □ *vi,vt* **1** [VP2A,C] give out ~ or vapour: *~ing hot coffee. The kettle was ~ing (away) on the stove.* **2** [VP2C] move, work, etc under (or as if under) the power of ~: *a ship ~ing up the Red Sea; ~ at ten knots. The train ~ed into the station.* **3** [VP6A,22] cook, soften, clean, by the use of ~; *~ fish; ~ open an envelope,* use steam to soften the gum on the flap. **4** ***~ up,*** become misty with condensed ~: *The windows ~ed up.* ***be/get (all) ~ed up,*** (colloq) become excited and perhaps violent: *Now don't get all ~ed up over nothing!* **~er** *n* **1** ~ship. **2** vessel in which food is cooked by being ~ed. **~y** *adj* of, like, full of, ~: *~y windows; the ~y heat of the rainy season in the tropics.*

steed /stid/ *n* (liter or hum) horse.

steel /stil/ *n* **1** [U] hard alloy of iron and carbon or other elements, used for knives, tools, machinery, etc. **ˋ~-clad** *adj* covered with ~ armour. **ˈ~-ˋplated** *adj* covered with ~ plates; armoured. **ˋ~-works** *n* (often with *sing v*) factory where ~ is made. **~ band** *n* (as, orig, in Trinidad) band of players who use old oil drums, etc as percussion instruments. **~ wool,** fine ~ shavings (used for scouring and polishing). **2** ~ weapon, e g a sword, contrasted with a firearm: *an enemy worthy of one's ~,* (rhet or fig) one who will fight well. **cold ~,** ⇨ cold[1](1). □ *vt* [VP6A,15A,16A] harden: *~ oneself/one's heart (against pity/to do sth).* **~y** *adj* like ~ in hardness, polish, brightness, etc.

a steel band

steel·yard /ˈstiljɑd/ *n* balance(1) with an arm in two parts, the longer side being graduated for a weight which slides along it.

steen·bok /ˈstinbok/ *n* kind of small S African antelope.

steep[1] /stip/ *adj* (**-er, -est**) **1** (of a slope) rising or falling sharply: *a ~ gradient/path/descent; a ~ roof,* with a ~ pitch. **2** (colloq, of a demand) unreasonable; excessive: *It's a bit ~ that I should pay for all of you! £2.50 for this dictionary—isn't that a bit ~? That story's rather ~,* difficult to believe, exaggerated. **~·ly** *adv* **~·ness** *n* **~en** /ˈstipən/ *vt,vi* [VP6A,2A] make or become ~ or ~er. **ˋ~·ish** /-ɪʃ/ *adj* rather ~.

steep[2] /stip/ *vt,vi* [VP6A,14,2A] ***~ sth (in sth),*** **1** soak or bathe in liquid: *~ gherkins in vinegar,* to pickle them. **2** (fig) pervade with; get a thorough knowledge of: *~ed in ignorance/prejudice/vice; a scholar ~ed in the classics of ancient Greece and Rome.*

steeple /ˈstipl/ *n* high tower with a spire, rising above the roof of a church. ⇨ the illus at **church**. **ˋ~·chase** *n* cross-country horse-race or race on foot with obstacles such as fences, hedges and ditches. ⇨ *flat racing* at **flat**[2](1). **ˋ~·jack** *n* man who climbs ~s, tall chimney-stacks, etc to do repairs.

steer[1] /stɪə(r)/ *n* young (usu castrated) male of an

animal of the ox family, raised for beef. ⇨ bull[1](1), heifer, ox.

steer[2] /stɪə(r)/ *vt, vi* [VP6A,2A,C] direct the course of (a boat, ship, car, etc): *~ north; ~ by the stars;* (with passive force): *a ship that ~s (= is ~ed) well/easily/badly.* **~ clear of,** (fig) avoid. **'~-ing-gear** *n* [U] (of a ship) rudder and the mechanism controlling it. **'~-ing-wheel** *n* **(a)** (on a ship) wheel turned to control for rudder. **(b)** (on a motor-vehicle) wheel for ~ing (mounted on the *'~ing-column*). ⇨ the illus at motor. **~s·man** /-zmən/ *n* (*pl* -men) person who ~s a vessel.

steer·age /'stɪərɪdʒ/ *n* (*sing* only, or attrib) that part of a ship nearest the rudder; this section formerly used for providing for passengers travelling at the lowest fares (term now usually replaced by 'tourist class' or 'third class'). **'~-way** *n* forward progress needed by a vessel to enable her to be controlled by the helm.

stele /'stilɪ/ *n* (*pl* stel æ /-lɪ/) (Gk archaeology) upright slab or pillar, usu with a sculptured design or inscription.

stel·lar /'stelə(r)/ *adj* of stars: *~ light.*

stem[1] /stem/ *n* **1** part of a plant coming up from the roots; part of a leaf, flower or fruit that joins it to the main stalk or twig. ⇨ the illus at flower. **-stemmed** *suff* (with *adjj*) *'long-'~med, 'short-'~med, 'thick-'~med,* having long, short, thick, ~s. **2** ~-shaped part, e g the slender part of a wine-glass, between the base and the bowl, the part of a tobacco pipe between the mouthpiece and the bowl. **3** root or main part of a noun or verb from which other words are made by additions (esp inflectional endings). **4** main upright timber at the bow of a ship. ***from ~ to stern,*** throughout the whole length of a ship. □ *vi* (-mm-) **~ *from,*** arise from; have as origin.

stems

stem[2] /stem/ *vt* (-mm-) [VP6A] **1** check, stop, dam up (a stream, a flow of liquid, etc). **2** make headway against the resistance of: *~ the tide/current;* (fig) *~ the tide of popular indignation.*

stench /stentʃ/ *n* [C] horrid smell.

sten·cil /'stensl/ *n* [C] thin sheet of metal, cardboard, waxed paper, etc with letters or designs cut through it; lettering, design, etc printed by inking paper, etc through a stencil: *cut a ~,* e g by typing without the ribbon on a waxed sheet. □ *vt* (-ll-, US also -l-) [VP6A] produce (a pattern, wording, etc) by using a ~.

Sten gun /'sten gʌn/ *n* small kind of machine-gun, usu fired from the hip.

sten·ogra·phy /stə'nogrəfɪ/ *n* (dated) = shorthand. **sten·ogra·pher** /-fə(r)/ *n* writer of shorthand (*'shorthand-'typist* is the now usu word).

sten·torian /sten'tɔrɪən/ *adj* (of a voice) loud and strong.

step[1] /step/ *vi, vt* (-pp-) **1** [VP2C] move the foot, or one foot after the other (forward, or in the direction indicated): *~ across a stream; ~ into a boat; ~ on to/off the platform; ~ across to a neighbour's,* cross (the road) to his house. ***~ this way,*** (polite invitation to) follow sb somewhere, e g into a room. ***~ on the gas/~ on it,*** **(a)** (gas = gasoline) press down the accelerator pedal to increase speed. **(b)** (colloq) hurry. **'~·ping-stone** *n* **(a)** one of a number of flat stones placed in a shallow stream, so that it can be crossed with dry feet. **(b)** (fig) means of attaining sth: *a first ~ping-stone to success.* **'~-ins** *n pl* (dated sl) woman's undergarment put on by being ~ped into. **2** [VP2C,15B] (uses with *adverbial particles*): ***~ aside,*** **(a)** move to one side. **(b)** (fig) allow sb else to take one's place. ***~ down,*** (fig) resign (to make way for sb else). ***~ in,*** (fig) intervene (either to help or hinder). ***~ sth off/out,*** measure by taking steps: *~ out a distance of ten metres.* ***~ out,*** **(a)** walk faster, walk briskly. **(b)** (colloq) have a gay time, a busy social life. ***~ sth up,*** **(a)** (naut) fix (the foot of a mast) in its socket. **(b)** increase: *~ up production; ~ up the doses (of medicine); ~ up the campaign,* put more effort into it.

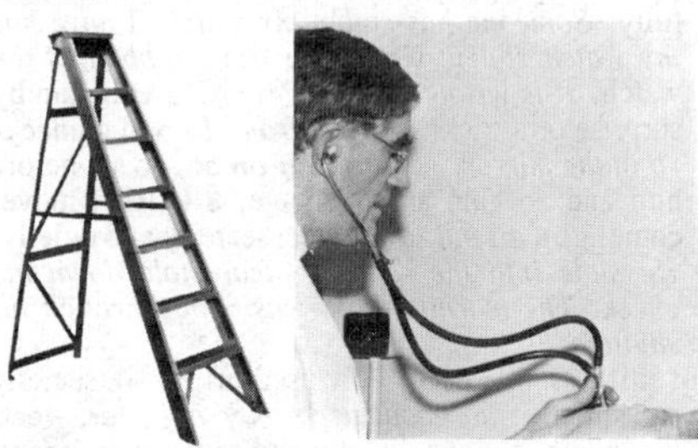

a step-ladder a stethoscope

step[2] /step/ *n* **1** act of stepping once; distance covered by doing this: *He was walking with slow ~s. The water was deeper at every ~. We must retrace our ~s,* go back. *It's only a few ~s farther. We have made a long ~* (fig, much progress) *towards success.* **watch one's ~,** be careful or cautious. ***~ by ~,*** gradually; by degrees. **'one-~, 'two-~** *nn* names of dances. **2** **('foot·)~,** sound made by somebody walking; way of walking (as seen or heard): *We heard (foot)~s outside. That's Lucy—I recognize her ~.* **3** ***be/get in/out of ~ (with),*** **(a)** put/not put the right foot to the ground at the same time as others (in walking, marching, dancing). **(b)** conform/not conform with other members of a group: *He's out of ~ with the rest of us.* ***keep ~ (with),*** walk or march in ~ (with). ***break ~,*** get out of ~. **4** one action in a series of actions with a view to effecting a purpose: *take ~s to prevent the spread of influenza; a false ~,* a mistaken action. *What's the next ~,* What are we to do next? *That would be a rash ~ to take.* **5** place for the foot when going from one level to another: *Mind the ~s when you go down into the cellar. They had to cut ~s in the ice as they climbed. The child was sitting on the bottom ~.* **~s, a pair of ~s, a '~-ladder** *nn* portable folding ladder with ~s, not rungs and usu a small platform at the top. **6** grade, rank; promotion: *When do you get your next ~ up?* When will you be promoted?

step- /step/ *pref* (used to show a relationship not

by blood but by a later marriage) **'~-child/-son/-daughter** *nn* child of an earlier marriage of one's wife or husband. **'~-brother/-sister** *nn* child of an earlier marriage of one's stepfather or stepmother. **'~-father/-mother/-parent** *nn* one's parent's later husband, wife.

steppe /step/ *n* [C] level, treeless plain, esp in S E Europe and central Asia.

stereo /'steriəʊ, 'stiər-/ *n* (abbr of *~phonic*) ~phonic record-player, radio set, etc.

stereo·phonic /ˌsteriə'fɒnik/ *adj* (of broadcast and recorded sound, using two separately placed loudspeakers) giving the effect of naturally distributed sound; (of apparatus) designed for recording or reproducing sound in this way: *a ~ recording.*

stereo·scope /'steriəskəʊp/ *n* [C] apparatus by which two photographs of sth, taken from slightly different angles, are seen as if united and with the effect of depth and solidity. **stereo·scopic** /ˌsteriəʊ'skɒpik/ *adj* of, by means of, a ~.

stereo·type /'steriətaip/ *n* [C,U] **1** (process of printing from a) printing-plate cast from a mould of a piece of printing set in movable type. **2** phrase, idea, belief, now unchanging and formalized. □ *vt* [VP6A] **1** make ~s of; print by the use of ~s. **2** (fig) (of phrases, ideas, etc) fixed in form; used and repeated without change: *~d greetings,* e g 'Good morning', 'How d'you do'?

ster·ile /'sterail *US:* 'sterl/ *adj* **1** not producing, not able to produce, seeds or offspring. **2** (of land) barren. **3** (fig) having no result; producing nothing: *a ~ discussion.* **4** free from living germs. **ste·ril·ity** /stə'riləti/ *n* [U] being ~. **ster·il·ize** /'sterḷaiz/ *vt* [VP6A] make ~: *The surgeon carefully sterilized his instruments. Should sexual maniacs be sterilized?* **ster·il·iz·ation** /ˌsterḷai'zeiʃn *US:* -ḷi'z-/ *n* [U].

ster·ling /'stɜliŋ/ *adj* **1** (of gold and silver) of standard value and purity; *of ~ gold. £20 stg* (*stg,* abbr of ~), twenty British pounds. **the '~ area,** group of countries which keep their reserves in British ~ currency and between which money can be transferred freely. **2** (fig) of solid worth; genuine: *~ sense/qualities. What a ~ fellow he is!* □ *n* British money: *payable in ~.*

stern[1] /stɜn/ *adj* (-er, -est) **1** demanding and enforcing obedience: *a ~ taskmaster.* **2** severe; strict: *a ~ face; ~ looks; ~ treatment/rebukes.* **~·ly** *adv* **~·ness** *n*

stern[2] /stɜn/ *n* [C] rear end of a ship or boat: *move out of dock ~ foremost.* ⇨ the illus at ship. **~-'wheeler** *n* steamer with a larger paddle-wheel at the ~ (instead of paddle-wheels at the sides).

ster·num /'stɜnəm/ *n* (anat) narrow bone in the front of the chest (also called *'breast-bone*) connecting the collar-bone and the top seven pairs of ribs. ⇨ the illus at skeleton.

ster·tor·ous /'stɜtərəs/ *adj* (of breathing or a person breathing) making a loud snoring sound. **~·ly** *adv*

stet /stet/ *vi* (Lat) direction to a printer, etc to disregard a correction in a manuscript or proof.

stetho·scope /'steθəskəʊp/ *n* instrument used by doctors for listening to the beating of the heart, sounds of breathing, etc. ⇨ the illus at step[2].

stet·son /'stetsn/ *n* man's hat with a high crown and a wide brim.

steve·dore /'stivədɔ(r)/ *n* man whose work is loading and unloading ships.

stew[1] /stju *US:* stu/ *vt,vi* [VP6A,15A,2A,C] cook, be cooked, in water or juice, slowly in a closed dish, pan, etc: *~ed chicken/fruit; '~ing pears,* suitable for ~ing but not for eating uncooked. ***let a person ~ in his own juice,*** do nothing to help him (when he is in trouble for which he is himself responsible). ***~ in one's own juice,*** suffer from trouble's of one's own making. ***let sb ~ (for a bit),*** let him continue suffering from the consequences of his own stupidity without offering help or sympathy. □ *n* **1** [C,U] (dish of) ~ed meat, etc: *have mutton ~ for supper; prepare a ~.* **2** ***be in/get into/a ~ (about sth),*** (colloq) a nervous, excited condition. **stewed** *adj* (sl) intoxicated.

stew[2] /stju *US:* stu/ *n* (usu **the ~s,** archaic) brothel.

stew·ard /'stjuəd *US:* 'stu-/ *n* **1** man who arranges for the supply of food, etc in a club, college, etc. **2** man who attends to the needs of passengers in a ship or airliner: *the 'baggage/'cabin/'deck, etc. ~.* **3** man responsible for organizing details of a dance, race-meeting, public meeting, show, etc: *~s of the Jockey Club. The hecklers were thrown out by the ~s.* **4** man who manages another's property (esp a large house or estate). **5 shop ~,** ⇨ shop(3). **~·ess** /ˌstjuə'des *US:* 'stuərdis/ *n* woman ~ (esp 2 above). **~·ship** /-ʃip/ *n* rank and duties of a ~(4); period of office.

stick[1] /stik/ *n* **1** thin branch broken, cut or fallen, from a bush, tree, etc: *gather dry ~s to make a fire; cut ~s to support the peas in the garden.* **2** such a branch cut to a convenient length, piece of cane cut, shaped, etc for a special purpose: *The old man cannot walk without a ~. Give that naughty boy the ~,* punish him by caning him. We have only a few ~s of furniture, only a few very roughly made articles of furniture of the simplest kind. **'hockey ~,** ⇨ hockey. ***have/get hold of the wrong end of the ~,*** be confused; misunderstand things completely. **the big ~,** (fig) threat of the use of force, e g in relationships between countries: *a policy of the big ~.* **3** slender, rod-shaped piece (of chalk, sealing-wax, charcoal, dynamite, celery, etc). **4** (colloq) person who is dull, stiff and reserved: *He's a dull/dry old ~.* **5** *the ~s,* (US colloq) the backwoods; rural areas far from cities. ***out in the ~s,*** away from the centre of things. □ *vt* (*pt,pp* ~ed) [VP6A] support with ~s(1): *Have you ~ed your peas yet?*

stick[2] /stik/ *vt,vi* (*pt,pp* **stuck** /stʌk/) (For special uses with *adverbial particles* and *preps,* ⇨ **7** below.) **1** [VP6A,15A] push (sth pointed) (into, through, etc): *~ a fork into a potato. The cushion was stuck full of pins.* **~ a pig,** (in sport) kill one with a spear. **2** [VP2C] (of sth pointed) be, remain, in a position by the point: *The needle stuck in my finger. I found a nail ~ing in the tyre.* **3** [VP15A, B,2A,C] (cause to) be or become joined or fastened with, or as with, paste, glue or other substance: *~ a stamp on a letter/a placard on a hoarding. These stamps have stuck (together).* ***be/get stuck with (sb/sth),*** (sl) permanently involved with; unable to escape from: *It looks as if I'm stuck with the job of clearing up this mess.* **'~-ing-plaster** *n* [U] plaster for ~ing on and protecting a cut, injury, etc. **4** [VP15A] (colloq) put (in some position or place), esp quickly or carelessly: *He stuck his pen behind his ear/his hands in his pockets/the papers in a drawer.* **5** [VP2A,C] (also in the passive) ***~ (in),*** be or become fixed; fail to work properly: *The key stuck in the lock,* could not be turned or withdrawn. *The bus (was) stuck in the mud. Don't get stuck in the bog. The door has stuck,* e g as the result of being newly painted. **~ *in one's throat,*** (of a proposal, etc) be difficult to accept; (of words) be difficult to utter (because of unwillingness, etc). **ˈ~-in-the-mud** *adj* slow, unprogressive. □ *n* person of this kind: *Our headmaster is an old ~-in-the-mud.* **6** [VP6A] (colloq) bear; endure: *How can you ~ that fellow? I can't ~ it any longer.* ⇨ 7, *~ it out,* below. *S~ to it!* (used as a cry of encouragement meaning 'Bear the conditions bravely', etc. **7** [VP2C,3A,15B] (special uses with *adverbial particles* and *preps*):

stick around, (colloq) hang about, stay in or near a place: *S~ around; we may need you.*

stick at sth, **(a)** stop short of, hesitate at: *Don't ~ at trifles, He ~s at nothing,* allows no feelings of doubt, no scruples, to stop him. **(b)** keep on with sth: *He ~s at his work ten hours a day.*

stick sth down, **(a)** (colloq) put down: *S~ it down anywhere you like.* **(b)** (colloq) write down. **(c)** fasten with paste, etc: *~ down (the flap of) an envelope.*

stick on sth, remain on: *Can you ~ on a horse?* ***~ sth on,*** fasten to with paste, etc: *~ on a label.* Hence, **ˈ~-on** *attrib adj*: *~-on labels* (as contrasted with *tie-on* labels). ***~ it on,*** (sl) make very high charges: *The hotel keepers ~ it on during the (busy) season.*

stick sth out, (cause to) project, stand out: *with his chest stuck out; a rude boy ~ing his tongue out at his sister. Don't ~ your head out of the carriage window.* ***~ it out,*** (colloq) endure hardship, etc until the end. ⇨ 6 above. ***~ one's neck out,*** ⇨ neck(1). ***~ out for sth,*** refuse to give way until one gets (sth demanded): *They're ~ing out for higher wages.*

stick to sb/sth, **(a)** be faithful to (one's ideals, a friend, etc); remain determined: *~ to a resolution.* **(b)** continue at: *~ to a task until it is finished; ~ to a timetable,* make no changes in what has been agreed. ***~ to one's guns,*** ⇨ gun(1).

stick together, (colloq) (of persons) remain loyal or friendly to one another.

stick up, be upright, project upwards: *The branch was ~ing up out of the water.* ***~ sb/sth up,*** (sl) threaten to shoot sb in order to rob: *~ up a bank.* Hence, **ˈ~-up** *n* ***~ your hands up, ~ 'em up,*** raise you hands (so that resistance is not intended). ***~ up for sb/oneself/sth,*** defend, support: *~ up for one's friends.*

stick with sb/sth, remain loyal to, continue to support: *~ with a friend/an ideal.*

sticker /ˈstɪkə(r)/ *n* **1** one who, or that which, sticks, e g a persevering person. ⇨ stick[2](7). **2** adhesive label to be stuck on sth.

stick·ler /ˈstɪklə(r)/ *n* ***~ for,*** person who insists upon the importance of sth (e g accuracy, discipline, formality, etc).

sticky /ˈstɪkɪ/ *adj* (-ier, -iest) **1** that sticks or tends to stick to anything that touches it: *~ fingers/toffee; a ~ road,* e g deep in wet mud. ***a ~ wicket,*** (cricket) soft wet area which makes batting difficult. ***be on a ~ wicket,*** (fig) in a situation that is difficult to deal with. **2** (sl) ***come to a ~ end,*** die in an unpleasant and painful way; *have a ~ (= unpleasant, difficult) time.* **3** (colloq) making, likely to make, objections, be unhelpful, etc: *The bank manager was ~ about letting her have an overdraft.* **stick·ily** /-əlɪ/ *adv* **sticki·ness** *n*

stiff /stɪf/ *adj* (-er, -est) **1** not easily bent or changed in shape: *a ~* (i e starched) *collar; a sheet of ~ cardboard; have a ~ leg/back,* not easily bent; *feel ~ after a long walk,* have ~ muscles and joints; *lying ~ in death.* ***keep a ~ upper lip,*** show firmness of character (by not complaining when in pain or trouble). **ˈ~-ˈnecked** *adj* obstinate. **2** hard to stir, work, move, etc: *stir the flour and milk to a ~ paste;* hard to do; difficult: *a ~ climb/examination. The book is ~ reading.* **3** (of manners, behaviour) formal, unfriendly, haughty: *get a ~ reception; be rather ~ with one's neighbours; give sb a ~ bow.* **4** great in degree: *a ~* (= strong) *breeze; a ~* (= high) *price; a ~ glass of rum/a ~ drink,* strong in alcoholic content. □ *adv* thoroughly; to the point of exhaustion: *It bored me ~,* bored me very much. *She was scared ~,* very badly scared. □ *n* (sl) **1** corpse: *Take this ~ to the mortuary.* **2** ***You big ~!*** (sl) You utter fool! **~·ly** *adv* **~·ness** *n* **~en** /ˈstɪfn/ *vt,vi* [VP6A,2A] make or become ~. **~·en·ing** /ˈstɪfnɪŋ/ *n* [U] material used to ~en a substance or object. **~·ener** /ˈstɪfn̩ə(r)/ *n* sth used to ~en.

stifle /ˈstaɪfl/ *vt,vi* **1** [VP6A,2A] give or have the feeling that breathing is difficult: *They were ~d by the heat. The heat was stifling. The smoke filled the building and almost ~d the firemen.* **2** [VP6A] suppress; put down; keep back: *~ a rebellion; ~ a yawn/a cry/one's laughter.*

stigma /ˈstɪgmə/ *n* [C] **1** (*pl* -mas /-məz/) (fig) mark of shame or disgrace: *the ~ of illegitimacy.* **2** (*pl* -mata /stɪgˈmɑtə/) marks resembling those made by the nails on the body of Jesus at His crucifixion, said to have appeared on the body of St Francis of Assisi and others. **3** (*pl* -mas) that part of the pistil of a flower which receives the pollen. ⇨ the illus at flower.

stig·ma·tize /ˈstɪgmətaɪz/ *vt* [VP16B] describe (sb) scornfully (*as*): *be ~d as a coward and a liar.*

stile /staɪl/ *n* means, not a gate, to enable persons on foot to get over or through a fence, hedge, etc but keeping cattle out. ⇨ *turnstile* at turn[2](6). ***help a lame dog over a ~,*** ⇨ dog[1](2).

sti·letto /stɪˈletəʊ/ *n* (*pl* -tos, -toes /-təʊz/) small dagger with a narrow tapering blade. **~ heel,** (on a woman's shoes) high, thin and (usu) made of metal.

still[1] /stɪl/ *adj, adv* **1** without movement or sound; quiet: *Please keep ~ while I take your photograph. How ~ everything is!* ***the ~ small voice,*** the voice of conscience. **ˈ~-ˈlife** *n* [U] representation of non-living things (e g fruit, flowers, etc) in painting; [C] (*pl* ~-lifes) painting of this kind. **ˈ~-birth** *n* child or foetus dead at birth. ⇨ *live-birth* at live[1](4). **ˈ~-born** *adj* (of a child) dead at birth. **2** (of wines) not sparkling; not containing gas. □ *n* **1** (poet) deep silence: *in the ~ of the night.* **2** [C] ordinary photograph selected from, and contrasted with, a motion picture film: *~s from a new film,* e g as used for advertising in the press. □ *vt* [VP6A] cause to be ~ or at rest; make calm. **~y** *adj* (poet) calm; quiet. **~·ness** *n*

still[2] /stɪl/ *adv* **1** (usu mid position, but may occur after a direct object) even to this or that time: *He is ~ busy. He ~ hopes/is ~ hoping for a letter from her. Will he ~ be here when I get back? In spite of his faults she ~ loved him/loved him ~.* Cf *still* and *yet*: *Is your brother here yet,* Has he arrived? *Is your brother ~ here,* Hasn't he left? **2** (with a comp) even; yet; in a greater degree: *Tom is tall but Mary is ~ taller/taller ~. That would be better ~/~ better.* **3** nevertheless; admitting that: *He has treated you badly: ~, he's your brother and you ought to help him.*

still[3] /stɪl/ *n* [C] apparatus for making liquors (brandy, whisky, etc) by distilling. **ˈ~-room** *n* house-keeper's storeroom in a large house.

stilt /stɪlt/ *n* one of a pair of poles, each with a support for the foot at some distance from the bottom, used to raise the user from the ground: *walk on ~s.*

stilted /ˈstɪltɪd/ *adj* (of liter style, talk, behaviour, etc) stiff and unnatural; too formal. **~·ly** *adv*

Stil·ton /ˈstɪltən/ *n* rich, creamy cheese with a green-blue mould in it.

stimu·lant /ˈstɪmjʊlənt/ *n* [C] drink (e g coffee, brandy), drug, etc that increases bodily or mental activity; sth that spurs one on (e g praise, hope of gain).

stimu·late /ˈstɪmjʊleɪt/ *vt* [VP6A,14,17] ***~ sb (to sth/to do sth),*** excite; rouse; quicken thought or feeling: *~ sb to further efforts; ~ sb to make greater efforts.* **stimu·lat·ing** *adj*

stimu·lus /ˈstɪmjʊləs/ *n* (*pl* **-li** /-laɪ/) [C] sth that stimulates: *work harder under the ~ of praise; a ~ to further exertions.*

sting[1] /stɪŋ/ *n* **1** [C] sharp, often poisonous, pointed organ of some insects (e g bees, wasps, gnats): *The ~ of a scorpion is in its tail.* **ˈ~·ray** *n* broad, flat, tropical fish which can cause severe wounds with its sharp spines. **2** hairs projecting from the surface of the leaves of plants (esp *ˈ~ing-nettles*), which cause pain to the fingers, etc when touched. **3** [C] sharp pain caused by the ~ of an insect or by nettles, etc; place of a wound made by a ~: *Her face was covered with ~s. Have you any ointment to put on these ~s?* **4** [C, U] any sharp pain of body or mind: *the ~ of a whip/the northeast wind/hunger/remorse. His service* (in tennis) *has no ~ in it,* is weak.

sting[2] /stɪŋ/ *vt,vi* (*pt,pp* **stung** /stʌŋ/) **1** [VP6A, 2A] prick or wound with a sting or as with a sting; have the power to ~: *A hornet stung me on the cheek. The blows of the cane stung the boy's fingers. Not all nettles ~.* **2** [VP6A,15A] cause sharp pain (to): *He was stung by his enemy's insults. Anger stung* (= roused) *him to action.* **3** [VP2A] (of parts of the body) feel sharp pain: *His fingers were still ~ing from the caning he had had.* **4** ***~ sb (for sth),*** (colloq) charge him an excessive price (for sth); swindle sb: *He was stung for £5,* had to pay this sum. *How much did they ~ you for?* **~er** *n* (esp) smart, painful blow. **~·less** *adj* having no ~.

stingy /ˈstɪndʒɪ/ *adj* (**-ier, -iest**) spending, using or giving unwillingly; niggardly; miserly: *Don't be so ~ with the sugar!* **stin·gily** /-dʒəlɪ/ *adv* **stin·gi·ness** *n*

stink /stɪŋk/ *vi,vt* (*pt* **stank** /stæŋk/ or **stunk** /stʌŋk/, *pp* **stunk**) **1** [VP2A,3A] ***~ (of sth),*** have a horrid and offensive smell: *That fish ~s. Her breath stank of garlic.* ***cry ~ing fish,*** condemn one's own goods, etc. **2** [VP15B] ***~ sb/sth out,*** **(a)** drive out by means of sth evil-smelling: *~ out a fox,* e g by sending smoke into its hole. **(b)** fill a place with ~s: *You'll ~ the place out with your cheap cigars!* □ *n* [C] **1** horrid smell. ***raise/kick up a ~ (about sth),*** (colloq) cause trouble or annoyance, e g by complaining. **2** (*pl;* schoolboy sl) chemistry (as a subject of study). **~er** *n* (sl) **1** letter intended to convey strong disapproval, reproach etc. **2** person who arouses strong dislike. **3** (colloq) sth difficult: *The biology paper* (i e in an examination) *was a ~er.*

stint /stɪnt/ *vt,vi* [VP6A,14] ***~ sb (of sth),*** restrict (sb) to a small allowance: *She ~ed herself of food in order to let the children have enough. Don't ~ the food.* □ *n* **1** (usu) ***without ~,*** without limit, without sparing any effort. **2** [C] fixed or allotted amount (of work): *do one's daily ~.*

sti·pend /ˈstaɪpend/ *n* [C] (esp clergyman's) salary. **sti·pen·di·ary** /staɪˈpendɪərɪ *US:* -dɪerɪ/ *adj* receiving a ~, not working without pay: *a ~iary magistrate,* paid magistrate in a large town (appointed by the Home Secretary) dealing with police court cases. □ *n* (*pl* **-ries**) ~iary magistrate.

stipple /ˈstɪpl/ *vt* [VP6A] draw or paint with dots instead of lines.

stipu·late /ˈstɪpjʊleɪt/ *vt,vi* **1** [VP6A,9] state, put forward, as a necessary condition: *It was ~d that the goods should be delivered within three days.* **2** [VP3A] ***~ for sth,*** insist upon (as part of an agreement): *~ for the best materials to be used.* **stipu·la·tion** /ˈstɪpjʊˈleɪʃn/ *n* [C] sth ~d; condition: *on the stipulation that....*

stir[1] /stɜ(r)/ *vi,vt* (**-rr-**) **1** [VP6A,2A,C] be moving; cause to move: *Not a leaf was ~ring,* There was no wind to move the leaves. *A breeze ~red the leaves. Nobody was ~ring in the house,* Everyone was resting. *She is not ~ring yet,* is still in bed. *You had better ~ yourself,* get busy, be active. *I haven't ~red out all morning,* haven't left the house. ***not ~ an eyelid,*** remain unmoved, showing no alarm or concern. ***not ~ a finger,*** make no effort to do things; give no help. ***~ one's stumps,*** (colloq) make haste, walk faster. **2** [VP6A,15B] ***~ sth (up),*** move a spoon, etc round and round in liquid, etc in order to mix it thoroughly: *~ one's tea; ~ the porridge; ~ milk into a cake mixture.* ***~ the fire,*** use the poker in it. **3** [VP6A,14,15B] ***~ sb to sth, ~ sth up,*** excite: *The story ~red the boy's imagination. Discontented men ~red the crew to mutiny/~ed up trouble among the crew. He wants ~ring up,* needs to be roused from lethargy. ***~ the blood,*** rouse to excitement or enthusiasm. **4** [VP2A,C] be roused: *Pity ~red in his heart.* □ *n* (usu *sing* with *a*) commotion; excitement: *The news caused quite a ~ in the village.* **~·ring** *adj* exciting: *~ring tales of adventure; live in ~ring times.* **~·ring·ly** *adv*

stir[2] /stɜ(r)/ *n* (sl) prison: *in ~ for six months.*

stir·rup[1] /ˈstɪrəp *US:* ˈstɜəp/ *n* [C] foot-rest, hanging down from a saddle, for the rider of a horse. ⇨ the illus at harness. **ˈ~-cup** *n* drink (of wine, etc) offered to sb mounted on a horse ready for departure.

stir·rup[2] /ˈstɪrəp *US:* ˈstɜəp/ *n* (anat) bone in the ear. ⇨ the illus at ear.

stitch /stɪtʃ/ *n* **1** [C] (in sewing) the passing of a needle and thread in and out of cloth, etc; (in knitting) one complete turn of the wool, etc over the needle. **2** the thread, etc seen between two consecutive holes made by a needle; result of a single movement with a threaded needle, knitting-needle, etc: *make long/neat, etc ~es; put a few*

~*es in a garment; drop a* ~, allow a loop to slip off the end of a knitting-needle; *put* ~*es into/take* ~*es out of a wound.* ***have not a ~ on,*** (colloq) be naked. ***A ~ in time saves nine,*** (prov) A small piece of work done now may save a lot of work later. **3** (in compounds) particular kind of ~: *a* ˋ*button-hole* ~*; a* ˋ*chain-*~, etc. **4** (*sing* only) sharp pain in the side (as caused sometimes by running too soon after a meal). □ *vt,vi* [VP6A, 15A,B,2A,C] sew; put ~es in or on.

stoat /stəʊt/ *n* small furry animal larger than a rat; weasel; ermine (in its summer coat of brown).

stock[1] /stɒk/ *n* **1** [C,U] store or goods available for sale, distribution or use, esp goods kept by a trader or shopkeeper. ***(be) in/out of ~,*** be available/not available: *The book is in/out of* ~. *Have you any linen sheets in* ~? ˋ**~-list** *n* list of goods, etc available. ˋ**~-room** *n* room in which ~ is kept. ***take ~,*** examine and make a list of goods in ~; Hence, ˋ**~-taking** *n*: *The annual* ~*-taking starts tomorrow,* e g in a draper's shop. ***take ~ of,*** (fig) review (a situation); estimate (sb's abilities, etc). ˈ**~-in-**ˋ**trade** *n* [U] everything needed for a trade or occupation. **2** (attrib use, from **1** above) usually kept in ~ (and therefore usually obtainable): ~ *sizes in hats,* commonly or regularly used; hackneyed: ~ *arguments/comparisons;* ~ questions/ answers. *She's tired of her husband's* ~ *jokes.* ~ **company,** company of actors who have a ~ (or repertoire) of plays which they perform. **3** [C,U] supply of anything: *a good* ~ *of information; get in* ~*s of coal and coke for the winter.* ˋ**~-piling** *n* purchase (esp by a Government) of ~s of raw materials or goods not easily available from local sources (e g tin, rubber, needed in war). **4** [U] (ˋ**live-**)**~,** farm animals: *fat* ~, ~ fit for slaughter as food: *fat-*~ *prices.* ˋ**~-breeder/farmer** *n* farmer who breeds or raises cattle. ˋ**~-car** *n* railway truck for carrying cattle. ˋ**~-car racing** *n* racing of ordinary models as sold generally. ˋ**~-yard** *n* enclosure where cattle are kept temporarily, e g at a market, or before being slaughtered. **5** [C,U] money lent to a government in return for interest; shares in the capital of a business company: *have £5000 in the* ~*s; invest one's money in (a) safe* ~. ˋ**~-broker** *n* man whose business is the buying and selling of ~(s). ˋ**~ exchange** *n* place where ~s and shares are publicly bought and sold; (esp) *the London S*~ *Exchange.* ˋ**~-holder** *n* (chiefly US) shareholder. ˋ**~-jobber** *n* member of a ~-exchange from whom a ~broker buys and to whom he sells. ˋ**~-list** *n* publication with current prices of ~s(5) and shares. **6** [U] line of ancestry: *a woman of Irish* ~*/of Puritan/farming, etc* ~. **7** ***~s and stones,*** lifeless things. ˈ**~-**ˋ**still** *adv* motionless. ˋ**laughing-~,** target or object or ridicule. **8** [U] raw material ready for manufacture: ˋ*paper* ~, e g rags, etc to be made into paper. **9** [U] liquid in which bones, etc have been stewed; juices of meat and vegetables, used for making soup, gravy, etc. ˋ**~-cube** *n* cube of dehydrated ~. ˋ**~-fish** *n* fish (esp cod) split open and dried in the air without salt, a staple food in some countries. ˋ**~-pot** *n* one in which ~(9) is made or stored. **10** [C] base, support, or handle of an instrument, tool, etc: *the* ~ *of a rifle/plough/ whip; the* ~ *of an anchor,* the crossbar. ***lock, ~ and barrel,*** (fig) completely. **11** [C] lower part of a tree trunk. **12** [C] growing plant into which a graft is inserted. **13** (*pl*) framework supporting a ship while it is being built or repaired. ***on the ~s,*** under construction; in preparation. **14** (*pl*) wooden framework with holes for the feet in which wrongdoers were formerly locked in a sitting position. **15** [C] wide band of stiff linen worn around the neck by men in former times (like the modern tie). **16** sort of garden plant with single or double brightly coloured sweet-smelling flowers.

stock[2] /stɒk/ *vt* [VP6A,14] supply or equip with; have a stock of; keep in stock: ~ *a shop with goods; well* ~*ed with the latest fashions in hats. Do you* ~ *raincoats? He has a memory well* ~*ed with facts.* **~·ist** /-ɪst/ *n* one who ~s (certain goods) for sale.

stock·ade /stɒˋkeɪd/ *n* [C] line or wall of upright stakes, built as a defence. □ *vt* (usu *pp*) defend with a ~.

stock·in·ette /ˈstɒkɪˋnet/ *n* [U] elastic machine-made knitted fabric (esp as used for underclothing).

stock·ing /ˋstɒkɪŋ/ *n* [C] tight-fitting covering of nylon, silk, cotton, wool, etc for the foot and leg, reaching to or above the knee: *a pair of* ~*s.* ⇨ tights. ***in one's ~ feet,*** wearing ~s or socks but not shoes.

stocky /ˋstɒkɪ/ *adj* (-ier, -iest) (of persons, animals, plants) short, strong and stout. **stock·ily** /-əlɪ/ *adv* in a ~ manner: *a stockily built man.*

stodge /stɒdʒ/ *n* [U] (sl) heavy and solid food. **stodgy** /ˋstɒdʒɪ/ *adj* **1** (of food) heavy and solid: *a stodgy meal.* **2** (of books, etc) written in a heavy, uninteresting way (overweighted with facts, details, etc); (of persons) having a heavy personality; dull and unenterprising.

stoep /stup/ *n* (S Africa) terraced veranda; porch or steps outside the front entrance of a house.

stoic /ˋstəʊɪk/ *n* person who has great self-control, who bears pain and discomfort without complaint. **sto·ical** /-kl/ *adj* of or like a ~. **sto·ically** /-klɪ/ *adv* **sto·icism** /ˋstəʊɪsɪzm/ *n* [U] patient and uncomplaining endurance of suffering, etc.

stoke /stəʊk/ *vt,vi* [VP6A,15B,2A,C] ***~ (sth) up,*** put (coal, etc) on the fire of (an engine, furnace, etc); attend to a furnace: ~ *(up) the furnace;* ~ *(up) twice a day.* ˋ**~-hole/-hold** *nn* place where a ship's furnaces are ~d. **stoker** *n* workman who ~s a furnace, etc; mechanical device for feeding a furnace with fuel.

stole[1] /stəʊl/ *n* **1** strip of silk or other material worn (round the neck with the ends hanging down in front) by priests of some Christian Churches during services. ⇨ the illus at vestment. **2** woman's wrap worn over the shoulders.

stole[2]**, stolen** *pt,pp* of steal.

stolid /ˋstɒlɪd/ *adj* not easily excited; slow to show the feelings. **~·ly** *adv* **~·ness, sto·lid·ity** /stəˋlɪdətɪ/ *nn* [U].

stom·ach /ˋstʌmək/ *n* **1** [C] bag-like part of the alimentary canal into which food passes to be digested: *It is unwise to swim on a full* ~*/work on an empty* ~. ⇨ the illus at alimentary. ˋ**~-pump** *n* pump with a flexible tube, inserted into the ~ through the mouth (for use, e g in a case of poisoning). **2** (genteel word for) belly, abdomen. ˋ**~-ache** *n* pain in the belly, esp the bowels. **3** [U] appetite. ***have no ~ for sth,*** be disinclined to do or agree with sth, (because one disapproves of it): *have no* ~ *for bull-fighting.* □ *vt* [VP6A] (usu neg in interr) endure; put up with: *How can you* ~ *the violence in so many films today?*

stomp /stɒmp/ *vi* [VP2C] ~ ***about,*** stamp, tread, heavily. □ *n* (jazz music for a) dance with a heavy beat.

stone /stəʊn/ *n* **1** [U] (often attrib) solid mineral matter which is not metallic; rock (often with a defining word as prefix, as *ˋsand~, ˋlime~*): *a wall made of ~; ~ walls/buildings; ~ jars*, made of *ˋ~ware*, ⇨ below; *have a heart of ~*, (fig) be hard-hearted. **the ˋS~ Age,** period of culture when weapons and tools were made of ~ (before the use of metals was known). **ˈ~-ˋblind/-ˋcold/-ˋdead/-ˋdeaf/-ˋsober** *adjj* completely blind, etc. **ˋ~-breaker** *n* person who breaks up ~, esp for road-making; machine for crushing ~. **ˋ~-mason** *n* man who cuts, prepares and builds with ~. **ˋ~-pit** *n* quarry for ~. **ˈ~-ˋwall** *vt* (cricket) be excessively cautious when batting so that runs come slowly; (fig) (in Parliament) obstruct progress by making long speeches, etc. Hence, **ˈ~-ˋwalling** *n* **ˈ~-ˋwaller** *n* person given to this. **ˋ~-ware** *n* [U] pottery made from clay and flint. **ˋ~-work** *n* [U] masonry; part(s) of a building made of ~. **2** [C] piece of ~(1) of any shape, usu broken off: *a road covered with ~s; a fall of ~s down a hillside.* ***leave no ~ unturned (to do sth),*** try every possible means. ***throw ~s at,*** (fig) attack the character of: *Those who live in glass houses should not throw ~s,* (prov) If your own character is not beyond reproach you should not attack the character of others. ***within a ˋ~'s throw (of),*** very close (to). **3** [C] **(precious) ~,** jewel; diamond. **4** [C] piece of ~ of a definite shape, for a special purpose (usu in compounds): *a ˋgrave~*, ⇨ grave[2]; *ˋstepping-~s*, ⇨ step[1]; *ˋtomb~s*, ⇨ tomb; *ˋmill~s*, ⇨ mill[1]. **5** [C] sth round and hard like a ~, esp **(a)** the hard shell and nut or seed of such fruits as the apricot, peach, plum and cherry. ⇨ the illus at fruit. **ˋ~-fruit** *n* fruits of this kind. **(b)** (usu **ˋhail-~**) small frozen drop of rain: *hail with ~s as big as peas.* **(c)** small hard object that has formed in the bladder or kidney: *have an operation for ~.* **ˋgall-~,** ⇨ gall[1](1). **6** (not US; *pl* unchanged) unit of weight, 14 lb: *two ~ of flour. A man who weighs 20 stone is certainly over normal weight.* □ *vt* **1** [VP6A,15A] throw ~s at: *Christian martyrs who were ~d to death.* **2** [VP6A] take the ~s(5 (a)) out of (fruit): *~d dates.* **~-less** *adj* without ~s esp of fruit(5 (a)) above. **stoned** *adj* (colloq) under the influence of (usu) soft drugs; very drunk.

stony /ˋstəʊnɪ/ *adj* (-ier, -iest) **1** having many stones: *~ soil/ground;* covered with stones: *a ~ path/road.* **2** hard, cold and unsympathetic: *a ~ heart; ˈ~-ˋhearted; a ~ stare; ~ politeness.* **3** (sl) **ˈ~(-ˋbroke),** completely without money; penniless. **ston·ily** /-əlɪ/ *adv* in a ~(2) manner: *stonily polite.*

stood /stʊd/ *pt,pp* of stand[2].

stooge /studʒ/ *n* person who, in variety entertainment, is made fun of by a comedian; (colloq) person used as an assistant (to perform unpleasant jobs or duties that may incur blame, punishment, etc). □ *vi* ~ ***for sb,*** act as a ~.

stool /stul/ *n* **1** seat without a back or arms, usu for one person; *sitting on ~s at the bar drinking cocktails; a piˋano-~.* ***fall between two ~s,*** lose an opportunity through hesitating between two courses of action. **2** **(ˋfoot-)~,** low support on which to rest the feet. **3** [U] (med) solid excrement: *send a specimen of one's ~s to the doctor,* e g to be tested for amoebic infection; (old use) privy; place for emptying of the bowels: *go to ~.* **4** **ˋ~-pigeon** *n* pigeon used as a decoy; (fig) person acting as a decoy, e g one employed by the police to trap a criminal.

stoop[1] /stup/ *vi,vt* **1** [VP2A,C,4A,6A] bend the body forwards and downwards; bend the neck so that the head is forward and down: *~ing with old age; ~ to pick sth up. ~ one's head to get into a car.* **2** [VP3A] ~ ***to sth,*** (fig) lower oneself morally: *~ to folly/cheating. He's a man who would ~ to anything,* who has no moral scruples. □ *n* (usu *sing*) ~ing position of the body: *walk with a ~,* as when very old or ill.

stoop[2] /stup/ *n* (in N America) porch or unroofed platform or set of steps at the entrance to a house. ⇨ stoep.

stop[1] /stɒp/ *n* [C] **1** stopping or being stopped: *The train came to a sudden ~. This train goes from London to Leeds with only two ~s.* ***put a ~ to sth, bring sth to a ~,*** cause it to ~ or end: *I'll put a ~ to this nonsense. Traffic was brought to a complete ~.* **2** place at which buses, trams, etc stop regularly or (*reˋquest ~*) when requested to do so: *Where's the nearest ˋbus-~?* **3** (music) key or lever (e g in a flute) for regulating pitch; row of pipes (in an organ) providing tones of one quality; knob or lever working such a row of pipes. ***pull out all the ~s,*** (fig) appeal to all the emotions; make a great effort. **4** (in writing and printing) mark of punctuation, esp *full ~.* **5** (in a camera) device for regulating the size of the aperture through which light reaches the lens. **6** (in phonetics) consonant produced by the sudden release of air which has been held back (e g /p, b, k, g, t, d/). **7** device that stops the movement of sth at a fixed point, e g a peg of wood to prevent an ill-fitting window from rattling. **8** (compounds) **ˋ~-cock** *n* valve inserted in a pipe by which the flow of liquid or gas through the pipe can be regulated: *A water-pipe has burst—where's the ~cock?* **ˋ~-gap** *n* temporary substitute. **ˋ~-press** *n* (not US) latest news inserted in a newspaper already on the printing machines. **ˋ~-watch** *n* watch with a hand that can be started and stopped when desired, used to time events such as races to a fraction of a second. **~-page** /ˋstɒpɪdʒ/ *n* [C] **1** condition of being stopped up, ⇨ **6** above; obstruction. **2** stopping(7): *~page of leave/pay,* (esp in the armed forces, e g as a form of punishment). **3** interruption of work (in a factory, etc as the result of strike action.) **~-per** *n* object which fits into and closes an opening, esp the mouth of a bottle or pipe. ***put the ~pers on (sth),*** suppress it.

stop[2] /stɒp/ *vt,vi* (-pp-) **1** [VP6A] put an end to (the movement or progress of a person, thing, activity, etc): *~ a car/a train/a runaway horse. The earthquake ~ped all the clocks.* **2** [VP6A,B,14] ~ ***sb (from) (doing sth),*** prevent; hinder: *What can ~ our going/~ us from going if we want to go? Can't you ~ the child (from) getting into mischief? He will certainly go—there's no one to ~ him.* **3** [VP6A,D] leave off; discontinue (doing sth): *~ work. We ~ped talking. Why doesn't he ~ beating his wife?* **4** [VP2A,3,4A] break off; discontinue: *The rain has ~ped. The clock/His heart has ~ped. It has ~ped raining. We ~ped to have a rest. We ~ped (in order) to talk.* Cf *We ~ped talking.* **5** [VP2A,3,4A] come to rest; halt: *The train ~ped. Does this train ~ at*

Crewe? ~ ***dead,*** ~ suddenly. ~ ***short at sth,*** limit one's actions, etc: *Will our neighbours ~ short at war?* **6** [VP6A,15A,B] ~ ***sth (up),*** fill or close (a hole, opening, etc): *~ a leak in a pipe; ~ up a mouse-hole; have a tooth ~ped,* have a cavity filled; *~ one's ears,* (fig) refuse to listen; *~ the way,* prevent progress. **7** [VP6A,14] cut off; keep back or refuse to give (sth normally supplied): *~ (payment of) a cheque,* order the bank not to cash it; *~ sb's wages. The bank has ~ped payment,* is unable to meet its obligations. ~ ***sth out of sth,*** deduct sth from (wages, salary, etc). **8** [VP2A,B,C] (colloq) stay: *~ at home. Are you ~ping at this hotel?* ~ ***off (at/in),*** break a journey for a short period: *~ off at a store to buy sth.* ~ ***off/over (at/in),*** break a journey for a stay: *~ (off) overnight in Edinburgh.* **'~-over** *n* (attrib): *'~-over ticket,* one that permits a journey to be broken in this way. ~ ***up (late),*** stay up, not go to bed until late. **9** (music) produce desired note(s) by pressing fingers on strings (e g of a violin), or over holes (e g in a flute). **~·ping** *n* filling for a dental cavity. ⇨ 6 above.

stor·age /'stɔrɪdʒ/ *n* [U] (space used for, money paid for) the storing of goods: *put one's furniture in ~; keep fish in cold ~;* (attrib) *'~ tanks,* e g for oil; *'~ heater,* electric radiator which stores heat (accumulated during off-peak periods).

store /stɔ(r)/ *n* **1** [C] quantity or supply of sth kept for use as needed: *lay in ~s of coal for the winter; have a good ~ of provisions in the house.* **2** [U] ***in ~,*** **(a)** kept ready for use; for future use: *That's a treat in ~,* a pleasure still to come. **(b)** destined (*for*); coming to: *Who knows what the future has in ~ for us?* **3** (*pl*) goods, etc of a particular kind, or for a special purpose: *naval and military ~s; marine ~s* (but note: *'marine-'~ dealer*). **4** [C] **'~(-house),** place where goods are kept; warehouse: *The book is a ~-house of information.* **'~·room** *n* one in which household supplies are kept. **5** [C] (chiefly US but ⇨ 6 below) shop: *a 'clothing ~; ~ clothes,* bought from a ~, ready to wear, not tailor-made. **6** (*pl*) shop selling many varieties of goods: *the big department ~s of London; the 'Army and 'Navy S~s; a general ~s,* (esp) village shop selling a variety of goods. ⇨ also *chain-~* at chain(4). **7** [U] ***set great/little/no/not much ~ by,*** consider of great/little, etc value or importance. □ *vt* [VP6A,15B] ~ ***sth (up),*** **1** collect and keep for future use; *Do all squirrels ~ up food for the winter?* **2** put (furniture, etc) in a warehouse, etc, for safe keeping. **3** furnish, equip, supply: *a mind well ~d with facts.*

storey (US = **story**) /'stɔrɪ/ *n* (*pl* -reys, (US) -ries) floor or level in a building: *a house of two ~s,* i e with rooms on the ground floor and one floor upstairs. **-storeyed** (US = **stor·ied**) /-'stɔrɪd/ *adj* having the number of ~s indicated by the prefixed number: *a six-~ed building.*

stor·ied /'stɔrɪd/ *adj* (liter) made famous in legend or stories: *the ~ Rhine.*

stork /stɔk/ *n* large, long-legged, usu white wading-bird (some of which build their nests on the tops of high buildings). ⇨ the illus at water.

storm /stɔm/ *n* **1** [C] occasion of violent weather conditions: *a 'thunder-/'wind-/'rain-/'dust-/'sand-~; cross the Channel in a ~. The forecast says there will be ~s.* ***a ~ in a teacup,*** much excitement about sth trivial. **'~-beaten** *adj* damaged by ~s. **'~-bound** *adj* unable to continue a journey, voyage, etc unable to go out, because of ~s. **'~-centre** *n* centre of a ~ or (fig) of a disturbance or trouble. **'~-cloud** *n* heavy rain-cloud accompanying, or showing the likelihood of, a ~. **'~-cone/-signal** *n* one hoisted as a warning of high wind. **'~-lantern** *n* one for use outdoors, made so that the light is well protected from wind. **'~-proof** *adj* able to resist ~s. **'~-tossed** *adj* damaged or blown about by ~s. **2** violent outburst of feeling: *a ~ of protests/cheering/applause/abuse.* ***bring a ~ about one's ears,*** do or say sth that rouses strong opposition, indignation, etc. **3** ***take by ~,*** capture by a violent and sudden attack. **'~-troops** *n pl* troops trained for violent attacks. **'~-trooper** *n* one of these. □ *vi,vt* **1** [VP2A,3A] ~ ***(at),*** give violent expression to anger; shout angrily. **2** [VP15A,B, 2C] force (a way) into a building, etc; [VP6A] capture (a place) by sudden and violent attack: *The men ~ed (their way) into the fort/~ed the fort.* **~y** *adj* (-ier, -iest) **1** marked by strong wind, heavy rain or snow or hail: *~y weather; a ~y night/crossing.* **2** marked by strong feelings of indignation, anger, etc: *a ~y discussion/meeting; ~y scenes during the debate.* **~·ily** /-əlɪ/ *adv*

story[1] /'stɔrɪ/ *n* [C] (*pl* -ries) **1** account of past events: *the ~ of Columbus; stories of ancient Greece.* **2** account of imaginary events: *a 'ghost ~; a children's '~-book; a ~-book ending,* a happy one (as in most stories for children). *The ~ goes that...,* People are saying that.... **'~-teller** *n* person who tells stories. **3** (journalism) any descriptive article in a newspaper; an event, situation, etc suitable for such an article. **4** (esp by and to children) untrue statement: *Don't tell stories, Tom.*

story[2] /'stɔrɪ/ *n* ⇨ storey.

stoup /stup/ *n* **1** (old use) drinking-vessel; flagon. **2** stone basin for holy water on the wall of a church or near the porch.

stout /staʊt/ *adj* (-er, -est) **1** strong, thick, not easily broken or worn out: *~ shoes for mountain-climbing.* **2** determined and brave: *offer a ~ resistance to the enemy; a ~ fellow; a ~ heart.* Hence, **'~-'hearted** *adj* courageous. **3** (of a person) rather fat; tending to fatness: *She's growing too ~ to walk far.* □ *n* [U] strongest kind of dark beer. **~·ly** *adv* **~·ness** *n*

stove[1] /stəʊv/ *n* [C] closed apparatus burning wood, coal, gas, oil or other fuel, used for warming rooms, cooking, etc. **'~-pipe** *n* pipe for carrying off smoke from a ~.

stove[2] /stəʊv/ ⇨ stave[2].

stow /stəʊ/ *vt* [VP6A,15A,B] ~ ***sth (away);*** ~ ***sth into sth/sth with sth,*** pack, esp carefully and closely: *~ cargo in a ship's holds; ~ things away in the attic; ~ clothes into a trunk/~ a trunk with clothes.* **'~·away** *n* person who hides himself in a ship or aircraft (until after it starts) in order to make a journey without paying.

straddle /'strædl/ *vt,vi* **1** [VP6A] sit or stand across (sth) with the legs widely separated: *~ a ditch/a seat/a horse/a fence.* **2** [VP2A] stand with the legs wide apart.

strafe /strɑf/ *vt* [VP6A] (colloq) **1** bombard. **2** punish; scold.

straggle /'strægl/ *vi* [VP2A,C] **1** grow, spread, in an irregular or untidy manner: *a straggling village; vines straggling over the fences.* **2** drop behind while on the march; stray from the main body. **strag·gler** /ˈstræglə(r)/ *n* person who ~s(2). **strag·gly** /ˈstræglɪ/ *adj* straggling.

straight[1] /streɪt/ *adj* **1** without a bend or curve; extending in one direction only: *a ~ line/road; ~ hair,* with no curls in it. **2** parallel to (sth else, esp the horizon); level: *Put the picture ~. Is my hat on ~?* **3** in good order; tidy: *put a room ~.* ***put sth ~,*** make it tidy: *Please put your desk ~ before you leave the office.* ***put the record ~,*** give an accurate account of events, etc. **4** (of a person, his behaviour, etc) honest, frank, upright: *give a ~ answer to a question,* answer frankly; *keep ~,* avoid wrongdoing, live as a good citizen. *He is perfectly ~ in all his dealings. His wife will keep him ~* (= help him to live honestly) *when he is released from prison.* ⇨ straight[2](4). **5** (phrases) **a ~ fight,** (in politics) one in which there are only two candidates. **a ~ play,** an ordinary drama (contrasted with variety). **a ~ tip,** (e g about the likely winner of a race, an investment in shares), one (said to come) from a direct and reliable source. ***keep a ~ face,*** refrain from smiling or laughing. ***vote the ~ ticket,*** ⇨ ticket(3). **6** (of alcoholic drinks) neat, i e without added (soda-)water: *Two ~ whiskies, please.* **~en** /ˈstreɪtn/ *vt,vi* [VP6A,15B,2A,C] make or become ~: *~en a piece of wire/one's tie. His figure has ~ened out.* **~·ness** *n*

straight[2] /streɪt/ *adv* **1** directly; not in a curve or at an angle: *The smoke rose ~ up. Keep ~ on. Look ~ ahead. The drunken man couldn't walk ~. Can you shoot ~,* aim accurately? **2** by a direct route; without turning aside; without delay: *Come ~ home. He went ~ to Rome without staying in Paris. He went ~ from school into his father's business.* ***come ~ to the point,*** make a prompt and clear statement of what is meant, wanted, etc. **3** ***~ away/off,*** immediately. ***~ out,*** without hesitation or deliberation: *I told him ~ out that I thought he was mistaken.* **4** ***go ~,*** (fig) live an honest life (esp after having been dishonest).

straight[3] /streɪt/ *n* (usu *sing* with *def art*) condition of being straight; straight part of sth, esp the final part of a track or race-course, near the winning-post: *The two horses were together as they entered the final ~.*

straight·for·ward /streɪtˈfɔwəd/ *adj* **1** honest; without evasion: *a ~ explanation.* **2** easy to understand or do: *written in ~ language; a ~ problem in algebra.* **~·ly** *adv*

straight·way /streɪtˈweɪ/ *adv* at once; immediately.

strain[1] /streɪn/ *n* **1** [C,U] condition of being stretched; force exerted: *The rope broke under the ~. Engineers calculate the ~s and stresses of a bridge. What is the breaking ~ of this cable,* the ~ that will break it? **2** [C,U] sth that tests and strains one's powers; severe demand on one's strength, etc: *the ~ of sleepless nights. The payment of the lawyer's bills was a great ~ on my resources. Do you suffer from the ~ of modern life? He has been under severe ~.* **3** [U] exhaustion; fatigue: *suffering from mental/nervous ~; suffer from ˈover~.* **4** [C] sprain; injury caused by twisting a joint, etc. **5** (poet; usu *pl*) music, song, verse (of the kind indicated): *the ~s of an organ; the martial ~s of the band of the Royal Marines.* **6** [C] manner of speaking or writing: *in a lofty/cheerful/dismal ~; and much more in the same ~,* the same general tendency. **7** tendency in a person's character: *There is a ~ of insanity in the family/of mysticism in her.* **8** breed (of animals, insects, etc); line of descent: *~s of mosquitoes that are resistant to D D T; a spaniel of good ~.*

strain[2] /streɪn/ *vt,vi* **1** [VP6A,15A] stretch tightly by pulling (*at*): *~ a rope to breaking-point; a dog ~ing at its lead.* **2** [VP6A,16A] make the greatest possible use of; exert one's powers: *~ every nerve* (*to do sth*), do one's utmost; *~ one's eyes/ears/voice,* look/listen/speak to the best of one's power. ⇨ 3 below. **3** [VP6A] injure or weaken by ~ing(2): *~ a muscle; ~ one's heart,* injure it by over-exertion; *~ one's eyes,* by using them too much, or on small print, in poor light, etc; *~ one's voice,* by speaking or singing too long or too loudly. **4** [VP2A,C] ***~ (at/on),*** make an intense effort; *The wrestlers ~ed and struggled. We ~ed at the oars.* ***~ after effects,*** make exaggerated efforts to get effects: *There is no ~ing after effects in this writer's work.* **5** [VP6A] (fig) stretch the meaning of: force beyond a limit or what is right: *~ the belief/credulity of one's listeners;* ask too much of it; *~ one's authority/rights,* apply them in a way that is beyond what is allowable or reasonable; *~ the meaning of a word.* **6** [VP15A] (liter) hold tightly; squeeze: *She ~ed the boy to her bosom.* **7** [VP6A,15B] pass (liquid) through a cloth, or a network of fine wire, etc; separate solid matter in this way: *~ the soup; ~ off the water from the vegetables.* **8** ***~ at sth,*** be too scrupulous or hesitant about accepting sth. **9** **~ed** (*pp*) (esp of feelings and behaviour) forced; unnatural; as if forced: *~ed cordiality; a ~ed laugh.* **~ed relations,** marked by loss of patience, irritability, risk of quarrelling. **~er** *n* sieve or other device by means of which solid matter is separated from liquid: *a ˈtea-~er,* for keeping back tea-leaves when tea is poured out from a teapot.

strait[1] /streɪt/ *adj* (old use) narrow (rare except in: *~ gate,* ⇨ Matt 7: 14). **ˈ~-jacket,** long-sleeved jacket used to bind the arms of a mentally ill person to the body and prevent him from struggling; (fig) sth that prevents growth or development. **ˈ~-ˈlaced** *adj* severely virtuous; having a strict attitude towards moral questions; puritanic. **~en** /ˈstreɪtn/ *vt* (usu in *pp*) ***in ~ed circumstances,*** in poverty.

strait[2] /streɪt/ *n* **1** narrow passage of water connecting two seas or two large bodies of water (*pl* or *sing* with proper names): *the S~s of Gibraltar; the Magellan S~.* **2** (usu *pl*) trouble; difficulty: *be in financial ~s; in great ~s.*

strand[1] /strænd/ *n* (poet or rhet) sandy shore of a lake, sea or river. □ *vi,vt* **1** [VP6A,2A] (of a ship) (cause to) run aground. **2** ***be (left) ~ed,*** (of a person) be left without means of transport, in a difficult position, without money or friends: *be ~ed in a foreign country.*

strand[2] /strænd/ *n* [C] **1** any of the threads, hairs, wires, etc twisted together into a rope or cable, or in a textile material; tress of hair. **2** (fig) line of development (in a story, etc): *May I pick out one ~ in that narrative?*

strange /streɪndʒ/ *adj* (-r, -st) **1** not previously known, seen, felt or heard of; (for this reason) surprising: *hear a ~ noise; in a ~ land. What ~* (= unusual) *clothes you're wearing! Truth is ~r than fiction. She says she feels ~,* not in her usual condition, perhaps rather dizzy, etc. ***~ to say…,*** It is surprising that…. **2** (*pred*) ***~ to sth,*** fresh or unaccustomed to: *The village boy was ~ to city life. He is still ~ to the work*, has not yet learnt his new job. **~·ly** *adv* **~·ness** *n*

stran·ger /ˈstreɪndʒə(r)/ *n* person one does not know; person in a place or in company that he does not know; *The dog always barks at ~s. You're quite a ~*, (colloq) It's a long time since we met. *I am a ~ in this town*, do not know my way about. *He is no ~ to misfortune*, (fig) has had experience of it.

strangle /ˈstræŋgl/ *vt* [VP6A] kill by squeezing the throat of; hinder the breathing of: *This stiff collar is strangling me*, is so tight that it squeezes my neck. **ˈ~·hold** *n* (usu fig) deadly grip: *The new tariffs have put a ~hold on our trade with them.* **stran·gu·la·tion** /ˈstræŋgjʊˈleɪʃn/ *n* [U] strangling or being ~d.

strap /stræp/ *n* strip of leather or other flexible material (often with a buckle) to fasten things together or to keep sth (e g a wrist-watch) in place. **ˈ~-hanger** *n* standing passenger in a bus, train, etc who holds on to a ~ with a loop (hanging from the roof) when all the seats are occupied. □ *vt* (-pp-). **1** [VP6A,15B] **~ *sth on/up***, fasten or hold in place with a ~: *~ on a wrist-watch; ~ up a suitcase*, using ~s and buckles. **2** beat with a ~. **~·ping** *adj* big, tall, healthy-looking: *a ~ping girl.*

strata /ˈstrɑtə/ ⇨ stratum.

strat·agem /ˈstrætədʒəm/ *n* [C,U] (use of a) trick or device to deceive sb (esp the enemy in war).

stra·tegic /strəˈtidʒɪk/, **stra·tegi·cal** /-kl/ *adj* of, by, serving the purpose of, strategy: *a ~ retreat; a ~ link in a line of defence; ~ bombing*, e g of industrial areas and communications; *~ materials*, those essential for war. **stra·tegi·cally** /-klɪ/ *adv* **stra·tegics** *n* [U] science or art of strategy.

strat·egy /ˈstrætədʒɪ/ *n* [U] the art of planning operations in war, esp of the movements of armies and navies into favourable positions for fighting; skill in managing any affair. ⇨ tactic(2). **strat·egist** /-dʒɪst/ *n* person skilled in ~.

strat·ify /ˈstrætɪfɑɪ/ *vt,vi* (*pt,pp* -fied) **1** [VP6A] arrange in strata: *stratified rock. English society is highly stratified.* **2** [VP2A] form into strata. **strat·ifi·ca·tion** /ˈstrætɪfɪˈkeɪʃn/ *n* arrangement in strata.

stratified rock

strato·sphere /ˈstrætəsfɪə(r)/ *n* layer of atmospheric air between about 10 and 60 km above the earth's surface.

stra·tum /ˈstrɑtəm/ *n* (*pl* -ta /-tə/) horizontal layer of rock, etc in the earth's crust; social class or division: *Students in Britain come from various strata in society.*

straw /strɔ/ *n* **1** [U] dry cut stalks of wheat, barley, rice and other grains, as material for making hats, mats, etc or bedding for cattle, or thatching roofs, etc: *a ~ mattress*, one stuffed with ~. ***make bricks without ~***, make sth without all the necessary materials. ⇨ Exod 5: 7. ***a man of ~***, imaginary person, easily overcome, set up as an opponent. **ˈ~·board** *n* [U] coarse cardboard made of ~ pulp. **ˈ~-coloured** *adj* pale yellow. **2** [C] single stalk or piece of ~; thin tube of other material for sucking up liquid: *suck lemonade through a ~.* ***catch at a ~, clutch at ~s***, try any expedient, however useless (like a drowning man clutching at a ~). ***not care a ~***, not at all. ***not worth a ~***, worth nothing. ***a ~ in the wind***, a slight hint that shows which way things may develop; hence, **a ~ vote**, attempt to discover public opinion on a topic of current interest by an unofficial poll (e g as made by a newspaper). **the last ~**, an addition to a task, burden, etc, that makes it intolerable. □ *vt* spread ~ on; cover with ~.

straw·berry /ˈstrɔbrɪ *US:* -berɪ/ *n* (*pl* -ries) [C] (perennial, low-growing plant having) juicy red fruit with tiny yellow seeds on its surface, eaten raw and in jam. ⇨ the illus at fruit. **ˈ~ mark**, reddish birthmark on the skin.

stray /streɪ/ *vi* [VP2A,C] wander (from the right path, from one's companions, etc); lose one's way: *Don't ~ from the point.* □ *n* **1** ~ed animal or person (esp a child). ***waifs and ~s***, homeless children. **2** (attrib) having ~ed: *~ cats and dogs; killed by a ~ bullet*, killed by chance, not purposely; occasional; seen or happening occasionally: *The streets were empty except for a few ~ taxis.*

streak /strik/ *n* [C] **1** long, thin, usu irregular line or band: *~s of lean and fat*, e g in meat; *like a ~ of lightning*, very fast. **2** trace or touch (*of*): *There's a ~ of vanity/cruelty in his character.* **3** brief period: *The gambler had a ~ of good luck*, won for a time. ***hit a winning ~***, have a series of successes (in gambling, etc). □ *vt,vi* [VP6A,15A] **1** mark with ~s: *white marble ~ed with brown.* **2** [VP2C] (colloq) move very fast (like a ~ of lightning): *The children ~ed off as fast as they could.* **~y** *adj* (-ier, -iest) marked with, having, ~s: *~y bacon*, with ~s of fat and lean in it.

stream /strim/ *n* **1** river or brook; current. ***go up/down ~***, move up/down the river. ***go with the ~***, (fig) do or think as the majority of people do, be carried along by the course of events. **2** steady flow (of liquid, persons, things, etc): *a ~ of blood/curses. S~s of people were coming out of the railway station.* **ˈ~·line** *vt* make more efficient (by simplifying, getting rid of, wasteful methods, etc): *~line production*, e g in a factory. **ˈ~·lined** *adj* **(a)** having a shape that offers least resistance to the flow of air, water, etc: *~lined cars.* **(b)** having nothing likely to impede progress: *~lined controls/methods.* **~ of consciousness**, continuous conscious experience of an individual; (in literature) technique of writing novels to indicate this, e g as in James Joyce's *Ulysses*. **3** (education) (division of a) class of children in age groups according to ability and intelligence; *bright boys and girls in the ˈA-stream.* □ *vi* **1** [VP2A,C] flow freely; move continuously and smoothly in one direction: *Sweat was ~ing down his face. His face was ~ing with sweat.* **2** [VP2C] float or wave (in the wind): *The flag/Her long hair ~ed in the wind.* **3** [VP6A] place (children) in ~s(3). **~er** *n* **1** long narrow flag; long narrow ribbon of paper. ~ **headline,** (US) = *banner* headline. ⇨ banner. **2** column of light shooting out in the aurora. '~**·let** /-lət/ *n* small ~ or brook.

street /strit/ *n* town or village road with houses on one side or both: *meet a friend in the ~; cross the ~; a* '*~-map/-plan of York.* Cf *a road-map of Yorkshire.* '~**·car** *n* (esp US) tram-car. ~ **door** *n* door which opens (usu directly) on to the ~. (If there is a garden *front door* is preferred). ***the man in the ~,*** typical citizen. ***not in the same ~ (as),*** not nearly so good (as). ***~s ahead of,*** (colloq) far ahead of. ***(not) up my ~,*** (colloq) (not) within my area of knowledge, interests, etc. ***go on the ~s,*** earn one's living by prostitution. '~**-girl,** '~**-walker** *nn* prostitute.

strength /streŋθ/ *n* [U] **1** quality of being strong: *a man/horse of great ~; the ~ of a rope,* its ability to resist strain; *the ~ of our army; get back one's health and ~ after an illness. She hasn't the ~/hasn't ~ enough to walk upstairs. How is the ~ of alcoholic liquors measured?* ***on the ~ of,*** encouraged by, relying upon: *I employed the boy on the ~ of your recommendation.* **2** that which helps to make sb or sth strong: *God is our ~.* **3** power measured by numbers of persons present or persons who can be used: *The enemy were in (great) ~,* Their numbers were great. *The police force is 500 below ~,* needs 500 more men. ***be/bring sth up to ~,*** the required number: *We must bring the police force up to ~.* **~en** /'streŋθn/ *vt,vi* [VP6A,2A] make or become strong(er).

strenu·ous /'strenjʊəs/ *adj* using or needing great effort; energetic: *~ work; ~ workers; make ~ efforts; lead a ~ life.* **~·ly** *adv* **~·ness** *n*

strep·to·coc·cus /ˌstreptə'kokəs/ *n* (*pl* -ci /-kaɪ/) any of a group of bacteria which causes serious infections and illnesses.

strep·to·my·cin /ˌstreptəʊ'maɪsɪn/ *n* antibiotic medical preparation.

stress /stres/ *n* **1** [U] pressure; condition causing hardship, disquiet, etc: *times of ~,* of trouble and danger; *driven into harbour by ~ of weather; under the ~ of poverty/fear/excitement.* **2** [U] (and with *indef art*) weight or force: *a school that lays ~ on foreign languages.* **3** [C,U] (result of) extra force, used in speaking, on a particular word or syllable: *In 'strategic' the ~ is on the second syllable. S~ and rhythm are important in speaking English. You must learn where to place the ~es.* '~**-mark** *n* mark (e g ' (principal or main ~) and ˌ (secondary ~) as used in this dictionary) that indicates the ~ on a syllable. **4** [C,U] (in mechanics) tension; force exerted between two bodies that touch, or between two parts of one body. □ *vt* [VP6A] put ~ or emphasis on: *He ~ed the point that....*

stretch /stretʃ/ *vt,vi* **1** [VP6A,15A,B,16A,22] make wider, longer or tighter, by pulling; be or become wider, etc when pulled: *~ a rope tight; ~ a rope across a path; ~ a pair of gloves,* e g to make them fit better; *~ one's neck,* e g to see over the heads of people in a crowd; *~ one's arms/legs/oneself/one's muscles,* extend the limbs, etc and thus tighten the muscles; *~ out one's arm for a book.* ***~ one's legs,*** exercise oneself by walking as a relief from sitting or lying. **2** ***~ (oneself) out (on),*** lie on at full length: *They were ~ed out on the lawn. He ~ed himself out on the sands.* **3** [VP6A] make (a word, law, etc) include or cover more than is strictly right; exert beyond what is right: *~ the law/one's principles/a point in sb's favour,* ⇨ point[1](9); strain to the utmost; *~ one's powers,* work very hard or too hard. ***be fully ~ed,*** working to the utmost of one's powers. **4** [VP2A,B,C] extend: *forests ~ing for hundreds of miles; a road ~ing away across the desert.* □ *n* [C] **1** act of ~ing or being ~ed: *by a ~ of authority/language.* ⇨ 3 above. *The cat woke and gave a ~. He got up with a ~ and a yawn.* ***by 'any/'no ~ of the imagination,*** however much one may try to imagine sth. ***at full ~,*** fully ~ed(3): *The factory was/The workers were at full ~.* **2** unbroken or continuous period of time or extent of country, etc: *a beautiful ~ of wooded country;* (sl) *do a two-year ~ in prison.* ***at a ~,*** continuously: *Can you work for six hours at a ~?* **3** straight side of a track or course (for racing). **~er** *n* **1** framework of poles, canvas, etc for carrying a sick, injured or wounded person. '~**er-bearer** *n* person who helps to carry a ~er. '~**er-party** *n* number of persons with ~ers (to carry an injured or wounded person). **2** device for ~ing things (e g gloves, shoes).

strew /stru/ *vt* (*pt* ~ed, *pp* ~ed or strewn /strun/) [VP6A,14] ***~ sth (on/over sth), ~ sth with sth,*** scatter (sth) over a surface; (partly) cover (a surface) (with sth scattered): *~ flowers over a path; ~ a path with flowers.*

strewth /struθ/ = struth.

stri·ated /straɪ'eɪtɪd *US:* 'straɪeɪtɪd/ *adj* striped; furrowed.

stricken /'strɪkən/ *adj* (*pp* of strike; used pred) affected or overcome: *'terror-~,* overcome by terror; very much frightened; *~ in years,* very old; *~ with fever/pestilence, etc; 'fever-~,* afflicted with fever, etc.

strict /strɪkt/ *adj* (-er, -est) **1** stern; demanding obedience or exact observance: *a ~ father; ~ discipline; be ~ with one's children; keep a ~ hand over the children; a ~ rule against smoking,* e g at a petrol station. **2** clearly and exactly defined; precisely limited: *tell sb sth in ~est confidence; in the ~ sense of the word; the ~ truth.* **~·ly** *adv* in a ~ manner: *Smoking is ~ly prohibited.* **~·ness** *n*

stric·ture /'strɪktʃə(r)/ *n* [C] **1** (often *pl*) severe criticism or blame: *pass ~s (up)on sb.* **2** (med) contraction of a tube-like part of the body, causing a diseased condition.

stride /straɪd/ *vi,vt* (*pt* strode /strəʊd/, *pp* (rare) stridden /'strɪdn/) **1** [VP2C] walk with long steps: *~ along the road; ~ off/away.* **2** ***~ over/across sth,*** pass over in one step: *~ over a ditch.* **3** [VP6A] = bestride. □ *n* [C] (distance covered in) one long step: *walk with vigorous ~s.* ***make great ~s,*** make good and rapid progress. ***take sth in one's ~,*** do it without special effort.

stri·dent /'straɪdnt/ *adj* (of sound) loud and harsh; shrill: *the ~ notes of the cicadas.* **~·ly** *adv*

stridu·late /'strɪdjʊleɪt *US:* 'strɪdʒʊleɪt/ *vi* [VP2A] make shrill grating sounds (esp of insects such as crickets). **stridu·la·tion** /ˌstrɪdjʊ'leɪʃn/ *n*

strife /straɪf/ *n* [U] quarrelling; state of conflict: *industrial ~* (between workers and employers).

strike[1] /straɪk/ *n* **1** act of striking(5): *the numerous ~s in the coalmines; a ~ of bus-drivers;* (attrib) *take ~ action.* ***be (out) on ~; come/go out on ~,*** be engaged in, start, a ~. ***a general ~,*** by workers in all or most trades, etc. '~**-pay** *n* money paid to strikers from trade-union funds (during a ~ officially recognized by a union). '~

fund *n* special fund to supplement ~-pay. '**~-leader** *n* worker or official who leads a ~. '**~-breaker** *n* worker brought in or coming in to take the place of a striker. '**~-bound** *adj* unable to function because of a ~: *The docks were ~-bound for a week.* **2** act of striking (oil, etc) in the earth: *a lucky ~*, a fortunate discovery. **3** hostile sortie of aircraft.

strike[2] /straɪk/ *vt,vi* (*pt,pp* struck /strʌk/) (⇨ stricken, above) (For special uses with *adverbial particles* and *preps*, ⇨ 17 below.) **1** [VP6A,12C,14,2A,C,3A] hit; give a blow or blows to; aim a blow at: *He struck me on the chin.* (note use of *def art*). *He struck the table with a heavy blow. He struck his knee with his hand/struck his hand upon his knee. He seized a stick and struck at me. Who struck the first blow*, started the fight? *The ship struck a rock. That tree was struck by lightning.* ***~ at the root of sth,*** attack trouble, evil, etc at its source. ***S~ while the iron is hot,*** (prov) Act promptly while action is likely to get results. ***a '~/'striking force,*** military force ready to attack at short notice. ***within 'striking distance,*** near enough to reach or attack easily. **2** [VP6A,2A] produce (a light) by striking or scraping: *~ sparks from a flint; ~ a match,* cause it to burst into flame by scraping it on a surface; *~ a light*, produce one in this way. *These matches are damp*they won't ~.* **3** [VP6A] come upon, discover (by mining, drilling, etc): *to ~ gold.* ***strike oil,*** (**a**) discover oil by drilling. (**b**) (fig) have good fortune; find a means of getting rich. ***~ it rich,*** win wealth suddenly. **4** [VP6A,2A] (cause to) sound: *~ a chord on the piano. This clock ~s the hours. The clock has just struck (four). The/His hour has struck,* (fig) the critical moment has come or gone. ***~ a note of,*** give an impression (of the kind indicated): *The prime minister struck a note of warning against over-optimism.* **5** [VP2A,3A] ***~ (for/against),*** (of workers, etc) stop working for an employer (in order to get more pay, shorter hours, better conditions, etc or as a protest against sth): *~ for higher pay/against bad working conditions.* ⇨ strike[1](1). **6** [VP6A,16A] impress; have an effect upon the mind: *How does the idea/suggestion ~ you? The plan ~s me as ridiculous. What struck me* (= The impression I had) *was that he was not telling the truth. An idea suddenly struck me*, came to me, with an immediate response. **7** [VP16A, or 2D with object and *as* omitted] have an effect on the body or mind: *The room ~s (you as) warm and comfortable when you enter. The prison cell struck cold and damp*, was felt as cold and damp by anyone entering it. **8** [VP6A] produce by stamping or punching: *~ a coin/medal/medallion.* **9** [VP6A] achieve, arrive at, by reckoning or weighing: *~ an average; ~ a balance between anarchy and authoritarian rule/between licence and repression.* ***~ a bargain (with sb),*** reach one by agreement; conclude one. **10** [VP6A] come upon; find: *~ the track/the right path.* **11** [VP2C] set out, go (in a certain direction): *We struck (off)* (= turned and went) *into the woods. The boys struck (out) across the fields. The explorers struck out* (= started, set out) *at dawn.* **12** [VP22] cause (sb) to be, suddenly and as if by a single stroke: *be struck blind. I was struck all of a heap,* (colloq) astounded. **13** [VP14] ***~ fear/terror/alarm into sb,*** fill, afflict, with fear, etc: *Attila struck terror into the people of eastern Europe. The bombing attack struck fear into their hearts.* **14** [VP6A] lower or take down (sails, tents). ***~ one's flag,*** lower it (as a signal that one surrenders a ship, fortress, etc to the enemy). ***~ tents/camp,*** pack up tents, etc. **15** [VP6A] ***~ a cutting,*** take a cutting from a plant and insert it in soil to ~ root. ***~ root,*** put out roots. **16** [VP6A] hold or put the body in a certain way to indicate sth: *~ an attitude of defiance; ~ a pose.* **17** [VP2C,3,15B] (special uses with *adverbial particles* and *preps*):

strike sb down, (formal) hit so that he falls to the ground; (fig): *He was struck down in the prime of life*, e g of sb who was assassinated.

strike sth off, (**a**) cut off with a blow, e g of an axe. (**b**) print: *~ off 1 000 copies of a book.* ***~ sth off (sth),*** remove: *~ sb's name off a list. The doctor's name was struck off the Medical Register*, was cancelled, e g because of professional misconduct.

strike out, (**a**) use the arms and legs vigorously in swimming: *~ out for the shore.* (**b**) aim vigorous blows: *He lost his temper and struck out wildly.* (**c**) follow a new or independent path, a new form of activity: *~ out on one's own/in a new direction.* ***~ sth out/through,*** cross out, put a line or lines through: *~ out a word/name/item.*

strike (sth) up, begin to play: *The band struck up (a tune).* ***~ up sth (with sb),*** begin (perhaps casually) a friendship or acquaintance: *The two boys quickly struck up a friendship. She struck up an acquaintance with a fellow passenger during the cruise.* ***~ (up)on sth,*** have suddenly or unexpectedly: *~ (up)on an idea/a plan.*

striker /'straɪkə(r)/ *n* (**a**) worker who strikes(5). (**b**) (football) player in an attacking position. ⇨ the illus at football.

strik·ing /'straɪkɪŋ/ *adj* **1** attracting attention; arousing great interest. **2** that strikes(4): *a ~ clock.* **~·ly** *adv* in a ~ manner: *a ~ly beautiful woman.*

string[1] /strɪŋ/ *n* **1** [C,U] (piece or length of) fine cord for tying things, keeping things in place, etc; narrow strip of other material used for the same purposes: *a ball of ~; a piece of ~; ~ and brown paper for a parcel.* ***tied to one's mother's/wife's apron-~s,*** ⇨ apron. (US) '**shoe ~s,** ⇨ lace(2). **2** [C] = *bow~*, ⇨ bow[1](1). ***have two ~s to one's bow,*** have an alternative means of achieving one's purpose. ***the first/second ~,*** the first/the alternative person or thing relied upon for achieving one's purpose. **3** [C] tightly stretched length of cord, gut or wire, e g in a violin or guitar, for producing musical sounds. **the ~s,** the instruments of the violin family in an orchestra; *a ~ quartet*, (music for a) quartet of four ~ed instruments. ***keep harping on one ~/on the same ~,*** keep talking or writing on one subject. '**~ 'orchestra/'band** *n* one composed of ~ed instruments. **stringed** /'strɪŋd/ *adj* **~ed instruments,** violins, etc with ~s. **4** [C] ~s used for causing puppets to move. ***have sb on a ~,*** have him under one's thumb, under control. ***pull (the) ~s,*** control the actions of other people (as if they were puppets on ~s). ***no ~s (attached), without ~s,*** (colloq; of help, esp of money, e g given by one country to another) without conditions about how the help is to be used. **5** [C] series of things threaded on a ~: *a ~ of beads/pearls/onions;* number of things in, or as in, a line: *a ~ of* *abuses/curses/lies; a ~ of horses,* number of horses kept for racing. ⇨ stud². **6** tough fibre or ~-like substance. **~ bean,** kind of bean of which the pod is used as a vegetable. **ˋheart~s,** ⇨ heart(7). **~y** *adj* (-ier, -iest) like ~; having tough fibres: *~y meat,* tough.

string² /strɪŋ/ *vt,vi* (*pt,pp* strung /strʌŋ/) **1** [VP6A] put a string or strings on (a bow, violin, tennis racket, etc). **2** (*pp*) ***strung (up),*** (of a person, his senses, nerves) made tense, ready, excited, etc: *The athlete was strung up before the important race. He is a very highly strung person,* is very sensitive, neurotic. **3** [VP6A] put (pearls, etc) on a string. **4** [VP15A,B] tie or hang on a string, etc: *~ up lanterns among the trees/lamps across a street.* **5** [VP2C,15B] (special uses with *adverbial particles*): ***~ sb along,*** deliberately mislead sb into the belief that he/she will benefit, etc: *He doesn't intend to marry the girl—he's just ~ing her along.* ***~ along with sb,*** maintain a relationship with sb for as long as it suits one, without making genuine commitments. ***~ out,*** be, become, spread out at intervals in a line. ***~ sth out,*** cause this to happen: *horses strung out towards the end of a long race.* ***~ sb up,*** (sl) put him to death by hanging. ***~ sth up,*** ⇨ 4 above.

strin·gent /ˋstrɪndʒənt/ *adj* **1** (of rules) strict, severe; that must be obeyed: *a ~ rule against smoking.* **2** (of the money-market) tight; difficult to operate because of scarcity of money. **~·ly** *adv* **strin·gency** /-nsɪ/ *n*

strip /strɪp/ *vt,vi* (-pp-) [VP6A,14,15B,22] ***~ sth (from/off sth), ~ sth/sb (of sth),*** take off (coverings, clothes, parts, etc): *~ the bark off a tree/ ~ a tree of its bark. The bandits ~ped him naked/~ped him of his clothes. They ~ped the house of all its furnishings. They ~ped off their clothes and jumped into the lake.* ***~ sth down,*** (e g of an engine) remove detachable parts (for overhaul, etc). **ˈ~-ˋtease, ˋ~-show** *nn* cabaret or theatrical entertainment in which a woman takes off her garments one by one. Hence, **ˋ~per** *n* woman who does this. **ˈ~-ˋpoker** *n* game of poker in which the loser of each hand must take off one garment. **2** [VP14] ***~ sb of sth,*** deprive of property, etc: *~ a man of his possessions/titles, etc.* **3** [VP6A] *~ a gear/screw,* tear the cogs/ thread from it (by misuse, etc); *~ a machine,* dismantle it. **4** [VP6A] squeeze out the last milk from (a cow's udder); obtain (milk) in this way. □ *n* [C] **1** long narrow piece (of material, land, etc): *a ~ of garden behind the house; a ~ of paper; an ˋair~,* ⇨ air¹(7). **ˋ~-lighting** *n* method of lighting, using long tubes instead of bulbs. **~ cartoon** *n* newspaper (often one of a series) made up of a number of drawings in a row. ⇨ *comic ~* at comic. **2** (mod colloq) clothes worn by players in a team: *the colourful ~ of many football teams.*

string instruments

stripe /straɪp/ *n* [C] **1** long, narrow band (usu of the same breadth throughout) on a surface different in colour, material, texture, etc: *a white tablecloth with red ~s; the tiger's ~s.* **the Stars and S~s,** the national flag of the US. **2** (often a V-shaped) badge worn on a uniform, showing rank, e g of a soldier: *How many ~s are there on the sleeve of a sergeant?* **3** (old use) blow with a whip (*stroke* is now the usu word). **striped** /stræɪpt/ *adj* marked with ~s(1): *~d material,* e g for clothing. **stripy** *adj* having ~s: *a stripy tie.*

strip·ling /ˈstrɪplɪŋ/ *n* young man not yet fully grown.

strive /straɪv/ *vi* (*pt* strove /strəʊv/, *pp* striven /ˈstrɪvn/) **1** [VP2A,3A] **~ *with/against sth/sb,*** struggle. **2** [VP3A,4A] **~ *for/to do sth,*** make great efforts. **striver** *n* person who tries hard.

strode /strəʊd/ *pt* of stride.

stroke[1] /strəʊk/ *n* [C] **1** (act of striking or dealing a) blow: *kill a man with one ~ of one's sword; the ~ of a hammer; 20 ~s of the lash.* **2** one of a series of regularly repeated movements, esp as a way of swimming or rowing: *swimming with a slow ~; the ˋbreast-/ˈside-/ˈback-~; a fast/slow ~* (in rowing). **3** (in a rowing crew) oarsman nearest the boat's stern who sets the rate of striking the oars. ⇨ the illus at eight; ⇨ bow[3](2). **4** single movement of the upper part of the body and arm(s), esp in games, e g cricket, golf. **5** single effort; result of this: *That was a good ~ of business. I haven't done a ~ of work today. What a ~ of luck!* What a piece of good fortune! ***at a/one ~,*** with one effort and immediately. **6** (mark made by a) single movement of a pen or brush: *with one ~ of the pen; thin/thick ~s.* **7** sound made by a bell striking the hours: *on the ~ of three,* at three o'clock. *He was here on the ~,* punctually at the time appointed. **8** sudden attack of illness in the brain, with loss of feeling, power to move, etc: *a paralytic ~.* ⇨ also *sun~* at sun(4). □ *vt* (*pt,pp* ~d) [VP6A] act as ~(3) to: *~ the Oxford boat.*

stroke[2] /strəʊk/ *vt* [VP6A,15B] pass the hand along a surface, usu again and again: *~ a cat/one's beard.* **~ *sb the wrong way,*** irritate him instead of soothing him. **~ *sb down,*** mollify him, cause him to be no longer irritated. □ *n* act of stroking; stroking movement.

stroll /strəʊl/ *n* [C] quiet, unhurried walk: *have/go for a ~.* □ *vi* [VP2A,C] go for a ~. **~er** *n*

strong /stroŋ *US:* strɔŋ/ *adj* (-er, -est) **1** (opp of *weak*) having power to resist; not easily hurt, injured, broken, captured, etc; having great power of body or mind: *a ~ stick,* not easily broken; *a ~ fort,* not easily captured; *a ~ wind; a ~ will/imagination/determination; have ~ nerves,* be not easily frightened, worried, etc; *~ eyes; feel quite ~ again,* in good health after an illness; *a ~ army; an army 500 000 ~,* numbering 500 000; *a ~ candidate,* one likely to be well supported, etc; *~* (= deeply held or rooted) *beliefs/convictions.* ***as ~ as a horse,*** physically powerful. ***one's ~ point,*** that which one does well. **ˋ~-arm,** (of methods, tactics, etc) violent; bullying. **ˋ~-box** *n* one that is ~ly built for keeping valuables. **ˋ~-hold** /-həʊld/ *n* (a) fort. (b) (fig) place where a cause or idea has ~ support: *a ~hold of Protestantism.* **ˈ~-ˋminded** /ˈmaɪndɪd/ *adj* having a mind that is capable and vigorous: *a ~-minded woman,* e g one of those who, in GB, claimed equality with men before this was obtained. **ˋ~-room** *n* one built with thick walls and (usu) a thick steel door (e g in a bank) for storing valuables. **2** having a large proportion of the flavouring element: *~ tea/coffee.* **3** having a considerable effect on the mind or the senses: *the ~ light of the tropics; a ~ smell of gas; ~ bacon/butter/cheese/onions. His breath is rather ~,* is ill-smelling. **~ language** *n* forcible expressions, esp words that are blasphemous or abusive. **4 ~ drink,** containing alcohol, e g gin, rum. ⇨ *soft drink* at soft(9). **5** (*adverbial* use) ***going ~,*** (colloq) continuing (the race, activity, etc) vigorously; continuing in good health: *aged 90 and still going ~.* ***come/go it (rather/a bit) ~,*** (colloq) go to greater lengths than is right; exaggerate somewhat. **6 ~ verb,** one that forms the past tense by a vowel change (e g *sing, sang*), not by adding *-d, -ed* or *-t.* **7** (comm; of prices) rising steadily: *Prices/Markets are ~.* **8 ~ form,** (of the pronunciation of some words) form occurring in a stressed position. ⇨ weak(5). **~·ly** *adv* in a ~ manner: *I ~ly advise you to go.*

stron·tium /ˈstrontɪəm *US:* -nʃɪəm/ *n* [U] soft silver-white metallic element (symbol **Sr**): *~ 90,* component of the fall-out from nuclear explosions.

strop /strop/ *n* leather strap for sharpening razors, e g as used by barbers. □ *vt* (-pp-) [VP6A] sharpen on a ~.

strophe /ˈstrəʊfɪ/ *n* [C] (lines of verse recited during a) turn from right to left of the chorus in ancient Greek drama; one section of a choral ode.

strove /strəʊv/ *pt* of strive.

struck /strʌk/ *pt,pp* of strike[2].

struc·ture /ˈstrʌktʃə(r)/ *n* **1** [U] way in which sth is put together, organized, etc: *the ~ of the human body; molecular ~; sentence ~.* **2** [C] building; any complex whole; framework or essential parts of a building: *The Parthenon was a magnificent marble ~.* **struc·tural** /ˈstrʌktʃərl/ *adj* of a ~, esp the framework: *structural alterations to a building,* e g combining two rooms into one; *structural steel,* i e bars, beams, girders, for use in building. **struc·tur·ally** /-rḷɪ/ *adv*: *The building is structurally sound.*

stru·del /ˈstrudl/ *n* kind of tart made of fruit, etc rolled up in puff pastry and baked: *a slice of apple ~.*

struggle /ˈstrʌgl/ *vi* [VP2A,B,3A,4A] **~ *against/with,*** fight, make great efforts: *~ against difficulties; ~ for influence/power. The thief ~d in the policeman's arms/~d to get free.* □ *n* [C] struggling; contest: *the ~ for freedom; not surrender without a ~.*

strum /strʌm/ *vi,vt* (-mm-) [VP2A,B,C,3A,6A] **~ *(on),*** play music, play (on a musical instrument) carelessly or monotonously (and esp without skill): *~ (on) the banjo; ~ a tune on the piano.* □ *n* sound of *~ming: the ~ of a guitar.*

strum·pet /ˈstrʌmpɪt/ *n* (archaic) prostitute.

strung /strʌŋ/ *pt,pp* of string[2].

strut[1] /strʌt/ *n* [C] piece of wood or metal inserted in a framework and intended to strengthen it by bearing weight or resisting pressure in the direction of its length.

strut[2] /strʌt/ *vi* (-tt-) [VP2A,C] walk (*about, along, in, out, into a room, etc*) in a stiff, self-satisfied way. □ *n* such a way of walking.

strych·nine /ˈstrɪknin/ *n* [U] strong poison (used in very small doses to stimulate the nerves).

stub /stʌb/ *n* [C] **1** short remaining end of a pencil, cigarette or similar object: *The dog has only a ~ of a tail,* a very short one. **2** counterfoil: *the ~s of a cheque-book.* □ *vt* (-bb-) **1** [VP6A] *~ one's toe,* strike it against sth. **2** [VP15B] ***~ sth out,*** extinguish (esp a cigarette) by pressing it against sth hard.

stubble /ˈstʌbl/ *n* [U] ends of grain plants left in the ground after harvest; sth suggesting this, e g a short stiff growth of beard: *three days' ~ on his chin.* **stub·bly** /ˈstʌblɪ/ *adj* of or like ~: *a stubbly beard.*

stub·born /ˈstʌbən/ *adj* obstinate; determined; difficult to deal with: *~ soil,* difficult to plough, etc; *a ~ illness.* ***as ~ as a mule,*** extremely obstinate. **~·ly** *adv* **~·ness** *n*

stubby /ˈstʌbɪ/ *adj* (-ier, -iest) short and thick: *~ fingers.*

stucco /ˈstʌkəʊ/ *n* (*pl* -cos, -coes /-kəʊz/) [C,U] (kinds of) plaster or cement used for covering and decorating ceilings or wall surfaces. □ *vt* (*pt,pp* -coed; -coing) coat with ~.

stuck /stʌk/ *pt,pp* of **stick**[2].

stuck-up /ˈstʌk ˋʌp/ *adj* (colloq) conceited; insolently refusing to be companionable.

stud[1] /stʌd/ *n* **1** small two-headed button-like device put through button-holes to fasten a collar, shirt-front, etc. **2** large-headed nail or knob, usu one of many, on the surface of sth (e g a gate or shield), as ornament or protection: *reˋflector ~s,* used on roads to mark out lanes (and reflecting light from headlamps at night). □ *vt* (-dd-) (usu *pp*) ***~ded with,*** having (sth) set in or scattered on the surface: *a crown ~ded with jewels; a sea ~ded with islands/the sails of yachts.*

stud[2] /stʌd/ *n* number of horses kept by one owner for a special purpose (esp breeding or racing). **ˋ~-book** *n* register of the pedigrees of horses. **ˋ~-farm** *n* place where horses are bred. **ˋ~-mare** *n* mare kept for breeding purposes.

stu·dent /ˈstjudnt *US:* ˋstu-/ *n* **1** (GB) (undergraduate or post graduate) person who is studying at a college, polytechnic or university: *ˋmedical ~s;* (US also) boy or girl attending school. **2** anyone who studies or who is devoted to the acquisition of knowledge: *a ~ of bird-life/nature/theology.*

stu·dio /ˈstjudɪəʊ *US:* ˋstu-/ *n* (*pl* -dios /-dɪəʊz/) **1** well-lit workroom of a painter, sculptor, photographer, etc. **ˋ~ couch,** couch that can be used as a bed. **2** room or hall where cinema plays are acted and photographed; (*pl*) all the ~s of a cinema company, with the office buildings, etc. **3** room from which radio or T V programmes are regularly broadcast or in which recordings are made. **ˋ~ audience,** audience in a ~, to provide applause, laughter, etc.

stu·di·ous /ˈstjudɪəs *US:* ˋstu-/ *adj* **1** having or showing the habit of learning. **2** painstaking; deliberate: *with ~ politeness.* **~·ly** *adv* **~·ness** *n*

study[1] /ˈstʌdɪ/ *n* (*pl* -dies) **1** [U and in *pl*] devotion of time and thought to getting knowledge of, close examination of, a subject, esp from books: *fond of ~: give all one's leisure time to ~; make a ~ of the country's foreign trade. My studies show that....* **2** [C] sth that attracts investigation; that which is (to be) investigated; *humane studies. The proper ~ of mankind is man. His face was a ~,* was well worth observing closely. **3** ***be in a brown ~,*** musing, unaware of people, happenings, etc near one. **4** room used by sb (e g in his home) for reading, writing, etc: *You will find Mr Green in the/his ~.* **5** sketch etc made for practice or experiment; piece of music played as a technical exercise. **6** [U] (old use) earnest effort: *Her constant ~ was how to please her husband.*

study[2] /ˈstʌdɪ/ *vt,vi* (*pt,pp* -died) **1** [VP6A,8, 15A,2A,B,4A] give time and attention to learning or discovering sth: *~ medicine. He was ~ing for the medical profession/~ing to be a doctor.* **2** [VP6A] examine carefully: *~ the map.* **3** [VP6A, 4A] give care and consideration to: *~ the wishes of one's friends/only one's own interests.* **4** (*pp*) **studied,** intentional, deliberate: *a studied insult.*

stuff[1] /stʌf/ *n* **1** [C,U] material or substance of which sth is made or which may be used for some purpose (often fig); [U] material of which the name is uncertain, unknown or unimportant; material of poor quality: *You take too much doctor's ~,* (colloq) pills, medicine, etc. *We're short of ˋgreen/ˆgarden ~,* vegetables. *He is not the ~ heroes are made of,* is not likely to be a hero, to act heroically. *Do you call this ~ beer? We must find out what ~ he is made of,* what sort of man he is, what his character is. ***S~ and nonsense!*** That's foolish talk! **2** (sl uses) *That's the ~ to give 'em,* That's how to treat them, etc. ***Do your ~,*** Show what you can do, etc. ***know one's ~,*** be expert in what one claims to be able to do, etc. **3** [U] (old use) woollen cloth: *a ~ gown.*

stuff[2] /stʌf/ *vt* **1** [VP6A,14,15B] ***~ sth with sth/sth into sth; ~ sth up,*** fill tightly with; press tightly into: *~ a bag with feathers; ~ feathers into a bag; ~ oneself with food,* overeat; *a head ~ed with facts/silly romantic ideas; ~ (up) one's ears with cotton-wool; ~ up a hole. My nose is ~ed up,* full of mucus (as when one has a cold). ***a ~ed shirt,*** (sl) a pretentious or pompous person. **2** [VP6A,14] (colloq) make (sb) believe what is not true: *He's ~ing you with silly ideas.* **3** [VP6A,14] put chopped up and specially flavoured food into (a bird, etc) before cooking it: *a ~ed turkey; ~ed veal.* **4** [VP6A] fill the empty carcass of (a bird, an animal, etc) with enough material to restore it to its original shape, e g for exhibition in a museum: *a ~ed tiger/owl.* **5** [VP2A,6A] overeat: *When will that boy stop ~ing (himself)?* **6** (sl) *If you don't like it you can ~ it,* will just have to put up with it. **7** ⚠ (vulg sl) have sexual intercourse (with a woman). **~·ing** *n* [U] material for ~ing, e g cushions, birds, ⇨ 3,4 above. ***knock the ~ing out of sb,*** **(a)** take away his conceit or self-confidence. **(b)** (of an illness, etc) weaken; make tired.

stuffy /ˈstʌfɪ/ *adj* (-ier, -iest) **1** (of a room) badly ventilated. **2** (colloq) sulky; ill-tempered. **3** (colloq, of a person) easily shocked or offended. **4** dull; formal. **stuff·ily** /-əlɪ/ *adv* **stuffi·ness** *n*

stul·tify /ˈstʌltɪfaɪ/ *vt* (*pt,pp* -fied) [VP6A] cause to seem foolish or to be useless; reduce to absurdity: *~ efforts to reach agreement.* **stul·ti·fi·ca·tion** /ˈstʌltɪfɪˋkeɪʃn/ *n*

stumble /ˈstʌmbl/ *vi* [VP2A,C,3A] **1** strike the foot against sth and almost fall: *~ over the root of a tree. The child ~d and fell.* ***~ across/upon sth,*** find unexpectedly or by accident. **ˋstumbling-block** *n* obstacle; sth that causes difficulty or hesitation. **2** ***~ along/across/about, etc,*** move or walk in an unsteady way. **3** speak in a hesitating way, with pauses and mistakes: *~ over one's words; ~ through a recitation.* □ *n* act of stumbling.

stump /stʌmp/ *n* [C] **1** part of a tree remaining in the ground when the trunk has fallen or has been cut down. **~ oratory/speeches,** speeches of the kind once made by orators standing on the ~ of a tree (often implying rant and demagogy). ***on the ~,*** (colloq) engaged in political speech-making, agitation, etc. **2** anything remaining after the main part has been cut or broken off or has worn off, e g an amputated limb, a worn-down tooth, the useless end of a pencil, cigar, etc; (hum) leg. ***stir one's ~s,*** (colloq) move quickly. **3** (cricket) one of the three upright pieces of wood at which the ball is bowled: *send the middle ~ flying; draw ~s,* end play. ⇨ the illus at **cricket**. □ *vi,vt* **1** [VP2C] walk (*along, about, etc*) with stiff, heavy movements. **2** [VP6A] (colloq) be too hard for; leave at a loss: *All the candidates were ~ed by the second question.* **3** [VP6A] go about (a district, the country) making ~ speeches ⇨ the *n*, **1** above. **4** [VP6A] (cricket) end the innings of (a batsman) by touching the ~s with the ball while he is out of his crease. ⇨ **crease(2)**. **5** [VP15B,2C] **~ *(sth) up,*** (sl) pay or give money required; produce (a sum of money): *Mr Green has had to ~ up (£50) for his son's debts.* **~er** *n* (colloq) question that ~s(2); difficult or embarrassing question.

stumpy /ˈstʌmpɪ/ *adj* (**-ier, -iest**) short and thick: *a ~ little man; a ~ umbrella.*

stun /stʌn/ *vt* (**-nn-**) [VP6A] **1** make unconscious by a blow, esp one on the head; knock senseless: *The blow ~ned me.* **2** shock; confuse the mind of: *He was ~ned by the news of his father's death.* **~·ning** *adj* (colloq) splendid; ravishing: *What a ~ning hat!* **~·ning·ly** *adv* **~·ner** *n* (colloq) delightful, attractive, person, object, etc.

stung /stʌŋ/ *pt,pp* of **sting**[2].

stunk /stʌŋk/ *pp* of **stink**.

stunt[1] /stʌnt/ *n* [C] (colloq) sth done to attract attention; *advertising ~s,* e g sky-writing by an aircraft; *~ flying,* aerobatics. *That's a good ~,* a clever idea (for getting publicity, etc). **ˈ~ man,** person employed to perform ~s (involving risk, etc) as a stand-in for an actor in films, etc.

stunt[2] /stʌnt/ *vt* [VP6A] check the growth or development of: *~ed trees; a ~ed mind.*

stu·pefy /ˈstjupɪfaɪ *US:* ˈstu-/ *vt* (*pt,pp* **-fied**) [VP6A] make clear thought impossible: *stupefied with drink/amazement. He was stupefied by what happened.* **stu·pefac·tion** /ˌstjupɪˈfækʃn *US:* ˌstu-/ *n* [U] state of being stupefied.

stu·pen·dous /stjuˈpendəs *US:* stu-/ *adj* tremendous; amazing (in size, degree): *a ~ error/achievement. What ~ folly!* **~·ly** *adv*

stu·pid /ˈstjupɪd *US:* ˈstu-/ *adj* **1** slow-thinking; foolish: *Don't be ~ enough to believe that.* **2** in a state of stupor. □ *n* (colloq) ~ person: *I was only teasing, ~!* **~·ly** *adv* **~·ity** /stjuˈpɪdətɪ *US:* stu-/ *n* [U] being ~; [C] (*pl* **-ties**) ~ act, utterance, etc.

stu·por /ˈstjupə(r) *US:* ˈstu-/ *n* [C,U] almost unconscious condition caused by shock, drugs, drink, etc: *in a drunken ~.*

sturdy /ˈstɜdɪ/ *adj* (**-ier, -iest**) strong and solid; vigorous: *~ children; offer a ~ resistance; ~ common sense.* **stur·dily** /-əlɪ/ *adv*: *a sturdily built bicycle.* **stur·di·ness** *adv*

stur·geon /ˈstɜdʒən/ *n* kinds of large fish valued as food, from which caviare is obtained.

stut·ter /ˈstʌtə(r)/ *vi,vt n* = stammer. **~er** *n* person who ~s. **~·ing·ly** *adv*

sty[1] /staɪ/ *n* (*pl* **sties**) pigsty. ⇨ **pig(1)**.

sty[2] (also **stye**) /staɪ/ *n* (*pl* **sties, styes**) inflamed swelling on the edge of the eyelid.

Styg·ian /ˈstɪdʒɪən/ *adj* (as) of the River Styx or Hades (the lower world in Gk myth); hence, dark; gloomy.

style /staɪl/ *n* **1** [C,U] manner of writing or speaking (contrasted with the subject matter); manner of doing anything, esp when it is characteristic of an artist or of a period of art: *written in a delightful ~. The ~ in this book is more attractive than the matter. What do you know about the Norman/decorated/perpendicular, etc ~s of architecture?* **2** [U] quality that marks out sth done or made as superior, fashionable or distinctive. ***in ~:*** *do things in ~,* not in a commonplace way; *live in (grand) ~,* with servants, luxuries, etc; *drive up in ~,* e g in a very fine car, not a taxi; *living in a ~ beyond his means,* in a way that he cannot afford. *Did they live in European ~ when they were in Japan?* **3** [C,U] (esp) fashion in dress, etc; *the latest ~s in hats/in hair-dressing.* **4** [C] general appearance, form or design; kind or sort: *made in all sizes and ~s; this ~, £1.50.* **5** [C] right title (to be) used when addressing sb: *Has he any right to assume the ~ of Colonel?* **6** [C] implement used in ancient times for scratching letters on wax-covered surfaces. **7** [C] (bot) part of the seed-producing part of a flower. ⇨ the illus at **flower**. □ *vt* [VP6A] **1** describe by a specified ~(5): *Should he be ~d 'Right Honourable' or merely 'Esquire'?* **2** design: *new cars ~d by the Italian experts; an electric cooker brilliantly re-~d,* re-designed. **styl·ish** /-ɪʃ/ *adj* having ~(2,3); fashionable: *stylish clothes.* **sty·lish·ly** *adv*: *stylishly dressed.* **styl·ish·ness** *n*

sty·list /ˈstaɪlɪst/ *n* **1** person, esp a writer, who achieves a good or original literary style. **2** (comm, etc) person who is concerned with the styles of decorating, clothes, etc: *a ˈhair-~,* woman's hairdresser. **sty·lis·tic** /staɪˈlɪstɪk/ *adj* of style in writing. **styl·is·ti·cally** /-klɪ/ *adv*

sty·lize /ˈstaɪlaɪz/ *vt* represent or treat (art forms, etc) in the particular, conventional style.

sty·lus /ˈstaɪləs/ *n* (*pl* **-luses** /-ləsɪz/) (esp, mod use) needle-like point (diamond or sapphire) used to cut grooves in records or to reproduce sound from records.

sty·mie /ˈstaɪmɪ/ *n* (in golf) situation on the green when an opponent's ball is between one's own ball and the hole. □ *vt* put (one's opponent or his ball, or oneself) in this difficulty; (fig) check; hinder.

styp·tic /ˈstɪptɪk/ *n, adj* (substance) checking the flow of blood: *a ~ pencil,* stick of this (e g as used on a cut made while shaving).

Styx /stɪks/ *n* (Gk myth) river that encircles Hades, where the spirits of the dead exist: *cross the ~,* die.

sua·sion /ˈsweɪʒn/ *n* [U] persuasion (rare except in): *moral ~,* persuasion based on moral grounds, not force.

suave /swɑv/ *adj* smooth and gracious in manner; **~·ly** *adv* **suav·ity** /-ətɪ/ *n* [U] quality of being ~; (*pl*) instances of being ~; ~ utterances, etc.

sub[1] /sʌb/ *n* (colloq, abbr of) **1** submarine. **2** substitute. **3** subscription. **4** subaltern. **5** sub-lieutenant. **6** sub-editor.

sub[2] /sʌb/ *n* (colloq) part of wages, paid in advance: *ask the manager for a sub.*

sub·al·tern /ˈsʌbltən *US:* səˈbɔltərn/ *n* (GB) commissioned army officer of lower rank than a captain. ⇨ App 9.

sub·atomic /ˈsʌbəˋtomɪk/ *adj* of, relating to, any of the particles smaller than an atom.

sub-com·mit·tee /ˋsʌb kəmɪtɪ/ *n* committee formed from members of a main committee.

sub·con·scious /ˈsʌbˋkonʃəs/ *adj* of those mental activites of which we are not (wholly) aware: *the ~ self.* □ *n* **the ~,** ~ thoughts, desires, impulses, etc collectively. **~·ly** *adv* **~·ness** *n*

sub·con·ti·nent /ˈsʌbˋkontɪnənt *US:* -ntn̩-/ *n* mass of land large enough to be regarded as a separate continent but forming part of a larger mass: *India and Pakistan are often called the S~.*

sub·con·tract /ˈsʌbˋkontrækt/ *n* contract which is for carrying out a previous contract or a part of it. □ *vt, vi* /ˈsʌbkənˋtrækt *US:* -ˋkontrækt/ [VP6A,2A] give or accept a ~. **~or** /ˈsʌbkənˋtræktə(r) *US:* -ˋkontræk-/ *n* person who accepts a ~.

sub·cu·taneous /ˈsʌbkjuˋteɪnɪəs/ *adj* under the skin; ~ *parasites,* living under the skin; *a ~ injection.*

sub·di·vide /ˈsʌbdɪˋvɑɪd/ *vt, vi* [VP6A,2A] divide into further divisions. **sub·di·vi·sion** /ˈsʌbdɪˋvɪʒn/ *n* [U] sub-dividing; [C] sth produced by subdividing.

sub·due /səbˋdju *US:* -ˋdu/ *vt* [VP6A] **1** overcome; bring under control: *~ savage tribes/one's passions.* **2** make quieter, softer, gentler: (esp *pp*) *~d voices/lights; a tone of ~d satisfaction in his voice.*

sub·edit /sʌbˋedɪt/ *vt* act as an assistant editor of (a newspaper, etc) **sub·edi·tor** /-tə(r)/ *n*

sub·fusc /ˈsʌbˋfʌsk/ *adj* rather dark in colour; (fig colloq) unimpressive.

sub·head·ing /ˋsʌbhedɪŋ/ *n* [C] words showing the contents of part of an article, etc e g in a newspaper.

sub·hu·man /ˈsʌbˋhjumən/ *adj* less than human; more like an animal than a human being.

sub·ject[1] /ˋsʌbdʒɪkt/ *adj* **1** under foreign government, not independent: *a ~ province; ~ tribes.* **2** **~ to,** owing obedience (to): *We are ~ to the law of the land.* **3** **~ to,** having a tendency (to); prone to: *Are you ~ to colds? The trains are ~ to delays when there is fog.* **4** **~ to,** (*adj, adv*) conditional(ly) upon: *The plan is ~ to confirmation. The arrangement is made ~ to your approval.* ***~ to contract,*** (legal) conditional upon the signing of a contract. ***~ to prior sale,*** conditional upon no sale having been made before a further offer is made, before the date of the auction, etc.

sub·ject[2] /ˋsʌbdʒɪkt/ *n* **1** any member of a State except the supreme ruler: *British ~s; French by birth and a British ~ by marriage.* ⇨ **citizen,** (usu preferred in republics). **2** sth (to be) talked or written about or studied: *an interesting ~ of conversation; a ~ for an essay; the ~ of a poem/picture.* ***change the ~,*** talk about sth different. ***on the ~ of,*** concerning, dealing with: *While we are on the ~ of money, may I ask when you will repay that loan?* ˋ**~ matter** *n* [U] matter treated of in a book or speech (contrasted with style). **3** person, animal or thing (to be) treated or dealt with, to be made to undergo or experience sth: *a ~ for experiment/dissection.* **4** ***~ for,*** circumstance, etc that gives cause (for): *a ~ for pity/ridicule/congratulation.* **5** person with the tendencies (usu undesirable) specified: *a hyˋsterical ~.* **6** (gram) word(s) in a sentence about which sth is predicated, e g *book* in 'There is a book on the table' and *they* in 'Did they come early?' **7** (music) theme on which a composition (or one of its movements) is based.

sub·ject[3] /səbˋdʒekt/ *vt* [VP14] **~ *sb/sth to,*** **1** bring, get (a country, nation, person) under control: *Ancient Rome ~ed most of Europe to her rule.* **2** cause to undergo or experience; expose: *~ oneself/one's friends to criticism/ridicule; ~ a man to torture. As a test the metal was ~ed to great heat.* **sub·jec·tion** /səbˋdʒekʃn/ *n* [U] ~ing or being ~ed: *The ~ion of the rebels took several months. The tribes lived in a state of ~ion/were kept/held in ~ion for half a century.*

sub·jec·tive /səbˋdʒektɪv/ *adj* **1** (of ideas, feelings, etc) existing in the mind, not produced by things outside the mind; not objective: *Did he really see a ghost or was it only a ~ impression?* **2** (of art and artists, writing, etc) giving the personal or individual point of view or feeling (opp to realistic art, writing, etc). **3** (gram) of the subject. **~·ly** *adv* in a ~ manner: *An examination paper in arithmetic can be marked objectively, but a literary essay can be marked only ~ly,* i e on the personal impression of the examiner. **sub·jec·tiv·ity** /ˈsʌbdʒekˋtɪvətɪ/ *n* [U].

sub·join /sʌbˋdʒɔɪn/ *vt* [VP6A] add at the end: *~ a postscript to a letter.*

sub judice /ˈsʌb ˋdʒudɪsɪ/ (Lat) under judicial consideration, not yet decided (and for this reason, in GB, not to be commented upon).

sub·ju·gate /ˋsʌbdʒʊgeɪt/ *vt* [VP6A] subdue; conquer. **sub·ju·ga·tion** /ˈsʌbdʒʊˋgeɪʃn/ *n* [U].

sub·junc·tive /səbˋdʒʌŋktɪv/ *adj* (gram) expressing a condition, hypothesis, possibility, etc. □ *n* the ~ mood; form of a verb in this mood.

sub·lease /ˈsʌbˋlis/ *vt, vi* [VP6A,2A] lease to another person (a house, land, etc which one has oneself leased); sublet. □ *n* lease of this kind.

sub·let /ˈsʌbˋlet/ *vt, vi* (-tt-) [VP6A,2A] **1** rent to sb else (a room, house, etc of which one is a tenant). **2** give part of (a contract, e g for building a factory) to sb else.

sub·lieu·ten·ant /ˈsʌbləˋtenənt *US:* -luˋt-/ *n* naval officer with rank next below that of a lieutenant. ⇨ App 9.

sub·li·mate /ˋsʌblɪmeɪt/ *vt* [VP6A] **1** (chem) convert from a solid state to vapour by heat and allow to solidify again (in order to purify it). **2** (psych) unconsciously change (emotions and activities arising from the instincts) into higher or more desirable channels. □ *n, adj* (substance) refined by being ~d. **sub·li·ma·tion** /ˈsʌblɪˋmeɪʃn/ *n*

sub·lime /səˋblɑɪm/ *adj* **1** of the greatest and highest sort; causing wonder or reverence: *~ scenery/heroism/self-sacrifice.* **2** extreme; astounding (as of a person who does not fear the consequences): *What ~ conceit/impudence/indifference!* □ *n* **the ~,** that which fills one with awe or reverence. ***from the ~ to the ridiculous,*** from what is noble, etc to what is absurd. **~·ly** *adv* in a ~ manner: *He was ~ly unconscious* (= completely ignorant) *of how foolish he looked.* **sub·lim·ity** /səˋblɪmətɪ/ *n* [U and in *pl;* -ties] ~ quality or qualities: *the sublimity of the Alps; the sublimities of religion.*

sub·lim·inal /ˈsʌbˋlɪmɪnl/ *adj* below the threshold of consciousness; of which one is not consciously aware: *~ advertising,* as when an advertisement is projected on to a cinema or TV screen for a fraction of a second and is noted only by the subconscious mind and is not consciously seen.

sub·mar·ine /ˈsʌbməˋrin *US:* ˋsʌbmərin/ *adj* existing, designed for use, under the surface of the sea: *~ plant life; a ~ cable.* □ *n* ship which can be submerged to operate under water. **sub·mari·ner** /sʌbˋmærɪnə(r)/ *n* member of a ~'s crew.

a submarine

sub·merge /səbˋmɜdʒ/ *vt,vi* **1** [VP6A] put under water; cover with a liquid. **2** [VP2A] sink out of sight; (of a submarine) go down under the surface. **sub·merged** *adj* under the surface of the sea, etc: *~d rocks; a wreck that is ~d at high tide; the ~d tenth,* (formerly used for) that part of the population always in debt or living in extreme poverty. **sub·merg·ence** /səbˋmɜdʒəns/, **sub·mer·sion** /sæbˋmɜʃn *US:* -ʒn/ *nn* submerging or being ~d. **sub·mers·ible** /səbˋmɜsəbl/ *adj* capable of submerging.

sub·mission /səbˋmɪʃn/ *n* **1** [U] act of submitting; acceptance of another's power or authority: *The rebels made their ~ to the President. The enemy were starved into ~,* compelled to submit by hunger. **2** [U] obedience; humility: *with all due ~,* with profound respect. **3** [C,U] (legal) theory, etc submitted to a judge or jury: *My ~ is that...; In my ~,... I submit* (3) *that....*

sub·miss·ive /səbˋmɪsɪv/ *adj* yielding to the control or authority of another: *~ to advice. Marian is not a ~ wife.* **~·ly** *adv* **~·ness** *n*

sub·mit /səbˋmɪt/ *vt,vi* (-tt-) **1** [VP6A,14] *~ oneself to,* put (oneself) under the control of another: *~ oneself to discipline. Should a wife ~ herself to her husband?* **2** [VP6A,14] *~ sth (to),* put forward for opinion, discussion, decision, etc: *~ plans/proposals, etc to a city council; ~ proofs of identity.* **3** [VP9] (legal) suggest, argue (usu deferentially): *Counsel ~ted that there was no case against his client.* **4** [VP3A] *~ (to),* surrender; give in; abstain from resistance: *~ to the enemy/ill treatment/separation from one's family.*

sub·nor·mal /ˈsʌbˋnɔml/ *adj* below normal: *~ temperatures.*

sub·or·bital /sʌbˋɔbɪtl/ *adj* of less duration or distance than one orbit.

sub·or·di·nate /səˋbɔdɪnət *US:* -dṇət/ *adj* **1** *~ (to),* junior in rank or position; less important: *in a ~ position.* **2** *~ clause,* (gram) dependent clause; clause which, introduced by a conjunction, serves as a *noun, adj* or *adv.* □ *n* person in a ~ position; person working under another. □ *vt* /səˋbɔdɪneɪt *US:* -dṇeɪt/ [VP6A,14] *~ sth (to),* treat as ~; make ~ (to). **subordinating conjunction,** (gram) one that introduces a ~ clause, e g *because, if, as.* **sub·or·di·na·tion** /səˈbɔdɪˋneɪʃn *US:* -dṇˋeɪʃn/ *n* subordinating or being ~d. **sub·or·di·na·tive** /səˋbɔdɪnətɪv *US:* -dṇeɪtɪv/ *adj* subordinating.

sub·orn /səˋbɔn/ *vt* [VP6A] induce (a person) by bribery or other means to commit perjury or other unlawful act. **sub·or·na·tion** /ˈsʌbɔˋneɪʃn/ *n* [U].

sub·poena /səˋpinə/ *n* (*pl* -nas) [C] (legal) written order requiring a person to appear in a law court. □ *vt* (*pt,pp* -naed) [VP6A] summon with a ~: *be ~ed/~ing as witness.*

sub rosa /ˈsʌb ˋrəʊzə/ (Lat) (of communications, etc) in strict confidence.

sub·scribe /səbˋskraɪb/ *vi,vt* **1** [VP2A,3A,6A,14] *~ (sth) to/for,* (agree to) pay (a sum of money) in common with other persons (to a cause, for sth): *He ~s liberally to charities. He ~ed £5 to the flood relief fund. How many shares did you ~ for in the new company?* **2** [VP3A] *~ to sth,* (a) agree to take (a newspaper, periodical, etc) regularly for a specified time. (b) agree with, share (an opinion, view, etc). *~ for a book,* agree before it is published to buy a copy or copies. **3** [VP6A] (formal) write (one's name, etc) at the foot of a document: *~ one's name to a petition. He ~s himself J L Smith, not John L Smith,* that is the usual form of his signature, e g on cheques. **sub·scriber** *n* person who ~s (esp to funds, newspapers). **sub·scrip·tion** /səbˋskrɪpʃn/ *n* **1** [U] subscribing or being ~d: *The monument was erected by public subscription.* **2** [C] sum of money ~d (for charity, for receiving a newspaper, magazine, etc), or paid for membership of a club. **subscription concert/dance,** one that is given when the costs are ~d in advance.

sub·se·quent /ˋsʌbsɪkwənt/ *adj ~ (to),* later; following: *~ events; ~ to this event.* **~·ly** *adv* afterwards.

sub·serve /sʌbˋsɜv/ *vt* [VP6A] serve as a means in helping or promoting (an end, a purpose).

sub·ser·vi·ent /səbˋsɜvɪənt/ *adj ~ to,* **1** giving too much respect to: *S~ shopkeepers are not so common as they used to be.* **2** useful as a means to a purpose; subordinate or subject to. **~·ly** *adv* **sub·ser·vi·ence** /-əns/ *n* [U].

sub·side /səbˋsaɪd/ *vt* [VP2A] **1** (of flood water) sink to a lower or to the normal level. **2** (of land) sink, e g because of mining operations. **3** (of buildings) settle lower down in the ground, e g because of a clay subsoil that shrinks in a dry season. **4** (of winds, passions, etc) become quiet(er) after being violent: *The storm began to ~.* **5** (hum) (of a person) go down slowly: *~ into a chair.* **sub·sid·ence** /səbˋsaɪdns/ *n* [C,U] act or process of subsiding(2,3); instance of this.

sub·sidi·ary /səbˋsɪdɪərɪ *US:* -dɪerɪ/ *adj ~ (to),* serving as a help or support but not of first importance: *a ~ company,* one that is controlled by a larger one. □ *n* (*pl* -ries) ~ company; ~ thing or person.

sub·sidy /ˋsʌbsədɪ/ *n* [C] (*pl* -dies) money granted, esp by a government or society, to an industry or other cause needing help, or to an ally in war, or (e g *food subsidies*) to keep prices at a desired level. **sub·si·dize** /ˋsʌbsɪdaɪz/ *vt* [VP6A] give a ~ to: *subsidized industries.* **sub·si·diz·ation** /ˈsʌbsɪdaɪˋzeɪʃn *US:* -dɪˋz-/ *n* [U].

sub·sist /səbˋsɪst/ *vi* [VP2A,3A] *~ (on),* exist; be kept in existence on: *~ on a vegetable diet/on charity.* **sub·sis·tence** /-təns/ *n* [U] existence; means of existing: *a bare ~ence wage,* one that is only just enough to enable a worker to exist; *my means of ~ence,* how I make a living; *ˋ~ence crops,* those grown, e g by peasants, for consumption (contrasted with *ˋcash crops,* those sold for money); *on a ˋ~ence level,* on a standard of living barely adequate for remaining alive.

sub·soil /ˋsʌbsɔɪl/ *n* [U] layer of soil that lies

immediately beneath the surface layer.

sub·sonic /ˈsʌbˋsonɪk/ *adj* (of speed) less than that of sound; (of aircraft) flying at ~ speed. ⇨ **supersonic.**

sub·stance /ˋsʌbstəns/ *n* **1** [C,U] (particular kind of) matter: *Water, ice and snow are not different ~s; they are the same ~ in different forms.* **2** [U] most important part, chief or real meaning, of sth: *an argument of little ~; the ~ of a speech. I agree in ~ with what you say, but differ on some small points.* **3** [U] firmness; solidity: *This material has some ~,* is fairly solid or strong. **4** [U] money; property: *a man of ~,* e g a property owner; *waste one's ~,* spend one's money unwisely.

sub·stan·dard /ˈsʌbˋstændəd/ *adj* below average standard.

sub·stan·tial /səbˋstænʃl/ *adj* **1** solidly or strongly built or made. **2** large; considerable: *a ~ meal/ improvement/loan.* **3** possessing considerable property; well-to-do: *a ~ business firm; ~ farmers.* **4** practical; in the main; in essentials: *We are in ~ agreement.* **5** real; having physical existence: *Was what you saw something ~ or only a ghost?* **~ly** /-ʃl̩ɪ/ *adv*: *Your efforts contributed ~ly* (= considerably) *to our success.*

sub·stan·ti·ate /səbˋstænʃɪeɪt/ *vt* [VP6A] give facts to support (a claim, statement, charge, etc). **sub·stan·ti·ation** /səbˈstænʃɪˋeɪʃn/ *n*

sub·stan·ti·val /ˈsʌbstənˋtɑɪvl/ *adj* (gram) of the nature of a substantive: *a ~ clause,* a clause functioning as a noun.

sub·stan·tive /ˋsʌbstəntɪv/ *adj* having an independent existence; real; actual: *Almost all of Great Britain's Colonies now have the status of ~ nations.* **a ~ motion,** (in a debate) an amendment which, having been carried, becomes the subject of further discussion; ~ /səbˋstæntɪv/ *rank,* (GB) permanent rank (in the army, etc). □ *n* (gram) noun.

sub·sta·tion /ˋsʌbsteɪʃn/ *n* branch or subordinate station, e g for the distribution of electric current.

sub·sti·tute /ˋsʌbstɪtjut *US:* -tut/ *n* person or thing taking the place of, acting for or serving for another: *Is chicory a satisfactory ~ for coffee? S~s for rubber can be made from petroleum.* □ *vt,vi* [VP6A,14,3A] **~ *(sth/sb) (for),*** put, use or serve as a ~: *~ margarine for butter. Mr X ~d for the teacher who was in hospital.* **sub·sti·tu·tion** /ˈsʌbstɪˋtjuʃn *US:* -ˋtuʃn/ *n* [U].

sub·stra·tum /ˈsʌbˋstrɑtəm *US:* -ˋstreɪt-/ *n* (*pl* -ta /-tə/) **1** level lying below another: *a ~ of rock.* **2** foundation: *The story has a ~ of truth,* is based upon facts (though perhaps at first sight seeming false).

sub·struc·ture /ˋsʌbstrʌktʃə(r)/ *n* foundation; supporting part. ⇨ **superstructure.**

sub·sume /səbˋsjum *US:* -ˋsum/ *vt* [VP6A,14] **~ *sth under,*** include (an example, etc) under a rule or in a particular class.

sub·tend /səbˋtend/ *vt* (geom) (of a chord, the side of a triangle) be exactly opposite to (an arc or angle).

sub·ter·fuge /ˋsʌbtəfjudʒ/ *n* [C] trick, excuse, esp one used to evade trouble or sth unpleasant; [U] trickery.

sub·ter·ranean /ˈsʌbtəˋreɪnɪən/ *adj* underground: *a ~ passage; ~ fires.*

sub·title /ˋsʌbtɑɪtl/ *n* secondary title (of a book); translation of the dialogue of a foreign language film, printed on the film.

subtle /ˋsʌtl/ *adj* **1** difficult to perceive or describe because fine or delicate: *a ~ charm/flavour; ~ humour; a ~ distinction.* **2** ingenious; complex: *a ~ argument/design.* **3** quick and clever at seeing or making delicate differences; sensitive: *a ~ observer/critic.* **sub·tly** /ˋsʌtl̩ɪ/ *adv* **~ty** *n* (*pl* **-ties**) [U] the quality of being ~; [C] ~ distinction, etc.

sub·topia /ˈsʌbˋtəʊpɪə/ *n* [U] (part of the country where there is a) monotonous urban sprawl of standardized buildings, etc; (result of such a) tendency to urbanize the country.

sub·tract /səbˋtrækt/ *vt* [VP6A,14] **~ *sth (from),*** take (a number, quantity) away from (another number, etc): *~ 6 from 9.* **sub·trac·tion** /səbˋtrækʃn/ *n* [U] the process of ~ing; [C] instance of this: *Two from five is a simple ~ion.*

sub·tropi·cal /ˈsʌbˋtropɪkl/ *adj* bordering on the tropics; nearly tropical; of ~ areas: *a ~ climate; ~ plants.*

sub·urb /ˋsʌbɜb/ *n* [C] outlying residential district of a town or city: *the ~s,* all these districts collectively. **sub·ur·ban** /səˋbɜbən/ *adj* **1** of or in a ~: *~an shops.* **2** (derog) having the good qualities of neither town nor country people; narrow in interests and outlook. **sub·ur·bia** /səˋbɜbɪə/ *n* [U] (usu derog) (kind of life lived by, characteristic outlook of, people in) ~s (collectively).

sub·ven·tion /səbˋvenʃn/ *n* subsidy; grant of money in aid.

sub·vers·ive /səbˋvɜsɪv/ *adj* tending to subvert: *speeches that are ~ of peace and order; ~ propaganda.*

sub·vert /sʌbˋvɜt/ *vt* [VP6A] destroy, overthrow (religion, a government) by weakening people's trust, confidence, belief: *~ the monarchy.* **sub·ver·sion** /səbˋvɜʃn *US:* -ˋvɜʒn/ *n* [U].

sub·way /ˋsʌbweɪ/ *n* [C] **1** underground passage or tunnel, e g one to enable people to get from one side of a busy street to another: *Cross by the ~.* **2** (US) underground railway in a town (GB, *the Underground* or, colloq, *the tube*).

suc·ceed /səkˋsid/ *vi,vt* **1** [VP2A,3A] **~ *(in),*** do what one is trying to do; gain one's purpose: *~ in life; ~ in (passing) an examination. The attack ~ed.* **2** [VP6A,16B] come next after and take the place of: *Who ~ed Churchill as Prime Minister?* **3** [VP2A,3A] **~ *(to),*** inherit; have (a title, position, etc) on the death of sb: *~ to an estate. On George VI's death, Elizabeth II ~ed (to the throne).*

suc·cess /səkˋses/ *n* **1** [U] succeeding; the gaining of what is aimed at: *meet with ~.* ***Nothing succeeds like ~,*** (prov) S~ in one case is likely to be followed by ~ in other cases. **2** [U] good fortune; prosperity: *have great ~ in life.* **3** [C] sb or sth that succeeds; example of succeeding: *The plan was a great ~. He has had three ~es and one failure,* e g of a dramatist. *The army has had several ~es* (= victories) *recently.* **~·ful** /-fl/ *adj* having ~: *~ful candidates; ~ in everything.*

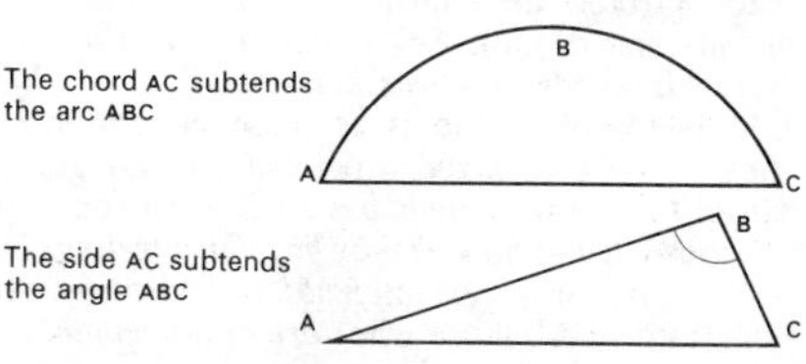

~·fully /-flɪ/ *adv*

suc·cession /sək`seʃn/ *n* **1** [U] the coming of one thing after another in time or order: *the ~ of the seasons.* ***in ~,*** one after the other. **2** [C] number of things in ~: *a ~ of wet days/defeats.* **3** [U] (right of) succeeding to a title, the throne, property, etc; person having this right: *Who is first in ~ to the throne?* **the Apostolic S~,** the unbroken passing of spiritual authority through the bishops from the Apostles of Jesus or of a Pope from St Peter. **`~ duty,** tax on inherited property.

suc·cess·ive /sək`sesɪv/ *adj* coming one after the other in an uninterrupted sequence: *The school team won five ~ games.* Cf *five games running.* **~·ly** *adv*

suc·ces·sor /sək`sesə(r)/ *n* person or thing that succeeds another: *the ~ to the throne; appoint a ~ to a headmaster.*

suc·cinct /sək`sɪŋkt/ *adj* expressed briefly and clearly; terse. **~·ly** *adv* **~·ness** *n*

suc·cour (US = **-cor**) /`sʌkə(r)/ *n* [U] (liter) help given in time of need. □ *vt* [VP6A] give help to (sb in danger or difficulty).

suc·cu·bus /`sʌkjʊbəs/ *n* female demon supposed to have sexual intercourse with a sleeping man. ⇨ incubus.

suc·cu·lent /`sʌkjʊlənt/ *adj* **1** (of fruit and meat) juicy; tasting good: *a ~ steak.* **2** (of stems, leaves) thick and fleshy; (of plants) having ~ stems and leaves. □ *n* ~ plant, e g a cactus. **suc·cu·lence** /-əns/ *n* [U].

suc·cumb /sə`kʌm/ *vi* [VP2A,3A] ***~ to,*** yield (to temptation, flattery, etc); die: *~ to one's injuries.*

such /sʌtʃ/ *adj* (no comp or superl; not placed between the *indef art* and its *n;* note, in the examples, the place of *such* after *no, some, many, all*) **1** of the same kind or degree (as): *~ words (as those); no ~ words (as those); poets ~ as Keats and Shelley; ~ poets as Keats and Shelley; ~ people as these; people ~ as these; on ~ an occasion/on an occasion ~ as this; Harrison, or some ~ name. Some ~ plan was in his mind. All ~ possibilities must be considered. I have met many ~ people. I've never heard of ~ a thing! I hope I never have ~ an experience again.* **2** ***~ as it is,*** used to suggest that sth is of poor quality, of little value, etc: *You can use my bicycle, ~ as it is.* ***~ as to (+ inf),*** of a degree or kind that would or might: *Your stupidity is ~ as to fill me with despair. His illness is not ~ as to cause anxiety.* **3** ***~ that, ~... that:*** *His behaviour was ~ that everyone disliked him. S~ was the force of the explosion/The force... was ~ that all the windows were broken.* **4** (Cf the positions of ~ and *so* in these examples): *Don't be in ~ a hurry,* in so much of a hurry, in so great a hurry. *I haven't had ~ an enjoyable evening* (= so enjoyable an evening) *for months.* **5** (intensive, esp in exclamatory sentences): *It was ~ a long time ago! You gave me ~ a fright! We've had ~ a good time!* Cf What a fright you gave me! What a good time we've had! **6** (pred use) this, that, these, those (as already stated, etc): *S~ is not my intention. S~ were his words. S~ was her reward. S~ is life!* Life is like that, life is as these circumstances show it to be! □ *pron* ~ person(s) or thing(s): *I haven't many specimens but I will send you ~ as* (= those that) *I have. I may have hurt feelings but ~* (= that) *was certainly not my intention. All ~es* (rare = All those who) *are of my opinion.... He is a brilliant scholar and is everywhere recognized as ~,* as a brilliant scholar. *Down with anarchists and all ~,* all persons of that kind! **`~·like** *adj* (colloq) of the same kind; similar: *I have no time for concerts, theatres, cinemas and ~like.*

suck /sʌk/ *vt,vi* **1** [VP6A,15A,B] ***~ sth (from/out of, etc),*** draw (liquid) into the mouth by the use of the lip muscles: *~ the juice from an orange; ~ poison out of a wound;* (fig) *~ in knowledge.* **2** [VP6A,22] draw liquid or (fig) knowledge, information, etc from: *A baby ~s its mother's breast.* Cf The mother was nursing her baby at the breast. *She ~ed the orange dry.* **`~·ing-pig** *n* young pig still taking its mother's milk. **3** [VP6A] hold (sth) in the mouth and lick, roll about, squeeze, etc with the tongue: *~ a toffee. The child still ~s its thumb.* **4** [VP2C] perform the action of ~ing: *The baby was ~ing away at the empty feeding-bottle. The old man was ~ing at his pipe.* **5** [VP6A,15B] ***~ sth up,*** absorb: *plants that ~ up moisture from the soil.* **6** [VP15A] (of a whirlpool, etc) engulf, pull in: *The canoe was ~ed (down) into the whirlpool.* **7** ***~ up (to),*** (schoolboy sl) try to please by flattery, offers of service, etc. □ *n* act or process of ~ing: *have/take a ~ at a lollipop.* ***give ~ to,*** allow (a baby) to ~ at the breast (but *nurse* and *suckle* are more usu).

sucker /`sʌkə(r)/ *n* [C] **1** one who, that which, sucks. **2** organ in some animals enabling them to rest on a surface by suction. **3** rubber device, e g a concave rubber disc, that adheres by suction to a surface (and can be used to cause articles to adhere in this way). **4** unwanted shoot (new growth) coming up from the roots of a tree, shrub, etc. **5** (colloq) person foolish enough to be deceived by unscrupulous tricksters, advertisements, etc.

suckle /`sʌkl/ *vt* [VP6A] feed with milk from the breast or udder. **suck·ling** /`sʌklɪŋ/ *n* baby or young animal still being ~d. ***babes and sucklings,*** innocent children.

suc·tion /`sʌkʃn/ *n* [U] **1** action of sucking; removal of air, liquid, etc from a vessel or cavity so as to produce a partial vacuum and enable air-pressure from outside to force in liquid or dust: *Some pumps and all vacuum-cleaners work by ~.* **2** similar process, e g in a rubber disc with a concave surface, a fly's foot, causing two surfaces to be held together.

sud·den /`sʌdn/ *adj* happening, coming, done, unexpectedly, quickly, without warning: *a ~ shower; a ~ turn in the road.* □ *n* (only in) ***all of a ~,*** unexpectedly. **~·ly** *adv* **~·ness** *n*

suds /sʌdz/ *n pl* froth, mass of tiny bubbles, on soapy water.

sue /su/ *vt,vi* ***sue for,*** **1** [VP6A,14] make a legal claim against: *sue a person for damages,* for money in compensation for loss or injury. **2** [VP14,3A] beg; ask: *sue (the enemy) for peace; suing for mercy; sue for a divorce,* in a law court.

suede, suède /sweɪd/ *n* [U] kind of soft leather made from the skin of goats, with the flesh surface rubbed into a soft nap: (attrib) *~ shoes/gloves.*

suet /`suɪt/ *n* [U] hard fat round the kidneys of sheep and oxen, used in cooking. **~y** *adj* like, containing, ~.

suf·fer /`sʌfə(r)/ *vi,vt* **1** [VP2A,3A] ***~ (from),*** feel or have pain, loss, etc: *~ from* (= often have) *headaches; ~ing from loss of memory. His business ~ed while he was ill,* His business did not do well. *You will* ~ (= be punished) *one day for your insolence!* **2** [VP6A] experience, undergo (sth unpleasant): ~ *pain/defeat/adversity;* ~ *death,* lose one's life, e g as a condemned criminal or as a martyr. **3** [VP17A] allow, permit (which are more usu words): *S~ little children to come unto Me* (biblical style). **4** [VP6A] tolerate; put up with: *How can you* ~ *such insolence?* ***~ fools gladly,*** be patient with foolish people. **~er** /ˈsʌfṛə(r)/ *n* person who ~s. **~·able** /ˈsʌfṛəbl/ *adj* bearable. **~·ing** *n* **1** [U] pain of body or mind: *How much ~ing there is in the world!* **2** (*pl*) feelings of pain, unhappiness, etc: *They laughed at the prisoner's ~ings.*

suf·fer·ance /ˈsʌfṛns/ *n* [U] ***on ~,*** with permissions implied by the absence of objection: *He's here on* ~, allowed to be here but not wanted.

suf·fice /səˈfaɪs/ *vi,vt* **1** [VP2A,3A] ~ ***for,*** be enough (which is more usu): *Will £10* ~ *for your needs? Your word will* ~, I am content to accept your promise. *S~ it to say that...* (= It ~s to say), I will content myself by saying that.... **2** [VP6A] meet the needs of: *One meal a day won't* ~ *a growing boy.*

suf·fi·cient /səˈfɪʃnt/ *adj* enough: *Is £10* ~ *for the expenses of your journey? Have we* ~ *food for ten people?* **~·ly** *adv* **suf·fi·ciency** /-nsɪ/ *n* (usu with *indef art*) ~ quantity: *a sufficiency of fuel.*

suf·fix /ˈsʌfɪks/ *n* (abbr *suff* used in this dictionary) letter(s), sounds or syllable(s) added at the end of a word to make another word, e g *y* added to *rust* to make *rusty*, or as an inflexion, e g *-en* in *oxen.* ⇨ prefix and App 3.

suf·fo·cate /ˈsʌfəkeɪt/ *vt,vi* **1** [VP6A,2A,C] cause or have difficulty in breathing: *The fumes almost ~d me. He was suffocating with rage.* **2** [VP6A] kill, choke, by making breathing impossible. **suf·fo·ca·tion** /ˌsʌfəˈkeɪʃn/ *n*

suf·fra·gan /ˈsʌfrəgən/ *n* ~ **bishop, bishop ~,** bishop who is consecrated to help the bishop of a see by managing part of the diocese.

suf·frage /ˈsʌfrɪdʒ/ *n* **1** [C] (formal) vote; consent expressed by voting. **2** [U] franchise; right of voting in political elections: *When was the* ~ *extended to all women in Great Britain? Is there universal* ~ *in your country,* Have all adults the right to vote? **suf·fra·gette** /ˌsʌfrəˈdʒet/ *n* woman who, in the early part of the 20th c, agitated for women's ~ in GB.

suf·fuse /səˈfjuz/ *vt* [VP6A] (esp of colours, tears) spread slowly over the surface of: *eyes ~d with tears; the evening sky ~d with crimson.* **suf·fu·sion** /səˈfjuʒn/ *n* [U].

sugar /ˈʃʊgə(r)/ *n* [U] sweet substance obtained from the juices of various plants, esp (**ˈcane-~**) from the **ˈ~-cane** and (**ˈbeet-~**) from the **ˈ~-beet,** used in cooking and for sweetening tea, coffee, etc. **ˌ~-ˈcoated** *adj* coated with ~: *~-coated pills.* **ˈ~ daddy** *n* (colloq) rich, usu elderly, man who is generous to a young woman in return for sexual favours or friendship. **ˈ~-loaf** *n* hard lump of ~ in the form of a cone, as sold in former times. **ˈ~-refinery** *n* establishment where raw ~ is refined. **ˈ~-tongs** *n pl* small tongs for taking lumps (cubes) of ~ at table. □ *vt* [VP6A] sweeten or mix with ~. **sugary** *adj* tasting of ~; (fig, of music, etc) too sweet.

sug·gest /səˈdʒest *US:* səgˈdʒ-/ *vt* **1** [VP6A,C,9,14] ~ ***sth/(to sb),*** ~ ***doing sth,*** propose; put forward for consideration, as a possibility: *I ~ed a visit/~ed going/that we should go to the theatre. I* ~ *we go to the theatre. What did you* ~ *to the manager?* **2** [VP6A] bring (an idea, possibility, etc) into the mind: *The white look on his face ~ed fear,* caused others to think that he was frightened. **3** [VP14] (reflex) come into the mind: *An idea ~s itself to me,* has occurred to me. **~·ible** /-əbl/ *adj* that can be influenced by ~ion; that can be ~ed.

sug·ges·tion /səˈdʒestʃən *US:* səgˈdʒ-/ *n* **1** [U] ~ing: *at the ~ion of my brother; on your ~ion. S~ion is often more effective than persuasion.* **2** [C] idea, plan, etc that is ~ed: *These ~ions didn't appeal to me.* **3** [C] slight indication: *He speaks English with a ~ion of a French accent.* **4** [U] process of bringing an idea into the mind through association with other ideas. **hypnotic ~ion,** putting ideas or impulses into the mind of a person who is hypnotized. **sug·ges·tive** /səˈdʒestɪv *US:* səg-/ *adj* **1** tending to bring ideas, etc into the mind: *~ive remarks.* **2** tending to ~ sth improper or indecent: *~ive jokes.* **sug·ges·tive·ly** *adv*

sui·cide /ˈsuɪsaɪd/ *n* **1** [U] self-murder: *commit* ~; [C] instance of this: *three ~s last week;* [C] person who commits ~. **2** [U] action destructive to one's interests or welfare: *political* ~, that makes continuance in office, etc, impossible; *economic* ~, e g adoption of policies that ruin the country's economy. **sui·cidal** /ˌsuɪˈsaɪdl/ *adj* of ~; very harmful to one's own interests: *a man with suicidal tendencies; a suicidal policy.*

suit[1] /sut/ *n* **1** [C] set of articles of outer clothing of the same material: *a* ~ *of armour; a man's* ~, jacket (waistcoat) and trousers; *a woman's* ~, coat and skirt; a *ˈtrouser-~*, woman's ~ of jacket and trousers; *a two-/three-piece* ~, of two/three garments; *a ˈdress* ~, a man's evening dress. **ˈ~-case** *n* portable flat-sided case for clothes, used when travelling. **2** [C] (formal) request made to a superior, esp to a ruler: *grant sb's ~; press one's* ~, beg persistently. **3** [C] (liter or old use) asking a woman's hand in marriage: *plead/press one's* ~ *with a young woman.* **4** (**ˈlaw-**)**~,** case in a law court; prosecution of a claim: *bring a* ~ *against sb; be a party in a ~; a criminal/civil* ~. **5** [C] any of the four sets of cards (spades, hearts, diamonds, clubs) used in many card games: ***a long ~,*** many cards of one ~, e g ace, king, 10, 8, 6, in one player's hand. ***follow ~,*** (**a**) play a card of the ~ that has been led. (**b**) (fig) do what sb else has done. **~·ing** *n* (shop term for) material for clothing: *gentlemen's ~ings,* material for men's suits.

suit[2] /sut/ *vt,vi* **1** [VP6A,2A] satisfy; meet the needs of; be convenient to or right for: *The seven o'clock train will* ~ *us very well. Does the climate* ~ *you/your health? Will Thursday* ~ *(you),* be convenient? ~ ***oneself,*** do what one chooses to do; act according to one's own wishes. **2** [VP6A] (esp of articles of dress, styles of dressing the hair, etc) look well; be appropriate for: *Does this hat* ~ *me? That colour does not* ~ *your complexion. It doesn't* ~ *you to have your hair cut short.* **3** ~ ***sth to,*** make fit or appropriate: ~ *the punishment to the crime;* ~ *one's style to one's audience.* ~ ***the action to the word,*** carry out the promise (threat, etc) at once. **4** (*pp*) ***be ~ed (to/for),*** be fitted, have the right qualities: *Is Western democracy ~ed to/for all the nations of Asia? That man is not ~ed for teaching/to be a teacher. Jack and his wife seem well ~ed to one another,* likely to be and remain on good terms.

suit·able /ˈsutəbl/ *adj* right for the purpose or occasion: *clothes ~ for cold weather; a ~ place for a picnic.* **suit·ably** /-əblɪ/ *adv* **suit·abil·ity** /ˈsutəˈbɪlətɪ/ *n* **~·ness** *n*

suite /swit/ *n* [C] **1** group of personal attendants of an important person (e g a ruler). **2** complete set of matching articles of furniture: *a dining-room ~*, i e a table, chairs, a sideboard; *a drawing-room/bedroom ~*. **3** set of rooms (e g in a hotel, a bedroom, a sitting-room and a bathroom). **4** (music) orchestral composition made up of three or more related parts.

suitor /ˈsutə(r)/ *n* **1** person bringing a lawsuit. ⇨ suit[1](4). **2** man courting a woman. ⇨ suit[1](3).

sulfa /ˈsʌlfə/ *adj*: *~ drugs,* ⇨ sulphonamides.

sul·fate ⇨ sulphate.

sul·fide ⇨ sulphide.

sul·fona·mides (US) ⇨ sulphonamides.

sul·fur, sul·fur·ic, sul·fur·ous, etc (US) ⇨ sulphur, sulphuric, sulphurous, etc.

sulk /sʌlk/ *vi* [VP2A,C] be in a bad temper and show this by refusing to talk. **the ~s** *n pl* condition of ~ing: *be in the ~s; have (a fit of) the ~s.* **~y** *adj* (-ier, -iest) having a tendency to ~; unsociable: *as ~y as a bear; be/get ~y with sb about a trifle.* **~·ily** /-əlɪ/ *adv* **~i·ness** *n*

sulky /ˈsʌlkɪ/ *n* (*pl* -kies) light two-wheeled carriage for one person, drawn by one horse.

sul·len /ˈsʌlən/ *adj* **1** silently bad-tempered; unforgiving: *~ looks.* **2** dark and gloomy; dismal: *a ~ sky.* **~·ly** *adv* **~·ness** *n*

sully /ˈsʌlɪ/ *vt* (*pt,pp* -lied) [VP6A] (usu fig) stain or discredit: *~ sb's reputation.*

sulpha /ˈsʌlfə/ *n* ⇨ sulphonamides.

sul·phate /ˈsʌlfeɪt/ *n* [C,U] salt of sulphuric acid: *~ of copper,* blue vitriol; *~ of magnesium,* Epsom salts.

sul·phide /ˈsʌlfaɪd/ *n* [C,U] compound of sulphur and another element: *hydrogen ~,* (**H_2S**) sulphuretted hydrogen, a gas with a smell like that of rotten eggs.

sul·phona·mides /sʌlˈfonəmaɪdz/ *n pl* group of drugs (synthetic chemical compounds, also called *the ˈsulpha drugs*) acting as anti-bacterial agents.

sul·phur (US = **sul·fur**) /ˈsʌlfə(r)/ *n* light-yellow non-metallic element (symbol **S**) that burns with a bright flame and a strong smell, used in medicine and industry. **~·etted** /ˈsʌlfjʊˈretɪd/ *adj* having ~ in combination: *~etted hydrogen,* (**H_2S**). **sul·phu·reous** (US = **sul·fu-**) /sʌlˈfjʊərɪəs/ *adj* of, like, containing ~. **sul·phu·ric** (US = **sul·fu-**) /sʌlˈfjʊərɪk/ *adj* **~ic acid,** oily, colourless, very strong acid (**H_2SO_4**) important in many industries. **~·ous** /-əs/ *adj* of, containing, ~.

sul·tan /ˈsʌltən/ *n* Muslim ruler, esp of the former Ottoman Empire. **~·ate** /ˈsʌltəneɪt/ *n* position, period of rule of, a ~; territory ruled by a ~: *the S~ate of Muscat and Oman.* **sul·tana** /slˈtɑnə *US:* -ˈtænə/ *n* wife, mother, sister or daughter of a ~.

sul·tana /slˈtɑnə *US:* -ˈtænə/ *n* [C] kind of small seedless raisin used in puddings and cakes.

sul·try /ˈsʌltrɪ/ *adj* (-ier, -iest) (of the atmosphere, the weather) hot and oppressive; (of a person's temper) passionate. **sul·trily** /-trəlɪ/ *adv* **sul·tri·ness** *n*

sum /sʌm/ *n* **1** (also **sum total**) total obtained by adding together items, numbers or amounts. **2** problem in arithmetic: *good at sums; do a sum in one's head.* **3** amount of money: *win a large sum at the Casino; save a nice little sum out of one's wages each week.* **4 in sum,** in a few words. □ *vt, vi* (-mm-) [VP15B,2C] ***sum (sb/sth) up,*** (**a**) give the total of. (**b**) express briefly (the chief points of what has been said); *The judge summed up (the evidence).* (**c**) form a judgement or opinion of: *He summed up the situation at a glance,* realized it at once. *She quickly summed him up,* judged his character, etc. **ˈsumming-ˈup** *n* (*pl* summings-up) judge's review of evidence, arguments, etc, in a law-case.

su·mac(h) /ˈsumæk/ *n* (kinds of) shrub or small tree, the dried leaves being used in tanning and dyeing.

sum·mary /ˈsʌmṛɪ/ *adj* **1** brief; giving the chief points only: *a ~ account.* **2** done or given without delay or attention to small matters: *~ justice/punishment/methods.* □ *n* (*pl* -ries) brief account giving the chief points. **sum·mar·ily** /ˈsʌmṛḷɪ *US:* səˈmerḷɪ/ *adv* **sum·mar·ize** /ˈsʌmṛɑɪz/ *vt* [VP6A] be or make a ~ of.

sum·mat /ˈsʌmət/ *n* (sl and dial) something.

sum·ma·tion /səˈmeɪʃn/ *n* **1** addition. **2** summing up.

sum·mer /ˈsʌmə(r)/ *n* (in countries outside the tropics) the warmest season of the year, May or June to August in the northern hemisphere: *in (the) ~; in the ~ of 1975; this/next/last ~;* (attrib) *~ weather; the ~ holidays; a ~ cottage/house,* for use during the ~; *a girl of ten ~s,* (liter) ten years of age. **ˈ~-house** *n* shelter with seats in a garden, park, etc. **ˈ~ school** *n* course of lectures, often at a university, during the ~ vacation. **ˈ~·time** *n* the season of ~. **ˈ~ time** *n* time as recognized in some countries where clocks are put forward one hour so that darkness falls an hour later, giving long light evenings during the ~ months. ⇨ *daylight saving* at daylight. **Indian ~,** ⇨ Indian(3). □ *vi* [VP2C] spend the ~: *~ at the seaside/in the mountains.* **~y** *adj* characteristic of, suitable for, ~: *a ~y dress.*

sum·mit /ˈsʌmɪt/ *n* [C] highest point; top: *reach the ~,* of a mountain; (fig) *the ~ of his ambition/power, talks at the ~.* **ˈ~ talk/meeting,** (mod use) at the highest level (i e between heads of States).

sum·mon /ˈsʌmən/ *vt* **1** [VP6A,14,17] ***~ sb (to sth/to do sth),*** demand the presence of; call or send for: *~ shareholders to a general meeting; ~ sb to appear as a witness,* e g in a law court; *~ the garrison of a fort to surrender. The debtor was ~ed,* i e to appear in a law court. *The Queen has ~ed Parliament,* ordered members to assemble. **2** [VP15B] ***~ sth up,*** gather together; call up: *one's courage/energy for a task/to do sth.*

sum·mons /ˈsʌmənz/ *n* (*pl* -es) [C] **1** order to appear before a judge or magistrate; document with such an order: *issue a ~. The ~ was served by a bailiff.* **2** command to do sth or appear somewhere: *send the commander of the garrison a ~ to surrender.* □ *vt* [VP6A] serve a ~(1) on.

sump /sʌmp/ *n* **1** inner casing of a petrol engine containing lubricating oil. **2** hole or low area into which waste liquid drains.

sump·ter /ˈsʌmptə(r)/ *n* (old use) (often *ˈ~-horse, ˈ~-mule*) horse or mule for carrying burdens; pack-animal.

sump·tu·ary /ˈsʌmptjʊərɪ *US:* -tʃʊerɪ/ *adj* (attrib only) (of laws) controlling or limiting private expenditure of money (on what is considered extravagant, etc).

sump·tu·ous /ˈsʌmptʃʊəs/ *adj* magnificent; costly-looking: *a ~ feast; ~ clothes.* **~·ly** *adv* **~·ness** *n*

sun /sʌn/ *n* **1 the sun,** the heavenly body from which the earth gets warmth and light. ⇨ the illus at planet. ***rise with the sun,*** get up at dawn. ***the midnight sun,*** the sun as seen in the arctic and antarctic regions. **2 the sun,** light and warmth from the sun: *sit in the sun; have the sun in one's eyes; draw the curtains to shut out/let in the sun.* ***under the sun,*** (anywhere) in the world: *the best wine under the sun.* ***have/give sb a place in the sun,*** (fig) space and conditions favourable to development. **3** [C] any fixed star with satellites: *There are many suns larger than ours.* **4** (compounds) **ˈsun·baked** *adj* made hard by the heat of the sun: *sunbaked fields.* **ˈsun·bathe** *vi* expose one's body to sunlight. **ˈsun·beam** *n* ray of sunshine; (colloq) cheerful and happy person (esp a child). **ˈsun·blind** *n* window shade, esp an awning outside a window. **ˈsun-bonnet/-hat** *nn* hat or (usu linen) bonnet made so as to shade the face and neck from the sun. **ˈsun·burn** *n* [C,U] (place where there is a) darkening of the skin caused by the sun, or reddening and blistering caused by too much exposure to the sun. **ˈsun·burnt, ˈsun·burned** *adjj* having sunburn. **ˈsun·burst** *n* sudden burst of sunlight (through broken clouds) **ˈsun·dial** *n* device that shows the time by the shadow of a rod or plate on a scaled dial. **ˈsun·down** *n* sunset. **ˈsun·downer** *n* (in Australia) tramp who habitually arrives (at a sheep farm, etc) at nightfall; (colloq) drink (usu of sth alcoholic) at sundown. **ˈsun-drenched** *adj* exposed to great light and heat from the sun: *sun-drenched beaches along the Riviera.* **ˈsun-dried** *adj* (of fruit, etc) dried naturally, by the sun, not by artificial heat. **ˈsun-fish** *n* large fish almost spherical in shape. **ˈsun-flower** *n* tall garden plant with large golden-rayed flowers. ⇨ the illus at flower. **ˈsun-glasses** *n pl* glasses of dark-coloured glass to protect the eyes from bright sunshine. **ˈsun-god** *n* sun worshipped as a god. **ˈsun-helmet** *n* hat specially made to protect the head from the sun in the tropics. **ˈsun-lamp** *n* lamp that gives out ultra-violet rays with effects like those of the sun, used for artificial sun-bathing. **ˈsun·light** *n* [U] the light of the sun. **ˈsun·lit** *adj* lighted by the sun: *a sunlit landscape.* **ˈsun-lounge,** or, less usu **ˈsun-parlour/-porch** *nn* made with glass sides and so situated as to admit much sunlight. **ˈsun-ray** *n* ultra-violet ray used on the body: (attrib) *ˈsun-ray treatment.* **ˈsun·rise** *n* (time of) the sun's rising: *start at sunrise.* **ˈsun-roof** (or, less usu **ˈsunshine-roof**) *n* panel on the roof of a saloon car which slides back to admit sunshine. **sunˈset** /-set/ *n* (time of) the sun's setting. **ˈsun·shade** *n* parasol (like an umbrella) to keep off the sun; awning of a shop window. **ˈsun·shine** *n* [U] light of the sun. **ˈsun-spot** *n* (astron) dark patch on the sun at times, often causing electrical disturbances and interfering with radio communications; (colloq) place that has a sunny climate (e g for holidays). **ˈsun·stroke** *n* [U] illness caused by too much exposure to the sun, esp on the head. **ˈsun·tan** *n* browning of the skin from exposure to sunlight: *ˈsuntan lotion/oil.* **ˈsun-trap** *n* warm sunny place (sheltered from wind). **ˈsun-up** *n* (colloq) sunrise. **ˈsun-worship** *n* worship of the sun as a deity; (colloq) fondness for sun-bathing. □ *vt* (-nn-) [VP6A] put in, expose (*oneself*) to, the rays of the sun: *The cat was sunning itself on the path.* **sun·less** *adj* receiving little or no sunlight; without sun; dark: *a sunless day/room.* **sunny** *adj* (-ier, -iest) **1** bright with sunlight: *a sunny room; sunny days.* **2** cheerful: *a sunny smile/disposition.* **sun·nily** /-əlɪ/ *adv*

a sundial

sun·dae /ˈsʌndɪ/ *n* (*pl* ~s) portion of ice-cream with crushed fruit, fruit-juice, nuts, etc.

Sun·day /ˈsʌndeɪ/ *n* the first day of the week, a day of rest and worship among Christians. ***one's ~ clothes/best,*** (colloq, e g among manual workers) best clothes, not used for working in. **ˈ~ school,** one (in a church, etc) attended by children on ~s for religious teaching. ***a month of ~s,*** a long period of time.

sun·der /ˈsʌndə(r)/ *vt* (old use, or liter) [VP6A] keep apart; sever. □ *n* (only in) ***in ~,*** = asunder.

sun·dries /ˈsʌndrɪz/ *n pl* various small items not separately named.

sun·dry /ˈsʌndrɪ/ *adj* various: *on ~ occasions.* ***all and ~,*** everybody and anybody.

sung /sʌŋ/ *pp* of song.

sunk /sʌŋk/ *pt,pp* of sink².

sunk·en /ˈsʌŋkən/ *pp* of sink² esp 5.

sunny /ˈsʌnɪ/ *adj* ⇨ sun.

sup¹ /sʌp/ *vi,vt* (-pp-) [VP2A,C,6A,15B] (esp Scot and N Eng) drink in small amounts; take (liquid) into the mouth a little at a time: (esp Scot) *Sup (up) your broth.* □ *n* small quantity (of liquid): *a sup of ale. I've had neither bite nor sup* (= neither food nor drink) *for six hours.*

sup² /sʌp/ *vi* (-pp-) [VP3A] ***sup on/off,*** (rare) take supper (on, off): *sup on bread and cheese.* ***He that sups with the devil must have a long spoon,*** (prov) Caution is needed in dealings with someone of doubtful character.

super /ˈsupə(r)/ *n* (colloq) = supernumary; superintendent (of police). □ *adj* (sl) superlative; of great size, striking appearance, etc; (colloq) excellent; splendid.

super·abun·dant /ˈsupərəˈbʌndənt/ *adj* very abundant; more than enough. **super·abun·dance** /-əns/ *n*

super·an·nu·ate /ˈsupərˈænjʊeɪt/ *vt* **1** [VP6A] give a pension to (an employee) when he is old or unable to work; dismiss (sb) because of age or weakness. **2** (*pp,* **~d,** as *adj*) too old for work or use; (colloq) old-fashioned or out of date. **super·an·nu·ation** /ˈsupərˈænjʊˈeɪʃn/ *n*

su·perb /suˈpɜb/ *adj* magnificent; first class. **~·ly** *adv*

super·cargo /ˈsupəkɑgəʊ/ *n* (*pl* -goes /-gəʊz/) person on a merchant ship who manages the sale of the cargo, etc.

super·charger /ˈsupətʃɑdʒə(r)/ *n* device used in an internal-combustion engine to force extra oxygen into the cylinders. **ˈsuper·charged** *adj* fitted with a ~.

super·cili·ous /ˈsupəˋsɪlɪəs/ *adj* showing contemptuous indifference: *nose high in the air, looking like a ~ camel.* **~·ly** *adv* **~·ness** *n*

super·ero·gation /ˈsupərˈerəˋgeɪʃn/ *n* the doing of more than is required or expected: (usu) *a work of ~.*

super·fat·ted /ˈsupəˋfætɪd/ *adj* (chiefly of soap) containing a larger than usual proportion of fat.

super·fi·cial /ˈsupəˋfɪʃl/ *adj* **1** of or on the surface only: *a ~ wound; ~ area.* **2** not thorough or profound: *a ~ book; have only a ~ knowledge of a subject; a ~ mind.* **~ly** /-ʃlɪ/ *adv* **~·ity** /ˈsupəˈfɪʃɪˋælətɪ/ *n* [U].

super·fi·cies /ˈsupəˋfɪʃiz/ *n* (*pl* unchanged) **1** surface; surface area. **2** outward appearance.

super·fine /ˋsupəfɑɪn/ *adj* **1** unusually fine in quality. **2** unnecessarily refined or subtle: *a ~ distinction.*

su·per·flu·ous /suˋpɜflʊəs/ *adj* more than is needed or wanted. **~·ly** *adv* **super·flu·ity** /ˈsupəˋfluətɪ/ *n* (*pl* -**ties**) [C,U] (an amount that is) more than is needed: *have a superfluity of good things.*

super·hu·man /ˈsupəˋhjumən/ *adj* exceeding ordinary human power, size, knowledge, etc: *by a ~ effort; an apparition of ~ size.*

super·im·pose /ˈsupr̩ɪmˋpəʊz/ *vt* [VP6A,14] put (one thing) on top of sth else: *a map of Great Britain ~d on a map of Texas,* e g to show comparative size.

super·in·tend /ˈsupr̩ɪnˋtend/ *vt,vi* [VP6A,2A] manage; watch and direct (work, etc). **~·ence** /-əns/ *n* [U] ~ing: *under the personal ~ence of the manager.* **~·ent** /-ənt/ *n* person who ~s; manager; police officer above a chief inspector in rank.

su·perior /səˋpɪərɪə(r)/ *adj* **1** better than the average: *~ cloth; a girl of ~ intelligence; ~ grades of coffee.* **2** greater in number: *The enemy attacked with ~ forces/were ~ in numbers.* **3 ~ to,** **(a)** better than: *This cloth is ~ to that.* **(b)** higher in rank or position than. **(c)** not influenced by; not giving way to: *~ to flattery; rise ~ to temptation.* **4** priggish; supercilious: *'I never apologize', he said, with a ~ air.* □ *n* **1** person of higher rank, authority, etc than another, or who is better, etc than another (in sth): *my ~s in rank. Napoleon had no ~ as a general.* **2** (in titles) *the Father S~,* abbot; *the Mother S~,* abbess. **~·ity** /səˈpɪərɪˋorətɪ *US:* -ˋɔr-/ *n* [U] state of being ~: *the ~ity of one thing to another; his ~ity in talent.* **ˋ~ity complex,** (pop use) aggressive or domineering attitude as a defence against a feeling of inferiority.

su·per·la·tive /suˋpɜlətɪv/ *adj* **1** of the highest degree or quality: *a man of ~ wisdom.* **2** (gram) *the ~ degree,* the form of an *adj* or *adv* expressing the highest degree, e g *best, worst, most foolish(ly).* □ *n* ~ form of an *adj* or *adv.* ***speak in ~s,*** use language expressing extreme opinions and feelings; exaggerate.

super·man /ˋsupəmæn/ *n* (*pl* -**men**) man having more than ordinary human powers and abilities, e g as imagined by sb writing about the future of mankind.

super·mar·ket /ˋsupəmɑkɪt/ *n* large self-service store selling food, household goods, etc.

su·per·nal /sjuˋpɜnl *US:* su-/ *adj* (liter) heavenly; divine: *~ loveliness.*

super·natu·ral /ˈsupəˋnætʃərl/ *adj* spiritual; of that which is not controlled or explained by physical laws: *~ beings,* e g angels and devils. **the ~,** ~ agencies, phenomena, etc. **~·ly** *adv*

super·nor·mal /ˈsupəˋnɔml/ *adj* beyond what is normal.

super·nu·mer·ary /ˈsupəˋnjumərərɪ *US:* -ˋnuməreri/ *n* (*pl* -**ries**), *adj* (person or thing) in excess of the normal number; (esp) person engaged for odd jobs; actor who has only a small part, e g in crowd scenes.

super·scrip·tion /ˈsupəskrɪpʃn/ *n* [C] word(s) written at the top of or outside sth, e g the address on the envelope of a letter.

super·sede /ˈsupəˋsid/ *vt* [VP6A] take the place of; put or use sb or sth in the place of: *Motorways have ~d ordinary roads for long-distance travel.* **super·session** /ˈsupəˋseʃn/ *n*

super·sonic /ˈsupəˋsonɪk/ *adj* (of speeds) greater than that of sound; (of aircraft) able to fly at ~ speed.

super·sti·tion /ˈsupəˋstɪʃn/ *n* [C,U] (idea, practice, etc founded on) unreasoning belief in magic, witchcraft, etc; irrational fear of what is unknown or mysterious: *sunk in ignorance and ~.* **super·sti·tious** /ˈsupəˋstɪʃəs/ *adj* of, showing, resulting from, ~; believing in ~s: *superstitious beliefs/ideas/people.* **super·sti·tious·ly** *adv*

super·struc·ture /ˋsupəstrʌktʃə(r)/ *n* structure built on the top of sth else; parts of a ship above the main deck.

super·tax /ˋsupətæks/ *n* [C,U] tax on (the taxation of) incomes (additional to income tax) above a certain level.

super·vene /ˈsupəˋvin/ *vi* [VP2A] come or happen as a change from or interruption of (a condition or process).

super·vise /ˋsupəvɑɪz/ *vt,vi* [VP6A,2A] watch and direct (work, workers, an organization). **super·vi·sor** /-zə(r)/ *n* person who ~s. **super·vi·sion** /ˈsupəˋvɪʒn/ *n* supervising: *under the supervision of,* ~d by. **super·vis·ory** /ˈsupəˋvɑɪzərɪ/ *adj* supervising: *supervisory duties.*

su·pine /ˋsupɑɪn *US:* səˋpɑɪn/ *adj* **1** lying flat on the back, face upwards. ⇨ **prone(1)**. **2** inactive; slow to act; indolent. **~·ly** *adv*

sup·per /ˋsʌpə(r)/ *n* [C,U] last meal of the day: *have cold meat for ~; eat very little ~; have a good ~; late ~s after the theatre.* **~·less** *adj* without ~: *go to bed ~less.*

sup·plant /səˋplɑnt *US:* -ˋplænt/ *vt* [VP6A] **1** supersede: *Trams in London have been ~ed by buses.* **2** take the place of (sb), esp after getting him out of office: *The Prime Minister was ~ed by his rival. She has been ~ed in his affections by another woman.* **~·er** *n* person who ~s another.

supple /ˋsʌpl/ *adj* easily bent or bending; not stiff: *the ~ limbs of a child; a ~ mind,* quick to respond to ideas. **~·ness** *n*

sup·ple·ment /ˋsʌpləmənt/ *n* [C] **1** sth added later to improve or complete, e g a dictionary. **2** extra and separate addition to a newspaper or other periodical: *The Times Literary S~; the Observer colour ~.* □ *vt* /ˋsʌpləment/ [VP6A,15A] make an addition or additions to: *~ one's ordinary income by writing books.*

sup·ple·men·tary /ˈsʌpləˋmentrɪ/ *adj* **1** additional; extra: *~ estimates,* e g for additional expenditure: *~ benefit,* (in GB) extra money granted by the State to people in need. **2** (of an angle) making with another a total of 180°.

sup·pli·ant /ˈsʌplɪənt/ *n, adj* (formal) (person) asking humbly for sth: *kneel as a ~ at the altar,* i e praying to God; *in a ~ attitude.*

sup·pli·cate /ˈsʌplɪkeɪt/ *vt,vi* [VP6A,14,17,2C] (formal and liter) make a humble petition to sb: *~ sb to help; ~ sb's protection; ~ for pardon.* **sup·pli·cant** /ˈsʌplɪkənt/ *n* person who ~s; suppliant. **sup·pli·ca·tion** /ˌsʌplɪˈkeɪʃn/ *n* [C,U] humble prayer.

sup·ply /səˈplaɪ/ *vt* (*pt,pp* -lied) [VP6A,14] ***~ sth to sb, ~ sb with sth,*** **1** give or provide (sth needed or asked for): *~ gas/electricity to domestic consumers; ~ consumers with gas, etc. Families supplied daily,* (a tradesman's notice meaning) We take orders every day (e g for meat) and deliver to the houses of our customers. **2** meet (a need): *Should the government ~ the need for more houses,* help to provide them (e g by giving subsidies or making loans)? □ *n* **1** [U] ~ing; [C] (*pl* -lies) that which is supplied; stock or amount of sth which is obtainable: *Have you a good ~ of reading matter for the train journey,* plenty of books, magazines, etc? *We shall be receiving new supplies of shoes next week,* (e g of a shop) new stocks. ***~ and demand,*** quantities available and quantities asked for (thought of as regulating prices). ***in short ~,*** scarce (which is the more usu word). **2** (*pl*) (esp) stores necessary for some public need, e g the armed forces: *ˈmedical supplies.* **Minister of S~,** (formerly in GB) minister responsible for production of material for the armed forces. **3** ***be/go on ~,*** work as a temporary substitute, e g for a teacher or clergyman: (attrib) *a ˈ~ teacher.* **4** (*pl*) (GB) grant of money by Parliament for cost of government. **S~ Day,** (in the House of Commons) day on which approval of the Estimates (of expenditure) is asked for. **5** (*pl*) allowance of money to a person: *Tom's father cut off the supplies.* **sup·plier** *n* person or firm ~ing goods, etc.

sup·port /səˈpɔt/ *vt* [VP6A] **1** bear the weight of; hold up or keep in place: *Is this bridge strong enough to ~ heavy lorries? He hurt his ankle, so he had to be ~ed home,* someone had to help him to walk home. **2** strengthen; help (sb or sth) to go on: *~ a claim/a political party; ~ing troops,* held in reserve to help those who are fighting; *a hospital ~ed by voluntary contributions; a theory that is not ~ed by the facts; an accusation not ~ed by proofs; a ˈ~ing actor,* one who takes a part secondary to that of the leading actor; *a ˈ~ing film,* secondary to the main feature film. **3** provide for: *He has a large family to ~.* **4** endure: *I can't ~ your impudence any longer.* □ *n* **1** [U] ~ing or being ~ed: *This bridge needs more ~. I hope to have your ~ in the election. The proposal obtained no/little/not much ~. Mr X spoke in ~ of the motion. The divorced wife claimed ~* (i e a regular financial contribution) *for her children from her ex-husband. The hippie was found without visible means of ~,* with no apparent resources (money, work) on which to live. ***in ~,*** (of troops) in reserve, ready to give ~. **2** [C] sb or sth that ~s: *Dick is the chief ~ of the family,* earns the money for the family. **ˈprice ~s,** (US) subsidies, e g paid by the government to farmers. **~·able** /-əbl/ *adj* that can be ~ed(**3**); endurable. **~er** *n* person who ~s; device that ~s.

sup·pose /səˈpəʊz/ *vt* **1** [VP9,6A,25] let it be thought that; take it as a fact that: *Let us ~ (that) the news is true. S~ the world were flat. Everyone is ~d to know the rules,* It is assumed, taken for granted, that we all know the rules. *I don't ~ for one/a minute that...,* I don't believe that.... **2** [VP9,6A,25] guess; think: *What do you ~ he wanted? All her neighbours ~d her to be/~d that she was a widow. You'll be there, I ~. 'Will he come?'—'Yes, I ~ so'/'No, I ~ not'/'No, I don't ~ so'. I ~ you want to borrow money again.* **3** [VP6A] (forming an imper, or used to make a suggestion or proposal): *S~ we go* (= Let's go) *for a swim.* **4** [VP6A] require as a condition; imply: *Creation ~s a creator.* **5** ***be ~d to,*** **(a)** be expected or required to (by customs, duty, etc): *Is he ~d to clean the outside of the windows or only the inside?* **(b)** (colloq) (in the neg) not be allowed to: *We're not ~d to play football on Sundays.* **sup·pos·ing** *conj* if: *Supposing it rains, what shall you do?* **sup·posed** *adj* accepted as being so: *his ~d generosity. The ~d beggar was really a police officer in disguise.* **sup·pos·ed·ly** /-ɪdlɪ/ *adv* according to what is/was ~d.

sup·po·si·tion /ˌsʌpəˈzɪʃn/ *n* **1** [U] supposing: *This newspaper article is based on ~,* on what the writer supposes to be the case: not on fact. We mustn't condemn him on mere ~. **2** [C] sth supposed; guess: *Our ~s were fully confirmed.* ***on this ~, on the ~ that,*** supposing that this is the case.

sup·posi·tory /səˈpɒzɪtrɪ *US:* -tɔrɪ/ *n* (*pl* -ries) medical preparation (in a soluble capsule) inserted into the rectum or vagina and left to dissolve.

sup·press /səˈpres/ *vt* [VP6A] **1** put an end to the activity or existence of: *~ a rising/the slave trade.* **2** prevent from being known or seen: *~ the truth/a yawn/one's feelings. ~ a newspaper,* prevent its publication. **sup·press·ion** /səˈpreʃn/ *n* ~ing: *a policy of ~ion,* e g of ~ing movements for independence or for freedom. **sup·press·ive** *adj* tending to ~; designed to ~. **sup·press·or** /-sə(r)/ *n* sth that ~es; (esp) a device fitted to electric apparatus to prevent interference with radio and television reception: *fit a ~ to an electric motor.*

sup·pu·rate /ˈsʌpjʊreɪt/ *vi* [VP2A] (formal) form pus, fester. **sup·pu·ra·tion** /ˌsʌpjʊˈreɪʃn/ *n*

supra·na·tional /ˌsuprəˈnæʃnl/ *adj* above nations or states: *a ~ authority,* one that might be created for world government.

su·preme /səˈprim/ *adj* **1** highest in rank or authority: *the S~ Commander; the S~ Court,* highest in one of the States of the US or in the whole of the US; *the S~ Soviet,* the legistature of the USSR; *the S~ Being,* God. **2** most important; greatest: *make the ~ sacrifice,* lay down one's life (e g in war). **~·ly** *adv* in a ~ manner: *~ly happy.* **su·prem·acy** /səˈpreməsɪ/ *n* [U] ***supremacy over,*** being ~ over; highest authority: *His supremacy was unchallenged.*

sur·charge /ˈsɜtʃɑdʒ/ *n* **1** payment demanded in addition to the usual charge, e g as a penalty for a letter with insufficient postage paid on it. **2** excessive or additional load. **3** mark overprinted on a postage-stamp changing its value. □ *vt* **1** [VP6A] overload. **2** [VP6A,15A] demand a ~(**1**) on or in.

surd /sɜd/ *n* (math) quantity, esp a root (√), that cannot be expressed in finite terms of ordinary numbers or quantities.

sure /ʃʊə(r)/ *adj* **1** (pred only) free from doubt; having confidence; knowing and believing; having, seeming to have, good reason for belief: *I think he's coming, but I'm not quite* ~. *You're* ~ *of* (= certain to receive) *a welcome. I'm not* ~ *whether I have a copy/where I left my copy/when I lost it. I'm not* ~ *why he wants it.* **be/feel ~ (about sth),** have no doubts (about): *I think the answer's right, but I'm not* ~ *(about it). Smith's a good man for the job, but I'm not so* ~ *about Robinson.* **be/feel ~ of sth/that...,** have confidence: *Are you* ~ *of your facts? Can we be* ~ *of his honesty/that he's honest?* **be/feel ~ of oneself,** have self-confidence. **Well, I'm ~!** (exclamation of surprise). **be ~ to,** (colloq) **be ~ and,** don't fail to: *Be* ~ *to write and give me all the news.* **to be ~,** **(a)** it is admitted, granted: *She's not pretty, to be* ~, *but she's very intelligent.* **(b)** exclamation of surprise: *Well, to be* ~*!* **make ~ that/of sth, (a)** feel ~: *I made* ~ *he would be here.* **(b)** satisfy oneself; do what is necessary in order to feel ~. to get sth, etc: *I think there's a train at 5.15, but you'd better make* ~, e g by looking up trains in a timetable. *There aren't many seats left for this concert; you'd better make* ~ *of one/make* ~ *that you have one today.* **2** (attrib and pred) proved or tested; reliable; trustworthy: *no* ~ *remedy for colds;* ~ *proof; send a letter by a* ~ *hand/a* ~ *messenger.* **'~-'footed** *adj* not likely to stumble or slip. *adv* **1 ~ enough,** certainly, in fact: *I said it would happen, and* ~ *enough it did happen.* **for ~,** (usu colloq) certainly. **2 as ~ as,** as certain as: *as* ~ *as fate; as* ~ *as my name's Bob.* **3** (colloq, esp US) certainly: *It* ~ *was cold.* **~·ness** *n*

sure·ly /ˈʃʊəlɪ/ *adv* **1** (usu placed with the *v*) with certainty: *He will* ~ *fail. He was working slowly but* ~. **2** (placed either with the subject, usu preceding it, or at the end of the sentence, often indicating either confidence or incredulity) if experience or probability can be trusted: *S~ this wet weather won't last much longer! You didn't want to hurt his feelings,* ~*! S~ I've met you before somewhere.* **3** (esp US) (in answers) certainly; undoubtedly: *'Would you be willing to help?'—'S~!'* (*Certainly* is more usu in GB usage.)

surety /ˈʃʊərətɪ *US:* ˈʃʊərtɪ/ *n* (*pl* **-ties**) **1** (old use) sureness. **of a ~,** certainly. **2** [C,U] (sth given as a) guarantee; person who makes himself responsible for the conduct or debt(s) of another person: *stand* ~ *for sb.*

surfing

surf /sɜf/ *n* [U] waves breaking in white foam on the seashore, on sand-banks or reefs. **~·ing, '~-riding** *nn* sport in which one balances oneself on a long narrow board while being carried along by heavy ~. **'~-board** *n* board used for this sport. **'~-boat** *n* boat specially built for use in ~.

sur·face /ˈsɜfɪs/ *n* [C] **1** the outside of any object, etc; any of the sides of an object: *Glass has a smooth* ~. *A cube has six* ~*s.* **2** top of a liquid, esp of a body in water, e g the sea: *The submarine rose to the* ~. *Most people consider* ~ *vessels* (= ordinary ships) *to be more vunerable than submarines.* **3 '~ mail,** mail sent by vehicles or ships moving on the earth's ~: *S~ mail is cheaper than airmail.* **'~-to-'air,** (of missiles, etc) fired or launched from the ground or from ships, and aimed at aircraft. **4** outward appearance; what is seen or learnt from a quick view or consideration: *You must not look only at the* ~ *of things. His faults are all on the* ~. *When you get below the* ~, *you find that he is warm-hearted and considerate.* **5** (attrib) of the ~ only: ~ *politeness;* ~ *impressions,* received quickly or casually, with no depth of thought, observation, etc; '~ *noise,* e g from a disc, made by the stylus or needle. □ *vt,vi* **1** [VP6A] give a ~ to: ~ *a road with gravel/tarmac.* **2** [VP6A,2A] (of a submarine, skin-diver, etc) (cause to) come to the ~.

sur·feit /ˈsɜfɪt/ *n* (usu with *indef art*) too much of anything, esp food and drink: *have a* ~ *of curry while in Madras;* a feeling of discomfort resulting from a ~. □ *vt* [VP6A,14] (cause to) take too much of anything: ~ *oneself with fruit; be* ~*ed with pleasure.*

surge /sɜdʒ/ *vi* [VP2C] move forward, roll on, in or like waves: *The floods* ~*d over the valley. The crowds* ~*d out of the sports stadium. Anger* ~*d (up) within him.* □ *n* [C] forward or upward movement; onrush: *the* ~ *of the sea; a* ~ *of anger/pity.*

sur·geon /ˈsɜdʒən/ *n* **1** doctor who performs operations. **'dental ~** *n* dentist qualified in surgery. **'house ~** *n* one of the staff of a hospital. **2** medical officer in the navy: *'~-com'mander.*

sur·gery /ˈsɜdʒərɪ/ *n* (*pl* **-ries**) **1** [U] the science and practice of treating injuries and disease by manual and instrumental operations: *qualified in both* ~ *and medicine.* **2** [C] (GB) doctor's or dentist's room where patients come to consult him: ~ *hours, 4p m to 6p m; political* ~, (colloq) where constituents can consult their member of Parliament.

sur·gi·cal /ˈsɜdʒɪkl/ *adj* of, by, for, surgery: ~ *treatment;* ~ *instruments; a* ~ *boot,* one specially designed to fit a deformed foot. **~·ly** /-klɪ/ *adv*

sur·ly /ˈsɜlɪ/ *adj* (**-ier, -iest**) bad-tempered and unfriendly. **sur·lily** /-əlɪ/ *adv* **sur·li·ness** *n*

sur·mise /səˈmɑɪz/ *vt,vi* [VP6A,9,2A] guess, conjecture: *She* ~*d as much.* □ *n* /ˈsɜmɑɪz/ [C] guess: *You were right in your* ~.

sur·mount /səˈmɑʊnt/ *vt* **1** [VP6A] overcome (difficulties); get over (obstacles). **2** (passive) **be ~ed by/with,** have on or over the top: *a spire* ~*ed by a weather-vane.* **~·able** /-əbl/ *adj* that can be overcome or conquered.

sur·name /ˈsɜneɪm/ *n* [C] person's hereditary family name: *Smith is a very common English* ~. ⇨ *given name* at **give**[1]**(11)**, *Christian name* at Christian and also forename.

sur·pass /səˈpɑs *US:* -ˈpæs/ *vt* [VP6A,15A] do or be better than; exceed; excel: ~ *sb in strength/speed/skill. The beauty of the scenery* ~*ed my expectations.* **~·ing** *adj* matchless: *of* ~*ing beauty.* **~·ing·ly** *adv* in a way that is not ~ed: ~*ingly ugly.*

sur·plice /ˈsɜplɪs/ *n* loose-fitting (usu white) gown with wide sleeves worn by (some) priests (over a cassock) during church services. ⇨ the illus at vestment. **sur·pliced** *adj* wearing a ~.

sur·plus /ˈsɜpləs/ *n* **1** [C] amount (of money) that remains after needs have been supplied; excess of receipts over expenditure, ⇨ **deficit**; amount (of anything) in excess of requirements: *Brazil had a ~ of coffee last year. Articles ~ to our requirements will be sold by auction.* **2** (attrib) exceeding what is needed or used: *~ labour,* workers for whom there are no jobs; *a sale of ~ stock; ~ population,* in excess of what is thought desirable, or for which there is insufficient food, employment, etc.

sur·prise /səˈprɑɪz/ *n* **1** [C,U] (feeling caused by) sth sudden or unexpected: *His failure did not cause much ~/was not a great ~. What a ~! To my ~/To the ~ of everyone, his plan succeeded. We have some ~s in store for you. He looked up in ~.* ***take sb by ~,*** catch him unprepared, at a time when he is not expecting to be seen, etc. ***take a fort (town, etc) by ~,*** capture by making an unexpected attack. **2** (attrib) unexpected; made, done, etc, without warning: *a ~ visit/attack.* □ *vt* **1** [VP6A] give a feeling of ~ to: *You ~ me! She was more ~d than frightened.* **2** ***be ~d,*** experience ~: *We were ~d at the news/~d to hear the news. I'm ~d (to learn that) he didn't come. We were ~d at finding the house empty. It's nothing to be ~d about/at. I shouldn't be ~d if it rained this afternoon,* It seems to me likely that it will rain. **3** [VP6A] come upon suddenly, without previous warning; take by ~; *~ the enemy,* attack them when they are off their guard; *~ a burglar in the act of breaking into a house.* **4** ***~ sb into doing sth,*** hurry him into doing sth, e g by making a sudden challenge. **sur·pris·ing** *adj* causing ~. **sur·pris·ing·ly** *adv* **sur·prised** *adj* showing or feeling ~. **sur·pris·ed·ly** /-ɪdlɪ/ *adv* in a ~d manner.

sur·real·ism /səˈrɪəl-ɪsm/ *n* [U] 20th-century movement in art and literature that aims at expressing what there is in the subconscious mind (so that a painting may depict a number of unrelated objects as seen in a dream). **sur·real·ist** /-ɪst/ *n* artist, writer, etc of this movement. **sur·real·is·tic** /səˌrɪəˈlɪstɪk/ *adj* of ~.

sur·ren·der /səˈrendə(r)/ *vt,vi* **1** [VP6A,14,2A] ***~ (to),*** give up (oneself, a ship, a town, etc) to the enemy, the police, etc): *We shall never ~. We advised the bandits to ~ (themselves) to the police.* **2** [VP6A] yield up under pressure or from necessity; abandon possession of: *We shall never ~ our liberty. He ~ed his insurance policy,* gave up his rights under the policy in return for a lump sum of money (called the *~ value* of the policy). **3** [VP14] ***~ (oneself) to,*** yield or give way to (a habit, emotion, influence, etc): *He ~ed (himself) to despair and committed suicide.* □ *n* ~ing or being ~ed: *demand the ~ of a town/of all firearms; ~ value,* ⇨ 2 above. *No ~!* Let us not ~!

sur·rep·ti·tious /ˌsʌrəpˈtɪʃəs *US:* ˌsɜəp-/ *adj* (of actions) done secretly or stealthily. **~ly** *adv*

sur·rey /ˈsʌrɪ *US:* ˈsɜɪ/ *n* (*pl* -reys) (US) light, four-wheeled horse-drawn carriage with two seats.

sur·ro·gate /ˈsʌrəgeɪt *US:* ˈsɜə-/ *n* deputy, esp of a bishop. ⇨ **suffragan**.

sur·round /səˈrɑʊnd/ *vt* [VP6A] be, go, all round, shut in on all sides: *a house ~ed with trees. We are ~ed with/by dangers. The troops were ~ed,* had enemy forces all round them. □ *n* floor between the walls and the carpet; its covering: *a linoleum ~.* **~·ing** *adj* which is around about: *York and the ~ing countryside.* **~·ings** *n pl* everything around and about a place; conditions that may affect a person: *living in pleasant ~ings. You don't see animals in their natural ~ings at a zoo.*

sur·tax /ˈsɜtæks/ *n* [C,U] (levying of) additional tax on personal incomes beyond a certain level. □ *vt* impose ~ on.

sur·veil·lance /sɜˈveɪləns/ *n* [U] close watch kept on persons suspected of wrongdoing, etc: *under police ~.*

sur·vey /səˈveɪ/ *vt* [VP6A] **1** take a general view of: *~ the countryside from the top of a hill.* **2** examine the general condition of: *The Prime Minister, in his speech at the Guildhall, ~ed the international situation.* **3** measure and map out the position, size, boundaries, etc of (an area of land, a country, coast, etc): *~ a parish/a railway.* **4** examine the condition of (a building, etc): *Have the house ~ed before you offer to buy it.* **~·ing** *n* [U] the work of ~ing(**3,4**): *ˈland-~ing; a ˈ~ing ship,* used for ~ing coasts; instruction in the principles of making surveys(**3**). □ *n* /ˈsɜveɪ/ [C] **1** general view: *make a general ~ of the situation/subject.* **2** piece of land-surveying; map or record of this: *an aerial ~ of East Africa,* made by photography from aircraft: *the ordnance ~ of Great Britain,* ⇨ **ordnance**. **~or** /səˈveɪə(r)/ *n* **1** person who ~s(**3**) land, etc. **2** person who ~s and values buildings, etc. **3** official inspector: *~or of weights and measures; the ~or of highways.* **quantity s~or,** ⇨ **quantity**.

sur·vival /səˈvɑɪvl/ *n* **1** [U] state of continuing to live or exist; surviving: *~ after death,* of the spirit after the death of the body; *the ~ of the fittest,* the continuing existence of those animals and plants which are best adapted to their surroundings, etc; (attrib) *a ˈ~ kit,* package of necessities for a person after a disaster, etc (e g at sea). **2** [C] person, custom, belief, etc that has survived but is looked upon as belonging to past times.

sur·vive /səˈvɑɪv/ *vt,vi* [VP6A,2A] continue to live or exist; live or exist longer than; remain alive after: *~ an earthquake/shipwreck; those who ~d. The old lady has ~d all her children. I hope I shall never ~ my usefulness,* continue to live (or to hold a position) after I have ceased to be useful. **sur·vivor** /-və(r)/ *n* person who has ~d: *send help to the survivors of the earthquake.*

sus·cep·tible /səˈseptəbl/ *adj* **1** easily influenced by feelings; impressionable: *a girl with a ~ nature; a ~ young man,* one who easily falls in love. **2** ***~ to,*** sensitive to; easily affected by: *~ to flattery/kind treatment; ~ to pain.* **3** ***~ of,*** capable of, that can receive or be given: *Is your statement ~ of proof?* **sus·cep·ti·bil·ity** /səˌseptəˈbɪlətɪ/ *n* (*pl* -ties) **1** [U] sensitiveness: *~ to hay fever/hypnotic influences.* **2** (*pl*) sensitive points of a person's nature: *We must avoid wounding their susceptibilities,* not say or do anything that might hurt their feelings.

sus·pect /səˈspekt/ *vt* **1** [VP6A,9,25] have an idea or feeling (concerning the possibility or likelihood of sth): *He ~ed an ambush. She has more intelligence than we ~ed her to possess. I ~ (that) he's a liar* (less usu *~ him to be a liar*). **2** [VP6A] feel doubt about: *~ the truth of an account.* **3** [VP6A,14] ***~ sb (of sth),*** have a feeling that sb may be guilty (of): *He is ~ed of telling lies.* □ *n* /ˈsʌspekt/ person ~ed of wrongdoing, disloyalty, etc: *Are political ~s kept under police observation in your country?* □ *pred adj* /ˈsʌspekt/ of doubtful character; ~ed: *His statements are ~.*

sus·pend /səˈspend/ *vt* **1** [VP6A,14] ***~ sth (from),*** hang up (from): *lamps ~ed from the ceiling.* **2** (passive) (of solid particles, in the air or other fluid medium) be or remain in place: *dust/smoke ~ed in the still air.* **3** [VP6A] stop for a time; delay; keep in an undecided state for a time: *~ payment,* stop payment (e g when bankrupt); *~ a rule; ~ judgement,* postpone giving one; (of a person) *in a state of ~ed animation,* alive but unconscious. (fig, joc; of institutions, committees, etc) temporarily inactive. *He was fined £50 with a ~ed sentence/~ed execution of sentence,* the payment of the fine being not required for a time, i e while he continues to observe the law. **4** [VP6A] announce that (sb) cannot be allowed to perform his duties, enjoy privileges, etc for a time; *~ a (professional) football player,* e g because of repeated breaches of the rules.

sus·pender /səˈspendə(r)/ *n* **1** ***~s; a pair of ~s,*** (GB) (now rarely used) elastic band for keeping up a sock or stocking. ˈ**~ belt,** light garment worn round the waist, with clasps for keeping up stockings. **2** (*pl;* US) pair of straps (*braces* in GB) worn over the shoulders to keep up trousers.

sus·pense /səˈspens/ *n* [U] uncertainty, anxiety (about news, events, decisions, etc): *We waited in great ~ for the doctor's opinion. Don't keep me in ~ any longer.*

sus·pen·sion /səˈspenʃn/ *n* [U] suspending or being suspended: the ~ of a member of Parliament, e g for abuse of Parliamentary privileges; ⇨ suspend(4); *the ~ of a motor-vehicle,* the springs, shock absorbers, etc. ˈ**~ bridge** *n* bridge suspended on or by means of steel cables supported from towers. ⇨ the illus at bridge.

sus·pi·cion /səˈspɪʃn/ *n* **1** [C,U] feeling that a person has when he suspects; suspecting or being suspected; feeling that sth is wrong: *I have a ~ that he is dishonest. I resent your ~s about my motives. He was looked upon with ~. He was arrested on (the) ~ of having stolen the money. His behaviour aroused no ~. Don't lay yourself open to ~. Don't let ~ fall on you/Don't fall under ~.* ***above ~,*** of such good reputation that ~ is out of the question. **2** (*sing* with *indef art*) slight taste or suggestion: *There was a ~ of sadness in her voice/of garlic in the stew.*

sus·pi·cious /səˈspɪʃəs/ *adj* having, showing or causing suspicion. *The affair looks ~ to me. He's a ~ character,* There is reason to suspect that he is dishonest, etc. ***(be/feel) ~ about/of sb/sth,*** have suspicions about: *The police were not ~ of his movements.* **~·ly** *adv*

sus·tain /səˈsteɪn/ *vt* [VP6A] **1** keep from falling or sinking: *Will this light shelf ~ (the weight of) all these books?* **2** (enable to) keep up, maintain: *~ing food,* that gives strength; *~ an argument/attempt; ~ a note,* continue to sing or play the note without faltering; *make a ~ed effort.* **3** suffer; undergo: *~ a defeat. The pilot ~ed severe injuries when his plane crashed.* **4** (legal) uphold; give a decision in favour of: *The court ~ed his claim/~ed him in his claim.*

sus·ten·ance /ˈsʌstɪnəns/ *n* [U] (nourishing quality of) food or drink: *There's more ~ in cocoa than in tea.*

sut·ler /ˈsʌtlə(r)/ *n* (in former times) camp-follower selling provisions to soldiers.

sut·tee /ˈsʌti/ *n* Hindu widow who cremated herself on the funeral pyre of her husband; practice (now illegal) of doing this.

su·ture /ˈsutʃə(r)/ *n* seam formed in sewing up a wound; thread used for this.

su·ze·rain /ˈsuzəreɪn *US:* -rɪn/ *n* State or ruler in relation to a country over which it or he has some control or authority; (formerly) feudal overlord. **~ty** /ˈsuzərntɪ/ *n: under the ~ty of.*

svelte /svelt/ *adj* (F) (of a woman) slender and graceful.

swab /swob/ *n* **1** mop or pad for cleaning, e g floors, decks. **2** sponge, bit of absorbent material, etc for medical use, e g taking a specimen from the throat for testing infection; specimen (e g of mucus) so taken: *take ~s from children suspected of having diphtheria.* □ *vt* (-bb-) [VP6A,15B] clean with a ~: *~ down the decks; ~ up water that has been upset on the floor.*

swaddle /ˈswodl/ *vt* [VP6A] bind (a baby) with long narrow strips of cloth (as was formerly the custom). ˈ**swaddling-clothes,** the strips of cloth used: *still in his swaddling-clothes,* (fig) still not free from restraining influences.

swag /swæg/ *n* [U] **1** (sl) stolen goods; things obtained dishonestly. **2** (Australia) bundle of personal belongings carried by a vagrant.

swag·ger /ˈswægə(r)/ *vi* [VP2A,C] walk or behave in a self-important or self-satisfied manner. □ *n* ~ing walk or way of behaving: *with a ~.* □ *adj* (sl) very chic. **~er** *n*

swain /sweɪn/ *n* (poet or archaic) young rustic man (esp regarded as a lover): *lasses and their ~s;* (joc) lover.

swal·low[1] /ˈswoləʊ/ *n* kinds of small, swift-flying insect-eating bird with a forked tail, which migrates to warm countries, e g to England every summer, and is associated with the beginning of summer. ⇨ the illus at bird. ***One ~ doesn't make a summer,*** (prov) It is unwise to form a judgement on the basis of a single instance. ˈ**~ dive** *n* dive with the arms outspread till close to the water. ˈ**~-tailed** *adj* (of butterflies, birds) with a deeply forked tail; (of a man's coat) with long tails (as of an evening dress coat).

swal·low[2] /ˈswoləʊ/ *vt,vi* [VP6A,15B,2C] **1** ***~ (up),*** cause or allow to go down the throat: *~ one's food,* eat it quickly; work the muscles of the throat as when ~ing sth (to give relief to some kind of emotion): *He ~ed hard,* e g as if ~ing an insult; ⇨ 3 below. **2** ***~ (up),*** take in; exhaust; cause to disappear; use up: *earnings that were ~ed up by lawyers' bills. The earth seemed to ~ them up,* They suddenly disappeared. *The aircraft was ~ed (up) in the clouds.* **3** (fig uses) *~ an insult/affront,* accept it meekly; *~ sth whole,* believe it without argument, doubt. *~ one's words,* take them back, express regret for them; *~ a story,* believe it too easily; *~ the bait,* (of a person) accept a proposal, an offer, etc made to tempt one to do sth. □ *n* act of ~ing; amount ~ed at one time.

swam /swæm/ *pt* of swim.

swami /ˈswɑmɪ/ *n* Hindu religious teacher; (loosely) mystic, yogi.

swamp /swomp/ *n* [C,U] (area of) soft wet land; marsh. □ *vt* **1** [VP6A] flood, soak, with water: *A* *big wave* ~*ed the boat. Everything in the boat was* ~*ed.* **2** [VP14] ~ ***with,*** (fig) overwhelm: *We are* ~*ed with work. The firm is* ~*ed with orders,* i e for their goods. **~y** *adj* (-ier, -iest).

swan /swɒn/ *n* large, graceful, long-necked (usu white) water-bird. ⇨ the illus at **water**. **ˈ~ dive,** (US) = swallow-dive. **ˈ~-song** *n* (from the old belief that a swan sang sweetly when about to die) last performance, appearance, work before death of a poet, musician, etc. **ˈ~'s-down** *n* [U] **(a)** soft underfeathers of ~s. **(b)** kind of thick cotton cloth with a soft nap on one side. □ *vi* (-nn-) [VP2C] (colloq) ~ ***off/around, etc*** move, go in a leisured, often aimless manner, esp of a privileged person or one who need not work: *I suppose you're* ~*ning off to Paris for the weekend. The boys are* ~*ning around Austria on a mountaineering holiday.*

swank /swæŋk/ *vi* [VP2A,C] (colloq) swagger; behave or talk in a boastful way; show off. □ *n* [U] ~ing behaviour: *wear a gold wrist-watch just for* ~; [C] person who ~s. **~y** *adj* smart; characteristic of a person who ~s: *a* ~*y sports car; Jill and her* ~*y friends.*

swap /swɒp/ *vt,vi* (-pp-) = **swop**.

sward /swɔd/ *n* [U] (liter) turf.

sware /sweə(r)/ (old) *pt* of **swear**.

swarm¹ /swɔm/ *n* [C] colony, large number, of insects, birds, etc moving about together: *a* ~ *of ants/locusts; a* ~ *of bees,* cluster of honeybees when migrating with a queen bee to establish a new colony; ~*s of children in the parks.* □ *vi* **1** [VP2A] (of bees) move or go in large numbers round a queen bee for emigration to a new colony. **2** [VP3A] ***be*** ~***ing with,*** ~ ***with,*** (of places) be overrun or crowded: *The beaches were* ~*ing with bathers. The stables* ~*ed with flies.* **3** [VP2C] be present in large numbers; move in a ~: *When the rain started the crowds* ~*ed into the cinemas. Beggars* ~*ed round the rich tourists.*

swarm² /swɔm/ *vt* [VP6A,15B] ~ ***(up),*** climb by clinging with the arms and legs.

swarthy /ˈswɔðɪ/ *adj* having a dark complexion.

swash·buck·ler /ˈswɒʃbʌklə(r)/ *n* bully; boastful fellow who behaves recklessly. **swash·buck·ling** /ˈswɒʃbʌklɪŋ/ *adj* reckless and boastful. □ *n* [U] behaviour of a ~.

swas·tika /ˈswɒstɪkə/ *n* [C] kind of cross emblematic of the sun, good fortune or Naziism. ⇨ the illus at **cross**.

swat /swɒt/ *vt* (-tt-) slap with a flat object: ~ *a fly.* □ *n* **1** slap of this kind: *Give that fly a* ~. **2** flexible device on a handle for ~ting (flies, etc): *a* ˈ*fly-*~ (also ˈ*fly-swatter*).

swath /swɒθ/ *n* (*pl* -s) **1** ridge of grass, wheat, barley, etc lying after being cut. **2** space left clear after one passage of a mower.

swathe /sweɪð/ *vt* [VP6A,15A] wrap or bind up: *He came out of hospital with his leg still* ~*d in bandages.*

sway /sweɪ/ *vi,vt* **1** [VP2A,C,6A,15A] (cause to) move, first to one side and then to the other; swing: *The branches of the trees were* ~*ing in the wind. Don't* ~ *your hips at me, you hussy!* **2** [VP6A] control or influence; govern the direction of: ~*ed by his feelings; a speech that* ~*ed the voters.* □ [U] **1** ~ing movement. **2** rule or control: *the peoples who were under the* ~ *of Rome,* were ruled by Rome (in ancient times).

swear /sweə(r)/ *vt,vi* (*pt* **swore** /swɔ(r)/, or old use, **sware** /sweə(r)/, *pp* **sworn** /swɔn/) **1** [VP6A,7,9] say solemnly or emphatically: *He swore to tell the truth/swore that he would tell the truth. I could have sworn that there was somebody in the next room,* I felt certain of this. **2** [VP6A, 15A,B] take an oath; cause (sb) to take an oath. ~ ***sb in,*** cause him to take the oath of office. ~ ***sb to secrecy,*** make him ~ to keep sth secret. ~ ***a witness,*** administer the oath to him. ***sworn enemies*** enemies who can never be reconciled. ***sworn friends/brothers,*** very close friends. **3** [VP3A] ~ ***by sth,*** **(a)** appeal to as a witness or witnesses: ~ *by all the gods that...;* ~ *by all that one holds dear.* **(b)** (colloq) use and have great confidence in: *He* ~*s by quinine for malaria.* ~ ***off sth,*** (colloq) declare that one will give up, stop using: *He swore off smoking when the doctors said it caused lung cancer.* ~ ***to sth,*** say emphatically: *He swore to having paid for the goods,* said emphatically that he had done so (when accused of not having done so). *I think I've met that man somewhere but I wouldn't* ~ *to it,* am not very confident of having met him. **4** [VP6A,14] make an affirmation after having taken an oath: ~ *an accusation/a charge against sb; sworn evidence/statements.* **5** [VP2A,B,C,3A,22] ~ ***(at sb),*** use curses and profane language: *The captain swore at his crew. Don't teach my parrot to* ~*, please. He swore himself hoarse,* continued ~ing until he was hoarse. **ˈ~-word** *n* word used in ~ing. **~er** *n* person who ~s(5).

sweat /swet/ *n* **1** [U] moisture that is given off by the body through the skin: *wipe the* ~ *off one's brow.* **ˈ~-band** *n* **(a)** band of absorbent material inside a hat. **(b)** cloth tied round the forehead, wrist, etc to absorb ~. **ˈ~ shirt** *n* = T-shirt. ⇨ T. **2** (with *indef art*) condition of a person or animal (esp a horse) when covered with ~: *be in a* ~. *They say that a good* ~ *will cure a cold.* ***be in a cold*** ~***,*** in a state of fear or anxiety. ***all of a*** ~***,*** (colloq) wet with ~; anxious or frightened. **3** (colloq, *sing* only) hard work: *This job is a frightful* ~. **4** [C] ***an old*** ~***,*** (sl) soldier with many years' service; (by extension) person with many years' experience of his job. **5** [U] moisture on the surface of anything, e g condensation on an inner wall. □ *vt,vi* **1** [VP2A] give out ~(1,5): *The long hot climb made him* ~. **2** [VP6A,15B] give out (sth that comes out of a surface). ~ ***blood,*** (fig) work like a slave. ~ ***out a cold,*** get rid of it by ~ing. **3** [VP6A] (cause to) ~: *The doctor* ~*ed his patient. Don't* ~ *your horse.* **4** [VP6A,2A,C] (cause to) work hard: ~ *one's workers.* **~ed goods,** produced by ~ed labour. **~ed labour,** the labour of underpaid workers. **ˈ~-shop** *n* workshop where ~ed labour is used. **~y** *adj* (-ier, -iest) **1** damp with ~: ~*y underwear.* **2** causing one to ~: ~*y work.*

sweater /ˈswetə(r)/ *n* knitted jacket or jersey, usu of thick wool, worn by athletes before or after exercise; similar woolly garment (not necessarily thick or heavy) worn for warmth.

swede /swid/ *n* kind of turnip.

sweep¹ /swip/ *n* **1** **ˈ~(-up/-out),** act of sweeping with, or as with, a broom, etc: *Give the room a good* ~*-out. Let's have a thorough* ~*-up.* ***make a clean*** ~ ***of sth,*** get rid of what is unwanted completely: *They made a clean* ~ *of their old furniture and bought new things. In forming his new Cabinet the Prime Minister has made a clean* ~. **2**

sweeping movement: *with a ~ of his arm/scythe.* **3** space covered by a sweeping movement; range of such a movement: *The knight killed everyone who came within the ~ of his sword.* **4** long unbroken stretch, esp curved, on a road, river, coast, etc or of sloping land: *a fine ~ of country.* **5** steady uninterrupted flow: *the ~ of the tide.* **6** (ˋ**chimney-**)**~,** man whose work is sweeping soot from chimneys. **7** long oar worked by a rower who stands, for steering or moving a boat, e g a sailing-boat when there is no wind. **8** long pole mounted as a lever for raising a bucket from a well. **9** ˋ**~(-stake),** form of gambling on horse-races, the money staked by all those who take part being divided among those who have drawn numbered tickets for the winners (usu the first three).

sweep[2] /swip/ *vt,vi* (*pt,pp* **swept** /swept/) **1** [VP6A,15A,B,22,2A] ***~ sth from sth, ~ sth (of sth), ~ sth up/away, etc*** clear (dust, dirt, etc) away with, or as with, a brush or broom; clean by doing this: *~ the dust from the carpets; ~ the carpets/the floor/the yard; ~ the chimney (free of soot); ~ up dead leaves from the garden paths; ~ up the crumbs; ~ the crumbs under the carpet/ into a corner/into a dustpan.* **2** [VP6A,15A,B] clean or clear away as with a broom; push away: *~ the seas of pirates. The current swept the logs along. The wind swept my hat off/the clouds away. Many bridges were swept away by the floods. We were almost swept off our feet by the waves.* ***~ all before one,*** have complete uninterrupted success. ***~ the board,*** **(a)** win all the money on the table when gambling. **(b)** win all the prizes; have every possible success. ***be swept off one's feet,*** (fig) be overcome by feeling, filled with enthusiasm, e g an audience by a great singer. ˈ**swept-**ˋ**back** *adj* **(a)** (of aircraft wings) attached so that they are at an acute angle to the axis of the aircraft. **(b)** (of hair) arranged so that it is combed or brushed away from the face. **3** [VP2C,6A] pass over or along, esp so as to overcome obstacles; move quickly over or with a rush. *A huge wave swept over the deck. A blizzard swept the country. The big tanks swept over the enemy's trenches. The wind swept along the street.* **4** [VP2C] move in a dignified or stately manner; go majestically: *She swept out of the room. The big car swept up the drive to the entrance of the palace.* **5** [VP2C] extend in an unbroken line, curve or expanse: *The road ~s round the lake. The coast ~s northwards in a wide curve.* **6** [VP6A] pass over (as if) to examine or survey: *The searchlights swept the sky. Her eyes swept the room.* **7** [VP6A] move along lightly and quickly: *His fingers swept the keys of the piano. Her dress swept the ground.* **8** [VP12A] make (a bow, curtsey) with a ~ing movement: *She swept him a curtsey.* **~er** *n* **1** person or thing that ~s: *ˋstreet ~ers; a ˋcarpet-~er.* **2** (football) defender who covers the backs, tackling any opponent who passes them. **~ing** *adj* far-reaching; taking in very much: *~ing changes/ reforms; a ~ing statement/ generalization,* with no limitations or exceptions; *a ~ing* (= complete) *victory; ~ing* (= very great) *reductions in prices,* e g at a sale. **~·ing·ly** *adv* **~ings** *n pl* dust, rubbish, scraps, etc, collected by ~ing: *a heap of ˋstreet ~ings.*

sweet /swit/ *adj* (**-er, -est**) **1** (opp of *sour*) tasting like sugar or honey: *Do you like your tea ~? It tastes ~,* has a ~ taste. ***have a ~ tooth,*** like things that taste ~. **~ wine,** wine with a ~ or fruity flavour (contrasted with *dry* wine). **2** fresh and pure: *~ milk; keep a room clean and ~; ~ breath; ~ water,* fit to drink (contrasted with brackish water, etc). **3** having a fragrant smell, like roses: *The garden is ~ with thyme. Don't the roses smell ~!* ˈ**~-**ˋ**scented** *adj* having a ~ smell. **4** pleasant or attractive: *a ~ face; a ~ voice; a ~ singer,* sb having a ~ voice; *a ~ little girl; a ~ temper;* ˈ*~-*ˋ*tempered. It was ~ to hear people praise me so much. What a ~ little poodle you have! Isn't the baby ~!* **5** (phrases) ***at one's own ~ will,*** as and when one pleases, with no one to give orders or advice. ***be ~ on (sb),*** (colloq) very fond of, in love with. **6** (compounds) ˋ**~·bread** *n* pancreas of a calf or lamb used as food. ˈ**~-**ˋ**briar/-**ˋ**brier** *n* wild rose with ~-scented leaves and single pink flowers. ˋ**~·heart** *n* either of a pair of lovers: *David and his ~heart.* ˋ**~·meat** *n* piece of ~-tasting food (usu made of sugar or chocolate); fruit preserved in sugar. ˈ**~** ˋ**pea** *n* garden plant (an annual) with brightly-coloured, ~-scented flowers. ˋ**~ potato** *n* tropical climbing plant with thick edible roots, cooked as a vegetable. ˈ**~** ˋ**william** *n* garden plant with flowers in close clusters, often parti-coloured. □ *n* [C] **1** (US = *candy*) small piece of sth ~ (boiled sugar, etc chocolate, etc). **2** (US = *~ dessert*) dish of ~ food (puddings, tarts, jellies, trifles, etc) as one of the courses of a meal. (In GB *dessert* usu means a course of fresh fruit, nuts, etc.) **3** (*pl*) delights; pleasures: *taste the ~s of success; enjoy the ~s of life while one is young.* **4** (as a form of address) darling: *Yes, my ~.* **~·ly** *adv* **~·ness** *n* **~·ish** /-ɪʃ/ *adv* rather ~. **~en** /ˋswitn/ *vt,vi* [VP6A,2A] make or become ~. **~·en·ing** /ˋswitnɪŋ/ *n* [C,U] that which ~ens; sth ~ used in cooking, etc.

swell /swel/ *vi,vt* (*pt* ~ed /sweld/, *pp* **swollen** /ˋswəʊlən/, rarely ~ed) **1** [VP6A,15B,2A,C] (cause to) become greater in volume, thickness or force: *Wood often ~s when wet. The river was swollen with melted snow. His face began to ~,* e g from toothache. *He/His heart was ~ing with pride. The boy's eyes were swollen with tears. These small items help to ~ the total.* ***have/suffer from a swollen head,*** be conceited. Hence, ˋ**swollen-headed** *adj* **2** [VP2A,C,6A,15B] ***~ (out),*** have, cause to have, a curved surface: *The sails ~ed out in the wind. The wind ~ed the sails.* □ *n* **1** gradual increase in the volume of sound: *the ~ of an organ.* **2** (*sing* only) slow rise and fall of the sea's surface after a storm (with large but unbroken waves): *There was a heavy ~ after the storm.* **3** (dated colloq) smartly dressed person; person of distinction or ability: *What a ~ you look in that new suit!* ***come the heavy ~ over sb,*** (sl) try to appear great and important and in this way impress him. □ *adj* (colloq) **1** smart, fashionable: *Who are your ~ friends? He took her to a ~ dinner party.* **2** (esp US) excellent; first-rate: *He's a ~ tennis player.* **~·ing** *n* **1** swollen place on the body, e g the result of a knock or blow or toothache. **2** increase in size.

swel·ter /ˋsweltə(r)/ *vi* [VP2A] be uncomfortably warm; suffer from the heat: *a ~ing hot day.*

swept /swept/ *pt,pp* of sweep[2].

swerve /swɜv/ *vi,vt* [VP2A,C,4A,6A] (cause to) change direction suddenly: *The car ~d to avoid knocking the boy down. Don't ~ from your pur-*

pose. □ *n* [C] swerving movement; (esp) turn or curve of a ball in the air.

swift[1] /swɪft/ *adj* (-er, -est) quick; fast; prompt: *~ of foot;* (liter) able to run fast; *a ~ revenge; ~ to anger,* (formal) quickly becoming angry. **~·ly** *adv* **~·ness** *n*

swift[2] /swɪft/ *n* sorts of small insect-eating bird with long wings, similar to a swallow. ⇨ the illus at bird.

swig /swɪg/ *vt,vi* (-gg-) [VP6A,15B,2A,C] (colloq) take drinks of: *~ging beer; ~ off a glass of rum.* □ *n* long drink: *take a ~ at a bottle of beer,* have a drink direct from the bottle.

swill /swɪl/ *vt,vi* **1** [VP6A,15B] ***~ sth (out),*** rinse; wash by pouring liquid into, over or through: *~ out a dirty tub.* **2** [VP6A] (colloq) drink greedily: *The workmen were ~ing tea when they ought to have been working.* □ *n* **1** [C] rinsing: *Give the bucket a good ~ out.* **2** [U] waste food, mostly liquid, e g as given to pigs.

swim /swɪm/ *vi,vt* (*pt* swam /swæm/, *pp* swum /swʌm/; -mm-) **1** [VP2A,B,C] move the body through water by using arms, legs, fins, the tail, etc: *Fishes ~. We swam all afternoon. Let's go ~ming. He swam across the river. When the boat upset they had to ~ for it,* save themselves by ~ming. ***~ with the tide/the stream,*** do as the majority do (taking the easiest course). **ˈ~·ming bath** *n* (usu indoor) pool for ~ming in. **ˈ~ming pool** *n* outdoor pool for ~ming in. **ˈ~·ming costume, ˈ~-suit** *nn* close-fitting one-piece garment worn by girls and women for ~ming. **ˈ~-ming-trunks** *n pl* short garment worn by boys and men for ~ming. **2** [VP6A] cross by ~ming: *~ the English Channel;* take part in (a race) in this way: compete with (sb) in this way: *~ a race; ~ two lengths of the pool;* cause (an animal) to ~, *~ one's horse across a river.* **3** [VP3A] ***~ with; ~ in/on,*** be covered (with), overflowing (with), or (as if) floating (in or on): *eyes ~ming with tears; meat ~ming in gravy.* **4** [VP2A] seem to be moving round and round; have a dizzy feeling: *The room swam before his eyes. His head swam.* □ *n* **1** act or period of ~ming: *have/go for a ~.* **2** (*sing* with *def art*) main current of affairs. ***be in/out of the ~,*** be/not be taking part in, aware of, what is going on. **~·mer** *n* person who ~s. **~·ming·ly** *adv* easily and without trouble: *We're getting along ~mingly. Everything went ~mingly,* without obstruction or delay of any kind.

swindle /ˈswɪndl/ *vt,vi* [VP6A,14] ***~ sth out of sb; ~ sb out of sth,*** cheat; get (money, etc out of sb) by cheating: *~ money out of sb; ~ sb out of his money. Some people are easily ~d.* □ *n* [C] piece of swindling; sth sold, etc that is less valuable than it is described to be: *This new radio set is a ~; the quality of the sound is bad.* **swin·dler** /ˈswɪndlə(r)/ *n* person who ~s.

swine /swaɪn/. *n* (*pl* unchanged) **1** (old use, or liter) pig. **ˈ~·herd** *n* man who (formerly) looked after ~ (when they were out in the woods, etc). **2** ⚠ (abusive, vulg derog) disgusting person. **swin·ish** /-ɪʃ/ *adj* beastly and disgusting.

swing /swɪŋ/ *vi,vt* (*pt,pp* swung /swʌŋ/) **1** [VP2A,B,C,6A,15A,B,22] (of sth having one end or one side fixed and the other free) move, cause to move, forwards and backwards or in a curve: *His arms swung as he walked. He was ~ing his arms. The door swung shut/swung to. The big ape swung (itself) from branch to branch.* ***~ for sb/sth,*** (colloq) be hanged (for murder). ***no room to ~ a cat in,*** (of an enclosure) very small; having very little space for movement. ***~ the lead,*** ⇨ lead[1](3). **2** [VP6A,C] walk or run with a free easy movement (the arms ~ing freely): *The soldiers advanced at a ~ing trot.* **3** [VP2A] dance to or play ~ music. **4** [VP2C,15A,B] turn, cause to turn, in a curve: *He swung (= turned quickly) round and faced his accusers. The car swung round the corner.* □ *n* **1** ~ing movement: *the ~ of the pendulum.* **2** strong rhythm. ***in full ~,*** active; in full operation. ***go with a ~,*** **(a)** (of music, poetry) have a good rhythm. **(b)** (fig) (of an entertainment, event, etc) proceed smoothly, without delays, etc. **~ (music),** (1930's) orchestral jazz, usu played by big bands. **3** [C] seat held by ropes or chains for ~ing on; act, period, of ~ing on such a seat. **~·ing** *adj* (all senses colloq) (of persons) fond of, leading, a gay life, following the latest fashions, etc: *a ~ing chick,* = girl; (of a couple) well-matched; (of places) providing gaiety, everything that is up-to-date and 'with it': *~ing London,* in the late 1960's.

swinge /swɪndʒ/ *vt* (archaic) strike hard. **~·ing** *part adj* huge; very forcible: *~ing damages,* e g awarded by a judge in a law suit; *~ing taxation.*

swipe /swaɪp/ *vt* (colloq) **1** [VP6A,15A,3A] hit hard: *The batsman ~d the ball into the grandstand. He ~d at the ball and missed it.* **2** [VP6A] (colloq, usu hum) steal. □ *n* swinging blow: *have/take a ~ at the ball.*

swirl /swɜl/ *vi,vt* [VP2C,15B] (of water, air, etc) (cause to) move or flow at varying speeds, with twists and turns: *dust ~ing about the streets;* carry (sth) *off, away,* in this way. □ *n* **1** ~ing movement; eddy: *a ~ of dust.* **2** (US) twist or curl: *a hat with a ~ of lace round it.*

swish /swɪʃ/ *vt,vi* **1** [VP6A,15B] ***~ sth (off),*** move (sth) through the air with a hissing or brushing sound; cut (sth off) in this way: *The horse ~ed its tail. He ~ed his whip/~ed off the tops of the thistles with his whip.* **2** [VP2A] make, move with, a sound like that of sth moving through the air: *Her long silk dress ~ed as she came in.* □ *n* sound of, sound suggesting, sth being ~ed: *We heard the ~ of a cane.* □ *adj* (colloq) smart; expensive and fashionable: *a ~ restaurant.*

switch /swɪtʃ/ *n* [C] **1** device for making and breaking a connection at railway points (to allow trains to go from one track to another). **ˈ~·man** /-mən/ *n* (*pl* -men) man in charge of railway ~es. **2** device for making and breaking an electric circuit: *a two-way ~,* one of a pair that can be used for turning electric current on or off from two points (e g at the bottom and the top of a staircase). **ˈ~·board** *n* panel with numerous ~es, esp for making connections by telephone or operating electric circuits. **3** thin twig or easily bent shoot cut from a tree, e g as used for urging a horse on. **4** bunch of false hair used by a woman to make her hair appear thicker or longer. **5** **ˈ~·back** *n* **(a)** *~back (railway),* one that twists and turns up and down steep slopes, esp the kind seen in amusement parks (US = *roller-coaster*). **(b)** *~back road,* road with numerous ups and downs. **6** transfer; change-over: *a ~ from Government securities to equities* □ *vt,vi* **1** [VP15B] ***~ sth on/off,*** use a ~(1) to turn (electric current) on/off: *~ the light/radio, etc on. Don't ~ off yet, please.* **2** ***~ sb on,*** (sl, esp *pp*) cause sb to feel happy, excited;

That music really ~*es me on! He's really* ~*ed on,* (a) is thoroughly involved in up-to-date kinds of entertainment, styles of clothes, etc. (b) is under the influence of hallucinatory drugs. **3** [VP6A, 15B] move (a train, tram, etc) on to another track: ~ *a train into a siding.* **4** [VP6A,15A] ~ ***(to),*** ~ ***(over to),*** shift; change: ~ *the conversation (to a less embarrassing subject);* ~ *over to modern methods.* **5** [VP6A] whip or flick with a ~(3). **6** [VP6A,15A] swing (sth) round suddenly; snatch suddenly: *The cow* ~*ed* (more usu *swished) her tail. He* ~*ed it out of my hand.*

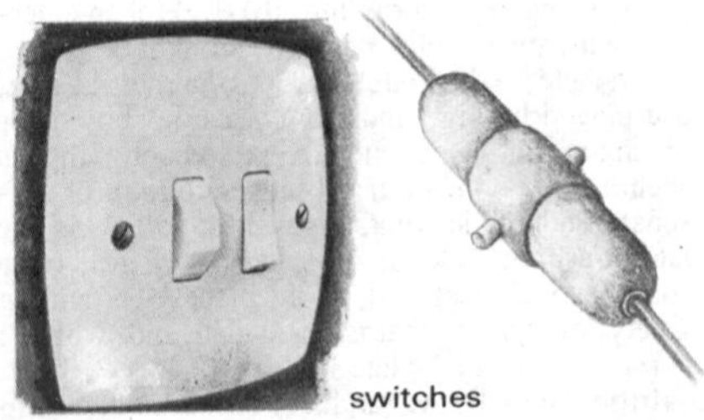
switches

swivel /ˈswɪvl/ *n* ring and pivot or ring with a linked hook to a chain joining two parts so that one can turn round without turning the other: *a* ˈ~*-chain/-hook,* provided with a ~; *a* ˈ~*-chair/-gun,* one that can rotate on a pivot. □ *vt,vi* (-ll-, US also -l-) [VP6A,15B,2A,C] turn on or as on a ~: *He* ~*led round in his chair/*~*led his chair round to see who had come in.*

swiz /swɪz/ *n* (colloq) bitter disappointment; fraud.

swizzle /ˈswɪzl/ *n* (colloq) (kinds of) mixed alcoholic drink served in a tall glass. ˈ**~-stick** *n* glass rod for stirring such a drink.

swob /swob/ *n, vt* (-bb-) = swab.

swol·len /ˈswəʊlən/ *pp* of swell, esp as *adj*: *a* ~ *ankle.*

swoon /swun/ *vi* [VP2A] faint. □ *n* fainting fit.

swoop /swup/ *vi* [VP2A,C] ~ ***down (on),*** come down on with a rush: *The eagle* ~*ed down on its prey. The soldiers* ~*ed down on the bandits,* attacked them suddenly. □ *n* ~ing movement; sudden attempt to snatch and carry off sth. ***at one (fell)*** ~, in one sudden swift attack or movement.

swop (also **swap**) /swop/ *vt,vi* (-pp-) [VP6A, 15A,2A] (colloq) exchange by barter: ~ *foreign stamps;* ~ *yarns,* tell one another stories (of adventure, etc). ~ ***places with sb,*** exchange seats. ***Don't*** ~ ***horses in mid-stream,*** (prov) If changes are needed, make them before the crisis is reached. □ *n* exchange by barter: *I think your hat would suit me—shall we try a* ~*?*

sword /sɔd/ *n* long steel blade fixed in a hilt, used as a weapon, or worn by army officers, etc as part of a uniform or as court dress. ***cross*** ~***s with,*** (fig) dispute with. ***draw/sheathe the*** ~, (rhet) begin/end a war. ***put to the*** ~, (formal) kill. ***at the point of the*** ~, under threat of violence. ˈ**~-cane/-stick** *n* ~-blade enclosed in a hollow walking-stick. ˈ**~-cut** *n* (scar left by a) wound given with a ~-edge. ˈ**~-dance** *n* dance over ~s laid on the ground, or one in which ~s are waved or clashed. ˈ**~-fish** *n* large sea-fish with a long ~-like upper jaw. ⇨ the illus at sea. ˈ**~-play** *n* [U] fencing; (fig) repartee; lively arguing. ˈ**~s-man** /-zmən/ *n* (*pl* -men) man skilled in the use of a ~ (usu with *adjj*): *a good* ~*sman.* ˈ**~s-man-ship** /-mənʃɪp/ *n*

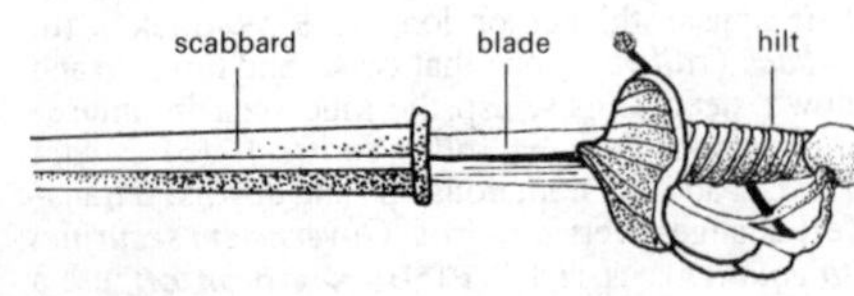

a sword

swore, sworn ⇨ swear.

swot /swot/ *vi,vt* (-tt-) [VP2A,C,3A,15B] (not US) ~ ***(for sth),*** study hard (for an examination, etc). ~ ***sth up,*** work hard at; revise: ~ *up one's geometry.* □ *n* **1** person who ~s. **2** hard work: *What a* ~*!*

swum /swʌm/ *pp* of swim.

swung /swʌŋ/ *pt,pp* of swing.

syb·ar·ite /ˈsɪbərɑɪt/ *n* person who is devoted to comfort and luxury and is considered effeminate. **syb·ar·itic** /ˈsɪbəˈrɪtɪk/ *adj* luxurious; characteristic of a ~.

syca·more /ˈsɪkəmɔ(r)/ *n* **1** [C] large tree valued for its wood (in GB a kind of maple-tree; in US a kind of plane, also called a 'buttonwood'; in Egypt and Syria a kind of fig-tree). **2** [U] valuable hard wood of the ~.

syco·phant /ˈsɪkəfənt/ *n* person who tries to win favour by flattering rich or powerful people. **~ic** /ˈsɪkəˈfæntɪk/ *adj*

syl·lable /ˈsɪləbl/ *n* minimum rhythmic unit of spoken language consisting of a vowel or sustained consonant often accompanied by unsustained consonant(s); similar unit of written language: *'Arithmetic' is a word of four* ~*s.* **-syl·labled** *suff* having a stated number of ~s: *'Sycophant' is a three-*~*d word.* **syl·la·bary** /ˈsɪləbərɪ *US:* -berɪ/ *n* [C] (*pl* -ries) list of characters (e g in Japanese) representing ~s. **syl·labic** /sɪˈlæbɪk/ *adj* of or in ~s. **syl·labi·cate** /sɪˈlæbɪkeɪt/, **syl·lab·ify** /sɪˈlæbɪfɑɪ/ (*pt,pp* -fied), **syl·la·bize** /ˈsɪləbɑɪz/ *vvt* divide into ~s. **syl·labi·ca·tion** /sɪˈlæbɪˈkeɪʃn/, **syl·labi·fi·ca·tion** /sɪˈlæbɪfɪˈkeɪʃn/ *nn* (system of) division into ~s.

syl·la·bus /ˈsɪləbəs/ *n* (*pl* -buses /-bəsɪz/ or -bi /-bɑɪ/) outline or summary of a course of studies; programme of school lessons.

syl·lo·gism /ˈsɪlədʒɪzm/ *n* [C] form of reasoning in which a conclusion is reached from two statements, e g: *All men must die; I am a man; therefore I must die.* ⇨ premise(2). **syl·lo·gis·tic** /sɪləˈdʒɪstɪk/ *adj* in the form of nature of a ~.

sylph /sɪlf/ *n* one of a class of female nature spirits believed to inhabit the air (cf *nymph,* spirit of the woods, etc); (hence) slender, graceful girl or woman. ˈ**~-like** *adj* slender and graceful.

syl·van, sil·van /ˈsɪlvən/ *adj* (liter) of trees and woodland; ~ *scenes; a* ~ *retreat,* e g a cottage in a forest.

sym·bio·sis /ˈsɪmbɪˈəʊsɪs/ *n* [U] (biol) harmonic association of different organisms, etc: *the tall Dingas of the southern Sudan, living in* ~ *with their magnificent cattle.*

sym·bol /ˈsɪmbl/ *n* [C] sign, mark, object, etc looked upon as representing sth: *mathematical* ~*s,* e g ×, ÷, +, −; *phonetic* ~*s. White is a* ~ *of purity. The Cross is the* ~ *of Christianity.* **~ic**

/sɪm`bolɪk/, **~i·cal** /-kl/ *adjj* of, using, used as, a ~. **~i·cally** /-klɪ/ *adv* **~·ize** /`simbḷɑɪz/ *vt* [VP6A] be a ~ of; make use of a ~ or ~s for. **~·iz·ation** /ˌsɪmbḷɑɪ`zeɪʃn *US:* -ḷɪ`z-/ *n* **~·ism** /`sɪmbḷ-ɪzm/ *n* **1** [U] representation of ideas by the use of ~s; literary and artistic movement (late 19th c) that used artistic invention to express sensually ideas, emotions, abstractions in place of realism. **2** [C] system of ~s used to represent a particular group of ideas.

sym·me·try /`sɪmətrɪ/ *n* [U] (beauty resulting from the) right correspondence of parts; quality of harmony or balance (in size, design, etc) between parts: *The bump on the left side of her forehead spoilt the ~ of her face.* **sym·met·ric** /sɪ`metrɪk/, **sym·met·ri·cal** /-kl/ *adjj* having ~; (of a design) having (usu two) exactly similar parts on either side of a dividing line. **sym·met·ri·cally** /-klɪ/ *adv*

sym·path·etic /ˌsɪmpə`θetɪk/ *adj* having or showing sympathy; caused by sympathy: *~ looks/words; a ~ face/heart; a ~ audience; be/feel ~ to/towards sb.* **sym·path·eti·cally** /-klɪ/ *adv*

sym·path·ize /`sɪmpəθɑɪz/ *vi* [VP2A,3A] ~ ***(with),*** feel or express sympathy (with): *~ with sb in his afflictions. Tom's parents do not ~ with his ambition to go on the stage,* do not give him their approval and encouragement. **sym·path·izer** *n* person who ~s, e g one who supports a cause or political party.

sym·pathy /`sɪmpəθɪ/ *n* (*pl* **-thies**) **1** [U] (capacity for) sharing the feelings of others, feeling pity and tenderness: *send sb a letter of ~; feel ~ for sb; have no ~ with sb's foolish opinions. I have some ~ with their views,* share them to some extent. ***in ~ with,*** agreeing with, approving of: *We are all in ~ with your proposals. Will the bus workers strike in ~ with* (= to show their ~ for) *the railway workers?* **2** (*pl* in a few usages): *a man of wide sympathies,* with a great capacity for fellow-feeling. *You have my sympathies. My sympathies are with the miners in this dispute,* I'm on their side.

sym·phony /`sɪmfənɪ/ *n* [C] (*pl* **-nies**) (long and large-scale) musical composition in (usu) three or four parts (called *movements*) for (usu a large) orchestra. **sym·phonic** /sɪm`fonɪk/ *adj* of, having the character of, a ~.

sym·po·sium /sɪm`pəʊzɪəm/ *n* (*pl* **-siums** or **-sia** /-zɪə/) collection of essays, etc (e g forming a book) by several persons on a problem or subject; conference for discussion of a subject.

symp·tom /`sɪmptəm/ *n* **1** change in the body's condition that indicates illness: *A persistent cough may be a ~ of tuberculosis.* **2** sign of the existence of sth: *The Government must not ignore these ~s of discontent among their own supporters.* **symp·to·matic** /ˌsɪmptə`mætɪk/ *adj* serving as a ~: *Headaches may be ~atic of many kinds of trouble.* **symp·to·mati·cally** /-klɪ/ *adv*

syna·gogue /`sɪnəgog/ *n* [C] (building used for an) assembly of Jews for religious teaching and worship.

syn·chro·flash /ˌsɪŋkrəʊ`flæʃ/ *n* (usu attrib) device for simultaneous flashlight and opening of the shutter of a camera: *~ photography/attachments for a camera.*

syn·chro·mesh /ˌsɪŋkrəʊ`meʃ/ *n* system of gear-changing (esp in motor-vehicles) so that the parts revolve at the same speed and so change smoothly.

syn·chron·ize /`sɪŋkrənɑɪz/ *vt,vi* [VP6A,2A] (cause to) happen at the same time, agree in time, speeds, etc: *~ the sound-track of a film with the movements seen; ~ all the clocks in a building.* **syn·chron·iz·ation** /ˌsɪŋkrənɑɪ`zeɪʃn *US:* -nɪ`z-/ *n*

inside a synagogue

syn·chro·tron /`sɪŋkrəʊtron/ *n* apparatus for accelerating electrons.

syn·co·pate /`sɪŋkəpeɪt/ *vt* [VP6A] (of music) change the rhythm of; displace the normal beats or accents of, e g as in some jazz. **syn·co·pa·tion** /ˌsɪŋkə`peɪʃn/ *n*

syn·cope /`sɪŋkəpɪ/ *n* (med term for) fainting; brief loss of consciousness from fall of blood-pressure.

syn·dic /`sɪndɪk/ *n* member of a committee (for business purposes) of a university or other organization).

syn·di·cal·ism /`sɪndɪkḷ-ɪzm/ *n* [U] theory that political power should be in the hands of trade unions and that these unions should own and manage the industries in which their members work. **syn·di·cal·ist** /-ɪst/ *n* supporter of ~.

syn·di·cate /`sɪndɪkət/ *n* **1** business association that supplies articles, cartoons, etc to periodicals. **2** combination of commercial firms associated to forward a common interest. □ *vt* /`sɪndɪkeɪt/ [VP6A] publish (articles, strip-cartoons, etc) in numerous periodicals through a ~**(1)**. **syn·di·ca·tion** /ˌsɪndɪ`keɪʃn/ *n*

syn·drome /`sɪndrəʊm/ *n* (med) number of symptoms which collectively indicate an often abnormal condition of the body or mind.

synod /`sɪnod/ *n* [C] meeting of church officers to discuss and decide questions of policy, government, teaching, etc.

syn·onym /`sɪnənɪm/ *n* word with the same meaning as another in the same language but often with different implications and associations. **syn·ony·mous** /sɪ`nonɪməs/ *adj*

syn·op·sis /sɪ`nopsɪs/ *n* (*pl* **-opses** /-siz/) summary or outline (of a book, play, etc). **syn·op·tic** /sɪ`noptɪk/ *adj* giving a ~: *the synoptic Gospels,* those of Matthew, Mark and Luke (similar in contents, order, etc). **syn·op·ti·cally** /-klɪ/ *adv*

syn·tax /`sɪntæks/ *n* [U] (ling) (rules for) sentence-building. **syn·tac·tic** /sɪn`tæktɪk/ *adj* of ~. **syn·tac·ti·cally** /-klɪ/ *adv*

syn·thesis /`sɪnθəsɪs/ *n* (*pl* **-theses** /-siz/) [C,U] combination of separate parts, elements, substances, etc into a whole or into a system; that which results from this process: *produce rubber from petroleum by ~.* **syn·thetic** /sɪn`θetɪk/ *adj* **1** produced by ~: *synthetic rubber,* artificially made. **2** pertaining to ~: *synthetic chemistry.* **3** (of a language) containing, tending to form, many compound words: *German is a synthetic lan-*

guage. **syn·theti·cally** /-klɪ/ *adv*

syph·ilis /ˈsɪflɪs/ *n* [U] infectious venereal disease. **syph·il·itic** /ˈsɪflˈɪtɪk/ *adj* pertaining to, suffering from, ~. □ *n* person affected with ~.

syphon *n* = siphon.

syr·inga /sɪˈrɪŋgə/ *n* shrub with strong-scented white flowers (popularly called the mock-orange); botanical name of the lilac genus.

syr·inge /sɪˈrɪndʒ/ *n* kinds of device for drawing in liquid by suction and forcing it out again in a fine stream, used for washing out wounds, injecting liquids into the body, in spraying plants, etc: *a hypodermic ~; a garden ~.* □ *vt* [VP6A,15B] clean, inject liquid into, with a ~; apply (liquid) with a ~.

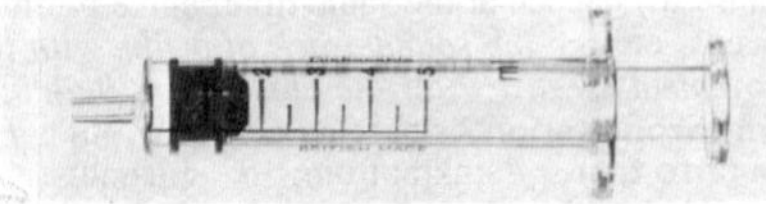

a syringe

syrup /ˈsɪrəp *US:* ˈsɜəp/ *n* [U] thick sweet liquid made from sugar-cane juice or by boiling sugar with water: *pineapple tinned in ~; ˈcough ~,* ~ with medicine in it to relieve a cough: *fruit ~,* ~ flavoured with fruit juices. **~y** *adj* of or like ~; (fig, e g of music) too sweet.

sys·tem /ˈsɪstəm/ *n* **1** group of things or parts working together in a regular relation: *the ˈnervous ~; the diˈgestive ~; a ˈrailway ~. The poison has passed into his ~,* his body as a whole. *Too much alcohol is bad for the ~.* ⇨ the illus at respiratory. **2** ordered set of ideas, theories, principles, etc: *a ~ of philosophy; a ~ of government; a good ~ of teaching languages; a comˈputer ~; ˈ~-building/ˈ~-built houses,* built of prefabricated sections, put together on the site. **3** [U] orderliness: *You mustn't expect good results if you work without ~.* **~·atic** /ˈsɪstəˈmætɪk/ *adj* methodical; based on a ~: *a ~atic attempt.* **~·ati·cally** /-klɪ/ *adv* **~·atize** /ˈsɪstəmətaɪz/ □ *vt* [VP6A] arrange according to a ~; make into a ~. **~·ati·za·tion** /ˈsɪstəmətaɪˈzeɪʃn *US:* -tɪˈz-/ *n*

Tt

T, t /tiː/ (*pl* **T's, t's** /tiːz/) the twentieth letter of the alphabet; used before names of various objects shaped like the letter T: *a ˈT-bandage; a ˈT-shirt,* short-sleeved, close-fitting, collarless usu cotton shirt worn informally; *a ˈT-square,* ⇨ square¹(7).

ta /tɑː/ *int* (colloq) (used by children or, childishly, by adults) thank you.

tab /tæb/ *n* **1** small piece or strip of cloth, etc fixed to a garment, etc as a badge or distinguishing mark or (as a loop) for hanging up a coat, etc; binding at the end of a shoe-lace, etc. **2** (colloq) account; check: (esp) ***keep a tab/tabs on sth/sb,*** keep an account of, keep under observation: *keep a tab on the expenses.*

tab·ard /ˈtæbəd/ *n* short, sleeveless outer garment (worn in former times, e g by a knight over his armour, or by a herald).

tabby /ˈtæbɪ/ *n* (*pl* **-bies**) **ˈ~(-cat),** cat, esp female, with grey or brown stripes.

tab·er·nacle /ˈtæbənækl/ *n* **1** (in the Bible) **the T~,** the portable structure used by the Israelites as a sanctuary during their wanderings before they settled in Palestine. **2** place of worship, e g a Baptist Church or Mormon temple.

table /ˈteɪbl/ *n* [C] **1** piece of furniture consisting of a flat top with (usu four) supports (called legs): *a ˈdining-~; a ˈdressing-~; a ˈtea-~; a ˈbilliard-~.* ***at ~,*** having a meal: *They were at ~ when we called.* **ˈ~-cloth** *n* one (to be) spread on a ~. **ˈ~-knife** *n* steel knife for use at ~. **ˈ~-lifting/-rapping/-turning** *nn* lifting/rapping, etc of a ~, apparently without physical exertion, occurring while people sit at a ~ during a spiritualistic seance. **ˈ~-linen** *n* [U] ~-cloths, napkins, etc. **ˈ~-mat** *n* one to be placed under a hot dish on a ~. **ˈ~·spoon** *n* large spoon for serving food at ~ from a dish, etc. **ˈ~·spoon·ful** *n* as much as a ~spoon holds. **ˈ~-talk** *n* conversation during a meal. **ˈ~ tennis** *n* game (formerly called *ping-pong*) played with bats and balls, similar to tennis, on a ~. **ˈ~-ware** *n* [U] dishes, silver, cutlery, etc used for meals. **2** (*sing* only) people seated at a ~: *a ~ of card-players; King Arthur and his Round T~,* his knights; *jokes that amused the whole ~.* **3** (*sing* only) food provided at ~: *He keeps a good ~,* provides good meals. **4 ˈ~(-land)** /-lænd/, plateau; extensive area of high, level land. **5** [C] list, orderly arrangement, of facts, information, etc (usu in columns): *a ~ of contents,* summary of what a book contains; *multiplication ~s; a railway ˈtime~.* **6** (phrases) ***lay sth on the ~.*** (in Parliament) postpone (a measure, report, etc) indefinitely. ***turn the ~s on sb,*** gain a position of superiority after having been defeated or in a position of inferiority. **7** [C] (in the Bible) flat slab of stone, wood, etc; tablet(1); what is written or inscribed on such a ~: *the ~s of the law,* the ten commandments given to Moses by God. □ *vt* [VP6A] **1** lay (a proposal, etc) on the ~ (⇨ 6 above); *~ a motion/a Bill/an amendment,* submit for discussion. **2** put in the form of a ~(5).

tab·leau /ˈtæbləʊ/ *n* (*pl* **-leaux** /-ləʊz/) (often **ˈ~ vivant** /ˈviːvɔ̃ *US:* viːˈvɑ̃/) representation by living persons of a picture or scene, without words or action, esp on a stage or platform; dramatic situation suddenly brought about.

table-d'hôte /ˈtɑːbl ˈdəʊt/ *n* (F) (of a restaurant meal) at an inclusive fixed price: *a ~ lunch.* ⇨ à la carte.

tab·let /ˈtæblət/ *n* **1** flat surface with words cut or written on it, e g one fixed to a wall in memory of sth or sb. **2** number of sheets of writing-paper fastened together along one edge. **3** lump of hard soap; small flattened pellet of compressed medicine: *two ~s of aspirin;* flat, hard sweet: *throat ~s,* to be sucked to relieve a cough, sore throat, etc. **4** (old use) flat sheet of wood, stone, etc for cutting words on (e g as used in ancient Rome).

tab·loid /ˈtæblɔɪd/ *n* newspaper with many pictures, strip cartoons, etc and with its news presented in concentrated form and easily understood: (attrib) *~ journalism.*

ta·boo /təˈbuː *US:* tæˈbuː/ *n* **1** [C,U] (among some primitive races) something which religion or custom regards as forbidden, not to be touched, spoken of, etc: *That tree is under (a) ~.* **2** [C] general agreement not to discuss sth, do sth. □ *adj* under ~: *Questions and problems that were once ~ are now discussed openly. Unkind gossip ought to be ~.* '**~ words,** those which convention prohibits (e g most of those marked ⚠ in this dictionary). □ *vt* [VP6A] forbid, esp on moral or religious grounds.

ta·bor /ˈteɪbə(r)/ *n* small drum, esp one used to accompany a pipe or fife.

tabu·lar /ˈtæbjʊlə(r)/ *adj* arranged or displayed in tables(5): *a report in ~ form.*

tabu·late /ˈtæbjʊleɪt/ *vt* [VP6A] arrange (facts, figures, etc) in tables(5), in lists or columns. **tabu·la·tor** /-tə(r)/ *n* machine, device, that ~s. **tabu·la·tion** /ˌtæbjʊˈleɪʃn/ *n*

tacit /ˈtæsɪt/ *adj* unspoken; understood without being put into words: *~ consent/agreement.* **~·ly** *adv*

taci·turn /ˈtæsɪtɜn/ *adj* (in the habit of) saying very little. **~·ly** *adv* **taci·tur·nity** /ˌtæsɪˈtɜnətɪ/ *n* [U].

tack /tæk/ *n* **1** small, flat-headed nail (e g as used for securing some kinds of carpet or linoleum to a floor): '*tin-~*, of iron coated with tin; '*thumb-~* (US) = drawing-pin. **2** long, loose stitch used in fastening pieces of cloth together loosely or temporarily. **3** sailing-ship's direction as fixed by the direction of the wind and the position of the sails: *on the port/starboard ~*, with the wind on the port/starboard side. ***on the right/wrong ~,*** (fig) following a wise/unwise course of action. **4** [U] (among sailors) *hard ~*, hard ship's biscuits. □ *vt,vi* **1** [VP6A,15A,B] fasten with ~s(1): *~ down the carpet.* **2** [VP6A,15A,B] fasten with ~s(2): *~ a ribbon on to a hat; ~ down a fold;* (fig) *~ an appeal for money on to a speech,* add one. **3** [VP2A,C] sail in a zigzag course; make a ~ or ~s(3): *~ing about; ~ to port.*

tackle /ˈtækl/ *n* **1** [C,U] set of ropes and pulleys for working a ship's sails, or for lifting weights, etc. **2** [U] equipment, apparatus, for doing sth: '*fishing ~*, a rod, line, hooks, etc. **3** [C] act of seizing and bringing down an opponent with the ball (in Rugby and American-style football). □ *vt,vi* **1** [VP6A,14] deal with, attack (a problem, a piece of work): *I don't know how to ~ this problem,* how to start on it. ***~ sb about/over sth,*** speak to sb frankly (about a matter). **2** [VP6A,2A] seize, lay hold of, sb, e g a thief, a player who, in Rugby, has the ball: *He ~s fearlessly.*

tacky /ˈtækɪ/ *adj* sticky; not yet dry: *The paint/varnish is still ~.*

tact /tækt/ *n* [U] (use of) skill and understanding shown by sb who handles people and situations successfully and without causing offence: *show ~/have great ~ in dealing with people.* **~·ful** /-fl/ *adj* having or showing ~. **~·fully** /-flɪ/ *adv* **~·less** *adj* lacking ~. **~·less·ly** *adv* **~·less·ness** *n*

tac·tic /ˈtæktɪk/ *n* **1** expedient; means of achieving an object. **2** (*pl* often with *sing v*) art of placing or moving fighting forces for or during battle. ⇨ strategy; (fig) plan(s) or method(s) for carrying out a policy: *win by surprise ~s; These ~s are unlikely to help you.* **tac·ti·cal** /-kl/ *adj* of ~s: *~al exercises; a ~al error.* ⇨ strategic. **tac·ti·cally** /-klɪ/ *adv* **tac·ti·cian** /tækˈtɪʃn/ *n* expert in ~s.

tac·tile /ˈtæktaɪl *US:* -təl/, **tac·tual** /ˈtækʃəl/ *adjj* of, experienced by, the sense of touch: *a ~ organ/reflex.*

tad·pole /ˈtædpəʊl/ *n* form of a frog or toad from the time it leaves the egg to the time when it takes its adult form. ⇨ the illus at amphibian.

tael /teɪl/ *n* Chinese ounce (= $1\frac{1}{3}$ oz avoirdupois), esp of silver as a former monetary unit.

taf·feta /ˈtæfɪtə/ *n* [U] thin, shiny, rather stiff silk material; similar material of linen, rayon, etc.

taff·rail /ˈtæfreɪl/ *n* rail round a ship's stern.

Taffy /ˈtæfɪ/ *n* (colloq) (Welsh pronunciation of *Davy* = David) Welshman.

taffy /ˈtæfɪ/ *n* (US) toffee.

tag /tæg/ *n* **1** metal or plastic point at the end of a shoe-lace, string, etc. **2** label (e g for showing prices, addresses) fastened to or stuck into sth. **3** phrase or sentence often quoted: *Latin tags.* **4** any loose or ragged end. '**question tags,** (gram) phrases such as *isn't it, won't you, are there,* added to statements. **5** [U] game in which one child chases and tries to touch another. □ *vt,vi* (-gg-) **1** [VP6A] fasten a tag(2) to. **2** [VP14] ***tag sth on (to),*** fasten, attach. **3** [VP2C] ***tag along/behind/after,*** follow closely: *children tagging after their mother. Tag along with us* (= Come with us) *if you like.* **4** [VP15A,B] join: *tag old articles together to make a book.*

tail /teɪl/ *n* **1** movable part (from the end of the backbone) at the end of the body of a bird, animal, fish or reptile: *Dogs wag their ~s when they are pleased.* ***turn ~,*** run away. ***~s up,*** (of persons) in good spirits. **2** sth like a ~ in position: *the ~ of a kite/comet/aircraft/cart/procession;* (attrib) *a ~* (= following) *wind.* '**~-board** *n* board, usu on hinges, forming the back part of a cart or truck. ˌ**~-ˈcoat** *n* (colloq *~s*) man's evening coat with divided tapering skirt. ˌ**~-ˈend** *n* (usu with *def art*) final part: *at the ~-end of the procession.* '**~·gate** *n* door or flap at the rear of a motor-vehicle which can be opened for loading and unloading. '**~-light** *n* light at the end of a train, tram or other vehicle. '**~·piece** *n* decoration printed in the blank space at the end of a chapter, etc. '**~-spin** *n* spiral dive of an aircraft in which the ~ makes wider circles than the front. ***the ~ of the eye,*** the outer corner: *watching me from the ~ of his eye.* **3** (*pl*) **(a)** side of a coin opposite to that in which there is the head of a monarch. ⇨ head[1](3). **(b)** (colloq) ~-coat: *Am I to wear a dinner-jacket or ~s?* **4** (colloq) sb employed to follow and watch sb, e g a suspected criminal: *put a ~ on sb.* □ *vt,vi* **1** [VP3] ***~ after sb,*** follow close behind. **2** [VP6A] ***~ a person,*** follow him closely, e g because he is suspected to be a criminal. **3** [VP2C] ***~ off/away,*** **(a)** become smaller in number, size, etc. **(b)** (of remarks, etc) end in a hesitating or inconclusive way. **(c)** fall behind or away in a scattered line. **-tailed** /teɪld/ *suff* (in compounds) ˌ*long-ˈ~ed,* ˌ*short-ˈ~ed,* having a long/short ~. **~·less** *adj* having no ~: *a ~less cat.*

tailor /ˈteɪlə(r)/ *n* maker of (esp outer) garments: *go to the ~'s to be measured for a suit/an overcoat.* ˌ**~-ˈmade** *adj* (esp of a woman's coat and skirt) made by a ~, with special attention to exact fit; (fig) appropriate, well-suited: *He seems ~-made for the job.* □ *vt* **1** [VP6A] cut out and sew: *a well-~ed suit.* **2** [VP15A] adapt: *~ed for a* *special purpose/to a particular audience.*

taint /teɪnt/ *n* [C,U] trace of some bad quality, decay or infection: *There was a* ~ *of insanity in the family. Is the meat free from* ~? □ *vt,vi* [VP6A,2A] make or become infected: *~ed meat.* **~·less** *adj* without ~; pure.

take¹ /teɪk/ *vt,vi* (*pt* took /tʊk/, *pt* taken /ˈteɪkən/) (For use with a large number of *nn,* ⇨ 15 below. For special uses with *adverbial particles* and *preps* ⇨ 16 below.) **1** [VP6A,15A] get or lay hold of with the hand(s) or any other part of the body, e g the arms, teeth or with an instrument (Cf *leave/let go of,* as opposite in meaning): ~ *sb's hand;* ~ *sth on one's back;* ~ *a man by the throat;* ~ *sb in one's arms,* put one's arms round him, embrace him; ~ *sth up* (= pick it up) *with one's fingers/a pair of tongs;* ~ *a person's arm,* put, rest, one's hand on his arm, e g to support him or be supported by him. ***~ hold of sth,*** grasp or seize it. **2** [VP6A,15A,2A] capture; catch (sb or sth) by surprise or pursuit; win (in a contest, etc): ~ *a town/a fortress,* in war; ~ *500 prisoners; be ~n prisoner/captive,* be caught and be made a prisoner. *The rabbit was ~n in a trap. The major's bull took* (= was awarded) *the first prize at the agricultural show. How many tricks did you* ~, i e win, e g at a card game such as whist or bridge? *Be careful not to* ~ *cold,* become ill with a cold (*catch cold* is more usu). ***~ sb's fancy,*** please, delight: *The new play really took the public's fancy.* ***~ sb at a disadvantage,*** be approached, attacked, etc when unready, in a unfavourable situation, etc. ***be ~n ill,*** (passive only) become ill, catch an illness. ***~ sb unawares/by surprise,*** approach or discover sb doing sth when he is unaware of one's presence, that one sees him, etc. **3** [VP6A] use; use or borrow without permission; steal; avail oneself of: *Someone has ~n my hat,* i e by mistake. *Who has ~n my bicycle,* borrowed or stolen it? *He ~s whatever he can lay his hands on.* **4** [VP6A,15A, B,12A,13A] carry sth, accompany sb away from a place: ~ *letters to the post;* ~ *the luggage upstairs;* ~ *a friend home in one's car;* ~ *the dog out for a walk;* ~ *one's wife to the cinema. Please* ~ *these things in/out/away/back/home, etc. Shall I* ~ *your message to her/~ her your message? T~ her some flowers. He took me a new way to the coast,* by a route that was new to me. **ˈ~-home ˋwages/ˈpay,** (colloq) net sum after deduction of national insurance contribution, income tax, etc. **5** [VP6A,15A] get, have; eat or drink; allow oneself: ~ *a holiday/a walk/a bath/a quick look round/a deep breath;* ~ *a chair/a seat,* sit down; ~ *medical/legal advice,* get the advice of a doctor/lawyer; ~ *driving lessons;* ~ (= hire) *a taxi;* ~ (= rent) *a cottage at the seaside for the holidays. Let's go into the garden and* ~ *the air,* have some fresh air. *Will you* ~ *tea or coffee? I'll* ~ (= buy) *2 lb of your Kenya coffee. Why don't you* ~ *a wife,* (old use) marry? *You should* ~ *a partner into the business/~ your brother into the business.* **6** [VP6A,15A,16B] accept; receive: *Will you* ~ *£150 for the car,* sell it for this sum? *This small café ~s £100 a week,* This is the total of the receipts. ⇨ takings below. (From the C of E marriage service) *Do you* ~ *this man to be your lawful wedded husband? You must* ~ *us as you find us,* not expect exceptional treatment, consideration, etc (while you are with us). *He will* ~ *no nonsense,* will not allow any. *I'm not taking any more or your insults,* I refuse to listen to them. ***~ one's chance,*** trust to one's luck; accept whatever may come or happen: *She'll have to* ~ *her chance with the other applicants for the job.* ***~ a chance (on sth),*** accept the possibility of not getting sth: *I'm ready to* ~ *a chance on finding him at home,* will call hoping to find him there. ***~ one's chance,*** attempt sth though aware of the possibility of failing. ***~ it from me; ~ my word for it,*** believe me when I say: *T~ it from me, there'll be some big changes made in the coming year.* ***be able to ~ it; can ~ it,*** be able to endure suffering, punishment, attack, etc without showing weakness, readiness to admit defeat, etc. **7** [VP6A] subscribe to; receive and pay for regularly: *Which newspapers do you* ~? **8** [VP6A,15A,B] make a record of: ~ *notes of a lecture;* ~ *sth down in shorthand;* ~ *a letter,* from dictation; ~ *(down) a broadcast on tape,* i e using a tape-recorder; ~ *a photograph.* [VP2A] *He does not* ~ *well,* It is difficult to ~ good photographs of him. **9** [VP6A,15A] need, require: *The work took four hours. These things* ~ *time. How long will this job* ~ *you/How long will you* ~ *over this job? The wound took a long time to heal.* ***~ one's time (over sth),*** **(a)** not hurry; use as much time as one needs: *Take your time over the job, and do it well.* **(b)** (ironic) use more time than is reasonable: *The workmen are certainly taking their time over the job.* ***It ~s two to make a quarrel,*** (prov) suggesting that each of two parties to a quarrel may be at fault. ***~ a lot of doing,*** need much effort, skill, etc. **10** [VP14,22] ***~ sb/sth for...; ~ sb/sth to be...,*** suppose; conclude; infer; consider to be: *I took you to be an honest man. Do you* ~ *me for a fool? Even the experts took the painting for a genuine Rembrandt.* ***~ it (from...) that,*** assume: *I* ~ *it that we are to come early. You may* ~ *it from me that...,* be confident because I tell you.... ***~ sth for granted,*** ⇨ grant, *v*(2). **11** [VP6A] find out (by inquiry, measurement, etc): *The doctor took my temperature. Has the tailor ~n your measurements for that new suit? Did the police* ~ *your name and address?* **12** [VP22,16B] treat or regard in a specified way: ~ *it/things easy,* not work too hard or too fast; ~ *things coolly/calmly,* not get excited; ~ *sth ill/amiss,* resent it. *I should* ~ *it kindly* (= be grateful to you) *if....* ***~ sth as read,*** agree that it is unnecessary to read, e g the minutes of the previous meeting. **13** [VP6A] accept responsibility for: ~ *evening service,* (at church) conduct it; ~ *a class,* be in charge, give the class its lesson, etc. **14** [VP2A] be successful: *Green's second novel did not* ~, did not become popular; have the required effect: *That smallpox injection did not* ~. *The dye doesn't* ~ *in cold water,* is ineffective. **15** (with *nn*) (For other examples, ⇨ the *n* entries) ***~ account of sth,*** (= ~ sth into account), ⇨ account¹(7). ***~ advantage of sb/sth,*** ⇨ advantage. ***~ aim,*** ⇨ aim¹(2). ***~ the biscuit/the cake,*** ⇨ biscuit, cake. ***~ care,*** ⇨ care¹(2). ***~ a chair,*** ⇨ 5 above. ***~ a/one's chance,*** ⇨ 6 above. ***~ charge (of),*** ⇨ charge¹(5). ***~ courage,*** ⇨ courage. ***~ a degree,*** obtain a degree(5). ***~ (a) delight/an interest/(a) pleasure/(a) pride in sth,*** be, show that one is, delighted/interested, etc. ***~ a dislike to sb,*** ⇨ dislike. ***~ effect,*** ⇨ effect(1). ***~ an examination,*** be tested on one's knowledge or ability. **~ exception to,** ⇨ exception(3). ***not/never take one's eyes off,*** ⇨ 16 below. ***~ a fancy to; ~ the fancy of,*** ⇨ fancy[1](3). ***~ fright (at sth),*** become frightened. ***~ a gamble (on sth),*** do sth knowing it is risky. ***~ a hand at,*** ⇨ hand[1](13). ***~ sb in hand,*** accept responsibility for him (esp to improve his behaviour). ***~ (fresh) heart; ~ sth to heart,*** ⇨ heart(2). ***~ heed,*** pay attention. ***~ a/the hint,*** ⇨ hint. ***~ (one's) leave (of sb),*** ⇨ leave[2](3). ***~ the liberty of; ~ liberties with,*** ⇨ liberty(2). ***~ a liking to,*** become fond of. ***~ one's/sb's mind off (sth),*** ⇨ mind[1](2). ***~ no notice (of),*** ⇨ notice(3). ***~ an oath,*** ⇨ oath(1). ***~ offence (at sth),*** ⇨ offence(2). ***~ the opportunity of doing/to do sth,*** recognize a favourable moment and act. ***~ (holy) orders,*** become a priest, etc. ***~ (great) pains (over sth/to do sth),*** ⇨ pains. ***~ part (in),*** ⇨ part[1](4). ***~ place; ~ the place of,*** ⇨ place[1](10). ***~ the risk of; ~ risks,*** ⇨ risk(1). ***~ a seat,*** ⇨ 5 above. ***~ silk,*** ⇨ silk(3). ***~ stock,*** ⇨ stock[1](1). ***~ one's time (over sth),*** ⇨ 9 above. ***~ trouble (over sth); ~ the trouble to do sth,*** ⇨ trouble, *n*(3). ***~ umbrage (at),*** ⇨ umbrage. ***~ my word for it,*** ⇨ 6 above. **16** [VP3A,2C,15B] (special uses with *adverbial particles* and *preps*):

be taken aback, ⇨ aback.

take after sb, resemble (esp a parent or relation) in features or character: *Your daughter does not ~ after you in any way.*

take sth apart, separate sth (machinery, etc) into its (component) parts.

take (away) from, lessen, weaken, diminish: *That foolish indiscretion took away from his public image. These faults to some extent ~ (away) from his credit as a biographer.* ***~ sth/sb away (from sb/sth),*** remove: *Not to be ~n away,* e g books from a library. *The child was ~n away from school,* not allowed to attend. *What ~s you away so early,* Why are you leaving so early? *If your mother should be ~n from you,* If (according to context) she should die, be put in a mental home, etc.

take sth back, **(a)** retreat or withdraw (what one has said) as an admission of error, as an apology, etc: *I ~ back what I said.* **(b)** agree to receive back: *Shopkeepers will not usually ~ back goods after they have been paid for.* ***~ sb back (to),*** carry or conduct to an earlier period: *These stories took him back to his childhood days,* (fig) brought them back to his mind.

take sth down, **(a)** write down: *The reporters took down the speech.* **(b)** lower; get by lifting down from (a shelf, etc): *~ down a book from the top shelf; ~ down the curtains/pictures from the walls; ~ down a mast.* **(c)** dismantle; pull down; get into separate parts: *~ down a crane/the scaffolding round a building; ~ down a partition.* ***~ sb down a peg (or two),*** humble; lower the pride of: *That fellow needs to be ~n down a peg.*

take from, ⇨ *take (away) from* above.

take sth in, **(a)** receive (work) to be done in one's own house for payment: *The poor widow earns money by taking in washing/sewing.* **(b)** (⇨ 7 above) pay for and receive regularly: *~ in journals/periodicals.* **(c)** reduce the size, area, length or width of (a garment, sail, etc): *This dress needs to be ~n in* (= made smaller) *at the waist. Orders were given to ~ in sail.* ⇨ *~ up the slack* at slack[2](1). **(d)** comprise; include, e g in one's journey or route: *a motor-coach tour that ~s in six European capitals.* **(e)** take (territory, common land, etc) into one's possession; (re)claim: *A good deal of Romney Marsh was ~n in from the sea by monks.* **(f)** understand; absorb; digest mentally: *They listened to my lecture, but how much did they ~ in, I wonder? We need more time to ~ in the situation,* form a correct idea of it. **(g)** see at a glance; see at once: *She took in every detail of the other woman's clothes. He took in the scene at a glance.* **(h)** listen to, watch, with excitement: *The children took in the whole spectacle open-mouthed.* ***~ sb in,*** **(a)** receive, admit: *make a living by taking in guests/lodgers; ~ a traveller in for the night.* **(b)** deceive; get the better of by a trick: *Don't let yourself be ~n in by these politicians. He was badly ~n in when he bought that second-hand car.* ***~ a lady in to dinner,*** (on a formal occasion) offer her one's arm, conduct her from the drawing-room to the dining-room, and sit beside her at table. Cf *~ a lady out to dinner,* e g to a restaurant.

take sb/sth into…, ~ sth into account, ⇨ account(7). ***~ a person into one's confidence,*** ⇨ confidence(1). ***~ sth into one's head,*** ⇨ head[1](19).

take off, **(a)** make a start in jumping. **(b)** (of an aircraft) leave the ground and rise: *The big plane took off easily.* Hence, **'~-off** *n* **(a)** (also *jump-off,* esp in show jumping) place at which the feet leave the ground in jumping. **(b)** (of aircraft) leaving the ground and rising: *a smooth ~-off.* ⇨ *touch-down* at touch[2](11). ***~ sth off,*** **(a)** remove: *~ off one's hat. I ~ off my hat to the President,* (fig) salute him to show my admiration for what he has done, said, etc. *Why don't you ~* (= shave) *off that silly little moustache? The surgeon took off* (= amputated) *his leg.* **(b)** withdraw (from service): *The 7a m express to Bristol will be ~n off next month,* will not run. ***~ sth off (sth),*** **(a)** lift and move to another position: *T~ your hand off my shoulder.* **(b)** deduct: *~ 50p off the price.* ***~ sb off,*** **(a)** conduct; lead away somewhere: *He was ~n off to prison. She took me off to see her garden. The crew were ~n off* (= rescued from) *the wrecked ship by the lifeboat.* **(b)** ridicule by imitation; mimic; burlesque: *Alice is clever at taking off the headmistress.* Hence, **'~-off** *n* caricature; burlesque imitation of sb's behaviour: *a good ~-off of the Prime Minister.* ***not/never ~ one's eyes off sth/sb,*** look at constantly: *He never took his eyes off her,* looked at her all the time. ***~ one's mind off (sth),*** ⇨ mind[1](2).

take on, **(a)** (sub-standard colloq) become excited or agitated; make a fuss: *She took on something dreadful when I said she'd told a pack of lies.* **(b)** (colloq = 'catch on') become popular; have a vogue: *We introduced a new sports car last year but it never took on.* ***~ sth on,*** **(a)** undertake; charge oneself with: *~ on extra work/heavy responsibilities.' You've ~n on too much.* **(b)** assume; put on (a quality, appearance): *The chameleon can ~ on the colours of its background.* ***~ sb on,*** **(a)** accept as an opponent: *~ sb on at golf/billiards; ready to ~ on all comers,* play against, fight, anyone who accepts a challenge. **(b)** engage: *~ on twenty more workers.* **(c)** (of a train, etc) allow to enter: *The bus stopped to ~ on some children.* **(d)** (of trains, etc) carry too far, past the destination: *I fell asleep in the train*

and was ~n on to York.
take sth out, **(a)** extract; remove: have one's appendix/a tooth ~n out. *How can I ~ out* (= remove) *these inkstains from my blouse?* **(b)** obtain; procure (sth issued): *~ out an insurance policy/a driving licence/a summons/a patent.* ***~ sb out,*** **(a)** conduct; accompany: *~ the children out for a walk; ~ one's wife out for dinner,* i e at a restaurant. **(b)** (in card games): *~ one's partner out,* make a higher bid (than that which he/she has made), e g by calling 5 spades over 5 hearts, or 3 no trumps over 3 spades. ***~ it out in sth,*** accept as recompense or compensation: *The innkeeper couldn't pay me the £10 he owed me but let me ~ it out in drinks and cigars.* ***~ it out of sb,*** leave him weak and exhausted: *His recent illness/All that hard work has ~n it out of him.* ***~ it out on sb,*** vent one's anger, disappointment, etc on (usu) sb else: *He came home angry at losing his job and took it out on his wife.*
take sb over, carry from one place to another: *Mr White took me over to the island in his launch.* ***~ sth over,*** assume control of; succeed to the management or ownership of (a business, etc): *Was it in 1948 that the Government took over the railways in Great Britain,* nationalized them? *When Mr Green retired his son took over the business.* Hence, **'~-over** *n* change of control of a firm or company, e g after another has made a successful bid to buy its stock: *a '~over bid.* ***~ over (from sb),*** accept duties, responsibilities, etc: *The new Chancellor took over* (i e from his predecessor) *yesterday.*
take to sth, **(a)** adopt as a practice or hobby, as a means of livelihood; get into a habit: *~ to gardening when one retires; ~ to drink(ing),* get into the habit of taking alcoholic liquor; *~ to the road,* become a tramp (or, in former times a highwayman); (of a circus, etc) go on tour from town to town giving shows. **(b)** take refuge in; use as a means of escape: *~ to flight,* run away; *~ to the woods/the jungle/the heather,* go to the woods, etc, to avoid capture. *The crew took to the boats when the torpedo struck the ship.* ***~ to one's heels,*** ⇨ heel[1](1). ***~ to sth/sb,*** conceive a liking for: *Has the baby ~n to its new nursemaid? That boy will never ~ to cricket.*
take sth up, **(a)** lift up; raise: *~ up one's pen/book/gun; ~ up a carpet.* **(b)** (of trains, taxis, etc; more usu *~ on*) stop to allow (passengers) to enter. **(c)** absorb (a liquid): *Blotting-paper ~s up ink.* **(d)** dissolve (solids): *How much water is needed to ~ up a pound of salt?* **(e)** interest oneself in; engage in (sth) (as a hobby, business, etc): *~ up photography/market gardening.* **(f)** pursue further; begin afresh (sth left off, sth begun by sb else): *Harry took up the tale at the point where John had left off.* **(g)** occupy (time, space): *This table ~s up too much space. My time is fully ~n up with writing.* **(h)** (comm) advance money (on a mortgage); accept (a Bill of Exchange); subscribe for (shares, etc) at the time of issue. **(i)** catch the end of and make secure: *~ up a dropped stitch.* **'~-up spool** *n* (on a ciné projector, tape-recorder, etc) spool on to which film, tape, etc is wound from the spool having the film, tape, etc that is being used. ***~ sth up with sb,*** speak or write to: *I will ~ the matter up with the Ministry,* e g by asking for information, or by making a protest. ***~ sb up,*** make a protegé of; help: *The young soprano was ~n up by the famous conductor,* He encouraged and helped her in her career. ***be ~n up with sb/sth,*** be much interested in: *He seems to be very much ~n up with that tall Swedish girl.* ***~ sb up sharp/short,*** interrupt and correct (a speaker): *He took me up short when I suggested that....* ***~ up one's residence at,*** (formal) proceed to occupy: *The new ambassador has ~n up his residence* (in the Embassy).
take sth upon oneself, assume responsibility; undertake: *You mustn't ~ upon yourself the right to make decisions.*

take[2] /teɪk/ *n* **1** amount (of money) taken. **2** (film industry) scene that has been or is to be photographed. **3** act of taking.

taker /ˈteɪkə(r)/ *n* one who, that which, takes, esp one who takes a bet: *There were no ~s,* No one was willing to take bets.

tak·ing /ˈteɪkɪŋ/ *adj* attractive; captivating. □ *n* (*pl*) money taken in business; receipts.

talc /tælk/ *n* [U] soft, smooth mineral that can be split into thin transparent plates. **'~ powder** *n* toilet powder (usu perfumed) made from ~.

tal·cum /ˈtælkəm/ *n* **'~ powder,** = talc powder.

tale /teɪl/ *n* [C] **1** story: *'fairy-~s; ~s of adventure. It tells its own ~,* explains itself, requires no comment or explanation. **2** report; account. ***tell ~s,*** tell sth about another person that he wishes to be kept secret, e g his wrongdoing. Hence, **'~-bearer/-teller** *nn* person who tells ~s. **'~-bearing/-telling** *nn* **3** (old use) total found by counting: *The ~ of dead and wounded was 60.*

tal·ent /ˈtælənt/ *n* **1** [C,U] (particular kind of) natural power to do sth well: *a man of great ~; local ~,* (usu amateur) musicians, actors, etc of a district; *a '~ scout,* (colloq) person who watches out for persons of ~ for films, the theatre, sports, etc; *have a ~ for music/not much ~ for painting; an exhibition of local ~,* of works, e g paintings, by people of a district or locality. **2** [C] measure of weight, unit of money, used in ancient times among the Greeks, Romans, Assyrians, etc. **~ed** *adj* having ~; gifted: *a ~ed musician.*

tal·is·man /ˈtælɪzmən *US:* -ɪsm-/ *n* [C] (*pl* -men) sth that is thought to bring good luck, e g a trinket or ring.

talk[1] /tɔk/ *n* **1** [C,U] conversation; discussion: *I've had several ~s with the headmaster about my boy. There's too much ~* (= ~ing) *and not enough work being done.* **2** ***the ~ of the town,*** sth or sb everyone is ~ing about. ***be all ~,*** said of sb who ~s a lot but does not get results. **'small ~,** conversation on everyday but not important topics. **3** [C] informal speech: *give a ~ to the Women's Institute on one's travels in Asia.*

talk[2] /tɔk/ *vi,vt* (*pt,pp* ~ed) **1** [VP2A,B,C,3A, 15B] ***~ (to sb) (about sth),*** say things; speak to give information; discuss sth, etc: *He was ~ing to* (less often *with*) *a friend. What are they ~ing about* (less often *of*)? *We ~ed all afternoon/for two hours. Were they ~ing in Spanish or in Portuguese?* ***be/get oneself ~ed about,*** (in some contexts) be made the subject of gossip: *You'll get yourself ~ed about if you go on being so foolish.* ***~ at sb,*** speak to sb without paying attention to his replies: *I don't like people who ~ at me instead of with me.* ***~ away,*** continue ~ing: *They were still ~ing away at midnight.* ***~ back (to sb),*** (often *answer back*) reply defiantly. ***~ big,*** brag; boast. ***~ down an aircraft,*** ~ by radio to the pilot while he is about to make a landing, giving him instructions, etc. **~ *down to sb,*** ~ in a way that suggests that the speaker is superior, e g by using condescendingly simple words, etc: *It's unwise for a lecturer to ~ down to his audience.* **~*ing of,*** while on the subject of: *T~ing of travel, have you been to Munich yet?* **~ *sth over,*** discuss it. **~ *round sth,*** ~ about a subject without reaching the point or a conclusion. **~ *to sb,*** (colloq) scold; reprove: *This new suit fits badly—I'll have to ~ to my tailor about it.* Hence, **ˈ~-ing-to** *n* scolding: *The teacher gave the lazy boy a good ~ing-to.* **2** [VP2A] have the power of speech: *Can the baby ~ yet?* **3** [VP6A] be able to use (a language): *~ English/Spanish.* **4** [VP6A] discuss: *~ business, ~ shop,* ⇨ shop(2). *We ~ed music all evening.* **ˈ~-ing-point,** topic likely to cause discussion; argument likely to persuade or convince sb. **5** [VP6A] express in words: *~ sense/ nonsense/treason.* **6** [VP14,22] bring into a certain condition by ~ing: *~ oneself hoarse,* ~ until one is hoarse. **~ *sb into/out of doing sth,*** persuade sb to do/not to do sth: *She ~ed her husband into having a holiday in France. He ~ed his wife out of buying a new hat.* **~ *sb over/round,*** persuade sb to agree to or to accept sth: *We ~ed them over to our way of thinking.* **7** [VP2A] (various uses): *Don't do anything indiscreet—you know how people ~,* gossip. *Has the accused man ~ed yet,* given information, e g under coercion or threats? *Some parrots can ~,* imitate the sounds of human speech. **~a·tive** /ˈtɔkətɪv/ *adj* fond of ~ing. **~er** *n* **1** (esp with an *adj*) person who ~s: *a good/ poor, etc ~er. What a ~er that woman is!* How fond she is of ~ing! **2** person who ~s a lot but does not get results: *He's a mere ~er.*

talkie /ˈtɔkɪ/ *n* [C] (dated colloq term for a) talking-picture (-film) (used when these were a novelty). **the ~s,** (colloq) cinema films with spoken dialogue.

tall /tɔl/ *adj* (-er, -est) **1** (of persons) of more than average height; (of objects such as a ship's mast, a flagpole, a church spire, a tree whose height is greater than its width, but not of mountains) higher than the average or than surrounding objects: *She is ~er than her sister. She wears high heels to make herself look ~er. That yacht has a very ~ mast.* **ˈ~·boy** (GB; US = *highboy*) *n* bedroom chest of drawers 5 or 6 ft high. **2** of a specified height: *Tom is six foot ~.* **3** (colloq) excessive, exorbitant. **a ~ order,** an unreasonable request; a task difficult to perform. **a ~ story,** one that it is difficult to believe. **~·ish** /-ɪʃ/ *adj* rather ~.

tal·low /ˈtæləʊ/ *n* [U] hard (esp animal) fat used for making candles, etc.

tally /ˈtælɪ/ *n* [C] (*pl* -lies) (in the past) stick with notches cut in it, to show quantities of goods delivered, etc or money owing; either half of such a stick split lengthwise; ticket, label, etc used for identification. **ˈ~-clerk** *n* clerk who checks cargo, etc e g at the docks. **ˈ~·man** /-mæn/ *n* (*pl* -men) person who sells goods and collects weekly payments. □ *vi* (*pt,pp* -lied) [VP2A,3A] **~ *(with),*** (of stories, amounts, etc) correspond; agree: *The two lists do not ~. Does your list ~ with mine? The stories of the two men tallied.*

tally-ho /ˈtælɪ ˈhəʊ/ *int* huntsman's cry on catching sight of the fox.

Tal·mud /ˈtælmʊd *US:* ˈtɑl-/ *n* compendium of Jewish law and teaching.

talon /ˈtælən/ *n* claw of a bird of prey, e g an eagle.

talus /ˈteɪləs/ *n* sloping mass of fragments at the foot of a cliff or precipice.

ta·male /təˈmɑlɪ/ *n* Mexican dish of chopped meat, red peppers, etc steamed in corn (= maize) husks.

tam·ar·ind /ˈtæmərɪnd/ *n* (edible fruit of a) tropical tree.

tam·ar·isk /ˈtæmərɪsk/ *n* [C] evergreen shrub with feathery branches, often planted in sandy soil near the sea.

tam·bour /ˈtæmbʊə(r)/ *n* rolling front for a T V set or the top of a writing-desk, made of narrow strips of wood glued to canvas.

tam·bour·ine /ˈtæmbəˈrin/ *n* small, shallow drum with metal discs in the rim, played by striking with the knuckles and shaking it at the same time. ⇨ the illus at percussion.

tame /teɪm/ *adj* **1** (of animals) brought under control and/or accustomed to living with human beings; not wild or fierce: *a ~ monkey. The deer in the park are very ~.* **2** (of a person) spiritless; submissive; docile: *Her husband is a ~ little man.* **3** dull: *a ~ baseball match. The story/film, etc has a ~ ending.* □ *vt* [VP6A] make ~: *~ a lion.* **tamer** *n* (usu in compounds) person who ~s: *a ˈlion-~r.* **tam·able** /-əbl/ *adj* that can be ~d, converted from a savage state. **~·ly** *adv* **~·ness** *n*

Tam·many /ˈtæmənɪ/ *n* **~ (Hall),** central organization of the Democratic Party in New York City; (attrib) of their politics, members, etc.

tam-o'-shan·ter /ˈtæm ə ˈʃæntə(r)/ **tammy** /ˈtæmɪ/ *nn* round, woollen or cloth cap fitting closely to the forehead.

tamp /tæmp/ *vt* [VP15B] **~ *sth down,*** tap or drive down by repeated light blows: *He ~ed down the tobacco in his pipe.*

tam·per /ˈtæmpə(r)/ *vi* [VP3A] **~ *with,*** meddle or interfere with; make unauthorized changes in: *Someone has been ~ing with the lock/the seal of this letter.*

tan /tæn/ *n, adj* yellowish brown; brown colour of sunburnt skin: *tan leather shoes/gloves; get a good tan* (on one's skin). □ *vt, vi* (-nn-) [VP6A,2A] **1** (of an animal's skin) make, be made, into leather (by treatment with tannic acid, etc). ***tan sb's hide,*** (sl) give him a good beating. **2** make or become brown with sunburn: *return from the holidays with a tanned face. Some people tan quickly.* **tan·ner** *n* workman who tans skins. **tan·nery** /ˈtænərɪ/ *n* (*pl* -ries) place where skins are tanned.

tan·dem /ˈtændəm/ *n* **ˈ~ (bicycle),** bicycle made for two persons to ride on one behind the other, with pedals for both. □ *adv* (of horses in harness or two persons on a ~ bicycle) one behind the other: *drive/ride ~.*

tang /tæŋ/ *n* sharp taste or flavour, esp one that is characteristic of sth: *the salt ~ of the sea air.*

tan·gent /ˈtændʒənt/ *n* straight line touching but not cutting a curve. ⇨ the illus at circle. ***go/fly off at a ~,*** (fig) change suddenly from one line of thought, action, etc to another.

tan·ger·ine /ˈtændʒəˈrin *US:* ˈtændʒərin/ *n* [C] small, sweet-scented, loose-skinned orange.

tan·gible /ˈtændʒəbl/ *adj* **1** that can be perceived by touch. **2** clear and definite; real: *~ proof; the ~ assets,* e g of a business company, its buildings, machinery, etc but not its goodwill. **tan·gibly**

/-əblɪ/ *adv* **tan·gi·bil·ity** /ˌtændʒəˈbɪlətɪ/ *n*

tangle[1] /ˈtæŋl/ *n* [C] **1** confused mass (of string, hair, etc): *brush the* ~*s out of a dog's hair. The kitten has made a* ~ *of my ball of wool.* **2** confused state: *The traffic was in a frightful* ~. □ *vt,vi* **1** [VP6A,15B,2A,C] make or become confused, disordered: ~*d hair.* **2** [VP3A] ~ ***with sb,*** (colloq) be/become involved in a fight or quarrel with: *I shouldn't* ~ *with Peter—he's bigger than you.*

tangle[2] /ˈtæŋgl/ *n* [U] (kinds of) seaweed with long leathery fronds.

tango /ˈtæŋgəʊ/ *n* (*pl* -gos /-gəʊz/) (music for a) S American dance with strongly marked rhythm and a wide variety of steps.

a tank

tank /tæŋk/ *n* **1** (usu large) container for liquid or gas: *the* ˈ*petrol-*~ *of a car; a* ˈ*rain-water* ~, e g for storing rain-water from roofs; *a ship's* ~*s*, the compartments into which the double hull is divided, to contain fuel-oil, fresh water, etc. ˈ**~-car,** large (usu cylindrical) ~ for carrying petroleum, etc by rail. **2** (in India, Pakistan, etc) large, artificial (usu rectangular) pool for storing water. **3** armoured fighting vehicle with guns, moving on caterpillar tracks. ˈ~ *trap*, deep ditch or other obstruction built to hinder or stop the advance of ~s. □ *vi* ***get*** ~***ed up,*** (sl) get drunk (on beer). **~er** *n* ship or aircraft with ~s for carrying petroleum as freight; heavy road vehicle with a large cylindrical ~ for carrying oil, milk or other liquid in bulk.

tank·ard /ˈtæŋkəd/ *n* large drinking mug, esp one for beer.

tan·ner[1] /ˈtænə(r)/ *n* (sl) British silver coin, former value sixpence, 6d (now worth 2½p).

tan·ner[2] /ˈtænə(r)/ **tan·nery,** ⇨ tan.

tan·nic /ˈtænɪk/ *adj* ~ **acid,** = tannin.

tan·nin /ˈtænɪn/ *n* [U] acid obtained chiefly from the bark of oak and other trees, and used in preparing leather, dyeing, the manufacture of ink, etc.

tan·noy /ˈtænɔɪ/ *n* (P) type of loudspeaker or loudspeaker system, e g as used for public-address systems.

tansy /ˈtænzɪ/ *n* herb with yellow flowers and bitter leaves, used in medicine and cooking.

tan·ta·lize /ˈtæntəlaɪz/ *vt* [VP6A] raise hopes that cannot (yet) be realized; keep just out of reach sth that sb desires: *a tantalizing smell of food.*

tan·ta·lus /ˈtæntələs/ *n* stand with a locking device for decanters (brandy, etc).

tan·ta·mount /ˈtæntəmaʊnt/ *adj* ~ ***to,*** equal in effect to: *The Queen's request was* ~ *to a command.*

tan·trum /ˈtæntrəm/ *n* [C] fit of bad temper or anger: *He's in one of his* ~*s again.*

tap[1] /tæp/ *n* **1** device for controlling the flow of liquid or gas from a pipe, barrel, etc. (Cf *valve* for controlling flow *through* a pipe; cf *faucet*, the usu word in the US): *turn the tap on/off. Don't leave the taps running*, i e turn them off. ***on tap,*** (of beer, etc) in a barrel with a tap, ready to be drawn off; (hence, fig) available when needed. ˈ**tap-room** *n* (in an inn, etc) room in which barrels are stored and cheaper drinks sold. ˈ**tap-root** *n* chief descending root of a plant, tree, etc (going straight down for moisture). **2** plug used to close the opening of a cask. □ *vt* (-pp-) [VP6A,14,15B] ***tap (off) sth (from sth).*** **1** draw out liquid through the tap of a (barrel): *tap a cask of cider; tap (off) cider from a cask;* cut (the bark of a tree) and get (the sap, etc): *tap rubber-trees; tap sugar-maples*, e g in Canada. **2** extract or obtain (sth from sb or sth): *tap a man for money/information; tap a telephone/wire/line*, make a connection so as to intercept messages: *My phone is being tapped.* **3** furnish (a cask, etc) with a tap.

tap[2] /tæp/ *n* [C] **1** quick, light blow: *a* ~ *on the window/at the door.* ˈ**tap-dancing** *n* stage-dancing with rhythmical tapping of the foot, toe or heel. **2** (*pl*) (US armed forces) last signal of the day (by drum or bugle) for lights to be put out. □ *vt,vi* (-pp-) [VP6A,15A,2A,C] give a tap or taps (to): *tap a man on the shoulder; tap at/on the door; tap one's foot on the floor impatiently.*

tape /teɪp/ *n* [C,U] **1** (piece, length of) narrow strip of material used for tying up parcels, etc or in dressmaking: *three yards of linen* ~*; do up the* ~*s of an apron into neat bows.* ˈ**~-measure** *n* length of ~ or strip of thin, flexible metal or of strengthened cloth graduated for measuring things with. ˈ**~-worm** *n* kinds of many-jointed, long, flat worm that lives during its adult stage as a parasite in the intestines of man and other animals. **2** (ˈ**ticker-**)~, narrow strip of paper on which telegraph instruments automatically print news, etc. ˈ**insulating** ~, strip of sticky cloth used for insulating electrical connections, etc. **mag**ˈ**netic** ~, strip of a plastic material magnetized to record sound or vision. ˌ**red** ˈ~, ⇨ red, *adj*(3). ˈ~ **deck,** ~ recorder (without amplifiers or speakers) as a component in a hi-fi system. ˈ**~-recorder** *n* apparatus for recording sound on, and playing sound back from, this kind of ~. **3** length of ~ stretched between the winning-posts on a race-track: *breast the* ~, reach and pass this ~. □ *vt* [VP6A] **1** fasten, tie together, with ~. **2** record (sound) on magnetic ~. **3** (colloq) ***have sth/sb*** ~***d,*** understand it/him thoroughly.

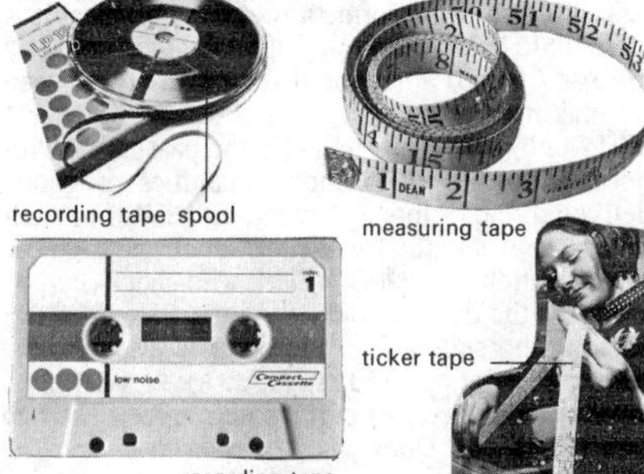

tapes

taper[1] /ˈteɪpə(r)/ *n* [C] length of thread with a covering of wax, burnt to give a light; very slender candle.

taper[2] /ˋteɪpə(r)/ *vt,vi* [VP6A,15B,2A,C] make or become gradually narrower towards one end: *One end ~s/is ~ed off to a point.*

tap·es·try /ˋtæpɪstrɪ/ *n* [C,U] (*pl* **-ries**) (piece of) cloth into which threads of coloured wool are woven by hand to make designs and pictures, used for covering walls and furniture. **tap·es·tried** *adj* hung, decorated, with ~: *tapestried walls.*

tapi·oca /ˈtæpɪˋəʊkə/ *n* [U] starchy food (in the form of hard, white grains) from the root of the cassava plant.

ta·pir /ˋteɪpə(r)/ *n* pig-like animal of Central and S America with a long, flexible nose.

tapis /ˋtæpi *US:* tæˋpi/ *n* (F) (only in) ***on the ~,*** under consideration; under discussion.

taps /tæps/ ⇨ **tap**[2]**(2)**.

tap·ster /ˋtæpstə(r)/ *n* person employed to draw and serve beer, spirits, etc. ⇨ *tap-room* at **tap**[1]**(1)**.

tar[1] /tɑ(r)/ *n* [U] black substance, hard when cold, thick and sticky when warm, obtained from coal, etc used to preserve timber (e g in fences and posts), in making roads, etc. **tar·mac·adam** /ˈtɑməˋkædəm/ *n* mixture of tar and crushed stone, used for road surfaces. **ˋtar·mac** *n* mixture of tar and gravel, as used for paths, road surfaces and runways for aircraft. □ *vt* (**-rr-**) [VP6A] cover with tar. ***tar and feather sb,*** put tar on him and then cover with feathers as a punishment, ***tarred with the same brush,*** having the same faults.

tar[2] /tɑ(r)/ *n* **(Jack) tar,** (dated term for a) sailor.

tara·diddle /ˋtærədɪdl *US:* ˈtærəˋdɪdl/ *n* (colloq) untruth; fib.

tar·an·tella /ˈtærənˋtelə/, **tar·an·telle** /-ˋtel/ *nn* [C] (music for a) rapid, whirling Italian dance for two persons.

ta·ran·tula /təˋræntjʊlə *US:* -tʃʊlə/ *n* large, hairy, poisonous spider of S Europe; other kinds of spider.

tar·boosh /tɑˋbuʃ/ *n* brimless felt cap like a fez, worn by some Muslim men.

tardy /ˋtɑdɪ/ *adj* (**-ier, -iest**) **1** slow; slow-moving; coming or done late: *~ progress/repentance; ~ in offering help.* **2** (US) late: *be ~ for school.* **tar·dily** /-əlɪ/ *adv* **tar·di·ness** *n*

tare[1] /teə(r)/ *n* (Biblical; usu *pl*) weed growing among corn.

tare[2] /teə(r)/ *n* allowance made to a purchaser for the weight of the vehicle carrying the commodity he has brought or for the weight of the container in which the commodity is packed, in cases where the commodity is weighed together with the vehicle or container; weight of a motor-vehicle, etc without fuel.

tar·get /ˋtɑgɪt/ *n* **1** sth to be aimed at in shooting-practice; any object aimed at. ⇨ the illus at **archery**. **2** thing, plan, etc against which criticism is directed: *This book will be the ~ of bitter criticism.* **3** objective (set for savings, production, etc); total which it is desired to reach.

tar·iff /ˋtærɪf/ *n* [C] **1** list of fixed charges, esp for meals, rooms, etc at a hotel; price-list. **2** list of taxes on goods imported or (less often) exported; tax on a particular class of imported goods: *raise ~ walls against foreign goods,* (try to) exclude them by means of import taxes; *~ reform,* movement (esp in GB, 19th century) to get rid of inequalities in ~s.

tar·mac /ˋtɑmæk/ *n* ⇨ **tar**[1].

tarn /tɑn/ *n* small mountain lake.

tar·nish /ˋtɑnɪʃ/ *vi,vt* [VP6A,2A] (esp of metal surfaces) lose, cause the loss of, brightness: *The damp atmosphere has ~ed the gilt. Chromium does not ~ easily. His reputation is ~ed.* □ *n* dullness; loss of polish.

taro /ˋtɑrəʊ/ *n* (*pl* **-ros** /-rəʊz/) kinds of tropical plant with a starchy root used as food, esp in the Pacific islands.

tar·pau·lin /tɑˋpɔlɪn/ *n* [C,U] (sheet or cover of) canvas made waterproof, esp by being tarred: *cover the goods on the lorry with a ~.*

tar·pon /ˋtɑpon *US:* -pən/ *n* large fish found in the warmer parts of the Atlantic Ocean.

tarra·diddle *n* = taradiddle.

tar·ra·gon /ˋtærəgən *US:* -gon/ *n* [U] herb with sharp-tasting leaves, used in salads and for flavouring vinegar (*~ vinegar*).

tarry[1] /ˋtɑrɪ/ *adj* covered, sticky, with tar.

tarry[2] /ˋtærɪ/ *vt* (now liter) **1** [VP2A,B,C] stay, remain, lodge: *~ a few days at/in a place; ~ (behind) for sb.* **2** be slow in coming, going, appearing.

tar·sal /ˋtɑsl/ *adj* (anat) of the bones in the ankle. □ *n* (anat) bone in the ankle. ⇨ the illus at **skeleton**.

tar·sus /ˋtɑsəs/ *n* (*pl* **tarsi** /-sɪ/) collection of seven small bones in the ankle.

tart[1] /tɑt/ *adj* acid; sharp in taste; (fig) sharp: *~ fruit; a ~ flavour; ~ humour; a ~ manner/disposition.* **~·ly** *adv* **~·ness** *n*

tart[2] /tɑt/ *n* **1** fruit pie. **2** circle of pastry cooked with fruit or jam on it.

tart[3] /tɑt/ *n* (sl) girl or woman of immoral character; prostitute. □ *vt* [VP15B] ***~ sth/sb up,*** (colloq) make gaudy; add meretricious attractions to: *a ~ed-up country cottage,* e g a workman's cottage bought by sb from a town, and painted, decorated, etc in a way out of harmony with the surroundings.

tar·tan /ˋtɑtən/ *n* [U] Scottish woollen fabric woven with coloured crossing stripes; [C] particular pattern of ~, e g of a Scottish clan. ⇨ the illus at **kilt**.

tar·tar[1] /ˋtɑtə(r)/ *n* [U] **1** chalk-like substance deposited on the teeth. **2** substance deposited on the sides of casks from fermented wine. **cream of ~,** purified form of this, used with baking soda to make baking powder. **~ic** /tɑˋtærɪk/ *adj*: *~ acid,* acid of ~, found in the juice of grapes, oranges, etc (used in making baking powder, etc).

tar·tar[2] /ˋtɑtə(r)/ *n* rough, violent, troublesome person. ***catch a ~,*** have to deal with a person of this kind, esp one who is more than one's match.

tar·tar[3] /ˋtɑtə(r)/ *n* **~ sauce,** cold mayonnaise with chopped onions, herbs, gherkins and pickles, served with some kinds of fish and with croquettes.

task /tɑsk *US:* tæsk/ *n* [C] piece of (esp hard) work (to be) done: *set a boy a ~. She finds housekeeping an irksome ~.* ***take sb to ~ (about/for sth),*** scold him: *It's wrong of you to take the child to ~ for such trifling offences.* **ˋ~-force** *n* specially organized unit (of warships, etc) for a special purpose. **ˋ~-master/-mistress** *nn* one who imposes ~s, esp a strict overseer. □ *vt* [VP6A] (of a ~) put a strain on: *Mathematics ~s that boy's brain.*

tas·sel /ˋtæsl/ *n* bunch of threads, etc tied together at one end and hanging (from a flag, hat, etc) as an ornament. ⇨ the illus at **kilt**. **~·led** (US = **~ed**) *adj* having a ~ or ~s.

taste[1] /teɪst/ *n* **1** (with *def art*) sense by which flavour is known: *sweet/sour to the* ~. '~ **bud** *n* group of cells in the tongue for this sense. **2** [C,U] quality of a substance made known by this sense, e g by putting some on the tongue: *Sugar has a sweet* ~. *I don't like the* ~ *of this mixture. This medicine has no/very little/not much/a queer* ~. ***leave a bad ~ in the mouth.*** (liter and fig) be followed by a feeling of dislike or disgust. **3** (usu *sing* with *indef art*) small quantity (of sth to eat or drink, or fig): *Won't you have a* ~ *of this cake/wine? Give him a* ~ *of the whip,* enough to be a sample of what it feels like to be whipped. **4** [C,U] ~ ***(for),*** liking or preference for: *He has a* ~ *for Manilla cigars. She has expensive* ~*s in clothes. There's no accounting for* ~*s,* We cannot explain why different people like different things. *Abstract art is not to his* ~*/not to the* ~ *of everyone.* **5** [U] ability to enjoy beauty, esp in art and literature; ability to form judgements about these; ability to choose and use the best kind of behaviour: *She has excellent* ~ *in dress/dresses in perfect* ~. *His behaviour was in good/bad* ~, pleasing/displeasing to people of ~. *It would be bad* ~ *to refuse their invitation.* **~·ful** /-fl/ *adj* showing good ~(5). **~·fully** /-flɪ/ *adv* in a ~ful manner: *~fully decorated with flowers.* **~·less** *adj* **1** (of food) having no ~ or flavour. **2** without ~(5); in bad ~. **~·less·ly** *adv* **tasty** *adj* (-ier, -iest) having a pleasant flavour; pleasing to the ~. **tast·ily** /-əlɪ/ *adv*

taste[2] /teɪst/ *vt,vi* **1** [VP6A,2A] (not in the progressive tenses; often with *can, could*) be aware of the taste of sth: *Can you* ~ *anything strange in this soup? If you have a bad cold you cannot* ~ *(anything).* **2** [VP3A,2D] ~ ***(of),*** have a particular taste or flavour: ~ *sour/bitter/sweet. It* ~*s too much of garlic/spice.* **3** [VP6A] test the ~ of: *The cook* ~*d the soup to see whether he had put enough salt in it.* **4** [VP6A] experience: ~ *happiness/the joys of freedom.* ~ ***of,*** (liter) know; experience: *The valiant* ~ *of death but once.* **taster** *n* person who is employed to judge teas, wines, etc by ~: *A professional wine-taster does not swallow the samples he* ~*s.*

tat[1] /tæt/ *vi,vt* (-tt-) do tatting; make by tatting.

tat[2] /tæt/ *n* (sl) coarse canvas or shabby cloth.

tat[3] /tæt/ *n* ⇨ **tit**[2].

ta ta /ˈtæ ˋtɑ/ *int* (baby language) goodbye □ *n* (*pl*) walk: *go* ~*s.*

tat·ter /ˋtætə(r)/ *n* (usu *pl*) rag; piece of cloth, paper, etc torn off or hanging loosely from sth: *in* ~*s,* in tags or torn strips; *tear sb's reputation to* ~*s,* (fig) destroy it. **~ed** *adj* ragged. **~·de·ma·lion** /ˈtætədəˋmeɪlɪən/ *n* sb dressed in ~s.

tat·ting /ˋtætɪŋ/ *n* [U] (art or process of making a) kind of handmade knotted lace-work used for trimming.

tattle /ˋtætl/ *vi,vt* [VP2A] chatter, gossip, prattle. □ *n* [U] idle talk. **tat·tler** /ˋtætlə(r)/ *n* person who ~s.

tat·too[1] /təˋtu *US:* tæˋtu/ *n* (*pl* -**toos**) **1** (sing only) beating of drum(s) to call soldiers back to quarters; hour at which a ~ is sounded: *beat/sound the* ~. **2** [C] continuous tapping: *He was beating a* ~ *on the table with his fingers.* **3** [C] public entertainment, usu at night (often *torchlight* ~) with music, marching and pageantry, by soldiers.

tat·too[2] /təˋtu *US:* tæˋtu/ *vt* [VP6A] mark (sb's skin) with permanent designs or patterns by pricking it and putting in dyes or stains; put (a design, etc) on the skin thus: *The sailor had a ship* ~*ed on his arm.* □ *n* [C] (*pl* -**toos**) mark or design of this kind.

tatty /ˋtætɪ/ *adj* (-ier, -iest) (sl) untidy and shabby looking. **tat·tily** /-əlɪ/ *adv*

taught /tɔt/ *pt,pp* of teach.

taunt /tɔnt/ *n* [C] remark intended to hurt sb's feelings; contemptuous reproach: *endure the* ~*s of a successful rival.* □ *vt* [VP6A,14] ~ ***sb with sth,*** attack (sb) with ~s: *They* ~*ed the boy with cowardice/with being a coward.* **~·ing·ly** *adv*

Taurus /ˋtɔrəs/ *n* (astrol) second sign of the zodiac. ⇨ the illus at zodiac.

taut /tɔt/ *adj* (of ropes, nerves, etc) tightly stretched: *haul a rope* ~. **~·ly** *adv* **~·ness** *n*

taut·ol·ogy /tɔˋtolədʒɪ/ *n* [U] the saying of the same thing again in different ways without making one's meaning clearer or more forceful; needless repetition; [C] (*pl* -**gies**) instance of this. **tauto·logi·cal** /ˈtɔtəˋlodʒɪkl/ *adj*

tav·ern /ˋtævən/ *n* (old use) inn; public house for the supply of food and drink (to be consumed on the premises).

taw /tɔ/ *n* [C] marble(3).

taw·dry /ˋtɔdrɪ/ *adj* (-ier, -iest) showy, brightly coloured or decorated, but cheap or in bad taste: ~ *jewellery/dresses.* **taw·drily** /-əlɪ/ *adv* **taw·dri·ness** *n*

tawny /ˋtɔnɪ/ *adj* brownish yellow.

tawse /ˋtɔz/ *n* [C] (Scot) leather strap for punishing children.

tax /tæks/ *n* **1** [C,U] (sum of) money (to be) paid by citizens (according to income, value of purchases, etc) to the government for public purposes: *state/local taxes; levy a tax on sth; direct taxes,* i e on income; *indirect taxes,* e g paid when one buys goods; *How much income tax did you pay last year? He paid £50 in taxes.* '**tax-collector** *n* official who collects taxes. '**tax-payer** *n* person who pays taxes. ˈ**tax-**ˋ**free** *adj* **(a)** not subject to taxation. **(b)** (of dividends or interest) on which tax has been deducted before distribution. **2** ***a tax on,*** (*sing* only) sth that is a burden or strain: *a tax on one's strength/health/patience.* □ *vt* **1** [VP6A] put a tax on; require (a person) to pay a tax: *tax luxuries/incomes/rich and poor alike.* **2** [VP6A] be a tax on: *tax a person's patience,* e g by asking him many silly questions. **3** [VP14] ***tax sb with sth,*** accuse: *tax sb with neglect of/with having neglected his work.* **4** (legal) examine and decide, e g costs of a lawsuit. **tax·able** /-əbl/ *adj* capable of being taxed. **tax·abil·ity** /ˈtæksəˋbɪlətɪ/ *n* **tax·ation** /tækˋseɪʃn/ *n* [U] (system of) raising money by taxes; taxes (to be) paid: *reduce taxation; grumble at high taxation.*

taxi /ˋtæksɪ/ *n* (*pl* ~s) (also '**~-cab,** usu abbr to *cab,* esp in US) motor-car, esp one with a ~meter, which may be hired for journeys. '**~-meter** *n* (usu abbr to *meter*) device which automatically records the fare during a journey in a ~. '**~ rank,** place where ~s wait to be hired. □ *vi,vt* [VP2C,15A] (of an aircraft) (cause to) move on wheels along the ground (or on floats, etc on the surface of water): *The plane* ~*ed/was taxiing across the tarmac.*

taxi·dermy /ˋtæksɪdɜmɪ/ *n* [U] art of preparing and stuffing the skins of animals, birds and fish so that they look as they did when living. **taxi·der-**

mist /-ɪst/ *n* person who practises ∼.

tea /ti/ *n* **1** [U] (dried leaves of an) evergreen shrub of eastern Asia, Africa, etc; drink made by pouring boiling water on these leaves: *a pound of tea; Ceylon/China, etc tea; a cup of tea; make (the) tea,* prepare it. ***not my cup of tea,*** not the sort of thing I like. **ˈtea-bag** *n* small porous bag holding enough tea-leaves for use in a teacup. **ˈtea-break** *n* (in an office, factory, etc) short period when work is stopped for tea drinking. **ˈtea-caddy** *n* (*pl* **-dies**) air-tight box in which to keep a supply of tea for daily use. **ˈtea-cake** *n* flat, sweetened cake, usu eaten hot with butter at tea. **ˈtea-chest** *n* large wooden box in which tea is packed for export. **ˈtea-cloth** *n* **(a)** cloth to be spread on a tea-table or tea-tray. **(b)** cloth used for drying cups, etc when they are washed. **ˈtea-cosy** *n* cover for keeping the contents of a teapot warm. **tea·cup** /ˈtikʌp *with short* i *as in 'speaker'*/ *n* cup in which tea is served. ***a storm in a teacup,*** a lot of commotion about sth trivial. **ˈtea-dance** *n* (in an hotel, etc) afternoon tea at which the guests dance. **ˈtea-garden** *n* **(a)** garden in which tea and other refreshments are served to the public. **(b)** tea plantation. **ˈtea-gown** *n* woman's loose gown (as formerly worn at tea, etc). **ˈtea·house** *n* (in Japan and China) restaurant where tea is served. **ˈtea-kettle** *n* one in which water is boiled for making tea. **ˈtea-leaf** *n* (usu *pl;* **-leaves**) one of the leaves in a teapot after tea has been made, or left in a teacup: *tell sb's fortune from the tea-leaves in her cup.* **ˈtea-party** *n* social gathering for afternoon tea. **tea·pot** /ˈtipot *with short* i *as in 'speaker'*/ *n* vessel in which tea is made. **ˈtea·room** *n* restaurant in which tea and light refreshments may be obtained. **ˈtea-service/-set** *nn* set of cups, saucers, plates, with a teapot, milk-jug, etc. **ˈtea-spoon** *n* small spoon for stirring tea. **ˈtea·spoon-ful** /-fl/ *n* as much as a teaspoon can hold. **ˈtea-strainer** *n* device for keeping back tea-leaves. **ˈtea-table** *n* (usu small) table at which tea is served: (attrib) *tea-table conversation.* **ˈtea-things** *n pl* (colloq) tea-set as needed for a meal: *put the tea-things on the table.* **ˈtea-time** /ˈti tɑɪm *with short* i *as in 'speaker'*/ *n* time at which tea is usu taken in the afternoon: *tea-time music from the B B C.* **ˈtea-tray** *n* one on which a tea-set is used or carried. **ˈtea-trolley** *n* tea-wagon. **ˈtea-urn** *n* urn in which water is boiled for making tea in quantity, e g in a café. **ˈtea-wagon** *n* small table on wheels, used for serving tea. **2** [C,U] occasion (in the late afternoon) at which tea is drunk: *We have tea at half-past four. They were at tea when I called. The waitress has served twenty teas since four o'clock.* **high tea,** meal taken between lunch and supper if a dinner is not taken in the evening (usu a more substantial meal than afternoon tea as taken by people who have dinner in the evening).

teach /titʃ/ *vt,vi* (*pt,pp* **taught** /tɔt/) [VP6A,11, 12A,13A,17,20,21,2A,B,C] give instruction to (sb); cause (sb) to know or be able to do sth; give to sb (knowledge, skill, etc); give lessons (at school, etc); do this for a living: *∼ children; ∼ French/history, etc; ∼ a child (how) to swim. He has taught his dog to perform some clever tricks. Who taught you German? She is ∼ing the piano to several of the village children. He ∼es for a living. He has been ∼ing four hours already this morning.* **ˈ∼·ing-machine** *n* mechanical device which provides learners with material of varying complexity to be followed at the pace they find satisfactory: *I will ∼ you (not) to…,* (colloq, used as a threat) I will let you know the risk or penalty of…. **ˈ∼-in** *n* (colloq) discussion of a subject of topical interest (as held in a college, with students, staff and other speakers). **∼·able** /-əbl/ *adj* that can be taught. **∼er** *n* person who ∼es. **∼·ing** *n* **1** [U] work of a ∼er: *earn a living by ∼ing.* **2** (usu *pl*) that which is taught; *the ∼ings of Jesus.*

teak /tik/ *n* tall, evergreen tree of India, Burma, Malaysia, etc; [U] its hard wood, used for making furniture, in shipbuilding, etc.

teal /til/ *n* (*pl* unchanged) kinds of small wild duck living on rivers and lakes.

team /tim/ *n* [C] **1** two or more oxen, horses, etc pulling a cart, plough, etc together. **2** number of persons playing together and forming one side in some games, e g football, cricket, hockey and sports, e g relay races; (by extension) group of people working together: *the players in my ∼,* my fellow players. **ˈ∼-work** *n* [U] combined effort; organized co-operation: *succeed by means of good ∼-work.* **∼ spirit,** spirit in which each member of a ∼ thinks of the success, etc of the ∼ and not of personal advantage, glory, etc. □ *vi* [VP2C] ***∼ up (with),*** (colloq) make an effort in co-operation (with); work together (with). **∼·ster** /ˈtim-stə(r)/ *n* driver of a ∼ of animals; (mod use, US) truck-driver.

tear[1] /tɪə(r)/ *n* [C] drop of salty water coming from the eye: *Her eyes filled with ∼s. The sad story moved us to ∼s,* made us cry. *The girl burst into ∼s,* ∼s began to flow from her eyes. *They all laughed till ∼s came.* **ˈ∼-drop** *n* single ∼. **ˈ∼-gas** *n* [U] gas that causes severe watering of the eyes: *ˈ∼-gas bombs,* as used by the police to disperse a mob of demonstrators, unruly crowds, etc. **∼·ful** /-fl/ *adj* crying; wet with ∼s: *a ∼ful face; ∼ful looks.* **∼·fully** /-flɪ/ *adv* **∼·less** *adj* without ∼s, not weeping: *The mother stared at her dead baby in ∼less grief,* grief that was too deep for ∼s.

tear[2] /teə(r)/ *vt,vi* (*pt* **tore** /tɔ(r)/, *pp* **torn** /tɔn/) **1** [VP6A,15A,B,22,3A] pull sharply apart or to pieces; make (a rent in sth), damage, by pulling sharply: *∼ a sheet of paper in two/∼ it to pieces/ to bits; ∼ sth up,* ∼ it into small pieces: *∼ one's dress on a nail; ∼ a hole in one's jacket; wearing old and torn clothes; ∼* (= hurt, injure, cause to bleed) *one's hand on a nail. He tore* (= pulled violently) *at the wrapping of the parcel. He tore his hair with rage. He tore the parcel open.* **2** [VP6A,15A,B] cause (sth) to be out of place (*down, off, away, etc*) by pulling sharply: *∼ a page out of a book/a notice down from a notice-board/a leaf from a calendar. She could scarcely ∼ herself away from the scene,* make up her mind to leave. *He could not ∼ himself away from his book,* couldn't put it down. **3** [VP6A] (usu passive) destroy the peace of: *a country torn by civil war; a heart torn by grief.* ***torn between,*** painfully distracted by having to choose between (conflicting demands, wishes, etc). **4** [VP2A] become torn: *This material ∼s easily. As I pulled the sheet out of the typewriter it tore.* **5** [VP2C] go in excitement or at great speed: *The children tore out of the school gates/were ∼ing about in the playground. He tore down the hill.* **ˈ∼·away** *n* aggressive youth. □ *n* [C] torn place, rent, e g in a coat.

tease /tiz/ *vt* **1** [VP6A,15A] make fun of (sb) playfully or unkindly; worry with questions, etc; annoy: *She ~d her father about his bald head. You must never ~ a child because it stutters. Molly was teasing the cat,* e g by pulling its tail. **2** [VP6A,15B] pick into separate fibres; fluff up the surface of (cloth, etc) by doing this: *~ flax.* □ *n* person who is fond of teasing others: *What a ~ she is!* **teaser** *n* **1** person who often ~s or who is fond of teasing. **2** (colloq) difficult question or task; puzzling problem. **teas·ing·ly** *adv* in a teasing manner; in order to ~.

tea·sel, tea·zel, teazle /ˈtizl/ *n* (kinds of plant with) large prickly flower with hooked points (used formerly for teasing cloth, etc).

teat /tit/ *n* nipple(**2**). ⇨ the illus at domestic.

tec /tek/ *n* (sl abbr for) detective.

tech /tek/ *n* (abbr for) technical college; polytechnic.

tech·ni·cal /ˈteknɪkl/ *adj* of, from, technique; of, connected with, special to, one of the mechanical or industrial arts (e g printing, weaving) or with methods used by experts and artists: *~ terms/difficulties; a pianist who has ~ skill but not much feeling; a ˈ~ college,* for engineering, etc. **~ly** /-klɪ/ *adv* **~·ity** /ˌteknɪˈkælətɪ/ *n* (*pl* **-ties**) ~ word, phrase, point, etc: *The two architects were discussing building ~ities. The judge explained the legal ~ities of the case to the jury.*

tech·ni·cian /tekˈnɪʃn/ *n* expert in the technique(s) of a particular art, etc; highly skilled craftsman or mechanic.

Tech·ni·color /ˈteknɪkʌlə(r)/ *n* (P) process of colour photography used for cinema films.

tech·nique /tekˈnik/ *n* **1** [U] technical or mechanical skill in art, music, etc. **2** [C] method of doing sth expertly; method of artistic expression in music, painting, etc.

tech·noc·racy /tekˈnokrəsɪ/ *n* [C,U] (*pl* **-cies**) (state where there is) organization and management of a country's industrial resources by technical experts. **tech·no·crat** /ˈteknəkræt/ *n* supporter, member, of a ~.

tech·nol·ogy /tekˈnolədʒɪ/ *n* [U] study, mastery and utilization of manufacturing methods and industrial arts; systematic application of knowledge to practical tasks in industry: *study engineering at a college of ~.* **tech·nol·ogist** /-dʒɪst/ *n* expert in, student of, ~. **tech·no·logi·cal** /ˌteknəˈlodʒɪkl/ *adj* of ~: *technological advances/problems.*

techy /ˈtetʃɪ/ = tetchy.

teddy bear /ˈtedɪ beə(r)/ *n* child's toy bear stuffed with soft material.

Teddy boy /ˈtedɪ bɔɪ/, (also **Ted** /ted/) *n* (GB) teenager (in the 1950's and early 1960's), who expressed opposition to authority by engaging in vicious gang fights and wore clothes like those worn during the reign of Edward VII (1901—10).

Te Deum /teɪ ˈdeɪəm/ *n* (music for a) Latin hymn beginning *Te Deum laudamus* (meaning 'We praise thee, O God'), sung at morning service and on special occasions of thanksgiving.

tedi·ous /ˈtidɪəs/ *adj* tiresome; wearying; uninteresting: *a ~ lecture(r); ~ work.* **~·ly** *adv* **~·ness** *n* **te·dium** /ˈtidɪəm/ *n* [U] ~ness; monotony; boredom.

tee /ti/ *n* **1** (golf) place from which a player starts in playing a hole; small pile of sand, etc on which the ball is placed before the player drives; specially shaped piece of wood or rubber used instead of such a pile of sand. **ˈtee-shirt** *n* = *T-shirt.* ⇨ T. **2** mark aimed at in certain games, such as quoits. ***to a tee,*** perfectly; exactly. □ *vt,vi* **1** [VP6A,15B] ***tee (up),*** put the ball on a tee(**1**); (fig) arrange; organize: *Get your travel agents to tee everything up.* **2** [VP2A] ***tee off,*** drive from a tee.

teem[1] /tim/ *vi* [VP2C] **1** be present in large numbers: *Fish ~ in this river.* **2** ***~ with,*** have in great numbers: *The lakeside ~ed with gnats and mosquitoes. His head is ~ing with bright ideas.*

teem[2] /tim/ *vi* [VP2A,C] ***~ (down),*** (of rain) fall heavily; pour: *It was ~ing with rain/a ~ing wet day. The rain was ~ing down.*

teens /tinz/ *n pl* the numbers 13 to 19: *girls in their ~,* between the ages of 13 and 19 inclusive: *She's still in/not yet out of her ~,* is under 20. **teen·age** /ˈtineɪdʒ/ *n* (attrib) *teenage fashions,* for persons in their ~. **teen·ager** /ˈtineɪdʒə(r)/ *n* boy or girl in his or her ~; (loosely) young person up to 21 or 22 years of age: *a club for teenagers.*

teeny /ˈtinɪ/ *adj* = tiny.

tee·ter /ˈtitə(r)/ *vi* [VP2C] stand or walk unsteadily: *~ing on the edge of disaster.*

teeth /tiθ/ *pl* of tooth.

teethe /tið/ *vi* [VP2A] (used only in progressive tenses, and as gerund and pres part) (of a baby) be getting its first teeth. **ˈteething troubles,** discomfort, slight illnesses, etc of a baby while its first teeth are coming through; (fig) troubles which may occur during the early stages of an enterprise.

tee·to·tal /tiˈtəʊtl/ *adj* not drinking, opposed to the drinking of, alcoholic liquor. **~·ler** (US also **~er**) /-tl̩ə(r)/ *n* person who abstains completely from alcoholic liquor.

tee·to·tum /tiˈtəʊtəm/ *n* top spun with the fingers, esp a four-sided one with letters on it.

teg /teg/ *n* sheep in its second year.

tegu·ment /ˈtegjʊmənt/ *n* [C] (more usu *integument*) natural covering of (part of) an animal body, e g a turtle's shell.

tele·cast /ˈtelɪkɑst *US:* -kæst/ *n, vt* broadcast by television.

tele·com·muni·ca·tions /ˌtelɪkəˌmjunɪˈkeɪʃnz/ *n pl* communications by cable, telegraph, telephone, radio or T V.

tele·gram /ˈtelɪgræm/ *n* [C] message sent by telegraphy.

tele·graph /ˈtelɪgrɑf *US:* -græf/ *n* means of, apparatus for, sending messages by the use of electric current along wires or by radio. **ˈ~-post/-pole** *nn* post supporting wires for the ~. **ˈ~-line/-wire** *n* wire along which messages (including telephone messages) travel. **bush ~** *n* sending of messages over long distances by smoke signals, beating of drums, etc. □ *vi,vt* [VP6A,12A,13A,11,2A] send (news, etc) by ~: *Shall I ~ or telephone? He ~ed (to) his brother.* (Note: *send a telegram* and *send a cable* are commoner than the use of the *v.*) **tel·egra·pher** /təˈlegrəfə(r)/ *n* skilled operator whose work is to send and receive messages by ~. **~ic** /ˌtelɪˈgræfɪk/ *adj* sent by, suitable for, connected with, the ~: *a ~ic address,* abbreviated address or brief registered address, for use in telegrams. **~i·cally** /-klɪ/ **tel·egra·phese** /ˌtelɪgrɑˈfiz *US:* -græˈf-/ *n* [U] style used in telegrams (with unessential words omitted). **tel·egra·phist** /təˈlegrəfɪst/ *n* = ~er. **tel·egra·phy** /təˈlegrəfɪ/ *n* [U] art, science, process, of sending and receiving messages by ~, of constructing ~ic apparatus, etc.

te·lem·etry /təˈlemətrɪ/ *n* [U] the automatic transmission and measurement of data from a distance by radio, etc e g from unmanned space vehicles or probes.

tele·ol·ogy /ˌtelɪˈɒlədʒɪ/ *n* theory, teaching, belief, that events and developments are due to the purpose or design that is served by them (opposed to the mechanistic theory of the universe). **teleo·logi·cal** /ˌtelɪəˈlɒdʒɪkl/ *adj* **tele·ol·ogist** /ˌtelɪˈɒlədʒɪst/ *n* believer in ~.

tel·epa·thy /təˈlepəθɪ/ *n* [U] **1** transference of thoughts or ideas from one mind to another at a distance without the normal use of the senses. **2** (pop use) ability to be immediately aware of the thoughts and feelings of others (not necessarily at a distance). **tele·pathic** /ˌtelɪˈpæθɪk/ *adj* **tel·epa·thist** /təˈlepəθɪst/ *n* person who studies or believes in ~ or who claims to have telephathic powers.

tele·phone /ˈteləfəʊn/ *n* (usu abbr to *phone* in speech) [U] means, system, of transmitting the human voice by electric current, usu through wires (usu called *telegraph wires,* not ~ *wires*) supported by poles (usu called *telegraph poles,* not ~ *posts*); [C] apparatus (with receiver and mouthpiece) for this purpose: *You're wanted on the phone. Mr Green is on the phone just now,* is using the ~. *Will you answer the phone,* Please, pick up the receiver and answer. ˈ**~ booth,** (also ˈ*phone booth* or *call-box*), small enclosure with a coin-operated public ~. ˈ**~ directory,** (also ˈ*phone book*) list of names with numbers and addresses. ˈ**~ exchange,** place where ~ connections are made. □ *vt,vi* [VP6A,12A,13A,11,12, 2A,4A] send (a message to sb) by ~: *I'll phone you tomorrow. He phoned (through) to say that.... It's Mary's birthday today—we must phone her a greetings telegram,* send her a greeting ('Happy Birthday') by asking for such a telegram to be sent (and usu received by ~). *Please phone (to) the office and say I can't come in today.* **tel·eph·ony** /təˈlefənɪ/ *n* [U] method, process, of sending and receiving messages by ~. **tel·ephon·ist** /təˈlefənɪst/ *n* operator in a ~ exchange.

tele·photo /ˌtelɪˈfəʊtəʊ/ *n* **1** **~ lens,** = telescopic lens. **2** (colloq abbr of) ~graph. **~·graph** /-grɑf *US:* -græf/ *n* **(a)** photograph made with a ~ lens. **(b)** picture transmitted and received by ~graphy. **tele·pho·togra·phy** /ˌtelɪfəˈtɒgrəfɪ/ *n* [U] **1** process of photographing distant objects, etc using a ~ lens. **2** process of transmitting and receiving charts, pictures, etc over a distance.

tele·prin·ter /ˈtelɪprɪntə(r)/ *n* telegraph instrument for sending messages (typed by an operator at the sending end), which are re-typed automatically and almost simultaneously on a machine at the other end.

tele·promp·ter /ˈtelɪprɒmptə(r)/ *n* TV device by which a speaker can read a line by line enlargement of his script, so that he seems to speak spontaneously.

tele·scope /ˈteləskəʊp/ *n* tube-like instrument with lenses for making distant objects appear nearer and larger. ˈ**radio** ˈ**~,** ⇨ radio-. □ *vt,vi* [VP6A,2A] make or become shorter by means of or in the manner of sections that slide one within the other: *When the trains collided, the first two cars of one of the trains ~d/were ~d.* **tele·scopic** /ˌteləˈskɒpɪk/ *adj* **1** of, containing, able to be seen with, a ~: *a telescopic lens,* extra lens attached to a camera to enable distant objects and scenes to be photographed (and now often called a *telephoto lens*); *a telescopic sight,* (on a rifle, to magnify the target); *a telescopic view of the moon,* seen through a ~. **2** having sections which slide one within the other: *a telescopic aerial,* e g as part of a portable radio receiver.

tele·type·writer /ˌtelɪˈtaɪpraɪtə(r)/ *n* (US) = teleprinter.

tele·vi·sion /ˈtelɪvɪʒn/ *n* **1** [U] (abbr TV, or colloq *telly* /ˈtelɪ/) process of transmitting a view of events, plays, etc (while these are taking place, or from films or tapes on which records have been made) by radio to a distant ~ receiving set with synchronized sound: *Did you see the boat race on (the) ~?* **2** [C] ˈ**~ (set),** apparatus for receiving and showing this transmission. **tele·vise** /ˈteləvaɪz/ *vt* [VP6A] send views of by ~: *The Olympic Games were televised.*

tel·fer /ˈtelfə(r)/ = telpher.

telex /ˈteleks/ *n* system of communication using teleprinters.

tell /tel/ *vt,vi* (*pt,pp* told /təʊld/) **1** [VP6A,13A, 12A,11,20,21] ***~ sth (to sb), ~ sb sth,*** make known (in spoken or written words); give information concerning or a description of: *He told the news to everybody in the village. I told him my name. T~ me where you live. I can't ~ you how happy I am,* can't find words that are adequate. *He told me (that) he was coming. So I've been told,* I've already been told that. *If he asks, ~ him. Don't ~ me it's too late!* (used to express surprise or alarm) *I'll ~ you what...,* used meaning 'Here's a suggestion, idea, etc that may help'. *I ~* (= assure) *you, he's thoroughly dishonest!* ***I told you so,*** I warned you that this would happen, etc and now you see that I'm right: *Things have gone wrong but please don't say 'I told you so!'* ˈ***You're ~ing*** ˈ***me!*** I know this—and there was no need at all for you to ~ me! ***T~ me another!*** I don't believe you. ***~ the world,*** (colloq) ~ everybody: *We all know you're clever, but do you have to ~ the world,* be so emphatic about it? **2** [VP6A,13A,12A,15A] utter; express with words: *~ a lie; ~ the children a tale/story. 'When in doubt, ~ the truth', said Mark Twain.* ***~ the tale,*** (colloq) ~ a pitiful story in order to get sympathy, etc. ***~ tales about sb,*** make known sb's secrets, misconduct, etc in a malicious way. **3** [VP17A] order; direct: *Do what I ~ you. You must do what you're told. T~ him to wait. He was told to start at once.* **4** [VP6A,14] (esp with *can/could/be able to*) know apart; distinguish: *Can you ~ Tom from his twin brother? They look exactly the same—how can you ~ which is which?* **5** [VP6A,2A] learn by observation; make out; become aware (of sth): *How do you ~ which of these buttons to press?* ***~ the time,*** (be able to) read (or say) the time from a clock, etc: *Can Mary ~ the time yet? Can you ~ me what time it is?* ⇨ App 4. ***You can never ~, You never can ~,*** never be sure, e g because appearances are often deceptive. ***there is/was, etc no ~ing,*** it is impossible or difficult to know: *There's no ~ing what may happen/where she's gone/what he's doing, etc.* **6** [VP6A,15B] (old use) count. ***~ one's beads,*** say one's prayers (counting beads on a rosary) ***~ sb off (for sth/to do sth),*** **(a)** count one by one and give orders: *Ten men were told off for special duty/to clean the latrines.* **(b)**

(colloq) give a list of sb's misdoings; scold him: *That fellow needs to be told off. He told the office boy off for making so many careless mistakes.* **7** [VP2A,3A] **~ (on/upon sb),** have a marked effect on: influence the result of: *All this hard work is ~ing on him,* is affecting his health. *Every blow ~s.* **8** [VP2A,3A] **~ (on sb),** (colloq) reveal a secret; inform against: *John told on his sister.* ⇨ *tale-bearer* at **tale(2)**. *You promised not to ~ and now you've done so!* **~er** *n* **1** person who receives and pays out money over a bank counter. **2** man who counts votes, e g in the House of Commons. **~·ing** *adj* effective; impressive: *a ~ing speech/argument/blow.* **~·ing·ly** *adv* **~·tale** /ˈtelteɪl/ *n* person who ~s about another's private affairs, makes known a secret, etc; circumstances, etc that reveal a person's thoughts, activities, etc (often attrib): *a ~tale blush; the ~tale cigar ash on the carpet,* that made known the fact that someone had been smoking a cigar.

telly /ˈtelɪ/ *n* (colloq abbr for) television.

tel·pher /ˈtelfə(r)/ *n* conveyance for goods, suspended from overhead wire cables, usu driven by electricity; transportation system of this kind, e g for rock from a quarry.

Tel·star /ˈtelstɑ(r)/ *n* (P) communications satellite used (commercially) for the transmission of telephone messages and TV.

te·mer·ity /tɪˈmerətɪ/ *n* [U] rashness.

tem·per¹ /ˈtempə(r)/ *n* **1** state or condition of the mind: *in a good ~,* calm and pleasant; *in a bad ~,* angry, impatient, etc. ***get/fly into a ~,*** become angry. ***keep/lose one's ~,*** keep/fail to keep one's ~ under control. ***out of ~ (with),*** angry (with). **-tem·pered** /ˈtempəd/ *adj* (in compounds) having or showing a certain kind of ~: *a ˈgood-/ˈsweet-/ˈfiery-/ hot-, etc ˋ~ed man.* **-tem·per·ed·ly** *adv* (in compounds) *good-~edly.* **2** [U] degree of hardness, toughness, elasticity, of a substance, esp of steel.

tem·per² /ˈtempə(r)/ *vt,vi* **1** [VP6A] give the required temper(2) to (e g steel) by heating and cooling; bring (e g clay) to the required condition by moistening, mixing, kneading, etc; [VP2A] come to the required condition as the result of treatment. **2** [VP6A,15A] soften or modify; mitigate: *~ justice with mercy,* be merciful when giving a just punishment.

tem·pera /ˈtempərə/ *n* [U] = distemper, esp as used in fresco painting.

tem·pera·ment /ˈtemprəmənt/ *n* **1** [C,U] person's disposition or nature, esp as this affects his way of thinking, feeling and behaving: *a girl with a nervous/an artistic ~. The two brothers have entirely different ~s. Success often depends on ~.* **2** [U] (without an *adj*) kind of disposition that is easily excited, passionate, not easily controlled or restrained, e g as in some actresses and opera singers. **tem·pera·men·tal** /ˈtemprəˋmentl/ *adj* **1** caused by ~: *a ~al dislike for study.* **2** subject to quickly changing moods: *a ~al tennis player,* one whose playing changes according to his mood. **tem·pera·men·tally** /-tlɪ/ *adv*

tem·per·ance /ˈtemprns/ *n* [U] **1** moderation, self-control, in speech, behaviour and (esp) in the use of alcoholic drinks. **2** total abstinence from alcoholic drinks: (attrib) *a ˋ~ society/league,* for the restriction or abolition of the use of alcoholic drinks; *a ˋ~ hotel,* (formerly) one where such drinks are not supplied.

tem·per·ate /ˈtemprət/ *adj* **1** showing, behaving, with temperance(1): *Be more ~ in your language, please.* **2** (of climate, parts of the world) free from extremes of heat and cold: *the north ˋ~ zone,* between the Tropic of Cancer and the arctic zone. **~·ly** *adv* **~·ness** *n*

tem·pera·ture /ˈtemprətʃə(r) *US:* ˋtempərtʃʊər/ *n* [C,U] degree of heat and cold: *In Hawaii there are no extremes of ~. The nurse took the ~s of all the patients,* measured their body ~s with a thermometer. ***have/run a ~,*** have a fever.

tem·pest /ˈtempɪst/ *n* [C] violent storm; (fig) violent agitation: *A ~ of laughter swept through the crowd.* **ˋ~-swept/-tossed** *adjj* (liter) swept, etc by ~s. **tem·pes·tu·ous** /temˋpestʃʊəs/ *adj* (of the weather and fig) violent; stormy: *in a ~uous mood; a ~uous political meeting.*

tem·plate, tem·plet /ˈtemplət/ *nn* pattern or gauge (usu a thin board or metal plate) used as a guide in cutting or drilling metal, wood, etc.

temple¹ /ˈtempl/ *n* **1** building used for the worship of a god (esp ancient Greek, Roman, Egyptian and modern Hindu, Buddhist, etc). **2** (applied occasionally to a) place of Christian worship (*church* and *chapel* being the usu words): *a Mormon ~.* **3** any of the three successive religious centres of the Jews in ancient Jerusalem. **4 Inner/Middle T~,** two Inns of Court in London. ⇨ **inn(2)**.

a Hindu temple

temple² /ˈtempl/ *n* flat part of either side of the forehead. ⇨ the illus at **head**.

tem·plet /ˈtemplət/ *n* ⇨ **template**.

tempo /ˈtempəʊ/ *n* (*pl* ~s or, in music, **tempi** /-pɪ/) (I) **1** rate of movement or activity: *the tiring ~ of city life. This long strike has upset the ~ of production.* **2** speed at which music is (to be) played.

tem·poral /ˈtempərl/ *adj* **1** of, existing in, time: *~ conjunctions,* e g *when, while.* **2** of earthly human life; of this physical life only, not spiritual: *the ~ power of the Pope,* i e as head of the Vatican State; *the lords ~* (= the peers of the realm) *and the lords spiritual* (= the bishops). **~·ity** /ˈtempəˋrælətɪ/ *n* (usu *pl;* **-ties**) secular possessions: *the temporalities of the Church.* **~ty** /ˈtempərltɪ/ *n* laity.

tem·por·ary /ˈtemprɪ *US:* -pərerɪ/ *adj* lasting for, designed to be used for, a short time only: *~ employment; a ~ bridge.* **tem·por·ar·ily** /ˈtemprlɪ *US:* ˈtempəˋrerəlɪ/ *adv* **tem·por·ari·ness** *n*

tem·por·ize /ˈtempəraɪz/ *vi* [VP2A] delay making a decision, giving an answer, stating one's purpose, etc; act so as gain time: *a temporizing* *politician/ commander of the armed forces.*

tempt /tempt/ *vt* [VP6A,17,14] **1** (try to) persuade (sb) to do sth wrong or foolish: *Nothing could ~ him to such a course of action/to take such a step. He was ~ed into making a false step,* doing sth unwise. **2** attract (sb) to have or do sth: *The warm weather ~ed us to go for a swim. She ~ed the child to have a little more soup. What a ~ing* (= attractive) *offer!* **3** (old use, biblical) test. **~ *Providence,*** take a risk. **~·ing·ly** *adv* **~er** *n* person who ~s; (esp) **the T~er,** Satan, the Devil. **temp·tress** /-trəs/ *n* woman who ~s.

temp·ta·tion /temp`teɪʃn/ *n* **1** [U] tempting or being tempted: *the ~ of easy profits; yield/give way to ~; put ~ in sb's way.* **2** [C] that which tempts or attracts: *The sight of the purse on the table was a strong ~ to the poor child. Clever advertisements are ~s to spend money.*

ten /ten/ *n, adj* ⇨ App 5. the number 10. ***ten to one,*** very probably: *Ten to one he will arrive late.* **tenth** /tenθ/ *n, adj* the next after the 9th; one of 10 equal parts. **tenth·ly** *adv* **`ten·fold** *adv* ten times as many or much. **`ten·pence** *n* (GB decimal coin with the) value of ten pennies.

ten·able /`tenəbl/ *adj* **1** that can be defended successfully: *His theory is hardly ~.* **2** (of an office or position) that can be held (*by* sb *for*): *The lectureship is ~ for a period of three years.* **ten·abil·ity** /ˌtenə`bɪlətɪ/ *n*

ten·acious /tə`neɪʃəs/ *adj* holding tightly, refusing to let go: *a ~ memory; ~ of our rights.* **~·ly** *adv* **~·ness** *n* **ten·ac·ity** /tə`næsətɪ/ *n*

ten·ant /`tenənt/ *n* person who pays rent for the use of land, a building, a room, etc: *evict ~s for non-payment of rent; ~ farmers,* who cultivate farms which they do not own. □ *vt* (usu passive) occupy as a ~: *houses ~ed by railway workers.* **ten·ancy** /-ənsɪ/ *n* [U] **1** use of land, etc as a ~: *during his tenancy of the farm.* **2** (with *indef art*) length of time during which a ~ uses land, etc: *hold a life tenancy of a house.* **ten·an·try** /`tenəntrɪ/ *n* (collective *sing*) all the ~s occupying land and houses on one estate.

tench /tentʃ/ *n* edible European freshwater fish; carp.

tend[1] /tend/ *vt* [VP6A] watch over; attend to: *shepherds ~ing their flocks;* (esp US) *~ store,* serve customers.

tend[2] /tend/ *vi* [VP2C,4A] be inclined to move; have a direction: *Prices are ~ing upwards. He ~s to pitch the ball too high. Don't set examples that ~ to undermine morality. He ~s towards atheism.* **ten·dency** /`tendənsɪ/ *n* [C] (*pl* -cies) turning or inclination, leaning: *Business is showing a ~ency to improve. There was a strong upward ~ency in oil shares yesterday,* prices ~ed upwards.

ten·den·tious /ten`denʃəs/ *adj* (of a speech, a piece of writing, etc) having an underlying purpose, aimed at helping a cause; not impartial: *Countries at war often send out ~ reports,* reports designed to show their cause in a favourable light, win sympathy, etc. **~·ly** *adv* **~·ness** *n*

ten·der[1] /`tendə(r)/ *adj* **1** delicate; easily hurt or damaged; quickly feeling pain: *~ blossoms,* e g easily hurt by frosts; *touch sb on a ~ spot,* one that hurts when touched; *a ~ subject,* (fig) one that has to be dealt with carefully to avoid hurting people's feelings; *a person of ~ age/years,* young and immature; *have a ~ conscience; a ~ heart,* easily moved to pity; Hence, **ˈ~-`hearted** *adj* **`~·foot** *n* (*pl* -foots) new-comer to the sort of country where there is rough living, hardship, etc. **2** (of meat) easily chewed; not tough: *a ~ steak.* **`~·loin** *n* [U] ~ part of the loin of beef or pork; undercut of sirloin. **3** kind, loving: *~ looks; ~ care; ~ parents; bid sb a ~ farewell.* **~·ly** *adv* **~·ness** *n*

ten·der[2] /`tendə(r)/ *n* **1** person who looks after, watches over, sth: *a ma`chine-~; a `bar~,* ⇨ bar[1](13). **2** small ship attending a larger one, to carry stores, put on or take off passengers, etc. **3** wagon for fuel and water behind a steam locomotive.

ten·der[3] /`tendə(r)/ *vt, vi* **1** [VP6A,12A,13A] offer; present: *~ money in payment of a debt. He ~ed his resignation to the Prime Minister/his services to the Government.* **2** [VP2A,3A] **~ *(for),*** make an offer (to carry out work, supply goods, etc) at a stated price: *~ for the construction of a new motorway.* □ *n* [C] **1** statement of the price at which one offers to supply goods or services, or to do sth: *invite ~s for a new bridge; put in/make/ send in a ~ for sth; accept the lowest ~.* **2 legal ~,** form of money which must, by law, be accepted in payment of a debt: *Are copper coins legal ~ for a sum in excess of £10?*

ten·don /`tendən/ *n* [C] tough, thick cord that joins muscle to bone; sinew.

ten·dril /`tendrɪl *US:* -drəl/ *n* [C] thread-like part of a plant, e g a vine, that twists round any nearby support.

ten·ement /`tenəmənt/ *n* [C] **1 `~(-house),** large house for the use of many families at low rents. **2** (legal) any dwelling-house; any kind of permanent property.

tenet /`tenet *US:* `tenɪt/ *n* [C] principle; belief; doctrine.

ten·ner /`tenə(r)/ *n* (colloq) ten pounds in GB money; ten-pound note.

ten·nis /`tenɪs/ *n* [U] game for two or four players

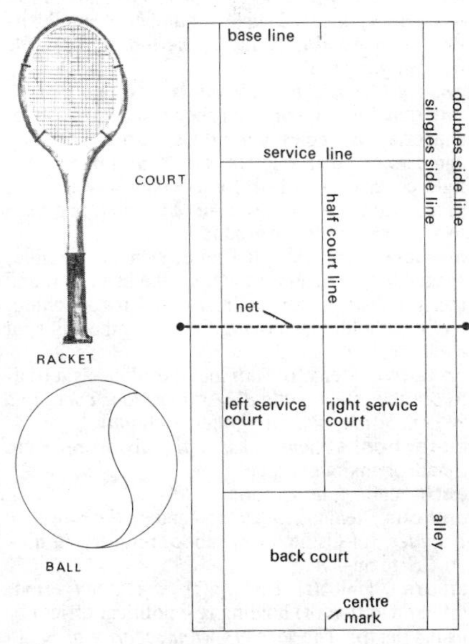

tennis

who hit a ball backwards and forwards across a net. **ˋ~-court** *n* marked area on which ~ is played. **ˈ~-ˋelbow** *n* inflammation of the elbow caused by playing ~.

tenon /ˋtenən/ *n* end of a piece of wood shaped to go into a mortise to make a joint.

tenor[1] /ˋtenə(r)/ *n* (usu *sing* with *def art*) general routine or direction (*of* one's life); general meaning, thread, drift (*of* a speech, etc): *She knew enough Spanish to get the ~ of what was being said.*

tenor[2] /ˋtenə(r)/ *n* **1** (music for, singer with, the) highest normal adult male voice: (attrib) ~ *voice; the ~ part.* **2** (of instruments) with a range about that of the ~ voice: *a ~ viola/saxophone.*

ten·pins /ˋtenpɪnz/ *n pl* **1** (with *sing v*) game like *ninepins* with ten skittles instead of nine. **2** (with *pl v*) the pins used. **3** (attrib) ~ *bowling.*

tense[1] /tens/ *adj* tightly stretched; strained to stiffness: ~ *nerves; faces ~ with anxiety; a moment of ~ excitement. We were ~ with expectancy,* Our nerves were ~, keyed up; *There was a ~ atmosphere,* People had a feeling of nervous strain and an attitude of expectancy. □ *vt,vi* [VP6A,2A] make or become ~; stiffen: *He ~d his muscles for the effort.* **be/get ~d up,** feel nervous strain: *He's always ~d up before a game/an exam.* **~·ly** *adv* **~·ness** *n*

tense[2] /tens/ *n* verb form that shows time: *the present/past, etc ~.*

ten·sile /ˋtensaɪl *US:* ˋtensl/ *adj* **1** of tension: *measure the ~ strength of wire,* e g to find the load it will support without breaking. **2** capable of being stretched.

ten·sion /ˋtenʃn/ *n* [U] **1** state of, degree of, being tense: *If you increase the ~ of that violin string it will break.* **2** stretching or being stretched. **3** mental, emotional or nervous strain; condition when feelings are tense, when relations between persons, groups, states, etc are strained: *racial ~(s) in Africa; political ~.* **4** voltage: *Keep away from those high ~ wires or you'll be electrocuted.* **high ~ battery,** one made up of a number of small batteries connected in series. ⇨ **series. 5** expansive force of gas or vapour.

tens·ity /ˋtensətɪ/ *n* = *tenseness.* ⇨ tense[1].

tent /tent/ *n* (usu portable) shelter made of canvas supported by poles and ropes, esp as used by campers, scouts, soldiers, etc. **ˋoxygen ~,** air-tight cover (over a bed) for a person who is being given extra oxygen. **ˋ~-peg** *n* wooden peg used to secure a rope to the ground.

ten·tacle /ˋtentəkl/ *n* [C] long, slender, flexible, snake-like, boneless growth on the head or round the mouth of certain animals used for touching, feeling, holding, moving, etc. ⇨ the illus at mollusc.

ten·ta·tive /ˋtentətɪv/ *adj* made or done as a trial, to see the effect: *only a ~ suggestion; come to a ~ conclusion; make a ~ offer.* **~·ly** *adv*

ten·ter·hooks /ˋtentəhʊks/ *n pl* (only in) **on ~,** in a state of anxious suspense.

tenth /tenθ/ *n, adj* ⇨ ten.

tenu·ous /ˋtenjʊəs/ *adj* thin; slender: *the ~ web of a spider;* (of distinctions) subtle. **ten·uity** /tɪˋnjuːətɪ *US:* teˋnu-/ *n*

ten·ure /ˋtenjʊə(r) *US:* -jə(r)/ *n* [C,U] (period, time, condition of) holding (e g political office) or using (land): *The farmers want security of ~,* to be secure in their tenancies. *The ~ of office of the President is four years.*

tepee /ˋtipi/ *n* cone-shaped tent of skins or bark of the American Indians; wigwam.

tepid /ˋtepɪd/ *adj* lukewarm (liter and fig). **~·ly** *adv* **~·ness** *n* **~·ity** /teˋpɪdətɪ/ *n*

ter·cen·ten·ary /ˈtɜsenˋtinərɪ *US:* tɜˋsentn̩erɪ/, **ter·cen·ten·nial** /ˈtɜsenˋtenɪəl/ *nn* 300th anniversary: (attrib) ~ *celebrations.*

ter·gi·ver·sate /ˋtɜdʒɪvəseɪt/ *vi* (formal) make a complete change in one's opinions, principles, etc; make conflicting statements. **ter·gi·ver·sa·tion** /ˈtɜdʒɪvəˋseɪʃn/ *n*

term /tɜm/ *n* [C] **1** fixed or limited period of time: *a long ~ of imprisonment; during his ~ of office as President.* **2** (of schools, universities, etc) one of the periods (usu three) into which the academic year is divided: *the spring/summer/autumn ~; end-of-~ examinations; during ˋ~(-time).* **3** (legal) period during which a Court holds session. **4** (*pl*) conditions offered or agreed to: *enquire about ~s* (i e prices) *for a stay at a hotel; ~s of surrender,* e g offered to a defeated enemy; *~s of reference,* ⇨ reference(1). ***come to ~s/make ~s (with) sb,*** reach an agreement. ***come to ~s with sth,*** accept, become resigned to: *come to ~s with a difficult situation.* ***do sth on one's own ~s/sb else's ~s,*** on conditions that one/sb else decides: *If he agress to help, it will be on his own ~s.* **5** (*pl*) relations: ***be on good/friendly/bad ~s (with sb),*** be friendly, etc with him: *I didn't know you and she were on such good ~s,* were such good friends. ***on equal ~s,*** as equals. ***not be on speaking ~s with sb,*** ⇨ speak(2). **6** words used to express an idea, esp a specialized concept: *technical/scientific/legal ~s. In box-office ~s* (as expressed in financial, or box-office receipts) *the film was a failure.* **7** (*pl*) mode of expression: *He referred to your work in ~s of high praise/in flattering ~s. How dare you speak of her in such abusive ~s?* ***a contradiction in ~s,*** a statement that contradicts itself. **8** (maths) part of an expression joined to the rest by + or −: *The expression $a^2 + 2ab + b^2$ has three ~s.* □ *vt* [VP23] name; apply a ~ to: *He has no right to ~ himself a professor.*

ter·ma·gant /ˋtɜməgənt/ *n* noisy, quarrelsome woman; shrew.

ter·min·able /ˋtɜmɪnəbl/ *adj* that may be terminated.

ter·minal /ˋtɜmɪnl/ *adj* **1** of, taking place, each term(1,3): ~ *examinations/accounts.* **2** of, forming, the point or place at the end: ~ *cancer,* uncurable; ending in death; *the ˋ~ ward,* (in a hospital) for persons who cannot be cured and must soon die. □ *n* **1** end of a railway line, bus line, etc; centre (in a town) used by passengers departing for, or arriving from, an airport: *the ˈWest ˈLondon ˋAir T~.* **2** point of connection in an electric circuit: *the ~s of a battery.* **ter·min·ally** *adv*

ter·min·ate /ˋtɜmɪneɪt/ *vt,vi* [VP6A,2A,15A] bring to an end; come to an end: ~ *sb's contract; ~ a pregnancy; the word that ~s a sentence. The meeting ~d at 10 o'clock. Many adverbs ~ in -ly.*

ter·mi·na·tion /ˈtɜmɪˋneɪʃn/ *n* **1** [C,U] ending: *the ~ of a contract; ~ of pregnancy,* abortion; *put a ~ to sth; bring sth to a ~.* **2** [C] final syllable or letter of a word (as in inflexion or derivation).

ter·mi·nol·ogy /ˈtɜmɪˋnolədʒɪ/ *n* [C,U] (*pl* -gies) (science of the) proper use of terms(6); terms used in a science or art: *problems of ~: medical/ grammatical ~.* **ter·mi·no·logi·cal** /ˌtɜmɪnəˈlodʒɪkl/ *adj* of ~: *a terminological inexactitude,* (hum) an untruth.

ter·mi·nus /ˈtɜmɪnəs/ *n* [C] (*pl* -ni /-naɪ/ or -nuses /-nəsɪz/) station at the end of a railway line; end of a tram, bus or air route.

ter·mite /ˈtɜmaɪt/ *n* insect (popularly but wrongly called *white ant*), found chiefly in tropical areas, very destructive to timber, textiles, etc and which makes large hills of hard earth. ⇨ the illus at insect.

tern /tɜn/ *n* sea-bird like a gull, but usu smaller and swifter in flight.

Terp·si·chorean /ˌtɜpsɪkəˈrɪən/ *adj* of (the Muse of) dancing: *the ~ art.*

ter·race /ˈterəs/ *n* **1** level(led) area of ground with a vertical or sloping front or side; a series of these, separated by sloping banks, rising one above the other, e g as a method of irrigation on a hillside. **2** flight of wide, shallow steps (e g for spectators at a sporting event such as a football match, or on the banks of the Ganges at Benares, used by bathers). **3** continuous row of houses in one block, e g along the top of a slope (often as part of a postal address): *6 Olympic T~, Glasgow.* **4** (US) porch, paved area, adjacent to a house, used as an outdoor living area. □ *vt* [VP6A] (usu *pp*) form into ~s; make ~s in: *a ~d lawn; ~d houses,* (long line of) houses joined together, sometimes with an alley in the rear for access to the backyards.

irrigation terraces

terra-cotta /ˈterə ˈkotə/ *n* [U] hard, reddish-brown pottery (used for vases, small statues, ornamental building material, etc): (attrib) *a ~ vase;* the colour reddish-brown.

terra firma /ˈterə ˈfɜmə/ *n* [U] (Lat) dry land, solid land (contrasted with water): *glad to be on ~ again.*

terra in·cog·nita /ˈterə inˈkognɪtə/ *n* (Lat) unknown territory, e g on maps of unexplored areas.

ter·rain /teˈreɪn *US:* tə-/ *n* stretch of land, esp with regard to its natural features: *difficult ~ for heavy armoured vehicles.*

ter·ra·pin /ˈterəpɪn/ *n* kinds of fresh-water tortoise and turtle; (esp) *the diamond-back ~,* valued as food.

ter·res·trial /təˈrestrɪəl/ *adj* **1** of, on, living on, the earth or land: *the ~ parts of the world.* **2** of the earth (opposed to *celestial*): *a ~ globe,* representing the earth.

ter·rible /ˈterəbl/ *adj* **1** causing great fear or horror: *a ~ war/accident. He died in ~ agony.* **2** causing great discomfort; extreme: *The heat is ~ in Baghdad during the summer.* **3** (colloq) extremely bad: *My room was in a ~ state of disorder. What ~ food they gave us!* **ter·ribly** /-əblɪ/ *adv* (colloq) extremely: *How terribly boring he is!*

ter·rier[1] /ˈterɪə(r)/ *n* kinds of small and active dog, esp the kind that digs into burrows to pursue its prey.

ter·rier[2] /ˈterɪə(r)/ *n* (colloq) member of the Territorial Army.

ter·rific /təˈrɪfɪk/ *adj* **1** causing fear; terrible. **2** (colloq) very great; extreme: *driving at a ~ pace.* **ter·rifi·cally** /-klɪ/ *adv* (colloq) extremely.

ter·rify /ˈterɪfaɪ/ *vt* (*pt,pp* -fied) [VP6A,15A] fill with fear: *The child was terrified of being left alone in the house. She was terrified out of her wits. What a ~ing experience!*

ter·ri·torial /ˌterɪˈtɔrɪəl/ *adj* **1** of land, esp land forming a division of a country: *~ possessions; have ~ claims against a State,* claim part of its territory. **~ waters,** the sea near a country's coast, over which special rights are claimed, e g for fishing. **2 T~,** of any of the US Territories: *T~ laws.* **3** (GB) (often *T~*) of the force of mostly non-professional soldiers organized for the defence of Great Britain and trained in their spare time: *the T~ Army.* □ *n* member of the T~ Army.

ter·ri·tory /ˈterətrɪ *US:* -tɔrɪ/ *n* (*pl* -ries) **1** [C,U] (area of) land, esp land under one ruler or Government: *Portuguese ~ in Africa.* **2** [C] land or district; [U] extent of such land, etc: *This salesman travels over a large ~. How much ~ does he travel over? Mating blackbirds will defend their ~* (= the area which they regard as belonging to themselves) *against intruders.* **3** (US) district not admitted as a State but having its own law-making body: *Until 1959 Hawaii was a T~, not a State.*

ter·ror /ˈterə(r)/ *n* **1** [U] great fear: *run away in ~; be in ~ of one's life,* fear that one will lose one's life. ***strike ~ into sb,*** fill him with ~. Hence, **ˈ~-struck, ˈ~-stricken** *adjj* struck, filled, with ~. **2** [C] instance of great fear; (sth or sb that causes) great fear: *have a ~ of fire. This added to our ~s.* **3** [C] (colloq) troublesome person: *This child is a perfect ~,* a great nuisance. **ˈ~·ism** /-ɪzm/ *n* use of violence and intimidation, esp for political purposes. **ˈ~·ist** /-ɪst/ *n* supporter of, participant in, ~ism. **ˈ~·ize** /-aɪz/ *vt* [VP6A] fill with ~ by threats or acts of violence.

terse /tɜs/ *adj* (of speech, style, speakers) brief and to the point; concise. **~·ly** *adv* **~·ness** *n*

ter·tian /ˈtɜʃn/ *adj* (of fever) marked by paroxysms which occur every other day.

ter·ti·ary /ˈtɜʃərɪ *US:* -ʃɪerɪ/ *adj* third in rank, order, occurrence, importance: *the T~ period,* (geol) the third period in the formation of rocks; *~ burns/syphilis,* a severe stage.

tery·lene /ˈterəlin/ *n* [U] (GB) (P) (fabric made from) kinds of man-made fibre.

tes·sel·lated /ˈtesḷeɪtɪd/ *adj* formed of small, flat pieces of stone of various colours (as used in mosaic): *a ~ pavement.*

test /test/ *n* [C] (often attrib) examination or trial (of sth) to find its quality, value, composition, etc; trial or examination (of sb, his powers, knowledge, skill, etc): *methods that have stood the ~ of time; an endurance ~,* e g for a new aero-engine; *a ˈblood ~,* e g at a hospital, for infection, etc. *a ˈ~ bore,* hole bored into the ground or sea-bed to learn whether there is mineral ore, oil, etc: *~ bores in the North Sea. a ~ in arithmetic; an inˈtelligence ~.* **a ˈ~ case,** (in law) one that shows the principle involved (even though it may not be important in itself). **ˈ~ drive** *n* drive in a car one thinks of buying, to judge its qualities, worth, etc. Hence, **ˈ~-drive** *vt* **ˈ~ pilot** *n* one who flies newly built aircraft to try their qualities, performance, etc. **a ˈdriving ~,** an examination of one's ability to drive a car in the way required by law. ***put sth to the ~,*** submit it to conditions, etc, that will show its qualities, etc. **ˈ~ match** *n* one of the matches in any of the cricket or Rugby tours arranged between certain countries. **ˈ~-tube** *n* slender glass tube, closed at one end, used in chemical ~s and experiments. **ˈ~-tube baby,** baby whose early development took place in a laboratory (after artificial insemination) and is later implanted in the womb. □ *vt* [VP6A,15A] put to the ~; examine: *have one's eyesight ~ed; ~ ore for gold; a well-~ed remedy. The long climb ~ed* (= was a ~ of) *our powers of endurance.*

tes·ta·ment /ˈtestəmənt/ *n* **1** [C] (often ***last Will and T~***) statement in writing saying how sb wishes his property to be distributed after his death. **2 Old T~, New T~,** the two main divisions of the Bible. **tes·ta·men·tary** /ˈtestəˈmentrɪ/ *adj* of, connected with, given in, a ~(1).

tes·tate /ˈtesteɪt/ *n, adj* (person) who has made a testament (and died leaving it in force). **tes·ta·tor** /teˈsteɪtə(r) *US:* ˈtesteɪtər/ *n* man who has made a testament. **tes·ta·trix** /teˈsteɪtrɪks/ *n* woman testator.

tes·ticle /ˈtestɪkl/ *n* (anat) each of the two glands of the male sex organ that secrete spermatozoa.

tes·tify /ˈtestɪfaɪ/ *vt,vi* (*pt,pp* -fied) **1** [VP2A,3A, 9] ***~ that/to sth, ~ against/in favour of sth,*** bear witness, give evidence: *He testified under oath that he had not been at the scene of the crime. The teacher testified to the boy's ability. Two witnesses will ~ against her and three will ~ on her behalf.* **2** [VP6A] serve as evidence of: *Her tears testified her grief.*

tes·ti·mo·nial /ˈtestɪˈməʊnɪəl/ *n* **1** written statement testifying to a person's merits, abilities, qualifications, etc e g as sent with an application for a position. **2** sth given to sb to show appreciation of services, usu sth subscribed for by several or many colleagues.

tes·ti·mony /ˈtestɪmənɪ *US:* -məʊnɪ/ *n* [U] **1** declaration, esp in a law court, testifying that sth is true: *The witness's ~ is false. Several men were called in to bear ~ to what the police officer said.* **2** declarations; statements: *According to the ~ of the medical profession, the health of the nation is improving.*

tes·tis /ˈtestɪs/ *n* (*pl* -tes /-tiz/) = **testicle.**

testy /ˈtestɪ/ *adj* (-ier, -iest) quickly or easily annoyed; impatient. **tes·tily** /-əlɪ/ *adv* **tes·ti·ness** *n*

teta·nus /ˈtetn̩əs/ *n* [U] disease marked by stiffening and tightening of some or all of the muscles which are normally under conscious control: *~ of the lower jaw* (colloq called *lockjaw*).

tetchy /ˈtetʃɪ/ *adj* (-ier, -iest) peevish; irritable. **tetch·ily** /-əlɪ/ *adv* **tetchi·ness** *n*

tête-à-tête /ˈteɪt ɑ ˈteɪt/ *n* private meeting between two persons; their talk: *have a ~ with sb; have a ~ talk.* □ *adv* in a ~: *He dined ~ with the Prime Minister.*

tether /ˈteðə(r)/ *n* rope or chain by which an animal is fastened while grazing. ***at the end of one's ~,*** (fig) at the end of one's powers, resources, endurance, etc. □ *vt* [VP6A,15A] fasten with a ~: *He ~ed his horse to the fence.*

Teu·ton /ˈtjutn *US:* ˈtutn/ *n* member of any of the Teutonic nations. **~ic** /tjuˈtonɪk *US:* tu-/ *adj* of the Germanic peoples (including Scandinavian and Anglo-Saxon races).

text /tekst/ *n* **1** [U] main body of a book or printed page (contrasted with notes, diagrams, illustrations, etc): *too much ~ and not enough pictures.* **2** [C] original words of an author, apart from anything else in a book: *a corrupt ~,* one that, perhaps because of mistakes in copying, is no longer in its original form. **3** [C] short passage, sentence, esp of Scripture, as the subject of a sermon or discussion. **4** (usu **~·book** /ˈteksbʊk/) book giving instruction in a branch of learning: *an algebra ~book.* **tex·tual** /ˈtekstʃʊəl/ *adj* of, in, a ~: *~ual errors; ~ual criticism.*

tex·tile /ˈtekstaɪl/ *attrib adj* of the making of cloth: *~ processes; the ~ industry;* woven; suitable for weaving: *~ fabrics/materials.* □ *n* [C] ~ material.

tex·ture /ˈtekstʃə(r)/ *n* [C,U] **1** the arrangement of the threads in a textile fabric: *cloth with a loose/close ~.* **2** arrangement of the parts that make up sth: *the ~ of a mineral.* **3** tissue: *a skin of fine/coarse ~.* **tex·tured** *pp* (in compounds): *ˈcoarse-/ˈthin-ˈ~d.*

thal·ido·mide /θəˈlɪdəmaɪd/ *n* [U] (P) sedative drug which caused some women to give birth to deformed babies (esp with undeveloped limbs).

than /ðən *rarely heard strong form:* ðæn/ *conj* **1** introducing the second part of a comparison: *John is taller ~ his brother. I have never met anyone cleverer ~ you.* ***different... than,*** ⇨ different. **2** (with a *transitive v* the form of a *pron* after *than* depends upon the sense of the complete sentence. Note the words in parenthesis in these examples): *I know you better ~ he (does),* i e ~ he knows you. *I know you better ~ him,* i e ~ I know him. *I like her no better ~ he (does),* i e ~ he likes her. *I like her no better ~ him,* i e ~ I like him. **3** (with an *intransitive v* the *pron* after *than* is often in the object form, in both colloquial and written English, even though the subject form is required by formal grammar. This is esp so when the *pron* is followed by *all*): *He is several years older ~ me. He is wiser ~ us all.* **4** (in phrases) ***no other ~,*** (used as an equivalent to a construction with an emphatic *pron*): *It was no other ~ my old friend Jones,* i e it was Jones himself. ***nothing else ~,*** only, entire(ly): *His failure was due to nothing else ~* (= was entirely due to) *his own carelessness. What he told you was nothing else ~ nonsense,* was complete nonsense. ***rather ~,*** ⇨ rather(1). ***sooner ~,*** ⇨ soon(3,5).

thane /θeɪn/ *n* member of a class of persons who (in the early period of English history) gave military service in return for land.

thank /θæŋk/ *vt* **1** [VP6A,14] ***~ sb (for sth),*** express gratitude: *~ a person for his help. There's no need to ~ me.* ***T~ you,*** the usual formula for 'I ~ you.' ***No, ~ you,*** formula used to decline an offer. (Note that the 'No' is essential; *'T~ you'* is used for acceptance and may mean 'Yes, please.') [VP11] *T~ Heaven (that) you've come. T~ God she's safe.* **2** [VP14,17] (in peremptory requests, future tense): *I'll ~ you for that book,* please give it to me. *I'll ~ you to be a little more polite/to mind your own business.* □ *n* (now only in *pl* except in *~-offering* and with suffixes as below): (expression of) gratitude: *kneel and give ~s to God; give ~s,* (esp) say grace, ~ God for food (at a meal). *No, ~s,* colloq formula of refusal. ***~s to,*** as the result of; owing to: *T~s to your help we* *were successful.* **small ∼s to,** used ironically: *We were successful, but small ∼s to you,* you gave us no help. **'∼-offering** *n* offering made, e g to a charity, a religious organization, as an expression of gratitude. **'∼s-'giving** *n* **(a)** expression of gratitude, esp to God; form of prayer for this. **(b)** (US) (also **'T∼s-'giving Day**) day set apart each year for ∼s to God for His goodness (usu the fourth Thursday in November). **∼ful** /-fl/ *adj* grateful: *Be ∼ful for small mercies. You should be ∼ful to have/that you have escaped with minor injuries.* **∼fully** /-fḷɪ/ *adv* **∼ful·ness** *n* **∼less** *adj* not feeling or expressing gratitude; (of actions) not arousing gratitude or winning appreciation: *a ∼less task,* one which brings no ∼s, appreciation or reward.

that[1] /ðæt/ (*pl* those /ðəʊz/) *adj, pron* (contrasted with *this, these*) **1** *Look at ∼ man/those men. What is ∼? What are those? What was ∼ noise? What noise was ∼? Is ∼ you, Mary? Are those children yours? Is ∼ what you really think? T∼'s what he told me. This book is much better than ∼ (one). These are much better than those. Life was easier in those days/at ∼ time,* then, during that period. *So ∼'s ∼!* (formula used to indicate finality, the end of a discussion, an argument, etc). **2** (as antecedent to a *rel pron,* expressed or omitted): *All those (∼) I saw were old. Those who do not wish to go need not go. It's a different kind of car from ∼* (= kind of car) *(which) I am used to. Throw away all those (which are) unfit for use. Those* (= People who were) *present at the ceremony were.... There are those who say* (= some people who say).... **3** (with a *pl n,* considered as a collective *sing*): *What about ∼ five pounds you borrowed from me last month? When do you intend to repay ∼ sum of five pounds?* **4** (*That* and a possessive cannot be used together. Note the construction used when ∼ and a possessive are both needed): *I don't like ∼ new secretary of his. Well, how's ∼ bad leg of yours getting on?* □ *adv* (colloq) to such a degree; so: *I can't walk ∼ far,* = as far as ∼. *I've done only ∼ much,* i e as much as is shown, indicated, etc. *It's about ∼ high,* i e as high as ∼. *I was ∼ (= so) angry I could have hit him,* i e I wanted to hit him. *It isn't all ∼ cold,* e g not so cold that a fire is needed, that you should need an overcoat, etc according to context.

that[2] /ðət *rarely heard strong form:* ðæt/ *conj* **1** introducing *n* clauses: *She said (∼) she would come. It so happens ∼ I know the man. The trouble is ∼ we are short of money. I will see to it ∼ everything is ready.* **2** ***so ∼; in order ∼,*** (introducing clauses of purpose): *Bring it nearer (so) ∼ I may see it better. I will give up my claim so ∼/in order ∼ you may have the property.* **3** (introducing clauses of manner): *His behaviour was such ∼/was so bad ∼ we all refused to receive him in our homes.* **4** (introducing clauses of condition): *supposing ∼; on condition ∼.* **5** (introducing clauses of reason or cause) ⇨ **not(4)**, and **now**, *conj.* **6** (rhet) in exclamations: *Oh, ∼ I could be with you again!* How I wish...! *Oh, ∼ I should live to see my own son sent to prison as a thief!* How sad it is ∼...!

that[3] /ðət *rarely heard strong form:* ðæt/ *rel pron* (*pl* unchanged; used in defining or restrictive clauses; not preceded by a pause or a comma; often preferred to *which* for things; often preferred to *whom* and often used in place of *who*) **(a)** (as the subject of the *v* in a clause): *The letter ∼ came this morning is from my father. Those dogs ∼ attacked your sheep ought to be shot. The man ∼* (*who* is preferred) *sold you that camera is a rogue. The man ∼* (*who* is preferred) *looks after the school garden is nearly sixty.* **(b)** (Although *who* is usually preferred to *that, that* is preferred to *who* after superlatives, *only, all, any,* and *it is* or *it was*): *Newton was one of the greatest men ∼ ever lived. He's the cleverest man ∼ ever taught in our school. You're the only person ∼ can help me. Any boy ∼ wants to succeed must work hard. Ask Mr Green, or any other person ∼ is likely to know. It is Mrs White ∼ makes the decisions in that family, not her meek little husband.* **(c)** (as the object of the *v* in the clause; *whom* is to be avoided; the *pron* ∼ is usually suppressed): *The fountain pen (∼) you gave me is very useful. The books (∼) I sent you will help you in your studies. Is this the best (∼) you can do? The people (∼) you met yesterday were amused by your stories.* **(d)** (after an expression of time. Cf *when, rel adv*): *during the years (∼) he had been in the army; the year (∼) my father died; the evening (∼) we went to the theatre.* **(e)** (as the object of a *prep; whom* is to be avoided; *that* is usually suppressed, and the *prep* follows the *v*): *All the people (∼) I wrote to agreed to come. Is this the book (∼) you were looking for? The photographs (∼) you were looking at were taken by my brother. The man (∼) I was talking to had just arrived from Canada. Where's the man (∼) you borrowed it from?*

thatch /θætʃ/ *n* [U] (roof covering of) dried straw, reeds, etc; (colloq) thick hair of the head. □ *vt* [VP6A] cover (a roof, etc) with ∼.

thaw /θɔ/ *vi,vt* [VP6A,15B,2A,C] ***∼ (out),*** **1** *It is ∼ing,* The temperature has risen above freezing-point (so that snow and ice begin to melt). **2** (cause anything frozen to) become liquid or soft again: *∼ out the radiator,* (of a car); *leave frozen food to ∼ before cooking it.* **3** (of persons, their behaviour) (cause to) become less formal, more friendly: *After a good dinner he begun to ∼. A bottle of wine helped to ∼ (out) our guests.* □ *n* (usu *sing*) (state of the weather causing) ∼ing: *Let's go skating before the ∼/a ∼ sets in.*

the /ðə *strong form:* ði/ *def art* **1** (used as a less specific form of *this, these, that, those,* applied to person(s), thing(s), event(s), etc already referred to or being discussed. Note the changes from the *indef art* to the *def art* in these sentences): *An old man and an old woman once lived in a small hut by a river near a forest. One day the old man left the hut and went into the forest to gather wood. The old woman went to the river to wash clothes.* **2** (used when the situation is sufficient to make clear who or what is referred to): *Please take these letters to the post office,* i e the post office near by, the post office of this district. *Please close the window,* i e the window that is open. *Shall we have a walk by the river?* e g in London, the River Thames. **3** (used with a *n* when it stands for sth unique): *the sun; the moon; the year 1939; the universe.* **4** (used with *nn* such as *sea, sky, wind* (as in **2** above) when there is no *adj*): *The sea was calm. There's an aeroplane in the sky. Isn't the wind strong!* (Note that the use of an *adj* to describe the sea, wind, etc may make the use of the *indef art* possible: *There was a calm sea* (cf *The* *sea was calm) when I crossed from Dover to Calais. What a stormy-looking sky! There was a cold wind.* (cf *The wind was cold.*) **5** (used with a *n* if it is modified by a phrase or clause that makes it unique): *the top of the blackboard; the back of the house; the left side of the road; the books I have on my desk.* (In many phrases the *def art* is or may be omitted: *from beginning to end; from (the) top to (the) bottom; in (the) future.*) **6** (used with the superl): *the best way to get there; the tallest of the five men; the most interesting book I have ever read.* (The *def art* is not needed in the predicate after the *v 'be'* when the superl is used without a *n*: *It is wisest* (= *the* wisest plan is) *to avoid the centre of the town.* When *most* means 'very', the *def art* is not used: *The story was most exciting. This is a most useful reference book.*) ⇨ most[2](3). **7** (used before **(a)** names of seas and oceans: *the Mediterranean, the Red Sea; the Atlantic (Ocean), the Indian Ocean.* **(b)** names of rivers and canals: *the Nile; the river Thames; the Suez Canal.* **(c)** *pl* geographical names: *the Alps; the Philippines; the West Indies; the Netherlands.* **(d)** in a few geographical names: *the Sudan; the Sahara.*) **8** (used with *adjj* and participles to denote all members of a class): *the rich; the young; the dead, the dying, and the wounded,* e g after a battle, all those who are dead, dying or wounded. **9** (used with an *adj* it is equivalent to an abstract *n*): *the sublime and the beautiful,* sublimity and beauty. **10** (used formerly with names of diseases, now usually ommitted except with colloq or sl *pl*): *suffering from the creeps/the dumps/the fidgets/the blues/the horrors.* Survivals of the older use: *suffering from (the) gout. The child has (the) measles.* **11** Note: *to play the piano/the violin/the banjo, etc,* but (with names of games): *to play tennis/football/cards/chess/billiards. etc.* **12** (used with a *sing common n* to denote the whole class): *Is it true that the owl cannot see well in daylight?* (In colloq style, the use of the *pl*, without the *def art*, is more usu: *Is it true that owls cannot...?*). **13** (used in a similar way with names of inventions. In this case the use of the *def art* with the *sing n* is usu in both liter and colloq styles): *We don't know who invented the wheel. The telephone is a most useful invention.* **14** (used with *nn* expressing a unit): *This car does thirty miles to the gallon,* i e to each gallon of petrol. *These apples are small; there are seven or eight to the kilo,* i e to each kilo. *Our gardener is paid by the hour,* i e so much for each hour's work. □ *adv* by so much; by that amount; (used before an *adj* or *adv* in the comparative degree to indicate that two things increase or decrease in a parallel way, or that one increases in a degree equal to that by which another decreases): *The more he has the more he wants. The more he reads the less he understands.*

the·atre (US = **the·ater**) /ˈθɪətə(r)/ *n* **1** building or arena (*open-air* ~) for the performance of plays, for dramatic spectacles, etc: *go to the ~ to see a Shakespeare play.* **ˈ~-goer** *n* person who frequently goes to ~s. **2** hall or room with seats in rows rising one behind another for lectures, scientific demonstrations, etc. **ˈoperating ~,** room (in a hospital, etc) where surgical operations are performed. **3** scene of important events: *Belgium has often been a ~ of war.* **4** (usu *sing* with *def art*) dramatic literature or art; the writing and acting of plays, esp when connected with one author, country, period, etc: *a book about the Greek ~. Henry James's plays did not make good ~,* were not satisfactory when presented on the stage. **the·atri·cal** /θɪˈætrɪkl/ *adj* **1** of or for the ~: *theatrical scenery/performances; a theˈatrical company,* of actors. **2** (of behaviour, manner, way of speaking, persons, etc) designed for effect; showy, not natural. □ *n* (usu *pl*) (usu amateur) dramatic erformance **the·atri·cally** /-klɪ/ *adv*

thee /ði/ *pron,* ⇨ thou.

theft /θeft/ *n* [C,U] (the act of, an instance of) stealing.

their /ðeə(r)/ *adj* of them: *They have lost ~ dog. They have a house of ~ own.* **theirs** /ðeəz/ *pron*: *That dog is ~s, not ours. It's a habit of ~s,* one of ~ habits.

the·ism /ˈθi-ɪzm/ *n* [U] belief in the existence of one God, creator and ruler of the universe, but without the denial of revelation. ⇨ deism. **the·ist** /ˈθi-ɪst/ *n* believer in ~. **the·is·tic** /θiˈɪstɪk/, **the·is·ti·cal** /-kl/ *adjj*

them /ðəm *strong form:* ðem/ *pron,* ⇨ they.

theme /θim/ *n* [C] **1** topic; subject of a talk or a piece of writing. **2** (esp US) (subject set for a) student's essay. **3** (music) short melody which is repeated, expanded, etc e g in a sonata or symphony. **ˈ~ song,** one that is often repeated in a musical play, film, etc.

them·selves /ðəmˈselvz/ *pron* **1** (reflex): *They hurt ~. They kept some for ~. They did the work by ~,* without help. *They were by ~* (= alone, without company) *when I called.* **2** (emphat): *They ~ have often made that mistake.*

then /ðen/ *adv* **1** at the time (past or future): *We were living in Wales ~. I was still unmarried ~.* ***(every) now and ~,*** ⇨ now(3). ***~ and there, there and ~,*** ⇨ there[1](5). **2** (used to modify a *n*): *the ~ Lord Mayor,* the Lord Mayor at that time. **3** (used after a *prep*): *from ~* (= from that time) *onwards; until ~; since ~.* **4** next; after that; afterwards: *We'll have fish first, and ~ roast chicken. We had a week in Rome and ~ went to Naples.* **5** (usu at the beginning or end of a sentence) in that case; that being so: *A: 'It isn't here.'—B: 'It must be in the next room, ~.' You say you don't want to be a doctor.—T~ what do you want to be?* **6** furthermore; and also: *T~ there's Mrs Green—she must be invited to the wedding. And ~, you must remember....* **7 *Now ~,*** used to call attention, or to express a warning, make a protest, etc: *Now ~, what are you boys doing in my orchard?*

thence /ðens/ *adv* (formal; rare in spoken English) from there; for that reason. **~·forth** /ˈðensˈfɔθ/, **~·for·ward** /ˈðensˈfɔwəd/ *advv* from that time onwards.

the·oc·racy /θiˈokrəsɪ/ *n* [C,U] (*pl* -cies) (country with a) system of government in which the laws of the State are believed to be the laws of God; (hence) government by priests or a priestly class. **theo·cratic** /ˈθiəˈkrætɪk/ *adj*

the·odo·lite /θiˈodəlɑɪt *US:* -dḷ-/ *n* instrument used by surveyors for measuring horizontal and vertical angles.

the·ol·ogy /θiˈolədʒɪ/ *n* [U] formation of a series of theories about the nature of God and of the foundations of religious belief. **theo·lo·gian** /ˈθiəˈləʊdʒən/ *n* advanced student of ~. **theo·logi·cal** /ˈθiəˈlodʒɪkl/ *adj: a theological lecture/*

discussion. **theo·logi·cally** /-klɪ/ *adv*

the·orem /ˈθɪərəm/ *n* **1** statement which logical reasoning shows to be true. **2** (maths) statement for which a reasoned proof is required.

the·or·etic, -i·cal /θɪəˈretɪk, -kl/ *adjj* based on theory, not on practice or experience. **theor·eti·cally** /-klɪ/ *adv*

the·ory /ˈθɪərɪ/ *n* (*pl* -ries) **1** [C,U] (explanation of the) general principles of an art or science (contrasted with practice): *Naval officers must understand both the ~ and practice of navigation. Your plan is excellent in ~, but would it succeed in practice?* **2** [C] reasoned supposition put forward to explain facts or events: *Darwin's ~ of evolution.* **3** [C] sth conjectured, not necessarily based on reasoning: *He has a ~ that wearing hats makes men bald. In ~, three things could happen,* There are three possibilities. **the·or·ist** /ˈθɪərɪst/ *n* person who forms theories. **the·or·ize** /ˈθɪəraɪz/ *vi* [VP2A,3A] ~ ***(about sth),*** form theories.

the·os·ophy /θiˈosəfɪ/ *n* [U] any of several systems of philosophy which aim at a direct knowledge of God by means of spiritual ecstasy and contemplation. **the·os·oph·ist** /-fɪst/ *n* believer in ~. **theo·sophi·cal** /ˈθiəˈsofɪkl/ *adj*

thera·peutic, -cal /ˈθerəˈpjutɪk, -kl/ *adj* connected with the art of healing, the cure of disease: *take ~ baths at a spa.* **thera·peutic(s)** /ˈθerəˈpjutɪk(s)/ *n* (usu with *sing v*) branch of medicine concerned with remedial agents in illness and in health.

ther·apy /ˈθerəpɪ/ *n* [U] curative treatment, esp of a kind indicated by a preceding word: *radio ~; occupational ~,* the curing of an illness by means of occupations that exercise certain muscles; psycho~. **thera·pist** /ˈθerəpɪst/ *n* specialist in ~.

there[1] /ðeə(r)/ *adv of place and direction* (contrasted with *here*) **1** in, at or to, that place: *We shall soon be ~. We're nearly ~,* have nearly arrived. *Put the box ~, in that corner. I've never been to Rome but I hope to go ~ next year.* **2** (front position, in exclamatory style; always stressed, and not to be confused with *there + to be,* dealt with below; ⇨ here(2), and [VP2C]; used with inversion of subject and *v* if the subject is a *n*, but not if the subject is a *pers pron*): *T~ goes the last bus! T~ it goes! T~ come the rest of the party! T~ they come!* **3** (used to call attention; always stressed): *T~'s the bell ringing for church. T~'s a good boy!* (used to give praise or encouragement.) *You have only to turn the switch and ~ you are,* i e you get the desired result. *T~'s a fine, ripe pear for you!* See what a fine, ripe pear this is! *T~'s gratitude for you!* Note how grateful he, she, etc is! Used either sincerely or ironically. **4** at, in connection with, that point (in an action, story, argument, etc): *Don't stop ~! T~* (i e on that point) *I disagree with you. T~ you are mistaken. T~ comes the difficulty.* **5** (in phrases): ***all ~,*** ⇨ all[2](1). ***here and ~,*** ⇨ here(5). ***~ and back,*** to a place and back again: *Can I go ~ and back in one day?* ***over ~,*** (indicating a place farther than is indicated by ~ alone): *I live here, Mr Green lives ~, and Mr Brown lives over ~, on the other side of the river.* ***then and ~, ~ and then,*** at that time and place. Cf *here and now.* **6** (in colloq style only, after a *n* or *pron,* for emphasis): *Hi! You ~! That woman ~ is eating a lot!* **7** (used after *preps* and *advv*): *Put them in/under/near, etc ~. Pass along ~, please!* (used to request people to move along in a crowded street, bus, etc).

there[2] /ðeə(r)/ *adv* (used to introduce a sentence of which the *v*, esp the *v 'be'*, normally precedes its subject, which is usually *indef. There* is almost always unstressed.) **1** (with the *v 'be'*): *T~'s a man at the door.* Cf *The man is at the door. T~ can be no doubt about it. I don't want ~ to be any misunderstanding. T~'s no stopping him,* It is impossible to stop him. **2** (with other *vv*, esp *seem* and *appear*): *T~ seems (to be) no doubt about it. T~ appeared to be no one who could answer our inquiries. T~ comes a time when….*

there[3] /ðeə(r)/ *int* (always stressed) **1** (used, chiefly to children, to soothe or comfort): *T~! T~! Never mind, you'll soon feel better.* **2** (used to suggest that the speaker was right in sth, or to indicate triumph, dismay, etc according to the context): *T~, now! What did I tell you,* You now see that I was right! *T~! You've upset the ink!*

there·about(s) /ˈðeərəbaʊt(s)/ *adv* (usu preceded by *or*) bear that place, number, quantity, degree, etc: *in Rye or ~; £5/15 lb/3 o'clock or ~.*

there·after /ðeərˈɑftə(r) *US:* -ˈæf-/ *adv* (formal) afterwards.

there·by /ðeəˈbaɪ/ *adv* (formal) by that means; in that connection.

there·fore /ˈðeəfɔ(r)/ *adv* for that reason.

there·in /ðeərˈɪn/ *adv* (archaic) in that place; in that; in that particular.

there·in·after /ˈðeərɪnˈɑftər *US:* -ˈæf-/ *adv* (chiefly legal) in that part which follows.

there·of /ðeərˈov/ *adv* (formal) of that; from that source.

there·to /ðeəˈtu/ *adv* (formal) to that; in addition to that.

there·under /ðeərˈʌndə(r)/ *adv* (formal) under that.

there·upon /ˈðeərəˈpon/ *adv* (formal) than; as the result of that.

there·withal /ˈðeəwɪðɔl/ *adv* (archaic) in addition; besides.

therm /θɜm/ *n* [C] (100 000 GB thermal units as a) unit of heat as used for measuring the consumption of gas (coal-gas or natural gas).

ther·mal /ˈθɜml/ *adj* of heat: *~ springs,* of warm or hot water; *the ˈ~ barrier,* barrier to the use of high speeds (in flying) caused by increased friction of the air on the surfaces of the aircraft; *a ˈ~ ˈpower station,* one using heat (from coal, oil) (contrasted with a hydro-electric power station). □ *n* rising current of warm air (as needed by a sailplane to gain height).

ther·mi·onic /ˈθɜmɪˈonɪk/ *adj* of that branch of physics that deals with the emission of electrons at high temperatures. **~ valve** (US = **~ tube**) *n* system of electrodes arranged in a glass or metal envelope exhausted of air.

thermo- /ˈθɜməʊ/ (in compounds) of heat. **ˈ~-dy·ˈnam·ics** *n pl* [U] (usu with *sing v*) science of the relations between heat and mechanical work. **ˈ~-ˈnu·clear** *adj* (e g of weapons) of, using, the high temperatures released in nuclear fission: *the ~-nuclear bomb,* the hydrogen bomb. **ˈ~-ˈplas·tic** *n, adj* (substance) which can at any time be made plastic by the application of heat. **ˈ~-ˈset·ting** *adj* (of plastics) becoming permanently hard after being heated and shaped. **ˈ~·stat** /ˈθɜməstæt/ *n* [C] device for automatically regulating temperature by cutting off and restoring the supply of heat (e g in central heating, refrigerators, air-conditioning). **~·static** /ˈθɜmə`stætɪk/ *adj* of a ~stat: *~static control.*

ther·mom·eter /θə`momɪtə(r)/ *n* instrument for measuring temperature. ⇨ App 5.

ther·mos /`θɜmos/ *n* (also `~ **flask**) (P) vacuum flask. ⇨ **vacuum**.

the·sau·rus /θɪ`sɔrəs/ *n* (*pl* -ri /-raɪ/ or -ruses /-rəsɪz/) lexicon or encyclopaedia, esp a collection of words, phrases grouped together according to similarities in their meanings.

these /ðiz/ ⇨ **this**.

the·sis /`θisɪs/ *n* (*pl* theses /-siz/) statement or theory (to be) put forward and supported by arguments, esp a lengthy written essay submitted (as part of the requirements) for a university degree.

Thes·pian /`θespɪən/ *adj* connected with the drama: *the ~ art,* the drama.

thews /θjuz/ *n pl* (liter) muscles: *~ and sinews,* bodily strength.

they /ðeɪ/ *pers pron* (subject form, *pl,* of *he, she, it*): *T~* (= People in general) *say that the government will have to resign. What a lot of questions ~* (= those in authority) *ask in this census form!* **them** /ðəm *strong form:* ðem/ *pers pron* (object form of *they*): *Give them to me. It was very kind of them,* They were very kind.

thick /θɪk/ *adj* (-er, -est) **1** (opp of *thin*) of relatively great or a specified measurement in diameter, from one side to the other, or from the front to the back: *a ~ slice of bread; a ~ line; ice three inches ~; ~ print,* of ~ lines. **ˈ~-`skinned** *adj* (fig) not sensitive to reproach or insults; stolid. **2** having a large number of units close together: *~ hair; a ~ forest; in the ~est part of the crowd. The corn was ~ in the fields.* **ˈ~-`set** *adj* **(a)** having a short, stout body; solidly built. **(b)** (of a hedge) with bushes, etc closely planted. **3** *~* ***with,*** abounding or packed with: *The air was ~ with dust/snow.* **4** (of liquids) semi-solid: *~ soup;* (of vapour, the atmosphere) not clear; dense: *a ~ fog. The weather is still ~.* **5** (of voices) obstructed, e g because one has a cold. **6** stupid; dull. **ˈ~-`headed** *adj* stupid. **7** (colloq) intimate: *They're very ~ together. John is very ~ with Anne now. They're as ~ as thieves,* (prov) very friendly. **8** (various colloq uses) ***a bit ~, rather/a little too ~,*** beyond what is reasonable or endurable: *Three weeks of heavy rain is a bit ~.* ***give sb a ~ ear,*** give him a blow that causes his ear to swell. ***lay it on ~,*** (sl) be profuse, esp in paying compliments. □ *n* [U] **1** most crowded part; part where there is greatest activity: *in the ~ of the fight. We were in the ~ of it.* ***through ~ and thin,*** under any kind of conditions, good or bad. **2** ~ part of anything: *the ~ of the thumb.* □ *adv* ~ly: *You spread the butter too ~. The snow/dust lay ~ everywhere. His blows came ~ and fast,* rapidly and in large numbers. **~·ly** *adv* **~en** /`θɪkən/ *vt,vi* make or become ~: *~en the gravy. The plot ~ens,* becomes more complex. **~·en·ing** /`θɪkn̩ɪŋ/ *n* [U] material or substance used to ~en sth; process of becoming ~(er) or making sth ~(er). **~·ness** *n* **1** [U] quality or degree of being ~: *four centimetres in ~ness; a ~ness of four centimetres.* **2** [C] layer: *one ~ness of cotton-wool and two ~nesses of felt.*

thicket /`θɪkɪt/ *n* [C] mass of trees, shrubs, undergrowth, growing thickly together.

thief /θif/ *n* (*pl* thieves /θivz/) person who steals, esp secretly and without violence. ⇨ **bandit, burglar,** *robber* at rob. **thieve** /θiv/ *vi,vt* [VP2A] be a ~; [VP6A] steal (sth). **thiev·ery** /`θivərɪ/ *n* theft. **thiev·ish** /-ɪʃ/ *adj* having the habit of stealing; thief-like. **thiev·ish·ly** *adv*

thigh /θaɪ/ *n* [C] **1** part of the human leg between the knee and the hip. ⇨ the illus at **leg**. `**~-bone** *n* bone of this part of the leg; femur. **2** corresponding part of the hind legs of other animals.

thimble /`θɪmbl/ *n* cap (of metal, etc) used to protect the end of the finger when pushing a needle through cloth, etc. **~·ful** /-fʊl/ *n* (colloq) sip, very small quantity (of a liquid).

thin /θɪn/ *adj* (-ner, -nest) **1** (opp of *thick*) having opposite surfaces close together; of small diameter: *a ~ slice of bread; a ~ sheet of paper; ~ boards; a ~ piece of string; a ~ stroke,* of the pen, etc. **ˈ~-`skinned** *adj* (fig) sensitive to criticism; easily offended. **2** lacking density: *a ~ mist. He seemed to vanish into ~ air,* disappear mysteriously without leaving a trace. **3** (opp of *fat*) having not much flesh: *rather ~ in the face. Your illness has left you very ~.* **4** not full or closely packed: *a ~ audience,* with more seats empty than occupied. *'Your hair's getting rather ~ on top, sir', said the barber.* **5** (of liquids) lacking substance; watery: *~ gruel; ~ beer,* weak; *~ wine,* lacking body; *~ blood,* as when weakened by illness, living in a tropical climate, etc. **6** lacking in some important ingredient; poor: *~ humour; a ~ excuse,* not very convincing; *a ~ disguise,* easily seen through; *a ~ story,* one that contains nothing very exciting; one that does not convince (as an excuse, etc). **7** (colloq) ***have a ~ time,*** uncomfortable, distasteful. □ *adv* so as to be ~: *You've spread the butter very thin.* □ *vt,vi* (-nn-) [VP6A, 15B,2A,C] make or become ~: *War and disease had ~ned (down) the population. He ~ned out the seedlings,* pulled up some of them to allow the others to grow better. *We had better wait until the fog ~s,* becomes less dense. *At last the crowd ~ned.* **~·ly** *adv* in a ~ manner: *Sow the seed ~ly.* **~·ness** /`θɪnnəs/ *n*

thine /ðaɪn/ ⇨ **thy**.

thing /θɪŋ/ *n* **1** any material object: What are those ~s on the table? There wasn't a ~ (= nothing) *to eat. She's too fond of sweet ~s,* sweet kinds of food. **2** (*pl*) belongings; articles of which the nature is clear (or thought to be clear) from the context: *Bring your swimming ~s* (= your swimming-suit, towel, etc) *with you. Have you packed your ~s* (= clothes, etc) *for the journey? Put your ~s* (= hat, coat, etc) *on and come for a walk.* **3** subject: *There's another ~* (= something else) *I want to ask you about.* **4** that which is non-material: *spiritual ~s. He values ~s of the mind more than ~s of the body.* ***be `seeing ~s,*** have hallucinations. **5** circumstance; event; course of action: *That only makes ~s* (= the situation) *worse. You take ~s* (= happenings) *too seriously. I must think ~s over,* consider what has happened, what has to be done, etc. *What's the next ~ to do,* What must be done next? *It's just one of those ~s,* sth that can't be helped, explained, remedied, etc (according to context). T~s (= The state of affairs) *are getting worse and worse. Well, of all ~s!* (expressing surprise, indignation, etc, at what has been done, suggested, etc). ***for `one ~,*** used to introduce a reason: *For one ~, I haven't any money; for* *another....* ***Taking one ~ with another***, considering various circumstances, etc. **6** (used of a person or an animal, expressing an emotion of some kind): *She's a sweet little ~/a dear old ~. Poor ~, he's been ill all winter.* **7** (*sing* with *def art*) just what will be best in the circumstances: *A holiday in the mountains will be the very ~ for you. That's not at all the ~ to do*, is most unsuitable, inappropriate. *He always says the right/wrong ~*, makes the most suitable/unsuitable remark or comment. ***quite the ~***, quite fashionable. **8** (phrases) ***The '~ 'is,*** the question to be considered is: *The ~ is, can we get there in time? The ~ is* (= The most important factor is) *to make your views quite clear to everyone.* ***(the) first ~*** (in the morning, etc), before anything else; early: *We must do that first ~.* ***the 'general/'common/'usual '~,*** the common practice. ***a near ~,*** a narrow escape (from an accident, missing a train, etc). ***an understood ~,*** sth that has been/is accepted. ***do one's ~,*** (colloq) do sth which one does well, or which one feels an urge to do; act without inhibition. ***have a ~ about,*** (colloq) be obsessed by. **9** (*pl* with an *adj* following) all that can be so described: *~s Japanese*, Japanese customs, art, etc. **10** (legal) *~s personal/real*, personal/real property.

thing·amy, thing·ummy /ˈθɪŋəmɪ/, **thing·ama·bob, thing·uma·bob** /ˈθɪŋəməbob/, **thing·uma·jig** /ˈθɪŋəmədʒɪg/ *nn* (colloq) person or thing whose name one forgets or is not known (used in the same way as *what's-his-name, what d'you call it*).

think[1] /θɪŋk/ *vi,vt* (*pt,pp* thought /θɔt/) (For special uses with *adverbial particles* and *preps*, ⇨ 8 below.) **1** [VP2A,B,C,6A] (with cognate object) use, exercise, the mind in order to form opinions, come to conclusions: *Are animals able to ~? You should ~* (= not be hasty) *before doing that. Do you ~ in English when you speak English, or translate mentally? Let me ~ a moment,* Give me time before I answer. *He may not say much but he ~s a lot. Do you ever ~ great thoughts?* ***~ aloud,*** utter one's thoughts as they occur. **2** [VP9,25] consider; be of the opinion: *Do you ~ it will rain? Yes, I ~ so. No, I ~ not. It's going to rain, I ~. I suppose you ~ you're clever? We thought her quite a clever girl. The child thought there was no harm in plucking flowers in your garden. Do you ~ it likely? They had been thought (to be) lost. It will be better, don't you ~, to start early. I thought it better to stay away.* ***~ fit.*** ⇨ fit[1](2). **3** [VP10] (neg with *can/could*) imagine, form a conception of: *I can't ~ what you mean. I can't ~ where she has gone off to/how she did it/why she left. You can't '~ how glad I am to see you. You can't '~ what a sharp tongue she has!* **4** [VP9] have a half-formed intention: *I ~ I'll go for a swim.* **5** [VP10] reflect: *She was ~ing (to herself) how strange the children were.* **6** [VP11] expect, intend: *I never thought to see you here! Little did he ~ that we should be watching him! Who would have thought to see you here! He ~s to deceive us. I thought as much,* That is what I expected or suspected. **7** [VP25,14] bring into a mental condition by ~ing: *Stop worrying or you'll ~ yourself silly!* **8** [VP3A,15B] (special uses with *adverbial particles* and *preps*): ***think about sth,*** **(a)** examine, consider (esp a plan, idea, to see whether it is desirable, practicable, etc): *She's ~ing about emigrating to Canada. Please ~ about the proposal and let me have your views tomorrow.* **(b)** recall; reflect upon: *She was ~ing about her childhood days.*

think of sth, **(a)** consider; take into account: *We have a hundred and one things to ~ of before we can decide. You ~ of everything!* **(b)** consider, contemplate (without reaching a decision or taking action): *We're ~ing of going to Venice for Easter. I did ~ of visiting him, but I've changed my mind.* **(c)** imagine: *Just ~ of the cost/danger! To ~ of his not knowing anything about it!* Isn't it surprising! **(d)** have, entertain, the idea of (often with *could, would, should,* and *not* or *never,* with *dream* as a possible substitute for *think*): *Surrender is not to be thought of. I couldn't ~ of such a thing. He would never ~ of letting his daughter marry a fellow like you. I never thought of looking/never thought to look for the book under the cushions.* **(e)** call to mind; recall: *I can't ~ of his name at the moment.* **(f)** put forward; suggest: *Who first thought of the idea? Can you ~ of a good place for a weekend holiday?* ***~ highly/well/not much/little, etc of sb/sth,*** (not in the progressive tenses), have a high/good/poor, etc opinion of: *His work is highly thought of by the critics. He ~s the world of her, ~s* she's wonderful, loves her dearly. ***~ nothing of,*** consider insignificant or unremarkable: *Barbara seems to ~ nothing of walking 10 or 20 miles a day.* ***~ better of sb,*** have a higher opinion of (than to...): *I had always thought better of you than to suppose you could be so unkind.* ***~ better of sth,*** reconsider and give up: *What a foolish idea! I hope you'll ~ better of it.*

think sth out, consider carefully and make a plan for: *It seems to be a well-thought out scheme. That wants ~ing out,* needs careful consideration.

think sth over, reflect upon, consider further (before reaching a decision, etc): *Please ~ over what I've said. I'd like more time to ~ things over.*

think sth up, devised, conceive, invent (a scheme, etc): *There's no knowing what he'll ~ up next.*

think[2] /θɪŋk/ *n* (colloq) occasion of, need for, thinking: *If that's what he wants, he's got another ~ coming,* will need to think again.

think·able /ˈθɪŋkəbl/ *adj* conceivable: *It's not ~* (more usu *It's un~*) *that....*

thinker /ˈθɪŋkə(r)/ *n* person who thinks (usu with an *adj*): *a great/shallow ~.*

think·ing /ˈθɪŋkɪŋ/ *adj* who think: *the ~ public,* those people who think (about public affairs, etc); *all ~ men* (usu meaning 'all men who share the views of the speaker'). □ *n* thought; way of reasoning: *do some hard ~,* think deeply. *You are of my way of ~,* You think as I do. *He is, to my (way of) ~* (i e in my opinion), *the best living novelist. Can I bring you round to my way of ~,* get you to think as I do, agree with me? ***put one's '~-cap on,*** (colloq) think about a problem, etc.

third /θɜd/ *adj, n* next after the second (in place, time, order, importance, etc); one of the three equal divisions of a whole: *the ~ month of the year,* i e March; *on the ~ of April; on the ~ floor* (US = fourth floor); *every ~ day; the ~ largest city in France; Edward the T~,* Edward III, the ~ king of this name; *get a ~* (= ~ class university degree) *in history; one-~ of a litre.* ***~ degree,***

prolonged or hard questioning, use of torture (as used by the police in some countries to get confessions or information). **a ~ party,** another besides the two principals: (attrib) *~-party insurance/risks,* of/to a person other than the person insured, which the insurance company undertakes to meet. **~ rail,** conductor rail (carrying current). **ˈ~-ˋrate** *adj* of poor quality. **ˈ~-ˋrater** *n* person who is ~-rate. **the T~ World,** the developing countries not aligned with the great power blocs. **~·ly** *adv*

thirst /θɜst/ *n* [U, and with *indef art* as in examples] **1** feeling caused by a desire or need to drink; suffering caused by this: *The horse satisfied its ~ at the river. This kind of work gives me a ~. They lost their way in the desert and died of ~.* **2** (fig) strong desire (*for*, or, liter and biblical, *after*): *a ~ for knowledge; satisfy one's ~ for adventure.* □ *vt* [VP2A,3A] **~ *(for)*,** have ~; be eager (for); *~ for* (biblical, *after*) *revenge.* **thirsty** *adj* (-ier, -iest) having or causing ~: *be/feel ~y. Some kinds of food make one ~y. Tennis is a ~y game on a hot day. The fields are ~y for rain.* **~·ily** /-əlɪ/ *adv*

thir·teen /ˈθɜˋtin/ *adj, n* ⇨ App 4. the number 13, XIII; one more than 12. **thir·teenth** /ˈθɜˋtinθ/ *adj, n* next after the twelfth; one of ~ equal parts.

thirty /ˋθɜtɪ/ *adj, n* ⇨ App 4. the number 30; XXX. **thir·ti·eth** /ˋθɜtɪəθ/ *adj, n* next after the 29th; one of ~ equal parts.

this /ðɪs/ (*pl* **these** /ðiz/) *adj, pron* (contrasted with *that, those*) **1** *Look at ~ box/these boxes. What's ~? What are these? Are these books yours? Are these your children? Is ~ what you want? T~ (one) is larger than that. These are better than those. Do it like ~,* i e in ~ way, as shown here, etc. *Life is difficult these days,* nowadays. *He will be here ~ day week,* a week (from) today, in a week's time. *Where were you ~ day last year,* a year ago today? *What's all ~?* (colloq) What's the trouble? What's happening? **2** (with a *pl n,* considered as a collective *sing*): *That's something I've been wanting ~ many a day,* for a long time. **3** (*T~* and a possessive cannot be used together. Note the construction used when ~ and a possessive are both needed): *T~ new pen of mine doesn't leak as the old one did. T~ boy of yours seems very intelligent.* **4** (in narrative) a certain: *Then ~ funny little man came up to me. We all ended up at ~ pub.* □ *adv* (colloq) to ~ degree; so: *It's about ~ high. Now that we have come ~ far* (= as far as ~).... *Can you spare me ~ much* (= as much as ~)? *I know ~ much* (= what I am about to state), *that his story is exaggerated.*

thistle /ˋθɪsl/ *n* [C] (sorts of) wild plant with prickly leaves and yellow, white or purple flowers. **ˋ~-down** *n* [U] fluff of ~ flowers, carrying the seed.

thither /ˋðɪðə(r) *US:* ˋðɪθər/ *adv* (old use) to that place; in that direction. ***hither and ~,*** here and there; in all directions.

tho' /ðəʊ/ *adv, conj* = though.

thole /θəʊl/ *n* (also **ˋ~-pin**) pin or peg in the gunwale of a boat to keep an oar secure; one of two pins between which an oar is held. ⇨ rowlock.

thong /θoŋ/ *n* narrow strip of leather, e g as a fastening, the lash of a whip.

tho·rax /ˋθɔræks/ *n* **1** part of an animal's body between the neck and the belly, e g in a man, the chest. **2** middle of the three main sections of an insect (bearing the legs and wings). ⇨ the illus at insect.

thorn /θɔn/ *n* **1** [C] sharp-pointed growth on the stem of a plant. ⇨ the illus at flower. ***a ~ in one's flesh/side,*** (fig) constant source of annoyance. **2** [C,U] (usu in compounds) kinds of shrub or tree with ~s: *ˋhaw~; ˋblack~.* **thorny** *adj* (-ier, -iest) **1** having ~s. **2** (fig) full of trouble and difficulty; causing argument; *a ~y problem/subject.*

thor·ough /ˋθʌrə *US:* ˋθɜəʊ/ *adj* complete in every way; not forgetting or overlooking anything; detailed: *a ~ worker; receive ~ instruction in English; give a room a ~ cleaning; be ~ in one's work.* **ˋ~-going** *adj* ~; complete; uncompromising. *a ~-going revision.* **~·ly** *adv* **~·ness** *n*

thor·ough·bred /ˋθʌrəbred *US:* /ˋθɜə-/ *n, adj* (animal, esp a horse) of pure breed; high-spirited, thoroughly trained (and fig of a person).

thor·ough·fare /ˋθʌrəfeə(r) *US:* ˋθɜə-/ *n* [C] road or street, esp one much used by the traffic and open at both ends: *Broadway is New York's most famous ~. No ~,* (as a sign) Not open to the public; no way through.

those /ðəʊz/ *pl* of that.

thou /ðaʊ/ *pron* (old or liter form of) you (*sing*). **thee** /ði/ *pron* object form of ~.

though /ðəʊ/ *conj* **1** (also **al~** /ɔlˋðəʊ/) in spite of the fact that; notwithstanding the fact that: *Al~ it was so cold, he went out without an overcoat.* Cf *but:* It was very cold, but he.... *T~ they are so poor, they are always neatly dressed. He passed the examination al~ he had been prevented by illness from studying.* **2** (also *al~, even ~*; in older English and in liter style sometimes with the *v* in the subjunctive mood) even if: *strange ~ it may appear/al~ it may appear strange,* even if it appears strange. *He will never be dishonest even ~ he (should) be reduced to poverty. T~ he slay me* (biblical style, = Even if he should kill me), *yet will I follow him.* **3** **what ~,** (old use) what does it matter if: *What ~ the way be long,....* **4** **as ~,** ⇨ *as ~/as if* at **as**[2](11). **5** (introducing an independent statement) and yet; all the same: *He will probably agree, ~ you never know,* and yet one can never be certain. *I'll try to come, ~ I don't think I shall manage it.* □ *adv* (used absolutely, in the sense **5** above) however: *He will probably agree; you never know, ~. He said he would come; he didn't, ~.*

thought[1] /θɔt/ *pt,pp* of **think**[1].

thought[2] /θɔt/ *n* **1** [U] (power, process of) thinking: *He spends hours in ~. He was lost/deep in ~,* thinking so deeply as to be unaware of his surroundings, etc. **2** [U] way of thinking characteristic of a particular period, class, nation, etc: *Greek/working-class/scientific/modern ~.* **3** [U] **~ *(for)*,** care, consideration: *after serious ~. He often acts without ~. The nurse was full of ~ for her patient.* **take ~ for,** be concerned about. **4** [C,U] idea, opinion, intention, formed by thinking: *His speech was full of striking ~s. Please write and let me have your ~s on the matter. That boy hasn't a ~ in his head. He keeps his ~s to himself,* does not tell anyone what he thinks. *She says she can read my ~s. He had no ~* (= intention) *of hurting your feelings. You must give up all ~ of marrying Tom. I had some ~ of going* (= had half intended to go) *to Spain this summer.* ***on***

'***second*** **'~s,** after further consideration. **'~-reader** *n* person who claims to know people's ~s. **'~ transference,** = telepathy. **5** (with *indef art*) a little: *You should be a ~ more considerate of other people.* **~·ful** /-fl/ *adj* **1** full of ~; showing ~: *~ful looks.* **2** considerate; thinking of, showing ~(3) for, the needs of others: *a ~ful friend. It was ~ful of you to warn me of your arrival.* **~-fully** /-flɪ/ *adv* **~·ful·ness** *n* **~·less** *adj* **1** careless; unthinking: *Young people are often ~less for the future.* **2** selfish; inconsiderate (*of* others): *a ~less action.* **~·less·ly** *adv* **~·less·ness** *n*

thou·sand /'θaʊznd/ *adj, n* the number 1 000, ⇨ App 4; (loosely, exaggerated style) a great number: *A ~ thanks for you kindness. He made a ~ and one excuses.* ***a ~ to one (chance),*** a remote possibility. ***one in a ~,*** a rare exception. **thou·sandth** /'θaʊznθ/ *adj, n* **~·fold** /-fəʊld/ *adj, adv* a ~ times (as much or many).

thrall /θrɔl/ *n* [C,U] (condition of being a) slave: (fig) *He is ~ to his passions.* **thral·dom** /-dəm/ *n* [U] slavery.

thrash /θræʃ/ *vt,vi* **1** [VP6A] beat with a stick, whip, etc: *Stop ~ing that donkey, you cruel boy! He ~ed the boy soundly,* gave him a thorough beating. *He threatened to ~ the life out of me.* **2** [VP6A] (colloq) defeat (a team, etc) in a contest. **3** [VP15B] ***~ sth out,*** **(a)** clear up (a problem, etc) by discussion. **(b)** arrive at (the truth, a solution, etc) by discussion. **4** [VP6A,15A,2C] (cause to) toss, move violently: *The whale ~ed the water with its tail. The swimmer ~ed about in the water. The gale made the branches of the trees ~ against the windows.* **5** = thresh. **~·ing** *n* [C] (esp) beating; *give sb/get a good ~ing;* defeat, e g in games.

thread /θred/ *n* **1** [C,U] (length of) spun cotton, silk, flax, wool, etc esp for use in sewing and weaving: *a reel of silk ~; a needle and ~; gold ~,* ~ with gold wire wound round it. ***hang by a ~,*** be in a dangerous or precarious state. **2** sth very thin, suggesting a ~: *A ~ of light came through the keyhole.* **3** [C] chain or line (connecting parts of a story, etc): *lose the ~ of one's discourse/argument; gather up the ~s of a story,* bring parts of it together and relate them to one another; *pick up/resume the ~s,* continue (after an interruption). **4** spiral ridge round a screw or bolt. □ *vt* **1** [VP6A] pass a ~ through the eye of (a needle); put (beads, pearls, etc) on a ~; make (a chain of beads, etc) thus: *~ a film,* put it in place (e g in a ciné-projector, ready for showing it on a screen). **2** [VP15A] ***~ one's way through,*** find, pick, one's way (through a crowd, streets, etc). **3** (of hair) streak: *black hair ~ed with silver,* with streaks of silver hair in it. **'~·bare** /-beə(r)/ *adj* **1** (of cloth) worn thin; shabby: *a ~bare coat.* **2** (fig) much used and therefore uninteresting or valueless; hackneyed: *~bare jokes / sermons/ arguments.* **'~·like** *adj* resembling a ~; long and slender.

threat /θret/ *n* [C] **1** statement of an intention to punish or hurt sb, esp if he does not do as one wishes: *utter a ~ (against sb); carry out a ~; be under the ~ of expulsion,* e g from a university. **2** sign or warning of coming trouble, danger, etc: *There was a ~ of rain in the dark sky.* **~en** /'θretn/ *vt,vi* **1** [VP6A,14,17] ***~ sb (with sth); ~ to do sth,*** use (~s) to or towards; utter a ~ of: *~en an employee with dismissal; ~en an enemy; ~en to murder sb. They ~ened revenge. The race was ~ened with extinction,* It seemed possible that all people of this race would die. **2** [VP6A,2A] give warning of: *The clouds ~ened rain. It ~ens to rain.* **3** [VP2A] seem likely to occur or come: *Knowing that danger ~ened, the sentry kept an extra careful watch.* **~·en·ing·ly** *adv*

three /θri/ *adj, n* the number 3. ⇨ App 4: *a ~-act play,* one with ~ acts. **'~-'cornered** *adj* triangular: *a ~-cornered contest/fight,* with ~ contestants or competitors, e g in a Parliamentary election. ⇨ *straight fight* at straight[1](5). **'~-'D,** (abbr for) *~-dimensional.* ⇨ below. **'~-'decker** *n* **(a)** old type of sailing-ship with ~ decks. **(b)** kind of sandwich with ~ layers of bread and two layers of filling. **(c)** novel in ~ volumes (common in the 18th and 19th cc). **'~-di'mensional** *adj* (abbr *~-D*) having, or appearing to have, ~ dimensions (length, breadth and depth); stereoscopic. **'~-'figure** *adj* (of numbers) between 100 and 999 (inclusive). **~-halfpence** /θri 'heɪpəns *US:* 'hæfpens/ *n* (before 1971, now *one and a half pence,* 1½p) the sum of 1½d. **~-halfpenny** /θri 'heɪpnɪ *US:* hæfpenɪ/ *adj* costing 1½d (old GB currency). **~·pence** /'θrəpəns *US and alternative GB decimal:* 'θri-pens/ *n* the sum of ~pence (old currency, 3d; decimal currency 3p). **~·penny** /'θrəpnɪ *US and alternative GB decimal:* 'θri-penɪ/ *adj* costing or worth ~pence, 3d or 3p: *a ~penny bit/piece,* former GB coin worth 3d. **'~-'lane** *adj* (of a roadway) marked for ~ lanes of traffic (the centre lane for overtaking). **'~-'piece** *n, adj* set of ~ garments (man's jacket, waistcoat and trousers, or woman's jacket, skirt/ trousers and blouse); set of furniture (usu sofa and two armchairs). **'~-'ply** *adj* **(a)** (of wool, thread) having ~ strands. **(b)** (of wood) having ~ layers glued together. **'~-'legged** /-'legɪd/ *adj* **(a)** having ~ legs: *a ~-legged stool.* **(b)** (of a race) one in which the competitors run in pairs, the right leg of one runner being tied to the left leg of the other. **~-'quarter** *n* (Rugby football) team member who plays between the half-backs and the full-back. □ *adj* (of a portrait) down to the hips. Cf *a full-length portrait* at full (7). **'~-'score** *n* sixty. **'~·some** /-səm/ *n* game of golf played by ~ persons. **'~-'storey(ed)** *adj* (of a building) having ~ storeys. **'~-'wheeled** *adj* having ~ wheels.

thren·ody /'θrenədɪ/ *n* (*pl* -dies) song of lamentation; funeral song.

thresh /θreʃ/ *vt,vi* [VP6A,15A,2A] beat the grain out of (wheat, etc); beat wheat, etc for this purpose: *~ corn by hand. Have the farmers started ~ing yet?* **'~·ing-floor** *n* part on which grain is ~ed out. **'~·ing-machine** *n* one for ~ing grain. **~er** *n* **1** ~ing-machine; person who ~es. **2** large shark with a long tail.

thresh·old /'θreʃhəʊld/ *n* [C] **1** stone or plank under a doorway in a dwellinghouse, church, etc: *cross the ~.* **2** (fig) entrance, start, beginning: *He was on the ~ of his career. Are we at the ~ of an era when war will have been abolished?* **3** (pysch) limit: *above/below the ~ of consciousness,* above/below the limit at which we are aware of things. ⇨ subliminal.

threw /θru/ *pt* of throw[1].

thrice /θraɪs/ *adv* (rarely used) three times.

thrift /θrɪft/ *n* [U] care, economy, in the use of money or goods. **thrifty** *adj* (-ier, -iest) **1**

economical; using ~. **2** (US) = thriving. **~·ily** /-əlɪ/ *adv* **~·less** *adj* without ~; wasteful. **~-less·ly** *adv* **~·less·ness** *n*

thrill /θrɪl/ *n* [C] (experience causing an) excited feeling passing like a wave along the nerves: *a ~ of joy/pleasure/horror. It gave her quite a ~ to shake hands with the Princess. This film will give you the ~ of a lifetime,* excite you as you have never been excited before. □ *vt,vi* [VP6A] cause a ~ or ~s in: *The film ~ed the audience. We were ~ed with horror/joy.* **2** [VP2A,C] feel a ~ or ~s: *We ~ed at the good news. She ~ed with delight when the handsome pop star kissed her. There was a ~ing finish to the race.* **~er** *n* novel, play or film in which excitement and emotional appeal are the essential elements (not necessarily a crime or detective story).

thrive /θraɪv/ *vi* (*pt* throve /θrəʊv/ or (rarely) ~d, *pp* thriven /ˈθrɪvən/) [VP2A,3A] ~ ***(on sth),*** prosper; succeed; grow strong and healthy: *A business cannot ~ without good management. Children ~ on good food. He has a thriving business.*

thro', thro /θru/ = through.

throat /θrəʊt/ *n* **1** front part of the neck; ⇨ the illus at head; *grip sb by the ~; cut one's ~,* e g intending to commit suicide or (fig) destroy one's own opportunities. **2** passage in the neck through which food passes to the stomach and air to the lungs: *A bone has stuck in my ~.* ***force/thrust sth down sb's ~,*** try to make sb accept one's views, beliefs, etc, try to make people accept them. ***stick in one's ~,*** (fig) not be readily acceptable. **-~ed** in compounds: *a red-~ed bird.* **throaty** *adj* (-ier, -iest) uttered deep in the ~: *a ~y voice,* gutteral.

throb /θrob/ *vi* (-bb-) [VP2A,C] (of the heart, pulse, etc) beat, esp beat more rapidly than usual: *His head ~bed,* He had a bad headache. *His wound ~bed with pain. Her heart was ~bing with excitement.* □ *n* [C] ~bing or vibration: *~s of joy/pleasure; the ~ of distant gun-fire.* **~·bing** *adj* that ~s: *the ~bing (sound of) machinery.*

throe /θrəʊ/ *n* (usu *pl*) sharp pain, esp of child-birth; (colloq) *in the ~s of struggling with an examination/packing one's luggage.*

throm·bo·sis /θromˈbəʊsɪs/ *n* [U] coagulation of blood in a blood-vessel or in the heart.

throne /θrəʊn/ *n* [C] **1** ceremonial chair or seat of a king, queen, bishop, etc. **2 the ~,** royal authority: *come to the ~,* become king/queen; *united in loyalty to the T~,* to the Sovereign.

throng /θroŋ *US:* θrɔŋ/ *n* crowd. □ *vt,vi* [VP6A, 4A,2C] crowd: *The railway stations were ~ed with people going away for their holidays. People ~ed to see the new play.*

throstle /ˈθrosl/ *n* song-thrush.

throttle /ˈθrotl/ *vt,vi* **1** [VP6A] seize (sb) by the throat and stop his breathing; choke; strangle: *~ the nightwatchman and then rob the bank. The tyrant ~d freedom in his country.* **2** [VP6A,15B, 2C] control the flow of steam, petrol vapour, etc in an engine; lessen the speed of (an engine) by doing this. ***~ down,*** slow down the engine. □ *n* **ˈ~ (-valve)** valve controlling the flow of steam, petrol vapour, etc in an engine: *open out the ~; close the ~; with the ~ full open.*

through[1] (US = **thru**) /θru/ *adv* (⇨ the *v* entries; specimens only here) **1** from end to end, beginning to end, side to side: *They wouldn't let us ~,* e g pass ~ the gate. *Did your brother get ~,* e g the examination? *He slept the whole night ~,* all night. *His trousers are ~* (= have holes or rents in them) *at the knees. Read the book ~ carefully.* ***all ~,*** all the time (while sth was happening, etc): *I knew that all ~.* **2** to the very end. ***be ~ (with),*** **(a)** finish (with): *When will you be ~ with your work?* **(b)** (colloq) have had enough of; be tired of: *I'm ~ with this job; I must find something more interesting.* ***go ~ with sth,*** continue until it is finished or completed. ***see sth ~,*** be present at, help in, a series of events, etc until the end. ***~ and ~,*** in all parts; completely: *He's a reliable man ~ and ~. You're wet ~/~ and ~,* Your clothes are thoroughly wet. **3** all the way to: *This train goes ~ to Paris,* There is no need to change trains. *Book your tickets/luggage ~ to Vienna.* **4** (telephoning) **(a)** (GB) connected: *I will put you ~ to the manager,* connect you. *You're ~,* Your telephone connection has been made. **(b)** (US) finished; not wishing to continue the call. **5** (used, in the sense of 3 above, to modify *nn*): *a ~ train to Paris; ~ tickets/passengers/fares; ~ traffic,* road traffic which is going ~ a place (contrasted with local traffic). **ˈ~·put** /-pʊt/ *n* output; amount of material put ~ a process. **ˈ~·way** (US also **ˈthru·way**) *n* ~ express way. ⇨ express[1](2).

through[2] (US also **thru**) /θru/ *prep* **1** (of places) from end to end or side to side of; entering at one side, on one surface, etc and coming out at the other: *The River Thames flows ~ London. The burglar came in ~ the window. The road goes ~ the forest. There is a path ~* (= across) *the fields. She passed a comb/her fingers ~ her hair. He was looking ~ a telescope. We can see ~ glass.* **2** (fig uses; ⇨ the *v* entries; specimens only here): *He went ~/has come ~* (= experienced) *many hardships. He soon got/went ~* (= got to the end of, spent the whole of) *his fortune. We must go ~* (= examine) *the accounts. He got ~* (= passed) *the examination. He saw ~* (= was not deceived by) *the trick.* **3** (of time) from beginning to end of: *He won't live ~ the night,* He will die before morning. *The children are too young to sit ~ a long sermon.* **4** (US) up to and including: *We'll be in London from Tuesday ~ Saturday.* **5** (indicating the agency, means or cause): *I learnt of the position ~ a newspaper advertisement. The accident happened ~ no fault of yours. We lost ourselves ~ not knowing the way. It was all ~ you* (= It was your fault) *that we were late.* **6** without stopping for: *Don't drive ~ a red light.*

through·out /θruˈaʊt/ *adv* right through; in every part; in all ways or respects: *The coat is lined with fur ~. The woodwork in the house was rotten ~.* □ *prep* all or right through; from end to end of: *~ the country; ~ the length and breadth of the land; ~ the war.*

throve /θrəʊ/ *pt* of thrive.

throw[1] /θrəʊ/ *vt,vi* (*pt* threw /θru/, *pp* thrown /θrəʊn/) (For special uses with *adverbial particles* and *preps,* ⇨ 11 below) **1** [VP2A,6A,15A,B,12A, 13A] cause (sth) to go through the air, usu with force, by a movement of the arm or by mechanical means: *He ~s well. He can ~ a hundred yards. Don't ~ stones at my dog! He threw the ball to his sister. Please ~ me that towel. He threw the ball up and caught it. He seized the man and threw him to the ground. The drunken man was thrown out. He threw an angry look at me/me an angry look.* **2**

[VP15A,B] put (articles of clothing) (*on, off, over,* etc) quickly or carelessly: ~ *off one's clothes/disguise:* ~ *a scarf over one's shoulders.* **3** [VP15A,B] move (one's arms, legs, etc) (*out, up, down, about*) violently: ~ *one's chest out;* ~ *up one's arms;* ~ *one's head back. You'll never learn to swim properly while you* ~ *your legs and arms about so wildly.* **4** [VP6A] **(a)** (of a horse) cause the rider to fall to the ground: *Two of the jockeys were* ~*n in the second race.* **(b)** (of a wrestler) force (an opponent) to the floor. **(c)** (of a snake) cast (its skin). **(d)** (of animals) bring forth (young). **5** [VP6A] (of dice) ~ on to the table (after shaking them in sth); get by doing this: ~ *three sixes.* **6** [VP6A] twist (silk) into threads. **7** [VP6A] shape (round pottery on a potter's wheel. **8** (sl) ~ ***a party,*** give a (dinner, cocktail, etc) party. ~ ***a fit,*** have a fit. ⇨ fit[3](2). **9** ~ ***sth open (to),*** [VP22] **(a)** make (e g a competition) open to all persons. **(b)** allow the general public to enter (e g gardens which are usually closed). **10** [VP6A] (with *nn,* to which cross-references are given): ~ ***cold water (on...),*** ⇨ cold[1](1). ~ ***doubt upon,*** ⇨ doubt(1). ~ ***light (up)on,*** ⇨ light[1](6). ~ ***dust in sb's eyes,*** ⇨ dust[1](1). ~ ***down the gauntlet,*** ⇨ gauntlet. ~ ***a sop to Cerberus,*** ⇨ sop. ~ ***one's weight about,*** ⇨ weight. **11** [VP15B,3C] (special uses with *adverbial particles* and *preps*):

throw sth about, scatter: *Don't* ~ *waste paper about in the park. He's* ~*ing his money about,* (fig) spending it recklessly.

throw oneself at, **(a)** rush violently at. **(b)** force one's attentions on; behave without restraint in an effort to win the love of.

throw sth away, **(a)** lose by foolishness or neglect: ~ *away an advantage. My advice was* ~*n away upon him,* wasted. **(b)** (of words spoken by actors, broadcasters, etc) utter in a casual way, with conscious under-emphasis. Hence, **ˈ~-away** *n* sth that may be ~n away (e g a printed handbill); sth of small value, discarded when used: (attrib) *a* ~*-away ballpen; a* ~*-away line, to be uttered casually, without emphasis.*

throw back, show characteristics of, revert to, a remote ancestor. Hence, **ˈ~-back** *n* (example of) reversion to an ancestral type. ~ ***sb back (up)on sth,*** (often passive) force sb to go back to (because nothing else is available): *After this failure to get help we were* ~*n back upon our own resources.*

throw oneself down, lie down at full length.

throw sth in, **(a)** supply sth extra, without an addition to the price: *You can have the piano for £60, with the stool* ~*n in.* **(b)** put in (a remark, etc) casually. **(c)** (football) ~ the ball in after it has gone out of play. Hence, **ˈ~-in** *n* ~ ***in one's hand,*** give up an attempt to do sth; confess one's inability to do sth. ~ ***in one's lot with sb,*** decide to share his fortunes. ~ ***in the towel/sponge,*** (colloq) (from boxing) admit defeat. ~ ***oneself into sth,*** begin to work vigorously at.

throw sb/sth off, manage to get rid of; become free from: ~ *off a cold/a troublesome acquaintance/one's pursuers.* ~ ***sth off,*** produce or compose, easily, as if without effort: ~ *off an epigram/a few lines of verse.*

throw oneself (up)on sb/sth, place one's reliance on: ~ *oneself (up)on the mercy of one's captors/the court/the judge.*

throw sth out, **(a)** utter (esp casually): ~ *out a hint/suggestion;* ~ *out a challenge.* **(b)** reject (a Bill in Parliament, etc). **(c)** build as an extension: ~ *out a new wing,* e g to a hospital or other large building. ~ ***sb out,*** **(a)** (cricket, of a fielder) get (a batsman) out by ~ing the ball and hitting the wicket. **(b)** disconcert or distract (sb whose attention is concentrated on sth) so that he makes an error, has to stop, etc: *Keep quiet for a while or you'll* ~ *me out in my calculations.*

throw sb over, desert, abandon: ~ *over an old friend/one's girlfriend.*

throw sth together, assemble hastily: *That last textbook of his seems to have been* ~*n together,* written or compiled carelessly and hurriedly. ~ ***people together,*** bring together: *Chance had* ~*n us together at a skiing resort.*

throw sth up, **(a)** vomit (food). **(b)** resign from: ~ *up one's job.* ~ ***sb up,*** show prominently; produce: *The country seldom* ~*s up a great musical genius.* ~ ***up one's hands (in horror),*** express horror by doing this.

throw[2] /θrəʊ/ *n* [C] throwing; distance to which sth is or may be thrown: *a well-aimed* ~, e g cricket, to get a batsman out; *a* ~ *of the dice; a record* ~ *with the hammer* (as a competition in athletic sports). ***within a ˈstone's ~ (of),*** quite near (to).

thru /θru/ (US) ⇨ through.

thrum /θrʌm/ *vt,vi* (-mm-) [VP6A,3A] ~ ***(on) sth,*** play monotonously or idly on (a stringed instrument): ~ *(on) a guitar;* ⇨ strum; tap or drum idly with the fingers: ~ *on the table.*

thrush[1] /θrʌʃ/ *n* [C] sorts of songbird, esp the kind called *ˈsong-~,* or *throstle.*

thrush[2] /θrʌʃ/ *n* inflammatory throat disease, chiefly among children.

thrust /θrʌst/ *vt,vi* (*pt,pp* ~) [VP6A,15A,B,2A,C] push suddenly or violently; make a forward stroke with a sword, etc: *He* ~ *his hands into his pockets/a dagger into his enemy's heart/a coin into the beggar's hand. We had to* ~ *our way through the crowd. They* ~ *themselves forward/past into the bus. Some people have greatness* ~ *upon them,* i e obtain renown without their own effort. *He has* ~ *himself into a well-paid position,* obtained one by ruthless methods. □ *n* **1** [C] act of ~ing; (in war) strong attempt to push forward into the enemy's positions; (in debate, etc) attack in words; hostile remark aimed at sb. **2** [U] stress or pressure on a neighbouring part of a structure (e g an arch); force directed forward in a jet-engine as a reaction to the ejection rearward of gases. **~er** *n* (esp) person who ~s himself or herself forward (to win an advantage, etc).

thru·way /ˈθruweɪ/ *n* (US) ⇨ through[1].

thud /θʌd/ *n* dull sound as of a blow on sth soft: *The bullet entered his brain and he fell with a* ~ *to the carpet.* □ *vi* (-dd-) [VP2C] strike, fall, with a ~: *Bullets* ~*ded into the sandbags behind which we were sheltering.*

thug /θʌg/ *n* violent criminal; murderous ruffian. **~·gery** *n* [U].

thumb /θʌm/ *n* short, thick finger set apart from the other four. ⇨ the illus at arm. ***under sb's ~,*** under his influence and control. ***rule of ~,*** method or procedure based on experience and practice. ***T~s up!*** exclamation of satisfaction or triumph. **~-nail sketch,** portrait on a small scale; hasty word-picture. **ˈ~·screw** *n* **(a)** (also **ˈ~-nut**) one that can be turned easily with the ~ and a finger. (b) old instrument of torture which squeezed the ~s. '~-stall n sheath to cover an injured ~. '~-tack n (US) drawing-pin. □ vt 1 [VP6A] turn over (pages, etc); make dirty by doing this: *~ the pages of a dictionary; a well-~ed book.* 2 **~ a lift,** ask for (and get) a free ride in a motor-vehicle (by signalling to the driver). **~ one's nose at sb, cock a snook at him.** ⇨ snook.

thump /θʌmp/ vt,vi [VP6A,15A,22,2,2A,C,3A] strike heavily, esp with the fists; deliver heavy blows: *He ~ed (on) the door. She ~ed the cushion flat. His heart was ~ing with excitement. The two boys began to ~ one another. He was ~ing the keys of the piano/~ing out a tune on the piano,* playing noisily. *I'd love to ~ a big drum.* □ n [C] (noise of, or as of, a) heavy blow (esp one given with the fist): *I dislike being given a friendly ~ on the back. The baby fell out of its cot with a ~.* **~·ing** adj (colloq) of great size. □ adv (colloq) extremely: *What a ~ing great lie!*

thun·der /ˈθʌndə(r)/ n [U] 1 noise which usu follows a flash of lightning: *a loud crash/a long roll of ~. There's ~ in the air,* ~ seems likely. *We haven't had much ~ this summer.* '**~·bolt** n flash of lightning with a crash of ~; (fig) unexpected and terrible event. '**~·clap** n crash of ~; sth that comes like ~; sudden, terrible event, bad news, etc. '**~·storm** n storm of ~ and lightning, usu with heavy rain. '**~·struck** adj (pred; fig) amazed. 2 (with *pl*) loud noise like or suggesting ~: *the ~ of the guns; ~s of applause.* **steal sb's ~,** spoil his attempt to be impressive by anticipating him. □ vi,vt 1 [VP2A,C] (impersonal): *It was ~ing and lightening.* 2 [VP2C] make a noise like ~: *Someone was ~ing at the door,* beating at it. *The train ~ed through the station. The juggernauts ~ed past.* 3 [VP2C,3A,15B] speak in a loud voice, attack violently in words. **~ against/out,** utter (threats, etc) violently: *The reformers ~ed against gambling. How dare you ~ out your orders at me?* **~er** n (esp) *the T~er,* one of the names of the god Jupiter. **~·ing** adj, adv = thumping: *He was in a ~ing* (= violent) *rage.* **~·ous** /-əs/ adj making a noise like, sounding like, ~: *~ous applause.* **thundery** adj (of weather) giving signs of ~.

thu·rible /ˈθjʊərəbl US: ˈθʊər-/ n censer.

Thurs·day /ˈθɜzdɪ/ n fifth day of the week.

thus /ðʌs/ adv in this way; so: *~ far,* to this point.

thwack /θwæk/ vt, n = whack.

thwart[1] /θwɔt/ n seat across a rowing-boat for an oarsman.

thwart[2] /θwɔt/ vt [VP6A] obstruct, frustrate: *~ sb's plans; be ~ed in one's ambitions/aims.*

thy /ðaɪ/ adj (old use) your. **thine** /ðaɪn/ adj (old use) (before a vowel sound) your: *thine uncle.* □ pron yours: *Is this mine or thine?* **thy·self** /ðaɪˈself/ reflex, emph pron (old use) yourself.

thyme /taɪm/ n [U] kinds of plant with fragrant aromatic leaves, growing wild and in gardens, used in cookery.

thy·roid /ˈθaɪrɔɪd/ n '**~ (gland),** gland in the front part of the neck, producing a substance which affects the body's growth and activity. ⇨ the illus at head.

ti·ara /tɪˈɑrə/ n [C] 1 coronet for a woman. 2 triple crown worn by the Pope.

tibia /ˈtɪbɪə/ n (*pl* -biae /-bɪi/) (anat) shin-bone; inner and thicker of the two bones between the knee and the foot. ⇨ the illus at skeleton.

tic /tɪk/ n involuntary, spasmodic twitching of the muscles (esp of the face).

tick[1] /tɪk/ n [C] 1 light, regularly repeated sound, esp of a clock or watch. '**~-~** n (child's word for a) clock or watch. '**~-'tock** n ~ing sound (of a clock, etc). 2 (colloq) moment: *I'll be with you in two ~s. Half a ~!* Just a moment! 3 small mark (often ✓) put against names, figures, etc in a list or to show that sth is correct. 4 '**~-tack** n system of signalling (a kind of hand semaphore) used by bookmakers' assistants on race-courses. □ vi,vt 1 [VP2A,C] (of a clock, etc) make ~s(1): *The child put the watch to its ear and listened to it ~ing. The (taxi)meter was ~ing away.* **What makes him/it ~,** (colloq) What makes him/it function, act, behave like that etc? 2 [VP15B] (of a clock): *~ away the minutes,* mark their passing with ~s(1). 3 [VP2C] **~ over,** (of an internal-combustion engine) operate slowly with gears disconnected (and the vehicle stationary). 4 [VP6A, 10B] **~ sth (off),** put a ~(3) against: *~ off a name/the items on a list.* **~ sb off,** (colloq) rebuke, scold him: *get ~ed off; give sb a good '~ing-'off.*

tick[2] /tɪk/ n small spider-like parasite that fastens itself on the skin, e g of dogs, and sucks blood. ⇨ the illus at arachnid.

tick[3] /tɪk/ n 1 [C] outside cover of stout striped linen for a mattress, bolster or pillow. 2 [U] (also **~·ing**) material used for ~s.

tick[4] /tɪk/ n [U] (colloq) credit(5): *buy goods on ~; get ~.*

ticker /ˈtɪkə(r)/ n [C] 1 telegraphic machine which automatically prints news (esp stock market prices) on paper tape (called '**~-tape**): *get a ~-tape reception,* e g in New York City, of a visiting celebrity in a procession through the streets, be welcomed with streamers of ~-tape thrown from office windows, etc. ⇨ the illus at tape. 2 (colloq) watch. 3 (sl) heart: *a dicky ~,* a weak heart.

ticket /ˈtɪkɪt/ n [C] 1 written or printed piece of card or paper giving the holder the right to travel in a train, bus, ship, etc or to a seat in a cinema, concert hall, etc: *Do you want a single or a return ~* (US = *one-way* or *round-trip ~*)? *Admission by ~ only,* (as a notice outside a hall, etc). '**~-collector** n person who collects ~s (esp railway ~s). 2 piece of card or paper, label, attached to sth and giving information, e g about the price, size of clothing, etc. 3 (US) list of candidates to be voted on, belonging to one political party: *vote the straight ~,* cast the ballot on strict party lines. 4 printed notice of an offence against traffic regulations (e g a parking offence): *get a ~.* 5 **the ~,** (colloq) the proper thing to do: *That's just the ~. That's not quite the ~.* 6 **~ of leave,** (GB) permission given to a prisoner or convict who has served part of his sentence to have his liberty with certain restrictions, e g reporting regularly to the police: (attrib) *a '~-of-'leave man.* ⇨ parole. 7 certificate listing the qualifications of a pilot, a ship's mate, etc. □ vt [VP6A] put a ~(2) on; mark with a ~.

tick·ing /ˈtɪkɪŋ/ n ⇨ tick[3].

tickle /ˈtɪkl/ vt,vi 1 [VP6A,2A] excite the nerves of the skin by touching lightly, esp at sensitive parts, often so as to cause laughter: *~ sb in the ribs. The rough blanket ~s (me).* 2 [VP6A] please (one's sense of humour, etc): *The story ~d her fancy. I* *was ~d to death/~d pink,* (colloq, very amused and delighted) *at the news. They ~d his vanity by praising his work to the skies.* **3** [VP2A,6A] have, feel, cause, an itching or tingling sensation: *Pepper ~s if it gets into the nose. My nose ~s. It ~d my nose.* **tick·ler** /ˈtɪklə(r)/ *n* (esp) puzzling question or situation. **tick·lish** /ˈtɪklɪʃ/ *adj* **1** (of a person) easily made to laugh or wriggle when ~d. **2** (of a problem, piece of work, etc) needing delicate care or attention: *a ticklish question; in a ticklish situation.*

ti·dal /ˈtaɪdl/ *adj* of a tide or tides: *a ~ river/estuary/harbour,* in which the tide rises and falls. **a ˈ~ wave,** (pop use) great ocean wave, often destructive of life and property, e g one that is (thought to be) caused by an earthquake; (fig) great wave of popular feeling (enthusiasm, indignation, etc).

tid·dler /ˈtɪdlə(r)/ *n* (colloq) **1** very small fish. **2** young small child. **3** (GB) (colloq) $\frac{1}{2}$p coin.

tid·bit /ˈtɪdbɪt/ *n* = **titbit.**

tid·dley /ˈtɪdl̩ɪ/ *adj* (colloq) **1** small; negligible. **2** tipsy; slightly drunk.

tid·dly·winks /ˈtɪdlɪwɪŋks/ *n* [U] game in which players try to make small discs or counters jump into a tray or cup in the centre of a table by pressing them on the edge with a larger disc.

tide /taɪd/ *n* **1** [C,U] regular rise and fall in the level of the sea, caused by the attraction of the moon: *at high/low ~; washed up by the ~(s); spring* (= maximum) *and neap* (= minimum) *~s.* **ˈ~·mark** *n* highest point reached by a ~ on a beach. **ˈ~·way** *n* channel where ~s run; ebb or flow in such a channel. **2** [C] flow or tendency (of public opinion, feeling, etc): *We must not ignore the rising ~ of public discontent. The Socialists hoped for a turn of the ~,* that public opinion might turn in their favour. **3** (old use) season (now only in compounds, as *ˈEaster~, ˈeven~, ˈWhitsun~*) □ *vt* [VP15B] **~ *sb over (sth),*** get over: help him to get through or survive (a period of difficulty, etc): *He sold his car to ~ over his period of unemployment,* to provide money for his needs. *She needs more coal to ~ her over the winter. Will £5 ~ you over until you get your wages?*

tid·ings /ˈtaɪdɪŋz/ *n pl* (now liter; used with *sing* or *pl v*) news: *The ~ came too late. Have you heard the glad ~?*

tidy /ˈtaɪdɪ/ *adj* (-ier, -iest) **1** arranged neatly and in order; having the habit of placing and keeping everything in its right place: *a ~ room/desk; a ~ boy; ~ habits.* **2** (colloq) considerable; fairly large (esp of money): *a ~ sum of money; cost a ~ penny,* quite a lot of money. □ *n* (*pl* -dies) receptacle for odds and ends: *a ˈhair-~,* e g on a dressing-table for hair from a hair-brush; *a ˈsink-~,* for bits of kitchen waste. □ *vt,vi* [VP6A,15B, 2A,C] **~ *(up),*** make ~: *I must ~ myself,* make myself look ~. *You'd better ~ up (the room) before the guests arrive.* **ti·dily** /ˈtaɪdəlɪ/ *adv* **ti·di·ness** *n*

tie[1] /taɪ/ *n* [C] **1** sth used for fastening; rod or beam holding parts of a structure together; (US) railway sleeper, ⇨ *sleeper*(2) at **sleep**[2]; (fig) sth that holds people together: *the ties of friendship; family ties; ties of blood.* **2** sth that takes up one's attention and limits one's freedom of action: *Mothers often find their small children a tie.* **3** equal score in a game, etc: *The game ended in a tie, 2—2. The tie will be played off* (= will be replayed) *on Saturday.* **4** (music) curved line joining two notes of the same pitch that are to be played or sung as one. ⇨ the illus at **notation. 5** = **necktie.**

tie[2] /taɪ/ *vt,vi* (*pres part* **tying,** *pt,pp* **tied**) **1** [VP6A,15A,B] fasten or bind (with string, rope, wire, etc): *tie a man's feet together; tie up a parcel; tie a branch down; tie a dog to the street railings.* **2** [VP6A,15B] ***tie sth (on),*** fasten by means of the strings, etc of: *tie an apron (on); tie on a label.* Hence, **ˈtie-on,** *attrib adj*: *a tie-on label.* **3** [VP6A,15A] arrange (a ribbon, etc) in the form of a bow or knot: *tie one's shoe-laces; tie a ribbon/scarf; tie the ribbon in(to) a bow.* **4** [VP6A,15A] make by tying: *tie a knot in a piece of string.* **5** [VP2A] be fastened: *Does this sash tie in front or at the back?* ***tie sb down,*** restrict sb's freedom: *He's not in a hurry to get married; he doesn't want to get tied down. Young children do tie a woman down, don't they?* ***tie sb down to sth,*** restrict sb to (the terms of a contract, etc). ***tie oneself down to sth,*** accept limits to one's freedom of action. ***tie (sth) in with sth,*** link, be linked, with: *Doesn't this tie in with what we were told last week?* Aren't the two things linked, connected? ***tie sth up,*** **(a)** invest (capital) so that it is not easily available, e g because of legal restrictions. **(b)** ensure that (property, e g land, buildings) can be used, sold, etc only under certain (usu legal) conditions. ***be/get tied up (with sth/sb),*** **(a)** be, get, involved (with sth/sb) so that one has no time for other things: *I'm afraid I can't help you now—I'm too tied up with other things.* **(b)** be, become, linked with: *Isn't this company tied up with Vickers-Armstrong?* Hence, **ˈtie-up** *n* link; merger; partnership. **tied house,** public-house controlled by a brewery. ⇨ free[1](3). **6** [VP2A,3A] ***tie (with) (for),*** (of players, teams, candidates in a competitive examination) make the same score (as); equal in points, marks, etc: *They tied for first place (in the examination). We tied with Wrexham in the last game.*

tier /tɪə(r)/ *n* row (esp of seats), shelf, etc esp one of a number parallel to and rising one above another, e g in a theatre or stadium: *a first/second ~ box,* in a theatre.

tiff /tɪf/ *n* slight quarrel (between friends or acquaintances): *Alice has had a ~ with her boyfriend.*

tif·fin /ˈtɪfɪn/ *n* (in the East) midday meal.

ti·ger /ˈtaɪgə(r)/ *n* large, fierce animal of the cat family, yellow-skinned with black stripes, found in Asia (and also called the jaguar and puma). ⇨ the illus at **cat.** **ˈ~-lily** *n* garden lily with orange flowers spotted with black or purple. **~·ish** /-ɪʃ/ *adj* like, cruel as, a ~. **ti·gress** /ˈtaɪgrəs/ *n* female ~.

tight /taɪt/ *adj* **1** fastened, fixed, fitting, held, closely: *a ~ knot. I can't get the cork out of the bottle—It's too ~. The drawer is so ~ that I can't open it. These shoes are so ~ that they hurt.* **ˌ~-ˈlipped** *adj* keeping the lips firmly together; saying little or nothing; (fig) grim-looking. **2** closely or firmly put together; put together in a small space: *a ~ joint;* (esp in compounds) made so that sth cannot get out or in: *ˌwater-/ˈair-ˈ~.* **3** packed so as to occupy the smallest possible space or to get in as much as possible: *Make sure that the bags are filled/packed ~.* **4** (colloq) having had too much alcoholic drink: *He gets ~ every pay-day.* **5** fully stretched: *a ~ rope.* **ˈ~-rope** *n* one on which acrobats perform feats. **6** produced by pressure; causing difficulty. ***in a ~ corner/spot,*** (usu fig) in a difficult or dangerous situation. ***a ~ schedule,*** one that it is difficult to keep to. ***a ~ squeeze,*** condition of being uncomfortably crowded: *We got everyone into the bus, but it was a ~ squeeze.* **7** (of money) not easily obtainable, e g on loan from banks: *Money is ~. The money-market is ~,* It is possible to borrow money only by paying a high rate of interest. **8** **~-ˋfisted,** stingy; miserly. **ˈ~-ˋlaced** *adj* = strait-laced. ⇨ **strait**[1]. **ˋ~-wad** /-wɒd/ *n* (sl) stingy person. □ *adv* = ~ly: *squeeze/hold sth ~.* ***sit ~,*** ⇨ **sit(1)**. **~·ly** *adv* **~·ness** *n* **~en** /ˋtɑɪtn/ *vt,vi* [VP6A,15B,2A,C] make or become ~(er): *~en (up) the screws; ~en the ropes of the tent. It needs ~ening up.* ***~en one's belt,*** (hum) go without food (when there is little or none available); become frugal.

tights /tɑɪts/ *n pl* **1** close-fitting garment covering the hips, legs and feet, as worn by girls and women. **2** skin-tight garment covering the legs and body, worn by acrobats, ballet-dancers, etc.

tike /tɑɪk/ *n* = **tyke**.

tilde *n* **1** /ˋtɪldə/ the mark (˜) placed over Spanish *n* when it is pronounced *ny* /nj/ (as in *cañon*). **2** /tɪld/ the mark (~) as used in this dictionary to indicate the use of the headword in entry.

tile /tɑɪl/ *n* (usu square or oblong) plate of baked clay for covering roofs, walls, etc, often, e g Dutch, Italian and Portuguese ~s, painted with designs or pictures. ***be (out) on the ~s,*** (sl) on a debauch. ***have a ~ loose,*** (sl) be rather mad. □ *vt* [VP6A] cover (a roof, etc) with ~s.

till[1] /tɪl/ (also **until** /ʌnˋtɪl/. The choice between *till* and *until* is chiefly a matter of usage and balance. *Until* is often preferred when its clause or phrase comes first.) *conj* up to the time when: *Go straight on until you come to the post-office and then turn left. Let's wait ~ the rain stops. Until you told me, I had heard nothing of what happened. She won't go away ~ you promise to help her.* □ *prep* up to the time when; up to; down to: *I shall wait ~ ten o'clock/next Monday, etc. Good-bye ~ tomorrow. Until now I knew/Until then I had known nothing about it. He works from morning ~ night, day after day. He lived at home until soon after his father's death. You had better wait ~ he gets back.*

till[2] /tɪl/ *n* money-drawer in a shop; cash-register: *The boy was caught with his hand in the ~,* caught stealing.

till[3] /tɪl/ *vt* [VP6A] cultivate (land). **~·age** /ˋtɪlɪdʒ/ *n* [U] act or process of ~ing; ~ed land. **~er** *n* person who ~s.

tiller /ˋtɪlə(r)/ *n* lever (like a long handle) used to turn the rudder of a small boat.

tilt /tɪlt/ *vt,vi* **1** [VP6A,15A,B,2A,C] (cause to) come into a sloping position (as by lifting one end); tip: *Don't ~ the table. T~ the barrel (up) to empty it. The table ~ed (over) and the plates slid off it to the floor.* **2** [VP2A,3A] ***~ (at),*** (in former times, of men on horseback) ride (at another) with a lance; (fig) attack in speech or writing: *The reformer ~ed at gambling and other abuses.* ***~ at windmills,*** fight imaginary enemies (from the story of Don Quixote). □ *n* [C] **1** ~ing; sloping position. **2** act of ~ing with a lance: *have a ~ at sb,* (fig) attack him (in a friendly sort of way) in a debate, etc. ***(at) full ~,*** at great speed; with great force: *The boy ran full ~ into me.* **ˋ~-yard** *n* place where ~ing was practised in former times.

tilth /tɪlθ/ *n* depth of soil affected by cultivation; tilled land: *rake a seed-bed to a good ~,* until there is a depth of fine, crumbly soil.

tim·ber /ˋtɪmbə(r)/ *n* **1** [U] wood prepared for use in building, etc: *ˋ~-merchants; a ˋ~-yard,* place where ~ is stored, bought and sold, etc; *dressed ~,* sawn, shaped and planed ready for use. **2** [U] growing trees (sometimes *standing ~*) thought of as containing wood suitable for building, carpentry, etc: *cut down/fell ~; put a hundred acres of land under ~,* plant with trees for ~. *The fire destroyed thousands of acres of ~.* **3** [C] large piece of shaped wood, beam, forming a support (e g in a roof or a ship). **4** [U] (in fox-hunting) wooden fences and gates. **5** [U] person's qualities (as fitting him for a position): *a man of real ministerial ~,* likely to make a good minister. **~ed** /ˋtɪmbəd/ *adj* (of buildings) made of ~ or with a framework of ~.

timbre /tæ̃br *with unsyllabic* r *US:* ˋtɪmbər/ *n* characteristic quality of sound produced by a particular voice or instrument.

tim·brel /ˋtɪmbrəl/ *n* tambourine.

time[1] /tɑɪm/ *n* **1** [U] all the days of the past, present and future: *past, present and future ~. The world exists in space and ~.* **2** [U] the passing of all the days, months and years, taken as a whole (sometimes personified as *(old) Father T~*): *T~ will show who is right. T~ waits for no man,* (prov). **3** [U] (also with *indef art* and *adj*) portion or measure of ~: *Six o'clock is a point of ~; six hours is a period of ~. What a (long) ~ you have been! That will take ~,* cannot be done soon or quickly. *I have no/not much ~ for sport. We have no ~ to lose,* We must hurry. *He spent a lot of ~ (in) getting ready. Take your ~ over it,* Don't hurry. *There is no ~ to lose,* haste is necessary. *We were pressed for ~,* had not enough ~, were forced to hurry. *It will take me all my ~ to do this,* (colloq) will tax my powers, require all my abilities. ***behind ~,*** **(a)** late: *The train is ten minutes behind ~.* **(b)** behindhand: *He's always behind ~ with his payments.* ***for the ~ being,*** ⇨ **be**[3]**(4)**. ***on ~,*** up to ~, not late, punctual(ly): *The train is/came in on ~.* ***in no ~,*** very soon; very quickly. ***~ immemorial, ~ out of mind,*** a period of ~ longer than any one can remember. ***gain ~,*** obtain extra ~ by making excuses, deliberately using slow methods, etc. ***all the ~,*** **(a)** during the whole of the ~ in question: *I looked all over the house for that letter, and it was in my pocket all the ~,* while I was searching. **(b)** at all times; first and last: *He's a business man all the ~,* has no other interests in life. ***half the ~,*** **(a)** as in: *He did the work in four hours; I could have done it in half the ~,* in two hours. **(b)** for long periods of ~; (loosely) very often; nearly always: *He says he works hard, but he's day-dreaming half the ~.* **4** [U] point of ~ stated in hours and minutes of the day: *What ~ is it? What is the ~? The child can now tell the ~.* **5** [U] ~ measured in units (years, months, hours, etc): *The winner's ~ was 11 seconds. He ran the mile in record ~,* in a period of ~ shorter than that of any previous runner. ***keep good/bad ~,*** (of a clock or watch) show the hour (in)correctly. ***the ~ of day,*** the hour as shown by a clock. ***pass the ~ of day***

(*with...*), exchange a greeting, say 'Good morning!', etc. **6** [C,U] point or period of ~ associated with, or available or suitable for, a certain event, purpose, etc: *at the ~ you're speaking of; by the ~ we reached home; last ~ I was there; every ~ I looked at her. It is 'lunch-~. There is a ~ for everything. Now's your ~* (= opportunity). *It's ~ I was going/~ for me to go,* I ought to leave now. *It's ~ somebody taught you to behave yourself. I must bide my ~,* be patient, wait for a suitable ~. *T~ is up,* The ~ allowed for something is ended. ***(work, etc) against ~,*** with the greatest speed (because only a limited amount of ~ is available). the same ~, **(a)** together, as *to laugh and cry at the same ~.* **(b)** notwithstanding; nevertheless. ***from ~ to ~, at ~s,*** occasionally; now and then. ***at all ~s,*** always. ***at your/his, etc ~ of life,*** at your/his, etc age. ***My/His, etc ~ is drawing near,*** I am/He is, etc near a ~ of crisis, of some important happening, etc (according to the context). ***in ~,*** **(a)** not late; early enough: *We were in ~ for the train/to catch the train. We arrived in good ~,* with ~ to spare. **(b)** sooner or later; after the passing of an indefinite period of ~: *You will learn how to do it in ~.* ***in the nick of ~,*** ⇨ nick[1](2). ***near her ~,*** (of a woman) soon to give birth to a child. ***do ~,*** (colloq) undergo a period of imprisonment. ***serve one's ~,*** **(a)** work as an apprentice for an agreed number of years: *The boy has served half his ~.* **(b)** = do ~. **7** [C] (Cf *twice*) occasion: *this/that/next/another ~; the ~ before last; for the first/last ~. He failed five ~s. I've told you a dozen ~s,* (= very often, repeatedly) *not to do that.* ***at 'one ~,*** during a period of past ~, known but not mentioned: *At one ~ I used to go mountain-climbing every summer.* ***at other ~s,*** on other occasions. ***~ and again; ~s without number,*** again and again; repeatedly. ***many a ~; many ~s,*** often; on many occasions. ***one/two, etc at a ~,*** one/two, etc on each occasion; separately: *Hand them to me two at a ~.* **8** (*pl*) used to indicate multiplication (but note that *twice* is used instead of *two ~s*). *Three ~s five is/are fifteen,* 3 × 5 = 15. *Yours is ten ~s the size of mine/ten ~s as large as mine.* **9** [C] (often *pl*) period of ~, more or less definite, associated with certain events, circumstances, persons, etc: *in Stuart ~s,* when the Stuart kings ruled; *in the ~(s) of the Stuarts; in ancient/prehistoric ~s; the good old ~s,* (more usu *days*) the past, viewed as preferable to the present. *Mr X was head of the school in my ~,* when I was there. *The house is old but it will last my ~,* will serve me for the rest of my life. **10** [C] (often *pl*) the conditions of life, the circumstances, etc of a period characterized by certain qualities, etc: *We lived through terrible ~s during the war years. T~s are good/bad,* (often meaning that it is easy/difficult to make a living). ***ahead of one's ~, born before one's ~,*** having ideas too much in advance of, too enlightened for, the period in which one lives. ***at the 'best of ~s,*** even when conditions are good: *He's an irritating fellow even at the best of ~s.* ***behind the ~s,*** antiquated; having out-of-date ideas, etc. ***have a good ~,*** enjoy oneself. ***have the ~ of one's life,*** (colloq) experience a period of exceptional happiness or enjoyment. **11** [U] **Greenwich/local/summer/standard ~,** ⇨ these words. **12** (music) measurement depending upon the number of rhythmic beats in successive bars of a piece of music: *'common ~,* two or four beats in a bar; *'waltz ~,* for dancing; also, the rate (or *tempo*) at which a piece of music is to be played. ***in/out of ~,*** in/not in accordance with the time of the music. ***in double-quick ~,*** very quickly. ***beat ~,*** show the ~ (*tempo,* etc) by movements made with the hand or a stick (*baton*). ***keep ~,*** sing or dance in ~. **13** (compounds) **'~-ball** *n* one which slides down a staff (at an observatory to show a fixed ~, usu noon or 1 p m). **'~-bomb** *n* designed to explode at some ~ after being dropped, placed in position, etc. **'~-card/-sheet** *n* one for a record of workmen's hours of work. **'~-expired** *adj* (of soldiers and sailors) having completed the period of service. **'~-exposure** *n* exposure of a photographic film for a ~ longer than half a second (contrasted with a 'snap'). **'~-fuse** *n* one that has been made to burn for a given ~, e g to explode a bomb. **'~-honoured** (US = **-honored**) *adj* respected because of its antiquity. **'~·keeper** *n* **(a)** one who, or that which, records the ~ spent by workers at their work. **(b)** (of a watch, etc) one that keeps ~ well, etc; *a good/bad ~keeper.* **'~-lag** *n* interval of ~ between two connected phenomena or events (e g between a flash of lightning and the thunder), or between two or more places on the earth. **'~-limit** *n* limited period of ~; last moment of this: *set a ~-limit for the completion of a job.* **'~·piece** *n* clock. **'~-saving** *adj* serving to save ~: *a ~-saving idea.* **'~-server** *n* one who acts, not according to principles, but according to self-interest, esp one who is always trying to please powerful people. **'~-serving** *adj* behaving as a ~-server: *~-serving politicians.* **'~-signal** *n* signal (e g a series of pips) for indicating the ~ (in a radio programme). **'~-switch** *n* switch set to operate at a desired ~ (e g to turn a heating system on or off). **'~·table** *n* list showing the days or hours at which events will take place, work will be done, etc, esp a list showing the ~s at which trains, ships, etc will arive and depart. **'~-work** *n* [U] work (esp manual work) paid for by the hour or day (contrasted with *piece-work*).

time[2] /taɪm/ *vt* **1** [VP6A,15A] choose the time or moment for; arrange the time of: *He ~d his journey so that he arrived before dark. The remark was well/ill ~d,* made at a suitable/an unsuitable moment. **2** [VP6A] measure the time taken by or for (a race, runner, an action or event). **3** [VP6A] regulate: *~ one's steps* (in dancing) *to the music; ~ the speed of a machine.* **tim·ing** *n* act of determining or regulating the (order of) occurrence of an action, event, etc to achieve the desired results: *a 'timing device;* (theatre) speed of dialogue/cues, etc: *The timing of last night's performance was excellent.* **~·less** *adj* (liter) unending; not to be thought of as having duration.

time·ly /'taɪmlɪ/ *adj* (**-ier, -iest**) occurring at just the right time; opportune. **time·li·ness** *n* [U].

timid /'tɪmɪd/ *adj* easily frightened; shy: *That fellow is as ~ as a rabbit.* **~·ly** *adv* **~·ity** /tɪ'mɪdətɪ/, **~·ness** *nn* [U].

tim·or·ous /'tɪmərəs/ *adj* timid. **~·ly** *adv*

tim·othy /'tɪməθɪ/ *n* [U] **'~ (grass),** grass grown as fodder for cattle.

tim·pani /'tɪmpənɪ/ *n pl* set of kettledrums (e g of an orchestra). ⇨ the illus at percussion. **tim·pan·ist** /'tɪmpənɪst/ *n* player of a kettledrum.

tin /tɪn/ *n* **1** [U] soft, white metal (symbol **Sn**) used in alloys and for coating iron sheets. **ˈtin·foil** *n* tin in the form of foil (thin pliable sheets), used for wrapping and packing tobacco, confectionery, etc. ***a (little) tin god,*** (colloq) sth or sb mistakenly given great veneration or worship. ***a tin hat,*** (sl) steel helmet (as worn by soldiers in modern times). **ˈtin-plate** *n* [U] sheet iron coated with tin (used in the canning industry). **ˈtinsmith** *n* worker in tin-plate. **ˈtin·tack** *n* short nail of tinned iron. **2** [C] (in US and now often in GB *can*) tin-plated container for food, etc esp one made so as to be airtight: *a tin of sardines/oil.* Cf *a can of beer.* **ˈtin-opener** *n* device for opening tins. **3** [U] (sl) money. □ *vt* (-nn-) [VP6A] **1** put a coating of tin on. **2** (= *can*) pack (food, tobacco, etc) in tins(2): *tinned peaches.* **tinny** *adj* of or like tin (e g in sound): *a tinny piano.*

tinc·ture /ˈtɪŋktʃə(r)/ *n* **1** medical substance dissolved in alcohol: *~ of iodine/quinine.* **2** (with *indef art*) slight flavour or suggestion (*of*). □ *vt* give a ~(2) of (sth) to: *views ~d with heresy.*

tin·der /ˈtɪndə(r)/ *n* [U] material (e g dry, scorched linen, etc) that easily catches fire from a spark. **ˈ~-box** *n* box containing ~, flint and steel (as used in former times for kindling fire).

tine /taɪn/ *n* point, prong (e g of a fork, harrow, etc); branch of a deer's antler. ⇨ the illus at **large**. **-tined** *suff* (in compounds) having the number or kind of ~s indicated: *a three-~d hayfork.*

ting /tɪŋ/ *vi, vt, n* (cause to make, make, a) clear, ringing sound.

tinge /tɪndʒ/ *vt* [VP6A,14] ***~ sth (with),*** **1** colour slightly (with red, etc). **2** (esp in *pp*) affect slightly: *admiration ~d with envy.* □ *n* slight colouring or mixture (*of*): *There was a ~ of sadness in her voice/of irony in his remark.*

tingle /ˈtɪŋgl/ *vi* [VP2A,C] have a pricking or stinging feeling in the skin; (fig) be stirred: *His cheek ~d from the slap she had given him. His fingers ~d with the cold. The children were tingling with excitement.* □ *n* tingling feeling: *have a ~ in one's finger-tips.*

tin·ker /ˈtɪŋkə(r)/ *n* **1** tin-plate worker who travels from place to place and repairs kettles, pans, etc. ***not care/give a ~'s cuss/damn,*** not care in the least. **2** ~ing: *have an hour's ~ at the radio set,* try to mend it. □ *vi* [VP2A,C,3A] work in an amateurish or inexpert way (at): *~ (away) at a broken machine. Please don't ~ with my car engine.*

tinkle /ˈtɪŋkl/ *vi, vt* [VP2A,C,6A] (cause to) make a succession of light, ringing sounds, e g of a small bell. □ *n* (*sing*) such sounds: *the ~ of a bell/of falling glass/of ice being stirred round in a glass.*

tinny /ˈtɪnɪ/ *adj* ⇨ **tin**.

tin pan alley /ˈtɪn pæn ˈælɪ/ *n* composers, players and publishers of popular music (as a group).

tin·sel /ˈtɪnsl/ *n* [U] **1** glittering metallic substance made in sheets, strips and threads, used for ornament: *trim a Christmas tree/a dress with ~.* **2** superficial brilliance; cheap, showy brilliance. **~ly** /-slɪ/ *adj* trimmed with, suggesting, ~. □ *vt* (-ll-, US also -l-) trim with ~.

tint /tɪnt/ *n* (esp pale or delicate) shade or variety of colour: *~s of green in the sky at dawn; an artist who excels at ˈflesh-~s.* □ *vt* [VP6A,22] give a ~ to; put a ~ on; tinge.

tin·tin·nabu·la·tion /ˌtɪntɪˌnæbjʊˈleɪʃn/ *n* tinkling of bells.

tiny /ˈtaɪnɪ/ *adj* (-ier, -iest) very small.

tip[1] /tɪp/ *n* [C] **1** pointed or thin end of sth: *the tips of one's fingers/the ˈfinger-tips; the tip of one's nose; asparagus tips. The bird measured 12 centimetres from tip to tip,* from the tip of one wing to the tip of the other. ***(have sth) on the tip of one's tongue,*** (be) just going to say (it). **ˈtip·toe** *adv* ***on tiptoe,*** on the tips of one's toes: *be/wait on tiptoe with excitement.* □ *vi* [VP2A,C] walk on tiptoe: *She tiptoed to the bedside of the sleeping child.* **ˌtip-ˈtop** *adj, adv* (colloq) first-rate: *a tip-top hotel/dinner. You've done tip-top.* **2** small piece put at the end of sth: *cigarettes with filter-tips.* □ *vt* (-pp-) supply with a tip(2): *filter-tipped cigarettes.*

tip[2] /tɪp/ *vt, vi* (-pp-) **1** [VP6A,15A,B,2A,C] ***tip (sth) up,*** (cause to) rise, lean or tilt on one side or at one end: *The table tipped up. Tip the barrel up and empty it.* ***tip sth (over),*** (cause to) overbalance or overturn: *Careful! You'll tip the canoe over.* ***tip the scale (at),*** **(a)** be just enough to cause one scale or pan (of a balance) to go lower than the other; (fig) be the deciding factor (for or against). **(b)** weigh: *He tipped the scale at 140 lb.* **tip-up seat,** seat with a hinge, e g the kind used in cinemas, etc to allow people to pass freely. **2** [VP15A,B] ***tip sth out (of sth)/into sth,*** empty (the contents of sth) out of/into: *No rubbish to be tipped here,* a warning put up in open spaces. *She tipped the slops out of the bucket into the sink. He was tipped out of the cart into the ditch. Which is better, to incinerate the rubbish from our towns or to tip it into disused quarries?* □ *n* (not US) place where rubbish may be tipped(2): *the municipal ˈrefuse tip;* hill of waste material from a coalmine, etc; (colloq) untidy place: *They live in a tip.*

tip[3] /tɪp/ *vt* (-pp-) [VP6A] **1** touch or strike lightly: *His bat just tipped the ball. He tipped his hat to the squire,* touched it (as an informal greeting, instead of raising it). **ˌtip-and-ˈrun** *adj* (of a raid by robbers, etc) in which there is a brief attack followed by a quick escape. **2** [VP6A,12C] give a tip to (1,2 below): *tip the porter 20p.* ***tip sb off,*** (colloq) give him a warning or a hint. Hence, **ˈtip-off** *n* hint or warning: *give the police a tip-off.* ***tip sb the wink,*** (colloq) give sb a sly or secret warning. ***tip the winner,*** name the winner (usu of a horse-race) before the event takes place. □ *n* [C] **1** gift of money to a porter, waiter, servant, etc for personal services (or from an uncle to a schoolboy nephew, etc): *leave a tip under/on one's plate,* e g at a restaurant. **2** piece of advice on how to do sth, esp information about the probable winner of a horse-race, on the future value of shares (on the Stock Exchange, etc): *a tip for the Derby. If you take my tip* (= advice) *you'll make a lot of money.* **3** light blow; tap.

tip·pet /ˈtɪpɪt/ *n* (word now seldom used for a) scarf or long fur worn by a woman round the neck and shoulders with the ends hanging down to the waist in front; similar article of dress worn by judges, clergy, etc. ⇨ the illus at **vestment**.

tipple /ˈtɪpl/ *vi, vt* **1** [VP2A] be in the habit of drinking (too much) alcoholic liquor. **2** [VP6A] drink (wine, spirits, etc). □ *n* [U] alcoholic drink; (hum) any kind of drink: *John's favourite ~ is coca-cola; mine is sherry.* **tip·pler** *n*

tip·staff /ˈtɪpstɑf *US:* -stæf/ *n* sheriff's officer.

tip·ster /ˈtɪpstə(r)/ *n* person who gives tips about races. ⇨ **tip**[3]**(2)**.

tipsy /ˈtɪpsɪ/ *adj* (colloq) slightly drunk.

tip·toe /ˈtɪptəʊ/ *adv, vt, vi* ⇨ tip[1].

ti·rade /taɪˈreɪd/ *n* long, angry or scolding speech.

tire[1] /taɪə(r)/ *n* (usu US spelling of) tyre.

tire[2] /ˈtaɪə(r)/ *vt,vi* [VP6A,15B,2A,3A] make or become weary, in need of rest or uninterested: *The long walk ~d the child/~d him out/made him ~d. The long lecture ~d the audience. She never ~s of talking about her clever son.* ***be ~d of,*** have had enough of, be exhausted with: *be ~d of boiled eggs,* have had too many of them, or too often. **tired** /ˈtaɪəd/ *adj* weary in body or mind: *He was a ~d man when he got back from the long climb.* ***~d out,*** completely exhausted. **tired·ness** *n* **~·less** *adj* **1** not easily ~d: *a ~less worker.* **2** ceaseless; continuing a long time: *~less energy.* **~·less·ly** *adv* ˈ**~·some** /-səm/ *adj* troublesome; tedious.

tire[3] /taɪə(r)/ *vt* (archaic) = attire. ˈ**~-woman** *n* (archaic) lady's maid. ˈ**tiring-room** *n* dressing-room for actors in a theatre.

tiro, tyro /ˈtaɪərəʊ/ *n* (*pl* -ros /-rəʊz/) beginner; person with little experience.

tis·sue /ˈtɪʃu/ *n* **1** [C,U] (any kind of) woven fabric. **2** [C,U] mass of cells and cell-products in an animal body: *ˈmuscular/conˈnective ~.* **3** ˈ**~ paper,** thin, soft paper for wrapping things, protecting delicate articles, etc; *ˈtoilet ~,* soft paper for use in the W C; *ˈface ~s,* for use in wiping off lip-stick, face-cream, etc. **4** [C] (fig) web or network; series: *a ~ of lies.*

tit[1] /tɪt/ *n* kinds of small bird: *titmouse; titlark; tomtit; long-tailed tit,* etc. ⇨ the illus at bird.

tit[2] /tɪt/ *n* ***tit for tat,*** blow for blow.

tit[3] /tɪt/ *n* ⚠ (vulg sl) teat; nipple; woman's breast.

Ti·tan /ˈtaɪtn/ *n* **1** (in Greek legend) one of a family of giants who once ruled the world. **2** (*titan*) person of super-human size, strength, intellect, etc. **ti·tanic** /taɪˈtænɪk/ *adj* immense.

ti·ta·nium /taɪˈteɪnɪəm/ *n* [U] dark-grey metallic element (symbol **Ti**) used in alloys.

tit·bit /ˈtɪtbɪt/ *n* [C] choice and attractive bit (*of* food, news, gossip, etc).

tit·fer /ˈtɪtfə(r)/ *n* (Cockney rhyming sl—tit for tat) hat.

tithe /taɪð/ *n* [C] **1** tenth part of farm produce formerly given by ancient custom for the support of (Church of England) parish priests. ˈ**~-barn** *n* barn in which ~s were stored. **2** (rhet) tenth part.

tit·il·late /ˈtɪtɪleɪt *US:* ˈtɪtḷeɪt/ *vt* [VP6A] stimulate or excite pleasantly. **tit·il·la·tion** /ˈtɪtɪˈleɪʃn/ *n*

titi·vate (also **tit·ti-**) /ˈtɪtɪveɪt/ *vt,vi* [VP6A,2A] (colloq) adorn; make smart: *She was titivating (herself) before the mirror.*

title /ˈtaɪtl/ *n* **1** [C] name of a book, poem, picture, etc. ˈ**~-page** *n* page at the front of a book giving the ~, the author's name, etc. ˈ**~-role** *n* part in a play that gives the play its name: *a performance of 'Othello' with Olivier in the ~-role,* with Olivier as Othello. **2** [C] word used to show a person's rank, occupation, status, etc, e g Lord, Prince, Professor, Dr, Miss, Esquire. **3** [C,U] ***~ to sth/ to do sth,*** (legal) right or claim, esp right to the possession of a position, property: *What ~ has he to the throne? Has he any ~ to the land?* ˈ**~-deed** *n* document proving a ~ to property. **4** ˈ**credit ~s,** (or *credits*), names of persons (e g script-writers, producers, camera men) responsible for a cinema film or T V production, shown at the beginning or end of the film, etc. **titled** /ˈtaɪtld/ *adj* having a ~ of nobility: *a ~d lady,* e g a duchess.

tit·mouse /ˈtɪtmaʊs/ *n* (*pl* -mice /-maɪs/) ⇨ **tit**[1].

tit·ter /ˈtɪtə(r)/ *vt* [VP2A], *n* (give a) silly, half-suppressed little laugh.

tittle /ˈtɪtl/ *n* ***not one jot or ~,*** not a particle; not even a very little bit. **tittle-tattle** /ˈtɪtl tætl/ *n, vi* gossip.

titu·lar /ˈtɪtjʊlə(r) *US:* -tʃʊ-/ *adj* **1** held by virtue of a title: *~ possessions.* **2** existing in name but not having authority or duties: *the ~ ruler; ~ sovereignty.*

tizzy /ˈtɪzɪ/ *n* (*pl* -zies) ***be in a ~,*** (colloq) in a nervous state.

T-junction /ˈti dʒʌŋkʃn/ *n* one where two roads, wires, pipes, etc meet to form a T.

TNT /ˈti en ˈti/ *n* (= *tri*nitro*t*oluene) powerful explosive.

to /*usual form before consonants:* tə *before vowels and strong-form:* tu/ *prep* **1** in the direction of; towards: *walk to work; go to the grocer's; fall to the ground; off to London; point to sth; hold sth (up) to the light; on the way to the station; twenty miles to Dover; sitting with his feet to the fire; turn to the right; going from town to town/place to place, etc. Scotland is to the north of England.* **2** (fig uses) towards (a condition, quality, etc): *a tendency to laziness; slow to anger; all to no purpose.* **3** (introducing the *indirect object,* as in VP13A): *To whom did you give it? Who did you give it to? The man I gave it to has left.* **4** as far as: *from beginning to end; from first to last; faithful to the end/last; fight to the last gasp; wet to the skin; frozen to the marrow; count (up) to ten; shades of colour from red to violet; moved to tears by the sad story.* **5** before: *a quarter to six; ten to two.* ⇨ past. **6** until: *from Saturday to Monday; from morning to night. I didn't stay to the end of the meeting. He was conscious to the last.* **7** (indicating comparison, ratio, reference): *He's quite rich now to what he used to be. It's nothing to what it might be. I prefer walking to climbing. We won by six goals to three. The picture is true to life/ nature. This is inferior/superior to that. Draw it to scale.* □ *part* (marking the *infin*) **1** (⇨ VP7,17; used after many *vv* but not after *can, do, may, must, shall, will*): *He wants to go. He wants me to go.* **2** (with *adv* functions, purpose, result, outcome): *They came (in order) to help me. He lived to be ninety. We make our goods to last,* i e so that they will last. **3** (limiting the meanings of *adjj* and *advv*): *I'm ready to help. The book is easy to understand. He's old enough to go to school. She's too young to marry. This coffee's too hot to drink,* to be drunk. **4** (indicating a subsequent fact; ⇨ VP4B): *The good old days have gone never to return,* and will never return. *He awoke to find himself* (= and found himself) *in a strange room.* **5** (with an *adjectival* function); *John was the first to arrive,* who arrived first. **6** (used with an *infin* as a *n*): *It is wrong to steal. To err is human, to forgive divine.* **7** (as a substitute for the *infin*): *We didn't want to go but we had to. I intended to go, but forgot to. He often does things you wouldn't expect him to.* □ *adv part* /tu *no weak form*/ **1** to or in the usual or required position, esp to a closed or almost closed position: *Push the door to. Leave the door to,* almost closed. **2** ***to and fro,*** ⇨ fro. **3** ⇨ come(15), bring(6), and fall[2](14).

toad /təʊd/ *n* frog-like animal that lives on land

except when breeding. ⇨ the illus at amphibian. **ˈ~-in-the-ˈhole** *n* sausages baked in batter. **ˈ~-stool** *n* kinds of umbrella-shaped fungus, some of them poisonous. ⇨ the illus at fungi.

toady /ˈtəʊdɪ/ *n* obsequious flatterer. □ *vi* [VP2A, 3A] **~ *(to sb)*,** flatter in the hope of advantage or gain: *~ to the boss.*

toast[1] /təʊst/ *n* [U] (slice of) bread made brown and crisp by heating at a fire, etc: *a poached egg on ~; two slices of ~.* **ˈ~-rack** *n* for holding slices of dry ~. □ *vt, vi* [VP6A,2A] **1** make or become brown and crisp by heating. **ˈ~ing-fork** *n* fork with a long handle used for holding bread in front of a fire. **2** warm (oneself, one's toes, etc) before a fire. **~er** *n* device (usu electric) for ~ing bread.

toast[2] /təʊst/ *vt* [VP6A] wish happiness, success, etc to (sb or sth) while raising a glass of wine: *~ the bride and bridegroom.* □ *n* [C] act of ~ing; person, etc ~ed: *propose a ~ to the bridesmaids; drink a ~; respond/reply to the ~,* e g of the speeches made after a wedding to and by the bride and bridegroom. **ˈ~-master** *n* person who announces the ~s at a banquet at which there are distinguished guests.

to·bacco /təˈbækəʊ/ *n* [U] (plant having) leaves which are dried, cured and used for smoking (in pipes, cigars, cigarettes) or as snuff; (*pl*, for kinds of ~ leaf): *This is a mixture of the best ~s.* **~·nist** /təˈbækənɪst/ *n* dealer in ~.

to·bog·gan /təˈbɒgən/ *n* long, narrow sledge without runners for sporting purposes. □ *vi* [VP2A,C] go down a snow- or ice-covered slope on a ~.

tobogganing

toby-jug /ˈtəʊbɪ ˈdʒʌg/ *n* drinking-mug shaped like a man, wearing a three-cornered hat.

toc·cata /təˈkɑtə/ *n* (music) composition for a keyboard instrument (organ, piano, etc) in a free style, designed to show the performer's technique.

toc·sin /ˈtɒksɪn/ *n* [C] (bell rung to give a) signal of alarm (now chiefly fig).

to·day /təˈdeɪ/ *adv, n* **1** (on) this day: *T~ is Sunday. Have you seen ~'s newspaper? We're leaving ~ week/a week ~,* in one week's time. **2** (at) this present age or period: *the writers/the young people of ~.*

toddle /ˈtɒdl/ *vi* [VP2A,C] walk with short, uncertain steps as a baby does; (colloq) walk: *~ off/round to see a friend.* **tod·dler** /ˈtɒdlə(r)/ *n* baby who can ~.

toddy /ˈtɒdɪ/ *n* [C,U] (*pl* **-dies**) **1** (drink of) alcoholic spirits (esp whisky) and hot water. **2** fresh or fermented sap of some kinds of palm-trees.

to-do /tə ˈdu/ *n* ado; fuss; commotion: *What a ~!* What a lot of excitement and talk!

toe /təʊ/ *n* **1** each of the five divisions of the front part of the foot; ⇨ the illus at leg; similar part of an animal's foot: *turn one's toes in/out,* i e in walking. ***tread/step on sb's toes,*** (fig) offend his feelings or prejudices. ***from top to toe,*** from head to foot, completely. ***on one's toes,*** (fig) alert, ready for action. ***on tiptoes,*** ⇨ tip[1](1). **ˈtoe-cap** *n* outer covering of the toe of a shoe or boot. **ˈtoe-hold** *n* small, insecure foothold (e g when climbing a cliff). **ˈtoe-nail** *n* nail of the toe of a human being. **2** part of a sock, shoe, etc covering the toes. □ *vt* [VP6A] touch, reach, with the toes. ***toe the line,*** **(a)** stand with a toe on the starting-line ready for a race. **(b)** (fig) obey orders given to one as a member of a group or party.

toff /tɒf/ *n* (dated GB sl) well-dressed or distinguished-looking person.

toffee, toffy /ˈtɒfɪ *US:* ˈtɔfɪ/ *n* (*pl* -fees, -fies) (US = *taffy* /ˈtæfɪ/) [C,U] (piece of) hard, sticky sweet made by boiling sugar, butter, etc.

tog /tɒg/ *vt* (-gg-) [VP15B] ***tog oneself up/out (in),*** (colloq) put on smart clothes. **togs** *n pl* (colloq) clothes: *put on one's best togs.*

toga /ˈtəʊgə/ *n* loose flowing outer garment worn by men in ancient Rome.

to·gether /təˈgeðə(r)/ *adv* **1** in company: *They went for a walk ~. We are working ~. Are they living ~,* e g of a man and a woman—Are they living as husband and wife? ***~ with,*** as well as; in addition to; and also: *These new facts, ~ with the evidence you have already heard, prove the prisoner's innocence.* **2** so as to be in the same place, to be in contact, to be united: *Tie the ends ~. He nailed the boards ~ and made a crate. The angry teacher knocked the heads of the two boys ~. Put them ~ and see which is larger. The leader called his men ~.* ***put your/our, etc heads ~,*** consult with each other (to find a solution to sth, make plans, etc). **3** at the same time: *All his troubles seemed to come ~.* **4** without interruption; in continuous succession: *They sat talking for hours ~. He has been away from school for weeks ~ through illness.* **~·ness** *n* comradeship; feeling of unity.

togs /tɒgz/ *n pl* ⇨ tog.

toggle /ˈtɒgl/ *n* short piece of wood (like a peg) (to be) put through a loop (to fasten two things together, e g as used instead of a button on a coat).

toil /tɔɪl/ *vi* [VP2A,B,C,4A] work long or hard (at a task); move with difficulty and trouble: *~ up a steep hill.* □ *n* [U] hard work: *after long ~.* **~er** *n* hard worker. **ˈ~·some** /-səm/ *adj*

toilet /ˈtɔɪlət/ *n* **1** process of dressing, arranging the hair, etc: *She spent only a few minutes on her ~.* **2** (attrib) *a ˈ~ set, ˈ~ articles,* such things as a hair-brush, comb, hand-mirror, etc. **ˈ~-powder** *n* [U] talc. **ˈ~-table** *n* dressing-table (with a mirror or mirrors). **3** (old use) (style of) dress or costume: *They went to the garden party to display their summer ~s.* **4** (e g in hotels, offices) lavatory; water-closet. **ˈ~-paper** *n* for use in a lavatory. **ˈ~-roll** *n* roll of ~-paper.

toils /tɔɪlz/ *n pl* nets; snares: (usu fig) *caught in the ~ of the law.*

To·kay /təʊˈkeɪ/ *n* [U] kind of sweet, rich Hungarian wine.

to·ken /ˈtəʊkən/ *n* [C] **1** sign, evidence, guarantee or mark: *A white flag is used as a ~ of surrender. I am giving you this watch as a ~ of my esteem/affection.* ***in ~ of,*** as evidence of. **ˈbook/ˈrecord/ˈgift ~,** receipt (usu on an attractive card) for payment of money, exchangeable for a book/

record, etc of the value stated. **2** (attrib) serving as a preliminary or small-scale substitute: *The enemy offered only a ~ resistance,* did not resist seriously. **~ money,** coins of low intrinsic value, e g as formerly issued and used by traders, but exchangeable for coins of standard value. **~ payment,** payment of a small part of what is owed, made to show that the debt is recognized. **~ strike,** for a few hours only (as a warning that a long strike may follow). **~ vote,** Parliamentary vote of money for government purposes, it being understood that a larger sum may be taken without further discussion or voting.

told /təʊld/ *pt,pp* of **tell**.

tol·er·ate /ˈtɒləreɪt/ *vt* [VP6A,C] **1** allow or endure without protest: *I won't ~ your impudence/your doing that.* **2** endure the society of: *How can you ~ that rude fellow?* **tol·er·able** /ˈtɒlrəbl/ *adj* that can be ~d; fairly good: *tolerable food; in tolerable health.* **tol·er·ably** /-əblɪ/ *adv* in a tolerable manner or degree: *feel tolerably* (= fairly) *certain about sth.* **tol·er·ance** /ˈtɒlərns/ *n* [U] quality of tolerating opinions, beliefs, customs, behaviour, etc different from one's own: *religious/racial tolerance.* **tol·er·ant** /-rnt/ *adj* having or showing tolerance: *Mr X is not very tolerant of criticism/contradiction,* does not endure it easily. **tol·er·ant·ly** *adv* **tol·er·ation** /ˈtɒləˈreɪʃn/ *n* [U] tolerance, esp the practice of allowing religious freedom.

toll[1] /təʊl/ *n* [C] **1** payment required for the use of a road, bridge, harbour, etc. **ˈ~-bar/-gate** *n* bar/gate across a road at which a ~ is payable. **ˈ~-house** *n* house for the man in charge of a ~-bar. **2** (fig) sth paid, lost or suffered: *the ~ of the roads,* deaths and injuries from traffic accidents. *The war took a heavy ~ of the nation's manhood.* **3** **ˈ~ call** *n* telephone call for which the rates are higher than for local calls.

toll[2] /təʊl/ *vt,vi* [VP6A,2A] (of a bell) (cause to) ring with slow, regular strokes: *The funeral bell ~ed solemnly. Whose death is being ~ed?* □ *n* (*sing* only) ~ing stroke, of a bell.

toma·hawk /ˈtɒməhɔk/ *n* light axe used as a tool and a weapon by N American Indians. □ *vt* strike with a ~.

tom·ato /təˈmɑtəʊ *US:* təˈmeɪtəʊ/ *n* (*pl* -toes /-təʊz/) [C] (plant with) soft, juicy, red or yellow fruit usu eaten with meat, in salads, and in sauces: (attrib) *ˈ~ juice.* ⇨ the illus at **vegetable**.

tomb /tum/ *n* place dug in the ground, cut out of rock, etc for a dead body, esp one with a monument over it. **ˈ~·stone** *n* stone set up over a ~.

tom·bola /tɒmˈbəʊlə/ *n* [C] (*pl* ~s) (now usu called *bingo*) kind of lottery with sums of money or small fancy articles as prizes.

tom·boy /ˈtɒmbɔɪ/ *n* girl who likes rough, noisy games and play.

tom·cat /ˈtɒmkæt/ *n* male cat.

tome /təʊm/ *n* large, heavy book.

tom·fool /ˈtɒmˈful/ *n* stupid person; (attrib) stupid: *a ~ speech.* **~·ery** /-ərɪ/ *n* [U] senseless behaviour; [C] (*pl* -ries) stupid joke.

tommy-gun /ˈtɒmɪ gʌn/ *n* submachine-gun (light kind that can be carried and used by one man).

tommy-rot /ˈtɒmɪ ˈrɒt/ *n* (colloq) utter foolishness: *You're talking ~. That's all ~.*

to·mor·row /təˈmɒrəʊ/ *adv, n* (on) the day after today: *If today is Monday, ~ will be Tuesday and the day after ~ will be Wednesday. Don't wait until ~. Where will he be ~ morning/afternoon/evening/night? The announcement will appear in ~'s newspapers. What will the men and women of ~* (= of the next few years) *think of us?* **~ week,** eight days hence.

tom-tit /ˈtɒm ˈtɪt/ *n* kind of small bird. ⇨ **tit**[1].

tom·tom /ˈtɒmtɒm/ *n* (kind of) African or Asian drum, esp a long and narrow kind, beaten with the hands.

ton /tʌn/ *n* **1** measure of weight (2 240 lb in GB, 2 000 lb in the US); *metric ton,* 2 204·6 lb or 1 000 kg. ⇨ App 5. **2** measure of the internal capacity (100 cu ft) or carrying capacity (40 cu ft) of a ship. **3** (colloq) large weight, quantity or number: *He has tons of money.* **4 the ton,** speed of 100 mph: *Will your motor-bike do the ton?* **ˈton-up,** (attrib): *ton-up boys,* motor-cyclists who like high speeds.

to·nal /ˈtəʊnl/ *adj* of tone or tones; of ~ity. **~·ity** /təʊˈnælətɪ/ *n* (*pl* -ties) (music) character of a melody, depending upon the scale in which it is written, the key in which it is developed, etc.

tone[1] /təʊn/ *n* **1** [C] sound, esp with reference to its quality, pitch, duration, feeling, etc: *the sweet ~(s) of a violin; speak in an angry/entreating ~. The doctor's ~ was serious.* **ˈ~-arm** *n* tubular arm connecting the sound-box of the old-fashioned kind of gramophone to the horn. Cf modern *pick-up arm.* **ˈ~-ˈdeaf** *adj* unable to distinguish between differences of pitch. **ˈ~-poem** *n* musical composition for an orchestra, illustrating a poetic idea, legend, etc. **2** [C] the pitch aspect of a (usu stressed) syllable; rise, fall, etc of the pitch of the voice in speaking: *In 'Are you ill?' there is usu a rising ~ on 'ill'; in 'He's ill', there is usu a falling ~ on 'ill',* **3** (*sing* only) general spirit, character, morale, of a community, etc: *The ~ of the school is excellent. The next speaker gave a serious/flippant ~ to the discussion. There was a ~ of quiet elegance in the room,* The furnishings, etc gave this impression. **4** [C] shade (of colour); degree (of light): *a carpet in ~s of brown; a picture in warm ~s,* in shades suggesting warmth. **5** (music) any one of the five larger intervals between one note and the next which, together with two semi-~s, make up an octave. **6** [U] proper and normal condition of (parts of) the body: *good muscular ~; recover mental ~.* **-toned** *adj* having a particular kind of ~(1): *silver-~d trumpets.* **~·less** *adj* lacking colour, spirit, etc; dull: *answer in a ~less voice.* **~·less·ly** *adv*

tone[2] /təʊn/ *vt,vi* **1** [VP6A] give a particular tone of sound or colour to. **2** [VP15B,2C] ***~ (sth) down,*** make or become less intense: *The excitement ~d down. The artist ~d down the cruder colours in his painting. You'd better ~ down some of the offensive statements in your article.* ***~ (sth) up,*** make or become more vigorous, intenser, brighter, etc: *Exercise ~s up the muscles.* **3** ***~ in (with),*** (esp of colours) be in harmony: *These curtains ~ in well with your rugs.*

tong /tɒŋ/ *n* Chinese secret society.

tonga /ˈtɒŋgə/ *n* light, two-wheeled horse-drawn vehicle used in India, Pakistan, etc.

tongs /tɒŋz/ *n pl* (often ***a pair of ~***) one of various kinds of usu hinged tool for taking up and holding sth: *ˈsugar ~; ˈcoal ~; ˈice ~.* ***be/go at it hammer and ~,*** ⇨ hammer(1).

tongue /tʌŋ/ *n* **1** [C] movable organ in the mouth, used in talking, tasting, licking, etc: *The doctor* *asked me to put out my* ~. *Don't put your* ~ *out at me, you saucy child!* ☞ the illus at mouth. ***have sth on the tip of one's*** ~, ☞ tip¹(1). ***find one's*** ~, become able to speak again (after being too shy to do so). ***have one's*** ~ ***in one's cheek,*** say sth that one does not intend to be taken seriously. ***have lost one's*** ~, be too shy to speak. ***have a ready*** ~, be fluent, quick to answer questions, etc. ***hold one's*** ~, be silent, saying nothing. ***keep a civil*** ˈ~ ***in one's head,*** not be rude. ˈ**~-tied** *adj* silent; unable or unwilling to speak through shyness, fear, etc. ˈ**~-twister** *n* word or succession of words difficult to utter quickly and correctly. **2** [C] language: *one's mother* ~, one's native language; *the German* ~. **3** [C,U] animal's ~ as an article of food: *boil an* ˈ*ox-*~; *ham and* ~ *sandwiches.* **4** sth like a ~ in shape or function, e g the clapper of a bell, the strip of leather under the laces of a shoe, a jet of flame (which licks things), a long promontory (*a* ~ *of land*). **-tongued** *adj* (in compounds) having a ~ of the kind indicated: *a sharp-*~*d woman.*

tonic /ˈtonɪk/ *n, adj* **1** (sth, e g, medicine) giving strength or energy: *the* ~ *quality of sea air; get a bottle of* ~ *from the doctor. Praise can be a mental* ~. *The good news acted as a* ~ *on us all,* cheered us up. ˈ~ **water,** (usu bottled) water with quinine: *a gin and* ~ (as an aperitif). **2** (music keynote. ˈ~ ˈ**sol-**ˈ**fa** /ˈsol ˈfɑ *US:* ˈsəʊl/ *n* (in teaching singing) method of showing musical notes by syllables, e g *sol, fa, doh.*

to·night /təˈnɑɪt/ *adv, n* (on) the night of today: *last night,* ~, *and tomorrow night; after* ~; ~*'s radio news.*

ton·nage /ˈtʌnɪdʒ/ *n* **1** internal cubic capacity of a ship (1 ton = 100 cu ft). **2** cargo-carrying capacity of a ship stated in tons (of 40 cu ft). **3** total ~(1) of a country's merchant shipping. **4** charge per ton on cargo, etc for transport.

ton·sil /ˈtonsl/ *n* either of two small oval masses of tissue at the sides of the throat, near the root of the tongue: *have one's* ~*s out,* have them removed by a surgeon. ☞ the illus at head. **~·itis** /ˈtonslˈɑɪtɪs/ *n* [U] inflammation of the ~s.

ton·sorial /tonˈsɔrɪəl/ *adj* (often hum, e g *the* ~ *art*) of a hairdresser and his work.

ton·sure /ˈtonʃə(r)/ *n* shaving of the top of the head of a person about to become a monk or priest; part of the head that has been shaved in this way. □ *vt* give the ~ to.

ton·tine /ˈtontin/ *n* annuity shared by subscribers to a loan, the shares increasing as the subscribers die, till the last subscriber gets all that is left.

too /tu/ *adv* **1** also; as well, in addition (usu with end position but placed immediately after the word it modifies if there is a risk of ambiguity): *I, too, have been to Paris,* e g I, as well as he, you, etc. *I've been to Paris, too,* e g to Paris as well as to Rome, Milan, etc. *She plays the piano, and sings, too,* plays the piano and also sings. *Sally, too,* (= Sally, as well as Mary, etc) *plays the piano.* (Cf the construction in negative sentences: *I know the answer, too.* Neg: *I don't know the answer, either.*) **2** moreover; nevertheless: *There was frost last night, and in May too!* **3** (*adv of degree,* modifying *adjj* and *advv*) in a higher degree than is allowable, required, etc: *We've had too much rain lately. You're driving too fast for safety. These shoes are much too small for me. It's too hot for work/too hot to work. It's too difficult a task for me. That's too small a box/That box is too small to hold all these things.* (Note that *too* is used to modify a participle that is adjectival, with a participle that is purely verbial, *too much* is preferred in formal style. Cf: *He was too tired to go any farther. I hope you were not too (much) disturbed by all the noise we made. I'm not too (much) bothered by his criticisms.*) **4** (phrases) ***go/carry sth too far,*** ☞ far²(2). ***all too soon/quickly, etc,*** sooner, more quickly, etc than is desired: *The holidays ended all too soon.* ***none too soon, etc,*** not at all too soon, etc: *We were none too early for the train,* We caught the train with very little time to spare. ***one too many,*** ☞ many(1). ***have one too many,*** take more than one can drink and remain sober. ***be too much for,*** ☞ much¹. ***only too*** (+ *adj*), ☞ only²(2).

took /tʊk/ *pt* of take¹(1).

tool /tul/ *n* **1** instrument held in the hand(s) and used by workmen, e g gardeners and carpenters. **maˈchine** ˈ~ *n* ☞ machine. **2** person used by another for dishonest purposes: *He was a mere* ~ *in the hands of the dictator.* □ *vt* **1** [VP6A] ornament (the edges of a book-cover) with designs pressed on with a heated ~. **2** [VP2C] ~ ***up,*** provide a factory with machine-~s (e g as needed for a particular kind of work.

toot /tut/ *n* [C] short, sharp warning sound from a horn, whistle, trumpet, etc. □ *vi,vt* [VP2A,6A] (cause to) give out a ~ or ~s.

tooth /tuθ/ *n* (*pl* teeth /tiθ/) **1** each of the hard, white, bone-like structures rooted in the gums, used for biting and chewing; ☞ the illus at mouth: *have a* ~ *out* (US, *have a* ~ *pulled*), i e by a dentist; *have all one's own teeth/a fine set of artificial teeth.* ***armed to the teeth,*** completely and elaborately armed. ***cast sth in a person's teeth,*** reproach him with it. ***escape by the skin of one's teeth,*** have a narrow escape. ***fight*** ~ ***and nail,*** fiercely, with a great effort. ***get one's teeth into sth,*** attack (a job) vigorously. ***have a sweet*** ~, be fond of sweet food. ***lie in one's teeth/throat,*** lie shamelessly. ***long in the*** ~, (originally of horses, because gums recede with age) old. ***show one's teeth,*** take up a threatening attitude. ***in the teeth of,*** against the full force of; in opposition to. ˈ**~·ache** *n* (*sing* only, with or without *a/the*) ache in a ~ or teeth. ˈ**~·brush** *n* one for cleaning the teeth. ˈ**~·paste/·powder** *n* [U] for cleaning the teeth. ˈ**~·pick** *n* short, pointed piece of wood, etc, for removing bits of food from between the teeth. **2** ~-like part, esp of a comb, saw or rake. ☞ the illus at gear. ˈ**fine-**ˈ~ **comb,** one with fine teeth set closely together (as used for combing lice and nits from hair). ***go over/through sth with a fine-*~ *comb,*** examine it closely and thoroughly. **3** (*pl,* colloq) effective force: *When will the new legislation be given some teeth,* be made effective? **~ed** /tuθt/ (attrib) having teeth (e g of the kind named): *a saw-*~*ed wheel.* **~·less** *adj* without teeth. ˈ**~·some** /-səm/ *adj* (rare) (of food) pleasant to the taste.

tootle /ˈtutl/ *vi, n* toot softly or continuously, as on a flute.

top¹ /top/ *n* **1** (usu *sing* with *def art*) highest part or point: *at the top of the hill; the hilltop; at the top of the page; line 5 from the top.* ***on top,*** above: *The green book is at the bottom of the pile and the red one is on top.* ***on (the) top of,*** (**a**) over, resting on: *Put the red book on (the) top of the others.*

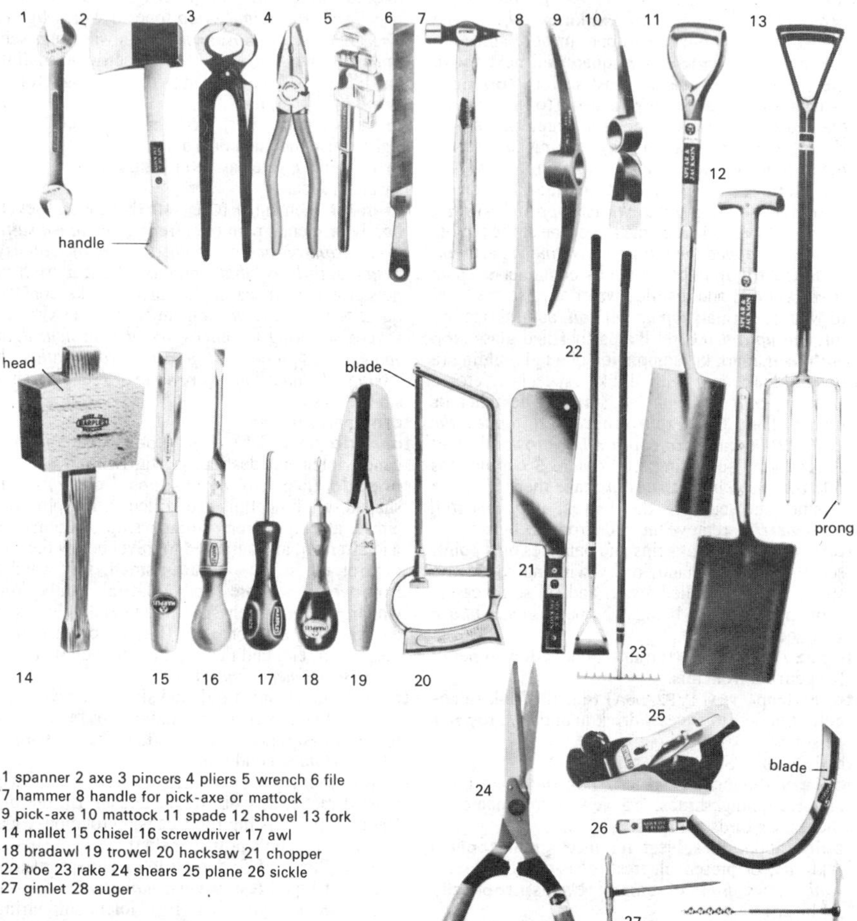

1 spanner 2 axe 3 pincers 4 pliers 5 wrench 6 file 7 hammer 8 handle for pick-axe or mattock 9 pick-axe 10 mattock 11 spade 12 shovel 13 fork 14 mallet 15 chisel 16 screwdriver 17 awl 18 bradawl 19 trowel 20 hacksaw 21 chopper 22 hoe 23 rake 24 shears 25 plane 26 sickle 27 gimlet 28 auger

tools and implements

(**b**) in addition to: *He borrowed £50 from me for the journey and then, on top of that, asked me if he could borrow my car, too.* ***from top to bottom,*** completely. ***from top to toe,*** from head to foot. ***blow one's top,*** (colloq) explode in rage. **2** upper surface, e g of a table: *polish the top of a table/the `table top; put the luggage on the top of the car.* ***go over the top,*** (mil) go over the front of a trench to attack the enemy; (fig) act quickly after a period of doubt or hesitation. ***on top of the world,*** (colloq) extremely happy, satisfied with everything: *I'm feeling on top of the world today!* **3** highest rank, foremost (or most important) place: *He came out at the top of the list,* e g of examination results. *Our host placed us at the top* (= the upper end) *of the table,* the part for honoured guests. ***come to the top,*** (fig) win fame, success, etc. ***reach/be at the top of the ladder/tree,*** the highest position in a profession, career, etc. **4** utmost height or degree: ***shout at the top of one's voice,*** ⇨ voice, *n*(3); ***to the top of one's bent,*** ⇨ bent[1]. **5** (motoring) ***in top,*** in top (the highest) gear: *What will the car do in top?* **6** (often *pl*) leaves, etc of a plant grown chiefly for its root: *`turnip tops.* **7** ***the big top,*** very large circus tent. **3** (attrib, and in compounds) highest in position or degree: *on the top shelf; at top speed; in top gear; the top right-hand corner; charge top prices.* **`top-boot** *n* boot with a high top, usu reaching to just below the knee. **`top-coat** *n* overcoat. ***be top dog,*** (sl) victor, master. ⇨ underdog. **`top drawer** *n* the highest social class: *She's out of the top drawer/is very top-drawer.* **'top-`dress** *vt* apply (manure, etc) to the surface of (ground) instead of ploughing or digging it in; Hence, **'top-`dressing** *n*: *give a field a top-dressing of lime.* **'top-`flight/-`notch** *attrib adjj* (colloq) first-rate; best possible: *top-flight French authors.* **'top-`gallant** *adj, n* mast, sail, etc immediately above the topmast and topsail. **'top `hat** *n* tall silk hat. **'top-`hat,** (attrib use) for highly-paid business executives, etc: *a top-hat insurance policy,* usu paid for by the employer. **'top-`heavy** *adj* over-weighted at the top so as to be in danger of falling. **'top-`hole** *adj* (dated sl) excellent; first-rate. **`top·knot** *n* knot of hair, bunch of feathers, etc on the top of the head. **top people,** those at the top of their profession, holding the highest positions, etc: *Not all top people read 'The Times'.* **'top-'ranking** *adj* of the highest rank. **'top·mast** *n* upper mast (clamped to the mainmast). **'top·sail** *n* square sail next above the lowest. **'top secret,** most secret. **'top·most** /-məʊst/ *adj* highest. **top·less** *adj* (of a woman's garment) leaving the breasts bare: *a topless dress/swimsuit;* (of a woman) wearing such a garment: *topless waitresses in California.*

top[2] /tɒp/ *vt* (-pp-) [VP6A] **1** provide a top for; be a top for; be a top to: *a church topped by/with a steeple.* **2** [VP6A] reach the top of; be at the top of: *When we topped the hill we had a fine view.* **3 top (sth) up,** fill up (a partly empty container): *top up a car battery,* add distilled water to raise the level to what is normal; *top up with oil,* add lubricating oil; *top up a drink,* refill a partly filled glass. ***top (sth) out,*** mark the completion of a tall building (a tower block, etc) with drinks, speeches, etc: *a 'topping-'out ceremony.* **4** surpass, be taller or higher than: *Our exports have just topped the £80 000 000 mark.* ***to top it all,*** to crown all, add the last (and surprising, etc) touch. **5** cut the tops off: *lift and top beets/turnips,* take them from the ground and cut off the leaves; *top and tail gooseberries,* remove the ends from the berries.

top[3] /tɒp/ *n* toy that spins and balances on a point, set in motion by hand, or by winding round it a string which is pulled away, and (in some cases) kept in motion by being whipped. ***sleep like a top,*** soundly.

to·paz /'təʊpæz/ *n* [U] transparent yellow mineral; [C] gem cut from this.

tope /təʊp/ *vi,vt* [VP2A,6A] (dated) drink (alcoholic liquors) to excess; drink habitually. **toper** *n* person who ~s.

topi /'təʊpɪ *US:* təʊ'pi/ *n* sun-helmet.

topi·ary /'təʊpɪərɪ *US:* -ɪerɪ/ *adj*: *the '~ art,* the art of clipping shrubs, e g yew, into ornamental shapes, e g birds, animals.

topic /'tɒpɪk/ *n* subject for discussion. **topi·cal** /-kl/ *adj* of present interest; of ~s of the day: *a ~al 'news film,* of current events. **topi·cally** /-klɪ/ *adv*

top·ogra·phy /tə'pɒgrəfɪ/ *n* [U] (description of the) features, e g rivers, valleys, roads, of a place or district. **topo·graphi·cal** /'tɒpə'græfɪkl/ *adj* **topo·graphi·cally** /-klɪ/ *adv*

top·per /'tɒpə(r)/ *n* (colloq) top hat.

top·ping /'tɒpɪŋ/ *adj* (colloq) excellent. **~·ly** *adv*

topple /'tɒpl/ *vi,vt* [VP2A,C,6A,15B] (cause to) be unsteady and overturn: *The chimney ~d and fell. The pile of books ~d over/down. The dictator ~d from power.*

tops /tɒps/ *n pl* (usu **the tops**) (colloq) the very best.

topsy-turvy /'tɒpsɪ 'tɜvɪ/ *adj, adv* in confusion; upside down: *The whole world is/has turned ~.* **~·dom** /-dəm/ *n* condition of being ~.

toque /təʊk/ *n* (woman's) small, brimless, close-fitting hat.

tor /tɔ(r)/ *n* small hill, rocky peak (esp in place-names on Dartmoor, S W England): *Hay Tor.*

torch /tɔtʃ/ *n* **1** piece of wood, twisted flax, etc treated with oil, soaked in tallow, etc for carrying or using as a flaming light; (fig) sth that gives enlightenment: *the ~ of learning; hand on the ~,* keep knowledge, etc alive. ***carry a ~ for,*** endure unrequited love for. **'~-race** *n* (in ancient Greece) performance of runners who handed lighted ~es to others in relays. **'~·light** *n* light of a ~ or ~es: *a ~light procession/tattoo,* one in which lighted ~es are used. **'~-singer** *n* woman who sings sentimental love-songs. **2** (GB) electric hand-light and battery; (US) blow-lamp (for welding, etc).

tore /tɔ(r)/ *pt* of **tear**[2].

tor·ea·dor /'tɒrɪədɔ(r) *US:* 'tɔr-/ *n* Spanish bull-fighter (usu mounted on a horse).

torii /'tɔrɪi/ *n* gateway at the entrance to a Shinto shrine in Japan.

tor·ment /'tɔment/ *n* [C,U] (sth that causes) severe bodily or mental pain or suffering: *be in ~; suffer ~(s) from an aching tooth; the ~s of jealousy. What a little ~ that child is!* What a frightful nuisance it is (because it worries, asks constant questions, etc). □ *vt* /tɔ'ment/ [VP6A,15A] cause severe suffering to; annoy: *~ed with neuralgia/hunger/mosquitoes. Stop ~ing your father by asking silly questions.* **tor·men·tor** /-tə(r)/ *n* sb or sth that ~s.

torn /tɔn/ *pp* of **tear**[2].

tor·nado /tɔ'neɪdəʊ/ *n* (*pl* -does /-dəʊz/) hurricane; violent and destructive whirlwind.

tor·pedo /tɔ'pidəʊ/ *n* (*pl* -does /-dəʊz/) cigar-shaped self-propelling shell filled with explosives, aimed at ships (from surface ships, submarines and aircraft), and launched to travel below the surface of the sea. **'~-boat** *n* small, fast warship from which ~es are fired. **'~-tube** *n* tube from which ~es are discharged. □ *vt* [VP6A] attack or destroy with a ~ or ~es; (fig) attack (a policy, institution, etc) and make it ineffective: *Who ~ed the Disarmament Conference?*

tor·pid /'tɔpɪd/ *adj* **1** dull and slow; inactive. **2** (of animals that hibernate) not moving or feeling. **~·ly** *adv* **~·ness, ~·ity** /tɔ'pɪdətɪ/, **tor·por** /'tɔpə(r)/ *nn* ~ condition.

torque /tɔk/ *n* **1** [C] necklace, collar or armband of twisted metal, as worn by the ancient Britons and Gauls. **2** [U] twisting force causing rotation, e g as exerted on a ship's propeller shaft.

tor·rent /'tɒrənt *US:* 'tɔr-/ *n* [C] **1** violent, rushing stream of liquid (esp water): *mountain ~s; ~s of rain; rain falling in ~s.* **2** (fig) violent outpouring: *a ~ of words/abuse/insults.* **tor·ren·tial** /tə'renʃl/ *adj* of, like, caused by, a ~: *~ial rain.*

tor·rid /'tɒrɪd *US:* 'tɔr-/ *adj* (of the weather, a country) very hot; tropical: *the '~ zone,* part of the earth's surface between the tropics(**1**). **~·ity** *n* [U] extreme heat.

tor·sion /'tɔʃn/ *n* [U] act or process of twisting; state of being twisted.

torso /'tɔsəʊ/ *n* (*pl* ~s) (statue of a) human body without head, arms and legs.

tort /tɔt/ *n* (legal) private or civil wrong for which the wronged person may get redress in a law court.

tor·tilla /tɔ'tijə/ *n* pancake omelette (Mexican style).

tor·toise /'tɔtəs/ *n* slow-moving, four-legged land (and fresh-water) varieties of turtle with a hard shell. ⇨ the illus at **reptile**. **'~-shell** *n* outer shell, esp the kind with yellow and brown markings, of some sea-turtles, used for making combs, fans, cigarette-cases, etc.

tor·tu·ous /'tɔtʃʊəs/ *adj* full of twists and bends: *a ~ path;* (fig) not straightforward; devious: *a ~ argument/policy/politician.* **~·ly** *adv*

tor·ture /'tɔtʃə(r)/ *vt* [VP6A,16A] cause severe suffering to: *~ a man to make him confess sth; ~d with anxiety.* □ *n* **1** [U] torturing; infliction of severe bodily or mental suffering: *put a man to the ~, ~ him* (esp to get a confession or to make him supply information); *instruments of ~.* **2** [C,U] pain so inflicted or suffered; method of torturing: *suffer ~ from toothache; the ~s of the damned,* i e in Hell. **tor·turer** *n*

Tory /ˈtɔrɪ/ *n* (*pl* -ries) = Conservative. **~·ism** /-ɪzm/ *n*

tosh /toʃ/ *n* (sl) nonsense.

toss /tos *US:* tɔs/ *vt,vi* **1** [VP6A,12A,13A,15B] throw up into or through the air; jerk: *~ a ball to sb; ~ sth aside/away. The horse ~ed its rider,* caused the rider to fall to the ground. *He ~ed the beggar a coin/~ed a coin to the beggar. The horse ~ed its head. She ~ed her head back,* i e with a suggestion of contempt, indifference, etc. *He was ~ed by the bull.* ***~ (up) a coin, ~ up,*** send a coin spinning up in the air and guess which side will be on top when it falls. ***~ sb for sth,*** use the method of ~ing a coin to decide sth: *Who's to pay for the drinks? Let's ~ up/Let's ~ for it.* **ˈ~-up** *n* ~ing of a coin; (hence) sth about which there is doubt: *It's a ~-up whether he will get here in time.* **2** [VP2C,6A,15A,B] (cause to) move restlessly from side to side or up and down: *The ship (was) ~ed about on the stormy sea. The sick child ~ed about in its sleep all night. The branches were ~ing in the wind.* **3** ***~ sth off,*** **(a)** drink sth straight down. **(b)** produce sth quickly and without much thought or effort: *~ off an epigram/a newspaper article.* □ *n* [C] **1** ~ing movement: *a contemptuous ~ of the head; take a ~,* (esp) be thrown from the back of a horse. **2** ***win/lose the ~,*** guess correctly/incorrectly when a coin is ~ed up (esp at the beginning of a game).

tot[1] /tot/ *n* **1** (often **tiny tot**) very small child. **2** (colloq) small glass of liquor.

tot[2] /tot/ *vt,vi* (-tt-) [VP15B,2C] ***tot (sth) up,*** (colloq) add up: *expenses totting up to £5; tot up a column of figures.*

to·tal /ˈtəʊtl/ *adj* complete; entire: *~ silence; be in ~ ignorance of sth. What are your ~ debts? There was a ~ eclipse of the sun.* **~ war,** war in which all the resources of a country (manpower, industry, etc) are involved. □ *n* ~ amount: *Our expenses reached a ~ of £20. What does the ~ come to?* □ *vt,vi* (-ll-, US also -l-) [VP6A,2C] find the ~ of; reach the ~ of; amount to: *The visitors to the exhibition ~led 15 000. It ~s up to £16.* **~ly** /ˈtəʊtl̩ɪ/ *adv* completely: *~ly blind.* **~·ity** /təʊˈtælətɪ/ *n* entirety; (esp) period during which an eclipse is ~.

to·tali·tar·ian /ˈtəʊˈtælɪˈteərɪən/ *adj* of a system in which only one political party and no rival loyalties are permitted: *a ~ State,* e g Germany under Hitler. **~·ism** /-ɪzm/ *n*

to·tal·iz·ator /ˈtəʊtl̩aɪzeɪtə(r) *US:* -tl̩ɪz-/ *n* machine for registering bets (esp on horses and greyhounds) with a view to dividing the total amount (less tax) among those who bet on the winners.

tote[1] /təʊt/ *n* (colloq abbr of) **totalizator.**

tote[2] /təʊt/ *vt* [VP6A] (sl) carry (esp a gun): *He ~s a six-shooter.*

to·tem /ˈtəʊtəm/ *n* [C] natural object, esp an animal, considered, esp by N American Indians, to have a close connection with a family group. **ˈ~-pole** *n* one on which is carved or painted a series of ~s.

tot·ter /ˈtotə(r)/ *vi* [VP2A,C] **1** walk with weak, unsteady steps; get up unsteadily: *The wounded man ~ed to his feet.* **2** be almost falling; seem to be about to collapse: *The tall chimney-stack ~ed and then fell.* **tot·tery** *adj* unsteady; insecure.

tou·can /ˈtukæn/ *n* kinds of tropical American bird with brightly coloured feathers and an immense beak. ⇨ the illus at **rare.**

touch[1] /tʌtʃ/ *n* **1** [C] act or fact of touching: *I felt a ~ on my arm. Even the slightest ~ will break a soap-bubble.* ***at a ~,*** if touched, however lightly. **2** [U] (sense giving) feeling by touching: *soft/rough to the ~,* when touched; *the cold ~ of marble.* **ˈ~·stone** *n* sth used as a test or standard (of purity, etc); criterion. **3** [C] stroke made with a brush, pen, etc: *add a few finishing ~es* (to a drawing or any piece of work): *give a horse a ~ of the spurs.* **4** [C] ***~ (of),*** slight quantity, trace: *a ~ of frost in the air; have a ~ of the sun,* slight sunstroke; *a ~ of irony/bitterness in his remarks; have a ~* (= a slight attack) *of rheumatism.* **5** [C] style or manner of touching the keys, strings, etc of a musical instrument, etc of workmanship (in art): *the ~ of a master,* expert style, e g in painting; *a sculpture with a bold ~; have a light ~,* e g on a piano, a typewriter; *the ˈNelson ~,* the bold way of dealing with a situation characteristic of Nelson. **ˈ~-type** *n* type without looking at the typewriter keyboard (because familiar with it). **6** [U] communication. ***in/out of ~ (with),*** in/not in regular communication (with); having/not having information about: *keep in ~ with old friends; be out of ~ with the political situation.* ***lose ~ (with),*** be out of ~ (with): *If we correspond regularly we shan't lose ~.* **7** (football) part of the pitch outside the side-lines: *The ball is in/out of ~.* **ˈ~-lines** *n pl* side lines of the field of play. ⇨ the illus at **football.** **8** ***a near ~,*** a narrow escape. **ˈ~-and-ˈgo** *adj* risky; of uncertain result: *It was ~-and-go whether the doctor would arrive in time. It was ~-and-go with the sick man,* uncertain whether he would live. **9** ***a soft/easy ~,*** (sl) sb from whom one can beg or borrow easily. ⇨ *~ sb for sth,* at **touch**[2]**(11).**

touch[2] /tʌtʃ/ *vt,vi* (For special uses with *adverbial particles* and *preps,* ⇨ **11** below.) **1** [VP6A,15A,B,2A] (cause to) be in contact with; be separated from at one or more points by no space or object; bring a part of the body (esp the hand) into contact with: *One of the branches is ~ing the water. The two estates ~ (each other),* have, in part, a common boundary. *Can you ~* (= reach with your hand) *the top of the door? The mountains seemed to ~ the clouds. Visitors* (e g in a museum) *are requested not to ~ the exhibits. He ~ed me on the arm/shoulder,* e g to attract my attention. *He ~ed his hat to me/~ed his hand to his hat,* as a greeting, instead of raising his hat. *I merely ~ed the eggs together and they cracked. The thermometer ~ed 35°C yesterday.* ***~ bottom,*** **(a)** reach the bottom: *The water isn't deep here; I can just ~ bottom,* i e with my feet. **(b)** (fig) reach the lowest point of misfortune, depravity, etc. ***~ the spot,*** (colloq) do exactly what is needed (to bring relief, etc): *A glass of iced lager ~es the spot on a hot day.* ***~ wood,*** ~ sth made of wood to avert ill luck: *I've never been in a road accident—~ wood.* **2** [VP6A] apply a slight or gentle force to: *He ~ed the bell,* rang it by pressing the button. *He ~ed the keys of the piano.* **3** [VP6A] (usu in neg) compare with; be equal to: *No one can ~ him as* an actor of tragic roles. *There's nothing to ~ mountain air for giving you an appetite.* **4** [VP6A] (usu neg) take (food, drink): *He hasn't ~ed food for two days.* **5** [VP6A] affect (a person or his feelings); concern: *The sad story ~ed us/our hearts. We were all ~ed with remorse/pity when we heard what had happened.* **6** [VP6A] have to do with: *As a pacifist I refuse to ~* (= invest money in) *shares of armament firms. What you say does not ~ the point at issue. The question ~es your interests closely.* **7** [VP6A] injure slightly: *The apple-blossom was ~ed by the frost. The valuable paintings were not ~ed by the fire.* **8** (*pp* **~ed**) slightly mad or deranged: *He seems to be a bit ~ed.* **9** [VP6A,15A] rouse painful or angry feeling in; wound: *The remark ~ed him to the quick. You've ~ed his self-esteem. You've ~ed him on a tender place* (liter or fig). **10** [VP6A] deal with; cope with; get a result from: *Nothing I have used will ~* (= get rid of) *these grease spots. She couldn't ~* (= even begin to answer) *the first two questions in the biology paper,* i e in an examination. **11** [VP3A,2C,15B] (special uses with *adverbial particles* and *preps*): ***touch at,*** (of a ship) call at: *Our steamer ~ed at Naples.*

touch down, **(a)** (Rugby football) ~ the ball on the ground behind the opponent's goal line. **(b)** (of aircraft) come down to land; alight. Hence, **ˋ~-down** *n*

touch sb for sth, (sl) get money from (by begging): *He ~ed me for a fiver* (i e £5).

touch sth off, discharge (a cannon, etc); (fig) cause to start: *The arrest of the men's leaders ~ed off a riot.*

touch (up)on sth, treat (a subject) briefly.

touch sth up, make small changes in (a picture, a piece of writing) to improve it, give the finishing touches, etc.

touch·able /ˋtʌtʃəbl/ *adj* that may be touched.

touch·ing /ˋtʌtʃɪŋ/ *adj* pathetic; arousing pity or sympathy. □ *prep* concerning. **~·ly** *adv*

touchy /ˋtʌtʃɪ/ *adj* (-ier, -iest) easily or quickly offended. **~·ily** /-əlɪ/ *adv* **~i·ness** *n*

tough /tʌf/ *adj* **1** (of meat) hard to cut or get one's teeth into. **2** not easily cut, broken or worn out: *as ~ as leather. T~ rubber is needed for tyres.* **3** strong; able to endure hardships: *~ soldiers.* **4** (of persons) rough and violent: *a ~ criminal.* ***a ~ customer,*** (colloq) a person likely to cause trouble, unlikely to submit to control or discipline. **5** stubborn; unyielding. ***be/get ~ (with sb)***: *The employers got ~ with/adopted a get-~ policy towards their workers.* **6** hard to carry out; difficult: *a ~ job/problem.* **7** ***~ luck,*** (colloq) bad luck. □ *n* (also **~ie**) (colloq) ~(4) person. **~·ly** *adv* **~·ness** *n* **~en** /ˋtʌfn/ *vt, vi* make or become ~.

tou·pee /ˋtupeɪ *US:* tuˋpeɪ/ *n* patch of false hair worn to cover a bald spot; small wig.

tour /tʊə(r)/ *n* **1** journey out and home again during which several or many places are visited: *a round-the-world ~; a motor-coach ~ of Europe; conducted ~s,* made by a group conducted by a guide. **2** brief visit to or through: *a ~ of the palace/house.* **3** period of duty (at a military or naval station overseas); interval between passage-paid home leaves (⇨ leave²(1)) in service abroad: *a ~ of three years as a lecturer in the University of Ibadan.* **4** round of (official) visits to institutions, units, etc: *The Director leaves tomorrow on a ~ of overseas branches.* **5** number of visits to places made by a theatrical company, etc: *take a company on ~ to perform three of Shakespeare's plays.* □ *vt,vi* [VP6A,2A,C] make a ~ (of): *~ western Europe. They are ~ing in Spain. The play will ~ the provinces in the autumn.* **~·ing** *n, adj*: *a ˋ~ing car,* one suitable for ~ing; *a ˋ~ing party.* **~·ist** /-ɪst/ *n* **1** person making a ~ for pleasure: *London is full of ~ists in summer.* **2** (attrib) of or for ~s: *a ˋ~ist agency; a ˋ~ist ticket,* one issued on special terms, e g at a lower price; *ˋ~ class,* (on liners, airliners) second class. **~ism** /ˋtʊər-ɪzm/ *n* [U] organized ~ing: *Some countries obtain large sums of foreign exchange from ~ism,* from the money brought in by ~ists.

tour de force /ˈtʊə də ˋfɔs/ *n* (F) feat of strength or skill.

tour·na·ment /ˋtʊənəmənt *US:* ˋtɜn-/ *n* [C] **1** series of contests of skill between a number of players: *a ˋtennis/ˋchess ~.* **2** (in the Middle Ages) contest between knights on horseback, armed with blunted weapons.

tour·ney /ˋtʊənɪ/ *n* = **tournament(2)**.

tour·ni·quet /ˋtʊənɪkeɪ *US:* ˋtɜnɪkɪt/ *n* device for stopping a flow of blood through an artery by twisting sth tightly around a limb.

tousle /ˋtaʊzl/ *vt* [VP6A] put (esp the hair) into disorder by pulling it about, rubbing it, etc; make untidy: *a girl with ~d hair.*

tout /taʊt/ *n* person who worries others to buy sth, use his services, etc, esp one who sells information about race-horses: *a ˋticket ~,* e g selling tickets for a major football match at a greatly inflated price. □ *vi* [VP2A,3A] **~ *(for),*** act as a ~: *There were men outside the railway station ~ing for the hotels.*

tout en·sem·ble /ˈtut õˋsõbl *with unsyllabic* l *US:* onˋsombl/ *n* (F) sth viewed as a whole; its general effect.

tow¹ /təʊ/ *vt* [VP6A,15A,B] pull along by a rope or chain: *tow a damaged ship into port; tow a broken-down car to the nearest garage.* **ˋtow-(-ing)-line/-rope** *nn* one used in towing. **ˋtow-(-ing)-path** *n* path along the bank of a river or canal for use in towing, e g by horses pulling canal boats. □ *n* [C,U] towing or being towed: *have/take a boat in tow. Can we give you a tow? The lorry was on tow. He usually has his family in tow,* (colloq) has them with him.

tow² /təʊ/ *n* [U] coarse and broken fibres of flax, hemp, etc (for making rope).

to·ward(s) /təˋwɔd(z) *US:* tɔrd(z)/ *prep* **1** approaching; in the direction of: *walking ~ the sea; sit with one's back turned ~ the window; drifting ~ war; first steps ~ the abolition of armaments.* **2** as regards; in relation to: *Are his feelings ~ us friendly? What will the Government's attitude be ~ the plan?* **3** for the purpose of (helping): *We must save money ~ the children's education.* **4** (of time) near: *~ the end of the century; ~ evening.*

towel /ˋtaʊl/ *n* [C] piece of cloth or absorbent paper for drying or wiping sth wet (e g one's hands or body): *a ˋbath-~; a ˋroller-~,* an endless one on a revolving bar. **ˋ~-rack/-horse** *nn* wooden frame for hanging ~s on. **ˋ~-rail** *n* (usu metal) rail for a ~ (e g near a wash-basin). ***throw in the ~,*** ⇨ **throw¹(11)**. □ *vt* (-ll-, US -l-) dry or rub (oneself) with a ~. **~·ling** (US = **~ing**) *n* [U] material for ~s.

tower /ˈtaʊə(r)/ *n* **1** tall, usu equal-sided (esp square) or circular building, either standing alone (e g as a fort, *the T~ of London*) or forming part of a church, castle or other large building (e g a college). ⇨ the illus at church. **2** (fig) ***a ~ of strength,*** a person who can be relied upon for protection, strength or comfort in time of trouble. **3** **ˈwater ~,** ~ that supports a large tank for the storage and distribution of water at high pressure. **ˈ~-block** *n* high block of flats or offices. □ *vi* [VP2C] rise to a great height, be very tall, esp in relation to the height of the surroundings: *the skyscrapers that ~ over New York.* ***~ above sb,*** (fig, of eminent persons) greatly exceed in ability, in intellectual or moral qualities: *a man who ~s above his contemporaries.* **~·ing** *adj* (esp): *in a ~ing rage,* violently angry.

town /taʊn/ *n* **1** centre of population larger than a village, esp one that has not been created a city (and often used in contrast to *country*): *Would you rather live in a ~ or in the country?* (In GB the word ~ is used much more frequently than *city,* even when the place actually is a city, the word *city* being used chiefly in connection with local government affairs.) ⇨ city(1). ***paint the ~ red,*** ⇨ red(1). **2** (attrib) **~ centre,** area around which public buildings, e g the town hall, the public library, are grouped. **~ clerk,** official who keeps ~ or city records and advises on certain legal matters. **~ council,** governing body of a ~. **~ councillor,** member of a ~ council. **~ crier,** employee who makes public announcements. **ˈ~-gas** *n* manufactured gas for domestic and industrial use. **~ hall,** building with offices of local government and usu a hall for public events (meetings, concerts, etc). **ˈ~ house,** house in ~, belonging to sb who also has a house in the country. **3** (preceded by a *prep,* and without the *def* or *indef art*) the business, shopping, etc part of a ~ (contrasted with the suburbs, etc): *go to ~ to do some shopping. He's in ~ today. I'm going down ~ this afternoon.* ⇨ downtown. ***go out on the ~,*** go out and enjoy the entertainment facilities of a ~. ***go to ~,*** (sl) act, behave, without inhibitions, e g by spending lavishly, having a spree. **4** (without the *def* or *indef art*) the chief city or ~ in the neighbourhood (esp, in England, London): *He is spending the weekend in ~. He went up to ~ from Leeds. Mr Green is not in ~/is out of ~.* ***a man about ~,*** a fashionable man who spends much time amusing himself (esp in London). **5** (*sing* with *def art*) the people of a ~: *The whole ~ was talking about it.* ***the talk of the ~,*** ⇨ talk[1](2). **6** (*sing* with *def art*) ~s in general: *Farm workers are leaving the country in order to get better paid work in the ~.* **7** **ˈ~s·folk** *n pl* **(a)** (with *def art*) the people of the ~ referred to. **(b)** (without *art*) people who live in ~s. **ˈ~s·people** *n pl* = ~sfolk. **ˈ~s·man** /-zmən/ *n* (*pl* -men) **(a)** man who lives in a ~. **(b)** (often *ˈfellow-ˈ~sman*) person who lives in one's own ~.

town·nee /taʊˈniː/ *n* **1** (US also **townie, towny**) (university sl) inhabitant of a university town who is not a member of the university. **2** /ˈtaʊnɪ/ (contemptuous) person who lives in a ~ and is ignorant of rural things.

town·ship /ˈtaʊnʃɪp/ *n* **1** (US, Canada) subdivision of a county having certain powers of government; district six miles square in US surveys of land. **2** (S Africa) area, suburb, for houses, etc, of non-Europeans. **3** (Australia) site laid out for a town.

tox·aemia (also **tox·emia**) /tokˈsiːmɪə/ *n* [U] blood-poisoning.

toxic /ˈtoksɪk/ *adj* of, caused by, a toxin; poisonous. **~·ity** /tokˈsɪsətɪ/ *n* quality or degree of being ~: *study the ~ity of insecticides.* **toxi·col·ogy** /ˌtoksɪˈkolədʒɪ/ *n* [U] branch of medical science dealing with the nature and effects of poisons. **toxi·col·ogist** /-dʒɪst/ *n* student of, expert in, toxicology.

toxin /ˈtoksɪn/ *n* [C] poisonous substance, esp one formed by bacteria in plants and animals and causing a particular disease.

toy /tɔɪ/ *n* **1** child's plaything; small thing meant for amusement rather than for serious use. **2** (attrib) *toy dog/spaniel, etc,* small kinds kept as pets; *toy soldier,* one made as a toy(1). **ˈtoy·shop** *n* shop where toys are sold. □ *vi* [VP3A] ***toy with sth,*** **1** amuse oneself (with); think not very seriously about: *He toyed with the idea of buying a yacht.* **2** handle carelessly or absent-mindedly: *toying with a pencil.*

trace[1] /treɪs/ *n* [C] **1** mark, sign, etc showing that sb or sth has been present, that sth has existed or happened: *~s of an ancient civilization. The police were unable to find any ~ of the thief. We've lost all ~ of them,* don't know where they are. **2** very small amount: *The post mortem showed ~s of arsenic in the intestines.* **ˈ~ elements,** elements of which a ~ is necessary for the development of animal or plant life and without which growth is poor (e g manganese in the soil, for wheat and oats).

trace[2] /treɪs/ *vt,vi* **1** [VP6A,15B] ***~ sth (out),*** draw, sketch, the course, outline, etc, of: *~ out the site of an old castle; ~ (out) one's route on a map.* **2** [VP6A] copy (sth), e g by drawing on transparent paper the lines, etc on (a map, design, etc) placed underneath. **3** [VP6A] write slowly and with difficulty: *He ~d the words laboriously.* **4** [VP6A,15A,B] follow or discover (sb or sth) by observing marks, tracks, bits of evidence, etc: *The criminal was ~d to Glasgow. I cannot ~* (= cannot find, do not think I received) *any letter from you dated 1st June.* ***~ (sth/sb) back (to sth),*** **(a)** find the origin of by going back in time: *He ~s his descent back to an old Norman family. His fear of dogs ~s back/can be ~d back to a childhood experience.* **(b)** find the origin of by going back through evidence: *The rumour was ~d back to a journalist,* It was discovered that he had started it. **5** [VP6A] discover the position, size, etc of (sth) from its remains: *Archaeologists have ~d many Roman roads in Britain.* **~·able** /-əbl/ *adj* capable of being ~d (*to*). **tracer** *n* (often *ˈ~r bullet/shell*) projectile whose course is made visible by a line of flame or smoke left behind it. **ˈ~r element,** radioactive element which, when introduced into sth, can be ~d by the use of a Geiger counter. **trac·ing** *n* reproduction (of a map, design, etc) made by tracing(1). **ˈtracing-paper** *n* [U] strong transparent paper on which tracings are made.

trace[3] /treɪs/ *n* [C] either of the leather straps, ropes, etc by which a wagon, carriage, cart, etc is pulled by a horse. ⇨ the illus at harness. ***kick over the ~s,*** (fig) become undisciplined; refuse to accept control.

tracery /ˈtreɪsərɪ/ *n* [C,U] (*pl* -ries) ornamental

arrangement of designs (e g as made by frost on glass, or of stonework in a church window); decorative pattern. ⇨ the illus at **window**.

tra·chea /trəˈkɪə *US:* ˈtreɪkɪə/ *n* (*pl* -cheae /-kɪɪ/) (anat) windpipe. ⇨ the illus at **respiratory**.

tra·choma /trəˈkəʊmə/ *n* [U] contagious eye disease causing inflammation of the inner surfaces of the eyelids.

track /træk/ *n* [C] **1** line or series of marks left by a vehicle, person, animal, etc in passing along; path or rough road made by persons/animals: *~s in the snow,* e g footprints; *follow the ~s left by a bear; the broad ~* (= the wake, the line of foam) *of a steamer; ˈsheep-~s across the moor; a ~ through the forest.* ***be on sb's ~/on the ~ of sb,*** be in pursuit of: *The police are on the ~ of the thief. I'm on his ~.* ***cover up one's ~s,*** conceal one's movements or activities. ***have a one-~ mind,*** habitually follow the same line of thought; give all one's attention to one topic. ***keep/lose ~ of sb/sth,*** keep in/lose touch with; follow/fail to follow the course or development of: *read the newspapers to keep ~ of current events.* ***make ~s,*** (colloq) depart (usu in a hurry); run away. ***make ~s for,*** (colloq) go towards: *It's time we made ~s for home.* ***in one's ~s,*** (sl) where one stands, there and then: *He fell dead in his ~s.* ***off the ~,*** (fig) away from the subject; following a wrong line of action. ***go (off)/keep to the beaten ~,*** ⇨ **beaten**. **2** course; line taken by sth (whether marked or not): *the ~ of a storm/comet/spacecraft.* **3** set of rails for trains, etc: *single/double ~,* one pair/two pairs of rails: *The train left the ~,* was derailed. ***on/from the wrong side of the (ˌrailroad) ~s,*** (US) on/from the part of a town that is socially inferior, the part lived in by poor people. **4** path prepared for racing (e g made of cinders, clinkers, etc): *a ˈmotor-racing/ˈcycling/ˌrunning ~;* (*attrib*) *ˈ~-racing; ˈ~ events,* e g running races, contrasted with *field* events such as jumping, throwing the discus. **ˈ~ suit** *n* loose-fitting warm suit worn by an athlete while not taking part in ~ events. **5** endless belt used instead of wheels on some tractors, military tanks, etc. □ *vt* **1** [VP6A,15A,B] follow the ~ of: *~ an animal to its den.* **ˈ~·ing station** *n* one which, by radar or radio, maintains contact with space-vehicles, etc. ***~ sb/sth down,*** find by searching: *~ down a bear/a reference.* ***~ out,*** trace (the course or development of sth) by examining ~s. **2** (cinema, TV) move a camera (mounted on a mobile platform) while taking a long shot (called *a ˈ~ing shot*). **~ed** *adj* having ~s(**7**): *~ed vehicles.* **~er** *n* person, esp a hunter, who ~s wild animals. **ˈ~er dog,** dog used in pursuing persons escaping from justice. **~·less** *adj* having no ~s(**3**): *~less forests.*

tract¹ /trækt/ *n* **1** stretch or area (*of* forest, farmland, etc): *the wide ~s of desert in N Africa.* **2** system of related parts in an animal body: *the diˈgestive/reˈspiratory ~.*

tract² /trækt/ *n* short printed essay on sth, esp a moral or religious subject.

tract·able /ˈtræktəbl/ *adj* easily controlled or guided. **trac·ta·bil·ity** /ˌtræktəˈbɪlətɪ/ *n*

trac·tion /ˈtrækʃn/ *n* [U] (power used in) pulling or drawing sth over a surface: *electric/steam ~.* **ˈ~-engine** *n* engine used for pulling heavy loads.

trac·tor /ˈtræktə(r)/ *n* powerful motor-vehicle used for pulling agricultural machinery (ploughs, drills, etc), or other heavy equipment.

trad /træd/ *n* [U] (colloq abbr of *traditional*) (esp) jazz (of the 1920's and 1930's) played by a small group with simple rhythms and much improvisation; revival of this in the 1950's.

trade¹ /treɪd/ *n* **1** [U] buying and selling of goods; exchange of goods for money or other goods; [C] particular branch of this: *Great Britain does a lot of ~ with some countries and not much with others. T~ was good last year. He's in the ˈcotton/ˈfurniture/ˌbook, etc ~.* **ˈstock-in-ˈ~,** ⇨ **stock¹(1)**. **the ~,** (colloq) those, esp the brewers, engaged in the manufacture and sale of alcoholic liquors. **ˈ~·mark** *n* design, special name, etc used to distinguish a manufacturer's goods from others; (fig) distinguishing characteristics: *He leaves his ~mark on all his undertakings.* **ˈ~ name** *n* name given by manufacturers to a proprietary article. **ˈ~ price** *n* the price charged by a manufacturer or wholesaler to a retailer. **ˈ~ show** *n* private exhibition of a new film to those who may rent it, and to film critics. **ˌ~(s)-ˈunion** *n* organized association of workers in a ~ or group of ~s, formed to protect their interests, improve their conditions, etc. **ˌ~-ˈunionism** *n* this system of association. **T~ Union Congress,** (abbr **TUC**) association of British ~ unions. **ˌ~-ˈunionist** *n* member of a ~-union. **ˈ~-wind** *n* strong wind blowing always towards the equator from the SE and NE. **the T~s,** these winds. **2** occupation; way of making a living, esp a handicraft: *He's a weaver/mason/carpenter/tailor by ~. Shoemaking is a useful ~. The school teaches many useful ~s.* **ˈ~s·folk, ˈ~s·people** *nn* persons engaged in ~; shopkeepers (and their families). **ˈ~s·man** /-zmən/ *n* (*pl* -men) shopkeeper.

trade² /treɪd/ *vi,vt* **1** [VP2A,C,3A] engage in trade(**1**); buy and sell: *~ in furs and skins; ships that ~ between London and ports in the Mediterranean. Britain ~s with many European countries.* **ˈtrad·ing estate,** (usu large) planned industrial area rented to manufacturers. **ˈtrad·ing stamp,** (= gift coupon) coupon given to customers with purchases, exchangeable for various articles or cash. **2** [VP14] ***~ sth (for sth),*** exchange; barter: *They ~d knives for gold dust. The boy ~d his knife for a cricket bat.* **3** [VP15B] ***~ sth in,*** hand over (a used article) in part payment for a new purchase: *He ~d in his 1970 car for a new model.* Hence, **ˈ~-in** *n* **4** [VP3A] ***~ (up)on,*** take a wrong advantage of, use, in order to get sth for oneself: *~ upon sb's sympathy; ~ upon one's past reputation.* **5** (US) shop: *Which stores do you ~ at,* do your shopping? **trader** *n* merchant.

tra·di·tion /trəˈdɪʃn/ *n* [U] (handing down from generation to generation of) opinions, beliefs, customs, etc; [C] opinion, belief, custom, etc handed down: *The stories of Robin Hood are based mainly on ~(s). It is a ~ in that family for the eldest son to enter the army and for the second son to become a lawyer.* **~al** /-nl/ *adj* **~·ally** /-nļɪ/ *adv* **~·al·ism** /-nļ-ɪzm/ *n* (excessive) respect for ~, esp in religious matters. **~·al·ist** /-nļ-ɪst/ *n* person who attaches great importance to ~.

tra·duce /trəˈdjus *US:* -ˈdus/ *vt* [VP6A] (formal) slander. **tra·ducer** *n* slanderer.

traf·fic /ˈtræfɪk/ *n* [U] **1** (movement of) people and vehicles along roads and streets, of aircraft in the sky: *There was a lot of/not much ~ on the roads* *yesterday. T~ in large towns is controlled by ~ lights. The ~ control tower at an airport uses radar screens.* '~ **circle,** (US) = roundabout. '~ **indicator** = trafficator. ⇨ the illus at motor. '~ **warden,** ⇨ warden. **2** transport business done by a railway, steamship line, airline, etc. **3** illicit trading: *the ~ in liquor; the illegal drug ~.* □ *vi* (-ck-) [VP3A] ***~ in sth (with sb),*** trade: *~ in hides (with...).* **traf·ficker** *n* (usu in a bad sense) trader: *a 'drug ~ker.*

traf·fi·ca·tor /ˈtræfɪkeɪtə(r)/ *n* device (usu a flickering amber light) used on a motor-vehicle to indicate the direction in which the vehicle is about to turn.

tra·gedy /ˈtrædʒədɪ/ *n* (*pl* -dies) **1** [C] play for the theatre, cinema, TV, of a serious or solemn kind, with a sad ending; [U] branch of the drama with this kind of play. **2** [C,U] very sad event, action, experience, etc, in real life. **tra·gedian** /trəˈdʒidɪən/ *n* writer of, actor in, ~. **tra·gedi·enne** /trəˈdʒidɪˈen/ *n* actress in ~.

tra·gic /ˈtrædʒɪk/ *adj* of tragedy: *a ~ actor/event.* **tragi·cally** /-klɪ/ *adv*

tragi-com·edy /ˈtrædʒɪ ˈkɒmədɪ/ *n* (*pl* -dies) drama, event, that is a mixture of tragedy and comedy. **ˈtragi-ˈcomic** /ˈkɒmɪk/ *adj*

trail /treɪl/ *n* [C] **1** line, mark or series of marks, drawn or left behind by sb or sth that has passed by: *a ~ of smoke,* (from a railway steam-engine); *vapour ~s,* as left in the sky by high-flying aircraft; *a ~ of destruction,* e g left by a violent storm. *The wounded tiger left a ~ of blood.* **2** track or scent followed in hunting. ***hot on the ~ (of),*** close behind. **3** path through rough country. ***blaze a ~,*** ⇨ blaze³. □ *vt,vi* **1** [VP6A,15A,B, 2A,C] pull, be pulled, along: *The child was ~ing a toy cart. Her long skirt was ~ing along/on the floor.* **2** [VP6A,15A] follow the ~ of: *~ a wild animal/a criminal.* **3** [VP2C] (of plants) grow over or along the ground, etc: *roses ~ing over the walls;* (of persons) walk wearily: *The wounded soldiers ~ed past us. The tired children ~ed along behind their father.* **~er** *n* **1** transport-vehicle hauled by a tractor or truck; van or caravan drawn by a motor-vehicle (used for living in when parked). **2** ~ing plant. **3** series of short extracts from a cinema or TV film to advertise it in advance.

train¹ /treɪn/ *n* **1** [C] (locomotive and) number of railway coaches, wagons, etc joined together: *'passenger/ˈgoods/ˈfreight ~s; take the 1.15am ~ to town; travel by ~; get into/out of a ~; get on/off a ~; have lunch on the ~. The ~ is in/is waiting,* is at the station. *He missed/just caught his ~.* '~ **ferry,** for carrying ~s over water (e g from England to France). '~**·man** /-mən/ *n* (*pl* -men) (US) member of the crew operating a ~. **2** number of persons, animals, carriages, etc, moving in a line: *a ~ of camels; the 'baggage ~; persons in the king's ~,* in his retinue of attendants. **3** series or chain: *A knock at the door interrupted my ~ of thought. What an unlucky ~ of events! War often brought pestilence in its ~.* **4** part of a long dress or robe that trails on the ground behind the wearer. '~**-bearer** *n* attentant who holds up, or helps to hold up, such a ~. **5** line of gunpowder leading to a place where material has been placed for an explosion (e g in a mine), to be lit at a safe distance; hence, ***in ~,*** in readiness.

train² /treɪn/ *vt,vi* **1** [VP6A,14,17,2C,3A] ***~ sb/sth for sth/to be sth,*** give teaching and practice to (e g a child, a soldier, an animal) in order to bring to a desired standard of behaviour, efficiency or physical condition: *~ (up) children to be good citizens; ~ a horse for a race/performing seals for a circus. Very little escapes his ~ed eye. He was ~ed for the ministry,* to be a minister in the Church. *There is a shortage of ~ed nurses. They are ~ing for the boat-race. He usually ~s on (a diet of) beer and beefsteak.* **2** [VP6A,15A] cause to grow in a required direction: *~ roses against/over a wall.* **3** [VP6A,14] ***~ sth (up)on sth,*** point, aim: *~ a gun upon the enemy's positions.* **~ee** /treɪˈni/ *n* person undergoing some form of (usu industrial) ~ing. **~er** *n* **1** person who ~s (esp athletes, horses for races, animals for the circus, etc). **2** *'~er aircraft,* one used for ~ing pilots. **~·ing** *n* [U] ~ing or being ~ed. ***in/out of ~ing,*** in/not in good physical condition (e g for athletic contests). ***go into ~ing,*** ~ oneself. '~**·ing-college** *n* (old use) one for ~ing teachers (now *college of education*). '~**·ing-ship** *n* one for ~ing boys in seamanship.

traipse /treɪps/ *vi* = trapse.

trait /treɪt/ *n* [C] distinguishing quality or characteristic: *Two ~s in the American character are generosity and energy.*

trai·tor /ˈtreɪtə(r)/ *n* ***~ (to),*** person who betrays a friend, is disloyal to a cause, his country, etc. ***turn ~,*** become a ~. **~·ous** /-əs/ *adj* treacherous; of or like a ~: *~ous conduct.* **~·ous·ly** *adv* **trai·tress** /ˈtreɪtrəs/ *n* woman ~.

tra·jec·tory /trəˈdʒektərɪ/ *n* (*pl* -ries) curved path of a projectile (e g a bullet, missile).

tram /træm/ *n* **1** (also '~**-car;** = US *'street-car*) electric car plying as public transport, running (usu) along public roads or streets, on rails flush with the road surface. '~**·line** *n* line of rails for ~s; route served by ~s. **2** four-wheeled car used in coalmines.

tram·mel /ˈtræml/ *vt* (-ll-; US -l-) [VP6A] hamper; make progress difficult. □ *n* (always *pl*) sth that ~s: *the ~s of routine/etiquette/superstition.*

tramp /træmp/ *vi,vt* **1** [VP2A,C] walk with heavy steps: *He ~ed up and down the platform waiting for the train.* **2** [VP2A,B,C,6A] walk through or over (esp for a long distance): *~ through the mountains of Wales; ~ over the moors. They ~ed (for) miles and miles/~ed all day. He enjoys ~ing the hills.* □ *n* **1** (with *def art; sing* only) sound of heavy footsteps: *I heard the ~ of marching soldiers.* **2** long walk: *go for a ~ in the country.* **3** person (usu homeless) who goes from place to place and does no regular work: *There's a ~ at the door begging for food.* **4** (sl) prostitute. **5** '~**(-steamer),** cargo boat which goes to any port(s) where cargo can be picked up.

trample /ˈtræmpl/ *vt,vi* **1** [VP6A,15B] ***~ sth (down),*** tread heavily on with the feet; crush under the feet: *The children have ~d (down) the flowers/~d the grass down. You wouldn't like to be ~d to death by elephants.* **2** [VP3A] ***~ on,*** tread heavily on: *~ on sb's toes/feelings.* **3** [VP2C] ***~ about,*** walk about heavily. □ *n* sound, act, of trampling.

tram·po·line /ˈtræmpəlin/ *n* [C] sheet of strong canvas on a spring frame, used by gymnasts for acrobatic leaps.

trance /trɑns *US:* træns/ *n* **1** sleep-like condition:

be/fall/go into a ~. **2** abnormal, dreamy state; hypnotic state: *send sb into a* ~.

tran·quil /ˈtræŋkwɪl/ *adj* calm; quiet: *a ~ life in the country.* **~ly** /-wɪlɪ/ *adv* **~·lity** (US also **~-ity**) /træŋˈkwɪlətɪ/ *n* [U] ~ state. **~·lize** (US also **~·ize**) /-ɑɪz/ *vt* [VP6A] make ~. **~·li·zer** (US also **~·izer**) *n* drug that ~lizes; sedative.

trans- /trænz-/ *pref* ⇨ App 3.

trans·act /trænˈzækt/ *vt* [VP6A,14] ~ ***sth with sb,*** conduct, carry through (business, etc with sb).

trans·ac·tion /trænˈzækʃn/ *n* **1** [U] (*sing* with *def art*) transacting: *the ~ of business.* **2** [C] piece of business: *cash ~s; the bank's ~s in stocks and shares.* **3** (*pl*) (records of the) proceedings of (esp a learned society, e g its meetings, lectures): *the ~s of the Kent Archaeological Society.*

trans·al·pine /trænˈzælpɑɪn/ *n, adj* (person living) beyond the Alps (esp as viewed from Italy).

trans·at·lan·tic /ˈtrænzətˈlæntɪk/ *adj* beyond the Atlantic; crossing the Atlantic: *a ~ voyage/flight;* concerning (countries on) both sides of the Atlantic: *a ~ treaty/trade agreement.*

tran·scend /trænˈsend/ *vt* [VP6A] go or be beyond or outside the range of (human experience, reason, belief, powers of description, etc).

tran·scen·dent /trænˈsendənt/ *adj* surpassing; excelling: *a man of ~ genius.* **tran·scen·dence** /-dəns/, **tran·scen·dency** /-dənsɪ/ *nn*

tran·scen·den·tal /ˈtrænsenˈdentl/ *adj* **1** not based on experience or reason; going beyond human knowledge; that cannot be discovered or understood by practical experience; known by intuition. ⇨ empirical. **2** (pop use) vague; not clear to ordinary minds. **~ly** /-tlɪ/ *adv* **~·ism** /-tl-ɪzm/ *n* [U] ~ philosophy; doctrine that knowledge may be obtained by a study of the mental processes, apart from experience. **~·ist** /-tl-ɪst/ *n* believer in ~ism.

trans·con·ti·nen·tal /ˈtrænzˈkontɪˈnentl/ *adj* crossing a continent: *a ~ railway.*

tran·scribe /trænˈskrɑɪb/ *vt* [VP6A] copy in writing, esp write (sth) in full from shorthand notes. **tran·script** /ˈtrænskrɪpt/ *n* [C] sth ~d. **tran·scrip·tion** /trænˈskrɪpʃn/ *n* **1** [U] transcribing: *errors in transcription.* **2** [C] sth ~d, esp into a special form of writing: *phonetic transcriptions.* **3** (broadcast made from a) recording (on a disc or tape): *the B B C transcription service.*

tran·sept /ˈtrænsept/ *n* [C] (either end of the) transverse part of a cross-shaped church: *the north/south ~ of the cathedral.* ⇨ the illus at church.

trans·fer[1] /ˈtrænsfɜ(r)/ *n* [C,U] (instance of) transferring; document that transfers sth or sb; drawing, plan, etc transferred from one surface to another; ticket that allows a passenger to continue his journey on another bus, etc. **ˈ~ fee,** sum paid for a ~ (esp of a professional footballer to another club).

trans·fer[2] /trænsˈfɜ(r)/ *vt,vi* (-rr-) [VP6A,14,3A] ~ ***(sb/sth) from... to,*** **1** change position, move: *The head office has been ~red from York to London. He has been ~red from the Manchester branch to the London branch. The dog has ~red its affection to its new master.* **2** hand over the possession of (property, etc to): *~ rights to sb.* **3** convey (a drawing, design, pattern, etc) from one surface to another (e g from a wooden surface to canvas). **4** change from one train, bus, etc to another; move from one occupation, position, etc to another: *He has ~red to an infantry regiment.* **~·able** /-əbl/ *adj* that can be ~red: *~able accounts,* of money that may be ~red from one currency to another. *Railway tickets are not ~able.* **~·abil·ity** /ˈtrænsˈfɜrəˈbɪlətɪ/ *n* [U]. **~-ence** /ˈtrænsfərəns *US:* trænsˈfɜəns/ *n* ~ing or being ~red, esp from one job to another.

trans·fig·ure /trænsˈfɪgə(r) *US:* -gjə(r)/ *vt* [VP6A] change the shape and appearance of, esp so as to make glorious, exalted or idealized. **trans·figur·ation** /ˈtrænsˈfɪgəˈreɪʃn *US:* -gjəˈr-/ *n* change of this sort, esp **the Transfiguration,** that of Jesus, as described in the Bible. ⇨ Matt 17.

trans·fix /trænsˈfɪks/ *vt* [VP6A] **1** pierce through: *~ a leopard with a spear.* **2** cause (sb) to be unable to move, speak, think, etc; paralyse the faculties of: *He stood ~ed with fear/horror/amazement.*

trans·form /trænsˈfɔm/ *vt* [VP6A,14] ~ ***sth into sth,*** change the shape, appearance, quality or nature of: *Success and wealth ~ed his character. A steam-engine ~s heat into energy. A caterpillar is ~ed into a butterfly.* **~·able** /-əbl/ *adj* that can be ~ed. **trans·form·ation** /ˈtrænsfəˈmeɪʃn/ *n* [U] ~ing or being ~ed; [C] instance of this: *His character has undergone a great ~ation since he was converted.* **~er** *n* sb or sth that ~s, e g apparatus that increases or decreases the voltage of an electric power supply.

trans·fuse /trænsˈfjuz/ *vt* [VP6A] transfer (sth, esp the blood of one person to another). **trans·fu·sion** /trænsˈfjuʒn/ *n* [U] act or process of transfusing; [C] instance of this: *The injured man was given a blood transfusion.*

tran·ship /trænˈʃɪp/ *vt* = transship.

trans·gress /trænzˈgres/ *vt,vi* **1** [VP6A] go beyond (a limit or bound): *~ the bounds of decency.* **2** [VP6A] break (a law, treaty, agreement). **3** [VP2A] sin; offend against a moral principle. **trans·gression** /trænzˈgreʃn/ *n* [U] ~ing; [C] instance of this; sin. **~or** /-sə(r)/ *n* person who ~es; sinner.

tran·si·ent /ˈtrænzɪənt *US:* ˈtrænʃnt/ *adj* lasting for a short time only; brief: *~ happiness; a ~ success.* □ *n* (US) guest (in a hotel, boarding-house, etc) who is not a permanent resident. **tran·si·ence** /-əns/, **tran·si·ency** /-nsɪ/ *nn*

tran·sis·tor /trænˈzɪstə(r)/ *n* [C] **1** small electronic device, often used in place of a thermionic valve, used in radio sets, hearing aids and other kinds of electronic apparatus: (attrib) *a portable ~ (set).* **2** ~ set; ~ radio. **~·ized** /-ɑɪzd/ *adj* fitted with ~s instead of valves: *a ~ized computer.*

tran·sit /ˈtrænsɪt/ *n* [U] **1** conveying or being conveyed, across, over or through: *goods lost/delayed in ~,* while being carried from one place to another. **ˈ~ camp,** one for the use of persons (esp soldiers) who are in ~ from one place to another. **ˈ~ visa,** visa allowing passage through (but not a stay in) a country. **2** apparent passage of a heavenly body, e g a planet, across the disc of another one, e g of Venus across the sun.

tran·si·tion /trænˈzɪʃn/ *n* [C,U] changing, change, from one condition or set of circumstances to another: *the period of ~ in Africa,* e g when countries there were becoming self-governing states. *Adolescence is the ~ period/the period of ~ between childhood and manhood. The frequent ~s from cold to warm weather this spring have caused illness.* **~al** /-nl/ *adj* **~·ally** /-nlɪ/ *adv*

tran·si·tive /ˈtrænsətɪv/ *adj* (gram) (of a verb) taking a direct object.

tran·si·tory /ˈtrænsɪtrɪ *US:* -tɔrɪ/ *adj* transient.

trans·late /trænzˈleɪt/ *vt* [VP6A,14] **~ *sth (from... into),*** **1** give the meaning of (sth said or written) in another language: *~ an English book into French; ~d from (the) Italian. The poems don't ~ well.* **2** interpret, clarify (sb's behaviour, etc): *How would you ~ his silence,* What do you think it signifies? **3** remove (a bishop) to a different see; (in the Bible) take to heaven without death. **trans·lat·able** /-əbl/ *adj* **trans·la·tor** /-tə(r)/ *n* person who ~s (esp sth written). Cf *interpreter* for sth spoken. **trans·la·tion** /ˈtrænzˈleɪʃn/ *n* [U] translating: *errors in translation;* [C] sth ~d: *make/do a simultaneous translation into French.*

trans·lit·er·ate /trænzˈlɪtəreɪt/ *vt* [VP6A,14] **~ *sth (into...),*** write (a word, passage) in the characters of a different language or system: *~ Greek into Roman letters; ~ English words into phonetic symbols.* **trans·lit·er·ation** /ˈtrænzˈlɪtəˈreɪʃn/ *n* [C,U] transliterating; sth ~d.

trans·lu·cent /trænzˈlusnt/ *adj* allowing light to pass through but not transparent (as ordinary glass is): *Frosted glass is ~.* **trans·lu·cence** /-sns/, **trans·lu·cency** /-snsɪ/ *nn*

trans·mi·gra·tion /ˈtrænzmaɪˈgreɪʃn/ *n* [U] migration; (esp) ***~ of the soul,*** the passing of the soul at death into another body.

trans·mission /trænzˈmɪʃn/ *n* **1** [U] transmitting or being transmitted: *the ~ of news/disease/a radio or TV programme.* **2** [C] clutch, gears and drive which transmit power from the engine to (usu) the rear axle (of a motor-vehicle).

trans·mit /trænzˈmɪt/ *vt* (-tt-) [VP6A,14] **~ *sth (to...),*** **1** pass or hand on; send on: *~ a message by radio; ~ a disease. Parents ~ some of their characteristics to their children.* **2** allow through or along: *Iron ~s heat.* **~·ter** *n* sb or sth that ~s, esp (part of a) telegraph or radio apparatus for sending out signals, messages, music, etc.

trans·mog·rify /trænzˈmɒgrɪfaɪ/ *vt* (*pt,pp* -fied) [VP6A] (hum) cause to change completely in appearance or character, esp in a magical or surprising way. **trans·mog·ri·fi·ca·tion** /ˈtrænzˈmɒgrɪfɪˈkeɪʃn/ *n*

trans·mute /trænzˈmjut/ *vt* [VP6A,14] **~ *sth (into...),*** change the shape, nature or substance of: *We cannot ~ base metals into gold.* **trans·mut·able** /-əbl/ *adj* that can be ~d. **trans·mu·ta·tion** /ˈtrænzmjuˈteɪʃn/ *n*

trans·oceanic /ˈtrænzˈəʊʃɪˈænɪk/ *adj* beyond or crossing an ocean: *the ~ migrations of birds.*

tran·som /ˈtrænsəm/ *n* horizontal bar of wood over the top of a door or window. **ˈ~(-window),** hinged window over a door or other window; (US) fanlight.

trans·par·ent /trænˈspeərnt/ *adj* **1** allowing light to pass through so that objects (or at least their outlines) behind can be distinctly seen: *~ window-panes; ~ silk.* ⇨ translucent. **2** about which there can be no mistake or doubt: *a ~ lie; a man of ~ honesty.* **3** clear; easily understood: *a ~ style of writing.* **~·ly** *adv* **trans·par·ence** /-rns/ *n* [U] state of being ~. **trans·par·ency** /-rnsɪ/ *n* (*pl* -cies) **1** [U] = transparence. **2** [C] diagram, picture, etc (usu in a frame) on photographic film, made visible by light behind it (so that it may be projected on to a screen).

tran·spire /trænˈspaɪə(r)/ *vi,vt* **1** [VP2A] (of an event, a secret) become public; come to be known: *It ~d that the President had spent the weekend golfing.* **2** [VP2A] (colloq) happen. **3** [VP6A] (of the body, plants) give off, pass off (moisture, Vapour). **tran·spi·ra·tion** /ˈtrænspəˈreɪʃn/ *n* transpiring(3); loss of water vapour, e g from the surface of leaves.

trans·plant /trænsˈplɑnt *US:* -ˈplænt/ *vt,vi* **1** [VP6A,2A] take up (plants, etc) with their roots and plant in another place: *~ young cabbage plants. Some seedlings do not ~ well.* **2** transfer (tissue, or an organ, e g a heart or kidney) from one body to another. **3** [VP6A] (fig, of people) move from one place to another. □ *n* /ˈtrænsplɑnt *US:* -plænt/ instance of ~ing(2): *a ˈkidney ~.* **trans·plan·ta·tion** /ˈtrænsplɑnˈteɪʃn *US:* -plæn-/ *n*

trans·po·lar /ˈtrænzˈpəʊlə(r)/ *adj* across the polar regions: *~ flights from London to Tokyo.*

trans·port[1] /ˈtrɑnspɔt *US:* ˈtræn-/ *n* **1** [U] conveying or being conveyed; means of conveyance: *the ~ of troops by air; road ~; water-borne ~,* by ship. *My car is being repaired so I am without ~/without means of ~ at present.* **2** (attrib) of or for carrying, conveying: *London's ~ system; ~ charges.* **a ˈ~ café,** one used by long-distance lorry drivers, etc. **3** [C] **(ˈtroop-)~** ship or aircraft for carrying troops and supplies. **4** (often *pl*) ***in a ~/in ~s of,*** (liter) filled with, carried away by, strong feelings of (delight, rage, etc).

trans·port[2] /trɑnˈspɔt *US:* træn-/ *vt* **1** [VP6A, 15A] carry (goods, persons) from one place to another: *~ goods by lorry.* **2** [VP6A,15A] (in former times) send (a criminal) to a distant colony as a punishment: *~ed to Australia.* **3 *be ~ed with,*** (liter) be overcome with, carried away by (strong emotion): *On hearing of the victory, the nation was ~ed with joy.* **~·able** /-əbl/ *adj* that can be ~ed or conveyed. **trans·por·ta·tion** /ˈtrɑnspɔˈteɪʃn *US:* ˈtræn-/ *n* [U] ~ing or being ~ed: *The criminal was sentenced to ~ation for life.*

trans·porter /trɑnˈspɔtə(r) *US:* træn-/ *n* person or thing that transports, e g a travelling crane, or a long vehicle for carrying motor-vehicles from a factory, or a conveyor belt. **ˈ~ bridge,** high bridge with a suspended deck, e g that across the harbour in Sydney, Australia.

trans·pose /trænˈspəʊz/ *vt* [VP6A,14] **1** cause (two or more things) to change places. **2** (music) put into another key. **trans·po·si·tion** /ˈtrænspəˈzɪʃn/ *n* [C,U] transposing or being ~d.

trans·ship /trænˈʃɪp/ *vt* (-pp-) [VP6A] transfer from one ship or conveyance to another. **~·ment** *n*

tran·sub·stan·ti·ation /ˈtrænsəbˈstænʃɪˈeɪʃn/ *n* doctrine that the bread and wine in the Eucharist are changed into the body and blood of Christ.

trans·verse /trænzˈvɜs/ *adj* lying or placed across: *a ~ engine,* one placed parallel, instead of at right angles, to the axles of a car. **~·ly** *adv*

trans·vest·ism /trænzˈvest-ɪzm/ *n* (psych) abnormal desire to dress in clothing of the other sex. **trans·ves·tite** /-taɪt/ *n* person who practises ~.

trap /træp/ *n* **1** device for catching animals, etc: *a ˈfly-~; a ˈmouse-~; caught in a ~;* (fig) plan for deceiving sb; trick or device to make sb say or do sth he does not wish to do or say: *The employer set a ~ for the man by putting marked money in the* *till. Our soldiers pretended to run away and the enemy, in pursuing them, fell into a ~.* **2** U-shaped or other section of a drain-pipe which retains liquid and so prevents return flow of sewer gas (e g under the pan of a lavatory). **3** light, two-wheeled vehicle pulled by a horse or pony. **4** **'~('-door),** hinged door or opening in roof, ceiling, floor or the stage of a theatre. **5** (sl) mouth: *Shut your ~!* **6** device (e g a box) from which an animal or object can be released, e g greyhounds at the start of a race, or clay pigeons, balls, etc. **'~-shooting,** the sport of shooting at clay pigeons or balls released by springs into the air. □ *vt* (-pp-) [VP6A,15A] take in a ~; capture by a trick. **~·per** *n* person who ~s animals, esp fur-bearing animals.

tra·peze /trəˈpiz *US:* træ-/ *n* horizontal bar or rod supported by two ropes, used by acrobats and for gymnastic exercise.

figure having two sides parallel; (US) = *trapezoid.* ⇨ the illus at quadrilateral.

trap·ezoid /ˈtræpəzɔɪd/ *n* (geom) (GB) four-sided figure having no sides parallel; (US) = *trapezium.* ⇨ parallelogram. ⇨ the illus at quadrilateral.

trap·pings /ˈtræpɪŋz/ *n pl* (fig) ornaments or decorations, esp as a sign of public office: *He had all the ~ of high office but very little power.*

Trap·pist /ˈtræpɪst/ *n* member of an order of monks noted for refraining from speaking and for other austerities.

traps /træps/ *n pl* (colloq) personal belongings; baggage: *pack up your ~s.*

trapse (US = **traipse**) /treɪps/ *vi* [VP2A,B,C] (colloq) trudge wearily: *~ round the shops buying food for the family.*

trash /træʃ/ *n* [U] **1** worthless material or writing. **2** (US) rubbish; refuse: *a ˈ~-can* (GB = *dustbin*). **3** (US) worthless people: *white ~,* (abusive term for) poor white population in the Southern States. **trashy** *adj* worthless: *~y novels.*

trauma /ˈtrɔmə *US:* ˈtraʊmə/ *n* (*pl* -mata /-mətə/ -mas /-məz/) morbid condition of the body produced by a wound or injury; (psych) emotional shock, often leading to neurosis. **trau·matic** /trɔˈmætɪk *US:* traʊ-/ *adj* of a wound or injury; of or for the treatment of a wound or injury; (of an experience) distressing and unforgettable.

tra·vail /ˈtræveɪl *US:* trəˈveɪl/ *n* (archaic) pains of childbirth: *a woman in ~.*

travel /ˈtrævl/ *vi,vt* (-ll-; US -l-) **1** [VP2A,B,C, 4A] make (esp long) journeys: *~ round the world; ~ (for) thousands of miles; (for) three months; ~ (over) the whole world.* **2** [VP3A] ***~ (in sth) (for sb),*** go from place to place as a salesman: *He ~s in cotton goods. He ~s* (i e as a salesman) *for a London publisher.* **ˈ~ agent,** person who makes arrangements for ~, by selling tickets, reserving accommodation, etc. Hence, **ˈ~·agency/-bureau** *nn* **3** [VP2A,B,C] move; go: *Light ~s faster than sound. Cars are assembled as they ~ from one part of a workshop to another.* **3** [VP2C] pass from point to point: *The general's eyes ~led over the enemy's positions. Her mind ~led over recent events.* **~·ling,** (US = **~·ing**) *n* [U] *ˈ~ling expenses; a ˈ~ling bag/dress,* used or designed for ~ling. □ *n* **1** [U] ~ling: *T~ was slow and dangerous in olden days. He is fond of ~.* **ˈ~ sickness** *n* (euphem for) diarrhoea (as caused by eating food to which one is not accustomed); sea sickness or airsickness. **2** (in compounds) **ˈ~-soiled/-stained/-worn,** soiled, etc, by ~. **3** (*pl*) journeys, esp abroad; book about such journeys and experiences: *write a book about one's ~s.* **4** extent of the movement of a mechanical part, e g the shuttle of a loom. **ˈ~ling fellowship,** grant of money for educational ~. **~·led,** (US = **~ed**) *adj* **1** having made many long journeys: *a ~led man.* **2** used by people who ~: *a much ~led part of the country.* **~·ler,** (US = **~er**) /ˈtrævlə(r)/ *n* **1** person on a journey. **ˈ~ler's cheque** (US **ˈ~er's check**), one issued by a bank, tourist agency, etc, for the convenience of ~lers. **2** (often *comˈmercial ~ler*) ~ling salesman. **trav·elogue** (also **-log**) /ˈtrævlɒg *US:* -lɔg/ *n* film or lecture describing ~s.

tra·verse /ˈtrævɜs/ *vt* [VP6A] travel across; pass over: *Searchlights ~d the sky. The railway ~s hundreds of miles of desert.* □ *n* [C] **1** mountaineering) sideways movement across the face of a precipice, steep slope of ice, etc from one point where ascent or descent is possible to another; place where this is necessary. **2** change of direction in a trench to prevent the enemy from firing along it.

trav·esty /ˈtrævəstɪ/ *n* [C] (*pl* -ties) parody; imitation or description of sth that is, often on purpose, unlike and inferior to the real thing: *His trial was a ~ of justice.* □ *vt* (*pt,pp* -tied) [VP6A] make or be a ~ of: *~ a person's style of writing.*

trawl /trɔl/ *n* [C] **1** **ˈ~(-net),** large wide-mouthed net to be dragged along the sea-bottom. **2** (US) **ˈ~ line** (also *setline*) long sea-fishing line to which are attached many short lines with hooks. □ *vi,vt* [VP2A] fish with a ~; [VP6A] drag along the sea-bottom: *~ a net.* **~er** *n* boat, fisherman, that ~s.

a trawler

tray /treɪ/ *n* flat piece of wood, metal, etc with raised edges, for holding light articles, e g *a ˈpen-~,* or carrying things, e g *a ˈtea-~*; container on a writing-desk for papers, etc. **ˈin-/ˈout-tray,** for papers, letters, etc coming in/ready to be posted, filed, etc.

treach·er·ous /ˈtretʃərəs/ *adj* **1** false or disloyal (to a friend, cause, etc). **2** deceptive; not to be relied upon: *~ weather. The ice is ~,* appears to be strong but may break. *My memory is ~.* **~·ly** *adv* **treach·ery** /ˈtretʃərɪ/ *n* (*pl* -ries) [U] being ~; (*pl*) ~ acts.

treacle /ˈtrikl/ *n* [U] thick, sticky, dark liquid produced while sugar is being refined (US = *molasses*). **treacly** /ˈtriklɪ/ *adj* like ~; thick and sweet; (fig) excessively sweet: *treacly sentiments.*

tread /tred/ *vi,vt* (*pt* trod /trɒd/, *pp* trodden /ˈtrɒdn/) **1** [VP2C,3A] ***~ (on sth),*** walk, put the foot or feet down (on): *~ on sb's toes. Don't ~ on the flower beds. She trod lightly so as not to wake* *the baby.* ~ ***on air,*** be light-hearted and gay, transported with joy. ~ ***on sb's corns/toes,*** (fig) offend him. ~ ***on sb's heels,*** (liter and fig) follow closely after. **2** [VP6A,15A,B] stamp or crush; push (down, etc) with the feet: ~ *out a fire in the grass;* ~ *grapes,* when making wine; ~ *(out) the juice from grapes;* ~ *the earth round the roots.* **3** [VP6A] make by walking: *The cattle had trodden a path to the pond.* **4** [VP6A] walk along: (fig) ~ *a dangerous path,* follow a risky course of action; ~ *the boards,* (rhet) be an actor; ~ *a measure/a minuet,* (old use) dance. ~ ***water,*** keep oneself afloat in deep water by moving the feet up and down (as if working the pedals of a bicycle). □ *n* **1** way or sound of walking: *with a heavy/loud* ~. **2** part of a step or stair on which the foot is placed. **'~-mill** *n* appliance or apparatus for producing circular motion by the movements of a person or animal walking on the steps (or treads) of a wheel or a sloping endless belt (e g the kind formerly used in prisons as a punishment); (fig) monotonous routine. **3** grooved part of a tyre which touches the ground: *Good* ~*s minimize the risk of skidding.* ⇨ retread.

treadle /'tredl/ *n* pedal or lever that drives a machine, e g a lathe or sewing-machine, worked by pressure of the foot or feet. □ *vi* [VP2A] work a ~.

trea·son /'trizn/ *n* [U] treachery to, betrayal of, one's country or ruler; disloyalty; betrayal of trust. **~·ous** /'triznəs/, **~·able** /'triznəbl/ *adjj* **~·ably** /-nəblı/ *adv*

treas·ure /'treʒə(r)/ *n* **1** [C,U] (store of) gold and silver, jewels, etc; wealth: *The pirates buried their* ~. **'~-house** *n* building where ~ is stored. **'~-trove** *n* [U] ~ found hidden in the earth and of unknown ownership. **2** highly valued object or person: *The National Gallery has many priceless 'art* ~*s. She says her new secretary is a perfect* ~. *My* ~*!* (as a term of endearment). □ *vt* **1** [VP6A,15B] ~ ***sth (up),*** store for future use: ~ *memories of one's courtship days;* ~ *sth up in one's memory.* **2** [VP6A] value highly: ~ *sb's friendship. He* ~*s the watch his father gave him.* **treas·urer** /'treʒərə(r)/ *n* person in charge of money, etc belonging to a club or society.

treas·ury /'treʒərı/ *n* (*pl* **-ries**) **1 the T~,** (in GB) department of State controlling public revenue. **First Lord of the T~,** the Prime Minister. **the 'T~ Board/Lords of the T~,** officers in charge of public revenue (usu the Prime Minister, the Chancellor of the Exchequer, and three others). **the 'T~ Bench,** bench in the House of Commons occupied by members of the Cabinet. **'~ bill,** (GB) bill of exchange issued by the T~ to raise money for temporary needs. **'~ note,** currency note issued by the US T~; (formerly) currency note issued by the British T~ (now replaced by Bank of England notes). **2** place where funds are kept; funds of a society, organization, etc: *The* ~ *of our tennis club is almost empty.* **3** person, book, etc looked upon as containing valuable information or as a valued source: *The book is a* ~ *of information. Palgrave's 'Golden T~' has long been valued as an anthology of poetry.*

treat /'trit/ *vt,vi* **1** [VP15A,16B] act or behave towards: *He* ~*s his wife badly. Don't* ~ *me as (if I were) a child. You must* ~ *them with more consideration.* **2** [VP16A] consider: *We had better* ~ *it as a joke,* instead of taking it seriously. **3** [VP6A] discuss; deal with: *The lecturer* ~*ed his subject thoroughly. The problem has been* ~*ed by numerous experts.* **4** [VP3A] ~ ***of,*** (formal) be about: *The essay/lecture/book* ~*s of the progress of cancer research.* **5** [VP6A] give medical or surgical care to: *Which doctors are* ~*ing her for her illness? How would you* ~ *a case of rheumatism/* ~ *sb ill with influenza?* **6** [VP6A] put (a substance) through a process (in manufacture, etc): ~ *a substance with acid/wood with creosote.* **7** [VP6A,14] ~ ***sb/oneself (to sth),*** supply (food, drink, entertainment, etc) at one's own expense (to): ~ *one's friends to oysters and champagne. I shall* ~ *myself to a good weekend holiday. It's my turn to* ~ *today.* **8** [VP3A] ~ ***with sb,*** discuss or arrange (sth with sb): ~ *with the enemy for peace. If we are to* ~ *with you, it must be on equal terms.* □ *n* **1** [C] sth that gives pleasure, esp sth not often enjoyed or sth that comes unexpectedly: *What a* ~ *to get into the peace and quiet of the country! It's a great* ~ *for her to go to the opera.* **a children's ~, a school ~,** excursion arranged for a party of children, e g a Sunday-school class. **2** act of ~ing(7): *This is to be my* ~, I'm going to pay. ***stand*** ~**,** (colloq) bear the expense of the entertainment.

treat·ise /'tritız *US:* -tıs/ *n* book, etc that deals systematically with one subject: *a* ~ *(up)on ethics.*

treat·ment /'tritmənt/ *n* [C,U] (particular way of) treating sb or sth; what is done to obtain a desired result: *Is the* ~ *of political prisoners worse than it used to be? He soon recovered under the doctor's* ~. *That dog has suffered from cruel* ~. *He has tried many* ~*s for skin diseases. They are trying a new* ~ *for cancer. She is still under* ~ *in hospital.*

treaty /'tritı/ *n* (*pl* **-ties**) **1** [C] (formal) agreement made and signed between nations: *a 'peace* ~*; enter into a* ~ *of commerce (with).* **'~ port,** one that a country is bound by ~ to keep open for foreign trade. **2** [U] agreement or negotiation between persons: *be in* ~ *with sb for...; sell a house by private* ~, instead of by public auction or other method.

treble[1] /'trebl/ *adj, n* three times as much or many (as): *He earns* ~ *my salary.* **'~ 'chance,** method of competing in football pools by predicting all the drawn games (these having higher points value), and then wins for away and home matches (these having less value). □ *vt,vi* [VP6A,2A] make or become ~: *He has* ~*d his earnings/His earnings have* ~*d during the last few years.*

treble[2] /'trebl/ *n* (boy's voice with, instrument that takes, the) highest part in a piece of music; of this part: ~ *pitch.*

tree /tri/ *n* **1** perennial plant with a single self-supporting trunk of wood with (usu) no branches for some distance above the ground: *cut down* ~*s for timber.* ⇨ bush, shrub. ***at the top of the*** ~**,** at the top of one's profession. ***up a ('gum-)*~,** (colloq) cornered; in a position from which escape is difficult. **'family ~,** diagram or list showing or giving family descent. **'~-fern** *n* fern that grows to the size of a tree. **2** piece of wood for a special purpose: *a 'boot-/'shoe-~,* for keeping a boot or shoe in shape while not being worn; *an 'axle-~,* connecting two opposite wheels. □ *vt* [VP6A] cause to take refuge up a ~: *The hunter was* ~*d by the bear. The dog* ~*d the cat.* **~·less** *adj* without ~s: *the* ~*less plains of Argentina.*

tre·foil /ˈtrifɔɪl/ *n* kinds of three-leaved plant, e g clover; ornament or design like a threefold leaf, e g as in stonework.

trek /trek/ *vi* (-kk-) [VP2A,B,C] (in S Africa) make a long journey, esp by ox-wagon. □ *n* journey of this kind; any long, hard journey. ⇨ **safari**.

trel·lis /ˈtrelɪs/ *n* light upright structure of strips of wood, etc esp as used for supporting climbing plants. □ *vt* [VP6A] furnish with, support on, a ~.

tremble /ˈtrembl/ *vi* [VP2A,B,C,4B] **1** shake involuntarily (as from fear, anger, cold, physical weakness, etc): *His voice ~d with anger. We were trembling with cold/excitement.* **2** move to and fro: *The bridge ~d as the heavy lorry crossed it. The ground ~d under our feet.* **3** be in a state of agitation: *I ~ to think what has happened to him,* am deeply worried. She ~d for his safety. ***in fear and trembling,*** in a state of frightened anxiety. □ *n* shudder; uncontrollable shaking: *There was a ~* (more usu *a tremor*) *in his voice. He was all of a ~,* (colloq) was trembling all over.

tre·men·dous /trəˈmendəs/ *adj* **1** very great; enormous; powerful: *a ~ explosion; travelling at a ~ speed.* **2** (colloq) extraordinary: *He's a ~ eater/talker,* eats/talks to an extraordinary degree; splendid, first rate: *a ~ concert/performance/meal.* **~·ly** *adv*

trem·olo /ˈtremələʊ/ *n* (*pl* -los /-ləʊz/) trembling or vibrating effect in singing, or in the playing of a bowed musical instrument.

tremor /ˈtremə(r)/ *n* [C] **1** shaking or trembling: *the ~ of a leaf,* e g in a breeze; *ˈearth ~s,* as during an earthquake. **2** thrill: *A ~ of fear went through the audience when the assassin fired at the President.*

tremu·lous /ˈtremjʊləs/ *adj* **1** trembling: *in a ~ voice; with a ~ hand.* **2** timid; nervous. **~·ly** *adv*

trench /trentʃ/ *n* [C] ditch dug in the ground, e g for the draining of water, for a latrine, as a protection for soldiers against the enemy's fire: *dig ~es for irrigation; ~ warfare,* fought in and from ~es; *a ˈ~-coat,* soldier's waterproof coat. ˈ**~ fever,** infectious fever transmitted by lice among soldiers living in ~es. □ *vt,vi* **1** [VP6A] surround with a ~; fortify with a ~ or ~es; make ~es in: *~ a field,* for draining. **2** [VP3A] **~ *upon,*** encroach upon (which is much more usu): *Visitors ~ed upon my spare time last week.*

trench·ant /ˈtrentʃənt/ *adj* (of language) vigorous; incisive: *~ wit; a ~ speech.* **~·ly** *adv* **trench·ancy** /-ənsɪ/ *n*

trencher /ˈtrentʃə(r)/ *n* large wooden plate on which food was formerly served or carved; (mod use) such a plate used for slicing bread on. ˈ**~·man** /-mən/ *n* (*pl* -men) *a good/poor ~man,* person who usu eats a lot/a little.

trend /trend/ *n* [C] general direction; tendency: *The ~ of the coastline is to the south. Is the ~ of modern thought away from materialism? The ~ of prices is still upwards.* ***set the ~,*** start a style, etc which others follow. Hence, ˈ**~-setter,** ˈ**~-setting** *nn* □ *vi* [VP2C] have a certain ~: *The road ~s towards the west.* **trendy** *adj* (-ier, -iest) showing, following, the latest ~s of fashion, etc.

tre·pan /trɪˈpæn/ *vt* (-nn-) make a round hole in (the skull) with a cylindrical saw (as an operation to relieve pressure on the brain).

tre·phine /trɪˈfin *US:* -ˈfaɪn/ *vt* (word now more generally used for) trepan. □ *n* surgical saw used for trepanning.

trepi·da·tion /ˌtrepɪˈdeɪʃn/ *n* [U] alarm; excited state of mind.

tres·pass /ˈtrespəs/ *vt* **1** [VP2A,3A] **~ *(upon),*** go on to privately owned land without right or permission: *~ upon sb's (private) property. No ~ing!* (a sign put up on privately owned land as a warning). **2** [VP3A] **~ *upon,*** encroach upon, make too much use of: *~ upon sb's time/*

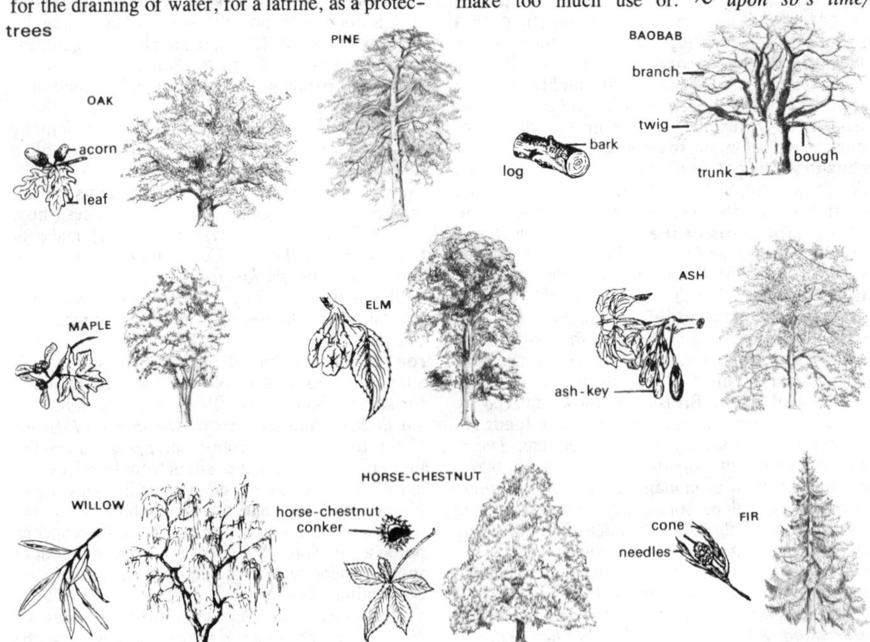

hospitality/privacy. **3** [VP2A,3A] (old use, and biblical) do wrong; sin: *'as we forgive them that ~ against us.'* □ *n* [U] ~ing(1); [C] instance of this. **2** [C] (old use, and biblical) sin; wrong: *'Forgive us our ~es.'* **~er** *n* person who ~es(1): *T~ers will be prosecuted.*

tress /tres/ *n* (poet or liter) **1** (*pl*) hair (esp of a woman's or girl's head): *her beautiful golden ~es.* **2** plait or braid of hair.

trestle /ˈtresl/ *n* horizontal beam of wood with two legs at each end, used in pairs to support planks, a table top, a workman's bench, etc. **ˈ~-ˈtable** *n* one made by laying planks on ~s. **ˈ~-ˈbridge** *n* bridge supported by a framework of timber or steel. ⇨ the illus at bridge.

trews /truz/ *n* (with *sing v*) close-fitting tartan trousers.

tri- /traɪ-/ *pref* three. ⇨ App 3.

triad /ˈtraɪæd/ *n* group or set of three closely related persons or things.

trial /ˈtraɪl/ *n* **1** [U] testing, trying, proving; [C] instance of this: *give sth a ~,* use it to learn about its qualities, value, etc; *give a new typist a ~,* give her a chance to show her skill; *have a ~ of strength with sb,* a contest to learn who is stronger. *We shall put the machine to further ~,* test it further. *The ship performed well during her ~s.* ***on ~,*** **(a)** for the purpose of testing: *Take the machine on ~ and then, if you like it, buy it.* **(b)** when tested: *The new clerk was found on ~ to be incompetent.* ***~ and error,*** method of solving a problem by making tests until error is eliminated. **2** (attrib) for the purpose of testing: *a ~ flight,* e g of a new aircraft; *a ~ trip/voyage; a ~ order,* e g for goods that are to be tested. **3** [C,U] examination in a law court before a judge (or judge and jury): *The judge conducted four ~s in one day. The ~ lasted a week.* ***be/go on ~ (for sth),*** be tried in a court of law (for an offence). ***bring sb to ~, bring sb up for ~, put sb on ~,*** cause him to be tried in a court of law. ***stand (one's) ~,*** be tried. **4** [C] sth or sb troublesome or annoying, esp thought of as a test of one's patience: *That mischievous boy is a ~ to his teachers. Life is full of little ~s.*

tri·angle /ˈtraɪæŋgl/ *n* **1** plane figure with three straight sides; any three points not in a straight line. **2** musical instrument made of a steel rod in the shape of a ~, struck with another steel rod. ⇨ the illus at percussion. **3** group of three. ***the eternal ~,*** the situation existing when two persons are in love with another of the opposite sex. **tri·angu·lar** /traɪˈæŋgjʊlə(r)/ *adj* **1** in the shape of a ~. **2** in which there are three persons, etc: *a triangular contest in an election,* with three candidates.

tribal /ˈtraɪbl/ *adj* of a tribe or tribes: *~ loyalties; ~ dances.* **~·ism** /ˈtraɪbl-ɪzm/ *n*

tribe /traɪb/ *n* **1** racial group, esp one united by language and customs, living as a community under one or more chiefs: *the Indian ~s of America; the twelve ~s of ancient Israel.* **2** (bot, zool) group of plants or animals, usu ranking between a genus and an order. **3** (usu contemptuous) group of persons, etc of one profession: *the ~ of politicians.* **ˈ~s·man** /-zmən/ *n* (*pl* -men) member of a ~(1).

tribu·la·tion /ˈtrɪbjʊˈleɪʃn/ *n* [C,U] (cause of) trouble, grief: *The war was a time of ~ for all of us. He bore his ~s bravely.*

tri·bu·nal /traɪˈbjunl/ *n* [C] place of judgement; board of officials or judges appointed for special duty, e g to hear appeals against high rents, for exemption from military service: (fig) *the ~ of public opinion.*

tri·bune[1] /ˈtrɪbjun/ *n* **1** official chosen by the common people of ancient Rome to protect their interests. **2** (later use) popular leader; demagogue.

tri·bune[2] /ˈtrɪbjun/ *n* raised platform for speakers addressing an assembly (e g that used in the French National Assembly).

tribu·tary /ˈtrɪbjʊtərɪ *US:* -terɪ/ *adj* **1** (of a state, ruler, etc) paying tribute(1) to another. **2** (of a river) flowing into another. □ *n* (*pl* -ries) ~ state, ruler, river, etc.

trib·ute /ˈtrɪbjut/ *n* [C,U] **1** (usu regular) payment which one government or ruler exacts from another: *Many conquered nations had to pay ~ to the rulers of ancient Rome.* ***lay sb under ~,*** force payment of ~ from. **2** sth done, said or given to show respect or admiration: *By erecting this statue we have paid (a) ~ to the memory of the founder of our college. The actress received numerous floral ~s,* bunches of flowers.

trice[1] /traɪs/ *n* ***in a ~,*** in an instant.

trice[2] /traɪs/ *vt* [VP15B] ***~ sth up,*** haul up and secure (*a sail, the boom*) in place with rope.

trick /trɪk/ *n* [C] **1** sth done in order to deceive, to outwit or outdo, sb; sth done to make a person appear ridiculous: *The wearing of white clothes is a common ~ of soldiers fighting in snow-covered country. He got the money from me by a ~.* ***the ~s of the trade,*** ways of attracting customers, gaining advantages over rivals, etc. **2** mischievous act, practical joke: *The children are always up to amusing ~s. That was an unfair ~.* ***play a ~ on sb,*** ⇨ play[2](3). ***a dirty ~,*** a contemptible action. **3** feat of skill or dexterity: *conjuring ~s. Does your dog know any ~s? Are you clever at card ~s?* ***do the ~,*** (sl) accomplish one's purpose: *One more turn of the screwdriver should do the ~,* fasten the screw securely. ***a ~ worth two of that,*** (colloq) a better way of doing it (than yours). ***(soon) get/learn the ~ of it,*** learn the knack (which is the more usu word) of doing it, managing it, etc. **4** strange or characteristic habit, mannerism, etc: *He has a ~ of pulling his left ear when he is thinking out a problem.* **5** (cards played in) one round (of bridge, etc): *take/win a ~,* win one round. **6** (among sailors) period of duty at the helm (usu two hours): *take one's ~ at the wheel.* □ *vt* **1** [VP6A,14] ***~ sb (into/out of),*** deceive; swindle: *You've been ~ed. He ~ed the poor girl out of her money/~ed her into marrying him by pretending that he was rich.* **2** [VP15B] ***~ sth out/up,*** decorate, dress, ornament. **~·ery** /-ərɪ/ *n* [U] deception; cheating. **~·ster** /-stə(r)/ *n* person who makes a practice of of ~ing people; swindler. **tricky** *adj* (-ier, -iest) **1** (of persons and their actions) deceptive: *a ~y politician.* **2** (of work, etc) requiring skill; full of hidden or unexpected difficulties: *a ~y problem/job.*

trickle /ˈtrɪkl/ *vi,vt* [VP2A,C,15A] (cause to) flow in drops or in a thin stream: *Blood ~d from the wound. The tears ~d down her cheeks. He was trickling oil into the bearings of the machine. People began to ~ out of the theatre to catch the last train home.* □ *n* weak or thin flow: *The stream had shrunk to a mere ~.* **ˈ~ charger,** device for the slow continuous charging of an accumulator (from the mains).

tri·col·our (US = **-color**) /ˈtrɪkələ(r) *US:* ˈtraɪkʌlər/ *n* flag of three colours in stripes of the same width, esp, **the T~,** the French national flag.

tri·cycle /ˈtraɪsɪkl/ *n* three-wheeled cycle.

tri·dent /ˈtraɪdnt/ *n* spear with three points (as carried by Neptune); this as a symbol of sea-power.

a trident

tried /traɪd/ ⇨ **try**[1].

tri·en·nial /traɪˈenɪəl/ *n, adj* (sth) lasting for, happening or done every, three years.

trier /ˈtraɪə(r)/ *n* ⇨ **try**[1].

trifle /ˈtraɪfl/ *n* **1** thing, event, etc of little value or importance: *It's silly to quarrel over ~s. The merest ~ upsets that man,* He easily gets out of temper, etc. ***not stick at ~s,*** not allow small things to interfere with one's plans, etc. **2** small amount of money: *It cost me only a ~.* **3 a ~,** (*adv*) somewhat, a little: *This dress is a ~ too short. Isn't the meat a ~ tough?* **4** [C,U] sweet dish made of cream, white of eggs, cake, jam, etc: *make a ~; eat too much ~.* □ *vi,vt* **1** [VP3A] ***~ with,*** play idly with, behave lightly or insincerely towards: *He's not a man to be ~d with,* he must be given serious attention. *It's wrong of you to ~ with the girl's affections,* make her think that you love her when you don't *Don't ~ with your food: either eat it or leave it.* **2** [VP3A] ***~ away,*** fritter away (which is more usu): *~ away one's time/energies/money.* **trif·ling** /ˈtraɪflɪŋ/ *adj* unimportant: *a trifling error; of trifling value. It's no trifling matter,* is serious. **tri·fler** /ˈtraɪflə(r)/ *n* person who ~s.

trig·ger /ˈtrɪgə(r)/ *n* lever for releasing a spring, esp of a firearm: ***be quick on the ~,*** quick to shoot. ***have one's finger on the ~,*** be in full control, esp of military operations. **ˈ~-happy** *adj* (sl) ready to use violence, e g by shooting, at slight provocation. □ *vt* [VP15B] ***~ sth off,*** be the immediate cause of (sth serious or violent): *Who/What ~ed off the rebellion?*

trig·on·om·etry /ˌtrɪgəˈnomətrɪ/ *n* [U] branch of mathematics that deals with the relations between the sides and angles of triangles.

tri·lat·eral /ˌtraɪˈlætərl/ *adj* three-sided: *a ~ agreement/treaty.*

trilby /ˈtrɪlbɪ/ *n* (*pl* -**bies**) **ˈ~ (hat),** (man's) soft felt hat.

trill /trɪl/ *n* [C] **1** quavering sound; shaky or vibrating sound made by the voice or as in bird song. **2** (music) quick alternation of two notes a tone or a semitone apart. **3** speech sound (e g Spanish *r*) uttered with a ~. □ *vi,vt* [VP6A,2A,C] sing or play (a musical note) with a ~; pronounce with a ~: *The canary was ~ing away in its cage. Can you ~ the sound r as in Spanish?*

tril·lion /ˈtrɪlɪən/ *n, adj* (GB) million million million; (US, F) million million. ⇨ **App 4.**

tril·ogy /ˈtrɪlədʒɪ/ *n* [C] (*pl* -**gies**) group of three plays, novels, operas, etc to be performed, read, etc in succession, each complete in itself but having a common subject.

trim /trɪm/ *adj* (**-mm-**) in good order; neat and tidy: *a ~ ship/cabin; a ~ little garden.* □ *n* [U] ~ state; readiness; fitness: *Everything was in good/proper ~. The crew is in/out of ~ for the boat-race. We must get into (good) ~ for the sports meeting.* □ *vt,vi* (**-mm-**) **1** [VP6A,15A,22] make ~, esp by taking or cutting away uneven, irregular or unwanted parts: *~ one's beard/the wick of a lamp.* **2** [VP6A,14] ***~ sth (with...),*** decorate or ornament (a hat, dress, etc): *a hat ~med with fur; ~ a dress with lace.* **3** [VP6A] make (a boat, ship, aircraft) evenly balanced by arranging the position of the cargo, passengers, etc; set (sails) to suit the wind. **4** [VP2A] hold a middle course in politics; change one's views, policy, etc in an effort to win popular approval: *a politician who is always ~ming.* **~mer** *n* person or thing that ~s. **~ming** *n* [C] sth used for ~ming(2): *lace ~mings.* **~·ly** *adv*

tri·maran /ˈtraɪməræn/ *n* boat with three parallel hulls. ⇨ **catamaran.**

tri·nitro·tolu·ene /ˌtraɪˌnaɪtrəʊˈtoljʊin/ *n* [U] (usu **TNT**) high explosive.

trin·ity /ˈtrɪnətɪ/ *n* group of three. **the T~,** (in Christian teaching) union of three persons, Father, Son and Holy Ghost, one God. **ˈT~ House,** British institution which licenses pilots of ships, maintains lighthouses, marks wrecks, etc. **ˌT~ ˈSunday,** Sunday after Whit Sunday. **ˈT~ term,** university term beginning after Easter.

trin·ket /ˈtrɪŋkɪt/ *n* ornament or jewel of small value: small fancy article.

trio /ˈtriəʊ/ *n* (*pl* ~**s**) group of three; (musical composition for) group of three singers or players.

trio·let /ˈtriəʊlet/ *n* poem of 8 (usu 8-syllabled) lines, and two rhymes.

trip /trɪp/ *vi,vt* (**-pp-**) **1** [VP2A,C] walk, run or dance with quick, light steps: *She came ~ping down the garden path.* **2** [VP2A,C,3A,15B] ***~ over sth,*** catch one's foot, etc in an obstacle and stumble: *He ~ped over the root of a tree.* ***~ (sb) (up),*** (cause to) stumble or make a false step: *He ~ped up and nearly fell. The wrestler ~ped (up) his opponent. That lawyer is always trying to ~ the witness up,* (fig) trying to make him contradict himself; be inaccurate, etc. **3** [VP2C] ***~ out,*** (sl) take a ~(3 below). **4** (old use) ***~ a measure,*** dance with quick light steps. □ *n* [C] **1** journey, esp a pleasure excursion: *a ~ to the seaside; a weekend ~; a holiday/honeymoon ~ to Venice.* **2** fall or stumble; (fig) fault or error: *a ~ of the tongue* (*slip* is more usu). **ˈ~ wire** *n* wire stretched along the ground, working a trap when an animal, etc trips against it. **3** psychedelic experience resulting from taking a hallucinatory drug. **~·per** *n* **1** person making a (usu short) excursion for pleasure: *weekend ~pers.* **2** (colloq) person who ~s out(3). **~·ping** *adj* light and quick. **~·ping·ly** *adv*

tri·par·tite /ˌtraɪˈpatɑɪt/ *adj* **1** (of an agreement) in which three parties have a share. **2** having three parts.

tripe /traɪp/ *n* [U] **1** part of the wall of the stomach of an ox or cow used as food: *a dish of stewed ~ and onions.* **2** (sl) worthless talk, writing, ideas etc: *Stop talking ~!*

triple /ˈtrɪpl/ *adj* made up of three (parts or parties): *the T~ Alliance,* one of several military alliances (in European history) between three countries; *~ time,* (music) of 3 or 9 beats to the bar; *the ~ crown,* the Pope's tiara. □ *vt,vi* [VP6A,2A] make, become, be, three times as much or many: *He ~d his income. His income ~d.*

trip·let /ˈtrɪplət/ *n* **1** (*pl*) three children born at one birth: *One of the ~s is ill.* **2** set of three.

trip·lex /ˈtrɪpleks/ *adj* triple; threefold: *~ glass,* (P) unsplinterable glass (as used in motor-cars, etc) made of a sheet of plastic material between two sheets of glass.

trip·li·cate /ˈtrɪplɪkət/ *adj* of which three copies are made. □ *n* one of three like things, esp documents: *drawn up in ~,* one original and two copies. □ *vt* /ˈtrɪplɪkeɪt/ [VP6A] make in ~.

tri·pod /ˈtraɪpod/ *n* three-legged support, e g for a camera; stool, table, etc, resting on three legs.

tri·pos /ˈtraɪpos/ *n* (GB) (list of successful candidates in) examination for an honours degree at Cambridge University: *the History/Classics, etc ~.*

trip·per /ˈtrɪpə(r)/ *n* ⇨ trip.

trip·tych /ˈtrɪptɪk/ *n* picture or carving on three (usu hinged) panels fixed side by side, e g of religious subjects in a Christian church.

tri·reme /ˈtraɪrim/ *n* ancient (esp Greek) warship with three tiers of oars on each side.

tri·sect /ˈtraɪˈsekt/ *vt* [VP6A] divide (a line, an angle, etc) into three (esp equal) parts.

trite /traɪt/ *adj* (of remarks, ideas, opinions) commonplace; not new. **~·ly** *adv* **~·ness** *n*

tri·umph /ˈtraɪʌmf/ *n* **1** [C,U] (joy or satisfaction at a) success or victory: *return home in ~; shouts of ~; score a resounding ~ over one's enemies; recount all one's ~s.* **2** [C] (in ancient Rome) procession and ceremony in honour of a victorious general. □ *vi* [VP2A,3A] ***~ (over...),*** win a victory (over); show joy because of success: *~ over opposition/adversity,* overcome it; *~ over a defeated enemy.* **tri·um·phal** /traɪˈʌmfl/ *adj* of, for, a ~; expressing ~: *erect a ~al arch,* one built to commemorate a victory. **tri·um·phant** /traɪˈʌmfnt/ *adj* (rejoicing at) having ~ed. **tri·um·phant·ly** *adv*

tri·um·vir /traɪˈʌmvə(r)/ *n* (in ancient Rome) each of three men holding an office jointly. **tri·um·vir·ate** /traɪˈʌmvɪrət/ *n* set of ~s.

tri·une /ˈtraɪjun/ *adj* three in one: *the ~ Godhead,* the Trinity.

trivet /ˈtrɪvɪt/ *n* (usu three-legged or three-footed) stand or support for a pot or kettle on or by a fire; iron bracket to be hooked on to the bars of a fire-grate. ***as right as a ~,*** in good condition or health; in satisfactory circumstances.

triv·ial /ˈtrɪvɪəl/ *adj* **1** of small value or importance: *a ~ offence; a ~ loss; raise ~ objections against a proposal.* **2** commonplace; humdrum: *the ~ round,* the ordinary course of everyday events, duties, etc. **3** (of a person) trifling; lacking seriousness; superficial: *Don't marry that ~ young man, please.* **~ly** /-ɪəlɪ/ *adv* **~·ity** /ˈtrɪvɪˈæləti/ *n* [U] state of being ~; [C] (*pl* -ties) ~ idea, event, etc: *talk/write ~ities.*

tro·chee /ˈtrəʊki/ *n* metrical foot of one stressed (or long) and one unstressed (or short) syllable, as in: *ˈLife is / ˈbut an / ˈempty / ˈdream.* **tro·chaic** /trəʊˈkeɪɪk/ *adj*

trod, trod·den /trod, ˈtrodn/ ⇨ tread.

trog·lo·dyte /ˈtrogləˌdaɪt/ *n* cave-dweller in ancient times.

troika /ˈtrɔɪkə/ *n* [C] **1** small Russian carriage drawn by a team of three horses abreast. **2** triumvirate (of political leaders).

Tro·jan /ˈtrəʊdʒən/ *n, adj* (inhabitant) of ancient Troy: *the T~ war,* between the Greeks and the Trojans, as described by Homer. ***work like a ~,*** work very hard.

troll[1] /trəʊl/ *n* (in Scandinavian mythology) supernatural being, a giant, or, in later tales, a mischievous but friendly dwarf.

troll[2] /trol *US:* trəʊl/ *vt,vi* [VP2A,C] fish with rod and line by pulling bait through the water behind a boat: *~ for pike.*

trol·ley /ˈtrolɪ/ *n* (*pl* ~s) **1** two- or four-wheeled handcart. **2** small, low truck running on rails, e g one worked by a handlever, used by workers on a railway. **3** (often **ˈtea-~**) small table on castors (small wheels) used for serving food. **4** small contact-wheel between a tram-car or bus (called *a ˈ~-bus*) and an overhead cable; (US) electric street-car (GB = *tram*).

trol·lop /ˈtroləp/ *n* slatternly woman, esp a woman of bad character.

trom·bone /tromˈbəʊn/ *n* large brass musical instrument with a sliding tube. ⇨ the illus at brass. **trom·bon·ist** /tromˈbəʊnɪst/ *n* ~ player.

troop /trup/ *n* [C] **1** company of persons or animals, esp when moving: *a ~ of schoolchildren; a ~ of antelope(s).* **2** (*pl*) soldiers: *find billets for the ~s.* ⇨ trooper below. **ˈ~-carrier** *n* ship or large aircraft for transporting ~s. **ˈ~·ship** *n* ship for transporting ~s. **3** unit of cavalry, armoured vehicles or artillery (under the command of a lieutenant). **4** company of boy scouts. □ *vi,vt* **1** [VP2C] (with *pl subject*) come or go together in a group: *children ~ing out of school.* **2** ***~ the colour,*** (GB) carry the colour (flag) through the ranks of a regiment. ***~ing the colour,*** such a ceremony (esp as on the Sovereign's birthday). **~er** *n* **1** soldier in a cavalry or armoured regiment. **2** (US) member of state police force (now using a motor-vehicle). ***swear like a ~er,*** swear fluently.

trope /trəʊp/ *n* figurative use of a word (as of *tread* in 'The years like great black oxen tread the world').

trophy /ˈtrəʊfɪ/ *n* [C] (*pl* -phies) **1** sth kept in memory of a victory or success (e g in hunting, sport, etc). **2** prize, e g for winning a tournament: *ˈtennis trophies.*

tropic /ˈtropɪk/ *n* **1** line of latitude 23°27′ north (*T~ of Cancer*) or south (*T~ of Capricorn*) of the equator. **2 the ~s,** the parts of the world between these two latitudes. **tropi·cal** /-kl/ *adj* of, or as of, the ~s: *a ~al climate; ~al fruits.* **tropi·cally** /-klɪ/ *adv*

trot /trot/ *vi,vt* (-tt-) **1** [VP2A,B,C] (of horses, etc) go at a pace faster than a walk but not so fast as a gallop. **2** [VP2A,C] run with short steps; (colloq, hum) go (at an ordinary speed): *Well, I must be ~ting off home. You ~ along!* Go away! **3** [VP15B] ***~ sth out,*** (hum) produce; bring out: *~ out one's knowledge,* e g to get admiration. **4** [VP15A,B] cause to: *~ a person off his legs,* take him round, e g sight-seeing, until he is exhausted; *~ sb round,* take him round with one (e g shopping). □ *n* (*sing* only) **1** ~ting pace: *go at a steady ~.* ***on the ~,*** (sl) one after the other: *five whiskies on the ~.* ***be on the ~, keep sb on the ~,*** **(a)** (colloq) busy on one's feet, moving from one task to another: *I've been (kept) on the ~ all morning and I'm exhausted.* **(b)** (sl) be running away (esp from prison or the police). ***be on the ~,*** (US = *have the ~s*), (colloq) have diarrhoea. **2** period of ~ting: *go for a ~*. **~·ter** *n* **1** horse bred and trained to ~. **2** (usu *pl*) pig's or sheep's foot as food.

troth /trəʊθ *US:* trɔθ/ *n* [U] (archaic) ***in ~,*** truly, upon my word; *plight one's ~,* pledge one's word/esp promise to marry.

trou·ba·dour /ˈtrubədɔ(r)/ *n* travelling poet and singer in France and Italy, 11th to 13th cc.

trouble /ˈtrʌbl/ *vt,vi* **1** [VP6A] cause worry, discomfort, anxiety or inconvenience to: *be ~d by bad news; ~d with a nasty cough. What ~s me is that...* **2** [VP17,14] ***~ sb to do sth; ~ sb for sth,*** put sb to the inconvenience of doing sth. **(a)** (with *may/might,* a polite request): *May I ~ you to pass the salt, please. May I ~ you for a match?* **(b)** (with *I'll, I must,* a sarcastic or ironic request): *I'll ~ you to be quiet. I must ~ you to remember your manners.* **3** [VP2A,C,4A] (esp in neg and interr) bother or inconvenience oneself: *Don't ~ to meet me at the station. Don't ~ about that. Oh, don't ~, thanks. Why should I ~ to explain?* **4** [VP6A] agitate; disturb: (esp *pp*) *a ~d countenance; ~d looks.* ***fish in ~d waters,*** try to gain an advantage from a confused state of affairs. □ *n* **1** [C,U] worry; anxiety; discomfort; unhappiness; difficulty; possible punishment: *Her heart was full of ~. She's always making ~ for her friends. He has been through much ~/has had many ~s. He has a lot of family/domestic ~(s). Don't be nasty to her; she has enough ~s as it is. His ~s are over now* (sometimes said of a person who dies). *The ~ is that...,* The difficulty is that.... *What's the ~ now?* What unfortunate thing has happened? ***in ~,*** suffering, or likely to suffer, misfortune, anxiety, etc, e g because one has done wrong. ***ask/look for ~,*** (colloq) behave in such a way that ~ is likely: *It's asking for ~ to associate with criminals.* ***get into ~,*** do sth that will bring unhappiness, punishment, etc. ***get sb into ~,*** cause sb to be in ~. ***get a girl into ~,*** (colloq) make her pregnant. **2** [C] sb or sth that causes ~(1): *I don't want to be any ~* (= nuisance) *to you. Some dishes are very enjoyable to eat but a great ~ to prepare. I find it a great ~ to get up at 6a m.* **3** [U] care; attention; (extra) work; inconvenience: *Did the work give you much ~? I don't like putting you to* (= causing you) *so much ~. Thank you for all the ~ you've taken to help my son. It will be no ~,* will not inconvenience me. **4** [C,U] political or social unrest: *ˈLabour ~(s)* (e g strikes) *cost the country enormous sums last year. They've been having a good deal of ~/a lot of ~s in South Africa.* **5** [C, U] illness: *ˈliver ~; ˈmental ~; ˈchildren's ~s.* **6** (compounds) **ˈ~-maker,** person who stirs up discontent (e g in industry). **ˈ~-shooter,** person employed in conciliating and arbitrating between parties in conflict (e g in industry), or in detecting and correcting faults (esp in machinery). **ˈ~·some** /-səm/ *adj* causing ~: *a ~some child/headache/problem. Her cough is very ~some today.* **troub·lous** /-əs/ *adj* (liter) disturbed; unsettled: *live in troublous times.*

trough /trof *US:* trɔf/ *n* **1** long, open (usu shallow) box for animals to feed or drink from. **2** long open box in which a baker kneads dough for bread. **3** *~ of the sea,* long hollow between two waves. **4** (met) region of lower atmospheric pressure between two regions of higher pressure.

trounce /traʊns/ *vt* [VP6A] beat; thrash; defeat; reprimand: *Our team was ~d on Saturday.* **trounc·ing** *n* beating; reprimand: *give sb a good trouncing.*

troupe /trup/ *n* company, esp of actors or of members of a circus. **trouper** *n* member of a theatrical ~: *He's a good ~r,* a loyal, hard-working and uncomplaining colleague.

trouser /ˈtraʊzə(r)/ *n* **1** ***~s; pair of ~s,*** two-legged outer garment for a man or boy, reaching from the waist to the ankles. ⇨ shorts, slacks. **2** (attrib) of or for ~s: *ˈ~ buttons/pockets.*

trous·seau /ˈtrusəʊ/ *n* outfit of clothing, etc, for a bride.

trout /traʊt/ *n* (*pl* unchanged) **1** freshwater fish valued as food and for the sport of catching it (with rod and line). **2** (dated GB colloq; usu *old ~*) unpleasant or interfering woman.

trove /trəʊv/ *n* ⇨ treasure(1).

trow /trəʊ/ *vt* (archaic or hum) think, believe.

trowel /ˈtraʊl/ *n* **1** flat-bladed tool for spreading mortar on bricks or stone, plaster on walls, etc. **2** hand-tool with a curved blade for lifting plants, etc. ⇨ the illus at tool.

troy /trɔɪ/ *n* [U] British system of weights, used for gold and silver, in which one pound = 12 ounces: *This spoon weighs 4 oz ~.* ⇨ App 5.

tru·ant /ˈtruənt/ *n* **1** child who stays away from school without good reason. ***play ~,*** stay away thus. **2** (attrib) (of persons, their conduct, thoughts, etc) wandering; idle; shirking (duty, etc). **tru·ancy** /-ənsɪ/ *n* (*pl* -cies) [U] playing ~; [C] instance of this.

truce /trus/ *n* [C] (agreement for the) stopping of fighting for a time (e g to take away the wounded).

truck[1] /trʌk/ *n* **1** (GB) open railway wagon for heavy goods. **2** (orig US) lorry. **3** porter's two-wheeled barrow (for moving heavy objects).

truck[2] /trʌk/ *n* [U] **1** barter; exchange. ***have no ~ with,*** have no dealings with. **2** **ˈgarden-~,** (US) fresh garden produce (vegetables, fruit) grown for the markets. **3** (*ˈ~ system*) payment of wages in goods instead of money.

truckle[1] /ˈtrʌkl/ *vi* [VP3A] ***~ to,*** submit in a timid or cowardly way: *This country will never ~ to bullies.*

truckle[2] /ˈtrʌkl/ *n* **ˈ~-bed,** low, wheeled bed that can be pushed under another when not in use.

trucu·lent /ˈtrʌkjʊlənt/ *adj* looking for, desiring, a fight; violent. **~·ly** *adv* **trucu·lence** /-ləns/, **trucu·lency** /-lənsɪ/ *nn*

trudge /trʌdʒ/ *vi* [VP2A,B,C] walk wearily or heavily: *trudging through the deep snow. He ~d 20 miles.* □ *n* long tiring walk.

true /tru/ *adj* (-r, -st) **1** in accordance or agreement with fact: *Is it ~ that you are going to Rome? Is the news ~?* ***come ~,*** (of a hope, dream) really happen, become fact. **2** ***~ (to),*** loyal, faithful: *be ~ to one's word/promise,* do what one has promised to do. **ˌ~-ˈblue** *n, adj* (person who is) of uncompromising principles, firmly loyal. **ˌ~-ˈborn** *adj* legitimate. **ˌ~-ˈhearted** *adj* loyal. **ˈ~-love** *n* one who loves truly/is truly loved. **3** in accordance with reason or received standards; genuine; rightly so named: *T~ friendship should last for ever. The frog is not a ~ reptile. Who was the ~ heir to the throne?* **4** ***~ to type,*** accurately conforming to its type or class: *Plants grown from seed are not always ~ to type.* **5** accurately fitted or placed: *Is the wheel/*

post ~? **6** exact; accurate: *a ~ copy of a document; a ~ pair of scales.* □ *n* (only in) ***out of ~,*** not in its exact or accurate position: *The axle (beam, door) is out of ~.* □ *adv* (with certain *vv*) truly: *aim ~; breed ~*(4); *tell me ~.* □ *vt* [VP15B] ***~ sth up,*** make, adjust so as to be ~(5): *~ up a wheel.*

truffle /ˈtrʌfl/ *n* kind of fungus that grows underground, used for flavouring savoury food dishes, pâté.

trug /trʌg/ *n* (GB) shallow basket made of strips of wood, used by gardeners.

tru·ism /ˈtru-ɪzm/ *n* [C] statement that is obviously true and need not have been made: *It's a ~ to say that your body was once much smaller than it is now.*

truly /ˈtrulɪ/ *adv* **1** truthfully: *speak ~.* **2** sincerely: *feel ~ grateful; yours ~* (used at the close of a letter, before the signature). **3** genuinely; certainly: *a ~ beautiful picture; a ~ brave action.*

trump[1] /trʌmp/ *n* [C] **1** (in card games such as whist, bridge) each card of a suit that has been declared as having higher value than the other three suits: *Hearts are ~s.* ⇨ declare(1). ***play one's ~ card,*** (fig) make use of one's most valuable resource, means of gaining one's ends (esp after trying other means). ***turn up ~s,*** (colloq) **(a)** have a better result than was expected. **(b)** have a stroke of good luck. **2** (colloq) excellent fellow; person who is full of resource, is generous, etc. □ *vt,vi* **1** [VP6A] play a ~ card on: *~ the ace of clubs.* **2** [VP15B] (usu passive) ***~ sth up,*** invent (an excuse, a false story, etc) in order to deceive sb: *He was arrested on a ~ed-up charge.*

trump[2] /trʌmp/ *n* (liter) (sound made by a) trumpet. ***the last ~; the ~ of doom,*** the trumpet call which will, some people believe, be sounded on the Last Day, the day when everyone will be judged by God.

trump·ery /ˈtrʌmpərɪ/ *adj* showy but of little value: *~ ornaments.*

trum·pet /ˈtrʌmpɪt/ *n* **1** musical wind-instrument of brass. ⇨ the illus at brass. ***blow one's own ~,*** (fig) praise oneself. **2** sound (as) of a ~. **3** sth suggesting a ~ in shape or use (e g the corona of a daffodil). □ *vt,vi* **1** [VP6A,15B] (old use, rhet) proclaim, make known, (as) by the sound of ~s; (fig) celebrate: *~ (forth) sb's heroic deeds.* **2** [VP2A,C] (esp of an elephant) make loud sounds. **~er** *n* person who plays a ~.

trun·cate /trʌŋˈkeɪt *US:* ˈtrʌŋkeɪt/ *vt* [VP6A] shorten by cutting the tip, top or end from: *a ~d cone/pyramid.*

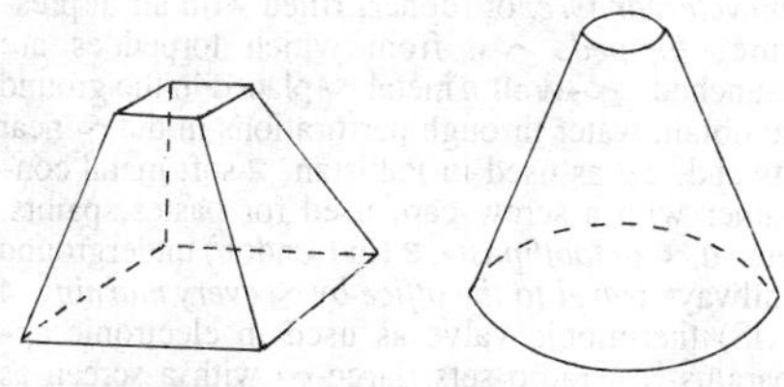

a truncated pyramid and cone

trun·cheon /ˈtrʌntʃən/ *n* short thick club (esp one used by the police).

trundle /ˈtrʌndl/ *vt,vi* [VP6A,15A,B,2C] (esp of sth heavy or awkward in shape) move or roll: *The porter ~d his barrow along the platform. The child was trundling a hoop along the pavement.* **ˈ~ bed,** (US) = truckle bed.

trunk /trʌŋk/ *n* [C] **1** main stem of a tree (contrasted with the branches). ⇨ the illus at tree. **2** body without head, arms or legs; main part of any structure. **3** large box with a hinged lid, for clothes, etc while travelling. **4** long nose of an elephant ⇨ the illus at large. **5** (*pl*) man's garment covering the lower part of the ~(2), worn by athletes, acrobats and for swimming. **ˈ~ hose** *n* short wide breeches worn by men (16th and 17th cc). **6** (US) = boot(2) of a car. **7** (attrib) **ˈ~-call** *n* telephone call to a distant place, with charges according to distance. **ˈ~-line** *n* **(a)** main line of a railway. **(b)** long-distance telephone line. **ˈ~-road** *n* main road.

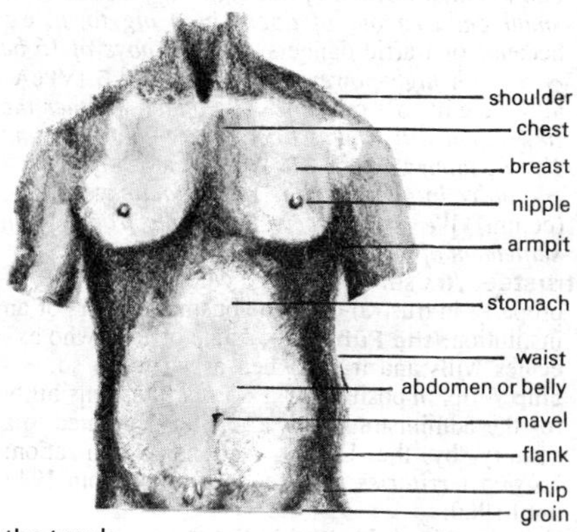

the trunk

truss /trʌs/ *n* [C] **1** (GB) bundle (of hay, straw). **2** framework supporting a roof, bridge, etc. **3** padded belt worn by a person suffering from hernia. □ *vt* [VP6A,15B] ***~ sth (up),*** **1** tie or fasten up: *~ hay; ~ up a chicken,* pin the wings to the body before boiling or roasting it. *The policemen ~ed up the struggling criminal with rope,* tied his arms to his sides. **2** support (a roof, bridge, etc) with a ~ or ~es(2).

trust[1] /trʌst/ *n* **1** [U] ***~ (in),*** confidence, strong belief, in the goodness, strength, reliability of sth or sb: *put one's ~ in God. A child usually has perfect ~ in its mother. She hasn't/doesn't place much ~ in his promises.* ***on ~,*** **(a)** without proof; without close examination: *You'll have to take my statement on ~.* **(b)** on credit. **2** [U] responsibility: *a position of great ~.* **3** [C] (legal) property held and managed by one or more persons (*trustees*) for the benefit of another or others; [U] the legal relation between the trustee(s) and the property; the obligation assumed by the trustee(s): *By his will he created ~s for his children. This property is not mine; it is a ~. I am holding the property in ~ for my nephew.* **ˈ~-money, ˈ~ fund** *nn* money held in ~. **4** [C] association of business firms for the achievement of various objects, e g reducing competition, maintenance of prices. **5** **ˈbrains ~,** ⇨ brain. **~·ful** /-fl/, **~·ing** *adjj* ready to have ~ in others; not suspicious. **~·fully** /-flɪ/, **~·ing·ly** *advv* **ˈ~·worthy** *adj* worthy of ~;

dependable. **ˋ~·worthi·ness** *n* **trusty** *adj* (old use) ~worthy: *a ~y servant/sword.* □ *n* convicted criminal given special privileges because of good behaviour in prison.

trust[2] /trʌst/ *vt,vi* **1** [VP6A] have trust(1) in; believe in the honesty and reliability of: *He's not the sort of man to be ~ed/not a man I would ~. Can you ~ his account of what happened?* **2** [VP3A] ***~ in sb,*** have confidence in; believe that he will act for the best: *~ in God. I can't put ~ in our prime minister.* ***~ to sth,*** have reliance on: *Don't ~ to chance. You ~ to your memory too much.* **3** [VP14] = entrust (the more usu word). **4** [VP15A,B,17] allow (sb) to do sth, have sth, go somewhere, etc without anxiety, knowing that he will act sensibly, etc: *Do you ~ your young daughters to go to pop concerts with any sort of men? He may be ~ed to do the work well. We can't ~ that boy out of our sight. It's unwise to ~ small children out of doors in a big town,* e g because of traffic dangers. *Should boys of 16 be ~ed with high-powered motor-bikes?* **5** [VP6A] allow credit to a customer: *I wonder whether the newsagent will ~ me; I need some cigarettes and I've no money on me.* **6** [VP7A,9] earnestly hope: *I ~ you're in good health. You're quite well, I ~,* (comm) *We ~ to receive a cheque from you in settlement of this account.*

trustee /trʌˋsti/ *n* person who has charge of property in trust(3) or of the business affairs of an institution. **the Public T~,** state official who executes wills and trusts when asked to do so. **~-ship** /-ʃɪp/ *n* position of a ~; (esp) responsibility for the administration of a territory, granted to a country by the United Nations Organization: *ˋ~ship territories,* e g the Cameroons from 1947 until 1960.

truth /truθ/ *n* (*pl* ~s /truðz/) **1** [U] quality or state of being true: *There's no ~/not a word of ~ in what he says.* **2** [U] that which is true: *tell the ~.* ***to tell the ~,...,*** (formula used when making a confession): *To tell the ~, I forgot all about your request.* ***in ~,*** (liter) truly, really. **3** [C] fact, belief, etc accepted as true: *the ~s of religion/science.* **~·ful** /-fl/ *adj* **1** (of persons) in the habit of telling the ~. **2** (of statements) true. **~·fully** /-fl̩ɪ/ *adv* **~·ful·ness** *n*

try[1] /traɪ/ *vi,vt* (*pt,pp* **tried**) **1** [VP2A,B,7A] (Note that *try to + inf* is often replaced by *try and + inf* in colloq style, esp in the imperative, but *don't try to* and *didn't try to* are not replaced by *don't try and* and *didn't try and*) make an attempt: *I don't think I can do it, but I'll try. I've tried till I'm tired. He's trying his hardest,* using his utmost efforts. *Try to get here early. Try to/Try and behave better. He didn't try to do it.* **2** [VP3A] ***try for sth,*** make an attempt to get or win (esp a position): *try for a scholarship/a position in the Civil Service.* **3** [VP6A,B,10] use sth, do sth, as an experiment or test, to see whether it is satisfactory: *Have you tried sleeping on your back as a cure for snoring? Won't you try* (= buy and use) *this new kind of detergent? Try how far you can jump/whether you can jump across this stream. Try knocking at the back door if nobody hears you at the front door. Please try me for the job,* let me do it as an experiment. ⇨ trial(1). [VP15B] ***try sth on,*** **(a)** put on (a garment, show, etc) to see whether it fits, looks well, etc: *go to the tailor's to have a suit tried on.* **(b)** (colloq) make a bold or impudent attempt to discover whether sth will be tolerated: *It's no use your trying it/your games/tricks on with me,* I shall stand no nonsense from you. Hence, **ˋtry-on** *n* (colloq) an attempt of this sort. [VP15B] ***try sth out,*** use it, experiment with it, in order to test it: *The idea seems good but it needs to be tried out.* **ˋtry-out** *n* preliminary test of ability, qualification, etc, e g of an athlete. ***try one's hand at sth,*** ⇨ hand[1](5). **4** [VP6A,15A] inquire into (a case) in a court of law: *He was tried and found guilty. He will be tried for murder. Which judge will try the case?* ⇨ trial(3). **5** [VP6A] put a strain on; cause to be tired, exhausted, out of patience, etc: *Small print tries the eyes. Don't try his patience too much. His courage was severely tried.* **tried** *adj* that has been tested; reliable: *a tried friend/remedy.* **trier** *n* person who tries hard, who always does his best. **try·ing** *adj* (⇨ 5 above) distressing; putting a strain on, e g the temper, one's patience: *a trying person to deal with; have a trying day,* one during which one's temper, patience, etc are tried; *work that is trying to the eyes.*

try[2] /traɪ/ *n* **1** attempt: *Let me have a try at it. He had three tries and failed each time.* **2** (Rugby) touching down the ball behind the opponents' goal-line (with a score of three points).

tryst /trɪst/ *n* (archaic) (time and place for, agreement to have, a) meeting, esp between lovers: *keep/break ~* (*with* sb).

Tsar /zɑ(r)/, **Tsa·rina** /zɑˋrinə/ *nn* ⇨ Czar.

tsetse /ˋsetsɪ/ *n* **ˋ~(-fly)** blood-sucking fly (in tropical Africa) carrying and transmitting (often fatal) disease in cattle, horses, etc. ⇨ the illus at insect.

T-shirt /ˋti ʃ3t/ *n* ⇨ T, t.

T-square /ˋti skweə(r)/ ⇨ square[2](7).

tub /tʌb/ *n* **1** large open vessel, usu round, made of wood, zinc, etc used for washing clothes, holding liquids, growing plants in, etc: *a rain-water tub.* **ˋtub-thumper** *n* mob orator. **2** (also *ˋtubful*) as much as a tub holds: *a tub of water.* **3** (colloq) bath-tub; (GB) bath: *have a cold tub before breakfast; prefer a tub to a shower.* **4** (colloq) clumsy slow boat. □ *vt* (-bb-) [VP6A] have a bath in a tub.

tuba /ˋtjubə *US:* ˋtu-/ *n* large musical instrument of brass, of low pitch. ⇨ the illus at brass.

tubby /ˋtʌbɪ/ *adj* (-ier, -iest) shaped like a tub; fat and round: *a tubby little man.*

tube /tjub *US:* tub/ *n* **1** long hollow cylinder of metal, glass or rubber, esp for holding or conveying liquids, etc: *ˋboiler ~s; the ˋinner ~ of a bicycle/car tyre,* of rubber, filled with air at pressure; *torˋpedo ~s,* from which torpedoes are launched. **ˋ~-well** *n* metal ~ placed in the ground to obtain water through perforations in the ~ near its end, e g as used in Pakistan. **2** soft metal container with a screw-cap, used for pastes, paints, etc: *a ~ of toothpaste.* **3** (in London) underground railway: *travel to the office by ~ every morning.* **4** (US) thermionic valve as used in electronic apparatus, e g radio sets; large ~ with a screen as used in a television set. **5** hollow ~-shaped organ in the body: *the bronchial ~s.* **tub·ing** *n* [U] material in the form of a ~: *five feet of rubber/copper tubing.* **tu·bu·lar** /ˋtjubjʊlə(r) *US:* ˋtu-/ *adj* **1** *a tubular bridge,* a rectangular ~ through which a railway, etc passes. **2** having, consisting of, ~s or tubing: *a tubular boiler,* in which water or steam is heated as it passes through many ~s; *tubular furniture*, with parts made of metal tubing; *tubular scaffolding*. **~less** *adj* having no inner ~: *~less tyres.*

tu·ber /ˈtjubə(r) *US:* ˈtu-/ *n* [C] enlarged part of an underground stem with buds from which new plants will grow, e g a potato, Jerusalem artichoke, yam, etc.

tu·ber·cu·lo·sis /tjuˈbɜkjʊˈləʊsɪs *US:* tu-/ *n* [U] (common abbr **T B**) wasting disease affecting various parts of the body's tissues, esp the lungs: *pulmonary* ~, consumption. **tu·ber·cu·lous** /tjuˈbɜkjʊləs *US:* tu-/, **tu·ber·cu·lar** /tjuˈbɜkjʊlə(r) *US:* tu-/ *adjj* of, affected by, ~.

tub·ing, tu·bu·lar ⇨ **tube.**

tuck /tʌk/ *n* **1** [C] flat, stitched fold of material in a garment, for shortening or for ornament: *make/put in/take out a ~ in a dress/the sleeve of a shirt.* **2** [U] (GB, sl) food, esp the cakes, pastry, etc that children enjoy. ˈ**~-shop** *n* shop (esp at a school) where ~ is sold. ˈ**~-ˈin** *n* full meal: *The boys had a good ~-in.* □ *vt,vi* **1** [VP15A,B] draw together into a small space; put or push into a desired or convenient position: *He ~ed up his shirt-sleeves. She ~ed the ends of her hair into her bathing-cap. Your shirt's hanging out, Ned; ~ it in at once*, put it inside your trousers. *He sat with his legs ~ed up under him. The bird ~ed its head under its wing. The map is ~ed away in a pocket at the end of the book. She ~ed the child up in bed*, pulled the bed-clothes up round the child. *She took off her shoes and stockings, ~ed up* (= rolled or turned up) *her skirt, and waded across the stream.* **2** [VP2C,3A] **~ in,** eat heartily. **~ into sth,** eat heartily of: *He ~ed into the cold ham.*

tucker /ˈtʌkə(r)/ *n* piece of lace, linen, etc, worn (in the 17th and 18th cc) to cover a woman's neck and shoulders. ***one's best bib and ~,*** (colloq) one's best or finest clothes.

Tues·day /ˈtjuzdɪ *US:* ˈtu-/ *n* third day of the week, next after Monday.

tuft /tʌft/ *n* bunch of feathers, hair, grass, etc growing or held together at the base. **~ed** *adj* having ~s; growing in a ~ or ~s.

a tug-boat

tug /tʌg/ *vt,vi* (-gg-) [VP6A,15A,B,2A,C,3A] pull hard or violently; pull hard (*at*): *The child was tugging her toy cart round the garden/tugging it along behind. We tugged so hard that the rope broke. The kitten was tugging at my shoe-lace.* □ *n* [C] **1** sudden hard pull: *The naughty boy gave his sister's hair a tug. I felt a tug at my sleeve. Parting from his family was a tug (at his heart-strings)*, It was difficult to leave them. ***tug of war,*** contest in which two teams pull against each other on a rope. **2** ˈ**tug(-boat),** small powerful boat for towing ships, etc.

tu·ition /tjuˈɪʃn *US:* tu-/ *n* [U] (fee for) teaching: *have private ~ in mathematics.*

tu·lip /ˈtjulɪp *US:* ˈtu-/ *n* bulb plant with, in spring, a large bell-shaped or cup-shaped flower on a tall stem.

tulle /tjul *US:* tul/ *n* [U] soft, fine, silk net-like material for veils and dresses.

tumble /ˈtʌmbl/ *vi,vt* **1** [VP2A,C] fall, esp quickly or violently: *~ down the stairs/off a horse or bicycle/out of a window/over the roots of a tree. The baby is just learning to walk and he's always tumbling over.* **2** [VP2A,C] move up and down, to and fro, in a restless or disorderly way: *The puppies were tumbling about on the floor. The sick man tossed and ~d in his bed. I was so tired that I threw my clothes off and ~d into bed.* **3** [VP2C] be in a weak state (as if ready to fall): *The old barn is tumbling to pieces.* ˈ**~-down** *attrib adj* dilapidated; likely to collapse: *What a ~-down old house you live in!* **4** [VP15A,B] cause to fall; upset: *The accident ~d us all out of the bus.* **5** [VP6A] put into a state of disorder: *~ one's bed-clothes/sb's hair or clothes.* **6** [VP3A] ***~ to sth,*** (colloq) grasp, realize (an idea, etc): *At last he ~d to what I was hinting at.* □ *n* [C] **1** fall: *have a nasty ~.* **2** confused state: *Things were all in a ~.* ˈ**~-weed** *n* (US) plant which grows in desert areas and, when withered, breaks off and is rolled about by the wind.

tum·bler /ˈtʌmblə(r)/ *n* **1** flat-bottomed drinking-glass without a handle or stem, ⇨ **goblet.** **2** part of the mechanism of a lock which must be turned by a key before the lock will open. **3** kind of pigeon that turns over in flight. **4** acrobat.

tum·brel, tum·bril /ˈtʌmbrəl, -brɪl/ *n* cart, esp the kind that carried prisoners to the guillotine during the French Revolution.

tu·mes·cent /tjuˈmesnt *US:* tu-/ *adj* swelling; swollen. **tu·mes·cence** /-sns/ *n*

tu·mid /ˈtjumɪd *US:* ˈtu-/ *adj* (of parts of the body) swollen; (fig, of a style of writing, etc) bombastic. **~·ity** /tjuˈmɪdətɪ *US:* tu-/ *n*

tummy /ˈtʌmɪ/ *n* (*pl* -**mies**) (colloq; used by and to children) stomach; belly.

tu·mour (US = **tu·mor**) /ˈtjumə(r) *US:* ˈtu-/ *n* diseased growth in some part of the body.

tu·mult /ˈtjumʌlt *US:* ˈtu-/ *n* [C,U] **1** uproar; disturbance: *the ~ of battle.* **2** confused and excited state of mind: *in a ~; when the ~ within him had subsided.*

tu·mul·tu·ous /tjuˈmʌltʃʊəs *US:* tu-/ *adj* disorderly; noisy and violent: *a ~ welcome.* **~·ly** *adv*

tu·mu·lus /ˈtjumjʊləs *US:* ˈtu-/ *n* (*pl* -li /-laɪ/) mound of earth over a (usu ancient) grave.

tun /tʌn/ *n* large cask for beer, wine, etc; measure of capacity (252 gallons).

tuna /ˈtjunə *US:* ˈtunə/ *n* (*pl* with or without *s*) tunny.

tun·dra /ˈtʌndrə/ *n* [C] wide, treeless plain of the arctic regions (of Russia, Siberia), marshy in summer and frozen hard in winter.

tune /tjun *US:* tun/ *n* **1** [C] succession of notes forming a melody (of a song, hymn, etc): *whistle a popular ~; ~s that are easy to remember.* **2** [U] quality of having a well-marked melody: *Some of this modern music has very little ~ in it.* **3** [U] ***in/out of ~,*** at/not at the correct pitch: *sing/play in ~. The piano is out of ~. The piano and the violin are not in ~.* **4** [U] (fig) harmony; harmonious adjustment: *be in/out of ~ with one's surround-*

ings/companions. **5** (fig uses) ***change one's ~, sing another ~,*** change one's way of speaking, behaviour, etc, or one's attitude to others (e g from insolence to respect). ***to the ~ of,*** to the amount of (usu with the suggestion that the sum is very high or exorbitant): *He was fined* (e g for a motoring offence) *to the ~ of £30.* □ *vt,vi* **1** [VP6A] adjust the strings, etc (of a musical instrument) to the right pitch: *~ a guitar.* [VP2C] ***~ up,*** (e g of a player or players in an orchestra) ~ a musical instrument: *The orchestra were tuning up when we entered the concert-hall.* **ˈtuning-fork** *n* small steel instrument, which produces a musical note of fixed pitch when struck. **2** [VP2C] ***~ in (to),*** **(a)** adjust the controls of a radio to a particular frequency/station: *~ in to the B B C World Service. You're not properly ~d in.* **(b)** (fig) be aware of what other people are saying, feeling, etc: *He's not very well ~d in to his surroundings.* **3** [VP6A] adjust or adapt the engine of a motor-vehicle so that it gives its best, or a special, performance. **tuner** *n* **1** (in compounds) person who ~s musical instruments: *a ˈpiano-tuner.* **2** (part of) a radio etc which receives the signals. ⇨ *amplifier* at amplify, *loud-speaker* at loud(1). **~·ful** /-fl/ *adj* having a pleasing ~; melodious. **~·fully** /-fḷɪ/ *adv* **~·ful·ness** *n*

tung-oil /ˈtʌŋ ɔɪl/ *n* [U] oil (from a tree) used chiefly in varnishing woodwork.

tung·sten /ˈtʌŋstən/ *n* [U] grey metal (symbol **W**) used in making steel and the filaments of electric lamps.

tu·nic /ˈtjunɪk *US:* ˈtu-/ *n* **1** close-fitting jacket as worn by policemen, soldiers, etc. **2** loose blouse or coat for a woman or girl, gathered at the waist with a belt, and reaching down to, or below, the hips. **3** loose, short-sleeved or sleeveless outer garment reaching to the knees, as worn by ancient Greeks and Romans.

tun·nel /ˈtʌnl/ *n* underground passage (esp through a hill or mountain, for a road, railway, etc); underwater passage (e g the proposed Channel ~ between England and France). □ *vi,vt* (-ll-, US also -l-) **1** dig a ~ (through/into) sth; dig a ~ or ~s through (sth).

tunny /ˈtʌnɪ/ *n* (*pl* -nies or unchanged) large sea-fish (the tuna) used as food, valued for the sport of catching it.

tup /tʌp/ *n* male sheep; ram.

tup·pence /ˈtʌpns *US:* -pəns/ *n* (colloq, esp of pre-decimal currency) twopence. **tup·penny** /ˈtʌpnɪ *US:* -pənɪ/ *adj* costing ~; (fig) of trifling value.

tu quo·que /ˈtju ˈkwəʊkwɪ *US:* ˈtu ˈkwəʊkweɪ/ *n* (Lat) (phrase used as a retort) So are you! So did you!

tur·ban /ˈtɜbən/ *n* **1** man's headdress made by winding a length of cloth round the head (as worn in some Asian countries). **2** woman's close-fitting hat with little or no brim. **~ed** *adj* wearing a ~: *a ~ed Sikh.*

tur·bid /ˈtɜbɪd/ *adj* **1** (of liquids) thick; muddy; not clear: *~ waters/rivers.* **2** (fig) disordered; confused: *a ~ imagination; ~ thoughts.* **~·ness, ~·ity** /tɜˈbɪdətɪ/ *nn*

tur·bine /ˈtɜbɑɪn/ *n* engine or motor whose driving-wheel is turned by a current of water, steam or air. ⇨ the illus at air.

tur·bo·jet /ˈtɜbəʊˈdʒet/ *n* (aircraft with a) turbine engine that delivers its power in the form of a jet of hot gases (no propellers being needed on the aircraft).

tur·bo·prop /ˈtɜbəʊˈprop/ *n* (aircraft with a) turbine engine that uses its power, from hot gases, to turn a propeller.

tur·bot /ˈtɜbət/ *n* large, flat sea-fish valued as food.

tur·bu·lent /ˈtɜbjʊlənt/ *adj* violent; disorderly; uncontrolled: *~ waves/passions; a ~ mob.* **~·ly** *adv* **tur·bu·lence** /-ləns/ *n*

turd /tɜd/ *n* (not in polite use) ball or lump of excrement: *ˈsheep ~s.*

tu·reen /tjʊˈrin *US:* tʊ-/ *n* deep dish with a lid, from which soup, vegetables, etc are served at table.

turf /tɜf/ *n* **1** [U] soil-surface with grass-roots growing in it: *strip the ~ off a field; make a lawn by laying ~* (instead of sowing grass-seed). **the ~,** the race-course; the occupation of profession of horse-racing. **ˈ~ accountant, ~ commission agent,** bookmaker, ⇨ book[1](8). **2** (*pl* ~s or turves /tɜvz/) piece of ~ cut out; (in Ireland) (piece of) peat. □ *vt* **1** [VP6A] cover or lay (a piece of land) with ~. **2** [VP15B] ***~ sb or sth out,*** (GB sl) throw out.

tur·gid /ˈtɜdʒɪd/ *adj* **1** swollen; bloated. **2** (of language) pompous; full of high-sounding words. **~·ly** *adv* **~·ity** /tɜˈdʒɪdətɪ/ *n*

Turk /tɜk/ *n* **1** native or inhabitant of Turkey. **2** (hum, esp of a child) lively, uncontrollable person: *You little ~!*

tur·key /ˈtɜkɪ/ *n* (*pl* -keys) [C] large bird valued as food; the illus at fowl; [U] its flesh; (US sl) a flop. ***cold turkey,*** **(a)** sudden withdrawal from, or hangover after taking, narcotics. **(b)** frank, determined statement of truth (usu about sth unpleasant). ***talk ~,*** (US sl) talk frankly and bluntly.

Tur·kish /ˈtɜkɪʃ/ *n, adj* (language) of Turkey or the Turks. **ˌ~ ˈbath,** of hot air or steam, followed by a shower and massage. **ˌ~ deˈlight,** sweetmeat of jelly-like substance covered with powdered sugar. **~ towel,** one made of rough absorbent cloth.

tur·meric /ˈtɜmərɪk/ *n* [U] (E Indian plant with a) root which is used, in powdered form, as a colouring substance and a flavouring (esp in making curries).

tur·moil /ˈtɜmɔɪl/ *n* [C,U] (instance of) trouble, agitation, disturbance: *The town was in a ~ during the elections.*

turn[1] /tɜn/ *n* **1** act of turning; turning movement: *a few ~s of the handle; a ~ of Fortune's wheel,* a change of fortune. ***on the ~,*** about to change: *The milk is on the ~,* about to turn sour. *The tide is on the ~.* ***done to a ~,*** (from the use of a ~spit) cooked just enough, neither underdone nor overdone. **2** change of direction: *sudden ~s in the road.* ***at every ~,*** (fig) very frequently: *I've been coming across old friends at every ~ during this reunion. He was frustrated at every ~,* every time he tried to achieve his aim. **3** change in condition: *The sick man/My affairs took a ~ for the better/worse. His illness took a favourable ~.* **4** occasion or opportunity for doing sth, esp in one's proper order among others: *It's your ~ to read now, John. Wait (until it is) your ~. My ~ will come* (sometimes meaning 'I shall have my time of success, triumph, revenge, etc', according to context). ***(do sth) ~ and ~ about,*** (of two persons) first one and then the other; alternately. ***by ~s,***

(of persons, groups, actions) in rotation; one after the other: *She went hot and cold by ~s. They laughed and cried by ~s.* **in ~,** (of two persons) = ~ and ~ about; (of more than two persons) in succession: *The boys were summoned in ~ to see the examiner.* **out of ~,** before or after the permitted time: *You mustn't speak out of (your) ~.* **take ~s at sth, take ~s about,** do it in ~: *Mary and Helen took ~s at sitting up with their sick mother,* Mary sat up first, Helen next, and so on. **5** action regarded as affecting sb. ***One good ~ deserves another,*** (prov) Help, kind service, etc should be repaid. ***(do sb) a good/bad ~,*** be/not be helpful. **6** natural tendency: *a boy with a me'chanical ~,* interested in, clever at, mechanical things. *He has a gloomy ~ of mind.* **7** purpose; special need. **serve one's ~,** meet one's requirements: *I think this book will serve my ~.* **8** short period of activity: *I'll take a few ~s (=* have a walk) *round the deck before I go to bed. I'll take a ~ at the oars now if you want a rest.* **9** short performance on the stage (esp of a variety theatre, or similar entertainment for sound or TV broadcasts), e g a song, dance, juggling feat, display of skill: *Grock used to be a star ~ at the circus.* **10** (colloq) nervous shock: *The news gave me quite a ~.*

turn[2] /tɜn/ *vt, vi* (For uses with *adverbial particles* and *preps,* ⇨ 7 below.) **1** [VP6A,15A,B,2A,C,4A] (cause to) move round a point; (cause to) move so as to face in a different direction: *The earth ~s round the sun. The wheels of the car were ~ing slowly. What ~s the wheels? He ~ed away from me. He ~ed his back on me,* ⇨ back[1](1). *He ~ed his back to the wall. He ~ed his head (round) and looked back. He ~ed to look at me. He ~ed (to the) left. It's time we ~ed and went back home. He was idly ~ing the pages of a magazine. The car ~ed (round) the corner. Be careful how you ~ that corner. Please ~ your eyes (=* look) *this way. The mere thought of food ~ed his stomach,* upset his stomach, made him feel ill. *His stomach ~ed at the sight of food. When does the tide ~,* begin to flow in/out? *This tap ~s easily. It's easy to ~ this tap. Nothing will ever ~ him from (=* cause him to change) *his purpose.* **~ one's mind/thoughts/attention to sth,** direct one's mind, etc to: *Please ~ your attention to something more important.* **~ one's hand to sth,** (be able to) undertake (a task, etc): *He can ~ his hand to most jobs about the house,* can deal with them. **~ sth to account,** ⇨ account[1](3). **~ a deaf ear to sth,** refuse to listen to: *They ~ed a deaf ear to my request for help.* **~ sb's flank, ~ the flank of sb,** pass round an enemy's position so as to attack it in the flank or rear: (fig) outwit sb; defeat him in debate, etc. **~ the corner,** (fig use) ⇨ corner(1). **~ the scale(s),** ⇨ scale[3](1). **2** [VP6A,14,15A,B,2A,C,3A] ***~ (sth) into sth,*** (cause to) change in nature, quality, condition, etc: *Frost ~s water into ice. Caterpillars ~ into (=* become) *butterflies. This hot weather has ~ed the milk,* made it sour. *His hair has ~ed grey. Anxiety ~ed his hair white. The leaves are beginning to ~,* change colour (as in autumn). *Could you ~ this piece of prose into verse/this passage into Greek? He has ~ed traitor,* become a traitor. *T~ the dog loose,* let it go free, e g by releasing it from a chain. **~ sb's head,** unsettle him, make him vain: *The excessive praise the young actor received ~ed his head.* **~ sb's brain,** upset him mentally. **3** [VP6A] reach and pass: *He has ~ed (=* reach the age of) *fifty. It has just ~ed two,* is just after two o'clock. **4** [VP6A] shape (sth, wood or metal) on a lathe, etc: *~ brass; an engine-~ed cigarette-case; ~ a bowl on a potter's wheel;* (fig) give a graceful form to: *~ an epigram/a compliment; a well-~ed phrase/sentence; a well-~ed ankle;* (with passive force) *wood/metal that ~s (=* can be ~ed) *easily.* **5** [VP6A] remake (a garment) so that the inner surface becomes the outer surface: *I'll have this old overcoat ~ed.* **~ one's coat,** ⇨ coat(1). **'~coat** *n* person who deserts one party to join another, esp to win profit, advantage, safety, etc. **6** (compounds) **'~cock** *n* person employed to ~ water on or off (at the main). **'~key** *n* keeper of the keys in a prison; jailer. **'~pike** *n* (formerly in GB) gate kept closed across a road and opened on payment of a toll; (mod use, US) toll road for fast traffic. **'~spit** *n* dog or servant who turned the spit on which meat, etc used to be roasted. **'~stile** *n* revolving gate that admits, lets out, one person at a time. **'~-table** *n* flat circular platform, e g one on which discs are played, or on which a railway locomotive is turned round. **7** [VP14,15B,2C,3A] (special uses with *adverbial particles* and *preps*):

turn (sb) about, (cause to) ~ to one side or in a different direction: *About ~!* (as a military command, in drills, etc).

turn sb adrift, send sb away without help or support: *He ~ed his son adrift in the world,* sent him away from home and refused to help him.

turn (sb) against sb, (cause to) become hostile to: *She ~ed against her old friend. He tried to ~ the children against their mother.*

turn (sb) aside (from), (more usu ~ *away*) (cause to) ~ to one side or in a different direction.

turn (sb) away, (cause to) ~ in a different direction so as not to face sb/sth; refuse to look at, welcome, help, admit (to a place): *She ~ed away in disgust. He ~ed away a beggar. We had to ~ away hundreds of people,* e g from a stadium, because all seats were sold.

turn (sb/sth) back, (cause to) return the way one has come: *It's getting dark—we'd better ~ back. We were/Our car was ~ed back at the frontier.*

turn (sth) down, **(a)** (cause to) fold down: *~ down one's coat collar; a ~-down collar; ~ down the bed-clothes.* **(b)** reduce (the flame or brilliance of a gas- or oil-lamp, stove, etc) by ~ing a wheel or tap: *~ down the lamps.* **(c)** place (a playing-card) on the table face downwards. **~ sb/sth down,** refuse to consider (an offer, a proposal, or the person who makes it): *He tried to join the police force but was ~ed down because of poor physique. He asked Jane to marry him but she ~ed him down/~ed down his proposal.*

turn in, (colloq) go to bed. ***~ in on oneself/itself,*** withdraw from contact with others; become a recluse; (of a country) become isolationist. **~ sb in,** (colloq) surrender sb to the police. ***~ (sth) in,*** (cause to) fold or slant inwards: *His toes ~ in. He ~ed his toes in.* **~ sth in,** (colloq) give back to those in authority: *You must ~ in your equipment* (e g uniform) *before you leave.*

turn (sth) inside out, (cause to) become inside out: *The wind ~ed my old umbrella inside out. He ~ed his pockets inside out in search of his keys.*

turn off, change direction; leave (one road) for

another: *Is this where we ~ off/where our road ~s off for Hull?* **~ sth off,** stop the flow of (liquid, gas, current) by ~ing a tap, switch or other control: *~ off the water/lights/radio/T V.* **~ (sb) off,** (sl) (cause sb to) lose interest, desire, etc: *He/This music really ~s me off!*

turn sth on, start the flow of (liquid, gas, current) by ~ing a tap, switch, etc: *T~ the lights/radio on. She's fond of ~ing on the charm,* (fig) using her charm to influence people. **~ (sb) on,** have, give to sb, great pleasure or excitement: *Some girls ~ on easily. What kind of music ~s you on? Some psychedelic drugs ~ you on very quickly,* change your mental or emotional state. **~ on sth,** depend on: *The success of a picnic usually ~s on the weather.* **~ on sb,** become hostile to; attack: *The dog ~ed on me and bit me in the leg.*

turn out (well, etc), prove to be; be in the end: *Everything ~ed out well/satisfactory. The day ~ed out wet. As it ~ed out...,* As it happened in the end.... **~ (sth) out,** (cause to) point outwards: *His toes ~ out. He ~ed his toes out.* **~ sth out,** **(a)** extinguish by ~ing a tap, switch, etc: *Please ~ out the lights/gas-fire before you go to bed.* **(b)** empty (a drawer, one's pockets, a room, etc) when looking for sth, when cleaning sth: *~ out all the drawers in one's desk; ~ out the attic,* to get rid of unwanted articles, etc. **~ sb/sth out,** produce, e g manufactured goods: *Our new factory is ~ing out large quantities of goods. The school has ~ed out some first-rate scholars.* **~ (sb) out, (a)** (cause people to) assemble for some event, or for duty: *The whole village ~ed out to welcome the princess. Not many men ~ed out for duty.* **~ out the guard,** summon them from the guard-room for duty. ⇨ guard[1](3). **(b)** (colloq) (cause sb to) get out of bed. **~ sb out (of/from sth),** expel by force, threats, etc: *~ sb out of his job/chair; ~ out a tenant* (= from his house) *for not paying the rent.* **~ed out,** (of a person, equipment, etc) dressed, equipped: *a well-~ed out young man. She was beautifully ~ed out,* elegantly dressed. Hence, **ˈ~-out** *n* **(a)** persons who have ~ed out (assembled): *There was a good ~-out at the meeting.* **(b)** occasion when one ~s out (empties, etc) a drawer, etc: *The drawers in my desk are full of old papers—it's time I had a good ~-out.* **(c)** equipment; way in which sth is equipped; clothes and accessories worn together; equipage (carriage and horses): *The duke, who prefers horses to cars, drove to the races in a smart ~-out.* **(d)** output (the more usu word) of manufactured goods, etc.

turn (sb/sth) over, (cause to) fall over, upset; change the position of: *The car (was) ~ed right over,* completely upset. *He ~ed over in bed. The nurse ~ed the old man over and gave him an injection in the left buttock.* **~ sth over,** do business to the amount of: *Mr Smith/His business ~s over £500 a week.* **~ sth over in one's mind,** think about sth (before making a decision). **~ sth/sb over (to sb),** give the control or conduct of sth to: *I've ~ed over the management of my affairs to my brother. He's ~ed over his business to his successors. The thief was ~ed* (= handed) *over to the police.* Hence, **ˈ~-over** *n* **(a)** amount of money ~ed over in business within a period of time or for a particular transaction: *a profit of £1 000 on a ~over of £10 000; sell goods at low prices hoping for a quick ~over,* quick sales and quick replacement of stock. **(b)** rate of renewal: *There is a higher ~over of the labour force in unskilled trades than in skilled trades,* unskilled workers leave and are replaced more quickly. **(c)** tart made by folding over half of a circular piece of pastry over the other half, with jam, meat, etc inside.

turn (sth/sb) round, (cause to) face another way, be in another direction: *T~ round and let me see your profile. T~ your chair round to the fire.* Hence, **ˈ~-round** *n* (esp of a ship or aircraft) process of getting it ready for the return voyage or flight: *a ~-round of 24 hours in Southampton,* e g for an Atlantic liner.

turn to, get busy: *The design staff ~ed to and produced a set of drawings in twenty-four hours.* **~ to sb,** go or apply to: *The child ~ed to its mother for comfort. She has nobody to ~ to.*

turn up, (a) make one's appearance; arrive: *He promised to come, but hasn't ~ed up yet. My typist hasn't ~ed up this morning—I hope she isn't ill.* **(b)** be found, esp by chance: *The book you've lost may ~ up one of these days.* **(c)** (of an opportunity, etc) happen; present itself: *Like Mr Micawber, he's still waiting for something* (e g a job, a piece of good luck) *to ~ up.* **~ (sth) up, (a)** (cause to) slope upwards: ~ (= roll) *up one's shirt sleeves.* **(b)** expose; make visible: *The share of a plough ~s up the soil. The ploughman ~ed up some buried treasure/an old skull.* **~ sb up,** (colloq) cause to vomit; disgust: *The stink from the slaughter-house ~ed me up.* **~ up one's nose at sth,** (fig) express a superior and critical attitude towards: *She ~ed up her nose at the suggestion.* **ˈ~-up** *n* **(a)** turned fold at the bottom of a trouser-leg. **(b) ~-up (for the book),** surprising and unexpected event: *Fancy seeing you after all these years. What a ~-up for the book!*

turn upon, ⇨ ~ on above, (= attack).

turner /ˈtɜnə(r)/ *n* person who works a lathe. ⇨ turn[2](4).

turn·ing /ˈtɜnɪŋ/ *n* place where a road turns, esp where one road branches off from another: *Take the first ~ on/to the right.* **ˈ~-point** *n* (fig) point in place, time, development, etc which is critical: *reach a ~-point in history/in one's life. There was a ~-point in the negotiations yesterday.*

tur·nip /ˈtɜnɪp/ *n* [C] (plant with a) large round root used as a vegetable and as food for cattle.

tur·pen·tine /ˈtɜpəntɑɪn/ *n* [U] oil obtained from certain trees, used as a solvent in mixing paint and varnish, and in medicine.

tur·pi·tude /ˈtɜpɪtjud *US:* -tud/ *n* [U] wickedness; depravity.

turps /tɜps/ *n* [U] (colloq abbr for) turpentine.

tur·quoise /ˈtɜkwɔɪz/ *n* [C] (colour of a) greenish-blue precious stone.

tur·ret /ˈtʌrət/ *n* **1** small tower, esp at a corner of a building or defensive wall. **2** steel structure protecting gunners, often made so as to revolve with the gun(s): *a warship armed with twin-gun ~s.*

turtle[1] /ˈtɜtl/ *n* sea-animal with a soft body protected by a hard shell like that of a tortoise. ⇨ the illus at reptile. ***turn ~,*** (of a ship) turn upside down; capsize. **ˈ~-necked** *adj* (of a garment, esp a sweater) having a high, close-fitting collar.

turtle[2] /ˈtɜtl/ *n* (usu) **ˌ~-ˈdove,** kinds of dove, esp a wild kind noted for its soft cooing, and its affection for its mate and young.

turves /tɜvz/ *n pl* ⇨ turf.

tush /tʌʃ/ *int* used as an expression of contempt or impatience.
tusk /tʌsk/ *n* long-pointed tooth, esp one coming out from the closed mouth, as in the elephant, walrus or wild boar. ⇨ the illus at **large, sea.**
tus·sah /ˈtʌsə/ *n* (US) = **tussore.**
tussle /ˈtʌsl/ *n, vi* [VP2A,3A] ~ ***(with),*** (have a) hard struggle or fight.
tus·sock /ˈtʌsək/ *n* clump or hillock of growing grass.
tus·sore /ˈtʌsɔ(r)/ *n* [U] strong coarse silk.
tut /tʌt/, **tut-tut** /ˌtʌt ˈtʌt/ *int* used to express impatience, contempt, rebuke. □ *vt* (**-tt-**) [VP6A] express impatience, etc by using this word: *He tut-tutted the idea.*
tu·te·lage /ˈtjutḷɪdʒ *US:* ˈtu-/ *n* [U] guardianship: *a child in* ~; (period of) being under ~.
tu·te·lar, tu·te·lary /ˈtjutələ(r) *US:* ˈtu-, -lərɪ *US:* -lerɪ/ *adj* serving as a guardian or protector; of a guardian: ~ *authority.*
tu·tor /ˈtjutə(r) *US:* ˈtu-/ *n* **1** private teacher, esp one who instructs a single pupil or a very small class, sometimes one who lives with the family of his pupil(s). **2** (GB) university teacher who guides the studies of a number of students. □ *vt* [VP6A, 15A,16A] **1** teach as a ~: ~ *a boy in Latin.* **2** train, exercise restraint over: ~ *one's passions;* ~ *oneself to be patient.* **~ial** /tjuˈtɔrɪəl *US:* tu-/ *adj* of a ~ of his duties: *~ial classes.* □ *n* period of instruction given by a college ~: *attend a ~ial.*
tutti-frutti /ˈtutɪ ˈfrutɪ/ *n* (portion of) ice-cream with chopped nuts and various fruits.
tutu /ˈtutu/ *n* short skirt with many layers of stiffened fabric worn by women dancers in classicai ballet.
tux·edo /tʌkˈsidəʊ/ *n* (*pl* **-dos** /-dəʊz/) (US) dinner-jacket.
twaddle /ˈtwodl/ *n* [U] foolish talk. □ *vi* [VP2A] talk or write ~: *Stop twaddling!* **twad·dler** *n*
twain /tweɪn/ *n* (archaic) two.
twang /twæŋ/ *n* **1** sound of a tight string or wire being pulled and released: *the* ~ *of a guitar.* **2** harsh, nasal tone of voice: *speak with a* ~. □ *vt, vi* [VP6A,2A] (cause to) make this kind of sound: *The bow ~ed and the arrow whistled through the air. He was ~ing a banjo.*
'twas /twoz *weak form:* twəz/ = it was.
tweak /twik/ *vt* [VP6A] pinch and twist: *Wouldn't you like to* ~ *that rude fellow's nose/ears?* □ *n* act of ~ing.
tweed /twid/ *n* **1** [U] (often attrib) thick, soft, woollen cloth, usu woven of mixed colours: *a* ~ *hat/coat.* **2** (*pl*) (suit of) clothes made of ~: *dressed in Scottish ~s.*
'tween /twin/ *adv, prep* between, esp **ˈ~-decks,** between decks.
tweeny /ˈtwinɪ/ *n* (*pl* **-nies**) (old use) young girl servant who helps both in cooking and housework.
tweet /twit/ *n, vi* (of a bird) chirp.
tweeter /ˈtwitə(r)/ *n* loudspeaker for reproducing high notes. ⇨ **woofer.**
tweez·ers /ˈtwizəz/ *n pl* (also ***a pair of*** ~) tiny pair of tongs for picking up or pulling out very small things, e g hairs from the eyebrows.
twelfth /twelfθ *with simultaneous* f *and* θ/ *adj, n* next after the 11th; one of twelve equal parts. **ˌ~ ˈman,** (in cricket) reserve player. **ˈ~-night,** eve of the festival of Epiphany, celebrated with festivities.
twelve /twelv/ *adj, n* the number 12, XII. ⇨ **App** 4. **the T~,** the ~ apostles of Jesus. **ˈ~-month** *n* (*sing* with *indef art*) year: *I haven't seen her for nearly a ~month.* □ *adv: this day ~month,* a year ago; a year from now (in the future).
twenty /ˈtwentɪ/ *adj, n* the number 20, XX. ⇨ **App 4. twen·ti·eth** /ˈtwentɪəθ/ *adj, n* next after the 19th; one of 20 equal parts.
'twere /twɜ(r)/ contraction of *it were* (archaic for *it would be*).
twerp = **twirp.**
twice /twɑɪs/ *adv* two times: ~ *as much/as many. I've been there once or* ~. *He's* ~ *the man he was,* ~ as well, strong, confident, capable, etc. ***think ~ about doing sth,*** hesitate, think carefully, before deciding to do it. ***a ~-told tale,*** a well-known one.
twiddle /ˈtwɪdl/ *vt, vi* **1** [VP6A] twist or turn idly or aimlessly: ~ *one's thumbs.* **2** [VP3A] ~ ***with sth,*** play idly: ~ *with one's hair/a ring on one's finger.*
twig¹ /twɪg/ *n* [C] small shoot on or at the end of a branch (bush, plant). ⇨ the illus at **tree. ~gy** *adj* having many ~s: *support plants with ~gy sticks.*
twig² /twɪg/ *vt, vi* (**-gg-**) [VP6A,2A] (GB colloq) observe; notice; understand: *I soon ~ged what he was up to,* saw the trick he was trying to play.
twi·light /ˈtwɑɪlɑɪt/ *n* [U] **1** faint half-light before sunrise or after sunset: *go for a walk in the* ~. **2** (fig) remote period about which little is known: *in the* ~ *of history.*
twill /twɪl/ *n* [U] strong cotton cloth woven so that fine diagonal lines or ribs appear on the surface. **~ed** *adj* (of cloth) woven in this way.
'twill /twəl/ contraction of *it will.*
twin /twɪn/ *n* **1** either of two children or other offspring born together of the same mother: *one of the ~s;* (attrib) ~ *brothers.* **2** usu (attrib) completely like, closely associated with, another: *a steamer with* ~ *propellers,* two identical propellers; ~ *beds,* two identical single beds; *a ˈ~-set,* woman's jumper and long sleeved cardigan of the same colour and style.
twine /twɑɪn/ *n* [U] thin strings made by twisting two or more yarns together. □ *vt, vi* [VP15A,B, 2A,C] twist; wind: ~ *flowers into a garland; vines that* ~ *round a tree. She ~d her arms round my neck.*
twinge /twɪndʒ/ *n* [C] sudden, sharp pain: *a* ~ *of toothache/rheumatism/conscience.*
twinkle /ˈtwɪŋkl/ *vi* [2A,C] **1** shine with a light that gleams unsteadily: *stars that* ~ *in the sky.* **2** (of eyes) sparkle; (of eyelids, feet in dancing, etc) move rapidly up and down, to and fro: *Her eyes ~d with amusement/mischief.* □ *n* **1** [U] twinkling light: *the* ~ *of the stars/of a distant light.* **2** sparkle; rapid twitching: *There was a mischievous* ~ *in her eyes.* **twink·ling** /ˈtwɪŋklɪŋ/ *n* (*sing* only) ***in a twinkling of an eye,*** in an instant.
twin·ned /twɪnd/ *attrib adj* paired (with): *a town in England* ~ *with a town in France,* (for cultural, educational, etc exchanges).
twirl /twɜl/ *vt, vi* [VP6A,16A,2A,C] **1** (cause to) turn round and round quickly: *She ~ed the mop to get the water out of it. He sat ~ing his thumbs.* **2** curl: *He ~ed his moustache (up).* □ *n* rapid circular motion.
twirp, twerp /twɜp/ *n* (sl) contemptible or insignificant person.
twist /twɪst/ *vt, vi* **1** [VP6A,15A,B] wind or turn (a number of threads, strands, etc) one around the

other: ~ *pieces of straw into a rope. She ~ed the girl's hair round her fingers to make it curl.* **2** [VP6A] make (a rope, a garland, etc) by doing this. **3** [VP6A,15A,B,16A] turn, esp by the use of force; turn the two ends of (sth) in opposite directions; turn one end of (sth): ~ (more usu *wring*) *a wet cloth,* to squeeze out the water; ~ *the cap off a fountain-pen/a tube of toothpaste. If you use too much force, you'll* ~ *the key,* bend it out of shape. *His features were ~ed* (= distorted) *with pain. He fell and ~ed his ankle. She ~ed her head round as she reversed the car into the garage.* ~ **sth off,** break off by ~ing: ~ *off the end of a piece of wire.* ~ **sb's arm,** (a) force it round to cause pain. (b) (fig, colloq) put (friendly or unfriendly) pressure on him to do sth. ~ **sb round one's little finger,** (colloq) get him to do what one wants him to do. **4** [VP6A,15A] force (sb's words) out of their true meaning: *The police tried to* ~ *his words into a confession of guilt.* **5** [VP6A,15A,2A,C] give a spiral form to (a rod, column, etc); receive, have, move or grow in, a spiral form: *~ed columns,* as in architecture. **6** [VP2A,C] turn and curve in different directions; change position or direction: *The road ~s and turns up the side of the mountain. The thief ~ed out of the policeman's grip and ran off. The injured man ~ed about in pain.* **7** [VP6A,2A] (of a ball, esp in billiards) (cause to) take a curved path while spinning. **8** [VP2A] dance the ~, ⇨ 6 below. □ *n* **1** [C] ~ing or being ~ed: *The bully gave the little boy's arm a* ~. *Give the rope a few more ~s. There are numerous ~s in the road over the pass.* **2** [C] sth made by ~ing: *a rope full of ~s* (= kinks, coils); *a* ~ *of paper,* a paper packet with screwed-up ends. **3** [C,U] thread, yarn, rope, etc made by ~ing together two or more strands, esp certain kinds of silk thread and cotton yarn; coarse tobacco made by ~ing dried leaves into a roll. **4** motion given to a ball to make it take a curved path. **5** peculiar tendency of mind or character: *He has a criminal* ~ *in him.* **6** dance (popular in the 1960's) in which there is ~ing of the arms and hips. **~er** *n* **1** (colloq) dishonest person. **2** difficult task, problem, etc: *a* ˋ*tongue-~er,* word or phrase difficult to pronounce. **twisty** *adj* (-ier, -iest) **1** having many ~s: *a ~y road.* **2** not straightforward: *a ~y politician.*

twit¹ /twɪt/ *vt* (-tt-) [VP6A,14] tease sb (usu in jest) (with or about sth): ~ *a man about the state he was in after a drinking bout.*

twit² /twɪt/ *n* (sl) contemptible fool; idiot.

twitch /twɪtʃ/ *n* [C] **1** sudden, quick, usu uncontrollable movement of a muscle; tic. **2** sudden quick pull: *I felt a* ~ *at my sleeve.* □ *vi,vt* **1** [VP2A,C,6A] (cause to) move in a ~(1): *The dog's nose ~ed as it passed the butcher's shop. His face ~ed with terror. The horse ~ed its ears.* **2** [VP15A,B] jerk; give a ~(5) to: *The wind ~ed the paper out of my hand.*

twit·ter /ˋtwɪtə(r)/ *vi* [VP15A,B] (of birds) chirp; make a succession of soft short sounds; (of persons) talk rapidly through excitement, nervousness, etc. □ *n* **1** chirping: *the* ~ *of sparrows.* **2** (of persons) (colloq, esp in) ***(all) of a ~,*** in an excited state.

ˈtwixt /twɪkst/ *prep* (liter) = betwixt.

two /tu/ *n, adj* **1** the number 2. ⇨ App 4. ***break/cut sth in two,*** into two parts. ***put two and two together,*** infer sth from what one sees, hears, learns, etc. ***by twos and threes,*** two or three at a time. ***Two can play at that game,*** used as a threat of retaliation. **2** (compounds) **ˈtwo-ˋedged** *adj* (of a sword) having a cutting edge on each side; (fig, of an argument, etc) having two possible (and contrary) meanings. **ˈtwo-ˋfaced** *adj* (fig) insincere. **ˋtwo·fold** *adj, adv* double, doubly. **ˈtwo-ˋhanded** *adj* (of a sword) needing two hands to use it; (of a saw, etc) to be used by two persons, one at each end. **ˋtwo·pence** /ˋtʌpns *US:* ˋtupens/ *n* sum of two pence (esp pre-decimal currency). **ˋtwo·penny** /ˋtʌpnɪ *US:* ˋtupenɪ/ *adj* costing twopence (2d or 2p): *There are no twopenny fares on the London buses.* **ˈtwopenny ˋpiece,** GB coin worth two new pence (2p). **ˈtwopenny-ˋhalfpenny** /ˈtʌpnɪ ˋheɪpnɪ *US:* ˈtupenɪ ˋhæfpenɪ/ *adj* (old use) (a) worth or costing 2½d. (b) (colloq) almost worthless; petty. **ˈtwo-ˋpiece** *n* set of garments of similar or matching material, e g skirt and jacket, trousers and jacket; bra and briefs (for swimming); (attrib) *a two-piece suit.* **ˈtwo-ˋply** *adj* of two strands or thicknesses: *two-ply wool/wood.* **ˈtwo-ˋseater** *n* car, aircraft, etc with seats for two persons. **ˋtwo-step** *n* (music for a) kind of dance in march time. **ˋtwo-timing** *adj* (sl) deceitful; engaged in double-crossing. **ˈtwo-ˋway** *attrib adj* (a) (of a switch) allowing current to be switched on or off from either of two points. (b) (of a road or street) in which traffic may move in both directions. Cf *one-way street.* (c) (of radio equipment, etc) for both sending and receiving.

ˈtwould /twʊd/ contracted form of *it would.*

ty·coon /taɪˋkun/ *n* **1** title given (not by the Japanese) to the hereditary commander-in-chief of the Japanese army in former times; shogun. **2** (mod colloq use) wealthy and powerful business man or industrialist: *ˋoil ~s.*

ty·ing /ˋtaɪɪŋ/ *pres part* of **tie²**.

tyke, tike /taɪk/ *n* cur; (as a term of abuse) low fellow.

tym·pa·num /ˋtɪmpənəm/ *n* (*pl* -na /-nə/) (anat) **1** eardrum. **2** middle ear.

type¹ /taɪp/ *n* **1** [C] person, thing, event, etc considered as an example of a class or group: *Abraham Lincoln was a fine* ~ *of American patriotism/of the American patriot.* **2** [C] class or group considered to have common characteristics: *men of this* ~. *Her beauty is of the Italian* ~. *They claim to make good Burgundy* ~ *wine/wine of the Burgundy* ~ *in Australia.* [U] *A cowardly bulldog is not true to* ~. **3** [U] letters, etc cast in blocks of (usu) metal, for use in printing; any fount of these; [C] one of these blocks: *The printers are short of ~/certain ~s. Wooden* ~ *is/Wooden ~s are sometimes used for printing posters. The material is now in* ~, has been set ready for printing. *The examples in this dictionary are in italic* ~. **4** (compounds) **ˋ~·script** *n* typewritten copy (prepared for printing, etc). **ˋ~·setter** *n* worker or machine that sets ~ for printing. **ˋ~·write** *vt,vi* (*pt* -wrote /-rəʊt/, *pp* -written /-rɪtn/) = type (the usual word now): *a ~written letter* (more usu: *a ~d letter*). **ˋ~·writer** *n* machine with which one prints letters on paper, using the fingers on a keyboard.

type² /taɪp/ *vt,vi* [VP6A,2A] **1** use a typewriter; write with a typewriter: ~ *a letter. She ~s well.* **2** [VP6A] determine the type(2) of sth: ~ *a virus;* ~ *her blood.* **ty·pist** /ˋtaɪpɪst/ *n* person who ~s.

type·cast /ˈtɑɪpkɑst *US:* -kæst/ *vt* (*pt,pp* unchanged) [VP6A] (theatre) cast (a person) for a part which he/she has the reputation of doing well or which seems to fit his/her own personality.

ty·phoid /ˈtɑɪfɔɪd/ *n* [U] ~ **(fever),** infectious disease which attacks the intestines, caused by bacteria taken into the body with food or drink.

ty·phoon /tɑɪˈfun/ *n* [C] violent hurricane of the kind that occurs in the western Pacific.

ty·phus /ˈtɑɪfəs/ *n* [U] infectious disease marked by fever, great weakness and the appearance of purple spots on the body.

typi·cal /ˈtɪpɪkl/ *adj* ~ ***(of),*** serving as a type; representative or characteristic. **~ly** /-klɪ/ *adv*

typ·ify /ˈtɪpɪfɑɪ/ *vt* (*pt,pp* **-fied**) [VP6A] be a symbol of; be representative of.

ty·pist /ˈtɑɪpɪst/ *n* ⇨ **type**[2].

ty·pogra·phy /tɑɪˈpogrəfɪ/ *n* [U] art or style or printing. **ty·pogra·pher** /tɑɪˈpogrəfə(r)/ *n* **ty·po·graphic** /ˌtɑɪpəˈgræfɪk/ *adj* **ty·po·graphi·cally** /-klɪ/ *adv*

ty·ran·ni·cal /tɪˈrænɪkl/, **tyr·an·nous** /ˈtɪrənəs/ *adjj* of or like a tyrant; acting like a tyrant; obtaining obedience by force or threats.

tyr·an·nize /ˈtɪrənɑɪz/ *vi,vt* [VP6A,3A] ~ ***(over),*** rule cruelly and unjustly: *~ over the weak. He ~s his family.*

tyr·anny /ˈtɪrənɪ/ *n* (*pl* **-nies**) **1** [U] cruel or unjust use of power; [C] instance of this; tyrannical act. **2** [C,U] (instance of, country with, the) kind of government existing when a ruler has complete power, esp when this power has been obtained by force and is used unjustly: *live under a ~.*

ty·rant /ˈtɑɪərnt/ *n* cruel or unjust ruler, esp one who has obtained complete power by force.

tyre (US = **tire**) /tɑɪə(r)/ *n* band of metal or rubber on the rim of a wheel, esp (*pneumatic ~*) the kind on bicycle and motor-car wheels. ⇨ the illus at **bicycle, motor.**

tyro /ˈtɑɪərəʊ/ *n* = tiro.

tzar /zɑ(r)/, **tza·rina** /zɑˈrinə/ *nn* ⇨ **czar.**

tzetze /ˈsetsɪ/ *n* ⇨ **tsetse.**

Uu

U, u /ju/ the 21st letter of the English alphabet. **ˈU-boat** *n* German submarine. **ˈU-ˈturn,** one of 180° (by a car, etc): *No U-turns!* (as a traffic notice in towns, on motorways).

ubiqui·tous /juˈbɪkwɪtəs/ *adj* present everywhere or in several places at the same time. **ubiquity** /juˈbɪkwətɪ/ *n* [U] quality of being ~.

ud·der /ˈʌdə(r)/ *n* bag of a cow, goat or other animal, from which milk comes, esp a large one with two or more teats. ⇨ the illus at **domestic.**

ugh /*This usu suggests a sound like* ɜ *made with the lips either spread or rounded very strongly and one's facial expression showing disgust*/ *int* used to indicate disgust.

ugly /ˈʌglɪ/ *adj* (**-ier, -iest**) **1** unpleasant to look at; hideous: *~ persons/furniture/surroundings.* **2** threatening; unpleasant: *The sky looks ~,* suggests bad weather. *He's an ~ customer,* (colloq) a dangerous person, one who may be difficult to deal with. *The news in today's newspapers is ~,* suggests unpleasant possibilities, e g of war. **ug·lify** /ˈʌglɪfɑɪ/ *vt* (*pt,pp* **-fied**) make ~. **ug·li·ness** *n*

ukase /juˈkeɪs/ *n* (formerly) edict of the Czarist Russian government; (mod use) arbitrary order.

uku·lele /ˌjukəˈleɪlɪ/ *n* Hawaiian four-stringed guitar.

ul·cer /ˈʌlsə(r)/ *n* open sore forming poisonous matter (on the outside or inside surface of the body); (fig) corrupting influence or condition. **~·ous** /-əs/ *adj* **~·ate** /-eɪt/ *vt,vi* [VP6A,2A] form, convert or be converted into, an ~. **~·ation** /ˌʌlsəˈreɪʃn/ *n*

ulna /ˈʌlnə/ *n* (*pl* **-næ** /-ni/) (anat) inner of the two bones of the forearm. ⇨ the illus at **skeleton.**

ul·ster /ˈʌlstə(r)/ *n* long, loose, belted overcoat.

ul·terior /ʌlˈtɪərɪə(r)/ *adj* situated beyond; beyond what is first seen or said. **~ motive,** motive other than what is expressed or admitted.

ul·ti·mate /ˈʌltɪmət/ *adj* last, furthest, basic: *~ principles/truths; the ~ cause,* beyond which no other cause is known or can be found; *the ~ deterrent* (used of nuclear weapons). **~·ly** *adv* finally; in the end.

ul·ti·ma·tum /ˌʌltɪˈmeɪtəm/ *n* (*pl* **-tums, -ta** /-tə/ [C] final statement of conditions to be accepted without discussion, e g one sent to a foreign government and threatening war if the conditions are not accepted.

ul·timo /ˈʌltɪməʊ/ *adj* (abbr **ult**) (formerly used in business letters) of the month before the current month: *Thank you for your letter of the 10th ult.*

ultra- /ˈʌltrə/ *pref* ⇨ **App 3.**

ul·tra·mar·ine /ˌʌltrəməˈrin/ *adj, n* brilliant pure blue (colour).

ultra·mon·tane /ˌʌltrəmonˈteɪn/ *adj* favouring the absolute authority of the Pope in matters of faith and discipline.

ul·tra·sonic /ˌʌltrəˈsonɪk/ *adj* relating to sound waves beyond the range of normal human audibility.

ul·tra·vio·let /ˌʌltrəˈvɑɪələt/ *adj* of the invisible part of the spectrum beyond the violet. **~ rays,** invisible rays (in sunlight, light from mercury-vapour lamps, etc) which have an effect upon the skin, curing certain skin diseases, forming vitamins, etc.

ul·tra vires /ˌʌltrə ˈvɑɪəriz/ *adj, adv* (Lat) beyond the powers or authority granted by law.

ulu·late /ˈjuljʊleɪt/ *vi* [VP2A] howl; wail loudly. **ulu·a·tion** /ˌjuljʊˈleɪʃn *US:* ˌʌl-/ *n*

um·ber /ˈʌmbə(r)/ *adj, n* yellowish-green (colouring substance). **burnt ~,** reddish-brown.

um·bili·cal /ʌmˈbɪlɪkl/ *adj* ˈ**~ cord,** cord connecting a foetus at the navel with the placenta. ⇨ the illus at **reproduce.**

um·brage /ˈʌmbrɪdʒ/ *n* [U] (only in) ***take ~ (at),*** feel that one has been treated unfairly or without proper respect.

um·brella /ʌmˈbrelə/ *n* folding frame (with a stick and handle), covered with cotton, silk, etc used to shelter the person holding it from rain; ⇨ *sunshade* at **sun(4), parasol;** (in some countries) such a device, used as a symbol of rank; (fig) screen of fighter aircraft, e g flying over bombers to protect them against enemy aircraft; political protection: *under the ~ of the UNO.*

um·laut /ˈʊmlaʊt/ *n* (in Germanic languages) vowel change shown by two dots over the vowel (as in the German plurals *Männer*, of *Mann*, and *Füsse*, of *Fuss*).

um·pire /ˈʌmpaɪə(r)/ *n* person chosen to act as a judge in a dispute, to see that the rules are obeyed in cricket, baseball, tennis, netball and other games. Cf *referee* for football and boxing. □ *vt,vi* [VP6A,2A] act as ~: *~ a cricket match.*

ump·teen /ˈʌmpˈtin/ *adj* (sl) many. **ump·teenth** /ˈʌmpˈtinθ/ *adj*: *for the ~th time*, for I don't know how many times.

'un /ən/ *pron* (colloq) one: *He's a good 'un*, a good fellow. *That's a good 'un*, a good specimen, joke, etc.

un- /ʌn/ *pref* (⇨ App 3; specimens only here). **1** (before *adjj* and *advv*) not: *uncertain(ly); unwilling(ly).* **2** (before *vv*) do the opposite of, reverse the action of, what is indicated by the *v*: *unscrew; unroll; undress, unlock.* **3** (before *nn*) indicating absence of: *uncertainty; unwillingness.*

un·abashed /ˈʌnəˈbæʃt/ *adj* not abashed, embarrassed or awed.

un·abated /ˈʌnəˈbeɪtɪd/ *adj* (of a storm, etc) (continuing) as strong, violent, etc as before.

un·able /ʌnˈeɪbl/ *adj* (*pred* only) ***~ to do sth,*** not able to.

un·accom·pan·ied /ˈʌnəˈkʌmpənɪd/ *adj* **1** without a companion: *~ luggage*, sent separately, the owner not travelling with it. **2** (music) performed without an accompaniment.

un·ac·count·able /ˈʌnəˈkaʊntəbl/ *adj* in a way that cannot be accounted for or explained. **un·ac·count·ably** /-əblɪ/ *adv*

un·ac·cus·tomed /ˈʌnəˈkʌstəmd/ *adj* **1** ***~ to,*** not accustomed to: *~ as I am to speaking in public.* **2** not usual; strange: *his ~ silence.*

un·adopted /ˈʌnəˈdɒptɪd/ *adj* (esp of a road) not taken over for maintenance by the local authorities.

un·ad·vised /ˈʌnədˈvaɪzd/ *adj* without advice; (esp) not discreet or wise; rash. **~·ly** /ˈʌnədˈvaɪzɪdlɪ/ *adv* rashly.

un·af·fec·ted /ˈʌnəˈfektɪd/ *adj* **1** free from affectation; sincere. **2** ***~ by,*** not affected by.

un·alien·able /ʌnˈeɪlɪənəbl/ *adj* that cannot be taken away or separated: *~ rights.*

un·al·loyed /ˈʌnəˈlɔɪd/ *adj* (of pleasure) pure; unmixed.

un·al·ter·ably /ʌnˈɔltərəblɪ/ *adv* in a way that cannot be changed.

un-Ameri·can /ˈʌn əˈmerɪkən/ *adj* not in accordance with the American (ie US) character; opposed to American customs, ideas, etc.

un·aneled /ˈʌnəˈnild/ *adj* (archaic) not having been anointed by a priest before death; not having received extreme unction.

unani·mous /juˈnænɪməs/ *adj* in, showing, complete agreement: *The country is ~ in support of the Government's policy. He was elected by a ~ vote. The proposal was accepted with ~ approval.* **~·ly** *adv* **una·nim·ity** /ˈjunəˈnɪmətɪ/ *n* [U] complete agreement or unity.

un·an·nounced /ˈʌnəˈnaʊnst/ *adj* without having been announced: *He walked into the room ~*, no one having told the persons there who he was, that he had arrived.

un·an·swer·able /ˈʌnˈɑnsṛəbl *US:* -ˈæn-/ *adj* (esp) against which no good argument can possibly be brought: *His case is ~.*

un·an·swered /ˈʌnˈɑnsəd *US:* -ˈæn-/ *adj* not replied to: *~ letters;* not returned: *~ love.*

un·ap·proach·able /ˈʌnəˈprəʊtʃəbl/ *adj* (esp, of a person) difficult to approach (because too stiff or formal): *The new manager is an ~ sort of man.*

un·armed /ˈʌnˈɑmd/ *adj* without weapons or means of defence.

un·asked /ˈʌnˈɑskt *US:* -ˈæs-/ *adj* (esp) without being requested: *She's always ready to help and often does so ~. Many of the contributions to the relief fund were ~ for.*

un·as·sum·ing /ˈʌnəˈsjumɪŋ *US:* -ˈsu-/ *adj* not pushing oneself forward; not drawing attention to oneself; modest. **~·ly** *adv*

un·at·tached /ˈʌnəˈtætʃt/ *adj* **1** not connected or associated with a particular person, group, organization, etc; independent. **2** not married or engaged to be married.

un·at·tended /ˈʌnəˈtendɪd/ *adj* **1** without attendants or escort. **2** not attended to; with no one to give care or attention to: *Would you leave small children at home ~ while you went to the cinema?*

un·avail·ing /ˈʌnəˈveɪlɪŋ/ *adj* without effort or success.

un·avoid·able /ˈʌnəˈvɔɪdəbl/ *adj* that cannot be avoided. **un·a·void·ably** /-əblɪ/ *adv*: *He was unavoidably absent.*

un·aware /ˈʌnəˈweə(r)/ *adj* (*pred*) ***~ of sth/that…,*** not knowing; not aware: *He was ~ of my presence/that I was present.* **un·awares** /-ˈweəz/ *adv* **1** by surprise; unexpectedly: *take sb ~s.* **2** without being aware; unconsciously: *She probably dropped the parcel ~s.*

un·backed /ˈʌnˈbækt/ *adj* **1** (of a proposal, etc) not supported. **2** (of a horse in a race) having no bets placed on it.

un·bal·anced /ˈʌnˈbælənst/ *adj* (esp of a person, the mind) disordered; not sane or normal.

un·bar /ʌnˈbɑ(r)/ *vt* (-rr-) remove bars from (a gate, etc); (fig) throw open: *~ all the professions to women.*

un·bear·able /ʌnˈbeərəbl/ *adj* that cannot be borne or tolerated: *I find his rudeness ~.* **un·bear·ably** /-əblɪ/ *adv* in a way that cannot be endured: *unbearably hot/impudent.*

un·beaten /ˈʌnˈbitn/ *adj* (esp) not having been beaten, defeated or surpassed: *an ~ record for the 1 000 metres race; an ~ team.*

un·be·com·ing /ˈʌnbɪˈkʌmɪŋ/ *adj* **1** not suited (to the wearer): *an ~ dress.* **2** ***~ to/for,*** not appropriate or befitting. **~·ly** *adv*

un·be·known /ˈʌnbɪˈnəʊn/, **un·be·knowns** /-nst/ *adj, adv* (colloq) not known (*to*), without the knowledge of: *He did it ~st to me*, without my being aware of it.

un·be·lief /ˈʌnbɪˈlif/ *n* [U] (esp) lack of belief, state of not believing, in God, religion. **un·be·liever** /ˈʌnbɪˈlivə(r)/ *n* (esp) person who does not believe in God, religion. **un·be·liev·ing** *adj* not believing; doubting. **un·be·liev·ing·ly** *adv*: *look at sb unbelievingly*, in a way that shows doubt.

un·bend /ʌnˈbend/ *vi,vt* (*pt,pp* unbent /-ˈbent/ or -ed) **1** [VP2A] behave in a way free from strain, formality; become relaxed: *In the classroom the teacher maintains discipline but after class he ~s.* **2** [VP6A] relax: *~ one's mind.* **~·ing** *adj* (esp) firm in purpose, in not changing decisions, etc: *have an ~ing attitude*, make no concessions, etc.

un·bi·assed (also **-biased**) /ˈʌnˋbɑɪəst/ *adj* not biassed; impartial.

un·bid·den /ˈʌnˋbɪdn/ *adj* (formal) uninvited; not requested or ordered.

un·bind /ʌnˋbɑɪnd/ *vt* (*pt,pp* -bound /-ˋbɑʊnd/) [VP6A] free from fastenings, bindings, etc.

un·blush·ing /ʌnˋblʌʃɪŋ/ *adj* (esp) shameless: *the ~ corruption of some politicians.*

un·born /ʌnˋbɔn/ *adj* not yet born; future: *~ generations.*

un·bosom /ʌnˋbʊzəm/ *vt* [VP6A,14] ***~ oneself (to sb),*** tell, reveal (one's sorrows, etc): *She rushed off to ~ herself to her mother.*

un·bounded /ʌnˋbɑʊndɪd/ *adj* boundless; without limits: *~ ambition.*

un·bowed /ʌnˋbɑʊd/ *adj* not bowed or bent; not conquered or subdued: *His head is bloody but ~.*

un·bridled /ʌnˋbrɑɪdld/ *adj* (esp, fig) not controlled: *~ insolence/passions; an ~ tongue.*

un·bro·ken /ʌnˋbrəʊkən/ *adj* (esp) **1** (e g of a horse) not tamed or subdued. **2** not interrupted: *six hours of ~ sleep.* **3** (of records, etc) not beaten or surpassed.

un·buckle /ʌnˋbʌkl/ *vt* [VP6A] loosen, undo, the buckle(s) of.

un·bur·den /ʌnˋbɜdn/ *vt* [VP6A,15A] ***~ sb/sth of sth,*** relieve of a burden: *~ one's heart/conscience,* e g by talking about one's troubles, making a confession; *~ oneself to a friend,* find relief by speaking to him about one's feelings, etc: *~ oneself of a secret,* tell it to sb.

un·but·toned /ʌnˋbʌtnd/ *adj* with the buttons not fastened; (fig) relaxed; (feeling) free from formality.

un·called-for /ʌnˋkɔld fɔ(r)/ *adj* neither desirable nor necessary: *~ insults. Such comments are ~.*

un·canny /ʌnˋkænɪ/ *adj* unnatural, mysterious; weird: *an ~ noise; ~ shapes in the darkness.* **un·can·nily** /-əlɪ/ *adv*

un·cared-for /ʌnˋkeəd fɔ(r)/ *adj* not looked after; neglected: *~ children; an ~ garden.*

un·ceas·ing /ʌnˋsisɪŋ/ *adj* incessant; going on all the time. **~·ly** *adv*

un·cer·emo·ni·ous /ˈʌnˈserəˋməʊnɪəs/ *adj* (esp) informal; lacking in courtesy. **~·ly** *adv* **~·ness** *n*

un·cer·tain /ʌnˋsɜtn/ *adj* **1** changeable; not reliable: *~ weather; a man with an ~ temper.* **2** not certainly knowing or known: *be/feel ~ (about) what to do next/~ of/about/as to/one's plans for the future; a lady of ~ age,* (usu hum) one whose age cannot be guessed (perhaps because she tries to look younger than she is). **~·ly** *adv* **~ty** /-tntɪ/ *n* (*pl* -ties) **1** [U] state of being ~. **2** [C] sth which is ~: *the uncertainties of adequate reward in the profession of an actor.*

un·chari·table /ʌnˋtʃærɪtəbl/ *adj* (esp) severe or harsh (in making judgements of the conduct of others): *offer an ~ explanation of/put an ~ interpretation on sb's actions.*

un·charted /ʌnˋtʃɑtɪd/ *adj* **1** not marked on a map or chart: *an ~ island.* **2** not explored and mapped: *an ~ sea.*

un·checked /ˈʌnˋtʃekt/ *adj* not checked or restrained: *an ~ advance; ~ anger.*

un·chris·tian /ʌnˋkrɪstʃən/ *adj* **1** not Christian; contrary to Christian principles. **2** (colloq) inconvenient and unreasonable: *Why do you call on me at this ~ hour?* (e g at 5a m).

un·civil /ʌnˋsɪvl/ *adj* (esp) impolite.

un·clad /ʌnˋklæd/ *adj* not clothed; naked (the usu word)

un·claimed /ˈʌnˋkleɪmd/ *adj* that has not been claimed: *~ letters/parcels* (at the post-office, a lost property office, etc).

uncle /ˋʌŋkl/ *n* **1** brother of one's father or mother; husband of one's aunt: *my ~ Tom. Yes, ~!* **2** (hum) pawnbroker. **3 U~ Sam,** personification of the US. ***talk to sb like a Dutch ~,*** ⇨ Dutch, *adj* (3).

un·clean /ʌnˋklin/ *adj* (esp, Jewish law) ceremonially impure, e g the pig.

un·clouded /ʌnˋklɑʊdɪd/ *adj* (esp fig) bright; serene: *a life of ~ happiness.* Cf *cloudless,* as in *a cloudless sky.*

unco /ˋʌŋkəʊ/ *adj* (Scot) strange; unusual: *an ~ sight.* □ *adv* remarkably: (esp) *the ~ good,* religious people who are rigid in their views and behaviour.

un·col·oured (US = **-colored**) /ʌnˋkʌləd/ *adj* (esp, fig) not exaggerated or heightened in description: *an ~ description of events.*

un-come-at-able /ˈʌnkʌmˋætəbl/ *adj* (colloq) not easy to get to; not accessible.

un·com·mit·ted /ˈʌnkəˋmɪtɪd/ *adj* ***~ (to),*** not committed or bound (to a course of action, etc); free, independent: *the ~ countries,* those not allied to or bound to either of the power blocs of the modern world.

un·com·mon /ʌnˋkɒmən/ *adj* unusual; remarkable. **~·ly** *adv* (esp) remarkably: *a ~ly intelligent boy.*

un·com·pro·mis·ing /ʌnˋkɒmprəmɑɪzɪŋ/ *adj* not ready to make any compromise; unyielding; firm: *an ~ member of the Tory party.*

un·con·cerned /ˈʌnkənˋsɜnd/ *adj* **1** ***~ in sth,*** not involved in. ***~ with sth/sb,*** not (emotionally) concerned with. **2** free from anxiety; untroubled. **un·con·cern·ed·ly** /-ˋsɜnɪdlɪ/ *adv*

un·con·di·tional /ˈʌnkənˋdɪʃnl/ *adj* absolute; not subject to conditions: *The victors demanded ~ surrender.* **~ly** /-nḷɪ/ *adv*

un·con·di·tioned /ˈʌnkənˋdɪʃnd/ *adj* not subject to conditions; (esp) *~ reflex,* instinctive response to a stimulus.

un·con·scion·able /ʌnˋkɒnʃṇəbl/ *adj* unreasonable; not guided by conscience; excessive: *You take an ~ time dressing.*

un·con·scious /ʌnˋkɒnʃəs/ *adj* not conscious (all senses): *~ humour,* not intended as humour by the speaker or writer; *be ~ of having done wrong.* □ *n* **the ~,** (psych) that part of one's mental activity of which one is unaware, but which can be detected and understood through the skilled analysis of dreams, behaviour, etc. **~·ly** *adv* **~·ness** *n*

un·con·sid·ered /ˈʌnkənˋsɪdəd/ *adj* **1** (of words, remarks) spoken, made, etc without proper consideration or reflection. **2** disregarded (as if of little value or worth).

un·cork /ʌnˋkɔk/ *vt* [VP6A] draw the cork from (a bottle).

un·couple /ˈʌnˋkʌpl/ *vt* [VP6A] unfasten: *~ hounds from the leash/a locomotive from a train.*

un·couth /ʌnˋkuθ/ *adj* (of persons, their behaviour) rough, awkward, uncultured. **~·ly** *adv* **~-ness** *n*

un·cover /ʌnˋkʌvə(r)/ *vt* [VP6A] **1** remove a cover or covering from; (fig) disclose; make known: *The police have ~ed a plot against the President.* **2** (mil) expose to attack: *By a sudden movement we ~ed the enemy's right flank.* **3** (old use) take off one's hat or cap.

un·crossed /ˈʌnˋkrost *US:* -ˋkrɔst/ *adj* (esp, of a cheque) not crossed. ⇨ **cross**[2]**(2)**.

un·crowned /ˈʌnˋkraʊnd/ *adj* **1** (of a king, etc) not yet crowned. **2** having the power but not the title or name of a king, etc.

unc·tion /ˋʌŋkʃn/ *n* [U] **1** act of anointing with oil, esp as a religious rite. **ˈExtreme ˋU~,** the anointing of a dying person by a priest (of the Orthodox and Roman Catholic Churches). **2** (pretended, insincere) earnestness in speaking, tone of voice: *She related the scandal with great ~.*

unc·tu·ous /ˋʌŋktʃʊəs/ *adj* excessively smooth (and esp insincere) in speech or manner. **unc·tu·ous·ly** *adv*

un·cut /ˈʌnˋkʌt/ *adj* (of a book) with the outer folds of the pages not trimmed or cut; (of a story, film, etc) not abridged.

un·dated /ˈʌnˋdeɪtɪd/ *adj* not having a date: *an ~ cheque; ~ stocks,* with no specified date for redemption.

un·daunted /ˈʌnˋdɔntɪd/ *adj* not daunted; fearless.

un·de·ceive /ˈʌndɪˋsiv/ *vt* [VP6A] cause to be no longer deceived or in error.

un·de·cided /ˈʌndɪˋsɑɪdɪd/ *adj* not decided; not yet having made up one's mind: *She was ~ whether to go to a concert or the cinema.*

un·de·clared /ˈʌndɪˋkleəd/ *adj* **1** (of goods liable to customs duty) not declared or shown to the customs officers. **2** not announced or made known: *~ war.*

un·de·fended /ˈʌndɪˋfendɪd/ *adj* (esp of a lawsuit) in which no defence is offered.

un·de·mon·stra·tive /ˈʌndɪˋmonstrətɪv/ *adj* reserved; not in the habit of showing feelings of affection, interest, etc.

un·de·ni·able /ˈʌndɪˋnɑɪəbl/ *adj* that cannot be denied; undoubtedly true: *of ~ worth/value.* **un·de·ni·ably** /-əblɪ/ *adv*

un·de·nomi·na·tional /ˈʌndɪˈnomɪˋneɪʃnl/ *adj* not connected with any particular religious sect: *~ education/schools.*

un·der[1] /ˋʌndə(r)/ *adv* **1** in or to a lower place, position, etc: *The ship went ~,* sank. *Can you stay ~* (= ~ the water) *for two minutes?* ***down ~,*** (used in GB, colloq) Australia and New Zealand. **2** (used to modify *nn*) subordinate; lower in rank, etc: *ˋ~-gardeners; ˈ~ˋsecretary.*

un·der[2] /ˋʌndə(r)/ *prep* **1** in or to a position lower than: *The cat was ~ the table. It is shady ~ the trees. There's nothing new ~ the sun,* (prov), nothing new anywhere. *We passed ~ several bridges. The soldiers were standing ~* (= at the foot of) *the castle wall. The village nestles ~* (= at the foot of) *the hill.* **2** in and covered by: *The part of an iceberg ~ the water is much larger than the part above the water. He hid his face ~ the bedclothes. Her hair came out from ~ her hat.* **3** less than; lower (in rank) than: *children ~* (opp *over/above*) *fourteen years of age; books for the ˈ~-ˋtens* (opp *over-tens*), children under ten; *incomes ~* (opp *over/above*) *£1 000; run a hundred metres in ~ ten seconds; ~ half an acre; no one ~* (opp *above/over*) (*the rank of*) *a captain; speak ~ one's breath,* in a whisper. ***~ age,*** ⇨ **age. 4** (indicating various conditions): *road ~ repair,* being repaired; *~ discussion,* being discussed; *fifty acres ~* (= planted with) *wheat; ~ sentence of* (= sentenced to) *death; living ~ an assumed name; England ~ the Stuarts,* during the times of the Stuart kings and queens: *be ~ the impression that,* have the idea or belief that: *The book is listed ~ biology,* within that classification. **5** weighed down by (lit and fig): *marching ~ a heavy load; sink ~ a load of grief (taxation, etc).*

under- /ˋʌndə(r)/ *pref* ⇨ App 3.

under·act /ˈʌndərˋækt/ *vt,vi* [VP6A,2A] act with too little spirit, energy, emphasis, etc: *~ the part of Hamlet. The star overacted; the other players ~ed.*

under·arm /ˋʌndərɑm/ *adj, adv* (cricket, tennis) with the hand kept below the level of the elbow: *~ bowling; bowl/serve ~.*

under·belly /ˋʌndəbelɪ/ *n* (*pl* **-lies**) under surface of an animal's body, e g as a cut of meat, esp pork.

under·bid /ˈʌndəˋbɪd/ *vt* (*pt,pp* unchanged) ⇨ **bid**[1]**(1)**. **1** make a lower bid than (sb else). **2** (card games, bridge) bid less on (a hand of cards) than its strength warrants.

under·bred /ˈʌndəˋbred/ *adj* ill bred; vulgar.

under·brush /ˋʌndəbrʌʃ/ *n* [U] = **undergrowth** (which is more usu).

under·car·riage /ˋʌndəkærɪdʒ/ *n* landing gear of an aircraft. ⇨ the illus at **air**.

under·charge /ˈʌndəˋtʃɑdʒ/ *vt* [VP6A] charge too little for (sth) or to (sb). □ *n* /ˋʌndətʃɑdʒ/ charge that is too low or small.

under·clothes /ˋʌndəkləʊðz *US:* -kləʊz/ *n pl* clothing worn under a suit, dress, etc; next to the skin. **under·cloth·ing** /ˋʌndəkləʊðɪŋ/ *n* [U] = ~.

under·cover /ˈʌndəˋkʌvə(r)/ *adj* secret; surreptitious: *an ~ agent,* person who associates with suspected criminals, etc to get evidence against them, or who acts as a spy, e g during a war; *~ payments,* e g made in order to bribe sb.

under·cur·rent /ˋʌndəkʌrənt *US:* -kɜənt/ *n* [U] current of water flowing beneath the surface; (fig) tendency (of thought or feeling) lying below what is apparent: *an ~ of opposition/melancholy.*

under·cut[1] /ˋʌndəkʌt/ *n* [U] meat cut from the under side of sirloin.

under·cut[2] /ˈʌndəˋkʌt/ *vt* (*pt,pp* unchanged; **-tt-**) [VP6A] (comm) offer (goods, services) at a lower price than competitors.

under·de·vel·oped /ˈʌndədɪˋveləpt/ *adj* not yet fully developed: *~ muscles/countries.*

under·dog /ˋʌndədog *US:* -dɔg/ *n* (fig, usu with *def art*) poor and helpless person who usu gets the worst of an encounter, a struggle, etc: *plead for the ~,* for sb who is oppressed.

under·done /ˈʌndəˋdʌn/ *adj* (esp of meat) not completely cooked throughout.

under·esti·mate /ˈʌndərˋestɪmeɪt/ *vt* [VP6A] form too low an estimate of: *~ the enemy's strength.* □ *n* /-mət/ [C] estimate which is too low.

under·ex·pose /ˈʌndərɪkˋspəʊz/ *vt* [VP6A] (photo) expose (a plate or film) for too short a time. **under·expo·sure** /-ˋspəʊʒə(r)/ *n*

under·fed /ˈʌndəˋfed/ *adj* having had too little food.

under·floor /ˋʌndəflɔ(r)/ *adj* (of systems for heating buildings) with the source of heat placed under the floor(s).

under·foot /ˈʌndəˋfʊt/ *adv* under one's feet; on the ground: *It is very hard ~,* e g when the ground is frozen hard.

under·gar·ment /ˋʌndəgɑmənt/ *n* [C] article of underclothing.

under·go /ˈʌndəˋgəʊ/ *vt* (*pt* **-went** /-ˋwent/, *pp* **-gone** /-ˋgon *US:* -ˋgɔn/) [VP6A] experience;

pass through: *The explorers had to ~ much suffering. The new aircraft underwent its tests well.*

under·grad·uate /ˌʌndəˈgrædʒʊət/ *n* university student working for a bachelor's degree: (attrib) ˈ~ *work/studies; in his* ˈ~ *days.*

under·ground /ˈʌndəgraʊnd/ *attrib adj* **1** under the surface of the ground: *London's ~ railways; ~ passages/caves.* **2** secret, esp of a secret political movement or one for resisting enemy forces in occupation of another country: *~ workers.* □ *adv* (also) /ˌʌndəˈgraʊnd/ (in the senses of the *adj*): *He went ~* (= into hiding) *when he heard the police were after him.* □ *n* (in the senses of the *adj*): *travel in London by ~*, i e the ~ railway (US = *subway*); *a member of the French ~*, the secret resistance movement during World War Two.

under·growth /ˈʌndəgrəʊθ/ *n* [U] shrubs, bushes, low trees, growing among taller trees.

under·hand /ˌʌndəˈhænd/ *adv* secret(ly); deceitful(ly); sly(ly): *play an ~ game; ~ methods; behave in an ~ way.* **~ed** *adj* = ~.

under·hung /ˌʌndəˈhʌŋ/ *adj* (attrib) (of the lower jaw) projecting beyond the upper jaw.

under·lay /ˈʌndəleɪ/ *n* [U] material (felt, rubber, etc) laid under a carpet or mattress (to preserve its condition).

under·lie /ˌʌndəˈlaɪ/ *vt* [VP6A] **1** be or lie under. **2** form the basis of (a theory, of conduct, behaviour, doctrine).

under·line /ˌʌndəˈlaɪn/ *vt* [VP6A] draw a line under (a word, etc); (fig) emphasize. □ *n* /ˈʌndəlaɪn/ line drawn under a word or words.

under·ling /ˈʌndəlɪŋ/ *n* (usu contemptuous) person in an unimportant position under another or others.

under·man·ned /ˌʌndəˈmænd/ *adj* (of a ship, factory, etc) having not enough men to do all the work that needs to be done.

under·men·tioned /ˌʌndəˈmenʃnd/ *adj* mentioned below or later (in an article, etc).

under·mine /ˌʌndəˈmaɪn/ *vt* [VP6A] **1** make a hollow or tunnel under; weaken at the base: *cliffs ~d by the sea.* **2** weaken gradually: *His health was ~d by drink. The President's enemies are spreading rumours to ~ his authority.*

under·neath /ˌʌndəˈniθ/ *adv, prep* beneath; below; at or to a lower place.

under·nour·ished /ˌʌndəˈnʌrɪʃt *US:* -ˈnɜɪʃt/ *adj* not provided with sufficient food for good health and normal growth. **under·nour·ish·ment** *n*

under·pants /ˈʌndəpænts/ *n pl* (US) short undergarment worn over the loins and thighs.

under·pass /ˈʌndəpɑs *US:* -pæs/ *n* [C] section of a road that goes under another road or railway. ⇨ overpass, flyover.

under·pay /ˌʌndəˈpeɪ/ *vt* (*pt,pp* -paid /-ˈpeɪd/) [VP6A] pay (workmen, etc) inadequately. **~ment** *n*

under·pin /ˌʌndəˈpɪn/ *vt* (-nn-) place a support of masonry, etc under (a wall, etc); (fig) support, form the basis for (a case, an argument, etc).

under·popu·lated /ˌʌndəˈpopjʊleɪtɪd/ *adj* (of a country or area) having a small population in view of its size or natural resources.

under·privi·leged /ˌʌndəˈprɪvlɪdʒd/ *adj* not having had the educational and social advantages enjoyed by more fortunate people, social classes, nations, etc.

under·proof /ˌʌndəˈpruf/ *adj* containing less alcohol than proof spirit. ⇨ proof[1](5).

under·pro·duc·tion /ˌʌndəprəˈdʌkʃn/ *n* [U] production of goods in insufficient quantity or below full capacity.

under·quote /ˌʌndəˈkwəʊt/ *vt* [VP6A] quote lower prices for goods than (others).

under·rate /ˌʌndəˈreɪt/ *vt* [VP6A] place too low a value or estimate on: *~ an opponent*, fail to realize his abilities, strength, etc.

under·sec·retary /ˌʌndəˈsekrətrɪ *US:* -terɪ/ *n* (*pl* -ries) assistant secretary, esp (*Parliamentary U~*) member of the Civil Service and head of a Government Department.

under·sell /ˌʌndəˈsel/ *vt* (*pt,pp* -sold /-ˈsəʊld/) [VP6A] sell (goods) at a lower price than (competitors).

under·sexed /ˌʌndəˈsekst/ *adj* having less sexual desire or potency than normal.

under·sher·iff /ˈʌndəʃerɪf/ *n* sheriff's deputy.

under·shoot /ˌʌndəˈʃut/ *vt* (*pt,pp* -shot /-ˈʃot/) (of an aircraft) *~ the runway*, land short of it. ⇨ overshoot.

under·shot /ˌʌndəˈʃot/ *adj* (of a mill wheel) worked by water that passes under it.

under·sign /ˌʌndəˈsaɪn/ *vt* [VP6A] sign (a letter, etc) at the foot: *We, the ~ed*, We whose signatures appear below.

under·sized /ˌʌndəˈsaɪzd/ *adj* of less than the usual size; stunted or dwarfish.

under·slung /ˌʌndəˈslʌŋ/ *adj* (in a vehicle) having springs attached to the axles from below.

under·staffed /ˌʌndəˈstɑft *US:* -stæft/ *adj* having too small a staff: *The school/hospital is badly ~.* ⇨ undermanned.

under·stand /ˌʌndəˈstænd/ *vt,vi* (*pt.pp* -stood /-ˈstʊd/) **1** [VP6A,C,8,10,2A] know the meaning, nature, explanation, of (sth): *~ French/figures/a problem. He didn't ~ me/what I said. You don't ~* (= realize) *what a difficult position I'm in. A good teacher must ~ children. I cannot ~ his robbing his friend/why he robbed his friend. It is easy to ~ his anger/why he was angry.* ***make oneself understood,*** make one's meaning clear: *Can he make himself understood in Russian?* ***(Now), ~ me,*** phrase often used to preface a warning or threat. ***~ one another,*** (of two persons, parties) be clearly aware of one another's views, feelings, intentions: *The employers and workers have not reached an agreement yet, but at least they ~ one another.* **2** [VP9,17] learn (from information received); infer; take for granted: *I ~ that you are now married. Am I to ~ that you refuse? I understood him to say that he would cooperate.* ***give sb to ~,*** cause sb to believe or have the idea (that): *We were given to ~ that free accommodation would be supplied.* **3** [VP6A] supply (a word or phrase) mentally: *In the sentence 'He is taller than I', the verb 'am' is to be understood after 'I'.* **~·able** /-əbl/ *adj* that can be understood: *His reluctance to agree is ~able.* **~ing** *adj* (good at) ~ing or realizing other persons' feelings or points of view; having or showing insight: *with an ~ing smile. Please be ~ing; do not scold the child.* □ *n* **1** [U] power of clear thought. **2** [U] capacity for sympathizing, seeing from another's point of view, etc. **3** (often with *indef art*, but rarely *pl*) agreement; realization of another's views or feelings towards oneself: *reach/come to an ~ing with sb.* ***on this ~ing,*** on this condition. ***on the ~ing that...,*** on condition that....

under·state /ˌʌndəˈsteɪt/ *vt* [VP6A] fail to state fully or adequately; express in excessively restrained language: *They exaggerated the enemy's losses and ~d their own. She ~d her age on the census form.* **~·ment** /ˈʌndəsteɪtmənt/ *n* [U] understating; [C] statement that expresses an idea, etc, too weakly: *To say that the boy is rather clever is an ~ment,* e g of a boy who is very brilliant.

under·stock /ˌʌndəˈstok/ *vt* [VP6A] equip with less stock than is desirable: *Is the farm ~ed,* Could it support more animals, etc than it now has?

under·strap·per /ˈʌndəstræpə(r)/ *n* (contemptuous) underling; official, employee, of low rank, little importance.

under·study /ˈʌndəstʌdɪ/ *n* (*pl* -dies) person learning to, able to, take the place of another (esp an actor). □ *vt* (*pt,pp* -died) [VP6A] study (a part in a play) for this purpose; act as ~ to (an actor): *He is ~ing Macbeth/~ing the leading actor in the play.*

under·take /ˌʌndəˈteɪk/ *vt* (*pt* -took /-ˈtʊk/, *pp* -taken /-ˈteɪkn/) **1** [VP6A,7A] ~ ***(to do) sth,*** make oneself responsible for; agree (to do sth): *Gladstone undertook the premiership when he was 82 years old. He undertook to finish the job by Friday.* **2** [VP6A] start (a piece of work). **3** [VP7A,9] affirm; promise: *I can't ~ that you will make a profit.* **under·tak·ing** /ˌʌndəˈteɪkɪŋ/ *n* [C] **1** work that one has ~n to do; task or enterprise. **2** promise; guarantee.

under·taker /ˈʌndəteɪkə(r)/ *n* one whose business is to prepare the dead for burial or cremation and manage funerals. Cf (US) *mortician.* □ *n* /ˈʌndəteɪkɪŋ/ this business.

under the counter /ˌʌndə ðə ˈkaʊntə(r)/ *adj* ⇨ counter[1].

under·tone /ˈʌndətəʊn/ *n* [C] **1** low, quiet, tone: *talk in ~s,* with subdued voices. **2** underlying quality: *an ~ of discontent/hostility/sadness.* **3** thin or subdued colour.

under·took /ˌʌndəˈtʊk/ *pt* of undertake.

under·tow /ˈʌndətəʊ/ *n* (current caused by the) backward flow of a wave breaking on a beach: *The swimmer was caught in an ~ and carried out to sea.*

under·value /ˌʌndəˈvælju/ *vt* [VP6A] value at less than the true worth. **under·valu·ation** /ˌʌndəˌvæljuˈeɪʃn/ *n*

under·vest /ˈʌndəvest/ *n* (*GB*) (*US* = *vest*) garment worn next to the skin under a shirt.

under·water /ˈʌndəwɔtə(r)/ *adj* below the surface of the water: ~ *swimming,* e g with a snorkel.

under·wear /ˈʌndəweə(r)/ *n* [U] underclothing.

under·went /ˌʌndəˈwent/ *pt* of undergo.

under·world /ˈʌndəwɜld/ *n* **1** (in Gk myths, etc) place of the departed spirits of the dead. **2** part of society that lives by vice and crime.

under·write /ˌʌndəˈraɪt *vt* (*pt* -wrote /-ˈrəʊt/, *pp* -written /-ˈrɪtn/) [VP6A] undertake to bear all or part of possible loss (by signing an agreement about insurance, esp of ships); engage to buy all the newly issued stock in (a company) not bought by the public. **under·writer** *n* one who ~s policies of (esp marine) insurance: *an ~r at Lloyd's.*

un·de·signed /ˌʌndɪˈzaɪnd/ *adj* (esp) not premeditated or done on purpose; not foreseen.

un·de·sir·able /ˌʌndɪˈzaɪərəbl/ *adj* objectionable; (esp of persons) of a kind not to be welcomed in society. □ *n* ~ person.

un·de·ter·red /ˌʌndɪˈtɜd/ *adj* not deterred or discouraged: *~ by the weather/by failure.*

un·de·vel·oped /ˌʌndɪˈveləpt/ *adj* not developed: ~ *land,* not yet used (for agriculture, industry, building, etc).

un·did /ʌnˈdɪd/ *pt* of undo.

un·dies /ˈʌndɪz/ *n pl* (colloq) women's underclothes.

un·dis·charged /ˌʌndɪsˈtʃɑdʒd/ *adj* (of a cargo) not unloaded; (of a debt) (not paid); (esp, of a bankrupt person or firm) not relieved of a further liability to pay money still owing to creditors. ⇨ discharge[2](5).

undo /ʌnˈdu/ *vt* (*pt* undid /ʌnˈdɪd/, *pp* undone /ʌnˈdʌn/) [VP6A] **1** untie, unfasten, loosen (knots, buttons, etc): *My shoe-lace has come undone.* **2** destroy the result of; bring back the state of affairs that existed before: *He has undone the good work of his predecessor. What is done cannot be undone.* **3** (usu passive, and now old use) bring to disaster; ruin the prospects, reputation or morals of: *'Alas, I am undone!' she sobbed out, as the bad baronet left her bedroom.* **un·do·ing** *n* (cause of) ruin: *Drink was his ~ing. He went to the moneylenders, to his complete ~ing.* **un·done** *adj* not done; not finished: *leave one's work undone. We have left undone those things which we ought to have done.*

un·dock /ʌnˈdok/ *vt,vi* [VP6A,2A] uncouple (a module, etc) from a spacecraft: *The astronauts had some difficulty in undocking the lunar module.*

un·dom·es·ti·cated /ˌʌndəˈmestɪkeɪtɪd/ *adj* not trained or interested in household affairs: *His wife/Her husband is, alas, quite ~.*

un·doubted /ʌnˈdaʊtɪd/ *adj* certain; accepted as true: *There is an ~ improvement in the patient's condition.* **~·ly** *adv*

un·dreamed /ʌnˈdrimd/, **un·dreamt** /ʌnˈdremt/ *adjj* (usu) **~-of,** not thought of; not imagined: *earn ~-of wealth; ~-of beauties.*

un·dress /ʌnˈdres/ *vt,vi* **1** [VP6A] remove the clothes of: *Jane ~ed her doll.* **2** [VP2A] take off one's clothes: *~ and get into bed.* □ *n* (often attrib) (esp mil) uniform for ordinary (non-ceremonial) occasions.

un·due /ˈʌnˈdju *US:* -ˈdu/ *adj* improper; more than is right: *with ~ haste; exercise an ~ influence upon sb.* **un·duly** /ˈʌnˈdjulɪ *US:* -ˈdulɪ/ *adv* in an ~ manner: *unduly pessimistic.*

un·du·late /ˈʌndjʊleɪt *US:* -dʒʊ-/ *vi* [VP2A,C] (of surfaces) have a wave-like motion or look: *a field of wheat undulating in the breeze; undulating land,* that rises and falls in gentle slopes. **un·du·la·tion** /ˌʌndjʊˈleɪʃn *US:* -dʒʊ-/ *n* [U] wave-like motion or form; [C] one of a number of wave-like curves or slopes.

un·dy·ing /ʌnˈdaɪɪŋ/ *adj* everlasting; never-ending: *~ love/hatred/fame.*

un·earned /ˈʌnˈɜnd/ *adj* **1** not gained by work or service: *~ income,* e g from investments, or land or property that is inherited; *~ increment,* increase in the value of property, e g houses, land, not due to the owner's expenditure or efforts, e g because of a rise in the value of land. **2** not deserved: *~ praise.*

un·earth /ʌnˈɜθ/ *vt* [VP6A] discover and bring to light: *~ new facts about the life of Shakespeare; ~ a buried treasure. The dog has ~ed some bones.*

un·earth·ly /ʌnˈɜθlɪ/ *adj* **1** supernatural. **2** mysterious; ghostly; frightening: *~ screams.* **3** (colloq) unreasonable: *Why do you wake me up at this ~ hour?*

un·easy /ʌnˈizɪ/ *adj* uncomfortable in body or mind; troubled or anxious: *have an ~ conscience; be ~ in one's mind about the future; pass an ~ night,* sleep badly. *We grew ~ at their long absence.* **un·eas·ily** /ʌnˈizl̩ɪ/ *adv* **un·easi·ness** *n* **un·ease** /ʌnˈiz/ *n* (liter) = uneasiness.

un·eaten /ʌnˈitn/ *adj* (of food, a meal) set out but left unused.

un·edu·cated /ʌnˈedʒʊkeɪtɪd/ *adj* not educated; suggesting lack of education (or the kind of education or social background considered desirable): *He has an ~ mind/voice.*

un·em·ploy·able /ˌʌnɪmˈplɔɪəbl/ *adj* that cannot be employed.

un·em·ployed /ˌʌnɪmˈplɔɪd/ *adj* not being used: *~ capital;* not working, not able to get work: *~ men; the ~,* those for whom there is no work or who are temporarily without work.

un·em·ploy·ment /ˌʌnɪmˈplɔɪmənt/ *n* **1** [U] state of being unemployed: *U~ is a serious social evil.* **2** amount of unused labour: *There is more ~ now than there was six months ago.* **3** (attrib): *ˈ~ insurance; ~ pay/benefit,* money paid from insurance funds to a worker who cannot get employment.

un·end·ing /ʌnˈendɪŋ/ *adj* everlasting; unceasing; (colloq) frequently repeated: *She's tired of your ~ grumbles.* **~·ly** *adv*

un·en·light·ened /ˌʌnɪnˈlaɪtnd/ *adj* uneducated; not well-informed; (in some contexts) prejudiced or superstitious.

un·equal /ʌnˈikwl/ *adj* **~ (to sth),** **1** not equal. **2** (esp of work such as writing) not of the same quality throughout; variable. **3** not strong, clever, etc enough: *I feel ~ to the task.* **~·ly** /-kwl̩ɪ/ *adv*

un·equal·led /ʌnˈikwld/ *adj* unmatched; unrivalled.

un·equivo·cal /ˌʌnɪˈkwɪvəkl/ *adj* clear; having one only possible meaning.

un·err·ing /ʌnˈɜrɪŋ/ *adj* accurate: *fire with ~ aim; strike an ~ blow.* **~·ly** *adv*

un·ex·ampled /ˌʌnɪgˈzɑmpld *US:* -ˈzæm-/ *adj* of which there is no other example that can be compared with it: *the ~ heroism of our soldiers.*

un·ex·cep·tion·able /ˌʌnɪkˈsepʃn̩əbl/ *adj* beyond criticism; altogether admirable.

un·fail·ing /ʌnˈfeɪlɪŋ/ *adj* never coming to an end; meeting one's expectations at all times: *his ~ good humour/patience; an ~* (= loyal) *friend.* **~·ly** *adv* at all times: *~ly courteous.*

un·fair /ʌnˈfeə(r)/ *adj* not right or fair; unjust: *~ treatment/competition.* **~·ly** *adv* **~·ness** *n*

un·faith·ful /ʌnˈfeɪθfl/ *adj* not true to one's duty, a promise, etc; (esp) not faithful to marriage vows: *Her husband is ~ to her.* **~·ly** /-flɪ/ *adv* **~·ness** *n*

un·fal·ter·ing /ʌnˈfɔltr̩ɪŋ/ *adj* not wavering or hesitating: *with ~ steps/courage.* **~·ly** *adv*

un·fam·il·iar /ˌʌnfəˈmɪlɪə(r)/ *adj* **1 ~ (to),** not well known: *That face is not ~ to me,* I feel that I know it, have seen it before. **2 ~ with,** not acquainted with: *He is still ~ with this district.*

un·fath·om·able /ʌnˈfæðm̩əbl/ *adj* so deep that the bottom cannot be reached; too strange or difficult to be understood. **un·fath·omed** /ʌnˈfæðmd/ *adj* (of a person's character) not understood; (of a crime, etc) not solved; (of ocean depths, etc) not measured.

un·feel·ing /ʌnˈfilɪŋ/ *adj* **1** hard-hearted; unsympathetic. **2** not able to feel. **~·ly** *adv*

un·feigned /ʌnˈfeɪnd/ *adj* not pretended; genuine (which is more usu); sincere: *He showed ~ satisfaction at the boy's success.* **~·ly** *adv* openly and sincerely.

un·fit /ʌnˈfɪt/ *adj* **~ (for sth/to do sth),** not fit or suitable: *He is ~ for business/~ to be a doctor. This road is ~ for heavy traffic. He was rejected* (e g for military service) *as medically ~.* □ *vt* (-tt) [VP14] **~ sb for sth,** make ~ (which is more usu): *A bad attack of lumbago ~ted him for work in the garden.*

un·flag·ging /ʌnˈflægɪŋ/ *adj* not showing signs of weariness; uninterrupted: *work with ~ energy.*

un·flap·pable /ʌnˈflæpəbl/ *adj* (colloq) unlikely to get into a flap; never upset in a crisis. ⇨ flap[1](4).

un·flinch·ing /ʌnˈflɪntʃɪŋ/ *adj* fearless; resolute.

un·fold /ʌnˈfəʊld/ *vt,vi* [VP6A,2A,C] **1** (of sth folded) open out: *~ a newspaper/a prospectus.* **2** reveal, make known; become known or visible: *as the story ~s (itself). She ~ed to him her plans for the future. The landscape ~ed before us.*

un·for·get·table /ˌʌnfəˈgetəbl/ *adj* that cannot be forgotten: *an ~ experience.*

un·for·tu·nate /ʌnˈfɔtʃʊnət/ *adj* unlucky: *an ~ expedition;* regrettable: *an ~ remark/lack of good manners.*

un·founded /ʌnˈfaʊndɪd/ *adj* without foundation: *~ rumours.*

un·fre·quented /ˌʌnfrɪˈkwentɪd/ *adj* seldom visited.

un·friend·ly /ʌnˈfrendlɪ/ *adj* not friendly; unfavourable.

un·frock /ˌʌnˈfrok/ *vt* [VP6A] (of a priest guilty of bad conduct) dismiss from the priesthood.

un·fruit·ful /ʌnˈfrutfl/ *adj* not bearing fruit; without results or success.

un·furl /ʌnˈfɜl/ *vt,vi* [VP6A,2A] unroll, spread out: *~ the sails.*

un·fur·nished /ʌnˈfɜnɪʃt/ *adj* (esp) without furniture: *rooms/a house to let ~.*

un·gain·ly /ʌnˈgeɪnlɪ/ *adj* clumsy; awkward; ungraceful.

un·gated /ˌʌnˈgeɪtɪd/ *adj* not having a gate or gates: *An ~ level crossing is dangerous.*

un·gen·er·ous /ʌnˈdʒenrəs/ *adj* not generous; unkind.

un·god·ly /ʌnˈgodlɪ/ *adj* **1** not religious; not giving reverence to God; sinful. **2** (colloq) annoying; shocking. **3** (colloq) unreasonable: *Why did you phone me at this ~ hour?*

un·gov·ern·able /ʌnˈgʌvn̩əbl/ *adj* that cannot be controlled: *~ passions; a man with an ~ temper.*

un·grate·ful /ʌnˈgreɪtfl/ *adj* **1** not showing gratitude. **2** (of a task) not pleasant or agreeable.

un·guarded /ʌnˈgɑdɪd/ *adj* (esp of a person and what he says) careless; indiscreet: *In an ~ moment, he gave away most important secrets.*

un·guent /ˈʌŋgwənt/ *n* [C,U] any soft substance used as an ointment (e g for soothing skin injuries) or for lubrication.

un·hal·lowed /ʌnˈhæləʊd/ *adj* **1** not made holy: *buried in ~ ground,* not consecrated by the Church. **2** wicked; impious: *with ~ joy.*

un·hand /ʌnˈhænd/ *vt* [VP6A] (archaic) let go; take the hands off: *'Unhand me, villain!' she cried.*

un·happy /ʌn`hæpɪ/ *adj* (-ier, -iest) **1** not happy. **2** not suitable or tactful: *an ~ comment.*

un·healthy /ʌn`helθɪ/ *adj* harmful to bodily or mental health; (colloq) dangerous.

un·heard /ʌn`hɜd/ *adj* not heard; not allowed a hearing. ***go ~,*** **(a)** not be heard. **(b)** have no-one willing to listen to it: *Her request for help went ~.* **un·heard-of** /ʌn`hɜd ov/ *adj* extraordinary; without an earlier example.

un·hinge /ʌn`hɪndʒ/ *vt* [VP6A] take (a door, gate, etc) from the hinge(s); cause (sb's mind, brain) to be off its balance: *His mind is ~d,* He is mentally ill.

un·holy /ʌn`həʊlɪ/ *adj* **1** wicked; sinful. **2** (colloq) unreasonable.

un·hook /ʌn`hʊk/ *vt* [VP6A] **1** undo the hooks of (a dress, etc): *Please ~ my dress, darling,* esp of a dress fastened with hooks at the back. **2** release from a hook: *My dress is caught on a nail—please ~ me.*

un·hoped-for /ʌn`həʊpt fɔ(r)/ *adj* unexpected: *an ~ piece of good fortune.*

un·horse /'ʌn`hɔs/ *vt* [VP6A] throw from a horse's back; cause to fall from a horse.

uni·corn /`junɪkɔn/ *n* (in old stories) horse-like animal with one long horn; (heraldry) representation of this with a lion's tail.

un·iden·ti·fied /'ʌnɑɪ`dentɪfɑɪd/ *adj* which cannot be identified: *The dead man is still ~.* **~ flying object,** (abbr **U F O**) ⇨ *flying saucer* at flying.

uni·form /`junɪfɔm/ *adj* the same; not varying in form, quality, etc: *sticks of ~ length; to be kept at a ~ temperature.* □ *n* [C,U] (style of) dress worn by all members of an organization, e g the police, the armed forces: *the blue ~(s) of the police; the khaki ~(s) of the army.* **in ~,** wearing such dress: *He looks handsome in ~.* **~ed** *adj* wearing ~: *the ~ed branch of the police,* contrasted with those who wear plain clothes, e g detectives. **~·ly** *adv* **~·ity** /'junɪ`fɔmətɪ/ *n* [U] ~ condition; condition of being the same throughout.

unify /`junɪfɑɪ/ *vt* (*pt,pp* -fied) [VP6A] **1** form into one; unite. **2** make uniform. **uni·fi·ca·tion** /'junɪfɪ`keɪʃn/ *n* [U] ~ing or being unified: *Work for the unification of Europe.*

uni·lat·eral /'junɪ`lætrl/ *adj* of, on, affecting, done by, one side or party only: *a ~ declaration of independence,* (abbr U D I); *~ repudiation of a treaty,* by one of the parties that signed it, without the consent of the other party or parties. **~ly** /-rl̩ɪ/ *adv*

un·im·peach·able /'ʌnɪm`pitʃəbl/ *adj* that cannot be questioned or doubted: *~ honesty; news from an ~ source.*

un·in·formed /'ʌnɪn`fɔmd/ *adj* (esp) not having, made without, adequate information: *~ criticism.*

un·in·hib·ited /'ʌnɪn`hɪbɪtɪd/ *adj* without inhibitions; free from the social and moral restraints usual among conventional people.

un·in·spired /'ʌnɪn`spɑɪəd/ *adj* without inspiration; dull: *an ~ lecture/lecturer.*

un·in·ter·ested /ʌn`ɪntrɪstɪd/ *adj* **1** having, showing no interest. **2** having no personal concern in sth.

union /`junɪən/ *n* **1** [U] uniting or being united; joining or being joined; [C] instance of this: *the ~ of the three towns into one; the Universal Postal U~,* of countries for the purpose of interchanging mail services to mutual advantage; *the U~ of Soviet Socialist Republics* (abbr **U S S R**) **the U~,** **(a)** of England and Scotland (in 1706). **(b)** the United States of America: *the President's address to the U~,* to all US citizens. **the U~ Jack,** the British flag. **2** [U] state of being in agreement or harmony: *live in perfect ~;* [C] instance of this: *a happy ~,* e g a happy marriage. **3** [C] association formed by the uniting of persons, groups, etc, esp **a trade ~,** ⇨ trade[1](1). **4** (old use; GB) workhouse built by two or more parishes for administration of the poor-laws. **5 the U~,** general club and debating society at some universities: *The debate of the Oxford U~ is to be broadcast.* **6** [C] coupling for connecting rods or pipes. **7** (US) *~ suit,* combinations(4). **~·ist** /-ɪst/ *n* [C] **1** member of a trade ~; supporter of trade ~s. **2 U~·ist, (a)** (GB politics) person who, before the Irish Free State was established, opposed the granting of independence to Ireland. **(b)** supporter of the Federal Government of the US during the Civil War; opponent of secession.

unique /ju`nik/ *adj* having no like or equal; being the only one of its sort. **~·ly** *adv* **~·ness** *n*

uni·sex /`junɪseks/ *adj* (of clothes) of a style designed for, or to be worn by, both sexes.

uni·son /`junɪsn/ *n* [U] concord or agreement: *sing in ~,* all singing the same notes, not harmonizing; *act in ~ (with others).*

unit /`junɪt/ *n* [C] **1** single person, thing or group regarded as complete in itself: (mil) *an armoured ~; ~s of the US Sixth Fleet. The family is often taken as the ~ of society.* **2** quantity or amount used as a standard of measurement: *The metre is a ~ of length. The monetary ~ of Great Britain is the pound.* **3** smallest whole number; the number 1. **4** (various) **`kitchen ~,** article of kitchen equipment, e g a sink, draining board, with cupboards, that can be fitted with others of similar design and appearance along a wall. **'~ `furniture,** articles of furniture of similar design, materials, etc, to be used together. **'~ `trust,** trust(3) that invests in a large number and wide variety of stocks and issues certificates (called *~s*) on which dividends are payable.

Uni·tar·ian /'junɪ`teərɪən/ *n* member of a Christian church which rejects the doctrine of the Trinity and believes that God is one person. □ *adj* of the ~s: *the U~ Church.* **~·ism** /-ɪzm/ *n*

unite /ju`nɑɪt/ *vt,vi* **1** [VP6A,2A] make or become one; join: *~ one country to another; the common interests that ~ our two countries,* that bring them together. *England and Scotland ~d in 1706.* **2** [VP2A,3A,4A] **~ *(in sth/to do sth),*** act or work together: *Let us ~ in fighting/~ to fight poverty and disease.* **united** *adj* **1** joined in spirit, by love and sympathy: *a ~d family.* **2** resulting from association for a common purpose: *make a ~d effort; present a ~d front to the enemy; the U~d Nations.* **3** joined politically: *the U~d Kingdom; the U~d States of Mexico.* **united·ly** *adv*

unity /`junətɪ/ *n* (*pl* -ties) **1** [C,U] the state of being united; (an) arrangement of parts to form a complete whole: *The figure on the left spoils the ~ of the painting. the dramatic unities; the unities of place, time and action,* the use of the same scene throughout, the limitation of the duration of the play to one day, or the time taken to act it, the use of one single plot, with nothing irrelevant to that plot. **2** [U] harmony, agreement (of aims, feelings, etc): *in ~ with others; live together in ~; political ~.*

uni·ver·sal /ˈjunɪˋvɜsl/ *adj* of, belonging to, done by, all; affecting all: *War causes ~ misery. The cinema provides ~ entertainment.* ***a ~ joint,*** one that permits the turning of connected parts in all directions. ***a ~ rule,*** one with no exceptions. **~ suffrage,** suffrage extending to all members of a community. **~ time,** ⇨ Greenwich. **~ly** /-slɪ/ *adv* **~·ity** /ˈjunɪvɜˋsælətɪ/ *n* [U].

uni·verse /ˋjunɪvɜs/ *n* **1 the U~,** everything that exists everywhere; all the stars, planets, their satellites, etc; the whole creation and the Creator; mankind. **2** [C] system of suns and stars: *a new telescope that may reveal new ~s.*

uni·ver·sity /ˈjunɪˋvɜsətɪ/ *n* (*pl* -ties) (colleges, buildings, etc of an) institution for the advancement and dissemination of knowledge, conferring degrees and engaging in academic research; members of such an institution collectively; (attrib) *a ~ student; a ~ don; the ~ boat-race.*

un·kempt /ʌnˋkempt/ *adj* untidy; (esp of the hair) uncombed.

un·kind /ʌnˋkaɪnd/ *adj* lacking in, not showing, kindness: *an ~ remark.* **~ly** *adv* in an ~ manner: *Don't take it ~ly if…,* Don't think I intend to be ~ if….

un·know·ing /ʌnˋnəʊɪŋ/ *adj* not knowing; unaware. **~·ly** *adv* in ignorance; unawares.

un·known /ʌnˋnəʊn/ *adj* not known or identified: *the tomb of the ~ warrior,* of an ~ soldier (in Westminster Abbey) buried there in memory of those killed in World Wars I and II; *an ~ quantity,* of which the value, etc is not known.

un·learn /ˈʌnˋlɜn/ *vt* [VP6A] get rid of (ideas, habits, etc); learn to give up (sth one has previously learnt).

un·leash /ʌnˋliʃ/ *vt* [VP6A] let go from a leash: *~ a dog.*

un·leav·ened /ˈʌnˋlevnd/ *adj* (of bread) made without yeast.

un·less /ənˋles/ *conj* if not; except when: *You will fail ~ you work harder. U~ bad weather stops me, I go for a walk every day.*

un·let·tered /ʌnˋletəd/ *adj* uneducated; unable to read.

un·like /ʌnˋlaɪk/ *adj, prep* not like; different from: *This design is ~ the former edition.*

un·like·ly /ʌnˋlaɪklɪ/ *adj* not likely to happen or be true: *an ~ event/hypothesis.*

un·listed /ˈʌnˋlɪstɪd/ *adj* (comm, of stocks) not quoted on one of the recognized Stock Exchanges.

un·load /ʌnˋləʊd/ *vt,vi* **1** [VP6A,2A] remove a load from: *~ a ship;* remove (cargo) from: *~ cargo. The ship is ~ing.* **2** [VP6A] get rid of (sth not wanted): *Many investors ~ed* (= sold) *their shares in S African companies.*

un·looked-for /ʌnˋlʊkt fɔ(r)/ *adj* unexpected; for which one is not prepared.

un·loose /ʌnˋlus/ *vt* [VP6A] let loose; make free.

un·man /ʌnˋmæn/ *vt* (-nn-) [VP6A] weaken the courage and self-control of: *The news of his friend's death ~ned him for a while.*

un·man·ly /ʌnˋmænlɪ/ *adj* **1** weak; cowardly. **2** effeminate.

un·man·ned /ˈʌnˋmænd/ *adj* having no crew: *an ~ aircraft with remote control; send an ~ spacecraft to Mars.*

un·man·nered /ʌnˋmænəd/, **un·manner·ly** /ʌnˋmænəlɪ/ *adjj* discourteous; having bad manners.

un·mask /ʌnˋmɑsk *US:* -ˋmæsk/ *vt,vi* [VP6A,2A] remove a mask (from): *The revellers ~ed at midnight,* took off their masks. **2** [VP6A] show the true character or intentions of: *~ a traitor/hypocrite; ~ a villain/villainy.*

un·match·able /ʌnˋmætʃəbl/ *adj* that cannot be matched or equalled. **un·matched** /ʌnˋmætʃt/ *adj* without an equal.

un·mean·ing /ʌnˋminɪŋ/ *adj* without meaning or purpose.

un·meas·ured /ʌnˋmeʒəd/ *adj* (esp) without limit or restraint: *~ abuse.*

un·men·tion·able /ʌnˋmenʃn̩əbl/ *adj* so bad, shocking, etc that it may not be spoken of.

un·mind·ful /ʌnˋmaɪndfl/ *adj* **~ *(of),*** forgetful; oblivious; heedless: *~ of the time/the need to hurry.*

un·mis·tak·able /ˈʌnmɪˋsteɪkəbl/ *adj* clear; about which no mistake or doubt is possible: *Are black clouds an ~ sign of rain?* **un·mis·tak·ably** /-əblɪ/ *adv*

un·miti·gated /ʌnˋmɪtɪgeɪtɪd/ *adj* complete; absolute: *an ~ scoundrel; an ~ evil,* sth which has no accompanying advantages whatever. *You ~ ass!*

un·moved /ʌnˋmuvd/ *adj* (esp) not moved in feelings; undisturbed; indifferent: *He remained ~ by her entreaties for pity.*

un·natu·ral /ʌnˋnætʃərl/ *adj* not natural or normal: *A mother who is cruel to her children is ~.* **~·ly** *adv: He expected, not ~ly, that his father would help him.*

un·nec·ess·ary /ʌnˋnesəsrɪ *US:* -serɪ/ *adj* not necessary; superfluous. **un·nec·ess·ar·ily** /ˈʌnˈnesəˋserl̩ɪ/ *adv* in an ~ manner.

un·nerve /ʌnˋnɜv/ *vt* [VP6A] cause to lose self-control, power of decision, courage.

un·not·iced /ʌnˋnəʊtɪst/ *adj* not observed or noticed: *The event passed ~. Are you going to let the insult pass ~?*

un·num·bered /ʌnˋnʌmbəd/ *adj* **1** more than can be counted. **2** having no number(s): *~ tickets/seats,* e g at a concert-hall.

un·ob·trus·ive /ˈʌnəbˋtrusɪv/ *adj* not too obvious or easily noticeable; discreet.

un·of·fi·cial /ˈʌnəˋfɪʃl/ *adj* not official: *an ~ strike,* not authorized by the union; *~ news,* not officially confirmed.

un·or·tho·dox /ʌnˋɔθədoks/ *adj* not in accordance with what is orthodox, conventional, traditional: *~ teaching methods.*

un·pack /ʌnˋpæk/ *vt,vi* [VP6A,2A] take out (things packed): *~ one's clothes;* take things out of: *~ a suitcase.*

un·par·al·leled /ʌnˋpærəleld/ *adj* having no parallel or equal; matchless: *an ~ achievement/disaster.*

un·par·lia·men·tary /ˈʌnˈpɑləˋmentrɪ/ *adj* (of language, conduct) not suitable (because abusive, disorderly) for Parliament.

un·pick /ʌnˋpɪk/ *vt* [VP6A] take out the stitches from (sth); take out (stitches).

un·placed /ˈʌnˋpleɪst/ *adj* (esp) not one of the first three in a race or competition.

un·play·able /ʌnˋpleɪəbl/ *adj* (of a ball, in games) that cannot be played; (of ground) not fit to be played on.

un·pleas·ant /ʌnˋpleznt/ *adj* disagreeable. **~·ness** *n* [U] ~ or disagreeable feeling; bad feeling (between persons); [C] quarrel, disagreement: *a slight ~ness.*

un·prac·tised /ʌnˈpræktɪst/ *adj* having little experience, inexpert; unskilled.

un·prece·dented /ʌnˈpresɪdentɪd/ *adj* without precedent; never done or known before. **~·ly** *adv*

un·preju·diced /ʌnˈpredʒədɪst/ *adj* free from prejudice.

un·pre·ten·tious /ˈʌnprɪˈtenʃəs/ *adj* modest; not trying to seem important.

un·prin·cipled /ʌnˈprɪnsəpld/ *adj* without moral principles; unscrupulous; dishonest.

un·print·able /ʌnˈprɪntəbl/ *adj* too rude or indecent to be printed.

un·privi·leged /ʌnˈprɪvl̩ɪdʒd/ *adj* (euphem for) poor; of the lowest social level; not having the material goods, education and other advantages of the well-to-do. ⇨ underprivileged.

un·pro·fessional /ˈʌnprəˈfeʃnl/ *adj* (esp of conduct) contrary to the rules or customs of a profession.

un·prompted /ʌnˈpromptɪd/ *adj* (of an answer, action) spontaneous; not said, done, etc as the result of a hint, suggestion, etc.

un·pro·vided /ˈʌnprəˈvɑɪdɪd/ *adj* **1** *~ for,* without provision having been made for: *The widow was left ~ for,* No means of support had been left for her on her husband's death. **2** *~ with,* not provided with: *schools ~ with books and equipment.*

un·pro·voked /ˈʌnprəˈvəʊkt/ *adj* without provocation: *~ aggression/attacks.*

un·quali·fied /ʌnˈkwolɪfɑɪd/ *adj* **1** not limited or restricted; absolute: *~ praise; an ~ denial.* **2** *~ as sth/to do sth,* not qualified: *~ to speak on the subject.*

un·ques·tion·able /ʌnˈkwestʃn̩əbl/ *adj* beyond doubt; certain. **un·ques·tion·ably** /-əblɪ/ *adv*

un·ques·tioned /ʌnˈkwestʃənd/ *adj* not questioned or disputed: *I cannot let your statement pass ~,* I must dispute its truth.

un·ques·tion·ing /ʌnˈkwestʃənɪŋ/ *adj* (esp) given, done, without question or protest: *~ obedience.*

un·quiet /ʌnˈkwɑɪət/ *adj* (formal) restless; uneasy; disturbed: *live in ~ times.*

un·quote /ʌnˈkweʊθ/ (*v*, imper only) (in a telegram, a telephoned message, etc) end the quotation; close the inverted commas: *The rebel leader said (quote) 'We shall never surrender' (unquote).*

un·ravel /ʌnˈrævl/ *vt,vi* (-ll-; US -l-) [VP6A,2A] **1** separate the threads of; pull or become separate: *The cuff of my jumper has ~led. The baby ~led the knitting that her mother left on the chair.* **2** make clear; solve: *~ a mystery/plot.*

un·real /ʌnˈrɪəl/ *adj* imaginary; visionary; illusory.

un·reas·on·able /ʌnˈriznəbl/ *adj* not governed by reason; immoderate; excessive: *make ~ demands.*

un·reas·on·ing /ʌnˈriznɪŋ/ *adj* not using or guided by reason.

un·re·lent·ing /ˈʌnrɪˈlentɪŋ/ *adj* not becoming less in intensity, etc: *~ pressure/attacks.* ⇨ *relentless* at relent.

un·re·li·able /ˈʌnrɪˈlɑɪəbl/ *adj* that cannot be relied on; untrustworthy.

un·re·lieved /ˈʌnrɪˈlivd/ *adj* (esp) without anything to vary monotony: *a plain black dress ~ by a touch of colour or trimming of any kind; ~ boredom/tedium.*

un·re·mit·ting /ˈʌnrɪˈmɪtɪŋ/ *adj* unceasing: *~ care/efforts. The doctor was ~ in his attention to the case.*

un·re·quit·ed /ˈʌnrɪˈkwɑɪtɪd/ *adj* not returned or rewarded: *~ love/service.*

un·re·serv·ed·ly /ˈʌnrɪˈzɜvɪdlɪ/ *adv* without reservation or restriction; openly: *speak ~; trust sb ~.*

un·rest /ʌnˈrest/ *n* [U] (esp) disturbed condition(s): *social ~,* e g because of widespread unemployment or poverty: *political ~.*

un·re·strained /ˈʌnrɪˈstreɪnd/ *adj* not checked or held in.

un·re·stricted /ˈʌnrɪˈstrɪktɪd/ *adj* without restriction(s); (esp of a road) not having a speed limit for traffic.

un·ri·valled (US = **-ri·valed**) /ʌnˈrɑɪvld/ *adj* having no rival (*in* courage, etc); unequalled: *an ~ reputation.*

un·ruffled /ʌnˈrʌfld/ *adj* calm; not upset or agitated: *He remained ~ by all these criticisms.*

un·ruly /ʌnˈrulɪ/ *adj* (-ier, -iest) not easily controlled; disorderly: *an ~ child.*

un·said /ʌnˈsed/ *adj* not expressed: *Some things are better left ~.*

un·sa·voury (US = **-sa·vory**) /ʌnˈseɪvərɪ/ *adj* (esp) nasty; disgusting: *~ stories/scandals; a man with an ~ reputation.*

un·say /ˈʌnˈseɪ/ *vt* (*pt,pp* -said /-ˈsed/) [VP6A] (liter) take back (sth that has been said); retract (which is the usu word).

un·scathed /ʌnˈskeɪðd/ *adj* unharmed; unhurt.

un·scramble /ˈʌnˈskræmbl/ *vt* (of a scrambled message) restore to a form that can be understood.

un·scripted /ʌnˈskrɪptɪd/ *adj* (e g of a broadcast talk or discussion) not read from a prepared script.

un·scru·pu·lous /ʌnˈskrupjʊləs/ *adj* not guided by conscience; not held back (from doing wrong) by scruples. **~·ly** *adv*

un·seas·oned /ʌnˈsizənd/ *adj* (of wood) not matured; (of food) not flavoured with seasoning.

un·seat /ˈʌnˈsit/ *vt* [VP6A] **1** remove from office: *Mr X was ~ed at the General Election,* lost his seat in the House of Commons. **2** throw from a horse: *Several riders were ~ed at the water-jump,* e g in a steeplechase.

un·seem·ly /ʌnˈsimlɪ/ *adj* (of behaviour, etc) not suitable or proper.

un·seen /ʌnˈsin/ *adj* not seen; invisible. □ *n* **1 the ~,** the spiritual world. **2** [C] passage to be translated, without preparation, from a foreign language into one's own language: *German ~s.*

un·settle /ʌnˈsetl/ *vt* [VP6A] make troubled, anxious or uncertain: *~d weather,* uncertain, changeable weather.

un·sex /ˈʌnˈseks/ *vt* [VP6A] deprive of the attributes of one's sex. **~ed** *adj* (of e g chicks) not yet separated according to sex.

un·sight·ly /ʌnˈsɑɪtlɪ/ *adj* displeasing to the eye: *~ advertisements in the countryside.* **un·sight·li·ness** *n*

un·skilled /ʌnˈskɪld/ *adj* (of work) not needing special skill; (of workers) not having special skill or special training.

un·soph·is·ti·cated /ˈʌnsəˈfɪstɪkeɪtɪd/ *adj* naive; simple-minded; inexperienced: *There are very few ~ girls about today.*

un·sound /ʌnˈsɑʊnd/ *adj* not in good condition; unsatisfactory: *an ~ argument. The structure/building is ~.* **of ~ mind,** unbalanced in mind; mentally disordered.

un·spar·ing /ʌnˈspeərɪŋ/ *adj* liberal; holding nothing back: *be ~ in one's efforts; ~ of praise.*

un·speak·able /ʌnˈspikəbl/ *adj* that cannot be

expressed or described in words: *~ joy/ wickedness.*

un·spot·ted /ʌnˋspɒtɪd/ *adj* (of reputation) without stain; pure.

un·stop /ʌnˋstɒp/ *vt* (-pp-) [VP6A] (esp) free from obstruction; open (sth that is stopped up): *~ a drain.*

un·strung /ʌnˋstrʌŋ/ *adj* (esp) with little or no control over the nerves, mind or emotions.

un·stuck /ʌnˋstʌk/ *adj* not stuck or fastened: *The flap of the envelope has come ~.* ***come (badly) ~,*** (colloq) be unsuccessful; fail to work according to plan: *Our plan has come ~.*

un·stud·ied /ʌnˋstʌdɪd/ *adj* (of behaviour) natural; not aimed at impressing other persons.

un·sung /ʌnˋsʌŋ/ *adj* not celebrated (in poetry or song): *an ~ hero.*

un·swerv·ing /ʌnˋswɜvɪŋ/ *adj* (esp of aims, purposes) not changing; straight: *~ loyalty/devotion; pursue an ~ course.* **~·ly** *adv*

un·syl·labic /ˈʌnsɪˋlæbɪk/ *adj* of a speech sound, not sustained enough to make a syllable, e g in the word *little* the first /l/ is unsyllabic and the second is usu syllabic.

un·think·able /ʌnˋθɪŋkəbl/ *adj* such as one cannot have any real idea of or belief; not to be considered.

un·think·ing /ʌnˋθɪŋkɪŋ/ *adj* thoughtless; done, said, etc without thought of the effect: *in an ~ moment.* **~·ly** *adv*

un·thought-of /ʌnˋθɔt ov/ *adj* quite unexpected; not imagined.

un·tidy /ʌnˋtaɪdɪ/ *adj* (-ier, -iest) (of a room, desk, etc) in disorder; (of a person) slovenly; not neat.

un·til /ənˋtɪl/ *prep, conj* ⇨ till.

un·time·ly /ʌnˋtaɪmlɪ/ *adj* occurring at a wrong or unsuitable time, or too soon: *an ~ remark. He came to an ~ end,* died before he had completed his life's work.

un·tir·ing /ʌnˋtaɪərɪŋ/ *adj* **1** continuing to work without getting tired: *She seems to be ~.* **2** continuing as if never causing tiredness: *his ~ efforts.*

unto /ˋʌntu *weak form:* ˋʌntə/ *prep* (old or liter) to.

un·told /ʌnˋtəʊld/ *adj* (esp) too many or too much to be counted, measured, etc: *a man of ~ wealth.*

un·touch·able /ʌnˋtʌtʃəbl/ *n, adj* (member) of the lowest caste in India.

un·to·ward /ˈʌntəˋwɔd *US:* ʌnˋtɔrd/ *adj* (formal) unfavourable; unfortunate; inconvenient: *There were no ~ incidents.*

un·truth /ʌnˋtruθ/ *n* [U] lack of truth; [C] (*pl* ~s /-ˋtruðz/) untrue statement; lie. **~·ful** /-fl/ *adv* **~·fully** /-flɪ/ *adv*

un·tu·tored /ʌnˋtjutəd *US:* -ˋtu-/ *adj* untaught; ignorant.

un·used[1] /ʌnˋjuzd/ *adj* not made use of; not put to use; never having been used.

un·used[2] /ʌnˋjust/ *adj* ***~ to,*** not accustomed to: *The children are ~ to city life.*

un·ut·ter·able /ʌnˋʌtrəbl/ *adj* unspeakable.

un·var·nished /ʌnˋvɑnɪʃt/ *adj* (esp of accounts, descriptions) plain; straightforward: *the ~ truth; give an ~ account of what happened.*

un·veil /ʌnˋveɪl/ *vt,vi* **1** [VP6A,2A] remove a veil from; remove one's veil. **2** [VP6A] disclose; reveal; (trade use) show publicly for the first time: *Several new models were ~ed yesterday at the Motor Show.*

un·voiced /ˈʌnˋvɔɪst/ *adj* (of thoughts, etc) not expressed or uttered.

un·wieldy /ʌnˋwildɪ/ *adj* awkward to move or control because of shape, size or weight. **un·wieldi·ness** *n*

un·wind /ʌnˋwaɪnd/ *vt,vi* (*pt,pp* -wound /-ˋwaʊnd/) **1** [VP6A,2A] wind off (what has been wound up); become unwound. **2** [VP21] (colloq) relax after a period of tension, exhausting work, etc. ⇨ wind[4](6).

un·wit·ting /ʌnˋwɪtɪŋ/ *adj* unknowing; unaware; unintentional. **~·ly** *adv*: *If I hurt your feelings it was ~ly.*

un·writ·ten /ˈʌnˋrɪtn/ *adj* not written down: *the ~ songs of the countryfolk,* folksongs not to be found in writing or print. ***an ~ law,*** one based on custom or tradition, but not precisely stated anywhere.

un·zip /ʌnˋzɪp/ *vt* (-pp-) unfasten or open by pulling a zip fastener: *~ a portfolio.*

up /ʌp/ *adv part* (contrasted with *down.* ⇨ the *v* entries for combinations with *up.* Specimen entries only here.) **1** to or in an erect or vertical position (esp as suggesting readiness for activity): *He's already up,* out of bed. *I was up late* (= did not go to bed until late) *last night. She was up all night with a sick child. It's time to get up,* out of bed. *He got up* (= stood up) *to ask a question. He jumped up* (i e to his feet) *from his chair. Up with you!* Get up! Stand up! *Up with them!* Put, bring, etc them up! *Parliament is up,* no longer sitting, no longer in session. *His blood was up,* His passions were roused. ***What's up,*** (colloq) What's going on, happening? *There's something up,* Sth unusual is happening, being planned, etc. ***up and about,*** out of bed and active (esp of a person recently ill). **2** to or in a high(er) place, position, degree, etc: *Lift your head up. Pull your socks up. The tide's up,* in. *He lives three floors up. Prices are still going up,* rising. *He's well up in Greek,* has made good progress. **3** to a place of importance; (in England) to London; to Oxford or Cambridge; to a place in or to the north: *He has gone up to London for the day. When are you going up to Oxford? He lives up in the Lake District. We're going up to Edinburgh. The case was brought up before the High Court. He was up before the magistrate for being drunk while in charge of a car.* **4** (used vaguely, in a way similar to the use of *down, round, over, across*) to the place in question, or in which the speaker is, was, will be: *He came up* (*to me*) *and asked the time. She went straight up to the door.* **5** (with *vv* to indicate completeness, finality): *The stream has dried up,* has become completely dry. *We've eaten everything up. Time's up,* The allowed time is ended. *When is your leave up?* When must you return to duty? *Tear it up. Lock/Tie/Fasten/Chain/Nail it up,* Make it fast, secure, safe, etc by locking, tying, etc. **6** (with *vv* to indicate an increase in intensity, etc): *Speak/Sing up!* (i e with more force). *Her spirits went up,* rose. *Blow the fire up.* **7** (attrib uses with *nn*): *the ˋup train* (to London); *the ˋup line/platform* (used by up trains); *an ˋup stroke,* e g of the pen when writing the letter l. **8** ***up against,*** faced with (difficulties, obstacles, etc). ***be up before,*** appear in court (before a magistrate, etc). ***up and down,*** **(a)** backwards and forwards; to and fro: *walking up and down the station platform.* **(b)** so as to rise and fall: *The float bobbed up and down on the water.* Hence, **ups and downs,** (usu fig) alternations of good and bad fortune. ***on the up and up,*** (colloq) steadily improving. **up for, (a)** being tried (for an offence, etc): *up for exceeding the speed limit.* **(b)** being considered for; on offer: *The contract is up for renewal. The house is up for auction/sale.* ***well up on,*** well informed about; expert in: *He's well up on this subject.* **up to, (a)** occupied or busy with: *What's he up to? He's up to no good. What tricks has she been up to,* playing? **(b)** equal to: *I don't feel up to going to work today. This new book of Green's isn't up to his last,* is not as good. *He's not up to his work/to the job,* not good enough for the job. **(c)** as far as: *up to now/then; count from one up to twenty.* **(d)** required, looked upon as necessary, from: *It's up to us* (= It is our duty) *to give them all the help we can.* ***all up (with),*** ⇨ all²(2). **'up-and-`coming,** (of a person) making good progress, likely to succeed, in his profession, career, etc: *an up-and-coming young MP.* □ *prep* (in the senses of the *adv*): *climb up a mountain; walk up the stairs; sail up* (towards the source of) *a river; travel up country,* away from the coast; *walk up* (= along) *the road.* □ *vi, vt* (-pp-) **1** (hum or colloq use only) rouse oneself: get or jump up: *She upped and threw the teapot at him.* **2** increase: *up the price; up an offer.*

up- /ʌp-/ *pref* in an upward direction.

up·beat /ˈʌp bit/ *n* (music) unaccented beat, esp at the end of a bar (e g when the conductor's hand is raised).

up·braid /ʌp`breɪd/ *vt* [VP6A,14] **~ *sb (for doing sth/with sth),*** scold, reproach.

up·bring·ing /ˈʌpbrɪŋɪŋ/ *n* [U] training and education during childhood: *He owed his success to the good ~ his parents had given him.*

up·coun·try /ˈʌp`kʌntrɪ/ *adj, adv* (esp in a large thinly populated country) towards the interior; inland: *~ districts; travel ~.*

up·date /ˈʌp`deɪt/ *vt* [VP6A] bring up to date: *~ a dictionary/textbook.*

up·grade /ˈʌp`greɪd/ *vt* [VP6A] raise to a higher grade. □ *n* /ˈʌpgreɪd/ (esp) ***on the ~,*** improving; making progress.

up·heaval /ʌp`hivl/ *n* [C] great and sudden change: *a volcanic ~; political/social ~s.*

up·held /ʌp`held/ *pt,pp* of **uphold**.

up·hill /ˈʌp`hɪl/ *adj* sloping upward; ascending: *an ~ road;* (fig) difficult; needing effort. ***an ~ task,*** very difficult one. □ *adv* up a slope: *walk ~.*

up·hold /ʌp`həʊld/ *vt* (*pt,pp* **upheld** /-`held/) [VP6A] **1** support or approve (a person, his conduct, a practice, etc): *I cannot ~ such conduct.* **2** confirm (a decision, a verdict).

up·hol·ster /ʌp`həʊlstə(r)/ *vt* [VP6A] provide (seats, etc) with padding, springs, covering material, etc; provide (a room) with carpets, curtains, cushioned seats, etc: *~ a settee in tapestry; ~ed in/with velvet; a well-~ed lady,* (colloq) rather fat. **~er** *n* person whose trade is to ~. **~y** /-stərɪ/ *n* [U] (materials used in, business of) ~ing.

up·keep /ˈʌpkip/ *n* [U] (cost of) keeping sth in good order and repair: *£450 for rent and ~,* e g of a house. *The ~ of this large garden is more than I can afford.*

up·land /ˈʌplənd/ *n* (often *pl*) higher part(s) of a region or country (not necessarily mountainous): (attrib) *an ~ region.*

up·lift /ʌp`lɪft/ *vt* [VP6A] (fig, not liter) raise (spiritually or emotionally): *His soul was ~ed by the Bach cantatas.* □ *n* /ˈʌplɪft/ [U] socially or mentally elevating influence; moral inspiration.

up·most /ˈʌpməʊst/ *adj* = **uppermost**.

upon /əˈpon/ *prep* on (which is more usual. *Upon* is the only normal form in): *~ my word, once ~ a time.*

up·per /ˈʌpə(r)/ *adj* (contrasted with *lower*) higher in place; situated above: *the ~ lip; the ~ arm; one of the ~ rooms.* **~ case,** ⇨ case²(2). **the ~ class,** ⇨ class(3). **the ~ storey,** (fig, colloq) the brain: *wrong in the ~ storey,* mentally disordered. ***have/get the ~ hand of,*** have/get an advantage or control of. **the U~ House,** (in Parliament) the House of Lords. **the ~ ten (thousand),** *the aristocracy.* **`~-cut** *n* (boxing) a blow delivered upwards with the arm bent inside an opponent's guard. □ *n* part of a shoe or boot over the sole. ***be (down) on one's ~s,*** be at the end of one's financial resources. **`~·most** /-məʊst/ *adj* highest; predominant: *Thoughts of the holidays were ~most in their minds.* □ *adv* on, to, at, the top or surface: *It's not always wise to say whatever comes ~most,* whatever comes to the top of one's thoughts.

up·pish /ˈʌpɪʃ/ *adj* (colloq) self-assertive, conceited: *Don't get ~ with me! Don't be too ~ about it!* **~·ly** *adv* **~·ness** *n*

up·pity /ˈʌpətɪ/ *adj* (colloq) uppish.

up·right /ˈʌp-rɑɪt/ *adj* **1** erect; placed vertically (at an angle of 90° to the ground): *an ~ post; stand/hold oneself ~; set a post ~.* **an ~ piano,** with the strings vertical, not horizontal as in a grand piano. **2** honourable; straightforward in behaviour: *an ~ man/judge; be ~ in one's business dealings.* □ *n* [C] ~ support in a structure; ~ post. **~·ly** *adv* **~·ness** *n* [U].

up·ris·ing /ˈʌp`rɑɪzɪŋ/ *n* [C] revolt; rebellion.

up·roar /ˈʌp-rɔ(r)/ *n* [U] (with *indef art*) (outburst of) noise and excitement; tumult: *The meeting ended in (an) ~.* **~i·ous** /ʌp`rɔrɪəs/ *adj* very noisy, esp with loud laughter and great good humour: *We were given an ~ious welcome. They burst into ~ious laughter.* **~i·ous·ly** *adv*

up·root /ʌp`rut/ *vt* [VP6A] pull up with the roots: *The gale ~ed numerous trees. After he had lived in New York for 20 years his employer ~ed him and sent him to Chicago.*

up·set /ʌp`set/ *vt,vi* (*pt,pp* **upset**; -tt-) **1** [VP6A, 2A] tip over; overturn: *Don't ~ the boat. The boat ~. The cat has ~ its saucer of milk.* **2** [VP6A] trouble; cause (sb or sth) to be disturbed: *~ the enemy's plans; ~ one's stomach by eating too much rich food. The sight of physical suffering ~s her. She is easily ~ emotionally.* □ *n* /ˈʌpset/ [C] **1** ~ting or being ~: *have a `stomach ~. She's had a terrible ~,* e g an emotional shock. *You can imagine what an ~ we have had with the builders and decorators in the house all week.* **2** (sport) unexpected result.

up·shot /ˈʌpʃot/ *n* (*sing* with *def art*) outcome; result: *What will be the ~ of it all?*

up·side-down /ˈʌpsɑɪd `daʊn/ *adv* with the upper side underneath or at the bottom; (fig) in disorder: *The boy pretended he could read, but he was holding the book ~. The house was turned ~ by the burglars,* Everything was left in disorder.

up·stage /ˈʌp`steɪdʒ/ *adj* (colloq) uppish; uppity. □ *adv* (theatre) towards the back of the stage. □ *vt* [VP6A] divert attention from sb else to oneself; force out of the spotlight.

up·stairs /ˈʌpˋsteəz/ *adv* **1** to or on a higher floor: *go/walk* ~. **2** (attrib) belonging to, situated on, an upper floor: *an* ~ *room*.

up·stand·ing /ʌpˋstændɪŋ/ *adj* standing erect; strong and healthy: *fine* ~ *children*.

up·start /ˋʌpstɑt/ *n* (often attrib) person who has suddenly risen to wealth, power or higher social position, esp one whose behaviour causes resentment: ~ *officials in government offices*.

up·stream /ˈʌpˋstrim/ *adv* up a river; against the stream or current.

up·surge /ˋʌpsɜdʒ/ *n* surging up (of emotion): *an* ~ *of anger/indignation*.

up·take /ˋʌpteɪk/ *n* (usu) ***quick/slow on the* ~,** (colloq) quick/slow to understand (sth said or hinted at).

up·tight /ˈʌpˋtɑɪt/ *adj* (sl) extremely tense; nervous: ~ *about an interview/examination*.

up-to-date /ˈʌp tə ˋdeɪt/ *adj* (no hyphens when *pred*) of the present time; of the newest sort. **ˈup-to-the-ˋminute** *adj* very modern; latest.

up·town /ˈʌpˋtɑʊn/ *adj, adv* (US) to or in the upper (the residential or non-business, non-commercial) part (of a town): ~ *New York; go* ~.

up·turn /ˋʌptɜn/ *n* upward turn; change for the better: *an* ~ *in business/employment/production*.

up·ward /ˋʌpwəd/ *adj* moving or directed up: *the* ~ *trend of prices; an* ~ *glance*. □ *adv* (often **~s**) towards a higher place, level, etc: *Is civilization still climbing* ~*s? The boat was on the beach, bottom* ~, upside-down. ***~s of,*** more than: ~*s of 50 people*.

ura·nium /jʊˋreɪnɪəm/ *n* [U] heavy white metal (symbol **U**) with radioactive properties, a source of atomic energy.

Ura·nus /jʊˋreɪnəs/ *n* (astron) planet seventh in order from the sun. ⇨ the illus at planet.

ur·ban /ˋɜbən/ *adj* of or in a town: *the over-crowded* ~ *areas of England;* ~ *guerillas,* ⇨ guerilla. **~·ize** /-ɑɪz/ *vt* [VP6A] change from a rural to an ~ character. **~·iz·ation** /ˈɜbənɑɪˋzeɪʃn *US:* -nɪˋz-/ *n* [U].

ur·bane /ɜˋbeɪn/ *adj* polite; polished in manners; elegant. **~·ly** *adv* **ur·ban·ity** /ɜˋbænətɪ/ *n* [U] refinement; politeness; (*pl;* **-ties**) courteous manners.

ur·chin /ˋɜtʃɪn/ *n* troublesome small boy; mischievous small boy; (often **ˋstreet-~**) poor destitute child.

urge /ɜdʒ/ *vt* **1** [VP6A,15B] ***~ sb/sth on(ward)/ forward,*** push or drive on: *With whip and spur he* ~*d his horse on(ward). The foreman* ~*d his workmen on*. **2** [VP14,17] ***~ sb to sth/to do sth,*** request earnestly; try to persuade: *The shopkeeper* ~*d me to buy a hat. 'Buy it now,' he* ~*d. 'Prices will soon rise.' Agitators* ~*d the peasants to revolt*. **3** [VP14] ***~ sth (up)on sb,*** press (on sb) requests and arguments: *He* ~*d on his pupils the importance of hard work*. □ *n* (rarely *pl*) strong desire: *He has/feels an* ~ *to travel*.

ur·gent /ˋɜdʒənt/ *adj* **1** needing prompt decision or action: *An SOS is an* ~ *message. It is most* ~ *that the patient should get to hospital. The earthquake victims are in* ~ *need of medical supplies*. **2** (of a person, his voice, etc) showing that sth is ~; persistent in making a demand. **~·ly** *adv* **ur·gency** /-dʒənsɪ/ *n* [U] need for, importance of, haste or prompt action: *a matter of great urgency*.

uric /ˋjʊərɪk/ *adj* of urine.

urine /ˋjʊərɪn/ *n* [U] waste liquid which collects in the bladder and is discharged from the body. **uri·nal** /ˋjʊərɪnl/ *n* **1** (ˋ*bed urinal*) vessel into which ~ may be discharged (by sb ill in bed). **2** (*public urinal*) place for the convenience of men who need to discharge ~. **uri·nate** /ˋjʊərɪneɪt/ *vi* discharge ~. **uri·nary** /ˋjʊərɪnrɪ *US:* -nerɪ/ *adj* of ~: *urinary infection*.

urn /ɜn/ *n* **1** vase, usu with stem and base, esp as used for holding the ashes of a person whose body has been cremated. **2** large metal container in which a drink such as tea or coffee is made or kept hot, e g in cafés and canteens.

urns

us / *usu* əs; *strong form:* ʌs; *after 'let' in invitations:* s/ *pron* object form of *we*.

usage /ˋjuzɪdʒ *US:* ˋjus-/ *n* **1** [U] way of using sth: treatment: *Machines soon wear out under rough* ~. **2** [C,U] body of conventions governing the use of a language (esp those aspects not governed by grammatical rules): *a guide to English grammar and* ~. *Do you have difficulty in learning the finer points of* ~*? Such* ~*s are not characteristic of educated speakers*. **3** [C,U] agreed codes of behaviour: *Industrialization and urbanization influence social* ~*(s)*.

use¹ /jus/ *n* **1** [U] using or being used; condition of being used: *the use of electricity for lighting; learn the use of tools; a room for the use of teachers only; for use only in case of fire; bought for use, not for ornament*. **in use,** being used. **out of use,** not being, no longer, used. ***come into use,*** begin to be used: *When did the word 'transistor' come into common use?* ***go/fall out of use,*** be no longer used: *The custom has gone out of use*. ***make (good/the best) use of,*** use (well/in the best way): *You must make good use of any opportunities you have of practising English*. **2** [C,U] purpose for which sth or sb is or may be employed; work that sth or sb is able to do: *a tool with many uses; find a use for sth; put sth to a good use; have no further use for sth. I have no use for* (fig, dislike, have no patience with) *people who are always grumbling*. **3** [U] value; advantage: *Is this of any use to you? It's no use your pretending/no use for you to pretend that you didn't know the rules. There isn't much use for that sort of thing nowadays*. **4** [U] power of using: *lose the use of one's legs,* become a cripple, unable to walk. **5** [U] right to use: *give a friend the use of one's bike*. **6** [U] usage; familiarity through continued practice: *In these cases use is the best guide*. **use·ful** /ˋjusfl/ *adj* **1** helpful; producing good results: *A spade is a useful tool. Are you a useful member of society?* **2** (colloq) capable, efficient: *He's a useful member of the team*. **use·fully** /-flɪ/ *adv* **use·ful·ness** *n* **use·less** *adj* **1** of no use; worthless: *A car is useless without petrol*. **2** without result; ineffectual: *It's useless to argue with* *them.* **use·less·ly** *adv* **use·less·ness** *n*

use[2] /juz/ *vt* (*pt,pp* used /juzd/) **1** [VP6A,16A,14] employ for a purpose: *You use your legs when you walk. You use a knife to cut bread. A hammer is used for driving in nails. When persuasion failed they used force. May I use* (= quote) *your name as a reference,* e g in an application for a post. **2** [VP6A,15B] ***use sth (up),*** consume: *How much coal did we use last winter? He has ~d up all his strength.* **3** [VP15A] behave towards: *Use others as you would like them to use you. He thinks himself ill used,* considers that he is badly treated. **used** /juzd/ *adj* no longer new; second/third-, etc hand: *used cars,* cars offered for sale after they have been used and are no longer in new condition. **us·able** /ˋjuzəbl/ *adj* that can be used, that is fit to be used. **user** *n* sb or sth that uses: *There are more telephone users in the USA than in any other country.*

used /just/ *anom fin* (irregular *pt* and *pp* of use) *pt,* followed by a *to*-infinitive; neg use(d)n't /ˋjusnt/, *used not* (and, colloq, *didn't use*); indicating a constant or frequent practice in the past, or, in the construction *there ~ to be,* the existence of sth in the past: *That's where I ~ to live when I was a child. Life isn't so easy here as it ~ to be. You ~ to smoke a pipe, use(d)n't you* (or *didn't you*)? *There ~ to be some trees in this field, use(d)n't there/didn't there?*

used to /ˋjust tə *before vowel sounds:* tu/ *adj* accustomed to: *He's quite ~ hard work/working hard. I'm not ~ being spoken to in that rude way. You will soon be/get ~ it.*

usher /ˋʌʃə(r)/ *n* **1** person who shows people to their seats in theatres, cinemas, etc. **2** doorkeeper in a law court, etc. **2** (old use, or hum) assistant schoolmaster. □ *vt* **1** [VP15B,14] lead, conduct: *The girl ~ed me to my seat* (in a cinema). **2** [VP15B] ***~ sth in,*** herald, announce: *The change of government ~ed in a period of prosperity.* **~·ette** /ˌʌʃəˋret/ *n* girl or woman ~(1).

usual /ˋjuʒʊəl/ *adj* such as commonly happens; customary: *Tea is the ~ drink of English people. He arrived later than ~. As is ~ with many picnickers, they left a lot of litter behind them. When the accident happened, the ~ crowd quickly gathered.* **~ly** /ˋjuʒḷɪ/ *adv* in the ordinary way: *What do you ~ly do on Sundays?*

usurer /ˋjuʒṛə(r)/ *n* person whose business is usury.

usurp /juˋzɜp/ *vt* [VP6A] wrongfully take (sb's power, authority, position): *~ the throne.* **~er** *n* person who does this. **usur·pa·tion** /ˌjuzɜˋpeɪʃn/ *n* [C,U] (instance of) ~ing.

usury /ˋjuʒṛɪ/ *n* [U] (practice of) lending money, esp at a rate of interest considered to be too high; such high interest. **usuri·ous** /juˋzjʊərɪəs *US:* -ˋʒʊ-/ *adj* of ~: *a usurious transaction; a usurious rate of interest.*

uten·sil /juˋtensl/ *n* instrument, tool, etc esp for use in the house: ˋ*household ~s,* e g pots, pans, brushes; ˋ*writing ~s,* e g paper, pens, ink.

uterus /ˋjutərəs/ *n* (anat) womb. ⇨ the illus at reproduce. **uter·ine** /ˋjutərɪn/ *adj* of the ~.

utili·tarian /juˌtɪlɪˋteərɪən/ *adj* **1** characterized by usefulness rather than by beauty, truth, goodness. **2** of the U~s and their ideas. □ *n* **U~,** supporter of ~ism. **~·ism** /-ɪzm/ *n* [U] political and moral theory that the best rule of life is to aim at 'the greatest happiness of the greatest number,' actions being considered right or wrong according as they help or hinder the achievement of this aim.

util·ity /juˋtɪlətɪ/ *n* (*pl* -ties) **1** [U] quality of being useful: (attrib) ˋ*~ van/truck,* one that can be used for various purposes. **2** [C] **(public) ~,** public service such as the supply of water, electricity, gas, or a bus or railway service.

util·ize /ˋjutɪlaɪz *US:* -tḷaɪz/ *vt* [VP6A] make use of; find a use for. **util·iz·able** /-əbl/ *adj* that can be ~d or put to a useful purpose. **util·iz·ation** /ˌjutɪlaɪˋzeɪʃn *US:* -tḷɪˋz-/ *n* [U] utilizing or being ~d.

ut·most /ˋʌtməʊst/ *adj* most extreme; greatest: *in the ~ danger; of the ~ importance; with the ~ care.* □ *n* (*sing* only) the most that is possible: *do one's ~; exert/enjoy oneself to the ~. That is the ~ I can do.*

Uto·pia /juˋtəʊpɪə/ *n* [C] imaginary perfect social and political system. **Uto·pian** /-pɪən/ *adj* (also with small *u*) attractive and desirable but impracticable: *a ~n scheme for giving all old people a pension of £100 a week.*

ut·ter[1] /ˋʌtə(r)/ *adj* complete; total: *~ darkness; an ~ scoundrel. She's an ~ stranger to me.* **~·ly** *adv* **1** completely. **2** to the depths of one's being: *She ~ly detests him.*

ut·ter[2] /ˋʌtə(r)/ *vt* [VP6A] **1** make (a sound or sounds) with the mouth: *~ a sigh/a cry of pain.* **2** say: *the last words he ~ed.* **3** put (false money, etc) into circulation. **~·ance** /ˋʌtṛəns/ *n* **1** (*sing* only) way of speaking: *a clear/defective/very rapid ~ance.* **2** [C] sth said; spoken word or words. **3** [U] *give ~ance to* (*one's feelings, etc*), express in words.

ut·ter·most /ˋʌtəməʊst/ *adj, n* = utmost: *the ~ ends of the earth.*

uvula /ˋjuvjʊlə/ *n* small piece of fleshy matter hanging from the back of the roof of the mouth. ⇨ the illus at mouth. **uvu·lar** /-lə(r)/ *adj* of the ~.

ux·ori·ous /ʌkˋsɔrɪəs/ *adj* excessively fond of one's wife. **~·ly** *adv* **~·ness** *n*

Vv

V, v /vi/ *n* (*pl* V's, v's) **1** the 22nd letter of the English alphabet; the Roman numeral 5. ⇨ App 4. **2** V-shaped thing; *the V sign,* sign made by the hand with the palm outwards and the first and second fingers spread to form a V (for *victory*). **V 1, 2** /ˌvi ˋwʌn, ˋtu/, flying bomb. ⇨ doodlebug.

vac /væk/ *n* (colloq, abbr of) vacation (2).

va·cancy /ˋveɪkənsɪ/ *n* (*pl* -cies) **1** [U] condition of being empty or unoccupied. **2** [C] unoccupied space; blank: *look over the edge of a cliff into ~.* **3** [U] lack of ideas or intelligence; lack of concentration. **4** [C] position in business, etc for which sb is needed: *good vacancies for typists and clerks.*

va·cant /ˋveɪkənt/ *adj* **1** empty: *gaze into ~ space.* **2** not occupied by anyone: *a ~ room,* e g in a hotel; *apply for a ~ position,* e g in an office. ~ **possession,** phrase used in advertisements of houses, etc declaring that the buyer can enter into immediate occupation. **3** (of time) not filled with any activity; leisured. **4** (of the mind) unoccupied with thought; (of the eyes) showing no signs of thought or interest: *with ~ looks; a ~ stare/expression.* **~·ly** *adv*

va·cate /veɪˋkeɪt *US:* ˋveɪkeɪt/ *vt* [VP6A] **1** give up living in: *~ a house/rented rooms.* **2** leave unoccupied: *~ one's seat.* **3** (formal) give up possession or use of.

va·ca·tion /vəˋkeɪʃn *US:* veɪ-/ *n* **1** (formal) vacating: *His ~ of a good position in the Civil Service was unwise.* **2** [C] weeks during which universities and law courts stop work: *the long ~; the summer ~; the Christmas ~.* **3** [C] (esp US) any time or period of rest and freedom from work. ***on ~,*** on holiday. □ *vi* [VP3A] **~ *at/in,*** (US) spend a holiday: *~ing in Florida.* **~·ist** /-ʃn̩-ɪst/ *n* (US) person on ~(3).

vac·ci·nate /ˋvæksɪneɪt *US:* -sn̩eɪt/ *vt* [VP6A,14] **~ *sb (against sth),*** protect (sb) (against smallpox, etc) by injecting vaccine. **vac·ci·na·tion** /ˌvæksɪˋneɪʃn/ *n* [C,U] (instance of) vaccinating or being ~d.

vac·cine /ˋvæksin *US:* vækˋsin/ *n* [C,U] substance from the blood of a cow, used to protect persons from smallpox by causing them to have a slight, but not dangerous, form of the disease.

vac·il·late /ˋvæsɪleɪt/ *vi* [VP2A,3A] **~ *(between),*** waver; hesitate; be uncertain (in opinion, etc): *~ between hope and fear.* **vac·il·la·tion** /ˌvæsɪˋleɪʃn/ *n* [C,U] (instance of) vacillating.

vacu·ous /ˋvækjʊəs/ *adj* (formal) showing or suggesting absence of thought or intelligence: *a ~ expression/stare/remark/laugh.* **~·ly** *adv* **vacu·ity** /vəˋkjuətɪ/ *n* (*pl* **-ties**) [U] state of being ~; (*pl*) ~ remarks, acts, etc.

vac·uum /ˋvækjʊəm/ *n* (*pl* **-uums** or, in science, **-uua** /-jʊə/) space completely empty of substance or gas(es); space in a container from which the air has been pumped out. **ˋ~ cleaner,** apparatus which takes up dust, dirt, etc by suction. **ˋ~ flask/bottle,** one having a ~ between its inner and outer walls, keeping the contents at an unchanging temperature. ⇨ thermos. **ˋ~ pump,** **(a)** pump to create a partial ~ in a vessel. **(b)** pump in which a partial ~ is used to raise water. **ˋ~ tube/valve,** sealed glass tube with an almost perfect ~ in it, for observing the passage of an electric charge.

vade-mecum /ˌveɪdɪ ˋmikəm/ *n* [C] small handbook which can be carried about and used for reference.

vaga·bond /ˋvægəbond/ *adj* having no fixed living-place; habitually wandering: *live a ~ life; ~ gipsies.* □ *n* ~ person; tramp.

va·gary /ˋveɪgərɪ/ *n* [C] (*pl* **-ries**) strange, unusual act or idea, esp one for which there seems to be no good reason: *the vagaries of fashion/of the human reason.*

va·gina /vəˋdʒɑɪnə/ *n* (anat) passage (in a female mammal) from the external genital organs to the womb (colloq *ˋbirth canal*). ⇨ the illus at reproduce. **vag·inal** /vəˋdʒɑɪnl/ *adj*

va·grant /ˋveɪgrənt/ *adj* leading a wandering life: *~ tribes/musicians;* wandering: *lead a ~ life; ~ thoughts.* □ *n* ~ person; vagabond or tramp. **va·grancy** /-rənsɪ/ *n* [U] being a ~.

vague /veɪg/ *adj* (**-r, -st**) **1** not clear or distinct: *~ outlines; ~ demands. I haven't the ~st idea what they want.* **2** (of persons, their looks, behaviour) uncertain, suggesting uncertainty (about needs, intentions, etc). **~·ly** *adv* **~·ness** *n*

vain /veɪn/ *adj* (**-er, -est**) **1** without use, value, meaning or result: *a ~ attempt; ~ hopes/promises.* **2 *in ~,*** **(a)** without the desired result: *try in ~ to do sth. All our work was in ~.* **(b)** without due reverence, honour or respect: *take the name of God in ~,* usu the word 'God' irreverently; *take a person's name in ~,* use it lightly, disrespectfully. **3** having too high an opinion of one's looks, abilities, etc; conceited: *He's as ~ as a peacock. She's ~ of her beauty.* **ˌ~·ˋglory** *n* extreme vanity or pride in oneself. **ˌ~·ˋglorious** *adj* full of ~glory; conceited and boastful. **~·ly** *adv* **1** in ~. **2** in a conceited manner.

val·ance, val·ence /ˋvæləns/ *n* [C] short curtain, frill, round the frame or canopy of a bedstead.

vale /veɪl/ *n* (liter except in place-names) valley.

val·edic·tion /ˌvælɪˋdɪkʃn/ *n* [C] (words used in) saying farewell.

val·edic·tory /ˌvælɪˋdɪktərɪ/ *adj* relating to, in the nature of, a farewell: *a ~ speech* (esp US, at the graduating exercises of a college).

val·ence[1] /ˋvæləns/ *n* = valance.

va·lence[2], **va·lency** /ˋveɪləns, -lənsɪ/ *nn* (chem) capacity of an atom or atoms to combine with another or others.

val·en·tine /ˋvæləntɑɪn/ *n* (letter, card, etc, usu anonymous, sent on St V~'s Day, 14 Feb, to a) sweetheart.

val·erian /vəˋlɪərɪən/ *n* [U] kinds of small perennial plant with strong-smelling pink or white flowers; root of this used medically.

valet /ˋvælɪt/ *n* manservant who looks after his master's clothes; employee in a hotel who dry-cleans or presses clothes. □ *vt* [VP6A] act as ~ to: *The hotel has a good ~ing service.*

val·etu·di·nar·ian /ˌvælɪˌtjudɪˋneərɪən *US:* -ˌtudn̩ˋeər-/ *adj* of poor health; unduly troubled about, almost wholly occupied with, the state of one's health. □ *n* ~ person.

val·iant /ˋvælɪənt/ *adj* brave. **~·ly** *adv*

valid /ˋvælɪd/ *adj* **1** (legal) effective because made or done with the correct formalities: *a ~ claim/marriage.* **2** (of contracts, etc) having force in law: *~ for three months; a ticket ~ for one single journey between London and Dover.* **3** (of arguments, reasons, etc) well based; sound: *raise ~ objections to a scheme.* **~·ly** *adv* **~·ity** /vəˋlɪdətɪ/ *n* [U] state of being ~. **vali·date** /ˋvælɪdeɪt/ *vt* [VP6A] make ~: *~ate a claim.*

va·lise /vəˋliz *US:* vəˋlis/ *n* small leather bag for clothes, etc during a journey; soldier's kitbag.

val·ley /ˋvælɪ/ *n* (*pl* **-leys**) stretch of land between hills or mountains, often with a river flowing through it. ⇨ the illus at mountain.

val·our (US = **valor**) /ˋvælə(r)/ *n* [U] bravery, esp in war. **val·or·ous** /ˋvælərəs/ *adj* brave.

valse /væls/ *n* (F) waltz.

valu·able /ˋvæljʊbl/ *adj* of great value, worth or use: *a ~ discovery.* □ *n* (usu *pl*) sth of much value, e g articles of gold, jewels.

valu·ation /ˌvæljʊˋeɪʃn/ *n* [U] process of deciding the value of sth or sb; [C] the value that is decided upon: *The surveyors arrived at widely different ~s. It is unwise to accept a person at his own ~,* the opinion which he has of himself.

value /ˈvælju/ *n* **1** [U] quality of being useful or desirable: *the ~ of walking as an exercise.* **2** [U] worth of sth when compared with sth else: *This book will be of great/little/some/no ~ to him in his studies.* **3** [C,U] worth of sth in terms of money or other goods for which it can be exchanged: *Is the ~ of the American dollar likely to decline? Does this volume give you good ~ for your money? The property is going down in ~ all the time. Market ~s rose sharply last week.* ˈ**~-ˌadded tax,** (abbr **VAT**) tax on the rise in ~ of a product at each stage of manufacture and marketing. ⇨ *purchase tax* at purchase¹(1). **4** [U] what sth is considered to be worth (contrasted with the price obtainable): *I've been offered £50 for my old car but its ~ is much higher.* **5** (various) **(a)** (in music) full time indicated by a note: *Give the note its full ~.* **(b)** (in art) relation of light and shade. **(c)** (in language) meaning; effect: *use a word with all its poetic ~.* **(d)** (*pl*) standards: *moral/ethical ~s.* □ *vt* [VP6A,15A,16B] **1** estimate the money ~ of: *He ~d the house for me at £9 500.* **2** regard highly; have a high opinion of: *~ sb's advice. Do you ~ her as a secretary?* **~·less** *adj* without ~; worthless. **valuer** *n* person whose profession is to estimate the money ~ of property, land, etc.

valve /vælv/ *n* **1** (sorts of) mechanical device for controlling the flow of air, liquid, gas or electrons in one direction only: *the inlet/outlet ~s of a petrol or steam engine; the ~ of a bicycle tyre.* ⇨ the illus at bicycle. **2** structure in the heart or in a blood-vessel allowing the blood to flow in one direction only. **3** (ˈ**radio**) **~,** (US = *tube*) vacuum tube used in a radio, allowing the flow of electrons from cathode to anode: (attrib) *a six-~ set,* radio receiving set with six ~s. **4** device in musical wind instruments, e g a cornet, for changing the pitch by changing the length of the column of air. **val·vu·lar** /ˈvælvjʊlə(r)/ *adj* of the ~s of the heart or blood-vessels: *valvular disease of the heart.*

va·moose, va·mose /væˈmus/ *vi* (US sl) go away quickly.

vamp¹ /væmp/ *n* upper front part of a boot or shoe. □ *vt, vi* **1** [VP6A,15B] repair (a boot or shoe) by putting a new ~ on. **~ *sth up,*** (fig) make sth from odds and ends: *~ up some lectures out of old notes.* **2** [VP6A,2A] make up (a tune) for a song; improvise a musical accompaniment to a song or dance.

vamp² /væmp/ *n* (abbr of *vampire*) seductive woman who uses her attractions to exploit men. □ *vt* [VP6A] (of a ~) exploit or allure (a man).

vam·pire /ˈvæmpɑɪə(r)/ *n* **1** reanimated corpse that leaves its grave at night and sucks the blood of sleeping persons; ruthless ill-disposed person who preys on others. **2** ˈ**~ (bat),** sorts of blood-sucking bat. ⇨ the illus at small.

van¹ /væn/ *n* **1** covered or roofed motor-vehicle for carrying and delivering goods: *the* ˈ*baker's van; a* ˈ*furniture van.* **2** (GB) roofed railway carriage for goods: *the* ˈ*luggage van.* **3** caravan, e g as used by gipsies.

van² /væn/ *n* **1** front or leading part of an army or fleet in battle. ˈ**van·guard** *n* advance party of an army, etc as a guard against surprise attack. **2** those persons who lead a procession or (fig) a movement: *in the van of scientific progress.*

va·na·dium /vəˈneɪdɪəm/ *n* [U] hard grey metallic element (symbol **V**) used in some steel alloys.

Van·dal /ˈvændl/ *n* one of a Germanic tribe that overran Gaul, Spain and N Africa in the 4th and 5th cc and sacked Rome in 455 AD. ⇨ Goth.

van·dal /ˈvændl/ *n* person who wilfully destroys works of art or public and private property, spoils the beauties of nature, etc. **~·ism** /-dḷ-ɪzm/ *n* [U] behaviour characteristic of ~s.

vane /veɪn/ *n* **1** arrow or pointer on the top of a building, turned by the wind so as to show its direction. **2** blade of a propeller, sail of a windmill, or other flat surface acted on by wind or water.

van·guard /ˈvængɑd/ *n* ⇨ van²(1).

va·nilla /vəˈnɪlə/ *n* **1** [C] (pods or beans of) plant with sweet-smelling flowers. **2** [U] flavouring substance from ~ beans or synthetic product used for it: *~ custard; two ~ ices.*

van·ish /ˈvænɪʃ/ *vi* [VP2A] suddenly disappear; fade away gradually; go out of existence: *Your prospects of success have ~ed. The thief ran into the crowd and ~ed from sight.* ˈ**~·ing cream,** cosmetic cream quickly absorbed into the skin. ˈ**~·ing point,** (in perspective) point at which all parallel lines in the same plane appear to meet.

van·ity /ˈvænətɪ/ *n* (*pl* **-ties**) **1** [U] conceit; having too high an opinion of one's looks, abilities, etc: *do sth out of ~; tickle sb's ~,* do or say sth that pleases his conceit; *injured ~,* resentment caused by some slight or humiliation. ˈ**~ bag/case,** bag or case carried by the owner for a small mirror, cosmetics, etc. **2** [U] worthlessness; quality of being unsatisfying, without true value: *the ~ of pleasure;* [C] vain, worthless thing or act: *the vanities of life.*

van·quish /ˈvæŋkwɪʃ/ *vt* [VP6A] defeat, subdue, overcome.

van·tage /ˈvɑntɪdʒ *US:* ˈvæn-/ *n* **1** advantage: ˈ*~-ground, point of ~.* ⇨ coign. **2** (in tennis) first point scored after deuce.

vapid /ˈvæpɪd/ *adj* tasteless; uninteresting: *~ conversation; the ~ outpourings/speeches of the politicians.* **~·ly** *adv* **~·ness** *n* **va·pid·ity** /vəˈpɪdətɪ/ *n* [U] state of being ~; (*pl;* **-ties**) ~ remarks.

va·por·ize /ˈveɪpərɑɪz/ *vt, vi* [VP6A,2A] convert into, become, vapour. **va·por·iz·ation** /ˌveɪpərɑɪˈzeɪʃn *US:* -rɪˈz-/ *n*

va·por·ous /ˈveɪpərəs/ *adj* **1** full of, like, vapour. **2** (old use) full of idle fancies; unsubstantial.

va·pour (US = **va·por**) /ˈveɪpə(r)/ *n* **1** [U] steam; mist; gaseous form to which certain substances may be reduced by heat: ˈ*water ~.* ˈ**~-bath** *n* (enclosed space or apparatus for a) bath in ~ or steam. ˈ**~ trails,** ⇨ trail(1). **2** [C] unsubstantial thing: sth imagined: *the ~s of a disordered mind.* **3** (*pl* with *def art;* hum, old use) depression of mind; deep melancholy: *suffering from the ~s.*

vari·able /ˈveərɪəbl/ *adj* varying; changeable: *~ winds; ~ standards; ~ costs,* (accounting) costs that go up or down according to the quantity of goods produced. *His mood/temper is ~.* □ *n* [C] ~ thing or quantity; factor which may vary, e g in an experiment. **vari·ably** /-əblɪ/ *adv* **~·ness** *n* **vari·abil·ity** /ˌveərɪəˈbɪlətɪ/ *n* [U] quality of being ~; tendency to vary.

vari·ance /ˈveərɪəns/ *n* [U] ***at* ~,** in disagreement; having a difference of opinion: *The two sisters have been at ~ for years. We are at ~ among ourselves/at ~ with the others.*

vari·ant /ˈveərɪənt/ *adj* different or alternative: ~

spellings of a word (e g 'tire' and 'tyre'). □ *n* ~ form (e g of spelling).

vari·ation /ˈveərɪˋeɪʃn/ *n* **1** [C,U] (degree of) varying or being variant: *~(s) of pressure/ temperature; ~s in public opinion.* **2** [C] (music) simple melody repeated in a different (and usu more complicated) form: *~s on a theme by Mozart.* **3** [U] (biol) change in bodily structure or form caused by new conditions, environment, etc; [C] instance of such change.

vari·col·oured (US = **-col·ored**) /ˋveərɪkʌləd/ *adj* of various colours.

vari·cose /ˋværɪkəʊs/ *adj* (esp in) ˋ~ **vein,** vein that has become permanently swollen or enlarged.

var·ied /ˋveərɪd/ *adj* **1** of different sorts; diverse: *~ opinions; the ~ scenes of life.* **2** full of changes or variety: *a ~ career.*

varie·gated /ˋveərɪgeɪtɪd/ *adj* marked irregularly with differently coloured patches: *The leaves of geraniums/The flowers of pansies, are often ~.* **varie·ga·tion** /ˈveərɪˋgeɪʃn/ *n*

var·iety /vəˋraɪətɪ/ *n* (*pl* **-ties**) **1** [U] quality of not being the same, or not being the same at all times: *a life full of ~. We demanded more ~ in our food.* **2** (*sing* only) number or range of different things: *for a ~ of reasons; a large ~ of patterns to choose from.* **3** (biol) subdivision of a species. **4** [C] kind or sort which differs from others of the larger group of which it is a part: *rare varieties of early postage stamps. There are now several varieties of spaniel.* **5** [U] kind of entertainment consisting of singing, dancing, acrobatic feats, short plays, etc as given in music-halls (GB), some night-clubs and hotels, and for broadcasting: *a ˋ~ entertainment; a ˋ~ theatre; ˋ~ artists.* (US = *vaudeville*).

vari·form /ˋveərɪfɔm *US:* ˋvær-/ *adj* of various forms.

vari·orum /ˋveərɪɔrəm/ *adj* (only in) ˋ~ **edition,** edition, e g of a Shakespeare play, with the notes of various commentators.

vari·ous /ˋveərɪəs/ *adj* (usu attrib) different; of a number of different sorts: *for ~ reasons; at ~ times; a criminal who is known to the police under ~ names.* **~·ly** *adv*

var·let /ˋvɑlət/ *n* (archaic) rascal.

var·mint /ˋvɑmɪnt/ *n* (colloq, form of *vermin,* old use, or dial) mischievous person or animal: *You little ~!* (e g said playfully to a mischievous child).

var·nish /ˋvɑnɪʃ/ *n* [C,U] (particular kind of) (liquid used to give a) hard, shiny, transparent coating on the surface of sth, esp woodwork or metalwork; (fig) false or deceiving appearance: *scratch the ~ on a table; a ~ of good manners;* ˋ*nail-~,* for fingernails. □ *vt* [VP6A] put a coating of ~ on: *~ a piece of furniture/an oil-painting. Some women ~ their toe-nails.*

vars·ity /ˋvɑsətɪ/ *n* (*pl* **-ties**) (GB colloq) university.

vary /ˋveərɪ/ *vi,vt* (*pt,pp* **-ried**) [VP2A,6A] be, become, cause to become, different: *~ing prices; prices that ~ with the season. They ~ in weight from 3 lb to 5 lb. You should ~ your diet.*

vas·cu·lar /ˋvæskjʊlə(r)/ *adj* of, made up of, containing, vessels or ducts through which blood, lymph or sap flows: *~ tissue.*

vase /vɑz *US:* veɪs/ *n* [C] vessel of glass, pottery, etc for holding cut flowers, or as an ornament.

vases

va·sec·tomy /vəˋsektəmɪ/ *n* (*pl* **-mies**) simple surgical operation to make a man sterile.

vas·eline /ˋvæsļin/ *n* [U] (P) yellowish substance, petroleum jelly, almost without taste or smell, used as an ointment or lubricant.

vas·sal /ˋvæsl/ *n* (in feudal times) person who held land in return for which he vowed to give military service to the owner of the land; feudal tenant; (fig) humble dependant: (attrib) *a ~ state,* one subject to another. ˋ**~·age** /-sļ-ɪdz/ *n* [U] state of being a ~; servitude.

vast /vɑst *US:* væst/ *adj* immense; extensive: *~ sums of money; a ~ expanse of desert.* **~·ly** *adv* **~·ness** *n*

vat /væt/ *n* tank or great vessel for holding liquids, esp in distilling, brewing, dyeing and tanning.

Vati·can /ˋvætɪkən/ *n* **the ~,** the residence in Rome of the Pope; centre of Papal government.

vaude·ville /ˋvɔdəvɪl/ *n* [U] ⇨ variety(4).

vault[1] /vɔlt/ *n* **1** arched roof; series of arches forming a roof. ⇨ the illus at crypt. **2** underground room or cellar (with or without an arched roof) as a place of storage (ˋ*wine-~s*), or for burials (e g under a church, or in a cemetery), or for safe-keeping of valuables: *keep one's jewels in the ~ at the bank.* **3** ~-like covering: (poet) *the ~ of heaven,* the sky. **~ed** *adj* built with, having, a ~ or ~s; in the form of a ~: *a ~ed roof/ chamber.*

vault[2] /vɔlt/ *vi,vt* [VP2A,B,C,6A] jump in a single movement, with the hand(s) resting on sth, or with the help of a pole: *~ (over) a fence. The jockey ~ed into the saddle.* ˋ**~·ing-horse** *n* apparatus for practice in ~ing. □ *n* jump made in this way. **~er** *n* person who ~s.

vaunt /vɔnt/ *vi,vt, n* (liter) boast. **~er** *n* **~·ing·ly** *adv*

veal /vil/ *n* [U] flesh of a calf as food.

veer /vɪə(r)/ *vi* [VP2A,C] (esp of the wind, fig of opinion, talk) change direction: *The wind ~ed round to the north.*

veg·etable /ˋvedʒtəbl/ *adj* of, from, relating to, plants or plant life: *the ~ kingdom; ~ oils.* □ *n* [C] plant, esp of the sort used for food, e g potatoes, cabbages, ⇨ the illus on p 970.

veg·etar·ian /ˈvedʒɪˋteərɪən/ *n* person who, for humane or religious reasons or for his health's sake, eats no meat: (attrib) *a ~ diet; ~ principles.*

veg·etate /ˋvedʒɪteɪt/ *vi* [VP2A] live as plants do, without mental effort or intellectual interests; lead a dull life with little activity or interest.

veg·eta·tion /ˈvedʒɪˋteɪʃn/ *n* [U] plants generally and collectively: *the luxuriant ~ of the tropical forests; a desert landscape with no sign of ~ anywhere.*

ve·he·ment /ˋviəmənt/ *adj* **1** (of feelings) strong, eager; (of persons, their speech, behaviour, etc) filled with, showing, strong or eager feeling: *a*

man of ~ character; ~ desires/passions. **2** violent: *a ~ wind.* **~·ly** *adv* **ve·he·mence** /-məns/ *n*

ve·hicle /ˋviɪkl/ *n* [C] **1** any conveyance (usu wheeled, e g a cart, lorry, motor-car, but also a sledge) for goods or passengers on land. Cf *craft* for water, space. **2** means by which thought, feeling, etc can be conveyed: *Art may be used as a ~ for/of propaganda.* **ve·hicu·lar** /viˋhɪkjʊlə(r)/ *adj* related to, consisting of, conveyed by, ~s: *The road is closed to vehicular traffic.* **a vehicular language,** one used as a ~ for communication between people with different languages, e g English in Nigeria.

veil /veɪl/ *n* [C] **1** covering of fine net or other material to protect or hide a woman's face, or as part of a headdress: *She raised/dropped/lowered her ~.* ***take the ~,*** become a nun. **2** (fig) sth that hides or disguises: *a ~ of mist; commit murder under the ~ of patriotism,* do so under the pretence of patriotism. ***draw a ~ over sth,*** be discreet or secretive about: *Let us draw a ~ over what followed.* □ *vt* [VP6A] put a ~ over; (fig) conceal: *Not all Muslim women are ~ed. He could not ~ his distrust.* **~·ing** *n* [U] light material used for making ~s; such material used as a ~.

vein /veɪn/ *n* **1** blood-vessel along which blood flows from all parts of the body to the heart. ⇨ the illus at **respiratory**. ⇨ **artery(1)**. **2** one of the ~-like lines in some leaves or in the wings of some insects; a coloured line or streak in some kinds of stone, e g marble; (fig): *There is a ~ of melancholy in his character.* **3** crack or fissure in rock, filled with mineral or ore; lode or seam: *a ~ of gold.* **4** mood; train of thought: *in a ˋmerry/ˈmelanˋcholic/iˋmaginative ~. He writes humorous songs when he is in the (right) ~.* **~ed** /veɪnd/ *adj* having, marked with, ~s.

veldt, veld /veldt/ *n* [C,U] (stretch of) grassland of the S African plateau.

vel·lum /ˋveləm/ *n* [U] parchment.

vel·oci·pede /vəˋlosɪpid/ *n* early kind of bicycle with pedals on the front wheel; (US) child's tricycle.

vel·oc·ity /vəˋlosətɪ/ *n* [U] **1** speed; quickness. **2** rate of motion: *at the ~ of sound; ˋmuzzle ~,* the speed of a bullet as it leaves the muzzle of a gun.

ve·lours, ve·lour /vəˋlʊə(r)/ *n* [U] fabric like velvet (of silk or silk and cotton).

vel·vet /ˋvelvɪt/ *n* [U] cloth wholly or partly made of silk with a thick soft nap (⇨ **nap**[2]) on one side: (attrib) *a ~ frock; a ~ tread,* (fig) soft and quiet. ***an iron hand in a ~ glove,*** ruthlessness concealed by good manners, soft speech, etc. **~·een** /ˈvelvɪˋtin/ *n* [U] cotton imitation of ~. **vel·vety** *adj* smooth and soft like ~.

ve·nal /ˋvinl/ *adj* **1** (of persons) ready to do sth

dishonest (e g using influence or position) for money: ~ *judges/politicians.* **2** (of conduct) influenced by, done for, (possible) payment: ~ *practices.* **~ly** /-nlɪ/ *adv* **~·ity** /viˈnælətɪ/ *n* quality of being ~.

vend /vend/ *vt* [VP6A] (chiefly legal) sell; offer for sale (esp small wares). **ˈ~·ing machine,** coin-operated slot machine for the sale of small articles, e g cigarettes and food. **~ee** /venˈdi/ *n* person to whom sth is sold. **~er, ~or** /-də(r)/ *nn* seller: *ˈnewsvendor,* seller of newspapers.

ven·detta /venˈdetə/ *n* hereditary feud between families in which members of each family commit murders in revenge for previous murders.

ve·neer /vɪˈnɪə(r)/ *n* **1** [C,U] (thin layer of) fine quality wood glued to the surface of cheaper wood (for furniture, etc). **2** (fig) surface appearance (of politeness, etc) covering the true nature: *a ~ of Western civilization.* □ *vt* [VP6A] put a ~ on: *~ a deal desk with walnut.*

ven·er·able /ˈvenr̩əbl/ *adj* **1** deserving respect because of age, character, associations, etc: *a ~ scholar; the ~ ruins of the abbey.* **2** (Church of England) title of an archdeacon; (Church of Rome) title of a person in process of being canonized.

ven·er·ate /ˈvenəreɪt/ *vt* [VP6A] regard with deep respect: *They ~ the old man's memory.* **ven·er·ation** /ˈvenəˈreɪʃn/ *n*

ve·nereal /vɪˈnɪərɪəl/ *adj* of, communicated by, sexual intercourse: *~ diseases.*

Ve·ne·tian /vɪˈniʃn/ *adj* of Venice. **~ blind,** window screen made of many horizontal strips (slats of wood or plastic material) that can be adjusted to let in light and air as desired.

ven·geance /ˈvendʒəns/ *n* [U] **1** revenge; the return of injury for injury: *seek ~ upon sb (for an injury); take ~ on an enemy.* **2** ***with a ~,*** (colloq) thoroughly; to a greater degree than is normal, expected or desired: *The rain came down with a ~.*

venge·ful /ˈvendʒfl/ *adj* showing a desire for revenge; vindictive.

ve·nial /ˈvinɪəl/ *adj* (of a sin, error, fault) excusable; not serious.

ven·ison /ˈvenɪsn/ *n* [U] deer meat.

venom /ˈvenəm/ *n* [U] poisonous fluid of certain snakes; (fig) hate; spite. **~ed** /ˈvenəmd/ *adj* (fig) full of malice or hate: *~ed remarks.* **~·ous** /ˈvenəməs/ *adj* deadly; spiteful: *~ous snakes/criticism.* **~·ous·ly** *adv*

ve·nous /ˈvinəs/ *adj* **1** of the veins: *~ blood,* (contrasted with arterial blood). **2** (bot) having veins: *a ~ leaf.*

vent /vent/ *n* **1** hole serving as an inlet or outlet for air, gas, liquid, etc, e g a hole in the top of a barrel, for air to enter as liquid is drawn out. **ˈ~-hole** *n* hole for the escape of air, smoke, etc. **2** (trade use) slit in the back of a coat or jacket. **3** means of escape: *The floods found a ~ through the dykes.* **4** (*sing* only) outlet for one's feelings. ***give ~ to,*** (fig) give free expression to: *He gave ~ to his feelings in an impassioned speech.* □ *vt* [VP6A,14] ***~ sth on sb/sth,*** find or provide an outlet for: *He ~ed his ill-temper upon his long-suffering wife.*

ven·ti·late /ˈventɪleɪt *US:* -tl̩eɪt/ *vt* [VP6A] **1** cause (air) to move in and out freely: *~ a room/the galleries of a coalmine.* **2** (fig) make (a question, a grievance) widely known and cause it to be discussed. **ven·ti·la·tor** /ˈventɪleɪtə(r) *US:* -tl-/ *n* device for ventilating. **ven·ti·la·tion** /ˈventɪˈleɪʃn *US:* -tl̩ˈeɪʃn/ *n* [U] ventilating or being ~d: *the ventilation shaft of a coalmine.*

ven·tricle /ˈventrɪkl/ *n* cavity in the body; hollow part of an organ, esp of the heart. ⇨ the illus at respiratory.

ven·tril·oquism /venˈtrɪləkwɪzm/ *n* [U] art of producing voice-sounds so that they seem to come from a person or place at a distance from the speaker. **ven·tril·oquist** /-kwɪst/ *n* person skilled in ~.

ven·ture /ˈventʃə(r)/ *n* [C,U] undertaking in which there is risk: *(do sth)* ***at a ~,*** without definite aim or deliberation; at random. □ *vt,vi* **1** [VP6A,15A,16A,3A] take the risk of, expose to, danger or loss: *~ one's life to save sb from drowning; ~ too near the edge of a cliff; ~ on a perilous journey. Will you ~ on a slice of my homemade cake?* ***Nothing ~, nothing gain/have,*** (prov) One cannot expect to achieve anything if one risks nothing. **2** [VP6A,7A] go so far as, presume, dare: *~ (to put forward) an opinion; ~ a guess. I ~ to disagree/to suggest that....* **ven·turer** *n* (esp) *Merchant Venturers,* merchants who, in former times, took part in trading ~s to distant countries. **ˈ~·some** /-səm/ *adj* **1** (of persons) ready to take risks; daring. **2** (of acts, behaviour) involving danger; risky. **ven·tur·ous** /ˈventʃərəs/ *adj* = adventurous.

venue /ˈvenju/ *n* (pop use) rendezvous; meeting-place; (sport) place fixed for a contest or match.

Venus /ˈvinəs/ *n* **1** (Roman myth) goddess of love and beauty. **2** (astron) planet second in order from the sun. ⇨ the illus at planet.

ver·acious /vəˈreɪʃəs/ *adj* (formal) true; truthful. **~·ly** *adv* **ver·ac·ity** /vəˈræsətɪ/ *n* [U] truth; truthfulness.

ve·ran·dah, ve·randa /vəˈrændə/ *n* roofed and floored open space along the side(s) of a house, sports pavilion, etc (US often called *porch*).

verb /vɜb/ *n* word or phrase indicating what sb or sth does, what state sb or sth is in, what is becoming of sth or sb.

ver·bal /ˈvɜbl/ *adj* **1** of or in words: *a ~ error; have a good ~ memory,* be able to remember well the exact words of a statement, etc. **2** spoken, not written: *a ~ statement/explanation.* **3** word for word, literal: *a ~ translation.* **4** of verbs: *a ~ noun* (e g *swimming* in the sentence 'Swimming is a good exercise'). **~ly** /ˈvɜblɪ/ *adv* in spoken words, not in writing.

ver·bal·ize /ˈvɜbəlaɪz/ *vt* put into words.

ver·ba·tum /vɜˈbeɪtɪm/ *adv* word for word, exactly as spoken or written: *report a speech ~; a ~ report.*

ver·bena /vɜˈbinə/ *n* kinds of herbaceous plant of which garden varieties have flowers of many colours.

ver·bi·age /ˈvɜbɪɪdʒ/ *n* [U] (use of) unnecessary words for the expression of an idea, etc: *The speaker lost himself in ~.*

ver·bose /vɜˈbəʊs/ *adj* using, containing, more words than are needed: *a ~ speech/speaker/style.* **~·ly** *adv* **~·ness, ver·bos·ity** /vɜˈbosətɪ/ *nn* [U] state or quality of being ~.

ver·dant /ˈvɜdnt/ *adj* **1** (liter) (esp of grass, vegetation, fields) fresh and green: *~ lawns.* **2** (fig) inexperienced; unsophisticated. **ver·dancy** /-dnsɪ/ *n*

ver·dict /ˈvɜdɪkt/ *n* [C] **1** decision reached by a jury on a question of fact in a law case: *The jury* *brought in a* ~ *of guilty/not guilty.* **open ~,** ⇨ open[1](6). **2** decision or opinion given after testing, examining, or experiencing sth: *the* ~ *of the electors. The popular* ~ (= The opinion of people in general) *was that it served him right.*

ver·di·gris /ˈvɜdɪgrɪs/ *n* [U] green substance formed on copper, brass and bronze surfaces (as rust is formed on iron surfaces).

ver·dure /ˈvɜdʒə(r)/ *n* [U] (liter) (fresh green colour of) growing vegetation: *the* ~ *of (the trees in) spring.*

Verey /ˈverɪ/ *adj* ~ **light,** ⇨ Very.

verge /vɜdʒ/ *n* **1** [C] edge; border (e g strip of ground at the side of a road, grass edge of a lawn). **2** (*sing* with *def art*). ***be on the ~ of; bring (sb) to the ~ of,*** very close to, on the border of: *The country is on the* ~ *of disaster. She was on the* ~ *of bursting into tears.* □ *vi* [VP3A] ~ ***(up)on,*** approach closely, border upon: *verge on bankruptcy. Such ideas* ~ *on foolhardiness.*

verger /ˈvɜdʒə(r)/ *n* **1** (C of E) official with various duties (e g opening pews for worshippers). **2** officer who carries a staff before a bishop in a cathedral, a vice-chancellor in a university, etc.

ver·ier, ver·iest ⇨ very[1](2).

ver·ify /ˈverɪfaɪ/ *vt* (*pt,pp* -fied) [VP6A] **1** test the truth or accuracy of: ~ *a report/statement;* ~ *the figures/details of a report.* **2** (of an event, etc) show the truth of; bear out: *Subsequent events verified my suspicions.* **veri·fi·able** /ˈverɪfaɪəbl/ *adj* that can be verified. **veri·fi·ca·tion** /ˌverɪfɪˈkeɪʃn/ *n* ~ing or being verified; proof or evidence.

ver·ily /ˈverḷɪ/ *adv* (archaic) really; truly.

veri·si·mili·tude /ˌverɪsɪˈmɪlɪtjud *US:* -tud/ *n* [U] appearance, semblance, of truth; [C] sth that seems to be true.

veri·table /ˈverɪtəbl/ *adj* real; rightly named.

ver·ity /ˈverətɪ/ *n* (*pl* -ties) **1** [U] (old use) truth (*of* a statement, etc). **2** [C] sth that really exists; true statement: *the eternal verities,* fundamental moral principles; laws of God.

ver·mi·celli /ˌvɜmɪˈselɪ/ *n* [U] paste of white flour made into long slender threads, like spaghetti but much thinner.

ver·micu·lite /vɜˈmɪkjʊlaɪt/ *n* form of mica, which, when heated, expands into threads, used for heat insulation in buildings and for growing seeds and cuttings.

ver·mi·form /ˈvɜmɪfɔm/ *adj* worm-like in shape: *the* ~ *appendix.* ⇨ the illus at alimentary.

ver·mi·fuge /ˈvɜmɪfjudʒ/ *n* substance taken to purge the intestines of worms.

ver·mil·ion /vəˈmɪlɪən/ *adj, n* bright red (colour).

ver·min /ˈvɜmɪn/ *n* [U] (with *pl v,* but not with numerals) **1** wild animals (e g rats, weasels, foxes) harmful to plants, birds and other animals. **2** parasitic insects (e g lice) sometimes found on the bodies of human beings and other animals. **3** human beings who are harmful to society; persons who prey on others. ˋ**~·ous** /-əs/ *adj* **1** infested with fleas, lice, etc: *~ous children.* **2** caused by insect ~: *~ous diseases.*

ver·mouth /ˈvɜməθ *US:* vərˈmuθ/ *n* [U] white wine flavoured with herbs, drunk as an aperitif (often in cocktails).

ver·nacu·lar /vəˈnækjʊlə(r)/ *adj* (of a word, a language) of the country in question: *the* ~ *newspapers in India,* those in the various languages (except English) of India; *a* ~ *poet,* one who uses a ~ language. □ *n* [C] language or dialect of a country or district: *the ~s of the USA.*

ver·nal /ˈvɜnl/ *adj* (liter) of, in, as in, the season of spring. **the ~ equinox,** about 21st March.

ver·onal /ˈverənl/ *n* [U] (P) sleep-inducing drug: *take two* ~ *tablets.*

ve·ron·ica /vəˈronɪkə/ *n* kinds of herb or shrub with blue, purple, pink or white flowers.

ver·sa·tile /ˈvɜsətaɪl *US:* -tl/ *adj* interested in and clever at many different things; having various uses: *a* ~ *genius/inventor; a* ~ *mind.* **ver·sa·til·ity** /ˌvɜsəˈtɪlətɪ/ *n*

verse /vɜs/ *n* **1** [U] (form of) writing arranged in lines, each conforming to a pattern of accented and unaccented syllables: *prose and* ~*; written in* ~*; a* ~ *translation of Homer's 'Odyssey'; blank* ~, without rhymes at the end of the lines. **2** [C] group of lines of this kind forming a unit in a rhyme scheme: *a poem/hymn of five ~s.* **3** [C] one ~ line with a definite number of feet or accented syllables: *quote a few ~s from Tennyson.* **4** one of the short numbered divisions of a chapter in the Bible. ***give chapter and ~ (for sth),*** supply the exact reference (for a statement, an authority one quotes, reports, etc).

versed /vɜst/ *adj* ~ ***in,*** skilled or experienced in: *well* ~ *in mathematics/the arts.* ⇨ *conversant with* at conversant.

ver·sify /ˈvɜsɪfaɪ/ *vt,vi* (*pt,pp* -fied) [VP6A] put into verse: ~ *an old legend;* [VP2A] write verses. **ver·si·fier** *n* maker of verses. **ver·si·fi·ca·tion** /ˌvɜsɪfɪˈkeɪʃn/ *n* [U] art of ~ing; style in which verse is written; metre.

ver·sion /ˈvɜʃn *US:* ˋvɜʒn/ *n* [C] **1** account of an event, etc from the point of view of one person: *There were contradictory ~s of what happened/of what the Prime Minister said.* **2** translation into another language: *a new* ~ *of the Bible.*

verso /ˈvɜsəʊ/ *n* (*pl* -sos /-səʊz/) any left-hand page of a book ⇨ recto; reverse side of a medal or coin.

verst /vɜst/ *n* (obs) Russian measure of length, 3 000 ft, a little more than 1 000 metres.

ver·sus /ˈvɜsəs/ *prep* (Lat) (in law and sport; often shortened to *v* in print) against: (legal) *Robinson* v *Brown;* (cricket) *Kent* v *Surrey.*

ver·te·bra /ˈvɜtɪbrə/ *n* (*pl* -brae /-bri/) any one of the segments of the backbone. ⇨ the illus at skeleton. **ver·te·brate** /ˈvɜtɪbrət/ *n, adj* (animal, bird, etc) having a backbone.

ver·tex /ˈvɜteks/ *n* (*pl* vertices /-tɪsiz/) highest point; top; point of a triangle, cone, etc opposite the base.

ver·ti·cal /ˈvɜtɪkl/ *adj* (of a line or plane) at a right angle to the earth's surface or to another line or plane: *a* ~ *cliff; a* ~ *take-off aircraft,* one that can rise ~ly, not needing a runway. ⇨ horizontal. □ *n* ~ line: *out of the* ~, not ~. **~ly** /-klɪ/ *adv*

ver·tices /ˈvɜtɪsiz/ *n pl* ⇨ vertex.

ver·tigo /ˈvɜtɪgəʊ/ *n* [U] (formal) dizziness. **ver·tigin·ous** /vɜˈtɪdʒɪnəs/ *adj* of, causing, ~.

verve /vɜv/ *n* [U] enthusiasm, spirit, vigour (esp in artistic or literary work).

very[1] /ˈverɪ/ *attrib adj* **1** itself and no other; truly such: *This is the* ~ *thing I want! At that* ~ *moment the phone rang. You're the* ~ *man I want to see.* **2** (rare; emphasizing the nature of the *n* with which ~ is used): *A verier rogue there never was! He's the veriest rogue unhung!* **3** extreme: *at the* ~ *end/beginning.* **4** (equivalent to an emphatic

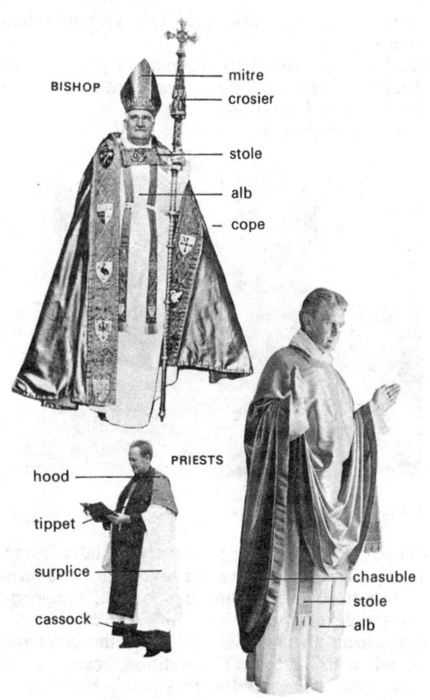

vestments

or intensive *pron* in *-self* or *-selves*): *He knows our ~ thoughts,* i e our thoughts themselves, even our innermost thoughts. *The ~ idea of being sent abroad* (i e the idea alone, quite apart from the reality) *delighted him.*

very[2] /ˈverɪ/ *adv* **1** (used intensively with *advv, adjj* and *part adjj*): *~ quickly/carefully/soon, etc; ~ much/little; ~ amusing/interesting, etc; ~ small/cold/useful, etc.* (Note that when the *pp* is part of a passive *v* phrase, *much,* or *very much* is preferred, and that when it is the complement of *be, seem, feel,* ~ is used): *I wasn't much surprised at the news. He wasn't much interested in the news.* Cf *He was/seemed ~ interested.* **~ well,** often used to indicate agreement or assent (often after persuasion or argument, or in obedience to a command, request, etc): *V~ well, doctor, I'll give up smoking. Oh, ~ well, if you insist.* **2** (with a superl, or *own*) in the highest possible degree: *the ~ best quality; the ~ first to arrive; six o'clock at the ~ latest. You can keep this for your ~ own.*

Very, Verey /ˈverɪ/ *adj* **ˈ~ light,** (P) coloured signal flare fired from a *ˈ~ pistol,* e g as a signal of distress from a ship.

ves·icle /ˈvesɪkl/ *n* (anat) small cavity, cyst or swelling. **ves·icu·lar** /vəˈsɪkjʊlə(r)/ *adj* of ~s: *vesicular disease.*

ves·pers /ˈvesperz/ *n pl* church service in the evening; evensong; (attrib, *sing*) *the vesper bell,* rung for ~s.

vessel /ˈvesl/ *n* [C] **1** hollow receptacle, esp for a liquid, e g a cask, tub, bucket, bowl, bottle, cup. **2** ship or large boat. **3** ⇨ *blood-~* at blood[1](7).

vest[1] /vest/ *n* [C] **1** (GB) undergarment worn on the upper part of the body next to the skin. **2** (trade use in GB; ordinary use in US) short, sleeveless garment worn by men under a jacket (*waistcoat* being the usual name in GB): *coat, ~ and trousers; a ~-pocket* (i e very small) *camera.*

vest[2] /vest/ *vt,vi* **1** [VP14] ***~ sth in sb, ~ sb with sth,*** furnish or give as a fixed right: *~ a man with authority/rights in an estate. In some countries authority is said to be ~ed in the people,* i e the people possess final authority on matters of government, etc. *In the US Congress is ~ed with the power to declare war.* **~ed interests/rights,** (e g in trade or manufacture) which are by law securely in the possession of a person or a group of persons. **2** [VP3A] ***~ in,*** (of property, etc) be ~ed in: *power/authority that ~s in the Crown.* **3** [VP6A] (old use, or poet) clothe.

ves·tal /ˈvestl/ *n* **~ (virgin),** one of the maidens dedicated to the service of the goddess Vesta in ancient Rome, vowed to chastity. □ *adj* pure; chaste.

ves·ti·bule /ˈvestɪbjul/ *n* **1** lobby or entrance hall to a building (e g where hats and coats may be left). **2** porch of a church. **3** (US) enclosed space at the end of a railway coach.

ves·tige /ˈvestɪdʒ/ *n* [C] **1** trace or sign; small remaining bit of evidence of what once existed: *Not a ~ of the abbey remains. There is not a ~ of truth in the report.* **2** (anat) organ, or part of one, which is a survival of sth that once existed: *A human being has the ~ of a tail.* **ves·tigial** /veˈstɪdʒɪəl/ **vest·ment** /ˈvestmənt/ *n* garment, esp one worn by a priest in church; ceremonial robe.

ves·try /ˈvestrɪ/ *n* (*pl* -tries) **1** part of a church where vestments are kept and where the clergy and members of the choir robe themselves. ⇨ the illus at church. **2** room in a non-conformist church used for Sunday School, prayer meetings, business meetings, etc. **3** (Anglian Church) (council of) ratepayers of a parish, or their representatives, assembled to discuss parish business. **ˈ~·man** /-mən/ *n* (*pl* -men) member of a ~.

ves·ture /ˈvestʃə(r)/ *n* (poet) clothing. □ *vt* clothe.

vet /vet/ *n* (colloq abbr for) veterinary surgeon. □ *vt* (-tt-) [VP6A] (colloq) **1** give (sb) a medical examination. **2** (GB) examine closely and critically, e g sb's past record, qualifications, etc: *He must be thoroughly vetted before he's given the job.*

vetch /vetʃ/ *n* kinds of plant of the bean family used, wild or cultivated, as fodder for cattle.

vet·eran /ˈvetṛən/ *n* **1** person who has had much or long experience, esp as a soldier: *~s of two World Wars;* (attrib) *a ~ teacher;* (of cars) of the years before 1916: *a ~ Rolls Royce.* **2** (US) any ex-service man. **ˈV~s Day,** 11th November, commemorating the armistice (1918) in World War I.

vet·erin·ary /ˈvetrɪnərɪ *US:* -nerɪ/ *adj* of or concerned with the diseases of (esp farm and domestic) animals: *a ~ surgeon/college.*

veto /ˈvitəʊ/ *n* (*pl* -toes) constitutional right of a sovereign, president, legislative assembly or other body, or a member of the United Nations Security Council, to reject or forbid sth; statement that rejects or prohibits sth: *exercise the ~; put a ~ on sth,* forbid it. □ *vt* [VP6A] put a ~ on: *The police ~ed the procession that the workers wanted. John's parents ~ed his plan to buy a sports car.*

vex /veks/ *vt* [VP6A] **1** annoy; distress; trouble: *His silly chatter would vex a saint. She was vexed that I didn't help her. He was vexed at his failure.* **a vexed question,** a difficult problem that causes much discussion. **2** (poet, rhet) put (the sea) into commotion: *vexed by storms.* **vex·ation** /vek`seɪʃn/ *n* [U] state of being vexed; [C] sth that vexes: *the little vexations of life; constant vexations from our neighbours.* **vex·atious** /vek`seɪʃəs/ *adj* annoying: *vexatious rules and regulations.*

via /`vɑɪə/ *prep* (Lat) by way of: *travel from London to Paris via Dover.*

vi·able /`vɑɪəbl/ *adj* able to exist; capable of developing and surviving without outside help: *Is the newly-created State ~?* **vi·abil·ity** /'vɑɪə`bɪlətɪ/ *n*

vi·aduct /`vɑɪədʌkt/ *n* long bridge (usu with many spans or arches) carrying a road or railway across a valley or dip in the ground.

vial /`vɑɪəl/ *n* small bottle, esp for liquid medicine.

via media /'vɑɪə `midɪə/ (Lat) middle course between extremes.

vi·ands /`vɑɪəndz/ *n pl* (formal) articles of food; provisions.

vibes /vɑɪbz/ *n* (colloq abbr for) vibraphone.

vi·brant /`vɑɪbrənt/ *adj* thrilling; vibrating: *the ~ notes of a 'cello.*

vi·bra·phone /`vɑɪbrəfəʊn/ *n* (music) instrument like an xylophone but with metal bars and tone sustained by electronic resonators.

vi·brate /vɑɪ`breɪt *US:* `vɑɪbreɪt/ *vi,vt* **1** [VP2A, 6A] (cause to) move rapidly and continuously backwards and forwards: *The house ~s whenever a heavy lorry passes.* **2** [VP2A,C] (of stretched strings, the voice) throb; quiver: *The strings of a piano ~ when the keys are struck. His voice ~d with passion.*

vi·bra·tion /vɑɪ`breɪʃn/ *n* **1** [U] vibrating movement: *The ship's engines even at full speed cause very little ~.* **2** [C] single movement to and fro when equilibrium has been disturbed: *20 ~s per second.*

vi·brato /vɪ`brɑtəʊ/ *n* (music) throbbing or tremulous effect in singing and the playing of stringed and wind instruments with minute and rapid variations in pitch.

vicar /`vɪkə(r)/ *n* **1** (C of E) clergyman in charge of a parish the tithes of which were partly or wholly payable to another person or body (e g a college) for whom or which the ~ acts. **2** (R C Church) deputy; representative: *the ~ of Christ,* the Pope; *cardinal ~,* Pope's delegate acting as the bishop of the diocese of Rome. **~·age** /`vɪkərɪdʒ/ *n* ~'s residence.

vi·cari·ous /vɪ`keərɪəs *US:* vɑɪ`k-/ *adj* **1** done, undergone, by one person for another or others: *the ~ sufferings of Jesus; a ~ ruler; feel a ~ pleasure/satisfaction,* e g when sth is done for you or which is sth you would like to do. **2** deputed; delegated: *~ authority.* **~·ly** *adv*

vice[1] /vɑɪs/ *n* [C,U] **1** (any particular kind of) evil conduct or indulgence in depraving practices: *Gluttony is just as much a ~ as is drunkenness.* **2** (in a horse) bad habit (e g kicking) which makes control difficult: *He said the horse was free from ~/had no ~s.*

vice[2] (US = **vise**) /vɑɪs/ *n* [C] apparatus with strong jaws in which things can be held tightly while being worked upon: *as firm as a ~,* immovable.

vice[3] /vɑɪs/ *n* (colloq abbr for) vice-president, vice-captain, etc.

vice[4] /vɑɪs/ *prep* (Lat) (formal) in place of: *Mr Smith has been appointed chief accountant ~ Mr Brown, who has retired.*

vice- *pref* ⇨ App 3.

a vice

viceroy /`vɑɪsrɔɪ/ *n* (e g formerly in India) person governing as the deputy of a sovereign. **vice·reine** /vɑɪs`reɪn *US:* `vɑɪsreɪn/ *n* ~'s wife. **vice·regal** /vɑɪs`rigl/ *adj* of a ~.

vice versa /'vɑɪsɪ `vɜsə/ *adj* (Lat) the other way round; with the terms or conditions reversed: *We gossip about them and ~,* they gossip about us.

vi·cin·ity /vɪ`sɪnətɪ/ *n* (*pl* **-ties**) **1** [U] nearness; closeness of relationship: *in close ~ to the church.* **2** [C] neighbourhood: *the northern vicinities of the capital. There isn't a good school in the ~.*

vi·cious /`vɪʃəs/ *adj* **1** of vice[1]; given up to vice[1]: *~ practices/habits; a ~ life.* **2** spiteful; given or done with evil intent: *a ~ kick/look.* **3** (of a horse) having bad habits such as biting, kicking, bolting. **4** having faults, corrupt: *a ~ argument.* **'~ `circle,** state of affairs in which a cause produces an effect which itself produces the original cause, e g *War breeds hate, and hate leads to war again.* **'~ `spiral,** continuous rise in one thing (e g prices) caused by a continuous rise in sth else (e g wages). **~·ly** *adv* **~·ness** *n*

vi·ciss·itude /vɪ`sɪsɪtjud *US:* -tud/ *n* [C] change, esp in sb's fortunes: *His life was marked by ~s,* e g changes from wealth to poverty, success to failure.

vic·tim /`vɪktɪm/ *n* **1** living creature killed and offered as a religious sacrifice. **2** person, animal, etc suffering injury, pain, loss, etc because of circumstances, an event, the ill-will of sb, etc: *He is the ~ of his brother's anger/of his own foolishness. A fund was opened to help the ~s of the earthquake. Thousands were ~s of the plague in the Middle Ages.* **~·ize** /-ɑɪz/ *vt* [VP6A] make a ~ of; single out for ill treatment because of real or alleged misconduct, etc: *Trade union leaders claimed that some of their members had been ~ized,* e g by being dismissed. **~·iz·ation** /'vɪktəmɑɪ`zeɪʃn *US:* -mɪ`z-/ *n*: *The strikers said they would return to work if they were promised that there should be no ~ization,* that none of their leaders (or ringleaders) should be ~ized.

vic·tor /`vɪktə(r)/ *n* person who conquers or wins.

vic·toria /vɪk`tɔrɪə/ *n* **~ plum,** juicy, sweet-flavoured plum, changing from green to yellow and red.

Vic·tor·ian /vɪk`tɔrɪən/ *n, adj* (person) of, living in, the reign of Queen Victoria (1837—1901): ~ *authors/manners/dress.*

vic·tory /`vɪktrɪ/ *n* [C,U] (*pl* -ries) (instance, occasion, of) success (in war, a contest, game, etc): *gain/win a ~ over the enemy; lead the troops to ~.* **vic·tori·ous** /vɪk`tɔrɪəs/ *adj* having gained the ~; triumphant. **vic·tori·ous·ly** *adv*

vict·ual /`vɪtl/ *vt,vi* (-ll-; US also -l-) (formal) **1** [VP6A] supply with provisions (of food): ~ *a ship.* **2** [VP2A] take in provisions: *The ship ~led at Colombo.* □ *n* (usu *pl*) food and drink; provisions. **~·ler** (US also **~er**) /`vɪtḷə(r)/ *n* trader in ~s. **licensed ~ler,** (GB) public-house keeper who is licensed to sell food, spirits, beer, etc to be consumed on the premises.

vi·cuña /vɪ`kjunə/ *n* animal of the central Andes somewhat like, but much smaller than, a camel, with soft, delicate wool.

vide /`vɑɪdɪ/ *v* (Lat) (imperative form used in references). **'~ `infra,** see below. **'~ `supra,** see above.

vide·licet /vɪ`dilɪset *US:* -`del-/ *adv* (common abbr *viz,* usu spoken as *namely*) that is to say; namely.

video /`vɪdɪəʊ/ *n T V.* **`~-tape,** magnetic tape for recording sound and vision, e g of television programmes; *~(-tape) recordings.*

vie /vɑɪ/ *vi* [VP3A] ***vie with sb/for sth,*** rival or compete: *The two boys vied with one another for the first place.*

view[1] /vju/ *n* **1** [U] state of seeing or being seen: field of vision: *The speaker stood in full ~ of the crowd,* could see them and could be seen by them. *Clouds came down and the hill tops passed from our ~,* could no longer be seen. ***in ~ of,*** considering, taking into account: *In ~ of the facts, it seems useless to continue.* ***on ~,*** being shown or exhibited: *The latest summer fashions are now on ~ in the big shops.* ***come into ~,*** become visible: *As we rounded the bend the lake came into ~.* ***come in ~ of,*** be able to see: *As we rounded the bend, we came in ~ of the lake.* **2** [C] (picture, photograph, etc of) natural scenery, landscape, etc: *a house with fine ~s over valleys and mountains; an album of ~s,* e g photographs. **3** [C] opportunity to see or inspect sth; occasion when there is such an opportunity: *a private ~,* e g of paintings, before public exhibition. **4** [C] personal opinion; mental attitude; thought or observation (on a subject): *She had/expressed strong ~s on the subject of equal pay for men and women. Your ~s on the situation are not helpful. He holds extreme ~s,* e g in politics. *He took a poor ~ of my conduct,* regarded it unfavourably. ***meet/fall in with sb's ~s,*** agree with, accept, his ideas, opinions, etc. **5** aim; intention; purpose. ***with a/the ~ to/of,*** with the intention or hope: *with a ~ to facilitating research; with the ~ of saving trouble.* **6** (compounds) **`~·point, point of ~,** ⇨ **point**[1](4). **`~-finder** *n* device in a camera showing the area, etc that will be photographed through the lens.

view[2] /vju/ *vt* [VP6A] look at; examine; consider: *The subject may be ~ed in various ways. Has the matter been ~ed from the taxpayers' standpoint?* ***an order to ~,*** written authority to look over a house, etc with the idea of buying it: *The house agents gave me an order to ~.* **~er** /`vjuə(r)/ *n* (esp) *television ~ers,* persons watching a television programme. **~·less** *adj* **1** (rhet or poet) invisible. **2** (US) without ~s (= opinions).

vigil /`vɪdʒɪl/ *n* **1** [U] staying awake to keep watch or to pray: *keep ~ over a sick child;* (*pl*) instances of this: *tired out by her long ~s.* **2** eve of a religious festival, esp when observed with prayer and fasting.

vigi·lance /`vɪdʒɪləns/ *n* [U] watchfulness; keeping watch: *exercise ~.* **`~ committee,** (chiefly US) self-appointed group of persons who maintain order in a community where organization is imperfect or has broken down.

vigi·lant /`vɪdʒɪlənt/ *adj* watchful; on the look-out for danger of any kind. **~·ly** *adv*

vigi·lante /ˈvɪdʒɪ`læntɪ/ *n* member of a vigilance committee.

vi·gnette /vɪ`njet/ *n* [C] **1** ornamental design, esp on the title-page of a book, or at the beginning or end of a chapter. **2** picture of a person's head and shoulders with the background gradually shaded off. **3** short sketch of a person's character.

vig·our (US = **vigor**) /`vɪgə(r)/ *n* [U] mental or physical strength; energy; forcefulness (of language). **vig·or·ous** /`vɪgərəs/ *adj* strong; energetic. **vig·or·ous·ly** *adv*

Vik·ing /`vɑɪkɪŋ/ *n* any of the Scandinavian sea-robbers who raided the coasts of Europe during the 8th, 9th and 10th cc.

vile /vɑɪl/ *adj* **1** shameful and disgusting: ~ *habits/language; the ~ practice of bribery.* **2** (colloq) bad: ~ *weather.* **3** (old use) valueless: *this ~ body,* i e contrasted with the soul or spirit. **~·ly** /`vɑɪllɪ/ *adv* **~·ness** *n*

vil·ify /`vɪlɪfɑɪ/ *vt* (*pt,pp* -fied) [VP6A] slander; say evil things about (sb). **vil·ifi·ca·tion** /ˈvɪlɪfɪ`keɪʃn/ *n*

villa /`vɪlə/ *n* **1** (in GB) (usu as part of the address) detached or semi-detached house or esp one on the outskirts of a town: *No 13 Laburnum Villas.* **2** country house with a large garden, esp in Italy or S France.

vil·lage /`vɪlɪdʒ/ *n* place smaller than a town, where there are houses and shops, and usu a church and school: (attrib) *the ~ post-office.* **vil·lager** /`vɪlɪdʒə(r)/ *n* person who lives in a ~.

vil·lain /`vɪlən/ *n* **1** (esp in drama) wrongdoer; wicked man. **2** (playful use) rascal; mischievous child, etc: *The little ~ hid my slippers.* **3** = villein. **~·ous** /vɪlənəs/ *adj* characteristic of a ~; evil; (colloq) bad: *Tony's ~ous handwriting.* **vil·lainy** *n* (*pl* -nies) [U] evil conduct; (*pl*) evil acts.

vil·lein /`vɪleɪn/ *n* feudal serf in the Middle Ages. **~·age** /`vɪlɪnɪdʒ/ *n* [U] state of being a ~; serfdom.

vim /vɪm/ *n* [U] (colloq) energy: *feel full of vim. Put more vim into it!*

vin·ai·grette /ˈvɪnɪ`gret/ *n* [U] **~ sauce,** dressing (for green salads, etc) of vinegar and olive oil, flavoured with herbs.

vin·di·cate /`vɪndɪkeɪt/ *vt* [VP6A] show or prove the truth, justice, validity, etc (of sth that has been attacked or disputed): ~ *a claim/one's title to a privilege;* ~ *one's veracity/judgement; Events have ~d his judgement/actions.* **vin·di·ca·tion** /ˈvɪndɪ`keɪʃn/ *n* [U] vindicating or being ~d; [C] instance of this: *speak in vindication of one's conduct.*

vin·dic·tive /vɪn`dɪktɪv/ *adj* unforgiving; having or showing a desire for revenge. **~·ly** *adv* **~·ness** *n*

vine /vɑɪn/ *n* [C] climbing plant whose fruit is the

grape; any plant with slender stems that trails, e g melons, or climbs (e g peas, hops). **~·yard** /ˈvɪnjəd/ *n* [C] area of land planted with grape-~s. **vin·ery** /ˈvaɪnərɪ/ *n* (*pl* -ries) greenhouse for ~s.

vin·egar /ˈvɪnɪɡə(r)/ *n* [C] acid liquor (made from malt, wine, cider, etc) used in flavouring food and for pickling. **~y** /ˈvɪnɪɡərɪ/ *adj* like ~; (fig) sour-tempered.

vino /ˈviːnəʊ/ *n* (*pl* -noes /-nəʊz/) (colloq) (kinds of) wine of unstated origin; cheap popular wine.

vi·nous /ˈvaɪnəs/ *adj* of, like or due to wine.

vin·tage /ˈvɪntɪdʒ/ *n* **1** (rarely *pl*) (period or season of) grape harvesting: *The ~ was later than usual last year.* **2** [C,U] (wine from) grapes of a particular year: *of the ~ of 1959; rare old ~s; a ~ year*, one in which good wine was made; *~ wines*, from ~ years. **3** (by extension; attrib) of a period in the past and having a reputation for high quality: *a ~ car*, one built between 1916 and 1930, ⇨ veteran; sports car more than 30 years old.

vint·ner /ˈvɪntnə(r)/ *n* wine-merchant.

vi·nyl /ˈvaɪnɪl/ *n* (kinds of) tough, flexible plastic, used for clothing, coverings and binding books.

viol /ˈvaɪəl/ *n* (usu six-)stringed instrument of the Middle Ages from which the modern violin was developed.

vi·ola[1] /vɪˈəʊlə/ *n* tenor violin, of larger size than the ordinary violin.

vi·ola[2] /ˈvaɪələ/ *n* kinds of plant including pansies of one colour only (not variegated) and violets.

vi·ol·ate /ˈvaɪəleɪt/ *vt* [VP6A] **1** break (an oath, a treaty, etc); act contrary to (what one's conscience tells one to do, etc). **2** act towards (a sacred place, sb's seclusion, etc) without proper respect: *~ sb's privacy.* **3** commit rape upon. **vi·ol·ation** /ˌvaɪəˈleɪʃn/ *n* [U] violating or being ~d: *act in violation of a treaty;* [C] instance of this: *violations of the rights of the citizens/the right of free speech, etc.*

vi·ol·ent /ˈvaɪələnt/ *adj* **1** using, showing, accompanied by, great force: *a ~ wind/attack; ~ blows; ~ passions; in a ~ temper; ~ abuse; a ~* (= extreme) *contrast.* **2** caused by ~ attack: *meet a ~ death.* **3** severe: *~ toothache.* **~·ly** *adv* **vi·ol·ence** /-əns/ *n* [U] state of being ~; ~ conduct: *crimes/acts of violence; robbery with violence; an outbreak of violence*, rioting, etc. ***do violence to,*** (fig) be a breach of: *It would do violence to his principles to work on Sundays.*

vi·olet /ˈvaɪələt/ *n* **1** [C] small wild or garden plant with sweet-smelling flowers. **2** [U] bluish-purple colour of wild ~s.

vi·olin /ˌvaɪəˈlɪn/ *n* four-stringed musical instrument played with a bow, ⇨ the illus at **string**. **~·ist** /-ɪst/ *n* player of a ~.

vi·olon·cello /ˌvaɪələnˈtʃeləʊ/ *n* (*pl* -los) (usu abbr **cello** /ˈtʃeləʊ/) bass violin held between the player's knees. ⇨ the illus at **string**. **vi·olon·cel·list** /-ˈtʃelɪst/ *n* (usu abbr **cellist**) ~ player.

vi·per /ˈvaɪpə(r)/ *n* kinds of poisonous snake, esp *the common ~*, the adder (the only poisonous kind in GB); (fig) spiteful and treacherous person.

vir·ago /vɪˈrɑːɡəʊ/ *n* (*pl* -gos or -goes /-ɡəʊz/) violent and bad-tempered woman who scolds and shouts.

vir·gin /ˈvɜːdʒɪn/ *n* girl or woman (and in recent use, man) who has not experienced sexual union. **the (Blessed) V~ (Mary),** (abbr **BVM**), the mother of Jesus Christ. □ *adj* **1** pure and chaste: *the V~ Queen*, Elizabeth I of England. **the ~ birth,** the doctrine that Jesus was miraculously conceived by the V~ Mary. **2** pure and untouched: *~ snow.* **3** in the original condition; unused: *a ~ forest*, one in its natural state, no trees having been felled; *~ soil*, soil never before used for crops; (fig) a mind open to receive new ideas. **~·ity** /vəˈdʒɪnətɪ/ *n* [U] state of being a ~; ~ condition.

vir·ginal[1] /ˈvɜːdʒɪnl/ *adj* of, suitable for, a virgin.

vir·ginal[2] /ˈvɜːdʒɪnl/ *n* (often *pl*) square spinet without legs used in the 16th and 17th cc (and also called *the ~s/a pair of ~s.*

Vir·ginia /vəˈdʒɪnɪə/ *n* [U] kinds of tobacco produced in the State of V~, US; *~ cigarettes.* **~ creeper,** ornamental vine often grown on walls, with large leaves which turn scarlet in the autumn.

Virgo /ˈvɜːɡəʊ/ *n* sixth sign of the zodiac. ⇨ the illus at zodiac.

vir·gule /ˈvɜːɡjuːl/ *n* diagonal mark (/), used to separate alternatives (as in *and/or*).

vir·ile /ˈvɪraɪl *US:* ˈvɪrl/ *adj* **1** having or showing strength, energy, manly qualities: *~ eloquence; a ~ style (of writing); live to a ~ old age.* **2** (of men) sexually potent. **vir·il·ity** /vɪˈrɪlətɪ/ *n* [U] masculine strength and vigour; sexual power: *young Italians, chatting up girls on the beaches, and eager to prove their virility.*

vi·rol·ogy /vaɪəˈrɒlədʒɪ/ *n* [U] the study of viruses and virus diseases.

virtu /vɜːˈtuː/ *n* (only in) **articles/objects of ~,** art objects interesting because of fine workmanship, antiquity, rarity, etc.

vir·tual /ˈvɜːtʃʊəl/ *adj* being in fact, acting as, what is described, but not accepted openly or in name as such: *the ~ head of the business; a ~ defeat/confession.* **~ly** /-tʃʊlɪ/ *adv*

vir·tue /ˈvɜːtʃuː/ *n* **1** [C,U] (any particular kind of) goodness or excellence. ***make a ~ of necessity,*** do sth pretending it to be an act of ~ when one really does it under compulsion. ***V~ is its own reward*** (prov). *Patience is a ~. Is patriotism always a ~? Our climate has the ~s of never being too hot or too cold.* **the cardinal ~s,** prudence, fortitude, temperance, justice. **the theological ~s,** faith, hope, charity. **2** [U] chastity, esp of women: *a woman of easy ~*, one who is promiscuous. **3** [U] efficacy; ability to produce a definite result: *Have you any faith in the ~ of herbs to heal sickness?* **4** excellence; advantage: *The great ~ of the scheme is that it costs very little.* **5 by/in ~ of,** by reason of; because of: *He claimed a pension in ~ of his long military service.* **vir·tu·ous** /ˈvɜːtʃʊəs/ *adj* having or showing ~. **vir·tu·ous·ly** *adv*

vir·tu·oso /ˌvɜːtʃʊˈəʊzəʊ *US:* -ˈəʊsəʊ/ *n* (*pl* -sos or -si /-ziː *US:* -siː/) person with special knowledge of, or taste for, works of art; person skilled in the methods of an art, esp one who plays a musical instrument with great skill: (attrib) *a ~ performer.* **vir·tu·os·ity** /ˌvɜːtʃʊˈɒsətɪ/ *n* [U] skill of a ~.

viru·lent /ˈvɪrʊlənt/ *adj* (of poison) strong; deadly; (of ill feeling, hatred) bitter; (of words, etc) full of ill feeling; (of diseases, sores) poisonous. **~·ly** *adv* **viru·lence** /-ləns/ *n*

vi·rus /ˈvaɪərəs/ *n* [C] any of various poisonous elements, smaller than bacteria, causing the spread of infectious disease: *the ~ of rabies; ~ diseases;* (fig) moral poison: *infected with the ~ of heresy.*

visa /ˈviːzə/ *n* [C] stamp or signature put on a passport to show that it has been examined and approved by the officials of a foreign country which the owner intends to visit (ˋ*entrance* or ˋ*entry* ~) or leave (ˋ*exit* ~). □ *vt* [VP6A] put a ~ on: *get one's passport ~ed* /ˈvɪzəd/ *before going to Poland.*

vis·age /ˈvɪzɪdʒ/ *n* [C] (now chiefly liter) face (of a human being). **-vis·aged** /ˈvɪzɪdʒd/ *suff* (in compounds) having the kind of ~ indicated: *gloomy-~d funeral directors.*

vis-à-vis /ˈviz ɑ ˈvi *US:* ˈviz ə ˈvi/ *adv, prep* **1** facing (one another): *sit ~ in a train.* **2** (fig) in relation to; compared with.

vis·cera /ˈvɪsərə/ *n pl* internal organs of the body, esp the intestines. **vis·ceral** /ˈvɪsərl/ *adj* of the ~.

vis·cid /ˈvɪsɪd/, **vis·cous** /ˈvɪskəs/ *adjj* sticky; semi-fluid. **vis·cos·ity** /vɪsˈkɒsətɪ/ *n* [U] being viscous.

vis·count /ˈvɑɪkaʊnt/ *n* nobleman higher in rank than a baron, lower than an earl. **~·ess** /-es/ *n* wife of a ~; woman who is a ~ in her own right. **~cy** /-tsɪ/ *n* (*pl* -cies) title, rank, dignity, of a ~.

vise /vɑɪs/ *n* US spelling of vice[2].

visé /ˈvizeɪ/ *n, vt* (US) = visa.

vis·ible /ˈvɪzəbl/ *adj* that can be seen; that is in sight: *The eclipse will be ~ to observers in western Europe.* **vis·ibly** /-əblɪ/ *adv* in a ~ manner: *She was visibly annoyed.* **vis·ibil·ity** /ˈvɪzəˈbɪlətɪ/ *n* [U] being ~; (esp) condition of the atmosphere for seeing things at a distance: *The aircraft turned back because of poor visibility.*

vi·sion /ˈvɪʒn/ *n* **1** [U] power of seeing or imagining, looking ahead, grasping the truth that underlies facts: *the field of ~*, all that can be seen from a certain point; *the ~ of a poet/prophet; a man of ~.* **2** [C] sth seen, esp by the mind's eye or the power of imagination, or sth seen during sleep or in a trance-like state: *The lake, in the morning mist, was a ~. Have you ever had ~s of great wealth and success? We must not laugh at the romantic ~s of youth.*

vi·sion·ary /ˈvɪʒnrɪ *US:* -ʒnerɪ/ *adj* **1** existing only in a vision or the imagination; unpractical; fanciful: *~ schemes/scenes/plans.* **2** (of persons) having ~ ideas; dreamy. □ *n* ~ person.

visit /ˈvɪzɪt/ *vt, vi* **1** [VP6A] go to see (sb); go to (a place) for a time: *~ a friend; ~ Rome. His rich relatives seldom ~ him.* [VP2C] (US) stay: *~ing in Paris; ~ing at a new hotel.* **2** [VP6A] (chiefly US) go to in order to inspect or examine officially: *Restaurant and hotel kitchens are ~ed regularly by officers of public health.* **3** [VP3A] (chiefly US) ***~ with,*** talk with: *She loves ~ing with her neighbours and having a good gossip.* **4** [VP14] ***~ sth on sb,*** (biblical use) punish. ***~ the sins of the fathers upon the children,*** make the children suffer for their parent's failings. □ *n* act of ~ing; time of ~ing: *pay a ~ to a friend/a patient, a prospective customer; go on a ~ to the seaside; a ~ of several hours; during her first ~ to her husband's parents.* **~·ing** *n* paying ~s; making calls (on people): ˋ*~ing hours at a hospital; We are not on ~ing terms,* not sufficiently well acquainted to ~ one another. ˋ**~·ing-card** *n* (usu abbr to *card*), ⇨ card[1](1). ˋ**~·ing-list** *n* list of persons to be ~ed. **visi·tor** /ˈvɪzɪtə(r)/ *n* person who ~s; person who stays at a place: *summer ~ors,* e g at a holiday resort; *the ~ors' book,* one in which ~ors sign their names, e g at an hotel or a place of public interest.

visi·tant /ˈvɪzɪtənt/ *n* **1** (liter) visitor, esp an important or supernatural one. **2** migratory bird: *a rare ~ to these shores.*

visi·ta·tion /ˈvɪzɪˈteɪʃn/ *n* **1** [C] visit, esp one of an official nature or one made by a bishop or priest: *a ~ of the sick,* made by a clergyman as part of his duties. **2** [C] trouble, disaster, looked upon as punishment from God: *The famine was a ~ of God for their sins.*

vi·sor /ˈvɑɪzə(r)/ *n* **1** (in former times) movable part of a helmet, covering the face. ⇨ the illus at armour. **2** peak of a cap. **3** (ˋ**sun-**)**~,** oblong sheet of dark-tinted glass hinged at the top of a windscreen in a car to lessen the glare of bright sunshine.

vista /ˈvɪstə/ *n* [C] **1** long, narrow view: *a ~ of the church spire at the end of an avenue of trees.* **2** (fig) long series of scenes, events, etc which one can look back on or forward to: *the ~s of bygone times; a discovery that opens up new ~s.*

vis·ual /ˈvɪʒʊəl/ *adj* concerned with, used in, seeing: *~ images. She has a ~ memory,* is able to remember well things she sees. **~ aids,** (e g in teaching) e g pictures, film-strips, cinema films. **~ly** /ˈvɪʒʊəlɪ/ *adv* **~·ize** /-ɑɪz/ *vt* [VP6A] bring (sth) as a picture before the mind: *I remember meeting the man two years ago but can't ~ize him,* recall what he looked like. **vis·ual·iz·ation** /ˈvɪʒʊəlɑɪˈzeɪʃn *US:* -lɪˈz-/ *n*

vi·tal /ˈvɑɪtl/ *adj* **1** of, connected with, necessary for, living: *wounded in a ~ part.* **the ~ force/principle,** that which is assumed to account for organic life. **~ statistics, (a)** relating to the duration of life, and to births, marriages and deaths. **(b)** (mod colloq) woman's measurements at bust, waist and hips. **2** supreme; indispensable: *of ~ importance; a ~ necessity.* **vi·tals** *n pl* ~ parts of the body, esp the lungs, heart and brain. **~ly** /ˈvɑɪtḷɪ/ *adv* **~·ism** /-ɪzm/ *n* belief that there is a controlling force in living things which is distinct from chemical and physical forces (opp of *mechanism*). **~·ist** /-ɪst/ *n* person who believes in ~ism.

vi·tal·ity /vɑɪˈtælətɪ/ *n* [U] vital power; capacity to endure and perform functions: *Can an artificial language have any ~?*

vi·tal·ize /ˈvɑɪtḷɑɪz/ *vt* [VP6A] fill with vitality; put vigour into.

vit·amin /ˈvɪtəmɪn *US:* ˈvɑɪt-/ *n* [C] any of a number of organic substances which are present in certain food-stuffs and are essential to the health of man and other animals: *illnesses* (e g scurvy, rickets) *caused by ~ deficiency;* ˋ*~ tablets.*

vi·ti·ate /ˈvɪʃɪeɪt/ *vt* [VP6A] lower the quality of; weaken or destroy the force of: *~d blood; the ~d air of an overcrowded room. This admission ~s your argument/claim.*

vit·reous /ˈvɪtrɪəs/ *adj* of or like glass: *~ rocks,* hard and brittle: *~ enamel,* used instead of porcelain.

vit·rify /ˈvɪtrɪfɑɪ/ *vt, vi* (*pt, pp* -fied) [VP6A, 2A] change, be changed, into a glass-like substance.

vit·riol /ˈvɪtrɪəl/ *n* [U] sulphuric acid; any of the salts of sulphuric acid: *blue ~,* copper sulphate; (fig) sarcasm. **~ic** /ˈvɪtrɪˈɒlɪk/ *adj* (fig, of words, feelings) biting; full of invective: *a ~ic attack on the President; ~ic remarks.*

vit·uper·ate /vɪˈtjupəreɪt *US:* vɑɪˈtu-/ *vt* [VP6A] abuse in words; curse; revile. **vit·uper·at·ive**

/vɪˋtjupṛətɪv *US:* vɑɪˋtupəreɪtɪv/ *adj* abusive. **vit·uper·ation** /vɪˈtjupəˋreɪʃn *US:* vɑɪˈtu-/ *n* [U] abusive language; severe scolding.

viva /ˋvivə/ *n* ⇨ viva voce.

vi·vace /vɪˋvɑtʃeɪ/ *adv* (music) briskly.

vi·va·cious /vɪˋveɪʃəs/ *adj* lively; high-spirited; gay: *a ~ girl.* **~·ly** *adv* **vi·vac·ity** /vɪˋvæsətɪ/ *n* [U].

viva voce /ˈvɑɪvə ˋvəʊsɪ/ *adj, adv* oral(ly): *a ~ examination.* □ *n* ~ examination or test.

vivid /ˋvɪvɪd/ *adj* **1** (of colours, etc) intense; bright: *a flash of lightning; a ~ green hat.* **2** lively; active: *a ~ imagination.* **3** clear and distinct: *a ~ description of an event; have ~ recollections of a holiday in Italy.* **~·ly** *adv* **~·ness** *n*

vi·vipar·ous /vɪˋvɪpərəs *US:* vɑɪ-/ *adj* having offspring which develop within the mother's body (not from eggs).

vivi·sect /ˈvɪvɪˋsekt/ *vt* [VP6A] operate or experiment on (living animals) for scientific research. **vivi·sec·tion** /ˈvɪvɪˋsekʃn/ *n* [U] ~ing; [C] instance of this. **vivi·sec·tion·ist** /-ʃṇ-ɪst/ *n* person who ~s; person who considers vivisection justifiable.

vixen /ˋvɪksn/ *n* female fox; bad-tempered quarrelsome woman. **~·ish** /ˋvɪksṇ-ɪʃ/ *adj* scolding; bad-tempered.

viz /vɪz/ (Lat *videlicet,* usu read as *namely*) that is to say; namely.

vi·zier /vɪˋzɪə(r)/ *n* official of high rank in some Muslim countries, esp the old Turkish empire.

vo·cabu·lary /vəˋkæbjʊlərɪ *US:* -lerɪ/ *n* (*pl* -ries) **1** total number of words which (with rules for combining them) make up a language: *No dictionary could list the whole ~ of a language.* **2** [C,U] (range of) words known to, or used by, a person, in a trade profession, etc: *a writer with a large ~.* **3** [C] book containing a list of words; list of words used in a book, etc, usu with definitions or translations.

vo·cal /ˋvəʊkl/ *adj* of, for, with or using, the voice: *the ~ chords,* ⇨ chord(3); *the ~ organs,* the tongue, lips, etc; *~ music,* to be sung; *a ~ score,* musical score, e g of an opera, giving the vocal parts in full. *Anger made the shy girl ~,* helped her to express her feelings by speaking. **~ly** /ˋvəʊkḷɪ/ *adv* **~·ist** /ˋvəʊkḷ-ɪst/ *n* singer. ⇨ *instrumentalist* at instrumental. **~·ize** /-ɑɪz/ *vt* say or sing; voice(2).

vo·ca·tion /vəʊˋkeɪʃn/ *n* **1** (*sing* only) feeling that one is called to (and qualified for) a certain kind of work (esp social or religious): *The nursing of the sick, said Florence Nightingale, is a ~ as well as a profession.* **2** [U] special aptitude (*for*): *He has little or no ~ for teaching.* **3** [C] person's trade or profession. **~al** /-nl/ *adj* of or for a ~(3): *~al guidance,* advice on the choice of a ~.

voca·tive /ˋvokətɪv/ *n, adj* (word, case) used (e g in Lat, not in English) in addressing a person. In *Et tu, Brute* (= And you, Brutus), *Brute* is in the ~ case.

vo·cif·er·ate /vəˋsɪfəreɪt *US:* vəʊ-/ *vt,vi* [VP6A, 2A] say loudly or noisily; shout. **vo·cif·er·ation** /vəˈsɪfəˋreɪʃn *US:* vəʊ-/ *n* shouting; yelling. **vo·cif·er·ous** /vəˋsɪfərəs *US:* vəʊ-/ *adj* noisy; yelling: *a vociferous crowd.*

vodka /ˋvodkə/ *n* [U] strong Russian alcoholic drink distilled from rye and also other vegetable products.

vogue /vəʊg/ *n* **1** current fashion; sth currently being done or used: *Are small hats still the ~? The ~s of the 18th century seem amusing today.* **2** popularity; popular use or acceptance: *M's novels had a great ~ ten years ago, but are not read today.* ***be in/come into; be/go out of ~,*** be/become (un)fashionable, (un)popular. *When did the miniskirt come into/go out of ~?* ***all the ~,*** popular everywhere; the latest fashion.

voice /vɔɪs/ *n* **1** [U] sounds made when speaking or singing: *He is not in good ~,* not speaking or singing as well as usual. **2** [C] power of making such sounds: *He has lost his ~,* cannot speak or sing properly, e g because of a bad cold. **3** [C,U] sounds uttered by a person, esp considered in relation to their quality: *in a loud/soft/shrill/rough, etc ~. I did not recognize her ~. The choir boys have sweet ~s. They gave ~ to their indignation.* ***lift up one's ~,*** (old use) sing, speak. ***shout at the top of one's ~,*** shout as loudly as one can. ***with one ~,*** (liter) unanimously. **4** [U] ***have/demand a ~ in sth,*** a right to express an opinion on: *I have no ~ in the matter.* **5** [C] anything which may be compared or likened to the human ~ as expressing ideas, feelings, etc: *the ~ of Nature; the ~s of the night; the ~ of God,* conscience. **6** [U] (in phonetics) sound produced by vibration of the vocal cords, not with breath only, as for vowel sounds and the consonants /b, d, ð, z/, etc. **7** (gram) the contrast between *active* and *passive* as shown in the sentences: *The dog ate the meat* and *The meat was eaten by the dog.* □ *vt* [VP6A] **1** put into words: *The spokesman ~d the feelings of the crowd.* **2** utter (a sound) with ~(6): *~d sounds* (e g /d, v, ŋ/). **-voiced** *adj* (in compounds) having the kind of ~ indicated: *rough-~d.* **~·less** *adj* **1** having no ~; unable to utter words. **2** (of consonants) uttered without ~(5): *The sounds, /p, tʃ, f/ are ~less.*

void /vɔɪd/ *adj* **1** empty; vacant. **2** **~ *of,*** without: *a subject ~ of interest; a proposal ~ of reason.* **3** ***null and ~,*** (legal) without force; invalid: *The agreement, not having been signed, was null and ~.* □ *n* [C] space: *There was an aching ~ in his heart,* (fig) a feeling of sadness caused by the loss of someone he had loved. □ *vt* [VP6A] (legal) make ~(3).

voile /vɔɪl/ *n* [U] thin, light dress material.

vol·atile /ˋvolətɑɪl *US:* -tl/ *adj* **1** (of a liquid) that easily changes into gas or vapour. **2** (of a person, his disposition) lively; changing quickly or easily from one mood or interest to another. **vol·atil·ity** /ˈvoləˋtɪlətɪ/ *n*

vol·cano /volˋkeɪnəʊ/ *n* (*pl* -noes or -nos /-nəʊz/) hill or mountain with openings (⇨ crater) through which gases, lava, ashes, etc, come up from below the earth's crust (in *an active ~*), or may come up after an interval (in *a dormant ~*), or have long ceased to come up (in *an extinct ~*). **vol·canic** /volˋkænɪk/ *adj* of, from, like, a ~.

vole /vəʊl/ *n* rat-like animal: *a ˋfield-~,* one like a mouse; *a ˋwater-~,* large water-rat.

vo·li·tion /vəˋlɪʃn *US:* vəʊ-/ *n* [U] act, power, of using one's own will, of choosing, making a decision, etc: *do sth of one's own ~.* **~al** /-nl/ *adj*

vol·ley /ˋvolɪ/ *n* [C] **1** hurling or shooting of a number of missiles (stones, arrows, bullets, etc) together. **2** number of oaths, curses, questions, directed together, or in quick succession, at sb. **3** (tennis) stroke which returns the ball to the sender before it touches the ground. **ˈhalf-ˋ~,** return of the ball as soon as it touches the ground. **ˋ~-ball** *n* game in which players on each side of a high net try to keep a ball in motion by hitting it with their hands back and forth over the net without letting it touch the ground. □ *vt, vi* **1** [VP2A,C] (of guns) sound together: *The guns ~ed on all sides.* **2** [VP6A,2A] return a tennis-ball across the net before it touches the ground.

volt /vəʊlt/ *n* [C] (abbr **v**) unit of electrical force; force that would carry one ampere of current against one ohm resistance. **~-age** /ˋvəʊltɪdʒ/ *n* electrical force measured in ~s.

volte-face /ˈvolt ˋfɑs/ *n* complete change; act of turning round to the opposite way of standing or to the opposite way of thinking: *make a complete ~.*

vol·uble /ˋvoljʊbl/ *adj* talking, able to talk, very quickly and easily; (of speech) fluent. **vol·ubly** /-jʊblɪ/ *adv* **vol·ubil·ity** /ˈvoljʊˋbɪlətɪ/ *n*

vol·ume /ˋvoljum *US:* -jəm/ *n* **1** book, esp one of a set of books; number of sheets, papers, periodicals, etc bound together: *an encyclopedia in 20 ~s.* ***speak ~s for,*** supply strong evidence of: *His donations to charity speak ~s for his generosity.* **2** [U] amount of space (expressed in cubic metres, etc) occupied by a substance, liquid or gas; cubic contents of a container, etc: *the ~ of a cask; the ~ of wine in a cask.* **3** [C] large mass, amount or quantity: *the ~ of business/work, etc;* (esp *pl*) rounded masses of steam or smoke: *V~s of black smoke belched out from the chimneys.* **4** [U] (of sound) power; sonority: *a voice of great ~. Your radio has a ~ control.*

vol·umi·nous /vəˋlumɪnəs/ *adj* **1** (of writing) great in quantity: *a ~ work/history;* (of an author) producing many books. **2** occupying much space: *a ~ correspondence; ~ skirts.*

vol·un·tary /ˋvoləntrɪ *US:* -terɪ/ *adj* **1** doing or ready to do things, willingly, without being compelled; (sth) done thus: *~ work/service; a ~ statement/confession; ~ workers/helpers.* **2** carried on, supported by, ~ work and gifts: *a ˋ~ school,* one supported by ~ contributions, not by the State, etc. **3** (of bodily, muscular, movements) controlled by the will (opp of *involuntary*). □ *n* [C] (*pl* **-ries**) organ solo, esp one played not as part of a church service. **vol·un·tar·ily** /ˋvoləntrḷɪ *US:* ˈvolənˋterḷɪ/ *adv*

vol·un·teer /ˈvolənˋtɪə(r)/ *n* **1** person who offers to do sth, esp sth unpleasant or dangerous. **2** soldier who is not conscripted: (attrib) *a ~ corps.* □ *vt, vi* [VP6A,7A,2A,3A] ***~ sth/to do sth/for sth,*** offer voluntarily; come forward as a ~: *He ~ed some information/~ed to get some information. How many of them ~ed? He ~ed for the campaign.*

vol·up·tu·ary /vəˋlʌptʃʊərɪ *US:* -ʊerɪ/ *n* person who gives himself up to luxury and sensual pleasures.

vo·lup·tu·ous /vəˋlʌptʃʊəs/ *adj* of, for, arousing, given up to, sensuous or sensual pleasures: *~ music/beauty/thoughts/sensations.* **~·ly** *adv* **~-ness** *n*

vo·lute /vəˋljut *US:* vəˋlut/ *n* spiral scroll, esp as on Ionic and Corinthian capitals. ⇨ the illus at column. **vo·luted** *adj* decorated with, having, ~s: *a ~d sea-shell.*

vomit /ˋvomɪt/ *vt, vi* **1** [VP6A,15B,2A] bring back from the stomach through the mouth; throw up from the mouth: *He ~ed everything he had eaten. He was ~ing blood. He began to ~.* **2** [VP6A] send out in large quantities: *factory chimneys ~ing smoke.* □ *n* [U] food that has been ~ed.

voo·doo /ˋvudu/ *n* [U] debased form of religion, made up of sorcery and witchcraft, practised by some Negroes in the West Indies, esp Haiti. **~-ism** /-ɪzm/ *n*

vo·racious /vəˋreɪʃəs/ *adj* very hungry or greedy; desiring much: *a ~ appetite; a ~ reader,* one who devours many books. **~·ly** *adv* in a ~ manner: *He ate his food ~ly.* **vo·racity** /vəˋræsətɪ/ *n*

vor·tex /ˋvɔteks/ *n* (*pl* **-texes** or **vortices** /-tɪsiz/) **1** mass of whirling fluid or wind, esp a whirlpool. **2** (fig) whirl of activity; system, pursuit, viewed as sth that tends to absorb things, engross those who engage in it: *be drawn into the ~ of politics/war; the ~ of social life/pleasure.*

vo·tary /ˋvəʊtərɪ/ *n* (*pl* **-ries**) person who gives up his time and energy to sth, esp to religious work and service: *Of the two leaders, one claimed to be a ~ of peace and the other was known to be a ~ of golf.*

vote /vəʊt/ *n* **1** (right to give an) expression of opinion or will by persons for or against sb or sth, esp by ballot or by putting up of hands: *give one's ~ to the more handsome candidate. Do women have the ~* (i e the franchise) *in your country? I'm going to the polling-booth to record/cast my ~. Mr X proposed a ~ of thanks to the principal speaker,* asked the audience to show, by clapping their hands, that they thanked him. *The Government received a ~ of confidence,* a majority of ~s was in its favour, to show confidence in its policies, etc. ***put sth to the ~,*** decide it by asking for ~s. **2** total numbers of ~s (to be) given (e g at a political election): *Will the Labour ~ increase or decrease at the next election?* **3** money granted, by ~s, for a certain purpose: *the Army ~.* □ *vi, vt* **1** [VP3A] ***~ for/against sb/sth,*** support/oppose by voting. ***~ on sth,*** express an opinion on sth by voting. **2** [VP6A,12B,13B] ***~ sb/sth (for sth),*** grant money (to sb): *~ a sum of money for Education. Parliament ~d Charles I £100 000 for the Army.* **3** [VP15B] ***~ sth down,*** defeat by ~s: *~ down* (= reject) *a proposal.* ***~ sth through,*** support, approve: *~ a Bill through.* **4** [VP25] (colloq) declare, by general opinion: *The new teacher was ~d a fine fellow,* The children gave this as their opinion. **5** [VP9] suggest, propose: *I ~ (that) we avoid him in future.* **voter** *n* person who ~s; person who has the right to ~. **~-less** *adj* having no ~; not having the right to ~.

vo·tive /ˋvəʊtɪv/ *adj* offered or consecrated in connection with the fulfilment of a vow: *There were numerous ~ tablets on the walls of the church.*

vouch /vaʊtʃ/ *vi* ***~ for sb/sth,*** be responsible for, express one's confidence in (a person, his honesty, the truth of a statement, etc): *I am ready to ~ for him/for the truth of his story/for his ability to pay.*

voucher /ˋvaʊtʃə(r)/ *n* receipt or document showing payment of money, correctness of accounts, etc: *hotel/meal ~s,* (e g as bought from travel agencies) showing that payment has been made in advance. **ˋgift ~,** supplied with some articles (e g petrol, cigarettes), to be exchanged for 'free' gifts. **ˋluncheon ~,** one supplied by some employers, exchangeable for all or part of a meal (at restaurants which have agreed to accept them).

vouch·safe /vaʊtʃˋseɪf/ *vt* [VP6A,7A,12C] (formal) be kind enough to give (sth), *to do* (sth): *He ~d (me) no reply. He ~d to help.*

vow /vaʊ/ *n* solemn promise or undertaking: *ˋmarriage vows; a vow of chastity; under a vow of celibacy/silence,* having solemnly undertaken not to marry/speak about sth; *break a vow; perform a vow,* do what one promised. □ *vt* **1** [VP6A,7A,9] make a vow; promise or declare solemnly: *He vowed to avenge the insult/that he would avenge the insult. She vowed never to speak to him again. They were forced to vow obedience.* **2** [VP9] (old use, 17th to 18th c) declare: *I vow, child, you are vastly handsome!*

vowel /ˋvaʊḷ/ *n* vocal sound made without audible stopping of the breath; letter or symbol used to represent such a sound (e g the letters *a, e, i, o, u;* the symbols /i, ɪ, e, æ, ɑ, o, ɔ, ʊ, u, ʌ, ɜ, ə/).

vox /voks/ *n* (Lat) voice. **vox populi** /ˈvoks ˋpopjʊlaɪ/, the voice of the people; public opinion.

voy·age /ˋvɔɪdʒ/ *n* journey by water, esp a long one in a ship: *a ~ from London to Australia; make/go on/send sb on a ~; on the ~ out/home; on the outward/homeward ~.* □ *vi* [VP2A,C] go on a ~: *~ through the South Seas.* **voy·ager** /ˋvɔɪədʒə(r)/ *n* person who makes a ~ (esp of those who, in former times, explored unknown seas).

vo·yeur /vwɑˋjɜ(r)/ *n* person who gets pleasure from looking at sexual objects or the sexual activities of others, esp in secret.

vul·can·ite /ˋvʌlkənɑɪt/ *n* [U] hard plastic made from rubber and sulphur. **vul·can·ize** /ˋvʌlkənɑɪz/ *vt* [VP6A] treat (rubber) with sulphur at great heat to harden it. **vul·can·iz·ation** /ˈvʌlkənɑɪˋzeɪʃn *US:* -nɪˋz-/ *n*

vul·gar /ˋvʌlgə(r)/ *adj* **1** ill mannered; in bad taste: *~ language/behaviour/ideas; a ~ person; a ~ display of wealth.* **2** in common use; generally prevalent: *~ errors/superstitions.* **a ~ fraction,** one written in the usual way (e g ¾), contrasted with a decimal fraction. **the ~ herd,** (contemptuous) the masses of ordinary people. **the ~ tongue,** the language commonly spoken by the people (formerly, in England, English contrasted with Latin). **~·ly** *adv* **vul·garian** /vʌlˋgeərɪən/ *n* ~ person, esp a rich person whose manners and tastes are bad. **~·ism** /ˋvʌlgərɪzm/ *n* [C] word, phrase, expression, etc used only by ignorant persons; [U] ~ behaviour. **~·ity** /vʌlˋgærətɪ/ *n* (*pl* ,-ties) [U] ~ behaviour; (*pl*) ~ acts, utterances, etc. **~·ize** /ˋvʌlgərɑɪz/ *vt* [VP6A] make ~. **~·iz·ation** /ˈvʌlgərɑɪˋzeɪʃn *US:* -rɪˋz-/ *n* [U].

Vul·gate /ˋvʌlgeɪt/ *n* **the V~,** Latin version of the Bible made in the 4th c.

vul·ner·able /ˋvʌlnṛəbl/ *adj* that is liable to be damaged; not protected against attack: *find sb's ~ spot; a position ~ to attack; people who are ~ to criticism.* **vul·ner·abil·ity** /ˈvʌlnṛəˋbɪlətɪ/ *n*

vul·pine /ˋvʌlpɑɪn/ *adj* of, like, a fox; crafty.

vul·ture /ˋvʌltʃə(r)/ *n* **1** kinds of large bird, usu with head and neck almost bare of feathers, that lives on the flesh of dead animals. ⇨ the illus at prey. **2** greedy person who profits from the misfortunes of others.

vulva /ˋvʌlvə/ *n* opening of the female genitals.

vy·ing /ˋvɑɪɪŋ/ ⇨ vie.

Ww

W, w /ˋdʌbḷju/ (*pl* **W's, w's**) the 23rd letter of the English alphabet.

wad /wod/ *n* **1** lump of soft material for keeping things apart or in place, or to stop up a hole (e g felt used to keep powder and shot in position in an old-fashioned gun). **2** collection of documents or banknotes folded or rolled together. □ *vt* (-dd-) stuff with a wad; hold in place with a wad; line (a garment, etc) with soft material (usu cotton or wool): *a wadded jacket/dressing-gown/quilt.* **wad·ding** /ˋwodɪŋ/ *n* [U] soft material, esp raw cotton or felt, used for packing, lining things, etc.

waddle /ˋwodl/ *vi* [VP2A,C] walk with slow steps and a sideways roll, as a duck does: *The stout old man ~d across the road.* □ *n* (*sing* only) this kind of walk.

wade /weɪd/ *vi,vt* [VP2A,C,6A] **1** walk with an effort (through water, mud or anything that makes progress difficult); walk across (sth) in this way: *He ~d through the weeds on the bank and then into and across the stream. Can we ~ the brook,* cross it by wading? *The boy ~d through the dull book.* **ˋwading bird,** long-legged water-bird that ~s (opp to web-footed birds that swim). **2 ~ in,** make a vigorous attack. **~ into sth,** attack sth vigorously. **wader** *n* **1** wading bird (⇨ above). **2** (*pl*) waterproof boots reaching the hips, used by anglers when wading in streams.

wadi /ˋwodɪ/ *n* (*pl* -dis) (in the Middle East, Arabia, northern Africa) rocky watercourse dry except after a heavy fall of rain.

wa·fer /ˋweɪfə(r)/ *n* **1** thin flat biscuit (e g as eaten with ice-cream). **2** small round piece of bread used in Holy Communion. **3** piece of paper (formerly a round flat piece of paste) used for fastening papers or holding them together or instead of a seal.

waffle[1] /ˋwofl/ *n* small cake made of batter baked in a special kind of griddle (*a ˋ~-iron*) with two parts hinged together.

waffle[2] /ˋwofl/ *vi* [VP2A,C] (GB colloq) talk vaguely, unnecessarily, and without much result: *How that man does ~ on! What's she waffling about now?* □ *n* [U] utterance which (even when it sounds impressive) means little or nothing.

waft /woft *US:* wæft/ *vt* [VP6A] carry lightly and smoothly through the air or over water: *The scent of the flowers was ~ed to us by the breeze.* □ *n* [C] **1** breath of air, scent, etc. **2** waving movement.

wag[1] /wæg/ *vt,vi* (-gg-) [VP6A,2A,C] (cause to) move from side to side or up and down: *The dog wagged its tail. The dog's tail wagged. Don't wag your finger at me,* show disapproval in this way. *The news set tongues/chins/beards wagging,* caused people to talk (esp of sth scandalous). **ˋwag·tail** *n* kinds of small bird with a long tail that wags constantly when the bird is standing. □ *n* wagging movement: *with a wag of the tail.*

wag[2] /wæg/ *n* merry person, full of amusing sayings and fond of practical jokes. **wag·gery** /ˈwægərɪ/ *n* (*pl* **-ries**) [U] behaviour or talk or a wag; (*pl*) acts, remarks, etc of a wag. **wag·gish** /ˈwægɪʃ/ *adj* of or like a wag; done in a joking way: *waggish tricks/remarks.* **wag·gish·ly** *adv* **wag·gish·ness** *n*

wage[1] /weɪdʒ/ *n* **1** (now usu *pl* except in certain phrases and when attrib) payment made or received (usu weekly) for work or services: *His ~s are £20 a week. We expect a fair day's ~ for a fair day's work. He takes his ~s/his ˈ~-packet home to his wife every Friday. The postal workers have asked for a ˈ~ increase/rise of £5 a week.* ⇨ fee(1), pay[1], salary. **living ~,** one which allows a man to live without fear of hunger and hardship. **minimum ~,** guaranteed basic level for ~s in an industry or country. **ˈ~-earner** *n* person who works for ~s (contrasted with the salaried classes). **ˈ~-freeze,** ⇨ freeze, *n*(2). **2** (old use; *pl* in form with *sing v*) reward or requital: *The ~s of sin is death.*

wage[2] /weɪdʒ/ *vt* [VP6A] carry on, engage in (*war, a campaign*).

wa·ger /ˈweɪdʒə(r)/ *vt,vi* [VP6A,11,14,12C,2A] bet: *~ 50p on a horse. I'm ready to ~ you a pound that....* □ *n* bet: *lay/make a ~; take up* (= accept) *a ~.*

waggle /ˈwægl/ *vt,vi* = wag[1].

wag·gon (US usu **wagon**) /ˈwægən/ *n* **1** four-wheeled vehicle for carrying goods, pulled by horses or oxen. ⇨ cart. ***on the (ˈwater) ~,*** (colloq) not drinking alcoholic liquors. **2** (US = *freight car*) open railway truck (e g for coal). **3** **ˈtea-~** *n* name sometimes used for *tea-trolley.* **ˈstation-~** *n* = estate-car. **~er** *n* man in charge of a ~ and its horses. **~·ette** /ˌwægəˈnet/ *n* (dated) four-wheeled horse-drawn pleasure vehicle with side seats facing each other.

wa·gon-lit /ˈvægõ ˈli *US:* ˈvægõ/ *n* (*pl* **wagons-lit**) sleeping-car (as on European railways).

wag·tail /ˈwægteɪl/ ⇨ wag[1].

waif /weɪf/ *n* homeless person, esp a child: *~s and strays,* homeless and abandoned children.

wail /weɪl/ *vi,vt* [VP2A,B,C,6A] **1** cry or complain in a loud, usu shrill, voice: *~ (over) one's misfortunes; an ambulance racing through the streets with sirens ~ing. She was ~ing for her lost child.* **2** (of the wind) make sounds like a person ~ing. □ *n* ~ing cry; lament: *the ~s of a newborn child.*

wain /weɪn/ *n* (old use, or poet) large farm wagon. **Charles's W~,** the constellation of stars also called the Plough and the Great Bear.

wain·scot /ˈweɪnskət/ *n* wooden panelling (usu on the lower half of the walls of a room). **~ed** *adj* lined with ~: *a ~ed room.*

waist /weɪst/ *n* **1** part of the body between the ribs and the hips; ⇨ the illus at trunk: *wear a sash round the ~; measure 30 inches round the ~. The workmen were stripped to the ~,* were wearing nothing above the ~. *That man has no ~,* is so stout that he has no narrowing at the ~ as in a normal figure. **ˈ~-band** *n* band on a garment (e g a skirt) fitting round the ~. **ˌ~-ˈdeep** *adj, adv* up to the ~: *~-deep in the water; wade ~-deep into a stream.* **ˌ~-ˈhigh** *adj, adv* high enough to reach the ~: *The wheat was ~-high.* **ˈ~-line** *n* line round the body at the smallest part of the ~: *a girl with a neat ~-line.* **2** that part of a garment that goes round the ~; (US *ˈshirt-~*) garment, or part of a garment, covering the body from the shoulders to the ~. **3** middle and narrow part: *the ~ of a ship,* between the forecastle and quarterdeck; *the ~ of a violin/an hour-glass.* **~·coat** /ˈweɪskəʊt *US:* ˈweskət/ *n* close-fitting sleeveless garment worn under a coat or jacket, buttoned down the front (called *vest* by tailors, and in the US).

wait[1] /weɪt/ *n* **1** act or time of waiting: *We had a long ~ for the bus. I don't like these long ~s.* **2** [U] ***lie in ~ for,*** (less usu) ***lay ~ for,*** be in hiding in order to attack, etc: *The highwayman lay in ~ for the stage-coach.* **3** (*pl*) **the ~s,** persons who go from house to house singing carols at Christmas.

wait[2] /weɪt/ *vi,vt* **1** [VP2A,B,C,3A,4A] ***~ (for sb/sth),*** stay where one is, delay acting, until sb or sth comes or until sth happens: *Please ~ a minute. W~ for me, please. How long have you been ~ing? We are ~ing for the rain to stop. We are ~ing for better weather. We ~ed* (in order) *to see what would happen. They say that everything comes to those who ~.* ***keep sb ~ing,*** fail to meet him or be ready at the appointed time: *His wife never keeps him ~ing.* ***~ up (for sb),*** stay up, not go to bed. **No ~ing,** warning (indicated by the sign ⊘) that motor-vehicles must not stop at the side of the roadway. **2** [VP6A] (= *await*) ~ for; ~ and watch for: *He is ~ing his opportunity. He always expects me to ~ his convenience,* until it is convenient for him (to do sth). *You must ~ your turn,* ~ until it is your turn. **3** [VP6A,14] defer, postpone (a meal): *Don't ~ dinner for me.* **4** [VP3A] ***~ (up)on sb,*** **(a)** act as a servant to, fetch and carry things for. ***~ on sb hand and foot,*** attend to his every need: *A Japanese wife was formerly expected to ~ upon her husband hand and foot.* **(b)** (old use) pay a visit to: *Our commercial agent will ~ upon you next Monday.* **5** [VP3A] ***~ at/on,*** act as a servant at table, serving food, clearing away dishes, etc: *~ at table* (US = *~ on table*). **6** **ˈ~·ing list,** list of persons who cannot be served, treated, etc now, but who will be served, etc later, if possible: *put sb on a ~ing-list for theatre tickets/an appointment, etc.* **ˈ~·ing-maid** *n* (old use) woman servant ~ing on her mistress. **ˈ~·ing-room** *n* room in a railway-station, etc used by people who are ~ing for trains; room (e g in a doctor's or dentist's house or office) where people ~ until they can be attended to. **~er** *n* man who ~s at table in a restaurant, hotel dining-room, etc. **~·ress** /ˈweɪtrəs/ *n* woman ~er.

waive /weɪv/ *vt* [VP6A] (say that one will) not insist on (a right or claim): *~ a privilege/the age-limit.* **waiver** /ˈweɪvə(r)/ *n* (legal) (written statement) waiving (a right, etc): *sign a waiver of claims against sb.*

wake[1] /weɪk/ *vi,vt* (*pt* **woke** /wəʊk/ or **~d,** *pp* **~d, woke,** or **woken** /ˈwəʊkən/) **1** [VP2A,C,4B] ***~ (up),*** stop sleeping: *What time do you usually ~ (up)? I woke early. Has the baby ~d/woken yet? He woke up with a start. He woke to find himself in prison.* **2** [VP6A,15B] ***~ sb (up),*** cause to stop sleeping: *Don't ~ the baby. The noise woke me (up). They were making enough noise to ~ the dead.* **3** [VP6A,15B] ***~ sb (up),*** stir up; rouse from inactivity, inattention, etc: *He needs someone to ~ him up,* stir him from his sloth, stir him to activity. *The incident ~d memories of his schooldays.* **4** [VP6A] disturb with noise; cause to re-echo: ~ *echoes in a mountain valley.* **wak·ing** *adj* being awake: *in his waking hours,* while awake; *waking or sleeping,* while awake or asleep. **waken** /ˈweɪkən/ *vt,vi* [VP6A,2A] (cause to) ~. **~·ful** /-fl/ *adj* unable to sleep; with little sleep: *pass a ~ful night.*

wake[2] /weɪk/ *n* **1** (usu *pl;* often **ˋW~s Week**) annual holiday in N England, esp in the manufacturing towns of Lancashire. **2** (in Ireland) all-night watch by a corpse before burial, with lamentations and drinking of alcoholic liquor.

wake[3] /weɪk/ *n* track left by a ship on smooth water, e g as made by propellers. ***in the ~ of,*** after; following: *Traders came in the ~ of the explorers.*

wale /weɪl/ *n* alternative spelling (esp US) of **weal**[2] or **welt**.

walk[1] /wɔk/ *n* [C] **1** journey on foot, esp for pleasure or exercise: *go for a ~; have a pleasant ~ across the fields. The station is a short ~/ten minutes' ~ from my house.* **2** manner or style of walking: *His horse slowed to a ~,* i e after trotting or galloping. *After running for two miles he dropped into a ~,* began to walk. *I recognized him at once by his ~,* his way of walking. **3** path or route for walking: *my favourite ~s in the neighbourhood.* **4** ***~ of life,*** calling, profession, occupation: *They interviewed people from all ~s of life.*

walk[2] /wɔk/ *vi,vt* **1** [VP2A,B,C] (of persons) move by putting forward each foot in turn, not having both feet off the ground at once, ⇨ **run**; (of animals) move at the slowest pace, ⇨ **trot, gallop**: *We ~ed five miles. Shall we ride or ~? How old are babies when they learn to ~? He was ~ing up and down the station platform.* **ˋ~-about** *n* **1** (Australian sl, of aborigines in the desert) journey. **2** (recent use) occasion when a celebrity ~s round meeting people informally. ***~ away from,*** beat easily in a contest: *Smith ~ed away from all his competitors,* beat them easily. Hence, **ˋ~·away** *n* easily won contest. (⇨ ~over below). ***~ away with sth,*** win sth easily: *Newcombe ~ed away with the match.* ***~ off with sth,*** (colloq) carry off; take (either on purpose or unintentionally): *Someone has ~ed off with my umbrella.* ***~ into,*** (sl) **(a)** eat heartily of: *~ into a meat-pie.* **(b)** abuse; scold. **(c)** (colloq) meet with through inattention: *He just ~ed into the ambush.* ***~ on,*** play a non-speaking part on the stage: (attrib) *a* ˈ~-ˋ*on part.* ***~ out,*** (colloq) go on strike: *The men in this factory ~ed out yesterday.* Hence, **ˋ~-out** *n* (workers') strike. ***~ out on sb,*** (sl) leave him (at a time when he is expecting help, etc). ***~ out with sb,*** (dated colloq) court; have as a sweetheart: *The cook is ~ing out with one of the tradesmen.* **ˋ~-over** *n* easy victory; contest in which there is little or no opposition: *The race was a ~-over for Jones.* ***~ up,*** **(a)** invitation to enter (e g as given by men outside a circus). **(b)** ~ along: *as I was ~ing up Oxford Street.* **(c)** ~ upstairs. Hence, *a ˋ~-up flat,* one in a building without a lift. **(d)** approach: *A stranger ~ed up to me and asked me the time.* **2** [VP6A,15A,B] cause to ~: *Horses should be ~ed for a while after a race. He ~ed his horse up the hill. He put his arm round me and ~ed me off.* ***~ sb off his feet/legs,*** tire him out by making him ~ far. **3** [VP6A] go over on foot: *I have ~ed this district for miles round.* **4** (with various *nn*: *~ the boards,* be an actor; *~ the wards,* be a medical student; *~ the plank,* (of a person captured by pirates in former times) be compelled to ~ blindfolded into the sea along a plank laid over the ship's side; *~ the streets,* (formerly) be a prostitute (*a ˋstreet-~er*) **~er** *n* person who ~s, esp for exercise or enjoyment. **~·ing** *n* (in compounds) *ˋ~ing-shoes* strong ones for ~ing in; *ˋ~ing-stick,* stick used in, or carried while, ~ing; *ˋ~ing-tour,* holiday spent ~ing from place to place.

walkie-talkie /ˈwɔkɪ ˋtɔkɪ/ *n* (colloq) portable two-way radio set.

wall /wɔl/ *n* **1** continuous, usu vertical, solid structure of stone, brick, concrete, wood, etc forming one of the sides of a building or room, or used to enclose, divide or protect sth (including land): *The castle ~s are very thick. Hang the picture on that ~. Some old towns have ~s right round them. Dry-stone ~s* (i e of stones not fixed in mortar) *extend across the moors in some parts of England. Fruit trees are often trained against garden ~s for protection and warmth.* ***with one's back to the ~,*** in a position where retreat or escape is impossible; at bay. ***be/go up the ~,*** (sl) be/become furious, distracted. ***bang/run one's head against a (brick) ~,*** attempt to do sth that is clearly impossible. ***see through a brick ~,*** have wonderful vision or insight. **2** (fig) sth suggesting or resembling a ~: *a ~ of fire; a mountain ~; the ~s of the chest,* the enclosing tissue and ribs; *the abdominal ~.* **3** side (contrasted with the centre) of the street: (chiefly fig) ***go to the ~,*** be pushed aside as weak or helpless, get the worst of it in competition. ***push/drive sb to the ~.*** **4** (compounds) **ˋ~-flower** *n* **(a)** common garden plant with (usu) brownish-red or orange sweet-smelling flowers. **(b)** woman who sits out dances because of a lack of partners. **ˋ~-painting** *n* [C] painting on a ~, esp a fresco. **ˋ~·paper** *n* [U] paper, usu with a coloured design, for covering the ~s of rooms. □ *vt* **1** (usu *pp*) surround with a ~ or ~s: *~ed cities; a ~ed garden.* **2** [VP15B] ***~ sth up/off,*** fill or close up with bricks, etc: *~ up a window/opening; ~ off part of a room.*

wal·laby /ˋwɔləbɪ/ *n* (*pl* **-bies**) sorts of small kangaroo.

wal·lah, walla /ˋwɔlə/ *n* (formerly, in India) person employed about or concerned with sth: *ˋbox-~,* pedlar; *ˋpunkah-~,* servant who worked a punkah.

wal·let /ˋwɔlɪt/ *n* **1** folding pocket-case, usu leather, for papers, banknotes, etc. **2** (archaic) bag (used by pilgrims, beggars, etc) for carrying personal necessaries, food, etc on a journey.

wall-eyed /ˈwɔl ˋaɪd/ *adj* having eyes that show an abnormal amount of white (e g as caused by a squint).

wal·lop /ˋwɔləp/ *vt* (sl or hum) beat severely; hit hard. □ *n* **1** heavy blow; crash: *Down he went with a ~!* **2** (sl) beer. **~·ing** *adj* big; thumping: *What a ~ing lie!* □ *n* defeat: *Our football team got a ~ing.*

wal·low /ˋwɔləʊ/ *vi* [VP2A,C] roll about (in mud, dirty water, etc): *pigs ~ing in the mire;* (fig) take gross delight in (sth sensual): *~ing in sensual pleasures.* ***be ~ing in money,*** (colloq) be very rich. □ *n* place to which animals (e g buffaloes) go regularly to ~.

Wall Street /ˋwɔl strit/ *n* (used for) the American money-market: *Shares rose sharply on ~*

yesterday; the ~crash, (1929).

wal·nut /ˈwɔlnʌt/ *n* [C] (tree producing a) nut with an edible kernel in a hard shell; [U] the wood of this tree, used (esp as a veneer) for making furniture.

wal·rus /ˈwɔlrəs/ *n* large sea-animal of the arctic regions with two long tusks, ⇨ the illus at **sea**: *a ~ moustache,* (colloq) one of which the ends come downwards like the tusks of a ~.

waltz /wɔls *US:* wɔlts/ *n* [C] (music in ¾ time for a) ballroom dance. □ *vi, vt* **1** [VP2A,C] dance a ~: *She ~es divinely.* **~ *in/out/into/out of,*** dance (in, out, etc) gaily: *She ~ed into the room and out again.* **2** [VP15A] cause to ~: *He ~ed her round the room.*

wam·pum /ˈwɔmpəm/ *n* [U] shells threaded like beads and used as ornaments by N American Indians (and formerly used as money).

wan /wɔn/ *adj* (-nn-) **1** (of a person, his looks, etc) looking ill, sad, tired, anxious: *a wan smile.* **2** (of light, the sky) pale; not bright. **wan·ly** *adv* **wan·ness** /ˈwɔnnəs/ *n*

wand /wɔnd/ *n* **1** slender stick or rod as used by a conjurer, fairy or magician; baton(2). **2** rod or staff carried as a symbol of authority (e g by an usher, steward or sheriff on ceremonial occasions).

wan·der /ˈwɔndə(r)/ *vi, vt* **1** [VP2A,B,C,6A] go from place to place without any special purpose or destination: *~ over the countryside; ~ up and down the road aimlessly; ~ (through/over) the world. Harry ~ed in to see me this morning,* paid me a casual visit. **2** [VP2A,C] leave the right path or direction: *Some of the sheep have ~ed away,* are lost. *We ~ed (for) miles and miles in the mist.* **3** [VP2A,C] be absent-minded; allow the thoughts to go from subject to subject: *Don't ~ from the subject/point. His mind is ~ing. Don't let your thoughts ~. His mind/thoughts ~ed back to his college days.* **~er** *n* person or animal that ~s. **~·ings** *n pl* **1** long travels; journeys: *tell the story of one's ~ings.* **2** confused speech during illness (esp high fever).

wan·der·lust /ˈwɔndəlʌst/ [U] strong desire to travel.

wane /weɪn/ *vi* [VP2A] **1** (of the moon) show a decreasing bright area after full moon. ⇨ **wax**²**(1)**. **2** become less or weaker: *His strength/influence/reputation is waning.* □ *n* esp ***on the ~,*** process of waning.

wangle /ˈwæŋgl/ *vt* [VP6A] (sl) get, arrange sth, by using improper influence, by trickery, plausible persuasion, etc: *~ an extra week's holiday.* □ *n* act of wangling: *get sth by a ~.*

want¹ /wɔnt/ *n* **1** [U] lack; scarcity; state of being absent: *The earthquake victims are suffering for ~ of food and medical supplies. The plants died from ~ of water. Your work shows ~ of thought/care.* **2** [U] need; absence of some necessary thing: *The house is in ~ of repair. We may one day be in ~,* very poor. **3** [C] (usu *pl*) desire for sth as necessary to life, happiness, etc; thing to be desired: *He is a man of few ~s. We can supply all your ~s. The book, said the reviewer, using an old cliché, meets a long-felt ~,* was sth that had been needed for a long time.

want² /wɔnt/ *vt, vi* **1** require; be in need of; lack: *W~ed, cook for small family. Will you ~ anything more, Sir? Tell the office-boy that I ~ him,* tell him to come to me. *You won't be ~ed* (= Your services will not be required) *this afternoon. These plants are drooping—they ~ water. That man ~s a wife to look after him,* needs to marry a woman who will look after him. *I don't ~* (= I object to having) *women meddling in my affairs. Do you ~* (= Would you like to have) *this box opened?* **ˈ~-ad** *n* (colloq) (usu short) advertisement (in a newspaper, etc) wanted, for a job, etc. **2** [VP6A,7A,17] wish for; have a desire for (⇨ **wish**, *v*(7); *want* is used for sth which it is possible to obtain; *wish for* is used for sth unlikely to be obtained, or obtainable only in exceptional circumstances): *She ~s a holiday. She ~s to go to Italy. She ~s me to go with her. He is ~ed by the police,* i e because he is suspected of wrongdoing. *I don't ~ there to be any misunderstanding.* **3** [VP6A,E,7A] need, ought (as in the notes to the examples): *Your hair ~s cutting,* needs to be cut. *You ~* (= ought) *to see your solicitors about that problem. What that naughty boy ~s* (= needs to be given) *is a good beating. That sort of thing ~s some doing,* (colloq) needs effort, skill, etc (because it is not an easy matter). **4** [VP2A] (progressive tenses only) (with non-human subject) ***be ~ing,*** be missing or lacking: *A few pages of this book are ~ing. The infinitive of the verb 'must' is ~ing.* ***be ~ing (in sth),*** (with human subject): *He's ~ing in courtesy,* is impolite. ***be found ~ing***: *He was put to the test and found ~ing,* inadequate. *He/It was tried and found (to be) ~ing,* unequal to a standard or to a need. **5** [VP6A] (impers) fall short by: *It ~s one inch of the regulation length. It ~s half an hour to the appointed time.* **6** [VP2A,3A] be in want (⇨ **want**¹**(3)**): *We mustn't let our soldiers ~* (= suffer poverty or hardship) *in their old age.* **~ *for nothing,*** have all one needs. **~·ing** *prep* without; in the absence of: *W~ing mutual trust, friendship is impossible.*

wan·ton /ˈwɔntən/ *adj* **1** playful; irresponsible; capricious: *~ breeze; in a ~ mood.* **2** unchecked; luxuriant; wild: *a ~ growth* (of weeds, etc); *in ~ profusion.* **3** wilful; serving no useful purpose: *~ destruction/damage; a ~ insult.* **4** immoral; unchaste: *a ~ woman;* lewd, licentious: *~ thoughts.* □ *n* unchaste woman. □ *vi* [VP2A,C] be ~ in behaviour: *the wind ~ing with the leaves.* **~·ly** *adv* **~·ness** *n*

war /wɔ(r)/ *n* **1** [C,U] (state created by) the use of armed forces between countries or (ˈ*civil war*) rival groups in a nation: *We have had two world wars in this century.* ***at war,*** in a state of war: *They were at war with three great countries.* ***carry the war into the enemy's camp,*** attack (instead of being satisfied to defend). ***declare war (on),*** announce that a state of war exists (with another state). ***go to war (against),*** start fighting. ***have been in the wars,*** (used colloq or hum) have suffered injury (e g as the result of an accident). ***make*** (rhet)***/wage war on,*** engage in fighting against. **2** (compounds) **ˈwar-baby** *n* (*pl* **-babies**) illegitimate child with a soldier as father and attributable to conditions during a war. **ˈwar-bride** *n* bride of a soldier during a war. **ˈwar-cloud(s)** *n* state of affairs that seems to threaten war. **ˈwar-cry** *n* (*pl* **-cries**) word or cry shouted as a signal in battle; catch-word (e g used by a political party) in any kind of contest. **ˈwar-dance** *n* one by tribal warriors before going into battle, to celebrate a victory, or (in peace) to represent fighting. **ˈwar-god** *n* god (e g Mars) worshipped as giving victory in war. **ˋwar·head** *n* (of a torpedo, shell, etc) explosive head (contrasted with a dummy charge as used in practice, etc). **ˋwar-horse** *n* (rhet) horse used in battle; charger. **ˋwar-lord** *n* (rhet) great military leader, esp a Chinese general in the period of civil wars, early 20th c. **ˋwar·monger** /-mʌŋgə(r)/ *n* person who advocates or stirs up war. **ˋWar Office,** (formerly in GB) State department in charge of the Army, under the Secretary of State of War. (Now named *Ministry of Defence*). **ˋwar-paint** *n* **(a)** paint put on the body before battle by some primitive people; (fig) full, ceremonial dress: *The General was in full war-paint.* **(b)** (sl) make-up (cosmetics). **ˋwar-path** *n* (only in) ***on the war-path,*** ready for, engaged in, a fight or quarrel. **ˋwar-ship** *n* ship for use in war. **ˋwar-torn** *adj* exhausted by, worn out in, war. **ˋwar-widow** *n* woman whose husband has been killed in war. **3** [U] science or art of fighting, using weapons, etc: *trained for war; the art of war,* strategy and tactics. **4** (fig) any kind of struggle or conflict: *the war against disease; the wars of the elements,* storms, natural calamities; *a war of nerves/words.* □ *vi* **(-rr-)** fight; make war: *warring for supremacy; warring* (= rival) *creeds/ideologies.* **ˋwar·fare** /ˋwɔfeə(r)/ *n* [U] making war; condition of being at war; fighting: *the horrors of modern warfare.* **war·like** /ˋwɔlaɪk/ *adj* ready for, suggesting, war: *warlike preparations;* fond of war: *a cruel, warlike people.* **war·time** /ˋwɔtaɪm/ *n* [U] time when there is war: *in wartime;* (attrib) *wartime regulations/rationing.*

warble /ˋwɔbl/ *vi,vt* [VP2A,C,6A] (esp of birds) sing, esp with a gentle trilling note: *larks warbling high up in the sky; a blackbird warbling from a branch.* □ *n* warbling; bird's song. **war·bler** /ˋwɔblə(r)/ *n* (kinds of) bird that ~s.

ward /wɔd/ *n* **1** ***keep watch and ~,*** guard and protect. **2** [U] state of being in custody or under the control of a guardian: *a child in ~*; [C] person under the guardianship of an older person or of law authorities. **3** division of a local government area, each division being represented by one Councillor. **4** division of, separate room in, a building, esp a prison or a hospital: *the fever/isolation/children's ~; the casual ~* (in former times, for occasional, not the regular, inmates of a workhouse). **5** notch in a key; corresponding part in a lock. □ *vt* [VP15B] ***~ sth off,*** keep away, avoid: *~ off a blow/danger.*

war·den /ˋwɔdn/ *n* **1** person having control or authority: *the ~ of a youth hostel.* **ˋair-raid ~,** (during World War II in GB) member of a civilian organization with various duties during air-raids. **ˋtraffic ~,** (e g in London) person responsible for controlling the parking of cars in streets, squares, etc at parking meters. **2** (old use except in a few cases) title of certain governors or presidents: *the W~ of Merton College, Oxford.* **3** (US) = **warder.**

war·der /ˋwɔdə(r)/ *n* (GB) man acting as guard in a prison; jailer. **war·dress** /ˋwɔdrəs/ *n* woman ~.

ward·robe /ˋwɔ-drəʊb/ *n* **1** cupboard (*ˋbuilt-in-~*) or movable cupboard-like piece of furniture with pegs, shelves, etc for a person's clothes. **2** stock of clothes: *My ~ needs to be renewed,* I must buy some new clothes. **3** stock of costumes of a theatrical company.

ward·room /ˋwɔdrʊm *US:* -rum/ *n* living and eating quarters for commissioned officers in a warship except the commanding officer.

ware[1] /weə(r)/ *n* **1** (in compounds) manufactured goods: *ˋsilver~; ˋiron~; ˋhard~.* **2** (*pl*) articles offered for sale: *advertise one's ~s.* **~·house** /ˋweəhaʊs/ *n* building for storing goods before distribution to retailers; storehouse for furniture (on bahalf of owners). □ *vt* [VP6A] store in a ~house.

ware[2] /weə(r)/ *vt* [VP6A] (in imper) look out for; be cautious about; beware of: *W~ wire!* (warning to riders in a fox-hunt that there is barbed wire on a fence, etc).

war·fare /ˋwɔfeə(r)/ ⇨ **war.**

war·ily, wari·ness ⇨ **wary.**

warm[1] /wɔm/ *adj* **(-er, -est) 1** having a fairly high degree of heat (between *cool* and *hot*); (of clothing) serving to keep the body ~: *Come and get ~ by the fire. It was ~, but not hot, yesterday. Put your ~est clothes on before you go out in the snow. Red, yellow and orange are called ~ colours.* ***~ work,*** **(a)** work or activity that makes one ~. **(b)** strenuous or dangerous activity or occupation. ***make things ~ for sb,*** make things unpleasant, make trouble for him; punish him. ***~ blood,*** that of mammals and birds (ranging from 36°C—42°C). Hence, **ˈ~-ˋblooded** *adj* **(a)** having ~ blood; not cold-blooded like snakes, etc. **(b)** having feelings and passions that are easily roused. **2** enthusiastic, hearty: *give sb a ~ welcome; a ~ friend/supporter.* **3** sympathetic; affectionate: *He has a ~ heart.* Hence, **ˈ~-ˋhearted** *adj* kind and sympathetic. **4** (of scent in hunting) fresh; recently made and easily followed by the hounds; (in children's games, when an object is hidden and searched for) close to the object: *You're getting ~,* near to what is being sought. **~·ly** *adv* in a ~ manner: *~ly dressed; thank sb ~ly.* **warmth** /wɔmθ/ *n* [U] state of being ~: *He was pleased with the ~th of his welcome. He answered with ~th,* with some emotion (of pleasure, resentment, etc, according to context).

warm[2] /wɔm/ *vt,vi* [VP6A,15B,2A,C] ***~ (sth) up,*** make or become warm or warmer: *~ oneself/one's hands by the fire. Please ~* (*up*) *this milk. The milk is ~ing* (*up*) *on the stove. He ~ed up* (= became more animated, enthusiastic) *as he went on with his speech.* ***~ to one's work/task, etc,*** become more interested; like it more. **ˋ~-ing-pan** *n* round metal pan with a lid and a long handle, (formerly) holding hot coals and used for ~ing the inside of a bed before it was occupied. □ *n* **1** (usu *sing* with *indef art*) act of ~ing: *Come by the fire and have a ~.* **2 British ~,** short thick overcoat worn by army officers. **~er** *n* (usu in compounds) sth which ~s: *a ˋfoot-~er,* a container with burning charcoal or hot water.

warn /wɔn/ *vt* [VP6A,14,11,15,17] give (sb) notice of possible danger or unpleasant consequences; inform in advance of what may happen: *He was ~ed of the danger. We ~ed them not to go skating on such thin ice. You've been ~ed. He ~ed me that there were pickpockets in the crowd/~ed me against pickpockets.* ***~ sb off,*** give him notice that he must go or stay away, e g from private property. **~·ing** *adj* that ~s: *He gave me a ~ing look. They fired some ~ing shots.* □ *n* **1** [C] that which ~s or serves to ~: *He paid no attention to my ~ings. Let this be a ~ing to you,* let this accident, misfortune, etc teach you to be careful in future. *There were gale ~ings to shipping along the coast.* **2** [U] action of ~ing; state of being ~ed: *You should take ~ing* (= be ~ed) *from what happened to me. The speaker sounded a note of ~ing,* spoke of possible danger. *The enemy attacked without ~ing.* **3** [U] (⇨ **notice(2)**, which is more usu) ***give sb ~ing,*** announce that employment is to end: *She gave her cleaner a month's ~ing* (*notice* is more usu).

warp /wɔp/ *vt,vi* [VP6A,2A] (cause to) become bent or twisted from the usual or natural shape: *The hot sun ~ed the boards. Some discs ~ in very hot weather. His judgement/disposition is ~ed,* biased because of possible advantage for himself. □ *n* [C] **1** twisted or bent condition in timber, etc, caused by uneven shrinking or expansion. **2** threads over and under which other threads (the *woof*) are passed when cloth is woven on a loom.

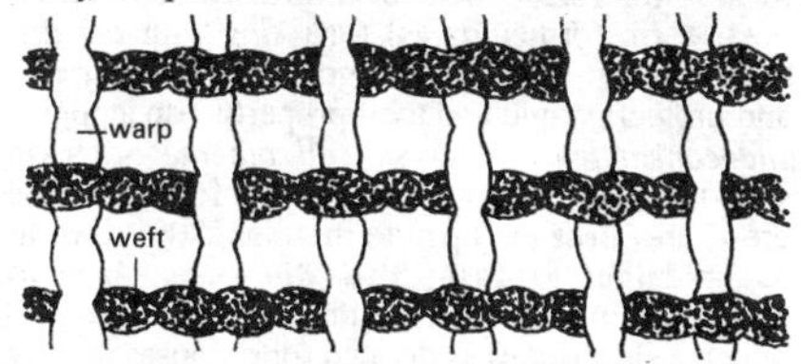

war·rant /ˋwɒrənt *US:* ˋwɔr-/ *n* **1** [U] justification or authority: *He had no ~ for saying so/for what he did.* **2** [C] written order giving official authority for sth: *a ~ to arrest a suspected criminal. The ˋdeath-~ has been signed. A ~ is out for his arrest/against him. Here are the ~s for your dividends,* ie on shares. **3** [C] certificate appointing a man as a ~ officer. ˋ**~ officer** *n* member of the armed forces, eg a sergeant-major in the army, a boatswain in the navy, with rank below commissioned officers and above non-commissioned officers. ⇨ App 9. □ *vt* **1** [VP6A] be a ~(1) for: *Nothing can ~ such insolence. His interference was certainly not ~ed.* **2** [VP6A,9,25] guarantee (the more usu word); (colloq) assure: *This material is ~ed (to be) pure silk. I'll ~ him an honest and reliable fellow. I can't ~ it to be/~ that it is genuine. He'll be back, I ~* (= assure) *you, when the money's paid out.* **war·ran·tee** /ˈwɒrənˋti *US:* ˈwɔr-/ *n* person to whom a warranty is made. **war·ran·tor** /ˋwɒrəntɔ(r) *US:* ˈwɔr-/ *n* person who makes a warranty. **war·ranty** /ˋwɒrəntɪ *US:* ˋwɔr-/ *n* [C] (*pl* -ties) authority; (written or printed) guarantee (eg to repair or replace defective goods): *What ~y have you for doing this? Can you give me a ~y of quality for these goods? The car is still under ~y.*

war·ren /ˋwɒrən *US:* ˋwɔrən/ *n* [C] area of land in which there are many burrows in which rabbits live and breed; (fig) (usu over-populated) building or district in which it is difficult to find one's way about: *lose oneself in a ~ of narrow streets.*

war·rior /ˋwɒrɪə(r) *US:* ˋwɔr-/ *n* (liter, rhet) soldier; fighter: (attrib) *a ~ race.*

wart /wɔt/ *n* small hard, dry growth on the skin; similar growth on a plant. ˋ**~-hog** *n* kinds of African pig with two large tusks and ~-like growths on the face.

wary /ˋweərɪ/ *adj* (-ier, -iest) cautious; in the habit of looking out for possible danger or trouble: *be ~ of giving offence/of strangers; keep a ~ eye on sb; a ~ old fox.* **war·ily** /-əlɪ/ *adv* **wari·ness** *n*

was /*usual form:* wəz; *strong form:* wɒz *US:* wʌz/ ⇨ **be**[1].

wash[1] /wɒʃ *US:* wɔʃ/ *n* **1** (*sing* only, usu with *indef art*) act of washing; being washed: *Will you give the car a ~/a ˈ~-ˋdown, please.* ***have a ~ and brush up,*** wash oneself and make oneself tidy. **2** (*sing* only) clothing, sheets, etc to be washed or being washed; place (laundry) where they are being washed: *She has a large ~ this week. She was hanging out the ~. All my shirts are at the ~. When does the ~ come back from the laundry?* **3** (*sing* with *def art*) movement or flow of water; sound made by moving water: *the ~ of the waves; the ~ made by a steamer's propeller(s).* **4** [U] thin, weak or inferior liquid: *This soup is a mere ~,* is too watery, has no flavour or substance. **5** [U] kitchen liquid with waste food (eg vegetable peelings and scraps) to be given to pigs. **6** (usu in compounds—⇨ under the first element) liquid prepared for a special purpose: *ˋwhite~,* for putting on walls; *ˋmouth-~,* for disinfecting; *ˋeye~.*

wash[2] /wɒʃ *US:* wɔʃ/ *vt,vi* **1** [VP6A,15B,22,2A] make clean with or in water or other liquid: *~ one's hands/clothes. W~ them clean. Go and ~ yourself. I must ~ before dinner. He never ~es* (ie ~es himself) *in cold water.* ***~ one's hands of sth/sb,*** say one is no longer responsible for. ***~ one's dirty linen in public,*** ⇨ linen. ***~ sth down,*** clean by ~ing, esp by using a stream or jet of water (eg from a hose): *~ down a car/the decks of a ship.* ***~ sth away/off/out,*** remove by ~ing: *~ dirty marks off a wall; ~ out blood stains.* ***be/look/feel ~ed out,*** (fig, colloq) pale and tired; exhausted. ***~ sth up,*** ~ dishes, cutlery, etc after a meal: *~ up the dinner things; help one's wife to ~ up.* Hence, ˈ**~·ing-ˋup** *n* (Note: *up* indicates that a number of dishes, etc are to be ~ed. For a single article *up* is not used: *Please ~ this plate*). ***(all) ~ed up,*** (colloq) ruined. **2** [VP2A] (of materials) be capable of being ~ed without damage or loss of colour: *Does this material ~ well? That argument/excuse will not ~,* (fig) will not bear examination, is weak. **3** [VP6A] (of the sea or a river) flow past or against: *The sea ~es the base of the cliffs.* **4** [VP15B] (of moving liquid) carry away, or in a specified direction: *He was ~ed overboard by a huge wave. All this timber has been ~ed up* (ie carried up on to the beach) *by the waves. The cliffs are being gradually ~ed away by the sea.* ***~ sth down (with),*** swallow (liquid) with: *My lunch was bread and cheese ~ed down with beer.* ***~ed out,*** **(a)** (of games such as cricket, of horse-races, etc) made impossible, cancelled, by heavy rain or flooding. **(b)** (of roads, etc) made impassable by heavy rain, floods, etc. **5** [VP6A,15A] scoop out: *The water had ~ed a channel in the sand.* **6** [VP2C] go flowing, sweeping or splashing (*along, out, in, into, over,* etc): *We heard the waves ~ing against the sides of our boat. Huge waves ~ed over the deck.* **~·able** /-əbl/ *adj* that can be ~ed without being spoiled.

wash- /wɒʃ *US:* wɔʃ/ (in compounds; often used as a substitute for *washing*). ˋ**~-basin** *n* basin for holding water in which to wash one's face and hands. ˋ**~-board** *n* board with ridges on it, on which clothes are washed (at home). ˋ**~-bowl** *n* (US) = ~-basin. ˋ**~-day** *n* day on which clothes were washed (at home). ˋ**~-hand-basin** *n* =

~-basin. ˈ~-**drawing** *n* one made with a brush in a black or neutral water-colour. ˈ~-**hand-stand** *n* = ~-stand. ˈ~-**house** *n* room or out-building equipped for washing. ˈ~-**leather** *n* [C,U] (piece of) chamois leather, used for cleaning and polishing windows and other surfaces. ˈ~-**out** *n* **(a)** place in a railway or road where a flood or heavy rain has carried away earth, rock, etc and interrupted communications. **(b)** (colloq) useless or unsuccessful person; complete failure or fiasco. ˈ~-**room** *n* (US) lavatory (esp in a public building, etc). ˈ~-**stand** *n* (now old-fashioned, except in houses where there is no piped supply of water to bathrooms or bedrooms) piece of furniture with a basin, jug, etc for washing in a bedroom. ˈ~-**tub** *n* large wooden tub in which to wash clothes.

washer /ˈwɒʃə(r) *US:* ˈwɔ-/ *n* **1** machine for washing clothes, or (ˈ*dish-~*) dishes. **2** ˈ~-**woman,** laundress. **3** small flat ring of metal, plastic, rubber or leather for making a joint or screw tight. ⇨ the illus at **bolt**.

wash·ing /ˈwɒʃɪŋ *US:* ˈwɔ-/ *n* [U] **1** washing or being washed. **2** clothes being washed or to be washed: *hang out the ~ on the line to dry.* ˈ~-**day** *n* = wash-day, ⇨ **wash-**. ˈ~-**machine** *n* power driven machine for washing clothes. ˈ~ **soda** *n* sodium carbonate, used, dissolved in water, for washing clothes or dishes. ˈ~-ˈ**up** *n* ⇨ *wash up* at **wash**[2]**(1)**.

washy /ˈwɒʃɪ *US:* ˈwɔ-/ *adj* (of liquids) thin, watery; (of colours) faded-looking; pale; (of feeling, style) lacking in vigour.

wasp /wɒsp *US:* wɔsp/ *n* kinds of flying insect of which the common kind has a narrow waist, black and yellow stripes and a powerful sting in the tail. ⇨ the illus at **insect**. ˈ~-ˈ**waisted** *adj* slender at the waist. ~·**ish** /-ɪʃ/ *adj* irritable; ill tempered; sharp in making retorts.

was·sail /ˈwɒseɪl/ *n* (archaic) time of drinking and merry-making; spiced ale or other liquor drunk at such a time.

wast·age /ˈweɪstɪdʒ/ *n* [U] amount wasted; loss by waste.

waste /weɪst/ *adj* **1** (of land) that is not or cannot be used; no longer of use; barren: ~ *land,* not occupied or used for any purpose. ˈ~·**land** /-lænd/ *n* **(a)** barren, desolate or unused land. **(b)** land ravaged by war, etc: *Vietnam reduced to ~land by bombing and shelling.* **(c)** (fig) life, society, looked upon as culturally and spiritually barren. ***lay ~,*** destroy the crops in, ravage (e g territory occupied in war). **2** useless; thrown away because not wanted: *~-paper; ~ products,* unwanted after a manufacturing process. □ *vt,vi* **1** [VP6A,14,2A] ***~ sth (on sth),*** make no use of; use without a good purpose; use more of (sth) than is necessary: *~ one's time and money; ~ one's words/breath,* talk without making any impression (on sb). *All his efforts were ~d,* had no result. ***W~ not, want not,*** (prov) If you do not ~ your money, etc you are unlikely to be in need. **2** [VP6A] make (land) waste; ravage. **3** [VP6A,2A, C] (cause to) lose strength by degrees: *He's wasting away. Consumption is a wasting disease. His body was ~d by long illness.* **4** [VP2A] be ~d: *Turn that tap off—the water is wasting.* □ *n* **1** [U] wasting or being ~d: *There's too much ~ in this house. It's a ~ of time to wait any longer. What a ~ of energy!* ***go/run to ~,*** be ~d: *What a pity to see all that water running to ~!* e g instead of being used for generating electric current. **2** [U] ~ material; refuse. ˈ~-**basket/-bin,** (US), ˈ~-ˈ**paper-basket** (GB) *nn* basket or other container for scraps of paper, etc. ˈ~-**pipe** *n* pipe for carrying off used or superflous water. **3** (with *pl*) area of ~ land: *the ~s of the Sahara;* dreary scene: *a ~ of waters.* **waster** *n* (colloq) wastrel. ~·**ful** /-fl/ *adj* causing ~; using more than is needed: *~ful habits/processes; ~ful expenditure.* ~·**fully** /-flɪ/ *adv*

wast·rel /ˈweɪstrəl/ *n* good-for-nothing fellow; wasteful person.

watch[1] /wɒtʃ/ *n* **1** [U] act of watching, esp to see that all is well. ***be on the ~ (for),*** be watching for (sth or sb, or esp possible danger). ***keep ~ (on/over),*** look out for danger, etc. ˈ~-**dog** *n* dog kept to protect property, esp a house. ˈ~-**tower** *n* high tower from which to keep ~, e g in a forest, to look for forest fires, or a fortified observation post. **2** (in former times) (usu *sing* with *def art*) body of men employed to go through the streets and protect people and their property, esp at night: *the constables of the ~; call out the ~.* **3** (in ships) period of duty (4 or 2 hours) for part of the crew. **the first ~,** 8p m to midnight. **the middle ~,** midnight to 4a m; **the** ˈ**dog-~es,** 4p m to 6p m and 6p m to 8p m; either of the halves into which a ship's crew is divided for purposes of duty (called the *starboard* and *port ~es* from the positions of the men's bunks in former times). ***on ~,*** on duty in this way. ***keep ~,*** be on ~. **4** (old use) period of wakefulness in the night: *in the ~es of the night,* while one lies awake. ˈ~ **night service,** church service at midnight, New Year's Eve. ~·**ful** /-fl/ *adj* on the ~; wide-awake. ~·**fully** /-flɪ/ *adv* ~·**ful·ness** *n* ~·**man** /-mən/ *n* (*pl* -men) **1** (old use) member of the ~**(2)**. **2** (mod use) man employed to guard a building (e g a bank, block of offices, factory) against thieves, esp at night. ~-**word** /-wɜd/ *n* **1** password. **2** slogan.

watch[2] /wɒtʃ/ *vt,vi* **1** [VP2A,B,C,3A,4,6A,8,10, 15A,18,19] look at; keep the eyes on: *W~ me carefully. W~ what I do and how I do it. We sat there ~ing the cricket. Are you going to play or only ~? He ~ed to see* (= ~ed in order to see) *what would happen. I ~ed her cross the street,* looked at and saw this action from start to finish. *I sat ~ing the shadows creep across the floor,* looked at and saw this happening (but not necessarily from start to finish). *My solicitor is ~ing the case for me/holds a ~ing brief for me,* is present in court during the case to protect my interests. ***~ one's step,*** **(a)** be careful not to fall or stumble. **(b)** be careful not to make an error, let sb win an advantage, etc, e g in negotiations. ***~ one's time,*** (more usu *bide*) wait for the right time. ***~ the time,*** keep your eye on the time (e g to avoid being late for sth). ***~ (for sth),*** look out for: *There's a policeman ~ing outside,* i e for anything suspicious: *The doctor told her to ~* (= be on the look-out) *for symptoms of measles.* ***~ (over) sth,*** guard; protect: *Will you ~ (over) my clothes while I have a swim?* **2** [VP2A] (old use) remain awake: *~ all night at the bedside of a sick child.* ~·**er** *n* person who ~es.

watch[3] /wɒtʃ/ *n* small timepiece that can be carried in the pocket or worn on the wrist (cf *clock*): *What time is it by your ~?* ˈ~-**glass** *n* disc covering the face of a ~. ˈ~-**guard/-chain** *n* strap or chain for securing a ~ to the clothing. ˈ~-**key** *n* separate key for winding a ~. ˈ~**-maker** *n* person who makes or repairs ~es.

water[1] /ˈwɔtə(r)/ *n* (*pl* only as in examples below) **1** liquid **(H_2O)** as in rivers, lakes, seas and oceans: *W~ is changed into steam by heat and into ice by cold. Fish live in (the) ~.* ***by ~,*** by boat, ship, barge, etc. ***in deep ~(s),*** experiencing or undergoing difficulty or misfortune. ***in smooth ~,*** making smooth or easy progress. ***on the ~,*** in a boat, etc: *Let's go on the ~ this warm afternoon.* ***under ~,*** flooded: *The fields were under ~ after the heavy rain.* ***be in/get into hot ~,*** have/get into trouble (esp because of foolish behaviour, etc). ***cast/throw one's bread upon the ~(s),*** do a good action without requiring reward, although later some unexpected return may come. ***drink the ~s,*** go to a spa where there are mineral ~s and drink them for one's health. ***go through fire and ~ (for sb/sth),*** undergo severe hardship and trials. ***hold ~,*** (of a theory) be sound when tested. ***keep one's head above ~,*** avoid (esp financial) troubles or misfortunes. ***make ~,*** **(a)** pass urine from the bladder. **(b)** (of a ship) have a leak. ***spend money, etc like ~,*** extravagantly. ***throw cold ~ on*** (a plan, etc), discourage (it). ***tread ~,*** ⇨ tread, *vi,vt*(4). ***like a fish out of ~,*** feeling uncomfortable, behaving awkwardly, because of unaccustomed surroundings, an unfamiliar situation, etc. ***Still ~s run deep,*** (prov) Beneath a quiet manner there may be depths of emotion, knowledge, cunning, etc. ***written in ~,*** (of a name, reputation, etc) soon forgotten; transient. ***~ on the brain/knee, etc,*** morbid accumulation of fluid. ***the ~s of forgetfulness,*** oblivion. **ˈtable/ˈmineral ~s,** with a mineral ingredient, bottled for use at table. **ˈback~,** ⇨ back[4](3). **2** the state of the tide: *at high/low ~; high/low ˈ~ mark.* ***in low ~,*** (fig) short of money. **3** (*pl*) seas as indicated by a preceding word: *in Korean ~s,* on the seas near Korea; *a ship for service in Home ~s,* on the seas near the country to which the ship belongs. **4** (usu *pl*) mass of ~: *the (ˈhead-)~s of the Nile,* the lake from which it flows. *The ~s of the lake flow out over a large waterfall.* **5** solution of a substance in ~: *ˈlavender-~; ˈrose-~, etc.* **6** ***of the first ~,*** of the finest quality: *a diamond of the first ~.* **7** (in compounds) ˈ~**-bird** *n* kinds of bird that swim or wade in ~. ˈ~**-biscuit** *n* thin, hard biscuit made of flour and ~, usu eaten with butter and cheese. ˈ~**-blister** *n* blister on the skin containing a colourless liquid, not blood. ˈ~**-borne** *adj* **(a)** (of goods) carried by ~. **(b)** (of diseases) passed on by the use of contaminated drinking-~. ˈ~**-bottle** *n* **(a)** glass container for ~ at table or in a bedroom. **(b)** metal flask (US = *canteen*) for use by a soldier, scout, etc. ˈ~**-buffalo** *n* the common domestic buffalo of India, Indonesia, etc. ⇨ the illus at domestic. ˈ~**-butt,** ⇨ butt[1](2). ˈ~**-cart** *n* cart with a tank for ~, either for sale or for sprinkling on dusty roads, etc. ˈ~**-cannon,** high-pressure hose, for forcing a jet of ~, e g to disperse rioters. ˈ~**-chute** *n* sloping channel leading to ~, down which boats, toboggans, etc slide, e g at a fun fair. ˈ~**-closet** *n* (common abbr **WC**) small room with a pan in which matter evacuated from the bowels may be flushed down a drain-pipe by ~ from a cistern. ˈ~**-colour** (US = **-color**) *n* **(a)** (*pl*) paints (to be) mixed with ~, not oil. **(b)** picture painted with ~-colours. **(c)** (*pl* or *sing*) the art of painting such pictures. ˈ~**-course** *n* (channel of a) brook or stream. ˈ~**-cress** *n* [U] creeping plant that grows in running ~, with hot-tasting leaves used in salads. ˈ~ **diviner,** ⇨ diviner. ˈ~**-fall** *n* [C] fall of ~, esp where a river falls over rocks or a cliff. ˈ~**-finder** *n* dowser, ⇨ dowsing. ˈ~**-fowl** *n* (collective *pl*) ~birds, esp those that swim, considered as suitable for shooting by sportsmen. ˈ~**-front** *n* land at the ~'s edge, esp the part of a town facing the sea, the harbour, a lake, etc. ˈ~**-glass** *n* [U] thick liquid used for coating eggs to keep them in good condition. ˈ~**-hen** *n* = moorhen. ˈ~**-hole** *n* shallow depression in which ~ collects (esp in the bed of a river otherwise dry, and to which animals go to drink). ˈ~**-ice** *n* [C] frozen ~ with sugar and fruit-juices or other flavouring. ˈ~**-jacket** *n* case filled with ~ and fitted over part of a machine which is to be kept cool. ˈ~ **jump** *n* obstacle (in show-jumping, steeplechases) of a ditch or water, usu with a fence, over which horses jump. ˈ~**-level** *n* surface of ~ in a reservoir or other body of ~, esp as a datum for measurement. ˈ~**-lily** *n* kinds of plant with broad, flat leaves floating on the surface of the ~, and white, blue or yellow flowers. ˈ~**-line** *n* line along which the surface of the ~ touches a ship's side: *the load ~-line,* when the ship is loaded; *the light ~-line,* when the ship is empty of cargo. ˈ~**-logged** /-lɒgd *US:* -lɔgd/ *adj* **(a)** (of wood) so saturated with ~ that it will barely float. **(b)** (of a ship) so full of ~ that it will barely float. **(c)** (of land) thoroughly soaked with ~. ˈ~**-main** *n* main pipe in a system of ~-supply. ˈ~**-man** /-mən/ *n* (*pl* -men) boatman; man who manages a boat for hire; ferryman. ˈ~**-mark** *n* **(a)** manufacturer's design in some kinds of paper, seen when the paper is held against light. **(b)** mark which shows how high ~ (e g the tide, a river) has risen or how low it has fallen. ˈ~**-melon** *n* large, smooth-skinned melon with juicy pink or red flesh; trailing plant bearing such melons. ˈ~**-mill** *n* mill whose machinery is turned by ~-power. ˈ~**-nymph** *n* nymph associated with a river, lake, etc. ˈ~**-polo** *n* [U] game played by two teams of swimmers who try to throw a ball into a goal. ˈ~**-power** *n* [U] power obtained from flowing or falling ~, used to drive machinery or generate electric current. ˈ~**-proof** *adj* which does not let ~ through: *~proof material.* □ *n* ~proof coat; raincoat. □ *vi* make ~proof. ˈ~**-rat/-vole** *n* rat-like animal frequenting ~. ˈ~**-rate** *n* (GB) charge made (usu quarterly) for the use of ~ from a public ~-supply. ˈ~**-shed** *n* line of high land separating river systems; (fig) dividing line between events which take different courses. ˈ~**-side** *n* margin of the sea, a river, lake, etc: *go for a stroll along the ~side.* ˈ~**-skiing** *n* the sport of skiing on ~ while being towed at speed by a fast motor-boat. ˈ~**-skin** *n* skin bag for carrying ~. ˈ~**-softener** *n* device or substance for removing the causes of hardness in ~. ˈ~**-spaniel** *n* kind of spaniel that can be trained to swim out and bring back ~fowl, etc shot down by sportsmen. ˈ~**-spout** *n* **(a)** pipe or spout from which ~ is discharged, e g rainwater from a roof. **(b)** whirlwind over the sea which draws up a whirling mass of ~ so as to look like a funnel-shaped column of ~ going up to the clouds. ˈ~**-supply** *n* system of providing and storing ~, amount of ~ stored, for a district, town, building, etc. ˈ~**-table** *n* level below which the ground is saturated with ~: *The ~table has been lowered by drought.* **ˈ~-tight** *adj* **(a)** made, fastened, etc so that ~ cannot get in or out: *~tight boots/joints/compartments in a ship.* **(b)** (fig, of an agreement, etc) drawn up so that there can be no escape from any of the provisions; leaving no possibility of misunderstanding. **ˈ~-tower** *n* one which supports a large tank which secures pressure for distributing a ~-supply. **ˈ~-waggon** (US = **-wagon**) *n* = ~-cart: *on the ~-waggon,* ⇨ **waggon(1).** **ˈ~-way** *n* navigable channel (e g a canal, channel up a river where the ~ is deep enough for ships). **ˈ~-wheel** *n* one turned by a flow of ~, used to work machinery. **ˈ~-wings** *n pl* floats worn on the shoulders by a person learning to swim. **ˈ~-works** *n* (with *sing* or *pl v*) **(a)** system of reservoirs, pumping stations, ~-mains, etc for supplying ~. **(b)** ornamental fountains. **(c)** (colloq) (working of the) bladder: *Are your ~works all right?* Can you pass urine normally? **(d)** (colloq) tears: *turn on the ~works,* shed tears: *Let's not have the ~works again!* Let's not have another outburst of tears! **ˈ~-worn** *adj* (of rocks, etc) made smooth by the action of ~.

water² /ˈwɔtə(r)/ *vt,vi* **1** [VP6A] put water on; sprinkle with water: *~ the lawn/the plants/the streets.* **~-ing-can** /ˈwɔtrɪŋ kæn/ *n* container with a long spout, used for ~ing plants. **~-ing-cart** /ˈwɔtrɪŋ kɑt/ *n* one with a tank and a sprinkler for ~ing roads (to settle the dust, clean them). **2** [VP6A] give water to: *~ the horses.* **3** [VP2A] (of the eyes or mouth) fill with water; have much liquid: *The smoke made my eyes ~. The smell from the kitchen made my mouth ~,* aroused my appetite. **4** [VP15B] ***~ sth down,*** add water to: *This whisky has been ~ed (down). The story has been ~ed down,* (fig) weakened, e g by making details less vivid. **5** [VP6A] (fin) increase (a company's debt or nominal capital) by issuing new shares without increasing the assets. **6 ~ed** (*pp* as *adj*) supplied with water: *a country ~ed by numerous rivers.* **~ed silk,** manufactured so that there are wavy markings on the surface. **7 ~-ing-place** /ˈwɔtrɪŋ pleɪs/ *n* **(a)** water-hole; place to which animals go to drink. **(b)** spa. **(c)** seaside resort.

Wat·er·loo /ˈwɔtəˈlu/ *n* ***meet one's ~,*** be finally and crushingly defeated in a contest (esp after a period of success).

wat·ery /ˈwɔtərɪ/ *adj* (-ier, -iest) **1** of or like water; (esp of cooked vegetables) containing, cooked in, too much water: *~ soup/cabbage.* **2** (of colour) pale. **3** (of the eyes or lips) running with, covered with, water. **4** suggesting that there will be rain: *a ~ moon/sky.*

watt /wɒt/ *n* unit of electrical power: *a 60 ~ light-bulb.*

wattle¹ /ˈwɒtl/ *n* **1** structure of sticks or twigs

birds 5

woven over and under thicker upright sticks, used for fences, walls, etc. ˈ**~ and ˋdaub,** this structure covered with clay, for walls and roofs. **2** kinds of Australian acacia supplying such twigs, with golden flowers adopted as the national emblem.

wattle[2] /ˋwɒtl/ *n* red flesh hanging down from the head or throat of a bird, esp a turkey. ⇨ the illus at **fowl**.

wave /ˋweɪv/ *vi, vt* **1** [VP2A,3] move to and fro, up and down: *flags/branches waving in the wind.* **2** [VP6A,15A,12A,13A] cause (sth) to move in this way (e g to make a signal or request, to give a greeting, etc): *~ one's hand at sb; ~ to sb; ~ one's umbrella/a flag. She ~d (me) a greeting. She ~d goodbye to us.* **3** [VP15B] cause (sb) to move in a certain direction by waving: *The officer ~d his men on/~d them to advance. He ~d us away.* **~ sth aside,** (fig) dismiss: *My objections were ~d aside.* **4** [VP2A] (of a line or surface, of hair) be in a series of curves (〰): *Her hair ~s beautifully.* **5** [VP6A] cause to be in a series of curves: *She's had her hair permanently ~d.* □ *n* [C] **1** long ridge of water, esp on the sea, between two hollows (or troughs, furrows); such a ridge curling over and breaking on the shore. **the ~s,** (poet) the sea. ***in ~s,*** in successive lines like sea-~s: *The infantry attacked in ~s.* **2** act of waving(3 above); waving movement: *with a ~ of his hand,* e g as a signal. **3** curve like a ~ of the sea: *the ~s in a girl's hair. She has a natural ~ in her hair.* **4** steady increase and spread: *a ~ of enthusiasm/indignation; a ˋcrime ~; a ˋheat ~,* a period of weather with temperatures much higher than usual and over a large area. **5** ~-like motion by which heat, light, sound or electricity is spread or carried. **ˋ~-length** *n* distance between the highest point (the crest) of one ~ and that of the next (esp with reference to wireless telegraphy). **long/medium/short ~s,** ~s used in broadcasting: *a short-~ transmitter.* **wavy** *adj* (-ier, -iest) having ~-like curves: *a wavy line; wavy hair.*

wa·ver /ˋweɪvə(r)/ *vi* [VP2A,C] **1** move uncertainly or unsteadily: *~ing shadows/flames.* **2** be or become unsteady; begin to give way: *His courage ~ed. He ~ed in his resolution. The line of troops ~ed and then broke.* **3** hesitate: *~ between two opinions.* **~er** *n* person who ~s.

wax[1] /wæks/ *n* [U] soft yellow substance produced by bees (*ˋbeeswax*) and used for making honeycomb cells; kinds of substance similar to beeswax (e g as obtained from petroleum): such material bleached and purified, used for making candles, for modelling, etc: (attrib) *a wax candle; a wax doll,* one with the head made of wax; *ˋparaffin wax; ˋcobblers'-wax,* kind of resin used on thread; *ˋear-wax,* substance secreted in the ears. **ˋwax-chandler** *n* maker or seller of candles.

'wax-paper *n* paper that is waterproofed with a layer of wax. **'wax·work** *n* object modelled in wax, esp the form of a human being with face and hands in wax, coloured and clothed to look like life and to be exhibited: *go to see the waxworks at Madame Tussaud's,* a place in London famous for waxworks. **'sealing-wax,** ⇨ seal, *v*(1). □ *vt* [VP6A] cover, polish or treat with wax: *wax furniture/a wooden floor/linoleum. He waxes his moustache,* treats it with a cosmetic wax. **waxen** /'wæksn/ *adj* **1** (old use; now usu *wax*) made of wax. **2** like wax: *a waxen complexion.* **waxy** *adj* like wax; having a smooth, pale surface; like wax in texture: *waxy potatoes.*

wax[2] /wæks/ *vi* **1** [VP2A] (esp of the moon, contrasted with *wane*) show a larger bright area. **2** [VP2D] (old use) become: *wax merry/lyrical/eloquent.*

wax[3] /wæks/ *n* (sl) fit of anger: *be in/get into/put sb into a wax.* **waxy** *adj* angry.

way /weɪ/ *n* **1** road, street, path, etc: (in compounds) *'highway; 'railway; 'byway; a way across the fields; a covered* (= roofed) *way; the Appian Way,* a Roman road in Italy. **'clear~,** ⇨ clear[1](1). *There's no way through. My friend lives across/over the way,* on the other side of the street (or road). ***pave the way for,*** prepare for, prepare people to accept (reforms, etc). **the permanent way,** complete length of railroad track. **the six-foot way,** the space left between each pair of rails and the next on a railway. **the Way of the Cross,** a series of paintings, carvings, etc (usu in or near a church) illustrating the progress of Jesus to Calvary. **2** route, road (to be) used (*from* one place *to* another): *Which is the best/right/quickest/shortest, etc way there/from A to B? Can you find your way home? We lost the way/our way in the dark. Which is the way in/out? The longest/farthest way round/about is the nearest way home,* (prov) Short cuts are often delusive. *We'd better stop and ask someone the way. He made/pushed/fought/felt his way out/back, etc. We had to pick our way along the muddy path.* ***go one's way(s),*** depart. ***go out of one's way (to do sth),*** make a special effort: *He went out of his way to be rude to me/to help me.* ***lead the way,*** go in front as leader; show by example how sth may be done. ***make one's way in life/in the world,*** succeed. ***make the best of one's way,*** go as fast as one can. ***take one's way*** (*to, towards*), go. ***pay one's way,*** **(a)** keep out of debt. **(b)** pay one's share of expenses instead of letting others pay. ***the parting of the ways,*** (fig) the time when an important decision must be made as to future plans, etc. ***by way of,*** via; using a route through: *He came by way of Dover.* ***out of the way,*** exceptional, uncommon: *He has done nothing out of the way yet.* **'out-of-the-'way,** (attrib use) remote: *an out-of-the-way place/corner.* **3** (*sing* only) being engaged in going or coming; time spent on this: *They're still on the way. I'll buy some on the/my way home. They sang songs to cheer the way. He's on the way to success. She's got another child on the way,* (colloq) is pregnant again. ***by the way,*** **(a)** during a journey. **(b)** (fig) incidentally; in passing (often used to introduce a remark not connected with the subject of conversation). ***on the way out,*** (fig; colloq) about to become out of date, out of fashion. **4** [C] method or plan; course of action: *the right/wrong/best, etc way to do/of doing a thing. Is this the way to do it/the way you do it? Do it (in) your own way if you don't like my way. The work must be finished (in) one way or another.* ***Where there's a will there's a way,*** (prov) If we want to do sth, we will find a method of doing it. ***ways and means,*** methods, esp of providing money. ***have/get one's own way,*** get/do what one wants. ***go/take one's own way,*** act independently, esp contrary to the advice of others. **5** (*sing* only) distance between two points; distance (to be) traversed: *It's a long way off/a long way from here. The roots go a long way down. Your work is still a long way off perfection,* is far from being perfect. *Your work this week is better by a long way,* much better. *This will go a long way* (= will be very helpful) *in overcoming the difficulty. Your demands are way* (= a long way, far) *above what I can accept.* **'way-a'head** *adj* (colloq) advanced: *way-ahead art/fashions.* **'way-'out** *adj* (colloq) advanced; ahead of fashion; eccentric: *way-out clothes.* **6** [C] direction: *He went this/that/the other way. Look this way, please. He couldn't look my way,* towards me. *Such opportunities never come/fall my way,* come to me. *You've got your hat on the wrong way,* e g back to front. *He's in a fair way to succeed,* is making progress in the right direction. ***put sb in the way of (doing) sth,*** help him to make a start: *A kind friend put him in the way of earning a living.* **7** (colloq; *sing* only; not stressed) neighbourhood: *He lives somewhere London way,* near London. *The crops are looking very well our way,* in our part of the country. **8** [U] advance in some direction; progress (esp of a ship or boat). ***be under way, have way on,*** (of a ship) be moving through the water. ***gather/lose way,*** gain/lose speed: *The boat slowly gathered way.* ***get under way,*** start to move forward. ***give way,*** (of oarsmen) row hard. ***make way,*** (liter, fig) advance. **9** [U] space for forward movement, for passing ahead; freedom to go forward: *Don't stand in the way. Tell that boy not to get in the way. Tell him to stand out of the/my way. Clear the way!* ***be/put sth out of harm's way,*** in a safe place. ***get sth out of the way,*** settle it, dispose of it. ***give way (to sth/sb),*** ⇨ give[1](10). ***make way (for),*** allow space or a free passage: *All traffic has to make way for a fire-engine.* ***put sb out of the way,*** put him in prison, kill him (secretly), or otherwise get rid of him. ***put sb in the way of (sth),*** give him the opportunity of securing, e g a good bargain. ***see one's way (clear) to doing sth,*** see how to do it; (esp) feel justified in doing sth: *I don't see my way clear to helping you. I don't see my way clear to recommending you for the job.* ***right of way,*** ⇨ right[3](2). **10** [C] custom; manner of behaving; personal peculiarity: *the good old ways; English/Chinese, etc ways of living; the way of the world,* what appears to be justified by custom. *It's not his way to be mean,* Meanness is not in his nature. *It's disgraceful the way he drinks,* His habit of (excessive) drinking is disgraceful. *I don't like the way* (= manner in which) *he looks at me. She has a (winning) way with her,* wins the confidence and affection of people by her manner of behaviour. *Don't take offence—it's only his way,* a manner of behaving that has no special significance. ***to 'my way of thinking,*** in my opinion. **the way,** (colloq; adverbial use) as; in the manner that: *He doesn't* *do it the way I do.* ***mend one's ways,*** improve one's manners, behaviour, etc. **11** [C] respect; point or detail: *He's a clever man in some ways. Can I help you in any way? He is in no way* (= not at all) *to blame. They are in no way similar. The work was well done in one way,* to a limited extent but not on the whole. He's an amusing fellow in his (own) way. What have we in the way of food, What food is there (e g in the house, for the next meal, etc)? **12** [C] condition, state, degree: *Things are in a bad way. She was in a terrible way,* much agitated. **ˋ*any way,*** in either case; in any case or event. ***each way/both ways,*** (in backing horses) to win, to get a place in the first three. ***in the ˋfamily way,*** (colloq) pregnant. ***in a small way,*** on a small scale: *live in a small way,* simply, without ostentation; *a printer in a small way.* ***have it both ways,*** choose first one and then the other of alternatives in order to suit one's convenience, argument, etc. **13** ordinary course: *do sth in the way of business.* **14** ***by way of,*** **(a)** as a substitute for or as a kind of: *say sth by way of apology/introduction.* **(b)** for the purpose of, with the intention of: *make inquiries by way of learning the facts of the case.* **(c)** in the course of: *by way of business.* ⇨ also 2 above. **15** (*pl*) structure of heavy timber on which a ship is built and down which it slides when launched. ⇨ *slipway* at **slip**[1]**(6)**. **16** (compounds) **ˋway-bill** *n* list of goods being conveyed by a carrier, with instructions about their destinations, etc. **ˋway·farer** /-feərə(r)/ *n* (liter) traveller, esp on foot. **ˋway-faring** /-feərɪŋ/ *adj* travelling: *a wayfaring man.* **ˋway·side** *n* side of a road: (attrib) *wayside flowers.*

way·lay /weɪˋleɪ/ *vt* (*pt,pp* -**laid** /-ˋleɪd/) [VP6A] (wait somewhere to) attack, rob (sb); accost (sb) unexpectedly (usu with a request): *He was waylaid by bandits. He waylaid me with a request for a loan.*

way·ward /ˋweɪwəd/ *adj* self-willed; not easily controlled or guided: *a ~ child; a child with a ~ disposition.*

we /wi/ *pron* **1** used by a speaker or writer referring to himself and another or others (with object form *us*). **2** used by a royal person in proclamations instead of *I,* and by the writer of an unsigned article in a newspaper, etc.

weak /wik/ *adj* (-**er**, -**est**) **1** (opp of *strong*) lacking in strength; easily broken; unable to resist hard wear or use, attack, etc: *too ~ to walk; ~ in the legs; a table with ~ legs; a ~ defence; a ~ team; the ~ points of an argument/plan; the ~er sex,* woman. **ˈ~-ˋkneed** *adj* (fig) lacking determination; ~ in character. **2** (of the senses, etc) below the usual standard: ~ (more usu *poor*) *sight and hearing; a ~ heart.* Hence, *ˈ~-ˋeyed, ˈ~-ˋsighted, ˈ~-ˋminded, ˈ~-ˋheaded.* **3** (of mixed liquids or solutions) watery; having little of some substance in relation to the water, etc: *~ tea/beer; a ~ solution.* **4** not good; not efficient: *~ in spelling/grammar/Latin.* **5** (gram) **~ verb,** one inflected by additions to the stem, not by vowel change (as *walk, walked,* contrasted with *run, ran* and *come, came*). **~ form** (of the pronunciation of some common words), form occurring in an unstressed position, usu by the use of a different vowel sound or by the absence of a vowel sound or consonant (e g /ən/ or /n/ for *and,* as in *bread and butter* /bred n ˋbʌtə(r)/). **~en** /ˋwikən/ *vt,vi* [VP6A,2A] make or become ~(er). **~·ling** *n* ~ person or animal. **~·ly** *adv* in a ~ manner. □ *adj* delicate in health; not robust: *a ~ly child.* **~·ness** *n* **1** [U] state of being ~: *the ~ness of old age; the ~ness of a country's defences.* **2** [C] fault or defect of character: *We all have our little ~nesses.* **3** ***have a ~ness for,*** a special or foolish liking for: *He has a ~ness for stewed eels/brandy/pretty typists.*

weal[1] /wil/ *n* [U] well-being (chiefly in): *~ and woe,* good and bad fortune; *for the public/general ~,* the welfare of all.

weal[2] /wil/ *n* [C] mark on the skin made by a blow from a stick, whip, etc.

weald /wild/ *n* (GB) stretch of open country, formerly forest: *the Sussex ~.*

wealth /welθ/ *n* [U] **1** (possession of a) great amount of property, money, etc; riches: *a man of ~; acquire great ~.* **2** (*sing* only with *indef* or *def art*) great amount or number of: *a book with a ~ of illustrations; the ~ of phrases and sentences to illustrate meanings in this dictionary.* **wealthy** *adj* (-**ier**, -**iest**) having ~(**1**); rich. **~·ily** /-əlɪ/ *adv*

wean /win/ *vt* **1** [VP6A] accustom (a baby, a young animal) to food other than its mother's milk. **2** [VP14] **~ *sb from sth,*** cause (sb) to turn away (from a habit, bad companions, etc).

weapon /ˋwepən/ *n* sth designed for, or used in, fighting or struggling (e g swords, guns, fists, a strike by workmen): *Whether a gun is a ~ of offence or a ~ of defence depends upon which end of it you are at. Are tears a woman's ~?* **~·less** *adj* without ~s.

wear[1] /weə(r)/ *n* [U] **1** wearing or being worn; use as clothing: *a suit for everyday ~; a coat that has been in constant ~. This carpet will stand any amount of hard ~. This coat is beginning to look the worse for ~,* shows signs of having been worn for a long time, so that it is no longer in a good or useful condition. **2** damage or loss of quality from use: *These shoes are showing (signs of) ~.* ***~ and tear,*** damage, loss in value, from normal use. **3** capacity to endure: *There's not much ~ left in these shoes,* they cannot be worn much longer. **4** (chiefly in compounds or in terms used by tradesmen) things to wear: *ˋunder~; ˋfoot~; ˋladies'/ˋmen's ~; a shop that specializes in ˋchildren's ~.*

wear[2] /weə(r)/ *vt,vi* (*pt* **wore** /wɔ(r)/, *pp* **worn** /wɔn/) **1** [VP6A,22,15B] have on the body, carry on one's person or on some part of it; (of looks) have on the face: *He was ~ing a hat/spectacles/a beard/heavy shoes/a ring on his finger/a troubled look/a flower in his buttonhole/a wristwatch. This is a style that is much worn now,* that is in fashion now. *She never ~s green,* i e green clothes. *She used to ~ her hair long,* used to have long hair. *The house wore* (= had) *a leglected look.* ***~ the crown,*** **(a)** be a monarch. **(b)** be a martyr. **2** [VP2C,D,4,22,15A,B] (cause to) become less useful or to be in a certain condition, by being used: *I have worn my socks into holes. This material has worn thin. The stones were worn by the constant flow of water. This old overcoat is much worn,* is much the worse for wear. **~ *away,*** become impaired, thin, weak, as the result of constant use: *The inscription on the stone had worn away,* the words were difficult to read. **~ *sth away,*** consume or impair sth by constant use, etc: *The foot-*

steps of thousands of visitors had worn away the steps. **~ down,** become gradually smaller, thinner, weaker, etc: *The heels of these shoes are ~ing down.* **~ sth down,** cause to ~ down. **~ sb/sth down,** weaken by constant attack, nervous strain, etc: *These noisy children do ~ me down! We wore down the enemy's resistance.* **~ off,** pass away: *The novelty will soon ~ off.* **~ sth off,** cause to pass away by degrees; be rubbed off by friction: *~ the nap off a piece of velvet.* **~ (sth) out,** (cause to) become useless, threadbare, exhausted: *Cheap shoes soon ~ out. My shoes are worn out. His patience had/was at last worn out. He has worn out* (= outstayed) *his welcome.* **~ sb out,** exhaust, tire out: *I'm worn out by all this hard work. That fellow ~s me out with his silly chatter.* Hence, **'worn-'out** *attrib adj: a worn-out coat.* **3** [VP6A] make (a hole, groove, etc) in by rubbing or attrition: *~ holes in a rug/one's socks. In time a path was worn across the field.* **4** [VP2B,2A,C] endure continued use; remain in a certain condition: *Good leather will ~ for years. This cloth has worn well/badly. Old Mr Smith is ~ing well,* still looks well in spite of his advanced age. *What a well-worn joke!* **5** [VP2C] **~ on/away, etc,** (of time) go slowly or tediously; pass gradually: *as the evening wore on; as winter wore away; as his life wore towards its close.* **~er** *n* person who is ~ing sth. **~·able** /-əbl/ *adj* that can be, or is fit to be, worn. **~·ing** *n* (gerund): *'~ing apparel,* clothes. □ *adj* tiring: *a ~ing day.*

weary /ˈwɪərɪ/ *adj* (-ier, -iest) **1** tired: *~ in body and mind; feel ~; be ~ of someone's constant grumbling.* **2** causing tiredness: *a ~ journey/wait; after walking ten ~ miles.* **3** showing tiredness: *a ~ sigh.* □ *vt,vi* [VP6A,14,2A,3A] **~ sb (with sth), ~ of sth,** make or become ~: *~ sb with requests; ~ of living all alone; wearied with marching and climbing.* **wear·ily** /-əlɪ/ *adv* **weari·ness** *n* **weari·some** /ˈwɪərɪsəm/ *adj* tiring; long and dull.

wea·sel /ˈwizl/ *n* small, fierce animal with red-brown fur, living on rats, rabbits, birds' eggs, etc.

weather[1] /ˈweðə(r)/ *n* [C] **1** conditions over a particular area and at a specific time with reference to sunshine, temperature, wind, rain, etc. (⇨ climate, used with reference to a long period of time, e g a season): *He stays indoors in wet ~. She goes out in all ~s* (*pl* here = all kinds of ~). *Many crops depend on the ~.* **be/feel under the ~,** (colloq) indisposed; unwell. **keep a/one's ~ eye open,** be on the alert; be on the look-out (for trouble, etc). **make good/bad ~,** (used by sailors) meet with good (bad) ~. **make heavy ~ of sth,** find it troublesome, trying, difficult. **under stress of ~,** because of storms, etc. **2** (compounds) **'~-beaten** *adj* bearing marks or signs which come from exposure to the sun, wind, rain, etc: *a ~-beaten face.* **'~-boarding/-boards** *nn* horizontal boards each of which overlaps the one below to cause rain to run off and so keep the wall, etc, from becoming damp. **'~-bound** *adj* unable to make or continue a journey because of bad ~. **'~-bureau** *n* office where the ~ is studied and where ~ forecasts are made; meteorological office. **'~-chart/-map** *n* diagram showing details of the ~ over a wide area. **'~·cock** *n* ~-vane in the shape of a cock. **'~ forecast** *n* = forecast. **'~-glass** *n* barometer. **'~·man** /-mæn/ *n* (*pl* -men) (colloq) man who reports and forecasts the ~. **'~-proof** *adj* able to stand exposure to the ~, to keep out rain, snow, wind, etc. **'~-ship** *n* one stationed at sea to make observations of the ~. **'~-station** *n* one where the ~ is observed. **'~-vane** *n* = vane(1).

weather[2] /ˈweðə(r)/ *vt,vi* **1** [VP6A] come through successfully: *~ a storm;* (fig) *~ a crisis.* **2** [VP6A] sail to the windward of: *~ a cape.* **3** [VP6A] expose to the weather: *~ wood,* leave it in the open air until it is properly shrunk and ready for use. ⇨ season, *v*(1). **4** [VP6A,2A] discolour, be discoloured, (cause to) become worn by the weather: *rocks ~ed by wind and water; ~ed limestone.*

weave /wiv/ *vt,vi* (*pt* wove /wəʊv/, *pp* woven /ˈwəʊvn/) **1** [VP6A,15A,B,2A] **~ sth (up) into sth, ~ sth from sth,** make (by hand or by machine) (threads) into cloth, etc; make (cloth, etc) from threads; work at a loom: *~ cotton yarn into cloth; ~ threads together; woven from/of silk;* make (garlands, baskets, etc) by a similar process: *~ flowers into a wreath; ~ a garland of flowers.* **2** [VP6A,15A] (fig) put together, compose (a story, romance, etc): *~ a story round an incident; ~ a plot.* **get weaving (on sth),** (sl) make an energetic start (on a task, etc). **3** [VP2C] twist and turn: *The driver was weaving (his way) through the traffic. The road ~s through the valleys.* □ *n* style of weaving: *a loose/tight/coarse/plain, etc ~.* **weaver** *n* person whose trade is weaving cloth at a loom.

web /web/ *n* [C] **1** network (usu fig): *a web of lies/deceit/intrigue.* **2** ⇨ the illus at arachnid. sth made of threads by a spider or other spinning creature: *a spider's web,* ⇨ cobweb. **3** skin joining the toes of some waterbird, e g ducks, geese, bats and some water-animals (e g frogs). Hence, **'web-'footed/-'toed** *adjj* **webbed** *adj* having the toes joined by webs. ⇨ the illus at fowl.

web·bing /ˈwebɪŋ/ *n* [U] strong fabric (usu coarse woven) used in belts, upholstery, binding the edges of rugs, etc.

wed /wed/ *vt,vi* (*pt,pp* wedded) [VP6A,14,2A] **1** marry. **2** unite: *simplicity wed to beauty.* **wedded to,** devoted to; unable to give up: *He is wedded to his own opinions and nothing can change him.*

we'd /wid/ = we had/would.

wed·ding /ˈwedɪŋ/ *n* marriage ceremony (and festivities connected with it): *attend/invite one's friends to a ~; the ~ dress.* **'~ breakfast** *n* meal for the bride and bridegroom, their relatives, friends, etc between the ~ ceremony and departure for the honeymoon. **'~-cake** *n* cake distributed to guests and sent in small portions to absent friends. **'~-ring** *n* ring placed on the bride's (and in some cases the groom's) finger and worn by her/him afterwards. **silver/golden/diamond ~,** 25th/50th/60th or 75th anniversary of a ~.

wedge /wedʒ/ *n* **1** V-shaped piece of wood or metal, used to split wood or rock (by being hammered), to widen an opening, or to keep two things separate. **the thin end of the ~,** (fig) a small change or demand likely to lead to big changes or demands. **2** sth shaped like or used like a ~: *a ~ of cake,* e g cut from a large round cake; *seats arranged in a ~,* so as to form a triangle. □ *vt* [VP6A,15A,22] fix tightly (as) with a ~; keep in place with a ~: *~ packing into a crack; ~ a door open,* by placing a ~ under it. *I was so tightly ~d between two fat women that it was difficult for me* *to get up and leave the bus.*

wed·lock /ˈwedlɒk/ *n* [U] condition of being married: *born in lawful* ~, born of married parents; *born out of* ~, illegitimate.

Wednes·day /ˈwenzdɪ/ *n* fourth day of the week.

wee[1] /wi/ *adj* very small: *just a wee drop of brandy in my coffee.* ***a wee bit,*** (adverbial) a little: *She's a wee bit jealous.* ***the wee folk,*** the fairies. ***the wee hours,*** (US) the hours after midnight. □ *n* (Scot) ***bide a wee,*** stay for a short time.

wee[2], **wee-wee** /(ˈwi) wi/ *n* (used by and to small children) urine: *do a wee-wee.* □ *vi* urinate.

weed /wid/ *n* [C] **1** wild plant growing where it is not wanted (e g in a garden, or in a field of wheat): *My garden is running to* ~*s,* is overgrown with ~s. ˈ**~-killer** *n* substance used to kill ~s. **2** (fig) thin, tall, weak-looking person or horse. **3** (dated sl) cigar; cigarette; tobacco; (mod sl) marijuana. □ *vt,vi* **1** [VP6A,2A] take ~s out of (the ground): ~ *the garden; be busy* ~*ing.* **2** [VP15B] ***~ sth/sb out,*** remove, get rid of (what is unwanted, or of lower value than the rest): ~ *out the herd,* get rid of the inferior animals. **weedy** *adj* (-ier, -iest) **1** full of, overgrown with, ~s. **2** tall, thin and weak: *a* ~*y young man*; (of a person's character) feeble.

weeds /widz/ *n pl* ˈ**widow's ~,** black clothes as formerly worn by a widow for mourning.

week /wik/ *n* **1** any period of seven days; (esp) seven days from Saturday midnight to Saturday midnight: *this/last/next* ~; *this day* ~, one week from today; *this Monday* ~, one week from Monday next; *for the last/next six* ~*s; a six weeks' holiday; tomorrow* ~, eight days from today; *yesterday* ~, eight days ago; *three* ~*s ago yesterday,* twenty-two days ago; *the working* ~, (usu) Monday to Friday or Saturday. *What day of the* ~ *is it?* Cf What's the date? ***~ in, ~ out,*** for ~s in succession. ˈ**~·ˈend** *n* Saturday and Sunday (as a period of rest or holiday): *a* ~*end visit to the country; spend the* ~*end with friends.* □ *vi* spend a ~end: *I'm* ~*ending at Brighton.* ˈ**~·ˈender** *n* person spending the ~end away from home. **2** the working days of the ~. ˈ**~·day** /-deɪ/ *n* any day except Sunday: *I'm always busy on* ~*days.* (attrib) *Are there any* ~*day services in the church?* **~·ly** *adj, adv* (happening) once a ~, every ~; of, for or lasting a ~: *a* ~*ly wage of £20;* ~*ly visits.* □ *n* periodical published once a ~.

ween /win/ *vt* (archaic) be of the opinion (*that*).

weeny /ˈwinɪ/ *adj* (-ier, -iest) (often ˈ*teeny-*ˈ~) (colloq) tiny.

weep /wip/ *vi,vt* (*pt,pp* **wept** /wept/) [VP2A,B, C,4B,3A,6A] cry; let tears fall from the eyes: ~ *for joy;* ~ *over one's misfortunes. She wept to see him in such a terrible state. She wept (over) her sad fate. She wept bitter tears. She wept herself to sleep.* **~·ing** *adj* (of trees, e g the birch and willow) having drooping branches.

wee·vil /ˈwivl/ *n* small beetle with a hard shell, feeding on and infesting stores of grain, nuts and other seeds.

weft /weft/ *n* cross-threads taken over and under the warp in weaving.

weigh /weɪ/ *vt,vi* **1** [VP6A,15B,2C] measure (by means of a scale, balance, etc) how heavy sth is: *He* ~*ed himself on the scales. He* ~*ed the stone* (= estimated how heavy it was) *in his hands.* ***~ sth out,*** distribute in definite quantities; take a definite quantity of: *She* ~*ed out flour, sugar and butter for a cake.* ***~ in,*** (of a jockey, boxer, etc) be ~ed before a race or contest. ***~ in (with),*** produce (arguments, facts, etc) triumphantly; bring (them) to bear on a discussion. ˈ**~-bridge** *n* ~ing-machine with a platform on to which vehicles, etc can be driven to be ~ed. ˈ**~-ing-machine** *n* machine for ~ing objects that are too large for a simple balance or scale. **2** [VP2B] show a certain measure when put on a scale, etc: ~ *10 kilos/a ton/nothing, etc.* **3** [VP2C] (of a machine, etc) be capable of taking, designed to take, objects up to a specified weight: *This machine will* ~ *up to 5 tons.* **4** [VP6A,14,15B] ***~ sth (with/against sth),*** compare the importance, value, etc of (one thing and another): ~ *one plan against another.* ***~ sth (up),*** consider carefully, assess: ~ (*up*) *the consequences of an action;* ~ *one's words,* consider/choose them carefully; ~ *the pros and cons.* **5** [VP15A,3A] ***~ sth down,*** pull or bring down; depress: *The fruit* ~*ed the branches down.* ***~ sb down,*** depress; make tired, troubled, etc: ~*ed down with sorrow/cares/anxieties.* ***~ on sb/sth,*** cause concern, anxiety (because of importance, seriousness): *The problem/responsibility* ~*s heavily on him/his mind.* ***~ with,*** influence: *evidence that did not* ~ *with the judges; the point that* ~*s with me.* **6** ***~ anchor,*** raise the anchor and start a voyage.

weight /weɪt/ *n* **1** [U] force with which a body tends towards the centre of the earth. **2** [U] how heavy a thing is; this expressed in some scale (e g tons, kilogrammes) as measured on a scale, weighing-machine, etc (⇨ App 5): *Are bananas sold by* ~ *or at so much a piece? That man is twice my* ~. *My* ~ *is 70 kilos. The two boys are (of) the same* ~. *He is your superior both in size and in* ~. ***under/over ~,*** weighing too little/too much. ***pull one's ~,*** ⇨ pull[2](2). ***put on ~,*** (of a person) become heavier. ***throw one's ~ about,*** (colloq) be domineering or conceited; try to bully people. **3** (not *pl,* but with *indef* or *def art*) load to be supported: *The pillars have a great* ~ *to bear/have to support the* ~ *of the roof. That's a great* ~ *off my mind. He has a great* ~ *of responsibility.* **4** [U] (degree of) importance or influence: *arguments of great* ~; *opinions that carry* ~; *considerations that had great* ~ *with me.* **5** [C] piece of metal of known ~ used in scales for weighing things: *an ounce/100 grammes/2 lb, etc* ~; heavy object for various purposes: *a clock worked by* ~*s; keep papers down with a* ~ (ˈ*paper*-~). *The doctor said he must not lift* ~*s.* ˈ**~-lifting** *n* gymnastic feat of lifting great ~s. **6** [U] system of units, scale or notation, for expressing ~: *troy/avoirdupois* ~. □ *vt* **1** [VP6A] put a ~ or ~s(5) on; add ~ to; make heavy: ~ *a walking-stick with lead,* e g to make it useful as a weapon; (fig): *Circumstances are* ~*ed in his favour,* give him an extra advantage. **2** ***~ sb down,*** burden with: *He was* ~*ed down with packages.* **3** [VP6A] treat (a fabric) with a mineral substance to make it seem stronger: ~*ed silk.* **~·less** *adj* having no ~, e g because of absence of gravity. **~·less·ness** *n*: *become accustomed to* ~*lessness in a spacecraft.* **weighty** *adj* (-ier, -iest) **1** of great ~; burdensome. **2** influential; important: ~*y considerations/arguments.* **~·ily** /-əlɪ/ *adv* **~i·ness** *n*

weir /wɪə(r)/ *n* [C] wall or barrier across a river to control the flow of water; fence of stakes or branches in a stream as a trap for catching fish.

a weir

weird /wɪəd/ *adj* **1** unnatural; unearthly; connected with fate: *~ shrieks from the darkness of the ruined castle.* **2** (colloq) strange; difficult to understand or explain: *What ~ shoes women sometimes wear!* **~·ly** *adv* **~·ness** *n* **weirdie** /ˋwɪədɪ/ *n* (sl) eccentric person, esp one who is very unconventional in behaviour, dress and appearance.

wel·come /ˋwelkəm/ *adj* **1** received with, giving, pleasure: *a ~ visitor/rest; ~ news; make a friend ~*, show him that his coming is ~. *A loan would be very ~ to me just now.* **2 ~ to, (a)** ungrudgingly permitted: *You are ~ to borrow my bicycle. He is ~ to the use of my library. Anyone is ~ to my share*, may have it. **(b)** (ironic) permitted to have sth burdensome or unwanted: *If anyone thinks he can do this job any better, he's ~ to it/~ to try!* I'll gladly let him have it. **(c)** absolved of the need to express thanks: *You are ~ to it* (usu shortened to) *You're ~.* **3** (as an interjection) *W~ home! W~ to England!* □ *n* [C] greeting, response by word or action, when sb arrives, when an offer is received, etc: *They gave us/We received a warm/cold/enthusiastic, etc ~. The heartiest of ~s awaited us.* □ *vt* [VP6A,15A] show pleasure or satisfaction at sth, at the arrival of sb or sth; greet (in the manner indicated): *~ a friend to one's home; ~ a suggestion warmly/coldly.*

weld /weld/ *vt,vi* **1** [VP6A,15A,B] join (pieces of metal) by hammering or pressure (usu when the metal is softened by heat) or fusing by the use of an oxyacetylene flame or an electric arc; make by doing this; ⇨ the illus at oxyacetylene: *~ the pieces of a broken axle; ~ parts together;* (fig) *arguments that are closely ~ed.* **2** [VP2A] (of iron, etc) be capable of being ~ed: *Some metals ~ better than others.* □ *n* ~ed joint. **~er** *n* workman who ~s.

wel·fare /ˋwelfeə(r)/ *n* [U] condition of having good health, comfortable living and working conditions, etc: *work for the ~ of the nation; be solicitous for sb's ~; child/infant/social ~; ˋ~ work*, organized efforts to improve the ~ of those who need help; *a ˋ~ officer*, one who engages in public ~ work. **the W~ State,** name applied to a country with State-financed social services, e g health, insurance, pensions.

wel·kin /ˋwelkɪn/ *n* (poet) sky: *make the ~ ring*, make the air re-echo with shouts.

well[1] /wel/ *n* **1** shaft, usu lined with brick or stone, for obtaining water from an underground source: *drive/sink a ~.* ˋ**~-water** *n* water from a ~. **2** hole bored for mineral oil: *the ˋoil-~s of Iran.* **3** (old use, or in place-names) spring or foundation of water; (fig) source. ˋ**~-head** *n* source of a spring or fountain. **4** deep, enclosed space in a building, often from roof to basement, for a staircase or lift. **5** (GB) railed space for barristers, etc in a law court. **6** ˋ**~-deck** *n* space on the mai deck of a ship, enclosed by bulwarks and highe decks. □ *vi* [VP2C] **~ out (from/of),** flow, lik water from a ~: *The blood was ~ing out (fron the wound).* **~ over,** overflow. **~ up (in),** rise like water in a ~: *Tears ~ed up in her eyes. Thei anger ~ed up.*

well[2] /wel/ (comp better, superl best) *adv* **1** in good, right or satisfactory manner (placed after th v, and after the direct object if the v is transitive) *The children behaved ~. They are ~-behave children. The house is ~ situated. He speak English ~. W~ done! W~ run! W~ played* (cries indicating satisfaction, praise, etc). *I hop everything is going ~* (= satisfactorily) *with you Do these two colours go ~ together,* Do they harmonize, look satisfactory side by side? *Does thi colour go ~ with that colour?* **do ~,** succeed make progress; prosper: *Simon has done ~ a school this term. Peter is doing ~ in Canada.* **be doing ~,** (progressive tense only) making a goo recovery (from illness, etc): *Both mother and bab are doing ~.* **do oneself ~,** provide oneself wit good things, esp comforts and luxuries. **do ~ by sb,** treat him with generosity. **do ~ out of,** mak a profit from sb or sth. **2** with praise or approval *think/speak ~ of sb. It speaks ~ for your teachin that all your pupils passed the examination,* thi fact is evidence that your teaching was good **stand ~ with sb,** be in his favour: *He stands ~ with his employers,* They like him, think highly o his abilities, etc. **3** fortunately. **be ~ out of sth** be out of an affair without loss, etc: *You are ~ ou of it,* may consider yourself fortunate to be out o the affair. *I wish I was ~ out of this business,* tha I could free myself from it without misfortune. **~ off,** fortunately situated: *He doesn't know when h is ~ off,* does not realize how fortunate he is *These people are very ~ off,* rich. **come off ~ (a)** (of a person) have good fortune; be lucky. **(b** (of an event) have a satisfactory outcome. **do ~ to** (+ inf), used to suggest either good judgemen or good luck: *He did ~ to leave the country befor the revolution started. You would do ~* (= I would be wise for you) *to say nothing about wha happened. You did ~ to come and help.* **4** (mi position) with good reason, justice or likelihood fairly; advisably: *You may ~ be surprised. W might ~ make the experiment. I couldn't very ~ refuse to help them,* It would have been difficult unreasonable, etc, to have done so. *You may quit ~* (= with good reason) *give illness as an excuse We may as ~ begin at once. It may ~ be that...* It is likely or possible that.... **5 may (just) as ~,** ⇨ may(4). **(a)** with equal reason, advantage, justification, etc: *You might just as ~ say that whit is black* (*as say that...*). *Our holidays were ruine by the weather; we might just as ~ have stayed a home!* **(b)** without worse consequences; *You ma as ~ tell me the truth,* i e because if you don't tel me, I shall certainly hear it from others. **be just a ~,** with no loss of advantage, no need for regret *It's just as ~ I didn't lend him the money.* **6** (en position) thoroughly; completely: *Examine th account ~ before you pay it. Shake the bottle ~* **7** to a considerable extent: *He was leaning ~ back/forward in his chair. His name is ~ up in th list,* near the top. *He must be ~ past forty/~ ove forty years of age. He is ~ up in* (= has a goo knowledge of) *business matters. It's ~ worth try* *ing.* **~ away,** (a) making good progress: *We're ~ away,* have made a good start. (b) (colloq) on the way to being slightly drunk, to becoming hilarious, etc. **8 as ~ (as),** in addition (to): He gave me money as ~ as advice. He gave me advice, and money as ~. We shall travel by night as ~ as by day, both by night and by day. *Give me those as ~,* = those, too. **9** (with another *adv*) **pretty ~,** almost: *You're pretty ~ the only person who's willing to help.* □ *pred adj* **1** in good health: *be/look/feel/get ~. I'm quite ~, thank you.* Cf (US) *I'm fine, thank you.* **2** in a satisfactory condition: *All's ~ that ends ~. We're very ~ where we are. All is not ~ in the world nowadays.* **It's all very ~...,** formula (used ironically) to indicate discontent, dissatisfaction, disagreement, etc: *It's all very ~ (for you) to suggest a holiday in Italy, but how am I to find the money?* **3** advisable; desirable: *It would be ~ to start early. It would be just as ~ for you to ask your employer's permission.* **4** lucky; fortunate: *It was ~ for you that nobody saw you.* □ *int* **1** (expressing astonishment) *W~, who would have thought it? W~, ~! I should never have guessed it!* **2** (expressing relief): *W~, here we are at last!* **3** (expressing resignation): *W~, it can't be helped. W~, there's nothing we can do about it.* **4** (expressing understanding or agreement): *Very ~, then, we'll talk it over again tomorrow.* **5** (expressing concession): *W~, you may be right.* **6** (used to resume a story, etc): *W~, as I was saying,...; W~, the next day....* □ *n* [U] that which is good: *wish sb ~,* wish him good fortune, success, etc. **let ~ alone,** not change what is already satisfactory.

well- /wel/ **1** (as an inseparable prefix): **'~-'being** *n* [U] welfare; health, happiness and prosperity: *have a sense of ~-being,* good bodily health; *work for the ~-being of the nation.* **'~-doer** *n* virtuous person. **'~-'doing** *n* [U] virtuous conduct; good deeds. **'~-nigh** *adv* almost: *It's ~-nigh impossible. He was ~-nigh drowned.* **'~-to-'do** *adj* wealthy. **'~-wisher** *n* person who wishes well to one, to a cause, etc. **2** (compounds with numerous participles and words in *-ed,* usu hyphened when attrib (before a *n*), but not hyphened when *pred* except when the compound has acquired a restricted sense): **'~-ad'vised,** prudent; wise: *a ~-advised action.* **'~-ap'pointed,** having all the necessary equipment: *a ~-appointed expedition.* **'~-'balanced,** sane, sensible. **'~-'born,** of a family with good social position. **'~-'bred,** of good upbringing. **'~-con'ducted,** characterized by good organization and control: *a ~-conducted meeting.* **'~-con'nected,** connected by blood or marriage with families of good social position or to rich or influential people. **'~-dis'posed (towards),** having kind feelings (towards); ready to help. **'~-'favoured,** (old use) good-looking. **'~-'found,** = ~-appointed. **'~-'founded,** based on facts, having a foundation in fact; *~-founded suspicions.* **'~-'groomed,** carefully tended; neat; meticulously dressed. **'~-'grounded,** (a) = ~-founded. (b) having a good training in or knowledge of the groundwork of a subject. **'~-'heeled,** (sl) rich. **'~-in'formed,** (a) having wide knowledge. (b) having access to reliable information: *in ~-informed quarters.* **'~-in'tentioned,** aimed or aiming (often or usu unsuccessfully) at good results. **'~-'knit,** compact; firmly jointed, not loose-made (esp of a person or his body). **'~-'known,** widely known. **'~-'lined,** (of a purse, colloq) full of money. **'~-'marked,** definite; distinct. **'~-'meaning,** = ~-intentioned. **'~-'meant,** done, said, etc, with good intentions. **'~-'read,** having read much; having a mind well stored with information as the result of wide reading. **'~-'rounded,** complete and symmetrical. **'~-'set,** = ~-knit. **'~-'spoken,** (a) speaking well, politely, in refined language. (b) spoken well. **'~-'timed,** done, said, at the right or a suitable time. **'~-'tried,** (of methods, remedies) tested and proved useful. **'~-'turned,** (of a compliment, phrase, verse) gracefully expressed. **'~-'worn,** much used; (esp) commonplace; trite.

wel·ling·ton /'welɪŋtən/ *n* **~ (boot),** high waterproof boot reaching to the knee.

Welsh /welʃ/ *n, adj* (the language) of the people of Wales. **'~ 'rabbit,** (occ *~ rarebit*) melted cheese on hot toast.

welsh /welʃ/ *vi, vt* [VP2A,6A] (of a bookmaker) go away without paying (winners of bets laid with him). **~er** *n*

welt /welt/ *n* [C] **1** strip of leather to which the sole and the upper part of a shoe are stitched. **2** = weal[2].

wel·ter[1] /'weltə(r)/ *vi* [VP2C] roll; wallow; be soaked or steeped (in blood, etc). □ *n* general confusion; disorderly mixture or aimless conflict: *the ~ of creeds/political beliefs; a ~ of meaningless verbiage.*

wel·ter[2] /'weltə(r)/ *adj*: *a '~ race,* for horses with heavy-weight riders. **'~-weight,** (esp boxing) boxer weighing between 135 and 147 lb or (61 to 66·6 kg).

wen /wen/ *n* [C] harmless, usu permanent, tumour on the scalp or other part of the body; (fig) abnormally large or overgrown urban area: *the great wen,* London.

wench /wentʃ/ *n* **1** (old use) girl or young woman. **2** (formerly, esp of a country girl) servant-girl: *a buxom ~; a fine strapping ~.* □ *vi* [VP2A] associate with prostitutes.

wend /wend/ *vt* (old use, only in) **~ one's way (home),** go, make one's way.

went /went/ *pt* of go[1].

wept /wept/ *pt,pp* of weep.

were /wɜ(r)/ *pt* of be[1].

we're /wɪə(r)/ = we are.

were·wolf /'wɜwʊlf *US:* 'wɪər-/ *n* (*pl* -wolves /-wʊlvz/) (in myths) human being turned into a wolf.

weren't /wɜnt/ = were not.

wert /wɜrt/ *v*: *thou ~,* (archaic) you were.

Wes·leyan /'wezlɪən/ *n, adj* (member) of the Methodist Church founded by John Wesley in the 18th c.

west /west/ *n* **1** (*sing* with *def art*) point of the horizon where the sun sets; that part of the world, of a country, etc, in this direction: *Bristol is in the ~ of England.* **the W~,** (a) Europe and the continent of America (contrasted with Asia). (b) (world politics) Western Europe and America (contrasted with the USSR and China). (c) the part of the US between the Mississippi River and the Pacific Ocean. (d) ~ern part of any country. **'~-north-'west, '~-south-'west,** ⇨ the illus at compass. **2** (attrib) coming from the ~: *a ~ wind;* towards, at, in the direction of the ~: *on the*

~ *coast;* ~ *longitude.* **the W~ End,** part of London with the largest and most fashionable shops, theatres, etc. Hence, **ˌ~-ˈend** *adj:* *~-end theatres/department stores.* **the ˈ~ country,** part of England ~ of a line from the Isle of Wight to the mouth of the River Severn. Hence, **ˈ~-country** *adj* of, from, characteristic of the ~ country. **W~ Central,** (abbr **WC**) London postal districts. □ *adv* towards the ~: *sail/travel ~.* **go ~,** (hum) die. **~ of,** farther ~ than. **ˈ~·ward** /-wəd/ *adj* towards the ~: *in a ~ward direction.* **~·ward(s)** /-wəd(z)/ *adv: travel ~ward(s).*

west·er·ly /ˈwestəlɪ/ *attrib adj* towards the west; (of winds) from the west. □ *adv* towards the west.

west·ern /ˈwestən/ *adj* of, in, from, characteristic of, the west: *the W~ Hemisphere,* including Europe and America; *~ science,* of Europe and America; *the W~ Empire,* that part of the old Roman Empire with Rome as its capital. □ *n* [C] film or novel dealing with life in the ~ part of the US in the times of the wars with the Red Indians, or one with cowboys, rustlers, sheriffs, etc. **~er** *n* native of the West, esp of the ~ US. **~·ize** /-ɑɪz/ *vt* [VP6A] introduce ~ civilization into. **~·iz·ation** /ˌwestənɑɪˈzeɪʃn *US:* -nɪˈz-/ *n* **ˈ~·most** /-məʊst/ *adj* farthest west.

wet /wet/ *adj* (**wetter, wettest**) **1** covered or soaked with water or other liquid: *wet clothes/roads. Her cheeks were wet with tears. Did you get wet,* e g in the rain? *We got wet to the skin,* Our clothes were soaked through. *Your coat is wet through,* from one side to the other. **ˌwet ˈblanket,** ⇨ blanket(1). **ˌwet ˈdock** *n* one (that can be) filled with water, able to float a ship. **ˈwet-nurse** *n* woman employed to suckle another's child. **ˌwet ˈpaint,** paint recently applied, not yet dry. **2** rainy: *wet weather; the wettest summer for 20 years.* **3** (US) not prohibiting or opposing the sale and use of alcoholic drinks: *a wet State.* **4** (sl, of a person) ineffectual; spiritless. □ *n* **1 the wet,** rain: *Come in out of the wet.* **2** [U] moisture. □ *vt* (**-tt-**) [VP6A] make wet: *The baby has wet(ted) its bed again.* ***wet one's whistle,*** ⇨ whistle, *n*(3). **wet·ting** *n* becoming or being made wet: *get a wetting,* e g in heavy rain.

wether /ˈweðə(r)/ *n* castrated ram.

we've /wiv/ = we have.

whack /wæk *US:* hwæk/ *vt* [VP6A] strike (sb or sth) with a hard blow; thwack. □ *n* **1** (sound of a) hard blow. **2** (sl) share: *Have you all had a fair ~?* **~ed** *adj* (colloq) (of a person) worn out; tired. **~·ing** *n* beating: *give a naughty child a ~ing.* □ *adj* (colloq) big of its kind: *a ~ing lie.* □ *adv* very: *a ~ing great lie.* **~er** *n* sth big of its kind.

whale /weɪl *US:* hweɪl/ *n* **1** kinds of large sea-animal some of which are hunted for their oil and flesh (used for pet foods). ⇨ the illus at sea. **ˈ~-bone** *n* thin, horny springy substance from the upper jaw of some kinds of ~. **2** (colloq) ***a ~ of (a good time),*** an exceedingly (good time); no end of (a good time). □ *vi* [VP2A] hunt ~s: *go whaling; the whaling industry.* **ˈwhaling-gun** *n* one used for firing harpoons at ~s. **whaler** /ˈweɪlə(r) *US:* ˈhw-/ *n* man or ship engaged in hunting ~s.

whang /wæŋ *US:* hwæŋ/ *vt* (colloq) strike heavily and loudly. □ *n* ~ing sound or blow. □ *adv* (colloq) exactly: *hit the target ~ in the centre.*

wharf /wɔf *US:* hwɔrf/ *n* (*pl* ~s or **wharves** /wɔvz/) wooden or stone structure at which ships are moored for (un)loading cargo. **ˈ~·age** /-ɪdʒ/ *n* [U] (money paid for) accommodation at a ~.

what /wot *US:* hwot/ *adj* **1** (interr) asking for a selection from an indefinite number (⇨ which): *W~ books have you read on this subject? Tell me ~ books you have read recently. W~ time is it? Ask him ~ time it is. W~ size/colour/shape, etc do you want?* **2** (exclamatory): *W~ a good idea! W~ genius you have!* **3** the... that; any... that; as much/many... as: *Give me ~ books* (= the books, any books, that) *you have on the subject. W~ little* (= The little that) *he said on the subject was full of wisdom. W~ few friends* (= The few friends that) *I have here have been very kind to me.* □ *pron* (interr) ~ thing(s): *W~ happened? Tell me ~ happened. W~ is he,* W~ is his occupation? ***~ for,*** for ~ purpose: *W~ is this tool used for? W~ did you do that for,* (colloq) Why did you do that? **ˌ~-ˈfor** *n* (colloq) punishment: *He gave the naughty boy ~-for.* **~... *like,*** (used to ask for a description, for details, etc): *W~'s the weather like this morning? W~'s the new neighbour like?* ***~ if,*** ~ will, would, be the result if: *W~ if it rains while we are a long way from shelter? W~ if the rumour is true?* ***~ though,*** ~ does it matter if: *W~ though we are poor, we still have each other.* ***~ about/of,*** **(a)** ~ news is there about.... **(b)** ⇨ about[3](4), of(10). ***Well, ~ of it?*** (or, mod colloq) ***So ~?*** (used to admit that sth is true, but questioning the inference (to be) made from it.) ***and ~ not,*** and other things of the same kind. ***or ~ have you,*** used to indicate that there are other things, etc: *Then there are bills for gas and electricity and ~ have you.* **ˈ~-not** *n* piece of furniture with open shelves for small ornaments, odds and ends. ***I know ~...,*** I have an idea, a suggestion to make.... ***I/I'll tell you ~...,*** Here's a suggestion.... ***know ~'s ~,*** have common sense; know how to distinguish useful things from useless, good things from bad, etc. **ˈ~-d'you-call-him/-her/-it,** etc /ˈwot ʃʊ kɔl ɪm *etc*/; **ˈ~'s-his/-her/-its, etc -name,** used as substitutes for a name that one cannot recall. □ *rel pron* that which; the thing(s) which: *W~ he says is not important. Do ~ you think is right. W~ the country needs most is wise leadership. When people say that they know ~ they like, they really mean that they like ~ they know,* They like ~ they are familiar with. *It's a useful book and, ~ is more, not an expensive one.* **~ *with... and (~ with),*** between various causes: *W~ with overwork and (~ with) undernourishment he fell ill.*

what·e'er /wotˈeə(r) *US:* hw-/ (poet for) **whatever.**

what·ever /wotˈevə(r) *US:* hw-/ *adj* **1** (emphatic for *what*) of any sort, degree, etc: *W~ nonsense the newspapers print, some people always believe it. Take ~ measures you consider best.* **2** (placed after a *n* in a negative context, giving emphasis to the negative): *There can be no doubt ~ about it. I have no intention ~* (= not the least intention) *of resigning.* □ *pron* **1** no matter what: *You are certainly right, ~ others may say. Keep calm, ~ happens.* **2** anything or everything that: *Do ~ you like. W~ I have is at your service.* **3 or ~,** (colloq) (usu at the end of a list of similar *nn* or *adjj*) or anything at all: *He'd have difficulty in learning any language—Greek, Chinese, or ~.*

what·so·e'er /ˌwotsəʊˈeə(r) *US:* ˈhw-/ (poet for)

what·so·ever /ˈwotsəʊˋevə(r) *US:* ˈhw-/ (emphatic for) **whatever**.

wheat /wit *US:* hw-/ *n* [U] (plant producing) grain from which flour (as used for bread and pastry products) is made: *a field of ~.* ⇨ the illus at **cereal**. **~en** /ˋwitn *US:* ˋhw-/ *adj* of ~: *~en flour/bread.*

wheedle /ˋwidl *US:* ˋhw-/ *vt* [VP6A,14] make oneself pleasant to sb, flatter or coax, to get sth one wants: *The girl ~d a pound out of her father/~d her father into buying her a bicycle.*

wheel /wil *US:* hwil/ *n* **1** circular frame or disc which turns on an axle (as on carts, cars, bicycles, etc and for various purposes in machines). ⇨ the illus at **bicycle**. ***~s within ~s,*** (fig) complicated motives and influences; indirect and secret agencies, all interacting. ***put one's shoulder to the ~,*** help a cause or undertaking. ***the man at the ~,*** the driver (at the steering-~ of a car, etc). **ˋ~·barrow** *n* small vehicle with one ~ and two handles for moving small loads. **ˋ~·base** *n* distance between the axles of a motor-vehicle. **ˋ~-chair** *n* chair with large ~s for the use of sb unable to walk. **ˋ~·house** *n* small enclosed place on a ship (old style sailing-ship, a small river-launch, a tug, etc), to shelter the pilot or steersman. **ˋ~·wright** *n* man who makes and repairs (esp waggon and cart) ~s. **2** (old use) bicycle. **3** *ˋpotter's ~,* ⇨ **potter**[2]; *ˋpaddle-~,* ⇨ **paddle**[1]**(3)**. **4** [C] motion like that of a ~; motion of a line of men as on a pivoted end, esp as a military evolution: *a right/left ~.* □ *vt,vi* **1** [VP6A, 15A,B] push or pull (a vehicle with ~s): *~ a bike up a hill; ~ a barrow;* convey (sb or sth) in a vehicle with ~s: *~ the rubbish out to the dump.* **2** [VP2A,C,6A,15B] (cause to) turn in a curve or circle: *The sails of the windmill were ~ing round. The seagulls were ~ing in the air above me. Right/Left ~!* (an order given to a column of men, esp troops, to change their line of route to the right (left)).

wheeze /wiz *US:* hwiz/ *vi,vt* **1** [VP2A,B,C] breath noisily, esp with a whistling sound in the chest (as when suffering from asthma); (of a pump, etc) make a similar sound. **2** [VP15B] ***~ sth out,*** utter with such sounds: *The asthmatic old man ~d out a few words. A barrel-organ was wheezing out an old tune.* □ *n* [C] **1** sound of wheezing. **2** (dated school sl) trick; bright idea. **wheezy** *adj* breathing, speaking, uttered, with ~s: *a fat and wheezy old dog; a wheezy old pump.* **wheez·ily** /-əlɪ/ *adv* **wheezi·ness** *n*

whelk /welk *US:* hwelk/ *n* kinds of marine mollusc (like a snail) with a spiral shell, some used as food. ⇨ the illus at **mollusc**.

whelp /welp *US:* hwelp/ *n* **1** young dog, lion, tiger, bear, wolf, fox, etc. **2** ill-bred boy or youth. □ *vi* give birth to ~s**(1)**.

when /wen *US:* hwen/ *interr adv* **1** at what time; on what occasion: *W~ can you come? W~ did that happen? I don't know ~ that happened.* **2** (after a prep) what time: *Till ~ can you stay? Since ~ has he been missing?* □ *rel adv* (with *day, time,* etc as antecedent) at or on which: *Sunday is the day ~ I am least busy. There are times ~ joking is not permissible. It was one of those cold, wet evenings ~ most people stay indoors.* □ *conj* **1** at or during the time that: *It was raining ~ we arrived. He raised his hat ~ he saw her. W~ speaking French, I often make mistakes.* **2** although: *He walks ~ he might take a taxi.* **3** since; considering that: *How can I help them to understand ~ they won't listen to me?* **4** at or during which time: *The Queen will visit the town in May, ~ she will open the new hospital.*

whence /wens *US:* hwens/ *adv* (old use) **1** (in questions) from what place or cause: *Do you know ~ she came? W~ comes it that…,* How is it that…? **2** (in statements) from which place: *the land ~ they are come.* **3** to the place from which: *Return ~ you came.* **ˈ~·so·ˋever** *adv, conj* from whatever place, cause or origin.

when·ever /wenˋevə(r) *US:* hw-/ *adv* **1** at whatever time; no matter when: *I'll discuss it with you ~ you like to come.* **2** on any occasion; as often as; every time that: *W~ that man says 'To tell the truth', I suspect that he's about to tell a lie.* **3** ***or ~,*** (colloq) or at any time: *He might turn up on Monday, or Friday, or ~, and expect to be given a meal.*

where /weə(r) *US:* hweə(r)/ *interr adv* **1** in or to what place or position; in what direction; in what respect: *W~ does he live? I wonder ~ he lives. W~ shall we be* (i e What will be our situation) *if another world war breaks out?* **2** (with a *prep* following the *v*) what place: *W~ does he come from? W~ are you going to? W~ did we get up to,* i e What point did we reach? □ *rel adv* **1** (with *place,* etc as antecedent) in or at which: *She would like to live in a country ~ it never snows. That's the place ~ the accident occurred.* **2** (with no antecedent) in, at or to the place in which; in the direction in which: *W~ there is no rain, farming is difficult or impossible. I found my books ~ I had left them. That's ~* (i e the point in respect of which) *you are mistaken.* **ˈ~·aˋbouts** *adv* in or near what place: *W~abouts did you find it? I wonder ~abouts he put it.* □ *n* (ˋ*~abouts*) (with *sing* or *pl,v*) place ~ sb or sth is: *Her present ~abouts is/are unknown.* **ˈ~·ˋas** *conj* **1** (esp legal) considering that. **2** but in contrast; while on the other hand: *Some people like fat meat, ~as others hate it.* **ˈ~·ˋat** *adv* (old use) at or upon which. **ˈ~-ˋby** *adv* by what; by which: *He devised a plan ~by he might escape.* **ˋ~·fore** *adv* (old use) why. □ *conj* for which reason; why. □ *n pl*: *the whys and the ~fores,* the reasons. **ˈ~·ˋin** *adv* (formal) in what; in which; in what respect: *W~in am I mistaken?* **ˈ~·ˋof** *adv* (formal) of what; of which. **ˈ~-ˋon** *adv* on which; on what. **ˈ~·so·ˋever** *adv* (emphatic for) *~ver.* **ˈ~·ˋto** *adv* (old use) to what; to which; to what end (= purpose). **ˈ~·ˋunto** *adv* (old use) = *~to.* **ˈ~·uˋpon** *adv* after which; and then. **wher·ever** /ˈweərˋevə(r) *US:* ˈhw-/ *adv* in, to, at, whatever place; at those places: *Sit ~ver you like. He comes from Boula, ~ver that may be,* from a place called Boula, and I have no idea where it is. **ˈ~·ˋwith** *adv* (old use) with that; with which. **ˋ~·withal** /-wɪðɔl/ *adv* (old use) = *~*with. □ *n* (*sing* with *def art*) (colloq) money needed for a purpose: *I should like to buy a new car but haven't got the ~withal.*

wherry /ˋwerɪ *US:* ˋhw-/ *n* (*pl* **-ries**) light, shallow rowing-boat for carrying passengers and goods on rivers.

whet /wet *US:* hwet/ *vt* **(-tt-)** [VP6A] sharpen (a knife, axe, etc); (fig) sharpen or excite (the appetite, a desire). **ˋ~·stone** *n* shaped stone used for sharpening tools, e g scythes.

whether /ˋweðə(r) *US:* ˋhw-/ *conj* **1** (introducing

an indirect question; ⇨ VP10,21; often replaced by *if* in colloq style except when there is possible confusion with a true conditional clause): *I don't know ~ she will be able to come. I wonder ~/if it's large enough.* (Note that when there are two indirect questions with *or*, ~ is repeated after *or*: *I wonder ~ we shall be in time for the last bus or ~ we shall have to walk home.*) Compare ~ and *if* in these sentences: *Send me a telegram letting me know ~ I am to come,* i e saying 'Come' or 'Don't come'. *Send me a telegram if I am to come,* i e only if I am to come, no telegram being needed if I am not to come. **2** (introducing an infinitive phrase; ⇨ VP8,20): *I don't know ~ to accept or refuse. Would you advise me ~ to accept the offer (or not)?* **3** (Clauses and infinitive phrases introduced by ~ are used with preparatory *it*): *It's doubtful ~ we shall be able to come.* (Such clauses and phrases may be subjects or complements): *The question was ~ to take the children to the funeral or to leave them at home. W~ to pay the price demanded was a question that worried him a long time.* (Such a clause may be the object of a *prep*): *Everything depends upon ~ we have enough money. I am not interested in ~ you like the plan or not.* (A clause introduced by ~ may be used in opposition to a *n*): *I am in doubt ~ I ought to give this plan my approval. The question ~ we ought to call in a specialist was answered by the family doctor.* **~ or no,** in either case: *You may rely upon my help, ~ or no,* e g ~ the others agree to help, or refuse to help.

whew /hju *or similar sounds roughly breathed out*/ *int* cry used (often in joke) to express consternation, dismay, fatigue or surprise.

whey /weɪ *US:* hweɪ/ *n* [U] liquid part of sour milk after separation of curds (for cheese).

which /wɪtʃ *US:* hwɪtʃ/ *interr adj* (asking for selection from two, or from a group, esp from possibilities thought of as limited in number; ⇨ what) **1** *W~ way shall we go—up the hill or along the river bank? W~ way* (= How) *shall we do it? W~ Jones do you mean; Jones the baker or Jones the postman? W~ foreign languages have you studied? Tell me ~ ones you want.* **2** (*rel adj*, formal, and rare except after a *prep*; preceded by a comma) and this; and these: *I told him to go to a doctor, ~ advice he took,* and this advice he took. *Don't call between 1 o'clock and 2 o'clock, at ~ time I am usually having lunch.* □ *interr pron* ~ thing(s); ~ person(s): *W~ is taller, Tom or Dick? W~ of the boys is the tallest? W~ of you wish to go with me? Tell me ~ of them is better. Please advise me ~ to take. The twins are so much alike that I never know ~ is ~,* i e I cannot distinguish one from the other. □ *rel pron* (in mod use, of things only, not of persons; ⇨ that) **1** (in defining or restrictive clauses, often replaced by *that;* used with no selective meaning; no pause before the clause and not set off by commas) **(a)** (with the *rel pron* as the subject of the *v* in the clause): *Take the book ~ is lying on that table. The house ~ is for sale is at the end of the street. The river ~ flows through London is called the Thames.* **(b)** (with the *rel pron* as the object of the *v* in the clause; in spoken English usually suppressed): *Was the book ~ you were reading a novel?* **(c)** (with the *rel pron* as the object of a *prep;* replaceable by *that,* with the *prep* following the *v;* if ~ is used, the *prep* should precede): *The photographs at ~ you were looking/The photographs (that) you were looking at were all taken by my brother. The hotel at ~ we stayed/The hotel we stayed at was both cheap and comfortable. The book to ~ I wanted to refer/The book I wanted to refer to was not in the library. The shop opposite ~ the car is parked is a grocer's.* **2** (in non-defining or non-restrictive clauses, rare in the spoken language but common in the written language; ~ is not replaceable by *that;* the clause is preceded by a pause and is set off by commas) **(a)** (referring to an antecedent *n*): (*i*) (with the *rel pron* as the subject of the clause): *This house, ~ is to be sold by auction next month, was built about fifty years ago. The meeting, ~ was held in the park, was attended by five hundred people.* (*ii*) (with the *rel pron* as the object of the *v* in the clause): *These apple-trees, ~ I planted three years ago, have not yet borne any fruit. This desk, ~ I bought second-hand, is made of oak.* (*iii*) (with the *rel pron* as the object of a *prep*): *His car, for ~ he paid £800, is a five-seater saloon. Their house, at ~ I have often stayed, is just outside Dorking.* **(b)** (in non-defining clauses that refer to a clause or sentence, not to a *n*): *It was raining hard, ~* (= and this) *kept us indoors. He said he had lost the book, ~* (= but this) *was untrue.* (The clause may occasionally precede the sentence to ~ it refers): *Moreover, ~ you may hardly believe, the examiners had decided in advance to fail half the candidates!*

which·ever /wɪtʃˈevə(r) *US:* hw-/ *adj, pron* **1** the one which: *Take ~ you like best. W~ (of you) comes in first will receive a prize.* **2** no matter which: *W~ of the three sisters you choose to marry, you will have a good wife. Does British foreign policy remain the same, ~ party is in power?* **ˈwhich·so·ˈever,** (emphatic for) ~.

whiff /wɪf *US:* ˈhwɪf/ *n* [C] **1** slight puff or breath (*of* sth): *a ~ of fresh air; the ~* (= smell) *of a cigar. Give her another ~ of chloroform. He stopped work to have a few ~s,* a short smoke (of a pipe, etc). **2** (colloq) small cigar. □ *vt, vi* [VP6A] blow or puff lightly.

Whig /wɪg *US:* hwɪg/ *n* member of a political party in GB which upheld the authority of Parliament (against the sovereign) during the 17th and 18th cc, their place being taken in the 19th c by the Liberals.

while /waɪl *US:* hwaɪl/ *n* (period of) time: *Where have you been all this ~? I haven't seen him for a long ~/for this long ~ past. We're going away for a ~. I'll be back in a little ~,* soon. *He was here a short ~ ago.* **once in a ~,** occasionally. **worth (one's) ~,** worth the time spent in doing it, etc: *It isn't worth ~ going there now,* i e it would be a waste of time to go. *He will make it worth your ~,* i e will pay or reward you in some way. □ *vt* (only in) **~ away,** pass the time in a leisurely way: *~ away the time; ~ a few hours away.* □ *conj* **1** during the time that; for as long as; at the same time as: *He fell asleep ~ (he was) studying his grammar book. W~ in London he studied music. W~* (= As long as) *there is life there is hope.* **2** (implying a contrast) whereas: *Jane was dressed in brown ~ Mary was dressed in blue.* **3** (implying a concession) although: *W~ I admit that the problems are difficult, I don't agree that they cannot be solved.* **whilst** /waɪlst *US:* hwaɪlst/ *conj* = ~.

whim /wɪm *US:* hwɪm/ *n* [C] sudden desire or

idea, often sth unusual or unreasoning: *only a passing ~*, an idea, a desire, that will soon pass; *full of ~s. His every ~ is complied with.*

whim·per /ˈwɪmpə(r) *US:* ˋhw-/ *vi,vt* **1** [VP2A] utter weak frightened or complaining sounds, e g a baby when ill, a dog when frightened of punishment. **2** [VP6A] utter in a ~ing voice. □ *n* [C] ~ing cry; sobbing sound.

whimsy, whim·sey /ˈwɪmzɪ *US:* ˋhw-/ *n* (*pl* **-sies, -seys**) **1** [C] whim; fanciful idea or wish. **2** [U] quaintness; odd or fanciful humour. **whim·si·cal** /ˈwɪmzɪkl *US:* ˋhw-/ *adj* full of whimsies; quaint. **whim·si·cally** /-klɪ/ *adv* **whim·si·cal·ity** /ˈwɪmzɪˋkæləti *US:* ˈhw-/ *n* [U] quality of being whimsical; [C] (*pl* **-ties**) caprice; quaint fancy.

whin /wɪn *US:* hw-/ *n* [U] furze; gorse.

whine /wɑɪn *US:* hwɑɪn/ *n* [C] long-drawn complaining cry or high-pitched sound (e g as made by a miserable dog, a siren, a motor or a shell in flight). □ *vi,vt* **1** [VP2A,C,4A] make such cries; utter complaints, esp about trivial things: *The dog was whining outside the door/whining to come into the room. If that child doesn't stop whining, I'll drown it!* **2** [VP6A,15B] utter with a ~ or ~s: *beggars whining (out) requests for alms.* **whiner** *n* animal or person that ~s.

whinny /ˈwɪnɪ *US:* ˋhw-/ *n* (*pl* **-nies**) gentle neigh. □ *vi* (*pt,pp* **-nied**) make such a sound.

whip[1] /wɪp *US:* hwɪp/ *n* [C] **1** lash (length of cord, strip of leather, etc) fastened to a handle, used for urging a horse on, or for punishing. ***have the ~ hand (over sb),*** have mastery over; be in a position to control. **ˋ~·cord** *n* **(a)** tightly twisted cord used for the lashes of ~s. **(b)** kind of hard-wearing worsted fabric. **2** (also **ˈ~per-ˋin**) (fox-hunting) servant who controls the hounds. **3** organizing secretary of a political party (in GB and US) with authority over its members to maintain discipline and secure attendance at parliamentary debates and divisions(**6**); order given by such a secretary to members of his party to attend a debate and vote. ***a three-line ~,*** urgent order of this kind, with three underlines. *The ~s are off,* members may vote as they wish. **4** preparation of eggs, cream, etc beaten or whipped(**2**): *prune ~*. **~py** *adj* flexible; springy.

whip[2] /wɪp *US:* hwɪp/ *vt,vi* (**-pp-**) **1** [VP6A,15A,B] strike with a whip; beat or flog: *~ a horse/a child; ~ a top,* ⇨ **top**[3]. *The rain was ~ping the window-panes,* beating against them. *The driver ~ped the horses on.* **2** [VP6A] beat (eggs, cream, etc) with a fork or other utensil to mix thoroughly or to make stiff: *~ped cream.* **3** [VP6A] (colloq) defeat. **4** [VP15B,2C] take, be taken, move, be moved, suddenly: *He ~ped off his coat. He ~ped out a knife. The thief ~ped the jewels off the counter. The thief ~ped round the corner and disappeared in the crowd.* ***~ round for subscriptions, etc,*** appeal to friends, members of a club, etc for subscriptions (esp to help sb who has suffered a loss, etc), for money to buy a gift, etc. Hence, **ˋ~-round** *n* such an appeal. **5** [VP6A] bind (a stick, a rope-end, etc) with a close, tight covering of thread or string; sew (a seam, the edge of a piece of cloth) with stitches that pass over and over. **~·ping** *n* [C] beating with a whip as a punishment. **ˋ~·ping-boy** *n* (in olden times) boy educated with a prince and ~ped when the prince deserved punishment; (hence) scapegoat. **ˋ~-ping-post** *n* post to which persons were tied to be ~ped. **ˋ~·ping-top** *n* = **top**[3].

whip·per-in /ˈwɪpər ˋin *US:* ˋhw-/ ⇨ **whip**[1]**(2)**.

whip·per-snap·per /ˋwɪpə snæpə(r) *US:* ˋhw-/ *n* young insignificant person who intrudes upon people and behaves as if he were important.

whip·pet /ˋwɪpɪt *US:* ˋhw-/ *n* dog that looks like a small greyhound, used for racing.

whip-poor-will /ˋwɪp pʊə wɪl *US:* ˋhwɪp pər/ *n* small American bird whose call (made at night or twilight) is imitative of its name.

whir /wɜ(r) *US:* hw-/ = **whirr**.

whirl /wɜl *US:* hwɜl/ *vt,vi* **1** [VP15A,B,2C] (cause to) move quickly round and round: *The wind ~ed the dead leaves about. The leaves came ~ing down in the autumn wind. The dancers ~ed round the room.* **2** [VP15A,B,2C] (cause to) move or travel rapidly (*off, away,* etc): *The telegraph poles ~ed past us as the train gathered speed. Our friends were ~ed away in Jack's sports-car.* **3** [VP2A,C] (of the brain, the senses) seem to go round and round; (of thoughts) be confused: *His head ~ed.* □ *n* (*sing* only) **1** ~ing movement: *a ~ of dust/of dead leaves. His brain was in a ~,* (fig) a confused state. **2** rapid succession of activities, etc: *the ~ of modern life in a big city; a ~ of social engagements,* e g cocktail parties, receptions. **3** (compounds) **ˋ~·pool** *n* place where there are ~ing currents (circular eddies) in the sea, etc (usu drawing floating objects towards its centre). **ˋ~·wind** *n* swift circling current of air in a funnel-shaped column: *Sow the wind and reap the ~wind,* (prov) Do wrong and, as a result, bring severe punishment upon oneself.

whirli·gig /ˋwɜlɪgɪg *US:* ˋhw-/ *n* **1** kinds of spinning top, ⇨ **top**[3]. **2** revolving motion: *the ~ of time,* the changes of fortune that come with time.

whirr /wɜ(r) *US:* hwɜ/ *n* (*sing* only) sound (as) of a bird's wings moving quickly, or of wheels, etc turning fast: *the ~ of an aircraft's propellers.* □ *vi* (**-rr-**) [VP2A,C] make such sounds: *A bird ~red past.*

whisk /wɪsk *US:* hw-/ *n* **1** small brush for removing dust (from clothes, etc). **(ˋfly-)~,** brush made of hair for flapping flies away from one's person. **2** device (e g coiled wire) for whipping eggs, cream, etc. **3** light brushing movement (e g of a horse's tail). □ *vt,vi* **1** [VP15B] ***~ sb/sth off/away,*** brush quickly and lightly: *~ the flies off.* **2** [VP6A] move or sweep quickly through the air: *The cow ~ed her tail.* **3** [VP15B] take (sb) quickly and suddenly: *They ~ed him off to prison. I was ~ed up to the top floor in an express lift.* **4** [VP6A] = whip[2](2): *~ eggs.*

whisker /ˋwɪskə(r) *US:* ˋhw-/ *n* **1** (*pl*) hair allowed to grow on the sides of a man's face. ⇨ **beard(1), moustache. 2** one of the long, stiff hairs growing near the mouth of a cat, rat, etc. **~ed** *adj* having ~s.

whis·key /ˋwɪskɪ *US:* ˋhw-/ *n* (*pl* **-keys**) US and Irish spelling of **whisky**.

whisky /ˋwɪskɪ *US:* ˋhw-/ *n* (*pl* **-kies**) (GB and Canadian spelling) [C,U] strong alcoholic drink distilled from malted grain (esp barley or rye); drink of this: *Two whiskies, please.*

whis·per /ˋwɪspə(r) *US:* ˋhw-/ *vi,vt* **1** [VP2A,3A,6A,14,19] speak, say (sth), using the breath but no vibration of the vocal cords: *~ (a word) to sb; ~ (to sb) that.* **ˋ~·ing-gallery,** gallery in which a sound made at one point may be heard at another far off (owing to acoustic peculiarities). **2** [VP6A, 15B] tell privately or secretly; (esp) put (a story, slander) into circulation: *The story is being ~ed about the neighbourhood. It is ~ed that he is heavily in debt.* **'~ing campaign,** systematic attack on sb by passing from person to person malicious statements, etc. **3** [VP2A,C] (of leaves, the wind, etc) make soft sounds; rustle: *The wind was ~ing in the pines.* □ *n* **1** ~ing sound or speech: *He answered in a ~. They were talking in ~s.* **2** ~ed remark; sth ~ed secretly; rumour: *W~s are going round that the firm is likely to go bankrupt.* **~er** *n*

whist /wɪst *US:* hwɪst/ *n* card-game for two pairs of players. **'~-drive** *n* series of games played by several sets of partners at different tables, certain players after each round passing to the next table.

whistle /'wɪsl *US:* 'hw-/ *n* **1** (usu steady) clear note made by forcing air or steam through a small opening, or made by the wind; tuneful sound made by some kinds of bird (e g the blackbird): *We heard the ~ of a steam-engine.* **'~-stop** *n* (US) short stop (during a journey made by a politician) for electioneering purposes (e g to speak to voters in a rural district): (attrib) *a ~-stop tour.* **2** instrument for producing such sounds: *the referee's ~; a 'steam-~,* sounded by a jet of steam. **3** (only in) ***wet one's ~,*** (colloq) have a drink. □ *vi,vt* **1** [VP2A,C] make a ~(1) (e g by blowing through the rounded lips or by using a ~(2): *The engine/The driver ~d before reaching the level-crossing. The wind ~d through the rigging/up the chimney, etc.* **~ *for sth,*** wish in vain for: *I owe my butcher £10, but he can ~ for it,* I shan't pay him. **2** [VP2A,C,6A] produce a tune in this way: *~ a tune. The boy was whistling (away) merrily.* **3** [VP6A,15A,16A] make a signal (to) by this means: *He ~d his dog back/~d to his dog to come back to him.* **4** [VP2A,C] pass swiftly with a whistling sound: *The bullets/arrows ~d past our ears.*

whit /wɪt *US:* hwɪt/ *n* (only in) ***not a ~, no ~,*** not the least, not at all: *There's not a ~ of truth in the statement. I don't care a ~.*

Whit /wɪt *US:* hwɪt/ *n* ⇨ **Whitsun.**

white[1] /waɪt *US:* hwaɪt/ *adj* **1** of the colour of fresh snow or common salt: *His hair has turned ~. Her face went ~,* pale. ***bleed ~,*** drain of wealth, strength, etc. **2** of ~ men (⇨ below): *~ civilization.* **3** (special uses, compounds) **'~ alloy,** any of various alloys that are cheap imitations of silver. **'~ ant,** termite. **'~-bait** *n* [U] small fish, the young of several varieties, eaten fried when small (about 2 inches long). **'~ bear,** polar bear. **'~-caps** *n pl* waves at sea with ~ foam on their crests. **'~-'collar,** used as a symbol of non-manual labour: *~ collar jobs/workers; ~-collared employees.* ⇨ *black-coated* at black(4), *blue-collared* at blue[2](7). **~ coffee,** with milk added. **'~ 'elephant/'ensign/'feather,** ⇨ these nouns. **~ flag,** symbol of surrender. **~ heat,** temperature at which metals become ~; (fig) intense passion. Hence, **'~-'hot** *adj* **the 'W~ House,** the official residence of the President of the US, Washington, DC. **~ lead** *n* poisonous compound of lead carbonate, used in paints. **~ lie,** lie considered to be harmless, esp one told for the sake of being polite: *She tells enough ~ lies to ice a wedding-cake!* **'~-'lipped** *adj* having ~ lips, esp with fear. **'~-'livered** *adj* cowardly. **'~ 'magic,** ⇨ magic. **'~ man** /-mən/ *n* (*pl* -men) member of one of the races inhabiting, or having formerly inhabited, Europe. **'~ 'meat,** poultry, veal, pork. **'~ 'metal,** ~ alloy. **'~ 'paper,** (GB) report issued by the Government to give information. **the ~ scourge,** tuberculosis. **'~d 'sepulchre,** (from Matt 23: 27) person who appears to be righteous but is in fact wicked; hypocrite. **~ sheet,** ~ robe of a penitent: *stand in a ~ sheet,* confess sin. **~ slave,** ~ girl who is forced to be a prostitute, esp one who is tricked into going to a foreign country by promises of employment: *the '~-'slave traffic.* **'~-thorn** *n* hawthorn. **~ tie,** ~ bow tie worn with men's full evening dress; (short for) full evening dress: *Is it dinner jacket or ~ tie?* **'~-wash** *n* [U] mixture of powdered lime or chalk and water, used for coating walls, ceilings, etc; (fig) means used to cover or hide sb's errors, faults, etc. □ *vt* put ~wash on (a wall, etc); (fig) try to make (sb, his reputation, etc) appear blameless by covering up his faults, etc.

white[2] /waɪt *US:* hwaɪt/ *n* **1** [U] ~ colour: *dressed in ~.* **2** [C] ~ man. **3** [C,U] colourless part round the yolk of an egg: *Take the ~s of two eggs.... There's too much ~ of egg in this mixture.* **4** [C] the ~ part of the eyeball: *Don't fire until you see the ~s of their eyes,* until they are very close. **~·ness** *n* **whiten** /'waɪtn *US:* 'hw-/ *vt,vi* [VP6A,2A] make or become ~.

White·hall /waɪt'hɔl *US:* hw-/ *n* (street in London where there are) Government offices; (hence) British Government (policy).

whiten·ing /'waɪtn̩ɪŋ *US:* 'hw-/ *n* [U] = **whiting**[2].

whither /'wɪðə(r) *US:* 'hw-/ *adv* (old use) where; (current use, much rhet, in journalism) what is the likely future of: *W~ Ulster? W~ the pound sterling?* **'~so·'ever** *adv* (old use) to whatever place; anywhere at all.

whit·ing[1] /'waɪtɪŋ *US:* 'hw-/ *n* (*pl* unchanged) kinds of small sea-fish used as food.

whit·ing[2] /'waɪtɪŋ *US:* 'hw-/ *n* [U] powdered white chalk used in whitewashing, and for polishing silver, etc.

whit·low /'wɪtləʊ *US:* 'hw-/ *n* small inflamed place on a finger or toe, esp near the nail.

Whit·sun /'wɪtsn *US:* 'hw-/ *n* (also *'Whit 'Sunday*) 7th Sunday after Easter, the feast of the Pentecost. **~·tide** /-taɪd/ *n* ~ and the weekend or the following week (often called *'Whit 'Monday, 'Whit 'Tuesday, etc*).

whittle /'wɪtl *US:* 'hw-/ *vt,vi* **1** [VP15B,2C,3A] **~ *sth away,*** cut thin slices or strips off, e g wood. **~ *at sth,*** cut at sth in this way: *He was whittling at a piece of wood.* **~ *sth down,*** reduce the size of by cutting away slices, etc; (fig) reduce the amount of: *They won't dare to ~ down our salaries.* **2** [VP6A,15A] make or shape by whittling: *The boy ~d a whip handle from a branch/~d a branch into a whip handle.*

whiz /wɪz *US:* hwɪz/ *vi* [VP2C] (-zz-), *n* [U] (make the) sound of sth rushing through the air: *The arrows/shells ~zed past.*

whizz-kid /'wɪz kɪd/ *n* (sl) bright, inventive young person with progressive ideas who achieves rapid success.

who /hu/ *interr pron* (used as the subject, and only of persons; object form **whom** /hum/) **1** *Who is that man? Who are those men? I wonder who those people are. Who broke the window? Do you know who broke the window? Who do you think he* *is?* **2** (*Whom* is used in formal and literary style, but is usually replaced by *who* in ordinary colloq style): *To whom did you give it? Who did you give it to? Who(m) did you see? Who(m) do you think I met in the post-office this morning? I don't know to whom I ought to address the request. I don't know who I ought to address the request to. Who else did you see?* □ *rel pron* **1** (in defining, or restrictive, clauses; ⇨ **that³**, which sometimes replaces *who*): *This is the man who/These are the men who wanted to see you.* (After *there* + *to be* the *rel pron 'who'* is often omitted: *There's somebody (who) wants you on the telephone. There was a man (who) called to see you while you were out.*) **2** (*Whom* is often replaced by *that* except after a *prep;* the *prep* may be placed at the end and *that* used for *whom*): *That is the man (whom) I met in London last year. That is the man about whom we were speaking. That's the man (that) we were speaking about. I know the man (whom) you mean.* **3** (in non-defining clauses, not replaceable by *that;* clause set off by the use of commas or placed in parentheses): *My wife, who has been abroad recently, hopes to see you soon. My brother, whom you met the other day, has recently written a book on Indian art. These new neighbours, to whom I was introduced yesterday, have come here from Yorkshire.* **4** (independent relative): *Whom* (= Those whom) *the gods love die young.*

whoa /wəʊ *US:* hwəʊ/ *int* ⇨ **wo.**

who'd /hud/ = who had/would.

who·dun·it /ˈhuˋdʌnɪt/ *n* (sl) (= *who done it,* illiterate for *who did it*) detective or mystery story.

who·ever /huˋevə(r)/ *pron* any person who; the person who: *W~ says that is wrong. W~ else may object, I shall approve.*

whole /həʊl/ *adj* **1** not injured or damaged; unbroken: *You're lucky to escape with a ~ skin. There isn't a ~ plate,* (= a plate that is not chipped, cracked, broken, etc), *in the house.* (Because ~ also means 'all' (⇨ 3 below), ~ is sometimes placed after the *n.* Cf: *He swallowed the plum ~,* without chewing it. *He ate the ~ loaf,* all of it. *The ox was roasted ~,* without being cut up into joints. *They ate the ~ ox,* all of it. *Snakes swallow their victims ~.*) ***go the ~ hog,*** ⇨ **hog. 2** entire; complete: *I waited for her a ~ half hour.* **~ number,** undivided quantity; integer. **ˋ~-meal, ˈ~-ˋwheat,** flour containing everything in the grain, nothing extracted. **~ milk,** milk from which no constituent (e g cream) has been extracted. **3** (attrib only, with a *sing n,* preceded by the *def art* or a *possessive*) all that there is of; complete: *I want to know the ~ truth about this matter. The ~ country* (= Everyone in the country) *was anxious for peace. I didn't see him the ~ evening. He gave his ~ attention* (= all of his attention) *to the problem. You haven't eaten the ~ lot* (= all of it, all of them), *have you?* ***do sth with one's ~ heart,*** do it with concentrated efforts, undivided attention. Hence, **ˈwhole-ˋhearted(ly),** *adj, adv* **4** (attrib with a *pl n*) not less or fewer than; nothing less than: *It rained for three ~ days. Give your ~ energies to the task. W~* (= Complete) *regiments surrendered to the enemy.* **5** (old use; biblical) in good health; well: *They that are ~ need not a physician. His hand was made ~.* □ *n* thing that is complete in itself; all that there is of something: *Four quarters make a ~. A ~ is greater than any of its parts. The ~* (= All) *of my money was stolen. He spent the ~ of that year in Pakistan. Is the land to be divided up or sold as a ~?* ***on the ~,*** taking everything into consideration. ***(taken) as a ~,*** (considered) all together, not separately. **wholly** /ˈhəʊllɪ/ *adv* completely; entirely: *Few men are wholly bad. I wholly agree with you.*

whole·sale /ˈhəʊlseɪl/ *n* (usu attrib) selling of goods (esp in large quantities) to shopkeepers, for resale to the public. ⇨ **retail**: *sell by ~* (US *at ~*); *~ prices; a ~ dealer.* □ *adj, adv* on the ~ plan; (fig) on a large scale: *Our business is ~ only. We buy goods ~. There was a ~ slaughter when the police opened fire.* **ˋwhole·saler** *n* one who sells by ~.

whole·some /ˈhəʊlsəm/ *adj* healthy; favourable to the health (bodily or moral); suggesting good health: *~ food/ exercise/ surroundings; a ~ appearance; ~ advice.*

who'll /hul/ = who will.

whom /hum/ ⇨ **who.**

whoop /hup/ *n* [C] **1** loud cry: *~s of joy.* **2** gasping sound heard during a fit of coughing. **ˋ~-ing-cough** *n* [U] children's disease with gasping coughs and long, noisy indrawing of breath. □ *vi, vt* utter a loud cry or yell: *to ~ with joy.* ***~ it up*** /wup *US:* hwʊp/, (sl) have a hilarious time.

whoopee /ˈwʊpi/ *n* ***make ~,*** (sl) take part in noisy rejoicing.

whop /wop *US:* hwop/ *vt* (-pp-) [VP6A] (sl) beat; defeat. **~·per** *n* anything unusually big, esp a big lie. **~·ping** *adj* very large of its kind: *a ~ping lie.* □ *adv* very: *a ~ping big fish.*

who're /ˈhuə(r)/ = who are.

whore /ˈhɔ(r)/ *n* (contemptuous term for a) prostitute. **ˋ~-monger** /-mʌŋgə(r)/ *n* (old use) man who fornicates.

whorl /wɜl *US:* hwɜl/ *n* ring of leaves, petals, etc round a stem of a plant; one turn of a spiral, e g as seen on the shell of a mollusc or on a fingerprint: *identify a criminal by the ~s of his fingerprints.* **~ed** *adj* having ~s; arranged in ~s.

whorls

who's /huz/ = who is/has.

whose /huz/ *poss pron* (⇨ **who**) of whom; of which. **1** *W~ house is that? I wonder ~ house that is.* **2** (rel defining clause): *Is that the man ~ house was broken into by burglars last week? The boy ~ father complained to me is very stupid.* **3** (*W~* is sometimes used in place of the usual *of which,* but it is often better to use a different construction, as shown below): *the house ~ windows are broken,* the house with the broken windows; *that dictionary ~/of which the cover has come off,* that dictionary without a cover. **4** (rel, non-defining clause): *Members of the Fire Service, ~ work is often dangerous, are paid less than mem-*

bers of the Police Force. Mr X, ~ car I borrowed for this journey, is a rich lawyer.

who·so /ˈhusəʊ/, **who·so·ever** /ˈhusəʊˈevə(r)/ *pron* (old use) = whoever.

why /wɑɪ *US:* hwɑɪ/ *adv* **1** (interr) for what reason; with what purpose: *Why was he late? Do you know why he was late? Tell me why. Why not let her do as she likes?* **2** (rel *adv*): *The reasons why he did it are obscure. This is (the reason) why I left early. Why you should always arrive late I don't know.* □ *int* **1** (expressing surprise) *Why, it's quite easy! A child could do it!* **2** (expressing protest): *Why, what's the harm?* ie there's no harm in it, is there? □ *n* (*pl* whys) reason or cause: *the whys and the wherefores.*

wick /wɪk/ *n* [C,U] (length of) thread through a candle; (strip of) woven material by which oil is drawn up in some cigarette lighters, an oil-lamp or oil-stove to burn: *trim the ~ of an oil-lamp.*

wicked /ˈwɪkɪd/ *adj* **1** (of a person, his acts) bad; wrong; immoral: *It was ~ of you to torment the poor cat.* **2** spiteful; intended to injure: *a ~ blow.* **3** roguish; mischievous: *She gave me a ~ look.* **~·ly** *adv* **~·ness** *n*

wicker /ˈwɪkə(r)/ *n* [U] (usu attrib) twigs or canes woven together, usu for baskets and furniture: *a ~ chair.* **ˈ~·work** *n* [U] things made of ~.

wicket /ˈwɪkɪt/ *n* [C] **1** **ˈ~(-ˈdoor/-ˈgate),** small door or gate, esp one at the side of, or made in, a larger one. **2** small opening (e g one with a sliding window) at which tickets are sold. **3** (cricket) either of the two pairs of three stumps (with cross-pieces called *bails*) at which the ball is bowled, ⇨ the illus at cricket; stretch of grass between two ~s: *take a ~,* defeat a batsman. *A soft ~* (= soft ground between ~s) *helps the bowler. Surrey were four ~s down,* Four of their batsmen were out. *We won by six ~s,* won with seven of our batsmen not out. ***keep ~,*** act as ~-keeper. **ˈ~-keeper** *n* player who stands behind the ~ to stop balls not struck by the batsman, to catch batsmen out, etc. **3** (US) croquet hoop.

wide /wɑɪd/ *adj* (-r, -st) **1** measuring much from side to side or in comparison with length; broad: *a ~ river; a road twelve feet ~.* **2** of great extent; comprehensive: *a man with ~ interests,* interested in many subjects; *the ~ world; the ~ Atlantic; a ~ selection of new books.* **3** fully opened: *She stared at him with ~ eyes. Open your mouth ~.* **4** far from what is aimed at or from a specific point: *a ~ ball,* (in cricket) one judged by the umpire to be out of the batsman's reach. *Your answer was ~ of the mark.* **5** (sl) shrewdly aware of business chances; unscrupulous: *~ boys.* □ *adv* **1** far from the point aimed at: *The arrow fell ~ of the mark.* **2** fully: *He was ~ awake. The window was ~ open.* **ˈ~-aˈwake** *adj* (fig) alert, vigilant: *a ~-awake young woman,* one who realizes what is going on, etc and is not easily deceived. **3** over a large area: *travel far and ~.* **ˈ~·spread** *adj* (esp) found, distributed, over a large area. **~·ly** *adv* **1** at ~ intervals: *~ly scattered.* Cf *scattered far and ~.* **2** to a large extent or degree: *~ly different; differing ~ly in opinions.* **3** over a large area: *It is ~ly known that....* **widen** /ˈwɑɪdn/ *vt,vi* [VP6A, 2A] make or become ~(r): *ˈroad-~ning in process.*

wid·geon /ˈwɪdʒən/ *n* kind of wild freshwater duck.

widow /ˈwɪdəʊ/ *n* woman who has not married again after her husband's death. **~er** *n* man who has not married again after his wife's death. **wid·owed** /ˈwɪdəʊd/ *adj* made into a ~ or ~er: *~ed by war.* **ˈ~·hood** /-hʊd/ *n* state of, time of being, a ~.

width /wɪtθ/ *n* **1** [U] quality or state of being wide: *a road of great ~;* (fig) *~ of mind/intellect/views.* Cf *broadminded, broad views.* **2** measurement from side to side: *a ~ of 10 metres; 10 metres in ~.* **3** [C] piece of material of a certain ~: *join two ~s of cloth; curtain material of various ~s.*

wield /wild/ *vt* [VP6A] have and use: *~ an axe; ~ power/authority/control.*

Wie·ner schnit·zel /ˈvinə ˈʃnɪtsl/ *n* (G) veal cutlet dressed with bread crumbs and eggs.

wie·ner·wurst /ˈvinəvɜst/ *n* (G) (often abbr to *wiener*) smoked pork or beef sausage.

wife /wɑɪf/ *n* (*pl* wives /wɑɪvz/) **1** married woman, esp in relation to her husband: *Smith and his ~; the baker's ~; a club for young wives.* **common-law ~,** ⇨ common[1](1). **2** (old use) woman (not necessarily married), esp one who is old and uneducated. ***old wives' tales,*** foolish or superstitious stories, usu traditional. ⇨ also *fish~* at fish[1](2), *house~* at house[1](7). **ˈ~·like, ~·ly** *adjj* of, like, suitable for, a ~: *~ly virtues/duties.*

wig /wɪg/ *n* head-covering of false hair (as worn to hide baldness, and by actors, barristers and judges, and formerly worn as a fashionable ornament in Europe during the 17th and 18th cc). ⇨ the illus at judge. **wig·ged** /wɪgd/ *adj* wearing a wig.

wig·ging /ˈwɪgɪŋ/ *n* (colloq) scolding: *get/give sb a good ~.*

wiggle /ˈwɪgl/ *vt,vi* [VP6A,2A] (cause to) move with quick, short, side-to-side movements: *The baby was wiggling its toes. Stop wiggling and sit still.* □ *n* wiggling movement.

wight /wɑɪt/ *n* (archaic) person; human being: *a luckless ~.*

wig·wam /ˈwɪgwæm *US:* -wɑm/ *n* hut or tent made by fastening skins or mats over a framework of poles, as formerly used by N American Indians.

wild /wɑɪld/ *adj* **1** (of animals) not tamed or domesticated; living in natural conditions (e g lions, giraffes, wolves); ⇨ the illus at cat, large, small; (of plants) growing in natural conditions; not cultivated: *~ flowers; a reserve for the preservation of ~ life,* area where ~ animals, birds, etc are protected and helped to survive; (attrib): *a ~-life sanctuary.* **ˈ~·cat** *attrib adj* reckless, unsound, impracticable: *~cat schemes,* esp in finance and commerce; *a ~cat strike,* unofficial and irresponsible strike (by workers). **ˈ~-fowl** *n* (esp) birds ordinarily shot or hunted as game, e g ~ ducks and geese, quail, pheasants. **ˈ~-ˈgoose** *attrib adj*: *a ~-goose chase,* a foolishly useless enterprise. ***sow one's ~ oats,*** ⇨ oat(1). **2** (of horses, game birds, etc) easily startled; hard to get near: *The deer/pheasants are rather ~.* **3** (of persons, tribes, etc) uncivilized; savage. **4** (of scenery, areas of land, etc) desolate; waste; unsettled: *~ scenery; ~, mountainous areas.* **5** violent; uncontrolled; stormy: *You'd better stay indoors on a ~ night like this. What ~ weather we're having!* **6** excited; passionate; distracted: *There were sounds of ~ laughter. He was ~ with anger. It made her ~* (= filled her with anger) *to see such cruelty. The anxiety drove them almost ~,* mad. **7** ***be ~ about sth/sb,*** (colloq) have a strong desire for; be madly enthusiastic about: *The silly girls were ~ about the famous pop star.* **8** disorderly; out of control: *a state of ~ confusion; a room in ~ disorder; settle down after a ~ youth.* ***run ~,*** be without check, restraint of training: *They allow their children to run ~*, allow them to amuse themselves in any way they like, with no control of any kind. **ˈ~·fire** *n* [U] (chiefly in) ***spread like ~fire,*** (of reports, rumours, etc) very fast. **9** reckless; done or said without reflection or consideration: *a ~ guess/scheme; ~ shooting,* without taking aim. □ *adv* in a ~ manner; *shoot ~.* □ *n* (*pl* with *def art*) uncultivated (and often uninhabited) areas: *the ~s of Africa; go out into the ~s.* **~·ly** *adv* in a ~ manner: *rush about ~ly; talk ~ly,* e g in an exaggerated way; *a ~ly exaggerated account.* **~·ness** *n*

wilde·beest /ˈwɪldəbist/ *n* = gnu. ⇨ the illus at large.

wil·der·ness /ˈwɪldənəs/ *n* (rarely *pl*) **1** wild uncultivated waste land. **2** desolate expanse: *a ~ of waters. From his attic window he looked out over a ~ of roofs.*

wile /waɪl/ *n* (usu in *pl*) trick; bit of cunning: *fall a victim to the ~s of an unscrupulous rogue; the ~s of the Devil.* □ *vt* [VP14] (rare) trick, entice: *~ sb into doing sth; ~ sb away.* (*Wile* is also used for *while*): *~ away the time,* etc.

wil·ful (US also **will-**) /ˈwɪlfl/ *adj* **1** (of a person) obstinate; determined to have one's own way: *a ~ child.* **2** intentional; for which compulsion, ignorance or accident is no excuse: *~ murder/negligence/waste/disobedience.* **~ly** /-flɪ/ *adv* **~·ness** *n*

will[1] /l *strong form:* wɪl/ *anom fin* (often shortened to 'll in speech; *neg ~* not or won't /wəʊnt/; *pt,* conditional would /*after 'I, he, she, we, you, they':* d, *elsewhere:* əd *strong form:* wʊd/, *neg* would not or wouldn't /ˈwʊdnt/) **1** (used as an *aux* of the future tense): *If today is Monday, tomorrow ~ be Tuesday. You'll be in time if you hurry. You won't be in time unless you hurry.* (*Would* replaces ~ to show future in the past). *I wonder whether it ~ be ready. I wondered whether it would be ready. You'll be in Oxford this time tomorrow.* **2** (used with the first person (*I, we*) to express willingness, consent, an offer or a promise): *All right, I'll come. I won't do it again. We'll pay back the money soon.* (*Would* replaces ~ to show future in the past). *I said I would do it. We said we would help them.* **3** (used with the 2nd person and in reported speech with the 1st, 2nd and 3rd persons, in questions, marking requests, and often equivalent to *please*): *W~ you come in? Pass the salt, ~ you?* Please pass the salt. *Would I come in, she wanted to know. Would you/he come back later, she asked.* **4** (used in *affirm* sentences, always with stress (never *'ll* or *'d*), indicating insistence or inevitability): *He ˈ~ have his own way,* insists on this. *Boys ˈ~ be boys,* We cannot expect them to behave except as boys naturally behave. *Accidents ˈ~ happen,* They are to be expected from time to time. *That's just what you ˈwould say,* what you might be expected to say. *Of course it ˈwould rain on the day we chose for a picnic,* We might expect such treatment from Fate. **5** (used in the neg to indicate refusal): *He won't/wouldn't help me. This window won't open,* cannot be opened. **6** (used to indicate that sth happens from time to time, that sb is in the habit of doing sth, that sth is natural or to be expected): *He'll sit there hour after hour looking at the traffic go by. Sometimes the boys would play a trick on their teacher. Occasionally the machine will go wrong without any apparent cause.* **7** (used to indicate probability or likelihood): *This'll be the book you're looking for, I think. She would be about 60 when she died. 'I want someone to do a lot of typing for me'—'Will I do?'* Am I likely to be suitable for the job? **8** (*Would* is used with the 2nd and 3rd persons to form conditional statements and questions): *They'd be killed if the car went over the cliff. They'd have been killed if the car had gone over the cliff.* **would rather,** ⇨ rather(1). **9** (*Would* is used with the 1st person to form conditional statements expressing the speaker's will or intention): *We would have come if it hadn't rained.*

will[2] /wɪl/ *vt* (*pt* would (will[1]), no other forms used) (all old uses) **1** [VP6A] wish: *Let him do what he ~. What would you?* **2** [VP9] (the subject *I* is often omitted) used to express wishes: *Would (that) it were otherwise! Would* (= I would) *to God (that) I had not agreed! Would that they were safe home again!* **3** [VP5] choose; desire: *the place where he would be. Come whenever you ~* (i e ~ or wish to come). Cf will[3] with which will[2] is closely connected. **ˈwould-be** *attrib adj* used to indicate what is desired, aspired to, or intended: *would-be authors,* persons who aspire to be authors.

will[3] /wɪl/ *vt, vi* (*pt, pp ~ed*) **1** [VP6A] make use of one's mental powers in an attempt to do sth or get sth: *We cannot achieve success merely by ~ing it.* **2** [VP2A] exercise will-power: *W~ing and wishing are not the same thing.* **3** [VP6A,9] intend unconditionally: *God has ~ed it so. God ~s that man should be happy.* **4** [VP7,14,15A] influence, control or compel, by exercising the will: *Can you ~ yourself to keep awake/into keeping awake? It would be convenient if we could ~ ourselves across lands and oceans.* **5** [VP12A,13A] ***~ sth to sb; ~ sb sth,*** leave (property, etc) (to sb) by means of a will and testament: *He ~ed most of his money to charities. I hope my uncle has ~ed me that fine painting.*

will[4] /wɪl/ *n* **1** (*sing* with *def art*) mental power by which a person can direct his thoughts and actions, and influence those of others: *the freedom of the ~.* **2** [C] (also **ˈ~-power**) (with or without the *indef art,* but not *pl*): control exercised over oneself, one's impulses: *He has no ~ of his own,* is easily influenced by others. *W~ can conquer habit. He has a strong/weak ~. He showed a strength of ~ that overcame all obstacles.* **-willed,** (in compound *adjj*) having the kind of ~ indicated: *ˈstrong-ˈ~ed; ˈweak-ˈ~ed.* **3** (*sing* only) determination; desire or purpose: *The ~ to live helps a patient to recover. She has a boundless ~ to please,* is full of desire to please. ***Where there's a ~ there's a way,*** (prov) If one has the determination to achieve sth, a way of doing so will be found. ***take the ~ for the deed,*** understand and be grateful for the fact that one wants to help, etc although unable to do so. ***of one's own free ~,*** without being required or compelled: *You did it of your own free ~,* ***at ~,*** whenever and however one pleases: *You may come and go at ~.* ***tenant at ~,*** (legal) one who can be required to give up (land, a house, etc). **4** (*sing* with *indef art*) energy; enthusiasm: *work with a* ~. **5** (with a possessive) that which is desired or determined upon: *God's ~ be done. He has always had his ~* (or, more colloq, *his own way*). *What is your ~* (more usu, *What do you want*)? **6 good/ill ~,** kind/unkind disposition or feeling: *feel no ill will towards anybody. 'Peace on earth and good ~ towards men.'* **7** [C] (also ***last ~ and testament***), ⇨ testament(1). **~·ful** *adj* (US spelling of) wilful.

wil·lies /ˈwɪlɪz/ *n pl* (sl) feeling of unease or nervousness: *This gloomy old house gives me the ~.*

will·ing /ˈwɪlɪŋ/ *adj* **1** ready to help, to do what is needed, asked, etc: *~ workers. He's quite ~ to pay the price I ask.* **2** done, given, etc readily, without hesitation: *~ obedience.* **~·ly** *adv* **~·ness** *n* [U].

will-o'-the-wisp /ˈwɪl ə ðə ˈwɪsp/ *n* moving light seen at night over marshy ground; (more usu fig) sth or sb that one pursues unsuccessfully because it or he is difficult to grasp or reach.

wil·low /ˈwɪləʊ/ *n* [C] **ˈ~(-tree),** kinds of tree and shrub with thin, easily bent branches; [U] twigs of this tree used for weaving into baskets; its wood, used for making cricket bats, etc. **ˈ~-pattern** *n* Chinese design (with a ~-tree, a river, etc) in blue upon white china (seen on plates, etc). **~y** *adj* (of persons) lithe and slender.

willy-nilly /ˈwɪlɪ ˈnɪlɪ/ *adv* willingly or unwillingly; whether wanted or unwanted.

wilt[1] /wɪlt/ *v* old form of will[2], used with thou.

wilt[2] /wɪlt/ *vi,vt* [VP6A,2A] (of plants, flowers) (cause to) droop, lose freshness; (of persons) become limp.

Wil·ton /ˈwɪltən/ *n* kind of carpet.

wily /ˈwɑɪlɪ/ *adj* (-ier, -iest) full of wiles; cunning: *a ~ old fox.*

wimple /ˈwɪmpl/ *n* linen covering arranged in folds about the head, cheeks, chin and neck, worn by women in the Middle Ages, and still by some nuns.

win /wɪn/ *vt,vi* (*pt,pp* won /wʌn/) (-nn-) **1** [VP6A,12B,13B,15A,2A] get by means of hard work, perseverance, struggle, as the result of competition, gambling, etc; do best (in a fight, etc): *win a race/a battle/a war/a scholarship/a prize/fame and fortune. Which side won? She has a nature that quickly won her the friendship of her colleagues. He soon won a reputation for himself. We've won! He won 50p from me at cards.* ***win the day/the field,*** (older use) be victorious. ***win free/ clear/ out/ through,*** make one's way through, out, etc; free oneself, get out of a difficult position, etc by effort. ***win hands down,*** (colloq) succeed easily. **ˈwin·ning-post** *n* post marking the end of a race. **2** [VP6A,15B,17] ***win sb over (to sth),*** (less usu) ***win sb to do sth,*** persuade (sb) by argument; gain the favour of: *We won him over to our view.* **3** [VP6A] reach by effort: *win the summit/the shore.* □ *n* [C] success in a game, competition, etc: *Our team has had five wins this summer.* **win·ner** *n* person, animal, thing, that wins. **win·ning** *adj* **1** that wins: *the winning horse.* **2** persuasive; gaining confidence and friendship: *a winning smile.* **win·nings** /ˈwɪnɪŋz/ *n pl* (esp) money won in betting, gambling, etc.

wince /wɪns/ *vt* [VP2A,C] show bodily or mental pain or distress (by a movement or by loss of composure): *He ~d under the blow/at the insult. He didn't ~ when the knife slipped and cut his thumb.* □ *n* wincing movement: *without a ~.*

win·cey·ette /ˈwɪnsɪˈet/ *n* [U] strong material of wool and cotton, or wool, used for shirts, etc.

winch /wɪntʃ/ *n* windlass; stationary machine for hoisting or pulling. □ *vt* [VP6A,15B] move by using a ~: *The sailplane was ~ed off the ground,* pulled along by means of a ~ until it rose into the air: *We can ~ out these big tree roots,* get them out by using a ~.

a windmill

wind[1] /wɪnd/ *n* **1** [C,U] (often *sing* with *def art;* with *much, little,* etc when the reference is to degree or force; with *indef art* or in *pl* when the reference is to the kind of ~, etc; ⇨ the examples) air in motion as the result of natural forces: *a north ~,* blowing from the north; *warm ~s from the south. The ~ blew my hat off. He ran like the ~,* very fast. *The ~ is rising/falling,* becoming stronger/weaker. *There's no/not much/a lot of ~ today.* ***fling/throw caution/prudence, etc to the ~s,*** abandon it, take no thought of it. ***get/ have the ~ up,*** (sl) become/be frightened. ***raise the ~,*** (sl) obtain the money needed. ***put the ~ up sb,*** (sl) cause him to feel frightened. ***see/find out how the ~ blows,*** what people are thinking, what is likely to happen. ***sail close/near to the ~,*** ⇨ sail[2](1). ***take the ~ out of sb's sails,*** prevent him from doing or saying sth by doing it or saying it before him; take away his advantage suddenly. ***there is/was sth in the ~,*** being secretly prepared or plotted. **2** (*pl*) the cardinal points: *The house stands on a hilltop, exposed to the four ~s of heaven,* ~s from all directions. *My papers were blown to the four ~s,* in all directions. **3** [U] breath needed for running or continuous exertion: *The runner soon lost his ~,* became out of breath. *He stopped to recover/get back his ~.* ***get one's second ~,*** recover the ability to breathe regularly after a first period of breathlessness. ***sound in ~ and limb,*** in excellent physical condition. **4** [U] scent carried by the ~ (as indicating where sth is): ***get ~ of,*** (fig) hear a rumour of, begin to suspect. **5** [U] empty words; meaningless or useless talk: *Don't listen to the politicians—they're all ~.* **6** [U] gas formed in the bowels and causing discomfort: *The baby is suffering from ~.* ***break ~,*** expel ~ from the bowels or stomach. **7** (*sing* with *def art*) orchestral ~-instruments: *the ˈwood~,* e g flutes, oboes. **8** (compounds) **ˈ~-bag** *n* (colloq) person who talks a lot but says nothing interesting. **ˈ~-break** *n* hedge, fence, line of trees, etc to break the force of the ~ and give protection. **ˈ~-cheater** (US = **ˈ~-breaker**) *n* close-fitting garment for the upper part of the body, designed to give protection against the ~. **ˈ~-fall** *n* [C] **(a)** fruit (e g an apple) blown off a tree by the ~. **(b)** (fig) unexpected piece of good fortune, esp money coming to sb. ˈ~-**flower** *n* anemone. ˈ~-**gauge** *n* instrument for measuring the force of the ~. ˈ~-**instrument** *n* musical instrument in which sound is produced by a current of air (e g an organ, a flute, a cornet). ⇨ the illus at brass. ˈ~-**jammer** *n* (colloq) merchant sailing-ship. ˈ~·**mill** *n* mill worked by the action of the ~ on sails which revolve. ***fight/tilt at ~mills,*** (from the story of Don Quixote) fight imaginary enemies; try to put right imaginary wrongs. ˈ~·**pipe** *n* passage for air from the throat to the lungs. ⇨ the illus at respiratory. ˈ~·**screen** (US = ˈ~·**shield**) *n* screen of glass in front of a motor-vehicle, etc. ⇨ the illus at motor. ˈ~-**screen-wiper** *n* ⇨ *wiper* at wipe. ˈ~-**sock** *n* canvas sleeve flown at the top of a pole (e g on an airfield) to show the direction of the ~. ˈ~·**swept** *adj* exposed to the ~s; blown bare by strong ~s: *a ~swept hillside.* ˈ~-**tunnel** *n* structure through which air is forced (at controlled speeds) to study its effects on (models of) aircraft, etc. ~·**less** *adj* without ~: *a ~less day.* ~·**ward** /-wəd/ *adj, adv* (side) in the direction from which the ~ blows; (side) exposed to the ~. □ *n* ~ward side: *Let's get to ~ward of that tannery* (to avoid the bad smell). **windy** *adj* (-ier, -iest) **1** with much ~: *a ~y day; ~y weather; a ~y hilltop,* open to the ~. **2** wordy, ⇨ 5 above. **3** (sl) frightened. ~·**ily** /-əlɪ/ *adv* ~·**i·ness** *n*

wind² /wɪnd/ *vt* (from wind¹) (*pt,pp* ~ed /ˈwɪndɪd/) [VP6A] **1** detect the presence of by scent: *The hounds ~ed the fox. The deer ~ed the stalkers.* **2** exhaust the wind(3) of; cause to breathe fast: *He was quite ~ed by the long climb/by running to catch the bus.* **3** give an opportunity of recovering the breath to: *We stopped to ~ our horses.*

wind³ /waɪnd/ *vt* (*pt,pp* ~ed, or, by confusion with wind⁴ below, wound /waʊnd/) [VP6A] sound by blowing: *~ a horn/a blast on the horn.*

wind⁴ /waɪnd/ *vi,vt* (*pt,pp* wound /waʊnd/) **1** [VP2A,B,C,15A] go, (cause to) move, in a curving, spiral, or twisting manner: *The river ~s (its way) to the sea. We climbed the ~ing* (= spiral) *staircase. The path ~s up the hillside. She wound herself/her way into his affections,* won his affections by her clever ways. **2** [VP6A,15A,B] twist (string, wool yarn, etc) into a ball, or round or on to sth: *~ (up) wool into a ball; ~ yarn; ~ thread on to a reel; ~ in the line,* e g a fishing-line on to a reel. ***~ sth off,*** unwind it. ***~ sb round one's (little) finger,*** make him do whatever one wants him to do. **3** [VP14,15A] ***~ sth round sb/sth, ~ sb/sth in sth,*** fold or wrap closely; embrace: *~ a shawl round a baby; ~ a baby in a shawl. She wound her arms round the child. She wound the child in her arms.* ˈ~·**ing-sheet** *n* shroud; sheet (to be) wound round a corpse. **4** [VP6A,15B] ***~ sth (up),*** turn (a handle, e g of a windlass); raise (sth) by doing this: *~ a handle; ~ up ore from a mine/a bucket from a well.* **5** [VP6A,15B] ***~ sth (up),*** tighten the spring of (a watch or clock), raise the weights that operate a clock (to put or keep the watch or clock in motion): *If you forget to ~ (up) your watch it will stop—unless it is a self-~ing watch,* i e one that is wound up automatically by movements of the wrist. **6** ***be wound up (to),*** be (emotionally) excited (esp in passive), ⇨ unwind: *He was wound up to a high pitch of excitement. Expectation was wound up to a high pitch. She was wound up to a fury.* **7** [VP2C,15B] ***~ (sth) up,*** come or bring to an end: *It's time for him to ~ up his speech,* come to a conclusion. *He wound up by declaring that his efforts would be continued. They wound up the evening by singing some folk-songs.* ***~ up a business company,*** put everything in order before dissolving it. ***~ up one's affairs,*** put them in order before bringing them to an end. □ *n* [C] single turn in ~ing string, ~ing up a clock, etc.

wind·lass /ˈwɪndləs/ *n* machine for pulling or lifting things (e g water from a well) by means of a rope or chain which is wound round an axle; winch.

win·dow /ˈwɪndəʊ/ *n* opening in a wall or roof of a building, the side of a ship, car, etc to let in light and air: ⇨ the illus on p 1006. ˈ~-**box** *n* long narrow box fixed to a ~-sill in which to grow plants. ˈ~-**dressing** *n* art of arranging goods attractively in shop-~s; (fig) (art of) making an impressive display of one's work, abilities, qualities, etc. ˈ~ ˈ**envelope** *n* one with a transparent part in the front through which an address on the paper inside may be read. ˈ~-**pane** *n* pane of glass for or in a ~. ***go ˈ~-shopping,*** look at goods displayed in shop-~s (for interest, but not necessarily with the idea of buying anything). ˈ~-**sill** *n* ⇨ sill. ***a ~ on the world,*** (fig) means of learning about coming into contact with, other countries: *The English language is a ~ on the world for people who cannot afford to travel.*

windy /ˈwɪndɪ/ ⇨ wind¹.

wine /waɪn/ *n* [U] **1** alcoholic drink made from the fermented juice of grapes: *a barrel/bottle/glass of ~; French ~(s),* (*pl* for different kinds of ~). ***new ~ in old bottles,*** a new principle that is too strong to be held back by old forms. ˈ~·**glass** *n* glass designed for drinking ~ from. ˈ~·**press** *n* one in which grapes are pressed. ˈ~·**skin** *n* whole skin of a goat, etc sewn up and used formerly for holding ~. **2** fermented drink resembling ~, made from other fruits or plants: *currant/cowslip/palm, etc ~.* □ *vt* (esp) ***~ and dine sb,*** entertain at a meal with ~: *We were ~d and dined at the firm's expense.*

wing /wɪŋ/ *n* **1** either of the two organs of a bird by which it flies; one of the similar organs of an insect; one of the surfaces by which an aircraft is supported in the air. the illus at air, bird. ***clip a person's ~s,*** limit his movements, activities, expenditure, etc. ***lend/add ~s to,*** cause to go fast: *Fear lent him ~s,* made him run off fast. ***take (to itself) ~s,*** disappear, vanish: *As soon as we go on a holiday, our money seems to take ~s.* ***take sb under one's ~,*** take him under one's protection; give him care and guidance. ˈ~-**nut/-screw,** = thumb-nut. ˈ~-**span/-spread** *nn* measurement across ~s when these are extended. **2** part of an object, building, etc which projects or is extended from one of its sides (e g the part of a motor-vehicle covering a wheel, called a *fender* in US): *a ˈ~ chair,* an upholstered chair with arms as high as the back; *add a new ~ to a hospital. The north ~ of the house was added 50 years ago.* **3** (mil) either of the flanks of an army or fleet; unit placed to guard a flank. **4** those members of a political party holding more extreme views than those of the majority: *the radical ~ of the Labour Party.* Hence, ˈ**left-**/ˈ**right-**ˈ~**er**. **5** unseen areas to the right and left of the stage of a theatre; the scenery

windows

there: *We were allowed to watch the performance from the* ~*s.* **6** flying. ***on the*** ~, in flight: *shoot a bird on the* ~. ***take*** ~, start flying. **7** sth like a ~ in appearance or position, e g certain seeds (esp of the maple and sycamore). **8** (also ~**er**) (football, hockey) forward player whose place is either side of the centre. the illus at football. **9** (GB; R A F) formation of two or more squadrons; (*pl*) pilot's badge: *get one's* ~*s.* **'~-com'mander,** air-force officer. ⇨ App 9. □ *vt,vi* **1** [VP6A] give ~s to; lend speed to: (usu fig) *Fear* ~*ed his steps.* **2** [VP2C,15A] fly; travel on ~s: *The planes* ~*ed (their way) over the Alps.* **3** [VP6A] wound (a bird) in the ~; (colloq) wound (a person) in the arm. **~ed** *adj* having ~s: *the* ~*ed god,* Mercury; *a* ~*ed Victory,* a statue of the goddess of victory with ~s. **~less** *adj* without ~s. **~er** *n* person who plays in a position on the ~s. ⇨ 8 above.

wink /wɪŋk/ *vi,vt* **1** [VP2A,3A,15B] ~ ***(at),*** close and open (one's eyes, or more usu one eye); get rid of (tears) by doing this: *She* ~*ed at me,* e g as a sign of secret amusement, or to call my attention to sth, or as a private signal of some kind. *He* ~*ed a tear away.* ~ ***at sth,*** purposely avoid seeing; deliberately ignore (a piece of misconduct, a transgression). **2** [VP2A,C] (of a star, light, etc) shine or flash intermittently, at very short intervals: *A lighthouse was* ~*ing in the far distance.* **'~ing lights,** (colloq '~**ers**) (red or amber) lights (at the rear or on the sides of a motor-vehicle) that flash in this way, to indicate the direction of a turn. □ *n* **1** act of ~ing, esp as a signal or hint. ***tip sb the*** ~, (sl) give him such a signal. ***A*** ~ ***is as good as a nod,*** A hint, etc given by a wink is as effective as a more obvious signal. **2** very short time: *I didn't sleep a* ~*/didn't have a* ~ *of sleep,* didn't sleep at all. **forty ~s,** a short sleep (esp during the day).

winkle /'wɪŋkl/ *n* sea snail used as food; periwinkle. □ *vt* [VP15B] ~ ***sb/sth out,*** extract, force or pull out (as a ~ is picked or pulled out of its shell with a pin).

win·ner, win·ning ⇨ win.

win·now /'wɪnəʊ/ *vt* [VP6A,15A,B] use a stream of air to separate dry outer coverings from (grain): ~ *wheat;* blow (husks, chaff) away from grain in this way: ~ *the chaff away/out/from the grain;* (fig) ~ *truth from falsehood.*

win·some /'wɪnsəm/ *adj* (of a person, his appearance) attractive; pleasing; bright: *a* ~ *smile/manner.* **~·ly** *adv* **~·ness** *n*

win·ter /'wɪntə(r)/ *n* season between autumn and spring (Nov or Dec to Feb in the northern hemisphere): ~ *sports,* e g ice-skating, skiing; ~ *wheat,* planted in the autumn and harvested in the following spring or summer; ~ *quarters,* (esp) to which troops retired for the ~ (in former times). **'~ garden,** glass-enclosed area with plants, etc e g as the lounge of a hotel. □ *vi* [VP2C] pass the ~: ~ *in the south; the* ~*ing quarters of wild geese.* **~y, win·try** /'wɪntrɪ/ *adjj* of or like ~; cold: *a wintry sky/day; wintry weather;* (fig) *a wintry smile/greeting,* one lacking in warmth or liveliness.

wipe /waɪp/ *vt,vi* [VP6A,15A,B,22] clean or dry (sth) by rubbing with a cloth, paper, the hands, etc: ~ *the dishes;* ~ *one's hands on a towel;* ~ *one's face;* ~ *sth dry;* ~ *one's eyes,* dry the tears.

Take this handkerchief and ~ your nose, David. ***~ the floor with sb,*** ⇨ floor¹(1). ***~ the slate clean,*** make a new start, with past errors, enmities, etc forgotten. ***~ sth away,*** remove (e g tears) by wiping. ***~ sth off,*** **(a)** remove by wiping: *~ off a drawing from the blackboard.* **(b)** get rid of: *~ off a debt.* ***~ sth out,*** **(a)** clean the inside of: *~ out a jug; ~ out the bath.* **(b)** get rid of; remove: *~ out a disgrace; ~ out old scores,* forget old quarrels, etc; *~ out an insult* (esp by vengeance). **(c)** destroy completely: *a disease that almost ~d out the population of the island.* ***~ sth up,*** take up (liquid, etc) by wiping: *~ up spilt milk; ~ up a mess.* □ *n* act of wiping: *Give this plate a ~.* **wiper** *n* sth that ~s or is used for wiping: *a ˋwindscreen-wiper,* for wiping rainwater from the windscreen. ⇨ the illus at motor.

wire /waɪə(r)/ *n* **1** [C,U] (piece or length of) metal drawn out into the form of a thread: *ˋtelephone ~(s); copper ~; barbed ~* (⇨ the illus at barb); *~ rope,* made by twisting strands of ~ together; *~ netting,* made by weaving ~ (used for fences, fruit cages, etc). ***pull (the) ~s,*** (usu fig) use secret or indirect influence to gain one's ends, manage a political party, etc; hence **ˋ~-puller** *n* **a live ~, (a)** ~ charged with electric current. **(b)** (fig) active, vigorous person. **ˋ~-cutters** *n pl* tool for cutting ~. **ˈ~-ˋhaired** *adj* (esp of a dog) with stiff or wiry hair. **ˋ~ tapping,** tapping of telephones, ⇨ tap¹, *v*(2). **wire wool** *n* [C,U] (pad of) fine ~ for cleaning pots and pans. **ˋ~-worm** *n* kinds of worm-like larva destructive to plants. **2** [C] (colloq, esp US) telegram: *send sb a ~; send off a ~. Let me know by ~ what time to expect you.* □ *vt,vi* **1** [VP6A,15A,B] fasten with ~: *~ two things together;* put ~(s) in or on; put (beads, pearls, etc) on fine ~. **2** [VP6A] install electrical circuits (in a building, to provide lighting, power, etc): *Has the house been ~d for electricity yet?* **3** [VP6A] catch, snare (birds, rabbits, etc) with ~. **4** [VP6A,16,11] (colloq, esp US) telegraph: *He ~d (to) his brother to buy oil shares. He ~d me that he would be delayed.* **5** [VP2C] ***~ in,*** (dated colloq) get to work energetically. **wir·ing** *n* [U] (esp) system of ~s for electric current. **wiry** *adj* (-ier, -iest) like ~; (of persons) lean and with strong sinews.

wire·less /ˋwaɪələs/ *adj* without the use of wire(s), esp: *~ telegraphy.* □ *n* [U] **1** ~ telegraphy: *send a message by ~; a ~* (now more usu *radio*) *officer or operator.* **2** (sound) radio (which is now the usu word): *a ˋ~ set,* receiving set for broadcasts; *listen to a concert over the ~.*

wis·dom /ˋwɪzdəm/ *n* [U] **1** quality of being wise. **ˋ~-tooth** *n* (*pl* -teeth) ⇨ the illus at mouth. back tooth, usu coming through after 20 years of age: *cut one's ~-teeth,* reach the age when one has discretion, etc. **2** wise thoughts, sayings, etc: *the ~ of the ancients/our ancestors.*

wise¹ /waɪz/ *adj* (-r, -st) having or showing experience, knowledge, good judgement, prudence, etc: *~ men/acts. He was ~ enough not to drive when he was feeling ill. 'I don't agree', he said, with a ~ shake of the head,* i e suggesting that he was ~. *It's easy to be ~ after the event,* to know, after sth has happened, what one failed to see in advance. ***be none the ~r,*** be no better informed: *He came away none the ~r,* knowing no more than before. ***be/get ~ to sb/sth,*** (sl) be/become aware of: *get ~ to what's happening/to the ways of business men, etc.* ***put sb ~ to sb/sth,*** inform him of (what is happening, etc). **ˋ~·acre** *n* dull and boring person who pretends to be much ~r than he is. **ˋ~·crack** *n* (sl) smart, witty saying or remark. □ *vi* make ~cracks. **~·ly** *adv*

wise² /waɪz/ *n* (*sing* only; old use) way, manner: *in no ~; in this ~.*

wish /wɪʃ/ *vt,vi* **1** [VP9] (*that* usu omitted and with a *pt* in the clause) have as an unfulfilled desire or a desire that cannot be fulfilled: *I ~ I knew what is happening. I ~ I were rich. I ~ I were a bird. She ~ed she'd stayed at home,* was sorry that she had not stayed at home. **2** [VP15A] have as a desire: *She ~ed herself home* (= ~ed that she was at home) *again. They ~ed the voyage at an end. He began to ~ himself* (= ~ that he was) *out of the affair. She could have ~ed him further,* was so annoyed that she ~ed he wasn't there. **3** ***~ sb well/ill,*** hope that he may have good/ill fortune, etc: *He ~es me well. I ~ nobody ill.* **4** [VP12A, 13A] say that one hopes for: *~ sb a pleasant journey; ~ happiness to all one's friends;* express as a greeting: *~ sb good morning/goodbye.* **5** [VP7A, 17, rarely VP6A with pron] want: *She ~es to be alone. Do you really ~ me to go? I ~ there to be no misunderstanding on this matter. What do you ~? Well, if you ~ it...,* if that is what you want me to do, etc. **6** [VP3A] ***~ for,*** have a desire for, pray for (esp sth unlikely to be obtained or achieved, or sth that can be obtained only by good fortune or in exceptional circumstances): *She has everything a woman can ~ for,* suggesting unusual good fortune. *How he ~ed for an opportunity to go abroad!,* suggesting small likelihood of getting one. *The weather was everything they could ~ for,* again suggesting unusual good fortune. *What more can you ~ for?* Cf *He would like a glass of cold water,* and *How he ~ed for a glass of cold water,* the second sentence suggesting that there was little likelihood of his getting one. **7** [VP2A] express a desire: *Let's ~! Doing is better than ~ing.* **ˋ~-bone** *n* forked bone above the breastbone of a fowl, pulled in two by two persons, the person getting the longer part having the right to the magic fulfilment of any wish. **ˋ~-ing-cap** *n* (in fairy tales) cap which secures to the wearer the fulfilment of any wish. **8** ***~ sb/sth on sb,*** (colloq) transfer to sb (esp with the idea of getting rid of sb/sth unwanted or disliked). *I wouldn't ~ my mother-in-law on anyone,* suggesting that she is intolerable. *We had the Jones children ~ed on us for the weekend.* □ *n* **1** [C,U] desire; longing: *He has no/not much ~ to go. She expressed a ~ to be alone. He disregarded his father's ~es. I hope you will grant my ~.* ***If ~es were horses, beggars might ride,*** (prov) If things could be obtained merely by ~ing for them, poor people would soon be rich. ***The ~ is father to the thought,*** (prov) We are apt to believe sth because we ~ it were true. **2** [C] that which is ~ed for: *She got her ~.* **~·ful** /-fl/ having or expressing a ~; desiring. ***~ful thinking,*** thinking or believing that sth is true because one ~es it were true. **~-fully** /-flɪ/ *adv*

wishy-washy /ˋwɪʃɪ wɒʃɪ *US:* wɔʃɪ/ *adj* (of soup, tea, etc) thin; weak; (of talk, persons) lacking in spirit or vigour; sloppy.

wisp /wɪsp/ *n* [C] small bundle, bunch or twist: *a ~ of straw/hay; a ~ of hair;* spiral or ribbon: *a ~*

of smoke/steam. **wispy** *adj* like a ~; slight.

wis·teria /wɪˋstɪərɪə/ *n* (kinds of) climbing plant with a woody stem and long drooping clusters of pale purple or white flowers and seeds in long pods, often grown on walls or over pergolas.

wist·ful /ˋwɪstfl/ *adj* sad and longing; having, showing, moved by, a rather unsatisfied and often vague desire: *~ eyes; a ~ expression; in a ~ mood.* **~ly** /-flɪ/ *adv* in a ~ manner: *She looked ~ly at the photographs of herself when she was young and beautiful.*

wit[1] /wɪt/ *n* **1** (*sing* or *pl*) intelligence; understanding; quickness of mind: *He hadn't the wits/hadn't wit enough to realize what to do in the emergency.* ***at one's wit's end,*** not knowing what to do or say. ***out of one's wits,*** greatly upset; distracted; mad: *You'll drive me out of my wits if you go on behaving in this way.* ***have a ready wit,*** be quick to make clever and amusing remarks. ***have/keep one's wits about one,*** be quick to see what is happening, alert and ready to act. ***live by one's wits,*** live by clever, not always honest, methods (as opportunities arise). **2** [U] clever and humorous expression of ideas; liveliness of spirit: *Our teacher/Our teacher's conversation is full of wit. His writings sparkle with wit.* **3** [C] person noted for his wit(**2**). **witty** *adj* (-ier, -iest) full of humour: *a witty girl/remark.* **wit·tily** /-əlɪ/ *adv* **wit·ti·cism** /ˋwɪtɪsɪzm/ *n* [C] witty remark. **wit·less** *adj* stupid.

wit[2] /wɪt/ *v* (arch except in) ***to wit,*** (in legal documents) namely; that is to say.

witch /wɪtʃ/ *n* woman said to use magic, esp for evil purposes; (fig) fascinating or bewitching woman. **ˋ~·craft** *n* [U] sorcery; use of magic. **ˋ~-doctor** *n* male ~; medicine-man (esp among primitive peoples). **ˋ~-hunt** *n* (mod colloq use) searching out and persecution (e g of persons said to be disloyal or untrustworthy). **~·ery** /ˋwɪtʃərɪ/ *n* [U] **1** ~craft. **2** fascination; charm. **~·ing** *adj* bewitching: *the ~ing hour of night,* the time when ~es are active; midnight.

witch-elm, witch-hazel ⇨ wych.

with /wɪð/ *prep* **1** (equivalent to constructions with the *v 'have'*) having; carrying; characterized by: *a cup ~ a broken handle; a coat ~ two pockets; a girl ~ blue eyes; a baby ~ no clothes on; a woman ~ an angry look in her eyes; ~ your permission.* ***~ child*** (of a woman), ***~ young*** (of an animal), pregnant. **2** (to indicate what is used for filling, covering, etc): *Fill the box ~ sand. The lorry was loaded ~ timber. The sack was stuffed ~ straw. The hills were covered ~ snow.* **3** (to indicate the means or instrument): *write ~ a pen; take sth ~ both hands; walk ~ a crutch; cut sth ~ a knife; see sth ~ your own eyes; ~ the help of your friends; ~ your help.* **4** (to indicate accompaniment or relationship): *live ~ your parents; go for a walk ~ a friend; discuss a problem ~ somebody; spend the day ~ one's uncle; mix one substance ~ another; put one thing ~ others. I shall be ~ you in a few minutes. Is there anyone ~ you or are you alone? The general, (together) ~ his staff officers, will inspect the camp.* ***in ~,*** in association ~; mixed up ~: *She's in ~ the wrong crowd,* e g of a girl whose companions are drug addicts. **5** (to indicate antagonism, opposition): *fight/argue/struggle/quarrel, etc ~ sb; have an argument ~ sb; in competition ~; a battle ~ savages; at war ~ the Romans. Fall out ~,* ⇨ fall[2](14); *have it out ~ sb,* ⇨ have[4](9). **6** (to indicate cause) because of; owing to: *silent ~ shame; trembling ~ fear/rage; shaking ~ cold; a face wet ~ tears.* **7** (to indicate manner): *do sth ~ an effort/~ a light heart/~ one's whole heart/~ joy/~ pleasure; standing ~ his hands in his pockets; win ~ ease,* easily; *fight ~ courage,* courageously; *~ a roar/a growl/a shout of triumph; receive sb ~ open arms.* **8** in the same way or direction as; at the same time as: *A tree's shadow moves ~ the sun. W~ the approach of sunset it becomes chilly. Do you rise ~ the sun,* i e at dawn? **9** (to indicate care, charge or possession): *Leave the child ~* (= in the care of) *its aunt. I have no money ~ me. The next move is ~ you. It rests ~ you to decide/The decision rests ~ you,* i e you must decide. **10** in regard to; concerning: *be patient ~ them; sympathize ~ her; bear/put up ~* (= endure) *sb or sth; have dealings/business ~ sb. What do you want ~ me? What's your business ~ him? It's a habit ~ some people. We can't do anything/can do nothing ~ him,* cannot influence, control, make use of, him. *It's holiday time ~ us now. The first object ~ him* (= His first object) *is always to make a profit. Away ~ him!* Send or take him away! *Down ~ the door!* (and many other exclamatory sentences in the pattern *adv + with + n* or *pron*). **11** (to indicate separation): *Let us dispense ~ ceremony,* i e not be ceremonious. *I parted ~ her at the gate. He has broken ~ his best friend.* **12** (to indicate agreement, harmony): *He that is not ~ me* (= on my side) *is against me. I'm ~ you* (= in agreement or sympathy ~ you) *in what you say. I (dis)agree ~ you. I can't go along ~ you on that question,* can't agree or co-operate with you. *Does this blue go well ~ this green?* ***be/get/~ it,*** (sl) become aware of what is popular and up to date: (attrib) *ˋ~-it clothes.* **13** in spite of; notwithstanding (the possession of): *W~ all her faults he still liked her. He failed ~ the best of intentions to win the sympathy of his pupils.*

withal /wɪðˋɔl/ *adv* (archaic) moreover; as well. □ *prep* (always after the object) with: *What shall he fill his belly ~?*

with·draw /wɪðˋdrɔ/ *vt,vi* (*pt* -drew /-ˋdru/, *pp* -drawn /-ˋdrɔn/) **1** [VP6A,14] ***~ sth/sb from...,*** pull or draw back; take out or away: *~ money from the Bank/dirty banknotes from circulation; ~ a boy from school,* not allow him to attend. *The workers threatened to ~ their labour,* to go on strike. **2** [VP6A,2A] take back (a statement, an accusation, an offer): *He refused to ~ (the offending expression),* e g after calling sb a liar. **3** [VP6A,14,2A,C] (cause to) move back or away: *~ troops from an exposed position; ~ from society. After dinner the ladies withdrew,* left the dinner-table and went to another room. *Our troops had to ~.* Cf *The enemy had to retreat.* **~al** /-ˋdrɔḷ/ *n* [U] ~ing or being withdrawn; [C] instance of this. **with·drawn** *adj* (of persons, their looks) retiring; unsociable; abstracted.

withe /wɪθ/, **withy** /ˋwɪðɪ/ *nn* [C] tough but easily bent twig or branch, esp of willow or osier used for binding bundles, e g of firewood.

wither /ˋwɪðə(r)/ *vt,vi* **1** [VP6A,15B,2A,C] ***~ (sth) up, ~ (away),*** (cause to) become dry, faded or dead: *The hot summer ~ed (up) the grass. Her hopes ~ed (away).* **2** [VP6A] cause (sb) to be covered with shame or confusion: *She ~ed him* *with a scornful look/gave him a ~ing look.* **~·ing·ly** /ˋwɪðɪŋlɪ/ *adv*

with·ers /ˋwɪðəz/ *n pl* highest part of the back of a horse, etc between the shoulder-blades (where the strain of the collar is taken). ⇨ the illus at **dog, domestic**.

with·hold /wɪðˋhəʊld/ *vt* (*pt,pp* -held /-ˋheld/) [VP6A,14] **~ sth (from...),** keep back; refuse to give: *He tried to ~ the truth from us. I shall ~ my consent.*

with·in /wɪðˋɪn/ *prep* inside; not beyond: *remain ~ call/reach,* near by; *live ~ one's income,* not spend more than one's income; *~ an hour,* in less than an hour; *~ a mile of the station.* □ *adv* (old use) inside: *decorate a house ~ and without* (now usu *inside and outside*).

with·out /wɪðˋaʊt/ *prep* **1** not having; not with; free from; lacking: *You can't buy things ~ money. Do you ever travel ~ a ticket? I once did it ~ being caught. The rumour was ~ foundation. He was working ~ any hope of reward. She went out ~* (= not wearing) *a hat.* **~ *fail,*** certainly. **do ~,** ⇨ do[2](15). **~ *doubt,*** admittedly; certainly. **2** (usu before gerunds) *He can't speak German ~ making mistakes,* He speaks German incorrectly. *Can you make an omelette ~ breaking eggs? Can you do it ~ his knowing,* so that he will not know? *He passed ~ seeing me,* and did not see me. *He passed ~ my seeing him,* and I did not see him. *He left ~ so much as saying* (= left and did not even say) *that he was sorry/~ even a thank-you.* ***go ~ saying,*** be too obvious, too well known, etc to need saying. **3** (old use) outside. □ *adv* (liter or old use) outside; to, at, or on, the outside; out of doors.

with·stand /wɪðˋstænd/ *vt* (*pt,pp* -stood /-ˋstʊd/) [VP6A] resist; hold out against (pressure, attack): *~ a siege; shoes that will ~ hard wear.*

withy /ˋwɪðɪ/ *n* (*pl* -thies) ⇨ **withe.**

wit·less /ˋwɪtləs/ *adj* ⇨ **wit**[1].

wit·ness /ˋwɪtnəs/ *n* **1** (often **ˋeye-~**) person who was actually present at an event and should, for this reason, be able to describe it; person who gives evidence under oath in a law court. **ˋ~-box** (US also **ˋ~-stand**) *n* enclosure in a law court in which ~es stand while giving evidence. **2** [U] evidence; testimony; what is said about sb, an event, etc: *give ~ on behalf of an accused person at his trial.* ***bear ~ to sth,*** **(a)** speak in support of, e g sb's character. **(b)** be evidence of: *The tests bear ~ to the quality of this new car.* **3** person who adds his own signature to a document to testify that another person's signature on it is genuine. **4** sb or sth that is a sign or proof of sth: *My clothes are a ~ to my poverty.* □ *vt,vi* **1** [VP6A] be present at and see: *~ an accident.* **2** [VP3A] **~ *to sth/doing sth,*** give evidence (in a law court): *~* (= testify) *to the truth of a statement. Mr X ~ed to having seen the accused near the scene of the crime.* **3** [VP6A] be a ~(3) to the signing of (an agreement, a will, etc): *~ a signature.* **4** [VP6A] give evidence of; show: *Her pale face ~ed the agitation she felt.*

wit·ti·cism /ˋwɪtɪsɪzm/ ⇨ **wit**[1].

wit·ting·ly /ˋwɪtɪŋlɪ/ *adv* knowingly; intentionally.

witty /ˋwɪtɪ/ *adj* (-ier, -iest) ⇨ **wit**[1].

wive /waɪv/ *vi,vt* [VP6A,2A] (archaic) take a wife; marry.

wives /waɪvz/ *pl* of **wife.**

wiz·ard /ˋwɪzəd/ *n* **1** magician. **2** person with amazing abilities: *a financial ~,* person able to make money with amazing ease. □ *adj* (schoolboy sl) wonderful; excellent. **~ry** /-drɪ/ *n* [U] magic (which is more usu).

wiz·ened /ˋwɪznd/ *adj* having a dried-up appearance; shrivelled: *a ~ old man; an old man with a ~ face; ~ apples.*

wo, whoa /wəʊ/ *int* (used chiefly to a horse) stop.

woad /wəʊd/ *n* [U] (plant from which is obtained a) kind of blue dye.

wobble /ˋwobl/ *vi,vt* [VP2A,C,6A] (cause to) move unsteadily from side to side; (fig) be uncertain (in opinions, in making decisions, etc): *This table ~s. The front wheels of that car ~. Don't ~ the desk. He ~d between two opinions. Her voice sometimes ~s on high notes,* Her high notes are not always steady. **wob·bler** /ˋwoblə(r)/ *n* sb or sth that ~s. **wob·bly** /ˋwoblɪ/ *adj* not firm or steady; inclined to ~: *a wobbly chair. He's still a bit wobbly on his legs after his long illness.*

woe /wəʊ/ *n* (chiefly poet; sometimes hum) **1** [U] sorrow; grief; distress: *a tale of woe. Woe (be) to...,* A curse upon.... **2** (*pl*) causes of woe; troubles: *poverty, illness and other woes.* **woe·ful** /-fl/ *adj* sorrowful; causing woe; regrettable: *woeful ignorance.* **woe·fully** /-flɪ/ *adv* **woe·be·gone** /ˋwəʊbɪgon *US:* -gɔn/ *adj* dismal(-looking): *What woebegone looks!*

woke, woken ⇨ **wake**[1].

wold /wəʊld/ *n* [C,U] (area of) open uncultivated country; down or moor.

wolf /wʊlf/ *n* (*pl* **wolves** /wʊlvz/) wild, flesh-eating animal of the dog family, hunting in packs. ***cry ~,*** raise false alarms: *You've cried ~ too often* (suggesting that genuine cries for help will in future be ignored). ***a ~ in sheep's clothing,*** person who appears friendly but is really an enemy. ***keep the ~ from the door,*** be able to buy enough food for oneself and one's family. **ˋ~'s-bane** *n* aconite. **ˋ~-cub** *n* **(a)** young ~. **(b)** junior boy scout. **ˋ~-hound** *n* large dog originally bred for hunting wolves. **ˋ~ whistle** *n* whistle or other sound (e g made by a man in the street) expressing admiration of a woman's physical charms. □ *vt* [VP6A,15A] eat quickly and greedily: *~ (down) one's food.* **~·ish** /-ɪʃ/ *adj* of or like a ~: *a ~ish appetite.*

wolf·ram /ˋwʊlfrəm/ *n* tungsten; tungsten ore.

woman /ˋwʊmən/ *n* (*pl* **women** /ˋwɪmɪn/) **1** adult female human being: *men, women and children; a single* (= unmarried) *~; a ~ of the world,* one with experience of society, not young and innocent: (attrib; to be preferred to *lady*) *a ˈ~ ˋdoctor* (*pl ˈwomen ˋdoctors*); *a ˈ~ ˋdriver* (*pl ˈwomen ˋdrivers*); (compounds) *ˋ~-hater,* a hater of women; *a ˋcountry-~; a ˋneedle-~,* etc. **2** (without article) the female sex; any ~: *W~ is usu physically weaker than man.* **3** [C] man with characteristics thought of as typically feminine: *All the old women in the Cabinet ought to resign now that war has broken out.* **4** (*sing* with *def art*) feminine emotions: *There is something of the ~ in his character. All the ~ in her rebelled against the treatment she was receiving.* **5** (archaic) female attendant of a queen or noblewoman: *The queen sent one of her women to fetch a doctor.* **ˋ~·hood** /-hʊd/ *n* [U] **1** (collective) women in general. **2** the state of being a ~: *She had now grown to/reached ~hood.* **~·ish** /-ɪʃ/ *adj* **1** (of a man) like a ~ (in feeling, behaviour, etc). **2** (of things) more suitable for women than men: *~ish clothes.* **~·ize** /-ɑɪz/ *vi* pursue women (esp for casual sexual intercourse). **~·izer** *n* man who does this: *He's an incurable ~izer.* **'~·'kind** *n* women in general. **'~·like, ~·ly** *adjj* like a ~; suitable or right for a ~: *~ly modesty/compassion.* **women·folk** /ˈwɪmɪnfəʊk/ *n pl* women; women of one's family.

womb /wum/ *n* (anat) organ in a female mammal in which offspring is carried and nourished while developing before birth: (fig) *It still lies in the ~ of time,* is sth which the passage of time will reveal. ⇨ the illus at reproduce.

wom·bat /ˈwombæt/ *n* Australian animal (looking like a small bear), the female of which has a pouch for its young.

won /wʌn/ ⇨ win.

won·der /ˈwʌndə(r)/ *n* **1** [U] feeling caused by sth unusual, surprising or inexplicable; surprise combined with admiration, bewilderment, etc: *They were filled with ~. We looked at the conjurer in silent ~.* ***no/little/small ~,*** it is not/hardly surprising: *No ~ you were so late. He was taken ill, and no/little ~, considering that he had been overworking for years.* **'~-struck** *adj* overcome with ~. **'~·land** /-lænd/ *n* (a) fairyland. (b) [C] country that is remarkable in some way (e g because of abundant natural resources). **2** [C] thing or event that causes such feeling: *Walking on the moon is one of the ~s of our times.* ***signs and ~s,*** miracles. ***work ~s,*** work with remarkable results, perform miracles. ***a nine days' ~,*** sth which arouses great interest or admiration for a short time. ***for a ~,*** it is surprising (because unusual, unexpected, etc): *For a ~ he paid back the money he had borrowed.* ***It is a ~ (that),*** It is surprising that: *It's a ~ (that) you didn't lose your way in the dark.* ***What a ~,*** How surprising! □ *vi,vt* **1** [VP2A,3A,4B] **~ *(at sth),*** be filled with ~(1); marvel; feel surprised: *Can you ~ at it,* Isn't it natural, to be expected, etc? *I don't ~ at her refusing to marry him. It's not to be ~ed at,* is sth one might expect. *I ~ 4(at the fact that) he wasn't killed,* am surprised that he wasn't killed. *I shouldn't ~ if...,* shouldn't be surprised if.... *I ~ed to hear her voice in the next room.* **2** [VP2A, 3A] **~ *(about sth),*** feel curiosity; ask oneself: *I was ~ing about that. I was just ~ing.* **3** [VP8,10] ask oneself: *I ~ who he is/what he wants/why he is late/whether he will come/whose it is. I was ~ing how to get there quickly/where to spend the weekend, etc.* **~·ing·ly** /ˈwʌndrɪŋlɪ/ *adv* **~·ful** /-fl/ *adj* causing ~; surprising: *We've been having ~ful weather recently. What a ~ful memory she has!* **~·fully** /-flɪ/ *adv* **~·ment** /-mənt/ *n* [U] surprise. **won·drous** /ˈwʌndrəs/ *adj* (archaic, or liter) ~ful. □ *adv* (only with *adjj*) ~fully: *wondrous kind.*

wonky /ˈwoŋkɪ/ *adj* (GB sl) **1** infirm; unreliable: *a ~ chair,* one that might break. **2** tottery; in poor health: *She still feels a bit ~ after that attack of 'flu.*

wont /wəʊnt *US:* wɔnt/ *n* (*sing* only) what sb is accustomed to doing. *He went to bed much earlier than was his ~,* than he usually did. ***use and ~,*** established custom. □ *pred adj* (usu ***be ~ to***) accustomed: *He was ~ to say* (= It was his custom to say, He often said) *that all boys are lazy.* **~ed** *attrib adj* customary; usual.

won't /wəʊnt/ = will not.

woo /wu/ *vt* (*pt,pp* wooed) **1** [VP6A] ***woo a woman,*** (old use) try to win her hand in marriage; court. **2** try to win (fame, fortune, success, sleep). **wooer** *n* one who woos.

wood /wʊd/ *n* **1** [U] (with *indef art,* and *pl* only when meaning *kind, sort, variety*) hard solid substance of a tree below the bark: *Tables are usually made of ~. Put some more ~ on the fire. He was chopping ~ for the fire. Teak is a hard (kind of) ~ and pine is a soft (kind of) ~.* (attrib): *~ floors/pavements,* made of blocks of ~. Cf *wooden,* used for articles made of ~. **2** [C] (often *pl*) area of land covered with growing trees (not so extensive as a forest): *a ~ of beech(-trees); a house in the middle of a ~; go for a walk in the ~(s).* ***out of the ~,*** (fig) free from troubles or difficulties: *We're not yet out of the ~,* still have difficulties to face. ***be unable to see the ~ for the trees,*** (fig) be unable to get a clear view of the whole because of too many details. **3** (sing with *def art*) ***in/from the ~,*** the cask or barrel: *wine in the ~; drawn from the ~.* **4** (compounds, from **1** above) **~ alcohol** *n* kind of alcohol distilled from ~ (also called *methyl alcohol*) used as a fuel and a solvent. **'~-block** *n* block of ~ from which ~cuts are made. **'~·cut** *n* print from a design, drawing, picture, etc cut on a block of ~. **'~-louse** *n* (*pl* -lice) kinds of small, wingless, insect-like creature living in decaying ~, damp soil, etc. **'~·pecker** *n* kinds of bird that clings to the bark of trees and taps or pecks it to find insects. **'~·pile** *n* pile of ~, esp for fuel. **'~-shed** *n* shed for storing ~ (esp for fuel). **'~-pulp** *n* [U] ~ shredded to pulp as the material for making paper. **'~·wind** *n* wind-instrument of ~ in an orchestra. **'~·work** *n* [U] (a) things made of ~, esp the ~en parts of a building (e g doors, stairs). (b) art of making things of ~; carpentry. **'~·worm** *n* (a) ~-eating larva that bores into ~. (b) [U] damage caused by ~worm. **5** (compounds, from **2** above) **'~·bine** *n* wild honeysuckle. **'~·cock** *n* kinds of game bird, brown with a long, straight bill, short legs and tail, found in ~land and valued as food. **'~·craft** *n* [U] knowledge of forest conditions, skill in finding one's way in ~s and forests, esp as used in hunting, etc. **'~·cutter** *n* man who cuts down trees. **'~·land** /-lənd/ *n* [U] land covered with trees; ~s: (attrib) *~land scenery.* **'~·man** /-mən/ *n* (*pl* -men) forester; ~-cutter. **'~s·man** /-zmən/ *n* (*pl* -men) (esp US) = ~man. **~ed** *adj* covered with growing trees: *~ed country,* abounding in trees. **~en** /ˈwʊdn/ *adj* **1** (attrib) made of ~: *a ~en leg; ~en walls* (fig, of the old ~en warships, thought of as a defence); *a '~en-head,* ⇨ block-head. Hence, **'~en-'headed** *adj* stupid. **2** stiff, clumsy, awkward (as if made of ~): *a ~en* (= inexpressive) *smile. His manners were extremely ~en.* **woody** *adj* (-ier, -iest) **1** ~ed: *a ~y hill-side.* **2** of or like ~: *the ~y stems of a plant.*

wooer /ˈwuə(r)/ *n* ⇨ woo.

woof /wuf/ *n* cross threads in a woven fabric; weft.

woofer /ˈwʊfə(r)/ *n* (radio) speaker designed to produce low notes.

wool /wʊl/ *n* [U] **1** soft hair of sheep, goats and some other animals (e g the llama and alpaca); thread, yarn, cloth, clothing, made from this: *wear ~* (i e clothing made of ~) *next to the skin; the '~ trade; '~ merchants; imports of ~ from Australia; 'knitting-~,* ~ yarn for knitting. **dyed**

in the ~, dyed before spinning and weaving; (fig) thorough-going, out-and-out: *a dyed-in-the-~ Tory*, person who is strongly convinced that Tory principles, etc are the best. ***much cry and little ~,*** much talk with little result; fuss about trifles. ***pull the ˈ~ over sb's eyes,*** deceive or trick him. **ˈ~-gathering** *adj, n* absent-minded(ness). **the ˈ~-sack,** ~-stuffed cushion on which the Lord Chancellor sits in the House of Lords: *reach the ~sack*, become Lord Chancellor. **2** material similar in appearance or texture to ~; *cotton-~*, raw cotton (US = *cotton-batting*). **3** (person's) thick curly hair. ***lose one's ~,*** (colloq) get angry. **~·len** (US = **~en**) /ˈwʊlən/ *attrib adj* made of ~: *~len cloth/blankets;* of ~ fabrics: *~len manufacturers/merchants.* **~·lens** (US = **~ens**) *n pl* ~len fabrics; cloth, flannel, blankets, etc, made of ~. **~ly** (US also **~y**) /ˈwʊlɪ/ *adj* (**-ier, -iest**) **1** covered with, made of, looking like, ~: *~ly hair; a ~ly coat.* **2** (fig, of the mind, ideas, arguments) confused; not clear; not incisive. □ *n* (*pl* **-lies**) (colloq) ~len garment, esp a sweater: *Put an extra ~ly on when you go out.*

word /wɜd/ *n* **1** sound or combination of sounds (or the written or printed symbols) forming a unit of the grammar or vocabulary of a language: *When we speak we put our thoughts into ~s. I have no ~s to* (= cannot adequately) *express my gratitude. W~s failed him,* He could not express his thoughts, his emotion, etc in ~s. ***a play (up)on ~s,*** a pun. ***be not the ~ for it,*** not an adequate or satisfactory description: *Warm's not the ~ for it* (i e *hot* is perhaps a better ~)! ***not get a ~ in edgeways,*** ⇨ edgeways. ***(repeat sth) ~ for ~,*** exactly, with no changes or omissions. ***(translate sth) ~ for ~,*** literally. Cf *a free translation.* ***in a/one ~,*** briefly; to sum up. ***by ~ of mouth,*** in spoken, not written, ~s. **2** [C] sth said; remark or statement: *He didn't say a ~ about it. I don't believe a ~ of the story. Mr A will now say a few ~s,* make a few remarks, give a short address. *Don't waste ~s on that fellow,* don't try to persuade, convince, warn, etc him. ***eat one's ~s,*** admit that one was wrong: take one's ~s back and apologize. ***have a ~ with sb,*** speak to him. ***have ~s (with sb),*** quarrel: *They've had ~s, I hear.* ***have the last ~,*** make the final remark in an argument, esp by making a retort to which there is no good answer. ***say/put in a good ~ (for sb),*** speak on his behalf (to support or defend). ***suit the action to the ~,*** do at once what one has said one will do (e g of a threat). ***take sb at his ~,*** act on the belief that he means what he says. ***big ~s,*** boasting. ***on/with the ~,*** as soon as sth has been said. ***a ~ in/out of season,*** a piece of advice given when it is welcome and helpful (unwelcome and interfering). ***the last ~ on*** (a subject), statement, etc which includes the latest views and information: *The last ~ has not yet been said on this subject,* There will be further facts, views, etc. ***the last ~ (in sth),*** the latest, most up-to-date, etc, in: *Our motor-coach tours of Scotland are the last ~ in comfort and convenience.* **3** (*sing*, without *def art*) news; information: *Please send me ~ of your safe arrival. Please leave ~ for me at the office. W~ came that I was wanted at the office.* **4** (*sing* only, with a possessive) promise; assurance. ***be as good as one's ~,*** do what one promises: *Don't worry—I'm sure he'll be as good as his ~.* ***give sb one's ~ (that...),*** promise: *The goods will arrive on time—I give you my ~.* ***keep/break one's ~,*** do/fail to do what one has promised to do. ***take sb's ~ for it,*** believe what he says: *I have no proof, but you may take my ~ for it.* ***take sb at his ~,*** believe that he is telling the truth, that he will keep a promise. ***my ~ upon it,*** (old use) on my honour. ***upon my ~,*** **(a)** on my honour. **(b)** used as an exclamation of surprise. **5** (*sing* only) command; order; spoken signal: *The officer gave the ~ to fire. His ~ is law,* His orders must be obeyed. *You must give the ~ before you can pass.* ⇨ *password* at pass[1](10). **6** (in the Christian religion) **the W~ of God; God's ~,** the Scriptures, esp the Gospel: *preach the W~ to the heathen.* **7** (compounds) **ˈ~·book** *n* vocabulary; list of ~s with meanings, etc. **ˈ~-division** *n* dividing of the spelling of a ~, e g at the end of a line on a page. **ˈ~-painter** *n* person who can describe vividly in ~s. **ˌ~-ˈperfect** *adj* knowing, able to repeat, a poem, a part in a play, etc by heart. **ˈ~-picture** *n* vivid description in ~s. **ˈ~-splitting** *n* sophistry; making of distinctions of meaning, etc that are subtle. □ *vt* [VP6A] express in ~s: *a well-~ed letter. The suggestion might be ~ed more politely.* **~·ing** *n* (*sing* only) way in which sth is expressed; choice of ~s to express meaning: *A different ~ing might make the meaning clearer.* **~·less** *adj* without ~s; not put into ~s: *~less grief.* **wordy** *adj* (**-ier, -iest**) using, expressed in, a large number of ~s, esp unnecessary ~s: *a ~y telegram; ~y warfare,* i e argument. **~·ily** /-əlɪ/ *adv* **~i·ness** *n*

wore /wɔ(r)/ *pt* of wear[2].

work[1] /wɜk/ *n* **1** [U] use of bodily or mental powers with the purpose of doing or making sth (esp contrasted with play or recreation); use of energy supplied by steam, electric current, etc: *Are you fond of hard ~? The ~ of building the new school took six months. It was the ~ of a moment* (= Only a moment was needed) *to turn the key in the lock and make him a prisoner. It was terribly hard ~ getting to the top of the mountain. This is the ~ of an enemy,* An enemy has done this. *Machines now do much of the ~ formerly done by man.* ***make hard ~ of sth,*** make it seem more difficult than it is. ***make short ~ of sth,*** finish it quickly. ***set/get to ~ (on sth/to do sth),*** begin; make a start. ***set/go about one's ~,*** start doing it: *You're not setting about your ~ in the right way.* ***at ~ (on sth),*** busy or occupied with (indicating uncompleted ~, ~ in progress). ***all in the day's ~,*** (used to indicate that sth is) normal; what is usual or to be expected. **2** [U] what a person does to earn a living; employment: *What time do you get to (your) ~ every day? The men were on their way to ~. It was difficult to find ~ during the depression.* ***in/out of ~,*** having/not having employment: *He has been out of ~ for a year. He'll be glad to be in regular ~ again.* Hence, (attrib) **ˌout-of-ˈwork.** ***at ~,*** at one's place of employment: *He's at ~ now, but he'll be back at six.* **3** [U] sth to be done, not necessarily connected with a trade or occupation, not necessarily for payment: *I always find plenty of ~ that needs doing in my garden. I have some ~ for you to do.* **4** [U] things needed or used for ~: *She took her ~* (e g her sewing materials) *out on the verandah.* **ˈ~-bag/-basket/-box** *nn* bag, etc for holding such things, esp for sewing. **5** [U] that which is produced by ~: *The ~ of famous silversmiths and sculptors may be seen in museums. What a beautiful piece of ~! The villagers sell their ~* (e g needlework, wood-carvings, metal articles) *to tourists.* ⇨ also compounds such as **stone~** and **wood~**. **6** (*pl;* also *sing* with *indef art*) product of the intellect or the imagination: *the ~s of Shakespeare; the ~s of Beethoven.* ⇨ **opus**; *~s of art; a new ~* (= musical composition) *by Benjamin Britten; a new ~* (= book) *on modern art.* **7** (*pl,* and with *pl v*) moving parts of a machine: *the ~s of a clock or watch. There's something wrong with the ~s.* **8** (*pl* in form but often treated as a *sing n*) building(s) where industrial or manufacturing processes are carried on: *a 'gas-~s; an 'iron-~s; a 'brick-~s. The 'steel-~s were closed for the Christmas holidays.* **'~s council/committee,** joint council of representatives of employers and employees to deal with problems of management, labour relations, etc. **9 public ~s,** the building of roads, dams, embankments; other engineering operations (by government departments, etc): *the Ministry of Public Building and W~s,* (until 1971) government department (now part of the Department of the Environment) responsible for these operations. **10** (*pl v*) (cf *'earth~s, 'out~s*) defensive structures; fortifications: *The ~s were thought to be impregnable.* **11** (compounds) **'~-bench** *n* table at which a mechanic does his ~. **'~·book** *n* book with outlines of a subject of study, with questions to be answered (in blank spaces, in writing), for notes, etc. **'~·day** *n* day for ~; day which is not a Sunday or a holiday. **'~ force** *n* total number of men working in a particular factory, etc. **'~·house** *n* **(a)** (formerly, in GB) public institution for homeless paupers in a parish or union of parishes. ⇨ *poor-house* and *poor law* under **poor(1)**. **(b)** (US) place where those who have committed small crimes are confined and made to work. **'~-in** *n* occasion when workers continue to ~ in a factory to protest against proposed dismissal, closure of the factory, etc. **'~·man** /-mən/ *n* (*pl* **-men**) **(a)** man who earns a living by physical labour or at machines, etc. **(b)** person who works in a specified way: *a skilled/quick, etc ~man.* **'~·man·like** *adj* characteristic of a good ~man. **'~·man·ship** /-mənʃɪp/ *n* [U] quality as seen in sth made: *articles of poor/excellent ~manship;* person's skill in doing ~. **'~·out** *n* [C] (esp US) practice, trial, test; period of exercise (esp by athletes). **'~-people** *n pl* ~men. **'~·room** *n* room in which ~ is done. **'~·shop** *n* room or building in which things (esp machines) are made or repaired. **'~-shy** *adj* disinclined to work; lazy. **'~-study** *n* (*pl* **-dies**) study of how ~ may be done efficiently and economically (e g by observing the sequence of movements in an operation, time needed, etc). **'~·table** *n* (esp) table with drawers for sewing materials, etc. **~·a·day** /ˈwɜkədeɪ/ *adj* commonplace; dull: *this ~aday world/life.*

work[2] /wɜk/ *vi,vt* (*pt,pp* **~ed** or **wrought** /rɔt/) (For uses with *adverbial particles* and *preps,* ⇨ **10** below. For uses with *wrought,* ⇨ **wrought**). **1** [VP2A,B,C,3A,4A] do work; engage in physical or mental activity: *He's been ~ing hard all day. The men in this factory ~ 40 hours a week. Most people have to ~ in order to live,* i e to earn a living. *He isn't ~ing now,* e g because unemployed or retired. *Have British statesmen always ~ed for peace? He's ~ing at* (= studying) *Latin and Greek. Green is ~ing on* (= writing) *a new novel. This man ~s in leather,* is a craftsman in leather. *He has always ~ed against* (= opposed) *reform.* **~ to rule,** ⇨ **rule(1)**. **2** [VP2A,C] (of a machine, apparatus, bodily organ, plan, method, etc) do what it is designed to do; have the desired result; function; operate: *The lift/elevator/bell/telephone is not ~ing. The gears ~ smoothly. This machine ~s by electricity. My brain doesn't seem to be ~ing well today. Will this new plan/scheme/method ~? The charm ~ed. It ~ed like a charm.* **3** [VP6A,15A] cause to ~; set in motion: *He ~s his wife/himself too hard. Don't ~ yourself/your poor wife to death. She was ~ing the treadle of her sewing-machine. This machine is ~ed by steam/electricity.* **4** [VP6A] produce or obtain as the result of effort: *~ wonders/a cure/harm/mischief.* **~ one's passage,** earn it by ~ing: *He ~ed his passage from England to Australia,* by ~ing on the ship. **~ one's way (through college, etc),** have a paid job, while studying to meet costs: *He's ~ing his way through medical school.* **~ one's will (on sb),** make him do what one wants him to do. **~ it,** (sl) bring sth about (by scheming, etc): *I'll ~ it if I can,* e g by using influence, cajolery, etc. **5** [VP6A] operate; control; be employed in the management of: *~ a mine. This salesman ~s the North Wales area,* travels there as a salesman. **6** [VP2C,D,15A,B,22] (cause to) move into, reach, a new state or position, usu by degrees or with a succession of small movements: *Your shirt has ~ed out,* has come out from above the top of your trousers. *One of the screws has ~ed loose. The rain had ~ed through the roof,* had penetrated it slowly. *Can you ~ the stone into place,* e g when building a stone wall? *The men ~ed their way forward. Many months later the splinter ~ed out of her arm,* came out after travelling through the flesh from the point at which it had entered. *The wind has ~ed round to the south,* changed direction by degrees. **7** [VP6A] make or shape by hammering, kneading, pressure, etc: *~ clay,* knead it with water; *~ dough,* (when making bread). ⇨ **wrought** for *wrought iron.* **8** [VP2A] ferment; move in an agitated way: *The yeast began to ~,* to ferment, e g in dough. *His face/features began to ~ violently,* twitch, etc in a way showing agitation. **9** [VP6A,14] make by stitching; embroider: *~ a design on a cushion-cover/one's initials on a handkerchief.* **10** [VP2C,3A,14,15B] (special uses with *adverbial particles* and *preps*):

work away (at sth), continue to ~: *He's been ~ing away at this job since breakfast.*

work in/into, (⇨ 6 above) penetrate; find a way in/into: *The dust has ~ed in everywhere,* e g into a house during a sandstorm. **~ sth in/into,** introduce; find a place for: *Can't you ~ in a few jokes/~ a few jokes into your lecture?*

work sth off, get rid of; dispose of; deal with: *~ off arrears of correspondence/superfluous energy/one's excess weight.*

work on sb/sth, ⇨ ~ *upon* below.

work out, **(a)** be capable of being solved: *This sum/problem will not ~ out.* **(b)** be, turn out, in the end: *How will things ~ out? The situation ~ed out quite well. The total ~s out at £10. How much does it ~ out at,* What's the total? **(c)** ⇨ 6 above. **(d)** exercise, train (for a contest): *The* *champion is ~ing out in the gym this morning.* Hence, ˋ~-**out** *n* period, form, of training. ***~ sth out,*** **(a)** calculate: *I've ~ed out your share of the expenses at £5.* **(b)** get results for: *I can't ~ out these algebra problems.* **(c)** devise; invent; develop in detail: *a well-~ed out scheme. They've ~ed out a method of sending a spacecraft to Mars. You must ~ out your own salvation,* find a way of saving yourself by your own efforts. **(d)** solve: *He was ~ing out some coded messages.* **(e)** (usu passive) exhaust by using, operating, etc: *That silver-mine is now ~ed out,* has no more ore. ***work up to sth,*** advance steadily to a high level: *The orchestra was ~ing up to a crescendo.* ***~ sth up,*** **(a)** make by degrees; bring to an efficient or satisfactory condition: *~ up a business.* **(b)** excite; stir up: *~ up the feelings of an audience.* ***~ sb/oneself up (into),*** rouse to a high point (of excitement, etc): *He ~ed himself/everyone up into a frenzy/rage/state of hysteria. The audience was really ~ed up by this time.* ***~ (up)on sth,*** (⇨ 8 above) excite, influence: *Will the high figure for unemployment ~ on the conscience of the Government? The sufferings of the refugees ~ed/wrought upon our feelings so much that we gave them all the help we could.* ⇨ also 1 above: *~ on a new novel, etc.*

work·able /ˋwɜkəbl/ *adj* that can be worked; that will work; practicable: *The silver-mine is no longer ~,* it cannot be worked (e g because it is flooded, or because the ore is exhausted). *Is the proposed scheme ~,* feasible?

worker /ˋwɜkə(r)/ *n* person who works; (attrib) *~ bees* (contrasted with the drones).

work·ing /ˋwɜkɪŋ/ *n* **1** mine, quarry, etc or part of it, which is being, or has been, worked: *The boys went exploring in some disused ~s,* e g the shafts of an old tin-mine. **2** the way sth works, or the result of this: *the ~s of conscience; the principles that guide the ~s of the human mind.* **3** (attrib) (in various senses of the *v*) *the ~ day,* **(a)** workday (as opposed to a day of rest). **(b)** number of hours worked on a normal day: *a ~ day of eight hours;* ˋ*~ clothes,* worn while ~; *a ~ drawing/plan,* one made as a guide for building, construction, etc; *a ~ hypothesis,* one formulated for a theory, etc: *~ capital,* money needed for carrying on a business, etc. *The Government has a ~ majority,* one that is sufficient. ˋ~ **party,** (esp) committee appointed to secure efficiency in an industry, or one appointed (e g by a government department) to study and report on a question. **a ~ breakfast/lunch/dinner,** one at which persons discuss business, etc: *The Prime Minister and some of his colleagues had a ~ breakfast to discuss the crisis in the docks.* **in ~ order,** able to function properly, do what is required; going smoothly: *put a machine in ~ order. Everything is in ~ order.* ˋ**~-out,** **(a)** calculation of results; elaboration of details: *the ~-out of a plan.* **(b)** execution: *Don't interfere with them in the ~-out of their scheme.* □ *part adj* engaged in work: *the ~ classes,* those engaged in manual work: *a ~-class family; a hard-~ woman.*

world /wɜld/ *n* **1** the earth, its countries and people; heavenly body that may resemble it: *the Old W~,* Europe, Asia and Africa; *the New W~,* America; *the Roman W~,* that part known to the ancient Romans; *the English-speaking ~,* those parts where English is the mother tongue of the inhabitants; *make a journey round the ~; to the ~'s end,* to the farthest distance possible. *Are there any other ~s besides ours? The whole ~/All the ~ knows...,* It is widely or generally known.... ***make a noise in the ~,*** be widely talked of; become famous. ***make one's way in the ~,*** succeed. ***a citizen of the ~,*** a cosmopolitan person. **2** (as **1** above; used attrib) affecting, used by, intended for, extending over, the ~: *a ~ language,* one that is or will be used, or is designed for use, in all or most parts of the ~: *English is a ~ language now. Esperanto was designed as a ~ language. Which countries today can be called ~ powers,* countries whose policies, etc affect all parts of the ~? *We've had two ~ wars in this century.* **the W~ Bank,** international bank established in 1945 for providing loans for development when private capital is not available (officially the *International Bank for Reconstruction and Development*). ˈ**~-ˋold** *adj* as old as the ~. ˈ**~-ˋwide** *adj* found in, spread over, all parts of the ~: *~-wide fame.* **3** time, state or scene of existence: *this ~ and the next,* life on earth and existence after death; *the ~ to come,* existence after death; *the lower ~,* hell, Hades; *bring a child into the ~,* beget one or give birth to one. ˈ**~-ˋweary** *adj* tired of existence. **4** the universe; everything: *Is this the best of all possible ~s?* ***in the ~,*** at all, in existence: *Nothing in the ~ would please me more. Who in the ~* (= Who ever, Who on earth) *is that fellow?* ***for all the ~ like sb/sth,*** exactly like: *She's for all the ~ like a woman I knew 20 years ago, in looks, behaviour, everything.* ***be all the ~ to sb,*** be everything to: *She's all the ~ to him,* He lives for her alone. ***for the ~,*** on any account: *I wouldn't hurt her feelings for the ~.* ***be/feel on top of the ~,*** elated (because of success, good health, etc). ***sth out of this ~,*** sth sublime, magnificent. ***carry the ~ before one,*** have quick and complete success. ***to the ~,*** (sl) utterly: *He was tired/drunk to the ~.* ***a ~ of sth,*** a great number or quantity of; very much/many: *My holiday did me a ~ of good. There was a ~ of meaning in the look she gave him. There's often a ~ of difference between promise and achievement.* **5** the material things and occupations of life (contrasted with the spiritual). ***the ~, the flesh, and the devil,*** the various temptations that face us. ***make the best of both ~s,*** the material and spiritual. ***forsake/renounce the ~,*** devote one's life to spiritual things. **6** human affairs; active life: *know/see the ~,* have experience of life; *a man of the ~,* person who has had experience of life, knows the ways of men, is tolerant, etc; *take the ~ as one finds it,* adapt oneself to things, not try to reform people, etc. *How goes the ~ with you,* How are your affairs going? **7** persons, institutions, etc connected with a special social class or special interests: *the ~ of sport/art; the ˋracing/ˆscientific ~;* all that concerns or belongs to a specified sphere: *the ˋanimal/ˆmineral/ˆvegetable ~.* ⇨ **kingdom(3). 8** average society, fashionable society, their opinions, customs, etc: *the great ~,* fashionable society. *All the ~ and his wife were at the ball,* all those who claim positions in high society. *What will the ~ say,* What about public opinion; can we defy it, etc? **~·ly** *adj* **1** material: *my ~ly goods,* my property. **2** temporal; of the affairs of this life (esp the pursuit of pleasure, contrasted with spiritual): ~*ly wisdom,* prudence, etc which enables one to obtain material gains and advantages. **3** (also ˈ~*ly-*ˋ*minded*) concerned with, interested in, material things. **~·li·ness** *n*

worm /wɜm/ *n* **1** kinds of small, boneless, limbless, creeping creature, esp (ˋ**earth-~**) the kind living in the ground, or the kinds living as parasites in the intestines, etc of animals. ⇨ *hookworm* at hook(1), *tapeworm* at tape. ˋ**~-cast** *n* tubular pile of earth pushed up by an earth~ on the ground. ***the ~ of conscience,*** remorse. **2** (in compounds) used as a name for larvae, insects, etc: ˋ*silk~;* ˋ*glow~.* ˋ**~-eaten** *adj* full of ~ holes; (fig) antiquated. ˋ**~-hole** *n* hole left in wood, fruit, etc by ~s. **3** (fig) insignificant or contemptible person. ***Even a ~ will turn,*** (prov) There are limits to patience. **4** spiral part of a screw. ˋ**~-gear** *n* arrangement in which a wheel with teeth gears with the ~(4) of a revolving spiral. □ *vt* **1** [VP15A,B] ***~ oneself/one's way in/into/through...,*** move slowly, or by patience, or with difficulty: *He ~ed himself/his way through the undergrowth. He ~ed himself into favour/into her confidence.* ***~ sth out of sb,*** extract (by persistent questioning, etc): *He ~ed the secret out of me.* **2** [VP6A] rid of parasitic ~s: *I think we'd better ~ the cat,* e g by giving it a powder or pill. **wormy** *adj* having many ~s; damaged by ~s; like a ~.

worm·wood /ˋwɜmwʊd/ *n* [U] kinds of perennial plant with a bitter flavour, used in the preparation of vermouth and absinthe and in medicine; (fig) bitter mortification and its cause.

worn /wɔn/ *pp* of wear[2].

worri·some /ˋwʌrɪsəm *US:* ˋwɜ-/ *adj* troublesome; worrying.

worry /ˋwʌrɪ *US:* wɜɪ/ *vt,vi* (*pt,pp* -ried) **1** [VP6A,14,15A,17] trouble; give (sb, oneself) no peace of mind; cause anxiety or discomfort to: *~ sb with foolish questions. The noise of the traffic worried her. What's ~ing you? Her child has a bad cough and it rather worries her. I have a bad tooth that is ~ing me. Don't ~ yourself about the children; they're old enough to take good care of themselves. He'll ~ himself to death,* make himself ill by ~ing. *She was always ~ing her husband for more money/~ing him to give her more money.* **2** [VP2A,B,C,3A] ***~ (about/over sth),*** be anxious, uneasy, troubled: *Don't ~ about trifles. You have no cause to ~. What's the use of ~ing? Don't ~ trying to find it—it'll turn up one day.* ***~ along,*** (colloq) manage to get along in spite of troubles. **3** [VP6A] (esp of dogs) seize with the teeth and shake: *The dog was ~ing the rat.* **4** [VP15B] *~ out a problem,* attack it again and again until one solves it. □ *n* (*pl* -ries) **1** [U] condition of being troubled: *show signs of ~.* **2** [C] (usu *pl*) sth that worries; cause of anxiety: *Is your life full of worries? Money worries and little domestic worries have made him look old. What a little ~ that child is!* **wor·ried** *adj* troubled; anxious: *He has a worried look.* **~·ing** *adj* full of ~; causing ~: *have a ~ing time.* **~·ing·ly** *adv*

worse /wɜs/ *adj* (independent comparative; ⇨ bad, worst) **1** *Your work is bad but mine is much ~. We couldn't have had ~ weather for our journey. Is there anything ~ than war/a ~ catastrophe than war/a catastrophe ~ than war? You are making things ~. He escaped with nothing ~ than a few scratches.* ***the ~ for wear,*** badly worn as the result of long wear; (fig) exhausted: *He looks the ~ for wear after only a year in office.* **2** (*pred* only) in(to) less good health or condition or circumstances: *The doctor says she is much ~ today. I'm glad you don't feel any ~. He fell into the river but is none the ~.* □ *adv* (⇨ badly, worst) **1** *He is behaving ~ than ever. He has been taken ~,* has become more seriously ill. ***none the ~,*** not less: *I like a man none the ~ for being outspoken.* ***~ off,*** (⇨ *badly off* at bad[1]; *better off* at better[2](1); *well off* at well[2](2)) more badly situated; in ~ circumstances. **2** (used to intensify): *It's raining ~* (= more heavily) *than ever. She hates me ~* (= more strongly) *than before.* □ *n* ~ thing(s): *I have ~ to tell. The first news was bad, but ~ followed. There has been a change for the ~ in the patient's condition. Things seem to be going from bad to ~ nowadays.* **worsen** /ˋwɜsn/ *vt,vi* [VP6A,2A] make or become ~.

wor·ship /ˋwɜʃɪp/ *n* [U] **1** reverence and respect paid to God: *places of ~,* churches and chapels; *hours of ~,* times of church services; *public ~,* church service(s). **2** admiration and respect shown to or felt for sb or sth: *the ~ of success; hero ~. She gazed at the film star with ~ in her eyes.* **3** ***your/his W~,*** (GB) title of respect used to/of a magistrate or mayor: *his W~ the Mayor of Chester.* □ *vt,vi* (-pp-; US -p-) [VP6A,2A,B] give ~(1,2) to: *~ God;* attend church service: *the church where she had ~ped for ten years.* **~·per** (US = **~er**) *n* **~·ful** /-fl/ *adj* (in GB titles of respect, e g to justices of the peace, aldermen) worthy of respect; honourable.

worst /wɜst/ *adj* (independent superlative; ⇨ bad, worse): *the ~ storm for five years; the ~ dinner I've ever eaten; the ~* (= most intense) *frost this winter.* □ *adv* (independent superlative; ⇨ badly, worse) most badly: *Tom played badly, Harry played worse and I played ~.* □ *n* ~ part, state, event, etc: *You must be prepared for the ~,* the ~ possible news, outcome, etc. *The ~ of the storm is over. She keeps cheerful, even when things are at their ~.* ***If the ~ comes to the ~,*** If the ~ happens. ***get the ~ of it*** (in a fight etc), be defeated. ***the ~ of it is that...,*** The most unfortunate part of the affair is that.... ***at (the) ~,*** if the ~ happens. ***do your ~/let him do his ~,*** used as expressions of defiance. □ *vt* [VP6A] defeat; get the better of: *He ~ed his enemy.*

wor·sted /ˋwʊstɪd/ *n* [U] twisted woollen yarn or thread; cloth made from this.

worth /wɜθ/ *pred adj* **1** having a certain value; of value equal to: *I paid only £300 for this used car but it's ~ much more. It's not ~ more than two pounds.* ***~ (one's) while,*** ⇨ while. ***for what it is ~,*** without any guarantee or promise concerning it: *That's the news I heard—I pass it on to you for what it is ~.* ˈ**~·ˋwhile** *adj* that is ~ the time, etc needed: *a ~while experiment.* ⇨ while. **2** possessing; having property to the value of: *What's the old man ~? He died ~ a million pounds.* ***for all one is ~,*** (colloq) with all one's energy; making every effort: *He was running for all he was ~.* **3** ~ (+ *-ing*) giving a satisfactory or rewarding return for: *The book is well ~ reading. It's hardly ~ troubling about. He says life wouldn't be ~ living without friendship.* □ *n* [U] **1** value; what sb or sth is ~: *books/discoveries, etc of great/little/not much ~; know a friend's ~.* **2** (usu /wəθ/) quantity of sth of a specified value: *a*

ˋpound's ~ of apples; fifty ˋpence ~ of copper coins; a ˋpenny~ of sweets. It's not ~ the paper its printed on. **~·less** *adj* having no value. **~-less·ly** *adv* **~·less·ness** *n*

worthy /ˈwɜðɪ/ *adj* (-ier, -iest) **1** **~ *(of sth/to be sth),*** deserving: *a cause ~ of support; behaviour ~ of praise; nothing ~ of mention; a man who is ~ to have a place in the team. He found a ~ enemy/an enemy ~ of his sword,* one brave or strong enough. **2** (often ironic or used with a patronizing effect) having merit; deserving respect: *a ~ gentleman. She says she helps only the ~ poor* (in contrast to those people who, she thinks, are poor through their own laziness, etc). □ *n* **1** (old use) person of some distinction (in his own country or during a certain period): *an Elizabethan ~,* i e during the reign of Queen Elizabeth I. **2** (hum or ironic) person who appears to be distinguished: *Who's the ~ who has just arrived? Who are the worthies on the platform?* **worth·ily** /-əlɪ/ *adv* **worthi·ness** *n*

wot /wot/ (1st and 3rd *p sing* of an archaic *v*) know(s): *God wot,* God knows.

wot·cher /ˈwotʃə(r)/ *int* (GB sl) (as a greeting) (= What cheer!) Hullo!

would ⇨ will[1].

wouldst /wʊdst/ *v* old form used with *thou*: *Thou ~,* You would.

wound[1] /wund/ *n* [C] **1** hurt or injury to the living tissue of the body, caused by cutting, shooting, tearing, etc, esp as the result of attack (*injury* being more usu for the result of an accident): *a ˋknife ~ in the arm; a ˋbullet ~. The dog was licking its ~s,* e g after a fight with another dog. **2** injury to a plant, tree, etc in which the bark is cut or torn. **3** pain given to a person's feelings: *a ~ to his pride/vanity.* □ *vt* [VP6A] give a ~ to: *Ten soldiers were killed and thirty ~ed.* Cf *hurt* or *injured* in an accident. *He felt ~ed in his honour/affections.*

wound[2] /waʊnd/ *pt,pp* of wind[4].

wove, wo·ven ⇨ weave.

wow[1] /waʊ/ *n* (sl) tremendous success: *The new play at the National Theatre's a wow.* □ *int* expressing wonder, admiration, etc.

wow[2] /waʊ/ *n* [U] varieties in the pitch of sound reproduced from a disc or tape, caused by fluctuations in speed (from the motor). ⇨ flutter, *n*(3).

wrack /ræk/ *n* [U] **1** seaweed thrown up on the shore by the waves (and used for manure, etc). **2** = rack[4](2).

wraith /reɪθ/ *n* apparition of a person seen shortly before or after his death.

wrangle /ˈræŋgl/ *vi* [VP2A,3A] **~ *(with sb/about/over sth),*** [C] take part in a noisy or angry argument. □ *n* such a noise, etc.

wran·gler /ˈræŋglə(r)/ *n* (at Cambridge) person placed in the first division of the mathematical tripos.

wrap /ræp/ *vt,vi* (-pp-) **1** [VP6A,15A,B] **~ *sth (up) (in sth),*** put round; cover or roll up (in): *~ a child in a shawl; ~ up sth in tissue paper; ~ oneself in a blanket; ~ up a business deal,* (trade use) finalize it. *The mountain top was ~ped in mist. You'd better ~ (yourself) up well before you go out,* put on an overcoat, scarf, etc. *Why does he ~ up his meaning in such obscure language,* Why doesn't he express his meaning clearly? **2** [VP14] **~ *sth round sth,*** wind or fold as a covering or protection; pack: *W~ plenty of paper round it. W~ this shawl round your shoulders.* **3** ***be ~ped up in,*** (a) be packed or enclosed in; (fig) be concealed in: *The affair is ~ped (up) in mystery.* (b) be deeply interested in: *He is ~ped up in his work/studies.* (c) be deeply devoted to: *She is ~ped up in her children,* devotes all her time, care, attention, etc to them. □ *n* outer garment or covering (e g a scarf, cloak, fur or rug); outer covering: (trade use) *keep sth under ~s,* conceal it; *take off the ~s,* place on public view (e g a new model of a car). **~·per** *n* (esp) **1** piece of paper (to be) ~ped round a newspaper or other periodical, a book etc (esp for sending by post); cover of loose paper, etc for a book. **2** light dressing-gown. **~·ping** *n* **1** [C] sth used for covering or packing: *the ~pings of a mummy.* **2** [U] material for covering or packing sth: *Put plenty of ~ping round the cups and saucers when you pack them.*

wrath /roθ *US:* ræθ/ *n* [U] (liter) great anger; indignation. **~·ful** /-fl/ *adj* **~·fully** /-flɪ/ *adv*

wreak /rik/ *vt* [VP6A,14] **~ *sth on sb,*** give expression to; give effect to: *~ one's fury upon sb; ~ havoc/vengeance upon sb.*

wreath /riθ/ *n* (*pl* ~s /riðz/) **1** flowers or leaves twisted or woven together into a circle (worn on the head as a garland, or placed on a coffin, a grave, a memorial to the dead, etc). **2** ring, spiral or curling line (*of* smoke, mist, etc).

wreathe /rið/ *vt,vi* **1** [VP6A] (esp in *pp*) cover, encircle: *~d with flowers; hills ~d in mist; a face ~d in smiles.* **2** [VP14] (reflex) **~ *itself round,*** wind: *The snake ~d itself round the branch.* **3** [VP14] **~ *sth into...,*** make (flowers, etc) (into a wreath). **4** [VP2A,C] (of smoke, mist, etc) move in the shape of a wreath.

wreck /rek/ *n* **1** [U] ruin or destruction, esp of a ship by storms: *save a ship from ~;* (fig) *the ~ of one's hopes/plans;* [C] instance of this: *The storm caused ~s all along the coast.* **2** [C] ship that has suffered ~(1): *Robinson Crusoe obtained food and supplies from the ~.* **3** [C] vehicle, building, etc that has been badly damaged or fallen into ruin; person whose health has been destroyed: *The car was a worthless ~ after the collision. He is a mere ~ of his former self. If these anxieties continue she will become a nervous ~.* □ *vt* [VP6A] cause the ~ of: *The ship/train was ~ed.* **~·age** /ˈrekɪdʒ/ *n* [U] ~ed material, fragments: *The ~age of the aircraft was scattered over a wide area.* **~·er** *n* **1** person employed to recover a ~ed ship or its contents. **2** (US) person employed to demolish old buildings. ⇨ *housebreaker* at house[1](7). **3** person who, in former times, tried from the shore to bring about shipwreck (e g by showing false lights) in order to plunder the cargo, etc.

wren /ren/ *n* kinds of small short-winged songbird.

wrench /rentʃ/ *n* [C] **1** sudden and violent twist or pull: *He gave his ankle a ~,* twisted it by accident. *He pulled the handle off with a single ~.* **2** (pain caused by a) sad parting or separation: *Separation from her children was a terrible ~.* **3** tool for gripping and turning nuts, bolts, etc; spanner. ⇨ the illus at tool. □ *vt* **1** [VP6A,15A,22] twist or pull violently: *~ the door open; ~ sth from sb; ~ sth out of his hand; ~ a door off its hinges. She ~ed herself from the villain's clutches.* **2** [VP6A] injure (e g one's ankle) by twisting. **3** [VP6A] (fig) distort (facts, the meaning of a sentence, etc).

wrest /rest/ *vt* **1** [VP15A] ~ ***sth from/out of,*** take (sth) violently away: *~ a knife from sb/~ it out of his hands.* **2** [VP14] ~ ***sth from,*** get by effort: *~ a confession of guilt from sb; ~ a living from marginal land.* **3** twist or pervert (facts, the meaning of sth).

wrestle /ˈresl/ *vi* [VP2A,C,3A] ~ ***(with sb),*** struggle with sb (as a sport) and try to throw him to the ground without hitting him: *~ with sb;* (fig) *~ with a problem/a temptation/one's conscience.* **wres·tler** /ˈreslə(r)/ *n* person who ~s.

wretch /retʃ/ *n* **1** unfortunate and miserable person. **2** contemptible, mean person. **3** (playfully or affectionately) rogue.

wretched /ˈretʃɪd/ *adj* **1** miserable: *lead a ~ existence in the slums; living in ~ poverty. This aching tooth makes me feel ~.* **2** causing misery: *~ houses.* **3** of poor quality; bad: *~ weather/food.* **4** (with *nn* implying blame) that causes dismay (because excessive): *the ~ stupidity of the nation's leaders.* **~·ly** *adv* **~·ness** *n*

wrick, rick /rɪk/ *vt* [VP6A] sprain or twist slightly: *~ one's ankle/a muscle in one's back.* □ *n* [C] sprain: *give one's back a ~; have a ~ in the neck.*

wriggle /ˈrɪgl/ *vi,vt* **1** [VP2A,C,3A] move with quick, short, twistings; move along in this way: *The worm ~d as Jim put it on the fish-hook. Small children ~ in their seats when they are bored. The eel ~d out of my fingers. He ~d out of* (= escaped from) *the difficulty. He ~d (his way) through the thick hedge. My criticism made him ~,* feel uncomfortable. **2** [VP6A,15B,22] move with a wriggling motion: *~ one's toes; ~ oneself free,* get free (e g from ropes round the body): *~ one's way out.* □ *n* wriggling movement. **wriggler** /ˈrɪglə(r)/ *n* (esp) larva of a mosquito.

wright /raɪt/ *n* (rare except in compounds) workman, maker. ⇨ *play~* at **play**[1](5), *ship~* at **ship**[1](3), *wheel~* at **wheel(1)**.

wring /rɪŋ/ *vt* (*pt,pp* **wrung** /rʌŋ/) **1** [VP6A] twist; squeeze: *~ a hen's neck,* to kill it; *~ a person's hand,* clasp it warmly. ~ ***one's hands,*** squeeze them together (indicating despair, sorrow, etc). **2** [VP15A,B] ~ ***sth out;*** ~ ***sth out of/from sth,*** twist and squeeze sth tightly; force out (esp water) by doing this: *~ out wet clothes; ~ out the water from one's swimming-trunks. They wrung a confession from her,* (fig) forced her to confess, by persuasion, threats, etc. ***~ing wet,*** (of clothes, etc) so wet that water can be wrung from them. □ *n* [C] squeeze: *Give it another ~.* **~er** /ˈrɪŋə(r)/ *n* = **mangle**[1].

wrinkle[1] /ˈrɪŋkl/ *n* small fold or line in the skin (esp of the kind produced by age) or on the surface of sth: *She's beginning to get ~s round her eyes. Her new dress fits without a ~. She ironed out the ~s in her dress.* □ *vt,vi* [VP6A,15A,2A] make, get, have, ~s in: *~ up one's forehead,* e g in perplexity; *~d with age. The front of this dress ~s.* **wrinkly** /ˈrɪŋklɪ/ *adj*

wrinkle[2] /ˈrɪŋkl/ *n* [C] (colloq) useful hint or suggestion: *give sb a ~.*

wrist /rɪst/ *n* joint between the hand and the arm: *He took me by the ~.* ⇨ the illus at arm. **ˈ~-band** *n* band of a shirt-sleeve fitting round the ~. **ˈ~-watch** *n* one worn on the ~. **~·let** /ˈrɪstlət/ *n* band or ornament for the ~.

writ /rɪt/ *n* **1** witten order issued in the name of a ruler or sb in authority to an official to do or not to do sth: *a ~ of habeas corpus; a ~ for the arrest of sb.* **2 Holy W~,** the Bible.

write /raɪt/ *vi,vt* (*pt* **wrote** /rəʊt/, *pp* **written** /ˈrɪtn/) **1** [VP2A,B,C] make letters or other symbols (e g ideographs) on a surface, esp with a pen or pencil on paper: *learn to read and ~; ~ on both sides of the paper. I've been writing (for) three hours. Are we to ~ in ink or in pencil?* **2** [VP6A] put down (on paper) by means of words, etc: *~ words/Chinese characters/shorthand; ~ one's name; ~ a cheque/a certificate/an application* (by filling in the spaces with words, figures, etc); *~* (= fill) *three sheets.* **3** [VP2C,15B] ~ ***sth down,*** **(a)** put down (on paper) in words: *You'd better ~ the address/~ it down before you forget it.* **(b)** (more usu *mark down*) reduce the nominal value of (stock, goods, etc); reduce in value or price. ~ ***sb down as,*** describe as: *I'd ~ him down as a fool.* ~ ***in for sth,*** apply by letter for. ~ ***off (for sth),*** order by post: *~ off for another dozen bottles of claret.* ~ ***sth off,*** **(a)** compose quickly and easily: *~ off an account of a sports meeting.* **(b)** cancel; recognize that sth is a loss or failure: *~ off a debt; ~ off £500 for depreciation of machinery. He has just written off a new car,* damaged it beyond repair, so that the insurers regard it as a loss. Hence, **ˈ~-off** *n*: *The burnt-out airliner was a complete ~-off,* had no value whatever. ~ ***sth out,*** ~ the whole of; ~ in full: *~ out a copy of an agreement; ~ out a cheque.* ~ ***sth up,*** **(a)** bring up to date; complete: *~ up one's diary. I must ~ up my notes of the lecture.* **(b)** overstate the value of (assets). **(c)** describe, ~ about, (an event) elaborately: *The journalist wrote up the affair for his paper.* **(d)** ~ a description giving praise: *A friendly critic wrote up the acting of the leading players.* Hence, **ˈ~-up** *n* written account or record of an event. **4** [VP6A,2A] do the work of an author; compose for publication: *~ a novel; ~ for the newspapers; make a living by writing.* **5** [VP2A,B,C,12A,13A,4A] ~ and send a letter (*to,* or colloq without *to*): *He promised to ~ (to) me every week. He ~s home/~s to his parents regularly. He wrote me that he was staying with his brother in York. He wrote me an account of his visit. I wrote to let them know that I was coming.* **6** (usu passive) show clear signs of: *He had trouble/honesty written on his face.* ***written*** (also ***writ,*** archaic form of the *pp*) ***large,*** easily or clearly recognizable.

writer /ˈraɪtə(r)/ *n* **1** person who writes: *the ~ of this letter.* **~'s cramp,** cramp of the muscles in the hand, causing difficulty in writing. **2** author. **3** (GB) clerk in some government offices; naval rating who does office work.

writhe /raɪð/ *vi* [VP2A,C] twist or roll about in pain; (fig) suffer mental agony: *~ under insults.*

writ·ing /ˈraɪtɪŋ/ *n* **1** [U] (in the senses of the *v* 'write'): *busy with his ~; put sth down in ~. His ~* (= *ˈhand~*) *is difficult to read.* **ˈ~-desk** *n* desk (usu with drawers) for ~ at. **ˈ~-ink** *n* ink for ~ (contrasted with printing-ink). **ˈ~-paper** *n* [U] (esp) paper cut to the size usual for letters. **2** (*pl*) literary work: *the ~s of Swift.*

writ·ten /ˈrɪtn/ ⇨ **write**.

wrong /rɒŋ *US:* rɔːg/ *adj* (contrasted with *right*) **1** not morally right; unjust: *It is ~ to steal. It was ~ of you/You were ~ to borrow his bicycle without asking his permission.* **2** mistaken; unsuitable; improper: *He has six ~ answers in his arithmetic.*

Can you prove that I am/that my opinions are ~? You're doing it the ~ way. We got into the ~ train. We came the ~ way/took a ~ turning. This is the ~ side of the cloth, not the side intended to be seen. ***~ side out,*** with the ~ side outside. ***be caught on the ~ foot,*** be caught when one is not ready. ***get out of bed on the ~ side,*** said of sb who is in a bad temper when he gets up. ***have/get hold of the ~ end of the stick,*** have a completely mistaken idea or impression. ***in the ~ box,*** in an awkward position. ***on the ~ side of*** (40, etc), older than. **ˈ~-ˈheaded** *adj* perverse and obstinate. **ˈ~-ˈheadedly** *adv* **3** out of order; in a bad condition: *There's nothing ~ with the engine—perhaps there's no petrol in the tank. There's something ~ with my digestion. What's ~ with that?* (colloq, as a rhetorical question, meaning 'That's quite all right, isn't it?') □ *adv* (usu end position) in a ~ manner: *guess ~. You've spelt my name ~.* Cf *~ly spelt. They told me ~.* Cf *~ly informed. You've got it ~,* have misunderstood, miscalculated, etc. ***go ~,*** **(a)** take the ~ path or road. **(b)** have a bad or poor result; fail: *All our plans went ~.* **(c)** (colloq) (of a machine, etc) break down. **(d)** take to immorality: *What's the best way to help young girls who go ~?* □ *n* **1** [U] what is morally ~; [C] ~ action: *know the difference between right and ~; do ~,* do what is ~; sin. *Two ~s don't make a right.* **ˈ~ˈdoer** *n* person who does ~. **ˈ~ˈdoing** *n* [U] doing ~; crime; sin. **2** [U] injustice; unjust treatment; [C] instance of this; unjust action: *suffer ~; do ~ to sb. You do me ~,* treat me unjustly. *They have done me a great ~. She complained of the ~s she had suffered.* **3 *in the ~,*** in the position of being responsible for an error, for having caused a quarrel, etc: *He admitted that he was in the ~,* that the fault, etc was his. *They tried to put me in the ~,* to make it seem that the fault, etc was mine. *You are both in the ~,* each of you is in error. □ *vt* [VP6A] treat unjustly; be unfair to: *He ~ed me when he said that I was envious. His deeply ~ed wife deserves our help and sympathy.* **~·ful** /-fl/ *adj* unjust; unlawful: *~ful dismissal* (from employment). **~·fully** /-fḷɪ/ *adv* **~·ly** *adv* in a ~ manner (used esp before a *pp*): *~ly informed/directed/accused.*

wrote /rəʊt/ ⇨ write.

wroth /rəʊθ *US:* rɔθ/ *adj* (pred only; poet, biblical, or in mod use hum) angry; indignant.

wrought /rɔt/ *pt,pp* of **work**² **1** beaten into shape: *~ iron.* ⇨ *cast iron* at **cast**¹(3). **2** (older use, or liter; used for *worked* in a small number of contexts; ⇨ **work**²(10), *work (up)on sth* = excite): *Their sufferings ~ upon our feelings.* **ˈ~-ˈup** *adj* over-excited; extremely agitated.

wrung /rʌŋ/ ⇨ wring.

wry /rɑɪ/ *adj* **(wrier, wriest)** pulled or twisted out of shape: *make a wry face,* usu to show disappointment or disgust; *a wry smile,* a forced smile that indicates disappointment. **wry·ly** *adv*

wych- (also **wich-, witch-**) /wɪtʃ/ *pref* used in names of trees: *ˈ~-elm; ˈ~-hazel.*

wynd /wɑɪnd/ *n* (Scot) alley in a town in Scotland.

Xx

X, x /eks/ *n* (*pl* **X's, x's** /ˈeksɪz/) **1** the 24th letter of the English alphabet. **2** symbol for the Roman numeral 10. ⇨ App 4. **3** (algebra) first unknown quantity; (fig) factor or influence about which there is uncertainty.

xeno·phobia /ˈzenəˈfəʊbɪə/ *n* [U] irrational hatred or fear of strangers or foreigners.

Xerox /ˈzɪərɔks/ *n, vt* [VP6A] (P) = photocopy.

Xmas /ˈkrɪsməs/ *n* common abbr (in writing) for Christmas.

X-ray /ˈeks reɪ/ *n* (now the usual term for *Röntgen rays*) (apparatus for using a) form of short-wave ray that penetrates solids and makes it possible to see into or through them; photograph taken by this means: (attrib) *have an X-ray (examination); an X-ray diagnosis; X-ray photography.* □ *vt* [VP6A] examine, treat, photograph, with X-rays.

xylo·nite /ˈzɑɪlənɑɪt/ *n* [U] (P) celluloid.

xylo·phone /ˈzɑɪləfəʊn/ *n* musical instrument of parallel wooden bars, graduated in length, which produce different notes when struck with small wooden hammers. ⇨ the illus at percussion.

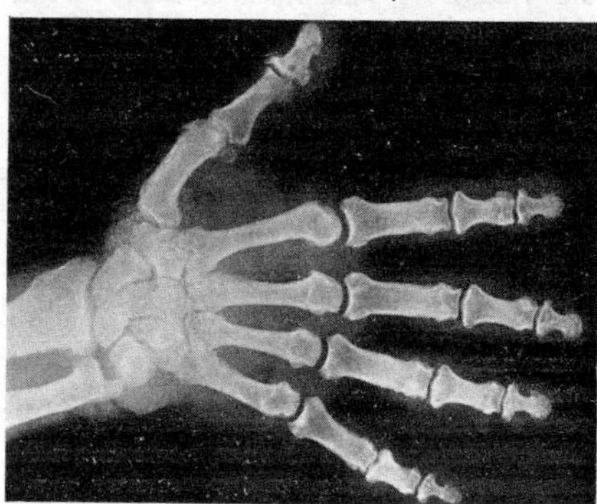

an X-ray photograph of the hand

Yy

Y, y /wɑɪ/ *n* (*pl* **Y's, y's** /wɑɪz/) the 25th letter of the English alphabet.

yacht /jɔt/ *n* **1** light sailing-boat built specially for racing. **ˈ~-club** *n* club for ~-owners. **ˈ~s·man** /-smən/ *n* (*pl* **-men**) person who makes a hobby of sailing. **2** (usu privately-owned, usu motor-driven) vessel kept by a wealthy person for pleasure-cruising. □ *vi* [VP2A] travel or race in a ~. **~·ing** *n* [U] the art, practice or sport of sailing ~s.

yah /jɑ/ *int* used to express derision.

ya·hoo /jɑˈhu/ *n* name given by Swift (in *Gulliver's Travels*) to members of a race of inferior human beings with the habits of animals: hence, detestable person with bestial habits.

yak /jæk/ *n* long-haired ox, wild or domesticated, of Central Asia.

yam /jæm/ *n* [C] **1** (edible tuber of) kinds of tropical climbing plant. ⇨ the illus at **vegetable**. **2** (US) kind of sweet potato.

yam·mer /ˈjæmə(r)/ *vi* (US colloq) **1** complain peevishly; whine. **2** talk volubly or foolishly.

yank /jæŋk/ *vt* [VP6A,15A,B] give a sudden sharp pull to: *~ out a tooth. Tom ~ed the bed-clothes off his young brother and told him to get up.*

Yank /jæŋk/ *n* (sl) (abbr of) *Yankee.*

Yan·kee /ˈjæŋkɪ/ *n* **1** native of New England (US). **2** (in the American Civil War) native of any of the Northern States. **3** (colloq, in GB, Europe) US citizen: (attrib) *~ inventions.*

yap /jæp/ *vi* (-pp-) [VP2A] **1** (esp of dogs) utter short, sharp barks. **2** (sl) talk noisily or foolishly: *Stop yapping!* □ *n* short, shrill bark.

yard[1] /jɑd/ *n* **1** (usu unroofed) enclosed or partly enclosed space near or round a building or group of buildings, often paved: *a ˈfarm~; a ˈcattle-~; the school ~,* used as a playground; (US) area of land laid out as a garden round a house. **2** (usu in compounds) enclosure for a special purpose: *the ˈrailway ~s/ˈmarshalling ~s,* area where trains are made up, where coaches, wagons, etc are stored; *a ˈtan-~* where tanning is carried on. ⇨ also *back ~* at **back**[4](3), *dock~* at **dock**[1], *ship~* at **ship**[1](3), *vine~* at **vine**(2). **3 the Y~,** (colloq abbr for) *New Scotland Y~.*

yard[2] /jɑd/ *n* **1** (⇨ App 5) unit of length, 3 feet or 36 inches: *Can you still buy cloth by the ~ in Britain?* **ˈ~-ˈmeasure** *n* rod, tape, etc one ~ long, marked in feet, inches, quarters, etc. **ˈ~-stick** *n* (fig) standard of comparison. **2** long, pole-like piece of wood fastened to a mast for supporting and spreading a sail. ⇨ the illus at **barque**. **ˈ~-arm** *n* either end of such a ~. ***man the ~s,*** place men along the ~s, stand along the ~s, as a form of salute.

yarn /jɑn/ *n* **1** [U] fibres which have been spun for knitting, weaving, etc esp woollen ~. **2** [C] (colloq) story; traveller's tale. ***spin a ~,*** tell a story; make up a story: *The beggar spun a long ~ about his misfortunes.* □ *vi* [VP2A,C] tell ~s: *We stayed up ~ing until midnight.*

yar·row /ˈjærəʊ/ *n* common perennial herb with flat clusters of small flowers.

yash·mak /ˈjæʃmæk/ *n* veil worn in public by some Muslim women in some countries.

yaw /jɔ/ *vi* (of a ship or aircraft) turn unsteadily off the right course. □ *n* such a turn.

yawl /jɔl/ *n* **1** sailing-boat with two masts, the second being a short one near the stern. **2** ship's boat with four or six oars.

yawn /jɔn/ *vi* [VP2A,C] **1** (usu involuntarily) open the mouth wide as when sleepy or bored. **2** be wide open: *a ~ing fissure. A gulf ~ed at our feet.* □ *n* [C] act of ~ing(1).

yaws /jɔz/ *n pl* contagious tropical skin disease.

ye[1] /ji/ *pron* old form of you: *Ye fools! How d'ye do* /ˈhaʊ dɪ ˈdu/?

ye[2] /ji/ (old written form of) *the* (still seen on signboards over some shops and inns): *Ye Olde Bull and Bush.*

yea /jeɪ/ *adv, int* (archaic) yes. □ *n* aye: *Yeas and nays,* ayes and noes.

yeah /jeə/ *adv* (sl) yes.

year /jɜ(r) *US:* jɪər/ *n* **1** time taken by the earth in making one revolution round the sun, about 365¼ days. **2** period from 1 January to 31 December (also called the *calendar ~*): *in the ~ 1865; last ~; this ~; next ~; the ~ after next; New Y~'s Day,* 1 January. ***~ in ~ out,*** ~ after ~. ***all the ~ round,*** at all times of the ~. ***this ~ of grace, of our Lord,*** any named ~ after the birth of Jesus: *in the ~ of our Lord, 1975.* **3** any period of 365 consecutive days: *It is just a ~ since I arrived here. He's twenty ~s of age. He became blind in his twelfth ~,* at the age of 11. **ˈ~-book** *n* book issued once a ~ giving information (reports, statistics, etc) esp about trade or commerce. **ˈ~-ˈlong** *adj* continuing for a ~: *a ~-long struggle.* **4** period of one ~ associated with sth: *the academic ~,* for schools, colleges and universities (beginning, in GB and US, in the autumn); *the financial/fiscal ~,* (in GB, for making up accounts, etc from the beginning of April). **5** (*pl*) age; time of life: *a boy of ten ~s; young for her ~s,* looking young although not young in age; *reach ~s of discretion.* **~·ly** *adj, adv* (taking place) every ~; once a ~.

year·ling /ˈjɜlɪŋ *US:* ˈjɪər-/ *n* animal between one and two years old: (attrib) *a ~ colt.*

yearn /jɜn/ *vi* [VP3A,4A] **~ *(for sth/to do sth),*** long for with tender feeling, affection, etc: *He ~ed for a sight of the old, familiar faces. He ~ed to return to his native land.* **~·ing** *n* [U] (*pl*) strong desire; tender longing. **~·ing·ly** *adv*

yeast /jist/ *n* [C] substance used in brewing beer, and in the making of bread. **yeasty** *adj* frothy like ~.

yell /jel/ *vi, vt* **1** [VP2A,C] utter a loud sharp cry or cries as of pain, excitement, etc: *~ with fright/laughter.* **2** [VP6A,15B] **~ *sth (out),*** say in a ~ing voice: *~ (out) an order/oath; ~ one's defiance.* □ *n* loud sharp cry: *a ~ of terror; the college ~,* (US) particular kind of shout or cheer used at a college to encourage a team, etc. *They greeted us with ~s of hate.*

yel·low /ˈjeləʊ/ *n, adj* **1** the colour of gold or the yolk of a hen's egg. **~ fever,** infectious tropical disease causing the skin to turn ~. **ˈ~-flag** *n* flag coloured ~ displayed by a ship or hospital which is in quarantine. **the ~ press,** newspapers which present news in a sensational way. **2** (often **ˈ~-bellied**) (colloq) cowardly: *He has a ~ streak in him.* □ *vt, vi* [VP6A,2A] (cause to) become ~: *The leaves of the book were ~ed/had ~ed with age. The leaves of the trees are ~ing.* **~·ish** /-ɪʃ/ *adj* rather ~. **~·ness** *n*

yelp /jelp/ *vi* [VP2A], *n* (utter a) short, sharp cry (of pain, anger, excitement, etc): *The dog ~ed/gave a ~ when I trod on its paw.*

yen[1] /jen/ *n* (*pl* unchanged) unit of currency in Japan.

yen[2] /jen/ *n* (US, colloq) yearning (*for* sth). □ *vi* yearn (*to do* sth).

yeo·man /ˈjəʊmən/ *n* (*pl* -men) **1** working farmer who owns his land (contrasted with tenant farmers and those who own large farms which they do not work themselves). ˋ~ **service,** long and efficient service; help in time of need. **2 ~ of signals,** (GB) naval petty officer in the branch concerned with signalling by visual means (flags, etc); (US) petty officer with clerical duties. **3 *Y~ of the Guard,*** (GB) member of a royal bodyguard with ceremonial duties at the Tower of London, and elsewhere on special occasions. **4** member of the ~ry. **~ry** /-nrɪ/ *n* (collective for) volunteer cavalry force raised from farmers, etc.

yes /jes/ *particle* (contrasted with *no*) expressing agreement, affirmation, consent, etc: *'Can you read this?' 'Yes.'* (Note that *yes* is used in answer to an interrogative-negative if the complete answer is affirmative: *'Don't you like it?'—'Yes'* (= 'Yes, I do like it') *'Isn't she beautiful!'—'Yes, isn't she?' 'Waiter!'—'Yes, sir.'* 'What do you want, sir?' □ *n*: *Answer with a plain 'Yes' or 'No'.*

yes·ter- /ˋjestə(r)/ *pref* (on) the day, year, etc before this, chiefly poet except in ˋ~*day* (⇨ below): *Where are the snows of* ˋ~*-year?*

yes·ter·day /ˋjestədɪ/ *adv, n* (on) the day just past; (on) the day before today: *He arrived ~. Y~ was Sunday. Where's ~'s (news)paper? Why were you away from work the day before ~? Where were you ~ morning/afternoon/evening?* Cf *last night. She left home ~ week,* eight days ago.

yet /jet/ *adv* **1** (in neg and conditional contexts and in contexts indicating ignorance or uncertainty; usu in end position, but also immediately after *not*; ⇨ already(2)) by this or that time; up to now; up to then: *They are not here yet/not yet here. We have had no news from him yet. We have not yet had news from him. At 2 o'clock they had not yet decided how to spend the afternoon. I wonder whether they have finished the work yet.* **2** (in interr and neg contexts; ⇨ already and still) so far; up to this/that time: *Has your brother arrived yet? Need you go yet? We needn't do it just yet.* **3** (in affirm sentences) still: *Be thankful you are yet alive* (*Still* is the more usu word). *Go at once while there is yet time,* while it is not too late. *This problem is yet* (= still) *more difficult. I have yet* (= still) *more exciting news for you.* **4** at some future time; before all is over: *The enemy may win yet/may yet win if we relax our efforts. He may surprise us all yet.* **5 as yet,** up to now or then: *As yet we have/had not made any plans for the holidays. The scheme has worked well as yet.* **nor yet**: *I don't like the red one nor the brown one,* nor the brown one either. □ *conj* but at the same time; nevertheless: *She's vain and foolish, and yet people like her. He worked hard, yet he failed. It is strange, yet (it is) true. He's a wealthy, yet honest, business man.*

yeti /ˋjetɪ/ *n* name of a hairy, man-like animal reported to live in the highest part of the Himalayas.

yew /ju/ *n* [C] ˋ**yew(-tree),** evergreen, berry-bearing tree with dark-green leaves, often used for garden hedges; [U] wood of this tree (formerly used for making bows).

Yid·dish /ˋjɪdɪʃ/ *n* international language spoken by Jews, a form of old German with words borrowed from several modern languages, used as a vernacular in Eastern Europe and by emigrants. (The language used in Israel is modern Hebrew.)

yield /jild/ *vt,vi* **1** [VP6A] give a natural product, a result or profit: *trees that ~ fruit; investments ~ing 10 per cent.* **2** [VP2A,3A,6A,15A,B] **~ (to sb/sth),** give way (to); cease opposition: *We will never ~ to force. The disease ~ed to treatment. He ~ed to temptation.* **~ (up) sth (to sb),** give up; surrender: *~ a fort; ~ ground to the enemy.* **~ up the ghost,** (liter or rhet) die. □ *n* [C,U] amount produced: *a good ~ of wheat. What is the ~ per acre? The ~s on his shares have decreased this year,* The dividends are lower. **~·ing** *adj* easily giving way or bending; (fig) not obstinate. **~·ing·ly** *adv*

yip·pee /ˋjɪpɪ/ *int* cry of joy or elation.

yippy, yip·pie /ˋjɪpɪ/ *n* (*pl* -pies) member of the Youth International Party (1968), with ideals similar to those of the hippies.

yob, yobo, yobbo /job, ˋjobəʊ/ *n* (sl) idle, objectionable teenager.

yodel /ˋjəʊdl/ *vt,vi* (-ll-; US also -l-) sing (a song), utter a musical call, with frequent changes from the normal voice to high falsetto notes, in the manner of Swiss mountaineers. □ *n* ~ling song or call. **~·ler** (US also **~er**) *n* person who ~s.

yoga /ˋjəʊgə/ *n* [U] Hindu system of meditation and self-control intended to produce mystical experience and the union of the individual soul with the universal spirit. **yogi** /ˋjəʊgɪ/ *n* (*pl* -gis) teacher of, expert in, ~.

yo·gurt, yo·ghurt, yo·ghourt /ˋjogət *US:* ˋjəʊgərt/ *n* [U] fermented liquor made from milk.

yo-heave-ho /ˈjəʊ ˋhiv həʊ/ *int* cry (formerly) used by sailors when pulling together (e g to raise a sail).

yoke /jəʊk/ *n* **1** shaped piece of wood placed across the necks of oxen pulling a cart, plough, etc. **2** (*pl* unchanged) two oxen working together: *five ~ of oxen.* **3** (Roman history) arch of three spears (a symbol of the ~ placed on oxen) under which defeated enemies were made to pass; hence, (fig) *pass/come under the ~,* acknowledge and accept defeat; *throw off the ~* (of servitude, etc), rebel; refuse to obey; *the ~ of a ˋtyrant.* **4** shaped piece of wood to fit a person's shoulders and support a pail at each end. **5** (dressmaking) part of a garment fitting round the shoulders and from which the rest hangs; top part of a skirt, fitting the hips. □ *vt,vi* [VP6A,15A] **1** put a ~ on (oxen): *~ oxen together; ~ oxen to a plough.* **2** unite: *~d to an unwilling partner; ~d in marriage.*

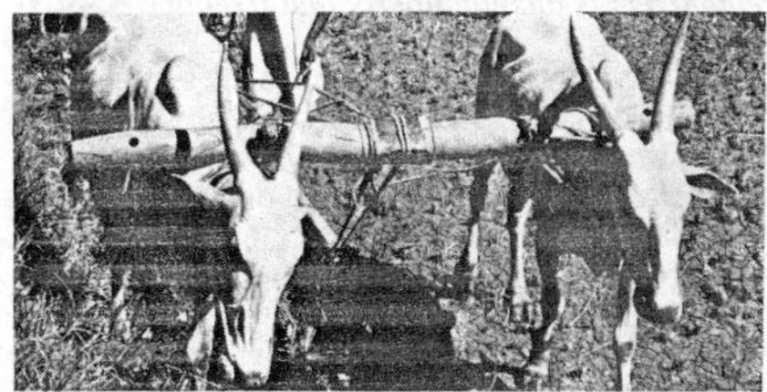

yoked oxen

yokel /ˋjəʊkl/ *n* simple-minded countryman.

yolk /jəʊk/ *n* [C,U] yellow part of an egg: *Beat up the ~s of three eggs.*

yon /jon/ *adj, adv* (archaic or dial) yonder.

yon·der /ˋjondə(r)/ *adj, adv* (liter) (that is, that can be seen) over there: *~ group of trees.*

yore /jɔ(r)/ *n* [U] (only in) ***of ~,*** formerly; in olden days; of long ago.

you /ju/ *pron* **1** the person(s) addressed: *You are my friend. Does he know you? This is for you.* **2** (colloq; used as an *indef pron*) one; anyone: *It is much easier to cycle with the wind behind you. You never know,* One can never be certain about things. **3** (preceding a *n*, esp in vocatives): *you boys;* (in exclamations): *You silly idiot! You bloody fool!*

young /jʌŋ/ *adj* **(-er, -est) 1** (contrasted with *old*) not far advanced in life, growth, development, etc; of recent birth or origin: *a ~ woman/tree/animal/nation, etc.* **2** still near its beginning: *The evening/century is still ~.* **3 ~er,** (used before or after a person's name, to distinguish that person from another; contrasted with *elder*): *the ~er Pitt; Pliny the Y~er.* **4** (used before a person's name to distinguish esp a son from his father): *The Y~ Pretender* (grandson of James II). *Y~ Jones is always ready to help his old parents.* **5** as a familiar or condescending form of address: *Now listen to me, ~ man/my ~ lady!* **6** having little practice or experience (in sth): *~ in crime.* **7 ~ and old,** everyone; *the ~,* ~ people; children: *books for the ~.* □ *n* offspring; ~ ones (of animals and birds): *The cat fought fiercely to defend its ~,* its ~ offspring. *Some animals quickly desert their ~.* ***with ~,*** (of an animal) pregnant. **~·ish** /ˈjʌŋgɪʃ/ *adj* fairly ~; somewhat ~. **~·ster** /ˈjʌŋstə(r)/ *n* child, youth, esp a boy.

your /jɔ(r) *US:* jʊər/ *adj* **1** belonging to, relating to, you: *Show me ~ hands. You'll see the post-office on ~ right,* i e ~ right side. **2** (often indicating polite interest, or disapproval or contempt, or used to suggest that sth is not so good, remarkable, etc as is claimed): *So this is what ~ experts said, is it? This is ~ famous English beer, is it?*

you're /jɔ(r) *US:* jʊər/ = you are.

yours /jɔz *US:* jʊərz/ *pred adj, pron* **1** of you: *Is that book ~? I borrowed a book of ~.* **2** (at the end of a letter): *~ truly/sincerely; faithfully ~.*

your·self /jɔˈself *US:* jʊərˈself/ (*pl* **-selves** /-ˈselvz/ *reflex pron: Did you hurt ~?* □ *emphat pron: You ~ said so. You said so ~.* ***(all) by ~,*** **(a)** alone. **(b)** without help.

youth /juθ/ *n* (*pl* ~s /juðz/) **1** [U] the state or time of being young: *the enthusiasm of ~; the friends of one's ~; in my ~,* when I was young. **2** (*pl*) young man: *As a ~ he showed no promise of becoming a great pianist. Half a dozen ~s were standing at the street corner.* **3** (collective) young men and women: *the ~ of the nation; a ˈ~ hostel,* ⇨ **hostel**; *a ˈ~ centre/club,* club (usu provided by a voluntary organization) for the leisure time activities of young people. **~·ful** /-fl/ *adj* young; having the qualities, etc, of young people: *a ~ful appearance.* **~·fully** /-fl̩ɪ/ *adv* **~·ful·ness** *n*

you've /juv/ = you have.

yowl /jaʊl/ *vi* howl; wail.

yoyo /ˈjəʊjəʊ/ *n* toy in the shape of a top with a groove for string, the top moving up and down the string by movement of the fingers: *The exchange rate is going up and down like a ~.*

yucca /ˈjʌkə/ *n* plant with sword-shaped evergreen leaves and large, white, lily-like flowers.

yule /jul/ *n* (also **ˈ~-tide**) Christmas. **ˈ~-log** *n* log of wood burnt on Christmas Eve.

Zz

Z, z /zed *US:* zi/ *n* (*pl* **Z's, z's** /zeds *US:* ziz/) the last letter of the English alphabet.

zany /ˈzeɪnɪ/ *n* (*pl* **-nies**) (formerly) character in comedies, etc; (mod use) half-witted person; foolish joker. □ *adj* foolish; mad.

zeal /zil/ *n* [U] enthusiasm: *show ~ for a cause; work with great ~.* **~·ous** /ˈzeləs/ *adj* full of, acting with, showing, ~: *~ous to please one's employer; ~ous for liberty and freedom.* **~·ous·ly** *adv*

zealot /ˈzelət/ *n* person who shows great and uncompromising enthusiasm for a religion, a party, a cause, etc; fanatic. **~ry** /-trɪ/ *n* [U].

zebra /ˈzibrə/ *n* horse-like wild animal of Africa, with dark stripes on its body. ⇨ the illus at **large**. **ˌ~ ˈcrossing,** street-crossing marked with broad white stripes, at which pedestrians have priority over traffic. ⇨ **panda**.

zebu /ˈzibju/ *n* domestic animal like an ox, with a hump on its shoulders, used in Asia and E Africa.

zee /zi/ *n* (US) name of the letter z.

Zen /zen/ *n* form of Buddhism asserting that enlightenment comes from meditation and intuition, with less dependence upon the scriptures.

zen·ana /zɪˈnɑnə/ *n* (India and Persia) part of a house in which women of high-caste families were formerly secluded.

zen·ith /ˈzenɪθ *US:* ˈzinɪθ/ *n* part of the sky directly overhead; (fig) highest point (of one's fame, fortunes, etc): *at the ~ of his career.* **~al** *adj: ~al projection,* map obtained by projecting[2](6). ⇨ the illus at **projection**.

zephyr /ˈzefə(r)/ *n* west wind; (poet) soft, gentle breeze.

zep·pe·lin /ˈzepəlɪn/ *n* rigid airship used by the Germans in World War I.

zero /ˈzɪərəʊ/ *n* **1** the figure 0; nought. ⇨ **App 4. 2** the point between the positive (+) and negative (−) on a scale, esp on a thermometer (⇨ **App 5**): *The thermometer fell to ~ last night. It was ten degrees below ~* (e g −10°C or −10°F). **absolute ~,** ⇨ **absolute(5)**. **ˈ~ hour,** (mil) time at which operations are to begin: *Z~ hour was 3a m.*

zest /zest/ *n* [U] **1** great interest or pleasure; gusto: *He entered into our plans with ~.* **2** (often with *indef art*) pleasing or stimulating quality or flavour: *The possibility of danger gave (a) ~ to the adventure.*

zig·zag /ˈzɪgzæg/ *n* [C] line or path which turns right and left alternately at sharp (equal or unequal) angles: (attrib) *a ~ path up the hillside.* □ *adv* in a ~. □ *vi* **(-gg-)** go in a ~: *The drunken man ~ged down the street.*

zinc /zɪŋk/ *n* [U] hard, bluish-white metal (symbol **Zn**) used in alloys and in coating iron sheets and wire to give protection against rust.

zin·nia /ˈzɪnɪə/ *n* kinds of garden plant with bright-coloured flowers.

Zion /ˋzaɪən/ *n* the Jewish homeland, esp as a symbol of Judaism; Israel. **~·ism** /-ɪzm/ *n* political movement for the establishment of an independent state for the Jews; (today) movement concerned with the development of Israel. **~·ist** /-ɪst/ *adj, n*

zip /zɪp/ *n* sound as of a bullet going through the air, or of the sudden tearing of cloth. □ *vt* (-pp-) [VP6A,22] open or close by means of a zip-fastener: *She zipped her bag open.* **zip·per, zip, zip-fastener** /ˋzɪp fɑsnə(r) *US:* fæs-/ *nn* device for locking together two toothed metal or plastic edges by means of a sliding tab, used for fastening articles of clothing, bags, etc.

zip code /ˋzɪp kəʊd/ *n* (US) = postcode.

zither /ˋzɪðə(r)/ *n* musical instrument with many strings on a flat sounding-board, played with a plectrum or the fingers.

zo·diac /ˋzəʊdɪæk/ *n* **1** belt of the heavens extending about 8° on each side of the path followed by the sun and containing the path of the principal planets, divided into 12 equal parts known as the *signs of the ~*, named after 12 groups of stars. **3** diagram of the ~, used in astrology.

zone /zəʊn/ *n* **1** belt, band or stripe going round, and distinguished by colour, appearance, etc. **2** one of the five parts into which the earth's surface is divided by imaginary lines parallel to the equator (the ˋ*torrid, N & S* ˋ*temperate,* and the ˋ*frigid ~s*). **3** area with particular features, purpose or use: *the war ~; within the ~ of submarine activity,* i e where, during a war, submarines are active; *the* ˋ*danger ~; a* ˋ*parking ~; smokeless ~s,* (usu urban) areas in which only smokeless fuels may be used (in homes, factories, etc). **4** (US) particular area in which certain postal, telephone, etc rates are charged. □ *vt* [VP6A] encircle, mark, with, into, or as with a ~ or ~s; divide into ~s. **zonal** /-nl/ *adj* relating to, arranged in, ~s. **zon·ing** *n* (in planning urban areas) designation of areas for various uses, e g shopping, residential, industrial.

zoo /zu/ *n* zoological gardens: *take the children to the zoo.*

zo·ol·ogy /zəʊˋɒlədʒɪ/ *n* [U] science of the structure, forms and distribution of animals. **zo·ologi·cal** /ˈzəʊəˋlɒdʒɪkl/ *adj* of ~: *zoological gardens,* park (usu public) in which many kinds of animals are kept for exhibition. **zo·ol·ogist** /zəʊˋɒlədʒɪst/ *n* expert in ~.

zoom /zum/ *n* **1** [U] (low, deep humming sound of the) sudden upward flight of an aircraft. **2 ~ lens,** (on a camera), one with continuously variable focal length. □ *vi* [VP2A,C] **1** (of aircraft) move upwards at high speed: (fig) *Prices ~ed,* rose sharply. **2** (of a camera with a ~ lens): *~ in/out,* cause the object being photographed to appear nearer/further.

zo·ophyte /ˋzəʊəfaɪt/ *n* plant-like sea animal (e g a sea anemone, coral).

zoot suit ˋzut sut/ *n* one with a knee-length jacket and tight-fitting trousers (as worn by some jazz enthusiasts and West Indians in the 1940's).

zou·ave /zuˋɑv/ *n* member of a French infantry-corps originally formed of Algerians.

zounds /zaʊndz/ *int* (old use) cry of anger, indignation, protest, etc.

zuc·chini /zuˋkinɪ/ *n* (*pl* ~s or unchanged) (esp US) = courgeette. ⇨ the illus at vegetable.

1
Aries (the Ram)
21st March–20th April

2
Taurus (the Bull)
21st April–20th May

3
Gemini (the Twins)
21st May–20th June

4
Cancer (the Crab)
21st June–20th July

5
Leo (the Lion)
21st July–19th/22nd Aug

6
Virgo (the Virgin)
20th/23rd Aug–22nd Sept

7
Libra (the Scales)
23rd Sept–22nd Oct

8
Scorpio (the Scorpion)
23rd Oct–21st Nov

9
Sagittarius (the Archer)
22nd Nov–20th Dec

10
Capricorn (the Goat)
21st Dec–20th Jan

11
Aquarius (the Water Carrier)
21st Jan–19th Feb

12
Pisces (the Fishes)
20th Feb–20th March

the zodiac

Appendix 1 IRREGULAR VERBS

Note: Full phonetic transcriptions of the irregular past tense and part participle forms are given in the entries on the infinitive forms in the dictionary.

Infinitive	Past Tense	Past Participle
abide	abode, abided	abode, abided
arise	arose	arisen
awake	awoke	awake, awoke
be	was	been
bear	bore	borne, born
beat	beat	beaten
become	became	become
befall	befell	befallen
beget	begot	begotten
begin	began	begun
behold	beheld	beheld
bend	bent	bent, bended
bereave	bereaved, bereft	bereaved, bereft
beseech	besought	besought
beset	beset	beset
bet	bet, betted	bet, betted
betake	betook	betaken
bethink	bethought	bethought
bid	bade, bid	bidden, bid
bide	bode, bided	bided
bind	bound	bound
bite	bit	bitten, bit
bleed	bled	bled
blend	blended, blent	blended, blent
bless	blessed, blest	blessed, blest
blow	blew	blown
break	broke	broken
breed	bred	bred
bring	brought	brought
broadcast	broadcast, broadcasted	broadcast, broadcasted
build	built	built
burn	burnt, burned	burnt, burned
burst	burst	burst
buy	bought	bought
cast	cast	cast
catch	caught	caught
chide	chid	chidden, chid
choose	chose	chosen
cleave	clove, cleft	cloven, cleft
cling	clung	clung
clothe	clothed	clothed
come	came	come
cost	cost	cost
creep	crept	crept
crow	crowed	crowed
cut	cut	cut
dare	dared	dared
deal	dealt	dealt
dig	dug	dug
dive	dived; (US) dove	dived
do	did	done
draw	drew	drawn
dream	dreamed, dreamt	dreamed, dreamt
drink	drank	drunk
drive	drove	driven
dwell	dwelt	dwelt
eat	ate	eaten
fall	fell	fallen
feed	fed	fed
feel	felt	felt
fight	fought	fought
find	found	found

flee	fled	fled
fling	flung	flung
fly	flew	flown
forbear	forbore	forborne
forbid	forbade, forbad	forbidden
forecast	forecast, forecasted	forecast, forecasted
foreknow	foreknew	foreknown
foresee	foresaw	foreseen
foretell	foretold	foretold
forget	forgot	forgotten
forgive	forgave	forgiven
forsake	forsook	forsaken
forswear	forswore	forsworn
freeze	froze	frozen
gainsay	gainsaid	gainsaid
get	got	got, (US) gotten
gild	gilded, gilt	gilded
gird	girded, girt	girded, girt
give	gave	given
go	went	gone
grave	graved	graven, graved
grind	ground	ground
grow	grew	grown
hamstring	hamstringed, hamstrung	hamstringed, hamstrung
hang	hung, hanged	hung, hanged
have	had	had
hear	heard	heard
heave	heaved, hove	heaved, hove
hew	hewed	hewed, hewn
hide	hid	hidden, hid
hit	hit	hit
hold	held	held
hurt	hurt	hurt
inlay	inlaid	inlaid
keep	kept	kept
kneel	knelt	knelt
knit	knitted, knit	knitted, knit
know	knew	known
lade	laded	laden
lay	laid	laid
lead	led	led
lean	leant, leaned	leant, leaned
leap	leapt, leaped	leapt, leaped
learn	learnt, learned	learnt, learned
leave	left	left
lend	lent	lent
let	let	let
lie	lay	lain
light	lighted, lit	lighted, lit
lose	lost	lost
make	made	made
mean	meant	meant
meet	met	met
melt	melted	melted, molten
miscast	miscast	miscast
misdeal	misdealt	misdealt
misgive	misgave	misgiven
mislay	mislaid	mislaid
mislead	misled	misled
misspell	misspelt	misspelt
misspend	mispent	misspent
mistake	mistook	mistaken
misunderstand	misunderstood	misunderstood
mow	mowed	mown, (US) mowed
outbid	outbade, outbid	outbidden, outbid
outdo	outdid	outdone
outgo	outwent	outgone
outgrow	outgrew	outgrown
outride	outrode	outridden
outrun	outran	outrun

outshine	outshone	outshone
overbear	overbore	overborne
overcast	overcast	overcast
overcome	overcame	overcome
overdo	overdid	overdone
overhang	overhung	overhung
overhear	overheard	overheard
overlay	overlaid	overlaid
overleap	overleapt, overleaped	overleapt, overleaped
overlie	overlay	overlain
override	overrode	overridden
overrun	orerran	overrun
oversee	oversaw	overseen
overset	overset	overset
overshoot	overshot	overshot
oversleep	overslept	overslept
overtake	overtook	overtaken
overthrow	overthrew	overthrown
overwork	overworked	overworked, overwrought
partake	partook	partaken
pay	paid	paid
prove	proved	proved, proven
put	put	put
read	read /red/	read /red/
rebind	rebound	rebound
rebuild	rebuilt	rebuilt
recast	recast	recast
redo	redid	redone
relay	relaid	relaid
remake	remade	remade
rend	rent	rent
repay	repaid	repaid
rerun	reran	rerun
reset	reset	reset
retell	retold	retold
rewrite	rewrote	rewritten
rid	rid, ridded	rid, ridded
ride	rode	ridden
ring	rang	rung
rise	rose	risen
rive	rived	riven, rived
run	ran	run
saw	sawed	sawn, (sawed)
say	said	said
see	saw	seen
seek	sought	sought
sell	sold	sold
send	sent	sent
set	set	set
sew	sewed	sewn, sewed
shake	shook	shaken
shave	shaved	shaved, shaven
shear	sheared	shorn, sheared
shed	shed	shed
shine	shone /ʃon/, (US) /ʃəʊn/	shone /ʃon/, (US) /ʃəʊn/
shoe	shod	shod
shoot	shot	shot
show	showed	shown, showed
shred	shredded	shredded
shrink	shrank, shrunk	shrunk, shrunken
shrive	shrove, shrived	shriven, shrived
shut	shut	shut
sing	sang	sung
sink	sank	sunk, sunken
sit	sat	sat
slay	slew	slain
sleep	slept	slept
slide	slid	slid, slidden
sling	slung	slung
slink	slunk	slunk

slit	slit	slit
smell	smelt, smelled	smelt, smelled
smite	smote	smitten
sow	sowed	sown, sowed
speak	spoke	spoken
speed	sped, speeded	sped, speeded
spell	spelt, spelled	spelt, spelled
spend	spent	spent
spill	spilt, spilled	spilt, spilled
spin	spun, span	spun
spit	spat	spat
split	split	split
spoil	spoilt ,spoiled	spoilt, spoiled
spread	spread	spread
spring	sprang	sprung
stand	stood	stood
stave	staved, stove	staved, stove
steal	stole	stolen
stick	stuck	stuck
sting	stung	stung
stink	stank, stunk	stunk
strew	strewed	strewn, strewed
stride	strode	stridden, strid
strike	struck	struck, stricken
string	strung	strung
strive	strove	striven
sunburn	sunburned, sunburnt	sunburned, sunburnt
swear	swore	sworn
sweep	swept	swept
swell	swelled	swollen, swelled
swim	swam	swum
swing	swung	swung
take	took	taken
teach	taught	taught
tear	tore	torn
tell	told	told
think	thought	thought
thrive	throve, thrived	thriven, thrived
throw	threw	thrown
thrust	thrust	thrust
tread	trod	trodden, trod
unbend	unbent	unbent
unbind	unbound	unbound
underbid	underbid	underbidden, underbid
undergo	underwent	undergone
understand	understood	understood
undertake	undertook	undertaken
undo	undid	undone
upset	upset	upset
wake	woke, waked	woken, waked
waylay	waylaid	waylaid
wear	wore	worn
weave	wove	woven, wove
wed	wedded	wedded, wed
weep	wept	wept
win	won	won
wind	winded, wound	winded, wound
withdraw	withdrew	withdrawn
withhold	withheld	withheld
withstand	withstood	withstood
work	worked	worked
wring	wrung	wrung
write	wrote	written

Appendix 2 COMMON ABBREVIATIONS

Note: This list includes abbreviations that occur in newspapers, timetables, etc. For abbreviations of parts of speech etc used in the text of the dictionary, ⇨ the inside covers of this book.
The use of capital or lower case letters indicates the more common usage but some abbreviations can be written in either style. Full points are often used in abbreviations though they are usually omitted in modern style.
Those abbreviations and acronyms that may be spoken, usually in a colloquial context, are given with phonetic transcriptions or stress marks, e g 'AG`M is pronounced /ˈeɪ dʒi ˋem/.

'A-bomb atomic bomb
`A-level advanced level (examination)
'A `A Alcoholics Anonymous; Automobile Association
'A A `A Amateur Athletics Association; American Automobile Association
'A `B (US) Bachelor of Arts
'A B `C Australian Broadcasting Commission
'a `c alternating current
a/c account
acc(t) account
ack(n) acknowledge(d)
ad(vt) advertisement
'A `D *Anno Domini* in the year of the Lord
'A D `C Aide-de-camp
add(r) address
Afr Africa(n)
'A G `M Annual General Meeting
'a `m *ante meridiem* before noon
amp ampere(s)
anon anonymous
ANZAC /ˋænzæk/ Australia and New Zealand Army Corps
'A P `B (US) All points Bulletin (for missing or wanted person)
appro /ˋæprəʊ/ approval
approx approximately
Apr April
arr arrival; arrives
assoc associate; association
asst assistant
Aug August
'A `V Audio-Visual; Authorised Version (of the Bible)
Av(e) Avenue
'A W O `L absent without leave

b born; bowled
'b & `b bed and breakfast
'B `A (GB) Bachelor of Arts; British Airways.
Barr Barrister
'B B `C British Broadcasting Corporation
'B `C Before Christ; British Council
'B `D Bachelor of Divinity
bk book
bldg(s) building(s)
'B `M British Museum
'B M `A British Medical Association
B Mus Bachelor of Music
'b `o body odour; box office
Br Brother
Brig Brigadier
Brit Britain, British
Bro(s) brother(s)
'B `S (US) Bachelor of Science
B Sc /ˈbi es ˋsi/ (GB) Bachelor of Science
'B S `T British Summer Time
Bt; Bart Baronet
B Th U British Thermal Unit
'B V `M *Beata Virgo Maria* Blessed Virgin Mary

C Centigrade; (Roman) 100
c cent(s); century; *circa* about; cubic
ca *circa* about, approximately
C A Chartered Accountant
Cantab /ˋkæntæb/ *Cantabrigiensis* of Cambridge University
Capt Captain
Card Cardinal
CAT /kæt/ College of Advanced Technology
Cath Catholic
'C B `C Canadian Broadcasting Corporation
'C B `S (US) Columbia Broadcasting System
'c `c cubic centimetre(s)
cc *capita* chapters; centuries
'C `D *Corps Diplomatique* Diplomatic Service
Cdr Commander
Cdre Commodore
CENTO /ˈsentəʊ/ Central Treaty Organisation
cert certificate; certified
'c `f *confer* compare with
cg centigram
c h central heating
'C `H Companion of Honour
ch(ap) chapter
'Ch `B Bachelor of Surgery
'c h `w constant hot water
C I Channel Islands
'C I `A (US) Central Intelligence Agency
'C I `D (GB) Criminal Investigation Department
'c i `f cost, insurance, freight
'C-in-`C Commander-in-Chief
cl class; centilitre(s)
cm centimetre(s)
Co (comm) Company
'C `O Commanding Officer
c/o care of
'C O `D Cash on Delivery
'C of `E /ˈsi əv ˋi/ Church of England
C O I (GB) Central Office of Information
Col Colonel
Coll College
concl concluded; conclusion
Cons (GB) Conservative (political party)
cont contents; continued
Co-op /ˋkəʊ op/ Co-operative (Society)
Corp Corporation
Coy (mil) Company
cp compare with
C P Cape Province; Communist Party
Cpl Corporal
'c p `s cycles per second
Cres(c) Crescent
C S Civil Servant; Civil Service

ˈC S ˋE (GB) Certificate of Secondary Education
ˈC S ˋT (US) Central Standard Time
cu cubic
cwt hundredweight

D Roman 500
d *denarius* penny; died
D-day Day on which a course of action is planned to start; ⇨ D-day in the dictionary
ˈD ˋA (US) District Attorney
dbl double
ˈD ˋC (US) District of Columbia
ˈd ˋc direct current
ˈD ˋD Doctor of Divinity
ˈD D ˋT (*D*ichloro-*d*iphenyl-*t*richloroethane) insecticide
Dec December
dec deceased
deg degree(s)
Dem Democrat
dep departs; departure; deputy
Dept Department
ˈD ˋG *Dei Gratia* by the grace of God; Director General
diag diagram
diff difference; different
Dip Diploma
Dip Ed /ˈdɪp ˋed/ Diploma in Education
Dir Director
ˈD ˋJ dinner jacket; disc jockey
D Litt /ˈdiˋlɪt/ Doctor of Letters/Literature
D M *Deutschmark* /ˋdɔɪtʃmɑk/ German currency
ˈD N ˋA *deoxyribose nucleic acid* basic constituent of the gene
dol dollar(s)
doz dozen
D Phil /ˈdi ˋfɪl/ Doctor of Philosophy
Dr Debtor; Doctor; Drive (i e small road)
dr dram(s)
D Sc /ˈdi es ˋsi/ Doctor of Science
ˈD ˋT; (the) d ts /ˈdi ˋtiz/ *delirium tremens* 'trembling delirium' (extreme state of alcoholism)
dupl duplicate
ˈD ˋV *Deo Volente* God being willing

E east
Ed edited by; editor; edition; education; educated
ˈE E ˋC European Economic Community (the Common Market)
EFTA /ˋeftə/ European Free Trade Association
ˈe ˋg *exempli gratia* for example, for instance
encl enclosed
E N E east northeast
Eng Engineer(ing); England; English
ˈE ˋP extended-playing (record)
ˈE ˋR *Elizabeth Regina* Queen Elizabeth
E S E east southeast
ˈE S ˋP Extra-Sensory Perception
Esq Esquire
ˈE S ˋT (US) Eastern Standard Time
e t a estimated time of arrival
et al /ˈet ˋæl/ *et alii* and other people; *et alia* and other things
etc; &c /ˈetˋsetrə/ *et cetera* and the rest, and all the others
e t d estimated time of departure
et seq /ˈet ˋsek/ *et sequens* and the following
eve evening

excl excluding; exclusive
ext exterior; external

F Fahrenheit; Fellow
f foot; feet; female; feminine
ˈF ˋA Football Association
ˈF A ˋO Food and Agriculture Organisation
ˈF B ˋA Fellow of the British Academy
ˈF B ˋI (US) Federal Bureau of Investigation; Federation of British Industries
ˈF ˋD *Fidei Defensor* Defender of the Faith
Feb February
Fed Federal; Federated; Federation
fem female; feminine
fig figurative; figure
fl fluid; floor
fm fathom(s)
ˈF ˋM Frequency Modulation
ˈF ˋO (GB) Foreign Office
ˈf o ˋb free on board
fol(l) following
for foreign
Fr Father; Franc; France; French
Fri Friday
ˈF R ˋS Fellow of the Royal Society
ft foot; feet
fur furlong(s)
furn furnished
fwd forward

g acceleration due to gravity; gram(s)
gal(l) gallon(s)
GATT /gæt/ General Agreement on Tariffs and Trade
ˈG ˋB Great Britain
ˈG ˋC George Cross
ˈG C ˋE (GB) General Certificate of Education
Gdn(s) Garden(s)
Gen General
Ger German(y)
ˈG H ˋQ General Headquarters
ˈG ˋI (US) enlisted soldier
Gk Greek
ˈG L ˋC Greater London Council
gm gram(s)
ˈG ˋM General Manager
ˈG M ˋT Greenwich Mean Time
ˈG N ˋP Gross National Product
gov(t) government
Gov Governor
ˈG ˋP General Practitioner (Medical Doctor)
ˈG P ˋO General Post Office
gr grade; grain; gross; group
grad graduate(d)
gt great

h height; hour
ha hectare(s)
h & c hot and cold (water)
ˋH-bomb Hydrogen bomb
H E high explosive; His/Her Excellency; His Eminence
H F High Frequency
H H His Holiness
H M His/Her Majesty
ˈH M ˋS His/Her Majesty's Ship
H of C House of Commons
H of L House of Lords
Hon Honorary; Honorable
hosp hospital

'H 'P Hire Purchase; Horse Power
'H 'Q Headquarters
hr hour(s)
HRH His/Her Royal Highness

I Island; Roman one
ib; ibid *ibidem* in the same place
i/c in charge
'ICB'M Inter-Continental Ballistic Missile
'i 'e *id est* which is to say, in other words
'I H 'S *Iesous* (Greek for) Jesus (Christ)
'I M 'F International Monetary Fund
in inch(es)
Inc Incorporated
incl including; inclusive
Ind India(n); Independent
inf *infra* below
info /'ɪnfəʊ/ information
infra dig /'ɪnfrə 'dɪg/ *infra dignitatem* beneath one's social dignity
'I N R 'I *Iesus Nazarenus Rex Iudaeorum* Jesus of Nazareth, King of the Jews
Inst Institute
inst *instante* of this month
int interior; internal; international
intro introduction
'I O 'U I owe you
'I 'Q *Intelligence Quotient* comparative measure of intelligence
'I R 'A Irish Republican Army
Ire Ireland
Is Islands
It(al) Italy, Italian

Jan January
J C Jesus Christ
Jnr; Jr Junior
'J 'P Justice of the Peace
Jul July
Jun June; Junior

kg kilogram(s)
'K G 'B Intelligence Agency of the USSR
km kilometre(s)
'K 'O knock-out
'k p 'h kilometres per hour
kw kilowatt(s)

L lake; little; Roman 50; (GB) Liberal (political party)
l left; length; line
'L 'A Legislative Assembly; Los Angeles
Lab (GB) Labour (political party)
lang language
Lat Latin
lat latitude
'l b 'w leg before wicket (cricket term)
Ld Lord
l h left hand
Lib (GB) Liberal (political party); Liberation
lit literal(ly); literature; literary
ll lines
'LL 'B Bachelor of Laws
'L M 'T (US) Local Mean Time
loc cit /'lok 'sɪt/ *loco citato* in the place mentioned
long longitude
'L 'P long-playing (record)
'L S 'D *lysergic acid diethylamide* drug inducing hallucinations
£ s d /'el es 'di/ *librae, solidi, denarii* pounds, shillings, pence (former G B currency system)
'L S 'T (US) Local Standard Time
Lt Lieutenant
Ltd Limited
lux luxury

M Member
m male; married; metre(s); mile(s); million
'M 'A Master of Arts
Maj Major
Mans Mansions
Mar March
masc masculine
math /mæθ/ (US) mathematics
maths /mæθs/ (GB) mathematics
max maximum
'M 'B Bachelor of Medicine
'M B 'E Member of (the Order of) the British Empire
'M 'C (US) Marine Corps; Master of Ceremonies; (US) Member of Congress; Military Cross
'M C 'C (GB) Marylebone Cricket Club (the governing body of English cricket)
Mc Megacycle(s)
'M 'D Doctor of Medicine
Med(it) Mediterranean
METO /'mitəʊ/ Middle East Treaty Organisation
mg milligram(s)
Mgr Monsignor
'M I '5 (GB) National Security Division of Military Intelligence
min minimum
misc miscellaneous
mkt market
ml mile(s), millilitre(s)
mm millimetre(s)
'M 'O Mail Order; Medical Officer; Money Order
mod moderate; modern
mod cons /'mod 'konz/ modern conveniences
Mon Monday
'M 'P Member of Parliament (House of Commons); Military Police
m p g miles per gallon
m p h miles per hour
MS(S) manuscript(s)
M Sc /'em es 'si/ Master of Science
Mt Mount

N north
NAAFI /'næfɪ/ (GB) Navy, Army and Air Force Institute
nat national; native; natural
NATO /'neɪtəʊ/ North Atlantic Treaty Organisation
'N 'B *nota bene* take special note of
'N C 'O Non-Commissioned Officer
N E northeast
'N H 'S (GB) National Health Service
N N E north northeast
N N W north northwest
no(s) number(s)
non-U /'non 'ju/ not upper class; not in vogue; vulgar
Nov November
nr near
'N S 'P C 'C (GB) National Society for the Prevention of Cruelty to Children
N T New Testament
N W northwest

N Y New York
N Z New Zealand

O Officer
ˈO A ˋU Organisation for African Unity
ob *obiit* died
Oct October
ˈO E ˋD Oxford English Dictionary
ˈO H M ˋS (GB) On Her/His Majesty's Service
ˋO-level (GB) Ordinary level (examination)
o n o or nearest offer
op opus; operation
op cit /ˈop ˋsɪt/ *opere citato* in the work mentioned
opp opposite
orch orchestra(1); orchestrated
O T Old Testament
Oxon /ˋoksn/ *Oxoniensis* of Oxford University; Oxfordshire
oz ounce(s)

P Parking
p page; penny, pence; per
p a *per annum* per year
ˈP ˋA Personal Assistant; Press Association; Public Address (System)
para(s) paragraph(s)
Parl Parliament(ary)
ˈP A Y ˋE pay as you earn
ˈP ˋC Police Constable; (GB) Privy Councillor; (US) Peace Corps
pd paid
ˈP D S ˋA People's Dispensary for Sick Animals
ˈP ˋE physical education
PEN /pen/ International Association of Writers
ˈP ˋG Paying Guest
Ph D /ˈpi eɪtʃ ˋdi/ Doctor of Philosophy
Pk Park
pkt packet
Pl Place
ˈP ˋM Prime Minister
ˈp ˋm *post meridiem* after noon; per month
P O Personnel Officer; Petty Officer; Post Office; Postal Order
ˈP ˋO Box Post Office Box
ˈP O ˋE Port of Entry
pop popular; population
poss possible; possibly
ˈP O ˋW Prisoner of War
pp pages
ˈp ˋp *per procurationem* by the authority of; representing (definition 5)
ˈP P ˋS *post postscriptum* additional postscript
pr pair; price
ˈP ˋR Public Relations
Pres President
ˈP R ˋO Public Records Office; Public Relations Officer
pro /prəʊ/ professional
pro tem /ˈprəʊ ˋtem/ *pro tempore* for the time being
Prof (*informally* /prof/) Professor
pron pronounced; pronunciation
Prot Protestant
Prov Province
Ps Psalm
ˈP ˋS Postcript
ˈP S ˋT (US) Pacific Standard Time
pt part; payment; pint; point
ˈP ˋT Physical Training
ˈP T ˋA Parent-Teacher Association
Pte (GB) Private (soldier)
P T O Please turn over
Pty Proprietary
Pvt (US) Private (soldier)
p w per week
ˈP ˋX please exchange; post exchange (US equivalent of NAAFI)

ˈQ ˋC Queen's Counsel
ˈQ E ˋD *quod erat demonstrandum* which had to be proved
qt quart
Qu Queen; Question
ˈq ˋv *quod vide* which may be referred to

R River; Royal
r radius; right
ˈR ˋA Rear-Admiral; Royal Academy; Royal Academician
RADA /ˈrɑdə/ Royal Academy of Dramatic Art
ˈR A ˋF (*also* /ræf/) Royal Air Force
ˈR A ˋM Royal Academy of Music
ˈR ˋC Red Cross; Roman Catholic
ˈR C ˋM Royal College of Music
Rd Road
rec(d) received
ref referee /ref/; reference; refer(red)
Reg *Regina* Queen
Rep Repertory /rep/; Representative; Republic(an)
res residence; resigned; reserved
resp respectively
ret(d) retired
rev revolution
Rev(d) Reverend
r h right hand
ˈR I ˋP *requiescat/requiescant in pace* may he/they rest in peace
rly railway
rm room
R M Royal Marines
ˈR ˋN Royal Navy
r p m revolutions per minute
ˈR S ˋM Regimental Sergeant Major; Royal Schools of Music
ˈR S V ˋP *répondez s'il vous plaît* please reply
ˈR S ˈP C ˋA Royal Society for the Prevention of Cruelty to Animals
rt right
Rt Hon Right Honourable
Rt Rev Right Reverend
R (S) V Revised (Standard) Version (of the Bible)
R U Rugby Union

S south
s second(s); shilling(s)
S A South Africa
s a e stamped addressed envelope
SALT /sɔlt/ Strategic Arms Limitation Talks
Sat Saturday
sc *scilicet* namely
s/c self-contained
Sch School
sci science
S E southeast
SEATO /ˋsitəʊ/ South East Asia Treaty Organisation
sec second(ary); secretary
Sen Senate; Senator; Senior

Sept September
ˈS ˋF Science Fiction
sgd signed
Sgt Sergeant
SHAPE /ʃeɪp/ Supreme Headquarters of Allied Powers in Europe
Sn(r) Senior
Soc Society
Sol Solicitor
sp special; spelling
Sp Spain, Spanish
sp gr specific gravity
Sq Square
Sr Senior; Sister
ˈS R ˋN State Registered Nurse
ˈS ˋS Steamship
S S E south southeast
S S W south southwest
St Saint; Street
Sta Station
ˈS T ˋD subscriber trunk dialling (telephone)
Str Strait; Street
sub(s) subscription; substitute
Sun Sunday
Supt Superintendent
S W southwest

T temperature
t time; ton(s)
ˈT ˋB Tuberculosis
Tech /tek/ Technical (College)
tel telephone
temp temperature; temporary /temp/
Ter(r) Terrace; Territory
Thurs Thursday
ˈT K ˋO technical knock-out
ˈT N ˋT (*Tri-nitro-toluene*) explosive
trans translated
treas treasurer
T U Trade Union
ˈT U ˋC (GB) Trades Union Congress
Tues Tuesday
ˈT ˋV television

U Union; Upper; upper class, fashionable, polite, ⇨ non-U above
ˈU A ˋR United Arab Republic
ˈU D ˋI unilateral declaration of independence
UFO /ˈjufəʊ/ unidentified flying object
ˈU H ˋF ultra high frequency
ˈU ˋK United Kingdom
ˈU ˋN United Nations
UNESCO /juˋneskəʊ/ United Nations Educational, Scientific and Cultural Organisation
UNICEF /ˈjunɪsef/ United Nations International Children's Emergency Fund (or United Nations Children's Fund)
Univ University
UNO /ˈjunəʊ/ United Nations Organisation
UNRRA /ˈʌnrə/ United Nations Relief and Rehabilitation Administration
UNRWA /ˈʌnwə/ United Nations Relief and Works Agency
ˈU ˋS United States
ˈU S ˋA United States of America; United States Army
ˈU S A ˋF United States Air Force
ˈU S ˋN United States Navy
ˈU S ˋS United States Ship
ˈU S S ˋR Union of Soviet Socialist Republics

V Roman 5; Victory; Volt
v very; verse; *vide* see, refer to
V A Vice-Admiral
V & A /ˈvi ən ˋeɪ/ Victoria and Albert (Museum in London)
vac /væk/ vacation
VAT /væt/ Value Added Tax, ⇨ value (3)
ˈV ˋC Vice Chairman; Vice Chancellor; Vice Consul; Victoria Cross; Vietcong
ˈV ˋD Venereal Disease
ˈV ˋE Day Victory in Europe (end of Second World War in Europe: 8.5.1945)
Ven Venerable
ˈV H ˋF very high frequency
Vic Victoria
ˈV I ˋP very important person
viz /vɪz/ *videlicet* namely
vocab vocabulary
vol volume
V P(res) Vice-President
vs versus
V S (US) Veterinary Surgeon
ˈV S ˋO (GB) Voluntary Service Overseas

W west
w watt(s); week; width; with
WASP /wosp/ (US) White Anglo-Saxon Protestant
ˈw ˋc water closet, ⇨ water[1](7)
W C C World Council of Churches
w e f with effect from
ˈW H ˋO /hu/ World Health Organization
W I West Indian; West Indies; Women's Institute
wk week; work
Wm William
W N W west northwest
ˈW ˋO Warrant Officer
ˈw p ˋb waste paper basket
w p m words per minute
ˈW R A ˋC Women's Royal Army Corps
ˈW R A ˋF Women's Royal Air Force
ˈW R N ˋS *also* /renz/ Women's Royal Naval Service
W S W west southwest
wt weight

X Roman 10; a kiss; an unknown number, thing, name, etc
Xmas Christmas

Y Yen (Japanese currency)
ˈY H ˋA Youth Hostels Association
ˈY M C ˋA Young Men's Christian Association
yr year; your
ˈY W C ˋA Young Women's Christian Association

Appendix 3 **AFFIXES**

Note: Many affixes have more than one pronunciation form or stress pattern. This often depends on the form of the word to which it is attached. ⇨ the entries in the dictionary for full phonetic transcriptions of the vocabulary given as examples in this appendix.

a-[1] /eɪ-, ə-, æ-/ *pref* not, without: *amoral; aseptic; atheist.*
a-[2] /ə-/ *pref* **1** (∼ + *n* = *adv*) in: *abed;* on, at: *field; ashore.* **2** (∼ + *v* = *adv*) in the state of, in the process of: *asleep; ablaze.* **3** (old use) (∼ + *gerund* = *adv*) in the act of: *a-running; a-singing.*
ab- /æb-, əb-/ *pref* from, away from: *absent; abduct.*
-able (also **-ible**) /-əbl/ *suff* **1** (*n* + ∼ = *adj*) showing qualities of: *fashionable; responsible.* **2** (*v* + ∼ = *adj*) that can be, fit to be: *eatable; reducible.* **-ably, -ibly** /-əblɪ/ *adv*
ad- /əd-, æd-/ *pref* to, towards: *advance; adjoin.*
-ade /-eɪd, -ɑd/ *suff* (used to form a *n*): *blockade; lemonade; façade.*
aer(o)- /eər(ə- *etc*)/ *pref* of aircraft: *aerodynamics; aeronaut.*
-age /-ɪdʒ, -ɑʒ/ *suff* (used to form a *n*): *breakage; postage; sabotage.*
-al /-l, -əl/ *suff* **1** (*n* + ∼ = *adj*): *magical; verbal.* **-ally** /-l̩ɪ, -əlɪ/ *adv* **2** (*v* + ∼ = *n*): *recital; survival.*
ambi- /æmbɪ- *etc*/ *pref* both, double, two: *ambiguous; ambidextrous.*
an- /æn-, ən-/ *pref* not, without: *anaesthetic; anonymous.*
-an /-ən, -n/ *suff* (*proper n* + ∼ = *n* or *adj*, ⇨ App 6): *Lutheran; Mexican.* ⇨ also -ian below.
-ana ⇨ -iana
-ance: (also **-ence**) /-əns, -ns/ *suff* (*v* + ∼ = *n*): *assistance; confidence.*
-ant (also **-ent**) /-ənt, -nt/ *suff* **1** (*v* + ∼ = *adj*): *significant; different.* **2** (*v* + ∼ = *n*): *assistant; deterrent.*
ante- /æntɪ-/ *pref* in front of: *anteroom;* before, previous to: *antenatal.*
anthrop(o)- /ænθrəp(ə- *etc*)/ *pref* of man, of mankind: *anthropoid; anthropology.*
anti- /æntɪ-/ *pref* **1** opposed to, against: *anti-social; antiseptic.* **2** instead of: *anti-hero.*
arch- /ɑk-, ɑtʃ-/ *pref* first, chief, head: *archetype; archbishop.*
-arian /-eərɪən/ *suff* practiser of: *disciplinarian; vegetarian.*
-ary /-ərɪ, -rɪ/ *suff* **1** (used to form an *adj*): *planetary; reactionary.* **2** (*pl* -aries) (used to form a *n*): *dictionary; functionary.*
astr(o)- /æstr(ə- *etc*)/ *pref* of the stars, of outer space: *astronomy; astronaut.*
-ate *suff* **1** /-ət, -ɪt/ (used to form an *adj*): *affectionate: passionate.* **-ately** /-ətlɪ, -ɪtlɪ/ *adv* **2** /-ət, -ɪt/ (used to form a *n*): *directorate; electorate;* **3** /-eɪt/ (used to form a *v*): *gyrate; stimulate.* **4** /-eɪt/ (chem) salt formed by the action of an acid on a base: *phosphate; nitrate.*
-ation ⇨ -tion
-ative /-ətɪv/ *suff* (used to form an *adj*, usu from an '-ate' *v*): *illustrative; quantitative.*
-atively /-ətɪvlɪ/ *adv*
-ator /-eɪtə(r)/ *suff* object or person carrying out the action of an '-ate' *v*: *percolator; stimulator.*
audio- /ɔdɪəʊ-/ *pref* of hearing, of sound: *audio-visual; audio-frequency.*
aut(o)- /ɔt(ə- *etc*)/ *pref* **1** of oneself: *autobiography; autograph.* **2** without help, independent of others: *automatic; autocrat.*
be- /bɪ-/ *pref* **1** (∼ + *v* = *v*) all over, all around, in all directions: *bedeck; bespatter.* **2** (∼ + *n* or *adj* = *v*) make, become: *befriend; belittle.* **3** (∼ + *vi* = *vt*): *bemoan; bewail.*
bi- /bɑɪ-/ *pref* **1** occurring twice in one period: *bi-monthly; bi-annual.* **2** occurring once in a period of two: *bicentenary; biennial.* **3** having two: *bilingual; biped.*
bibli(o)- /bɪblɪ(ə- *etc*)/ *pref* of books: *bibliography; bibliophile.*
bio- /bɑɪ(ə- *etc*)/ *pref* of life, of living organisms: *biography; biology; biotic.*
by- (also **bye-**) /bɑɪ-/ *pref* of secondary importance, incidental: *by-election; bye-law; by-product.*
cent(i)- /sent(ɪ- *etc*)/ *pref* a hundred, a hundredth part: *Centigrade; centimetre.*
chron(o)- /kron(ə- *etc*)/ *pref* of time: *chronology; chronometer.*
-cide /-sɑɪd/ *suff* (used to form a *n*) killing, killer: *suicide; insecticide.*
co- /kəʊ- *etc*/ *pref* together, jointly, equally: *cohabit; co-operate; co-education.*
con- (also **col-, com-, cor-**) /kon-, kən-, *etc*/ *pref* with, together: *conduct; collaborate; combine; correlate.*
contra- /kontrə-/ *pref* against, opposite to: *contraception; contradict.*
-cracy /-krəsɪ/ *suff* (*pl* -cracies) (used to form a *n*) government or rule by, class characterized by: *democracy; aristocracy.*
-crat /-kræt/ *suff* (used to form a *n*) member or supporter of a '-cracy': *democrat; aristocrat.* **-cratic** /-krætɪk/ *adj*: *democratic; aristocratic.*
-cy (also **-acy**) /-(ə)sɪ/ *suff* (*pl* -(a)cies) (used to form a *n*) condition, quality: *accuracy; infancy; supremacy.*
-d ⇨ -ed
de- /di-, dɪ-/ *pref* (used with a *v*) the negative, reverse, opposite of: *depopulate; defrost; defuse.*
demi- /demɪ-/ *pref* half, partly: *demimonde; demigod.*
di- /dɑɪ-, dɪ-/ *pref* twice, double: *dilemma; dioxide.*
dia- /dɑɪə-/ *pref* through, across: *diameter; diagonal; diaphragm.*
dis- /dɪs-/ *pref* (used with a *v*) the negative, reverse, opposite of: *disbelieve; disorder; disagree.*
-dom /-dəm/ *suff* (used to form a *n*) **1** a condition, state: *boredom; freedom.* **2** domain: *kingdom; officialdom.*

-ed (also **-d**)/ *After* p, k, tʃ, f, θ, s *pronounced* -t; *after* t, d *pronounced* -ɪd; *otherwise pronounced* -d. *Exception* 'used', ⇨ use²/ *suff* **1** (used to form *pt* and *pp* of a *v*): *laughed; acted; washed.* **2** (*n* + ∼ = *adj*) having the characteristics of: *diseased; talented; cracked.*

-ee /-i/ *suff* (*v* + ∼ = *n*) **1** person affected by the action of the *v*: *employee; payee.* **2** person acting: *absentee; refugee.* **3** (*n* + ∼ = *n*) diminutive: *bootee; coatee.*

-eer /-ɪə(r)/ *suff* (*n* + ∼ = *n*) person concerned with the *n*: *auctioneer; mountaineer.*

electr(o)- /ɪlektr(ə- *etc*)/ *pref* concerned with, caused by electricity: *electrocute; electromagnet.*

en- /ɪn-, en-/ (also **em-** /ɪm-, em-/) *pref* **1** (∼ + *n* or *v* = *v*) put in, on: *encase; endanger; emplane.* **2** (∼ + *n* or *adj* = *v*) make into, cause to be: *enlarge; enrich; empower.*

-en /-ən, -n/ *suff* **1** (used to form the *pp* of some *vv*) *broken; eaten; hidden.* **2** (n + ∼ = *adj*) made of: *golden; wooden.* **3** (adj + ∼ = *v*) make, cause to be: *blacken; sadden.*

-ence ⇨ -ance

-ent ⇨ -ant

equi- /ikwɪ- *etc*/ *pref* equal, the same: *equidistant; equivalent.*

-er /-ə(r)/ *suff* **1** (*v* + ∼ = *n*) person who carries out the action of the *v*: *runner, sleeper.* **2** (*n* + ∼ = *n*) practiser of: *astronomer; philosopher.* **3** (also **-r**) (used to form the *comp* of an *adj*): *stronger; rarer; thinner.* ⇨ also -ier.

-ery /-ərɪ, -rɪ/ (also **-ry** /-rɪ/) *suff* (*pl* -eries) (*n* or *v* + ∼ = *n*) **1** place where an action is carried out: *bakery; fishery.* **2** art of, practice of: *cookery; pottery.* **3** state, quality, character: *rivalry; snobbery.*

-es (also **-s**) /-ɪz/ *suff* **1** (used to form *pl* of a *n* ending in /s, z, ʃ, ʒ/): *pieces; judges.* **2** (used to form *3rd pers sing pres t* of a *v* ending in /s, z, ʃ, ʒ/): *washes; urges.*

-ese /-iz/ *suff* **1** (*proper n* + ∼ = *adj*) of a place or a country: *Burmese;* (the *adj* may also be used as a *n*, ⇨ App 6): person or language: *Japanese.* **2** (used to form a *n*) in the (literary) style of: *journalese.*

-esque /-esk/ *suff* (*n* + ∼ = *adj*) in the manner, style of: *statuesque; picturesque.*

-ess /-əs, -ɪs, -es/ *suff* (*n* or *v* + ∼ = *n*) female: *lioness; actress.*

-est /-ɪst/ *suff* (also **-st**) (used to form the *superl* of an *adj* or *adv*): *fastest; barest; wettest.*

-ette /-et/ *suff* (*n* + ∼ = *n*) **1** diminutive: *cigarette; kitchenette.* **2** female: *usherette; suffragette.* **3** imitation: *flannelette; leatherette.*

ex- *pref* **1** /ɪks-, eks-, ɪgz-, egz-/ out, out of, from: *exclaim; extract.* **2** /eks-/ former, at one time: *ex-wife; ex-president.*

extra- /ekstrə-/ *pref* outside, beyond, especially: *extramarital; extramural, extrasensory.*

-fic /-fɪk/ *suff* (used with a '-fy' *v* to form an *adj*): *horrific; specific.*

-fied /-faɪd/ ⇨ -fy

-fold /-fəʊld/ *suff* (*cardinal numeral* + ∼ = *adj*) **1** multiplied by: *tenfold; hundredfold.* **2** of (so many) parts: *twofold.*

fore- /fɔ(r)-/ *pref* before, in front of: *foretell; foreground.*

-form /-fɔm/ *suff* (used to form an *adj*) having the shape or character of: *uniform; cuneiform.*

-ful *suff* **1** /-fl/ (*n* or *v* + ∼ = *adj*) full of, having the quality of: *eventful; peaceful.* **2** /-fʊl/ (*n* + ∼ = *n*) amount that fills; *handful; mouthful.*

-gamy /-gəmɪ/ *suff* (used to form a *n*) of marriage: *monogamy; polygamy.* **-gamous** /-gəməs/ *adj*

ge(o)- /dʒi(ə- *etc*)/ *pref* of the earth: *geography; geology.*

-gon /-gən, -gon/ angle, corner: *polygon; pentagon.*

-gram /-græm/ *suff* (used to form a *n*) sth written down or drawn: *telegram; monogram; diagram.*

-graph /-grɑf *US:* -græf/ *suff* (used to form a *n*) sth written down, of writing: *autograph; telegraph.* **-graphy** /-grəfɪ/ *n*: *calligraphy; orthography.*

hem(o)- (also **haem(o)-**) /himə-, hemə-/ *pref* of the blood: *hemoglobin; hemorrhage.*

heter(o)- /hetər(ə- *etc*)/ *pref* the other, the opposite, different: *heterogeneous; heterosexual.*

hom(o)- /hom(ə- *etc*), həʊm-/ *pref* the same: *homogeneous; homosexual.*

-hood /-hʊd/ *suff* (*n* + ∼ = *n*) status, rank, condition of life: *boyhood; brotherhood.*

hydr(o)- /hɑɪdr(ə- *etc*)/ *pref* of water: *hydrant; hydro-electric.*

hyper- /hɑɪpə(r)-/ *pref* to a large or extreme degree: *hypercritical; hypersensitive.*

-ial /-ɪəl, -l/ *suff* (*n* + ∼ = adj) characteristic of: *dictatorial; palatial.* **-ially** /-ɪəlɪ, -l̩ɪ/ *adv*

-ian /-ɪən, -n/ *suff* **1** (*proper n* + ∼ = *n* or *adj*, ⇨ App 6): *Brazilian; Shakespearian.* **2** (used with an '-ics' *n* to form a *n*) specialist in: *optician; pediatrician.*

-(i)ana /-(ɪ)ɑnə/ *suff* (used with words ending in '-ian' or '-an' to form a *collective n*) collection of facts, objects, etc relating to: *Victoriana; Africana.*

-ible ⇨ -able

-ic /-ɪk/ *suff* (*n* + ∼ = *adj*): *poetic; romantic.* **-ical** /-ɪkl/ *adj* **-ically** /-ɪklɪ/ *adv*

-ics /-ɪks/ *suff* (used to form a *n*) science or specific activity: *physics; politics; athletics.*

-ide /-ɑɪd/ *suff* (used to form a *n*) (chem) chemical compound: *chloride; sulphide.*

-ie ⇨ -y

-ier ⇨ -y

-ies ⇨ -y.

-(i)fy /-(ɪ)fɑɪ/ *suff* (*pt* and *pp* -(ɪ)fied /-(ɪ)fɑɪd/) (*n* or *adj* + ∼ = *v*) make into, cause to be, bring to a state of: *beautify; terrify; solidify.*

in- (also **il-**, **im-**, **ir-**) /ɪn-, ɪl-, ɪm-, ɪr-/ *pref* **1** (∼ + *v* = *v* or *n*) in, on: *intake; imprint.* **2** (∼ + *adj* = *adj*) not: *infinite; illicit; immoral; irrelevant.*

-ing /-ɪŋ/ *suff* (*v* + ∼ = *pres p* and *gerund*): *talking; thinking.*

inter- /ɪntə(r)-/ *pref* between, from one to another: *international; interplanetary.*

intra- (also **intro-**) /ɪntrə-/ *pref* inside: *intravenous; intra-uterine; introspection.*

-ise ⇨ -ize

-ish /-ɪʃ/ *suff* **1** (*national name* + ∼ = *adj*, ⇨ App 6): *Irish; Spanish.* **2** (n + ∼ = *adj*) resembling, in the manner of: *childish; devilish.* **3** (*adj* + ∼ = *adj*) somewhat, near to: *reddish; twentyish.*

-ism /-ɪzm/ *suff* (used to form a *n*) **1** showing qualities typical of: *Americanism; heroism.* **2** specific doctrine, principle or movement: *Buddhism; Communism.*

ist /-ɪst/ *suff* (*n* + ∼ = *n*) **1** agent of an '-ize' *v*: *dramatist; publicist.* **2** follower, practiser of an '-ism': *industrialist; fascist.* **3** person concerned with a specific activity or thing: *tobacconist; motorist.*

-ite /-ɑɪt/ *suff* **1** (*proper n* + ∼ = *n*) follower, devotee of a person or organisation: *Labourite.* **2** (chem) specific chemical substance: *anthracite; dynamite.*

-ities ⇨ -ity

-ition ⇨ -tion

-itis /-ɑɪtɪs/ *suff* (med) (used to form a *n*) inflammation of: *appendicitis; tonsillitis.*

-ity /-ətɪ/ *suff* (*pl* -ities) (used with an *adj* to form a *n*): *crudity; oddity.*

-ive /-ɪv/ *suff* (*v* + ∼ = *adj*) having a tendency towards, quality of: *active; constructive.*

-ize (also **-ise,** which is not used in this dictionary, but is equally acceptable) /-ɑɪz/ *suff* (used to form a *v*) **1** cause to be, make like, change into: *computerize; dramatize.* **2** act with the qualities of: *criticize; deputize.*

-less /-ləs/ *suff* (*n* + ∼ = adj) without: *treeless; spiritless.* **-lessly** /-ləslɪ/ *adv* **-lessness** /-ləsnəs/ *n*

-let /-lət/ *suff* (*n* + ∼ = *n*) diminutive: *piglet; booklet.*

-like /-lɑɪk/ *suff* (*n* + ∼ = *adj*) resembling, in the manner of: *childlike; godlike.*

-ling /-lɪŋ/ *suff* **1** (used to form a *n*) diminutive: *duckling; fledgeling.* **2** (used to form a *n*) person connected with (often used disparagingly): *hireling; underling.*

-logue /-log *US:* -lɔg/ *suff* (used to form a *n*) sth spoken: *dialogue; travelogue; monologue.*

-logy /-lədʒɪ/ *suff* (*pl* -logies) (used to form a *n*) branch of learning: *biology; sociology.*

-ly /-lɪ/ *suff* **1** (*n* + ∼ = *adj*) having the qualities of: *cowardly; scholarly.* **2** (*n* + ∼ = *adj* or *adv*) regular occurrence: *hourly; yearly.* **3** (*adj* + ∼ = *adv*) in the manner of the *adj*: *happily; stupidly.*

macro- /mækrə(ʊ)-/ *pref* relatively large, extending: *macrocosm; macrobiotic.*

mal- /mæl-/ *pref* bad, wrong, not: *maladjusted; malnutrition.*

-man *suff* **1** /-mən/ (used to form a *n*) dweller in: *Irishman; countryman.* **2** /-mən, -mæn/ (*n* + ∼ = *n*) sb connected by a specific activity to: *guardsman; doorman; businessman.*

-mania /-meɪnɪə/ *suff* (used to form a *n*) abnormal behaviour, excessive enthusiasm: *kleptomania; bibliomania.* **-maniac** /-meɪnɪæk/ sb affected by a '-mania': *kleptomaniac.*

matri- /meɪtrɪ- mætrɪ-/ *pref* mother: *matriarch; matricide.*

mega- /megə-/ *pref* **1** large: *megalith.* **2** one million: *megaton.*

-ment /-mənt/ *suff* (*v* + ∼ = *n*) result or means of an action: *development; government.* **-mental** *adj* **-mentally** *adv: governmental(ly).*

-meter /-mɪtə(r)/ *suff* (used to form a *n*) a means of measuring: *speedometer.*

-metre /-mitə(r)/ *suff* (used to form a *n*) a (specified) part of a metre: *centimetre.*

micro- /mɑɪkr(ə- *etc*)/ *pref* **1** relatively small: *microfilm; microwave.* **2** of examining or reproducing small quantities: *microscope; microphone.*

milli- /mɪlɪ-/ *pref* a thousandth part of: *milligram; millimetre.*

mis- /mɪs-/ *pref* bad, wrong, not: *misconduct; misdirect; mistrust.*

-monger /-mʌŋgə(r)/ *suff* (used to form a *n*) sb who deals in: *fishmonger; scandalmonger.*

mono- /mon(ə- *etc*)/ *pref* one, a single: *monosyllable; monotone.*

-most /-məʊst/ *suff* (*prep* or *adj of position* + ∼ = *superl adj*) *inmost; outermost.*

multi- /mʌltɪ-/ *pref* many: *multistage; multi-coloured.*

neo- /ni(ə- *etc*)/ *pref* new, revived, later: *neologism; neo-classical.*

-ness /-nəs/ *suff* (*adj* + ∼ = *n*) a quality, state, character: *dryness; silliness.*

neur(o)- /njʊər(ə- *etc*)/ *pref* of the nervous system: *neuralgia; neurology.*

non- /non-/ *pref* not: *nonsense; non-stop.*

-oid /-ɔɪd/ *suff* (used to form an *adj* or *n*) resembling in shape: *asteroid; rhomboid.*

-or /-ə(r), ɔ(r)/ *suff* (*v* + ∼ = *n*) sb or sth that carries out the action of the *v*: *governor; elevator; lessor.*

-ories ⇨ -ory

ortho- /ɔθ(ə- *etc*)/ *pref* correct, standard: *orthodox; orthopaedic.*

-ory /-ərɪ, -rɪ *US:* -ɔrɪ/ *suff* (*pl* -ories) **1** (used to form a *n*) place where specific activity is carried on: *laboratory; observatory.* **2** (used to form an *adj*): *compulsory; illusory.*

-osis /-əʊsɪs *etc*) *suff* (used to form a *n*) a process, change: *hypnosis; metamorphosis.*

-ous /-əs/ *suff* (*n* + ∼ = *adj*) having the qualities of: *poisonous; zealous.* **-ously** /-əslɪ/ *adv* **-ousness** /-əsnəs/ *n*

out- /ɑʊt-/ *pref* **1** located outside: *outhouse; outpost.* **2** surpassing, to a greater extent: *outnumber; outmanoeuvre.* **3** with the various senses of 'out' as defined in the dictionary: *outcry; outspoken.*

over- /əʊvə(r)-/ *pref* **1** across, above: *overland; overhead.* **2** to excess, too much: *overcharge; overwork.* **3** with the various senses of 'over' as defined in the dictionary: *overthrow; overpower.*

pale(o)- (also **palaeo-**) /pælɪ(ə- *etc*)/ *pref* of ancient times: *paleolithic; paleontology.*

pan- /pæn-/ *pref* all, throughout: *panchromatic; Pan-African.*

patri- /peɪtrɪ- pætrɪ-/ *pref* father: *patriarch; patricide.*

-philia /-fɪlɪə/ *suff* (used to form a *n*) excessive love of: *Anglophilia; bibliophilia.* **-phile** /-fɑɪl/ *n* lover of.

-phobia /-fəʊbɪə/ *suff* (used to form a *n*) excessive fear of: *claustrophobia; xenophobia.* **-phobic** *adj* **-phobe** *n* fearer of.

-phone /-fəʊn/ *suff* (used to form a *n*) means of reproducing sound: *megaphone; telephone.* **-phonic** /-fonɪk/ *adj: stereophonic.*

phon(o)- /fə(ʊ)n(ə- *etc*)/ *pref* of sound: *phonetic; phonology.*

photo- /fəʊt(ə- *etc*)/ *pref* **1** of light: *photo-electric.* **2** of photography: *photocopy; photogenic.*

physi(o)- /fɪzɪ(ə- *etc*)/ *pref* of the body, of living things: *physiotherapy; physiology.*
poly- /polɪ- *etc*/ *pref* many: *polygamy; polysyllabic.*
post- /pəʊst- *etc*/ *pref* after: *postscript; posthumous; post-graduate.*
pre- /pri- *etc*/ *pref* before: *prefabricate; premature; pre-recorded.*
pro- /prəʊ-/ *pref* **1** supporting, in favour of: *pro-Chinese; pro-revolutionary.* **2** acting as: *pro-Vice-Chancellor.*
proto- /prəʊt(ə- *etc*)/ *pref* first, original, basic: *prototype; protoplasm.*
pseud(o)- /sjud(ə- *etc*) *US:* su-/ *pref* false, fake: *pseudonym: pseudo-intellectual.*
psych(o)- /sɑɪk(ə- *etc*)/ *pref* of the mind: *psychiatry; psycho-analysis.*
quasi- /kweɪsɑɪ-/ *pref* almost, seemingly: *quasi-serious; quasi-explanation.*
re- /ri- *etc*/ *pref* again: *re-echo; reinstate.*
retro- /retr(ə- *etc*)/ *pref* backwards, behind: *retrospective; retro-rocket.*
-ry ⇨ -ery
-s /*After* p, t, k, f, θ *pronounced* s; *otherwise* z/ *suff* **1** (used to form the *pl* of a *n*): *pots; stars.* **2** (used to form *3rd pers sing pres t* of a *v*): *breaks; sees.*
-scape /-skeɪp/ *suff* (*n* + ~ = *n*) a stretch of scenery: *landscape; moonscape.*
-scope /-skəʊp/ *suff* (*n* + ~ = *n*) means of observing or showing: *microscope; stroboscope.*
self- /self-/ *pref* of one's self, alone, independent: *self-taught; self-service.*
semi- /semɪ-/ *pref* half, partially, midway: *semi-circular; semi-detached; semi-final.*
-ship /-ʃɪp/ *suff* (*n* + ~ = *n*) **1** state of being, status, office: *friendship; ownership; professorship.* **2** skill, proficiency as: *musicianship; scholarship.*
-sion ⇨ -tion
soci(o)- /səʊsɪ(ə- *etc*)/ *pref* of society: *sociology; socio-economic.*
-some /-səm/ *suff* (used to form an *adj*) likely to, productive of: *quarrelsome; meddlesome.*
-sphere /-sfɪə(r)/ *suff* spherical, of a sphere: *hemisphere; atmosphere.*
-ster /-stə(r)/ *suff* **1** (*n* + ~ = *n*) sb connected with the *n*: *songster; gangster.* **2** (*adj* + *n* = n) sb with the qualities of the *adj*: *youngster.*
sub- /sʌb- *etc*/ *pref* **1** under: *subway; subsoil.* **2** secondary, lower in rank: *sub-committee; sub-species.* **3** not quite: *sub-tropical: subnormal.* **4** (used with a *v*) secondary repetition: *sublet; subdivide.*
super- /supə(r)-/ *pref* **1** above, over: *superstructure; superimpose.* **2** superior to, more than: *superhuman; supernatural.*
sym- (also **syn-**) /sɪm-, sɪn- *etc*/ *pref* sharing with, together: *sympathy; synchronize.*
-t /-t/ *suff* (used to form the *pt* and *pp* of some *vv*): *burnt; lent; slept.*
techn(o)- /tekn(o- *etc*)/ *pref* of applied science: *technocracy; technology.*
tele- /telɪ- *etc*/ *pref* of linking across distances: *telepathy; television.*
theo- /θi(o- *etc*)/ *pref* of God: *theocracy; theology.*
thermo- /θɜm(ə- *etc*)/ *pref* of heat, of temperature: *thermostat; thermometer.*
-tion /-ʃn/ (also **-sion** /-ʃn, -ʒn/; **-ation** /-eɪʃn/; **-ition** /-ɪʃn/) *suff* (*v* + ~ = *n*): *relation; confession; adhesion; hesitation; competition.* **-tional** /-nl/ *adj* **-tionally** /-nlɪ/ *adv*
trans- /trænz- *etc*/ *pref* **1** across: *trans-atlantic; trans-continental.* **2** to a changed state: *transplant; transform.*
tri- /trɑɪ- *etc*/ *pref* three: *triangle; tricolour.*
-tude /-tjud *US:* -tud/ *suff* (used to form a *n*) condition: *magnitude; exactitude.*
-ule /-jul/ *suff* (used to form a *n*) relative smallness: *capsule; globule.*
ultra- /ʌltrə-/ *pref* beyond, to excess: *ultraviolet; ultra-liberal.*
un- /ʌn-/ *pref* **1** (used with an *adj* or *n*) not: *unable; untruth.* **2** (used with a *v*) negative, reverse, opposite of: *uncover; unpack.*
under- /ʌndə(r)-/ *pref* **1** located beneath: *undercurrent; undergrowth.* **2** not enough: *underestimate; undersized.* **3** lower in rank, importance: *undersecretary; understudy.*
uni- /junɪ-/ *pref* one, the same: *uniform; unisex.*
up- /ʌp-/ *pref* to a higher or better state: *uphill; upgrade.*
-ure /-jʊə(r), -jə(r) *etc*/ *suff* (used to form a *n*) act, process, condition: *closure; legislature.*
vice- /vɑɪs-/ *pref* sb who is next in rank to and may act for another: *vice-consul; vice-president.*
-ward /-wəd/ *suff* (used to form an *adj* or *adv*) in the direction of: *backward; eastward; homeward;* **-wards** /-wədz/ *adv*
well- /wel-/ pref (~ + *pp* of a *v* = *adj*) fortunately, properly, thoroughly: *wellborn; wellinformed; wellworn.*
-wise /-wɑɪz/ *suff* (*n* or *adj* + ~ = *adv*) **1** in the manner of: *crosswise; crabwise.* **2** (colloq) in connection with: *disciplinewise; accommodationwise.*
-worth /-wɜθ, -wəθ/ *suff* (used to form a *n*) using the amount of: *poundsworth; daysworth.*
-worthy /-wɜðɪ/ *suff* (*n* + ~ = *adj*) deserving of: *praiseworthy; blameworthy.* **-worthily** *adv*
-y¹ (also **-ey**) /-ɪ/ *suff* (*n* + ~ = *adj*) *dusty; bushy; clayey.* **-ier** /-ɪə(r)/ *comp* **-iest** /-ɪɪst/ *superl* **-ily** /-əlɪ/ *adv*
-y² (also **-ie**) /-ɪ/ *suff* (*n* + ~ = *n*) pet name or familiar name: *piggy; doggie; daddy; Susie.* ⇨ also App 7.

Appendix 4 NUMERICAL EXPRESSIONS

The following section will give you help in the reading, speaking and writing of numbers and expressions which commonly contain numbers.

1 Numbers

Note: a/one (as in e g 'a/one hundred'): 'a /ə/ hundred' is a less formal usage than 'one /wʌn/ hundred'.

CARDINAL	ORDINAL
1 one /wʌn/	1st first /fɜst/
2 two /tu/	2nd second /ˋsekənd/
3 three /θri/	3rd third /θɜd/
4 four /fɔ(r)/	4th fourth /fɔθ/
5 five /fɑɪv/	5th fifth /fɪfθ/
6 six /sɪks/	6th sixth /sɪksθ/
7 seven /ˋsevn/	7th seventh /ˋsevnθ/
8 eight /eɪt/	8th eighth /eɪtθ/
9 nine /nɑɪn/	9th ninth /nɑɪnθ/
10 ten /ten/	10th tenth /tenθ/
11 eleven /ɪˋlevn/	11th eleventh /ɪˋlevnθ/
12 twelve /twelv/	12th twelfth /twelfθ/
13 thirteen /ˈθɜˋtin/	13th thirteenth /ˈθɜˋtinθ/
14 fourteen /ˈfɔˋtin/	14th fourteenth /ˈfɔˋtinθ/
15 fifteen /ˈfɪˋftin/	15th fifteenth /ˈfɪfˋtinθ/
16 sixteen /ˈsɪkˋstin/	16th sixteenth /ˈsɪkˋstinθ/
17 seventeen /ˈsevnˋtin/	17th seventeenth /ˈsevnˋtinθ/
18 eighteen /ˈeɪˋtin/	18th eighteenth /ˈeɪˋtinθ/
19 nineteen /ˈnɑɪnˋtin/	19th nineteenth /ˈnɑɪnˋtinθ/
20 twenty /ˋtwentɪ/	20th twentieth /ˋtwentɪəθ/
21 twenty-one /ˈtwentɪˋwʌn/	21st twenty-first /ˈtwentɪˋfɜst/
22 twenty-two /ˈtwentɪˋtu/	22nd twenty-second /ˈtwentɪˋsekənd/
23 twenty-three /ˈtwentɪˋθri/	23rd twenty-third /ˈtwentɪˋθɜd/
30 thirty /ˋθɜtɪ/	30th thirtieth /ˋθɜtɪəθ/
38 thirty-eight /ˈθɜtɪˋeɪt/	38th thirty-eighth /ˈθɜtɪˋeɪtθ/
40 forty /ˋfɔtɪ/	40th fortieth /ˋfɔtɪəθ/
50 fifty /ˋfɪftɪ/	50th fiftieth /ˋfɪftɪəθ/
60 sixty /ˋsɪkstɪ/	60th sixtieth /ˋsɪkstɪəθ/
70 seventy /ˋsevntɪ/	70th seventieth /ˋsevntɪəθ/
80 eighty /ˋeɪtɪ/	80th eightieth /ˋeɪtɪəθ/
90 ninety /ˋnɑɪntɪ/	90th ninetieth /ˋnɑɪntɪəθ/
100 a/one hundred /ə, wʌn ˋhʌndrəd/	100th a/one hundredth /ə, wʌn ˋhʌndrədθ/
1000 a/one thousand /ə, wʌn ˋθɑʊznd/	1000th a/one thousandth /ə, wʌn ˋθɑʊznθ/
10 000 ten thousand /ˈten ˋθɑʊznd/	10 000th ten thousandth /ˈten ˋθɑʊznθ/
100 000 a/one hundred thousand /ə, wʌn ˈhʌndrəd ˋθɑʊznd/	100 000th a/one hundred thousandth /ə, wʌn ˈhʌndrəd ˋθɑʊznθ/
1 000 000 a/one million /ə, wʌn ˋmɪlɪən/	1 000 000 a/one millionth /ə, wʌn ˋmɪlɪənθ/

SOME MORE COMPLEX NUMBERS

101 a/one hundred and one /ə, wʌn ˈhʌndrəd n ˋwʌn/
152 a/one hundred and fifty-two /ə, wʌn ˈhʌndrəd n ˈfɪftɪ ˋtu/
1 001 a/one thousand and one /ə, wʌn ˈθɑʊznd n ˋwʌn/
2 325 two thousand, three hundred and twenty-five /ˈtu ˈθɑʊznd, ˈθri ˈhʌndrəd n ˈtwentɪ ˋfɑɪv/
15 972 fifteen thousand, nine hundred and seventy-two /ˈfɪˈftin ˈθɑʊznd, ˈnɑɪn ˈhʌndrəd n ˈsevntɪ ˋtu/
234 753 two hundred and thirty-four thousand, seven hundred and fifty-three /ˈtu ˈhʌndrəd n ˈθɜtɪ ˈfɔ ˈθɑʊznd, ˈsevn ˈhʌndrəd n ˈfɪftɪ ˋθri/

		US, France	GB and other European countries
1 000 000 000	10^9	a/one billion /ə, wʌn ˋbɪlɪən/	a/one thousand million(s) /ə, wʌn ˋθɑʊznd ˋmɪlɪən(z)/
1 000 000 000 000	10^{12}	a/one trillion /ə, wʌn ˋtrɪlɪən/	a/one billion /ə, wʌn ˋbɪlɪən/
1 000 000 000 000 000	10^{15}	a/one quadrillion /ə, wʌn kwoˋdrɪlɪən/	a/one thousand billion(s) /ə, wʌn ˈθɑʊznd ˋbɪlɪən(z)/
1 000 000 000 000 000 000	10^{18}	a/one quintillion /ə, wʌn kwɪnˋtɪlɪən/	a/one trillion /ə, wʌn ˋtrɪlɪən/

VULGAR FRACTIONS	DECIMAL FRACTIONS
$\frac{1}{8}$ an/one-eighth /ən, wʌn ˋeɪtθ/	0·125 (nought) point one two five /(ˈnɔt) pɔɪnt ˈwʌn tu ˋfɑɪv/
$\frac{1}{4}$ a/one quarter /ə, wʌn ˋkwɔtə(r)/	0·25 (ˈnought) point ˈtwo ˋfive

$\frac{1}{3}$ a/one third /ə, wʌn ˋθɜd/	0·33	('nought) point 'three three
$\frac{1}{2}$ a/one half /ə, wʌn hɑf US: hæf/	0·5	('nought) point ˋfive
$\frac{3}{4}$ three-quarters /'θri ˋkwɔtəz/	0·75	('nought) point 'seven ˋfive

Notes: 1 In the spoken forms of vulgar fractions, the versions 'and a half/quarter/third' are preferred to 'and one half/quarter/third' whether the measurement is approximate or precise. With more obviously precise fractions like $\frac{1}{8}$, $\frac{1}{16}$, 'and one eighth/sixteenth' is normal. Complex fractions like 3/462, 20/83 are spoken as 'three over four-six-two; twenty over eight-three', especially in mathematical expressions, e g 'twenty-two over seven' for 22/7.

2 When speaking ordinary numbers we can use 'zero', 'nought' or 'oh' /əʊ/ for the number 0; 'zero' is the most common US usage and the most technical or precise form, 'oh' is the least technical or precise, In using decimals, to say 'nought point five' for 0·5 is a more precise usage than 'point five'.

3 In most continental European countries a comma is used in place of the GB/US decimal point. Thus 6·014 is written 6,014 in France. A space is used to separate off the thousands in numbers larger than 9999, e g 10 000 or 875 380. GB/US usage can also have a comma in this place, e g 7,500,000. This comma is replaced by a full point in continental European countries. e g 7.500.000. Thus 23,500·75 (GB/US) will be written 23.500,75 in France.

COLLECTIVE NUMBERS

6 a half dozen/half a dozen
12 a/one dozen (24 is two dozen *not* two dozens)
20 a/one score
144 a/one gross /grəʊs/
three score years and ten (Biblical) = 70 years, the traditional average life-span of man.

ROMAN		ARABIC	ROMAN	ARABIC
I	i	1	LX	60
II	ii	2	LXV	65
III	iii	3	LXX	70
IV (IIII)	iv (iiii)	4	LXXX	80
V	v	5	XC	90
VI	vi	6	XCII	92
VII	vii	7	XCV	95
VIII	viii	8	XCVIII	98
IX	ix	9	IC	99
X	x	10	C	100
XI	xi	11	CC	200
XII	xii	12	CCC	300
XIII	xiii	13	CD	400
XIV	xiv	14	D	500
XV	xv	15	DC	600

ROMAN		ARABIC	ROMAN	ARABIC
XVI	xvi	16	DCC	700
XVII	xvii	17	DCCC	800
XVIII	xviii	18	CM	900
XIX	xix	19	M	1000
XX	xx	20	MC	1100
XXI	xxi	21	MCD	1400
XXV	xxv	25	MDC	1600
XXIX	xxix	29	MDCLXVI	1666
XXX	xxx	30	MDCCCLXXXVIII	1888
XXXIV		34	MDCCCXCIX	1899
XXXIX		39	MCM	1900
XL		40	MCMLXXVI	1976
L		50	MM	2000

A letter placed after another letter of greater value adds, e g VI = 5 + 1 = 6. A letter placed before a letter of greater value subtracts, e g IV = 5 − 1 = 4. A dash placed over a letter multiplies the value by 1000; thus $\bar{X}$ = 10 000 and $\bar{M}$ = 1 000 000. The alternative IIII is seen only on some clock faces (⇨ the illus at **dial**), and iiii is seen only in the preliminary pages of some books.

2 Mathematical Expressions

Below are some of the more common symbols and expressions used in mathematics, geometry and statistics; in the cases where alternative ways of saying the expressions are given, both are equally common but generally the first is more formal or technical and the second less formal or technical.

$+$ plus/and
$-$ minus/take away
$\pm$ plus or minus/approximately
$\times$ (is) multiplied by/times (*or when giving dimensions* by)
$\div$ (is) divided by
$=$ is equal to/equals
$\neq$ is not equal to/does not equal
$\simeq$ is approximately equal to
$\equiv$ is equivalent to/is identical with
$<$ is less than
$\not<$ is not less than
$\leqslant$ is less than or equal to
$>$ is more than
$\not>$ is not more than
$\geqslant$ is more than or equal to
% per cent
∞ infinity

$\propto$ varies as/is proportional to
3:9::4:16 three is to nine, as four is to, sixteen, ⇨ **proportion (5)**
$\in$ is an element of (a set)
$\notin$ is not an element of (a set)
$\emptyset$ *or* {} is an empty set
$\cap$ intersection
$\cup$ union
$\subset$ is a subset of
$\Rightarrow$ implies
$\log_e$ natural logarithm *or* logarithm to the base e /i/
$\sqrt{}$ (square) root
$\sqrt[3]{}$ cube root
x^2 x /eks/ squared
x^3 x /eks/ cubed
x^4 x /eks/ to the power four/to the fourth

π pi /paɪ/ = 22/7
r /ɑ(r)/ = radius of circle
πr^2 pi r squared /'paɪ ɑˋskweəd/ (formula for area of circle)
n! n /en/ factorial
$\int$ the integral of
$\angle$ angle
∟ right angle
Δ triangle
$\parallel$ is parallel to
$\perp$ is perpendicular to
° degree, ⇨ **degree (1)**
′ minute (of an arc), ⇨ minute[1](2); foot *or* feet (unit of length)
″ second (of an arc), ⇨ second[3](1); inch *or* inches (unit of length)

Appendix 4 NUMERICAL EXPRESSIONS

THE GREEK ALPHABET

Many letters of the Greek alphabet are commonly used in statistics and other branches of mathematics. Here is a complete list of the letters:

capitals	*small letters*	*name*
Α	α	alpha /`ælfə/
Β	β	beta /`bitə *US:* `beɪtə/
Γ	γ	gamma /`gæmə/
Δ	δ	delta /`deltə/
Ε	ϵ	epsilon /ep`sɑɪlən *US:* `epsɪlon/
Ζ	ζ	zeta /`zitə *US:* `zeɪtə/
Η	η	eta /`itə *US:* `eɪtə/
Θ	θ	theta /`θitə *US:* `θeɪtə/
Ι	ι	iota /ɑɪ`əʊtə/
Κ	κ	kappa /`kæpə/
Λ	λ	lambda /`læmdə/
Μ	μ	mu /mju/
Ν	ν	nu /nju *US:* nu/
Ξ	ξ	xi /ksɑɪ/
Ο	o	omicron /əʊ`mɑɪkrən *US:* `omɪkron/
Π	π	pi /pɑɪ/
Ρ	ρ	rho /rəʊ/
Σ	σ, ς	sigma /`sɪgmə/
Τ	τ	tau /tɑʊ/
Υ	υ	upsilon /jup`sɑɪlən *US:* `jupsɪlon/
Φ	φ	phi /fɑɪ/
Χ	χ	chi /kɑɪ/
Ψ	ψ	psi /psɑɪ/
Ω	ω	omega /`əʊmɪgə *US:* əʊ`megə/

3 Computer Numbers

Cheque books, business accounts, etc have long strings of numerals. If such a number has to be read aloud, the numerals are spoken as separate digits (1-9, 0=/əʊ/) grouped rhythmically into pairs. Doubled numerals may be read separately or as e g 'double six'.

05216472 'oh 'five/'two 'one/'six 'four/'seven`two

As mentioned earlier, 0 can also be read as 'zero' (formal) or 'nought' (informal). ⇨ also binary

4 Measurements (Inanimate)

Traditionally GB and US measurements have been made in inches, feet, yards, miles, etc, but there is now a gradual move towards the metric system of millimetres, metres, kilometres, etc. Examples of both are given below. (For tables of weight, measurement, etc and conversion tables, ⇨ App 5) Even if the move towards metrication is completed in the near future, there will remain a vast amount of literature in which the other units are used.

in	inch(es)	sq in	square inch(es)	cu in	cubic inch(es)
ft	foot/feet	sq ft	square foot/feet	cu ft	cubic foot/feet
yd	yard(s)	sq yd	square yard(s)	cu yd	cubic yard(s)
-	mile(s)	-	square mile(s)	-	-
mm	millimetre(s)	mm^2	square millimetre(s)	mm^3	cubic millimetre(s)
cm	centimetre(s)	cm^2	square centimetre(s)	cm^3, cc	cubic centimetre(s)
m	metre(s)	m^2	square metre(s)	m^3	cubic metre(s)
km	kilometre(s)	km^2	square kilometre(s)	-	-

(⇨ square[1](4) for difference between e g 'four square feet' and 'four feet square')

DISTANCE

London to New York is three thousand four hundred and forty-one miles. (3 441 miles)

London to New York is five thousand five hundred and six kilometres. (5 506 km)

There is a speed limit of thirty miles per/an hour. (30 mph)

There is a speed limit of fifty kilometres per/an hour. (50 kph)

That ship has a top speed of fifteen knots. (1 knot = 1 nautical mile per hour)

HEIGHT / DEPTH

Mount Everest is twenty-nine thousand and twenty-eight feet high. (29 028 ft)

Mount Everest is eight thousand eight hundred and forty-eight metres high. (8 848 m)

The airliner is flying at a height/an altitude of twenty thousand feet. (20 000 ft)

The airliner is flying at a height/an altitude of six thousand metres. (6 000 m)

The sea's average depth is twelve thousand feet or two and half miles. (12 000 ft)

The sea's average depth is three thousand seven hundred metres. 3 700 m

DIMENSION

This room is sixteen foot/feet (wide) by twenty-five (foot/feet) (long). (16ft × 25ft *or* 16′ × 25′)

This room is three metres (wide) by eight and half (metres) (long). (3m × 8·5m)

AREA

We need five thousand square foot/feet of office space. (5 000 sq ft)

We need six hundred square metres of office space. (600 sq m)

Scotland has an area of thirty thousand, four hundred and five square miles. (30 405 sq miles) ⇨square[1](4)

Scotland has an area of seventy-six thousand, two hundred and thirty-five square kilometres. (76 235 sq km)

The house is for sale with ten acres of grounds.

The house is for sale with four hectares of grounds.

VOLUME

You'll need thirty (cubic) feet/foot of sand to mix with the cement. (30 cu ft) ⇨ cubic

You'll need a (cubic) metre of sand to mix with the cement. (1 m^3)

TEMPERATURE

The ordinary GB temperature scale for everyday use has been Fahrenheit. With metrication, the use of Centigrade (which has long been common in scientific usage) is becoming widespread.

FAHRENHEIT	CENTIGRADE
Water freezes at thirty-two degrees Fahrenheit. (32°F)	*Water freezes at nought degrees Centigrade.* (0°C)
Last night we had nine degrees of frost. (23°F)	*Last night the temperature was five degrees below zero.*(−5°C)
It was ninety-five in the shade this morning. (95°F)	*It was thirty-five in the shade this morning.* (35°C)

ATHLETICS

He holds the record for the fifteen hundred metres (colloq *'the metric mile'*). (1 500 m)

She ran for her country in the two hundred metres women's hurdles. (200 m)

Our team was narrowly beaten in the four by four hundred metres relay. (4 × 400 m)

Our captain won the high jump with a jump of two point oh five metres (2·05 m), *and threw the javelin a national record of eighty-three point four four metres* (83·44 m).

SWIMMING

I swam for Britain in the eight hundred metres freestyle. (800 m)

She came second in the women's hundred metres back-stroke. (100 m)

TENNIS

Smith won the first set six four/by six games to four (6-4). *The scoring in the final game was: fifteen love* (15-0), *fifteen all* (15-15), *thirty fifteen* (30-15), *forty fifteen* (40-15), *forty thirty* (40-30), *deuce* (40-40), *advantage Smith, game to Smith. Smith went on to win the match by three sets to two* (3-2).

ASSOCIATION FOOTBALL (SOCCER)

In the first leg the half-time score was one all (1-1). *In the second half only Italy scored and won the match two one/by two goals to one* (2-1). *The full time score in the return match was nil all/a goalless draw/a no goal draw* (0-0), *but Brazil scored two magnificent goals in extra time to win the Cup two nil* (2-0).

RUGBY FOOTBALL (RUGGER)

Wales beat Scotland sixteen five/by sixteen points to five (16-5). *For Wales, Owen scored two tries* (8 points), *Price converted one* (2 points), *and kicked two penalty goals* (6 points). *Scotland's score came from a penalty* (3 points) *and a dropped goal* (2 points), *both kicked by Frazer.*

HORSE-RACING

The Derby is run over a distance of twelve furlongs/one mile four furlongs/one and a half miles/a mile and a half. (12 fur = $1\frac{1}{2}$ miles)

The favourite in the Grand National was Never Say Die *at five to two.* (5-2, betting stake; *The odds on* Never Say Die *were five to two.*)

5 Measurements (Human)

HEIGHT, ETC

i Note that 'tall', not 'high', is used. Feet and inches are used, or metres and centimetres if the metric system is employed.

My wife is five foot/feet six (inches) (tall). (5ft 6in/5′6″)	*My wife is one metre sixty-eight (centimetres) (tall).* (1m 68cm/1·68m)

ii Measurements round parts of the body are in inches or centimetres:

She is 36-24-36. (i e 36 inches round the bust, 24 inches round the waist, 36 inches round the hips)	*She is 91-61-91.* (i e 91 centimetres round the bust, 61 centimetres round the waist, 91 centimetres round the hips)

WEIGHT

In GB weight has traditionally been given in stones and pounds, and in the US in pounds only. The metric system uses kilos/kilograms.

I weigh twelve stone eleven (pounds)/a hundred and seventy-nine pounds. (12st 11lb/179lb)	*I weigh eighty-one kilos* (81 kg).

AGE

I have three children. The eldest is nine (years old), the middle one is five and a half and the youngest is four. I'm thirty-three. How old are you?

6 Time of day

Note: When times are quoted, specified precisely or 'read' from a digital clock, the second form given below is more common.

GB

7.00 seven o'clock/seven a m /ˈeɪˋem/ *or* seven p m /ˈpiˋem/
8.15 a quarter past eight/eight fifteen
9.45 a quarter to ten/nine forty-five
4.30 half past four/four thirty/(colloq) half four
5.10 ten (minutes) past five/five ten
6.25 twenty-five (minutes) past six/five and twenty past six/six twenty-five
6.35 twenty-five (minutes) to seven/five and twenty (minutes) to seven/six thirty-five
5.40 twenty (minutes) to six/five forty
3.50 ten (minutes) to four/three fifty
7.55 five (minutes) to eight/seven fifty five
9.57 three minutes to ten/nine fifty-seven
2.03 three minutes past two/two oh three

US

The system used is similar to that used in GB except that *after* is usual where GB has *past*:

5.10 ten after five
5.15 a quarter after five
9.30 'nine thirty' is more usual than 'half past nine'

of is common where GB has *to*:

7.45 a quarter of eight
7.55 five of eight

TWENTY-FOUR HOUR CLOCK

Used originally in military orders etc, but now increasingly used in travel timetables.

07.00 ('oh) 'seven `hundred hours = 7.00 a m
10.30 'ten `thirty = 10.30 a m
12.00 'twelve `hundred hours = midday/noon
13.45 'thirteen 'forty-`five = 1.45 p m
15.15 'fifteen 'fi`fteen = 3.15 p m
19.00 'nine'teen `hundred hours = 7.00 p m
22.50 'twenty-'two `fifty = 10.50 p m
23.05 'twenty-'three 'oh `five = 11.05 p m
24.00 'twenty-'four `hundred hours = midnight

7 Dates

2000 BC 'two thousand /'bi`si/'
55 BC 'fifty-five /'bi`si/'

AD is usually reserved only for the earlier years: AD 55 '/'eɪ`di/ fifty-five'; but 1066, not AD 1066 Queen Elizabeth I 1558-1603: 'Queen Elizabeth the first reigned from fifteen (hundred and) fifty-eight to sixteen (hundred and) three/sixteen oh three.

GB

1(st) January 1975: 'the first of January nineteen seventy-five', often abbreviated to 1 Jan '75 (Feb, Mar, Apr, May, Jun, July, Aug, Sept, Oct, Nov, Dec) or to numbers only eg 1/1/75. Sometimes Roman numbers are used for the month, e g 27 ii 40.

US

May 4, 1975: 'May fourth, nineteen seventy-five.' In numbers only: 5.4.75 (GB = 4.5.75).

8 Money

For monetary tables ⇨ App 5

Note: In referring to the new GB penny, the population as a whole has not yet adopted one regular set of forms, and it is too early to say whether some forms are more or less common or colloquial than others. The expressions below are all heard.

GB	US
I paid a penny/ one p for it. (1p)	*I bought it for a cent.* (1¢)
It's ten pence/ten p a cup. (10p)	*It's ten cents a cup.* (10¢)
The cheapest seats are fifty pence/fifty p each. (50p)	*The cheapest seats are half a dollar/*(sl) *half a buck each.* (50¢)
They'll charge you a pound/ (sl) *a quid membership fee.* (£1)	*They'll charge you a dollar/* (sl) *a buck membership fee.* ($1)
I was given one (pound) fifty (pence) change. (£1.50)	*I was given a dollar fifty/one fifty/* (sl) *one and a half bucks change.* ($1.50)
The return ticket is thirteen (pounds) twenty-seven (pence). (£13.27)	*The return ticket is thirteen (dollars) twenty-seven (cents).* ($13.27)

Note: The penny and cent signs (p, ¢) are *never* shown with the pound and dollar signs (£, $) when writing down a sum of money:
e g £6.25 and $6.25 are right
£6.25p and $6.25¢ are wrong

9 Telephoning

Each digit is spoken separately, i e no figure above nine is used. 0 is pronounced /əʊ/. In US usage, 'zero' (and sometimes 'nought') may replace 'oh'. The figures are usually grouped rythmically in pairs (pairing from the right), though there is a tendency to use rhythmic triplets, especially for six-figure numbers. If the two digits of a pair are the same, it is usually spoken as 'double three' etc. An exception is the GB emergency call 999 which is always '*nine 'nine `nine.*

6638 'double 'six, 'three `eight
but
3668 'three 'six, 'six `eight (not usu 'three 'double 'six `eight)

677 'six, 'double `seven
but
667 'six, 'six `seven (or 'double 'six `seven)

In numbers which include an STD (Subscriber Trunk Dialling) code number, the code is to be separated by a pause:
01-629 8494 'oh 'one‖'six, 'two 'nine|'eight 'four| 'nine `four
037 181-679 'oh 'three 'seven|'one 'eight 'one‖'six 'seven `nine

10 Chemical Formulae

In chemical formulae full-size and reduced-size numbers, and capital and lower case letters are not distinguished orally.

NaCl /'en eɪ si `el/
$2H_2 + O_2 = 2H_2O$ /'tu eɪtʃ 'tu plʌs 'əʊ tu 'ikwlz 'tu eɪtʃ tu `əʊ/

Appendix 5 WEIGHTS AND MEASURES

The Metric System

METRIC				GB & US
		length		
10 millimetres (mm)	=	1 centimetre (cm)	=	0·3937 inches (in)
100 centimetres	=	1 metre (m)	=	39·37 inches or 1·094 yards (yd)
1000 metres	=	1 kilometre (km)	=	0·62137 miles or about ⅝ mile
		surface		
100 square metres (sq m)	=	1 are (a)	=	0·0247 acres
100 ares	=	1 hectare (ha)	=	2·471 acres
100 hectares	=	1 square kilometre	=	0·386 square miles
		weight		
10 milligrams (mg)	=	1 centigram (cg)	=	0·1543 grains
100 centigrams	=	1 gram	=	15·4323 grains
1000 grams	=	1 kilogram	=	2·2046 pounds
1000 kilograms	=	1 tonne	=	1·9684 cwt
		capacity		
1000 millilitres (ml)	=	1 litre	=	1·75 pints (= 2·101 US pints)
10 litres	=	1 dekalitre	=	2·1997 gallons (=2·63 US gallons)

Avoirdupois Weight

GB & US				METRIC
		1 grain (gr)	=	0·0648 grams (gm)
437½ grains	=	1 ounce (oz)	=	28·35 grams
16 drams (dr)	=	1 ounce	=	28·35 grams
16 ounces	=	1 pound (lb)	=	0·454 kilograms (kg)
14 pounds	=	1 stone	=	6·356 kilograms
2 stone	=	1 quarter	=	12·7 kilograms
4 quarters	=	1 hundredweight (cwt)	=	50·8 kilograms
112 pounds	=	1 cwt	=	50·8 kilograms
100 pounds	=	1 short cwt	=	45·4 kilograms
20 cwt	=	1 ton	=	1016·04 kilograms
2000 pounds	=	1 short ton	=	0·907 metric tons
2240 pounds	=	1 long ton	=	1·016 metric tons

Troy Weight

system of weights used in England for gold, silver and precious stones

GB & US				METRIC
24 grains	=	1 pennyweight (dwt)	=	1·555 grams
20 pennyweights	=	1 ounce	=	31·1 grams
12 ounces	=	1 pound (5760 grains)	=	0·373 kilograms

Apothecaries' Weight

used by pharmacists for mixing their medicines; they buy and sell drugs by Avoirdupois weight

GB & US				METRIC
20 grains	=	1 scruple	=	1·296 grams
3 scruples	=	1 drachm	=	3·888 grams
8 drachms	=	1 ounce	=	31·1035 grams
12 ounces	=	1 pound	=	373·24 grams

Linear Measure

GB & US				METRIC
		1 inch (in)	=	25·3995 millimetres (mm)
12 inches	=	1 foot (ft)	=	30·479 centimetres (cm)
3 feet	=	1 yard (yd)	=	0·9144 metres (m)
5½ yards	=	1 rod, pole, or perch	=	5·0292 metres
22 yards	=	1 chain (ch)	=	20·1168 metres
220 yards	=	1 furlong (fur)	=	201·168 metres
8 furlongs	=	1 mile	=	1·6093 kilometres (km)
1760 yards	=	1 mile	=	1·6093 kilometres
3 miles	=	1 league	=	4·8279 kilometres

Square Measure

GB & US		METRIC
	1 square inch (sq in)	= 6·4516 sq centimetres
144 sq inches	= 1 sq foot	= 929·030 sq centimetres
9 sq feet	= 1 sq yard	= 0·836 sq metres
484 sq yards	= 1 sq chain	= 404·624 sq metres
4840 sq yards	= 1 acre	= 0·405 hectares
40 sq rods	= 1 rood	= 10·1168 ares
4 roods	= 1 acre	= 0·405 hectares
640 acres	= 1 sq mile	= 2·599 sq kilometres

Cubic Measure

GB & US		METRIC
	1 cubic inch	= 16·387 cubic centimetres
1728 cubic inches	= 1 cubic foot	= 0·028 cubic metres
27 cubic feet	= 1 cubic yard	= 0·765 cubic metres

Surveyors' Measure

GB & US		METRIC
7·92 inches	= 1 link	= 20·1168 centimetres
100 links	= 1 chain	= 20·1168 metres
10 chains	= 1 furlong	= 201·168 metres
80 chains	= 1 mile	= 1·6093 kilometres
10 square chains	= 1 acre	= 0·405 hectares

Nautical Measure

used for measuring the depth and surface distance of seas, rivers, etc

GB & US		METRIC
6 feet	= 1 fathom	= 1·8288 metres
608 feet	= 1 cable	= 185·313 metres
6,080 feet	= sea (or nautical) mile (1·151 statute miles)	= 1·852 kilometres
3 sea miles	= 1 sea league	= 5·550 kilometres
60 sea miles	= 1 degree	
360 degrees	= 1 circle	

The speed of one sea mile per hour is called a *knot*

Liquid Measure of Capacity

GB		US	METRIC
4 gills	= 1 pint	= 1·201 pints	= 0·5679 litres
2 pints	= 1 quart	= 1·201 quarts	= 1·1359 litres
4 quarts	= 1 gallon	= 1·201 gallons	= 4·5435 litres

Apothecaries' Fluid Measure

used by pharmacists for measuring medicines

GB & US		METRIC
60 minims	= 1 fluid drachm (dram)	= 3·552 millilitres
8 fluid drachms	= 1 fluid ounce	= 2·841 centilitres
20 fluid ounces	= 1 pint	= 0·568 litres
8 pints	= 1 gallon	= 4·546 litres

Dry Measure of Capacity

GB & US		METRIC GB	METRIC US
	1 gallon	= 4·5435 litres	4·404 liters
2 gallons	= 1 peck	= 9·0870 litres	8·810 liters
4 pecks	= 1 bushel	= 36·3477 litres	35·238 liters
8 bushels	= 1 quarter	= 290·7816	281·904 liters

Circular or Angular Measure

60 seconds (″)	= 1 minute (′)	60 degrees	= 1 sextant
60 minutes	= 1 degree (°)	90 degrees	= 1 quadrant or right angle (∟)
45 degrees	= 1 oxtant	360 degrees	= 1 circle or circumference

The diameter of a circle	= the straight line passing through its centre
The radius of a circle	= ½ × the diameter
The circumference of a circle	= 22/7 × the diameter

Appendix 5 WEIGHTS AND MEASURES

Temperature Equivalents

	FAHRENHEIT (F)	CENTIGRADE (C)
Boiling Point	212°	100°
	194°	90°
	176°	80°
	158°	70°
	140°	60°
	122°	50°
	104°	40°
	86°	30°
	68°	20°
	50°	10°
Freezing Point	32°	0°
	14°	−10°
	0°	−17·8°
Absolute Zero	−459·67°	−273·15°

To convert Fahrenheit temperature into Centigrade: subtract 32 and multiply by 5/9 (five ninths).
To convert Centigrade temperature into Fahrenheit: multiply by 9/5 (nine fifths) and add 32.

Money

also ⇨ App 4**(8)**

GB: £ p (pounds and pence).
100 pence (100p) = 1 pound (£1)

	(amount)	(coin)
½p	a halfpenny /ˈheɪpnɪ/, half a penny	a halfpenny /ˈheɪpnɪ/
1p	a penny, (colloq) one p /pi/	a penny
2p	twopence /ˈtʌpns/, two pence, (colloq) two p /pi/	a twopenny /ˈtʌpnɪ/ piece
5p	five pence	a fivepenny piece
10p	ten pence	a tenpenny piece
50p	fifty pence	a fifty pence piece
		(note)
£1	a pound, (sl) a quid	a pound note
£5, £10, £20	five/ten/twenty pounds; (sl) five/ten/twenty quid	a five/ten/twenty pound note; (sl) a fiver/tenner
£3·82	three pounds eighty-two pence	

US; $ ¢ (dollars and cents)
100 cents (100¢) = 1 dollar ($1)

	(amount)	(coin)
1¢	a cent	a penny
5¢	five cents	a nickel
10¢	ten cents	a dime
25¢	twenty-five cents	a quarter
50¢	half a dollar, (sl) half a buck	a half-dollar
		(note)
$1	a dollar, (sl) a buck	a dollar bill
$5, $10, $20	five/ten/twenty dollars; (sl) five/ten/twenty bucks	a five/ten/twenty dollar bill
$3·82	three dollars eighty-two cents	

Time

60 seconds	= 1 minute	4 weeks, or 28 days	= 1 lunar month
60 minutes	= 1 hour	52 weeks, 1 day; or 13 lunar months, 1 day	= 1 year
24 hours	= 1 day		
7 days	= 1 week	365 days, 6 hours	= 1 (Julian) year

Number of Days in the Month

30 days have September,
April, June and November;
All the rest have 31,
Excepting February alone,
Which has but 28 days clear
And 29 in each leap year.

Speed

Light travels at 186 300 miles per second; 300 000 metres per second
Sound travels at 1130 feet per second; 330 metres per second; 770 miles per hour (the 'sound barrier')

Appendix 6 **GEOGRAPHICAL NAMES**

COUNTRIES OF THE WORLD

Notes:

1 The list consists of both sovereign independent countries and dependent states forming such countries: e g *Malaysia,* a sovereign nation, is a federation of *Malaya, Sabah* and *Sarawak; England, Scotland* and *Wales* make up *Great Britain;* the *United Kingdom* is the union of *Great Britain* and *Northern Ireland.*

2 Some countries have different words for the *adjective* and the *person;* in these cases both are given, e g *Swedish; Swede.*

Adjective: I admire *Swedish* architecture.
He sang a *Japanese* song.
Person: My mother is a *Swede.*
A *Japanese* has joined our class.

3 Words for the *person* ending in '-ese', and *Swiss,* remain unchanged in the plural:
I know many *Japanese.*
The *Swiss* have arrived.

4 In some cases, the *adjective* is also the word for the country's language:
I am learning to speak *Malay.*

COUNTRY	ADJECTIVE; PERSON
Afghanistan /æfˈgænɪˋstɑn *US:* -ˋstæn/	Afghan /ˋæfgæn/; Afghanistani /-nɪ/
Albania /ælˋbeɪnɪə/	Albanian /-nɪən/
Algeria /ælˋdʒɪərɪə/	Algerian /-rɪən/
Andorra /ænˋdɔrə/	Andorran /-rən/
Angola /æŋˋgəʊlə/	Angolan /-lən/
Anguilla /æŋˋgwɪlə/	Anguillan /-lən/
Antigua /ænˋtigə/	Antiguan /-gən/
Argentina /ˈɑdʒənˋtinə/ (also *The Argentine* /ˋɑdʒəntɑɪn/)	Argentinian /-ˋtɪnɪən/ Argentine
Australia /ɔˋstreɪlɪə *US:* ɔˋs-/	Australian /-lɪən/
Austria /ˋɔstrɪə *US:* ˋɔs-/	Austrian /-strɪən/
(The) Bahamas /bəˋhɑməz *US:* -ˈheɪm-/	Bahaman /-mən/
Bahrain /bɑˋreɪn/	Bahraini /-ˋreɪnɪ/
Bangladesh /ˈbæŋgləˋdeʃ/	Bengali /beŋˋgɔlɪ/; Bangalee /ˈbæŋgəˋli/
Barbados /bɑˋbeɪdəs/	Barbadian /-dɪən/
Belgium /ˋbeldʒəm/	Belgian /-dʒən/
Bermuda /bəˋmjudə/	Bermudan /-dən/
Bhutan /buˋtɑn/	Bhutani /-nɪ/
Bolivia /bəˋlɪvɪə/	Bolivian /-vɪən/
Botswana /botˋswɑnə/	Setswana /set-/; Motswana /mot-/, (pl) Batswana /bɑt-/
Brazil /brəˋzɪl/	Brazilian /-lɪən/
Brunei /ˋbrunɑɪ/	Bruneian /bruˋnɑɪən/
Bulgaria /bʌlˋgeərɪə/	Bulgarian /-rɪən/
Burma /ˋbɜmə/	Burmese /ˈbɜˋmiz/
Burundi /bʊˋrʊndɪ/	Burundian /-dɪən/
Cameroon /ˈkæməˋrun/	Cameroonian /-nɪən/
Canada /ˋkænədə/	Canadian /kəˋneɪdɪən/
Chad /tʃæd/	Chadian /-dɪən/
Chile /ˋtʃɪlɪ/	Chilean /-lɪən/
China /ˋtʃɑɪnə/	Chinese /ˈtʃɑɪˋniz/
Colombia /kəˋlombɪə/	Colombian /-bɪən/
Congo /ˋkoŋgəʊ/	Congolese /ˈkoŋgəˋliz/
Costa Rica /ˈkostə ˋrikə/	Costa Rican /-kən/
Cuba /ˋkjubə/	Cuban /-bən/
Cyprus /ˋsɑɪprəs/	Cyprian /ˋsɪprɪən/; Cypriot /ˋsɪprɪət/
Czechoslovakia /ˈtʃekəʊ-sləˋvækɪə/	Czech /tʃek/, Czechoslovak /ˈtʃekəʊ-ˋsləʊvæk/, Czechoslovakian /-kɪən/
Dahomey /dəˋhəʊmɪ/	Dahomeyan /-mɪən/
Denmark /ˋdenmɑk/	Danish /ˋdeɪnɪʃ/; Dane /deɪn/
Dominica /dəˋmɪnɪkə/	Dominican /-kən/
Ecuador /ˋekwədɔ(r)/	Ecuadorian /ˈekwəˋdɔrɪən/
Egypt /ˋidʒɪpt/	Egyptian /ɪˋdʒɪpʃn/
El Salvador /el ˋsælvədɔ(r)/	Salvadorean /ˈsælvəˋdɔrɪən/
Ethiopia /ˈiθɪˋəʊpɪə/	Ethiopian /-pɪən/
Fiji /ˈfiˋdʒi *US:* ˋfidʒi/	Fijian /ˈfiˋdʒiən *US:* ˋfidʒɪən/

Finland /`fɪnlənd/	Finnish /`fɪnɪʃ/; Finn /fɪn/
France /frɑns/	French /frentʃ/; Frenchman /`frentʃmən/
Gabon /gə`bõ *US:* gə`bɔ̃/	Gabonese /'gæbə`niz/
(The) Gambia /`gæmbɪə/	Gambian /-bɪən/
German Democratic Republic /'dʒɜmən demə'krætɪk rɪ`pʌblɪk/	(East) German /`dʒɜmən/
(Federal Republic of) Germany /'fedr̩l rɪ'pʌblɪk əv `dʒɜmənɪ/	(West) German /`dʒɜmən/
Ghana /`gɑnə/	Ghanaian /gɑ`neɪən/
Gibraltar /dʒɪ`brɔltə(r)/	Gibraltarian /'dʒɪbrɔl`teərɪən/
Great Britain /'greɪt `brɪtn/	British /`brɪtɪʃ/; Briton /`brɪtn/
Greece /gris/	Greek /grik/
Grenada /grɪ`neɪdə/	Grenadian /-dɪən/
Guatemala /'gwɑtə`mɑlə/	Guatemalan /-lən/
Guinea /`gɪnɪ/	Guinean /-nɪən/
Guyana /gɑɪ`ænə/	Guyanese /'gɑɪə`niz/
Haiti /`heɪtɪ/	Haitian /`heɪʃn/
Holland (also *The Netherlands*) /`holənd/	Dutch /dʌtʃ/; Hollander /`holəndə(r)/, Dutchman /`dʌtʃmən/
Honduras /hon`djʊərəs *US:* -`dʊə-/	Honduran /-rən/
Hong Kong /'hoŋ `koŋ/	
Hungary /`hʌŋgərɪ/	Hungarian /hʌŋ`geərɪən/
Iceland /`ɑɪslənd/	Icelandic /ɑɪs`lændɪk/; Icelander /-də(r)/
India /`ɪndɪə/	Indian /-dɪən/
Indonesia /'ɪndə`nizɪə *US:* -`niʒə/	Indonesian /-zɪən *US:* -ʒn/
Iran (formerly *Persia*) /ɪ`rɑn/	Iranian /ɪ`reɪnɪən/
Iraq /ɪ`rɑk/	Iraqi /ɪ`rɑkɪ/
(The Republic of) Ireland /`ɑɪələnd/	Irish /`ɑɪrɪʃ/; Irishman /`ɑɪrɪʃmən/
Israel /`ɪzreɪl/	Israeli /ɪz`reɪlɪ/
Italy /`ɪtəlɪ/	Italian /ɪ`tælɪən/
Jamaica /dʒə`meɪkə/	Jamaican /-kən/
Japan /dʒə`pæn/	Japanese /'dʒæpə`niz/
Java /`dʒɑvə/	Javanese /'dʒɑvə`niz/
Jordan /`dʒɔdn/	Jordanian /dʒɔ`deɪnɪən/
Kashmir /kæʃ`mɪə(r) *US:* `kæʃmɪə(r)/	Kashmiri /kæʃ`mɪərɪ/
Kenya /`kenjə *US:* `kinjə/	Kenyan /-jən/
Khmer (formerly *Cambodia*) /`kmeə(r)/	Khmer
Korea /kə`rɪə/	Korean /-rɪən/
Kuwait /kʊ`weɪt *US:* -`wɑɪt/	Kuwaiti /-tɪ/
Laos /`lɑ-os/	Laotian /`lɑʊʃn *US:* leɪ`əʊʃn/
Lebanon /`lebənən/	Lebanese /'lebə`niz/
Lesotho /lə`səʊtəʊ/	Sesotho /sə-/; Mosotho /mə-/, (*pl*) Basotho /bə-/
Liberia /lɑɪ`bɪərɪə/	Liberian /-rɪən/
Libya /`lɪbɪə/	Libyan /-bɪən/
Liechtenstein /`lɪktənstɑɪn/	Liechtenstein; Liechtensteiner /-nə(r)/
Luxemburg /`lʌksmbɜg/	Luxemburg; Luxemburger /-gə(r)/
Madagascar /'mædə`gæskə(r)/	Madagascan /-kən/
Malawi /mə`lɑwɪ/	Malawian /-wɪən/
Malaya /mə`leɪə/	Malay /mə`leɪ/
Malaysia /mə`leɪzɪə *US:* -`leɪʒə/	Malaysian /-zɪən *US:* -ʒn/
Mali /`mɑlɪ/	Malian /-lɪən/
Malta /`mɔltə/	Maltese /mɔl`tiz/
Mauritania /'morɪ`teɪnɪə *US:* 'mɔr-/	Mauritanian /-nɪən/
Mauritius /mə`rɪʃəs *US:* mɔ-/	Mauritian /-`rɪʃn/
Mexico /`meksɪkəʊ/	Mexican /-kən/
Monaco /`monəkəʊ/	Monegasque /'monə`gæsk/
Mongolia /moŋ`gəʊlɪə/	Mongolian /-lɪən/; Mongol /`moŋgl/
Montserrat /'montsə`ræt/	Montserratian /-`ræʃn/
Morocco /mə`rokəʊ/	Moroccan /-kən/
Mozambique /'məʊzæm`bik *US:* -zm-/	Mozambiquean /-`bikən/
Nauru /'nɔ`ru/	Nauruan /-`ruən/
Nepal /nɪ`pɔl/	Nepalese /'nepə`liz/
(The) Netherlands /`neðələndz/	Dutch /dʌtʃ/; Dutchman /`dʌtʃmən/
New Zealand /'nju `zilənd *US:* 'nu/	New Zealand; New Zealander /-də(r)/
Nicaragua /'nɪkə`rægjʊə *US:* -`rɑgwə/	Nicaraguan /-ən/
Niger /nɪ`ʒeə(r)/	Nigerien /nɑɪ`dʒɪərɪən/
Nigeria /nɑɪ`dʒɪərɪə/	Nigerian /nɑɪ`dʒɪərɪən/
Norway /`nɔweɪ/	Norwegian /nɔ`widʒən/
Pakistan /'pɑkɪ`stɑn *US:* `pækɪstæn/	Pakistani /-nɪ *US:* 'pækɪ`stænɪ/

Panama /ˈpænəˋmɑ *US:* ˋpænəmɑ/	Panamanian /ˈpænəˋmeɪnɪən/
Papua /pəˋpjʊə *US:* ˋpæpjʊə/	Papuan /-ən/
Paraguay /ˋpærəgwɑɪ/	Paraguayan /ˈpærəˋgwɑɪən/
Peru /pəˋru/	Peruvian /-ˋruvɪən/
(The) Philippines /ˋfɪlɪpinz/	Philippine /ˋfɪlɪpin/; Filipino /ˈfɪlɪˋpinəʊ/
Poland /ˋpəʊlənd/	Polish /ˋpəʊlɪʃ/; Pole /pəʊl/
Portugal /ˋpɔtʃʊgl/	Portuguese /ˈpɔtʃʊˋgiz/
Rhodesia /rəˋdiʒə *US:* -ˋdiʃə/	Rhodesian /-ən/
Rumania /ruˋmeɪnɪə/	Rumanian /-nɪən/
Russia /ˋrʌʃə/	Russian /-ʃn/
Rwanda /ruˋwændə/	Rwandan /-dən/
Sabah /ˋsʌbə/	Sabahan /ˋsʌbəhən/
Samoa /səˋməʊə/	Samoan /-ən/
San Marino /ˈsæn məˋrinəʊ/	San Marinese /ˈmærɪˋniz/
Sarawak /səˋrɑwæk/	Sarawakian /ˈsærəˋwækɪən/
Saudi Arabia /ˈsɑʊdɪ əˋreɪbɪə/	Saudi Arabian /-bɪən/
Senegal /ˈsenɪˋgɔl/	Senegalese /ˈsenɪgəˋliz/
(The) Seychelles /ˋseɪʃelz/	Seychellois /seɪˋʃelwa/
Sierra Leone /sɪˈerə lɪˋəʊn/	Sierra Leonean /-nɪən/
Singapore /ˈsɪŋgəˋpɔ(r) *US:* ˋsɪŋəpɔr/	Singaporean /ˈsɪŋgəˋpɔrɪən/
Somalia /səˋmɑlɪə/	Somalian /-lɪən/; Somali /-lɪ/
South Africa /ˈsɑʊθˋæfrɪkə/	South African /-kən/
Spain /speɪn/	Spanish /ˋspænɪʃ/; Spaniard /ˋspænjəd/
Sri Lanka (formerly *Ceylon*) /ˈsrɪ ˋlæŋkə/	Ceylonese /ˈseləˋniz/
(The) Sudan /suˋdɑn/	Sudanese /ˈsudəˋniz/
Sumatra /suˋmɑtrə/	Sumatran /-trən/
Swaziland /ˋswɑzɪlænd/	Swazi /ˋswɑzi/
Sweden /ˋswidn/	Swedish /ˋswidɪʃ/; Swede /swid/
Switzerland /ˋswɪtsələnd/	Swiss /swɪs/
Syria /ˋsɪrɪə/	Syrian /-rɪən/
Tahiti /tɑˋhitɪ/	Tahitian /-ˋhiʃn/
Taiwan (formerly *Formosa*) /tɑɪˋwɑn/	Taiwanese /ˈtɑɪwəˋniz/
Tanzania /ˈtɑnzəˋnɪə/	Tanzanian /-nɪən/
Tibet /tɪˋbet/	Tibetan /-tn/
Thailand (formerly *Siam*) /ˋtɑɪlænd/	Thai /tɑɪ/
Tobago /təˋbeɪgəʊ/	Tobagonian /ˈtəʊbəˋgəʊnɪən/
Togo /ˋtəʊgəʊ/	Togolese /ˈtəʊgəˋliz/
Tonga /ˋtɒŋə/	Tongan /-ən/
Trinidad /ˋtrɪnɪdæd/	Trinidadian /ˈtrɪnɪˋdeɪdɪən/
Tunisia /tjuˋnɪzɪə *US:* tuˋniʒə/	Tunisian /-ən/
Turkey /ˋtɜkɪ/	Turkish /ˋtɜkɪʃ/; Turk /tɜk/
Uganda /juˋgændə/	Ugandan /-dən/
(The) Union of Soviet Socialist Republics /ˈjunɪən əv ˈsəʊvɪət ˈsəʊʃəlɪst rɪˋpʌblɪks/	Russian /ˋrʌʃn/
(The) United States of America /juˈnɑɪtɪd ˈsteɪts əv əˋmerɪkə/	American /-kən/
Uruguay /ˋjʊərəgwɑɪ *US:* -gweɪ/	Uruguayan /-gwɑɪən *US:* -gweɪən/
Venezuela /ˈvenəˋzweɪlə/	Venezuelan /-lən/
Vietnam /ˈvɪətˋnæm *US:* -ˋnɑm/	Vietnamese /ˈvɪetnəˋmiz/
(The) West Indies /ˈwest ˋɪndɪz/	West Indian /-dɪən/
Yemen /ˋjemən/	Yemeni /-nɪ/
Yugoslavia /ˈjugəʊˋslɑvɪə	Yugoslavian /-vɪən/; Yugoslav /ˋjugəʊslɑv/
Zaire /zɑˋɪə(r)/	Zairean /-rɪən/
Zambia /ˋzæmbɪə/	Zambian /-bɪən/

THE UNITED KINGDOM OF GREAT BRITAIN (GB) AND NORTHERN IRELAND (NI)

COUNTIES AND SHIRES

The usual American pronunciation of '-shire' is /-ʃɪər/. Where the suffix '-shire' is usually omitted from the name of a county it is given in parentheses.

The common written abbreviations of the names of the counties are given in parentheses and transcribed only when they are used in spoken English

ENGLAND /ˋɪŋglənd/

Note: By the Local Government Act of 1972, the boundaries of the English Counties were redrawn: those counties marked* ceased to function as official areas; those marked† were newly established.

† Avon /ˈeɪvən/
Bedfordshire (*Beds*) /ˈbedfədʃə(r)/
Berkshire (*Berks*) /ˈbɑkʃə(r) *US:* ˈbɜk-/
Buckinghamshire (*Bucks*) /ˈbʌkɪŋəmʃə(r)/
Cambridgeshire (*Cambs*) /ˈkeɪmbrɪdʒʃə(r)/
Cheshire (*Ches*) /ˈtʃeʃə(r)/
† Cleveland /ˈklivlənd/
Cornwall (*Corn*) /ˈkɔnwl/
* Cumberland (*Cumb*) /ˈkʌmbələnd/
† Cumbria /ˈkʌmbrɪə/
Derbyshire /ˈdɑbɪʃə(r) *US:* ˈdɜbɪ-/
Devon(shire) /ˈdevn(ʃə)(r)/
Dorset(shire) (*Dors*) /ˈdɔsɪt(ʃə)(r)/
Durham (*Dur*) /ˈdʌrəm *US:* ˈdɜəm/
Essex (*Ess*) /ˈesɪks/
Gloucestershire (*Glos*) /ˈglostəʃə(r)/
Hampshire (*Hants* /hænts/)/ˈhæmpʃə(r)/
† Hereford and Worcester /ˈherɪfəd n ˈwʊstə(r)/
* Herefordshire /ˈherɪfədʃə(r)/
Hertfordshire (*Herts* /hɑts/) /ˈhɑ(t)fədʃə(r)/
† Humberside /ˈhʌmbəsɑɪd/
* Huntingdonshire (*Hunts* /hʌnts/) /ˈhʌntɪŋdənʃə(r)/
† Isle of Wight (*I of W*) /ˈɑɪl əv ˈwɑɪt/
Kent /kent/
Lancashire (*Lancs* /læŋks/) /ˈlæŋkəʃə(r)/
Leicestershire (*Leics*) /ˈlestəʃə(r)/
Lincolnshire (*Lincs* /lɪŋks/) /ˈlɪŋkənʃə(r)/
London (County of) /ˈlʌndən/
† Manchester (County of) /ˈmæntʃɪstə(r)/
† Merseyside /ˈmɜzɪsɑɪd/
* Middlesex (*Middx*) /ˈmɪdlseks/
Norfolk (*Norf*) /ˈnɔfək/
Northamptonshire (*Northants*/nɔˈθænts/) /nɔˈθæmptənʃə(r)/
Northumberland (*Northd*) /nɔˈθʌmbələnd/
Nottinghamshire (*Notts* /nots/) /ˈnotɪŋəmʃə(r)/
Oxfordshire (*Oxon* /ˈoksn/) /ˈoksfədʃə(r)/
* Rutland(shire) /ˈrʌtlənd(ʃə)(r)/
Shropshire (*Salop* /ˈsæləp/) /ˈʃropʃə(r)/
Somerset(shire) (*Som*) /ˈsʌməset(ʃə)(r)/
Staffordshire (*Staffs* /stæfs/) /ˈstæfədʃə(r)/
Suffolk (*Suff*) /ˈsʌfək/
Surrey (*Sy*) /ˈsʌrɪ *US:* ˈsɜɪ/
Sussex (*Sx*) /ˈsʌsɪks/
† Tyne and Wear /ˈtɑɪn n ˈwɪə(r)/
Warwickshire (*Warks*) /ˈworɪkʃə(r) *US:* ˈwɔr-/
† West Midlands /ˈmɪdləndz/
* Westmorland /ˈwestmələnd/
Wiltshire (*Wilts* /wɪlts/) /ˈwɪltʃə(r)/
* Worcestershire (*Worcs*) /ˈwʊstəʃə(r)/
Yorkshire (*Yorks*) (North, South and West) /ˈjɔkʃə(r)/

WALES /weɪlz/

Anglesey /ˈæŋglsɪ/
Brecknockshire (*Brec*) /ˈbreknokʃə(r)/
(also Breconshire /ˈbrekənʃə(r)/)
Caernarvonshire (*Caern*) /kəˈnɑvənʃə(r)/
Cardiganshire (*Cards*) /ˈkɑdɪgənʃə(r)/
Carmarthenshire (*Carm*) /kəˈmɑðnʃə(r)/
Denbighshire /ˈdenbɪʃə(r)/
Flintshire /ˈflɪntʃə(r)/
Glamorgan(shire) (*Glam*) /gləˈmɔgən(ʃə)(r)/
Merionethshire /ˈmerɪˈonɪθʃə(r)/
Monmouthshire (*Mon*) /ˈmonməθʃə(r)/
Montgomeryshire (*Montgom*) /məntˈgʌmrɪʃə(r)/
Pembrokeshire (*Pemb*) /ˈpembrʊkʃə(r)/
Radnorshire (*Rad*) /ˈrædnəʃə(r)/

Note: By the Local Government Act of 1972, the above thirteen Welsh Counties are replaced by the following eight:

Clwyd /ˈkluɪd/
Dyfed /ˈdʌvɪd/
Glamorgan (Mid, South and West) /gləˈmɔgən/
Gwent /gwent/
Gwynedd /ˈgwɪnəð/
Powys /ˈpɑʊɪs/

SCOTLAND /ˈskotlənd/

Note: From May 1975 the following counties are replaced by a system of regions.

Aberdeenshire /ˈæbəˈdinʃə(r)/
Angus /ˈæŋgəs/
Argyllshire /ɑˈgɑɪlʃə(r)/
Ayrshire /ˈeəʃə(r)/
Banffshire /ˈbænfʃə(r)/
Berwickshire /ˈberɪkʃə(r)/
Bute(shire) /ˈbjut(ʃə)(r)/
Caithness /ˈkeɪθnes/
Clackmannanshire /klækˈmænənʃə(r)/
Dumbartonshire /dʌmˈbɑtnʃə(r)/
Dumfriesshire /dʌmˈfrisʃə(r)/
East Lothian /ˈləʊðɪən/
Fife /ˈfɑɪfʃə(r)/
Inverness-shire /ˈɪnvəˈnesʃə(r)/
Kincardineshire /kɪnˈkɑdɪnʃə(r)/
Kinross-shire /kɪnˈrosʃə(r)/
Kirkcudbrightshire /kɜˈkubrɪʃə(r)/
Lanarkshire /ˈlænəkʃə(r)/
Midlothian /mɪdˈləʊðɪən/
Morayshire /ˈmʌrɪʃə(r)/
Nairnshire /ˈneənʃə(r)/
Orkney /ˈɔknɪ/
Peeblesshire /ˈpiblʃə(r)/
Perthshire /ˈpɜθʃə(r)/
Renfrewshire /ˈrenfruʃə(r)/
Ross and Cromarty /ˈros n ˈkromətɪ/
Roxburghshire /ˈroksbrəʃə(r)/
Selkirkshire /ˈselkɜkʃə(r)/
Stirlingshire /ˈstɜlɪŋʃə(r)/
Sutherland /ˈsʌðələnd/
West Lothian /ˈləʊðɪən/
Wigtownshire /ˈwɪgtənʃə(r)/
Zetland /ˈzetlənd/

NORTHERN IRELAND /ˈnɔðən ˈɑɪələnd/

Antrim /ˈæntrɪm/
Armagh /ɑˈmɑ/
Down /dɑʊn/
Fermanagh /fəˈmænə/
Londonderry /ˈlʌndənderɪ/
Tyrone /tɪˈrəʊn/

THE REPUBLIC OF IRELAND

PROVINCES AND COUNTIES

THE PROVINCE OF LEINSTER /ˋlenstə(r)/
Carlow /ˋkɑləʊ/
Dublin /ˋdʌblɪn/
Kildare /kɪlˋdeə(r)/
Kilkenny /kɪlˋkenɪ/
Leix /liʃ/
Longford /ˋloŋfəd *US:* ˋlɔŋ-/
Louth /lɑʊð/
Meath /miθ/
Offaly /ˋofəlɪ/
Westmeath /westˋmiθ/
Wexford /ˋweksfəd/
Wicklow /ˋwɪkləʊ/

THE PROVINCE OF MUNSTER /ˋmʌnstə(r)/
Clare /kleə(r)/
Cork /kɔk/
Kerry /ˋkerɪ/
Limerick /ˋlɪmərɪk/
Tipperary /ˈtɪpəˋreərɪ/
Waterford /ˋwɔtəfəd/

THE PROVINCE OF CONNAUGHT /ˋkonɔt/
Galway /ˋgɔlweɪ/
Leitrim /ˋlitrɪm/
Mayo /ˋmeɪəʊ/
Roscommon /rosˋkomən/
Sligo /ˋslɑɪgəʊ/

PART OF THE PROVINCE OF ULSTER /ˋʌlstə(r)/
Cavan /ˋkævn/
Donegal /ˋdonɪgɔl/
Monaghan /ˋmonəhən/

THE COMMONWEALTH OF AUSTRALIA
/oˋstreɪlɪə *US:* ɔˋs-/

STATES AND TERRITORIES

(*Australian Capital Territory:* Canberra /ˋkænbərə/)

New South Wales (*NSW*) /weɪlz/
Northern Territory (*NT*)
Queensland (*Qld*) /ˋkwinzlənd/
South Australia (*S Aus* or *S Austr*)
Tasmania (*Tas*) /tæzˋmeɪnɪə/
Victoria (*Vic*) /vɪkˋtɔrɪə/
Western Australia (*W Aus* or *W Austr*)

NEW ZEALAND /nju ˋzilənd *US:* nu/

PROVINCIAL DISTRICTS

Auckland /ˋɔklənd/
Canterbury /ˋkæntəbrɪ *US:* -berɪ/
Hawke's Bay /ˈhɔks ˋbeɪ/
Marlborough /ˋmɑlbrə/
Nelson /ˋnelsn/
Otago /əʊˋtɑgəʊ/
Taranaki /ˈtærəˋnɑkɪ/
Wellington /ˋwelɪŋtən/

CANADA /ˋkænədə/

PROVINCES AND TERRITORIES

Alberta (*Alta*) /ælˋbɜtə/
British Columbia (*BC*) /kəˋlʌmbɪə/
Labrador (*Lab*) /ˋlæbrədɔ(r)/
Manitoba (*Man*) /ˈmænɪˋtəʊbə/
New Brunswick (*NB*) /ˋbrʌnzwɪk/
Newfoundland (*ND* or *Nfd*) /ˈnjufəndˋlænd *US:* ˈnu-/
Nova Scotia (*NS*) /ˈnəʊvə ˋskəʊʃə/
Ontario (*Ont*) /onˋteərɪəʊ/
Prince Edward Island (*PEI*) /ˈprɪns ˈedwəd ˋɑɪlənd/
Quebec (*Que*) /kwɪˋbek/
Saskatchewan (*Sask*) /səˋskætʃəwən/
Yukon Territory /ˋjukon/
North West Territories (*NWT*)

THE UNITED STATES OF AMERICA
/əˋmerɪkə/

STATES

Alabama (*Ala*) /ˈæləˋbæmə/
Alaska (*Alas*) /əˋlæskə/
Arizona (*Ariz*) /ˈærɪˋzəʊnə/
Arkansas (*Ark*) /ˋɑkənsɔ/
California (*Cal* or *Calif*) /ˈkælɪˋfɔnɪə/
Colorado (*Colo*) /ˈkoləˋrɑdəʊ/
Connecticut (*Conn*) /kəˋnetɪkət/
Delaware (*Del*) /ˋdeləweə(r)/
District of Columbia (*DC*) /kəˋlʌmbɪə/
Florida (*Fla*) /ˋflorɪdə *US:* ˋflɔr-/
Georgia (*Ga*) /ˋdʒɔdʒə/
Hawaii /həˋwɑii/
Idaho (*Id*) /ˋɑɪdəhəʊ/
Illinois (*Ill*) /ˈɪləˋnɔɪ/
Indiana (*Ind*) /ˈɪndɪˋænə/
Iowa (*Ia*) /ˋɑɪəwə/
Kansas (*Kan*) /ˋkænzəs/
Kentucky (*Ken* or *Ky*) /kenˋtʌkɪ/
Louisiana (*La*) /luˈiziˋænə/
Maine (*Me*) /meɪn/
Maryland (*Md*) /ˋmeərɪlənd/
Massachusetts (*Mass*) /ˈmæsəˋtʃusɪts/
Michigan (*Mich*) /ˋmɪʃɪgən/
Minnesota (*Minn*) /ˈmɪnɪˋsəʊtə/
Mississippi (*Miss*) /ˈmɪsɪˋsɪpɪ/
Missouri (*Mo*) /mɪˋzʊərɪ/
Montana (*Mont*) /monˋtænə/
Nebraska (*Nebr* or *Neb*) /nəˋbræskə/
Nevada (*Nev*) /nəˋvɑdə *US:* -ˋvædə/
New Hampshire (*NH*) /ˋhæmpʃə(r)/
New Jersey (*NJ*) /ˋdʒɜzɪ/
New Mexico (*NM*) /ˋmeksɪkəʊ/
New York (*NY*) /ˋjɔk/
North Carolina (*NC*) /ˈkærəˋlɑɪnə/
North Dakota (*ND*) /dəˋkəʊtə/
Ohio (*O*) /əʊˋhɑɪəʊ/
Oklahoma (*Okla*) /ˈəʊkləˋhəʊmə/
Oregon (*Ore* or *Oreg*) /ˋorɪgən US: ˋɔr-/
Pennsylvania (*Penn* or *Pa*) /ˈpenslˋveɪnɪə/
Rhode Island (*RI*) /ˈrəʊd/
South Carolina (*SC*) /ˈkærəˋlɑɪnə/
South Dakota (*SD*) /dəˋkəʊtə/
Tennessee (*Tenn*) /ˈtenəˋsi/
Texas (*Tex*) /ˋteksəs/
Utah (*Ut*) /ˋjutɑ/
Vermont (*Vt*) /vəˋmont/
Virginia (*Va*) /vəˋdʒɪnɪə/
Washington (*Wash*) /ˋwoʃɪŋtən *US:* ˋwɔʃ-/
West Virginia (*W Va*) /vəˋdʒɪnɪə/
Wisconsin (*Wis*) /wɪsˋkonsɪn/
Wyoming (*Wy* or *Wyo*) /wɑɪˋəʊmɪŋ/

Appendix 7 COMMON FORENAMES

Note: Pet names are either shown after the name from which they are formed or listed separately with a note on their origins. Many of the names listed which consist of a single syllable have pet name forms produced by adding /ɪ/ to the pronunciation and -y or -ie to the spelling, and doubling the final consonant if the preceding vowel is short:

e g Fred, Freddy /ˋfredɪ/; Hugh, Hughie /ˋhjuɪ/;
Jean, Jeannie /ˋdʒinɪ/; Rose, Rosie /ˋrəʊzɪ/.

Men

Abraham /ˋeɪbrəhæm/
Adam /ˋædəm/
Adrian /ˋeɪdrɪən/
Alan, Allan, Allen /ˋælən/
Albert /ˋælbət/; Al /æl/
Alexander /ˌælɪgˋzɑndə(r) *US:* -ˋzæn-/; Alex /ˋælɪks/
Alfred /ˋælfrɪd/; Alf /ælf/
Andrew /ˋændru/; Andy /ˋændɪ/
Aneurin /əˋnɑɪərɪn/
Angus /ˋæŋgəs/
Anthony, Antony /ˋæntənɪ/
Arnold /ˋɑnld/
Arthur /ˋɑθə(r)/
Barry /ˋbærɪ/
Bartholomew /bɑˋθoləmju/; Bart /bɑt/
Basil /ˋbæzl/
Benjamin /ˋbendʒəmɪn/; Ben /ben/
Bernard /ˋbɜnəd/; Bernie /ˋbɜnɪ/
Bert /bɜt/ (from *Albert, Gilbert, Herbert, Hubert*)
Bill /bɪl/ (from *William*)
Bob /bob/ (from *Robert*)
Boris /ˋborɪs *US:* ˋbɔr-/
Brian, Bryan /ˋbrɑɪən/
Bruce /brus/
Carl /kɑl/
Cecil /ˋsesl *US:* ˋsisl/
Charles /tʃɑlz/; Chas /tʃæz/
Christian /ˋkrɪstʃən/
Christopher /ˋkrɪstəfə(r)/; Chris /krɪs/
Claud(e) /klɔd/
Clement /ˋklemənt/
Clifford /ˋklɪfəd/; Cliff /klɪf/
Clive /klɑɪv/
Colin /ˋkolɪn/
Cyril /ˋsɪrl/
Daniel /ˋdænɪəl/; Dan /dæn/
David /ˋdeɪvɪd/; Dave /deɪv/
Dean /din/
Dennis, Denis /ˋdenɪs/
Derek /ˋderɪk/
Desmond /ˋdezmənd/; Des /dez/
Dick /dɪk/ (from *Richard*)
Dominic /ˋdomɪnɪk/
Donald /ˋdonəld/; Don /don/
Douglas /ˋdʌgləs/; Doug /dʌg/
Duncan /ˋdʌŋkən/
Edgar /ˋedgə(r)/
Edmund /ˋedmənd/
Edward /ˋedwəd/; Ed /ed/
Enoch /ˋinok/
Eric /ˋerɪk/
Ernest /ˋɜnɪst/; Ernie /ˋɜnɪ/
Eugene /juˋdʒin/
Ewen /ˋjuən/
Felix /ˋfilɪks/
Francis /ˋfrɑnsɪs *US:* ˋfræn-/; Frank /fræŋk/
Frederick /ˋfredrɪk/; Fred /fred/
Gareth /ˋgærəθ/
Gary /ˋgærɪ/
Gavin /ˋgævɪn/
Gene /dzin/ (from *Eugene*)
Geoffrey /ˋdʒefrɪ/; Geoff /dʒef/
George /dʒɔdʒ/
Gerald /ˋdʒerld/; Gerry /ˋdʒerɪ/
Gerard /ˋdʒerəd/
Gilbert /ˋgɪlbət/
Giles /dʒɑɪlz/
Glen /glen/
Godfrey /ˋgodfrɪ/
Gordon /ˋgɔdn/
Graham /ˋgreɪəm/
Gregory /ˋgregərɪ/; Greg /greg/
Guy /gɑɪ/
Harold /ˋhærld/; Harry /ˋhærɪ/; Hal /hæl/
Harvey /ˋhɑvɪ/
Henry /ˋhenrɪ/
Herbert /ˋhɜbət/
Hilary /ˋhɪlərɪ/
Horace /ˋhorɪs *US:* ˋhɔr-/
Howard /ˋhɑʊəd/
Hubert /ˋhjubət/
Hugh /hju/
Humphrey /ˋhʌmfrɪ/
Ian /ˋiən/
Isaac /ˋɑɪzək/
Ivan /ˋɑɪvən/
Ivor /ˋɑɪvə(r)/
Jack /dʒæk/ (from *John*)
Jacob /ˋdʒeɪkəb/
James /dʒeɪmz/
Jason /ˋdʒeɪsn/
Jeffrey /ˋdʒefrɪ/; Jeff /dʒef/
Jeremy /ˋdʒerəmɪ/; Jerry /ˋdʒerɪ/
Jerome /dʒəˋrəʊm/
Jim /dʒɪm/ (from *James*)
Jocelyn /ˋdʒoslɪn/
John /dʒon/
Jonathan /ˋdʒonəθən/
Joseph /ˋdʒəʊzɪf/; Joe /dʒəʊ/
Joshua /ˋdʒoʃʊə/
Julian /ˋdʒulɪən/
Justin /ˋdʒʌstɪn/
Keith /kiθ/
Kenneth /ˋkenɪθ/; Ken /ken/
Kevin /ˋkevɪn/
Kit /kɪt/ (from *Christopher*)
Laurence, Lawrence /ˋlɔrns/; Larry /ˋlærɪ/
Leo /ˋliəʊ/
Leonard /ˋlenəd/; Len /len/
Leslie /ˋlezlɪ/; Les /lez/
Lewis /ˋluɪs/
Lionel /ˋlɑɪənl/
Louis /ˋluɪ *US:* ˋluɪs/; Lou /lu/
Luke /luk/
Malcolm /ˋmælkəm/
Mark /mɑk/
Martin /ˋmɑtɪn *US:* -tn/
Matthew /ˋmæθju/; Matt /mæt/
Maurice /ˋmorɪs *US:* ˋmɔr-/
Max /mæks/

Michael /ˋmɑɪkl/; Mick /mɪk/; Mike /mɑɪk/
Miles /mɑɪlz/
Nathaniel /nəˋθænɪəl/; Nat /næt/
Neil /nil/
Neville /ˋnevl/
Nicholas /ˋnɪkḷəs/; Nick /nɪk/
Ned /ned/ (from *Edward*)
Nigel /ˋnɑɪdʒl/
Noel /ˋnəʊḷ/
Norman /ˋnɔmən/
Oliver /ˋolɪvə(r)/
Oscar /ˋoskə(r)/
Oswald /ˋozwld/
Patrick /ˋpætrɪk/; Pat /pæt/; Paddy /ˋpædɪ/
Paul /pɔl/
Percy /ˋpɜsɪ/
Peter /ˋpitə(r)/; Pete /pit/
Philip /ˋfɪlɪp/; Phil /fɪl/
Quentin /ˋkwentɪn *US:* -tn/
Ralph /rælf/
Randolph /ˋrændolf/
Raymond /ˋreɪmənd/; Ray /reɪ/
Reginald /ˋredʒɪnld/; Reg /redʒ/
Rex /reks/
Richard /ˋrɪtʃəd/
Robert /ˋrobət/
Robin /ˋrobɪn/
Rodney /ˋrodnɪ/; Rod /rod/
Roger /ˋrodʒə(r)/
Ronald /ˋronld/; Ron /ron/
Roy /rɔɪ/
Rudolf /ˋrudolf/
Rupert /ˋrupət/
Samuel /ˋsæmjʊəl/; Sam /sæm/
Sandy /ˋsændɪ/ (from *Alexander*)
Seamus /ˋʃeɪməs/
Sean /ʃɔn/
Sidney /ˋsɪdnɪ/; Sid /sɪd/
Simon /ˋsɑɪmən/
Stanley /ˋstænlɪ/; Stan /stæn/
Stephen, Steven /ˋstivn/; Steve /stiv/
Ted /ted/ (from *Edward*)
Terence /ˋterns/; Terry /ˋterɪ/
Theodore /ˋθɪədɔ(r)/; Theo /ˋθɪəʊ/
Thomas /ˋtoməs/; Tom /tom/
Timothy /ˋtɪməθɪ/; Tim /tɪm/
Toby /ˋtəʊbɪ/
Tony /ˋtəʊnɪ/ (from *Anthony*)
Trevor /ˋtrevə(r)/
Vernon /ˋvɜnən/
Victor /ˋvɪktə(r)/; Vic /vɪk/
Vincent /ˋvɪnsnt/
Vivian /ˋvɪvɪən/
Walter /ˋwɔltə(r)/
Wayne /weɪn/
Wilfred /ˋwɪlfrɪd/
William /ˋwɪlɪəm/; Will /wɪl/

Women

Ada /ˋeɪdə/
Agatha /ˋægəθə/
Agnes /ˋægnɪs/; Aggie /ˋægɪ/
Alexandra /ˋælɪkˋzɑndrə *US:* -ˋzæn-/
Alice /ˋælɪs/
Alison /ˋælɪsn/
Amanda /əˋmændə/
Amy /ˋeɪmɪ/
Angela /ˋændʒələ/
Ann, Anne /æn/
Annabel /ˋænəbel/
Anthea /ˋænθɪə/
Audrey /ˋɔdrɪ/
Barbara /ˋbɑbrə/; Babs /bæbz/
Beatrice /ˋbɪətrɪs/
Belinda /bəˋlɪndə/
Bella /ˋbelə/ (from *Isabella*)
Beryl /ˋberl/
Bess /bes/ (from *Elizabeth*)
Betsy /ˋbetsɪ/ (from *Elizabeth*)
Betty /ˋbetɪ/ (from *Elizabeth*)
Brenda /ˋbrendə/
Bridget /ˋbrɪdʒɪt/
Carol, Carole /ˋkærl/
Caroline /ˋkærḷɑɪn/
Carolyn /ˋkærḷɪn/
Catherine /ˋkæθrɪn/; Cathy /ˋkæθɪ/
Cecilia /səˋsilɪə/
Cecily /ˋsesḷɪ/
Celia /ˋsilɪə/
Charlotte /ˋʃɑlət/
Chloe /ˋkləʊɪ/
Christina /krɪˋstinə/
Christine /ˋkrɪstin/; Chris /krɪs/
Clare /kleə(r)/
Constance /ˋkonstns/; Connie /ˋkonɪ/
Cynthia /ˋsɪnθɪə/
Daisy /ˋdeɪzɪ/
Daphne /ˋdæfnɪ/
Dawn /dɔn/
Deborah /ˋdebṛə/; Debby /ˋdebɪ/
Deirdre /ˋdɪədrɪ/
Denise /dəˋniz/
Diana /dɑɪˋænə/
Dolly /ˋdolɪ/ (from *Dorothy*)
Dora /ˋdɔrə/
Doreen /ˋdɔrin/
Doris /ˋdorɪs *US:* ˋdɔr-/
Dorothy /ˋdorəθɪ *US:* ˋdɔr-/
Edith /ˋidɪθ/
Eileen /ˋɑɪlin/
Elaine /ɪˋleɪn/
Eleanor /ˋelənə(r)/
Eliza /ɪˋlɑɪzə/ (from *Elizabeth*)
Elizabeth /ɪˋlɪzəbəθ/
Ellen /ˋelən/
Elsie /ˋelsɪ/ (from *Elizabeth*)
Emily /ˋeməlɪ/
Emma /ˋemə/
Erica /ˋerɪkə/
Ethel /ˋeθl/
Eunice /ˋjunɪs/
Eva /ˋivə/
Eve /iv/
Evelyn /ˋivḷɪn/
Fanny /ˋfænɪ/ (from *Frances*)
Felicity /fəˋlɪsətɪ/
Fiona /fɪˋəʊnə/
Flora /ˋflɔrə/
Florence /ˋflorns *US:* ˋflɔr-/
Frances /ˋfrɑnsɪs *US:* ˋfræn-/; Fran /fræn/
Freda /ˋfridə/
Geraldine /ˋdʒerəldin/
Gertrude /ˋgɜtrud/; Gertie /ˋgɜtɪ/
Gillian /ˋdʒɪlɪən/; Gill /dʒɪl/
Gladys /ˋglædɪs/
Gloria /ˋglɔrɪə/
Grace /greɪs/
Gwendoline /ˋgwendəlɪn/; Gwen /gwen/
Harriet /ˋhærɪət/
Hazel /ˋheɪzl/

Heather /ˋheðə(r)/
Helen /ˋhelən/
Hilary /ˋhɪlərɪ/
Hilda /ˋhɪldə/
Ida /ˋɑɪdə/
Ingrid /ˋɪŋgrɪd/
Irene /ɑɪəˋrinɪ *US:* ˋɑɪərin/
Iris /ˋɑɪərɪs/
Isabel, Isobel /ˋɪzəbel/
Isabella /ˈɪzəˋbelə/
Ivy /ˋɑɪvɪ/
Jane /dʒeɪn/
Janet /ˋdʒænɪt/
Janice /ˋdʒænɪs/
Jacqueline /ˋdʒækəlɪn/; Jackie /ˋdʒækɪ/
Jean /dʒin/
Jennifer /ˋdʒenɪfə(r)/; Jenny /ˋdʒenɪ/
Jessica /ˋdʒesɪkə/; Jess /dʒes/
Jill /dʒɪl/ (from *Gillian*)
Joan /dʒəʊn/
Joanna /ˋdʒəʊænə/
Jocelyn /ˋdʒoslɪn/
Josephine /ˋdʒəʊzəfin/; Jo /dʒəʊ/
Joy /dʒɔɪ/
Joyce /dʒɔɪs/
Judith /ˋdʒudɪθ/; Judy /ˋdʒudɪ/
Julia /ˋdʒulɪə/
Julie /ˋdʒulɪ/
Juliet /ˋdʒulɪət/
June /dʒun/
Karen /ˋkærən/
Katherine /ˋkæθrɪn/; Kate /keɪt/; Kathy /ˋkæθɪ/
Kay /keɪ/
Kitty /ˋkɪtɪ/ (from *Katherine*)
Laura /ˋlɔrə/
Lesley /ˋlezlɪ/
Lilian /ˋlɪlɪən/
Lily /ˋlɪlɪ/
Linda /ˋlɪndə/
Lisa, Liza /ˋlɑɪzə *US:* ˋlisə/ (from *Elizabeth*)
Liz /ˋlɪz/ (from *Elizabeth*)
Lois /ˋləʊɪs/
Lorna /ˋlɔnə/
Louise /luˋiz/
Lucy /ˋlusɪ/
Lydia /ˋlɪdɪə/
Lynn /lɪn/
Mabel /ˋmeɪbl/
Madeleine /ˋmædlɪn/
Madge /mædʒ/ (from *Margaret*)
Maggie /ˋmægɪ/ (from *Margaret*)
Mamie /ˋmeɪmɪ/ (from *Mary*)
Mandy /ˋmændɪ/ (from *Amanda*)
Marian /ˋmærɪən/
Margaret /ˋmɑgrət/
Margery /ˋmɑdʒərɪ/; Margie /ˋmɑdʒɪ/
Marjorie /ˋmɑdʒərɪ/
Marlene /mɑˋlin/
Martha /ˋmɑθə/
Maria /məˋrɪə/
Marie /məˋri, ˋmɑrɪ/
Marilyn /ˋmærlɪn/
Marion /ˋmærɪən/
Mary /ˋmeərɪ/
Maud /mɔd/
Maureen /ˋmɔrin/
Mavis /ˋmeɪvɪs/
Maxine /mækˋsin/
May /meɪ/ (from *Mary*)
Meg /meg/ (from *Margaret*)
Michelle /mɪˋʃel/
Mildred /ˋmɪldrɪd/
Millicent /ˋmɪlɪsnt/; Milly /ˋmɪlɪ/
Miranda /mɪˋrændə/
Miriam /ˋmɪrɪəm/
Moira /ˋmɔɪrə/
Molly /ˋmolɪ/ (from *Mary*)
Monica /ˋmonɪkə/
Muriel /ˋmjʊərɪəl/
Myra /ˋmɑɪərə/
Nancy /ˋnænsɪ/
Naomi /ˋneɪəmɪ/
Natalie /ˋnætəlɪ/
Nelly /ˋnelɪ/ (from *Eleanor; Helen*)
Nora /ˋnɔrə/
Olive /ˋolɪv/
Olivia /əˋlɪvɪə/
Pamela /ˋpæmələ/; Pam /pæm/
Patience /ˋpeɪʃns/
Patricia /pəˋtrɪʃə/; Pat /pæt/
Paula /ˋpɔlə/
Pauline /ˋpɔlin/
Pearl /pɜl/
Peg /peg/ (from *Margaret*)
Penelope /pəˋneləpɪ/; Penny /ˋpenɪ/
Philippa /ˋfɪlɪpə/
Phoebe /ˋfibɪ/
Phyllis /ˋfɪlɪs/
Polly /ˋpolɪ/
Priscilla /prɪˋsɪlə/
Prudence /ˋprudns/
Rachel /ˋreɪtʃl/
Rebecca /rəˋbekə/
Rita /ˋritə/ (from *Margaret*)
Rosalie /ˋrəʊzəlɪ/
Rosalind /ˋrozəlɪnd/
Rose /rəʊz/
Rosemary /ˋrəʊzmərɪ *US:* -merɪ/
Ruth /ruθ/
Sally /ˋsælɪ/ (from *Sarah*)
Samantha /səˋmænθə/
Sandra /ˋsɑndrə *US:* ˋsæn-/
Sarah /ˋseərə/
Sharon /ˋʃærən *US:* ˋʃɑr-/
Shirley /ˋʃɜlɪ/
Sheila /ˋʃilə/
Sonia /ˋsonɪə/
Sophia /səˋfɑɪə/
Sophie /ˋsəʊfɪ/
Stella /ˋstelə/
Stephanie /ˋstefənɪ/
Susan /ˋsuzn/; Sue /su/; Susie /ˋsuzɪ/
Suzanne /suˋzæn/
Sylvia, Silvia /ˋsɪlvɪə/
Teresa, Theresa /təˋrizə/; Tess /tes/; Tessa /ˋtesə/
Tina /ˋtinə/ (from *Christina*)
Tracy /ˋtreɪsɪ/
Ursula /ˋɜsjʊlə/
Vanessa /vəˋnesə/
Vera /ˋvɪərə/
Veronica /vəˋronɪkə/
Victoria /vɪkˋtɔrɪə/; Vicky /ˋvɪkɪ/
Viola /ˋvɑɪələ/
Violet /ˋvɑɪələt/
Virginia /vəˋdʒɪnɪə/
Vivien /ˋvɪvɪən/
Wendy /ˋwendɪ/
Winifred /ˋwɪnɪfrɪd/; Winnie /ˋwɪnɪ/
Yvonne /ɪˋvon/
Zoe /ˋzəʊɪ/

Appendix 8 THE WORKS OF WILLIAM SHAKESPEARE (1564-1616)

Note: The list below includes the approximate date of composition, full title and common abbreviation; phonetic transcriptions are provided where necessary.

Plays

1590–1	The First Part of King Henry VI (*1 Hen VI*)
	The Second Part of King Henry VI (*2 Hen VI*)
	The Third Part of King Henry VI (*3 Hen VI*)
1592–3	The Tragedy of King Richard III (*Rich III*)
	The Comedy of Errors (*Com Err*)
1593–4	Titus Andronicus (*Titus A*) /ˈtɑɪtəs ænˋdronɪkəs/
	The Taming of the Shrew (*Tam Shr*)
1594–5	The Two Gentlemen of Verona (*Two Gent*) /vəˋrəʊnə/
	Love's Labour's Lost (*Love's L L*)
	Romeo and Juliet (*Rom & Jul*) /ˈrəʊmɪəʊ ən ˋdʒulɪət/
1595–6	The Tragedy of King Richard II (*Rich II*)
	A Midsummer Night's Dream (*Mid N D*)
1596–7	The Life and Death of King John (*K John*)
	The Merchant of Venice (*Mer of Ven*) /ˋvenɪs/
1597–8	The First Part of King Henry IV (*1 Hen IV*)
	The Second Part of King Henry IV (*2 Hen IV*)
1598–1600	Much Ado about Nothing (*M Ado*)
	As You Like It (*As You L It*)
	Twelfth Night, or, What You Will (*Tw N*)
	The Life of King Henry V (*Hen V*)
	Julius Cæsar (*Jul Cæs*) /ˈdʒulɪəs ˋsizə(r)/
1600–1	Hamlet, Prince of Denmark (*Haml*) /ˋhæmlət/
	The Merry Wives of Windsor (*Merry W*) /ˋwɪnzə(r)/
1601–2	Troilus and Cressida (*Tro & Cr*) /ˈtrɔɪləs n ˋkresɪdə/
	All's Well that Ends Well (*All's Well*)
1604–5	Measure for Measure (*Meas for Meas*)
	Othello, the Moor of Venice (*Oth*) /əˋθeləʊ/
1605–6	King Lear (*K Lear*) /lɪə(r)/
	Macbeth (*Macb*) /mækˋbeθ/
1606–7	Antony and Cleopatra (*Ant & Cleop*) /ˈæntənɪ ən ˈkliəˋpætrə/
1607–8	Coriolanus (*Cor*) /ˈkorɪəˋleɪnəs *US:* ˈkɔr-/
	Timon of Athens (*Tim of Ath*) /ˈtɑɪmən əv ˋæθnz/
1608–10	Pericles, Prince of Tyre (*Per*) /ˋperɪkliz/
	Cymbeline (*Cymb*) /ˋsɪmbəlin/
	The Winter's Tale (*Wint T*)
1611–12	The Tempest (*Temp*)
1612–13	The Famous History of the Life of King Henry VIII (*Hen VIII*)

Poems

(Date given is that of first printing)

1593	Venus and Adonis (*Ven & Ad*) /ˈvinəs n əˋdəʊnɪs *US:* əˋdonɪs/
1594	The Rape of Lucrece (*Lucr*) /luˋkris/
1601	The Phoenix and the Turtle (*Phoen & T*)
1609	Sonnets (*Sonn*)
1609	A Lover's Complaint (*Lover's Comp*)

Appendix 9 **RANKS IN THE ARMED FORCES**

ARMY

Officers

GB	**US** (United States Army: USA)
'Field `Marshal (FM)	'General of the `Army (GEN)
`General (Gen)	`General (GEN)
Lieu'tenant-`General (Lt-Gen)	Lieu'tenant-`General (LTG)
'Major-`General (Maj-Gen)	'Major-`General (MG)
'Briga`dier (Brig)	'Briga`dier-`General (BG)
`Colonel (Col)	`Colonel (COL)
Lieu'tenant-`Colonel (Lt-Col)	Lieu'tenant-`Colonel (LTC)
`Major (Maj)	`Major (MAJ)
`Captain (Capt)	`Captain (CPT)
Lieu`tenant (Lieut)	'First-Lieu`tenant (1LT)
'Second-Lieu`tenant (2nd-Lt)	'Second-Lieu`tenant (2LT)
Note: Lieutenant /lef`tenənt/	*Note: Lieutenant* /lu`tenənt/

Non-Commissioned Officers

GB	US
`Warrant Officer (WO)	'Chief `Warrant Officer (CWO)
	`Warrant Officer (WO)
`Staff-Sergeant (Staff-Sgt)	'Sergeant-'Major of the `Army (SGM)
	Com'mand 'Sergeant-`Major (CSM)
`Sergeant (Sgt)	'First-`Sergeant (1SG)
	'Master-`Sergeant (MSG)
	'Sergeant 'First `Class (SFC)
	`Staff-Sergeant (SSG)
	`Sergeant (SGT)
`Corporal (Cpl)	`Corporal (CPL)
'Lance-`Corporal (Lance-Cpl)	
`Private (Pte)	'Private 'First `Class (PFC)
	`Private (PVT)

NAVY

Officers

GB (Royal Navy: RN)	**US** (United States Navy: USN)
'Admiral of the `Fleet	'Fleet `Admiral
`Admiral (Adm)	`Admiral (ADM)
'Vice-`Admiral (Vice-Adm)	'Vice-`Admiral (VADM)
'Rear-`Admiral (Rear-Adm)	'Rear-`Admiral (RADM)
`Commodore (Cdre)	`Commodore (CDRE)
`Captain (Capt)	`Captain (CAPT)
Com`mander (Cdr)	Com`mander (CDR)
Lieu'tenant-Com`mander (Lt-Cdr)	Lieu'tenant-Com`mander (LCDR)
Lieu`tenant (Lt)	Lieu`tenant (LT)
'Sub-Lieu`tenant (Sub-Lt)	Lieu'tenant `Junior Grade (LTJG)
'Acting 'Sub-Lieu`tenant (Actg Sub-Lt)	`Ensign (ENS)
	'Chief 'Warrant `Officer (CWO)
`Midshipman	`Midshipman
Note: Lieutenant /lə`tenənt/	*Note: Lieutenant* /lu`tenənt/

Non-Commissioned Officers

GB	US
'Fleet 'Chief 'Petty `Officer (FCPO)	`Warrant Officer (WO)
	'Master 'Chief 'Petty 'Officer of the `Navy (MCPO)
	'Senior 'Chief 'Petty `Officer (SCPO)
'Chief 'Petty `Officer (CPO)	'Chief 'Petty `Officer (CPO)
'Petty `Officer (PO)	'Petty `Officer (PO)
'Leading `Seaman (LS)	`Seaman (SN)
'Able `Seaman (AB)	
'Ordinary `Seaman (OD)	
'Junior `Seaman (JS)	'Seaman Ap`prentice (SA)

Appendix 9 **RANKS IN THE ARMED FORCES**

AIR FORCE

Officers

GB	US
('Royal `Air Force: RAF)	(U'nited `States `Air Force: USAF)
'Marshal of the 'Royal `Air Force	'General of the `Air Force
'Air 'Chief `Marshal	`General (GEN)
'Air `Marshal	Lieu'tenant-`General (LTG)
'Air 'Vice-`Marshal	'Major-`General (MG)
'Air `Commodore (Air Cdre)	'Briga'dier-`General (BG)
'Group `Captain (Gp Capt)	`Colonel (COL)
'Wing Com`mander (Wing Cdr)	Lieu'tenant-`Colonel (LTC)
`Squadron Leader (Sqn Ldr)	`Major (MAJ)
'Flight Lieu`tenant (Flt Lt)	`Captain (CAPT)
`Flying Officer (FO)	'First-Lieu`tenant (1LT)
'Pilot `Officer (PO)	'Second-Lieu`tenant (2LT)
Note: Lieutenant /lef`tenənt/	*Note: Lieutenant* /lu`tenənt/

Non-Commissioned Officers

GB	US
`Warrant Officer (WO)	'Chief `Warrant Officer (CWO)
	`Warrant Officer (WO)
'Flight `Sergeant (FS)	'Chief 'Master-`Sergeant (CMSGT)
	'Senior 'Master-`Sergeant (SMSGT)
	'Master-`Sergeant (MSGT)
'Chief Tech'nician (Chf Tech)	'Technical-`Sergeant (TSGT)
`Sergeant (Sgt)	'Staff-Sergeant (SSGT)
`Corporal (Cpl)	`Sergeant (SGT)
'Junior Tech`nician (Jnr Tech.)	
'Senior `Aircraftman (SAC)	'Airman 'First `Class (A1C)
'Leading `Aircraftman (LAC)	
`Aircraftman	'Airman `Basic (AB)

MARINES

Officers

GB	US
('Royal Ma`rines: RM)	(U'nited 'States Ma`rine Corps: USMC)
`General (Gen)	`General (GEN)
Lieu'tenant-`General (Lt-Gen)	Lieu'tenant-`General (LTG)
'Major-`General (Maj-Gen)	'Major-`General (MG)
	'Briga'dier-`General (BG)
`Colonel (Col)	`Colonel (COL)
Lieu'tenant-`Colonel (Lt-Col)	Lieu'tenant-`Colonel (LTC)
`Major (Maj)	`Major (MAJ)
`Captain (Capt)	`Captain (CPT)
Lieu`tenant (Lieut)	'First-Lieu`tenant (1LT)
'Acting-Lieu`tenant (Actg-Lt)	
'Second-Lieu`tenant (2nd-Lt)	'Second Lieu`tenant (2LT)
Note: Lieutenant /lef`tenənt/	*Note: Lieutenant* /lu`tenənt/

Non-Commissioned Officers

GB	US
`Warrant Officer (WO)	'Sergeant-`Major (SGM)
	'Master 'Gunnery-`Sergeant (MGSGT)
'Colour `Sergeant (C/Sgt)	'First-`Sergeant (1SGT)
	'Master-`Sergeant (MSGT)
	'Gunnery-`Sergeant (GSGT)
`Sergeant (Sgt)	'Staff-Sergeant (SSGT)
	`Sergeant (SGT)
`Corporal (Cpl)	`Corporal (CPL)
Marine (Mne)	'Lance-`Corporal (LCPL)
	'Private 'First `Class (PFC)
'Junior Ma`rine (J/Mne)	Private (PVT)

Appendix 10 **BOOKS OF THE BIBLE**

Old Testament

Genesis (*Gen*) /ˋdʒenɪsɪs/
ExodusM (*Exod*) /ˋeksədəs/
Leviticus (*Lev*) /lɪˋvɪtɪkəs/
Numbers (*Num*) /ˋnʌmbəz/
Deuteronomy (*Deut*) /ˈdjutəˋronəmɪ *US:* ˈdu-/
Joshua (*Josh*) /ˋdʒoʃjʊə/
Judges (*Judg*) /ˋdʒʌdʒɪz/
Ruth /ruθ/
I Samuel (*I Sam*) /ˋsæmjʊəl/
II Samuel (*II Sam*) /ˋsæmjʊəl/
I Kings (*I Kgs*) /kɪŋz/
II Kings (*II Kgs*) /kɪŋz/
I Chronicles (*I Chron*) /ˋkronɪklz/
II Chronicles (*II Chron*) /ˋkronɪklz/
Ezra /ˋezrə/
Nehemiah (*Neh*) /ˈniɪˋmɑɪə/
Esther /ˋestə(r)/
Job /dʒəʊb/
Psalms (*Ps*) /sɑmz/
Proverbs (*Prov*) /ˋprovɜbz/
Ecclesiastes (*Eccles*) /ɪˈklizɪˋæstiz/
Song of Solomon /ˈsoŋ əv ˋsoləmən *US:* ˈsɔŋ/
or Song of Songs (*S of S*)
Isaiah (*Isa*) /ɑɪˋzɑɪə *US:* ɑɪˋzeɪə/
Jeremiah (*Jer*) /ˈdʒerɪˋmɑɪə/
Lamentations (*Lam*) /ˈlæmənˋteɪʃnz/
Ezekiel (*Ezek*) /ɪˋzikɪəl/
Daniel (*Dan*) /ˋdænɪəl/
Hosea (*Hos*) /həʊˋziə/
Joel /ˋdʒəʊl/
Amos /ˋeɪmos *US:* -məs/
Obadiah (*Obad*) /ˈəʊbəˋdɑɪə/
Jonah /ˋdʒəʊnə/
Micah /ˋmɑɪkə/
Nahum /ˋneɪhəm/
Habbakuk (*Hab*) /ˋhæbəkək *US:* həˋbækək/
Zephaniah (*Zeph*) /ˈzefəˋnɑɪə/
Haggai (*Hag*) /ˋhɑgeɪɑɪ *US:* ˋhɑgɪɑɪ/
Zechariah (*Zech*) /ˈzekəˋrɑɪə/
Malachi (*Mal*) /ˋmæləkɑɪ/

The Apocrypha /əˋpokrɪfə/

Tobit /ˋtəʊbɪt/
Judith /ˋdʒudɪθ/
Wisdom /ˋwɪzdəm/
Ecclesiasticus /ɪˈklizɪˋæstɪkəs/
Baruch /ˋbeərək/
I Maccabees /ˋmækəbiz/
II Maccabees /ˋmækəbiz/

New Testament

St Matthew (*Matt*) /ˋmæθju/
St Mark /ˋmak/
St Luke /ˋluk/
St John /ˋdʒon/
Acts /ækts/
Romans (*Rom*) /ˋrəʊmənz/
I Corinthians (*I Cor*) /kəˋrɪnθɪənz/
II Corinthians (*II Cor*) /kəˋrɪnθɪənz/
Galatians (*Gal*) /gəˋleɪʃnz/
Ephesians (*Eph*) /ɪˋfiʒnz/
Philippians (*Phil*) /fɪˋlɪpɪənz/
Colossians (*Col*) /kəˋloʃnz/
I Thessalonians (*I Thess*) /ˈθesəˋləʊnɪənz/
II Thessalonians (*II Thess*) /ˈθesəˋləʊnɪənz/
I Timothy (*I Tim*) /ˋtɪməθɪ/
II Timothy (*II Tim*) /ˋtɪməθɪ/
Titus (*Tit*) /ˋtɑɪtəs/
Philemon (*Philem*) /fɪˋlimən/
Hebrews (*Heb*) /ˋhibruz/
James (*Jas*) /dʒeɪmz/
I Peter (*I Pet*) /ˋpitə(r)/
II Peter (*II Pet*) /ˋpitə(r)/
I John /dʒon/
II John /dʒon/
III John /dʒon/
Jude /dʒud/
Revelation (*Rev*) /ˈrevəˋleɪʃn/
or Apocalypse /əˋpokəlɪps/